P9-DGI-493

1989
Britannica
Book of the Year

Encyclopædia Britannica, Inc.
Chicago
Auckland/Geneva/London/Madrid/Manila/Paris
Rome/Seoul/Sydney/Tokyo/Toronto

EDITOR
Daphne Daume

EDITORIAL STAFF
David Calhoun
Charles Cegielski
Karen Jacobs Justin
Arthur Latham
Elizabeth B. Luft
Melinda Shepherd
Medical Subjects
Ellen Bernstein
Linda Tomchuck
Bibliographical Research
Leah Hotimlanska

EDITORIAL CONSULTANT
Bruce L. Felknor

ADVISER
Martin E. Marty

CORRESPONDENTS
Joan Harris, Toronto
Harold DeWeese, Sydney
Rinzo Sakauchi, Tokyo
Sergio A. Sarmiento,
Mexico City
J. Amaral, Rio de Janeiro

ART DIRECTOR
Cynthia Peterson
PLANNING ANALYST
Marsha Check
SENIOR PICTURE EDITOR
Holly Harrington
PICTURE EDITORS
Kathryn Creech
Cathy Melloan
April A. Oswald
LAYOUT ARTISTS
Curtis E. Hardy
Dale Horn
ART PRODUCTION SUPERVISOR
Richard A. Roiniotis
ART STAFF
Amy I. Brown
Daniel M. Delgado
Patricia L. Henle
LeNair Hunt

MANAGER, CARTOGRAPHY
Gerzilla Leszczynski
CARTOGRAPHY STAFF
Steven Bogdan
Chandrika Kaul
Phyllis A. Kawano
Laurie J. Purkiss

DIRECTOR, YEARBOOK
PRODUCTION AND CONTROL
J. Thomas Beatty

MANAGER, COPY DEPARTMENT
Anita Wolff
SENIOR COPY EDITORS
Julian Ronning
Barbara Whitney
COPY STAFF
Elizabeth A. Blowers
Linda A. Cifelli
Madolynn Cronk
Ellen Finkelstein
Patrick Joyce
Elizabeth Laskey
Lorraine Murray
A. Laurie Palmer
Thomas J. Riggs
John Scanlon
Joan E. Sebastian
Carol Smith

MANAGER, PRODUCTION
CONTROL
Mary C. Srodon
PRODUCTION CONTROL STAFF
Marilyn L. Barton
Vernetta McCoy
Yvonne G. Pua

MANAGER, COMPOSITION
AND PAGE MAKEUP
Melvin Stagner
COORDINATOR, COMPOSITION
AND PAGE MAKEUP
Philip Rehmer
COMPOSITION STAFF
Duangnetra Debhavalya
Morna Freund
John Krom, Jr.
Thomas Mulligan
Gwen Rosenberg
Tammy Tsou
PAGE MAKEUP STAFF
Michael Born, Jr.
Griselda Cháidez
Arnell Reed
Danette Wetterer

DIRECTOR, EDITORIAL COMPUTER
SERVICES
Michelle J. Brandhorst
COMPUTER SERVICES STAFF
Steven Bosco
Barbara Staffen
Vincent Star

MANAGER INDEX DEPARTMENT
Frances E. Latham
SENIOR INDEX EDITOR
Lisa Strubin
INDEX STAFF
Jean Getty Klein
Steven M. Monti

LIBRARIAN
Terry Miller
ASSOCIATE LIBRARIAN
Shantha Uddin
CURATOR/GEOGRAPHY
David W. Foster
ASSISTANT LIBRARIAN
Robert Lewis

SECRETARIAL STAFF
Dorothy Hagen
Catherine E. Johnson

EDITORIAL ADMINISTRATION
Philip W. Goetz, *Editor in Chief*
Michael Reed, *Managing Editor*
Karen M. Barch, *Executive Director
of Editorial Production*
Carl Holzman, *Director of Budgets
and Controller*

ENCYCLOPÆDIA BRITANNICA, INC.
Robert P. Gwinn, *Chairman
of the Board*
Peter B. Norton, *President*

©1989 BY ENCYCLOPÆDIA BRITANNICA, INC.

Copyright Under International Copyright Union
All Rights Reserved Under Pan American and Universal Copyright Conventions
by Encyclopædia Britannica, Inc.

Library of Congress Catalog Card Number: 38-12082
International Standard Book Number: 0-85229-504-9
International Standard Serial Number: 0068-1156

No part of this work may be reproduced or utilized in any form or by any means, electronic or
mechanical, including photocopying, recording, or by any information storage and retrieval system,
without permission in writing from the publisher.

BRITANNICA BOOK OF THE YEAR

(Trademark Reg. U.S. Pat. Off.) Printed in U.S.A.

THE UNIVERSITY OF CHICAGO
*The Britannica Book of the Year is published with the editorial advice
of the faculties of the University of Chicago.*

CONTENTS

CALENDAR 1989

JANUARY

1 New Year's Day
 Tenth anniversary of the establishment of diplomatic relations between the United States and China
7 Coptic Orthodox Christmas
13 125th anniversary of the death of Stephen Foster, U.S. composer
15 Adults Day in Japan
16 Martin Luther King Day, a U.S. federal holiday
19 150th anniversary of the birth of Paul Cézanne, French painter
21 30th anniversary of the death of Cecil B. DeMille, U.S. motion picture pioneer
26 Australia Day, commemoration of the first British settlement (1788)

FEBRUARY

2 20th anniversary of the death of Boris Karloff, British actor who created the role of Frankenstein's monster
6 Chinese New Year's Day, which ushers in the Year of the Snake
7 Mardi Gras, festival on the eve of Ash Wednesday, the first day of Lent
11 Tenth anniversary of the seizure of power in Iran by the followers of Ayatollah Ruhollah Khomeini
 150th anniversary of the birth of J. Willard Gibbs, U.S. physicist and chemist
14 Valentine's Day in U.S.
20 Official U.S. observance of George Washington's birthday

MARCH

3 World Day of Prayer
12 75th anniversary of the death of George Westinghouse, U.S. inventor and industrialist
17 St. Patrick's Day
19 Palm Sunday
20 60th anniversary of the death of Marshal Ferdinand Foch, renowned French commander of Allied troops during World War I
26 Easter in Western churches
 Tenth anniversary of the historic peace treaty negotiated by U.S. Pres. Jimmy Carter and signed in Washington, D.C., by Anwar as-Sadat for Egypt and by Menachem Begin for Israel

APRIL

5 25th anniversary of the death of Douglas MacArthur, celebrated U.S. Army general during World War II and the Korean War
6 175th anniversary of the abdication of Emperor Napoleon Bonaparte, who then went into exile on Elba but died on St. Helena in 1821
7 Projected first day of Ramadan; for Muslims, start of a monthlong fast
9 30th anniversary of the death of Frank Lloyd Wright, U.S. architect
20 Jewish festival of Passover
30 Easter in Eastern Orthodox churches
 200th anniversary of the inauguration of George Washington as first president of the United States

MAY

1 May Day, observed in many countries as Labour Day
7 'Id al-Fitr, Muslim festival ending the fast of Ramadan
14 Mother's Day in U.S.
16 Tenth anniversary of the death of A. Philip Randolph, U.S. civil rights activist and labour leader
22 Victoria Day in Canada
24 15th anniversary of the death of Duke Ellington, U.S. jazz musician and composer
27 25th anniversary of the death of Jawaharlal Nehru, first prime minister of India after it gained independence in 1947
29 U.S. observance of Memorial Day

JUNE

8 Chinese Dragon Boat Festival
10 Queen Elizabeth II participates in Trooping the Colour, part of her official birthday celebration
11 125th anniversary of the birth of Richard Strauss, German composer
12 Philippine Independence Day (1898)
18 Father's Day in U.S.
 Tenth anniversary of the signing in Vienna of the SALT II accords
22 20th anniversary of the death of Judy Garland, U.S. entertainer
28 75th anniversary of the murder of Austrian Archduke Francis Ferdinand and his wife in Sarajevo (modern Yugoslavia), an event that touched off World War I

JULY

1 Canada Day
2 500th anniversary of the birth of Thomas Cranmer, English Protestant reformer
4 Independence Day in U.S. (1776)
10 Tenth anniversary of the death of Arthur Fiedler, for 50 seasons maestro of the Boston Pops Orchestra
14 Bicentennial of the French Revolution, which began with the storming of the Bastille and led to the overthrow of the ancien regime. The Eiffel Tower was erected for the centenary of the revolution
17 Tenth anniversary of the resignation of Pres. Anastasio Somoza and his departure from Nicaragua

AUGUST

3 Islamic New Year's Day
6 Peace Festival in Hiroshima, Japan
8 15th anniversary of Richard Nixon's announcement that he would resign as president of the United States the following day
12 25th anniversary of the death of Ian Fleming, British novelist who created the character James Bond
17 20th anniversary of the death of Ludwig Mies van der Rohe, German-born architect
21 30th anniversary of Hawaii's joining the U.S. as its 50th state
27 Tenth anniversary of the assassination of Lord Mountbatten of Burma by Irish Republican Army terrorists

SEPTEMBER

1 50th anniversary of Germany's invasion of Poland. The attack marked the beginning of World War II
4 Labor Day in U.S.
11 Coptic Orthodox New Year
12 15th anniversary of the overthrow of Emperor Haile Selassie, who had ruled Ethiopia for 44 years
14 175th anniversary of the "Star Spangled Banner." In 1931 the U.S. adopted it as its national anthem. Korean festival of Chusok
23 50th anniversary of the death of Sigmund Freud, Austrian neurologist and founder of psychoanalysis
30 Rosh Hashana, Jewish New Year's Day

OCTOBER

1 40th anniversary of the People's Republic of China
9 Thanksgiving Day in Canada
 Yom Kippur, Jewish Day of Atonement
 U.S. observance of Columbus Day
12 Columbus Day
15 25th anniversary of the death of Cole Porter, U.S. songwriter
24 United Nations Day
26 Tenth anniversary of the assassination of Pres. Park Chung Hee by the head of the Korean Central Intelligence Agency
29 60th anniversary of "Black Tuesday," when the U.S. stock market collapsed and the country was plunged into the Great Depression

NOVEMBER

4 Tenth anniversary of the seizure of the U.S. embassy in Tehran by Iranian militants
7 Anniversary of the Bolshevik Revolution in Russia (1917)
11 Veterans Day in U.S., Remembrance Day in Canada. Originally called Armistice Day, it commemorated the end of World War I and honoured those who died in the war
18 Bicentennial of the birth of Louis-Jacques-Mandé Daguerre, French inventor of the first practical photographic process
23 Thanksgiving Day in U.S.
24 125th anniversary of the birth of Henri de Toulouse-Lautrec, French painter

DECEMBER

5 Birthday of King Bhumibol Adulyadej, who ascended the throne of Thailand in 1950; a national holiday
12 Centenary of the death of Robert Browning, English poet who lies buried in the Poet's Corner in Westminster Abbey, London
14 15th anniversary of the death of Walter Lippmann, U.S. political commentator
22 350th anniversary of the baptism of Jean Racine, French dramatic poet
23 First day of Hanukkah, Jewish Festival of Lights
25 Christmas Day
26 Boxing Day, observed especially in Britain and its former colonies

From Marx to Madison:
Socialism's Cultural Contradictions

BY JAMES O'TOOLE

Marx-Lenin: Groucho Marx and John Lennon
—Graffito on a wall in Prague

"A revolution is taking place here. Not everyone realizes it, but that's what it is—a revolution!" Those words were proclaimed in Moscow (significantly, at an American-style press conference) by Mikhail P. Vyshinsky, deputy justice minister of the U.S.S.R., on the eve of the June 1988 extraordinary meeting of the Soviet Communist Party. Over the next four momentous days—days that may not have "shaken the world" but certainly did send tremors throughout Soviet society—party General Secretary Mikhail Gorbachev engineered sweeping reforms of his country's economic and political institutions which, he claimed, constituted "a revolution without bullets." In 1985 Gorbachev's Chinese counterpart in all but title, Deng Xiaoping (Teng Hsiao-p'ing), had dubbed similar changes being wrought in his own Communist country "China's second revolution." Today, the drift of events in the Soviet Union and China so threatens orthodox Marxists in both countries that they are sounding alarums about the danger of "creeping capitalism."

Meanwhile, in the West, conservatives have come to power during the last decade in such welfare states as Britain, West Germany, The Netherlands, Canada, and Finland. Indeed, throughout the Western world, long-term voting trends have been running against the left. For example, the French Communist Party, which once commanded 28% of the vote, now considers itself fortunate to garner a tenth of the ballots cast. In recent European elections the total vote for the left (including Socialists, Communists, and Greens but excluding the centrist Social Democratic parties of Britain and Portugal) has exceeded 50% only in Spain, Greece, and Sweden. More significant, perhaps, has been the unprecedented right turn by the socialist parties of France, Spain, and Italy. Once Marxist in orientation, their policies now sound much like those of the U.S. Democratic Party. As we shall see, the key to understanding the different dilemmas of both Communism and democratic socialism is found in the recent ascendancy of *political pluralism,* the advantages of which were first noted by James Madison 200 years ago.

The failures of democratic socialism in Europe, coupled with the retreat from Marxist orthodoxy in China and the U.S.S.R., have led many observers to conclude that

socialism in all its forms is in a state of terminal decline. Indeed, the editors of *Fortune* magazine already have announced the "Death of Socialism." In this view, socialism is a burnt-out case, ready for Trotsky's "ash heap of history." After a century and a half in which socialism has been the world's preeminent intellectual idea, what, in Lenin's name, is happening?

New Look in the East. Current happenings in the world's two dominant Marxist countries look very much like the stuff of revolutions—perhaps even *democratic, capitalist revolutions* complete with "bourgeois" American pizzas for sale in Moscow's Red Square, "spiritually polluting" rock concerts disturbing the serenity of Beijing's (Peking's) Forbidden City, "parasitical" entrepreneurs launching "new ventures" right across the Eurasian landmass, and signs of "subversive" political pluralism aborning from Leningrad to Shanghai. It would be revolutionary, indeed, if the two largest centrally planned economies were to give way to the dictates of free market supply and demand, and even more revolutionary if the polities of these two single-party nations were to become rooted in laws debated and enacted by democratically elected officials, implemented by government agencies free of Communist Party "guidance," and upheld by independent judiciaries willing—finally—to enforce the freedoms of press, assembly, religion, and union organization long "guaranteed" by Marxist regimes.

There are hints of such in Gorbachev's vaunted *glasnost* (openness) and *perestroika* (restructuring). Nonetheless, most Western observers remain skeptical, if not cynical, and are prudently adopting a wait-and-see attitude. But even if the current reforms ultimately fall short by Western standards, recent events in the U.S.S.R. and China constitute the most significant alterations of Communist ideology and practice since that fateful October in 1917 when V. I. Lenin's Bolsheviks seized power in the world's first Communist revolution. In these two nations, where the practice of Communism has come to be equated with ruthless totalitarianism, the current repudiation of Stalinism, the tentative dismantling of doctrinaire Leninism, and the questioning of Marxist fundamentalism is the cover story not only of the year but of the era.

One can now buy designer jeans with a Visa card in China (in the U.S.S.R., Mrs. Gorbachev uses American Express), and such pragmatic changes are news if for no other reason than that they may herald the formation of a truly global economy. But, more important, the changes also might presage an end to the cold war (could it be mere chance that the Moscow reforms have coincided

---

James O'Toole is university associates' chair in the Graduate School of Business, University of Southern California.

with a significant thaw in U.S.-Soviet relations?), greater personal freedom and a higher standard of living for some two billion people who live under Communism, and, perhaps, greater political autonomy for the nations of Eastern Europe. The reforms have personal ramifications as well. At the end of the Soviet party conference, a Soviet worker was asked what would now be different in his life. He answered with a single word: "Hope."

The Technological Imperative. While reasonable people may hope for such changes, it is unreasonable to assume that the political agendas of the Marxist states are identical with those of the West. Both Gorbachev and Deng have stated explicitly that the intent of their reforms is to increase the efficiency of their national economies. But to accomplish even this limited aim, they have had to confront an issue Marxists have long sought to avoid: dealing with the choice between equality and efficiency. The late economist Arthur Okun argued that every increment of social equality a nation gains comes at the cost of an increment in economic efficiency. Thus, in Mao's relentlessly egalitarian China, the price the Chinese paid was an economy that was arguably the least efficient among all the industrializing nations. Now the leaders of the U.S.S.R. and China are proposing to trade off a bit of equality (by providing financial incentives) in order to gain as much efficiency as they can.

Political economists have long understood that there is another key trade-off which the Communist world has yet to confront: liberty versus equality. The relative social equality and economic security of Chinese and Soviet citizens have been purchased at a terrible price in terms of political and economic freedom. While failing to address this issue directly, Gorbachev has at least recognized the relationship between the sorry state of the Soviet economy and the absence of democracy in the society. He knows that the Soviet Union must modernize its technological and industrial infrastructure immediately or fall irreversibly behind its Western competitors. And he recognizes that the sine qua non of that change is political liberalization.

Gorbachev on the Spot. The French social critic Raymond Aron once posed a rhetorical question that Gorbachev has doubtless asked himself of late: "Why is it that the Soviet Union alone can eternally escape the dynamics of evolution?" One possible answer to that

Soviet leader Mikhail Gorbachev addresses an assembly of delegates at the 19th All-Union Communist Party Conference. More than 70 delegates delivered speeches during the four-day convention, which moved toward restructuring the Soviet government and initiating both political and economic reforms.
TASS/SOVFOTO

question has been offered by Bernard-Henri Levy, former Marxist enfant terrible of French politics (and now an anti-Communist media guru), who says, "Marxism is, literally, counterrevolutionary thought."

That "counterrevolution" is waged by all manner of means, as Gorbachev has discovered. The Brookings Institution's Ed Hewett explains that Gorbachev's reforms immediately encountered resistance from planners and administrators who stood to lose power; from workers who were threatened by the loss of job security; from managers who now were to be held responsible for the performance of their enterprises; and from the 6% of Soviet citizens who belong to the party. The latter were being asked to give up some of their power and privileges but, beyond these self-serving concerns, they were also being asked to abandon their most cherished beliefs. When Gorbachev faced the 5,000 delegates in the Palace of Congresses in June and asked them to question the basic tenets of Marxism-Leninism, it was as if the pope had convened the College of Cardinals and asked them to recant their beliefs in the Holy Trinity, the Virgin Birth, and the miracle of transubstantiation.

For over 150 years, those who have called themselves socialists have agreed fully on only one principle: *free market systems create intolerable levels of social and economic inequality.* Those who adhere to the dominant Soviet interpretation of Marxism-Leninism have believed that the pursuit of equality necessitates making market forces subservient to three political mechanisms: (1) state planning; (2) state ownership of the means of production; and (3) party control of the state. Stating these basic tenets throws into sharp relief several fundamental ideological contradictions created by the Gorbachev reforms: Isn't "market socialism" an oxymoron? Doesn't the creation of

---

The Cultural Contradictions of Socialism

The contradictions of capitalism . . . have to do with the disjunction between the kind of organization and the norms of self-realization that are now central in the culture. The two realms which had historically been joined to produce a single character structure . . . have now become unjoined. The principles of the economic realm and those of the culture now lead people in contrary directions. These contradictions have arisen primarily in American and other Western societies. It is not at all clear that the communist world, with its drive for efficiency and its promise of self-realization, is immune to these contradictions. We shall have to wait and see when (or if) a consumer society is achieved in the Soviet Union.

—Daniel Bell

From *The Cultural Contradictions of Capitalism*, by Daniel Bell. Copyright © 1976 by Daniel Bell. Reprinted by permission of Basic Books, Inc., Publishers.

even a smidgeon of private enterprise lead to inequality? Doesn't democracy preclude party control over the state? And, if the answers are yes to the above, then isn't reform merely another word for capitalism?

Gorbachev's problem was to convince the party delegates that the correct answers to those thorny questions were *nyet*, *nyet*, *nyet*, and *nyet*. He sought first to assure the delegates that the reforms were designed to "save the system." Then he tried to get off the ideological hook—as he had previously attempted to do in his book *Perestroika*—by drawing a distinction between socialism, the current "temporary" condition of Soviet society, and communism, a classless system yet to come:

> Socialism has nothing to do with equalizing. Socialism cannot ensure conditions of life and consumption in accordance with the principle "From each according to his ability, to each according to his needs." This will be under communism. Socialism has a different criterion for distributing social benefits: "From each according to his ability, to each according to his work."

To the assembled delegates, this "socialism" probably sounded a great deal like capitalism. Gorbachev then added to their ideological confusion when he called for "full-blooded and unconditional democracy," which would seem to put him at odds with the teachings of Lenin. Although Gorbachev offered the delegates the requisite words about the continued "guiding role of the party," the underlying music they heard must have sounded as if it had been composed by Western democratic socialists or, at the very least, by revisionist Czechoslovak or Hungarian Communists.

Indeed, the roots of democratic socialism that seem to inform some of Gorbachev's proposals are not in Marxism-Leninism at all but in the writings of such 19th-century "utopians" as Pierre-Joseph Proudhon, Charles Fourier, and Robert Owen. Unlike the dour troika of Marx, Engels, and Lenin, these idealistic socialists were democrats who believed capitalists could be convinced that reform was in their self-interest. While the utopians shared the troika's fervent belief in the goal of equality, they also believed that equality should be achieved through such democratic reforms as laws establishing humane working conditions and through forming worker-owned cooperatives. Of course, the 5,000 students of Marxism gathered in the Palace of Congresses knew that the dyspeptic Mr. Marx had dismissed all this as pie-in-the-sky dreaming and disdainfully applied the term utopian to his democratic rivals. Gorbachev sought to cover his left flank by assuring the delegates—using a code they all understood—that "We need no social utopias." (Significantly, he called for "pluralism" in his next breath! If nothing else, Gorbachev is the equal of any Western politician in his ability to walk a tightrope.)

Ideological Limits to Change. Nonetheless, Gorbachev found himself constrained ideologically from presenting the conferees with the very facts that would have supported his call for reform most persuasively. He could not say that the democratic socialists had been proved right in that the growth of state regulation in the West had belied the inevitability of capitalism's downfall, or that the ruling classes had proved ready (if not always willing) to reform the system rather than see it destroyed. And he could not tell the delegates that the Western welfare state had improved the lot of workers beyond the subsistence level to which Marx had said they were fated (or that their standard of living today is far higher than that of those privileged to live under Communism).

Gorbachev also was not free to call attention to certain telling ironies. For starters, there was Marx's prediction that capitalism would become so complex that it would require central planning. The irony, of course, is that the Soviet economy has become too complex for planners, and it is Communism that now requires the liberated guidance of the free market's "invisible hand." He could not say (at least not with the chief party ideologue, Comrade Egor Ligachev, sitting beside him on the dais) that both Marx's dialectic and his materialism had been proved wanting. Borrowing the notion of the historical dialectic from the philosopher Georg W. F. Hegel, Marx had predicted that society would march inexorably forward from capitalism to Communism, just as it had progressed from feudalism to capitalism. While Marx was right when he forecast the growth of giant multinational businesses (a truly remarkable prediction in the 1860s), few of the other "inevitabilities" of his dialectical explanation of history have occurred as he foretold.

His "materialism" has fared only slightly better. Marx believed that all of human behaviour could be explained by "scientifically observable" physical causes and, in the words of the historian Jacques Barzun, "of all material causes the . . . economic, being closest and most common, is the most persuasive." Thus, according to Marx, we are all slaves to economic determinism. As Barzun writes, "Surely the whole point of [Marx's] contrasting 'scientific' socialism with utopianism is that, where the latter is a plan depending on the goodwill of men to carry out, the former represents the inevitable course of history." But there was Gorbachev at the conference *plan in hand*—worse, a plan that contradicted the "inevitable course of history"! Because Marx's shade was floating around the Palace of Congresses, Gorbachev could not offer the conferees evidence that the recent course of history in the Western world had *not* been preordained but had been created as an expression of the collective, democratic will of the voters. Gorbachev was barred by Marxist dialectic from making the Western politician's best argument for change: *the people want it*.

Nor, in calling for the creation of small, cooperative enterprises and the devolution of political power along the lines advocated by the utopian socialists, could Gorbachev call attention to what was, perhaps, Marx's biggest error—namely, the abolition of private property. Marx had argued that economic injustice is caused by the private ownership of capital, all of which, according to Marx, was owned by the wealthiest 10% of the population. As the philosopher Mortimer Adler argues, "If that is the case, then the remedy is not the abolition of private ownership, but rather overcoming its concentration by diffusing its ownership." Marx proposed doing the opposite, lumping the ownership of the means of production in the hands of the state and thus "concentrating all economic and political power in the hands of the central government and its bureaucrats—a totalitarian state in which all workers may be equal but in which none is free."

Worker ownership is one way of resolving the Marxian contradiction identified by Adler. The welfare state is another, and so is the progressive free enterprise management philosophy practiced by such firms as Volvo and SAS in Sweden and Herman Miller, Motorola, and NCR in the U.S. Duke University's Thomas Naylor, author of *Gorbachev's Strategy*, has had lengthy discussions with Soviet managers and economists who claim to be much taken by this progressive movement in Western management, particularly by the Swedish experience. But Gorbachev could not mention these alternatives *even as he proposed adopting key aspects of each*.

Reforms in the U.S.S.R. and China have engendered freedoms once associated solely with the West. The U.S.S.R. has tolerated Western businesses and ideals, allowing Soviets to enjoy the taste of pizza (top left) and victory at a local beauty pageant (right). In China rock groups such as Fu Ban (above) now play to crowds in Beijing's (Peking's) Forbidden City.

(TOP LEFT) NOVOSTI/SOVFOTO; (RIGHT) V. SHONE—GAMMA/LIAISON; (BOTTOM LEFT) A. KELER—SYGMA

Gung Ho in Wenzhou. China, too, suffers from ideological barriers to reform, although the country is some ten years ahead of the Soviet Union in its efforts to de-Stalinize its economy. In 1976 China was a depressed, backward third world state. A decade later, the streets and shops from Guilin (Kweilin) in the south to Harbin in the north are abuzz with entrepreneurial action à la Hong Kong, and Chinese youth dress like their overseas counterparts, listen to rock music, and watch Western movies. Output of private enterprise in China has grown by 80% per year in the 1980s and now accounts for nearly a quarter of all retail sales.

Unlike the Soviets, the Chinese take to free enterprise like Peking duck to pancakes. Traditional Chinese culture has always been congenial to individual risk-taking, so the Chinese have been remarkably amenable to the opportunities for entrepreneurialism created by Deng's reforms. In sharp contrast, Russians (who for centuries paid absolute obeisance to the Orthodox Church and to the tsar) typically remain risk-averse and tend to respond to Gorbachev's call for entrepreneurialism by waiting for someone to give them orders.

Nonetheless, it is easy to overstate the results of Deng's reforms. In 1987 China's private sector still accounted for only about 5% of all urban employment, and some 85% of industrial output was still regulated by state planning. And while it is true that on economic matters the Chinese are far less rigid than the Soviets (recall Deng's famous line, "It doesn't matter if the cat is black or white as long as it catches mice"), there are limits to how far the Communist Party of China will go. For example, the city of Wenzhou (Wen-chou) was given carte blanche to liberalize its economy, and the experiment became such a success that over 60% of the city's industrial output soon was produced by the private sector, and the city's standard

of living came to be among the highest in China. The experiment was cut short by conservatives like Premier Li Peng (Li P'eng), who accused the city's capitalists of being "parasites."

The Threat of Pluralism. In terms of political freedom, China may be slipping behind the Soviet Union. While the Chinese people are relatively free to speak their minds (as long as they don't broadcast their ideas), there are still no independent voluntary associations, no independent media, and no free labour markets. Party chief Zhao Ziyang (Chao Tzu-yang), while the chief architect of the economic reforms, nevertheless goes out of his way to contrast appropriate, party-controlled "consultative socialist democracy" with the inappropriate "anarchy of mass democracy."

Increasingly, however, the Chinese leadership is finding it difficult to keep the lid on reform. For example, Chinese astrophysicist Fang Lizhi (Fang Li-chih) has become a constant irritant to the system. Like the dissident physicist Andrey Sakharov in the U.S.S.R., Fang attracts vast audiences of sympathetic students when he argues that democracy is the mother's milk of modernism: "Only freedom of speech will be able to break the tyranny of a 'one-party voice' and bring about the realization of political pluralism" needed for scientific and technological progress. Market reforms are of as little interest to Fang as they are to Poland's Lech Walesa, who, in May 1988, opposed the Polish version of *perestroika*. Free markets—while desirable—aren't the issue, Walesa said. What was needed were "real reforms," specifically, *pluralism*; "Without pluralism, no country can catch up with the 21st century."

But it is pluralism that is most threatening to conservatives like Li Peng, Ligachev, and Polish Communist Party chief Wojciech Jaruzelski. So they resist the tide.

They put the brakes on here and there. For example, they limit the access of their citizens to photocopying machines because the machines might be used for samizdat—for the unofficial, uncontrolled, and uncensored spread of political ideas. Thus Soviet professionals and technicians have far less access to copiers than do Western teenagers, and the spread of technical knowledge is also severely constrained. The Communist world will need a xerographic revolution before it can have a computer revolution, and the consequence will be a true political revolution with unpredictable and threatening ramifications.

Thus Marxism faces a choice of death by democracy or death by technological obsolescence. Not coincidentally, "the other socialism" in the democratic West is also faced with a dilemma that threatens its extinction. Its paramount achievement, the welfare state, creates a middle class indifferent to socialism.

Decline of Democratic Socialism. Most Western socialists are not burdened with the freight of dialectical materialism, but they nonetheless avow many of the same goals as orthodox Marxists: greater economic equality, less class differentiation, more far-reaching welfare provisions, full employment, more public goods, and a smoothing out of the business cycle. In the 1950s and 1960s, the rapid postwar expansion of the Western economies allowed democratic socialists to pursue those ends by skimming off the dividends of growth. But when most Western economies stagnated in the late '60s, socialists were forced to pay for the welfare state by raising taxes. This produced two untoward consequences: it removed financial incentives needed to encourage hard work and entrepreneurial activity (thus further exacerbating the financial crisis), and it raised the ire of the burgeoning middle class, whose votes were becoming increasingly important to the socialists.

The only other financing mechanism available to the socialists was the nationalization of industry, which was seen as a "tool" for the redistribution of wealth and power (as the French Socialist leader François Mitterrand put it in 1976). But using this tool proved to be a reform without benefit, as Mitterrand discovered when his program of high taxation and nationalization drove the French economy from prosperity to crisis in three years. And Mitterrand was not alone; by the late 1970s, big spending, left-leaning governments in Italy, Britain, and Scandinavia (and the United States) all presided over economies in disarray.

The voters then revolted. Forced by public pressure to move to the centre, democratic socialists nonetheless have enjoyed only mixed success of late at the polls. The only socialist governments in power in Europe are in Spain,

Greece, and Sweden (socialists share power or participate in minority governments in France, Austria, Denmark, Norway, and Italy). Viewed against this background, Messrs. Deng and Gorbachev are seen by many not as brave helmsmen sailing their little reforms into the teeth of a gale of Marxist orthodoxy but, rather, as passengers on a sinking ship called socialism, a ship whose manifest includes every socialist leader from the most crimson Marxist to the palest pink democrat. This interpretation of current events can be given considerable weight by reference to a host of related occurrences around the globe during the last decade:

• Everywhere one looks, governments of all political stripes have been "privatizing" once-nationalized industries.

• Throughout the developed world, taxes are being reduced and entrepreneurialism and venture capital are being encouraged.

• Socialist governments in democratic countries have turned their backs on the basic tenets of socialism, the rhetoric of class struggle, and the idea that free markets are inimical to social justice.

• Leftist intellectuals are aiming rhetorical brickbats not only at Soviet-style Communism but at traditional Western European socialism as well.

• Such third world countries as India and Indonesia—once hotbeds of socialism—have begun to emulate the market-oriented policies of the third world's most successful countries: Taiwan, Hong Kong, Singapore, and South Korea.

• Die-hard Marxist regimes in Mozambique, Kampuchea, and Vietnam are creating openings to Western capitalism. There is soon to be a Club Med in Da Nang.

And then there is Mrs. T's capitalist revolution.

Capitalism Triumphant? The record of Britain's Conservative Prime Minister Margaret Thatcher during her three terms in office could well be advanced as the strongest single example of capitalism's triumph over socialism. When Thatcher came to power in 1979 after Britain's strike-ridden "winter of discontent," her country had long been plagued by "the British disease"—some two decades of drooping productivity, stagflation, declining standard of living, and diminishing exports. Almost immediately upon accepting the queen's call to form a government, Thatcher cut the marginal tax rate of 83% (on incomes over £24,000) to 60% and put into motion a decade-long program of privatization of state-owned industry. The results have been impressive. Since 1981 Britain's economy has grown at a real rate of 3% per annum (second only to Japan's). Inflation is down and Britain's share of world markets is up. Industry has rebounded: British Steel—which had set a world record for the

Socialism v. Capitalism: Which System Performs Better?

Market-oriented economy	Per capita GNP[1]	Female life expectancy at birth	% Population age 25+ completed primary education	Persons per telephone receiver	Centrally directed economy	Per capita GNP[1]	Female life expectancy at birth	% Population age 25+ completed primary education	Persons per telephone receiver
West Germany	12,080	78.1	100%	1.5	East Germany	11,180	75.4	100%	4.4
Austria	10,000	76.4	100%	2.0	Hungary	7,890	73.2	98.7%	7.2
Puerto Rico	5,190	79.0	92.0%	4.3	Cuba	2,690	76.1	60.4%	19
Taiwan	3,750	75.9	77.0%	3.2	China	300	70.7	55.5%	149
South Korea	2,370	71.8	85.7%	4.5	North Korea	860	72.0	...	2,000
Thailand	810	67.7	79.5%	53	Burma	200	55.0	44.2%	710
Côte d'Ivoire	740	54.0	24.7%	97	Guinea	320	41.8	...	310
Kenya	300	54.7	41.4%	74	Tanzania	240	50.7	10.6%	195
United States	18,300	78.1	92.5%	2.0	Soviet Union	8,410	73.3	99.8%	9

Note: The table compares neighbouring countries that are broadly similar ethnically, industrially, and in terms of natural resources but that have quite different economic systems. The capitalist economies outperform socialist ones rather easily on economic measures and marginally on social measures.
[1]Per capita gross national product estimates for the centrally planned economies are not strictly comparable with Western estimates.

largest corporate loss in 1980 ($4 billion), is now one of the world's most efficient steel producers. Most British subjects have fared as well as the economy. Between 1979 and 1987, car ownership in Britain rose from 54 to 66%, homes with telephones increased from 67 to 81%, home ownership jumped from half to two-thirds of all families, and the share of the population qualifying as middle class grew from 30 to 40%.

To some degree, Mrs. T's British *perestroika* was achieved by breaking the backs of the trade unions. Since 1979 union membership in the U.K. has dropped from 51 to 37% of the work force, and days lost through industrial action have fallen from 29.4 million to fewer than 2 million. Part of this decline was due to legislation curbing union power and part to the enormous growth of Britain's new high-tech, service, and financial industries whose work forces tend not to be organized. Not coincidentally, there has been an entrepreneurial renaissance in Britain—specifically, in southern England. For instance, the city of Oxford, once as famous for being the Detroit of England as for its university, is now the Boston of England, ringed with high-tech startups.

Most remarkable, Thatcher's success was based also on the introduction of a 19th-century "utopian socialist" idea: she won over a great section of the working class to the Tories by making employees owners of the newly privatized firms (stock ownership in Britain has risen from 7 to 21% of the population). Still there are a few nagging by-products of Thatcher's revolution. The fruits of her efforts have been slow to trickle up to the country's industrial heartland; such manufacturing cities as Manchester, Liverpool, and Glasgow have declined while most cities in the south have grown affluent. Moreover, the gulf between rich and poor, always a serious issue in class-ridden Britain, has widened. While fully 10% of the working class has joined the middle class, those left behind are worse off financially now than they were under socialist governments. Presently, the U.K. has chronic double-digit unemployment and the distinction of being the first European country to have U.S.-style social problems, ranging from second-generation welfare families to gangs, drugs, child abuse, and racial conflict.

Even though 30% of British labour union members voted Conservative in the 1987 election, the Tories did not garner a majority of the votes cast, and Thatcher's personal popularity, as measured by the polls, is in long-term decline. Some have sought to explain this phenomenon as a peculiarly British quirk, a paradoxical penchant of Britons to punish the person who cured

them. But one can identify a pattern in the behaviour of Western voters that is consistent with the U.K. experience. For instance, across the Channel, Europe's only other successful ideological free-market politician, Jacques Chirac, suffered at the hands of French voters in 1988 after enacting a series of Thatcherite reforms. Thus, in the last two French election years, voters first punished the socialists for nationalizing over 10% of the economy and then, two years later, punished the conservatives for threatening social entitlements (and for a lack of ethics that included selling off state-owned companies to a hard core of Chirac's campaign contributors).

Welfare State Survives . . . and Thrives. It is important to understand that the decade-long revolt at the polls against left-wing governments was *not* against the benefits of the welfare state, or even against the philosophy of welfare statism. Rather, the reaction was against the enormous costs of the programs and the inefficient and ineffective ways in which they were administered. As for the four pillars of the welfare state—health, education, pensions, and welfare (a category that includes unemployment compensation and aid to poor families)—those programs were sacrosanct. The conservatives who came to power in the late '70s and '80s understood this. Like Thatcher and Ronald Reagan in the U.S., they cut taxes, privatized firms, deregulated industries, and trimmed the power of the unions. Thus conservatives moved to "counter socialism" without touching democratic socialism's only real accomplishment.

The pattern has been the same almost everywhere in the developed world: voters favour the freedom and efficiency that come with entrepreneurialism, privatization, and reduction of taxes and regulations while at the same time favouring the welfare state and governmental efforts to decrease inequalities and inequities caused by the market. Thus, while socialism may be moribund, it probably cannot be said that laissez-faire capitalism is ascendant. For while Communist and traditional leftist parties (like Britain's Labourites) have lost ground almost everywhere, the big gainers have not been the major conservative parties. A few quixotic parties like the Austrian Freedom Party on the right and the Greens on the left have gained ground, but most of the protest vote has gone to centrist parties like Bettino Craxi's Socialists in Italy. In effect, voters in democratic countries seem to be rejecting both the ideological left *and* the ideological right.

The International Cultural Revolution. Significantly, the current "demise of socialism" comes hard on the heels of a similarly ballyhooed "death of capitalism" a decade

DRAWING BY OLIPHANT; © 1987 UNIVERSAL PRESS SYNDICATE.
REPRINTED WITH PERMISSION. ALL RIGHTS RESERVED

"Where did we go wrong?"

10

earlier. The "illogical" coexistence of the observed decline of *both* doctrinaire capitalism and doctrinaire socialism may indicate a common cause of the "morbidity" of both ideologies. Indeed, the most cogent explanation offered for capitalism's purported decline contains elements of an equally convincing explanation for socialism's presumed fatal malaise. Over a decade ago, Daniel Bell and other American neoconservatives suggested that capitalism's undoing was caused by "cultural modernism," the intellectual movement that reached its zenith in the works of such avant-garde thinkers and artists as Freud, Picasso, Joyce, and Stravinsky before degenerating in the 1960s into what the neoconservatives called "hedonism." By placing the individual (as opposed to the community) at the centre of things, modernism, according to Bell, created demands for instant gratification that were contradictory to the self-sacrifice required by capitalism.

Today it is popular culture, now global instead of Western, material instead of intellectual, that is undercutting *all* ideologies, beginning with the least flexible: doctrinaire Marxism. Popular culture—as represented by British rock, American films and television sitcoms, Japanese cars, Italian fashions, Scandinavian design, worldwide mass advertising, globally standardized hotel-restaurant-apartment-supermarket-office architecture, multinational corporations, international Olympic and professional sports, and a transnational system of finance and banking—is not only knocking the socialist movement for a loop, it also is changing values in non-Communist Asia, Africa, and Latin America, undermining traditional societies, challenging authoritarian governments, and altering the way Westerners think about politics, society, and economics.

Let me illustrate the point: On a 1986 trip to the once industrial city of Ghent in Belgium, I came across a square that I had first visited some 25 years earlier. On that first trip, the square had been grimy and dominated by the run-down, turn-of-the-century headquarters of the Socialist Party and its affiliated unions. Not only had the building been in keeping with the surrounding architecture, the pronouncements that had emanated from its bureaus rang true to the young students with whom I had drunk beer at the time. A quarter of a century later, that still-grimy Socialist Party building remained on that same venerable square, but now it was surrounded by boutiques, discos, chic restaurants, and an American-style supermarket. To the generation that frequented them, the rhetoric of socialism had little relevance.

Paradoxically, the goals of the long-dead men and women who had built the Socialist Party headquarters had been realized in Ghent. The city's satanic mills were gone, class differences had all but disappeared, a welfare state provided health services and education, and the standard of living of the average Belgian was quite high. In short, the social and economic equality sought by the early socialists existed to a degree they had never thought possible, at least not without a revolution to destroy "bourgeois freedoms."

A revolution did in fact, occur. It was a revolution unanticipated by those on the left (and often opposed by those on the right). It came about as a result of peace and prosperity, of technological change and the growth of a service economy, of free market entrepreneurialism, of a liberal democracy enacting key parts of the socialist agenda, and, perhaps most important, as a result of the spread of popular culture. Because of these changes, the young people of Ghent—like the youth of most of the free world—had a new social consciousness. But it was not the class consciousness envisioned by socialists.

Thus socialism's steep descent—like that of capitalism a decade earlier—may be part of a much larger international transformation, of a magnitude last experienced during the Industrial Revolution. Changes taking place in the Communist countries (and complementary events around the globe) might be explained by the emergence of a worldwide *cultural revolution* fueled by the new technologies of communication—inexpensive television sets, radios, tape recorders, and video players, sophisticated, computerized telephones, communications satellites and fax machines, photocopiers and jet airplanes. The effects of the international cultural revolution are most obvious in the emerging trend toward global homogenization, a process that has accelerated dramatically in the last dozen years.

Within living memory, each of the world's cities and countries was (materially, at least) unique. One could never have confused the sights of China with those of the Congo, or the look of Chichicastenango with that of Copenhagen. Today, buildings in Frankfurt look like buildings in Fresno. Toyotas clog the streets of Stockholm and Singapore. Stumble into a remote Indonesian village and Sony televisions and Nestlé chocolate will make you feel at home. Most dramatic has been the rise of suburbia. While the central cities of Paris, Budapest, San Francisco, and Stockholm retain marks of their glorious pasts, the *suburbs of these cities are all identical.* And as pollsters around the world are discovering, *there are few socialists there.*

The global cultural revolution has led to a notable convergence among the world's politico-economic systems, particularly in the developed countries. The once vast differences in governmental policies and economic structure that distinguished, say, Sweden from Japan in the 1930s are narrowing rapidly. If one sets aside the short-term changes that occur in the policies of all governments, one can discern several trends common to most Western democracies. The first we have already discussed: the rise—and apparent permanence—of the welfare state. The second (again, one anticipated by the remarkable Daniel Bell) has been a marked decline in ideology in the politics and governance of Western democracies; from the Antipodes to Scandinavia, we are all centrists now.

The third trend: most advanced nations have evolved two-tier economies. One tier, comprised of small- and medium-sized farms and firms, represents the classic free market. Most Western nations consider the invisible hand of the market as the most appropriate constraint on this petty capitalistic activity. In contrast, the large enterprises of the second tier are seen as multipurpose organizations serving social, political, and technological as well as economic ends. Hence, all nations exert public control over large corporations, whether by state ownership, government regulation, or cooperative arrangements between management, government, and, frequently, unions. In every democracy, where the market works well it is given the freedom to function (as when establishing the price and supply of shoes, shirts, and shampoo). Equally, there is agreement that government action is legitimate in areas where the market fails to be self-regulating (as in internalizing the costs of pollution or ensuring worker safety).

The last—and most important—trend is political pluralism. No way has been found to organize a complex, technologically advanced society other than to provide freedom of association to disparate organized groups—religious, ethnic, professional, special interest, and so forth. Pluralism protects and empowers individuals by allowing them to organize voluntarily with like-minded people; it

is beneficial to society as a whole because it promotes the expression of healthy differences of opinion. It serves as a major vehicle of progress and change and a bulwark against the power of the state.

Marxist Parallels. The last two of these trends— economic bifurcation and pluralism—now seem to be infiltrating Communist systems as well. Hungary, Yugoslavia, and China are developing small first tiers of privately owned farms, shops, and factories that are left free to operate under the discipline of supply and demand (and the appropriateness of central planning in the second tier is now being tentatively questioned). While *speculative* ownership of second-tier corporations is still roundly rejected, *worker* ownership is becoming the preferred mode. Almost all large firms are worker-owned in Yugoslavia; most Hungarian farms are *cooperatives* rather than state *collectives;* and in China, where agriculture is more cooperative than collectivist, some industrial workers now own shares in the firms where they work. Gorbachev is attempting to dismantle the original (and still the largest) economy not structured in this fashion. If he succeeds, only a few Stalinist states (Romania, Bulgaria, Albania, North Korea) will lack vital first-tier economies.

Much more threatening to Communist rulers than free markets is the spectre of democracy because it is through the door of pluralism that counterideological cultural values enter the system. Opening a closed system to even one independent group can—and usually does—quickly lead to demands for the rights of other groups and, ultimately, to questioning of the party's authority. It is significant that the only Marxist states where there are no demands for reform are small countries like Albania and North Korea that have been completely sealed off from contaminating external influences. Hence, the risk Gorbachev and Deng run when they allow the modicum of freedom needed to stimulate innovation and revitalize their economies is that their systems will get "out of control." That condition of being "out of control" is what Westerners recognize as a functioning democracy. To the totalitarian, of course, it is tantamount to anarchy.

Pluralism and Individualism. Pluralism is particularly dangerous to the Communist nations today because the first external influences that sneak into a totalitarian system are the values of the popular culture. At base, these values are individualistic. They do not constitute direct demands for capitalism (as those on the right claim) or against Communism (as those on the left fear). Instead, the demand is for the immediate satisfaction of the individual's material wants and his or her right to self-expression. Ironically, popular culture is the most egalitarian movement in history—more so than Communism—because it says to each and every person: "*You* are entitled. Do *your* own thing. Get *yours* now." It is that set of values, and not capitalist ideology, that neither China nor the U.S.S.R. has been able to hold at bay.

Here we must give Marx his due: over a century ago, he argued that the search for new markets "chases the bourgeoisie over the whole surface of the globe," and this process breaks down nationalism and creates what he called "cosmopolitanism." Marx was on target when he then concluded that global capitalism "creates a world after its own image." One can explain the decline of Marxism and the rise of the international cultural revolution by using this Marxist logic. In *Das Kapital,* Marx argues that new classes evolve as the result of changing technology, and that the new classes change the order of social relations. One might say that today's revolutionary class is the middle class of the developed world, together with

Throngs of shoppers jam the aisles and counters at a department store in Shanghai. Today's shopper in China can buy almost anything—from designer watches to Kentucky Fried Chicken.
J. P. LAFFONT—SYGMA

its growing counterparts in the Eastern bloc. In the Soviet Union itself there is now an expanding educated and "cosmopolitan" middle class demanding a kind of freedom that Marx had not anticipated. To Marx, freedom had to do with entire classes possessing the means to achieve their basic material needs. But the middle classes of the Soviet Union have had their basics fairly well satisfied, and now they want to vote, to travel, to wear blue jeans, to watch foreign films. whatever. Popular culture has brought demands for individualism—a development with which the delegates at the Moscow party conference were completely unprepared to cope.

"A Word Is Not a Sparrow." The same Chinese who only yesterday were Red Guards wearing drab, ill-fitting Mao jackets and parading "capitalist roaders" in humiliating dunce caps through the streets of Shanghai are, today, "Chuppies," preoccupied with the pursuit of the "eight new things" (colour television sets, "boom boxes," designer watches, electric fans, motorbikes, cameras, refrigerators, and washing machines). Like the pop singer Madonna (herself a hit among China's peasants and workers), Mao's children have turned into material girls and boys. A symbolic break in the dike of Maoism came in 1980 when an enterprising worker in Shanghai's #8 Plastic Factory extruded his country's first "flying saucer toy" in defiance of the central plan. It was no time at all between the first launching of a Frisbee across Nanking Road and the first munching of a Colonel Sanders chicken leg in Beijing. In the Soviet Union, the war was lost in May 1988 when a Pepsi commercial featuring the pop culture idol Michael Jackson appeared on Moscow television.

Once breached, the Soviet and Chinese systems will never be the same. While the path from Big Brother to Big Mac is not a straight one, there can be little question that Michael Jackson is a far more subversive threat to Marxist orthodoxy than Ronald Reagan, and the showing of "Dallas" on Chinese television does more to undermine collectivist thinking than would an airing of Milton Friedman's series about capitalist economics, "Free to Choose." If that were not the case, party ideologues would not be fighting the cultural trends so vigorously. If the demands for change came from a few ideologically oriented intellectuals who wanted to watch Milton Friedman on TV, they could be packed off to the

Gulag. But *this* is a serious threat: it comes not from the University of Chicago but from Hollywood, speaking to the masses in a language they can understand.

Chinese and Soviet leaders are quite aware that materialistic demands go directly to the soft underbelly of the Communist system. That is why the recent resurgences of Maoist orthodoxy in Deng's China have been characterized by attacks not on the market pricing of goods but on the "spiritual pollution" emanating from the West. Chinese rightists like Li Peng and Deng Liqun (Teng Li-ch'ün) can live with a reduction in agricultural collectivism, and Soviet conservatives like Ligachev can bite the bullet on bankruptcies, but they are threatened to the core by the "decadence" symbolized by miniskirts, discos, blow dryers, and Barbie dolls. Thus, in both China and the Soviet Union, the prime targets for Marxist "conservatives" (everyone else's leftists) are cultural and not economic. For as certainly as holding hands leads to snuggling, "pollution" from the West leads to demands for artistic freedom at home, and that leads to criticism of the party. Open the door to The Who and wham, next thing somebody is demanding secret ballots!

Thus Deng and Gorbachev have been behaving like ballroom dancers: every two steps taken toward the liberalization of culture and the arts have been accompanied by artful backsliding and sidestepping. As a result, the cultural climate in the two countries has alternated between what the Chinese call "warm breezes and cold winds." Arthur Miller is allowed to direct his *Death of a Salesman* in Beijing, but the Chinese rock star Cui (Ts'ui) Jan is jailed for singing songs with protest lyrics. Soviet avant-garde artists are allowed to sell their paintings at a Sotheby's auction (but to Westerners only), yet Aleksandr Solzhenitsyn's writings are still banned. Why? Because, as the old Russian expression goes, "A word is not a sparrow. Once it flies, you can't catch it."

Harking back to Daniel Bell and his contradictions of capitalism, we must keep in mind that this ongoing cultural revolution is not one that pleases all Westerners. Much like a contemporary Soviet or Chinese conservative, America's Irving Kristol wrote in 1978 that "the enemy of liberal capitalism today is not so much socialism as nihilism." This nihilism (or hedonism, as Bell had called it) was represented by books, films, and television shows that glorified the popular culture's opposition to the traditional Judeo-Christian values of family and hard work and to the institutions of "liberal bourgeois" society. But Western democratic societies have proved far more resilient than expected. A decade later, these same bourgeois societies have encapsulated popular culture and

co-opted it. Michael Jackson now *works for* Pepsi and Walt Disney.

Will the Marxists learn from the West's experience? Probably not. As the citizens of the Communist states begin to go shopping in capitalism's cultural cafeteria, Marxist conservatives are echoing Kristol. And they have every reason to be quaking in their boots, for the Communist countries have none of the institutionalized flexibility that allowed the West to ride out the popular cultural storm.

Western Socialism After the Cultural Revolution. While orthodox Marxists fight a rearguard action against the international cultural revolution, Western socialists are regrouping, but they have a way to go before recovering the ground lost in the last decade. By the mid-1980s socialists were in retreat in nearly every democratic nation. The new, educated middle class had grown weary of the excesses of the socialists' chief ally, the labour unions, and conservatives had robbed them of their only tools, taxation and nationalization. Worse, the socialists were left without a strategy, without an identity, and without clear ideas about how to overcome their decline. Only one thing was certain: after the cultural revolution, no political party that promised single-minded pursuit of equality could succeed in a free election in the West. In the late 1980s the electorate demanded not only equality but also liberty, not only industrial efficiency and economic growth but also a concomitant improvement in the quality of life.

In Britain the Labour Party has attempted to counter Thatcher's successful capture of the high ground of liberty by claiming that socialism offers a greater sum total of freedom than does capitalism. Updating the Marxian notion of "freedom to," Labourite Roy Hattersley argues that being free do to something is a useless right unless one has the wherewithal to exercise it. For example, the right to decent housing is hollow if a citizen lacks the money to buy or rent a house. Hence, Hattersley proposes that socialists champion a political principle proposed by the Harvard philosopher John Rawls, namely, that the benefits of society must be distributed *un*equally in favour of the least advantaged. This is, of course, the principle underlying affirmative action. As attractive as this philosophy is to the intelligentsia, it has proved controversial and difficult to put into practice, and it has not caught on with the electorate in any nation.

A more promising strategy has been to borrow the page on efficiency from the capitalists' book. In 1988 France's centrist Socialist prime minister, Michel Rocard, came to power on the promise of running the economy more efficiently than the conservatives. His argument was simple: If capitalist economies, left to their own devices, do not grow fast enough to support the welfare state, then government involvement in the economy is justified to avoid a greater evil: the socially divisive need to partition a shrinking economic pie. The model of business-government partnership most frequently cited by Rocard and the new breed of socialists is Sweden's. Sweden has Western Europe's highest taxes, largest public sector, most generous welfare state, most powerful unions, and highest level of social and economic equality—all factors conservatives would claim lead to the loss of political freedom and economic efficiency. Yet Sweden also has Europe's lowest rate of unemployment, many of the continent's most successful large corporations, a dynamic entrepreneurial sector, and a standard of living and degree of political freedom comparable to those of the United States. Democratic socialists argue that this accomplishment is a product of Sweden's quasi-socialistic

---

Glasnost in the Soviet Press

Excerpt from a letter published in the March 1988 issue of the Soviet magazine *Ogonyok*; reprinted in the *New York Times,* April 24, 1988.

. . . having published Vasily Aksyonov's article, Communists wanted to know whether it is true that he writes on behalf of Soviet citizens. I say yes, it is true. I thank God that in this world there exists America, which won't allow this plague of socialism to spread.

—(Signed) A. Petrov
Naberezhny Chelny, U.S.S.R.

system, the key elements of which include such *free market practices* as private ownership of corporations, pro-growth regulatory policies, and conservative fiscal and monetary policies, *coupled with an active governmental role* in support of research and development and high-tech ventures, active programs of worker training, and laws that encourage labour-management cooperation.

Advocates of government-business cooperation argue that this system is not only superior to Marxism's stifling controls, it is also more efficient than laissez-faire capitalism. They point out that the most successful post-World War II economies—Sweden and West Germany in Europe; Japan, South Korea, Taiwan, and Singapore in Asia—have been ones in which government played an active role in creating the conditions for long-term growth. Advocates of such policies argue that the government-business partnerships found in West Germany, Sweden, and Japan have given those economies a significant competitive leg up on the U.S. with its decentralized, lassez-faire system of education, training, and research and development. They believe it is not only legitimate for the state to support the formation of private capital, to regulate abuses by corporations, to provide social goods (infrastructure), and to channel national resources in order to make private corporations more competitive in world markets, *it is a necessity because this will lead to greater social justice as well.* The new socialist argument is that countries where there is a strong business-government partnership have fewer of the social problems associated with poverty amid plenty that bedevil the United States and Britain.

This new socialism seems to be catching on. The clearest political trend in the West over the last few years has been the rise of a new breed of "centrist" socialist leader. France's Rocard, Spain's Felipe González, Italy's Craxi, Sweden's Ingvar Carlsson, Austria's Franz Vranitzky, New Zealand's David Lange, and Australia's Robert Hawke have modeled their careers not on those of doctrinaire leftists but on that of former West German chancellor Helmut Schmidt, perhaps the century's most politically moderate, and influential, socialist. If one adds to this list the Social Democratic leaders David Owen of Britain and Aníbal Cavaço Silva of Portugal (who have separated themselves almost entirely from the socialist label), this group constitutes a lion's share of the most popular, influential, and imaginative politicians in the West.

The trick, of course, is to draw the appropriate line between useful government support and counterproductive government interference. The Swedes, with their small, homogenous society, seem to have got the mix right—*for them.* But the proper mix appears to vary from country to country and to be continually changing as social, political, and technological environments change. In truth, neither Western socialists nor conservatives have found *the* formula for social justice and economic growth.

The central failure of Marxist ideology—the belief that there is a single "scientific" solution to the affairs of mankind—brings home a fundamental truth, that the wellspring of social justice is found not in any one ideology but in the continuing byplay of competing ideas in a pluralistic society. By observing the halting transformations of China and the U.S.S.R., Westerners have come to realize that their own frustrating and messy democratic systems have created a greater sense of social justice than ever before existed.

Not Marxism but Madisonism. What shall we call this dynamic emerging order? Many terms seem *almost* accurate: social capitalism, welfare state capitalism, safety-net capitalism, and social entrepreneurialism come to mind. Such conjoining of opposites might lead one to conclude that Marx and Hegel were right: perhaps the thesis (capitalism) did battle with the antithesis (socialism) to produce the current synthesis (capitalistic socialism or socialistic capitalism). But Hegel and Marx envisioned violent confrontations between systems resulting in the emergence of a new order. After all, feudalism had been swept away; why not capitalism as well?

In hindsight, we see that Hegel was not the most prescient of early 19th-century social prognosticators. Rather, it was James Madison who most accurately anticipated the way change would occur in the soon-to-be-industrialized Western world. Whereas most social thinkers of his era (including Marx and Adam Smith) had described systems in which men and women *must* do good, Madison envisioned no single-focused future for the new nation he and his fellow authors of *The Federalist Papers* were creating. In today's jargon Madison was a "process man," and the process he favoured was similar to the one we see at work today throughout the Western world: pluralism. It was Madison who first saw that social justice ensues from the free interplay of competing groups and ideas. And pluralism has become even more important in the late 20th century than it was in Madison's day. The more advanced a society becomes—the more it must deal with the interrelated complexities of the global economy, high technology, and the international cultural revolution—the less it is held together by the traditional bonds of family, religion, community, ethnicity, and shared beliefs. Pluralism thus becomes the only effective mechanism for reconciling the adversarial issues found in a modern society—conflicts between those who seek greater political and market freedom and those who seek equality and economic security, between those who want greater industrial efficiency and economic growth and those who desire a higher quality of life.

All the great domestic political and economic issues facing any advanced nation—including the Soviet Union—can be mapped as conflicts between groups with these different values and goals. The genius of Western democracies is that they have arrived at ways of getting as much of all of these values as possible. A pluralistic society attempts to satisfy *all* competing interests. Because no system is perfect, all the various constituents in a democratic society will never be fully satisfied. Yet, because the system treats the values of all the constituents as legitimate, democracy is the only condition that modern men and women accept as just.

And what is justice? As long as people have different and changing values, there can be no final answer. Democracy is, now and forever, a dynamic process, the goal of which is to keep striking a creative balance somewhere near the moving centre. But the only way to find the centre is through the turbulent, conflict-ridden pluralistic process. The citizens of Western nations have learned to pay the price of political turbulence, flux, and tumult in order to achieve the continual economic renewal, social justice, and institutional legitimacy that emerge from Madison's miraculous process. Now the question is whether the entrenched leaders of the Marxist states will accept the unpredictability and uncontrollability of democracy in order to overcome the technological stasis, social injustices, and institutional illegitimacy of their societies. They will not *want* to do so—that is certain—but, ultimately, they may be *forced* to accept democracy as the international cultural revolution creates irresistible pressures for change. After all, that is the way of all true revolutions.

Gombrich, Sir Ernst Hans Josef

A British art historian, Sir Ernst Gombrich was enormously influential in disseminating widely not only appreciation but also understanding of the visual arts. He was born March 30, 1909, in Vienna and was educated there at the Theresianum and the University of Vienna. In 1936 he went to London, where he joined the faculty of the University of London as research assistant at the Warburg Institute. With the outbreak of World War II in 1939, he joined the radio monitoring service of the BBC. In 1946 he returned to Warburg as senior research fellow. He became lecturer in 1948, reader in 1954, and special lecturer in 1956. He was appointed director of Warburg in 1959 and also professor of history of the classical tradition.

He held a variety of collateral and visiting chairs in other institutions, including that of Slade professor of fine art at Oxford (1950–53) and others at Harvard University, Cornell University, Ithaca, N.Y., the University of Pennsylvania, the University of Cambridge, and University College, London. He was treasurer of the British Museum. Among his many honours were the Erasmus Prize (1975) and an honorary degree from the University of Chicago (1975). In 1987 he was appointed to the Order of Merit. His book *The Story of Art* (1950) was a standard text for two generations of college students. Among his many other works were *Art and Illusion: A Study in the Psychology of Pictorial Representation* (1960), *Norm and Form: Studies in the Art of the Renaissance* (1966), *The Sense of Order: A Study in the Psychology of Decorative Art* (1979), and *Reflections on the History of Art* (1987).

CURTIS LINTINGA

Goodall, Jane

British ethologist Jane Goodall's studies of chimpanzees in the wild made great contributions to the knowledge of human evolution as well as primate behaviour. Born April 3, 1934, in London, she dreamed of being able to observe animals in their native state. Although an excellent student, she left school at age 18 to work until she could save enough money to go to Africa. When she reached her savings goal, she went to Kenya and came into contact with the anthropologist Louis S. B. Leakey, who hired her as his secretary. Under Leakey's supervision she held appropriate odd jobs and, eventually, Leakey suggested that she try a long-term study of chimpanzees.

In 1960 she established her base on Lake Tanganyika within the Gombe Stream Game Reserve, where a band of some 100 chimpanzees lived freely but with government protection from poachers. Over the years her minute observation of the chimps' behaviour and social life broke much new ground, including the notable revelations that these apes used crude tools and that, far from being exclusively herbivorous, they killed and ate insects, fowl, and even smaller simians.

A few years after the start of her study, *National Geographic* magazine sent a photographer, Baron Hugo van Lawick, to Kenya to record her work. He and Goodall were married in 1964. They were later divorced and she married Derek Bryceson, a member of Tanzania's parliament and director of the country's national parks.

In 1965 she was awarded a Ph.D. from the University of Cambridge. From 1970 through 1975 she was visiting professor of psychiatry and human biology at Stanford (Calif.) University. Her writings, several of which were illustrated by her first husband, include *My Friends the Wild Chimpanzees* (1967), *Innocent Killers* (1970), *In the Shadow of Man* (1971), *The Chimpanzees of Gombe* (1986), and *My Life with the Chimpanzees* (1988).

MANNI MASON'S PICTURES

Hawking, Stephen

Despite devastating physical handicap, Stephen Hawking not only was generally acknowledged to be Einstein's successor as the world's preeminent living theoretical physicist but also showed himself a superb communicator to lay readers of extremely difficult physical concepts. Hawking was born Jan. 8, 1942, in Oxford, England. From childhood, his intelligence was almost intuitive in its instant grasp of the way things worked. He had concluded that astronomy would be his specialty before he graduated from University College, Oxford, in 1962. While pursuing graduate studies at the University of Cambridge, where he earned a Ph.D. in 1966, he became afflicted with amyotrophic lateral sclerosis, a progressive, incurable neuromuscular disease. With support from his tutor and the language student whom he married in 1965, he refocused his life and adapted with nearly superhuman determination to his growing physical immobilization.

Hawking's numerous contributions to physics—particularly in relativity theory, quantum mechanics, and the physics of black holes—earned him many high honours. In 1974 the Royal Society elected him one of its youngest fellows. He became professor of gravitational physics at Cambridge in 1977 and two years later was appointed Cambridge's Lucasian professor of mathematics, the position once held by Isaac Newton. His publications include *General Relativity: An Einstein Centenary Survey* (1979), *Superspace and Supergravity* (1981), and *The Very Early Universe* (1983). His *A Brief History of Time: From the Big Bang to Black Holes* (1988) was notable for its comprehensibility to nonscientists.

Kennan, George Frost

A U.S. diplomat, historian, and author, George Kennan spent his life in international affairs. He was born Feb. 16, 1904, in Milwaukee, Wis., and received an A.B. from Princeton University in 1925. After training with the U.S. Foreign Service, he was posted as vice-consul to Germany in 1927. He attended a special school on Russian history, politics, and language (1929–31) run by the Foreign Service in Berlin. He went to Moscow in the entourage of the first U.S. ambassador in 1933 and became third secretary the next year. He held consular and other assignments in Vienna, Moscow, and Berlin, becoming first secretary in Berlin in 1940.

He was assigned to Lisbon as counselor to the American Legation and in 1944 went to London as counselor to the U.S. delegation to the European Advisory Commission looking at postwar relations among the Allies. After serving as minister-counselor in Moscow (1945), he

COURTESY OF GEORGE F. KENNAN

was named director of the State Department's Policy Planning Staff (1947) and was made long-range adviser and counselor to the department in 1949. He spent about two years at the Institute for Advanced Study, Princeton University, and then served as ambassador to the U.S.S.R. (1952). He returned to the Institute for Advanced Study, where he was named a permanent professor in 1956. He remained there, with occasional interruptions to teach elsewhere and to serve during the Kennedy administration as ambassador to Yugoslavia. In 1974 he received emeritus status. His influential 1947 article in *Foreign Affairs,* signed "X," outlined the policy of containment of the Soviet Union. His books include *American Diplomacy 1900–1950* (1951), *On Dealing with the Communist World* (1964), *Memoirs* (1972), and *Bismarck: The Man and the Statesman* (1987).

Samuelson, Paul

A highly influential economist, author, educator, and Nobel laureate, Paul Samuelson was unexcelled as an interpreter of economic theory to college students for 40 years and to the highest levels of government and the U.S. public for nearly as long. Born May 15, 1915, in Gary, Ind., Samuelson earned a bachelor's degree from the University of Chicago in 1935 before going on to Harvard University to study economics under Alvin Hansen, the leading Keynesian of the day. There he earned a Ph.D. in 1941 as well as a number of academic honours. His dissertation, published as *Foundations of Economic Analysis* (1947), became an instant classic. While still a graduate student at Harvard, Samuelson accepted a teaching position at the Massachusetts Institute of Technology, where he remained from 1940, becoming a full professor in 1947.

Samuelson's position on the economic spectrum was essentially that of a moderate liberal and definitely not that of an unalloyed Keynesian, a posture that the business community usually found reassuring. His cogent, articulately stated views made him a powerful voice in economic policy. He was a consultant to the RAND Corporation from 1948 to 1975 and was appointed by U.S. Pres. John F. Kennedy to the Council of Economic Advisers and by Pres. Lyndon B. Johnson to the Federal Reserve Board. His impact on society was recognized in 1970 with the Nobel Prize for Economics.

Samuelson's long-running *Newsweek* column and articles in other popular publications informed a generation and more of Americans. Among his books were *Economics: An Introductory Analysis* (1948), still a standard work; *Readings in Economics* (1955); *Linear Programming and Economic Analysis* (1958); and *Collected Scientific Papers* (1966–86, 5 vol.).

REUTERS/BETTMANN NEWSPHOTOS

Chronology of 1988

JANUARY

2   **Canada and U.S. sign trade pact.** Canadian Prime Minister Brian Mulroney and U.S. Pres. Ronald Reagan signed a historic trade agreement that would make Canada and the U.S. the largest free-trade area in the world. The agreement would require ratification by passage through the legislatures of both countries.

3   **Israel to expel Palestinians.** The Israeli Army ordered the deportation of nine Palestinians from the Gaza Strip and West Bank after accusing them of being "chief instigators" of repeated violence in the occupied territories. Some two dozen Palestinians had been killed since anti-Israel demonstrations began on Dec. 9, 1987. All nine men marked for permanent exile were in prison when informed of the deportation order. Their cases could be appealed to a military review board and then, if necessary, to the Israeli Supreme Court. On January 5 the U.S. sided with other members of the UN Security Council in calling the planned deportations a violation of human rights. Undeterred by such criticism, and aware that Egypt and Jordan would not accept any of the deportees, Israel exiled four of the five West Bank Palestinians to Lebanon on January 13. When demonstrators continued to attack Israeli troops with stones and homemade firebombs, Israel officially resorted to beatings, which it said were more humanitarian than shootings.

4   **Witness says soldier shot Aquino.** A worker at Manila International Airport testified in court that he had been an eyewitness to the murder of Benigno Aquino, Jr., on Aug. 21, 1983. The man said he had been driving a tractor about 15 m (50 ft) from the aircraft stairs when he saw a soldier shoot Aquino in the neck as he was being led to the tarmac by two other soldiers. The testimony dramatically confirmed the contention of the prosecution, which had insisted, both before and after the 1985 trial of 25 soldiers and one civilian, that Aquino was the victim of a military assassination. Widespread belief that then president Ferdinand Marcos had taken steps to ensure that all the defendants would be found innocent was one of several major developments that finally forced Marcos into exile in February 1986. Another factor was the presidential election which Marcos claimed to have won but which many people firmly believed had been won by Aquino's widow, Corazon Aquino. The Supreme Court subsequently ordered a new murder trial, saying Marcos had rigged the outcome of the first one.

7   **East German leader visits France.** Erich Honecker, general secretary of East Germany's Socialist Unity (Communist) Party, arrived in Paris for an official visit, the first by an East German leader. Although there was no plan to sign any agreement, the meeting was seen as a small first step toward ending what French Pres. François Mitterrand called a fundamentally artificial split between East and West. French Prime Minister Jacques Chirac remarked that mutual confidence is as important as arms control and that "the destruction of the wall that inhumanly divides Berlin is an essential step in the reestablishment of that confidence." Honecker had previously visited West Germany, Belgium, and The Netherlands, but he had never gone to France, Britain, or the U.S., which together share responsibility for West Berlin.

8   **Salvadoran judge bars amnesty.** A judge of the First Criminal Court in Zacatecoluca, El Salvador, refused to grant amnesty to five national guardsmen who were serving 30-year sentences after being convicted of murdering four U.S. churchwomen in 1980. Three of the five had sought release under a general political amnesty that was part of a broad peace plan for Central America. The judge ruled that the murders were common crimes, not political offenses. In a parallel case, however, two guardsmen convicted of murdering two U.S. land-reform advisers in 1981 were granted amnesty by a different judge. On January 26 a military appeals court announced that three men charged with the slaying of six Americans and seven others in 1985 had committed political crimes or common crimes associated with political crimes and, consequently, qualified for amnesty. U.S. officials and spokesmen for human rights groups strongly condemned the amnesty, even though it had been approved by five Central American presidents in August 1987.

12   **Suriname ends military rule.** Suriname's National Assembly ended seven years of military rule by electing 50-year-old Ramsewak Shankar to a five-year term as president of the South American republic. Henck Arron, who had been prime minister when the military seized power in 1980, was elected vice-president. Shankar was the choice of a three-party coalition that won 40 of the 51 seats in elections to the National Assembly in November 1987. The military was expected to play a significant role in the government for the indefinite future.

13   **Chiang Ching-kuo dies in Taiwan.** Chiang Ching-kuo, president of the Chinese Nationalist government in Taiwan, died in Taipei after a long period of ill health. Chiang had been elected president in 1978, three years after his father, Chiang Kai-shek, died. Chiang had initiated far-reaching political and social reforms before his death and had overseen Taiwan's extraordinary economic development during his nearly ten years in office. He also approved the election of Lee Teng-hui, a native of Taiwan, as his vice-president and automatic successor. Zhao Ziyang (Chao Tzu-yang), head of the Communist Party of China, paid an unexpected tribute to anti-Communist Chiang, praising him for his unswerving commitment to a reunified China.

14   **U.S. jet fighters to leave Spain.** The U.S. announced that it would withdraw 72 F-16 jet fighters from the Torrejón de Ardoz air base near Madrid, as the Socialist government of Prime Minister Felipe González Márquez had long demanded. Spain, however, indicated a willingness to negotiate a new defense treaty that would allow U.S. Navy ships continued access to the port of Rota, near Gibraltar, and permit U.S. military planes use of smaller air bases, one at Morón, the other at Zaragoza. In addition, the U.S. would retain use of nine communications installations. Other details of the agreement were of less significance. In 1986 González had won approval of a referendum endorsing Spanish participation in NATO by pledging to reduce the U.S. military presence in the country. The removal of the three F-16 squadrons fulfilled that promise. The U.S. would also gradually cut by some 40% the 12,500 servicemen it had stationed in Spain. On February 23 the U.S. and Italy announced that the 72 F-16s would probably be transferred to an already existing base in Italy.

18   **Mutiny quelled in Argentina.** About 2,000 Argentine soldiers ended a three-day mutiny at Monte Caseros camp when they captured Lieut. Col. Aldo Rico and about 100 fellow rebels. There was no immediate report on the number of casualties sustained during the three-hour battle. Rico, who had led a revolt against the government of Pres. Raúl Alfonsín in April 1987, escaped from house arrest and seized control of the

Authorities question passers-by and inspect the mangled car from which Colombian Attorney General Carlos Hoyos had been kidnapped by drug traffickers. His body was found hours later in a wood near Medellín.

EL COLOMBIANO—SYGMA

camp after being informed he was about to be transferred to a military prison. Rico had vigorously opposed the prosecution of high military officers accused of violating human rights during the eight-year "dirty war" that preceded Alfonsín's election and the end of military rule in December 1983. Between 9,000 and 30,000 people "vanished" during the years the country was ruled by the military.

24 **Haiti reports election results.** One week after the presidential election, and seven weeks after the first attempt to elect a president had been interrupted because of violence, Haiti's electoral council announced that 57-year-old Leslie F. Manigat had been elected president with 50.38% of the popular vote. The government of Lieut. Gen. Henri Namphy reported that 35% of the eligible voters had cast ballots, but those who boycotted the election insisted the turnout was considerably lower. There were also claims of wholesale election irregularities. On January 16, the eve of the election, the capital was brought to a virtual standstill by a general strike. A U.S. Department of State spokesman had earlier warned that the election, because of "flaws" in the procedures, would not meet congressional requirements for the resumption of U.S. aid to Haiti. On February 7 Manigat, a former professor of political science, took the oath of office.

25 **Colombian attorney general slain.** Colombia's attorney general, Carlos Hoyos, was kidnapped and slain near Medellín by local drug traffickers. Colombian drug lords reportedly controlled 80% of the cocaine smuggled into the U.S. Two of Hoyos's bodyguards were also killed in the ambush. Hoyos had gone to Medellín to investigate the release from prison of Jorge Luis Ochoa Vásquez, who was wanted by U.S. authorities and was said to be the second most important person in the Medellín drug cartel. Members of the drug operation had vowed total war against anyone seeking to extradite Colombians to the U.S. to face trial. A minister of justice, 21 judges hearing drug cases, and various journalists were among those murdered by drug traffickers in recent years.

26 **Australia celebrates bicentennial.** Australia celebrated its bicentennial with characteristic joviality,

reenacting the arrival of Capt. Arthur Phillip in Sydney Harbour in 1788. The exiled British convicts aboard Phillip's 11 ships were the first Europeans to settle permanently on the continent. Some of Australia's Aborigines were on hand to protest "the white invasion" of their land, but many others stood shoulder to shoulder with white Australians, excited by the sight of the prince and princess of Wales, who represented Queen Elizabeth II, the nation's chief of state. The huge crowds also included tens of thousands of new Australians, immigrants from all over the world.

27 **Thailand turns away refugees.** Thai officials invited reporters to the southeastern province of Trat to witness a boatload of Vietnamese refugees being escorted back out to sea. They had come, as many others before them had come, from Kampuchea. Thailand, apparently feeling it had to take effective action to stem the tide of refugees pouring into the country, inaugurated its stern policy without first notifying the United Nations High Commissioner for Refugees. Thai newspapers had been reporting public anger over the refugee problem and had accused UN officials of encouraging refugees to seek asylum in Thailand.

28 **Sandinistas and *contras* meet.** Officials of Nicaragua's Sandinista government and leaders of the guerrilla movement met for two and a half hours in San José, Costa Rica, to discuss conditions for ending their civil conflict. The government's basic offer was

a guarantee of full political rights to rebels who laid down their arms. The rebels, however, demanded extensive changes in the constitution, the departure of foreign military advisers, immediate amnesty for all political prisoners, and the exclusion of military personnel from government affairs. Hopes were not high that the two sides would resolve their profound differences in the near future. Some observers believed that the Sandinistas were not likely to endorse any agreement that would jeopardize their hold on power, and that the *contras* did not want to weaken U.S. support for their cause by agreeing to a cease-fire without a satisfactory accord on all major issues.

30 **Poland announces price increases.** The Polish government announced a substantial increase in prices, which it said were needed to "limit state subsidies and to accelerate the transition to a market economy." Overall, food prices would increase about 40%, housing and rail fares 50%, gasoline 60%, diesel fuel 100%, liquor 46%, and tobacco 40%. The increases would mean that the expenses of most workers would rise an estimated 36%. The government, however, planned to offset this burden with wage increases of nearly 40%. The following day there were sporadic antigovernment protests, notably in Warsaw and Gdansk. Further price increases, planned for April 1, would raise the price of coal 200% and the cost of gas, electricity, and central heating 100%. A government-sponsored referendum seeking approval of even greater economic austerity had been rejected by the voters in November 1987.

31 **Greece and Turkey reach accord.** Prime Minister Andreas Papandreou and Turkish Prime Minister Turgut Ozal ended a meeting in Davos, Switz., after pledging to work together to promote peace and cooperation between their two traditionally hostile nations. The two countries, both members of NATO, had been on the verge of war in March 1987 over oil and mineral rights in the Aegean Sea. Although the 1974 proclamation of the Turkish Republic of Northern Cyprus (the northern third of the island) had never been accepted by Greece or Greek Cypriots, the two leaders promised to meet at least once a year to discuss mutual problems and foster a more amicable relationship between their two countries.

KOK—GAMMA/LIAISON

A woman in a Polish market posts a price tag on a ring of sausages. The Polish government raised the prices of necessities between 40 and 200% in order to "limit state subsidies and to accelerate the transition to a market economy."

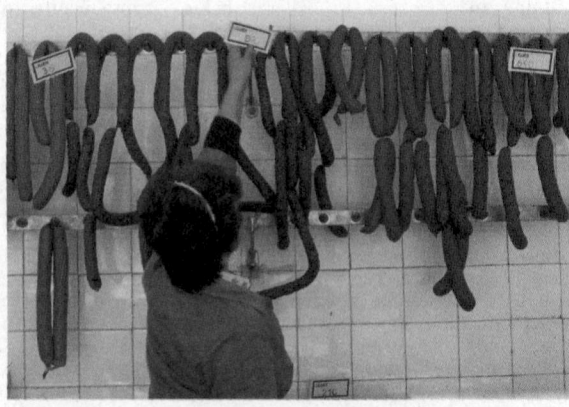

FEBRUARY

4 **Philippine rebels arrested.** Gen. Renato de Villa, chief of staff of the Philippine armed forces, confirmed that 20 suspected Communist rebels had been captured in raids on safe houses around Manila and that a coded list of those who had contributed at home or abroad to the rebel cause had also been seized. Two of those arrested were believed to be members of the Central Committee of the outlawed Communist Party; two others were taken to be regional finance officers. The raids, planned with the help of an informer, also uncovered a rebel field hospital and a number of items used in sophisticated computer-assisted communications systems. At the end of March several other high-ranking rebels were captured, including Rafael Baylosis, alleged general secretary of the Communist Party; Romulo Kintanar, commander of the New People's Army; and Benjamin de Vera, the NPA's logistics officer and a member of the Central Committee of the Communist Party.

5 **U.S. indicts General Noriega.** The U.S. government announced that Panamanian Gen. Manuel Noriega had been indicted by federal grand juries in Miami and Tampa, Fla., on charges of taking millions of dollars in bribes from notoriously violent drug traffickers. Noriega then protected the drug operation and guaranteed the use of secured airstrips in Panama from which illegal drugs could be flown to the U.S. Noriega's involvement with drugs had long been known to U.S. authorities, but a decision was reportedly made to do nothing in order to protect so-called U.S. national security interests. After the indictments were unsealed, U.S. officials attempted to work out an agreement with Noriega that would remove him from the country and restore power to Pres. Eric Delvalle, but the negotiations ended in failure. When, on February 25, Noriega was dismissed as commander of the Defense Forces, he simply ignored Delvalle's order, as did also the officer named to replace him. In the early hours of the morning of February 26 the National Assembly, meeting in emergency session, voted to oust Delvalle; Manuel Solís Palma then took the oath of office as president. Later that day seven Latin-American foreign ministers concluded a three-day meeting of the Group of Eight in Colombia after voting to suspend Panama's participation in its economic and political discussions. On February 27 the military attempted to arrest Delvalle, but he had already gone into hiding.

10 **Bangladesh election a disaster.** During nationwide nonpartisan elections for positions in 4,376 village governments in Bangladesh, about 200 persons were killed and thousands were injured as rival factions fought one another with guns, clubs, rocks, and homemade bombs. In some areas the situation was so out of control that voting had to be suspended. There did not appear to be any connection between the village violence and repeated demands by antigovernment groups that Pres. H. M. Ershad resign. Ershad, however, became the object of vituperation when parliamentary and municipal elections were held on March 3. An alliance of 21 opposition parties urged voters to stage a general strike and to boycott the election which, it was said, would be meaningless anyway because of blatant fraud. Foreign journalists reported that the boycott was highly successful and that patent fraud made the election a political farce. Early returns, according to the election commission, indicated that Ershad's Jatiya Party had won a massive majority in the 300-seat Parliament.

14 **Stroessner wins reelection.** Gen. Alfredo Stroessner, leader of Paraguay's Partido Colorado, was routinely elected to an eighth term as president of the nation. Antigovernment forces claimed that the election had been vitiated by fraud. Although the opposition had no realistic hope of altering the political status quo, large numbers vented their political frustrations by rendering their ballots invalid or by simply refusing to participate in the election, despite a law requiring all citizens to cast ballots if they had reached age 18. Paraguay's main opposition newspaper and radio station had been closed by the government, but the Roman Catholic Church's radio station partially filled the void by reporting statements and activities of the opposition throughout the day.

18 **Boris Yeltsin loses post.** Boris Yeltsin, who had criticized the slow pace of Soviet reform in October 1987 and consequently lost his position as head of the Communist Party in Moscow, was removed from the Politburo by the party's Central Committee. The announcement of Yeltsin's demotion was a major news story because only 20 persons (13 voting, 7 nonvoting) made up the Politburo, and Yeltsin had been nominated to that position by Mikhail Gorbachev, the general secretary of the Communist Party. Yeltsin, it appeared, was being demoted for being too zealous in promoting Gorbachev's own program. He also had attacked Egor Ligachev, second only to Gorbachev in the party's hierarchy, for being too cautious and hesitant in pushing for implementation of badly needed reforms.

Kennedy joins U.S. high court. Anthony M. Kennedy, who had been a judge of the U.S. Court of Appeals for the 9th Circuit in San Francisco, became an associate justice of the U.S. Supreme Court. He replaced Lewis Powell, Jr., who had retired in June 1987. Kennedy, confirmed by the Senate (97–0) on February 3, was President Reagan's third choice to fill the vacancy. The first nominee, Judge Robert Bork, had been rejected by the Senate (58–42) in October 1987 after an acrimonious public debate. Opponents did not want Bork, an advocate of "judicial restraint," to cast the swing vote when liberal and conservative justices were evenly split on important constitutional issues. Reagan's second nominee, Judge Douglas Ginsburg, acknowledged that he had occasionally used marijuana as a student and as a teacher; he then requested that his name be withdrawn from further consideration.

21 **Greek Cypriots choose leader.** George Vassiliou, a millionaire businessman, defeated Glafkos Clerides in a close runoff election for the presidency of Cyprus. Vassiliou, a political independent, won with the support of the powerful Communist Party. Both candidates had promised to step up efforts to reunify the country, which had been split in 1974 when the Turkish Cypriots declared the northern third of the island a separate republic. On February 28 Vassiliou took the oath of office, replacing Pres. Spyros Kyprianou, who had been eliminated from the contest when he finished third in the first-round election held on February 14.

STEPHEN FERRY—GAMMA/LIAISON

Gen. Alfredo Stroessner (centre) of Paraguay's Partido Colorado was elected to an eighth presidential term amid opposition charges of vote fraud.

23 **Armenian unrest worries Moscow.** Soviet news media reported that a worrisome breach of public order was taking place among ethnic Armenians in the southern part of the country. The focus of the unrest was Nagorno-Karabakh Autonomous Oblast, an administrative division of the Azerbaijan Soviet Socialist Republic. For reasons of transportation, the region had been made part of Azerbaijan rather than part of the Armenian Soviet Socialist Republic, even though its population was overwhelmingly Armenian. The Armenians were now demanding that their ethnic identity be strengthened by redrawing borders so that most Armenians would belong to the same republic. Soviet officials in Moscow, however, knew all too well how dangerous to national unity it could be if any ethnic group—and there were scores of them in the Soviet Union—were allowed to dictate government policy. On February 27 leaders of the Armenian community agreed to suspend demonstrations for one month to give Mikhail Gorbachev the opportunity he had requested to study the problem.

24 **South Africa imposes new curb.** The South African government, invoking a 20-month-old national emergency decree, imposed an immediate ban on all activities by the United Democratic Front and 16 other antiapartheid organizations. They were all prohibited from "carrying on or performing any acts whatsoever." The ban was apparently meant to neutralize organizations as such rather than individuals. Leaders of the opposition vowed to defy the ban and warned that such actions would lead to further violence. Anglican Archbishop Desmond Tutu said that white South Africans must realize that they are at a crossroads. He then added: "If they don't stop this government soon, and there's not much hope that they will, we are heading for war."

Court protects outrageous satire. The U.S. Supreme Court voted 8–0 to overturn a lower court award of $200,000 to the Rev. Jerry Falwell for emotional distress. The case involved *Hustler* magazine which, in what Chief Justice William Rehnquist referred to as a parody that was "doubtless gross and repugnant in the eyes of most," depicted Falwell as an incestuous drunk. The Supreme Court justices concluded that the First Amendment guarantee of free speech protected even grossly offensive remarks about public figures as long as the material was not presented as factual. The court noted that political cartoons, even those that have been "slashing and one-sided" and would be judged to be offensive and insulting by disinterested persons, have played a significant role in U.S. political history. They have, therefore, always been considered legitimate expressions of free speech.

25 **Roh Tae Woo assumes office.** Roh Tae Woo became president of the Republic of Korea's Sixth Republic during a ceremony at the National Assembly in Seoul. He replaced Chun Doo Hwan, who did not run for reelection in December 1987. It was the first peaceful transfer of power since Syngman Rhee, the first president of independent Korea, took office in 1948. Roh promised that privilege and corruption would not be tolerated during his single five-year term. The following day the government granted amnesty to 7,234 people, 1,731 of whom were political detainees. On February 11 the president-elect had named Lee Hyun Jae as prime minister.

29 **Senegal racked by violence.** Abdou Diouf, president of Senegal and head of the Socialist Party, declared a state of emergency in the capital city of Dakar in an effort to suppress riots set off by his reelection the day before. Police then moved onto the campus of Dakar University and against the headquarters of defeated candidate Abdoulaye Wade of the Democratic Party. Before order was restored, the police had made numerous arrests and angry crowds had set fire to vehicles. Unofficial government reports gave Diouf about 77% of the popular vote, Wade 21%, and two other candidates the remainder. The opposition charged the government with wholesale election fraud.

MARCH

2 **Deaths reported in Azerbaijan.** A Soviet official confirmed that a number of people had recently been killed in Sumgait, the site of Armenian riots in the Azerbaijan Soviet Socialist Republic. According to unofficial reports, there were 17 fatalities. The Soviet official had earlier acknowledged that military forces had been sent to the area to quell the unrest and that a nighttime curfew had been imposed to limit the possibility of further violence. Observers believed the situation in Azerbaijan was the most serious outbreak of nationalist unrest since the consolidation of the Soviet Union some 65 years earlier. The Armenians were demanding that their region of Azerbaijan be incorporated into the neighbouring Armenian Soviet Socialist Republic.

NATO allies meet in Belgium. Leaders of the 16 nations comprising NATO began a two-day meeting in Brussels, the first gathering of such high-ranking government officials in six years. Their purpose was to discuss future arms control policies vis-à-vis the Soviet Union. In their final communiqué, the Western leaders reaffirmed their unity of purpose and the need to maintain an appropriate mix of adequate nuclear and conventional forces that would be kept up to date as the need arose. Before departing for Europe, President Reagan had declared that the U.S. would never sacrifice the interests of its allies while negotiating further arms control agreements with the Soviet Union. In December 1987 the two countries had signed a historic accord in Washington, D.C., that would, when ratified, provide for the elimination of two classes of intermediate-range weapons systems from each nation's nuclear arsenal.

10 **Suharto elected to fifth term.** Indonesian President Suharto, facing no opposition, was elected to a fifth five-year term by the People's Consultative Assembly (MPR). Suharto's choice for vice-president was known to be Brig. Gen. Sudharmono, who had become the president's closest adviser while serving as his chief of staff for 15 years. He was also chairman of Golkar ("functional groups"), which dominated the government but was not technically a political party. On March 2 Golkar and regional representatives appointed to the MPR nominated Sudharmono for the vice-presidency. Two days earlier, however, Jailani Naro, president of the United Development Party (PPP), had been nominated for the same office by the PPP. The stage was set for unexpected turmoil. Just moments after Suharto was elected, Brig. Gen. Ibrahim Saleh leaped onto the dais and disrupted the proceedings. He appeared to have taken upon himself the role of expressing the discontent of certain fellow officers with the selection of Sudharmono, with Golkar, and with the political tradition that required Naro to voluntarily step aside. Even though he had no hope of being elected, Naro refused to withdraw until the last moment. Sudharmono was then elected unopposed.

11 **Wanton attacks continue in Sri Lanka.** Sri Lankan police reported that as many as 30 masked gunmen had attacked a bus near the northern town of Anuradhapura and killed at least 17 passengers with gunfire and hand grenades. Most of those killed or wounded were identified as Tamils. The ambush was presumed to be an act of retaliation for two incidents earlier in the month. On March 3 Tamils wearing army uniforms suddenly appeared in the doorways of five Sinhalese homes in Morawewa and proceeded to machine-gun the children and adults inside. Two days later Tamil rebels struck again, this time exploding a mine under a truck in Sittaru. The death toll from the two attacks was put at 39. The Tamils, who were predominantly Hindu and constituted a small minority of Sri Lanka's population, had been demanding for several years that areas in the Northern and Eastern provinces of the country be designated Tamil homelands.

13 **Political murders make a farce of Colombian elections.** Municipal elections, intended to prove to Colombia's leftist insurgents that they could participate in a democratic government, became a mockery when the leftist Patriotic Union, according to early returns, won only 14 of more than 1,000 mayoral races. The outcome was predictable because 29 of the Patriotic Union's 87 mayoral candidates, and more than 100 Union candidates running for the office of municipal councillor, were

A billboard in Indonesia bears slogans for President Suharto's reelection campaign. Although Suharto won easily, his choice of vice-president was initially challenged.
ROBERT NICKLESBERG—GAMMA/LIAISON

murdered during the six months preceding the election. Leftist guerrillas added to the violence by retaliating with bombings and assassinations. Fear of rightist paramilitary groups was also a major factor in keeping many people at home on election day, especially in poor rural areas. Unlike the Patriotic Union, the M-19 guerrilla forces and members of the National Liberation Army had continued to fight rather than accept the government's offer to test the democratic process.

16 **IRA mourners murdered at graveside.** Three persons were killed in Belfast, Northern Ireland, and dozens of others wounded when a Protestant terrorist hurled four hand grenades into a crowd of about 5,000 mourners attending the Roman Catholic burial of three Irish Republican Army (IRA) guerrillas. The IRA members, reportedly on a bombing mission, had been slain in Gibraltar by undercover British agents. When the grenades began to explode, many mourners raced after the assailant, ignoring the shots fired in their direction. The gunman, believed to be a member of a paramilitary Protestant gang, was captured and severely beaten before officers of the Royal Ulster Constabulary arrested him. For years the outlawed IRA had been fighting to unite Northern Ireland, which was part of the United Kingdom and predominantly Protestant, with the Republic of Ireland, which was overwhelmingly Roman Catholic. On March 19 two armed British soldiers in civilian clothes were pulled from their car near another IRA funeral and were severely beaten and then shot to death. British authorities said the two men were on their way to an assignment outside Belfast and came upon the funeral by chance. When the men realized their dangerous predicament, they tried to escape by driving directly into the funeral cortege.

Lieut. Col. Oliver North indicted. U.S. Marine Lieut. Col. Oliver North was indicted by a U.S. federal grand jury on charges of conspiracy to defraud the government. The multiple accusations were all connected with North's role in the sale

of U.S. weapons to Iran during 1985–86 and the clandestine transfer of money from those sales to *contra* insurgents fighting Nicaragua's Sandinista government. Also indicted were Rear Adm. John Poindexter, North's superior at the National Security Council (NSC), who in earlier testimony took complete responsibility for authorizing the diversion of funds to the *contras;* Richard Secord, a retired major general in the Air Force, who was suspected of personally profiting from the Iran-*contra* arms deal; and Albert Hakim, an Iranian-American businessman, who served as middleman in the financial transactions and the delivery of supplies to the *contras.* Each defendant faced a different set of charges. North, for example, was accused of obstructing a presidential inquiry by shredding classified documents. Lawrence Walsh, a 76-year-old former judge who began investigating the Iran-*contra* affair after being named special prosecutor, stated that the work of the grand jury was not yet finished. On March 11 Robert McFarlane, Poindexter's predecessor at the NSC, pleaded guilty to four misdemeanour counts of withholding information from congressional committees investigating the Iran-*contra* affair and agreed to serve as a prosecution witness in criminal proceedings. On March 18 North announced that he had submitted his resignation to the Marine Corps because he might require testimony and records "from the highest-ranking officials of our government." On March 24 all four defendants pleaded not guilty in a federal district court to charges of conspiracy, theft, and fraud.

18 **Panama declares state of urgency.** The Panamanian government declared a state of urgency, indicating it was prepared to suspend constitutional rights to restore public order. On March 16 there had been an unsuccessful coup directed against Gen. Manuel Noriega, the de facto ruler of the country. The nation was also plagued by a series of strikes and demonstrations that were, for the most part, spontaneous reactions to the government's failure to issue paychecks to hospital personnel, dock workers, public utilities employees, and

tens of thousands of other civil servants. The Reagan administration had deliberately created the financial crisis in order to disrupt Panama's economy so severely that Noriega, who had been indicted in U.S. courts on charges of drug trafficking, would be compelled to relinquish power. There was, however, no indication that economic pressure by itself would loosen Noriega's hold on the country.

20 **Duarte's party loses election.** El Salvador's political future became even more unpredictable when Pres. José Napoleón Duarte's centrist Christian Democratic Party lost its majority in the 60-seat national Legislative Assembly and suffered staggering losses in municipal elections all across the country. Marxist guerrillas belonging to the Farabundo Martí National Liberation Front attempted to disrupt the election by setting off six bombs in the capital city of San Salvador on the eve of the balloting. They also succeeded in halting virtually all highway traffic and in blowing up electrical lines, which cut off the power supply to 80% of the country. In recent weeks the guerrillas had also killed one mayor and kidnapped at least four others, had blown up the offices of two mayors and dozens of public buildings, and had burned voting cards. Despite such intimidation, many Salvadorans went to the polls to support the right-wing Nationalist Republican Alliance (ARENA). After a controversial recount, the Central Election Council announced that ARENA had won 30 assembly seats, the Christian Democrats 23, and the conservative National Conciliation Party 7. The presidential election scheduled for 1989 would profoundly affect the nation's future.

21 **Sandinistas and *contras* meet.** For the first time, top-ranking members of Nicaragua's Sandinista government and leaders of the *contra* guerrillas met face to face to begin implementation of the Central American peace plan that had been signed by five regional presidents in August 1987. Defense Minister Humberto Ortega Saavedra headed the Sandinista delegation and Adolfo Calero was chief spokesman for the *contras.* Nicaragua's Roman Catholic primate and the secretary-general of the Organization of American States were also present as witnesses. Both sides in the conflict quickly agreed to a cease-fire during their scheduled three days of negotiations in Sapoá, a Nicaraguan town near the Costa Rican border. Prospects for an end to the six-year-old civil war appeared to improve on March 24 when the bitter rivals agreed to continue their talks through the end of the month. Even more important was the signing of an accord that extended the truce through the end of May. In addition, the government promised in writing to grant amnesty to several categories of prisoners, to permit unrestricted freedom of expression, to allow exiles to return home without facing recriminations, and to guarantee full participation in all elections. For their part, the *contras* pledged to restrict their soldiers to specified enclaves within Nicaragua and to accept only humanitarian aid through neutral organizations.

Nicaraguan Defense Minister Humberto Ortega (left) signs a cease-fire agreement with the *contras,* with João Baena Soares, the secretary-general of the OAS (centre), and Nicaragua's Miguel Cardinal Obando y Bravo (right) as witnesses.
AFP PHOTO

23 **Iraq uses toxic gas in Gulf war.** Iran reiterated its accusation that Iraq was making use of toxic weapons in the stalemated 7¹/₂-year-old Persian Gulf war in direct violation of the Geneva Protocol on Gas Warfare signed in 1925. Iran urged the United Nations to send a mission to Halabjah to confirm that some 5,000 civilians had been killed with cyanide and mustard gas when Iraq launched a counterattack to retake the city. A member of the International Institute of Strategic Studies in London, after studying photographs of the victims, said he was "very much persuaded" they had died of chemical agents. According to generally accepted figures, the death toll during the war already exceeded one million.

29 **Six Meese aides resign.** Six top officials of the U.S. Department of Justice resigned their posts after indicating they could not continue to serve under Attorney General Edwin Meese as long as he was being investigated by a special prosecutor. The resignations reportedly stunned Meese and members of the Reagan administration, but the president reaffirmed his "full confidence" in Meese, a longtime friend. Those leaving the Justice Department included Deputy Attorney General Arnold Burns, Assistant Attorney General William Weld, and four of their top assistants. All were said to feel that Meese's legal problems were severely tarnishing the reputation of the agency and disrupting its work. Among

other things, the special prosecutor was probing Meese's ties to Wedtech Corp., a New York military contractor accused of making payoffs to obtain huge government contracts.

31 **South Korea rocked by scandal.** Chun Kyung Hwan, brother of South Korea's former president Chun Doo Hwan, was arrested on charges of influence peddling, tax evasion, illegal reclamation of land, and embezzlement of a vast sum of money while head of Saemaul, a government rural development program. Reports of a criminal investigation had dominated the news for weeks, but the actual arrest of Chun and three associates rocked the nation. Two days earlier five others had been taken into custody, including two of Chun's brothers-in-law. The prosecutor's office revealed that it was still collecting and evaluating evidence of possible bribery and illegal transfers of money outside the country.

Rebels gain in Ethiopia. Ethiopian Pres. Mengistu Haile Mariam publicly acknowledged that government forces were engaged in grim combat against rebel forces in the northern provinces of Eritrea and Tigrai. Calling the escalating conflict a new challenge to the nation's sovereignty, Mengistu noted that the rebels had inflicted numerous casualties, had disrupted communications, and had destroyed public and private trucks, including United Nations convoys carrying food to drought-stricken areas in the north. Relief officials estimated that the lives of as many as seven million people were threatened by the drought. The rebels, who had recently captured three Soviet military advisers, were seeking greater autonomy and a more liberal form of government than that offered by Mengistu's one-party Marxist regime.

APRIL

2 **Honasan escapes from prison.** Gregorio Honasan, a former colonel in the Philippine Army, escaped from a Navy prison ship where he had been confined for leading an unsuccessful coup against Pres. Corazon Aquino in August 1987. Military officers reported that the elite detachment guarding Honasan had been won over by bribes and persuasion and escaped with Honasan in two rubber boats. One week later a lieutenant colonel who had directed an assault on a government television station during the attempted coup escaped on the way back to confinement after a dental appointment.

5 **Kuwaiti plane hijacked.** A reported eight Arabic-speaking gunmen hijacked a Boeing 747 Kuwaiti airliner on a flight from Thailand to Kuwait and ordered the pilot to divert the plane to Iran. The hijackers threatened to kill three members of the Kuwaiti royal family along with other passengers unless Kuwait released 17 Arab terrorists who were in prison for killing 6 persons, wounding 80, and damaging the French

and U.S. embassies in 1983. On April 8, after the gunmen reportedly acquired additional weapons in Iran, the plane was flown to Beirut, but Lebanese officials refused permission to land. The aircraft was then flown to Cyprus, where two Kuwaiti passengers were murdered. On April 13 the plane landed in Algeria. Six days later, after long negotiations, the terrorists allowed the last 24 passengers, who had not been released with 79 others in Iran, Cyprus, or Algeria, to depart. Seven members of the flight crew were also allowed to leave. The hijackers were apparently given free passage out of the country.

Dalai Lama rejects China's offer. The Dalai Lama, the spiritual leader of Tibetan Buddhism, rejected China's offer to return to Tibet provided he abandon his demands for Tibetan independence. The Dalai Lama, however, suggested that some sort of compromise might be worked out in face-to-face meetings with Chinese leaders. The Dalai Lama had fled to India in 1959 after a failed rebellion against Chinese rule. When China's Ch'ing dynasty fell in

1912, Tibet declared its independence, but Chinese troops occupied the country in 1950. The two most violent anti-Chinese upheavals in recent months occurred in September 1987 and in March 1988.

8 **Soviets to leave Afghanistan.** Diego Cordovez, the under secretary-general of the United Nations, announced in Geneva that full agreement had been reached on the withdrawal of all 115,000 Soviet troops from Afghanistan within nine months. Soviet forces had invaded the country on Dec. 27, 1979. The four-part settlement would be signed by Afghanistan and Pakistan; the latter represented the insurgents whom it had supported against the Soviet-backed Afghan government. The U.S. and the Soviet Union would also sign the document as guarantors that the treaty would be observed. Among other things, the future of Afghanistan would be decided by the Afghans themselves, but the country would be committed to neutrality in international affairs. An estimated one million Afghans had lost their lives in the civil war and five million had been made homeless.

Honduras declares emergency. Honduran Pres. José Azcona Hoyo declared a state of emergency in Tegucigalpa, the nation's capital, and in San Pedro Sula, the country's industrial centre and second largest city. The previous night about 2,000 university students had attacked the U.S. embassy annex and set fire to 25 cars in the parking lot. The violence was touched off by news that a Honduran citizen suspected of being a major drug trafficker had been seized and summarily put on a predawn flight to the Dominican Republic. From there he was extradited to the U.S. to face trial. Five of the rioters were reported killed by police who used bullets, tear gas, and nightsticks in an attempt to restore order.

10 **Pakistani ammunition depot explodes.** Explosions at a Pakistani ammunition depot located between Rawalpindi and Islamabad showered the twin cities with rockets, grenades, mortars, and artillery shells. At least 100 people were believed to have died during the series of explosions, large and small, that continued for several hours. Although initial reports suggested the devastation had been triggered by an accident, Pres. Mohammad Zia-ul-Haq did not rule out the possibility of sabotage.

13 **China ends national congress.** China concluded the annual meeting of its National People's Congress after approving the appointment of Li Peng (Li P'eng) as premier and formally sanctioning new policies that were expected to have a significant impact on economic development. Private enterprise was officially approved, as was also the selling of land-use rights. The future role of Communist Party officials in the operation of industrial enterprises was not clearly delineated, but factory directors would be given far greater authority, with corresponding responsibilities, to make their factories profitable and more efficient. China also reorganized its central government. New ministries were established and the work of others redefined; the bureaucracy was trimmed; and younger men were named to posts that gave them authority to formulate policies. The changes wrought by the congress were broadly viewed as being among the most significant since the establishment of the government in 1949.

Italy gets new government. Ciriaco De Mita, Italy's new prime minister, presented his 32-member Cabinet to Pres. Francesco Cossiga for approval. The new coalition, headed by the Christian Democrats, included Socialists, Social Democrats, Republicans, and Liberals—the same five-party alliance that comprised the government of Prime Minister Giovanni Goria before he resigned on March 11. De Mita's government would be Italy's 48th since the end of World War II.

16 **Abu Jihad slain in Tunisia.** Khalil al-Wazir, better known by his nom de guerre Abu Jihad, was assassinated at his home in a suburb of Tunis, Tunisia. He was the senior military officer of the Palestine Liberation Organization (PLO) and considered second only to Yasir

China's newly appointed premier, Li Peng (Li P'eng), addresses the annual meeting of the National People's Congress, calling for continued economic and political reforms.
F. ANDERSON—GAMMA/LIAISON

Arafat in the PLO hierarchy. Although rival Arab groups had been blamed for previous attacks on prominent Palestinian leaders, in this case Israeli commandos were considered the most likely assassins. Israeli leaders, adhering to a general policy of not commenting on any Israeli commando operation, refused to discuss the matter. Ezer Weizman, however, a Cabinet minister without portfolio and a leading proponent of peace talks with the Palestinians, denounced the killing, saying it would not silence terror and might possibly intensify it.

18 **U.S. and Iran clash in Gulf.** During a confrontation in the Persian Gulf, the U.S. Navy sank or damaged an Iranian missile patrol boat, three large armed speedboats, and two frigates while losing one Cobra gunship. All the Iranian vessels had reportedly first

fired on U.S. ships or aircraft. The battle followed the destruction of two Iranian oil platforms by six U.S. Navy ships. The U.S. contended that those attacks were in response to damage sustained by a U.S. Navy frigate on April 14 when it hit an Iranian mine. On April 19 a tanker flying the flag of the United Arab Emirates was set ablaze by Iranian gunboats, but no casualties were reported. The French Navy also reported the sighting of newly laid Iranian mines. On April 26 Saudi Arabia announced it was severing diplomatic relations with Iran. Among other reasons, Saudi Arabia cited Iranian attacks against its ships in the Persian Gulf.

Israel convicts Demjanjuk. John Demjanjuk, a 68-year-old retired autoworker from the U.S., was convicted by an Israeli court of committing war crimes in the Treblinka death camp. Demjanjuk, despite his repeated denials, was identified as "Ivan the Terrible," the man who operated the Nazi gas chamber in the Polish camp where hundreds of thousands of Jews were put to death. On April 25 Demjanjuk was sentenced to die by hanging.

20 **Japanese-Americans get apology.** The U.S. Senate, after heated debate, voted 69–27 in favour of giving $20,000 and an official apology to each Japanese-American interned by government orders during World War II. Only those internees still living would benefit financially from the legislation, which would take final form after small differences between the Senate and House versions were reconciled in committee. The 1942 presidential order, which was signed by Franklin D. Roosevelt and later acknowledged to have been a clear violation of the U.S. Constitution, affected 77,000 U.S. citizens and some 43,000 legal and illegal alien residents.

23 **Bomb kills scores in Lebanon.** A truck loaded with about 135 kg (300 lb) of TNT killed scores of people when it was detonated in a crowded produce market in Tripoli, Lebanon. It was the worst such incident in the war-

B. BISSON—SYGMA
Tunisian officers bear the coffin of Abu Jihad, the Palestine Liberation Organization's second-in-command, who was assassinated at his home in Tunis.

torn country in three years. No one took responsibility for the attack, but members of the city's coordination committee considered the Lebanese Forces, a Christian militia, to be the prime suspect. The leader of the militia was known to harbour deep animosity toward Syria, whose soldiers controlled Tripoli.

25 **Polish strikers get pay raise.** Transportation workers in Bydgoszcz, Poland, negotiated a 63% wage increase after staging a 12-hour wildcat strike that crippled the city's transportation system. The workers were apparently organized by local leaders of the government-endorsed labour union that had been established to supplant Solidarity, the once powerful but now outlawed independent federation of labour unions. During a rally on April 22, steelworkers in Stalowa Wola threatened to strike if the government did not accede to their demands for higher wages and free trade unions. By April 29 the labour unrest had spread to other areas of the country. The

government's determination to maintain public order, to curtail rampant inflation, and to promote free market pricing for basic commodities raised the spectre of an ominous confrontation between the Communist regime and the country's increasingly defiant work force. Polish voters had already expressed their dissatisfaction in November 1987 when they failed to support the austerity program proposed by Gen. Wojciech Jaruzelski, Poland's premier.

26 **Roh Tae Woo suffers setback.** The Democratic Justice Party (DJP), led by Pres. Roh Tae Woo, captured 125 of 299 seats in elections to South Korea's National Assembly. The DJP was victorious in 87 of the nation's 224 constituencies and was awarded 38 of the 75 seats apportioned among the major political parties. It would be the first time since independence that a South Korean president would have to deal with a legislature his party did not control. The Party for Peace and Democracy, led

by Kim Dae Jung, finished second with 70 seats (54 plus 16). Its strong showing would make it the largest of the opposition parties, a position formerly held by the Reunification Democratic Party (RDP). Under the leadership of Kim Young Sam, the RDP won 59 seats (46 plus 13). The New Democratic Republican Party, controlled by former prime minister Kim Jong Pil, won 35 seats (27 plus 8). Of the 10 remaining constituencies, 9 went to independents and one to a member of the Hangyore Democratic Party.

29 **Thai Parliament dissolved.** Prem Tinsulanond, prime minister of Thailand, dissolved his Cabinet and Parliament after 32 members of his coalition government refused to back legislation that would protect U.S. copyrights of artistic and literary works. Thailand had a thriving market for pirated music and videocassettes. Those who opposed the legislation accused their colleagues of yielding to U.S. bullying. New elections were scheduled for July 24.

MAY

8 **Mitterrand wins reelection.** French Pres. François Mitterrand, leader of the Socialist Party, was elected to a second seven-year term, soundly defeating Jacques Chirac, the candidate of the Rassemblement pour la République (Rally for the Republic), a neo-Gaullist party. Mitterrand's margin of victory was about 2.5% greater than it was in 1981 when he captured 51.8% of the popular vote in defeating Valéry Giscard d'Estaing, the incumbent president. Mitterrand's latest triumph was especially remarkable because his party had suffered a severe setback in March 1986 when it lost control of the National Assembly. At that time Mitterrand was compelled to appoint Chirac prime minister, a political anomaly that precipitated a temporary constitutional crisis. On May 10 Mitterrand named Michel Rocard, a moderate Socialist, prime minister. Two days later, when Rocard named his Cabinet, it became evident that Socialists would control all the important ministries. On May 14 Mitterrand dissolved the National Assembly, as expected, and called for elections on June 5 and 12. He hoped thereby to increase the 215-seat Socialist representation in the 577-seat assembly.

Borja wins Ecuador election. Rodrigo Borja Cevallos, a 52-year-old lawyer and candidate of the Democratic Left Party, won the presidency of Ecuador in a runoff election against Abdalá Bucaram Ortiz of the Roldosista Party. Borja, who had run unsuccessfully in 1979 and 1984, was scheduled to begin his four-year term on August 10, succeeding Pres. León Febres Cordero, who had attacked the country's severe economic problems with a program of austerity. Borja was expected to control a majority in the 71-seat Congress because his party held 31 seats and a coalition of 8 Christian Democrats was expected to support him. Borja and Bucaram, both representing the centre-left in Ecuador's

political spectrum, pledged during the campaign to launch new programs to help the poor and underprivileged.

9 **Kurdish rebels attack Turks.** Kurdish rebels, renewing their drive for an independent "Kurdistan" that would comprise their traditional homelands in Iran, Iraq, Turkey, U.S.S.R., and Syria, were reported to have killed at least 25 civilians in recent attacks on two villages in southeastern Turkey. Because the Turkish government did not officially recognize the Kurds as people with a separate identity, it refused to discuss independence with those they referred to as "mountain Turks." The government, however, was trying to quell the unrest by spending millions of dollars to develop

Kurdish areas. It had also dispatched tens of thousands of armed personnel into the field in an attempt to curb the activities of the separatist guerrillas. An estimated 15 million Kurds were living in lands with large Kurdish populations.

15 **Soviets begin Afghan pullout.** The Soviet Union began to withdraw its 115,000 troops from Afghanistan, tacitly admitting that its eight-and-a-half-year effort to defend the Communist government in Kabul against U.S.-supported Muslim guerrillas had failed. More than 13,300 Soviet soldiers had been killed and some 35,500 wounded. The Afghan guerrillas indicated they would not cease attacking the Soviets during their planned nine-month withdrawal and

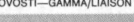

NOVOSTI—GAMMA/LIAISON

A flower-bedecked Soviet tank attracts the attention of passersby as it wends its way through a town in Afghanistan during the withdrawal of Soviet forces that began on May 15.

U.S. Pres. Ronald Reagan and his wife, Nancy, appear with Soviet leader Mikhail Gorbachev, his wife, Raisa, and other guests at the departure ceremony held in honour of the president's visit to the U.S.S.R.

J. LANGEVIN—SYGMA

would, moreover, continue fighting until the Communist regime headed by Najibullah was overthrown.

16 **Yugoslavia imposes controls.** Yugoslavia activated planned limits on the size of wage increases even though the move was certain to anger the working class. Wage controls and strict limits on government spending were two of the conditions laid down by the International Monetary Fund in exchange for $430 million in credits and, among other things, a rescheduling of the payment of some $21 billion to Western creditors. The nation's economic problems included an inflation rate of 170% and an unemployment rate of 15%.

Algeria and Morocco renew ties. Algeria and Morocco agreed to mend the diplomatic rift that occurred in 1976 when Spain abandoned the region known as Spanish Sahara. At that time Morocco claimed the northern two-thirds of the territory and Mauritania the other third. Algeria entered the picture by supporting the claims of the indigenous Saharawis and providing arms and bases in Algeria for their military force, the Polisario Front. After Mauritania withdrew its claim in 1979, Morocco and the Polisario Front continued to fight. Among several reasons given for the improved relations between Morocco and Algeria were a desire to facilitate international efforts to settle the conflict and a wish to restore Arab unity.

21 **Moscow demotes two leaders.** Tass, the official Soviet news agency, reported that the two Communist Party leaders in the southern republics of Armenia and Azerbaijan had been replaced. The announcement came after efforts to stifle months of civil unrest had proved ineffective. On May 17 some 100,000 protesters in the capital of Armenia had to be dispersed by Soviet troops. Two days later about twice that number gathered for a peaceful demonstration. The unrest began in February when ethnic Armenians living in Azerbaijan began resorting to boycotts and demonstrations

to press demands that the borders of the two republics be redrawn so that their region of Azerbaijan would become part of the Armenian Republic.

22 **Hungarian leader replaced.** Karoly Grosz was named general secretary of Hungary's Communist Party by members of the party's new Central Committee. Grosz, who had been appointed prime minister by the Council of Ministers in June 1987, replaced Janos Kadar, who rose to power as party leader in 1956. During the years that followed, Kadar had made Hungary one of the Eastern bloc's most prosperous nations. Even so, there appeared to be general agreement that a new leader was needed to revitalize the nation's sluggish economy. Although Grosz was a political conservative, he was known to favour new economic policies and appeared willing to grant businesses greater autonomy in order to foster economic growth.

23 **U.S.S.R. plans basic changes.** The Central Committee of the Communist Party of the Soviet Union called for changes in the nation's political system. The aim was to "draw broad sections of the population into running all state and public offices and to complete the formation of a socialist law-based state." The restructuring of the Soviet system, which had been vigorously advocated by Soviet leader Mikhail Gorbachev, would include limits on the length of time party and government officials would remain in their posts. Another change would expand the authority of popularly elected legislatures and require competitive elections by secret ballot. Similar changes would affect the election of party officials. The Communist Party would continue to formulate the nation's policies, but its involvement in the management of government agencies and economic enterprises and its intrusion into the daily life of the people would be greatly reduced.

26 **Vietnam to withdraw troops.** The Vietnamese government announced that it would withdraw

50,000 of its estimated 120,000 troops from Kampuchea before the end of the year. Vietnam had taken over control of the country in 1978. According to Western sources, Vietnam had already withdrawn about half its 40,000–50,000 troops stationed in Laos. It was not clear how much pressure, if any, the Soviet Union was exerting on Vietnam to seek an end to the conflict in Southeast Asia.

Libya ends war with Chad. Col. Mu'ammar al-Qadhdhafi, Libya's chief of state, declared an end to Libya's 20-year-old war with Chad, its neighbour to the south. Although Qadhdhafi said he would recognize the Chad government, he did not say Libya had relinquished its claim to the Aozou Strip, the 110,000 sq km (43,000 sq mi) of desert land that Libya and Chad had been fighting over.

29 **Reagan and Gorbachev hold summit.** President Reagan arrived in Moscow for his fourth meeting with Soviet leader Mikhail Gorbachev. They had previously met in Geneva (November 1985), Reykjavík, Iceland (October 1986), and Washington, D.C. (December 1987). Both leaders publicly acknowledged that fundamental differences continued to exist, but they also noted that the prospects for better understanding and future cooperation were improving. On May 31 representatives of the U.S. and U.S.S.R. signed nine separate agreements dealing with such diverse subjects as nuclear testing and student exchanges. The following day Reagan and Gorbachev exchanged formal documents ratifying the Intermediate-range Nuclear Forces (INF) Treaty.

Zia dissolves Assembly. Pakistani Pres. Mohammad Zia-ul-Haq dismissed Prime Minister Mohammad Khan Junejo and his Cabinet and dissolved the National Assembly. Zia accused the legislature of failing to maintain law and order and of not hastening the creation of an Islamic society in Pakistan. Zia also announced that elections to the Assembly would be held within 90 days, as the constitution prescribed. Candidates, moreover, would be allowed to campaign as representatives of political parties rather than as mere individuals. Zia, an army general, had seized power in a bloodless coup in 1977. After seven years of martial law, he named Junejo civilian prime minister.

Pope names new cardinals. Pope John Paul II increased membership in the College of Cardinals to 161 with 25 new appointments. Of that number, 11 were selected from Europe, 3 from Africa, 3 from North America, 3 from South America, and 2 from India. The other three resided, respectively, in Australia, Hong Kong, and Lithuania. All were considered to be conservative in matters of church doctrine. During the formal installation of the new cardinals in Rome on June 28, Bishop Sladkevicius of Lithuania would become the second cardinal residing in the Soviet Union. Julijans Cardinal Vaivods of Latvia had been elevated to the cardinalate in 1983. The most important responsibility of the College of Cardinals is to elect a pope's successor.

JUNE

5 **Russian Orthodox Church celebrates millennium.** The Russian Orthodox Church began a year-long celebration to commemorate its 1,000th anniversary. The church credited Prince Vladimir I of Kiev with having established a permanent Byzantine church after his conversion to Christianity. The celebration had additional significance because Soviet leader Mikhail Gorbachev had given the church greater autonomy when he met with church leaders on April 29. On June 9 church authorities officially adopted the new government guidelines that gave priests the right to direct their churches and to engage in charitable works.

6 **South African blacks strike.** More than a million blacks in South Africa began a three-day strike in protest against a government crackdown on antiapartheid groups in February and against proposed laws to curb the power of black labour unions. Even though strikes had been banned two years earlier when the government declared a state of emergency, officers of the Congress of South African Trade Unions and the National Congress of Trade Unions ordered their members to walk off their jobs. The strike was especially effective in Johannesburg and Durban. In Pretoria, the capital, buses were reported to be half empty. On June 8, the last day of the strike, employers and union officials agreed to negotiate any changes affecting the rights of the labour unions.

7 **Bangladesh officially adopts Islam.** The Parliament of Bangladesh approved a constitutional amendment that made Islam the official state religion. About 87% of the country's 105 million people were Muslims and some 12%, Hindus. The Jatiya Party had formally proposed the amendment at the request of Pres. H. M. Ershad, who had gone on record as saying he did not intend to go further and make Bangladesh an Islamic state.

Arab leaders meet in Algeria. Leaders of the Arab world convened in Algiers to discuss support for the Palestinians who were fighting Israeli occupation of the West Bank and Gaza Strip. Together they pledged to provide the Palestinians with "all necessary help and assistance in all necessary forms," but each nation would decide for itself how it would fulfill this commitment. Yasir Arafat's request that the Palestine Liberation Organization, which he headed, be given exclusive responsibility for handling the funds was disregarded. The Arab leaders criticized the Middle East peace initiative undertaken by U.S. Secretary of State George Shultz as "slow and ineffective" but did not condemn the peace process itself.

10 **Seoul blocks student march to DMZ.** South Korean riot police were called out to prevent several thousand students armed with pipes, clubs, and firebombs from marching north to the demilitarized zone to meet with North Korean students at Panmunjom. The fighting was especially intense at Yonsei University. South Korean Pres. Roh Tae Woo had been seeking ways to broaden contacts with the Communist regime in Pyongyang and thereby hasten the day when divided Korea would be reunited. He insisted, however, that negotiating with North Korea was the right and responsibility of the government, not of individuals. Leaders of South Korea's opposition parties agreed. On June 11 a small group of students forced their way into the Combined Central Government Complex in Seoul. They were able to inflict moderate damage with firebombs before being arrested.

12 **France elects National Assembly.** The Socialist Party of French Pres. François Mitterrand and Prime Minister Michel Rocard failed to win the majority it sought in elections to the National Assembly. Official figures gave the Socialists 276 of the 577 seats, with 289 needed for outright control. A coalition of neo-Gaullists and conservatives captured 271 seats and the Communists 27, 8 fewer than they had in the previous legislature. The extreme right, represented by Jean-Marie Le Pen's National Front, suffered a devastating defeat when it lost all but one of the 32 seats it had previously controlled. Le Pen himself failed to carry his Marseille constituency. The remaining two seats would be occupied by delegates from French Polynesia.

15 **Greek and Turkish leaders meet.** Turkish Prime Minister Turgut Ozal and Greek Prime Minister Andreas Papandreou concluded three days of intense talks outside Athens. Both hoped they had taken the first step toward ending the decades of hostility and suspicion that had characterized relations between the neighbouring countries. Ozal's visit to Greece, the first by a Turkish leader in 36 years, was to be followed by a Papandreou visit to Turkey, perhaps in autumn. During the discussions no concrete agreements were reached, nor were any expected. The Turkish occupation of the northern third of Cyprus remained a highly emotional issue, but both sides were willing for the present to leave the matter in the hands of the United Nations. After the meeting Papandreou remarked that dialogue had replaced war, and that in itself, he said, was a great achievement. In March 1987 the two nations, both members of NATO, had been on the brink of war over oil rights in the Aegean Sea.

20 **Haitian general seizes power.** Lieut. Gen. Henri Namphy, who for two years had ruled Haiti before Leslie Manigat became civilian president earlier in the year, seized power and declared himself president of a new military government. Manigat was reported to have landed safely in neighbouring Dominican Republic with members of his family. On June 15 Manigat had refused Namphy's demand that certain high-ranking officers be reassigned. Two days later tensions increased when Manigat fired the general. After taking over the presidential palace, Namphy, wearing a steel helmet and carrying a submachine gun, addressed the nation. He declared: "Everyone is now in the Army because it is this Army that is going to lead this country as it has to be led." He also dissolved the National Assembly and picked an 11-member Cabinet consisting only of military officers.

S. KOGURE—GAMMA/LIAISON

Fighting erupted at South Korea's Yonsei University when South Korean riot police blocked a student march to the demilitarized zone to meet with North Korean students.

21 **Group of Seven meets in Toronto.** Leaders of the seven major industrialized democracies (Canada, France, Italy, Japan, the U.K., the U.S., and West Germany) concluded their annual economic meeting in Toronto after agreeing on policies designed to foster continued economic growth. There was also a consensus that special concessions were needed to lighten the pressure on poor nations burdened with the repayment of heavy debts. Once again President Reagan pleaded in vain for an end to government farm subsidies by the year 2000. There was general agreement that such aid distorted prices and created other problems, but most members of the Group of Seven preferred a more gradual transition to free market prices.

Canada charges Soviets with spying. During a news conference in Toronto, Canadian Prime Minister Brian Mulroney was asked to comment on reports that 17 Soviet diplomats had been expelled or barred from reentering the country because they had engaged in industrial and commercial espionage. Mulroney replied: "I will confirm that indeed the government of Canada took such action last week in regard to the improper and unacceptable behaviour by representatives of the Soviet government in Canada." A Canadian official said that this case was completely separate from one involving a Canadian who had been recently charged with spying for the Soviet Union. The man was accused of passing on secret documents and information obtained from a U.S. Navy station in Newfoundland.

22 **Vietnam names new leader.** Hanoi radio announced that 71-year-old Do Muoi had been elected chairman of the Council of Ministers on the first day of a regular session of the National Assembly. He replaced Pham Hung, who had died of a heart attack in March. Muoi was the third-highest-ranking member of the 13-member Politburo, which determines policy. During

European Communities Pres. Jacques Delors (far left) poses with the Group of Seven—the leaders of the seven major industrialized democracies—during their annual meeting.
DIANA WALKER—GAMMA/LIAISON

the meeting Vo Van Kiet, who had been Hung's temporary replacement, reported that serious food shortages existed in the northern provinces because production had failed to keep pace with population growth. His proposed solution included decentralized management and material incentives for farmers.

28 **Soviet Communist Party holds pivotal conference.** In his opening speech to a special conference of nearly 5,000 Communist Party officials, Soviet party chief Mikhail Gorbachev declared that a basic restructuring of the Soviet political system was the only hope for solving the nation's economic and social problems. Among other changes Gorbachev proposed a new type of presidency, whose occupant would oversee domestic and foreign affairs and head

the important Defense Council. Such a president would be elected by a new broadly based Congress, not by popular vote as some had proposed. Gorbachev also endorsed popularly elected legislatures with sufficient power to carry out reforms. He rejected the idea of alternative political parties and the redrawing of republic borders to satisfy the demands of Armenians living in Azerbaijan. Nonetheless, Gorbachev appeared to lean toward greater regional economic independence. On June 30, in a dramatic departure from traditional protocol, Vladimir Melnikov called for the dismissal of 78-year-old Pres. Andrey Gromyko and three other top officials. The unprecedented personal humiliation inflicted on Gromyko and the others was shown on television that evening. On July 1 the delegates approved most of the changes Gorbachev had proposed.

JULY

3 **U.S. Navy downs Iranian airbus.** The U.S. missile cruiser *Vincennes* shot down an Iranian airbus over the Persian Gulf, killing all 290 persons aboard. The midmorning tragedy occurred within minutes of a skirmish between Iranian gunboats and two U.S. naval vessels, the *Vincennes* and the frigate *Montgomery*. According to initial reports, the airbus was mistaken for a hostile F-14 jet fighter flying through an air corridor between Bandar-e 'Abbas, Iran, and the United Arab Emirates. How the radar image of a large airbus could have been mistaken for that of an F-14 was but one of many questions that set off heated denunciations of the U.S. action and an extensive U.S. investigation of the incident. On July 11 the U.S. announced it would pay compensation to the families of all those who died. On August 19 Secretary of Defense Frank Carlucci said no navy personnel would be disciplined, even

though the crew had made mistakes due to "stress, task fixation, and unconscious distortion of data." A report released by Carlucci and Adm. William Crowe, Jr., chairman of the Joint Chiefs of Staff, said Iran had to share the blame. Crowe made a point of the fact that the unidentified aircraft had taken off from an airfield used by both military and commercial aircraft and that seven warnings from the *Vincennes* over both commercial and military frequencies had gone unanswered. He said it was unconscionable that Iran would permit a commercial plane to fly directly into the midst of an ongoing sea battle. He concluded: "I believe that, given the operating environment, Captain Rogers acted reasonably and did what his nation expected of him in defense of his ship and crew."

French cardinal counters Lefebvre. Jean-Marie Cardinal Lustiger, archbishop of

Paris, celebrated a traditional Latin mass in Notre Dame Cathedral, the first such Sunday liturgy in the celebrated 12th-century landmark in 20 years. Lustiger urged the 5,000 worshipers not to follow Archbishop Marcel Lefebvre, an ultraconservative, who had been excommunicated on June 30 for consecrating four bishops in defiance of a Vatican prohibition. Lefebvre, who had established his own seminary in Switzerland, was supported by a small group of priests whose bases of operation included a 17th-century church on the Left Bank of the Seine. Lefebvre was so uncompromisingly opposed to mass in the vernacular and to other innovations adopted by Rome after the second Vatican Council that he referred to such changes as satanic and the work of the Antichrist. Lefebvre's excommunication created a schism of worrisome proportions because some 500,000 lay people, mostly in France, had rallied to his banner.

Carlos Salinas de Gortari was elected president of Mexico despite a serious challenge by Cuauhtémoc Cárdenas.
GREG SMITH—GAMMA/LIAISON

5   **Meese announces resignation.** U.S. Attorney General Edwin Meese III announced he would soon leave government service now that "false allegations" against him had been put to rest. A short time earlier special prosecutor James C. McKay had concluded a 14-month criminal investigation of Meese's affairs. When McKay filed his sealed report with a special panel of appellate judges in the nation's capital without recommending indictment, Meese claimed he had been cleared of all charges. On July 18 McKay's report was made public. Meese was basically exonerated of wrongdoing in two major government scandals that had been the chief focus of the investigation. The first concerned Meese's role in a $1 billion Iraqi pipeline project. McKay concluded there was insufficient evidence to show that federal laws against bribing foreign officials had been violated. In the second case, which involved Wedtech Corp., a military contractor, the evidence was likewise deemed insufficient to prove that Meese had taken bribes or illegal gratuities. McKay, however, concluded that Meese had willfully filed a false federal tax return in 1985, but he believed Meese intended to pay the taxes eventually. For that and other reasons, McKay decided not to bring criminal charges. Richard Thornburgh, a two-time governor of Pennsylvania, was sworn in as the new attorney general on August 12.

6   **Mexican election generates turmoil.** Mexican voters went to the polls in record numbers to elect a successor to Pres. Miguel de la Madrid and to fill all 64 seats in the Senate and the 500 seats in the Chamber of Deputies. Although the ruling Partido Revolucionario Institucional (PRI; Institutional Revolutionary Party) had not lost a presidential, senatorial, or gubernatorial election since 1929, there was widespread preelection belief that the PRI was facing a very serious challenge. After suspicious delays, the Federal Electoral Commission finally announced on July 13 that Carlos Salinas de Gortari, the PRI candidate, had been elected president with 50.4% of the vote. Cuauhtémoc Cárdenas, candidate of the left-wing National Democratic Front,

was given 31.1%, and Manuel Clouthier, standard bearer of the right-of-centre Partido Acción Nacional (PAN; National Action Party), was given 17.1%. On July 16 an estimated 200,000 people marched on the National Palace in Mexico City in support of Cárdenas, who claimed the government had resorted to blatant fraud to cheat him out of the presidency. After two months of heated debate and numerous efforts by the opposition to have the official election results nullified, the electoral college formally certified Salinas as the new president on September 10. The PAN cast 85 negative votes, while all 136 members of the National Democratic Front walked out of the proceedings.

7   **Roh Tae Woo favours closer ties with North Korea.** South Korean Pres. Roh Tae Woo revealed a basic change in foreign policy by declaring in a nationally televised speech that he would henceforth permit family visits, student exchanges, and trade with Communist North Korea. He also encouraged other nations to improve relations with the regime in Pyongyang. On August 15 Roh suggested that he and Kim Il Sung hold face-to-face talks, but it did not seem likely that Kim would accept an invitation he had previously declined. On August 19 legislators from both sides met in Panmunjom. Chon Kum Chol, North Korea's chief delegate, summarized his opinion of the meeting by saying that "the attitude of the South was not sincere." The meeting ended on August 22 without even a date being set for further discussions. More amicable talks being held in Tokyo ended on August 26 in a deadlock. The main discussions had centred on the size of parliamentary delegations that might hold a joint session sometime in the future. The North was insisting on some 1,000 delegates, the South on a much more modest number.

8   **Lee Teng-hui to head Kuomintang.** Lee Teng-hui, president of Taiwan, was elected chairman of the ruling Nationalist Party (Kuomintang). The bestowing of the party chairmanship on the chief executive, the first native of Taiwan to hold either office, appeared

ALVIN CHUNG—SYGMA

Taiwan's president, Lee Teng-hui, was elected chairman of the ruling Nationalist Party. He was the first native of Taiwan to hold either office.

to guarantee that Lee would continue the process of democratization begun by his predecessor, the late Chiang Ching-kuo. On July 14, 12 of the 31 members of the Central Standing Committee were replaced by persons who were generally younger and more committed to change than their predecessors. On July 20 Lee appointed 15 new members to his Cabinet; for the first time, the contingent of eight ministers from Taiwan Province gave local people a majority in the top hierarchy of the government. In another precedent-shattering move, the Ministry of Finance was given to a woman, economist Shirley Kuo.

20   **Khomeini ends war with Iraq.** Ayatollah Ruhollah Khomeini, the spiritual leader of Iran, called a halt to Iran's eight-year war with neighbouring Iraq. In a radio statement delivered in his name, Khomeini accepted United Nations Security Council Resolution 598, which called for a cease-fire. The ayatollah then remarked, "Taking this decision was more deadly than taking poison." Khomeini had vowed to wage war until total victory was achieved and Iraqi Pres. Saddam Hussein overthrown. UN Secretary-General Javier Pérez de Cuéllar announced he would immediately send a military mission to Tehran and Baghdad to work out details of a formal cease-fire. The following day Hussein said he would not be satisfied with anything less than a comprehensive peace agreement that went way beyond a mere cessation of hostilities. The cost of the war had been staggering for both sides. An estimated 1 million people had been killed, 1.7 million wounded, and 1.5 million turned into refugees. In addition, the warring nations had spent about $400 billion to carry on the conflict and had suffered major damage to their most important cities. On August 8 Iran finally agreed to hold direct talks with Iraq in order to implement a cease-fire. Hostilities formally ended on August 20.

23   **U Ne Win relinquishes power.** The powerful chairman of Burma's only political party, U Ne Win, resigned under intense pressure after 26 years of brutal rule. Speaking before

a special session of the Burma Socialist Program Party, Ne Win said the student-led riots, which caused the closing of Burma's universities, had prompted his resignation from the party. After leading a successful coup against U Nu in 1962, Ne Win had introduced socialist and isolationist policies that proved disastrous. On July 26 U Sein Lwin, who was said to have led a brutal crackdown in March that resulted in the deaths of an estimated 100 students, became party chairman. On July 27 Sein Lwin was also elected president, replacing U San Yu, who had resigned along with Ne Win. On August 3 the new president imposed martial law in Rangoon after Buddhist monks joined students in a peaceful march of protest against the new leadership. On August 8 tens of thousands of Burmese marched in the capital and 14 other cities. At least 36 persons were killed the following day as the protest marches spread to some two dozen cities. On August 11 government troops once again attacked unarmed protesters. The next day, unable to stifle the protests, Sein Lwin resigned his posts.

25 **Kampuchean talks get under way.** For the first time since 1979, the year Vietnamese troops overthrew the terrorist regime of Pol Pot's Khmer Rouge in Cambodia (now called Kampuchea), representatives of all the warring factions met in Bogor, Indon., to consider ways of ending the long conflict. There were also delegates from Laos and from the six nations making up the Association of Southeast Asian Nations (ASEAN), which had condemned Vietnam when it first occupied its neighbour to the west. Although China, which had long berated Vietnam for its military invasion, and the Soviet Union, which had backed Vietnam, gave joint assurances that they would support a peace plan, there were grave doubts that a settlement could be reached. On one side were the Kampuchean and Vietnamese officials; on the other, three groups of guerrillas at odds among themselves. After endless wrangling, the talks in Bogor ended on July 28 without even an agreement among the delegates to meet again.

28 **Search for MIAs to resume.** U.S. officials announced that Vietnam had agreed, after four days of talks in Hanoi, to undertake "joint investigative, survey, and excavation activities" with the U.S. to determine the fate of 1,758 U.S. military personnel still listed as missing in action (MIA) inside Vietnam during the war. The U.S. also maintained a list of 547 Americans missing in Laos, 83 in Kampuchea, and 6 in China. U.S. officials had for years told Hanoi authorities that no normalization of relations between the two countries was possible until the MIA issue and the problem created by Vietnam's occupation of Kampuchea were satisfactorily settled. A spokesman for the U.S. Pacific Command said: "There is no doubt that the leaders of Vietnam have information about the fate of many missing Americans. We are pushing for that information." Despite sporadic reports to the contrary, U.S. officials entertained no strong belief that any American was still being held in Vietnam against his will.

31 **Jordan abandons West Bank.** In a dramatic television address, King Hussein of Jordan abandoned all claims to the West Bank, leaving it up to the Palestine Liberation Organization (PLO) to decide what should now be done. In a single stroke Hussein appeared to dissociate himself completely from the Palestinians who in December 1987 began a violent uprising against Israeli forces occupying the West Bank and Gaza Strip. Hussein pointedly noted that "Jordan is not Palestine," even though Jordan had ruled the West Bank between 1948 and the end of the 1967 Arab-Israeli war. The king, however, reaffirmed his support for the Palestinian cause and expressed confidence that an "independent Palestinian state will be established on the occupied Palestinian land after its liberation, God willing." On July 28 Hussein had hinted at what was to follow. He canceled a $1.3 billion development plan for the West Bank. On July 30 he dissolved the lower house of Parliament, which represented Palestinian interests in the occupied West Bank. On August 4 Jordan announced that it would stop paying the salaries of the majority of its employees in the West Bank. The decision affected about 21,000 Palestinians, including teachers, health workers, and municipal employees. Yasir Arafat, chairman of the PLO, said on August 9 that Hussein had not consulted him before making his decision about cutting Jordan's ties to the West Bank. Two weeks later Arafat announced that the PLO would assume responsibility for paying the salaries of civil servants in the West Bank.

AUGUST

2 **South Africa proposes truce.** During secret U.S.-sponsored peace talks in Geneva, South Africa proposed an August 10 cease-fire in Angola, hoping that an interruption of hostilities would allow it to withdraw from Angola and from South West Africa/Namibia before UN-supervised elections were held in Namibia in June 1989. South African Foreign Minister Roelof Botha said the offer was firm provided Cuba pulled out its estimated 47,000 troops from Angola and provided the seven African National Congress camps in Angola were dispersed before the election in Namibia. Angola and Cuba immediately expressed anger over the public revelation of proposals still being discussed in secret. Nonetheless, South Africa, Angola, and Cuba agreed on August 5 to "a sequence of steps to achieve peace in southwestern Africa." On August 8 the three nations endorsed an immediate cease-fire.

5 **Oliver North trial delayed.** Gerhard Gesell, a federal district court judge, announced in Washington, D.C., that the trial of Oliver North would be postponed to give both defense and prosecuting attorneys additional time to study thousands of classified documents that could be relevant to the case. Gesell set no new trial date. North was charged with having conspired to secretly transfer to the Nicaraguan *contras* profits from the sale of U.S. weapons to Iran. The *contras* were fighting to overthrow the Sandinista government. John Poindexter, former head of the National Security Council, faced similar charges, but he was to be tried separately. President Reagan had earlier dismissed speculation about a possible presidential pardon for the two men, saying he believed neither had committed any crime. The postponement of the trial meant that a verdict would not be rendered until after Reagan had left office.

12 **Somalis flee civil war.** Kenneth Bleakley, U.S. deputy assistant secretary of state for international refugees, arrived in Addis Ababa, Eth., hoping to evaluate the condition of 300,000 Somali refugees who had crossed the border into Ethiopia to avoid the ravages of a fierce civil war. An Ethiopian official informed Bleakley that he would not be allowed to visit the arid region of Ogaden, where the refugees had settled. The International Red Cross had also been denied access to the area. The government of Somali Pres. Muhammad Siyad Barrah, who belonged to the Marehan clan, was at war with the Somali National Movement—members of the rival Isaak clan, who were demanding greater equality and a more democratic government.

14 **Soviet pullout on schedule.** Lieut. Gen. Boris Gromov, commander of Soviet troops in Afghanistan, reported from Kabul that not a single Soviet soldier remained in 25 of the country's 31 provinces. He also confirmed that the pullout of all Soviet forces would be completed as scheduled by mid-February 1989, even though Afghan guerrillas had captured the capital of Qonduz Province shortly after the Soviets departed. Mohammad Najibullah, Afghanistan's leader, and Prime Minister Mohammad Hassan Sharq pleaded for world pressure on the guerrillas to end the fighting by accepting a role in a coalition government. There was no indication the *mujahideen* were willing to accept such a compromise.

16 **Polish miners go on strike.** Thousands of Polish miners went on strike at the large July Manifesto Mine in Upper Silesia to demand higher pay and the legal restoration of Solidarity, the labour federation that had been outlawed in 1981 with the imposition of martial law. Within a few days, spreading work stoppages threatened to plunge the nation into a crisis rivaling that of the early 1980s. On August 23 Lech Walesa, leader of the Solidarity movement, called for a dialogue with the government to defuse the growing tension. On August 31, after talks with high officials, Walesa called for an

Shipyard strikers raise their hands in support of Solidarity. Strikes throughout Poland led to crisis conditions. The government responded by imposing strict security measures.

G. MERILLON—GAMMA/LIAISON

end to the strikes. The next day, workers at the Gdansk shipyard returned to work. By September 3, despite serious misgivings on the part of numerous workers, most striking miners, dockworkers, and bus drivers had returned to their jobs.

17 **Zia-ul-Haq dies in crash.** Pakistani Pres. Mohammad Zia-ul-Haq was killed when the air force C-130 turboprop aircraft he was on mysteriously crashed shortly after taking off from Bahawalpur. Arnold Raphel, the U.S. ambassador to Pakistan, Brig. Gen. Herbert Wassom, the chief U.S. military attaché, and ten senior Pakistani Army officers were among the 29 others also killed in the crash. Ghulam Ishaq Khan, the 73-year-old leader of Pakistan's Senate, assumed the post of caretaker president as prescribed in the constitution. That evening he informed the nation that the constitution remained in effect and a presidential election would be held as scheduled in mid-November. Benazir Bhutto, Zia's chief political opponent, allegedly told reporters she did not regret Zia's death. Zia had overthrown her father, Prime Minister Zulfikar Ali Bhutto, in

1977 and had had him hanged two years later. During the weeks following the crash, experts examined all the available evidence but were unable to determine why the aircraft went down.

19 **Civilian to lead Burma.** One week after U Sein Lwin resigned as president of Burma and as chairman of the nation's only political party, Maung Maung, one of two civilians in the Cabinet, was picked as his successor. Sein Lwin had ordered the military to shoot hundreds of protesters after he replaced Ne Win on July 27. It was not clear whether Ne Win or the military had forced Sein Lwin to step down. The appointment of a civilian leader was welcomed, but it did not mollify the students and their supporters, who were demanding an end to one-party rule, the lifting of martial law, the freeing of student leaders and political prisoners, and compensation for those killed or injured during the protests. On August 24 Maung Maung lifted martial law and proposed a referendum on one-party rule. The next day hundreds of thousands of demonstrators moved through the streets of Rangoon demanding that the nation's leaders resign. As the unrest continued, fear began to mount that the country could be facing anarchy because the opposition had no obvious leader.

22 **Thousands killed in Burundi.** The Burundi government reported that at least 5,000 people had been killed during a week of ethnic violence between the majority Hutu tribe and the smaller, wealthier Tutsi tribe, which controlled the armed forces and ruled the country. No casualty figures were released, but the Hutus presumably suffered greater losses because their machetes and spears were no match for the helicopters and modern weapons used by government troops. A government spokesman blamed the slaughter on Hutu tribesmen in Rwanda, who, he said, had incited fellow Hutus in Burundi to attack the Tutsi.

23 **Baltic republics challenge Moscow.** Tens of thousands of demonstrators marched in the capitals of Estonia, Latvia, and Lithuania to protest the 1939 pact between Nazi Germany and the Soviet Union that led to Soviet annexation of the three Baltic republics in 1940. During the peaceful

ANIS HAMDANI—GAMMA/LIAISON

The remains of Pakistani Pres. Mohammad Zia-ul-Haq rest beneath a profusion of colour.

protests, which had been sanctioned by the authorities, various speakers emphatically denied that the people of the Baltic states had ever willingly accepted Soviet rule. There were also emotional calls for total independence from the Soviet Union.

Reagan signs trade bill. President Reagan signed a massive omnibus trade bill that had reached final form only after three years of intense debate and numerous revisions. Most sections that had been criticized as protectionist had been eliminated. The bill was essentially a consolidation and reshaping of already accepted remedies for dealing with unfair trade practices abroad and for surges in imports that were deemed detrimental to U.S. companies. For the first time, U.S. trade policy not only was defined in terms of tariffs, subsidies, and quotas but was extended to include such matters as currency surpluses, third world debt, restrictions on security-sensitive exports, and the bribing of foreigners in order to secure sales.

25 **Iran and Iraq begin talks.** The foreign ministers of Iran and Iraq met in Geneva to begin the first face-to-face peace negotiations since the two countries went to war in 1980. Javier Pérez de Cuéllar, secretary-general of the United Nations, moderated the talks at the UN's European headquarters. Although Pérez de Cuéllar was hopeful when the peace discussions got under way, he was unable to persuade the two sides to begin carrying out the ten-point Persian Gulf peace plan approved by the UN Security Council in 1987. It soon became clear that no comprehensive settlement would emerge in the immediate future.

West Germany identifies U.S. spy. West German officials identified Clyde L. Conrad, a former U.S. Army sergeant, as the key figure in an espionage network that had been operating in Europe for at least 14 years. Before obtaining an honourable discharge in 1985, Conrad had access to sensitive documents that he allegedly passed on to Hungarian intelligence agents, who then shared the information with the Soviet government. On August 26 Swedish authorities revealed that two Hungarian-born Swedes arrested in Göteborg on August 23 had admitted being members of the spy ring. West Germany and the U.S. acknowledged that over the years Conrad and his associates had provided the Eastern bloc with very valuable information.

30 **Chile to hold plebiscite.** Chile's ruling military junta announced that a national plebiscite would be held on October 5 to decide whether Pres. Augusto Pinochet Ugarte would begin a new eight-year term on March 11, 1989, or remain in office for another year and then call an election to choose his successor. The announcement provided another occasion for antigovernment demonstrations in Santiago, during which 3 persons were killed, more than 20 were injured, and hundreds were arrested. Leaders of 16 antigovernment factions pledged to work vigorously to defeat Pinochet at the ballot box in early October.

SEPTEMBER

3 **Singapore holds election.** In parliamentary elections, Singapore's ruling People's Action Party (PAP), under the leadership of 64-year-old Prime Minister Lee Kuan Yew, won control of all but one of the 81 seats in the national legislature. The election had been called 15 months ahead of schedule while Singapore's 2.7 million people were enjoying conspicuous prosperity. Lee said the election results were a vote of confidence in the new generation of parliamentarians who would lead the nation in the future. The prime minister had already designated Goh Chok Tong, his 46-year-old deputy, as his successor. PAP's overwhelming victory tended to obscure a growing resentment over the government's heavy-handed control of the press and its apparent determination to control people's lives. The opposition, which was poorly organized but had hoped to do better than it did, took comfort in the fact that Francis Seow had come very close to winning a seat in Parliament. Earlier in the year Seow had been jailed for 72 days for meeting with a U.S. diplomat to discuss local politics.

5 **Chun Kyung Hwan found guilty.** Chun Kyung Hwan, the brother of former South Korean president Chun Doo Hwan, was convicted in Seoul on eight counts involving embezzlement, bribery, influence peddling, and tax evasion. He was then sentenced to seven years in prison and fined nearly $5.8 million. Chun's misdeeds occurred while he was president of the Saemaul Headquarters, a rural development program that critics charged became a political tool to compel support for the president. Eleven others tried at the same time received sentences ranging from one to three years. Five, however, had their sentences suspended. The trial became a highly emotional event and gave birth to demands that Chun Doo Hwan also be put on trial, along with his wife, Lee Soon Ja, for alleged corruption.

Brezhnev in-law goes on trial. Yury Churbanov, the son-in-law of the late Soviet leader Leonid Brezhnev, and eight others went on trial in Moscow on charges of corruption and bribery. Many believed the trial was a deliberate effort to focus on the Brezhnev era, which had been officially branded as a period of stagnation. On September 8 Churbanov pleaded guilty to abusing his powers as first deputy interior minister, but he denied the charge that from 1976 to 1982 he had taken bribes amounting to more than $1.1 million. A conviction of large-scale bribery carried with it the possibility of a death sentence.

10 **Sri Lanka yields to Tamils.** Sri Lanka announced that Pres. J. R. Jayawardene had signed an executive order merging the country's Northern and Eastern provinces. The decree met a major demand of militant Tamils fighting to have their region of Sri Lanka recognized as their homeland. This concession to the largely Hindu Tamils angered many Sinhalese, who were

Chun Kyung Hwan, brother of former South Korean president Chun Doo Hwan, was convicted of crimes he committed while serving as head of a government program.
HYUNGWANG KANG—GAMMA/LIAISON

predominantly Buddhists. Resentment was especially intense among Buddhist and Muslim Sinhalese living in the southern part of Eastern Province because they had no desire to be dominated by a group that comprised a distinct minority in the country. On September 12 the capital came to a virtual standstill following a mostly silent campaign of intimidation directed at businesses and government workers. The extremist anti-Indian group of Sinhalese who presumably organized the strike had been blamed for past acts of terrorism, including political murders.

18 **Greens gain in Sweden.** In national elections, the Greens Environmental Party became the first new party in 70 years to win representation in Sweden's 349-seat Riksdag (parliament). During the campaign they promised to protect the environment by making pollution and energy more costly and to reduce the taxes of low-income families. They also pledged to support only the program of the Greens and not to become part of any coalition government. Official results gave the ruling Social Democratic Party of Prime Minister Ingvar Carlsson 156 seats (loss of 3). The Communists, natural allies of the Socialists, captured 21 seats (plus 2). With the strength of the Socialist bloc virtually undiminished, the 20 seats won by the Greens came at the expense of the non-Socialist opposition. The Conservatives won 66 seats (minus 10), the Liberals 44 (minus 7), and the Centre 42 (minus 2). The total representation of the non-Socialists was thus four seats fewer than that of the ruling Social Democrats.

Military seizes power in Burma. Burma's civilian president, Maung Maung, was overthrown in a military coup led by Gen. Saw Maung, the minister of defense and head of the Army. Saw Maung quickly banned all antigovernment protests, imposed a nighttime curfew, outlawed gatherings of more than five persons, and ordered striking workers back to their jobs. The new government, however, said it was committed to holding multiparty general

elections in accord with a promise made by the previous regime on September 10. Violence nonetheless continued, with no indication that the opposition was prepared to abandon its demand that a neutral interim government be installed to run the country until elections were held. Amid the chaos, there was no way to assess accurately the number of casualties, but official estimates of the number of people killed in Rangoon after September 18 totaled at least 450. The call for a new interim government and for honest multiparty elections had gained support on September 6 when all 187 foreign ministry workers belonging to Burma's ruling party canceled their membership. On September 9 at least 200 members of the Air Force joined the opposition. On September 27 U Aung Gyi, a retired army officer, was named chairman of an opposition alliance. On October 3 thousands of government workers, facing arrest or dismissal if they defied an ultimatum, returned to work.

Namphy ousted in Haiti. Noncommissioned officers from Haiti's Presidential Guard overthrew Lieut. Gen. Henri Namphy, who had returned to power in June following a military coup. The Presidential Guard then nominated Lieut. Gen. Prosper Avril for head of state. Avril accepted, saying he did so "to save the country from anarchy and chaos." Rumours of an impending coup had been rife in the capital after Namphy appeared to ignore recent attacks on churches, hospitals, private radio stations, and ordinary citizens. In an attack on a Roman Catholic church on September 11, at least 12 persons were killed and more than 70 wounded. The dreaded Tontons Macoutes, a group of paramilitary thugs organized in the late 1950s, were believed responsible for the unprovoked slaughter.

21 **Japanese emperor gravely ill.** The Japanese government announced that the Cabinet would soon ask Crown Prince Akihito to assume the official duties of his ailing father, 87-year-old Emperor Hirohito. The 54-year-old heir to the chrysanthemum throne had assumed some of the duties of emperor a year earlier when Hirohito underwent intestinal bypass surgery. Since that time Hirohito had passed through several medical crises but had never regained his earlier vigour.

Armenian unrest continues. The Soviet Union declared the equivalent of a state of emergency in the area of Azerbaijan dominated by ethnic Armenians clamouring for union with the Armenian republic. The official news agency TASS reported that cars had been set ablaze, shots fired, and the police and military "humiliated." To quell the unrest, a curfew was imposed in Stepanakert, the capital of Nagorno-Karabakh, an administrative district within the Azerbaijan republic that was home to some 135,000 ethnic Armenians. They comprised about 80% of the region's population. Measures used to suppress similar unrest in Yerevan, the capital of Armenia, included the deployment of troops and

armoured vehicles around government and Communist Party buildings as well as in large city squares. A similar show of force in 16 other locales indicated that the government had no intention of yielding to the protesters' demands.

23 **Lebanon in presidential crisis.** Lebanese Pres. Amin Gemayel, having come to the end of his six-year term, appointed a caretaker military government after the National Assembly was unable to elect a successor. Gemayel, a Maronite Christian, had first tried to form a Cabinet of Christian and Muslim politicians, but he did not succeed. Muslim leaders had warned that the formation of a Cabinet before a president was chosen could plunge the country into new chaos. Gemayel moved ahead, however, citing a 1952 precedent; in 1952 a military government had taken charge while the presidency was vacant for 12 days. The head of the new Cabinet, Maj. Gen. Michel Aoun, was named prime minister and minister of defense and information. He also retained his post as commander of the Army. All religious factions fighting in the civil war were represented in the six-member Cabinet, but the three Muslims refused to serve. A rival Muslim government was soon formed under the leadership of Selim al-Hoss, prime minister when Gemayel's term expired. Both governments claimed to be the nation's only legitimate authority, and both declared they were only attempting to create the proper conditions for an election.

Deaver sentenced for perjury. Michael Deaver, at one time deputy chief of staff in the Reagan administration, was given a suspended three-year sentence, placed on probation, and fined $100,000 for lying to a federal grand jury about his lobbying activities after leaving the White House staff. He was also ordered to perform 1,500 hours of community service and was forbidden to lobby government officials for profit for a period of three years. Federal district court judge Thomas Jackson, rejecting the prosecution's demand that Deaver be imprisoned, said that Deaver's acknowledged alcoholism "does not excuse but it helps to explain" why he had repeatedly lied under oath.

27 **U.S. reforms welfare system.** Representatives of the U.S. Senate, House of Representatives, and the White House approved the final version of a welfare bill that was the first major revision of the nation's welfare system in more than half a century. On September 29 the Senate passed the legislation 96–1; the House followed suit the next day with a vote of 347–53. Sen. Daniel Patrick Moynihan (Dem., N.Y.), chief author of the revision, said Congress had redefined the whole question of dependency. Welfare, Moynihan said, "is no longer to be a permanent or even extended circumstance. It is to be a transition to employment, and it is to be accompanied by child support from the absent parent." Among other things, the new legislation would require individual states to set up education and training programs in order to receive federal funds for welfare. Most welfare recipients would be required to enter these programs or to work.

28 **Kuwait addresses third world debts.** Speaking to the UN General Assembly, Sheikh Jabir al-Ahmad al-Jabir as-Sabah, the emir of Kuwait, called the debts of third world nations the single most important question affecting relations between rich and poor countries. He then proposed a three-point plan for dealing with the problem. First, he suggested that creditor nations consider writing off the interest on loans to very poor nations and possibly part of the principal also. Second, he urged the International Monetary Fund and the World Bank to show more flexibility and to reconsider the "stringent conditions" they have imposed before agreeing to help less developed countries. He then called for expansion and regulation of scientific and technical assistance to poor nations and efforts to conserve their natural and human resources.

Spain approves U.S. bases. The U.S. State Department announced that the U.S. and Spain had negotiated an agreement that would permit the three U.S. bases at Rota, Zaragoza, and Morón to continue their operations for eight more years. Unlike previous agreements, this accord included no U.S. commitment to assist Spain economically or militarily. The government of Prime Minister Felipe González had earlier insisted that the U.S. remove 72 F-16 jets from a base near Madrid within 3½ years. Italy then consented to accept the three squadrons when the time came to redeploy them.

Reagan vetoes textile bill. President Reagan vetoed a trade bill that would have strictly limited U.S. imports of textiles and certain footwear. Reagan called the proposed legislation "protectionism at its worst." He also remarked: "Only improved competitiveness can truly protect [U.S.] jobs, yet there is nothing in this bill that would encourage domestic industries to become more competitive." On October 3 the bill died when the Senate failed to override the veto.

29 **U.S. revives shuttle program.** The U.S. space shuttle *Discovery* was successfully launched from Cape Canaveral, Fla., with five veteran astronauts aboard. It was the first U.S. attempt at manned spaceflight since Jan. 28, 1986, when seven astronauts lost their lives after the shuttle *Challenger* exploded about 73 seconds into the flight. Although the *Discovery* had undergone hundreds of modifications since the *Challenger* tragedy, doubts and worries about the future of the shuttle program were not totally put to rest until the *Discovery* and its crew returned safely to Earth on October 3.

30 **China to tighten controls.** After a five-day meeting of the Central Committee of China's Communist Party, Premier Li Peng (Li P'eng) told a gathering of dignitaries that the nation's economy was getting out of control and that the central government would begin tightening some of the controls it had loosened earlier. He noted that China faced many current problems, the most conspicuous of which was inflation coupled with excessive increases in prices. Li remarked: "We must firmly do away with economic overheating, slow down overly rapid industrial growth, and proceed to maintain a reasonable growth rate." With the encouragement of party leader Zhao Ziyang (Chao Tzu-yang), private farming had increased dramatically, central controls on industry had been relaxed, and free markets had been allowed to determine to a significant degree the price of goods and services. Although inflation had been officially calculated at 24%, some believed the actual rate, especially in large cities, was perhaps twice that high. In recent weeks panic buying, runs on banks, and heavy borrowing by industries and local governments had contributed to social unrest and to uncertainty about the future.

OCTOBER

1 **Gorbachev becomes president.** Mikhail Gorbachev, general secretary of the Communist Party of the Soviet Union, consolidated his power by being unanimously elected chairman of the Presidium of the Supreme Soviet (president). The previous day the Central Committee of the Communist Party had dismissed three veteran members of the Politburo and accepted the retirement of Andrey Gromyko, who had served for decades as foreign minister before being named president. In other significant changes, Anatoly Dobrynin, longtime ambassador to the U.S., lost his post as Central Committee secretary; Vladimir Kryuchkov was named head of the security and intelligence agency; and Egor Ligachev, who held the second highest post in the party and had publicly questioned certain Gorbachev policies, was appointed head of a party commission on agriculture. On October 12 Gorbachev declared that "all agriculture, the entire agrarian sector" should move in the direction of privately leased farms, which had begun as experiments in several regions of the country and had proved successful. Gorbachev did not call for an end to state farms and collectives, but he seemed to want these transformed into service centres for small leased farms.

2 **Pakistan approves party labels.** The Pakistani Supreme Court overturned a decree of the late Pres. Mohammad Zia-ul-Haq that had prohibited candidates in the November 16 election from identifying themselves as members of an opposition political party. This meant that politicians could not appeal for votes as members of an

antigovernment party. The court ruling, it was generally acknowledged, significantly enhanced the election prospects of Benazir Bhutto, who had been Zia's chief political rival and whose father had been overthrown by Zia in 1977 and later hanged.

4 **Honduras wants *contras* expelled.** In a speech to the UN General Assembly, Honduran Foreign Minister Carlos López Contreras urged the UN to create an international peacekeeping force to patrol his country's borders and relocate outside the country an estimated 11,000 Nicaraguan rebels and their 12,000 family members. López suggested the use of Canadian, Spanish, and West German troops. There had been a noticeable increase in the number of *contras* crossing the border after the U.S. Congress cut off military aid. López also requested that a much smaller number of Salvadoran rebels be similarly evacuated. U.S. Assistant Secretary of State Elliott Abrams called the suggestion "an intelligent proposal," but he doubted it would be physically possible to get the rebels out of Honduras.

5 **Pinochet loses plebiscite.** Gen. Augusto Pinochet Ugarte, president of Chile, failed to receive sufficient votes in a national plebiscite to extend his term an additional eight years. Had Pinochet won the simple yes-or-no plebiscite, he planned to resign from the military and run the country as a civilian when his new term commenced in March 1989. Even though Pinochet lost the plebiscite, he was permitted, according to the new constitution, to remain in office until a successor was elected, probably in December 1989. Incomplete returns indicated that "no" votes comprised about 55% of the total cast. The following day Pinochet publicly acknowledged defeat and pledged to respect the result of the plebiscite and see to it that others respected it also. Although there were clamours for Pinochet's immediate resignation, there was also talk of reconciliation and the need to come together to prepare for the transition from tough military rule to a civilian government and greater democracy.

Brazil adopts new charter. After nearly two years of often intense wrangling, Brazil adopted a new constitution that was viewed as a giant step away from dictatorship and toward democracy. The new charter strengthened civil rights, guaranteed the right of workers to strike, and institutionalized social programs. It also lowered the voting age from 18 to 16, abolished censorship, invested state and municipal governments with broader authority, and gave Congress extensive powers to determine national economic policies. In November 1989, for the first time since 1960, Brazil would elect a new president by direct popular vote. The new constitution, moreover, abolished the president's right to decree new laws. Knowing this, Pres. José Sarney's government became, in the words of an angry critic, "a factory of decrees." The October 4 issue of the *Official Gazette*, about four times its normal size, contained a mass of new decrees and appointments. Although no group was entirely satisfied with the new constitution, many viewed it as a monumental change for the better and an end to more than two decades of military rule.

6 **Klan groups heavily fined.** A federal jury in Atlanta, Ga., found the Invisible Empire Knights of the Ku Klux Klan, the Southern White Knights, and 11 members of those organizations guilty of violently disrupting a January 1987 civil rights march in Forsyth County. During the trial, former Klansmen testified that they had been directed to show up at the "brotherhood march" to incite violence. When the jury's verdict was unsealed on October 25, the court ordered each of the two organizations to pay $400,000 to the 50 plaintiffs. In addition, David Holland, the grand dragon of the Southern White Knights, was ordered to pay $50,000 in damages. The smallest fine imposed on an individual was $1,000. Morris Dees, who represented the plaintiffs, acknowledged that racial violence would not cease until people's hearts and minds changed. Until that happened, he said, lawsuits were the best alternative.

10 **Czechoslovak premier resigns.** Lubomir Strougal, premier of Czechoslovakia for 18 years, and Peter Colotka, the deputy premier, resigned their respective offices. They stepped down presumably because their views were not in harmony with those of Milos Jakes, the leader of the country's Communist Party. The next day the entire Cabinet of Ministers submitted their resignations, and Ladislav Adamec was named Strougal's successor. He was expected to promote change at a more gradual pace than that championed by Strougal. There were, in addition, five new appointments to the Presidium. Taken together, the changes placed Jakes in an advantageous position for carrying out his programs.

11 **Bank charged with money laundering.** The U.S. government indicted 9 executives and 76 other employees of the Bank of Credit and Commerce International S.A. (BCCI) and its holding company, BCCI Holdings. The Luxembourg-based institution operated in more than 70 countries and had assets in excess of $20 billion. The indictment charged that BCCI—the institution as such, not merely individual officers or employees—had conspired with cocaine traffickers to launder millions of dollars derived from a drug network that stretched from Europe to the U.S. to Colombia. The indictment came after a two-year undercover operation that involved U.S. Customs Service agents who passed themselves off as experts in money laundering and acted as intermediaries in the transfer of $14 million between the drug dealers and the bank.

12 **Brazil to protect rain forest.** In a televised address, Brazilian Pres. José Sarney announced that his government was initiating a series of steps that would put an end to the rapid destruction of the rain forests in the Amazon River basin. Sarney said he was moved to act when he learned that more than 6,000 fires had been set in a single day by landowners attempting to clear the land. Environmentalists were especially elated to learn that preservation of the forests along the Atlantic coast would be given high priority. The forests, believed to have once covered some 365,000 sq km (140,000 sq mi), now covered about 10,500 sq km (4,000 sq mi). Pressure to stop the wholesale destruction of the forests had also come from the World Bank, which had furnished Brazil with large sums of money for development projects.

Military contractor fined $115 million. U.S. authorities announced that the Sundstrand Corp. had agreed to plead guilty to charges of fraud against the U.S. Department of Defense involving overcharging on military contracts and billing the government for such things as country club fees and babysitters. The company also agreed to pay $115 million in fines and penalties. Anton Valukas, the U.S. attorney in Chicago who directed the two-year investigation, stated in a news conference that the government had been overcharged millions of dollars in various conspiracies between 1980 and 1986. Although no individuals were named in the indictment, prosecutors admitted that government officials might have received illegal gratuities from the contractor. A grand jury would later be convened to decide if indictments against company and government employees were warranted.

14 **Senate approves genocide treaty.** Forty years after Pres. Harry Truman proposed an international treaty to outlaw genocide, the U.S. Senate gave approval to legislative changes in the U.S. criminal code that would make it possible for the U.S. to become, as 97 other countries had already become, a signatory to the treaty. The treaty itself had been approved by the Senate, as the Constitution required, in February 1986, but a dispute over the imposition of capital punishment had halted the legal process. Certain senators continued to insist on the death penalty as an appropriate penalty for genocide; others, as a matter of principle, were opposed to it. The impasse was overcome when it was finally agreed that the crime of genocide—"the intent to destroy, in whole or in part, a national, ethnic, racial, or religious group"—would, in the most flagrant cases, be punishable by a fine of up to $1 million and life imprisonment. For attempting to cause permanent mental impairment through torture or drugs, and for similar crimes, the penalty could be a $1 million fine and up to 20 years in prison.

15 **U.S. promises more aid while using bases in Philippines.** The Philippines and the U.S. reached basic agreement on terms that would govern continued U.S. operation of military bases in the Philippines through September 1991. The accord called for a U.S. payment of $481 million in economic, military, and developmental assistance in both 1990 and 1991, the final two years of an agreement already in effect. The prenegotiation figure had been $180 million a year. The Subic Bay Naval Station

was the U.S. Navy's principal repair and supply centre for its Asian fleet, and Clark Air Base north of Manila was the home of the 13th Air Force and a major ammunition depot. In recent years the voices of Filipinos demanding the total removal of U.S. military bases had been growing increasingly more strident.

17 **Mexico to get U.S. loan.** The U.S. announced it would provide debt-ridden Mexico with up to $3.5 billion in short-term loans to help it cope with urgent economic problems arising from a sharp drop in oil prices. Long-term loans from the World Bank and the International Monetary Fund were expected to be approved, but it would take several months at least to work out the details of such large-scale assistance. The previous largest U.S. loan to a Latin-American country was $1.8 billion made to Mexico in 1982. A U.S. Treasury official noted that Mexico had slashed its annual inflation rate from 150% to a current 10% and had done a better job than many other debtor nations in repaying its loans on schedule.

18 **Roh Tae Woo addresses UN.** South Korean Pres. Roh Tae Woo, in an address to the UN General Assembly, called for an international conference to help lessen tensions on the Korean Peninsula and lay the groundwork for the eventual reunification of Korea. Rho suggested that China, Japan, the Soviet Union, and the U.S. join North and South Korea in such a conference. Rho used the occasion to recall his declaration of July 7, which, among other things, called for greater mutual respect and cooperation between North and South Korea and improved relations with the world community. He also renewed his offer to meet Kim Il Sung at any time to "explore together possible avenues of compromise acceptable to both sides." As both Korean governments held only observer status at the UN, Roh had to gain approval to speak. The next day North Korea's deputy foreign minister told the Assembly there was little hope in the foreseeable future for improved relations with South Korea. He then repeated an earlier proposal made by his government

Imelda Marcos, wife of former Philippine president Ferdinand Marcos, is escorted to a federal court in New York City, where she was to face charges of racketeering.
A. TANNENBAUM—SYGMA

that both parts of Korea become equal partners in a confederal republic that would represent all of Korea at the United Nations and in foreign affairs.

21 **U.S. indicts Marcos.** The U.S. government indicted Ferdinand Marcos, former president of the Philippines, his wife, Imelda, and eight associates, charging them with racketeering. A federal grand jury in New York City decided there was sufficient evidence to conclude that Marcos had used more than $100 million he had embezzled while president of the Philippines to buy three buildings in New York City. Marcos's illegal dealings outside the U.S. were relevant under U.S. law because such activities were shown to be part of a pattern of racketeering involving U.S. institutions, especially as the criminal activity continued in the U.S. after Marcos left his homeland in February 1986. The indictment also charged Marcos with fraudulently borrowing $165 million from U.S. banks. The Marcoses were ordered to appear in a New York City court on October 31 to be arraigned or face arrest "like anyone else." Federal officials

acquainted with the case estimated that, if convicted, the Marcoses could forfeit at least $250 million in assets. On October 31 Imelda Marcos pleaded not guilty to racketeering charges. After a friend posted her $5 million bond, she was allowed to rejoin her husband in Hawaii. A doctor had certified that Marcos was too ill at the time to travel to New York for his arraignment.

22 **U.S. passes tough drug bill.** The U.S. Congress, in its final act before adjournment, passed a comprehensive drug bill aimed at reducing both the supply and the consumption of illegal drugs. The legislation placed new emphasis on the treatment of addicts, on educational programs, and on the so-called recreational use of drugs. It also sanctioned the death penalty in the case of murders committed by anyone involved in two or more continuing illegal drug operations. A similar fate awaited anyone guilty of killing a police officer while engaged in a drug-related crime. A Senate provision that would have subjected workers in the aviation, railroad, motor carrier, mass transit, and nuclear power industries to random drug testing was eliminated. Sen. Warren Rudman (Rep., N.H.), chief author of the bill, called the legislation "probably the first comprehensive assault on drugs in our nation's history."

24 **Helmut Kohl visits Moscow.** West German Chancellor Helmut Kohl arrived in Moscow to discuss with Soviet leader Mikhail Gorbachev ways of improving relations between their two countries. Early in the visit Gorbachev declared that the ice had been broken and that discussions were leading in the right direction. Kohl expressed optimism about the future, but he pointed out that the large number of Eastern bloc troops along his nation's border and Warsaw Pact superiority in short-range nuclear weapons aimed at West Germany were issues of overriding importance to his country. Kohl suggested that the ultimate goal of East-West negotiations should be an overall reduction in military might and a gradual shift to weapons not designed for large-scale offensive actions or for surprise attacks.

NOVEMBER

1 **Israeli election inconclusive.** After an intense campaign, Israeli voters gave Prime Minister Yitzhak Shamir's Likud bloc a narrow victory over the Labour Party of Foreign Minister Shimon Peres, but neither party had sufficient representation in the Knesset (parliament) to form a government. Four years earlier Israel's two major parties had found themselves in virtually the same situation. They resolved the problem by agreeing to form a coalition with Peres serving as prime minister and Shamir as foreign minister for 25 months; the two then exchanged offices during the second half of the term. The result was often bitter disagreement. The far-right religious parties gained most in the recent election

and hoped to persuade Shamir to accept their tough demands as the price for their support. Shamir could then form a coalition and rule without help from the Labour Party.

8 **Bush wins U.S. presidency.** George Bush, candidate of the Republican Party, was elected 41st president of the United States. The vice president-elect, J. Danforth Quayle, was a senator from Indiana. Although the Bush-Quayle ticket won about 54% of the popular vote, the Republican margin of victory in the electoral college was far more conclusive. When the final tallies were announced, Gov. Michael Dukakis of Massachusetts and his Democratic

running mate, Sen. Lloyd Bentsen of Texas, had won only 10 of the 50 states and the District of Columbia. The Democratic Party, however, retained control of both the Senate and the House of Representatives. Political analysts saw in this a general endorsement of the status quo coupled with a desire on the part of the electorate to give the Democrats a strong voice in formulating national and international policies. The news media and the general public found the campaign rhetoric both uninspiring and unusually nasty, with more attention frequently given to insignificant matters and to tearing down the opposition than to serious consideration of the major issues facing the nation.

15 **Arafat proclaims Palestinian state.** Yasir Arafat, chairman of the Palestine Liberation Organization (PLO), announced the establishment of an independent Palestinian state with Jerusalem as its capital. The pronouncement came during a speech to the Palestine National Council, the Palestinians' parliament in exile, which was meeting in Algiers. Arafat stated that a 1947 United Nations plan that made provision for an Arab and a Jewish state offered a basis for "international legitimacy." His declaration had no immediate practical consequences because the West Bank, Gaza Strip, and the Arab sector of Jerusalem, which presumably would be the core of any Palestinian state, were all occupied by Israeli troops. An important implication of Arafat's speech was his apparent willingness to recognize, for the first time, the state of Israel.

16 **Bhutto's party wins plurality.** The Pakistan People's Party (PPP), led by Benazir Bhutto, won 92 of 215 contested seats in elections to Pakistan's National Assembly. The Islamic Democratic Alliance finished second with 55 seats. The remaining seats were won by independents and members of minority parties. Two days later Bhutto asked acting president Ghulam Ishaq Khan for the opportunity to form a coalition government. The president had constitutional authority to select anyone as prime minister, but he decided to give Bhutto the opportunity she had requested. On December 2, after receiving promises of support from non-PPP politicians, Bhutto was installed as prime minister and became the first woman, at least in modern times, to rule an Islamic nation. Rejecting the advice of conservative Muslim clerics, Khan had defended Bhutto's constitutional right to the prime ministership. In this matter, he said, theology and government are clearly separate realms. Khan then lifted the state of emergency imposed in August when then president Mohammad Zia-ul-Haq died in a plane crash. Khan also accepted the resignations of all current ministers and presidential advisers so that Bhutto would have a free hand in choosing those she would be working with.

Estonia asserts political rights. The Supreme Soviet of the Republic of Estonia approved a constitutional amendment that gave Estonia the right to ignore any Soviet law it deemed to be an infringement of its own local authority. Although the action underscored sharp differences with the central government in Moscow, it was far less than a declaration of independence. It did, however, signal strong opposition to Moscow's plan to set economic and social policies for the entire country, with or without the approval of local governments. Latvia and Lithuania, the two other Baltic republics, were also opposed to certain planned changes, but they did not appear disposed to challenge Moscow as vehemently as Estonia. On December 7 Estonia's Supreme Soviet voted 150–91 to reconfirm its earlier stand.

21 **Canadians reelect Mulroney.** In parliamentary elections Canadian Prime Minister Brian Mulroney's

Canadian Prime Minister Brian Mulroney's party, the Progressive Conservatives, won a decisive victory in the November parliamentary elections.
M. PONOMAREFF—GAMMA/LIAISON

Progressive Conservatives (PCs) won 170 of the 295 seats in the House of Commons. The victory of the PCs assured Mulroney of another term as prime minister and virtually guaranteed ratification of the controversial U.S.-Canadian free-trade agreement that had been tentatively approved by both countries on October 4. The issue of free trade had dominated the campaign. Many of the Canadians who voted for John Turner's Liberal Party or for the New Democratic Party led by Edward Broadbent felt free trade with the U.S. was tantamount to a sellout of Canadian national interests. Annual trade between the two countries was thought to be about $150 billion.

22 **U.S. unveils Stealth bomber.** During a rollout ceremony at U.S. Air Force Plant 42 in the Mohave Desert in California, news media personnel and members of Congress were given a restricted view of the B-2 Stealth bomber. The aircraft, developed by Northrop Corp. under tight security, was designed to penetrate Soviet airspace undetected and seek out underground command centres and mobile missile launchers. Although the Stealth had not yet flown, the Air Force planned to purchase 132 at a cost of at least $500 million each.

23 **Chun Doo Hwan apologizes to nation.** Chun Doo Hwan, former president of South Korea, apologized to the nation for the misdeeds and abuse of power that occurred during his tenure in office. He also announced that he would surrender all his personal assets to the state, including his home, and would not hesitate to accept any kind of punishment as long as he was allowed to remain in his homeland. Chun's statement came after opposition parties began demanding that he, his wife, and certain relatives and close friends be prosecuted for their alleged misdeeds. When it became apparent that Chun's apology had not appeased his severest

critics, Pres. Roh Tae Woo appealed for clemency and forgiveness.

Protests banned in Yugoslavia. Officials in Serbia's autonomous province of Kosovo outlawed all public assemblies and forbade organized groups of demonstrators to enter Pristina, the provincial capital. The announcement was meant to curb protests by ethnic Albanians, a majority in Kosovo, who were demanding an end to Serbian "interference" in their local affairs. The Albanians, chanting patriotic slogans and carrying Yugoslav flags, had marched repeatedly to protest mandated changes in their local Communist Party leadership and in their province's constitutional status. The nation's high inflation rate, its huge foreign debt, and other economic problems were also creating social turmoil in other parts of the country. According to news reports, about 25% of the people were unable to pay their utility bills and faced a cutoff of natural gas, electricity, and water.

Hungary chooses prime minister. The Central Committee of Hungary's Communist Party announced the selection of Miklos Nemeth as prime minister. After formal approval by Parliament, he would replace Karoly Grosz, who had taken over the party leadership from Janos Kadar in May. Rezso Nyers, an advocate of economic change, was nominated for the new post of state minister in charge of economic affairs. He had reportedly declined the prime ministership when the conditions he laid down were rejected.

24 **OPEC to control oil output.** After days of heated debate, the 13 nations belonging to OPEC reached agreement on oil-production quotas that were intended to lower production from 23 million to 18.5 million bbl per day for a period of six months. If the quotas were observed, the average price of oil was expected to rise from about $12 per barrel to nearly $18 per barrel. Under pressure from Arab leaders, Iran agreed to allow Iraq to match its daily production of about 2.6 million bbl. Iraq then agreed to operate within the quota system for the

FILIP HORVAT—PICTURE GROUP

Ethnic conflict between Serbs and Albanians in the autonomous province of Kosovo led Yugoslav officials to ban all public assemblies there.

first time since 1986. Even though past OPEC agreements were often violated, oil experts believed there was a better than usual chance that this one would hold.

Iran and Iraq exchange POWs. In the first exchange of Iranian and Iraqi prisoners of war since a cease-fire was declared on August 20, 52 Iraqis and 19 Iranians were repatriated by the International Committee of the Red Cross. The exchange took place four days behind schedule and involved fewer than half the average number of soldiers scheduled to be moved each day for a period of ten days. Only the sick and wounded were included in the exchange agreement, but each soldier had the right to request asylum. With Iran claiming that several thousand Iraqis had received asylum, and with unspecified numbers declared no longer sick, the Red Cross was hard pressed to carry out its mission.

27 **Jorge Blanco convicted.** Salvador Jorge Blanco, president of the Dominican Republic from 1982 to 1986, and two businessmen were convicted of corruption and sentenced to 20 years in prison. The three were also fined a total of $17.3 million, $5 million of which represented overcharges for police and military supplies. Because Jorge Blanco was living in Atlanta, Ga., he was tried in absentia and, for that reason, could not legally present a defense or have witnesses appear on his behalf. When Jorge Blano returned home on November 30 to file an appeal, he was immediately arrested.

DECEMBER

1 **Mexico wants debt relief.** Carlos Salinas de Gortari, shortly after taking the oath of office as president of Mexico, declared that his country could no longer consider repayment of its enormous foreign debt its top priority. "This is not demagoguery or an admonition," he said. "It is a reasoned argument that derives from the needs of my people and the enormous effort we have made." He then added, "But I declare emphatically and with conviction that the interests of Mexicans are above the interests of creditors." Foreign bankers conceded that Mexico needed both debt relief and additional credits.

2 **Argentine soldiers try to free convicted officers.** An estimated 500 Argentine soldiers seized control of an infantry school outside Buenos Aires and tried to capture a prison where senior military officers convicted of human rights abuses were being held. The government immediately ordered troops to subdue the rebels. A colonel who claimed to be the leader of the revolt told reporters that his sole aim was "to restore military honour to the army and to review the trials that punished the just." The revolt ended on December 5 with the surrender of the colonel and his followers. On December 20 the commander of Argentina's Army resigned, yielding to demands made by the disgruntled rebels. Pres. Raúl Alfonsín then appointed a replacement, pointedly refusing to submit the appointment to the rebels for their approval.

4 **Red Cross aids starving Sudanese.** The International Committee of the Red Cross began flying food into two famine-ravaged towns in southern Sudan. It took a year of frustrating negotiations before the Red Cross got permission from the central government to deliver the badly needed supplies. During that time thousands of Sudanese died of starvation. The Khartoum government, located in the north, had long resisted because it did not want to alleviate the sufferings in the south, where rebel forces of the Sudan People's Liberation Army were based. One Red Cross flight carried food to Wau, which was held by government forces. The other went to Akon, which was controlled by insurgents.

Pérez elected in Venezuela. Carlos Andrés Pérez, candidate of the Acción Democrática Party, was elected president of Venezuela. His closest rival among numerous other candidates was Eduardo Fernández of the Social Christian Party. Incomplete returns indicated that Pérez had won an absolute majority of the popular vote. Pérez had already served as president from 1974 to 1979, but constitutional law did not permit him to campaign again for the presidency during the following two five-year terms. Pérez said his first priority after assuming office in February 1989 would be to renegotiate payment of his country's $32 billion foreign debt.

5 **Roh Tae Woo revamps Cabinet.** South Korean Pres. Roh Tae Woo replaced 20 of the 24 ministers in his Cabinet in an apparent effort to distance himself from his disgraced predecessor, Chun Doo Hwan. Roh named Kang Young Hoon, a retired army general, prime minister; he replaced Lee Hyun Jae. Cho Soon, a professor at Seoul National University and the author of books on South Korea's economic development, was named deputy prime minister and minister of economic planning. Despite such wholesale changes, Roh was still criticized by political opponents for retaining or appointing ministers with military backgrounds or with opinions that were considered more hard-line than democratic.

7 **Gorbachev to cut military.** During an address to the General Assembly of the United Nations, Soviet leader Mikhail Gorbachev announced unilateral cuts in Soviet military strength. Gorbachev pledged to reduce Soviet military power by 500,000 men and 10,000 tanks over the next two years, remove about half of the Soviet tanks deployed in Eastern Europe, and withdraw a major portion of the Soviet forces stationed along the Chinese border. Although the announced cuts were applauded by Western nations, they noted that compared with NATO the Soviets would still have overwhelming superiority in conventional forces. Gorbachev's announcement was not only a great diplomatic success; the approximately 10% cut in Soviet military might promised to save the U.S.S.R. a vast sum of money at a time when money was sorely needed.

Quake devastates Armenia. An earthquake that measured 6.9 on the open-ended Richter scale virtually destroyed several cities in the Armenian S.S.R. Initial reports from the scene were so spotty that officials in Moscow were at first unaware of the magnitude of the calamity. Soon, however, rescue teams, equipment, medicines, food, and clothing were arriving in Armenia from all over the world. The final death toll was put at 25,000, far lower than originally feared. When Soviet leader Mikhail Gorbachev visited the scene, after a hasty departure from New York City, he castigated those responsible for the shoddy construction of the buildings. Thousands were killed when the buildings split in half or fell apart.

12 **North Korea names premier.** North Korea's official news agency announced that Yon Hyong Muk, a member of the Communist Party's Politburo, had replaced Li Gun Mo as premier. Li, who had held the office since December 1986, was reportedly in poor health. The Supreme People's Assembly also approved the appointment of Han Song Ryang as secretary of the party's Central Committee. The changes were made during a special meeting of the assembly, which presumably also dealt with the broader political problem created by its closest allies, China and the Soviet Union, which were rapidly improving relations with South Korea.

A. MORVAN—GAMMA/LIAISON

PLO leader Yasir Arafat attends a press conference in Geneva, where he formally renounced terrorism and recognized Israel's right to exist.

Homes devastated by the remains of a jetliner, Pan Am flight 103, were only part of the tragedy that resulted when a bomb exploded aboard the Boeing 747, causing it to crash in Lockerbie, Scotland.

JOHN PAUL—GAMMA/LIAISON

14 **U.S. to hold talks with PLO.** In a dramatic turn of events, Secretary of State George Shultz announced that the U.S. was now prepared to begin "a substantive dialogue with PLO representatives." Shultz explained that the PLO had finally met U.S. conditions for such talks by unequivocally stating that it accepted UN Security Council Resolutions 242 and 338, recognized Israel's right to exist in peace and security, and renounced terrorism. The previous day, during a special session of the UN in Geneva, Yasir Arafat, the chairman of the PLO, had said much the same thing, but he had used words that were judged by the U.S. to be too ambiguous and therefore susceptible to different interpretations. Arafat removed the ambiguities the following day. The UN had voted to convene a special session in Geneva after the U.S. on November 26 refused to grant Arafat a visa to enter the U.S. The State Department cited Arafat's membership in the PLO, which was classified as a terrorist organization.

Strike paralyzes Spain. At least 70% of Spain's work force participated in a national strike that was described as the nation's largest work stoppage since 1934. When pleas by Prime Minister Felipe González Márquez to negotiate rather than strike went unheeded, it was clear that dissatisfaction with the policies of the Socialist government were broad and deep. For several years the unions had complained that the government's anti-inflation policies and the nation's steady economic boom had not benefited ordinary workers. The unions demanded new elections or at least new government policies that would reward workers as much as businessmen. On December 21, addressing a special session of the Cortes (parliament), González ruled out new elections but admitted he had underestimated the depth of discontent throughout the country. He then called for discussions to resolve the workers' grievances.

15 **Hanoi returns remains of 38 U.S. servicemen.** During a ceremony at the Hanoi airport, Vietnamese officials turned over the remains of 38 individuals who were believed to be U.S. servicemen still classified as missing in action during the Vietnam war. Each of the 38 metal caskets was draped with an American flag and placed aboard

an air force plane by a U.S. military honour guard. The U.S. Army Central Identification Laboratory in Hawaii would undertake the slow and tedious task of attempting to identify the remains.

19 **Sri Lanka elects president.** Prime Minister Ranasinghe Premadasa was elected president of Sri Lanka with 50.9% of the popular vote, according to figures released on December 20 by the National Election Commission. Sirimavo Bandaranaike, a former prime minister, was given 44.9% of the vote. Charging fraud, she vowed to challenge the results before the Supreme Court. A ten-member group that monitored the election stated that "the problem of general intimidation during the election was unprecedented." On December 3 Pres. Junius Richard Jayawardene announced that he would dissolve Parliament on December 20 and advance elections by six months so his successor would have a new legislature in February 1989.

21 **Bomb kills 259 on Pan Am flight.** A Pan Am Boeing 747, on a flight from London to New York City, crashed in a Scottish village after a bomb exploded on the aircraft while it was flying over Scotland at 9,500 m (31,000 ft). In addition to the 259 persons aboard the plane, perhaps 11 others on the ground also lost their lives. A laboratory examination of a ripped suitcase and selected parts of the aircraft confirmed beyond doubt that the plane had been destroyed by plastic explosives. Scotland Yard and the FBI began "a criminal inquiry of international dimensions" to determine when and how the bomb got on the plane and who was responsible for putting it there. The U.S. government also announced a reward of up to $500,000 for information leading to the prosecution of anyone responsible for destroying the plane. The investigation was expected to continue until the case was solved or until there was no glimmer of hope of ever tracking down the guilty party or parties.

22 **Accords on Africa signed.** Angola, Cuba, and South Africa signed two accords that would grant independence to South West Africa/Namibia and remove Cuban troops from neighbouring Angola. The formal settlement, which was signed at the United Nations in

the presence of U.S. Secretary of State George Shultz, came only after years of difficult negotiations. The first accord required South Africa to give up control of Namibia; the second obliged Cuba to withdraw all its estimated 50,000 troops from Angola by July 1, 1991. Because the U.S. and South Africa emphatically confirmed that their support for the Angolan rebel forces of Jonas Savimbi would continue until Angola made peace with the rebels, the meeting ended on a bitter note. The foreign minister of South Africa, for instance, challenged the Cuban foreign minister to a debate on each country's human rights records after the Cuban accused South Africa and the U.S. of causing "enormous destruction and tens of thousands of deaths" by supporting the rebels. The South African also said he was prepared to name many black African presidents who had asked that his nation's troops remain in Namibia until the last Cuban soldier had departed.

Shamir forms government. Nearly two months after national parliamentary elections, Israeli Prime Minister Yitzhak Shamir's newly formed coalition government formally assumed power. Urged on by recent political developments, especially the decision of the U.S. to begin talks with the PLO, Shamir's Likud bloc and the Labour Party of former prime minister Shimon Peres set aside their differences and agreed to join together in a new coalition. Before that point was reached, both groups were involved in heated intraparty squabbles over the conditions of the political alliance.

23 **U.S. readies trade penalties.** An aide to U.S. trade representative Clayton Yeutter announced that the U.S. wanted to "make sure the Europeans knew exactly where they stood" if they imposed their announced January 1 ban on imports of U.S. meat from animals treated with growth hormones. President Reagan had already signed an executive order authorizing 100% duty on $100 million of annual imports from the European Communities (EC) if the ban went into effect. The EC ban and the U.S. threat of retaliation were manifestations of broader disagreements over trade policies and efforts by the EC to create a single market in Europe by 1992. The Europeans were similarly concerned about the effects of the new free-trade pact entered into by the U.S. and Canada. Both the EC and the U.S. realized that their annual trade of $150 billion could be jeopardized if current and future problems were not satisfactorily resolved.

24 **Canada approves free trade.** Canada's House of Commons voted 141–111 in favour of the Canada-U.S. free-trade agreement that was scheduled to go into effect at the beginning of the new year. The vote was definitive, but several pro forma matters still required action before the ten-year accord was technically ratified. Many who favoured the free-trade agreement believed it had worldwide significance because it might encourage other nations to lower their tariffs and remove other restrictions on international trade.

Major Revisions from the 1989 *Macropædia*

The purpose of this section is to introduce to continuing *Book of the Year* subscribers selected *Macropædia* articles or portions of them that have been completely revised or written anew. It is intended to update the *Macropædia* in ways that cannot be accomplished fully by reviewing the year's events or by revising statistics annually, because the *Macropædia* texts themselves—written from a longer perspective than any yearly revision—supply authoritative interpretation and analysis as well as narrative and description.

Three articles have been chosen from the 1989 print-

ing: the wholly new *Physical and human geography* section of MEXICO; the extensively revised sections of PRE-COLUMBIAN CIVILIZATIONS dealing with the Lowland Maya and Andean civilizations; and—also extensively revised—the section of The History of Western ARCHITECTURE on *20th-century architecture*. All are the work of distinguished scholars and represent the continuing dedication of the *Encyclopædia Britannica* to bringing such works to the general reader. A bibliographical updating of the *Macropædia* begins on page 61.

Mexico

Mexico, or the United Mexican States (Spanish: Estados Unidos Mexicanos), is a federal republic located in North America. Sharing a common border throughout its northern extent with the United States, the country is bounded on the west and south by the Pacific Ocean, to the east by the Gulf of Mexico and the Caribbean Sea, and on the southeast by Guatemala and Belize. Roughly triangular in shape, Mexico covers an area of 756,066 square miles (1,958,201 square kilometres). While it is more than 1,850 miles (3,000 kilometres) across the country from northwest to southeast, the width varies from less than 135 miles at the Isthmus of Tehuantepec to more than 1,200 miles in the north.

Physical and human geography

THE LAND

Relief. Mexico is located in one of the Earth's most dynamic tectonic areas. It is a part of the circum-Pacific "Ring of Fire," a region of active volcanism and frequent seismic activity. Towering peaks, such as Citlaltépetl (also called Orizaba; 18,701 feet [5,700 metres]) and Popocatépetl (17,883 feet [5,452 metres]), are extremely young in geologic terms (late Tertiary) and are examples of the volcanic forces that built much of the central and southern parts of the country. Mexico is situated on the western, or leading, edge of the huge North American Plate, whose interaction with the Pacific, Cocos, and Caribbean plates has, over geologic time, given rise to the earth-building processes of the area. The complexity found in southern Mexico's physiography is due to the interaction among these tectonic plates, which produces numerous and severe earth movements. It is in this dynamical but often unstable physical environment that the Mexican people have built their nation.

On the basis of geologic history and surface configuration,

Mexico can be divided into eight major landform regions. The largest, and most important for human habitation, is the Mexican Plateau. Extending from the Isthmus of Tehuantepec northward to the U.S. border, this region consists of a central plateau and its dissected borders. The central plateau tilts gently upward from the north toward the south. At its northern end the plateau is about 4,000 feet above sea level, and it rises to more than 8,000 feet south of Mexico City. Throughout the plateau, flattish intermontane basins and *bolsones* (ephemeral interior drainage basins) are interrupted by mountainous outcrops.

The central plateau is divided into two major parts. The Mesa del Norte begins near the U.S. border and ends near San Luis Potosí. In this arid, lower part of the Mexican Plateau, interior drainage (that is, without outlet to the ocean) predominates, and there are few permanent streams. The Mesa Central stretches from San Luis Potosí to just south of Mexico City. Formed largely by volcanic action, the surface of the Mesa Central is higher (7,000 to 9,000 feet above sea level), moister, and generally flatter than the Mesa del Norte. The Mesa Central is divided into a series of fairly level intermontane basins separated by eroded volcanic peaks. The largest valleys, such as those of Mexico, Puebla, and Guadalajara, rarely exceed 100 square miles in area, while many others are quite small. The basins are generally fertile; the traditional breadbasket of the country, the Guanajuato Basin, is located in the northern part of the Mesa Central. Many of the basins were sites of major lakes that were drained to facilitate European settlement. Around Mexico City the weak, structurally unstable soils that remain have caused buildings to shift on their foundations and over many years to sink slowly into the ground.

The Mexican Plateau is flanked by dissected mountainous borders. To the west is the largely volcanic Sierra Madre Occidental, with an average height of 8,000 to

The Mexican Plateau

9,000 feet. It has been highly incised by westward-flowing streams that eroded a series of deep canyons, or *barrancas,* the most spectacular of which is the Barranca del Cobre ("Copper Canyon"), Mexico's Grand Canyon. The Sierra Madre Oriental, a range of folded mountains formed of shales and limestones, is situated on the eastern side of the Mexican Plateau. With average elevations similar to those of the Sierra Madre Occidental, this highly dissected highland region has peaks exceeding 12,000 feet. The Neo-Volcánica Cordillera (also called the Transverse Volcanic Axis), with spectacular snow-capped peaks such as Popocatépetl, Ixtacíhuatl (17,342 feet [5,286 metres]), and Toluca (14,954 feet [4,558 metres]), forms the southern boundary of the Mexican Plateau.

Coastal lowlands

East and west of the Mexican Plateau lie the country's coastal lowlands. The Gulf Coastal Plain extends some 900 miles along the Gulf of Mexico from the Texas border to the Yucatán Peninsula. Characterized by lagoons and low-lying swampy areas east of the abrupt escarpment formed by the Sierra Madre Oriental, the triangular northern portion of the plain is more than 100 miles wide near the U.S. border but tapers toward the south. North of Tampico, an outlier of the Sierra Madre Oriental reaches the sea and interrupts the continuity of the Gulf Coastal Plain. South from there the plain is narrow and irregular, widening at the northern end of the Isthmus of Tehuantepec and then encompassing the horizontal limestone formations that underlie the Yucatán Peninsula.

The Pacific Coastal Lowlands, much narrower and less well defined than their east coast counterpart, begin near the Mexicali Valley in the north and terminate near Tuxpan, some 900 miles to the south; despite their name, for most of this distance the lowlands face the Gulf of California. Bounded on the east by the steep-sided Sierra Madre Occidental, the Pacific Coastal Lowlands are a series of coastal terraces, mesas, and small basins interspersed with riverine deltas and restricted coastal strips. Parts of this arid region have become important sites of irrigated agricultural production.

Baja California

An isolated strip of extremely arid land, the Baja California Peninsula is nearly 800 miles long but seldom more than 100 miles wide. The central core of the peninsula is a huge granitic fault block with peaks of more than 9,000 feet above sea level in the San Pedro Martír and Sierra de Juárez. The gently sloping western side of these mountain ranges is in contrast to the steep eastern escarpment, which makes access from the Gulf of California extremely difficult.

The Balsas Depression, which takes its name from the major river draining the region, lies immediately south of the Mexican Plateau. The depression is formed of small, irregular basins interrupted by hilly outcrops, which gives this hot, dry area a distinctive physical landscape.

The Southern Highlands are a series of highly dissected mountain ranges and plateaus. On their southwestern side, approximately from Puerto Vallarta to the Gulf of Tehuantepec, are a series of ranges known collectively as the Sierra Madre del Sur. These relatively low (7,000 to 8,000 feet above sea level) crystalline mountains often reach the sea to create a rugged coastal margin, part of which is known as the Mexican Riviera. Picturesque coastal sites, such as Ixtapa-Zihuatanejo, Acapulco, and Puerto Escondido, are favourite tourist destinations, while the less hospitable inland basins provide a difficult environment for traditional peasant farmers. Farther northeast is the Mesa del Sur, with numerous stream-eroded ridges and small, isolated valleys some 4,000 to 5,000 feet above sea level. The Oaxaca Valley is the largest and most densely settled of these valleys. With its predominantly Indian population, it is one of the most picturesque yet poorest parts of Mexico.

A low-lying, narrow constriction of land, the Isthmus of Tehuantepec reaches an elevation of less than 900 feet. Its hilly central area is bordered on either side by narrow coastal plains.

The Chiapas Highlands, an extension of the mountain ranges of Central America, are composed of a series of fault block mountains surrounding a high rift valley. The low, crystalline Sierra de Soconusco range lies along the Pacific coast. To the northwest and paralleling the coast is the rift valley of the Grijalva River. A group of highly dissected, folded, and faulted mountains is located between the valley and the Tabasco Plain, a southeastern extension of the Gulf Coastal Plain.

To the northeast of the Tabasco Plain and extending into the Gulf of Mexico is the Yucatán Peninsula. The peninsula's limestone terrain is generally flat to rolling and seldom exceeds 500 feet in elevation. There is little surface drainage, and subterranean erosion has produced caverns and sinkholes, the latter being formed when cavern roofs collapse. The islands of Cozumel and Mujeres lie off the peninsula's northeastern tip.

Drainage. Because of its climatic characteristics and arrangement of landforms, Mexico has few major rivers or natural lakes. The largest are found in the central part of the country. The Lerma River has its headwaters in the Toluca Basin, west of Mexico City, and flows westward to form Lake Chapala, the country's largest natural lake. The Santiago River then flows out of the lake to the northwest, crossing the Sierra Madre Occidental on its way to the Pacific. The eastward-flowing Moctezuma-Pánuco river system, which drains much of the eastern portion of the Mesa Central, has carved gorges through the Sierra Madre Oriental to reach the Gulf of Mexico. Lakes Pátzcuaro and Cuitzeo, west of Mexico City, are remnants of the numerous lakes that once were found in the Mesa Central.

The Balsas River and its tributaries drain the Balsas Depression as well as much of the southern portion of the Mesa Central. Dammed where it crosses the Sierra Madre del Sur, the Balsas is a major source of hydroelectric power. Farther southeast, the Grijalva-Usumacinta river system drains most of the humid Chiapas Highlands. Together with the Papaloapan River, which enters the Gulf of Mexico south of Veracruz, the Grijalva and Usumacinta account for about 40 percent of the total volume of Mexico's rivers.

In the north aridity and interior drainage limit the size and number of rivers. By far the most important stream in this part of the country is the Río Bravo del Norte (Rio Grande in the United States), which forms part of the international border. The Conchos River, a tributary of the Río Bravo, drains much of the Mesa del Norte. Because the Sierra Madre Occidental and the Sierra Madre Oriental originate close to the coastal margins, streams on the west and east coasts are short and steep. Along the Pacific Coastal Lowlands the Yaqui, Fuerte, and Culiacán rivers have been dammed and support major irrigated acreages. Aridity in Baja California and the porous limestones that underlie the Yucatán Peninsula cause these regions to be virtually devoid of permanent surface streams.

Soils. In the tropical areas of southern Mexico, lateritic soils predominate. Throughout southeastern Mexico, leaching produces infertile reddish or yellow soils high in iron oxides and aluminum hydroxides. The richest soils in the country are the chenozem-like volcanic soils found in the Mesa Central. Deep, easily crumbled, and rich in base minerals, these dark soils have been, in some areas, farmed continuously for several centuries. Because of their excellent drainage and good structural properties, they can be used for crops even on extremely steep slopes, but overuse has caused serious sheet erosion and exposure of tepetate (a lime hardpan) in many areas. In the arid north, gray-brown desert soils occupy the largest expanses. High in lime and soluble salts, these soils can be extremely productive when irrigated, but salt buildup is sometimes a serious problem.

Volcanic soils

Climate. Because of its topographic diversity and latitudinal range, Mexico has a wide array of climatic conditions, often occurring over short distances. More than half of the country lies south of the Tropic of Cancer. In these areas, tropical maritime air masses from the Gulf of Mexico, the Caribbean, and the Pacific, which are attracted by the relatively low pressures that occur over the land, are the main sources of precipitation that is heaviest during the period from May through August. Tropical hurricanes, which are spawned in oceans on both sides of the country, are common in the coastal lowland areas during the months of August through October. The climates

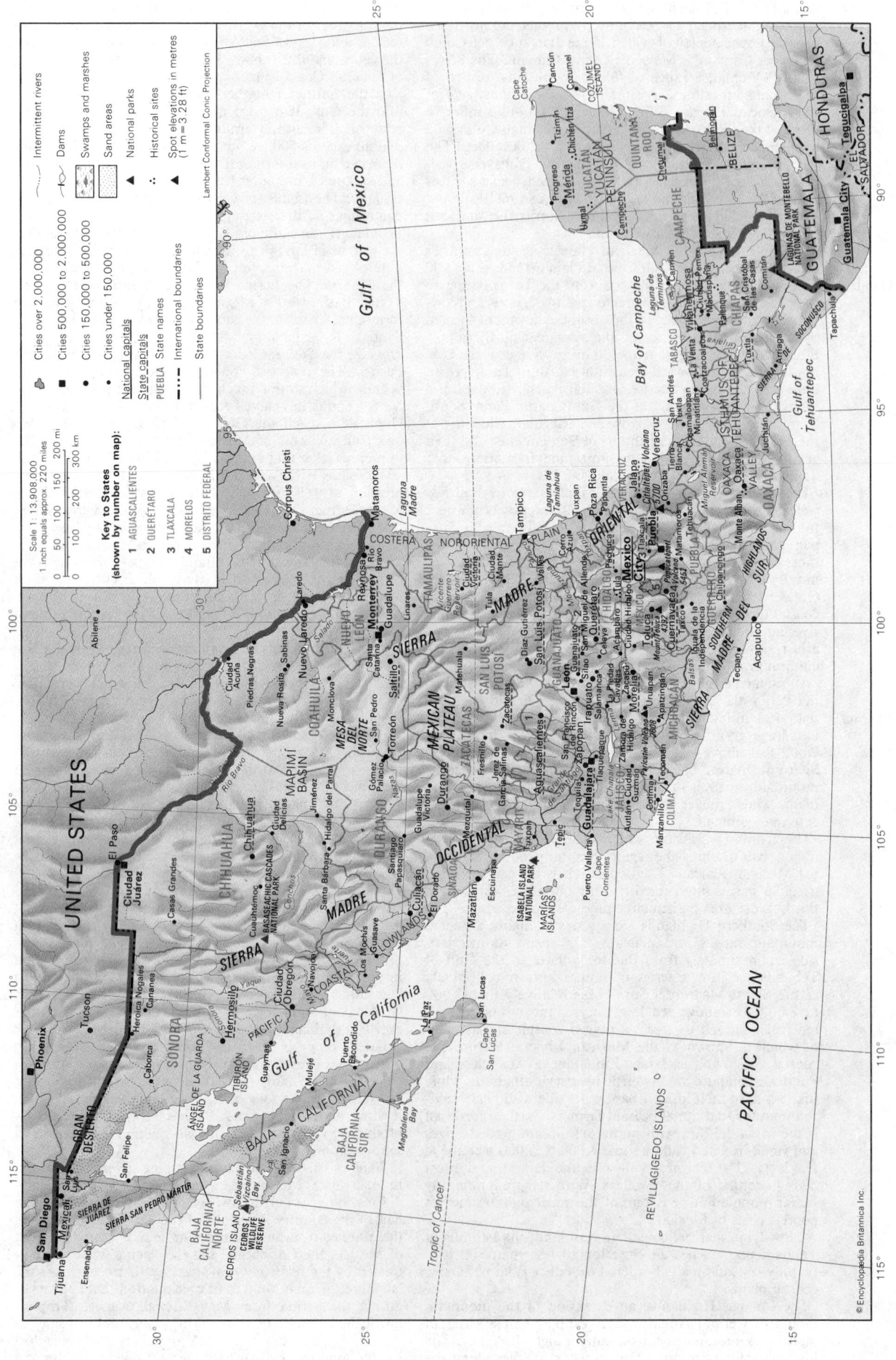

© Encyclopædia Britannica, Inc.

in northern Mexico, situated latitudinally within one of the world's great desert regions, are strongly influenced by the semipermanent Pacific subtropical anticyclone, which minimizes precipitation.

Within the tropics temperature variations from season to season are small, often only about 10° F (5° C) between the warmest and coldest months. In these areas winter is defined as the rainy rather than the cold season. Because elevation rather than latitude is the primary climatic influence in southern Mexico, several vertical climatic zones are recognized. In the Mexican tropics, from sea level to just over 3,000 feet, is the *tierra caliente* ("hot land"), with uniformly high temperatures. Veracruz, located on the Gulf of Mexico, for example, has an average daily temperature of approximately 77° F (25° C). The *tierra templada* ("temperate land") extends to about 6,000 feet. Located at an elevation of more than 4,600 feet, Jalapa has an average daily temperature of 66° F (19° C). *Tierra fria* ("cold land") extends as high as 11,000 feet. Pachuca, at just under 8,000 feet, has an average annual temperature of 59° F (15° C). Above the *tierra fria* are the *paramos,* or alpine pastures, while the *tierra helada* ("frozen land"), or permanent snow line, in central Mexico is found between 13,000 and 14,000 feet.

North of the tropics, temperature ranges increase substantially and are greatest in the north central portion of the Mesa del Norte. In the northern interior, summer and winter temperatures are extreme. The highest temperatures in the country, exceeding 110° F (43° C), occur in July and August in central Baja California and in the northern Sonoran and Chihuahuan deserts. Outside of the high mountainous areas of northern Mexico and the north central portion of the Mesa del Norte, the lowest temperatures normally do not descend below 32° F (0° C).

Rainfall   Most of Mexico lacks adequate precipitation at least during a part of the year. With the exception of the highland areas of the Sierra Madre Occidental, the Sierra Madre Oriental, and the Gulf Coastal Plain, all of the area north of the Tropic of Cancer generally receives less than 20 inches (500 millimetres) of precipitation annually and is classified climatically as either tropical desert or tropical steppe. Nearly all of Baja California, much of Sonora state, and large parts of Chihuahua state receive less than 10 inches of rainfall yearly. Much of central and southern Mexico receives less than 40 inches of precipitation annually, most from May through August, and is classified as having tropical savanna or highland savanna climates. Only the Gulf Coastal Plain and the adjacent mountains, from roughly Tampico southward to Villahermosa, the Chiapas Highlands, and the southern part of the Yucatán Peninsula receive abundant rainfall year-round. In combination with uniformly high temperatures, this creates a tropical rain forest climate in these areas.

Plant and animal life. The tropical deserts of Baja California, Sonora, and north central Mexico are characterized by sparse desert scrub vegetation. On the higher portions of the Sonoran and Chihuahuan steppes, as well as in much of Coahuila and Tamulipas, there have evolved distinctive ecosystems composed of short grasses, scattered shrubs, and a variety of cacti and other succulents. Sonora and Chihuahua are the archetypes for flora groups that bear their names. The boojum tree is unique to a limited portion of Sonora and central Baja California.

Most of the Sierra Madre Occidental and large parts of the Mesa Central, including its dissected borders, originally were covered by forests of coniferous, evergreen deciduous, and deciduous trees. Similar forests extended southward into the Southern Highlands. Long periods of human occupation in these regions have decimated most of the natural vegetation. Major areas of coniferous forests are found at higher elevations in the Sierra Madre Occidental. The semiarid Balsas Depression has a tropical scrub vegetation composed of shrubs, low deciduous trees, and scattered cacti.

The high-precipitation zones of the Gulf Coastal Plain, the adjacent east-facing mountain slopes, the Chiapas Highlands, and the southern part of the Yucatán Peninsula are dominated by tropical rain forest, or selva, vegetation. These dense stands of broadleaf evergreen trees of varying heights are among the most luxuriant and diversified in the world. Valuable tropical hardwoods, as well as ferns, epiphytes, and a variety of palms, make these selva areas of particular interest. A large portion of the Pacific coastal area, from Mazatlán to the Guatemalan border, is covered by tropical deciduous or semi-deciduous forests, which lack the variety and density of tropical rain forests.

Mexico sits astride the commonly accepted boundary dividing North and Middle American animal species and, therefore, has a diverse array of fauna, especially in the selva regions of the south. The rain forests of the Gulf Coast and Chiapas Highlands and the semi-deciduous forests of the Pacific coast still provide a largely undisturbed habitat for monkeys, parrots, jaguars, tapirs, anteaters, and other tropical species. In contrast, the natural wildlife of northern Mexico was severely affected by the introduction of European grazing animals more than 400 years ago. While rabbits, snakes, and armadillos abound in the deserts and steppes, larger animals such as deer, pumas, and coyotes are found mainly in isolated or mountainous areas. Countless ducks and geese migrate into the northern part of the Sierra Madre Occidental to winter. A millennium of human habitation has brought about the decimation of natural fauna throughout much of the Mesa Central and parts of the Southern Highlands, especially in the Oaxaca Valley.

Settlement patterns. *Traditional regions.* Because of distinctive differences in physical environment, ethnic and racial characteristics, and settlement histories, specific cultural areas have evolved. Mexico traditionally has been divided between the Spanish-mestizo north and the Indian-mestizo south. This corresponds roughly to the pre-Columbian boundary that separated the highly developed Indian cultures of the Mesa Central and the south from the more primitive groups to the north.

Northern Mexico is a sparsely populated area with isolated clusters of settlement; it can be divided into four separate cultural regions. The largest region is the North, which closely corresponds in area to the Mesa del Norte. Mining and ranching were introduced there by the Spanish in the 16th and 18th centuries, respectively, and these industries have continued to characterize the region, though modern irrigation projects and industrialization programs

Chip and Rosa Maria de la Cueva Peterson

Volcanic peak of Ixtacíhuatl overlooking a field of corn shocks in the agricultural region of Puebla state in the Mesa Central of Mexico.

along the border with the United States have diversified the economy.

The Northeast stretches from Tampico to the U.S. border and inland to the Sierra Madre Oriental. The Indian population of the area was eliminated by early European settlers, who established farms and ranches in the area. Although it was long one of the country's poorest regions, the emerging petroleum and steel industries and the development of irrigation projects along the Río Bravo del Norte have greatly improved the region's economic condition.

The Northwest is an extensive region lying west of the crest of the Sierra Madre Occidental and stretching southward from the U.S. border to northern Nayarit state. This physiographically complex area had a substantial Indian population before the Spanish conquest, and the Tarahumara and Seri are among the Indian peoples still found in isolated parts of the region. As in the North, mineral resources originally attracted the Spanish, but agriculture, especially ranching, now characterizes the region.

Baja California, historically one of the more isolated parts of Mexico, is largely a desert, with major concentrations of settlement in urban areas at both ends of the peninsula. The original Indian population, scattered and culturally poorly developed, was decimated by diseases introduced by missionaries in the late 18th century. Europeans and mestizos established themselves in farming communities at oases, originally at sites such as San Ignacio and Mulejé.

Southern Mexico was much more strongly influenced by its Indian heritage than was the northern part of the country. **The Central region** The cultural core of the nation has been the Central region, which includes the central and eastern portions of the Mesa Central and its surrounding highlands. This was the centre of the Aztec Empire as well as numerous other Indian homelands. It became the core of New Spain and the political and economic capital of Mexico. In addition to being the primary centre of urbanization, this is also one of the nation's most important agricultural areas. Numerous basins, such as those of Mexico, Toluca, Puebla, and Morelos, are densely settled. Racial mixing has been intense in this region, but Indian groups are still found in the more isolated portions of Michoacán, Mezquital, Puebla, and Toluca. Nowhere is the contrast between modern urban Mexico and traditional rural Indian lifestyles sharper than in this region.

The West region is centred on the city of Guadalajara and encompasses the state of Jalisco along with portions of Colima, Nayarit, Aguascalientes, Zacatecas, and Guanajuato states. With its relatively high rural population, fertile basins, and access to the Pacific, it was historically the most important agricultural region in the nation. The Guanajuato Basin has long been called the "breadbasket of Mexico." Despite its agricultural prominence, a large number of small urban centres, such as Querétaro, Salamanca, Irapuato, and León, are developing industrially while Manzanillo has become the most important port on the Pacific. Many of the things often thought of as distinctively Mexican—such as tequila, mariachi music, and the ornate embroidered sombrero and charro costume—originated in the West.

The Balsas cultural region, which closely corresponds to the physiographic area of the same name, is arid, hot, and sparsely settled. Cattle ranching has been the mainstay of the economy, although subsistence-level slash-and-burn agriculture is widely practiced by impoverished peasant farmers.

The Southern Highlands, encompassing much of the states of Michoacán, Guerrero, and Oaxaca, is poverty-stricken. This region has the highest concentration of Indians in the country; and the Zapotec, Mixtec, and other Indian groups farm *minifundia* (small plots of land), using traditional methods. The picturesque, "crazy-quilt" landscape that results belies the widespread poverty. Modern coastal tourist centres, such as Acapulco and the more recently developed Puerto Escondido, are a marked contrast to the traditional rural life-styles of the region.

The Gulf Coast region includes the coastal zones of Veracruz and Tabasco as well as the adjacent east-facing slopes of the Sierra Madre Oriental. The population of the coastal area is overwhelmingly mestizo, but Indian groups are found in the mountains north of Veracruz. Veracruz, the cultural centre of this region, has long been the country's major non-petroleum port. Cattle ranching and commercial agriculture are important components of the rural economy. The southern parts of the region were disease-infested, swampy, and nearly devoid of settlement until the Papaloapan and Grijalva-Usumacinta river projects allowed commercial exploitation of the rich alluvial soils.

Most of the Chiapas region is relatively isolated from the rest of Mexico. Commercial agriculture, particularly cotton production, is practiced on the Soconusco (Pacific) coast, while livestock grazing and subsistence agriculture are important elsewhere. Indian peoples are the majority in the northern highlands around San Cristóbal de las Casas, but mestizos are the dominant population in the southern half of the region.

The centre of the lowland Maya civilization, the Yucatán has a predominantly Indian rural population. This low-lying area is known for its archaeological sites, such as Chichén Itzá, Uxmal, and Tulum. Mérida, the only major city in the region, was the centre for the production of henequen (a type of *Agave*), which led to a regional economic boom in the late 1800s. In the tropical rain forests to the south, the sparse population depends on subsistence agriculture or hunting and gathering. **The Yucatán**

Rural settlement. Before the arrival of Europeans, the indigenous population was highly concentrated in the Central, West, and Southern Highland regions. The Spanish settled in existing Indian communities in order to exploit their labour in agriculture and mining. As a result, these areas have remained the most densely populated throughout Mexico's history.

Away from this central core, settlement was sparse and was attracted to specific opportunities, such as mines, mission sites, or military outposts. Mining had the largest impact on population redistribution. Silver-mining towns, such as Durango, San Luis Potosí, Aguascalientes, Pachuca, and Zacatecas, were founded in the middle to late 1500s and represented the first settlements outside the central core. By contrast, it was not until the mid-1800s that large-scale ranching was introduced into northern Mexico. This clustered pattern of settlement, with large areas effectively devoid of population, has characterized the nation's rural settlement pattern.

Urban settlement. Urbanization is taking place at a rapid pace in Mexico. While the largest urban places are growing the most rapidly in absolute numbers, small- and intermediate-sized cities have the highest percentage increases. By the mid-1980s the country had more than 100 urban centres with 50,000 or more people. The major axis of urbanization stretches as a narrow band across central Mexico from Puebla to Guadalajara, but the growth of the northern border cities has been the most spectacular.

Within the hierarchy of Mexican urban places, Mexico City is the undisputed primary city. It is the political, economic, social, educational, and industrial capital of the nation. With a population of almost 10,000,000 in the mid-1980s, it is the largest city in the world (see MEXICO CITY). **Major cities**

Guadalajara is the nation's second largest urban area. It is a much more traditional city in structure and appearance than is Mexico City. As the regional capital of Jalisco and much of the West, Guadalajara is a major market centre and has developed a substantial industrial base. With a well-respected university and medical school, it is also a major educational and cultural centre.

Monterrey developed as the iron and steel centre of the nation. Because the modern city dates only to the beginning of the 20th century, and because much of its growth is recent, it is singularly unremarkable in appearance, and the arid Mesa del Norte provides a stark, somewhat barren setting. High-grade coal from the nearby Sabinas fields was a major consideration in siting the steel industry in Monterrey. A number of heavy industries also have been located in the urban area. As the centre of the National Action Party (PAN), Monterrey is a stronghold of political conservatism.   (ERNST C. GRIFFIN)

The History of Western
Architecture

20th-century architecture

THE MODERN MOVEMENT

Before World War II. The Modern movement was an attempt to create a nonhistorical architecture of functionalism in which a new sense of space would be created with the help of modern materials. A reaction against the stylistic pluralism of the 19th century, the Modern movement was also coloured by the belief that the 20th century had given birth to "modern man," who would need a radically new kind of architecture.

Austria and Germany

The Viennese architect Adolf Loos opposed the use of any ornament at all and designed purist compositions of bald, functional blocks such as the Steiner House at Vienna (1910), one of the first private houses of reinforced concrete. Peter Behrens, having had contact with Olbrich at Darmstadt and with Hoffmann at Vienna, was in 1907 appointed artistic adviser in charge of the AEG (Allgemeine Elektricitäts Gesellschaft), for which he designed a turbine factory (1909) at Berlin. Behrens strongly affected three great architects who worked in his office: Walter Gropius, Le Corbusier, and Ludwig Mies van der Rohe.

In Germany, Gropius followed a mechanistic direction. His Fagus Works factory at Alfeld-an-der-Leine in Germany (1911) and the Werkbund exposition building at the Cologne exhibition (1914) had been models of industrial architecture in which vigorous forms were enclosed by masonry and glass; the effect of these buildings was gained by the use of steel frames, strong silhouette, and the logic of their plans. There were no historical influences or expressions of local landscape, traditions, or materials. The beauty of the buildings derived from adapting form to a technological culture.

Gropius succeeded van de Velde as director of the ducal Arts and Crafts School at Weimar in 1919. Later called

By courtesy of the Museum of Modern Art, New York

Hôtel Tassel, Brussels, by Victor Horta, 1892–93.

the Bauhaus, it became the most important centre of modern design until the Nazis closed it in 1933. While he was at Weimar, Gropius developed a firm philosophy about architecture and education, which he announced in 1923. The aim of the visual arts, he said, is to create a complete, homogeneous physical environment in which all the arts have their place. Architects, sculptors, furniture makers, and painters must learn practical crafts and obtain knowledge of tools, materials, and forms; they must become acquainted with the machine and attempt to use it in solving the social problems of an industrial society. At the Bauhaus, aesthetic investigations into space, colour, construction, and elementary forms were flavoured by Cubism and Constructivism. Moving the school to Dessau in 1925, Gropius designed the pioneering new Bauhaus (1925–26) in which steel frames and glass walls provided workshops within severely Cubistic buildings. Gropius assembled a staff of modern teachers, including the artists László Moholy-Nagy, Wassily Kandinsky, Paul Klee, Marcel Breuer, and Adolf Meyer, whose projects, such as the 116 experimental standardized housing units of the Törten Estate at Dessau, Ger. (1926–28), bore a highly machined, depersonalized appearance. In France, Tony Garnier caught the modern currents in materials, structure, and composition when he evolved his masterful plan for a *Cité industrielle* (1901–04), published in 1917, in which reinforced concrete was to be used to create a modern city of modern buildings. . . .

The mechanistic philosophy of Gropius

The Futurist movement counted among its members another early 20th-century urban planner, the Italian architect Antonio Sant'Elia. Influenced by American industrial cities and the Viennese architects Wagner and Loos, he designed a grandiose futuristic city, entitled "Città nuova" ("New City"). He conceived of the city as a symbol of the new technological age. It was an affirmative environment for the future, however, in opposition to the negating inhuman Expressionistic city of the future conceived by Fritz Lang in the 1926 film classic *Metropolis*.

Centred in Germany between 1910 and 1925, Expressionist architects, like the painters who were part of the Brücke and Blaue Reiter groups, sought peculiarly personal and often bizarre visual forms and effects. Among the earliest manifestations of an Expressionistic building style were the highly individual early works of Hans Poelzig, such as the Luban Chemical Factory (1911–12) and the municipal water tower (1911) of Posen, Ger. (now Poznan, Pol.), which led to his monumental, visionary "space caves," such as the project for the Salzburg Festival Theatre (1920–21) and the Grosses Schauspielhaus, built in Berlin (1919) for Max Reinhardt's Expressionistic theatre. These later works by Poelzig show the influence of the structural audacity of Max Berg's Centenary Hall at Breslau, Ger. (now Wrocław, Pol.; 1912–13), with its gigantic reinforced concrete dome measuring 213 feet in diameter. The second generation of Expressionists centred their activities in postwar Germany and The Netherlands. Distinctly personal architectural statements were given form in such dynamically sculptured structures as the Einstein Observatory in Potsdam (1920), by Erich Mendelsohn; the anthroposophically based design by Rudolf Steiner for the Goetheanum in Dornach, Switz. (1925–28); the Eigen Haard Estates (housing development) at Amsterdam (1921), by Michel de Klerk; and Fritz Höger's (1877–1949) Chilehaus office building in Hamburg (1922–23), with its imperative thrust of mass and acute angularity.

Expressionism in Germany

As Germany was the centre of Expressionism, Paris was the stronghold of the advocates of a new vision of space, Cubism, which Georges Braque and Pablo Picasso developed in 1906. Forms were dismembered into their faceted components; angular forms, interpenetrated planes, trans-

Casa Milá, Barcelona, by Antonio Gaudí, 1905–10.
Archivo Mas, Barcelona

parencies, and diverse impressions were recorded as though seen simultaneously. Soon architectural reflections of the Cubist aesthetic appeared internationally. Interior spaces were defined by thin, discontinuous planes and glass walls; supports were reduced to slender metal columns, machine finished and without ornamentation; and Cubistic voids and masses were arranged programmatically in asymmetric compositions.

The Dutch de Stijl movement was influenced by Cubism, although it sought a greater abstract purity in its geometric formalism. Organized in Leiden in 1917, the painters Piet Mondrian and Theo van Doesburg and the architects Jacobus Johannes Oud and Gerrit Thomas Rietveld were counted among its members. Their Neoplastic aesthetic advocated severe precision of line and shape, austerely pristine surfaces, a Spartan economy of form, and purity of colour. Rietveld's Schroeder House, built in 1924 at

By courtesy of Walter Gropius/Bauhaus Archive

Fagus Works, Alfeld-an-der-Leine, Ger., by Walter Gropius, 1911.

Utrecht, was a three-dimensional parallel to Mondrian's paintings of the period. Van Doesburg's work for the Bauhaus art school at Weimar brought the influence of Dutch Neoplasticism to bear upon Gropius and Mies, whose plans for houses at times markedly resembled van Doesburg's paintings. Meanwhile Oud collaborated with van Doesburg for a time and vigorously proclaimed the new style in housing developments he built at Rotterdam (after 1918), Hook of Holland (1924–27), and Stuttgart, Ger. (1927).

Cubism and the related movements of Futurism, Constructivism, Suprematism, and Neoplasticism, like any artistic styles, might have faltered and fallen into a merely decorative cliché, as at the Paris Exposition of 1925, but for Gropius, Mies van der Rohe, and Le Corbusier.

Gropius was succeeded at the Bauhaus in 1930 by Mies van der Rohe, whose training as a mason was supplemented by the engineering experience he had gained from 1908 to 1911 in the office of Behrens; both of these elements of his education were synthesized in his project for the Kröller House in The Hague (1912). Influenced by van Doesburg's de Stijl, Mies's natural elegance and precise orderliness soon revealed themselves in unrealized projects for a brick country house, a steel and glass skyscraper, and a glazed, cantilevered concrete-slab office building (1920–22). He directed the Weissenhof estate project of the Werkbund Exposition at Stuttgart (1927), contributing the design for an apartment house. Such practical problems failed to show his talent, which was not fully known until he designed the German pavilion for the International Exposition at Barcelona in 1929. The continuous spaces partitioned with thin marble planes and the chromed steel columns drew international applause. His Tugendhat House at Brno, Czech. (1930), along with Le Corbusier's Savoye House, epitomized the Modern domestic setting at its best.

The Swiss-French architect Charles-Édouard Jeanneret, known as Le Corbusier, gave the new architecture, sometimes referred to as the International Style, a firm foundation by writing the strong theoretical statement, *Vers une architecture* (*Towards a New Architecture*), published in 1923. It revealed a world of new forms—not classical capitals and Gothic arches but ships, turbines, grain elevators, airplanes, and machine products, which Le Corbusier said were indexes to 20th-century imagination. His love of machines was combined with a belief in communal authority as the best means of accomplishing social reforms, and Le Corbusier directed his attention toward the problems of housing and urban patterns. An architectural attack, using standardized building components and mass production,

Mies van der Rohe's contribution

Le Corbusier's support of the International Style

Centenary Hall, Breslau, Ger. (now Wrocław, Pol.), by Max
Berg, 1912–13.
Dyckerhoff & Widmann

was required. His sociological and formal ideas appeared
in a Cubist project for Domino housing (1916), and his
aesthetic preferences led him, after World War I, to develop an extreme version of Cubist painting that he and
the painter Amedée Ozenfant called Purism. Returning to
architecture in 1921, he designed a villa at Vaucresson, Fr.
(1922), the abstract planes and strip windows of which revealed his desire to "arrive at the house machine," that is,
standardized houses with standardized furniture. In 1922
he also brought forth his project for a skyscraper city of
3,000,000 people, in which tall office and apartment buildings would stand in broad open plazas and parks with the
Cubist spaces between them defined by low row housing.

Much of his work thereafter—his Voisin city plan, his
Pavilion of the New Spirit at the Paris Exposition of
1925, his exhibit of workers' apartments at the Werkbund
Exposition at Stuttgart (1927), and his influential but
unexecuted submittal to the League of Nations competition—was a footnote to that dream of a new city. The
villa, Les Terrasses, at Garches, Fr. (1927), was a lively
play of spatial parallelepipeds (six-sided solid geometric
forms the faces of which are parallelograms) ruled by horizontal planes, but his style seemed to culminate in the
most famous of his houses, the Savoye House at Poissy,
Fr. (1929–30). The building's principal block was raised
one story above the ground on pilotis (heavy reinforced-
concrete columns); floors were cantilevered to permit long
strip windows; and space was molded plastically and made
to flow horizontally, vertically, and diagonally until, on
the topmost terrace, the whole composition ended in a
cadenza of rounded, terminating spaces. Gaining greater
facility in manipulating flowing spaces, Le Corbusier designed the dormitory for Swiss students at the Cité Uni-
versitaire (1931–32) in Paris.

Early   In the period after the Revolution the Soviet Union
Soviet ar-   at first encouraged modern art, and several architects,
chitecture   notably the German Bruno Taut, looked to the new government for a sociological program. The Constructivist
project for a monument to the Third International (1920)
by Vladimir Tatlin was a machine in which the various
sections (comprising legislative houses and offices) would

rotate within an exposed steel armature. A workers' club
in Moscow (1929) had a plan resembling half a gear, and
the Ministry of Central Economic Planning (1928–32),
designed by Le Corbusier, was intended to be a glass-filled
slab but, because of Stalin's dislike of modern architecture,
was never completed. Its foundation later was used for an
outdoor swimming pool.

Modern European styles of architecture were subjected
to official disfavour in the Soviet Union in the 1930s,
as Stalin's government adopted classical monuments—
such as Boris Mikhaylovich Iofan's winning design for the
Palace of the Soviets (1931), which was intended to pile
classical colonnades to a height of 1,365 feet and have a
colossal statue of Lenin at its summit. With its gigantic
Corinthian columns, the building for the Central Committee of the Communist Party at Kiev (1937) showed an
overbearing scale.

After 1930 the Modern movement spread through Europe. In Switzerland Robert Maillart's experiments with
reinforced concrete attained great grace in his Salginato-
bel Bridge (1930). Finland's Alvar Aalto won a competition for the Municipal Library at Viipuri (now Vyborg,
U.S.S.R.) in 1927 with a building of glass walls, flat roof,
and round skylights (completed 1935; destroyed 1943);
but he retained the traditional Scandinavian sympathy for
wood and picturesque planning that were evident in his
Villa Mairea at Noormarkku (1938–39), the factory and
housing at Sunila (1936–39, completed 1951–54), and his
later civic centre at Säynätsalo (1950–52). Aalto and other
Scandinavians gained a following among those repelled
by severe German modernism. Sweden's Erik Gunnar
Asplund and Denmark's Kay Fisker, Christian Frederick
Møller, and Arne Jacobsen also brought regional character into their modern work. In The Netherlands, Johannes Andreas Brinkman and Lodewijk Cornelis van der
Vlugt, at the Van Nelle Tobacco Factory in Rotterdam
(1929–30), aimed at more mechanistic, universal form.
In England, refugees from Germany and other countries,
alone or with English designers, inaugurated a radical
modernism—for example, the apartment block known as
Highpoint I, Highgate, London (by Berthold Lubetkin and
the Tecton group, 1935).

The locus for creative architecture in the United States
remained the Middle West, although Californians such as
the brothers Charles Sumner Greene and Henry Mather
Greene struck occasional regional and modern notes, as
in the Gamble House at Pasadena, Calif. (1908–09). The

By courtesy of Sonnenobservatorium Einsteinturm, Potsdam

Einstein Observatory, Potsdam, E.Ger., by Erich Mendelsohn,
1920.

Schroeder House, Utrecht, Neth., by Gerrit T. Rietveld, 1924.
Dr. Franz Stoedtner

second generation of architects of the Chicago school, such as William G. Purcell, G.G. Elmslie, and William Drummond, disseminated Middle Western modern architecture throughout the United States.

The "prairie style" of Frank Lloyd Wright

The greatest of all these new Chicago architects was Frank Lloyd Wright. His "prairie architecture" expressed its site, region, structure, and materials and avoided all historical reminiscences; beginning with its plan and a distinctive spatial theme, each building burgeoned to its exterior sculptural form. Starting from Richardson's rustic, shingle houses and making free use of Beaux-Arts composition during the 1880s and 1890s, Wright hinted at his prairie house idiom with the Winslow House at River Forest, Ill. (1893), elaborated it in the Coonley House at Riverside, Ill. (1908), and, ultimately, realized it in 1909 in the flowing volumes of space defined by sculptural masses and horizontal planes of his Robie House at Chicago. Meanwhile, he scored a triumph with his administration building for the Larkin Company at Buffalo in 1904 (destroyed 1950), which grouped offices around a central skylighted court, sealed them hermetically against their smoky environs, and offered amenities in circulation, air conditioning, fire protection, and plumbing. In its blocky fire towers, sequences of piers and recessed spandrels were coupled together in a powerful composition. Wright was, however, ignored by all except a select following. The buildings of the single figure who gave international distinction to early 20th-century American architecture remained the cherished property of personal clients, such as Aline Barnsdall, for whom Wright designed the Hollyhock House at Los Angeles (1918–20).

Wright's *Autobiography* (1943) recorded his frustrations in gaining acceptance for organic architecture. The first edition summarized the chief features of that architecture: the reduction to a minimum in the number of rooms and the definition of them by point supports; the close association of buildings to their sites by means of extended and emphasized planes parallel to the ground; the free flow of space, unencumbered by boxlike enclosures; harmony of all openings with each other and with human scale; the exploitation of the nature of a material, in both its surface manifestations and its structure; the incorporation of mechanical equipment and furniture as organic parts of structure; and the elimination of applied decoration. There were also four new properties: transparency, which was obtained through the use of glass; tenuity, or plasticity of mass achieved through the use of steel in tension, as in reinforced concrete; naturalism, or the expression of materials; and integration, in which all ornamental features were natural by-products of manufacture and assembly.

The Millard House at Pasadena, Calif. (1923), exemplified many of these principles; its concrete-block walls were cast with decorative patterns. Taliesin East, Wright's house near Spring Green, Wisc., went through a series of major rebuildings (1911, 1914, 1915, and 1925), and each fitted the site beautifully; local stone, gabled roofs, and outdoor gardens reflected the themes of the countryside. A period of withdrawal at Taliesin afforded Wright several years of intensive reflection, from which he emerged with fabulous drawings for the Doheny ranch in California (1921), a skyscraper for the National Life Insurance Company at Chicago (1920–25), and St. Mark's Tower, New York City

Organic architecture in the United States

Hedrich-Blessing photo

Robie House, Chicago, by Frank Lloyd Wright, 1909.

(1929). The last was to have been an 18-story apartment house comprising a concrete stem from which four arms branched outward to form the sidewalls of apartments cantilevered from the stem to an exterior glass wall. Unexecuted like most of Wright's most exciting projects, St. Mark's Tower testified to his revolutionary thinking about skyscraper architecture. His ideas gained a wide hearing in 1931 when he published the Kahn lectures he had delivered at Princeton in 1930. In keeping with the needs of the United States during the Depression, Wright turned his attention to the low-cost house, designing a "Usonian house" for Herbert Jacobs near Madison, Wisc. (1937), and a quadruple house, "the Sun houses," at Ardmore, Pa. (1939). These exemplified the residences he intended for his ideal communities, such as rural, decentralized Broadacre City (1936), which was Wright's answer to European schemes for skyscraper cities.

At about the same time, Wright produced four masterpieces: Fallingwater, Bear Run, Pa. (1936), the daringly cantilevered weekend house of Edgar Kaufmann; the administration building of S.C. Johnson & Son, in which brick cylinders and planes develop a series of echoing spaces, culminating in the forest of graceful "mushroom" columns in the main hall, and the Johnson House (1937), aptly called Wingspread, both at Racine, Wisc.; and Taliesin West at Paradise Valley, near Phoenix, Ariz. (begun 1938), where rough, angular walls and roofs echo the desert valley and surrounding mountains. With increasing sensitivity to local terrain and native forms and materials, Wright stated more complex spatial and structural themes than European modernists, who seldom attempted either extreme programmatic plans or organic adaptation of form to a particular environment. Eventually, Wright himself developed a more universal geometry, as he revealed in the sculptural Solomon R. Guggenheim Museum at New York City (1956–59).

The emblem of business, the office building, continued to suffer from demands for unique, distinctive towers. Harvey Wiley Corbett, a New York architect, admitted that publicity was the ruling motivation. Sometimes a business with nationwide suboffices developed a corporate iconography; Sears, Roebuck and Company, Bell Telephone, Howard Johnson, A & P, and the various gasoline companies were recognizable instantly. The Gothic skyscraper, popularized by Gilbert's Woolworth Building, was the style used by Raymond Hood for his winning entry in the *Chicago Tribune* competition (1922). Some buildings gained attention through their classical ornament; others were Renaissance palaces. About 1920 some architects developed simple cubical forms, and the stepped ziggurat was popularized by renderers, notably Hugh Ferriss, and such painters as Georgia O'Keeffe, John Marin, and Charles Sheeler. This soaring and jagged form received legal support from the New York City zoning law of 1916 and economic justification from the fact that, in order to obtain rentable, peripheral office space in the upper floors, where the banks of elevators diminished, whole increments of office space had to be omitted. These cubical envelopes were not without ornament at their crests, as in Hood's American Radiator Building in New York City (1924–25), suitably described as "one huge cinder incandescent at the top." Such decoration might be chic, as in New York City's Barclay–Vesey (telephone company) Building, where Ralph Walker re-created the Art Deco interiors of the Paris Exposition of 1925. In San Francisco, Miller, Pflueger, & Cantin used Chinese ornament to enliven their telephone building (1926). Paradoxically, one archaeological find led to simpler buildings when, about 1930, Mayan pyramids inspired Timothy Pflueger in his work on the 450 Sutter building in San Francisco. Clifflike blocks arose in Chicago, the Daily News and Palmolive buildings (1929) being the best examples; New York City acquired a straightforward expression of tall vertical piers and setback cubical masses in the Daily News Building (1930), by the versatile Hood, who had run the course from Gothic to modern form. The bank and office building of the Philadelphia Savings Fund Society (1931–32) by George Howe and William Lescaze, a Swiss architect, gave the skyscraper its first thoroughly 20th-century form,

and Hood, again, produced a counterpart in New York City, the McGraw-Hill Building (1931). Few of these, including the Empire State Building (1931), did anything to solve urban density and transportation problems; indeed, they intensified them. Rockefeller Center, however, begun in 1929, was, with its space for pedestrians within a complex of slablike skyscrapers, outstanding and too seldom copied.

American industry showed some inclination to respect function, materials, and engineering between the world wars, as was evident in Joseph Leland's glazed, skeletal buildings for the Pressed Steel Company at Worcester, Mass. (1930). Occasionally, a traditional architect had produced an innovation, such as Willis Polk's (1867–1924) Hallidie Building at San Francisco (1918). With the aid of Ernest Wilby, the engineering firm of Albert Kahn created a work of architectural merit in Detroit's Continental Motors Factory (about 1918). The National Cash Register, United States Shoe Company, National Biscuit, Sears, Roebuck and Company and various automobile companies, such as Ford, sponsored Functional architecture.

Rockefeller Center indicated that by 1930 there was a move toward simple form, which was presaged by the architecture of the TVA (Tennessee Valley Authority). European modernism gained a firm following in the United States as some of its best practitioners emigrated there. Eliel Saarinen, who won second prize in the *Chicago Tribune* competition, gained the acclaim of Sullivan and other architects. He settled in Bloomfield Hills, Mich., a Detroit suburb, where he established a school of architecture at the Cranbrook Academy. Saarinen designed its new buildings, gradually freeing himself from historical reminiscences of his native Scandinavia. He remained sensitive to the role of art in architecture, best revealed by his use of the sculpture of the Swede Carl Milles. The Austrian

By courtesy of New York News Inc.

The Daily News Building, New York City, by Raymond Hood, 1930.

Crown Hall, Illinois Institute of Technology, Chicago, by Mies van der Rohe, 1952–56.

Hedrich-Blessing photo

architect Richard Neutra established a practice in California, notable products of which were the Lovell House at Los Angeles (1927–28) and the Kaufmann Desert House at Palm Springs (1946–47).

A modern architecture exhibit in the Museum of Modern Art, New York City, in 1932, recorded by the architectural historian Henry-Russell Hitchcock and the architect Philip Johnson in the book *International Style; Architecture Since 1922,* familiarized Americans with the International Style. After 1933, as modernists fled the Soviet Union, Germany, and Italy, the United States received Gropius, Breuer, and Mies. Gropius joined the architectural school of Harvard University and established an educational focus recalling the Bauhaus.

After World War II. Initially, the leading interwar architects of modernism, Gropius, Mies van der Rohe, Le Corbusier, Wright, and Aalto, continued to dominate the scene. In the United States, Gropius, with Breuer, introduced modern houses to Lincoln, Mass., a Boston suburb, and formed a group, The Architects Collaborative, the members of which designed the thoroughly modern Harvard Graduate Center (1949–50). Mies became dean of the department of architecture at the Illinois Institute of Technology at Chicago in 1938 and designed its new campus. Crown Hall (1952–56) marked the apogee of this quarter-century project.

Not all the immigrants remained in the United States. Aalto, whose work first appeared on the American scene in the Finnish pavilion at the New York World's Fair and again in the Massachusetts Institute of Technology's Baker Dormitory (1947–49), returned to Finland. The European who might have contributed most was Le Corbusier. The United Nations buildings at New York City, for which he was a member of a 10-man commission headed by New York architect Wallace Harrison, is a token of the new forms he might have suggested for American cities. His plan for rebuilding Saint-Dié, Fr. (1945), was the inspiration for many city-planning proposals made after mid-century.

Beginning with private houses by Hood, Lescaze, Edward Stone, Neutra, Gropius, and Breuer during the 1930s, American Modernism gradually supplanted the historical styles in a range of building types, including schools and churches; for example, Eliel Saarinen's simple, brick Christ Lutheran Church (1949–50) at Minneapolis, Minn.

After World War II, big industry turned to Modern architects for distinctive emblems of prestige. The Connecticut General Life Insurance Company hired one of the largest modern firms, Skidmore, Owings, and Merrill, to design their new decentralized headquarters outside Hartford, Conn. (1955–57). Lever Brothers turned to the same firm for New York City's Lever House (1952), in which the parklike plaza, glass-curtain walls, and thin aluminum mullions realized the dreams of Mies and others in the 1920s of freestanding crystalline shafts. Designed by Eliel

Saarinen's son Eero, the General Motors Technical Center (1948–56) at Warren, Mich., was compared with Versailles in its extent, grandeur, and rigorous conformity to an austere, geometric aesthetic of Miesian forms. The Harrison and Abramovitz's tower for the Aluminum Company of America at Pittsburgh (1954) advertised its own product, as did Skidmore, Owings, and Merrill's Inland Steel Building at Chicago (1955–57). Perhaps the most chaste of all was the Seagram Building (1954–58) at New York City, designed by Mies and Philip Johnson. Wright alone avoided the rectilinear geometry of these office buildings.

Ben Schnall

Lever House, New York City, by Skidmore, Owings, and Merrill, 1952.

The United States as the centre of the International Style

Architecture as a commercial and industrial symbol

Church of Notre-Dame-du-Haut, Ronchamp, Fr., by Le Corbusier, 1950–55.
George Holton—Photo Researchers/EB Inc.

In 1955 he saw his Price Tower rise at Bartlesville, Okla., a richly faceted, concrete and copper fulfillment of the St. Mark's Tower he had designed more than 25 years earlier.

Advent of Formalism

About 1952 there was a significant shift within Modernism from what had come to be called Functionalism, or the International Style, toward a monumental Formalism. There was increasing interest in highly sculptural masses and spaces, as well as in the decorative qualities of diverse building materials and exposed structural systems. Wright's Guggenheim Museum is a manifestation of this aesthetic. Those who had focused their attention on the rectilinear portions of Le Corbusier's Savoye House and Unité d'Habitation apartments at Marseille (1946–52), tended to ignore the plastic sculpture on the roofs of those buildings; to such people, Le Corbusier's highly individual buildings at Chandigarh, India (begun 1950), and the cavernous space in the lyrical church of Notre-Dame-du-Haut at Ronchamp, Fr., seemed to be examples of personal whimsy. Pier Luigi Nervi in Italy gave structural integrity to the complex curves and geometry of reinforced-concrete structures, such as the Orbetello aircraft hangar (begun 1938) and Turin's exposition hall (1948–50). The Spaniard Eduardo Torroja, his pupil Felix Candela, and the American Frederick Severud followed his lead. Essentially, each attempted to create an umbrella roof the interior space of which could be subdivided as required, such as Torroja's grandstand for the Zarzuela racetrack in Madrid (1935). Mies constructed rectilinear versions of such a space in Crown Hall and in his Farnsworth House at Plano, Ill. (1946–50), while Philip Johnson allowed a single functional unit, the brick-cylinder utility stack, to protrude from his precise glass house at New Canaan, Conn. (1949). Other designers used curvilinear structural geometry, best indicated by Matthew Nowicki's (1910–49) sports arena at Raleigh, N.C. (1952–53), in which two tilted parabolic arches, supported by columns, and a stretched-skin roof enclose a colossal space devoid of interior supports. In 1949 Nowicki had challenged Louis Sullivan's precept, form follows function, with another, form follows form, a dictum that freed architecture from programmatic expression. Hugh Stubbins' congress hall, at Berlin (1957), and Eero Saarinen's Trans World Airlines terminal at John F. Kennedy International Airport, New York City (1956–62), were outstanding examples of these dynamically monumental, single-form buildings the geometric shapes and silhouettes of which were derived from mathematical computation and technological innovation. International competitions for the opera house at Sydney (1957) and a government centre at Toronto (1958) were won by the Dane Jørn Utzon and the Finn Viljo Revell, respectively. Both architects were exponents of the new monumentalism.

These designs posed problems in structural engineering and in scale, but many architects, such as the American Minoru Yamasaki in the McGregor Building for Wayne State University at Detroit (1958), attempted to make structure become decorative, while the decorative screen, as used by Edward Durell Stone at the U.S. embassy in New Delhi (1957–59), offered a device for wrapping programmatic interiors within a rich pattern of sculptured walls.

Latin-American developments

Mexico and South America broke their bonds to French, Spanish, and Portuguese academic design during the 1930s. Le Corbusier's influence became partially strong in Brazil, where the Brazilian Oscar Niemeyer and other architects designed the Corbusier-inspired Ministry of Education and Public Health at Rio de Janeiro (1937–42). Brazil's Lúcio Costa, Affonso Reidy, and Niemeyer; Mexico's Felix Candela, Juan O'Gorman, José Villagran Garcia, and Luis Barragán; and Venezuela's Carlos Raúl Villanueva were the vanguard of Latin-American architectural modernism. Whole communities such as Caracas and São Paulo essentially were rebuilt during the 1950s, and new cities, such as Brasília, the capital of Brazil, and "university cities," such as those of Mexico and Venezuela, were conceived and erected. In Mexico there was avid support for modern design in buildings such as the Presidente Juárez housing at Mexico City (1950) by Mario Pani and Salvador Ortega. In Colombia, after World War II, enormous strides were made in thin-shelled reinforced-concrete construction. In Brazil, dramatic complexes were erected from concrete by Reidy, such as the school and gymnasium at Pedregulho housing at Rio de Janeiro (1953) and Rio's Museum of Modern Art (1960–67).

After 1959, office buildings for administrative headquarters of large corporations followed the 1955–57 suburban-campus model of Skidmore, Owings, and Merrill's Connecticut General Life Insurance Company or, if urban, the towerlike form, often with strong structural expression (Torre Velasca, Milan, by Belgiojoso, Peressutti, and Rogers, 1959) or the slab form, usually emphasizing glazed walls (Mannesmann Building, Düsseldorf, by Paul Schneider-Esleben, 1959), but they rarely achieved an urban composition such as the 1962 Place Ville-Marie, built at Montreal by the Chinese-born American architect I.M. Pei.

Air transportation, trade exhibitions, and spectator sports summoned the often awesome spatial resources of modern technology. The stadiums for the 1964 Olympics at Tokyo by Tange Kenzō, Rome's Pallazzi dello Sport done by Nervi (1960), Eero Saarinen's Dulles International Airport at Chantilly, Va. (1958–62), and Chicago's exposition hall, McCormick Place, by C.F. Murphy and Associates (1971) are examples of the colossal spaces achieved in reinforced

concrete or steel and glass. International exhibitions seldom offered comparable architecture. At the New York World's Fair (1964) the Spanish pavilion by Javier Carvajal and the Japanese pavilion by Maekawa Kunio were buildings of merit. There were also several notable examples at Montreal's Expo 67: the West German pavilion by Frei Otto, the U.S. pavilion by R. Buckminster Fuller, and the startling Constructivist apartment house, Habitat 67, by the Israeli Moshe Safdie, in association with David, Barott, and Boulva, whose 158 precast-concrete apartment units were hoisted into place and post-tensioned to permit dramatic cantilevers and terraces.

World's fairs continued to provide a setting for occasionally distinguished examples of modern structures that demonstrated innovations in building technology.

The architecture of South and Southeast Asia as well as of Japan has been decisively influenced by Western architects, particularly Le Corbusier. The leading figure in Japan was Tange Kenzō, whose many powerful buildings of rough concrete include the Peace Centre, Hiroshima (1949–55), and St. Mary's Roman Catholic Cathedral at Tokyo (1965). His disciples included the so-called Metabolism Group, led by Kikutake Kiyonori, Maki Fumihiko, and Otaka Masato. Their work, characterized by a dynamic science-fiction quality expressive of fluidity and change, culminated in the Osaka Expo 1970, with constructions such as Tange's giant space frame, known as the Theme Pavilion, and Kikutake's Landmark Tower.

Much significant architecture in the postwar period was sponsored by cultural centres and educational institutions, such as Berlin's philharmonic hall (1963) by Hans Scharoun. Louis I. Kahn, in his design for the Richards Medical Research Building (1960), gave the University of Pennsylvania in Philadelphia a linear programmatic composition of laboratories, each served by vertical systems for circulating gases, liquids, and electricity. Paul Rudolph's art and architecture building (1963) at Yale University in New Haven, Conn., gathered its studios, galleries, classrooms, and light wells on 36 interpenetrating levels distributed over six stories. The Morse and Stiles colleges (1962), also at Yale, were designed by Eero Saarinen and set a new standard for multiple-entry urban dormitories. Even the traditionalist campuses of New England preparatory schools gained modern architecture, such as the art building and science building at Phillips Academy in Andover, Mass., by Benjamin A. Thomson (1963) and the dormitories at St. Paul's School in Concord, N.H., by Edward Larrabee Barnes (1965).

The innovations in educational architecture were international. In England, distinctive educational architecture arrived at Hunstanton Secondary School, Norfolk (1949–54), by Peter and Alison Smithson. An example of what became known as the New Brutalism, this building was influenced by Mies van der Rohe. Most New Brutalist buildings, however, owed more to Le Corbusier's late work—for example, the gray concrete masses of Denys Lasdun's University of East Anglia, Norfolk (1962–68)—while James Stirling's History Faculty, Cambridge (1964–67), brought a neo-Constructivist element to the Brutalist tradition. Canada gained the Central Technical School Arts Center by Robert Fairfield Associates (1964) and Scarborough College by John Andrews, with Page and Steele (1966), both at Toronto. Italian innovative educational architecture is exemplified in Milan's Instituto Marchiondi (1959) by Vittoriano Viganò. Led by disciples of Le Corbusier, the Japanese built Waseda University (1964), which was designed by Katsuo Ardo, and Maekawa Kunio's Gakushuin University (1964), both in Tokyo.

Some of the new educational settings proposed solutions to what was undoubtedly the mid-20th century's greatest problem, its urban environment. The high-rise, dense campus at Boston University by José Luis Sert and the skyscraper towers of MIT's earth-sciences building (1964) by I.M. Pei, as well as Harvard's behavioral sciences building (1964) by Minoru Yamasaki, were imaginative single buildings responding to urban circumstances. The Air Force Academy at Colorado Springs, Colo., and the Chicago Circle Campus of the University of Illinois (1965), both by the firm of Skidmore, Owings, and Merrill with Walter A. Netsch as the principal designer (1956), and the Salk Institute for Biological Studies at La Jolla, Calif., by Louis I. Kahn (1966), all offered intimations of a new city built around a cultural, educational centre.

No comparable concentration of intensive, harmonious urban architecture was achieved for cities, even though, after 1955, the building of new cities produced some remarkable examples such as Vällingby, Swed.; Brasília, the new capital of Brazil; Cumbernauld, in Scotland; and Chandīgarh, in India; and some remarkable renovations of old cities, as in Eastwicks in Philadelphia (Reynolds Metals Co.; plans by Constantinos Doxiadis, 1960) and Constitution Plaza in Hartford, Conn. (Charles DuBose, with Sasaki, Walker & Associates 1964), and New York's Lincoln Center for the Performing Arts (1962). By this time, however, it was beginning to be felt that the application of Modern movement principles had caused visual damage to historic cities and had also failed to create a humane environment in new cities. It was at this moment that the postmodernist era began.

(ALBERT BUSH-BROWN/ DAVID J. WATKIN)

POSTMODERNISM

The 1960s saw the rise of dissatisfaction with consequences of the Modern movement, especially in North America, where its failings were exposed in two influential books, Jane Jacobs' *The Death and Life of Great American Cities* (1961) and Robert Venturi's *Complexity and Contradiction in Architecture* (1966). Jacobs highlighted the destruction of urban coherence wrought by the utopian iconoclasm of the Modern movement, whereas Venturi implied that Modern buildings were without meaning because they were designed in a simplistic and puritan way that lacked the irony and complexity which enrich historical architecture. This dissatisfaction was translated into direct action in 1972 with the demolition of several 14-story slab blocks that had been built only 20 years earlier from designs by Yamasaki as part of the award-winning Pruitt-Igoe housing development in St. Louis, Mo. Similar apartment blocks in Europe and North America were demolished in the following decades, but it was at St. Louis that the postmodernist era was begun.

Venturi's *Learning from Las Vegas* (with Denise Scott Brown and Steven Izenour) was also published in 1972.

Peter Aaron/ESTO

Portland Public Service Building, Oregon, by Michael Graves, 1980–82.

World's fair architecture

Educational architecture

New cities

Wit and
historical
reference
in
buildings

In seeking to rehumanize architecture by ridding it of the restricting purism of the Modern movement, the authors pointed for guidance to the playful commercial architecture and billboards of the Las Vegas highways. Venturi and his partner John Rauch reintroduced to architectural design elements of wit, humanity, and historical reference in buildings such as the Tucker House, Katonah, N.Y. (1975), and the Brant-Johnson House, Vail, Colo. (1976). These owed something to Lutyens, who, as a master of paradox and complexity, exercised a deep appeal for Venturi and for his followers, such as Charles Moore and Michael Graves. Graves's Portland Public Service Building, Portland, Ore. (1980–82), and Humana Tower, Louisville, Ky. (1986), have the bulk of the modern skyscraper yet incorporate historical souvenirs such as the colonnade, belvedere, keystone, and swag. Like Moore's Piazza d'Italia, New Orleans (1975–80), and Alumni Center, University of California at Irvine (1983–85), these confident and colourful buildings are intended to reassure the public that it need no longer feel that its cultural identity is threatened by modern architecture. That mood was encapsulated in Venice in 1980 when a varied group of American and European architects, including Venturi, Moore, Paolo Portoghesi, Aldo Rossi, Hans Hollein, Ricardo Bofill, and Léon Krier, provided designs for an exhibition organized by the Venice Biennale under the title, "The Presence of the Past." These key architects of postmodernism represented several different outlooks but shared the ambition of banishing the fear of memory from modern architectural design.

The many American architects in the 1970s and '80s who adopted a populist language scattered with classical souvenirs included Philip Johnson and his partner John Burgee and the prolific Robert Stern. Johnson and Burgee designed the AT&T Building, New York City (1978–84), a skyscraper with a Chippendale skyline. Their School of Architecture Building, University of Houston (1982–85), is inspired by Ledoux's project for a House of Education at Chaux (1773–79). Stern's Observatory Hill Dining Hall, University of Virginia, Charlottesville (1982–84), is in a cheerful Jeffersonian classicism, while his Prospect Point Office Building, La Jolla, Calif. (1983–85), incorporates Spanish Colonial references. Many postmodernist architects were either trained by or began their careers as modernists, and many elements of Modernism carried over into postmodernism, especially in the work of architects such as Graves, Venturi, and Richard Meier.

Rejecting the playful elements in such buildings as kitsch,

Interior of the Clore Gallery at the Tate Gallery, London, by James Stirling, 1980–87.
Angelo Hornak

some architects, notably Allan Greenberg and John Blatteau, chose a more historically faithful classical style, as in their official reception rooms of the U.S. Department of State in Washington, D.C. (1984–85). The most complete instance of historical accuracy is probably the J. Paul Getty Museum, Malibu, Calif. (1970–75), designed by the Los Angeles partnership of Langdon and Wilson, who relied on archaeological advice to achieve the authentic character of a Roman villa at Herculaneum.

A similar duality existed in this period in Britain, where the populist style of Graves was paralleled in the work of
Pupkewitz/Rapho

Les Espaces d'Abraxas, Marne-la-Vallée, by Ricardo Bofill, 1978–83.

Terry Farrell (TV-am Studios, Camden Town, London, 1983), and of James Stirling (Clore Gallery at the Tate Gallery, London, 1980–87), while undeviating classicism was pursued by Quinlan Terry (Riverside Development, Richmond, Surrey, 1986–88), Julian Bicknell (Henbury Rotunda, Cheshire, 1984–86), and John Simpson (Ashfold House, Sussex, 1985–87). The spirit of classical urban renewal was represented in France by Christian Langlois's Senate Building, rue de Vaugirard, Paris (1975), and the Regional Council Building in Orléans (1979–81). Urban preoccupations have been more dramatically expressed in France by Ricardo Bofill's vast housing developments, such as Les Espaces d'Abraxas, Marne-la-Vallée, near Paris (1978–83). The gargantuan scale of this columnar architecture of prefabricated concrete pushes the language of classicism to its limits and beyond.

Neo-rationalism

A third branch of postmodernism was represented by a neorationalist or elementalist approach that echoes the stripped classicism of the 19th and early 20th century. This movement was again in part a reaction to changes in the urban environment by the combination of commercial pressure and Modern movement ideology. Neorationalism originated in Italy where the architect Aldo Rossi published an influential book, *L'architettura della città* (1966; *The Architecture of the City*), Rossi's Modena Cemetery (1971–77) exhibits both his austerely fundamental classicism and his concern for contextualism, since it echoes features of the local farms and factories of Lombardy.

Neorationalist ideals have also been realized in the Italian-speaking Swiss canton of Ticino: for example, in the work of Mario Campi (Casa Maggi, Arosio, 1980); Mario Botta; and Bruno Reichlin and Fabio Reinhardt, whose Casa Tonino, Torricella (1972–74), is a pristine stripped Palladian essay in white concrete. Close to this work is a group of buildings in the Basque region, including the School at Ikastola (1974–78) by Miguel Garay and José-Ignacio Linazasoro; Casa Mendiola at Andoian (1977–78) by Garay; and the Rural Centre at Cordobilla (1981) by Manuel Iniguez and Alberto Ustarroz. The projects of the German architect Oswald Matthias Ungers—for example, his Stadtloggia in the Hildesheim marketplace (1980)—promoted the same kind of rationalist contextualism in Germany. They have been influential on the design of infill buildings in other historic towns in West Germany, Italy, and France. The Viennese architect Hans Hollein also contributed to this vein of radical eclecticism, as in his sophisticated interiors in the Austrian Travel Bureau, Vienna (1978), which distantly recall the city of Otto Wagner and Josef Hoffmann. The urban work of the Belgian architect Rob Krier has been related to this movement, as can be seen in his housing in the Ritterbergstrasse, West Berlin (1978–80). His brother, Léon Krier, has been influential for his iconlike drawings of city planning schemes in a ruthlessly simple classical style and for his polemical attacks on what he sees as the destruction by modern technology of civic order and human dignity.

The 1920s revivalist element in the neorationalist movement is demonstrated in the United States in the work of Richard Meier, for example in his Smith House, Darien, Conn. (1965–67), inspired by Le Corbusier's Citrohan and Domino houses, and his more complex High Museum, Atlanta (1980–83). Helmut Jahn's Bank of the South West, Houston (1982), recalls the Art Deco glass skyscraper, while the prolific Kevin Roche, originally a minimalist trained in the 1950s by Eero Saarinen, returned to the heroic formalism of the early skyscrapers for his Morgan Bank headquarters, New York City (1983–87), a 48-story skyscraper resting on a 70-foot-high entrance loggia of coupled granite columns.

Western influences in Asian architecture

In Japan, Isozaki Arata and Yamashita Kazumasa led the move away from Brutalism and Metabolism toward a postmodernism inspired by Charles Moore—for example, Isozaki's Tsukuba Centre building, Tsukuba Science City, Ibaraki (1983), and Yamashita's Japan Folk Arts Museum, Tokyo (1982). In India, Charles Correa led a parallel shift away from high-rise mass-housing of the Le Corbusier type. In the 1950s he worked in the International style, as in his hotel of white concrete at Ahmadabad, but in later low-rise housing and in his book, *The New Landscape* (1985), he demonstrated the virtues of a return to the more indigenous building types of the Third World.

The spirit of technology is, by contrast, celebrated in the Centre Pompidou, Paris (1971–77), by Renzo Piano and Richard Rogers. With its services and structure exposed externally and painted in primary colours, this exhibition centre can be seen as an outrageous joke in the historic centre of Paris. Though defiantly "modern," it has a postmodernist flavour as a playful statement of the modernist belief, going back at least to Viollet-le-Duc, in the truthful exposure of the structural bones of a building. Rogers repeated the theme in his Lloyd's Building, London (1984–86), but Stirling's addition to the Staatsgalerie, Stuttgart, W.Ger. (1977–82), is a key postmodernist building in the Venturi sense: that is, it makes ironic references to the language of Schinkel without accepting the fundamental principles of classicism. (DAVID J. WATKIN)

Pre-Columbian Civilizations

Meso-American civilization

LATE CLASSIC LOWLAND MAYA (600–900)

Settlement pattern. There is still controversy over whether the Late Classic sites built by the lowland Maya were actually cities or whether they were relatively empty ceremonial centres.

The common people built their simple pole-and-thatch dwellings on low earthen mounds to keep them dry during the summer rains. Thus, total mapping of a particular site should always include not only masonry structures but also house mounds as well. So far, only a few Maya sites have been so mapped. The mightiest Maya centre of all, Tikal in northern Petén, has a total of about 3,000 structures ranging from the tiny mounds up to gigantic temple pyramids; these are contained, however, within an area of six square miles. The Tikal population has been estimated from this survey to be 10,000–11,000 people, but perhaps as many as 75,000 within an even wider area could have belonged to Tikal.

Tikal

This sounds very much like a city, but the evidence actually can be differently interpreted. First, at the time of the conquest the Maya generally buried their dead beneath the floors of houses, which were then abandoned. Thus, an increase in number of house mounds could just as easily indicate a declining population in which the death rate exceeded the birth rate. Second, the appearance of even such a tremendous centre as Tikal is quite different from that of such true cities as Teotihuacán. An ordinary Maya family typically occupied two or three houses arranged around a rectangular open space. These were grouped into unplanned hamlets near good water and rich, well-drained soils. A survey of Petén has shown that for every 50 to 100 dwellings there was a minor ceremonial centre; this unit has been called a zone. Several zones formed a district for which a major centre like Tikal acted as the ceremonial and political nucleus. Neither Tikal nor any other such centre shows signs of town planning or neatly laid out streets.

Ecological factors

There are also ecological factors that must have set certain limits upon the potential for urban life in the Maya lowlands. Slash-and-burn cultivation would have made for widely settled populations; and, as has been argued, the uniformity of the lowland Maya environment would

A prisoner pleading for mercy before his captors, detail of
a mural at Bonampak, Chiapas state, Mexico; original *c.* AD
800, Late Classic Maya; watercolour copy by Antonio Tejeda.

Peabody Museum, Harvard University; photograph by Hillel Burger

have worked against the growth of strong interregional
trade, always a factor in urban development. Yet these
statements must be qualified. It is known that raised-field,
or chinampa-type, farming was used in many places and
at many times in the Maya lowlands. This would have
allowed for greater population concentration. It is also
known that there was a brisk trade in some commodities
from one lowland Maya region to another.

What, then, can be concluded about lowland Maya ur-
banism? Clearly, the urban form, even at a metropolis
such as Tikal, was not as large or as formally developed as
it was at highland Teotihuacán. At the same time, a centre
whose rulers could draw upon the coordinated efforts of
75,000 people must inevitably have had some of the functions of a true city—in governance, religion, and trade, as
well as in the development of the arts and intellectual life.

Major sites. While there are some important differences
between the architecture of the Central and Northern
subregions during the Late Classic, there are many features shared between them. A major Maya site generally
includes several types of masonry buildings, usually constructed by facing a cement-and-rubble core with blocks
or thin slabs of limestone. Temple pyramids are the most
impressive, rising in a series of great platforms to the temple superstructure above the forests. The rooms, coated
with white stucco, are often little more than narrow slots
because of the confining nature of the corbeled vaults, but
this was probably intentional, to keep esoteric ceremonies
from the public.

The so-called palaces of Maya sites differ only from the
temple pyramids in that they are lower and contain a great
many rooms. Their purpose still eludes discovery; many
scholars doubt that they really served as palaces, for the
rooms are damp and uncomfortable, and there is little or
no evidence of permanent occupation. The temples and
palaces are generally arranged around courts, often with
inscribed stelae and altars arranged in rows before them.
Leading from the central plazas are great stone causeways,
the function of which was probably largely ceremonial.
Other features of lowland sites (but not universal) are
sweathouses, ball courts, and probably marketplaces.

There are more than 50 known sites that deserve to be
called major. Most are in the Central Subregion, with
probably the greatest concentration in northern Petén,
where Maya civilization had its deepest roots. Tikal is the
largest and best-known Classic site of the Central Subre-

gion. It is dominated by six lofty temple pyramids, one
of which is some 230 feet high, the tallest structure ever
raised by the Meso-American Indians. Lintels of sapodilla
wood still span the doorways of the temple superstructures
and are carved with reliefs of Maya lords enthroned amid
scenes of great splendour. Some extraordinary Late Classic
tombs have been discovered at Tikal, the most important
of which produced a collection of bone tubes and strips
delicately incised with scenes of gods and men. Ten large
reservoirs, partly or entirely artificial, supplied the scarce
drinking water for the residents of Tikal.

Other important sites of northern Petén include Uaxac-
tún, Naranjo, Nakum, and Holmul, of which only the first
has been adequately excavated. To the southeast of Petén
are two Maya centres—Copán and Quiriguá—that show
notable differences with the Petén sites. Copán is located
above a tributary of the Motagua River in western Honduras in a region now rich in tobacco. Its architects and
sculptors had a ready supply of a greenish volcanic tuff far
superior to the Petén limestone. Thus, Copán architecture
is embellished with gloriously baroque figures of gods,
and its stelae and other monuments are carved with an
extraordinary virtuosity. Copán also has one of the most
perfectly preserved ball courts in Meso-America. Quiriguá
is a much smaller site 30 miles north of Copán. While its
architectural remains are on a minor scale, it is noted for
its gigantic stelae and altars carved from sandstone.

The principal watercourse on the western side of the
Central Subregion is the Usumacinta River, originating
in the Guatemalan highlands and emptying into the Gulf
of Mexico. For much of its course the Usumacinta is
lined with such great Maya ceremonial centres as Piedras
Negras and Yaxchilán. Even more renowned is Bonampak, a satellite of Yaxchilán located on a tributary of the
Usumacinta. The discovery in 1946 of the magnificent
murals embellishing the rooms of an otherwise modest
structure astounded the archaeological world. From floors
to vault capstones, its stuccoed walls were covered with
highly realistic polychrome scenes of a jungle battle, the
arraignment of prisoners, and victory ceremonies. These
shed an entirely new light on the nature of Maya society,
which up until then had been considered peaceful.

In the hills just above the floodplain of the Usumacinta
lies Palenque, the most beautiful of Maya sites. The architects of Palenque designed graceful temple pyramids
and "palaces" with mansard-type roofs, embellished with
delicate stucco reliefs of rulers, gods, and ceremonies. The
principal structure is the Palace, a veritable labyrinth of
galleries with interior courts; over it looms a four-story
square tower that may have served as both lookout and
observatory. A small stream flowing through the site was
carried underneath the Palace by a long, corbel-vaulted
tunnel. The temples of the Cross, Foliated Cross, and
Sun were all built on the same plan, the back room of
each temple having a kind of sanctuary designed like the
temple of which it was a part. It can be supposed that all
three temples served the same cult. The most extraordinary feature of Palenque, however, was the great funerary
crypt discovered in 1952 deep within the Temple of the
Inscriptions. Within a sarcophagus in the crypt were the
remains of an unusually tall ruler, accompanied by the
richest offering of jade ever seen in a Maya tomb. Over
his face had been fitted a mask of jade mosaic, while a
treasure trove of jade adorned his body.

Northward from the Central Subregion, in the drier and
flatter environment of the Yucatán Peninsula, the character of lowland Maya civilization changes. Just north of
Petén is the Río Bec zone, as yet little explored but noted
for temple pyramids and palaces with flanking false towers fronted by unclimbable "stairways" reaching dummy
"rooms" with blank entrances. Río Bec structures are
carved with fantastic serpents in deep relief, a feature that
becomes even more pronounced in the Chenes country to
the northwest, in the modern state of Campeche. There
Maya architects constructed frontal portals surrounded by
the jaws of sky serpents and faced entire buildings with a
riot of baroquely carved grotesques and spirals.

This elaborate ornamentation of buildings is far more
restrained and orderly in the style called Puuc, so named

The
Bonampak
murals

from a string of low hills extending up from western Campeche into the state of Yucatán. The Puuc sites were for the Northern Subregion what the Petén sites were for the Central, for they are very numerous and clearly were the focal point for Maya artistic and intellectual culture. Uxmal is the most important Puuc ceremonial centre and an architectural masterpiece. It has all of the characteristics of the Puuc style: facings of thin squares of limestone veneer over a cement-and-rubble core; bootshaped vault stones; decorated cornices around columns in doorways; engaged or half-columns repeated in long rows; and lavish use of stone mosaics in upper facades, emphasizing sky-serpent faces with long, hook-shaped noses, as well as frets and latticelike designs of crisscrossed elements.

The nearby centre of Kabah, connected to Uxmal by a ceremonial causeway, has an extraordinary palace completely faced with masks of the Sky Serpent. Other major Puuc sites are Sayil, with a multistoried palace, and Labná. The Puuc style reaches east across the Yucatán Peninsula, for at Chichén Itzá, a great site that was to occupy centre stage during the Toltec occupation of the Northern Subregion, there are several buildings strongly Puuc in character.

Puuc sites may be said to represent a lowland Maya "New Empire" in the sense that their apogee occurred in the 9th and 10th centuries, a time during which the great Petén, or Central Subregion, centres were in decline or had collapsed. Just how late Puuc sites remained active, with major constructions being dedicated, remains something of a question. In about 1000 a major change took place in northern Yucatán. It was marked by the construction of a number of Toltec-style temples and palaces at Chichén Itzá, a site that also has many Puuc-style edifices. It is not known if Toltec Chichén Itzá existed contemporaneously with such Puuc sites as Uxmal and Labná, and if so, for how long. Eventually, Chichén Itzá appears to have dominated northern Yucatán, lasting well into the Postclassic Period (about 1250). Questions also surround the bringers of Toltec-style architecture to Chichén Itzá. They may have been either central Mexican Toltecs or Gulf coast peoples who probably were Maya-speakers and who had adopted central-Mexican ways. In this connection, it should be noted that Puuc sites were under several influences from Gulf-coast Mexico, particularly from central Veracruz.

Maya art of the Late Classic. Maya art, at the height of its development, was fundamentally unlike any other in Meso-America, for it was highly narrative, baroque, and often extremely cluttered, unlike the more austere styles found elsewhere. It is essentially a painterly rather than sculptural tradition, and it is quite likely that even stone reliefs were first designed by painters. Much of this art has disappeared for all time because of the ravages of the

wet, tropical environment on such perishable materials as wood, painted gourds, feathers, bark, and other substances. There must have been thousands of bark-paper codices, not one of which has survived from Classic times.

Following the downfall of Teotihuacán, Maya artists were free to go their own way. Magnificently carved stelae and accompanying altars are found at most major sites, the greatest achievement in this line being found at Copán, where something approaching three-dimensional carving was the rule. Palenque and Yaxchilán specialized in graceful bas-reliefs placed as tablets or lintels in temple pyramids and palaces. In the Northern Subregion, however, the sculptor's art was definitely inferior in scope and quality and shows strong influence from alien, non-Maya cultures.

A few wooden objects have somehow survived. Particularly noteworthy are the massive wooden lintels of Tikal, with scenes of lords and their guardian deities, accompanied by lengthy hieroglyphic texts. In ancient times, wood carvings must have been vastly more common than sculptures. The wet climate has also destroyed innumerable examples of mural art.

Maya pottery can be divided into two groups: (1) the pots and pans of everyday life, usually undecorated but sometimes with geometric designs, and (2) grave offerings. Vessels meant to accompany the honoured dead were usually painted or carved with naturalistic and often macabre scenes. To achieve polychrome effects of great brilliance, the Maya potters painted in semitranslucent slips over a light background, then fired the vessels at a very low temperature. Relief carving was carried out when the vessels were leather-hard, just before firing.

The most precious substance of all to the Maya was jade, to which their craftsmen devoted great artistry. Jade was mainly fashioned into thin plaques, carved in relief, or into beads. In the absence of metal tools, jade was worked by applying abrasives and water with cane or perhaps other pieces of jade.

The Maya calendar and writing system. It is their intellectual life that established the cultural superiority of the Maya over all other American Indians. Much of this was based upon a calendrical system that was partly shared with other Meso-American groups but that they perfected into a tool capable of recording important historical and astronomical information. Most Maya inscriptions that have been interpreted are calendrical inscriptions. Since the late 1950s, it has been learned that the content of Classic Maya inscriptions was far more secular than had been supposed. For many years specialists believed that the inscriptions recorded little more than the passage of time and that, in fact, the Maya were time worshipers; but it has been shown that certain inscriptions recorded the birth, accession, marriage, and military victories of ruling dynasties. One very significant advance in following dynastic histories and plotting political territoriality was the discovery in 1958 of "emblem glyphs," symbols standing for royal lineages and their domains.

Yet it would be misleading to contend that the hurly-burly of Maya court affairs and conquests was all that mattered, for some texts must have been sacred and god-oriented. At Palenque, in the similar temples of the Cross, Foliated Cross, and Sun, the dates inscribed on the tablets in the sanctuaries fall into three groups. The very latest seem to refer to events in the lives of reigning monarchs. An earlier group must deal with distant but real ancestors of those kings, while the very earliest fall in the 4th millennium BC and apparently describe the birth of important gods to whom the respective temples were dedicated and who may have been regarded as the progenitors of Palenque's royal house.

The meaning of many non-calendrical signs and even of complete clauses is not known, but there is a difference between this and assigning an actual Maya word to an ancient glyph or a sentence to a glyphic clause. While it is certain that the language of the Classic inscriptions was Mayan, it is also certain that it was more archaic than any of the Mayan languages spoken at the time of the conquest, six centuries after the Classic downfall. The three extant Maya codices, none dating earlier than

Uxmal (margin note)

Wood carvings (margin note)

Peabody Museum, Harvard University

Ruins of the palace at Sayil, a Puuc site, Yucatán state, Mexico; Late Classic Maya.

The Maya codices

1100, contain a strong phonetic component, in fact a kind of syllabary, which can be successfully read as Yucatec-Maya, but the Classic peoples of the Central Subregion more likely spoke an ancestor of the Cholan branch of Maya. Furthermore, Maya hieroglyphic writing covers the entire span from about AD 250 to the conquest, during which time both the language or languages and the writing system itself must have undergone extensive evolution.

In writing systems in general, there is usually a development from pictographic signs, in which a picture stands for a word or concept, through logographic systems, in which words are still the basic unit but phoneticism is employed to reduce ambiguities (as in Chinese), to phonetic syllabaries, and finally to alphabets. Probably most Classic Maya hieroglyphs are logograms with a mainly ideographic orientation, and it seems that there was a considerable degree of flexibility in how the words and sentences could be written. By the Postclassic, this had been codified into a much more rigid system closely resembling that of Japanese, in which a well-defined syllabary can supplement or even replace logograms. There are approximately 300 to 500 logograms in Classic Maya (the number varies according to how one separates affixes from so-called main signs), but it will probably be many years before the majority of these are satisfactorily deciphered. Great progress, however, may be expected in unraveling their meaning in specific contexts.

(MICHAEL D. COE/GORDON R. WILLEY)

Maya mathematics included two outstanding developments: positional numeration and a zero. These may rightly be deemed among the most brilliant achievements of the human mind. The same may also be said of ancient Maya astronomy. The duration of the solar year had been calculated with amazing accuracy, as well as the synodical revolution of Venus. The Dresden Codex contains very precise Venusian and lunar tables and a method of predicting solar eclipses.

Maya chronology consisted of three main elements: a 260-day sacred year (*tzolkin*) formed by the combination of 13 numbers (1 to 13) and 20 day names; a solar year (*haab*), divided into 18 months of 20 days numbered from 0 to 19, followed by a five-day unlucky period (Uayeb); and a series of cycles—*uinal* (20 *kins,* or days), *tun* (360 days), *katun* (7,200 days), *baktun* (144,000 days), with the highest cycle being the *alautun* of 23,040,000,000 days. All Middle American civilizations used the two first counts, which permitted officials accurately to determine a date within a period defined as the least common multiple of 260 and 365: 18,980 days, or 52 years.

The Long Count

The Classic Maya Long Count inscriptions enumerate the cycles that have elapsed since a zero date in 3114 BC. Thus, "9.6.0.0.0," a *katun*-ending date, means that nine *baktun*s and six *katun*s have elapsed from the zero date to the day 2 Ahau 13 Tzec (May 9, AD 751). To those Initial Series were added the Supplementary Series (information about the lunar month) and the Secondary Series, a calendar-correction formula that brought the conventional date in harmony with the true position of the day in the solar year.

Both Classic and recent Maya held the *tzolkin* as the most sacred means of divination, enabling the priests to detect the favourable or evil influences attached to every day according to the esoteric significance of the numbers and the day-signs. (JACQUES SOUSTELLE)

Classic Maya religion. It has been denied that there was any such thing as a pantheon of deities in Classic times, the idea being that the worship of images was introduced by the Toltec or Itzá invaders, or both, in the Postclassic. Several gods who played significant roles in the Postclassic codices, however, can be identified on earlier Maya monuments. The most important of these is Itzamná, the supreme Maya deity, who functioned as the original creator god, as well as lord of the fire and therefore of the hearth. In his serpent form he appears on the ceremonial bar held in the arms of Maya rulers on Classic stelae. Another ophidian deity recognizable in Classic reliefs is the Feathered Serpent, known to the Maya as Kukulcán (and to the Toltecs and Aztecs as Quetzalcóatl). Probably the most ubiquitous of all is the being known as Bolon

Tzacab (first called God K by archaeologists), a deity with a baroquely branching nose who is thought to have functioned as a god of royal descent; he is often held as a kind of sceptre in rulers' hands.

The Classic Maya lavished great attention on their royal dead, who almost surely were thought of as descended from the gods and partaking of their divine essence. Many reliefs and all of the pictorial pottery found in tombs deal with the underworld and the dangerous voyage of the soul through that land. Classic Maya funerary ceramics show that this dark land was ruled by a number of gods, including several sinister old men often embellished with jaguar emblems, the jaguar being associated with the night and the nether regions.

Human sacrifice

The Classic, as well as the Postclassic, Maya practiced human sacrifice, although not on the scale of the Aztecs. The victims were probably captives, including defeated rulers and nobles. Self-sacrifice or self-mutilation was also common; blood drawn by jabbing spines through the ear or penis, or by drawing a thorn-studded cord through the tongue, was spattered on paper or otherwise collected as an offering to the gods. (MICHAEL D. COE/GORDON R. WILLEY)

The four main categories of documents that provide knowledge of the Maya civilization and its religion are: archaeological remains; native books in hieroglyphic writing; books in native languages written in Latin script by learned Indians; and early accounts written in Spanish by conquerors or priests.

From surviving temples, tombs, sculpture, wall paintings, pottery, and carved jades, shells, and bone, a significant amount of valuable information can be gained; *e.g.,* representations of godheads and ritual scenes. Perhaps the most important archaeological source, however, is the hieroglyphic texts carved on stone monuments or stone or bone artifacts and painted on pottery. These, insofar as they can be translated, provide descriptions of ceremonies and beliefs.

Three native hieroglyphic books of pre-Columbian date survived the Spanish conquest: the Dresden, Madrid, and Paris codices, named for the cities in which they are now housed. Written on bark paper, they deal with astronomical calculations, divination, and ritual. They appear to be Postclassic copies of earlier Classic originals.

After the Spanish conquest, books were written by learned Indians who transcribed or summarized hieroglyphic records. Such is the case of the *Books of Chilam Balam,* in Yucatec Maya, and of the *Popol Vuh,* in Quiché, a highland Maya language. The former consist of historical chronicles mixed with myth, divination, and prophecy, and the latter (which shows definite central Mexican influences) embodies the mythology and cosmology of the Postclassic Guatemalan Maya. The *Ritual of the Bacabs* covers religious symbolism, medical incantations, and similar matters.

The most important of the early accounts written by the Spanish themselves is Diego de Landa's *Relación de las cosas de Yucatán* ("On the Things of Yucatán"), which dates to about 1566. It describes Postclassic rather than Classic religion, but given the deeply conservative nature of Maya religion, it is highly probable that much of this description is pertinent for the earlier period. Landa's account is also an excellent description of other aspects of Maya life in 16th-century Yucatán.

To these archaeological, ethnohistorical, and historical sources may be added the observations of modern ethnologists about the present-day Maya. Thus, in the Guatemalan highlands, the 260-day calendar still survives, as do ancient prayers to and information about Maya gods.

It is likely that a simpler religion of nature worship prevailed in Early Formative times. This probably began to undergo modification during the Middle Formative, as astronomical knowledge became more precise. Certainly by the Late Formative (300 BC, if not earlier), with the appearance of major centres and pyramid and temple constructions, an elaborate worldview had evolved. Deified heavenly bodies and time periods were added to the earlier-conceived corn and rain gods. Concepts derived from priestly speculation were imposed upon the simpler

religious beginnings. Religion became increasingly esoteric, with a complex mythology interpreted by a closely
organized priesthood.

Creation.   The Maya, like other Middle American Indians, believed that several worlds had been successively
created and destroyed before the present universe had
come into being. The Dresden Codex holds that the end of
a world will come about by deluge: although the evidence
derived from Landa's *Relación* and from the Quiché *Popol
Vuh* is not clear, it is likely that four worlds preceded the

present one. People were made successively of earth (who,
being mindless, were destroyed), then of wood (who, lacking souls and intelligence and being ungrateful to the gods,
were punished by being drowned in a flood or devoured
by demons), and finally of a corn gruel (the ancestors of
the Maya). The Yucatec Maya worshiped a creator deity
called Hunab Ku, "One-God." Itzamná ("Iguana House"),
head of the Maya pantheon of the ruling class, was his
son, whose wife was Ix Chebel Yax, patroness of weaving.

Myths about the creation of man

Four Itzamnas, one assigned to each direction of the
universe, were represented by celestial monsters or two-
headed, dragonlike iguanas. Four gods, the Bacabs, sustained the sky. Each world direction was associated with
a Bacab, a sacred ceiba, or silk cotton tree, a bird, and a
colour according to the following scheme: east–red, north–
white, west–black, and south–yellow. Green was the colour
of the centre.

The main act of creation, as stated in the *Popol Vuh,*
was the dawn: the world and humanity were in darkness,
but the gods created the Sun and the Moon. According to
other traditions, the Sun (male) was the patron of hunting and music, and the Moon (female) was the goddess
of weaving and childbirth. Both the Sun and the Moon
inhabited the earth originally, but they were translated to
the heaven as a result of the Moon's sexual license. Lunar
light is less bright than that of the Sun because, it was said,
one of her eyes was pulled out by the Sun in punishment
for her infidelity.

Because the Maya priests had reached advanced knowledge of astronomical phenomena and a sophisticated
concept of time, it appears that their esoteric doctrines
differed widely from the popular myths.

Cosmology.   The Maya believed that 13 heavens were
arranged in layers above the earth, which itself rested on
the back of a huge crocodile or reptilian monster floating
on the ocean. Under the earth were nine underworlds,
also arranged in layers. Thirteen gods, the Oxlahuntiku,
presided over the heavens; nine gods, the Bolontiku, ruled
the subterranean worlds. These concepts are closely akin
to those of the Postclassic Aztec, but archaeological evidence, such as the nine deities sculptured on the walls of
a 7th-century crypt at Palenque, shows that they were part
of the Classic Maya cosmology.

Time was an all-important element of Maya cosmology.
The priest-astronomers viewed time as a majestic succession of cycles without beginning or end. All the time
periods were considered as gods; time itself was believed
to be divine.

The gods.   Among the several deities represented by
statues and sculptured panels of the Classic period are
such gods as the young corn god, whose gracious statue is
to be seen at Copán, the sun god shown at Palenque under
the form of the solar disk engraved with anthropomorphic
features, the nine gods of darkness (also at Palenque), and
a snake god especially prominent at Yaxchilán. Another
symbol of the corn god is a foliated cross or life tree
represented in two Palenque sanctuaries. The rain god
(Chac) has a mask with characteristic protruding fangs,
large round eyes, and a proboscis-like nose. Such masks
are a common element in Puuc architecture.

Agricultural and astral deities

The three hieroglyphic manuscripts, especially the Dresden Codex, depict a number of deities whose names are
known only through Postclassic documents. Itzamná, lord
of the heavens, who ruled over the pantheon, was closely
associated with Kinich Ahau, the sun god, and with the
moon goddess Ix Chel. Though Itzamná was considered
an entirely benevolent god, Ix Chel, often depicted as an
evil old woman, had definitely unfavourable aspects.
The Chacs, the rain gods of the peasants, were believed to

The corn god (left) and the rain god, Chac. Drawing from the
Madrid Codex (Codex Tro-Cortesianus), one of the Mayan
sacred books. In the Museo de América, Madrid.
By courtesy of the Museo de America, Madrid

pour rain by emptying their gourds and to hurl stone axes
upon the earth (the lightning). Their companions were
frogs (*uo*), whose croakings announced the rains. Earth
gods were worshiped in the highlands, and wind gods were
of minor importance in Maya territory.

The corn god, a youthful deity with an ear of corn in his
headdress, also ruled over vegetation in general. His name
is Ah Mun, and he is sometimes shown in combat with
the death god, Ah Puch, a skeleton-like being, patron of
the sixth day-sign Cimi ("Death") and lord of the ninth
hell. Several other deities were associated with death; *e.g.,*
Ek Chuah, a war god and god of merchants and cacao
growers, and Ixtab, patron goddess of the suicides.

In Postclassic times, central Mexican influences were
introduced; *e.g.,* the Toltec Feathered Serpent (Quetzalcóatl), called Kukulcán in Yucatán and Gucumatz in the
Guatemalan highlands.

The ancient Maya's attitude toward the gods was one of
humble supplication, since the gods could bestow health,
good crops, and plentiful game or send illness and hunger.
Prayers and offerings of food, drink, and incense (*pom*)
were used to placate the gods. A strong sense of sin and
a belief in predestination pervaded the Maya consciousness. Man had to submit to the forces of the universe.
The priests, because of their astronomical and divinatory
knowledge, determined favourable days for such under-
takings as building houses and hunting.

Death.   As was noted above, the Classic Maya buried
the dead under the floors of their houses. High priests or
powerful lords were laid to rest in elaborate underground
vaults. The dead were believed to descend to the nine
underworlds, called Mitnal in Yucatán and Xibalba by the
Quiché. There is no evidence of a belief among the Maya
in a heavenly paradise. The modern Lacandón, however,
believe that the dead live forever without work or worry
in a land of plenty located somewhere above the earth.

Eschatology.   The present world, the Maya believed, is
doomed to end in cataclysms as the other worlds have
done previously. According to the priestly concept of time,
cycles repeat themselves. Therefore, prediction was made
possible by probing first into the past and then into the
future: hence the calculations, bearing on many millennia,
carved on temples and stelae. Evil influences were held
to mark most of the *katun* endings. The *Chilam Balam*
books are full of predictions of a markedly direful character. The priests probably believed that the present world
would come to a sudden end, but that a new world would
be created so that the eternal succession of cycles should
remain unbroken.

The end of the world

Sacrifice.   Sacrifices made in return for divine favour
were numerous: animals, birds, insects, fish, agricultural

Forms of sacrifice

products, flowers, rubber, jade, and blood drawn from the tongue, ears, arms, legs, and genitals. Evidence of human sacrifice in Classic times includes two Piedras Negras stelae, an incised drawing at Tikal, the murals at Bonampak, various painted ceramic vessels, and some scenes in native manuscripts. Only in the Postclassic era did this practice become as frequent as in central Mexico. Toltec-Maya art shows many instances of human sacrifice: removal of the heart, arrow shooting, or beheading. At Chichén Itzá, in order to obtain rain, victims were hurled into a deep natural well (cenote) together with copper, gold, and jade offerings. Prayers for material benefits (which were usually recited in a squatting or standing position), fasting and continence (often for 260 days), and the drawing of blood from one's body often preceded important ceremonies and sacrifices.

These practices had become so deeply rooted that, even after the Spanish conquest, Christian–pagan ceremonies occasionally took place in which humans were sacrificed by heart removal or crucifixion. The last recorded case occurred in 1868 among the Chamula of Chiapas.

The priesthood. Bejeweled, feather-adorned priests are often represented in Classic sculpture. The high priests of each province taught in priestly schools such subjects as history, divination, and glyph writing. The priesthood, as described by Landa, was hereditary. *Ahkin,* "he of the sun," was the priests' general title. Specialized functions were performed by the *nacom*s, who split open the victims' breasts, the *chac*s who held their arms and legs, the *chilan*s who interpreted the sacred books and predicted the future. Some priests used hallucinatory drugs in their roles as prophets and diviners.

Rites. Ritual activities, held on selected favourable days, were complex and intense. Performers submitted to preliminary fasting and sexual abstinence. Features common to most rites were: offerings of incense (*pom*), of balche (an intoxicating drink brewed from honey and a tree bark), bloodletting from ears and tongues, sacrifices of animals (human sacrifices in later times), and dances. Special ceremonies took place on New Year's Day, 0 Pop, in honour of the "Year-Bearer"; *i.e.,* the *tzolkin* sign of that day. Pottery, clothes, and other belongings were renewed. The second month, Uo, was devoted to Itzamná, Tzec (fifth month) to the Bacabs, Xul (sixth) to Kukulcán, Yax (10th) to the planet Venus, Mac (13th) to the rain gods, and Muan (15th) to the cocoa-tree god. New idols were made during the eighth and ninth months, Mol and Ch'en, respectively.

The ritual ball game | Both the Classic and Postclassic Maya practiced a typically Middle American ritual ball game, as evidenced by numerous grandiose ball courts at Tikal, Copán, and Chichén Itzá. No court, however, has been found at Mayapán, and Landa does not mention that game. It appears, therefore, that the Yucatec had ceased to play it, while it remained of the utmost importance in central Mexico.

Archaeological remains at Uxmal and Chichén Itzá point to phallic rites, doubtless imported into the Yucatán from the Gulf coast. The *Chilam Balam* books strongly condemn the Mexican immigrants' sexual practices, which were quite alien to Maya tradition.

Sorcery. Ahmen, "he who knows," was the name given to sorcerers and medicine men, who were both prophets and inflicters or healers of disease. They made use of a mixture of magic formulas, chants, and prayers and of traditional healing methods, such as administering medicinal herbs or bleeding. Belief in witchcraft is widespread among present-day Maya Indians, as it most probably was in pre-Columbian times.

The evolution of Maya religion parallels that of Mexican religions from the Classic to the Postclassic era, with the sun worship and human sacrifice complex gaining importance as it did in Mexico proper.

The profoundly original feature of Maya religious thought, in comparison with that of other pre-Columbian civilizations, is the extraordinary refinement of mathematical and astronomical knowledge, inextricably mixed with mythological concepts. Even the most learned Aztec priests never reached the intellectual level of their Maya counterparts of the 1st millennium, nor did they conceive of the eternity of time and of its "bearers," the divinized time periods. The ancient Maya may be said to have been among the very few people in history (along with the Zurvanites of Iran) who worshiped time.

The simple, naturalistic religion of the corn-growing peasants, however, subsisted apart from the priesthood's abstract speculations and has partly survived to this day among the Christianized Maya Indians or the unevangelized Lacandón. (JACQUES SOUSTELLE/ GORDON R. WILLEY)

Society and political life. There is a vast gap between the lavishly stocked tombs of the Maya elite who ran the ceremonial centres and the simple graves of the peasantry. Careful measurements of the skeletons found in tombs and graves have also revealed that persons of the Maya ruling class were much taller than the tillers of the soil who provided them tribute. It is likely that this gulf was unspannable, for throughout Meso-America the rulers and nobility were believed to have been created separately from commoners.

The most revealing testimony to this royal cult is the temple pyramid itself, for almost every one explored has a great tomb hidden in its base. On death, each ruler might have been the object of ancestor worship by members of his lineage, the departed leader having become one with the god from whom he claimed descent. Ancestor worship, in fact, seems to be at the heart of ancient and modern society and religion among the Maya.

The ordinary folk may have participated in the ceremonies of even the greatest Maya centres. The modern highland Maya have a complex ceremonial life in which a man advances through a series of *cargos,* or "burdens," each one of which brings him greater prestige, costs him a great deal of money, and requires that he reside in the otherwise nearly empty centre for a year at a time carrying out his religious duties. The same may have prevailed in Classic times, though all activities were then under the direction of a hereditary and divine elite class, long since destroyed by the Spaniards.

Warfare apparently was a continuing preoccupation of the Maya lords. Translations of hieroglyphic inscriptions show that in some cases such warfare led to territorial aggrandizement and the domination of one centre or polity by another; however, the principal purpose of war appears to have been to gain captives for slavery and sacrifice. | Warfare

It has often been said that the Maya realm was a theocracy, with all power in the hands of the priests. That this is a misconception is apparent from the monuments themselves, which show kings, queens, heirs, and war prisoners, but no figures surely identifiable as priests. In 16th-century Yucatán, the priesthood was hereditary, and it is reported that younger sons of lords often took on that vocation. Quite probably such a class was also to be found among the Late Classic Maya, but neither for the Maya nor for any other Classic civilization of Meso-America can the term theocracy be justified.

The collapse of Classic Maya civilization. In the last century of the Classic period, Maya civilization went into a decline from which it never recovered. Beginning about 790 in the western edge of the Central Subregion, such ceremonial activity as the erection of stelae virtually came to a standstill. During the next 40 years this cultural paralysis spread gradually eastward, by which time the great Classic civilization of the Maya had all but atrophied. A date in the Maya calendar corresponding to 889 is inscribed on the last dated monuments in the Central Subregion; soon after the close of the 9th century it is clear that almost all of this region was abandoned.

For this event, which must have been one of the greatest human tragedies of all time, there are few convincing explanations. It now seems that the Classic Maya civilization in the region of its greatest development went out "not with a bang but a whimper." Massive foreign invasions can be discounted as a factor, but non-Maya elements did appear in the west at the same time as ceremonial activity terminated. These became the inheritors of whatever was left of the old civilization of the Central Subregion after AD 900, having established trading colonies and even a few minor ceremonial centres on its peripheries.

Whatever incursions did take place from the west were piecemeal and probably the result of the general decline, rather than its cause. Similarly, there is little reason to believe that there were peasant revolts on a general scale. The only real fact is that most of the inhabitants of the Central Subregion went elsewhere. Probably some were absorbed by such still flourishing ceremonial centres of the Northern Subregion as Uxmal and Kabah, while others might have migrated up into the congenial highlands of Chiapas and Guatemala. Although a population explosion and severe ecological abuse of the land must have played their role in the tragedy, the full story of the decline and fall of this brilliant aboriginal civilization remains to be told. (MICHAEL D. COE/GORDON R. WILLEY)

The nature of Andean civilization

The coastal desert
The coastal desert was inhabited for millennia by fishermen, and many of their settlements have been studied by archaeologists. The people in these communities were familiar with the sea and depended heavily on its products, but from very early times they also used and possibly cultivated native varieties of cotton. Textiles have been the major art form in the Andes for thousands of years. It is known that these textiles—found preserved in the coastal sands—have woven into them a wealth of information on Andean peoples; and, while the information in the textiles still cannot be read, it is believed that they will eventually be as revealing as have been the Meso-American codices.

In modern Peru irrigation eventually may permit the cultivation of the lower reaches of most rivers. Still, it is useful to note that of some 50 rivers descending from the Andean glaciers to the Peruvian coast, only three have water flowing through them year-round. Such an ambitious irrigation scheme would be most productive only if the waters were tapped quite high on the western slope and if several rivers were connected through canals high in the Andes, thus allowing the scarce waters of three or four valleys to be pooled into a single one as needed. Rumours of such a project reached the first Spaniards in Peru: in the final decade before the invasion, the Inca were said to be planning to bore through a mountain in what today is northern Chile, so that water from the Amazonic watershed would flow westward to the deserts and thus alter the continental divide.

Archaeologists, particularly non-Peruvian scholars, have concentrated on the study of coastal peoples: they have found that sites are more accessible along the Pan-American Highway; that the hot and dry climate presents none of the challenges of the high altitudes; and that the remains, mummified in the desert sands, are immediately rewarding. Pottery finds have portrayed such things as fishing or warfare, diseases, weapons, cultivated plants, and differences in rank and in sexual habits among the Andeans. Usually this evidence has been recovered by professional grave looters but sometimes also by archaeologists themselves. One of the most remarkable of the latter type of finds is the grave of a Moche leader that was discovered near the village of Sipan on the northern coast of Peru in the mid-1980s. Since the mid-20th century architectural studies of ceremonial and political centres have allowed researchers to follow changes in the location and the architectural features of important Andean cities. Distance from the sea and the degree of dependence on maritime products, the proximity to irrigation waters from the highlands, and the repeated efforts to control militarily more than a single irrigated valley have all received attention from archaeologists.

A major question remains: did these coastal polities extend upward to the Andean highlands to control areas beyond the slopes where the irrigation works tapped the rivers? The Peruvian historian María Rostworowski has pointed to similarities, found in colonial administrative papers, between coastal places-names and personal names in the Cajamarca Highlands, an area due east and above the coastal political entities. The colonial papers have not explained the presence of such distant colonies, but they have introduced a topic fundamental to understanding Andean success: given the apparently inhospitable environments of both the desert coast and the nearby high Andes, how could so many separate societies have fed such enormous populations and constructed highways, palaces, and temples in what were clearly urban centres for so many centuries?

AGRICULTURAL ADAPTATION

One answer to this question was suggested in the 1930s by the German geographer Carl Troll. His solution took into account a unique aspect of Andean ecology: the greatest population concentration (more than 1,000,000 people) and the highest agricultural productivity occurred around Lake Titicaca, which is some 12,500 feet above sea level. Nowhere else in the world—not even in Tibet or Nepal—has cultivation been so successful at such a high altitude. The effort to understand the ramifications of this paradox is far from complete, but Troll's insights have proved fertile: (1) The fields and terraces clustered around the lake were located just a few degrees south of the Equator, where daytime temperatures are truly tropical. (2) At this altitude climatic contrasts are not so much seasonal as diurnal, i.e., summer by day and winter by night. Contrasts of 55° to 70° F (30° to 40° C) within a single 24-hour period are not uncommon, and nearly 300 nights of frost per year have been recorded on the high, windy plateau (puna) surrounding the lake. (3) Populations settled in such circumstances seem to have endured as others have survived in the Arctic, the Kalahari, and the Gobi, but it is clear that in the Andes a far denser population fared much better than have groups in other environmentally harsh regions, acquiring with time an intimate familiarity with the agricultural and pastoral possibilities of high altitude.

Tuber cultivation
These peoples cultivated many varieties of tubers, of which only the potato has achieved widespread use in the world. But since the soils at this altitude were easily exhausted, "second- and third-year" tubers had to be domesticated to take advantage of the nutrients left unused in the soil. Then, as now, it was usual to allow the ground to rest—for six, eight, or even 10 years—after which some of the "rested" acreage was returned to cultivation annually, a rotation pattern that is still familiar to the local people.

The upper elevation limit of cultivation has varied throughout the centuries, as the climate has fluctuated. Thus, considerable effort was invested in the development of ever more frost-resistant varieties of tubers. Modern observers have noted that tubers grown close to and above about 13,000 feet were mostly of the pentaploid varieties, bitter hybrids resulting from selection and crossing by the grower. Although they usually required additional nurture and processing that were beyond the procedures familiar today, the bitter varieties represented a gain in total productivity.

Terracing
A significant improvement in agriculture was the construction of massive terraces, which not only extended the cultivated area but also created protected microclimates where particular varieties could flourish. It has been suggested that an "amphitheatre" found in the Cuzco region was actually an experimental field where the concentric terraces reproduced tiny variations in the upland environment. When the use of highland irrigation and raised-ridged fields are taken into account, it becomes clear that these upland populations were highly familiar with, and respectful of, the potential for high-altitude agriculture and were intent on gaining additional acreage in circumstances that elsewhere would not have seemed worth the effort.

Another incentive for settlement at high altitudes was the presence of glacier-fed pastures for alpaca herds. The llama—it and the alpaca were the two camelids domesticated by the Andean peoples—could live at altitudes ranging from sea-level to those in the high mountains. The alpaca's habitat, however, was much narrower; it did best above 13,000 feet, and its preference for a swampy range was catered to by pastoralists. It has been found that even today alpaca-herding is a full-time occupation, almost impossible to combine with agriculture. While Andean herders did belong to wider ethnic groups, they tended to be specialists, relying for their food staples on their kinsmen closer to Lake Titicaca.

Present-day distribution and use of these animals (known

collectively as camelids) tends to mask their importance in pre-Columbian times. A European inspector, reporting in the 1560s on the camelid wealth of a single Aymara chiefdom near Lake Titicaca, claimed, "I have heard of an Indian who is not even a lord, one don Juan Alanoca of Chucuito, who has more than 50,000 head." Such control of vast herds, combined with the hundreds of varieties of high-altitude tubers and grains, helps to explain the density of Andean populations.

THE COLD AS A RESOURCE

Beyond such skilled manipulation of the natural geography there lay an awareness of frost. As noted above, in the high Andes frost can occur almost every night of the year. Elsewhere people have endured the cold; in the Andes the cold was transformed into a positive and even creative factor.

It is not known when this step was taken. For at least 1,000 years people in the Andes have been aware that the sharp alternation between tropical noon and arctic midnight can be utilized. Any animal or vegetable tissue exposed to this daily contrast can be processed into nutritive products that keep for decades, and the process can be achieved either at the household or the state level.

Food preservation and storage

Chuño is the name popularly used for processed tubers, but a rich vocabulary for tubers exists in the Quechuan (Andean) languages: there is a separate term for each plant and for each mode of preparation. Chuño cannot be made where a diurnal temperature extreme is absent; thus, north of modern Cajamarca in northern Peru no chuño is prepared, since nocturnal frosts are rare or absent. Animal tissues also can be handled in this manner. After 1532 European meats were added to those of local birds, fish, and camelids. The name for these preserved meats is charqui, or jerky (*ch'arki* in Quechua), the one Andean word that has made its way into common English usage.

Such food reserves allowed both the peasants and the state to compensate for natural and man-made calamities. They filled thousands of warehouses—many of which are still extant—that were built in ways and places so as to use the tiny differences of exposure to the sun, winds, and humidity. Those built by the state or by the ethnic lords along the more than 15,500 miles of roads provided food for both human and camelid porters, for the armies, and for priests traveling to the many shrines.

The presence of such large stores made possible the incredible forays of Spaniards like Diego de Almagro, who reached Chile from Cuzco across thousands of miles of deserts and snow-covered mountains. As late as 1547, 15 years after the Spanish invasion, one Spaniard, Polo de Ondegardo, reported that he had fed 2,000 soldiers for seven weeks with the food still stored above Xauxa, which had been the first European capital. A detailed archaeological study of an Inca storage system was made by the American anthropologist Craig Morris, who found almost 500 warehouses at Huánuco Pampa. There were some 1,000 warehouses at Xauxa and many more near Cuzco, the Inca capital.

THE HIGHLANDS AND THE LOW COUNTRIES

The cultivators of high-altitude tubers and lowland crops—the plants of which seem botanically far apart at first glance—were actually in continuous contact. This point was stressed by the pioneer Peruvian archaeologist Julio C. Tello and was later verified by foreign scholars. The inhabitants all along the Andean highlands were aware of the diverse populations and climates of the Pacific

coastal deserts to the west and of the Amazon lowlands to the east. The Chilean researcher Lautaro Núñez has traced the several societies who inhabited a single valley: products and settlement patterns changed through the centuries, but at all times each successive ethnic group accumulated resources from diverse ecological niches into a single system.

By adding written Spanish sources to the information provided by archaeologists, it is possible to explain further the density of the Andean population and its great productivity. Throughout the Andes, south of Cajamarca, political units large and small were characterized by a dispersed settlement pattern. The preferred location of the seat of power frequently was at very high altitudes, almost at the upper limit of cultivation, and kinsmen of these highlanders were settled permanently at three, five, or even 10 days' walk from the political centres. The German anthropologist Jürgen Golte has stressed that the agricultural calendar permitted such absences, since crops matured at different dates according to altitude; but many outliers were too far away from the political and demographic nucleus to permit seasonal migrations. The outlier communities could be large or small and could be established on the dry Pacific shore or in wet Amazonic enclaves. The Lupaca (Lupaqa), an Aymara-speaking polity whose political centre was located on the puna on the shores of Lake Titicaca, controlled outliers on both slopes.

Dispersed settlement pattern

Other ethnic groups reached in only one direction. For example, the two lords of the Karanga (Caranga), on what today is the highest part of the Bolivian High Plateau, do not seem to have controlled any outliers of their own on the Amazonic slope. Their main puna farms and most of their subjects lived above 12,000 feet, and their camelid herds were pastured even higher. The Karanqa also controlled corn (maize) fields at less lofty altitudes in what today is Chilean territory, several days' walk away. Farther west and closer to the coast were their fruit and coca-leaf gardens. Finally, even farther north, across the Atacama Desert near the modern city of Arica, the Karanqa had their "own" fishers.

One unexpected feature of such outliers is that they were usually multiethnic: several political centres shared settlements of salt miners, fishers and seaweed gatherers, cultivators of hot peppers and coca leaves, and timber cutters and honey gatherers. The political mechanisms by which conflicting groups could reach truces, even if temporary, or the means by which caravans moved with safety when connecting the central settlements with their multiple outliers are still not known.

This diverse pattern of settlement and political control and of pooling dispersed resources and populations has been named "Andean ecological complementarity," or the "vertical archipelago." Such complementarity went beyond the efficient control of the nocturnal cold and of the high altitude. Even if many details of how it worked still escape understanding, it is obvious that each ethnic group was able to diversify the risks that would have existed if each had been concentrated in any of the separate Andean ecological tiers. Beyond defensive strategies, in ecological complementarity it is possible to detect new opportunities that would permit massive storage of a wide range of foods going beyond those grown locally. Eventually there emerged dense populations and large polities like the Inca. It is notable that the foci of Andean civilizations across the centuries—Chavín, Huari (Wari), Tiahuanaco (Tiawanaku), Cuzco—were all located on the high puna.

(GEOFFREY H. S. BUSHNELL/JOHN V. MURRA)

Bibliography: Recent Books

The following list encompasses some 175 recent books that have been judged significant contributions to learning and understanding in their respective fields. Each citation includes a few lines of commentary to indicate the general tenor of the work. The citations are organized by subject area, using the ten parts of the *Propædia* as an outline.

Matter and Energy

Martin Sherwood and Christine Sutton (eds.), *The Physical World* (1988), a beautifully illustrated exploration of physical and chemical phenomena as manifested in everyday life.

Barry Parker, *Search for a Supertheory: From Atoms to Superstrings* (1987), a nonmathematical discussion of the theories trying to explain the universe and the workings of its parts.

Kenneth S. Krane, *Introductory Nuclear Physics* (1987), an accessible, comprehensive treatment of the subject.

I.R. Kenyon, *Elementary Particle Physics* (1987), an overview of theoretical issues and experimental techniques.

Hans-Georg Elias, *Mega Molecules: Tales of Adhesives, Bread, Diamonds, Eggs, Fibers, Foams, Gelatin, Leather, Meat, Plastics, Resists, Rubber, and Cabbages and Kings* (1987; originally published in German, 1985), a readable, comprehensive treatment of molecular biology, with a lively history of polymers.

Charles K. Adams, *Nature's Electricity* (1987), a broad though brief survey of naturally occurring electricity, with an explanation of basic theoretical issues.

Michael I. Sobel, *Light* (1987), a nontechnical introduction to the physical theories of light, with a historical perspective.

Wallace Tucker and Karen Tucker, *The Dark Matter: Contemporary Science's Quest for the Mass Hidden in Our Universe* (1988), an accessible general introduction to the concepts of a closed universe.

Nathan Cohen, *Gravity's Lens: Views of the New Cosmology* (1988), a readable exposition of the theory of the universe, with an explanation of modern measuring techniques.

Edward Harrison, *Darkness at Night: A Riddle of the Universe* (1987), a historical exploration of scientific views on the darkness of the night sky.

Stephen W. Hawking, *A Brief History of Time: From the Big Bang to Black Holes* (1988), a readable examination of the theories of the origin, nature, and evolution of the universe.

George Greenstein, *The Symbiotic Universe: Life and Mind in the Cosmos* (1988), a discussion of the Anthropic Principle of cosmology, summarizing the alternative points of view.

The Earth

David Lambert and the Diagram Group, *Field Guide to Geology* (1988), a comprehensive, well-illustrated discussion of the geologic processes of creation and evolution of the Earth.

Claude Allègre, *The Behavior of the Earth: Continental and Seafloor Mobility* (1988; originally published in French, 1983), a well-illustrated historical survey of complex geologic phenomena, written for the general reader.

John Gribbin, *The Hole in the Sky: Man's Threat to the Ozone Layer* (1988), a concise, readable summary of the atmospheric condition and the scientific and social controversy around it.

Lyall Watson, *The Water Planet: A Celebration of the Wonder of Water* (1988), a beautifully illustrated survey of the Earth's water, its properties, and its uses.

Jay S. Fein and Pamela L. Stephens (eds.), *Monsoons* (1987), a comprehensive discussion of the specific weather conditions and their biologic and social impact.

Hubert H. Lamb, *Weather, Climate & Human Affairs* (1988), a readable analysis of the multitude of factors influencing the changing climate on the Earth.

Cliff Ollier, *Volcanoes* (1988), an informative examination of vulcanism and landforms associated with volcanoes.

James P.M. Syvitski, David C. Burrell, and Jens M. Skei, *Fjords: Processes and Products* (1987), a study of complex interaction of geologic, biologic, physical, and chemical aspects of deep estuaries.

Preston Cloud, *Oasis in Space: Earth History from the Beginning* (1988), an interdisciplinary treatment of Earth history.

Life on Earth

R.J. Berry and A. Hallam (eds.), *The Encyclopedia of Animal Evolution* (1987), an attractively illustrated large-format compendium, reflecting current scientific research.

Robert L. Carroll, *Vertebrate Paleontology and Evolution* (1987), a comprehensive review of the history of backboned animals.

John A. Burton, *The Collins Guide to the Rare Mammals of the World* (1988), a collection of basic information about almost 1,200 endangered species, fully illustrated in colour.

Stephen A. Wainwright, *Axis and Circumference: The Cylindrical Shape of Plants and Animals* (1988), an original. mechanistic but nonmathematical, approach to morphology and biophysics.

Jeremy Burgess, Michael Marten, and Rosemary Taylor, *Microcosmos* (1987), a beautifully illustrated description of the ways to study biologic processes through microscopic procedures.

Mary L. Baker, *Whales, Dolphins, and Porpoises of the World* (1987), a clearly written and excellently illustrated (by the author) systematic study of all cetaceans.

Mark L. Winston, *The Biology of the Honey Bee* (1987), a well-illustrated, comprehensive, and readable survey of apiculture and the ecology, entomology, and behaviour of bees.

Irene Elia, *The Female Animal* (1988), an interpretative exploration of the biologic role and evolution of female reproductive behaviour.

Felicity A. Huntingford and Angela K. Turner, *Animal Conflict* (1987), a balanced survey of aggressive behaviour in animals.

J.R. Krebs and N.B. Davies, *An Introduction to Behavioural Ecology*, 2nd ed. (1987), an examination of the role of behaviour in ecological survival and of the impact of ecology on behaviour.

John Fisher, *Wild Flowers in Danger* (1987), a study of endangered representatives of European flora.

Frederick F. Gilbert and Donald G. Dodds, *The Philosophy and Practice of Wildlife Management* (1987), a discussion of cultural, social, and biologic aspects of management and preservation of nondomesticated animals.

John Hay, *The Immortal Wilderness* (1987), an outline of environmental concerns in view of findings in natural history.

Marius Jacobs, *The Tropical Rain Forest: A First Encounter*, ed. by Remke Kruk *et al.* (1988; originally published in Dutch, 1981), a posthumously completed important and concerned treatment of many aspects of rain forest ecology.

Bryan G. Norton, *Why Preserve Natural Variety?* (1987), a broad readable treatment of philosophical implications and policies of the preservation of species.

Human Life

Sidney Fox, *The Emergence of Life: Darwinian Evolution from the Inside* (1988), an independent theory of the origin of life and the author's firsthand account of underlying research.

Roger Lewin, *Bones of Contention: Controversies in the Search for Human Origins* (1987), an insider's account of developments, personalities, and contradictions in paleoanthropology.

Jayne Gackenbach (ed.), *Sleep and Dreams* (1987), an accessible exploration of the neurological fundamentals of sleep.

Myron Winick *et al.* (eds.), *The Columbia Encyclopedia of Nutrition* (1988), an informative, well-organized compendium of facts based on mainstream specialist opinion.

Serge Gracovetsky, *The Spinal Engine* (1988), a review of accepted knowledge about the human spine and a presentation of some new ideas about its functions.

Stevan E. Hobfoll, *The Ecology of Stress* (1988), a survey of research on psychological stress and its prevention.

Bruce Bridgeman, *The Biology of Behavior and Mind* (1988), a study of physiology of the brain and its mental activity.

Wanda Wyrwicka, *Brain and Feeding Behavior* (1988), a study of psychological aspects of appetite and its suppression, digestion, food preferences, and nutritional disorders.

Rima D. Apple, *Mothers and Medicine: A Social History of Infant Feeding, 1890–1950* (1987), an exploration of social practices that stimulated the development of a special branch of medicine.

Inge B. Corless and Mary Pittman-Lindeman (eds.), *AIDS: Principles, Practices & Politics* (1988), an important collection of authoritative facts, for the lay reader.

William H. Masters, Virginia E. Johnson, and Robert C. Kolodny, *Crisis: Heterosexual Behavior in the Age of AIDS* (1988), a controversial discussion of the epidemiology of the disease and preventive measures.

Diane Richardson, *Women and AIDS* (1988), an informative outline of the problem.

Lee Gutkind, *Many Sleepless Nights: The World of Organ Transplantation* (1988), an emotional account of this very modern branch of medicine, providing historical information.

Sherwin B. Nuland, *Doctors: The Biography of Medicine* (1988), a history of medicine based on the lives of its prominent practitioners.

Robert H. Blake, *Rationing Medicine* (1988), a well-written treatment of serious problems with health care allocation.

George J. Annas, *Judging Medicine* (1988), a balanced analysis of bioethical and legal problems of modern medicine, such as are involved in organ transplantation, human experimentation, surrogate motherhood, etc.

Dana Ullman, *Homeopathy: Medicine for the 21st Century* (1988), a nontechnical, informative though partisan overview of an alternative to conventional medicine.

Laura Betzig, Monique Borgerhoff Mulder, and Paul Turke (eds.), *Human Reproductive Behaviour: A Darwinian Perspective* (1988), a cross-cultural study of the evolution of human reproduction and behavioral patterns surrounding it.

Fred Dretske, *Explaining Behavior: Reasons in the World of Causes* (1988), a scholarly, though brief, exploration of the philosophy of mind, for philosophically minded readers.

Paul C. Horton, Herbert Gewirtz, and Karole J. Kreutter (eds.), *The Solace Paradigm: An Eclectic Search for Psychological Immunity* (1987), a collection of essays probing the nature of consolation and analyzing its role in human development.

Mary Warnock, *Memory* (1987), an examination of philosophical perspectives of memory and its role in personal identity.

Human Society

Julian Burger, *Report from the Frontier: The State of the World's Indigenous Peoples* (1987), a comprehensive examination of native tribal societies that exist as minorities among larger populations and undergo traumatic acculturation.

Ernest S. Burch, Jr., *The Eskimos* (1988), a beautifully illustrated ethnographic exploration of a complex culture.

Garry Marvin, *Bullfight* (1988), a detailed original treatment of the highly structural cultural phenomenon.

John D'Emilio and Estelle Freedman, *Intimate Matters: A History of Sexuality in America* (1988), a survey of gender relations as a cultural component and a means of social control.

Ruth F. Chadwick (ed.), *Ethics, Reproduction, and Genetic Control* (1987), a nontechnical survey of genetic engineering and alternative reproductive technologies.

Philip Silverman (ed.), *The Elderly as Modern Pioneers* (1987), a well-organized collection of analyses of characteristics of aging.

Anthony Storr, *Solitude: A Return to the Self* (1988), a study of the psychological aspects of solitude.

Frances Gies and Joseph Gies, *Marriage and the Family in the Middle Ages* (1987), a clearly written broad social history.

Ruth Macklin, *Mortal Choices: Bioethics in Today's World* (1987), an insightful study of the modern profession of bioethics dealing with complex issues surrounding health care.

David Crystal, *The Cambridge Encyclopedia of Language* (1987), a well-organized and accessible survey of modern linguistics and the state of living languages.

Barry Glassner and Julia Loughlin, *Drugs in Adolescent Worlds: Burnouts to Straights* (1987), an analysis of social conditions under which drug abuse exists.

Bonnie Menes Kahn, *Cosmopolitan Culture: The Gilt-Edged Dream of a Tolerant City* (1987), a cross-cultural sociological study of hospitality to strangers and minorities as a prerequisite for harmonious development of a great city.

Hans Singer, John Wood, and Tony Jennings, *Food Aid: The Challenge and the Opportunity* (1987), a thoughtful study of agricultural assistance as a tool of development.

James O. Grunebaum, *Private Ownership* (1987), a historical study of philosophical views on property ownership.

Jack Donnelly and Rhoda E. Howard (eds.), *International Handbook of Human Rights* (1987), a collection of interpretive discussions on the civil and human rights situation in 19 countries of Europe, Asia, and America.

Randolph C. Kent, *Anatomy of Disaster Relief: The International Network in Action* (1987), a systematic examination of agencies and organizations, their strengths and weaknesses.

Anatoly Gromyko and Martin Hellman (eds.), *Breakthrough: Emerging New Thinking: Soviet and Western Scholars Issue a Challenge to Build a World Beyond War* (1988), a collection of opinions by American and Soviet scholars on the possibility of a common security system.

Robert E. Osgood, *The Nuclear Dilemma in American Strategic Thought* (1988), a nontechnical, insightful comparative study of opinion on the subject of strategic nuclear deterrence.

Stephen Nathanson, *An Eye for an Eye?: The Morality of Punishing by Death* (1987), an analytical survey of ethical, philosophical, and social controversy around capital punishment.

Roberta Kevelson, *The Law as a System of Signs* (1988), an interpretive nontechnical study of the basic philosophy of law and its interaction with other aspects of the ethical system.

Norman L. Cantor, *Legal Frontiers of Death and Dying* (1987), a thoughtful treatment of such issues as the right to die, life preservation, and certification of death in the general system of medical ethics.

David Harman, *Illiteracy: A National Dilemma* (1987), a historical examination of many complex aspects of the problem.

J.A. Laponce, *Languages and Their Territories* (1987; originally published in French, 1984), a broad survey of psychological, social, economic, and political issues of bilingualism.

Art

Harold Schechter, *The Bosom Serpent: Folklore and Popular Art* (1988), an interpretative, readable study finding the roots of modern popular arts, as reflected in horror cinema, comics, and popular literature, in the traditional folklore.

Frances Borzello, *Civilizing Caliban: The Misuse of Art, 1875–1980* (1987), a thought-provoking case study of the role of superior 19th-century art works in the broad social culture.

Cecelia Tichi, *Shifting Gears: Technology, Literature, Culture in Modernist America* (1987), a broad interpretation of 20th-century culture and literature, analyzing the "mechanistic" imagery and style pervading them.

Sven Birkerts, *An Artificial Wilderness: Essays on 20th-Century Literature* (1987), a collection of in-depth critical reviews of the works of 30 modern novelists.

Alastair Fowler, *A History of English Literature* (1987), a wide-ranging commentary with analysis of literary technicalities.

Rosalind Miles, *The Female Form: Women Writers and the Conquest of the Novel* (1987), an examination of women writers and characters in 19th- and 20th-century literature.

Noel Perrin, *A Reader's Delight* (1988), a collection of expository discussions of 40 books that the author considers to have been undeservedly neglected by critics and readers.

Sam Smiley, *Theatre, the Human Art* (1987), a treatment of philosophy, history, practices, trends, and business of the art.

Lee Strasberg, *A Dream of Passion: The Development of the Method* (1987), a nontechnical autobiographical book by the prominent theoretician and philosopher of theatre and acting.

George C. Izenour, *Theater Technology* (1988), a beautifully illustrated monograph on all aspects of theatre construction, machinery, lighting, and scenery.

Ethan Mordden, *The Hollywood Studios: House Style in the Golden Age of the Movies* (1988), a historical overview of the important role of the film industry and its personalities.

William Luhr (ed.), *World Cinema Since 1945* (1987), a broad, well-written historical reference source outlining developments in more than 30 countries.

Michael Winship, *Television* (1988), an illustrated history of both the industry and the genre, including interviews.

Mary Louise Serafine, *Music as Cognition: The Development of Thought in Sound* (1988), a systematic philosophical analysis of aesthetics of music and its place in developmental psychology.

Robert R. Craven (ed.), *Symphony Orchestras of the World: Selected Profiles* (1987), a comprehensive, inclusive, well-organized reference work.

Nicholas Cook, *A Guide to Musical Analysis* (1987), a penetrating nontechnical survey of analytical techniques and methods used to interpret music.

Doreen Yarwood, *A Chronology of Western Architecture* (1987), an accessible, well-illustrated discussion of architectural styles.

Charles Jencks, *Post-Modernism: The New Classicism in Art and Architecture* (1987), an original illustrated exploration of painting, sculpture, and architecture of the 1970–80s.

Virginia Jackson *et al.* (eds.), *Art Museums of the World*, 2 vol. (1987), a well-organized encyclopaedic reference source on more than 120 museums in almost 50 countries.

Alastair Duncan (ed.), *The Encyclopedia of Art Deco* (1988), an expert, well-illustrated overview of architecture, painting, sculpture, and design of furniture, glass, and ceramics.

Technology

Wiebe E. Bijker, Thomas P. Hughes, and Trevor J. Pinch (eds.), *The Social Construction of Technological Systems* (1987), a collection of essays exploring sociological, historical, and political aspects of technology.

Trevor I. Williams, *The History of Invention* (1987), a very browsable chronological anthology illustrating developments from early tools to space rockets.

Daniel R. Headrick, *The Tentacles of Progress: Technology Transfer in the Age of Imperialism, 1850–1940* (1988), an effective study of social and political consequences of technological power.

Peter Ellis Jones, *Oil: A Practical Guide to the Economics of World Petroleum* (1988), an interdisciplinary survey of technology, management, and geography of the oil industry.

Michelle Adato *et al.*, *Safety Second: The NRC and America's Nuclear Power Plants* (1987), an important, concise discussion of problems in regulating the nuclear power industry.

J.A. Bennett, *The Divided Circle: A History of Instruments for Astronomy, Navigation, and Surveying* (1987), a beautifully illustrated history of measuring instruments.

B.L. Turner II and Stephen B. Brush, *Comparative Farming Systems* (1987), an interdisciplinary collection of case studies exploring the productive agricultural systems of the world.

Colin Tudge, *Food Crops for the Future: The Development of Plant Resources* (1987), a survey of the problems of providing the world population with reliable food resources.

Carl F. Jordan (ed.), *Amazonian Rain Forests: Ecosystem Disturbance and Recovery: Case Studies of Ecosystem Dynamics Under a Spectrum of Land Use-Intensities* (1987), an important analysis of long-term ecological imbalance caused by intrusion of technology.

John Hoyt Williams, *A Great & Shining Road: The Epic Story of the Transcontinental Railroad* (1988), a well-researched, reliable history of the first transcontinental railroad.

Franck Blackler and David Oborne (eds.), *Information Technology & People: Designing for the Future* (1987), a review of societal effects of information technology and an evaluation of the technology's penetration into the home life of individuals.

Charles Piller and Keith R. Yamamoto, *Gene Wars: Military Control over the New Genetic Technologies* (1988), a balanced though polemic examination of the application of genetic engineering in chemical and biological warfare.

Matthew Evangelista, *Innovation and the Arms Race: How the United States and the Soviet Union Develop New Military Technologies* (1988), a survey of technological innovations in arms development and their role in arms control.

John Watkinson, *The Art of Digital Audio* (1988), an authoritative survey of digital sound reproduction.

Peter R. Bond, *Heroes in Space: From Gagarin to Challenger* (1987), an informative illustrated review of the quarter-of-a-century history of manned space flight.

Religion

Leonard Swidler (ed.), *Toward a Universal Theology of Religion* (1987), a collection of papers providing an exchange between religious scholars on the ecumenical religious experience.

Robert Alter and Frank Kermode (eds.), *The Literary Guide to the Bible* (1987), a collection of authoritative scholarly interpretations, with a glossary of biblical and literary terms.

Jeannine Gramic and Pat Furey (eds.), *The Vatican and Homosexuality: Reactions to the "Letter to the Bishops of the Catholic Church on the Pastoral Care of Homosexual Persons"* (1988), a collection of vocal opinion in response to the doctrinal document, reflecting the complexity of the issues involved.

Thomas A. Shannon and Lisa Sowle Cahill, *Religion and Artificial Reproduction: An Inquiry into the Vatican "Instruction on Respect for Human Life in Its Origin and on the Dignity of Human Reproduction"* (1988), an analysis of the doctrinal treatment of an important contemporary issue.

Ursula King (ed.), *Women in the World's Religions, Past and Present* (1987), a book of essays discussing women's contribution in different religions.

Joachim Wach, *Introduction to the History of Religions*, ed. by Joseph M. Kitagawa and Gregory D. Alles, trans. from German (1987), a first substantial collection in English of the writings of a prominent religious historian.

Alan Sponberg and Helen Hardacre (eds.), *Maitreya, the Future Buddha* (1988), a collection of specialist interdisciplinary essays exploring the image of Buddha in the history of religions.

Richard W.L. Guisso and Chai-Shin Yu (eds.), *Shamanism: The Spirit World of Korea* (1988), a collection of descriptions of various rituals and functions of shamans in everyday life.

Emil L. Fackenheim, *What Is Judaism?: An Interpretation for the Present Age* (1987), an examination of the meaning of religious issues by a contemporary Jewish philosopher.

David Rosenberg (ed.), *Congregation: Contemporary Writers Read the Jewish Bible* (1987), a collection of interpretative literary essays, testifying to the infinite appeal of the Book.

Peter Calvocoressi, *Who's Who in the Bible* (1987), an original and readable, if not all-inclusive, dictionary providing information on biblical characters.

Alister McGrath, *The Intellectual Origins of the European Reformation* (1987), an exploration of developments in late medieval theology.

J. Gordon Melton (ed.), *The Encyclopedia of American Religions, Religious Creeds: A Compilation of More than 450 Creeds, Confessions, Statements of Faith, and Summaries of Doctrine of Religious and Spiritual Groups in the United States and Canada* (1988), a massive, comprehensive compendium.

Charles Wei-Hsun Fu and Gerhard E. Spiegler (eds.), *Movements and Issues in World Religions: A Sourcebook and Analysis of Developments Since 1945: Religion, Ideology, and Politics* (1987), a collection of scholarly analyses of interactive roles of various religions in the general sociopolitical framework.

The History of Mankind

George Holmes (ed.), *The Oxford Illustrated History of Medieval Europe* (1988), a well-organized, authoritative compendium.

Dian H. Murray, *Pirates of the South China Coast, 1790–1810* (1987), an intriguing historical account of the undermining of legal power under the Ch'ing dynasty by a local pirate force.

W. Theodore de Bary, *East Asian Civilizations: A Dialogue in Five Stages* (1988), a study of the contribution of various Asian traditions in the development of the powerful civilization.

Nigel Davies, *The Aztec Empire: The Toltec Resurgence* (1987), a substantial interpretive history of a Central Mexican culture.

Frank B. Tipton and Robert Aldrich, *An Economic and Social History of Europe, 1890–1939* (1987), and *An Economic and Social History of Europe from 1939 to the Present* (1987), a comprehensive survey placing Europe and its smaller countries in broad historical perspective.

F.W.J. Hemmings, *Culture and Society in France, 1789–1848* (1987), a readable, informative history of the period focusing on literature, theatre, and art up to the 1848 Revolution.

Paul Kennedy, *The Rise and Fall of the Great Powers: Economic Change and Military Conflict from 1500 to 2000* (1987), an impressive, readable analysis of over four centuries of economic, political, military, and diplomatic history.

Eric Hobsbawm, *The Age of Empire, 1875–1914* (1987), a broad description of the processes in cultural, social, economic, and political spheres that culminated in World War I.

Eric Foner, *Reconstruction, 1863–1877* (1988), a substantial history of political and social forces that developed as a result of the American Civil War and the abolition of slavery.

William K. Klingaman, *1919: The Year Our World Began* (1987), an engaging history of events that took place within one year and were pivotal in determining the development of civilization in this century.

Ferenc Fehér and Agnes Heller, *Eastern Left, Western Left: Totalitarianism, Freedom, and Democracy* (1987), a study of the evolution of reciprocal influences between Eastern and Western political forces.

Charles R. Morris, *Iron Destinies, Lost Opportunities: The Arms Race Between the U.S.A. and the U.S.S.R., 1945–1987* (1988), a balanced history of the ongoing strategic noncombat confrontation between the superpowers, with an exploration of possible outcomes of the arms race.

Flora Lewis, *Europe: A Tapestry of Nations* (1987), a cogent, effective survey of European history and present-day realities.

Silviu Brucan, *World Socialism at the Crossroads: An Insider's View* (1987), an expert evaluation of the past, present, and future of the Soviet bloc countries.

Anthony D'Agostino, *Soviet Succession Struggles: Kremlinology and the Russian Question from Lenin to Gorbachev* (1988), an innovative historical study of Soviet political organization and developments in Soviet power.

Stanley G. Payne, *The Franco Regime, 1936–1975* (1987), an important, massive reexamination of the Spanish Civil War, fascist Spain, and its role in World War II.

Edwina Moreton (ed.), *Germany Between East and West* (1987), an analysis of relations between the two German states.

Primo Levi, *The Drowned and the Saved* (1988; originally published in Italian, 1986), a remarkably humane and desperate memoir of a victim of a Nazi concentration camp, written shortly before the author's death in 1987.

Nicholas Gage, *Hellas, a Portrait of Greece* (1987), an informed travelogue with an insight into the social life and customs of modern Greece.

T.J. Winnifrith, *The Vlachs: The History of a Balkan People* (1987), an original, scholarly but accessible study of a little-known contemporary people and their unusual language.

James Paul Allen and Eugene James Turner, *We the People: An Atlas of America's Ethnic Diversity* (1988), an excellent analysis of American ethnicity presented in the form of a well-organized reference work.

Howard J. Wiarda, *Latin America at the Crossroads: Debt, Development, and the Future* (1987), an expert observation of the economic, social, and political conditions.

Edy Kaufman, *Crisis in Allende's Chile: New Perspectives* (1987), a well-organized history of the Latin-American country.

James S. Olson (ed.), *Dictionary of the Vietnam War* (1988), a balanced, well-documented reference source on almost everything and everyone associated with the subject from 1945 to 1975.

Edwin O. Reischauer, *The Japanese Today: Change and Continuity* (1987), an expert survey of characteristics of modern Japanese society.

Witold Rodzinski, *The People's Republic of China: A Concise Political History* (1988), a balanced, though Marxist, authoritative and readable overview by a diplomat.

Rosanne Klass (ed.), *Afghanistan, the Great Game Revisited* (1987), an important survey of Afghanistan history, political and social structure, culture, and economics, with an analysis of Soviet aspirations there.

Marion Farouk-Sluglett and Peter Sluglett, *Iraq Since 1958: From Revolution to Dictatorship* (1987), a well-written critical analysis of the political situation in the country since the defeat of the monarchy.

Ghassan Salame (ed.), *The Foundations of the Arab State* (1987), a collection of analyses of the long-term development of the Arab political structure.

Edem Kodjo, *Africa Tomorrow* (1987; originally published in French, 1985), a concerned treatment of Africa's problems with an engaging, if idealistic, prescription for the future.

Human Sciences Research Council, *The South African Society: Realities and Future Prospects* (1987), a work by a group of white South African scholars who collaborated in the reevaluation of the South African ideology.

The Branches of Knowledge

Harry Edwin Eiss, *Dictionary of Mathematical Games, Puzzles, and Amusements* (1988), a well-arranged, compact source of information on this intellectual recreation.

Paul Hoffman, *Archimedes' Revenge: The Challenge of the Unknown* (1988), an entertaining review of mathematical topics pertaining to modern science and technology.

Ronald N. Giere, *Explaining Science: A Cognitive Approach* (1988), a readable exploration of the philosophical structure of scientific thinking and the resulting knowledge.

Timothy Ferris, *Coming of Age in the Milky Way* (1988), an informative overview of the history of Western science.

Heinz R. Pagels, *The Dreams of Reason: The Computer and the Rise of the Sciences of Complexity* (1988), an authoritative examination of the role of computers in the development of areas of research that had been too complex for the human brain.

John D. Barrow, *The World Within the World* (1988), a discussion of traditional and contemporary branches of physics and a dichotomous relationship of theories and experiments.

Robert L. Forward and Joel Davis, *Mirror Matter: Pioneering Antimatter Physics* (1988), an explanation of antimatter and the possibilities, still hypothetical, of its technological application.

Henry C. Tuckwell, *Elementary Applications of Probability Theory* (1988), a look at the techniques based on the theory of probability, and their use in biology and technology.

Charles W. Finkl (ed.), *The Encyclopedia of Field and General Geology* (1988), an illustrated reference overview for both the practitioner and the informed lay reader.

S. Warren Carey, *Theories of the Earth and Universe: A History of Dogma in the Earth Sciences* (1988), a survey of the developments in geology with an emphasis on the interpretative nature of many modern concepts and theories.

Ernst Mayr, *Toward a New Philosophy of Biology: Observations of an Evolutionist* (1988), an analysis of the philosophical concepts underlying the process of biologic change.

Carolyn Marvin, *When Old Technologies Were New: Thinking About Electric Communication in the Late Nineteenth Century* (1988), an informative appraisal of the growth of the electricity-based technologies such as telecommunications.

Michael Collins, *Liftoff: The Story of America's Adventure in Space* (1988), a history of American astronautics written by a veteran of spaceflight.

Wendy Ashmore and Robert J. Sharer, *Discovering Our Past: A Brief Introduction to Archaeology* (1988), an exploratory overview of the science, its fieldwork, collection, analysis, and laboratory techniques.

Frank Wilczek and Betsy Devine, *Longing for the Harmonies: Themes and Variations from Modern Physics* (1988), an original exploration of the concept of philosophical harmony between arts and sciences.

People of 1988

BIOGRAPHIES

Akihito, Crown Prince

Japanese Crown Prince Akihito, heir to Japan's Chrysanthemum Throne, came into the limelight in 1988 when his father, 87-year-old Emperor Hirohito, became gravely ill on September 19. Three days later the crown prince became de facto regent. Akihito was born on Dec. 23, 1933, the first son of Emperor Hirohito and Empress Nagako. In 1944 he reached the age when imperial princes were commissioned in the military, but the emperor did not allow his son to accept a commission. After World War II Akihito went to school with commoners at Gakushuin High School; his father had been educated by private tutors. In 1952 Akihito was invested as heir to the Japanese throne and entered Gakushuin University in Tokyo, where he majored in political science. The next year he made his first trip abroad to attend the coronation of Queen Elizabeth II in London.

In 1959 Akihito attracted world media attention when he became the first crown prince in Japanese history to marry a commoner. His bride, Michiko Shoda, was the daughter of a flour-milling magnate and a graduate of a Roman Catholic university for women in Tokyo. The couple have had two sons, Hiro and Aya, who were sent to the University of Oxford, and a daughter named Nori.

Although Akihito was quiet, reserved, and somewhat shy by nature, he was at ease with foreigners. He spoke fluent English, having been educated in part by an American woman Quaker imposed by the U.S. after the war. In his youth Akihito enjoyed tennis and horseback riding. Marine biology became such an absorbing hobby that the crown prince published several academic treatises on goby fish. Under the postwar constitution the emperor and other members of the imperial family were entrusted with ceremonial duties but were allowed no political role. The emperor, however, remained the highest ranking priest in Shinto, the indigenous religion of Japan. As direct descendants of Amaterasu Omikai, the sun goddess who created the universe, Akihito and his father fulfilled the duty of performing Shinto rituals before the sacred shrines on the imperial palace grounds. When Akihito ascended the throne, he would carry on the centuries-old traditions of the imperial family. He and his empress would also introduce change, however, a natural manifestation of their education and the times in which they were living. (HIDEAKI KASE)

Allais, Maurice

The 1988 Nobel Memorial Prize in Economic Science was awarded to 77-year-old Maurice Allais, a French economist known for developing theories that allow increased understanding of market behaviour and the efficient use of resources. Allais was the first French citizen to win the Economics Prize. Assar Lindbeck, chairman of the selection committee, said, "Allais is not only the father of the new French school of economics, but he is also a giant within the world of economic analysis."

While the Nobel selection committee cited as crucial to their choice the Frenchman's basic market theories, they also stressed the important implications of his work regarding state-run monopolies, especially in terms of making investment and pricing decisions. His principles had been a guiding force for planning state enterprises in terms of prices rather than by direct (often politically determined) regulation. Indeed, Allais's theories offered to large state monopolies—institutions often reluctant to adhere to marketplace machinations—the opportunity to apply efficient market economics principles.

Allais was born in Paris on May 31, 1911. He first studied economics at the École Polytechnique, Paris, then at the École Nationale Supérieure des Mines de Paris. In 1937 he began working for the French state-owned mine administration. Several years later he became a professor and director of the economic research institute at the École Nationale Supérieure des Mines de Paris, where he remained. In the late 1940s Allais was appointed director of research at the National French Research Council. In 1977 he was named an officer of the Legion of Honour. He planned to use the $403,000 Nobel Prize to continue advanced research.

Allais said he was shocked to have won. While he knew his name had been considered in the past, he had given up hope of receiving the coveted prize. The committee acknowledged that the award was long in coming, both because some of Allais's most important works are extremely long and complicated and because they are in French. Perhaps a comment once made by Nobel laureate Paul Samuelson best expressed the Frenchman's contribution: "Had Allais's earliest writings been in English, a generation of economic theory would have taken a different course." (BONNIE OBERMAN)

Ashdown, Paddy

On July 28, 1988, Paddy Ashdown became the first elected leader of Britain's new Social and Liberal Democratic Party (SLD), formed earlier in the year when the Liberals and the Social Democratic Party (SDP) voted to merge. Ashdown defeated his rival, Alan Beith, the former deputy leader of the Liberals, by 41,401 votes (71.9%) to 16,202 (28.1%).

JANE BOWN—CAMERA PRESS/GLOBE PHOTOS

Jeremy John Durham Ashdown was born on Feb. 27, 1941, in New Delhi, India. His father had been a (British) officer in the Indian Army. When Ashdown was five, his family returned to Northern Ireland. Ashdown acquired the name "Paddy" at Bedford School (80 km [50 mi] from London) because of his Irish accent, which he later lost. At 18 Ashdown joined the Marines, subsequently becoming a commando with the Special Boat Squadron. He served in the Far East during the 1960s (where he also took a first-class degree in Mandarin at Hong Kong University) and in Northern Ireland in the early 1970s. He was recruited by the Foreign Office in 1971 and worked there for four years, first on the Far East desk in London and then at the UN in Geneva as first secretary.

In 1976 Ashdown resigned from the Foreign Office in order to pursue a political career as a Liberal. In 1983 he won the West Country constituency of Yeovil from the Conservatives. He was initially appointed as the Liberals' trade and industry spokesman but was switched subsequently to education. Ashdown was never regarded as an outstanding performer in the House of Commons; he did, however, develop an attractive style on television, using his good looks and conversational manner effectively. When the former Liberal and SDP leaders, David Steel and Robert Maclennan, decided not to contest the leadership of the new party, Ashdown's public image helped him secure an emphatic win over Beith.

Ashdown immediately made it clear that, while he intended to lead the SLD as a progressive party, he would resist any attempt to conclude a deal with the Labour Party; instead, he announced that his ambition was to replace Labour as the main non-Conservative force in British politics. He was not deterred by opinion polls during the second half of 1988, which showed, on average, Labour's support to be 38% and the SLD's to be only 8%—down by almost two-thirds from the 22% that the alliance of Liberals and SDP secured in the 1987 general election. (PETER KELLNER)

Baker, Kenneth Wilfred

In 1988 Kenneth Baker accomplished the second of two signal achievements for U.K. Prime Minister Margaret Thatcher. As secretary of state for education, he piloted a radical Education Reform Bill onto the statute book. This removed many of the powers of local education authorities over state schools, gave parents greater rights over the running of those schools, and, through a national core curriculum, gave the government greater say in what should be taught. Three years earlier, as minister for local government, Baker had steered through Parliament another controversial bill, abolishing the Greater London Council.

Baker was born on Nov. 3, 1934, in Newport, Monmouth, and educated at St. Paul's School, London, and Magdalen College, Oxford. He was first elected to Parliament in 1968 at a by-election. He lost the seat (Acton, in west London) in 1970 but was almost immediately adopted to defend a large Conservative majority at Marylebone, in central London. Baker's close association with Edward Heath, then prime minister, culminated in his becoming Heath's political

RICHARD OPEN—CAMERA PRESS/GLOBE PHOTOS

private secretary in 1974. A year later, however, Heath was voted out of the Conservative leadership by the party's MPs.

When Thatcher became party leader in February 1975, Baker was cast into the political wilderness. In January 1981, however, she appointed him minister for information technology, a high-profile post that gave him the chance to promote the wider use of electronic and computer technology in schools and industry. In September 1984 Baker was appointed minister for local government. The government's plans for abolishing the Greater London Council had run into strong resistance, both from the GLC, which ran a lively campaign in its own defense, and from the House of Lords, but Baker succeeded where his predecessors had failed. In May 1986 he became secretary of state for education.

As a result of his achievements, Baker came to be seen as a possible successor to Thatcher. He was the choice of moderate (rather than rightwing) Conservative MPs, who regarded him as a skillful but ideologically shallow politician. In one respect, at least, Baker differed from Thatcher. She never claimed any great interest in cultural matters, whereas Baker established a formidable reputation as a poetry enthusiast.

(PETER KELLNER)

Bentsen, Lloyd Millard, Jr.

Michael Dukakis, already certain of the Democratic nomination for president, announced on July 12, 1988, that Sen. Lloyd Bentsen of Texas would be the nominee for vice-president. On July 21 the Democratic national convention nominated Bentsen by acclamation. The choice was a surprise because of Bentsen's reputation

ADAM SCULL—RANGEFINDERS/GLOBE PHOTOS

as a conservative, but he emerged from the often nasty campaign as probably the least disliked national candidate and demonstrated his skills as a public speaker, persuader, and fund-raiser. Debating the Republican vice-presidential candidate, Dan Quayle *(q.v.)*, in Omaha, Neb., on October 5, Bentsen scored no overwhelming victory but offered a response to Quayle's self-comparison with John F. Kennedy that proved unanswerable. Allowed by Texas law to run as both a national and a state candidate, Bentsen on November 8 was elected to his fourth term in the U.S. Senate. The unsuccessful Dukakis-Bentsen ticket lost Texas and every other former Confederate state, however, as Republicans attacked Dukakis—but not Bentsen—for alleged deficiencies in patriotism and in firmness on crime and defense.

Bentsen, whose father was a millionaire landowner, was born on Feb. 11, 1921, in Mission, Texas, and was raised in nearby McAllen. In 1942 he received a law degree from the University of Texas and joined the U.S. Army. He became a commissioned pilot, served in combat, and in 1945 was discharged as a colonel and established a law practice in McAllen. He served as a judge in Hidalgo County from 1946 to 1948 and as a member of the U.S. House of Representatives from 1949 to 1955, voting with most other Texas Democrats except for his support of a bill to end poll taxes. In 1955, apparently hoping to become a millionaire before reentering politics, he borrowed money from relatives and formed the Consolidated American Life Insurance Co.—later called Lincoln Consolidated, Inc.—with himself as president and offices in Houston.

In 1970 Bentsen—believed to be a millionaire—ran for the U.S. Senate. In the Democratic primary he defeated Ralph Yarborough, considered an antibusiness liberal, and in the general election he defeated the Republican candidate, George Bush *(q.v.)*. Reelected to the Senate in 1976 and 1982, he became chairman of the Finance Committee in 1987. He gained respect as a fund-raiser, although his decision in early 1987 to have breakfast with lobbyists who contributed to his reelection campaign raised ethical questions. Though called a conservative, Bentsen voted as often as not with the majority of Democratic senators.

(CHARLES JOHNSON TAGGART)

Bergman, Ingmar

Ingmar Bergman, the director of more than 75 plays, maker of some 50 feature and TV films, and winner of honours and medals galore, among them three Academy Awards, had a momentous 1988. Bergman celebrated his 70th birthday on July 14 in regal style on his Swedish island retreat of Fårö. The year 1988 also saw the publication in English of his 1987 memoirs, *Laterna Magica (The Magic Lantern)*. In the book he told of his turbulent personal and professional experiences from earliest childhood to his harmonious marriage in 1971. For the English version alone his publishers paid a record eight-figure advance, making Bergman a multimillionaire and allowing him to drop filmmaking for good.

Ernst Ingmar Bergman was born in Uppsala, Sweden, the son of a Lutheran pastor. He shot his first film, *Crisis*, in 1945, a year after he wrote his earliest original script, for Alf Sjöberg's *Frenzy* (U.S. title *Torment*). With *Crisis* he began his regular practice of having a stock company of actors, who performed for him onstage and in his films. With occasional exceptions, Bergman devoted himself to making films ("his mistress") and staging plays ("his wife") in Sweden. Many of his films gained international admiration, including *The Seventh Seal* (1957), *Wild Strawberries* (1957), and the six-part television drama *Scenes from a Marriage* (1972). In the theatre he worked first in Helsingborg and then in Göteborg, Malmö, and finally Stockholm, at the Royal Dramatic Theatre, or "Dramaten" (*see* THEATRE: *Sidebar*), where he became director in 1963.

After a devastating experience with the tax

inspector in 1976, which led to a wrongful arrest, subsequent nervous breakdown, and self-imposed exile in West Germany, Bergman began to stage plays in German in Munich. There he also shot the anti-Nazi film *The Serpent's Egg* (1977). Later he was fully exonerated and placated by a remorseful Swedish government. Back at Dramaten in 1986 he staged memorable productions of August Strindberg's *Miss Julie* and of *Hamlet*, both of which had successful international tours.

Forced by overwork and a troublesome hip to "take it easy" and shelve a planned production of Euripides' *Bacchae*, Bergman was well enough in 1988 to stage a brilliantly streamlined all-star production of Eugene O'Neill's *Long Day's Journey into Night*, which proved to be the highlight of the season at the Nobel-Foundation-sponsored international symposium on Strindberg and O'Neill. With the aid of a walking stick, he embarked on rehearsals of Shakespeare's *A Winter's Tale*, as indefatigable as ever. (OSSIA TRILLING)

Berlin, Irving

On May 11, 1988, more than two dozen show business stars gathered at Carnegie Hall in New York City to honour Irving Berlin on his 100th birthday. The gala salute to the Broadway composer was staged by the American Society of Composers, Authors, and Publishers (ASCAP), which Berlin had founded in 1914 along with

AP/WIDE WORLD

Victor Herbert and John Philip Sousa. Although Berlin had maintained a professional silence since the early 1960s, he agreed to a birthday celebration that would benefit Carnegie Hall and ASCAP. (Berlin and his wife, Ellin, did not attend but planned to watch a telecast of the event.)

Berlin was so prolific that organizers of the gala had to divide the event into four segments: Americana, swing, Broadway, and Hollywood. Among the evening's highlights were the Army Chorus performing parts of the extraordinarily successful 1942 World War II revue *This Is the Army;* a special song composed by Leonard Bernstein; and "Puttin' on the Ritz," a song-and-dance tribute to Fred Astaire, for whom Berlin did some of his most sophisticated writing. The array of stars who performed Berlin works included Marilyn Horne ("God Bless America"), Michael Feinstein ("I Love a Piano"), Rosemary Clooney ("White Christmas" and "Count Your Blessings [Instead of Sheep]"), Ray Charles ("How Deep Is the Ocean?" and "What'll I Do?"), Shirley MacLaine ("There's No Business like Show Business"), and Willie Nelson ("Blue Skies").

Israel Baline was born in Siberia on May 11, 1888, the youngest son of a Jewish cantor. He was five years old when his family immigrated to New York's Lower East Side. After his first job as a paper boy, he became a singing waiter and soon began composing. "Alexander's Ragtime Band" (1911) made him famous, and by 1924 he was America's preeminent popular songwriter. Unable to read notes, he learned

music by ear, and the only key in which he ever learned to play was F sharp.

An ardent patriot, a painter (watercolours), an avid poker player, and a very private person, Berlin by 1988 was an American institution. Thirty years earlier the *New York Times* had labeled him "safely and sentimentally, . . . the greatest popular songwriter who ever lived."

(BONNIE OBERMAN)

Birt, John

At a time when British television was facing a future of multichannel competition, with threats of commercial ratings wars and—some warned—falling standards, one senior figure, at least, embodied in the popular eye the idea of old-fashioned rigour. Yet it was part of the paradox of John Birt, deputy director general of the British Broadcasting Corporation (BBC) since April 1987 with particular charge over its journalism, that he was nevertheless one of the younger breed of television executives. When the unexpected call to the BBC came, he was director of programming at one of the most ratings-conscious of the commercial Independent Television (ITV) network's stations, London Weekend Television (LWT).

Born in Liverpool on Dec. 10, 1944, and educated at a strict Roman Catholic school there, Birt went to St. Catherine's College, Oxford, to study engineering. Though he gained his degree, a combination of Oxford's and the 1960s culture set him on another path. He made films, married an artist, and, on joining Granada Television in 1968, worked first on a youth entertainment show (with Germaine Greer). A year later, as joint editor of the cutting-edge public affairs program "World in Action," he produced one of the landmark episodes of that youth-driven era: a headline-making debate on morality between the editor of *The Times*, a former attorney general, Bishop Trevor Huddleston—and rock singer Mick Jagger, lately acquitted of a drug charge.

Birt moved to London Weekend in 1971 as producer of "The Frost Programme" and later was David Frost's producer for the interviews with Richard Nixon. Meanwhile, he founded the weekly hour-long political program "Weekend World." He went on to become LWT's director of programs for five years and ran a vigorous schedule of populist entertainment. But it was the detailed research and austere interviewing style he developed with "Weekend World" presenter Peter Jay, together with their critique of existing journalism ("the Jay-Birt thesis"), that led the BBC's new director general, Michael Checkland, to appoint Birt. His charge was to weld the BBC's journalism into a cohesive body and to restore confidence after a series of legal and political controversies.

Inevitably, his approach aroused internal suspicions. Eighteen months later, with the first new programs just hitting the screen, the controversies had died down, but the fruits of the new philosophy were still not ripe.

(PETER FIDDICK)

Black, Sir James Whyte

For his revolutionary approach to drug design and for his development of the two key medicines propranolol and cimetidine, British pharmacologist Sir James Black, with American researchers Gertrude Elion and George Hitchings (*qq.v.*), was awarded the 1988 Nobel Prize for Physiology or Medicine. Black's prizewinning research began in the 1950s while he was working as a senior pharmacologist with the British firm Imperial Chemical Industries. He set out to develop a drug that would relieve angina pectoris, the spasms of deep pain felt in the chest when the heart does not receive sufficient oxygen. Earlier scientific research had indicated that cells within the human body contain isolated target areas, called receptor sites, that are stimulated by specific natural chemicals circulating in the bloodstream. In turn, these receptors, when stimulated, trigger particular physiological responses within the body. In the heart muscle the so-called beta receptors, when

stimulated by the hormones epinephrine and norepinephrine (also known as adrenaline and noradrenaline, respectively), cause the heart rate to quicken and increase the strength of heart contractions, thus increasing the heart's demand for oxygen. Angina pectoris results when this increased demand for oxygen is not met.

Black reasoned that a "beta blocker"—a drug that could block the beta receptor sites—would lessen the stimulating effect of the hormones, thereby reducing the heart's oxygen demand and relieving anginal pain. In 1964 he succeeded in designing the beta-blocking drug propranolol, the drug currently used to treat angina, heart attacks, other kinds of heart disease, high blood pressure, and migraines. A decade later, as a researcher at a British laboratory of SmithKline Beckman, Black used a similar strategy to develop a drug that blocks the histamine receptors that govern the secretion of gastric acid in the stomach. The introduction of that drug, cimetidine, marked the beginning of a new era in the successful treatment of stomach and duodenal ulcers.

Black was born in Uddingston, Scotland, on June 14, 1924. He received a medical degree in 1946 from the University of St. Andrews, where he became an assistant lecturer in physiology. He took a teaching position with the University of Malaya in 1947 and remained there until 1950, when he left to teach at the University of Glasgow. He joined Imperial Chemical Industries as a senior pharmacologist in 1958. In 1964 Black became head of biologic research for Smith Kline & French Laboratories (a subsidiary of SmithKline Beckman) in Welwyn Garden City, England. In 1973 he returned briefly to the academic world as professor and head of the department of pharmacology at University College in London. He left in 1978 to become director of therapeutic research at Wellcome Research Laboratories in Kent. Black was knighted in 1981. From 1984 he was a professor of analytic pharmacology at King's College Hospital Medical School, University of London.

(CAROLYN D. NEWTON)

Bochco, Steven

If 1988 proved anything to executives in network television, it was that they sorely needed more Steven Bochcos. In a year that saw the viewership of network television continue to fall and that of the competition—cable television and video home rental—continue to rise, Bochco produced and co-wrote two series that ranked high in the Nielsen ratings: "Hooperman," a 30-minute ABC show about an offbeat San Francisco cop; and "L.A. Law," a 60-minute NBC show about a diverse group of lawyers in a large Los Angeles firm. While they praised both shows for their intelligent and provocative stories, critics were especially effusive about "L.A. Law," citing its unique blend of the sexy (a daring depiction of bed-hopping characters) and the serious (a thoughtful treatment of social-legal issues). To them and millions of other viewers, Bochco's work showed that network television was still capable of imaginative programming, which, if not art, was at least worth spending prime time with. The youthful-looking Bochco, whose 40-plus years were betrayed only by his salt-and-pepper-coloured hair, said that the secret to his success was that "I'm willing to take the risk that some people will not like what I do."

Bochco first took that kind of risk in 1980, when he and Michael Kozoll wrote and produced "Hill Street Blues," an NBC series that focused on the private lives of the characters working in an inner-city police station. Though it was frank and unconventional enough to antagonize the network censors, the series did not attract the attention of many viewers until it won eight Emmy awards in 1981. It then went on to build a large and loyal audience and to earn a total of 26 Emmys, 6 of which went to Bochco. In 1985, however, Bochco's unwillingness to trim the cost of the show—estimated at about $1.4 million per episode—led the producing company, MTM Enterprises, to fire him.

Joining 20th Century Fox in 1986, he originated "L.A. Law," which, like "Hill Street," featured multiple characters and multiple story lines.

Bochco was born in New York City on Dec. 16, 1943, and attended Carnegie Institute of Technology (now called Carnegie Mellon University), Pittsburgh, Pa. Helped by his father-in-law, a show business lawyer, he broke into writing for television with Universal in 1966, eventually doing scripts for such police shows as "Columbo," "Delvecchio," and "McMillan and Wife." During a break in his television work in the early 1970s, he wrote the screenplay for *Silent Running*, which, when filmed, departed so completely from his original conception that he decided to become a producer to protect his writing.

(MICHAEL AMEDEO)

Borja Cevallos, Rodrigo

On Aug. 10, 1988, Rodrigo Borja Cevallos was inaugurated as president of Ecuador for a four-year term, becoming the country's third democratically elected leader since the end of military rule in 1979. The first round of presidential elections on January 31 had proved inconclusive, with ten candidates vying for the nation's highest office. However, Borja had led the field with 24.6% of the valid vote against the 17.6% won by his nearest rival, Abdalá Bucaram Ortiz. In the second round on May 8, Borja emerged with a narrow majority, taking some 52.8% of valid votes. While both candidates represented left-of-centre parties and promised to reverse the pro-U.S. policies of Pres. León Febres Cordero, Bucaram's volatile personality and populist rhetoric raised fears that the military would intervene in the event of his victory. Thus some observers suggested that Borja won the election because he was seen as the lesser of two evils. His detractors notwithstanding, Borja was certainly the more seasoned of the two politicians; his victory was a milestone in a distinguished political career spanning 30 years.

Borja was born in Quito, Ecuador, on June 19, 1935. He took a first degree in politics and science at the Central University of Ecuador, winning the university's best graduate prize, and in 1960 he was awarded a doctorate in law. Borja's peers had already recognized his leadership abilities, having elected him president of the university's Law School Association in 1958. He came to political prominence in 1968 as a founding member of the Izquierda Democrática (ID), a party he represented as a congressional deputy in 1962–82. Affiliated with the Socialist International, the ID became the largest party in Ecuador's highly factionalized political scene. Borja served as professor of political science at the Central University from 1963 until his presidential inauguration in 1988.

When Borja ran for president in 1978, he came in fourth in the first round of voting and was eliminated from the race. In the 1984 elections he was a convincing first-round leader with 36% of the total vote, but he lost the second round by three percentage points to the more flamboyant and aggressive Febres Cordero.

President Borja promised a government of national consensus to deal with Ecuador's severe economic problems, the most pressing of which were rising inflation, falling oil revenues, and the foreign debt. Shortly after taking office, his government introduced an economic austerity program prior to opening negotiations with the International Monetary Fund. The measures were received as a pragmatic response to the crisis.

(JANET KRENGEL)

Bubka, Sergey

Sergey Bubka could sprint so fast and throw things so far that some people insisted the Soviet pole vaulter could be the best decathlete the world had ever seen. However, it would be difficult to dominate the decathlon the way he crushed all opposition in the pole vault, where he had made the world record his private toy since 1984. "I love the pole vault because . . . one must not only run and jump, but one must think," Bubka said. His records, indeed, were a tribute to the blend of tactics and athleticism.

His leap of 6.06 m (19 ft 10½ in) on July 10, 1988, at Nice, France, was his second world record in five weeks and his ninth in barely four years. Bubka was unable to clear the mystical 6.1-m (20-ft) barrier either afterward or 2½ months later at the Olympic Games in Seoul, South Korea, but witnesses swore he had vaulted that high. He just had not set the crossbar that high.

Once in 1984, when a competitor cleared 5.91 m (19 ft 4¾ in) to break Bubka's record briefly, he took it back on his next jump, soaring 5.94 m (19 ft 5¾ in). His country rewarded him with a bonus worth about $385 every time he broke a world record. The 21 cm (8¼ in) that Bubka had piled onto the record since 1984 represented a greater gain in 4 years than other pole vaulters had achieved in the previous 12.

Bubka first cleared 6 m (19 ft 8¼ in), long an unimaginable height, in Paris on July 13, 1985, four days after the birth of his first child, Vitaly. The boy was named for Bubka's coach, Vitaly Petrov, whom he followed at the age of 15 to Donetsk, a city in the Ukraine. Bubka, born Dec. 14, 1963, had grown up 135 km (85 mi) away in the coal-mining town of Voroshilovgrad. He began pole vaulting at nine and rejoined Petrov soon after the coach's transfer to better facilities and the divorce of Bubka's parents.

Bubka introduced himself to the world at the 1983 world track and field championships in Helsinki, Fin., where he astonished his competitors by winning his event at 5.7 m (18 ft 8¼ in). From there, he changed the standards of his event and won the admiration of his country. He was named the Soviet Union's top sportsman three years in a row in 1984–86.

Bubka was not exceptionally big at 1.83 m (6 ft) tall and weighing 79.8 kg (176 lb), but his speed and strength enabled him to use poles that were unusually long and stiff for better catapulting action. Other vaulters, lacking Bubka's muscular upper body and swift approach to the vaulting pit, could not bend the bigger poles. Bubka also gripped his pole at least 15¼ cm (6 in) higher than his competitors.

(KEVIN M. LAMB)

Bush, George Herbert Walker
In 1988 George Bush became the first incumbent vice-president to be elected president of the United States since Martin Van Buren in 1836. He quickly bested all of the other Republican candidates in the primaries, and by April 26 he had the pledges of a majority of the delegates-elect to the Republican national convention. However, the probable Democratic nominee, Massachusetts Gov. Michael Dukakis (q.v.), led in the polls, and Bush was widely perceived as an errand boy for Pres. Ronald Reagan and as lacking Reagan's machismo. A national newsmagazine called his problem "the wimp factor."

Unanimously nominated by the convention in New Orleans, La., on August 17, Bush began campaigning vigorously against Dukakis, calling him a "liberal," deficient in patriotism and lacking firmness on defense and crime. One of his themes concerned a convicted murderer who escaped after having been released from prison under a Massachusetts prison furlough program during Dukakis's term. Ten months later he was arrested for raping a woman and stabbing a man. Though accused of negative campaigning, Bush managed to create a tough, independent image, and polls showed him pulling steadily ahead. Debating Dukakis in Winston-Salem, N.C., on September 25 and in Los Angeles on October 13, Bush neither surprised nor was surprised. On November 8 he received 54% of the popular vote to carry 40 states with 426 of the 538 electoral votes. Within a few weeks he had announced several major appointments, many of them from the long out-of-favour Eastern wing of the Republican Party.

Bush was born in Milton, Mass., on June 12, 1924. His father, Prescott Bush, soon moved the family to Greenwich, Conn.; he would become a town official and later a U.S. senator. George Bush served in the U.S. Navy from 1942 to 1945, rising from enlisted man to pilot; he saw action in the Pacific and was decorated for bravery. In 1948 he received a B.A. from Yale University and went to work for Dresser Industries in Odessa, Texas. In 1950 he founded an oil-properties firm, which was merged into the Zapata Petroleum Corp. in 1953. The following year he helped to organize some of Zapata's machinery interests as the Zapata Off-Shore Co., serving as president of the firm from 1956 to 1964 and chairman of the board from 1964 to 1966.

A resident of Houston, Texas, by 1960, Bush served in the U.S. House of Representatives from 1967 to 1971 and ran unsuccessfully for the U.S. Senate in 1964 and 1970. Pres. Richard Nixon appointed him ambassador to the United Nations in 1971 and designated him to be chairman of the Republican National Committee in 1973. Pres. Gerald Ford appointed him chief of the liaison office (ambassador) in Beijing (Peking; 1974–75) and director of central intelligence (1976–77). He sought the presidential nomination in 1980 and was elected vice-president on the ticket with Reagan in 1980 and 1984.

(CHARLES JOHNSON TAGGART)

Campeau, Robert
Campeau Corp.'s 1986 acquisition of Allied Stores Corp., combined with the 1988 acquisition of Federated Department Stores Inc., made one of Canada's largest real estate development companies into one of the largest retailing chains in the U.S. Robert Campeau, the owner of Campeau Corp., intended to retain such high-prestige, high-margin stores as Bloomingdale's. The sale of other retailers, such as Brooks Brothers, I. Magnin, Filene's of Boston, and Foley's of Houston, Texas, coupled with the issuance of "junk bonds," helped pare down the huge debt incurred in the two takeovers. By combining shopping-mall development with ownership of retail stores, Campeau planned to take in both rent and retail revenue as owner of the mall itself and of the leading department store there.

Campeau was born in Sudbury, Ont., on Aug. 3, 1923. He dropped out of school and took a job as a machinist with International Nickel in Sudbury. He worked in war production plants in Ottawa before becoming a carpenter in the heavy construction industry in 1949. After building his own home, Campeau sold the house to a contractor and used the profit to become a builder. He eventually built almost 20,000 homes in the Ottawa area, and in 1953 he incorporated Campeau Construction Corp. Ltd. Expanding into commercial and multiuse complexes, Campeau built some 40% of the office space in Ottawa. Soon his subsidiaries manufactured, marketed, and exported building materials and components. In 1969 Campeau sold his company and moved to Toronto. He repurchased Campeau Corp. in 1972, however, and expanded it into a major development corporation.

Campeau's experiences with the Canadian financial markets were not as rewarding. His biggest business setback came in 1980 when he attempted to take over the Royal Trust Co., one of Canada's largest financial institutions. His attempt was blocked by an alliance of Toronto businessmen. In another struggle over stock, Campeau initiated a legal battle with his son Jacques over voting rights to two million shares of Campeau Corp.

Although he continued to reside in Canada, Campeau preferred to conduct his business in the U.S., which he believed had better securities regulation, better enforcement of its securities law, and a much more open economy than Canada with far less government interference. Campeau considered Canada and the U.S. to be one market, and he viewed himself as a North American entrepreneur.

(DIANE LOIS WAY)

Cárdenas, Cuauhtémoc
Cuauhtémoc Cárdenas achieved international recognition in the 1988 presidential and congressional elections in Mexico for his vigorous challenge to the 59-year grip on power of the Partido Revolucionario Institutional (PRI). A former member of the PRI, Cárdenas led a breakaway faction in 1987 known as the Democratic Current, calling for more democracy and challenging the president's right to nominate his successor. After the nomination of Carlos Salinas de Gortari as PRI presidential candidate, Cárdenas announced his own candidacy and chose to stand for the Authentic Party of the Mexican Revolution (PARM), an offshoot of the PRI. His leftist, populist campaign soon attracted other small but influential parties, which united to form the National Democratic Front (FDN). As the July 6 elections drew nearer, the Mexican Socialist Party (PSM), a coalition of the independent left, withdrew its presidential candidate and committed itself to Cárdenas.

Born in 1934 and educated as a civil engineer, Cárdenas gained governmental experience as deputy minister of agriculture, as governor of his home state of Michoacán, and as a senator. He was a stilted, rather boring speaker, but his Indian name, his parentage (his father was the revered president Lázaro Cárdenas, who nationalized the oil industry in 1938 and handed out parcels of the best farming land to peasant cooperatives), and his serious, unsmiling face combined to make him seem more Mexican than his foreign-educated opponent. He was able to capitalize on the unpopularity of the government's economic austerity policies, which had led to a massive decline in living standards in the 1980s. He called for populist economic policies, such as the suspension of foreign debt servicing, higher incomes, and an end to corruption.

The PRI claimed to have won the elections, but suspicions of irregularities were heightened by alleged computer malfunctions that delayed the announcement of results for several days. The electoral commission finally awarded Cárdenas 31% of the vote, compared with just over 50% for Salinas and 17% for Manuel Clouthier of the Partido Acción Nacional (PAN). But the PRI party machine would never be the same again. Cárdenas refused to recognize Salinas as president-elect and called on all parties to support him in creating a unified political opposition to win fresh elections. In October he announced the formation of a new party, the Party of the Democratic Revolution (PRD), which would attract broad leftist membership.

(SARAH CAMERON)

Chapman, Tracy
For someone who was virtually unknown to popular music fans at the beginning of 1988, becoming the number one artist on the Billboard charts by August was quite a feat. However, considering that the artist was Tracy Chapman, a black female singer-songwriter whose music was most often described as "folk," this rise to the top was nothing short of amazing. Perhaps the most remarkable aspect of the debut album Tracy Chapman was its content; her lyrics speak of racism, domestic violence, poverty, hatred, and helplessness, and the album lacks high-tech musical embellishment—Chapman's acoustic guitar is the main accompaniment to her expressive alto voice.

Chapman's songs are not autobiographical, but she admitted that there "are parts of me in all the songs that I write." Born in 1964, Chapman grew up in a mostly black neighbourhood in Cleveland, Ohio. Her parents were divorced, and Chapman's mother raised her and a sister single-handedly. The music of Mahalia Jackson, Neil Diamond, and Marvin Gaye was frequently on the turntable in their home. Chapman began experimenting with musical instruments herself, and at 11 she discovered the guitar. Through a program called A Better Chance, she won a scholarship to the Wooster School in Danbury, Conn., a progressive prep school where political and social injustices were not ignored and students were encouraged to discuss such problems. Chapman began singing in coffeehouses, and the school's chaplain, recognizing her talent, took up a collection to buy her a better guitar. She earned another scholarship and

enrolled at Tufts University, Medford, Mass. While performing at a campus rally, Chapman was urged by a classmate to play for his father, a music-publishing executive. She did, was offered a contract to make an album, and signed the contract after graduating from Tufts.

Although the darker side of the human condition had certainly been dealt with before in pop music, such a topic was not considered marketable in the 1980s. *Tracy Chapman* was not synthesizer-dominated dance music or head-banging heavy metal—it did not belong to any so-called marketable genre—yet in 1988 Chapman joined well-established rock stars in performing successful benefit concerts for imprisoned South African political activist Nelson Mandela and for Amnesty International's Human Rights Now! world tour. Chapman strengthened the growing contingent of popular musicians who were using their influence to educate people about the lack of human rights and basic human necessities in the world.

(ELIZABETH LASKEY)

Choonhavan, Chatichai

The unexpected refusal of Thailand's prime minister of eight years, Prem Tinsulanond, to continue in office after the July 1988 general election led to the appointment of Chatichai Choonhavan to take his place. The leader of Chart Thai, the party that had gained more seats than any other, 66-year-old Chatichai was the first elected member of Parliament to become prime minister since 1976. A gregarious, wealthy man with various business interests, he presented a contrast to the reserved, frugal Prem. Chatichai's six-party coalition promoted private enterprise at a time when Thailand's economy was doing better than ever before. Taking advice from his group of young academic advisers, Chatichai favoured better trade relations with Indochina, regarded as hostile since the Communist takeovers of the mid-1970s. In November he became the first Thai prime minister to visit Laos since 1979.

Chatichai, whose main interest as a child was music, joined the Army at the insistence of his father, Pin Choonhavan, a general who led the 1947 coup that brought Field Marshal Pibul Songgram to power. Pin served as deputy prime minister, but he and Pibul were ousted in 1957. Chatichai's part in an unsuccessful coup to return them led to his being sent abroad to a string of unimportant diplomatic posts. He returned in the early 1970s and helped found Chart Thai in 1974. He became an MP and foreign minister the next year. Later he was associated with some financial failures. A finance company he headed foundered in the late 1970s, and in 1981, when he was industry minister, an oil deal he arranged fell apart when prices dropped.

His first months in power were marked by controversies over some of his ministers. One was Interior Minister Pramarn Adireksarn, who suggested opening casinos, widely disapproved of in Buddhist Thailand. The government survived a no-confidence motion in October brought against a deputy interior minister who had allegedly used government equipment to dig a well for his own use. Chatichai still faced major challenges, however. One was to keep his fractious coalition together; the other was to fend off the military, headed by the politically ambitious army commander in chief, Chaovalit Yongchaiyuth. (JUDITH L. CLARKE)

Clancy, Tom

Although he would not consider his life as exciting as that of his main character, Jack Ryan, novelist Tom Clancy became privy to top-secret information, talked with U.S. Pres. Ronald Reagan, and was declared the undisputed "darling" of the U.S. military. All of these achievements were accomplished after 1984, when an unlikely publisher, the Naval Institute Press, decided to print *The Hunt for Red October.* It was the institute's first work of fiction that became not only a best-seller but also required reading at the war colleges. A fast-paced thriller, *The Hunt for Red*

October featured the combination of high-tech weaponry and military strategy that became the hallmark of Clancy's work.

A newspaper article recounting an attempted defection to the West by *Storozhevoy,* a Soviet frigate, provided the basis for *Red October.* Clancy conducted his own insatiable hunt to find the information needed to build his novel. He used Norman Polmar's *Guide to the Soviet Navy, Combat Fleets of the World,* and Harpoon, a war game. Instead of a frigate he chose a submarine, and his success was measured by the fact that it almost was not published because of the controversy over whether he had used classified information.

Controversy continued to surround Clancy in his later works. *Red Storm Rising,* with Larry Bond, a former intelligence officer, as coauthor, depicted World War III erupting between the Soviets and NATO. Again his information appeared to be highly classified. For *Patriot Games,* based on an imagined terrorist incident involving the British royal family, he was criticized for working too closely with the FBI. *The Cardinal of the Kremlin* depicted a Soviet space-defense research site so accurately that the CIA asked him to leave out the description. Common to all his novels was a clearly drawn theme of good triumphing over evil.

Thomas L. Clancy, Jr., was born in 1947 in Baltimore, Md. He admitted that he was not a good student while attending Roman Catholic schools because he immersed himself in technology and military history. At Loyola College in Baltimore he was an English major. It was at this time, however, that fate made a decision for him. His desire to fight in Vietnam was frustrated when he was dismissed from an officer's training program because of poor eyesight. He changed his course, married and had four children, and put his writing on hold. Finally, when he became successful as an insurance agent, he found the time to write.

(SUSAN MARTS MYERS)

Crawford, Michael

In 1988 Michael Crawford brought music to the fears of Broadway theatregoers. As the title character in Andrew Lloyd Webber's *Phantom of the Opera,* a record-breaking box-office hit, Crawford played a disfigured and haunted composer who, from his lair in the bowels of the Paris Opera House, plots and promotes the career of a beautiful, virginal chorus girl with whom he is obsessively in love. Though forced to wear a starkly ominous mask on one side of his face and deathly white and garishly red makeup on the other, Crawford managed to act sensually and sing passionately; he transformed the phantom—the homicidal subject of a novel and five nonmusical films—into a sympathetic threat, a mix of Cary Grant, Mario Lanza, and Mephistopheles. While critics were mixed on the show's merits, most praised Crawford's performance, agreeing in spirit with the *New York Times* that "when he is on stage—or over the stage in one of his gymnastic feats of daredevilry—he electrifies the evening." The power he generated as the phantom earned him almost a million dollars and a Tony award for best lead actor in a musical.

He made his debut on Jan. 19, 1942—born Michael Dumbell-Smith in Salisbury, England. After choir school, he studied as a soprano under Benjamin Britten and sang in the composer's *Let's Make an Opera* and *Noyes Fludde*—work that made the teenager intent on pursuing a show business career. Later he showed a sense of humour by taking his stage name from a Crawford's biscuit box and by making his London debut in the comedy *Come Blow Your Horn* (1962). In subsequent comedic roles on stage and screen, Crawford established himself as an actor who loved to get physical. In *Black Comedy,* his 1967 Broadway debut, he tumbled down a flight of stairs every night and eventually injured his neck and tore five tendons slamming into a door.

Crawford showed the same intensity in his return to musical work. In 1969 he practiced

DAVID PARKER—ALPHA/GLOBE PHOTOS

soft-shoe dancing night and day to win the part as the singing shop assistant in the movie *Hello Dolly!* Helped by singing lessons, he later took roles in a succession of London musicals, including the tightrope-walking lead in *Barnum* (1981–85), for which he won the Olivier award—the British equivalent of the Tony.

His stage work caught the eye—and ear—of Lloyd Webber, and Crawford landed the lead in the London production of *Phantom* (1986). His stunning performance earned him another Olivier in 1986 and created publicity for the play's New York run. After Broadway, Crawford hoped to play the phantom again, giving his tender loving scares to audiences in a movie version. (MICHAEL AMEDEO)

De Benedetti, Carlo

Although Carlo De Benedetti's financial interests included banking, insurance, publishing, high fashion, food processing, metalworks, and automobile components, he remained best known as the man who rescued Olivetti & Co. from near oblivion. When he took over Olivetti in 1978 (investing $17 million of his own), it was famous for its elegantly designed typewriters and for losing $6 million a month. By 1983 Olivetti showed a net profit of $160 million. In 1984 AT&T acquired 25% of Olivetti for $260 million, and by the late 1980s Olivetti was Europe's leading personal computer company.

In January 1988 De Benedetti acquired control of 18.6% of the Société Générale de Belgique and made a bid "to create the first European-scale holding company," with himself in charge. It looked for a while as if he would soon "own Belgium," as people were saying, but a rallying of "old boys" blocked the bid and De Benedetti returned home, far from sheepishly. Later in 1988 he won control over Italy's second largest private bank and the Mondadori publishing house. Profits at Olivetti, however, were down from their 1987 high, and De Benedetti planned to reorganize his flagship firm.

De Benedetti was born in Turin, Italy, on Nov. 14, 1934. When he was one year old, his family moved into the same apartment building as the Agnelli family, who owned Fiat S.p.A., and he went to school with Umberto Agnelli, later vice-president of Fiat.

In 1972 De Benedetti bought a virtually defunct tanning company in Turin with "four walls and not even one employee" because it was already quoted on the Milan stock exchange. After merging it with his father's pipe-manufacturing company, he became one of the first entrepreneurs in Italy to encourage the small investor to buy shares. When word of De Benedetti's significant success reached Fiat headquarters, he was asked by Fiat to become

CAMERA PRESS/GLOBE PHOTOS

their managing director in 1976. He accepted on the condition that Fiat purchase his family firm in exchange for Fiat shares. After only 100 days, however, the giant company issued a short communiqué saying that De Benedetti would be leaving because of "disagreements on company policies." His error, it seemed, had been to say that one-third of Fiat's management could be sent home. De Benedetti had an even shorter run as vice-president of Milan's Banco Ambrosiano (November 1981–January 1982), which he called "the worst mistake I ever made." The bank was declared bankrupt in a major scandal five months later.

(GEORGE ARMSTRONG)

De Mita, Luigi Ciriaco

Luigi Ciriaco De Mita did not emerge on the national political stage with a drumroll as the new prime minister of Italy in 1988. Even before he was chosen for the demanding role of chairman (secretary-general) of Italy's largest party, the Christian Democrats (CD), De Mita had long been on that stage. He appeared first as part of the chorus (a party councillor from 1956), then as a member of the chorus with a sword (1963 as MP), and next as a player given words in a *recitativo* (minister for industry, minister for foreign trade, minister for the Mezzogiorno; 1973–79). An Italian party leader need not have star quality nor be a public figure. A CD leader, however, must be acceptable to a coalition of some of the eight ironclad party factions and, ideally, a skillful administrator of party affairs. De Mita met those two requirements in 1982 and was reelected party chairman in 1986 with the backing of 60% of the party conference.

De Mita was born in Nusco, in the Neapolitan hinterland, on Feb. 2, 1928. He obtained a scholarship to the Università Cattolica in Milan, where he took his degree in law. When he took over the party leadership, it seemed as if the CD political amalgamation was coming unstuck after 33 years in power. Candidates chosen by De Mita as possible prime ministers had failed to persuade the other parties to join the CD in another coalition, and Pres. Alessandro Pertini asked the Republican leader, Giovanni Spadolini, to try his luck. The result was that in June 1981 the CD party for the first time joined a coalition that was not headed by one of its own men. After 17 months Spadolini was replaced by Amintore Fanfani, a Christian Democrat, but 8 months later another "outsider," Socialist leader Bettino Craxi, representing a party one-third the size of De Mita's, was chosen as prime minister. Craxi held onto the post for nearly four years. Those years allowed Craxi to enhance his personal power and that of his party, to De Mita's regret. Even follow-

ing the 1987 elections, De Mita eschewed the premiership for eight months while his protégé, Giovanni Goria, was prime minister.

In April 1988 De Mita was finally sworn in as prime minister. His refusal to give up chairmanship of the party at the same time caused irritation among those wanting to step into his shoes. "Nothing has come easily to me in my life," De Mita once said. It might seem an odd remark from someone who could have been prime minister eight years earlier, but it was an honest if somewhat oblique confession that his first love was his party, its continuity, and its success.   (GEORGE ARMSTRONG)

Deisenhofer, Johann

In 1982 West German biochemist Johann Deisenhofer and colleague Robert Huber (*q.v.*) collaborated with another West German researcher, Hartmut Michel (*q.v.*), to study the structure of a bacterial protein complex. The complex, called a photosynthetic reaction centre, was known to play a central role in initiating a simple type of photosynthesis, the process by which green plants and certain other organisms convert light energy to chemical energy. The products of photosynthesis are used by virtually all living things as a source of energy for vital functions, including growth, repair, reproduction, and movement. In 1985 the three researchers succeeded in determining the exact arrangement of the more than 10,000 atoms composing the protein complex. Their achievement was recognized three years later, when they were awarded the 1988 Nobel Prize for Chemistry.

Deisenhofer was born in Zusamaltheim, Bavaria, now in West Germany, on Sept. 30, 1943. He attended the Max Planck Institute for Biochemistry in Martinsried, West Germany, where he received his doctorate in 1974. He worked there until 1987, when he left to join the scientific staff at the Howard Hughes Medical Institute in Dallas, Texas.

The three scientists studied the structure of a protein complex that bridges the membrane of a photosynthetic bacterium. The protein is called a membrane-bound protein because it extends from the outside of the bacterial cell through the cell membrane to the cellular interior. The protein's specialized structure allows it to absorb light energy from the cell's surroundings and use that energy to transfer electrons and hydrogen ions (electrically charged hydrogen atoms) through the cell membrane to the inside of the cell. The bacterium uses the resulting difference in concentrations of electrons and hydrogen ions inside and outside the cell to manufacture adenosine triphosphate (ATP), an energy-rich molecule that functions as the carrier of chemical energy in many cellular processes. Although the bacterium's form of photosynthesis is simpler than that in plants, the laureates' discovery increased the scientific community's understanding of the mechanisms of photosynthesis in general and was a possible step toward the development of artificial photosynthetic materials that could harness solar energy by a process similar to natural photosynthesis.

(CAROLYN D. NEWTON)

Ditka, Mike

In five months Chicago Bears coach Mike Ditka went from induction into the Professional Football Hall of Fame to a heart attack to his second award as National Football League (NFL) coach of the year and fifth divisional championship. The Bears won 12 and lost 4 despite the absence for at least two games of 13 starters who retired, changed teams, or were injured. Seven of those 13 had been in Pro Bowls. "Challenges are what motivate," Ditka said.

Although he was in 1982 a surprising choice of founder George Halas to coach the Bears, Ditka became a national figure in his first coach-of-the-year season, 1985. His 18–1 team won the Super Bowl by a record 46–10 margin and, as in 1988, the Bears stood for work ethic and the underdog. His won–lost record of 73–31 in the 1982–88 regular season gave Ditka the

highest career winning percentage (.702) among active NFL coaches.

The fiery-tempered taskmaster, who broke his hand pounding a metal cabinet in anger after a 1983 loss, eventually became better known for what he wrote on clipboards than for how far he threw them. Fans identified with his bold decisions to use 138.5-kg (305-lb) defensive tackle William Perry at fullback, to try Hall of Fame halfback Walter Payton at quarterback, and to go for first downs more often than not on fourth-and-two. The country embraced him as a motivational speaker and advertising spokesman.

Ditka received more than 12,000 cards and letters after his mild heart attack on November 2. He was back in his office eight days later and on the sideline at a Bears game on November 13.

On July 30 Ditka became the Hall of Fame's first tight end, a position Halas, as Bears coach, virtually created for him. Tight ends were essentially third tackles before Halas put Ditka in the passing game. Ditka's 75 catches in 1964 remained an NFL record for tight ends until Kellen Winslow broke it in 1980. Despite limited speed, Ditka averaged 14.3 yd per catch in six Bear seasons, a high figure even by current more wide-open standards. He caught 427 passes for 5,913 yd and 43 touchdowns in 12 NFL seasons.

Michael Keller Ditka was born Oct. 18, 1939, in Carnegie, Pa., the son of a steelworker in the Pittsburgh area. He hated losing even as a child, once taking the ball from the pitcher on his baseball team because he thought he could do better. He nearly quit football as a 59-kg (130-lb) sophomore at Aliquippa (Pa.) High School, but he gained 14 kg (30 lb) before his junior year and went on to an All-America career at Pittsburgh as a tight end, defensive end, middle linebacker, and punter. He was the NFL's rookie of the year in 1961 and made the Pro Bowl the next five years. He finished his playing career with two years at Philadelphia and four at Dallas and then served as an assistant coach for Dallas from 1973 to 1981.

(KEVIN M. LAMB)

Donaldson, Sam

For Americans taking part in, or just taking stock of, the presidential campaigns of 1988, there was good news and bad news: Sam Donaldson was on TV more than usual. ABC-TV newsman Donaldson—whose pushy and irreverent style was loved by some and loathed by others—left his White House beat to report on the national party conventions. He continued as an acid commentator on "This Week with David Brinkley." Donaldson's detractors saw him as tall, dark, and irksome, a man who delighted in seizing the spotlight by yelling out hostile and sometimes crude questions to presidents and would-be presidents alike. To his admirers he was a passionate, no-nonsense pursuer of the truth. Not surprisingly, Donaldson viewed himself in that light, writing in his 1987 book, *Hold On, Mr. President,* that he had but one goal: "to find out what's *really* going on." Whatever his motives, there was no doubt that his approach helped make him both a distinct TV personality and a successful reporter—a rare combination.

Donaldson, who was born on March 11, 1934, in El Paso, Texas, spent his early years in radio. While attending Texas Western College (now the University of Texas at El Paso), he worked at El Paso radio stations, reading news, doing interviews, and as host of his own show. Years later he said the "real freedom and romance in broadcasting is . . . in radio."

Donaldson worked in television during the 1960s and immediately ruffled feathers. In an editorial for Washington's CBS affiliate, Donaldson criticized the U.S. Federal Communications Commission for not approving new broadcasting outlets for Austin, Texas, where the only television station was owned by Pres. Lyndon Johnson's wife. Infuriated, the president tried to have him fired—but failed.

In 1967 Donaldson graduated to the network at ABC. He aggressively covered the Vietnam war and Watergate, but he did not achieve the status of a household name until he became a White House correspondent in 1977. His greatest coup came when his nagging questions forced a reluctant Pres. Jimmy Carter to reveal an impending Middle East peace agreement. Later it was Donaldson's questions that induced Pres. Ronald Reagan to call the Soviet Union an "evil empire" and to admit that the U.S. sought to overthrow Nicaragua's Sandinistas.

Donaldson inspired fear and respect. In May 1988, with Republican George Bush down in the polls, Bush's campaign aides were nevertheless upbeat. The reason: ABC had just announced that Donaldson would be covering the campaign of Democrat Michael Dukakis.

(MICHAEL AMEDEO)

Downey, Morton, Jr.

Stalking across the stage, attacking the air with thrusts of his fist and jabs at his index finger, the sneering talk-show host would put his face right up to that of his startled guest and shout: "Shut up, you old hag," "zip it, buddy," or some other command or epithet that showed even less of a kinder, gentler nature. His anger would send the young studio audience into a howling, foot-stomping frenzy, which would culminate in chants of "Mort! Mort! Mort!" In 1988 that scene was a regular occurrence on the five-day-a-week "Morton Downey Jr. Show," which, just a month after its nationwide debut in June, became the highest rated late-night program in syndication since "Mary Hartman, Mary Hartman." The key to the show's success was, of course, the chain-smoking 55-year-old Morton Downey, Jr., who offered viewers a combination of theatrical meanness and reactionary populism—a right-wing Phil Donahue with fangs. To some, Downey's show was journalism from the gut—pure television. To others, it was journalism from the gutter—pure televenom. Downey claimed that he needed his boorishness to "break away the Madison Avenue veneer that all these experts come on the show with nowadays. You get them angry enough, they'll blow their stack and tell you what they really think."

Downey was the first child of popular crooner Morton Downey and dancer Barbara Bennett (sister of actresses Constance and Joan). His parents were divorced when he was nine, forcing Downey and his brothers and sister to live with their paternal grandparents. Thereafter Downey had largely a poor relationship with his father and almost no relationship with his mother.

After dropping out of New York University, Downey worked as nightclub singer, a

MICHAEL FERGUSON—GLOBE PHOTOS

songwriter, a political lobbyist, a co-owner of a professional basketball team, and a campaign aide to boyhood acquaintances John and Robert Kennedy. Disillusioned with liberalism, he joined the National Right to Life Organization in 1974 and soon became its director. Six years later he was briefly the presidential candidate of the organization's American Independent Party.

In late 1987 Downey left Chicago's radio station WMAQ, where he had been an outspoken talk-show host, to introduce "The Morton Downey Jr. Show" on New Jersey's cable TV superstation WWOR. He was an instant hit. Within a month he was accused of slapping a gay rights activist during an emotional exchange on the show. The resulting publicity made it certain that Downey's scream-screen television would soon go national. (MICHAEL AMEDEO)

Dukakis, Michael Stanley

When Gary Hart withdrew as a candidate for the Democratic presidential nomination on May 8, 1987, polls showed Gov. Michael Dukakis of Massachusetts narrowly leading all the other candidates except the supposedly unelectable Jesse Jackson. In 1988 Dukakis won the primary in New Hampshire on February 16 and

AP/WIDE WORLD

the two largest of the primaries held on March 8 (Super Tuesday). Now the clear leader, he made people listen to his claims of managerial competence and of knowing how to make government an engine of real economic growth. By June 7 a majority of the delegates-elect to the Democratic national convention were pledged to him, and on July 20, in Atlanta, Ga., more than two-thirds of the delegates to the convention voted to give him the nomination. Public opinion polls showed him leading George Bush (q.v.), the certain Republican candidate, by 17 percentage points.

Then things began to come apart. Attacked by Bush as a "liberal," deficient in patriotism and soft on crime and defense, Dukakis at first seemed uncertain how to respond. He accused Bush of negative campaigning but responded in kind. Dukakis's tendency to appear aloof became an increasing problem. There were no surprises in the televised presidential debates in Winston-Salem, N.C., on September 25 and in Los Angeles on October 13. In Fresno, Calif., on October 30, hitting back at last at Bush's jibes about the "L" word, Dukakis offered a positive definition of liberalism. He embarked on a whirlwind tour of the nation and seemed to be gaining some support, but in the election on November 8, he carried only ten states and the District of Columbia.

Dukakis was born in Brookline, Mass., on Nov. 3, 1933. His father, a doctor, and his

mother had emigrated from Greece. He received a B.A. from Swarthmore College in 1955 and served in the Army from 1955 to 1957. In 1960 he received a law degree from Harvard. He served in the state House of Representatives (1963–70), ran unsuccessfully for lieutenant governor in 1970, and was moderator of a syndicated television show, "The Advocates" (1971–73). Massachusetts's weak economy helped Dukakis win the governorship over an incumbent Republican in 1974, but he failed to improve it and was defeated for reelection in 1978 by Edward King, an antitax maverick Democrat. Elected governor again in 1982, Dukakis seemed less aloof and more persuasive than in earlier campaigns. In his second term Massachusetts's economy suddenly boomed. He was overwhelmingly reelected in 1986.

(CHARLES JOHNSON TAGGART)

Eisner, Michael

In the decades following the death of Walt Disney in 1966, the Disney companies fell into a slump, corporate raiders were eyeing the property, and the Magic Kingdom seemed doomed. The appointment of Michael Eisner as chairman and chief executive officer in late 1984 miraculously turned the situation around. In his first four years at the helm of the nearly 60-year-old Disney empire, annual revenues more than doubled and profits increased almost fourfold. The theme parks in California, Florida, and Japan—still the company's most profitable segment—raised their prices and saw attendance mushroom. Plans were also under way for a 1992 opening of Euro Disneyland near Paris. Eisner was also credited with the remarkable success of Disney's movie studio, which was the highest-grossing Hollywood studio for several months at the beginning of 1988. Three years earlier it had been ranked ninth. The success was due, in part, to films released under Disney's Touchstone label, including *Down and Out in Beverly Hills; Good Morning, Vietnam; Three Men and a Baby; Big Business;* and *Who Framed Roger Rabbit.*

Eisner was born in New York City on March 7, 1942. He was raised on Manhattan's Upper East Side and educated in private schools. He began premedical studies at Denison University, Granville, Ohio, but found that he preferred literature and theatre. After graduation he worked for six weeks as a clerk at NBC, then briefly at CBS, and then spent ten years at ABC. There he climbed the corporate ladder, becoming vice-president of daytime programming, vice-president of programming planning and development, and finally senior vice-president of prime-time production and development. He was credited with taking ABC to first

ROBERT NESE—GLOBE PHOTOS

place in the ratings. In 1976 he became president and chief operating officer at Paramount Pictures, where he spent eight years and oversaw the production of such movie blockbusters as *Saturday Night Fever, Raiders of the Lost Ark,* and *Terms of Endearment.*

In September 1984 Eisner joined Walt Disney Productions, which was renamed the Walt Disney Co. in 1986. As a result of his first years with Disney, the company's appeal to adults was enhanced while the mainstays of the children's attractions were revitalized. According to the vice-chairman of the board and Walt Disney's nephew, Roy E. Disney, the changes that Eisner made were the right ones: "We've become an idea company again."

(FRANCINE SHONFELD SHERMAN)

Elion, Gertrude Belle

In 1945, when U.S. drug researcher Gertrude Elion joined George Hitchings (*q.v.*) at the Burroughs Wellcome Research Laboratories in Tuckahoe, N.Y., the two scientists embarked on a program of custom-designing drugs to attack only certain abnormal cells and disease-causing microorganisms in the human body. Their method of formulating target-specific agents represented a radical departure from the trial-and-error approach toward drug research taken by many of their colleagues. Over the more than 40 years that they worked together, Elion and Hitchings developed numerous medicines, including drugs for treating leukemia, gout, malaria, and autoimmune disorders. However, it was primarily for their innovative research philosophy that they were selected, with British pharmacologist Sir James Black (*q.v.*), to receive the 1988 Nobel Prize for Physiology or Medicine. Said the Nobel Committee, "[The three researchers] introduced a more rational approach based on the understanding of basic biochemical and physiological processes," and this approach "has had a more fundamental significance" than their development of individual drugs.

Elion was born on Jan. 23, 1918, in New York City. In 1937 she earned a bachelor's degree in biochemistry from Hunter College, and for the next seven years she worked in several laboratories and taught high-school chemistry and physics. In 1941 she received a master's degree from New York University. Elion joined the Burroughs Wellcome labs in 1944 and started her long collaboration with Hitchings a year later. Although she embarked on a doctorate program at Brooklyn Polytechnic Institute while working, she left the program when she learned that she would have to give up her job for full-time study in order to earn a degree. She became emeritus scientist with the Wellcome Research Laboratories in Research Triangle Park, N.C., in 1983.

In the 1940s, when Elion and Hitchings began their prizewinning work, most drug researchers set out to discover new drugs rather than design them. Researchers sought out natural compounds, altered their chemical structures in various ways, and then applied the altered forms to infected animals in hopes of finding a substance that would damage the infecting organism without causing excessive harm to the host animal. Elion and Hitchings, on the other hand, began by examining the difference between the biochemistry of normal human cells and that of cancer cells, viruses, bacteria, and parasites. They then used the information they acquired to formulate drugs targeted specifically for the abnormal cells or pathogenic microorganisms. Their drugs killed or inhibited the reproduction of only those pathogens, leaving the host's normal cells undamaged. A number of the compounds that they developed were included in the World Health Organization's list of mankind's most essential drugs.

(CAROLYN D. NEWTON)

Elliott, John Dorman

John Elliott, the federal president of the Australian Liberal Party, spent 1988 waiting in the wings for the opportunity to enter the centre stage as leader of the Liberal Party in Parliament. He consolidated his position in the business and political worlds, emerging as both a beneficiary of the October 1987 stock market crash and the sage political leader of the extra-parliamentary conservatives. Within six months of the crash, Elliott was estimated to have increased his personal fortune from $20 million to $90 million and had made his company one of Australia's richest firms.

Elliott, born Oct. 3, 1941, was one of Australia's most successful entrepreneurial businessmen. Using his accounting, commerce, and business expertise, he became managing director of Henry Jones (IXL) in 1972, before the creation of Elders IXL in 1981. In seven years Elliott turned Elders from a pastoral enterprise into a giant multinational, with diversified interests including the popular beer Foster's Lager.

Although parodied by his political opponents as primarily interested in beer and football, Elliott was a shrewd businessman who used the Foster's label to make an assault on the world beer market while at the same time protecting his local base and reputation by involvement with one of Australia's most successful football teams. From 1975 to 1988 Elliott was vice-president of the Victorian branch of the Liberals, and in 1988, as federal president, Elliott did not hesitate to flagellate the weaker members of his own political side.

Using sporting imagery, Elliott announced to his surprised party that they had not deserved to win the 1985 elections because they lacked both leadership and teamwork. He compared the Liberals unfavourably with the victorious Australian Labor Party, noting that "a champion team will always beat a team of champions." Elliott clearly signaled that he was not prepared to remain outside the parliamentary arena indefinitely. Should it be necessary, he would not hesitate to enter Parliament with a view to becoming prime minister in the interests of the conservative coalition and the nation as a whole. While supporters of the Liberal parliamentary leader, John Howard, deplored the open canvassing of Elliott as a future prime minister, many of the rank and file in the community believed that only a strong populist leader could beat Prime Minister Bob Hawke at his own game.   (A. R. G. GRIFFITHS)

Endo, Shusaku

Shusaku Endo was not unique in Japan because he had won the Akutagawa Prize for literature in 1955. What set him apart from other celebrated authors was his Roman Catholicism and the central role it played in much of what he wrote. On quite another level, he had won fame as a practical jokester. In addition, he organized a dramatic troupe of totally inexperienced persons who somehow managed to perform *Romeo and Juliet, Hamlet,* and even an opera. Endo also declared that a troupe he sent to New York gave a "highly acclaimed performance at some off-off Broadway theatre."

Endo was born in Tokyo on March 27, 1923. His father, a banker, moved the family to Port Arthur (Lu-shun) in Manchuria, China, then to Kobe, where Shusaku delighted his devout Catholic mother by being baptized. He majored in French at Keio University in Tokyo and then went to France in 1950 to study French Catholic novelists at the University of Lyon. His religious conversion marked him for life—at least as a novelist—because to be Catholic in Japan was to belong to a distinct minority. The trauma of his mother's untimely death and the importance to him of his Catholic training could be seen in his writings, which reveal a deep concern with the image of the Virgin Mary and the impact of Christianity on Japan in the early 17th century.

Among his most read works was "White Men," a short story based on his personal experiences in France; it was honoured with the Akutagawa Prize. *The Sea and Poison* (1957) was a problem novel, dealing with the war crimes of Japanese doctors during the Pacific war. It focused on the "pagan" mentality of the

JOHN REARDON—CAMERA PRESS/GLOBE PHOTOS

Japanese, especially the absence of a sense of original sin. This theme was developed more fully in *Silence* (1966), a historical novel of the Japanese persecution of early Christians; *By the Dead Sea* (1973); and *Samurai* (1980), which vividly delineated the responses of "samurai" converts in Mexico and Europe and their later tragic homecoming.

Endo's emphasis seemed to have gradually moved from criticism of Japan's "pagan mentality" to a sympathetic appreciation of Japanese efforts to clothe Christianity in Japanese attire. Endo also wrote several humorous novels, such as *Wonderful Fool* (1959) and *Mr. Gourd* (1961), and innumerable immensely popular light essays. French and English translations of some of his novels were also very well received.

(SHOICHI SAEKI)

Fay, Michael

On July 17, 1987, wealthy New Zealand merchant banker Michael Fay issued a challenge from the Mercury Bay Boating Club of Whitianga, N.Z., to the current America's Cup holder, the San Diego (Calif.) Yacht Club, to defend the title. This announcement caught the yachting world and most of the general public by surprise. Since 1958 the race had been held approximately every four years. Fay decided, however, that he wanted to have the race run only 18 months after Dennis Conner and his San Diego team recaptured the cup from the Australians on Feb. 4, 1987. What followed was a series of legal maneuvers and various interpretations of the America's Cup's historic Deed of Gift—the governing document of the

BERG & ASSOCIATES

regatta—that were designed to give each of the competitors an edge.

Initially, the San Diego Yacht Club ignored the challenge and continued with business as usual, looking to May 1991 as the next race date. Fay sailed into court, however, and persuaded New York State Supreme Court Justice Carmen Ciparick, in the state where the deed was overseen, to uphold his challenge, citing a passage from the Deed of Gift that says, "Any organized Yacht Club of a foreign country . . . shall always be entitled to the right of sailing a match for this Cup." Conner thus was forced to fight it out at sea, but rather than sulk he delivered a counterpunch by choosing to race against Fay's $3 million 41-m (133-ft) monohull boat, *New Zealand,* with an 18-m (60-ft) twin-hull catamaran, *Stars & Stripes.* This matchup was seen as giving Conner a distinct advantage, and Fay cried foul. This time, however, Judge Ciparick came down on the side of Conner, saying that under the Deed of Gift very little is said about the characteristics of qualifying yachts and that "the provisions of the deed lack the requisite clarity, as to whether the challenger's choice of boat in effect dictates that of the defender." The race was on, and both parties agreed that the best-of-three competition would take place off San Diego beginning September 7.

As was expected, Conner's catamaran defeated Fay 2–0. Fay then went back to court to try to have the entire race declared illegal, which would force San Diego to forfeit the cup. A ruling was expected in early 1989.

Michael Fay was born on April 10, 1949, in Auckland, N.Z. He established a highly successful banking business. Since Fay was the grandson of a judge, it was ironic that the future of his efforts to take the America's Cup home to New Zealand depended on another member of the judiciary. If the decision should go against him, Fay vowed to return in 1991.

(ANTHONY L. GREEN)

Filmon, Gary Albert

Successful businessman Gary Filmon became leader of the Progressive Conservative Party in Manitoba, and thereby leader of the opposition in the Manitoba legislature, on Dec. 10, 1983. Fending off challenges to his party leadership in 1986 and 1987 earned him the right to lead the Conservatives in the April 26, 1988, provincial election. Although the Tories won one seat fewer than they had held before the election was called, they still had enough seats to form a minority government. Thus Filmon capped his political career by becoming Manitoba's 19th premier on May 9.

Born on Aug. 24, 1942, Gary Albert Filmon attended the University of Manitoba, receiving a B.Sc. in civil engineering (1964) and an M.Sc. (1967). He worked for five years as a consulting engineer. In 1969 he joined his father-in-law in business at Success Business College in Winnipeg, and in 1971 he purchased the college. In 1974–75 Filmon was president of the Association of Canadian Career Colleges. He found business both stimulating and challenging, and his favourite people were always those who took risks and made investments, created things and made them grow. He saw hard work, risk-taking, self-reliance, and self-determination as the important elements in life.

Politics, he believed, was much like business, and he applied business techniques to his political life. Plodding and methodical, he worked long hours and insisted on efficient scheduling. He was a member of the Winnipeg City Council (1975–79), serving as chairman of the Works and Operations Committee. Elected to the Manitoba legislature to represent first the riding of River Heights (1979–81) and then the riding of Tuxedo, he was minister of consumer and corporate affairs and environment (1981) and minister of housing in the last Cabinet of former Manitoba premier Sterling Lyon.

Filmon won the post of party leader after Lyon's retirement because of his popularity with the urban delegates. However, the 1988 election left his party in the legislature composed mostly of rural members. This, coupled with the fact that the Tories held power by only a narrow margin (the Tories held 25 seats; the Liberals, 20; and the New Democrats, 12), meant Filmon needed to exercise great caution to keep from being defeated in a no-confidence vote. Styling himself a fiscal conservative and a social progressive, Filmon endorsed middle-of-the-road policies and practiced moderate pragmatism in his political dealings. (DIANE LOIS WAY)

Fugard, Athol

The year 1988 was a busy one for South African playwright, director, and actor Athol Fugard. In April his play *The Road to Mecca* opened in New York City at the Promenade Theatre. Not only did reviews cite his meticulous direction, they also alluded to his sensitive dialogue, clever wit, and, as an actor, superb portrayal of a Dutch Reformed pastor named Marius Byleveld, a rural clergyman who epitomizes white South African ideology.

Soon afterward Fugard participated in a symposium sponsored by the First New York International Festival of the Arts. In discussing both popular and critical reactions to his work, this white dissident long harassed by his native government said he had found an extraordinary degree of sensitivity on the part of audiences to the subtleties and complexities of South African politics, a subject with which he was fascinated and that he had treated in such a way as to change the face of modern theatre. (In *The Road to Mecca* there were no black characters onstage, but their struggles were apparent in every interaction.) Then, at summer's end, Fugard agreed to appear in a television soap opera called "One Life to Live." He played a disabled old sea captain who lived in an abandoned lighthouse.

This versatile man was born in the remote Karroo district of South Africa in 1932 to Anglo-Irish and Afrikaner parents. He studied philosophy and social anthropology at the University of Cape Town. His first play, *No Good Friday,* was produced when he was 27.

In 1964 Fugard and his actress wife, Sheila Meiring, went to Port Elizabeth to help a group of nonwhite actors form an amateur drama group called the Serpent Players. They produced works by Machiavelli, Brecht, Sophocles, and others. Fugard's own work was enriched by this experience. His angry trilogy—*The Blood Knot* (1961), *Hello and Goodbye* (1968), and *Boesman and Lena* (1970)—is about the lives of poor people who lived in Port Elizabeth. His *People Are Living There* (1968) is about life in a cheap Johannesburg boardinghouse.

Fugard's work with the Serpent Players also enabled him to understand the black South African viewpoint, an insight that resulted in the early 1970s plays *The Coat, Sizwe Bansi Is Dead,* and *The Island.* Actors John Kani and Winston Ntshona were coauthors of the latter two. In 1980 *A Lesson from Aloes,* starring James Earl Jones, was considered a triumphant portrayal of the South African environment that had been Fugard's inspiration.

The Road to Mecca was a personal as well as professional triumph for Fugard. It was the first play he had written after a several-year bout with alcoholism. (BONNIE OBERMAN)

Giuliani, Rudolph William

In the great tradition of other big city "crime busters," Rudolph Giuliani, U.S. attorney for the southern district of New York, launched a campaign in 1983 to rid New York City of drug dealers and mob bosses. In 1986 Giuliani used the 1970 Racketeer Influenced and Corrupt Organizations Act to obtain a single conviction of eight top Mafia leaders. His pioneering use of RICO to prosecute entire organizations rather than individuals drew national attention and set the stage for an expanded definition of racketeering. Giuliani's office applied RICO in 1987 in an explosive government corruption scandal involving the military contractor Wedtech.

In May 1986 Giuliani had used long-neglected securities laws from the 1930s against investment banker Dennis Levine and arbitrageur Ivan Boesky in an insider-trading scandal that rocked Wall Street. Two years later Giuliani unveiled the largest-ever insider-trading case against the investment firm Drexel Burnham Lambert Inc. and its star "junk bond" dealer, Michael Milken. In December 1988 Drexel pleaded guilty to several other criminal charges in order to avoid a racketeering indictment. Perhaps Giuliani's most controversial use of RICO was in October 1988 when he filed charges against former Philippine president Ferdinand Marcos and his wife, Imelda.

Giuliani was born on May 28, 1944, into a fiercely anti-Mafia Italian family in Brooklyn, N.Y. After graduating (1968) from New York University law school, he clerked for a federal district judge, and in 1970 he became an assistant U.S. attorney in the New York office that he was later to head. His aggressive cross-examination techniques and tenacity as a prosecutor were portrayed in the film *Prince of the City* (1981) and earned him a job as associate attorney general (1981–83), the third highest position in the U.S. Justice Department.

Giuliani's aggressive nature and brilliant use of the media, notably his mastery of the 20-second "sound bite," drew criticism from all sides. While the prosecutor in Brooklyn claimed that Giuliani used his Washington connections to eclipse that office's investigations, others charged that his high profile was paving the way for a career in politics. Indeed, in 1988 he publicly considered and then rejected a run for the U.S. Senate, and he was widely touted to run against New York Mayor Edward Koch in 1989. Giuliani, however, shrugged off such speculation, arguing that publicity was simply a weapon in his personal war against crime.

(MELINDA SHEPHERD)

Gorbachev, Mikhail Sergeyevich

By late 1988, less than four years after his election as general secretary of the Central Committee (CC) of the Communist Party of the Soviet Union (CPSU) on March 11, 1985, Mikhail Gorbachev had become one of the megastars of world politics. A man whose speeches were once as dreary and devoid of ideas as those of Leonid Brezhnev, his leader, he had turned into a silver-tongued propagandist for radical political and economic reform of the Soviet Union and a complete restructuring of the U.S.S.R.'s relations with the outside world. In fact, he had become a political visionary.

By skilled political maneuvering he had, by late 1988, produced a Politburo and CC Secretariat that were likely to support his plans for *perestroika* (restructuring), *glasnost* (openness), and democratization. However, given the presence of Egor Ligachev (*q.v.*) and Gen. Viktor Chebrikov, both with less radical ideas on change, at the core of the Soviet leadership, Gorbachev was not unassailable.

Mikhail Gorbachev, the son of Russian peasants, was born on March 2, 1931, in the village of Privolnoye, in Stavropol territory in the northern Caucasus. He studied law at Moscow State University between 1950 and 1955. He joined the CPSU in 1952. After graduation he returned to Stavropol and made a career in the Komsomol, the Young Communist movement. In 1963 he transferred to the party apparatus, rising to become party first secretary of Stavropol in 1970. In 1971 he was elected a member of the CC of the CPSU.

His breakthrough to national party affairs occurred in 1978 when he succeeded Fedor Kulakov as CC secretary for agriculture. In 1979 he was elected a candidate member of the Politburo and in the following year a full member. At 49 he was by far the youngest member of the party leadership's inner core. The aged and ailing Brezhnev was succeeded as CPSU first secretary by two other aged and ailing leaders, but after the death of Konstantin Chernenko in 1985, Gorbachev fought off a challenge from Grigory Romanov and Viktor Grishin to gain the country's most powerful position. In October 1988 he also became Soviet president.

In late 1988 Gorbachev's standing abroad was higher than at home. Four summit meetings with U.S. Pres. Ronald Reagan confirmed his stature as a world leader, and many foreign trips enhanced his reputation as a political charmer. In a major speech to the UN in December, he announced a unilateral reduction of 500,000 Soviet troops over the next two years and the withdrawal of 10,000 tanks from Eastern Europe. (MARTIN MCCAULEY)

Griffith Joyner, Florence

Her uniform was standard issue, not one of her signature body stockings with one leg cut off and bright, eye-riveting colours, but Florence Griffith Joyner still stole the show. She ran so fast that her long hair straightened behind her like a kite's tail. She led the others by so far that she started smiling only two-thirds into the 100-m race. Even so, her gold-medal time of 10.54 sec in the 1988 Olympics nearly broke her own world record.

The victory on September 25 at Seoul, South Korea, won Griffith Joyner her first of four Olympic running medals, the most ever by a woman. She won at 200 m in a world-record 21.34 sec, 0.37 sec faster than the record that had stood nine years. She gained a third gold on the U.S. women's 4 × 100-m relay team and a silver in the 4 × 400-m relay. She won the Jesse Owens Award as the best athlete in U.S. track and field.

Griffith Joyner began training for the Olympic 400 m in November 1987, but when she ran a 100 in less than 11 seconds in early 1988, she said, "I knew the speed was there, so we decided to run the 100 and 200." She dazzled the world at the U.S. Olympic trials July 16 with more than her purple and chartreuse racing togs. Her 10.49-sec semifinal in 37.8°C (100° F) heat blasted 0.27 sec off Evelyn Ashford's four-year-old world record for 100 m.

Griffith Joyner's dramatic improvement at age 28 spawned rumours about performance-enhancing drugs. She passed all her drug tests, however, and attributed her new speed to distance training for the 400 and weight training that gave her the fastest starts in memory.

Florence Delorez Griffith was born Sept. 21, 1959, in Los Angeles. She grew up in the city's public housing projects after her parents were divorced. When she visited her father in the Mojave Desert, she chased jackrabbits, and when she started racing formally at age seven, she outran boys. She went to California State University at Northridge to study English. Coach Bob Kersee lured her to the track team, and he coaxed her to follow him when he went to UCLA in 1980.

In 1982 she was NCAA champion at 200 m. She won the Olympic silver medal at that distance in 1984, when international fans first called her "Fluorescent Flo" for her colourful outfits and 15-cm (6-in) fingernails, fastidiously decorated with paintings and rhinestones. On Oct. 10, 1987, she married Al Joyner, the 1984 Olympic triple-jump winner. Joyner's sister, Jackie Joyner-Kersee, double-gold winner in the 1988 Olympics, was married to Kersee. After the Olympic trials, Griffith Joyner changed coaches from Kersee to Joyner, who was more encouraging of her shift in specialties to the 100. (KEVIN M. LAMB)

Grosz, Karoly

On May 22, 1988, 58-year-old Karoly Grosz became the new general secretary of the Hungarian Socialist Workers' (Communist) Party (HSWP), succeeding Janos Kadar, who had led the country since the failed uprising in 1956, when he was put into power by the U.S.S.R. This time, however, the Soviet Union reportedly had no say in the matter. Party veteran Grosz had been appointed prime minister by Kadar in June 1987 with the expectation that, by imposing harsh economic measures in an effort to revive Hungary's economy, Grosz would make himself unpopular and would not pose a threat to Kadar's leadership. Grosz's energetic but pragmatic style earned him allies in the

DOD MILLER—CAMERA PRESS/GLOBE PHOTOS

party leadership instead, and when the national party conference was held, Grosz was elected general secretary. The unprecedented elections of Grosz and other members of the Central Committee were generally welcomed by the Hungarians, and the mood in Budapest could have been described as euphoric.

Grosz was a recent convert to reformist thinking. Throughout most of his career, he had been considered a Communist bureaucrat who adhered closely to the party line. Born in Miskolc, Hung., on Aug. 1, 1930, he started his career as a printer before graduating from Eotvos Lorand University in Budapest and becoming a teacher. Shortly thereafter he joined the Hungarian Young People's Federation and became that organization's secretary. In the mid-1950s Grosz was chief editor of the daily newspaper *North Hungary,* and from 1958 to 1981 he edited *Eszak Magyarotszag,* a Miskolc daily. In 1961 Grosz became secretary of the party committee of Hungarian Radio and Television. He served on the HSWP Central Committee's agitation and propaganda department, both as deputy leader (1968–73) and as leader (1974–79), supervising most of the Hungarian media. He later served as first secretary of the Borsod County Party Committee (1979–84). In 1984 he was elected first secretary of the Budapest Party Committee, a post he held until he was named prime minister. Grosz became a member of the Politburo in 1985.

In July 1988 Grosz visited the U.S., becoming the first Hungarian leader in 42 years to do so. In his meeting with Pres. Ronald Reagan, Grosz discussed his interests in economic ventures and a variety of other projects, including the expansion of an exchange program for U.S. and Hungarian high-school and college students. However, some of his reform measures in his own country, such as a new personal income tax, unique in the Communist world, caused public resentment. (EDWARD PAUL MORAGNE)

Hawke, Robert James Lee

The Australian Labor Party (ALP) prime minister of Australia, Bob Hawke, had difficulty at the beginning of 1988 deciding whether his biggest political threat came from the opposition parties in the Parliament, the Liberal-National coalition, or from his heir apparent, Paul Keating. By the end of the year, he had vanquished one and quieted the other. Hawke, who became prime minister in 1983, entered the bicentennial year with the tide of public opinion apparently running against his party. The ALP performed badly in by-elections and lost the state of New South Wales to the Liberals.

In the wake of the downturn in the prime minister's performance, Keating, the brilliant and ambitious treasurer, was openly canvassed

as an imminent potential replacement. Hawke, however, alternately raised Keating's hopes by praising him and dashed them by suggesting other candidates for party leader. The prime minister also vacillated between hinting at retirement and promising to stay on indefinitely. Keating's frustrations surfaced, and the public discussion of whether Keating would remain in Parliament if Hawke chose to remain leader indefinitely further damaged the ALP. By October 1988 the tide turned for Labor as the Liberals were unable to make appropriate headway in the Victorian state election, and with public opinion firmly behind him, Hawke was delighted to have Australia's largest trade union, the Shop Distributive and Allied Employees' Association, call upon him to stay as prime minister "for many more elections yet." Hawke immediately hinted that he would stay on well beyond the next election, and Keating's chances of becoming prime minister were further reduced when the New South Wales ALP president, John MacBean, said that party members, trade unionists, and the general community did not view the treasurer as a potential prime minister "while Bob Hawke wants to stay." Whatever the parliamentary party thought, public opinion popularity polls continued to rate Hawke twice as likeable as his rivals in both the opposition and the ALP, and Hawke's great personal charisma and common touch were assets no party could lightly jettison.

Hawke was born on Dec. 9, 1929, at Bordertown, South Australia. After a career as a trade union advocate, he entered Parliament in 1980 and in 1983 was appointed party leader just in time to lead the ALP to victory in the federal elections. (A. R. G. GRIFFITHS)

Hershey, Barbara

Twenty years after her film debut at age 20, Barbara Hershey had become, after a lengthy apprenticeship, an actress of international acclaim, whose ability to handle roles with a wide technical and emotional range was undisputed. In May 1988, in Cannes, France, she received her second consecutive award for best actress, a prize she shared with her two leading coactresses for their powerful roles in Chris Menges's *A World Apart.* Hershey portrayed a middle-class mother and committed antiapartheid journalist in South Africa in 1963. In 1987 she won for her portrayal of a hard-edged Louisiana bayou woman in Andrey Konchalovsky's *Shy People.*

Hershey was born in Los Angeles on Feb. 5, 1948. She began television acting at age 17 and at 20 made her film debut in *With Six You Get Egg Roll.* During the late '60s and the '70s she appeared in several films, including Frank Perry's *Last Summer,* James Bridges's *The Baby Maker,* and Martin Scorsese's (*q.v.*) *Boxcar Bertha.* In the '70s she went through what she called her "dark period"—a time of no work and unreturned phone calls—but dur-

ADAM SCULL—RANGEFINDERS/GLOBE PHOTOS

ing the '80s she climbed quietly into the big time, demonstrating rare talent and bringing true intelligence to her varied roles. As one reviewer noted, Hershey was "both so technically dazzling and self-effacing that the personality within the actress is in danger of disappearing inside the work." Woody Allen said: "She's got a built-in attractive quality that immediately makes the character come to life. It's an earthy sensuality, a natural sensuality." Her commitment and talent were obvious in films as varied as *The Right Stuff; Hoosiers; The Natural;* Allen's *Hannah and Her Sisters,* which some said was her true maturing role; and *Tin Men,* where she played Danny DeVito's badly used wife, her sense of betrayal handled so cleverly that it allowed the film's comedy to succeed.

These parts led to her prizewinning roles and to the long-desired part of Mary Magdalene in the highly controversial Scorsese film *The Last Temptation of Christ.* (It was Hershey who had given Nikos Kazantzakis's book to Scorsese more than 20 years earlier when they were working together on *Boxcar Bertha.*) Clearly, Hershey would continue to get opportunities to challenge her abilities as an actress. Film audiences around the world could expect to watch her meet the challenge and move onward.

(BONNIE OBERMAN)

Hershiser, Orel

Even after he finished the 1988 National League season with a major-league record of 59 consecutive scoreless innings pitched, Orel Hershiser said, "I'm not great in my own mind." Even after he shut out the New York Mets to win the National League championship series for his Los Angeles Dodgers, four games to three,

FOCUS ON SPORTS

Hershiser was the same guy who collected bubble gum cards into adulthood and said he was "always just the kid trying to make the lineup." Even after he won the decisive fifth game 5–2 in the Dodgers' World Series upset of the Oakland Athletics, Hershiser could not seem to believe he was really a star.

From Sept. 5, 1988, the first complete game in his 59-inning streak, through the Series clincher on October 20, Hershiser won eight games, lost none, and had a .46 earned run average. He pitched seven shutouts and 10 scoreless innings of a 16-inning game. He also saved a game when the Dodgers' relief ace was suspended in the championship series. He even tied a World Series record by batting 1.000 in three at-bats.

It was a feat for Hershiser to downplay and others to admire. "Never in our lifetime will anyone accomplish what Orel accomplished this year," Dodger teammate Kirk Gibson said. "Nobody has ever been in such a groove." Besides earning unanimous acclamation as the National League Cy Young Award winner for the pitcher of the year, Hershiser was named World Series most valuable player and *The Sporting News* major league player of the year.

Orel Leonard Hershiser IV was born Sept. 16, 1958, in Buffalo, N.Y. His family moved fre-

quently, eventually to Cherry Hills, N.J., while his father climbed from sales to part ownership of a printing business. "I had to explain my name a lot," said Hershiser, whose older of two sons, Orel V, goes by the name Quinton. A family name, Orel means "eagle" in Slavic.

Hershiser's pitching was not impressive enough to earn a full scholarship at Bowling Green (Ohio) State University, and it took him five minor-league seasons to reach the Dodgers in late 1983. He blossomed in 1985 with a 19–3 record, leading the league with an .864 winning percentage.

The 1988 season, his fifth, was the fourth time he ranked in the top three in NL earned run average. He led the league with eight shutouts and 267 innings pitched, tied for first with 23 victories and 15 complete games, ranked third with a 2.26 earned run average, and allowed opposing batters a .213 average. After a 23–8 season, his career won-lost record was 83–49 with an earned run average of 2.77. His scoreless streak broke by one inning the record set in 1968 by another Dodger pitcher, Don Drysdale.

(KEVIN M. LAMB)

Hick, Graeme Ashley

From the time he arrived in England from his native Zimbabwe in 1984, Graeme Hick was established as the most exciting young talent in world cricket. Remarkably, he made that reputation solely on his record-breaking achievements for Worcestershire in county cricket because, under the current qualification laws for overseas-born players in English cricket, Hick would have to wait until 1991 (when he would be 25) before he could play test matches for England.

After only three and a half seasons in county cricket, Hick had already scored 26 first-class centuries and topped 7,000 runs. In 1986, at the age of 20, he became the youngest player to score 2,000 runs in an English season, and in 1988 he became only the eighth player ever to score 1,000 first-class runs before the end of May. His unbeaten 405 against Somerset in May was only 19 runs short of the highest innings in English cricket, made by Archie MacLaren in 1895. However, Hick's talent might best be measured by the strenuous—and so far unsuccessful—efforts that had been made by the England authorities to change the qualification laws so that he would be available to play for his adopted country before 1991.

Tall and immensely strong, Hick learned cricket under the critical eye of his father in Harare. From an early age he showed he had the ability and the concentration to play big innings; he made his first century at the age of six and scored seven centuries and averaged 216 for his school under-14 team. At the age of 17 he was selected for the Zimbabwean national team for the ICC World Cup (for non-test-playing countries) in England in 1983, and the following year he joined Worcestershire on a special scholarship, making his debut in county cricket that year. Worcestershire quickly recognized his talent, and in 1985 he played half of the county's first-class games before establishing himself as a regular member of the team in 1986.

A right-handed batsman and useful off-break bowler, Hick possessed a batting talent based on an upright classical technique, great power, and extraordinary concentration. Once in, he rarely made mistakes, and it seemed that only a combination of frustration at not being able to match his talent against the best in the world until 1991 and boredom at having nothing left to achieve in county cricket could stop the quiet Zimbabwean's seemingly inevitable progress toward a place on the list of all-time greats.

(ANDREW LONGMORE)

Hitchings, George Herbert

For more than 40 years U.S. biochemist George Hitchings and colleague Gertrude Elion (*q.v.*) worked together at the Burroughs Wellcome Research Laboratories in New York and North Carolina to formulate drugs targeted at specific cancer cells and disease-causing microorganisms. For their pioneering approach to drug

design and their development of numerous essential drugs, the two scientists, with British researcher Sir James Black (*q.v.*), were honoured with the 1988 Nobel Prize for Physiology or Medicine. The award was one of only a few in the history of the Nobel Prizes that had recognized researchers in the commercial drug industry.

Hitchings was born on April 18, 1905, in Hoquiam, Wash. He received his bachelor's and master's degrees from the University of Washington, and in 1933 he earned a Ph.D. in biochemistry from Harvard University, where he remained as an instructor until 1939. For three years he taught at Western Reserve University. In 1942 he joined the Burroughs Wellcome Research Laboratories in Tuckahoe, N.Y. He became emeritus scientist with the Wellcome Research Laboratories in Research Triangle Park, N.C., in 1975.

By designing compounds that interfered with the vital functions or replication of specific pathogens, Hitchings and Elion succeeded in developing drugs that combat some of mankind's most common diseases. In the 1950s they formulated thioguanine and 6-mercaptopurine (6MP), which proved effective in treating childhood leukemia. In 1957 they altered 6MP to produce a less toxic compound, azathioprine, which was used to treat various autoimmune disorders and to control rejection of transplanted organs. In the early 1960s, as a result of further work on 6MP, they created allopurinol, used to relieve gout, and later they invented the antimalarial drug pyrimethamine. They also developed trimethoprim, used to treat urinary- and respiratory-tract infections. In 1977 the researchers synthesized acyclovir, the first drug to prove effective against viral herpes. Other scientists used the principles established by Elion and Hitchings to formulate azidothymidine (AZT), the only drug approved in the U.S. as of 1988 for the treatment of AIDS.

(CAROLYN D. NEWTON)

Huber, Robert

From 1982 to 1985 West German biochemist Robert Huber, managing director of the Max Planck Institute for Biochemistry in Martinsried, West Germany, directed the structural analysis of a bacterial protein complex that has been called "the heart of photosynthesis." (Photosynthesis is the process by which green plants and certain other organisms harness the energy of sunlight to synthesize chemical compounds and carry out various life functions.) By 1985 Huber and two West German colleagues, Johann Deisenhofer and Hartmut Michel (*qq.v.*), had succeeded in describing the complete structure of the protein. For their accomplishment the three scientists received the 1988 Nobel Prize for Chemistry. Said the Nobel committee, "They are the first to succeed in unraveling the full details of how [such a] protein is built up, revealing the structure of the molecule atom by atom." Although the kind of photosynthesis that was studied by the three researchers is simpler than that in plants, the laureates' work helped scientists understand the mechanisms of photosynthesis in general.

Huber was born in Munich on Feb. 20, 1937, and received his doctorate from the Munich Technical University. In 1972 he took a position as head of the Max Planck Institute for Biochemistry in Martinsried, where he remained for four years. In 1976 he left to teach chemistry at the Technical University, returning to the institute in 1987.

Preparatory work for the prizewinning research was done by Michel, who isolated and crystallized the protein complex, a cluster of four individual proteins intertwined in a three-dimensional tangle. Then in 1982 Michel collaborated with Huber and Deisenhofer to analyze the protein's exact shape and pattern. The researchers were able to map the position of each atom within the complex by means of X-ray diffraction, a technique in which Huber was an internationally recognized expert. In this procedure scientists deduce the atomic structure of a

crystal by analyzing the manner in which the crystal's atoms scatter a beam of X-rays.

(CAROLYN D. NEWTON)

Itami, Juzo

Moviemaker Juzo Itami, like all Japanese, was preoccupied with death, food, sex, and money. After making his directorial debut at age 50, he attempted to revitalize Japanese cinema with these universal concerns. After finishing high school he became a boxer, a commercial designer, a translator, a TV documentarist, an essayist, an afternoon talk-show host, and eventually an actor. After the death of his father-in-law, he and his wife, Nobuko Miyamoto, had to learn how to conduct the complex ritual for a Japanese funeral. Inspired by this experience, he mortgaged his house to produce *The Funeral* (1984), an award-studded movie that satirized traditional taboos and shattered box-office records. His second effort, *Tampopo* (1986), was an amusing look at Japanese homage to food and the quest for the perfect bowl of *ramen* noodles.

His first two movies attracted the tax collectors, who took a huge chunk of his earnings. That experience inspired his third and fourth films, *A Taxing Woman*, I and II. Itami and Miyamoto did their homework well, hounding the tax office, recording statistics, and gathering sob stories and explanations. Both films were spiced with humour and the cold realities of life.

Itami, considered Japan's foremost film satirist, was born in Kyoto on May 15, 1933, the son of Mansaku Itami, pioneer director, scriptwriter, and film producer. Itami was so in awe of his father's talents that he could not believe he was sufficiently gifted to follow in his father's footsteps. Gradually, however, he gained confidence in a variety of movie roles in such foreign films as *5 Days in Peking* (1963) and *Lord Jim* (1965), in domestic movies, and in the TV superdrama "47 Ronin." Itami's attempt to produce movies in which the Japanese could see themselves as in a mirror fell short of expectations, he felt, because sometimes the messages were lost or distorted. His latest attraction was to horror films, which he called "pure cinema." He did not, however, direct his fifth film, *Sweet Home*—"a haunted house horror film." Future projects were to include a film about tragically funny misunderstandings born of Japanese and U.S. cultural differences.

Itami and his wife, 12 years his junior and heroine of all his movies, had two sons. At home Itami played the guitar, watched movies, and prepared his favourite foods with champagne and caviar. Somehow he also found time to produce 26 books, including 15 collections of essays, translations, and film diaries, as well as a book on French cuisine. (KAY K. TATEISHI)

Jakes, Milos

On Dec. 17, 1987, the Central Committee of the Communist Party of Czechoslovakia elected Milos Jakes to the most important job in the party—and therefore in Czechoslovakia—that of secretary-general. On Oct. 10, 1988, Jakes announced the resignation of Lubomir Strougal as prime minister and as a member of the Presidium, the inner circle of party leaders. Although Jakes had kind words for Strougal, Western observers believed that the two had been rivals for years. Both had achieved prominence after the Soviet invasion of 1968 ended the "Prague Spring" (which both called the "crisis period"), an experiment in radical relaxation of the party's control of cultural and economic matters. Neither wanted anything like a repetition of that experiment, but Strougal, in 1987, had worked with economists on a policy of reduced economic planning and greater reliance on market forces. Jakes, then chairman of the Central Committee's National Economic Committee, apparently assumed responsibility for implementing the new policy, but observers saw little real effort was being made. Thus Jakes seemed to be resisting Soviet leader Mikhail Gorbachev's policies of *glasnost* (openness) and *perestroika* (restructuring).

CAMERA PRESS/GLOBE PHOTOS

Jakes was born in Ceske Chalupy, Czech., on Aug. 12, 1922. He studied electrical engineering in Zlin (now Gottwaldov), becoming an apprentice engineer in 1937. In 1945 he joined the Communist Party, which was rapidly signing up new members, and became a leader at the local level. Later he studied at the College of Party Education in Moscow. He was an employee of the Central Committee of the Communist Party of Czechoslovakia (1958–63), chairman of the Central Administration for the Development of a Communal Economy (1963–66), deputy minister of the interior (1966–68), and chairman of the party's Central Control and Auditing Commission (1968–77). After the Soviet invasion, it was his commission that reviewed what party members had done during the "crisis period." Thousands were expelled. In 1977 Jakes joined the Central Committee and became chairman of its Committee on Agriculture and Food. He increased food production by promoting entrepreneurship without ending planning. As chairman of the National Economic Committee (1981–87), by contrast, he supervised a stagnant national economy.

(CHARLES JOHNSON TAGGART)

Jordan, Michael

Both literally and figuratively, Michael Jordan has soared higher than any basketball guard before him. His leaping drives to the basket elevated the National Basketball Association with him. More than merely the league's most valuable player in 1987–88, he was "Air Jordan," the headliner who combined the heat of exciting performance with the coolness of class personality. After only four professional seasons, the Chicago Bulls' 1.98-m (6-ft 6-in), 89.9-kg (198-lb) dynamo was perhaps the most recognized U.S. athlete.

Jordan performed his high-wire act not only without a net but also without a wire. He had won two NBA Slam Dunk championships and divided the prize money among his teammates. His midair blend of ballet and ballistic "just happens," Jordan said, declaring that he did not plan or practice it. "If I thought about a move, I'd probably make a turnover. I just look at a situation in the air, adjust, create, and let instinct take over."

No NBA player besides 2.18-m (7-ft 2-in) centre Wilt Chamberlain had ever scored 3,000 points in a season before Jordan did it in 1986–87, averaging 37.1 points a game. He set a league record April 16, 1987, by scoring 23 consecutive points against Atlanta. He led the league again with 35 points a game in 1987–88, when he failed to score more than 20 points in only 3 of 82 games. Jordan was much more than a scoring machine, however. "Every time you see

him, he does something different," Sacramento coach Jerry Reynolds said.

No NBA player had blocked more than 100 shots and stolen more than 200 balls in the same season until Jordan did so in 1986–87. He repeated these achievements in the 1987–88 season, when his 259 steals (3.2 per game) led the league and his 131 blocked shots (1.6 per game) led the team. He became the second NBA scoring champion ever to make the league's all-defense team, which he said meant more to him than his second straight appearance on the all-NBA team. In addition he was voted most valuable player of the All-Star game, in which he led both teams with 40 points and four blocked shots. As Jordan kept getting improbably better, the Bulls improved their won-lost record by at least ten games in each of his first three full seasons.

Jordan was born Feb. 17, 1963, in Brooklyn, N.Y., but grew up in Wilmington, N.C., where he did not make Laney High School's varsity basketball team until his junior year. In college he made the winning shot for North Carolina in the 1982 national championship game. He was All-America the next two seasons and left school after his junior year, leading the U.S. basketball team to a gold medal in the Olympic Games before joining the Bulls in 1984.

(KEVIN M. LAMB)

Kennedy, Anthony

He lacked sex appeal. That, in essence, was how many conservatives felt about Arthur Kennedy when Pres. Ronald Reagan nominated him to the U.S. Supreme Court in November 1987. While his decisions and written opinions as a federal appeals judge in California were generally regarded as conservative, he personally did not show the ideological fervour for conservative political and legal causes that characterized Robert Bork, Reagan's first choice for the court vacancy, who was rejected by the Senate 58–42 just weeks before Kennedy's nomination. Nevertheless, Kennedy's reputed pragmatism and open-mindedness helped make him acceptable to Senate liberals and moderates, who, in February 1988, joined their colleagues in approving him 97–0.

To the relief of the right, the new associate justice—who had been dubbed "Bork without a bite" during the confirmation hearings—proved consistently, if quietly, conservative during his first months on the job, joining the other two Reagan appointees and Justice Byron White in eight of nine 5–4 votes. His most significant vote enabled the court to order new arguments on whether it should overturn a 1976 civil rights decision that permitted minorities to use a Reconstruction law as a remedy against private acts of discrimination. Kennedy's voting fed the conservatives' hope—and the liberals' fear—that the court was shifting farther to the right.

Kennedy was born in Sacramento, Calif., on July 23, 1936. According to one of his friends, "When we were growing up, if any of us were going to do something naughty, Tony would go home." Indeed, the young Kennedy was so quiet and studious that his flamboyant father—a lawyer and lobbyist, a devout churchgoer, and a dedicated poker player—once offered him $100 if he could get himself arrested.

Rather than break the law, Kennedy broke into law in the early 1960s. After two years with a law firm in San Francisco, the Harvard University graduate returned to Sacramento to take over his father's law practice. He was a success, though colleagues said that the intellectual Kennedy abhorred the glad-handing and backslapping required for the firm's lobbying work. In the early 1970s he drafted the tax-limitation initiative known as Proposition 1 for California Gov. Ronald Reagan. Appreciating his work, the governor later recommended him to Pres. Gerald Ford, who appointed Kennedy to a seat on the U.S. Court of Appeals for the Ninth Circuit in 1976. He remained there until his appointment to the Supreme Court.

(MICHAEL AMEDEO)

Lawson, Nigel Thomas

During 1988 the success or failure of Margaret Thatcher's third term as U.K. Conservative prime minister depended in large measure on the performance of her chancellor of the Exchequer, Nigel Lawson. On March 15 he unveiled a bold budget, reforming personal taxation. (He had reformed company taxation in his 1984 budget.) Lawson's measures included a reduction in the standard rate of income tax from 27 to 25% and a cut in the top rate from 60 to 40%. Critics accused him of giving money to the rich rather than using it to alleviate poverty or tackle social problems. Lawson, however, said that the extra incentives to high-earners would do the economy more good and eventually generate a higher tax yield.

The fact that Lawson was able to cut taxes at all owed much to the buoyancy of the U.K. economy, which was growing at more than 4% a year. Lawson, who had been chancellor since 1983, was widely credited by other Conservatives for this achievement—as he had been for delivering higher output and lower unemployment in 1986 and 1987, thus helping the Conservatives to win their third consecutive election victory in June 1987. The corollary of this, however, was that Lawson would get the blame if the economy turned sour. By the summer of 1988 there were clear danger signs. Inflation was starting to rise, and Britain's trade deficit was growing alarmingly. It seemed that the buoyancy of the economy was being generated in part by a massive credit expansion, itself a product of earlier Lawson measures to liberalize the operations of London's financial markets. Lawson pushed base interest rates up, in a series of steps, from 7 to 12% in hopes of preventing the economy from overheating. As 1988 ended, it was unclear whether the chancellor would achieve a "soft landing" for the economy or whether it would dive into recession.

Lawson was born on March 11, 1932, in Hampstead, north London. He won a first-class degree at Christ Church, Oxford, and worked subsequently as a financial journalist on the *Financial Times* and *Sunday Telegraph*. Lawson edited the weekly political magazine *Spectator* from 1966 to 1970. He entered the House of Commons in 1974, where he quickly established a reputation as one of the brightest and most confident, but also most abrasive and sometimes arrogant, of Conservative MPs.

(PETER KELLNER)

Lederman, Leon Max

From 1960 to 1962, while affiliated with New York City's Columbia University, U.S. physicist Leon Lederman and two colleagues, Melvin Schwartz and Jack Steinberger (*qq.v.*), conducted a landmark experiment in particle physics. The results of their work, done at the Brookhaven National Laboratory on Long Island, N.Y., were to have far-reaching consequences in the research and theory of their field. In order to carry out the experiment, the three scientists devised a method for producing the first laboratory-made beam of high-energy neutrinos—elusive subatomic particles that have no detectable mass and no electric charge and that travel at the speed of light. Such high-energy neutrino beams became a basic research tool in the study of subatomic particles and nuclear forces. During the course of their experiment, the researchers also identified a previously unknown type of neutrino. This discovery played a central role in the formulation of the currently accepted theory describing the relationships between the various fundamental particles that make up all matter.

More than two decades later, in 1988, the Royal Swedish Academy of Sciences recognized the ground-breaking achievements of Lederman and his co-workers by awarding them the Nobel Prize for Physics. The laureates were cited both for their development of a method for producing high-energy neutrinos in the laboratory and for their discovery of the new neutrino.

Lederman was born in New York City on July 15, 1922. He received his doctorate in physics from Columbia University in 1951 and joined the faculty at Columbia, where he was a full professor from 1958. Lederman also served as U.S. representative to the International Committee on Future Accelerators and, from 1967 to 1970, as a member of the high-energy-physics advisory panel to the Atomic Energy Commission. He was director of Nevis Laboratories in Irvington, N.Y., from 1962 to 1979. From 1979 he was director of the Fermi National Accelerator Laboratory in Batavia, Ill. In recent years he outspokenly supported construction in the U.S. of the Superconducting Super Collider, planned as the largest accelerator ring ever built.

The Brookhaven experiment was designed to answer a critical question in particle physics. It already had been known that when neutrinos interact with matter, they may create either of two types of particles: electrons (fundamental particles with a negative electric charge) or electron-like particles known as muons (mu mesons). It was not clear, however, whether this fact necessarily indicated the existence of two distinct types of neutrinos. The laureates' work established that this was indeed the case. By virtue of their association with the muons seen in neutrino-matter interactions, the new neutrinos were named muon neutrinos.

Discovery of the muon neutrino led theorists to hypothesize a number of different particle "families" within the world of subatomic particles. Theorists used these family classifications to develop a scheme, called the standard model, for classifying all fundamental particles.

(CAROLYN D. NEWTON)

Lee Teng-hui

Lee Teng-hui became the first native Taiwanese to head the Republic of China government in Taiwan when he succeeded Chiang Ching-kuo (*see* OBITUARIES) as president when the latter died on Jan. 13, 1988. Lee also became acting chairman of the ruling party, the Kuomintang (KMT). His election as KMT chairman at the party's 13th congress in July further strengthened his position. Popular and well respected by virtually all segments of society, Lee carried on his predecessor's democratic reforms and anti-Communist policies. He promoted parliamentary reforms designed to rejuvenate the legislature and urged a more flexible approach when dealing with political and diplomatic challenges. Lee brought Taiwan back into such international organizations as the Asian Development Bank. He also facilitated travel to China for family reunions and promoted more people-to-people contacts with the mainland in such fields as trade, culture, and sports. All the while, Taiwan continued to enjoy steady economic growth and ever greater democracy.

Born near Tamsui, Taiwan, on Jan. 15, 1923, Lee belonged to a Hakka family whose ancestors came from Fujian (Fukien) Province. He received his Ph.D. in agricultural economics from Cornell University, Ithaca, N.Y., in 1968. As a professor at National Taiwan and Chengchi universities and in various important capacities at the Joint Commission on Rural Reconstruction, he contributed much to Taiwan's agricultural development. He promoted farmers' associations, irrigation systems, agricultural mechanization, and the Agricultural Development Act, which balanced agricultural and industrial development. As mayor of Taipei (1978–81) and governor of Taiwan Province (1981–84), he carried out the construction of freeways and reservoirs, oversaw the modernization of sewage disposal, introduced regional planning and agricultural reforms, and contributed greatly to the renovation of rural villages. Enjoying strong U.S. support, Lee upheld the one-China policy and opposed the independence of Taiwan. Firmly committed to Taiwan's security and welfare and to the rule of law, Lee steadfastly rejected the Chinese Communist formula for reunification— "one country, two systems"—insisting that Taiwan and the mainland should be reunited eventually on the basis of freedom, democracy, and an equitable distribution of wealth.

(WINSTON L. Y. YANG)

Lefebvre, Archbishop Marcel

Archbishop Marcel Lefebvre ordained four bishops on June 30, 1988, against the wishes of the Vatican. He was automatically excommunicated. He and his followers were thus in a state of schism—cut off from communion with the Roman Catholic Church.

Lefebvre was born Nov. 29, 1905, in Turcoing, northern France. Ordained priest in 1929, he joined a missionary order, the Holy Ghost Fathers, and worked in Libreville, Gabon, as a theology teacher. He was a Vatican diplomat in West Africa and (1952–62) the first archbishop of Dakar in Senegal. Present at the second Vatican Council (1962–65) as superior general of his order, he was one of the leaders of the minority. The chapter of the Holy Ghost Fathers insisted on his resignation in 1968.

Lefebvre then began a new free-lance life as the outspoken champion of the defeated minority of Vatican II. In 1970 he established a seminary at Ecône in Switzerland, where he denounced the council's openness to the modern world. His tone became increasingly strident. He held that the values of the French Revolution had invaded the church: liberty was expressed in the pernicious doctrine of religious liberty; equality in the notion of collegiality, which undermined—he said—papal primacy; and fraternity in ecumenism, which blurred important distinctions between Christians. Sometimes Freemasonry or Marxism was named as the villain of the piece.

On June 29, 1976, Lefebvre ordained 13 priests at Ecône and was "suspended"—a technical term meaning that from then on his sacramental acts would be illicit. But he was not deterred and was optimistic at first about Pope John Paul II, whom he met early in the new pontificate. Protracted negotiations with Joseph Cardinal Ratzinger (1984–87) suggested that the Vatican was ready to make concessions to him. In 1984 permission was given for mass to be celebrated according to the 1962 missal. This especially worried the French bishops, who had to struggle to defend the liturgy of Vatican II.

By May 1988 Lefebvre had before him an agreement that gave him almost all he wanted. He signed it—and then reneged the next day. From then on schism was inevitable. It was the first schism to be seen on television. Some of his followers drifted back to Rome, encouraged by the Vatican's generous treatment of them. Lefebvre and his hard-line followers were increasingly isolated, and no one knew what would happen to the movement after his death.

(PETER HEBBLETHWAITE)

Li Peng

China's economic problems reached crisis proportions in 1988 about the time Li Peng (Li P'eng) was officially promoted from acting to full-fledged premier. Soaring inflation (as high as 40% in some cities), widespread corruption, nepotism, and bureaucratic inefficiency forced Chinese leaders into confrontation over the direction of economic policy. The clash of wills enhanced Li's influence and reduced the authority of Zhao Ziyang (Chao Tzu-yang), the Communist Party general secretary and the protégé of China's paramount leader, Deng Xiaoping (Teng Hsiao-p'ing). The leadership eventually adopted Li's more measured approaches to cope with inflation and other economic problems and rejected Zhao's sweeping restructuring of the economy. Zhao had favoured an aggressive strategy of economic change, including decontrol of prices to allow market forces to play a larger role in the distribution of goods and services. He also urged devaluation of the artificially overvalued Chinese currency, rapid economic development of coastal provinces, and greater private ownership to make China's lumbering economy more efficient. The speed and radical nature of these changes created social unrest, inflation, and industrial strikes. Li's go-slow approach called for continued price controls on certain commodities, reduced local economic autonomy, agricultural sufficiency, and measures to curb inflation. These included

higher interest rates, a tightening of the money supply, and public spending cutbacks. Food shortages forced officials in some cities to adopt rationing. The role of the free market and local economic decision making thus suffered serious setbacks under Li's leadership.

Born in Chengtu (Ch'eng-tu), Sichuan (Szechwan) Province, in 1928, Li Peng joined the Communist Party in 1945 and attended the Moscow Power Institute in the early 1950s. In 1979 he was appointed vice-minister of China's power industry. Elected to the party's Central Committee in 1982, he became vice-premier in 1983 in charge of education, energy, transportation, and economic development. He was elected to the Secretariat of the party's Central Committee and the ruling Political Bureau in 1985 and to the Standing Committee of the Political Bureau in 1987. Li was expected to play an important role in the planned 1989 Chinese-Soviet summit meeting, the first such in almost 30 years.   (WINSTON L. Y. YANG)

Ligachev, Egor Kuzmich
Regarded as a conservative brake on Soviet leader Mikhail Gorbachev's ambitious plans for radical political and economic reform in the Soviet Union, Egor Ligachev was demoted by the plenum of the Central Committee (CC) of the Communist Party of the Soviet Union (CPSU) of Sept. 30–Oct. 1, 1988. His loss was underlined at the 71st anniversary celebrations of the October Revolution on November 7 when Gorbachev, Premier Nikolay Ryzhkov, and Moscow party boss Lev Zaikov formed the top trio.

Ligachev, a Russian, was born on Nov. 29, 1920. After graduating from the Moscow Aviation Institute in 1943, he joined the CPSU in 1944. From 1943 to 1949 he worked as an engineer, and in the latter year he became a party official in Novosibirsk. He held a variety of party and government posts in Novosibirsk and Tomsk, rising in rank until in 1983 he was named secretary of the CC Secretariat. In 1985 he became a member of the Politburo. In December 1987 Ligachev stated that he chaired meetings of the CC Secretariat and Gorbachev those of the Politburo. This confirmed his status as second in command in the U.S.S.R. only to Gorbachev.

Under Gorbachev, Ligachev consistently espoused a less radical approach to reform. A particular target was the media, especially the outspoken *Moscow News*. When Gorbachev was on holiday in the summer of 1987, Ligachev seized the opportunity, together with the then head of the KGB, Gen. Viktor Chebrikov, to sound a warning against too radical change. Ligachev played a leading role in the dismissal of Boris Yeltsin, the aggressive pro-radical-reform first party secretary of Moscow. Subsequently, a violent altercation took place between the two at the CC plenum in November 1987. Whereas Yeltsin castigated party officials for their privileges and abuse of power, Ligachev denied that they enjoyed any privileges.

CAMERA PRESS/GLOBE PHOTOS

In August 1988 Ligachev, again while Gorbachev was on holiday, once more warned against the danger of radical reform. However, when Ligachev himself was on holiday in September 1988, Gorbachev called a CC plenum and pushed through drastic personnel changes. Ligachev was caught off guard and was made chairman of the CC commission on agrarian affairs.   (MARTIN MCCAULEY)

Lorenzo, Frank
Frank Lorenzo found himself in 1988 at the centre of an ongoing controversy that had started in the early 1980s. As chairman of Houston-based Texas Air Corp. (TAC), which owned Eastern Airlines, and with his reputation well established as a hard-nosed union buster, Lorenzo was embroiled in a bitter fight with the International Association of Machinists, the union whose members serviced Eastern's jets. By midyear both Lorenzo and TAC had undergone investigations by the U.S. Transportation Department, and the Federal Aviation Administration had proposed fining Eastern $823,500 for safety violations.

Born in New York City on May 19, 1940, Francisco Anthony Lorenzo grew up in the borough of Queens. His father, a hairdresser and beauty shop owner, and his mother had emigrated from Spain. Lorenzo earned a B.A. in economics from Columbia University, New York City, in 1961 and an M.B.A. from Harvard in 1963. From 1963 to 1965 he worked as a financial analyst for TWA, and he was manager of the financial analysis department at Eastern Airlines from 1965 to 1966.

With a former Harvard Business School classmate, Robert J. Carney, he formed an airline consulting firm, Lorenzo, Carney & Co., and in 1969 they set up Jet Capital, a holding company with Lorenzo as chairman. In 1971 Jet Capital devised a recapitalization program that saved Texas International Airlines (TIA) from going bankrupt, and by August 1972 Lorenzo had become TIA's president and chief executive officer. In 1977 Lorenzo instituted what he called "peanut fares." These half-price fares, which nearly quadrupled TIA's earnings by mid-1978, were instrumental in radically changing the industry's rate structure.

Lorenzo wasted no time in taking advantage of the new climate in the industry following passage of the Airline Deregulation Act of 1978. In June 1980 he formed TAC, and in September he announced the creation of a subsidiary, New York Air, a shuttle carrier service. In October 1981 he won control of Continental Airlines, merging it with TAC in October 1982 and laying off 15% of its work force in March 1983; on Sept. 24, 1983, he announced that Continental was seeking reorganization under federal bankruptcy laws. After returning Continental to profitability, he acquired Eastern Airlines in November 1986, and with the purchase of People Express in December 1986, he had captured 20.1% of the U.S. market.
                    (EDWARD PAUL MORAGNE)

Louganis, Greg
When Greg Louganis retired from competitive diving after 13 years, there were flecks of gray at his temples and a blizzard of gold on his résumé. He had won 47 national championships and 13 championships in world competitions. His last victories, in the 3-m springboard and 10-m platform at the 1988 Olympic Games in Seoul, South Korea, made him the first man ever to win both gold medals in successive Olympics. It was the fifth time he had taken both golds in Olympic, World Cup, or world championship competition, something no man had done until Louganis did it first in 1982.

At 28, Louganis planned to move to lower and brighter stages. He performed as a stand-up comedian a few days after the Olympics in September. He had studied acting for nine years and was well-reviewed in his modern dance and jazz debut in October 1987, 24 years after he began studying dance at age three.

His dancing, tumbling, and acrobatics train-

ing as a child made Louganis a distinctively graceful diver who leaped higher than most divers, twisted his body through apparently effortless airborne contortions, and landed with no more than a trace of a splash. Unbeatable as he seemed, however, he had to win his last Olympic springboard title less than 24 hours after banging the back of his head on the diving board.

"It shook my confidence a lot," Louganis said, but Gregory Louganis already had overcome so much. He was the son of unmarried high-school students, born Jan. 29, 1960, and adopted nine months later by Frances and Peter Louganis. As a child he suffered from dyslexia and stuttering and was subjected to racial taunts because of his dark skin (his biologic father was Samoan). As an adult he conquered alcoholism. As a competitor he was kept out of the 1980 Olympics by his country's boycott.

Louganis's first coach was former Olympic champion Sammy Lee. In 1976, at 16, Louganis won an Olympic silver medal in the platform. After enrolling at the University of Miami, Fla., for its drama program, he transferred in 1981 to the University of California at Irvine, closer to his home in the San Diego suburb of El Cajon and to the Mission Viejo club, where Ron O'Brien became his coach.

In 1983 Louganis set 3-m springboard records with a 99-point dive and 755.49-point total. His platform record of 717.41 points came in 1986. He won the Jesse Owens International Trophy as amateur athlete of the year in 1987, and he had won 118 of 151 major events when he hit his head on the board in the Olympic competition.

With five stitches in his head, Louganis won his second Olympic springboard gold on September 20. One week later, in the platform final, he needed an impressive 85.57 points on his last dive to win another gold. He scored 86.70.   (KEVIN M. LAMB)

McCarthy, William Joseph
In Washington, D.C., on July 15, 1988, William J. McCarthy emerged from a meeting of the General Executive Board (GEB) of the International Brotherhood of Teamsters, Chauffeurs, Warehousemen and Helpers of America and told reporters that the GEB had elected him to finish the term—ending in 1991—of Jackie Presser (*see* OBITUARIES) as president of the union. The announcement was a surprise because reporters had expected the GEB to elect Weldon Mathis, who was secretary-treasurer, acting president, and an ally of Presser. The reporters' next surprise came when one of them asked McCarthy how the GEB had divided between him and Mathis, and McCarthy said it was none of the reporter's business. This was a marked change from the style of Presser, who had cherished good public relations—but had been unable to overcome the Teamsters' reputation as a corrupt union with ties to organized crime. On June 28 Rudolph Giuliani (*q.v.*), U.S. attorney for the Southern District of New York, had sued Presser, Mathis, McCarthy, and the other 15 members of the GEB for corruption. At the time of his death on July 9, Presser had been under indictment for ghost employment.

McCarthy, after assuming his new office, fired John Climaco, a close associate of Presser and Mathis, as the union's general counsel. He also held discussions on how to democratize the Teamsters, one of a minority of unions in North America in which officers were not elected directly and served five years, the longest term allowed by U.S. law. The decision of a majority of the union members who returned mail ballots to endorse George Bush for U.S. president was seen as a victory for McCarthy, a Bostonian who was opposed to Michael Dukakis.

McCarthy was born in Boston on July 2, 1919. He joined the Teamsters at the age of 17, becoming a shop steward in 1941, business agent of Teamsters Local 25 in Boston in 1947, and president of Local 25 in 1955. He held that job while rising both in the International and in a federation of locals in New England called

AP/WIDE WORLD

Joint Council 10. In 1969 he became a member of the GEB and in 1971 vice-president of the International. Trucking executives who bargained with him learned to respect his toughness. He was believed to have opposed two agreements made by the Presser-Mathis leadership with national organizations of truckers early in 1988. The agreements were defended as necessary in a deregulated market but had little support from members. (CHARLES JOHNSON TAGGART)

Mahfouz, Naguib
A man who once called himself "a fourth- or fifth-rate writer" was awarded the 1988 Nobel Prize for Literature. Naguib Mahfouz, a 77-year-old Egyptian novelist, playwright, and screenwriter, was the first Arabic writer to receive the coveted literary award. His books describe the search for human values in settings as diverse as the ancient Nile Delta of the pharaohs and the back alleys of modern Cairo. The Nobel academy praised him as an author whose work is "rich in nuance—now clear-sightedly realistic, now evocatively ambiguous . . . an Arabian narrative art that applies to all mankind. . . . His work speaks to us all."

Egyptian officials had not always agreed, banning his books for a time because of Mahfouz's outspoken support of the late Pres. Anwar as-Sadat's peace treaty with Israel. Particular works—*The Thief and the Dogs* (1961), *Chatting on the Nile* (1966), and *Miramar* (1967)—not only attacked the military coup that brought Gamal Abdel Nasser to power in 1952 but also dealt with social issues involving women and political prisoners. *Children of Gebelawi* (1959) remained banned because of its controversial treatment of religion.

Nevertheless, he was a popular writer who masterfully expressed the rhythms of city life and broad social concerns. A prime example of his novellas is *A Houseboat on the Nile* (1966). His achievement as a short-story writer is clearly demonstrated in *God's World* (1973). About a dozen of Mahfouz's books were translated into English, although not all remained in print. He had written some 40 novels and short-story collections, as well as several plays and more than 30 screenplays.

Despite past controversies over his work, Egypt's leaders hailed Mahfouz's selection. The choice was also applauded by Israeli officials, who considered Mahfouz a good neighbour. His monumental masterwork, *The Cairo Trilogy* (1956–57), had been translated into Hebrew and published in Israel. This depiction of Cairo, which established Mahfouz's reputation as a writer, had been compared to Dickens's London.

Mahfouz was born in Cairo on Dec. 11, 1911, and worked in the cultural section of the Egyptian civil service from 1934 to 1971, when he retired. After the Nobel announcement, requests for rights to translate his works were received from around the world. Unable to travel to Stockholm to receive the award because of poor health, Mahfouz nevertheless said, "If the urge to write should ever leave me, I want that day to be my last." (BONNIE OBERMAN)

Mayor Zaragoza, Federico
At the end of 1987, Federico Mayor Zaragoza, a 53-year-old Spanish biochemist and intellectual, took over as director general of the United Nations Educational, Scientific and Cultural Organization (Unesco). He replaced Amadou Mahtar M'Bow of Senegal, who, after 13 years at the helm, was accused of politicizing Unesco and leading an anti-Western campaign. During M'Bow's term Western nations had been pitted against third world countries over innumerable issues, and the U.S., Britain, and Singapore had left the organization.

Born Jan. 27, 1934, in Barcelona, Mayor earned his doctorate in pharmacology at the University of Madrid in 1958. After studying biochemistry at Trinity College, Oxford, in 1966–67, he engaged in research for several years. In 1974–75 he served as Spain's under secretary for education and science and became founding director of the Severo Ochoa Centre of Molecular Biology at the Autonomous University of Madrid. He was elected to the Cortes (parliament) in 1977 and named chairman of the education and science commission of the Chamber of Deputies as well as an adviser on such matters to the prime minister. He joined Unesco as M'Bow's chief deputy in 1978. After three years he resigned as a result of irreconcilable differences with the Senegalese director, although he acted as special adviser to M'Bow in 1983–84.

As early as 1986, Mayor had described his plan for restructuring Unesco. He felt the organization should concentrate on a few major global programs while cooperating with individual governments or regions in the fields of science, education, and culture. To be nominated to the directorship, Mayor battled through five ballots in Unesco's 50-member executive board, but he was confirmed with an overwhelming 142 votes in the 158-member-state general convention. While the new leader was friendly toward the West, as of mid-1988 critics saw an unchanged program and asserted that Mayor was moving too slowly and timidly in cleaning up Unesco's administration. Defenders said he was moving as quickly as possible to remake what had become a personal fiefdom into an organization intent on upholding its charter. It remained to be seen whether Mayor could accomplish his goals: the prompt return of countries that had withdrawn; the restoration of Unesco's original principles; the restructuring of management; and, perhaps most important, the rejuvenation of a greatly demoralized staff. (BONNIE OBERMAN)

Michel, Hartmut
Three West German biochemists—Johann Deisenhofer, Robert Huber (qq.v.), and Hartmut Michel—were awarded the 1988 Nobel Prize for Chemistry for deciphering the atom-by-atom structure of a protein complex, called a photosynthetic reaction centre, that is crucial to the process of photosynthesis in certain bacteria. It is by means of photosynthesis that green plants and certain other organisms convert the radiant energy of sunlight to the chemical energy needed to carry out various life processes. The three scientists arrived at their results in 1985, but it was Michel's preliminary work, carried out over the four-year period from 1978 to 1982, that cleared the way for the scientists' award-winning achievement.

Michel eliminated the greatest technical hurdle of the project by developing a means of isolating and crystallizing the protein complex, an accomplishment previously considered impossible by many scientists. Putting the protein into the form of large, well-ordered crystals enabled researchers for the first time to analyze the reaction centre's structure. From 1982 to 1985 Michel collaborated with Deisenhofer and Huber to map, by means of X-ray diffraction, the locations of the thousands of atoms making up the protein. They also pointed out similarities between the bacterial reaction centre and the comparatively more complex photosynthetic system of plants, thus adding to scientific knowledge of the nature of photosynthesis in general.

Michel was born in Ludwigsburg, West Germany, on July 18, 1948. He received his doctorate in 1977 from the University of Würzburg. In 1979 Michel joined the research staff at the Max Planck Institute for Biochemistry in Martinsried, where he did his prizewinning work. In 1987 he became head of the institute's new division for biophysics in Frankfurt am Main. (CAROLYN D. NEWTON)

Miller, Jonathan Wolfe
The often-heard description of Jonathan Miller—actor, man of letters, director of dramatic and music theatre, TV producer and presenter, and doctor of medicine (who qualified, after graduating from St. John's College, Cambridge, in 1959)—as a "Renaissance man" was no exaggeration. His career in medicine and the arts culminated in 1988 in his becoming artistic director of the Old Vic, at the invitation of its Canadian owner, Ed Mirvish.

After a spell in the doldrums, this historic playhouse was regaining its former glowing reputation, thanks largely to his efforts. He had added to its lustre in earlier years when, under Laurence Olivier, he directed such star-spangled National Theatre plays as *The Merchant of Venice* (1970). After the company moved to the South Bank, he staged a colourful *The Marriage of Figaro* (1974) during his three-year period as associate director.

His first season at the Old Vic was largely successful. Miller blamed the failure of any new work on the philistinism of the audience and the mistaken notion that what tourists liked was what counted. Despite poor audiences, his spectacular production of Racine's *Andromache* achieved recognition in the form of *Drama* magazine's Best Designer award for scene designer Richard Hudson. The controversial penultimate item, his "anticolonialist" staging of *The Tempest*, with black actors and singers as the "natives" and Swedish star Max von Sydow as Prospero, was an echo of an earlier experiment at the Mermaid Theatre in 1970. Nothing daunted, Miller followed the year's closing production, the guest visit of the Scottish Opera's *Candide* by Leonard Bernstein, which he and John Wells had staged, with news of an even more adventurous program for 1989. It was to open with *King Lear*, directed by himself, and end with a new production of Wedekind's erotic *Lulu*, staged by Anglo-German directorial whiz kid Peter Zadek.

LIONEL CHERRUAULT—CAMERA PRESS/GLOBE PHOTOS

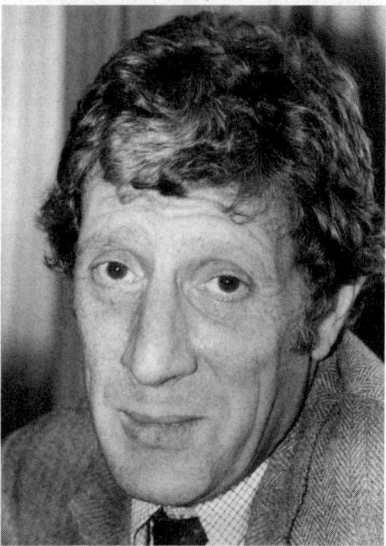

Born in London on July 21, 1934, Miller was the son of a surgeon father and a novelist mother (Betty Bergson). He made his professional stage debut at the Edinburgh Festival in 1961 as actor and coauthor in the satirical review *Beyond the Fringe.* Miller prided himself on the intellectual interests of a Cambridge graduate, who could write a learned treatise as readily as he could stage a play or create a TV program like *The Body in Question,* a history of medicine that became a best-selling book. His musical theatre work took him all over Britain—to Kent Opera, to Glyndebourne, and to the English National Opera, where he was associate director—as well as to Italy, Germany, and Los Angeles, where he planned to do Kurt Weill's *Mahagonny* in 1989.

(OSSIA TRILLING)

Mitterrand, François Maurice

When François Mitterrand defeated Prime Minister Jacques Chirac to win reelection to the French presidency on May 8, 1988, he accomplished a feat that only Charles de Gaulle had previously achieved in 1965. And when he named Michel Rocard (*q.v.*), his chief rival within the Socialist Party and partisan of a "renewed" socialism, as the new prime minister, he surprised no one. In the first months of his second seven-year term, Mitterrand sought to establish France as a leader in the European Communities (EC), improve relations with the Soviet Union, and build a stronger political alliance with other EC countries, particularly West Germany.

The year 1981 had constituted a turning point in French history when, after 23 years of uninterrupted rule by right-wing Gaullist politicians, Mitterrand became the first Socialist president. In his first term Mitterrand tried to gain the confidence of his often skeptical critics and prove his stature as a world statesman. He initiated the nationalization of several industries, notably banking; increased government social spending; worked more closely than his predecessors with NATO; and decentralized the rigid French system of local government. Mitterrand called legislative elections soon after his victory, and a new leftist majority in the National Assembly made it possible for Prime Minister Pierre Mauroy to put into effect the reforms Mitterrand promised. The economy declined, however, and the government devalued the franc three times in the first three years. In July 1984 Mitterrand chose Laurent Fabius to replace Mauroy as prime minister and moved the country toward greater austerity. Although Mitterrand had for the first time included Communists in the government in 1981, this change in policy contributed to a split in the "union of the left" that he had engineered, and the four Communist ministers resigned. In the legislative elections of March 1986, the parties of the right seized control of the National Assembly and established an unprecedented "cohabitation" of a leftist president and a right-wing prime minister, Chirac. This often awkward situation lasted until May 1988, when the newly reelected Mitterrand again called elections and the Socialists regained a working majority.

Mitterrand was born into a bourgeois family on Oct. 26, 1916, at Jarnac (Charente). He represented Nièvre in the National Assembly (1946–58, 1962–81) and the Senate (1959–62), and from 1959 to 1981 he served as mayor of Chateau-Chinon. After a brilliant ministerial career under the Fourth Republic, Mitterrand ran against President de Gaulle in 1965, forcing an unexpected runoff. In 1966 Mitterrand dominated the Federation of the Democratic and Socialist Left, and when that coalition failed he was chosen to lead the Socialists. By 1981 he had transformed the formerly unimportant Socialist Party into a political force, replacing the Communists as the majority party of the left.

(JEAN KNECHT)

Morrison, Toni

In April 1988, when it was announced that *Beloved,* the story of a group of slaves struggling to survive before and after the U.S. Civil War, had won the 1987 Pulitzer Prize for fiction, author Toni Morrison could not say it was a dream come true. She began writing in the 1960s only because she felt stifled by her marriage. She did not imagine then that the outcome would be best-selling novels with a strong impact on the literary scene.

Morrison was born Chloe Anthony Wofford on Feb. 18, 1931, in Lorain, Ohio. In 1949, after graduating from high school with honours, she attended Howard University, Washington, D.C., and received her B.A. degree in 1953. She then enrolled at Cornell University, Ithaca, N.Y., for graduate work in English, receiving a master's degree in 1955. After teaching English "theory, pronunciation, and grammar" to undergraduates at Texas Southern University for two years, she became an English instructor at Howard University in 1957.

During her tenure at Howard, she married Jamaican architect Howard Morrison. In 1964 she got a divorce, resigned from Howard University, and moved with her two children to Syracuse, N.Y., where she took a job as a textbook editor for a subsidiary of Random House. By 1967 Morrison was a senior editor at Random House, editing, on the average, six or seven books a year, including the autobiographies of boxer Muhammed Ali and black activist Angela Davis.

The Bluest Eye, Morrison's first novel, was published in 1969 and received good reviews. It was followed in 1973 by *Sula,* published also in condensed form in *Redbook* and nominated for the 1975 National Book Award in the fiction category. *Song of Solomon* (1977) became a best-seller, won the National Book Critics Circle Award for fiction in 1978, and was the first novel written by a black author to be chosen as a full selection of the Book-of-the-Month Club since Richard Wright's *Native Son.* Morrison's fourth novel, *Tar Baby* (1981), got its author on the cover of *Newsweek.* In addition to winning the Pulitzer Prize, *Beloved* was nominated for the National Book Award, the National Book Critics Circle Award, and the Ritz Hemingway Award. Morrison had also written one play, *Dreaming Emmett.*

(EDWARD PAUL MORAGNE)

Namaliu, Rabbie

In July 1988 Rabbie Namaliu became Papua New Guinea's fourth prime minister since independence. His rise to power had its origins in the instability of the government of Prime Minister Paias Wingti, which had been weakened by internal divisions and embarrassed by a major timber scandal. In connection with the latter, a Commission of Inquiry announced findings of corruption and perjury against Ted Diro, former commander of the military forces and, as leader of the People's Action Party, a coalition partner of Wingti.

Faced by a vote of no confidence and the defection of Diro and his supporters, Wingti tried to form a coalition with Michael Somare, the nation's first prime minister. This failed; Somare retired and was replaced as leader of the Pangu Pati by Namaliu. A further attempt by Wingti to join with the Pangu Pati also failed, and on July 4, a little more than one week after becoming leader of the opposition, Namaliu was sworn in as prime minister.

Namaliu's two main objectives were to secure constitutional amendments that would help to generate stability in the nation's politics—a move that had the full support of the parliamentary opposition—and a renewed attempt to grapple with the country's law and order problem. In his first weeks of office, Namaliu appointed a committee of ministers to investigate the broad policy issues of law and order, initiated legislation that would broaden the powers of district courts, and established an anticorruption force. He declared his support for capital punishment for major crimes and justified this viewpoint in terms of traditional law.

Namaliu was born in 1947 on the island of New Britain in the Bismarck Archipelago. He graduated from the University of Papua New Guinea in 1970 and then received a master's degree from the University of Victoria, British Columbia. He returned briefly to the University of Papua New Guinea but soon moved into the political arena with his appointment as principal private secretary to Somare, then chief minister and later prime minister of Papua New Guinea when the nation gained its independence in 1975. Namaliu remained in government employment, serving as a district commissioner and as chairman of the Public Service Commission, until he was elected to Parliament representing Kokopo on New Britain in 1982. In Parliament he was a member of Pangu Pati and held the portfolios of foreign affairs and primary industry. (BARRIE MACDONALD)

Nolan, Christopher

Although he can hear and see perfectly, Christopher Nolan spent his first 11 years communicating with his family only with an elaborate system of eye signals. His sister and parents knew that a fierce intelligence was trapped inside this boy, and they shared his frustration at his inability to speak. Nolan suffered severe brain damage at birth that left him speechless and paralyzed. A new drug, Lioresal, provided him with enough muscle control to type, which he accomplished with what he called a "unicorn rod," a stick attached to a band strapped to his forehead. His mother, Bernadette, helped to steady his head so that he could strike the right keys.

Under the Eye of the Clock, Nolan's autobiographical novel, won Britain's prestigious Whitbread Prize for 1987. The book was selected over new works by Seamus Heaney and Richard Ellman and brought Nolan to the attention of a much wider public throughout the British Isles and elsewhere. The novel, written in the third person, tells the story of Joseph Meehan, whose life story is a barely disguised version of the author's. Nolan had a fine ability to look at himself from a distance. His autobiography is never bitter, although it recounts some of his more traumatic moments in the world of "normal" children. The reader is introduced to some of Nolan's heroes, including several teachers, a school headmaster, and his curate, who found ways to surprise his stubborn muscles into taking communion. Nolan's prose style, like his poetic style, is adventurous. He does not hesitate to coin new words or phrases when he finds existing ones to be insufficient.

Nolan was born Sept. 6, 1965, in Mullingar, Ireland. To make life easier for the young handicapped boy, his family moved from the country to a home on the outskirts of Dublin. In *Under the Eye of the Clock* he remembers the simpler life on the farm. It was only one of the things that his family sacrificed for Nolan's sake, and the boy shows his appreciation in vivid and touching sections of the novel.

Nolan first received the attention of Britain's press after winning prizes from the British Spastics Society. He went on to submit some of his writings to a London publishing house. These became his first book, *Dam-Burst of Dreams.* Published in 1981, it is a collection of plays, stories, poems, and autobiographical material that led readers and critics to make comparisons between Nolan and such writers as W. B. Yeats, Dylan Thomas, and James Joyce.

(FRANCINE SHONFELD SHERMAN)

Otto, Kristin

For winning six Olympic gold medals, East German swimmer Kristin Otto won a gold crown. It was the most valuable athlete trophy for the 1988 summer Olympic Games at Seoul, South Korea, the Paek Sang crown designed after the headgear of ancient Korean warriors.

Before Otto no woman had ever won more than four gold medals at a single Olympics, a record that seven athletes had shared. "She's best because she works harder than the rest," East German coach Wolfgang Richter said. "She cannot stand to lose."

Otto also was the most versatile woman ever

CAMERA PRESS/GLOBE PHOTOS

to swim competitively, with the possible exception of retired American Tracy Caulkins. Otto had won world or Olympic championships in the backstroke, butterfly, freestyle, and individual medley. She did not set any world records at the Olympics, but she defeated record holders when she came from behind to win the 100-m butterfly, and she shocked the field in the 50-m freestyle, where she had ranked only 11th in the world. Otto's winning time of 25.49 sec shaved a remarkable 0.46 sec off her previous best in the event.

On September 19–25 the tall blonde went to the victory stand nearly every day. She won all six events she entered. Her other individual victories were in the 100-m freestyle and the 100-m backstroke. She also swam the lead leg in East Germany's 4 × 100-m freestyle relay victory and the backstroke leg in the 4 × 100-m individual medley relay. She led an East German team that won 10 of the 15 women's gold medals in swimming.

Otto might have been as successful in the 1984 Olympics if her country had not boycotted them. When she cracked a vertebra later that year, it looked as though her career was over. She spent nine months in a neck brace, and physicians advised her to give up sports, but she returned to compete in the 1986 world championships and won four gold medals and two silvers.

Otto grew up in Leipzig, East Germany's second largest city, where her mother was a physiotherapist and her father a college physics professor. She entered a special sports school when she was 11 after East Germany's comprehensive scouting program identified her as a swimming prospect. In 1982 at age 18, as part of her country's 4 × 100-m medley relay team, she set her first world record. After the Olympics she returned home to complete her internship with a radio station, the first of three years of training required for becoming a journalist.

(KEVIN M. LAMB)

Pérez de Cuéllar, Javier
United Nations Secretary-General Javier Pérez de Cuéllar in 1988 presided over the UN during one of its most productive and successful years. He played a key role in arranging both the formal cease-fire and the initiation of the peace talks that occurred between Iran and Iraq in August 1988. He had been working diligently throughout his tenure in office to end that bitter eight-year-old conflict. In August he arranged the first meeting since 1985 between the president of Cyprus, who was of Greek heritage, and the leader of Cyprus's Turkish population. The UN's peacekeeping forces (*q.v.*), who were

active during the year in many parts of the world, were recognized for their effectiveness when they were awarded the 1988 Nobel Prize for Peace.

Pérez de Cuéllar was born on Jan. 19, 1920, in Lima, Peru, the son of a prosperous businessman and a descendant of Spanish nobility. He studied law at Catholic University in Lima, receiving his degree in 1943. The next year he joined the Peruvian diplomatic service. He became a member of Peru's delegation to the first session of the UN General Assembly in 1946. During subsequent years he served, successively, as first secretary at the Peruvian embassies in France, the United Kingdom, Bolivia, and Brazil. He was then promoted to counselor and served again in Brazil.

In 1962, after serving as director of the legal and personnel departments at the Ministry of Foreign Relations, Pérez de Cuéllar was promoted to the rank of ambassador. He served as Peru's ambassador to Switzerland from 1964 to 1966 and became his country's first ambassador to Moscow in 1969 and its permanent representative to the UN in 1971.

From 1979 to 1981 Pérez de Cuéllar served as the UN under secretary-general for special political affairs. He was elected to his first term as secretary-general on Dec. 15, 1981, succeeding Kurt Waldheim. Sworn into office on Jan. 1, 1982, Pérez de Cuéllar became the first Latin American and the second non-European to occupy that post. With the unanimous recommendation of the UN Security Council, he was appointed by the UN General Assembly to a second term on Jan. 1, 1987. As the top UN official he headed a staff of some 15,000, based mainly in New York and Geneva. He received praise for his appointments of women to key UN posts. (EDWARD PAUL MORAGNE)

Quayle, James Danforth
In New Orleans, La., on Aug. 17, 1988, the Republican national convention nominated George Bush (*q.v.*) for president of the United States, as expected. The convention's only surprise had occurred the previous day, when Bush selected Dan Quayle, a rather obscure member of the U.S. Senate from Indiana, to be the vice-presidential nominee. Affable and youthfully handsome, Quayle had no enemies and was on good terms with Republicans who did not regard Bush as a true conservative. However, Quayle impressed many as inexperienced, intellectually shallow, and a beneficiary of help from powerful relatives. Nominated by acclamation of the convention on August 18, he then was confronted with reports that a friend of his family had helped him get into the Indiana Na-

GLOBE PHOTOS

tional Guard in 1969, when he otherwise might have had to serve in Vietnam. Quayle defended his Guard service and essentially treated the matter as a nonissue, and interest in it waned. An interview published in the *Boston Globe* on August 29, in which Quayle acknowledged ignorance about the drug problem, raised other questions, however. On October 5, debating the Democratic vice-presidential nominee, Lloyd Bentsen, in Omaha, Neb., he was asked three times what he would do if he succeeded to the presidency. He first said he would pray and call the president's advisers. The third time he compared his own experience to that of John F. Kennedy, evoking a patronizing response from Bentsen. Polls indicated that many who had intended to vote for the Bush-Quayle ticket had changed their minds. Quayle traversed the U.S. discussing Bush's proposals and the alleged deficiencies of the Democratic ticket, but mostly before friendly audiences, and he made few speeches in the campaign's last week. On November 8 the Bush-Quayle ticket got 54% of the vote, but a later Gallup Poll indicated that 4% of those voting had voted against that ticket because of Quayle.

James Danforth ("Dan") Quayle was born on Feb. 4, 1947, in Indianapolis, Ind., the city from which his maternal grandfather, Eugene Pulliam, ran a newspaper empire. Dan's father, James C. Quayle, bought control of the *Huntington* (Ind.) *Herald-Press* from Pulliam in 1963. In 1969 Dan Quayle was graduated from DePauw University, Greencastle, Ind. He served as a welder and a journalist in the Indiana National Guard (1969–75) while attending Indiana University Law School (graduated in 1974) and working for Indiana's attorney general (1970–71), governor (1971–73), and Department of Revenue (1973–74). In 1974 he practiced law in Huntington and became general manager of the *Herald-Press*. He served in the U.S. House of Representatives (1977–81), his first election being a surprising victory over an incumbent Democrat. Elected to the U.S. Senate in 1980, with much evangelical Protestant support, he cosponsored the Job Training Partnership Act of 1982 and was chairman of a committee on the Senate's organization. He was easily reelected in 1986. (CHARLES JOHNSON TAGGART)

Rakowski, Mieczyslaw
The appointment of Mieczyslaw Rakowski as prime minister on Sept. 28, 1988, took everybody in Poland by surprise. Viewed as an opportunist and a staunch opponent of the free trade union Solidarity, he was not generally popular. Although a hard-line Communist, he was convinced that far-reaching economic reforms were badly needed in Poland and that the free market economy should be introduced. Ministers in his Cabinet were also committed to the reform program, and one of them, the minister of industry, was a party member who had made a fortune as a private businessman.

In his inaugural speech as prime minister, Rakowski said: "To be consistent in rebuilding our economy means in effect that enterprises will go under, that thousands of people will face the necessity of changing their workplace or even of a temporary job hunt." One of his first "economic" moves was to close down the unprofitable Lenin Shipyard in Gdansk, the cradle of Solidarity. This was widely recognized as a political rather than an economic move and met strong protest by the shipyard's employees, one of whom was Lech Walesa (*q.v.*).

Rakowski was born on Dec. 1, 1926, at Kowalewko in Bydgoszcz Province, the son of a farmer. In 1955 he was graduated from the Institute of Social Science, and two years later he obtained a doctorate. Between 1945 and 1949 he served as an officer in the Polish Army.

In 1946 he joined the Communist Party, and from 1975 he was a member of the party's Central Committee. Between 1958 and 1982 he worked as editor in chief of the prestigious weekly *Polityka*. In those years Rakowski was, in the eyes of popular opinion, a "liberal-minded" party man.

ZOLTAN POLYA—CAMERA PRESS/GLOBE PHOTOS

In 1981 he became vice-president of the Council of Ministers and was appointed the chairman of the regime's committee dealing with Solidarity. Subsequently, the popular image of Rakowski as a liberal changed completely, especially after a television appearance at the Lenin Shipyard in which he displayed considerable arrogance and contempt toward workers. After his appointment in 1985 as a deputy speaker of the Sejm (parliament), his political career seemed to decline. However, at the end of 1987 a secret document called "Rakowski's view" was circulated, including an accurate appraisal of the Polish political and economic situation. This was the beginning of his successful bid to gain power.   (K. M. SMOGORZEWSKI)

Reagan, Ronald Wilson

The last full year of Ronald Reagan's presidency began with top marks on his six-month physical exam. By the time he readied the reins of office for George Bush (q.v.), his political health was just as rosy. His approval rating had climbed to one of the highest levels of his eight years in office.

In January his physician certified that Reagan showed no recurrence of colon cancer and no intestinal polyps. In April, however, he had worries of a different sort with the publication of advance excerpts of a "kiss and tell" book, *Speaking Out*, by former deputy press secretary Larry Speakes. Revelations included the news that Speakes had constructed his own presidential "quotes" after such events as Reagan's first meeting with Soviet leader Mikhail Gorbachev (q.v.) in 1985 and the Soviet downing of a South Korean airliner in 1983.

For the Record: From Wall Street to Washington, by former White House chief of staff Donald Regan, caused more ripples. Regan disclosed that First Lady Nancy Reagan was a powerful player in the administration and strongly influenced by astrology, to the point of its affecting the president's schedule. The White House did not deny that astrological projections were considered in planning, especially concerning travel, but the president assured reporters, "No policy or decision in my mind has ever been influenced by astrology."

The spotlight soon shifted to the Reagans' first trip to Moscow (May 29–June 2) for the fourth summit with Gorbachev. In Helsinki, Fin., en route to the summit, Reagan spoke out against Soviet failure to live up to the 1975 Helsinki Final Act on human rights. The president again pressed the issue face-to-face with Gorbachev, which contributed to the amicable but somewhat cool tone to their meetings. Although minor accords on arms control were negotiated in Moscow, the network news seemed to devote more time to the tension evident between Nancy Reagan and Raisa Gorbachev, the Soviet leader's wife. Reagan met Gorbachev again in December when the latter spoke before the UN in New York.

By late summer much of the nation's attention had turned to presidential candidates Bush

and Michael Dukakis (q.v.). On May 11, at a Republican fund-raiser, Reagan had endorsed Bush's presidential bid. Some observers called the endorsement lukewarm and pointed out that it came when Bush had all but clinched the nomination. Nevertheless, Reagan was greeted with wild cheers of gratitude at the party's national convention in August. Reagan proved that he was still an enthusiastic and skilled campaigner as the election frenzy moved into high gear after Labor Day.

As the January inauguration day drew close, Reagan was securing another place for himself in history—this time in a rather odd category. He would become the first president since James Monroe elected in a year divisible by 20 not to die in office.

Reagan was born in Tampico, Ill., on Feb. 6, 1911. He received a B.A. from Eureka (Ill.) College (1932) and then worked as a sportscaster in Iowa. In 1937 he became a motion-picture actor under contract to Warner Brothers. He was governor of California from 1967 to 1975 and was first inaugurated as U.S. president in 1981.
                                    (BETSY R. ELLIOT)

Rocard, Michel

In his autobiography, *Le Coeur a l'ouvrage,* published only a few weeks before he was chosen prime minister of France, Michel Rocard admitted that he was first "mobilized" by the desire to build a stronger Europe. In fact, in 1949 the 19-year-old Rocard had joined the National Federation of Socialist Students in the SFIO (the French branch of the Workers' International) because of its commitment to European unity.

Michel-Louis-Léon Rocard was born on Aug. 23, 1930, in the Parisian suburb of Courbevoie. He attended the Institute for Political Studies in Paris and the prestigious National School of Administration before taking a post in the finance ministry in 1958. During the controversy over Algerian independence in the same year, he broke away from the SFIO to found the left-wing Autonomous Socialist Party (PSA). In 1960 the PSA merged with smaller splinter groups to form the Unified Socialist Party (PSU), of which Rocard later served as national secretary (1967–73). He ran for president in 1969, but he received less than 3.7% of the vote and instead became a delegate to the National Assembly (1970–73).

In 1974 Rocard supported the call for a "union of the left" by François Mitterrand (q.v.), leader of the Socialist Party (PS), the renamed successor to the SFIO. After Mitterrand lost the 1974 election to Pres. Valéry Giscard d'Estaing by a small margin, Rocard rejoined the Socialists, serving on the party's executive committee from 1975. Rocard, who was reelected to the National Assembly in 1978, failed to oust Mitterrand as PS leader at a chaotic party congress in 1979 and became, in effect, opposition leader within the PS.

Rocard abandoned his own bid for the presidency in 1981 to support Mitterrand's successful campaign. He served as minister of economic planning (1981–83) and minister of agriculture (1983–85) under Prime Minister Jacques Mauroy, but he resigned in 1985 amid accusations that Mitterrand had backed away from his Socialist beliefs in seeking greater austerity. As Mitterrand's chief rival for party leadership, Rocard gained increasing national attention and support. In an early bid for the presidency in 1988, Rocard promised to "govern differently," but when Mitterrand announced he would run for reelection, Rocard again gave up his own campaign. In the end, Rocard's willingness to compromise paid off, and on May 10 he was named prime minister.

Rocard represented the desire for a new *ouverture* (openness) in the French government, and he sought to include more centrists and civilians without previous government experience. Although he achieved a notable success in June with a new accord on strife-torn New Caledonia, the triumph was short-lived. In the autumn only 37% of the French electorate turned out

JULIEN QUIDEAU—CAMERA PRESS/GLOBE PHOTOS

to vote on Rocard's hard-won accord. Several prolonged strikes in the public sector, many of which led to violent confrontations with police, also cast some doubt on Rocard's ability to accomplish his goals.   (JEAN KNECHT)

Roh Tae Woo

Having come to power on the promise of restoring harmony through compromise, South Korean Pres. Roh Tae Woo found himself presiding over a political scene scarcely less turbulent than that of 1987. Although the summer Olympic Games in Seoul were not disrupted, students took to the streets both before and after the Games to vociferously denounce the president and his administration. The most unruly demonstrations occurred in August when student activists, increasingly more leftist, fought police who were preventing them from marching to the North Korean border to meet Communist students and to demand reunification of the peninsula. In July Roh had offered to meet North Korean Pres. Kim Il Sung "anywhere, any time," and in August he declared himself willing to travel to Pyongyang.

Roh, who was born on Dec. 4, 1932, was an army general when he retired in 1981. Four years later he was chosen chairman of the Democratic Justice Party (DJP). He was elected president on Dec. 16, 1987, and inaugurated Feb. 25, 1988. The new president had received only 35.9% of the vote and might have lost if either of his two main opponents, Kim Dae Jung and Kim Young Sam, had dropped out of the race. Roh's position was further weakened when the DJP won only 33.9% of the vote

AFP PHOTO

in the National Assembly elections on April 26. It won 125 seats; the opposition parties, 164. Before the elections Roh had sought to defuse antigovernment feeling by orchestrating the retirement from politics of his unpopular predecessor, Chun Doo Hwan, whose brother had been arrested two weeks earlier for corruption. Roh's government also apologized for the violent suppression of the 1980 uprising at Kwangju. These measures, however, did not placate the new Assembly, which pushed ahead with investigations that led to the indictment of several more members of Chun's family.

In a dramatic televised appearance on November 23, Chun apologized to the nation for the misdeeds that had occurred during his rule and said he would surrender all his personal assets to the state. He then went into rural exile. Roh was widely believed to have persuaded Chun that he had no viable alternative. Roh doubtless hoped that Chun's address would satisfy those demanding that past wrongs be righted. Until that was done, it would be difficult for him to concentrate on South Korea's future.   (ROBERT WOODROW)

Sakamoto, Ryuichi

When Japanese rock musician Ryuichi Sakamoto shared the 60th Hollywood Academy Award with two fellow composer-musicians for the best film score—in Bernardo Bertolucci's *The Last Emperor*—he confessed: "My wife didn't really want me to be selected. She thought it would inflate my ego." The world of music was where Sakamoto wanted to be since introducing "techno-pop" rhythm in 1978. As the keyboard player of the three-member Yellow Magic Orchestra (YMO), Sakamoto demonstrated Japanese new wave music by playing in harmony with prerecorded and computerized synthesizer sounds.

Born in Tokyo on Jan. 17, 1952, the son of a magazine editor and a musically inclined mother, Sakamoto studied classical music at the prestigious Tokyo Arts University. In 1977 he formed the YMO, which broke up five years later. He then went solo. In 1983 he composed the musical score for director Nagisa Oshima's *Merry Christmas, Mr. Lawrence*. Sakamoto was one of the leading characters, the nihilist POW camp commander. Although the film score won the Golden Globe Award, it was Sakamoto's cold deadpan face that drew Japanese commercial interest. He signed contracts for watch, wine, camera, cosmetics, and insurance company ads and showed up on posters and in TV commercials. He was even recruited to appear in samurai armour as well as in business suits and was featured in a boudoir scene with a Brazilian actress.

Sakamoto loved music, be it classical, jazz, pop, or rock—anything musical. The new generation so respected his literary ability that he established his own publishing house, Honhondo, which first published a volume of his conversations with philosophers Shinji Takahashi and Sozo Omori. His literary background came from his father, Kazuki, former editor of the liberal literary magazine *Bungei*. With his singer-songwriter wife, Akiko Yano, who was responsible for many of his records and albums, Sakamoto produced "Front Life," "Field Work," "Risky" and the albums *Yellow Magic Orchestra, Solid-State Survivor*, and *Public Pressure*. Among his recent concerts were Sakamoto Plays Sakamoto in Tokyo shortly after the Academy Award honour and Neo Geo in New York.

(KAY K. TATEISHI)

Salinas de Gortari, Carlos

On July 6 Carlos Salinas de Gortari, of the ruling Partido Revolucionario Institucional (PRI), was elected president of Mexico with 50.4% of the vote, the smallest majority ever gained by a PRI candidate. His election was surrounded by controversy and allegations of fraud; his opponents refused to recognize his victory; and there were wild and violent scenes in Congress when he was officially declared president-elect. He took office on December 1 for a six-year

AP/WIDE WORLD

term with the political battle still raging and was expected to face the most vociferous opposition of any PRI president. He would also have to cope with the loss of a rubber-stamp Congress, with the PRI occupying only 260 of the 500 seats. Salinas accepted the outcome as a "mandate for change," but it clearly came as a blow to the PRI old guard.

Although born in Mexico City on April 3, 1948, Salinas came from a family with strong ties to the northern state of Nuevo León, where he spent much of his childhood. His father, Raúl Salinas Lozano, senator for Nuevo León and former commerce minister, and his mother, Margarita, were both economists, and Carlos grew up in an atmosphere of intellectual debate on politics and economics. He first joined the PRI at the age of 18 when he was studying economics at the autonomous National University of Mexico (UNAM). He went on to do graduate work at Harvard University, earning master's degrees in public administration in 1973 and political economy in 1976. In 1978 he was awarded a Ph.D. in political economy and government.

Salinas's first government job was as an economic analyst at the Ministry of Finance, and he went on to win eight promotions in eight years, in 1979 becoming general director of economic and social policy in the Budget and Planning Ministry. At this time he became close to Miguel de la Madrid Hurtado, who was budget minister, and in 1981 he campaigned behind the scenes to secure him the presidential nomination. When de la Madrid was elected in 1982, Salinas was rewarded with the position of minister of budget and planning. In that position, he began the economic liberalization program that he hoped to complete as president, and from mid-1986 he was in firm charge of economic policy.

Although universally acknowledged to have a first-class mind with an infallible memory, Salinas during the election campaign appeared to have a limited capacity to inspire his followers. Voters saw him as a foreign-educated technocrat, and he was a favourite target for cartoonists.   (SARAH CAMERON)

Saw Maung

Few people outside Burma's reticent official circles had heard of Gen. Saw Maung before he became president on Sept. 18, 1988. Even afterward, few details of his career were known. Installed as head of state following a military coup, Saw Maung was believed by Western diplomats in Rangoon to be a front man for U Ne Win, the autocratic ruler of Burma for 26 years until July 23, when he resigned as chairman of the Burma Socialist Program Party.

Three days later he handed over power to his longtime hard-line associate Sein Lwin. At the time, Ne Win's action had seemed to be the result of pressure from rebellious students and others dissatisfied by his inept and repressive rule. Later, however, wide currency was given to the notion that the wily Ne Win had engineered the takeover by Sein Lwin, his replacement on August 19 by the moderate civilian Maung Maung, and Saw Maung's seizure of power.

Gen. Saw Maung, armed forces chief of staff from 1986, was minister of defense in Sein Lwin's 18-day Cabinet. Younger than most of Ne Win's inner circle (he turned 60 in December 1988), he had been known for his loyalty to the leader. Like other followers of Ne Win, he had little formal education, having become an apprentice electrician at age 16. He joined the Army as a private in 1945, was made sergeant the following year, and was commissioned in 1952. An infantryman, he rose steadily over the next 30 years in field-command and state-security positions, becoming army vice chief of staff in 1983.

Saw Maung abolished the whole apparatus of state, including Parliament. He announced a nine-member Cabinet with only one civilian. Dissidents were ruthlessly suppressed in a bloody street massacre witnessed by observers from the U.S. embassy. The government acknowledged 99 dead on the first day and 240 more by the end of the week, but diplomats put the figure at more than 1,000. Troops cleared the streets, pressing demonstrators into the military as unpaid forest porters. At least 1,000 students fled to the hills for training as separatist insurgents. Saw Maung insisted that elections scheduled by Maung Maung would be held, but only after law and order were restored. To replace Ne Win's Burma Socialist Program Party, the National Unity Party was established.

(ROBERT WOODROW)

Schwartz, Melvin

Three Americans—Leon Lederman (*q.v.*), Melvin Schwartz, and Jack Steinberger (*q.v.*)—received the 1988 Nobel Prize for Physics for work they did while at Columbia University, New York City, in the early 1960s. The physicists were recognized both for their development of a method for generating a beam of high-energy neutrinos—subatomic particles with no electric charge and essentially no mass—and for their discovery of a new type of neutrino. It was Schwartz, then a graduate student of Steinberger, who first proposed a way in which the researchers could use a beam of high-energy protons to create a neutrino beam. Since the Nobel laureates' award-winning research, which exploited a new particle accelerator at the Brookhaven National Laboratory, Upton, N.Y., neutrino beams had become an important and widely used tool in high-energy-physics research. They were used to understand supernova explosions and to probe the so-called weak force, or weak interaction, one of the four basic forces in nature.

Schwartz was born on Nov. 2, 1932, in New York City. In 1958 he earned a Ph.D. in physics from Columbia University, where he remained as a faculty member until 1966. That year he became a professor of physics at Stanford University. While on the Stanford faculty, Schwartz founded Digital Pathways, Inc., a small company in Mountain View, Calif., that designed computer-security systems. In 1983 Schwartz left Stanford to become full-time chairman and chief executive of the company.

Because neutrinos rarely interact with other forms of matter, they had been extremely difficult to detect. (It was estimated that from a sample of ten billion neutrinos traveling through matter for a distance equal to the Earth's diameter, only one neutrino would interact with some particle of that matter.) Neutrinos are produced naturally in certain radioactive-decay processes but in such small numbers and with such scattered trajectories that they are of little use as tools in laboratory research.

Acting on Schwartz's suggestion, the three

researchers set out to increase the statistical probability of neutrino interactions by creating a beam containing hundreds of billions of neutrinos and sending the beam through a detector of solid matter. The scientists used the accelerator at Brookhaven to produce high-energy protons that were then fired at a beryllium target. Bombardment of the beryllium produced a stream of particles, including particles called pions (pi mesons) that, as they traveled, decayed into muons (mu mesons) and neutrinos. The stream of particles from the beryllium target was passed through a steel barrier 13.4 m (44 ft) thick that filtered out all particles but the neutrinos. The pure neutrino beam entered a ten-ton aluminum detector, wherein a few neutrinos interacted with the aluminum atoms and were detected. By analyzing these interactions, the scientists learned that the neutrino beam comprised a new type of fundamental particle—the muon neutrino.   (CAROLYN D. NEWTON)

Scorsese, Martin

As early as 1975, Martin Scorsese admitted his ambition "to make the New Testament. . . . After all, I must do one religious picture." His "religious picture," *The Last Temptation of Christ,* appeared in 1988 and sparked one of the bitterest theological debates in years.

Scorsese was born on Nov. 17, 1942, in New York City. Frail health limited his childhood activities, but he enjoyed sketching and going to the movies with his father. When he was 14, Scorsese enrolled in a junior seminary. Although he was later expelled, Scorsese remained a devout Roman Catholic and still aspired to the priesthood. He applied to several Roman Catholic universities but was turned down and instead went to New York University, where he found his "true vocation." He immersed himself in the art of filmmaking and won several awards for his student films. During the early 1970s Scorsese reevaluated his view of Roman Catholicism after hearing a priest champion the Vietnam war as a holy cause. He dissociated himself from the church, but critics still found him to be "perhaps the most innately religious of major American filmmakers." Faith, guilt, and sin could certainly be identified as powerful aspects of such films as *Mean Streets* (1973), *Taxi Driver* (1976), and *Raging Bull* (1980).

The Last Temptation of Christ, based on Nikos Kazantzakis's 1955 novel, portrays Christ as tormented and unsure of his role as the Messiah. The most controversial scene in the movie shows Christ imagining he is married to Mary Magdalene and having sexual relations with her. Scorsese felt he was depicting Christ

GLOBE PHOTOS

as a human being with ordinary human desires; the religious right felt he was depicting Jesus as a "sex-crazed mental defective."

Scorsese, anticipating controversy, held a preview screening for religious leaders, but most fundamentalist groups refused to attend, having previously read a bootleg copy of an outdated script that contained a large amount of material that did not make it into the final-cut film. Conservative Christians organized protests, boycotts, and advertising campaigns condemning the film. Universal Pictures (the film's distributor) replied with ads citing constitutional freedoms of religion and expression. The protests turned ominous when an ultra-right religious group staged an anti-Semitic demonstration outside the home of the Jewish chairman of MCA (Universal's parent company), Lew Wasserman. Many moderate religious leaders who actually saw the film did not find reason to condemn it; their characterizations of it ranged from brilliant to boring. Ironically, the backlash surrounding the film's release might be better remembered than the film itself.   (ELIZABETH LASKEY)

Serota, Nicholas

Aged just 42, Nicholas Serota in September 1988 became director of the Tate Gallery in London. His appointment, surprising yet appropriate, followed his 12 years of being the innovative and successful director of London's Whitechapel Art Gallery, where he established a reputation as a champion of contemporary art, mounting many major exhibitions devoted to leading artists of the 1980s. He also presided over the highly praised £1.7 million extension to the Whitechapel.

Serota was born April 27, 1946, and was educated at Cambridge University and the Courtauld Institute of Art, University of London. For three years he worked for the Arts Council as a regional art officer and exhibitions officer before being named director of the Museum of Modern Art, Oxford (1973–76). He moved to the Whitechapel in 1976 and remained its director until 1988. Under his directorship the Whitechapel concentrated on exhibitions of contemporary art, introducing several of the leading artists of the 1980s to the British art scene. He was a coorganizer of the influential "New Spirit in Painting" at the Royal Academy, perhaps the major exhibition to date of the art of the 1980s. Because of Serota's interest in the art of the present and recent past, his directorship at the Tate was likely to be controversial as he attempted to expand the gallery's collection of contemporary art and ensure its prominent installation. He was also to preside over the raising of £34 million to fund the gallery's proposed expansion and the construction of museums devoted to 20th-century art, to sculpture, and to New Art on an adjoining site.

Though not an eminent art historian or scholar, as were his recent Tate predecessors, Serota represented a new generation of art administrators. His command of contemporary art—together with his museum experience—was expected to herald a new image for the gallery, perhaps transforming it into a lively centre of New Art.   (SANDRA MILLIKIN)

Sopinka, John

Canadian Prime Minister Brian Mulroney broke with recent tradition when he appointed a practicing lawyer, not a sitting judge, to be a justice of the Supreme Court of Canada. John Sopinka, one of Canada's best and most expensive civil litigation attorneys, was sworn in on June 23, 1988, as Ontario's newest representative on the court. He was expected to assume the role of authority on commercial and financial law played by his predecessor, Mr. Justice Willard Estey.

From the time he was called to the bar in 1960, Sopinka's law practice consistently encompassed difficult and controversial cases. He was counsel for several royal commissions, including the Ontario Human Rights Commission Inquiry into Minority Hiring Practices in Toronto (1971), the Canadian Committee on Aviation Safety (1979–81), and the Commission

of Inquiry into the Royal Canadian Mounted Police Relationship with the Department of National Revenue. In 1986 Sopinka represented the Yukon and the Northwest Territories in a challenge to the Meech Lake accord, a proposed constitutional amendment having as one of its provisions the requirement that all existing provinces agree to the entrance of any new province into the confederation. He said his most personally satisfying case was one in which he represented a nurse wrongfully accused in connection with four infant deaths at a Toronto hospital.

Born in Broderick, Sask., on March 19, 1933, Sopinka grew up in Hamilton, Ont., and attended the University of Toronto. He received his B.A. degree in 1955 and his LL.B. in 1958. He wrote two books on courtroom practice, *The Law of Evidence in Civil Cases* (1974; with Sidney Lederman) and *The Trial of an Action* (1981). While attending the university, Sopinka played professional football for the Toronto Argonauts (1955–57) and the Montreal Alouettes (1957–58). He retained his interest in sports, serving as a director of Hockey Canada and as chairman of the Ontario Task Force on Equal Opportunity in Athletics (1983).

Expected to be progressive on human and equality rights, Sopinka stated that he assumed his role with no preconceived ideas. However, he was emphatic in his belief that judges should voice opinions on issues of public importance.   (DIANE LOIS WAY)

Steinberger, Jack

In the early 1960s, while at Columbia University, New York City, German-born physicist Jack Steinberger collaborated with American colleagues Leon Lederman and Melvin Schwartz (qq.v.) in a unique particle-physics experiment. In order to attempt the experiment, however, the three researchers had to accomplish something else that had never been done before—the generation in the laboratory of a high-energy beam of elusive subatomic particles called neutrinos. Once this technical hurdle was overcome, the experiment they conducted culminated in the discovery of a new type of subatomic particle, the muon neutrino. It was for these two achievements in invention and discovery that the physicists were awarded the 1988 Nobel Prize for Physics.

Steinberger was born in Bad Kissingen, Germany, on May 25, 1921. He immigrated to the U.S. in 1934. His first degree, from the University of Chicago, was in chemistry, but during World War II Steinberger turned to physics while working at the Radiation Laboratory at the Massachusetts Institute of Technology. After the war he returned to the University of Chicago, where for his Ph.D. in physics he studied subatomic particles called muons (mu mesons) produced in cosmic rays and showed that the muon decays into an electron and two neutrinos (one of which would later be shown in his prizewinning work with Lederman and Schwartz to be the muon neutrino). After his graduation in 1948, Steinberger taught at the University of California at Berkeley until 1950 and then at Columbia University until 1971. From 1968 Steinberger was a staff physicist at the European Laboratory for Particle Physics (CERN) in Geneva.   (CAROLYN D. NEWTON)

Suleymanoglu, Naim

Naim Suleymanoglu set world weight-lifting records under three names, four including "Pocket Hercules," the nickname that charmed the world during the 1988 summer Olympic Games at Seoul, South Korea, in September. There Suleymanoglu set and reset world records in the 60-kg (132-lb) weight class in the snatch (152.5 kg [336.3 lb]), clean and jerk (190 kg [419 lb]), and total lifts (342.5 kg [755.2 lb]—more than the Olympic heavyweight champion's total in 1956). The previous records in the clean and jerk and total lifts were held by Naum Shalamanov. That was Suleymanoglu's name in Bulgaria, his native country, from which he escaped in 1986.

Suleymanoglu was born Naim Suleimanov in the mountain village of Ptichar, Bulg., on Jan. 23, 1967. He was one of two million Turks in the country of nine million, leftovers from the Ottoman Empire, which ruled Bulgaria until the late 19th century. After gaining independence, Bulgaria banned the Turkish language, closed the Islamic mosques and schools in Turkish communities, and forced Turks to change their names to Bulgarian ones in an assimilation campaign that even rewrote cemetery headstones. In 1985 Naim Suleimanov became Naum Shalamanov.

The name change was the last straw. "To take away your name is to take away your character," Suleymanoglu said. At a December 1986 banquet at the world weight-lifting championships in Melbourne, Australia, he left his table and did not return. While Bulgarian officials announced that terrorists had kidnapped him, he stayed in the Melbourne house of a Turkish man before surfacing four days later at the Turkish embassy and asking for asylum. He flew to the Turkish capital, Ankara, in the private jet of Prime Minister Turgut Ozal. He received immediate Turkish citizenship and another name, the Turkish Suleymanoglu.

His father, a miner, was barely 1.52 m (5 ft) tall, his mother 1.41 m (4 ft 7½ in). Suleymanoglu grew only to 1.52 m (4 ft 11 in). He was a 1.14-m (3-ft 9-in) ten-year-old when he began lifting weights. He was assigned to a special sports school two years later and, at the age of 14, came within 2.5 kg (5.5 lb) of a world record. He set his first world record soon after his 15th birthday and would have been a 16-year-old favourite for three Olympic gold medals if Bulgaria had not boycotted the 1984 Games.

Turkey valued its new national hero enough to pay Bulgaria more than $1 million to waive the Olympic rule barring athletes from participating for three years after changing nationality. His three Olympic gold medals were Turkey's first in weight lifting.   (KEVIN M. LAMB)

Superman
For Superman, 1988 marked five decades of flying high. Packed into red and blue tights that made him look like a human flag, and trailed by a billowy, bright red cape that a count would have killed for, this man of flight, might, and invulnerability had fought for Truth, Justice, and the American Way wherever the need had arisen—in media as varied as comics and movies. In honour of his anniversary, *Time*

GEORGE REEVES PORTRAYING SUPERMAN
IN THE TELEVISION SERIES; PHOTOGRAPH, GLOBE PHOTOS

wrote a cover story, Collier Books published *Superman at Fifty* in paperback, CBS aired a prime-time television special, and towns across the U.S. held celebrations. Ironically, however, he received his highest praise from highbrows, who saw him as a quintessential American immigrant, a metaphor for an angel of God. Those fans were among the millions who had enabled the man of steel to generate a lifetime income of more than $1 billion.

Superman was conceived in 1934 by Jerry Siegel, a high school student in Cleveland, Ohio. Siegel made him a being from the planet Krypton who had crash landed in the U.S. Midwest, where he grew up discovering and mastering superhuman abilities. In between deeds for the common good, the adult Superman would assume the identity of wimpy Clark Kent, who was pining away for Lois Lane, who had eyes only for Superman. Siegel took his idea to a classmate, artist Joe Shuster, and the two of them created a dozen comic strips exploiting it.

Their conception did not fly until Detective Comics (DC) turned their strips into the first issue of *Action Comics* (June 1938). With that, a superstar was born. *Action* reached a monthly circulation of half a million issues, which led DC, in 1939, to give Superman his own comic (while keeping him in *Action*). The new publication was soon selling one and a quarter million copies per issue. The next year Superman took to the airwaves on the Mutual Radio Network; that show and his newspaper comic strip created a loyal following of many millions more.

Initially a wisecracking tough guy with extraordinary strength, Superman gradually acquired godlike powers, including vision that could see into another dimension and breath that could blow out a faraway star. As he became more super, however, his personality became more bland, and the result—a white-bread kind of Superman—was especially evident in the popular TV series of the 1950s and the four hit movies of the late 1970s and early 1980s (although in the fourth he went through a synthetic Kryptonite-induced identity crisis during which he performed evil acts). With Superman's comic circulation dipping to only 100,000 in 1986, DC adopted the radical changes of a more vulnerable Superman and a less wimpy Clark Kent. While the move doubled sales, the question of whether it would propel Superman to new heights of popularity was, in 1988, up in the air.   (MICHAEL AMEDEO)

Thatcher, Margaret Hilda
When U.K. Conservative Prime Minister Margaret Thatcher first reached the pinnacle of British politics in May 1979, few people believed that she would still be there nine years and two general elections later. On Jan 3, 1988, she set a new record as the country's longest-serving prime minister in the century, overtaking both Herbert Asquith (8 years and 241 days [1908–16] and Winston Churchill (8 years and 238 days [1940–45 and 1951–55]). In two major interviews Thatcher dismissed speculation that she might soon retire. She told *The Sunday Times* that no suitable successor was yet in sight, and *The Times* that she expected to remain prime minister for a fourth parliamentary term—which meant until 1995, if the Conservatives were to win the next general election.

On May 21 Thatcher delivered a speech to the General Assembly of the Church of Scotland, where she quoted St. Paul and other biblical sources to support her belief that voluntary action is better than state intervention to relieve poverty and other social problems. This speech was intended to counter criticism that her policies promoted individual greed rather than any spirit of community. In another major speech, on September 27, she countered another criticism: that she lacked concern for the environment. She argued that the impact of the "greenhouse effect" had not been fully appreciated and that new policies would be needed "for energy production, for fuel efficiency and for reforestation." In subsequent interviews she argued the case for producing more electricity

from nuclear power rather than from the burning of coal.

On the international stage Thatcher was at her most active during the final third of the year. On September 20 in Bruges, Belgium, she spoke out against the idea of European union, preferring each nation to maintain as much sovereignty as possible. During the first week of November, Thatcher visited Poland, where she held talks with Lech Walesa (*q.v.*), the leader of Solidarity, as well as with members of the Polish government. As 1989 opened, with a new president of the United States about to be installed, Thatcher could claim to be by far the most senior among the world's major heads of government. At 63—she was born on Oct. 25, 1925, in Grantham, Lincolnshire—she intended to retain that position for several more years.
          (PETER KELLNER)

UN Peacekeeping Forces
The 1988 Nobel Peace Prize was awarded to the United Nations peacekeeping forces, so recognized because they "represent the manifest will of the community of nations to achieve peace through negotiations and the forces have, by their presence, made a decisive contribution toward the initiation of actual peace negotiations." While the Nobel committee noted that armed strife in areas of conflict did not always cease as a result of the forces' presence, the level of confrontation was clearly reduced.

For 40 years thousands of troops recruited from several participating countries had been deployed in various trouble spots around the globe. The peacekeeping forces had carried out 14 missions, of which the most well-known was in the Middle East, where approximately 300 troops in Beirut, Lebanon, and in the Sinai monitored the 1948 armistice between the new Jewish state of Israel and neighbouring Arab nations.

Early in 1949 a small UN military observer group was sent to supervise an Indian-Pakistani cease-fire in the Jammu-Kashmir area. In 1964, 2,100 troops were sent to Cyprus to maintain a buffer between Greek and Turkish regions. More than a thousand observers on Syria's Golan Heights supervised a cease-fire with Israel following the 1973–74 war. In 1978, following an Israeli invasion of southern Lebanon, almost 6,000 troops ensured peace and security for the withdrawing Israeli forces.

In April 1988 about 50 observers were sent to Afghanistan to monitor the Soviet troop withdrawal. Peacekeeping forces were headquartered in Kabul and in Islamabad, Pak. In the summer 350 troops based in Tehran and Baghdad monitored the August 20 cease-fire in the Iran-Iraq war, observed troop withdrawals, and helped with prisoner-of-war exchanges.

This was not the first time that the Nobel Peace Prize had been awarded to a UN organization. In 1954 and 1981 the UN High Commissioner for Refugees received the prize for its various activities aiding refugees around the world. In 1965 the prize was awarded to the UN International Children's Fund (UNICEF). Outside observers of the UN said that such missions as those performed in 1988 represented the type of peace initiative for which the UN was originally founded. Surely the celebration in 1988 of the UN's 40th anniversary was enhanced by this award. Prior to the announcement of the prize and in keeping with its most important mission, plans to deploy peacekeeping forces to South West Africa/Namibia and to Western Sahara were already under way.
          (BONNIE OBERMAN)

Vargas Llosa, Mario
When Mario Vargas Llosa announced that he would be willing to run for president in Peru's 1990 elections, he entered a new arena. As one of Latin America's preeminent authors, he had long been known as an opinion shaper for his books that deal with contemporary political issues. Once a supporter of Cuba, Vargas Llosa since the 1970s had sought to portray himself as a centrist—defending democracy from the ex-

tremes of both right and left. In 1987 he stepped into the political limelight with his opposition to the government's attempt to nationalize private banks. Speaking for the conservatives, he accused Pres. Alan García Pérez of endangering democracy by attempting to "concentrate too much power in the hands of the government." Prior to that he had been chairman of a special governmental investigation into the murders of eight journalists in Peru's ongoing guerrilla war. Citing the "moral obligation" of a Latin-American writer to be "involved in civic activities" and not simply to make pronouncements from the safety of the sidelines, Vargas Llosa expressed a determination to prevent the election of a Marxist president. He agreed to run as a candidate of the right-wing Democratic Front, a coalition of his own Liberty Movement and the centre-right Popular Action and Popular Christian parties.

Vargas Llosa was born March 28, 1936, in Arequipa, Peru. He was a journalist in Peru in the 1960s before moving to Paris to work with Agence France-Presse and as a broadcaster on Latin-American affairs with Radiodiffusion-Télévision Française. He was a lecturer in Latin-American literature at Queen Mary College and Kings College in London and had been a visiting professor in the U.S. and Puerto Rico.

Known for their complex structures and combination of description and dialogue, his novels were often based on personal experience and on his abhorrence of violence and corruption. *La ciudad y los perros* (1963; *The Time of the Hero*, 1966), based on two years at Leoncio Prado Military Academy, was attacked by the military, and copies were burned at the school. *La casa verde* (1966; *The Green House*, 1968) was drawn from Vargas Llosa's childhood in the jungle town of Piura, Peru. The epic *War of the End of the World* (1984), based on an apocalyptic religious movement in 19th-century Brazil, indicated his shifting political perspective. While his earlier novels criticized a corrupt society, it condemned both the religious fanatics of Canudos and the government that sent 4,000 soldiers to subdue them—resulting in the destruction of the area and the deaths of nearly 40,000 people. Recent novels included *El hablador* (1987) and *Elogio de la madrasta* (1988). (ELLEN FINKELSTEIN)

Vassiliou, George
George Vassiliou, a political unknown, combined business acumen and personal history to win the support of the most powerful Communist party in any Western democracy and went on in 1988 to wrest the presidency of Cyprus from the man who had held the office for 11 years.

Vassiliou was born in Famagusta on May 21, 1931, of parents distinguished both as doctors and as left-wing intellectuals. His parents moved to Hungary after World War II to arrange medical assistance for Communists fighting in the Greek civil war. His father went on to Greece, and young George, then a medical student in Geneva, joined his mother in Budapest. In Hungary he abandoned medicine for economics, and later he studied marketing in England. In 1962 he started a one-man business in Cyprus, the Middle East Research Centre. It became the biggest market research bureau in the Middle East and made Vassiliou a millionaire.

Vassiliou was mentioned, among others, as a possible compromise candidate for centre and left-wing groups opposed to Pres. Spyros Kyprianou in the 1983 election. However, Kyprianou secured an election pact with AKEL, the (Communist) Progressive Party of the Working People, which consistently polled around 30% of the vote. With AKEL's support he won a new five-year term but, once elected, he ignored the pact. Furious, the AKEL leaders began to plot his downfall, and Vassiliou again caught their eye. In July 1987 AKEL threw its support behind Vassiliou as an independent candidate. The other independent candidate, former foreign minister Nicos Rolandis—another self-made millionaire—stood down and

put his small Liberal Party behind Vassiliou to attract centre-right voters. Vassiliou defined himself as his own man by defying AKEL on two key issues. He backed a new customs union between Cyprus and the European Communities and took a moderate stand on the island's two British military bases, which AKEL wanted removed.

In a first-round poll in February, right-wing Rally Party leader Glafcos Clerides won the most votes, but Vassiliou edged past Kyprianou into second place, ousting him from the contest and the presidency. In a hard-fought second round a week later, Vassiliou narrowly beat Clerides to become president. Attempts to federate the hostile Greek- and Turkish-Cypriot populations had been stalemated for 14 years. Within months of his election, Vassiliou persuaded the Turkish Cypriot leader, Rauf Denktash, to meet him in Geneva, and the two continued secret talks in Nicosia. Their new objective was a draft agreement on federation by mid-1989. (THOMAS O'DWYER)

Walesa, Lech
Eight years after signing the Gdansk agreement that established the free trade union Solidarity, Lech Walesa was invited to Warsaw for talks with Poland's minister of the interior to discuss preparations for a roundtable dialogue between the government and the opposition. Workers represented by Walesa, until then officially an "unperson," would thereby have something to say about the country's future. He made the recognition of Solidarity as a free trade union a condition for his participation in the discussions. Hoping that talks with the government would lead to some agreement, he helped to end strikes in September in some factories and coal mines, and he counseled against a strike when the government announced its decision to close the Lenin Shipyard. However, the government showed little goodwill, and the talks were repeatedly postponed. In late November, Walesa appeared on Polish television in a debate with the head of the official unions.

Walesa in 1988—as some said—was much more of a politician but less of a workers' spokesman than he had been eight years earlier. His popularity and authority among young workers was not as great as it was among those who with him had created the Solidarity movement, but he remained a potent symbol for all Poles who were longing for democracy and freedom. His realistic approach to politics made him distrustful of the government's intentions but—on the other hand—also made him tough with the radical wing of Solidarity. He was not an extremist and regarded strikes as a weapon of last resort.

Walesa, the son of a carpenter, was born Sept. 29, 1943, at Popowo, northwest of Warsaw. His education was limited to elementary and a three-year vocational school. In 1961 he began work as an electrician in an agricultural machinery centre, but in 1967 he moved to the Lenin Shipyard in Gdansk. After the tragic events in 1970, when the Army fired on demonstrating workers, he became involved in a clandestine movement fighting for free trade unions. For this he was dismissed from the shipyard in 1976, but he returned during the strike in August 1980 and was enthusiastically greeted by his fellow workers. He became a leader of striking workers and represented them in negotiations with the government on the right to organize unions. Thus was Solidarity born. On Dec. 13, 1981, martial law was imposed, Solidarity outlawed, and its most active members interned. Walesa spent 11 months in confinement. Returning to Gdansk, he was permitted to resume his work as an electrician in the shipyard. In 1983 he was awarded the Nobel Prize for Peace. (K. M. SMOGORZEWSKI)

Watkins, James D.
When retired admiral James D. Watkins reluctantly replaced W. Eugene Mayberry as chairman of U.S. Pres. Ronald Reagan's 13-member AIDS (acquired immune deficiency syndrome)

AP/WIDE WORLD

commission in late 1987, he had many preconceptions about the disease and how the spread of it should be handled. As a military engineer and later chief of naval operations, he knew little about AIDS and had little sympathy for the male homosexuals who were contracting it. As a Roman Catholic, Watkins believed that homosexuality is a sin, and he endorsed the military's ban on homosexuals.

Watkins began to rethink his attitudes toward AIDS when he saw firsthand that the disease was not confined to the homosexual community and that its effects touched the lives of many Americans. "I never realized what was out there in the way of bigotry and hatred," said Watkins, who came to believe that the government should enact new federal antidiscrimination laws and confidentiality statutes that would protect those infected with AIDS from the loss of jobs and ensure a greater response to testing. "People simply will not come forward to be tested or will not supply names of sexual contacts for notification if they feel they will lose their jobs and homes based on an HIV-positive test," Watkins said.

Watkins proposed further AIDS education in the schools and suggested that the surgeon general be given policymaking powers. The commission called for more than 3,000 new treatment centres for intravenous-drug abusers, a group that by the end of 1988 constituted one-fourth of all AIDS patients in the U.S. According to Watkins's figures, intravenous-drug abusers were responsible for 70% of heterosexually transmitted cases, yet only 12% received care at treatment centres.

The commission produced a 269-page final report that included 579 recommendations that could cost $3 billion to implement. Commenting on the progress that had been made up to the time of the report, Watkins said, "The system has failed. It is not working well, and we had better get with it."

James David Watkins was born on March 7, 1927, in Alhambra, Calif. He received a B.S. degree in 1949 from the U.S. Naval Academy and an M.S. degree in 1958 from the Naval Postgraduate School. He advanced through the ranks of the U.S. Navy to become an admiral in 1979. As an engineer he worked on the controversial "Star Wars" missile-defense system. (ANTHONY L. GREEN)

Williams, Richard
The animation director of the film *Who Framed Roger Rabbit* almost rejected the project because he did not believe it would be possible realistically to mix cartoon characters with live actors. However, Richard Williams was able to combine more than 1,000 optical illusions to make the inhabitants of Toontown three-dimensional

figures that interacted effectively with humans. This achievement was the work of 326 animators, who drew the cartoons onto the 82,080 frames of film by hand. What Richard Williams created in *Roger Rabbit* was a milestone in the history of animation.

Born in Toronto in 1933, Williams decided as a small child to become an animator. Upon seeing Walt Disney's *Snow White and the Seven Dwarfs,* he was fascinated that cartoons could walk, talk, and even think. He studied the basics of animation by reading all he could find on the subject, and at the age of 15 he traveled to Los Angeles to visit the Disney Studios. There he was told to learn to draw, and so he returned to Toronto and enrolled in the Ontario College of Art to study painting. Four years later he went to Spain to become a painter.

In 1955 Williams moved to London and resumed his career as an animator. His desire was to combine painting with animation—to make serious art move. While at the Ontario College of Art, he had financed his painting by animating television commercials; in London he became Britain's premier director of animated commercials. Williams also did animation for feature films, creating the opening sequences for such movies as *What's New Pussycat?, Casino Royale,* and *A Funny Thing Happened on the Way to the Forum.* He won acclaim for his openings for the *Pink Panther* films.

Over the years Williams won 240 awards for his work in animation. His first animated film, *The Little Island* (1958), which took more than three years to draw, won a British Academy Award and acclaim at the Venice Film Festival. In 1972 Williams won a U.S. Academy Award for his version of Dickens's *A Christmas Carol.* Always a perfectionist, he began work in 1965 on his full-length animated feature *The Thief and the Cobbler,* a tale based on the *Arabian Nights;* however, by the end of 1988 he had completed only 15 minutes of its animation.

(DIANE LOIS WAY)

Wilson, August

With the 1988 Broadway production of *Joe Turner's Come and Gone,* Pulitzer Prize-winning playwright August Wilson was firmly established as one of the most significant writers of the day. Wilson, who considered himself a black nationalist, thought that black Americans had "the most dramatic story of all mankind to tell." *Joe Turner* was the latest installment in a series of ten plays, each to be set in a different decade of the 20th century, that he intended to write. Through his plays Wilson hoped to expose and explore the collective black experience in the U.S. *Joe Turner,* which was set in a Pittsburgh, Pa., boardinghouse in 1911, was his most ambitious yet.

Wilson was born in 1945 and was reared with his three older sisters and two younger brothers in a two-room cold-water apartment in the Hill district of Pittsburgh. His father, a white baker of German descent, chose not to live with his family. His proud black mother raised her six children, temporarily relying on welfare until she was able to support her family as a cleaning woman. Wilson, who found the racist attitudes he encountered in school unconducive to his creativity, interests, and learning abilities, dropped out of the ninth grade at age 15. He enlisted in the U.S. Army in 1962 and was honourably discharged a year later.

A major turning point in Wilson's life occurred on April 1, 1965, the day he bought a typewriter and began writing poetry. His early poems were influenced by Dylan Thomas and the Black Power movement. Several of them were published in *Black World* and *Black Lines* in the early 1970s. About the same time he cofounded the black activist theatre company Black Horizon on the Hill, which produced several of his early plays. Although these plays were not commercially successful, they were instrumental in making Wilson resolve to write the "best play ever written." Out of this effort came the award-winning *Ma Rainey's Black Bottom* (1981), the story of blues singers in 1927

Chicago. His next play, *Fences* (1983), opened on Broadway in March 1987. This production, with veteran actor James Earl Jones as a disillusioned former baseball player in the 1950s, won not only the Antoinette Perry (Tony) Award for best play of the 1986–87 season but also the New York Drama Critics Circle Award for best play and the 1987 Pulitzer Prize for drama. In addition to being successful in the U.S., Wilson's plays were staged in Australia, Britain, and Japan; *Ma Rainey* was translated into Chinese.

In late 1987 the Yale Repertory Theater, which had done pre-Broadway productions of Wilson's earlier plays, staged *The Piano Lesson* (set in 1936). At about that same time, Wilson began work on a play set in 1968, *Two Trains Running.*   (EDWARD PAUL MORAGNE)

Witt, Katarina

In Budapest, Hung., on March 26, Katarina Witt said an emotional farewell to international amateur figure skating after proving herself to be the undisputed queen of the ice. It was a bittersweet moment as the charismatic East German skater wiped away a tear while the fans saluted her second gold medal triumph within a month.

She mesmerized an enraptured Hungarian audience with a masterly interpretation of the opera heroine Carmen, richly punctuated with well-centred spins, perfectly landed triple jumps, and highly intricate footwork. One judge awarded her a maximum 6 for presentation, each of the other eight giving her a 5.9.

Her final world championship triumph followed her second Olympic Games victory three weeks earlier in Calgary, Alta., when Witt, master manipulator of the big occasion, became the first figure skater since Norway's Sonja Henie in the 1930s to defend successfully the women's Olympic title. By that time she had acquired that rare kind of worldwide support and admiration that transcends national affiliations.

Born at Karl-Marx-Stadt, East Germany, on Dec. 3, 1965, Witt became a pupil of Jutta Müller, and they developed a winning rapport that resulted in eight consecutive national titles (1981–88); six straight European crowns (1983–88); world titles in 1984, 1985, 1987, and 1988; and Olympic gold medals in 1984 and 1988. She was outpointed only once in free skating during her last six seasons—when she lost the world title in 1986 to Debi Thomas of the U.S.

Though Witt owed her success to all-around ability, her major forte was her free skating. Throughout her career she repeatedly turned apparent defeat into victory by coming from behind during that part of the competition.

Gracefully slim and undeniably glamorous, Witt gained a commanding presence of a kind that caused many people to be fascinated by her actions off the ice as well as on. Turning professional during the summer of 1988, she made guest appearances in touring theatrical skating shows while pursuing studies in dramatic art in East Berlin.   (HOWARD BASS)

Wörner, Manfred

On Dec. 11, 1987, Manfred Wörner was elected secretary-general of the North Atlantic Treaty Organization (NATO) by consensus of the North Atlantic Council, NATO's policy-making body. The election of Wörner, the first citizen of West Germany to become secretary-general, was seen as recognition of that nation's contribution to NATO's budget and its position as host to other members' soldiers.

On July 1, 1988, in Brussels, Wörner began his five-year term in a job that involved supervising NATO's civilian activities and presiding over the North Atlantic Council. He had insisted on the importance of nonnuclear forces and on the need for a more even balance in such forces between NATO and the Warsaw Pact, which had long enjoyed nonnuclear superiority. With reluctance he supported the treaty made by the U.S. and the U.S.S.R. in 1987 to destroy intermediate-range nuclear missiles, and he said that neither the U.S. nor NATO should reduce

nuclear forces further until nonnuclear forces were trimmed by the Warsaw Pact.

Wörner was born in Stuttgart, Germany, on Sept. 24, 1934. He studied law at the University of Heidelberg, the University of Paris, and the University of Munich from 1953 to 1957. He joined the Christian Democratic Union (CDU) in 1956 and became a member of the civil service of the *Land* of Baden-Württemberg in 1957. In 1961 he received a Ph.D. in law from the University of Munich for a dissertation on the legal problems caused by stationing soldiers in friendly countries. He served as parliamentary adviser to the legislature of Baden-Württemberg from 1962 to 1964 and as a member of the Bundestag (federal parliament) from 1965 to 1988. He joined the nation's Air Force Reserve in 1966 and became a respected pilot. He was deputy chairman of those members of the Bundestag who belonged to the CDU and the affiliated Christian Social Union (CSU) from 1969 to 1971, chairman of the CDU/CSU's working group on defense from 1972 to 1976, chairman of the Bundestag's committee on defense from 1976 to 1980, and again deputy chairman of the CDU/CSU in the Bundestag from 1980 to 1982. In 1982 the CDU/CSU, then in opposition, formed a coalition with a smaller party to become a majority in the Bundestag and elected Helmut Kohl as chancellor. Kohl designated Wörner for the unpopular job of minister of defense, in which office he remained after elections in 1983 and 1987. In 1987 Kohl—at first quietly but by August overtly—advocated Wörner's election as secretary-general of NATO.   (CHARLES JOHNSON TAGGART)

Zurbriggen, Pirmin

In an age of increasing specialization in alpine skiing, Switzerland's Pirmin Zurbriggen defied the odds as an outstanding all-rounder. His charm, pleasant demeanour, exemplary behaviour, and sense of fair play endeared him to a worldwide legion of fans.

His career was not yet over, yet Zurbriggen in 1988 already ranked among the sport's all-time greats. His record almost certainly would have been even better but for a form lapse in 1986, when his concentration was interrupted by a serious illness to his sister Heidi, temporarily halting her own promising skiing career.

Happily, Zurbriggen's thirst for more success on the snow was not yet quenched. As of early 1989, his major accomplishments were winning the World Cup overall title three times—1984, 1987, and 1988; gaining world championship titles in four disciplines—downhill and combined in 1985 and giant slalom and super giant slalom in 1987; and, the honour he cherished most, winning the downhill gold medal in the Olympic Games in 1988.

Swiss head coach Karl Frehsner said in 1988: "It is a rare privilege to have an exceptional talent like Zurbriggen on my team. There isn't really anything anyone can teach him now. He is a natural and does everything right by instinct."

In the 1987 World Cup he became only the second man to win four titles in the same season—downhill, giant slalom, super giant slalom, and overall. This equaled the achievement of Frenchman Jean-Claude Killy in 1968.

In the 1987 alpine world championships at Crans-Montana, Switz., Zurbriggen gained two gold medals, for giant slalom and super giant slalom, and two silvers, for downhill and alpine combination. In that same winter's World Cup series, he won 11 races—5 downhill, 3 giant slalom, a super giant slalom, and 2 combination events.

Zurbriggen began racing on the World Cup circuit in December 1980, at the age of 17. He won his first race in 1982 in a giant slalom—two years before winning the first of his three overall titles.

Quiet and unassuming, this hotelier's son from the small Alpine village of Saas-Almagell in the Swiss Valais, where he was born on Feb. 4, 1963, was a devout Roman Catholic who made numerous pilgrimages to Lourdes.

(HOWARD BASS)

OBITUARIES

Abubakar III, Nigerian potentate and religious leader (b. March 15, 1903, Sokoto, Nigeria—d. Nov. 1, 1988, Sokoto?), celebrated his 50th anniversary as the 16th sultan of Sokoto in June 1988. He was born on the day that British troops defeated the army of Sultan Attahiru I and began their occupation of northern Nigeria. Abubakar was also caliph, or spiritual leader, of an estimated 50 million Muslims in Nigeria and beyond its borders; he reigned as the leading Islamic figure in Africa south of the Sahara. After receiving a traditional Islamic education, Abubakar became scribe (1929) of the Denge district and learned the responsibilities of the traditional ruler of the country from his uncle, Sultan Hassan, whom Abubakar accompanied to Britain in 1934. He was appointed sultan in 1938; during World War II he enlisted some of his followers for Britain's Burma campaign, for which he was knighted in 1954, six years before Nigeria became independent. Throughout his rule, Abubakar emphasized the importance of education. He advocated education for girls when to do so was unpopular; he urged older students to go to Britain when northern Nigeria had no higher education; and he held weekly study groups in his own library for his subjects. An ascetic who wore turbans and robes and championed religious tolerance, Abubakar also spoke out against Western-educated intellectuals who failed to value their African heritage.

Addams, Charles Samuel, U.S. cartoonist (b. Jan. 7, 1912, Westfield, N.J.—d. Sept. 29, 1988, New York, N.Y.), delighted readers of *The New Yorker* magazine for more than five decades with cartoons depicting the ghoulish antics performed by the peculiar residents of a cobwebbed Victorian mansion. His cast of misfits inspired the television series "The Addams Family" (1964–66). As a youth Addams was fascinated by coffins and especially skeletons. He attended Colgate University, Hamilton, N.Y. (1929–30), and the University of Pennsylvania (1930–31) before enrolling in the Grand Central School of Art in New York City. In 1932 he published his first cartoon in *The New Yorker* magazine, but it was not until the appearance of his 1940 sketch showing a lady skier whose downhill tracks led to a tree and continued in perfect parallel lines with one on each side of the tree that his reputation was secured. Addams's carefully crafted creations featured bats, spiders, broomsticks, snakes, cobwebs, and quirky characters. The master of black humour also contributed to such magazines as *Life, Colliers,* and *Cosmopolitan* and published such books as *Monster Rally* (1950), *Nightcrawlers* (1957), *Dear Dead Days* (1959), *Black Maria* (1960), and *Chas Addams Favorite Haunts* (1976). Exhibitions of his works were mounted at the Fogg Art Museum in Cambridge, Mass., the University of Pennsylvania Museum, and the Metropolitan Museum of Art in New York City.

Adler, Lawrence James, Hungarian-born Australian businessman (b. Nov. 2, 1931, Budapest, Hung.—d. Dec. 13, 1988, Sydney, Australia), arrived in Australia in 1950 as a penniless refugee unable to speak English, yet he rose to head a business empire that made him one of the ten richest men in the country. Adler, who changed his name from Laszlo to Lawrence when he fled post-World War II Hungary, worked as a Melbourne railway labourer, a taxi driver, and a janitor. In 1960 he founded the Fire and All Risks Insurance Co. (later renamed FAI Insurance, Ltd.), which eventually grew into Australia's largest general insurer. The bulk of Adler's wealth, however, came from his shrewd, aggressive stock investments. In 1987 he had acquired almost 15% of the British merchant bank Hill Samuel, which succumbed in a takeover by another bank just prior to the October 1987

crash. Adler's profits in the deal pushed FAI to a precrash value of more than $A 1.7 billion.

Albery, Sir Donald (Arthur Rolleston), British theatre manager (b. June 19, 1914, London, England—d. Sept. 14, 1988, Monte Carlo, Monaco), introduced British theatregoers to the works of such playwrights as Samuel Beckett and Brendan Behan, produced a string of hit musicals, notably *Oliver!* (1960), and helped build the London theatre into a prime tourist attraction. Albery was born into a family with strong ties to the stage. His grandfather was playwright James Albery; his grandmother was actress and theatre manager Mary Moore (Lady Wyndham); and his father, Sir Bronson Albery, was the founder of what became the Society of West End Theatres and was general manager of a half-dozen theatres that were passed on to Donald in 1962. Albery was general manager of the Sadler's Wells Ballet (now the Royal Ballet) from 1941 to 1945. His first production of a play was Graham Greene's *The Living Room* (1953). It was followed by two decades of hits including *Waiting for Godot* (1955); *The Rose Tattoo, A Taste of Honey, The Hostage,* and *The World of Suzie Wong* (all in 1959); *Fings Ain't Wot They Used T' Be* and *A Passage to India* (both in 1960); *Beyond the Fringe* and *Celebration* (both in 1961); and *Who's Afraid of Virginia Woolf?* (1964). He also mounted many productions in New York and served (1958–78) in Britain as a director of Anglia Television. Albery was knighted in 1977.

Almirante, Giorgio, Italian politician (b. June 27, 1914, Salsomaggiore, Italy—d. May 22, 1988, Rome, Italy), as a founder (1948) and first secretary (1948–50 and 1969–87) of the right-wing Italian Social Movement (MSI), pursued a campaign of aggressive anti-Communism. His low-key style brought respectability to the neo-Fascist MSI, which remained Italy's fourth largest political party with 5.9% of the vote in the 1987 election. During World War II Almirante served in the Army in North Africa as war correspondent for the Fascist daily *Il Tevere* ("The Tiber"). In 1943 he joined the Ministry of Culture in the Italian Social Republic, Benito Mussolini's last government in northern Italy. Almirante came out of hiding after World War II when a 1946 amnesty for minor Fascist officials was announced. In 1948 he was elected to the Chamber of Deputies (lower house) as a member for the new MSI. He was ousted as secretary-general of the MSI in 1950, but he reclaimed control in 1969. The Chamber of

VEZIO SABATINI—MARKA/GLOBE PHOTOS

Deputies suspended Almirante's parliamentary immunity in 1979 and charged him with reviving the outlawed Fascist Party; he escaped prosecution when he was promptly reelected to Parliament, and the immunity-lifting process had to begin again. He was twice accused of aiding right-wing terrorists (1981 and 1984), but the charges were dropped in a 1987 general amnesty. Almirante, who relinquished control of the MSI in December 1987, died two days after his frequent rival Pino Romualdi, another founding MSI member and editor of the party newspaper, succumbed to cancer. They were buried together in an openly Fascist funeral that was broadcast live on national television.

Alvarez, Luis Walter, U.S. experimental physicist (b. June 13, 1911, San Francisco, Calif.—d. Sept. 1, 1988, Berkeley, Calif.), won the 1968 Nobel Prize for Physics for his work with liquid-hydrogen bubble chambers, which he used to detect the reactions of resonance particles, subatomic particles that have extremely short lifetimes and occur only in high-energy nuclear collisions. Alvarez, who earned a B.S. (1932), M.S. (1934), and Ph.D. (1936) from the University of Chicago, joined the faculty of the University of California at Berkeley. He became professor of physics in 1945 and served in that capacity until 1978. While conducting research at the Massachusetts Institute of Technology during the 1940s, Alvarez developed a radar beam narrow enough to be used by a ground technician to guide a fog-enshrouded airliner in for landing. Besides the development of the ground-controlled landing approach system, Alvarez also devised linear radar antennas and a method for aerial bombing using radar to locate targets. During World War II he worked at the Los Alamos (N.M.) Laboratory, where he helped develop the atomic bomb, and after the war he designed the first proton linear accelerator. At the Lawrence Berkeley Laboratory, Alvarez was dubbed the "prize wild-idea man" because his scientific pursuits were so varied. In one of these efforts, he used cosmic rays in an attempt to find hidden treasure chambers at the Chephren pyramid at Giza, Egypt. The detectors placed under the pyramid, however, did not illuminate an area that contained less stone, and thus there was little likelihood of a hidden chamber. With his son Walter, Alvarez developed an impact theory proposing that the extinction of dinosaurs took place some 65 million years ago when an asteroid or a comet struck the Earth, precipitating the mass extinction of dinosaurs, together with hundreds of other species.

Ameche, Alan Dante ("THE HORSE"), U.S. football player (b. June 1, 1933, Kenosha, Wis.—d. Aug. 8, 1988, Houston, Texas), as a star fullback scored the decisive one-yard touchdown that gave the Baltimore Colts professional football team a 23–17 sudden-death victory over the New York Giants for the 1958 National Football League title. Ameche, who set a national record by rushing for 3,212 yd while playing at the University of Wisconsin, won the 1954 Heisman Trophy, college football's most coveted award. During his six seasons (1955–60) with the Baltimore Colts, he was voted rookie of the year (1955), was named All Pro (1955–58), and played in Pro Bowl games (1956, 1957, 1958, and 1959) until an acute Achilles tendon injury ended his career. Ameche retired after the 1960 season. An excellent blocker and power runner, Ameche was given the nickname "the Horse" for the way he worked on the practice field. During his professional career Ameche rushed for 4,045 yd in 964 carries for a 4.2-yd average. He scored 44 touchdowns and caught 101 passes. In 1975 Ameche was inducted into the National Football Foundation's College Football Hall of Fame.

Arias Madrid, Arnulfo, Panamanian politician (b. Aug. 15, 1901, Penonomé, Colombia—d. Aug. 10, 1988, Miami, Fla.), served as the president (1940–41, 1949–51, and for 11 days in 1968) of Panama; he was deposed by the military in each of his three short terms in office. Arias Madrid was educated at the University of Chicago and Harvard Medical School with the financial help of his elder brother Harmodio, who was Panama's president in 1932. Arias Madrid became interested in politics during the late 1920s and served as ambassador to France and England before being elected president in 1940. During his 12-month term in office, Arias Madrid instituted his country's social security system, gave the vote to women, and strengthened labour laws. When he scrapped the constitution and extended his presidential term in office to six years, however, he was ousted by the military. Though he was elected president of Panama again in 1948, the election results were thrown out. Eighteen months later the results were finally recognized, but Arias Madrid was deposed (1951) when he again tried to revoke the constitution. His 1964 presidential bid was believed marred by fraud at the ballot boxes, and though he was elected president in 1968, he served only 11 days before being ousted by the military. Arias Madrid narrowly lost the 1984 election to the official party's candidate in what many of his supporters claimed was fraud. In exile in Miami, Arias Madrid opposed the military regimes of Gen. Omar Torrijos, who died in a plane crash in 1981, and his successor, Gen. Manuel Antonio Noriega.

Armstrong, Henry (HENRY JACKSON), U.S. boxer (b. Dec. 12, 1912, Columbus, Miss.— d. Oct. 24, 1988, Los Angeles, Calif.), reigned for a few months in 1938 as featherweight, lightweight, and welterweight professional boxing champion, thereby becoming the only fighter ever to hold three world titles simultaneously. Armstrong, a phenomenal puncher, was dubbed "Homicide Hank, the Human Buzz-Saw." After winning 58 of his 62 fights as an amateur, Armstrong turned professional in 1931 and for a time fought under the name Melody Jackson. Armstrong won (Oct. 29, 1937) the world featherweight (57.2 kg [126 lb]) crown by knocking out Pete Sarron. He captured by decision (May 31, 1938) the welterweight (66.7 kg [147 lb]) championship crown held by Barney Ross, and he defeated (Aug. 17, 1938) Lou Ambers by decision to capture the lightweight (61.3 kg [135 lb]) title. Late in 1938 Armstrong resigned the featherweight championship without having defended the title, and on Aug. 22, 1939, he lost the lightweight crown in a 15-round rematch with Ambers. Armstrong defended his welterweight title 18 times before losing the title to Fritzie Zivic in a 15-round bout on Oct. 4, 1940. After being knocked out in the 12th round by Zivic in a rematch for the title the following year, Armstrong fought for four more years without a title fight. Armstrong, who was inducted into the Boxing Hall of Fame in 1954, was ordained a Baptist minister after his retirement from the ring and spent much of his life as an evangelist and as director of the Henry Armstrong Youth Foundation. He published his autobiography, *Gloves, Glory and God,* in 1956.

Ashton, Sir Frederick William Mallandaine, British ballet choreographer (b. Sept. 17, 1904, Guayaquil, Ecuador—d. Aug. 18, 1988, Eye, Suffolk, England), was principal choreographer (1935–70), associate director (1952–63), and director (1963–70) of the renowned Royal Ballet, where he created a distinctly British style of dance in neoclassical ballets of exquisite charm and lyricism. As a boy in Lima, Peru, Ashton was inspired to seek a dancing career after seeing the celebrated ballerina Anna Pavlova perform. Despite his parents' fierce opposition, in 1924 he left a position at a London import-export firm to study ballet with Léonide Massine. Ashton then studied with Marie Rambert, who encouraged him to create *The Tragedy of Fashion,* a short ballet for the 1926 revue *Riverside Nights.*

In 1932 he choreographed *Regatta* for Ninette de Valois's Vic-Wells Ballet (which became the Sadler's Wells Ballet in 1940 and the Royal Ballet in 1956). Ashton devised ballets for most of the great companies of Europe and the U.S., but the Royal Ballet remained the showcase for his most innovative pieces, such as *Les Patineurs* (1937), *Ondine* (1958), *La Fille Mal Gardée* (1960), and *Enigma Variations* (1968). In his first full-length ballet, *Cinderella* (1948), Ashton combined dance of classic simplicity with the broad humour of traditional pantomime. His finest interpreter, Margot Fonteyn, epitomized the elegant, almost poetic British style in such collaborative efforts as *Symphonic Variations* (1946), *Daphnis and Chloe* (1951), and *Marguerite and Armand* (1963). Ashton retired from his administrative duties with the Royal Ballet in 1970, but he continued to create new works for the troupe's repertory, most notably *A Month in the Country* (1976) and the ballet film *Tales of Beatrix Potter* (1971). In 1985 he assisted in a painstaking reconstruction of *Romeo and Juliet,* which he had originally created for the Royal Danish Ballet in 1955. As a dancer Ashton excelled in character roles, notably as Carabosse in *The Sleeping Beauty,* the timid Ugly Stepsister in *Cinderella,* and Mrs. Tiggy-Winkle in *Tales of Beatrix Potter.* He was created Commander of the Order of the British Empire in 1950, knighted in 1962, and made a Companion of Honour in 1970.

Astorga, Nora, Nicaraguan diplomat (b. 1949, Managua, Nicaragua—d. Feb. 14, 1988, Managua), as one of the key Sandinista guerrillas, helped engineer the revolution that overthrew the regime of Anastasio Somoza Debayle in 1979 and later served (1986–88) as Nicaragua's chief delegate to the United Nations. Astorga studied at Catholic University in Washington, D.C. While earning a law degree from the

AP/WIDE WORLD

Universidad Centroamericana in Managua, she became involved with the Frente Sandinista de Liberacíon Nacional. She married, had two children, and served as a corporate lawyer for a construction firm—a perfect cover for her clandestine activities. She earned her reputation as a "Mata Hari" when on March 8, 1978, International Women's Day, she lured the deputy commander of Somoza's National Guard, Gen. Reynaldo Pérez Vega, an alleged torturer and womanizer, to her room. When the general began to disrobe, three of her *compañeros* burst out of hiding, supposedly to kidnap, question, and then exchange him for prisoners; however, when he resisted, they killed him. Astorga later described the incident by saying, "It was not murder but political justice." She escaped to a Sandinista training camp and became com-

mander of a military squad. After the Sandinistas took power in July 1979, she was appointed chief special prosecutor for the trials of some 7,500 members of Somoza's National Guard. In 1984 the U.S. refused to accept her appointment as ambassador to Washington because of her involvement in the death of General Pérez Vega, who apparently had connections with the U.S. Central Intelligence Agency. She served as deputy foreign minister from 1984 until her appointment to the UN. As chief delegate to the UN she was instrumental in winning Security Council support for the World Court decision calling U.S. aid to the *contras* illegal. In 1986 she missed seven weeks of work after a mastectomy; she succumbed to cancer.

Balthasar, Hans Urs von, Swiss Roman Catholic theologian (b. Aug. 12, 1905, Lucerne, Switz.— d. June 26, 1988, Basel, Switz.), rejected the right-wing traditionalism of French schismatic Marcel Lefebvre (*see* BIOGRAPHIES) and the leftwing progressivism of Swiss theologian Hans Küng in favour of a deeply personal spirituality. Balthasar penned more than 60 books on such diverse topics as the theology of history, the early Christian Church Fathers, classical literature, and modern aestheticism. He wrote much of his early work as a rebuttal to the writings of his friend and rival Swiss Protestant theologian Karl Barth. Balthasar studied philosophy at the Universities of Vienna, Berlin, and Zürich, where he received a Ph.D. in 1929. He was ordained a Jesuit priest in 1936 and taught school in Basel (1940–48) before leaving the Jesuits in 1950 to found a secular institute in Basel with the Christian mystic Adrienne von Speyr. Balthasar, greatly admired by Pope John Paul II, was awarded the Paul VI international prize in 1984 and was made a cardinal in 1988; he died two days before his investiture.

Bearden, Romare Howard, U.S. collagist and painter (b. Sept. 2, 1914, Charlotte, N.C.—d. March 11, 1988, New York, N.Y.), extracted elements of Cubism and combined them with photographic images and painted cut paper to produce extraordinary canvases, which explored such themes as jazz and folk music, urban and rural life, rituals of baptism and voodoo, and home life and street action, relevant to black life and culture in the U.S. Though Bearden planned to study medicine, he began sketching cartoons in college for the *Afro-American,* a black weekly newspaper, and found his artistic niche. From 1936 to 1937 he studied with George Grosz at the Art Students League in New York City. After serving in the Army during World War II, he met art dealer Samuel Kootz, who sponsored his first important one-man show in New York City. He then studied at the Sorbonne and traveled extensively in Europe. Bearden was a celebrated black collagist and the nation's foremost exponent of the medium; he was instrumental in helping younger artists find an outlet for their works both by serving as a mentor and by founding the Cinque Gallery, together with Norman Lewis and Ernest Crichlow. From 1970 to 1980 he created 342 collages, 128 oils on paper, 24 drawings, 25 prints, 5 tapestries, 4 murals and mosaics, and dozens of illustrations. Some of his most famous collages include "The Block," "Patchwork Quilt," and "Family."

Bellisario, Marisa, Italian business executive (b. July 9, 1935, Ceva, Italy—d. Aug. 4, 1988, Turin, Italy), as the dynamic managing director (1981–88) of Italtel, the state-owned manufacturer of telecommunications equipment, transformed the lumbering colossus with a deficit of 700 billion lire into a streamlined profitable firm in less than three years. Bellisario was one of the few top businesswomen in Italy, and her tough but fair management technique was often cited as a model for other struggling state-held industries. Bellisario studied economics at the University of Turin and joined the electronics division at Olivetti SpA in 1960. She remained head of electronics product and operations plan-

ning when Olivetti sold the division to General Electric in 1964 and when the latter sold it to Honeywell in 1969. In 1972 Bellisario returned to Olivetti as director of corporate planning, and in 1979 she was sent to the U.S. as president of the Olivetti Corp. of America. She was recalled to Italy in 1980 and the next year was offered the task of saving the nearly bankrupt Italtel. Bellisario encouraged product diversification, increased exports, and cut the staff by one-third without antagonizing the unions. In 1987 Fiat rejected a merger with Italtel, allegedly because of Bellisario's left-wing politics, but a few days before her death Bellisario signed a lucrative licensing agreement with Fiat.

Bourne, Geoffrey, Australian-born anatomist and nutritionist (b. Nov. 17, 1909, Perth, Western Australia—d. July 19, 1988, New York, N.Y.), was an international authority on nutrition who wrote widely renowned historical overviews on hunger, notably *Nutrition and the War* (1940) and *Starvation in Europe* (1943). He was more closely identified, however, with his extraordinary work with primates as director of the Yerkes Regional Primate Research Center at Emory University in Atlanta, Ga. (1962–78). Bourne appeared on U.S. television and described, on the "Johnny Carson Show," how he taught chimpanzees to communicate by typing on a computer; he popularized his studies in works such as *Ape People* (1971), *Primate Odyssey* (1974), and *The Gentle Giants: The Gorilla Story* (1975). After receiving a B.Sc. (1931) and D.Sc. (1935) from the University of Western Australia, he worked as an anatomist and a biochemist in Australia before teaching histology at the University of London and physiology at the University of Oxford, where he earned a Ph.D. in 1943. During World War II he served as a nutritional adviser to the British forces in Burma and rose to the rank of lieutenant colonel. He was a reader in histology at London Hospital Medical College (1947–57) before immigrating to the U.S. to become professor and chairman of anatomy at Emory University in 1957. After retiring as director of Emory's primate centre in 1978, he became vice-chancellor and professor of nutrition at St. George's University School of Medicine in Grenada. He was in charge of scores of U.S. medical students rescued from there in 1983 after a coup by a revolutionary council precipitated an invasion led by U.S. military forces.

Boxer, Mark (CHARLES MARK EDWARD BOXER), British editor and cartoonist (b. May 19, 1931, England—d. July 20, 1988, London, England), skewered the foibles and pretensions of the British upper middle class in caricatures and single-frame "pocket cartoons" under the pseudonym "Marc," yet he remained a respected magazine and newspaper editor within the society he satirized. Boxer's deftly drawn cartoons, many of which featured the trendy social-climbing couple the Stringalongs, appeared daily in *The Times* (1969–83), *The Guardian* (1983–86), and *The Daily Telegraph* (1986–88). He also contributed whimsical social and political caricatures to such periodicals as *New Statesman* and *The New Yorker.* Boxer was briefly expelled from the University of Cambridge when he published an irreverent poem in the student magazine *Granta,* of which he was editor. He quit Cambridge soon after to study layout and design at a London fashion magazine and to draw cartoons for *The Tatler.* After working as art director of *Queen* (1957–61), he was named editor of the new *Sunday Times* colour supplement. Boxer later served as director (1964–66) and assistant editor (1966–79) of *The Sunday Times.* In 1983 Boxer was hired by Condé Nast Publications as editor of *The Tatler,* and in 1987 he was promoted to editor in chief of *Vogue* and editorial director of Condé Nast.

Boyington, Gregory ("PAPPY"), U.S. pilot (b. Dec. 4, 1912, Coeur d'Alene, Idaho—d. Jan. 11, 1988, Fresno, Calif.), was a colourful World

AP/WIDE WORLD

War II flying ace who shot down 28 enemy Japanese planes and in 1943 organized the legendary Black Sheep Squadron. His unit comprised 49 replacement and inactive pilots who in 84 days of combat shot down 98 Japanese planes over Kahili, Bougainville, and Rabaul in the South Pacific and annihilated or damaged at least 130 other enemy aircraft on the ground. Boyington, a 1934 graduate of the University of Washington, enlisted in the U.S. Marine Corps in 1936 and became a pilot the following year. He was a lieutenant and flight instructor at Pensacola (Fla.) Naval Air Station when he resigned from the Marines to join Gen. Claire L. Chennault's American Volunteer Group, the Flying Tigers, in China, where he became an ace after shooting down six Japanese planes. He rejoined the Marines in 1942 after the Japanese attack on Pearl Harbor, and after briefly serving in an administrative capacity, he organized the 212 Squadron, one of the most renowned fighting units during the war. On Boyington's last mission, Jan. 3, 1944, he shot down 3 aircraft, bringing his total to 26 (later corrected to 28), including his 6 kills with the Flying Tigers. His bullet-ridden aircraft was shot down on the same day, and he was picked up by a Japanese submarine, which transported him to a prison camp in Japan, where he remained for 20 months. Though his fate was unknown, the U.S. government awarded him the Medal of Honor in 1944. He was released from prison in 1945 and retired with the rank of colonel in 1947. For a time he was dogged by alcoholism, but he later recovered and chronicled his memoirs in *Baa Baa Black Sheep* (1958), which was made into a popular television program. Boyington was also the recipient of the Navy Cross.

Brewster, Kingman, Jr., U.S. educator and diplomat (b. June 17, 1919, Longmeadow, Mass.—d. Nov. 8, 1988, Oxford, England), as president (1963–77) of Yale University was best remembered for his support of students protesting the Vietnam war and for an admissions policy that permitted the enrollment of more blacks and the admission in 1969 of undergraduate women to the men's university. Brewster, who graduated from Yale University in 1941, earned a law degree from Harvard University in 1948. He served (1950–60) as professor of law at Harvard before being appointed provost at Yale in 1960 by A. Whitney Griswold. After the latter's death in 1963, Brewster became acting president of Yale; the appointment was made permanent later that year. Brewster became the first Yale president who was also a lawyer and the first since 1900 not to hold a Ph.D. During his tenure Brewster also started a school of black studies and led a Yale antiwar demonstration in Washington, D.C. His leniency toward antiwar

protesters, however, led to a serious financial erosion due to the withdrawal of the support of alumni who disagreed with his views. In 1977 Brewster was named ambassador to Great Britain by Pres. Jimmy Carter, a post he held until 1981. Brewster then returned to private law practice in London for a New York-based firm until he was appointed (1986) master of University College, Oxford, a post he held until his death.

Brockway, (Archibald) Fenner Brockway, BARON, British politician (b. Nov. 1, 1888, Calcutta, India—d. April 28, 1988, Watford, Hertfordshire, England), as a passionate socialist devoted his life to such prominent 20th-century causes as world peace, anticolonialism, and nuclear disarmament. Brockway was the son of missionaries and espoused liberal beliefs from an early age, notably in his support for the Boers in the South African War (1899–1902). He became a convert to socialism in 1907 after interviewing Keir Hardie (founder of the Labour Party) for a London newspaper, and by 1912 Brockway was editor of the weekly *Labour Leader.* After being jailed as a draft resister during World War I, Brockway fought for prison reform and served as chairman (1923–28) of the No More War Movement and War Resisters' International. As a member of the Independent Labour Party (ILP; Labour's left-wing offshoot), Brockway was ILP general secretary (1923–26 and 1933–39), chairman (1931–33), and political secretary (1939–46), but he returned to the Labour Party in 1946. He represented Labour

JANE BOWN—CAMERA PRESS/GLOBE PHOTOS

in Parliament (1929–31 and 1950–64), where his fight for independence for British African colonies earned him the nickname "the member for Africa." After reluctantly accepting a life peerage in 1964, Brockway continued to crusade for various causes in the House of Lords (an institution he tried to have abolished). His many books included a defense of Indian nationalism, *The Indian Crisis* (1930); a study of race relations, *This Shrinking Explosive World* (1967); and four autobiographical volumes, the last of which, *98 Not Out,* was published in 1986.

Calvo Serer, Rafael, Spanish intellectual (b. 1916, Valencia, Spain—d. April 19, 1988, Pamplona, Spain), was a vehement apologist for Gen. Francisco Franco's regime until he switched his allegiance to exiled pretender Don Juan de Borbón. Calvo Serer taught history at the University of Madrid. As a youth he joined the powerful Roman Catholic organization Opus Dei, whose members strive for Christian perfection and pledge to uphold Christian ideals in their chosen profession. In 1939 he helped found the Superior Council of Scientific Investigations (a hard-line Roman Catholic group that dominated Spanish culture under Franco),

and he was editor of its influential periodical, *Arbor*. During the 1950s Calvo Serer opposed an apparent decline in conservative ideals and turned his support to Don Juan. As publisher of the newspaper *Madrid* from 1966, Calvo Serer offered a forum for all anti-Franco sentiments. His 1968 editorial in favour of Charles de Gaulle's retirement was widely seen as a demand for Franco to step down, and the newspaper was banned for several weeks. It was finally shut down in 1971, and Calvo Serer fled to Paris, where he wrote a succession of monarchist editorials for French and Latin-American newspapers. In 1974 he formed an anti-Franco coalition, the Democratic Junta, with exiled Communists. He was arrested on his return to Spain in June 1976, but he was released within days. Later that year the Spanish Supreme Court ruled that *Madrid* had been seized illegally, and Calvo Serer was awarded more than $4.4 million in damages.

Caniff, Milton A., U.S. cartoonist (b. Feb. 28, 1907, Hillsboro, Ohio—d. April 3, 1988, New York, N.Y.), was dubbed the "Rembrandt of the comic strip" and was credited with helping to elevate the comics to an art form as the creator of "Terry and the Pirates," an action-filled, suspense-packed strip that featured the seductive Dragon Lady. After graduating from Ohio State University with a degree in fine arts, Caniff moved in 1932 to New York City, where he created such strips as "The Gay Thirties" and "Dickie Dare" for the Associated Press. He was hired by the *New York News* in 1934 to sketch a strip with a blood-and-thunder formula, and he introduced "Terry and the Pirates" on October 22 that same year. In 1946, when Caniff was unable to obtain ownership of the strip, he abandoned "Terry and the Pirates," which was taken over by George Wunder and was drawn by him until it ended in 1973. Caniff founded his own strip, "Steve Canyon," in 1947, and his square-jawed hero was a huge success, appearing in syndication in more than 500 newspapers throughout the world. Caniff was one of the original founders of the National Cartoonists Society in 1946 and served as an inspiration to hundreds of cartoonists who borrowed heavily from his superb techniques.

Carradine, John (RICHMOND REED CARRADINE), U.S. actor (b. Feb. 5, 1906, New York, N.Y.—d. Nov. 27, 1988, Milan, Italy), was a versatile performer whose sunken cheeks, imposing height, and stentorian voice made him ideally suited to portraying villains in both westerns and horror films. The indefatigable Carradine appeared in more than 200 films and gave some of his most memorable performances in *Stagecoach* (1939) as a gambler, *The Grapes of Wrath* (1940) as a former preacher, *Hitler's Madman* (1943) as a Nazi general, *The Adventures of Mark Twain* (1944) as the writer Bret Harte,

AP/WIDE WORLD

and *The Ten Commandments* (1956) as Aaron. As a member of John Ford's stock company of character actors, Carradine also appeared in such films as *Mary of Scotland* (1936), *Drums Along the Mohawk* (1939), and *The Man Who Shot Liberty Valance* (1962). His preference for Shakespearean roles prompted him to return to the theatre. He also amused spectators as he donned a wide-brimmed hat and red-satin-lined cape to traverse the streets of New York and Los Angeles reciting Shakespeare; in Hollywood he was affectionately known as the "bard of the Boulevard." Carradine starred at least three times as Dracula and also appeared in such films as *The Invisible Man* (1933), *Bride of Frankenstein* (1935), *The Hound of the Baskervilles* (1939), and *Blood and Sand* (1941). Some of his most recent films included *The Shootist* (1976), *The Sentinel* (1977), and his last one, *The Return of the Three Musketeers*, which had not yet been released. Carradine was also the patriarch of an acting family; four of his five sons—David, Robert, Keith, and Bruce—acted in films and on television.

Carter, Billy (WILLIAM ALTON CARTER III), U.S. personality (b. March 29, 1937, Plains, Ga.—d. Sept. 25, 1988, Plains), was a self-styled "beer-drinking good ol' boy" who rose to national prominence when his older brother, Jimmy, was elected president of the U.S. in 1976. Carter, a peanut farmer and proprietor of "Billy Carter's filling station" in Plains, delighted in embellishing his image as a Georgia redneck. He turned his celebrity status to his advantage by hiring an agent and making public appearances for $5,000 each. He even sold his name to a brewing company that marketed the short-lived Billy beer. However, his antics shed a dark cloud over the White House in 1978 when he became an apologist for Libya and in 1980 when evidence came to light that he had agreed "under protest" to register as a Libyan agent and admitted receiving $220,000 from the government of Libya's Mu'ammar al-Qadhdhafi. Although a subcommittee of the Senate Judiciary Committee concluded that Billy's activities had had no influence on U.S. policy, his actions were an acute embarrassment to the president, who nonetheless refused to distance himself from his irrepressible brother. In 1981 Billy was forced to sell his Plains property, including his gas station, to pay federal taxes and to satisfy local bankers. After his home was auctioned, Carter moved his family to Haleyville, Ala., and joined Tidwell Industries as a sales representative. In 1985, while serving as vice-president of Scott Housing Systems, Inc., he entered a guilty plea on behalf of the company on charges that it had participated in padding invoices. The company was fined $10,000 and was ordered to make restitution to the Veterans Administration. Carter had suffered from pancreatic cancer for a year before his death.

Carver, Raymond, U.S. writer (b. May 25, 1938, Clatskanie, Ore.—d. Aug. 2, 1988, Port Angeles, Wash.), whose realistic writings about the working poor mirrored his own life, which was shadowed by alcoholism, a broken marriage, poverty, and the cancer that took his life. Carver, who got married a year after finishing high school, supported his wife and two children by working as a janitor, a farm worker, and a delivery boy. In 1958 he began attending Chico (Calif.) State College and, after taking a creative writing course, he became serious about a writing career. He published his first short story, "Pastoral," and his first poem, "The Brass Ring," while studying at Humboldt State College, Arcata, Calif., from which he graduated in 1963. His first success as a writer came in 1967 when the story "Will You Please Be Quiet, Please?" was selected for the anthology *Best American Short Stories*. Despite his literary success, Carver never found personal happiness, and he began to drink heavily. A minimalist writer whose hard-biting prose chronicled the lives of the working poor in his native Pacific Northwest, Carver was credited with reviving

the short story as a literary genre. Despite his heavy dependence on alcohol, Carver continued to turn out short stories. His first volume of poetry, *Near Klamath*, was published in 1968. It was followed by collections of short stories including *Put Yourself in My Shoes* (1974), *What We Talk About When We Talk About Love* (1981), and *Cathedral* (1984). After conquering his drinking problem in 1982, Carver, who had taught at the University of California at Santa Cruz for several years, won a Mildred and Harold Strauss Living Award (1983), with a $35,000 annual stipend, which freed him to concentrate on his writing full time. Shortly after *Where I'm Calling From* appeared in 1988, Carver was inducted into the American Academy and Institute of Arts and Letters.

Char, René, French poet (b. June 14, 1907, L'Isle-sur-la-Sorgue, France—d. Feb. 19, 1988, Paris, France), was a Surrealist during his youth, but after World War II he wrote poetry that juxtaposed austere language with dense, contradictory ideas and images. Char drew much of the nature imagery that permeated his poetry from rural Vaucluse (a region in southeastern France), where he spent most of his life. In 1929 he sent a copy of *Arsenal*, his first volume of poems, to Paul Éluard, who invited him to Paris and introduced him to André Breton, the nominal leader of the Surrealists. Char collaborated with Éluard and Breton on the verse collection *Ralentir travaux* (1930), and he became friends with artists Pablo Picasso, Georges Braque, and Joan Miró, all of whom illustrated his work. During his years in Paris, Char composed one of his finest groups of poems, *Le Marteau sans maitre* (1934), which was later set to music (1954) by Pierre Boulez. Char fought in Alsace at the outbreak of World War II, but he returned to Vaucluse when France was defeated. In 1942, suspected of being a Communist because of his left-wing Surrealist friends, he escaped and led a Resistance unit in the Alps. He was seriously wounded in 1944, fled to Algeria to serve on the North Africa Allied Council, and then fought with the liberation forces in Vaucluse. After the war, Char published a collection of antiwar poems, *Seuls demeurent* (1945), and his poetic journal of the war years, *Feuillets d'Hypnos* (1946). His subsequent volumes were compiled into *Oeuvres complètes* in 1983.

Chiang Ching-kuo, Chinese politician (b. March 18, 1910, Ch'i-k'ou, Zhejiang [Chekiang] Province, China—d. Jan. 13, 1988, Taipei, Taiwan), as the son and political heir of Generalissimo Chiang Kai-shek, served as president (1978–88) of Taiwan and chairman of the ruling Nationalist Party, the Kuomintang (KMT). As president, Chiang was a pragmatic leader who instituted sweeping political, social, and economic reforms. He ended 38 years of martial law, widened freedoms of speech, assembly, and press, allowed the formation of opposition political parties, and encouraged natives of Taiwan to join the KMT. He also permitted family visits to China. His "Ten Major Construction Projects" transformed Taiwan into a modern economic power. As a youth in China, he was arrested for participating in revolutionary activities, and in 1925, two years after his father visited the Soviet Union, he went to Moscow, where he studied at Sun Yat-sen University. He denounced his father's dissolution of the Nationalist-Communist alliance in a bloody showdown (1927). Chiang was then selected for advanced studies at the Central Tolmachev Military and Political Institute in Leningrad. In 1935 he married a Soviet woman. In 1937, after his father formed a united front with the Communists to oppose the Japanese invaders, Chiang was able to return to China. He then claimed he had been forced to criticize his father and had, in effect, been held hostage in the Soviet Union. After the Communists gained control of the mainland in 1949, father and son moved to Taiwan, where Chiang Kai-shek relocated the seat of the Nationalist government. Chiang became involved with political train-

ing in the Army and with security and intelligence operations. In 1952 he was elected to the KMT's Central Committee and became head of the Chinese Youth Corps. From 1965 to 1969 he served as minister of national defense, and in 1972 he became president of the Executive Yuan (premier). After his father's death in 1975, he was named chairman of the KMT's Central Committee. Three years later he was elected president of Taiwan, succeeding Yen Chia-kan. In 1979 the U.S. ended formal relations with Taiwan in order to establish diplomatic ties with China. Chiang proved, during the years that followed, to be a much more skillful and popular leader than many had expected.

Cournand, André Frédéric, French-born physician (b. Sept. 24, 1895, Paris, France—d. Feb. 19, 1988, Great Barrington, Mass.), shared the 1956 Nobel Prize for Physiology or Medicine with Dickinson W. Richards and Werner Forssmann for their discoveries concerning heart catheterization and circulatory changes. Cournand, who graduated from the Sorbonne in 1915, served in the French Army before completing his medical studies at the University of Paris. In 1930 he immigrated to New York City to study chest diseases with Richards at Bellevue Hospital, and the two perfected a method of catheterization using the heart catheter invented by Forssmann, who in 1929 had demonstrated how a catheter could be maneuvered through a vein in his elbow into his heart. This procedure enabled physicians to examine the diseased human heart and to make more accurate diagnoses of underlying anatomic defects. In 1934 Cournand joined the faculty of the College of Physicians and Surgeons of Columbia University, New York City, a post he held until 1964, when he became emeritus professor of medicine. He and Richards continued to collaborate on improvements in diagnosis and theory until Richards's death in 1973.

Cunningham, Glenn, U.S. track star (b. 1910, Elkhart, Kan.—d. March 10, 1988, Menifee, Ark.), reigned as the ranking middle-distance runner in the U.S. during the 1930s, a feat that was all the more impressive because he had been severely burned at the age of seven when a stove exploded in his schoolroom, killing his older brother. Cunningham, threatened with the amputation of both of his legs, began exercising his limbs and recovered so spectacularly that on June 16, 1934, he set a new world record for the mile—4:06.7. Cunningham used running as a therapy for his leg burns and easily won the first high school mile race he entered. While attending the University of Kansas, he set a U.S. record for the mile with a time of 4:11.1. As a member of the 1932 Olympic team, he finished fourth in the 1,500-m run in Los Angeles, and in the 1936 Berlin Olympics he won a silver medal. In all, Cunningham captured 21 of the 31 mile races on the indoor track at Madison Square Garden, New York City, and established six world records in the mile and the 1,500-m races and another at 1,000 yd. His personal best time for the mile was 4:04.4. Cunningham, who earned a Ph.D. in physical education from New York University in 1938, retired from sports in 1940 to teach at Cornell College, Mount Vernon, Iowa. He later purchased a ranch in Kansas, where, besides raising his own 12 children, he cared for some 9,000 troubled youths or orphans. Cunningham was the recipient of the Sullivan and Helms trophies in 1933.

Daniel, Yuly Markovich (NIKOLAY ARZHAK), Soviet writer (b. 1925, Moscow, U.S.S.R.—d. Dec. 30, 1988, Moscow), with Andrey D. Sinyavsky was convicted of anti-Soviet slander in a sensational 1966 trial that marked the beginning of literary repression under Leonid I. Brezhnev, general secretary of the Communist Party. Daniel had smuggled several anti-Stalinist short stories to Paris, where they were published as *This Is Moscow Speaking, and Other Stories* (1962) under the pseudonym Nikolay Arzhak. He was arrested in September 1965,

less than a year after Brezhnev's rise to power. At Daniel and Sinyavsky's four-day joint trial, which was closed to the public, no evidence was allowed on their behalf, and dozens of Soviet and Western writers protested the convictions. Daniel was sentenced to five years of hard labour and Sinyavsky to seven years. After his release in September 1969, Daniel lived quietly in Kaluga, near Moscow. He was later allowed to return to Moscow, and in July 1988, in the new spirit of *glasnost* (openness), several of his poems were published in the Soviet Union for the first time.

Daniels, Billy (WILLIAM DANIELS), U.S. singer (b. 1915, Jacksonville, Fla.—d. Oct. 7, 1988, Los Angeles, Calif.), was a polished showman who dazzled nightclub audiences with his renditions of such all-time favourites as "That Old Black Magic," "On the Sunny Side of the Street," and "When You're Smiling." Daniels launched his career as a singing waiter in Harlem during the Depression and by 1948 had reached stardom with his recording of "That Old Black Magic," which sold more than nine million copies. During the 1950s and '60s he performed throughout the U.S.; he was especially popular in Las Vegas, Nev. Daniels also appeared on the Broadway stage in *Golden Boy* (1964) and *Hello, Dolly!* (1975), in London in *Bubbling Brown Sugar* (1977), and in such films as *Rainbow 'Round My Shoulder, When You're Smiling,* and *Sunny Side of the Street.* Even after two coronary bypass operations (1982 and 1987), Daniels continued to perform, gaining critical acclaim for his craftsmanship.

Dart, Raymond Arthur, Australian-born anatomist and paleoanthropologist (b. Feb. 4, 1893, Brisbane, Australia—d. Nov. 22, 1988, Johannesburg, South Africa), was credited with having found the link between apes and humans with his 1924 identification of an early human fossil skull in Africa. Though his announcements were received skeptically by fellow scientists, who then believed that humans had evolved in China, the correctness of Dart's *Australopithecus africanus* ("South African ape") species was later proved. Subsequent African discoveries by such anthropologists as Phillip Tobias, the Leakey family, and Donald Johanson underscored Dart's work and indicated that the creatures he identified lived more than two million years ago. Dart, who graduated (1913) with honours in biology from the University of Queensland, received (1917) his M.D. from Sydney University and served (1917–19) as a captain in the Australian Army Medical Corps in Europe. He was (1919–22) senior demonstrator in anatomy at University College, London, spent a year in the U.S. as a Rockefeller Foundation fellow, returned to London as a lecturer, and served as both professor of anatomy (1923–58) and medical faculty dean (1926–43) at the medical school of the University of the Witwatersrand, Johannesburg. The skull Dart tagged as early human was from a cave near Taung, a village at the edge of the Kalahari Desert, 644 km (400 mi) southwest of Johannesburg; it was kept at the Transvaal Museum in Pretoria. After World War II Dart led expeditions that opened other major African fossil sites. Since 1966 he had been a visiting professor at the Institute for the Study of Human Potential in Philadelphia. In addition to many scholarly articles, he wrote *Adventures with the Missing Link* (1959), an autobiography.

Day, Dennis (EUGENE DENIS McNULTY), U.S. singer (b. May 21, 1917, New York, N.Y.—d. June 22, 1988, Brentwood, Calif.), was a golden-voiced Irish balladeer who delighted radio and television audiences while portraying the dim-witted adolescent tenor who served as a foil for comedian Jack Benny. He was especially favoured for his renditions of such songs as "Danny Boy," "Clancy Lowered the Boom," and "Peg o' My Heart." After joining "The Jack Benny Program" in 1939, he adopted the professional name of Dennis Day. He was said to

AP/WIDE WORLD

have landed the job when he made an off-the-cuff wisecrack; when Benny called out, "Oh, Dennis," he replied, "Yes, please." Day stayed with the radio show until its last broadcast in 1955 and reprised his role for Benny's weekly television program (1950–64). Besides starring on his own radio program, "A Day in the Life of Dennis Day" (1946–51), he was a regular on such television variety shows as "All Star Revue," "Hour Glass," and "The RCA Victor Show." Day also had roles in the films *Music in Manhattan* (1944) and *The Girl Next Door* (1953). A shrewd businessman, Day founded his own television production company, operated a restaurant chain, and invested in oil wells and stocks.

Dearden, John Francis Cardinal, U.S. prelate of the Roman Catholic Church (b. Oct. 15, 1907, Valley Fall, R.I.—d. Aug. 1, 1988, Southfield, Mich.), was spiritual leader (1958–80) of 1.2 million Roman Catholics in the Detroit archdiocese and was viewed as a progressive leader, instrumental in shaping the liturgical changes that evolved from the second Vatican Council (1962–65). After graduating (1928) from St. Mary Seminary in Cleveland, Ohio, he was ordained a priest in 1932. During the 1940s Dearden served as rector and philosophy professor at St. Mary's before being named bishop of Pittsburgh in 1950. In 1958 he became archbishop of Detroit and, after Pope Paul VI restored the lay diaconate in 1967, Dearden revitalized the archdiocese's shrinking clergy by ordaining 13 married laymen as deacons. From 1966 to 1971 Dearden served as president of the National Conference of Catholic Bishops, and in 1969

AP/WIDE WORLD

he was elevated to cardinal. A central figure during the second Vatican Council, Dearden gained national prominence for his innovative approach to the new liturgy. He was criticized, however, when he closed 56 of the 269 schools in the archdiocese in 1970 after an amendment was added to the Michigan constitution barring all public aid to nonpublic schools; his actions caused widespread discontent because at that time he was serving as head of the bishops' conference. During the mid-1970s Dearden headed a church committee that spent two years studying social issues; hearings and debates involved 1,350 delegates. In 1976 the group adopted a five-year, 182-point "Call for Action" agenda that was submitted to the Conference of Bishops. Dearden retired in 1980 but continued in his role as apostolic administrator until 1981.

Diamond, I. A. L. (ITEK DOMMNICI), U.S. screenwriter (b. June 27, 1920, Ungheni, Rom.—d. April 21, 1988, Beverly Hills, Calif.), teamed up with director Billy Wilder to produce such memorable motion pictures as *Love in the Afternoon* (1957), *Some Like It Hot* (1959), and *The Apartment* (1960), for which he won an Academy Award for best screenplay. While attending Columbia University, New York City, Diamond began writing for *The Columbia Spectator* and at the same time adopted the initials I. A. L. (Interscholastic Algebra League) as his legal name, although he also answered to Iz or Isadore. He wrote scripts for such films as *Murder in the Blue Room* (1944) and *Always Together* (1947) before embarking on a 30-year collaboration with Wilder. The two successfully combined witty dialogue with mature sexual situations and introduced adult entertainment to Hollywood. Their most successful scripts explored male-female relationships and combined cynicism with sentiment. Some of their other films included *Irma La Douce* (1963), *The Fortune Cookie* (1966), *The Private Life of Sherlock Holmes* (1970), *Avanti!* (1972), *The Front Page* (1974), and *Buddy Buddy* (1981).

Doko Toshio, Japanese businessman (b. 1896, Okayama Prefecture, Japan—d. Aug. 4, 1988, Tokyo, Japan), was instrumental in revitalizing Japanese manufacturing after World War II, most notably as president (1965–72) and chairman (1972–76) of Toshiba Corp. and as chairman (1974–80) of one of Japan's four main business organizations, the powerful Keidanren, comprising about 110 industry-wide groups representing some 800 corporations. After graduating from Tokyo Technical Higher School (now Tokyo Institute of Technology), he worked as a turbine designer for the Ishikawajima Shipyard. As president (1950–60) of Ishikawajima Heavy Industries, he revamped the firm in order to benefit from heavy U.S. procurement during the Korean War. Doko later presided over the newly merged Ishikawajima-Harima Heavy Industries Co. Ltd. and oversaw the construction of the *Idemitsu maru,* the world's largest tanker during the 1960s. When he took the helm at Toshiba, he revived worker and management morale and steered the company to prosperity. In 1981 Doko was named chairman of the prime minister's advisory council on administrative reform. In 1983 his group submitted a plan that recommended the division of the state-run Japan National Railways into several private companies; the measure was implemented in 1987.

Dorati, Antal, Hungarian-born composer and conductor (b. April 9, 1906, Budapest, Hung.—d. Nov. 13, 1988, Gerzensee, Switz.), led major symphony orchestras around the world and made more than 500 recordings in a career that exceeded 50 years. The son of musicians—his father was a violinist with the Budapest Philharmonic Orchestra, and his mother was a teacher of piano and violin—Dorati first studied piano at the age of five and then was a student (1920–24) of composers Bela Bartok and Zoltan Kodaly at the Liszt Academy in Budapest. Upon graduation, Dorati was named assistant director

of the Budapest Royal Opera and then assistant director (1928) of the Dresden (Germany) State Opera before serving as director (1929–32) of the Münster (Germany) State Opera. He then was principal conductor (1933–40) of the Ballet Russe de Monte Carlo, with which he toured in Europe and the U.S. In 1941 he immigrated to the U.S. to serve as musical director (1941–45) of the newly formed American Ballet Theatre. He was conductor (1945–49) of the Dallas (Texas) Symphony Orchestra, where his reputation grew both for forcefully building a symphony and for performing world premieres of works by such composers as Paul Hindemith, Benjamin Britten, and Bartok. Dorati, who became a naturalized U.S. citizen in 1947, was also conductor of the Minneapolis (Minn.) Symphony Orchestra (1949–60), the BBC Symphony Orchestra, London (1963–66), the Stockholm Philharmonic (1966–70), the National Symphony Orchestra, Washington, D.C. (1970–77), the Detroit Symphony (1977–81), and, simultaneously, the Royal Philharmonic Orchestra, London (1975–79). His own compositions and arrangements spanned his conducting career. Dorati, known for a no-nonsense manner on and off the podium, published his autobiography, *Notes of Seven Decades,* in 1979. He was knighted in 1984.

Drees, Willem, Dutch politician (b. July 5, 1886, Amsterdam, Neth.—d. May 14, 1988, The Hague, Neth.), as prime minister of The Netherlands (1948–58), laid the foundations for the modern welfare state, relinquished control over the Dutch East Indies (now Indonesia), and abandoned traditional Dutch neutrality to establish military and economic alliances, most notably the North Atlantic Treaty Organization and the European Economic Community. Drees joined the Social Democratic (later Labour) Party at the age of 18 and worked as a stenographer in Parliament (1906–19). He served on the municipal council in The Hague from 1913 until 1941. In 1933 he was elected to the Second (principal) Chamber of the States-General. During World War II Drees was arrested for anti-German activities and was briefly interned (1940–41) in the Buchenwald concentration camp; he joined the resistance movement after his release. As minister of social affairs (1945–48) and then as prime minister, Drees introduced such social welfare programs as old-age pensions, unemployment compensation, and national health care. In 1948 Drees sent troops to the Dutch East Indies, which had declared its independence in 1945, in order to reestablish Dutch sovereignty. The action was widely supported in The Netherlands, but it attracted international condemnation, and in 1949 Drees reluctantly acknowledged the independence of Indonesia. Drees retired in 1958 after the coalition he headed broke apart in a dispute over proposed tax increases. In 1971 he denounced the increasingly leftist Labour policies and resigned from the party.

Evans, Gil (IAN ERNEST GILMORE GREEN), Canadian-born jazz composer and orchestrator (b. May 13, 1912, Toronto, Ont.—d. March 20, 1988, Cuernavaca, Mexico), was a superb improviser who began a fruitful collaboration with Miles Davis during the 1940s and arranged such masterpieces as "Moondreams" and "Boplicity" for Davis's nine-piece orchestra, which featured trumpet, trombone, french horn, tuba, alto sax, baritone sax, piano, bass, and drums and was credited with ushering in the "cool" school of jazz during the 1950s. Evans created luminescent floating arrangements that defied categorization as dance music or as entertainment and thus transformed American composing and arranging. Earlier in his career, Evans had performed with Claude Thornhill's band, but it was his arrangements for such Davis albums as *Miles Ahead, Porgy and Bess,* and *Sketches of Spain* that assured his reputation. In later years Evans fronted his own bands and embraced rock music, incorporating tough rock rhythms with an electric sound.

Eyskens, Gaston, Belgian economist and politician (b. April 1, 1905, Lier, Belgium—d. Jan. 3, 1988, Louvain, Belgium), was prime minister of Belgium three times (1949–50, 1958–61, and 1968–72) and was instrumental in granting independence (1960) to the Belgian Congo (now Zaire). He studied economics at the University of Louvain and at Columbia University, New York City, and then returned to Louvain in 1931 to teach economics. In 1939 he entered Parliament as a member of the Catholic (later Social Christian) Party, serving as minister of finance from 1945 until 1949, when he was chosen to head a new coalition government. This government fell in 1950 during the controversy over the possible restoration of exiled King Leopold III. Eyskens returned to the Finance Ministry, but he was recalled as prime minister in 1958. He successfully negotiated an end to a complicated dispute involving the right of students to attend either state or parochial schools without undue financial burdens, but economic problems, coupled with the high cost of the Congo's independence, forced him to institute new austerity measures. He was defeated in the 1961 election but continued in the Finance Ministry until 1968, when he was again named prime minister. In the early 1970s he lessened tensions between the Flemish-speaking population in the north and the French-speaking Walloons in the south by granting each group cultural autonomy. In 1971 he presided over constitutional reforms that granted greater autonomy to Flanders and Wallonia, but friction resurfaced over the issue of regionalization. Eyskens failed to solve the dispute and resigned in November 1972. The following year he became president of the Kredietbank in Brussels.

Faure, Edgar Jean, French politician (b. Aug. 18, 1908, Béziers, France—d. March 30, 1988, Paris, France), was one of France's most durable politicians; he was prime minister twice (1952 and 1955–56) but achieved his greatest success when he became minister of education in 1968 after the student rebellion of May–June 1968 and instituted sweeping university reforms. Faure received degrees in Russian and law at the age of 19 and practiced law in Paris until 1942, when he joined Gen. Charles de Gaulle's forces in Algeria as director of legislative services. Faure was a member of the International Military Tribunal at the Nürnberg trials in 1945, and he was elected (1946) to the National Assembly as a member of the centrist Radical Party. From 1949 to 1958 he was in almost every Cabinet formed, holding portfolios of finance (1949–50, 1953–54, and 1958), budget (1950–51), justice (1951–52), and foreign affairs (1955). He was prime minister for 40 days in 1952 and again for 11 months in 1955–56. When de Gaulle came to power in 1958, Faure left the Cabinet to serve in the

CAMERA PRESS/GLOBE PHOTOS

Senate (1959–66) and teach law at the University of Dijon (1962–66). He negotiated French diplomatic recognition of China in 1964. He returned to the Cabinet as minister of agriculture (1966–68) and then was education minister (1968–69). In the latter post Faure broke with tradition by consulting a special commission of teachers, parents, and students. The resulting legislation called for greater autonomy for each university and more decision-making power for students, faculty, and parents. Although Faure was not included in Pres. Georges Pompidou's government in 1969, he remained in the National Assembly until 1978, and he represented France in the European Parliament (1979–81). Faure refused a post in Pres. François Mitterrand's Cabinet in 1981. Faure, who also wrote detective novels under the pseudonym Edgar Sanday, was elected to the Académie Française in 1978.

Ferrari, Enzo, Italian sports car manufacturer (b. Feb. 18, 1898, Modena, Italy—d. Aug. 14, 1988, Modena), as the autocratic president of Ferrari SpA, built luxury sports cars and Formula One racers of formidable speed and quality. Ferrari demanded handcrafted detail in every automobile that bore his name. Although fans clamoured to buy the powerful road cars, fewer than 4,000 cars per year were produced during the 1980s, when prices topped $100,000. Ferrari, who studied engineering in technical school, raced test cars for a small automobile company in Milan after World War I. He drove for Alfa Romeo in the 1920s, and in 1929 he formed a racing stable, Scuderia Ferrari, which remained Alfa Romeo's official team even after Ferrari ceased to drive in 1932. In 1939 Ferrari severed the team's connection with Alfa Romeo and founded Ferrari SpA, but government restrictions delayed production of the first cars under the Ferrari name until 1946. Between 1952 and 1988 Ferrari's bright red Formula One automobiles won a record 93 Grand Prix races, 8 constructors' titles, and 9 drivers' championships, while Ferrari sports cars garnered 13 world championships and 9 victories in the grueling 24-hour race at Le Mans, France. Although Ferrari sold 50% of the business to Fiat SpA in 1969, he remained president until 1977 and retained control over the Ferrari racing team until his death.

Ferreira Aldunate, Wilson, Uruguayan politician (b. Jan. 28, 1918, Nico Perez, Uruguay—d. March 15, 1988, Montevideo, Uruguay), as leader of the liberal Blanco Party, the largest opposition party in the country, was a vociferous opponent of the military government that seized power in 1973. Ferreira was narrowly defeated in the 1971 presidential election by the Colorado Party candidate, Juan María Bordaberry. Ferreira, who served in Congress for 34 years and was agriculture minister from 1963 to 1967, contended that the 1971 election was fraudulent and demanded a recount. Bordaberry was installed as president the following year. After the legislature was dissolved in 1973, Ferreira went into exile and lived in Argentina, Spain, and Britain but continued to campaign against human rights abuses in Uruguay. The dictatorship tried to kidnap him in Argentina, and 12 newspapers that reported on his activities were closed. When Ferreira returned to Uruguay in 1984, he was immediately arrested and jailed by the military, who feared that his powerful influence would inhibit their negotiated exit from power. He was released from prison after the election and resumed his post as president of the Blanco Party. Though he lost some favour within the party for his stand on military amnesty, he would have been eligible to run in the presidential election scheduled for 1989.

Feynman, Richard Phillips, U.S. theoretical physicist (b. May 11, 1918, New York, N.Y.—d. Feb. 15, 1988, Los Angeles, Calif.), was a brilliant theoretician who together with Julian S. Schwinger and Shinichiro Tomonaga shared the 1965 Nobel Prize for Physics for redefining the

AP/WIDE WORLD

basic principles of quantum electrodynamics. The trio worked independently, and Feynman ingeniously constructed simple diagrams, now called Feynman diagrams, to graphically represent interactions of particles. Feynman earned a Ph.D. in physics from Princeton University in 1942 and was immediately recruited to work on the atomic bomb project, first at Princeton (1942–43) and then at Los Alamos, N.M. (1943–45). Together with Hans Bethe, Feynman devised a top secret formula for predicting the energy yield of a nuclear weapon; their calculations remained classified. He joined the faculty at Cornell University, Ithaca, N.Y., in 1945 and stayed there until 1950, when he became professor of physics at the California Institute of Technology. He remained there for the rest of his professional career. Among Feynman's greatest scientific achievements was his use of a mathematical approach to formulate a theory for liquid helium, which helped physicists understand its many properties. His work with Murray Gell-Mann resulted in a theory that accounted for most of the phenomena associated with the so-called weak interaction of subatomic particles, and he later provided an explanation for the behaviour of electrons in high-energy collisions. Feynman became a highly successful author in 1985 with his best-selling autobiography, *Surely You're Joking, Mr. Feynman!*, and in 1986 he became known to the general public as a member of the presidential commission investigating the space shuttle explosion. During a simple yet illuminating demonstration, he placed one of the shuttle's O-ring seals, the critical seals in the rocket booster, in a glass of ice water and squeezed it with a small clamp. Its failure to spring back into shape demonstrated that the rings were not resilient enough to maintain their shape after being subjected to cold. He maintained that this simple experiment could have averted the shuttle disaster. He received the Albert Einstein Award in 1954 and was the author of a magnificent physics text, *Lectures on Physics* (3 vol., 1963–65).

Fisher, Alan Wainwright, British labour leader (b. June 20, 1922, Birmingham, England—d. March 20, 1988, England), as general secretary (1968–82) of the National Union of Public Employees (NUPE), improved pay for local government, sanitation and sewage, and National Health Service workers. By planning "dirty-jobs" strikes in 1971, he captured public sympathy for the work done by members of NUPE and built the union into a powerful force. Fisher left school in 1939 to become a junior clerk at the local office of NUPE, then a small, embattled splinter union that was beginning to grow militant in its demands for better pay. Fisher became a district organizer in 1953 and general secretary in 1968. Wry and unauthoritative in private, he became a fiery speaker. Under his leadership, membership grew from 150,000 to

more than 700,000, making NUPE the fifth largest union in the Trades Union Congress (TUC). His well-orchestrated strategies and his popularity as an intelligent firebrand were intensified when he selected a former press officer of TUC as NUPE's director of research and when he named women to several executive seats. Fisher also presided over the 1978–79 "winter of discontent," when NUPE staged a series of disruptive strikes in an attempt to force the government to increase earnings beyond the 5% limit that had been established the previous July. Fisher retired in 1982.

Ford, Edmund Brisco, British geneticist (b. April 23, 1901, Papcastle, Cumberland, England—d. Jan. 22, 1988, Oxford, England), was a leading figure in the study of the genetics of natural selection and was the founder of the science of ecological genetics. While attending the University of Oxford (1923–27), he conducted research with Julian Huxley on the genetic control of growth in freshwater crustaceans and with R. A. Fisher on genetic adaptations found in natural populations. Ford combined genetic experiments in the laboratory with quantitative observations of butterfly and moth populations in nature. His techniques, which included marking and recapturing animal specimens in the wild to estimate population change, became basic to what he called ecological genetics. In 1940 Ford speculated that genetic polymorphisms (consistent variations between members of a single species) are maintained when the variations are equally advantageous to the species. He applied this theory to the four human blood groups (A, B, AB, and O) in 1945 and theorized that the groups are balanced by their susceptibilities to different diseases. Ford joined the Oxford faculty in 1927, serving as director of the genetics laboratory (1952–69) and professor of ecological genetics (1963–69), and became emeritus professor in 1969. His books include *Butterflies* (1945), *Ecological Genetics* (1964), and *Genetics and Adaptation* (1976).

Franco, Carmen Polo de (CARMEN POLO Y MARTÍNEZ VALDÉS DE FRANCO), Spanish consort (b. July 9, 1900, Oviedo, Spain—d. Feb. 6, 1988, Madrid, Spain), was thought to be the force behind many of the puritanical religious and social strictures imposed on Spain during the repressive regime (1939–75) of her husband, Francisco Franco. She was born into a middle-class provincial family and had a strict Roman Catholic education. She married Franco (over her parents' objections) in October 1923 and was thereafter his constant companion and adviser. As the wife of the chief of state, she was widely admired and emulated for her elegant fashions, her religious devotion, and her public deference to her husband. After her only daughter's marriage in 1950, Doña Carmen (as she was popularly known) grew in importance, often shielding her husband from outside influences and occasionally pressuring him on political decisions. She was frequently criticized for the apparent contradiction between her lavish spending on jewelry and designer clothes and the censorship and austere morality that she espoused. She retired from public life after Franco's death in 1975, but she remained a figurehead for his supporters.

Freeman, Cynthia (BEA FEINBERG), U.S. author (b. 1915?, New York, N.Y.—d. Oct. 22, 1988, San Francisco, Calif.), rocketed to the top of the best-seller list with such romance novels as *A World Full of Strangers* (1975), *Fairytales* (1978), *Days of Winter* (1977), *Come Pour the Wine* (1980), and *No Time for Tears* (1981), all penned under the pseudonym Cynthia Freeman. She launched her writing career at the age of 50, and though she never garnered critical acclaim, Freeman acquired a huge and enthusiastic readership with her tales of Jewish immigrants in the U.S. Her novels were translated into 33 languages and sold more than 20 million copies. Her last book, *The Last Princess*, appeared in 1988.

Frenay, Henri, French soldier (b. Nov. 19, 1905, Lyon, France—d. Aug. 6, 1988, Porto-Vecchio, Corsica, France), was a leading figure in the French Resistance during World War II and a longtime opponent of Gen. Charles de Gaulle. Frenay attended the military academy at Saint-Cyr (1924–29) and advanced to the rank of captain in 1934. He was captured by the Germans in June 1940 but escaped within days, and in 1941 he resigned from the Army to establish the Resistance group Combat in Lyon. Although he opposed de Gaulle's growing political power, Frenay was a central member of the unified National Liberation Movement and published the influential underground newspaper *Combat.* In 1943 Frenay escaped to Algiers, where he served in the government-in-exile as commissioner of prisoners and deportees, a post he retained as a minister in the postliberation provisional government (1944–46). Frenay retired in 1946 to become a business executive, but he remained an outspoken critic of de Gaulle and was a founding member of the Socialist Party.

Frobe, Gert, German actor (b. Feb. 25, 1913, Zwickau, Saxony, Germany—d. Sept. 5, 1988, Munich, West Germany), epitomized an archvillain after playing the cruel title character in the 1964 James Bond film *Goldfinger* but also appeared in many different character roles in more than 100 films. Before World War II Frobe worked in the German theatre as a violinist, a set designer, and an actor. During the war he was a medical orderly in the Red Cross in Vienna. Frobe returned to the stage after the war and made his film debut (1948) in *Berliner Ballade.* Despite his versatility, exemplified by his zany performance as a Prussian general in *Those Magnificent Men in Their Flying Machines* (1965), Frobe's heavyset, small-eyed appearance and wide identification with such parts as Auric Goldfinger or a Nazi soldier increasingly limited him to roles as a "heavy."

Fuchs, Klaus Emil Julius, German-born British physicist (b. Dec. 29, 1911, Rüsselsheim, Germany—d. Jan. 28, 1988, East Germany), confessed to passing U.S. and British atomic research secrets to the Soviets, thus enabling them to develop an atomic bomb at least one year earlier than they might otherwise have done. While attending the University of Kiel, Fuchs joined (1930) the German Communist Party and engaged in underground anti-Nazi activities. He fled to France (1933) and then to Great Britain (1934), where he completed his Ph.D. in physics at Edinburgh University. Fuchs was briefly interned as an enemy alien in 1940, but he was released to participate in nuclear research at the University of Birmingham. He became a British citizen in 1942, and in 1943 he was one of several British physicists sent to the U.S. to work on the first atomic bomb. After the war he was appointed head of the theoretical physics division of the British Atomic Energy Commission's research centre at Harwell. When he was arrested in 1950 (on evidence obtained by the U.S. Federal Bureau of Investigation), Fuchs confessed that he had been passing detailed top secret information on the theory and design of the atomic bomb to the Soviet Union since 1943. He was charged with four counts of espionage under the British Official Secrets Act, pleaded guilty, and was sentenced to 14 years' imprisonment (the maximum sentence). Fuchs was released in 1959 and immigrated to East Germany, where he was granted citizenship and hailed as a hero. He worked at the East German Central Institute for Nuclear Research from 1959, serving as its director from 1974 until his retirement in 1979.

Gaekwad, Fatesinghrao, Indian potentate (b. April 2, 1930, Baroda, India—d. Sept. 1, 1988, Bombay, India), was the former maharajah of Baroda and was reputedly one of the world's richest men. Known as "Jackie Baroda," Gaekwad was the last of a family of princes that dated to his great-great-great-grandfather, who had inherited the princedom as a poor 13-year-

old cousin from a distant village. Gaekwad himself inherited (1951) the title and wealth then estimated at £15 million when his father was deposed. Gaekwad was educated by English tutors and entered national politics in 1957, serving as a member of Parliament for ten years. In the regional Gujarat government, he was (1967–71) minister of health, fisheries, and jails. Besides founding (1956) the Baroda Rayon Corp., he was also part owner of other Indian manufacturing concerns. He played cricket (1946–59), became president (1963) of the Board of Control for Cricket in India, and managed teams (1978, 1982) that revived India's cricket competitions with Pakistan. Gaekwad, revolted after a two-month shooting safari in the Belgian Congo (now Zaire) in the early 1950s, became an ardent conservationist, serving the World Wildlife Fund and establishing a zoo on the palace grounds. When Indira Gandhi abolished (1971) the titles and legendary privileges of Indian princes, Gaekwad protested but adapted. His palace was to be converted into a museum and arts centre.

Galbreath, John Wilmer, U.S. real estate developer and sportsman (b. Aug. 10, 1897, Derby, Ohio—d. July 20, 1988, Galloway, Ohio), amassed a fortune by rehabilitating old company towns and then showcased his Midas touch in horse racing, winning the Kentucky Derby with Chateaugay in 1963 and Proud Clarion in 1967; he extended his winning streak as co-owner (1946–85) of the Pittsburgh Pirates professional baseball team, which captured World Series championships in 1960, 1971, and 1979. Galbreath graduated from Ohio State University and launched his real estate business in Columbus, Ohio. He later acquired major holdings in New York, Pittsburgh, Pa., and Los Angeles. During the 1930s he became involved in horse racing, and in 1935 he purchased Darby Dan Farm, which expanded to 1,620 ha (4,000 ac) and produced his Derby winners. Galbreath also held the distinction of winning the Epsom Derby in England with Roberto in 1972; he became the only owner ever to win both the Epsom and Kentucky Derbies. Another of his horses, Little Current, captured the Preakness and Belmont Stakes in 1974. Besides being co-owner of the Pirates, he was president (1950–69) of the team until his son, Dan, succeeded him. In 1986 *Forbes* magazine estimated his fortune and that of his son at $400 million.

Gascon, Jean, Canadian actor and director (b. Dec. 21, 1921, Montreal, Que.—d. April 20, 1988, Stratford, Ont.), as one of the most prominent figures in Canadian theatre, was a seasoned actor and the founder in 1951 of the Théâtre du Nouveau Monde. In 1952 he also helped found the École du TNM, which later became the National Theatre School. While studying medicine, Gascon was also an actor, gaining attention for his performances with Les Compagnons de St. Laurent (1942–45). He perfected his acting techniques in France and was at home in both French and English productions. Gascon spent 19 seasons at the Stratford Festival and served (1969–74) as its artistic director. He appeared in *Henry V* (1956) at the festival and directed *Othello* (1959), *The Comedy of Errors* (1964), and *The Misanthrope* (1981) at Stratford. For his longtime contributions to the theatre and the arts, he was made an Officer (1967) and then Companion (1974) of the Order of Canada.

Ghaffar Khan, (Khan) Abdul, Pashtun leader (b. 1890?, Utmanzai, India—d. Jan. 20, 1988, Peshawar, Pak.), as a Muslim disciple of Mohandas K. Gandhi, was dubbed "the Frontier Gandhi" for his devotion to nonviolent nationalist agitation and to cooperation between Hindus and Muslims. A prominent leader of the Pashtuns (or Pathans; a Muslim ethnic group of Pakistan and Afghanistan), Ghaffar Khan devoted himself to the struggle against British rule in India. He joined (1920) the Khilafat movement, which sought closer spiritual ties between Indian Muslims and the Turkish sultan. The

following year he was elected president of a district Khilafat committee in his native North-West Frontier. He was repeatedly jailed in the 1920s, but he maintained Gandhi's principles of nonviolent noncooperation. In 1930 he founded the Khudai Khitmatgar ("Servants of God"), or Red Shirt Movement, which worked with the Indian National Congress in the campaign for a free, unified India. When partition became inevitable, Ghaffar Khan fought for an independent Pashtun state (Pakhtunistan) in the North-West Frontier, and in 1948 the new Pakistani government imprisoned him. He was released in 1954, but he was jailed again several times during the next decade. In the mid-1960s he went into exile in Afghanistan, where he wrote his memoirs, *My Life and Struggle* (1969), and continued to agitate for Pashtun autonomy. He returned to Pakistan in 1972 and was soon arrested, but he was finally released in 1976. His death was observed in India with an official five-day period of national mourning.

Gibb, Andy (ANDREW ROY GIBB), British-born pop singer (b. March 5, 1958, Manchester, England—d. March 10, 1988, Oxford, England), embarked on a successful solo singing career during the late 1970s and early 1980s with such smash hits as "I Just Want to Be Your Everything," "Love Is Thicker than Water," "Shadow Dancing," and "Everlasting Love." Gibb followed his older brothers, the Bee Gees, to stardom, beginning his solo career in Australia while his brothers were gaining an international following. During the 1981–82 television season he served as host of the program "Solid Gold," and in 1982 he starred on Broadway in *Joseph and the Amazing Technicolor Dreamcoat.* He was dismissed from the cast the following year; his career took a downward turn; and he admitted that he had a serious addiction to cocaine. After treatment for his addiction, he filed for bankruptcy in 1987 but was scheduled to make a comeback in 1988 after having signed a recording contract with Island Records. Gibb, who had complained of stomach pains, died suddenly of natural causes due to an inflammation of the heart, probably caused by a virus.

Gillars, Mildred Elizabeth ("AXIS SALLY"), U.S. propagandist (b. November 1900, Portland, Maine—d. June 25, 1988, Columbus, Ohio), became a notorious figure during World War II, appearing on German radio with her English-language propaganda broadcasts aimed at destroying Allied morale by suggesting that soldiers' wives and girl friends on the home front were unfaithful to them. As hostess of the popular music and talk show "Home, Sweet Home," which was beamed to U.S. troops in Europe and North Africa, she earned the nickname "Axis Sally" for her Nazi propagandizing. After the war she was found in Berlin, living in the cellars of bombed-out buildings, by U.S. military officials, who sent her to the U.S. for trial in 1948. She was found guilty of treason and served 12 years in a federal prison at Alderson, W.Va. Gillars later admitted that after arriving in Berlin in 1934 she had fallen in love with a German named Max Otto Koischwitz, who had persuaded her to begin the broadcasts. After her release from prison in 1961 she lived quietly in Columbus, where she taught music at a kindergarten.

Goldsmith, Raymond William, Belgian-born economist (b. Dec. 23, 1904, Brussels, Belgium—d. July 12, 1988, Hamden, Conn.), was an internationally respected authority in his field and was instrumental in devising ways to measure wealth, especially balance sheets that recorded and tracked the flow of capital among various segments of the economy. After earning a Ph.D. from the University of Berlin in 1927, Goldsmith studied at the London School of Economics and Political Science before immigrating to the U.S. in 1934. He worked for several U.S. government agencies, including the Securities and Exchange Commission (1934–41) and the War Production Board (1942–46),

and in 1946 he was a member of the U.S. government mission on German currency reform. He was adviser to numerous foreign governments, including those of such less developed countries as India and Brazil. From 1960 until 1974 Goldsmith was professor of economics at Yale University. He was the author of such works as *The Changing Structure of American Banking* (1933), *The National Balance Sheet of the United States, 1953–1980* (1981), and *Comparative National Balance Sheets: A Study of 20 Countries, 1688–1978* (1985).

Goossens, Leon Jean, British musician (b. June 12, 1897, Liverpool, England—d. Feb. 12, 1988, Tunbridge Wells, Kent, England), employed brilliant styling that elevated the oboe from near obscurity to unparalleled prominence. The youngest son of conductor Eugene Goossens II, Leon began his musical studies at age ten. Two years later (1909) he played his first orchestral engagement as third-chair oboist with the Liverpool Philharmonic, conducted by Sir Thomas Beecham. Goossens later performed at Covent Garden (1924) and then (1932) with the London Philharmonic Orchestra under Beecham's direction. When Goossens's family moved to London (1911), he enrolled at the Royal College of Music. In 1913 he joined the Queen's Hall Orchestra; he was first-chair oboist until 1915, when he volunteered for the infantry during World War I. After the war Goossens returned to Queen's Hall Orchestra and was appointed professor of oboe at the Royal College of Music (1923) and also at the Royal Academy of Music. During the 1920s he played solo engagements in Europe and abroad, amazing audiences with the lighter, more flexible, sweeter, and softer sound he was capable of producing on an often shrill instrument. His phrasing was brilliant, and the richness of his tone inspired such leading composers as Benjamin Britten, Sir Edward Elgar, and Ralph Vaughan Williams to write works for the oboe, thus expanding the slim solo repertoire for that instrument. He was made a Commander of the Order of the British Empire in 1950. In 1962 an automobile accident severely injured Goossens's lips, teeth, and jaw. Four years later, after mastering a new technique, he resumed performing and played solos until he was well into his 80s.

Gorshkov, Sergey Georgyevich, Soviet admiral (b. Feb. 26 [Feb. 13, old style], 1910, Kamenets-Podolsky, Ukraine, Russia—d. May 13, 1988, U.S.S.R.), as commander in chief of the Soviet Navy (1956–85), transformed its small coastal fleet into a world sea power. Gorshkov joined the Navy at the age of 17, graduated from the Frunze Naval College (1931), and spent most of his early career commanding ships in the Black Sea. He was commander of the Azov and Danube flotillas during World War II, and after the war he served as chief of staff (1948–51) and commander (1951–55) of the Black Sea Fleet. Gorshkov became an admiral in 1953 and supreme commander of the Soviet Navy only three years later. He was ordered to replace the Navy's surface fleet with submarines, but Gorshkov argued that the traditionally land-based Soviet Union would need a balanced conventional fleet, including more powerful warships, to be accepted as a world power. This view prevailed after the 1962 Cuban missile crisis, and Gorshkov coordinated a massive shipbuilding program that included not only sophisticated warships and nuclear-armed submarines but also an expanded merchant marine, a global deep-sea fishing fleet, and advanced scientific research vessels. A member of the Communist Party from 1942, Gorshkov became a full member of the Central Committee in 1961. By the time he retired in 1985, Gorshkov had received the title Hero of the Soviet Union (1965) and every available decoration, including five Orders of Lenin. His book *The Sea Power of the State* (1979) was widely admired in the West.

Grandi, Dino, CONTE DI MORDANO, Italian politician and diplomat (b. June 4, 1895, Mor-

dano, Italy—d. May 21, 1988, Bologna, Italy), was a dedicated Fascist who orchestrated foreign policy under Benito Mussolini; he later opposed the Italian-German alliance, however, and in 1943 led a faction in the Grand Council that deposed Mussolini. Grandi, trained as a lawyer, joined the Fascist gangs that terrorized the Italian countryside after World War I. At the national Fascist congress in 1921, he failed to gain a prominent post in the Fascist movement but became a member of the party's General Directorate. Grandi was a leader in the 1922 March on Rome that brought Mussolini to power. He then served in the Chamber of Deputies as a party member. As foreign minister (1929–32) and ambassador to Britain (1932–39), he encouraged stronger ties with the League of Nations and helped soothe British opposition to the Italian conquest of Ethiopia (1935–36). He was recalled from Britain in 1939 when Adolf Hitler reportedly objected to his pro-British sympathies. While serving in the Cabinet as minister of justice and president of the Chamber of Fasces and Corporations, he held negotiations with King Victor Emmanuel III against Mussolini. On the night of July 24–25, 1943, Grandi successfully persuaded the Grand Council to dismiss Mussolini for mishandling the war. Grandi was condemned to death in absentia by a Fascist tribunal in 1944, but he had already fled to Portugal. Although he ran a successful business in Brazil from 1948, he returned to Italy in 1973. His death coincided with, and was completely overshadowed by, those of postwar neo-Fascist leaders Giorgio Almirante (*q.v.*) and Pino Romualdi.

Grant, George Parkin, Canadian philosopher (b. Nov. 13, 1918, Toronto, Ont.—d. Sept. 27, 1988, Halifax, Nova Scotia), achieved national acclaim in 1965 with the publication of his pessimistic *Lament for a Nation: The Defeat of Canadian Nationalism*, a 97-page book that secured his position as one of the country's great thinkers. In this slender volume Grant decried the decision made by Liberal Prime Minister Lester Pearson to allow cruise missile testing over Canada. Grant later cautioned about "the dictatorship of technology" and how Canadian nationalism could become endangered through the adoption of U.S. business goals. One of the country's most eminent and respected social philosophers, Grant was educated at Queen's University, Kingston, Ont., and in England at the University of Oxford, where he was a Rhodes scholar. He taught philosophy at Dalhousie University, Halifax (1947–60), before becoming (1961) chairman of the department of religion at McMaster University, Hamilton, Ont. He remained there until 1980, when he returned to Dalhousie University as a professor of political science and classics. Some of his other influential works include *Technology and Empire: Perspectives on North America* (1969), *English-Speaking Justice* (1974; reprinted 1978, 1985), and *Technology and Justice* (1986).

Hamengkubuwono IX, Indonesian potentate (b. April 12, 1912, Yogyakarta, Java, Dutch East Indies [now Indonesia]—d. Oct. 2, 1988, Washington, D.C.), as the ninth sultan of Yogyakarta from 1940 until his death, was a benign ruler who was revered by the nation for his personal commitment to modern democratic values. Educated at the University of Leiden, Neth., he returned to Yogyakarta in 1940 to succeed his father, who had named him, the fifth son, hereditary heir. He thus became ruler of the cultural capital of Java and, as governor of the special district of Yogyakarta, the head of its civil administration. In 1942 Hamengkubuwono actively opposed the Japanese when they invaded what was then called the Dutch East Indies. After Japan's surrender and Indonesia's declaration of independence from Dutch rule in 1945, Hamengkubuwono played a pivotal role in establishing the new republic. He and others fought the Dutch until 1949, when they gave up hope of reestablishing control and acknowledged Indonesia's independence. After the

war Hamengkubuwono served under President Sukarno as minister of state (1946–49), defense minister (1949–53), and deputy prime minister (1950–51), and from 1973 to 1978 he held the office of vice-president under President Suharto. After retiring from national politics in 1978, he continued to serve as governor of Yogyakarta. Because Hamengkubuwono did not designate a hereditary successor, elders of a special court would choose one of his children.

Hamilton, Sir (Charles) Denis, British newspaper editor (b. Dec. 6, 1918, South Shields, Durham, England—d. April 7, 1988, London, England), as editor (1961–67) of *The Sunday Times* (London), editor in chief (1967–81) of Times Newspapers Ltd., and chairman (1979–85) of the news service Reuters Ltd., led the postwar campaign for broader coverage and more innovative journalism in British newspaper reporting. He recruited talented young reporters, delegated almost unlimited freedom to his senior editors, encouraged investigative reporting, expanded business coverage, and added the first colour Sunday supplement. After serving on Field Marshal B. L. Montgomery's staff during World War II, Hamilton was personal assistant (1946–50) to the British newspaper magnate Lord Kemsley and editorial director (1950–58) of Kemsley Newspapers Ltd., which owned *The Sunday Times*. Hamilton remained with the newspaper when Kemsley sold out to the Canadian publisher Roy (later Lord) Thomson in 1959, and in 1961 Hamilton became editor of *The Sunday Times*. Thomson bought *The Times* in 1967 and promoted Hamilton to editor in chief in charge of both newspapers. When Hamilton failed to overcome union resistance to modernization in 1978, Thomson ceased publication for almost a year. In 1981, after Thomson sold the financially troubled newspapers to Australian publisher Rupert Murdoch, Hamilton resigned. He was a trustee of the British Museum from 1969 and was knighted in 1976.

Hamilton, Hamish (JAMES HAMILTON), British publisher (b. Nov. 15, 1900, Indianapolis, Ind.—d. May 24, 1988, London, England), founded a quality publishing house in 1931 and during a 50-year career published works by some of the most renowned authors in Britain, the U.S., and France. Hamilton studied modern languages and law at Caius College, Cambridge, and gained national attention as a champion oarsman in the Grand Challenge Cup (1927 and 1928) and the Olympic Games (1928). In 1926 he became London office manager of the New York-based publisher Harper & Brothers, and five years later Harper helped him establish Hamish Hamilton Ltd. Hamilton legally changed his name to Hamish (Gaelic for James) to avoid conflict with another publisher. Hamilton was a hands-on publisher and lavished personal attention on his authors, including such Americans as James Thurber, John Gunther, Raymond Chandler, J. D. Salinger, and William Styron. His British authors included Nancy Mitford, Cecil Woodham-Smith, and Angela Thirkell. Hamilton also published works by Albert Camus and Jean-Paul Sartre. In 1965 Hamilton sold the firm to Thomson Publications, but he remained at the helm until 1981.

Hargreaves, Roger, British cartoonist (b. 1935, Cleckheaton, Yorkshire, England—d. Sept. 12, 1988, Kent, England), turned potato-shaped doodles into whimsical characters best known in the enormously popular "Mr. Men" series of books for children. As a youth Hargreaves worked in his father's laundry in Yorkshire. After his father died, Hargreaves took a job with a local advertising agency, began a career as a copywriter, moved to London, and became a successful creative director. In the early 1970s, to amuse his four children and to fight his own boredom, he used a black felt-tipped pen to draw simple figures he customized and named to match their personalities, including Mr. Tickle, Mr. Happy, Mr. Nosey, Mr. Greedy,

and Mr. Grumpy. These characters also appeared as BBC cartoons and in a comic strip in the *Daily Mirror*. Each one, the star of its own thin paperback book, had positive and negative characteristics that even very young children could understand. Hargreaves's little "Men" spawned more than 700 products, from T-shirts to food cartons, and paved the way for a "Little Miss" (Helpful, Bossy, Sunshine, Lazy, and so forth) series. Together the two series reached worldwide sales of 85 million books and were published in 20 languages.

Harty, (Fredric) Russell, British writer and television personality (b. Sept. 5, 1934, Blackburn, Lancashire, England—d. June 8, 1988, Leeds, England), charmed audiences with his intelligence, wit, and audacity, particularly as an irreverent talk-show host with London Weekend Television (LWT; 1972–80) and the BBC (1980–88). Harty received a scholarship to the University of Oxford (B.A. 1957; M.A. 1961) and taught English at Giggleswick Boys School in North Yorkshire (1958–64) and at the City University of New York (1964–66). In 1967 he became a producer for BBC radio, and two years later he moved to television as producer of the LWT arts program "Aquarius." After "Russell Harty Plus" debuted on LWT in 1972, Harty's air of spontaneity, quirky interviewing style, and North Country speech patterns soon earned him a popular following. He moved to the BBC in 1980 and appeared in documentaries and specials as well as on his live talk show. In 1987 he took on the popular Radio 4 talk show "Start the Week," interviewed celebrities for the BBC series "Favourite Things," and wrote a witty, anecdotal column, "Russell Harty's Notebook," for *The Sunday Times.* "Mr. Harty's Grand Tour," a humorous four-part tour of Europe, was broadcast on the BBC only a few weeks before his death.

Hayter, Stanley William, British-born printmaker and painter (b. Dec. 27, 1901, London, England—d. May 4, 1988, Paris, France), advanced the technique of intaglio printmaking with designs created in his influential workshop. Hayter not only expanded the boundaries of this traditional genre with his innovative use of colour and texture but also served as a link between the automatism of the early Surrealist artists and the dynamic spontaneity of the later Abstract Expressionist painters. After working (1922–25) as a research chemist for an oil company in the Persian Gulf, Hayter moved to Paris. There he became intrigued by Surrealism, particularly the visual free association used in automatic drawing, and by the intaglio technique of engraving a copper plate with a burin, the traditional engraver's tool. In 1927 Hayter established his studio, Atelier 17 (so named in 1933), where he investigated the creative possibilities of printmaking with such notable artists as Pablo Picasso, Joan Miró, and Alberto Giacometti. He abandoned the studio at the beginning of World War II, but he reestablished Atelier 17 in New York City. From 1940 until his return to Paris in 1950, Hayter taught printmaking at several U.S. colleges and also worked with such emerging American Abstract Expressionists as Jackson Pollock, Willem de Kooning, and Mark Rothko. In later years Hayter concentrated on painting and silk-screen prints. His writings include *New Ways of Gravure* (1949) and *About Prints* (1962). Hayter received the French Legion of Honour (1951) and was made Officer (1959) and Commander (1967) of the Order of the British Empire.

Heinlein, Robert Anson, U.S. science-fiction writer (b. July 7, 1907, Butler, Mo.—d. May 8, 1988, Carmel, Calif.), was a prolific author and master of the genre who produced such cult classics as *Starship Troopers* (1959), *Stranger in a Strange Land* (1961), *The Moon Is a Harsh Mistress* (1966), and *I Will Fear No Evil* (1970). Though many of his novels provoked controversy because of dire speculations about future societal changes, they were superb in the scientific realm, predicting the coming of the atom bomb, nuclear power plants, the water bed, moving sidewalks, and an electronic space defense shield. In one novel Heinlein coined the word grok, which meant intuitive understanding. Heinlein, who took up writing when tuberculosis cut short his naval career, began writing science-fiction stories for *Astounding Science Fiction* magazine before graduating to the *Saturday Evening Post* and elevating science fiction to a new sophistication. Some of his early novels captured the imagination with the prospect of space travel becoming a commonplace occurrence, while later novels broke the traditional molds of science fiction by exploring the future while questioning present values. Some of his other novels include *Rocket Ship Galileo* (1947), *Revolt in 2100* (1953), *Friday* (1982), *Job: A Comedy of Justice* (1984), and *The Cat Who Walks Through Walls: A Comedy of Manners* (1985). Heinlein was the recipient of a number of awards, among them an unprecedented four Hugo awards.

Holman, M(oses) Carl, U.S. civil rights leader (b. June 27, 1919, Minter City, Miss.—d. Aug. 9, 1988, Washington, D.C.), as president (1971–88) of the National Urban Coalition, an organization formed after the inner-city race riots of 1967, promoted the need for a mutual partnership between industry and government to foster inner-city development. The scholarly Holman graduated (1942) magna cum laude from Lincoln University, Jefferson City, Mo., earned (1944) an M.A. in English from the University of Chicago, and received (1954) a master of fine arts degree from Yale University. While

AP/WIDE WORLD

serving (1948–62) on the English and humanities faculty at Clark College, Atlanta, Ga., he joined students in founding (1960) *The Atlanta Inquirer*, an all-black journal. In 1962 Holman joined the staff of the United States Commission on Civil Rights, rising to deputy staff director in 1966. Two years later he became vice-president of programs at the National Urban Coalition; he was elevated to president in 1971. During his tenure as president, Holman advocated programs in housing, education, employment opportunities, job training, and economic development. He forged liaisons between black and Hispanic communities and was an influential behind-the-scenes organizer, effectively orchestrating meetings between individuals who were hesitant to discuss issues. During the 1980s Holman was active in developing programs to help minority and female children develop scientific, mathematical, and computer skills.

Household, Geoffrey Edward West, British writer (b. Nov. 30, 1900, Bristol, England—d. Oct. 4, 1988, Banbury, England), created the novel *Rogue Male* (1939), a psychological thriller about an aristocratic big-game hunter who tracks down a Hitler-like dictator but fails to kill him; the novel, a brilliantly crafted tale, set the standard for the genre. Household was educated at Clifton College, Bristol (1914–19), and at Magdalen College, Oxford (1919–22), where he won honours in English literature. In 1922 he secured a position as confidential secretary to the Bank of Romania in Bucharest, and there he learned the language and traditions. After four years he went to Spain, where he learned Spanish and local traditions. In 1929 Household went to New York City, where he found work writing articles for an encyclopaedia, but then he returned to England, where he found a job selling printer's ink throughout Europe, the Near East, and South America—all later settings for his novels. Household published *The Third Hour* (1937), a book of short stories, *The Salvation of Pisco Gabar* (1938), and *Rogue Male* before serving (1939–45) in the Intelligence Corps in Greece, Palestine, Syria, and Iraq and earning the rank of lieutenant colonel. Though he published more than 20 novels, collections of short stories, juvenile novels, and an autobiography, *Against the Wind* (1958), none ever matched the success of his "rogue" novel.

Houseman, John (JACQUES HAUSSMANN), U.S. actor (b. Sept. 22, 1902, Bucharest, Rom.—d. Oct. 31, 1988, Malibu, Calif.), was a commanding figure who made immeasurable contributions to radio, television, theatre, and the film industry; he was probably best known, however, for his portrayal of the crusty law professor Charles W. Kingsfield, Jr., in the film *The Paper Chase* (1973)—a role for which he won the Academy Award for best supporting actor in 1974—and the television series of the same name that followed. Houseman arrived in the U.S. by way of Argentina in 1924. He held a seat on the Chicago Board of Trade, but after the stock market crash of 1929, he moved to New York City and began writing, directing, and producing for the stage. He directed the 1934 world premiere of the Virgil Thomson opera *Four Saints in Three Acts* before cofounding (1937) the Mercury Theatre with Orson Welles. Houseman was coproducer of Welles's legendary 1938 radio broadcast, "The War of the Worlds," and he was instrumental in packaging Welles's 1941 film masterpiece, *Citizen Kane.* Houseman terminated his partnership with Welles in 1941 and served as director of the "Voice of America" during World War II. From 1945 to 1962 Houseman produced such notable films as *The Blue Dahlia* (1946), *The Bad and the Beautiful* (1953), *Lust for Life* (1956), and *All Fall Down* (1962). He also regularly commuted from Hollywood to New York City to direct such Broadway productions as *Lute Song* (1946), *King Lear* (1950), and *Coriolanus* (1954). In 1967 Houseman helped establish the school of drama at the Juilliard School, New York City, and became cofounder and longtime artistic director of the Acting Company, a touring repertory group. As an actor he appeared in such films as *Seven Days in May* (1964), *Rollerball* (1975), and *Ghost Story* (1981). Houseman's role as Professor Kingsfield led to his becoming a spokesman for Smith Barney, Harris Upham & Co., an investment concern, and he was suitably imperious in television commercials delivering the lines, "They make money the old-fashioned way. They *earn* it." His fourth volume of autobiography, *Unfinished Business: Memoirs, 1902 to 1988*, was published posthumously.

Howard, Trevor Wallace, British actor (b. Sept. 29, 1916, Cliftonville, Kent, England—d. Jan. 7, 1988, Bushey, Hertfordshire, England), was a meticulous craftsman who was admired for his wide range of characterizations on stage, on television, and in more than 70 motion pictures. He was best known for his portrayal of the sensitive doctor in love with a married woman in the bittersweet film *Brief Encounter* (1945). Howard made his professional acting debut in

1934 while still a student at the Royal Academy of Dramatic Art. He appeared regularly on the stage, notably in Shakespearean roles in Stratford and for two years in London's West End in *French Without Tears.* In World War II he served as an army paratrooper until a medical discharge in 1943 left him free to pursue his acting career. His third film, *Brief Encounter,* was followed by acclaimed roles in such motion pictures as *The Third Man* (1949), *The Heart of the Matter* (1953), and *Sons and Lovers* (1960), for which he received an Academy Award nomination for best actor. He garnered a British Academy Award for *The Key* (1958). In his later years Howard often portrayed a bluff, stiff-necked English military officer, notably in *Mutiny on the Bounty* (1962), *The Charge of the Light Brigade* (1968), and *Gandhi* (1982) and in a television adaptation of Paul Scott's *Staying On.* His last film appearance was in *White Mischief* (1988).

Hubbell, Carl Owen, U.S. baseball player (b. June 22, 1903, Carthage, Mo.—d. Nov. 21, 1988, Scottsdale, Ariz.), reigned as "King Carl," the phenomenal left-handed pitcher for the New York Giants professional baseball team, from 1928 to 1943 and—with a lifetime record of 253 wins, 154 losses, and a 2.97 earned run average (ERA)—was considered one of the sport's greatest pitchers. Hubbell, who specialized in throwing the screwball pitch, was admired for his precision, control, and consistency. He was the Giants' star pitcher during the 1930s and was affectionately dubbed "the Meal Ticket." In 1929 Hubbell had the distinction of pitching a no-hitter against the Pittsburgh Pirates. In 1933 he threw an 18-inning, 1–0 victory over the St. Louis Cardinals, but the hallmark of his career was his performance in the 1934 All-Star Game, when he struck out in succession Babe Ruth, Lou Gehrig, Jimmie Foxx, Al Simmons, and Joe Cronin, all of whom were later inducted into Baseball's Hall of Fame. In 1933 Hubbell had a 1.66 ERA when he pitched 46⅓ consecutive scoreless innings; he was named the National League's most valuable player that year and again in 1936, when he began his 24-consecutive-game winning streak, which overlapped into the 1937 season. Hubbell helped the Giants capture the National League pennant in 1933, 1936, and 1937 and the World Series against the Washington Senators in 1933, in which he won the first and last games of the series. Because of his heavy reliance on the screwball pitch, Hubbell began having elbow trouble in 1938, and in 1943 he retired as a player but remained in baseball as director of the Giants' farm system. In 1947 Hubbell was elected to the Hall of Fame.

Hulton, Sir Edward George Warris, British publisher (b. Nov. 29, 1906, England—d. Oct. 8, 1988, London, England), created (1938) the *Picture Post,* a weekly magazine that exerted widespread influence over a generation of Britons during World War II with its dramatic use of candid photographs and vigorous text. Hulton followed in the footsteps of his father, a onetime proprietor of the *Evening Standard* in London. After studying at Harrow and at Brasenose College, Oxford, where he was a prizewinning history scholar, Hulton twice (1927, 1931) ran unsuccessfully for Parliament as a Conservative. He became a barrister and then, in 1937, founded Hulton Press, which published such successful journals as *Farmer's Weekly, Housewife,* and *Lilliput.* During World War II Hulton provided funds for the Home Guard Training School and the 1941 Committee; he also organized support for the Beveridge Report on Full Employment (1942), which provided a blueprint for the welfare state. After the war, however, he rejoined the Conservative Party. The *Picture Post* covered the war, the slums of postwar Britain, early investigations of England's "colour bar," and the day-to-day life of Britons at home and on vacation. Hulton ceased publication of *Picture Post* in 1957 because of falling revenues, and in 1959 he sold

Hulton Press. His book, *When I Was a Child* (1952), was an autobiographical account of life in a wealthy, unhappy north country home. Hulton was knighted in 1957 and received the NATO Peace Medal in 1969.

Issigonis, Sir Alec (ALEXANDER ARNOLD CONSTANTINE), British auto designer (b. Nov. 18, 1906, Smyrna [now Izmir], Turkey—d. Oct. 2, 1988, Birmingham, England), created the Morris Minor and the Mini, Britain's most beloved cars of the 1950s and '60s, respectively. Issigonis, the son of a Greek-born father and a Bavarian-born mother, was evacuated with his parents (1922) by the Royal Navy from Greek-Turkish strife in Anatolia. The family moved to London, and Issigonis enrolled in Battersea Polytechnic to study engineering. He joined Morris Motors (1936) as a suspension designer; after working on special military projects during World War II, he continued to develop a front-wheel suspension that resulted in his almost single-handed production (1948) of the Morris Minor. The Minor was popular for its excellent steering and cornering qualities, its somewhat homely looks, and its rugged reliability. In response to the Suez energy crisis (1956) and the popularity of Germany's Volkswagen Beetle, Issigonis created (1959) a tiny car for what had become the British Motor Corp. The Mini, a 3-m (10-ft)-long automobile on 25-cm (10-in) wheels, could comfortably carry four passengers and zip in and out of city traffic while using a minimum amount of fuel. More than five million Minis had been sold by the late 1980s. Issigonis was knighted in 1969. He became a Commander of the Order of the British Empire in 1964 and a fellow of the Royal Society in 1967.

Janowitz, Morris, U.S. sociologist (b. Oct. 22, 1919, Paterson, N.J.—d. Nov. 7, 1988, Chicago, Ill.), served as chairman of the department of sociology at the University of Chicago (1967–72) and was internationally renowned for writings that explored the relationship between citizens and the military, notably *The Professional Soldier* (1960), *Sociology and the Military Establishment* (1959; revised 1965), and *The Military in the Political Development of New Nations* (1964). After earning a B.A. at New York University (1941), Janowitz served as senior propaganda analyst (1941–43) at the U.S. Department of Justice, Washington, D.C. He joined the faculty of the University of Chicago in 1947 as an instructor and the following year earned a Ph.D. there. He taught (1951–61) sociology at the University of Michigan until he returned to the University of Chicago in 1961. Janowitz collaborated with Bruno Bettelheim on the influential book *The Dynamics of Prejudice* (1950), which shed new light on the problem of racial and ethnic prejudice. Some of Janowitz's other works include *Social Change and Prejudice* (1964, with Bettelheim), *The Last Half Century: Societal Change and Politics in America* (1978), and *The Reconstruction of Patriotism: Education for Civic Consciousness* (1985).

Joffrey, Robert (ABDULLAH JAFFA ANVER BEY KHAN), U.S choreographer (b. Dec. 24, 1930, Seattle, Wash.—d. March 25, 1988, New York, N.Y.), was the founder and artistic director of the Joffrey Ballet, which became the country's third largest ballet ensemble. Joffrey, whose father was a native of Afghanistan and whose mother was Italian, was a lifelong asthmatic. He took up dancing as therapy for his condition and studied with Mary Ann Wells and later with Alexandra Fedorova and at the School of American Ballet. In 1948 Joffrey joined Roland Petit's Ballet de Paris, and from 1950 to 1953 he taught at New York's High School for the Performing Arts. In 1952 he created his first ballet, *Persephone,* and the following year he opened a school, the American Ballet Center. In 1956 Joffrey launched his own company, the Robert Joffrey Ballet Company, with the aid of Rebekah Harkness. The troupe of six dancers toured nationwide in a station wagon with a

NATE CUTLER—GLOBE PHOTOS

repertoire of four of Joffrey's ballets. Following disagreements on policy, Joffrey and Harkness dissolved the company in 1964, and in 1966 Joffrey founded the Joffrey Ballet, which came to enjoy international acclaim. As artistic director of the company, Joffrey was eclectic in his selection of works; his ensemble embraced the creations of such major European choreographers as Frederick Ashton, John Cranko, and Kurt Jooss, and he also reconstructed neglected or lost works, most notably Vaslav Nijinsky's 1913 *Le Sacre du printemps.* Joffrey had a keen eye for talented dancers and choreographers; he invited modern dance choreographers Twyla Tharp and Laura Dean to create works for his company. Joffrey's own creations, including *Gamelan* (1962), *Astarte* (1967), *Remembrances* (1973), and *Postcards* (1980), were also included in the company's repertoire.

John, Errol, Trinidadian-born actor and playwright (b. Dec. 20, 1924, Port-of-Spain, Trinidad—d. July 10, 1988, London, England), was best known for his play *Moon on a Rainbow Shawl,* a compassionate and often humorous study of people trapped in an impoverished Port-of-Spain slum and the painful but ultimately successful efforts of one man to escape. John won *The Observer's* prize for best new playwright (1957) and a Guggenheim fellowship (1958) in recognition of the play, which was produced first in London (1958) and then, in a slightly revised version, in New York City (1962). It was later performed in such diverse countries as Iceland, Hungary, and Argentina, and it became a classic school text in the West Indies. John, a founding member of the Whitehall Players in Port-of-Spain, pursued his acting career from 1950 in London, where in 1958 he portrayed Othello. He also had supporting roles in many Hollywood films, including *The African Queen.*

Johnson, Louis Albert, New Zealand poet (b. Sept. 27, 1924, Wellington, N.Z.—d. Nov. 1, 1988, Winchester, Hampshire, England), rejected the rural themes and parochial nationalism of traditional New Zealand poetry in favour of highly personal poems revolving around everyday suburban life and ordinary human relationships. From his early abstractionist poetry in *Stanza and Scene* (1945) to such later works as *Winter Apples* (1984), Johnson's constant poetic output became increasingly concrete and colloquial. From 1968 to 1980 Johnson lived overseas and traveled widely; in *Land like a Lizard* (1970), written during an extended stay in Papua New Guinea, he examined the spread of urban society and the attendant loss of innocence. As editor of the *New Zealand Poetry Yearbook* (1951–64) and *Antipodes New Writing* (1987), Johnson also championed regional Commonwealth poetry.

Jordan, Jim (JAMES EDWARD JORDAN), U.S. radio personality (b. Nov. 16, 1896, near Peoria, Ill.—d. April 1, 1988, Los Angeles, Calif.), became an American institution as the blundering yet well-intentioned Fibber McGee on the classic radio program "Fibber McGee and Molly," which aired from 1935 to 1957. Jordan, who was raised on a farm, married his childhood sweetheart, Marian Driscoll, in 1918. Four years later they made the vaudeville circuit, touring theatres and opera houses before launching their radio career in 1924. In 1931 they met Don Quinn, a radio writer, who starred them in his show "Smackout," based on a grocer who was always out of goods but never tall tales. In 1935 the show was purchased by Johnson's Wax, and "Fibber McGee and Molly" made its debut on April 16. The program, which relied on humour that was a second cousin to slapstick, convulsed audiences, who roared when McGee's overstuffed closet predictably deposited its contents on him. The format of the show was centred around various dilemmas that befell the cast of characters who entered 79 Wistful Vista, McGee's residence. McGee's wife, Molly, was played by Jordan's wife, Marian, and her gentle rejoinder to him, "Tain't funny, McGee," became a catchphrase. The show's successful formula also relied on the antics of such characters as Throckmorton P. Gildersleeve, Mayor La Trivia, and the Old Timer. Though the program was adapted for television in 1959, the Jordans did not reprise their roles.

Kapoor, Raj, Indian motion picture actor and director (b. December 1924, Peshawar, India [now in Pakistan]—d. June 2, 1988, New Delhi, India), was one of India's most beloved Hindi-language actors and an internationally recognized star throughout the Middle East, the Soviet Union, and China. Although Kapoor portrayed passionate romantic leads in his early films, his best-known characters were modeled on Charlie Chaplin's poor but honest tramp. Kapoor's motion pictures combined social commentary with romantic plots and elaborately staged film songs, many of which became popular hits. His use of sexual imagery often challenged traditionally strict Indian film standards. Kapoor began his career at Prithvi Theatres, the acting company founded by his father, the renowned actor Prithvi Raj Kapoor. Raj Kapoor's first major screen role was in *Aag* (1948), which he also produced and directed. He formed his own Bombay film studio, RK, in 1950 and the next year achieved romantic stardom in *Awara* (*The Vagabond*). Thereafter Kapoor wrote, produced, directed, and starred in such hits as *Barsaat* (1949), *Shri 420* (1955), *Jagte Raho* (1956), and *Mera Naam Joker* (1970). He also directed successful films starring his two brothers and his three sons. On May 2, 1988, during an awards ceremony at which he received the Indian film industry's highest honour, Kapoor suffered an acute asthma attack and collapsed. He died a month later.

Kiesinger, Kurt Georg, West German politician (b. April 6, 1904, Ebingen, Germany—d. March 9, 1988, Tübingen, West Germany), as chancellor of West Germany (1966–69) led the "grand coalition," which linked the ruling Christian Democratic Union (CDU) with the opposition Social Democrats (SPD). After studying law at the Universities of Tübingen and Berlin, Kiesinger practiced law in Berlin (1935–40). He joined (1933) the Nazi Party, but he was soon disillusioned and refused (1938) to join the Nazi lawyers' guild. After World War II Kiesinger was interned by the Allies for 18 months for his wartime participation in the German radio propaganda department, but he was never charged with any war crimes. In 1949 he was elected to the new West German Bundestag (federal parliament) as a member of Chancellor Konrad Adenauer's majority party, the CDU. Kiesinger actively promoted Adenauer's pro-West foreign policy, but he abruptly left the Bundestag in 1958 when Adenauer failed to reward his loyalty

CAMERA PRESS/GLOBE PHOTOS

with a ministry or ambassadorship. Kiesinger returned to Tübingen, where he was elected (1958) minister-president of the *Land* (state) of Baden-Württemberg. In 1966 he was unexpectedly recalled to Bonn to head the "grand coalition." Kiesinger's term as chancellor was marred by criticism of his former Nazi membership and by violent protests against the Emergency Powers Bill (1968), which granted the government special authority in security matters. Under his leadership, however, the fragile coalition improved the nation's faltering economy and eased relations with Eastern Europe. In 1969 the CDU was unable to form a government for the first time since 1949, and Kiesinger was supplanted by Willie Brandt's coalition of the SPD and the left-wing Free Democratic Party. Kiesinger was replaced as CDU leader in 1971 but remained in the Bundestag until 1980.

Killian, James Rhyne, Jr., U.S. government official and academic administrator (b. July 24, 1904, Blacksburg, S.C.—d. Jan. 29, 1988, Cambridge, Mass.), was instrumental in the formation in 1958 of the National Aeronautics and Space Administration (NASA) as both chairman of the President's Science Advisory Committee and as presidential assistant to Dwight D. Eisenhower from 1957 to 1959. Killian, who earned a B.S. in engineering and business administration from the Massachusetts Institute of Technology (MIT) in 1926, served as managing editor of *Technology Review*, a scientific journal published by the MIT alumni association, before holding a series of administrative positions at the institute. From 1945 to 1948 he served as vice-president of MIT, and in 1949 he became president, a post he held until 1959. When the Soviets launched Sputnik, the first artificial Earth satellite, in 1957, the U.S. reevaluated its science policy; Eisenhower chose Killian to establish priorities in research and development. After Killian helped coordinate the creation of NASA, he resigned his post as presidential adviser but continued to serve as a member of the President's Science Advisory Committee until 1961. He went on to serve as chairman of the Carnegie Commission on Educational Television (1965–67) and as chairman of the Corporation for Public Broadcasting (1973–74).

Kinnear, Roy Mitchell, British actor (b. Jan. 8, 1934, Wigan, Lancashire, England—d. Sept. 20, 1988, Madrid, Spain), was a short, heavyset, bald man best known for his comic roles on the stage, on the television series "That Was the Week That Was," and in such films as *Help!* and *The Three Musketeers*. Kinnear, who was educated at the Royal Academy of Dramatic Art, made his first stage appearance (1955) at the Newquay Theatre in Newquay, Cornwall. He joined the Theatre Workshop repertory company headed by director Joan Littlewood

in 1959 and made his London debut that year. During the 1960s Kinnear performed with the Royal Shakespeare Company and with the National Theatre. He entered films in 1961 and became best known as a droll, often lovable character actor. Kinnear's most recent stage role (1987) was as the Common Man in a London revival of *A Man for All Seasons*. He died after falling from a horse in Toledo, Spain, where he was filming *The Last Return of the Three Musketeers.*

Kluszewski, Ted (THEODORE BERNARD KLUSZEWSKI), U.S. baseball player (b. Sept. 10, 1924, Argo, Ill.—d. March 29, 1988, Cincinnati, Ohio), was a powerhouse hitter and first baseman who spent 11 of his 15 seasons as a player with the Cincinnati Reds professional baseball team and in 1954 led the National League in home runs with 49. In his last four seasons he played for the Pittsburgh Pirates, the Chicago White Sox, and the Los Angeles Dodgers. During his professional career he slammed 279 home runs and had a lifetime .298 batting average. In 1959 he made his only World Series appearance with the Chicago White Sox, and while the Sox lost the series to the Dodgers, Kluszewski belted three homers, slammed nine hits, and drove in ten runs in 23 times at bat.

Kolodin, Irving, U.S music critic and historian (b. Feb. 21, 1908, New York, N.Y.—d. April 29, 1988, New York), chronicled the history of the Metropolitan Opera in such detailed volumes as *The Metropolitan Opera: 1883–1935* (1936) and *The Story of the Metropolitan Opera, 1883–1950* (1953) and as the longtime music critic for the *Saturday Review* (1947–82) exerted a powerful influence on music. Kolodin worked for the *New York Sun* (1932–50) and became its chief music critic before writing program notes for the New York Philharmonic from 1953 to 1958. He taught criticism at the Juilliard School from 1968 to 1986, and after the original *Saturday Review* folded in 1982, he wrote articles for other publications. Some of his other volumes include *The Continuity of Music: A History of Influence* (1969), *The Interior Beethoven* (1975), and *The Opera Omnibus* (1976). At the time of his death, he was preparing a book on the first 100 years of the Metropolitan Opera.

Kuenn, Harvey Edward, U.S. baseball player and manager (b. Dec. 4, 1930, West Allis, Wis.—d. Feb. 28, 1988, Peoria, Ariz.), as a star shortstop and batting powerhouse with the Detroit Tigers professional baseball team (1952–60), earned laurels as the American League rookie of the year in 1953, his first full year with the team, and in 1959 was crowned batting champion with a .353 average. Kuenn was traded to the Cleveland Indians in 1960 and then played with the San Francisco Giants (1961–65), the Chicago Cubs (1965–66), and the Philadelphia Phillies (1966) before retiring as a player in 1966. He served as a coach for the Milwaukee Brewers from 1971 to 1982 and then managed the team from 1982 to 1983, leading them to their only American League pennant (1982). Kuenn was dismissed when the team finished fifth the following year. During his career he compiled a lifetime batting average of .303 with 2,092 hits, including 356 doubles and 87 home runs. He also slammed 671 runs batted in and scored 951 runs.

Laing, Hugh (HUGH SKINNER), British ballet dancer (b. 1911, Barbados—d. May 10, 1988, New York, N.Y.), possessed a superb dramatic stage presence and was especially noted for his interpretation of the ballets of Antony Tudor in performances with Ballet Theatre (later American Ballet Theatre) from 1939 to 1950 and the New York City Ballet from 1950 to 1952. Laing joined Marie Rambert's experimental Ballet Club in 1932, and Tudor created roles for him in such ballets as *The Planets* (1934), *The Descent of Hebe* (1935), *Jardin aux lilas* (1936), and *Dark Elegies* (1937). In 1938 he appeared exclusively in Tudor's short-lived London Bal-

let, and in 1939 Laing joined Tudor in the U.S. and became a star of Ballet Theatre, with Tudor choreographing roles for him in *Pillar of Fire* (1942), *Romeo and Juliet* (1943), *Dim Lustre* (1943), and *Undertow* (1945). While dancing with New York City Ballet he performed such new Tudor works as *The Lady of the Camellias* (1951) and *La Gloire* (1952). Laing also gave outstanding performances in Léonide Massine's *Aleko*, Jerome Robbins's *Facsimile* and *Age of Anxiety*, and George Balanchine's *Prodigal Son*. After making guest appearances with Ballet Theatre from 1954 to 1956, he retired from the stage and enjoyed a successful career as a fashion photographer.

L'Amour, Louis Dearborn, U.S. writer (b. March 22, 1908, Jamestown, N.D.—d. June 10, 1988, Los Angeles, Calif.), was the prolific and best-selling author of more than 100 books, most of them formula westerns that were highly popular because of their authentic portrayals of life on the frontier. L'Amour, who researched his novels extensively, was a globe-trotter who mined in the West, sailed aboard an East African schooner, lived with bandits in Tibet, and worked as an elephant handler, a professional boxer, and a fruit picker before embarking on a career as a writer. His books sold 200 million copies in 20 languages. After World War II he used the name Tex Burns since "L'Amour" seemed an unlikely name for an author of westerns. After *Hondo* was published in 1953 and became a blockbuster motion picture starring John Wayne, L'Amour wrote under his own name. Some of his best-sellers that later became motion pictures included *Kilkenny* (1954), *The Burning Hills* (1956), *Guns of the Timberland* (1955), and *How the West Was Won* (1963). The first novelist to receive a Congressional Gold Medal, L'Amour was working on his autobiography, *Education of a Wandering Man,* at the time of his death.

Lane, Dame Elizabeth Kathleen, British jurist (b. Aug. 9, 1905, England—d. June 17, 1988, Winchester, Hampshire, England), was the first woman judge appointed to the British High Court. She also headed the controversial inquiry (1971–73) that upheld the 1967 Abortion Act. Born Elizabeth Coulborn, she attended McGill University, Montreal, and became interested in a legal career while helping her husband prepare for his bar exams. She was called to the bar in 1940 and rose to queen's counsel in 1960. Lane held numerous distinguished positions, including commissioner of the crown courts at Manchester (1961–62) and county court judge (1962–65). Upon her appointment to the Family Division of the High Court in 1965, she was created Dame Commander of the Order of the British Empire. She retired from the bench in 1979 and published her autobiography, *Hear the Other Side,* in 1985.

Lassiter, Luther, U.S. billiards player (b. 1919, Elizabeth City, N.C.—d. Oct. 25, 1988, Elizabeth City), was considered by many to be the best nine-ball player of all time. Lassiter, who dropped out of school at the age of 16 to hustle pool, earned the nickname "Wimpy" because of his seemingly insatiable appetite for hot dogs and Orange Crushes, which he devoured with the same relish that the character Wimpy lavished on hamburgers in the "Popeye" comic strip. During his professional career, Lassiter competed in the Jansco brothers' all-around championships (1962–72) in Johnston City, Ill., and captured the straight pool title five times, the nine-ball title four times, and the one-pocket title once. He won the all-around title in 1962, 1963, and 1967. Lassiter, who also won the Billiard Congress of America's (BCA's) U.S. Open in 1967, was a member of the BCA Hall of Fame. He captured his last title, the Legendary Pool Players championship, in 1983.

Le Poulain, Jean, French actor (b. Sept. 12, 1924, Marseille, France—d. March 1, 1988, Paris, France), was a versatile performer, celebrated primarily for his comedic interpretations but also noted for his roles in tragedies. During his tenure (1986–88) as administrative director of the 308-year-old Comédie Française, Le Poulain used his considerable influence to enlarge the performing quarters of the Comédie Française and to institute a training program for young actors. Le Poulain spent much of his childhood in Indochina, where his father was a colonial administrator, but returned to France at the age of 19. He studied in small conservatories before being admitted to the National Conservatory of Theatre Arts in Paris, where he won first prize in comedy acting before graduating in 1949. After his application to the venerable Comédie Française was turned down, he joined the livelier Popular National Theatre. During the 1950s he performed more than 100 roles and directed classic French comedies. Le Poulain also directed and performed in contemporary dramas by such playwrights as Bertolt Brecht and Jean Cocteau. By the 1960s Le Poulain, known for his energy and grimaces, had become one of Paris's most respected and popular actors onstage, in films, and on radio and television. He published his autobiography, *Je rirai le dernier* ("I Will Have the Last Laugh"), the year before he was invited to join the Comédie Française as an actor. In 1986 he was named administrator of the company by Pres. François Mitterrand.

Lee, Jennie (JANET), BARONESS LEE OF ASHERIDGE (Mrs. ANEURIN BEVAN), British politician (b. Nov. 3, 1904, Lochgelly, Fife, Scotland—d. Nov. 16, 1988, London, England), as a member of Parliament and a staunch champion of the Labour Party, established the arts as a serious governmental concern. Jennie Lee, as she was best known, was the daughter of a coal miner with deep roots in the trade union movement and the Independent Labour Party (ILP). Lee won scholarships to the University of Edinburgh, where she earned an M.A. (1926) and a law degree (1927). She taught school until she was recognized for her spirited support of the ILP. Lee won election (1929) to the House of Commons as ILP candidate representing North Lanark and was the youngest MP. Failing reelection (1931), she turned to journalism and lecturing; during World War II she served with the Ministry of Aircraft Production and as a political correspondent; she was returned to Parliament (1945) as Labour Party representative from Cannock. In her marriage (1934) to MP and Labour Party leader Aneurin ("Nye") Bevan, Lee was a fervent political ally. After his death in 1960, she was appointed minister for the arts (1964). During her six-year tenure, government funding for the arts more than doubled, theatres and libraries were built, the film industry was strengthened, theatre censorship by the lord chamberlain was abolished, and the Open University was founded. Lee was made a privy councillor in 1966 and a life peer in 1970. She published two autobiographies, *Tomorrow Is a New Day* (1939) and *My Life with Nye* (1980).

Lemnitzer, Lyman Louis, general (ret.), U.S. Army (b. Aug. 29, 1899, Honesdale, Pa.—d. Nov. 12, 1988, Washington, D.C.), had a distinguished military career, highlighted by his service as commander of United Nations forces in the Korean War (1955–57), as chairman of the Joint Chiefs of Staff (1960–62), and as supreme allied commander in Europe (1962–69). Lemnitzer graduated from the U.S. Military Academy, West Point, N.Y., in 1920, from the Command and General Staff School, Fort Leavenworth, Kansas, in 1939, and from the Army War College, Carlisle, Pa., in 1940. He was instrumental in planning the African invasions in World War II and once was nearly apprehended by Vichy police in Algeria. A skilled diplomat, he participated in secret negotiations with Italy's Premier Pietro Badoglio that led to Italy's surrender (1943) to the Allies, and he also conducted secret talks with the German High Command that led (1945) to the surrender of German armies in Italy and southern Austria. At the age of 51 Lemnitzer qualified as a paratrooper, and in 1952 he took command of infantry troops in Korea. After serving as commander of all U.S. and UN forces in Korea and Japan, Lemnitzer returned to Washington, D.C., in 1957 and became army vice-chief of staff under Gen. Maxwell D. Taylor. After Taylor retired, Lemnitzer succeeded him and in 1960 was named chairman of the Joint Chiefs of Staff, a post he held until he was appointed supreme allied commander in Europe. Lemnitzer retired from active duty in 1969.

Lexcen, Ben (ROBERT MILLER), Australian yachtsman and marine architect (b. 1936, Newcastle, New South Wales, Australia—d. May 1, 1988, Sydney, Australia), designed *Australia II,* the first non-American yacht ever to win (1983) the prestigious America's Cup in that race's 132-year history. Lexcen, who had little formal education, was apprenticed at the age of 14 to a locomotive mechanic, but he eventually quit to build boats and sails. When he and his partner dissolved their sailmaking enterprise, he left his name (Bob Miller) with the company and had a friend's computer create a new six-letter surname for him. A self-taught boat designer and accomplished yachtsman, Lexcen represented Australia in the Soling class at the 1972 Olympic Games. He first learned of the America's Cup challenge in 1970 while traveling in the U.S. with Alan Bond, a self-made millionaire and sailing enthusiast, who commissioned Lexcen to design a boat that could beat the American entry. The final result was *Australia II,* a 12-m yacht with a radically new winged keel that improved the boat's stability and maneuverability. Lexcen suffered a heart attack in 1983 after accusations that he had not designed the revolutionary keel, but he ultimately received full credit for *Australia II*'s victory.

Loewe, Frederick ("FRITZ"), U.S. composer (b. June 10, 1904, Vienna, Austria—d. Feb. 14, 1988, Palm Springs, Calif.), together with lyricist Alan J. Lerner, created some of the most enduring and enchanting Broadway hits—including *Brigadoon* (1947), *Paint Your Wagon* (1951), *My Fair Lady* (1956), and *Camelot* (1960)—and the motion picture *Gigi* (1958), which won nine Academy Awards. Loewe, the son of an operetta tenor and an actress, began playing the piano at the age of 5 and at 13 became the youngest pianist to appear as soloist with the Berlin Symphony. Two years later he composed "Katrina," an enormous success that sold some two million copies of sheet music in Europe. He received advanced instruction from keyboard masters Ferruccio Busoni and Eugène d'Albert before moving to the U.S. with his father in 1924 to promote his career on the concert stage. His efforts proved unsuccessful, and for the next decade he held a variety of jobs, including prizefighter, prospector, and cowpuncher. After he joined the Lambs theatrical club, he met Lerner, and the two launched a nearly 20-year collaboration. Their first Broadway effort, *What's Up?* (1943), was unsuccessful, but it was followed by *The Day Before Spring* (1945), which enjoyed moderate acclaim. Their first solid hit was *Brigadoon,* which yielded "Almost Like Being in Love," and they went on to delight audiences with such memorable hit songs as "They Call the Wind Maria," "I Could Have Danced All Night," "The Rain in Spain" (which Loewe reputedly composed in ten minutes), "Get Me to the Church on Time," "Gigi," "Wouldn't It Be Lovely?," and "On the Street Where You Live." Their biggest and most dazzling success, *My Fair Lady,* was faithfully adapted from George Bernard Shaw's *Pygmalion* and enjoyed 2,717 performances on Broadway. The original Broadway cast recording sold more than five million copies, and the 1964 motion picture garnered eight Academy Awards. Such hits as *Brigadoon, Paint Your Wagon,* and *Camelot* were also successfully adapted to the screen— in 1954, 1969, and 1967, respectively. After the Broadway production of *Camelot,* Loewe and

Lerner disbanded their partnership until 1973, when they teamed up again to adapt *Gigi* for Broadway. After their last collaboration, on the film *The Little Prince* (1974), Loewe went into retirement.

Logan, Joshua Lockwood, U.S. director and playwright (b. Oct. 5, 1908, Texarkana, Texas—d. July 12, 1988, New York, N.Y.), was a multitalented theatrical genius who scored numerous Broadway triumphs as director of such classic hit shows as *Annie Get Your Gun* (1946), *Picnic* (1953), and *The World of Suzie Wong* (1958); he also displayed versatility by serving as both director and coauthor of the Broadway blockbusters *Mister Roberts* (1948); *South Pacific* (1949), which won the 1950 Pulitzer Prize for Drama; and *Fanny* (1954). Logan entered Princeton University in 1927 and soon organized the University Players, a summer stock group that performed on Cape Cod and boasted such members as James Stewart, Henry Fonda, and Margaret Sullavan. Logan spent his senior year in Moscow studying under the famed director Konstantin Stanislavsky. assumed various jobs during the Depression before making his Broadway directing debut with *To See Ourselves* (1935). However, it was his staging of *On Borrowed Time* (1938) and, even more importantly, *I Married an Angel* (1938) that secured his reputation and began his string of hits. During the 1950s Logan turned to directing motion pictures, adapting many of his smash hit Broadway musicals for the screen, among them *Picnic* (1956), *South Pacific* (1958), and *Fanny* (1961). Though critics felt that some of his films lacked a cinematic sensibility, many of them were huge successes with audiences, including *Bus Stop* (1956), *Sayonara* (1957), *Camelot* (1967), and *Paint Your Wagon* (1969). Logan published his autobiography, *Josh*, in 1976 and his memoirs, *Movie Stars, Real People, and Me*, in 1978.

Lower, Arthur Reginald Marsden, Canadian historian (b. Aug. 12, 1889, Barrie, Ont.—d. Jan. 7, 1988, Kingston, Ont.), chronicled the economic history of the Canadian timber industry in such books as *The Trade in Square Timber* (1932), *Settlement and the Forest Frontier in Eastern Canada* (1936), and *The North American Assault on the Canadian Forest* (1938) and later, in *Colony to Nation: A History of Canada* (1946; rev. 1964), attempted to establish a nationalistic pride to unite French and English Canadians. Lower's pioneering historical writings, which were peppered with lively social commentary, witticisms, and anecdotes, aroused controversy yet were widely read because of their fierce nationalistic persuasion. He was educated at the University of Toronto and at Harvard University, where he earned a Ph.D. in 1929. Lower served as professor at United College, University of Manitoba (1929–46), and as Douglas professor of Canadian history at Queen's University, Kingston (1947–59). Some of his other important works included *Evolving Canadian Federalism* (1958); *Canadians in the Making* (1958); an autobiography, *My First Seventy-Five Years* (1967); and his last work, *A Pattern for History* (1978). Lower was twice recipient of the Governor General's Medal (1947 and 1955), was winner of the Tyrrell Medal of the Royal Society of Canada (1947), and in 1968 was made a Companion of the Order of Canada.

MacBride, Sean, Irish statesman (b. Jan. 26, 1904, Paris, France—d. Jan. 15, 1988, Dublin, Ireland), was a onetime member of the Irish Republican Army (IRA) but later became an international human rights activist, an advocate of disarmament, and the winner of the 1974 Nobel Prize for Peace. MacBride's mother, the Irish actress and patriot Maud Gonne, was a founding member of the anti-British political party Sinn Fein. When his father was executed by the British for his part in the 1916 Easter Rising, MacBride and his mother returned to Ireland, where he joined the IRA. While working as a journalist for a conservative London newspaper, he secretly fought in the Irish rebellion, becoming IRA chief of staff in 1936. Although he continued to oppose the partition of Ireland, MacBride accepted the constitution of 1937 (which loosened Ireland's ties with the Commonwealth) and quit the IRA. He practiced criminal law from 1937, often defending accused IRA terrorists. MacBride was elected to the Dail (lower house of Parliament) in 1947 as a member of the Clann na Poblachta (Republi-

AP/WIDE WORLD

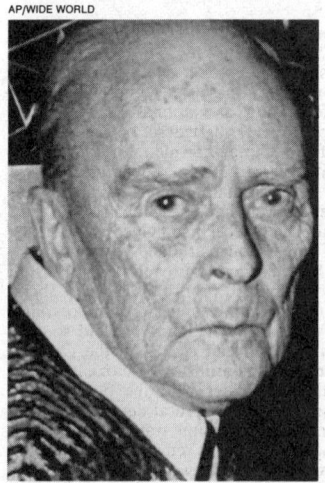

can Party), which he had founded the previous year. He was minister for external affairs (1948–51) in the coalition government that severed Ireland's last links with the Commonwealth and declared the country a republic in 1949. In this post he became increasingly involved in international affairs, serving as president (1950) of the Council of Foreign Ministers of the Council of Europe and vice-president (1948–51) of the Organization for European Economic Cooperation. After losing his seat in the Dail in 1957, MacBride devoted himself to his law practice and to promoting international human rights. He was cofounder (1961) and chairman (1961–75) of Amnesty International, secretary-general (1963–70) of the International Commission of Jurists, and chairman (1972–85) of the International Peace Bureau. He was named assistant secretary-general of the UN and UN commissioner for South West Africa/Namibia in 1973. In 1977 he was appointed chairman of a Unesco commission studying world communications problems, and from 1982 to 1984 he chaired an international committee studying Israeli actions in Lebanon. MacBride was the only person ever to win the Nobel Peace Prize, the Lenin Peace Prize (1977), and the American Medal of Justice (1978).

McCracken, James Eugene, U.S. singer (b. Dec. 16, 1926, Gary, Ind.—d. April 29, 1988, New York, N.Y.), possessed an extraordinary emotional intensity heightened by his dark-timbred tenor voice and for many years performed with the Metropolitan Opera, first in secondary roles but later as a star. McCracken studied with Wellington Ezekiel, who coached him for his professional debut (1952) at the Central City Opera, Colorado, in the role of Rodolfo in *La Bohème*. The following year he made his debut at the Metropolitan Opera in the small role of Parpignol in the same opera. Because he was limited to secondary roles, McCracken left the Met in 1957 to gain experience in Europe. The turning point in his career was his performance as Otello with the Washington (D.C.) Opera Society, a role he duplicated in the great opera houses of Europe in Zürich (1960), Vienna (1960), and London (1964). He returned triumphantly to the Met in 1963 as a star and took leading roles as Calaf in *Turandot*, the tragic clown in *Pagliacci*, the Hebrew champion in *Samson et Dalila*, and the heroes

of Verdi's *Aïda, Il Trovatore*, and *La Forza del destino*. McCracken and the Metropolitan Opera had another falling out in 1978 when, probably because of his considerable girth, he was denied the leading role in a televised production of *Otello* and a telecast of *Tannhäuser* was dropped abruptly. He left the company but returned to participate in the Met's centennial in 1983 and thereafter accepted singing engagements with the opera until illness forced him to cease performing near the end of the 1987–88 season.

McMahon, Sir William, Australian politician (b. Feb. 23, 1908, Sydney, Australia—d. March 31, 1988, Sydney), became prime minister of Australia in March 1971 but failed to hold the ruling coalition together and was voted out of office in December 1972. McMahon received his law degree from the University of Sydney and practiced law until 1939. After serving as a major in the Australian Army in World War II, he returned to Sydney to obtain a degree in economics. He was elected to the House of Representatives in 1949, the first year of the powerful Liberal-Country Party coalition. McMahon held increasingly important portfolios in the government, rising in 1966 to treasurer and deputy leader of the Liberals. In 1968

CAMERA PRESS/GLOBE PHOTOS

he lost his bid to become party leader and, therefore, prime minister, in part because of opposition from the Country Party (the coalition's junior partner). He was named foreign minister in 1969, and two years later he succeeded to the party leadership after an internal shake-up forced John Gorton to step down. As prime minister, McMahon supported SEATO (Southeast Asia Treaty Organization), withdrew Australian troops from Vietnam, and advocated stronger ties with other Southeast Asian nations. He was unable to overcome opposition from the Country Party leadership and from rivals within his own party, however, and in the 1972 elections the crumbling coalition was defeated by the Australian Labor Party led by Gough Whitlam. McMahon was replaced as party leader immediately after the election, but he remained in Parliament until his retirement in 1982. He was knighted in 1977.

Malenkov, Georgy Maksimilianovich, Soviet politician (b. Jan. 21 [Jan. 8, old style], 1902, Orenburg, Russia—d. Jan. 13?, 1988, Moscow?, U.S.S.R.), briefly succeeded Joseph Stalin as head of the Communist Party and, as prime minister (1953–55), advocated Soviet arms limitations, increased production of consumer goods, and incentives for collective farm workers. Born into a middle-class family, Malenkov volunteered in 1919 for the Red Army, joined the Communist Party in 1920, and within a year became a commissar of Bolshevik forces in Turkestan. In Moscow he studied engineering

CAMERA PRESS/GLOBE PHOTOS

at the Higher Technical Institute (1921), where he distinguished himself as a student party leader. After graduating in 1925, Malenkov was appointed as a secretary to Stalin, organization chairman of the Moscow Party committee (1930–34), and personnel chairman of the Central Committee (1934–39). Familiar with files of party members, Malenkov carried out purges of Stalin's enemies and was named to the Central Committee in 1939. During World War II he was responsible for production of military equipment; after the war he became a deputy prime minister and was named to the Politburo in 1946. Upon Stalin's death (1953), Malenkov became prime minister and top party leader but, within two weeks, he yielded the latter post to Nikita S. Khrushchev. When Malenkov's programs were not supported by other Soviet leaders, he resigned as prime minister (1955) but kept his seat in the Politburo and was named a deputy chairman of the Council of Ministers and minister of electric power stations. In 1957, during a power struggle over Khrushchev's destalinization program, Malenkov and two other close Stalin aides, Vyacheslav Molotov and Lazar Kaganovich, lost and were expelled from the Politburo, the Central Committee, and the Communist Party. Malenkov was sent to manage a hydroelectric power station in central Asia, and his name disappeared from major Soviet reference books. Following his retirement in 1963, he moved to Moscow and reportedly began to write his memoirs. He was named a Hero of Socialist Labour (1943) and was twice awarded the Order of Lenin.

Maravich, Pete ("PISTOL"), U.S. basketball player (b. June 22, 1947, Aliquippa, Pa.—d. Jan. 5, 1988, Pasadena, Calif.), was a brilliant athlete and crowd pleaser who held the record as the leading career and single-season scorer in major college basketball history, with 3,667 points in 83 games, for an average of 44.2. Maravich, who rarely let go of his basketball, was known to dribble the ball in aisles at movie theatres and to practice fingertip drills in bed. As a player (1967–70) at Louisiana State University (LSU), he was coached by his father, Press Maravich, and given wide latitude in his on-court antics. He earned the nickname "Pistol" for his penchant to shoot the ball and was remembered for his trademark sagging gray socks, floppy hair, and flamboyant ball handling. After his three-year stint at LSU, he was signed to a lucrative professional contract with the Atlanta Hawks. During his ten years with the National Basketball Association (NBA), he also played for the New Orleans (later Utah) Jazz and the Boston Celtics. Maravich captured the NBA scoring crown in 1977 with an average of 31.1 points per game, but he never played on a championship team. After retiring from professional basketball in 1980, he became a born-again Christian and began to be dedicated

to a health-food regimen. His career earnings enabled him to operate youth basketball camps with little concern for making a profit. Maravich had just finished playing a game of basketball with friends when he collapsed and died. An autopsy revealed that he had only one coronary artery, a rare heart defect that enlarges and weakens the heart owing to a continuous lack of oxygen to the heart muscle and that usually kills its victims before the age of 20. Maravich was inducted into the professional Basketball Hall of Fame in 1987.

Marchand, Jean, Canadian politician (b. Dec. 20, 1918, Champlain, Que.—d. Aug. 28, 1988, St.-Augustin, Que.), was a union firebrand who rose through the ranks to become president of the Confederation of National Trade Unions in 1961 before entering federal politics in 1965 as one of the "three wise men" of Quebec, together with Pierre Elliott Trudeau and Gérard Pelletier. After graduating from Laval University, Quebec, Marchand became a prominent union leader in Quebec and helped engineer the defeat of the Union Nationale government in 1960. In 1965 Prime Minister Lester B. Pearson persuaded Marchand to join the federal Liberal Party, but Marchand agreed to run for office only if Trudeau and Pelletier also did so. The three were elected and served in the Cabinet. Marchand began as minister for citizenship and immigration and later held the portfolios of manpower, forestry and rural development, regional economic expansion, transport, and environment. When Pearson retired from politics in 1968, Marchand was viewed as a likely successor, but instead Marchand propelled Trudeau into the race and a 16-year career as prime minister. A strong federalist, Marchand was a fierce promoter of bilingualism and strongly opposed separatism for Quebec. Marchand served in Trudeau's Cabinet until 1976, when he resigned to protest the government's refusal to allow French Canadian pilots the right to communicate with air traffic controllers in French. Marchand was named to the Senate in 1976 and served as speaker from 1980 until 1983, when he resigned to head the Canadian Transport Commission, a post he held until 1985. The following year Marchand was appointed to the Order of Canada.

Marshall, Sir John Ross, New Zealand politician (b. March 5, 1912, Wellington, N.Z.—d. Aug. 30, 1988, England), served briefly as prime minister of New Zealand in 1972 but achieved his greatest success in 1971 when, as minister of overseas trade, he stalled Britain's admission to the European Economic Community (EEC) until the EEC agreed to continue the importation of New Zealand dairy products for at least five years. Marshall, who studied law at Victoria University of Wellington, was called to the bar in 1936 and was first elected to Parliament in 1945. He held a wide variety of ministerial posts, including the portfolios for health (1951–54), justice (1954–57), industry and commerce (1960–69), and labour and immigration (1969–72). As deputy leader of the National Party from 1957, he was chosen to succeed retiring prime minister Sir Keith Holyoake in February 1972, but the party was defeated in the November general election by Norman Kirk's Labour Party. Marshall retired after he was ousted as leader of the opposition by his party rival, Robert David Muldoon, shortly before the National Party regained a majority in the 1975 election. Marshall was knighted in 1974.

Matthews, Burnita Shelton, U.S. judge (b. Dec. 28, 1894, Burnell, Miss.—d. April 25, 1988, Washington, D.C.), was named to the Federal District Court for the District of Columbia by Pres. Harry S. Truman in 1949, thus becoming the first woman to serve as a federal district judge. As a young woman she was sent to study voice and piano at the Conservatory of Music in Cincinnati, Ohio, although her real interest was in law. She later moved to Washington, D.C., and took a job at the Veterans Administration

in order to attend law school at night. In 1919 she graduated from National University Law School (later George Washington University) and became an active campaigner for women's rights. During her 30 years of practicing law, she helped draft bills for the National Woman's Party. When Matthews was named a judge, she had to overcome the prejudice of her fellow judges because of her sex. She became a senior judge in 1968, thus enabling her to reduce her court work load, though she heard cases until she was 88 years old.

Melen, Ferit, Turkish politician (b. 1906, Van, Turkey—d. Sept. 3, 1988, Ankara, Turkey), was twice minister of defense and served (1972–73) as prime minister of Turkey. Melen headed a military-approved coalition government noted for harsh measures, including martial law court trials and executions of political foes. After graduating from the School of Political Science of the University of Ankara, Melen returned to Van and began (1931) a steady climb through the ranks of the bureaucracy. He served (1933–43) as auditor in the Ministry of Finance and became (1944) director general of revenue before being elected (1950) to represent Van in Parliament as a member of the Republican People's Party (RPP). He also was minister of finance (1962–65). As the RPP moved to the left, Melen and 47 of his conservative colleagues resigned (1967) and formed the National Reliance Party, currently part of the Republican Reliance Party. After the Army ousted (1971) the democratically elected government of Suleyman Demirel, Turkey was ruled by a coalition government that included ministers from the National Reliance Party, the Justice Party, and the RPP. Melen was minister of defense until he was appointed (April 1972) prime minister. In 1975, under a new Demirel coalition, Melen again served as minister of defense, a post he held until 1977.

Menghistu Lemma, Ethiopian writer (b. August 1925, Addis Ababa, Eth.—d. July 1988, Addis Ababa), wrote poetry and witty, satiric plays in Amharic (the modern language of Ethiopia) in which he examined the difficulty of reconciling traditional values and customs with modern Western ideas. After receiving a Muslim education in Harar, Menghistu studied in Addis Ababa and at the London School of Economics (1953). He worked in government service, notably as first secretary at the Ethiopian embassy in India (1957–63), but he remained aloof from partisan politics. Menghistu's best-known plays, which he also translated into English, were published as *Snatch and Run, or Marriage by Abduction* (1963; first staged in 1962) and *Marriage of Unequals* (1970; staged in 1963). Menghistu also wrote critical essays in both Amharic and English and published a historically important transcription of his father's oral memoirs.

Miki, Takeo, Japanese politician (b. March 17, 1907, Donari, Japan—d. Nov. 13, 1988, Tokyo, Japan), served in the Diet (parliament) for 38 years before being named leader of the ruling Liberal-Democratic Party (LDP) and serving (1974–76) as prime minister of Japan. Miki, educated at Meiji University in Tokyo, also studied at universities in the U.S. He earned a law degree in 1937 and a few months later entered the Diet. A pragmatic politician, Miki publicly opposed the war with the U.S., and his career was not interrupted by the post-World War II U.S. occupation of Japan. Miki held numerous posts, serving as minister of communications (1947–48), transport (1954–55), and international trade and industry (1965–66). He was chairman of the Atomic Energy Commission (1961–62) and director of the Environmental Agency (1972–74) while also serving as deputy prime minister from 1972 to 1974, a post he resigned to protest Prime Minister Kakuei Tanaka's alleged financial irregularities and heavily financed electoral campaign. When Tanaka resigned in December 1974, the impeccable Miki became the LDP's compromise

AP/WIDE WORLD

candidate because the selection of either rival candidate, Masayoshi Ohira or Takeo Fukuda, would have split the party. During his tenure as prime minister, Miki adopted the policy of limiting defense spending to no more than 1% of gross national product, and he initiated the government inquiry into the Lockheed scandal, involving Tanaka, who allegedly accepted huge bribes from high executives in the Lockheed Aircraft Corp. After Tanaka's August 1976 indictment, the LDP suffered in the December 1976 general election, winning only 249 of the 511 seats in the Diet. Miki, who took responsibility for the party's poor showing at the polls, resigned his post as prime minister but remained a powerful leader within the party.

Milburn, Jackie (JOHN EDWARD THOMPSON MILBURN), British athlete (b. May 11, 1924, Ashington, Northumberland, England—d. Oct. 9, 1988, Ashington), as a mainstay of the association football (soccer) team Newcastle United from 1946 to 1956, scored more than 170 goals in 354 league appearances and led the team to the FA Cup championship in 1951, 1952, and 1955. "Wor Jackie," as Milburn was known to legions of fans, scored the only two goals in the 1951 FA Cup final, and in the 1955 final he scored in the first 45 seconds of play, a record time. He played for the English national team 13 times between 1948 and 1956, scoring ten goals in international matches. Milburn retired in 1956 and, after serving briefly as manager for Ipswich (1963–64), became a sports journalist with the *News of the World*.

Mitchell, John Newton, U.S. politician (b. Sept. 15, 1913, Detroit, Mich.—d. Nov. 9, 1988, Washington, D.C.), during his tenure as U.S. attorney general (1969–72) in the administration of Pres. Richard M. Nixon, authorized the infamous overnight break-in (June 16–17, 1972) at the headquarters of the Democratic National Committee at the Watergate, an office-apartment-hotel complex in Washington, D.C., and was instrumental in the subsequent cover-up of the wire-tapping and burglary. After earning a law degree from Fordham University law school in New York City, Mitchell joined the firm of Caldwell & Raymond and specialized in municipal and state bond financing. During World War II he served in the Navy as a torpedo boat commander. In 1967 Mitchell came to know Nixon when their law firms merged. Mitchell became a close political adviser to Nixon, and he successfully orchestrated Nixon's presidential campaign in 1968. As attorney general Mitchell became controversial because he backed two of Nixon's nominees to the Supreme Court who were rejected by the Senate as unqualified, approved wiretaps without court authorization (declared unconstitutional by the Supreme Court), prosecuted antiwar protesters, and brought suit to block publica-

tion of the classified Pentagon Papers on the Vietnam war (rejected by the Supreme Court). After resigning his post as attorney general in 1972 to become chairman of Nixon's reelection committee, Mitchell launched a "dirty tricks" campaign that included espionage, forged letters, and sabotage directed against Sen. Edmund Muskie of Maine, the Democratic front-runner for the presidency. On July 1, 1972, Mitchell resigned from the reelection committee when the Watergate scandal began unfolding. For his role in the scandal, Mitchell was indicted in 1974 on charges that he had conspired to plan the break-in and that he had obstructed justice and perjured himself during the cover-up. The scandal forced the resignation of President Nixon on Aug. 9, 1974. Mitchell was convicted in 1975 and sentenced to 2½ to 8 years in prison. He entered prison in 1977, and after his release on parole in 1979, he was disbarred.

Moore, Colleen (KATHLEEN MORRISON), U.S. actress (b. Aug. 19, 1900, Port Huron, Mich.—d. Jan. 25, 1988, Paso Robles, Calif.), epitomized the jazz-age flapper with her stylishly bobbed hair and short skirts in such silent motion pictures as *Flaming Youth* (1923), *Naughty But Nice* (1927), *Synthetic Sin* (1929), and *Why Be Good?* (1929). Moore, who launched her motion picture career in westerns as Tom Mix's leading lady, became the consummate flapper and also possessed a comedic talent which she showcased in such films as *Irene* (1926) and *Orchids and Ermine* (1927). Though she gave an excellent performance in *The Power and the Glory* (1933), opposite Spencer Tracy, she did not make a successful transition to the talkies, probably because the flapper era was waning. However, she was enormously rich when she retired and invested her fortune wisely under the tutelage of her husband, a stockbroker. She later married another stockbroker and became a successful author during the 1960s with her autobiography, *Silent Star;* an investment guide, *How Women Can Make Money in the Stock Market;* and *Colleen Moore's Doll House,* a book about her elaborate Fairy Castle, which was put on permanent display at the Museum of Science and Industry in Chicago. Her 100 film credits also included *So Big* (1925), *Lilac Time* (1928), and *Oh Kay* (1928).

Moses, Sir Charles Joseph Alfred, British-born Australian broadcasting executive (b. Jan. 21, 1900, Little Hulton?, Lancashire, England—d. Feb. 9, 1988, Sydney, Australia), ran a broadcasting empire for 30 years as chief executive of the Australian Broadcasting Commission (ABC). Moses graduated (1918) from the Royal Military College at Sandhurst, England, and was stationed with the British Army in Ireland before immigrating to Australia in 1922. After joining the staff at the ABC in 1930 as a radio sports announcer, he gained prominence as a news analyst, and in 1935 he was promoted to general manager of the entire broadcasting service. In this post Moses built the ABC into a nationwide media corporation. In 1956 he inaugurated Australia's first national television service just in time for the Melbourne Olympic Games. After his retirement from the ABC in 1965, Moses founded the Asian Broadcasting Union (which brought together broadcasters from across parts of Asia and the South Pacific) and served as its general director until 1977. He was made a Commander of the Order of the British Empire in 1954 and was knighted in 1961.

Murray, Henry Alexander, U.S. psychologist (b. May 13, 1893, New York, N.Y.—d. June 23, 1988, Cambridge, Mass.), developed a theory of human personality based on an individual's inborn needs, and the way people interact in a complex fashion with each other and with the physical and social environment. Murray, who majored in history at Harvard University, earned an M.D. in 1919 from Columbia University's College of Physicians and Surgeons, an M.A. in biology from Columbia, and a Ph.D.

in biochemistry from the University of Cambridge in 1927. His interest in psychology was sparked when he began reading the works of the eminent psychologist Carl Jung. He later visited Jung and credited him and Sigmund Freud with influencing his own work. With no formal training he began teaching psychology at Harvard University in 1927, and from 1929 to 1938 he served as director of the Harvard Psychological Clinic. One of Murray's most important contributions to analytical psychology was the development of the Thematic Apperception Test, which became an important tool in evaluating personality. By showing a person a series of 20 pictures, each depicting a different dramatic event which the subject was asked to interpret, Murray was able to evaluate personality, since studies proved that individuals are likely to interpret events according to their own experience or that of family or friends. He published his most important work, *Explorations in Personality,* in 1938, and after his retirement from Harvard in 1962, he continued to lecture and devote much of his time to the study of the works of Herman Melville. At the time of Murray's death he was preparing a book that was tentatively titled, *A Melville Mosaic: Morsels from the Unpublished Biography.*

Nevelson, Louise, U.S. sculptor (b. Sept. 23?, 1900, Kiev, Russia—d. April 17, 1988, New York, N.Y.), became one of the foremost artists in the U.S. with her mammoth environmental sculptures, made of wood and later of steel and other materials, which captured the essence of darkness and shadow. As a child she immigrated (1905) with her family to Rockland, Maine, where she experimented with scrap wood from her father's lumberyard. She later studied (1929–30) with Kenneth Hayes Miller at the Art Students League in New York City. She married businessman Charles Nevelson in 1920 and bore a son in 1922 but separated from them in 1931 when she went to Munich to study with Hans Hofmann. The following year Nevelson returned to the U.S. and assisted the muralist Diego Rivera on a mural project in New York City. In 1941 she held her first exhibition at the Karl Nierendorf Gallery but destroyed her entire exhibit when none of her works sold. She had another show in 1946 called "Ancient City," but it was not until the late 1950s when she abandoned figurative sculptures and began working in the abstract with wood that she received public acclaim. With such wall sculptures as "Gate of Eternity" (1958), "Nightscape" (1959), "Homage to 6,000,000" (1964), "Atmosphere and Environment I" (1966), and "Sky Gate—New York," her largest wall sculpture, at the World Trade Center (1978), she created a strong horizontal and vertical environment by using open-faced wooden boxes, stacked to make freestanding walls. Many of her works were defined in black or white paint. During the

LISA DUBOIS—GLOBE PHOTOS

1970s and '80s Nevelson worked in a variety of media, including black steel, Plexiglas, and Lucite, and received numerous commissions. In 1967 she had a major retrospective at the Whitney Museum of American Art, and in 1978 she was honoured when the Legion Memorial Square in the Wall Street area of Manhattan was renamed the Louise Nevelson Plaza, which showcased an entire outdoor environment of her black sculptures.

Nguyen Kim Dien, Philippe, Vietnamese prelate (b. March 13, 1921, Long Duc, Vinh Long Province, Vietnam—d. June 8, 1988, Ho Chi Minh City, Vietnam), as archbishop of Hue and, therefore, leader of the Roman Catholic Church in Vietnam, defied government efforts to control the church after Vietnam's reunification (1976). Dien, who was ordained in 1947, was appointed bishop of Cantho (1961), archbishop of Pario (1964), and archbishop of Hue (1968). After reunification he kept the Roman Catholic community together, despite seminary closures and the forced "reeducation" of many priests. In 1983 the government formed the Committee for the Solidarity of Patriotic Vietnamese Catholics, in an attempt to separate the Vietnamese Roman Catholic Church from papal authority. Dien was placed under house arrest in 1984 for his vigorous opposition to this committee. Two years later cardinals and bishops from 40 countries issued a formal protest when Dien was prevented from attending the 1986 Vatican Congregation for the Evangelization of Peoples. Dien died of heart failure while still under house arrest.

Noguchi, Isamu, U.S. sculptor (b. Nov. 17, 1904, Los Angeles, Calif.—d. Dec. 30, 1988, New York, N.Y.), skillfully blended the diverse philosophies and ideals of Eastern and Western cultures in highly polished abstract sculptures of wood, bronze, galvanized steel, and stone; his sculptures and meditative gardens became landmarks of 20th-century art. At the age of two, Noguchi accompanied his Japanese father and American mother to Japan. He was educated there until his mother sent him back (1918) to the U.S. to continue his studies. Noguchi served (1919–22) as an apprentice to Gutzon Borglum, who carved the Mount Rushmore National Memorial in South Dakota, but he entered Columbia University, New York City, as a premed student when Borglum declared that he would never succeed as a sculptor. Noguchi, however, soon left Columbia to study at the Leonardo da Vinci Art School in New York, where he copied classical Greek casts. Inspired by the works of Romanian sculptor Constantin Brancusi, Noguchi turned to Abstract Expressionism and moved to Paris to study with Brancusi. He returned to New York in 1929, staged his first of many one-man shows, and earned a living by making portrait busts. Noguchi, who constructed monumental sculptures as well as small, delicate lamps, was dedicated to the use of the elemental mediums of clay, wood, and stone—including basalt, granite and marble—and to developing a "oneness with stone." During the 1930s and throughout his life, Noguchi traveled extensively, learning calligraphy and brush drawing in China, studying the gardens in Japan, and developing a respect for the cultures of various countries in travels to England, France, Italy, Spain, Greece, India, Indonesia, and Mexico. In 1935 he designed the first of many sets and props for dancer Martha Graham; his commissions continued throughout his life. Some of his best-known sculptures include the low-relief symbol for freedom of the press that was installed above the main entrance of the Associated Press building in New York City; two bridges for Hiroshima's Peace Park; gardens for the Unesco building in Paris (1956–58); a marble garden for the Beinecke Rare Book and Manuscript Library at Yale University (1960–64); the Billy Rose Sculpture Garden for the Israeli Museum, Jerusalem (1960–65); a fountain for the Detroit Civic Centre Plaza (1975); and "A Bolt of Lightning" (1984), placed near the

Benjamin Franklin Bridge in Philadelphia, Pa. In 1985 Noguchi opened the Isamu Noguchi Garden Museum in a former factory in Long Island City, N.Y. Noguchi, the winner of the 1982 Edward MacDowell Medal for outstanding lifelong contribution to the arts, was awarded the National Medal of Arts by Pres. Ronald Reagan in 1987, and in 1988 he received the Order of the Sacred Treasure from the Japanese government.

Norstad, Lauris, general (ret.), U.S. Air Force (b. March 24, 1907, Minneapolis, Minn.—d. Sept. 12, 1988, Tucson, Ariz.), served (1956–63) admirably as supreme allied commander of U.S. and NATO forces in Europe during the sensitive 1961 Berlin crisis, when East Germany erected the Berlin Wall to seal off East Berlin from West Berlin. Norstad, a 1930 graduate of the U.S. Military Academy at West Point, N.Y., won his wings and became a member of the Air Corps in 1931. During World War II he held various command posts and was instrumental in planning the Allied invasion of North Africa in 1942. He personally went ashore with the assault forces and earned a Silver Star for gallantry. In 1943 Norstad was promoted to brigadier general, and two years later, as chief of staff of the newly created 20th Air Force, he helped engineer the devastating strategic air offensive against Japan by advanced Superfortress bombers. As commander of NATO he established a fast-moving multinational unit and stressed the need for tactical nuclear weapons as part of the alliance's arsenal. After his retirement from the military in 1963, Norstad joined Owens-Corning Fiberglass Corp. and served (1967–72) as its chairman and chief executive officer until his retirement.

Oliver, Sy (MELVIN JAMES OLIVER), U.S. jazz composer, arranger, and trumpeter, (b. Dec. 10, 1910, Battle Creek, Mich.—d. May 27, 1988, New York, N.Y.), created such dynamic and high-powered arrangements as "Yes Indeed!," "For Dancers Only," "Organ Grinder Swing," "Opus One," and "Easy Does It," which fueled the repertory of the swing bands of Jimmie Lunceford and Tommy Dorsey. Oliver performed with Cliff Barnett's Club Royal Serenaders, Zack Whyte and his Chocolate Beau Brummels, and Alphonso Trent's band before joining Lunceford's orchestra in 1933. Oliver's arrangements, many of which became jazz classics, helped define the band's virtuosity. He composed novelty numbers, sentimental vocals, and dramatic pieces, including "Dream of You," "Stomp It Off," and "Tain't What You Do." It was Oliver who was chiefly responsible for designing the arrangements of the vocal trio, a hallmark of the band, and he also served as one of the band's main trumpet soloists. In 1939 Oliver was lured to Dorsey's orchestra as an arranger, singer, and composer, and he became a resounding success. After serving in the Army (1943–45) as the leader of a band, he returned to Dorsey's orchestra but founded his own group in the late 1940s and continued to front various ensembles until he retired in 1984. Besides working for ten years at Decca Records as musical director, Oliver also wrote scores for television shows, recorded several albums, and continued to compose and arrange.

Olson, James Elias, U.S. business executive (b. Dec. 3, 1925, Devils Lake, N.D.—d. April 18, 1988, Short Hills, N.J.), as the aggressive chairman and chief executive officer (1986–88) of the American Telephone and Telegraph Co. (AT&T) played a vital role in restructuring the communications giant after its 1984 divestiture of the Bell telephone companies and guided the firm toward financial health by implementing cost-cutting and by reorganizing the computer division. Olson, who spent 44 years with Bell companies, began with a summer job cleaning silt out of telephone manholes and later served as an apprentice cable splicer before earning a degree in commerce in 1950 from the University of North Dakota. He then landed a man-

agement position with the company and gained a succession of quick promotions. In 1972 he was appointed president of the Indiana Bell Telephone Co. and two years later headed the Illinois Bell Telephone Co. He became executive vice-president of AT&T in 1977 and in 1979 was elected vice-chairman. In 1984 Olson was named chairman and chief executive officer of AT&T Technologies, and the following year he became president and chief operating officer. During his 20-month tenure as chairman of AT&T, Olson formulated a long-term strategy that, implemented by his dynamic leadership, began to revive the ailing company.

Onassis, Christina, U.S.-born heiress (b. Dec. 11, 1950, New York, N.Y.—d. Nov. 19, 1988, Buenos Aires, Arg.), as the daughter of Greek shipping magnate Aristotle Onassis, took command, upon her father's death in 1975, of the Onassis Group, with assets then estimated between $500 million and $1 billion. Her father and mother, Athina Livanos, divorced in 1960. In 1971, against her father's wishes, Onassis married millionaire Joseph Boker, who was 27 years her senior. Within months the two divorced, and in 1975 she wed Alexander Andreadis, a Greek shipping and banking heir. Their union was dissolved after 14 months, and in 1978 she married Sergey Kauzov, a Soviet shipping agent. Days after that marriage she fled to Greece, and the couple divorced in 1979. The year after her fourth marriage—to French businessman Thierry Roussel—Onassis gave birth to a daughter, Athina, who became her only consolation after her marriage to Roussel also failed. Onassis, who endured the death of her brother, Alexander, in 1973, also lost her father and mother within a 24-month period. Her much-publicized marriages and divorces were accompanied by accounts of her continual battles against weight. Her daughter was to inherit the bulk of the fortune, estimated at more than $1 billion, and Roussel would receive a $1.5 million annuity.

Orbison, Roy, U.S. singer (b. April 23, 1936, Vernon, Texas—d. Dec. 6, 1988, Hendersonville, Tenn.), was a vocalist, guitarist, and songwriter who became a seminal figure in the evolution of rock and roll. Orbison—easily recognizable with his trademark dark glasses, dark clothing, and black pompadour hairdo—possessed a surging falsetto voice with an incredible three-octave range. During his heyday in the early 1960s, he placed 22 songs on the top 100 singles chart, including "Only the Lonely," "Running Scared," "Crying," "Dream Baby," and "Oh, Pretty Woman," which sold more than seven million copies in 1964. Orbison began playing the guitar on the radio at the age of 8 and was in a country band at 14. He launched his pro-

AP/WIDE WORLD

fessional singing career as a country artist for Sun Records and achieved mild success with "Ooby Dooby" and "Go Go Go," but when he moved to Monumental Records, he quickly established a reputation with his mournful romantic songs. Some of his other hits included "Blue Bayou," "Mean Woman Blues," and "It's Over." After the death of his wife in a motorcycle accident in 1966 and the death in 1968 of two of his three sons in a house fire, Orbison's career plummeted in the U.S., although he continued to enjoy popularity in Britain. In recent years Orbison had enjoyed a comeback with a new generation of fans and along with George Harrison, Tom Petty, Bob Dylan, and Jeff Lynne formed the Traveling Wilburys. In 1980 Orbison earned a Grammy award for his collaboration with Emmylou Harris on "That Loving You Feeling Again." His contributions were recognized in 1987 when he was enshrined in the Rock and Roll Hall of Fame.

Ortega, Domingo (DOMINGO LÓPEZ ORTEGA), Spanish bullfighter (b. Feb. 25, 1906, Borox, Spain—d. May 8, 1988, Madrid, Spain), thrilled spectators with his elegant cape work and his uncanny ability to "read" each bull, talents that heightened the calibre and drama of his performances. From 1931 (when he faced 93 bulls in his first season) until his retirement in 1954, Ortega was one of Spain's most admired matadors. His artistry and daring influenced most bullfighters who came after him. Ortega, born into a family of labourers, began bullfighting in 1928 and made his professional debut in Madrid on Sept. 28, 1930. On March 8, 1931, he received the sword of the great bullfighter Francisco Vega during a ceremony in Barcelona that marked his debut as a champion matador. Ortega made his last appearance in the ring on Oct. 14, 1954. His book, *El Arte del Toreo* (1950; "The Art of Bullfighting"), increased public appreciation of his impassioned style and of bullfighting in general.

Parker, (James) Stewart, Irish playwright (b. Oct. 20, 1941, East Belfast, Ireland—d. Nov. 2, 1988, London, England), in innovative plays that captured the human dimension of Northern Irish conflict, focused on the abilities of ordinary Belfast people to survive—or not survive—the religious strife that was such a part of their lives. Born into the working class and a Protestant, Parker won scholarships to grammar school and Queen's University, Belfast, where he earned (1965) a master's degree in poetic drama. He taught English in the U.S. at Hamilton College, Clinton, N.Y. (1964–67), and at Cornell University, Ithaca, N.Y. (1967–69). In 1969 he returned to Belfast, becoming rock-music columnist for *The Irish Times* while he wrote plays for theatre, for radio, including *Minnie and Maisie and Lily Freed* and *The Iceberg,* and for television, including *Catchpenny Twist* and *Iris in the Traffic, Ruby in the Rain.* His first widely produced work for the stage, *Spokesong,* opened (1975) at the Dublin Theatre Festival and was produced the next year in London and, in 1979, in New York. Parker's later plays included *Northern Star* (1984), *Heavenly Bodies* (1986), and *Pentecost* (1987). While still a student, Parker contracted bone cancer, and one of his legs was amputated. He died soon after being diagnosed as having stomach cancer.

Paton, Alan (Stewart), South African English-language writer and political activist (b. Jan. 11, 1903, Pietermaritzburg, Natal—d. April 12, 1988, near Durban, South Africa), became his country's conscience with the publication of his first novel, *Cry, the Beloved Country* (1948), a passionate tale of racial injustice that heightened international awareness of South African apartheid. In South Africa he was equally renowned as an educator and prison reformer and as the leader of the multiracial Liberal Party (1958–68). Paton received degrees in science and education from the University of Natal and taught school for several years. As the principal (1935–48) of the Diepkloof Reformatory, which

housed several hundred black youths, he introduced controversial progressive reforms. While on a prison fact-finding tour of Europe and North America in 1948, Paton wrote *Cry, the Beloved Country.* Using a rhythmic tone and almost biblical language, he vividly portrayed the anguish suffered by an elderly black minister who must come to terms with his faith when his son is convicted of murdering a white man. The novel was adapted by Maxwell Anderson and Kurt Weill into the musical *Lost in the Stars* (1949; filmed 1974); a nonmusical motion

HY SIMON—GLOBE PHOTOS

picture, with a screenplay by Paton, appeared under the original title in 1952. In 1953 Paton founded the racially mixed Liberal Association (the Liberal Party from 1958), but he dissolved it in 1968 when multiracial political parties were outlawed. Although Paton was never arrested for his antiapartheid activities, his passport was confiscated from 1960 to 1970. In the 1980s he was often criticized for his opposition to economic sanctions. Paton's other literary works included a collection of short stories, *Debbie Go Home* (1961; U.S. title, *Tales from a Troubled Land*); a biography of the moderate South African politician Jan Hendrik Hofmeyr (1964); and two more novels, *Too Late the Phalarope* (1953) and *Ah, But Your Land Is Beautiful* (1981). The first volume of his autobiography, *Towards the Mountain* (1980), recorded his life up to the publication of *Cry, the Beloved Country.* A second volume, *Journey Continued,* was published shortly after his death.

Patterson, Frederick Douglass, U.S. educator (b. Oct. 10, 1901, Washington, D.C.—d. April 26, 1988, New Rochelle, N.Y.), made a vital contribution to the education of blacks as the president of Tuskegee Normal and Industrial Institute (1935–53) and as the founder in 1944 of the United Negro College Fund, which in 1988 boasted 42 member colleges and aided some 45,000 students with an annual income of $42 million. Patterson received a Ph.D. in veterinary medicine (1923) and a master of science degree (1927) from Iowa State College; in 1932 he earned a second Ph.D. from Cornell University, Ithaca, N.Y. He taught at Virginia State College in Petersburg before joining Tuskegee Institute in Alabama (1928), where he headed the veterinary division, served as director of the School of Agriculture, and then became the institute's third president. A prominent black leader, Patterson also devised another program in the mid-1970s, called the College Endowment Funding Plan, which depended on funds from private businesses that were matched with federal moneys. For his contributions to education, Patterson was awarded the Presidential Medal of Freedom in 1987.

Paul, Jean-Claude, Haitian army officer (b. 1939?, Haiti?—d. Nov. 6, 1988, La Boule,

Haiti), as a colonel in the Haitian Army, served as commander of the Dessalines Battalion in Port-au-Prince, the country's largest and most feared army unit. Paul was also linked to the Tontons Macoute, the hated private army of dictator Jean-Claude Duvalier, who was driven into exile in 1986. Paul and his troops were suspected of initiating widespread violence after Duvalier's ouster in an attempt to thwart moves toward democratization. In March 1988 Paul was indicted by a federal grand jury in Miami, Fla., on charges of conspiring to import cocaine into the U.S. Paul, a supporter of Haiti's military leader Lieut. Gen. Henri Namphy until the latter was ousted in a coup on Sept. 17, 1988, was dismissed from his army post on September 30. Though it was reported that Paul had died following a heart attack, there was some speculation that he may have been poisoned.

Pendleton, Clarence, U.S. government official (b. Nov. 10, 1930, Louisville, Ky.—d. June 5, 1988, San Diego, Calif.), served (1981–88) as the first black chairman of the U.S. Commission on Civil Rights and aroused controversy with his conservative opinions, including his disdain for affirmative action, his opposition to desegregation through busing, and his rejection of the concept of "comparable worth," requiring employers to pay employees an equal salary for different jobs judged, by various criteria, to be similar. Pendleton, who grew up in a Washington, D.C., ghetto, graduated from Howard University in 1954. He initially supported government sponsorship for blacks, and in 1968 he was named recreational coordinator for Baltimore's Model Cities program, a federally funded effort to revive poor neighbourhoods. After he moved to San Diego in 1972, however, he adopted the view that progress for blacks could best be achieved through private industry rather than public assistance, an opinion shared by Mayor Pete Wilson and Edwin Meese, a confidante of then California governor Ronald Reagan. With their backing he was appointed president of the San Diego Urban League, a post he held from 1975 until 1981, when Reagan became U.S. president and named him chairman of the U.S. Commission on Civil Rights.

Pham Hung, Vietnamese politician (b. June 11, 1912, Vinh Long Province, Vietnam—d. March 10, 1988, Ho Chi Minh City, Vietnam), was the first southern Vietnamese to reach the highest levels of the Communist Party Central Committee, or Politburo, and he was named prime minister of Vietnam in June 1987. Hung, an early follower of Ho Chi Minh, joined the Revolutionary Youth League soon after his expulsion from secondary school and was a founding member of Ho's Indochinese Communist Party in 1930. Hung was arrested by the French colonial authorities in 1931 and sentenced to death, but his sentence was commuted to life imprisonment on the infamous prison island of Poulo Condore (Con Son). He was freed during the 1945 uprising in which Ho's forces gained control of northern Vietnam. Hung held key posts in the Communist Party in southern Vietnam until the defeat of France (1954) and the subsequent legal division of the country, after which he entered the Politburo in North Vietnam. As chairman of the Central Office of South Vietnam (COSVN) from 1967, Hung directed Viet Cong guerrilla warfare and coordinated the 1968 Tet offensive. He was political commissar during the capture of Saigon (Ho Chi Minh City) in 1975, and the next year he was named a deputy prime minister in the first unified government. Hung served as interior minister and commander of the internal security force (1980–87) until government reformers chose him to replace Prime Minister Pham Van Dong.

Philby, Kim (HAROLD ADRIAN RUSSELL PHILBY), British intelligence agent (b. Jan. 1, 1912, Ambala, India—d. May 11, 1988, Moscow, U.S.S.R.), used his high rank within the Secret Intelligence Service (MI-6) to betray British and U.S. secrets to the Soviet Union for

more than 20 years. While attending the University of Cambridge in the 1930s, Philby, Guy Burgess, Donald Maclean, and Anthony Blunt were recruited as Soviet agents. Philby was a respected journalist when Burgess got him a job with MI-6 in 1940. As a trusted member of the Iberian counterespionage unit (1941–44) and head of the anti-Soviet section (1944–49), Philby had almost unlimited access to highly classified information, which he transmitted to the Soviet KGB. Philby went to Washington, D.C., in 1949 as MI-6 liaison with the Central Intelligence Agency (CIA). Two years later Burgess and Maclean, under suspicion as double agents, disappeared without a trace. In the ensuing scandal Philby was suspected of being the "third man" who had warned them, and the CIA demanded his dismissal, but MI-6 retained him as a free-lance agent. When his loyalty was questioned again in 1955, shortly before Burgess and Maclean surfaced in the Soviet Union, Philby was defended in Parliament by then foreign secretary Harold Macmillan. In 1963, while working as a journalist in Beirut, Lebanon, Philby vanished; six months later he reappeared in Moscow. Thereafter Philby rose to the rank of general in the KGB and wrote his autobiography, *My Silent War* (1968). A few weeks before his death the unrepentant Philby broke a 25-year silence by revealing details of his treachery during an interview with a British journalist. Philby was buried in Moscow with full military honours.

Ponge, Francis, French poet (b. March 27, 1899, Montpellier, France—d. Aug. 6, 1988, Le Bar-sur-Loup, France), crafted intricate prose poems concerning such everyday objects as rain, a butterfly, or an orange. Ponge sought to create a "visual equivalence" between language and subject matter by emphasizing word associations and puns and by manipulating the sound, rhythm, etymology, and typography of the words to mimic the essential characteristics of the object described. Ponge studied philosophy and law in Paris before serving in the Army during World War I. He was briefly involved with the Surrealist movement in the 1920s. Ponge joined the Communist Party in 1937 and became literary and art editor of the Communist weekly *Action* in 1944, but he left the party in 1947 to concentrate on writing and teaching at the Alliance Française (1952–64). He was best known for his collection *Le Parti pris des choses* (1942; *The Voice of Things,* 1972) and for the book-length poem *Le Savon* (1967; *Soap,* 1969). Ponge was made Commander of the Legion of Honour in 1959 and received the Académie Française grand prize for poetry in 1972 and the National Poetry Prize in 1981. He lived as a recluse for the last 20 years of his life.

Ponnelle, Jean-Pierre, French opera director and designer (b. Feb. 19, 1932, Paris, France—d. Aug. 11, 1988, Munich, West Germany), mounted audacious and often controversial productions for opera houses throughout Europe and the U.S. Although Ponnelle's unorthodox interpretations and complex staging scandalized many critics and audiences, his work remained in great demand. Ponnelle read philosophy and art history at the Sorbonne in Paris and studied art with the painter Fernand Léger. In 1952 Ponnelle designed the sets and costumes for the premiere of Hans Werner Henze's opera *Boulevard Solitude* in Hannover, West Germany. He worked as a designer until 1959, when he was called up for military service in French Algeria. On his return to Europe in 1961, he directed straight plays, and in 1962 he designed and directed the opera *Tristan und Isolde* in Düsseldorf, West Germany. Thereafter Ponnelle handled all aspects of the operas he staged, frequently mounting productions in different cities simultaneously. He was also an early supporter of international coproductions, in which a successful new staging was shared by two or more opera companies. Ponnelle adapted several operas for television, notably *Madame Butterfly* and *Rigoletto.*

Pressburger, Emeric (IMRE PRESSBURGER), Hungarian-born screenwriter (b. Dec. 5, 1902, Miskolc, Hung.—d. Feb. 5, 1988, Saxtead, Suffolk, England), wrote and produced innovative, visually striking motion pictures in collaboration with his longtime partner, British director Michael Powell, most notably *The Red Shoes* (1948). Pressburger studied engineering in Prague and Stuttgart, but in 1925 he went to Berlin, where he became a scriptwriter at the prestigious German film company Ufa. He settled in Britain in 1935 and launched his partnership with Powell with *The Spy in Black* in 1938. In 1941 Pressburger won an Academy Award for best original story for their third film, *The 49th Parallel* (U.S.; *The Invaders*). From 1943 Pressburger and Powell shared equal credit for writing, producing, and directing the 14 films that were released by their joint production company, The Archers. The team's most successful films, which were notable for their use of fantasy, lavish sets, and vivid colours, included *The Life and Death of Colonel Blimp* (1943), *A Canterbury Tale* (1944), *Black Narcissus* (1946), and *The Tales of Hoffmann* (1951). After The Archers was amicably disbanded in 1956, Pressburger wrote two novels, *Killing a Mouse on Sunday* (1961; filmed as *Behold a Pale Horse,* 1964) and *The Glass Pearls* (1966). He was named fellow of the British Film Institute in 1983.

Presser, Jackie, U.S. union leader (b. Aug. 6, 1926, Cleveland, Ohio—d. July 9, 1988, Lakewood, Ohio), as president (1983–88) of the 1.7 million-member International Brotherhood of Teamsters, led (1987) the nation's largest union back into the AFL-CIO after a 30-year exile, but his administration was dogged by allegations of links to organized crime. At the time of his death, he was facing federal charges of embezzlement and racketeering. Presser, the son of William ("Big Bill") Presser, a powerful president of the Ohio Conference of Teamsters and later international vice-president of the Teamsters, quit school after eighth grade and joined the Navy at the age of 17. After serving in World War II, Presser joined the staff of a restaurant workers' union in Cleveland and was elected president of the local in 1948. He later helped his father as a Teamsters organizer and in 1966 formed Teamsters Local 507 in Cleveland; it grew from a dozen paint company workers to a union boasting some 6,000 warehousemen. During the 1970s, while serving as vice-president of the Ohio Conference of Teamsters, Presser attempted to improve the organization's public image by sponsoring charitable activities and supporting government-sponsored job-retraining programs. After succeeding his father as international vice-president in 1976, he used his considerable influence to gain a union endorsement of Ronald Reagan in the U.S. presidential election. After Reagan's victory Presser was named labour cochairman for Reagan's inauguration. In 1983 Presser succeeded Roy

AP/WIDE WORLD

Williams, who resigned as Teamsters president after being convicted of conspiring to bribe a U.S. senator. A 1986 report issued by the White House Commission on Organized Crime concluded that Presser undoubtedly attained the presidency with assistance from the New York-based Genovese crime family. Presser, suffering from brain cancer, announced a four-month leave of absence as Teamsters president in May 1988. On June 28, the same day Presser was admitted to the hospital with a blood clot on his right lung, the U.S. Justice Department filed suit against him and other senior leaders of the Teamsters in an effort to place the union under the control of a government trustee.

Qoboza, Percy, South African journalist (b. Jan. 17, 1938, Johannesburg, South Africa—d. Jan. 17, 1988, Johannesburg), was an outspoken critic of apartheid and one of South Africa's most influential black newspaper editors. After studying theology in Basutoland (now Lesotho), Qoboza turned to journalism, joining the staff of the *World* in 1963. He became editor there in 1974 and turned the *World* into the largest-circulation black newspaper in South Africa. In 1975 he won a Nieman fellowship at Harvard University, where he gained a new perspective on race relations, and he returned to South Africa in 1976 deeply opposed to apartheid policies that he had previously accepted. A few months later he was briefly held for questioning about his editorial support of the Soweto rebellion. In October 1977 the *World* was banned, and Qoboza was detained without charge until March 1978. His case drew international attention, and he was awarded the Golden Pen of Freedom by the International Federation of Newspaper Publishers. Soon after his release he became editor of the *Post,* but a strike in 1980 forced the newspaper to shut down, and the government would not allow it to reopen. Qoboza then accepted a post as guest editor in residence (1980–81) at the *Washington* (D.C.) *Star.* In 1985 he became editor of the Johannesburg *City Press.*

Rabi, Isidor Isaac, U.S. physicist (b. July 29, 1898, Rymanów, Austria—d. Jan. 11, 1988, New York, N.Y.), was awarded the 1944 Nobel Prize for Physics for the invention (1937) of the atomic and molecular beam magnetic resonance method for registration of magnetic properties of atomic nuclei. This important discovery made possible precise measurements that were needed to develop the atomic clock, the laser, maser, and diagnostic scanning of the human body by nuclear magnetic resonance. Rabi immigrated to the U.S. with his parents when he was an infant. He studied chemistry before finding his niche in physics. After earning (1927) a Ph.D. in physics at Columbia University, New York City, he joined the faculty of his alma mater in 1929 and became professor of physics in 1937. During World War II he helped develop radar while working at the Radiation Laboratory of the Massachusetts Institute of Technology. He also helped arrange international conferences on peaceful uses of atomic energy in 1955, 1958, and 1964. As a U.S. representative to Unesco, he was instrumental in promoting the establishment of CERN, an international laboratory for high-energy physics. In the U.S. he was a founder of the Brookhaven National Laboratory, Upton, N.Y. Besides serving as a member of the General Advisory Committee of the Atomic Energy Commission from 1946 to 1956 and as its chairman from 1952 to 1956, he was also a science adviser to Pres. Dwight D. Eisenhower.

Raby, Albert, U.S. civil rights activist (b. Feb. 19, 1933, Chicago, Ill.—d. Nov. 23, 1988, Chicago), as the inspirational cochair of the Chicago Freedom Movement, persuaded Martin Luther King, Jr., to move his Southern civil rights movement to Chicago for several months in 1966; in 1983, as Harold Washington's campaign manager, he succeeded in making Washington Chicago's first black mayor.

Raby, a grade-school dropout, taught himself to read when he was a teenager. He later graduated (1960) from Chicago Teachers College, and from 1967 to 1969 he undertook graduate studies at the University of Chicago. He taught in Chicago public schools before leading antisegregation boycotts of the schools during the 1960s. Raby served in the Illinois constitutional convention in 1970 and directed the Peace Corps in Ghana from 1979 to 1982. He returned to Chicago, successfully managed Washington's mayoral campaign, and served on the Human Relations Commission until shortly after Washington's death in 1987. Like Washington, Raby succumbed to a heart attack on the eve of Thanksgiving.

Ramsey of Canterbury, Arthur Michael Ramsey, BARON, British ecclesiastic (b. Nov. 14, 1904, Cambridge, England—d. April 23, 1988, Oxford, England), was the 100th archbishop of Canterbury (1961–74) and a leader in the cause of Christian ecumenism. Ramsey graduated (1927) with first-class honours in theology from Magdalene College, Cambridge, where he was president of the Cambridge Union. After his ordination (1928) in the Church of England, he did parish work and taught at Lincoln Theological College (1930–36). Ramsey was a professor of divinity at the Universities of Durham (1940–50) and Cambridge (1950–52), and in 1952 he was named bishop of Durham. Four years later he was elevated to archbishop of York, the second highest position in the Church of England. In 1961 he succeeded Geoffrey Francis Fisher as archbishop of Canterbury (and, therefore, primate of all England and senior bishop of the worldwide Anglican Communion). Ramsey, sometimes criticized as an administrator, was a scholarly theologian. He endorsed liberal policies on such controversial subjects as immigration laws, capital punishment, and the rights of homosexuals; he was also highly critical of South African apartheid and of U.S. involvement in Vietnam. Ramsey traveled widely and served as president of the World Council of Churches (1961–68). For many years he argued (tirelessly but unsuccessfully) for a reunion of the Anglican and Methodist churches in Britain. In 1966 Ramsey went to Rome to talk with Pope Paul VI, the first official meeting between the leaders of the Anglican and Roman Catholic churches since their separation (1534) during the Reformation. Ramsey was created a life peer after his retirement in 1974.

Ravera, Camilla, Italian politician (b. June 18, 1889, Acqui Terme, Italy—d. April 14, 1988, Rome, Italy), was a leading figure in the Italian Communist Party (PCI) for more than 60 years and was one among a select group of nine persons named senator for life. Ravera taught school in Turin (1908–09), and in 1918 she joined the Italian Socialist Party (PSI). She gravitated toward the left wing of the PSI under the leadership of Antonio Gramsci, wrote a column for Gramsci's newspaper, *L'Ordine nuovo,* and edited the journal *La compagna.* Ravera remained loyal to Gramsci when his leftist faction split from the PSI (January 1921) and formed the PCI. She served on the PCI Central Committee (1922–30) and coordinated clandestine activities after the Fascist government outlawed the party and arrested Gramsci in 1926. Ravera was arrested in 1930 and sentenced by a special tribunal to 15 years in jail. She was imprisoned for five years and then remained in internal exile until 1943. Ravera was expelled from the PCI in 1943 because of her opposition to the 1939 Soviet-German nonaggression pact, but her party membership was reinstated in 1945. As a member of the Chamber of Deputies (lower house) from 1948 and later as the first woman elected to the Senate (upper house), she was a powerful advocate of women's rights. In 1983 Ravera was appointed senator for life by Pres. Sandro Pertini.

Ricci, Robert, French business executive (b. July 29, 1905, Paris, France—d. Aug. 8, 1988, Paris),

was a cofounder and the chief executive of the renowned Parisian couturier Nina Ricci, which was equally acclaimed for its elegant haute couture and for its perfumes. In 1932 Ricci established a fashion house with his mother, Marie Nielli ("Nina") Ricci, a dressmaker and designer for whom the firm was named. After World War II Robert Ricci concentrated on perfume design and created several classic fragrances, most notably "L'Air du Temps" in 1948. Ricci became managing director of the company in 1945 and took full control of the fashion business in the 1950s. After his mother's death in 1970 he successfully expanded the company's product lines into accessories and ready-to-wear fashions. Ricci opened the firm's first ready-to-wear retail boutique in 1979.

Rich, Irene (IRENE LUTHER), U.S. actress (b. Oct. 13, 1891, Buffalo, N.Y.—d. April 22, 1988, Hope Ranch, Calif.), abandoned her career as a successful real estate agent to became a popular star of the silent screen, appearing in scores of women-oriented melodramas in the 1920s opposite such stars as Lon Chaney, Ronald Colman, and Warner Baxter. In seven films she played the wife of Will Rogers. She later starred on radio for more than a decade in the Irene Rich Dramas, of which the most popular were "Dear John" and "Glorious One." Her trim figure and sophisticated bearing became identified with her longtime sponsor, Welch's grape juice. Rich returned to films during the late 1930s, usually portraying a mother. Some of her credits included *Jes' Call Me Jim* (1920), *They Had to See Paris* (1929), *The Champ* (1931), *Angel and the Badman* (1947), and her last two films, *Fort Apache* and *Joan of Arc* (1948). After appearing on Broadway in *As the Girls Go* (1948–50), Rich retired from show business.

Roman, Stephen Boreslav, Canadian mining executive (b. April 17, 1921, Kelky Ruskov, Slovakia [now Czechoslovakia]—d. March 23, 1988, Toronto, Ont.), was a shrewd businessman who amassed a fortune by risking his small savings on stock investments that gave him enough capital to purchase North Denison Mines, a speculative venture that he built into an empire. In 1954 he purchased claims to a uranium strike near Quirke Lake that proved to be the richest uranium mine in the world. As president and chairman of Denison Mines Ltd., he diversified his holdings into potash, coal, oil, and gas and became a vocal advocate of free enterprise and capitalism. In 1970 he sued Prime Minister Pierre Trudeau and Energy Minister J. J. Greene because the administration disallowed the sale of Denison to Continental Oil of Delaware. He was twice defeated (1972 and 1974) as a federal Progressive Conservative candidate for Parliament attempting to unseat Liberal minister Barnett Danson. In his later years he dedicated himself to the construction of the giant Cathedral of the Transfiguration in Unionville, which boasted a 20-story central tower. Roman donated the land and was the chief financier of the project.

Rooney, Arthur ("THE CHIEF"), U.S. sportsman (b. Jan. 27, 1901, Coultersville, Pa.—d. Aug. 25, 1988, Pittsburgh, Pa.), was the colourful, cigar-chomping owner of the Pittsburgh Steelers professional football team and was also famous for his legendary bets on horse races. He purchased the team, then known as the Pirates, in 1932 for $2,500 with funds he had won on the horses. In 1936 he reportedly parlayed a modest bet on a horse into a two-day winning streak that netted him more than $300,000. As owner of the Steelers, however, Rooney spent 40 years watching his lacklustre team struggle. In 1975, though, with a team that included Terry Bradshaw at quarterback, tackle Joe Greene, and running back Franco Harris, the Steelers captured the first of an unprecedented four Super Bowl victories. They also won Super Bowls in 1976, 1979, and 1980. In later years Rooney turned Steeler operations over to his sons, but at the time of his death he was chairman of the team.

Rose, George, British-born actor (b. Feb. 19, 1920, Bicester, England—d. May 5, 1988, near Sosúa, Dominican Republic), was a multitalented star on Broadway for some 40 years who excelled in comic roles ranging from Shakespeare to Gilbert and Sullivan; he garnered two Tony awards as the master of ceremonies in *The Mystery of Edwin Drood* and as Alfred P. Doolittle in a revival production of *My Fair Lady.* After appearing in bit parts at the Old Vic Theatre in London, Rose made his New York debut in the 1946 production of *Henry IV, Part 1.* His prized comic performance as Dogberry in the 1959 production of Shakespeare's *Much Ado About Nothing* earned him critical acclaim, but it was his 1961 eight-character role of the Common Man in Robert Bolt's *A Man for All Seasons* that secured his reputation. Some of Rose's other notable credits included *The Pirates of Penzance, My Fat Friend, The Devil's Disciple,* and *The Kingfisher,* which earned him a Drama Desk Award in 1979.

Ross, Lanny (LANCELOT PATRICK ROSS), U.S. radio personality (b. Jan. 19, 1906, Seattle, Wash.—d. April 25, 1988, New York, N.Y.), with his boyish good looks and clear tenor voice delighted radio listeners for a score of years. Known as the "idol of the airwaves," Ross starred in such programs as "Show Boat," "Troubadour of the Moon," "The Swift Show," and "The Lanny Ross Show." Although Ross earned a law degree from Columbia University, New York City, in 1931, his singing propelled him to stardom, and he earned five times more as a singer than he would have as a new attorney. He also appeared in such films as *College Rhythm, Melody in Spring,* and *The Lady Objects,* but his primary medium remained radio. His version of "Moonlight and Roses" became his signature song, and he sang professionally after his stint on radio ended.

Rothschild, Philippe de, BARON, French wine grower and Renaissance man (b. April 13, 1902, Paris, France—d. Jan. 20, 1988, Paris), built Château Mouton Rothschild into one of the greatest wineries in the world. When his father, a member of the British branch of the Rothschild banking family, made him manager of the dilapidated Bordeaux vineyard in 1922, the estate was still without electricity or running water. He scandalized other vintners in 1924 when he produced the first estate-bottled wine and again in the early 1930s when he introduced Mouton Cadet, a cheaper, blended brand of wine, which quickly became an international favourite. He continued to expand and improve the estate until he was imprisoned by the Vichy government during World War II. In 1943 he fled to London to join Gen. Charles de Gaulle's forces, serving with them as a liaison officer in the 1944 landing at Normandy. After the war his innovations for Mouton Rothschild included a

AP/WIDE WORLD

new label each year, designed by such artists as Picasso, Chagall, Dali, and Andy Warhol. In 1973 he achieved his life's goal when Mouton Rothschild was elevated to the highest wine ranking, premier cru. Rothschild also gained international renown as a champion yachtsman, bobsledder, and race-car driver, competing in several Grand Prix races and the 24-hour race at Le Mans during the 1920s. He also founded and directed (1928–31) the Théâtre Pigalle in Paris, published several translations of English poetry and plays as well as a volume of his own poetry, and produced early motion pictures, including *Lac aux Dames* (1932), one of the first French talkies.

Ruska, Ernst August Friedrich, German electrical engineer (b. Dec. 25, 1906, Heidelberg, Germany—d. May 27, 1988, West Berlin, West Germany), won the Nobel Prize for Physics in 1986 for the invention of the electron microscope. Ruska garnered half the award for his work, while Gerd Binning and Heinrich Rohrer shared the other half of the prize for developing the scanning tunneling microscope. Ruska studied engineering at the Technical University of Munich (1925–27) and at the Technical University of Berlin (1927–34), where he engaged in electron microscopy research. Earlier studies indicated that the resolving power of a conventional microscope was limited by the wavelength of visible light, so Ruska's team theorized that a highly focused beam of electrons (which have a much shorter wavelength) would achieve a higher magnification and yield far greater detail. The team developed a rough prototype in 1931 using two electromagnetic lenses to magnify the electron image. In 1933 Ruska unveiled an electron microscope that permitted magnification far greater than a light microscope could achieve. As a research engineer with Siemens-Reiniger-Werke AG from 1937, Ruska perfected the first commercially available electron microscope (1939). He remained at Siemens until 1955, when he became the director of the Institute for Electron Microscopy at the Fritz Haber Institute of the Max Planck Society. Ruska also taught electronic optics and microscopy at the Technical University of Berlin from 1949.

St. Johns, Adela Rogers, U.S. journalist, (b. May 20, 1894, Los Angeles, Calif.—d. Aug. 10, 1988, Arroyo Grande, Calif.), as a top-notch newspaperwoman for the Hearst chain, covered some of the most sensational stories of the century including the Lindbergh baby kidnapping, the trial of the kidnapper, Bruno Hauptmann, the abdication of Edward VIII, and the Leopold-Loeb murder trial. St. Johns, the daughter of renowned trial lawyer Earl Rogers, was weaned on courtroom drama. After attending Hollywood High School, she traveled before becoming a reporter and feature writer (1913) with the *San Francisco Examiner*. While working for the *Los Angeles Herald* (1914–18), the *Chicago American* (1928), and the *New York American* (1929), she secured her reputation as an adept "sob sister," a woman writer skilled in conveying the emotional angle of a story. She became known as "Mother Confessor of Hollywood" after writing profiles of some of the biggest stars of the 1920s for *Photoplay* magazine. St. Johns published short stories in such magazines as *McCall's, Ladies Home Journal,* and *Cosmopolitan*, the first of which, "The Black Cat," appeared in 1918. Such novels as *The Sky Rocket* (1923), *A Free Soul* (1924), and *A Single Standard* (1928) became motion pictures. Some of her other books include *How to Write a Short Story* (1952); *Affirmative Prayer in Action* (1957); *Final Verdict* (1962), a biography of her father; and *The Honeycomb* (1969) and *Love, Laughter, and Tears: My Hollywood Story* (1978), her two autobiographies. St. Johns was awarded the Presidential Medal of Freedom in 1970.

Salem, Mamdouh Muhammad, Egyptian politician (b. 1918, Alexandria, Egypt—d. Feb. 25, 1988, London, England), was prime minister of Egypt during Pres. Anwar as-Sadat's historic peace negotiations with Israel. Salem rose to the rank of general in the Alexandria police force before becoming police commander there in 1964. He served Pres. Gamal Abdel Nasser as a security aide and as the provincial governor of Asyut (1967–70), Gharbiyah (1970), and Alexandria (1970–71). Salem joined President Sadat's Cabinet in 1971 as minister of the interior and as a member of the Central Committee of the Arab Socialist Union (the sole political party), but within a few months he was raised to deputy prime minister. When widespread violent protests against food shortages and rising inflation broke out in 1975, Salem was asked to form a new government as prime minister. He remained a loyal supporter of Sadat's peace initiatives, forming a new Cabinet in 1977 as head of the first multiparty government. In 1978 Salem merged his Arab Socialist Party with Sadat's newly formed National Democratic Party, but he unexpectedly resigned his Cabinet post when he discovered that Sadat wanted to install a new government. Salem later assisted Sadat's successor, Pres. Hosni Mubarak, as a presidential adviser.

Saragat, Giuseppe, Italian politician (b. Sept. 12, 1898, Turin, Italy—d. June 11, 1988, Rome, Italy), was the founder of Italy's post-World War II anti-Fascist, anti-Communist Social Democratic Party (PSDI) and, as president of Italy from 1964 to 1971, supported Western democracies and improved housing, medical care, and education for Italians. Born into the middle class, Saragat studied economics and commerce at the University of Turin before working as a bank clerk (1919–26). He joined the Socialist Party in 1922 and became secretary of the Turin branch the year Benito Mussolini came to power. After living in exile in Vienna (1926–35) and then in Paris (1935–43), Saragat returned to Italy to join the partisans who were fighting the Germans after the fall of the Fascists. He was arrested and imprisoned by the Nazi forces occupying Rome but escaped (1944) and, after Rome's liberation later that year, served as minister without portfolio and ambassador to Paris (1945–46). Upon his return to Italy, Saragat was elected president of the Constitutional Assembly, which drafted Italy's postwar constitution. In 1947 he led a group that opposed aligning with the Communist Party and founded the PSDI, serving as its secretary until 1964 and again from 1975 to 1983, when he was elected president of the party for life. Saragat was twice (1947–49 and 1954–57) Italy's deputy prime minister, and he served as minister of foreign affairs (1963–64) before he was elected the nation's president.

Savary, Alain François, French politician (b. April 25, 1918, Algiers, Algeria—d. Feb. 17, 1988, Paris, France), resigned as education minister in 1984 after his proposed reform of the French educational system brought hundreds of thousands of protesters into the streets. Savary, who was educated in France, joined the Resistance in 1940 and led the group that liberated (1941) the French dependency of Saint-Pierre and Miquelon. He served as governor there (1941–43) before fighting with Gen. Charles de Gaulle's forces in Europe. Savary represented Saint-Pierre in the postwar government, but he soon broke with de Gaulle and joined the Socialist Party. He served as minister of Moroccan and Tunisian affairs in the 1956 Socialist government but resigned to protest the hijacking of a plane carrying Algerian nationalist leader Ahmed Ben Bella and Ben Bella's subsequent arrest. Savary's opposition to French colonialism led him to quit the Socialists (1958) in favour of a small leftist party, but in 1969 he was named first secretary of the reorganized Socialist Party, a position he held until François Mitterrand ousted him two years later. In 1981 President Mitterrand appointed Savary minister of education with a mandate to merge all public and private schools into a unified secular school system. Savary presented a bill in 1984 giving local authorities greater control over private schools, but protests by Roman Catholic educators and parent associations, backed by a mass demonstration of more than one million people who came from all over France to Paris on June 24, 1984, prompted Mitterrand to abandon the proposed legislation. Savary retired from politics the following month.

Scott, Sheila (SHEILA CHRISTINE HOPKINS), British aviator (b. April 27, 1927, Worcester, England—d. Oct. 20, 1988, London, England), broke more than 100 light-aircraft records between 1965 and 1972 and was the first British pilot to fly solo around the world. After attending a boarding school in Worcester, Scott became (1944) a trainee nurse at Haslar Naval Hospital. She went to London (1945) to accept a small part in a film and joined a repertory acting company, where she adopted her stage name; for the next 14 years she appeared in small stage, film, and television roles and worked as a model. In 1960 she earned her pilot's license, bought and repainted an old Royal Air Force biplane she named "Myth," and entered her first air race, from London to Cardiff, Wales. She took fifth place and proceeded to enter more races, winning (1960) the De Havilland Trophy and the award of the British Women Pilots' Association for her achievements that year. To pay for her flying, Scott became (1961) a demonstrator for U.S.-made Cessna and, later, Piper aircraft. She first flew around the world in 1966, covering nearly 50,000 km (31,000 mi) in 189 flying hours. She set records (1967) from London to Cape Town and in both North Atlantic and South Atlantic crossings; in 1971 she was first to solo in a light plane, Equator to Equator, over the North Pole. She wrote *I Must Fly* (1968) and *On Top of the World* (1973; published in the U.S. as *Barefoot in the Sky* in 1974). She was named an Officer of the Order of the British Empire in 1968.

Seefried, Irmgard, German-born singer (b. Oct. 9, 1919, Köngetried, Bavaria, Germany—d. Nov. 24, 1988, Vienna, Austria), was widely admired for her rich soprano voice and the charm she brought to a variety of operatic roles, particularly in works by Mozart and Richard Strauss. In 1944 Strauss personally requested that she sing the role of the Composer in a special performance of *Ariadne auf Naxos* in honour of the composer's 80th birthday. Seefried studied at the Augsburg Conservatory and made her professional debut in 1940 at the Aachen Opera. Although she performed throughout the world, her most significant work was as a member of the Vienna State Opera from 1943 until her retirement in 1976. Seefried became an Austrian citizen in 1946 after her marriage to Vienna Philharmonic violinist Wolfgang Schneiderhahn, with whom she gave frequent lieder recitals.

Shaplen, Robert Modell, U.S. journalist (b. March 22, 1917, Philadelphia, Pa.—d. May 15, 1988, New York, N.Y.), whose incisive reporting chronicling the frustrations and failures associated with anticolonial revolutions in Asia made him one of the most respected U.S. correspondents during a 50-year career reporting for the *New York Herald Tribune* (1937–43), *Newsweek* (1945–47), *Fortune* (1948–50), *Colliers* (1950–51), and *The New Yorker* (1952–88). Shaplen, who earned an M.S. from the Columbia University (New York City) School of Journalism, gave minute attention to detail and was credited with capturing the exotic sights, sounds, and texture of Asia as well as establishing a historical perspective based on his long experience. He was with Mao Zedong (Mao Tsetung) in the remote caves in the mountains of Yanan (Yen-an) in 1946, covered the rise and fall of Indonesia's President Sukarno during the 1960s, and was present at the fall of Saigon in 1975. Though many felt his criticism of U.S. involvement in Vietnam was too moderate, he later adopted a harsher view and recounted his 1984 journey to Vietnam and Kampuchea in

his last book, *Bitter Victory* (1986). Some of his other works included *A Corner of the World* (1949), *The Lost Revolution* (1965), *Time Out of Hand: Revolution and Reaction in Southeast Asia* (1969), and *A Turning Wheel* (1979).

Shen Congwen (Shen Ts'ung-wen), Chinese writer (b. Dec. 28, 1902, Feng-huang, Hunan Province, China—d. May 10, 1988, Beijing [Peking], China), vividly chronicled Chinese rural life during the violent era (1920s and '30s) of the warlords and was an outspoken champion of literary and intellectual independence, a view that led to his downfall when the Communists took power in 1949. Shen served in the military before writing his first work in 1924; he helped edit the magazines *Man's World* and *Red and Black* from 1927 to 1928. The prolific author penned lyrical poetry that explored nature, some 35 volumes of fiction that focused on the lives of the people in western Hunan, and one-act farces that poked fun at modern social conventions. He published his first major work, *Fengzi,* in 1932 and what many believe to be his most important work, *The Long River,* in 1943. After the Communists took control of mainland China, Shen was disgraced and forced to write a confession renouncing his works. In 1953 his books were burned and the printing plates destroyed. Such persecution caused him to attempt suicide. Afterward, Shen was given a post at the Museum of Chinese History, where he compiled the respected volume *The Bronze Mirrors of the Tang and Song Dynasties.* During the Cultural Revolution (1966–76) when traditional values were attacked and intellectuals were verbally and physically abused, Shen was sent to a labour camp, and many of his remaining books were sold as wastepaper. In 1978 he was given liberty to resume his literary pursuits, but by then he was unable to write seriously. Some of his other works include *The Art of Dragon and Phoenix, Border Town, Xiaoxiao, The Ox,* and *The Husband.* Two important collections of short stories appeared under the titles *Lamp of Spring* and *Black Phoenix.*

Shulman, Max, U.S. writer and humorist (b. March 14, 1919, St. Paul, Minn.—d. Aug. 28, 1988, Los Angeles, Calif.), was a master of satire who scored huge popular and critical successes with such novels as *The Many Loves of Dobie Gillis* (1951) and *Rally Round the Flag, Boys* (1957) and with the Broadway play *The Tender Trap* (1954), which comically portrayed the pitfalls of marriage and was made into a motion picture starring Frank Sinatra and Debbie Reynolds. While attending the University of Minnesota, Shulman edited the campus humour magazine and was persuaded by a talent scout to pursue a writing career after graduation. His first novel, *Barefoot Boy with Cheek* (1943), was a best-seller and was regarded as a classic of campus humour. While serving as a sergeant during World War II, he wrote *The Feather Merchants* (1944) and *The Zebra Derby* (1946); the latter poked fun at anxious civilians greeting returning veterans and anxious veterans coping with anxious civilians. Shulman's novel *The Many Loves of Dobie Gillis* inspired the television series featuring a feckless grocer's son, Dobie Gillis, and his romantic misadventures. Shulman served as scriptwriter for the series, which aired from 1959 to 1962. From 1954 to 1970 the irrepressible Shulman, who considered nothing sacred, was the author of a syndicated weekly column, "On Campus."

Siegel, Seymour, U.S. theologian (b. Sept. 12, 1927, Chicago, Ill.—d. Feb. 24, 1988, New York, N.Y.), was a religious liberal who helped shape contemporary Conservative Jewish theology and was especially instrumental in paving the way for the ordination of female rabbis with his learned writings. As head of the Committee on Jewish Law and Standards of the Rabbinical Assembly for more than a decade, he helped initiate in 1973 the practice of allowing women to be counted in a minyan, the quorum of ten or more adult Jews required for com-

munal worship. Previously, only men could be counted. This breakthrough paved the way for the body's decision some ten years later to allow women to serve as Conservative rabbis. Siegel, who spent 41 years with the Jewish Theological Seminary, wrote hundreds of articles and edited such important books as *Conservative Judaism and Jewish Law* (1977) and *Jewish Ethics and Contemporary Problems* (1980); at the time of his death he was preparing *Medical Ethics in a Jewish Perspective.* A political conservative with close ties to the Reagan administration, Siegel also served on the President's Commission on Ethics in Medicine and Biomedical Research and on the Advisory Council of the Republican National Committee.

Sitwell, Sir Sacheverell, 6TH BARONET, British poet (b. Nov. 15, 1897, Scarborough, Yorkshire, England—d. Oct. 1, 1988, Weston, England), was the youngest and most conventional of the three dilettantes Sitwell—the late poets Dame Edith and Sir Osbert were his sister and brother—who chronicled the London avant-garde during the 1920s. Sitwell was educated at Eton and Balliol College, Oxford. In 1919, one year after his first book of poems, *The People's Palace,* appeared, he and his siblings organized an exhibition of French art that introduced the works of Picasso and Modigliani to the British public. The first of his several dozen books of essays, *Southern Baroque Art* (1924), championed and drew attention to a subject few then knew about. Beginning in the 1930s and continuing through the 1960s, he wrote guidebooks that mixed fact with fancy in describing the exotic places he visited and things he saw. Sitwell unleashed his curiosity on the lives of such composers as Mozart, Liszt, and Scarlatti, and he also mused about and described flowers, birds, and festivals. Though his poems were considered good, he was disappointed in their lukewarm reception by critics and turned from poetry after the late 1930s until 1972, when he began publishing small books privately. In 1982 he published *An Indian Summer,* a volume of poems.

Solomon (SOLOMON CUTNER), British pianist (b. Aug. 9, 1902, London, England—d. Feb. 22, 1988, London), was a brilliant performer admired for his technical skill, his poetic interpretations, and his meticulous sense of pacing. A paralyzing stroke in 1956 abruptly ended his career. Solomon (he never used his full name professionally) was the son of a Polish immigrant tailor in London's East End. He started taking music lessons in 1910 and made his debut only one year later, playing Tchaikovsky's Piano Concerto No. 1 at London's Queen's Hall. In 1919, exhausted from almost constant touring and studying, Solomon retired to Paris for two years. He reappeared in 1921 in a triumphant London recital, where he reaffirmed his reputation as a mature virtuoso. He made his first trip to the U.S. in 1926 and returned there in 1939 to perform the world premiere of Sir Arthur Bliss's Piano Concerto (which was dedicated to him) at the New York World's Fair. During World War II he performed for Allied troops in Britain and abroad. Solomon made more than 100 classical recordings, including concertos and sonatas by Beethoven, Brahms, and Schumann. He was made Commander of the Order of the British Empire in 1946.

Sorabji, Kaikhosru Shapurji (LEON DUDLEY SORABJI), British composer (b. Aug. 14, 1892, Chingford, England—d. Oct. 15, 1988, England), distinguished himself among pianists by performing—and then banning both publication and performance of—his own complex, elaborately textured fusions of Eastern improvisations and European melodies. The son of a successful Parsi architect and a Sicilian-Spanish opera singer, Sorabji studied music privately and taught himself a piano technique considered unique for its intricate ornamentation and demands on physical endurance. His *Opus Clavicembalisticum* (1929–30) consisted of one

movement that lasted three hours. Sorabji wrote music reviews that championed such composer-performers as Busoni, Schoenberg, and Mahler. His two books, *Around Music* (1932) and *Mi Contra Fa: The Immoralisings of a Machiavellian Musician* (1947), were biting observations of Europe's musical scene in the early 1900s. After a few performances of his works, Sorabji stopped publishing his compositions and forbade (in the late 1930s) their performance. During the 1960s his private recordings of some of his piano music were broadcast in New York (1970) and California (1973), arousing renewed interest in this exotic, reclusive musician. In 1976 he permitted the first of what would become a few handpicked pianists to perform his works.

Stazewski, Henryk, Polish painter and graphic artist (b. Jan. 9, 1894, Warsaw, Poland—d. June 10, 1988, Warsaw), was a leader of the Polish Abstractionist painters during the 1920s and '30s and the guiding force in the post-World War II rebirth of Polish modern art. His work as a practitioner of Constructivism—Cubist-Futurist-inspired "constructed" art that celebrated machines and technology and used such modern industrial materials as plastic, steel, and glass—evolved into small, spare paintings and reliefs of lines and geometric shapes in pale colours or all-white, black, or gray designs. Educated (1913–19) at the Warsaw Academy of Fine Arts, Stazewski was a founding member of three Polish artist groups during the 1920s and was a member of the *Cercle et Carré* and Abstraction-Creation groups in Paris. During his frequent trips to Paris, Stazewski came into contact with Piet Mondrian, the best known artist of the Constructivist school. Although most of Stazewski's prewar works were destroyed during World War II, a large one-man show (1955) in Warsaw signaled the reemergence of both art in Poland and his own exhibitions, which continued into the early 1980s. Stazewski received Warsaw's Golden Cross of Merit (1955) and Ministry of Culture Prize (1965).

Steptoe, Patrick Christopher, British physician (b. June 9, 1913, Witney, Oxfordshire, England—d. March 21, 1988, Canterbury, England), was best known as the doctor who, together with British physiologist Robert Edwards, perfected in vitro ("test tube") fertilization of the human egg. The process involved extracting an egg from a woman's ovary using a procedure called laparoscopy, fertilizing the egg with sperm in a glass container, and then returning the embryo to the womb where, barring any problems, it developed normally. Their research resulted in the birth (July 25, 1978) of a perfectly formed baby girl, Louise Brown, the world's first "test-tube baby." Steptoe and Edwards were later credited with more than 1,000 such births including Louise Brown's younger sister. After graduating in 1939 from the University of London's St. George's Hospital Medical School, Steptoe joined the Royal Navy Volunteer Reserve, serving as a surgeon until his ship was sunk and he was taken prisoner by the Italians (1941). After his release in 1943, he returned to London to study obstetrics and gynecology. In 1951 he was named senior obstetrician and gynecologist at a hospital in Oldham, where he conducted research on sterilization and infertility. In 1967 he published the authoritative *Laparoscopy in Gynaecology* and the following year formed a partnership with Edwards. Steptoe became expert in using the laparoscope, a narrow tube with a built-in fibre light. He used the instrument to help Edwards harvest human eggs to be fertilized outside the womb. Their work, conducted in Steptoe's Centre for Human Reproduction at Oldham, raised a number of serious ethical questions. The two quietly collaborated until April 1978 when the news that a baby had been conceived outside the womb made headlines. Steptoe, who had been battling cancer for several years, died the day before he was to be made a Commander of the Order of the British Empire.

Stevens, Siaka Probyn, Sierra Leonean politician (b. Aug. 24, 1905, Tolubu, Sierra Leone—d. May 29, 1988, Freetown, Sierra Leone), dominated the political scene as the nation's prime minister (1967 and 1968–71) and longtime president (1971–85). Stevens survived in office despite attempted coups in 1971 and 1974, a burdensome national debt, and almost continual charges of gross mismanagement and governmental corruption. Stevens worked as a police officer, a mineworker, and a railway station master before founding the United Mineworkers Union in 1943. He studied industrial relations at the University of Oxford (1947–48) and represented the Sierra Leone People's Party in the Protectorate Assembly, becoming minister of lands, mines, and labour in 1953. After serving as deputy leader of the breakaway People's National Party (1958–60), he formed his own All People's Congress (APC) in 1960 and was opposition leader from 1961, when Sierra Leone achieved independence, until the APC won the 1967 election. Stevens was overthrown in a military coup only days after being sworn in as prime minister, but he was recalled from exile in Guinea after another coup 13 months later. He requested Guinean troops to quell the protests surrounding his installation as executive president in 1971, and in 1978 he declared Sierra Leone a one-party state. Stevens stepped down peacefully in 1985 in favour of his handpicked successor, but in 1987 he was put under house arrest on suspicion of plotting a coup attempt.

Strauss, Franz Josef, West German politician (b. Sept. 6, 1915, Munich, Germany—d. Oct. 3, 1988, Regensburg, West Germany), was the flamboyant, arch-conservative minister-president of the state of Bavaria and, as president of the Christian Social Union (CSU), had played a major role in rebuilding West Germany after World War II. Strauss distinguished himself early as a student, graduating (1939) from the University of Munich with highest honours. He was an artillery officer during World War II and was captured by U.S. forces shortly before the war ended. After his release he was administrator of a military school in Bavaria, and in 1946 he was elected head of the local government. Strauss helped to found the CSU and served (1949–78) as its candidate to the Bundestag (federal parliament) in Bonn. His forceful and colourful speeches, often peppered with Latin, caught the attention of Chancellor Konrad Adenauer, who named Strauss minister without portfolio (1953), minister for atomic affairs (1955), and minister of defense (1956). In the latter post, Strauss supported rearmament and played a leading role in rebuilding West Germany's armed forces. After the news magazine *Der Spiegel,* which had often criticized Strauss, published an article on a NATO exercise, Strauss became infuriated and had the magazine's publisher and editors arrested on charges of treason. The ensuing public outrage forced Strauss to resign (1962) from the government. He was later cleared of impropriety in the matter. Strauss returned (1966) to the Cabinet with a newly earned degree in economics and was named minister of finance in the coalition government of the Christian Democratic Union, the national party of which CSU was the Bavarian partner, and the Social Democratic Party. In 1978 Strauss resigned from the Bundestag and was elected minister-president of Bavaria; in 1980 he lost his bid to become chancellor of West Germany and returned to Bavaria.

Symington, (William) Stuart, U.S. politician (b. June 26, 1901, Amherst, Mass.—d. Dec. 14, 1988, New Caanan, Conn.), as the longtime Democratic senator (1953–76) from Missouri, was a staunch advocate of a strong national defense but became an outspoken critic of U.S. military involvement in Vietnam because he held that that war was irrelevant to U.S. security. Symington attended Yale University (1919–23), but it was not until 1946 that he was awarded a B.A. from that university. He was a successful

businessman before entering politics in 1945 as chairman of the Surplus Property Board in the administration of U.S. Pres. Harry S. Truman. Symington later served as assistant secretary of war, as secretary of the air force, and as chairman of the National Security Resources Board. In 1956 and 1960 Symington made unsuccessful bids to become the Democratic presidential candidate. In the Senate Symington was best remembered for his commitment to national defense. He warned in 1957 that the U.S.S.R. was assuming a dominant position in science and military power, a theory that was proved when the Soviets orbited their first Sputnik later that year, thus beating the U.S. in inaugurating the Space Age. During the 1970s he decried excessive secrecy by the U.S. concerning nuclear weapons stored on foreign soil, and he also opposed the Grumman F-14 fighter plane. Near the end of his fourth and last term in the Senate, Symington declared, "I'm tired of having old men in Government passing laws that force young men to do battle in causes that are not essential to the United States."

Szentkuthy, Miklos (MIKLOS PFISTERER), Hungarian writer (b. June 2, 1908, Budapest, Hung.—d. July 18, 1988, Budapest), wrote complex experimental fiction that explored the absurdity of life and the impossibility of imposing order on a chaotic world. After attending Budapest University, Szentkuthy taught secondary school in Budapest (1932–57). In 1934 he privately published the structureless "pseudonovel" *Prae,* and in the next five years he wrote two more avant-garde novels and began *Szent Orpheus breviáriuma* ("The Breviary of St. Orpheus"), a massive philosophical examination of the whole range of human experience. Szentkuthy's work was suppressed during a period of government censorship after World War II. Thereafter he wrote fictional biographies of such figures as Mozart and Goethe and did Hungarian translations of classic English literature, most notably a masterly edition of James Joyce's *Ulysses.* After Szentkuthy was officially rehabilitated in the 1970s, he resumed work on the multivolume *Szent Orpheus breviáriuma,* which he completed in 1984.

Szeryng, Henryk, Polish-born violinist (b. Sept. 22, 1918, Zelazowa Wola, Poland—d. March 3, 1988, Kassel, West Germany), was an internationally acclaimed virtuoso who was regarded as one of the most elegant exponents of the school of Romantic violin playing, with a repertory that showcased the music of such masters as Mozart, Bach, Vivaldi, Brahms, and Paganini.

AP/WIDE WORLD

Szeryng studied violin under Carl Flesch and Jacques Thibaud before making his concert debut in 1933 in four European capitals. He then spent four years studying composition as a student of Nadia Boulanger in Paris. After the Nazi invasion of Poland, Szeryng, fluent in

eight languages, served as liaison officer to the exiled Polish prime minister during World War II and helped find homes for refugees in Mexico. In 1943 he took up residence in Mexico when the government invited him to join the faculty at the National University in Mexico City; three years later he became a Mexican citizen. Szeryng helped support modern Mexican composers by performing their works, and he served as the country's goodwill ambassador. In 1971 Szeryng, who achieved eminence for concertos, rediscovered and recorded the Third Concerto in E Major of Paganini. Included in his 250 recordings are the complete works of Mozart for violin and orchestra.

Tarradellas i Joan, Josep, Catalan political leader (b. Feb. 19, 1899, Cervelló, Spain—d. June 10, 1988, Barcelona, Spain), led the struggle for an autonomous Catalonia as head of the Catalan government-in-exile (1939–77) and as interim president (1977–80). Tarradellas joined the campaign for Catalan autonomy in 1916 and entered the Generalitat (regional parliament) in 1931. During the Spanish Civil War (1936–39) he held several posts in the Catalan government, including minister of finance (1936) and prime minister (1936–37). After Gen. Francisco Franco captured Barcelona and abolished Catalan regional autonomy (1939), Tarradellas established a government-in-exile, based alternately in France, Switzerland, and Mexico, where he was elected president by the surviving deputies of the Generalitat in 1954. After Franco's death (1975) Tarradellas refused to return to Spain from his headquarters in France until King Juan Carlos assured him that Catalan autonomy would be forthcoming. On his triumphal return to Barcelona in 1977, Tarradellas was named president of the reestablished Catalan Generalitat, and in 1979 Catalonia was granted full constitutional autonomy within a unified Spain. Tarradellas retired from politics in 1980.

Tchicaya U Tam'si (GÉRARD FÉLIX TCHICAYA), Congolese poet (b. Aug. 25, 1931, Mpili, French Equatorial Africa—d. April 21, 1988, Bazancourt, France), penned extremely personal poetry that explored the cultural, economic, social, and political values that evolved in Africa as a result of French colonial rule and the policy of assimilation. Tchicaya ("the little bird who sings from home") rejected the assumption that European culture and civilization were superior to those of Africa. Using rich and varied imagery inspired by the music, dancing, and poetry of the Congo, he wrote several volumes of French poetry that captured the essence of his country and detailed the sufferings of its people. In 1946 Tchicaya went to Paris, where his father represented Moyen-Congo (the part of French Equatorial Africa that became independent Congo) in the National Assembly. After studying in Orléans and Paris, Tchicaya held a variety of menial jobs and published two poetry collections, *Le Mauvais sang* (1955) and *Feu de brousse* (1957; *Brush Fire,* 1964). As a producer at a Paris radio station (1957–60), he adapted traditional African stories, many of which were collected as *Légendes africaines* (1968). In 1960 Tchicaya went to Léopoldville (now Kinshasa, Zaire) as editor of the *Congo,* but the newspaper soon folded, and he returned to Paris as Congo's permanent representative at Unesco. Many of Tchicaya's poems appeared in English translation as *Selected Poems* (1970). He also wrote three avant-garde plays in the 1970s; a book of short stories, *La Main sèche* (1980); and a novel, *Les Cancrelats* (1980).

Tennant, Kylie (KATHLEEN TENNANT RODD), Australian writer (b. March 12, 1912, Manly, New South Wales, Australia—d. Feb. 28, 1988, Sydney, Australia), was best known for her earthy, slice-of-life novels, in which she depicted dispossessed and underprivileged Australians with sympathy and humour. She briefly attended the University of Sydney and held a variety of jobs before she published her picaresque first novel, *Tiburon* (1935), which was

awarded the S. H. Prior Memorial Prize. Tennant often gathered material by adopting the life-style of and associating with her intended subjects. She dressed as a man and traveled with unemployed migrants during the Great Depression before writing *The Battlers* (1941), which won both the Prior Memorial Prize and the Australian Literature Society's Gold Medal. She worked as a barmaid in the slums of Sydney while planning *Ride On, Stranger* (1943) and built boats in a fishing village for *Lost Haven* (1946). Researching *Tiburon,* she was arrested while posing as a prostitute, a disguise she used again for *The Joyful Condemned* (1953; later expanded as *Tell Morning This,* 1967). Tennant also wrote short stories and plays, most notably *Tether a Dragon* (1952), a prize-winning play about Australian Prime Minister Alfred Deakin. Her nonfiction included *Australia: Her Story* (1953), a popular history of the country; *Evatt: Politics and Justice* (1970), a biography of Australian chief justice Herbert V. Evatt; *All the Proud Tribesmen* (1960), a children's book about Aborigines; and *The Missing Heir* (1986), an autobiography.

Tinbergen, Nikolaas, Dutch-born British zoologist (b. April 15, 1907, The Hague, Neth.—d. Dec. 21, 1988, Oxford, England), shared the 1973 Nobel Prize for Physiology or Medicine with Konrad Lorenz and Karl von Frisch for their work in ethology, the study of animal behaviour under natural conditions. Tinbergen was particularly noted for his research on social patterns among sea gulls and for his development of comprehensive and ingenious experiments that provided scientific tests for sociobiological theories. Tinbergen, whose older brother, Jan, won the 1969 Nobel Prize for Economics, graduated (1932) from the University of Leiden and taught there (1933–49) except for a two-year period during World War II when he was imprisoned by the Nazi occupation forces. In 1949 he became a lecturer in the University of Oxford's newly formed department of animal behaviour; he was named professor of animal behaviour in 1966 and professor emeritus in 1974. Tinbergen applied to humans many of his findings on aggression, communication, and courtship behaviour in animals, and in the 1970s he devoted most of his time to the study of autism in children. His many influential books include *The Study of Instinct* (1951), *The Animal in Its World: Explorations of an Ethologist, 1932–72* (1972–73), and *Autistic Children: New Hope for a Cure* (1983). He was also a skilled nature photographer and an award-winning documentary filmmaker.

Trevelyan, Julian Otto, British artist (b. Feb. 20, 1910, Dorking, Surrey, England—d. July 12, 1988, London, England), was a founding member of the British Surrealist group in the 1930s. Trevelyan, who often incorporated miscellaneous objects into his paintings, infused much of his work with a sense of humour and fantasy. While attending (1928–30) the University of Cambridge, Trevelyan became so impressed by the dreamlike imagery of French Surrealism that he went to Paris to study (1931–34) at Stanley William Hayter's (*q.v.*) printmaking workshop, Atelier 17. Trevelyan exhibited Surrealist paintings and collages in a one-man show in London in 1935, and the next year he participated in the groundbreaking London International Surrealist Exhibition. After serving as a camouflage officer during World War II, Trevelyan taught at the Chelsea School of Art (1950–60) and the Royal College of Art (1955–63). His later work displayed a marked move toward primitivism. Trevelyan wrote several books, including an autobiography, *Indigo Days* (1957).

Truong Chinh (DANG XUAN KHU), Vietnamese politician (b. 1908, Ha Nam Hinh, Vietnam—d. Sept. 30, 1988, Hanoi, Vietnam), was twice (1941–56 and July–December 1986) general secretary of the Vietnamese Communist Party and the party's senior theoretician; he was instrumental in persuading (late 1960s) Vietnamese leaders to wage guerrilla, small-unit war rather than conventional battles against U.S. forces in Vietnam. As a teenager Truong Chinh was expelled from school for his political activities. He went to Hanoi to complete his secondary education, studied at the Hanoi College of Commerce, and was a founding member (1930) of the Communist Party of Indochina, which elected Ho Chi Minh its president and later formed the Viet Minh. Truong Chinh's writings for a party newspaper in Hanoi made him the leading propagandist against French colonial rule. He was arrested (1931) for subversion and sentenced to five years in prison. In the late 1930s he changed his name to Truong Chinh ("long march") in honour of Mao Zedong's (Mao Tse-tung's) Long March across China (1934). Truong Chinh returned to Hanoi as a party leader, and when the party was banned during World War II, he went underground (1940) and Ho went abroad. At the end of World War II (1945), the Viet Minh assumed power, but it was driven out of Hanoi in 1947. The party returned to prominence (1951) as the Vietnamese Workers' Party (Lao Dong), with Truong Chinh as general secretary. An eight-year war with France ensued, ending in 1954 with a French defeat and the end of colonial rule. As general secretary, Truong Chinh made land reform his top priority; his extreme measures, which reportedly led to the executions of as many as 50,000 peasants and party dissenters, led to his demotion in 1956. He resurfaced in 1958 and was appointed vice-premier of North Vietnam and president of the Scientific Research Council. After Ho's death in 1969, Truong Chinh, Le Duan, and Pham Van Dong formed the controlling triumvirate of North Vietnamese politics. In 1976, after the reunification of Vietnam, Truong Chinh served as chairman of the Standing Committee of the National Assembly and also of the committee to draft a new constitution. In 1986, after the death of his rival, Le Duan, Truong Chinh was appointed secretary-general, a post he held for only six months. He served as a party adviser until his death. Truong Chinh wrote *The Resistance Will Win* (1947), a primer for revolution, and he received the Order of Lenin in 1982.

Uhlenbeck, George Eugene, Dutch-born physicist (b. Dec. 6, 1900, Batavia, Java, Dutch East Indies [now Indonesia]—d. Oct. 31, 1988, Boulder, Colo.), codiscovered with Samuel A. Goudsmit the electron's spin, a revolutionary finding that proved to be vital in understanding the nature of atoms. Uhlenbeck and Goudsmit were working on their Ph.D. degrees at the University of Leiden when, in 1925, after ascertaining that electrons rotate about an axis, they theorized that an electron spins. In 1927 Uhlenbeck joined the faculty of the University of Michigan as an instructor in physics. He went back (1935) to The Netherlands as a professor at the State University of Utrecht but returned (1939) to the University of Michigan as professor of theoretical physics. From 1943 to 1945 he helped in the development of radar while working at the Radiation Laboratory at the Massachusetts Institute of Technology. In 1960 he was appointed professor and physicist at the Rockefeller Institute (later Rockefeller University), New York City, a post he held until his retirement in 1974. An expert on the theory of atomic structure and quantum mechanics, statistical mechanics, the kinetic theory of matter, and nuclear physics, Uhlenbeck published many influential papers on those subjects. He was the recipient of the National Medal of Science in 1977 and was co-winner of the Wolf Prize in 1979.

Ulanhu, Mongol nationalist (b. 1904, Banner of Tumd, Suiyuan Province, Mongolia—d. Dec. 8, 1988, Beijing [Peking], China), was a highly visible promoter of Mongolian rights from 1925, when he took part in the first Congress of the People's Revolutionary Council of Inner Mongolia, until his retirement in 1987. Ulanhu, educated in China and the Soviet Union, was at first dedicated to Inner Mongolian independence from Nationalist-ruled China. He later fought against the Japanese occupation of Inner Mongolia; sought improved relations with Outer Mongolia, the Mongolian People's Republic; and conducted underground work for the Communist Party of China. After the Communist victory in 1949, Ulanhu held a series of posts in the central government, but in 1967, at the height of the Cultural Revolution, he was branded a "ruler in an independent kingdom" and was stripped of office. After his rehabilitation in 1973, Ulanhu served on the party Central Committee and in the Political Bureau. From 1975 until his retirement, he was one of 18 deputy chairmen in the legislature, the National People's Congress.

Vineberg, Arthur Martin, Canadian heart surgeon (b. May 24, 1903, Montreal, Que.—d. March 26, 1988, Montreal), developed in 1950 the Vineberg procedure, a surgical method of revascularizing the heart by transplanting the left internal mammary artery into the heart wall in order to provide an alternate blood flow to the heart when blockages caused by atherosclerosis threaten to stifle circulation. Later Vineberg improved his technique by also transferring tissue, rich in blood vessels, taken from around the intestines to the heart. This tissue then develops new vascular connections with the heart muscle. Vineberg earned an M.S. from McGill University, Montreal (1928), and a Ph.D. (1933) in physiology. He studied in Paris and New York City before joining the staff of the Royal Victoria Hospital, Montreal, where in 1957 he was named head of the department of cardiac surgery. Vineberg was the author of *How to Live with Your Heart: The Family Guide to Heart Health* (1975), and at the time of his death he was preparing *The Complete Guide to Heart Health.*

Wankel, Felix, German engineer (b. Aug. 13, 1902, Lahr, Germany—d. Oct. 9, 1988, Lindau, West Germany), invented the revolutionary Wankel rotary engine, unique because it contained a rotor in the shape of a curved equilateral triangle in place of the moving pistons in standard combustion engines. Wankel showed a natural understanding of mechanisms and invented the Wankel engine without knowing how to drive a car or having earned an engineering degree. He sold scientific books to finance a small engineering workshop and to pay for correspondence courses and night classes. Wankel specialized in the sealing problems of conventional engines. He was hired (1933) by the Daimler-Benz Co. but was soon fired. Wankel then worked (1934–36) for Bayerisch Motorenwerke (BMW), where he developed an airplane engine with rotary valves that replaced conventional valves, resulting in a lighter, more efficient configuration. The German Air Ministry learned (1936) of his work and sought to enlist his skills for the Third Reich; Wankel reportedly persuaded Hermann Göring to build the Wankel Test Institute on the shores of Lake Constance in exchange for his continued research on pistonless, rotary engines. French occupation forces destroyed (1945) the institute, imprisoned Wankel for a short time, and forbade him to continue his work. In 1951 he joined NSU Motor Works, which produced his rotary automobile engine (1957). Many major corporations attempted to produce Wankel's engine; most successful were the Mazda automobile corporation in Japan and the Norton motorcycle company in Britain. Wankel received an honorary doctorate in engineering from the Technical University of Munich in 1969 and the Bavaria Order of Merit in 1973.

Wazir, Khalil Ibrahim al- (ABU JIHAD), Palestinian leader (b. Oct. 10, 1935, Ramleh, Palestine—d. April 16, 1988, Tunis, Tunisia), was believed to be the military strategist and second in command of the Palestine Liberation Organization (PLO). Wazir fled with his family from Palestine during the upheaval that accompanied Israeli independence (1948). He grew up

in the Gaza Strip, where he was educated by the United Nations Relief and Works Agency. He met Yasir Arafat in 1951 while attending college in Cairo, and together they organized anti-Israel guerrilla actions (Wazir was later expelled from Egypt for suspected terrorist activities). In 1958 they founded the militant organization al-Fatah, which merged (1964) with smaller groups to form the PLO, and Wazir took the nom de guerre Abu Jihad ("father of struggle"). As Arafat's deputy and a relative moderate within the PLO, Wazir often negotiated with PLO extremists who opposed Arafat's leadership and with countries that did not maintain official diplomatic relations with the PLO. He reportedly arranged arms purchases and planned military strategies for al-Fatah and for the PLO as a whole. After the PLO was expelled from Jordan in 1971, Wazir remained in Amman as an unofficial contact there until his own expulsion in 1986. He was assassinated in his home by unidentified commandos. Despite early denials, Israel later unofficially acknowledged involvement.

Williams, Edward Bennett, U.S. lawyer (b. May 31, 1920, Hartford, Conn.—d. Aug. 13, 1988, Washington, D.C.), was a polished criminal attorney who used his considerable courtroom expertise to defend such celebrated clients as Sen. Joseph McCarthy, Rep. Adam Clayton Powell, reputed mobster Frank Costello, CIA director Richard Helms, and John Hinckley, who attempted to assassinate Pres. Ronald W. Reagan. After gaining renown by winning cases that appeared hopeless, Williams entered the sports world as part owner and president (1965–85) of the Washington Redskins professional football team and as owner of the Baltimore Orioles, a professional baseball team. After graduating summa cum laude from Holy Cross College, Worcester, Mass., he served in the Army Air Force before earning a law degree from Georgetown University, Washington, D.C., in 1945. Williams joined the prestigious Washington law firm Hogan & Hartson and distinguished himself in daily courtroom appearances by enthralling juries with his rhetoric and by hammering away on points of law to gain acquittals for his clients. In 1949 he formed his own law firm and specialized in civil liberties and constitutional guarantees. Though many of his clients were controversial, Williams passionately defended every citizen's constitutional entitlement to legal representation; he elaborated on that belief in *One Man's Freedom* (1962). His most celebrated victory was in 1957 when he won acquittal for Teamster boss James Hoffa on charges of bribing a lawyer to garner confidential information from a U.S. Senate committee's files. Just a few weeks before his death, Williams, a senior partner in the firm of Williams & Connolly, was still practicing law and his own brand of "contest living," trying to defeat the cancer that finally claimed victory.

Williams, G(erhard) Mennen, U.S. government official and lawyer (b. Feb. 23, 1911, Detroit, Mich.—d. Feb. 2, 1988, Detroit), as six-term governor of Michigan (1949–60) enacted strong measures to ensure civil rights and later served as justice (1971–83) and chief justice (1983–86) of the state Supreme Court; he was also a federal official in the Departments of State and Justice. Williams, who was tagged with the nickname "Soapy" because his maternal grandfather was the founder of the Mennen soap and toiletries company, was nurtured in a staunch Republican family. He acquired a B.A. in 1933 from Princeton University, but while earning his law degree from the University of Michigan Law School, he became a liberal Democrat. After graduating in 1936 he served as an attorney for the Social Security Board and then as executive assistant to the U.S. attorney general (1939–40) and as a member of the criminal division of the U.S. Department of Justice (1940–41). As governor he was a highly visible politician with his polka-dot bow ties, crew cut, and amiable disposition and was active in national Democratic politics.

After Williams chose not to seek reelection in 1960, Pres. John F. Kennedy appointed him assistant secretary of state for African affairs, a post he held until 1966. His diplomatic service continued from 1968 to 1970 when he served as ambassador to the Philippines. Williams then returned to Michigan to serve as justice of the state Supreme Court; he retired from the bench as chief justice in 1986 at the mandatory retirement age of 75.

Woodhouse, Barbara, British animal trainer (b. May 9, 1910, Rathfarnham, County Dublin, Ireland—d. July 9, 1988, Great Missenden, Buckinghamshire, England), gained international recognition and unexpected television stardom on the British Broadcasting Corporation (BBC) series "Training Dogs the Woodhouse Way" (1980). Woodhouse, who held that the key to an obedient dog was a properly trained owner, had a lilting voice and an uncanny air of authority that brought dogs and owners alike under her spell. Born Barbara Blackburn, she demonstrated an exceptional affinity with animals from childhood and, after attending agricultural college (1927–30), she operated a riding school in Oxford. She developed an unorthodox but highly effective teaching method while studying horse training in Argentina (1934–37) and then

AP/WIDE WORLD

returned to Oxford to import and train Argentine polo ponies. After her marriage in 1940, Woodhouse raised cows and trained animals, particularly dogs, for motion pictures. In 1955 she appeared in *Love Me, Love My Dog,* the first in a series of short instructional films, and in 1979 she convinced the BBC to produce "Training Dogs the Woodhouse Way." Woodhouse was named female television personality of 1980, and the command "walkies" quickly became a popular catchphrase in Britain and the U.S. She wrote numerous books on animal training, most notably the best-seller *No Bad Dogs: The Woodhouse Way* (1982).

Wright, Sewall, U.S. geneticist (b. Dec. 21, 1889, Melrose, Mass.—d. March 3, 1988, Madison, Wis.), together with British scientists R. A. Fisher and J. B. S. Haldane, founded population genetics, the study of both experimental and theoretical consequences of Mendelian genetics (the scientific study of heredity in accordance with Mendel's laws) on the population level. His experimental work included investigations of the effects of inbreeding and crossbreeding among guinea pigs in order to improve stock, and he later used these animals to correlate the effects of gene action on coat colour. He was most prominently identified with his concept of genetic drift termed the Sewall Wright effect, which propounds that in small isolated populations the few individuals possessing a rare gene may not pass it on, and a new species may

result without natural selection playing a role. Wright also developed a mathematical foundation to synthesize the 19th-century theories of Charles Darwin, the father of evolution, and Gregor Mendel, the founder of genetic investigation. After Wright earned his Ph.D. in zoology from Harvard University (Sc.D., 1915), he conducted experimental work in animal genetics at the U.S. Department of Agriculture (1915–25), before serving on the faculties of the University of Chicago (1926–54) and the University of Wisconsin (1955–60). Wright wrote his masterpiece, *Evolution and the Genetics of Populations,* in 1968, at the age of 79.

Zia-ul-Haq, Mohammad, Pakistani military leader (b. Aug. 12, 1924, Jullundur, Punjab, India—d. Aug. 17, 1988, near Bahawalpur, Pak.), ruled Pakistan as chief martial-law administrator (1977–78) and president (1978–88) after the 1977 military coup in which he overthrew Prime Minister Zulfikar Ali Bhutto. Zia was commissioned from the Royal Indian Military Academy at Dehra Dun in 1945 and served with the British forces in Southeast Asia. After the partitioning of India in 1947, he transferred to the new Pakistani Army. He rose to brigadier general in 1969 and to major general in 1972 and was promoted by Bhutto to lieutenant general in 1975. Zia was named army chief of staff in 1976. After the elections of March 7, 1977, allegations that Bhutto's Pakistan People's Party (PPP) had engaged in ballot rigging led to widespread rioting, and in the ensuing disorder Zia seized power in a bloodless coup on July 5. Although he initially promised new elections within 90 days, he postponed the elections indefinitely, and after Pres. Fazal Elahi Chaudhry's term expired in August 1978, Zia became president. During his tenure Zia instituted a policy of islamization to bring Pakistan under strict Islamic law, banned political parties, and began a program of nuclear development. Western criticism aimed at Zia's regime peaked in April 1979 when Bhutto was executed despite international appeals for clemency. U.S. opposition faded during the 1980s when Pakistan accepted more than three million Afghan refugees following the 1979 Soviet invasion of Afghanistan, and Zia received substantial U.S. aid. Zia won a national referendum on islamization in December 1984, but the PPP won a majority in the long-awaited elections that were held in February 1985. In response, Zia restored a modified version of the 1973 constitution and later that year lifted martial law. In May 1988, however, he dismissed the government and announced new nonparty elections for later that year. Zia was killed along with several top army officers and the U.S. ambassador to Pakistan when the airplane in which they were traveling exploded in midair and crashed.

AP/WIDE WORLD

Events of 1988

Agriculture and Food Supplies

Drought in North America was the most prominent feature of the world agricultural situation in 1988. It not only reawakened concerns about short-term world food security by reducing world stocks of cereals and pushing up previously depressed grain prices but also fueled anxiety that the expected long-term impacts of global warming were already producing disruptive effects. Ironically, abundant rainfall in 1988 in some usually drought-prone areas of Africa was rekindling a serious threat to African food security by providing favourable breeding conditions for large swarms of locusts. An international meeting of trade ministers designed to give impetus to negotiations for a more liberalized world trade system was deadlocked when the European Communities (EC) and the U.S. failed to reach agreement on the objectives of major agricultural trade reforms. The year ended with the EC and the U.S. on the verge of a major trade war over the former's ban on imports of beef in which growth hormones were used.

World output of food and agricultural products failed to rise significantly in 1988 after falling slightly in 1987, according to estimates (in September) of the United Nations Food and Agriculture Organization (FAO). The result was a decline in per capita global production in both years. Drought caused North America to be the only major region to register a decline in agricultural output in 1988, pulling down overall production in the developed countries. Production also fell in those nations in 1987 but principally because of policies curbing output in both North America and Europe. By contrast, production in 1988 recovered strongly from 1987 declines in the less developed market economies of Asia, the Middle East (western Asia), and Africa, while gains in Latin America slowed. Modest gains were made in the Soviet Union and Eastern Europe after setbacks in 1987, and output also rose modestly in the Asian centrally planned economies, as weather was not as favourable to crops in China in 1988.

North American Drought. The drought in North America was described as the most pervasive early-season drought ever to strike the heart of the U.S. farm belt, comparable to the previous worst drought conditions, in 1934 and 1936, on record in both Canada and the U.S. In the U.S. January–August rainfall deficiencies and summer high temperatures were the second highest on record. By late July a peak of 40% of the U.S. was affected by severe-to-extreme drought conditions, and more than 70% of all

Table I. Selected Indexes of World Agricultural and Food Production
(1979–81 = 100)

Region or country	Total agricultural production						Total food production						Per capita food production					
	1983	1984	1985	1986	1987	1988¹	1983	1984	1985	1986	1987	1988¹	1983	1984	1985	1986	1987	1988¹
Developed countries	100	106	108	109	107	104	100	107	108	109	108	104	98	104	104	105	103	99
United States	88	102	107	100	98	89	90	102	108	102	99	89	87	98	102	97	93	82
Canada	109	108	113	123	114	99	109	108	112	123	114	100	105	104	107	115	106	92
Western Europe	103	109	107	108	109	108	103	109	107	108	109	108	102	108	105	106	107	106
Japan	99	108	108	107	102	100	99	110	110	109	104	102	97	107	107	105	100	97
Oceania	111	106	107	108	108	112	106	101	101	100	107	109	106	101	101	100	98	99
South Africa	81	89	94	98	102	104	79	89	94	99	102	104	74	80	83	85	86	85
Centrally planned economies	113	119	121	126	127	128	113	118	119	126	127	128	109	112	112	118	117	116
Eastern Europe	107	109	110	117	115	117	108	110	110	118	116	117	105	107	106	113	110	110
U.S.S.R.	109	109	110	117	116	118	109	110	110	118	118	119	107	106	106	112	110	111
China	122	134	132	136	141	141	120	128	129	136	140	139	115	122	122	126	128	126
Less developed countries	112	116	120	122	123	126	112	116	120	123	123	127	105	107	108	109	107	106
South and East Asia²	113	117	120	121	118	124	107	106	114	118	119	125	108	108	108	108	103	107
Bangladesh	107	109	114	114	112	109	108	110	113	114	114	110	99	98	98	97	94	89
Burma	122	128	137	140	139	144	123	129	137	141	141	146	116	119	125	125	123	125
India	117	120	123	123	118	127	119	121	123	124	119	128	112	112	112	111	104	111
Indonesia	114	125	127	128	130	135	115	127	127	130	131	137	108	117	116	116	115	118
Korea, South	102	108	110	108	104	107	102	109	111	110	105	109	98	103	103	100	94	96
Malaysia	106	118	130	135	143	150	107	123	140	145	156	165	100	112	124	125	133	137
Pakistan	109	117	123	132	135	141	113	116	119	127	130	136	103	102	102	107	107	110
Philippines	103	102	106	107	104	104	102	102	106	107	104	104	95	93	94	92	88	86
Thailand	114	116	123	119	114	121	114	117	122	117	114	121	108	108	110	104	100	105
Vietnam	115	122	125	130	133	137	115	122	124	130	133	136	108	113	113	116	115	116
Western Asia	107	106	113	117	117	121	107	106	114	118	119	125	99	96	100	101	98	99
Iran	109	113	115	119	130	135	109	113	115	119	121	120	100	101	100	100	99	96
Turkey	105	106	109	113	114	117	105	106	109	114	115	118	99	97	99	101	99	100
Africa³	101	102	112	116	115	120	101	102	112	117	114	119	101	104	105	105	92	93
Egypt	108	109	115	120	137	139	113	114	120	126	147	149	105	103	106	109	124	123
Ethiopia	101	90	98	106	103	113	100	91	99	108	104	115	93	83	87	93	87	93
Morocco	105	106	117	144	110	150	105	106	117	144	110	150	98	96	103	124	93	123
Nigeria	107	113	124	130	123	123	107	113	124	130	123	123	97	99	105	107	97	94
Sudan, The	106	99	118	119	106	119	102	94	116	118	103	118	94	84	101	100	85	94
Latin America	105	108	113	110	115	117	106	109	113	112	115	119	99	100	101	98	98	100
Argentina	104	108	105	108	104	106	104	108	106	108	105	106	100	101	98	99	94	93
Brazil	108	113	125	112	129	132	108	114	124	116	127	138	101	105	111	102	109	116
Colombia	100	103	103	108	113	117	100	104	106	111	118	121	93	96	95	97	101	102
Mexico	119	126	125	131	113	110	109	110	110	110	111	111	101	99	97	94	93	91
Peru	101	112	112	109	116	118	104	115	114	112	119	121	96	103	100	96	99	98
Venezuela	107	104	104	116	110	117	107	104	103	116	109	115	98	92	89	98	90	92
World	106	111	114	115	115	115	106	111	114	116	115	115	101	104	105	105	103	101

¹Preliminary.   ²Excludes Japan.   ³Excludes South Africa.
Source: Food and Agriculture Organization of the United Nations, *FAO Quarterly Bulletin of Statistics.*

U.S. counties were eventually affected. U.S. crop yields per acre of spring wheat were 51% below average, while those for corn were 36% and for soybeans 24% below average.

The consequences were a 29% decline in U.S. grain production and prospects of the largest one-year decline in world grain stocks ever recorded. The approximately 33% drop was estimated to result in stocks' equaling a little over 16% of total annual cereals use by the end of 1988–89. This would be the lowest since the 1972–74 world food crisis, when stocks ranged between 15 and 16.5% of consumption. The immediate impact upon world food security was not great because harvests were generally favourable outside North America and stocks were available to be drawn down in support of consumption and trade. Although grain prices rose sharply and placed a greater burden upon poorer countries heavily dependent upon food imports, they rose from an extremely depressed level and stood at a more "normal" level comparable to those in the early 1980s. The danger was that another poor grain harvest in 1989–90 could force more drastic cuts in grain consumption and send prices rocketing

Some FAO studies concluded, as a rough rule of thumb, that stocks equal to at least 17% of total annual grain consumption are necessary for maintenance of a "minimum safe level of world food security." This was a rough aggregate measure since the various possible distributions of gains and losses of production, consumption, and trade among food and feed grains and among countries can have markedly different impacts on food security and yet result in identical global stock-to-use ratios. To achieve that level of stocks without reducing grain consumption by either humans or livestock would probably require both a recovery in crop yields and an expansion in land devoted to grains comparable to the largest achieved in the last 30 years— 4.1% in 1973–74 in response to the 1972–74 crisis. The roughly 30 million ha (74 million ac) required represents about one-third of the land taken out of grain production around the world since 1981–82. The requirement is so large because, even before the drought, grain consumption

continued to rise while producers of wheat and coarse grains were cutting back output and relying upon stocks to make up the difference. Thus the need to expand area could be less in terms of food security if higher prices were to cause farmers to reduce the amount of grain they fed to their livestock.

Locust Plague. Until after the winter rains came in late 1987, the prospects had looked good for finally bringing under control in 1988 the explosive spread of locusts launched by the rains in 1985 that had ended the great African drought. Because of the rainfall the FAO, however, issued a warning in March that a "veritable plague" was developing in wide areas of western, northwestern, and northern Africa. The largest swarms originated in the western Sahara and northern Mauritania. By mid-1988 they had spread into North Africa and south and east into the Sahelian zone from Mauritania to the Red Sea. By autumn infestations were reported in the Arabian Peninsula, the Middle East, and Iran. Three waves of swarms flew west across more than 450 km (300 mi) of ocean to invade Cape Verde, and significant but controllable numbers aided by the wind reached the Caribbean and Suriname, although they were not considered a serious threat.

In October 32 of the afflicted countries met in Morocco, where they endorsed an FAO strategy that placed primary emphases on large-scale aerial spraying, attacking all phases of the locust's life cycle, and concentrating on strategic areas. In most countries the first priority had to be given to protecting vital food crops. Scarce resources limited the ability of many of them to attack the locusts in their breeding grounds, which were frequently located in remote and hard-to-reach areas. The conference also accepted a proposal by the U.S., later endorsed by the FAO Council, to create an international task force, popularly dubbed the "Green Helmet Force," to intercede rapidly in strategic infested areas, especially those where breeding takes place. Some of the difficulties inherent in cross-border operations by such a force were illustrated by the shooting down of a plane and the death of its U.S. crew when it was returning to Morocco after spraying locusts in Senegal.

The governments represented on the FAO Council concluded in November that, despite expenditures of more than $200 million on locust control since the beginning of the campaign, winning the battle could take two to three more years, and in the interim the plague could constitute a major threat to food security. FAO experts indicated that the outlook was for a continuation of the plague in western and northwestern Africa, an extension into the Middle East and eastern Africa, and an invasion of southwestern Asia by mid-1989. The most critical areas for battling the locust were expected to be along the Red Sea, especially in The Sudan, Saudi Arabia, North Africa, and the band comprising Mali, Niger, and Mauritania.

Commodity Developments. *Grains.* World grain production was expected (in December) to fall about 4% in 1988–89, the second consecutive season of smaller output, with the great bulk of the decline in coarse grains. Severe drought cut the output of grains sharply in North America, most especially coarse grains but also wheat. Ample carryover stocks from 1987–88 cushioned the impact, and supplies were expected to be sufficient to maintain grain consumption—which also for the second straight year exceeded production—and trade close to 1987–88 levels. World grain prices moved up strongly, reflecting the fact that world stocks of grain were likely to fall by the end of 1988–89 to levels not seen since the period of great scarcity in the early 1970s.

Wheat production was expected to decline only a lit-

Table II. World Cereal Supply and Distribution
In 000,000 metric tons

	1985–86	1986–87	1987–88	1988–89[1]
Production				
Wheat	500	530	504	503
Coarse grains	843	835	791	713
Rice, milled	320	319	309	320
Total	1,663	1,684	1,604	1,536
Utilization				
Wheat	496	523	534	535
Coarse grains	778	811	814	806
Rice, milled	321	323	317	322
Total	1,595	1,657	1,665	1,663
Exports				
Wheat	85	91	106	94
Coarse grains	83	84	83	90
Rice, milled	13	13	12	12
Total	181	188	201	196
Ending stocks[2]				
Wheat	168	175	146	113
Coarse grains	208	233	210	116
Rice, milled	54	50	42	41
Total	430	458	398	270
Stocks as % of utilization				
Wheat	33.8%	33.5%	27.3%	21.1%
Coarse grains	26.8%	28.7%	25.7%	14.4%
Rice, milled	16.9%	15.5%	13.3%	12.6%
Total	27.0%	27.6%	23.9%	16.2%
Stocks held by U.S. in %				
Wheat	30.9%	28.3%	23.5%	12.9%
Coarse grains	60.9%	65.6%	64.0%	45.2%
Rice	4.6%	3.4%	2.4%	2.7%
Total	42.1%	44.5%	42.6%	25.3%

[1] Forecast.
[2] Data not available for all countries, including parts of Eastern Europe and Asia. Series revised to include data for Chinese stocks, which especially affect estimates of rice, but continues to be adjusted only for changes in Soviet stocks.
Source: USDA, Foreign Agricultural Service, December 1988.

tle in 1988–89. Gains in the rest of the world, especially recovery in the Soviet Union, Eastern Europe, and the EC, nearly offset a 40% drop (to 15.7 million tons) in Canadian output and a 14% smaller U.S. crop (49.3 million tons). The EC was the only major wheat exporter that experienced favourable overall growing and harvesting conditions. Higher prices and smaller supplies available for export were expected to keep wheat consumption near that of 1986–87.

Global wheat stocks were forecast to fall again and to equal about 21% of total annual wheat use by the end of 1988–89, about equal to the low recorded at the end of 1972–73. Most of the predicted decline was expected to be in U.S. stocks, to about 14.5 million tons, compared with 50 million tons or more held during 1985–86 and 1986–87.

The U.S.-Soviet Long Term Grain Agreement (LTA), which expired at the end of September, was extended in November for two years. It continued to call for minimum annual Soviet purchases of four million tons each of wheat and corn (maize) and one million of corn or wheat or 500,000 tons of soybeans or soybean meal. Under the 1983–88 LTA, the Soviets always exceeded the minimum for corn but failed to buy sufficient wheat twice, claiming uncompetitive U.S. prices. The first U.S.-Soviet LTA was motivated by a desire on the U.S.'s part to predict Soviet purchases in order to avoid wide price swings and by a Soviet desire to assure access to grain. The LTA was honoured even during the 1977 U.S. embargo of trade with the U.S.S.R.. The Soviets also had agreements with Argentina to provide four million tons of coarse grains and 500,000 tons of soybeans annually between December save and November 1991, with Canada for 25 million tons of wheat and feedgrains between August 1986 and July 1991, with

China for 7.5 million tons of corn and 2.6 million tons of soybeans between 1986 and 1990, and, confidentially, with Hungary for perhaps 500,000 tons of corn and with France for wheat or barley.

World output of coarse grains was expected to fall nearly 10% in 1988–89. The drought helped cut U.S. coarse-grain production a staggering 74 million tons, or 34%. This 142 million-ton crop was the third consecutive smaller harvest since the peak total of 275 million tons in 1985–86. Drought also cut output in Canada, and in the Soviet Union it was resulting in pressures for reduced feeding of livestock and larger imports. Tight supplies and stronger prices for wheat intended for human consumption were stimulating coarse-grain trade by reducing the availability of wheat for feeding to livestock, especially in the Soviet Union and South Korea. Among major exporters the recovery in EC coarse-grain production put it in the best position to expand exports.

The prospect of strong expansion in trade in coarse grains and only a moderate decline expected in their global utilization implied a sharp, perhaps 45%, fall in world coarse-grain stocks by the end of 1988–89. Stocks of this magnitude would represent about 14.4% of utilization, comparable to those remaining after the 1983 U.S. corn blight and approaching the 12% reached at the end of 1973–74. Most of the decline was expected to be in U.S. stocks, forecast to fall nearly 72 million tons, or 60%.

Global rice production in 1988–89 was forecast to rise more than 4% despite a somewhat smaller crop in China and damage from floods in Bangladesh. Improved rainfall in southern and southeastern Asia led to higher rice yields than in 1987–88, when much of the region suffered from drought. Large crops were expected in India, Indonesia, and Thailand. Rice consumption in 1988–89 was expected

Table III. World Production of Oilseeds and Products

In 000,000 metric tons

	1986–87	1987–88[1]	1988–89[2]
Production of oilseeds	194.3	206.4	201.1
Soybeans	97.9	102.9	94.3
U.S.	52.8	52.3	41.2
China	11.6	12.2	11.0
Argentina	7.0	9.9	11.0
Brazil	17.3	17.8	20.0
Cottonseed	27.1	30.9	32.4
U.S.	3.5	5.2	5.4
U.S.S.R.	4.9	4.5	5.0
China	6.0	7.2	7.2
Peanuts	20.5	19.8	22.1
U.S.	1.7	1.6	1.9
China	5.9	6.2	5.8
India	6.1	4.8	7.3
Sunflower seed	19.3	20.6	21.3
U.S.	1.2	1.2	0.6
U.S.S.R.	5.3	6.1	6.3
Argentina	2.5	2.8	3.2
Rapeseed	19.5	23.0	21.8
Canada	3.8	3.9	4.2
China	5.9	6.6	5.7
EC	3.7	6.0	5.3
India	2.6	3.1	3.0
Flaxseed	2.7	2.3	1.8
Copra	4.8	4.4	4.7
Palm kernel	2.6	2.7	2.9
Crushings of oilseeds	161.2	165.1	167.2
Soybeans	85.0	83.9	82.9
Ending stocks of oilseeds	23.3	23.6	17.4
Soybeans	19.7	19.8	13.9
World production[3]			
Total fats and oils	62.0	64.0	...
Edible vegetable oils	48.4	50.4	51.5
Soybean oil	15.1	15.0	14.9
Palm oil	8.1	8.6	9.3
Animal fats	11.5	11.6	...
Industrial and marine oils	2.0	2.1	2.0
High-protein meals[4]	105.7	107.7	108.2
Soybean meal	66.8	66.5	65.5

[1] Preliminary.
[2] Forecast.
[3] Processing potential from crops in year indicated.
[4] Converted, on basis of product's protein content, to weight equivalent to soybeans of 44% protein content.
Source: USDA, Foreign Agricultural Service, June and December 1988.

Table IV. Livestock Numbers and Meat Production in Major Producing Countries

In 000,000 head and 000,000 metric tons (carcass weight)

Region and country	1987	1988[1]	1987	1988[1]
	Cattle and buffalo		Beef and veal	
World total	1,024.3	1,029.6	44.89	44.54
Canada	10.8	11.0	0.98	0.98
United States	99.0	97.8	10.88	10.80
Mexico	35.4	36.9	1.21	1.39
Argentina	50.8	50.5	2.70	2.57
Brazil	98.3	98.8	2.25	2.40
Uruguay	10.3	10.7	0.28	0.31
Western Europe	86.7	85.5	8.73	8.31
EC	79.2	78.0	8.06	7.67
Eastern Europe	36.5	36.5	2.59	2.49
U.S.S.R.	120.6	119.5	8.29	8.40
Australia	23.5	24.0	1.55	1.55
India	264.9	267.9	0.69	0.55
China	94.7	98.0	0.72	0.80
	Hogs		Pork	
World total	741.2	739.9	58.40	59.54
Canada	10.5	11.0	0.94	1.00
United States	54.4	56.0	6.52	7.10
Mexico	10.9	8.9	0.95	0.94
Western Europe	113.0	110.7	13.21	13.27
EC	103.6	101.4	12.08	12.13
U.S.S.R.	77.4	78.0	6.32	6.50
Japan	11.7	11.6	1.58	1.61
China	327.7	327.8	17.80	18.20
	Poultry		Poultry meat[2]	
World total	...	...	29.21	30.14
United States	...	...	9.11	9.47
Brazil	...	...	1.87	1.86
EC-12	...	...	5.71	5.95
U.S.S.R.	...	...	3.13	3.20
Japan	...	...	1.47	1.48
	Sheep and goats		Sheep, goat meat	
World total	693.0	701.4	5.55	5.76
			All meat	
Total	...	...	138.06	139.98

[1] Preliminary livestock numbers at year's end. Consists of 51 countries for beef and veal, 38 for pork, 51 for poultry meat, 30 for sheep and goat meat, and roughly the same coverage for animal numbers. Includes nearly all European producers, the most significant in the Western Hemisphere, and scattered coverage elsewhere.
Source: USDA, Foreign Agricultural Service, September and October 1988.

to exceed production for the fourth year in a row, resulting in the lowest stocks-to-consumption ratio since 1974–75.

Oilseeds. Drought in the U.S. and China was responsible for an expected (in December) 2.6% decline in world output of oilseeds in 1988–89. Brazil and Argentina responded to the 21% reduction in U.S. soybean production by expanded plantings of soybeans for harvest in early 1989, but total soybean production was still expected to be down more than 8% in 1988–89. The production of high-protein meals was expected to be maintained at about the 1987–88 level through a sharp drawdown of soybean stocks in the U.S. and the increased availability of other oilseeds. Oilseed prices showed strong increases in 1988 as evidenced by soybeans, rising to a peak of $350 per ton (c.i.f., Rotterdam, U.S. No. 2 yellow) before dropping back to about $313 later in the year as South American crop prospects became clearer. Stocks of both oilseeds and oilseed products were expected to fall in 1988–89.

Firm demand for livestock products, buoyed by strong economic growth in much of the world, led to a continued expansion of consumption of high-protein oilseed meals in 1987–88. However, tighter supplies and higher prices were expected to cut consumption in 1988–89. The rise in oilseed meal prices was reflected in prices for soybean meal (c.i.f., Rotterdam), which, after averaging $191 per ton in 1986–87, peaked at $317 per ton in June 1988 (average of $254 in 1987–88) before slipping to $254 per ton in November.

Production of edible vegetable oils in 1988–89 was likely to increase more rapidly than that of protein meals because gains in oilseed production were concentrated in seeds with greater oil content than soybeans. However, output was expected to be roughly in balance with consumption after exceeding consumption for the past four years. The steady decline since 1983–84 from an average of $722 per ton in world vegetable oil prices, as reflected in prices for soybean oil (f.o.b. Rotterdam), was reversed when prices bottomed out at $305 per ton in March 1987. They reached $600 per ton in July 1988 (average of $443 in 1987–88, compared with $324 in 1986–87) and then fell back to $431 per ton by November.

Meat and Livestock. The growth of world production of meat in major producing countries was expected (in October) to slow in 1988, with output of beef and veal actually declining slightly. Production of red meat (from cattle, pigs, and sheep) in 1987 proved higher, especially for pork, than early estimates, resulting in an overall increase in meat production of about 3%. World cattle numbers were estimated to have risen slightly in 1988 after declining a little over 1% in 1987.

Most of the cattle herd expansion was in countries producing primarily for their domestic markets, while the record for traditional beef exporters was mixed. The end did not appear to be in sight for the steady decline in recent years of the U.S. cattle inventory, which at the end of 1988 was estimated to be smaller than the 1961 herd. Production of beef and veal was leveling off in the EC, permitting a 25% reduction in government-held "intervention" stocks for the 12 months ended October 1988 to about 500,000 tons. EC agricultural ministers were said to be near agreement on restricting such government purchases of beef and veal to 200,000 tons annually.

The estimated increase in world pork production was led by recovery in Chinese output that resulted from policy adjustments and also by a larger U.S. output in response to strong prices over the past two years. The U.S., Brazil, and the EC were largely responsible for the growth in world output of poultry in 1988. Substantial gains in poultry out-

put, although from a still relatively small base, continued to be made in the Middle East. This increase contributed to a reduction of imports in what had been until recently a fast-growing import market.

The complicating influence of national trade policies on trade in livestock products was illustrated by a series of developments in 1988. The Japanese and the U.S. reached an agreement that would permit a substantial increase in Japanese beef and citrus imports over a three-year transitional period and beyond. Australian beef exports were also expected to benefit. The pact could also help increase Canadian beef exports to the U.S. by replacing U.S. beef bid away by high prices in Japanese meat markets. On the other hand, a General Agreement on Tariffs and Trade (GATT) panel found that Canada had improperly applied a duty on imports of beef from the EC. Should Canada accept the finding and resume buying EC beef, imports from countries such as the U.S., Australia, and New Zealand that had supplanted EC supplies would probably be reduced. In renegotiating its voluntary restraint agreement (VRA) with New Zealand, the EC reduced its limit on sheep imports from that country by 16%. EC member Portugal temporarily banned all imports of lamb from Australia and New Zealand in order to increase its own production. Australian and New Zealand beef exports were also restricted by VRAs with the U.S. designed to prevent the mandatory imposition of U.S. import quotas. The "trigger" level for mandatory quotas was raised 6% from 1987.

The restrictions on New Zealand's trade appeared particularly galling to its sheep farmers because of that country's recent unilateral elimination of various production incentives that had afforded producers significant protection. New Zealand was restructuring its sheep industry, and pro-

Table V. World Production and Stocks of Dairy Products[1]

Region and country	Production of cow milk[2]		
	1986	1987	1988[3]
	In 000,000 metric tons		
North America	81.3	81.6	83.4
United States	65.4	64.6	65.9
South America	21.3	23.3	23.1
Brazil	11.6	13.3	13.2
Western Europe	132.4	127.4	123.3
EC	116.2	111.6	107.8
France	28.1	27.1	26.1
West Germany	26.4	24.4	23.6
Italy	10.3	10.5	10.4
Netherlands, The	12.7	11.7	11.2
United Kingdom	16.2	15.4	14.6
Other Western Europe	16.1	15.8	15.5
Eastern Europe	43.3	43.5	42.9
Poland	15.7	15.5	15.0
U.S.S.R.	102.2	103.4	105.5
China	2.9	3.3	3.8
India	19.5	21.2	22.5
Australia/New Zealand[4]	14.4	13.7	14.2
Japan/South Africa	9.7	9.7	9.9
Total	426.8	427.1	428.6

Product/Region	Production		Year-end stocks	
	1987	1988[3]	1987	1988[3]
	In 000 metric tons			
Butter	6,584	6,474	1,451	938
EC	1,857	1,620	1,095	595
U.S.	501	545	67	86
Cheese	10,073	10,320	1,416	1,371
EC	4,161	4,263	847	890
U.S.	2,424	2,495	205	145
Nonfat dry milk	3,515	3,189	1,126	432
EC	1,675	1,332	783	194
U.S.	480	470	80	22

[1]Based on 38 major producing countries. Those not shown individually include (North America) Canada and Mexico; (South America) Argentina, Chile, Peru, and Venezuela; (EC) Belgium-Luxembourg, Denmark, Greece, Ireland, Portugal, and Spain; (Other Western Europe) Austria, Finland, Norway, Sweden, and Switzerland; and (Eastern Europe) Czechoslovakia, East Germany, and Yugoslavia.
[2]Buffalo milk included in 1986 totals.
[3]Preliminary.
[4]Year ended June 30 for Australia and May 31 for New Zealand.
Source: USDA, Foreign Agricultural Service, November 1988.

Japanese farmers protest the idea of rice importation from the United States. Because of the ban on rice imports, Japanese rice growers could command prices considerably higher than the world price.

AFP PHOTO

duction of sheep meat had declined, with the result that Australia, with production of about 600,000 tons of sheep meat, surpassed New Zealand for the first time in 1987. The Soviet Union was the leading producer with about 900,000 tons annually, and India's production approached that level, but neither of those countries was a significant exporter.

Dairy Products. World production of cow's milk by 38 major producing countries was estimated (in November) to have grown very little in both 1987 and 1988. Successive reductions in EC dairy quotas, designed to reduce budgetary expenditures on its common agricultural policy (CAP), brought about substantial reductions in EC dairy output. The accelerating expansion of U.S. dairy production was dampened by drought, which had the effect of raising feed prices.

The consumption of fluid milk, which averaged about 37% of milk production, may have grown 2% in 1988, largely because of recovery of output after the 1987 drought in India and continued rapid expansion in China. Milk production in China began from a very small base compared with that of other countries but had been increasing about 14% annually over the past four years. In those two countries about 80% of cow's milk produced was consumed in liquid form, compared with about 25–40% in most industrialized regions.

Prices for dairy products on international markets strengthened in 1988, reflecting a two-year reduction in output (except cheese) and stocks. Output of cheese continued to expand in response to the steady growth of consumption and imports buoyed by rising incomes in many markets. Nearly all of the decline in butter production was once again in the EC, though consumption was stagnating or declining in most countries. The EC's butter "mountain," which measured almost 2.3 million tons at its peak in 1983, continued to erode; EC butter stocks were reduced by 45% in 1988 and were expected to decline further in 1989.

The EC was also responsible for the bulk of the reduction in output and stocks of nonfat dry milk (NFDM). The EC's feeding of NFDM to calves—one million tons or more in recent years—was being drastically reduced. As stocks fell, export prices rose strongly. The U.S. became a commercial exporter of NFDM without government assistance for the first time in years when international prices

climbed above the domestic support level of $1,604 per ton in May 1988. By the fall of 1988 international prices for NFDM were in the $1,900–$2,000 range, compared with $890–$1,150 a year earlier. Less developed countries with limited financial resources, many of which traditionally had received NFDM in the form of food aid, were most affected by tighter supplies and higher prices for the product. By the end of 1988 no U.S. government-held stocks of NFDM were available for allocation to food-aid programs in fiscal 1989, and the EC's stocks were minimal. Thus a further reduction of imports of NFDM by less developed countries appeared likely in 1989.

Sugar. World output of sugar in 1988–89 was expected (in November) to expand because of large increases in

Table VI. World Production of Centrifugal (Freed from Liquid) Sugar			
In 000,000 metric tons raw value			
Region and country	1986–87	1987–88	1988–89[1]
North America	10.2	10.6	10.1
United States	6.1	6.6	6.1
Mexico	4.0	3.8	3.9
Caribbean	8.6	8.6	9.1
Cuba	7.2	7.3	7.8
Central America	1.8	1.7	1.8
South America	13.5	13.5	13.8
Argentina	1.1	1.2	1.3
Brazil	8.5	8.5	8.7
Colombia	1.3	1.3	1.4
Europe	21.8	20.5	21.3
Western Europe	15.9	14.9	16.3
EC	15.0	14.0	15.2
France	3.7	4.0	4.3
West Germany	3.5	3.0	3.4
Eastern Europe	5.8	5.6	5.0
Poland	1.9	1.8	1.8
U.S.S.R.	8.7	9.6	10.0
Africa and Middle East	10.1	10.3	10.2
South Africa	2.2	2.1	2.2
Turkey	1.5	1.8	1.6
Asia	24.7	24.9	26.5
China	5.8	4.8	5.1
India	9.5	10.0	10.7
Indonesia	2.0	2.1	1.8
Pakistan	1.4	1.9	2.1
Philippines	1.4	1.3	1.4
Thailand	2.6	2.7	3.3
Oceania	4.0	3.9	4.1
Australia	3.5	3.5	3.7
Totals			
Production	103.4	103.5	106.8
Consumption	103.9	105.1	107.0
Exports	28.1	27.6	28.2
Ending stocks	23.9	21.4	21.2[2]
Excluding U.S.	22.5	20.2	19.6

[1]Preliminary.
[2]Unofficial estimate by author in absence of data for U.S. imports and ending stocks.
Source: USDA, Foreign Agricultural Service, November 1988.

production in the EC and India, as well as in Thailand, Cuba, China, and the U.S.S.R., and despite smaller crops attributable to drought in the U.S., Eastern Europe, and Indonesia. World consumption of sugar in 1987–88 proved to be stronger than anticipated and was likely to continue expanding in 1988–89, especially in parts of Asia and the U.S.S.R. Sugar consumption continued to rise rapidly in Asia, where it started from a low per capita base and where in many countries both population and incomes were increasing rapidly.

With sugar consumption likely to exceed production for the third year in a row, a further decline of world stocks seemed probable, perhaps to a stocks-to-use ratio of less than 20%, the lowest since 1980–81. The average annual contract of freely traded sugar was about 6.7 cents per pound in 1987, compared with 6.1 cents in 1986. The monthly average price began climbing in the summer of 1986 and accelerated in the summer of 1988, partly on speculation about the effects of the drought on U.S. sugar production and uncertainty about Cuban sugar supplies. It reached 14 cents per pound in July 1988 but had eased to 10.3 cents by October.

World exports of sugar were likely to rise in 1988–89, in part because of larger U.S. sugar imports. The U.S. sugar import quota for 1988, originally set almost 25% lower than the 910,000-metric ton quota (raw value) of 1987, was later raised to about 958,000 tons because of rising consumption and expectations of a drought-reduced U.S. sugar crop. The 1989 quota was set in December at 1,125,000 tons. The U.S. in 1988 chose not to implement a program authorized by Congress in December 1987 designed to aid domestic sugar refiners and countries covered by the "Caribbean Initiative." The scheme had called for importing raw sugar at the domestic price (about 21.7 cents per pound at that time) and reexporting it as refined sugar at the world price (about 11.5 cents per pound).

The International Sugar Agreement (ISA) negotiated in September 1987 became operative in March 1988. Like the 1984 agreement, it provided a consultative mechanism but contained no economic provisions. A new market evaluation, consumption, and statistics committee was expected to enlarge the old agreement's monitoring and analysis role. U.S. voting rights in the ISA were suspended in November because it was $71,000 in arrears in support of the organization's administrative budget.

Coffee. World coffee production was expected (in December) to decline sharply in 1988–89, largely as a result of poor weather conditions in Brazil a year earlier. Nevertheless, global stocks were estimated at the beginning of 1988–89 to equal more than half of the coffee drunk annually. Coffee consumption appeared to be rising between 1 and 2% a year despite a steady drop in the U.S.

The composite indicator price (15-day moving average) of the International Coffee Agreement (ICA) had bottomed out at 96 cents a pound in July 1987. Following reimposition of export quotas totaling 56.4 million bags under the ICA in October 1987—at the beginning of the 1987–88 coffee year—prices climbed slowly but remained below the ICA's lower target boundary of $1.20 per pound. This resulted in two cuts in the quota of one million bags each that for a short time pushed prices above $1.20 per pound. By July prices were back below $1.15, and quotas were cut a final two million tons.

One result of the low coffee prices in 1987 was a trend away from low-quality Robustas generally used in producing instant coffee and toward increased use of mild Arabica coffees generally preferred for ground coffee. A shortage of Arabica, resulting from traditional ICA quota

allocations giving a large share to Robustas on the basis of market shares in the past, made Arabicas much more expensive than Robustas in 1987–88. As a result, importing countries successfully pushed for allocations under the 1988–89 export quotas that were based more on "objective criteria" that took account of recent levels of production, stocks, and trade. The 1988–89 global quota was set at 56 million bags (74% Arabicas) and could not be reduced by more than 3 million bags. New provisions were adopted to permit additional quota allocations of Arabicas when their prices exceeded those for Robustas by specified percentages. Thus, one million bags were allocated in November for countries producing Arabicas and another one million on December 22 when the composite indicator price stood at $1.21 per pound ($1.42 for Arabica and $1 for Robustas).

The current ICA was to expire at the end of September 1989, but negotiations for a new agreement were moving slowly. Both the U.S. and the EC indicated that they would not agree under any circumstances to a mere extension of the current ICA. Several major changes in the operation of the agreement were proposed, but at the year's end none seemed sure of adoption.

Cocoa. World cocoa production in 1988–89 was expected (in October) to exceed consumption for the fifth year in a row. The consequent buildup in cocoa stocks continued to drive down international prices for cocoa beans, which in the last months of 1987 had already fallen below the International Cocoa Agreement's (ICCA's) lower limit. Cocoa bean prices (New York futures, nearest three-month average) declined steadily from their most recent peak, an average of $1.06 per pound in 1984, to an average of 87 cents in 1987. The ICCO (ICCA Council) responded in January 1988 by authorizing purchases, exclusively from ICCA members, of 175,000 tons of cocoa beans by the ICCA buffer stock. By June the stock had been filled to its authorized 250,000-ton ceiling. Nevertheless, cocoa bean prices continued their downward slide, reaching an average of 54 cents per pound by September.

The September meeting of the ICCO became deadlocked when cocoa producers refused to accept consumer countries' insistence upon a 7% reduction in the agreement's lower limit, which required mandatory purchases for the buffer stock. This was the producers' condition for considering implementing supplementary provisions of the ICCA that could authorize countries to withhold up to a total of 120,000 tons of cocoa beans from the market.

Cotton. World cotton consumption continued to expand in 1987–88, although at a modest 1% rate, reflecting maintenance of a shift in consumer preference toward cotton that had partly originated in low cotton prices earlier. Rising incomes in many countries, especially in the U.S. and other industrialized markets, stimulated demand for textiles, despite strengthened prices influenced by the sharp drawdown in world stocks of cotton during 1986–87. Stocks, which had fallen nearly 27% in 1986–87 to 34.5 million bales, declined to 32.1 million bales during 1987–88 as cotton use exceeded production for the second year in a row. Cotton use was also favoured by strong price increases for polyester fibre resulting from short supplies of a key raw material used in its manufacture.

World export prices (Northern European "A" Index), down from their peak of 83.6 cents per pound in August 1987, still averaged 72.7 cents in 1987–88, providing incentive for the estimated (in December) nearly 5% expansion in 1988–89 world cotton output. Most of the gain was expected to come from the Soviet Union and India because weather problems thwarted another substantial increase in China. Export prices reflected the increase, fluctuating near

58 cents per pound during August through November. World trade in cotton fell from 25.9 million bales in 1986–87 to an estimated 23.7 million bales in 1987–88.

International Trade Policy. *Multilateral Trade Negotiations.* The midterm review of progress in the multilateral trade negotiations (MTN) sponsored by GATT was held in Montreal in December. The review was supposed to give direction and impetus to the remaining two years of negotiation of more liberalized trade across a broad range of activities. Although preliminary agreement was reached on a large number of matters, the talks foundered when the EC and the U.S. could not agree on the path that agricultural trade liberalization was to take. When several countries, especially the U.S., were unwilling to move forward without agreement on agriculture, the participants put on hold preliminary agreements reached on some 11 other subjects. Other unresolved issues concerned textiles, safeguards, and intellectual property rights. The participants agreed to extend the review and attempt to resolve their differences at a meeting to be held in Geneva in April 1989.

The dispute in agriculture centred both on the balancing of commitments to long-term agricultural reform against short-term measures to ameliorate the immediate effects of policies that distorted trade and on how far agricultural reform should ultimately go. The U.S. entered the review with its focus primarily on long-term reform. Its position was little changed from its October 1987 proposal in support of the "zero option," the virtual total elimination of trade-distorting support and protection of agriculture throughout the world. It later indicated willingness to ac-

Indian farmers stage a sit-in alongside the capitol buildings in New Delhi. Stricken by drought and floods, they were seeking relief from the government.
AFP PHOTO

cept a longer period for achieving reform than the ten years it had originally proposed, as well as some modifications to take account of food-security concerns of less developed countries. The U.S. had indicated that it would not oppose "decoupled" support for farmers—presumably some form of payment to farmers that did not affect production and trade in a major way. This left open some possibility of compromise with the EC based on the negotiation of the definition of what constituted a significantly trade-distorting policy.

The EC proved unwilling to move that far down the road to agricultural reform. Before the talks it argued that the U.S. position was excessive, was unrealistic, and went beyond the guidelines agreed upon for the negotiations, claiming the Punta del Este Declaration contained no reference to the total elimination of trade-distorting policies. (This declaration, which had established the MTN, had called for greater "discipline on the use of all direct and indirect subsidies and other measures affecting—directly or indirectly—agricultural trade, including the phased reduction of their negative effects and dealing with their causes.")

The EC was preoccupied with improving the short-term problems of high budget expenditures on agriculture resulting from agricultural surpluses and cutthroat market competition in the form of export subsidies and credits. It argued that it was essential to agree on short-term measures

Table VII. World Green Coffee Production

In 000 60-kg bags

Region and country	1986–87	1987–88[1]	1988–89[2]
North America	17,478	17,222	17,417
Costa Rica	2,566	2,450	2,700
El Salvador	2,275	2,541	2,100
Guatemala	2,843	3,020	2,800
Honduras	1,535	1,493	1,690
Mexico	5,297	4,717	5,100
South America	29,999	55,446	42,547
Brazil	13,900	38,000	25,000
Colombia	11,000	13,300	12,700
Ecuador	2,268	1,660	1,700
Africa	19,967	19,582	20,420
Cameroon	2,191	1,313	1,500
Côte d'Ivoire	4,405	3,410	4,400
Ethiopia	2,700	3,400	3,000
Kenya	1,822	2,088	1,830
Uganda	2,700	2,600	3,000
Zaire	1,875	1,970	1,900
Asia and Oceania	11,720	11,086	12,921
India	3,200	2,000	3,500
Indonesia	5,900	5,965	6,000
Total production	79,164	103,336	93,305
Exportable[3]	56,986	79,598	68,490
Beginning stocks	42,056	33,221	47,608
Exports	66,086	65,524	68,506

[1]Preliminary.
[2]Forecast.
[3]Production minus domestic use in exporting countries.
Source: USDA, Foreign Agricultural Service, December 1988.

Table VIII. World Cocoa Bean Production

In 000 metric tons

Region and country	1986–87	1987–88	1988–89[1]
North and Central America	103	119	119
South America	521	552	563
Brazil	365	400	400
Ecuador	77	71	80
Africa	1,111	1,154	1,260
Cameroon	123	129	125
Côte d'Ivoire[2]	611	650	700
Ghana[3]	228	180	225
Nigeria	100	145	160
Asia and Oceania	258	319	349
Malaysia	167	220	245
Total	1,993	2,143	2,292

[1]Forecast.
[2]Includes some cocoa marketed from Ghana.
[3]Includes cocoa marketed through Benin.
Source: USDA, Foreign Agricultural Service, October 1988.

Table IX. World Cotton Production

In 000,000 480-lb bales

Region and country	1986–87	1987–88	1988–89
Western Hemisphere	15.6	23.0	23.2
United States	9.7	14.8	15.2
Mexico	0.6	1.0	1.2
Brazil	3.0	3.4	3.5
Europe	1.4	1.2	1.6
U.S.S.R.	12.2	11.3	12.7
Africa	6.0	6.1	6.3
Egypt	1.9	1.6	1.6
Sudan, The	0.8	0.6	0.6
Asia and Oceania[1]	34.3	38.8	40.5
China	16.3	19.5	19.5
India	7.4	7.0	8.2
Pakistan	6.1	6.8	6.6
Turkey	2.4	2.5	3.0
Australia	1.0	1.3	1.2
Total	70.4	80.5	84.3

[1]Includes Middle East.
Source: USDA, Foreign Agricultural Service, December 1988

that would immediately freeze support for cereals, rice, sugar, fats and oils, dairy products, beef, and veal at 1984 levels and then reduce support by a specific percentage in 1990. Many analysts considered the EC approach to be tantamount to accepting fixed-market shares, for long an EC objective in past negotiations that the U.S. consistently had rejected.

The U.S. had indicated a willingness to negotiate short-term measures in response to an earlier attempt by the Cairns Group of nonsubsidizing exporters to bridge the gap between the U.S. and EC positions. However, the U.S. then had also insisted upon agreement on the character of long-term reform as a precondition for such negotiations. The talks were extended one day, but neither side would move from its basic position, and the review was suspended.

Growth Hormones. The EC and the U.S. at year's end appeared to be drifting into a major trade war over a dispute that initially involved perhaps 2% of the roughly $11 billion in annual agricultural trade in 1986 between the two regions. The EC on Jan. 1, 1989, banned the importation of beef and veal from cattle that had been administered hormones to promote growth.

The ban was based on the prior use of hormonal substances rather than on a level of hormone residue, which the U.S. had been willing to guarantee. It had been postponed for a year following U.S. protests backed up by a presidential proclamation that would have imposed retaliatory restrictions on certain agricultural imports from the EC. A new proclamation, announced on December 27, applied a 100% tariff on boneless beef, pork hams and shoulders, tomato sauce, instant coffee, low-alcohol beverages, fruit juices, and certain pet food products. Both sides said that they would continue to retaliate against actions taken by the other. The EC said that it intended to select countermeasures from a list of products that included fruit juice, dried fruit, nuts, honey, and canned sweet corn.

The U.S., citing the FAO Codex Alimentarius and findings of the U.S. Food and Drug Administration, claimed that the ban was an unfair nontariff barrier and that the EC had no scientific evidence that the particular hormones used by U.S. farmers represented health hazards. The EC did not argue the scientific merits of its action. Instead, it asserted the right of EC governments to adopt nondiscriminatory measures based on health considerations. In a conciliatory move the EC exempted pet food from its ban, while the U.S. dropped sausage casings from its list.

The domestic production of beef and veal using growth hormones became illegal in the EC in January 1988 following several cases involving the discovery of high levels

of hormone residues in domestically produced beef. Public concern was intensified during the year by scandals in several EC countries revealing the use of hormones in defiance of the ban, including those, ironically, that were effectively banned in the U.S. U.S. officials suggested that failure of the EC to control their use could provide legal justification for the U.S. to bar EC meat exports to the U.S. worth $450 million annually.

Canadian-U.S. Trade Agreement. Canadian Prime Minister Brian Mulroney made approval of the Canadian-U.S. free-trade agreement (FTA), initialed in October 1987, the central issue in a general parliamentary election in November 1988 that returned his party to power with a substantial majority. On December 30 Parliament completed ratification of the FTA, which had been approved by the U.S. Congress in September, and it was to become effective the first day of 1989.

In agricultural trade between the two countries, the FTA called for a ten-year phasing out of all tariffs; banned direct export subsidies; pledged no new quantitative restrictions on the grain trade as long as domestic grain supports were not raised; eliminated several, but not all, nontariff barriers; exempted each country from the other's meat import quotas; ended certain Canadian transportation subsidies for farm products; and created a binational panel to hear appeals concerning decisions made under each country's countervailing-duty and antidumping laws in cases such as those brought in recent years by U.S. hog producers and Canadian corn growers. Trade in agricultural commodities between the two countries totaled about $5 billion annually.

Food Aid. The drought contributed to a major reduction in the supply of grain available for food aid in 1988–89. It both sharply reduced grain surpluses in the U.S. that in recent years had served as an inducement for providing larger quantities of aid and made aid more expensive by pushing grain prices higher. In November the U.S. considered it necessary to authorize the release of up to 1.5 million tons of wheat from its Food Security Wheat Reserve to ensure the continued flow of food aid in fiscal 1989. The four million-ton reserve was designed to guarantee U.S. food-aid commitments and meet emergency requirements when time did not permit seeking congressional authorization. Fewer dairy products were available as a result of changes in policies in the EC and the U.S. that reduced dairy surpluses there.

Total pledges, as of the end of September, by 56 donors to the regular resources of the World Food Program (WFP) for the 1989–90 biennium equaled about $343 million, 25% of the agreed-upon target of $1.4 billion. Pledges amounting to $1,214,000,000 (76% commodities and 24% cash), 87% of the target, had been made by 80 donors for the 1987–88 biennium. As of the same date, pledges to the WFP's International Emergency Food Reserve in 1988 equaled 328,310 tons of cereals and 62,914 tons of other foods. Contributions for all of 1987 totaled 636,293 tons of cereals, 42% of which was donated specifically for Afghan refugees, and 60,030 tons of other foods.

The Food Aid Committee of the Wheat Trade Convention (WTC) under the International Wheat Agreement agreed to extend to June 30, 1991, the Food Aid Convention (FAC), due to expire in June 1989, thus coinciding with the expiration of the WTC. The FAC committed food-aid donors to providing a minimum of 7.6 million tons of cereals annually.   (RICHARD M. KENNEDY)

See also Gardening.
This article updates the *Macropædia* article The History of AGRICULTURE.

Table X. Shipments of Food Aid in Cereals

In 000 metric ton grain equivalent

Region and country	Average 1983–84, 1985–86	1986–87	1987–88[1]	1988–89[1]
Australia	424	368	330	330
Canada	992	1,240	1,100	900
EC	2,012	1,859	2,479	2,000
By members	945	912	1,064	...
By organization	1,067	947	1,415	...
Japan	397	495	490	380
Saudi Arabia	66	108	...	...
Sweden	80	74	70	70
United States	6,622	7,861	7,700	5,300
Others[2]	510	400	...	...
Total	11,103	12,405	12,549	9,357
Percentage to low-income food-deficit countries[3]	87%	83%	80%	85%

[1]Partly estimated.
[2]Includes Argentina, Austria, China, Finland, India, Norway, OPEC Special Fund, Spain, Switzerland, Turkey, and World Food Program, but not necessarily for all years.
[3]Per capita incomes under U.S. $790 in 1984.
Source: FAO, *Food Outlook*, November 1988.

FISHERIES

Although the total world catch for 1988 was predicted to rise again to more than 11 million metric tons, many of the fishing booms anticipated during 1987 either failed to meet expectations or collapsed entirely. The orange roughy fishery, which Australian and New Zealand vessel owners had entered into with such fervour, turned sour for at least one vessel owner when stocks were found to be at a low level, confirming marine scientists' revised stock assessments. All but three of a large fleet of scallopers, purpose-built or converted for Norwegian owners during 1986–87, lay tied up or bankrupt, largely because of problems involved in marketing the product in the U.S. One or two British fishing companies that entered the new Falkland Islands fisheries experienced severe problems, which onlookers attributed to lack of knowledge of the fishery: how to catch and, more important, how to process product to meet market requirements. One newly formed Scottish company went out of business, leaving behind debts amounting to several millions of pounds sterling for which, it was understood, the Falkland Islands government would take responsibility.

Japan also had its share of problems as far as catching was concerned when its overseas trawling fleet was effectively barred from operating in U.S. waters by being given a zero quota for all fish species in the U.S. 200-mi exclusive economic zone (EEZ). The principal target species for these vessels was Alaska pollack, used for the production of surimi (processed minced fish). Demand for surimi seemed to lose momentum in most markets except the U.S., where, as a result of the "americanization program," it was reported to be firm. Building and conversion of vessels designed for surimi, Alaska pollack fillet, and groundfish fillet production continued in the U.S. The North Pacific factory trawler fleet was increased to just over 40 ships by the addition of 4 new vessels, and 8 others were under construction. Although the surimi market in Europe experienced a downturn, Atli P. Dam, prime minister of the Faeroe Islands, was reported as saying that, "despite limited catch opportunities for blue whiting and the failure of one market, the home government is now directly involved in attempts to get definitive answers about the possibilities for using blue whiting products for food for fillets, minced fish, and surimi."

Demand for prawns, especially the cold-water species, continued unabated, and Iceland was compelled to introduce a quota system in order to prevent overfishing. The demand for whitefish species remained strong, although Iceland faced intense competition from Canada for the massive U.S. market for whitefish products. Canadian products, which in earlier years gained a reputation for inferior quality, had improved considerably, mainly as a result of better onboard handling and processing techniques and—more fundamentally—recognition of the need to enhance the level of the product and thus attract export markets.

Many traditional fishing nations complained during the year of limited fishing opportunities, caused by rigid implementation of fishing quotas, while the North Atlantic Fisheries Organization called for a reduction of fishing effort in order to conserve stocks. The reduced fishing opportunities of the past few years might be held responsible for the shipowners' move toward onboard processing. This, in turn, created difficulties for some shore-based processors who had to consider expanding their production range to include "added-value" products and ready-to-serve meals. Meanwhile, more fishing companies had been compelled to investigate other ways of keeping their vessels at sea, either by exploiting nontraditional species, especially those

A French fisherman holds a cod caught in waters off Newfoundland and several French islands. A French fishing crew was jailed briefly in a dispute between France and Canada over the right to fish in these waters, claimed by both governments.
RAY FENNELLY

whose stocks were not under pressure, or by taking up joint-venture or high-seas fishing opportunities (the latter being conducted in waters lying outside any national EEZ). One of Poland's biggest fishing companies, Gryf Deep-Sea Fishing Enterprise, which caught 202,000 tons of fish in 1987, had already begun to rebuild many of its vessels' fish-processing plants and planned to commence experiments with new fishing techniques in open waters.

Instructions to European Communities (EC) member states to reduce fishing capacity were mostly ignored, and EC-funded new-building and repair grants were drastically reduced or withdrawn. The effect of this action had yet to be felt in most European yards, since order books had been at a high level, and there was sufficient work in hand to allow most yards to complete the year without problems. Scottish yards were among the first to complain of hard times, and order books there were reported to be very low. Spanish orders for large freezer trawlers for the Falkland Islands fisheries tailed off, owing to the strict implementation of a fishing license system that limited the number of fishing opportunities around the Falklands and stabilized the fisheries. Instead, Spanish yards received a spate of orders for squid trawlers for operation in Moroccan waters.

Ironically, Norway, which continued to encourage foreigners to build at Norwegian yards, had failed to offer similar incentives to Norwegian owners. For the first time, orders for up to six new ships for Norwegian owners were placed in Spain. Nonetheless, Norway continued to enjoy a boom in construction for foreign owners, and by the end of the year one yard was scheduled to deliver two 55-m (180-ft)-overall-length freezer stern trawlers to French owners, the first fishing vessels ever built in Norway for France. Work undertaken in Norwegian yards to convert U.S. supply boats for fishing duties for U.S. owners was halted after U.S. yards complained to their government that a loophole in U.S. legislation enabled conversions to be carried out abroad, thus depriving them of valuable work. The loophole was closed during the summer, and Norway delivered its last conversion for U.S. owners.

During the year a new generation of fishing "giants" emerged—built for countries such as Ireland, West Germany, and The Netherlands—each of which cost over £10 million. For the time being, at least, these ships were dependent on exploiting nonpressure stocks of pelagic and semipelagic species such as mackerel, horse mackerel, and herring, but these species commanded low prices and were often consigned to fish-meal reduction plants. This raised questions about the long-term availability of these nonpressure stocks and the economic viability of the vessels. The Finnish shipyard Rauma Repola delivered to the U.S.S.R. the first two of a series of three 179.2-m (587.8-ft) fish factory ships, designed to act as mother ships to Soviet catcher vessels. These vessels were extensively equipped to produce canned, frozen, and ready-to-sell fish products. Each was fitted with more than 2.5 km (1.5 mi) of conveyors. At the other end of the scale, the first so-called micro-trawler designs were being made available by naval architects to owners wishing to beat the 10-m registered rule (this would be a vessel whose length between the foreside of the rudder stock and the forepart of the bow measured under 10 m [32.8-ft]) and thus evade the fishing quota restrictions imposed by EC and national legislation.

These could well be early signs of a new era in which fishing vessels would fall mainly into two categories: smaller, multipurpose coastal vessels of less than 12 m (39 ft) overall length, which would probably remain in the hands of individual skipper-owners or smaller-sized companies, and the larger, deep-sea types, which could operate worldwide, often in joint venture fishing activities, and which would be owned by larger national companies or even multinational conglomerates. Several large catcher/producer companies had already confirmed the likelihood of such a trend, since smaller and medium-sized companies tended not to have the financial resources necessary to sustain the enormous costs involved in operating fleets of large vessels in distant waters. Fewer still could afford to conduct trial fishing activities, with a view to opening up new fisheries or markets for non- or underutilized species. Those that could generally had their own brand labels and marketing, sales, and distribution networks.

While most technologically advanced fishing nations were complaining about their lot, others, notably in Africa and the Indian subcontinent, were reassessing the viability of their marine and freshwater fisheries and were introducing development plans, often including the introduction or further development of aquaculture for the production of high-value species such as shrimp. Infrastructural problems were also being studied, especially with regard to preservation and transportation of the product to urban areas, as well as to potentially lucrative export markets.

(VIVIANNE L. AERS)

This article updates the *Macropædia* article Commercial FISHING AND MARINE PRODUCTS.

FOOD PROCESSING

The consumer's appetite for novelties continued unabated, leading to a flood of new product launches by food companies in developed countries. In the U.K.—not highly innovative in comparison with the U.S. and some other European countries—introductions of brand name foods and drinks more than doubled over the previous year. Food industries in prosperous countries maintained the growth in production and profitability that began in 1981. The year was also a good one for the world's food machinery makers, who made particularly satisfactory sales in the U.S., West Germany, and France. China emerged as a significant buyer from Western companies. By contrast, problems in the Eastern bloc multiplied. *Pravda* reported widespread food shortages in the U.S.S.R.

Industry Structure and Trends. In the European Communities (EC), 1992 took on increasing significance as the date when tariff barriers between member states would be abolished and a single market throughout the Community created. The implications for Europe's fragmented food industry were profound, and the number of mergers and consolidations rose sharply as companies began to jockey for position in the expanded market. Belated measures taken the previous year to halt the growth of surplus stocks, the EC's notorious "food mountains," began to take effect. This was especially evident in the dairy sector, where production of butter and skim milk powder fell markedly, leading to fears of shortages.

It was paradoxical that, at a time when health consciousness among consumers had reached new peaks, a record number of food poisoning incidents worldwide were reported. In the U.K. in 1987 there were 30,000 reported incidents, 5,000 more than in 1986. In the U.S. between two million and four million people were infected annually with food-borne pathogens. Considerable publicity was given to an outbreak of listeriosis involving Swiss cheese, which temporarily caused strained trade relations between Switzerland and France.

New Products and Ingredients. Quorn, a fungal protein being made in the U.K. jointly by Ranks Hovis McDougall and ICI, appeared in the shops as a simulated meat ingredient in savory products. NutraSweet Co. of the U.S., originator of the artificial sweetener aspartame, which had revolutionized the low-calorie food and drink

Table XI. World Fisheries, 1986¹
In 000 metric tons

Country	Catch		Trade	
	Total	Inland	Imports	Exports
Japan	11,966.8	198.7	1,798.3	771.3
U.S.S.R.	11,260.0	926.9	537.5	824.0
China	8,000.1	3,363.5	201.2	186.3
Peru	5,609.6	28.2	0.7	750.2
Chile	5,571.6	1.0	0.1	1,290.8
United States	4,943.2	72.0	1,447.4	1,765.9
South Korea	3,102.5	56.9	134.9	529.4
India	2,925.3	1,204.8	—	84.1
Indonesia	2,521.2	607.0	56.0	91.0
Thailand	2,119.0	168.0	266.3	591.2
Philippines	1,916.3	538.5	69.3	61.2
Norway	1,898.4	0.4	128.8	625.6
Denmark	1,871.3	24.2	360.0	758.4
North Korea	1,700.0	100.0	—	23.3
Iceland	1,657.1	0.7	0.8	706.4
Canada	1,466.6	45.0	133.1	571.8
Mexico	1,303.7	93.0	13.5	62.3
Spain	1,303.5	27.2	330.6	218.8
Ecuador	1,019.3	0.9	—	268.8
France	850.0	29.6	608.7	224.7
Brazil	847.9	215.0	101.3	49.8
United Kingdom	847.8	13.2	820.3	349.9
Vietnam	800.0	230.0	—	25.0
Bangladesh	794.0	586.5	—	21.8
Poland	645.2	29.4	192.3	114.8
Burma	643.8	146.8	—	7.5
South Africa	628.7	0.8	116.1	46.9
Malaysia	616.3	9.2	238.3	182.9
Morocco	595.9	1.3	1.3	168.0
Turkey	579.8	40.3	0.5	22.5
Italy	547.6	43.9	546.6	107.4
The Netherlands	454.8	4.3	476.3	559.9
Argentina	420.3	8.5	7.9	162.8
Pakistan	414.9	83.2	0.1	36.3
Portugal	389.6	...	152.9	71.5
Faeroe Islands	353.7	—	3.4	127.4
New Zealand	339.6	...	8.1	158.2
Tanzania	309.9	265.8	0.1	0.3
Ghana	309.2	40.0	18.0	24.1
Venezuela	283.6	16.0	0.1	42.7
Romania	271.1	65.8	37.2	—
Nigeria	268.5	107.0	190.0	0.7
Senegal	255.4	15.0	24.6	94.0
Cuba	244.6	16.1	48.0	36.8
Other	6,589.1	1,687.2	4,489.4	1,742.3
World	91,456.8	11,111.8	13,560.0	14,559.0

¹Excludes whaling.
Source: United Nations Food and Agriculture Organization, *Yearbook of Fishery Statistics*, vol. 62 and 63.

market, launched Simplesse, a fat substitute made from egg and milk proteins which closely mimics the texture and mouthfeel of fat. Creamy Fish Protein (CFP), a paste made by treating fish flesh with enzymes, was launched in Japan by Asahi Denko. Unlike the processed minced fish product surimi, it contains no additives or preservatives and retains the original mineral content, which is lost in the surimi process. The first application of CFP was in combination with a soybean ingredient in a fabricated fish steak developed for the Japanese school lunch program.

New ingredients to aid the processor included Superset, a modified starch from National Starch of the U.S. which reduces the manufacturing time of jelly confectionery by 80%; Liquisweet, a natural sweetener produced from apples, being made by Premier Natural Foods of the U.K.; and Liquid Pure Malt, a caramel replacer made from roasted malt by Pure Malt Products Ltd. of the U.K. The first petition to be accepted for a food additive made by a fermentation process using a genetically engineered microorganism was filed with the U.S. Food and Drug Administration (FDA). It concerned Pfizer's fermentation-produced enzyme chymosin, claimed to be identical to natural chymosin, the active component of calf rennet used in cheese making.

Technology. Progress in the application of irradiation preservation was slowed by consumer resistance, restrictive legislation, and high cost. Fewer than 20 countries applied the technology on a commercial scale. The least controversial use was the sterilization of packaging materials for aseptically processed products. APV of the U.K. made available the first production-sized plants utilizing its ohmic heating technique for sterilizing food, which involves passing an electric current through the food; the electrical resistance of the food generates the necessary heat. The most promising application was in the treatment of large quantities of fruit, which otherwise could not be processed in bulk; fruit so treated could be kept for 12 months under ordinary conditions.

Packaging. New developments were mainly in the field of plastics, but canning continued to stage a modest comeback in certain sectors, notably beer and soft drinks. Metal Box of the U.K. introduced the Bi-Can, a two-compartment aerosol can for liquids and pastes. The product is contained in an inner plastic bag; the propellant is introduced through the base of the can and is never in contact with the product. A self-cooling can was tested in Japan, complementing the self-heating can introduced some years earlier. Like the latter, it has inner and outer containers, with a liquid and a solid in separate compartments between the two. To activate cooling, the base is pressed, causing the two chemical components to mix. The contents are chilled in two to three minutes.

The use of modified atmosphere packs for fresh meat, fish, vegetables, bakery goods, and pasta increased dramatically. After being loaded with product, the packs are evacuated and flushed with an inert gas such as nitrogen or carbon dioxide before being sealed, giving the product extra shelf life. The displacement of glass by polyethylene terephthalate (PET) accelerated. Sauces, salad dressings, and mincemeat were among products that moved out of glass into PET jars.

Companies. The westernization of China's culture and economy proceeded during the year as rapidly as a shortage of technological expertise and foreign exchange would allow. The seventh Coca-Cola factory there went into production in Beijing (Peking). Also in Beijing, Kentucky Fried Chicken Corp., in partnership with the local corporations governing commerce and tourism, opened what was said

Simplesse, developed by NutraSweet Co., is a fat substitute that is low in calories and has no cholesterol.
STEVE LEONARD

to be the world's largest fast-food restaurant, seating 500 customers and offering takeout service from a window on the street.

As EC market liberalization approached, Europe was the scene of much activity involving company mergers and expansions. The Swiss Nestlé group, the world's largest food company, acquired a major U.K. confectionery company, Rowntrees of York, for $4.5 billion. The U.K.'s largest confectionery company, Cadbury Schweppes, fearful of a takeover by General Cinema of the U.S., sold its three U.S. factories to Hershey Foods of the U.S. and licensed its brands to that company in an effort to make itself less attractive to the potential predator. BSN, a leading French food group, bought the long-established U.K. companies HP Foods and Lea & Perrins from Hanson Trust.

Co-operative Agricole de Céréales, a cooperative of 3,000 French farmers, joined forces with the food machinery company Alfa-Laval of Sweden to build one of the world's largest food-research centres at Vers-chez-les-Blanc in Switzerland. Arthur Guinness, Ireland's biggest brewer, invested $200 million in its 24-ha (60-ac) site in Dublin, which was acquired in 1760 for a yearly rent of $76 on a 10,000-year lease. Grand Metropolitan, a U.K. hotel and catering group, bought Pillsbury Co. of the U.S. for $5.7 billion. In the U.S., Kraft Inc. was sold to Philip Morris for $13.5 billion and RJR Nabisco, the nation's 19th largest industrial company, went to the buyout firm of Kohlberg, Kravis, Roberts & Co. for $24,880,000,000.

Legislation. The EC Council of Ministers agreed on food law proposals paving the way toward the liberalization of the internal food market planned for 1992. One related to food additives, another to materials that come into contact with food; two proposals on flavourings were also adopted. However, a European Court of Justice ruling in favour of Denmark's ban on nonreturnable beverage containers was judged bad for prospects of a unified market, although environmentalists were jubilant. New EC laws set maximum permissible levels for 61 pesticides in cereals, meat, dairy products, and a range of fruits and vegetables.

The Canton Court of Zürich, Switz., declared invalid NutraSweet Co.'s Swiss patent on an artificial sweetener blend. The decision was of crucial importance to DSM of The Netherlands and Tosoh Corp. of Japan, which had jointly built a factory in The Netherlands to manufacture

aspartame sweetener and were now free to exploit in Europe NutraSweet's original patents, which had expired in Europe although not in the U.S. France, the last major country to do so, finally approved aspartame.

The FDA cleared Sunette artificial sweetener, manufactured by Hoechst of West Germany, and permitted a higher allowable daily intake than that set in 1983 by a joint Food and Agriculture Organization-World Health Organization expert committee. Sunette, which was already approved in 20 countries including the EC, could now enter the world's largest single market for sweeteners.

The U.K. government's Food Advisory Committee called for a clampdown on the use of the word natural on food labels, claiming that consumers were frequently misled by current practices in labeling and advertising.

(ANTHONY WOOLLEN)

See also Environment; Health and Disease; Industrial Review: Beverages; Textiles; Tobacco.

This article updates the Macropædia article FOOD PROCESSING.

Anthropology

In the 25 years since it was first proposed, the "molecular clock" has become an important tool for interpreting the fossil record. The clock is based on the assumption that mutations in the nuclear DNA occur at a constant rate. (Nuclear DNA is that which is found in the nucleus of a cell as a component of the chromosomes.) The differences in the genetic characteristics of living species are thus proportional to the time since those species diverged from one another. Recently this molecular dating technique was applied to mitochondrial DNA (mtDNA) of individuals from different geographic human populations. Unlike nuclear DNA, the resulting branching diagram represented divergences exclusively in the female lineage (since only mothers contribute their mtDNA to their offspring). The African mtDNA was most diverse and therefore assumed to be the oldest. When the differences were converted to years, it was shown that the ancestral African "Eve" existed about 200,000 years ago. The first non-African populations diverged 90,000 to 180,000 years ago.

There are, however, problems with molecular dating. Mutation rates are based on estimates (for mtDNA it is up to ten times faster than for nuclear DNA), and it is assumed that the rate is constant (although now there is evidence that the clock runs more slowly in humans than in apes and monkeys). Moreover, when tracing back to an oldest population, it is impossible to determine whether it is a true original population. Also one can never be completely sure that the part of the genome (the genetic makeup of a species) that has been measured has not been, or is not being, affected by processes that affect the frequencies and characteristics of the genes. Other factors that can perturb the clock include the introduction of genes from other species via a virus and a number of processes working within the genome itself. In any case, while it is premature to conclude that modern humans originated approximately 200,000 years ago from an African population, it is intriguing that recent interpretation of the fossil record does not rule out that possibility.

There is general acceptance of fossil evidence that fully modern humans were in existence at least 100,000 years ago and that at least one of those populations was African. The 30,000-year-old Cro-Magnon people are now recognized as late arrivals in eastern Europe, long after modern Homo sapiens (now often referred to as Homo sapiens sapiens) had evolved in eastern and southern Africa. The

dating of these African fossils is in the range of 80,000–100,000 years ago. Moreover, a recent redating of the Qafzeh cave material in Israel places the structurally modern skulls found there in about the same time range.

These discoveries lead to interesting questions about the origin and dispersal of modern humans. Why did it take them some 50,000 years or more to reach Europe? And, if they existed simultaneously in the Middle East and sub-Saharan Africa, where was their point of origin? Or was there a point of origin? Until recently most paleoanthropologists supported the idea that H. sapiens evolved independently and more or less at the same time from the geographically widely dispersed Homo erectus populations. During the year this regional continuity model was being questioned. As an alternative, dispersal from one place of origin appeared to be a distinct possibility, and both the molecular and fossil evidence pointed to Africa as that place.

The question then arose as to the effect of the spread of H. sapiens sapiens on the Neanderthal people (Homo sapiens neanderthalensis), who were already living in Europe. Replacement seems to be the answer. While the incoming moderns might have incorporated the Mousterian tools of the Neanderthals into their culture (as was the case at Qafzeh), they did not necessarily incorporate their genes. Moreover, recent studies of Neanderthal anatomy reveal a creature biologically quite different from H. sapiens sapiens. The Neanderthals, it is suggested, were much stronger, less sexually differentiated, shorter lived, unable to make many of the sounds of human speech, and more mature at birth than were the forebears of modern humans. Moreover, in reexamining the cultural data, some paleolithic archaeologists suggested that, contrary to initial interpretations, Neanderthal burials do not show any signs of ritual; their tools do not show sophistication or diversity but show only reshaping through reuse; fire was used by them in only the most rudimentary ways; and there is no evidence that they stored food. This biologic and cultural demotion of the Neanderthals is consistent with evidence of the newly recognized greater antiquity of H. sapiens sapiens. While the two kinds of humans evidently coexisted for tens of thousands of years, it appears that wherever they came into actual contact, the Neanderthals were replaced by the modern form.

Some long-held views of Homo erectus were also being questioned. Was this hominid really unvarying in physical structure, both geographically throughout Africa and Eurasia and chronologically from its origin 1.6 million years ago until its more or less gradual disappearance 300,000 years ago? There is doubt on both counts. In fact, there is doubt that H. erectus ever existed in Europe. It appears to be an African and Asian form that, over an extensive period of time, shows substantial decreasing robustness as well as regional structural variations.

A recent new find from earlier in the fossil record, dated at 1.8 million years ago, has been designated OH62. Discovered at Olduvai Gorge in Tanzania in 1987, it is considered a Homo habilis, the first of that species to be found with the skull and limb bones in association. It was a very slight individual, about 0.9 m (3 ft) tall, with arms and legs of almost equal length. However, some anthropologists questioned the combination of a small, apelike body with a skull attributed to Homo. Critics suggested that perhaps OH62 is really an australopithecus of the less robust kind, Australopithecus africanus. This would be unusual for the Olduvai site, where only the robust form, A. boisei, has been found. Could its size therefore be attributed to sexual dimorphism within A. boisei? The fossil record once

again had provided more variability than could be accommodated by a simple linear descent model with only a few side branches. Certainly the dichotomy, apelike versus humanlike, is far too simplistic. Relatively large brains, some form of bipedalism, and even tool fabrication and use were characteristic of more than one species of hominid from the Pliocene and Pleistocene epochs.

There is now substantial evidence from the Swartkrans site in South Africa that the rugged form of australopithecus (*A. robustus*) made tools of both bone and stone. These tools are found in association with the skulls and now also with the hands and feet of this species. They are slight, gracile bones compared with the ruggedness of the face and jaws. According to some anthropologists, these hands were capable of the precision grip needed by a toolmaker, and the feet were those of a biped with an almost modern human gait. Because a small number of associated fragments of what is probably *H. erectus* are also found at Swartkrans, the possibility arises that it could have been the toolmaker. While that cannot be ruled out, there is little dispute that *A. robustus* is now known to have been physically capable of making and using tools.

In April 1987 a symposium was held to clarify the classification of the australopithecines since there are as many as six African species now attributed to that genus. The consensus phylogenetic scheme places *A. afarensis* near the common ancestry of all the later forms. One branch goes to *Homo* via *A. africanus,* and the other includes separate *A. robustus* and *A. boisei* lineages. The former is slightly older than the latter and is the first of these two lineages to become extinct. Both lineages derive from an *A. aethiopicus* group, which in turn comes from *A. afarensis.*

(HERMANN K. BLEIBTREU)

See also Archaeology.

This article updates the *Macropædia* article Human EVOLUTION.

Archaeology

Eastern Hemisphere. No particularly spectacular archaeological finds had been reported from the Old World as of late 1988. There continued to be acute concern over the destructive effect of pollution from factories, traffic, and tourism on ancient monuments. The situation around Cairo was particularly alarming, and in February a large chunk of the right shoulder of the Sphinx fell to the ground. It was estimated that on some days in the peak season there might be 10,000 tourists at Luxor. In the castle of the late Lord Carnarvon (who financed the excavation of the tomb of Tutankhamen in 1922), his grandson's butler discovered a cache of antiquities from the tomb. The Egyptian government wanted them back. The Italian government accused the Getty Museum of California of purchasing a large Greek statue reportedly taken illegally from the site of Morgantina in Sicily.

The number of new scientific procedures available for the recovery of information about the past continued to increase. One such technique yielded cautionary information during the year. Thanks to recent refinements in the method of radiocarbon age assaying, it had become possible to make remarkably sensitive and precise dating of very small samples. After much negotiation, the Vatican authorities agreed to submit three postage-stamp-sized samples of the cloth of the so-called Shroud of Turin. The shroud had for years been venerated as the burial cloth of Jesus, although the Roman Catholic Church had never accepted the identification as certain. The samples were assayed by three independent radiocarbon laboratories at the University of Arizona, the University of Oxford, and the Swiss Federal Institute of Technology. The tests showed that the cloth dates to between AD 1260 and 1390.

Pleistocene Prehistory. Perhaps the most interesting new information dealing with humankind in the Pleistocene was more of a paleontological than an archaeological nature, although chipped stone tools were involved. Fossil bones from the cave of Qafzeh, in Israel, were dated by the thermoluminescence technique to *c.* 92,000 years ago. The bones had already been identified as of essentially modern *Homo sapiens* type, heretofore not known to be earlier than *c.* 40,000 years ago beyond South Africa, and of somewhat uncertain date there. The Qafzeh evidence appeared to be firm and raised the question of where the *H. sapiens* species may have first developed.

A new excavation, undertaken jointly by Istanbul University and the University of California at Berkeley at the Yarimburgaz cave, just west of Istanbul, yielded typologically very early stone tools and many fossil animal bones. The geomorphologic estimate of the age of the pertinent strata was about 200,000 years ago. There was a reassessment of the great quantity of horse bones at the classic site of Solutré in France. It had been assumed that the horses had been stampeded over the cliff at the site, but the reassessment suggested careful butchery. In Australia stone tool and human remains, dating to *c.* 25,000 years ago, were taken as supporting evidence for the early age of the Lake Mungo skull, said to have a minimum age of at least 36,000 years.

Middle East. In Egypt the Royal Ontario Museum began work, after 100 years, at Sir Flinders Petrie's old site of Lahun, in al-Fayyum. In Jordan substantial clearances were made by the University of Chicago's Oriental Institute adjacent to the port area of al-'Aqabah, an important centre of medieval Arab overseas trade. Work continued at the impressive early village site of 'Ain Ghazal, near Amman. Reports from Israel included a description of work at the large Philistine site of Ekron, southwest of Jerusalem, where evidence of a large industrial complex was recovered. Despite the unsettled condition in the country, the *Newsletter* of the American Schools of Oriental Research listed 14 different expeditions willing to accept paying volunteers as workers. Local labourers in Israel were both difficult to find and costly, so paying volunteers were welcome.

No archaeological activity was reported from Lebanon, but work did proceed in Syria, especially in the northeast beyond the Euphrates River and usually in the context of salvage recovery before new dams were completed. The work of a joint University of Chicago and University of Melbourne, Australia, team adjacent to the dam site of al-Qitar, on the Euphrates, had to be terminated because of new dam construction, but a survey for a new site was undertaken upstream. Farther to the northeast, away from the salvage region, a Yale University expedition, at the large, many-layered mound of Tall Laylan, recovered an important archive of royal correspondence on cuneiform tablets. The excavator, Harvey Weiss, joined other scholars in entertaining the proposition that not everything involved in the early unfolding of literate urban civilization necessarily took place in southern Mesopotamia.

In Iraq there was salvage activity not only along the Tigris River north of the Eski Mosul dam but also at the sites of Nippur and Abu Salabikh, south of Baghdad. Both 3rd millennium BC and Parthian strata were cleared at Nippur, and Uruk levels at Abu Salabikh. In the north, interesting early village materials (*c.* 8000 BC) were recovered from small mounds in the salvage region by Japanese, Pol-

ish, and Scottish expeditions. Both foreign and domestic archaeologists were active in Turkey. New investigations were resumed at the site of Troy by a Tübingen (West Germany) University team and at Gordion by the University of Pennsylvania, and further attention was being given to the preclassical strata at Sardis. The joint Turkish-West German-U.S. excavations on the important early village site of Cayonu continued, and Metin Ozbek, the physical anthropologist of Hacettepe University, recovered valuable information on the burial habits and health of the Cayonu people from the skeletal remains. Recovery of the cargo of a sunken merchant ship at Ulu Burun on the southwestern coast of Turkey continued to yield a remarkable collection of artifacts, indicating the actual extent of overseas trade *c.* 1400 BC.

Later Prehistoric Europe. Geoarchaeological investigations in the Argive plain in Greece showed that the late Pleistocene-early Holocene positions of the coastal meadows, lakes, and the Aegean shoreline lay well inland of those of today. Also in Euboea, Greece, the Skotini cave yielded late prehistoric materials of *c.* 5300–3300 BC. On the island of Malta clearances of the ritual monuments of the so-called Temple Period (*c.* 3200–2500 BC) and of associated domestic remains were made. In the southeastern Gatas region of Spain, well known for its earlier rock art, new attention was being given to Copper and Bronze Age settlements.

ROBERTO SURO/THE NEW YORK TIMES

A worker digs at an ancient Roman wall uncovered on the Palatine Hill in Italy. The wall's discovery revealed that Rome was already a major city by the 7th or 6th century BC, a finding that called for a reassessment of early Roman history.

There was an informative report on the clearance of a dolmen at Haute-Suane, France, with a description of its contents. In Britain (as well as other Western European countries) increasing attention was being given to "wetland archaeology." Areas of fens, marshlands, and damp peat bogs had always been good contexts for the survival of ancient woodworking, basketry, and other organic materials. A fine example of such yields came from excavations at the Bronze Age site of Flag Fen, near Peterborough. In southwestern Wales new exposures were being made on an Iron Age hill fort and at the impressive Crickley Hill Fort in the Cotswolds.

The Greco-Roman World. Further clearances were made at the Sanctuary of Poseidon at Isthmia in Greece, aided by geophysical surface prospecting. Work was begun on the closed harbour of the Classical and Hellenistic town of Phalasarna in Crete. In Italy significant exposures were made on harbour installations at the Roman port of Cosa, where the remains of a winery, an amphora factory, and a water-distribution system were recovered. In Rome itself, excavations on the slope of the Palatine Hill revealed a wall that, its discoverers claimed, showed that Rome was already a dynamic city in the 7th to 6th century BC. Restoration of the mural paintings in the House of Menander in Pompei was proceeding well. In Tunisia excavations at Carthage continued around the early 5th-century AD city wall and Roman circus, both threatened by modern building activity.

East Asia and Africa. Little detailed information had been published concerning the year's archaeological activities in the Far East. It was clear that China was actively interested in exposing and caring for its more spectacular antiquities as tourist attractions. There was a report from Zaire on the investigations of Belgian ethnoarchaeologists in simulating the process of iron smelting, adjacent to furnace remains of *c.* 2,500 years ago.

(ROBERT J. BRAIDWOOD)

Western Hemisphere. The year 1988 was notable both for important new discoveries and for advances in the areas of applied technology and legal protection of cultural resources. In Peru controlled archaeological excavation revealed a totally undisturbed gold-filled royal tomb that was described as being nearly as rich as that of King Tut, and in Mexico archaeologists announced the discovery of what might be a new Mayan culture. Advances in applied technology permitted archaeologists to trace clues in international trade contacts as well as genetic relationships between preserved human remains. In the area of legislation and new government guidelines, the U.S. Forest Service announced a new and enlightened policy toward the treatment of Native American remains.

In Mexico and Peru major discoveries were disclosed after being kept secret for several years out of fear that the locations would be attacked by looters. From a mangrove swamp on the eastern Gulf coast of Veracruz, Fernando Winfield Capitaine, director of the Jalapa Museum, announced the discovery of what might be an ancient Mexican culture that could help define the origins of the Maya civilization. Discovered in 1986 and kept secret until May 1988, the evidence was described by scientists as a four-ton granite stele, or carved stone slab, and a 48-cm (19-in) clay figurine of a priest covered with the skin of a sacrificial victim in a previously unrecognized style. The two-metre (seven-foot)-tall stele was decorated with some numbers similar to Maya, but also with glyphs or word symbols in a previously unknown style. However, because the bar and dot numbers were in the Maya format, two dates could be read from the otherwise undecipherable inscriptions: AD

May 22, 143, and July 13, 156. These dates placed the new finds some 500 to 1,000 years after the time of the Olmec civilization and some 300 years before the rise of the Maya around AD 400. Because of the date, and because the finds came from an area 1,125 km (700 mi) northwest of the Maya heartland in the Yucatán Peninsula, the discoveries held the promise of bridging the gap between these two ancient cultures and might help to explain the origins of the enigmatic Maya civilization.

The discovery of the intact 1,700-year-old tomb in Peru, described as that of a "Peruvian King Tut," read like a movie script starring the dashing Hollywood archaeologist Indiana Jones. The sudden appearance in the Lima antiquities market of numerous exquisitely crafted gold and silver artifacts thought to have come from a recently looted tomb somewhere on the north coast of Peru, coupled with the diligent investigation by Peruvian officials aided by a tip from a looter cut out of the profits, led to a band of grave robbers who had been looting a heavily eroded and previously plundered mound and temple complex in the small Peruvian coastal village of Sipán, situated in the heartland of the pre-Inca coastal Moche culture (AD 100–700). A shoot-out following a predawn raid by Peruvian police left one of the looters dead. Walter Alva, director of the Bruning Archaeological Museum, Lambayeque, Peru, working with armed guards protecting both the site and the archaeologists and with support from the Peruvian government and the National Geographic Society, launched the controlled scientific excavation of what was being called the richest find of gold, silver, and other elaborate artifacts to be scientifically documented in the New World.

The excavation exposed an untouched 4.5 × 4.5-m (15 × 15-ft) chamber some 3.7 m (12 ft) down from the tip of the pyramid, within an adobe platform mound known locally as Huaca Rajada, which contained the undisturbed remains of a gold-covered "warrior priest" of the Moche, in addition to seven bodies (four women, two men, and a guard) thought to represent members of his family and servants, as well as a pet dog. Radiocarbon dated to AD 300, the burial had apparently been protected in antiquity by a guard who was killed and buried at the mouth of the chamber and who had his feet cut off, presumably to keep him at his post. Found with the bodies were over a thousand ceramic vessels—some containing food and drink for the use of the deceased in the afterworld—representing the largest cache of unlooted ceramic vessels ever found from the coast of Peru. Identified as a man about 1.65 m (5 ft 6 in) tall and in his early 30s, the warrior priest was found wrapped in 13 layers of cloth and shrouds, many decorated with gold objects, inside the first hardwood coffin documented in the New World. Covering the body were a gold mask, a gold knife, two necklaces of gold and silver peanuts, gold bells, and a gold shield weighing 900 g (2 lb).

In Haiti, Kathleen A. Deagan of the Florida State Museum used radioactive trace element analysis to show that 15th-century pig bones excavated from the northern coast of Haiti came from the Sevilla region of Spain, helping to demonstrate that the site was probably that of La Natividad, Columbus's long-lost first settlement in the New World. The colony was set up by Columbus in December 1492 after one of his ships, the *Santa Maria,* ran aground. Columbus instructed the stranded crewmen to build a fort and trade with the Indians until he returned, but he never came, and the colony members all died. The presence of strontium isotopes that matched samples from Spain helped to fingerprint the origin of the excavated colonial-era pig remains. In addition, the pig bones were found with those of a European rat not native to the New World,

Archaeologists in Peru examine artifacts from a 1,500-year-old tomb of the Moche civilization. The tomb was discovered intact and, like that of King Tut, contained one of the richest collections yet discovered of ancient artifacts.
AP/WIDE WORLD

together with colonial-era fragments of pottery. The projected large-scale excavation and study of the site promised to serve as a highlight of the forthcoming 500th anniversary of Columbus's voyage.

In 1984 archaeologists announced the discovery of hundreds of well-preserved human burials in a bog near Titusville, Fla., which also yielded the earliest evidence of weaving as well as well-preserved brain tissues. In 1988, after excavating and studying over 94 of the 8,000-year-old remains, a team of scientists announced some startling results. William H. Hauswirth of the University of Florida announced the identification of preserved DNA that held the promise of identifying kinship links between the buried individuals as well as possible genetic bonds with modern descendants of these ancient North Americans. In a related forensic study, David N. Finkle of the Florida State University team announced that 19% of the adult skeletons had broken bones suggesting a violent end.

William C. Noble and Jacqueline Crerar of McMaster University in Hamilton, Ont., announced evidence that added significantly to the scanty written record of Iroquois society and economy in the 17th century. Using clues that included traces of post molds suggesting pens or corrals, a preponderance of male deer bones, and a rise in the number of whelk shells being traded from the Chesapeake Bay area, the researchers pieced together a scenario of Iroquois-European relations that helped to clarify the Iroquois re-

sponse to European settlement. The new data suggest that they actively changed their settlement patterns and developed animal husbandry in the form of penned-in herds of deer, which were managed and selectively culled to maintain a well-stocked inventory of much-prized "chamois" deerskins; these, in turn, were traded with the Europeans for the whelks.

Within the U.S. the year was highlighted by changes in government policy toward the treatment of Native American burials. What had been considered primarily a Native American issue—the appropriate treatment and reburial of ancestral remains—was made more immediate to a broader domestic audience by the emotionally charged announcement of the return by Canada to the U.S., for honour guard reburial, of American dead from the War of 1812. For only the second time in its history, the Smithsonian Institution returned the human remains of Blackfoot Indians, which had been taken from a native burial ground in 1892 by a U.S. army surgeon, Z. T. Daniel. He had inadvertently helped the Blackfoot claim by leaving a letter that described in detail his efforts to evade dogs and tribal members at night as he stole the remains from the community burial ground for "scientific study." In another indication of the emerging federal perception that these human remains were indeed sacred to their Native American descendants, the U.S. Forest Service announced a major policy shift aimed at bringing its treatment of Native American remains more in line with that accorded to historic and Colonial Caucasian remains, such as the dead from the War of 1812. Henceforth the Forest Service would deal directly with Native American representatives when a burial ground was encountered, and whenever possible the remains would be left in place and protected from looters and development pressures. While the policy allowed for some scientific documentation, it also mandated that actions be reviewed and negotiated with Native American tribal representatives to develop a mutually acceptable program.   (JOEL W. GROSSMAN)

See also Anthropology.

Architecture

Britain's Prince Charles during the past year was once again one of the most stinging critics of modern architecture, and his remarks were, as always, widely reported and discussed. Speaking to an assembly of town planners in Britain late in 1987, he commented upon the new designs for the Paternoster Square site in London, adjacent to St. Paul's Cathedral. He concluded that architects had done more damage to London than did the German air force in World War II. He likened the St. Paul's precinct to "a basketball team standing shoulder to shoulder between you and the Mona Lisa."

The new designs for the site by Arup Associates were widely criticized for their increased density, required by the commercial pressures of the developers who wished to maximize rentable space. The conflict between developers, with their interest in financial return, and those who, like the prince, were concerned with amenity, conservation, and harmony between existing historic buildings and new buildings continued to rumble. One solution advocated by Prince Charles was a return to classical styles.

Certainly there was an active classical revivalist "school" in England, best represented by architect Quinlan Terry. His most significant monument to this style of architecture in Britain was the Howard Building at Downing College, Cambridge, completed in 1987, a structure that had as many vociferous promoters as it did detractors. Downing College was one of the most complete examples of early 19th-century Greek Revival architecture in England, the original building having been designed by William Wilkins (architect of the National Gallery in London). Terry was to provide, in a continuation of Wilkins's Greek Revival manner, a detached structure that would house a new lecture theatre and other facilities toward the west end of the college's dominant axis and next to an 1873 building by E. M. Barry. The building by Terry was, in fact, more Renaissance or Mannerist than neoclassical, with its Corinthian attached columns and pilasters on a high pedestal articulating the front and its Doric colonnade on the south facade. The whole, though contrived, was not without charm, and it stimulated much critical debate about the old classical architectural language.

Terry was also the architect for an even larger project, the new Richmond Riverside Development by the Thames River in southwest London. A commercial undertaking, it again excited controversy between those who claimed that it was merely a modern speculative development cloaked in classical facades and those who regarded Terry as one of the few architects of the 20th century able to use traditional classical forms in a fluent and correct manner.

The Richmond Riverside Development, which covered 1.4 ha (3.5 ac), had for many years been the subject of planning debates. Adjacent to the site were a number of important classical and Italianate buildings, all of which had to be respected in the new design. In the early 1980s the public voted in favour of the Terry scheme, rejecting a more conventional one, and certainly his design was unusual and harmonious, even if vulnerable to debate on "moral" issues of style. It provided more than 9,000 sq m (100,000 sq ft) of offices and more than 900 sq m (10,000 sq ft) of shops as well as some residential accommodations and automobile parking garages. The river frontage featured a formal garden with attractive traditional elements. All the facades were classical, but the sources ranged from the Greek and Roman to the Baroque, Palladian, and 18th-century English. One was even Venetian Gothic.

That architectural style could provoke reaction on a moral and ideological basis was clearly shown by the fiasco and controversy surrounding a new superstore in Warwick Road, West London. The Sainsbury's Homebase Store by architect Ian Pollard, a neo-Egyptian design slightly reminiscent of the manner of James Stirling but more like a stage set than a substantial building, was a pastiche of decoration, full of colour and wit. No sooner had the building been completed, however, than the client, expressing displeasure at the use of historical form and at the overall effect, required an almost immediate demolition. Apparently due to a failure of communication at the design stage between architect and client, one of the client's major objections was that the image of the store was at odds with the impression given by the architect's design.

A style that began as a legitimate and serious postmodernism in the hands of architects such as Michael Graves and Philip Johnson had by 1988 been debased by commercial speculators who reduced it to superficial pediments and arches that seemed to ornament every new shopping centre, warehouse, or gas station. Elements that could be intelligently and sensitively combined in the hands of a skilled architect could equally well be pasted onto a box by a developer. Consequently a polarization was occurring with serious classicists such as Terry on the one side and on the other a new younger group who were rejecting all forms of classical elements, once again, and returning to a "retro-modernism," a mode evidenced during the year by

an exhibition at the Museum of Modern Art in New York City called "Deconstructivist Architecture." This exhibition gathered the work of seven architects from Europe and the U.S. who designed in a jagged, angled mode more reminiscent of sculpture than building. This mode, described as analogous to dissonant electronic music, was described by Michael Graves as "slash and crash architecture."

One of the leading practitioners of this style was Frank O. Gehry, of Los Angeles, whose Aerospace Museum in that city, with its twisted facade and intersecting planes, typified the mode. Another good example was Gehry's Winton Guest House in Wayzata, Minn. The site occupied ten wooded acres; the existing main house dated from 1952 and was designed by Philip Johnson. Gehry built a 225-sq m (2,500-sq ft) two-bedroom guest house whose features were defined as a collection of separate sculptural elements; that is, each of the components was an individual room fragmented into a structural composition. For example, the living room, a skylit mass, had a high roof clad in black sheet metal. Other features were an unpainted metal tree-houselike sleeping loft, a plywood-clad garage/kitchen, and vaulted bedrooms shaped like fish and covered with pinkish limestone.

Cultural and Educational Buildings. The campus of Rice University, Houston, Texas, boasted buildings by many leading architects and reflected some of the leading ideas in architectural thought during the last ten years. Buildings by James Stirling-Michael Wilford & Associates and Cesar Pelli & Associates exemplified recent trends. Construction of the Shepherd School of Music, to be designed by Spanish architect Ricardo Bofill, was due to begin late in 1988. Bofill was best known for a dramatic large-scale housing project in Paris. The building at Rice was to cover 10,350 sq m (115,000 sq ft) on a prominent central campus site and would complement the original Italian Romanesque campus buildings of the early part of the 20th century.

Antoine Predock of Albuquerque, N.M., was selected to design the multifunctional C.L.A.B. Building at California State Polytechnic University, Pomona, following a limited competition. This structure would house the computer technology centre, with administrative and classroom facilities; the dominant triangular shape of the administrative tower was the distinguishing feature, setting apart the administrative area from the courtyard classroom building.

The Minneapolis (Minn.) Sculpture Garden, a joint project of the Walker Art Center and the Minneapolis Park and Recreation Board, opened in 1988 and would occupy a 2.8-ha (7-ac) site across from the Walker Art Center and the Guthrie Theatre complex. The site was donated and maintained by the city, but the exhibitions were to come from the Walker, which also commissioned several works of art for the project. The garden was designed by Edward Larrabee Barnes Associates with Peter Rothschild as landscape architect.

A new exhibition and assembly hall in Ulm, West Germany, on a site in the Cathedral Square, was designed by Richard Meier & Associates of New York City. The structure featured curving surfaces of stone and stucco that would contrast with the cathedral and involved a complete redesign of the square itself.

The Portland (Ore.) Center for the Performing Arts, occupying a downtown site in a city that boasted many fine examples of 1980s architecture, was a joint venture by three architectural firms—BOOR/A, Portland; the ELS Design Group, Berkeley Calif.; and Barton Myers Associates, Toronto (later moved to Los Angeles). The design for the centre won a *Progressive Architecture* award in 1984 and involved the renovation of the 1929 Paramount Theatre (which was transformed into the Arlene Schnitzer Concert Hall) and two new theatres and ancillary areas. The site occupied part of the Main Street mall, and the complex opened in August 1987. Echoes of the architecture of the existing First Congregational Church were evident in the new theatres, which used a lot of glass but also employed traditional shapes and brickwork. Pedimented facades and the use of coloured brick accents and glass-staired projections and entryways let passersby experience and share the excitement of nighttime lights and crowds.

The Arthur M. Sackler Gallery and the National Museum of African Art in Washington, D.C., both opened late in 1987 and formed part of the Smithsonian Institution. Both museums were built almost entirely underground. The location of the Museum of African Art was marked by domes, and the Sackler was topped by pyramidal roofs; the two were connected by an underground concourse. The original concept was to preserve the vistas to the famous Smithsonian "castle" and, therefore, only the entry pavilions were to be visible. The architect was Junzo Yoshimura of Japan, and the designs were executed by Boston architects Shepley Bullfinch Richardson and Abbott.

Commercial Buildings. A new terminal for United Airlines at O'Hare International Airport in Chicago was de-

TIMOTHY SOAR

Designed by Quinlan Terry, the Howard Building at Downing College, Cambridge, sparked much debate among critics over the use of the Classical style.

signed by Helmut Jahn of Murphy/Jahn and was dubbed "Terminal for Tomorrow." The architecture was reminiscent in effect of the "gateway" concept as associated in the past with major rail terminals, which made arrival or departure memorable and ceremonial. Jahn employed high-tech forms, including linear metal ceilings and metal truss roofs, skylights, and steel canopies over the counter areas. The terminal featured curving domed concourses; Concourse B, with its lofty vaulted hall, was particularly reminiscent of a 19th-century metal and glass train shed. The satellite structure forming Concourse C was symmetrical to the main terminal with the roof treatment similar to the vault in Concourse B. A rich and exciting tunnel between the concourses, 16 m (52 ft) wide at its narrowest point, was a riot of multicoloured serpentine glass and neon forms, creating spatial excitement and a sense of occasion.

A new resort and convention complex for Walt Disney World and Epcot Center at Lake Buena Vista, Fla., was designed by Michael Graves and begun early in 1988. The $375 million complex would ultimately include two luxury hotels and meeting spaces on a 60-ha (150-ac) site. The 12-story-high Walt Disney World Swan Resort would be topped by two 14-m (47-ft)-high whimsical swans, while the Dolphin Hotel and Convention Center would be crowned by a pair of 17-m (55-ft) dolphins. A crescent-shaped lagoon and landscaped walkway formed part of the complex, and the hotels were to be painted in cheerful blue-green and coral, with a banana-leaf pattern incised on the dolphins and waves on the swans. The complex was scheduled to open in 1989.

For Japanese publisher Obunsha, Foster Associates of London designed a £60 million headquarters in Tokyo that would combine museum, office, and restaurant functions. That firm was also carrying out various other Japanese projects including a private house, a radio station, and a clubhouse for golfers.

A new waterfront complex for Boston, called Rowes Wharf, was designed by Skidmore, Owings & Merrill of Chicago. It consisted of a main building with luxury housing, and piers and walkways projected into the sea, creating an environment reminiscent of the old Boston wharves.

Shops, offices, and marinas, as well as a water taxi pavilion and domed observatory, also formed part of the complex. The forms were highly ornamented, including sculptured precast concrete surfaces perceived by the designers as being harmonious with Boston's traditional building mode.

Construction of a 19-story office tower in Denver, Colo., began in 1988 and was dubbed by its designer, Anthony Pellecchia, "Il Campanile." Featuring arches and mock crenellations, the building was to be clad in concrete with accents of granite. Skidmore, Owings & Merrill was also the designer of the tallest building in Connecticut, planned for downtown Hartford. This was a 42-story, $200 billion commercial and office structure with a stepped-back design and a pointed roof.

Completion was planned for the autumn of 1988 of 75 State Street, Boston, a complex designed also by Skidmore, Owings & Merrill with architects Graham Gund Associates of Cambridge, Mass. The multiuse complex would feature a 31-story setback office tower whose surface would be enriched by five different kinds of granite cladding. A six-story courtyard atrium and grand hall, clad internally with five different marbles and making rich use of wood and bronze, completed the elaborate effect. Gold leaf chevrons would ornament the tops of the towers, providing a Neo-Art Deco effect.

A large development in Minneapolis by architects Ellerbe Associates of that city would incorporate Neo-Gothic- and Italian Renaissance-style structures of 1915 and 1919. The two-story retail arcade, known as La Salle Plaza, would connect a 54,000-sq m (600,000-sq ft) office tower of brick and limestone with the existing structures and would incorporate a new YMCA, arts centre, and motion picture theatre. The project comprised a mixture of modern shapes and historical detail, again in an effort to harmonize old and new.

The Atlanta, Ga., skyline was dominated by a new tower for IBM, designed by John Burgee with Philip Johnson of New York. It consisted of a monolithic block of granite crowned by a pyramid clad with copper and topped by a gold cupola. The 50-story tower formed the first completed phase of the new Atlantic Center development, which would eventually include a second tower, along with retail

MICHAEL MORAN

The California Aerospace Museum by Frank Gehry exemplifies "deconstructivism," a new twist in architecture that rejected all forms of classical elements and instead promoted an aleatoric style of purposeful randomness.

and parking areas. Setbacks, and the grouping of floors in bands of three, reduced the mass of the tower, and pseudo-Gothic detail contributed to the glamorous and rich effect.

On a much smaller scale a winery by Michael Graves in the Napa Valley of California made use of familiar postmodern elements, including segmented flat arches and massive columns and porticos. The winery itself featured an overscaled portico with massive engaged columns. The entrance to the complex for visitors was marked by a segmented flat arch and a single massive Tuscan column. The familiar Graves colours of buff and dark pinkish stucco with soft blue accents were repeated. The complex, which also included a house for the owners, was elegant and beautifully detailed.

Granite cladding was also chosen for a large speculative development in the City of London, known as Alban Gate and designed by architect Terry Farrell. This giant new office building would straddle London Wall itself and would replace a 1960s office block. Alban Gate, actually consisting of two separate buildings, would accommodate column-free financial dealing rooms on 3 of its 18 floors and a low-rise residential wing to the rear. Massing and colouring would distinguish the buildings from the other drab surroundings between the Barbican and the City. Aspects of the design were reminiscent of Art Deco monuments and of 1930s skyscrapers, and there were also echoes of U.S. architects, such as Michael Graves, Helmut Jahn, and the firm of Kohn Pedersen Fox.

In England one building of the 1960s, however, far from being demolished, received the accolade of being the first structure of that decade to be listed by the Department of the Environment. The Economist Building in St. James, one of the major postwar London modern architectural monuments, was designed by Peter and Alison Smithson and built between 1960 and 1964. It consisted of three separate structures that occupied a raised piazza in St. James. The three were clad with Portland stone and glass on a reinforced-concrete structure and were respectively 16, 8, and 4 stories high. The buildings were described as "exemplary in environmental sensitivity, spacial subtlety and high architectural quality."

Finally, a competition for a memorial to the 14 U.S. astronauts who lost their lives during space exploration was held in the United States. The Astronauts Memorial would be erected at the Kennedy Space Center in Florida. The successful design by Holt Hinshaw Pfau & Jones of San Francisco, selected from 756 applicants, consisted of a rotating plane of polished granite with the incised names of the fallen astronauts. The monument would be continually moving to allow a complex series of mirrors to project backlighting sunshine onto the cut-out names, while the highly polished front would reflect the passing clouds. The names of the fallen would be projected against the sky.

(SANDRA MILLIKIN)

See also Engineering Projects; Industrial Review: *Building and Construction.*

This article updates the *Macropædia* article The History of Western ARCHITECTURE.

Art Exhibitions and Art Sales

The year 1988 was marked by a number of notable art exhibitions composed of loans of major works from individual collections. Several were drawn from collections in the Soviet Union, often as part of cultural exchanges, and such shows allowed works not previously seen in the West to be enjoyed and studied.

The National Gallery in London exhibited "French Paintings from the U.S.S.R.: Watteau to Matisse" in the summer. This was the first major exhibition in London of paintings from the Hermitage Museum in Leningrad and the Pushkin Museum in Moscow, and it was without doubt one of the most impressive shows of masterpieces seen in London for some years. The paintings were drawn from over three centuries of art, and many had been acquired by Catherine the Great in the 18th century and by the Moscow merchants Savva Morozov and Sergey Shchukin in the 19th. Many were familiar works, and all were of extremely high quality. Among the artists represented were Boucher, Chardin, Ingrès, Cézanne, Picasso, and Matisse.

In Washington, D.C., the Smithsonian Institution/Hirschhorn Museum and Sculpture Garden exhibited "Russian and Soviet Paintings 1900–1930," lent by the State Tretyakov Gallery in Moscow and the State Russian Museum in Leningrad. Ninety paintings were shown, including many unfamiliar works. In contrast, the Hermitage at Leningrad and the Pushkin at Moscow exhibited "19th and 20th Century French Paintings from the Art Institute of Chicago and the Metropolitan Museum in New York." The show was organized in exchange for a loan of Dutch paintings. The Art Institute and the Metropolitan were able to exhibit a selection of 51 masterpieces of Dutch and Flemish paintings from the Hermitage, including works by Frans Hals, Van Dyck, Rubens, and Rembrandt.

"Painters by Painters: Portraits from the Uffizi Gallery" was an exhibition arranged by the National Academy of Design in New York City, which itself owned a fine collection of self-portraits by American artists. Fifty-three of the portraits owned by the National Academy of Design had been lent to museums in Milan and Florence in 1987, and in exchange this exhibition of 30 portraits dating from the 15th to the 20th century was lent by the Uffizi to a number of American museums, including the National Academy of Design and the Museum of Fine Arts in Houston, Texas. All but two of the portraits were self-portraits, and the subjects included Velásquez, Carlo Dolci, and Luca Giordano. An exchange between two museums in Boston and two in Düsseldorf, West Germany, was hailed as a major experiment. The Museum of Fine Arts and the Institute of Contemporary Art, both in Boston, selected works by nearly 30 artists representative of aspects of American art in the late 1980s. In exchange, the Städtische Kunsthalle and the Kunstsammlung Nordrhein-Westfalen chose works by the same number of artists currently active in Germany. The exhibition of American art was shown in Boston in the autumn and would then travel to Germany. After an autumn showing in Germany, the German art went on view at the two Boston museums in December 1988 and would remain there through January 1989. The set of exhibitions was referred to as "The BiNational."

Two common reasons for museums to lend large groups of works were to publicize private collections and to raise money. Eighty of the best-known works from the Phillips Collection in Washington, D.C., made a worldwide tour with such objectives. In particular, it was hoped the tour would raise funds for the construction of new galleries for temporary exhibitions. The traveling show included canvases by Cézanne, Picasso, Renoir, Van Gogh, and Matisse. The works were representative of the taste of the collector, Duncan Phillips, whose brilliance and intuitive approach to collecting were particularly apparent in the French works. The organizers of the exhibition made an attempt to re-create the atmosphere of the Phillips Gallery

itself. The exhibition was seen early in the year at the Art Gallery of South Australia in Adelaide, at the Hayward Gallery in London in the summer, and subsequently at museums in Frankfurt, West Germany, and in Madrid.

An exhibition at the Royal Academy in London of Old Master paintings from the Thyssen-Bornemisza collection was said to be the Academy's most successful show of its size, attracting 186,600 visitors. The exhibition of the private collection of Baron Thyssen, 53 paintings from the Villa Favorita in Lugano, Switz., sparked discussion in England about a possible gift of part of the collection, but the discussions were not fruitful. It was decided that the bulk of the collection would go to Spain, to be housed in the Palacio Villahermosa opposite the Prado in Madrid. Artists represented included Duccio, Hans Memling, Holbein the Younger, Caravaggio, Boucher, and Goya. The first public showing of Heinz Berggruen's collection of 19th- and 20th-century art, at the Musée d'Art et d'Histoire in Geneva, provided a fine insight into the choices made by a great art dealer for his own collection. The star of the show was "Les Poseuses" by Seurat, for which the collector was said to have been offered £35 million in recent months. There were also some fine paintings by Picasso, who had a close relationship with Berggruen for many years. Other artists included were Cézanne, Matisse, and Paul Klee. In 1984 the collector had given 90 paintings and drawings by Klee to the Metropolitan Museum of Art in New York City, which put the whole collection on view for the first time in a new gallery in the summer.

In Australia a number of art exhibitions celebrated the country's bicentenary. These included "Prints and Australia, Pre-settlement to Present" and "Shades of Light, Photography and Australia, 1939–1988," both at the Australian National Gallery in Canberra in the spring. "The Australian Bicentennial" was yet another major survey, this time of 20th-century art, shown from May to July at the Art Gallery of New South Wales in Sydney.

Denmark was the venue for the 19th Council of Europe exhibition, the theme of which was "Christian IVth and Europe." The exhibition was divided into various sections and shown in at least a dozen separate places. The main section, "Art Centres and Artists in Northern Europe," was on view at the Royal Museum of Fine Arts from March to September. In Venice in the spring the Fondazione Cini marked the 400th anniversary of the death of the painter Paolo Véronèse with an exhibition of 21 paintings and 54 drawings. A similar exhibition devoted to the artist, but including 50 paintings and 60 drawings, was on view at the end of the year at the National Gallery of Art in Washington, D.C. Viewers could enjoy the grand compositions and vibrant colours of the work of this fine Renaissance painter, best known for his decorative cycles.

The most important Paris exhibition in the spring was the large Degas show that opened in February at the Musée d'Orsay and was on view until May. It then moved to the new National Gallery of Canada in Ottawa and later to the Metropolitan Museum in New York City. The massive and complex exhibition was somewhat different at each venue. The catalog included 392 items, although the show in Paris had 284, and certain items on view in one venue were not seen at another. Degas enthusiasts or scholars could have benefited from a visit to each showing. A slightly later exhibition in the spring and summer at the Grand Palais in Paris was devoted to the influence of Japan on late 19th- and early 20th-century fine and applied arts in Europe. Entitled "Le Japonisme," the enormous show included many fine examples of Japanese art as well as European works influenced by the Japanese. Another notable show in

Paris, "The Real Fake Exhibition," was held at the Cartier Foundation. It included forgeries, counterfeits, imitations, pastiche, and other items showing forgers' practices in both fine art and industrial products.

"The Age of Chivalry" at the Royal Academy was probably the most popular exhibition held in London during the winter. The catalog for this enormous show devoted to English works of art from the 13th and 14th centuries had some 748 entries. Officially titled "The Age of Chivalry: Art in Plantagenet England 1200–1400," the exhibition was a somewhat theatrical attempt to enliven the history of the period by means of a stunning visual installation and with remarkable items on loan. For example, there was a stained glass window from Canterbury Cathedral depicting the miracles of St. Thomas Becket. Other examples of stained glass had also been lent, as well as illuminated manuscripts, sculpture, jewelry, ivories, textiles, pottery, and other works of art.

Later in the year, in the autumn, the Royal Academy mounted its largest ever show of sculpture, devoted to the work of Henry Moore. One hundred and twenty sculptures traveled to London from all over the world. Several of the pieces that were sent from Switzerland were said to be too large to travel by airplane, and a number of the pieces were so heavy that special wooden plinths had to be built so their weight would be spread evenly across the floors of the Academy. The show illustrated Moore's immense range during his almost 80 years of creativity. The centrepiece was his great "Madonna and Child" for the Church of St. Matthew at Northampton, moved for the first time since its installation. A much smaller but no less fine exhibition in London was "Treasures from the Royal Collection" at the Queen's Gallery, which marked the retirement of Sir Oliver Millar as director of the Royal Collection. Many of the queen's major paintings had been specially cleaned for the occasion.

In Germany, Stuttgart and West Berlin were the locations for a major exhibition devoted to the work of the sculptor Alberto Giacometti, the first retrospective of his work to be seen in Germany for ten years. The show emphasized that Giacometti was a talented painter, draftsman, and graphic artist as well as a sculptor. There were more than 260 items drawn from collections worldwide, many of them private. West Berlin marked its year as cultural capital of Europe with an exhibition in February at the Martin-Gropius-Bau devoted to the work of Joseph Beuys. Later in the year the same venue held a major exhibition devoted to modern art in Germany called "Stationen der Moderne." This illustrated the stages in the development of German modern art by reconstructing 20 major historical exhibitions, from the show devoted to "Die Brücke" in Dresden in 1910 to the "Land Art" show of 1969 in Berlin. Each reconstruction included either a representative selection of the works originally shown or, in the case of smaller shows, a total reconstruction.

Seventeenth-century Dutch landscape painting was the subject of a major show that was seen first in Amsterdam and later traveled to Boston and Philadelphia. As with the Degas show, some paintings were on view in one venue but not another. There were approximately 123 paintings, many of them key examples of the genre. A notable loan to the Boston showing was Govaert Flinck's "Landscape with Obelisk," previously attributed to Rembrandt and lent by the Isabella Stewart Gardner Museum in Boston to the Boston Museum of Fine Arts. This was only the second work ever lent by the Gardner Museum since its opening in 1903. Important works by Cuyp, Ruisdael, Hobbema, and Rembrandt were included.

Edgar Degas's portrait of "Mlle Hortense Valpinçon" was part of a vast exhibit shown in museums of France, Canada, and the U.S.

EDGAR DEGAS, *MLLE HORTENSE VALPINCON*, 1871 (OIL ON CANVAS, 29 5/16 × 43 5/8 IN), THE MINNEAPOLIS INSTITUTE OF ARTS, THE JOHN VAN DERLIP FUND

In Mexico City early in 1988 a large retrospective devoted to the work of the Mexican painter Rufino Tamayo, entitled "Rufino Tamayo: 70 Años de Creación," was at the Palacio de Bellas Artes and also at the Museo Rufino Tamayo. It was a spectacular show organized by Mexico's National Institute of Fine Arts and finally gave official recognition to one of Mexico's best-known and most prolific modern artists, who spent the years 1936–49 in virtual exile in New York and then in Paris. Tamayo, well known for his murals and frescoes, returned to Mexico in 1964. The exhibition provided a vast panorama of his work with over 600 items. A smaller version would travel to Madrid in the summer. Tamayo, still painting actively, finished a few of the works on show only days before the opening.

The Art Institute of Chicago marked the opening of its new Daniel F. and Ada L. Rice Building with the most comprehensive exhibition of the work of Paul Gauguin since 1906. The exhibition, which included about 250 paintings, sculpture, ceramics, prints, and drawings from collections around the world, was seen first at the National Gallery in Washington and later at the Grand Palais in Paris. A complementary exhibition was devoted to "Gauguin and His Circle in Brittany: The Prints of the Pont-Aven School." At the Kimbell Art Museum, Fort Worth, Texas, a show devoted to the early work of Poussin included 40 paintings and 60 drawings, again loans from important collections. The title was "Early Poussin in Rome: The Origins of French Classicism."

A large retrospective centennial exhibition was devoted to the work of Georgia O'Keeffe, known for her powerful and detailed still lifes, frequently of flowers. Items were chosen mainly from the estate of the artist, who died in 1986. O'Keeffe had become something of a cult figure since her death, and interest in her work was part of the general revival of interest in art from the southwestern states. The show, organized by and first shown at the National Gallery in Washington, later traveled to the Art Institute of Chicago in the spring, the Dallas (Texas) Museum of

PAUL GAUGUIN, *SPIRIT OF THE DEAD WATCHING*, 1892 (OIL ON BURLAP MOUNTED ON CANVAS, 28 1/2 × 36 3/8 IN), ALBRIGHT–KNOX ART GALLERY, BUFFALO, NEW YORK, A. CONGER GOODYEAR COLLECTION, 1965

"The Spirit of the Dead Watching" by Paul Gauguin was said to have been inspired by an incident during the artist's life. The life of Gauguin was reflected in a comprehensive exhibit of 250 paintings, sculptures, and graphics that opened a new wing at the Art Institute of Chicago.

Art in the summer, and the Metropolitan Museum in New York City in the late autumn and winter. The Guggenheim Museum in New York City celebrated 50 years of the Guggenheim Foundation with a show of over 400 works drawn from the museum's New York collection and also from the Venice collection of Peggy Guggenheim. This was the first time works from the two venues had been seen together. The exhibition included items by Picasso, Braque, and Mondrian. In honour of the show the 1959 spiral ramp, the main feature of the Wright interior, was restored to its original appearance.

An exhibition devoted to the work of the American artist and photographer Charles Sheeler (1883–1965), known particularly for his abstractions of industrial and machine images, was seen at Boston, at the Whitney Museum of Art, New York City, in the spring, and later at the Dallas Museum of Art. The show included approximately 90 paintings and drawings and the same number of photographs. Another show at New York City's Guggenheim Museum was devoted to the work of Josef Albers. There were 250 items in this large retrospective, including a fine and incisive self-portrait drawing of about 1917. The show, which marked the centenary of the artist's birth in Germany in 1888, included a substantial selection of works from his Bauhaus period as well as works drawn from his later career at Black Mountain College in North Carolina and at Yale. A major David Hockney exhibition, concentrating on his recent work from 1980–86 but considered a retrospective, was mounted by the Los Angeles County Museum of Art and seen later at the Metropolitan Museum in New York City and at the Tate Gallery in London.

An exhibition at the National Gallery in Washington devoted to Michelangelo was marked by the discovery of an unknown drawing by that artist that turned up on the back of another drawing as it was being prepared for exhibition. The drawing shows an openmouthed woman and was actually discovered by curators at the Uffizi Gallery in Florence on the reverse of Michelangelo's drawing of Cleopatra. It was behind a paper backing that had been glued to it in the 19th century and was discovered as the drawing was being restored. The image had been dimly visible when the drawing was held up to the light since at least the 1950s, but it was not until the cleaning of the sheet began in preparation for the Washington exhibition that the backing was removed. It was thought that the newly discovered drawing may have been a preliminary study for Cleopatra, although it showed her in a very different mood from the portrait on the front. Both drawings were said to date from the 1530s.　(SANDRA MILLIKIN)

ART SALES

Shrugging off the October 1987 stock market crash, the 1987–88 auction season was marked by conspicuous spending at the top of the market. Private collectors were to the fore, but since there was a fashion for bidding over the telephone, it was difficult to tell who the buyers were or even what part of the world they came from. The premium paid for exceptional rarity or quality seemed to be growing, but middle-quality goods were more difficult to shift, and a high proportion of unsold lots was recorded at many sales. Old Master paintings, for instance, were salable only if they were of high quality and in good condition. Impressionist and modern paintings were the exception. In the wake of the £24,750,000 paid for Van Gogh's "Sunflowers" the previous year, this field became the focus of interest for the rich. European buying was dominant, with Japan taking second place and Americans accounting for a much smaller proportion of purchases—a significant reversal of

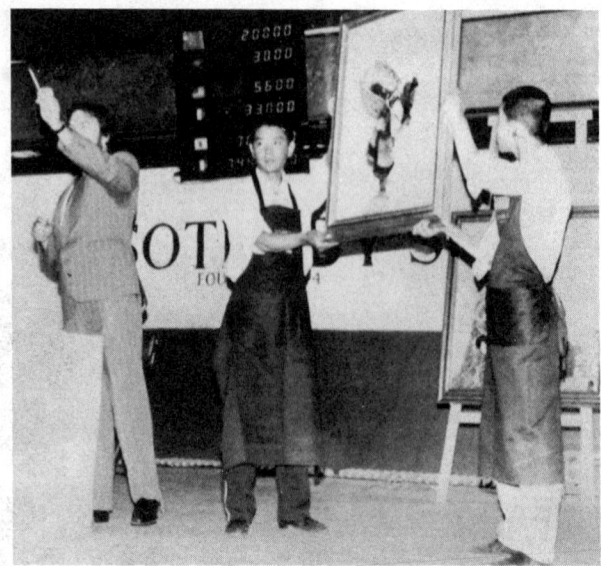

"Sunrise on the Summit of Mount Huang" is sold during Sotheby's auction in Beijing (Peking), their first in China. Proceeds were to go toward restoration of the Great Wall and the Italian city of Venice.
AP/WIDE WORLD

the traditional pattern. It was a Japanese buyer who paid $38 million for Picasso's "Acrobat and Young Harlequin" in November, setting a new auction record for a 20th-century work of art.

Sotheby's sold 104 individual lots for over $1 million in the course of the season and Christie's, 105. A 5th-century gold brooch shaped as an eagle and studded with garnets from the Comtesse de Behague's collection made F 14.4 million in Monaco, and a 14th-century porcelain vase with underglaze red decoration was sold from Jack Chia's collection in Hong Kong for HK$17.1 million. Christie's turnover for the season was up 10% at £639 million and Sotheby's, 3% at £865 million.

The first shock waves of the 1987 crash appeared to send money scurrying into collectors' items as a refuge. Within days of Black Monday, Christie's sold a copy of the Gutenberg Bible for $5,390,000, and an investor who had made a fortune selling the stock market short bid $6,380,000 for a pear-shaped diamond at Sotheby's, setting a new auction price record for a jewel. When Van Gogh's ravishing rendering of a bed of "Irises" sold for $53.9 million at Sotheby's in New York on November 11, the biggest auction price ever for anything, it was interpreted as a signal by those who had been hesitating, and they rushed to buy art. On November 20 in Paris, 41 paintings from the collection of Georges Renand, a department store magnate, made £17.9 million. Auction records were set for works of Modigliani, Rodin, Seurat, Utrillo, Vallotton, and Gromaire. By the time the London sales began in December, however, many people were losing their nerve. Degas's brilliant painting of two laundry girls ironing, "Les Blanchisseuses," was widely interpreted as cheap at £7,480,000. The Cubist Picasso that made £4,180,000 the next day, "Souvenir du Havre," 1912, was said to have crept over the owner's reserve price by only one bid.

Great works of art seem to come onto the market in bursts, and a great many were crammed into December 1987. A set of French Régence giltwood chairs and matching sofa made F 16,650, a pair of Girardon bronzes on boulle stands F 14 million, and a 12th-century manuscript decorated by the artists who worked on the Winchester Bible £1.3 million. The National Gallery in London spent

F 15,540,000 to acquire a mysterious "Winter Landscape" blanketed in snow by the great master of the German Romantic movement, Caspar David Friedrich. Lower down on the financial scale, however, anxiety was making itself felt. In many sales half the lots on offer were left unsold, and buyers were still in an anxious mood in January 1988. While Christie's managed to get $6.6 million for a quintessentially lavish Dutch still life painting by Jan Davidsz de Heem—possibly painted for Charles I of England—many of the important Dutch paintings consigned to Sotheby's by a property developer in financial trouble were left unsold.

In February the tide turned. Christie's got £3,960,000 in March for another Degas painting of laundresses. In New York in May Kazuo Fujii, a Tokyo dealer, set a new auction price record for postwar art when he paid $4,840,000 for one of the last paintings completed by Jackson Pollock before his death in 1956. At $4,180,000, Jasper Johns's "Diver" became the most expensive painting by a living artist ever sold at auction. One of the 27 known casts of Degas's three-quarters-life-size bronze "Petite Danseuse de 14 ans" broke all records for sculpture at $10,120,-000, while Giacometti's "Trois Hommes qui marchent" set an auction price record for 20th-century sculpture at $3,850,000.

By the time 24 French 18th-century paintings from Roberto Polo's collection were sold on May 30, Polo was on the run from his creditors, who made F 81.3 million from the collection. Chardin's "Le Chien Barbet" brought F 11 million. At London's summer sales, Monet's painting of his wife Camille half-submerged in a meadow of wild flowers, "Dans la prairie" of 1876, brought £14.3 million, and a pair of elegantly spotted leopards by Agasse, a 19th-century Swiss animal painter of hitherto modest reputation, £3,850,000.

Two features of the year were the strength of the Paris auction market, long overshadowed by London and New York, and the huge sums spent by Hong Kong, Taiwan, and other overseas Chinese collectors on art works in Chinese taste, most notably porcelains made for the imperial household, identified by reign marks, and modern Chinese paintings and jade.

Book Sales. During the 1987–88 season the auction rooms, and Sotheby's in particular, continued to dress up book sales in lavish catalogs, with the aim of tempting nonspecialists to buy at auction. They had some spectacular successes with the strategy—and some failures when new buyers failed to materialize and the hoped-for prices were too high for dealers.

Several outstanding collections, more than worthy of lavish cataloging, came on the market during the year, but that of the papal countess from California, Estelle Doheny, formed in the 1930s and 1940s, was the star attraction. At the first sale on Oct. 22, 1987, her Gutenberg Bible sold to Japan at $5,390,000, the highest auction price ever paid for a printed book; Quaritch of London paid $2,420,000 for a Netherlandish Bible in pictures of around 1460–70, each page printed from a separate block. At her manuscript sale on December 2, J. Paul Getty, Jr., paid £1,320,000 for a 12th-century commentary to the Gospels with six great English Romanesque illuminations. The first four sales from the collection made a total of $30.8 million.

On March 14, 1988, Sotheby's sold 67 books from the library formed by the 2nd Earl Spencer (1758–1834) and 23 from the collection of Richard Copley Christie (1834–1901) on behalf of Manchester University for a total of £1.8 million, amid howls of protest from bibliophiles over the breakup of the Spencer collection. Spencer's "Hyp-

nerotomachia," bound in gilt calf around 1550 for Jean Grolier, sold for £187,000 to Quaritch. The first sale from the collection of the London book dealer Philip Robinson on June 23 and the dispersal of the British Rail Pension Fund's books on September 27 were also landmarks, earning £1 million and £2.6 million, respectively. The railwaymen's treasures included the Doria atlas at £247,500 and a manuscript volume of Jane Austen juvenilia at £132,000.

Portugal recovered an illuminated chart of the Americas, Africa, and Europe by João Teixiera Albernaz I, the most noted Portuguese cartographer of the 17th century, from Sotheby's London at £330,000. France refused to allow Émile Zola's papers on the Dreyfus affair to leave France; Sotheby's had estimated their value at £600,000–£800,000, but the sale was finally canceled following a family squabble. The Spanish government secured a newly discovered set of Columbus letters, worth around £3 million on the open market, for 65 million pesetas by banning their export.

Illuminated manuscripts purchased in the 1880s by William Waldorf Astor were sold by his descendants for £4.3 million at Sotheby's in June, setting new auction price records for an English manuscript, a Flemish manuscript, and an Italian illuminated manuscript. The "Hours" and "Psalter" of Elizabeth de Bohun, countess of Northampton, of 1340–45 sold for £1,540,000, the "Book of Hours" illuminated in Bruges around 1522–23 for Cardinal Albrecht of Brandenburg for £1,210,000, and the "Great Hours" of Galeazzo Maria Sforza of 1461–66 for £770,000. Highlights in the Oriental field were the sale of 14 leaves from the Houghton "Shahnameh," the greatest 16th-century Persian illuminated manuscript, for £976,800 at Christie's on Oct. 11, 1988—a single leaf attributed to Muhammadi made £253,000—and the Donald and Mary Hyde collection of Japanese books and manuscripts, which made $5.8 million at Christie's on October 7, with a manuscript of Sei Shonagon's "Pillow Book" setting a price record for a Japanese book at $352,000.   (GERALDINE NORMAN)

This article updates the *Macropædia* articles The History of Western PAINTING; The History of Western SCULPTURE.

Astronomy

The year 1988 was exciting for astronomy, even if it could not offer an event as dramatic as the supernova of the previous year. Observations of that object, SN 1987A, continued throughout 1988, producing a wide range of insights into the explosive death of stars. Other discoveries about astronomical objects ranging in distance from the outermost planet, Pluto, to the most distant quasars and galaxies known provided new clues to the evolution of the solar system and of the universe.

Solar System. Of the nine known planets in the solar system, Pluto has been perhaps the least well studied. Observations of it have been made difficult by the fact that it is both the smallest and, usually, the most distant planet from the Sun. Pluto's orbit crosses that of Neptune, however, and during the late 1980s it was closer to the Sun and the Earth than at any other time in its 248-year orbital period. Exploiting this proximity, astronomers watching occultations of its moon Charon in 1987 made the first accurate measurement of Pluto's size, showing it to have a radius of about 1,145 km (710 mi). On June 9, 1988, there occurred a rare occultation, observable from Earth, of a relatively bright (12th-magnitude) star by Pluto. This event was watched simultaneously by astronomers in Australia and New Zealand and aboard NASA's Kuiper

Airborne Observatory. The starlight was first refracted by the planet's atmosphere and then blocked by the disk of the planet itself. From these observations, the astronomers found that Pluto's atmosphere extends at least 200 km (125 mi) above its surface. Furthermore, from the rate of extinction of the light, it appeared that much of the atmosphere comprises methane gas. The dilute, extended atmosphere of Pluto could be understood as a consequence of its small mass and radius, which result in a low surface gravity. Further, unexpected changes seen in the rate of extinction of the light may point to a stratified atmosphere, or one possessing sharp temperature variations. In June 1989, when the next stellar occultation by Pluto was to occur, these observations and theories concerning Pluto's atmosphere would be put to the test.

Stars. SN 1987A was the brightest supernova seen on Earth since the one observed by Johannes Kepler in 1604. The spectacular phenomenon, first noticed in the early morning of Feb. 24, 1987, represented the death of a massive blue supergiant star in the nearby Large Magellanic Cloud, a galaxy near our own Milky Way. It had been fading from view as an optical object since early 1987. Throughout 1988 X-rays and gamma rays were observed from the supernova. Steve Matz and collaborators from the U.S. Naval Research Laboratory, Washington, D.C., used the Earth-orbiting Solar Maximum Mission satellite to search for discrete gamma-ray lines, which might result from the decay of short-lived radioactive elements produced in the supernova explosion. Indeed, gamma-ray lines having energies of 847 keV (kiloelectron volts) and 1,238 keV were found, very close to the energies predicted for gamma rays emitted by decaying cobalt-56. The detected flux was in reasonably good agreement with theories suggesting that such nucleosynthesis decay products power the optical light emission from a supernova in the months following the initial explosion. These observations represented the first direct evidence for the hitherto theorized synthesis and dispersion of heavy elements in stellar explosions.

Another novel feature of the unfolding SN 1987A story was the detection of two glowing arcs of light centred on the supernova itself, the so-called light echo effect. The arcs were discovered by Arlin Crotts of the University of Texas at Austin using the Carnegie Institution's one-metre telescope at Las Campanas Observatory in Chile and were well photographed by David Malin and collaborators using the 3.9-m Anglo-Australian Telescope in July 1988. (One metre is about 39.4 in.) The rings appeared to be expanding at about 15 times the speed of light. Although this superluminal motion appeared to contradict the special theory of relativity, which asserts that no signal can move faster than the speed of light, the observations could be reconciled with the theory. Since the supernova occurred in a galaxy lying some 160,000 light-years from Earth, the expanding light echo could be understood as the scattering of light from dust clouds or bands lying in front of the supernova at distances from it of about 400 and 1,000 light-years. This geometry produced the appearance of rapidly moving arc-shaped light reflections, even though the light itself moved at a fixed speed.

While many theorists believed that a pulsar should have been formed in SN 1987A, none had been detected by the end of 1988. Nevertheless, about 450 pulsars were known throughout the Milky Way, believed to have been formed in similar supernova explosions. Pulsars are rapidly rotating magnetized neutron stars, objects as dense as the nucleus of an atom but with the mass of the Sun. Most have pulsation and rotation periods of about a second, but a few have periods of less than ten milliseconds (ten thousandths of

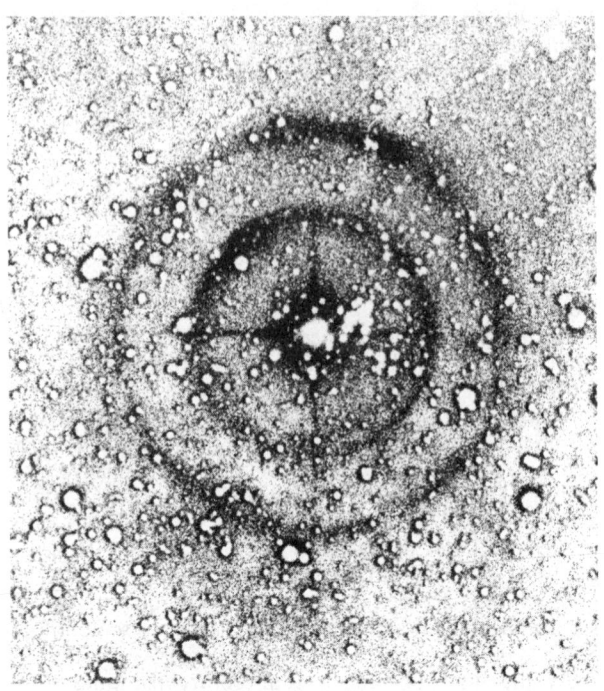

Two ring-shaped light echoes surround Supernova 1987A in a negative image processed from a telescopic photo taken in July. The echoes arise in two intervening clouds of dust being illuminated by light that left the exploded star in May 1987.
DAVID MALIN, ANGLO–AUSTRALIAN OBSERVATORY

a second). The fastest, called PSR 1937+214, spins on its axis more than 630 times per second. In 1988 the second fastest pulsar, PSR 1957+20, with a spin period of about 1.607 milliseconds, was discovered by Princeton University astronomers Andrew S. Fruchter, Daniel R. Stinebring, and Joseph H. Taylor. The object is in a binary star system, revolving in roughly nine hours about a common centre of mass with its companion star. Although several other binary pulsar systems are known, this was the first one found in which the companion actually eclipses the pulsar during each orbital revolution. The orbital period and pulsar velocity suggested that the companion star must have a very low mass, implying, under normal circumstances, a very small size. The observed eclipse duration, however, indicated that the companion star is large. The only way for the companion to eclipse the pulsar is if the pulsar itself is literally evaporating the surface of the companion star, expanding it far beyond its normal size. Rapid evaporation of companions may account for the existence of single millisecond pulsars, since the companion would "spin up" the pulsar by transferring mass to it and then ultimately disappear, leaving a lone, rapidly rotating pulsar.

Galaxies and Cosmology. In 1936 Albert Einstein suggested that if two objects were lined up, one behind the other, then light emitted from the more distant object could be deflected by the gravitational field of the closer one to form a ringlike image of the more distant object. This phenomenon, called the gravitational lens effect, would occur because gravity exerts a force on light as well as on mass. Deflection of the pointlike image of a distant star by the Sun had been seen as long ago as 1919 and, more recently, astronomers had discovered quasars gravitationally lensed by foreground galaxies to form images consisting of two or more blobs or arcs. No example of a complete, so-called Einstein ring, however, had ever been seen prior to 1988. Using the Very Large Array radio telescope in Socorro, N.M., Jacqueline Hewitt and collaborators from the Mas-

sachusetts Institute of Technology's Haystack Observatory produced an image of the radio source MG 1131+0456, which lies in the constellation Leo. Because of its high galactic latitude, the object is presumed to reside outside our own Galaxy. The resulting radio image was a sharp-edged ellipse some 2.2 by 1.6 arc seconds, accompanied by two bright compact sources. This radio object was similar to two optically luminous arcs, discovered in 1987, that lie in two distant clusters of galaxies. In this case, however, the ring is complete. For a ring to be observed, there must be an almost perfect alignment of the lensed object and of the lensing object with respect to the observer. Such an alignment apparently exists for this situation, thus allowing models to be made of the mass distribution in the presumed foreground, lensing galaxy.

The most distant objects ever seen in the universe are the quasi-stellar objects, or quasars. These objects look starlike on an optical photographic plate. Their light spectrum, however, does not indicate the presence of stars, only of hot emitting and absorbing gas. The distance to a quasar is determined by its redshift, the shift of its spectral lines toward the red. This effect is attributable to the expansion of the universe: the larger the redshift, the faster the object is receding from observers on Earth, the more distant the object is, and the farther back in time astronomers are seeing it, given the finite time it takes for light to travel from the object to Earth. In late 1987 astronomers Stephen Warren and Paul Hewett announced their discovery of the most distant quasar yet known. The object, discovered through the use of the 3.9-m Anglo-Australian telescope at Siding Spring, Australia, was designated Q0051−279 and has a redshift of 4.43. Depending on the current rate of expansion of the universe and on whether it is open (and will expand forever) or closed (and will collapse in the future), light from this quasar has traveled 12 billion to 16 billion years to reach Earth.

In early 1988 Simon Lilly of the University of Hawaii at Manoa announced discovery of the most distant galaxy found to date, one that has a redshift of about 3.4 and thus lies deep within the realm of the more distant quasars. The result followed from optical and infrared observations made with the 3.6-m Canadian-French-U.S. telescope and with the 3.8-m U.K. infrared telescope on Mauna Kea in Hawaii. Later in the year, using the 4-m telescope at Kitt Peak in Arizona, Kenneth Chambers of Johns Hopkins University, Baltimore, Md., and colleagues found an even

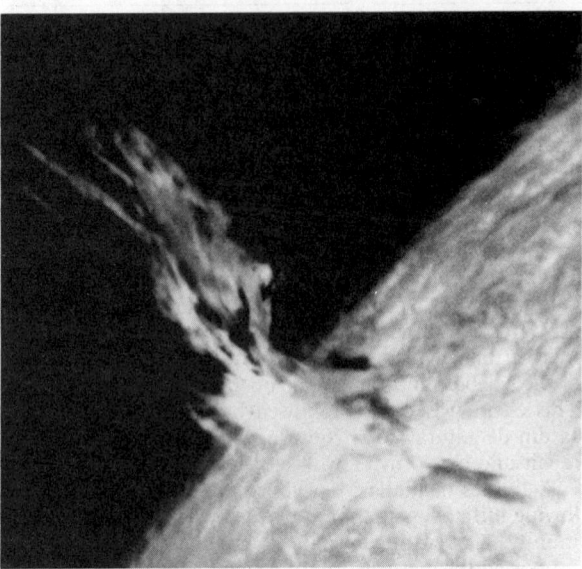

A flare bursts from the Sun's surface, reaching a height of about 129,000 kilometres (80,000 miles). The unusual amount of solar flares, plages, and sunspots seen in 1988 suggested to astronomers that the current solar cycle could become one of the most active yet known.
AP/WIDE WORLD

more distant quasar, 4C 41.17, with a redshift of about 3.87. Because these objects show at least one optical spectral line characteristic of stars, as well as an overall colour quite different from that of most quasars, astronomers concluded that they are galaxies. If the conclusion is correct, the finds would have great bearing on the origin and time of formation of galaxies. In many current models of the universe that invoke the presence of a great deal of dark or "missing" mass, formation of galaxies at such a high redshift (i.e., so early in time) was totally unexpected.

Long before the formation of galaxies, the universe is thought to have been expanding as a hot dense plasma consisting of particles and radiation mixed together in thermal equilibrium. Indeed, the most important clue to the big-bang picture of the origin of the universe, after the observed recession of galaxies and quasars, is the radiation left over. This radiation exists today as a virtually isotropic (uniform) background radiation field, the so-called 3 K, or microwave, background radiation. First detected in 1965, it was studied for more than two decades to ascertain in detail its uniformity over the sky and to measure its spectrum. Until 1988, results of those studies had conformed to the expected emission from hot matter—a "blackbody" radiation spectrum. In 1988 new measurements were made aboard a Japanese sounding rocket by a collaboration of scientists from Nagoya University headed by Satio Hayakawa and by Paul Richards and Andrew Lange of the University of California at Berkeley. The result showed deviations from the predicted blackbody spectrum, a bell-shaped curve, in the form of an excess of radiation at energies near the infrared. The implications of this finding were not clear. It may be that a burst of galaxy and star formation occurred early in the evolution of the universe or that dust was formed early to reradiate radiation into the infrared regime. Clarification of this puzzle would likely have to await launch of NASA's Cosmic Background Explorer spacecraft, expected in 1989. (KENNETH BRECHER)

See also Space Exploration.
This article updates the *Macropædia* articles The COSMOS; GALAXIES; The PHYSICAL SCIENCES: *Astronomy and Astrophysics;* The SOLAR SYSTEM; STARS AND STAR CLUSTERS.

Earth Perihelion and Aphelion, 1989

Jan. 1	Perihelion, 147,009,000 km (91,347,000 mi) from the Sun
July 4	Aphelion, 152,004,000 km (94,451,000 mi) from the Sun

Equinoxes and Solstices, 1989

March 20	Vernal equinox,	15:28[1]
June 21	Summer solstice,	09:53[1]
Sept. 23	Autumnal equinox,	01:20[1]
Dec. 21	Winter solstice,	21:22[1]

Eclipses, 1989

Feb. 20	Moon, total (begins 12:29[1]), visible in western North America, the Pacific Ocean, Australia, Asia, the Indian Ocean, and parts of Europe and Africa.
March 7	Sun, partial (begins 16:16[1]), visible in northwestern Mexico, western continental United States, western and central Canada, Greenland, extreme northeastern Asia, and Hawaii.
Aug. 17	Moon, total (begins 00:22[1]), visible in Europe, the Middle East, Africa, Antarctica, the Atlantic Ocean, South and Central America, North America (except Alaska), and the eastern Pacific Ocean.
Aug. 31	Sun, partial (begins 03:33[1]), visible in southeastern Africa, Madagascar, and parts of Antarctica.

[1]Universal time.
Source: *The Astronomical Almanac for the Year 1989* (1988).

Botanical Gardens and Zoos

Botanical Gardens. For a decade a number of smaller botanical gardens in Europe had been subjected to severe financial constraint, which in some instances caused their demise. However, a new optimism emerged when policies were reexamined and modified so that some of the older, smaller gardens that had been threatened were revitalized. In addition, during the last five years as many as 30 new botanical gardens had been opened throughout the world and more were planned. In Spain the Jardín Botánico de Córdoba arranged a conference on the propagation of Mediterranean plants, attended by 200 delegates, as part of the celebration to mark the opening of this new garden. This event was closely followed by the reopening of the Jardín de Altura Sierra Nevada, which had fallen into disrepair and closed in 1976.

Activities in the less developed countries expanded following initiatives sponsored by the botanical gardens community. Governments and other funding agencies also supported the construction of new botanical gardens in the tropics. Although the botanical garden, the Jardin de l'État, on the Indian Ocean island of Réunion became a public park, the French minister of agriculture formally opened the Floralies de l'Ocean Indien in October 1987, and two days later the inauguration of the Conservatoire Botanique de Mascarin took place. In China the Academia Sinica established a new botanical garden that would cultivate rare and endangered plants of Sichuan (Szechwan) Province, promote conservation, carry out scientific research, and initiate an educational program linked to tourism.

Following the publication in 1984 of a national strategy document by the Royal Australian Institute of Parks and Recreation detailing the need for regional botanical gardens, provisional planning proceeded for a new garden in the district of Sunraysia, which encompassed a large portion of northwestern Victoria and southwestern New South Wales. In southwestern Costa Rica, the once private Las Cruces Tropical Botanic Garden, now under the jurisdiction of the Organization of Tropical Studies, a consortium of academic institutes in Costa Rica and the United States, actively pursued a development program.

Within the framework of the International Union for Conservation of Nature and Natural Resources (IUCN), the Botanic Gardens Conservation Secretariat (BGCS) continued to provide support for the less well endowed botanical gardens in less developed countries. Advice on development and conservation programs was made available by linking directors and curators in such gardens with colleagues in established and successful botanical gardens. The twinning of gardens allowed cooperative conservation programs to be developed and provided the opportunity for a two-way exchange of personnel for training and study purposes. Several botanical gardens, including those in Bolivia, Gabon, and Papua New Guinea, joined the BGCS through the generous sponsorship of other member gardens.

A collection of endemic plant species from Mauritius was donated by Trinity College Botanic Garden, Dublin, to the Jersey Zoo in the Channel Islands. *Mimusops petiolaris, Dictyosperma album,* and *Ficus rubra*, all threatened Mauritian lowland species, were coupled with rare Mauritian reptiles to create a unique and important conservation exhibit.

During late January delegates at a meeting in the Azores, Portugal, considered urgent conservation measures for this group of Atlantic islands. In early September 1988 a conference titled "Conservation through Research" was held at Kirstenbosch Botanic Garden, Cape Town, South Africa, in collaboration with IUCN. Later in the month an international symposium of botanical gardens took place in Nanjing (Nanking), China.

A new directory of botanical gardens and arboretums of the world was scheduled for publication by IUCN in the near future; directory entries were extracted from the data base built up by IUCN.   (REGINALD IAN BEYER)

Zoos. The giant panda, *Ailuropoda melanoleuca,* the international symbol of wildlife protection, was once again a prominent and persistent headliner. In 1988, however, the publicity was particularly concerned with a bitter and unpleasant dispute that erupted among the very people who should be dedicated to the panda's preservation. There was a decreasing population of less than 1,000 in the wild, scattered in small, probably nonviable groups. They were subject to increasing loss of habitat and to possible starvation because of natural periodic diebacks of bamboo, virtually their only food. In 1988 the Chinese authorities acknowledged that poaching was a further serious threat, either accidentally, when pandas were caught in traps set for musk deer, or deliberately, because of a lucrative trade in panda hides. In February the authorities recovered 146 hides.

The situation in captivity was not much better, because few of the estimated 100 pandas in China, and the 16 outside China, had bred. China had stopped sending pandas as permanent gifts but allowed short-term loans for exhibition purposes. It was these loans, over which there was no international control or coordination, that caused the furor. "Rent-a-panda" exhibits were popular in the U.S., Canada, Ireland, Belgium, and The Netherlands. Those in favour argued that such exhibitions increased public perception of the plight of the panda and that part of the money raised contributed to conservation work in China. Others argued that these loans and their commercial exploitation could jeopardize conservation by removing possible breeders from an already small stock. In the U.S. the World Wildlife Fund and the main association of zoo professionals, the American Association of Zoological Parks and Aquariums, filed lawsuits in an effort to force the federal government to cancel the display of two pandas at the Toledo (Ohio) Zoo.

Some relief from panda-wrangling came in August when the Zoological Society of London sent its single male, Chia-Chia, to join a young female in Mexico. However, in September China announced a ban on lending giant pandas to the U.S. because the U.S. Department of the Interior refused to issue import permits to certain institutions wishing to bring in pandas. The ban, which also covered golden monkeys, did not affect other countries or U.S. contracts already in force.

The world population of California condors, *Gymnogyps californianus,* the largest bird in North America, rose from 27 to 28 (all in captivity) when on April 29 a chick hatched at the San Diego (Calif.) Wild Animal Park. The chick, a female named Molloko, was the first ever bred outside the wild. Weighing 191.4 g (6.75 oz) on hatching, she was hand-fed, and puppet condor heads were used to prevent imprinting on humans.

Good news also came for another animal on the edge of extinction, the black-footed ferret, *Mustela nigripes,* whose total known population, all in captivity in Sybille, Wyo., rose dramatically to 62 with the addition of 38 from 12 litters.

Two notable successes in the artificial manipulation of reproduction were reported from Dallas (Texas) Zoo: the

Molloko, the first California condor conceived and hatched in captivity, sidles up to a hand puppet that is used to help the youngster become accustomed to others of its kind. Molloko's home is the San Diego Wild Animal Park in California.

SAN DIEGO WILD ANIMAL PARK; PHOTOGRAPH, RON GARRISON

first known in vitro fertilization of a gorilla (*Gorilla g. gorilla*) ovum, using semen collected at postmortem and held frozen for several years; and the birth of a female Suni antelope, *Neotragus moschatus zuluensis,* as a result of intraspecific embryo transfer. In July the Cincinnati (Ohio) Zoo and Botanical Garden announced the birth of a common eland, *Taurotragus oryx,* the result of intraspecific split embryo transfer.

Progress in reintroduction projects involving zoos included the transfer of 40 Bali mynah, *Leucospar rothschildi,* to Indonesia; the release of red wolves, *Canis rufus,* into Alligator River (N.C.) and Cape Romain (S.C.) national wildlife refuges; addax, *Addax nasomaculatus,* to Bou-Hedma National Park, Tunisia; Arabian oryx, *Oryx leucoryx,* to Oman; and West Indian tree ducks, *Dendrocygna arborea,* to Parque Zoologico Nacional, Dominican Republic.

In June the new Indianapolis (Ind.) Zoo opened, and in July the Central Park Zoo in New York City was reopened after a five-year renovation. (P. J. OLNEY)

See also Environment; Gardening.

Chemistry

Hundreds of exciting developments and discoveries each year owe much of their success to research in the more than two dozen major fields of chemistry and some ten related areas. Three such achievements making the news during the past year were DNA fingerprinting, embryo cloning of dairy cattle, and a replacement for sperm-whale oil.

DNA Fingerprinting. A new identity test, DNA fingerprinting, virtually exploded upon forensics and paternity testing in 1988. It was developed in 1984 by Alec Jeffreys, a geneticist at the University of Leicester, England, from an idea he had while seeking genetic variations that would serve as markers of inherited diseases. Why, Jeffreys wondered, could not biochemical methods for visualizing variations in DNA also be used to establish identity?

DNA fingerprinting was first applied forensically in 1987 in the much-publicized case of Colin Pitchfork, who was subsequently found guilty of raping and strangling two 15-year-old girls in the Leicester countryside. More than 5,000 men living near Leicester were given the DNA test in the search for the guilty party. When DNA patterns derived from samples of Pitchfork's blood were compared with those from semen samples taken from the murder victims, there was a clear match. The first American whose guilt was determined with the help of the test was Tommie Lee Andrews, who in 1988 received concurrent terms for sexual battery, armed burglary, and aggravated battery. Following Andrews's sentence, at least seven rape and murder trials in the U.S. resulted in convictions based on DNA fingerprinting, and in late 1988 about another 100 suspects in criminal cases were being tested for possible court action.

DNA fingerprinting depends on delineating those regions of DNA molecules in human body cells that vary among individuals. Some of this DNA contains particular segments that are repeated many times in a way that distinctly differs from one person to the next. To perform an analysis, DNA is taken from a tiny amount of basically any type of tissue—semen, hair, blood, or skin, for example. It is then cut into fragments by restriction enzymes, proteins that cleave the molecules at specific locations. The fragments are sorted by size by means of gel electrophoresis. Those fragments that contain repeated DNA are tagged with radioactive probes that allow the fragments to be visualized as a pattern of bands on a piece of photographic film. Each band stands for a DNA fragment of a particular size. The natural DNA variations among individuals lead to variations in the sites of attack by the restriction enzymes. This in turn gives rise to individual variation in the lengths of the resulting DNA fragments—a variation termed restriction fragment length polymorphism (RFLP).

Using the Andrews case as an example, the RFLP banding patterns from the suspect's blood-cell DNA matched, band for band, the patterns from that of the sperm found on the last victim. On the other hand, the patterns derived from blood samples from the victim and from other people looked distinctively different. The odds of a person's having Andrews's DNA pattern was, some scientists said, as high as one in 30 billion people. In other words, he was beyond reasonable doubt the only man who could have left the sperm found on the final victim.

The reason that DNA fingerprinting can also be used to establish paternity is that the banding patterns are heritable. Roughly half the patterns will be shared by a child and his or her natural father.

Some observers termed DNA fingerprinting the most significant advance for forensics in the 20th century. The U.S. Federal Bureau of Investigation opened its own DNA fingerprinting laboratory in October and began training state and local forensic scientists in the technique. Several commercial labs in the U.S. also were equipped for DNA fingerprinting. (*See* LIFE SCIENCES: *Molecular Biology.*)

Embryo Cloning of Dairy Cattle. They were named Fusion and Copy. They were highly unusual because they were among the first reported calves brought into the world by a technique known as embryo cloning. Once refined, the technique could revolutionize the production of dairy cows perhaps as early as the mid-1990s. It is not animal cloning in the conventionally understood sense because it does not make copies from adult animals. It is nuclear transplantation for the purpose of cloning embryos.

The difficult, time-consuming research was being conducted by Neal First and colleagues at the University of Wisconsin at Madison and was being sponsored by the Research Division of W. R. Grace & Co. in conjunction with the American Breeders Service (ABS) Division of Grace headquartered in De Forest, Wis. The objective of the work was to remove much of the uncertainty of cattle breeding by producing genetically equivalent animals in quantity, with the ultimate goal of advancing the rate at which the desirable traits of genetically superior dairy cattle can be

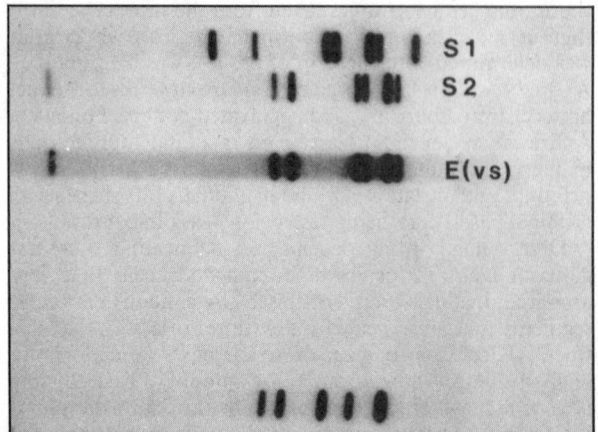

DNA fingerprints—S1 and S2—taken from the blood of two rape suspects are compared with one—E(vs)—from a sample of semen recovered from a rape victim. Suspect 2, when confronted with the matching evidence, confessed.

CELLMARK DIAGNOSTICS

produced for commercial dairy herds. A major attraction for the dairy farmer would be the availability of accurate data on desirable traits, including milk production, of various clonal lines of genetically equivalent animals that had been tested under normal husbandry conditions. In 1986 the average Wisconsin dairy cow produced 6,145 kg (13,534 lb) of milk. Once a cell line was developed for cows having a much higher capacity, animals would be produced from it. According to First, the average annual output from embryo-cloned cows in well-managed herds could increase to more than 11,804 kg (26,000 lb).

The Grace Research Division began funding the project in 1982. Originally several pairs of identical twin calves were produced by microsurgically splitting embryos and implanting the half-embryos into foster mothers. In the second stage of the research, a calf was born in 1986 as a result of maturing an egg and fertilizing it in vitro (in the test tube), culturing it in a sheep oviduct, and then implanting it in a recipient cow. Most recently, in the embryo-cloning stage, First's team started with individual bovine cells—fertilized eggs. Once each cell had divided to become a 16-cell embryo, the researchers removed individual embryo cells (each cell containing all the genetic information needed to produce a complete organism) and fused them with unfertilized egg cells whose genetic material and about half of the cytoplasmic contents had been removed. (The cytoplasm is everything in the cell outside the nucleus.) Some of these fused cells began dividing like ordinary fertilized eggs into a multicelled embryo, eventually reaching a stage in which they could be introduced into foster mothers.

Ideally, if all the embryonic cells from a 16-cell embryo could be successfully fused and cultured, the result would be 16 genetically equivalent embryos. These could be used to produce cows, be split up and fused once again at the 16-cell embryo state, or frozen as stock for later rounds of cloning. Thus the multiplication of one embryo could be carried on to potentially unlimited numbers. Currently the actual success rate of embryo cloning was still low. Fusion and Copy did not come from the same 16-cell embryo; the calves had different parents and thus were not genetically equivalent.

Another obstacle to be overcome was reflected in the fact that the research team surgically implanted the embryos that would become Fusion and Copy into sheep to incubate for a few days. They were then surgically removed

and nonsurgically transferred to surrogate mother cows. Incubating the embryos in sheep was a costly procedure that needed to be eliminated to reduce the overall expense of the technique. Some success was reported in performing the incubation stage in the test tube, but the efficiency was very poor.

Similar research on both sheep and cattle was being conducted by other investigators in the U.S., England, and Canada. Developing superior lines of meat-producing animals was a concurrent goal.

Plant Oil Brightens Sperm Whale's Future. In the 1970s the sperm whale's future was bleak. The creature made famous as Moby Dick was being hunted to extinction for the valuable oil in its body. The slaughter reached a peak in 1964 when 29,255 sperm whales died, their fat destined for refineries that turned sperm whale oil into cosmetics and transmission fluid additives. Fortunately, by the late 1980s two forces—one political, the other scientific—had worked to reverse the animal's fate. The International Whaling Commission decided that the sperm whale harvest would henceforth be set permanently at zero beginning with the 1986 season. The demand for sperm whale oil still existed, however, and some Japanese, Soviet, and Norwegian whalers continued hunting.

The sperm whale also got a break from an unexpected quarter, however. Seeds of the jojoba plant, which grows wild in the deserts of Baja California and the American Southwest, contain an oil chemically very similar to that of the sperm whale. Chemists had recognized the similarity for some time, but it was not until the mid-1970s that the efforts of American Indians succeeded in interesting industry in jojoba oil. A decade and a half later, the jojoba oil industry, though still small, was thriving, and the need for sperm whale oil was dropping fast.

About the time that sulfurized sperm whale oil was gaining popularity as a lubricant, botanists at the Boyce Thompson Southwestern Arboretum in Superior, Ariz., began cultivating test plots of various plants that grow wild in the neighbouring desert. From the acorn-size seeds of one of these plants, the jojoba (*Simmondsia chinensis*), they extracted a thick, waxy substance that was sent to the University of Arizona for analysis. There, analytical chemists determined that jojoba oil was a mixture of esters of long-chain alcohols and long-chain fatty acids and noted its similarity to sperm whale oil. Further tests pointed up close similarities in physical properties: both substances were superior lubricants, both withstood high pressures and temperatures without decomposing, and both contained natural antioxidants.

The results of this research went unapplied for some years until William P. Miller, a Cherokee and an employee in the U.S. Bureau of Indian Affairs, realized that jojoba might be a good candidate for cultivation on Indian reservations in the U.S. Southwest, where poverty was endemic. He persuaded members of the San Carlos Apache tribe in California to collect seeds from wild jojoba, got a local company to extract the oil (a fairly simple process), and had samples sent to dozens of industries that relied on sperm whale oil. Encouraged by the response, a few tribes and individual investors began planting small stands of jojoba in the early 1980s and embarked on a lengthy wait for the plant to mature and begin maximum seed production. In 1986 oil production from plantation-grown jojoba equaled that from wild-borne seeds for the first time.

More than 90% of the jojoba oil produced in the late 1980s went into cosmetics, shampoos, and other personal care products, whose manufacturers appreciated jojoba as one of the finest cosmetic oils available. Like sperm whale

oil, jojoba oil can be hydrogenated, converting it to a hard, white solid wax that tests have shown to be an excellent car and floor polish and a good protective coating for fresh vegetables. The other major application for jojoba oil was in specialty lubricants, such as bus transmission fluid. Short supplies were limiting its use in all applications, and the main challenge to the fledgling jojoba industry was to produce more oil as soon as possible.   (FRANK C. BIGGER)

This article updates the *Macropædia* articles AGRICULTURAL SCIENCES; BIOCHEMICAL COMPONENTS OF ORGANISMS; The Principles of GENETICS AND HEREDITY; The PHYSICAL SCIENCES: *Chemistry.*

Consumer Affairs

Continued worldwide growth of the consumer movement was evidenced in 1988 by increased consumer protection activity in the third world. The first consumer conference in Africa, held in Nairobi, Kenya, by the International Organization of Consumers Unions (IOCU), assembled consumer leaders from 11 African countries and produced a strongly worded declaration calling for consumer action on the continent. Regional consumer training courses in Ecuador, Peru, and Mexico strengthened contacts among 40 consumer organizations in Latin America and the Caribbean. In China 703 consumer organizations were functioning in December 1987, and 75% of Chinese provinces had established their own consumer organizations.

On March 15, 1988, consumer organizations commemorated World Consumer Rights Day by drawing attention to consumers' rights and responsibilities regarding the environment and by actively promoting the theme of sustainable development, which was highlighted in the 1987 Brundtland Report. The IOCU coordinated a global campaign to reduce the production and use of ozone-depleting chlorofluorocarbons (CFCs). The IOCU urged its member organizations to lobby their governments to ratify the Montreal Protocol, which targeted a global freeze in production of CFCs at 1986 levels and a 50% production cut by 1999. By mid-1988 the protocol had been ratified by some 50 countries, and several countries had begun phasing out use of CFCs at a pace faster than that spelled out by the protocol. West Germany pledged to reduce its use of CFCs in aerosols by 95% in three years, and Switzerland

and The Netherlands vowed to take similar action. Consumer organizations insisted that, in the meantime, CFC-containing products should be clearly labeled.

In an important step toward curbing global trade in hazardous products, the 158 member countries of the Food and Agriculture Organization (FAO) resolved to incorporate prior informed consent into the International Code of Conduct on Distribution and Use of Pesticides. The prior informed consent principle requires exporters of banned or severely restricted pesticides to inform and obtain permission from authorities of the importing country. The FAO decision was, in part, the result of the findings of the Pesticide Action Network (PAN), which revealed that extremely toxic pesticides, most of them banned or restricted in industrialized countries, were freely available in many third world countries.

The problems associated with international trade in toxic substances were highlighted by the discovery of toxic waste dumping in Nigeria, Togo, and other parts of West Africa and by the difficulties that ensue when ships removing the waste fail to find a country willing to accept their toxic cargo. The IOCU and its European counterpart, the Bureau Européen des Unions de Consommateurs (BEUC), together with a number of international environmental organizations, called for an immediate end to the exportation of industrial and toxic wastes to the third world.

The Uruguay round of negotiations under the General Agreement on Tariffs and Trade (GATT) focused renewed attention from the consumer movement on the negative effects of protectionist trade measures. At the World Food Conference organized by the president of the European Parliament in April, the IOCU and BEUC urged liberalization of agricultural trade. The groups maintained that agricultural support subsidies have increased food costs to consumers and have created surpluses that frequently distort the international market.

Global consumer-health campaigns continued to concentrate on three issues: the promotion of sound infant feeding practices, the rational use of medicines, and the movement to stop the promotion of tobacco. The 1988 edition of *State of the Code*, published by the International Baby Food Action Network and the IOCU, tabulated results on the implementation by countries and baby food companies of the 1981 World Health Organization (WHO)/United Nations Children's Fund (UNICEF) International Code of

BOB BYRD—THE LIGHT WORKS, INC.

Customers wait in line at the long row of checkout counters in Hypermart USA. The sprawling mall in a Dallas, Texas, suburb covered the area of five football fields. It offered customers an enormous variety of goods, low prices, and early experience with what might become an extremely successful retailing format.

Marketing of Breastmilk Substitutes. The study revealed that only 30 governments had adopted significant parts of the code into law, and that most manufacturers continued to supply hospitals with free or subsidized products. As a result, the original seven-year Nestlé products boycott, which ended in 1984, was reimposed in early October. The organizations behind this boycott asserted that Nestlé had broken the agreement to maintain the code signed in 1984. The new boycott was also extended to American Home Products.

In the U.S. two product liability cases set legal precedents. In June 1988 a federal court jury in Newark, N.J., awarded $400,000 to the husband of a woman who died of lung cancer. Though the court rejected charges that Philip Morris, Lorillard and Liggett Group conspired to conceal the health risks associated with smoking before 1966, the jury did find the cigarette maker 20% responsible for the woman's injuries because it failed to issue warnings about the possible health hazards associated with smoking before the government required warning labels on cigarette packages in 1966. The lawsuit, filed by Mr. and Mrs. Antonio Cipollone in 1983, after Rose Cipollone had lost a lung to cancer, was pursued by her husband after her death in 1984. Liggett was charged with guaranteeing, by express warranty, safety in advertisements before 1966 by using such slogans as L&M's "Just What the Doctor Ordered" and "Play Safe—Smoke Chesterfields." Liggett planned to appeal the verdict. The Newark jury broke new ground by explicitly linking cancer to smoking and placing 20% of the blame on Liggett. The jury ruled that the plaintiff bore 80% of the blame for her own death and awarded damages to her husband but none to her estate. The landmark verdict was expected to be used as a precedent in such states as Louisiana, Mississippi, and Texas, where damages were based on the degree of fault. The case also forced three tobacco companies to disclose thousands of pages of confidential documents revealing that the companies had known for many years that smoking was linked to cancer and other diseases.

On Dec. 11, 1987, a federal judge in Richmond, Va., ordered A. H. Robins, maker of the Dalkon Shield contraceptive device sold during the 1970s, to set aside $2,475,000,000 in its bankruptcy reorganization fund to compensate some 200,000 women who claimed injuries from using the intrauterine device. On Jan. 19, 1988, A. H. Robins announced that the board had accepted a $3,280,-000,000 takeover bid from American Home Products. The takeover, which was endorsed by Robins's shareholder committee on January 13, also had to be approved by Dalkon Shield claimants, who gave their consent on the weekend of January 16–17. American Home offered to pay the entire court-ordered $2,475,000,000 for claimants into a trust fund within one year of the settlement of Robins's bankruptcy case.

In October 1988, just as the new 1989-model cars rolled off the assembly line, the National Association of Attorneys General identified automobile manufacturers as their next regulatory target. The association's goals were to establish national automobile manufacturer guidelines that would monitor deceptive warranties, car performance, and price and safety advertising claims.

An expanded investigation by federal regulators was conducted into the sudden-acceleration problems experienced in automobiles, including 309,000 vehicles manufactured by Mercedes-Benz from 1984 through 1988. The National Highway Traffic Safety Administration conducted six investigations concerning the same problem in more than four million automobiles. Besides Mercedes, the other man-

ufacturers involved included Ford Motor Co., 3.2 million cars; General Motors Corp., 800,000 cars; Audi, 225,000 vehicles; Nissan, 183,000 cars; and Honda, 62,500 cars.

The "lemon laws" passed in 45 states during the preceding decade to protect new-car buyers were adopted as a model for new laws to protect buyers of used vehicles. "Lemon laws" for used vehicles were implemented in Connecticut, New York, Rhode Island, and the District of Columbia. In 1988 Massachusetts and Minnesota also adopted laws that required warranties for used cars and trucks.

Chrysler Corp. announced, in a print advertising campaign, the installation of driver-side air bags in six of its car lines, thereby becoming the first U.S. automobile manufacturer to offer this safety device as standard equipment. By the 1990 model year, passive restraints such as air bags would be required in all automobiles.

In September the U.S. Department of Health and Human Services created a nationwide data bank (approved by Congress in 1986) to identify incompetent health practitioners. The data bank, though not available to the public, would include information on disciplinary actions taken against physicians, dentists, nurses, therapists, and other licensed health professionals and was expected to be operational by 1989.

On September 1 the Expedited Funds Availability Act of 1987 went into effect guaranteeing customers of banks, savings associations, and credit unions timely access to money deposited by check. Congress passed this act after consumer groups complained that lost interest and unjustified overdraft charges cost depositors millions of dollars a year because many financial institutions were holding checks as long as two weeks before the depositor could gain access to the funds. Under the new rules, local checks written on a financial institution in the same metropolitan area or within the same Federal Reserve check-processing region had to be available within three business days; nonlocal checks could be held for as long as seven days after deposit.   (EDWARD MARK MAZZE; SUSAN LARK SNIJDER)

See also Economic Affairs: *World Economy;* Environment; Industrial Review: *Advertising.*

Crime, Law Enforcement, and Penology

Violent Crime. *Terrorism.* According to U.S. State Department officials, the number of reported terrorist incidents during 1988 was up by about one-third, compared with the previous record of 832, set in 1987. However, the State Department also noted a decrease in the number of spectacular terrorist attacks, such as airline hijackings. Tighter airport security and increasing intelligence cooperation between Western nations were credited.

Tight security surrounded the Olympic Games in Seoul, South Korea, in September, and the Games were held without incident. Fears that North Korea might seek to disrupt the Games were fueled in January by the televised confession of a woman said to be a North Korean agent. The woman, Kim Hyon Hui, admitted that she had assisted in planting a bomb on a South Korean airliner that vanished with 115 persons aboard near the coast of Burma on Nov. 29, 1987.

Another potential threat to the Olympics appeared in April with the reemergence after several years of the Japanese Red Army (JRA), a shadowy terrorist group with known ties to North Korea. The JRA was thought to be

John F. Lavery, former vice-president of Beech-Nut Nutrition Corp., leaves a federal court after sentencing. Lavery and Niels L. Hoyvald, the former president, received fines and prison terms for selling an apple juice for babies that was, in fact, not made from apples.
STEPHEN FERRY—GAMMA/LIAISON

responsible for a car bombing in front of a U.S. servicemen's club in Naples, Italy, on April 14 which killed five people. Police speculated that the attack had been planned to coincide with the second anniversary of the U.S. bombing of Libya.

On April 5 Kuwait Airways Flight 422 was hijacked while en route from Bangkok, Thailand, to Kuwait. For the next 15 days the plane made a tortuous journey from Mashhad in northeastern Iran to Larnaca, Cyprus, and finally to Algiers. The hijackers killed 2 of the 112 people originally aboard and threatened the lives of the rest if Kuwaiti authorities did not free 17 terrorists jailed in 1983 for bombing the U.S. and French embassies in the Gulf state. The ordeal ended on April 20 when the hostages were released in return for safe conduct out of Algeria.

On December 21 a Pan American World Airways 747 jetliner en route to the U.S. from Frankfurt, West Germany, via London crashed over the village of Lockerbie, Scotland, killing all 259 persons on board and 11 on the ground. Investigators determined that the crash was almost certainly caused by a bomb explosion on board, but at year's end there were no clues as to what persons or groups might have been responsible.

On April 16, while the hijack drama was in progress, Khalil al-Wazir (better known by his nom de guerre, Abu Jihad; see OBITUARIES), the military chief of the Palestine Liberation Organization (PLO), was gunned down in Tunis, Tunisia, by a team of masked assailants, presumed to be Israeli commandos. His death appeared to be part of a shadowy war between Israeli and PLO intelligence operatives. On February 14 a car bomb explosion in Limassol, Cyprus, killed three senior PLO officers. On March 7 three Palestinians seized a bus near Israel's secret nuclear plant at Dimona; the Palestinians and three Israeli passengers died before Israeli forces regained control.

In another covert war, between the white-dominated South African government and the opponents of apartheid, the European representative of the banned African National Congress, Dulcie September, was shot dead on March 29 outside her office in Paris. On April 7 Albie Sachs, a prominent South African lawyer and antiapartheid activist, was severely injured in a car bomb attack in Maputo, Mozambique. Both of these attacks were believed to be the work of South African-backed assassination squads. In September South African police were involved in storming a hijacked

bus during a visit by Pope John Paul II to Lesotho. Four hijackers, reported to be members of the Lesotho Liberation Army, seized the bus and some 70 passengers as they traveled to Maseru to see the pope. Three of the hijackers and two hostages were killed in the subsequent shoot-out; the fourth hijacker died in Lesotho police custody.

Allegations of wrongful conduct were made against members of the elite British Special Air Service (SAS), who on March 6 shot dead three members of an Irish Republican Army (IRA) bomb squad in Gibraltar. The IRA members were found to be unarmed, but it appeared that the SAS believed they were in possession of a remote control device to explode a nearby car bomb. The incident provoked a fierce debate about British antiterrorism policies, fueled by an SAS ambush in Northern Ireland on August 30 in which three IRA members were killed. In September a coroner's jury reviewing the Gibraltar shootings determined that the SAS had acted in "a lawful manner." One of the most shocking incidents in the Northern Ireland conflict occurred on March 19 when a group of mourners in an IRA funeral procession killed two young British soldiers whose car had become trapped in the crowd. The incident, which was captured by television cameras, followed an attack three days earlier on a crowd gathered around the graves of the three IRA members who had been killed in Gibraltar. A lone terrorist, Michael Stone, lobbed splinter grenades and fired pistol shots at the mourners, killing 3 people and injuring more than 60. He was rescued by police after being beaten and severely injured by the mourners.

Retribution for the shooting down of an Iranian Airbus by a U.S. warship that mistook the airliner for a hostile plane appeared to have been the motive for the July 11 terrorist attack on a Greek ferry carrying tourists; 9 people were killed and more than 80 injured. The Turkish prime minister, Turgut Ozal, narrowly escaped death in an assassination attempt on June 18. A lone gunman, Kartal Demirag, fired at Ozal as he was making a speech, wounding him in the hand. The assailant was said to belong to the ultra-right-wing Grey Wolves. On August 17 Pakistani Pres. Mohammad Zia-ul-Haq, five of his top generals, and the U.S. ambassador to Pakistan were among 30 people who died when their military plane crashed shortly after takeoff. A Pakistani military inquiry board blamed a "highly sophisticated form of sabotage," but the evidence was not conclusive.

Drug Trafficking. At their summit meeting in Toronto in June, the leaders of the seven largest industrial nations, under pressure from U.S. Pres. Ronald Reagan, agreed to the establishment of a special task force to fight global drug trafficking. The enormous power of drug traffickers was nowhere more evident than in Latin America, where drug merchants superseded many insurgent groups as the main threat to stability in the region. (*See* Special Report.) In the U.S. many cities reported a frightening burst of drug-related violence as rival groups fought over the lucrative drug market.

Murder and Violence. The U.S. Justice Department's two major measures of crime—the FBI's Crime Index and the Bureau of Justice Statistics (BJS) National Crime Survey—differed somewhat in their assessment of the extent of crime in the U.S. in 1987. The FBI's preliminary figures revealed a 2% rise in the overall rate of crime with variations among crime categories, while BJS found that the crime rate remained at a 14-year low, with no significant changes in most crime categories. The FBI's figures were based on the accumulation of data from 16,000 law-enforcement agencies, while BJS figures were based on
(*continued on page 146*)

Latin America and the Drug Trade

BY ETHAN A. NADELMANN

It is Latin America's great fortune, and misfortune, to be the world's leading producer of cocaine as well as a significant producer of marijuana and heroin. Bolivia and Peru grow most of the coca leaf that is ultimately converted into cocaine. Colombia has been the principal refiner and exporter of cocaine since the mid-1970s; during the 1980s it emerged as the third leading cultivator of the coca plant as well. Colombian and other Latin-American drug-trafficking organizations now export an estimated 100–200 tons of cocaine each year to the U.S., Western Europe, and elsewhere. Most of the marijuana consumed in the U.S. is produced in Latin America and the Caribbean, principally Mexico and Colombia and, to a lesser extent, Jamaica and Belize. Mexico also produces approximately one-third to one-half of the heroin

Ethan A. Nadelmann is assistant professor of politics and public affairs at the Woodrow Wilson School of Public and International Affairs, Princeton University.

consumed in the U.S.; in years past, its share of the U.S. market reached as high as 80%. Many other Latin-American countries produce relatively small amounts of these drugs for export; some, such as Brazil, may soon progress into the ranks of the major producers. Virtually every country in the region also serves as a transit point for illicit drugs and, increasingly, as a consumer.

The impact of the international drug business in Latin America is almost entirely a consequence of two factors: the magnitude of the market relative to that for most other Latin-American exports, and the illegality of the market. If consumer interest in these products were to dwindle, so too would the negative and positive consequences for Latin America. Alternatively, if they were legal, Latin America would possess little competitive advantage in the production of marijuana and heroin—which can be grown virtually anywhere—and its involvement in the cocaine trade would probably resemble international trade in legitimate agricultural commodities. The drugs, however, remain both illegal and in growing demand—with dramatic consequences for much of Latin America.

Economic Consequences. By and large, the international demand for marijuana and cocaine has proved to be an economic boon for Latin America, especially the principal source countries, Bolivia, Peru, and Colombia. Much but by no means all of the economic benefit has derived from the market's illegality. Government repression of the market has had much the same effect on the price of drugs as would a huge tax, except that the tax revenues are collected not by the government but by the illicit sellers. Hundreds of thousands of coca-farming families have earned far more than they would have from any

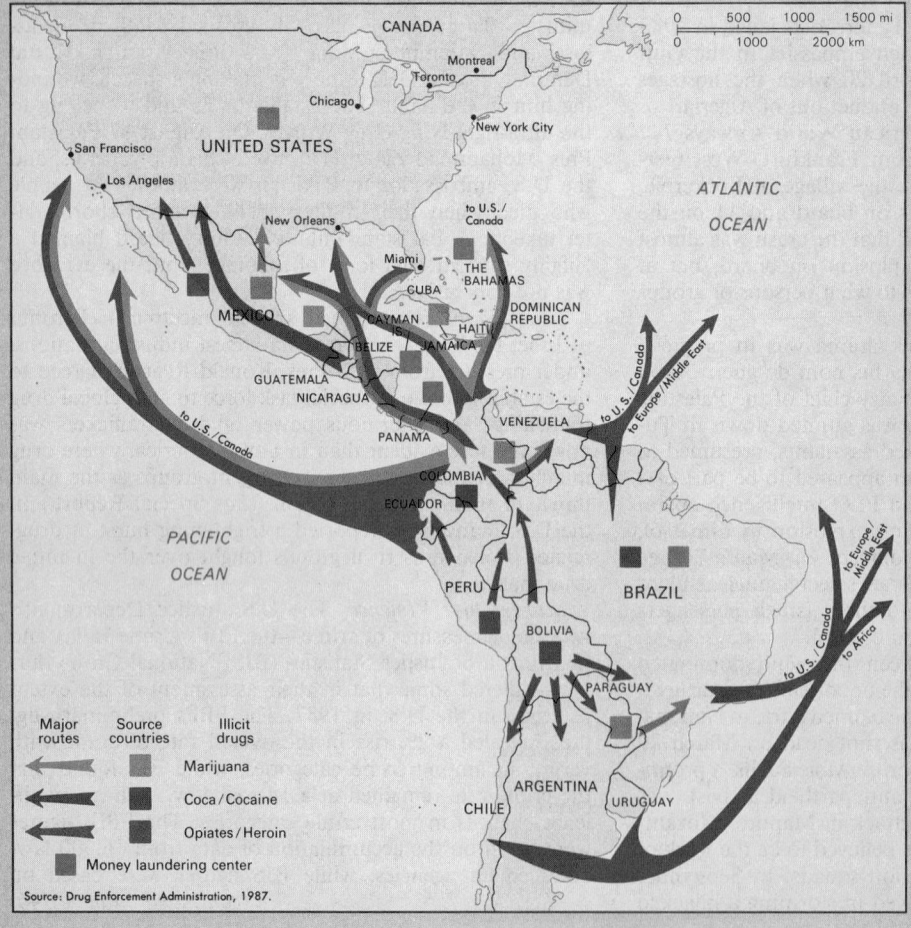

Drug operations in Latin America export an estimated 100–200 tons of cocaine to the U.S., Europe, and other regions. Latin America is now the world's leading producer of cocaine and a significant producer of marijuana and heroin. The drugs cut a path of death and destruction, not only where they are shipped but also in Latin America itself. There, huge profits lead to government corruption and violence against law enforcers and among rival druglords.

other crop. The same is true of the tens of thousands of marijuana growers in Mexico, Colombia, Jamaica, Belize, and elsewhere, as well as the thousands of Mexicans involved in producing illicit opium. Many others employed in sectors of the illicit drug markets ranging from refining to transport to security have supplemented or replaced meagre legitimate incomes. Countless corrupt officials have likewise profited from their informal tax on the drug market. The major traffickers, who are believed to invest most of their profits in safer havens outside their countries, are still obliged to spend substantial sums on production. And of course many others not directly involved in the drug business have benefited from its trickle-down effects.

Estimates of the market's total value remain highly speculative. The Bolivian government has estimated that the cocaine trade brings $600 million per year into its economy, more than all of its legitimate exports combined. Peru, which produces about the same amount of cocaine, probably earns a similar amount, although the drug accounts for a lesser proportion of its total exports. In both countries a large proportion of the coca money is distributed among the growers and other low-level participants in the market. Colombia is different in that it produces about a third as much coca leaf as Peru and Bolivia but is responsible for refining and exporting much of what is grown in those countries. It also was the principal supplier of marijuana to the North American market from the mid-1970s, when it surpassed Mexico, to mid-1986, when Mexico once again regained its preeminent position. Colombia's earnings from the drug traffic are distributed differently than in the two major coca-producing countries. There are fewer growers, but more people are involved in peripheral areas of the business. There are also more very wealthy traffickers, who are most likely to send large portions of their profits out of the country. The distribution of the wealth is thus not as progressive as in Peru and Bolivia, although the trickle-down effects may be more pervasive. All told, cocaine and marijuana exports generate between $1 billion and $2 billion a year in foreign currency for Latin Americans—excluding the billions invested outside the continent.

Political and Social Consequences. The economic benefits of the illicit drug traffic have been accompanied by tremendous corruption, lawlessness, and violence. Most Latin-American governments have long been plagued by corruption, in part because government salaries often have been insufficient to make ends meet, but it did not present overwhelming problems for the societies. During the past decade, however, the illegality and size of the drug business have stimulated a terrifying boom in corruption. Government officials ranging from common policemen to Cabinet ministers have been offered bribes many times their annual salaries, often for doing nothing more than looking the other way. Such bribes have often been accompanied by the suggestion or promise of violence if they are not accepted. The result has been an upset of the balance between corruption and functional government. Moreover, the limits on what could be bought have evaporated. Where once supreme court judges, top police and military officials, and Cabinet ministers were above such things, that is no longer the case. The combination of temptation and threat has become such that only the most courageous government officials can resist.

The ultimate degree of corruption is when government officials take the initiative in perpetrating crimes. This also has happened throughout much of Latin America. Policemen no longer merely accept bribes or extort from traffickers but engage in trafficking themselves. Provincial mayors and governors enter into partnerships with full-time drug traffickers. Even military officers, who in at least a few countries traditionally shunned drug corruption, have succumbed. This has occurred not just in the major drug-producing countries but throughout the continent.

Perhaps even worse than the corruption of governments has been the growth in the power of criminal groups. The two cannot, of course, be disentangled from one another, but they are distinct. In many Latin-American countries it is the drug-trafficking organizations rather than the government that represent the ultimate power in portions of the country if not the country as a whole. The heads of such organizations are seldom arrested. On the rare occasions when one is, those charged with guarding him understand that he retains the power to have their family members killed on command. Principled government officials know that ultimately the government cannot protect them or their families. In the U.S. it is almost unheard of for a federal judge or prosecutor to be killed. Even police rarely need to fear the vengeance of those they arrest. In Latin America not just police but prosecutors and judges have been killed by the dozens. In Colombia drug traffickers have killed a supreme court judge, an attorney general, a justice minister, a former chief of the drug-enforcement agency, and hundreds of lower-level judges, prosecutors, and police officials. If Bolivian and Mexican officials have not suffered to the same extent, it is probably at least partly because fewer of them have tried to stand in the way of the traffickers. As for informants, there is nothing in Latin America resembling the U.S. government's witness protection program. In the final analysis, what has eroded in many of the Latin-American countries—to the extent that it ever existed—is the ultimate authority of the state as symbol and enforcer of law and order.

Relations with the United States. The drug-related dilemmas confronting many Latin-American countries are to a considerable extent a function of the strong U.S. government interest in attacking the drug problem at its origins. Despite growing evidence that efforts to prevent the production and export of illicit drugs abroad are largely futile, international drug-control efforts continue to be regarded as a central component of U.S. drug policy. U.S. embassies in many Latin-American countries are directed to give top priority to the issue. Over 100 agents of the U.S. Drug Enforcement Administration are stationed throughout the region. Congress has repeatedly passed legislation making economic aid contingent upon foreign governments' cooperation in this area. Although many in Latin America bristle at the pressures applied by the U.S., all governments recognize that they must provide at least a modicum of cooperation. They thus have found themselves torn between trying to appease the U.S. and trying to minimize the harmful consequences of a drug problem that lies beyond their control.

Latin-American governments presently see little hope for a solution to their drug problems. The jobs and wealth generated by the illicit drug business are irreplaceable. Enhanced law-enforcement measures offer neither economic alternatives nor much competition to the drug traffickers. Only two alternatives offer any hope at all for Latin America's drug-related ills: a significant reduction in the world market for illicit cocaine, or the development of noncriminal justice approaches for regulating the global cocaine market; *i.e.,* legalization. Neither of these alternatives seems likely in the foreseeable future. By all indications, the drug problem in Latin America will get worse before it gets any better.

A dedication ceremony by the U.S. Customs Service heralds the latest weapon in the U.S. war on drugs, the "Blue Eagle." The plane was equipped with a radar system that could survey roughly 500,000 square kilometres (nearly 200,000 square miles) of air and ground.

AFP PHOTO

(continued from page 143)
a survey in which 99,000 people were interviewed about whether they had been victimized by crime. In a special report released in May, BJS found that U.S. rates for homicide, rape, and robbery were several times higher than the averages reported in European countries.

In the U.S.S.R., where crime statistics had long been suppressed, the new spirit of *glasnost* (openness) resulted in the publication of some revealing information. The overall recorded crime rate in the U.S.S.R. was said to have dropped by almost 9% during 1987, thanks largely to the antialcohol campaign introduced by Soviet leader Mikhail Gorbachev. However, Moscow police officials reported that juvenile delinquency had risen by 20% during the past five years.

A study of mass murder in the U.S. indicated that there had been a definite increase in this type of crime during the past decade, although it remained relatively rare. The researchers defined mass murder as the killing of four or more victims within a short period of time. The study showed that an average of three mass murders occurred in the U.S. each month. It estimated that more than 1,700 people had died as a result of mass murder over a ten-year period, compared with approximately 20,000 homicides occurring in the U.S. each year.

The increasing emphasis on victim rights in the U.S. was demonstrated in New York City in March in the widely publicized "preppy murder case." Robert E. Chambers, Jr., admitted killing Jennifer Levin on Aug. 26, 1986, after picking her up in a bar, but he insisted that her death had occurred accidentally during rough sex. After a 13-week trial, Chambers abruptly pleaded guilty to first-degree manslaughter in a plea bargain initiated by the Manhattan district attorney, Robert M. Morgenthau. Morgenthau indicated that Levin's parents had been consulted about the plea bargain. Such consultation with the victim, or the victim's family in homicide cases, was mandatory in 23 states and was becoming a common practice elsewhere.

Meeting in Lisbon in June, European justice ministers discussed a report that claimed one million children fell victim each year to pedophiles, prostitution racketeers, and traffickers in pornography. The report said that there had been a steep rise in recent years in the sexual abuse of children in both Europe and the third world. Children were bought or kidnapped from third world slums and sold through middlemen to clients in the developed countries.

Nonviolent Crime. *Political Crime and Espionage.* A long-awaited special prosecutors' report released in July concluded that U.S. Attorney General Edwin Meese "probably violated the criminal law" but that no prosecution was warranted. The special prosecutor's 14-month investigation focused on charges that the attorney general had assisted a New York defense contractor to win government contracts and was involved in plans to build an oil pipeline in Iraq. In the Soviet Union, Yury M. Churbanov, the son-in-law of the late Soviet leader Leonid Brezhnev, went on trial in September before the Soviet Supreme Court on charges of having accepted bribes of more than $1 million to protect corrupt police officials. Former Philippine president Ferdinand Marcos and his wife, Imelda, were indicted by a New York grand jury on racketeering charges involving the use of embezzled Philippine government funds to buy property in New York City.

A major stock market scandal in Japan implicated Prime Minister Noboru Takeshita and other government leaders. The scandal, which first broke in June, involved the activities of a real estate firm, Recruit Cosmos Co., which allegedly sold cheap unlisted shares on credit to relatives or associates of an impressive lineup of politicians, businessmen, and senior journalists and publishers. In September a South Korean court sentenced the brother of former president Chun Doo Hwan to seven years in prison for embezzling millions of dollars during President Chun's seven-year rule, which ended in February 1988. Growing corruption in China, much of it a product of the country's market-oriented economic reforms, sparked renewed efforts by Chinese leaders to expose those concerned. In August the nation's first 24-hour corruption hot line was set up in Beijing (Peking) by the Ministry of Supervision.

In March Mordechai Vanunu, a former Israeli technician who revealed secrets of Israel's nuclear arsenal to a British newspaper, was convicted of treason and espionage and sentenced to 18 years in prison. Vanunu's lawyers appealed the verdict to the Supreme Court, maintaining that Israeli courts had no jurisdiction in the case since Vanunu had been abducted in Rome by Israeli agents. West German authorities announced that in late August they had uncovered a major spy ring that had passed NATO secrets to the Eastern bloc via Hungary. A former sergeant with the U.S. Army's 8th Infantry Division in West Germany, Clyde Lee Conrad, was believed to be the central figure in the ring. He was arrested, together with seven suspected

accomplices, by police in West Germany and Sweden. Kim Philby (*see* OBITUARIES), a Soviet master spy who for many years worked undercover in the British Secret Intelligence Service (MI-6), died in Moscow in May at the age of 76.

White Collar Crime and Theft. In June the results of Operation Ill Wind, a two-year investigation of fraud and bribery in the handling of major U.S. military purchases, sent reverberations through the military-industrial complex. Conducted jointly by the FBI and the Naval Investigative Service, the inquiry was said to have uncovered schemes whereby past and present Pentagon officials, as well as employees and consultants of some of the nation's largest defense firms, paid bribes for inside information that gave companies an unfair advantage in bidding for multibillion-dollar defense contracts. In September the U.S. Securities and Exchange Commission (SEC) filed civil charges against six individuals in connection with an insider trading case involving the major securities firm of Drexel Burnham Lambert Inc. At the centre of the affair was Michael Milken, a senior executive vice-president of Drexel and head of its high-yield, or "junk," bond department. Much of the SEC's case was believed to rest on testimony to be provided by the now imprisoned takeover speculator Ivan Boesky. In a related criminal case, on December 21 Drexel agreed in principle to plead guilty to six felony charges and pay $650 million in penalties.

In February financier Licio Gelli was extradited from Switzerland to Italy to face charges relating to his alleged role in the 1982 collapse of Banco Ambrosiano, Italy's biggest private bank. Gelli, who had escaped from a top security prison in Geneva in 1983, was rearrested while trying to withdraw millions of dollars deposited in a bank by South American subsidiaries of Banco Ambrosiano. A number of officials of the Institute for Religious Works (the Vatican bank), including U.S. Archbishop Paul Marcinkus, were alleged to have been involved in the affair, but Italy's Constitutional Court ruled in June that they could not be arrested because a treaty made institutions of the Vatican City State immune from interference by Italian authorities. Two suspected computer hackers were arrested in Switzerland in September in connection with the unauthorized electronic transfer of about £15 million worth of Eurobonds from a Japanese investment bank in London.

The BJS released a study in March showing that 12.3 million cars, trucks, vans, and motorcycles, valued at $52 billion, had been stolen in the U.S. over a 13-year period. About 65% of the stolen vehicles were recovered, leaving losses estimated at $29 billion. The most likely people to be victimized by car thefts were black Americans, Hispanics, households headed by people under the age of 25, people in multiple dwelling units, central city residents, and low-income households.

Law Enforcement. The increasing importance of forensic evidence in law-enforcement work was stressed in a report issued in April by the U.S. National Institute of Justice. The report noted that police were about three times as likely to clear criminal cases if forensic evidence played a role in the investigation; prosecutors were less likely to enter into plea negotiations if they had fingerprints or other scientific evidence; and jurors found forensic evidence interesting, understandable, and trustworthy. Prosecutors in a number of U.S. jurisdictions reported that they had begun to use DNA fingerprinting techniques in criminal trials. This involved breaking DNA—the genetic material present in every human cell—into fragments. All humans, except identical twins, possess a unique distribution of fragments, which can be used for identification.

A number of police forces in Canada began to use a new form of computer technology to assist with criminal investigations. Dubbed HOLMES (Home Office Large Major Enquiry System), it was first developed in the U.K. during the hunt for a serial killer known as the Yorkshire Ripper. Using HOLMES, a search to connect pieces of information that would take many weeks manually could be done in a few seconds. In London the Metropolitan Police Force reported a steady increase in the number of assaults against its officers. These assaults rose by 33% in 1987, when about one in six of London's more than 27,000 police officers was assaulted in a way that required medical attention.

European police forces conducted discussions during the year about the effects of the plan to turn the European Communities into a single market in 1992. This, coupled with the eventual opening of a tunnel under the English Channel, was thought likely to bring about much closer collaborative ties between police forces throughout the EC. In Sweden controversy continued about the police investigation into the murder of Prime Minister Olof Palme in February 1986. The complex affair led to the resignation of the Swedish justice minister, Anna-Greta Leijon, in June. At year's end a suspect, who had been questioned in 1986 and released for insufficient evidence, was arraigned in the case. (*See* WORLD AFFAIRS [Western Europe]: *Sweden.*)

(DUNCAN CHAPPELL)

Prisons and Penology. Punitivism continued to dominate penological thought and practice in 1988, moderated chiefly by concern over the cost of imprisoning the growing number of convicts. In the U.S. privatization of prisons remained controversial, despite the successes claimed by the Corrections Corporation of America, the leading private prison corporation in the U.S., in managing prisons more humanely as well as more cheaply; by July the corporation had 11 contracts with five states, had helped a French consortium win an order to build private prisons in France, and was negotiating to bring its experience to the U.K.

Also controversial was electronic "tagging," which according to a report in June was being used in the surveillance of some 5,000 offenders sentenced to house arrest in four U.S. states. The proposed introduction of tagging in the U.K. was a principal subject of penological debate there in 1988, together with more rigorous forms of community service orders and other noncustodial penalties. Also debated in the U.K. was the proposed introduction of "day fines," fines expressed in terms of the offender's net income so as to equalize the effect. Day fines had been used in Sweden since 1931 and in several other countries from the 1970s.

Individual and regional variations in sentencing attracted criticism in France and the U.K., leading to proposals for curtailing judicial autonomy in sentencing. A majority of judges and lawyers in the British House of Lords were reported to favour abolition of the mandatory life sentence for murder, allowing judges to set different terms reflecting the degree of heinousness of the crime.

Capital Punishment. Amnesty International reported that a previously noted decline in the number of officially recorded executions worldwide had continued in 1986 but that the number had increased slightly in 1987. They stressed, however, that official figures gave little indication of the real number of people put to death by the state. Thus the fatal shooting of three IRA suspects in Gibraltar by British agents in March was seen by some critics as further evidence that the British government had not so much abolished the death penalty as "transferred executions . . . to the street." In June the House of Commons rejected restoration of the death penalty by 341 votes to 218.

A law-enforcement worker monitors a person under house arrest. Machines that enabled an officer, via telephone, to check an offender's whereabouts were helping alleviate prison crowding and reducing the need for new prison construction.

AP/WIDE WORLD

Opposition to capital punishment in the U.S. remained less clamorous than in the 1970s, but in June the Supreme Court overturned death sentences passed on three juvenile murderers, including Paula Cooper, sentenced for a murder committed when she was 15, and agreed to consider banning the death penalty for all juveniles on the grounds that it was "cruel and unusual punishment." Wholesale use of capital punishment continued to be reported from China, where some Western observers estimated that about 10,000 executions had taken place since the launching of the anticrime drive in 1983. Execution of an innocent man (and the imprisonment of 14 others) was proved at Vitebsk, U.S.S.R., when the police discovered the real murderer in March. In Islamic countries executions continued to be carried out in accordance with the Shari'ah law, though in January Mohammad Khan Junejo, prime minister of Pakistan, intervened to stay the execution by stoning of an adulteress. In February the family of an Irishwoman murdered at Taif, Saudi Arabia, waived their right to have her alleged murderers executed after conviction.

Prisons. As in previous years, rising crime rates in many countries led to overcrowded prisons, resulting in strain and deteriorating conditions. Despite government requests that courts make less use of jail, magistrates and judges exercised their judicial independence (and almost certainly reflected public opinion) by remanding to custody more often and sending more people to prison for longer terms. In what was described as a "magistrates' rebellion," John Hosking, chairman of the British Magistrates' Association, said magistrates had "very strong reservations" about the alternatives to custody proposed by the government. In the U.S. the use of alternatives to custody became an issue in the presidential election campaign; Republican George Bush persistently reminded voters that his Democratic opponent, Massachusetts Gov. Michael Dukakis, had presided over a prisoner furlough program and that at least one offender had committed a serious crime while at liberty.

The U.S. prison population rose faster than the crime rate, reaching nearly half a million in June. In the U.K., where prison numbers also reached record levels, widespread industrial action by prison staff in August was sparked by grievances over staff shortages at Holloway women's prison, London, but it developed into a dispute about overcrowding and understaffing throughout the British prison service. The government responded by opening two new temporary jails and by housing prisoners in police cells, often hundreds of kilometres away,

at an estimated nightly cost per prisoner (£163) more expensive than the Ritz Hotel (£145). Home Secretary Douglas Hurd's response to the longer-term problem of prison-population growth was to plan accelerated prison construction (with an element of privatization envisaged in a July Green Paper) and to provide new, more severe, noncustodial sentences. Plans for "air security" at British maximum-security prisons were announced in January after the escape of two prisoners by helicopter from Gartree maximum-security prison in December 1987.

Prison riots and disturbances were reported from many countries, including the U.S.S.R., where Soviet commandos stormed the jail at Komsomolsk-na-Amure in June after six prisoners had seized a guard and five women. A January siege at a prison near Pôrto Alegre, Brazil, led to the occupation of the prison by more than 350 police and the death of two prisoners. At Norrköping, Sweden, a man armed with a submachine gun forced his way into the prison in April and freed two inmates. Even more dramatic was the escape, also in April, of Col. Gregorio Honasan from the prison ship in Manila Bay where he was detained following his attempted coup in 1987; he left before dawn in a rubber dinghy with 13 members of the naval warfare unit detailed to guard him. In Madrid a prison governor, two doctors, and eight prison guards were themselves sent to prison for their involvement in the fatal beating of a suspected terrorist in 1978.

The government of Cuba, where the postrevolution per capita prison population had been among the highest in the world, announced a revision of the criminal code making some petty offenses punishable by fine instead of imprisonment. A reduction of 16% in the prison population of West Germany in the years 1983–87 was attributed not to government action but to a 1983 conference organized by the criminal law section of the German Lawyers' Association. The more than 200 judges, prosecutors, and administrators who attended were apparently persuaded that bail could be granted more freely and that imprisonment was useless as a method of treating offenders.   (C. R. M. DAVIES)

See also Law.

This article updates the *Macropædia* articles CRIME AND PUNISHMENT; POLICE.

Dance

North America. The key event of 1988 was the visit by the School of the Paris Opéra Ballet, directed by Claude Bessy, during the main company's New York appearances at the Metropolitan Opera House in June. Nearly 90 students and most of the faculty laid out the school syllabus for all but the youngest level. The process took more than six hours; the Juilliard Theater audience was the same intense group of professionals who turned out for the annual workshops of the School of American Ballet, a cosponsor of the Paris Ballet school's visit. The next day, the French students gave two breathtaking performances of a program that showcased their classical style, folk dance, mime, and musicality. Meanwhile, at the Met, the parent company, directed by Rudolf Nureyev, stressed very different values: discontinuity, glamour, technique as a replacement for fantasy.

For ballet dancers, the links between studio tradition and stage vision are the meaning of the art. In 1988 two leading U.S. classical companies made them a matter of public interest. American Ballet Theatre (ABT) instituted a School of Classical Ballet for advanced students, aged 12–19. (ABT's former school was dissolved during the 1980-

81 season.) The idea belonged to ABT's artistic director, Mikhail Baryshnikov, who had become an increasingly visible and impressive leader. ABT seemed to turn many corners in 1988. Its productions were marked by luxury (Christian Lacroix designed the costumes for the revival of *Gaîté Parisienne*), but they also reflected a coherent taste: decisive silhouettes, rich fabrics, brilliant palettes. In December the company gave the premiere of its new *Swan Lake*, designed by Pier Luigi Samaritani, who had also been responsible for ABT's sumptuous *La Bayadère*.

ABT also scored in choreography. Mark Morris's *Drink to Me Only with Thine Eyes*—a plotless étude with a stress on partnering, to a Virgil Thomson piano score—was arguably the best new ballet of the year by any U.S. company. ABT principal Clark Tippet emerged as a productive in-house choreographer with an excellent eye for dancers and a mature sensitivity to the needs of repertory. ABT also signed Twyla Tharp, choreographer of four works for ABT (three of them masterful portraits of Baryshnikov), as full-time artistic associate. Although Tharp did not dissolve her own company as a corporate entity, only seven of her dancers followed her. Finally, ABT grossed over $7 million during its eight-week Met season, another record.

At the New York City Ballet (NYCB), where fund-raising also soared to record levels, the year was rockier artistically. The company celebrated its 40th anniversary in two parts. During the spring it produced the $3.5 million American Music Festival (AMF), brainchild of co-ballet-master-in-chief Peter Martins, who choreographed 9 of its 24 new ballets (22 world premieres and 2 company premieres). The festival was intended to galvanize the dancers and explore future directions. The second celebration, marked by the opening gala of the fall season, reproduced the majestic all-Balanchine program that initiated NYCB in 1948 (*Concerto Barocco, Orpheus, Symphony in C*), thus accenting the company's continuity and, it was hoped, Balanchinean character. However, the AMF precipitated a fire storm of protest in the press, owing largely to its lack of focus, awkward musicianship, and implied condescension toward the independence of the ballerina.

NYCB's other co-ballet-master-in-chief, Jerome Robbins, pointedly made his "American" work—*Ives, Songs*—for the preceding season and did not take an active part in the AMF. Modern dance choreographers who did take part—Paul Taylor, Eliot Feld, Lar Lubovitch, Laura Dean—made the AMF's connection to Balanchine even more attenuated, and the AMF Balanchine works themselves (*Episodes, Western Symphony, Stars and Stripes, Who Cares?*) seemed peripheral in context. Martins continued to be publicly supported by his board of directors, who, for the first time in the company's life, were pressed to take an active role in its management. In this they were typical of their times. The 1988 National Roundtable for professional American dance companies, produced by Dance/USA, focused on problems that arise as companies pass from the autocratic control of their founders to consensus governance by boards of trustees, often driven more by market necessity than by artistic compulsion.

Perhaps the most surprising thing about 1988 was the extent of dance exchange between North America and the rest of the world, especially the Communist world. NYCB made its first tour to Japan since 1958, and ABT returned to Paris, with success, after an absence of 12 years. There was much U.S. travel to the U.S.S.R. Pacific Northwest Ballet's Francia Russell went to Leningrad to stage the Kirov's first Balanchine ballet, *Theme and Variations*. Fernando Bujones became the first U.S. male dancer to perform as a guest with the Bolshoi. The Dance Theatre of Harlem made a warmly received 30-day tour of Moscow, Tbilisi, and Leningrad. Dancers from Minneapolis, Minn., and Seattle, Wash., studied and performed in the U.S.S.R. by invitation of the Union of Theatrical Workers there.

An extraordinary number of dancers from abroad visited the U.S. One influx came in early summer for the first New York International Festival of the Arts, including Pina Bausch's Wuppertal Dance Theatre, the Frankfurt Ballet, and Astrakan from France, which performed Daniel Larrieu's *Waterproof* in the swimming pool of Columbia University. The Royal Danish Ballet made its first U.S. visit since 1982. Kirov stars Altynai Asylmuratova and Farukh Ruzimatov were guests with ABT and Bolshoi stars Andris Liepa and Nina Ananiashvili with NYCB; later, Liepa returned to begin a year with ABT. The city of Boston put on an homage to Maya Plisetskaya, featuring performances by the honouree with other Bolshoi dancers and by Baryshnikov, transcendent in the title role of *Apollo,* with members of ABT. The Moscow Classical Ballet Company and Zagreb Grand Ballet made debut tours.

Significant new works by U.S. choreographers included Paul Taylor's *Brandenburgs, Counterswarm, Speaking in Tongues,* and *Danbury Mix;* Merce Cunningham's *Five Stone Wind* and *Eleven;* Mark Morris's *Fugue and Fantasia* (Mozart), *Poulenc Sonatas,* and *Strict Songs;* Martha Graham's *Night Chant;* and Karole Armitage's *The Elizabethan Phrasing of the Late Albert Ayler.* The Joffrey Ballet reconstructed Balanchine's 1932 *Cotillon* ("lost" for four decades), persuasively mounted by Millicent Hodson and Kenneth Archer. The Martha Graham Dance Company and school put on a rare daylong seminar devoted to Graham's changing technique from the 1930s to the present. On stage the company reconstructed Graham's 1937 *Deep Song* and revived her 1940 *Letter to the World.*

Daniel Duell became head of Ballet Chicago after a bitter dispute effectively dissolved its antecedent, the Chicago City Ballet (CCB). Paul Mejia, former CCB artistic director, became director of the Fort Worth (Texas) Ballet. Ted Kivitt became artistic director of Northwest Ballet in Minneapolis, after it split off from Pacific Northwest in Seattle. Judith Jamison, former Ailey star, founded the Jamison Project, which made an exciting debut in repertory that included a remarkable new solo for Jamison by Garth Fagan. The Dance Notation Bureau completed its four-year project to notate 18 Balanchine ballets.

In Canada the Alberta Ballet and Les Grands Ballets Canadiens were featured in the Olympic Arts Festival,

JONATHAN PLAYER—THE NEW YORK TIMES

Natalia Makarova exchanges a rose for a kiss from her partner, Konstantin Zaklinsky, after a London peformance with the Kirov Ballet. Makarova was the first Russian dancer allowed to perform with a Soviet company after defecting to the West.

Wings of silk fan out from dancer Brygida Ochaim in her presentation of works inspired by Loie Fuller. Fuller, a turn-of-the-century American dancer, took Paris by storm with her innovative combinations of costumes, lighting, and sound.

MONROE WARSHAW—THE NEW YORK TIMES

held during the Winter Games in Calgary, Alta. Canadian Reid Anderson, formerly of the Stuttgart Ballet, was chosen permanent artistic director of the National Ballet of Canada, effective in 1990. Other new artistic directors included Henny Jurriens (Royal Winnipeg Ballet) and Bill James (Toronto's influential Dancemakers). Anik Bissonnette and Louis Robitaille of the Ballet de Montréal Eddy Toussaint starred in *Giselle* with the Odessa Ballet in the U.S.S.R. Irena Lavrova and Sabirian Yapparov of the Odessa Ballet performed in Canada with Eddy Toussaint in exchange. Canada's first Erik Bruhn Prize ($11,250) went to Errol Pickford (Great Britain's Royal Ballet) and Rose Gad Poulsen (Royal Danish Ballet); the prize was open to contestants from companies with which Bruhn had been associated.

Among the many deaths mourned were those of Robert Joffrey (*see* OBITUARIES), William Carter, Robert Blankshine, La Meri (Russell Meriwether Hughes), John Bernd, Maria-Thérèsa Duncan, Roberto Lorca, Robert D. Rodham, Jack Moore, David Cuevas, Colette C. Kaufman, Alexander Iolas, Eugene Hari, and James Selva in 1988 and Carmelita Maracci in late 1987.   (MINDY ALOFF)

Europe. The year 1988, formally designated "Year of Dance" in France on the recommendation of Unesco, was heralded by the award on New Year's Eve of the Legion of Honour to Nureyev, director of France's national company, the Paris Opéra Ballet. Former dancer Brigitte Lefèvre, the first dance delegate to the French Ministry of Culture, announced substantial increases in public funding and a new long-term development policy. Among the Year of Dance's major events was a four-week festival at Lyon (September–October) celebrating 400 years of dance in France from the time of Louis XIV to the latest in modern dance. Generous funding included free use of Lyon's

purpose-built dance house and ten other local theatres, and programs assembled regional companies from all over France as well as dancers from the Paris company. The Paris company's major production was Nureyev's commission of a new *Martyre de Saint Sébastien* staged by the American Robert Wilson to the Debussy music and Gabriele d'Annunzio text, premiered at Bobigny on March 25 and subsequently taken on the Paris Ballet's tour to New York.

Paris was host to the Leningrad Kirov Ballet before the Soviets went on to Dublin and London. Simultaneous visitors in the British capital in August were the Moscow Classical Ballet, which meant that, with concurrent London visits from the Australian Ballet and New York's Dance Theatre of Harlem, some 10,000 seats went on sale six nights a week for two weeks and, contrary to forecast, were almost all sold. Britain's Royal Ballet at this time was on an exchange visit to Australia as part of that country's bicentennial celebrations, having previously staged a London gala for the 90th birthday of founder-director Dame Ninette de Valois, at which three generations of British choreography were represented. Two months later, on August 18, the entire profession mourned the death of the Royal Ballet's founder-choreographer Sir Frederick Ashton (*see* OBITUARIES). Ashton's last task was to supervise the Royal Ballet's May 10 revival of his three-act fairy tale *Ondine,* with the company's youngest ranking ballerina, Maria Almeida, in the title role created in 1958 by Margot Fonteyn. At the opposite stylistic extreme, Dance Umbrella celebrated a tenth anniversary with a monthlong fall festival of modern dance involving 20 groups, from the U.S. and Australia as well as nearer home.

Benefiting from the new Soviet spirit of *glasnost* (openness), former Kirov ballerina Natalia Makarova was briefly reunited with her old company and director, Oleg Vinogradov, when she danced Odette in *Swan Lake* Act II with them in their London season on August 6. BBC Television jettisoned three hours of prime-time scheduling to relay the full evening program as it happened. This followed Makarova's venture into ballet production with her own staging of *Swan Lake* for London Festival Ballet, first given at Bradford, Yorkshire, on April 12 before being taken to London and Copenhagen, among other places. Much acclaimed by audiences, her version kept some of the traditional choreography but had major changes, including separate ballerinas for Odette and Odile, dropping most of the Act III character dances, and showing the evil von Rothbart as a cinematic projection.

Britain's modern dance companies, including the London Contemporary Dance Theatre and the renamed Rambert Dance Company, maintained regular touring dates and a healthy proportion of new work. Michael Clark and Company were cofunded from The Netherlands as well as Britain for a new production, *I Am Curious, Orange,* first staged in Amsterdam. Supposedly celebrating the tercentennial of William of Orange's accession to the English throne, its performance more closely resembled a promotional video for The Fall rock band, which appeared onstage with the dancers. The Netherlands' National Ballet and Netherlands Dance Theatre continued their complementary activities and received the National Ballet of Turkey on that company's first foreign tour. Repertory included *At the Fountainhead* by Ninette de Valois, who was instrumental in forming the Turkish company in 1960 and keeping it supplied with teachers. Netherlands Dance Theatre's choreographer-director Jiri Kylian, a native of Prague, had a work shown in the Czechoslovak capital for the first time when his *Evening Songs* to Dvorak music

Members of the American
Ballet Theatre perform
in the new production of
Leonide Massine's *Gaité
Parisienne.* A combination
of solid programming and
strong casting made 1988 a
momentous year for the ballet
company.
MARTHA SWOPE

was staged by the Prague Chamber Ballet (June 8). Earlier, this company, directed by Pavel Smok, was the first foreign company invited to share the stage in a Sadler's Wells Royal Ballet program in London, giving Smok's own *Kreutzer Sonata* (January 14), to music by Janacek.

Venezuela's Ballet de Caracas joined companies from the U.S. and the U.S.S.R. at the Madrid Autumn Festival. The Venezuelans premiered *George Sand,* a full-evening ballet by Vicente Nebrada to Liszt and Chopin music (September 29), with the title role danced by Spanish-born Trinidad Sevillano from London Festival Ballet. American Indian Dance Theatre, comprising dancers and musicians from 15 North American Indian tribes, performed authentic repertory in Europe for the first time at Rimini, Italy, on August 24. Also in Italy, Gian Carlo Menotti's Festival of Two Worlds at Spoleto was host to an International Dance Marathon divided between classical and jazz dance; one highlight was new choreography by Robert North to Menotti's own 1944 ballet music, *Sebastian.* The Arena at Verona saw the premiere on August 6 of *Zorba the Greek,* choreography after the Kazantzakis novel by Lorca Massine to Mikis Theodorakis's music, with Bolshoi Ballet star Vladimir Vasiliev in the title role.

A first Nordic Choreographers Competition was held in Oslo on May 14, organized through a professional working association developed between ballet directors in Denmark, Finland, Iceland, Norway, and Sweden. The prize was taken by Hlif Svavarsdottir, director of the small Icelandic Dance Company formed 15 years earlier by Britain's Alan Carter. Titled *About People,* her ballet used a free range of dance styles to specially written music by Thorkell Sigurbjørnsson. The annual festival built around the Royal Danish Ballet's historic Bournonville repertory included first Hans Christian Andersen Ballet Awards to Irek Mukhamedov (U.S.S.R.) and Sylvie Guillem (France) as best male and female dancers; to Kylian for choreography; and, for "outstanding contribution to ballet," divided between Ashton, Robbins, and the Danish-born Peter Martins. Increased attention to new work was evident from premieres of *The Song of the Earth* by Constantin Patsalas, to Mahler's song-symphony, and Robert North's *Elvira Madigan.*

The Irish National Ballet faced closing when public funding through the Irish Arts Council was withdrawn because of financial pressure, but it was replaced by a direct grant from government funds at the intervention of Prime Minister Charles Haughey. Having relocated his company from Belgium to Switzerland to become Béjart Ballet Lausanne, Maurice Béjart began operations at the new base and on tour, attracting significantly more praise for the dancers than for program content. A competition to discover new choreographic talent with a guarantee of production by Béjart resulted in prize money being divided equally among five finalists.

Deaths during the year included: Pierre Bos, Royal Ballet of Flanders soloist, in an air accident; Hans Brenaa, leading Bournonville specialist and teacher with Royal Danish Ballet; Gerda Karstens, outstanding Danish character dancer and mime; Deirdre O'Conaire, who took early retirement as soloist with Britain's Royal Ballet; John Regan, Irish choreographer, dancer, and teacher; and Dora Stratou, Greek folk-dance historian and founder of the Society for Greek Folk Dances and Songs. (NOËL GOODWIN)

See also Music; Theatre.

This article updates the *Macropædia* article The History of Western DANCE.

MARTHA SWOPE

Members of the Lar Lubovitch Dance Company dance to the music of Poulenc in Lubovitch's latest work, *Musette.* After a three-year period of experimentation, Lubovitch provided in *Musette* a sample of his considerable skill with more traditional choreography.

Disasters

The loss of life and property from disasters in 1988 included the following:

Aviation

January 2, Near Izmir, Turkey. A Boeing 737 jetliner crashed in mountainous countryside while attempting to land at the airport at Izmir; all 16 persons aboard lost their lives .

January 13, Northern Somalia. An air force helicopter on a routine inspection tour crashed while attempting to land; 12 officials were killed.

January 18, Chongqing (Ch'ung-ch'ing), China. An Ilyushin-18 domestic airliner crashed some eight kilometres (five miles) from the airport in Sichuan (Szechwan) Province; all 108 persons aboard the craft lost their lives.

January 18, Krasnovodsk, U.S.S.R. A Soviet TY-154 airliner apparently disintegrated while attempting to land and crashed; 11 persons were known dead and 12 others were injured.

January 19, Orchid Island, Taiwan. A British-built Britten-Norman 2 commuter plane crashed into a mountain on Orchid Island; of the 11 persons aboard, only one survived the crash.

February 8, Near Müllheim, West Germany. A twin-engine turboprop FA-4 Metroliner commuter airliner began disintegrating in midair after being struck by lightning; the craft crashed, and all 21 persons aboard were killed.

February 19, North Carolina. A commuter plane crashed moments after taking off from the Raleigh-Durham airport; all 12 persons aboard were killed.

February 25, Chico, Texas. An army helicopter carrying 18 soldiers burst into flames and crashed into a pasture; 10 soldiers were killed.

February 27, Surgut, Siberia, U.S.S.R. An Aeroflot Tu-134 airliner crashed while attempting to land and then caught fire and broke into pieces; the official news agency TASS reported that an unspecified number of the 51 persons aboard perished in the crash.

February 27, Kyrenia, Cyprus. A Boeing 727 Turkish chartered plane crashed into mist-enshrouded mountains some ten minutes before landing; all 15 persons aboard were killed.

March 1, Near Johannesburg, South Africa. A Brazilian-made turboprop passenger plane exploded in midair and plunged into a Coca Cola factory; all 17 persons aboard the aircraft died.

March 4, Near Machault, France. A French commuter airplane awaiting landing instructions hit high-tension power lines and crashed into a field during driving snow and rain; all 22 persons aboard were killed.

March 8, Near Fort Campbell, Kentucky. Two U.S. Army helicopters crashed after one of the UH-60 Blackhawks collided with one of three planes flying in formation during a night training exercise; 17 servicemen were killed.

March 17, Near Cúcuta, Colombia. A Colombian airliner carrying 137 persons crashed in a remote mountainous region minutes after take-off; there were no survivors.

April 12, Near Henneman, South Africa. A chartered DC-3 Dakota airliner, ferrying jockeys from races in Bloemfontein, crashed; all 23 persons aboard were killed.

Late April, Siberia. An L-410 carrying 17 persons crashed into a slope near Lake Baikal while attempting to land at the town of Bagdarin; all aboard were killed.

May 6, Near Bronnoysund, Norway. A four-engine de Havilland Canada Dash 7, with 36 persons aboard, crashed in rocky terrain, burst into flames, and was rocked by a series of small explosions; there were no survivors.

June 12, Near Posadas, Arg. A DC-9 jetliner, attempting to land at Posadas airport, crashed into a grove of eucalyptus trees in heavy fog; all 22 persons aboard were killed.

July 3, Persian Gulf. The U.S. Navy warship *Vincennes* shot down an Iran Air Airbus A300 passenger jet after incorrectly identifying the aircraft as an F-14 fighter plane; all 290 persons aboard were killed.

Fire officials sort through the luggage of an Air Vietnam passenger plane that was struck by lightning and then crashed outside of Bangkok, Thailand, killing 75 of the 81 passengers on board.

AP/WIDE WORLD

August 2, Sofia, Bulg. A Soviet-built Yak-40 airliner carrying 37 persons crashed moments after takeoff; 23 persons lost their lives.

August 17, Near Bahawalpur, Pak. A Pakistani Air Force C-130 plane exploded and crashed some three minutes after takeoff; the 30 persons aboard, all of whom were killed, included Pres. Mohammad Zia-ul-Haq of Pakistan, U.S. ambassador Arnold L. Raphel, U.S. Brig. Gen. Herbert M. Wassom, and five Pakistani Army generals. Sabotage had not been ruled out as a cause of the blast.

August 28, Ramstein, West Germany. Three Italian fighter jets collided during an air show at a U.S. military base, causing one of them to crash into a crowd of spectators and explode; 70 persons died as a result of the crash, and more than 150 others were hospitalized.

August 31, Mexico. A twin-engine commuter plane crashed in the Sierra Madre mountains during heavy rains; all 21 persons aboard lost their lives.

August 31, Arlington, Texas. A Boeing 727 jetliner crashed to the ground, broke in two, and erupted in flames shortly after taking off from the Dallas-Fort Worth International Airport; 13 persons died in the accident; 94 others escaped the burning wreckage by climbing through a charred hole in the roof, but two weeks later another person died of injuries.

September 9, Bangkok, Thailand. An Air Vietnam passenger plane carrying 81 persons crashed and exploded in a rice field while making its landing approach; 75 persons were killed in the crash, which reportedly occurred when the aircraft was struck by lightning.

September 15, Bahir Dar, Eth. A state-owned jetliner crashed and burst into flames shortly after takeoff after a flock of birds was sucked into its engines; 31 persons were killed in the accident. Of the 71 persons who escaped the wreckage, 12 were seriously injured.

October 1, Near Buenos Aires, Arg. A plane crashed shortly after takeoff; ten persons lost their lives.

October 7, Linfen, Shaanxi (Shensi) Province, China. A sight-seeing plane carrying 46 persons, most of them workers who were aboard as a reward for good performances, crashed into a hotel; the 4 survivors of the crash were injured, as were some hotel patrons.

October 17, Near Rome. A Ugandan Boeing 707 jetliner crashed, broke into three pieces, and burst into flames after trying to land in heavy fog; 32 of the 52 persons aboard were killed.

October 19, Near Ahmadabad, India. A Boeing 737 jetliner struck a tree, slammed into high-tension wires, and exploded while attempting to make its descent; of the 135 persons aboard the aircraft, only 5 survived.

October 19, Near Gauhati, India. A small Fokker Friendship turboprop plane carrying 34 persons slammed into a hill during a blinding rainstorm; there were no survivors.

October 25, Near Juliaca, Peru. A twin-engine

Fokker F-28 crashed moments after takeoff; 12 persons were killed, 1 was missing, and 56 others survived.

October 25, Southwestern Arizona. Two U.S. Marine Corps helicopters apparently collided during a night training flight in the desert some 200 km (125 mi) from Yuma; the ten men aboard both aircraft were killed.

December 11, Leninakhan, Armenian S.S.R. A Soviet military transport plane conducting a rescue mission in the earthquake-ravaged city of Leninakhan crashed while approaching that city; all 78 persons aboard were killed.

December 16, Australia. A twin-engine Mitsubishi MU2, carrying miners from the airstrip at the Bellview gold mine to the town of Kalgoorlie, crashed shortly after takeoff; all ten persons aboard were killed.

December 21, Lockerbie, Scotland. Pan Am Flight 103 en route to the U.S. from Frankfurt, West Germany, via London crashed into a residential area after a bomb exploded aboard the aircraft as it cruised at 9,500 m (31,000 ft); all 259 persons aboard were killed, and at least 11 persons on the ground lost their lives as the aircraft rained wreckage on the small Scottish town.

Fires and Explosions

January 1, Bangkok, Thailand. An early-morning fire gutted a hotel that apparently had no fire alarm or smoke-detector system; 13 persons were killed in the blaze.

January 25, Mangora, Pak. A bus exploded after a bomb detonated aboard the vehicle; 10 persons were killed, and 19 others were injured.

March 20, Lashio, Burma. A fast-spreading fire, which started in a residential kitchen, swept through 2,096 dwellings and two primary schools and killed at least 113 persons, many of them trapped in the rapidly spreading fire; 20,-000 others were left homeless, and 64 persons suffered severe burns.

April 10, Rawalpindi, Pak. An accidental fire triggered an explosion at an army ammunition depot in a densely populated area between the twin cities of Rawalpindi and Islamabad; at least 90 persons died, more than 1,000 others were wounded by falling stray shells and shrapnel, and some 200 army trucks were destroyed.

May 18, Osaka, Japan. A blazing fire aboard a Soviet cruise ship docked in Osaka Harbour claimed the lives of 11 persons and injured 35 others.

June 21, Al-Qusia, Egypt. A makeshift tent city, erected on the perimeter of the monastery of Deir al-Muharraq for the Feast of the Consecration of the Church of the Virgin, erupted in flames apparently when sparks from a food stall ignited a tent. The fire left hundreds of other tents in smoldering heaps and claimed the lives of 47 Christian pilgrims.

July 6, Off the east coast of Scotland. An explosion split a towering oil platform into a tangle of fallen metal; 167 lives were lost in

what officials termed the worst oil-rig disaster in North Sea history.

October 22, Shanghai, China. An explosion at a petrochemical refinery claimed the lives of 25 persons and injured 16 others.

November 9, Chembur, India. An explosion and fire at an oil refinery killed 22 persons and severely burned 9 others.

November 19, Kazakh S.S.R. A fast-burning fire in the stewards' compartment of a train claimed the lives of ten persons.

Early December, Near Algiers. A gas explosion at a date-processing plant claimed the lives of 18 persons and injured 8 others.

December 11, Mexico City. An explosion in a store selling illegal fireworks touched off a fire that charred a marketplace; 62 persons were killed, and at least 83 others were injured.

December 13, Monterrey, Mexico. A fire swept through a prison dormitory after an altar candle ignited a curtain; 20 prisoners lost their lives, and 6 others were injured.

December 16, Near Manila. An explosion in an illegal fireworks factory killed 11 persons and injured 20 others.

December 31, Chittagong, Bangladesh. A fire ignited a barge during a welding operation and spread to another barge; 33 persons were killed in the blaze.

Marine

January 4, Jumna River, Bangladesh. An overcrowded ferry collided with a barge and capsized; at least 11 persons were known dead, and 150 others were missing and feared drowned.

February 18, Northeastern India. A boat carrying more than 120 passengers capsized in shark-infested waters near the mouth of the Ganges River; at least 70 persons were feared dead.

April 21, Off the coast of Newfoundland. An explosion aboard the 18,000-ton tanker *Athenian Venture* broke the vessel apart and claimed the lives of 24 Polish crewmen and 5 of their wives.

May 5, Off the coast of the central Philippines. A ship that had been converted from a cargo launch sank, and at least 15 of the reported 200 persons aboard drowned.

May 8, Eastern India. A boat carrying 49 persons capsized in a reservoir on the border of Orissa and Andhra Pradesh states; there were only 8 survivors.

May 21, Off the coast of Chittagong. Fishing boats capsized in the Bay of Bengal, resulting in the deaths of 18 fishermen.

May 28, Off the coast of Indonesia. An overcrowded ferry carrying more than 200 passengers, 330 cows, and 100 metric tons of salt sank in the Java Sea; at least 200 persons were feared drowned.

July 12, Chang Jiang (Yangtse River), China. A ship carrying 556 metric tons of steel and iron capsized and sank; 10 sailors drowned, and 14 others were rescued.

July 15, Amazon River, Brazil. A ferry carrying more than 170 persons sank; 35 persons were known dead.

July 21, Sichuan Province. A ferryboat sailing on the Minjiang (Min-Chiang) from Yibin (Yipin) to Leshan sank after apparently hitting a rock; 24 persons were drowned, and 112 others were missing and feared dead.

July 23, Near Yokosuka, Japan. A Japanese submarine rammed a fishing boat, which immediately sank; of the 48 persons aboard the fishing boat, only 18 survived.

August 4, Vera Cruz, Mexico. A ferry transporting workers to a sulfur plant on the Coatzacoalcos River slammed into a cargo boat and sank; 17 persons aboard the ferry were killed, and 10 others were missing and feared drowned.

August 6, Bihar State, India. An overcrowded steam-powered ferry carrying 565 passengers tilted and sank in the rain-swollen Ganges River near Manihari Ghat; as many as 400 persons were feared lost in the turbulent river waters.

August 11, Bihar State. A boat traveling on the flooded Ganges River capsized near Begusarai; ten women lost their lives.

August 17, Zaire. A ferryboat traveling on Lake Tanganyika reportedly sank, and 50 persons were feared dead.

October 26, Southern Bangladesh. An overcrowded ferry carrying some 300 persons capsized and sank in strong currents in the estuary of the Meghna River; at least 200 persons were missing and feared drowned.

October 31, Off the northeastern coast of Japan. A South Korean fishing boat capsized in rough seas; all 27 crew members were missing and feared dead.

November 10, Atlantic Ocean. A British-owned oil tanker, the *Odyssey,* broke in two, caught fire, and sank during stormy weather; 27 crewmen were missing and presumed drowned.

November 11, New Delhi, India. A boat capsized, and at least 20 persons lost their lives.

Late November, Near Khartoum, The Sudan. A sailboat traveling on the Nile River capsized; 21 persons drowned.

December 27, Munshiganj, Bangladesh. A river ferry that was rammed by a cargo ship capsized and sank in the Dhaleswari River; 11 persons were known dead, and 250 others were missing and feared drowned.

Late December, Eastern India. A river ferry sank, and some 70 persons were feared drowned.

December 31, Off the coast of Rio de Janeiro, Brazil. A boat with a 15-person capacity capsized and sank as passengers ran to one side of the vessel as it laboured through heavy waves; though 40 persons were rescued, 53 others were known dead and 40 more were missing.

Mining

January 25, Near Las Esperanzas, Mexico. An explosion and fire in a coal mine trapped more than 140 miners underground; 88 miners escaped unharmed, 20 were injured—some seriously burned—and at least 34 were killed.

April 5, Northeastern China. A gas explosion in a coal mine claimed the lives of 12 persons.

Mid-April, Western China. A cave-in at an antimony mine killed 15 persons.

May 13, Near Virginia, Orange Free State, South Africa. An accident in a gold mine was precipitated when an elevator slammed into an obstruction; ten miners fell to their deaths.

May 29, Shaanxi Province. A gas explosion ripped through a coal mine, causing cave-ins and damage to the ventilation system; only 7 of some 50 miners in the cave survived the blast.

June 1, Borken, West Germany. An explosion in a coal mine trapped 57 miners in a shaft and seriously injured 8 on the surface; three days later 6 miners who had been trapped in a deep underground pocket of air were rescued, but all others were presumed dead.

Late October, Northeastern China. An underground explosion in a coal mine claimed the lives of 17 miners.

December 4, Near Budapest, Hung. An explosion in a coal mine killed 11 miners and injured 28 others, 4 of them seriously.

Miscellaneous

January 29, Kazakh S.S.R. A sewage reservoir burst and unleashed a giant wave of stagnant water and gravel that destroyed two bridges and led to an unspecified number of deaths.

March 2, China. Celebrations commemorating the Lantern Festival in the city of Xining (Hsi-ning), Qinghai (Tsinghai) Province, and in Lankao (Lan-k'ao) County, Henan (Honan) Province, resulted in the deaths of 25 persons, who were trampled by panicky crowds of revelers.

March 6, Near Necochea, Arg. A race car that blew a tire while competing in a Tourism class race jumped off the track and flew into a crowd of picnickers beside the racecourse; 16 spectators were killed in the incident.

March 10, Tripoli, Libya. A row of seats collapsed at a sports stadium after fearful soccer fans stampeded to avoid knife-wielding ruffians; at least 20 persons were dead and hundreds were injured in the skirmish.

March 12, Kathmandu, Nepal. A stampede sparked by soccer fans attempting to flee a hailstorm resulted in the deaths of some 80 persons, who were trampled.

May 2, Jammu, India. A new wing of a children's hospital collapsed, apparently because of a weak foundation; at least 14 persons were known dead, and at least 50 children and their parents were trapped under concrete.

May 12, Aguascalientes, Mexico. Four stories of a downtown building under construction collapsed and trapped as many as 40 persons beneath tons of concrete; at least 10 persons were known dead.

Mid–Late May, India. A two-week blistering heat wave claimed the lives of at least 450 persons and left hundreds of others ill in northern, central, and western areas of the country.

June 25, Lucknow, India. The roof of a house collapsed, killing 13 inhabitants.

July, India. Heavy monsoon rains were blamed for contaminated water that caused a serious outbreak of cholera and gastroenteritis; some 400 deaths were attributed to the flooding and disease.

July 3–10, Greece. A severe weeklong heat wave was blamed for the deaths of at least 56 persons, 4 of whom succumbed in raging forest fires that were presumably ignited by the intense heat.

July 3–12, Nanjing (Nanking), China. A ten-day killer heat wave claimed the lives of 83 persons, most of them elderly.

July 7, Brownsville, Texas. A three-story department store collapsed during a severe thunderstorm; 14 persons were killed.

July 19, Southern China. A severe heat wave accompanied by a drought was blamed for more than 1,440 deaths, many of them among the elderly and sick in Nanchang (Nan-ch'ang).

July 31, Butterworth, Malaysia. A pier on which thousands of people stood awaiting ferries

AP/WIDE WORLD

A group of children receive food from volunteers at a refugee centre in Nicaragua. At least 111 people were killed and thousands were left homeless after Hurricane Joan's high winds and rains tore through the Caribbean coast.

Survivors pick through rubble in Spitak, an Armenian town leveled by a devasting earthquake in December. The quake, which measured 6.9 on the Richter scale, laid waste much of the Armenian S.S.R. and, in terms of lives lost, was one of the worst of the century.
NOVOSTI—GAMMA LIAISON

to Pinang Island collapsed; at least 30 persons were killed, and some 445 others were injured.

August 15, Bombay, India. Locally brewed liquor laced with methyl alcohol claimed the lives of 23 persons.

August 19, Cairo. A five-story apartment building collapsed; 16 tenants were killed.

October 20, Jamshedpur, India. A stampede at a Hindu festival killed at least 14 persons.

Early November, Southern Turkey. At least 26 persons succumbed to poison mushrooms.

Late November, Northern China. Gas fumes at a chemical fertilizer factory killed 16 workers.

December 5, Yaoundé, Cameroon. Rumours that a vocational school under construction was about to collapse led to the deaths of at least 60 panicked students, who were either trampled to death or killed as they leaped out of windows.

Natural

January 2–8, U.S. A bone-chilling storm system gripped the Midwest and the East and delivered snow and strong winds that paralyzed much of the South; at least 33 deaths were attributed to the cold weather, 13 of them from exposure.

February 3, Huanuco Province, Peru. Torrential rains unleashed an avalanche of mud and rocks that buried a dozen vehicles and killed at least 30 persons.

February, Rio de Janeiro State. Monthlong torrential rains precipitated numerous floods and landslides of mud and rock, destroying shantytowns, killing more than 280 persons, and injuring 600 others.

February 12–13, U.S. A major snowstorm pummeled the South and the Northeast with up to a foot of snow that created hazardous driving conditions; at least 22 traffic fatalities were recorded.

February 18, Huancacalle-Pujyura, Peru. Several days of torrential rains touched off a mud slide that thundered down on sleeping residents of the village; at least 50 persons died.

February 22, Orange Free State. Heavy weekend rains produced flash floods that claimed the lives of at least 12 persons.

February 27, Near Fes, Morocco. Several days of heavy rains weakened a cliff, which collapsed onto a shantytown in an abandoned quarry; at least 31 persons were known dead.

March 7, Hakkari, Turkey. An avalanche claimed the lives of 19 persons.

March 11, Korak, Pak. An avalanche claimed the lives of 24 persons in a remote village.

March 15, Jammu and Kashmir, India. Heavy snow precipitated avalanches and landslides that claimed the lives of at least 76 persons.

March 18, Rio de Janeiro. Unrelenting rains triggered landslides of mud and boulders that crushed homes and inundated neighbourhoods with debris; hardest hit was the neighbourhood of Santa Teresa, where an avalanche demolished two wings of a home for the aged and buried more than 60 of its residents.

March 24–27, Buenos Aires. Four days of torrential rains resulted in 16 deaths.

April 23–24, Kenya. Heavy weekend rains precipitated severe flooding that claimed the lives of at least 13 persons.

Early May, Rabotak, Afghanistan. A gigantic mud slide destroyed the village and claimed the lives of at least 35 persons.

May 22, Fujian (Fukien) Province, China. Heavy rains triggered flash floods that killed 72 persons and injured 200 others.

Late May, Southeastern China. Severe rainstorms caused massive flooding that swamped farmlands and damaged tens of thousands of homes; at least 149 persons were known dead.

Early June, Central Cuba. Torrential rains triggered massive flooding and claimed the lives of at least 21 persons.

June 12, Ankara, Turkey. A powerful storm precipitated flash flooding that inundated the city's shantytowns, killing 13 persons.

June 23, Catak, Turkey. A landslide propelled by half a million tons of mud and rock vaulted down a rain-soaked mountain and engulfed a village; 64 persons were known dead, but some 200 others were also feared dead, many of them tourists who were stranded in restaurants or buses.

June 23, Jiangxi (Kiangsi), China. Incessant rain triggered a landslide that dumped tons of earth and rock on a small village; 17 persons were killed, 17 others were missing, and 34 were seriously injured.

July 10, Southwestern China. A brutal rainstorm unleashed a mud-and-rock slide that crushed a power station and swept away dozens of homes; more than 35 persons were killed.

July 16–17, Northeastern Brazil. Heavy rains battered the region and caused a landslide that swept away a hillside shantytown; at least 40 deaths were attributed to the storm.

July 29–30, Zhejiang (Chekiang) Province, China. A torrential rainstorm precipitated flash floods that claimed the lives of at least 264 persons; 50 others were missing and presumed drowned.

August, The Sudan. Torrential rains, which left an estimated two million people homeless, caused severe flooding when the swollen Nile River unleashed its water on surrounding areas; at least 90 deaths were attributed to the floods.

Mid-August, Nigeria. Torrential rains claimed the lives of 26 persons in Borno State and 50 others in Kano State.

August 21, Nepal and India. A devastating earthquake struck the Himalaya Mountain regions, precipitating landslides and floods that destroyed thousands of homes; more than 700 persons were killed in Nepal by official count (witnesses and news reports estimated 1,000), and more than 275 deaths were reported in India.

Late August–September, Bangladesh. Nearly three-quarters of the country was immersed in floodwaters after being pelted with the worst monsoon rains in 70 years; the government reported that more than 2,000 persons had died and many more were afflicted with waterborne diseases, including cholera and diarrhea, the latter claiming at least 100 lives. At least 30 million people were believed homeless.

Early–Mid-September, Southern China. Massive flooding in the Guangxi (Kwangsi) region and in Hunan and Hubei (Hupeh) provinces killed at least 170 persons, injured some 500 others, and left 110,000 homeless.

September 6, Morobe Province, Papua New Guinea. A huge mud slide occurred when a chunk of mountain collapsed; five villages were swept away, and at least 76 persons were known to have been killed.

September 11, Pune, India. A bolt of lightning struck an apartment block, which then thundered down on huts built below; 12 persons lost their lives.

September 12–17, Caribbean Sea and the Gulf of Mexico. The fiercest storm of the century, Hurricane Gilbert, ravaged Jamaica before churning across the Caribbean and slamming into the Yucatan Peninsula of Mexico, where an estimated 200 persons in four buses in Monterrey died after heavy winds and floodwaters washed the vehicles away. The hurricane, which also blasted the popular Mexican resorts of Cancún and Cozumel, was billed as probably the most destructive Atlantic storm to date, with damages topping $10 billion. The storm claimed at least 260 lives and spawned some 39 tornadoes in Texas.

September 22, Western Nepal. Flash floods killed at least 87 persons in the village of Darbang.

Late September, Southern Ethiopia. Heavy rain precipitated flash floods that claimed the lives of at least 41 persons and made 2,240 others homeless.

Late September–Early October, Northwestern India. A week of severe flooding inundated vast areas of the states of Punjab, Haryana, Himachal Pradesh, and Jammu and Kashmir; some 1,000 persons were feared dead.

October 2, Fredonia, Colombia. Heavy rains precipitated a landslide that buried several small farms and at least five vehicles; some 50 persons were feared dead.

October 3, Nîmes, France. A torrential rainfall claimed the lives of at least ten persons; dozens of others were missing and feared drowned.

October 10–18, Northern Vietnam. Heavy rains precipitated flooding that damaged homes and killed at least 27 persons.

October 19, Southern Bangladesh. A brutal storm packing high winds that churned up 4-m (15-ft)-high waves lashed the country's southern coastal cities; at least 35 persons were known dead, and an estimated 1,500 fishermen were reported missing.

October 22–27, The Caribbean coast of Central America. Hurricane Joan stormed into Nicaragua, smashing homes and unleashing severe floods and mud slides before hitting Costa Rica, Panama, Colombia, and Venezuela with relentless rain and high winds; at least 111 persons lost their lives in the storm, which weakened into Tropical Storm Miriam as it reached the Pacific. The latter storm battered El Sal-

vador with constant rain and high winds and left some 3,000 persons homeless.

October 24–25, The Philippines. Typhoon Ruby pounded the country with heavy rain and high winds that precipitated widespread flooding and landslides; the storm, which caused $45 million in damage to crops and destroyed $7.5 million in roads and bridges, also caused an interisland ferry carrying some 500 persons to sink. The number of deaths was estimated at near 500; 143 survived the sinking of the ferry by swimming, aided by lifejackets, to small islands, where they were rescued.

October 25, Kalingapatnam, India. A huge wave swept away 12 children bathing in the Bay of Bengal during a religious festival.

Late October, Central Vietnam. A storm lashed the country with heavy rains; at least 100 persons were killed, and 500,000 others were left homeless.

November 6, Southwestern China. An earthquake measuring 7.6 on the Richter scale devastated the counties of Lancang (Lan-ts'ang) and Menglian (Meng-lien); more than 1,000 persons were feared dead, and some 500,000 others were left homeless.

November 7, Central Philippines. Typhoon Skip, the second typhoon in two weeks to pound the country with high winds and torrential rains, caused mud slides and flooding and killed at least 129 persons.

Mid-November–Early December, Southern Thailand. Torrential monsoon rains precipitated widespread flooding exacerbated by excessive logging, which caused mud slides and timbers to crash down into villages; more than 400 people succumbed in flood-related incidents.

November 29, Bangladesh and Eastern India. The worst cyclone in 20 years struck Bangladesh, which was recovering from flooding that had inundated three-quarters of the country; as many as 3,000 persons were feared dead in the latest storm.

December 7, Armenian S.S.R. A catastrophic earthquake measuring 6.9 on the Richter scale devastated the cities of Leninakhan, Kirovakan, Spitak, Gurgak, Stepanavan, and Dzhadzhur; though initial estimates were that 55,000 persons had been killed under collapsed industrial complexes, schools, and apartment buildings, at the end of the year the government reported that about 25,000 persons had died. The temblor also killed six persons in Turkey.

Late December, Java, Indon. Torrential rains burst dams, causing floods and landslides that killed at least 40 persons.

Railroad

January 17, Heilongjiang (Heilungkiang) Province, China. Two trains collided head-on, killing 19 persons.

January 15, Nayarit, Mexico. A passenger train plowed into a bus as it crossed railroad tracks; 20 persons were killed, and 30 others aboard the bus were injured.

January 17, Hunan Province, China. A train caught fire when paint thinner being transported ignited; 34 persons lost their lives.

January 24, Yunnan Province, China. An express train traveling between Qiewu (Ch'iehwu) and Dengjiacun (Teng-chia-ts'un) stations derailed in the mountains of southern China; 90 persons were killed, and 66 others were injured.

March 24, Near Shanghai, China. Two passenger trains were involved in a head-on collision, and 12 persons were reported killed; one train was carrying a 193-member Japanese high school tour group.

June 4, Arzamas, U.S.S.R. A freight train packed with industrial explosives blew up as it entered the train station, killing at least 80 persons and injuring some 200 others; the force of the blast leveled some 150 homes and gouged a 50-m (164-ft) crater near the train station.

June 25, Near Havana. A passenger train crashed into a crowded bus during rush hour; 25 persons lost their lives, and 84 others were injured.

June 27, Paris. An eight-car Paris-bound train traveling at an estimated 80 km/h (50 mph)

Fishermen comb the waters of Lake Asthamudi for passengers from a train that had derailed while crossing a bridge near Quilon, India.
AFP PHOTO

collided head-on with a stationary four-car train at the Gare de Lyon railroad station after both its brakes and emergency brakes failed to operate; 59 persons were killed, but both engineers survived the crash by jumping out of their locomotives just prior to impact.

July 8, Near Quilon, India. A 14-car passenger train derailed while crossing a bridge, and nine of its cars and the locomotive plunged into Lake Asthamudi; at least 103 persons were killed, and 167 persons were injured.

July 9, El Quebrechal, Arg. A train collided with a flatbed truck at an unmarked crossing; 16 persons were killed in the crash.

August 16, Near Bologoye, U.S.S.R. The Avrora Express, a high-speed passenger train, was carrying some 800 passengers when 15 of its 18 cars derailed and burst into flames; 28 persons were killed, and 104 others were injured.

October 9, Lapovo, Yugos. The last two cars of an express passenger train traveling at full speed derailed as the train entered a train station and hit an engine of a parked freight train; at least 33 persons were killed, and 15 others were injured.

December 12, London. A fast-moving commuter train slammed into the rear of a stationary train at Clapham Junction, and a third, empty train plowed into the wreckage; the three-train pileup, which was attributed to a faulty signal mechanism, claimed the lives of 33 persons and injured more than 110 others.

December 23, Shenyang, China. A train traveling from Dandong (Tantung) to Beijing (Peking) struck a bus at an unmarked train crossing; 46 persons were killed in the collision.

Traffic

January 12, North West Frontier Province, Pakistan. A bus, speeding out of control, plunged into a river; 13 persons aboard lost their lives.

January 17, Dalbandin, Pak. Two buses collided head-on, and one of them, carrying a large supply of matches, burst into flames on impact; 24 persons were killed, and 30 others were injured.

January 18, Zhejiang Province, China. A bus fell into a stream, and 14 persons lost their lives.

January 29, Cape Province, South Africa. A bus carrying policemen to a gymnastic exhibition plunged off a mountain road in the Robinson Pass; 13 officers were killed, and 71 others were injured.

Mid-February, Ancash Province, Peru. An out-of-control bus plunged off a cliff in northern Peru; at least 14 persons were killed.

March 7, Henan Province, China. A bus plunged off a mountain road and fell into a deep gorge in Lingbao (Ling-pao) County; 39 persons were killed, and 17 others were injured.

March 13, Turkey. The collision of a truck

and a bus on the main highway between Ankara and Konya resulted in the deaths of 13 persons; 35 were injured in the accident.

March 16, Madhya Pradesh State, India. A bus carrying members of a Muslim wedding party swerved and smashed into a culvert after the driver lost control of the vehicle while trying to change a tape cassette; 90 persons lost their lives in the crash.

April 1, Seoul, South Korea. A speeding city bus with a punctured tire rammed into a concrete embankment before plunging into the Han River; 18 persons were killed, and 36 others were injured.

April 8, Near Lhasa, Tibet. A bus plunged off a winding mountain road after the driver lost control of the vehicle; 16 persons lost their lives in the crash.

April 10, Central Thailand. A crowded bus fell into an irrigation canal after a front tire blew out; 42 persons died, and 11 others were injured.

May 14, Carrollton, Ky. A pickup truck traveling on the wrong side of the highway slammed head-on into a school bus and exploded; 27 persons aboard the bus, which belonged to the First Assembly of God Church, were killed, and the driver of the truck was charged with murder.

May 20, Takli, Thailand. A truck loaded with stone plowed through railroad crossing gates and slammed into a seven-car passenger train; 24 persons, including the truck driver, were killed, and 30 others were injured.

June 16, Near Hyderabad, India. A bus slammed into a wall and burst into flames after a tire blew out; 27 persons aboard were killed, and 10 others were injured in the crash.

June 19, Near Meerut, India. A truck crashed into a passenger bus, causing 15 deaths and 25 injuries.

August 16, Near Eidfjord, Norway. A bus whose brakes had failed veered into a tunnel wall as the driver tried to ease the vehicle to a stop; 15 persons were killed in the crash.

September 25, Punjab, India. A bus slammed into a canal feeding a large hydroelectric plant; at least 60 persons were missing and feared drowned.

October 9, Assam, India. A bus skidded off a mountain road and fell into a river after the driver lost control of the vehicle; 38 persons were killed, and 16 others were injured.

October 12, Shaanxi Province, China. An overcrowded bus not equipped with windshield wipers fell off a narrow road into a deep irrigation ditch and burst into flames during a rainstorm; 43 of the 83 persons aboard were burned to death.

Early November, Near Srinagar, India. A bus skidded off a mountain road; 58 persons lost their lives.

Earth Sciences

GEOLOGY AND GEOCHEMISTRY

During 1988 the Space Science Board of the U.S. National Research Council published the seven-volume *Space Science in the Twenty-First Century: Imperatives for the Decades 1995–2015,* the comprehensive results of a study to determine the principal scientific issues facing the earth and space sciences. The volume *Mission to Planet Earth* (chairman, Don L. Anderson of the California Institute of Technology [Caltech]) outlined a unified program for studying the Earth from its deep interior to its fluid envelopes. The proposals emphasized the need for an integrated and interrelated set of satellite and surface observations of the environment on a global, consistent, repetitive, long-term basis. The primary research objectives comprised four themes, the first being to determine the composition, structure, and dynamics of the Earth's interior and crust and to understand the processes by which the Earth evolved to its present state and the second being to establish and understand the structure, dynamics, and chemistry of the oceans, atmosphere, and cryosphere (the Earth's frozen regions) and their interactions with the solid Earth. The other two themes involved interactions with the biosphere.

The report coincided with rapid advances in the understanding of the Earth's internal processes, reinforcing the conclusion that it was essential to study the Earth as a system. Geology and geochemistry are dependent on the physical behaviour of the Earth's interior. Results from seismic tomography, studies of the geoid, and fluid dynamic calculations were determining the nature of mantle convection, which controls the evolution of the lithosphere and crust. The nature of the hydrosphere and atmosphere depends on the outgassing of the mantle. Coupling of solid-earth processes and oceanic and atmospheric processes occurs on time scales of millions of years. The wide disparity of time scales and space scales represented by geophysics, geochemistry, fluid dynamics, and biologic processes on Earth could be addressed for the first time by large global data sets and modeling on high-speed supercomputers.

A technical achievement in computer modeling was the work of Michael Gurnis, Bradford Hager, and Arthur Raefsky of Caltech, who developed a numerical model to study the two-way dynamic feedback between continental drift and mantle convection, demonstrating that congregated continents initiate upwelling in the mantle, which is followed by breakup and dispersal of the continents. Raymond Jeanloz of the University of California at Berkeley reported a mineralogical explanation for deep-focus earthquakes based on experiments making use of diamond-anvil high-pressure apparatus. He found that mantle minerals could be made to fracture abruptly at very high pressures and about 600° C (1,100° F), but only with the hydrous mineral serpentine present; release of water in the dehydration reaction decreased the frictional forces within the sample, promoting fracture.

The proposed explosive impact of an extraterrestrial body on Earth 65 million years ago, leading to the extinction of dinosaurs and many other species, was an obvious example of interrelationship between earth and space sciences. Joanne Bourgeois of the University of Washington and her associates described coarse-grained sedimentary deposits at the Cretaceous-Tertiary boundary in Texas, which had been 75–100 m (245–330 ft) below sea level at the time of formation. They concluded that these sediments must have been formed by an enormous tsunami (sea wave), suggesting that the colliding body landed in the ocean. On the basis of laboratory shock-wave experiments, John O'Keefe and Thomas Ahrens of Caltech evaluated the effect of such an impact into limestones of the continental shelf. They calculated that the strike of a comet 50 km (30 mi) in diameter could produce an immediate hundredfold increase in the carbon dioxide (CO_2) content of the atmosphere, causing a greenhouse effect sufficient to raise the temperature by 20° C (36° F) in as little as ten days.

Increases in atmospheric CO_2 and methane (CH_4) assigned to human activity continued to raise serious concern about the greenhouse effect and future climates and spurred research into past climatic change. Until recently, explanations for ice ages tended to rely on physical processes that reinforced solar insolation cycles, but studies of deep ice cores taken from the Antarctic and Greenland ice sheets confirmed the significant role of chemical and biologic changes. Paleoclimatology, a topic that developed strongly with plate tectonics, provides the long-term basis for understanding climatic changes, but sources of data about the chemistry of ancient atmospheres have been few. After 14 years of drilling in Antarctica, a Soviet team recovered an ice core spanning 160,000 years. A shorter core (100,000 years) was obtained from Greenland. Analyses by geochemists from France and Switzerland of gases trapped in the ice layers demonstrated that the concentrations of CO_2, CH_4, and sulfate particles changed in synchrony with the temperature changes. During the warm interglacial periods, CO_2 and CH_4 increased while sulfate particles decreased. According to Claude Lorius of the Laboratory of Glaciology and Geophysics in St. Martin d'Heres, France, there was not enough information to sort out cause and effect. The situation was complicated by the role of the ocean as a sink for CO_2 and by the involvement of photosynthetic plankton.

In 1987 Robert Berner of Yale University and Gary Landis of the U.S. Geological Survey claimed that amber as old as 85 million years had trapped samples of the ambient atmosphere and that analysis of the samples showed the Cretaceous atmosphere to have contained 30% oxygen, compared with the present 21%. These results were disputed in 1988 by other groups on the grounds that air can diffuse through amber and that amber reacts with enclosed gas, altering its composition.

Whereas ice on Earth traps atmospheric gases, ice on the Uranian moons Ariel and Miranda may trap gases from the interior. David Janowski and Steven Squyres of Cornell University, Ithaca, N.Y., interpreted surface features that had been imaged by the Voyager 2 space probe in 1986 in terms of solid-ice volcanism, wherein very cold, plastic ice oozes up through major cracks to form round-topped ridges. They suggested that ammonia, methane, or carbon monoxide trapped in the ice may have rendered it locally buoyant.

Exploration of a major tension crack on Earth, the East Pacific Rise, by means of a side-scan sonar system revealed the existence of a huge, very young lava field about 1,300 km (800 mi) southwest of the Galápagos Islands. Ken Macdonald of the University of California at Santa Barbara and his associates reported that the lava covered 21,500 ha (53,000 ac) with an average thickness of 70 m (230 ft). The lava emerged at the ridge crest and flowed downslope for 20 km (12.4 mi). The eruption might be related to earthquake swarms recorded in that area of the Pacific in 1964, 1965, and 1969 and to a long plume of helium-3 discovered in 1972 in the ocean water southwest of the lava field.

A new field of high-temperature seafloor hydrothermal vents was discovered in September on the Gorda Ridge off the coast of Oregon. It was believed by many that these vent fields influence not only ocean chemistry but also climate and the greenhouse effect. Peter Rona of the U.S. National Oceanographic and Atmospheric Administration reported that the Navy's submersible *Sea Cliff* reached the vent field at a depth of 3,000 m (10,000 ft).

In a project sponsored by the U.S. Department of Energy (DOE), drilling began in July at the Valles Caldera, a large volcanic crater in New Mexico, with a view to sampling another type of mineral-forming system. Aqueous fluids, driven by a molten magma chamber five kilometres (three miles) below, circulate through pores and cracks in the rocks, transporting dissolved minerals that precipitate in favourable localities to form mineral deposits. Catching the mineralization process in operation in this way could aid prospecting for mineral deposits in other, fossil geothermal systems.

While DOE was having success with relatively shallow drilling and while the U.S.S.R. and West Germany continued to provide large budgets for scientific drilling projects deep into the continents, the Continental Scientific Drilling Program being supported by the U.S. National Science Foundation was halted in early 1988 for lack of funds. Earlier U.S. plans for ultradeep drilling had already been postponed for budgetary reasons, and it had been decided instead to bore the deepest scientific drill hole in the U.S. to a depth of five kilometres at Cajon Pass, Calif., near the San Andreas Fault. Insufficient funding forced many compromises during the first year of drilling, and by March 1988, when the hole was 3.5 km (2.2 mi) deep and still 1.5 km (0.9 mi) short of target, drilling was stopped for at least two years. Although useful information was gathered, the experiment was not deep enough to resolve the main objective, which was to investigate a paradox about heat flow and stress along the fault.   (PETER JOHN WYLLIE)

GEOPHYSICS

No great earthquakes, those of magnitude 8 or greater on the Richter scale, struck during 1988. Several shocks of magnitude 7 or greater did occur around the world, including the South Pacific, the Gulf of Alaska, the Himalayas, the Peruvian coast, the Philippines, and China. On November 6 one of the more deadly earthquakes of 1988, measuring 7.6, devastated the counties of Lancang

(Lan-ts'ang) and Menglian (Meng-lien) in southwestern China. More than 1,000 persons were feared dead, and hundreds of thousands were left homeless. Another killer quake struck with a magnitude of 6.9 on August 20 along the border between Nepal and India. In Nepal more than 700 persons were killed, and in northern Bihar, India, at least 275 lost their lives. By far the most disastrous earthquake of the year occurred on December 7 in the southern Soviet republic of Armenia near the Turkish border. The shock, which measured 6.9 and was followed four minutes later by an aftershock of magnitude 5.8, ravaged the northwestern Armenian cities of Leninakan, Kirovakan, Spitak, Yerevan, Stepanavan, and Dzhadzhur. More than 25,000 people were believed buried under collapsed schools, factories, and office and residential buildings, and possibly as many as a half million were left homeless.

The Ocean Drilling Program (ODP) continued in the Indian Ocean, where the scientific drilling ship *JOIDES Resolution* completed and reported on Leg 115 through Leg 120. On Leg 115, 900 m (3,000 ft) of seafloor cores were recovered from 22 holes drilled at 12 sites on the Mascarene Plateau and the Chagos Ridge between Madagascar and southwestern India. The cores contained important information concerning the motion of the Indian Plate with respect to recognized stationary hot spots during the Cenozoic Era (within the past 65 million years). These data also provided a better understanding of the processes that indicate climatic changes, glaciation, and the evolution of deep- and shallow-water patterns. On Leg 116 the distal Bengal Fan, which stretches southward from the Ganges-Brahmaputra delta more than 2,500 km (1,550 mi) into the Southern Hemisphere, was explored to clarify the history of distortion and sedimentation of the interplate region. Cores from ten holes at three sites provided a complete historical sequence for the past 17 million years, which indicated that the main phase of the Himalayan uplift occurred no later than the early Miocene Epoch (about 20 million years ago).

Leg 117 consisted of a transect across the northwestern Indian Ocean from the Oman continental margin to the Indus Fan, comprising 12 sites where a record 4,367 m (14,327 ft) of core were obtained from 25 boreholes. In this area the annual monsoon drives the nutrient-depleted surface water eastward, causing an upwelling of colder, nutrient-rich water along the east coast of Africa and the western Arabian Peninsula. Owing to the high rate of sed-

M. UGUEN—GAMMA/LIAISON

A man in Bhaktapur, Nepal, surveys damage caused by an earthquake that shook Nepal, eastern India, and Bangladesh. The area's losses were compounded by monsoon rains and massive landslides that disrupted communications and hindered rescue attempts.

imentation of organic matter, minerals of biologic origin, and windblown clastics from the deserts of Arabia and southern Asia, a very complete history was obtained from the cores. Subsequent analyses provided important information relating to the variations in monsoon strength, the rate of Himalayan uplift, and even the geometry of the Earth's orbit.

The deepest penetration to date into formations of the lower crust and upper mantle was accomplished on Leg 118 when 0.5 km (0.3 mi) of nearly continuous core was obtained from hole 735B on the east rim of the Atlantis II Fracture Zone, a prominent feature associated with the Southwest Indian Ridge. Though not the deepest hole, it was drilled in an area where there is little depositional overburden and the mantle is close to the ocean bottom.

The *JOIDES Resolution* sailed to the southern Indian Ocean on Leg 119 to gather data on its paleoceanic history, the geologic development of the Kerguelen Plateau, and the development of glaciation in East Antarctica. Two holes were drilled just to the southeast of Kerguelen Island near the northern end of the plateau, below the surface-water boundary, the Antarctic Convergence, which separates temperate from polar surface water. Evidence of the distribution of diatom species indicated that present oceanic circulation patterns were established during the late Miocene or early Pliocene, between 15 million and 8 million years ago. Four holes were then drilled 1,200 km (750 mi) to the south, at the southern end of the plateau, in deep water. These provided evidence of interglacial fluctuation during the past ten million years, which was correlated with that obtained from the final five holes drilled on the continental margin of Antarctica in Prydz Bay. Sediments retrieved there showed that glaciation proceeded in phases and that grounded ice occupied the bay in a series of advances and retreats during the past 40 million years.

Twelve holes were drilled at five sites across the central region of the Kerguelen Plateau on Leg 120. Although the work was carried out in rough seas and was hampered by several equipment failures, enough data were gathered to support the hypothesis that the plateau is of mid-oceanic volcanic origin rather than a continental remnant. Evidence was also recovered showing that much of the region was once above sea level and supported forests and other

vegetation. It had apparently been subsiding slowly for a long time until about 65 million years ago, when a cataclysmic volcanic or tectonic event caused a marked increase in the rate of subsidence.   (RUTLAGE J. BRAZEE)

HYDROLOGY

The dry conditions that in 1987 afflicted parts of the U.S., including the Northwest and Southeast, persisted into 1988 while spreading and worsening. By March the combined flow of the three largest U.S. rivers, the Columbia, Mississippi, and St. Lawrence, was 13% below normal, and streamflow in the southeastern U.S. was 54% below normal. At the end of May drought conditions extended into the central U.S. and Great Lakes states. The combined flow of the big three rivers was the second lowest in 60 years of record keeping. By midsummer the drought had spread to the northern plains. All-time record-low streamflows for July were experienced in the southeast and north-central states. Barge traffic on the Mississippi was severely curtailed, and hydroelectric power generation on the Columbia was reduced. In the St. Lawrence, which ten months earlier had experienced record-high flows, emerging sandbars posed a hazard to boats.

Great Lakes water levels continued their decline from record highs in 1986. By the end of May the level in Lake Superior was below normal for the first time since 1982. Pumping and evaporation continued to lower the level of Utah's Great Salt Lake. In late August the lake level was 1.36 m (4.45 ft) below the record-high 1,283.77 m (4211.85 ft) reached in June 1986.

Louisiana wetlands were disappearing beneath the ocean at the rate of 100–150 sq km (40–60 sq mi) annually owing to rising sea levels and land subsidence. If the trend continued, the Louisiana shoreline would move inland about 53 km (33 mi) over the next 50 years.

The *Water Reporter* for August 1988 indicated that U.S. water use was about one-third of the average annual streamflow. A national study by the U.S. Geological Survey showed water use to be 10% less in 1985 than in 1980. Severe water shortages were predicted for the Middle East where river systems were fully utilized. African watersheds tributary to the Nile River were experiencing severe drought. Live storage in Lake Nasser was predicted

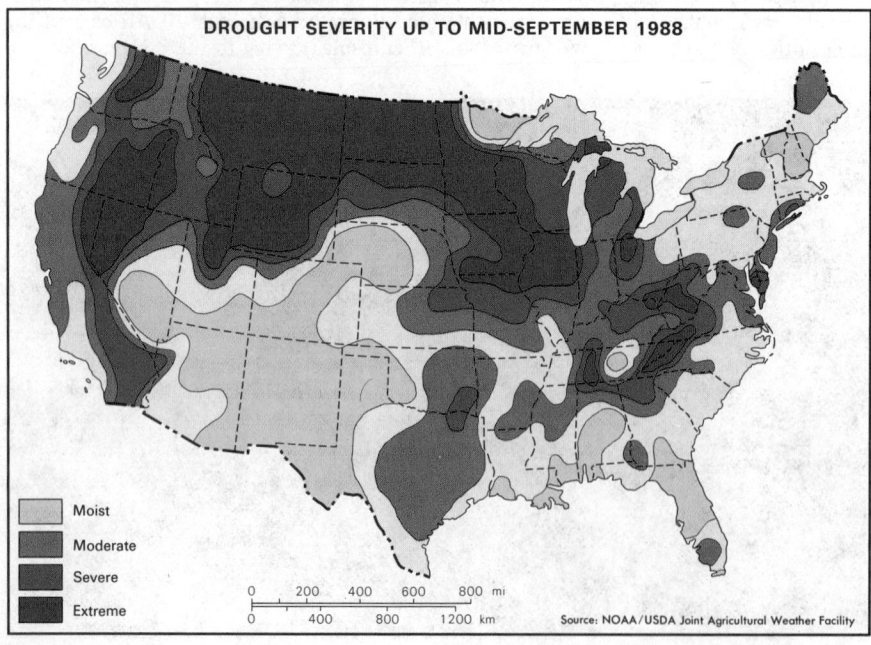

DROUGHT SEVERITY UP TO MID-SEPTEMBER 1988

Moist
Moderate
Severe
Extreme

0   200   400   600   800 mi
0   400   800   1200 km

Source: NOAA/USDA Joint Agricultural Weather Facility

During the summer of 1988 the United States suffered its worst drought since the Dust Bowl era more than 50 years earlier. The damage caused by the drought was increased by the summer's excessive heat.

to be depleted by July 1989 if current climate conditions persisted. The Aral Sea in the south-central Soviet Union, once the fourth largest lake in the world, was fast disappearing. Between 1960 and 1987 it shrank in area by 40%, largely because of the diversion of inflowing river water for agriculture.

Restrictions on groundwater pumping in Japan reduced land subsidence to the lowest levels since records began, according to Norio Tase of the University of Tsukuba. On the other hand, groundwater levels in Manila and in Bangkok, Thailand, dropped below sea level, resulting in seawater intrusion into aquifers; overpumping was lowering water levels at the rate of 4–10 m (13–33 ft) per year. Spain passed a national water law that declared all surface water and groundwater public property. The right to alter the water balance was vested solely in the national government and regulated by a national water board. Concerns in the U.S. over groundwater pumping and aquifer contamination were prompting federal and state lawmakers to draft legislation that would create groundwater protection programs and strategies. During the year the U.S. Congress debated a National Groundwater Research Act. A Latin American Groundwater Association, with headquarters in Cochabamba, Bolivia, was formed to monitor and control pollution of groundwater in Latin-American countries.

The theme of the 26th annual conference of the Universities Council on Water Resources was "Climate Change and Water Resources." Hydrologists were becoming increasingly interested in predicting the effects of climate change on the hydrologic cycle, and research activity on this topic was expected to increase. The World Meteorological Organization and the International Association of Hydrological Sciences supported a Global Energy and Water Cycle Experiment (GEWEX) with the objective of observing, understanding, and modeling processes of the global atmospheric water cycle and energy budget and their interaction with hydrologic processes at the land surface. This international research effort would eventually provide a tool for understanding the effect of changing atmospheric composition on the hydrologic cycle.

(BRUCE P. VAN HAVEREN)

METEOROLOGY

About 35% of the continental U.S. experienced severe drought conditions in 1988. The midwestern states suffered their worst dry conditions since 1936. Major crop areas received less than half the normal rainfall during the critical growing period from April through June. The last drought substantially worse and so early in the season occurred in 1934—the beginning of the dust-bowl era. Although the most acute phase of the drought began in April, abnormal dry conditions had existed in many areas—for example, in parts of the southeastern U.S.—for as long as four years. Below-normal rains in the central U.S. resulted in some of the lowest water levels for the Mississippi River system in 50 years.

While the spring and early summer were among the driest on record, the summer in the U.S., particularly the northern half, was one of the hottest. Parts of the Plains, the Midwest, and the lower Mississippi Valley endured their driest or hottest periods, or both, since records began in 1895. Forest fires damaged more than 1.6 million ha (4 million ac) nationwide, with large-scale devastation over areas of the Northwest and Rocky Mountains.

Western parts of the Soviet Union were also hot and dry in 1988. China showed the variability of weather, with some areas of the north-central and south-central regions receiving torrential rains and much of eastern and

southeastern China being abnormally dry. The monsoon in India, which had largely failed in 1987, came back in 1988 with the heaviest rains in 70 years. Bangladesh experienced one of the most devastating floods in its history; three-quarters of the land was under water, and loss of life was heavy. Torrential rains also caused extreme flooding in The Sudan in August.

After two years of very light hurricane activity, the 1988 Atlantic hurricane season produced 11 tropical storms, 5 of which reached hurricane intensity. The seventh storm of the season, Gilbert, became the most intense hurricane in recorded history in the Western Hemisphere. After Gilbert struck Jamaica on September 12, its central pressure fell from 960 millibars (mb; 28.35 in) to 885 mb (26.13 in) in a 24-hour period. By the evening of September 13, reconnaissance aircraft measured sustained winds of 280 km/h (175 mph) with gusts to 320 km/h (200 mph). The centre of Gilbert crossed the northeastern Yucatán Peninsula on September 14, the strongest hurricane to make landfall on the North American continent since Camille struck the Mississippi coast in 1969. Gilbert lost strength after crossing Yucatán and made landfall again in northeastern Mexico the evening of September 16. The death toll from Gilbert was at least 160, and damage was estimated at $10 billion.

The fifth hurricane of the season, Joan, struck Nicaragua on October 22 with sustained winds of 215 km/h (135 mph) after battering the northern parts of Colombia and Venezuela. At least 111 deaths and tens of thousands of homeless were reported as a result of the winds, flash floods, and mud slides in Central and South America. Joan was only the fourth hurricane known to have occurred so far south in the Caribbean since the late 1800s.

In the Pacific, Typhoon Ruby hit the Philippines in central Luzon on October 24–25 with winds as high as 225 km/h (140 mph) and extremely heavy rains. On November 29 a powerful cyclone struck Bangladesh, killing as many as 3,000.

The intense drought, heat, and other extreme weather triggered renewed concern over global climate changes caused by the greenhouse effect, whereby gases—primarily carbon dioxide—trap the Sun's radiant energy in the lower atmosphere and warm the air near the Earth's surface. Although there was vigorous debate among atmospheric

THE NEW YORK TIMES

A group of farm animals is led along the Nile riverbank. Agriculture on Egypt's Nile River delta was threatened by the rising waters of the Mediterranean Sea, which continuously cut back the shoreline.

scientists over direct linkage of the 1988 drought to the greenhouse effect, there was irrefutable evidence of the continued rise worldwide in levels of atmospheric carbon dioxide and other trace gases as a result of a century of human industry. Three major international organizations—the International Council of Scientific Unions, the UN Environment Program, and the World Meteorological Organization—issued a report calling for immediate action in developing policies for responding to climatic change. The report also urged approval and implementation of the Montreal Protocol on Substances that Deplete the Ozone Layer (see Sidebar). The international scientific community called for a reexamination of long-term energy strategies with the goal of achieving high end-use efficiency. They appealed for intensified development of nonfossil energy systems and for other measures to slow the rate of increase of carbon dioxide and trace gases in the atmosphere.

(ELBERT W. FRIDAY, JR.)

This article updates the Macropædia article CLIMATE AND WEATHER.

OCEANOGRAPHY

During the first half of 1988, some 9,000 common harbour seals out of a population of 15,000–16,000 along the North Sea coasts of The Netherlands, West Germany, Denmark, Sweden, and Norway died as the result of a highly contagious viral infection. Mortality rates in the Dutch Waddenzee were 60–70%. By autumn the disease had spread to the east coast of Great Britain, and the total number of seal deaths was estimated at about 12,000. The reported symptoms—lethargy and breathing difficulties—were similar to those in dogs infected with canine distemper virus, and it was hypothesized that this virus had somehow been introduced to the seal population after an outbreak of distemper in Arctic foxes on Baffin Island and subsequently in huskies in Greenland. The mode of transmission of the virus remained unexplained, however. One possibility was that harp seals abundant in northern seas had carried the virus into the North Sea. Examination of dead and seriously ill seals confirmed the presence of a virus and showed severe pneumonia and encephalitis. Later studies suggested that the virus was sufficiently different from canine distemper virus to be considered a new virus. Vaccination of an appreciable part of the wild population was considered impractical, although a small number of seals in a Dutch sanctuary were inoculated, and trials of a vaccine were to continue in captive seal populations. It was believed, however, that many seal pups exposed to the virus would develop natural immunity.

U.S. and Canadian oceanographers joined Soviet scientists in a series of studies of Siberian Lake Baikal, the world's deepest lake (1,620 m, or 5,314 ft) and also one of its largest. They measured temperature as well as dissolved oxygen, nutrients, and chlorofluorocarbons—industrial gases released in the last 50–70 years whose concentration in samples of deep ocean water indicates how long ago those waters were last at the surface. On the basis of the measurements, deep waters in Lake Baikal appeared to remain away from the surface for 10–15 years, five to ten times longer than had previously been thought. Such information helped in understanding how nutrients and pollutants were distributed and diffused throughout the lake and was thus of great utility in managing this unique natural resource.

In 1988 a U.S. oceanographic research vessel was given permission to work within the exclusive economic zone of the Soviet Union, the first such permission granted in a decade. U.S. and Soviet researchers studied a plateau in the far western Bering Sea believed to be the oldest feature in a chain of seamounts stretching southwestward toward Hawaii and including Loihi Seamount, an active submarine volcano showing unusual hydrothermal activity.

Hydrothermal vents are seafloor springs of water at a temperature as high as several hundred degrees Celsius. The vented water originates as seawater that percolates over an extended area into the seafloor to a depth where it is heated by and reacts chemically with the surrounding hot rock before rising back to the surface to emerge from localized vents. The vented water is rich in minerals, and many vents support communities of specialized marine life. During 1988 several new discoveries concerning such vents were reported. At Loihi Seamount hydrothermal vents

The Ozone Layer: A Fragile Shield

Ozone, a molecule made of three oxygen atoms (O_3), is one of the most important chemically active gases in the Earth's atmosphere. A natural layer of the gas, which exists mainly from 10 to 50 km (6 to 30 mi) above the Earth's surface, shields human beings and other life against damaging solar ultraviolet (UV) radiation. Research has demonstrated that increased UV radiation at the surface could cause skin cancer, cataracts, damage to the human immune system, and disruption of the biosphere.

In the mid-1970s two U.S. scientists theorized that man-made chlorine-containing compounds known as chlorofluorocarbons (CFCs), then in widespread use as spray-can propellants and refrigeration coolants and in other industrial products and processes, were depleting the ozone layer. More recently, CFCs also have been blamed for adding to the greenhouse effect believed to be responsible for global temperature rises and possible dramatic future climate changes.

Scientific concerns heightened in 1985 when researchers from the British Antarctic Survey discovered an austral springtime "hole," or thinning, in the ozone layer over Antarctica. An intensive study mounted in 1987 revealed that the Antarctic ozone layer decreased 40–50% that year. It concluded that the prime cause of the depletion appeared to be chemical, involving reactions of chlorine compounds, but that the unique meteorology during winter and spring over Antarctica set up the special conditions of an isolated air mass (polar vortex) and cold temperatures that allowed the chemistry to proceed. By 1988 a similar, though smaller, hole and a perturbed chlorine chemistry also had been confirmed over the Arctic.

In September 1987 the UN adopted the Montreal Protocol on Substances that Deplete the Ozone Layer. The protocol, ratified by 31 nations by the end of 1988, called for an early freeze on the use of key chlorinated compounds and a phased reduction through the 1990s. In October 1988 the Antarctic hole appeared less severe than it had the previous two years, but scientists attributed the moderation to year-to-year natural variations.   (ELBERT W. FRIDAY, JR.)

were found to be emitting water unusually rich in carbon and bicarbonate at the surprisingly low temperature of 30° C (86° F). The source of the excess carbon was unknown. The first vents to be discovered, in 1977, lie in the eastern Pacific; in 1985 additional vents were found at depths of 3,500 m (11,480 ft) along the Mid-Atlantic Ridge. Mineral deposits around the latter vents are much more extensive than around their Pacific counterparts, which occur along more rapidly spreading ridges at depths of about 2,500 m (8,200 ft). Nevertheless, during the year investigators reported the surprising finding that the temperature and chemical composition of the deep Atlantic vent water was very similar to that from Pacific vents.

Using the research submersible *Alvin*, researchers captured a fish first seen in 1977 at the Galápagos Rift, a volcanically active seafloor spreading centre in the East Pacific, but not caught on subsequent expeditions to the location. The new fish brought to four the number of species in its genus (*Bythites*); the three other species had been found in the North Atlantic. Again using *Alvin*, but this time at the Juan de Fuca Ridge off the coast of British Columbia, researchers employed a sensitive electronic camera to photograph vents solely by means of the light emitted from the vents, light too weak to be detected by the unaided human eye. Sunlight does not penetrate to the depth (about 2,000 m, or 6,560 ft) of these vents, and any magma hot enough to glow lies hundreds of metres below the seafloor. The source of the light remained unexplained.

(MYRL C. HENDERSHOTT)

See also Disasters; Energy; Environment; Life Sciences; Mining; Space Exploration.

This article updates the *Macropædia* articles ATMOSPHERE; The EARTH; EARTHQUAKES; The EARTH SCIENCES; FISHES; GEOCHRONOLOGY; Principles, Methods, and Instruments of MEASUREMENT AND OBSERVATION; OCEANS; PLATE TECTONICS; RIVERS; VOLCANISM.

Economic Affairs

Contrary to expectations, the world economy shrugged off the massive fall in share prices seen in October 1987 and turned in a sparkling performance in 1988. (*See* Special Report.) The growth of output accelerated, surpassing even the most optimistic forecasts; unemployment was reduced; living standards rose in most countries; and, despite a slight acceleration, inflation remained under control. At the same time, as world trade gained considerable momentum, international payment imbalances were reduced somewhat and came to be seen as less of a problem than before. World financial conditions were relatively stable, and the problem of world debt was managed successfully, with some small signs of movement in the right direction. Less developed countries shared in the achievements of 1988 to a greater extent than on many past occasions, although most continued to face major problems of poverty, debt, and structurally unbalanced economies.

All in all, as 1988 drew to a close there was considerable satisfaction about progress during the year, although there were some doubts about the sustainability of growth at a comparable rate in the new year. However, the fact that most—if not all—observers expected further, albeit slower, growth was perhaps the most remarkable feature of the year's achievements. It marked the sixth year of the current growth phase in the world economy, the longest period of continuous expansion since World War II. Nevertheless, instead of ending on a note of a major loss of momentum, a rapid acceleration in prices, and a rise in unemployment, all of which characterized the end of past (and shorter)

growth phases, the principal cause for concern in 1988 was a modest gain in the rate of inflation (from 3 to 3.3% in the industrialized countries) and a need for a gentle tightening of monetary policy to cut back the rate of economic growth from the exceptionally high level of 1987.

During 1988 the volume of world output was estimated to have risen by 3.8%, compared with an advance of 3.2% in 1987—nearly one percentage point above earlier expectations. Both developed and less developed countries grew at broadly the same rate; both did better than in the preceding year and exceeded the original forecasts. Among the industrialized countries, the fastest growth was recorded by Japan, which showed a 6% gain in gross national product (GNP), compared with 4.2% in 1987. Japan was followed by the U.K. with 5% (4% in 1987), Canada with 4.3% (4%), and the U.S., which was heading for a gain of 4% (3.4%).

Other large Western developed countries advanced a little less rapidly at around 3%, and all except Italy saw an acceleration in their growth. The same was true of the less developed countries, which were thought to have boosted their collective GNP by 3.7%, compared with 3.3% in 1987. However, performance varied greatly from country to country. Asian economies, including such high-growth countries as South Korea, Singapore, and Taiwan, did the best with 7–8%. At the other extreme were Middle Eastern countries and other oil exporters, where the weakness of oil prices restricted growth to around 1.5%.

Investment and private consumption had been the twin engines of economic buoyancy in the developed world. Overall investment expenditures appeared to have grown nearly twice as fast as in 1987, with countries such as the U.K. and the U.S. recording nearly a threefold gain. This was the result of several factors, including a significant improvement in corporate profits since the early 1980s, a diminishing margin of spare capacity, and a continuing high level of business confidence. Housing investments were also strong owing to relatively low interest rates and the good availability of credit. The strength of investment activities was a highly welcome feature of the year in that, by increasing capacity, these investments could reduce the danger of overheating and inflation and prolong the current growth phase of the world economy.

Consumer expenditure in the developed world probably rose by around 3.5% in volume terms during 1988, compared with 3.2% in 1987. This modest acceleration reflected overall growth in disposable incomes, resulting from higher employment, a rise in wages, and tax reductions in some countries. Thus in the U.S., employment was calculated to have grown by 2.5%, with growth rates of 1–2% in most other large countries. Hourly earnings rose rapidly, exceeding the rate of inflation in virtually all cases and ranging from 2.5% in Japan to 7–8% in the U.K. Tax cuts played a significant part in West Germany and in the U.K., where the spring budget provided for an income tax reduction of around £4 billion. It is for this reason that the U.K. saw the fastest rate of increase in consumer spending—about 5.8%, nearly twice as fast as the average for all developed nations.

The effect of this rapid growth in the two most important components of demand—business investment and consumer spending—was a strong recovery in industrial production and a further significant cut in the number of people out of work. Industrial output in the larger countries of the Organization for Economic Cooperation and Development (OECD) was thought to have expanded by around 5%, twice as fast as in the previous year. Manufacturers reported record order books, an increase in overtime worked, and lengthening delivery dates. Capacity utilization rates

Finance ministers from 24 developing nations meet in West Berlin to discuss the third world's economic situation. Many third world officials feared that the U.S. budget and trade deficits would drive up world interest rates and hurt their struggling economies.
AFP PHOTO

rose just about everywhere to historically high levels, and the attendant need to expand capacity played a key part in the investment boom.

There was a decline in unemployment for the fifth consecutive year. For 1988 the average unemployment rate of the developed world was estimated at 7%, compared with 7.5% in 1987 and a peak of 8.6% reached in 1983. This was still well above the rates of the 1970s, when the industrialized world's average unemployment rate stood at 4.2%, but hardly any commentator, government, or policymaker expected to match that figure in the foreseeable future. As usual, Japan had the lowest unemployment rate (2.5%), while Italy and France, with 12 and 10%, respectively, were well above the average.

Inflation was affected by a number of conflicting influences, resulting, on balance, in a modest strengthening of consumer prices. The principal favourable factor was the weakness of oil prices, which reduced energy costs. This was more than offset by an increase in most primary commodity prices, an acceleration in wage increases, and buoyant demand, which enabled manufacturers to improve their profit margins. The net result was a rise in consumer prices of some 3.5% in the developed world, compared with 3.2% in 1987. These were average yearly figures and masked a rather more pronounced upturn in inflation toward the end of 1988. In the final quarter of the year, price rises were running at around 4%, as against 3.5% 12 months previously, with some countries recording a rapid acceleration between the two quarters.

For the early part of 1988, monetary policies were fairly relaxed, reflecting governments' relative initial lack of concern about inflation and their desire to maintain growth in the wake of the stock market crash in October 1987. During the second half of the year, accelerating inflationary pressures were accompanied by modest upward movements in the cost of credit. This was true of the U.S., where the federal funds rate started edging up in April, and West Germany. The rise was anything but gentle in the U.K., with the Bank of England pushing up base rates from 7.5 to 13% over seven months. In terms of economic growth, fiscal policies in 1988 were broadly neutral. In the U.S., efforts to control the budget deficit were not expected to yield significant results, and the deficit for fiscal 1988 was put at $155 billion, up from $150 billion in the preceding

year. In West Germany the tax-relief package originally scheduled for 1990 provided strong support to economic growth but contributed to a further increase in the budget deficit. In the U.K. strong economic growth resulted in buoyant tax revenues, which allowed the government to introduce a cut in taxation as well as providing an increase in the budget surplus.

On the foreign trade and payments front, the year was characterized by strong growth in world trade, a modest reduction in payment imbalances, and an orderly readjustment of exchange rates. World trade grew by some 7.5%, as against 5.8% in 1987. Growth was rapid in most countries and was largely the result of buoyant domestic economic conditions. Less developed nations also recorded a respectable gain in trade of around 7%, partly because the weakness of oil prices had a positive effect on the volume of oil exports. During 1988 U.S. sales abroad rose at a rapid rate, which had the effect of reducing that country's current account deficit from $154 billion to around $130 billion. Japan, on the other hand, boosted its imports and engineered a cut in its surplus from $87 billion to $75 billion. There was a reduction in West Germany's positive current account balance, but the U.K. saw an explosion in the deficit from £2.5 billion to £15 billion as rapid domestic growth boosted imports and had an adverse effect on exports. Strong international approval of the U.K.'s fiscal policies and its high level of interest rates kept sterling strong against most currencies, especially the West German Deutsche Mark, the sterling value of which fell by some 7% during the year. Sterling's improvement against the dollar was less pronounced, which restricted the gain in its effective (average) rate to some 4% in the same period. The dollar lost heavily against the Japanese yen. Despite considerable fluctuation, the dollar stood its ground against the Deutsche Mark, with the result that its effective rate, which stood at 94.1 in the first quarter of 1988, was little changed at 93.8 in November. During the same period, the average rate of the West German currency declined just over 3%.

NATIONAL ECONOMIC POLICIES

Developed Market Economies. *United States.* Economic growth accelerated in the U.S. during 1988, confounding predictions of a recession. The GNP expanded at around

Table I. Real Gross Domestic Products of Selected OECD Countries				
% annual change				
Country	1985	1986	1987	1988*
United States†	3.0	2.9	2.9	2.75
Japan†	4.9	2.4	4.2	4.25
West Germany†	2.0	2.5	1.7	2.25
France	1.7	2.1	1.9	2.00
United Kingdom	3.6	3.3	4.5	3.50
Canada	4.3	3.3	3.9	4.00
Italy	2.9	2.9	3.1	2.50
Total major countries	3.2	2.8	3.1	3.00
Australia	5.5	1.8	4.4	3.50
New Zealand	2.8	1.3	0.2	−0.25
Austria	2.8	1.7	1.3	1.50
Belgium	1.4	2.4	1.8	2.00
Denmark	3.7	3.5	−0.9	0.00
Finland	3.5	2.4	3.6	3.25
Greece	3.0	1.3	−0.5	1.75
Iceland	3.4	6.3	6.5	0.50
Ireland†	−0.8	−1.6	3.1	0.25
Luxembourg	3.8	2.9	2.0	2.00
Netherlands, The	2.3	2.4	2.5	1.50
Norway	5.4	4.4	1.6	0.75
Portugal	3.3	4.3	5.0	4.25
Spain	2.3	3.3	5.2	4.00
Sweden	2.1	1.2	2.8	2.25
Switzerland	4.1	2.7	2.5	1.50
Turkey†	5.1	7.9	7.4	5.25
Total OECD countries	3.2	2.8	3.1	3.00

*OECD projection.   †GNP.
Source: OECD *Economic Outlook.*

4%, compared with an average of 3% for the previous two years. Nevertheless, despite strong growth, full capacity utilization, low unemployment, high export growth, and record business investment, the nation's economy remained under a cloud, and the dollar continued to be vulnerable because the high trade and budget deficits were still unresolved.

In spite of the stock market crash, the fourth quarter of 1987 rounded off the year on a strong note with an annualized 4.8% GNP growth rate, paving the way for a surprisingly robust 3.9% in the opening quarter of 1988. Although a slight loss of momentum was evident, a buoyant tone remained throughout the year. April–June growth of 3% was followed by a drought-induced slowdown to a more modest 2.6% in the third quarter. As the year drew to a close, the GNP was widely expected to grow between 3.5 and 4%. Without the effects of the drought, U.S. economic growth would have been closer to 5%, giving six years of sustained growth, the longest peacetime expansion since World War II.

All components of demand grew robustly with the exception of government spending. Average earnings rose by as much as 3.8%, reflecting the final phase of the federal income tax cuts and higher employment levels. A reasonably steady inflation rate improved disposable incomes, encouraging higher spending and lower savings. Personal consumption, having fallen by 2% immediately after the stock market crash, rose at an annualized 3.5% during the first nine months of the year. Government consumption grew at a slower pace for the second year in a row, reflecting the attempt to reduce the federal deficit. On the basis of incomplete data, it was estimated to have increased by only 0.75%, compared with 2.3% the year before and 3.8% in 1986.

The main engine of growth in the economy in 1988 was business investment, which rose by nearly 10% after remaining stagnant for two years. It was stimulated by a recovery in confidence after the October 1987 crash and a high level of capacity utilization. As corporate profitability grew and cash flows remained buoyant, industrialists were willing to expand their capital stock. Once again the housing sector remained weak, but business expenditure on industrial buildings put some life into the construction

sector. Exports, benefiting from the decline of the dollar during 1986 and 1987 and favourable economic conditions in the other major economies of the world, continued to grow at double-digit rates.

In light of this, it was not surprising that industrial output continued to expand throughout the year. The rate of expansion (5.5%) was noticeably faster than it had been the year before, reflecting a pickup in the autumn, especially in the auto industry. Another aspect of strong demand and higher industrial output was a steady increase in the capacity utilization rate to 83.5%, the highest level in more than eight years. Although higher output was achieved largely through longer working hours (one reason why earnings rose sharply earlier in the year), this did not prevent the unemployment rate from falling rapidly. Having stood at around 6% at the beginning of 1988, it fell to 5.3% by the summer—the lowest rate in 14 years. In the summer the unemployment rate edged up a little, but by October the June low had been equaled.

The concern of the financial markets and of the Federal Reserve Board (the Fed) about inflationary developments was not confirmed by an actual upsurge in the consumer price index. Compared with an average of 3.7% for the whole of 1987, the pace picked up slightly to 3.9% in the opening quarter of 1988, settling to just over 4% by July. Preliminary figures signaled an average of 4.4% for the year overall. Nevertheless, concern remained that with industry working at full capacity, labour costs accelerating, and the dollar weak, a steep upturn in the inflation rate was just around the corner. Analysts agreed that falling oil prices and a rise in the value of the dollar during the summer had masked the true underlying trends.

There was no doubt, however, that insufficient progress had been made in reducing the twin deficits—trade and budget. Responding to the competitive position of the dollar and strong economic growth in other major OECD countries, the export boom continued, but so did the U.S. appetite for imports. A 30% rise in exports, seasonally adjusted, during the first nine months was offset by a 13% surge in imports. The trend of the trade deficit was downward during the first nine months, but the rate of improvement was judged to be too slow to sustain the reduction into 1989 and beyond. The seasonally adjusted deficit (using the cost, insurance, and freight basis) for the January–September period came to $113.6 billion, down appreciably from the $119.2 billion deficit in the corresponding period of 1987. This pointed to an annual figure of around $145 billion, although the autumn figures indicated that it could drop as low as $137 billion. The current account deficit for 1988 was expected to decline significantly from the $154 billion recorded the year before. The U.S. net international debt rose by some $99 billion to a total of $368 billion, completing the transformation of the U.S. from a net creditor in 1984 to the world's leading debtor nation.

The fear within the financial markets was that while capital inflows were sufficient to fund the trade deficit, as the size of the debt grew and the world economy entered into a slower growth phase, capital inflows could fall short. This, in turn, would require much higher U.S. interest rates to attract capital, with serious economic implications for the U.S. and the rest of the world; *i.e.,* a full-blown recession. For most of the year the dollar remained on a slightly upward but volatile trend, but it came under pressure in September–October. In the aftermath of the presidential election, the dollar's decline gathered speed, reflecting concern that President-elect George Bush's economic advisers appeared to favour a further 15–20% fall in

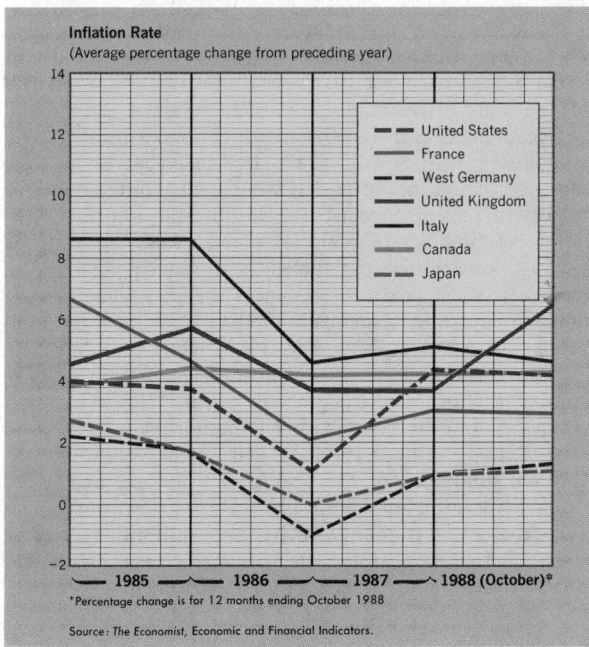

Inflation Rate
(Average percentage change from preceding year)

United States
France
West Germany
United Kingdom
Italy
Canada
Japan

1985   1986   1987   1988 (October)*

*Percentage change is for 12 months ending October 1988

Source: *The Economist,* Economic and Financial Indicators.

the currency against the yen and Deutsche Mark to sustain export growth and choke off imports.

The monetary policy was flexible from late 1987, while fiscal policy retained a slightly restrictive stance. Immediately after the October 1987 crash, the Fed relaxed its monetary policy and provided liquidity for the banking system to offset the deflationary effects of the financial crisis. The Fed cut its key federal funds rate (the rate at which it lends overnight funds to banks) by three-quarters of a point to 6.75%, helping to restore confidence and minimize the risk of a recession. The easier stance was continued into the spring, with the rate lowered to 6.5% by March. As it became clear that the earlier predictions of a sharp slowdown were exaggerated, a gradual tightening up in policy occurred, and the federal funds rate edged up by half a point to 7% in April. In early August the June unemployment figures showed a 14-year low of 5.3%, well below a level that Alan Greenspan, the chairman of the Fed, regarded as compatible with noninflationary expansion. The Fed then raised the discount rate from 6 to 6.5%, the first increase since September 1987. The federal funds rate soon followed suit, and the major banks raised their prime rates to 10%. At the end of November commercial banks raised their prime lending rates to 10.5%, fueling speculation that the Fed would raise its discount rate to dampen inflationary trends.

The federal budget deficit in fiscal 1988 (ended September 30) was $155 billion, slightly higher than the previous year's $150 billion but in line with the $156 billion target agreed upon with the Congress in the aftermath of the October crash. Given the robust economic growth rate, the fiscal policy was at best neutral but more likely marginally stimulatory. The budget deficit of 3.3% of GNP was not out of line with the West German deficit, but the extremely low U.S. savings rate forced dependence on external funds to finance the deficit and, despite the Gramm-Rudman legislation, the deficit was unlikely to be reduced significantly in the foreseeable future. President-elect Bush's "flexible

Table II. Percentage Changes in Consumer Prices in Selected OECD Countries						
Country	1983	1984	1985	1986	1987	1988*
United States	3.2	4.3	3.5	1.9	3.7	3.9
Japan	1.9	2.2	2.1	0.4	−0.2	0.5
West Germany	3.3	2.4	2.2	−0.2	0.2	1.0
France	9.6	7.4	5.8	2.7	3.1	2.5
United Kingdom	4.6	5.0	6.1	3.4	4.2	3.5
Italy	14.6	10.6	8.6	6.1	4.6	4.9
Canada	5.9	4.3	4.0	4.2	4.4	4.1
Austria	3.3	5.6	3.2	1.7	1.4	2.3
Belgium	7.7	6.3	4.9	1.3	1.6	1.0
Denmark	6.9	6.3	4.7	3.6	4.0	4.7
Finland	8.3	7.1	5.9	2.9	4.1	4.0
Greece	20.2	18.5	19.3	23.0	16.4	13.2
Iceland	86.5	30.9	31.9	22.2	18.3	25.0
Ireland	10.5	8.6	5.4	3.8	3.2	1.9
Luxembourg	8.7	4.6	4.1	0.3	−0.1	0.8
Netherlands, The	2.8	3.3	2.3	0.2	−0.5	0.6
Norway	8.4	6.2	5.7	7.2	8.7	7.2
Portugal	25.5	29.3	19.3	11.7	9.4	8.8
Spain	12.2	11.3	8.8	8.8	5.3	4.5
Sweden	8.9	8.0	7.4	4.3	4.2	5.4
Switzerland	3.0	3.0	3.4	0.7	1.5	1.8
Turkey	28.8	45.6	45.0	34.5	38.9	69.8
Australia	10.1	3.9	6.8	9.1	8.5	6.9
New Zealand	7.4	6.2	15.4	13.2	15.7	9.0

*Twelve-month rate of change.
Sources: OECD, Economic Outlook; Main Economic Indicators.

freeze" policy for tackling the deficit looked unconvincing to the financial markets, and they took their cue from Greenspan's warning that if the adjustments were delayed the cost would become inordinate. The dollar came under pressure, and it took concerted intervention by other Western governments to slow the steep fall.

United Kingdom. In the U.K. 1988 was the seventh successive year of rapid economic growth. Although the year opened on a somewhat uncertain note in the wake of the world stock market crash in October 1987, by the first quarter it was clear that the unexpected, and largely unjustified, fall in equity values would not have a significant effect on the performance of the real economy. Thus the volume of gross domestic product (GDP) rose at an annual rate of 4.1% in the first three months of the year, representing only a marginal slowdown from the gain seen in the last quarter of 1987. The second quarter registered a further advance of a similar magnitude and, as 1988 was drawing to a close, the indications were that the volume of GDP for the year as a whole would post an increase of 5%. This compared well with the exceptionally rapid growth of 4.7% in 1987 and an estimated 1988 growth rate of around 4% for the OECD as a whole.

Despite a sharp rise in interest rates in the second half of the year, investment activities remained strong and were estimated to have registered a volume gain of 9–10%, compared with 5.6% in 1987. The principal reasons for this remarkable performance were strong order books, a rapidly increasing capacity utilization ratio, improved corporate profitability in both 1987 and 1988, and a strong level of housing demand fueled by the easy availability of relatively cheap credit for much of the year. Thus private housing investment was estimated to have risen by 21%, some four times as fast as in 1987, while investment in the manufacturing sector was heading for a gain of 14%, compared with 5% in the preceding year.

At the same time, consumer demand in the U.K. grew rapidly. In December 1988 the gain in the volume of private consumption for the year as a whole seemed set to reach 5.8%, up from 5% in 1987. During 1988 just about every major determinant of private consumption moved in a positive direction. In the spring budget Nigel Lawson (*see* BIOGRAPHIES), the chancellor of the Exchequer, brought in a massive £4 billion cut in income tax, reducing the standard rate from 27 to 25% and the top rate from 60

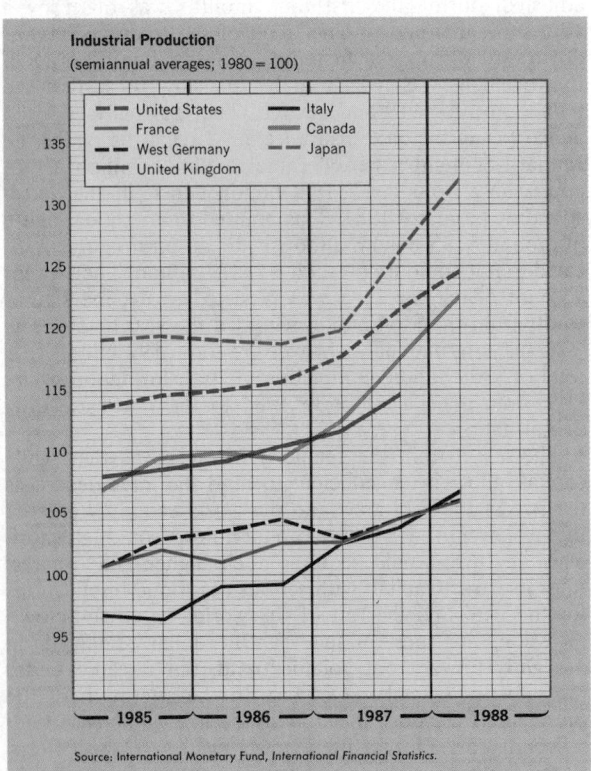

Industrial Production

(semiannual averages; 1980 = 100)

Source: International Monetary Fund, International Financial Statistics.

to 40%. Average earnings rose by some 8.5% during the year, beating price inflation by at least three percentage points. There was a significant and sustained fall in the level of unemployment, providing an additional boost to personal incomes. In fact, largely as a result of these factors, real personal disposable incomes were estimated to have risen by some 4.5%, as against 3.3% in the previous year. Consumer expenditures also benefited from a cutback in savings and the easy availability of credit. During the year as a whole, personal borrowing rose rapidly and, although the bulk of this went into financing house purchases, a significant proportion was translated into demand for goods. This trend was further strengthened by another reduction in the already low relative level of savings—down to 4% of personal disposable income, as compared with 5.5% in 1987 and 7% in 1986.

The boom in domestic demand had both positive and negative consequences. On the positive side, between December 1987 and October 1988 the seasonally adjusted number of unemployed fell by nearly 500,000 to 2,160,-000, the lowest level since May 1981. As a result, the unemployment ratio (the number of jobless as a percentage of the labour force) fell from 9.3 to 7.7%. Another encouraging feature was the continuing growth in productivity. During the first half of the year, output per person employed in manufacturing rose by some 7%, and the gain for the full 12 months was expected to top 6%, showing only a modest slowdown from the 7.3% advance achieved in 1987. Another positive development was the massive improvement in government finances. Despite the spring tax cuts, the 1988–89 fiscal year (ending in March 1989) was expected to provide a surplus of £10 billion, some £3 billion more than had been forecast in the spring. The two principal reasons for this were the continued strict control of public expenditure (in 1988–89 public expenditure as a proportion of GDP was set to fall to under 40% for the first time for over 20 years) and the faster-than-expected increase in tax revenue fueled by the rapid rise of corporate profits, personal incomes, and consumption.

On the other hand, faced with an investment and consumer boom, domestic industry could not cope, and much of the extra demand was channeled into imports. Although manufacturing output rose rapidly—by some 7%, as against 5.4% in 1987—the volume of imports for the year was thought to have grown by around 12%, compared with 7% in 1987. At the same time, a significant proportion of domestic output that would have gone abroad was diverted to the home market. As a result, export volumes, which registered a gain of more than 5% in 1987, managed an increase of only 2–2.5%. The effect of these developments, together with the movements in the exchange rate, was a current account deficit of £15 billion, compared with £2.6 billion in 1987 and a forecast of some £3 billion at the time of the April budget.

Table III. Standardized Unemployment Rates in Selected OECD Countries
% of total labour force, seasonally adjusted

Country	1983	1984	1985	1986	1987	1988*
Canada	11.8	11.3	10.5	9.6	8.9	7.50
United States	9.5	7.5	7.1	7.0	6.2	5.50
Japan	2.6	2.7	2.6	2.8	2.8	2.50
Australia	9.9	8.8	8.2	8.0	8.1	7.25
France	8.3	10.0	10.2	10.5	10.6	10.75
West Germany	8.0	8.2	8.3	8.0	7.9	8.00
Italy	9.8	9.8	9.6	10.3	11.0	11.50
Sweden	3.5	2.5	2.4	2.2	1.9	1.75
United Kingdom	12.6	11.5	11.7	11.8	10.4	9.50

*Partially estimated.
Source: OECD *Economic Outlook.*

The deteriorating external payments position and the growing inflationary pressures persuaded the government to take steps to moderate the growth in demand. After some public disagreement with the prime minister, the chancellor decided to achieve this objective almost entirely by raising interest rates. It was hoped that, given the large volume of outstanding credit, particularly mortgage finance, a significant increase in debt-servicing costs would cut back the growth in consumer spending. The government also expected that the financial consequences of higher interest rates would stiffen the backbone of employers against inflationary wage settlements. However, some analysts expressed concern that the rapid increase in interest rates could push the economy into recession. Certainly as the year drew to its close, there were indications that the interest rate hike was giving a temporary boost to the already strengthening pace of inflation. During the first quarter of 1988, inflation stood at 3.3%. In the second quarter it was up to 4.8% and—partly because of the increase in mortgage rates that resulted from the government's interest rate policy—by October the inflation rate had risen to 6.4%. All in all, the year as a whole was heading for an increase of 5%, as compared with 4.1% in 1987, exceeding the average OECD figure by more than two percentage points.

The external value of sterling strengthened during the year, partly as a result of general international confidence in the British government's handling of the economy (especially public finances) and the relatively high level of interest rates. The average sterling index showed a particularly strong rise in the second quarter, and by the end of November it was up to 78, as against an average of 74.9 in the closing quarter of 1987. The average year-on-year gain was expected to be in excess of 4%. There was a particularly strong rise against the West German Deutsche Mark (from an average of DM 2.99 in the final quarter of 1987 to DM 3.17 in the third quarter of 1988 and to DM 3.21 on December 30). The improvement against the dollar was only slightly less pronounced than that against the Deutsche Mark; at year's end the rate was $1.81, compared with a third-quarter average of $1.70 and a figure of $1.75 for the last quarter of 1987.

Japan. The Japanese economy turned in a highly satisfactory performance during 1988. The volume of GNP rose by just under 6%, representing a significant acceleration on the gain of 4.2% seen in 1987. In spite of this, inflationary pressures remained well under control, productivity grew at a rapid rate, and capacity kept up with demand. The already low level of unemployment saw a small decline. However, somewhat disappointingly, the still large and internationally unacceptable current account surplus recorded only a modest decrease. This put further strains on Tokyo's economic relations with its principal trading partners, which provided a difficult backdrop for the settling of specific trade disputes and complaints about unfair competition in a range of products.

Economic growth during the year was widely based, with most components of domestic demand doing better than in 1987. Growth in private consumption was stimulated by the continuing impact of the tax cuts introduced in the 1987–88 fiscal year, a relatively large wage hike in the spring of 1988, a significant rise in summer bonus payments, a reduction of about 0.5% in the savings rate, and continuing stability in retail prices. As a result, consumer spending rose rapidly during the first half of the year. Progress appeared to have been maintained in the subsequent six months, with the result that year-end estimates pointed to an overall gain in volume of approximately

5.5%. This was well above expectations and compared favourably with the gain of 3.9% secured in 1987.

Investment expenditures were also buoyant, although some key components displayed evidence of weakening as the year progressed. Housing purchases, in particular, were losing momentum during the second half, which depressed the gain for the entire year to an estimated 14%, compared with 20% during the preceding 12-month period. However, private plant and equipment investments—boosted by strong domestic and overseas demand, good corporate profitability, and the need for additional capacity—grew at a rapid rate throughout the year. All in all, the total for the year was thought to have been some 13% higher than in 1987, which had managed an increase of only 8.3%. Public consumption turned in a volume gain of some 2%, more than making up for the decline of 0.7% in 1987. Inventory stockpiling was also strong in 1988 after a year of relative weakness.

A remarkable feature of the economy was that this unexpectedly strong performance was secured without any serious sign of overheating. Although the buoyancy of the economy resulted in a predictable (and welcome) growth in imports, there was no evidence that the country's productive resources were unable to cope with demand. Thus industry managed to boost its output by some 9%, compared with an increase of only 3% recorded in 1987. Nevertheless, there were no signs of capacity shortages, largely because the investment boom had the effect of boosting capacity and improving labour productivity.

Partly because of this, but also because of favourable external trends, inflation remained under control. Wholesale prices, which benefited from the strengthening of the yen and the weakness of oil prices, were running below the previous year's level month by month, with the result that the average annual figure was set to register a drop (of around 1%) for the fourth successive year. This effect could also be seen in the index of import prices, which was heading for an annual decline of 4–5%. Retail prices, however, saw a modest rise of 0.7% in the wake of a 0.2% drop in 1987. This was well within the government's target range and was widely regarded as acceptable, given the 6% gain in GNP. One of the consequences of the strength of the economy was a tightening of the labour market. The unemployment rate of 2.8% recorded in 1987 was down to 2.4% by autumn of 1988 and was likely to average out at 2.5% for the year. Although this was still well above the 1% seen in the high economic growth era of the mid-1960s, there were some fears that, despite rapid productivity increases, it could signal a faster rate of wage and price inflation. Such fears were underlined when, for the first time since 1974, job offers exceeded the number of those seeking work.

A somewhat disappointing feature of the year was that, in spite of the rapid economic growth, Japan's huge and much criticized current account surplus saw only a modest cutback. Despite a stronger yen, the volume of goods and services exported was estimated to have risen by some 5%, compared with 3.4% in the previous year. At the same time, the volume of imports probably recorded a hike of 17%, nearly twice as large as the 9.1% achieved in 1987. However, because of the relative movement of import and export prices, the current account surplus was still estimated at $75 billion for the year, a relatively small reduction of the figure of $86.7 billion recorded in 1987.

Given the absence of any serious inflationary worries, the authorities maintained a relaxed and generally accommodating monetary policy. Thus the Bank of Japan's official discount rate remained firmly at 2.5%, and short term rates (the three-month Gensaki rate) were stable at 3.8% for the first three quarters of the year. During the autumn, however, a modest upward trend provoked some concern over the potentially inflationary effects of the tightening labour market. As already indicated, the external value of the yen gained some momentum, largely because of U.S. developments, particularly the continuing concern about the large U.S. budget and current account deficits. The yen performed relatively strongly in the first half of the year with the average rising to 127 yen to the dollar, compared with 136 yen in the closing quarter of 1987. By September, however, the rate was down to 137 yen, followed by a sharp recovery to 128 yen in late October. The last few months of 1988 were characterized by a degree of instability as foreign-exchange markets attempted to come to terms with the result of the U.S. presidential election. In November the dollar weakened further to 122 yen, but by the end of the year it had recovered slightly to 125 yen.

The year's good economic performance had a positive effect on corporate profitability; the latest surveys for the March–September period pointed to a profit hike of 25%. This, together with the absence of any storm clouds on the horizon, boosted the stock market to record levels. (See *Stock Exchanges*, below.) Its performance was significantly better than in most other countries, where year-end equity values were still well below their peak in 1987.

West Germany. During 1988 the West German economy outperformed most expectations, but as in every other year since 1980, it failed to match the average performance of the OECD area, which was heading for a 1988 GNP hike of 4%. Indicators of West German economic activity available to December 1988 pointed to a volume GNP gain of some 3.5% for the year. This represented a significant improvement both on early forecasts of a 1.5–2% advance and on the 1987 growth rate of 1.7%. A particularly satisfactory feature of 1988 was that, despite stronger growth, inflation accelerated only modestly and remained eminently manageable. Unemployment, however, stopped falling and leveled out at 8.8% (compared with 8.9% in 1987) as demographic trends offset the effects of job creation. The large current account deficit experienced

Table IV. Changes in Output in the Less Developed Countries

In %

Area	Annual average 1970–79	Change from preceding year				
		1983	1984	1985	1986	1987
All less developed countries	5.6	1.8	4.2	3.2	4.1	3.1
Oil-exporting countries	7.1	−1.5	0.9	—	0.3	−0.2
Non-oil less developed countries	5.1	3.4	5.9	4.8	5.9	4.5
Africa	4.4	−1.8	1.2	1.9	0.9	0.9
Asia	5.4	7.9	8.1	6.5	6.5	6.6
Europe	5.7	1.9	4.3	2.9	4.3	2.6
Middle East	7.3	—	0.4	−1.7	2.0	−1.0
Western Hemisphere	5.7	−2.5	3.5	3.1	4.0	2.3

Source: International Monetary Fund, *World Economic Outlook*.

Table V. Changes in Consumer Prices in the Less Developed Countries

In %

Area	Annual average 1970–79	Change from preceding year				
		1983	1984	1985	1986	1987
All less developed countries	18.1	32.9	38.6	38.9	29.9	40.3
Oil-exporting countries	12.0	24.1	20.3	14.7	21.6	33.2
Non-oil less developed countries	20.8	37.6	48.7	52.2	33.9	43.5
Africa	12.7	18.9	20.4	13.4	14.9	16.2
Asia	9.5	6.6	7.3	7.1	8.0	8.7
Europe	12.4	22.9	25.3	25.1	25.0	30.3
Middle East	11.6	12.2	14.8	12.2	11.3	16.3
Western Hemisphere	34.8	108.2	131.9	143.2	88.4	130.8

Source: International Monetary Fund, *World Economic Outlook*.

A group of Canadians carry banners and signs to protest the free-trade treaty between Canada and the United States. The treaty, supported by Prime Minister Brian Mulroney, was ratified by the Canadian Parliament in December.

KEVIN ARGUE—GAMMA LIAISON

a modest reduction, which made the Bonn government less subject to international pressure to introduce demand-boosting measures.

Contrary to expectations, the year started rather well, with the first-quarter GNP recording an average annual growth of 5.7%. Although a significant part of this was due to the unusually mild weather, which assisted the construction industry, other areas of activity also performed well. The most spectacular turnaround was seen in investment expenditures, which posted an annualized growth rate of more than 10%. There were also signs of an improvement in business confidence and investment intentions, largely because of the downward trend of interest rates in late 1987 and the unexpected strength of exports. The rate of growth in investment demand in subsequent months could not match the exceptional first-quarter performance, but at the end of 1988 it was estimated that the gain for the year would reach some 6.5%, as against only a 1.7% advance in 1987.

Consumer expenditure, which accounted for just under 60% of total GNP, also rose faster than had been anticipated. After a relatively disappointing start in the first quarter, growth became stronger, and West Germany experienced a modest acceleration of 3.5% (3.1% in 1987). This was partly due to a slight upturn in wage increases (which were not fully offset by faster inflation) and a cut in taxes under the 1986–88 tax-reduction program. The rise in wages averaged out at around 3%, some half a percentage point faster than in the previous year, but an increase in overtime working held the per capita increase to some 4%. At the same time, under the long-term tax-reduction program, some DM 14 billion worth of tax cuts were implemented, much of which went into consumption rather than boosting the savings ratio.

Not unexpectedly, the acceleration of economic growth resulted in a modest and easily manageable rise in the rate of inflation. During 1987 the cost-of-living index recorded an advance of only 0.2%, with both producer and import prices posting a significant decline. However, for most of 1988 consumer prices rose by 1%, with both producer prices and the cost of imported materials heading for the first increase since 1985. All in all, the government predicted a consumer price rise of 1–1.5%, relatively low by international standards but high by the yardstick of the previous two years.

It was largely for this reason that the West German authorities decided in June to push up interest rates. Thus, having been held at 3.25% since November 1987, the repurchase rate was raised in several steps from June 1988 to 4.25% in August. During the same period, the discount rate was raised from 2.5 to 3.5%, while in July the Lombard rate went up by half a percentage point from the 3.5% level established following the stock market crash in October 1987.

Apart from official concern about the slight increase in inflationary pressures, an increase in interest rates was also justified by exchange-rate considerations. During the first five months of the year, the rate for the dollar was broadly steady within the DM 1.60–DM 1.70 range, well above the level seen in late 1987. However, beginning in May the dollar strengthened considerably, and by August it had reached DM 1.90. Although this was a positive development for exporters, it fueled fears of inflation and caused some concern about its potentially adverse (and internationally troublesome) effect on the growth of imports. After some sharp short-term fluctuations following the U.S. presidential election in November, the rate at year's end was back to around DM 1.77, which was considered satisfactory in both Bonn and Washington.

The volume of merchandise exports rose rather better than expected, with the gain for 1988 estimated at 5.5%, as against 2.3% in the preceding year. Faster domestic consumption had a modest effect on import volume, pushing the growth rate from 4.9% in 1987 to 5.5% in 1988. A small increase in the already large trade surplus was likely to be more than offset by the rapid growth in the deficit on the invisible-payments account (interest receipts, tourism,

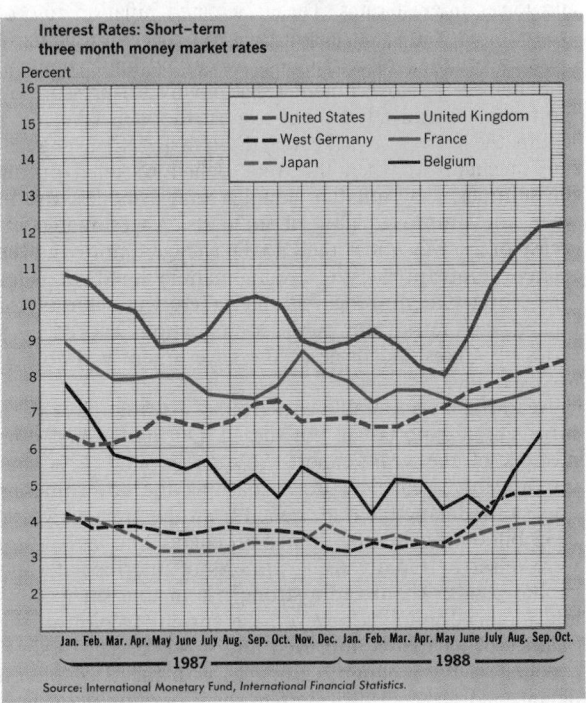

and so forth), with the result that the current account was expected to record a surplus for the year of $42 billion, some 5% less than the $44.6 billion recorded in 1987. Thus, unlike 1987, when economic growth was weak and the external surplus rose by 15%, in 1988 West Germany was seen as playing a more constructive role in underpinning the world economy and the reduction of international payment imbalances.

France. The French economy also performed much better than expected during 1988 and was on target with an expansion of nearly 3.5%, the highest rate since 1979, when it grew by 3.4%. Positive features in the strength of industrial investment, including stable inflation and exchange rates, were marred by two negative ones: the trade deficit and the high unemployment rate. The tone of economic policy remained cautiously restrictive, nurturing economic growth but avoiding excessive stimulation.

The year opened strongly despite expectations of a slowdown in the wake of the October stock market crash. After five years of austerity budgets, GDP growth accelerated to more than 1% in the first quarter, compared with an average of 0.7% in the previous six months. A spring slowdown that cut the growth rate to 0.6% was followed by renewed dynamism, leading to revised government predictions of 3.5% growth for the year as a whole—almost double the forecasts in the spring. Compared with expectations of a 5% increase, business investment rose by an estimated 14%, spurred by strong export demand and stable private consumption. In general terms, the contribution of consumer spending to economic growth continued the downward trend evident since 1987. Consumption by French households was largely unchanged during 1988; a slight decrease in the first half was offset by a recovery in the summer. Although wage increases remained modest, gently declining inflation and the proposed tax cuts in the summer budget improved consumer confidence, leading to a rise in borrowing levels.

Despite the rapid rate of economic activity, the inflation rate during the first half of 1988 accelerated from 2% in late 1987 to an annualized rate of 3.5%, but it stabilized and declined slightly under the impact of falling oil prices and lower interest rates. The anticipated inflation rate of around 3% for the year meant the gap between French and German inflation rates remained close and under control. This helped the government resist downward pressure on the franc (*i.e.,* an adjustment against the Deutsche Mark within the European Monetary System [EMS] exchange-rate mechanism) when the trade deficit rocketed during the summer. Low inflation coupled with a modest rise in wage rates improved unit labour costs. An estimated increase of 2% was under the OECD average, improving the relative competitiveness of French manufactured goods for the second year running. Although there was clamour for higher wage rates from public sector unions backed by a series of strikes and protests, the government was able to hold the line.

Against this favourable background it would have been surprising if exports had not surged. During the first nine months of the year, exports rose by around 12%, but imports increased even faster, dashing the government's hopes of reducing the trade deficit from the previous year's F 32 billion. Favourable trends on energy and agriculture were offset by rapidly rising imports of intermediate and capital goods. Thanks to a strong rise in tourism receipts and financial inflows, however, the current account of the balance of payments improved and was expected to show a deficit of F 15 billion, compared with the F 24 billion deficit recorded in 1987. Despite the economic buoyancy,

the underlying unemployment rate remained disappointingly high at approximately 10.2%, leaving some 2.6 million persons unemployed.

Overall economic policy guidelines established by the conservative government of Jacques Chirac in 1986 remained broadly unchanged under the new Socialist prime minister, Michel Rocard, whose budget proposals for 1989 retained the previous government's target of F 100 billion. Spending was planned to increase by 4.7% in nominal terms (or 2% after inflation). There were no new taxes except for reintroduction of the wealth tax, which was expected to raise a modest F 4 billion–F 5 billion, more than offset by F 24 billion in tax cuts divided between individual consumers and industry.

The monetary policy, too, remained largely unchanged over the year, the main objective being maintenance of France's parity within the EMS. Although the intervention rate was pushed up 0.75% to 8.25% in November 1987 in coordination with West Germany after the October crash, it was then lowered in stages to 7.25% by January. The new government in the summer cut interest rates by 0.25% to reduce the interest rate differentials between France and West Germany, but the rate rose again in October to end the year at 7.25%.

Less Developed Countries. Economic growth among the less developed countries during 1987 was slightly stronger than expected. Revised estimates pointed to a GDP growth of 3.4%, compared with earlier estimates of 3.2%. Despite the revision, it still represented a weaker rate of growth than the average of the previous four years. Projections based on incomplete data pointed to an estimated GDP growth of 3.75% for 1988. Given the robustness of growth in the industrialized countries and the general strength of commodity prices during 1988, the sluggishness in the rate of economic growth in the less developed countries was disappointing. International Monetary Fund (IMF) sources attributed this to four major factors. The first factor was

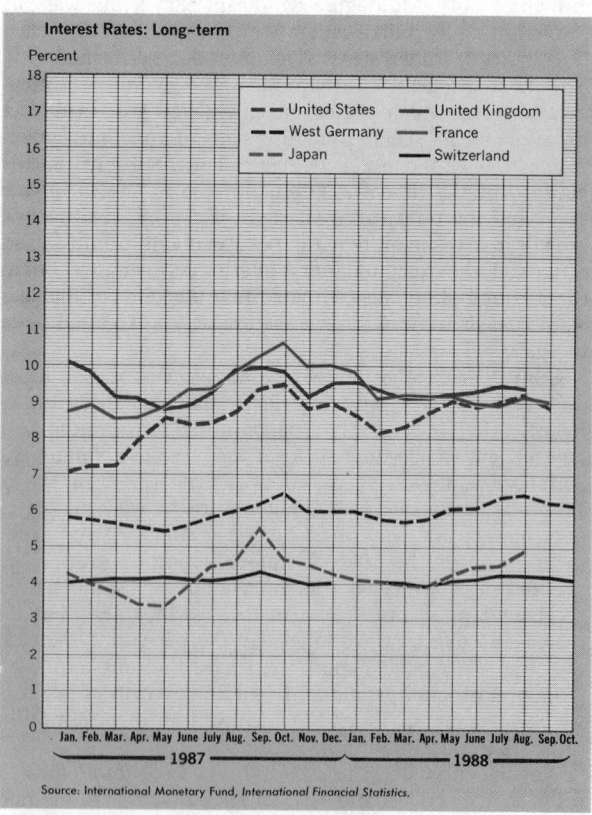

Interest Rates: Long-term

Source: International Monetary Fund, *International Financial Statistics.*

Clayton Yeutter, the U.S. trade representative, leaves a meeting at the General Agreement on Tariffs and Trade (GATT) talks where he had advocated that all nations eliminate their subsidies to farmers.
AFP PHOTO

the weak oil prices. The 10% average fall in the price of oil in nominal dollar terms (it was much higher in real terms) cut export earnings and reduced economic activity in oil-exporting countries. An indirect effect of weak oil prices was a drop in the remittances of many migrant workers and the negative impact on those countries that relied on this source of income. Second, the prices of some commodities, notably tea, coffee, and cocoa, went against the overall trend and fell. Exporters of these commodities thus experienced a decline in their terms of trade. Third, a firming in interest rates after a decline in late 1987 and early 1988 increased debt-servicing costs, partly offsetting the gains from higher export revenues. Fourth, higher inflation reduced disposable incomes, thus weakening demand and investment, and induced governments to adopt tighter policies to curb the inflationary forces.

In 1987, according to World Bank estimates, per capita income growth for the less developed world was 2.3%, compared with 2.8% the year before. The per capita growth rate in 1988 was expected to have improved slightly to around 2.5%, reflecting the underlying acceleration in the GDP rate. At this level, income per capita in the less developed world stood at around $655, compared with $12,850 for the developed world. Because the growth rate in the developed world's income per capita remained faster than that in the less developed world, the gap between the two continued to widen. This variation worsened between the different income groups and geographic regions. For example, in sub-Saharan Africa (excluding South Africa) GDP per capita stood at $450, 18% lower than in 1980. By contrast, East Asian income per capita, at $500, was 30% higher than in 1980.

Not surprisingly, among the less developed countries, exporters of manufactured goods were estimated to have grown fastest in 1988. This group benefited most from the strength of demand in the Western countries. Outstanding beneficiary countries included all the Asian newly industrialized countries, notably Hong Kong, South Korea, Singapore, and Taiwan. Growth in these countries as a whole was estimated to have been 6%. The recovery from previous years' drought also enabled output to rise rapidly in India and China. Eastern European countries were expected to remain stagnant.

Exporters of non-oil primary commodities benefited from improving terms of trade and higher demand from the industrialized countries. Asian exporters such as the Philippines saw additional benefits by widening the base of their exports to include some manufactured goods. By contrast, the primary-product exporters in Africa lagged behind in economic growth terms because of adverse terms of trade and the narrowness of their export base. The current account deficit for the oil-exporting less developed countries widened rapidly from an estimated $4 billion in 1987 to $23 billion in 1988. Reflecting the importance of this group as a whole, the current account balance of all less developed countries swung into an estimated deficit of $17.6 billion from a nominal surplus in 1987. The non-oil exporters' current account balance improved for the second year running and was expected to reach a surplus of $5 billion, compared with the previous year's surplus of $4.3 billion. The improvements in the current account balances of non-oil-exporting less developed countries were due to better terms of trade brought about by higher commodity prices and higher demand, generally from the industrialized countries.

Exports from less developed countries were thought to have increased by around 12% overall in dollar terms, reversing the previous year's 7% fall. Non-oil producers increased their exports by an estimated 17%—largely unchanged from 1987. There were few surprises in the import patterns. Oil producers faced import prices that had increased by an estimated 8% in dollar terms. This was largely due to the relative strengthening of the dollar during

Table VI. Balance of Payments on Current Account
In $000,000,000

Area	Annual average 1970–79	Change from preceding year				
		1983	1984	1985	1986	1987
All less developed countries	−87.3	−63.8	−34.1	−23.8	−47.6	4.4
Oil-exporting countries	−18.2	−18.7	−5.4	2.6	−35.7	−1.0
Non-oil less developed countries	−69.1	−45.1	−28.8	−26.5	−11.9	5.4
Africa	−21.7	−12.5	−7.4	−0.3	−7.0	−6.6
Asia	−17.5	−15.4	−4.2	−12.9	2.1	23.0
Europe	−8.6	−5.7	−3.5	−3.2	−1.7	0.2
Middle East	2.9	−19.3	−16.4	−2.6	−24.9	−2.9
Western Hemisphere	−42.4	−10.9	−2.6	−4.7	−16.1	−9.3

Source: International Monetary Fund, *World Economic Outlook*.

the first nine months of the year and the higher prices of manufactured goods. Thus in volume terms imports probably decreased slightly, continuing the trend established in previous years. By contrast, non-oil producers' imports increased by 17%, reflecting an improved economic position and the capacity to finance a higher import volume without increasing their trade deficits. In fact, the overall trade balance of non-oil less developed countries was estimated to have improved slightly during 1988 because of the fall in oil prices.

Total debts outstanding in the less developed world were at a standstill during 1987 at $886 billion and were thought to have increased slightly during 1988. However, the burden of debt still remained a very heavy one. In 1987 debt as percent of GDP stood at 38.5%. Although down from the 1986 figure of 41.2%, it was far above the 1980–85 average ratio of 29.3. The debt-service burden lightened slightly in 1987 and 1988 as export revenues increased. However, debt service as a percentage of exports of goods and services was more than 23.8% in 1987, compared with the 1980–85 average of 15.6%.

Efforts continued in the search for a "solution" to the problems of the highly indebted countries, especially those in Latin America. Several countries, including Argentina, Brazil, Chile, Nigeria, the Philippines, and Venezuela, negotiated to reschedule their repayments. Some, most notably Chile and Mexico, arranged "debt for equity" swaps, which would enable the creditors to sell the debt at a fraction of its original value in the world's major capital markets.

Since private international banks showed increasing reluctance to lend to the less developed countries, measures were taken to increase the inflow of resources through official channels. Net disbursements of official development assistance from member countries of the Development Assistance Committee (DAC) of the OECD amounted to $41.2 billion in 1987, which represented 0.34% of their GNP. Only five countries' disbursements exceeded the target of 0.7% of GNP set by the UN. Aid provided by non-DAC countries fell 9% during 1987. Although the drop in oil prices led to a cutback by most Arab countries, Saudi Arabia and Kuwait's aid as a percentage of GNP remained at a generous level of 3.7 and 1.3%, respectively.

Centrally Planned Economies. The 44th session of the Council for Mutual Economic Assistance (CMEA, or Comecon) was held in Prague, Czech., on July 5–7, 1988. It was attended by the heads of government of Bulgaria, East Germany, Mongolia, Poland, Romania, the Soviet Union, and Czechoslovakia, with the deputy prime ministers of Hungary and Vietnam and the vice-president of the Council of State and the Council of Ministers of Cuba. Also present were the secretary of Comecon, V. V. Sychev, and the vice-president of the Yugoslav Federal Executive Council. Representatives from Laos, Angola, Afghanistan, Yemen (Aden), Mozambique, Nicaragua, and Ethiopia took part as observers. The Czechoslovak premier, Lubomir Strougal, presided over the session.

The leaders of delegations discussed the issues that concerned their countries. Special importance was attached to the ongoing construction of the so-called integration projects, which included the opening up of the Yamburg gas field, the building of the "Progress" pipeline, and the Khmelnitsky nuclear power station.

The main discussion concentrated on the question of restructuring the mechanism of cooperation among the member states and on the question of "socialist economic integration." Cooperation among the member states was not developing quickly enough. The growth in trade had in

fact slowed, and in the majority of countries foreign debt had increased. Greater economic cooperation and a new and more effective approach to improving the distribution of labour was urgently needed. The session concluded that "the collective concept will be the basis for the coordination of economic policy in spheres connected with mutual cooperation and by those countries concerned in other spheres of socioeconomic development."

The session reached no decision on how to change the operating mechanism of the grouping. For the second year in a row, the radical restructuring of the economic mechanism was postponed because of the wide range of economic systems and management in the individual member

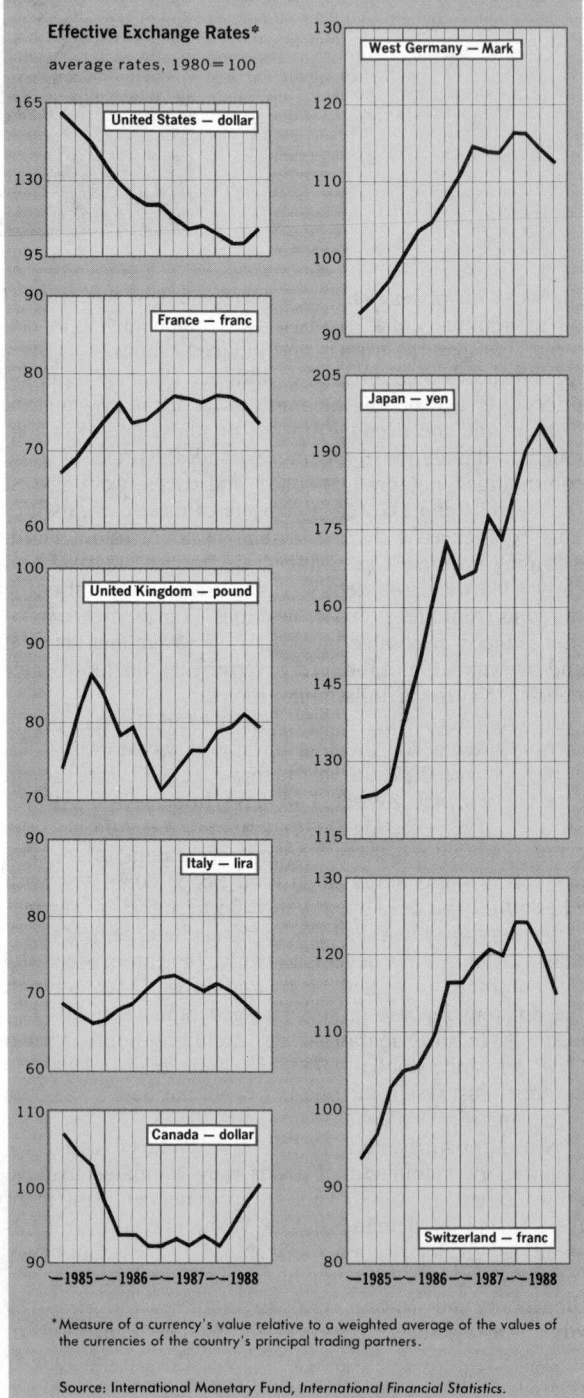

Effective Exchange Rates*
average rates, 1980=100

United States — dollar
France — franc
United Kingdom — pound
Italy — lira
Canada — dollar

West Germany — Mark
Japan — yen
Switzerland — franc

*Measure of a currency's value relative to a weighted average of the values of the currencies of the country's principal trading partners.

Source: International Monetary Fund, *International Financial Statistics.*

countries. On the one hand, Romania and, to some extent, East Germany were still guided by the old concept of "command economy" with the emphasis on central planning. Hungary and Poland tried to operate market economies, while the Soviet Union, Bulgaria, and Czechoslovakia occupied the middle ground. In this situation it was virtually impossible to find a common denominator. Consequently, no common policy was adopted, although there was theoretical agreement that new forms of economic relations based on enterprise initiatives would have to be extended with the intention of creating an integrated market. Romania, however, refused to be party to such an agreement, while Hungary expressed strong doubts about the ability of Comecon to reform itself.

After the meeting Soviet Premier Nikolay Ryzhkov said he believed the integrated market was an absolute necessity. He also expressed the opinion that Romania would in time recognize this. However, a senior member of the Romanian delegation, Ioan Stoian, stated that Romania had been pursuing its own policies for the last 25 years and saw no need to change its views.

There was no doubt that Comecon was suffering from a severe crisis of identity. A senior member of the Hungarian delegation, Miklos Nemeth, said that it was noticeable during the meeting that when different countries described the reforms that were needed in terms of price, convertibility, and markets, they did not mean or understand the same thing. The identity crisis was largely caused by the Soviet *perestroika* (restructuring). While Mikhail Gorbachev's policies had brought about little change as yet, they had undermined the fundamental system that governed Communist economies by, for example, introducing market concepts and the profit motive. Comecon internal trade agreements were based on political rather than market considerations. The main function of Comecon had been to ensure that heavy industries in the member countries were supplied with energy by the Soviet Union, which in return received their manufactured goods. Comecon could not find an attractive economic alternative to the existing system that would unite them and provide the economic impetus that *perestroika* required.

Nevertheless, the Prague session approved certain proposals for a phased restructuring of the mechanism for multilateral cooperation. The gradual creation of conditions for the free movement of goods, services, and other output was agreed on in principle by all member countries except Romania. The session also studied the existing differences and unrealized potential of the member countries. It was noted that the implementation of the comprehensive programs to stimulate scientific and technical progress had so far failed to improve the technology and quality of products in member countries.

The delegates acknowledged the increasing ties between the Comecon countries and Yugoslavia and expressed a willingness to expand cooperation between the Comecon countries and other socialist states. They also welcomed the signing of the joint declaration on the establishment of official relations between Comecon and the European Communities (EC). Comecon members confirmed their commitment to restructuring world economic ties and to the establishment of a new international economic order. Comecon would continue to try to broaden and improve cooperation with less developed countries so as to strengthen their economies and their political independence.

Ryzhkov stated that the Soviet Union's share of international trade did not match its economic or political status in the world. He criticized the level and management of Soviet foreign trade, as well as the division of labour among Comecon countries, which he said had exhausted its potential. Although Ryzhkov accepted that uniformity of economic conditions could be achieved only in the long term, he stated that free trade could be increased by the development of nonquota and border trade, agreements between individual regions of countries, and joint enterprises in state and cooperative sectors. Ryzhkov concluded that the new methods of economic cooperation would take place only on a totally voluntary basis through bilateral and multilateral accords between interested countries.

Problems concerning the Comecon countries were also discussed at the international conference organized by the Hungarian Academy of Science's Institute of World Economy. The conference, which was attended by 150 economists from both Eastern and Western countries, was held at the beginning of October 1988 in Sopron, Hung. Predictably, Romanian and East German economists declined to attend.

The debate focused on the reform of Comecon. The chairman of the institute, Kalman Pecsi, called for political as well as economic changes. He suggested the creation of a common market that would include some, but not all, members of Comecon as the first step toward a wider Eastern European market. Such smaller-scale regional integration would include Hungary, Poland, and perhaps Czechoslovakia, as well as Yugoslavia, which was not a full Comecon member but had had formal links with Comecon since 1964.

The head of the Soviet Section of the Comecon Economic Research Institute, Juri Shamray, presented a more cautious approach. He accused Pecsi of placing too much importance on markets and financial aspects of economic cooperation and stated that gradual integration of all Comecon countries would be a better solution. Shamray listed ways in which integration might be achieved: multinational socialist companies, competition for government tenders from other socialist countries, and special free-trade and production areas in border zones. In the past the Soviet Union had always strongly opposed the formation of regional organizations within Comecon.

INTERNATIONAL TRADE

The year 1988 saw a good increase in international trade, outstripping both initial expectations and the unexpectedly strong performance recorded in the previous year. According to the IMF World Economic Outlook released in the autumn, the volume of world trade was heading for an increase of 7.5% for the whole of 1988, compared with a rise of 5.8% in 1987. Although early world trade estimates would almost certainly be subject to substantial revision, there was little doubt that the outcome for 1988 was better than for 1987. Unexpected economic buoyancy in the OECD countries resulted in a good expansion of intra-OECD trade.

In terms of exports, the star performer was the U.S., which took full advantage of the strong growth of other developed economies and the improvement in competitiveness resulting from the long-term decline in the international value of the dollar. Thus its export volume was provisionally estimated to have risen by more than 20%, as against an increase of around 13% in 1987 and 7% in 1986. Japan and West Germany also saw a strong acceleration in the volume of shipments abroad. Japanese growth quickened from only 0.5% in 1987 to some 5%, whereas in West Germany there appeared to be an acceleration from 2.5 to 4%. In fact, most OECD countries did better than in 1987; the principal exception was the U.K., where strong domestic demand diverted potential exports to the home

market, resulting in serious deceleration in export growth from 5.7% in 1987 to 1.5% in 1988.

All in all, in 1988 exports by industrialized countries grew by 8%, compared with some 6% in the preceding year. Imports expanded at a similar rate—about 8–9%. This was a little faster than the growth rate of 7% seen in 1987 and was largely the result of the strong import performance of Japan and the U.K. British imports—estimated to have risen by more than 10%, as against 7.4% in 1987—were given a strong boost by the rapid advance of both investment and consumer demand, fueled by the large tax reductions implemented in the spring budget. Japanese imports also grew faster than in the preceding year, reflecting strong domestic economic activity and efforts by the authorities to open up the domestic market in the face of foreign criticisms of its trade policies. Other OECD countries as a group showed little change in growth rates, although the performance of individual countries varied widely.

Partial statistics available at the end of 1988 suggested a modest loss of buoyancy in less developed countries' exports, although the estimated growth rate (7%) was not far off the comparable gain for the industrialized world. This figure masked a considerable discrepancy between the performance of oil exporters and non-oil countries. Oil exporters, facing stronger demand for fuel, did relatively well, with an estimated gain in volume of 5%, as against a fall of 0.5% in 1987. Other less developed countries, however, could not match their exceptionally strong growth of more than 12% in 1987, although the indications were that non-oil producers would achieve a respectable growth rate of, perhaps, 9%.

This slowdown in export growth ruled out a significantly faster advance in imports by non-oil exporters for balance of payments reasons, although it was suggested that the previous year's volume gain of 8.5% would probably be matched. In 1987 imports by oil-exporting less developed countries had to be curbed (and fell by over 11% in volume) because the weakness of demand for oil reduced foreign-exchange earnings. Demand for energy improved in 1988, but high prices for manufactured items kept 1988 imports high in dollar terms. Overall, the increase in volume in the less developed world's import growth stood at around 8%, compared with 5% in 1987.

Taken as a bloc, the less developed world faced a small deterioration in terms of trade in the wake of an improvement in the previous year. This, however, was entirely the result of weak oil prices (an average drop of around 15% in dollar terms), which reduced the relative unit value of oil producers' exports by 13–14%. Against this, the prices of other commodities rose relatively rapidly. Food prices were strong partly in reaction to the U.S. drought, and the prices of a wide range of industrial imports, such as metals and minerals, exhibited a strong underlying trend throughout the year, mainly in response to buoyant demand from industrialized countries. Prices rose by some 10–15%, more

than twice as fast as in 1987. Export unit values of non-oil less developed countries were, therefore, estimated to have risen by around 5%, as against a drop of 2% in 1987. Unit values of industrialized countries' exports recorded only a modest growth of 2%. The net result of these changes was that the developed world saw a significant improvement in its terms of trade relative to oil producers but did relatively poorly against non-oil exporting less developed economies, which managed to improve their position in comparison to both groups of countries.

As a result of this, non-oil exporting less developed countries were likely to have seen an improvement in their trade balance. In 1987 this group had a trade surplus (on a balance of payments basis) of around $1 billion, but partial figures and trends for 1988 suggested a positive figure of $5 billion. Despite higher oil output, the oil producers faced a deterioration of around $15 billion in the trade surplus of $47 billion recorded in 1987.

The trade deficit of the industrialized world saw a sizable reduction; at the end of the year the total was heading for some $5 billion, as against $19 billion in 1987. As in 1987 the major deficit country was the U.S. A further significant negative contribution of around $28 billion came from the U.K., where trade performance deteriorated sharply as a result of domestic demand pressures. France was thought to have seen a deficit of around $10 billion, while other European OECD members, such as Austria, Portugal, Spain, Switzerland, and Greece, also witnessed a weaker trade performance and sizable foreign trade deficits. At the opposite end of the scale were Japan, which was heading for a slightly reduced but still massive trade surplus of around $95 billion, and West Germany, where an improved export performance pushed the surplus from $70 billion in 1987 to approximately $80 billion. Canada, which managed good growth in both the economy and foreign sales, also produced a surplus, as did The Netherlands.

Fears of increasing trade protectionism, which were prevalent in late 1987, were on the whole shown to have been misplaced by developments in 1988. Politicians in the Western world were given a strong reminder that protectionism, while appealing to a vocal minority, does not guarantee voter support. The Canadian elections were fought largely on the issue of the U.S.-Canadian free-trade agreement (providing for the abolition of tariffs over ten years). Despite a strong challenge from the Liberal opposition, the incumbent Progressive Conservative government retained power with a reduced but still substantial majority, and the agreement was approved. Trade protectionism also featured prominently in the U.S. presidential election campaign, but once again the candidates who argued for greater protection for U.S. industries and interests were easily defeated.

Another achievement of the year was the agreement to abolish and relax restrictions on trade in tropical products. This, together with a number of other related issues,

Table VII. Output of Basic Industrial Products in Eastern Europe, 1987

In 000 metric tons unless otherwise stated

Country	Anthracite (hard coal)	Lignite (brown coal)	Natural gas (000,000 cu m)	Crude petroleum	Electric power (000,000 kw-hr)	Steel	Sulfuric acid	Cement
Bulgaria	192	36,588	150	40	43,464	3,048	685.2	5,592
Czechoslovakia	25,740	100,668	24,564	144	85,825	15,420	1,264.0	10,368
East Germany	. . .	308,976	13,000	25	114,180	8,244	866.4	12,432
Hungary	2,364	20,484	258,108	1,920	29,676	3,624	573.6	4,152
Poland	193,008	73,200	180,240	179	145,836	17,148	3,146.4	16,092
Romania	51,500		36,300	10,713	. . .	. . .	. . .	. . .
U.S.S.R.	595,000	165,000	727,000	621,800	1,665,000	161,868	28,500.0	137,400

Source: UN, *Monthly Bulletin of Statistics;* national and industry sources.

had been the subject of tough bargaining among the General Agreement on Tariffs and Trade (GATT) members throughout the year and was expected to be confirmed at the midterm review of the Uruguay round of multilateral trade negotiations in Montreal on December 5–9. However, against a generally favourable backdrop, there were several disappointments. Despite intensive negotiations, several of the key issues set out two years earlier at Punta de Este, Uruguay, remained unresolved. The question of agricultural subsidies continued to be a highly sensitive and difficult issue. Arguments about the protection of intellectual property rights, where U.S. demands for action faced strong resistance from some less developed countries, were still a long way from resolution. Similarly, the commitment, made at the start of the Uruguay round, not to impose new restrictions on trade in breach of GATT rules and to eliminate existing barriers in this category seemed to remain more a pious expression of intent than practical policy. Free trade in services and an improved procedure for settling disputes also figured high on the agenda at the start of the Uruguay initiative but showed little progress.

Nor did the year see a letup in the volume and intensity of bilateral disputes concerning specific issues and products—all the more disappointing since in times of rapid trade growth most countries can afford to adopt a more relaxed approach to "unfair" trade practices. Thus the U.S. rejected Tokyo's appeal to lift restrictions on semiconductor imports imposed in 1986, despite a significant opening up of the Japanese market to imported semiconductors. At the same time, the U.S. and the EC were at loggerheads about a European move to ban the importation of meat from animals that had been treated with growth hormones. Other disputes included U.S. complaints about West German subsidies for the European Airbus in competition with Boeing and Japanese concern about Europe's new, tougher antidumping practices.

INTERNATIONAL EXCHANGE AND PAYMENTS

As in previous years, world debt, foreign payment imbalances, and uncertainties about the appropriate exchange rates for the major currencies remained the key issues on the international financial scene during 1988. However, the potential short- and long-term problems associated with these features seemed to be viewed less seriously than in 1987. This was largely attributable to a change in perception of the ability of the world's financial institutions to manage the associated problems and, therefore, their long-term sustainability. After the stock market crash of October 1987, an already dangerously overstretched international financial system had seemed to be threatened by a major new source of weakness and instability. As 1988 got under way, however, economic growth gained further momentum, debtor and less developed countries progressed comparatively well, and the world was not rocked by major exchange-rate instability or unacceptable fluctuations in interest rates.

The fact that there was some modest progress toward reducing payment imbalances also played a part in the emergence of a more confident view of the strength of world financial infrastructure. Thus for the first time in several years, the long period of downward exchange-rate adjustments appeared to have made an inroad into the U.S. trade and current account deficits. After rising steadily from $9 billion to $154 billion between 1982 and 1987, the U.S. current account deficit was cut some $25 billion in 1988—a modest enough achievement in absolute terms but significant in marking a change in trend. Similarly, the two major surplus countries, Japan and West Germany,

Table VIII. Soviet Trade with Eastern European Countries
In 000,000 rubles, current prices

Country	Exports			Imports		
	1985	1986	1987	1985	1986	1987
Bulgaria	6,434.7	6,787.8	6,276.3	6,040.0	6,191.3	6,551.7
Czechoslovakia	6,813.3	6,942.0	6,776.7	6,587.3	6,556.4	6,907.4
East Germany	7,651.7	7,884.2	7,635.9	7,553.0	7,128.1	7,093.2
Hungary	4,560.0	4,678.2	4,600.0	4,850.1	4,873.4	5,080.3
Poland	6,516.7	6,813.8	6,542.2	5,525.0	6,127.2	6,329.3
Romania	1,948.8	2,823.3	2,539.2	2,276.5	2,415.2	2,347.2

Source: U.S.S.R. Foreign Trade Statistics/Moscow.

Table IX. Soviet Crude Petroleum and Products Supplied to Eastern Europe
In 000 rubles

Country	1985	1986	1987
Bulgaria	2,211,090	2,256,362	1,910,394
Czechoslovakia	2,924,466	2,994,622	2,675,574
East Germany	3,106,406	3,126,569	2,860,031
Hungary	1,476,068	1,494,733	1,333,684
Poland	2,653,655	2,742,241	2,464,032
Romania	388,533	974,947	703,673

Source: U.S.S.R. Foreign Trade Statistics/Moscow.

also made a small move in the right direction. Japanese imports grew relatively fast during the year because of a stronger yen and efforts by the government to open up the domestic market to imports, which resulted in an estimated cut in the current surplus from $87 billion in 1987 to around $75 billion in 1988. West Germany also broke with recent tradition by posting an estimated $5 billion cut in its 1987 current account surplus of $45 billion. Other major changes in international payment balances included a massive deterioration in the U.K., caused by an unsustainably rapid rate of economic growth sucking in imports and diverting potential exports to the home market. This pushed the previous year's current account deficit of £2.5 billion to around £16 billion.

All in all, the industrialized world saw little change in its overall current account position; on the basis of the returns available at the end of 1988, it seemed that the full-year figure would be within a few billion dollars of the 1987 deficit of $43 billion. The position of the less developed world, however, saw some deterioration, with the previous year's near equilibrium being turned into a deficit on current account of $15 billion–$20 billion. Weak oil prices cut foreign earnings of the oil exporters, which resulted in a nearly sixfold increase in the deficit from $4 billion to $23 billion. This more than offset the advances made elsewhere in the less developed world. Primary product exporters managed to cut their collective deficit by around 25% to $13 billion, while exporters of manufactured goods were thought to have maintained their surplus at the previous year's level of $25 billion.

Exchange rates did not exhibit the kind of instability feared in the aftermath of the October stock market crash. Following the dramatic decline against most major currencies immediately after the crash, the dollar showed a good recovery during the first few months of 1988. This was followed by a period of relative stability until halfway through the year, when evidence of progress in cutting back the U.S. trade deficit exerted a strong upward influence on the dollar's international value. The U.S. currency rose strongly against sterling, the yen, and the Deutsche Mark, with the result that its trade-weighted average value gained 5 points to 99 between the first and third quarters of the year. After a temporary blip following the presidential election, the trade-weighted average was around 94 in the closing month of the year.

Notwithstanding the rise in the U.K.'s current account deficit, sterling gained strength against most currencies. In fact, in the late spring the rise in the external value of sterling became so pronounced that it gave rise to fears of a significant adverse effect on exports. It also gave rise to a temporary (but public) dispute between the prime minister and the chancellor of the Exchequer as to the use of interest rates in influencing exchange rates. During the third quarter of the year, sterling remained relatively stable, but there was a further upward trend in the closing months; the year as a whole registered a gain of around 4% in sterling's average trade-weighted value. There was a particularly rapid rise against the Deutsche Mark (up by 8% between the last quarter of 1987 and December 1988). The gain against the dollar was about 6% during the same period. Within the EMS, exchange rates remained relatively stable throughout 1988.

As usual, short-term fluctuations in currency values were influenced by interest-rate movements in the principal countries. During the year the broad trend of interest was upward, with most major OECD members taking steps to increase the cost of borrowing. This was done more for domestic economic, particularly anti-inflationary, reasons than with a view to influencing exchange rates. Faced with faster-than-expected economic growth and some concern about renewed inflationary pressures, most countries felt it necessary to put up lending rates to moderate economic growth. This was particularly true in the U.K., where the large balance of payments deficit and rising inflation forced the chancellor of the Exchequer to abandon his low-interest-rate policy in June in favour of a rapid succession of hikes in base rates. Thus between January and May base rates fluctuated between 7.5 and 8.5%, but between May and November there were five increases from 7.5 to 13%. In the U.S. interest rates were largely stable until spring, when the Fed began to tighten monetary policy. By year's end the Fed's discount rate stood at 6.5%, and major banks had raised the prime rate to 10.5%. West Germany also engineered a modest interest-rate rise of around one percentage point during the summer. In France there was a weak downward movement in the early months of the year, but in the autumn the government caused a small increase, largely to support the franc. In Japan the central bank's official discount rate remained at 2.5% throughout the year, with long-term rates strengthening marginally during the summer months.

Given the evidence of satisfactory world economic growth, a reduction in current account imbalances, and the absence of any major upheavals in international exchange and interest rates, it was not surprising that the annual meeting of the World Bank and the IMF, held in West Berlin in September, did not produce any major policy initiatives. Indeed, the underlying feature of the proceedings was one of quiet satisfaction if not complacency. Although there were the usual, almost obligatory, warnings about the dangers of inflation, international economic coordination was felt to be working well, and the existing pattern of foreign exchange was endorsed.

The assembled officials also concluded that, while still a major problem, the world debt situation had shown some signs of improvement. According to IMF estimates, the less developed countries' debts (excluding debts owed to the IMF) rose by about 4% to $1,218,000,000,000 by the end of 1987 and were expected to rise by rather less during 1988. Despite the increase in the total amount outstanding, the relatively good increase in exports resulted in a fall in the debt-to-export earnings ratio from 169% at the end of 1986 to 158% in 1987, with a further (estimated) decline

to 146% by the end of 1988. Part of the improvement was attributed to efforts by creditor countries to develop more flexible assistance packages on a case-by-case basis. IMF members announced a number of new initiatives to lessen debt problems for some debtors in particular difficulties, notably a complex package developed for 34 low-income countries in sub-Saharan Africa that would allow eligible countries to reduce the burden of debt servicing. The 34 countries in this group had official debts of $46 billion at the end of 1987, accounting for 70% of their total indebtedness. IMF officials estimated the cost of the package at around $500 million a year, with the bulk going to 20 of the poorest nations that were prepared to agree to the accompanying IMF-approved economic programs.

Another major debt initiative announced by the World Bank was a package of $1,250,000,000 in new loans for financial and trade reforms, low-cost housing, and power development in Argentina. Contrary to normal practice, the loan was agreed to by the World Bank before Argentina reached agreement with the IMF on the required economic measures, raising fears about a weakening IMF role and influence in ensuring the necessary economic discipline. A little later Argentina announced promises of investment credits of $9 billion from Italy and Spain available to 1992 and repayable in 20 years at a fixed annual rate of 1.75%. In a similar development the U.S. announced a $3.5 billion emergency loan for Mexico, which—in spite of making good progress with reforming its economy according to IMF prescription—had been hit by severe liquidity problems as a result of the fall in oil prices. Another development of importance was the decision of Brazil to resume interest payments on its loans and to erase arrears of $3 billion accumulated since February 1987. The new move was part of an agreement between Brazil and its large commercial creditors, which also involved new loans of $5.2 billion and a rescheduling of medium-term loans. The deal was welcomed as evidence of lessening militancy on the part of debtors.   (IEIS)

This article updates the *Macropædia* articles BANKS AND BANKING; ECONOMIC GROWTH AND PLANNING; GOVERNMENT FINANCE; INTERNATIONAL TRADE.

STOCK EXCHANGES

For the world's major stock exchanges, the 1987 October crash turned out to be a sharp correction rather than the first leg of a slump. At the end of a bumpy and hesitant journey during 1988, the exchanges ended the year higher than they had started it. With the notable exception of Japan, however, few exceeded their October 1987 levels (TABLE X). Fixed-income securities declined slightly, but commodity price indexes, in dollar terms, were mixed. They were characterized by sharply lower oil prices, weak prices for soft commodities, and generally higher prices for metals except gold and silver.

During the opening months of the year, share prices moved within a narrow range. Quick action taken by the economic policymakers to provide liquidity averted an immediate financial crisis. The ensuing lower interest rates were favourably received—in particular by the bond (fixed-interest securities) markets—but the outlook for consumers and producers was uncertain. However, by the spring better-than-expected economic statistics, a continuation of supportive monetary and fiscal policies, improving corporate profitability, and high liquidity of institutional investors provided further encouragement.

The gentle pace of recovery in stock price indexes was not matched by a rise in the volume of shares traded; typically, volumes remained 30–40% below 1987 levels.

Institutional investors remained cautious and did not increase their exposure to the equity or bond markets. Preference for cash remained high, reflecting the fact that the fundamental factors that caused the October crash had remained unsolved. Measures to reduce the U.S. budget deficit seemed unconvincing. The U.S. trade deficit also appeared likely to remain high, with little or no evidence of restrictive economic policies to curb the U.S. appetite for imports before the November presidential election. Short rallies during the summer and the autumn could not be sustained, and stock price indexes for major markets traded within a wide band, reacting aimlessly to the ebb and flow of mixed economic statistics.

Although the world's major stock exchanges were closely linked (as evidenced by the October crash) and were influenced by U.S. economic developments, Japan and to some extent the smaller exchanges in Europe and the Pacific basin succeeded in decoupling from Wall Street. As exchanges in New York City and London faltered in the spring, those in other European countries and in Japan continued to rise. Rapid economic growth in Europe, stimulated by business investment and export demand against a background of stable inflation, low interest rates, and stable exchange rates vis-à-vis the dollar, proved an attractive environment for corporate profits and dividends. It was also a favourable backdrop for takeovers, often financed by debt (instead of equity). The high level of corporate activity in the U.S. and Western Europe further improved the liquidity of the investment community but more significantly served as a reminder of the bargain levels of many share prices.

The diverging trends in international capital markets toward the end of 1988 signaled concern over the rapid rate of economic growth throughout the world. In Western Europe and the U.S. the risk of recession was giving way to fears of accelerating inflation. Furthermore, lack of credible policies in the U.S. for tackling the twin deficits—budget and trade—increased fears that the supply of external funds might decrease, forcing U.S. interest rates up sharply and thereby plunging the U.S. (and the world with it) into a deep recession. The U.K. economy appeared to have overheated, sending interest rates to crisis levels. Except in Japan the great bull market that had prevailed since 1982 had finally run out of steam and seemed unlikely to break out of its current range. The *Financial Times* Actuaries World Index was about 15% higher than the January level but 5% down from its peak in August. Excluding Japan, the index rose 10% during the year.   (IEIS)

United States. In the wake of the Oct. 19, 1987, crash, the stock market was subdued in 1988, as investors lost confidence in the market and in the performances of their brokerage firms. The lack of confidence in the market reduced average daily volume on the New York Stock Exchange (NYSE) to 161.5 million shares in 1988, down from 188.9 million in 1987, a decline of 14.5%. At least 15,000 jobs were lost on Wall Street. Stock prices moved listlessly within a relatively narrow range—first higher and then lower and then higher again—as investors anticipated a recession that did not occur. An extraordinary volume of merger and acquisition-bidding activity helped push the Dow Jones industrial average (DJIA) up to 2168.57, a gain of 11.8% for the year.

Meanwhile, the massive issuance of "junk" bonds, high-risk and high-yield debt offerings, drove bond prices down sharply. Inflation concerns caused banks to raise their prime rates four times, each time by a half point, bringing them by the year's end to 10.5%, the highest level in more than three years.

The stronger-than-expected economy was a major factor supporting stock prices, but rising interest rates slowed down the potential gains. Higher rates lured investors out of stocks and into Treasury bills and bonds, as well as into certificates of deposit from banks and savings institutions.

Among the significant developments in the stock market in 1988 were new defensive measures to prevent hostile takeovers of major corporations and the decline of portfolio insurance. The "poison put" was designed to curb highly leveraged corporate deals (those achieved by the use of large amounts of credit). The "poison put" allows investors to sell their bonds back to the issuer at a previously specified price in the event of any corporate restructuring that reduces the market value of the bonds. Portfolio insurance, or dynamic hedging, is a strategy that uses futures contracts to change automatically the relative size of a portfolio's positions in securities and cash as market circumstances change. As a result of the October 1987 crash, when liquidity in the market fell sharply, pension funds, which had covered about $70 billion of their assets with such insurance, dropped their coverage to less than $25 billion.

The volume of mergers and acquisitions in the U.S. rose to a record $282.4 billion in 1988 as a wave of massive transactions lifted the Wall Street takeover industry to its best year ever. The volume rose sharply from the 1987 total of $247.1 billion. One hundred and nineteen leveraged buyout offers were completed in 1988 for a total value of $37.7 billion, compared with 124 in 1987 for a value of $36.9 billion. In all, it was estimated that 3,310 merger and acquisition transactions were completed in 1988. The biggest deals completed were (1) Philip Morris, Inc., bought Kraft, Inc., for $13,440,000,000; (2) Campeau Corp. bought Federated Department Stores, Inc., for $6,510,000,000; (3) BATUS, Inc., bought Farmers' Group, Inc., for $5.2 billion; and (4) Eastman Kodak Co. bought Sterling Drug, Inc., for $5.1 billion. In December Kohlberg, Kravis reached agreement to acquire RJR Nabisco, Inc., for $25,760,000,000, the highest price on record for a U.S. corporate takeover.

The total number of initial public offerings (IPOs) in 1988 declined almost 50% to 278 from the 550 that came to market in 1987, a year in which many IPOs were stalled by the crash. The dollar volume of new offerings was approximately $30 billion, of which $17 billion was repackaged bonds in the form of closed-end investment trusts. The volume of new bond issues, excluding repackaged debt, climbed to more than $120 billion from $113.4 billion in 1987. Merrill Lynch & Co., Inc., ranked first among domestic securities underwriters in 1988 with $39.7 billion, 14.5% of the $273 billion overall brought to market in 1988. Second was Goldman, Sachs & Co. with $36.9 billion, while Salomon Brothers, Inc., ranked third with $33.9 billion. Drexel Burnham Lambert, Inc., underwrote $11.9 billion, 43% of the market in new junk bonds in 1988.

Trading volume in stocks listed on the NYSE was 40,438,346,358 shares, compared with 47,801,308,660 in 1987, a decline of 15.4%. Prices were generally higher, with 1,534 advances, compared with 810 in 1987, and only 679 declines, compared with 1,444 in 1987. Total issues traded were 2,263, compared with 2,279 in 1987. Bond volume was $7,594,664,000, compared with the prior year's figure of $9,726,244,000, a fall of 21.9%. In January the NYSE established program trading curbs for days when the DJIA moved more than 75 points. (Program trading is a strategy of trading simultaneously in the stock market and in stock index futures contracts in order to profit from discrepancies between the two markets.) In April the NYSE stopped

(continued on page 177)

Black Monday Revisited

BY SARAH HOGG

The crash of '87 left a blush on the cheeks of economic forecasters as well as egg on the faces of market traders. It was not that economists had failed to warn that trouble was in store. Although most of them had focused on the foreign exchange markets rather than stock markets, there had been a chorus of anxiety about the threat to world stability posed by the U.S.'s "twin deficits" on its federal budget and its trade balance.

Where the economic forecasters went wrong was in the aftermath of the stock market crash. The universal expectation at the end of October 1987 was that the world economy would be lucky to avoid a full-scale slump. It was easy to see why. Consumer spending—and, perhaps, property prices—were expected to be checked by the "wealth effect" of the fall in share prices. Investment in new factories and new products was expected to be held back, not only by fear that demand would stop growing but also by the impact on companies of a fall in equity values. In the event, however, in the 12 months after the crash, the world economy achieved its fastest rate of economic growth in four years. It was in industrial countries, where the crash was expected to have the most impact, that the growth spurt was most marked—and the forecasters were most taken by surprise. In September 1988, almost a year after the crash, the International Monetary Fund (IMF) estimated that output in the industrial world as a whole would be found to have grown nearly 4%, in real terms, that year. The countries supposedly most vulnerable to the vagaries of equity markets were no exceptions to this cheerful picture.

What Went Wrong. Take, to begin with, the United States. It was, after all, the eye of the stock market storm. The slide in share prices on Wall Street began in earnest on Oct. 14, 1987, accelerating to crisis-point on "Black Monday," October 19. The crash came after a long "bull market," which analysts later conceded had taken share prices way out of line with business or economic fundamentals. The gathering clouds before the storm were news of a worse-than-expected U.S. trade deficit in August 1987 and—arguably—a fear that tax changes passing through Congress might dent the takeover boom.

Most damaging of all, however, was the public quarrel between West Germany and the U.S. over interest rates. There had been some concern worldwide that inflationary pressures were reemerging, but central banks could not unilaterally raise their rates without threatening to destabilize currencies, which had been the subject of an international agreement that spring. When the rise in West German interest rates in September 1987 put upward pressure on U.S. rates, and it was suddenly apparent that equities were offering the worst-ever yield relative to bonds, the stock market slide became a rout.

Sarah Hogg is Business and Finance Editor of the Independent, *London.*

As if these economic difficulties were not enough to stunt growth, the high proportion of private investors in the U.S. were expected to act as a particularly rapid channel for a recession as their wealth and spending were diminished by the collapse in share values. Yet the U.S. managed remarkably strong growth in the year after the crash. The IMF had by September 1988 raised its estimate of U.S. growth in 1988 to some 4%.

The built-in barriers in the Tokyo stock market meant that Japan suffered a less spectacular fall in share prices during the crash. Since Japanese share prices had risen to multiples of company earnings that seemed fantastic by the standards of other major markets, it was thought that Tokyo's punctured stock market balloon would be particularly hard to reinflate. Ironically, the Tokyo market achieved the most vigorous postcrash recovery, exceeding precrash levels quite early in 1988. Economic growth was correspondingly strong; the IMF estimated that Japan would grow nearly 6% in 1988.

In London the stock market had been distracted by a hurricane the previous Friday, and pent-up selling on Black Monday made the slide all the more dramatic. At its low point just before the close on Monday, the London stock market was down a full 13% in a single day. In his annual autumn statement the following month, the chancellor of the Exchequer warned that prospects had taken a knock. Yet by summer 1988 he was complaining that the economy was growing too fast. The IMF's guess was that Britain's output would rise 4% in 1988; that was likely to prove to be an underestimate.

Even Australia—where the Sydney market fell some 29% during October 19–23—achieved a remarkably healthy economic recovery. On the back of stronger commodity prices, there was strong growth in industrial profitability in Australia in 1988.

Of course, there were other stock markets where the crash had a more bruising effect—most notably Hong Kong, where trading was suspended after Black Monday for the rest of the week. On the other hand, the fall in share prices in some European markets, such as Frankfurt, was seen even at the time as having remarkably little effect on those economies.

The Aftermath. Why were the forecasters caught out so badly? The first, and most important, reason was that they underestimated the underlying strength of most economies in 1987. The sharp fall in oil prices the previous year had been expected to give a boost to industrialized economies—even oil-producing Britain—but this kick start had been slow to take effect. The industrial economies grew only 2.7% in 1986—the slowest rate since the 1982 recession—and forecasters seemed to lose confidence in the bonus of cheaper energy. France and West Germany were particularly sluggish, and in 1987 the West German economy slowed down even more. Nevertheless, as the months went by, it became clear that growth had actually begun to accelerate by the summer of 1987. The benefits of cheaper oil had at last come through.

It was also probably true that the effect of looser monetary policies in the mid-1980s had been underestimated; in all the major economies, financial deregulation had played havoc with monetary measures. Although there was some tightening of monetary policy in the U.S., Britain, and West Germany in 1987, governments moved swiftly to loosen up after the crash. This was the second reason why the worst predictions of disaster were proved false. By early 1988 it was being argued in some countries—notably Britain—that monetary conditions had been loosened too much. In the weeks after the crash, however, the move

by the U.S. Federal Reserve Board to ensure sufficient liquidity in the financial system did much to steady market nerves.

While the regulators' inquests into market systems continued well into 1988, the robustness of economic growth in almost all the major economies was becoming plain. By the autumn most of the industrialized world was enjoying an investment boom. For the U.S., Japan, Britain, and Canada, the IMF forecast a rise in business investment of over 10% in 1988 as a whole.

The world economy did not, however, escape scot-free. Those countries that experienced the worst of Black Monday subsequently suffered something of a shakeout in their financial industries; low trading volumes after the crash, in both Britain and the U.S., for example, caused many of the big international securities houses to trim their staffs and their market operations. Questions about the behaviour and regulation of stock markets under pressure, particularly in New York City, remained unresolved. The role of new, computerized trading methods and the relationship between the stock markets and the options and futures markets, based mainly in Chicago, continued to be matters of concern. The growing phenomenon of takeovers and "leveraged buyouts" gave rise to fresh worries about the health of the system. Most important, however, was the fact that the basic economic problems that underlay stock market anxiety in 1987—the U.S. budget and trade deficits—persisted right up to and beyond the U.S. presidential election in November 1988.

Future Prospects. It was small wonder, therefore, that once George Bush was elected, the markets again began to question the viability of U.S. economic policy. Bush had insisted all through his campaign that he would not raise taxes, and all the old questions as to how the U.S. would close the gap in the federal budget came to the fore again. The White House was forced to admit, just after the election, that in fiscal 1990 (beginning in October 1989), the budget deficit would be some $132 billion—$32 billion more than permitted by the Gramm-Rudman Act.

As this problem reemerged from the clouds of electioneering, the dollar slipped sharply. Central banks again came to the rescue, buying dollars in the foreign exchange markets; this could be only a palliative. Although good or bad U.S. trade figures could alter the mood of the markets from month to month, it remained clear that the basic budget problem would not disappear with Pres. Ronald Reagan. In addition, it was being argued persuasively that the forecasters had not, after all, been so wrong.

Many people had said in 1987 that a dollar crisis was inevitable; in 1988 many still held that this had been averted only by the Louvre accord between the U.S. and other governments, notably Japan, West Germany, France, and Britain, to hold the dollar stable. Whether President Bush would recommit the U.S. to the Louvre rules was one big question. Another was whether the Louvre accord had merely switched the inevitable crash from the market in currencies to the market in equities. The third question, therefore, was whether one or the other of those markets would experience a repeat.

A year and a bit after Black Monday, there were plenty of people who feared that the intervening months of rapid growth were only the lull in the U.S. storm, but gloom was by no means universal. Japanese confidence remained strong, and Europe's remarkable burst of growth was a new and encouraging sign. The U.S., however, still retained a powerful influence over the world economy in general—and its stock markets in particular.

(continued from page 175)

program trading briefly as the daily limit was reached. The most active issues in terms of numbers of shares sold were AT&T, 421,583,300; IBM, 366,016,700; General Electric, 354,447,400; Exxon, 349,165,000; and Occidental Petroleum, 335,644,600.

The American Stock Exchange (Amex) market value index rose 17.5% for the year, but share turnover declined to 2,515,210,000, compared with 3,505,950,000 in 1987, a drop of 28.2%. Bond sales on the Amex totaled $604,950,-000 in 1988, compared with $684,965,000 in 1987, down 11.7%. Prices increased for 666 issues, up from 435 in 1987, and there were 395 declines, as contrasted with 617 during the previous year. Total issues traded were 1,095, up from 1,072 in 1987.

In the over-the-counter market the National Association of Securities Dealers automated quotation (Nasdaq) index rose 15% for the year, ending at 381.38. Nasdaq volume was 27,187,050,000, compared with 35,597,292,000 in 1987, a drop of 23.6%. The most active issues in the Nasdaq market were all in the high-technology fields. The leader by volume was Apple Computer, with a turnover valued at $15,306,087,000, followed by Intel Corp. at $12,-845,395,000 and MCI Communications at $7,803,959,000.

The Standard & Poor's Index of 500 stocks ranged between a high of 283.66 and a low of 242.63 during 1988, providing a 12.4% gain for the year. The composite index of 500 shares (TABLE XI) began the year at 250.48, continuing its recovery from the October 1987 crash. The index rose to 265.74 in March and after a brief interlude achieved 270.68 in June, well below the prior year's level of 301.38. The recovery continued during the last half of the year but did not reach the precrash high. The industrial index began to recover in January but rose irregularly to a level of 307.40, which was 17.5% below the level of 372.49 a year earlier. The high for 1988 was 326.84. Public utilities traded within a narrow range between 106.13 in January and 109.67 in September. The high for the year was 114.57. Financial stocks also showed modest gains, rising from 22.41 in January to 25.75 in September, 14.2% below the level of 30.02 achieved the previous year. The high for 1988 was 26.48. Transportation stocks traded at levels well below those of the prior year. By September, at 209.71, the index was 18.3% below the corresponding 1987 figure of 256.77. The high for the year was 229.61.

U.S. government bond yields in 1988 (TABLE XII) rose steadily during the first eight months of 1988 from 8.82% in January to 9.33% in August, well above the 1987 levels. In May the Treasury completed its quarterly financing with the sale of new 30-year bonds at an average yield of 9.17%, the highest in more than two years. After a decline in September, yields rose again in the last quarter of the year. At the year's end short-term rates exceeded long-term rates, historically a signal of an economic downturn. U.S. corporate bond yields (TABLE XIII) were more irregular than those of U.S. government bonds, beginning the year at 9.88% in January, declining in February and March, and then rising unevenly to a high of 10.11% in August before tapering off in September.

Sellers of options did well in 1988, while buyers had been the big winners in 1987. Option premiums started 1988 at lofty levels and declined throughout the first half. Trading volume on the Chicago Mercantile Exchange fell 7.5% in 1988 compared with 1987, mainly because of a 40% drop in stock-index futures trading at the futures exchange. The exchange said that 78,011,668 futures and futures options contracts were traded there in 1988, compared with 84,-367,214 in 1987. While volume dropped, the number of

contracts outstanding rose 18%. That gain was attributed largely to increased activity in the exchange's foreign currency futures.

The Securities and Exchange Commission (SEC) had an active year in 1988, responding to the concerns arising from the 1987 crash and an expanding inquiry into illegal trading activity by corporate insiders. In February the SEC issued its report on the October crash and called for limited regulatory changes. In May it moved to limit off-market trading by allowing the over-the-counter market to halt trading in a stock pending corporate news. This decision, giving Nasdaq the same power as the NYSE and Amex, made it possible for the first time to ban trading in a stock in all U.S. markets. The SEC imposed new rules that required funds to identify all charges in a standardized fee table that would be prominently located in prospectuses. The tables would specify how much the fees, sales charges, and expenses would affect a $1,000 investment over various periods of time. In September the SEC charged Drexel Burnham Lambert, Inc., Michael Milken, "father of the junk bond market," and others with insider trading and other securities violations. In December Drexel Burnham Lambert agreed to settle the investigation by pleading guilty to securities fraud and other criminal charges and paying a record $650 million in fines and restitution.

Canada. In Canada share prices were little changed in 1988 owing to a buoyant economy and a dollar that rose to levels high enough to threaten earnings of Canadian exporters. The central bank combated inflationary pressures by repeatedly raising interest rates. Both trends helped restrain gains in share prices. Against all expectations, the Canadian economy continued a six-year surge. Unemployment slid to a 14-year low, and capacity utilization reached its highest rate in seven years. The prime rate rose from 9.75 to 12.25%, the highest level in almost three years. The free-trade agreement entered into between Canada and the U.S. was expected by Canadian advocates to create a minimum of 250,000 new jobs, spur exports, and attract foreign investment.

The Toronto Stock Exchange's broadly based 300 composite index lagged behind the DJIA in 1988, but after the strength of the Canadian dollar compared with the U.S. dollar was taken into account, Canadian stocks outperformed their U.S. counterparts. The Toronto index ended the year at 3389.99, up 7.3% from the end of 1987 and up 13.9% from the crash. Total volume was 4,740,000,000 shares, down 35.9% from 1987, and the value of trading declined 36.8% to Can$63.3 billion. Financial services stocks were a leader in the Toronto index's overall gain, rising 19.2%. Mining stocks posted an annual gain of 21%, compared with a 35% jump in 1987. Oil and gas stocks rose 10.3%, while industrial products gained 7.3% and consumer products showed an increase of 7.1%. Canadian gold stocks fell as gold prices throughout the world dropped. The Toronto gold index fell 27.9%.

The Vancouver Stock Exchange suffered as investors lost interest in its highly speculative securities. The stock exchange index fell 31.1%, and volume declined about 28%. The Montreal exchange, however, showed a gain of 7.1% for the year. New common stock issues for the first nine months of the year slumped 88% from the same period in 1987, largely as a by-product of investor reaction to the October 1987 crash.

The deregulation of Canada's financial institutions continued. New rules allowed brokers to work out of affiliated banks and trust companies.   (IRVING PFEFFER)

Western Europe. Stock markets in Europe staged a good recovery during the early part of 1988, reflecting a better-than-expected rate of economic growth and corporate profitability. By the spring the recovery in the London Stock Exchange had petered out, while many smaller continental exchanges continued to do well. While London approached the end of 1988 only slightly above the level of 1987, the other large industrialized countries in Europe—France, West Germany, Italy, and Spain—registered gains between 20 and 35%. The smaller countries, such as Belgium, The Netherlands, Sweden, and Switzerland, enjoyed even more bullish conditions, notching gains between 35 and 40%.

Table X. Selected Major World Stock Price Indexes*

Country	1988 range† High	1988 range† Low	Year-end close	Percent change from 12/31/87
Australia	1658	1171	1487	+12.5
Austria	225	164	219	+20.9
Belgium	5566	3608	5566	+46.4
Denmark	269	181	272	+47.0
France	416	251	416	+40.5
West Germany	554	396	550	+23.9
Hong Kong	2773	2224	2687	+22.5
Italy	593	424	590	+10.9
Japan	30,159	21,217	30,159	+29.5
Netherlands, The	288	206	287	+34.7
Norway	468	328	468	+33.3
Singapore	1178	834	1039	+27.6
South Africa	1942	1387	1942	+35.5
Spain	302	226	274	+28.0
Sweden	3444	2149	3444	+54.0
Switzerland	604	467	604	+22.0
United Kingdom	1879	1738	1793	+8.5
United States	2184	1879	2169	+11.9

*Index numbers are rounded.
†Based on daily closing price.
Source: *The Financial Times.*

Table XI. U.S. Stock Market Prices

Month	Industrials (400 stocks) 1988	Industrials (400 stocks) 1987	Public utilities (40 stocks) 1988	Public utilities (40 stocks) 1987	Transportation (20 stocks) 1988	Transportation (20 stocks) 1987	Composite (500 stocks) 1988	Composite (500 stocks) 1987
January	288.36	296.10	106.13	120.09	192.20	212.07	250.48	264.51
February	296.46	318.18	110.67	119.87	199.03	224.37	258.13	280.93
March	308.04	334.65	107.24	117.65	212.88	227.30	265.74	292.47
April	305.78	335.43	104.12	109.97	209.54	222.25	262.61	289.32
May	297.39	336.10	103.11	108.06	197.57	231.31	256.12	289.12
June	312.78	349.58	109.86	112.63	211.33	247.20	270.68	301.38
July	310.87	362.36	108.49	110.93	210.37	256.09	269.05	310.09
August	303.12	384.94	107.89	117.70	203.10	268.34	263.73	329.36
September	307.40	372.49	109.67	114.98	209.71	256.77	267.97	318.66
October	...	323.13	...	111.73	...	226.47	...	280.16
November	...	280.11	...	106.49	...	188.23	...	245.01
December	...	277.68	...	102.36	...	185.50	...	240.96

Sources: U.S. Department of Commerce, *Survey of Current Business;* Board of Governors of the Federal Reserve System, *Federal Reserve Bulletin.* Prices are Standard & Poor's monthly averages of daily closing prices, with 1941–43 = 10.

Table XII. U.S. Government Long-Term Bond Yields

Month	Yield (%) 1988	Yield (%) 1987	Month	Yield (%) 1988	Yield (%) 1987
January	8.82	7.60	July	9.20	8.70
February	8.41	7.69	August	9.33	8.97
March	8.61	7.62	September	9.06	9.58
April	8.91	8.31	October	...	9.61
May	9.24	8.79	November	...	8.99
June	9.04	8.63	December	...	9.12

Source: U.S. Department of Commerce, *Survey of Current Business.* Yields are for U.S. Treasury bonds that are taxable and due or callable in ten years or more.

Table XIII. U.S. Corporate Bond Yields

Month	Yield (%) 1988	Yield (%) 1987	Month	Yield (%) 1988	Yield (%) 1987
January	9.88	8.36	July	9.96	9.42
February	9.40	8.38	August	10.11	9.67
March	9.39	8.36	September	9.82	10.18
April	9.67	8.85	October	...	10.52
May	9.90	9.33	November	...	10.01
June	9.86	9.32	December	...	10.11

Source: U.S. Department of Commerce, *Survey of Current Business.* Yields are based on Moody's Aaa domestic corporate bond index.

Michael Milken of Drexel Burnham Lambert faces criminal charges for violating securities and income tax laws. Milken, a Wall Street financier known primarily for junk bond trading and who had been connected with convicted arbitrageur Ivan Boesky, had been under investigation since 1986.

© CHARLES BORNIGER

On the whole the performance of the London market was disappointing—the *Financial Times*-Stock Exchange 100 Index (FT-SE 100) approached the end of 1988 only fractionally higher for the year. Most of the time it fluctuated aimlessly within a narrow range between 1750 and 1850. Trading volumes were an average 30% below the precrash levels, and there was little genuine long-term investment demand. More than any other stock exchange, London mirrored Wall Street and lacked a firm direction of its own.

The year opened on a relatively optimistic note following an almost 200-point (10%) gain in the final weeks of 1987, but in the absence of investment demand, the rally soon ran out of steam. The traditional prebudget run, coupled with a series of takeovers—the largest one being the bid by Nestlé for Rowntree—restored the market's poise. The FT-SE 100 Index consolidated at about 1850 during the summer and shrugged off a gradual tightening in monetary policy. A Wall Street rally, booming asset values, a steady exchange rate, and an optimistic outlook for corporate profitability maintained the market at this level for nearly three months.

In the late summer sentiment changed rapidly. The market fell by 100 points (5.5%), in response first to a worldwide coordinated rise in interest rates to ease the pressure on the dollar and second to surprisingly large U.K. trade-deficit figures. The government ordered a 1% increase in the base lending rates of commercial banks to 12%. A subsequent rally, based on the hope that this would be sufficient to slow down the economy, was short-lived. In late November there was a record £2.4 billion current account deficit, swiftly followed by another 1% rise in base rates. The FT-SE 100 plunged by nearly 50 points to well below 1780, but it rebounded slightly to close the year at 1793.

The Paris Bourse, after a weak opening that took the CAC General Index to a low of 251 (40 points below the October crash level), bounced back strongly. After a spring pause it raced up to 368 with only a short pause in late summer. The spring rally was influenced by a spate of takeovers and by the strength of the economy.

As in other countries, strong economic growth, a low inflation rate, and a stable franc against the West German Deutsche Mark provided a favourable scenario for the French market. It correctly predicted that corporate profitability would respond to the previous year's restructuring and investment to improve competitiveness and efficiency.

With the approaching presidential elections and accumulating evidence that the economy was growing much faster than expected, the Paris Bourse index shrugged off a spring weakness. Supported by additional takeovers, it rose by nearly 20% in the first six months of the year to 368 in June. The French fund managers and their international counterparts clamoured to catch the tide, sending the market still higher.

New York Stock Exchange Common Stock Index Closing Prices
Stock prices (Dec. 31, 1965 = 50)

High
Close
Low

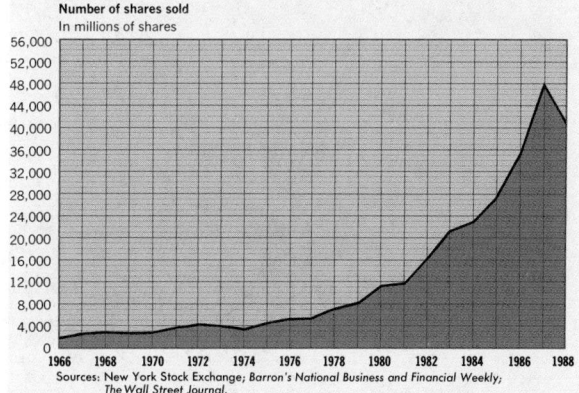

Number of shares sold
In millions of shares

Sources: New York Stock Exchange; Barron's National Business and Financial Weekly; The Wall Street Journal.

Having risen by nearly 40% since January, the market reached 397 in November. It succumbed to the dollar's weakness in the wake of the U.S. presidential election. The other factor that worried investors was the rising labour union militancy among public sector workers, who were demanding higher wages and a more socialistic economic policy. At the year's end the French market was nearly 10% below the spring 1987 peak but, given the encouraging economic outlook, it was far from moribund, rising to 416—the year's high—on December 30.

West German equities performed impressively during 1988. Once an initial weakness had been overcome and the investor's focus fell on the nation's strong economic fundamentals (improving corporate profitability, low interest rates, and low inflation), the market gained 85 points from the postcrash low of 396.

With the West German economy growing much faster than expected in the opening months of the year, assisted by a mild winter and higher consumer spending stimulated by DM 14 billion tax cuts, the outlook appeared to be good. With the slight rise of the dollar against the Deutsche Mark and an annual inflation rate at a modest 1%, exports soon rivaled consumer spending as an engine of economic growth. In the spring the second leg of the rise took the Frankfurt FAZ Aktien Index close to the psychologically important 500 level.

Revised economic forecasts of greater economic growth, falling interest rates in the bond market, and prospects of peace in the Persian Gulf leading to hopes of an order boom from Iran and Iraq provided a fertile backdrop for further rises. With the New York and London markets in the doldrums, Japan rather giddy, and France frothy with speculative issues, international investors preferred West German stocks, sending the FAZ Index up by another 6% before it peaked at 554 in December. This represented a

gain of 34% from the February low but was still a long way from the October 1987 high of 685 and the all-time high of 700 reached in November 1986.

On the smaller stock exchanges, although liquidity was poor, volumes low, and international investor interest limited, the gains during 1988 were among the highest. Belgium was a good example. The Brussels Bourse index rose by 42%, equaling the October 1987 level and coming within 5% of the all-time high. The Belgian stock prices staged the steepest rise anywhere in the world as the market was seized by a winter takeover frenzy.

The Netherlands suffered a fall of 40% in the October 1987 crash as foreign investors took fright and sold heavily. The open economy, dependence on international trade, and poor economic fundamentals made the Dutch stocks unattractive. When it became clear that the prompt coordinated response of the authorities had stabilized the situation, however, the Dutch stocks offered good value. The Amsterdam Stock Exchange bounced back 50 points (25%) before institutional investors could increase their participation. The summer rally, which took the Amsterdam General Index to 250—a gain of another 20% from the June level—was equally powerful but more broadly based. Unlike neighbouring Belgium, the Dutch stock market index at its best was 20% below the previous year's peak.

The experience of the Swiss stock exchanges was similar to that of The Netherlands and West Germany. Despite a steady and encouraging rise during the year, only half of the 40% loss suffered in the October 1987 crash was recovered.

The Scandinavian stock markets were generally higher during 1988 but remained below the previous year's peak. Norway's recovery was the weakest compared with those of Sweden and Denmark. The Oslo Stock Exchange was held back by lack of investor interest, competition from high-yield bonds, and weak oil prices. The Oslo Stock Exchange index tested the 420 level in March, June, and October, but on each occasion it failed to break through; the index retraced its steps back to 360–370 and at the year's end was far below the previous year's peak of 600.

The Swedish exchange, on the other hand—supported by stronger investor commitment, higher liquidity, and stronger corporate profitability—rose without interruption until July to 3120, within striking distance of the 1987 peak of 3270. After a short pause it moved up strongly but

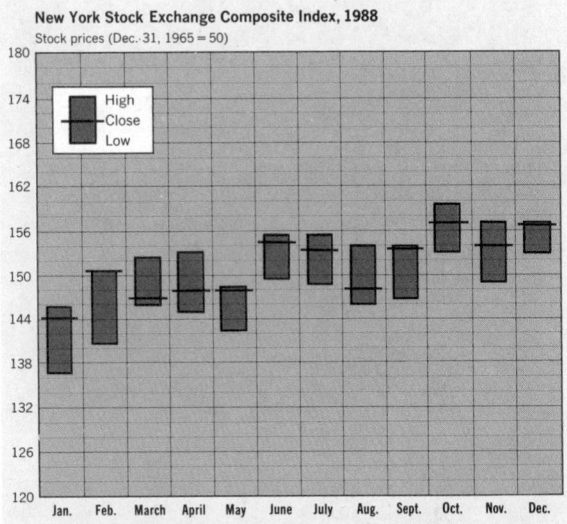

New York Stock Exchange Composite Index, 1988
Stock prices (Dec. 31, 1965 = 50)

High
Close
Low

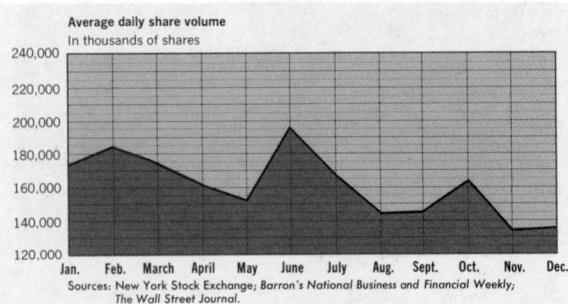

Average daily share volume
In thousands of shares

Sources: New York Stock Exchange; Barron's National Business and Financial Weekly; The Wall Street Journal.

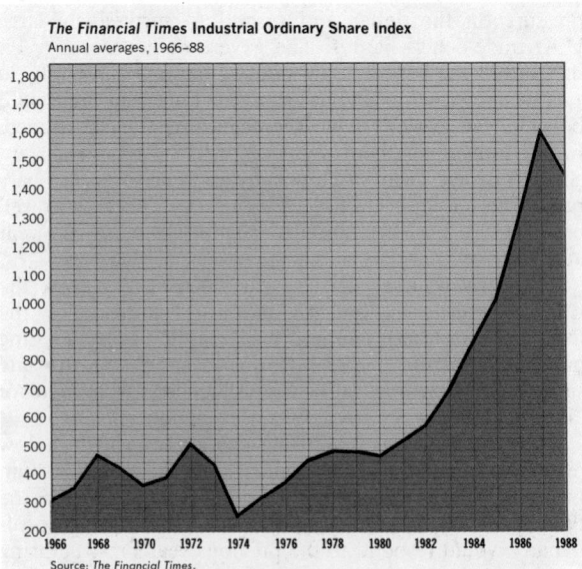

The Financial Times Industrial Ordinary Share Index
Annual averages, 1966–88

Source: The Financial Times.

could not break through the 3270 mark. In Denmark a spring rally was followed by a strong October performance, but the total gains for the year, at around 26%, left it far short of the previous year's peak.

The Austrian market showed considerable strength in the late summer. Although it largely escaped the October 1987 crash, falling by only 13%, it started sluggishly in 1988. In March a favourable outcome of a court case boosted the share prices of Montana (financial services, mining, and biochemical products) from 11,000 Schillings to more than 19,000 Schillings. This did not initially push up the prices of other shares but was later instrumental in waking up the Vienna Bourse. The Credit Aktien Index climbed rapidly to a high of 220, a gain of 34% from the low of 164 reached in February.

In Spain the Madrid Stock Exchange index rose strongly in the first six months of 1988 to a high of 300, an increase of 30% from January 1. Despite expectations that after a short summer pause the next stop would be 330, an all-time high, the market ran out of steam and fluctuated between 270 and 290.

Share prices in the Milan Stock Exchange were slow to recover from the October 1987 setback. By summer the Banco Commerciale Italiana Index was below the January level. Encouraged by predictions of 3.5% growth in the gross domestic product, steady inflation, weak oil prices, and the government's willingness to tackle the perennial public sector deficit, sentiment changed, however. Milan performed better than any other European exchange in October after a decision by the government to abolish the secret voting system in the Parliament. The index peaked just short of 600, 20% below the May 1987 level.

Other Countries. As the West's stock markets languished well below the 1987 peaks, Tokyo set new records. The October 1987 crash turned out to be a short, sharp correction. The shares soon recovered their poise and resumed their familiar rise. In less than three months the Nikkei Average Price Index passed the October 1987 peak and set a new record at 28,200 before consolidating. Tokyo decoupled itself from the rest of the world for three major reasons: its sheer size, good economic fundamentals, and the attitude of the Japanese investors. Even before the crash Tokyo had become the world's largest stock exchange, and in 1988 it steadily widened the gap between itself and the U.S. and the U.K. The sheer size and inflow of funds gave it a momentum of its own. With gross national product growth of 5.5% and an inflation rate of 0.6%, a public sector deficit of about 1%, and unit labour costs actually falling, Japanese exporters did not find it difficult to overcome further appreciations of the yen against the dollar. What held back the Tokyo market in the early autumn was the financial impact of a sale of government stocks in Nippon Telegraph & Telephone and also the emperor's health. Japanese investors did not wish to see the market soar away while the emperor was critically ill. By early December some of these worries had lifted sufficiently to enable the Nikkei average to break through the psychological barrier of 30,000 and end the year at a record 30,159.

Other Pacific Basin countries also experienced strong market gains. Strongly rising commodity prices, for wool tops in particular, helped Australia. After a 30% rise, however, the index peaked in the summer and consolidated at about 1450, well below the 1987 peak of 2305. Hong Kong's performance was limited, given the colony's close commercial ties with the U.K. and the U.S. The Hang Seng Index rose by 14% in the first six months but subsequently weakened, showing a 5% gain at the year's end. The Singapore Straits Industrial Index performed much

A man at the Tokyo foreign exchange market checks Japan's Nikkei average, an index of selected stocks. On December 7 the Nikkei average—aided by the U.S. dollar's recovery on the foreign market—had reached an unprecedented level of 30,050.82.
AFP PHOTO

better, recovering by as much as 64% in the summer but heading toward a more modest 25% gain at the year's end.

Commodity Markets. The overall trend of world commodity price indexes was upward during 1988. The *Economist* commodity price index, which measured spot prices in U.S. dollars and sterling for 28 internationally traded foodstuffs, nonfood agricultural products, and metals, rose by nearly 19% in dollar terms from the beginning of the year (in sterling terms a more modest 15%).

The price of crude oil, which was not included in the *Economist* index, was once again volatile. During 1988 the spot price of North Sea Brent fluctuated as high as $17 per barrel and as low as $11.50. From the end of 1987 to the end of 1988, the price of Brent crude oil fell by 20%. With demand remaining well below the high level of supply, prices fell steeply from around $16 per barrel in the summer as OPEC meetings failed to agree on a quota and a target price until November 27. The new targets of 18.5 million bbl per day for a six-month period from January 1989 with a price target of $18 per barrel marked the end of a major disagreement within OPEC. Although doubts remained on the willingness of individual members to stay within their quotas, oil prices firmed slightly to $15.80 per barrel at the year's end.

The two major sectors of the *Economist* index of dollar commodity prices rose at markedly different rates. The average 1988 level of the food index rose by 13%, while that of industrial raw materials gained 23%. Within the industrial raw materials component, nonfood agricultural prices rose by 14% and metals showed the highest gains at 37%.

Gold remained volatile but on a downward trend. During the opening months of the year, as it became clear that the world economy was not heading for a recession and also with the ending of the Gulf war, gold prices tumbled from around $480 to $420 per ounce. After a short-lived rally mirroring a recovery in oil prices, it steadily drifted, falling below the $400-per-ounce level in late September. Although a technical rise followed in November–December anticipating a recovery in oil prices, investors remained concerned about the weakness of the U.S. dollar and the willingness of the U.S. government to tackle its budget and trade deficits. At the year's end the price was 15% below the December 1987 peak of $502 per ounce.   (IEIS)

This article updates the *Macropædia* article MARKETS.

Education

The struggle to reduce or at least contain illiteracy remained the principal focus of education worldwide in 1988. That the need was not confined to less developed countries was shown by a report, *Social Europe,* produced by the European Commission. Based on an inquiry that began in 1984, it stated that one of every 20 Europeans was illiterate. The Commission had been alarmed for some time over the extent of illiteracy in Europe and its close relationship to unemployment. In Belgium, for example, it was found that 60% of those drawing unemployment benefits had barely completed primary education. The most urgently argued proposal to combat illiteracy—especially among adults—was radically to improve teacher training.

One heartening success story came from drought- and war-ravaged Ethiopia. In the Haile Selassie era more than 90% of the population had been illiterate. The new regime that seized power in 1974 made education a priority, launching a national literacy campaign in 1979. It was estimated that by 1988 some 70% of the people were literate, and more than 47 million books for beginners and those who had just attained literacy had been published. This was backed by the development of rural newspapers in the different languages used in the country. It was recognized, however, that the level of literacy reached was only "functional," and that more efforts were called for if the gains already made were not to slip away.

In the member countries of the European Communities (EC), there was growing concern among educators about what would happen in 1992, when the single European market was scheduled to come into existence. It appeared that the main effects on education would be through mutual recognition of degrees and professional qualifications and on the teaching of modern languages. In June the EC trade ministers agreed on a directive stating that lawyers, accountants, and engineers qualified in one EC country should have the right to work in all of them. It had already been established that qualified architects, doctors, and those in the pharmaceutical professions had a right to practice throughout the Community. The intention was that this directive should come into force by 1991. It would mean that each EC state recognized, as equivalent to its own, degrees and professional diplomas awarded by other member countries following a minimum of three years' study. EC citizens who qualified outside the Community would have to spend three years studying in their own country before being able to work elsewhere in the EC. Partly to complement this arrangement, two EC-wide schemes were developed: Erasmus, the European Action Scheme for the Mobility of University Students, and COMETT, the Community Action Program for Education and Training for Technology.

Unesco's session in June to approve the major priorities for the agency's future was of more than usual importance. The new director, Federico Mayor Zaragoza (*see* BIOGRAPHIES), elected in the autumn of 1987, was now in charge. His objective, he said, was "to do less to do better." This was inevitable because two years previously both the U.S. and the U.K. had left the organization after accusing its then director of mismanagement. Mayor proposed cutting back the main programs from 16 to 5—Education, Science, Culture, Communications, and Social Sciences. Some countries, including India and the U.S.S.R., feared that efficiency was being made an end in itself. The U.K. and U.S. were invited as observers, and it was evident that Mayor hoped to entice them back into the Unesco fold.

In Mikhail Gorbachev's Soviet Union, there were suddenly no inhibitions about discussing the state of education. Gennady Yagodin, president of the U.S.S.R. State Committee for Public Education, admitted publicly that half the schools in the country were without central heating, running water, or sewerage; a quarter of the children were in overcrowded schools, and many had to study in two shifts; and more than a million children were unable to go to kindergarten because there were no places for them. As to higher education, the Soviet Union—judging by the number of students per 10,000 population—had fallen from 9th in the world to 23rd over the past ten years. The proportion of national income spent on education fell to 4.2% in 1982 and had not increased since.

Both major candidates for the presidency in the U.S. general election promised that education would be a primary emphasis of their administrations. Republican George Bush emphasized aid for disadvantaged students, magnet schools, and promotion of state programs for excellence. Democrat Michael Dukakis stressed funds for prospective teachers, the financing of research centres, and increased availability of college loans. In the closing months of his presidency, Ronald Reagan selected Lauro F. Cavazos, the president of Texas Tech University, to replace William Bennett as secretary of education, and Bush, following his election, announced that Cavazos would retain his position in the new administration. Cavazos was the first Hispanic ever appointed to the Cabinet. Bennett, who had made headlines with his outspoken criticism of the U.S. educational system, joined another prominent critic, Allan Bloom, author of *The Closing of the American Mind,* to establish a foundation dedicated to teaching "the major works of the Western world" in literature, philosophy, and political theory. With both parties planning to make education a campaign issue, Congress in the spring passed a $7.5 billion education bill that reauthorized most federal elementary, secondary, and adult education programs through fiscal 1993 and established some new ones, among them programs aimed at dropout prevention, improving the basic skills of high school students, and introducing satellite technology into the schools.

In an unusual step, the U.S. Supreme Court decided to review a 1976 ruling that prohibited private schools from discriminating on the basis of race. If the justices overturned the earlier decision, it would be the first instance in modern times of an expansion of civil rights being reversed. The court let stand a lower court's refusal to require Tennessee to pay for continuing efforts to desegregate the Nashville public schools. A federal judge dismissed a lawsuit against the Los Angeles public schools on the grounds that little could be done to integrate a system with only 17% white students. In other cases relating to education, the Supreme Court determined that it is constitutional to require fundamentalist students to read textbooks that their parents consider "godless" and held that school officials have the right to censor student publications that are inconsistent with educational missions (the ruling did not affect college-level publications). Schools were told by the justices that they could not exclude students whose handicaps result in disruptive behaviour. Schools that received federal aid for handicapped students retained the right to suspend students for ten days when their behaviour might be dangerous to others. The cooling-off period would permit the exercise of due process relative to expulsion.

Primary and Secondary. A major Education Reform Act enacted in the U.K. in 1988 embodied much of the ideology of the Conservative government. It was passed in the teeth of opposition from the teachers' unions and educa-

tional administrators, although a number of its provisions enjoyed wide support. The most important of them, the establishment of a "national curriculum," marked a radical change in the English tradition. Until 1988 there had been no set curriculum with which schools had to comply, although in practice the secondary schools all prepared children for a national school-leaving examination given at age 16. The national curriculum had three compulsory subjects—English, mathematics, and science—and seven other "foundation" subjects. Children were to be tested at the ages of 7, 11, 14, and 16. The whole package reflected concern about levels of achievement in the schools and the fact that standards in Britain seemed to be a good deal lower than in West Germany and other continental countries.

The most controversial provisions concerned the permission given to schools to "opt out"; that is, to decide to be under the direct control of the Department of Education rather than under the local authority. In many ways the act was seen as an attack by central government on local government, which in practice had run the educational system. The government decided to break up the major local authority in England, the Inner London Education Authority, which had existed for over a hundred years. It was divided into 13 areas to be administered by local councils. The act also continued a process begun some years earlier of delegating financial power to schools' governing bodies.

This trend manifested itself in several other countries as well. Thus in New Zealand the Picot Report proposed a major shake-up in the administration of primary and secondary education. The government decided that each school should have a board of trustees—mostly parents—to run it as a "stand alone" unit. Prime Minister David Lange, who also took on the job of minister of education, initiated a series of reports on education. Besides the Picot Report, these included the Hawke Report on tertiary education and the Mead Report on early childhood education. In Australia education became a major political issue, especially in New South Wales, where a new Liberal government instituted a program of reforms. These involved major cuts in teaching staffs, although more money was allocated for maintenance, computers, and special and rural education. On the curricular side, the state proposed making math and science compulsory and eliminating subjects

catering to "transient life-styles," such as child psychology and peace studies.

The new French government under Pres. François Mitterrand announced in June that it was investing some F 1.2 billion in state education, F 350 million of which would go toward higher education. Mitterrand had promised that education and job training would be priorities of his government. In August the new minister for education, Lionel Jospin, announced changes in the schools. He hoped to drastically reduce the large numbers of children who were kept back after a bad report by helping them catch up without repeating a class. He wished to reduce the overlong school day, lighten the curriculum, and possibly lengthen the short school year. His views reflected a general anxiety in Western Europe over the state of language teaching; he proposed to introduce a foreign language at the primary stage and to encourage more secondary pupils to study two languages. Jospin also wanted to continue the expansion of technical and vocational education and to extend the range of vocational degrees, tailor-made to the needs of industry.

An unusually critical report on primary education, presented by the Cour des Comptes, appeared in France during the year. This venerable body of French magistrates, which reports on abuses in public spending every year, accused the Ministry of Education of gross mismanagement in the provision of primary teachers. The criticisms went back to 1981, when many of the 8,500 teaching posts added in that year had not been allocated to the schools that needed them most. Heads of primary schools in Paris were not called upon to teach, and in 1986 many schools had more than double the number of "replacement" teachers they needed. In particular, the report highlighted the plight of replacement teachers, often straight out of college, who were sent to the most difficult schools despite their lack of experience. The magistrates blamed the overrigid administration and overpowerful teachers' unions.

One of the more significant reports to appear in 1988 was that of the Kingman committee of inquiry into the teaching of English, commissioned by the U.K. Department of Education. To some extent, the establishment of the committee was a reaction to the views of right-wing Conservatives that it was high time to return to old-fashioned learning of grammar by rote. The report, which appeared in May, rejected this view, though it insisted that

AP/WIDE WORLD

Students at a Moscow middle school discuss the recent revisions of Soviet history textbooks. Teachers and students in the Soviet Union were being encouraged to talk openly about what once had been omitted from approved history books.

there was a "standard English," the rules of which could not be learned without rigorous application. The report's main criticism concerned the inadequacy of teacher training. The committee put forward a model of the English language that would serve as a basis of how teachers were to be trained and an indication of the broad attainment targets for children at 7, 11, and 16. At the same time, the views of so-called progressives who denied the very concept of "correct and incorrect language" were equally rejected. Teachers should cover grammar, punctuation, spelling, and syntax, but an understanding of concepts such as verb, noun, or sentence should be acquired "mainly through an exploration of the language pupils use rather than through exercises out of context."

Few countries had seen standards slip more conspicuously than Egypt, where a spiraling birthrate coupled with a scarcity of resources led to chronic overcrowding in schools, with classes of 60 or more. The minister of education, Ahmed Fathi Sorour, presented a five-year plan to halt the decline, and his proposals were approved by the Egyptian Cabinet in June. The plan proposed to attack classroom overcrowding by reducing compulsory education from nine years to eight, a move justified by the argument that pupils who had no desire to continue up to age 15 were absent anyway. A maximum class size of 40 was set, to be enforced by inspectors. More teachers would be hired and more schools built, with funding from the U.S. Agency for International Development. It was hoped that within five years every child in Egypt would go to school for a full day. The curriculum and the examination system were also revised; the General Secondary Certificate was condensed into a single examination containing elements of literature, science, and math, divided into ordinary and advanced levels. In-service training of some 15,000 primary teachers was an important part of the plan.

A survey of 13,500 U.S. teachers by the Carnegie Foundation for the Advancement of Teaching found that their morale had declined, even though they felt student achievement had improved. Most of the teachers believed that the national movement toward educational reform had benefited students more than it had promoted teacher well-being. Seven out of ten gave the schools a grade of "C" or lower. In a similar vein, the annual conventions of the two major U.S. teachers' unions concluded that much of what was wrong with the schools could be corrected if teachers were given more power to make decisions about curriculum, textbooks, and related matters. The Institute for Educational Leadership, in a report endorsed by the National Education Association and the American Federation of Teachers, urged troubled schools to pattern themselves after model schools with collegial staff relations, teacher involvement in decision making, and strong, sensitive administrators.

Despite this evidence of dissatisfaction with working conditions, strikes by teachers were rare when the schools opened in September. A contributing factor was the improvement in salaries. According to a RAND Corporation report, the average teacher salary was $25,240, representing an increase of 31% over the last five years. The same report also detected an improvement in teacher quality, which it attributed to stricter training requirements, testing of teachers to assure minimum competency, and the institution of minimum grade point averages for prospective teachers.

The U.S. Census Bureau reported an improvement in the high school dropout rate for black students; according to the bureau, it had declined from 27 to 17% between 1975 and 1985. Average Scholastic Aptitude Test (SAT) scores for minority students improved, although they were still lower than the national mean, and scores for minority students who took the American College Test (ACT) were also higher. However, overall SAT scores declined in 1988 for the first time since 1980. In November six major educational testing organizations issued a uniform set of guidelines designed to guard against bias and cultural discrimination. In a controversial move, Georgia mandated testing of all kindergarten pupils to determine their readiness to enter first grade.

Among the many reports on education published during the year, *The Science Report Card,* issued by the Educational Testing Service, found the state of science literacy among U.S. students "alarming and depressing"; half of 17-year-olds could not benefit from job training or perform work that required technical understanding. A study commissioned by the National Geographic Society showed that Americans 18 to 24 years old scored lowest among youth in nine countries in geographic knowledge (Swedes were first, followed by West Germans). The president of the society described them as a "lost generation . . . They haven't the faintest idea where they are." In a study conducted by the Ontario Institute of Education, female students in 20 nations were found to do as well as males in arithmetic, algebra, and statistics, but boys were stronger in geometry and measurement. Citing illiteracy and the growth of a permanent underclass as critical problems for the U.S., *American Potential: The Human Dimension,* a report issued by the Business-Higher Education Forum, called for action to assure a supply of skilled, adaptable, and committed workers. Similarly, an interim report of the Commission on Work, Family and Citizenship urged more attention to the needs of students who are not college-bound.

The Carnegie Foundation for the Advancement of Teaching, in a report on urban schools, concluded that reform had largely bypassed the cities. One of its recommendations, the subdivision of large urban districts to counter anonymity, was part of a reform of the Chicago public school system, the nation's third largest, enacted by the Illinois state legislature. Each school would have a local council, including parents, teachers, the principal, and neighbourhood residents, that would have the authority to hire or remove the principal and set the school budget. Other changes in the system, which Secretary Bennett had called the country's worst, included the reduction of administrative staff and the establishment of an oversight committee with power to discipline the central school board and staff. Principals would have increased authority but would not have tenure.

In September the Kenyan minister of education, Peter Aloo Aringo, announced that mandatory sex education was under consideration. Research had revealed that some 10,000 girls were dropping out of the educational system every year because of pregnancy. The minister said a draft syllabus and curriculum concerned with family life education would be introduced in 50 primary and secondary schools before being approved for use in all schools. Sex education also began to emerge as a school subject in China, again as part of an effort to contain population growth. Jointly sponsored by the State Education and Family Planning commissions, lessons on sex began in 13 provinces and municipalities, with the expectation that they would eventually be part of a nationwide campaign.

Higher Education. A report issued by the World Bank on education in sub-Saharan Africa raised many issues that applied equally to the Indian subcontinent and parts of Latin America and Asia. It noted the internal political

pressures for expanding higher education despite the sorry financial state of many less developed countries. In the past three decades there had been an almost unimaginable expansion of university education in Africa. In 1960 the continent had only 21,000 university students; by 1983 there were 437,000, plus 100,000 studying abroad. Surprisingly, the evidence pointed to the survival of colonial university structures, down to their increasingly inappropriate subject mix. Humanities and social sciences still accounted for about 60% of places in the average African university despite the near universal demand for more engineers and scientists. The result was serious graduate unemployment, and the World Bank report saw conditions worsening unless there was a radical change of approach. It recommended lower unit costs, student loans, and smaller enrollments in nonvocational subjects.

In European countries there was still a preponderance of arts subjects in higher education. This emerged at a conference in September of the "Europe region of Unesco" (which also included North America). It was noted that there had been a rise in the overall number of students as well as the proportion of young people in the 18–23 age group who were receiving higher education. The ratio of women students had also increased. In 1985 the proportion of students in the 18–23 age group worldwide had reached 28.5%, but there were wide variations; in Canada and the U.S. nearly half of this age group attended institutions of higher learning. In several of the developed countries, there was evidence of a wish to expand higher education following the cutbacks of previous years. In Australia, for example, a program of expansion was begun that would increase spending by 16% over the next three years. In Hungary the new Communist Party leader, Karoly Grosz, announced that the universities would be expanded. By contrast, expansion in China was curtailed. The original goal of 750,000 students in universities and junior colleges by 1990 was lowered to less than 700,000. The Australian Trade Commission, Austrade, began an effort to market Australian higher education courses to Asian countries.

The cost of four years of college reached about $80,-000 in some U.S. institutions. The average increase for the year was 7%. A study of private colleges showed that tuition had increased 80% between 1981 and 1987, while median family income rose 40% during the same period. An American Council on Education survey of 1984 college graduates found that those who had borrowed money to pay for their education devoted about 4% of their income to debt reduction. The average debt was $5,470. Student loans commonly were repaid over a ten-year period. Rising costs had not hurt college applications, however, and students often found that they could not gain admission to the college of their choice. As the small post-baby-boom generation reached college age, most institutions had expected the number of students to drop. Accordingly, many colleges curtailed admissions and recruited energetically. Instead of the expected slight decline in admissions, however, there was an increase to a record 12.5 million students. Contributing to the rise were a small increase in the percentage of high school graduates wanting to attend college and a major expansion in the number of mature part-time students.

A year after Bloom's best-selling *Closing of the American Mind* had lamented the lack of sound liberal arts teaching in U.S. colleges and universities, a round in the ongoing struggle between classicists and revisionists went to the revisionists. After two years of intense debate both on and off the campus, the Faculty Senate of Stanford University voted to replace the course in Western culture,

Terry Weeks, a social studies teacher at the Central Middle School in Murfreesboro, Tennessee, speaks at a news conference after receiving the 1988 National Teacher of the Year Award. The award is sponsored by the Encyclopædia Britannica Companies, *Good Housekeeping* magazine, and the Council of Chief State School Officers.
AP/WIDE WORLD

which required the study of 15 Western classics, with a new course called "Culture, Ideas and Values" (CIV). While six of the classics would be retained (the Bible and works by Plato, St. Augustine, Machiavelli, Rousseau, and Marx), CIV would also include works from non-European cultures and works by women and members of minority groups.

Students at Gallaudet University in Washington, D.C., the only institution of higher learning for the hearing impaired in the U.S., forced the resignation of a president-designate with normal hearing and the appointment of the 124-year-old institution's first deaf president. The choice of Elisabeth Ann Zinser, vice-president of academic affairs of the University of North Carolina at Greensboro, who was not hearing impaired and did not know sign language, sparked five days of demonstrations by students who claimed that a person with normal hearing could not understand their needs. Zinser resigned, and two days later the board of trustees named Irving King Jordan, who had been dean of the Gallaudet college of arts and sciences. The affair brought considerable public attention to the nascent movement for deaf rights and to the continuing dispute over whether the deaf should be encouraged to speak and to blend into the larger community or should rely primarily on signing.

Perhaps the most unexpected event of 1988 concerned the cancellation of history examinations in Soviet schools during the summer. It was decided that the textbooks should be revised to include a more realistic picture of the Stalinist period, but it became clear that Soviet history could not be rewritten overnight. In particular, historians were unsure how far they could take revelations about the consequences of forced collectivization and statistics on the victims of Stalin's purges. They also demanded access to hitherto unavailable archives. As one professor at Moscow's Institute of Marxism-Leninism commented in September: "Before you make rabbit stew you must at least have a rabbit."   (JOEL L. BURDIN; TUDOR DAVID)

See also Libraries; Motion Pictures.

This article updates the *Macropædia* articles History of EDUCATION; TEACHING.

Energy

Weather featured prominently among the events affecting energy in 1988. During the summer months the United States experienced a prolonged and widespread heat wave that was combined with severe drought in much of the West and Southeast. The resulting demand for air conditioning repeatedly broke records for electricity use in many regions of the country, and the drought brought the Mississippi River to the lowest level of flow in recorded history, which seriously interfered with the transportation of fuels. Low streamflows also reduced the output of hydroelectricity to 30% of normal in the western U.S., but the nation's electric utility industry was able to cope with all this without having to resort to extreme emergency measures. Argentina was not so lucky. Low water levels in that country in April reduced the availability of hydroelectricity at the same time that technical problems shut down two nuclear power stations, forcing the rationing of electricity.

Petroleum and Natural Gas. As in 1987, the Organization of Petroleum Exporting Countries (OPEC) struggled throughout the year to sustain the price of oil at the target

level it had set. The difficulties were partly OPEC's own doing and partly the result of external circumstances. Most OPEC members persisted in producing above the quotas that had been agreed upon, and production by non-OPEC countries also continued at high levels. The result was chronic oversupply and prices below the target level.

In April representatives of seven non-OPEC producing countries met with an OPEC committee in an attempt by OPEC to obtain their cooperation in reducing output and thus strengthening oil prices. The non-OPEC nations were willing to reduce their own production, but because the OPEC representatives were unable to guarantee that their countries would abide by the assigned quotas, the effort was ultimately fruitless. In May Mexico declined a formal invitation to join the cartel but repeated its willingness to cooperate in reducing production provided OPEC observed discipline in its own production by producing no more than the quotas.

In July the market was stunned by Iran's unexpected announcement that it would abide by the long-standing United Nations resolution calling for a cease-fire and the beginning of peace negotiations to bring an end to the Iran-Iraq war. The end to hostilities would allow both combat-

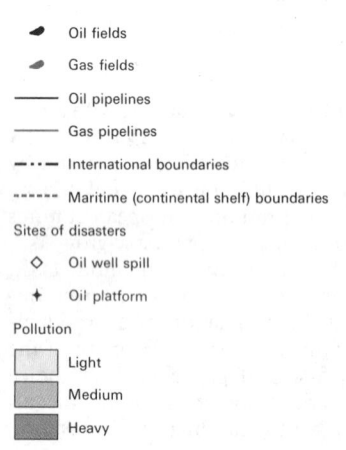

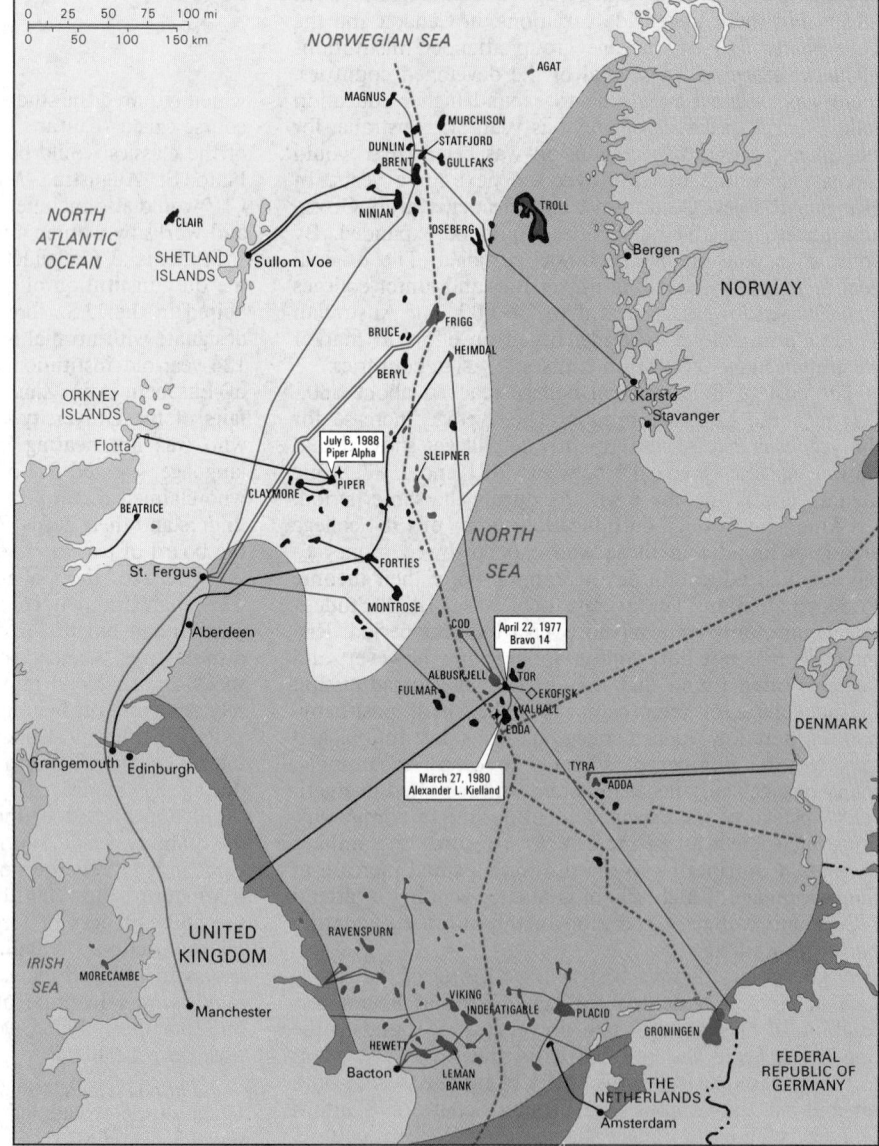

The rich reserves of petroleum and gas for which the North Sea has become world famous also have been the sources of environmental disasters that have made that area one of the most polluted regions in the world.

ants to turn their attention to reconstruction, which would require enormous sums that could be earned only by oil exports. On the other hand, peace also increased the possibility that the two countries could overcome their mutual animosity sufficiently to cooperate in abiding by OPEC production quotas. As negotiations dragged on while the cease-fire held, it was not apparent which outcome would prevail in the long term.

In the meantime, chronic oversupply and price weakness continued. During the summer the situation worsened as it became apparent that Saudi Arabia was disregarding its quota on a grand scale. The Saudis confirmed this with the announcement that they would produce whatever was necessary to preserve their market share, with the implied threat that they were ready if need be to precipitate another market collapse such as the one they had brought about in 1986. Prices sagged ominously, touching the 1986 level.

OPEC meetings during early fall grappled with the key issue: the demand by Iraq that its quota equal that of Iran. In the face of persistent Iranian refusal to agree to this parity, Iraq continued its refusal to accept any quota. The issue came to a head at a meeting in late November. During several days of frantic negotiating, rumours abounded and prices in the oil markets gyrated wildly. Finally a compromise was reached—Iraq would gain quota parity with Iran, but Iran would save face by retaining its assigned percentage of the total OPEC production quota. This was accomplished by persuading all other OPEC members to take small reductions in their quotas. The total was raised, however, and so all members' quotas increased.

The new agreement was to take effect on Jan. 1, 1989, and would apply only for the first half of the year. The agreement also specified a target price of $18 per barrel, a defeat for the Saudi proposal of $15. Oil markets promptly firmed, but it remained to be seen whether the higher quotas would remove the propensity of OPEC members to produce in excess of their assigned limits.

External developments during the year suggested that even with a resolution of the quota issue, OPEC's difficulties would not diminish. On the positive side for the organization, preliminary results of a new look at U.S. oil reserves and resources (undiscovered reserves) reduced estimates by more than one-third, and U.S. imports of crude oil reached an eight-year high. Elsewhere the news for OPEC was all bad. The Soviet Union announced in March that an oil field near the northeast coast of the Caspian Sea, discovered in 1979, had been evaluated as one of the world's largest. Also in March, Brazil announced the discovery of the world's largest offshore oil field in the Campos Basin off its southeast coast. The find made it likely that Brazil would become an oil exporter in the 1990s.

Continued improvements in the technology of finding and producing oil at ever greater ocean depths further contributed to the prospects for large supplies. The world's tallest offshore platform was installed in the Gulf of Mexico 520 km (330 mi) east of Corpus Christi, Texas. The mammoth structure was 490 m (1,615 ft) high from its base to the top of its derrick, stood in 410 m (1,353 ft) of water, and weighed 49,375 tons. The North Sea continued to yield significant new discoveries.

The record of oil events in 1988 was marred in July by a tragic occurrence on an oil-producing platform in the North Sea 192 km (120 mi) northeast of Aberdeen, Scotland. In the worst disaster in the history of world offshore oil operations, a series of explosions and fire in the middle of the night totally destroyed the platform and killed 167 of the 230 workers there. The last fire on the platform was not extinguished until 22 days later. The disaster resulted in the loss of production not only from the destroyed platform but from nearby platforms as well. The tragedy occurred only one day after a much smaller explosion on another North Sea platform. The two incidents reduced the total productive capability of the United Kingdom oil industry by almost 15%.

A "world class" natural gas discovery was made in the Gulf of Papua, 256 km (160 mi) west of Port Moresby, Papua New Guinea. The owners of the find faced a task of great difficulty, however, in putting the gas to commercial use. Because of its remote location, the only feasible means of marketing the gas would be liquefying it so that it could be transported to markets in Southeast Asia, but there was already an abundance of such remote gas in the Pacific available in liquefied form.

Electricity. The major event in the field of electric power was the decision by the British government to privatize the state-owned electric industry of England and Wales. The actual sale was expected to take two or three years to accomplish. This privatization move was by far the most controversial in a series of sales of state-owned industries by the government of Prime Minister Margaret Thatcher. The issues concerned the replacement of the existing organizational structure with a radically different one and the introduction of competition into the generation of electricity.

Among other developments in electric power, the submarine cable under the English Channel linking the electric grids of the United Kingdom and France reached operational status. The high-voltage, direct-current link was the largest of its type and could deliver 2,000 MW between the two grids—as much power as the output from a large generating station. In West Germany a record-size turbine generator went into service at the Brokdorf nuclear power plant in Schleswig-Holstein. It had a capacity of 1,330 MW.

Nuclear power continued to be the subject of intense controversy in many countries during the year. In the U.S. attention focused on two plants, both fully complete but unable to operate because local authorities would not cooperate in the demonstration of a workable emergency evacuation plan, necessary before an operating license could be obtained. Faced with the inability to recover any of its $2.1 billion investment in the plant at Seabrook, N.H., in the extreme southeastern corner of the state, New Hampshire's largest electric utility filed for bankruptcy in January. This action was the first by a public utility in the U.S. in 50 years; it did not, however, affect the ability of the company to continue normal operations.

A different approach was tried in New York State, where the Shoreham plant, on the north coast of Long Island 88 km (55 mi) east of New York City, remained finished but idle. By proposing that the plant be purchased by the state and decommissioned, the state government attempted to forestall any attempt by the utility to put it into operation. The proposal failed, however, and the ultimate solution of the problem remained elusive in the face of controversy over how the costs should be shared by taxpayers, stockholders, and customers.

Federal regulators attempted to resolve the impasse by considering the licensing of both plants for at least low-power operation, despite the absence of approved evacuation plans. In November U.S. Pres. Ronald Reagan signed an executive order directing a federal agency to assume the responsibility for emergency planning where state and local governments declined to do so. The fate of the plants nevertheless remained in limbo.

Nuclear plants elsewhere in the world met similar fates.

Sweden announced it would shut down two of its nuclear reactors in the mid-1990s, well ahead of their designed operating life; and a plant being built at Krasnodar in the northern Caucasus was abandoned by Soviet authorities in the face of local opposition stemming from the Chernobyl disaster of 1986.

In regard to nuclear fuel, the uranium mining industry of the U.S. lost its battle against foreign competition. The U.S. Supreme Court ruled that the U.S. Department of Energy was not required by law to prohibit the enrichment of imported uranium in order to safeguard the domestic uranium industry.

Other Developments. A solar-powered car set a world speed record of 77.9 km/h (48.7 mph) for such vehicles. The same car had won the world's first race for solar-powered cars in Australia the previous year, averaging 66.6 km/h (41.6 mph) over a 3,140-km (1,950-mi) course. Researchers at the University of Chicago achieved a new level of concentration of sunlight 60,000 times greater than the normal energy level of sunlight and three times higher than the level of concentration previously achieved. The advance opened the way for new processing uses of solar energy.

In Los Angeles the first service-station pump for methanol (methyl alcohol) was opened to the public. The pump dispensed a mixture of 85% methanol and 15% unleaded gasoline. Methanol offers the environmental advantage of an automotive fuel that produces much less air pollution than gasoline does.

The race to commercialize the epochal 1987 discovery of high-temperature superconducting materials continued in 1988. The fact that all resistance to the flow of electricity in a conductor can take place not only near the temperature of liquid helium but above the temperature of the much less expensive liquid nitrogen as well opened up a host of potential opportunities to generate, transmit, and use electricity in new ways and at lower costs. A Japanese institution began work on a ship propelled solely by the interaction of an onboard magnetic field and a current flowing through the surrounding seawater. Researchers throughout the world tackled the formidable problems involved in fabricating the new superconducting materials into wire.

The U.S. Department of Transportation announced a new program that would support projects to develop alternative fuels for transportation, such as ethanol, methanol, propane, and compressed natural gas. The action was taken in the face of increased air pollution in urban areas due to rising concentrations of auto-exhaust pollutants. To the extent that such pollution could be reduced, it would also be a contribution to meeting the problem of the "greenhouse effect," the possibility that the world may be entering an era of severe climatic change as a result of continuing accumulation of carbon dioxide in the Earth's atmosphere. Although the use of the alternate fuels would not eliminate the discharge of carbon dioxide in vehicle exhausts, it would significantly reduce such emissions.

(BRUCE C. NETSCHERT)

See also Engineering Projects; Industrial Review; Mining; Transportation.

This article updates the *Macropædia* articles ENERGY CONVERSION; FOSSIL FUELS.

Engineering Projects

Bridges. Two major events during 1988 made a significant impression on those bridge builders who favoured concrete over steel as their crossings' primary structural material. The first, at a location on France's Atlantic coastline, pleased them, for it showed how quickly and economically large bridges could be built of concrete. However, the second, in West Germany, sounded warning bells for those who advance concrete technology too far.

The first of the two, the Île de Ré Bridge, opened in the summer to link the island with the French west coast town of La Rochelle, 3 km (1.86 mi) away. An aesthetically pleasing structure, the bridge had 29 spans of 110 m (1 m = 3.3 ft) each, provided maximum clearance for shipping of 40 m, and cost a little under $50 million. Commendably, contractor Francis Bouygues needed only 19 months between design of the bridge and completion of construction.

This achievement was being hailed in France as a major civil engineering success. Among its most successful features were the raking pile foundation, which could be installed quickly, and a lightweight, cable-stayed launching gantry for placing the bridge's 798 precast concrete segments in

AFP PHOTO

Several solar-powered cars are tested during West Germany's "Solarmobile 1989," an exhibition in which 12 car designers introduced their new solar-powered models.

The Sunshine Skyway Bridge across Tampa Bay, Florida, is a cable-stayed bridge with support from a single row of cables that extend from its central pylons. A more traditional suspension bridge design would have utilized two parallel support cables suspended from bridge towers.

THE NEW YORK TIMES

rapid succession. Sitting on three piers, Bouygues's gantry built the deck on top of the outermost pier by lowering segments sequentially in pairs. The inner cantilever thus formed was eventually closed with already-completed deck; the outer cantilever was finished in mid-span to await the gantry as it advanced to the next pier, and the process began over again.

This process allowed the long bridge to be built quickly and safely, but the same could not be said of another technique, which came to grief near Frankfurt, West Germany. One engineer died and seven other people were seriously injured when the 360-m-long, seven-span Mainbrücke Stockstadt viaduct collapsed during construction in August.

West German contractors were building the 10.3-m-wide structure by casting the deck in 24-m-long sections behind one abutment, then sequentially jacking the completed deck sections prestressed together out over the bridge piers. The failure of the deck just before it was completed was viewed in West Germany as a major blow.

Those bridge builders who did not favour concrete could enjoy the formal opening of two major crossings in steel in 1988. The earlier of these was the first fixed link across the Inland Sea to join the Japanese main islands of Honshu and Shikoku. The multistructure crossing, accommodating both road and rail traffic, was opened in April and stood as a showpiece of Japanese engineering; it included bridges of suspension, cable-stayed, and truss design in its 12-km length.

Later in 1988 the second bridge to cross the Bosporus Straits was opened. Designed, as was the first, by the British consultancy Freeman Fox & Partners, it was built by a consortium that included firms from Japan, Italy, and Turkey. It was completed in a remarkably short time; 30 months was all that was required for the massive suspension bridge with its 1,090-m-long, 39.4-m-wide steel box deck to be built. Part of the secret of the bridge's success was the marrying of Japanese industriousness with British ingenuity. Former Freeman Fox partner William Brown took over as engineer for the structure and led its construction like an autocratic bridge builder of Victorian times.

Istanbul's need for a second crossing of the Bosporus was mirrored across the world in Vancouver, B.C., where the Canadians were building a second crossing of the Fraser River. The first, formerly the Annacis Bridge but renamed the Alex Fraser, was opened in 1986 and, at 465 m, became the world's longest cable-stayed span. The second, known as SkyTrain Bridge, would have a main stayed span 125 m shorter but was nonetheless an outstanding example of structural engineering.

SkyTrain's deck passed through the slender "bow" legs of two main towers slipformed in concrete; each tower top contained a concrete diaphragm from which a fan of 60 stays descended to support the deck. Intended to carry Vancouver's mass-transit railway, the bridge was scheduled to open in 1990.   (TY BYRD)

Buildings. Construction began in Hong Kong in 1988 on the new Bank of China building, which at 315 m would be the world's tallest building outside North America. While the structure consisted mainly of steel, the innovative framing and use of concrete with steel in a building of this type resulted in an economical design. The structure was bold in concept, being based on 5½ cubical modules, each 52 m square by 13 stories high, stacked on one another. The remaining height was accounted for by a five-story podium at the base of the building and a short pinnacle at the top. Each module had diagonal cross braces on each face, and the plan was also broken up into quadrants by diagonals. While the lowest module was a complete cube, one quadrant had been removed from the top of the next module. This process continued until only the south quadrant remained at the top. An unusual feature was the cross bracing, which assisted in carrying the vertical loads as well as resisting the large lateral forces that would result from wind and earthquake. The whole weight of the superstructure was carried down to the ground on the four corner columns, one of which, at 100,000 tons, was believed to be the heaviest ever single-column load in a building. These columns were driven into granite some 33 m below the surface, the foundation being concrete-filled caissons belled out to 12-m diameter at their base.

While perhaps not so innovative, construction was well under way on the giant World Trade Centre complex in east Beijing (Peking). This would eventually cover approx-

imately 400,000 sq m (1 sq m = 10.8 sq ft) and comprise a 38-story and a 6-story office block, an 18-story hotel, two 30-story apartment buildings, and an exhibition hall. The project was truly international; the main design was carried out in the U.S., the steel was supplied from Japan and China, and the main contractor came from France.

The new extension to the Louvre in Paris was of technical interest. While the main part was underground, it was topped by one 21.5-m-high and two smaller glass-clad pyramids. The building extended as deep as 15 m below ground, and the subsoil in the first 10 m consisted of sands and gravels with limestone below. Because of the water levels of the nearby Seine River, chemically protected permanent concrete cofferdams were anchored diagonally through to the limestone. The roof beams were to be left exposed, and to achieve a high standard of finish, the steel reinforcement to them was suspended from above to avoid the possibility of marking the face with spacer blocks. The main pyramid was clad with 666 diamond-shaped, double, ten-millimetre-thick pieces of glass specially developed to remove the greenish tint of normal glass and carried on a steel frame.

During the year work began on the 370-m-high telecommunications centre in Kuwait. This would be the tallest tower in the Middle East and one of the highest in the world. The central conical concrete shaft was to be 308 m high, with a public viewing platform at the 150-m level. At the 185-m level would be the main 25-m-high technical head. Atop the concrete shaft would be a 62-m-high steel mast housing the vertical antenna.

So far as wide-span structures were concerned, the Olympic Oval in Calgary, Alta., was honoured for excellence by the U.S. Prestressed Concrete Institute. In Britain there were two projects of note. One was a new superstore complex in London. A number of requirements led to a novel superstructure design. Roof trusses some 30 m long were supported at their ends on 7-m cantilevers. The supporting structure was anchored by tie-down rods to pile foundations. A 9.4-m-wide first-floor area extending along each side comprised a similar cantilever arrangement also tied down to the foundation and the roof.

The use of glue-laminated timber structures in Britain had been much less prevalent than in other parts of Europe and in North America. It was, therefore, interesting that it was used for the roof structure of a new recreation centre at Bournemouth. This had an 83-m × 48-m clear area spanned by 1-m-deep glue-laminated pinned arches that rose 2.5 m and were spaced at 4.6-m intervals. Other lower areas were roofed with curved glue-laminated beams spanning up to 13.25 m.

Responding to an upturn in volume, the U.K. construction industry was gearing itself to faster construction speed than it had previously achieved. Thus the first three phases of a 160,000-sq m development in London were built at rates of between 250 and 630 sq m per week, and the final phase was expected to be even faster.

(GEOFFREY M. PINFOLD)

Dams. While the worldwide rate of dam construction dropped from 300 to 200 dams per year, both developed and less developed countries continued to build dams to capture the floodwaters that would otherwise be lost to the sea. This rate of construction was exclusive of China, where dam construction exceeded 1,000 dams per year.

Worldwide, 80% of the dams were less than 30 m in height, and only 1% exceeded 100 m. The latter group, however, received most of the attention because of their impact on the environment and the need to resettle people from areas that would become flooded with their reser-

voirs. In the less developed countries, where the need for water was often urgent, there was much less construction. In India dams continued to be completed at the rate of four to six per year, and in Turkey three to four were completed annually. Some countries had accelerated their dam building to develop hydroelectric power, which, as a renewable resource, could replace the need to purchase imported fuel oil.

China completed a study of the development of the Leishui, a river that would provide 977 MW of power at 13 hydroelectric plants. The plan called for the completion of all the dams by the year 2000. Similarly, the development of the Hongshui (Hung-shu) called for ten dams to produce 11,120 MW of power in addition to supplying water for irrigation and providing for flood control.

In Brazil the filling of the Balbina Dam reservoir, with a capacity of 17 billion cu m (600 billion cu ft) raised environmental issues. The dam builders instituted an aggressive program to minimize the damage caused by the rising waters. Some 19,000 animals and reptiles were rescued, including boa constrictors, anteaters, armadillos, and hundreds of monkeys. Tribal Indians were relocated into new communities, which were provided with educational and health facilities not available to them in their original locations.

In another area the Brazilian government decided to abandon its plan to build the Babaquara Dam on the lower Xingu River, in the Amazon region. The dam was to have provided 6,500 MW of power but would have flooded 4,120 sq km (1,590 sq mi) of tropical forest.

The Greek government approved a billion-dollar multipurpose project consisting of five dams to develop 680 MW of power. The Mesochora Dam and the Mouzaki dams would be 135 m high and the Sykia Dam 150 m high. This project would provide for expansion of the irrigation system.

The Turkish Power Authority was pushing ahead with the designs of three major dams, primarily to generate power. The Dernier Dam was to be 247 m high and would produce 670 MW of power; the Borcka Dam, 140 m high, would provide 140 MW of power; and the Muratli Dam would be 49 m high and provide 115 MW.

Ghana initiated construction of two dams at Daboya and Pwalugh for hydropower development. Botswana completed its Gaborone water supply dam, which would provide water to the capital city of Gaborone with its population of 96,100. It was estimated that the water supply would be adequate only until 1995. Plans were being made to provide future water from neighbouring countries, including the transfer of water from the Limpopo River in South Africa.

Morocco's highest dam was inaugurated. It was a 144-m-high rock-fill dam and would provide 40 million cu m (140 million cu ft) of drinking water to the city of Marrakech, 140 km (87 mi) away. Irrigation water would also be provided to 35,000 ha (86,450 ac).

Algeria started construction of an earth-fill dam in Bordj Bou Arreridj Province to store 2 million cu m (70 million cu ft) of water. Two other dams, at Bayata and Qued Char, were being planned as part of the nation's five-year development plan. Work was being accelerated, meanwhile, as the severe drought reduced the stored water behind existing dams and water was being rationed. (T. W. MERMEL)

Roads. The traditional role of the road as a publicly financed facility was changing as highway administrators in industrialized and less developed nations alike turned to the private sector for funding. The "build-operate-transfer" (BOT) concept, under which a consortium of contractors

Major World Dams Under Construction in 1988[1]

Name of dam	River	Country	Type[2]	Height (m)	Length of crest (m)	Volume content (000 cu m)	Gross reservoir capacity (000 cu m)
Altinkaya	Kizilirmak	Turkey	E,R	195	634	16,000	5,763,000
Arachtas/Kalaritikos	Arachtos	Greece	E	185	238	1,500	1,840,000
Ataturk	Euphrates	Turkey	E,R	184	1,820	84,500	48,700,000
Bakun	Rajang	Malaysia	R	210	900	29,400	43,800,000
Balbina	Uatuma	Brazil	E,R	33	3,264	6,724	17,533,000
Barakshetra	Sapta Kasi	Nepal	G	239	640	7,677	8,500,000
Boguchany	Angara	U.S.S.R.	R	79	1,816	27,360	58,200,000
Boruca	Terraba	Costa Rica	E,R	267	700	43,000	14,960,000
Casa de Piedra	Rio Colorado	Argentina	E	56	10,000	16,500	4,000,000
Chapeton	Paraná	Argentina	E,G	35	224,000	296,200	60,600,000
Chisapani	Karnali	Nepal	E,R	210	850	35,000	15,000,000
Cipasang	Cimanuk	Indonesia	E,R	200	640	90,000	860,000
Corpus Posadas	Paraná	Argentina/Paraguay	E,G	65	8,474	18,200	13,000,000
Corumba	Corumba	Brazil	R	150	600	3,668	675,000
Dongfeng	Wujiang	China	A	168	251	622	1,020,000
Dongjiang	Laishui	China	A	157	438	943	8,120,000
Ertan	Yalongjiang	China	A	245	763	4,742	5,800
Garabi	Uruguay	Argentina/Brazil	E,G	60	3,960	19,884	5,810,000
Geheyan	Qingjiang	China	A	151	674	3,060	3,400,000
Guavio	Guavio	Colombia	E,R	246	380	16,800	950,000
Guayllabamba	Guayllabamba	Ecuador	A	165	413	704	105,000
Hrusov-Dunakiliti-Gabcikovo	Dunaj	Czechoslovakia/Hungary	E,G	29	31,500	18,340	199,000
Ilha Grande	Paraná	Brazil	E,G	29	7,060	11,573	30,000,000
Ingapata	Paute	Ecuador	G	166	430	1,600	413,000
Kabalebo	Kabalebo	Suriname	E,R	45	1,650	3,790	19,000,000
Kayraktepe	Goksu	Turkey	E,R	199	580	17,000	4,800,000
Kilickaya	Kelkit	Turkey	E,R	140	405	6,030	14,000,000
Kishau	Tons	India	E,R	253	360	18,400	2,400,000
Kouilou	Kouilou	Congo	A	137	345	390	35,000,000
Kumgang	North Itan	North Korea	E	215	1,120	N.A.	9,250,000
La Vueltosa	Caparo	Venezuela	E	118	1,200	15,000	5,300,000
Li Jia Xia	Huang He	China	A	175	382	3,030	760,000
Menzelet	Ceyhan	Turkey	E,R	151	420	8,530	19,500,000
Michihuao	Limay	Argentina	E	70	6,700	29,840	5,860,000
Pati	Paraná	Argentina	E,G	36	174,900	238,180	38,000,000
Piedra del Aquila	Limay	Argentina	G	174	795	2,764	12,800,000
Potrerillos	Mendoza	Argentina	E	146	550	17,120	860,000
Rocandor	Uruguay	Brazil/Argentina	E,R	78	1,598	9,940	33,580,000
San Roque	Agno	Philippines	E	210	1,130	43,150	990,000
Sardar Sarovar	Narmada	India	G	163	1,199	7,472	9,500,000
Tehri	Bhagirathi	India	E,R	261	570	22,750	2,600,000
Tian Sheng Qia	Hongshui	China	E,R	185	1,250	19,300	9,550,000
Tokuyama	Ibi	Japan	R	161	420	15,000	660,000
Urra II	Sinu	Colombia	R	170	275	23,500	34,300,000
Yacyreta-Apipe	Paraná	Paraguay/Argentina	E,G	43	69,600	81,000	21,000,000
Major World Dams Completed in 1987 and 1988[1]							
Bureya	Bureya	U.S.S.R.	G	139	810	3,561	20,900,000
Gallilo Ciego	Jequetepeque	Peru	E,R	120	750	15,000	573,600
Kara Kaya	Euphrates	Turkey	A	173	462	2,000	9,580,000
Khudoni	Inguri	U.S.S.R.	A	201	545	1,475	365,000
Lhakwar	Yamuna	India	G	204	440	2,800	580,000
Longyangxia	Huang He	China	A,G	172	342	1,750	24,700,000
Lower Usuma	Usuma	Nigeria	E	49	1,350	93,000	100,000
Planicie Banderita	Neuquen	Argentina	E	35	350	1,194	43,000,000
Rogun	Vakhsh	U.S.S.R.	E,R	335	660	75,500	13,300,000
São Felix (Serra da Mesa)	Tocantins	Brazil	E,R	160	1,950	34,000	55,200,000
Upper Wainganga	Wainganga	India	E	43	181	6,290	50,700,000
Warna	Warna	India	E,G	91	1,580	15,310	964,000

[1] Having a height exceeding 150 m (492 ft); or having a volume content exceeding 15 million cu m (19.6 cu yd); or forming a reservoir exceeding 14,800 × 10[6] cu m of capacity (12 million ac-ft).
[2] Type of dam: E = earth; R = rockfill; A = arch; G = gravity.

(T. W. MERMEL)

and financiers build a road or bridge, operate it as a toll facility to recoup their investment, and then turn it over to the government after a specified period, was gaining ground in the United States, Europe, and Asia.

Maintenance of aging and overused road networks continued to be a problem. The World Bank estimated that in 85 less developed countries one-quarter of the paved roads and one-third of the unpaved roads outside urban areas needed reconstruction, while 40% needed strengthening, at a total cost of $90 million.

In the U.S., 98% of the 68,500-km (1 km = 0.62 mi) Interstate System was open to traffic. More than 8,000 km were in unsatisfactory condition, however, and the cost of restoring the system to 1983 standards was estimated at $84 billion. California was preparing to build its first toll highway at a cost of $2 billion, one of eight toll roads in the U.S. to be partially financed by federal funds. Canada was planning to upgrade large segments of its Trans-Canada Highway after 20 years of service and was considering expanding its 840,000-km national highway system significantly.

In Chile 1,000 km of the main highway stretching south from the city of Puerto Montt opened up a previously inaccessible area of the country. A key segment of the Cochabamba–Santa Cruz Highway, serving one of the most productive agricultural areas in Bolivia, was opened. Argentina's 5,200-km Route 40, paved for only 800 km, was to be upgraded to a modern high-capacity highway.

China planned to build one million kilometres of roads by 1990. Construction was to begin in 1989 on the 345-km highway between Chengdu (Chengtu) and Chongqing (Chungking). A 142-km, $275 million expressway was under construction in the Beijing–Tianjin (Tientsin)–Tanggu (T'ang-ku) corridor, one of China's most industrialized and congested areas. The 302-km superhighway from Hong Kong to Guangzhou (Canton) was under construction and was expected to be completed in 1994.

A six-lane, 40-km elevated highway in Bangkok, Thailand, was to be privately built at a cost of $700 million. The last 202-km segment of the East-West Highway in Nepal, under construction since 1985, was to be completed in 1989.

A new financing program for Australia would assure improved access to the country's ports and terminals. Australia was building a privately financed and operated toll road near Newcastle, New South Wales.

A train emerges from Japan's recently opened Seikan tunnel, the world's longest undersea tunnel. About 54 kilometres (33 miles) long, it links Honshu, the main island, with the northern island of Hokkaido.
AP/WIDE WORLD

The United Nations recommended formation of an African Highway Development Association to coordinate the Trans-African Highway network. A bypass was to be built around Nairobi, Kenya, to reduce congestion. The Nigerian government awarded a $28 million contract to a consortium of Nigerian and Italian companies to build a 223-km expressway between Kaduna and Kano. The 146-km N'Djamena–Guelingdeng–Djermaya road in Chad, critical to the nation's north–south transportation, was to be paved. Malawi planned construction of a $108 million northern access corridor highway. Reconstruction of the major freeway linking Pretoria and Johannesburg in South Africa was in progress.

Construction of the first segment of the 41-km Amman–Dead Sea road in Jordan was under way. Turkey was planning an $8.6 billion network of 3,200 km of expressways, including the 140-km, $280 million motorway under construction from Edirne to Kinali.

More than 2,000 km of the 10,000-km Trans-European North-South Motorway (TEM) had been built by the end of 1988, and an additional 4,500 km were either being designed or under construction. In France the 72-km segment of the expressway between Clermont-Ferrand and Montmarault was opened to traffic. Finland implemented a $937 million, ten-year road and bridge rehabilitation program financed by the forestry industry.

(HUGH M. GILLESPIE)

Tunnels. Following a trend established in recent years, the demand for and interest in transport-related projects continued, especially in Europe, where the progress of the Channel Tunnel provided a focus of attention for financiers, engineers, the press, and the general public. This £5 billion, privately funded project would create by means of three tunnels, a service tunnel plus two operating tunnels, with diameters between 4.8 m and 7.6 m, the first fixed railway link between the United Kingdom and France.

When completed, these would be the world's longest undersea tunnels, 38 km under the Strait of Dover and 50 km long from portal to portal. The Seikan rail tunnel under the Tsugaru Strait in Japan, now open to traffic after 24 years of construction, was longer overall (54 km) but at 23.3 km was shorter undersea.

The first year of construction on the tunnel by Trans-manche-Link (TML), a joint venture of ten British and French construction groups, was a mixture of impressive achievements and some early setbacks, almost inevitable on such a huge and complex project with so many independently operated construction activities. Eleven tunnel-boring machines (TBMs) were to be employed, and four of them were installed and launched during the year.

Boring of the service tunnel, however, fell behind schedule on both sides of the Channel. The French were held up by delivery problems on the first TBM, a U.S. and Japanese prototype mixed-face machine, and encountered extraordinarily difficult ground almost immediately. Early progress was slow, but improved outputs were beginning to win back some of the four months lost in the waterlogged chalk strata. The second French TBM, a 300-ton, 5.7-m-diameter Mitsubishi slurry shield, was successfully boring the 3.2-km service tunnel back to the rail terminal site at Coquelles.

At Shakespeare Cliff, Dover, the British tunnelers had been targeted to bore five kilometres of the service tunnel by November 1. Progress was frustrated by the effect of groundwater percolation through tiny fissures in the chalk marls. This produced local instability in the tunnel roof, hindering the placement of the precast concrete linings behind the TBM. Nevertheless, as many as 145 m were bored in a full week.

In Denmark a decision was made to construct the 7,850,-000,000 kroner Great Belt Crossing, which would provide a 16-km fixed link across the waterways that separate Copenhagen from the rest of Europe. An eight-kilometre tunnel was to carry a twin-track railway under the Eastern Channel between Sprogo and Halsskor (Zealand), while a bridge would span the eight-kilometre Western Channel.

The linking of North Africa and Europe grew a step nearer when Spain and Morocco cooperated to produce feasibility studies for crossing the Strait of Gibraltar. Although only 13.8 km at its narrowest, the Strait would require a railway tunnel of some 50 km, with 27 km needed below sea level to achieve practical track gradients. These requirements were comparable to those of the Channel Tunnel, and the two governments would obviously take advantage of any information that emanated from that project.

In North America the continent's longest railway tun-

nel, 14.7 km, was completed. Passing beneath Cheops Mountain, Rodgers Pass, and Mt. MacDonald, the tunnel took the Canadian Pacific railroad between Calgary and Vancouver. The tunneling took six years and was accomplished by use of a combination of hard-rock TBM and conventional drill-and-blast methods.

(GEOFFREY J. NOBLETT)

This article updates the *Macropædia* articles BUILDING CONSTRUCTION; PUBLIC WORKS.

Environment

The political influence of environmentalist "green" parties waned during 1988 in much of Western Europe, but strong and outspoken groups emerged in the U.S.S.R. and several Eastern European countries.

The deaths from disease of large numbers of seals in the North Sea outraged public opinion and drew attention to the generally poor condition of the sea. Agreements were reached to end the dumping of waste in the North Sea and waste incineration at sea throughout the world. The scandal surrounding the discovery in Nigeria of a large dump of leaking drums of industrial wastes and subsequent efforts to dispose of them reinforced UN demands that the international trade in toxic wastes be strictly regulated.

The U.S. and the European Communities (EC) agreed to reduce production of chlorofluorocarbons (CFCs) to below the levels stipulated in the 1987 Montreal Protocol, mainly because these chemicals contributed strongly to the greenhouse effect. Scientists warned that the North American drought and severe floods, especially in The Sudan and Bangladesh, might be linked to the greenhouse warming, and by the latter part of the year it seemed probable that attempts would soon begin to reach an international agreement restricting emissions of carbon dioxide and other greenhouse gases.

In December the national science academies of the U.S. and the U.S.S.R. announced plans to form a joint Committee on Global Ecology Concerns. The committee hoped to provide an early warning mechanism for identifying long-range environmental and ecological problems.

INTERNATIONAL COOPERATION

In 1988 the World Bank reassessed its $6,860,000 program of development projects in light of the 1987 decision to consider their environmental consequences. On March 3 the bank's vice-president in charge of policy, giving the World Wildlife Fund's annual World Conservation Lecture in London, said the review covered 500 projects already begun and 300 that were being planned. The bank was especially concerned about problems arising from the greenhouse effect.

In September the bank held a meeting with the International Monetary Fund in Berlin at which the director of the bank's environmental department welcomed the increasing recognition by Western political leaders of the importance of environmental issues. He referred in particular to a speech highlighting environmental problems delivered to the Royal Society of London on September 27 by British Prime Minister Margaret Thatcher and to Chancellor Helmut Kohl's promise of major West German funding for projects in tropical countries that agreed to preserve their rain forests.

The UN Environment Program (UNEP) and the World Health Organization published joint reports in September on the pollution of air, water, and food. They estimated that 625 million people, mostly in less developed countries, were exposed to unacceptably high levels of sulfur dioxide and that another 550 million were exposed to levels close to the acceptable limit. Fewer than one-fifth of city dwellers, about 350 million people, were exposed to acceptable levels of dust and smoke, compared with 1,250,000,000 people living in unacceptable conditions and 200 million with smoke and dust levels approaching the acceptable limit. About 10% of the world's rivers were described as "polluted," the Ganges being probably the most polluted of all, and in China 25% of all lakes were eutrophic (deficient in oxygen). Brazil, China, India, Indonesia, Mexico, and Nigeria were among the countries in which major threats existed from water pollution. The levels of contamination of foodstuffs were generally well below danger limits in industrialized countries, although mercury and polychlorinated biphenyls (PCBs) were sometimes found in fish,

AP/WIDE WORLD

A boy hurries past a burning stretch of Brazil's Amazon Rain Forest. Brazilian landowners have burned tens of thousands of square kilometres to clear the forested land for farming and development, despite the concern among environmentalists about the enormity of the destruction and the vast emissions of carbon dioxide caused by the fires.

lead in canned foods, and aflatoxins in nuts and cereals. In less developed countries there were risks to health from organochlorine pesticides and aflatoxins.

Unusually heavy rains in North Africa led to enormous swarms of desert locusts in late 1987 and 1988. Despite concerted international efforts under the auspices of the UN Food and Agriculture Organization, the problem grew into the worst infestation since the 1950s, with billions of insects ravaging crops throughout the region. In October locusts were reportedly sighted on several Caribbean islands.

NATIONAL DEVELOPMENTS

U.K. On July 3 an EC directive came into force that required an environmental-impact assessment of any development likely to have a significant effect on the flora, fauna, or cultural heritage of the area concerned. The new rules covered many changes in land use previously exempt from planning controls, including oil and gas installations, opencast mines of more than 51 ha (125 ac), forestry, land drainage, fish farming, road building, and overhead power line construction.

The government was criticized for failing to provide adequately for the implementation of antipollution legislation or for environmental research. The 12th report of the Royal Commission on Environmental Pollution, published on February 24, said the pollution inspectorate had insufficient powers or funds to monitor industrial emissions and enforce the law, and the 1988 annual report of the Natural Environment Research Council, published on February 29, set out the consequences of the reduction in its income. A shortfall of £22 million predicted for 1989–90 was projected to rise to £38 million by 1993–94.

Hungary. It was announced in January that the government had formed an environmental ministry, headed by Laszlo Marothy. Hungary had the largest environmental movement in Eastern Europe, led by the Danube Circle.

Controversy continued to surround the proposed Czechoslovak-Hungarian Gabcikovo-Nagymaros River Barrage Scheme, involving the building of a dam and power station at Nagymaros. An artificial lake at Hrusov, east of Bratislava, and a northward diversion of the Danube along a 23-km (14-mi) concrete channel were also required in order to compensate for large changes in water level due to artificial waves produced by the complementary Czechoslo-

vak system, which was nearing completion. There were demonstrations by opponents in May; the Nagymaros Action Committee, comprising 15 pressure groups, held a scientific conference in early September; and on September 12 more than 20,000 people met in Lajos Kossuth Square in Budapest to protest against the scheme. In addition to the unofficial groups, opponents included the official Society for the Protection of the Environment, the Academy of Sciences, eight ministries including the Ministry of Health, and many members of Parliament. However, the Hungarian government would have been liable to pay about £600 million compensation to the Czechoslovak and Austrian governments if it withdrew, and in October it decided to proceed with the project.

Japan. The Environment Ministry on May 20 reported that Japan consumed more than 10% of the world total of CFCs, carbon dioxide emissions were increasing faster than those in any Western country, and rain was acidified throughout the country, but strict controls had held down emissions of sulfur dioxide and nitrogen oxides. The annual report said Japan accounted for 52% of the world total of imports of unprocessed tropical timber, mostly from Malaysia, making it a major force in the destruction of tropical forests. The ministry recommended the inclusion of environmental-impact assessments in all aid programs.

Sweden. In the September 18 general election the Greens won more than 4% of the vote, for the first time entitling them to 20 seats in the Riksdag (parliament). They had campaigned for increased spending on environmental programs and acceleration of the plan to close all Swedish nuclear power stations.

U.S. The first part of California's Safe Drinking Water and Toxic Enforcement Act, 1986, came into force in February and the second part in October. The act listed a total of 178 substances classed as carcinogenic or teratogenic and established heavy fines for industrial polluters. In June the Occupational Safety and Health Administration set new standards for exposure of workers to more than 400 industrial chemicals.

Recommendations for the reorganization of the Environmental Protection Agency (EPA) were published in September following a study by a committee of members of the EPA Science Advisory Board. Recommendations included creating an Environmental Research Institute to lead a national research program, setting up a council to

AP/WIDE WORLD

Drums of toxic waste sit near the Nigerian city of Koko, where an Italian firm had secretly dumped them. Because many industrialized nations were shipping toxic wastes to third world countries unable to handle them safely, the UN had begun talks aimed at drafting a treaty that would regulate the international shipment of hazardous wastes.

Extreme weather conditions such as the severe drought suffered by U.S. farmers (left) and the storms that triggered excessive flooding in Bangladesh (right) were linked by some scientists to the greenhouse effect and focused international attention on its implications.
(LEFT) ERIC HYLDEN—GAMMA/LIAISON; (RIGHT) CHIP HIRES—GAMMA/LIAISON

define the most important areas of concern, and changing the post of assistant administrator from a political to a career appointment. To finance this the committee recommended doubling the $317 million EPA annual budget over five years.

In June a congressional report and a separate report by Radioactive Waste Campaign, a New York-based environmental group, criticized the handling of hazardous and radioactive wastes by the Departments of Defense and Energy. In New Jersey a military arsenal had seriously contaminated groundwater with trichloroethylene, and the same chemical, as well as arsenic and heavy metals, from McClellan Air Force Base had led to the closure of 12 wells near Sacramento, Calif. In 1987 and 1988 safety concerns led to the closure of several nuclear-fuel-processing plants, including the Hanford facility at Richland, Wash., the Rocky Flats plant in Golden, Colo., and the Savannah River complex near Aiken, S.C. In October the reprocessing plant at Fernald, Ohio, was shut down by a strike amid charges that it had released radioactive particles into the air and dumped highly radioactive wastes into storm sewers. Waste leaking from buried drums at the Lawrence Livermore National Laboratory in California had contaminated groundwater, but the laboratory announced plans to build a waste-treatment plant and to start a $60 million cleanup of the burial site. A Department of Energy report released in December cited 155 instances of contamination at 16 nuclear weapons plants and laboratories and acknowledged that in some cases they constituted a serious threat to public health.

U.S.S.R. In February a new law came into force under which those who damaged the environment were held financially responsible and offending enterprises could be closed.

On June 30 at the Communist Party conference, a steelworker called for an emergency program to reduce air pollution in 60 cities. The following day the head of the environmental protection committee formed in January called for scientists, builders, and planners to be punished if their activities caused environmental damage.

It was reported in early July that the Estonian Communist Party had authorized the formation of a green movement, to be part of the international green movement. It would oppose nuclear power, start a news agency, and run candidates in local elections.

West Germany. By the end of 1987 the Green Party had split into three factions. At its three-day conference, held in Bonn in June 1988, no resolutions were passed and no executives were elected.

Environment ministers of East and West Germany agreed in July on a collaborative program for environmental improvement. The agreement did not include details of financing, however, or plans to clean up the Elbe River, for the pollution of which the West Germans held the East Germans almost wholly responsible.

The Greenhouse Effect. In late October 1987 an iceberg 6,500 sq km (2,500 sq mi) in area and 230 m (750 ft) thick broke away from the Ross Ice Shelf in Antarctica. Evidence that the ice cap was shrinking was presented in August: from satellite photographs at a meeting of the Geographical Congress in Sydney, Australia, and from studies on Signy Island at a conference on Antarctica, held in Hobart, Tasmania. In March a spokesman from the U.S. National Oceanographic and Atmospheric Administration told a conference in California that 1987 had been the warmest year in a phase of rapid warming and suggested a link between the especially warm years of 1980, 1983, and 1987 and the El Niño warming trend in the Pacific Ocean. The year 1988 was warmer even than 1987, and serious drought conditions contributed to widespread fires in the western U.S. Heavy rains in Australia and severe flooding in southern China, The Sudan, and Bangladesh, linked to the greenhouse warming, were associated with a trough in the El Niño cycle, called La Niña, that might bring cooler conditions later. (*See* EARTH SCIENCES.)

The implications of the greenhouse effect dominated a conference on "The Changing Atmosphere: Implications for Global Security," sponsored by the Canadian government with the support of UNEP and the World Meteorological Organization and held in Toronto June 27–30.

The more than 300 scientists and policymakers from 48 countries, the UN, and other international agencies who attended heard predictions that by the mid-2030s the warming would be most intense in high latitudes, the world's grain belts would become drier, and rises in sea level would affect people living in deltas and low-lying coastal areas. Large areas in low latitudes might become unsuitable for growing wheat, but corn (maize) yields might increase and rice yields might not be affected. The conference called for a "law of the atmosphere," the establishment of a "world atmosphere fund," and a global reduction in carbon dioxide emissions by 20% from 1988 levels by 2005.

The Ozone Layer. The 1987 Montreal Protocol came into force on December 16 after the EC filed its formal ratification notice. The treaty would freeze production of CFCs from July 1, 1989, reduce it by 20% from 1992, and cut it by a further 30% in 1998, but it soon became clear that a much larger reduction would be needed to stabilize the ozone layer. In Britain a report from the House of Lords Committee on the European Community published on August 2, and another from the Stratospheric Ozone Review Group published on October 4, called for an 85% reduction, and the government agreed to aim for this target as quickly as possible. In the U.S. the EPA called for a complete phasing out of CFCs. The West German Environment Ministry urged a reduction of 85–95% by the year 2000.

Major manufacturers, led by Du Pont de Nemours on March 25 and ICI on October 4, announced they would phase out production of CFCs. Many companies using CFCs said they would henceforth market only products they could label "ozone friendly."

In October 1987 the ozone layer over Antarctica was depleted by 97.5% at the 70-millibar level, and the depletion lasted three weeks longer than usual in November. In late 1987 and early 1988 a smaller "ozone hole" was observed in the Arctic, with a 50% depletion at a height of about 20 km (66,000 ft).

Further U.S. studies of data from the Nimbus-7 satellite were reported in March 1988 by the Ozone Trends Panel. Over middle and low latitudes a slight thinning of the ozone layer from 1978 halted in 1985 owing to increased

Contaminated medical syringes—like those found on Staten Island's Midland Beach—and such other pollutants as toxic chemicals and raw sewage were turning up along the U.S. coasts.
SUDHIR—PICTURE GROUP

solar activity, and the layer might thicken until 1991, when solar activity would decrease and the thinning might resume. Over the tropics, and especially North Africa, the National Center for Atmospheric Research reported an increase in ozone over land, coinciding with forest and grass fires, and a slight decrease over the oceans.

Antarctica. A convention to govern mining was adopted by 33 countries on June 22. Sponsoring governments would be held responsible for restoration of the environment by operators, and the convention would be administered by an Antarctic Minerals Resources Commission based in New Zealand.

In August a report by Bruce Manheim of the Environmental Defense Fund said McMurdo Sound was polluted by raw sewage, PCBs, and heavy metals including lead and cadmium from British bases and U.S. bases run by the National Science Foundation (NSF). Manheim said the NSF should have produced regulations on waste disposal under the Antarctic Conservation Act, 1978, but had issued only guidelines. He reported that all wastes were removed from Australian bases, sewage from Polish bases was filtered, and incinerator emissions were controlled at Australian and New Zealand bases.

Air Pollution. EC environment ministers agreed in December 1987 on limits to emissions from vehicles, but during 1988 several countries found the agreement unacceptable. Denmark wanted stricter standards than those proposed. In June France accepted a standard test cycle limit of eight grams of nitrogen oxides and hydrocarbons for cars of less than 1.4 litres capacity, but West Germany insisted on stricter standards after 1993, and in July France said it could not accept eight grams unless it was for five years. The Dutch wanted lower taxes to reduce by about 5% the purchase price of cars, in effect fitted with catalytic converters, emitting no more than five grams.

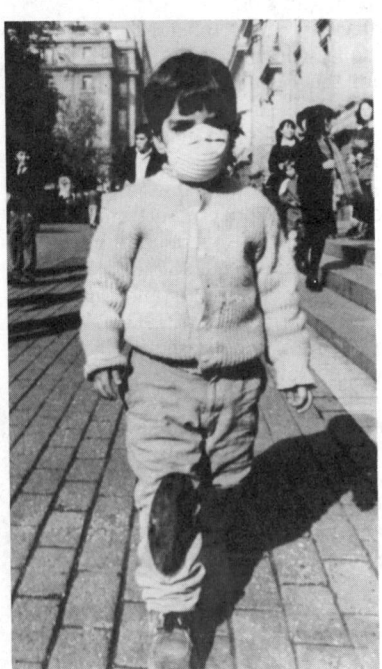

AFP PHOTO

A boy in Santiago, Chile, wears a surgical mask to protect himself from the noxious gases in the air. A lack of rain caused the city's air pollution to build to dangerous levels and hang overhead for days.

In April Canada discussed with the U.S.S.R. ways to decrease haze in the Arctic that was reducing visibility for aircraft. The haze was caused mainly by sulfur, of which 42% came from the U.S.S.R., 27% from Eastern Europe, 25% from Western Europe, and 6% from North America.

Qu Geping (Ch'ü Ko-p'ing), head of the Chinese State Environmental Protection Agency, was quoted in *China Youth News* on April 19 as saying that permitted levels for soot and sulfur dioxide were being exceeded in 60 cities. Beijing (Peking) residents were to be supplied with low-sulfur coal; factories would be required to install filters; and the city's 400,000 vehicles would have to be fitted with antipollution devices.

A report on the environment commissioned by the Polish government and published in March said that nearly 4.3 million tons of sulfur dioxide were being released annually, about 40% of it from the industrial region of Upper Silesia. If the trend continued, the report said, emissions would reach 7 million tons by 1990.

Acid Rain. During his visit to Washington on April 26–27, Canadian Prime Minister Brian Mulroney told Congress that acid rain had killed the fish in 15,000 Canadian lakes and a further 300,000 lakes were threatened. In May there were fears that dieback in maple trees south of Quebec might harm the maple syrup industry. In August U.S. Pres. Ronald Reagan agreed that U.S. nitrogen oxide emissions should be frozen at their 1987 level, in accordance with Canadian proposals.

In October 1987 the British Central Electricity Generating Board had announced a ten-year program to fit flue-gas desulfurization equipment to three power stations and so reduce sulfur dioxide emissions in Britain by 15%. In June 1988 at a meeting of EC environment ministers, the government agreed to go further and reduce its emissions to 20% below the 1980 level by 1993, 40% by 1998, and 60% by 2003. All new coal-fired power stations of more than 50 MW and possibly additional existing stations would be equipped with desulfurization units, and many smaller existing stations would be closed.

A Swiss report published in November 1987 said more than half the country's trees were diseased, and symptoms were spreading from conifers into broad-leaved species. The Jura region, where 61% of trees were sick or dying, was the most severely affected. A West German report, also published in November 1987, said the number of dead trees had decreased slightly in the country as a whole, although tree health had deteriorated in Saarland and Schleswig-Holstein. A 1987 survey by the British Forestry Commission indicated that in Britain climate might have more influence on tree health than pollution.

Freshwater Pollution. In Britain the Water Authorities Association and the Ministry of Agriculture, Fisheries and Food announced on June 6 that in 1987 there had been 3,890 pollution incidents, an increase of 13% from 1986. Effluent from silage and from intensive pig farms were the most common causes. EC rules on the quality of drinking water came into force in April 1988. Proposals to end or reduce fertilizer use in about 570,000 ha (1.4 million ac) of "nitrate protection zones" above aquifers or porous rocks in order to keep the nitrate content below the 50-mg-per-litre limit led to disagreements when the Department of the Environment refused to pay compensation demanded by farmers.

On May 20 Chinese police broke up demonstrations by more than 1,000 people who had camped on the slope of a dam at Guci, about 48 km (30 mi) from Beijing, to prevent the release into nearby fields of reservoir water contaminated by an oil refinery. The sluices were opened the following morning, and the authorities promised compensation to peasants who said they had been poisoned.

In Czechoslovakia the discovery in February of fish contaminated with up to ten times the permitted levels of PCBs led in August to a ban on the consumption of fish from a 2,000-sq km (5,180-sq mi) area in western Bohemia, including the Orlik reservoir on the Vltava River. The contamination was believed to have been caused by an industrial leak in October 1986.

Supplies of drinking water to some 23,000 residents of suburban Pittsburgh, Pa., were cut off after a storage tank at Floreffe, Pa., spilled about 3.3 million litres (860,000 gal) of diesel oil into the Monongahela River on January 2. The oil slick spread into West Virginia, and by January 10 it was 77 km (48 mi) long and had reached Steubenville, Ohio. The oil was eventually cleared by a combination of inflatable booms with deep skirts, activated carbon, and bentonite.

The first environmental discussions ever held between the U.S.S.R. and Mongolia took place in Ulan Bator in July and concerned Lakes Baikal and Huvsgul. Deforestation in Mongolia had decreased the flow of water in the Selenge River, which supplied about 60% of Baikal water.

Marine Pollution. The UN International Maritime Organization announced on January 11 that from the end of 1988 ships would be forbidden to dump plastics and other synthetic wastes overboard, and the dumping of food wastes and other garbage would be strictly controlled.

About 3,000 tons of oil escaped from an Italian tanker off the French coast in January and formed a slick 300 km (185 mi) long, contaminating beaches in Brittany. In early July municipal beaches in New York City and New Jersey were closed when sewage and medical debris, including syringes and vials of AIDS-infected blood, washed ashore. The resulting furor made such pollution problems a leading issue in the U.S. presidential campaign. The head of the Athens-based UNEP Mediterranean Action Plan said on July 26 that about 80% of Mediterranean beaches were clean and safe for bathing, compared with 65% in 1975, owing to the provision of more sewage-treatment facilities and better control of dumping. Industrial pollutants continued to reach the sea from the Rhône, Po, Nile, and Ebro rivers, but Italy had planned a $3.5 million program to clean the Po.

Environment ministers from seven countries bordering the North Sea agreed in November 1987 to end all dumping of toxic wastes in the sea by the end of 1989, to halt the incineration of wastes at sea by the end of 1994, and to reduce substantially the discharge of harmful substances into rivers, estuaries, and coastal waters. The incineration ban was extended to all seas by an agreement reached on October 6 at the annual meeting of the London Dumping Convention.

A large bloom of the toxic alga *Chrysochromulina polylepsis* killed tens of thousands of fish in the Baltic and northern North seas between mid-May and mid-June. High concentrations of plant nutrients in coastal waters were suspected of contributing to such blooms, which had been increasing for 25 years, but the cause remained unknown.

Toxic Wastes. In June UNEP Executive Director Mostafa Tolba said in Nairobi, Kenya, that UNEP was sponsoring a working group to establish the technical and legal details of a treaty to control international trade in toxic waste, which he hoped would be ready for ratification by March 1989. At the June meeting of EC environment ministers, however, Britain and France blocked moves to restrict shipments of wastes to third world countries and to enforce a 1987 EC directive that would ban such exports

unless the receiving country could deal with the material. The Norwegian authorities agreed in June to remove 15,000 tons of ash, originating in Philadelphia, that had damaged vegetation on the Guinean island of Kassa. Côte d'Ivoire legislated against waste dumping in its territorial waters, but Benin and Guinea-Bissau reportedly agreed to accept some wastes.

On June 5 the Nigerian authorities discovered 2,100 tons of wastes near Koko and seized the Italian ship *Piave,* which had dumped it. On inspection the waste was found to consist of about 10,000 drums, each containing 225 litres of flammable solvents and probably PCBs. The drums were unshaded, and there was risk of fire. Ambiente, the waste-handling subsidiary of the Italian state-owned company ENI, the original source of the waste, commissioned two German ships, the *Karin B* and *Deep Sea Carrier,* to remove the drums, together with about 2,000 tons of soil on which they had stood. The *Karin B* sailed from Koko on July 31 and the *Deep Sea Carrier* on August 15, but they were refused entry by Spain, France, Belgium, West Germany, Britain, and The Netherlands. On September 2 the Italian authorities said the wastes would be allowed into Italy and, despite vigorous local protests, arrangements were made for the *Karin B* to discharge at Livorno and the *Deep Sea Carrier* at Ravenna. In November the freighter *Pelicano,* which had been at sea for two years with 13 million kg (28 million lb) of toxic ash from Philadelphia, unloaded its cargo, but the final destination of the ash was not revealed. The 19-year-old ship, registered at various times in Liberia, The Bahamas, and Honduras, had been refused permission to dock by at least 11 countries.

The illegal import into Romania of 2,400 tons of industrial wastes through the free port of Sulina was reported in June to have led to the dismissal of the foreign trade minister and two other high officials and public reprimands or warnings to five others. Senior officials at the port and of the Chimica Bucharest Co. faced prosecution.

In Britain, the Inspectorate of Pollution reported on May 4 that of about 1,300 waste-disposal sites where leaks of methane from waste dumps presented a safety risk, 600 urgently needed gas controls, and there were 100 where gas had been detected at or near housing. The inspectorate estimated that 60% of the 4,000 dumps in use and 75% of those closed in the past ten years could also pose a threat. There were 14 occasions in 1987 when people had been evacuated from their homes because of such leaks. Plans to use 1.9 million tons a year of domestic waste from New York to generate methane in Cheshire and Cornwall brought local protests and, on June 10, a more formal objection from the Royal Commission on Environmental Pollution, and the scheme was dropped. Regulations to control the import of wastes came into force on November 14, in accordance with the 1984 EC Directive on the Transfrontier Shipment of Hazardous Wastes.

At a conference of science and technology ministers from Caribbean countries, held in Port of Spain, Trinidad, on March 12–13, alarm was expressed about the dumping of U.S. wastes. In early 1988 Haiti allowed 4,000 tons of waste from Philadelphia to be dumped on a beach near Gonaives, and the Turks and Caicos Islands were said to be negotiating waste-import deals with U.S. companies.

The U.S. EPA announced in August that four sites in Massachusetts and New Hampshire, where the Cannons Engineering Corp. dumped waste oils, solvents, and other toxic substances illegally, were to be cleaned up at a cost of $49 million. In September the U.S. Energy Department postponed indefinitely the scheduled opening of the Waste Isolation Pilot Plant near Carlsbad, N.M. The facility would be the first permanent repository for high-level radioactive wastes.

Radon. In Britain and the U.S. there were reports that radon levels in many homes were higher than had been estimated earlier. The British government set a maximum level of 400 and the U.S. a limit of 150 becquerels of radiation per cubic metre of air. The Institution of Environmental Health Officers later proposed that the British level be halved. The British National Radiological Protection Board reported in June that its study of 3,500 homes had led it to estimate that radon caused 1,500 of the 40,000 British lung cancer deaths a year. The U.S. Surgeon General's Office issued a "health advisory" in September declaring radon a national health hazard and recommending that all homes be tested. Of the 136,000 U.S. lung cancer deaths each year, it was estimated that up to 20,000 might be due to radon. In late September, however, evidence was presented at a meeting of the American Chemical Society disputing the connection between radon and lung cancer.

(MICHAEL ALLABY)

WILDLIFE CONSERVATION

The Scientific Committee of the International Whaling Commission (IWC) met on Dec. 15–17, 1987, to discuss Japan's new scientific whaling proposal, which involved killing 300 minke whales in the Antarctic. The meeting refused to endorse the research, and Britain proposed a condemnatory resolution and called for a postal ballot of IWC members, which passed in February 1988. On Dec. 22, 1987, however, a Japanese whaling ship had sailed for Antarctica, returning in April after killing 273 minke whales. The U.S. Department of Commerce declared Japan in violation of the moratorium on whaling in February, and in April it ended all Japanese fishing in U.S. waters. In May the IWC recommended that research whaling proposed by Norway and Iceland should not take place, but in June the U.S., in a bilateral agreement, endorsed a research kill of 68 fin whales and 10 sei whales by Iceland and negotiated with Norway over a new research proposal before removing its threat of sanctions for going against the moratorium. The IWC approved quotas for aboriginal whaling of 60 minkes and 23 fin whales for Greenland and 44 bowheads over three years for North American Eskimos. Although Japan did not present a new research

AP/WIDE WORLD

The Northern spotted owl was added to the endangered species list—an action that would end logging and development in parts of the bird's Pacific Northwest habitat.

proposal at the IWC meeting, its fleet was reported to be preparing to set out for Antarctica in November.

On January 14 it was reported that a specimen of *Exsul singularus* had been found in southern New Zealand. This five-centimetre (two-inch)-long fly, which was believed to be the rarest fly in the world, had not been seen since 1941. A new species of lemur, *Hapalemur aureus,* from southeastern Madagascar was reported in January. It was extremely rare and was endangered by the destruction of its rain forest home. Also in January, at an international workshop in Vietnam, an agreement was reached on a survival plan for a rare species of wild cattle, the kouprey (*Bos sauveli*). The kouprey survived in small numbers in remote areas of Vietnam, Laos, and Kampuchea, and the first priority was to establish transfrontier reserves.

In late February the captive breeding project for the giant tortoise (*Geochelone elephantopus*), which had started in 1965, released its 1,000th tortoise into the wild on the Galápagos Islands. In March, in the Virolin area of Colombia, the gorgeted wood quail (*Odontophorus strophium*) was rediscovered, having been known to science only from eight museum specimens, the last collected in 1981.

In Queensland conservationists continued the fight to save caves on Mt. Etna from being blasted by Queensland Cement Ltd. The caves were home to the vulnerable Australian ghost bat (*Macroderma gigas*) and Australia's largest breeding colony of little bent-winged bats (*Miniopterus australis*). Experienced cavers occupied the caves in April to stop the blasting, while a boycott was called on all products made by the cement company. Many of the caves had already been destroyed, and conservationists had been campaigning for more than 20 years to have Mt. Etna declared a national park.

On April 4 Thailand shelved plans to build the controversial Nam Choan Dam, saving the Thung Yai Wildlife Sanctuary from flooding. The area contained several rare mammals, and the flooding would have seriously affected the almost extinct white-winged wood duck (*Cairina scutulata*) and the green peafowl (*Pavo muticus*).

One of North America's rarest mammals, the black-footed ferret (*Mustela nigripes*), believed to be extinct in the wild, produced 38 pups in the second season of captive breeding. The colony now numbered more than 60, and reintroduction into the wild in the early 1990s seemed likely. On April 29 the first egg ever produced by a pair of captive California condors (*Gymnogyps californianus*) hatched at the San Diego (Calif.) Wild Animal Park. In addition to the chick, there were 27 California condors left alive, all in captivity. In May an expedition that set out to find the giant earwig (*Labidura herculeana*) and the giant ground beetle (*Aplothorax burchelli*) on Saint Helena in the Atlantic Ocean returned disappointed, and the insects were assumed to be extinct. In July a description was published of a newly discovered monkey from Gabon's equatorial rain forest, the sun-tailed guenon (*Cercopithecus solatus*).

The year was marked by several fires in protected areas. In early 1988 fire swept through the Walter T. Deininger National Park in El Salvador, causing wildlife to flee. Hundreds of animals, including endangered species, were shot or captured. The destruction was described as the country's greatest ecological tragedy in 20 years; most wildlife in the country was near extinction. Fire also damaged two-thirds of the 132,000-ha (326,000-ac) Emas National Park in central Brazil in August, killing an incalculable number of animals. In the U.S. about 45% of Yellowstone National Park's 890,000 ha (2.2 million ac) was burned—with about 8,000 ha (20,000 ac) virtually destroyed—and despite a massive fire-fighting effort, the fires did not die

out until the autumn brought snow. The fires renewed the argument between those who claimed that letting natural fires burn was environmentally beneficial and critics who blamed that policy for delays in fighting the fires and the resultant destruction. A government report issued in December concluded that the federal policy was basically sound but its execution had been flawed.

Poachers continued to take their toll of Africa's black rhinoceros. Zimbabwe, which with 2,000 rhinos had the biggest remaining population, intensified its antipoaching operations after having lost 427 rhinos over a four-year period. In Kenya, where poachers killed a rhino in a fenced private sanctuary in March, the president ordered game rangers to shoot poachers. Hong Kong announced new legislation on July 29 under which worked ivory could be imported only when proper permits had been issued by the Convention on International Trade in Endangered Species of Wild Fauna and Flora (raw ivory imports were already banned). This closed the loophole whereby Hong Kong traders had set up factories in Dubai, which had no restrictions on the trade, to carve illegally obtained raw ivory.

Between April and October in the Baltic and North seas, about 10,000 common, or harbour, seals (*Phoca vitulina*) died from a virus indistinguishable from the one that causes canine distemper. PCBs were suspected of contributing to the problem by damaging the immune system of the mammals. In September it was reported that Soviet scientists had also identified canine distemper virus as the cause of a mysterious illness among seals (*Phoca siberica*) in Lake Baikal in April.　　　　(JACQUI M. MORRIS)

See also Agriculture and Food Supplies; Botanical Gardens and Zoos; Energy; Life Sciences; Transportation.

This article updates the *Macropædia* article CONSERVATION OF NATURAL RESOURCES.

Fashion and Dress

The fashions of 1988 demanded a streamlined figure. The "leggy" look of 1987 no longer made the grade for 1988 styles. Slender figures were required for both the long and mannish and the short and feminine winter coats. The long coat, just above the ankles, was relaxed and casual in subdued colours—burnt orange, caramel, mole, or plain black. It was worn over tight pants or thermal pants. The short version, above the knee, was playful in shape and colour, the latter ranging from azalea pink to vivid turquoise. This coat, belted and flared, was featured with a narrow, above-the-knee skirt and opaque black hose.

For spring a raincoat, belted and with pushed-up sleeves, was worn unbuttoned at the top and looked more like a dress, particularly when worn with a dashing wide-brimmed fedora hat or a perky little straw boater. Many raincoats sported a knotted scarf that was tied at the neck, either in the front or back or, sometimes, at the waist. The fabric was lightweight acrylic, plain or in small patterns, checked or hair-lined, more or less tone on tone. Plain silk taffeta in muted shades looked juvenile and breezy. An oily and inky look provided a dramatic counterpart.

The new spring outfit featured unmatched separate pieces assembled to break the total look of the traditional suit, which slipped out of vogue. Tops were tailored with squared-off shoulders, mannish, and hitting mid-thigh level, leaving very little visibility for the withering skirt. Bermudas, instead of a skirt, were occasionally worn with a lengthened safari jacket. Swapping was the mood, and combinations from two different outfits were preferred to one that matched. A tweed jacket was paired with a plain

Floral patterns sprang into style in bold prints.
Brilliant colours and striking patterns typified
1988 fashions, as did great variety in hemlines,
which ranged from ultramini to ankle length.
NIALL MCINERNEY

linen or silk miniskirt. The fancy skirt was worn with a plain cotton or gabardine jacket.

The tailored jacket could be worn straight over the under lace "body," with a plain cotton T-shirt or with a long-sleeved poplin shirt trimmed with an embroidered flower spray on the front and on collar tips. The shirt collar was then worn over the jacket collar. Blouses became softer and more feminine, with shawl collars, cross-my-heart fichu effects, and elbow-length sleeves. Full summer tops were strapless or had a cuffed, off-the-shoulder neckline.

Stripes and dots, essentially black and white, made a big hit in knitwear for early spring, with the size of the stripes differing in the same outfit. The range went from the three-finger-wide stripe for the cardigan, to the two-finger-wide for the T-shirt, to hardly one-finger-wide for the clinging stretch pants covering the calf. Socks and even ballerinas were striped. Long-sleeved T-shirts were paired off with narrow miniskirts and even tights, all in various widths of stripes. The black and white stripe was longer lived than the black and white dot, though the latter was a clear winner in a strapless minidress with a flounced hemline. For beachwear the dots were transformed into gold pinpoints adorning a miniskirt and a long-sleeved brassiere top that bared one shoulder.

The bold minidress stole the show for the summer street look in Europe. The snug-fitting, black cotton stretch jersey sheath accentuated every curve as well as unwelcome bulges. The minidress was less popular in the U.S., however, and retailers were left with an abundance of unsold merchandise. Well-maintained, all-over suntans enabled black to triumph for a full-summer total look. The extra-tight black mini, with an off-the-shoulder neckline and occasional short sleeves, was worn with black ballerinas or stiletto-heel black pumps. The latest pump had an arrow-shaped front cut and rising sides. As a finishing touch to the total look, hair was pulled back, pinned high on the head, and topped with a dizzy flower.

Black was even more striking on the beaches. Ensembles varied from a one-piece outfit uncovering shoulders and knees to a two-piece outfit combining a brassiere sleeved top with a narrow miniskirt. As an alternative, a strapless top went with a pair of clinging, black over-the-knee stretch pants. These ensembles prevailed over pants or shorts for evening wear along the Mediterranean coast. Only a razor's edge divided these miniature outfits from the one-piece

swimsuit with giddy cutouts. Black was again prominent, highlighted with touches of white. Powerful metallic hues were also seen on the beaches, if not in the sea.

Spring parties twinkled with stupendous embroidery worthy of the Arabian Nights. Beads, pearls, strass, sequins, braid, or chenille turned each one of the corselet or fitted tops into a collector's piece. The well-above-the-knee skirt was gathered, draped, or flounced. At times the skirt was light and airy as a tulle "tutu," straight from one of Degas's portraits of a ballet dancer. An exhibition of Degas's works made a triumphant world tour in winter and left its mark on fashion. Floral prints, omnipresent for dressy clothes, appeared in vivid and dazzling chaotic combinations of patterns, sizes, and colours. Added to the prints were artificial flowers scattered on dresses or bunched on wide-brimmed hats. Bright yellow sunflowers borrowed from a Van Gogh painting rivaled huge pink roses.

A runner-up in the fashion field for daywear was the ankle-length skirt, also worn with an unmatched top. Softer, gathered and belted, in light wool, linen, or cotton for summer, it was usually worn with ballerinas or open sandals. The longer skirt gained momentum in the autumn when it was printed in muted tones of mustard, burgundy red, and pine-tree green. It was matched to a fitted plain jacket in one of the dominant print colours. The hemline problem was solved in early autumn by adopting ankle-length styles for daytime and above-the-knee lengths for evening.

To avoid the dangers of skintight clothes, pants that were far less mannish than before became a popular alternative. They were easy over the hips with unpressed pleats and cropped off above the ankles. In contrast to the mini outfits, long pants were mostly worn with softly tailored tops or shirts. One of the standbys was the black tailored jacket with silk lapels, the perennial "smoking" jacket that could be worn in identical pairs by male and female. Evening pant suits were in velvet, satin, or lace. Many had a high waistline. The ever popular denim was dressed up, and blue denim appeared jeweled and embroidered to the hilt, accessorized with sequins and silk chiffon. Denim was still stone-washed and occasionally patched, but it was considered very chic worn with a lingerie top or with mink and cashmere.

Gold caught the eye with necklaces made of large flat links surrounding high necklines. White enamel was out-

lined in gold for summer earrings featuring birds in flight, and black enamel shimmered with diamonds for winter. In the evening earrings continued to cascade, bracelets to jingle, and rings to multiply. Coloured stones, genuine and fake, adorned hats and suit lapels. The latest accessory in autumn was a gold Byzantine cross hanging on a cord to waist level.

In summer, wide rings were used to hold hair tight on top of the head in African slave style. Chignons were trimmed with barrettes and bows and, for dressier occasions, twisted and lacquered into large loops. Alternatively, hair, crinkly and tinted red, was loose on the shoulders.

Handbags, which shrank to doll size, were geometric in shape and electrifying in colour. Handles were short and were worn over the arm or held in the hand in a prim and proper manner.

The focus for makeup was on pale apricot and peach for face powder, lemon yellow for the upper eyelids, and bicolour lipstick. Blue-tinted contact lenses gave brown eyes a new appeal, but green lenses were considered more disquieting.　　　　　(THELMA SWEETINBURGH)

Men's Fashions. The "swinging '60s" in men's fashions were followed by the "sober '70s" and the "elegant '80s." Styles in 1988 reflected the elegance of the early '80s, beginning with the still-classic styling in suits, sports jackets, and contrasting jacket and trouser ensembles and with the blazer in its many modern variations, including a much wider choice of both cloth patterns and colours.

Men's fashions in the autumn/winter season assumed a more "dressed-up" look, with a trend favouring natural fibres, woolens, worsteds, and tweeds.

There was a resurgence of cotton and linen, sometimes blended with silk for tropical-weight summer suits. The European and American choice was the tropical suit with a sky blue background, decorated with a darker sea blue pinstripe. Denim jeans gave some ground to summer sports pants of cotton, linen, or blends of both of these natural fibres.

Knitwear lost some of its fashion favour, but knitted sports and T-shirts in cotton, linen, or man-made fibres became almost a universal summer uniform throughout the U.S. and Europe. Many of these shirts were emblazoned with advertising slogans or personal messages. Others fea-

tured embroidered motifs. For casual wear waxed cottons were used for jackets and trench coats.

Designer menswear became more fashionable during the year; the more successful designers were able to open their own retail outlets.

Throughout the year double-breasted styling continued to make inroads into business suits and to a lesser extent in topcoats. Topcoats and rainwear generally continued to be lighter in weight and longer, with many more 3/4 and 7/8 lengths appearing.

Toward the end of the year, the vest made a comeback in styles suitable for sportswear or business suits. Suspenders played a public as well as a supporting role. When jackets were removed, this colourful accessory was revealed in all its glory. Scarlet and daffodil yellow were the most popular shades.　　　　　(STANLEY H. COSTIN)

See also Industrial Review: *Furs.*

This article updates the *Macropædia* article DRESS AND ADORNMENT.

Gardening

The severe drought in the U.S. in 1988 affected nurserymen and gardeners as well as farmers in all sections of the country, although the Midwest and West were the most vulnerable. Possibly the best thing to come out of the crisis was a national awareness of the water problem and a better appreciation of this limited resource. Soil conservationists urged the use of mulches to preserve what little moisture the ground still had and advocated recycling water and giving first priority to vegetable gardens and woody plants. The drought also directed attention toward xeriscaping or dry-land gardening, utilizing plants that can grow with very little moisture. This style of gardening was especially popular—and needed—in the West and Southwest. Weather was also in the forefront in the U.K., where the effects of the October 1987 windstorm in southeastern England were still being assessed. Many fallen trees had not yet been cleared, and little replanting had been done. Lower yields in orchards in 1988 were attributed to the effects of the high winds.

In the U.K. the main horticultural event was the Gar-

DOD MILLER/THE NEW YORK TIMES

A British pensioner admires the gardens of the Chelsea Flower Show, a week-long event featuring extravagant gardens that contain exotic hybrids as well as familiar favourites.

den Festival in Glasgow, which opened at the end of April and continued for five months. This was the third in the series of such festivals in Britain and the first to be held in Scotland. As a festival it was a success with the local population, attracting over four million visitors; the garden dimension was also an improvement on earlier festivals, largely because there was a longer period of preparation but also because more experience had been gained in planting for such events. In The Netherlands a new public garden was opened in May at Castle Arcen in the southern province of Limburg. First planned by rose growers in the area as a show garden, it developed into a permanent exhibition of ornamental horticulture. Roses, however, remained dominant.

It was reported that demand for roses for the garden was declining in the U.K., but new varieties were still being produced. Among the top awards from the Royal National Rose Society, medals went to two climbing miniatures, a new group of roses. In the U.S., where at least $400 million was reportedly spent on rose growing each year, the All-America Rose Selections committee chose two miniature roses as outstanding varieties for 1989, the first time miniatures had been selected in the association's 50-year history. The medal winners were Debut, a showy red-blend miniature, and New Beginning, an orange-red rose that blooms throughout the summer. Both rosebushes are diminutive and the flowers about the size of 50-cent pieces.

Among the 1989 awards by Fleuroselect, an organization of European seed firms, a gold medal went to *Coreopsis grandiflora* Early Sunrise, a herbaceous perennial that can be raised from seed to flower in its first year. Bronze medals were given to *Dianthus* Telstar Crimson, an annual that also grows well in pots, *Lobelia* Compliment Scarlet, the first F_1 hybrid of this half-hardy perennial, and four varieties of African-French marigolds.

As members of the U.S. baby boom generation—now in their 30s and 40s—acquired homes in the suburbs, they also acquired gardens. The result was a boom in landscaping services and "instant gardens," expensive trees and shrubs, and the power tools—power mowers, clippers, and saws, mechanized leaf blowers and leaf chippers—that were rapidly replacing such old-fashioned tools as rakes. A study by the American Demographics Institute showed that this generation made the home the focus of living, and couples, often with two incomes, were willing to spend generously to support their newfound life-style. According to a Gallup Poll conducted for the National Gardening Association, couples in this age bracket spent an average of $226 per year on garden care in 1987, compared with a national average of $196. Some observers saw this trend as reflecting an urge to return to the land, but others attributed it simply to a desire to upgrade property values. In Europe the garden trade also remained buoyant. Results of a survey of the gardening market in West Germany showed an annual increase in total spending by gardeners in recent years, about half on plants and the rest on tools, equipment, and furniture. The main spenders were the middle-aged, a group growing in size throughout Europe.

Reflecting the desire for instant show, impatiens was the number one annual bedding plant in the U.S., according to a survey by Bedding Plants Inc. Not far behind it in popularity was the geranium. These two flowers had pushed aside the petunia, which held first place among gardeners for many years. Besides showy gardens, one of the fastest growing categories among hobbyists was herb gardening. The plants could be grown decoratively in garden settings and then dried for use in cooking. In Europe interest was growing in the use of ornamental sculpture in gardens, both

new works created for the purpose and antique statues, which could command high prices.

The world-famous fruit research station at East Malling in Kent, England, celebrated the 75th anniversary of its foundation. It was best known for its work on the classification of apple rootstocks, which had a profound effect on the fruit industry throughout the world.

(JOAN LEE FAUST; ELSPETH NAPIER)

See also Agriculture and Food Supplies; Botanical Gardens and Zoos; Life Sciences.

This article updates the *Macropædia* article GARDENING AND HORTICULTURE.

Health and Disease

As in other recent years, AIDS (acquired immune deficiency syndrome) dominated news of medicine and health in 1988. While researchers seemed no closer to finding a vaccine, there were some reports of success in the use of drugs to limit or even reverse the effects of the AIDS virus. Another hopeful sign, a decrease in the number of new cases of AIDS being reported among homosexuals, was counterbalanced by reports of increasing incidence of the disease in drug abusers.

Although overshadowed by the AIDS epidemic, important developments occurred in many fields of medicine during the year. Genetics researchers, having located the gene responsible for Duchenne muscular dystrophy, isolated and characterized its protein product, a step that could lead to a treatment for the disease. In a major devel-

BARBARA KINNEY—GAMMA/LIAISON

AIDS activists lie in front of the U.S. Food and Drug Administration's headquarters to protest the agency's time-consuming drug-approval process, which was preventing terminally ill patients from using potentially lifesaving experimental drugs.

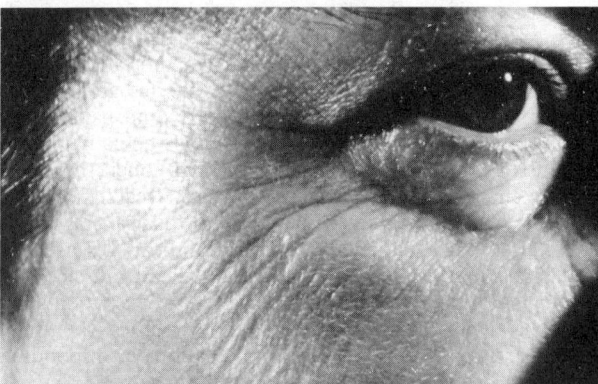
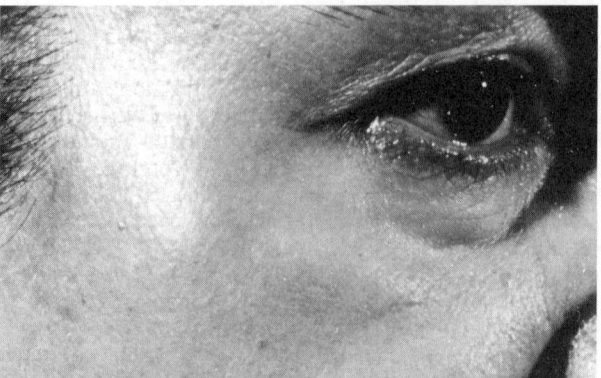

Fine wrinkles, scaly patches, and other conditions caused by sunlight (left) can be reduced by the prolonged use of Retin-A (tretinoin), a vitamin A derivative used in the treatment of acne.
PHOTOGRAPHS, JOHN J. VOORHEES, THE UNIVERSITY OF MICHIGAN MEDICAL CENTER

opment with implications for the study and treatment of human immunodeficiency diseases, three separate research teams in the U.S. and Canada successfully transplanted into laboratory mice functioning human immune system cells. Investigators studying the retrovirus called human T-cell lymphotropic virus, type 1 (HTLV-1), detected components of the virus in the blood and cerebrospinal fluid of patients with the paralytic condition known as chronic progressive myelopathy; the finding virtually confirmed the suspicion that HTLV-1 plays some part in this little-understood disorder, which occurs in clusters throughout Africa, India, Central and South America, and the Caribbean. Subsequently it was announced that routine screening of donated blood for HTLV-1 would be instituted in the U.S. The ethics of the use of fetal tissue for transplantation continued to be debated, and there was a bitter international controversy over a French drug that induces abortion.

AIDS. Although changed sexual practices in the U.S. and other developed countries seemed to be slowing the spread of AIDS among homosexuals, there were growing fears about the potentially devastating effects of the disease in African and other third world countries, where the pattern of transmission is predominantly heterosexual. By November 1988 a cumulative total of just over 124,000 cases had been reported to the World Health Organization (WHO), which estimated the actual total at more than 300,000 cases. WHO officials were particularly concerned that in some urban regions of sub-Saharan Africa, up to 25% of sexually active adults and a majority of female prostitutes were known to be infected.

In the U.S. controversy continued about who should be tested for antibodies to the AIDS virus, called human immunodeficiency virus (HIV), and how the results of positive tests should be handled. A report by University of Minnesota researchers indicated that hospital policies and practices varied widely around the country. State policies also varied. As of 1988 two U.S. states required all couples applying for marriage licenses to be tested. In one of them, Illinois, only 23 of the 146,000 people tested during the first 11 months of the program were found to be infected. The cost of finding those cases was estimated at $693,000 apiece, leading many to oppose the requirement as wasteful and ineffective.

New drugs for the treatment of AIDS continued to be tested in laboratories and hospitals around the world. In the U.S. numerous drugs were being tried, both alone and in combination with AZT (zidovudine; trade name, Retrovir), the only agent approved by the Food and Drug Administration (FDA) for treatment of the disease. During the year AZT, already shown to be helpful in certain groups of AIDS patients, was demonstrated to prolong life and improve symptoms in a new group, infants and children with AIDS. The drug was also known to have preventive value in some patients, and researchers were considering a program in which AZT would be administered to pregnant women infected with the virus in hopes of protecting fetuses exposed to the disease in the womb. One potentially promising new agent set to go into trials was soluble CD4, a substance made from a protein found on the surface of certain white blood cells, which functions as a receptor for HIV; the hypothesis was that large amounts of rCD4—made by recombinant DNA techniques—might serve as a decoy for the virus, diverting it from attacking the immune system cells that are its intended targets.

Many people with AIDS, believing the research efforts of the U.S. medical establishment to be inadequate, continued to seek alternative treatments available only through extensive "underground" networks. At one point during the year, the FDA banned the importation from Canada of dextran sulfate—an anticoagulant that had shown some activity against HIV—by groups distributing it to AIDS sufferers. Although the drug was being tested in the U.S., and trials in human subjects were scheduled to begin shortly, the FDA defended the ban on the grounds that the drug had not yet been approved for use against AIDS and might be harmful. An outcry from gay organizations and other concerned groups forced the agency to rescind its order with regard to this particular drug and to make official a policy, already in force unofficially, regarding importation of non-FDA-approved drugs. Under this policy, an individual in the U.S. could import from abroad small quantities of a drug—basically, about enough for a three-month supply—exclusively for his or her personal use. In a related development the Reagan administration announced in August that it was preparing a proposal to speed up the testing and evaluation of drugs for life-threatening illnesses. Subsequently, the FDA agreed to make another experimental AIDS drug, trimetrexate, more widely available, even though the agent had not yet received agency approval.

There were significant developments during the year in the detection of HIV infection prior to the development of AIDS. The first tests for AIDS had relied on detection of HIV antibodies in the bloodstream. Although important clinically and in the screening of blood donors, the test proved unreliable: detectable levels of antibody may not appear for up to a year after infection. Thus, some individuals shown to be seronegative (*i.e.*, having no antibodies in their blood) were actually infected. One new

technique, developed at the University of Geneva, reveals the presence of viral DNA directly and early—before the appearance of antibodies. A similar process, developed in France, was being used to detect HIV infection in infants who, although born to infected mothers, were seronegative and thus seemed to be free of the virus. Still another test was introduced to determine whether HIV-positive persons were shedding infectious virus; it was expected to be useful in monitoring the progress of drug treatments.

Cardiovascular Disease. An aspirin every other day may keep heart attacks away: That was the message from a nearly five-year study of 22,000 healthy physicians over age 40 conducted by Charles Hennekens and Harvard Medical School associates. The study, which was terminated early and rushed into print in the *New England Journal of Medicine,* showed that those who took one 325-mg aspirin tablet every other day had a dramatically reduced incidence of first heart attack compared with those taking a placebo drug (104 heart attacks in the aspirin-treated group versus 189 in the placebo group). Presumably, aspirin reduces the aggregation (clumping) of platelets in the blood, thereby preventing the formation of blood clots. Clots that form in the coronary arteries deprive the heart muscle of oxygen-laden blood, thus inducing heart attack.

While aspirin manufacturers immediately launched advertising campaigns to publicize the newly reported benefit of their product, the authors of the study and others worried that too many people might begin taking aspirin—not an innocuous drug—unsupervised by physicians. They noted that the group of men in the Harvard study was particularly healthy—with few smokers, for example—so that some typical cardiovascular risk factors were less apt to be present. In addition, they pointed to the increased risk of hemorrhagic stroke in those who took aspirin compared with those who took placebo (ten versus two).

The need for a cautious approach was underlined by a six-year study among 5,000 male British physicians, reported concurrently with the findings of the Harvard trial. Although the total number of deaths was 10% lower in those taking 500 mg of aspirin daily, the difference in mortality between aspirin and placebo groups was not statistically significant; furthermore, the incidence of heart attack and stroke was no lower in those taking aspirin. Whether the much larger dose explains the disparity between the U.S. and U.K. findings remained to be seen.

Further support for the efficacy of early measures to dissolve blood clots came from trials of two relatively new substances—anisoylated plasminogen streptokinase activator (APSAC; not available in the U.S.) and tissue plasminogen activator (t-PA; Activase). A multicentre study in Britain showed that APSAC, given to more than 1,000 patients within four hours of the onset of a heart attack, reduced the death rate after at least 30 days by 47%—from 12.2% in a group of patients given a placebo to 6.4% in the subjects given APSAC. Another study, conducted in the U.S., involved patients who had suffered acute pulmonary embolism (a blood clot in the lungs). Results of the study showed that t-PA caused the clot to break down rapidly in 82% of the patients, making the new drug appreciably more effective than the treatment formerly and routinely used for this life-threatening condition.

A once-popular scientific theory that further lost credibility during the year was that linking coronary heart disease with "Type A behaviour." For the past three decades, many cardiologists had believed that people with the so-called Type A personality, characterized by a hard-driving competitiveness, urgency, and aggression, were at higher risk of developing coronary disease than the calmer, more acquiescent Type B individuals. A study of 257 men suffering from heart disease, carried out at the University of California at Berkeley, showed a *lower* mortality rate in Type A individuals than in Type B's. The researchers suggested that some aspects of Type A behaviour, particularly the competitive response to challenge, may actually protect against death following a heart attack, although they cautioned that the question required further research.

New evidence emerged in 1988 on the way in which mental stress in patients with coronary heart disease can transitorily reduce oxygen supply to the heart muscle. Cardiologists at three U.S. centres found that their patients developed electrocardiogram (ECG) abnormalities when they were carrying out mathematical calculations or responding to psychological tests and even more pronounced changes when speaking to an audience on a sensitive personal matter. Most of these effects were "silent"; that is, not causing any apparent distress. Nevertheless, the researchers concluded that because mental stress may occur more frequently in daily life than stress from exercise (which induces still greater ECG abnormalities), it could be a significant and largely unrecognized factor in precipitating more severe coronary changes.

Cancer. In a highly unusual action, officials of the U.S. National Cancer Institute (NCI), in Bethesda, Md., announced the results of three studies on breast cancer treatment by letter, directly to 13,000 physicians, without first publishing them in a medical journal or presenting them at a scientific meeting. The studies concerned women with invasive, early-stage breast cancer in whom the disease had not spread to the lymph nodes. Contrary to much established practice, all three studies indicated that treating these "node negative" patients with adjuvant (additional) therapy—chemotherapy, hormonal therapy, or both—after primary therapy (surgery or radiation therapy) considerably increased their years of disease-free survival. Since adjuvant therapy is most effective when started early, NCI officials said they thought physicians should know of the new findings immediately.

A "meta-analysis" (a study that draws conclusions from analysis of existing data), conducted at the Harvard University School of Public Health and covering 21 separate, individual studies, concluded that there is a link between alcohol consumption and breast cancer—a strong association at intakes of 24 g (one ounce) per day and a weak association at lower levels of consumption. The investigators were unable, however, to establish a causal relationship and claimed that only 13% of all cases of breast cancer might be attributable to alcohol. The report was unusual in that the authors highlighted the possible beneficial effects of moderate drinking on the development of coronary heart disease and pointed out that these benefits may outweigh any increased chance of breast cancer. Because the incidence of cardiovascular disease is greater than that of breast cancer, they argued, the possible heightened risk of the latter should not be considered separately from the apparent protective effect of alcohol against cardiovascular disease.

Genetics. Work published by Louis Kunkel and co-workers at Harvard Medical School during 1988 furthered their characterization of the genetic defect in muscular dystrophy by showing that the differences between Duchenne muscular dystrophy (DMD) and Becker's muscular dystrophy, a similar disorder sometimes difficult to distinguish from DMD, could be accounted for by differing abnormalities in the muscle protein dystrophin, the product of the gene that is affected in the disease. In Duchenne muscular dystrophy, which affects one in 3,500 male births and is

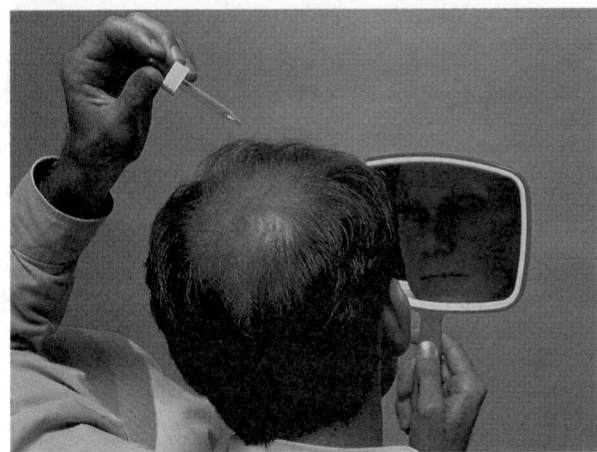

A man applies a few drops of Rogaine, a minoxidil-based drug, to his balding head. Approved by the U.S. Food and Drug Administration, minoxidil was proved effective in the treatment of some cases of male-pattern baldness.

TED THAI/TIME MAGAZINE

the more severe of the two disorders, dystrophin is virtually absent. In Becker's, which occurs later in life, dystrophin is present but altered. Kunkel's laboratory and others were working on ways to boost expression of dystrophin or find a substitute for it.

Obesity. New light was shed during the year on the long-standing scientific puzzle of why some people are more likely than others to become overweight and why obesity tends to run in families. One clue emerged from research on the Pima Indians, a southwestern American tribe being studied by investigators from the National Institutes of Health (NIH) in Phoenix, Ariz. The Pima are unusual in that by the age of 20 to 30 years, a majority are obese (*i.e.,* exceeding "desirable" body weight by 20% or more). Using a direct calorimeter, a special room-sized chamber that measures an individual's oxygen consumption and carbon dioxide production for up to 24 hours, the NIH team found that compared with individuals whose energy expenditure was shown to be high, subjects who demonstrated low energy expenditure had a fourfold risk of putting on as much as 7.5 kg (16.5 lb) over a two-year period. The researchers suggested that the "energy efficient" metabolic

pattern found in those with a reduced rate of energy expenditure may be an inherited trait.

This conclusion was supported by the results of a very different investigation, conducted in Cambridge, England, and Cambridge, Mass., into the energy intake and expenditure of infants born to lean and overweight women. This study revealed that an important factor behind the rapid weight gain during the first year of life in the offspring of obese mothers is reduced energy expenditure by the babies, particularly during physical activity.

Birth Control. The year 1988 saw two major steps toward contraception by immunization. WHO officials announced the results of an Australian trial of a vaccine directed against human chorionic gonadotrophin (HCG), the so-called pregnancy hormone, which begins to be produced in a woman's body shortly after conception. The new vaccine, a synthetic product made to resemble part of the HCG molecule, exerts an antifertility effect by virtue of antibodies whose production it induces. The vaccine was tried in 30 surgically sterilized volunteers. Two injections, given six weeks apart, led to the development of potentially contraceptive levels of antibody, and there were no significant adverse reactions. Because such a vaccine could be considered abortifacient, however, researchers elsewhere were developing an alternative. A team at the University of Connecticut reported that a vaccine against proteins in spermatozoa achieved a 100%, long-lasting but reversible contraception in guinea pigs; investigators believed the technique could be applied with equal success to humans.

One of the most highly publicized medical controversies of the year revolved around an abortion-inducing drug called RU 486, reported to be a safer as well as less expensive alternative to surgical abortion. In October, only one month after it had begun to market the drug in France, the manufacturer, Groupe Roussel Uclaf, halted its distribution. The action, a response to vehement protests on the part of antiabortion groups, caused a wave of counterprotests by family-planning agencies in the U.S., France, and elsewhere and organizations that included WHO and the World Congress of Gynecology and Obstetrics, which happened to be meeting in Brazil at the time the drug was withdrawn from the market. As a result of this international furor, the French government ordered Roussel to resume selling the drug. RU 486 had not yet been approved by the FDA and was not available in the U.S.

BRENT CLINGMAN/TIME MAGAZINE

A researcher holds up genetically immunodeficient mice that were injected with human white blood cells and that then developed immune systems identical or nearly identical to those of humans. Such mice held great promise for medical research, providing animal subjects for tests and studies unsafe for humans.

Cigarette Smoking. Discussion about the health hazards of smoking intensified in 1988. U.S. Surgeon General C. Everett Koop, in his annual report on smoking and health, stressed that nicotine is as addictive as heroin. Not only does it act directly on the brain, but it also affects the cardiovascular and skeletal muscle systems and various hormones. Many workplaces and public places had already begun to severely restrict or even ban smoking. They were being joined by hospitals, a small percentage of which, such as the University of Chicago Medical Center, instituted complete smoking bans. Federal authorities urged all hospitals to ban smoking.

During the summer the R. J. Reynolds Tobacco Co., a subsidiary of RJR Nabisco, began taking orders from retailers for Premier, the world's first "smokeless" cigarette. The device, which heats tobacco rather than burning it, reportedly produces almost no sidestream smoke. A heating element at the lighted end produces a tobacco-flavoured, nicotine-impregnated vapour that is drawn into the smoker's mouth when he or she puffs on the filtered end. Sales started in Phoenix, Ariz., Tucson, Ariz., and St. Louis, Mo., in October. Even before Premier reached cigarette counters, however, it had become a source of controversy and a target of public health officials. The surgeon general and representatives of the American Medical Association and the American Heart and American Lung associations urged the FDA to ban the device, but it was not immediately clear whether the agency had jurisdiction to do so.

Banishing Age? After studying 30 patients in a four-week, double-blind, randomized trial, a University of Michigan team reported that use of a topical acne medication called Retin-A (tretinoin) can diminish fine wrinkles and roughness and mottled pigmentation caused by sun damage on the face and elsewhere on the body. Most of the subjects suffered skin irritation as a side effect of the treatment, and their skin became more vulnerable to sunburn. Nevertheless, on the strength of a report published in the *Journal of the American Medical Association,* thousands of American women obtained prescriptions for the cream, and the manufacturer could not meet the demand. Imitations began appearing almost immediately. The FDA, by midyear, was issuing warnings against such products and advising caution on Retin-A itself, which had not yet been approved as an antiaging remedy. A follow-up to the study,

reported in December, suggested that skin improvement could be sustained with continued Retin-A treatment.

If women received encouragement from the news that a remedy for wrinkles might be at hand, many hundreds of thousands of bald men also had some cause for optimism. After several years of clinical trials, minoxidil (Rogaine), a drug originally formulated for treatment of high blood pressure, was licensed in a topical form as a treatment for some types of baldness. The degree of benefit derived seemed to be related to the progress of the condition; men just beginning to lose their hair had better results than those with more advanced hair loss. The duration of benefit was also limited; hair regrowth ceased when the drug was discontinued.   (BERNARD DIXON; GAIL W. MCBRIDE)

MENTAL HEALTH

The substantial psychological toll of war was underlined by publication of the U.S. Centers for Disease Control's Vietnam Experience Study. A four-year project covering some 15,000 veterans, the survey revealed few persistent adverse physical effects of the war. But it did reveal that 15–20 years afterward, serious psychological problems were more than twice as common in men who fought in Vietnam than in noncombat veterans who served elsewhere during the same period. Among the Vietnam vets, 5% suffered from generalized anxiety (compared with 3% of the noncombat controls) and 5% from major clinical depression (as against 2% of controls); 14% of the Vietnam veterans had alcohol abuse or dependence problems (as against 9% of controls), and some 15% had also suffered from combat-related post-traumatic stress disorder. One unexpected finding was that while former combatants who entered the military between 1965 and 1967 were twice as likely as controls to have problems today, the rates leveled off for those who enlisted after 1968. The authors of the study report speculated that changes in the "culture surrounding war" could explain these trends. The year 1968 saw the height of antiwar fervor in the U.S., and men who went to Vietnam after that date may have been less idealistic and thus less easily shocked by what they saw.

New evidence about the psychiatric consequences of the sexual and physical abuse of women came from a survey carried out in New Zealand. The study, whose participants were 2,000 women selected on a random basis, showed

JAMES D. WILSON—WOODFIN CAMP & ASSOCIATES

An art therapy class at a Veterans Administration hospital provides veterans with a tool for working through the psychological impact of war. A recent study by the U.S. Centers for Disease Control revealed that those who fought in Vietnam were more susceptible to severe psychological problems than were those noncombat veterans who served elsewhere during the same period.

that those who had been abused were significantly more likely to be identified as psychiatric cases and to have high scores in a psychopathology assessment interview. Of those who had been exposed to sexual abuse during childhood, 20% were found to have psychiatric disorders, mainly of the depressive variety, compared with 6.3% women who had no history of abuse. There was a similarly increased percentage among those who had been sexually or physically abused as adults. The psychiatrists who conducted the study suggested that the psychological consequences of abuse, largely neglected by social psychiatric research in the past, might help to explain why depressive and anxiety disorders are more common among women than men.

Bulimia nervosa, an eating disorder characterized by recurrent episodes of binge eating and purging, is another condition that is far commoner among females than males. Surveys suggested that it may affect 4 to 20% of young women in the U.S. and other developed countries. When interviewed about their eating behaviour, many patients described difficulty in achieving the sensation of fullness. Physicians studying the disorder differed over whether this apparent impairment of satiety in bulimics was psychological or physiological in origin. Researchers at the National Institute of Mental Health, Bethesda, Md., and the University of California at San Francisco decided to investigate the possibility that bulimia sufferers were deficient in the hormone cholecystokinin, which is released from the intestines after eating and is responsible for sending satiety signals to the brain. Studying 14 women with bulimia and 10 unaffected controls, before and after eating a meal, they found that the bulimia sufferers did not secrete cholecystokinin in response to eating and did not experience normal satiety. They also found that the condition responded well to antidepressant drugs, although another recent trial reported from the Royal Edinburgh (Scotland) Hospital indicated that, compared with antidepressant medications, weekly psychotherapy afforded more substantial and longer-lasting improvement.

Collaborative research among several California centers resulted in a significant advance in understanding autism, a potentially devastating condition in which children have major difficulties in communicating and fail to develop normal social awareness. Controversy over the cause of autism ranged from suspicion that aberrations in brain development were to blame to claims that early experiences were crucial. The most recent evidence was based on the application of magnetic resonance (MR) imaging to the study of brain structure and function. MR scans of 18 autistic patients aged 6 to 30 indicated that the condition is associated with anatomical abnormalities in the cerebellum, the brain structure whose main task is to control muscular coordination. How these abnormalities bear on the personality defects seen in autism—and, indeed, whether they occur concomitantly with more directly influential changes elsewhere in the brain—remained to be determined.

Despite the fact that recently developed drugs such as ranitidine (Zantac) could heal ulcers rapidly, without resort to surgery, long-term drug treatment might be necessary for some individuals. Clinicians at the University Hospital of South Manchester, England, set up a clinical trial of hypnotherapy in patients whose ulcers had recurred at least once over the previous six months. Once the ulcer had healed again, ranitidine therapy was continued for ten weeks, during which time half of the patients received seven sessions of hypnotherapy and used an audiotape at home for self-hypnosis. A year later every one of the control subjects had relapsed—compared with only about half of

those who underwent hypnotherapy. Hypnotically induced relaxation was particularly effective for some individuals, possibly even reducing the gastric acid secretion.

(BERNARD DIXON)

This article updates the *Macropædia* article MENTAL DISORDERS and Their Treatment.

DENTISTRY

Half of all U.S. schoolchildren have no decay in permanent teeth, according to a report by the National Institute of Dental Research (NIDR), which celebrated its 40th anniversary in 1988. The NIDR report detailed the results of a survey of 40,000 children aged 5–17 conducted during the 1986–87 school year at 970 schools around the country. Survey findings indicated that tooth decay and cavities had declined at a dramatic rate over the past 15 years and that the decline was generally uniform throughout the nation. Close to half of all the children surveyed had no decay in their permanent teeth (compared with 36% in a similar 1979–80 study and an estimated 28% in the 1970s). James P. Carlos, NIDR chief epidemiologist, cited three major factors behind the decline: fluoride in water, food, and toothpaste; good dental habits; and high-level dental care.

A significant amount of adult periodontal (gum) disease may be inherited, University of Minnesota School of Dentistry scientists told the annual meeting of the International Association for Dental Research in Montreal. Preliminary results from a study of 30 pairs of fraternal and identical twins suggested that genetic factors may account for 50 to 70% of chronic gum disease in adults. The researchers planned to gather additional data from twins reared together and those raised in different families to learn how genetic and environmental factors contribute to gum disease.

At the same meeting, scientists from the Forsyth Dental Center in Boston described a new method for the detection of gum disease, using a temperature probe. The device contained a tiny microprocessor that measured gum temperature, which can be an indication of the presence of periodontal disease. The Boston researchers predicted that the device would enable dentists to detect gum disease before extensive tissue damage had occurred and to monitor the progress of treatment.

Scientists from the NIDR reported in 1988 that human saliva contains substances that prevent the AIDS virus from infecting white blood cells. This discovery might explain why no cases had been documented in which the virus was transmitted through saliva. The researchers tested saliva from three healthy men who were not in any risk group for AIDS. In laboratory dishes the men's saliva prevented the AIDS virus from infecting lymphocytes, a type of white blood cell that is among the immune system cells attacked by the virus in the body. Philip Fox, who headed the research team, cautioned that the finding should not be interpreted as ruling out the possibility that an individual could get AIDS via an oral route, such as through deep kissing. Because of the small size of the sample, Fox planned to repeat the study with saliva from healthy women and children as well as saliva from AIDS patients.

(LOU JOSEPH)

VETERINARY MEDICINE

For a veterinary scientist to discover a means of identifying racehorses with winning potential is virtually equivalent to an alchemist's finding the philosopher's stone. Nevertheless, in 1988 a researcher at Tufts University School of Veterinary Medicine, Medford, Mass., claimed he had done just that. W. Robert Cook, a professor of surgery,

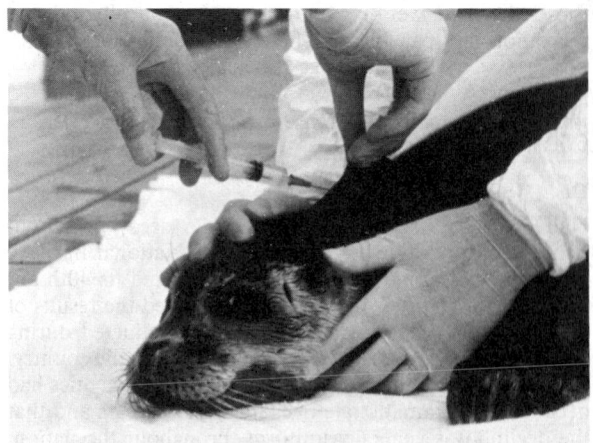

A harbour seal is treated for distemper, a common canine disease that had killed thousands of seals living in the North Sea.
PIETER 'T HART—SIPA

devised a simple method of diagnosing an inherited defect in the larynx (voice box) of foals that interferes with breathing and thus affects performance. By using his index fingers to palpate the throat over the larynx, Cook claimed to be able to assess the degree of muscle wasting (laryngeal palsy) and to score it on a scale correlated statistically with racehorse performance.

Endoscopy, the traditional method of detecting laryngeal palsy, is an invasive process that sellers of young blood-stock at auction do not often allow. Other investigators in the field were skeptical of Cook's findings. They denied his claim that the condition was inherited, maintaining that it might be due to a virus or the stress of exercise and could be corrected surgically.

Using scintigraphy, one of the latest techniques, another team, also from Tufts, studied one of the oldest problems in racehorses: exercise-induced pulmonary hemorrhage. The great exertions of a race can induce bleeding in the lungs that is sometimes so severe that blood may flood from the horse's nostrils. The condition affects performance in a similar way to palsy of the larynx, by restricting oxygen uptake. Scintigraphy involves injecting small amounts of radioisotopes into the bloodstream; sophisticated imaging equipment is then used to produce a computer-enhanced colour scan of lung function. The technique allowed the Tufts researchers to compare function before and after exercise and to assess the effect of bronchodilator drugs, which enlarge the airways. Previously, research on pulmonary hemorrhage was severely limited, depending solely on postmortem examinations and clinical surveys.

A new type of degenerative brain disease, spongiform encephalopathy, was identified during the year in cattle in the U.K. Related to scrapie in sheep and Creutzfeld-Jakob disease in humans, bovine spongiform encephalopathy (BSE), although small in incidence, was invariably fatal. Researchers suspected that the cause might be an unconventional viral agent acquired from another species, probably sheep. The means of transmission was believed to be concentrated cattle feeds that included offal from scrapie-infected sheep. BSE had not been found outside the U.K., but there were hints that it might be related to transmissible encephalopathy of mink in the U.S.

An outbreak of another viral disease devastated seal populations in the North Sea in 1988. Albert Osterhaus, a veterinary virologist at the Netherlands National Institute of Public Health and Environmental Hygiene, identified the cause as canine distemper, a common agent of infec-

tion in dogs. The seals were believed to have been infected by huskie dogs used in seal hunting in Greenland. A vaccine was developed but could be used only in sanctuaries because of the difficulty of catching seals in the wild. It was estimated that up to 80% of the seal population of Scandinavia and the U.K. might be lost.

(EDWARD BODEN)

See also Life Sciences; Populations and Population Movements; Social Security and Welfare Services.

This article updates the *Macropædia* articles DISEASE; MEDICINE.

Industrial Review

Industrial activity strengthened in 1987—an improvement that was sustained into 1988. Growth in the Western world reached 5.2%, with industrial output in the developed economies nearly 3% higher, the best annual increase since 1984. In the less industrialized economies, output rose a record 15%, even faster than the 11.6% of 1986. In the centrally planned economies, industrial production was 4.8% higher, the fifth successive year of near-5% growth.

Although the raw figures suggest that 1987 as a whole was a satisfactory year, it would be wrong to conclude that it was without difficulties. Only modest progress was made in correcting the major trade imbalance between the U.S. on the one hand and Japan and West Germany on the other. Also, despite the strengthening of activity during the year, the Dow Jones Industrial Average crashed on October 19, which sent other world stock markets plummeting. By the end of the year, the U.S. dollar had touched record lows against the yen and the Deutsche Mark.

Nevertheless, the world economy, helped by a postcrash relaxation of monetary policy, remained robust. In the first half of 1988, industrial production in the economies of the developed nations was 5% higher than it had been a year earlier. For the year as a whole, the latest projections from the International Monetary Fund suggested that world output would rise 3.8%, which would be the fastest rate of growth since the 1970s (except for 1984, when, as a result of U.S. fiscal expansion, output rose 4.5%). Within the industrial countries there was still a gap between the relatively fast-growing North American and Japanese economies and the relatively slow-growing European economies. Industrial

Table I. Annual Average Rates of Growth of Manufacturing Output, 1973–87
Percent

Area	1973–78	1978–81	1981–84	1985	1986	1987
World[1]: Market economies	2.2	1.5	2.2	3.5	3.2	5.2
Industrial countries	1.7	1.0	1.8	2.8	1.6	2.9
Less industrialized countries	5.9	3.9	4.0	6.7	11.6	15.2
Centrally planned economies[1]	7.6	3.3	4.0	4.6	4.9	4.8

[1] For definition see Table III.
Source: UN, *Monthly Bulletin of Statistics.*

Table II. Manufacturing Production in the U.S.S.R. and Eastern Europe[1]
1980 = 100

Country	1983	1984	1985	1986	1987
Bulgaria[2]	115	120	124	129	132
Czechoslovakia	107	111	115	119	122
East Germany[2]	112	117	122	127	131
Hungary	107	110	110	112	116
Poland	89	94	98	102	106
U.S.S.R.	112	116	121	127	...

[1] Romania not available.
[2] All industries.
Source: UN, *Monthly Bulletin of Statistics.*

output rose by about 4% in 1987 in the U.S., Canada, and Japan, whereas in Europe the rise was only about 2%. Within Europe some economies were growing rapidly: manufacturing output rose 12% in Ireland; 5–6% in Spain, Sweden, and the U.K.; and 4–5% in Finland and Portugal. Growth in West Germany, however, was under 1%, while industrial output declined in Austria, Denmark, Greece, and Yugoslavia.

Growth in the less industrialized nations, though strong in total, was far from uniform. The most rapid expansion was recorded by the newly industrializing economies of the Far East, particularly the "Four Dragons" (South Korea, where industrial output rose 19% in 1987, Hong Kong, Singapore, and Taiwan). Growth was also strong in the Philippines (14%), Malaysia (12%), and India (6%). Elsewhere the performance was weaker. The Latin-American economies continued to be held back by debt problems and the weakness of commodity prices, while for most African countries output per capita was not even rising.

In the case of the centrally planned economies, full figures were not available for the U.S.S.R. and Romania. Although the UN estimates suggested growth near 5% for the bloc as a whole—unchanged from 1986—individual countries appeared to have fared less well. Expansion was only 2–3% in Bulgaria and Czechoslovakia and 3–4% in East Germany, Hungary, and Poland. Among the centrally planned economies, only in Hungary was 1987 a year of faster growth than 1986.

At the world level the pattern of growth in production was remarkably well balanced. Not one of the major categories of manufacturing identified separately by the UN registered a drop in output and—even more impressively—growth in each category was at least as strong as in 1986. Light industries generally outperformed heavy industries, though not in the identified categories (food, textiles, clothing and footwear, and wood and paper industries). The explanation for this was to be found in the less developed countries, where output of light industries rose 22% in total but only 5–13% in the separate categories. This apparent discrepancy was explained by the very rapid growth of computer-based industries, particularly the assembly of microcomputers in the newly industrializing economies of Southeast Asia. Elsewhere the pattern of output was similar to that of the previous year. Within the developed economies there was a recovery in the output of base metals—reflecting a strengthening in their price—and a further contraction of the clothing and footwear industries in the face of competition from the third world. The centrally planned economies displayed their usual bias in favour of the heavy industries.

(GEOFFREY R. DICKS)

Table III. Index Numbers of Production, Employment, and Productivity in Manufacturing Industries
1980 = 100

Area	Relative importance[1] 1980	1987	Production 1986	1987	Employment 1986	1987	Productivity[2] 1986	1987
World[3]	1,000	1,000	117	123	...	...	...	...
Industrial countries	861	818	110	114	...	...	...	...
Less industrialized countries	139	182	136	157	...	...	...	...
North America[4]	282	283	115	121	...	...	...	...
Canada	22	21	117	...	...	...	...	...
United States	260	262	119	124	93	94	128	132
Latin America[5]	79	75	109	114	...	...	...	...
Argentina	12	...	92	...	...	...	...	...
Brazil	26	...	...	...	...	...	...	...
Mexico	18	...	102	...	91	...	112	...
Asia[6]	183	223	136	153	...	...	...	...
India	11	15	153	162	107	107	143	151
Japan	131	134	118	122	108	107	109	114
South Korea	6	12	203	242	...	...	...	...
Europe[7]	422	379	105	107	...	...	...	...
Austria	9	8	110	109	88	87	125	125
Belgium	13	12	106	107	...	...	...	...
Denmark	5	5	127	124	106	104	120	119
Finland	6	6	117	122	94	90	124	136
France	75	63	97	100	86	84	113	119
West Germany	114	103	107	108	92	92	116	117
Greece	4	3	100	98	...	...	...	...
Ireland	2	3	134	150	83	81	161	185
Italy	54	47	99	103	86	85	115	121
Netherlands, The	14	13	111	112	...	...	...	...
Norway	5	5	108	110	93	...	116	...
Portugal	3	3	122	127	...	...	...	...
Spain	23	21	105	111	...	...	...	...
Sweden	13	13	110	116	90	91	122	127
Switzerland	13	11	107	...	...	...	...	...
United Kingdom	58	53	104	110	78	77	133	143
Yugoslavia	10	10	117	116	...	...	...	...
Rest of the world[8]	34	30	...	...	...	...	...	...
Oceania	15	13	101	102	...	...	...	...
Australia	13	11	96	98	...	...	...	...
South Africa	8	7	95	99	94	95	101	104
Centrally planned economies[9]	...	...	126	132	...	...	...	...

[1] The 1980 weights are those applied by the UN Statistical Office; those for 1986 were estimated on the basis of the changes in manufacturing output since 1980 in the various countries.
[2] This is 100 times the production index divided by the employment index, giving a rough indication of changes in output per person employed.
[3] Excluding Albania, Bulgaria, China, Czechoslovakia, East Germany, Hungary, Mongolia, North Korea, Poland, Romania, the U.S.S.R., and Vietnam.
[4] Canada and the United States.
[5] South and Central America (including Mexico) and the Caribbean islands.
[6] Asian Middle East and East and Southeast Asia; including Japan, Israel, and Turkey.
[7] Excluding Albania, Bulgaria, Czechoslovakia, East Germany, Hungary, Poland, Romania, and the U.S.S.R.
[8] Africa and Oceania.
[9] These are not included in the above world total and consist of the European countries listed in note 7 above.

Table IV. Pattern of Output, 1984–87
Percent change from previous year

	World[1] 1984	1985	1986	1987	Developed countries 1984	1985	1986	1987	Less developed countries 1984	1985	1986	1987	Centrally planned economies[2] 1984	1985	1986	1987
All manufacturing	7	4	4	5	7	3	2	3	9	7	12	15	5	5	5	5
Heavy industries	8	4	3	4	9	4	1	3	9	5	11	9	6	6	6	5
Base metals	8	1	-2	4	9	1	-5	3	13	3	8	6	4	2	3	4
Metal products	10	6	4	4	10	5	1	3	12	7	17	11	7	7	7	7
Building materials, etc.	4	1	3	3	4	-1	1	1	5	5	8	7	3	3	5	4
Chemicals	6	3	4	5	7	3	3	4	7	5	8	8	4	3	4	3
Light industries	4	3	4	7	4	1	3	3	8	8	12	22	3	3	4	4
Food, drink, tobacco	3	3	3	4	2	2	2	2	7	5	3	5	3	5	5	5
Textiles	2	2	3	3	2	1	2	2	3	4	6	5	1	3	2	2
Clothing, footwear	3	0	1	1	2	-2	-1	-1	7	1	9	7	3	3	1	2
Wood products	5	1	4	5	5	0	5	6	5	1	2	7	4	4	5	2
Paper, printing	7	3	5	6	7	1	4	5	9	15	7	13	4	4	5	3

[1] Excluding Albania, China, North Korea, and Vietnam.   [2] Excluding China.

ADVERTISING

The candidates' television ads themselves became issues in the 1988 U.S. presidential election, as the campaigns of both Vice-Pres. George Bush and Massachusetts Gov. Michael Dukakis relied heavily on "negative advertising" that tore down the competition rather than building up the sponsor. Observers gave the edge to Bush in the war of the TV spots, pointing out that Dukakis's ads never developed a coherent theme. A Bush ad, aimed at a Massachusetts prisoner-furlough program, that showed convicts going through a revolving door was cited by some as one of the best political commercials ever made. Surveys indicated that voters deplored the use of negative advertising but were nonetheless influenced by it.

Hallmark Cards and R. J. Reynolds Tobacco Co. joined a growing list of advertisers offering prerecorded videocassettes free or at a reduced price with product purchases. This new type of premium was expected to create a $200 million annual business for home video companies by the end of 1989. Hallmark, which offered a "Creepy Classics" video for $4.95 with a $5 Hallmark purchase for Halloween, ordered 500,000 copies of the 30-minute tape, which was narrated by Vincent Price. Proctor & Gamble gave away more than one million videocassettes of a special edition of "Walt Disney Cartoon Classics" with the purchase of Ivory dishwashing liquid and Tide laundry detergent.

In May Soviet television aired its first hard currency-earning commercials, sponsoring a series featuring interviews with Americans by Soviet commentator Victor Pozner. PepsiCo and Visa International were the first U.S. advertisers on Soviet television. The favourable feedback encouraged the Soviets to accept other advertisements for this medium. In September 1988, during telecasts of the Olympic Games, PepsiCo aired six previously broadcast commercials featuring the pop singer Michael Jackson. Visa International also advertised during the Olympics. The telecasts showing these commercials reached nearly 200 million Soviet viewers.

In November U.S. Pres. Ronald Reagan vetoed a measure that would have reintroduced limits on advertising during children's television programming. The president considered the measure, which had passed Congress by a wide margin, to be an unconstitutional infringement on freedom of expression. The bill would have limited ads to 10.5 minutes an hour on weekends and 12 minutes on weekdays and would have required broadcasters to provide educational programs for children.

By a 6–3 vote in June, the U.S. Supreme Court ruled that lawyers could solicit clients through targeted direct mail to individuals known to have legal problems. The court found that targeted direct mail did not present any of the dangers of in-person solicitation, such as invasion of privacy and exertion of undue influence. This was the last restraint on lawyer advertising. The ruling rounded out a series of decisions begun in 1977 when the court ruled that some newspaper advertising by lawyers was protected by the First Amendment and could not be banned by states.

With controversies connecting athletes with drugs and steroids featured prominently in the news, some advertisers were giving second thought to the use of athletes in their commercials. In 1988 advertisers spent more than $500 million on celebrity athlete endorsements of their products. Many of these companies were now planning to sponsor tournaments and other events instead. The contracts that companies now used with their celebrity athletes contained clauses that let a company terminate an agreement if a player's actions reflected "moral turpitude."

NBC-TV sold out its commercial advertising time for Super Bowl XXIII three months before the football game was scheduled to take place in 1989. The cost for an average 30-second advertising spot was $675,000. The early sellout was part of NBC's sales strategy tying the sale of advertising time for the Super Bowl with the World Series and other events. The average 30-second commercial for the 1988 World Series cost $275,000.

Each year *Advertising Age* lists the top 100 national advertisers in the U.S. for the year before. In 1987 Philip Morris moved ahead of Proctor & Gamble as the nation's number one advertiser. Proctor & Gamble had been number one for 24 years. Philip Morris spent $1,560,000,000 in 1987 to Proctor & Gamble's $1,390,000,000. The increase in advertising spending by Philip Morris was mostly for its General Foods and Miller Brewing units. The next three largest advertisers in 1987 were General Motors, Sears, Roebuck & Co., and RJR Nabisco. General Motors was the only other national advertiser spending more than $1 billion in 1987. As a group, the top 100 national advertisers spent an average of 4.3% more in 1987 than in 1986.

The top 100 favoured network television among the 11 media measured by *Advertising Age*. Network television accounted for $6,670,000,000, or more than 20% of the $28 billion spent by the top 100 on all advertising (excluding couponing, in-store displays, direct marketing, special events, and promotions, which were not reported). Proctor & Gamble was the leading network television advertiser, although its $377.6 million was 15.6% below 1986. General Motors was number one in newspaper advertising with $174 million, while Philip Morris was the largest spender on magazine advertising. RJR Nabisco led in outdoor advertising, Proctor & Gamble in cable television, PepsiCo in spot television (Coca-Cola was 12th in spending in this medium), and the Franklin Mint in newspaper supplement advertising.

(EDWARD MARK MAZZE)

AEROSPACE

Air transport enjoyed a boom year in 1988, and the signs were that this would continue. All three major airframe manufacturers in the West—Boeing and McDonnell Douglas in the United States and Airbus Industrie in Europe—were stretched to capacity and beyond in trying to meet demand by the airlines, reflecting the upsurge in traffic and a huge aircraft reequipment program.

Expansion brought with it growing pains, however, as air-traffic controllers struggled to guide airliners through an increasingly complex and congested maze of airways. There was also congestion at many major airports as operators fought one another and the smaller, business-aviation users to secure reserved takeoff and landing times. In the U.S. airborne congestion was being overcome by the introduction of a massive new computer-based ATC (air-traffic control) system. In Europe the efficient flow of traffic was plagued by the continued inability of sovereign nations to weld together their separate ATC systems.

Such was the momentum of the industry that the financial crash of October 1987 had no permanent effect on the airlines or their reequipment plans. Twelve months later airliner production rates at the three major manufacturers had reached all-time highs. Despite vigorous growth, however, profitability remained low; one observer put the net income of the entire U.S. air-

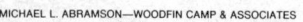
MICHAEL L. ABRAMSON—WOODFIN CAMP & ASSOCIATES

VideOcart, a promotional device developed by Information Resources Inc., is triggered by an electronic scanner to flash ads and messages to the consumer about a product close at hand. Ads are transmitted by radio waves to the cart from the store's computer.

Boeing introduces the world's largest airliner, a 747-400 jumbo jet, designed to hold 660 passengers.
BOEING COMPANY

line industry during its first nine years of deregulation (since 1978) as just sufficient to buy four Boeing 747s.

Predictably, it was Boeing that continued as the world's top producer, its top-of-the-range 747s emerging from the factory at the rate of one a week. The 757, until recently less in demand than the 767 launched almost at the same time, suddenly received a number of large orders, and by the end of September the company had sold 368, compared with 307 of the 767s. It was the relatively small 737, however, that emerged as the world's best-selling airliner.

McDonnell Douglas, meanwhile, continued to climb back from what many observers some years earlier had thought might be its disappearance from the airliner industry. Its MD-80 was an example of how an elderly airframe (the DC-9) could be continuously improved so as to maintain a front-rank position—in this case, as the leader in the 150-seat category. The 1970s-vintage DC-10 likewise grew into the MD-11; a first flight was scheduled for April 1989, and orders came in gradually over the year. At the biennial Farnborough (England) Air Show McDonnell Douglas showed off its MD-80/UDF (unducted fan) demonstrator aircraft. This was a "proof-of-concept" airplane for the company's proposed MD-90 airliner, to be powered by a pair of rear-mounted General Electric GE36 turbine engines driving two multiblade, contrarotating propellers. No one wanted to be first to try such a radically new propulsion method, however, and no sales had been recorded by October.

Boeing staged a unique publicity coup by rolling out two "new" aircraft (both, in fact, derivatives of old models) on the same January day: the long-awaited 747-400 and 737-400. However, the pressure by airlines for quick deliveries of proven aircraft and the static or declining price of oil resulted in the shelving by Boeing of its proposed 150-seat 7J7 UDF (unducted fan) transport, which would have been a competitor to the McDonnell Douglas MD-90.

Europe's Airbus A320 entered service in February, and by the year's end orders and options stood at more than 700, comfortably exceeding the 600 needed to break even financially. The A330 and A340 airliners (the first with two engines, the second with four, but otherwise closely similar to one another) were launched in June 1987, and orders for them continued to arrive at a slow but satisfactory rate. The advent of the A320 and A330/340 confirmed Airbus as an airframe company of the first rank, and during the year it was courted by both McDonnell Douglas and Lockheed during tentative discussions on possible cooperative ventures. Lockheed was thought to be particularly interested, since (apart from a few civil Hercules) it had left the commercial transport field with the termination of the L-1011 TriStar program in 1981 and now appeared anxious to return to this market.

Demand for new aircraft produced some huge orders. Delta Air Lines, for example, in September set about implementing its fleet-replacement policy for the 1990s with an order for a staggering 215 aircraft of different types, no fewer than 100 being for the McDonnell Douglas MD-88 medium-range transport.

The corporate aviation sector was also healthy, and sales were sufficient to permit the development of new, very fast turboprop models. However, corporate and company aviation operations suffered increasingly from pilot shortages as the airlines, because of their rapid expansion, sought new sources of manpower, holding out tempting employment packages that could not be equaled in the corporate sector.

By contrast, at the lower, fly-for-fun level, the situation continued to be little less than disastrous. Deliveries of piston-engined planes declined 37% from 1986. As a result, Cessna decided to pull out of that market, at least for the time being. Commercial helicopter manufacturers also continued to experience a downturn, paralleling the slump in the offshore oil industry.

The Soviet Union's *glasnost* (openness) policy emerged as a reality at the Farnborough Air Show with the appearance of its advanced new fighter, the MiG-29 Fulcrum. For the U.S.S.R. to show off a top weapon such as this in a Western event would have been inconceivable even a year earlier. *Glasnost* was also responsible for the visit in August by top U.S. defense officials, including Secretary of Defense Frank Carlucci, to the U.S.S.R., during which they were shown the new Blackjack bomber, a close rival in both mission and shape to the U.S.'s Rockwell B-1B bomber.

At the same time that the U.S. contingent was in the Soviet Union, the U.S. Air Force released a picture of one of its most secret new aircraft in development—the Northrop B-2, or "Stealth bomber." Later the delta-shaped craft, designed to be invisible to radar, was rolled out at Palmdale, Calif.   (MICHAEL WILSON)

AUTOMOBILES

World production of automobiles reached new highs in 1987. This healthy growth continued strongly in 1988. Most European manufacturers enjoyed substantial growth, defying the worst effects of the 1987 stock market slump. Even such traditional loss makers as Italy's Alfa Romeo, Renault of France, and Rover Group in Britain recorded large earnings gains.

Europe and Australia. During the first six months of 1988, every major European manufacturing nation except West Germany and Sweden recorded higher car production than in the same period of 1987. West German production was marginally lower at 2,540,000 cars, from 2,590,000, but Sweden fell from 227,000 to 213,000. However, both West Germany and Sweden shared the world expansion in output of commercial vehicles.

Car sales in domestic markets continued at or near peak levels in Britain, France, and Italy but slowed a little in West Germany. Sweden, Spain, Belgium, and The Netherlands also experienced further strong growth in domestic car registrations in 1988. Only The Netherlands had lower commercial vehicle sales. European car production in 1988 was expected to reach a record 12.5 million, up from the previous peak of 12.2 million in 1987.

For the long term there were still major challenges for Europe. As of 1988 it remained largely protected in one form or another against the full onslaught of Japanese imports. In Britain an informal but effective "understanding" restricted Japanese imports to no more than 11% of total automobile sales, and commercial vehicle sales were similarly constrained. France confined Japanese sales to about 3% of the total, while in Italy they were held below 1%. West Germany also maintained an effective, if unspecified, limitation. The formerly "open market" Swedes in 1988 began to investigate the possibility of voluntary restraint by Japanese manufacturers after Swedish manufacturers Volvo and Saab saw the Japanese virtually equal their combined share of the domestic market.

In 1988 Japan served notice that it planned to move into a traditional market of the Europeans, the exotic sports and luxury cars. Honda scored strongly in the U.S. with its Accura line, filling a pricing void between the U.S. luxury models and such

New 1989 Cadillac Coupe DeVilles and Sedan DeVilles await their final inspection at a plant in Michigan. General Motors was hoping that these bigger cars and other newly expanded models would strengthen its lagging position in the market.

PETER YATES

European cars as Jaguar, BMW, and Mercedes Benz. Posing the most serious future threat to Europe, however, appeared to be Japan's Toyota and Nissan. Both planned to introduce high-technology, wide-body luxury cars and high-performance, advanced-specification sports cars in 1989 or soon afterward. It seemed likely that these models would take sales from the Europeans in the U.S., traditionally Europe's most profitable export market.

In the small- and medium-sized car markets, Europe faced increasing competition, if not a threat, from South Korea, Taiwan, and Malaysia. The strongest of those was South Korea, where car output reached 793,000 in 1987, up from 158,000 in 1984. Commercial vehicle output in South Korea rose over the same three years from 107,000 to 187,000.

The loser of 1988 remained Australia, although both production and sales moved up slightly from the 20-year low of 1987. The Australian automobile industry was undergoing major restructuring at the urging of the Labor government of Prime Minister Bob Hawke. Toyota joined forces with General Motors (GM), and there was to be joint production of several models. Ford and Nissan also planned to share certain models in Australia, though no more formal links were envisioned.

Two of Europe's state-owned motor companies moved to the private sector in 1987–88. Fiat Group in Italy absorbed Alfa Romeo, and Rover Group, which included the successful Land and Range Rover four-wheel-drive vehicles, became part of the giant British Aerospace company.

DAF of The Netherlands merged with the formerly British government-owned Leyland Trucks in a new joint company, Leyland DAF. Sweden's Volvo took over Leyland Bus operations. General Motors moved out of the European heavy-truck market with the sale of its Bedford Truck operations to independent British group AWD. GM, however, continued to use the Bedford name in Britain for its light commercial vehicles.

Many new models were introduced in Europe in 1988, but there was little real innovation. The main features included more advanced electronics, more aerodynamic styling, and an expansion of multivalve engine choices and four-wheel-drive options.

The two most important model launches of the decade in Australia, the Holden Commodore and the Ford Falcon, followed the proven Australian formula of big six-cylinder engines in strong, conventionally engineered medium-large sedan and wagon body styles. The success of these models was expected to bear heavily on the future of an "independent" Australian automobile industry. Failure of either could mean that they would be the last Australian-designed models.   (JOHN R. WEINTHAL)

Japan. Toyota Motor Co. produced in mid-September 1988 its 60 millionth automobile, the first Japanese auto manufacturer to do so. During the year ended June 1988, it attained 93% of the profits it had gained in its peak year. Also in 1988 other leading automakers, including Nissan, Honda, and Mazda, either registered substantial gains in their profits or equaled their past records. Two factors that contributed to these outstanding performances were the brisk demand for luxury cars in the Japanese domestic market—new series of Mark II and Cresta from Toyota; Maxima, Laurel, and Cefiro from Nissan; and Persona from Mazda—and the success of all makers in adjusting to the strong yen by improving their productivity.

Under these circumstances, production in Japan of both cars and commercial vehicles during the January–July period of 1988 rose to 7,434,615 units, 3% above the corresponding period in 1987. Of this total, cars accounted for 4,768,227 units, a 4% rise, and commercial vehicles stood at 2,666,388 units, a 2.1% advance. This recovery followed a slight decline in 1987.

Domestic sales of cars and commercial vehicles, excluding "light vehicles" of 500 cc displacement or less, during the January–August period totaled 3,250,073

units, up 15.3% from the same period of 1987. A continuation of this pace would result in domestic sales of 4.7 million units during 1988, surpassing the previous record of 4,340,000 vehicles in 1987. Reflecting mainly a strong demand from the construction industry, sales of trucks, excluding light vehicles, surged to 899,821 units during the first eight months of 1988, a significant 19.3% advance. Truck sales had been sluggish in the early 1980s owing to the second oil crisis in 1979. Sales of light vehicles, both cars and trucks, totaled 1,141,096 units, up 3.7%.

The industry, however, suffered a downturn in exports. The total fell during the January–June period of 1988 to 3,592,556 vehicles, a 5.1% decline, following a drop of 4.5% registered in 1987. On the other hand, imports rose more rapidly than ever before, thanks partly to the growing demand for luxury foreign-made cars and partly to the restructuring and reorganizing measures taken by importers, distributors, and dealers. Imports jumped a dramatic 44% to 70,809 units during the first half of 1988. On the basis of that figure, it was estimated that total imports would top 140,000 units at the year's end, far surpassing the previous record of 110,771 units attained in 1987.

One fact that characterized 1988 was that several Japanese manufacturers began selling their foreign-made cars in Japan. They included Honda, Mazda, and Mitsubishi.   (MASATO MIYAHARA)

U.S. The year opened with General Motors Corp. holding a multimillion-dollar "Teamwork & Technology" extravaganza at New York's Waldorf-Astoria Hotel, an invitation-only showing of a dozen prototypes of future GM vehicles for 14,000 employees, stockholders, investment analysts, political and business leaders, and the news media. The event featured not only the vehicles but chairman Roger B. Smith and president Robert Stempel assuring those assembled that GM was on the road to recovery.

Soon after the exhibit ended, Ford Motor Co. reported that it had earned a record $4.6 billion in 1987, up from $3.3 billion in 1986. GM earned $3.6 billion, versus $2.9 billion a year earlier, and Chrysler Corp. earned $1,290,000,000, down from $1,390,000,000 in 1986.

When the 1988 model year drew to a close on September 30, GM again found itself upstaged by Ford. For the 1988 model year, Ford outsold Chevrolet in both cars and trucks combined for the first time in a nonstrike year since 1957. Ford had outsold Chevrolet in trucks but not in cars in 1987. Ford sold 1.5 million cars and 1.5 million trucks to Chevrolet's 1.4 million cars and 1.3 million trucks for the 1988 model year.

The top-selling vehicle in the industry for the 1988 model year was the Ford F-Series pickup truck, with sales of 588,452 units. The best-selling car was the Ford Escort, with sales of 381,330 units. In second place among cars was the Ford Taurus, with sales of 367,327 units. GM's best-sellers were the Chevrolet C/K series pickup truck, which finished second to Ford at 489,882 units, and the Chevrolet Cavalier, with sales of 301,809 units, which ranked it as the seventh-best-selling vehicle in the industry.

The top ten sellers for the 1988 model year were the F-Series truck, C/K truck, Escort, Taurus, Honda Accord (362,118), Ford Ranger truck (303,666), Cavalier, Hyundai Excel (267,099), Ford Tempo (264,548), and Chevrolet Celebrity (258,601).

For the 1988 model year, GM sales totaled 3.5 million units, down from 3.7 million in 1987. Ford sales rose to 2.1 million from 2,070,000 the previous year. Chrysler sales were at 1,050,000, up from 1,010,000 in 1987. Honda sold 360,035 U.S.-built cars in the 1988 model year, up from 316,812 a year earlier. Toyota sold 60,076 versus 37,308 a year earlier. Nissan sold 110,517 versus 123,113 in 1987, and Volkswagen totaled 36,159 against 65,671 a year earlier. Mazda, in its first year of U.S. production, sold 24,707.

The U.S. manufacturers sold 7,320,000 cars in 1988, down from 7,340,000 a year earlier. Import sales totaled 3,120,000, down from 3,180,000 a year earlier.

Truck sales were 5.1 million, up from 4.9 million in 1987. Total industry sales—cars and trucks, imports and domestics—were 15.5 million units, compared with 15.4 million for 1987.

With 1988 over, the automakers rolled out new vehicles for the 1989 model year, which began October 1. Ford's new entries were a restyled Ford Thunderbird and Mercury Cougar, both of which offered a version with a supercharged engine, and a high-performance version of the Taurus called the SHO, which featured a 24-valve, 3-litre, V-6 engine developed by Yamaha of Japan. Ford also brought out a longer version of its Aerostar minivan.

General Motors unveiled a Cadillac DeVille and a Fleetwood coupe that were each six inches longer than in 1987 and DeVille and Fleetwood sedans that were nine inches longer. The Fleetwood sedan had fender skirts. Buick restyled its Riviera and extended the length 28 cm (11 in).

Chevrolet revamped its import lineup. The subcompact Nova, built in Fremont, Calif., in a joint venture with Toyota, was renamed the Prizm; the Sprint, built by Suzuki of Japan for Chevrolet, was renamed the Metro; and the Spectrum, built by Isuzu of Japan, was to be renamed the Storm for 1990. Chevrolet also began marketing a longer, wider version of the Suzuki Samurai four-wheel-drive mini utility vehicle called Tracker. Chevrolet saved a few models for later in the model year; these included a new Corvette powered by a 32-valve V-8 engine developing 375 horsepower that was dubbed the "King of the Hill" and a replacement for the midsize Celebrity called the Lumina. The Lumina also was to feature a front-wheel-drive minivan with a plastic body. Pontiac planned to add a minivan called Transport.

Chrysler also saved its new models until midyear. They included a midsize Dodge Spirit and Plymouth Acclaim that eventually would replace the Aries and Reliant K-cars and a two-door sport coupe called the Plymouth Laser that was to be built at the joint-venture Chrysler/Mitsubishi Diamond-Star assembly plant in Normal, Ill. The Mitsubishi car was called the Eclipse.

Soon after the 1989 models were introduced, the U.S. government said that it would roll back its corporate average

A Nissan Gloria (right) edges past a Nissan Cedric on a Tokyo street. The Japanese car market was producing larger cars to meet the demand of the status-conscious consumer; however, those who bought larger cars would have to contend with Tokyo streets originally designed for handcarts.
DAVID E. SANGER/THE NEW YORK TIMES

fuel economy (CAFE) laws and require the automakers to obtain 26.5 miles per gallon (mpg) from their fleet of cars rather than the 27.5 mpg that had been on the books. In the annual competition for best mileage, the Chevrolet GEO Metro (formerly Sprint), with a 53-mpg city and 58-mpg highway rating by the U.S. Environmental Protection Agency, was the top-rated vehicle. Metro finished ahead of the Honda Civic CRX HF, which had a 50-mpg city and 56-mpg highway rating. The Metro was powered by a one-litre, three-cylinder engine, and the Civic by a 1.5-litre, four-cylinder engine; both had five-speed automatic transmission. At the other end of the mileage scale, the Aston Martin Lagonda, Saloon, Vantage, and Volante all tied for worst mileage at 8-mpg city and 11-mpg highway ratings from their 5.3-litre V-8 engines.

The year was one of numerous joint ventures. Chrysler and Fiat entered an agreement for Chrysler to market the Alfa-Romeo automobile line in the U.S. At the same time, Chrysler loosened its ties with Maserati of Italy and chose to focus on importing the TC convertible roadster developed jointly by the two rather than increase its equity interest in the firm. Volvo agreed to pay Ford $100 million for a 20% interest in Hertz, while GM announced an agreement with China National Automotive Industry Corp. of Beijing (Peking) to build two-litre, four-cylinder engines in that country. Ford and Nissan entered a pact to build front-wheel-drive minivans in Avon Lake, Ohio, and Volkswagen stopped building cars in the U.S. after having produced 1,197,411 at a plant in Pennsylvania since 1978.

Audi spent most of the year in and out of court defending itself against charges that certain 1978–86 model 5000 sedans with automatic transmission were subject to unintended acceleration. A proposed settlement was reached in which Audi agreed to pay owners from $300 to $2,000 provided they bought a new Audi, but a circuit court rejected the offer as unfair to those who did not want another Audi.

Chrysler became the first U.S. automaker to make driver-side air bag restraint systems standard in some of its cars. They included the Chrysler Fifth Avenue, Dodge Diplomat, Plymouth Gran Fury, Chrysler LeBaron convertible and coupe, and Dodge Daytona. Ford followed by making both a driver-side and passenger-side air bag restraint standard in its 1989 model Lincoln Continental.

All automakers increased their offerings of antilock brake systems. They used computer control to pump brakes automatically so as to avoid wheel lockup and loss of control in a panic stop regardless of the road surface. Many of the automakers also turned to new so-called bumper-to-bumper warranties on their cars in which all items except maintenance were covered for three years or 36,000–50,000 mi (57,924–80,450 km).

A surprise to many was a new twist in the incentive game. Chrysler tested a pilot program in two markets in which buyers of its 1988 or 1989 model cars or trucks could return the vehicle if they were dissatisfied for any reason within the first 30 days or 1,000 mi (1,609 km) of ownership. In one market buyers could get their money back, and in the other they were offered another vehicle of the same or a different line. Pontiac and Oldsmobile followed suit with a 30-day, 3,000-mi (4,827-km) program in which those who bought a 1989 model Pontiac Grand Prix or Oldsmobile Cutlass Supreme could return the car and apply the purchase price toward a new Pontiac or Oldsmobile. Those offers were not limited to test markets.   (JAMES L. MATEJA)

BEVERAGES

Beer. Asia was a centre of interest in brewing technical expertise in 1987 and 1988. Under a joint venture with the Chinese brewery in Zhao Qing (Chao Ch'ing), the U.S. brewer Pabst shipped 3,000 tons of brewing equipment to China via Singapore. The Steinecker Machine Co. of Freising, West Germany, provided 12 wet malt processing mills for breweries in China, and the British company Redler Ltd. sold £4 million of malting plant to the Dou Men (Tou Men) brewery, 160 km (100 mi) from Guangzhou (Canton).

In the English-speaking world a notable trend was the rapid increase in microbreweries or pub breweries. In the U.K., where a handful of pub breweries (or "brewpubs") had existed unchanged for 200 years, the number of small production units now exceeded 140. With changes in state legislation, brewpubs and microbreweries had spread across the U.S., although the largest concentration was in the Western states. There were an estimated 110 such operations in the U.S., 40 in Canada, and over 20 in Australia and New Zealand.

In England and Wales the compulsory closing of pubs and bars in the afternoon ended following the repeal of laws introduced during World War I, as a temporary measure to ensure that workers in war plants remained sober. Pubs were now allowed to remain open from 11 AM to 11 PM except on Sunday. Scotland had eliminated afternoon closing in 1976. For those preferring beer at home, the Japanese company Gekkeikan claimed to have developed a self-chilling can, double-walled to allow a pressure-activated coolant to circulate around the drink.

Probably the most expensive beer in the world was Domesday Ale, produced by the Cornish Brewery Co. in England to mark the 900th anniversary of the Domesday Book. The first bottle of the 15.8% alcohol-by-volume beer, containing 250 ml, was auctioned at Christie's in London for £1,000. (MICHAEL D. RIPLEY)

Spirits. The biggest factors in a generally depressed spirits market in 1988 were the continuing trend to white spirits and the rapid emergence of lower-alcohol products. The phenomenal growth of brands like De Kuyper's Original Peachtree and Malibu in the U.S. underlined the move away from dark, full-strength spirits.

The emergence of low-alcohol and lower-calorie beer, wine, and soft drinks contributed to the problems faced by the traditional spirits brands. The trend was illustrated by the decision of many Chinese spirit producers to reduce the alcohol content of their traditionally high-strength (55–65% alcohol by volume) brands. The share of the Chinese alcoholic beverage market held by spirits had dropped to 33% from the 1980 high of 58%.

In the U.S. the "hangover" from the massive 30% increase in federal tax imposed in 1986 was still in evidence, although the effect of stricter "driving while intoxicated" laws in many states was believed to be a more significant factor in the move toward fruity, lower-alcohol products. Cocktails and coolers were satisfying the U.S. consumer's demand for a sporty, lighter drink. However, the cooler market in the U.K. all but collapsed, despite massive initial promotion.

The market share of white spirits—light rum, vodka, and gin—increased in the U.K. to 34% in 1987, while whisky, which until the early 1980s had accounted for more than half the spirits market, reached an all-time low of 45%. Brandy's share rose slightly to 9%, reflecting growing consumer interest in brands at the premium end of the market. The liqueurs sector, the fastest growing, was pushing toward a 10% market share.

The harmonization of taxes in the European Communities (EC), scheduled for 1992, would mean a reduction in duty on spirits in the U.K. (amounting, for example, to over £2 on a bottle of whisky). However, it was expected that antialcohol forces would step up their demands for tighter restrictions. (ANTONY C. WARNER)

A general manager from the Great Wall Wine Co. holds up his company's product. China hoped to gain a respectable position in the world's wine market.
AP/WIDE WORLD

Wine. World output of wine in 1988 was estimated provisionally at approximately 302.4 million hectolitres (hl; 1 hl = 26.4 U.S. gal), considerably below actual 1987 production of 326 million hl. The greatest decrease was in the EC countries, where output, at 186 million hl, was 11.4% lower than in the preceding year. Italy remained the world's leading producer, with 69 million hl (75.8 million hl in 1987). The 1988 harvest was a little below the average of recent years, but the quality was said to be excellent. The French harvest, at 64.8 million hl, was also lower in quantity (70.5 million hl in 1987) but high in quality, with a very good sugar/acidity balance. It could become a memorable year, especially for Bordelais, Borgogne, and Champagne. Spain, the other major EC producer, reported output of 32.5 million hl.

Table V. Estimated Consumption of Beer in Selected Countries			
In litres[1] per capita			
Country	1985	1986	1987
East Germany	141.6	142.1	c. 145.0
West Germany	145.5	146.4	144.2
Czechoslovakia	130.8	133.4	130.0
New Zealand	115.2	120.8	121.7
Belgium	121.0	119.8	121.1
Austria	111.6	118.5	113.8
Denmark	121.26	125.78	118.05
Luxembourg	120.4	119.3	116.5
United Kingdom	108.9	108.1	110.5
Australia[2]	115.5	111.3	108.2
Hungary	92.4	99.4	100.2
United States	90.3	90.8	90.1
Netherlands, The	84.5	86.0	84.3
Canada[3]	81.6	81.1	...
Ireland	77.0	77.3	c. 75.0
Venezuela	59.5	60.7	72.4
Switzerland	69.2	69.4	69.3
Finland	61.7	65.4	68.1
Bulgaria	63.3	64.3	66.4
Spain	61.0	62.0	64.5
Colombia	52.3	54.7	56.3
Sweden	46.8	50.0	51.5
Norway	47.52	50.78	51.44
Yugoslavia	45.9	50.1	51.0
Cyprus	42.0	44.1	46.6

[1] One litre = 1.0567 U.S. quart = 0.8799 imperial quart.
[2] Years ending June 30.
[3] Years ending March 31.

Table VI. Estimated Consumption of Spirits in Selected Countries			
In litres[1] of pure alcohol per capita			
Country	1985	1986	1987
East Germany	4.8	4.9	c. 5.0
Hungary	5.4	5.3	4.7
Poland	4.6	4.7	4.7
Czechoslovakia	3.52	3.40	3.32
Finland	3.01	1.17	3.22
Spain	c. 3.0	c. 3.0	c. 3.0
Bulgaria	3.21	3.41	2.83
Canada[2]	2.61	c. 2.55	...
Luxembourg	c. 2.5	c. 3.5	c. 2.5
United States	2.72	2.45	2.41
Iceland	2.26	2.44	2.40
Cyprus	2.1	2.3	2.4
Japan	2.4	2.38	2.30
France[3]	2.33	2.34	2.30
West Germany	2.37	2.29	2.24
Belgium	2.12	1.98	2.15
Netherlands, The	2.24	2.21	2.07
Switzerland	2.18	2.08	2.04
Romania	c. 2.0	c. 2.0	c. 2.0
Yugoslavia	1.9	c. 2.0	c. 2.0
Sweden	2.06	2.12	1.96
United Kingdom	1.72	1.71	1.73
Ireland	1.8	1.7	c. 1.7
Soviet Union	3.1	1.9	1.6
Uruguay	1.5	1.5	1.6

[1] One litre = 1.0567 U.S. quart = 0.8799 imperial quart.
[2] Years ending March 31.
[3] Including aperitifs.

Table VII. Estimated Consumption of Wine in Selected Countries			
In litres[1] per capita			
Country	1985	1986	1987
Italy	84.8	73.3	79.0
France	79.7	76.4	75.1
Portugal	87.0	70.8	64.3
Luxembourg	57.3	55.4	58.5
Argentina	60.1	59.2	58.1
Spain	48.0	47.0	54.0
Switzerland	49.6	48.6	49.5
Chile	40.0	35.0	35.0
Austria[2]	34.3	32.8	32.1
Greece	37.3	23.7	31.8
Romania	c. 28.0	c. 28.0	c. 28.0
West Germany	25.6	23.3	25.8
Uruguay	24.3	22.0	25.7
Yugoslavia	17.4	27.5	c. 25.0
Belgium	22.7	21.7	23.0
Bulgaria	20.2	22.1	22.5
Hungary	24.8	23.2	21.5
Australia[2]	21.6	20.6	21.5
Denmark	20.71	19.82	20.63
New Zealand	14.3	16.2	15.3
Netherlands, The	14.96	14.90	14.61
Czechoslovakia	16.0	12.3	13.7
Cyprus	11.9	11.8	13.2
Sweden	11.70	11.96	11.83
United Kingdom	9.96	10.40	11.03

[1] One litre = 1.0567 U.S. quart = 0.8799 imperial quart.
[2] Years ending June 30.

Source: Produktschap voor Gedistilleerde Dranken, *Hoeveel alcoholhoudende dranken worden er in de wereld gedronken?*

Production rose in the Comecon countries, from 36.9 million hl in 1987 to an estimated 44.6 million hl in 1988. In the Soviet Union, the largest producer, output increased from 17.2 million hl to 20 million. Production fell in the U.S., however, to 16.7 million hl from 18.4 million. Australian wine growers had experienced freezes and rain in the last few years, seriously lowering output. The 3.4 million-hl harvest of 1988 would present great qualitative differences among regions. Africa and Asia showed a slight rise in output to 10.6 million hl.

Since 1950 production of wine had been tending more and more to outstrip consumption, but the situation was reversed in 1987, when production fell and consumption rose slightly. On the one hand, output was lowered by cutbacks in vineyards, especially in the EC but also in Australia, Argentina, California, and North Africa. On the other hand, consumption was bolstered by the appearance of new products such as wine coolers (especially in the U.S.) and by the emergence of new consumer countries, notably in Asia. Nevertheless, the situation remained troublesome, with stocks still at a high level.

(MARIE-JOSE DESHAYES)

Soft Drinks. Per capita consumption of soft drinks in the U.S. in 1987 climbed 3.5% to 46.6 gal (1 U.S. gal = 3.8 litres), and industry volume increased 4.5%, to 11,286,000,000 gal. Colas were still the fastest growing segment, but diet drinks, now representing about 25% of all soft drink sales, also showed strength. More consumers appeared to be buying diet soft drinks for the taste rather than the reduced calorie content. In 1988 saccharin and aspartame were still the only diet sweeteners available for use in soft drinks. Alitame and sucralose were being reviewed by the U.S. Food and Drug Administration, and the FDA was being petitioned to approve cyclamate for general use. The juice-added category, including both sugar and diet products, had made a strong initial showing, reaching a 5% share of the market in 1986, but slipped to less than a 4% share in 1987.

Food stores sold approximately 55% of all packaged soft drinks in the U.S., and sales in convenience stores were growing rapidly as the convenience-store industry expanded. However, vended distribution had outstripped industry growth throughout the '80s and appeared to be one of the strongest areas for growth in the future. Technological innovations, such as the dollar bill validator that provides change automatically, played a significant role in this increase.

While sales volume and per capita consumption continued to grow, the number of firms continued to shrink as the result of mergers and acquisitions. An increasing number of plants were owned by the franchise companies or large conglomerates. The industry continued its commitment to recycling. A number of states had passed legislation setting mandatory recycling goals. Some specified redemption values for containers, imposed a ban or tax on certain types of packaging, or combined these and other elements. Debate on mandatory recycling legislation in the U.S. Congress was expected in 1989.

(DWIGHT C. REED)

BUILDING AND CONSTRUCTION

Dollar outlays for new construction in the U.S. in 1988 fell below the levels achieved in 1987 and 1986. On the basis of reports of the U.S. Department of Commerce for the first eight months of the year, it appeared that construction spending in 1988 would be down about 1.1% to an estimated $343 billion. During the 1980s, except for the depression year of 1982, there had been widespread overbuilding of office and apartment buildings because of the tax benefits to be gained from their operation. However, the 1986 tax reform legislation greatly reduced these benefits, and this had a dampening effect on these two segments of the construction industry.

Housing starts in the U.S. fell sharply in 1987 and 1988. The major factor was the high vacancy rates for apartments, but there was also a decline in starts of single-family units. A 1987 study by the mortgage banking firm of Lomas and Nettleton Co. revealed that the average monthly payment for new homes, including taxes and insurance, rose 8% from $984 in 1986 to $1,063 in 1987, reflecting the increase in the average price of a new home financed with a conventional fixed-rate mortgage ($136,-000 in 1987). While the average price of a new home fluctuated somewhat in 1988, it reached $145,200 in August, presumably raising monthly payments further, even though mortgage rates were essentially unchanged. The high cost of housing, even for old homes, was excluding many middle-income people from the market.

The U.S. Department of Commerce Composite Construction Cost Index reached 114.4 (1982 = 100) in 1987. In 1988 it fluctuated between 114.9 and 116.1 on a monthly basis and stood at 115.9 in August. The rising costs of construction and land and the increased size of new homes built all contributed to the higher prices of new homes for sale in 1988.

One indication of the importance of the construction industry to the overall economy is the number of people it employs. This number rose significantly during the 1980s. In 1982 contract construction employed 3.9 million people and in 1987, over 5 million. The decline in construction activity in 1988 stopped this growth in employment, and this in turn adversely affected employment growth in the economy as a whole.

In Canada it appeared that the growth rate of gross domestic product (GDP) in 1988 could be lower than in 1986 and 1987. While business investment was expected to be relatively strong, the rate of increase in housing investment was forecast at about 1%, compared with almost 15% in 1986 and 1987. In Great Britain the outlook was reasonably good, although the significant growth in GDP that had been experienced in 1986 and 1987 was not expected to continue at the same levels. Forecasts of new investment indicated a healthy prospect for the building and construction industry.

Housing and business investment in West Germany rose only 1.7% in 1987, but it appeared that growth in 1988 could be slightly higher; much would depend on sustained consumer demand and continued stability in foreign exchange markets. In France housing investment was down in 1986 and 1987, but the outlook for 1988 was more favourable. Investment spending in Italy rose 2.7% in 1987, but the country's unfavourable trade position was expected to depress housing and business investment in 1988.

The Japanese economy was expected to continue expanding in 1988 and 1989, stimulated by investment in housing, which rose 20.6% in 1987, and in business, which increased by 8.2%. Because of the strong demand for housing, it was forecast that housing construction would continue at high levels.   (CARTER C. OSTERBIND)

BRENT CLINGMAN/TIME MAGAZINE

A housing site takes shape in front of an already crowded section of San Diego, California. The rapid growth and development of many metropolitan areas was making residents angry, and their protests forced some state governments to consider growth-restriction plans.

CERAMICS

U.S. ceramic industry sales for 1987 totaled just over $32 billion, and 1988 sales were expected to be strong. Advanced ceramic sales continued to grow, with electronic substrates, electronic packages, spark-plug insulators, and wear- and corrosion-resistant ceramics leading the way. Optical fibre sales declined, and automotive applications were still lagging behind earlier market forecasts. Sales of refractories showed strong growth, as did those of porcelain enamel, tile, and sanitary ware. The major factor in the growth of the ceramic industry was the overall strength of the U.S. economy, especially the building industry. The decline in the value of the dollar and the growing demand for advanced ceramics were also important factors in the industry's performance. Imports and competition from other materials were the major negative factors.

Buyouts, joint ventures, and cooperative developments occurred with increasing frequency as companies positioned themselves for emerging markets for advanced ceramics. Contributing importantly to the interest in advanced ceramics was their usefulness in advanced systems involving engines, electronics, and machine tools. This factor was creating a need for an advanced ceramic company to develop a business strategy that included input from the systems developers to allow the focused development of advanced ceramic components.

U.S. advanced ceramic consumption increased to $4.4 billion in 1987, and continued strong growth was forecast for 1988. Advanced structural ceramics accounted for 17% of the total. This segment consisted primarily of automotive heat engine components, cutting tools, wear- and corrosion-resistant industrial components, heat exchangers, aerospace and defense components, and bioceramics. Cutting tools and wear parts had the largest growth rates. Spark plug insulators showed substantial growth thanks to increased strength in the export market, while optical fibre consumption declined because of the completion of major long-distance communication lines. Although the automotive components market was well behind earlier market projections, turbocharger rotors, seal rings for direct-drive water pumps, exhaust-port liners, valves and valve-train components, and piston pins were either in use or expected to be in use within the next few years.

U.S. advanced electronic ceramic consumption in 1987 was estimated at $2.2 billion. Electronic packages, including substrates, accounted for 37%, capacitors for 27%, and thick film pastes for 11% of the total. The remainder included ferrites, piezoelectrics, and nonautomotive sensors. Aluminum oxide continued to dominate the substrate market, although beryllium oxide was used in about 5% of the applications because of its outstanding thermal conductivity. Aluminum nitride, silicon carbide, and glass ceramics, such as cordierite/mullite materials, were beginning to enter the market. These newer materials were developed to meet the demands of advanced integrated circuits.

Although there were no significant applications of high-temperature ceramic superconductors, the worldwide research-and-development efforts in regard to these materials remained intense. Progress in terms of new materials and improved fabrication techniques continued, and applications in areas such as magnetic-field sensors appeared likely in the near future.

Whiteware sales in the U.S. totaled $2.6 billion, 6% over 1986. Tile and sanitary ware demonstrated increased sales. Tableware sales declined, while those of glazed tile continued to show strong growth because of increased use in construction and remodeling. The strength of the construction industry was a major factor in the sales of sanitary ware and tile. The major factor in the decline of dinnerware and fine china sales was increased competition from imports.

Refractories sales recovered to $1.7 billion in 1987 and were expected to show continued strength in 1988. Contributing significantly to the recovery of the refractories industry was the strength of the steel industry. Sales of refractories revealed a major shift toward more expensive and more durable products, due to demands in the steel industry for better quality and higher productivity.

Porcelain enamel sales in the U.S. in 1987 increased almost 20% over 1986 to $4.6 billion, and 1988 sales were expected to be good. This strong performance was due mostly to increased sales of appliances.   (DALE E. NIESZ)

CHEMICALS

Chemical sales by producers in major chemical-manufacturing areas of the world (the United States, Western Europe, and Japan) were expected to be only about 1% higher in 1988 than in 1987, when they totaled $685 billion. As recently as 1985, sales were only $528 billion. These general figures, however, obscure considerably different growth rates among the different areas.

In Western Europe, for example, sales were 3% higher than the $367 billion registered in 1987. In Japan, however, the figure was expected to be close to 1% above the 1987 total of $166 billion. A strong surge in sales occurred in the United States. The $235 billion in chemical sales anticipated in 1988 would be 10.5% higher than the $212.7 billion in shipments of chemical and allied products reported by the Department of Commerce in 1987.

The increases, especially in the U.S., might have been greater had it not been for limitations of production capacity. Almost everywhere across the product spectrum of the U.S. industry, producers were running at relatively high operating rates. Also, shortages of key chemicals, including a vital feedstock, ethylene, were much in evidence. Prices were up substantially despite the lower cost of petroleum from which organic chemical feedstocks are derived.

The average operating rate for the U.S. chemical industry was 77% in 1986, according to the Federal Reserve System. In 1987 the rate exceeded 81%, and little change was likely in 1988. High operating rates resulted in a relentless advance in the chemical and allied products producer price index compiled by the U.S. Bureau of Labor Statistics. Switching to a new base year of 1982 = 100, the bureau reported that the index advanced to 106.4 in 1987 from a value of 102.6 in 1986. By mid-1988 the index had risen to 115.2.

Strong demand and high prices resulted in marked growth in profits and capital spending. Corporate profits for U.S. producers of chemical and allied products before taxes were $9.5 billion in 1986 and $13.5 billion in 1987, according to the Department of Commerce. Profits for 1988 were estimated to be about $20 billion. Expenditures for new plants and equipment were $16.8 billion and $16.4 billion in 1986 and 1987, respectively. In 1988, however, capital spending was estimated to have exceeded $18 billion.

The cumulative direct investment for chemical and allied products by U.S. concerns abroad increased to $26.9 billion in 1987 from $22.7 billion reported for 1986 by the Department of Commerce. The cumulative direct investment in the U.S. by foreign concerns for the same category, however, was much greater, expanding to $30.4 billion in 1987 from $23 billion in 1986 and $18.8 billion in 1985. This surge undoubtedly reflected the weakness of the dollar against some foreign currencies.

If the pace of 1988 investment was any indication, foreign investment in the U.S. was sure to grow. West German and Japanese companies invested heavily in the U.S. in 1988. West Germany's Bayer acquired Compugraphic and Denka Chemical, while BASF purchased the Latex division of Polysar. Schering bought the AZS Corp. A year earlier, in 1987, Bayer had acquired Wyrough & Loser, and Henkel had picked up Oxy Process Chemicals and Parker Chemical, while Hoechst, in the single largest transaction, had purchased the U.S. fibre giant Celanese.

Not to be outdone, Japanese firms spent more than $500 million on acquisitions of U.S. chemical process industry companies in 1987. Dainippon Ink & Chemicals acquired Reichhold Chemicals, and Fujikura Kasei obtained a stake in Polytribo. Also acquiring U.S. operations in whole or in partnership with U.S. companies were Ashai Glass, Mitsubishi Corp., Sumitomo Chemical, Takeda Chemical, and Yokohama Rubber.

The huge trade imbalance between Japan and the U.S. was a major factor in the thirst for U.S. investments, but other factors were also at work. In the case of West Germany, high labour costs deterred producers from investing in the homeland. Labour and benefit costs in West Germany were almost $20 per hour, while in the U.S. they were closer to $15 per hour. Power costs, an important factor in the electricity-hungry process industries, were also relatively high in West Germany compared with the rest of Europe and the U.S.

In 1987 U.S. chemical imports totaled $16.2 billion, a gain of 1.2% from 1986. Exports of chemicals by U.S. producers were much larger—$26.4 billion in 1987 and $22.8 billion in 1986, an increase of 16%. Exports in 1988 were estimated to be near $30 billion, while imports were estimated to be about $20 billion.

In their home markets chemical producers were looking for at least steady demand while counting on exports for much of their growth. West German producers maintained relatively flat domestic sales of $95 billion in 1987 and 1988, but export sales were estimated to have grown

more than 4% in 1988 over 1987, to $46 billion. Imports grew by about the same percentage, to $32 billion. Exports in the U.K. expanded by about 3%, to some $20 billion. Japanese producers, however, were expected to report total chemical sales in 1988 barely over the 1987 showing of $166 billion while exports stayed essentially flat at less than $17 billion in both years. Japanese chemical imports, however, were expected to come close to $15 billion in 1988, compared with $13 billion in 1987.

To maintain their position in world markets, producers for the most part were increasing capital spending appreciably. In 1987 companies in France, Italy, Japan, the United Kingdom, and West Germany spent about $13 billion. In 1988 the comparable figure was estimated to be near $14 billion. Relatively high capital spending was planned in a number of important chemical-producing nations. French producers invested about $2.5 billion in both 1987 and 1986. The Netherlands increased spending by $300 million, to more than $2 billion, and Italy raised expenditures by about 7% in 1988, to about $2 billion.

(JOHN M. WINTON)

ELECTRICAL

Manufacturers of electrical power and control equipment were grappling in 1988 with the increasing demand by users for fully integrated systems. To meet this demand at the control end of the market, the two U.S. automation giants, Allen-Bradley (part of Rockwell) and the Digital Equipment Corp. (DEC), joined forces. The combination of DEC's computers and Allen-Bradley's automation modules was expected to provide an integrated office-factory information and control system.

User demand for integrated power systems, particularly for "intelligent" buildings, led the British RTZ subsidiary RTZ-Pillar (a £1.6 billion building products company) to acquire the MK Electric group in a £200 million takeover battle with French electrical equipment manufacturer Legrand. Pillar Electrical was soon trying to acquire other firms that would make it the first British company to offer a complete, integrated range of products and systems for building services.

However, most of the news in the industry in 1988 was made by ABB, the world's largest electrical equipment manufacturing company, formed by the merger of the Swedish Asea and the Swiss Brown Boveri groups in August 1987. Efforts to increase efficiency and profitability quickly resulted in the shedding of 2,500 employees in Switzerland, 4,000 in West Germany, and others in Finland and Italy, totaling 20,000 lost jobs throughout the world. Thereafter, the group lost no time in strengthening its grip on world power markets.

In April 1988 ABB agreed with Westinghouse to set up two joint ventures in a $500 million deal covering the power-generation and power-transmission activities of both groups. In power generation the partnership planned to sell, service, and maintain steam turbines in North America. Westinghouse contributed its power-generation business, with 5,000 employees, to the joint venture but retained its nuclear activities. ABB brought about $100 million of North American power-generating sales to the deal but retained its other interests

in North America. In power transmission Westinghouse contributed all its transmission and distribution business, worth $1 billion, but ABB contributed only $400 million of its $5 billion activities in this business.

In October ABB set up a joint venture with Kraftwerk Union, a Siemens subsidiary, to meet the expected demand for intrinsically safe high-temperature gas-cooled reactor power stations. Siemens had an agreement with General Atomics in the U.S. to explore the prospects for commercialization of a 538-MW station based on the 330-MW Fort St. Vrain (Colo.) high-temperature reaction station. In December, however, it was announced that the Fort St. Vrain plant would be shut down because of operating problems.

One reason for ABB's moves in the power market was the forthcoming decentralization of some of the European electric utilities, notably the planned privatization of the British electricity supply industry in 1990. Another reason was the European Commission's proposed Public Procurement directive, planned to become law also in 1990. Under this directive, all major plant or equipment contracts for "public" services such as electricity supply, whether publicly or privately owned, would have to be widely advertised. This meant that current national purchasing policies would have to be abandoned.

Compared with events in Europe, the North American scene was relatively quiet. General Electric Co. (GE) recorded net earnings of $2,915,000,000 in 1987, a 17% increase over 1986, on total revenues of $40,515,000,000. The combined sales of industrial equipment and power systems, the two sectors that compare directly with other multinational electrical companies, totaled $9,702,000,000 ($9,973,000,000 in 1986), but the combined operating profits were only $173 million. However, sales in GE's aerospace and engines sectors reached $12,035,000,000 ($1,543,000,000 operating profit). Consumer products and major appliances produced sales of $9,763,000,000 and operating profits of $906 million. In 1987 GE spent $1.2 billion on research and development (R and D).

Company-sponsored R and D by Wes-

tinghouse Electric Corp. declined from $246 million in 1986 to $215 million in 1987. Sales were also down to $10,679,-000,000, compared with $10,731,000,000 in 1986, but net income increased from $671 million in 1986 to $739 million in 1987.

Among other large producers Britain's GEC had total sales of £5,553,000,000 in the year ended March 31, 1988, up £306 million from the previous year. Net income also rose £31 million to £451 million.

Siemens reported sales of DM 51.4 billion in the year ended Sept. 30, 1987, up 9% from the previous year, but net income after taxes fell by 13% to DM 1,275,000,-000. R and D expenditure rose from DM 5.4 billion to DM 6.2 billion.

(T. C. J. COGLE)

FURNITURE

A year after the stock market crash in October 1987, the furniture industry was doing well, if not setting any records. Based on a composite of 38 furniture stocks, analyzed by the industry publication *Furniture Today,* prices rose over the year from 570.12 to 652.06, or about 14%. According to the U.S. Department of Commerce, sales of U.S. furniture, home furnishings, and equipment stores were 9.2% higher than for the same period of 1987. In comparison, U.S. furniture shipments for 1988 were expected to rise only 1.5% for the full year, according to the American Furniture Manufacturers Association, largely because store inventories, as reported by the U.S. Census Bureau, were 14.8% higher than a year earlier. This would mean only $15.3 billion in furniture shipments.

The country's top retailers were led by the 105-store Levitz Furniture Corp., based in Florida, which had total revenues of $879.1 million in 1987. This was almost four times larger than the runner-up, Seaman Furniture Co. of New York with $260 million. Third was Rhodes, Inc., of Georgia with $239.6 million in furniture, bedding, and accessory sales. The major change in retailing was the amount of square footage given over to galleries, or stores-within-stores showing products by only one manufacturer. The growth of this phenomenon during the mid-1980s had

DIRECTIONAL, INC.

The exotic green colour and faux-lizard base of the keystone buffet designed by Vladimir Kagan exemplify the trendy art moderne style.

had a dramatic effect on the way furniture stores did business. According to the National Home Furnishings Association, 44.5% of retailers now had at least one gallery, and sales from galleries accounted for 23% of income.

Style trends could best be described as Romantic. Traditional and transition collections were dominated by such designer names as Ralph Lauren, Mark Hampton, and Mario Buatta, all of whom promoted a heavily decorated decor featuring flamboyant touches. These included Victorian wicker, tapestry upholstery, overstuffed footstools, and yards of chintz. Leading the continuing interest in the Country style was the eclectic Raymond Waites/Bettye Martin Gear collection. Even contemporary broke out of its beige, rectangular format into more romantic offerings, exemplified by Jay Spectre's art moderne-inspired collection and the work of Vladimir Kagan, who designed, for example, a keystone-shaped buffet in jade green lacquer with an imitation lizard base. Leather continued to gain market share; it was estimated that leather accounted for as much as 10% of the upholstered furniture business.

After 60 years of struggle, the April and October furniture markets in High Point, N.C., firmly established themselves as the biggest and most important in the world. Indicative was the fact that the National Home Furnishings Association, representing 3,500 U.S. retail companies, moved to High Point from the Chicago area. The Southern Furniture Exposition Building changed its name to the International Home Furnishings Center, a title that more properly reflected its scope. This building alone contained 232,250 sq m (2.5 million sq ft) of showroom space. In the High Point environs, there were over 557,400 sq m (6 million sq ft) of showrooms representing most U.S. manufacturers and firms from 53 other countries.

Two new furniture organizations were created during the year: the American Furniture Hall of Fame in Washington, D.C., with a mandate to collect and preserve American manufactured-furniture history, and the National Home Furnishings Foundation at High Point College, dedicated to the development of research and educational programs.   (ABBY CHAPPLE)

FURS

The fur industry worldwide experienced another difficult year in 1988, despite the importance of furs in the overall fashion picture. Although retail sales rebounded somewhat from the 1987 decline—the result of poor sales in the important months of November and December—they were still disappointing. At the wholesale level, the wide price swings in the pelt market since early 1987 caused losses in virtually every sector of the industry, making 1988 one of the worst years in memory from a profit standpoint. Fur-garment production declined in all the major manufacturing areas, a direct reflection of the heavy carryover of 1987 inventories by most retailers. Orders at all the international fairs early in 1988 lagged behind the previous year.

Lower prices in 1988 worked in retailers' favour, as did the disappearance of the previous year's high hemlines, which had caused many consumers to postpone purchases. Although retail activity improved

toward the end of the year, there were more than the usual number of insolvencies, and indications were that the international industry was undergoing further attrition. In Hong Kong, for example, many of the younger, more mobile operators found permanent employment in other industries.

The U.S. remained the largest consumer of furs, but Japan was catching up quickly. Imports of fur apparel into the U.S. declined in 1988. At year's end it appeared that the total would be well below the $477 million reached a year earlier.

World production of mink rose fractionally to about 35 million pelts, but prices fell sharply. The blue fox crop was reduced 20% by Finland, the largest producer, to 1.1 million pelts, reflecting a 40% drop in prices. Production of Swakara Karakul, on the other hand, rose 10% to about one million pelts because of a price improvement. As part of an omnibus trade measure, the U.S. Congress lifted an embargo against seven Soviet furs that had been in effect for 37 years. As a result, Americans could once again import unprocessed Soviet mink, marten, muskrat, fox, kolinsky, weasel, and ermine.

Animal rights groups stepped up their antifur activities in 1988, particularly in the U.S. and Canada. Having achieved some success in reducing the market for furs in Europe, several groups turned their attention to North America. At the same time, some conservationists were concerned that animal overpopulation could lead to environmental problems.   (SANDY PARKER)

GAMES AND TOYS

"Back to basics" was the phrase used to describe the mood of toy markets worldwide in 1988. The popularity during the previous year of expensive high-tech toys dwindled, and they were not replaced by any products or lines with potential "blockbuster" status. Products that as a result enjoyed a surge in popularity included such old favourites as Lego, Play-Doh, Monopoly, G.I. Joe, and Barbie.

The lack of dominance by expensive toys was reflected in the U.S. by sales volumes that showed a 13.4% increase in 1987 to 1,793,000,000 toys at the same time that the value of these at manufacturers' wholesale prices fell 1.5% to $8.2 billion, compared with $8.3 billion in 1986. The retail value of the market in 1987 was $12.5 billion. The U.K. toy market did enjoy an increase in sales value during 1987, to £921 million from £860 million a year earlier. One of the largest European toy markets, West Germany, experienced a 16.2% increase in imports in the period January–August 1987 to DM 797.9 million. Exports remained level at DM 616 million. Production for the first six months declined 1.2% to DM 751.1 million.

Europe, notably France and Italy, expressed concern over the high level of imported goods, particularly from China. In an effort to protect itself against Chinese imports, the French finally took legal action.

A number of multinational toy companies witnessed major changes in their fortunes during the year. Lego lost its monopoly over the plastic building block market after its four-year battle against Tyco Toys for infringement failed. Coleco Industries, Inc., and its principal U.S. subsidiary filed a petition under Chapter 11 of the U.S. bankruptcy code in July. The filing did not include the company's Canadian and other foreign subsidiaries. The company had never managed to regain stabilization following the decline in sales of the line that shot them to fame, Cabbage Patch Kids.

Mattel Inc., makers of Barbie, trimmed staffing levels in an effort to keep its head above water following substantial losses in the U.S. and U.K. Public and trade opposition in the U.K. caused the company to drop distribution of World of Wonder's interactive gun line, Lazer Tag.

Not all fortunes were bad. The British company Bluebird Toys expanded its base with the acquisition of Peter Pan Play-

SPECTRUM HOLOBYTE

Tetris, a computer game designed in the U.S.S.R., became available in the West. Against a moving background of Soviet locales, the player had to rotate the grouped coloured blocks falling from the top of the central panel and align them with those at the bottom.

things and Merit Toys, both British firms, to become the largest U.K. toy company. Across the Atlantic toy retailing saw a major move with the announcement that Sears, Roebuck and the hamburger giant McDonald's' were joining forces to open 20 to 40 McKid's stores throughout the U.S. during the next two years. The financial power of both companies seemed certain to pose a major challenge to Toys Я Us and Kids Я Us.

The 1988 New York's American International Toy Fair, generally regarded as the trend-setting yardstick for the year to come, provided some interesting developments. Products such as Fisher Price's Pocket Rockers, a cassette recorder with miniature cassettes that can be worn as jewelry; Tonka Corp.'s Dress N Dazzle, a range of dress-up costumes, jewelry, and cosmetics; and Lewis Galoob Toys Inc.'s Just Girls, a line of jazzy jewelry and cosmetics confirmed that toy makers clearly had not lost sight of potential sales afforded by an increasing sophistication at an earlier age.

Other new toys included Hasbro's Maxie fashion doll, an effort to compete with Barbie; Mattel's finger puppets called Boglins; and Tonka's Bone Age dinosaurs. Video games, dominated by the Japanese firm Nintendo, were expected to account for more than $1.5 billion in sales in 1988.

Among the action figures Kenner Parker's Ghostbusters enjoyed continued success, and a popular new entry was Playmates' Teenage Mutant Ninja Turtles, which live in sewers and eat pizza. One of the leading entries in the doll department was Mattel's Lil' Miss Makeup; wetting her cheeks and lips causes her makeup to be revealed.

The campaign in the U.S. against realistic-looking toy guns gathered momentum throughout the year and gained a foothold in Britain. The state of New York passed a bill banning the manufacture and sale of such guns, and this was followed swiftly by the introduction of a bill, debated in the U.S. House of Representatives, that could extend the ban to the entire nation.

(KATE STEVENS)

GEMSTONES

During 1988 the gemstone and jewelry market increased its turnover, in keeping with the almost explosive growth in retail trading in Western countries. In London shops the quality of goods offered was as high as usual, and buying, despite the stock market crash of October 1987, continued at a high level. This revival of the British market, coinciding to some extent with the revival of the British economy, was echoed in other major Western European countries and in the U.S. and Japan.

Christie's in Geneva held its most successful jewelry sale ever in May 1988, realizing a total of Sw F 51.8 million. Similar results were achieved by the other major houses. There was still a strong demand for Art Deco pieces, and it was expected that in coming years there would be an increased interest in older "fashion" jewelry, in which the stones were mostly glass and considerable use was made of plastic.

Despite the great increase in retail purchasing in the Western economies, there had not been much of a revival of the gemstone investment business, which had

been prominent in the early 1970s. There were a few signs that this unwelcome side of the trade might stage a comeback, but the gem trade was better equipped to deal with it.

A large number of unidentified people in the Far East were having great success in altering the colour of major gem species. In general, the stones originated in Sri Lanka or the Indochinese countries, and the treatment was carried out in Bangkok, Thailand. It was clear that any large, fine-coloured stone of the corundum (ruby and sapphire) group had to be regarded with suspicion. The trade worldwide had yet to decide what designation it would give to stones whose colour was known to have been altered.

No new gemstones appeared on the market, and there were no major improvements in the supply of established ones. Unrest in Sri Lanka did not seem to have had any lasting effect on the supply of stones from that country, and it remained to be seen whether recent political events in Burma would have an adverse effect. Fine stones from Burma had long reached the world markets via smuggling. Diamond from the new Argyle field in Australia was of good quality and provided a surprisingly large number of pink stones.

(MICHAEL O'DONOGHUE)

GLASS

The glass industry in the major industrial countries was characterized in 1988 by company consolidations and moderate investment in increased capacity to meet a further rise in demand. In the United States an all-time high of 428.5 million sq m (4.6 billion sq ft) of flat glass was achieved in 1987, and 1988 figures were expected to be only slightly lower. A growing gross national product, low unemployment, stabilized mortgage rates, an increased amount of disposable income, and a greater number of dual-income families contributed to a rise in the number of new homes, 78% of which were fitted with insulated or double-glazed windows. The market for low-emissivity and solar-control glasses was also advancing. Sales of flat glass also continued to increase in Western Europe, as they had since 1983.

There was comparable optimism among manufacturers of glass containers in Western Europe and North America. A recent study among British container manufacturers showed capacity and demand almost balanced. The total amount of recycled glass in the U.K. reached 245,000 metric tons. A significant development on the European mainland was cross-frontier investment such as the purchase by Saint-Gobain (France) of a substantial stake in Oberland Glas (West Germany). Technical improvements accompanied the renaissance in container demand, particularly in making products of light weight. For example, Ruhrglas of West Germany began operating the first RIS-8 (rotating individual section machine) for the production of ultralightweight containers.

In the U.S. new markets and increasing environmental concerns were expected to maintain the impetus for glass container production well into the 1990s. Premium beers, single-serving juices and soft drinks, bottled water, and microwavable foods were among the major growth areas. Also

in the U.S., through a joint labour-management program known as the Nickel-Solution Trust, glass-recycling programs were established in 22 states and the District of Columbia by the Glass Packaging Institute.

After the 14% increase in the sale of glass fibre for the reinforcement of plastics and composites in the U.S. in 1987, a relatively modest growth of 2.5% was expected in 1988 and a somewhat reduced pace in 1989. Elsewhere the main growth areas in 1987 were Japan and other Far Eastern countries.

The manufacture of domestic glassware in Europe and elsewhere appeared in 1988 to be enjoying a minor boom, with several British companies, for example, investing in new production facilities and introducing new working methods in this traditional industry. Most order books were full, and nontraditional markets, including Japan, were being investigated. The variety of special glasses for the electronic, chemical, optical, and communications industries represented less than 1% of the tonnage of glass produced in the Western world but more than 15% of the value. Sales of high-performance glasses were expected to increase dramatically by the year 2000 with the advent of new applications such as glass substrates for memory disks. (See Ceramics, above.)   (PETER J. DOYLE)

INSURANCE

Record catastrophic losses, which by mid-year exceeded the entire previous 12 months, tested the financial strength of worldwide insurance in 1988. That global reinsurance helped provide protection for large losses, however, was seen in the January payment of $350 million by Bermuda reinsurers for an earlier Texas chemical plant loss. Largest of the year's insured losses was the explosion of the Piper Alpha oil-drilling platform in the North Sea, resulting in 167 deaths and $1.4 billion in claims. Other catastrophies included a Brazilian oil platform blowout that cost $325 million; drought and forest fires in the U.S.; a 727 jet crash in Dallas, Texas, with 93 survivors; an airshow disaster in West Germany that killed 70 persons and injured hundreds; and a $200 million fire in the Chiado shopping district of Lisbon. Hurricane Gilbert caused havoc in Jamaica and Mexico, but the estimated $1.8 billion of insured losses would have been much greater if its full force had hit the U.S. mainland.

Despite such calamities, general insurance companies in the U.K. in 1987 reported their most favourable results since 1980. Premiums rose by 4.3% to almost £20 billion, with worldwide trading profit of £1.6 billion, or 8%. The preliminary figures to mid-1988 showed even larger profit gains. However, higher automobile insurance rates increased premiums by nearly 28%, and more than a million property claims were recorded for the widespread windstorm damages occurring late in 1987. Liability insurance problems also continued, with more strict liability imposed by EC directives on defective products, and many professions forming mutual insurance associations (even for insurance brokers). Lloyd's of London celebrated its tercentenary. Under its three-year accounting system, Lloyd's reported increased underwriting profit of £190 million on 1985 net

Smoke billows from the Piper Alpha oil-drilling platform in the North Sea after a catastrophic explosion tore the rig in two. The disaster, which killed 167, resulted in the year's largest insured losses, $1.4 billion in claims.

PRESS ASSOCIATION

premiums of £3 billion, but reduced overall profit (including investments) of £211 million.

The income of U.K. life insurance companies rose by almost 20% to £26 billion. New business was spurred after midyear by legislation permitting individual pension plans to substitute for government and employer pensions. The threat of AIDS deaths caused insurers to set aside £1 billion for increased claims during the next ten years. Implementation of the Financial Services Act forced life insurance advisers to sell the products of one insurer only or to meet independent "best advice" rules. The EC intensified its efforts to create freedom of services, including insurance, among its member countries. In France the previously announced divestiture of state-owned insurance companies was halted following formation of a left-wing government.

In the U.S. midyear results for property-liability insurance showed the effects of a softening market and rate reductions of about 20% in many commercial lines; net premiums rose only 2%, compared with 9% for personal insurance. Underwriting losses reported by A. M. Best Co. during the first half of 1988 totaled approximately $5 billion, offset by $13 billion of investment income for net operating income of $6 billion after taxes. Liability insurance problems eased somewhat, with tort reform laws instituted in many states and more "risk retention groups" offering competing coverage. A controversial lawsuit brought by 18 states claimed collusion by major insurers and a rating organization during the "liability insurance crisis" of recent years. In November California voters approved a proposition reducing automobile insurance rates by 20%, but the courts stayed enforcement of the rollback until challenges to its constitutionality were resolved. The Surety Association of America

predicted overall profitability for 1988 for contract bonds, following several years of large stock losses that caused some insurers to leave the business. Fidelity bonding results, with premiums up 20% in 1987, were expected to be less favourable; computer frauds and savings and loan companies were particular trouble spots.

Life insurance sales in the U.S. fell in 1988, reflecting consumer uncertainty in regard to two leading products — interest-sensitive universal life insurance and single-premium contracts. Legislation approved by Congress in October would limit the tax advantages of newly written single-premium policies and "modified endowments" (those with fewer than seven level annual premiums) and allow the Treasury Department to regulate reasonable mortality and expense charges. Health insurance costs continued to soar, with approximate increases of 20–25% in indemnity policies and 10–15% in health maintenance and other managed health care plans. Concern mounted over new accounting rules that might require employers to put postretirement health and welfare benefits on an accrual basis. The Medicare Catastrophe Coverage Act became law in July, providing broader protection against medical bankruptcy for the elderly and other Medicare recipients. With heightened public interest in long-term medical and custodial care, a few insurers were beginning to offer separate coverage or life insurance options permitting partial use of death benefits for such expenses.   (DAVID L. BICKELHAUPT)

IRON AND STEEL

Total world demand and production of crude steel increased by 3% in 1987 to a total of 737 million metric tons. The year started badly but improved so that at its end steel producers throughout the world were experiencing boom conditions. The

strong growth appeared likely to continue throughout 1988.

Many steel producers in industrialized countries had undertaken restructuring measures that allowed them to benefit greatly from the increase in demand. Prices for steel increased in almost all markets through 1987 and 1988, while costs remained stable or in some cases went down. Whereas, following 1986, the financial results of many steel producers were a cause of great concern, 1987 produced a dramatic turnaround from widespread loss to profit in a trend that continued through 1988.

The new optimism spurred investment, although it was likely to be directed toward further modernization in developed countries rather than toward any significant increase in capacity. This strategy arose from the experience of producers who had operated for the last ten years in a situation where chronic excess capacity depressed prices. It was also the result of an awareness that steel consumption in developed countries was on a downward trend. A continuing slow decline in consumption was anticipated, attributable in large measure to the use of higher strength but lighter steels and also to a certain amount of substitution by competing products, such as plastics and aluminum.

The worldwide trends in production were particularly marked in the U.S., where abnormally low production in 1986 was followed by growth of about 10% in 1987, with an additional 5% expected in 1988. Because of large cuts in steelmaking capacity, the utilization of plant increased from 64 to 80%. This much more efficient use of plant was reflected in financial results. Five of the largest U.S. steel producers reported substantial losses in 1986, but in all but one case they announced profits from 1987 operations. On the basis of figures reported for the first two quarters of 1988, all U.S. steel producers appeared to be on course for much better results in 1988. Despite this apparently healthy situation, the producers were calling for the extension of the import restrictions that were due to expire at the end of September 1989 after five years. The restrictions took the form of a series of bilateral agreements with exporting countries to limit deliveries to the U.S. market.

In Japan the steel industry also achieved a rapid return to profitability. The industry had suffered during 1986 and the first part of 1987 from the rapid appreciation of the yen. This reduced the industry's export potential and allowed a significant increase in imports. In crude steel equivalence, Japan's net trade balance in steel deteriorated from a 37 million-ton "surplus" in 1985 to one of 26 million tons in 1987. This situation had prompted efforts to streamline production facilities. The Japanese government's reaction to the appreciation of the yen had been to expand the domestic economy and promote spending on infrastructure. The result was an increase in domestic demand for steel so that during the most recently completed financial year, ended March 1988, steel production totaled 102 million tons, compared with 96 million tons in the previous year. Taken together with the efficiency measures already accomplished, this resulted in all the major Japanese steel pro-

ducers recording substantial profits during that period.

For the European Communities in total, the recovery to boom conditions was somewhat behind that of Japan and the U.S. Although certain countries, notably Spain and the U.K., benefited from strong economic growth during 1987, in the rest of the EC growth was much slower. As a result, production during 1987 was only marginally higher than in 1986. Even the recovery toward the end of 1987, which compensated for a weak beginning to the year, resulted from stronger export markets more than from internal demand. During 1988, however, growth accelerated in almost all the EC markets so that production was expected to increase by about 6% compared with the previous year. Prices increased as demand strengthened, and all EC steel producers were anticipating improved financial results.

The exceptional growth in the U.K. resulted in an increase in production of crude steel by 11.5% during 1987. British Steel had recorded three successive years of increasing profits, and in October 1988 the government announced its intention to sell all of its interest in the company before the end of the year. During 1987 the two French government-owned producers were merged to form Usinor-Sacilor, the largest European steel company and the world's second largest after Nippon Steel of Japan.

The trend of increased production continued in less developed and newly industrialized countries. South Korea extended its growth with the start-up of its new steelworks at Kwangyang, resulting in a 20% increase in the first eight months of 1988 over 1987. China experienced strong gains

and was planning a new steelworks in cooperation with overseas interests. Brazil also resumed a faster growth in production, with a 14% increase during 1988 compared with the previous year.

(IAN D. MATTHEWS)

MACHINERY AND MACHINE TOOLS

World production of metalworking machine tools in 1987 was valued at $31.3 billion, a 10% increase over 1986. Of this, $23.6 billion was attributed to cutting machines such as lathes, milling machines, and drill presses, while $7.7 billion was for forming machines, which include presses, shears, and bending machines.

The leading nations in machine-tool production in 1987 were Japan and West Germany, each with shipments valued at $6.4 billion. The Soviet Union produced shipments valued at $4 billion, followed by the U.S. with $2.6 billion, Italy with $2.2 billion, Switzerland with $1.5 billion, and East Germany with $1.3 billion.

West Germany, with machines valued at $3.3 billion, produced more machine tools for export than any other country; it was followed by Japan with $3 billion, Switzerland with $1.4 billion, East Germany with $1.2 billion, and Italy with $1 billion. The principal importing countries in 1987 were the U.S., with imports valued at $2 billion, followed by the Soviet Union with $1.6 billion and West Germany with $1.2 billion. For the year the U.S. experienced a machine-tool trade deficit of $1.4 billion. The leading consuming nations for machine tools in 1987, where consumption is defined as domestic production plus imports and minus exports, were the Soviet

Union at $5.3 billion, West Germany at $4.3 billion, the U.S. at $4 billion, Japan at $3.7 billion, Italy at $1.8 billion, and France at $1.2 billion.

In recent years the emphasis in machine tool design had been on providing increased productivity. This was accomplished in a number of different ways. Many machines were now offered with automatic part-handling systems to increase productivity. These mechanisms provided rapid removal of completed parts and quick delivery of new stock to the work-processing area.

Improved cutting tool materials became available to increase productivity. Such materials could prolong tool life and allow the tool to be used at increased production rates. Another feature of newly designed machinery was the concept of modularity, which allows complex machines to be built from less expensive pre-engineered building blocks yet facilitates the easy changeover of machinery to process different piece parts as production requirements change.

(JOHN B. DEAM)

MICROELECTRONICS

Worldwide sales of semiconductors were projected to increase 38.2% in 1988 owing to improvements in the economies of the U.S., Europe, and Japan. The increase, more than double that of the previous year, would raise the value of sales from $32.5 billion in 1987 to $45 billion in 1988. U.S. sales should experience a 35.3% increase from $10.3 billion in 1987 to $13.9 billion in 1988, according to World Semiconductor Trade Statistics (WSTS), an industry statistics group. This increase was tied to continued economic expansion, which in-

Table VIII. World Production of Crude Steel
In 000 metric tons

Country	1983	1984	1985	1986	1987	1988 Year to date	No. of months	Percent change 1988/87
World	663,200	710,320	719,410	714,500	737,460	—	—	—
U.S.S.R.	152,510	154,200	154,500	161,000[1]	161,400	[2]	[2]	[2]
Japan	97,170	105,580	105,280	98,275	98,510	70,013	8	+9.8
U.S.	76,760	84,500	79,240	73,750	81,000	60,700	8	+17.8
China	40,020	43,360	46,700	51,900	56,020	[2]	[2]	[2]
West Germany	35,730	39,390	40,500	37,140	36,250	27,060	8	+11.2
Italy	21,810	24,060	23,870	22,870	22,820	15,310	8	+1.5
France	17,580	19,000	18,820	17,900	17,690	12,456	8	+7.5
Czechoslovakia	15,020	14,830	14,960	15,110	15,400	4,014	3	+4.5
Poland	16,240	16,530	15,800	17,200	17,100	4,325	3	+8.7
U.K.	14,990	15,120	15,720	14,810	17,430	12,447	8	+11.5
Spain	13,010	13,500	14,230	11,980	11,810	7,680	8	−0.3
Romania	12,590	14,440	13,760	14,300	15,000[1]	[2]	[2]	[2]
Brazil	14,670	18,390	20,450	21,230	22,230	16,180	8	+14.0
Canada	12,830	14,700	14,650	14,080	14,740	10,238	8	+3.9
South Korea	11,920	13,030	13,540	14,560	16,780	12,780	8	+19.6
India	10,240	10,550	11,540	11,870	13,100	9,300	8	+7.7
Belgium	10,150	11,300	10,680	9,720	9,820	7,320	8	+15.5
South Africa	7,180	7,730	8,510	9,060	8,730	5,950	8	+2.2
East Germany	7,220	7,573	7,840	7,970	8,200	2,085	3	+3.2
Mexico	6,920	7,480	7,260	7,170	7,490	5,230	8	+8.9
Australia	5,680	6,300	6,410	6,670	6,100	3,910	8	−0.9
North Korea	6,100	6,500	8,400[1]	9,000	9,500[1]	[2]	[2]	[2]
Netherlands, The	4,480	5,740	5,520	5,280	5,080	3,640	8	+8.2
Austria	4,410	4,870	4,660	4,290	4,300	3,040	8	+8.3
Taiwan	5,030	5,010	5,090	5,550	5,790	3,860	8	0.0
Sweden	4,210	4,705	4,810	4,710	4,600	3,030	8	+8.0
Yugoslavia	4,130	4,290	4,470	4,520	4,370	2,950	8	+0.7
Hungary	3,620	3,750	3,620	3,730	3,500[1]	916	3	+1.7
Luxembourg	3,290	3,990	3,945	3,710	3,300	2,400	8	+8.9
Turkey	3,830	4,330	4,950	5,980	7,050	5,220	8	+14.5
Argentina	2,940	2,650	2,940	3,240	3,610	2,260	8	−4.6
Bulgaria	2,830	2,870	2,880	2,830	3,000	770	3	—
Finland	2,420	2,640	2,520	2,590	2,670	1,815	8	+6.4
Venezuela	2,320	2,770	3,055	3,460	3,720	2,480	8	+1.3
Iran	1,200[1]	1,200[1]	1,200[1]	1,200	1,250[1]	[2]	[2]	[2]
Greece	870	900	990	1,010	910	609	8	+5.0
Switzerland	840	980	990	1,010	870	[2]	[2]	[2]
Norway	900	920	940	850	850	572	8	+5.7

[1]Estimated. [2]1988 figures not yet available.
Sources: International Iron and Steel Institute; United Nations.

Table IX. World Production of Pig Iron
In 000 metric tons

Country	1983	1984	1985	1986	1987
World	457,830	489,740	498,955	488,840	510,600
U.S.S.R.	110,450	110,800	109,980	113,600	113,900
Japan	72,940	80,400	80,570	74,650	73,420
U.S.	44,210	47,090	45,760	39,770	43,570
China	37,380	40,000	43,540	47,000	51,000[1]
West Germany	26,600	30,200	31,530	28,590	28,120
France	13,500	14,710	15,070	13,710	13,240
Italy	10,310	11,630	11,660	11,900	11,370
Brazil	12,950	17,220	18,960	15,840	16,940
India	9,160	9,460	9,840	10,510	10,920
Czechoslovakia	9,470	9,560	9,560	9,600	9,790
Romania	8,180	9,560	9,210	9,500	9,500[1]
South Korea	8,020	8,760	8,830	9,000	11,080
U.K.	9,480	9,490	10,380	9,713	11,660
Poland	9,470	9,540	9,440	10,220	10,120
Canada	8,570	9,640	9,670	9,250	9,690
Belgium	8,070	9,010	8,750	8,090	8,230
South Africa	5,220	5,530	5,040	5,770	6,350
Spain	5,420	5,340	5,480	4,803	4,860
Australia	5,060	5,330	5,600	5,850	5,580
North Korea	5,500	5,750	7,750[1]	8,500[1]	8,800[1]
Netherlands, The	3,750	4,930	4,820	4,630	4,570
Mexico	3,540	3,870	3,530	3,730	3,690
Austria	3,320	3,745	3,700	3,350	3,420
Yugoslavia	2,840	2,850	3,110	3,070	2,940
Taiwan	3,420	3,290	3,430	3,740	3,770
Luxembourg	2,320	2,770	2,750	2,650	2,310
Hungary	2,060	2,100	2,100	2,080	2,110
Turkey	2,720	2,900	3,190	3,670	4,073
East Germany	2,210	2,360	2,580	2,625	2,760
Finland	1,900	2,030	1,900	1,980	2,060
Sweden	2,010	2,210	2,420	2,440	2,320
Bulgaria	1,630	1,580	1,710	1,600	1,660
Argentina	910	920	1,310	1,640	1,780
Norway	600	550	610	570	370
Chile	540	590	580	590	610
Venezuela	170	330	440	490	470

[1]Estimated.
Source: International Iron and Steel Institute; United Nations.

cluded the strongest growth in the electronics market in four years.

As economic uncertainties decreased, there was a rise in sales of communications equipment, computers, and industrial instrumentation, all heavy users of microchips. WSTS estimated an increase of 38.5% in chip sales in Japan, from $12.7 billion to $17.6 billion. Japan's semiconductor industry operated at near 100% capacity in 1988. Improved economic conditions and anticipation of the elimination of existing trade barriers between Common Market countries sparked growth in semiconductor sales in Europe. WSTS projected a 31.3% rise in semiconductor sales in Western Europe to $8.1 billion in 1988.

The increasing use of 32-bit microprocessors, particularly in new models of personal computers (PCs), also spurred the microelectronics market. The new PCs contained more semiconductors than older models, and sales of these new machines were brisk as buyers took advantage of their increased capabilities. The 32-bit chip processes much larger volumes of information at faster rates than does the 16-bit chip, the previous PC standard.

Rising sales of computers, along with a continuing trade dispute between the U.S. and Japan, created a shortage of dynamic random access memory (DRAM) chips. U.S. companies claimed that their Japanese counterparts, which made more than 90% of the world's DRAMs, deliberately cut production to create the shortage and push up prices. A shortage of 256-kilobit DRAMs was aggravated by a switch to more powerful one-megabit chips. Japanese manufacturers then found the one-megabit chips more difficult to make than anticipated. The subsequent shortage of one-megabit DRAMs delayed introduction of new-model and upgraded computers.

Japan's dominance of the manufacture of DRAMs and other chips spawned concern by both commercial and military users in the U.S. The latter feared that inability to obtain microchips for operation of advanced defense systems would jeopardize national security. This led to

the formation of Sematech (semiconductor manufacturing institute), an industry-government partnership to share the costs of developing new methods and equipment for making and testing microchips.

Among the new microelectronic devices expected to capture the attention of Sematech were application specific integrated circuits (ASIC) and reduced instruction set computing (RISC) chips. ASICs integrate several functions dedicated to a single application on the same chip. RISCs cannot handle as many programs as ordinary microprocessors, but they execute the instructions more quickly.

(WILLIAM J. CROMIE)

NUCLEAR INDUSTRY

Figures for 1987 released by the International Atomic Energy Agency (IAEA) during the year indicated that 23 new power-generating reactors were commissioned, adding 23,161 MW of electrical nuclear capacity to the world's systems. At the beginning of 1988 there were 417 reactors totaling 296,876 MW in 26 countries.

Antinuclear feeling resulting from the accident in 1986 at the Chernobyl nuclear power plant in the Soviet Union waned a little during 1988. To some extent it was replaced by growing concern over environmental effects of other large-scale power generation, which prompted many scientists to draw attention to the absence of combustion exhausts from nuclear power plants. Even in the Soviet Union it was decided not to scrap the RBMK (Chernobyl-type) reactor, and an advanced design was being produced. This would have a modified graphite block layout to eliminate the negative void coefficient at low power that caused Chernobyl to "run away." Among the many new safety features were to be the containment of all primary cooling circuit components and some form of excess containment pressure relief.

The Chernobyl accident led to new international agreements on the reporting of and emergency planning for nuclear incidents and the sharing of nuclear safety expertise. Several missions of the IAEA's Operational Safety Review Team were carried out dur-

ing the year to such countries as Sweden, France, Spain, Hungary, and Japan. The team checked operational safety, management, training, radiation protection, and emergency response capability in operating plants and reviewed the quality of all engineering design and the plans for operation in plants under construction.

A report from the Organization for Economic Cooperation and Development (OECD) Nuclear Energy Agency on the radiological consequences of the Chernobyl accident concluded that people living in those nations, even those in western and southern Europe, were unlikely to have been subjected to an additional radiation dose significantly greater than that received from one year's exposure to natural background radiation. The lifetime average risk to health for individuals was not changed to any noticeable extent, nor would the additional collective doses received make any noticeable difference in radiation-related health effects in any of the member countries.

Robert Gale, the Los Angeles bone marrow transplant specialist who went to the U.S.S.R. to help Soviet doctors treat the victims of the accident, stated that estimates of the total health effects (an additional 60,000 cases of cancer worldwide in the next 50–70 years, about half of which would be expected in the U.S.S.R., according to a U.S. Department of Energy study) were too pessimistic. His own view was that the number of cases would be ten times less.

A team from the Imperial Cancer Research Fund in Britain dismissed media scares of increased cancer incidence near nuclear establishments in the United Kingdom. In fact, the team found (presumably an irrelevant coincidence) that the numbers of cancer cases were lower near nuclear establishments. In the U.S., however, fears of nuclear pollution were revived by the revelation that several plants producing nuclear material for the military were structurally unsound, were poorly managed, and in some cases had contaminated surrounding areas. An Energy Department report estimated the cost of remedying the problem at $81 billion.

At a new public inquiry Britain's Central Electricity Generating Board began to argue its case for the second British pressurized-water reactor (PWR) at Hinkley Point in Somerset. The prototype fast-breeder reactor at Dounreay in Scotland achieved its highest ever fuel burnup, 20% of its fuel atoms undergoing fission, compared with its design target of 7.5%. Technical achievements at the research facility did not, however, impress the British government, which decided to remove funding for the fast-breeder reactor program. The owners, the U.K. Atomic Energy Authority, hoped to find other funding. An agreement for the marketing in Japan of British nuclear technology was signed with the Sumitomo Corp. during the year.

The troubled commercial prototype fast-breeder reactor at Creys-Malville in France remained out of service while the sodium leak in the refueling system was being investigated. Cracks were found in several components of the fuel-transfer system, which had to undergo extensive modifications.

An agreement was signed between

MARTIN MARIETTA

A solar-powered semiconductor chip affixed to the thorax of a European bee is like those to be placed eventually on aggressive africanized bees. The chip would help scientists study the bees' habits in an effort to discover a means of controlling their northward migration.

Tufts of weeds line the sidewalks of Pripyat, an abandoned town located near the Chernobyl nuclear power plant. Public concern after the catastrophic Chernobyl explosion caused setbacks in Soviet nuclear-power programs.

REUTERS/BETTMANN NEWSPHOTOS

Siemens's Kraftwerk Umvelt (KWU) division and the Soviet Union for cooperation on the development of a modular high-temperature gas-cooled reactor (HTGR). Another HTGR agreement was signed by ABB (a firm formed in 1987 by a merger of Sweden's Asea and Switzerland's Brown Boveri) with China, which was intended to lead to the start of a 100-MW project in China in which both ABB and Chinese industry would participate. A collaboration agreement was also signed between the U.S. champion of the gas-cooled reactor, GA Technologies, and Siemens/KWU. The GA modular HTGR won a design competition sponsored by the U.S. Department of Energy for one of two reactors it planned to build for operation in the late 1990s.

Negotiations between India and the U.S.S.R. for the construction of two 1,000-MW pressurized water reactors were held in 1988. India had previously built only pressurized-heavy-water reactors (PHWR). The order for the calandria (the tank holding the entire reactor) for the first of six Indian-designed 500-MW PHWRs was placed by the country's Nuclear Power Corp. with Walchandnagar Industries. The first 500-MW unit was to be ready by 1995.

Negotiations were held in Quebec during the year for the sale of a new type of 10-MW "heat only" nuclear reactor, a development of Atomic Energy of Canada's simple research reactor called Slowpoke. The plan was to supply space heating in the research hospital at Sherbrooke, using the reactor in place of the existing electric boilers. At the same time, the reactor was needed for the production of medical isotopes.

Allegations that the European nuclear-fuel-transport company Transnuklear had been paying bribes to utilities to obtain contracts and had illegally moved 321 drums of nuclear waste containing plutonium and cobalt-60 into West Germany from the Mol nuclear centre in Belgium caused a major scandal in West Germany and Belgium. Government inquiries were held in both countries. The resulting reorganization of the nuclear-fuel-cycle industry was intended to ensure that irradiated wastes from one country could not become mixed with those from another.

ABB joined forces with Westinghouse in the U.S. to supply fuel for boiling-water reactors (BWRs) in the U.S. Under the agreement, an ABB Atom BWR fuel group was established in Pittsburgh, Pa., and Westinghouse would supply BWR manufacturing and licensing services under subcontract to ABB Atom.

Confirmation of requirements for uranium enrichment services to the end of the century enabled the U.S. Department of Energy to undertake long-term planning of enrichment, including the deployment of atomic vapour laser isotope separation to ensure that low-cost enrichment would be available well into the next century. Japan announced the formation of a Mitsubishi, Hitachi, Toshiba consortium to develop the laser enrichment process based on research at the Japan Atomic Energy Research Institute. Permission to build a gas centrifuge uranium enrichment plant at the Rokkasho-mura fuel-cycle centre was given by the Japanese government to the Japan Nuclear Fuel Industry Co.

(RICHARD A. KNOX)

PAINTS AND VARNISHES

Recovery, consolidation, and strategically directed acquisitions continued to mark Western paint industries during 1988. With 1987 output at 5.3 million metric tons in Western Europe, some 4.5 million in the U.S., and 1.9 million in Japan, most Western markets were reaching maturity. Selling rather than making paint was the industry's current problem, and profitability remained a challenge. Specialization in high-tech areas, rather than high-volume bulk production, was seen as the key. Selective acquisitions and divestments were assuming ever greater significance.

Williams Holdings's 1987 purchase of both Crown Decorative Products and Berger Jenson Nicholson had polarized the U.K. market, concentrating about 55% of all decorative paints in the hands of just two companies, Imperial Chemical Industries (ICI) and the new Crown Berger Europe. Williams devoted most of the year to disposing of its unwanted holdings and then restructuring the rest. Crown's African and Asian subsidiaries were sold to Consolidated Paint of India, and Berger's 16 money-losing Australasian companies were acquired by ICI. At home Berger Elastomers went to Products Research and Chemical Corp. of California, and Berger Traffic Markings to Colas. With overcapacity in the decorative paint market, the ax fell on Berger's Bristol plant, the 200-year-old company that had pioneered emulsion paints in the 1950s.

Most acquisitions were designed to buy specific technologies or geographic market shares. By acquiring Italian can coatings manufacturer Attivalac and Du Pont's Spanish powder-coating business, ICI advanced not only its technical interests but its presence in southern Europe. More significant still was ICI's thrust into the European automotive market in conjunction with Du Pont. IDAC, their joint venture based at ICI's former Inmont factory at Bonn, West Germany, was intended as a challenge to the European market leaders BASF, Hoechst, and PPG. Aquabase, ICI's new water-based automotive topcoat which earned the company the 1988 Queen's Award for Technology, was one of the products to be made in Bonn.

The various EC directives on occupational hygiene and the environment were gradually becoming embodied in national legislation. Several of these were implemented in the U.K. during the year. The U.S. chose to follow the European example in banning organotin-containing antifouling paints for small pleasure boats.

(HELMA JOTISCHKY)

PHARMACEUTICALS

With little public fanfare, the U.S. pharmaceutical industry in 1988 achieved unprecedented success in influencing laws in other countries that "undermined patent protection" with the aim of bringing down drug prices. The Pharmaceutical Manufacturers Association played a leading role in this effort, but even more crucial was the appointment of Pfizer Inc. chairman Edmund Pratt, Jr., as chairman of the President's Advisory Committee for Trade Negotiations. This gave the industry input into U.S. trade pacts with foreign governments, the current negotiating round of the General Agreement on Tariffs and Trade, and the imposition of penalties on other nations. The Reagan administration persuaded the Canadian government to restore patent rights and to make this part of the U.S.-Canada trade pact signed and ratified during the year, and in Mexico and South Korea policies more amenable to U.S. practice were adopted to protect exports to the U.S.

Such efforts were less successful in Brazil, which was eventually hit with punitive tariffs. Another country of special concern was West Germany, where the Bundestag (parliament) had been moving toward passage of a law to reduce drug prices as a way of halting spiraling health care costs. Since U.S. multinational firms accounted for about a fifth of the $14 billion that

West Germans spent annually on drugs, there was an important market at stake.

These victories were not repeated at home, despite a momentary slowdown in the growth of approved generics (and some signs of intense price competition and regulatory problems with a few generic firms). Patents on profitable drugs were due to expire in 1989, 1991, 1992, and 1993. Other signs favourable to the generic portion of the industry included continued cost reductions by hospitals, institutions, and third-party payment plans and a 1991 effective date for the Medicare Catastrophic Coverage Act of 1988, whose drug-payment provisions called for use of generic drugs where available. Brand name drug manufacturers had been developing several strategies to maintain their marketing lead. Research was beginning to pay off in the areas of new delivery systems, prolonged-action versions of old drugs, drug implants, and combinations with other drugs, all aimed at prolonging patent life.

The research staffs of a few companies had delivered a series of promising new drugs. These included biogenetically engineered drugs that were beyond the capability of the "low tech" generic producers. Some 100 drug companies and research firms were currently engaged in research in this area, along with 84 organizations tied to government or academia. First to be commercialized had been insulin and human growth hormone, while the headline-catching drug in 1988 was t-PA, which dissolves the blood clots that produce often fatal heart attacks. t-PA was a product of Genentech Inc., a biogenetic research firm that, as a result of that one drug, became a pharmaceutical manufacturer of a stripe not hitherto encountered by the "establishment" manufacturers. Whatever their source, biogenetically engineered drugs for cancer, sexually transmitted diseases like AIDS and herpes, and viral diseases like the common cold and viral pneumonia appeared to be the "new wave" of the mid-1990s.   (DONALD A. DAVIS)

PLASTICS

The renewed growth of the plastics industry that started in 1984 continued and even accelerated in 1988; annual world consumption was running at around 90 million metric tons per year. Expansion was limited only by the ability of plants to fulfill unexpectedly high rates of demand, and in many cases customers went short. Especially in Europe, material suppliers, having suffered huge losses because of gross oversupply in the early 1980s, were reluctant to invest in new capacity. For the first time, the U.S. had to import ethylene—the base petrochemical for all the large-tonnage "commodity" thermoplastics—in order to maintain home deliveries. Prices everywhere rose accordingly.

The most surprising feature of 1988 was the renewed vitality of plastics such as low-density polyethylene and polystyrene, which had been regarded as mature. The industry had not fully agreed on the reasons. There had been little opportunity for stock building anywhere in the supply chain, so overall industrial buoyancy was seen as the most probable explanation. Another factor was the continuing substitution of commodity plastics for other materials; for example, the acute shortage

of high-density polyethylene in Europe was attributed in part to its successful use in natural gas mains in place of metal. Packaging was another sector in which plastics continued to penetrate new markets. The prospects for the replacement of metal cans and glass jars by multilayer polymer structures advanced during the year.

The continued unwillingness to invest in new capacity arose from a belief that a downturn in activity was likely in the next two or three years. However, polypropylene was a special case. For some time this versatile material had shown sustained, above-average growth in a number of fields, among them automotive components, rigid and flexible packaging, and carpet fibres. Western European polypropylene production was around 3.5 million tons in 1988, with plants working at capacity. (World demand approached ten million tons per year.) Based on company statements, projected European capacity for 1991 was well over 4.5 million tons per year. Although some of the plans might not materialize, fears of an eventual polypropylene surplus began to be voiced toward the end of 1988.

Restructuring had by no means run its course. The two major Italian chemical groups, Montedison and Enichem, announced a projected merger involving many of their interests, including those in plastics. In the U.S., General Electric, already a prominent manufacturer of engineering plastics, bought Borg-Warner Chemicals, the world's leading producer of ABS (acrylonitrile-butadiene-styrene).

Compared with the more mercurial commodities, the engineering plastics were relatively immune to the economic cycle. This was reflected in continued steady rather than spectacular growth for these materials in 1988, largely through substitution for metals in such products as automobiles. Their success was based on technical merit, high added value, and cost effectiveness, which easily offset their higher initial price. World demand for them was now over 1.5 million tons per year, and prospects remained excellent.

Composites (in which plastics are combined with other materials, such as fibreglass) also sustained their promise. In the U.S. alone, production was estimated at 1,250,000 tons, about 6% more than in 1987. A quarter of this went to the transportation industry, and construction and the marine industry each accounted for about another fifth.   (ROBIN C. PENFOLD)

PRINTING

The year 1988 was dominated by the takeover of the web offset division of AM International's Harris Graphics subsidiary by Heidelberger Druckmaschinen AG of West Germany. The world's largest manufacturer of printing machines thus also became the supplier of the widest range of printing machines to the world. Heidelberger had nosed out Komori Printing Machinery of Japan. In November, however, Komori took over the French manufacturers Machines Chambon, thus establishing a manufacturing base in the EC.

Personal computer (PC)-based desktop publishing systems providing graphic arts quality and integration into colour systems were proving successful. Bedford Computers using Unix-base and working with Sun

and Macintosh II PC systems were able to integrate into Crosfield Studio colour pagination systems. Teragon of Sweden developed a low-cost system bringing colour and phototypesetting together, with a first installation going to the French newspaper *L'Express.* In London *The Guardian* began printing on a new line of Koenig & Bauer Commander letterpress machines, an unusual move at a time when offset and flexo newspapers made all the headlines. In Japan, Tokyo Kikai Seisakusho installed an anilox flexo news press. Anilox dispenses with ink key settings and inks the whole plate by means of a cylinder roll.

MAN Roland joined the ranks of ultrafast sheetfed offset machines with the Roland 600 series of multicolour machines with a top speed of 12,000 sheets per hour. In small sheet work, Oliver of Japan introduced the ultimate push-button machine, making operation as simple as that of a copier. In the Soviet Union it was decided to extend phototypesetting capacity rapidly and to add 40 web offset printing presses, mostly from East Germany and India.

The Swiss manufacturers Bobst acquired 50% of the Italian rotogravure printers Schiavi. Du Pont acquired the marketing rights to Dainippon Printing's thermal colour proofing system. Robert Maxwell's Pergamon Press bought the "fattest" of the airline timetable titles, the OAG, from Dun & Bradstreet. His Maxwell Communications Corp. was now the second largest U.S. printer, after R. R. Donnelley.
                (W. PINCUS JASPERT)

RUBBER

The internationalization of tire production in the North American market was virtually completed in 1988, as Japan's Bridgestone bought Firestone Tire and Rubber Co. and Italy's Pirelli purchased Armstrong Tire. These two companies joined Japan's Sumitomo Rubber, which bought Dunlop, and Continental of West Germany, which bought General Tire, as owners of tire production facilities in North America. Bridgestone reportedly paid $2.6 billion to acquire Firestone, the second largest tire manufacturer in the U.S., strengthening its position as the world's third largest tiremaker and moving it past Michelin into second place among world rubber companies. (Goodyear was ranked first in both categories.)

Other major acquisitions during 1988 included the takeover of Polysar Ltd. of Canada, one of the largest synthetic rubber producers, by Nova Corp., also of Canada, for a reported $1.7 billion. In an attempt to thwart the takeover, Polysar sold its latex division, with an annual capacity of 220,000 tons, to BASF of West Germany for Can$500 million. Ente Nazionale Idrocarburi (ENI, the state chemical and energy company) and Montedison S.p.A. of Italy were combining units, including rubber. The union would create the world's seventh largest chemical company, to be called Enimont.

Degussa of West Germany purchased Ashland Chemical's carbon black business for $58.5 million, making it the second largest producer of this important ingredient in rubber processing. Mobay Chemical, a division of Bayer AG of West Germany, bought Denka Chemical, a major producer of polychloroprene rubber, and Rhone-

Poulenc of France bought the silicone business of Imperial Chemical Industries. Other acquisitions included Conap Inc., a manufacturer of adhesives and sealants, by American Cyanamid; the aircraft tire operations of BF Goodrich by Michelin; a management group buyout of BFG's engineered rubber products division; and Ceat Pneumatici by Marangoni Pneumatici and A.G. International in Italy. A Mohawk Rubber management group purchased that company from the Danaher Corp. for $71 million, and BFG was divesting its fabricated polymers division through the same type of buyout.

Joint ventures were also in vogue during 1988 as companies attempted to expand their markets and manufacturing bases. Dow Chemical and Exxon Chemical formed a 50-50 joint venture in styrenic thermoplastic elastomers, and an alliance between Continental and its General Tire subsidiary with Toyo Tire & Rubber and Yokohama Rubber of Japan was announced. Union Carbide and General Electric agreed to combine silicone businesses; Exxon Chemical and Japan Synthetic Rubber signed a joint technology pact covering ethylene-propylene rubber; Bridgestone formed a joint venture in Turkey with the Sabanci Group for passenger radials as well as truck and bus tires; and Michelin formed a joint venture with Okamoto Industries of Japan for the production of radial tires.

Among new plants and expansions, Goodyear was building a steel radial passenger and light truck tire plant in South Korea and expanding its Lawton, Okla., plant by 20%. Dunlop began building a 3,720-sq m (40,000-sq ft) truck tire facility in Buffalo, N.Y. Kumho Tire of South Korea planned to build a plant that would have an annual capacity of 15 million tires upon completion in 1995. Suppliers of materials to the rubber industry also had a good year. Polysar was spending $18.5 million to increase capacity for halogenated butyl rubbers at its Antwerp, Belgium, plant; Goodyear was building a powdered nitrile plant in Houston, Texas; Himont Inc. started construction on an 80,000-ton engineering resin and elastomer manufacturing facility in Ferrara, Italy; and Exxon Chemicals' $32 million expansion of its ethylene-propylene rubber operations in Baton Rouge, La., would bring capacity to 80,000 tons per year.

Natural rubber producers enjoyed a good year in 1988. The International Natural Rubber Agreement began its second round, and prices reached the upper limits of the accord for the first time. This necessitated selling off the more than 320,000 metric tons that had been stockpiled at lower prices, and prices remained firm. Synthetic rubber also showed strong growth during the year, with producers able to pass along price increases as consumption rose. Consumption of most rubbers increased over the previous year, with nitrile rubbers (14%), ethylene-propylene rubbers (10%), and polybutadiene rubbers (5.5%) posting the largest increases for general-purpose rubbers.

The effect of AIDS was reflected in the rubber industry as the price of latex concentrate, used for condoms and surgical gloves, more than tripled.

(DONALD SMITH)

SHIPBUILDING

The modest rise of 752,744 gross tons (gt) in the quarterly world order book figures in 1987 was the forerunner of continued acceleration, and the total for the second quarter of 1988 was 2,621,992 gt above a year earlier. Tonnage under construction and orders not begun stood at an encouraging 23,967,508 gt. This was the fifth successive rise in the quarterly order book figures since the low point reached in the March quarter of 1987, a significant indication that the most serious shipbuilding recession of the past few decades was ending.

The mood of increasing optimism among shipowners paradoxically contributed to gloom among some big shipbuilders of the Far East. The surge of global new-building prices led Hyundai Heavy Industries of South Korea to try to renegotiate its contractual arrangements for shipbuilding orders being carried out for the World-Wide Shipping Group of Hong Kong. The reasons were not hard to fathom. A ship that could be ordered in Korea in the second half of 1986 for a negotiated price of about $40 million cost some $65 million–$70 million in the second half of 1988. Other shipowners feared new-building contract renegotiation could become widespread. There were rumours of five other approaches to supplement contract prices.

The long-standing dispute between the EC and Far East shipbuilders about unfair prices quoted by the latter was brought to a head by the EC, which threatened to impose punitive port levies on unfairly underpriced Japanese and South Korean vessels visiting EC ports. As a result, Japan and the EC agreed to set a reference range for ship prices as part of a drive to bring stability to the world shipbuilding industry. The intention was to stop shipbuilders from quoting prices below the cost of production.

The mid-1988 figures showed that South Korea had overtaken Japan. Its order book represented 26.97% of world tonnage (6,463,876 gt), while Japan's order book, at 5,774,968 gt, was 24.09% of world tonnage. Third place was gained by the combined tonnages of the two Chinas (People's Republic 991,127 gt, Taiwan 669,500 gt). Behind the Far East shipbuilders came Yugoslavia (1,269,528 gt), Poland (1,030,067 gt), West Germany (984,163 gt), Italy (979,539 gt), Brazil (828,553 gt), and Finland (699,111 gt). The U.K. rose slightly to 15th place, but the tonnage involved was only 229,751 gt—equal to one large bulk carrier. The U.S. share of the world order book, at 0.1%, was even eclipsed by Malta. Thus over half the world's ships continued to be built in the Far East; with Japanese prices now approaching European levels, however, this might change.

In Europe as well as Japan the path toward restructuring of shipbuilding capacity was still being pursued. Portugal's Setenave yard was split into two enterprises; one, dealing with ship-repair work, was to be run by the Portuguese Lisnave yard, and the other, dealing with shipbuilding, by the West German shipbuilding consultants MPC Munchmeyer Petersen. In the U.K. the Norwegian Kvaerner Group took over the Govan yard of British Shipbuilders,

and other nationalized U.K. yards were put up for privatization.

The principal ship types under construction or on order remained broadly the same as in 1987: oil tankers 40.7%, bulk carriers 25.1%, and general cargo ships 18.1% of the total order book. However, the containership component of the general cargo ship total increased from 41.9 to 54.1%. Of the total order book of 23.9 million gt, 66.8% was for registration in countries outside those where the ships were built. This included 5.2 million gt for Liberia, 3.4 million gt for Panama, 1.2 million gt for Singapore, 1 million gt for the U.S.S.R., and 570,000 gt for The Bahamas.

(EDWARD CROWLEY)

TELECOMMUNICATIONS

New technology and the marketplace each strongly influenced the telecommunications industry in 1988. Progress in technology was symbolized by increasing development of the Integrated Services Digital Network (ISDN), a system that was designed to integrate voice, data, text, and video communications into a single worldwide network. This would be made possible by switching from analog to digital technology. Transmitting information as a series of on-off signals (digital) instead of as sound or electrical waves (analog) allows much more information to be sent over wires. The marketplace was demanding this increase and wanted the wires to be connected in larger networks for broader access. The end goal was a global network over which people could speak, send words and data, and receive television signals. It was a situation where the smallest machines ever made—microchips that handle digital signals—were revolutionizing the largest machine ever made—the international telephone network.

Development of the ISDN was taking place in three stages: existing telephone networks were being expanded and digitized; data and text services were being added to voice communications; and plans were being made to add video capability.

Large telecommunications systems already in existence were in the best position to dominate the ISDN. For example, in 1988 American Telephone and Telegraph (AT&T) operated the largest number of telephone lines. The combination of Alcatel (France) and ITT (U.S.) was the world's second largest telephone company. L. M. Ericsson of Sweden had more than 17 million lines in 66 countries—the largest geographic spread for a single system. Northern Telecom of Canada operated the first system originally conceived as an all-digital system.

For a global network to function, all the national telephone systems must adopt the same technical standards. The International Telegraph and Telephone Consultative Committee established such a standard. The European Commission urged its adoption by its 12 member nations, the U.S., and Japan.

In the U.S. the Federal Communications Commission (FCC) and the Congress began struggling with another technology and another set of standards in 1988. In September the FCC issued technical guidelines for high-definition television (HDTV), which was to replace conventional television with pictures of a quality currently seen only in

movie theatres. According to plan, HDTV would also provide stereophonic sound.

During the same month, the U.S. House of Representatives Subcommittee on Television and Finance held hearings to discuss the rules under which high-definition broadcast systems would operate and the potential effect that HDTV could have on the U.S. economy and foreign trade. HDTV signals can carry more information than conventional television signals; therefore, it would become increasingly difficult to find space on the already crowded transmission channels. Digitizing some of the signals could reduce this problem.

Not only communications airways but land and undersea telephone cables also showed signs of increased overcrowding in 1988. One solution was communications satellites. Successful launches in 1988 included three new satellites for the U.S., two for Japan, and three for European countries. The other solution was increased use of optical fibre cables, which, because they use the medium of light waves, can transmit much more information at a higher rate.

In 1988 AT&T completed laying an undersea optical fibre cable between the U.S. and Europe. It carried 37,800 telephone calls simultaneously, doubling the number of transatlantic calls that could be made at one time. A second optical fibre cable, to be laid in 1990, would double this again.

The bottleneck in transmitting voice and other signals by light involved a lack of optical switches and amplifiers to control the light. This still had to be done by electronic devices. Along undersea cables, for example, light signals had to be periodically converted to electronic signals for amplification in devices called repeaters and then converted back to light. Optical signals also had to be converted to electronic signals before the information they carried became available to business and home users. In 1988 several laboratories were testing optical devices that would eliminate the need for repeaters and converters.   (WILLIAM J. CROMIE)

TEXTILES

For many years the world textile trade, particularly in the industrially advanced countries, had suffered from the constant cycle of good and bad years. Good business led to overproduction, which led to a slump.

In the mid-1980s there had been growing optimism in the textile trade, based on the belief that the restructuring that had taken place throughout the industry had had the effect of flattening out these troughs and peaks. Whether this was correct would be decided by the events of the next few years. In 1988 there were signs of what the trade hoped would be only a temporary decline.

The older types of fabrics, which tended to be heavy and stiff, continued to lose ground, and world textile makers were looking toward what could be described as "engineered" textiles embodying specific characteristics. The waterproof but porous lightweight materials made from a lightweight fabric combined with a porous synthetic membrane were examples. Thus a skiwear manufacturer could produce garments that would allow perspiration to be transmitted through the fabric while still protecting the wearer from wind chill.

The trend toward a somewhat "unkempt" look provided a market for lower-quality fabrics, often produced in less developed countries. Manufacturers in those countries benefited from lower labour costs, but the developed countries, by concentrating on high-speed and increasingly automated production of higher quality products, were recovering a more competitive position.   (PETER LENNOX-KERR)

Wool. Prices were on a strongly rising trend in January 1988, and the market accelerated to establish a new record peak in April, when the Australian Wool Corporation's (AWC's) market indicator reached 1,257 cents. The rise from the start of the season amounted to 61% and from the beginning of 1988, to 37%. The average for the whole season was 1,003 cents, 59% more than in 1986–87.

The AWC stockpile was reduced from an opening 346,000 bales to a negligible 8,000 bales during the 1987–88 season. The AWC raised its floor price by an overall 35%, from 645 cents in 1987–88 to 870 for 1988–89. Wool market strength was most evident in Australia and South Africa, with fine merinos leading the price rise. New Zealand, biased more toward coarser crossbreds, benefited less from the fashion favouring finer apparel wools. The market indicator in New Zealand in 1987–88 averaged only 8.5% above 1986–87.

The world wool market fell about 10% from its April peak during the opening months of the 1988–89 season. The AWC market indicator subsequently fluctuated around 1,000 cents. Buoyant world demand for wool stemmed largely from Japan, China, and the U.S.S.R. Wool growers also gave credit to the International Wool Secretariat's promotional efforts.

World wool production in 1988–89 was provisionally estimated by the Commonwealth Secretariat at 3,188,000 metric tons greasy (1,842,000 tons clean), 2.3% higher than in 1987–88 and a new record.   (H. M. F. MALLETT)

Cotton. World cotton production was expected to decline between 1988 and 1989, with projected production of 86.4 million bales in 1988 dropping to 84.4 million bales in 1989. (One bale = 480 lb or *c*. 218 kg.) Somewhat anomalously, consumption was expected to rise from a 1988 level of 83.4 million bales to 87 million bales, although the U.S. anticipated a fall in consumption, as did the U.S.S.R. and Brazil. Stocks of cotton held in different parts of the world were currently running at some 32 million–35 million bales.

Egypt, one of the major cotton-producing countries and a supplier of high-quality fine cottons, was expecting its output to rise to 1.8 million bales in the 1988–89 season. However, some fluctuations in harvests could be predicted as a result of the year's unusual weather conditions, ranging from continuing drought to inundation.

Declines in raw cotton consumption in the first half of 1988 in the U.S., East Asia, and Europe resulted in lower cotton prices. This was likely to improve the competitive position of cotton as compared with synthetic fibres, and a recovery in the cotton trade was anticipated in the second half of the year, continuing into 1989. Also brightening the outlook for cotton was a shortage of ethylene glycol, the raw material used to make polyester fibres, which would push up polyester fibre prices.

The change in yarn-production systems from classical ring spinning to the comparatively recent rotor spinning system was forcing cotton growers to produce the finer fibres required by the new machines. Cotton breeders were making every effort to improve strains accordingly.
          (PETER LENNOX-KERR)

Silk. In the period 1987–88 China remained the world's largest producer of raw silk, with 35,800 metric tons in 1987. Worldwide demand for silk improved, and shortages became apparent at the end of 1987. Four official price rises took place, but demand persisted. Inside China consumption was buoyant, with such articles as silk bed quilts using large quantities of fibre and fabric.

Japan's government-held stock of raw silk continued to decline, and the stabilization price remained at 9,800 yen per kilogram. Demand there was also increasing with the consumption of more Western-style clothes in silk. Japan was the world's largest silk consumer at 19,000 tons. The silk trade now hoped that Japanese production would stabilize or increase and that production in countries such as Brazil and Colombia could be stepped up to meet rising demand.

Consumption per capita in Europe had increased from 23 g (0.81 oz) in 1976 to 28 g (0.99 oz) in 1986, and a considerable amount of new silk-processing equipment had been installed. Talk of European and U.S. protectionism died down as supply became the main problem. Spun silk became even harder to obtain than raw. Direct offers from China to Europe almost ceased, and the product was available only at inflated prices from third countries such as Hong Kong.

World production for raw silk in 1986, as calculated by the International Silk Association, was 62,622 tons.
          (ANTHONY H. GADDUM)

Man-Made Fibres. The restructuring of man-made fibre production in Europe, the U.S., and Japan resulted in the simplification of production programs and, it was assumed, the range of products made. This inevitably resulted in job losses and an apparent decline of certain producers. The main man-made fibre was now polyester. In 1987 the production of cellulosic fibres such as viscose rayon and acetate fell 0.2% to 2,835,000,000 kg (6,246,000,000 lb), but polyester production increased 2 1/2 times to 7,470,000,000 kg (16,457,000,000 lb). Production of all synthetic textile fibres rose almost 6% in the 1986–87 period to 13,770,000,000 kg (30,332,000,000 lb).

Modacrylic fibres were used mainly in flame-resistant materials when fire hazards needed to be minimized. As legislation establishing flammability standards was introduced, demand for these fibres was likely to increase. Aramid fibres, special high-performance fibres of the nylon family, were used in such applications as aerospace composites and ballistic protection and in others where immense strength was required. It was polyester, however, that made up the bulk of synthetic fibre production, and here flame resistance was being provided by special flame-resistant polyester fibres. Olefin fibres, used in the carpet trade as both pile and backing and

A man in Taiwan smokes a cigarette in front of posters promoting American brands. Currency gains over the U.S. dollar coupled with fewer trade restrictions increased Taiwan's demand for American-made imports.

HO CHING-TAI

also as a packaging material, were important, but there tended to be some confusion about how such materials should be divided into textile and nontextile fibres. Polyethylene, which was included in this category, had been greatly improved and was likely to compete in markets currently dominated by the aramids.

(PETER LENNOX-KERR)

TOBACCO

Despite the many efforts to discourage smoking, world tobacco production and consumption rose during 1988. The estimated 32 million people who produced the crop grew about 6.5 million tons—approximately 5% more than in 1987. Average farm-gate prices were little changed, signaling that supply was in line with demand. While consumption was static or falling in developed countries, it continued to rise in the populous third world, particularly in China, now firmly established as the world's biggest producer and consumer of tobacco. World production of cigarettes, still the most favoured form of tobacco consumption, edged up again in 1988, by some 1.5%, to a record of nearly 5.1 trillion.

Cigarette export trade rose strongly in 1988, as the U.S. used trade agreements to gain entry into such formerly closed monopoly markets as Japan, South Korea, and Taiwan. Imported cigarettes, predominantly from the U.S., were expected to capture about 12% of the huge Japanese market by the end of 1988. A novel feature of this assault was that the major weapons were brands formulated especially for Japan, a departure from the usual technique of pushing internationally known brands in export initiatives.

The industry viewed with dismay the projected denial, from 1992, of duty-free concessions to travelers crossing frontiers within the EC. It was feared that the loss of sales of cigarettes and luxury cigars that travelers could no longer buy cheaply at airport shops, aboard aircraft, and on ferries would only partly be made good by increased sales at travelers' destinations.

The first totally new cigarette-format product aimed at quieting the health controversy and making smoking socially more acceptable was being test marketed by

R. J. Reynolds in the U.S. It heated, rather than burned, tobacco, substantially reducing many of the compounds implicated in the health debate and producing virtually no smoke. The American Medical Association filed petitions with the U.S. Food and Drug Administration and state regulatory officials claiming that the new product should be treated as a "drug-delivery system" dispensing nicotine.

Meanwhile, tobacco farmers and traders were concerned to note that this innovative product needed only one-third as much tobacco as a conventional king-size cigarette. (MICHAEL F. BARFORD)

TOURISM

During 1988 demand for tourism services continued to grow. Global international arrivals increased to nearly 400 million, and the value of tourism receipts worldwide, which exceeded $150 billion in 1987, pushed ahead toward a total of $200 billion, including international fare payments.

Relatively stable prices for tourism services and rising disposable incomes in the world's main tourist-generating countries led to the industry's good performance in 1988. The strength of European currencies and the Japanese yen helped boost holiday taking by residents of Europe and Japan. By contrast, tourist flows from the U.S. dwindled as the U.S. dollar weakened through 1988, Europe especially being affected.

Europe and North America maintained their positions as the world's main international tourist-receiving markets in 1988. Their combined share of international arrivals was 80%. East Asia and the Pacific continued, as in 1987, to be the fastest growing region in terms of arrivals and receipts, helped by strong Japanese overseas travel and the Olympic Games held in Seoul, South Korea.

In Africa tourism arrivals surged in popular North African destinations such as Morocco and Tunisia in 1988, mostly as a result of low-priced packages negotiated by European tour operators. As the South African government moved to settle regional political issues, arrivals in that nation rose by 14%. In Senegal tourism marked up a healthy 6% increase. The exotic holiday island of Mauritius proved

its popularity with Europeans, recording a 15% increase in tourism.

In North America there was a marked strengthening of tourism in the U.S. The weakening dollar made U.S. trips especially attractive to visitors from Europe and Asia. Arrivals from East Asia and the Pacific were up by 28% and those from Western Europe by 25%, while the 33% rise in visits from Eastern Europe seemed a sure sign of *glasnost* (openness) at work. Tourism in Canada moved ahead more slowly, however, with a 4% rise in overall visits but only a 1% increase from the U.S. Caribbean destinations were helped mainly by European arrivals in 1988. Jamaica was among the popular Caribbean destinations whose tourism facilities were hard hit by Hurricane Gilbert in the fall.

In Central and South America 1988 was a mixed year for tourism. Mexico scored highly as a value-for-money destination for North American visitors, showing a 15% rise in arrivals. Venezuela experienced an 8% increase, but tourism in Uruguay and Argentina, as well as Panama, fell back compared with 1987.

Rapid economic development, combined with vigorous marketing and promotion, was seen as underpinning the continuing strong performance of tourism in East Asia and the Pacific. The region in 1988 enjoyed a share of just over 10% of world tourist arrivals. Many countries in the area benefited from the surge in Japanese overseas travel, which increased 25% over 1987. Bicentennial celebrations in Australia resulted in 28% more visitors than in 1987. In South Korea 19 new tourist hotels with 1,687 rooms were opened to meet increased demand from visitors to the Olympic Games; at least 16% more tourists visited South Korea in 1988 than in 1987. Singapore (14%), the Philippines (19%), China (20%), and Thailand (24%) were other regional destinations that prospered in 1988, though travel to Japan remained steady owing to the rising value of the yen.

Social and political factors affected tourism adversely in some countries of

AP/WIDE WORLD

Fireworks explode over the closing ceremonies of the Summer Olympics, an event that boosted travel to South Korea.

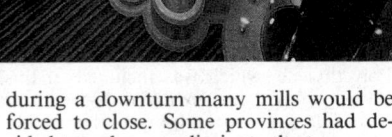

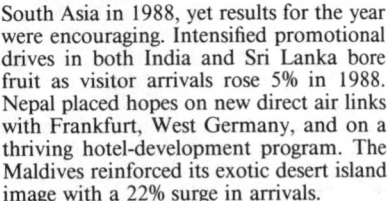

The *Sovereign of the Seas,* the world's largest cruise liner, sails into the port of Miami before embarking on her maiden voyage. The 268-metre (880-foot)-long floating resort was luxuriously designed with such architectural eye-openers as a five-story atrium (right) and two swimming pools.

PHOTOGRAPHS, FORT LAUDERDALE NEWS AND SUN-SENTINEL; (LEFT) JOHN CURRY; (RIGHT) SUSAN GARDNER

South Asia in 1988, yet results for the year were encouraging. Intensified promotional drives in both India and Sri Lanka bore fruit as visitor arrivals rose 5% in 1988. Nepal placed hopes on new direct air links with Frankfurt, West Germany, and on a thriving hotel-development program. The Maldives reinforced its exotic desert island image with a 22% surge in arrivals.

Europe, which accounted for 65% of world tourist arrivals, continued to prosper as a destination in 1988. Its residents traveled not only within the region but outside it as well, as could be seen from the 11.5% increase in North Atlantic air traffic in 1988 compared with the preceding year. Indifferent weather during the northern European summer stimulated demand for second holidays, and September appeared to be ready to supplant June as a peak holiday month. Among Mediterranean, sun-sea destinations, Turkey swung into fashion with the youth market, registering a 37% increase in arrivals. Cyprus (17%) and Spain (6%) also welcomed significant numbers of visitors. However, such other traditional Mediterranean, destinations as Greece, Italy, and Yugoslavia moved ahead by less than 3% compared with 1987. North of the Mediterranean U.S. travelers showed an interest in the cultural attractions of Poland and Czechoslovakia, where arrivals surged by 25 and 23%, respectively. The United Kingdom's dependence on the U.S. market was revealed as arrivals grew by only 2% over 1987, while Switzerland experienced a small decrease, reflecting a drop in both European and North American demand.   (PETER SHACKLEFORD)

WOOD PRODUCTS

Hardwood. The dominating factor in the world hardwood market in 1988 was increasing environmental pressure for sustained-yield management of the tropical rain forests. While statistics showed that most of the destruction was caused by the local population, the world timber industry was the object of considerable criticism.

In July the forestry department at the University of Oxford held a conference, sponsored by timber groups, that brought together environmental groups, experts from such organizations as the World Bank, and representatives of the timber industry. Among the findings were that population pressure in the third world could be expected to double in the next 20 years and that deforestation had no proven effect on the global climate, although regional effects were inevitable. Substantial funds would be required, however, for monitoring the effects of deforestation more closely.

Meanwhile, temperate hardwood producers had been increasing sales, notably in the U.S., which produced more than 16.5 million cu m (7 billion bd-ft) of hardwood lumber in 1987. Exports in 1988, running at some 1,688,400 cu m (730 million bd-ft), were expected to show a 7% increase over 1987.

Softwood. Following restructuring of the industry, Finland produced some 7.2 million cu m (305 million bd-ft) of softwood lumber in 1987 and expected a similar figure in 1988. Export sales were likely to reach about five million cubic metres (three billion board-feet). Production techniques had been modernized to allow more "tailor-made" cutting to customer specification. Similar developments had taken place in Sweden and in smaller North American mills. The first half of 1988 proved favourable for the sawmilling industry in the U.S. and Canada, but as the dollar strengthened, trading slowed down.

The wrangling between the U.S. and Canada continued. The Canadian provinces had to decide whether to maintain the 15% lumber export tax for U.S. sales or to increase stumpage fees fully or partially to offset the tax. The additional 15% sustained by the mills in Canada was estimated to bring total stumpage costs to Can$820 million in 1988, against Can$580 million in 1987. Two years earlier the stumpage bill had amounted to only Can$230 million. The additional costs had been absorbed relatively easily by the industry in 1988, but it was feared that

during a downturn many mills would be forced to close. Some provinces had decided to reduce or eliminate the tax.

Panel Products. Trade disagreements between the U.S. and Canada spilled over into plywood, where a bitter struggle had been fought to maintain technical standards. Plywood demand in North America and overseas remained good. In 1987 U.S. producers achieved a 7% increase in production to 2.2 billion sq m (23.7 billion sq ft; 3/8-in basis), in spite of a fall in housing starts in the U.S. However, such nonveneered boards as waferboard and oriented strand board continued to eat into the plywood market.

In the Far East, Indonesia continued to dominate the hardwood plywood market. Protectionist measures there and in other producing areas, such as Malaysia and the Philippines, meant minimum selling prices and restricted sales volumes. As less developed nations sought to add value to their wood products, additional protectionist measures were likely. Indonesia had already banned the export of ramin strips, which was read as a sign that it would build up its own moldings and furniture industries. In West Africa, Ghana was restricting log and lumber exports and stepping up its furniture and components production.

(JEAN CLARK CAMERON KLOOS)

See also Agriculture and Food Supplies; Consumer Affairs; Economic Affairs; Energy; Information Processing and Information Systems; Labour-Management Relations; Mining; Photography; Television and Radio; Transportation.

This article updates the *Macropædia* articles BEVERAGE PRODUCTION; ELECTRONICS; ENERGY CONVERSION; FORESTRY AND WOOD PRODUCTION; FURS, LEATHERS, AND HIDES; INDUSTRIAL GLASS AND CERAMICS; Chemical Process INDUSTRIES; Extraction and Processing INDUSTRIES; Manufacturing INDUSTRIES; Textile INDUSTRIES; INSURANCE; MARKETING AND MERCHANDISING; PRINTING, TYPOGRAPHY, AND PHOTOENGRAVING; TELECOMMUNICATIONS SYSTEMS; TOOLS.

Information Processing and Information Systems

Under pressure from computer customers, particularly corporations using mainframe computers from several manufacturers, the computer industry in 1988 turned its attention to intercomputer communication and standardization. As a result, one of the most significant events of the year was a conference in Baltimore, Md., where 50 computer makers from around the world demonstrated their machines communicating with one another in a $50 million network of 310 computers. The computers were interacting through use of a standard set of communications rules called Open Systems Interconnection (OSI). Developed by the same international standards-setting body that produces speed ratings for photographic film, OSI seemed certain to become the basis for networks of diverse computers in factories and offices. OSI networks are not likely to come into widespread use until the early 1990s, however; as of 1988 OSI-based products were expensive and not widely available.

Earlier in the year, an effort toward standardization was made in the area of computer operating systems, which control the flow of data within a computer. After purchasing a 20% stake in Sun Microsystems, a Mountain View, Calif., maker of workstation computers, AT&T said that it and Sun would together create a new "standard" version of the operating system called Unix, which was widely used by engineers. Though originally touted as a standard operating system—one that would run the same on any computer, regardless of manufacturer—Unix instead was available in several variations, not all of them compatible. AT&T, which developed Unix, said that the joint development with Sun would utilize the best in the various Unix

versions. AT&T's competitors, however, felt threatened by the move and, under IBM's leadership, banded together to form the Open Software Foundation, which promised to produce its own "standard" Unix.

One feature for which AT&T's new Unix was expected to be notable was the graphic means by which users issue commands to the computer. This so-called graphic user interface, which turns computer commands into on-screen symbols, would make Unix computers, which had always been difficult to use, simple enough to be operated by office workers.

AT&T and Sun unveiled the graphic interface of their forthcoming version of Unix in early 1988, but IBM rejected it, turning instead to the graphic Unix interface of one of the most interesting computers introduced in 1988, the NeXT computer. This machine was produced by the NeXT Computer Co., a creation of Apple Computer's cofounder Steven Jobs. Like the desktop computers used by engineers for computer-aided design, the NeXT ran Unix, had a 32-bit "brain," and offered a high-resolution, black-and-white display. Unlike most other computers available, however, the NeXT also had a built-in CD-ROM (compact disc–read only memory) player (the collected works of Shakespeare, stored on a CD-ROM, were included). The computer was also unique for its ability to produce concert-hall quality sound; at its introduction the computer played a duet with a violinist.

Because the NeXT computer was aimed at college students and professors, it carried a price tag of only $6,500, not counting educational discounts. The hitch, however, was that it would not be available until 1989.

While NeXT, IBM, AT&T, and Sun were all promoting the spread of graphic interfaces for computers, Apple in 1988 sued Microsoft for allegedly copying the graphic interface of its Macintosh model. Microsoft had, with IBM, jointly developed the operating systems for both the IBM

Computer Viruses

On March 2, 1988, Macintosh II computers running a new package for drawing pictures found their work suddenly interrupted by a message calling for world peace. The message marked the first time that commercially available software had been infected by an increasingly bothersome pest, the computer virus.

For some, the sudden message was only a slight bother since it disappeared in seconds. Others, however, found the virus had also destroyed their data. Later in the year, other viruses "infected" computers at federal agencies, prompting one U.S. congressman to call for a federal study of computer viruses.

Viruses have been around about as long as computer programs, but only recently have they begun to infect software in businesses and homes. Like their biologic namesakes, computer viruses are tiny and automatically reproduce themselves, usually by jumping from one infected program to another. They are written, mainly for Apple or IBM personal computers, by computer hackers whose motives range from mischief to malevolence. Some viruses only interrupt you with the display "I Want Cookie!" (proper response: type "Oreo"), while others wait until they have infected all of one's software—and then erase the computer's hard disk.

Viruses usually get into a computer system by

way of noncommercial computer programs, which are given away or sold at low cost at user group meetings or over electronic "bulletin boards." Personal computer users communicate with these bulletin boards by calling them with their computer's modem. The bulletin board serves as software exchange, but because many programs come from unknown sources, bulletin boards are a hotbed of viruses. The virus that infected the Macintosh II drawing program, for instance, had come from a bulletin board.

Computer virus infection can be prevented. Business users, particularly those on networks, can be banned from using anything other than commercial software. Home computer users, meanwhile, should never copy a noncommercial program onto a hard disk without testing it first. Since a virus will hop from an infected diskette to a healthy program the minute the infected program is started up, users should keep write-protect tabs on their healthy programs—and watch to see if any new program is trying to copy a part of itself onto a healthy diskette. A number of virus-buster programs for the Macintosh and IBM computers also recently became available. While these programs can "kill" most viruses, hackers are said to be busily developing new viral strains—just as a biologic virus will mutate to avoid destruction. (EDWARD S. WARNER)

personal computer (PC) and the latest line of IBM desktop computers, the PS/2s. Despite the lawsuit, Microsoft and IBM in late 1988 released a graphic version of the PS/2 operating system, a move that some expected would make these computers as easy to use as the Macintosh.

IBM's PS/2 computers were notable for their Micro Channel architecture, which involved an extra-wide path for carrying data within the computer. The Micro Channel data path permitted computers using it to communicate more rapidly with other computers and with the hard disks on which they store data. In 1988, however, the workings of IBM's Micro Channel design were replicated in computers developed by Tandy Corp. and Dell Computer Corp. It was perhaps inevitable that IBM's latest line of computers should have been finally "cloned," as was the earlier PC line, but this time IBM responded with a warning that any technology cloned by competitors—even the old PC technology—would require the competitor to pay royalties or face a lawsuit.

IBM's tough response was probably caused by the increasing competition of the high end of the desktop computer market, where computers were based on 32-bit processor chips such as the Intel Corp. 80386. Though IBM had several PS/2 models that used the 80386, sales of those computers were put at risk in 1988 when Sun Microsystems introduced a desktop computer that had the 80386 chip and ran both Unix and the PS/2 operating system. The new Sun computer was expected to sell for $8,000, thousands less than the most expensive PS/2s, and was aimed at office users. It was the first computer to be equipped with the AT&T/Sun graphic Unix interface.

One reason that office workers were taking an increased interest in high-performance desktop computers was that software was introduced in 1988 that allowed those machines to perform the sophisticated data management work that formerly could be assigned only to an expensive minicomputer. These new data management programs operated on networks of personal computers in which the most powerful PC acted as a "server," or shared filing cabinet, for the network's data.

Causing a business slowdown throughout the computer industry was a chronic shortage of computer memory chips. From the second quarter of 1987 to the same period in 1988, the spot market price of a 256-kilobit memory chip quadrupled to nearly $400. The big users of such chips, personal computer and workstation makers, were particularly affected by the shortage and consequent price increase, and several said that it had limited their production capacity. (EDWARD S. WARNER)

A major focus of attention of Japanese computer makers in 1988 was the supercomputer. Although Cray Research Inc. and Control Data Corp. continued to control the world market in these machines, they had become increasingly dependent on Japanese-made microchips, such as dynamic random access memory chips. Accordingly, some industry observers pointed out that Japanese firms were beginning to regard supercomputers as the next high-tech area in which to establish a dominant position.

The output of computers and their related equipment in Japan was valued at 4,408,023,000,000 yen in 1987, up 12.4% from the previous year. For January–June 1988 the value was 2,344,233,000,000 yen, up 16% from the corresponding period a year earlier. Of these totals, production of mainframes accounted for 1,153,056 units (up 12.1%), totaling 950,616,000,000 yen (up 21.2%) for the first half of 1988. (MASATO MIYAHARA)

This article updates the *Macropædia* article INFORMATION PROCESSING AND INFORMATION SYSTEMS.

Labour-Management Relations

Stability rather than innovation was the keynote of labour-management relations in 1988. In most countries industrial relations systems had adapted to the economic (and sometimes political) environment that followed the economic shocks of the late 1970s and early 1980s. The emphasis, at least in several countries, was increasingly on achieving higher productivity at the workplace, both by enhancing labour-management cooperation and by instituting more flexible employment arrangements and work practices.

United Kingdom. In Britain the Employment Act, 1988, received the royal assent on May 26. Its most controversial provision was, perhaps, that union members should not be disciplined by their unions for failing to follow a call to take part in industrial action (even when such action was lawfully taken). Members were also given the right to resist the calling of a strike by their union without a ballot.

It was not a good year for British trade unions. Early in 1988 the Ford Motor Co. renounced its intention to establish a plant at Dundee, Scotland (an area of high unemployment), after other unions said that they would not countenance the single-union agreement Ford had worked out with the plant's engineering union. The Trades Union Congress (TUC), which was unable to persuade Ford to change its plans, also had to resolve the issue of disciplinary action against one of its larger members, the 340,000-member Electrical, Electronic, Telecommunication and Plumbing Union. The EETPU had refused to obey a ruling by the TUC's disputes committee to withdraw from two of its controversial single-union, strike-free agreements. An EETPU ballot of its members, reported in July, showed a five-to-one majority in support of the union's executive. The EETPU was expelled at the TUC conference in September.

The September conference also decided against participating, for the time being, in the government's proposed £1.5 billion employment training scheme, on the grounds that the trainees' pay rates were insufficient, the quality of training was likely to be inadequate, there was no certainty of jobs at the end of training, and the scheme might not always be voluntary.

On a happier note, two substantial unions catering to technical, financial, and managerial workers merged in February to form the Manufacturing, Science, and Finance union (MSF), claiming 653,000 members. In October Clive Jenkins, joint general secretary of the MSF and past president of the TUC, unexpectedly announced his intention to move to Australia.

United States. In the saga of the mammoth trade bill, the provision dealing with workers affected by plant closures or layoffs was a major cause of Pres. Ronald Reagan's veto in May (a veto subsequently sustained by the Senate). Shortly afterward, however, these provisions were reintroduced in the form of a stand-alone bill, which duly passed in the Senate and the House. The bill was popular with the public, and when it became apparent that a second veto would not be upheld, Reagan allowed it to pass into law unsigned on August 3 as the Worker Adjustment and Retraining Act, 1988. The act required employers to give workers 60 days' advance notice before implementing either a layoff or a reduction in working hours of more than 50% that would be applicable for more than six months and that involved a minimum of 500 workers at one site or 50 or more employees if they constituted at least one-third of the

employees at the site. Limited as the application of the bill was likely to prove, it represented the first breach of the traditional U.S. "hire-at-will" principle.

The last of the big-three automakers in the bargaining round, Chrysler, concluded its deal with the United Automobile Workers in May. The main elements of the 28-month agreement (which did not include an increase in base pay) provided for two annual bonus payments, together with profit-sharing bonuses and job-security provisions. The union agreed to cooperate with management on reducing job classifications and work rules.

The International Brotherhood of Teamsters faced major difficulties in 1988. The Justice Department, following a recommendation by the Commission on Organized Crime, filed suit against the union in June, alleging undue criminal influence and deprival of members' rights. It also asked that the union be placed under trusteeship and that elections be held. In July the Teamsters' executive committee selected William J. McCarthy (*see* BIOGRAPHIES) to succeed Jackie Presser (*see* OBITUARIES) as union president.

Australia. In Australia a federal Industrial Relations Act replaced the Conciliation and Arbitration Commission with an Industrial Relations Commission, with somewhat enlarged responsibilities and powers. The act also pressed unions with fewer than 1,000 members to amalgamate within three years, facilitated such mergers, enhanced complementary arrangements for action by the Commonwealth and state tribunals, and arranged for certain union elections to be conducted independently at public expense.

The Commonwealth Commission handed down its national wage decision on August 12, providing wage increases of up to 3% and then, after not less than six months, $A 10 a week. The commission laid stress on a new structural efficiency principle, encouraging those involved to establish career paths for workers and ensure that working arrangements enhanced flexibility and met competitive requirements. In April the central employers' organization and the Australian Council of Trade Unions issued a joint statement on participative practices, emphasizing their commitment to the development of a more cooperative and productive industrial culture.

Continental Western Europe. The political uncertainties of early 1988 made for a relatively quiet time in labour relations in France. However, discontent over continued

AP/WIDE WORLD

Thousands of auto workers chant slogans and raise their hands in defiance during a demonstration at South Korea's Daewoo Motor Co. Earlier the plant had closed its doors to its workers after a breakdown in negotiations for higher wages.

austerity, notably in the public sector, mounted as the year went on and erupted in October in a wave of strikes by nurses, teachers, and workers in electricity, gas, the post office, and the Paris urban transport. One of the keenest thinkers among French trade union leaders, Edmond Maire, quit the leadership of the radical-socialist Confédération Française Démocratique du Travail, France's third largest union confederation, in November after 17 years in office.

The emphasis in collective bargaining in West Germany was on working time, with reductions in weekly hours being negotiated in several industries, including steel and construction, and in the public sector (excluding established civil servants). It was estimated that well over half of West German workers would be working less than 40 hours a week by April 1989. The reductions were generally secured without loss of weekly pay, but suggestions that senior civil servants and other highly paid employees should forgo full wage compensation for hours reductions launched quite a debate about the relationship between hours reductions and pay.

In Italy early 1988 was marked by numerous strikes involving railway workers, airport staff, ferry operators, customs officials, construction workers, journalists, and teachers. Both the labour minister and the trade union central organizations, which had limited control over the grass roots committees that called most strikes, proposed measures to regulate strikes.

In Spain the rift between the government and its traditional trade union ally, the socialist General Union of Workers (UGT), continued as the government pursued its hard-line policies on wages and public spending. In an unusual show of unity, in February the leaders of the UGT and its Communist rival, the Comisiones Obreras, announced an 11-point joint program that amounted to an attack on the wage moderation and increased labour flexibility sought by the government.

Though a tripartite pay agreement was arrived at in Portugal on January 25, neither the industrial employers' organization nor the Communist trade union centre (federation) signed it, and the Portuguese UGT later revoked it. There was considerable discord between the government and unions, marked by the biggest one-day general strike in the country's history, held on March 28 to protest government plans to liberalize rigid labour laws concerning dismissals and fixed-term contracts.

On January 1, three existing central employers' organizations in Norway came together in a new body, the Naeringslivets Hovedorganisation. In February inflationary dangers led the Norwegian Federation of Trade Unions to accept a two-year agreement establishing a limit of 5% on wage increases in 1988 and prohibiting wage drift. Agreement was also reached on reducing retirement age from 67 to 66 as a first step.

The European Communities (EC). The European Commission, anticipating the single internal market in 1992, suggested that a "minimum threshold of social rights" for workers be negotiated between European unions and employers' organizations, that all workers have a right to training over their working lives, and that increased worker participation in management be instituted. The Commission also revived its long-dormant project for a "European company," proposing that enterprises planning to operate in more than one EC country incorporate under a single European law instead of under different national laws.

Poland. Industrial relations in Poland were difficult in 1988. The government managed to overcome a wave of strikes in April and May and assumed emergency powers to

manage industry and, if deemed necessary, to freeze wages and prices. Further widespread strikes in August, however, led the government to enter into discussion with the trade union Solidarity (banned in 1982) concerning the economic crisis. On October 31 the government announced the closure of the Lenin Shipyard in Gdansk, birthplace and stronghold of Solidarity. A strike in November, called against the advice of Solidarity founder Lech Walesa, failed to change the government's decision. (R. O. CLARKE)

The views expressed in this article are the author's and should not be attributed to any organization with which he may be connected.

See also Economic Affairs: *World Economy;* Industrial Review.

This article updates the *Macropædia* article WORK AND EMPLOYMENT.

Law

Court Decisions. In 1988 the various judicial tribunals of the world decided a number of important cases, the most noteworthy of which, perhaps, were handed down by the U.S. Supreme Court and the European Court of Human Rights (ECHR). Significant cases mainly involved civil rights, including matters of free speech and picketing and rights of privacy; criminal law, particularly relating to juveniles; and other limitations on government.

Government Structure. Most U.S. legal scholars agreed that the most important decision rendered by the U.S. Supreme Court in 1988 was *Morrison* v. *Olson.* In 1978 Congress passed the Ethics in Government Act, which provided, among other matters, for the appointment of a special prosecutor to bring criminal actions against certain high-ranking governmental officials for alleged violations of federal criminal laws. These criminal laws, enacted by Congress and directed mainly at individuals in the executive branch of government, had been perceived by some as an unwarranted, and perhaps unconstitutional, effort by one branch of government to control another by criminalizing activities over which the two differed. The U.S. Constitution, of course, provides for a separation of powers that prohibits any of the three branches of government, executive, legislative, or judicial, from controlling any other.

In the case at hand, it was alleged that certain members of the Department of Justice, an important appendage of the executive branch, had withheld information from Congress and given it false and misleading testimony. Congress sought the appointment of a special prosecutor to investigate the matter. The Justice Department countered by alleging that it was the normal governmental agency to investigate and prosecute cases of this type and that Congress had arrogated to itself the authority that belonged to the executive. In a decision that surprised critical legal observers because of the size of the plurality, the Supreme Court held on a 7–1 basis that Congress had the authority to proceed as it had done. Justice Antonin Scalia dissented from the opinion, and Justice Anthony Kennedy did not participate in it.

In *Webster* v. *Doe,* the Supreme Court held that at least some actions of the director of central intelligence were subject to judicial review. The case involved the discharge of a CIA employee who confessed that he was a homosexual. A federal statute gives the CIA director the power to discharge any employee when the director "deems that such termination [is] necessary or advisable in the interests of the United States." The employee was discharged pursuant to the discretion provided by this law. However, the employee contended that the termination of employment was unfair in the circumstances, particularly because he was not given an opportunity to prove that his sexual preference did not constitute a security threat, and he sought declarative and injunctive relief in federal court. This action raised the issue of whether a court has the power to review this kind of CIA activity. The Supreme Court said it did but made plain that a balance must be struck between the constitutional rights of employees and the national security interests of the country. The case was, therefore, remanded to the trial court to effectuate this balancing of public and private interests. The importance of the decision was not this direct judgment but the holding that the CIA did not have unfettered discretion in cases of this type.

Free Speech. In *Ärzt für das Leben,* the ECHR was called upon to decide how the balance should be struck between the rights of demonstrators and counterdemonstrators, both of whom are guaranteed the right of peaceful assembly under article 11 of the Convention on Human Rights. The court held that the state, in this case Austria, was under a positive obligation to ensure that the rights of demonstrators are not disrupted by counterdemonstrators. The decision left doubts and queries in the minds of some legal observers, because the court emphasized that the state's duty is not merely to ensure that there is no interference but to make sure that counterdemonstrators do not inhibit the rights of demonstrators. The principal question left unanswered by the decision, in the view of some legal scholars, was: Who is a demonstrator and who is a counterdemonstrator under this formulation?

The U.S. Supreme Court, in *Boos* v. *Barry,* held unconstitutional a provision of the District of Columbia code that made it unlawful (1) to display within 500 ft (152.5 m) of a foreign embassy any sign tending to bring a foreign government into public odium or public disrepute, or (2) to congregate within 500 ft of any foreign embassy. In violation of this code, individuals congregated within 500 ft of the Soviet embassy carrying signs saying "Release Sakharov" and within 500 ft of the Nicaraguan embassy carrying signs that read "Stop the Killing." The legal question arose whether these activities could be punished. Although the Reagan administration, through the office of the attorney general, intervened in the case to support the constitutionality of the code, Justice Sandra Day O'Connor, sometimes identified with the positions of that administration, held, along with a majority of the court, that the statute violated the First Amendment to the Constitution, which guarantees free speech. In a ringing opinion, she opined that it is impermissible to bar free speech on public streets and sidewalks, "traditional fora that time out of mind have been used for purposes of assembly, communicating thoughts between citizens and discussing public questions." She stated that "[w]e have recognized that the First Amendment reflects a profound national commitment to the principle that debate on public issues should be uninhibited, robust, and wide open. . . ."

The most interesting, and perhaps the most important, case on free speech, *Attorney General* v. *The Observer Ltd.,* was handed down by the United Kingdom's Court of Appeal. The case involved the book *Spycatcher,* which contained confidential material that was published in the U.S. in breach of confidence. Thereafter, the U.K. attorney general sought to enjoin publication of the book in Australia, but the court denied the injunction. In its decision it balanced the interest of confidentiality with freedom of expression and tipped that balance in favour of the latter, perhaps because the information contained in the book already had become freely available.

"That'll be £74,692,437 and 48 P. How would you like to pay?"
A cartoonist provided a wacky view of the British Home Office's attempt to establish payment guidelines for the enforcement of financial penalties to compensate those who are illegally assaulted. The payment was to be made by the assailant to the victim.

GRIFFIN, DAILY MIRROR, LONDON

In *Hustler Magazine* v. *Falwell,* the U.S. Supreme Court held that the First Amendment to the Constitution prohibits a public figure from recovering damages for intentional infliction of emotional distress as a result of a parody, in the absence of proof of a false statement of fact made with actual malice. The case involved Jerry Falwell, a nationally known minister, who claimed to have been emotionally injured by an advertisement parody in *Hustler* magazine—labeled on the bottom, in small print, as an "ad parody—not to be taken seriously." The parody presented Falwell as recalling, in a supposed interview, that his "first time" was during a drunken incestuous rendezvous with his mother in an outdoor toilet. A jury found that the advertisement could not reasonably be understood as depicting an actual event, but it awarded Falwell substantial damages because of the emotional damage it had inflicted upon him. The Supreme Court ruled that public figures are not entitled to recover for emotional distress by reason of publication of a caricature, unless it contains a false statement of fact made with actual malice.

Not all important decisions, however, came down on the side of free speech as opposed to other public and private values. In *Muller* v. *Switzerland,* the ECHR found that the confiscation by the Swiss government of certain paintings found to be obscene and the criminal conviction of the artist did not constitute a violation of article 10 of the Convention on Human Rights. The court found, on balance, that the value of protecting morals was a legitimate aim of government that transcended freedom of expression, under the circumstances of particularly offensive portrayals. In *Hazelwood School District* v. *Kuhlmeier,* the U.S. Supreme Court held that a high school principal could delete from a school-sponsored newspaper materials that he reasonably found to be objectionable. Students had complained unsuccessfully that such "censorship" violated their First Amendment rights.

Criminal Law. In *Regina* v. *Board of Visitors for the Maze Prison,* the House of Lords, England's highest court, decided that a prisoner is not always entitled as of right to legal representation in a disciplinary matter before the Board of Visitors. The Board of Visitors is empowered to hear a wide range of matters concerning prison administration, some noncriminal, some criminal, and some merely

disciplinary. The case involved a prisoner charged with assaulting a prison officer. The court suggested, but did not squarely hold, that the prisoner would be entitled to legal counsel at his own expense, in accordance with article 6(3)(c) of the Convention on Human Rights, which provides that any person charged with crime has the absolute right to defend himself or herself through legal assistance of his or her own choosing. In the view of the House of Lords, this rule does not mean that legal assistance must be provided in all cases. The court rejected the idea that prisoners are entitled to legal representation as of right in hearings before the board that are criminal in scope. It said that it would not be rational to try to distinguish criminal from disciplinary proceedings, since both may result in some kind of punishment. In a subsequent case, *Regina* v. *Deputy Governor of Parkhurst Prison,* the House of Lords made it clear, however, that decisions made by the board are subject to judicial review. Prior to this decision, it had been believed that a prisoner's only remedy lay in an appeal to the home secretary.

The ECHR, in the case of *Bouamar* v. *Belgium,* invalidated Belgian legislation that permitted detention of juveniles for the purpose of educational supervision. The court held that the legislation violated article 5(4) of the Convention on Human Rights because there was no procedure under the legislation by which a detainee could obtain a speedy decision as to the legality of his or her incarceration.

In *California* v. *Greenwood,* the U.S. Supreme Court held that the Fourth Amendment to the Constitution does not prohibit a search and seizure, without warrant, of garbage bags placed outside the home on a curb for collection. The court said that the defendants could not claim that their privacy had been breached, since it is common knowledge that plastic garbage bags left along a public street are readily accessible to animals, scavengers, snoops, and other members of the public. It opined that the police cannot be expected reasonably to avert their eyes from the evidence of criminal activity that could have been observed by any member of the public.

In a stronger claim for breach of privacy, the ECHR ruled in *Re Schenk* that article 6(1) of the Convention on Human Rights does not prevent the admission of evidence in a criminal case based on an unauthorized tapping of the accused's telephone. The court said that the admissibility of illegally obtained evidence was a matter to be decided under national law. (WILLIAM D. HAWKLAND)

International Law. The most remarkable feature of 1988 was the cessation of all the major international wars, accompanied by a slight but perceptible increase in civil modes of dispute settlement, although domestic or quasi-domestic violence continued. To a considerable extent, this reflected greatly enhanced peacemaking activity by the UN, especially its secretary-general.

International Violence. The unilateral decision by the Soviets to withdraw from Afghanistan was followed in April by four treaties: between Afghanistan and Pakistan (on the principles of mutual relations, especially noninterference and nonintervention; and on the voluntary return of refugees); the U.S. and the U.S.S.R. (on international guarantees); and all four states (on the interrelationships for the settlement of the situation relating to Afghanistan). A UN good offices mission was established to assist in monitoring compliance and implementation of the settlement.

The Iran-Iraq war started the year with an ominous heightening of attacks on neutrals and civilians on the international waters of the Persian Gulf and its surrounding coasts. Iranian gunboats (not part of the Navy) attacked

neutral tankers while the Iranian Navy continued its correct but harshly enforced policy of interrogating neutral shipping, except when warned off by neutral escorting warships. The U.S. Navy, which was protecting U.S.-registered vessels, destroyed two Iranian oil platforms in reprisal for mines laid in international waters and struck by a U.S. frigate. In addition, an Iranian frigate was totally disabled by the U.S. A more serious incident was the shooting down in July by the USS *Vincennes* of an Iranian civil airliner on a routine flight across the Gulf, in the belief that it was a warplane. All 290 persons aboard were killed. The U.S. accepted responsibility and offered ex gratia compensation to the families of the victims. Then, on July 18, Iran unconditionally accepted UN Security Council Resolution 598 for a cease-fire, which, after detailed negotiation by the secretary-general, came into force on August 20. Negotiations for a permanent peace settlement then began, but difficulties soon emerged relating to sovereignty over the Shatt al-Arab waterway, Iranian inspection of Iraqi shipping until the conclusion of a peace treaty, and the exchange of prisoners of war.

The war in Western Sahara between Morocco and the Algerian-backed Popular Front for the Liberation of Saguia el Hamra and Río de Oro (Polisario Front) came close to ending on August 30, when both parties accepted a cease-fire plan drawn up by the UN secretary-general; this included a UN-supervised referendum to determine the area's future. A bloody attack by the Polisario in mid-September on the outer defensive wall built by Morocco, however, indicated that the cessation of hostilities was far from complete. In December a U.S. plane spraying against locusts was shot down over the Sahara, and another was damaged; the Polisario Front later apologized for what it claimed was a case a mistaken identity. The 1987 cease-fire between Libya and Chad was confirmed in October by an agreement to restore full diplomatic relations and to negotiate over the disputed Aozou Strip through a special committee of the Organization of African Unity. A cease-fire in Angola was announced in August, and in December Angola, Cuba, and South Africa signed two accords providing for withdrawal of Cuban troops from Angola and independence for South West Africa/Namibia. A cease-fire agreement was signed in March to end the civil war in Nicaragua, but the truce was not fully observed.

Violence continued in the Middle East. Israeli attacks in Lebanon brought positions of the UN Interim Force in Lebanon (UNIFIL) under fire. In April a Kuwaiti Airlines plane was hijacked by Muslim terrorists in an unsuccessful attempt to force the release of 17 prisoners convicted of involvement in 1983 bombings in Kuwait City. Two passengers were killed but the others were eventually released, and the hijackers were allowed to escape. Shortly before, in February and March, two antipiracy conventions had been adopted, one by the International Civil Aviation Organization on the Suppression of Unlawful Acts of Violence at Airports Serving Civil Aviation, and the other by the International Maritime Organization on the Suppression of Unlawful Acts Against the Safety of Maritime Navigation.

The continued use of poison gas by Iraq in the Iran-Iraq war was confirmed by a UN report in August and admitted by Iraq's foreign minister. The Security Council shortly afterward adopted a resolution threatening that "appropriate and effective measures will be taken" if such chemical weapons were used again by anyone anywhere. After the cease-fire, however, use of the gas against Kurdish rebels was stepped up.

International Adjudication. The international arbitration between Egypt and Israel over the 640-m (2,100-ft) Taba strip of beach at the head of the Gulf of Aqaba resulted in an award on September 29 in favour of Egypt. The Israeli government indicated that there was still room for disagreement and that it would not automatically transfer the whole of the disputed area to Egypt. The long-standing dispute between Denmark and Norway over the sea boundary between Greenland and Jan Mayen Island was taken to the International Court of Justice (ICJ) in August.

In April the ICJ gave an advisory opinion in a dispute between the UN and the U.S. The U.S. Anti-Terrorism Act declared illegal the maintenance of an office of the Palestine Liberation Organization (PLO) anywhere within U.S. jurisdiction. This would, if implemented (which it had not been), mean closing the office of the PLO mission to the UN, established after the UN conferred observer status on the PLO in 1974. The court held that there was a dispute relating to UN rights under the 1947 Headquarters Agreement, that the agreement contained an arbitration clause, and that therefore the U.S. was under an obligation to enter into arbitration. Later in the year, when the U.S. refused to grant a visa to Yasir Arafat to enter the U.S. to address the UN General Assembly (also a breach of the Headquarters Agreement), the Assembly adjourned to Geneva, where the address could be given without hindrance. On December 14, however, the U.S. announced that Arafat's statement recognizing Israel's right to exist, accepting UN Resolutions 242 and 338, and renouncing terrorism met its criteria and, accordingly, it authorized contact with the PLO.

The ECHR held in *Belios* v. *Switzerland* that contracting parties were not able to make unilateral reservations to the European Convention on Human Rights except in accordance with article 64. The Caribbean Economic Community received a request from the attorneys general of its 13 member states to set up a Caribbean Court of Appeal to replace the U.K. Privy Council; a decision would be taken at the Caricom summit meeting in July 1989. The French Conseil d'État in *Sapvin* dismissed a claim that the French state should be liable for its failure to enforce a French judgment in Spain by use of diplomacy or recourse to the ICU. The English Court of Appeal held that the state members of the International Tin Council (now insolvent) were not liable for its debts, but the judges described the conduct of the council as "fraudulent trading on a massive scale."

Diplomatic Immunities. The systematic implantation of listening devices in the new U.S. embassy building in Moscow was taken to international commercial arbitration under the Stockholm Chamber of Commerce. At the same time, Sweden made an official protest against bugging of its embassy in Moscow, and Norway complained that its Prague (Czech.) embassy was bugged. In Chile the Supreme Court ruled that two West German diplomats might be subjected to interrogation in criminal proceedings against them for violation of rights of privacy, contrary to their immunity under the Vienna Convention.

The return home of the third secretary at Vietnam's London embassy after he had brandished a gun at demonstrators was the normal consequence of such undiplomatic behaviour, but more serious retaliation was resorted to in other instances. Australia threatened to close the Yugoslav consulate in Sydney if a security guard, who had shot and wounded a Croatian demonstrator from inside the consulate, was not handed over to the Australian police within 24 hours. The threat was duly carried out, and all staff, including the guard, were flown home. After the Panamanian ambassador to Britain had hired seven security men to force an entry into his London consulate, which was

occupied by supporters of the ousted president of Panama, the U.K. government insisted that he waive his and his staff's diplomatic immunity to allow questioning by the police and even possible prosecution, on pain of expulsion; he complied. The English High Court, in *ex parte Samuel,* approved the British seizure of the abandoned former Kampuchean embassy, now occupied by squatters, and its sale, with the proceeds being held on behalf of the Kampuchean state. More dubious was the British reaction to the firing of shots by the Cuban commercial attaché against British secret service men following him outside his London flat. Not only was the diplomat expelled but the Cuban ambassador, who had nothing to do with the event, was summarily expelled on 24 hours' notice. An attaché at the Tunisian embassy in London was expelled for refusing to pay parking fines.

Territory and Sea. Morocco and Spain agreed in June that the two North African garrison towns of Cueta and Melilla should remain Spanish. The 1984 frontier treaty between Luxembourg and West Germany came into force.

The dispute between China and Vietnam over the Spratly Islands erupted again in an exchange of fire between warships of the two countries. A major dispute developed between Canada and France over the fishing limits around St. Pierre and Miquelon. (*See* WORLD AFFAIRS [North America]: *Canada.*)

The long-running dispute between Sweden and the U.S.S.R. over their overlapping economic zones in the Baltic was settled by a treaty signed in January whereby roughly one-quarter of the disputed area went to the U.S.S.R. and three-quarters to Sweden. Following two years of negotiations, the U.K. and Ireland signed a treaty in November on delimitation of the continental shelf, but it excluded the still unsettled questions of the territorial waters around Northern Ireland and around the uninhabited island of Rockall. The U.S. and Ireland extended their territorial seas to 12 mi.

A major international convention was agreed by 65 states to ban the burning of toxic waste at sea from 1995 unless scientific evidence in the meanwhile should indicate that this was unnecessary. In April the Maritime Safety Committee of the International Maritime Organization adopted detailed guidelines and standards for the removal of abandoned or disused offshore oil installations and structures on the continental shelf. The unauthorized presence of submarines in Swedish waters intensified during the year, but despite the greater readiness of the Swedish Navy to use depth charges, mines, and other weapons, none of the intruders was forced to the surface. The sinking or damaging of fishing boats by unidentified submarines in the Irish Sea continued to cause concern. It was claimed that NATO countries were now admitting responsibility and paying compensation. Previously, they had denied all knowledge.

General. Other important developments included approval by the EC Court of Justice of the extraterritorial effect of EC antitrust law (in the *Woodpulp* case); the adoption of the U.S.-Canada trade agreement; a joint Australia-New Zealand declaration to work toward a common market by 1990; a mutual recognition agreement between the EC and Comecon; and the conclusion of a convention on the regulation of Antarctic mineral resource activities. (*See* WORLD AFFAIRS [Polar Regions]: *Antarctica.*)

(NEVILLE MARCH HUNNINGS)

See also Crime, Law Enforcement, and Penology; World Affairs: *United Nations.*

This article updates the *Macropædia* articles CONSTITUTIONAL LAW; INTERNATIONAL LAW.

Libraries

There was no improvement in 1988 in the condition of West African libraries, faced with poor economic conditions and lack of hard currency. This seriously affected the acquisition of books and, more especially, of serials, lack of which isolates administrators, social scientists, and technologists, as well as the general public, from recent work elsewhere. Sierra Leone made brave attempts to establish a national information and library system and improve its university libraries, but the outlook for the project was not promising. Unesco had been attempting for ten years to replace the NATIS (National Information System) concept initiated by an intergovernmental conference in 1974 in favour of UNISIST (World System of Information in Science and Technology), introduced in 1971, largely the initiative of the International Council of Scientific Unions. On the world scene, however, UNISIST had been considered to be mainly of interest to developed countries, NATIS to less developed countries.

One of Unesco's outstanding successes was the "Major Programme VII Information Systems and Access to Knowledge," estimated to cost $17,290,400 over 1988–89, or about 5% of Unesco's total budget. One of the objectives of the program was the wider dissemination of knowledge about—and use of—modern technology for processing and transferring information; for example, establishing means for the uniform production of bibliographic information in libraries and information centres. As part of the program, work continued on developing appropriate software packages for microcomputers and on achieving the standardization of formats. The computer package IDS/ISIS had been installed in about a thousand locations. It was proposed that an expert meeting be held in Yugoslavia in order to select the most promising developments in the field of information technology for future work.

The program aimed at strengthening regional information networks, such as ASTINFO in Asia and the Pacific and INFOLAC in Latin America, the Caribbean, and the Arab states, and sought to encourage national participation in information sharing worldwide through the establishment of national coordination units and the appointment of liaison officers. With a view to improving information exchange, a revised edition of the Common Communication Format was made available, and there was an active program of translation into Unesco's various official languages. The program was also concerned with information practices within the UN organizations themselves, including the establishment of a Global Network of Scientific and Technological Information. At the other end of the scale were seminars on proposals for the founding of a new Alexandrian library and on the conservation and preservation of library materials in tropical climates.

The technological development of libraries continued in both industrialized and less developed countries. There was a danger that if academic and public libraries did not open their doors to technological change, they could become the dinosaurs of the 20th century. In some European countries, the separation of libraries and documentation centres—not only in content and practice but also in the training and outlook of staff—was a matter of concern. In general, the trend was toward the provision of information rather than, specifically, books, and the profession of librarian/information scientist was developing with an emphasis on information provision rather than library management, though conservation and preservation continued to be burning topics. Opportunities for librarians were increas-

ing in the private sector, even in less developed countries, as business became more technologically oriented and information more complex. The British government turned its attention to the profit-making capacities of the public library system in England (similar proposals for Wales, Northern Ireland, and Scotland were likely to follow). It was estimated that earned revenue could be more than doubled if charges were levied for many services now regarded as free, such as providing specially requested recent works, nonbook media, and various kinds of specialized information.   (P. HAVARD-WILLIAMS)

In the U.S. library groups, the national media, and legislators widely opposed the FBI's Library Awareness Program of surveillance for spies among library users. After a January informational meeting between the FBI and library representatives, it became generally known that the FBI had contacted staff in some 25 libraries, requesting alerts when suspicious patron behaviour occurred. Among groups condemning the program as a violation of intellectual freedom were the American Library Association, the Special Libraries Association, and the Association of Research Libraries. In November the FBI told a congressional subcommittee that the program was being confined to New York City and cooperation of librarians would be on a voluntary basis.

Public library circulation in the U.S. rose 6.3% from 1986 to 1987—the largest increase in ten years—according to 1988 figures from the University of Illinois annual survey. Academic and research libraries launched studies looking toward cooperative action to cope with soaring foreign journal costs. Driven partly by the falling dollar, subscription increases had decimated many book budgets. *Information Power: Guidelines for School Library Media Programs*—the first such guidelines since 1975—were published jointly by the Association for Educational Communications and Technology and the American Library Association's American Association of School Librarians. The guidelines stressed planning based on local needs. Children's librarians began to develop positive programs, such as tutoring, for the growing number of "latchkey" children of working parents left in their care.

The Chicago Public Library broke ground for the nation's largest municipal library, a 70,404-sq m (757,031-sq ft) classical structure to be completed in 1991. Queens College of the City University of New York dedicated a striking $60 million academic library building. Harvard opened its automated public catalog. Rights to Dewey Decimal Classification products were acquired for about $3.8 million by the Online Computer Library Center, which was to develop new computer-based applications of this most widely used classification system. (ARTHUR PLOTNIK)

This article updates the *Macropædia* article LIBRARIES AND LIBRARY SCIENCE.

Life Sciences

ZOOLOGY

Detailed observations and experimental studies of animals during 1988 revealed unusual and unanticipated phenomena, serving as a continuing reminder of the complexity of natural systems. In addition, fossil finds and interpretations advanced scientists' understanding of evolutionary possibilities and phylogenetic relationships.

Research on a colony of cliff swallows (*Hirundo pyrrhonota*) in Nebraska by Charles R. Brown and Mary Bomberger Brown of Yale University uncovered an unusual variation of a well-known reproductive strategy.

Nesting swallows were observed to transfer eggs from their own nests to other swallow nests to be raised by unsuspecting foster parents. Nest parasitism, in which female birds lay their eggs in another's nest, is common among some species, but this study represented one of the first observations of females actually carrying eggs in their mouths for the purpose of nest parasitism. The investigators estimated that more than 6% of the eggs in the large nesting colony were not in the nests of the genetic mothers. One possible advantage of having eggs in more than one nest is to increase the probability that some offspring will survive in the high-risk environment of rocky cliffs and canyons.

A study of marble salamanders (*Ambystoma opacum*) by David E. Scott of the University of Georgia's Savannah River Ecology Laboratory uncovered important connections between the conditions a larval salamander experiences in the aquatic habitat and the acquisition of adult traits related to reproductive output. Manipulation of larval densities in large field enclosures at several breeding sites over a three-year period demonstrated that larvae reared at low density under natural conditions grow faster than larvae reared at high density. They also attain larger body size, have a shorter larval period and higher probability of survival, and emerge from the pond with more body fat. The effects were due, in part, to differences experienced by the two groups in competing for limited food resources. In laboratory studies salamanders from low-density enclosures survived longer than those from high-density enclosures. In field populations adults from low-density larval environments returned to breeding sites at a larger size and earlier age, two traits associated with increased reproductive output. Variation in the number of days a breeding site holds water also exerts effects on larval traits that carry over to adults. The effects are most pronounced in drought years, when body size at metamorphosis is small and survivorship is low.

Recent prolonged droughts in many regions of the U.S. induced a variety of responses by animals. Potentially serious was the discovery of a new viruslike particle (VLP) that is transmitted by a mite and causes a disease in barley. In greenhouse experiments Nancy L. Robertson and Thomas W. Carroll of Montana State University found that seeds of diseased barley produced healthy plants; the infectious agent was not transmitted through soil or by means of common viral vectors such as aphids and leafhoppers. Following an outbreak of brown wheat mites (*Petrobia latens*) in Montana, however, barley crops became diseased. The researchers conducted experiments and used electron microscopy to document that the mite transmitted the VLP between diseased and healthy plants. Brown wheat mites are more prevalent in dry weather, and in the drought-stricken barley crop region they apparently reached population densities sufficient to cause the disease outbreak. The researchers also found that the VLP can pass from female mites to their eggs, thus allowing infected offspring to transmit the disease to healthy barley the following year.

In the field of anatomy, a new kind of imaging optics system was discovered in animals. Many arthropods have compound eyes of a simple type (apposition eyes) in which the visual units (ommatidia) are optically isolated and operate independently. In more advanced superposition eyes, the ommatidia cooperate to collect light to transmit a single image to the retina. True crabs and hermit crabs had been thought to possess apposition eyes, but D.-E. Nilsson of the University of Lund, Sweden, found many of them to have superposition eyes that handle light in a more complex manner than in any other superposition compound eyes yet described. The optical system, termed parabolic

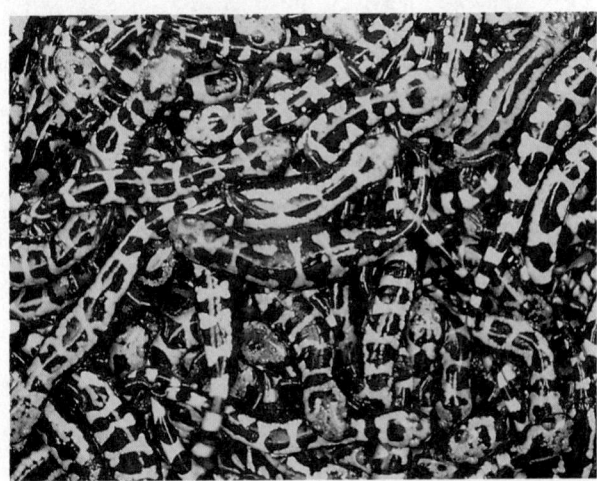

Dozens of marble salamanders mill about. A study of thousands showed that the population density of the salamanders' larvae had significant effects on their overall longevity and breeding success.

DAVID E. SCOTT, SAVANNAH RIVER ECOLOGY LABORATORY, UNIVERSITY OF GEORGIA

superposition, comprises a diversity of lens types, convex parabolic mirrors, and light-guiding structures.

The specifics of diet and feeding behaviour were determined for a highly endangered reptile, the hawksbill turtle (*Eretmochelys imbricata*), in the Caribbean Sea by Anne Meylan of the American Museum of Natural History, New York City. She found that the species feeds almost exclusively on sponges. The specialized diet includes some sponges that are toxic to other vertebrates, and the large amounts of silica present make the food equivalent to a diet of glass. The findings were important not only in understanding the turtle's natural history but also in identifying broader ecological interactions. The removal of sponges by hawksbills may influence the dynamics and species diversity of reef communities by providing open areas for settlement by other organisms.

Interpretations of fossil finds were responsible for several zoological advances. Elisabeth M. Brouwers of the U.S. Geological Survey, Denver, Colo., and associates reported that dinosaurs inhabited the Alaskan North Slope during the Upper Cretaceous, about 68 million to 70 million years ago. The region was one of mild-to-cold temperate deciduous forests, and because of the high latitude (70°–85° N) extreme seasonal variation occurred in solar insolation, temperature, and food supply for herbivores. Long migrations would have been necessary to reach warmer temperatures and evergreen food sources during winter, so the dinosaurs presumably remained at the high latitudes year-round and survived on marginal food sources. The evidence suggested that at least some dinosaurs were able to exist under seasonally cold, dark environmental conditions for months—a factor that would bear on extinction theories invoking dinosaurs' supposed inability to adapt to a cooling of the Earth's climate at the end of the Cretaceous.

Information was obtained about embryological development in early reptiles, a poorly known aspect of these animals because of the rarity of fossil embryo discoveries. P. Martin Sander of the University of Zürich, Switz., described the first known embryo of a nothosaur (genus *Neusticosaurus*) from Middle Triassic deposits (about 230 million years old) in southern Switzerland and northern Italy. When compared with other fossils of *Neusticosaurus*, the specimen reveals the changes in body proportions and morphology during embryological and juvenile development. Uncertainty existed about whether the nothosaur

laid eggs or was a live bearer, but John R. Horner of Montana State University and David B. Weishampel of Johns Hopkins University, Baltimore, Md., had no trouble making this distinction for two dinosaurs. They found embryos of two egg-laying species of ornithischian dinosaurs preserved inside their eggs in Upper Cretaceous deposits in Montana. Fossils of embryos, juveniles, and adults were found in association, thus permitting morphological comparisons of these developmental stages. Moreover, a comparison of embryo development in the two species revealed information about parental care. Examination of bone and tooth development indicated that one species (*Orodromeus makelai*, a hypsilophodontid dinosaur) was precocial, leaving the nest upon hatching. The structure of the other species (*Maiasaura peeblesorum*, a hadrosaurid dinosaur) confirmed an earlier suggestion that they were altricial, remaining in the nest and being fed by parents. Both types of hatchling behaviour are common in birds, but neither had been confirmed for egg-laying dinosaurs.

Fossil birds also contributed to an understanding of early vertebrate evolution. Peter Wellnhofer of the Bavarian State Collection of Paleontology and Historical Geology, Munich, West Germany, reported the identification of another specimen of the primitive extinct bird *Archaeopteryx* from the Upper Jurassic (about 150 million years ago) in Bavaria. The specimen is 10% larger than any of the other five specimens previously reported, and clear impressions of feather shafts provide additional direct evidence that *Archaeopteryx* had feathers. A fossil bird from Lower Cretaceous deposits (120 million to 130 million years old) in Spain yielded information on evolutionary links between *Archaeopteryx* and modern birds. J. L. Sanz of the Autonomous University, Madrid, J. F. Bonaparte of the Argentine Museum of Natural Sciences, Buenos Aires, and A. Lacasa of the Institut d'Estudis Ilerdencs, Lérida, Spain, reported that the specimen has primitive characteristics in some traits (pelvic girdle, hind limbs) and more advanced ones in others (a pygostyle, or tailbone, that is shorter than that of *Archaeopteryx* but longer than that in modern birds). (J. WHITFIELD GIBBONS)

Entomology. Jacqueline J. Belwood of the University of Florida and Glenn K. Morris of the University of Toronto found that the courtship calls of male katydids in Panama are used as beacons by foliage-gleaning bats to locate the insects as prey. A calling male was shown more likely to be eaten by a bat than one not calling or calling sporadically. By electronically analyzing calling songs, the researchers demonstrated that katydids living in clearings not inhabited by bats call often and over a broad range of frequencies. On the other hand, katydids living in forested areas with bats have reduced calling cycles and purer tones that are more difficult for bats to locate. To compensate for short songs, tree-dwelling male katydids use body vibrations as an inaudible signal to advertise their locations. The implication was that in bat-inhabited areas natural selection has operated on katydids to produce a compromise mating call that is less effective in attracting mates but also in attracting bat predators.

Parasitoid wasps, which lay their eggs on or in a host organism on which their larvae then feed, contributed to basic genetic research during the year in studies by Uzi Nur, John H. Werren, Thomas H. Eickbush, and co-workers of the University of Rochester, N.Y. Female wasps of the species *Nasonia vitripennis* lay both unfertilized eggs and fertilized ones. The eggs containing only maternal chromosomes become males; the ones containing both maternal and paternal chromosomes become females. The investigators found that an extra chromosome, contributed by some

males, carries a genetic element (called *psr,* for paternal sex ratio) that interferes with normal determination of sex. In eggs fertilized by a male carrying the *psr* chromosome, the other paternal chromosomes are somehow destroyed; these eggs in effect become unfertilized and thus develop into males instead of females. The *psr* chromosome itself, however, is retained and is thus available to be transmitted by the new male offspring. According to one interpretation, the *psr* element can be viewed as an example of a "selfish" or "parasitic" gene, one that has no function other than to further its own transmission and survival.

Research with honeybees gave evidence for the way in which males can influence future colony genetic structure and social behaviour. Studies indicated that division of labour within a honeybee colony is at least partly a consequence of the genetic makeup of individuals rather than strictly a result of environmental conditions, as previously theorized. Two independent studies, by Gene E. Robinson and Robert E. Page, Jr., of Ohio State University and by Peter C. Frumhoff and Jayne Baker of the University of California at Davis, tracked the hive occupations of nestmate honeybee workers having known, but different, paternal backgrounds. The level of involvement by particular workers in such hive chores as grooming, guarding, and disposing of dead bees was found to be related to their genetic background. The observed behaviour helped explain the way the specialized traits of workers, which are sterile females and thus cannot directly transmit their genetic makeup to offspring, might evolve in a social insect colony.

Africanized honeybees, expected to enter the U.S. from Mexico in 1989 or 1990, were found able to survive long periods at subfreezing temperatures. Thus, weather conditions seemed unlikely to inhibit their spread throughout North America. Africanized bees, a hybrid of native honeybees (originally introduced from Europe) and African bees accidentally released in Brazil in the 1950s, tend to replace native bees but do not produce honey as well. They are also more aggressive and, because of their group-attack behaviour, can sting humans and other animals to death. Basic ecological and behavioral studies on bees might prove vital to mounting suitable responses to what could become a serious economic problem for the honey industry and for agriculture dependent on insect pollinators.

Compounding the woes of U.S. beekeepers was the spread of the varroa mite (*Varroa jacobsoni*), which by

PETER JORDAN/TIME MAGAZINE

Workers tend traps used to capture Africanized bees. The aggressive strain has been spreading northward through Mexico and may enter the U.S. in 1989 or 1990.

mid-1988 was reported in as many as 13 states. The parasitic mite, of Asiatic origin, infests both adult bees and developing larvae, sucking their blood, and in two to three years can destroy an entire hive. Research concentrated on developing both chemical and biologic means to combat the parasite.   (ANNE R. GIBBONS)

This article updates the *Macropædia* article INSECTS.

Ornithology. Detailed reviews of ornithology and bird conservation in China were completed during the year. Whereas amateur bird-watching was almost unknown in China, in the late 1980s there were nearly 400 professional members of the Chinese Ornithological Society. Much contemporary work centred on the economic significance of such pest species as the tree sparrow and the yellow-breasted bunting. The pheasant family, with no fewer than nine species native to China, also attracted attention, most notably Cabot's tragopan. Concern was expressed over the declines seen in some pheasant species and in certain natural communities of birds; *e.g.*, those in the Changbai Shan (mountains) bordering North Korea.

Having been delayed during the Cultural Revolution, the conservation of Chinese birds surged forward after 1976. About 180 species were to appear in the Chinese *Red Data Book* of endangered birds; 97 rare species already received special protection by law. Many of the more than 460 nature reserves in China protected birds, but 17 particularly so. The special role that cranes enjoy in Chinese culture and folklore contributed strongly to their study and protection. Some reserves in the north were maintained for breeding cranes, particularly the red-crowned species; others in the south afforded sanctuary for wintering cranes, notably the Siberian crane. Of the world population of this last species, 80% wintered on the middle reaches of the Chang Jiang (Yangtze River). A special international crane workshop was held near Harbin in northeast China.

The world's rarest crane remained the North American whooping crane. During the winter of 1987–88, 135 were counted; only 16 birds had existed in 1941. Another highly endangered species, the California condor, was bred successfully in captivity for the first time. In late April an egg produced from captive mating hatched in an incubator at the San Diego (Calif.) Wild Animal Park.

The sanderling, an Arctic-breeding shorebird, was studied in its "winter" (austral summer) quarters in southern Africa. The observed percentage of first-year, adolescent birds fluctuated on a three-year cycle, coinciding with the rise and fall in lemming numbers in northern Siberia. It was suggested that Arctic foxes and other predators feed on lemmings in years of lemming abundance but subsist on eggs and chicks of such birds as the sanderling when lemmings are scarce. First-year sanderlings do not accumulate the large fat reserves that older birds develop between March and early May for the northward migration, because they do not breed until their second summer and thus remain in Africa. Adult sanderlings complete the 13,000-km (8,000-mi) northward migration in less than seven weeks. The journey involves three long flights broken by two stops to replenish fat reserves. Birds first cross the Sahara to the Mediterranean. From there some travel via the North Sea to Greenland or western Siberia, others via the Caspian Sea to eastern Siberia.

Female barn swallows prefer males with longer tails. Those that pair up with a better endowed male fledge more offspring each summer. This finding, reported by Anders Møller of the University of Uppsala, Sweden, was significant in that it was the first instance in which the preferences of females of a monogamous avian species were observed to promote the evolution of male sexual

ornaments. In polygamous bird species it long had been established that, owing to the pressure of sexual selection, males evolve extreme displays involving elongated, colourful feathers that are often moved in a ritual fashion. The birds of paradise of New Guinea and the manakins of South America are classic examples. Among the Swedish barn swallows the older males have longer tails and also return earlier from the south (perhaps because they are more experienced migrants). They also secure mates more speedily, thus allowing more time for egg-laying and for rearing the larger broods that result.

New bird species come to light only once or twice a year on average. A new antwren from Brazil, named the Rio de Janeiro antwren, was reported during the year by Luiz P. Gonzaga of the Federal University of Rio de Janeiro. A second new species, a type of parrotlet, was found in Peru.

(JEFFERY BOSWALL)

This article updates the *Macropædia* article BIRDS.

MARINE BIOLOGY

During the year an Intergovernmental Oceanographic Commission workshop on the biologic effects of marine pollution concluded that assessments of pollution episodes must include accurate measurements of suborganismic and organismic effects, which may help predict possible future deterioration, and effects on the human community, which may be useful indicators of socioeconomic consequences. The deaths of thousands of common seals in the North Sea beginning in April were attributed by Dutch scientists to an epidemic of a virus related to canine distemper virus, although pollution effects on the immune system could also have contributed. In the northern Adriatic, a study of oxygen-concentration data collected between 1911 and 1984 showed significant decreases on the sea bottom during August and September, probably caused by nutrient enrichment from land-based sources. Mass die-offs of bottom-living animals during this period were predicted.

It had been hypothesized that organic matter apparently lost from primary production may be used by bacteria, which in turn are consumed by heterotrophic microflagellates (certain microorganisms that obtain nourishment from the ingestion of complex organic compounds) and returned to the phytoplankton-zooplankton food chain—the so-called microbial loop. New studies in the Delaware Estuary contradicted this hypothesis and suggested that the primary effect of heterotrophic microbes is the mineralization of organic compounds to their inorganic constituents. Small animals that dwell in marine sediments traditionally had been thought to remain there, whereas occasional reports of their occurrence in the water column had been regarded as a passive effect of sediment erosion. In contrast, West German studies showed active emergence of some of these animals in seawater above intertidal sand. Nighttime high-tide swimming occurred in 87% of copepods, 67% of ostracods (copepods and ostracods are subclasses of crustaceans), and 42% of platyhelminths (flatworms), but nematodes (roundworms) and oligochaetes (a class of worms that includes earthworms) did not leave the sediment.

Studies in the Banda Sea and Aru Basin near Indonesia revealed in the upper 100 m (330 ft) of the water column the presence of organisms that normally dwell at greater depths (some below 1,000 m [3,300 ft]), a unique phenomenon attributed to strong and deep mixing of waters in this oceanic basin. New studies of the lantern fish *Benthosema pterotum* demonstrated that these important open-ocean, mid-water fish are abundant throughout the world, particularly in the Arabian Sea and Gulf of Oman, suggesting a potential new fisheries resource.

The whelk *Buccinum undatum* in Canadian waters was shown to exhibit pronounced body contortions as avoidance behaviour in the presence of its starfish predator *Leptasterias polaris*. This strong, chemically mediated escape reaction probably permits *B. undatum* to associate closely with *L. polaris* since both animals compete for the same bivalved mollusk prey in bottom sediments. A British study showed a remarkable adaptation of the prawn *Palaemon elegans*, which inhabits intertidal rock pools where dissolved oxygen levels may be very low. The prawns often lie on their sides at water's edge, appearing to exploit higher oxygen levels at the air-water interface. A newly described shrimp, *Rimicaris exoculata*, was reported to dominate the community of larger animals present at two hydrothermal vent sites on the Mid-Atlantic Ridge. They feed by ingesting free-living bacteria associated with sulfide particles on "black smoker" vent chimneys. (See *Molecular Biology*, below.)

(ERNEST NAYLOR)

This article updates the *Macropædia* articles CRUSTACEANS; FISHES; MOLLUSKS; etc.

BOTANY

The structure of the enzyme RuBPCase, or RuBisCO, shortened forms of ribulose-1,5-bisphosphate carboxylase/oxygenase, was extracted from the bacterium *Acaligenes eutrophus* and reported in the scientific literature in 1987. The work was considered pioneering since RuBPCase is not only the most abundant protein in plants but also the enzyme in photosynthetic organisms that binds atmospheric carbon dioxide and initiates its conversion to useful organic compounds. It was not until 1988, however, that a team of researchers at the University of California at Los Angeles published their results describing the three-dimensional structure of the enzyme from a higher plant, tobacco, at a resolution of 2.6 angstroms (one angstrom [Å] is a hundred-millionth of a centimetre). Because the enzyme consists of 16 subunits (8 large and 8 small polypeptide chains) that together contain 37,792 atoms, determination of the three-dimensional structure represented a remarkable achievement. Perhaps the most important aspect of the research was that it might lead ultimately to a better understanding of the way RuBPCase works and thus to the possibility of genetically engineered crops that carry out the initial photosynthetic reactions more efficiently.

In 1832 botanist A. P. de Candolle first described the competitive advantage one plant could achieve over another species by presumably manufacturing and then

FROM ANTHONY B. BLEECKER, *ET AL. SCIENCE*, VOL. 241 (AUG. 26, 1988), PP. 1086–1089, © 1988 by the AAAS; PHOTOGRAPH, KURT STEPNITZ, MICHIGAN STATE UNIVERSITY

A single mutant *Arabidopsis thaliana* seedling, its growth uninhibited by exposure to the plant hormone ethylene, towers over a stand of nonmutant seedlings. The isolation of ethylene-insensitive plant strains may lead to a better understanding of the compound's many important natural roles in the life of plants.

depositing substances in the soil that inhibit the growth and development of the second species. He was addressing what had been termed the soil sickness problem, and as a result of the observed antagonism, he postulated a theory of crop rotation such that each species of the sequence was chosen on the basis that it should not be inhibited by residues left in the soil by the preceding species. The imaginative thinking of Candolle has since blossomed into the subdiscipline of botany and agriculture called allelopathy (or allelochemics) and has broadened to include a vast array of plant metabolites, some of which are toxic to potential predators. By the late 1980s allelochemicals were considered to include all natural plant products that affect the growth, health, behaviour, or population biology of members of other species.

During the year a well-documented case of allelochemical interaction was demonstrated between a plant product, L-canavanine, and the development of a predator, the tobacco hornworm (*Manduca sexta*). An amino acid not naturally found in proteins, L-canavanine is closely related to the protein amino acid L-arginine and is apparently used by many higher plants for storage and transport of nitrogen. Hornworm larvae fed an artificial diet containing L-canavanine showed dramatic growth aberrations in the resultant pupae and adults. The plants that make L-canavanine, which include more than 1,000 legume species as well as other plants, thus appear to have the added benefit of a chemical defense against certain predators in the form of an endogenous, naturally occurring insecticide. Further study of allelochemicals, particularly the so-called secondary plant metabolites, could well lead to truly integrated pest management in crops.

Major advances in biology often come when diverse disciplines focus on model organisms. Examples of such organisms are the bacterium *Escherichia coli,* the fruit fly (vinegar fly) *Drosophila melanogaster,* and the laboratory mouse. All of these organisms have rapid reproductive cycles and are amenable to laboratory culture in large numbers. Among the higher plants, a short-life-cycle member of the cabbage family, *Arabidopsis thaliana,* has emerged as an important model for research in plant physiology and molecular genetics. Large numbers of *Arabidopsis thaliana* can be grown in petri dishes on agar, and the plants complete their life cycle in four to six weeks. The small, simple genome (genetic endowment) of the species makes it ideal for genetic studies.

Using *A. thaliana* plants, researchers at Michigan State University in 1988 isolated a mutant that is insensitive to the action of the gaseous compound ethylene, a naturally occurring plant hormone that regulates growth and development. Taking advantage of the rapid life cycle of the plant, they demonstrated that the insensitivity results from a single gene mutation and that the gene may well code for the ethylene receptor. Although much remained to be done, work with ethylene-resistant plants could lead to a more detailed understanding of the mode of action of ethylene, which affects, among other things, seed germination, seedling growth, plant senescence, and fruit ripening.

(PHILIP D. REID)

MOLECULAR BIOLOGY

Life in Deep, Cold, Dark Water. For almost all life forms on Earth, the need for energy is met, directly or indirectly, by sunlight. The cyanobacteria, algae, and higher plants are direct consumers of sunlight by means of photosynthesis. They use such pigments as the chlorophylls to trap and transform radiant energy, which then drives the synthesis of the complex molecules called carbohydrates from simple carbon dioxide and water. Practically all nonphotosynthetic organisms, human beings included, are secondary consumers of sunlight. They feed on plants, or on animals that have fed on plants, and obtain the energy they need by degrading the complex molecules, originally made by the plants, back into carbon dioxide and water. In a very real sense, plants feed on sunlight and everything else feeds on plants.

There are exceptions to this grand pageant of Sun-powered life. For example, bacteria called chemolithotrophs can derive all of their energy from the oxidation of inorganic substances such as sulfur, sulfides, or ferrous iron. Indeed, there are entire communities of organisms, some of which include worms half as long as a human being and clams as wide as a dinner plate, whose source of energy is entirely independent of the Sun. Over the last decade a number of such communities have been found living around deep-sea hydrothermal vents in both the Pacific and Atlantic oceans.

The initial discovery of these oases of life on the lightless seafloor was made in 1977 from the manned deep-diving submersible *Alvin.* The craft was being used to explore the Galápagos Rift in the eastern equatorial Pacific, where new crust is formed by the upwelling of hot lava. At intervals along the rift the pilots of the *Alvin* found the seafloor-equivalent of terrestrial geysers, where water that has been heated geothermally spurts from the surface. The temperature of terrestrial geysers is limited by the boiling point of water. At a pressure of one atmosphere, the atmospheric pressure at sea level, water boils at 100° C (212° F). In contrast, water issuing from deep-sea hydrothermal vents can be much hotter because the boiling point of water is markedly elevated with increasing pressure. At a depth of 3,000 m (about 10,000 ft), a typical depth for these vents, the pressure is more than 300 atmospheres. Water issuing from deep-sea vents has been measured at 363° C (685° F)—higher than the melting point of lead.

Water is a good solvent for salts, and the hotter the water, the greater its solvent properties. Water gushing from sea-floor vents is laden with dissolved minerals—so laden that when it encounters the near-freezing seawater at the ocean floor, the dissolved minerals precipitate, producing a dark, cloudy plume termed a black smoker. Among the dissolved minerals are sulfides; in fact, about 0.04% of the hot water by weight is sulfide. As the vent water becomes diluted and cooled by the cold seawater around it, an environment is created in which the water is at a temperature close to 10° C (50° F) and contains about 0.0012% sulfide, along with dissolved oxygen.

The oxidation of sulfide to sulfate is an energy-yielding process that, like the oxidation of sugars to carbon dioxide and water, can be harnessed by living cells. There exist chemolithotrophic microorganisms called sulfur bacteria that obtain all their energy from the oxidation of sulfide, or of elemental sulfur, to sulfate. The waters around the black smokers teem with such bacteria. These organisms play a role analogous to that of green plants on the Earth's surface, exploiting the available source of energy and, in turn, being exploited as an energy source by other organisms.

One of the more striking organisms in the Pacific vent communities is *Riftia pachyptila.* This metre-long worm lives within a tube from which it waves a highly vascular blood-red plume. The plume exposes a large surface area to the water, from which it efficiently extracts both oxygen and sulfide. Indeed, the blood of *Riftia* can concentrate sulfide as much as 30-fold from the surrounding water by virtue of a specialized sulfide-binding protein. This protein serves two essential functions. It extracts sulfide from the

water, and it sequesters, or chemically ties up, the sulfide to keep it from reacting with and thus inactivating such important proteins as cytochrome *c* oxidase, a vital enzyme in cell respiration. Free sulfide is even more toxic to many animals than cyanide, precisely because of its avidity for cytochrome *c* oxidase, and the cytochrome *c* oxidase of *Riftia* is not immune. The sulfide-binding protein in the blood of the worm keeps the concentration of free sulfide so low that little of it can diffuse into the body cells. Moreover, the worm's cells contain a second line of defense against sulfide, an enzyme called sulfide oxidase that rapidly detoxifies any sulfide that does manage to enter.

If the body cells of *Riftia* must be protected from the toxicity of sulfide, then how does the worm use sulfide to meet its energy needs? The answer lies in a large organ called the trophosome, which receives blood from the plume. The trophosome, which constitutes one-third of the weight of the worm, is filled with sulfur bacteria living in symbiotic association with the animal. The bacteria oxidize sulfide in the worm's blood and use the liberated energy to drive the synthesis of carbohydrates from carbon dioxide. Some of the sugars made by the bacteria are released to nourish the worm. *Riftia* thus supplies sulfide to its symbiotic partners, and they return sugar. The worm's life-style requires neither mouth nor gut and, indeed, it has neither.

One outstanding question concerns the method by which the bacteria release the sulfide from the sulfide-binding protein in the blood of *Riftia*. A possible answer is provided by the response of this protein to changes in acidity. If the protein's environment is changed from neutrality (pH = 7) to slightly acidic (pH = 5), the protein loses its affinity for sulfide. It may be that the symbiotic bacteria increase the acidity in their immediate vicinity and thus induce release of the sulfide from the binding protein.

Riftia is not unique in its ability to live off of the oxidation of sulfide. A few other members of the black-smoker communities, such as the giant clam *Calyptogena magnifica*, can do likewise. Furthermore, black smokers do not provide the only environments in which sulfide oxidation is the major potential source of energy. Muds often harbour sulfate-reducing bacteria, which produce substantial amounts of sulfide. Small vestimentiferan worms distantly related to *Riftia* are found in such muds, deriving their energy from the oxidation of sulfide. By 1988, more than a decade after the first discoveries of the vent communities, it was still not at all clear how *Riftia* and the other members of its bizarre ecosystem came to colonize the energy-rich oases created on the seafloor by the black smokers. Nor was it clear how, after a new hydrothermal vent is formed, it becomes colonized by organisms living at a far distant vent.

Many details of the remarkable adaptations that permit the vent communities to flourish remained to be studied. By their very existence, they were teaching that life is so incredibly tenacious and plastic that it may be expected wherever there is an exploitable energy source and liquid water. That lesson was reinforced by the recent discovery of hydrocarbon-seep communities. These ecosystems are based on organisms that have become adapted to obtaining their energy from the oxidation of hydrocarbons, both natural gas and oil, that seep upward from faults in the seabed. Some of the organisms, which also live in deep, dark waters, were shown to use symbiotic bacteria, which metabolize the hydrocarbons for them. It is clear that science has not yet fully plumbed the staggering diversity of life forms on the Earth.   (IRWIN FRIDOVICH)

A Closer Look at the Human Genome. As long ago as biblical days, people noticed that children tend to resemble their parents. This may seem obvious, but it establishes the most basic premise of genetics—that traits are heritable.

The First Patented Animal

In April 1988 the U.S. Patent and Trademark Office awarded a patent to Harvard University for a strain of genetically engineered mice. The animals in question, first developed more than four years earlier by Philip Leder and colleagues using recombinant DNA techniques, carry an altered form of a normal gene that renders them unusually susceptible to cancer. Ideally, these mice and other animals like them could provide invaluable tools for probing the causes of cancer and finding treatments. In fact, by the late 1980s the technology existed that would allow the introduction of virtually any engineered gene into any of a wide variety of animals, paving the way for the development of animal models for many human diseases. The possible benefits of this technology not only for medicine but also for agriculture and other endeavours appeared practically limitless.

Plants and microorganisms had been patented for years in the U.S., but the April award marked the first ever in the world for an animal. More than 20 other animal patent applications received by the Patent Office were under consideration. Proponents of animal patenting argued that patenting and commercialization of genetically engineered animals would facilitate their further development and use toward many positive ends. Opponents forewarned of a host of problems including limited availability of the engineered animals, exorbitant costs passed along to the public, and royalties to be paid by farmers and ranchers on the offspring of patented livestock. Moreover, some critics argued that the lure of high profits could spur companies to develop bizarre or even dangerous new animals. The need, simply stated, was to facilitate the benefits of this technology while avoiding its pitfalls.

(JUDITH L. FRIDOVICH-KEIL)

DRAWING BY D. REILLY; © 1988 THE NEW YORKER MAGAZINE, INC.

"It'll never work out. She's patented, he isn't."

It was not until the mid-19th century that the concept of heredity came under rigorous study in the hands of Gregor Mendel, a monk living in what is now part of Czechoslovakia. Although people had, perhaps inadvertently, practiced selective breeding of plants and animals for many centuries, it was Mendel who first described the passage of heritable traits from parents to offspring in terms of the passage of discrete entities. From his study of garden peas, Mendel noted that numerous observable traits, such as the texture and colour of ripe peas and the height of pea-plant stems, could be passed from generation to generation. The information that specified each of these heritable traits was determined to be discrete and thus constituted the original definition of a gene.

In the decades that followed Mendel's work, a further fundamental observation was made: not only were many traits inherited but some traits tended to be inherited together. It was not until 1913 that geneticist A. H. Sturtevant, then an undergraduate studying mutations in the fruit fly (vinegar fly) *Drosophila melanogaster*, realized that the frequencies with which various traits are found associated could be used to construct a genetic linkage map, indicating the positions of various genes relative to one another in some linear array. Sturtevant reasoned that if some biologic mechanism operates on the genetic material such that any gene has a finite chance of becoming uncoupled from any other gene, then the farther apart two genes appear on the linear genetic map, the more likely they are to be uncoupled and inherited independently. Conversely, the closer the genes, the more likely they are to be inherited together. The biologic mechanism postulated by Sturtevant is now known as recombination and involves the exchange of analogous regions of DNA between homologous chromosomes.

Constructing a genetic linkage map for a living organism requires much information concerning heritable traits and the relative frequencies with which the traits are inherited. For traditional traits, such as eye colour or blood type, such information can be difficult to obtain, especially for organisms that have long generation times and that bear small numbers of offspring. By these criteria, humans rank among the most difficult of species to study.

Since the advent of recombinant DNA technology, however, it has become possible to study the finer characteristics of genes themselves, not just the physical traits that they encode. Through these methods it was found, for instance, that even genes that encode as yet unknown traits may themselves be distinguished in molecular terms. In 1980 David Botstein and colleagues argued that a genetic linkage map of the human genome, or genetic endowment, could be constructed on the basis of the inheritance of the molecular characteristics of genes, as well as of the more familiar inheritance of directly observable traits.

One measure of the molecular characteristics of genes involves the use of enzymes known as restriction endonucleases, which cleave large pieces of DNA into smaller fragments. The exact points of cleavage, and thus the sizes of the fragments, depend on the sequence of the genetic building blocks, *i.e.,* the nucleotides, in the gene itself because the restriction endonucleases cleave DNA only at specific "recognition" sequences. DNA fragments generated in this way can be sorted according to size by the technique of gel electrophoresis and eventually viewed as a pattern of bands on a piece of photographic film, where each band represents a fragment of one particular size. The same gene from two different individuals may give different banding patterns, indicating minor differences (polymorphism) in the DNA sequences of these genes. The genetic variation revealed in this way is known as restriction fragment length polymorphism, or RFLP. A large number of specific human genes have been shown to exhibit such polymorphism. The inheritance of these polymorphic traits may be determined from the banding patterns of small samples of DNA taken from the individuals in question. RFLP, as a measure of heritable genetic variation, is therefore a convenient tool for the construction of a genetic linkage map for the human genome.

In late 1987 such a map was deduced. Helen Donis-Keller, working with 32 colleagues, published a genetic linkage map that in their estimation encompassed at least 95% of the DNA in the human genome. Construction of the map was based on the patterns of inheritance of over 400 polymorphic traits, including 393 RFLPs, as observed in 21 three-generation families. Although such a map represented the culmination of an immense effort, it was but a powerful springboard for future work.

A genetic linkage map may be viewed as a road map that marks the location of known landmarks, in this case either RFLPs or genes detected by the traits they encode. With such a map in hand, it becomes possible to locate new genes by virtue of their linkage with the known landmarks. Recent studies of the patterns of inheritance of randomly selected RFLPs in human families revealed that at least some of these RFLPs are detectably linked to the genetic loci (locations) responsible for a number of human diseases. Among them are retinoblastoma, Duchenne muscular dystrophy, Huntington's disease, cystic fibrosis, and familial Alzheimer's disease. Moreover, the knowledge of genetic linkage to known segments of DNA facilitated the molecular cloning (mass reproduction) of the genes responsible for several of these diseases. The isolation and study of such genes and the products they encode is essential if these and other genetically determined diseases are to be better understood and effectively treated.

Another offshoot of genetic linkage studies involves the use of RFLP analysis in the prenatal or presymptomatic diagnosis of individuals at risk for inherited diseases. Such an early-warning system may facilitate the use of preventive measures in treating many illnesses. In addition, it may find its way into applications of a more controversial nature, such as the genetic screening of applicants by health insurance providers or prenatal screening by means of amniocentesis. As with other new and powerful technological innovations, humankind's increasing ability to characterize the human genome will also test its moral and ethical abilities to act wisely upon that knowledge.

During the past two years, RFLP analysis and genetic linkage data made inroads in the realm of forensic medicine. Because of the large number of genetic loci shown to be polymorphic by RFLP analysis, it proved possible to construct a "DNA fingerprint" of any individual, given a small sample of blood, semen, or other tissue from which DNA may be isolated. Unlike blood-typing or other traditional forms of identification, DNA fingerprinting can distinguish any one person from virtually every other human on Earth. DNA fingerprint data were beginning to appear in the courtroom and seemed likely to become routine evidence within a few years. (*See* CHEMISTRY.)

(JUDITH L. FRIDOVICH-KEIL)

See also Earth Sciences; Environment.

This article updates the *Macropædia* articles Animal BEHAVIOUR; BIOCHEMICAL COMPONENTS OF ORGANISMS; The BIOLOGICAL SCIENCES; BIOSPHERE; CONSERVATION OF NATURAL RESOURCES; ECOSYSTEMS; The Principles of GENETICS AND HEREDITY; GEOCHRONOLOGY; Biological GROWTH AND DEVELOPMENT; PHOTOSYNTHESIS; PROTOPHYTES; REPRODUCTION AND REPRODUCTIVE SYSTEMS; SENSORY RECEPTION.

Literature

The 1988 Nobel Prize for Literature was awarded to Naguib Mahfouz, an Egyptian writer (*see* BIOGRAPHIES). He was the first Arab (and only the second African) to win the prize. His *Cairo Trilogy,* published in 1956 and 1957, was said to comprise "the first true novels in Arabic." His novels had been compared to those of Graham Greene, by Fatma Moussa-Mahmoud of Cairo University, with the interesting difference that Mahfouz was no traveler. He never absented himself (until his retirement in 1971, at the age of 60) from his job as a civil servant in the Egyptian government.

In the West he was little known to the reading public, although scholars were quick to report that there were "at least 50 doctoral theses" on Mahfouz in U.S. and European universities. His English publishers, Heinemanns, had decided in September (just before he won the prize) to give up their 20-year effort to sell his work in Britain; they had sold the rights to his titles to the American University of Cairo. The 77-year-old Mahfouz expressed pleasure at the Nobel tribute paid to Arabic literature, saying, "I thought the world had forgotten us." He supposed that the new European interest in his work might be attributed to the recent success of a translation of the *Cairo Trilogy* in France.

Western attention was drawn to Arabic literature and the difficulties endured by its novelists. An anthology from Saudi Arabia, *The Literature of Modern Arabia,* edited by Salma Khadra Jayyusi, contained work from six different countries, covering the whole 20th century. An Egyptian writer in London, Ahdaf Soueif, observed that the bulk of the pieces could be called "literature of protest," complaining of oppression.

Salman Rushdie, born in Bombay, met the force of Muslim censorship when his English novel, *The Satanic Verses,* was nominated for the U.K.'s Booker Prize. It was based on the story that the Devil misled the Prophet Muhammad into pub-

lishing some verses in the Koran, permitting devotion to three pagan goddesses. Rushdie's attitude to Islam displeased orthodox worshipers. His book was admired in Britain but banned in both Pakistan and India.

In France the Prix Goncourt was won by Erik Orsenna for his fourth novel, *L'Exposition coloniale.* The "colonial exhibition" of the title was taken to mean "exposure to the idea of the colonies"—exemplified by the concept of that colonial product, rubber. The novel concerned the part played by rubber in the lives of the characters and in European history.

ENGLISH

United Kingdom. Among the anniversaries commemorated during the year was that of the political disorders of 1968, dominated by students hostile to the U.S war in Vietnam. Ronald Fraser wrote a useful book, *1968: A Student Generation in Revolt,* largely the work of oral historians who had interviewed more than 100 people, from six different nations, who had been vigorously involved in the demonstrations and disruptions. Another valuable study was *Sixty-Eight: The Year of the Barricades* by David Caute, a playwright, novelist, and university historian with some sympathy for the protesting students.

The fate of Peter Wright's book *Spycatcher* continued to excite attention. The British government had forbidden the publication of this memoir, which was written by a former member of the Security Services, and had unsuccessfully attempted to prevent its publication in other countries. In October the law lords ruled that British newspapers had the right to publish the so-called "revelations" offered by Peter Wright; however, the lords' decision was taken to imply that, if the book was published in Britain, the government could seize the profits.

Some saw the case as an indication of the government's readiness to restrict free expression; others claimed that *Spycatcher* was a dishonourable work by a civil servant who had failed in his duty to keep silent about Security Service work. The argument was relevant to a book by John

Peter Carey
© JERRY BAUER

Costello, *The Mask of Treachery,* concerning the damage done to the nation's security by the double agent Anthony Blunt. This book revealed the names of several secret agents, and the government was expected to suppress it.

Dissatisfaction with the condition of English literature was noticeable. The jeremiads of the novelist D. J. Taylor were welcomed in several journals, fulminating against the provincialism of contemporary novelists, predictable and classbound—overpraised by reviewers and read with boredom. "Novels in this country are still written by literary gents (or gentlewomen) about literary gents and for literary gents," said Taylor. He singled out a foreign novelist, remarking that "he *matters,* in any discussion of European high culture, in a way in which English writers do not." Much attention was paid to a book written in the U.S., *A Sinking Island: The Modern English Writers,* by Hugh Kenner; it was a book (said Kingsley Amis) devoted to demonstrating that British literature "had been no good since 1895." Kenner's dismissive account of contemporary writing and his enthusiasm for not-so-modern "Modernists" (such as Ezra Pound) irritated some critics but amused others.

Fiction. The winner of the Booker Prize was *Oscar and Lucinda* by Peter Carey, an advertising copywriter from Australia. This long book concerned two people traveling in Australia during the last century; the Australian poet Peter Porter wrote admiringly that both Oscar and Lucinda were "idealists, believers, Puritans and, at the same time, addicted gamblers. . . . I have never read a better account in fiction of the mixture of misery, audacity and discipline which attended the founding of Australia." Another attraction was the picturesque image of a glass church, which Oscar and Lucinda carried into the outback on a barge.

The chairman of the judges, Michael Foot, preferred Rushdie's *Satanic Verses,* which joined *Oscar and Lucinda* and four other novels on the shortlist of finalists. "It is not a philosophical treatise," wrote Hyam Macooby; it was concerned with reconciling "the pluralist vision of India with the effective but limiting tunnel-vision of the West."

THOMAS HARTWELL—TIME MAGAZINE

Naguib Mahfouz

A more modest, but much admired, contender for the Booker Prize was *Nice Work* by David Lodge, a learned scholar of modern literature and a sharp humorist. His comedy concerned a similar scholar and her relationships with a failing industrialist and a successful merchant banker; more serious than usual, Lodge presented a lifelike impression of modern Britain. Bruce Chatwin, a travel writer, offered *Utz,* a brief, quirky study of a reclusive collector of porcelain in Czechoslovakia.

Penelope Fitzgerald's historical novel, *The Beginning of Spring,* had a theme appropriate for the Booker Prize; it concerned life in Moscow over a few weeks preceding the Russian Revolution. Well researched, it presented the society with verisimilitude, wit, and charm. The sixth contender for the prize was Marina Warner, with *The Lost Father,* the story of a London museum worker tracing the history of her family back to New York and to the Italy of Mussolini.

Other interesting and enjoyable novels seemed, for one reason or another, unsuitable for the Booker Prize. Doris Lessing published *The Fifth Child,* a story about a little boy who was different from the rest of his family, unloved and perhaps unlovable—certainly uneducable and dangerously violent; his decent, unloving mother stayed with him, while the rest moved away from home. This plain tale was as haunting as *The Turn of the Screw.*

Rather haunting, too, was Muriel Spark's witty novel *A Far Cry from Kensington,* the tale of an admirably intelligent, noncompetitive woman working in publishing and magazine production—and her steely hostility toward a pretentious and incompetent writer. Andrew Sinclair at last completed his trilogy about the Matter of Britain with *King Ludd* succeeding the first two novels, *Gog* and *Magog.* This was an evocation of Ludd, the Celtic god, of the King Ludd who built London, and of Captain Ludd, the leader of the machine-wrecking Luddites; the book mingled Sinclair's views on labour unions and technology with wide, willful impressions of the nation's history. John Arden, an admired playwright, published *Books of Bale,* a historical novel about a 16th-century cleric and dramatist who took the side of Protestant monarchs against Roman Catholic opponents. This man, Bale, eventually became a repressive Protestant bishop in Catholic Ireland.

Kingsley Amis's new comedy, *Difficulties with Girls,* returned to the characters of his 1960 novel, *Take a Girl Like You.* The sequel was set in 1967, with Patrick Standish, the susceptible hero of the first book, now married to the heroine and no longer able to "take" girls casually and wantonly but rather compelled to suffer difficulties with them.

Stephen Spender published, for the first time, an autobiographical novel written almost 60 years earlier. *The Temple* concerned the youthful male body, as appreciated by a handsome young Englishman in Germany during the golden summer of 1929; the sense of liberated homosexuality was mingled with the feverish political excitement of Nazism and Communism. The older Spender extensively rewrote the novel, setting the story in the more sombre Germany of 1932.

Doris Lessing
JIM WILSON—THE NEW YORK TIMES

Graham Greene published *The Captain and the Enemy,* noticed by critics as a fresh and youthful book. The hero was a boy who thought of his father as an enemy, the Devil, and who was rescued from his school by a romantic, untrustworthy captain, a rogue engaged in modern-style smuggling in Latin America. It was noticed in the London *Sunday Telegraph* that this story bore some resemblance to Greene's first published novel, *The Man Within,* written when he was only 21. That book was a historical novel about a boy who thought his father a devil—and who was rescued from his school by the captain of a smugglers' ship. Though popular in its time, this early novel had been disdained by the older Greene. It was assumed that the new book was a deliberate reworking of the same themes.

Biography. The most destructive biographical exercise was *Intellectuals* by Paul Johnson, a right-wing intellectual who was formerly a left-wing intellectual. He chose to denounce all the famous men whom he had once been accustomed to revere: Rousseau, Marx, Shelley, Tolstoy, Ibsen, Brecht, Sartre, and Bertrand Russell were all presented as selfish and immoral beings. This destructive mood was echoed by the reviewers of Michael Holroyd's industrious biography *Bernard Shaw: The Search for Love.* There was no love for Shaw in the book but a great deal of sneering at his late sexual development and his carefully constructed public image. *Bertrand Russell: A Political Life* by Alan Ryan similarly prompted antagonism toward this strong-willed and free-thinking philosopher. Respect was more apparent in the reviewers' response to Brian McGuinness's biography of another philosopher, *Wittgenstein, A Life: Young Ludwig 1889–1921.* Yet another philosopher, A. J. Ayer, showed loyalty in his biography *Thomas Paine.* Many of Paine's contemporaries felt that this strong-minded revolutionary and critic of the Bible went too far, but Ayer would urge him to go even further.

Among the anniversaries celebrated were those of Lord Byron and T. E. Lawrence. Michael Foot, the former leader of the Labour Party, produced *The Politics of Paradise: A Vindication of Byron.* He seemed to be trying to reconcile Byron, as a fellow left-winger, with his contemporary

William Hazlitt—another of Foot's heroes. Other useful contributions were *Byron's Travels* by Allan Massie and *Byron and Tragedy* by Martyn Corbett.

T. E. Lawrence, too, was properly honoured, notably in *A Touch of Genius* by Malcolm Brown and Julia Cave, two BBC employees who had worked on television appreciations of Lawrence. *The Mint,* his memoir of service in the postwar Army and the Royal Air Force, was reprinted, and a selection of his private letters appeared as *The Letters of T. E. Lawrence,* collected and edited by Malcolm Brown.

Poetry. There was a tendency, suggested Blake Morrison, for poets to overpublish. "Most poets publish a new collection of thirty or forty poems every three or four years," he wrote in the *London Review of Books.* "Some are more industrious even than that." He listed seven new books of too many poems, published too soon. It was argued that "you have to write the bad poem in order to write the good"; but why, asked Morrison, "do you have to put the mediocre ones between hard covers?"

From this "minimalist" point of view, it was natural to praise the small size of Ian Hamilton's *Fifty Poems,* which Hamilton described as "not much to show for 25 years in the business." These poems concerned personal experiences, grave and painful. Morrison noted that Hamilton the poet admitted his vulnerability, whereas in his prose he seemed a well-armoured "tough guy."

Hamilton himself noticed that the new volume *Collected Poems* by the late Philip Larkin was "somewhat cluttered with botch-ups, immaturities and fragments." The book's editor, Anthony Thwaite, had added something like 80 poems to Larkin's known tally; "The poems we already know him by and most admire," said Hamilton, "total a mere 85." Andrew Motion, who had written Larkin's biography, published a book of his own poems, *Natural Causes,* in which critics were happy to discern echoes of Larkin.

There was much discussion of another dead poet, T. S. Eliot, concerning his unfriendly (and ill-timed) references to Jews. The painful subject was thoroughly discussed in *T. S. Eliot and Prejudice* by Christopher Hicks. *The Letters of T. S. Eliot (1898–1922),* edited by Valerie Eliot, his second wife, were informative about his first marriage and his concern to adapt himself to English life.

The most popular poem of the year was *Whale* by Heathcote Williams, a useful, didactic treatise about the protection of whales, with photographic illustrations. It was televised and found to be very moving. Some critics thought it to be merely photograph captions or claimed that it "backed all the right animal causes but all the wrong poetic ones." (D. A. N. JONES)

United States. *Fiction.* The year 1988 was an election year for the United States. Paradoxically, while most citizens were looking forward to putting a new president in the White House, many of the best novels of the year were historical in orientation. Of these, one of the best and the longest, if not the most ponderous, appeared early in the year. This was *The Tenants of Time* by Long Island novelist Thomas Flanagan. Flanagan, who taught literature for many years at the University

of California at Berkeley, had moved to Long Island about a decade earlier and begun to write fiction about Ireland. His first novel, *The Year of the French* (1979), won him a National Book Critics Circle Prize. *The Tenants of Time,* his second book, focuses once again on Ireland, this time upon the little known, and quickly squelched, Clonbrony Wood rebellion of the mid-19th century. Flanagan found this little-known insurrection, and the subsequent effect it had upon Irish nationalism and British occupation, paradigmatic of the Irish situation. His multivoiced narrative dramatizes quite effectively the conflicting politics and passions and points of view in Ireland, London, and even as far away as New York.

In the spring William Kennedy, recipient of a Pulitzer Prize for his novel *Ironweed* (1983) and of a McArthur Award for his achievements as a fiction writer and essayist, published another novel in his series set in Albany, N.Y. *Quinn's Book* is historical fiction of a special sort. Daniel Quinn, former riverboat apprentice turned journalist, tells a love story that intertwines with the history of the age, particularly the Civil War and the political civil wars of Albany at the time. These events have a profound effect on the intimate life of Daniel and his beloved young Maud, a waif whom he befriends during the course of a natural disaster on the upper Hudson River. The book in certain ways was a sidestep away from the kind of dour quasi-naturalistic fiction Kennedy's readers had come to anticipate. Its broad, often bawdy, and genuinely warm, sometimes comical scenes took some critics by surprise.

Two other interesting writers who turned to history for their newest novels were Don DeLillo and Louise Erdrich. In *Libra* DeLillo, who had made a reputation for himself in recent years as one of the best poker-faced satirists of U.S. culture, took the material of the Warren Commission Report on the assassination of John F. Kennedy and transformed it into a historical novel of sorts, with Lee Harvey Oswald as the main character. In DeLillo's version of the events of November 1963, a small band of rogue agents within the CIA forge the plot to kill the president. His plot to en-

E. FEINBLATT—SYGMA

Anne Tyler

lighten a readership still befuddled on this question seems lively and plausible and is filled with odd, designing characters out of the pages of the Warren Report. Erdrich imaginatively constructs the history of Argus, N.D., and its surrounding territory in *Tracks,* her third novel on motifs begun in *Love Medicine* (1984) and continued in *The Beet Queen* (1986). The pivotal period around World War I when the local Indian tribes had to face the question of giving up old rituals for a town religion such as Catholicism assumes faces, souls, and a destiny in the characters of the tribal narrator turned Indian agent and Fleur, the woman with special powers who undoes the fates of a number of men from the woods and the town.

The Old West came to life once again in the work of Larry McMurtry, whose novel *Lonesome Dove* (1985) had won

© JERRY BAUER

Barbara Tuchman

the Pulitzer Prize several years earlier for its vivid evocation of a trail drive from Texas to Montana. In the autumn of 1988 McMurtry brought out another western novel, *Anything for Billy,* an entertaining and endearing treatment of Billy the Kid as seen through the eyes of a 19th-century dime novelist named Ben Sippy. This was McMurtry working in a minor key but succeeding, nonetheless, in demonstrating his narrative strengths.

Thomas Savage, by contrast, was virtually unknown, although *The Corner of Rife and Pacific,* set in the fictional town of Grayling, Mont., at the turn of the century, was his 13th book. A fine and compact little saga that shows a Montana family in turmoil and a town in transition, it deserved a wider readership than it probably would receive. Like the Erdrich book, it calls up the old landscape of the forgotten West in prose both beautiful and functional. *Fair and Tender Ladies,* an epistolary novel by North Carolina author Lee Smith, conjures up the Old East, specifically the hollows and mountain cabins of the mining area of southwestern Virginia from the beginning of the 20th century until almost the present. Told in the sprightly, undaunted, and intelligent voice of Ivy Rowe, it stands as a major achievement in Smith's writing career.

Of the novels that focused on contemporary life, almost none was as successful as

any one of the historical fictions. John Updike, for example, brought out *S.* (also an epistolary novel). While the book touched on history insofar as it reworked themes from Nathaniel Hawthorne's *Scarlet Letter,* it centred mainly on the adventures of a runaway New England housewife in the throes of joining a religious cult in Arizona, with mixed results. Even more disappointing was *Breathing Lessons,* the latest novel from the extraordinarily successful Baltimore writer Anne Tyler. Although the book sold as briskly as her previous novels and was, in fact, honoured with a nomination for the American Book Award for Fiction, a few critics found it quite listless and a serious falling off from such previous novels as *Dinner at the Homesick Restaurant* (1982) and *The Accidental Tourist* (1985).

Jay McInerney, whose *Bright Lights, Big City* (1984) had won him much acclaim and comment a few years earlier, brought out *Story of My Life,* a novel that was not highly regarded by many critics. Michiko Kakutani of the *New York Times* scolded him about lowering his own standards for fiction in this first-person narrative about a 20-year-old aspiring actress who feels abandoned by her rich father and dives with seeming relish into the world of yuppie sex and drugs.

Joy Williams published *Breaking and Entering,* a deftly composed but meandering novel about two young Floridians living on the wild side. Ellen Douglas (Josephine Haxton) brought out *Can't Quit You, Baby,* an intermittently successful treatment of race relations in a Mississippi middle-class household. The best novel set in the South that appeared in 1988 was Pete Dexter's *Paris Trout,* a dark study of the murder of a young black girl by a white shopkeeper in southern Georgia just after the Korean War. *Palm Latitudes,* a linguistically daring novel about Chicano women in Los Angeles by California novelist Kate Braverman, met with both highly positive and highly negative reviews. Among popular best-selling fiction, *Cardinal of the Kremlin* by adventure writer Tom Clancy (*see* BIOGRAPHIES) led the pack.

A few outstanding collections of short fiction were published during the year. The best of them, *Where I'm Calling From,* new and selected stories by Raymond Carver, came out only a few months before the distinguished author's death in early August. Another first-rate story writer, Hob Broun, died before the publication of his newest book, *Cardinal Numbers.* James Salter, one of the least known but most highly respected fiction writers in the country, brought out *Dusk and Other Stories.* Harold Brodkey's *Stories in an Almost Classical Mode* appeared to mixed notices. Mary Robison published *Believe Them,* a new collection of short fiction. Novelist Richard Elman collected his short fiction on revolutionary Nicaragua under the title *Disco Frito.* Two new young writers, Mary Gaitskill and Ethan Canin, saw the appearance of their first collections, *Bad Behavior Stories* and *Emperor of the Air,* respectively. Both books won wide acclaim. *Emperor of the Air* was reported to have sold 50,000 copies in hard cover, an extraordinary success for any work of serious fiction, let alone a collection of stories by a first-time author.

Nonfiction. History, both distant and recent, engaged the imaginations of nonfiction writers in 1988. Barbara Tuchman published *The First Salute,* in which an obscure incident in the American Revolutionary War becomes the jumping-off place for a book-length essay on the early days of the U.S. James McPherson won wide critical acclaim for his one-volume history of the Civil War period, *Battle Cry of Freedom.* David Brinkley's recollective account of the U.S. capital during the early 1940s, *Washington Goes to War,* had some popular success. Two former White House staffers, Richard Goodwin and Hodding Carter, came out with appraisals of the not-so-distant past, Goodwin with *Remembering America* about the 1960s, and Carter with *The Reagan Years.* The major work of historical and political import was former *New York Times* reporter Neil Sheehan's 700-page volume *A Bright Shining Lie: John Paul Vann and America in Vietnam,* a narrative that encompasses both the life story of a paradigmatic modern U.S. military figure and the progress and defeat of the U.S. war effort in Southeast Asia.

The private lives of two literary warriors came under scrutiny in 1988 in biographies of Truman Capote (*Capote* by Gerald Clarke) and John Cheever (*John Cheever* by Scott Donaldson). Cheever's son Benjamin edited *The Letters of John Cheever,* in which his father's tortured psychic life is fully displayed. These were conventional works, based on extensive interviews and thorough research. Less conventional was Philip Roth's first venture into autobiography, a dour, stolidly composed book called *The Facts.* Poet Karl Shapiro offered the first volume of his autobiography (*The Younger Son*), in which he treats himself in the third person, focusing on his youth and his military service in the Pacific during World War II. A book that effectively wove together elements of confession, travel, and social observation was fiction writer Mary Morris's *Nothing to Declare,* an account of a long sojourn in Mexico and Central America. A fine example of contemporary American nature writing was published by Dan O'Brien—

AP/WIDE WORLD

Richard Rhodes

Howard Nemerov
AP/WIDE WORLD

The Rites of Autumn: A Falconer's Journey Across the American West. In *The Dark Side of the Universe* physicist James Trefil takes readers on a journey through time from the birth of the cosmos to the end of all matter as it is known a quadrillion years from the present—in a popular but wholly intelligent series of chapters for the lay reader. Another well-written treatment of cosmology was Timothy Ferris's *Coming of Age in the Milky Way.* The end of a famous style seemed to be marked by Hunter Thompson's latest collection, *A Generation of Swine.*

Poetry and Criticism. Former poet laureate Richard Wilbur published his *New and Collected Poems* early in 1988. A second important collection, C. K. Williams's *Collected Poems, 1966–1986,* came out in the autumn. Philip Levine's latest book, *A Walk with Tom Jefferson,* appeared during the year, with the title poem a serious and successful attempt to fuse the poet's empathy for his economically depressed home town of Detroit with a spare narrative line. Another narrative poem, this one nearly 70 pages long, was Nicholas Christopher's *Desperate Characters,* though—unlike the Levine—this seemed more fashionable than enduring. Alabama poet Andrew Hudgins in *After the Lost War* offered a book-length narrative based on Civil War themes. Other established poets who brought out books were Donald Hall (*The One Day*), John Hollander (*Harp Lake*), James Merrill (*The Inner Room*), and James Schuyler (*Selected Poems*). Among younger poets, Donald Revell was represented with *The Gaza of Winter.* Two notable works of literary criticism to appear were Barbara Herrnstein Smith's *Contingencies of Value: Alternative Perspectives for Critical Theory* and poet-critic Robert Pinsky's *Poetry and the World.*

Awards and Prizes. A small controversy arose early in the year, when a number of black writers and poets, irritated that the novel *Beloved* by Toni Morrison (*see* BIOGRAPHIES) appeared to have been passed over for the American Book Award for 1987 (which went instead to *Paco's Story* by Larry Heinemann), signed a manifesto-like letter to the *New York Times Book Review* in which they agitated for a Pulitzer

Prize for the novel in question. As Pulitzer judge Julian Moynahan, writing later in the year in the *Rutgers Alumni Magazine,* observed, the Morrison novel was a clear choice for the prestigious award, though he feared at the time that the agitation might cause the prize committee to balk. They did not, and *Beloved* was awarded the Pulitzer Prize. The 1988 American Book Award for fiction went to *Paris Trout* by Pete Dexter and for nonfiction to *A Bright Shining Lie* by Neil Sheehan. Journalist Richard Rhodes won the Pulitzer general nonfiction award for *The Making of the Atomic Bomb.* In poetry the prize went to William Meredith for *Partial Accounts: New and Selected Poems.* The National Book Critics Circle awarded its fiction prize to *The Counterlife* by Philip Roth and its poetry award to *Flesh and Blood* by C. K. Williams. *World's End* by T. C. Boyle, a multilayered historical novel set in New York's Hudson River Valley, won the PEN/Faulkner Prize. McArthur Foundation Award winners in fiction were novelist Thomas Pynchon and story writer Andre Dubus. Howard Nemerov was named poet laureate of the United States, succeeding Richard Wilbur. (ALAN CHEUSE)

Canada. The worldview of many of the novels published in Canada in 1988 tended to be a bleak one. In Malcolm Lowry's last novel, *October Ferry to Gabriola,* the emphasis is on last things and the despair that sunders us from them. Janice Kulyk Keefer's first novel, *Constellations,* set on one of the outer rings of hell, it seems—cooler, perhaps, but lonely, as Pluto is lonely, being farther from the Sun—is a starkly beautiful evocation of nihilism and sterility. Neil Bissoondath's first novel, *A Casual Brutality,* is set on a fictional Caribbean island where protagonist and island together struggle to forge a new identity from the rich spoils of a colonial history. One of the more humorous novels of the year, by way of contrast, was Austin Clarke's *Proud Empires,* a tender yet tough rendering of a real island, Barbados, during the early 1950s.

The theme of identity also runs through Constance Beresford-Howe's most recent novel, *Prospero's Daughter,* in which a writer confuses his will with his imagination in an illusion of a freedom responsible only to itself—leading to consequences both predictable and startling. Morley Callaghan's *A Wild Old Man on the Road* tells of the sojourn of an aspiring journalist to Paris and the past, during which he meets with his literary hero, and the ultimate betrayal, that of oneself. In Doris Anderson's *Affairs of State,* the sojourn is through the labyrinths of Ottawa's bureaucracy by a woman fresh from academe and ripe for action.

Humour surfaces in *The Lyre of Orpheus,* Robertson Davies's latest romp among a cast of collegiate characters, pranksters grim and merry, playing games with them, the language, and stray ideas, while, through her *Cat's Eye,* Margaret Atwood coolly observes a young girl, and the woman she becomes, wielding metaphor like a rapier. Both books make one laugh, and each should be taken in its own way—Atwood's on an empty stomach, Davies's after a good meal.

Short-story collections were, on the whole, more upbeat in outlook than the

novels, although Mavis Gallant's ninth collection, *In Transit,* is characterized by people who, whether parents or children, husbands or wives or lovers, are hard to like. They are in turn abusive, dictatorial, and incompetent—and impossible to disown, for they are we, like it or not.

The battleground of family life also offers many targets for Timothy Findley's *Stones,* a barrage of the absurd and unlikely upon the walls of everyday life. Death and destruction become grounds for amusement in *Sins for Father Knox,* a collection of detective stories in which Josef Skvorecky includes sins against the genre itself among the original ten. In Dionne Brand's *Sans Souci and Other Stories,* the conflict of family members is set against, and often set off by, the exigencies of racism, migration, and cultural shock.

One way or another, poets were on the move in Canada during the year. They ran the gamut from Milton Acorn's avowedly anarchic *Hundred Proof Earth* to Carolyn Zonailo's zesty odes in *Zen Forest;* from bill bissett's *What We Have,* concrete and sound poems, both lyrical and satirical, to Patricia Young's *The Business of Shining,* poems in which the west-coast light, reflected from the sea, illuminates and deceives; from the *Entertaining Angels* that sport through Elizabeth Brewster's 11th collection to the entertaining mental and linguistic acrobatics of Yvonne Trainer's *Landscape Turned Sideways;* and from the *Infinite Worlds* of Louis Dudek, selections from 42 years of poetic exploration, to the traveling cosmos of Anne Szumagalski's *Journey/Journée,* in which all elements of poetics are in motion, in play, in question, and in doubt. In *Furious,* Erin Mouré's fine lines dissect the body politic as the body in love—the cutting edge, like paper's, stinging—while in *The End of Innocence* Gail Fox delineates sins we never knew we knew but recognize as our own, and Raymond Souster draws from history, *Asking for More.*

Daphne Marlatt and Betsy Warland went to Australia and, having returned, expose it in *Double Negative.* David Helwig went to China to learn *The Hundred Old Names* by which the Chinese refer to themselves and reflects upon them; Libby Oughton went from cellar to attic, *Getting the Housework Done* in time for a party; and Tom Konyves went to great lengths in refining his techniques in *Experimeter.*

(ELIZABETH WOODS)

FRENCH

The most notable event in French literature during the year was, incontestably, the publication of numerous works concerning the attitude of Martin Heidegger toward Nazism. "The Heidegger Affair," as it was labeled by the newspapers, was launched by the publication, in September 1987, of the work of Victor Farias, a longtime student of philosophy. The book, soberly entitled *Heidegger et le Nazisme,* contains documents that appear to show Heidegger as sympathetic to Nazism, notably letters that he wrote in 1934 when he was rector of the University of Freiburg.

The question quickly arose as to whether Heidegger should continue to be ranked as one of the great thinkers of the 20th century. Could a great thinker, in good conscience, come out in support of a bar-

Alain Robbe-Grillet
© JERRY BAUER

barous and bloody ideology? Everyone responded with his or her own opinion, all of them sensible but all of them different. The philosophers Jacques Derrida (*De l'esprit, Heidegger et la question*), Philippe Lacoue-Labarthe (*La Fiction du politique*), and Jean-François Lyotard (*Heidegger et "les Juifs"*) preferred to discuss the philosophical theses of Heidegger rather than his political association. The sociologist Pierre Bourdieu (*L'ontologie politique de Martin Heidegger*) reset Heideggerian discourse into the context of his era. Finally, in *Anatomie d'un scandale,* François Fédier dissected Farias's book, seeking to show the inadequacy and, perhaps, the falseness of the work. Nevertheless, the debate was far from being finished as 1988 drew to a close.

For those concerned with editorial boldness, the publication by Pierre-Marc de Biasi of the set of *Carnets de travail* ("Notebooks of Work") by Gustave Flaubert (1,000 pages of notes, reflections, and secrets) constituted a genuine achievement. In the domain of essays, among those released in anticipation of the bicentennial of the French Revolution an outstanding effort was *Condorcet, un intellectuel en politique* coauthored by Elisabeth and Robert Badinter. It is a skillful portrait of the man of convictions who was the marquis de Condorcet: active militant for civic equality for blacks and Protestants, fierce partisan for the abolition of the death penalty, and a man resolutely ahead of his times, wanting—for example—to apply the rigours of the physical sciences to the social sciences. Another successful biographical study was that of Claude Arnaud on a contemporary of Condorcet, *Chamfort,* famous for his *Maximes* but whose life—full of short, sudden breaks and contradictions—had remained little known. Among essays that were more specifically literary, Paul Bénichou's *Les Mages romantiques* analyzed, with spirit, the ideological influence that was exerted by the three great poets of French Romanticism—Lamartine, Vigny, Hugo—on their era.

Autobiographies provided some of the most interesting books of the year. *A cor et à cri* was Michel Leiris's addition to his

enterprise of laying bare the "I" (or "me") that he started 50 years earlier in *L'âge d'homme. L'angélique* by Alain Robbe-Grillet mixed memories of childhood, fantasies, and theoretical and personal reflections. Throughout *L'Invitation,* Claude Simon sprinkled comical details and direct political analyses and also employed his considerable talents for description. Also in a resplendent style, *Déconnection* by Claude Ollier paints an apocalyptic tableau of the contemporary world, which, according to the author, has brought into being nothing but violence, poverty, and a lack of culture.

Halfway between autobiography and novel, *Une femme* by Annie Ernaux was an attempt to resume the work of mourning that Ernaux had accomplished four years earlier over the figure of her father (*La Place*). This book, however, written soon after the death of her mother, is marked by a pervasive coldness; love and suffering are entirely contained in the extreme dryness of the style. The reader remains outside the story. In *Un détour par la vie,* Henri Thomas also confides in the reader, but in a manner more outrageous and complex than Ernaux's. In it, one is inside the story from the onset.

Erik Orsenna received the Prix Goncourt, the nation's highest literary award, for *L'Exposition coloniale.* On the sixth poll Orsenna had narrowly defeated Bernard-Henri Lévy, whose novel *Les Derniers Jours de Charles Baudelaire* had been widely favoured to win. Two weeks later Lévy's book won the Prix Interallié. The Prix Renaudot was awarded to exiled Haitian writer René Depestre for *Hadriana dans tous mes rêves.* Alexandre Jardin won the Prix Femina for his second novel, *Le Zèbre,* while Christiane Rochefort's *La Porte du fond,* which was shortlisted for the Femina, won the prestigious Prix Medici in a close vote over Patrick Deville's *Longuevue.*

If French professors increasingly preferred essays over novels, poetry seemed almost completely ignored. Rare were the authors who could boast, as did René Char (*see* OBITUARIES), of a relatively large readership. His last work, the somewhat disappointing *Eloge d'une soupçonnée,* was published several months after his death on February 19. Two books of high quality were written by less well-known poets: *L'Amour de loin* by Jacqueline Risset and *Pour une île à venir* by Benoît Conort.

(FRANÇOIS POIRIÉ)

Canada. Two of the outstanding novels of 1988 were written by an internationally renowned writer, Anne Hébert, and a 24-year-old author publishing a first piece of work, Christian Mistral. Hébert confirmed her remarkable talent in *Le Premier Jardin.* The novel depicts the homecoming of an actress, Flora Fontages, and her *recherche du temps perdu* after an extensive stay abroad. Hébert's readers were pleased to discover new subject matter couched in the now familiar style, with constant intertextual references to her earlier works, covering more than four decades. Totally different, in style as well as in theme, Mistral's *Vamp* is a harsh and disturbing rejection of modern society. Blending the approaches of the narrative and the essay, the novel is a direct and troubling portrayal of the contemporary world from the

Anne Hébert
CANAPRESS PHOTO SERVICE

point of view of a young man in his mid-20s drifting through deteriorating times.

Retrospective poetry collections continued to be popular. Pierre Morency's *Quand nous serons* (1967–78) is a quite readable text for the most part. In *Poésies complètes* (1955–87), more than 700 pages of diversified poetry, Michel Garneau succeeds beyond any doubt in his endeavour to convince us that *ce n'est pas la vie /qui est utile à la littérature* ("it is not life that serves literature") but rather the opposite.

For those interested in the origins of modern Québecois theatre, *Les Fridolinades 1938-1939-1940* should prove to be an important book since Gratien Gélinas's Fridolin was in many ways the forerunner of the main character in the author's seminal plays, *Tit-Coq* (1948). Jean Basile, on the other hand, surprised the theatrical community by writing a very unusual play, *Adieu . . . je pars pour Viazmal!* Long a reader of Chekhov, Basile presents his works as owing much to the Russian author; more than 15 of Chekhov's texts serve as the basis for this play, but even so the resulting work bears the distinctive stamp of Jean Basile.

In 1988 Quebec lost not only a major writer and "chansonnier" but also a man who for more than 40 years was a symbol of his people: Félix Leclerc. Another major loss was that of the scientist-writer Fernand Seguin, whose *Le Cristal et la chimère* as well as his many other works did so much to make the scientific world more widely accessible. (PIERRE HÉBERT)

GERMAN

West Germany, Austria, Switzerland. The trauma of urban terrorism in the 1970s was the dominant theme of new West German fiction. Peter-Jürgen Boock's *Abgang* owed its success to its background: it was written in prison, where its author was serving a life sentence for his involvement with the Red Army Faction. In Friedrich Christian Delius's *Mogadischu Fensterplatz,* the 1977 hijacking of a Lufthansa jet forms the setting for an outstanding psychological study of the mind of a hostage and also for a meditation on the chain of guilt and responsibility that

leads from Hitler to the Arab-Israeli conflict and ultimately to the hijacking itself. The 1977 events are the subject of Rainald Goetz's novel *Kontrolliert,* but there they serve as the focus of a highly personal, anarchic statement. In her *Heidelberger Novelle,* Eva Zeller uses a more recent event, the 1981 rocket attack on a U.S. general, for her study of the mentality of a so-called sympathizer, the daughter of a highly respectable Heidelberg family. Most ambitious is Christian Geissler's "romantic fragment" *kamalatta,* which relates the Red Army Faction's activities to the Greek struggle for independence from the Turks; linguistically impressive, it purports to offer an "aesthetics of resistance."

Another preoccupation was a critique of civilization, often with apocalyptic undertones. Ingomar Kieseritzky's much-admired *Buch der Desaster* is a black comedy in which two men try to outdo each other in recounting all the disasters of the 1980s. Both Michael Winter's *Rückkehr in die Metropolen* and Karin Scholten's *Longlife* are dystopic novels, the one an account of the modern city as the paradigm of an inhumane rationalism, the other a Huxley-like satire on medicine and advertising. Gabriele Wohmann's *Der Flötenton* is a post-Chernobyl piece of cultural pessimism; its theme of aging is repeated in Hartmut Lange's *Die Ermüdung.* In Michael Köhlmeier's *Spielplatz der Helden* the true story of a trans-Greenland expedition becomes a parable of social existence.

Köhlmeier's novel is also the account of the writing of a novel. Literature was the subject of a number of other works. Walter Kempowski's enormously entertaining *Hundstage* was its author's first venture outside his family history; its protagonist is a successful novelist concerned with his image rather than with reality. Hermann Lenz's *Seltsamer Abschied* continued the autobiographical series on Eugen Rapp; in the late 1960s he finds himself quite out of touch with literary fashions; only a few years later he is "discovered" by the fickle public once more. In Gertrud Leutenegger's *Meduse* the jellyfish of the title inspires a poetic evocation of transience.

Margrit Baur presented storytelling as a form of evasion in her *Geschichtenflucht;* its four main characters tell each other of their experiences, but all are concealing the essence of their own personalities. By contrast, Rosemarie Quadflieg's *Fabels Veränderung* describes a painter's preoccupation with the child he might have had; eventually it comes alive for him, a fiction that permanently changes his life. Thorsten Becker's *Die Nase* is a picaresque artist novel set in East Berlin, amusing and ultimately life-affirming in its message. Katherine Mansfield is the subject of Christa Moog's *Aus tausend grünen Spiegeln.*

Impressive collections of poetry were produced by Erich Fried (*Am Rand unserer Lebenszeit*), Ulla Hahn (*Unerhörte Nähe*), Robert Schindel (*Geier sind pünktliche Tiere*), and Ludwig Fels (*Blaue Allee, versprengte Tataren*).

East Germany. Historical themes continued to be popular. Hans-Peter Jaeck's *Kammerherr und König,* a novel on Voltaire's sojourn at the court of Frederick the Great, concerns the perennial tensions between intellectuals and politicians.

Volker Ebersbach's *Caroline,* the fictional biography of one of the most interesting women of the late 18th and early 19th centuries, Caroline Schlegel-Schelling, was further evidence of East Germany's renewed interest in the Romantic movement. Heinz-Jürgen Zierke's *Wibald der Mönch* went back to the times of Frederick Barbarossa. Turning to more recent history, Erik Neutsch continued his vast project on East Germany's development: *Nahe der Grenze* describes in orthodox terms the crisis year 1968 and the invasion of Czechoslovakia.

Back in the contemporary world, Hermann Kant's *Die Summe* satirized international conferences of writers; unlike Jaeck, he seems to be suggesting that it should all be left to the politicians. Manfred Pieske's *Die Traumfrau* treated male sexuality with unusual frankness in a study of repressions linked to tensions at work and the experience of an overbearing mother. Reinhart Heinrich mingled fantasy and scientific insight in his *Jenseits von Babel,* a kind of science fiction novel set in the present day. The most interesting novelty, however, was Brigitte Burmeister's *Anders,* a plea on behalf of the imagination, written in the manner of the French *nouveau roman.* Heinz Czechowski published a collection of elegiac poems, *Kein näheres Zeichen,* some of which were based on his journeys to France and Britain.

One substantial project began in which East and West collaborated: a critical edition of the works of Bertolt Brecht.

(J. H. REID)

SCANDINAVIAN

Denmark. Age and glances back were features of the year. Two small volumes of Hans Kirk's magazine writing were published: *En plads i verden og andre fortællinger* and *En kommis' dagbog,* both showing Kirk as an excellent realist. Some of Leif Panduro's short stories from the 1950s were published posthumously in 1987 in *Bare det hele var anderledes,* prefiguring his later observations of middle-class life. Anders Bodelsen wrote two volumes of stories, *Den blå time* (1987) and *Jeg kommer til at løbe,* the first close to the thriller genre, the second in a gentler mood and concerned with the meeting of generations. In her *Glemselens forår,* Dorrit Willumsen also ponders aging. A contrast in style is Peer Hultberg's *Slagne veje,* concentrated studies of people, largely American, in a modernist vein. Modernist, too, are Sven Holm's often surprising and disturbing portraits in *Under blodet.*

Among novels, the sensation was Lars Bukdahl's *Guldhornene,* a fantasy full of literary references and a gallery of characters that range from talking animals to Superman. Traditional novels appeared as well. Dea Trier Mørch's *Skibet i flasken* projects a small child's only half-comprehending perspective of World War II and the Liberation. Flashbacks to the 1950s are also in evidence in Klaus Rifbjerg's *Engel* (1987), a novel centred on a couple's two journeys to the South, in the 1980s and the 1950s, and including such typical Rifbjerg themes as the crisis of middle age, inhibition, repression, and neurosis. Juliane Preisler, established as a leading poet of her generation, made her prose debut in *Den lille* (1987).

Uffe Harder's poems *I denne verden* are about contact and communication—or their lack. In *Af jord,* Sten Kaalø repeated his experiment in writing modern hymns. Erik Stinus is less religious in *Det belejrede hjerte,* but he is a social moralist in the best sense, glimpsing suffering throughout the world, from Nicaragua to South Africa, from reindeer in Lapland to the bison of North America. Benny Andersen looks back in a collection of early poems, *Andre sider* (1987). Other glances back were the diaries or memoirs of distinguished writers. Thorkild Bjørnvig published his memoirs of postwar Germany in *Onsket. Erindringer 1946–48* (1987) and Villy Sorensen some of his diaries in *Tillob. Dagboger 1949–53.*

Marta Christensen received the Booksellers' Golden Laurel. (W. GLYN JONES)

Norway. Johannes Heggland confirmed his position as a superb master of Norwegian language and storytelling with the closing volume of the trilogy *Seglet og vinden,* entitled *Gullkalven,* and a major new work, *Meisterens søner.* Both novels take the reader back to a rapidly changing society in western Norway in the second half of the 19th century, combining psychological insight with cultural and economic history.

Anne Karin Elstad drew on her personal experience of suffering a severe stroke in her moving novel *Maria, Maria. . . .* Kaj Skagen's roman à clef about publishing, *Himmelen vet ingenting,* which caused a sensation, gives a pessimistic view of contemporary Norway. Marital tensions and the ambiguous complexities of a friendship between two boys are penetratingly analyzed in Tor Edvin Dahl's deeply pessimistic novel *Venner.* Friendship, adultery, jealousy, and feelings of guilt are ingredients in Tore Hamsun's complex psychological thriller *Rhapsody in Blue.* Fredrik Skagen launched his fifth successful thriller, *Menneskejegeren,* based on the adventures of his now familiar character Morten Martins, this time operating as an agent for MI5, the British Secret Service.

It was a rich year for literary biographies, with contributions from Kjartan Fløgstad on the modernist poet and actor Claes Gill in *Portrett av eit magisk liv,* Klaus Hagerup on his mother, Inger Hagerup, in *Alt er så nær meg,* and Espen Haavardsholm on Aksel Sandemose in *Mannen fra Jante.* There were autobiographical books from the poet Hans Børli, *Med øks og lyre,* and from the novelist Ebba Haslund, *Som plommen i egget,* as well as a remarkable autobiographical novel from the severely handicapped Finn Carling, *Gjensyn fra en fremtid.* Another autobiographical novel, Bjørg Vik's *Små nøkler store rom,* captures the atmosphere of everyday life in Oslo during the 1940s.

Knut Hamsun's works were analyzed in Arild Haaland's *Hamsun—spenninger og slør.* An unexpected bonus was the appearance of nine hitherto unpublished short stories by Hamsun, *Livsfragmenter.* Reflections on aging are given moving expression in Marie Takvam's collection of poems, *Aldrande drabantby,* and 375 poems by Ernst Orvil, published posthumously in *Siste dikt,* provide a last encounter with a master of the playful poetic paradox. A new literary periodical in English, *News from the Top of the World,* was launched. (TORBJØRN STØVERUD)

Sweden. The tercentenary year of the birth of Emanuel Swedenborg saw the reissuing of his dream diary, *Swedenborgs Drömbok,* edited by Lars Bergquist, as well as publication of the literary biographies *Hjalmar Söderberg, Ett författarliv* by Bure Holmbäck and *Gunnar Ekelöf, En biografi* by Carl Olov Sommar. In Sigrid Combüchen's *Byron,* the poet is seen through the eyes of close associates in a narrative purporting to present the researches of admirers preparing for his sesquicentennial celebrations in 1938. Bengt Pohjanen's *Dagning; röd!*—like Combüchen's book, fiction based on reality—presents the ministry of the preacher Toivo Korpela in northern Finland/Sweden in the 1930s.

In *Kärleksguden Frö. En levnadsteckning,* Torgny Lindgren freely elaborates on Old Norse legends of Frö, god of love, with illustrations by Peter Dahl. Young Peter Kihlgård centred his novel *Fadder Teiresias vår* on the blind Theban seer Tiresias, with many shifts in time and space. The year's three major fictional works, Kerstin Ekman's *Rövarna i Skuleskogen,* Sven Delblanc's *Änkan,* and Ulla Isaksson's *FödelseDagen,* all played with time. Ekman showed a being evolving over 500 years from troll to possessor of a soul. Delblanc subverted the *Lace*-genre (female daydreams of power) by writing about a 55-year-old widow who regains dazzling youth by means of a magic potion. In a hedonistic world without ethical principles, desire leads her to murder and incest. By contrast, Isaksson's widow struggles with dawning insights on her 75th birthday, counterpointed by flashbacks and the reactions of daughters simultaneously loving and resentful.

People rather than politics were important in 1988. In Kristian Petri's first novel, *Första rummet,* the narrator seeks to exorcise the memory of his mother's suicide. In *Skilda öden* Margareta Ekström, probably the foremost short-story practitioner, varied the theme of divorce. In *Erotik* the basically caring nature of the short stories on amorous love by 12 accomplished writers contrasted interestingly with a preceding volume from 1968, the heyday of sexual liberation.

Stig Larsson offered casually outspoken poems on existential issues in *Händ!* Göran Palm continued his Heinesque ironic critique of Sweden in *Fosterlandet i bitar;* Anders Olsson built *Bellerofontes resa* round a figure in the Odyssey. Novelist Per Gunnar Evander published his first poetry collection, *Fritt fall.* (KARIN PETHERICK)

ITALIAN

In a rich and interesting year that produced work of enduring quality in many fields, one main trend seemed to have come to full maturity. Experimentation with language was no longer carried out tentatively or for its own sake as a polemical statement but seemed to have become a regular feature of Italian writing. A new geography of Italian literature was emerging, as excellent works were produced from all over the country, all bearing the distinctive linguistic and cultural marks of their regions.

Italian-style thrillers—detective stories in which the writer's ideological or stylistic commitment prevails over the intrigue—were once again quite popular with critics and readers alike. Among these, *La troga*

by Giampaolo Rugarli was a somewhat surreal pastiche, modeled on Carlo Emilio Gadda's *Pasticciaccio* and set in Rome in the near future, where the deep corruption affecting the old city permeates everything, including language; *La notte dell'arciduca* by Oddone Camerana was a more consistently sombre story, set in 1910 Turin, of a father overcome by the enigmatic suicide of his son. In *Decrizioni criminali* by Carlo Cristiano Delcorno, narrative itself, shifting imperceptibly between past and present, fiction and autobiography, seemed to be affected by "criminal" dealings. A love story set within the frame of a thriller was the subject of *La trappola amorosa,* the well-received last novel of Giovanni Arpino, who died during the year. In a category of its own was *Porte aperte* by Leonardo Sciascia, a characteristically lucid and compelling dramatization of a legal case in which a judge stands firm against the Fascist regime.

Two Sicilian writers published works of impressive quality. Gesualdo Bufalino's *Le menzogne della notte* is a novel of remarkable clarity and firmness, in which four revolutionaries, sentenced to death for plotting against the Bourbons, spend their last night telling each other enigmatic stories. *Retablo* by Vincenzo Consolo is a linguistic tour de force, a travel journal and a picaresque novel at the same time, in which a Lombard painter and his Sicilian guide and servant travel together through 18th-century Sicily trying in vain to forget their unrequited loves. Equally complex in terms of structure, but written in an ostensibly easy, almost spoken, register, was *L'oro del mondo* by Sebastiano Vassalli, in which the narrator's present experiences as writer mingle with autobiographical memories and fictional reconstructions of the past to achieve a tragicomic picture of life in postwar Lombardy. Aldo Busi's fourth novel in four years, *Sodomie in corpo 11,* raised the usual stir: the book is an exuberant, detailed, and provoking first-person account of the narrator's homosexual experiences and intellectual ruminations between Morocco and Vienna, Tunisia and Prague, Kenya and Leningrad.

© JERRY BAUER

Leonardo Sciascia

If what distinguished Busi's work was the uncontrolled and undisguised presence of the self as the focus of his book, Antonio Tabucchi's main quality seemed to consist in his ability to control and conceal all authorial intrusion in his work. His new collection of "unfinished" short pieces, *I volatili del beato Angelico* (stories, letters, travel notes), offered yet again evidence of his consummate skill in producing brilliant variations on themes that the narrative, rather than making plain, complicates and renders more and more mysterious.

Among the revelations of the year were three women writers of unusual accomplishment. Marisa Volpi with *Nonamore,* a collection of short stories, provided some remarkably lucid portraits of women, seen not in their social and economic roles but in their complex psychological makeup. Fabrizia Ramondino's *Un giorno e mezzo,* set in September 1969, narrates the events of a weekend in the lives of a Neapolitan group of friends, mainly women. Against the student debates and political militancy of the period, the novel sensitively explores feelings, attitudes, and relationships in the decaying Neapolitan villa where the story is set. Particularly striking was the writer's natural command of language, the slow and musical, yet urgent, rhythm of narration. Ramondino's magic sense of language and reality was rightly compared to Elsa Morante's, yet her style seemed less artificial and therefore firmer and more convincing.

Finally, *Le strade di polvere* by Rosetta Loy, which won two of the most prestigious literary prizes of the year, is the story of a Piedmontese family through four generations in the 19th century. Against the distant background of the Risorgimento, the book describes with compelling vividness the private events that history never tells. A deep sense of the passing of time underlines the narrative, colouring even the moments of joy with sorrow and nostalgia, as if the narrator wished to resist—while at the same time narrating—the destiny that time has irrevocably brought to fulfillment.   (LINO PERTILE)

SPANISH

Spain. Cultural commentators seemed obsessed with the phenomenon of the "new Spanish novel." Some analysts insisted that the real resurgence of Spanish fiction, well under way at the time of Gen. Francisco Franco's death in 1975, had to wait for the Latin-American literary "boom" to level off in order to be widely noticed. In any case, prose fiction largely dominated the Spanish literary scene in 1988.

In this light, it is ironic that five years after the blockbuster performance of his *Mazurka para dos muertos* (1983), Camilo José Cela, arguably the dean of contemporary Spanish fiction, failed to satisfy most critics with *Cristo versus Arizona,* a plotless, spirally configured, picaresque monologue, breathlessly expressed in a single 238-page sentence, culminating in the episode of American frontier vengeance known as the Gunfight at the OK Corral. A much warmer reception was given to *Ciencias naturales,* the final volume of Rosa Chacel's epic trilogy of war and exile, 12 years in the making and completed in the author's 90th year. Leading a list of popular "new fiction" by younger women novelists

were Rosa Montero's *Amado amo,* about office politics and corporate power-brokering; Soledad Puértolas's *Todos mienten,* in which characters and narrator alike were chastised for misrepresenting their hollow lives; and Ana Rossetti's *Plumas de España,* a stylized documentary of absurdities in contemporary Andalusian life.

In his third novel, *Lady Pepa,* Jesús Ferrero abandoned the orientalism of earlier work and applied his aggressive, choppy style to settings that ranged from the Texas of Bonnie and Clyde to the darkest recesses of present-day Barcelona. Julio Llamazares, a poet turned novelist and a leading figure of the so-called Leonese School, enraptured critics and readers with his second novel, the year's surprise best-seller; with poetic images of a rural Spain that is fast disappearing, the ragged narrator of *La lluvia amarilla* describes his dying days as the last inhabitant of an abandoned village in the mountains of Aragón.

Among active established masters, Juan Goytisolo subverted all hierarchies of conventional narration in his mystical allegory *Las virtudes del pájaro solitario,* which oscillates between the 16th and 20th centuries and begins not on its first page but on its last. From a sawyer's catalog, Miguel Delibes took the title of his *377A, madera de héroe* (1987). The prestigious Planeta Prize, usually awarded to beginning novelists, went to Gonzalo Torrente Ballester for his pseudonymously submitted *Filomeno a mi pesar. Retornos,* Francisco Ayala's third volume of memoirs, dealing extensively with his experiences as professor at several major U.S. universities, earned him the National Prize for Spanish Letters.

(ROGER L. UTT)

Latin America. The major figures in Latin America during the year were the celebrities Mario Vargas Llosa (*see* BIOGRAPHIES), Carlos Fuentes, and Octavio Paz. The young Mexican novelist Luis Arturo Ramos, the Chilean Jorge Edwards, and the Puerto Rican Luis Rafael Sánchez also made contributions of international importance. Vargas Llosa published two novels, *El hablador* (late 1987), set in the Amazon and relating indigenous traditions, and *Elogio de la madrastra,* an experimental and erotic narrative in which the writer uses painting as a generator of the text. Fuentes, a polemical intellectual figure in Mexico, nevertheless received two international prizes: the Premio Cervantes (Spain, late 1987) and the annual literary prize of the Italo Latino Americano Institute. Octavio Paz published poetry and essays that appeared throughout the Hispanic world.

The major novel of the year in Mexico was Luis Arturo Ramos's sixth book, *Este era un gato* (late 1987), a subtle but accessible story set in Veracruz, where a U.S. Marine returns years after having participated in the invasion of the city in 1914. Fernando del Paso also published an important work, *Noticias del imperio* (late 1987), an ambitious and lengthy historical novel set during the Habsburg intervention in Mexico. Journalist Elena Poniatowska provided the novel *La "Flor de Lis." Muchacho en llamas* (late 1987) by Gustavo Sainz represents a return to his previous involvement with the 1960s Mexico of his early fiction. María Luisa Puga's *La forma del silencio* is an inti-

mate and feminist book. Carmen Boullosa published her first novel, the experimental *Mejor desaparecer.*

The most important literary event in Colombia was the publication of R. H. Moreno-Durán's complete trilogy, *Fémina Suite,* which had appeared in Spain as the novels *Juego de damas* (1977), *El toque de Diana* (1981), and *Finale capriccioso con Madona* (1983). Marco Tulio Aguilera Garramuño wrote his third novel, *Mujeres amadas,* the narrator-protagonist's reflections on love and writing. Manuel Mejía Vallejo's *La casa de las dos palmas* represented a culmination of his recent novels concerning small-town life in rural Antioquia. Héctor Sánchez published his 11th book, the satirical novel *El héroe de la familia.* Fernando Vallejo continued to publish his irreverent fiction, now set in Europe, with the novel *Los caminos a Roma. Ilona llega con la lluvia* by Alvaro Mutis continues the story of Maqroll, Mutis's lifelong obsession.

Two Chileans, Jorge Edwards in Chile and Ariel Dorfman in exile, published major works. Edwards's *El anfitrión,* hailed by some critics as his best work to date, is an approach to the theme of exile through fantasy. *Mascara,* published by Dorfman in English, is also a fantastic novel about sexual domination, power, and betrayal. Two notable postmodern experimental works appearing in Argentina were Ricardo Piglia's novel *Prisión perpetua* and Néstor Sánchez's short stories *La condición efímera.* The venerable Uruguayan writer Juan Carlos Onetti published a short novel, *Cuando entonces.* One of the most noteworthy books to appear in Central America was the Nicaraguan Sergio Ramírez's complex mystery novel *Castigo divino,* dealing with the politics of Nicaragua in the 1930s.

The interface between the North and South American continents was underscored by international literature prizes and translations. The "Letras de Oro" (based in Florida) awarded its novel prize for 1987–88 to the Puerto Rican Ana María Delgado for *La mitad de un día,* the short story prize to the Cuban-American

© JERRY BAUER

Carlos Fuentes

Manuel M. Serpa, and the poetry prize to the Chilean Ximena Alen-Fischer. The Uruguayan Hiber Contreras won the Casa de las Américas novel prize for *La cifra anónima.* The Juan Rulfo short story prize of Mexico was awarded to the Argentine writer Isidoro Blaisten.

Among other noteworthy books, the Puerto Rican Luis Rafael Sánchez's novel *La importancia de llamarse Daniel Santos* was an important experiment with popular culture. In Venezuela Denzil Romero published *La esposa del Dr. Thorne,* an imaginary biography of Bolívar's lover, Manuelita Saenz. The Cuban Virgilio Piñera's posthumous *El último fogonazo* appeared in print. The Peruvian literary scholar José Miguel Oviedo published a cerebral and sometimes dreamlike set of stories, *La vida maravillosa.* The Cuban novelist Severo Sarduy produced a volume of essays on Latin-American literature and the baroque, *Nueva estabilidad.* The year marked the death of one of Latin America's major poets, the Chilean Enrique Lihn. (RAYMOND LESLIE WILLIAMS)

PORTUGUESE

Portugal. The author of the year was Fernando Namora, an outstanding novelist who had been producing a steady flow of books for 50 years. He was publicly honoured throughout Portugal, although he was unable to attend the celebrations because of a severe illness. His work is remarkable for the sensitive, though dispassionate, way in which he deals with the problems of human resilience in the face of suffering and the deceptive changes of history.

The memories of Portugal's recent colonial past—a self-imposed taboo subject for some time—began to emerge in the work of new writers. Angela Caires, a brilliant newcomer, adopted a straightforward and colloquial style in her novel, *Daqui em Diante Só Há Dragões* ("From Now Onward There Are Only Dragons"), to tell the story of the white community at Ambriz, a coastal town in Angola, during the last years of colonial rule. In intermittent flashes the narrator builds up a pattern of memories of moving and amusing scenes that are described with the knowledge of hindsight. The pervasive humour of the narrative frequently attains a surrealistic level, making this book a delightful read.

Lídia Jorge, a well-established name as a great fiction writer, chose Mozambique for the setting of her latest novel, *A Costa dos Murmúrios* ("The Shore of Murmurs"). The self-contained narrative of the wedding of a young army officer at the time of the colonial war provides the basis for a subtle retelling from the wife's viewpoint of the strange events of that period as they are seen 20 years later. The complex intertwining of the two narratives leads into a deep exploration of thought and action, desire and fulfillment, enabling the reader to question the meaning of history and heroism through a web of coincidences that stand out as the symbols of a national enigma. (L. S. REBELO)

Brazil. Literature and literary criticism thrived during 1988, but the best-seller list was dominated by translations of foreign writers. Among the major works of fiction by young authors were Benito Barreto's *Os Guaianãs,* a two-volume epic novel

set just after the military coup d'état in 1964; Cristóvão Tezza's *Trapo,* a narrative about a "beat" poet's opus; and Renato Modernell's novel about the relationship between Middle Eastern oil and literature. Several established writers published new works, including Josué Montello, Nélida Piñon, Darcy Ribeiro, Antônio Olinto, Ignácio de Loyola Brandão, and Oswaldo Franca Júnior.

Collections of short fiction and *crônicas* (short prose sketches integrating elements of essay and fiction) were published by Millôr Fernandes, Luís Fernando Veríssimo, Domingos Pellegrini Júnior, Carlos Eduardo Novaes, Cyro de Mattos, and João Ubaldo Ribeiro. Dalton Trevisan's stories, *Pão e Sangue,* once again return to his artistic preoccupation with sex and crude violence. In *Os Dragões Não Conhecem o Paraíso* Caio Fernando Abreu paints a rather bleak picture of contemporary Brazil; the dedication is to young writers who have fallen victim to suicide or to AIDS.

João Cabral de Melo Neto's new poetry, *Crime Na Calle Redentor,* has a Spanish backdrop. Several works by the late Carlos Drummond de Andrade, including poetry and maxims about the Brazilian existence, were posthumously published.

Roberto Schwarz's collection of essays *Que Horas São?,* published in late 1987, included his 1985 censure of the "provincial foolishness" of members of the Brazilian concrete poetry movement through an analysis of Haroldo de Campos's poem "Póstudo." New studies of modernism included Carlos Sandroni's *Mário Contra Macunaíma,* a study of Mário de Andrade's relationship with his masterpiece, and Vasda Bonafini Landers's *De Jeca a Macunaíma,* which analyzed the premodernist tendencies of Monteiro Lobato. Renato Ortiz studied the influence of the recent massive industrialization on Brazilian culture, and José de Sousa Dantas published a study of the relationship between music and poetry since the 1930s.

The English translation of Clarice Lispector's important novel *The Passion According to G.H.* was prepared by Ronald W. Sousa. The *Dictionary of Brazilian Literature,* containing more than 300 English-language entries on individual authors and literary and cultural movements, was organized by Irwin Stern. (IRWIN STERN)

RUSSIAN

Soviet Literature. To say that the 27th congress of the Communist Party of the Soviet Union in 1986 triggered a cultural and ideological revolution would be no

Vasily Aksyonov
SOVFOTO

exaggeration. The 19th All-Union Party Conference, held June 28 to July 2, 1988, graphically proved it. Creative writing was at the peak of the sweeping change brought about by the new emphasis on *perestroika* (restructuring) and *glasnost* (openness).

Once taboos were removed, the Soviet reading public gained access to many firstrate books of the Stalinist period that had been suppressed. Newly released books included Boris Pasternak's *Doctor Zhivago,* Anna Akhmatova's *Requiem,* Aleksandr Tvardovsky's *Authorized by Memory,* and Vasily Belov's *The Beginnings.* Many of these previously banned works revealed by powerful artistic means the inception, consolidation, and cruel practices of Stalinism. These books analyzed with insight and compassion the correlation between revolution, socialism, and humanism—the basic social problem underlying the debate on *perestroika.*

Regrettably, contemporary literary criticism had not risen to the level of the books it studied. Assuming many of the functions of history and philosophy, literature led Soviet intellectual life, yet few critics could advise readers as they sought to understand the involved cultural process at work. Many experts turned Soviet literary history upside down by contrasting some trends and writers with others and by consolidating the newly found reputations at the expense of writers who were long-established. The role in literature of such well-known authors as Maksim Gorky, Mikhail Sholokhov, and Aleksandr Fadeyev was played down or even denied.

There were three trends predominant in Soviet literature of the late 1980s. There were dogmatics out to perpetuate the past and repel everything new. There were adventurous ultraleftists, who, in their noisy drive for progress, ended up, more often than not, in the ultraright bog. And there were those who sought a dynamic yet sober and circumspect renovation based on socialist principles.

Not only diehard conservatives but also false progressives threatened *perestroika.* Cultural primitivism and lack of genuine concern for Soviet literature accounted for bitter quarrels between many periodicals. Some critics branded as conservatives and enemies of *perestroika* such notable writers as Valentin Rasputin and Yury Bondarev, but they, along with many others, had written about the plight of the Soviet Union in those tragic years under Stalin. To misunderstand them and what they did to lay the groundwork for *perestroika* was to misinterpret the whole of Soviet literature. (FELIX KUZNETSOV)

Expatriate Russian Literature. Great diversity of themes and genres distinguished Russian émigré literature in 1988. The millennium of Christianity in Russia was celebrated in émigré periodicals and journals with articles on religious themes. Ten volumes of the collected works of Georges Florovsky were completed in a series that would eventually comprise 20 volumes.

The publication of works by Joseph Brodsky, Sasha Sokolov, Viktor Nekrasov, Vladimir Voinovich, and Aleksandr Galich in the Soviet Union intensified the old debate among émigrés over whether there are one or two Russian literatures. Speaking at a conference attended by both Soviet and émigré artists and intellectuals, Efim Etkind (whose critical study *The Trial of Iosif Brodsky* appeared in 1988) called for rewriting of the history of Russian literature, which, he believed, should be understood as a single historical entity. Adding another dimension to the debate, Wolfgang Kasack's encyclopaedic *Lexikon der russischen Literatur ab 1917*, which treats Russian literature since 1917 as a single entity, was published in a revised and updated Russian translation under the title *Russkaia literatura ot a do ia* ("Russian Literature from A to Z").

Many valuable items documenting literature in emigration appeared during the year: Yury Terapiano's *Literaturnaia zhizn ruskogo Parizha za polveka* ("Half a Century of Russian Literary Life in Paris"); the anthology *Russkie poety na zapade* ("Russian Poets in the West"); Dimitry Savitsky's *Niotkuda s lyubovyu* ("From Nowhere with Love"); *Free Voices in Russian Literature, 1950–1980*, edited by A. Sumerkin; and an index of articles from Russian émigré journals and collected works, *L'emigration russe. Revues et recueils, 1920–1980. Index general des articles.*

There had been a marked shift in the last few years from political themes to those of everyday life. Examples during the year were Natalia Medvedeva's novel *Mama, ia zhulika lyublyu!* ("Mama, I'm in Love with a Swindler!") and Julia Voznesenskaia's collection of erotic short stories, *Zhenskij dekameron* ("Women's Decameron"). Important prose fiction published in 1987–88 included Vasily Aksyonov's *Quest for an Island* and *V poiskah grustnogo bebi* (*In Search of Melancholy Baby*); and Vladimir Voinovich's controversial satirical novel *Moskva 2042* ("Moscow 2042"), *Antisovetskij Sovetskij Souiuz* ("Antisoviet Soviet Union"), and *Shapka* ("A Hat"), the last in the journal *Kontinent*. Aleksandr Solzhenitsyn's fourth volume of *Mart semnadtsatogo* ("The Seventeenth of March") continued his relentless research into the events leading to the Revolution. To commemorate his 70th birthday, the magazine *Strelec* declared 1988 "The Year of Solzhenitsyn." Yury Mamleev's long-awaited esoteric novel *Shatuny*, previously available only in French and English translations and samizdat, was published in Russian. Svetlana Allilueva published *Daliokaia muzyka* ("Distant Music").

Noteworthy poetry collections included Yury Ivask's *Igraiushchij chelovek* ("A Playing Man") and the first thoroughly researched collection of Vladimir Vysotsky's poetry, in three volumes.

(E. R. CZERWINSKI;
AGNIESZKA PERLINSKA)

EASTERN EUROPEAN LITERATURE

Soviet leader Mikhail Gorbachev's policy of *glasnost* touched every aspect of Soviet life in 1988, but it had yet to be felt in the countries of the Eastern European bloc. In Poland most of the controversial authors continued to be published underground by the Niezalezny Press. The most notable books published by the government were the four volumes of Tadeusz Rozewicz's collected poems and plays.

Harcourt Brace Jovanovich continued to offer English translations of some of the finest prose written in Yugoslavia. In 1988 it provided an excellent translation of Aleksandar Tisma's *The Use of Man*, which Barbara Finkelstein described in the *New York Times Book Review* as "a sad and extraordinary novel." Harper and Row performed the same service for one of Poland's most original prose stylists, Bruno Schulz (*Letters and Drawings of Bruno Schulz, with Selected Prose*, edited by Jerzy Ficowski). Through his account of the book in the *New York Times Book Review*, John Updike managed to raise Schulz into the pantheon of world writers.

Pope John Paul II was well served with an impressive volume of his dramatic works, *The Collected Plays and Writings on Theater* (1987), faithfully translated by Boleslaw Taborski. Stanislaw Lem, almost as popular, continued his personal odyssey among the stars with *Fiasco*, translated into English by Michael Kendel (1987). Vaclav Havel continued to be published outside his native Czechoslovakia; his famous character Vanek was celebrated in one volume—*The Vanek Plays: Four Authors, One Character*, eight plays by Havel (3), Pavel Kohout (3), Pavel Landovsky (1), and Jiri Dienstbier (1), edited by Marketa Goetz-Stankiewicz. Twenty-two essays written on the occasion of Havel's winning the Erasmus Prize in 1986 were published as *Vaclav Havel, or, Living in Truth* (1987). Polish-born Nobel laureate Czeslaw Milosz was similarly honoured in Canada with *Between Anxiety and Hope: The Poetry and Writing of Czeslaw Milosz*, edited by Edward Mozejko.

With the recent deaths of Stanislaw Grochowiak, Helmut Kajzar, and Ireneusz Iredynski, Poland's brightest talents of the mid-generation were silenced, and no new writers appeared to fill the vacuum. In Czechoslovakia Alena Vostra, best known for her avant-garde plays of the '60s, published a psychological detective novel, *Tanec na lede* ("Dancing on Ice"). A new collection of short stories about sexual awakening and political upheaval by Ivan Klima, *My First Love*, was published in English. A collection of five essays and two dialogues by Milan Kundera was translated by Linda Asher and published under the title *The Art of the Novel*. A belated translation of one of the great Hungarian writers of the 20th century, Milan Fust, appeared: *The Story of My Wife: Reminiscences of Captain Storr*, translated by Ivan Sanders.

The Canada-based poet George Faludy was experiencing something of a renaissance both abroad and in his native Hungary, where until recently he had been officially regarded as a nonperson. His autobiography, *My Happy Days in Hell*, and

his *Villon Ballads* were scheduled for release. The Hungarian translation of his autobiography was published in Hungary in 1987 by the Samizdat Press. In addition, a full-length biographical documentary film of the poet was released. In the West, Faludy's massive essay collection, *Notes from a Rainforest*, was published in the fall. Yugoslav Milorad Pavic's playful *Dictionary of the Khazars: A Lexicon Novel in 100,000 Words* was published in a fine translation by Christina Pribicevic-Zoric.

The millennium of Christianity in Russia was also celebrated in the Ukraine. Two volumes appeared in English: *A Thousand Years of Christianity in Ukraine: An Encyclopedic Chronology*, edited by Osyp Zinkewych and Andrew Sorokowskyj, and *One Thousand Years of Christianity in Ukraine: Papers from a Symposium*, edited by Marko Pavlyshyn. Other trends in the Ukraine included continued emphasis on the 1986 Chernobyl nuclear disaster (Yury Shcherbak's documentary novel *Chornobyl;* Ivan Drach's epic poem "Chornobylska Madonna") and publication of authors from the 1920s whose works had previously been censored.

(EDWARD J. CZERWINSKI;
AGNIESKZKA K. PERLINSKA)

JEWISH

Hebrew. Israeli fiction in 1988 featured the works of several new writers. These included Yoel Hoffman's novellas in *Sefer Yosef;* Meir Shalev's *Roman Russi;* Dan Benaya Seri's stylized Yemenite stories, *Tsiporei Tsel;* and short-story collections by Yitshak Ben-Yosef, Anar Shalev, and Tsur Shizef. In addition, significant works were published by established writers: *Shoshan Lavan, Shoshan 'Adom* by David Schitz, *haKala haNitshit* by Yitshak Orpax, and *Ta'atu'on* by Yitshak Ben-Ner—a novel inspired by the Arab *intifadeh* (uprising). Second volumes appeared by two rising writers: a collection of stories by Savyon Librecht, *Susim 'al Kvish Geha*, and *'Una*, a Holocaust novel by Dorit Peleg.

Eminent works of poetry included Ori Bernstein's *Ma Shenish'ar, Ma Shelo*, Maya Bejerano's *Retsef haShirim*, and Aharon Shabtai's *'Ahava*—a runaway bestseller. T. Carmi wrote *Shirim min ha-'Azuva*, and Ya'ir Hurvitz's *Tsipor Kelu'a* was published just before his premature death. Haim Gouri's selected poetry, 1945–87, appeared in *Heshbon Over*.

Critical studies were written by Avraham Holtz on S. Y. Agnon, Ziva Shamir on Hayyim Bialik, Dan Miron on turn-of-the-century writers, Hillel Barzel on early modern Hebrew poetry, Shmuel Werses on the development of modern Hebrew fiction, Avraham Balaban on Amos Oz, and Nurit Govrin on Devora Baron. Gershon Shaked published the third volume of his history of modern Hebrew fiction.

Other significant publications included a collection of essays by Amos Oz; the first volume of a planned two-volume biography of Agnon by Avinoam Barshai; the first three volumes of the collected plays of Hanoch Levin; Uriel Ofek's two-volume study of Hebrew children's literature, 1900–48 (published posthumously); and *Hayalim shel Mayim*, an anthology of contemporary Arab literature. Following a growing trend, Keter Publishing began a series on Arab literature in He-

brew translation. The 100th anniversary of Agnon's birth was celebrated worldwide in 1988. Mourned were Shimon Halkin, Ya'ir Hurvitz, and Zerubavel Gilead.

(WARREN BARGAD)

Yiddish. Poetry and short stories vied for pride of place in the world of Yiddish letters. Several compelling volumes of poetry and a festschrift honouring a language-corpus planner constituted the highlights of the year. A group of scholars and former students compiled *Mordkhe Schaechter and His Work,* celebrating the protean interests of the leading Yiddish-language standardizer of his generation. *The Eternal Moment* brought together materials from the literary estate of Switzerland's remarkable poet Leyzer Aykhenrand. From Montreal came the last books of M. M. Shaffir's verse, *A Bit of Consolation in My Misery* and *A Group of Poems.* He died on September 10.

My Yiddish was a provocative and revealing exploration of the wellsprings of Rokhl Boymvol's "Yiddishness." *Touching Time,* an assemblage of poems by Rivke Basman, was often sombre, while Rivke Kope seemed to be led by intellect and moved by nostalgia in *The Bread of My Desire.* Longing also provided the leitmotif for Yakov Tsvi Shargel's *Soothing Oils.* In his bilingual *Tree and Forest,* Yoysef Papiernikov demonstrated how trees are able to mirror humanity's mood and spirit. The serene reflectiveness of an earlier time continued to surface in M. Olitski's *Song and Essay.*

A plethora of short stories appeared: Meyir Yelin's *Tears of Fire in the Month;* Romanian writer Itsik Karo's *Years of Hope;* Maks Riyant's *The Trains Arrive on Time;* and Mordkhe Tsanin's anthology, *From the Other Side of Time.* Torn-Up *Roots* by Osher Stuschinski was a personal retracing of his life and travels through Poland and Cuba to safe harbour in the U.S. In a similar vein, Shloyme Vorzoger's *June 1941* describes the outbreak of World War II and the travails of Jewish refugees in the Soviet Union. Edited in Moscow by Arn Vergelis, *In Those Stormy Days* includes five authors discussing the October Revolution.

In literary criticism, Nakhman Blits's *A Journey into the Region of Night* is a mosaic of vignettes about memorable persons and places. Essayist Arn Shteynberg's *Ideas in Harmony* included both Yiddish and European letters among his analyses.

(THOMAS E. BIRD)

CHINESE

China. Chinese writers and critics in 1988 continued the drive toward more literary freedom and independence, even though the authorities attempted to restrain such dissident intellectuals and writers as Fang Lizhi (Fang Li-chih) and Wang Ruowang (Wang Jo-wang), who championed rapid democratization and fundamental political reforms. Rejecting the requirement that literature serve as a political tool of the Communist Party, Chinese writers and critics stressed the importance of literature's artistic aspects. The Chinese Association of Writers and Artists, which held its fifth congress in November, endorsed the need for artistic freedom. The association's bylaws were amended to stress that the association was designed to "serve" rather

than to "guide" writers and artists. Many, however, remained skeptical. With some works of dissident writers and some television programs attacked or banned, there seemed to be limits to China's openness to literary dissent.

Writers and journalists continued to expose the growing corruption, nepotism, malfeasance, hypocrisy, injustice, repression, and, especially, the suffering of the common people under Communist rule. A good example was Ma Bo's (Ma Po's) *Blood-Red Sunset,* a fictionalized memoir of his struggle and betrayal as a Red Guard during the Cultural Revolution. A tale of suffering, resistance, struggle, betrayal, and, ultimately, the protagonist's awakening to the tragic consequences of his deeds, it became an instant best-seller and sparked spectacular reactions. Zhang Shimin's (Chang Shih-min's) *Honorary Cross,* a portraying of the dark side of a model worker, was one of several works of fiction based largely on real experiences that became targets of lawsuits filed by people who claimed the authors had depicted them. The novel *Business Circles,* by Qian Shichang (Chien Shih-ch'ang) and Ou Weixiong (Ou Wei-hsiung), presented a vivid description of the impact of China's open-door policy and the problems created by the recent economic reforms.

Taiwan. The lifting of the ban on reprinting literary works from China and on travels to the mainland created a feverish interest in the mainland, including its art and literature, as the impact of Chinese literature from the mainland finally reached Taiwan. Some of Taiwan's native writers expanded their coverage to the mainland, while others continued to produce works of political and social criticism. Nearly all restrictions on free expression were eliminated. Even works describing or advocating self-determination or independence for Taiwan began to be published, as did works on human rights abuses, environmental issues, and problems between the mainlanders and Taiwanese natives.

Among works reflecting the new political consciousness were the native Taiwanese writer Lin Yang-min's political novels and stories, especially *The Career of the Great Leader,* which presented powerful political criticisms and attacks on human rights abuses. Other writers, such as Lin Shuang-pu and Shih Ming-cheng, published important works on similar themes. Several young women writers emerged, whose explorations of love and lust attracted wide attention. Works by Chang Man-chuan, Yang Hsiao-yün, and others portrayed women who, liberated from traditional values, sought new meanings of love and life.

(WINSTON L. Y. YANG)

JAPANESE

"Whom do you elect the literary Man of the Year?" "Haruki Murakami, of course," most editors and publishers in Japan should answer. Murakami's two novels *Norwegian Wood* and *Dance, Dance, Dance* were both immensely successful. By late 1988 *Norwegian Wood* had sold 2.8 million copies, a tremendous number for a writer still in his 30s. Murakami was not a newcomer, however, having been awarded the prestigious Tanizaki Prize for *The End of the World and the Hard-Boiled Wonderland* in 1985. His popularity among

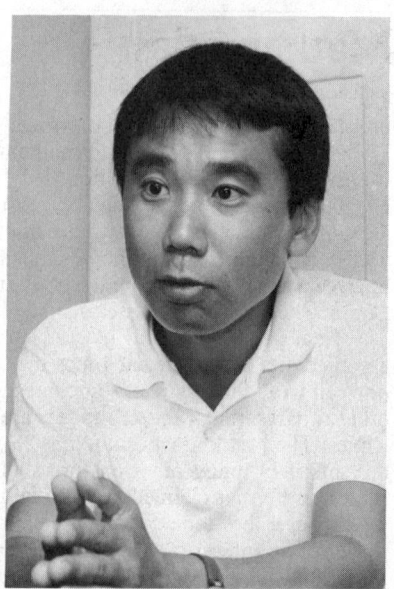

Haruki Murakami
KYODO NEWS SERVICE

young readers was reminiscent of F. Scott Fitzgerald, a writer whom Murakami had translated and edited. His main characters remained cool and detached, seeming to enjoy and despise Japanese affluence at the same time.

Several remarkable collections of short stories—a characteristically Japanese genre—appeared during the year, as well as tanka and haiku (short poetic forms). Yoshiko Shibaki's *Stories of Nara* impressed with its sensitive choice of locale (Nara was the capital of 8th-century Japan) and classical balance of feminine passion and restraint. The stories in Taku Miki's *Collection of Comic Stories* were both humorous and nostalgic, deeply embedded in the author's own boyhood. Mieko Kanai's clever combination of sophisticated vignettes, *Oh, Tama,* was awarded the Woman Writer's Prize. There was a certain literariness about Kanai's style of narration, but she successfully evoked the loneliness of uprooted urban inhabitants.

In biography, Nanami Shiono's *Machiavelli, My Friend* was an impressive achievement, both for its lively style and for the author's exhaustive researches into the background and psychological responses of this highly complex Florentine. Shiono had already written attractive biographical sketches of women of the Italian Renaissance. Hiroshi Matsumoto's *Tsutaya Juzaburo* opened up a new perspective on art of the Tokugawa period by revealing the hidden career of a "cultural producer" who sponsored and popularized several prominent Ukiyo-e painters.

Three senior literary critics died during the year: the genial haiku critic Kenkichi Yamamoto (b. 1907), the incisive, provoking polemicist Mitsuo Nakamura (b. 1911), and Shigeki Senuma (b. 1904), a literary biographer of sound scholarship.

(SHOICHI SAEKI)

See also Art Exhibitions and Art Sales: *Art Sales;* Libraries; Publishing.

This article updates the *Macropædia* article The History of Western LITERATURE and articles on the literatures of the various languages.

Mathematics

The major news event of 1988 in mathematics was a proof that turned out to be wrong. Early in the year Yoichi Miyaoka, a 38-year-old mathematician with Tokyo Metropolitan University, announced that he had proved Fermat's last theorem, perhaps the most famous open problem in mathematics. The entire mathematical community was electrified as word of the possible achievement spread. Six weeks later Miyaoka retracted his announcement when he realized there was an essential flaw in his argument.

Fermat's last theorem is not a theorem at all but rather a conjecture. Since ancient times it had been known that one can write the square of some integers as the sum of two other squares. (Such sets of integers are called Pythagorean triples. The best known example is $25 = 9 + 16$, but there are infinitely many other examples.) In the 17th century Pierre de Fermat claimed to have found a proof that this could never be done for higher powers; that is, an nth power of an integer can never be the sum of two, nonzero nth powers ($c^n = a^n + b^n$) when n is larger than two. Fermat wrote in the margin of a mathematics book that he had a marvelous proof but not enough room to write it down. That claim has challenged some of the best mathematicians during the ensuing centuries, yet it remains unproved (although it is known to be true for some values of n).

Miyaoka tried to prove the theorem by using analogies with geometry. The idea is simple: equations in number theory, in which one is interested only in integer values, also make sense in geometry when one uses all real (or complex) numbers to generate geometric objects (curves and surfaces). Facts about the resulting geometric objects should provide information about the integer solutions to these equations.

This idea was used successfully in 1983 by Gerd Faltings, then of Wuppertal University, West Germany, to prove another well-known conjecture proposed by number theorist Louis Mordell. Such analogies were subsequently used by Soviet mathematician A. N. Parshin to show that if a certain geometric inequality were true then the Fermat theorem would follow. Miyaoka attempted to prove the inequality. In this case, however, he discovered that the analogy between number theory and geometry was not quite perfect, and in one crucial step of his proof the analogy broke down.

This was not the first time that a respected mathematician had announced a false proof of the Fermat theorem. Several 19th-century mathematicians claimed proofs, only to discover that at one crucial step they had made an unwarranted assumption. In many cases the discovery of the mistake was the beginning of a fruitful inquiry into a whole new branch of mathematics. (Essentially all of modern algebraic number theory developed because of such a mistake.) In this case it was not yet clear whether Miyaoka's mistake would lead to any new mathematics.

The Fermat theorem is not the only famous problem for which false proofs have been offered. During the past five years, proofs for two other conjectures were announced and later retracted. In 1984 mathematicians believed for a time that the Riemann conjecture, over 100 years old, had been solved. The Riemann conjecture is a conjecture in number theory that, unlike the Fermat theorem, would have far-reaching consequences if proved. While there are many technical statements of the conjecture, one description is easy to understand. A prime is a positive integer that is divisible only by 1 and itself. Every integer can be factored completely into a product of primes, and if no factor occurs more than once, the integer is called square-free. The number 6 is square-free, while 18 is not. There are two kinds of square-free integers, those with an odd number of factors and those with an even number of factors, and one expects that there should be about the same number of each. The Riemann conjecture is essentially equivalent to this statement. It is the assertion that for all positive integers less than some large number N, the square-free integers of each kind are randomly distributed, as if one were flipping a coin to determine the type of each square-free integer. The mistake in the announced proof was discovered several months later.

In 1986 a proof was given for a famous conjecture made by Henri Poincaré more than 80 years earlier. Poincaré's conjecture deals with topology, the mathematics of spaces, and it proposes a set of specific criteria that would identify the three-sphere, which is the three-dimensional analogue of the surface of a ball. Again, after much initial excitement, the mistake was discovered buried deep within the proof.

Because mathematics is usually viewed as a subject whose truths are certain and absolute, it may seem surprising that there can be uncertainty and even disagreement about the validity of a proof. There is, of course, no disagreement about many results. For example, mathematicians proved long ago that it is impossible to divide a given angle into three equal angles using only a compass and straight edge according to fixed rules. The proof has been studied and refined, and each step in the argument is now easy to follow. But mathematics constantly grows and changes, forcing mathematicians to develop new ideas and new tools, which require time to understand fully. Part of the excitement lies in the fact that arriving at certainty requires making some wrong turns along the way.   (JOHN EWING)

This article updates the *Macropædia* articles GEOMETRY: *Topology;* NUMBER THEORY.

Military Affairs

The two most significant defense events of 1988 were the stabilization of the U.S.-Soviet conflict and the increasing destructiveness of conflicts in the third world, even though some of those might be ending. The first of these events was symbolized by the May 1988 Moscow summit meeting of U.S. Pres. Ronald Reagan and Soviet leader Mikhail Gorbachev (*see* BIOGRAPHIES). No major formal agreements were reached at this summit, although progress was made toward a START (strategic arms reduction talks) Treaty. (See *Arms Control and Disarmament,* below.) However, the U.S. and the Soviets informally agreed that their 40-year-old conflict had become a stabilized cold war.

The Soviet Union had built up a massive and very expensive military advantage over the U.S. Nevertheless, the Soviets remained unwilling to risk using this advantage to attempt to defeat the U.S. and its allies in a major conflict because of the uncertainties over the outcome of such a war. In particular, the uncertainties over the effects of the use of nuclear weapons remained an overwhelming deterrent to a major conflict between the two superpowers. In theory, the Soviet's military advantages should give them a good chance of victory. If the U.S.S.R. attempted to realize this advantage, however, it would run the risk of defeat or a victory that was too costly, and these potential risks outweighed the potential gains.

For these reasons the Soviets had limited their use of military forces to gaining political advantage in the third world. Despite some successes in establishing pro-

Soviet governments in such countries as Cuba, Angola, and Ethiopia, Moscow's gains had been limited and had been partly offset by countervailing U.S. intervention and by local opposition to externally imposed governments. In Afghanistan the U.S. and the Islamic powers had allied to aid the local resistance fighters with sophisticated weapons, sharply increasing the cost of the Soviet occupation. In addition, the economic and social costs of the Soviet empire were proving increasingly difficult to sustain in the U.S.S.R. and Eastern Europe. This created additional difficulties for Gorbachev in his efforts to achieve economic restructuring (*perestroika*).

The U.S. and its allies thus achieved a major strategic victory without fighting a major war. The original U.S. policy of containing the Soviet Union and of building up an alliance of four major world power centres (the U.S., Western Europe, Japan, and China) to contain the fifth power centre, the U.S.S.R., had worked. In addition, the U.S. containment strategy had looked toward an eventual change in the totalitarian political structures imposed in the U.S.S.R. and Eastern Europe by the Soviet dictator Joseph Stalin. This change was beginning under Gorbachev, although it could be reversed. Military analysts concluded that as long as the U.S. and its allies maintained defense forces adequate to support their containment strategy, the cold war would remain a relatively stable conflict.

In contrast, third world conflicts were increasing in frequency and destructiveness. While some of them were being ended, the widespread idea that peace was breaking out seemed overoptimistic. New conflicts were likely to occur, and they would further raise the level of violence in the third world. However, the two most destructive of the third world conflicts, the Soviet-Afghanistan war and the Iran-Iraq war, seemed to be winding down. The Soviets had invaded Afghanistan on Dec. 27, 1979, and fought a bitter nine-year war against the Afghan freedom fighters (the mujahideen), who received aid from the Islamic countries and the U.S. Soviet casualties were estimated at 49,000 and Afghan casualties at more than half a million, while more than five million Afghans had fled to Pakistan and Iran.

The Iran-Iraq war had begun with Iraq's Sept. 22, 1980, attack on Iran. The result was a total of more than one million casualties, partly caused by two new weapons systems. One of those systems was the short-range ballistic missile armed with a conventional high-explosive warhead. These missiles were used by both sides to bombard the other's capital in the "war of the cities." The other was chemical weapons, including nerve gas, used mainly by Iraq but also by Iran. Chemical weapons in the form of poisonous gases had been used in World War I, but afterward their use was limited by the 1925 Geneva Protocol, which banned the first use of chemical weapons but did permit them to be employed for retaliatory purposes. The use of chemical weapons in the Iran-Iraq war violated the protocol's no-first-use rule and also represented the first wartime employment of the deadly nerve gases that were developed after World War I.

Iraq's use of chemical weapons undermined the morale of Iran's soldiers, while Iraq's missile bombardment of Tehran, the Iranian capital, undermined civilian morale. In addition, Iraq's air attacks on tankers carrying Iranian oil exports, along with the U.S. and allied protection of tankers carrying Iraqi oil exports, undercut Iran's economic ability to carry on the war. Within about a year, Iraq turned its near defeat by Iran into an ability to force the latter to accept prewar boundaries.

During 1988 progress was made toward ending both

Table I. U.S./NATO–Soviet Strategic Nuclear Force Balance, June 1988

Weapons systems	Range[1] (km)	Payload[2] (000 kg)	Warheads, yield[3]	CEP[4]	Speed (Mach)	Number deployed
UNITED STATES Strategic Forces						
Intercontinental ballistic missiles (ICBM)						1,000
Minuteman II	11,300	0.7	1 × 1.2 mt	370	...	450
Minuteman III Mod 1	14,800	1.0	3 × 170 kt	220	...	211
Mod 2	12,900	1.1	3 × 335 kt	220	...	300
Peacekeeper (M-X)	11,000	3.2	10 × 300 or 400 kt	100	...	39
Submarine-launched ballistic missiles (SLBM; in 36 nuclear submarines)						640
Poseidon C-3	4,600	1.5	10 × 40 kt or 14 × 40 kt	450	...	256
Trident I/C-4	7,400	1.4	8 × 100 kt	450	...	384
Manned bombers and air-launched cruise missiles (ALCM)						
B-52G	4,600	29.5	20–24	...	0.95	167
B-52H	6,140	29.5	8–12 or 20–24	...	0.95	96
FB-111A	1,890	13.2	6	...	2.2	61
B-1B	4,580	61	30–38	...	1.25	99
AGM-86B ALCM	2,400	60	170–200 kt	...	0.66	1,650
Medium range manned bombers						
U.S. F-111 E/F	1,750	13.1	3	...	2.5	160
BRITAIN (Strategic and Theatre Nuclear Forces)[5]						
Submarine-launched ballistic missiles (SLBM; in 4 nuclear submarines)						
Polaris A-3	4,600	0.7	3 × 200 kt	900	...	64
Strike aircraft						
Tornado	1,390	6.8	...	...	0.95	210
FRANCE (Strategic and Theatre Nuclear Forces)[5]						
Submarine-launched ballistic missiles (SLBM; in 6 nuclear submarines)						
MSBS M-20/TN-60	3,000	...	1 × 1 mt	...	...	64
MSBS M-4/TN-70	4,400+	...	6 × 150 kt	...	...	16
MSBS M-4/TN-71	6,000+	...	6 × 150 kt	...	...	—
Intermediate-range ballistic missiles (IRBM)						
SSBS S-3D/TN-61	3,500	...	1 × 1 mt	...	...	18
Strike aircraft/Air to surface missiles (ASM)						
Mirage IVP	930	9.3	1 × 60/1 × 150 kt ASMP ASM	...	2.2	18
Mirage IIIE	960	19	2 × 15 kt	...	1.8	15
Super Etendard	650	2.1	2 × 15/1 × 150 kt ASMP ASM	...	1.0	64
SOVIET UNION Strategic Forces						
Intercontinental ballistic missiles (ICBM)						c. 1,500+
SS-11 Mod 1	9,500	0.9	1 × 1 mt	1,400	...	} 420
Mod 2/3	11–13,000	1.1	3 × 100–300 kt	1,100	...	
SS-13 Mod 2	9,400	0.6	1 × 600 kt	1,800	...	60
SS-16	9–10,000	...	3 × 150 kt	...	...	c. 100[6]
SS-17 Mod 3	10,000	2.9	4 × 500 kt	...	...	138
SS-18 Mod 4	11,000	7.6	10 × 500 kt	250	...	308
SS-19 Mod 3	10,000	3.4	6 × 550 kt	300	...	350
SS-24	10,000	3.6	8–10 × 100 kt	200	...	10
SS-25	10,500	0.7	1 × 550 kt	200	...	100
Submarine-launched ballistic missiles (in 63 nuclear plus 12 diesel submarines)						c. 978[7]
SS-N-5 Sark	1,400	...	1 × 1 mt	2,800	...	36
SS-N-6 Mod 1,2	2,400	0.7	1 × 500 kt–1 mt	1,300	...	} 256
Mod 3	3,000	0.7	2 × 500 kt	1,300	...	
SS-N-8 Mod 1	7,800	0.7	1 × 500 kt–1 mt	1,500	...	} 286
Mod 2	9,100	...	1 × 800 kt	900	...	
SS-N-17	3,900	1.1	1 × 500 kt	1,400	...	12
SS-N-18 Mod 1	6,500	...	3 × 500 kt	1,400	...	
Mod 2	8,000	...	1 × 500 kt–1 mt	900	...	} 224
Mod 3	6,500	...	5 × 500 kt	900	...	
SS-N-20	8,300	...	6 × 100 kt	500	...	100
SS-N-23	8,300	...	10 × 100 kt	900	...	64
Manned bombers and air-launched cruise missiles (ALCM)						c. 420
Tu-95 Bear A/H	5,690	11.3	2–3 + 8 AS-15 ALCM	...	0.9	170
Mya-4 Bison	5,100	15	4	...	0.94	5
Tu-26 Backfire B	4,430	12	4	...	1.92	358
AS-15 ALCM	1,600	...	250 kt	...	0.6	
Medium range manned bombers[8]						745
Tu-16 Badger	2,180	9	2	...	0.91	452
Tu-22 Blinder	1,500	10	2	...	1.4	160

[1] Range, for aircraft, is their radius of action in normal configuration, at optimum altitude, with a standard warhead, without in-flight refueling.
[2] Payload refers to a missile's throw weight or a bomber's weapons load.
[3] For MIRV and MRV the figure to the left of the multiplication sign gives the number of warheads and the figure to the right is the yield per warhead. For bombers, weapons per bomber are given.
[4] Circular Error Probable: the radius (in metres) of a circle within which at least half of the missile warheads aimed at a specific target will fall.
[5] British nuclear forces are under national control but may be assigned to NATO. French nuclear forces are controlled and targeted independently of NATO.
[6] Mobile SS-16 ICBM reported deployed, based on SS-20 V/IRBM.
[7] Includes 36 non-SALT/START counted SS-N-5 theatre missiles in 12 diesel submarines and 1 non-SALT/START counted SSBN.
[8] Total deployed worldwide. Of these, about half are allocated to Soviet Naval Aviation (some 240 Tu-16, 30 Tu-22, and 120 Tu-26). Two-thirds of the remaining strike bombers and ASM carriers are considered deployed against NATO. Tu-26 Backfire is now counted as strategic.
Sources: International Institute for Strategic Studies, *The Military Balance 1988–1989*; and *Aviation Week and Space Technology*. Figures for Soviet forces can only be estimates.

Table II. Approximate Strengths of Regular Armed Forces of the World

Country	Military personnel in 000s			Warships[1]			Jet aircraft[3]		Tanks[4]	Defense expenditure as % of 1986 GDP[5]
	Army	Navy	Air Force	Aircraft carriers/ cruisers	Submarines[2]	Destroyers/ frigates	Bombers and fighter-bombers	Fighters/ recon-naissance		
I. NATO										
Belgium	65.1	4.5	18.7	—		4 FFG	114 FB	36, 19 R	334	3.0
Canada[6]	22.5	10.0	23.1	—	3	4 DDG, 15 FF	149 FB, 33 MR	—	114	2.2
Denmark	17.0	5.4	6.9	—	4	3 FFG	95 FB	18	210	2.0
France[7]	280.9	66.5	95.0	2 CV, 1 CVV, 1 CG	14, 4 SSN, 6 SSBN	4 DDG, 11 DD, 24 FFG	18 B, 332 FB	205, 64 R, 53 MR	1,340	3.9
Germany, West	332.1	36.4	108.7	—	24	3 DDG, 4 DD, 6 FFG, 3 FF	629 FB	72 R, 19 MR	4,937	3.1
Greece	170.5	19.5	24.0	—	10	14 DD, 2 FFG, 5 FF	223 FB	74, 30 R	1,893	5.6
Italy	265.0	48.0	73.0	1 CVV, 3 CAH	9	4 DDG, 12 FFG, 10 FF	284 FB	30 R, 14 MR	1,720	2.2
Luxembourg	0.8	—	—	—			—	—	—	1.0
Netherlands, The	66.0	17.1	18.1	—	5	4 DDG, 12 FFG	213 FB	12 R, 13 MR	913	3.0
Norway	19.0	7.0	9.1	—	12	5 FFG	89 FB	—	122	3.1
Portugal	44.0	16.3	13.6	—	3	15 FF	91 FB	—	66	3.2
Spain	232.0	45.0[8]	32.5	2 CVV	8	7 DD, 8 FFG, 6 FF	110 FB	118, 16 R, 6 MR	838	2.2
Turkey	522.9	55.0	57.4	—	17	12 DD, 7 FF	484 FB	40, 28 R	3,600	4.8
United Kingdom	158.4	64.8[8]	93.5	3 CVV	11, 16 SSN, 4 SSBN	13 DDG, 34 FFG	441 FB	150, 27 R, 34 MR	1,170	4.9
United States	776.4	783.2[8]	603.6	4 BBG, 5 CVN, 10 CV, 9 CGN, 29 CG, 5 LHA, 7 LPH, 13 LPD, 32 LSD/T	88 SSN, 36 SSBN, 7 SSGN,	37 DDG, 32 DD, 56 FFG, 59 FF	361 SB, 297 B, 3,450 FB	2,451, 270 R, 345 MR/ASW	15,600	6.7
II. WARSAW PACT										
Bulgaria	115.0	8.8	34.0	—	4	3 FF	105 FB	150, 30 R	2,550	4.2
Czechoslovakia	145.0	—	52.0	—	—	—	170 FB	270, 12 R	3,400	4.9
Germany, East	120.0	15.0	37.0	—	—	19 FF	60 FB	270, 12 R	2,850	7.7
Hungary	77.0		22.0	—	—	—	15 FB	135, 10 R	1,300	3.7
Poland	230.0	19.0	92.0	—	4	1 DDG, 1 FF	225 FB	400, 35 R, 10 MR	3,950	3.7
Romania	140.0	7.5	32.0	—	—	1 DDG, 4 FF	120 FB	230, 20 R	1,860	1.3
U.S.S.R.	3,376.0	477.0[8]	1,228.0[9]	4 CVV, 2 CVH, 3 CGN, 29 CG, 5 CA	120, 77 SSN, 63 SSBN, 12 SSB, 50 SSGN, 16 SSG	37 DDG, 25 DD, 33 FFG, 133 FF	533 SB, 612 B, 3,170 FB	4,405, 490 R, 180 MR	53,300	15–17 20–25
III. OTHER EUROPEAN										
Albania	31.5	3.3	7.2	—	2	—	45	50	190	4.1
Austria	50.0	—	4.7	—	—	—	15 FB	8	170	1.3
Finland	30.0	2.7	2.5	—	—	—	—	66	150	1.4
Ireland	11.6	0.8	0.8	—	—	—	—	—	—	1.7
Sweden[10]	47.0/700.0	12.0	8.0	—	14	—	100 FB	211, 48 R	785	2.9
Switzerland[10]	20.0/560.0	—	3.0/45.0	—	—	—	135 FB	133, 18 R	850	2.0
Yugoslavia	144.0	11.0	33.0	—	5	3 FFG	165 FB	156, 70 R	1,570	3.1
IV. MIDDLE EAST AND MEDITERRANEAN; SUB-SAHARAN AFRICA; LATIN AMERICA[11]										
Algeria	120.0	7.0	12.0	—	4	3 FF	84 FB	123, 7 R	900	1.7
Egypt	320.0	20.0	10.5	—	12	1 DD, 4 FFG	175 FB, 9 B	227, 20 R	2,425	8.3
Iran[12]	305.0	14.5	35.0	—	—	3 DDG, 2 FFG	40 FB	10 F, 8 R	1,000	30.4
Iraq[12]	955.0	5.0	40.0	—	—	4 FFG	20 B, 181 FB	255, 5 R	4,500	31.7
Israel[10]	104.0/598.0	9.0/10.0	28.0/37.0	—	3	—	524 FB	14 R	3,850	18.9
Jordan	74.0	0.3	11.0	—	—	—	59 FB	35	980	15.5
Kuwait	16.0	2.1	2.2	—	—	—	27 FB	34	275	8.1
Lebanon[13]	...	...	...	—	—	—	—	—	—	...
Libya[14]	55.0	6.5	10.0	—	6	3 FFG	4 B, 206 FB	264, 13 R	1,800	6.8
Morocco	170.0	6.5	15.0	—	—	1 FFG	43 FB	21	173	5.1
Oman	20.0	2.5	3.0	—	—	—	35 FB	—	39	28.4
Qatar	6.0	0.7	0.3	—	—	—	23 FB	—	24	...
Saudi Arabia	38.0	7.8	16.5	—	—	8 FFG	83 FB	45, 10 R	550	22.4
Sudan, The	54.0	0.7	3.0	—	—	—	25 FB	16	175	...
Syria	300.0	4.0	100,000	—	3	2 FF	146 FB	302, 6 R	4,050	14.5
Tunisia	30.0	4.5	3.5	—	—	1 FF	12 FB	10	68	5.9
United Arab Emirates	40.0	1.5	1.5	—	—	—	19 FB	10	136	8.8
Yemen, North	35.0	0.6	1.0	—	—	—	33 FB	30	764	12.5
Yemen, South	24.0	1.0	2.5	—	—	—	77 FB	35	470	...
Angola[15]	91.5	1.5	7.0	—	—	—	62 FB	60	500	...
Ethiopia[16]	313.0	1.8	4.0	—	—	2 FF	138 FB	—	750	8.8

of these conflicts. Linked U.S.-Soviet and Pakistan-Afghanistan agreements committed the Soviets to the withdrawal of all of their military forces from Afghanistan by Feb. 15, 1989. Half of the estimated 115,000–135,000 Soviet occupation forces were to be withdrawn by Aug. 15, 1988, a commitment Moscow observed. Iran and Iraq agreed to a cease-fire, to withdraw to their prewar boundaries, and to negotiate a peace treaty. The UN and its secretary-general, Javier Pérez de Cuéllar (*see* BIOGRAPHIES), played an important role in negotiating these agreements, but it was not clear that they would be observed.

The Afghanistan agreements included the concept of "positive symmetry," meaning that if the Soviets continued to supply their puppet government in Kabul with military equipment, the U.S. would continue to supply the mujahideen with sophisticated weapons, including Stinger antiaircraft missiles, which had proved highly effective.

However, the Soviets claimed that this concept violated the agreements and suspended their troop withdrawals as the mujahideen gained control of the areas from which Soviet troops had withdrawn. The U.S.S.R. also launched a series of heavy bombing raids with Su-27 strike aircraft and the Tu-26 Backfire strategic bomber, the first combat use of the Backfire, and fired Scud-1 short-range ballistic missiles (SRBM) at mujahideen bases from sites around Kabul, the Afghanistan capital.

The U.S. responded to these actions by increasing weapons supplies to the mujahideen and insisting that the Soviets observe the Afghanistan agreements, including the positive symmetry provision. The incoming U.S. administration of President-elect George Bush seemed committed to a continuation of this policy. Afghanistan thus seemed set to provide the first major test of Gorbachev's new thinking in defense policy. To translate this new think-

	Military personnel in 000s			Warships[1]			Jet aircraft[3]			
Country	Army	Navy	Air Force	Aircraft carriers/ cruisers	Submarines[2]	Destroyers/ frigates	Bombers and fighter-bombers	Fighters/ recon-nais-sance	Tanks[4]	Defense expenditure as % of 1986 GDP[5]
Kenya	19.0	1.0	3.0	—	—	—	9 FB	—	76	3.7
Madagascar	20.0	0.5	0.5	—	—	—	12 FB	—	—	2.2
Mozambique[17]	35.0	0.7	1.0	—	—	—	66 FB	—	250	...
Nigeria	80.0	5.0	9.5	—	—	1 FFG	58 FB	—	132	1.3
Somalia	61.3	1.2	2.5	—	—	—	20 FB	38	293	11.0
South Africa[10]	75.0	7.5	13.0	—	3	—	12 B, 111 FB	33, 7 R	250	3.8
Tanzania	38.35	0.7	1.0	—	—	—	—	22	30	2.8
Zaire	22.0	1.5	2.5	—	—	—	—	8	50	1.6
Zimbabwe	46.0	—	1.0	—	—	—	7 B, 21 FB	7	43	7.0
Argentina	55.0	25.0[8]	15.0	1 CVS	4	6 DDG, 6 FFG	8 B, 109 FB	12 MR	425	1.5
Brazil	218.0	50.5[8]	50.7	1 CVS	7	10 DD, 6 FFG	31 FB	17, 27 MR	—	0.6
Chile	57.0	29.0[8]	15.0	—	4	6 DDG, 2 DD, 2 FFG	48 FB	16, 9 MR	171	4.7
Colombia	69.0	10.6[8]	6.7	—	2	4 FFG	15 FB	—	—	0.9
Cuba	145.0	13.5[8]	22.0	—	3	3 FF	36 FB	112	950	7.7
El Salvador	39.0	1.0	2.0	—	—	—	—	8	—	4.1
Mexico	105.5	26.0[8]	7.0	—	—	3 DD	—	11, 21 MR	—	0.5
Nicaragua	70.0	4.0	3.0	—	—	—	—	...	130	6.7
Peru	80.0	23.0[8]	15.0	2 CA	12	6 DD, 2 DDG, 4 FFG	19 B, 72 FB	26	300	3.3
Venezuela	34.0	10.0[8]	5.0	—	3	6 FFG	10 B, 70 FB	57	81	1.6
V. FAR EAST AND OCEANIA[11]										
Afghanistan[18]	50.0	—	5.0	—	—	—	18 B, 85 FB	30	450	...
Australia	32.0	15.8	22.6	—	6	3 DDG, 9 FFG	22 B, 33 FB	20 MR	103	2.7
Bangladesh	90.0	7.5	4.0	—	—	3 FF	52 FB	12	50	1.3
Burma	170.0	7.0	9.0	—	—	—	—	—	24	3.1
China	2,300.0	300.0[8]	470.0	—	107, 3 SSG, 3 SSN, 1 SSBN	19 DDG, 23 FFG, 11 FF	600 B, 600 FB	4,600, 260 R, 10 MR	9,000	2.6
India	1,200.0	52.0	115.0	2 CVV	13, 1 SSGN	5 DDG, 11 FFG, 13 FF	424 FB	275, 20 R, 8 MR	3,150	3.5
Indonesia	215.0	43.0[8]	27.0	—	2	6 FFG, 6 FF	29 FB	14, 9 MR	—	2.4
Japan	156.0	44.0	45.0	—	14	6 DDG, 30 DD, 3 FFG, 22 FF	80 FB	250, 10 R, 73 MR	1,170	1.0
Korea, North	750.0	39.0	53.0	—	21	1 FF, 1 FFG	80 B, 410 FB	266	3,000	...
Korea, South	542.0	54.0[8]	33.0	—	—	7 DDG, 4 DD, 18 FFG	284 FB	68, 10R	1,500	5.2
Laos	52.5	0.7	2.0	—	—	—	30 FB	—	30	...
Malaysia	90.0	12.5	12.0	—	—	2 FFG, 2 FF	38 FB	18	—	3.7
Mongolia	21.0	—	3.5	—	—	—	—	30	650	...
New Zealand	6.0	2.6	4.2	—	—	4 FF	22 FB	6 MR	—	2.0
Pakistan	450.0	16.0	17.6	—	6	7 DD	119 FB	209, 13 R, 3 MR	1,600	6.5
Philippines	65.0	23.0[8]	16.0	—	—	3 FF	—	10	—	1.7
Singapore	45.0	4.5	6.0	—	—	—	109 FB	42	—	6.6
Taiwan	270.0	65.5[8]	70.0	—	4	14 DDG, 12 DD, 10 FF	300 FB	5 R, 30 MR	309	5.8
Thailand	166.0	42.0[8]	48.0	—	—	4 FF, 1 FFG	18 FB	37, 9 MR	95	3.7
Vietnam	1,100.0	33.0[8]	12.0	—	—	6 FF, 1 FFG	40 FB	200	1,600	...

Note: Data exclude paramilitary, security, and irregular forces. Naval data exclude vessels of less than 100 tons standard displacement. Figures are for June 1988. Because of substantive changes in national forces and reassessments of evidence, data may not be comparable with previous editions.

[1]Aircraft carrier (CV); aircraft carrier, nuclear (CVN); small (CVS); V/STOL and helicopter carrier (CVV); general purpose amphibious assault ship (LHA); amphibious transport dock (LPD); amphibious assault ship (helicopter) (LPH); dock/tank landing ship (LSD/T); battleship (BBG); heavy cruiser (CA); guided missile cruiser (CG); guided missile cruiser, nuclear (CGN); helicopter cruiser (CAH); destroyer (DD); guided missile destroyer (DDG); frigate (FF); guided missile frigate (FFG); N denotes nuclear powered.
[2]Nuclear-powered attack submarine (SSN); ballistic missile submarine (SSB); guided (cruise) missile submarine (SSG); coastal (C); N denotes nuclear powered.
[3]Bombers (B), fighter-bombers (FB), strategic bombers (SB), reconnaissance fighters (R); maritime reconnaissance (MR). Data include jet combat aircraft from all services including naval and air defense. MR also includes propeller drive ASW and ECM aircraft; data exclude light strike/counter-insurgency (COIN) aircraft.
[4]Main battle tanks (MBT), medium and heavy, 31 tons and over.
[5]Figures are for Gross Domestic Product (GDP).
[6]Of Canada's other military personnel, approximately 29,000 are not identified by service.
[7]French forces were withdrawn from NATO command structure in 1966, but France remains a member of NATO.
[8]Includes marines.
[9]Figure includes the Strategic Rocket Forces (298,000) and the Air Defense Force (335,000), both separate services.
[10]Second figure is fully mobilized strength.
[11]Sections IV and V list only those states with significant military forces.
[12]Losses in Iran-Iraq war made remaining force estimates uncertain.
[13]Lebanon's civil war and division mean that there are no longer any truly national forces, only militias.
[14]Some advanced Libyan aircraft are maintained and manned by Soviet/Warsaw Pact crews, figures reflect losses in 1987 conflict with Chad.
[15]Plus 50,000 Cubans and 500 East Germans serving with Angolan forces.
[16]Ethiopia also has 5,000 Soviet, Cuban plus other Soviet bloc troops, Army includes a 150,000-strong People's Militia.
[17]Plus Cuban, Warsaw Pact, and Chinese advisers and technicians.
[18]Figures approximate, given Soviet occupation of Afghanistan. Excludes about 60,000 Soviet occupation troops, 5,000 Cubans/Czechoslovaks, and 130,000–240,000 mujahidin freedom fighters.

Sources: International Institute for Strategic Studies, 23 Tavistock Street, London, *The Military Balance 1988–1989, Strategic Survey 1987–88.*

ing into practice, the Soviets would have to observe the agreements, withdraw their troops from Afghanistan, and accept the replacement of their puppet, Pres. Mohammad Najibullah, by a freely elected government. Alternatively, the Soviets could continue their occupation of Afghanistan at the cost of returning the U.S.-Soviet relationship to one of confrontation. At year's end the U.S.S.R. continued to insist that it would observe the February deadline. Meanwhile, the Iran-Iraq cease-fire seemed to be holding. Agreements were also signed to end the war in Angola, although implementing them would be extremely difficult. (See *Africa South of the Sahara,* below.)

UNITED STATES

The U.S. all-volunteer armed forces in 1988 totaled 2,163,-200 personnel (203,000 women). Both retention rates and personnel quality remained at record highs. Defense spend-ing for fiscal 1988 at $285.4 billion represented some 6.4% of gross domestic product (GDP) and approximately 28% of the federal budget.

U.S. strategic nuclear forces (SNF) continued their modest modernization programs. The Strategic Air Command (SAC) had received 100 new Rockwell B-1B strategic bombers, although these planes continued to suffer from defects limiting their effectiveness, and three were lost in accidents.

The elderly B-52 bomber force remained at 167 B-52Gs and 96 B-52Hs (first deployed in 1959 and 1962, respectively). Of the B-52Hs, 60 carried 12 AGM-86B air-launched cruise missiles (ALCM) each, while 69 of the B-52Gs were equipped with the Harpoon air-to-surface missile (ASM) and were intended for a nonnuclear anti-shipping role. SAC also had 56 FB-111A medium-range nuclear bombers. Development of the advanced technology

(Stealth) bomber, the B-2, and the advanced cruise missile continued.

The land-based, fixed silo intercontinental ballistic missile (ICBM) force remained almost completely vulnerable to a Soviet attack. It consisted of 1,000 silos, containing MX Peacekeeper, Minuteman II, and Minuteman III missiles. The Peacekeeper, which was intended to modernize the ICBM force, was to have been deceptively based, but political pressures limited deployment to 50 Peacekeepers in vulnerable Minuteman silos. Of these large missiles, 39 were operational, each weighing 88,000 kg (195,000 lb) and carrying ten multiple independently targetable reentry vehicles (MIRV). The 511 Minuteman IIIs were modernized missiles, each carrying three MIRV. The 450 Minuteman II missiles were more than 20 years old. Development of the single-warhead Midgetman small ICBM (about 11,350 kg [25,000 lb]) continued, but the very high costs of this system made its deployment unlikely.

The ballistic missile nuclear submarine (SSBN) force totaled 36, carrying 640 submarine-launched ballistic missiles (SLBM). The eight new Ohio-class SSBN each carried 24 Trident I/C-4s, to be replaced by the Trident II/D-5 SLBM from 1989 onward. The test of a Trident II with 12 warheads was canceled so that these missiles would be counted in the START negotiations as carrying only eight MIRV each. Older SSBN included 12 Franklin class (96 Trident I/C-4s and 96 Poseidon C-3s) and 16 Madison and Lafayette class (96 Trident I/C-4s and 160 Poseidon C-3s). The deployment of submarine-launched nuclear cruise missiles continued, with seven nuclear cruise-missile submarines (SSGN) so equipped. Plans called for a total of about 750 BGM-109A Tomahawk sea-launched cruise missiles (SLCM). In addition, 2,300 conventionally armed Tomahawk SLCM were being deployed in order to give each vessel a mix of nuclear and conventionally armed missiles. Dispersing the nuclear SLCM would enhance their survivability.

The U.S. Navy at the end of 1988 totaled 239 principal surface ships, 88 nuclear-fueled submarines (SSN), and 585,000 personnel. These provided 14 carrier and 4 battleship groups (to rise to 15), each carrier having an attack wing of some 86 aircraft plus escorting surface vessels and SSN. Of the 13 modern (post-1955) aircraft carriers, 5 were nuclear powered. Modern aircraft included 372 F-14A Tomcat interceptors, 338 A-6 Intruder/Prowler and 270 F/A-18A Hornet strike planes, and 74 E-2C electronic

warfare/airborne early warning aircraft. A fourth World War II battleship, the *Wisconsin,* was recommissioned with Tomahawk SLCM. The 9 nuclear and 29 conventionally powered guided weapons (GW) cruisers included 11 new Ticonderoga-class ships equipped with the Aegis fleet air defense missile/radar system. One of these cruisers, the *Vincennes,* was on patrol in the Persian Gulf when it misidentified an Iranian airliner as an attacking aircraft and shot it down. Other major surface combatants included 37 GW and 31 gun/antisubmarine warfare (ASW) Spruance-class destroyers and 56 GW and 59 gun frigates.

The Marine Corps, with 198,200 personnel, was organized in three divisions, each with its air wing. Modern aircraft included 128 F/A-18 Hornet interceptor/strike aircraft, 70 A-6 Intruder strike aircraft, and 142 AV-8B Harrier vertical/short takeoff and landing (V/STOL) interceptor/strike aircraft.

The 603,600-strong Air Force had approximately 3,972 combat aircraft plus 902 in storage. Among modern types were 825 F-15 Eagle interceptors, 1,289 F-16 Falcon fighter-bombers, and 34 E-3A Sentry airborne warning and control systems (AWACS). Older types included 1,026 F-4 Phantom fighter-bombers/reconnaissance, 236 F-111A/D/E/F medium bombers, and 653 A-10A Thunderbolt ground-support aircraft.

The Army, with 776,400 personnel, formed 14 heavy divisions (about 16,000 men each)—4 armoured, 6 mechanized, 1 high-technology motor, 1 regular infantry, 1 air assault, and 1 airborne—plus 4 light infantry divisions (about 10,200 men each). The light infantry divisions were easier to transport and were intended as part of the Rapid Deployment Force for use outside NATO-Europe. Armour included 5,290 M-1/1A1 Abrams tanks and 4,013 M-2/3 Bradley mechanized infantry combat vehicles (MICV), plus some 9,270 M60A1/2 and M-60A3 tanks and 19,000 M-113 armoured personnel carriers (APC).

The major overseas deployments of U.S. forces, including those afloat, were in Europe (317,000 personnel), the Pacific/Far East (143,800), and Latin America (19,300).

U.S.S.R.

The Soviet military machine remained the world's most powerful, with about 5.1 million personnel plus some 55 million in reserves and 570,000 paramilitary personnel. Western, including U.S., estimates of Soviet defense spending put it at 15–17% of gross national product (GNP),

AP/WIDE WORLD

Two Iranians demonstrate a method for decontamination in chemical warfare. Both Iran and Iraq reportedly used chemical weapons in their eight-year war, violating the 1925 Geneva Protocol and representing the first wartime use of nerve gas.

The U.S. Air Force introduced its new B-2 Stealth bomber in November 1988 following seven years of research and development.
U.S. AIR FORCE

amounting to over $700 billion, and the total cost of the Soviet bloc at 20–25% of GNP. This was a massive burden on the Soviet economy, one that had increased steadily.

Gorbachev's campaign for *perestroika* was badly handicapped by this high level of defense spending. It could not be reduced without weakening the U.S.S.R.'s only claim to superpower status, military power, but, at the same time, it had to be reduced to obtain the resources needed to make restructuring work and to provide the long-term economic base for that power. Thus the Soviet government faced a difficult series of choices. This was the background of Gorbachev's December 7 speech to the UN, at which he announced a major unilateral cutback in Soviet conventional forces and a pullback of Soviet troops in Eastern Europe and along the Chinese border. However, observers pointed out that the reductions would still leave Soviet conventional forces stronger than those of the West, and the immediate resignation of Marshal Sergey Akhromeyev as chief of staff (ostensibly for reasons of health) suggested that even these cuts might be resisted by the military.

The Strategic Nuclear Forces Command, a separate service with 298,000 troops, further increased its superiority over U.S. forces in missile and warhead numbers and in warhead yields and accuracy. This gave the Soviets a first-strike capability that the U.S. would not have even after the year 2000. The figures shown in Table I underestimate the Soviet advantage because the U.S.S.R. also deployed 1,000–3,000 reload missiles for their ICBM, IRBM, and SLBM launchers. New systems being tested and deployed included two ICBM, the SS-24 and SS-25 (both mobile); one SLBM, the SS-N-23; and five long-range cruise missiles, all in the 3,000-km [1,860-mi] range. Sharp increases in SS-24 and SS-25 deployments brought these up to a total of 20 and 150, respectively. The five Typhoon-class SSBN, each carrying 20 SS-N-20 SLBM with MIRV, were the world's largest, displacing 23,000 tons each.

The strategic aviation force included the new Blackjack A, larger than the U.S. B-1B; 70 Bear-H, each carrying eight ALCM; and 178 Tu-26 Backfire B/Cs. Additional medium-range bombers included 120 Tu-22 Blinder A/Bs, 272 obsolete Tu-16 Badgers, and 450 Su-24 strike aircraft. Soviet strategic defensive forces were also large. The Air Defense Command (VVO) formed a separate service with some 520,000 personnel, 2,300 interceptors, and 8,600 SAM launchers at 1,200 fixed sites. The latest surface-to-air missile (SAM), the SA-X-12B, had an antitactical ballistic missile (ATBM) capability. Soviet upgrading of the antiballistic missile (ABM) system around Moscow, together with construction of other ABM radars, would enable the U.S.S.R. to field a nationwide ABM system.

The nearly two million-strong Army was organized into 52 tank, 150 motor rifle (mechanized), 18 artillery, and 7 airborne divisions (10,500–12,500 men each). Equipment—at much higher levels than for the U.S., its NATO allies, or China—included 53,000 tanks (modern types comprised 11,500 T-72/-80s and 9,900 T-64s, plus 31,900 older T-54/-55/-62s); 64,400 armoured fighting vehicles (AFV); and 31,300 artillery pieces, including new self-propelled 203-mm, 180-mm, 152-mm, and 130-mm guns.

Soviet Army forces continued to be deployed roughly two-thirds against NATO-Europe and one-third against China. There were three major strategic theatre commands (GTVD), subdivided into five regional theatres of military operations (TVD), and a central strategic reserve military district with 16 divisions. Soviet forces stationed in Eastern Europe included 20 divisions in East Germany, 2 in Poland, 5 in Czechoslovakia, and 4 in Hungary.

WARSAW PACT

Poland maintained the largest military forces of the Eastern European nations, totaling 406,000 personnel and including a 230,000-strong Army with 3,950 T-34/-54/-55/-72 main battle tanks (MBT) and a 92,000-strong Air Force with 625 combat aircraft (400 MiG-21U/-23 interceptors). Czechoslovakia's 197,000-strong forces, the second largest, comprised an Army of 145,000 with 3,400 T-54/-55/-72 tanks and an Air Force of 52,000 with 450 combat aircraft (270 MiG-21U/-23 interceptors).

East Germany's armed forces totaled 172,000, including an Army of 120,000 with 2,050 T-54/-55/-72 tanks (plus 800 in storage) and an Air Force of 37,000 with 330 combat aircraft, including 270 MiG-21/-23 interceptors. Hungary's armed forces, with 99,000 personnel, included an Army of 77,000 with about 1,300 T-54/-55/-72 tanks and an Air Force of 22,000 with 135 MiG-21/-23 interceptors. All four countries allocated much lower proportions of their GDP to defense than did the U.S.S.R.

NATO

The main effect of the superpower intermediate-range nuclear forces (INF) agreement signed on Dec. 8, 1987, was to increase fears of the European NATO nations that the U.S. was becoming less willing to couple its defense against a Soviet attack to that of Western Europe. Because the U.S. had agreed to withdraw all the modernized INF that had been deployed as a result of NATO's 1979 INF modernization, an important rung in the coupling ladder of escalation was to be removed, the rung represented by longer-range and shorter-range INF (LR/SR-INF) and by the 72 Pershing IA short-range ballistic missiles (SRBM)

operated by West Germany, with U.S. warheads. Other elements of NATO theatre nuclear forces (TNF) were being withdrawn as a result of a decision made in 1983. After all of these reductions were completed, by the early 1990s, NATO TNF would consist mainly of aircraft and artillery able to deliver either conventional or nuclear weapons.

The TNF leg of the NATO triad of conventional forces, TNF, and SNF would thus be weakened. In addition, the conventional leg of the NATO triad could well be weakened by U.S. reductions of conventional forces. President Reagan's Strategic Defense Initiative (SDI) was also seen as a potential shield behind which the U.S. could decouple itself from NATO-Europe. The decoupling issue thus seemed likely to remain a major one in the alliance, even though many NATO-Europe governments, notably West Germany, had pressed the U.S. to negotiate any possible reduction in INF. Similarly, many of those raising the decoupling issue had also resisted LR-INF and chemical weapons modernization. They had also opposed any halt in the reductions in NATO-Europe defense spending as a percentage of GDP. As Table II shows, U.S. defense spending as a percentage of 1986 GDP was, at 6.7%, approximately twice that of France and West Germany (3.9 and 3.1%) and more than three times that of Canada, Denmark, and Italy. Britain's defense spending, at 4.9% of GDP, was closer to that of the U.S.

The result of NATO-Europe's refusal to fund a stalwart conventional defense was that the new concepts for improving this defense remained paper concepts. The reality was that NATO could defend itself with conventional weapons for only a few days before it would have to use nuclear weapons to defeat a Soviet attack. On the crucial Central Front covered by the NATO guidelines area for the mutual and balanced force reductions (MBFR) negotiations (Norway to West Germany), the balance of forces, in terms of total war-mobilized divisions, gave the Soviet-Warsaw Pact forces an advantage of over 50% in MBT.

UNITED KINGDOM

Defense expenditure for 1987–88 totaled $31.9 billion (4.9% of 1986 GDP). The Army of 158,400 had 300 new Challenger and 870 Chieftain MBT plus 2,488 MICV/APC. The Royal Air Force (RAF), with 93,500 personnel, had about 553 combat aircraft. Some 300 of the new Tornado GR-1 multirole combat aircraft were being deployed in

fighter, ground attack, and reconnaissance models, replacing 150 Phantom fighters. Other modern aircraft included 51 Harrier GR-3/T-4 V/STOL, 132 Jaguar GR-1 ground-attack/ reconnaissance planes, and 34 Nimrod MR-2 maritime reconnaissance aircraft.

The Royal Navy was the third largest naval force in the world with 64,800 personnel, 27 attack submarines (16 nuclear), and 50 major surface combatants including 3 small carriers with Sea Harriers, 13 GW destroyers, and 34 general-purpose frigates. Royal Marine personnel totaled some 7,100.

FRANCE

Defense spending in 1988 was estimated at $31,880,000,-000. Modernization of France's national nuclear forces continued, with five SSBN operational, one being refitted, and one under construction. The M-20 SLBM was being replaced with the M-4. Medium-range and tactical nuclear forces were also being increased.

Military personnel had been reduced to a total of 456,-900 (280,900 in the Army). Equipment included 1,340 AMX-30 MBT (400 new AMX-30-B2), 816 AMX-10P/PC Milan MICV, and about 3,000 APC. These were organized in six armoured and two mechanized infantry divisions, plus a Rapid Action Force for overseas intervention consisting of one parachute, one air portable marine, one light armoured, one mountain, and one air mobile division (averaging 7,000–8,000 personnel each). The Air Force of some 95,000 personnel had 580 combat aircraft, the newer models including 123 Mirage F-1C and 58 Mirage 2000B/C-N interceptors plus 30 Mirage 5F and some 127 Jaguar A ground-attack fighters. The 66,500-strong Navy's 43 major surface combatants included 2 light carriers, 15 GW destroyers, 24 frigates, and 18 attack submarines.

WEST GERMANY

West Germany's defense budget amounted to $30,310,-000,000 in 1988. Standing armed forces totaled 488,700, more than half of them volunteers. The 332,100-strong Army included 12 divisions: 6 armoured, 4 armoured infantry, 1 mountain, and 1 airborne. Armour included 2,000 new Leopard 2 and 2,287 Leopard 1A1 MBT, plus about 2,130 MICV and 3,600 APC.

The Air Force had 108,700 personnel with 459 combat aircraft. These included 210 new Tornados, 222 older F-4

(LEFT) ERIKA SULZER-KLEINEMEIER; (RIGHT) ADN-ZB

Intermediate-range missiles are dismantled by U.S. (left) and Soviet (right) troops as directed by the intermediate-range nuclear forces (INF) treaty. It was the first arms control agreement to eliminate a whole class of nuclear weapons delivery systems.

Phantoms, and 171 Alpha Jet ground-attack fighters. The 36,400-strong Navy, designed for coastal warfare in the Baltic Sea, had 40 fast-attack craft equipped with guided missiles, 7 GW destroyers, 8 GW frigates, and 24 coastal submarines. The naval air arm consisted of 112 combat aircraft, including 98 Tornado attack/reconnaissance planes.

ARMS CONTROL AND DISARMAMENT

For arms control, 1988 was a year of contradictory developments. On the positive side was U.S. and Soviet ratification of the Dec. 8, 1987, INF treaty, which represented unprecedented progress in arms control and also a step toward START. The negative developments were technical ones that made successful arms control agreements even more difficult than in previous years and the weakening of existing agreements by continuing Soviet violations. Two of the most significant and easily understood were the development and deployment of two new ICBM (SS-24 and SS-25) instead of the one allowed under SALT II and the building of a massive ABM radar at Krasnoyarsk. In September Gorbachev offered to put the radar under international control for use in the peaceful exploration of space, but the U.S. continued to insist it should be dismantled.

The INF treaty was the first arms control agreement to eliminate a whole class of nuclear weapons delivery systems, ballistic missiles with ranges of 500 to 5,000 km. This treaty also introduced unprecedented on-site-inspection (OSI) measures and the monitoring of missile production facilities in a U.S. attempt to verify Soviet compliance with its limits. U.S. critics of the treaty argued that despite these provisions the Soviets could still keep a covert stockpile of INF missiles because the U.S. could inspect only those missile sites declared by the Soviets and could not inspect other sites where the U.S. suspected missiles were being deployed. Even so, the INF treaty marked a major shift in the standards for future superpower arms control agreements. These would make real reductions instead of establishing legalized planned building programs and would include much more intrusive verification provisions, including OSI and production monitoring.

The draft U.S.-Soviet START treaty reflected these new standards. It made real reductions in the strategic nuclear forces of each nation, cutting their warhead totals from about 12,000 to about 9,000, less than the popular description of the treaty as making a 50% reduction but still a large cut. The START treaty also contained unprecedented verification provisions, although it was not clear that even these would be completely effective.

Despite this progress, formidable obstacles remained to agreement on a START treaty. Technical barriers included the Soviet insistence that it limit the deployments of sea-launched cruise missiles (SLCM), a limit the U.S. rejected as impossible to verify, and the U.S. insistence that the treaty ban the deployment of mobile ICBM, a provision that the Soviets rejected. Continuing Soviet violations of existing arms control agreements raised the question of whether the Soviets would comply with a START treaty. The Soviet refusal to admit that their Krasnoyarsk ABM radar was a treaty violation and to dismantle it was becoming an increasingly serious obstacle. Progress in the nuclear and space talks (NST) was further limited by basic U.S.-Soviet differences on limits on weapons in space and additional limits on ABM.

Negotiations between NATO and the Warsaw Pact on reducing conventional forces in Europe were transferred from the moribund talks on MBFR to a new, larger forum called the conventional stabilizing talks (CST). The com-

plexity of such reductions made early progress toward an agreement unlikely, however.

The use of chemical weapons in the Iran-Iraq war focused new attention on the "poor man's nuclear weapons," which were cheap and difficult to control because the components also had many legitimate uses. At year's end the U.S. claimed that a plant in Libya was about to produce chemical weapons. Libya denied the charge, and the matter was certain to be discussed at an international conference on chemical warfare to be held in Paris in January 1989.

MIDDLE EAST

Syrian armed forces personnel totaled 404,000 with an Army of 300,000, comprising five armoured and three mechanized divisions. Equipment included 950 new T-72 and 3,100 T-54/-55/-62 MBT and 3,650 BMP/BTR-series MICV/APC. The separate Air Defense Command had 60,000 personnel manning 87 batteries with Soviet SA-2/-3/-6 SAM. The 40,000-strong Air Force had some 448 combat aircraft, including 15 MiG-29 Fulcrum, 30 MiG-25 Foxbat E, 80 MiG-23 Flogger E, 172 MiG-21 PF/MF interceptors, 60 MiG-23 Flogger F, and 33 Su-22 fighter-bombers. Defense spending totaled $1.6 billion in 1988.

Israel remained the region's strongest military power, especially in the quality of its weapons. Its defense spending burden ($5,710,000,000 for 1988), though considerably reduced, was still difficult to support, even with massive U.S. aid. Defense had consumed 18.9% of GDP in 1986, compared with 22.4% in 1984. With a population of only 4,466,000, Israel raised standing armed forces of 141,000 that would increase to 645,000 on mobilization. The Army of 104,000 formed, on mobilization, 12 armoured divisions and 7 mechanized infantry and 6 artillery brigades. These forces had some 3,850 MBT and 5,900 MICV/APC. The 28,000-strong Air Force had 676 combat aircraft, including 50 U.S. F/TF-15 Eagles, 145 U.S. F-16A/D Falcons, 170 Israeli Kfir C2/C7s, and 113 U.S. F-4E Phantom interceptor/fighter-bombers.

Egypt's armed forces totaled 445,000 personnel; defense spending was estimated at $5,640,000,000 in 1988-89. The nation's conversion from Soviet to Western equipment was continuing, with most of the Soviet equipment in reserve or rebuilt. The Army of 320,000 had 785 U.S. M-60A3 and 1,640 effective Soviet T-54/-55/-62 MBT. Effective aircraft for the 25,000-strong Air Force comprised 33 F-4E Phantoms, 16 Mirage 5E2 and 52 J-7 fighter-bombers, plus 33 F-16A Falcon and 16 Mirage 2000C interceptors. Jordan's small but effective Army (74,000 personnel) had some 1,000 MBT, and the Air Force (11,000) had 59 F-5E/F and 35 Mirage F-1CJ/EJ/BJ fighter-bombers.

Libya's forces remained numerically large, totaling 71,-500 personnel with 1,800 MBT and 500 combat aircraft. However, they performed poorly in the war between Libya and Chad.

SOUTH, EAST, AND SOUTHEAST ASIA

The Soviet occupation of Afghanistan was reduced in 1988, but border incidents between Afghanistan and Pakistan remained a potential danger. Despite increased U.S. military aid, Pakistan's armed forces totaled only 483,600 personnel, mainly an Army of 450,000 with 1,600 MBT (mostly Type-59). The Air Force comprised 17,600 personnel and 338 combat aircraft, including 39 F-16 Falcon and 62 Mirage 5 fighter-bombers. The defense budget in 1988-89 totaled $2,740,000,000.

India's armed forces in 1988 totaled some 1,367,000 personnel. The 1.2 million-strong Army had some 3,150 MBT, including 650 new T-72s. The Air Force of 115,000

had 714 combat aircraft, including 135 MiG-23 Flogger H and 40 Mirage 2000 fighter-bombers. Defense spending in 1988–89 amounted to $9,890,000,000.

China's forces were being reduced, but more slowly than had been thought, to 3.2 million. They were weak in modern equipment, and defense expenditure had been sharply reduced from its 1978 level of 12% to 5% of GNP.

China's nuclear stockpile was small, with limited numbers of comparatively old, vulnerable delivery systems. These included about 6 ICBM (DF-4/-5), 60 DF-3 IRBM, and 1 Xia-class SSBN with 12 CSS-N-3 SLBM (modified DF-3s). The Army had 2.3 million personnel but only 9,000 MBT (mostly T-59), while the 470,000-strong Air Force's 6,000 combat aircraft were modifications of old Soviet models, including 3,000 J-6/MiG-19 fighters.

Vietnam remained the largest active military power in Southeast Asia, with armed forces, mostly Army, totaling 1,252,000—the fourth largest army in the world. The Army had about 1,760 MBT, and the 12,000-strong Air Force had approximately 250 combat aircraft. Occupation forces in Kampuchea were being withdrawn, about 60,000 remaining at the end of 1988, but 50,000 troops remained in Laos.

North Korea's forces were so much larger than those of South Korea that concerns over the danger of a Northern invasion of the South remained significant. The balance was 842,000 personnel, 3,000 MBT, 1,400 APC, and 800 combat aircraft (mostly older types) for the North versus 629,000 personnel, 1,500 MBT, 850 APC, and 473 combat aircraft (mostly modern types) for the South.

Japan continued to exceed, marginally, its long-standing spending ceiling of no more than 1% of GNP on defense. Japan's 1988–89 defense expenditure was $29,630,000,000. Armed forces personnel totaled 245,000, including 156,-000 army personnel with 1,170 MBT. The air and naval forces had approximately 45,000 personnel each. Equipment included 80 Japanese-made F-1 fighter-bombers, 121 F-15J/DJ Eagle and 129 F-4/EJ Phantom fighter-bombers, 36 destroyers (16 GW), 25 frigates, and 14 submarines. Taiwan's forces, totaling 405,500 personnel, continued to provide a credible defense against China. The Army, with 270,000 personnel, had 309 MBT, and the 70,000-strong Air Force had 500 combat aircraft. Defense spending in 1988–89 was to total $6.7 billion.

AFRICA SOUTH OF THE SAHARA

An agreement to end the war in Angola was signed in December. (See WORLD AFFAIRS [Africa South of the Sahara]: *African Affairs.*) The agreement, negotiated by U.S. Assistant Secretary of State Chester A. Crocker, involved a complex plan for the phased withdrawal of Cuban troops from Angola and of South African troops from South West Africa/Namibia, and the holding of UN-supervised elections in Namibia. It remained unclear whether the parties to the agreement really intended to carry it out or what would become of the UNITA (National Union for the Total Independence of Angola) rebels, led by Jonas Savimbi and supported by South Africa.

The Angolan government's armed forces, totaling 100,-000 personnel with 500 MBT, had been reinforced by 50,000 Cuban military personnel, a sharp increase from the previous year's level of 25,000, and large quantities of Soviet military equipment. South Africa remained the region's dominant military power, with armed forces totaling 103,500 (rising to 558,500 on mobilization). Equipment included 250 MBT, 1,500 Ratel MICV, and 324 combat aircraft. Defense spending was estimated at $3,760,000,000 for 1988–89.

LATIN AMERICA

Although Costa Rica's Pres. Oscar Arias Sánchez received the 1987 Nobel Peace Prize for his Central American peace plan, the Arias plan failed to deal with the two basic causes of instability in Central America. These were depressed economic and social conditions, which encouraged revolutionary movements, and large-scale Soviet aid to those movements via their Cuban and Nicaraguan allies.

Central and Latin-American armed forces, primarily internal-security infantry troops with little equipment, were poorly paid and often poorly led. They were also small relative to the size and population of their countries, as is apparent from Table II, so the region was vulnerable to outside intervention. Costa Rica had no military forces and only a single Northern Border Security Battalion (9,500 personnel) of paramilitary forces. Honduras cut its total armed forces personnel to 18,700, and Guatemala's personnel totaled 42,000. El Salvador's armed forces totaled 55,000, mostly Army, supported by U.S. economic and military aid in its fight against some 6,000–7,000 rebel guerrillas, aided by Cuban and Nicaraguan personnel plus Soviet weapons and supplies.

In sharp contrast, the fifth party to the Arias plan, Nicaragua's Sandinista Pres. Daniel Ortega Saavedra, had increased his total armed forces to 77,000 personnel, with 130 Soviet T-54/55 tanks and some 45 Mi-8/-17/-24/-25 attack/assault helicopters. Nicaragua's anti-Sandinista guerrillas, the U.S.-backed *contras,* totaled 12,000–15,000 personnel. Equipment included the U.S.-supplied Stinger SAM. Cuba was the dominant Latin-American and Caribbean power, with armed forces further increased to 180,500 personnel, including major overseas deployments in Angola (50,000), Nicaragua (4,000), and Ethiopia (2,800).   (ROBIN RANGER)

See also Space Exploration.

This article updates the *Macropædia* article The Technology of WAR.

AP/WIDE WORLD

A soldier drives a "Rooikat," a new armoured tank developed by the South African Defence Force, which is equipped with 76-mm guns and can travel at speeds up to 120 kilometres (75 miles) per hour.

Mining

In conjunction with the September convention of the American Mining Congress in Denver, Colo., a National Mining Hall of Fame was established and the first group of honourees inducted. The hall and museum, the latter originally founded in 1977, were located at nearby Leadville, Colo. A group of 25 geologists, mining engineers, and businessmen who had shaped the field over the last 150 years were honoured. Best known of the nominees was U.S. Pres. Herbert Hoover, who in an 18-year career on four continents pursued a successful business as a mining engineer and consultant and in 1909 helped found *Mining Magazine,* which was still being published. Other nominees included Clarence King (1842–1901), founder of the U.S. Geological Survey, who first described systematically the mineral resources along the route of the Union Pacific Railroad; Herman Frasch (1851–1914), who invented the process that bears his name for the extraction of underground sulfur; and Daniel Jackling (1869–1956), who developed open-pit mining techniques and flotation processes for concentrating ores.

World mining output, as measured by United Nations production indexes, revealed continued recovery from the difficult years from 1980 to 1986 but showed few dramatic gains or losses through mid-1988. (*See* Table.) The strongest growth among the three main commodity groups was demonstrated by metals, fueled in part by rising consumption in the "newly industrializing countries," where relocation of manufacturing jobs from the older, developed nations and accompanying higher wages were creating new markets for industrial products. Petroleum output remained some 20% below 1980 levels, although coal, led by the centrally planned and less developed market countries, remained close to the metals sector. None of these gains was particularly dramatic, however, and mining as a whole continued to lose ground against manufacturing.

In 1987, the last year for which reasonably complete data were available, U.S. mine production of nonfuel mineral products gained about 8.5%, rising to some $25 billion in current prices and to an estimated $250 billion as processed metals and minerals. According to U.S. Federal Reserve Board (FRB) indexes, through the third quarter of 1988

the mining industry was utilizing about 83% of domestic production capacity, about the average for all industry, but its total capacity had grown only 26% in the last decade, compared with 65% for all industry. Not surprisingly, the lowest growth rate for all of the industrial sectors surveyed by the FRB was metal durable goods manufacturing, which had grown only 9.4% in capacity between 1977 and 1988. Mining's total contribution to the U.S. gross domestic product amounted to $85.4 billion, of which oil and natural gas represented just over three-quarters of the total, coal mining 14.9%, other nonmetallic minerals 6.4%, and metals only some 2.6% in 1987.

Rising prices in world markets encouraged producers of several important base metals (nickel, most notably, but also aluminum, copper, tin, lead, and zinc). Neither gold nor silver prices had received any significant impetus from the October 1987 New York Stock Exchange crash, and prices in late 1988 drifted 20% below those of a year earlier. There was some consensus that base metal prices were unlikely to show further gains during 1989, tin perhaps excepted because of efforts by the Association of Tin Producing Countries to reduce stocks, limit new production, and exert pressure on the two major nonmember producers, Brazil and China, to join ATPC efforts to restore world prices following the October 1985 International Tin Council debacle. (See *Business and Markets,* below.)

Exploration. The worldwide emphasis on gold exploration continued unabated during the year. Though there were sound business reasons for this, it had the effect of decreasing investment in the exploration and development of new reserves for other minerals. In Canada, for example, government economists at the September meeting of the Quebec Prospector's Association drew attention to the reduced reserves of many of the base metals upon which Canada's mining industry depended—copper, down 23% during 1980–86; lead, down 34%; zinc, down 30%. Because of the five- to seven-year lead time necessary for bringing an undeveloped deposit from the "greenfield" stage to that of a producing mine, the possibility of exhaustion of current workings before alternatives had been developed was seen to contain the potential for reduced output by the mid-1990s.

Similar concerns were evident in a survey drawn from a different body of evidence. The Metals Economics Group

Indexes of Production, Mining and Mineral Commodities
(1980 = 100)

	1983	1984	1985	1986	1987	1988 1st quarter	1988 2nd quarter
Mining (total)							
World[1]	85.0	88.2	87.1	90.0	91.6	89.4	...
Centrally planned economies[2]	105.1	106.9	108.6	112.3	114.1	114.6	114.8
Developed market economies[3]	98.5	103.1	105.5	103.2	104.3	107.4	102.8
Less developed market economies[4]	73.2	75.7	71.9	78.1	79.9	73.9	...
Coal							
World[1]	101.7	100.7	105.8	108.5	108.5	109.0	...
Centrally planned economies[2]	105.2	107.0	108.9	112.0	112.9	113.0	114.6
Developed market economies[3]	97.8	93.5	101.0	103.0	102.2	100.8	99.8
Less developed market economies[4]	114.1	124.1	132.0	139.0	139.4	162.7	...
Petroleum and natural gas							
World[1]	79.4	82.5	79.5	82.6	83.6	80.3	...
Centrally planned economies[2]	106.5	107.5	108.0	111.4	113.2	113.6	107.4
Developed market economies[3]	100.6	106.4	107.3	102.1	102.7	109.4	98.7
Less developed market economies[4]	70.1	72.2	67.5	73.8	74.9	67.5	...
Metals							
World[1]	97.3	103.9	108.1	109.7	113.4	114.2	...
Centrally planned economies[2]	92.9	93.2	95.5	97.6	99.4	100.2	100.4
Developed market economies[3]	96.2	106.4	110.0	111.6	116.2	115.0	117.6
Less developed market economies[4]	99.9	102.0	107.5	109.2	111.6	115.6	...
Manufacturing (total)	101.8	108.6	112.7	116.7	123.0	127.7	...

[1] Excluding Albania, China, North Korea, and Vietnam.
[2] Bulgaria, Czechoslovakia, East Germany, Hungary, Poland, Romania, and the U.S.S.R.
[3] North America, Europe (except centrally planned and Yugoslavia), Australia, Israel, Japan, New Zealand, and South Africa.
[4] Caribbean, Central and South America, Africa (except South Africa), Asian Middle East, East and Southeast Asia (except Israel and Japan), and Yugoslavia.
Source: UN, *Monthly Bulletin of Statistics* (November 1988).

analyzed the nonferrous metals exploration budgets of some 60 major international mining companies and found a deficit for the current year of approximately $350 million with respect to the same exploration budgets in 1987. Virtually all of the deficit, however, was in two countries: Canada, about $250 million, and Australia, about $80 million, both of which had shown recent strong growth in gold production.

Development. As noted above, the lead time needed for bringing a new mine on line is long. The investment required may be enormous, depending on the location; geologic setting; and the technology required for extracting, concentrating, and refining the ore and for transporting it to a suitable market. Some of the hazards associated with this process were illuminated at the September symposium of the Uranium Institute in London. Comparisons were offered of projections made in the mid-1970s for world uranium production, consumption, and industry structure a decade into the future—the mid-1980s—and of actual patterns as they had developed by that time. Optimistic projections of increased demand, upon which expensive exploration and development decisions had in part been based, were found to have been more than twice actual demand by the mid-1980s, mostly as a consequence of postponement or cancellation of new nuclear-power-generating capacity because of environmental and safety considerations.

The same uncertainties plagued governments that had to base national development plans on mineral development; Venezuela provided two instances during the year of major long-term mineral investments whose funding represented a substantial national commitment in a world commodity market that had shown great volatility in the last decade. The country, which once funded much of its national development from revenues generated by the petroleum industry, had accumulated $35 billion in foreign debt since 1976 and by 1989 had to manage much-reduced oil revenues and scarcer development capital with great prudence. Government officials announced during the year, after intense debate in the legislature, a long-term program for development of its growing aluminum industry that would increase annual alumina (Al_2O_3 concentrate) and refined aluminum metal capacities to three million and two million tons, respectively, by the end of the century. In addition, Petróleos de Venezuela (PDVSA), the national oil company, announced plans for commercial production of "Orimulsion," an emulsion of oil and water based on a heavy domestic crude oil reserve that would otherwise be unmarketable. The product, which took years of research to develop, was seen as a kind of liquid coal and was to be tested at power stations in the U.S., Canada, Japan, and Europe during the year. Venezuela hoped to develop a 600,000-bbl-per-day market by the mid-1990s.

Safety and Environment. Though two of the principal mining countries showed improvements during the year in the fatality rate for mining—the U.S. dropped in the first nine months to 74 from 101 for the same period in 1987, and South Africa in the first six months dropped from 361 to 265—the year also was marked by the outcome of a South African post mortem into the Ermelo Mines disaster that killed 35 black miners in 1987. The mine's managers and operators were found responsible. In October 1988, soon after the release of South Africa's six-month safety report, seven miners died of asphyxiation by fumes from burning polyurethane foam of the same kind found responsible for the deaths of 177 miners in the 1986 Kinross disaster. An expert panel had recommended the removal of all such foam from South African mines.

There was some good news from the South African industry, however, when the British Safety Council awarded its "Sword of Honour" to the Rossing uranium operation in South West Africa/Namibia for achieving 50 million man-hours of fatality-free operations. This was the best record in either South Africa or Namibia.

The most serious single accident of the year occurred at the Borken brown (low-grade) coal pit near Kassel, West Germany, on June 1. Damage to the mine was extensive and hindered both recovery of the bodies and a determination as to the cause. The final death toll was put at 51, although recovery of all of the bodies proved to be impossible.

Business and Markets. A World Bank report was issued during the year on the industrial minerals, those, that provide the basis for the world's construction industries, industrial and chemical processes, agriculture, and the like. These products tend to have a low unit value (cost per ton), to require little in the way of specialized mining techniques (removal or stripping is often the only method needed), and to reach their end uses after no more than a single processing step. They include sand, gravel, dimension stone, the natural fertilizers, and base chemicals such as salt and sulfur, but the classification also extends to electronic-grade quartz and industrial diamonds. The World Bank's study found that the best potential for profitable development of these minerals in the less developed countries was in those areas with a combination of favourable geologic potential, sizable domestic markets, and good access to ocean shipping (for export of the more valuable commodities). The countries identified by the Bank as having the best possibilities included Brazil, Mexico, Thailand, the Philippines, and Indonesia.

The default of the 24 (government)-member International Tin Council in October 1985 left £900 million owed to various creditors, whose claims had been refused by the governments comprising the ITC. In a ruling at the end of April 1988, the U.K. Court of Appeals in a far from unanimous decision denied the liability of the governments concerned, ruling that under international law, these governments and the ITC could be pursued only through the International Court of Justice at The Hague and that the U.K. would have to bring the case, which it appeared unlikely to do. The court, however, criticized ITC behaviour in very blunt language and indicated that ITC had at least a "moral obligation" to pay its creditors in full.

Technology. The U.S. Bureau of Mines appeared to be accepting the view that the decade-long decline in U.S. production levels and market share in favour of less expensive products from countries with lower labour costs was probably retrievable only by means of new technology. This view was probably the most tenable approach to current strategic planning since U.S. mineral reserves would remain depleted and low-grade compared with newer overseas mines, labour costs would remain high in comparison with those of the less developed countries, and the probable profitability levels of U.S. operations were not likely to justify the investment needed to replace aging capital equipment with new technology.

Therefore, the Bureau of Mines in its *Minerals Position of the United States—1988* stated that only the vigorous imposition of new technology had the realistic possibility of allowing the U.S. to achieve the 40% gain in productivity believed necessary to preserve the present U.S. position or retrieve past achievements. The bureau focused on a variety of approaches that over the next ten years might yield such gains in productivity: (1) reduction of repetitive movements of men and matériel to and from the mine

Workers enjoy a brief chat at a gold mine site in Kalgoorlie, one of the productive new areas in Australia. Reasonable prices and new technologies in prospecting and production generated handsome profits and a corresponding gold rush.
OLIVER STREWE—WILDLIGHT

face; (2) on-site extraction and processing of ores by chemical, bacteriologic, and other means; and (3) continuous mining of hard rock faces with new cutting techniques.

Prominent among examples of new technology announced during the year were a variety of tools depending on magnetism. In February operation of the world's largest magnetic separator began at Bingham Canyon, Utah; in West Germany test and demonstration installations for the use of maglev (magnetic levitation) haulage systems for mine work were developed; and in the U.K. studies were carried out on biomagnetic separation and concentration processes, in which heavy metal ions displaying magnetic characteristics accumulate around microorganisms and can then be manipulated with magnetic fields.

(WILLIAM A. CLEVELAND)

See also Earth Sciences; Energy; Industrial Review: Gemstones; Iron and Steel.

This article updates the Macropædia article Extraction and Processing INDUSTRIES.

Motion Pictures

English-Speaking Cinema: *United States.* The most controversial U.S. film of 1988 was unquestionably *The Last Temptation of Christ,* directed by Martin Scorsese (*see* BIOGRAPHIES), a rereading of the gospel story and an examination of the human aspect of Christ. Its scenes of Christ on the cross imagining an earthly life, including love and marriage, caused a furor wherever the film was shown, boosting the box-office sales of a sober motion picture that would otherwise have had considerably less commercial potential.

Among the runaway box-office hits of the year, *Who Framed Roger Rabbit* was a triumph of animation technique, combining cartoon characters with live performers in a comedy crime story. The box-office attraction of Eddie Murphy guaranteed the financial success of *Coming to America.* Sequels of earlier box-office champions—*Rambo III* and a lacklustre *Crocodile Dundee II*—fell short of commercial expectations. Also disappointing in commercial terms was Ron Howard's *Willow,* an artfully concocted fable, synthesized out of biblical lore, fairy tales, and films ranging from *The Wizard of Oz* to *Star Wars.* The occult horror genre was pleasantly demonstrated by Tim Burton's *Beetlejuice,* about sympathetic ghosts who were trying to

drive some unpleasant humans out of the home they had loved before they died.

Among the best comedies were Catlin Adams's *Sticky Fingers,* about two impoverished women musicians who come into possession of a pile of drug loot; Dan Aykroyd's *The Couch Trip,* playing with the fine line between sanity and insanity; John Waters's *Hairspray,* a comic view of lower-middle-class mores in early 1960s Baltimore, Md.; Mike Nichols's treatment of Neil Simon's army comedy, *Biloxi Blues;* and Ron Shelton's witty evocation of minor-league baseball, *Bull Durham.* During the year there was a boom in comedies about magical return to childhood: Rod Daniel's *Like Father, Like Son,* Paul Flaherty's *18 Again,* and Brian Gilbert's updating of the Victorian novel *Vice Versa* all had grown-ups and children changing roles. Penny Marshall's charming *Big* granted a child his wish to become a man.

Notable police thrillers included Dennis Hopper's *Colors,* a well-constructed and serious treatment of community law enforcement against street gangs in Los Angeles; James B. Harris's intelligent *Cop;* and James Glickenhaus's

GAMMA/LIAISON

Roger Rabbit is handcuffed to detective Eddie Valiant, played by actor Bob Hoskins, in *Who Framed Roger Rabbit*, a humorous detective film that combines cartoon characters with live action.

Shakedown, dealing with corrupt New York police profiting from drug dealers. In Martin Brest's *Midnight Run,* Robert de Niro displayed a comic talent as a bounty hunter taking his quarry back to New York cross country.

A renewed taste for dramatized biography brought Paul Schrader's *Patty Hearst;* Clint Eastwood's fine, low-key account of the jazz virtuoso Charlie Parker, *Bird;* Francis Ford Coppola's *Tucker: The Man and His Dream,* an overly sunny rendering of the frustrations of a visionary automobile designer; and Michael Apted's *Gorillas in the Mist,* about the anthropologist Dian Fossey, who did much to save the endangered gorilla before she was brutally murdered. Historic fact was also the basis of John Sayles's *Eight Men Out,* the story of the players on the Chicago White Sox baseball team who accepted bribes to throw the 1919 World Series.

Two of the most original films of the year were Alan Rudolph's *The Moderns*—a wry, stylish comedy about American bohemians in 1920s Paris—and David Mamet's *Things Change,* a quirky and charming comedy about a gentle old shoeshine man (an exquisite performance by the octogenarian Don Ameche) mistaken for a Mafia boss. Both Jonathan Demme's *Married to the Mob* and Paul Morrissey's *Spike of Bensonhurst* also successfully turned the rituals of heavy crime to comic use.

Among the outstanding films released late in the year were Alan Parker's *Mississippi Burning,* about the murders of three civil rights workers in Mississippi in 1964; Kevin Wade's comedy *Working Girl;* Barry Levinson's *Rain Man,* describing the relationship between an opportunistic hustler and his autistic brother; Lawrence Kasdan's *The Accidental Tourist,* about an emotionally constricted travel writer; David Zucker's crime spoof *The Naked Gun;* Oliver Stone's *Talk Radio,* about a controversial talk-show host; and Richard Donner's *Scrooged,* an update of Dickens's *A Christmas Carol.* Two animated features for children were George Scribner's *Oliver & Company,* also a Dickens adaptation, and Don Bluth's *The Land Before Time.*

At the annual awards ceremony of the Academy of Motion Picture Arts and Sciences in Los Angeles in March, Bernardo Bertolucci's *The Last Emperor* won nine Oscars—for best picture, best director, best screenplay adaptation, best cinematography, best editing, best original score, best art direction, best costume design, and best sound. The awards for best actor and actress went to Michael Douglas in *Wall Street* and Cher in *Moonstruck,* which also received the award for best original screenplay, and for best supporting players to Sean Connery in *The Untouchables* and Olympia Dukakis in *Moonstruck.* The best foreign-language film was Gabriel Axel's *Babette's Feast,* from Denmark.

Great Britain. A *Fish Called Wanda,* a farcical crime story directed by the 78-year-old Ealing comedy director Charles Crichton and written by and starring John Cleese, became the biggest commercial success in the history of British cinema. Britain was again prominent at the Cannes Festival, where the Jury Grand Prix went to Chris Menges's first feature film, *A World Apart,* from an autobiographical script by Shawn Slovo about the impact of South African apartheid on the 13-year-old daughter of white liberal activists. The international critics' prize was won by Terence Davies's *Distant Voices, Still Lives,* an extraordinary, expressionist, autobiographical reminiscence of life in a poor Liverpool family during and just after World War II.

Other notable productions of the year included Christine Edzard's six-hour scrutiny of *Little Dorrit,* telling the story twice from the different viewpoints of hero and heroine; John Schlesinger's appealing and unrepentantly old-

fashioned adaptation of Bernice Rubens's novel *Madame Sousatzka,* about an eccentric but dedicated old Russian piano teacher (Shirley MacLaine); and Peter Greenaway's idiosyncratic *Drowning by Numbers,* a philosophical farce. The actor Bob Hoskins made his debut as writer-director with *The Raggedy Rawney,* an odd little antiwar fable. Ken Russell made the characteristically eccentric *Salome's Last Dance,* which had Oscar Wilde as the audience of a production of his play by the inmates of a London brothel, and subsequently directed an effective horror picture from a story by Bram Stoker (author of *Dracula*), *The Lair of the White Worm.*

A growing number of directors grappled with present-day British realities: Franco Rosso's *The Nature of the Beast* looked at the depressed industrial North through the eyes of two young boys. Martin Stellman's *For Queen and Country* painted a grim picture of present-day, inner-city Britain from the viewpoint of a black Falklands war veteran (Denzel Washington). Mike Leigh's melancholy comedy *High Hopes* perceived the divisions in contemporary society in a working-class microcosm.

New Zealand. Two major films were distinguished by exceptional visual qualities. Vincent Ward's *The Navigator* was an imaginative and vividly realized fantasy about a group of Cumbrian peasants at the time of the Black Death who magically pass through earth and time to arrive in an Australasian city of the 1980s. Leon Narbey's *Illustrious Energy* was a spectacular study of Chinese prospectors in worn-out goldfields in 1895.

Australia. John Hillcoat's horrific *Ghosts of the Civil Dead,* set in a near future, imagined the human degeneration of both convicts and guards in a dangerously overcrowded prison. Mark Joffe made a striking debut with a stylish and exciting thriller, *Grievous Bodily Harm,* with action moving from moodish stormy cityscapes to vast rural panoramas. A new fashion for horror films rooted in Aboriginal legends and curses resulted in *The Dreaming* and James Bogle's effective *Kadaicha.*

Western Europe. *France.* Production-line thrillers and comedies continued to be the staple of the film industry. One of the year's biggest successes was a superior comedy; Etienne Chatiliez's *La Vie est un long fleuve tranquille* was the story of two large families—one pious and boringly

LEHR—SIPA

Solveig Dommartin (left) and Bruno Ganz star in Wim Wenders's *Wings of Desire*, a German movie about two angels sent to observe and comfort people in West Berlin.

respectable, the other rambunctiously disreputable—who discover that, through a mistake in the maternity ward, their children were switched 15 years earlier.

A remarkable range of generations was at work in the French cinema. The famous Dutch documentarist Joris Ivens became the first nonagenarian film director in history with *Une Histoire de vent,* shot in China and blending actuality with fantasy and film history to evoke impressions of a life that spans the century. The 80-year-old Jean Delannoy returned to theatrical filmmaking for the first time since 1972 to make a reverent and pedestrian biographical movie of the peasant saint of Lourdes, *Bernadette.*

From the middle generation Claude Chabrol, in *Une Affaire de femmes,* dramatized the case of the last woman to be guillotined in France, an amateur abortionist sacrificed to Vichy-era "morality." Agnès Varda conceived an intriguing diptych of films with the actress Jane Birkin; *Jane B. par Agnes V.* was a collage portrait of the actress, and *Kung Fu Master* a light drama about the infatuation of a divorcée for her son's 14-year-old classmate. Roger Planchon, an eminent theatrical director, made his film debut at 57 with an overstylish adaptation of Molière's *Dandin.* Among younger directors, Chantal Akerman of Belgium celebrated the English poet Sylvia Plath in *Letters Home.*

West Germany. No exceptional film emerged from West Germany during the year. Werner Herzog turned Bruce Chatwin's novel *Cobra Verde* into another of his characteristic exotic sagas of white men becoming crazed and tyrannical in the far-flung lands of the old colonial world. With limited success, Reinhard Hauff adapted a stage musical, *Line 1,* set on the subway and bringing together characters from the Berlin streets and the preoccupations of the German conscience. Wim Wenders's *Wings of Desire* told of two angels observing and comforting people in West Berlin.

Italy. The outstanding film of the year and winner of the Venice Festival's Golden Lion, Ermanno Olmi's *La leggenda del santo bevitore,* adapted a story by Joseph Roth as a parable about atonement. The fiasco of the year was undisputedly Franco Zeffirelli's absurd and simplistic biography *The Young Toscanini.*

Otherwise, the principal output of the Italian studios was horror pictures, including Dario Argento's ghoulish but well-produced *Opera,* and comedies. Among the latter, Maurizio Ponzi's contemporary version of *Volpone* was light and stylish.

Scandinavia. The major Scandinavian success of the year was Bille August's *Pelle the Conqueror,* the saga of the child of a poor Swedish worker struggling to survive in Denmark in the early years of the century. A Swedish-Danish coproduction, it won the Cannes Festival Grand Prix. On the lighter side a Swedish filmmaker, Joakim Ersgard, competed with Hollywood horror with *The Visitor,* while Suzanne Osten's successful comedy *Deadly Film* was set in a film studio serving the horror trade.

From Denmark, Sigfrid Aagaard's *Tomorrow It Is Over* was a charming, low-budget comedy about a village performance of the Kaj Munk high drama *Ordet* (once filmed by Carl Theo Dreyer). Erik Clausen's *Rami og Julie* retold the *Romeo and Juliet* story through the experience of a Palestinian guest worker and a local girl. From Norway, Per Blom's *Is-slottet (Ice Palace)* was a stylish, haunting story about the friendship of two girls, one of whom dies in the ice, leaving behind the mystery of her disappearance.

Finland's lively low-budget industry offered Aki Kaurismäki's *Hamlet Goes into Business,* a wry, satirical transference of the Hamlet story into the business world of present-day Finland; and Marjaana Mykkänen's admirable documentary on the Soviet rock scene, *From Russia with Rock,* showing the problems that energetic young musicians with highly developed and critical social awareness have in gaining acceptance.

Switzerland. The most interesting Swiss films of the year were low budget and socially critical. Richard Dindo's *Dani, Michi, Renato and Max* was an unfamiliar and unflattering picture of undercurrents in aseptic Swiss society: the investigation of the deaths of four young men apparently at the hands of the Zurich police. The establishment came in for more criticism in Bernard Safarik's *Stormy Paradise,* based on a true case and showing how inhumanely bureaucracies can victimize immigrants.

Spain. Spain's biggest international success in several years was Pedro Almodóvar's *Women on the Edge of a Nervous Breakdown,* which observed, with comic irony though not without warmth, women in marital crisis. Meanwhile, Spain's most costly film to date was Carlos Saura's lavish but tedious and ill-structured tale of the Conquistador Lope de Aguirre, *El Dorado.*

Portugal. Portugal continued to offer offbeat curiosities. The veteran Manoel de Oliveira displayed an unexpected sense of comedy in a grotesque film opera, *The Cannibals,* while João Botelho's *Tempos Difíceis* was a strange, stylized updating of Dickens's novel *Hard Times* to a modern Portuguese industrial town.

Greece. One of Greece's outstanding directors, Theo Angelopoulos, returned to his finest form with *Landscape in the Mist,* a tale of two illegitimate children who set off in search of the illusory father they have been told is living somewhere in Germany. With virtuoso photography by Giorgios Arvanitis, the film achieved moments of real cinematic magic.

Eastern Europe. *U.S.S.R.* The first films made under the new freedoms of *perestroika* (social restructuring) began to emerge during the year. Vassili Pitchul's *Little Vera* proved a sensation because of its frankness about the frustrations and violence of family life in a provincial industrial city. Pavel Chukrai's *Zina, Dear Zina* highlighted corruption and sexual inequality in a provincial factory, where a solitary woman strikes for justice. Sergey Soloviov's *Assa* was a surprising and lively rock thriller set in Yalta.

Studios in some of the outlying republics offered much of the most interesting work. From Georgia, Nodar Managadze's *Hey, Maestro!* was a strange, moody tale of a talented musician who becomes a dropout, piano tuner, and unwitting social observer; from the Ukraine, Yury Ilienko's *Straw Bells* was an unsparing account of invaders and traitors during the Nazi occupation; and from Estonia came an unexpected story about a complicated love affair between a woman and a much younger man, Arvo Ikho's *Birdwatcher.*

Poland. Krzysztof Kieslowski embarked on a series of films dedicated to the Ten Commandments. The first of these were *Short Film About Killing,* a devastating account of two violent deaths—a senseless murder and an official execution; and *Short Film About Love,* a drily comic account of a young man's infatuation with a voluptuous and somewhat sadistic woman.

Hungary. The new openness of the Socialist world was displayed in some remarkable documentaries, notably Pal Schiffer and Balint Magyar's *Magyar Stories,* in which the turbulent history of postwar Hungary was witnessed through the reminiscences of seven elderly village men. The most startling documentary revelation from Hungary's past, however, was *In Keeping with the Law,* in which Gyula and Janos Gulyas interviewed survivors of the Hun-

garian labour camps of the 1950s alongside people who had been responsible for their inhuman operation.

East Germany. Lothar Warnecke's *Einer Trage des Anderen Last* (*Bear Ye One Another's Burdens*) was a predictable, simplistic, but appealing fable about tolerance—the story of a hard-line young Communist and a priest obliged to share a room in a tuberculosis sanatorium in the early 1950s. *Interrogation of the Witness* (Gunther Scholz) was an interesting murder story, the investigation unveiling a middle-class world offering only frustrations for the young people involved in a crime of passion.

Yugoslavia. The issue of the Albanian border regions and their Muslim separatists provided the subject for two of the year's best motion pictures in Yugoslavia, Srdjan Karanovic's *Film with No Title*—a complex affair of film within film and a Romeo and Juliet story—and Zarko Dragojevic's more conventional debut drama, *The House by the Railway Tracks.*

Bulgaria. The country's major commercial success, Ludmil Staikov's *Time of Violence,* was a lavish, sweeping epic about the forced Islamization of Bulgarians by Turkish invaders in the 17th century. Rangel Vulchanov's *Where Do We Go from Here?* used a contest for admission to a drama school as a comic metaphor for society at large.

Middle East. *Egypt.* A first-time director, Yousri Nasrallah made a sophisticated, mature, and poetic semiautobiographical film about a middle-class family during the years from Gamal Abdel Nasser's revolution in 1952 to the political upheavals of the 1960s.

Israel. Nadav Levitan's *Stalin's Children* was an ironic, minimal-budget film about the fortunes of three hard-line Stalinist dogmatists—cobblers on a kibbutz—in the years of disillusionment. The traumas of the continuing war continued to preoccupy filmmakers, and both Yoel Sharon's *China Ranch* and Amos Gurman's *Himo, King of Jerusalem* were set in hospital wards where soldiers suffer the aftereffects of war traumas.

Latin America. *Argentina.* The tango, Argentina's national dance, continued its tradition of providing potent metaphors in Victor Dinenzon's *Open from 6 to Midnight,* which examined the complexities of human relationships in the microcosm of an evening dance class; in Fernando Solanas's reflection upon varied fates under dictatorship,

South; and in the lighter-weight *Tango Bar,* directed by Marcos Zurinaga.

Dominica. Agliberto Melendez's assured *A One Way Ticket* was an exposé of the corrupt traffic of illegal immigrants into the U.S. It was apparently Dominica's first film production.

Asia. *India.* The new school of Indian directors continued to strive after new subjects and new styles. Adoor Gopalakrishnan's *Monologue* presented a complex portrait of a frustrated young intellectual, his story related twice from different viewpoints. Buddhadeb Dasgupta's *Phera* was a stylish, atmospheric story of an aristocratic old stage artist, living in mournful, drunken, misanthropic disillusionment but retrieved by the friendship of a small boy. *Portrait of a Life,* a debut feature by Raja Mitra, made compulsive viewing out of a story of an academic obsession, a poor teacher who sets out to write the first Bengali dictionary and succeeds at the cost of his family, health, and, eventually, life.

Another first-time director, Mira Nair, adventurously shot her story of street children, *Salaam Bombay,* on actual locations and with the street children themselves. This highly accomplished film won the *Caméra d'Or* as best first film at the Cannes Festival.

Japan. Among the few notable productions of the year, Kiju Yoshida's *Onimaru* was an interesting, if somewhat passionless, attempt to translate *Wuthering Heights* to medieval Japan. *Door,* directed and co-written by Banmei Takahashi, was an effective psychological horror story about a woman terrorized by a door-to-door salesman. A sequel to the previous box-office success of director Juzo Itami (*see* BIOGRAPHIES), *Return of a Taxing Woman* was a morality tale in which a female tax investigator is pitted against racketeering entrepreneurs.

China. The new generation of Chinese directors continued to produce films of variety and quality. One of the best movies of the year, however, was the veteran Xie Jin's (Hsieh Chin's) *Hibiscus Town,* a saga (three hours in its full version) of the sufferings and privations of simple people—and the indestructibility of party dogmatists—through the purges, the Cultural Revolution, and beyond.

Zhang Yimou's (Chang Yi-mou's) *Red Sorghum* took the major prize at the Berlin Festival. A haunting saga of

PHOTOS, AP/WIDE WORLD

Willem Dafoe (centre), left, comforts children in his role as Jesus Christ in *The Last Temptation of Christ.* The movie drew widespread criticism from Christian activists, above, for its portrayal of Christ as a man tormented by earthly desires.

the Chinese countryside before and during the Japanese occupation, it moved smoothly and skillfully from a lyrical opening to a horrific finale of atrocities and killing. In *Far from the War,* a woman director, Hu Mei, showed an army veteran and "ideal" Communist experiencing problems fitting into unregimented civil life. Zhang Zeming's (Chang Tse-ming's) *Sun and Rain* was an innovation in that it dealt with the private lives of unremarkable contemporary young people. Perhaps the most surprising film to emerge from China, however, was *A Dead Man Visits the Living,* in which a young artist and the ghost of her dead lover tour the country in search of his murderess and discover a society that is far from ideal or idealistic.

Hong Kong. Ann Hui, previously known for modern dramas, made a spectacular two-part epic of the Ming Dynasty, *The Romance of Book and Sword.* The runaway success of the year, however, was Stanley Kwan's *Rouge,* a period (1900) ghost story involving a prostitute and a rich young man.

Taiwan. Now established as the country's most gifted director, Hou Hsiao-hsien chronicled the misadventures of a working-class urban family in *Daughter of the Nile,* a film of effortless elegance and subdued feeling. With *Rouge of the North,* the story of a woman's life in the oppressive society of the period between 1910 and 1935, Fred Tan established himself as a new director of considerable skill and understanding.

Africa. The first motion picture ever made in Guinea-Bissau, Flora Gomes's *Mortu Nega* was an ambitious panorama of the country's history from the war of independence against Portugal to the present day. The first Madagascan film, *Tabataba,* by Raymond Rajaonarivelo, told the story of a village's doubtful preparations for an event they hardly understood, the insurrection against the French in 1947.

The veteran Senegalese director Ousmane Sembene directed the masterly *The Camp of Thiaroye,* in coproduction with Algeria and Tunisia. An indictment of French colonialism, it recreated a real event in World War II in which the French authorities attempted to cheat black soldiers returning from the front of money due to them and met the threat of their rebellion with a massacre of the camp.

(DAVID ROBINSON)

Nontheatrical Motion Pictures. *Danish Symphonie* took top honours among nontheatrical films in 1988, capturing the Grand Prix at the prestigious International Industrial Film and Video Congress held in Dublin and the Best of Festival at Chicago's U.S. Industrial Film & Video Festival. Produced for the Copenhagen Handelsbank by Nordisk Film Commercial with P. G. Iinde as producer, the film promoted Danish exports.

At the American Film Festival in New York City, a Canadian National Film Board production, *To a Safer Place,* won the coveted Emily Award. In a sensitive story the film showed the healing of wounds of incest in a woman, the survivor.

Several U.S. scientific films captured high honours. At London's British Medical Festival, *The Cat That Drank and Used Too Much* won the Gold Award. Taking a positive approach to addiction, denial, and recovery, it was produced by FMS Productions, Santa Barbara, Calif.

A film by the Moody Institute of Science in Whittier, Calif., *Journey of Life,* was awarded the diploma of honour at the Beijing Scientific Festival in China. Time-lapse and high-speed cinematography were used to show the intricate propagation of plants. (THOMAS W. HOPE)

See also Photography; Television and Radio.
This article updates the *Macropædia* article MOTION PICTURES.

Museums

Museums during the year continued to face the need to balance economic demands and a lack of funds against their educational and public goals. On the one hand, museums had never been so popular; it was estimated that 75 million visitors had attended museums in the United Kingdom in 1987, and the projection for 1988 was 80 million. Changes in government policies, however, made funding more difficult as grants and subsidies were reduced. In the United States federal arts funding in 1988 included $21.9 million to the Institute for Museum Services, $37.4 million to the National Gallery of Art, and $230.2 million to the Smithsonian Institution. In Britain the Arts Council raised overall spending as part of a new three-year program that made some grants dependent on the ability of museums to raise funds. Bequests from affluent benefactors were also not sufficient. In addition, changes in U.S. and British tax laws did not encourage donors to give money or works of art to museums; owners of such works had more incentive to sell them at auction, pay the tax, and pocket the difference.

Corporate sponsorship remained an important area of funding, but the emphasis by corporations was more on loan exhibitions than on donations for general museum purposes. Many museums had introduced controversial admission fees or encouraged voluntary contributions for admission. Museum sales of books, posters, calendars, and souvenir items had also increased, and at some museums the sale of works from their collections was under discussion.

In London the Victoria and Albert Museum, which had

AP/WIDE WORLD

A curator from the Egyptian Antiquities Organization studies a 3,000-year-old board game from the Râmses II exhibit on display at the Boston Museum of Science.

It was announced in 1988 that the country house of Soviet author Boris Pasternak was to be a memorial museum. Pasternak was expelled from the Soviet Writers' Union after his novel *Doctor Zhivago* was published in the West in 1956, but he was posthumously reinstated in 1987.

PHIL TAUBMAN—THE NEW YORK TIMES

suffered since the introduction in 1985 of voluntary entrance charges, considered boosting attendance with major loan exhibitions, which had been discontinued in 1984. The British Museums Association designated 1989 as Museum Year and launched a five-year campaign to help local museums generate income.

The most significant new museum of 1988 was the National Gallery of Canada, which opened in Ottawa in May. The first permanent structure for its art collection, the $133 million granite and glass building was clearly celebratory, with 12,000 sq m (130,000 sq ft) of exhibition space, a 37-m (120-ft)-long Great Hall, and a silhouette intended to complement the nearby Canadian Parliament building. The Montreal Museum of Fine Arts launched a campaign to raise $25 million toward a new building. The federal and provincial governments each had already pledged $25 million.

The Art Institute of Chicago opened its new south wing, the Daniel F. and Ada L. Rice Building, in September. The $23 million, 12,000-sq m extension added 32% more space to the museum, and the 1,800-sq m (19,400-sq ft) Regenstein Hall could accommodate 700 visitors every half hour for special exhibitions. In Minnesota the Minneapolis Sculpture Garden, a 3-ha (7.5-ac), $12 million open-air facility, opened adjacent to the Walker Art Center. The Walters Art Gallery in Baltimore, Md., reopened its original 1904 building after extensive renovation.

The Massachusetts legislature passed a $35 million funding bill to establish the Massachusetts Museum of Modern Art in Williamstown. Meanwhile, in Roslyn Harbor, N.Y., friction led to an unprecedented call for the 13-year-old public Nassau County Museum of Fine Art to be turned over to a private, nonprofit group of administrators.

In New York City several museums appeared to have solved persistent problems. The long-time controversy over the removal of the Museum of the American Indian from inadequate quarters in upper Manhattan seemed close to a solution. Many of those involved reached a compromise in April that would move the museum to the downtown Custom House, which the federal government had recently renovated for $35 million. The Bronx Museum of the Arts completed a $5.8 million renovation project. The Pierpont Morgan Library purchased an adjacent brownstone mansion; the expansion would double the museum's available space. The medieval collection of the Metropolitan Mu-

seum of Art, housed in a complex of buildings called the Cloisters, celebrated its 50th anniversary by opening a renovated ground-floor treasury room. In its mid-Manhattan quarters, the Met opened its $8 million ancient Chinese art gallery.

In July it was revealed that the 184-year-old New York Historical Society, the first museum chartered in the state, had been the victim of major financial and administrative mismanagement. Its endowment had been depleted, and hundreds of objects had deteriorated owing to neglect.

On the West Coast petroleum executive Armand Hammer announced in January that his prestigious art collection, valued at $250 million and long promised to the Los Angeles County Museum of Art, would instead be placed in a new $30 million Hammer Museum of Art and Cultural Center under construction in Los Angeles. The Los Angeles County Museum of Art opened its Pavilion for Japanese Art, the fifth building in the museum complex, to house the Shin'enkan collection of scrolls and screen paintings, a gift of the Oklahoma collector Joe D. Price, who also donated $5 million toward construction costs. The Museum of Art in Santa Monica, Calif., opened in a newly renovated commercial building, which the museum would be permitted to purchase within seven years at half its market value.

In Edinburgh a major refurbishment of the Royal Museum of Scotland was completed, and the reopening in August of the first renovated gallery was devoted to a display of European decorative arts, 1200–1800. The Tate Gallery in London, under its new director, Nicholas Serota (*see* BIOGRAPHIES), opened its first provincial outpost in May with a museum in a previously derelict dock area of Liverpool. The Museum of the Moving Image opened in London in September and provided a detailed and complete account of the development of the moving image, from the early Chinese shadow play to television by satellite.

The first Italian museum devoted exclusively to modern art opened in Prato in June. The museum planned to build a permanent collection by purchasing works from the temporary exhibitions. In Paris the controversial pyramid in the front courtyard of the Louvre was dedicated in March.

(JOSHUA KIND; SANDRA MILLIKIN)

See also Art Exhibitions and Art Sales.
This article updates the *Macropædia* article MUSEUMS.

Music

Classical. In a world where truly to be a star meant being called either Madonna or Springsteen, it might be thought extraordinary—astonishing even—to find an essentially classical musician being honoured with the kind of enthusiasm more often reserved for such phenomena as the "heavy metal" troubadours of contemporary rock. When the classical musician in question was the multitalented Leonard Bernstein, however, the plaudits seemed less unexpected. "Lenny" (as he had long been known to fans worldwide) in 1988 celebrated his 70th birthday, looking and sounding 15 years younger. As the year progressed, he followed a schedule of visits and guest appearances that might have caused people half his age to blanch.

Individual strands of the maestro's peregrinations were finally drawn together at the 1988 Tanglewood Summer Festival in the Berkshire Hills of Massachusetts. The festival welcomed Bernstein as the guest of honour at a birthday celebration beamed to television stations throughout the world. New York City Opera general director Beverly Sills was the host of the evening's entertainment, which included such guest performers as cellists Yo-Yo Ma and Mstislav Rostropovich, the outstanding 16-year-old Japanese violinist Midori, and mezzo-soprano Christa Ludwig. The memorable evening concluded with the assembled company joining in a quietly moving performance of the closing scene from Bernstein's musical *Candide.* The celebration ended several days later with Bernstein himself taking the Boston Symphony through a Sunday afternoon birthday prom that included a performance of Tchaikovsky's Fifth Symphony as electrifying as any that even hardened followers of Tanglewood, the Boston Symphony, and Bernstein could remember.

Losses to the world of music in 1988 included those of cellist André Navarra; composers Adrian Cruft, Kenneth Leighton, Kaikhosru Sorabji, and William Wordsworth; conductors Antal Doráti and Yevgeny Mravinsky; harpists Martine Geliot and Lily Laskine; mezzo-soprano Annelies Burmeister; oboist Léon Goossens; opera designer and director Jean-Pierre Ponnelle; pianists Yury Egorov (a sadly premature victim of AIDS), Monique Haas, Ernest Lush, and Solomon; scholars Gerald Abraham and Hans Heinz Stuckenschmidt; sopranos Hilde Gueden and Irmgard Seefried; tenor James McCracken; and violinists Manoug Parikian and Henryk Szeryng. (*See* OBITUARIES.)

Symphonic and Instrumental. One of the year's most fascinating, some would argue important, premieres occurred more than 150 years after the composer's death. For the last ten years of his life, Ludwig van Beethoven had steadily accumulated sketches for what was to have been a final, tenth symphony. As he lay on his deathbed in Vienna in 1827, he had been intensely moved by the generosity of the Philharmonic Society in London and promised them, when he was well, this same tenth symphony.

When Beethoven died, the symphony was thought lost to posterity, the composer's sketchbooks containing little more than a few random jottings. By the time Brian Newbould, a professor from England's University of Durham, was putting the finishing touches to his impressive, if inevitably speculative, completion of Schubert's similarly unfinished Tenth Symphony, a second richly talented British academic, Barry Cooper of Aberdeen (Scotland) University, had already begun reassessing the evidence in libraries and private collections throughout Europe concerning Beethoven's Tenth.

His near-sensational conclusion was that although

The Eurythmics play to a capacity crowd during a benefit concert in which pop musicians gathered for a ten-hour 70th-birthday tribute to jailed South African antiapartheid leader Nelson Mandela.
AP/WIDE WORLD

Beethoven had not to any substantial degree progressed beyond sketches for the symphony's first movement, enough linked material did exist to re-create, at least in outline, that portion of the lost work. The finished score, some three-quarters of which could be attributed entirely to Beethoven and the remainder to Cooper, was finally premiered at London's Royal Festival Hall by Walter Weller and the Royal Liverpool Philharmonic Orchestra, creating a considerable stir in both academic and lay circles. It was believed that Beethoven, a celebrated reviser and refiner, would have made many changes to his sketches. What mattered, however, was that Cooper's completion actually *sounded* like Beethoven, the unexpected key scheme that he employed in particular having the undoubted stamp of authenticity.

A tighter performance than that heard at the London concert was subsequently committed to disc by Wynn Morris and no less a body than the prestigious London Symphony. The liner notes were in the form of a detailed, illustrated lecture by Cooper that enabled even the musically uneducated listener to reach his or her own conclusions and to hear at first hand precisely what secrets Beethoven's battered sketchbooks had yielded up after a century or more of silence.

In the U.S. the single most satisfying development on the symphonic front in the 1980s was conductor Herbert Blomstedt's appointment as music director of San Francisco's hitherto modestly regarded symphony orchestra. A musician of the old school—the antithesis of the whiz-kid baton twirlers whose stars so often blink and fail within months of their being appointed to positions of musical power—Blomstedt declared that his aim was to hone the San Francisco Symphony Orchestra to the highest European standards of warmth and unforced musicality while at the same time preserving the orchestra's superbly American pizzazz. An important London-Decca recording contract soon followed, and a number of exciting projects were announced, among them a full three-disc cycle of Danish composer Carl Nielsen's six symphonies.

Less happily, a number of British orchestras in 1988

suffered major defections and other problems. While André Previn's disagreements with London's Sir Thomas
Beecham-founded Royal Philharmonic Orchestra were not
terminal, it was felt advisable to retain his services in
a more titular manner and appoint pianist-conductor
Vladimir Ashkenazy in effect as his day-to-day successor. Elsewhere in the U.K., Michael Tilson Thomas, one-
time music director of the Buffalo (N.Y.) Philharmonic
Orchestra, moved to London and the city's London Symphony Orchestra. In sad contrast, the orchestra Sir John
Barbirolli left the New York Philharmonic Symphony in
1941 to save, Manchester's long-established Hallé Orchestra, suffered grave financial difficulties despite the efforts
of its fine conductor, Stanislaw Skrowaczewski, one-time
music director of the Minnesota Orchestra, and desperately
needed further support if it was to thrive into the 1990s.

Opera. Few young composers or musicians, amateur or
professional, active in the last decades of the 19th century
failed to be dazzled by the extraordinarily potent music
dramas of German master Richard Wagner. Many in their
maturity still fought to throw off Wagner's all-pervasive
harmonic influence. Others became "Perfect Wagnerites"
of the most fanatic kind, occasionally with disastrous results, and the master's operatic dramas and distasteful racial
theories (Wagner had been a lifelong anti-Semite) attracted
some appalling extramusical camp followers. Throughout
the 1930s Nazi Chancellor Adolf Hitler and his entourage
had been regular visitors to the all-Wagner Bayreuth Festival, but after 1945 Wagner's music, especially the *Ring*
cycle of four operas, inevitably fell into neglect.

It was remarkable then that in 1988 Wagner's music,
mercifully shorn of its political associations, was heard and
seen almost everywhere. Tied to a long-term recording
project, New York's Metropolitan Opera lavished much
time and energy on a James Levine-conducted survey of
the fabulous (and fabulously huge) *Ring* tetralogy. In Munich, West Germany, Sir Bernard Haitink was busily ta-
ping (as part of a recording contract) stage performances of
the same four operas in association with Bavarian Radio.
In Bayreuth itself the annual summer *Wagnerfest* regaled
its audience with, rather less than surprisingly, yet another
Ring, in this case in a thoroughly controversial expressionist production by Harry Kupfer. The cool, Corbusier-
like productions seen at Bayreuth during the 1950s and
1960s, with Wagner's grandsons in artistic control, had
been generally considered too spartan in concept and dramatic effect. Faced with Wagner *à l'avant-garde,* numerous
operagoers now spoke of a return to, if not the good old
days, at least a more aesthetically pleasant, arguably less
ambitious, approach to the master's mythic strivings.

Elsewhere, Claudio Abbado's tenure at Vienna's troubled State Opera got off to a promising start with a
critically acclaimed naturalistic production of Alban Berg's
still startling *Wozzeck.* The only real concern was how
well and for how long Abbado would survive the vendettas
and intrigues that remained as much a part of Viennese
musical life in 1988 as they were a century and more ago.
As Abbado's immediate predecessor, Lorin Maazel, wryly
put it, "If I were an insurance salesman I wouldn't offer
policies to anyone holding that job."

Among Europe's smaller opera companies, special palms
were again awarded to the Lyon (France) Opera, where a
lively regime headed by the English-born music director
John Eliot Gardiner continued to explore the byways of
19th-century French opera, unearthing on the way such
delights as André Messager's long-forgotten but exquisite
Fortunio. In England similar praise was garnered by the
enterprising managers of English National Opera North,

a traveling company active in the country's northern and
central regions, whose repertoire stretched from Mozart
and Tchaikovsky to Janacek's *Jenufa* and Prokofiev's as-
tringently entertaining *The Love for Three Oranges.*

Albums and Technical Developments. At a time when
the laser-read compact disc was busily consolidating its position as the world's leading music carrier, it was interesting
to note that, in marketing terms, the new *Wunderteknik*
had come about almost accidentally. As long ago as 1967,
electrical engineers at the Philips Co.'s experimental research station at Eindhoven, Neth., had been exploring
the possibilities of creating a viable, mass production laser-
read disc system. At the time, such discs were regarded as
having a primarily visual (that is, video) application. However, the first "laserdiscs," which combined digital sound
and vision, proved to be a costly commercial failure. In
1988 the technology was revived with the launch in Europe
of compact disc video (CDV), essentially a reintroduction
of the laserdisc but one that was concentrating wisely on
strictly musical subject matter and conforming to a brilliant technical dual standard whereby, armed with one of
the new-generation "two-play" CD decks, the consumer
could play CDVs on the same player as the regular sound-
only CDs.

Whether consumers were any more likely to become
hooked on the CDV than on the laserdisc remained to
be seen. Initial omens were mixed, with software costs remaining prohibitively high and the 30-cm (12-in)-diameter
discs—the same size, ironically, as the old long-playing
phonograph record—causing storage headaches for those
living in small homes or apartments.

Meanwhile, the sound-only compact disc went from
strength to strength as the vast majority of new classical
recordings appeared immediately on CD and back-catalog
reissues enriched the laser repertoire monthly. A particular breakthrough came with the decision by Angel-EMI
to launch the hitherto LP-only, Paris-sourced *Références*
series of archive recordings on CD, with sonic results that
could only be described as spectacular. A degree of surface
scratching permitting, old phonograph classics emerged, if
not like new, then easily as good as decent radio transmission of the early 1950s.

As the year drew to a close, a further point in favour of
the CD had become apparent, the music-per-dollar factor.
A very few dollars could buy more than an hour's music,
flawlessly reproduced on a single wear-proof disc. Many in
the industry envisioned an 80- and even 90-minute CD,
all at no extra cost.   (NICHOLAS HARPER)

Jazz. In 1988 Charlie Parker, the brilliant alto saxophonist who died in 1955 at the age of 34, received more
publicity than had ever come his way during his turbulent
life. This was due to *Bird,* a biographical film produced
and directed by Clint Eastwood. Hailed by some critics as
the best U.S. feature film with a jazz theme but less warmly
received by musicians and fans with firsthand knowledge of
Parker, *Bird* was most remarkable, from a musical standpoint, for the technological sleight-of-hand employed on its
sound track. In a complex process solos by Parker from his
recorded performances were isolated sonically from their
accompaniment. Then, while listening to Parker's playing
through headphones, prominent jazz musicians (a few of
whom had actually worked with Parker) overdubbed new
backgrounds in up-to-date sound. The result was eerie;
as star Forest Whitaker mimed Parker's playing, the saxophonist's sound emerged authentic but muffled, while
the new accompaniment seemed oddly askew. The film
spawned a host of reissues of vintage Parker recordings
and newly recorded tributes. A standout among these was

the boxed set of ten compact discs, *The Complete Charlie Parker on Verve;* featuring the best in modern sound restoration, it proved that, given equal attention, authentic Parker recordings could readily have been used in *Bird* in their entirety without resort to expensive and elaborate tricks.

Also celebrated during the year was Duke Ellington. In April the Smithsonian Institution's National Museum of American History announced its purchase, with the aid of a special congressional appropriation, of more than 3,000 pieces of music, film and television scripts, unissued recordings, business records, photographs, scrapbooks, and other memorabilia from the Ellington estate. The Ellington collection was to be housed in the museum's Archive Center and would be, it was announced, available for research in 1989. The continued viability of Ellington's music was demonstrated by the performance (and subsequent studio recording) of the composer's longest work, *Black, Brown and Beige,* in a newly revised edition at the JVC Jazz Festival in New York, and by a tribute concert at that city's Lincoln Center, which included the first live performance of Ellington's suite *Such Sweet Thunder.* The concert was part of a new annual series, "Classical Jazz at Lincoln Center," marking the first time that this prestigious cultural institution had placed its imprimatur on a jazz event.

Also conferring cultural prestige on jazz was the publication of *The New Grove Dictionary of Jazz,* a two-volume, 1,260-page cornucopia of reference information on almost all aspects of the music. Though criticized in some quarters for being overly concerned with academic classification and pigeonholing, the work no doubt was a milestone in scholarly research.

The Lincoln Center series also honoured drummer-composer Max Roach, but this was overshadowed by a jazz "first" scored by Roach. He became the recipient of the most coveted award in the arts and sciences, a MacArthur Foundation Fellowship. With no strings attached, the fellowships offer the recipient complete financial security for a period of years.

The international character of jazz was highlighted by frequent visits to the U.S. by foreign musicians. The Italian composer and pianist Giorgio Gaslini took a quintet to the Chicago Jazz Festival, which was celebrating its tenth birthday. The JVC New York Festival devoted a night to French jazz, featuring the brilliant pianist Martial Solal and avant-garde multi-instrumentalist Michel Portal. In addition, groups of Soviet jazzmen performed their own music and then joined forces in a jam session with U.S. friends at New York City's Village Gate—a taste of *glasnost* in Manhattan.

It was in another borough of New York City, Brooklyn, that stirrings of innovation were heard in 1988. A number of young jazz artists of note resided in Brooklyn, as did practitioners of other contemporary forms of Afro-American music. Having joined forces more or less informally, they felt ready to unveil some of the results in early December at the Brooklyn Academy of Music, under the name of M-Base. The group included saxophonists Steve Coleman and Greg Osby, pianist Geri Allen, and singer Cassandra Wilson. The Brooklyn phenomenon may or may not have been the long-awaited next wave of innovation in jazz, but it was interesting to note that such waves in the past had always had a community base. Other noted jazz players living in Brooklyn included saxophonist Branford Marsalis, trombonist Robin Eubanks, and bassist Kevin Bruce Harris.

The year took its toll of jazz talent, and deaths included arranger-composer Gil Evans (*see* OBITUARIES); tenor saxophonists Al Cohn, Warne Marsh, and Charlie Rouse; drummers Ray Bauduc, J. C. Heard, Dannie Richmond, and Sam Woodyard; and trumpeters Chet Baker and Billy Butterfield. Two notable arrangers who helped set the pace for the swing era died: Sy Oliver (*see* OBITUARIES), who wrote for Jimmie Lunceford and Tommy Dorsey, and Horace Henderson, a pianist, writer, and bandleader whose career paralleled but was overshadowed by that of his older brother Fletcher. Charles Delaunay, father of jazz discography, cofounder of the first record label devoted entirely to jazz (the French *Swing,* in 1937), founding editor of the periodical *Jazz Hot,* discoverer and biographer of guitarist Django Reinhardt, and founder of the Hot Club de France also died, as did Robert Donaldson Darrell, one of the first U.S. music critics to write perceptively about jazz, and the prominent British jazz critic Albert McCarthy.

Among the year's crop of jazz books, the autobiography of veteran bassist Milt Hinton, *Bass Line,* illustrated with the author's fine photographs, and Gary Giddins's *Satchmo,* a lavishly presented biography of Louis Armstrong, stood out.   (DAN M. MORGENSTERN)

Popular. During 1988 pop musicians became involved in political causes on a grander scale than ever before, and female singers, African music, and Irish styles gained

ROBERT R. McELROY—WOODFIN CAMP & ASSOCIATES

Sarah Reese (left), John Moulson (centre), and Igor Morozov perform in the opera *Dead Souls,* a new work by the Soviet composer Rodion Shchedrin.

prominence. An event that brought much of this together was the 70th birthday tribute concert for South African black nationalist Nelson Mandela, held at London's Wembley Stadium on June 11 and watched by a television audience of literally hundreds of millions throughout the world.

Live Aid (which raised money for the African famine) had been held at the same stadium three years earlier, with a parallel concert in Philadelphia, but it was never as directly political as this demand that the South African authorities free one of the world's best-known political prisoners as a major step in the dismantling of the apartheid system. The concert attracted such major stars as Whitney Houston, Dire Straits, Stevie Wonder, Sting, and Eurythmics, but it was most remarkable for its range of popular music. There were soul artists, rap artists, reggae artists, and African musicians, as well as collaborations between different groups. When the laid-back (but highly political) U.S. star Jackson Browne performed with musicians from West Africa and Jamaica, it was clear that the event was also a reflection of the growing spirit of internationalism in popular music.

Such idealism was reflected in the second major pop-political event of the year, Amnesty International's Human Rights Now! tour, in which five performers, including Bruce Springsteen, Sting, and Peter Gabriel, embarked on an unprecedented six-week series of concerts from London to Buenos Aires, Arg., via cities in Europe, Africa, Asia, and the Americas. The aim was to encourage worldwide support for the human rights organization and publicize the fact that this was the 40th anniversary of the UN's adoption of the Universal Declaration of Human Rights. When the tour reached Harare, Zimbabwe (where the show was dedicated to Nelson Mandela and to murdered black activist Steven Biko), Springsteen urged the many white South Africans in the audience not to join the Army "in a country at war with itself."

The impact of consciousness-raising (as opposed to money-raising) events is hard to judge but, inevitably, the show also had a commercial impact—particularly on the career of one black U.S. singer taking part. Tracy Chapman (*see* BIOGRAPHIES) was little known when she appeared at the Mandela show, but although she was a soloist armed only with an acoustic guitar, she faced the vast worldwide audience as confidently as if she were singing in a small club—then faced them again when she was asked to fill a gap in the proceedings after part of Stevie Wonder's equipment had been stolen. A few weeks earlier she had been playing to tiny audiences on the folk circuit, but by capturing the mood of the Mandela show, she almost instantly became a major star.

Chapman's was the most remarkable success story of a good year for new female singers, which also included Toni Childs and Debbie Gibson in the U.S. and Philadelphia expatriate Gail Ann Dorsey, Mica Paris, and Tanita Tikaram in Britain. Whitney Houston (whose "One Moment in Time" provided the theme for one U.S. network's coverage of the Olympic Games) remained the most popular female performer, though the classiest recording of the year was by Detroit soul star Anita Baker, with *Giving You the Best That I Got,* her long-awaited follow-up to the best-selling *Rapture.*

Appearing alongside Chapman at both the Mandela and Amnesty shows was the Senegalese singer Youssou N'Dour, whose presence indicated a second trend of the year—the growing popularity of African styles. Like many West African musicians, N'Dour had launched his career in the West in Paris, a city with a large African population

that had become a mecca for African musicians and those wanting to study the music.

Talking Heads, an inventive white U.S. band, traveled to Paris to record their new album, *Naked,* and were helped by Mory Kante from Mali, an exponent of the kora, an instrument that is a cross between a harp and a lute. Kante's own furious dance song "Ye Ke Ye Ke" became a massive hit in France, where he was now treated as a major celebrity. So too was Johnny Clegg, leader of the multiracial South African band Savuka, whose albums topped the French best-seller lists while he was still trying to establish his reputation elsewhere in the world. In the U.S. one of his antiapartheid songs was covered by Joan Baez, but in Britain he was expelled from the British Musicians Union because, as a British-born musician, he refused to stop working in South Africa—despite his multiracial band and political stance.

Clegg, the most successful South African of the year, was unable to appear at the Mandela show as a result of the expulsion. Also missing from both this and the Amnesty events, despite their high-profile work in both fields, were U2, the Irish group that had become firmly established as the most popular rock band in the world, with a vast following in the U.S. after the release of their album *The Joshua Tree* in 1987. They spent much of 1988 working on a new double album, *Rattle And Hum.*

The fashion for Irish music was also helped by a rousing album from the London Irish folk-punk group The Pogues, *If I Should Fall from Grace with God,* which showed that they had developed musical skills to match their wild energy. The finest Irish music of the year was provided by a collaboration between two very different Irish stars. Van Morrison, the "Belfast cowboy" famous for his "Celtic soul," performed and recorded with Ireland's best-known traditional instrumental band, The Chieftains, and the result was a refreshing, often startling treatment of well-known folk songs.

Morrison's renewed success reflected the continued interest in pop music heroes from the 1960s. Keith Richards of the Rolling Stones released his first-ever solo LP— which revealed that his guitar work was far better than his singing—and so did the Beach Boys' Brian Wilson, whose excellent new songs sounded as if they could have been written in the '60s. Other veterans still doing well included Steve Winwood, who was particularly successful in the U.S. with his LP *Roll with It,* and Pink Floyd.

George Michael, formerly with Wham!, scored a major solo success with *Faith,* as did the Australian band INXS with *Kick* and Michael Jackson with *Bad.* Heavy Metal groups continued to enjoy wide popularity, among them Def Leppard, Guns N' Roses, Ron Jovi, and Metallica.

(ROBIN DENSELOW)

See also Dance; Motion Pictures; Television and Radio; Theatre.

This article updates the *Macropædia* article The History of Western MUSIC.

Philately and Numismatics

Stamps. The market in quality stamps and postal history continued strong throughout 1988. With the support of the British Post Office and those of Jersey, Guernsey, and the Isle of Man, the Stamp Publicity Board (formerly the Stamp Collecting Promotion Council) launched its first major exhibition, Stampway to the World, held in Liverpool and designed to appeal to collectors and noncollectors of all ages. It was linked to the annual congress of the British

Four ornately carved carousel animals grace the block of new 25¢ stamps issued by the U.S. Postal Service, announcing October as National Stamp Collecting Month.

U.S. POSTAL SERVICE

Philatelic Federation, held in Liverpool in September to mark the centenary of the Liverpool Philatelic Society. Two collectors signed the Roll of Distinguished Philatelists at the congress: Geral J. Ellott of New Zealand, author of *New Zealand Postal Routes and Rates pre-1874*, and Paul H. Jensen of Norway, president of the Federation of Norwegian Philatelic Societies. The BPF Congress Medal for 1988 was awarded to C. Angus Parker. In an exceptional move, America's premier award, the Lichtenstein Medal, went to a British subject, John B. Marriott, keeper of the Royal Philatelic Collections at Buckingham Palace.

The auction market, concentrated in Great Britain and the U.S., continued to be active. Among the best realizations for single items were £52,800 for an 1854 Indian 4 annas inverted head error, cut to shape and fine used (Harmers of London, at whose salesroom this identical stamp was sold for £725 in 1954); £15,400 for a newly discovered Dockwra "PENNY/POST/PAID" letter of 1681 (Christie's/Robson Lowe, London); and $33,000 for a U.S. 1861 90 cents blue used with a 24 cents brown-lilac on cover (Christie's/Robson Lowe, New York) from the Augustine Heard correspondence. Important one-country collections sold included the Rhodesia "Double Heads" collection of Robert Gibbs of Saratoga, Calif. (Sotheby, London); at the same sale, a complete set of 22 black and white die proofs from the Waterlow archives made £78,100.

One and a half years after his arrest and release on bail, William Raife Wellsted, former curator of the National Postal Museum, London, was sentenced in November 1987 to two years' imprisonment after pleading guilty to charges of stealing stamps worth £27,000 from the museum and to false representation concerning a receipt for £1,500 issued on behalf of the museum.

Three major Fédération Internationale de Philatélie (FIP) international exhibitions were held between October 1987 and September 1988. Major awards were: at HAFNIA 87 in Copenhagen, the FIP Grand Prix d'Honneur to Rolf-Dieter Jaretzky (West Germany) for his specialized collection of Braunsweig (Brunswick), the Grand Prix International to Ronald A. G. Lee (Great Britain) for Cape of Good Hope, and the Grand Prix National to Peter Meyer (Denmark) for a study of Danish West Indies (now the U.S. Virgin Islands) issues; at FINLANDIA 88 in Helsinki, Fin., the FIP Grand Prix d'Honneur to Jaretzky for U.S. postmaster, carrier, and local stamps, the Grand Prix International to Guiseppe Barcella (Italy) for Parma 1856–60, and the Grand Prix National to Hiroyuki Kanai (Japan) for classic issues of Finland; at PRAGA 88 in Prague, Czech., the FIP Grand Prix d'Honneur to Albert Fillinger (France) for French armies of Louis XIV to Charles X, the Grand Prix International to Zbigniew Milkulski (Switz.) for imperial Russia, and the Grand Prix National to Fred W. Heffer (West Germany) for Czechoslovakia 1918–39.

(KENNETH F. CHAPMAN)

Coins and Paper Money. Canada's "maple leaf" was expected to capture at least half of the international market for gold bullion coins during 1988, despite strong competition from similar items issued by other nations. The Royal Canadian Mint estimated that sales of 1988-dated maple leafs could total approximately 1.4 million troy ounces of gold, worth at least Can$700 million. The maple leaf had become one of Canada's best-known export items. Other gold coins traded worldwide included the U.S. American eagle, the Mexican 50 pesos, and two newcomers from 1987—the Australian nugget and the U.K.'s Britannia.

In late summer Australia became the first large nation to market a bullion coin made of platinum; investors called the new issue the "koala." Canada followed suit by introducing a platinum—as well as a silver—maple leaf in November. The silver piece would compete with the silver American eagle, which had been the world's best-selling silver bullion coin since 1986. South Korea promoted the last of 24 coins commemorating the 1988 Summer Olympics in Seoul. Earlier, Canada had completed an 11-coin program honouring the Winter Olympics in Calgary. Other governments also minted 1988-dated Olympic coinage; for example, the U.S. sold two types of such commemoratives to raise millions of dollars for the training of U.S. athletes.

Legislation in the U.S. Congress calling for new designs on circulating coinage failed to become law in 1988, in large part because the chairman of the House subcommittee considering the measure believed the public did not want them. In August the Treasury said it would need more time to study the effect of another bill calling for new $1 coins to replace $1 Federal Reserve notes. Some experts said the change would save the government at least $50 million a year because a coin would last much longer in circulation than a paper dollar, but the Treasury said it wanted to conduct market research to determine whether people would use the coin. The Bank of England's one-pound paper note ceased to be legal tender in March, forcing British citizens to use a one-pound coin first issued in 1983. Canada announced it would no longer print a $1 note after June 30, 1989; a new dollar coin entered circulation in Canada in 1987. In The Netherlands a five-guilder coin replaced a five-guilder note, and Australia made plans to introduce a $2 coin and phase out its $2 bill. Australia already had a circulating $1 coin.

Rare-coin prices increased 14% in the 12 months ended June 1, according to a Wall Street securities firm, while a survey by the hobby newspaper *Coin World* indicated that

the market advanced a more modest 2.21% during 1987. Dealers reported that demand for rare coins in the top condition categories escalated during much of 1988, but the market for old coins worn from use remained soft. In November a U.S. $20 gold piece dated 1861 with a special tails-side design sold for $600,000 plus a $60,000 "buyer's fee"—the fourth highest coin-auction price on record. The rarity was part of a collection once owned by the late R. Henry Norweb, a U.S. ambassador, and his wife, the late Emery May. During July the U.S. Federal Trade Commission and the American Numismatic Association issued a brochure designed to help protect rare-coin investors. Among other things, the brochure advised would-be buyers to get second opinions about coin grade and to comparison shop. Hobbyists mourned the death in November of Richard S. Yeoman, whose *A Guide Book of United States Coins* had sold nearly 17 million copies.   (ROGER BOYE)

Photography

New cameras proliferated in 1988, continuing the trend of combining popular automated features with the versatility and sophistication of 35-mm single-lens-reflex (SLR) models. Also making its appearance was a new breed of futuristic-looking "bridge" cameras that attempted to combine point-and-shoot simplicity with traditional advantages of the SLR, especially zoom lenses. Culturally the year was marked by the vigorous production of photo books and exhibitions, including major retrospectives, theme-based projects, popular surveys, and group shows.

Photo Equipment. An outstanding new SLR was the Nikon F4 Professional, a model eight years in development, which combined popular high-technology features with ruggedness and reliability while retaining the Nikon F lens mount compatible with most Nikon lenses. An electronically controlled, vertical-travel, focal-plane shutter provided speeds up to $1/8000$ second and flash synchronization from $1/30$ to $1/250$ second, plus T and B settings. Exposure metering options included a five-segment, computer-controlled matrix system that could sense the difference between horizontal and vertical compositions and adjust the metering appropriately; traditional Nikon 60/40 centre-weighted metering; and spot metering.

Exposure modes for the F4 included manual, aperture-priority automatic, shutter-priority automatic, and programmed and high-speed programmed automatic. In manual any deviation from the metered exposure value (EV) was indicated in one-third EV increments in the viewfinder's liquid-crystal display (LCD) screen. The high-speed programmed automatic setting was biased in favour of faster shutter speeds, thus being especially suited for use with long-focal-length lenses to reduce motion blur. An exposure compensation dial allowed compensation in steps of one-third between plus and minus EV 2. In addition to through-the-lens flash metering, the F4 offered the possibility of automatic matrix-balanced fill flash with any of several Nikon-dedicated flash units. Manual focusing was assisted by an electronic range finder that could function in light as dim as EV -1, equivalent to illumination requiring an exposure of four seconds at $f/1.4$ with ISO 100 film. Rapid automatic focusing (AF) was available in single and continuous modes, the latter for tracking moving subjects as the camera automatically calculated the subject's anticipated position at the instant of exposure. A removable battery pack and handgrip operated a built-in motor drive providing a choice of four modes of operation.

Minolta, which stimulated the current boom in autofocus 35-mm SLRs with its Maxxum 7000 in 1985, introduced a new generation of that line with the Maxxum 7000i and its less advanced sibling, the 3000i (the "i" stood for "intelligence"). Increased sensitivity of its AF system allowed the 7000i to perform in levels as low as EV 0 in its continuous mode to track a moving subject even after the shutter was released and to detect subject motion, switching automatically to continuous focus as appropriate. A central horizontal and two vertical side AF sensors enlarged the AF area some 12 times and permitted the camera to focus accurately on both horizontal and vertical lines.

The 7000i, with a top shutter speed of $1/4000$ second, carried an impressive array of advanced features including a programmed autoexposure mode that shifted the selected aperture/shutter-speed combination in seven steps depending on the focal length of the lens used. Any of ten Creative Expansion Cards containing memory circuits plus microprocessors could be inserted into the camera to provide special programs such as exposure bracketing, fantasy effect, sports action, and close-up.

ANTHONY SUAU—BLACK STAR

"Kiro—The Final Stand," a photograph by Anthony Suau showing a mother in South Korea clinging to a policeman's shield after her son's arrest, won the World Press Photo of the Year Award in February.

Camera makers attempted to bridge the gap between snapshot cameras and interchangeable-lens SLRs with hybrid models of unusual ergonomic design. The Chinon Genesis, for example, was a true SLR having a built-in 35–80-mm $f/4.1$–6.4 zoom lens with macro capability while providing such customary point-and-shoot features as DX film coding; an infrared AF system; programmed automatic exposure; automatic loading, winding, and rewinding; and a built-in pop-up flash. The non-SLR Olympus Infinity SuperZoom featured a coupled direct optical viewfinder and an automatic-focus 38–105-mm $f/4.5$–5.6 power zoom lens with macro capability. The SuperZoom also included such convenience features as DX coding, programmed autoexposure, autowind and rewind, and a built-in multimode zooming flash.

Another hybrid, the Kyocera (Yashica) Samurai, attempted to rekindle interest in the half-frame 35-mm format, which doubles the number of exposures per roll. The fully automatic SLR had a body shape resembling a small video camera, a built-in 25–70-mm power zoom lens, and a built-in flash. Although the camera stimulated interest in Japan and the U.S., its outlook for success in the latter country appeared dubious because many U.S. photofinishers were unprepared to print from half-frame negatives.

Kodak introduced two significant colour negative films. One, Ektar 25 (ISO 25), was generally credited with being the sharpest and most fine-grained colour negative film to date. The other, Ektar 1000 (ISO 1000), provided considerable speed while retaining the quality of an ISO 400 film.

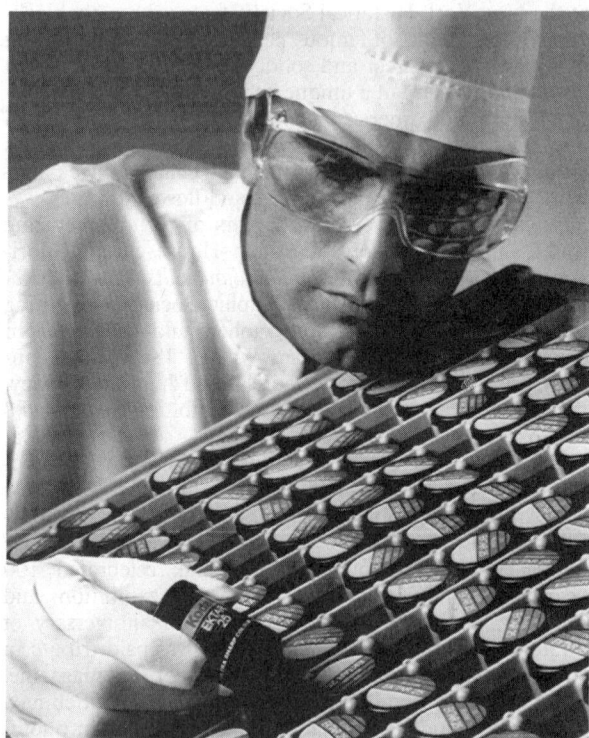

An Eastman Kodak worker checks a roll of Ektar 25, a new colour negative film designed by Kodak to produce the sharpest image of any colour film yet made.
AP/WIDE WORLD

Kodak also released a T-Max P3200 black-and-white film that some users found pushable (extendable in sensitivity) to ISO 6400 and higher, and made Kodachrome 200 and Ektachrome 100 professional films available for amateur consumers in versions that did not require refrigerated storage. Fuji introduced two improved professional daylight colour transparency films, E-6-processed Fujichrome 50D and 100D, and Fuji Neopan 1600, a higher speed version of Neopan 400. Agfa claimed significant improvement in colour saturations for its four new films: Agfa 100-XRC and Agfa 200-XRC colour negative films and Agfa CT100 and CT200 colour transparency films.

While many manufacturers continued to explore the potential of still video cameras in prototype, Canon introduced a production model of its RC-250 consumer all-electronic still camera. Shaped like a pair of binoculars and designed for point-and-shoot operation, it included a fixed-focus lens with built-in macro mode, automatic exposure, built-in flash, and a recording mode that yielded 50 images per magnetic floppy disk. The RC-250 could be connected directly to a TV set for picture playback.

Cultural Trends. Stimulating considerable controversy was the late Garry Winogrand's massive retrospective at the Museum of Modern Art, New York City, and the book *Winogrand: Figments from the Real World,* with text by John Szarkowski, curator of the show and long a friend and champion of the photographer. At his death, Winogrand left behind some 300,000 exposed but undeveloped negatives. Szarkowski, along with Tod Papageorge and Thomas Roma, put considerable effort into viewing contact sheets and selecting images to include in the exhibition, a task that raised questions about the ethics of making postmortem judgments for the photographer and about the state of Winogrand's talent in recent years.

Another retrospective, "Arnold Newman: Five Decades,"

AP/WIDE WORLD

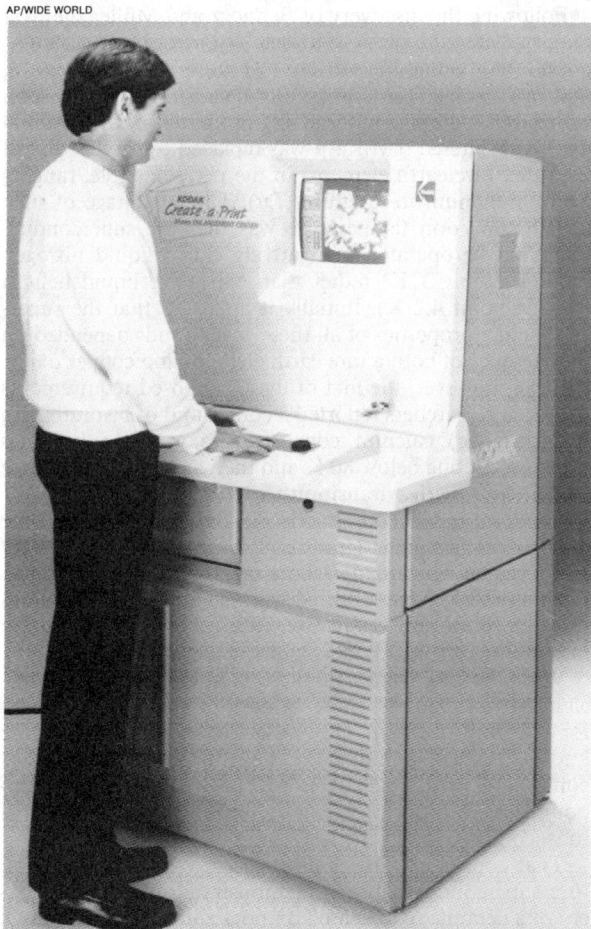

A man checks the monitor of a Kodak *Create-A-Print* photo machine, a device that enables a customer to make custom-designed colour prints from exposed 35mm film negatives.

at the New York Historical Society, featured mostly black-and-white portraits of famous people photographed during Newman's long career and solidly confirmed his powerful vision and mastery of a unique personal style. At the Whitney Museum of American Art, New York City, was shown a review of Robert Mapplethorpe's compelling, sometimes erotic work since 1970, which included collages, black-and-white and colour portraits, nudes, and flower still lifes.

An ambitious survey of 150 years of picture reporting was compiled by George Eastman House curator Marianne Fulton in *Eyes of Time: Photojournalism in America,* published by the New York Graphic Society. Presenting the work of some 200 photographers and ranging from daguerreotypes of the Mexican War of 1846–48 to contemporary photos by Susan Meiselas and James Nachtwey, the survey formed the basis of an exhibition at the 1988 Photokina in Cologne, West Germany. As part of the National Geographic Society's 100th anniversary, the Corcoran Gallery of Art, Washington, D.C., mounted "Odyssey: The Art of Photography at *National Geographic,*" a colourful but sprawling overview of the distinctive pictorial style established by that publication. Kodak celebrated 100 years of the snapshot, 1888 to 1988, with exhibitions and publicity, while on the eve of the 150th anniversary of photography's birth in 1839, the event was paid tribute in so many places, including an entire issue of *Life* magazine, that 1989 itself promised to be something of an anticlimax.

Discovery and reappraisal of hidden or forgotten photographic works made in Japan during the 1920s and 1930s reflected the continuing strong interest in the history of photography in that country. Typical of the trend was "Japan: 1920," an exhibition at the Tokyo Metropolitan Museum that reviewed the entire avant-garde culture of the decade and presented works by such photographers as Kozo Nojima, Kiyoshi Koishi, and Masao Horino.

The 1988 Pulitzer Prize for spot news photography was awarded to Scott Shaw of the *Odessa* (Texas) *American* for his widely published picture of a child, Jessica McClure, just after her rescue from a well where she had been trapped for more than two days. The Pulitzer for feature photography went to Michel duCille of the *Miami* (Fla.) *Herald* for his photographic essay on a housing project affected by drugs and urban decay. In the 31st annual World Press Photo Contest, the Photo of the Year Award was won by Anthony Suau of Black Star USA for his image of a Korean woman during a political demonstration. Chris Steele-Perkins, a London-based Magnum photographer, won the Oskar Barnack Award for a report on children with birth defects caused by the drug thalidomide.

At the 45th Pictures of the Year competition sponsored by the National Press Photographers Association and the University of Missouri School of Journalism, Anthony Suau won the Magazine Photographer of the Year title, Bill Greene of the *Boston Globe* was named Newspaper Photographer of the Year, and free-lancer Herman LeRoy Emmet received the Canon Photo Essayist Award for "Fruit Tramps," documenting itinerant farm workers.

English photographer Paul Graham won the 1988 W. Eugene Smith Grant in Humanistic Photography for his colour essay on "The New Europe." The International Center of Photography gave its Master of Photography award to 89-year-old Alfred Eisenstaedt for lifetime work as a photojournalist and a Certificate of Honor to Wu Yinxian, 88, a Beijing (Peking) photographer who documented the early career of Mao Zedong (Mao Tse-Tung) and the birth of contemporary China. (ARTHUR GOLDSMITH)

See also Motion Pictures.

This article updates the *Macropædia* article PHOTOGRAPHY.

Physics

Superconductivity. High-temperature superconductivity, the absence of electrical resistance in a substance at temperatures significantly above absolute zero (0 kelvins [K], or $-273°$ C), was again the dominant subject throughout physics in 1988 and indeed had a marked influence on research themes in chemistry, metallurgy, ceramics, and electronics engineering, among others. Nevertheless, despite enormous expenditure and activity, much of the initial optimism over the new ceramic superconductors remained unrealized. Although the original materials themselves were refined and purified, leading to cleaner superconducting behaviour, and although other materials having somewhat higher transition temperatures were found, the goal of room-temperature superconductivity seemed almost as elusive as before. Moreover, although the superconductors could be fabricated into thin films, thick films, high-density ceramic blocks, short fibres, and even single crystals, they had yet to find their first significant application. Finally, the origin and nature of superconductivity at temperatures in excess of 80 K was as much of a mystery as it was in 1986 when J. Georg Bednorz and K. Alexander Müller of the IBM Research Laboratory, Zürich, Switz., discovered the first of these materials—a compound of barium (Ba), lanthanum (La), copper (Cu), and oxygen (O) that makes the transition from normal to superconducting behaviour at a temperature below 35 K. (To convert kelvins to degrees Celsius, subtract 273; thus 35 K = $-238°$ C).

Following the discovery of Bednorz and Müller the next major advance came in 1987: the report of a similar compound, but containing yttrium (Y) rather than lanthanum, that has a transition temperature near 100 K. It was soon realized that the superconducting properties of the material were little altered if yttrium was replaced by almost any of the other rare earth elements in the periodic table, ranging from lanthanum to lutetium (Lu). The advantage of such a high transition temperature was that the superconductor could be operated in relatively cheap liquid nitrogen (boiling point 77 K) rather than expensive liquid helium (boiling point 4.2 K). Initially it appeared that the superconducting properties of all these compounds depended on the presence of both a rare earth element and copper oxide. In 1988, however, the first of these supposed requirements fell when researchers reported a compound of bismuth (Bi), strontium (Sr), calcium, copper, and oxygen that becomes superconducting below 80 K and then another, of the same constituents, with a transition temperature of 110 K.

Thallium-based compounds (Tl-Ba-Ca-Cu-O) were the next to display higher transition temperatures: reports of 125 K came from many laboratories, and possible transitions at 140 K were reported from some others. Thallium research, however, was hampered by the need for caution in handling this highly poisonous metal.

With the discoveries of these complex four- and five-element compounds came a flock of shorthand names for referring to them. The Y-Ba-Cu oxides soon became known as ibco, pointing the way for the bismuth-based compounds to be called bisco. The thallium-based compounds were more problematic, receiving such names as tobacco and tesco in the U.K and tabasco in the U.S.

That copper likewise is not necessary for high-temperature superconductivity was demonstrated with the discovery of a ceramic oxide based on potassium (K): Ba-K-Bi-O. Its transition temperature of 27 K, although low, was still higher than anything known before Bednorz and Müller's discovery.

Theoretical work on the superconducting behaviour of the new materials was active, though little understanding emerged. The behaviour of the previously known, lower temperature superconducting materials (all metal elements or alloys) was understood in terms of the BCS (Bardeen-Cooper-Schrieffer) theory, wherein electrons flow through the superconductor in pairs, the two negatively charged particles being bound together by the exchange of a phonon (a quantized vibration in the material's crystal lattice). One of the main successes of the BCS theory was in predicting the change in the transition temperature of a superconductor when one of its elements is replaced by an isotope. The isotope will be either lighter or heavier than the original element by one or more neutrons in the nucleus. In the new materials the observed isotope effects were much smaller than BCS predictions, although in some cases there was considerable disagreement among experimenters about the size of the differences. Not only did BCS theory appear unable to explain the isotope effects in the new materials, it also failed to explain the high transition temperatures achieved, since the electron-pairing force in the theory begins to be overwhelmed at a temperature of 40–50 K.

The elegance of a model based on pairing, however, was retained in most new theories, and there was some experimental support for doing so. Still, the question remained: what is being paired with what and how? There were at least three broad groups of theorists and theories. First, there was an extension of the BCS theory that used ideas borrowed from semiconductor physics—in particular, the notion that electric current can be considered to be carried by "holes" rather than electrons. A hole is a region of the material's crystal lattice wherein the removal of an electron creates a positively charged location that can move through the material like a real charged particle. The crystal structure of the high-transition-temperature superconductors contains layers of Cu-O planes that have holes; according to the theory, the holes are paired by the exchange of a phonon or other excitation of the Cu-O arrays.

A second theory involves pairing of electrons but proposes that around the pair are fluctuations of charge that can be quantized and described either as excitations or entities called plasmons. It was shown that the charge fluctuation method of pairing does lead to superconductivity.

Perhaps the most popular theoretical approach uses not fluctuations of charge but fluctuations of spin, the property of angular momentum assigned to subatomic particles.

Conventionally, the charge and spin of particles acting in crystalline solids are linked in a special way that imposes limits on particle behaviour. In the new theory the degrees of freedom allowed to the particles by charge and spin are separated, resulting in very strong electron-electron correlations. It is proposed that the charge is carried by entities known as holons and having a hole-like character, while spin is carried by spinons.

One driving force behind research into high-temperature superconductors was the range of possible applications that the materials promised. During the past year, however, the ceramics remained difficult to manufacture in useful forms without destroying their superconducting properties. Crucial to any high-power applications was the development of ways to fabricate the materials in forms having a high critical current, the maximum electric current the materials can support in the superconducting state. The most promising fabrication routes for achieving high critical currents were thin-film deposition techniques, resulting in polycrystalline superconductors that could carry currents in excess of 100,000 amp/sq cm. Such materials might play a role as interconnects in certain high-speed electronic circuitry or as the basis of sensitive magnetometers.

Search for New Forces. Since 1981 Australian researchers had been measuring the Earth's gravity at various points along descending mine shafts. After accounting for such known effects as density anomalies in nearby rock strata, they found that their measured value differed slightly from the traditional value calculated from Newton's law and in a way suggestive of a repulsive force acting over a range of a few hundred metres. In 1986 U.S. theorist Ephraim Fischbach proposed that the effect was caused by a previously unknown fifth force, a force separate from the known strong, weak, electromagnetic, and gravitational forces. After a reexamination of gravity measurements made in the early 1900s by Hungarian scientist Roland Eotvos, Fischbach found additional evidence that a fifth force exists and that its strength depends on the density of the nuclear protons and neutrons (baryon density) in the interacting masses. Soon other theorists developed alternate explanations, some of which included an additional, attractive sixth force.

The excitement generated by these experiments and theories inspired new research efforts in 1987 and 1988, though none of it proved definitive. Some experimenters carried out modern versions of Eotvos's work, measuring

© RICHARD DERK

An experimental electric motor built by researchers at Argonne (Illinois) National Laboratory was the first to exploit the new superconducting ceramics. Although the new materials were still too brittle and sensitive for practical use, scientists were progressing toward usable forms.

the forces on samples of materials having different baryon densities (such as copper and water, or beryllium and aluminum) placed close to large geologic masses like granite cliffs. Other researchers took gravity readings at points along the length of a tall television transmission tower, while still others dropped masses of different baryon densities in a vacuum chamber, looking for differences in their acceleration. One of the more recent experiments, reported in mid-1988, was a variation of the mine-shaft experiment conducted down a borehole in the Greenland ice sheet, where the uniformity of the surrounding ice mass reduced the possibility of the readings' being affected by local mass concentrations.

By the end of the year, though the excitement persisted, the only certainty to emerge from all the activity was that no one could prove or disprove whether the purported new force (or forces) is attractive or repulsive, how it depends on matter for its properties, or whether it even exists at all. Plans for more experiments were under way, including one that would compare the effects of the Earth's gravity on freely falling protons and antiprotons (the antimatter counterpart of protons) generated in the particle accelerator facilities at the European Laboratory for Particle Physics (CERN) in Switzerland. (S. B. PALMER)

This article updates the *Macropædia* articles GRAVITATION; MATTER: *Low-Temperature Phenomena;* The PHYSICAL SCIENCES: *Physics;* SUBATOMIC PARTICLES.

Populations and Population Movements

DEMOGRAPHY

World population stood at 5,111,900,000 as of mid-1988, according to United Nations medium ("most probable") estimates released in 1988, and was growing by just under 88 million, or 1.73%, a year. These figures were higher than the UN had projected for 1988 in its medium estimates prepared in the early 1980s, largely because of an unexpected rise since 1985 in the birthrate of China and a slower than projected decline in the fertility of India. The populations of China and India were estimated at 1,104,000,000 and 818.8 million, respectively, at mid-1988 and together accounted for 38% of total world population. The revised UN medium projections put world population at 6,250,400,000 in 2000 (up from 6,121,800,000 projected in the early 1980s) and 8,465,700,000 in 2025 (compared with 8,205,800,000 projected earlier). Between 1988 and 2025, 95% of world population growth would occur in the less developed countries of Africa, Asia (minus Japan), and Latin America, which together made up 77% of world population in 1988. The Population Reference Bureau estimated that annual natural increase (births minus deaths) averaged 2.1% in these countries about 1988, compared with 0.6% in the more developed countries. An estimated 45% of world population lived in urban areas about 1988.

U.S. Census Bureau estimates put the U.S. population (including armed forces overseas) at 246,113,000 on July 1, 1988, an increase of 2,198,000 over a year earlier. Close to 1.7 million of this gain was due to natural increase and the remainder to net immigration (legal plus illegal immigration into the country minus emigration from it). For its estimates, the Census Bureau put net illegal immigration at 200,000 a year. In 1988 black persons comprised 12.5% of the U.S. population (up from 11.7% in 1980) and Hispanics, 8.1% (up from 6.5% in 1980). The urban proportion of the total U.S. population about 1988 was 77%.

Birth Statistics. The National Center for Health Statistics provisionally estimated U.S. births in 1987 at 3,829,000, 2% more than the 3,756,547 births registered in 1986 and the highest annual number since 1964, the last year of the "baby boom" that began in 1947. The estimated birthrate was 15.7 per 1,000 population, and the fertility rate was 66.1 births per 1,000 women aged 15–44, both slightly above the final figures of 15.6 and 65.4 for 1986. The increase in numbers of births continued into 1988. For the 12-month period ended in May, there were 2% more births than reported for the comparable period a year earlier. However, the birthrate for this period was still 15.7, and the fertility rate, 66.2, was scarcely higher than the estimated rate for calendar 1987. Detailed data indicated that the increase in numbers of births resulted largely from a sharp rise in the number of women in their 30s, born during the peak baby boom years of 1947–57, coupled with continued, though slowing, increases in birthrates for women aged 30 and over.

The total fertility rate, which indicates the average number of lifetime births per woman if current fertility rates were to continue, was 1.8 for U.S. women as a whole in 1986, 1.7 for white women, and 2.2 for black women. The overall rate and the rate for white women had been below the "replacement" level of 2.1 births per woman since 1972. However, births continued to outstrip deaths in the U.S. because the number of women of childbearing age was currently inflated by those born during the baby boom. In 1986 the fertility rate per 1,000 women aged 15–44 was 93.9 for Hispanic women in the U.S., 48% higher than the rate of 63.3 for the non-Hispanic population. Births to unmarried women in the U.S. totaled 878,477 in 1986, 6% more than in 1985. Both the proportion of all births to unmarried women, 23%, and the birthrate per 1,000 unmarried women aged 15–44, 34, were the highest on record. The proportion of nonmarital births was 61% for black women and 16% for white women, but this racial difference was narrowing.

Estimates reported by the Population Reference Bureau put average birthrates per 1,000 population about 1988 at 28 for the world as a whole and 15 for more developed countries, both unchanged from a year earlier. The rate for less developed countries, 31, was down one point. China's birthrate was reported at 21 for 1987, the same as in 1986 but up from 18 in 1985. Regionally, birthrates about 1988 ranged from 44 per 1,000 population in Africa to 13 in Europe, both unchanged from the previous annual estimates. Also unchanged was the estimated total fertility rate for the world as a whole, 3.6 births per woman. The estimated average total fertility rate in less developed countries dropped one point to 4.1, although China's rate was still reported above replacement level at 2.4. The rise in China's total fertility rate was said to be due in part to some improvement in the country's economy. With higher incomes, many couples in the rural population were willing to pay the fines often levied on those who defied the government's one-child-per-couple policy. The government was also said to be relaxing its policy by allowing some rural couples with one girl to have another child.

India's current total fertility rate was estimated at 4.3 to 4.5 or more. The Population Reference Bureau pointed out that this was higher than the rate of 3.7 assumed for India by the late 1980s in the UN medium projections made early in the decade. Fertility declines were also slower than previously projected in other populous less developed countries such as Egypt, Pakistan, the Philippines, and Zaire. Only a few less developed countries had reduced fertility to or below the replacement level of 2.1: Cuba, South

Korea, Taiwan, the small nations of Hong Kong and Singapore, and one or two others. The proportion of children under age 15 was 37% for less developed countries as a whole, compared with 22% for more developed countries. This meant these countries had a large built-in potential for future population growth. The latest reported total fertility rates averaged 1.8 in Europe and North America (Canada and the U.S.) and 1.9 in more developed countries as a whole.

Death Statistics. The estimated number of deaths in the U.S. in 1987 reached a record annual high of 2,127,000. This reflected the increasing size of the population, especially for ages 65 and over. The "crude" death rate, at 8.7 per 1,000 population, remained about the same as in 1986. However, because of the continued decline in death rates for most age groups, the estimated age-adjusted death rate, 536 per 100,000 population, was again the lowest on record. Accounting for 87% of all deaths, the 15 leading causes of death in 1987 were:

	Causes of death	Estimated rate per 100,000 population
1.	Diseases of the heart	313.4
2.	Malignant neoplasms	196.1
3.	Cerebrovascular diseases	61.3
4.	Accidents and adverse effects	39.0
5.	Chronic obstructive pulmonary diseases	32.2
6.	Pneumonia and influenza	28.8
7.	Diabetes mellitus	15.6
8.	Suicide	12.7
9.	Chronic liver disease and cirrhosis	10.7
10.	Atherosclerosis	9.5
11.	Nephritis, nephrotic syndrome, and nephrosis	9.5
12.	Homicide and legal intervention	8.5
13.	Septicemia	8.1
14.	Conditions of the perinatal period	7.6
15.	Congenital anomalies	5.0

The estimated world death rate was unchanged from the previous year at 10 per 1,000 population. For less developed countries, the average of 10 (down one point) was almost as low as the average of 9 in more developed countries (also down one point) but, combined with their birthrate of 31, it resulted in a high rate of natural increase of 2.1% a year. At that rate a population doubles in 33 years. Kenya's estimated rate of natural increase was again highest of all countries at 4.1%, resulting from a birthrate of 54 and a death rate of 13. Natural increase was again reported to be negative (fewer births than deaths) in Denmark, Hungary, and West Germany.

World's 25 Most Populous Urban Areas[1]

Rank	City and Country	City proper Population	Year	Metropolitan area Population	Year
1	Tokyo, Japan	8,328,000	1988 est.	27,824,000	1985 est.
2	New York City, U.S.	7,262,700	1986 est.	18,053,800	1987 est.
3	Mexico City, Mexico	9,931,413	1985 est.	17,321,800	1985 est.
4	Osaka, Japan	2,647,000	1988 est.	15,891,000	1985 est.
5	São Paulo, Brazil	7,032,547	1985 est.	15,233,492	1985 est.
6	Los Angeles, U.S.	3,259,300	1986 est.	13,470,900	1987 est.
7	Shanghai, China	6,987,253	1986 est.	12,323,316	1986 est.
8	London, England	6,775,200	1986 est.	12,290,500	1986 est.
9	Buenos Aires, Arg.	2,924,000	1986 est.	10,750,000	1985 est.
10	Calcutta, India	3,305,006	1981 cen.	10,462,000	1985 est.
11	Paris, France	2,127,100	1986 est.	10,249,700	1986 est.
12	Rio de Janeiro, Brazil	5,090,700	1980 est.	10,190,384	1985 est.
13	Bombay, India	8,243,405	1981 cen.	10,137,000	1985 est.
14	Seoul, South Korea	2	2	9,790,000	1986 est.
15	Cairo, Egypt	6,052,836	1986 cen.	9,753,860	1986 cen.
16	Beijing, China	5,350,783	1986 est.	9,751,240	1986 est.
17	Moscow, U.S.S.R.	8,614,000	1987 est.	8,815,000	1987 est.
18	Rhine-Ruhr, W.Ger.	3	3	8,730,000	1986 est.
19	Tianjin, China	4,244,065	1986 est.	8,187,687	1986 est.
20	Chicago, U.S.	3,009,530	1986 est.	8,146,900	1987 est.
21	Nagoya, Japan	2,145,000	1988 est.	8,139,000	1985 est.
22	Jakarta, Indonesia	2	2	7,829,299	1985 est.
23	Manila, Philippines	1,987,000	1986 est.	7,561,000	1988 est.
24	Delhi, India	4,884,234	1981 cen.	6,993,000	1985 est.
25	Karachi, Pakistan	4,776,000	1981 cen.	6,673,000	1986 est.

[1]Ranked by population of metropolitan area.
[2]Administrative unit within which a separate city proper is not distinguished.
[3]An industrial conurbation within which no single central city is defined.

Infant Mortality. The provisional infant mortality rate for the U.S. in 1987 was down 4% from 1986 and the lowest on record: 10 deaths under one year of age per 1,000 live births. Detailed data showed that in 1985 that for black infants in the U.S., 18.2, was still nearly twice that for white infants, 9.3, a gap almost the same as in 1960. The latest worldwide estimates reported by the Population Reference Bureau indicated four-point declines in average infant mortality rates to 77 for the world as a whole and to 86 for less developed countries, while the rate of 15 for more developed countries was down one point from the previous annual estimate. Japan again reported the lowest national infant mortality rate, 5.2.

Life Expectancy. Life expectancy at birth for the total U.S. population in 1987 remained at the record high attained in 1986, 74.9 years. Provisional data showed slight rises for white males (72 to 72.1 years) and black females (73.6 to 73.8) and declines of 0.1 year to 78.8 for white females and 65.4 years for black males.

Estimated average life expectancy for the world as a whole, 63 years, and for more developed countries, 73, remained unchanged from the previous annual estimate, but it rose one year to 60 for less developed countries. Among regions, Africa, at 52 years, still had the lowest average life expectancy. Japan reported a record national high for men and women combined, 78 years, followed by Iceland, Sweden, and Switzerland at 77 years.

Marriage and Divorce Statistics. Between 1986 and 1987, the number of marriages in the U.S. rose by 21,000 to an estimated 2,421,000. However, this rise did not keep pace with population growth, and the marriage rate per 1,000 population fell from 10 to 9.9, the lowest since 1977. This was the third consecutive annual drop in the marriage rate, which had held fairly steady from 1980 to 1984. The Census Bureau reported that in 1987 the proportions of persons aged 30 to 34 who had never married were 15% for women and 23% for men.

From 1986 to 1987, the number of divorces in the U.S. edged down by 2,000 to 1,157,000. The divorce rate remained unchanged at 4.8 per 1,000 population. This represented a decline from the recent peak of 5.3 in 1979 and 1981 and was the lowest since 1975.

Surveys. Among reports issued for 19 of the 30 less developed countries to be covered in the Demographic and Health Surveys program of 1985–90, Thailand reported the highest proportion of married women of childbearing age currently using contraception, 66%. The proportions were also above 60% in Brazil (65%), Colombia (63%), and Sri Lanka (62%). Thailand also reported the lowest total fertility rate in the five years before the survey, 2.4 births per woman, followed by Sri Lanka (2.7) and Trinidad and Tobago (3.1). The six reporting sub-Saharan African countries were at the other extreme, with the lowest proportions of married women of reproductive age using contraception, all below 13%, and the highest total fertility rates, ranging from 6.2 in Ondo state in Nigeria to 7.1 in Mali.

(JEAN VAN DER TAK)

See also World Data.

INTERNATIONAL MIGRATION

In 1988 the major trends of economic and political dislocations in the third world continued to generate international migration. At the same time, political pressures in the industrialized countries operated to limit the rights of immigrants and asylum seekers.

European reception of refugees and immigrants continued to be problematic, with the origin of the migrants being an important factor. The West German Interior

Ministry reported in July that it expected 200,000 ethnic Germans from Eastern Europe to arrive in West Germany in 1988. The primary sources had been the Soviet Union and Poland, and the West German government was negotiating with Romania for the immigration of approximately 200,000 Romanians of German origin. Although Bonn had already paid Bucharest DM 8,000 per head to allow up to 12,000 German-speaking Romanians to leave each year over a ten-year period, West Germany wanted the process accelerated, and Romania sought a higher price. The West German government announced in July an increase of more than DM 1.3 billion in 1989 for accommodation and German lessons for ethnic Germans. There was growing tension inside West Germany over the cost of this resettlement program and over job competition as unemployment increased to 8.6%.

The Conservative government in Britain continued the process of restricting the rights of entry of both asylum seekers and immigrants from the New (nonwhite) Commonwealth. In July 1988 the immigration minister announced that as of September 1, people who sought political asylum in Britain would not have a right of appeal or a guarantee that their case would be referred by the home secretary to the United Kingdom Immigrant Advisory Service before deportation. In addition, Britain had delayed implementation of a 1987 agreement with the UN to provide monthly figures on the fate of people seeking asylum, despite the fact that all other countries in the European Communities had implemented it.

On August 1 the Immigration Act 1988 came into force. It required male Commonwealth citizens to show that they could maintain and accommodate their families without recourse to public funds before they were allowed entry. It also limited the right of appeal of people who had lived in Britain for less than seven years and were being deported for overstaying in breach of conditions attached to their stay, and it made overstaying a continuing criminal offense.

The number of people accepted for settlement in the U.K. in 1987 was 46,000—800 fewer than in 1986 and the lowest annual figure since Commonwealth citizens first became subject to control in 1962. There had also been a shift in the origin of those accepted; in 1977 immigrants from the Indian subcontinent accounted for 34.6% of all immigrants, but in 1987 this had fallen to 25.3%. During the same period, the figures for the Old Commonwealth rose from 9.5 to 15%, and other foreign acceptances increased from 27 to nearly 40%. The number of deportation orders issued in 1987 was 863, 67 more than in the previous year, and the number of illegal entrants actually deported totaled 438, compared with 304 in 1986.

In Hong Kong concern over the transfer of sovereignty to China in 1997 had apparently prompted thousands of residents to emigrate, mainly to the U.S., Canada, and Australia. A secret Hong Kong government report estimated that 48,000 residents were preparing to emigrate in 1988—rather than the original estimate of 27,000—up from 27,000 in 1987 and 13,000 in 1986. The emigrants were expected to be from the educated and professional groups in the colony.

Australia's 20-year consensus on a nonracial immigration policy was called into question in August by the leader of the opposition Liberal Party, John Howard. As part of his policy of "One Australia," Howard called for a reduction in the number of Asians entering the country. He asserted that present levels (2.6% of Australians were born in Asia) were "imposing social tension and a lack of social cohesion." The Liberal coalition partner, the National Party, declared that immigration must reflect Australia's "European heritage." Australia's Labor prime minister, Bob Hawke, rejected these calls and told Asian countries that Australia would not change its nonracial immigration policy. In the fiscal year ended in June, the government increased the number of immigrants allowed into the country from 120,000 to 132,000. Most of the increase was being taken up by business immigrants and skilled workers.

In the U.S. the yearlong amnesty for the estimated four million eligible illegal aliens expired on May 4, 1988. It was estimated that more than 1.4 million aliens had registered for temporary legal status, which they could obtain by proving they had resided in the U.S. continuously from Jan. 1, 1982. If they got over that hurdle and passed English-language and U.S. civics tests, they could become citizens after five years.   (LOUIS KUSHNICK)

REFUGEES

The year 1988 was characterized by the continuation of some long-standing refugee problems and the appearance of some new situations. The Horn of Africa and The Sudan remained major fields of operation for the UN High Commissioner for Refugees (UNHCR). About 57,300 Ugandans repatriated from The Sudan in the first nine months of the year, while Ethiopian refugees continued to return home from Djibouti, Somalia, and The Sudan. The flow of refugees from The Sudan into southwestern Ethiopia led to serious overcrowding in remote areas, and in mid-1988 refugees from northwestern Somalia began to arrive in southeastern Ethiopia, where there were some 275,000 persons receiving UNHCR assistance. Elsewhere in Africa, some 18,000 refugees had returned to Mozambique by October, but the influx of Mozambicans into neighbouring countries continued, particularly into Malawi, where there were about 600,000. Starting in August, some 65,000 persons arrived in Rwanda from Burundi.

In August an International Conference on the Plight of Refugees, Returnees and Displaced Persons in Southern Africa (SARRED) took place in Oslo. It resulted in a Declaration and Plan of Action, which proclaimed that apartheid and South Africa's policy of destabilization were the root causes of the refugee situation in the region, called for greater international burden sharing and solidarity, and stressed the importance of the link between relief, recovery, and development assistance.

The situation in Southeast Asia gave rise to considerable concern throughout the year. The number of Vietnamese arriving in Hong Kong, Malaysia, and Thailand increased dramatically. This led to serious security problems and placed a severe strain on existing facilities. A screening mechanism was established in mid-June in Hong Kong to ensure that the status of asylum seekers was clearly established and that those falling within the mandate of UNHCR were afforded international protection and appropriate assistance. The fate of the Kampucheans in Thailand remained uncertain as the closure of the Khao-I-Dang camp was postponed to allow resettlement processing to continue. Laotian asylum seekers continued to arrive in Thailand, but Laotians who had applied for repatriation or had been determined not to be refugees were allowed to return to Laos. The status of some 9,000 previously unregistered hill-tribe Laotians was regularized early in 1988.

The repatriation of Tamils from India to Sri Lanka constituted a major operation for UNHCR in 1988. During the first nine months, UNHCR assisted some 24,000 persons to return, while an additional 12,000 returned spontaneously.

Publishing

The year 1988 was one in which, on a world scale, business matters took second place to the manifold shifts in the eternal tensions between journalism and government. From the viewpoint of press freedom, there was, as always, good news and bad news.

The British government's long and unsuccessful battle to ban publication of *Spycatcher,* a book written by former security agent Peter Wright, was fought mainly in the Australian courts, but it was only after that saga was ended that the highest court in the U.K. itself freed three British newspapers from an injunction against reporting the contents of the book—now a world best-seller—imposed on them at the very outset. (*See* LAW: *Court Decisions.*)

In the Soviet Union the policy of *glasnost* (openness) continued to have dramatic effects on that nation's long-suppressed rights of expression. For the first time, the head of the press censorship bureau, Glavlit, gave an interview; in that interview, to *Izvestia,* he said: "Information that reveals a state secret or that could be detrimental to our country's interests is forbidden. As far as the rest is concerned, the formula is this: whatever is not forbidden is allowed." Three weeks later East Germany banned distribution of the Soviet magazine *Sputnik,* which was giving much space to changes in the U.S.S.R.

In China the swing to greater freedom perceived in recent years appeared to meet a conservative backlash. In India it took a widely supported protest campaign to force Prime Minister Rajiv Gandhi to withdraw a Defamation Bill that was believed to impose limitations far beyond its avowed aims. When the International Press Institute held its conference in Turkey, the prime minister of that nation, Turgut Ozal, was challenged to change a regime in which journalists faced, and in many cases received, jail sentences.

In South Africa in June the renewal of the emergency regulations governing the media greatly tightened the restrictions on reporting the continuing unrest in that nation. A proposal to register foreign journalists was withdrawn, but in November the pressures on South Africa's own press were symbolized by the closing for three months of the English-language newspaper the *Weekly Mail.*

Newspapers. Britain's 12th national daily newspaper, the *Post,* was launched on Nov. 10, 1988. It was the third such new title in as many years, and a new national Sunday newspaper, to be called the *Correspondent,* was announced for early 1989. Although this growth was a further symbol of the changes brought about by the British press's shift to technology requiring a smaller labour force, its true meaning was less clear. Within days the *Post*'s proprietor, Eddie Shah, was admitting that not enough had been spent on promoting the launch; in 1986 Shah had set the new wave rolling with *Today.* Another new entry during the year, the *North West Times,* which aimed at businessmen in the region around Manchester, failed to reach its 40,000-sales target and was folded after seven weeks.

The *Post*'s success or failure might also have been seen as symbolic of another aspect of the current British tabloid press scene. Announcing it as the "antisleaze" paper, Shah said that he had detected an audience antipathetic to the mass-market newspapers' increasing diet of topless women and purported revelations about the sex lives of celebrities. In December, however, after more than $12 million in losses and just 33 issues, the paper folded.

Such antipathy certainly seemed to be true of British courts. In November Koo Stark, an actress-turned-photog-

Three Vietnamese refugee children peer through the wires of their makeshift dwelling in a former Hong Kong factory building that had become home to more than 4,000 refugees from Southeast Asia.
AFP PHOTO

Afghans remained the largest single refugee population, with some 3.2 million in Pakistan and 2.1 million–2.3 million in Iran. Following the signing of the peace accord in Geneva in April, UNHCR signed agreements with Afghanistan and Pakistan specifying the conditions under which UNHCR would assist in repatriation. On the appointment of the UN coordinator for humanitarian and economic assistance to Afghanistan, UNHCR's plan was updated and incorporated into the overall UN relief and rehabilitation program.

In the Middle East and North Africa, UNHCR continued to implement programs. A chargé de mission's office was opened in Yemen (San'a') early in the year to monitor an assistance program for some 70,000 displaced persons from Yemen (Aden).

The refugee population in Latin America and the Caribbean remained relatively stable, with the numbers of those repatriating being offset by new arrivals. In Central America some 12,500 returned home, mainly Salvadorans, Nicaraguans, and Guatemalans, while some 4,500 Nicaraguans from the Pacific coast arrived in Costa Rica and Honduras in the first nine months of the year.

In Europe the numbers of asylum seekers continued to increase in many countries. UNHCR pointed to the need to prevent abuse of asylum procedures and to streamline such procedures, while maintaining adequate safeguards, in order to reduce the large backlogs and to work toward a global approach to the problems being faced. Major consultations among European governments and UNHCR, begun in 1985 in Geneva, continued with a meeting in Oslo in May. Canada accepted 9,600 persons for resettlement in the first half of 1988, while the U.S. accepted 3,400. Both, however, continued to receive large numbers of spontaneous asylum seekers. Canada adopted new legislation to reform its refugee-determination procedure, and the U.S. was in the process of adopting revised asylum regulations.

(UNHCR)

This article updates the *Macropædia* article POPULATION.

rapher, won four libel cases in a week, including £300,000 in damages from the *Sunday People,* for newspaper stories alleging that after her own marriage she had continued to meet with Prince Andrew and had dallied with another star's husband.

In general there was strategic activity rather than dramatic short-term action on the national press scene. The *Sunday Times* established its dominant position among the quality Sunday newspapers and added more sections, while the possibility of a takeover bid for Tiny Rowland's Lonrho empire flushed out several potential suitors for the *Observer,* which it owned. Rupert Murdoch, meanwhile, emerged with a stake in Pearson, parent group of the *Financial Times,* one of the world's most highly regarded business newspapers, exciting speculation that he might make a bid for it. Pearson, however, refusing even to contemplate joint ventures, formed an alliance with a Dutch publisher, and cash needs elsewhere seemed by the year's end to have diminished Murdoch's interest.

The *Guardian* in February undertook a radical redesign. While the growth of the *Independent* slowed, by its second anniversary it had moved into the 400,000-plus league, just below its rivals, the *Guardian* and *The Times.* The *Star,* weakest of the tabloids, continued to slide, and in the middle market *Today* strengthened its pitch for readers of the *Daily Mail* and *Daily Express,* while the *Mail* on Sunday continued to grow.

The most evident trend was toward the use of colour. In a flurry of autumn-season activity the *Independent, Daily Mail, Daily Express, Daily* and *Sunday Telegraph,* and *Observer* either launched new colour supplements or repositioned existing ones, and the three titles in Robert Maxwell's Mirror Group Newspapers increased their colour production.

Britain's growing awareness of its European dimension, sharpened by the approach of the implementation of the European Communities' single-market provisions in 1992, began to affect the newspaper industry. Pearson, after some French political resistance, took control of the French business newspaper *Les Echos,* and Robert Maxwell began to recruit staff and buy presses for his planned daily, *The European,* due to begin publication in 1989. The *Guardian,* having launched a summer Mediterranean edition printed in Marseille, France, and aimed at British tourists, shifted to Frankfurt, West Germany, as the base for a long-term European edition. The *Independent* forged editorial links with papers in France, Spain, and West Germany. The *Wall Street Journal,* on the other hand, announced cost-cutting plans to withdraw some of its European-based staff and to service more of the European edition from New York City.

On the other side of the world, the Murdoch empire strengthened itself in New Zealand, where in July Independent Newspapers, 40% owned by his News Limited, bought the *Sun* and the *Auckland Star* from the NS News group and closed the former. Murdoch, however, was precluded by ownership laws from becoming involved in a major shake-up in the land of his birth, Australia. There the misfortunes of the Fairfax empire in the wake of the 1987 stock market crash caused its head, Warwick Fairfax, to sell many of his interests and led to a battle to keep the leading newspapers, the *Sydney Morning Herald* and the *Age* of Melbourne, out of rival hands.   (PETER FIDDICK)

On the morning after his 1948 presidential election victory, a grinning Harry Truman held up a copy of the *Chicago Tribune*'s postelection front page with the premature headline "Dewey Defeats Truman." Four decades later a presidential election was again the story of the

U.S. Attorney General Edwin Meese addresses reporters outside the Justice Department where he had approved the merger of the business and production departments of the *Detroit Free Press* and the *Detroit News*.
AP/WIDE WORLD

year for U.S. newspapers, yet much had changed since Truman's day. For one thing, editors, having learned their lesson from 1948, had over the years become more cautious in announcing results. For another, the importance of newspapers in the election process continued to decline as the role of television increased. Both major candidates, Michael Dukakis and George Bush, timed their campaign speeches and events to catch the networks' evening newscasts; newspaper deadlines were not a top concern. In addition, whereas newspaper reporters once made up nearly all of the journalists attending the two major party nominating conventions, in 1988 more than half of the 15,000 or so media people at the Atlanta, Ga., and New Orleans, La., conventions were from television.

Newspaper endorsements also were not as significant a factor in elections as they once had been. In Truman's day the vast majority of U.S. dailies backed one candidate or another editorially, and voters sometimes took the endorsements seriously. In 1932, for instance, only 7.45% of newspapers responding to a survey by *Editor & Publisher,* a newspaper trade magazine, were either undecided about which candidate to back or deliberately neutral. In 1988 results of a similar *Editor & Publisher* survey indicated that 55.4% of U.S. dailies either were undecided or had a no-endorsement policy.

Though its influence in presidential politics may have waned, the newspaper industry continued to prosper. Total circulation in the U.S. reached 62,826,273, according to the 1988 *Editor & Publisher International Year Book,* an increase of 324,237, or 0.5%. That gain more than offset the loss of circulation due to a decline in the total number of daily newspapers, from 1,657 to 1,645.

The trend away from afternoon publication, which had begun in the 1970s, continued in 1988. There were 22 fewer afternoon newspapers than in 1987, 12 more morning dailies, and 2 more "all-day" newspapers (with new editions published throughout the day). In all, evening cir-

culation declined by 5.4%, from 25,060,911 to 23,702,466, while morning circulation rose 4.5%, from 37,441,125 to 39,123,807. The number of Sunday newspapers published in conjunction with a daily newspaper increased from 802 to 820. Total Sunday circulation increased 6.6%, from 58,-924,518 to 62,829,875.

Among the year's various newspaper mergers, acquisitions, and other transactions, one event stood out: the approval by U.S. Attorney General Edwin Meese of the largest "joint operating agreement" in newspaper history. The arrangement involved the Gannett Co.'s *Detroit News* (circulation 686,787) and the Knight-Ridder chain's *Detroit Free Press* (circulation 649,312), both of which had decided to take advantage of a federal law designed to preserve the editorial voice of a dying newspaper by allowing it to combine its business operations with those of a healthy competitor. Thus, JOA, as the shared monopoly was often abbreviated, was in effect an exemption from federal antitrust laws. At the beginning of 1988, there were JOAs in 21 U.S. cities, including Cincinnati, Ohio, San Francisco, and Seattle, Wash., and no application had ever been denied. The Detroit case, however, was by far the largest consolidation ever proposed, involving more than $300 million in annual advertising and circulation revenues. Local businessmen and civic leaders, fearing the increases in advertising rates and newsstand prices that usually accompany a shared monopoly, initially opposed the consolidation. In a preliminary ruling an administrative law judge determined that both newspapers could survive without the merger. Nevertheless, Knight-Ridder declared that its 157-year-old *Free Press* would stop publishing unless the request was approved, and Attorney General Meese complied. Opponents of the merger, however, appealed his decision, and in December the case was still in court.

The biggest sale of the year involved the *New York Post* (circulation 555,000), which was bought by Peter Kalikow, a local real estate developer, from Rupert Murdoch. The *Post* became the largest U.S. daily to have a female editor when Kalikow installed Jane Amsterdam, a former magazine editor, in the newspaper's top editorial position.

On November 14 Katherine W. Fanning, editor of the *Christian Science Monitor,* and two other editors resigned in protest against a diversion of funds to the church's cable television program and monthly news magazine. Richard J. Cattani was immediately named to replace Fanning.

The Pulitzer gold medal for public service, the most prestigious of the Pulitzer Prizes, was awarded to the *Charlotte* (N.C.) *Observer* for its articles revealing the misuse of funds by the television ministry of evangelist Jim Bakker. The prize for general news reporting was won jointly by the *Alabama Journal* for a series on infant mortality and by the *Lawrence* (Mass.) *Eagle-Tribune* for a total of 175 articles on prison furloughs. The furlough series spotlighted the case of a convicted murderer who went on a crime spree while on furlough from a Massachusetts prison. The incident was used by George Bush as a campaign issue against Massachusetts Gov. Michael Dukakis.

The Pulitzer for national reporting went to Tim Weiner of the *Philadelphia Inquirer* for a series on secret budget accounts at the U.S. Defense Department. The international reporting prize was given to Thomas Friedman, chief of the *New York Times*'s Jerusalem bureau, for his coverage of Israel. Dave Barry, a humour columnist for the *Miami* (Fla.) *Herald,* won the award for commentary. The prize for criticism went to Tom Shales, the *Washington Post*'s television critic. Doug Marlette of the *Atlanta Constitution* and the *Charlotte Observer* was cited for his editorial cartoons.   (DONALD MORRISON)

Magazines. The British magazine market was again dominated by a seemingly endless stream of new titles, monthly or weekly, aimed at women: *Essentials* (January); *More!* (April); *Hello!* (May); *New Woman* (July); *Marie Claire* (August); and *Riva* (September). Several of them had roots in Europe (*Hello!* and *Marie Claire*) and the U.S. (*New Woman*).

These new entries were increasingly characterized by the huge sums of money spent on their continuing promotion. One of the previous year's newcomers, *Bella,* from the West German publisher Bauer, became Britain's best-selling women's magazine in 1988, with claimed sales of 1.4 million, on a strategy of low price per issue and a promotion budget of about £1 million a month. When Reed introduced *Riva* in September, it had a £7 million budget for the launch, but seven weeks later, with half of that money spent, *Riva* became the first casualty of the new boom, having failed to reach its sales targets.

A U.S. import aimed at men, the monthly *GQ,* was launched in November. Even in the glossy leisure sector that it occupied, however, there were problems. *Landscape,* introduced in 1987, was folded into *Country Times,* which had been started by defectors from *The Field.*

In February *New Society,* a respected reporter on social issues, was merged with the left-wing weekly *New Statesman.* A downturn in advertising for jobs in the social services field was blamed. Another serious weekly, *The Listener,* published by the BBC since the 1920s, passed into joint ownership with the commercial ITV network, with Alan Coren, formerly of *Punch,* as editor. At *Punch* Coren's successor, David Taylor, lasted only until October, when the proprietors, United Newspapers, ousted him, appointed first one acting editor and then another, and laid off many staff members, giving rise to fears that their confidence in the veteran humorous weekly was in doubt.

(PETER FIDDICK)

The first issue of *Lear's,* a magazine for women over 40, appeared in February. The New York City-based publication—developed and published by Frances Lear—showed signs of success from the start.

In 1988 it seemed that almost anyone with a micro-computer could publish a magazine at home. During the year scores of new small periodicals were published in this fashion in the U.S., including *Desktop Publishing,* which told readers how it was done. Most desktop publishing systems were sold to offices, but only during the year did professional publishers begin to be convinced that there was something in the revolution for them.

Freedom of speech has limits, or so said a Texas jury, which ordered the magazine *Soldier of Fortune* to pay $9.4 million in damages to the family of a woman whose husband hired a killer through a classified advertisement in the magazine. *Soldier of Fortune* appealed the decision.

It was a year of ownership changes. A few of the deals included the sales of *Woman's Day* to Hachette, *Psychology Today* to P. T. Partner's, *Modern Bride* to Cahners, *Mother Earth News* to Owen Lipstein, and *Science Digest* to Time Inc. In purchasing *Woman's Day,* the French publisher Hachette entered the U.S. magazine business for the first time.

Travel magazines became one of the most popular new categories. In 1987–88 the public was introduced to *Trips* from the Banana Republic clothing store; *European Travel & Life,* which offered tips for the rich from the Rupert Murdoch group; *Travel Today,* which named inexpensive hotels, air fares, and so forth; and Conde Nast's *Traveler,* which went to the other extreme and rated the best of everything.

The Boston-based *Atlantic* won three National Magazine Awards—for feature writing, fiction, and public service. Among other winners of the prestigious annual prizes were *Parents* for general excellence for titles with more than one million circulation, *Traveler* for special interests, and *Life* for design and a single-topic issue.

Among the best new magazines of 1987–88 were *Birder's World,* with a self-explanatory title; *Celebrity Plus,* a challenge of sorts to *People* and *Us; The Quarterly,* a bright new literary review; and *Hippocrates,* covering medicine and health. Others included *Harrowsmith,* a Canadian import about country living; *Sports History;* and *Children's Magic Window Magazine.* As usual, the vast majority of entries were specialized and drew upon narrow interests, such as *Decorative Rug* and *Animation Magazine.*

The movement from print to home video continued for many magazines. Among them were Time Inc. with cassettes on sports, *Money* with a personal finance program, and *American Baby* with a show on cable TV. *Ebony* produced a show for both broadcast and cable.

(WILLIAM A. KATZ)

Books. Publishers Row in the U.S. seemed a lot like Wall Street in 1988, with mergers and takeovers (hostile and otherwise) making news throughout the year. During 1988 publishing eyes seemed trained on either the maneuverings of billionaires Robert Bass and Robert Maxwell, who bid against one another for control of Macmillan, or the noisy squabble over *The Uncollected Stories of John Cheever* that precipitated two lawsuits between Mary Cheever, widow of Pulitzer Prize-winning author John Cheever, and Academy Chicago, a small publishing house.

First, however, there was a 1988 sequel to the legal conflict between Random House and J. D. Salinger over *J. D. Salinger: A Writing Life* by Ian Hamilton, which Random House had proposed to publish in 1986 but which Salinger was able to stop because the court agreed that his letters had been improperly quoted. In November 1987 the U.S. Supreme Court refused to hear Random House's appeal of a lower court's injunction barring publication of the biography. In February 1988, though, the publisher announced

that an "entirely rewritten" version of the biography would be published in May under a new title, *In Search of J. D. Salinger.* The text of all quoted or paraphrased letters was removed.

Speculation about the future of Macmillan ran high throughout 1988. The corporate drama began on May 17 when the Robert M. Bass Group, which owned 9.1% of Macmillan, made an unsolicited bid of $64 a share to take control of the publisher. Two weeks later Macmillan announced a restructuring as a defense against the bid. The company divided into two separate publicly held firms: Macmillan Publishing, which would remain a trade publishing house, and Macmillan Information Co., which would consist of nonpublishing operations spun off as a dividend to stockholders; the latter move raised the company's stock value considerably. On June 6 Bass sued in Delaware Chancery Court to stop this action; simultaneously, Macmillan sued Bass for stock manipulation, fraud, and violation of securities laws. On July 14 (by which time Bass had sweetened his initial offer and Macmillan had formally rejected it) the Delaware court disallowed the Macmillan restructuring. The following week British publishing magnate Robert Maxwell joined the fray by offering $80 a share for Macmillan, $5 more than Bass's most recent offer. During the next month Macmillan rejected that and another offer from Bass. On September 9 Maxwell raised his offer to $84. Three days later Macmillan agreed to a $2,360,000,000 buyout by the investment firm Kohlberg, Kravis, Roberts and Co. (KKR), which would buy 94% of Macmillan's outstanding stock at $85 a share. Maxwell, who did not give up and whose offer for Macmillan was still in force, brought suit against KKR in the Delaware Chancery. In early November the Delaware court ruled against the KKR buyout, and Maxwell acquired Macmillan for $90.25 a share.

The other major merger of the year was an unexpected one that astonished the publishing industry: Random House, the book-publishing subsidiary of Advance Publications (owned by the Newhouse family), bought the Crown Publishing Group in August. Both firms were privately owned, and financial terms were not disclosed, although a price tag of several hundred million dollars was estimated. The acquisition almost certainly made Random House the largest U.S. trade-book publisher. Crown was founded in 1936 as the publishing arm of Outlet Book Co., a remainder house that with its subsidiary operations still accounted for two-thirds of Crown's total sales. The first Crown book, *The Book of Furniture and Decoration,* sold 273,662 copies before it went out of print in 1984. Other Crown best-sellers included the novels of Jean Auel and Judith Krantz as well as *The Joy of Sex* and *How to Avoid Probate.* In October Random House purchased Vanguard Press, which had published the first books of Saul Bellow and Dr. Seuss. In the same month, it began to digest its acquisitions by restructuring itself into six new divisions, selling its school and college divisions to McGraw-Hill.

Soon after McGraw-Hill made this purchase, the company announced plans to sell its trade-book group, which a company spokesperson said "no longer fits our long-term plans." McGraw-Hill would "continue to emphasize educational, professional and reference books." Of the firm's total 1987 revenues of $563.9 million, approximately $10 million were in trade-book sales.

Throughout the year Dodd, Mead, founded in 1839, was in dangerous financial straits. To retire "senior debt" in May, it sold to the Putnam Berkley Publishing Group some of its most lucrative assets, including its children's book division and the publishing rights to mysteries by

Agatha Christie, and in December, two weeks before its 150th anniversary, it went into liquidation.

Shifts in company fortunes also affected Stein & Day, which for the past several years had faced bankruptcy. In June 1987 the company ceased publishing, filing for protection under Chapter 11 of the Federal Bankruptcy Code. It offered a 1,200-title backlist and 50 unpublished works for sale, appraised in court at a value of between $5 million and $6 million. Among the best-sellers Stein & Day had published were Elia Kazan's *The Arrangement*, *Laughing All the Way* by Barbara Howar, *The Defense Never Rests* by F. Lee Bailey, and Jack Higgins's *The Eagle Has Landed*.

John Cheever's widow, Mary, was locked in legal battle with publisher Academy Chicago throughout 1988, and at the year's end one of the two lawsuits remained unresolved. Academy Chicago and Mary Cheever signed an August 1987 contract for Academy Chicago to publish *The Uncollected Stories of John Cheever*. Eventually, Academy Chicago decided to publish 68 stories in one volume in the fall of 1988. She, however, believed that the collection should be limited to a smaller number of stories. To force her to proceed with publication (through her lawyers she claimed the contract was invalid because Academy Chicago had not consulted her on the number of stories to be included), Academy Chicago filed in May for a declaratory judgment in the Circuit Court of Cook County, Illinois. At about the same time, she sued Academy Chicago in White Plains (N.Y.) District Court for copyright infringement. In September the Illinois Circuit Court ruled that the August 1987 contract was valid and enforceable, adding that Cheever would have to select some stories that Academy Chicago might publish and suggesting that 10 to 15 would be appropriate. The New York suit remained to be adjudicated.

In announcing its 1987 revenues, Simon & Schuster (a subsidiary of Gulf and Western), with total revenues of $1,075,000,000 for the year, laid claim to being the largest U.S. publisher. Many acquisitions over the past four years—worth a total of $1.2 billion, including five companies in 1984 (among them Prentice-Hall), three in 1985, and nine each in 1986 and 1987—had transformed Simon & Schuster from a trade-book publisher into an educational and professional information publisher. Its 1983 revenues as a trade publisher were $220.3 million; four years later only 6% of the firm's total sales were trade-oriented.

Two record-breaking book contracts were announced in 1988. Mary Higgins Clark, a mystery writer (*Where Are the Children?; Weep No More, My Lady*), signed a contract for five books with Simon & Schuster that would pay between $10.1 million and $11.6 million, depending on bonuses. The contract was inaccurately reported to have been the first eight-figure book deal ever; more lucrative book deals had been negotiated for Danielle Steel, Jackie Collins, and Stephen King (who signed a two-book, $10 million deal with New American Library in 1985). Houghton Mifflin paid $801,000 for a retelling of *Swan Lake* (due in fall 1989) by novelist Mark Helprin, to be illustrated by Chris Van Allsburg. The price was a record for a children's book. Best-sellers for 1987 in the U.S. were three novels—*The Tommyknockers* by Stephen King (Putnam, 1,405,-000 copies sold), *Patriot Games* by Tom Clancy (Putnam, 1,063,000), and *Kaleidoscope* by Danielle Steel (Delacorte, 1,015,000)—and the nonfiction *Time Flies* by Bill Cosby (Doubleday, 1,461,000), the only nonfiction title to sell more than one million copies.   (WILLIAM W. GOLDSTEIN)

See also Literature.
This article updates the *Macropædia* article PUBLISHING.

Race Relations

The state of race relations in 1988 was characterized by confrontation, competition, and the use by politicians and government officials of racial prejudices and fears for their own purposes. It was also characterized by rising ethnic conflicts and territorial disputes, as in the Nagorno-Karabakh region of Azerbaijan, whose return the Armenians had been demanding; the conflicts between ethnic Albanians and the Slav population, Serbs and Montenegrins, living in Kosovo, Yugos.; the dispute between Hungary and Romania over the Hungarian minority in Transylvania; and the conflicts in Tibet between Tibetans and the Chinese authorities.

Asia. In Malaysia political and economic conflicts took on racial overtones during late 1987. The University of Malaya's decision to abolish teaching in Chinese, Tamil, and English was met with demonstrations. The government's appointment of non-Mandarin-speaking senior staff in Chinese primary schools was seen by Chinese educators as an attempt to "erode Chinese culture" and to "destroy the primary schools from within." It was met by a boycott of classes by tens of thousands of Chinese pupils. The government responded by arresting a third of all opposition leaders, three Chinese members of the government's National Front coalition, and the chief of the independent television channel and also by banning all public meetings and four national newspapers.

In Fiji the civilian government created by the leader of the 1987 coup, Brig. Gen. Sitiveni Rabuka, continued to be under the control of forces claiming to represent the indigenous Fijians. General Rabuka vowed to ensure their political supremacy, to turn the island into a strong Christian nation, and to make efforts to convert the ethnic Indians—who slightly outnumbered the indigenous Fijians—to Christianity.

In Sri Lanka the Indian peacekeeping force, which was sent to implement the Indo-Sri Lanka Agreement to Establish Peace and Normalcy in Sri Lanka of July 1987, had grown from 6,000 to 50,000 men. They were seen as being no closer to subjugating the Tamil militants fighting for a separate Tamil state in the north and east of the country than when they first arrived.

In the Chinese city of Nanjing (Nanking) in December, thousands of Chinese workers and students attacked African students and destroyed their dormitories. The disorders, apparently set off when African men attempted to go to a dance with Chinese women, reflected long-simmering racial tensions between the two groups.

Australia. The official bicentennial celebrations of the arrival of the first white settlers further divided Australians along racial lines. Aboriginal groups declared 1988 a year of mourning for forebears killed by early white settlers. In January the Anti-Slavery Society issued a report entitled "Land and Justice: Aboriginals Today," which documented an appalling record of poverty, deprivation, and misery of the "dispossessed minority with second-class status": unemployment six times the national average; infant mortality four times the national average; and 90% of the Aborigines living in poverty.

Australia's record on Aboriginal education was equally damning. In 1987 only 8% of Aboriginal 20–25-year-olds were enrolled in higher education. The high-school dropout rate was massively greater than that of whites, and Aboriginal parents and educators throughout 1988 demanded separate schools because of racism in the white-controlled education system.

South Africa. On June 9 the government of South Africa announced its third successive yearlong state of emergency. It was estimated that 2,000–2,500 people were still held in detention without trial and would continue to be held under the above-mentioned state of emergency. In addition, the banning of 19 organizations would continue, as would the banning of antiapartheid newspapers, such as the weekly *New Nation*—owned by the Roman Catholic Church—and *South*. The restrictions on the activities of the media were strengthened by broadening the category of persons and organizations that could not be quoted and by curbing the activities of small local news agencies.

In May the International Commission of Jurists charged South Africa's security forces with widespread use of torture and violence—even against children. They concluded that in South Africa "an undemocratic government has extended the executive power of the state so as to undermine the rule of law and destroy basic human rights."

The October local government elections were characterized by a continuing increase in white support for the far-right Conservative Party—though not at the level Conservative Party officials had hoped for—and a large-scale black boycott of the elections. In Soweto, for example, the black turnout was about 10.8%. There were only about 1.5 million registered black voters in a population of 26 million. The boycott was effective despite a revised emergency decree making it an offense, punishable by a heavy fine or jail for up to ten years or imprisonment without the option of a fine, to call for a boycott of municipal elections. Sixteen church leaders, including Archbishop Desmond Tutu of the Anglican Church and Allan Boesak of the World Alliance of Reformed Churches, called for a boycott.

United States. The Census Bureau on August 31 issued a report that found that while white poverty declined modestly from 11 to 10.5% in 1987, black poverty rose by 2% to 33.1%, and Hispanic poverty rose from 27.3 to 28.2%. The report noted that 45.8% of black children were living in poverty.

A Carnegie Foundation for the Advancement of Teaching study, entitled "An Imperiled Generation," found that most of the more than ten million children trapped in schools characterized by high dropout rates, low morale, aging buildings, and overregulation were black and Hispanic. A recently published report found that white children made up no more than 3% of the school population in inner-city schools. The Census Bureau reported that whites were more than twice as likely as blacks to complete college.

The 1988 presidential election was seen to have been strongly affected by racism. The race for the Democratic nomination was clearly affected by attitudes of voters and the media and party officials to Jesse Jackson because he was black. During the campaign for president there was widespread recognition that racism played a central role in the law-and-order theme of the Republican campaign—particularly in connection with television advertisements concerning the rape of a white woman by a black convict on a furlough from a Massachusetts prison.

Two court decisions in October shed additional light on the state of race relations in the U.S. A New York State grand jury determined that black teenager Tawana Brawley had not been abducted and sexually assaulted by a group of racist white men in November 1987, as she had claimed. The case had exacerbated racial tensions in the state. Later in the month a federal jury ruled that two white supremacist groups and 11 individuals were responsible for violently disrupting a civil rights march in Forsyth County, Ga., and awarded almost $1 million in damages to the demonstrators who had filed the suit.

Western Europe. In France electoral support for the far-right, racist National Front dropped dramatically in the elections to the National Assembly and in the departmental elections. The NF vote fell from 4,375,894 cast for party leader Jean-Marie Le Pen in the first round of the presidential election on April 24 to 2,359,228 in the first round of the Assembly elections. Only one NF candidate was elected—and in October she was stripped of her party membership and was sitting as an independent right-wing

(LEFT) AP/WIDE WORLD; (ABOVE) JOSE LOPEZ—THE NEW YORK TIMES

Members of Congress stand by as U.S. Pres. Ronald Reagan (above) signs a bill that offers an apology and provides compensation to the many Japanese-Americans who were forced to live in internment camps such as that in Manzanar, California (left), during World War II.

member. The NF vote fell still further in the departmental elections—down to 5% from 15% in the second round of the presidential election in May. The NF put up candidates for nearly two-thirds of the Assembly seats and finished with only one success.

In Great Britain the Commission for Racial Equality declared that urgent action was needed in employment, education, and housing if the plight of black people was not to get even worse. They called for a stronger Race Relations Act and more resources.

Racial harassment in schools was found to be "widespread and persistent." Complaints of racial harassment to the police increased by 25%, and a new survey by the Scottish Council for Racial Equality found that more than 80% of Pakistanis and Indians had experienced racist abuse, with 58% of Indians reporting a physical attack.

In West Germany the 1987 Annual Report on Political Extremism found that the far right had grown from 22,100 to 25,200 since 1986. They found 69 far-right organizations—20 of them neo-Nazi—and 91 people were convicted for neo-Nazi offenses during the year. A nationwide poll suggested that 6% of West Germans were overtly anti-Semitic, a further 10–15% expressed unequivocally anti-Semitic prejudices, and another 15–20% revealed traces of anti-Semitism in their thinking. The poll found 60% would like to see an end to the discussion of Germany's fascist past—as would a growing percentage of young people.

In March the Bavarian State Opera orchestra won the right not to play Sir Kenneth MacMillan's ballet *Élite Syncopations,* with music by the black American composer Scott Joplin, under a law passed in 1937 by the Nazis. The law held that no German could be compelled to perform music written by a black person. (LOUIS KUSHNICK)

Religion

Moves by Soviet leaders to ease restrictions on religious activities gave an unexpected lustre to the Russian Orthodox Church's 1988 observance marking the thousandth anniversary of the coming of Christianity to Russia. The surprising change in the Soviet religious climate was perhaps the most significant development in a year that also saw the first major schism in Roman Catholicism in more than a century, a storm of protest over a controversial film about the life of Jesus, church tensions over women in leadership positions, and additional chapters in a continuing saga of scandals in the world of televangelism.

More than 500 dignitaries from 100 countries—including the archbishop of Canterbury, Robert Runcie, and the American evangelist Billy Graham—attended the Russian Orthodox festivities. The welcome extended to the large number of prominent religious leaders from outside the Soviet Union would have been unthinkable a few years earlier.

Observers credited Soviet leader Mikhail Gorbachev with extending his program of *glasnost* (openness) and *perestroika* (restructuring) to treatment of churches and religious believers. Church buildings and monasteries seized by the government decades before were returned to church control. Easter services were held in some houses of worship for the first time since the era of Joseph Stalin. During the year, Gorbachev had an unprecedented meeting with Patriarch Pimen, leader of the Russian Orthodox Church. Evidence of the new official Soviet openness to religion was also seen in the release of prisoners held for violations of laws restricting religious practices and in promises by Soviet officials to review restrictive laws. The Orthodox

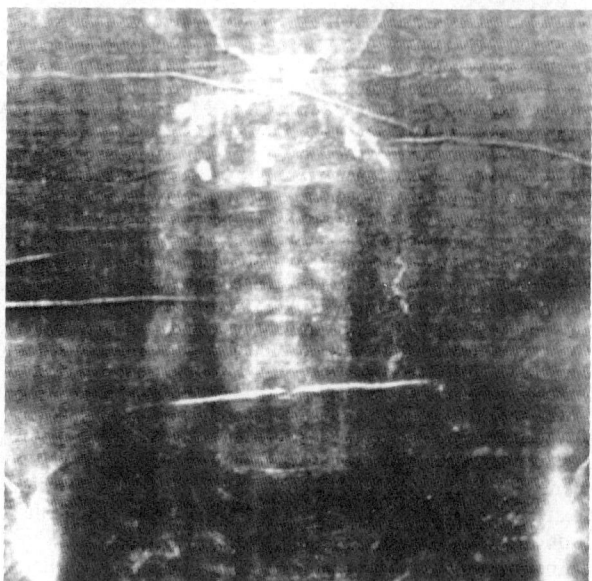

The image on the Shroud of Turin is believed by many to be that of Jesus Christ. Although for centuries the shroud was thought to be the burial cloth of Christ, radiocarbon dating showed that the shroud originated at a much later time.
AP/WIDE WORLD

church hierarchy reported a rise in enrollments at seminaries. Open Doors, a religious organization that in other years resorted to "Bible-smuggling" to make Scriptures available in Communist-dominated countries, announced that plans had been approved for it to ship one million Russian New Testaments into the Soviet Union. (See *The Orthodox Church,* below.)

In Switzerland rebel Roman Catholic Archbishop Marcel Lefebvre (*see* BIOGRAPHIES), 82, an opponent of the reforms of the second Vatican Council and a defender of the Latin Tridentine Mass, consecrated four bishops without the approval of Pope John Paul II. The action, which was formally proclaimed schismatic, led to Lefebvre's excommunication. The incident marked the first major split in Roman Catholicism since 1870, when the Old Catholics left the church over the doctrine of papal infallibility.

While Lefebvre and his followers represented rebellion on the right against Vatican teachings, Rome also sought to rein in its critics on the left. Charles Curran, an American priest and theologian earlier denied official approval to teach theology at Catholic University of America in Washington, D.C., continued to wage a fight for restoration of his teaching credentials. The writings on spirituality of another American priest, Matthew Fox, were judged unorthodox by Joseph Cardinal Ratzinger, the Vatican guardian of doctrinal orthodoxy. Dominican authorities imposed a "silencing" order on Fox at Ratzinger's direction. (See *Roman Catholic Church,* below.)

In Johannesburg offices of the South African Council of Churches and other church groups were bombed by unknown attackers. The explosion came shortly after South African church leaders had publicly committed themselves to a nonviolent strategy of civil disobedience. The church-state conflict in South Africa escalated in 1988, and senior government leaders unleashed scathing criticism against such church leaders as Anglican Archbishop Desmond Tutu and Allan Boesak of the Reformed Church. Liberal church groups in the United States and other Western nations continued to press for stronger sanctions against

(continued on page 291)

A Field Guide to Fundamentalisms

BY MARTIN E. MARTY

Incidents in American politics and religion during 1988 kept the word fundamentalism on page one of newspapers and on prime time television. While presidential candidate M. G. ("Pat") Robertson and fallen televangelist Jimmy Swaggart were technically Pentecostalists, the public identified them with fundamentalism. Commentators often treated the whole New Christian Right as fundamentalist, thus keeping the term on the public mind.

Incidents in world politics and religion similarly accented the trend that was making fundamentalism a household word. The inability of Iran to win the war with Iraq led analysts to measure how effective Ayatollah Ruhollah Khomeini's Shi'ite Islamic fundamentalism was at motivating an effective revolution in the Middle East. Headlines about battles between Muslims and Jews in the West Bank and the Gaza Strip furthered talk about Islamic fundamentalism and regularly labeled Israeli movements like the Gush Emunim, "the Party of God," as fundamentalist.

Fundamentalism showed up as a surprisingly strong accent in movements around the world. Many Protestants in Northern Ireland proudly called themselves fundamentalist. Extreme rightist groups in South Africa increasingly acquired the same designation. The term appeared in connection with Sikh revolts and with other religiopolitical movements throughout Asia. Most frequently, people linked it with efforts stringently to apply Shari'ah, Islam's holy law, in nations from Nigeria through Egypt to Malaysia.

Purist historians and linguists may protest the use of this American-born term to describe movements that differ radically from the Protestant Christianity on whose soil the term first appeared. Yet it is evident that in these cases, as so often, they will not find it possible to slow the spread of the word. The public, mass communicators, political scientists, and scholars of religion need some way to designate the rise and spread of a modern phenomenon.

Clues to a Phenomenon. A field guide to fundamentalisms opens with a reminder that commentators and leaders are speaking of *modern* fundamentalism. There have been fundamentalist-like movements all through history. For centuries Hindu parties responded to challenges much as modern fundamentalists do. One must ask why in the 20th century a new word or concept had to be invented for diverse movements and parties. Good words like "conservative," "traditional," "classic," and "orthodox" already existed. What occasioned the addition of another term?

The idea of *modern* fundamentalism provides a clue. People adopt or apply the term after movements feel uncommon threats. These challenges take many forms.

People whose ancestors led sheltered lives cannot keep their own values separate and intact when modernity—whatever form it takes—invades. Often cinema, television, radio, and the modern press bring signals and symbols that clash with the values and practices traditionalists cherish. Similarly, pluralism, the existence of many faiths among many peoples within the same nation or region, bewilders those who want homogeneity in order to preserve their values.

The attacks on tradition may also be intellectual. In the 19th-century United States, the impact of Darwinian evolutionary theory upset Protestants who took literally the Genesis account of origins. When scholars imported European styles of biblical criticism and questioned the literal truth of the Bible, conservatives reacted. Reaction is a second clue for spotting fundamentalism. Fundamentalists are people who were already conservative and traditionalist but who, to counter challenges, reacted and invented new, harder-line approaches.

The third clue in a field guide is in the word itself. When reactionaries want to hold their forts, to counterattack, or to spread the faith, they reach for "fundamentals." A series of pamphlets first published in 1910 in the United States was called *The Fundamentals*. It indicated what doctrines the authors and disseminators thought were at stake. When believers in these doctrines formed parties within denominations, a Baptist editor, Curtis Lee Laws, in 1920 urged that they be called fundamentalist. Partisans chose to call themselves thus, and their enemies, religious moderates and liberals and modernists, were glad to apply the word.

Reference to such "modernists" is a fourth clue. Fundamentalisms tend to arise when already challenged people sense that some within their culture are adapting, making compromises. When American Protestants in seminaries and pulpits found ways to blend faith and evolution or affirmed that biblical criticism was a better approach to the word of God, they seemed treasonous. When moderate Shi'ites, Sunni Muslims, or secular-minded Iranians or Egyptians began to tolerate other faiths or ideologies, people like the Ayatollah Khomeini or leaders of the Muslim Brotherhood took revenge on these "infidels."

The "fundamentals" differ vastly from religion to religion, from culture to culture. It is this diversity that led some critics to protest that it is confusing to speak of fundamentalism across the lines of nations, cultures, and faiths. Protestant fundamentalists in America and Northern Ireland stress certain doctrines such as biblical inerrancy or the second coming of Christ which are necessarily offensive to Sikhs or Muslims. All Muslims believe literally in an inerrant Qur'an, so they cannot use that as a fundamental belief. They stress not fundamental doctrines but practices, insisting that the religious law called Shari'ah be literally enforced. If it offends the rest of the world to see television portrayals of an adulterous couple being stoned or of someone chopping off the hand of a pickpocket, well and good; the practice is supposed to offend all but the true believers.

Matters of Style. If the content of fundamentalisms differ, so do the styles. One can sympathize with pacific American fundamentalists who find themselves linked by the press with the ayatollah. Similarly, Shi'ite Iranians or Israeli "ultras" seethe when the press lumps them with American Protestant intransigents. It is true, they have some superficially common interests. For instance, the one feature of modernity no fundamentalists seem to reject and most of them seem to rely upon is technology. The Iranian revolution fed on cassette tapes smuggled in from

Martin E. Marty is Fairfax M. Cone distinguished service professor of the history of modern Christianity at the University of Chicago and a senior editor of The Christian Century.

France during Khomeini's exile. American fundamentalists make use of television, computers, and rapid mailing techniques with a facility Catholics, Jews, and mainstream Protestants cannot match.

Beyond such coincidences, however, many choices divide fundamentalisms. Not all are belligerent, ready to resort to arms, as the Iranians or Muslim Brotherhood have been. Not all of them even try to change polity or policy through law. Through the first 50 years after 1920, American fundamentalists had the image of being · generally nonpolitical. As individuals, most were conservative on social issues but could be liberal on economic ones; many supported the New Deal. Fundamentalist-movement support of the prohibition of alcohol, efforts to prevent legalized gambling, and the organization of voters against the candidacy of the Catholic Democrat Alfred E. Smith in 1928 were exceptions.

During those years of political quiet, most non-fundamentalists ignored, dismissed, or disdained their fundamentalist neighbours. They were the nice people down the block who ran the grocery, paid their taxes, went to church twice a week, and would witness to Jesus if you gave them a chance. Or they were residents of the Bible Belt, rubes or hillbillies or hicks. Certainly they were throwbacks or fossils, the butt of jokes. In reaction, they eventually struck back, and right-wing political leaders saw in them a restless cohort waiting to be organized. Television preachers linked up with these politicians. Respectable candidates like Ronald Reagan appealed to them. They began with a politics based on resentment and quickly moved to a politics based on a desire to rule. Through fronts like the Moral Majority they asserted some power in the elections of the 1980s, and will continue to do so.

Here to Stay. Islamic fundamentalism will not disappear. It is winning in many African and South Pacific island nations. Not all of it will follow the pattern of Khomeini's revolution. Often such fundamentalism wins its way in parliaments and through ballots. At other times, its devotees must compromise for coexistence with secular or moderate parties. As decades pass, antifundamentalists, weary of terrorism or reacting against legislation, may blunt their force.

In the meantime, in pluralist societies like the United States fundamentalists are trying to make their intentions clear. More and more nonfundamentalists are observing and listening to them and learning to make distinctions among conservative religious parties. For instance, Pentecostalists join with fundamentalists in political causes but differ in some approaches to faith. They also believe in an inerrant Bible but are more ready to picture God speaking to them today. Evangelicals on the order of Billy Graham are often identified as fundamentalists; the two parties could sign up together as believers in what they regard to be the fundamental doctrines. Yet evangelicals are a more moderate group. Indeed, fundamentalists often attack them for compromising, even though they form coalitions with them for practical ends.

Fundamentalists tend to be frustrated when they do not prevail, whether by the sword of revolution, the pressure for legislation, or response to their witness. It is likely that around the world they will have to settle for living next door to people whose faiths differ radically from theirs. In every case, the rise, power, and spread of fundamentalisms have been astonishments on the modern scene. Nonfundamentalists in many nations will be busy for years trying to understand the impulses that give rise to these reactions and to the movements themselves.

(continued from page 289)

the South African government and divestment from companies with ties to South Africa.

Both Roman Catholic and Anglican church bodies struggled with conflicts over women's role in the church. In an apostolic letter, *Mulieris Dignitatem* ("On the Dignity of Women"), issued on the occasion of the Marian Year, Pope John Paul II called for an end to all discrimination against women in everyday life, even linking prejudicial attitudes against women to sin, but he reaffirmed the centuries-old ban against women priests. U.S. Roman Catholic bishops issued the first draft of a proposed pastoral letter on women and the church, "Partners in the Mystery of Redemption," which called sexism a sin but urged no startling changes in traditional practices. The U.S. bishops did, however, prod the church to study the question of eventual admission of women to the diaconate, an order subordinate to priesthood. Deacons have authority to perform most leadership tasks except presiding over the sacraments. The letter also recommended that women be regularly assigned to read Scriptures and assist at the altar, routine practices in many parishes although not formally provided for by the Vatican.

For the first time, a woman was elected bishop in a church of the worldwide Anglican Communion. Barbara Harris, a 58-year-old divorced black priest from Philadelphia, was selected as suffragan (assistant) bishop of the Episcopal diocese of Massachusetts. Her election came less than three months after participants in the Lambeth Conference, the once-a-decade gathering of the world's Anglican bishops, agreed to let each of the 27 provinces of the communion decide for itself whether to ordain women as priests and bishops. The bishop of London, Graham Leonard, chief opponent of women's ordination in the Church of England, said he and his followers would not recognize Harris as a bishop. Earlier, the General Convention of the Episcopal Church, the U.S. branch of Anglicanism, had approved a controversial "Episcopal Visitors" provision that would allow dissident parishes under the ministry of a woman bishop to request the services of a male bishop from outside the diocese. (See *Anglican Communion,* below.)

The United Methodist Church, which first elected a woman to the episcopacy in 1980, named its fourth and fifth woman bishops to preside over the denomination's Philadelphia and Minneapolis areas. One of the new leaders, Sharon Brown Christopher, was the first in history to have a "bishop's husband," the Rev. Charles Logsdon Christopher, at the time of her election.

Homosexuality continued to be an explosive issue in many religious bodies. Ministries to AIDS victims—many of them gay men—increased as the number of deaths from the deadly disease rose, but church leaders disagreed on whether to advocate openly the use of condoms to help prevent the spread of the sexually transmitted disease, since some feared that their constituencies would interpret this as condoning homosexual activity. The United Methodist Church voted to retain a ban on the ordination or appointment of "self-avowed practicing homosexuals" as pastors. The new Evangelical Lutheran Church in America, within weeks of its January 1 start-up with the merger of three denominations, became embroiled in a dispute over ordaining homosexuals. Three openly gay male seminarians who had been certified as qualified for ordination by committees in predecessor church bodies were eventually ruled ineligible by bishops of the new church. New guidelines were drawn up by the church's Division for Ministry forbidding all extramarital sexual activity by candidates for ordination. The United Church of Canada, on the other

"The Birth of Brahma with Reclining Vishnu on a Makara," a sandstone carving long missing from Thailand's Khmer temple of Phnom Rung, became the source of heated debate between Thai officials and those of the Art Institute of Chicago, where it was discovered. The museum, which obtained the piece legitimately, finally agreed to return it when a U.S. foundation promised to provide a work of comparable value.
AP/WIDE WORLD

hand, adopted a policy that made homosexuals eligible for the ordained ministry, despite warnings from opponents that the action could split the church. (See *Lutheran Communion; The United Church of Canada,* below.)

Conservative Christian groups mounted protests and a boycott of the motion picture *The Last Temptation of Christ.* The film by noted director Martin Scorsese (*see* BIOGRAPHIES) was based on a 1960 novel by Nikos Kazantzakis, who also wrote *Zorba the Greek.* The film's critics said it painted an inaccurate picture of a doubting Jesus. Objections were raised also because of the film's sexual content. Other church figures defended the film's speculations about the humanity of Jesus and his struggle with his mission as the Messiah.

Financial woes hit many religious organizations. The Presbyterian Church (U.S.A.) released a survey warning of a drastic income dip expected to come with the graying of the membership of mainline churches. As the World Council of Churches (WCC), composed of 300 Protestant and Orthodox churches in 100 countries, marked its 40th anniversary at a meeting in Hannover, West Germany, council leaders said the drop in the value of the U.S. dollar was causing budgetary strains. Although U.S. churches increased their donations to the council in Geneva, the value of the donations in Swiss francs decreased. The Vatican announced a record deficit and appealed to Roman Catholics worldwide to help erase the shortfall.

The problem of shrinking church resources in the United States was dramatized by the announcement by the Roman Catholic archdiocese of Detroit that it planned to close 43 of its 112 parishes—the most sweeping cutback by the Catholic Church in U.S. history. The closings, all in the inner city, were prompted not only by a drop in income but also by the movement of traditionally Catholic populations from urban areas to the suburbs, a shortage of priests, and the high cost of maintaining old church buildings. Critics accused the archdiocese of abandoning ministries to inner-city blacks. The National Council of Churches, made up of more than 30 Protestant and Orthodox bodies in the U.S., was forced to cut back staff and programs as a result of dwindling support from member churches. Council officials said the costly relocations of member churches away from the council's New York City headquarters were partly to blame. Lutheran offices moved to Chicago; Presbyterians established a new headquarters in Louisville, Ky.; and United Church of Christ officials were proposing a relocation to Cleveland, Ohio.

Personal scandals in the lives of television evangelists made news, as they had the previous year. Jimmy Swaggart of Baton Rouge, La., stepped down from his television pulpit after confessing to a moral lapse involving a prostitute. He was defrocked by the Assemblies of God after he refused to obey the terms of a two-year rehabilitation program. An Orthodox Jew from Toronto bought the assets of the troubled PTL ("Praise the Lord" or "People That Love") ministry for $65 million. In December former PTL leader Jim Bakker and a former aide, Richard Dortch, were indicted on federal charges of mail and wire fraud and conspiracy. In response to uproars over shady financial dealings by TV ministry entrepreneurs, the National Religious Broadcasters adopted new standards for auditing, governance, and accountability for its member groups.

A coalition of "mainstream" religious bodies, hoping to benefit from the plummeting ratings of evangelical broadcasters, started the Vision Interfaith Satellite Network, a cable channel with programming by Protestant, Catholic, Jewish, Mormon, and other groups. ACTS, a Southern Baptist-owned cable network, ran into financial troubles and was sold to private interests who promised to maintain a style of programming consistent with Southern Baptist values. In the ten-year campaign by fundamentalists to take control of agencies of the 14-million-member Southern Baptist Convention, the ultraconservative faction gained majorities on some seminary boards and denominational agencies. (See *Baptist Churches,* below.)

American Jewish groups that had long defended the State of Israel under almost any circumstances unleashed uncharacteristically sharp criticism against the Israeli government after Israeli troops began beating scores of young Palestinians suspected of taking part in an uprising to protest continued Israeli occupation of the West Bank and Gaza. (See *Judaism,* below; WORLD AFFAIRS [Middle East and North Africa]: *Israel.*)

New scientific tests showed that the Shroud of Turin—believed by many to be the burial shroud of Jesus Christ—was only six or seven centuries old and could not date to the time of Jesus. The famous relic, named for the city of Turin, Italy, where it was kept, shows what appears to be a photographic image of a crucified man. Sophisticated carbon-14 analysis indicated that the linen cloth could be dated to sometime between 1260 and 1390. Church officials said the faithful would probably continue to venerate the shroud, much as they would a masterwork of religious art.   (JEAN CAFFEY LYLES)

PROTESTANT CHURCHES

Anglican Communion. The possibility that a woman would be elected as bishop dominated discussion throughout the Anglican Communion in 1988. That possibility was realized on September 24 when the diocese of Massachusetts elected Barbara C. Harris as a suffragan, or assistant bishop.

This was the central issue for the Lambeth Conference of Anglican bishops in Canterbury, England, July 17–August 7. Held once every decade, the 1988 Lambeth Conference attracted more than 500 bishops from 27 Anglican provinces. Its chief task was preserving the unity of the Anglican Communion, whose nonhierarchical character gives complete autonomy to its provinces in such matters. Eight provinces, including the Episcopal Church in the U.S., had already adopted legislation permitting the ordination of women as priests and bishops. The conference approved a resolution urging respect for one another's decisions on the issue, "without such respect necessarily indicating acceptance of the principles involved."

The Church of England now ordained women to the diaconate but not the priesthood. Its July synod passed by a 299–216 vote the first stage of legislation that would open its priesthood to women. The figures still fell short of the two-thirds majority that the legislation would eventually require. The archbishop of Canterbury, Robert Runcie, announced that he favoured the ordination of women but said the time was not yet right for the Church of England to take the step.

Anticipating the election of a woman bishop, the Episcopal Church's General Convention passed an "Episcopal Visitors" resolution. If a particular parish could not accept a woman bishop in a diocese where one had been elected, the resolution would allow the presiding bishop to designate a male member of the House of Bishops as "episcopal visitor" to that parish. The convention also took action enabling the Philippine Episcopal Church to become an autonomous province of the Anglican

THE WITNESS; PHOTOGRAPH, MARY LOU SUHOR

In a controversial decision by the diocese of Massachusetts, the Rev. Barbara C. Harris became the first woman to be elected bishop of the Episcopal Church.

Communion. It had been a missionary jurisdiction of the U.S. church.

The Anglican Communion mourned the passing of two of its major leaders with the deaths of Arthur Michael Ramsey, the 100th archbishop of Canterbury (*see* OBITUARIES), and Festo Kivengere, Ugandan bishop and founder of African Evangelistic Enterprise. Kivengere, who died on May 18 in Nairobi, Kenya, had clashed with the Ugandan dictator Idi Amin in 1977 and eventually fled the country.

(DAVID E. SUMNER)

Baptist Churches. The American Baptist Churches in the U.S.A. (formerly Northern Baptists) successfully completed a campaign in 1988 that raised in excess of $31 million. Half would go toward starting 500 new churches in the U.S. and half for mission work overseas. The ABC/USA was reputed to be the most integrated of all the mainstream, traditionally white denominations. Many of the new churches would be in minority communities. During the year, Daniel Weiss was appointed as the denomination's general secretary.

By all accounts, the fundamentalist takeover of the Southern Baptist Convention begun in 1979 was completed ahead of schedule as 30,000 elected messengers (delegates) from 37,286 local churches gathered in San Antonio, Texas, in June 1988. By a small margin they elected fundamentalist Jerry Vines, copastor of the First Baptist Church in Jacksonville, Fla., as president. Conservatives, or fundamentalists, could continue to replace seminary administrators (though not faculty with tenure), missionaries, and agency employees with those who agreed with their insistence on biblical inerrancy, the belief that the Bible is literally authoritative in all matters.

Moderates saw the fundamentalists as making a radical departure from traditional Baptist beliefs. For instance, in one resolution moderates felt the fundamentalists were undercutting the "priesthood of every believer," generally accepted as a foundational Baptist tenet. To show their displeasure, about 200 moderates marched to the plaza in front of the Alamo, where they symbolically shredded the resolution. W. Randall Lolley, who had resigned in 1987 as president of Southeastern Baptist Theological Seminary after a struggle with inerrantist trustees, called the resolution "the most non-Baptist document I've ever seen."

Despite these disagreements, the decade-long concern about schism apparently could be laid to rest as many local churches took sides with the moderates, thus providing a certain stalemated stability. Meanwhile, for whatever reason, baptisms decreased in 1986, and membership rose by the smallest percentage since 1936. The Foreign Mission Board announced serious budget cuts.

The world entity of Baptists, the Baptist World Alliance, elected Denton Lotz, an American Baptist and former missionary, as executive secretary.

The National Baptist Convention, U.S.A., Inc., the largest black religious organization in the world, with 7.7 million members, began construction of its world headquarters in Nashville, Tenn. T. J. Jemison was president of the convention.

(NORMAN R. DE PUY)

Christian Church (Disciples of Christ). After adopting its 12-year priority "to develop vital congregations as dynamic faith communities in prophetic, redemptive and reconciling ministries to the whole world," the Disciples of Christ invited all members to participate in a churchwide planning conference, held in Lexington, Ky., in June 1988. The General Board affirmed several of the concerns and suggestions that emerged and approved a Priority Council to establish a priority plan.

Disciples' giving topped $25 million for the first time. Even so, giving fell short of projections made for 1988, resulting in across-the-board budget cuts for the general units of the church.

Members of the Hispanic Caucus withdrew temporarily from the Committee on Racial Ethnic Inclusiveness and Empowerment, claiming that current church structure inhibited their full participation. The top executive bodies of the Disciples and their partner church, the United Church of Christ, held a historic joint meeting in March. The Disciples continued their dialogue with the Roman Catholic Church and conversations with Christians in the Soviet Union and the World Alliance of Reformed Churches.

(AUDREY BERTINA LEE)

Churches of Christ. The bicentennial celebration of the birth of the religious reformer Alexander Campbell, Sept. 12, 1988, was marked by numerous efforts to unify the various branches of the Restoration movement and to restore Campbell's emphasis on knowledge of and obedience to the Scriptures.

The falling dollar had cut into European missions, but World Bible School, a correspondence outreach, was reaching into China, and World Christian Broadcasting covered a third of the globe with broadcasts in Russian, Chinese, Japanese, and English. New benevolent efforts included a program for battered wives at the Madison Church in Madison, Tenn.; numerous ministries to substance abusers; and Room at the Inn, which housed the homeless in Nashville, Tenn. Bering Drive Church in Houston, Texas, was among the churches serving the spiritual, psychological, and financial needs of AIDS victims.

The recent edition of *Where the Saints Meet* indicated a 3% increase in membership of U.S. churches of Christ since 1980. *The Worldly Church,* a book by three college professors in Texas, called on churches to examine the tendency toward secularization. (M. NORVEL YOUNG)

Church of Christ, Scientist. At its 1988 annual meeting held in Boston in June, the Christian Science Church focused on the denomination's continued commitment to spiritual healing. During the year, several parents faced legal challenges for having relied on Christian Science care for their children. Members were told that these legal challenges to spiritual healing were ironic, given that "one of the most significant contributions Christian Science has made to society has been its healing of children. It seems especially vital that society look beyond the assumption that there is only one method of care—conventional medical treatment."

A feature-length documentary film about church founder Mary Baker Eddy was completed. The *Christian Science*

Monitor expanded in two new areas: "World Monitor," an evening news program, made its debut on cable television's Discovery Channel, and a monthly magazine, *World Monitor,* began publication. (*See* PUBLISHING: *Newspapers.*)

Pearline Thompson succeeded to the one-year post of church president.

(NATHAN A. TALBOT)

Church of Jesus Christ of Latter-day Saints. With almost seven million church members at the end of 1988 and some 15,-000 local congregations in 100 countries, high officials increasingly communicated with members by means of statements of the First Presidency read at Sunday worship services. In 1988 statements were issued calling on all members "to commit themselves to the establishment of full civil equality for all of God's children"; discussing AIDS and emphasizing chastity before marriage, total fidelity in marriage, and abstinence from all homosexual behaviour; and reiterating the long-standing church policy of strict political neutrality.

The church demonstrated its commitment to ecumenical relief efforts by substantial contributions to the needs of the homeless in Salt Lake City, by entering into a cooperative arrangement with the American Red Cross to provide assistance to victims of disasters in the U.S. and its possessions, and by continued contributions to development programs abroad. The church played a major role in polio immunizations for more than a million children in Kenya and Côte d'Ivoire.

In June Elder Howard W. Hunter was sustained as president of the Council of the Twelve Apostles, the office next in line to the president of the church, succeeding Marion G. Romney, who died the previous month. In 1988 temples were under construction in Toronto; Las Vegas, Nev.; Portland, Ore.; and San Diego, Calif. In June the church was granted full legal recognition by Hungary. The Aba Nigerian Stake (diocese) was formed in May, the first stake in western Africa.

(LEONARD J. ARRINGTON)

Jehovah's Witnesses. During 1988 the Witnesses sponsored a series of "Divine Justice" conventions in over 90 countries. More than six million attended these four-day Bible seminars. A highlight was the release of a new Bible encyclopaedia, *Insight on the Scriptures.* The two-volume set, totaling 2,560 pages, contained articles about 3,000 persons and 1,000 places mentioned in the Bible. Also released was a 320-page commentary, *Revelation—Its Grand Climax at Hand!,* containing an explanation of every verse of this cryptic book.

Jehovah's Witnesses published over 30 million Bibles and religious books during 1987. To help persons apply the Bible, all Witnesses were encouraged to teach others on a one-to-one basis, and during 1987 they conducted weekly Bible-study sessions in three million households. Such methods had increased their membership by 50% since 1980 to 3,395,612 in 210 countries in 1987. To accommodate such increases, it was necessary during 1988 to enlarge or build new expanded administrative facilities in 24 countries. This work was done primarily by local Witnesses, supplemented by an international construction crew of 244 volunteers.

(FREDERICK W. FRANZ)

Lutheran Communion. A theme and subthemes for the eighth assembly of the Lutheran World Federation (LWF), to be held in 1990 in Curitiba, Brazil, were chosen in June 1988 by the LWF Executive Committee. "I Have Heard the Cry of My People" was to be the theme, and the four subthemes specified cries for life in communion, salvation, peace with justice, and a liberated creation.

With the situation in southern Africa an ongoing Lutheran concern, church representatives from the five Nordic countries met in Norway with counterparts from eight southern African countries to discuss economic and cultural cooperation. An explosion in February in Oshakati, South West Africa/Namibia, killed 27 people, including the 18-year-old daughter of Kleopas Dumeni, Lutheran bishop for the northern part of the country. LWF General Secretary Gunnar Stålsett and other LWF representatives met in Angola with leaders of the South West Africa People's Organization, the principal group in the fight for Namibian independence.

In the U.S. the new Evangelical Lutheran Church in America (ELCA)—which brought together about 5.3 million people belonging to three predecessor bodies—officially began operating at the beginning of the year. The ELCA faced its first major controversy when it became known early in the year that three seminarians who described themselves as "openly gay" had been declared eligible for a call to service in a parish or other setting. In the ELCA such a call is necessary before one can be ordained. After discussing the matter in closed session, the conference of ELCA bishops announced that all extramarital sexual activity would preclude ordination for anyone otherwise qualified.

The Lutheran-Roman Catholic Joint Commission held the third session in the third phase of its two-decade-old dialogue. It completed work on a paper, "Ascertaining the Wide-Ranging Agreement on Justification" (a major issue on which Lutherans and Roman Catholics split in the 16th century). In East Germany leaders and members of the eight Lutheran and United regional churches continued to press the government for better treatment of environmental and peace activists and of those wishing to leave the country.

The first women—about 100—were ordained as Lutheran pastors in Finland in 1988, as were the first two women in one of Indonesia's Lutheran denominations. The 2.6 million-member Lutheran Church-Missouri Synod in the U.S. was now the largest Lutheran denomination not ordaining women.

(THOMAS HARTLEY DORRIS)

Methodist Churches. In May 1988 Methodists all over the world celebrated the 250th anniversary of John and Charles Wesley's conversion. The focus of the celebrations was a service on May 24, the day of John Wesley's "Aldersgate experience," in St. Paul's Cathedral, London, attended by Queen Elizabeth II, together with representatives of world Methodism and leaders of other churches, including the archbishop of Canterbury and Basil Cardinal Hume. It was followed by an open-air service at Nettleton Court, near the site of the house in Aldersgate Street where Wesley felt his heart "strangely warmed."

The recommendation of the Joint Commission of the World Methodist Council and Lutheran World Federation to establish "full fellowship of Word and Sacraments" was given concrete expression in West Germany in a service of Holy Communion in the Lutheran St. Lorenz Church at Nürnberg in September 1987. The service brought together not only Methodists and Lutherans but also Reformed and United Churches. The fifth general assembly of the Council of Methodist Churches in Latin America was held in Quito, Ecuador, in February 1988.

The quadrennial General Conference of the U.S.-based United Methodist Church, the largest Methodist church in the world with 9.1 million members, met in St. Louis, Mo., in April. Among its principal decisions was an agreement to invest $20 million in a new university in Zimbabwe. In other actions, the General Conference formulated a new doctrinal statement for its Book of Discipline in which the Bible was reaffirmed as the primary authority, interpreted by "tradition, experience and reason, under the guidance of the Holy Spirit"; maintained its long-standing position that homosexuals are persons of "sacred worth" while reaffirming its ban against the ordination or appointment of active homosexuals; approved a new hymn book and psalter, in the process agreeing to maintain the use of the personal pronoun "His" in reference to God in 35 Psalms from which it had been removed by the Hymnal Revision Committee; and affirmed support for "In Defense of Creation," the statement by the Council of Bishops on the dangers of nuclear escalation.

The 1988 World Methodist Peace Prize was awarded to Gordon Wilson, whose daughter was killed and he himself injured in a bomb attack during a Remembrance Day parade at Enniskillen, Northern Ireland. He won worldwide respect for his televised statement that he bore no bitterness to the perpetrators.

(JOHN C. A. BARRETT)

Pentecostal Churches. In the wake of the sex and financial scandals involving Jim Bakker that made headlines in 1987, the Assemblies of God suffered a further blow in February 1988 when another of their televangelists, Jimmy Swaggart, confessed to sexual indiscretions. Although his home district slapped his hand with a three-month suspension, the denominational headquarters held Swaggart to the two-year rehabilitation program required by church law. When Swaggart refused to submit to this discipline, he was defrocked in April.

Despite this setback, Pentecostal denominations in the U.S. pushed forward with plans to evangelize the world during the last decade of the millennium. Looking toward the year AD 2000, the Assemblies of God adopted a plan for the 1990s called a "Decade of Harvest." Similarly, the Church of God (Cleveland, Tenn.) adopted a plan called "Project 2000," while the Pentecostal Holiness Church called its plan "Target 2000."

Some 200,000 Christians gathered on the Mall in Washington, D.C., in April in the first "Washington for Jesus" rally since 1980. In August over 15,000 delegates met in Fort Worth, Texas, to reelect Raymond

Crowley as general overseer of the Church of God (Cleveland, Tenn.).

Reinhard Bonnke announced to 20,000 followers in a crusade in Birmingham, England, that he would bring his 32,000-seat tent to Europe for one month annually, beginning in 1989. In Poland the Pentecostals organized the Pentecostal Church Synod with 86 local churches and 10,000 adherents. (VINSON SYNAN)

Reformed, Presbyterian, and Congregational Churches. During 1988 the World Alliance of Reformed Churches (WARC) devoted much of its energy to preparing for the 22nd General Council of the World Alliance of Reformed Churches, to be held in Seoul, South Korea, Aug. 15–27, 1989. Milan Opocensky was elected to replace Edmond Perret as general secretary when the latter retired in October 1989. Opocensky was an ordained minister of the Evangelical Church of the Czech Brethren and professor of Christian social ethics at the Comenius Faculty in Prague.

Beginning in 1988, the WARC took up the issue of human rights violations in Romania, drawing particular attention to the plight of ethnic minorities in that country and the planned destruction of 7,000 villages in the government's attempt to industrialize the country. In October the executive committee agreed to continue the suspension of the Dutch Reformed Church from full membership in the alliance for its continued support of South Africa's apartheid policies.

Two consultations for member churches in southern Africa were held in April. The first, "Church, Mission and Witness," focused on the role played by the Dutch Reformed Church and the South African government in directing the mission policies and influencing theological education of church members and pastoral candidates in the whole region of southern Africa. The second, a theological consultation on "Called to Witness to the Gospel Today," attempted to discern the theological contribution to be made by Reformed churches in the region, taking into account the cultural traditions of African peoples. The participants voted to establish a region of WARC member churches in southern Africa.

In September minority churches in Europe convened for a roundtable discussion of the issues—justice, peace, and the integrity of creation—to be addressed at the General Council. Discussions were held on disarmament, transforming national policies of deterrence to policies of mutual trust and cooperation, redistributing economic resources, and ways to protect the environment.

In October 1987 the WARC had welcomed five churches from Zaire to membership: the Evangelical Community in Zaire, the Protestant Community in Shaba, the Presbyterian Community in East Kasai, the Presbyterian Community in West Kasai, and the Reformed Presbyterian Community. All were members of Coreza (the Reformed Conference of Zaire). (JILL SCHAEFFER)

Religious Society of Friends. An event that drew Quakers from all parts of the world was the Triennial meeting of Friends World Committee for Consultation at the end of August 1988. For the first time, it was held in northern Asia, with the small group of Friends in Japan as hosts. One matter discussed at the Triennial was the call of the WCC for concerted action under the title "Justice, Peace, and the Integrity of Creation." Friends in The Netherlands had called for wholehearted involvement in this conciliar process by Quakers at the local, national, and international level, and this was endorsed by the world body.

Other events that drew the attention of Quakers internationally were the third UN Special Session on Disarmament in New York—where the permanent Quaker UN office was joined by Friends with specialist knowledge of disarmament from Switzerland, East Germany, Australia, and the U.K.—and a Mission and Service Conference held in Birmingham, England, in April. The year 1988 marked the tenth anniversary of the Leaveners, the British Quaker Youth Theatre, which celebrated by taking a production to the U.S.S.R., the first stage of an exchange with the Moscow Energy Institute Student Theatre. (DAVID FIRTH)

Salvation Army. In May 1988 the Salvation Army officially began work in Liberia, the 90th country in which the movement operated. During the year the Army's world leader, Gen. Eva Burrows, reviewed the movement's work in South Africa, Norway, South America, Japan, Switzerland, Australia, the U.S., Canada, Nigeria, and the U.K. and discussed its activities with many heads of state and government.

The national commander of the Salvation Army in the U.S. spoke on behalf of the general during the UN Special Session of the General Assembly devoted to disarmament. A Salvation Army officer also addressed the World Health Organization's London Conference on the Global Impact of AIDS. In the U.K. local initiatives included a campaign highlighting the dangers of alcohol abuse. The Salvation Army's public profile in Britain was enhanced by a seven-week television series, "Marching As to War," featuring its work.

Throughout the year the Salvation Army continued to provide help in the wake of natural and man-made disasters. Its work was recognized by the conferring of Rotary International's highest honour, the Rotary Award for World Understanding. (CHARLES KING)

Seventh-day Adventist Church. The heart team from the church's Loma Linda (Calif.) University celebrated its 25th year of international heart-surgery education in 1988 with programs in Zimbabwe and Kenya. The team conducted its first international surgical program in Pakistan in 1963. The church appointed an AIDS Committee to develop a position statement on the disease and to work with the church's world divisions and Adventist Development and Relief Agency (ADRA) in conducting AIDS education workshops.

After being closed two years, Adventist churches in Burundi reopened following a change in government there in October 1987. ADRA responded to major natural disasters in Venezuela and the Philippines with food, clothing, housing, and medical aid. ADRA also signed an agreement with China to establish a public-health project. Church officials continued negotiations on establishing a publishing facility in the U.S.S.R.

Adventist officials from the International Commission for the Prevention of Alcoholism met in Beijing (Peking) to discuss educational programs with representatives of China's medical and educational institutions. The church joined a coalition of religious denominations to help establish Vision Interfaith Satellite Network (VISN), which was to supply programming for cable television systems.

World membership totaled 5,384,417 on Dec. 31, 1987, an increase of 6.9% over 1986. The church was growing fastest in Africa and Central and South America. (ROBERT W. NIXON)

Unitarian (Universalist) Churches. The 1988 General Assembly of the Unitarian Universalist Association (UUA) drew over 2,200 registrants to Palm Springs, Calif., June 15–20. General resolutions were passed against censorship in public schools and for the right to die with dignity, housing for the homeless, conversion of the economy from military to human needs, and dealing constructively with the AIDS crisis.

The UU Church of the Larger Fellowship, serving over 2,000 isolated Unitarian Universalist groups in 60 countries, initiated several new programs during the year. Congregational giving in North America ($1,465,000 in 1984–85) rose to over $2 million in 1987–88, about 43% of the annual budget. Two new buildings were purchased on Beacon Hill, Boston, to serve the expanding needs of the denomination and its personnel.

The 1988 General Assembly of the Unitarian and Free Christian Churches met in Lancaster, England, in April. Resolutions were passed on social issues, education, and proposed tax legislation that would adversely affect the poorest in British society. Robert Inkson was made president of the movement; the first full-time development officer was appointed; and a new religious education program for children and young people was launched.

The 400-year-old Christian Unitarian movement of ethnic Hungarians living in the Transylvanian section of Romania was reportedly being persecuted by the government. Some 80,000 adherents had been told that their villages would be razed to make room for more farmland. Protests by North American Unitarian Universalists in the past had only accelerated persecution, but a new effort was being mounted. (JOHN NICHOLLS BOOTH)

The United Church of Canada. An issue that many members believed would split the church was debated at the 32nd General Council meeting in Victoria, B.C., in August 1988: the ordination of homosexuals and lesbians. In March a church-appointed committee had released a report recommending that gays and lesbians be eligible for ordination. Speaking on the second evening of the ten-day meeting, retiring moderator Anne Squire said, "The question is whether we can accept the ministry of gays and lesbians, or whether we can tolerate erecting barriers to ministry."

The Sessional (ad hoc) Committee assigned to bring a resolution to Council seemed to agree with Squire. Its submission that "All members . . . are eligible to be *considered* for ordered ministry" won approval from a majority of the nearly 400 clergy and lay delegates. The decision, however, did not please all pastors

and church members across Canada, and it remained to be seen whether threatened withdrawals would be carried out.

The election of Sang Chul Lee as moderator for the next biennium was warmly acclaimed. Lee was the first Korean to hold the office. In other actions at Victoria, the Council reaffirmed its 1980 stand on abortion and contraception; *i.e.,* that abortion is acceptable only in certain medical, social, and economic situations, and contraception is the only completely acceptable form of birth control. A resolution dealing with compensation to Japanese Canadians "for the injustices inflicted on them by Canada during and after World War II" was approved.

In October the United Church launched a weekly 30-minute television program on Vision TV (VTV), the interfaith cable network. The United Church presentation, "Spirit Connection," followed a magazine format and was directed to the church's constituency across Canada.

(NORMAN K. VALE)

United Church of Christ. A historic joint meeting of the United Church Board for Homeland Ministries and the United Church Board for World Ministries was held in Pasadena, Calif., in November 1988, signaling an intention to plan the mission work of the UCC, both international and domestic, from common theological and policy assumptions. Building on a long history of concern for peace and justice in sub-Saharan Africa, 22 leaders of the UCC spent three weeks in April visiting church and government leaders in Zimbabwe, Zambia, Angola, and Botswana.

More than 1,000 youth and young adults gathered in Grinnell, Iowa, in July for an assembly that included Bible study, leadership training, and worship. In late July the biennial assembly of the church's new Coordinating Center for Women in Church and Society was held in Bloomington, Ind. New curriculum resources were published by the United Church Board for Homeland Ministries.

Carrying out the partnerships voted by the General Synod, joint partnership committees had been developed with the Pentecostal Church of Chile, the Evangelical Church of the Union in East and West Germany, the United Church of Christ in the Philippines, and the Presbyterian Church of the Republic of Korea. In June the ministers of the UCC's 39 conferences met for a week at La Foret, a conference centre operated by the Rocky Mountain Conference. Planned as a retreat, the meeting focused on the development of spiritual disciplines, Bible study, and leadership training.

After 17 years, Reuben A. Sheares II left the position of executive director of the Office for Church Life and Leadership to become pastor of the Congregational Church of Park Manor in Chicago. Daniel F. Romero became general secretary for the Mission Program Unit of the United Church Board for World Ministries.

(AVERY D. POST)

ROMAN CATHOLIC CHURCH

Seen from the point of view of the Vatican, the eyes of the Roman Catholic Church were turned resolutely eastward in 1988. The coincidence of the millennium celebrations in Russia in June, a Polish pope who could grasp their significance, and the novel *glasnost* policies of Soviet leader Gorbachev all combined to make the *Ostpolitik* predominant. Personal participation of Pope John Paul II in the millennium celebrations was ruled out by Patriarch Pimen (he would have stolen the show), but he sent a top-level delegation of ten cardinals, and his secretary of state, Agostino Cardinal Casaroli, reported after a meeting with Gorbachev that they had discussed the idea of "putting contacts between our two states on a regular footing."

Pope John Paul had prepared for this apparent reconciliation by writing two letters on the millennium: the first was addressed to Patriarch Pimen and congratulated the Russian Orthodox Church on the anniversary; the second was directed to the Ukrainian Catholic Church in communion with Rome (the Uniates), who also had the right to celebrate their origins in the baptism of Prince Vladimir in 988. The Ukrainian Catholic Church was officially abolished and forcibly converted to Orthodoxy in 1946. The leader of the Ukrainians, Metropolitan Myroslav Lubachivsky, said he had forgiven the Russian Orthodox Church for this crime. There was no answer, but with the aid of Gorbachev, even that circle might be squared.

Even documents addressed to the universal church, such as the encyclical *Sollicitudo Rei Socialis* (February 19), had a bearing on the *Ostpolitik.* The letter was evenhanded in its critique of both capitalism (here called "liberalism") and Marxism. It contained a first hint that the church was taking up the ecology theme. It also recommended selling off superfluous church "ornaments" to feed the poor. There was no evidence of anyone actually doing this, and the suggestion sat ill with the Vatican's rather desperate appeal for funds in March.

The post-Vatican II expansion of the Roman Curia was one of the reasons why the Vatican was strapped for cash. In July a further "reform" of the papal bureaucracy was announced, but it amounted to

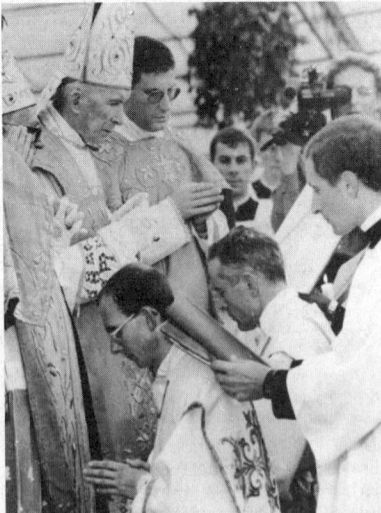

AFP PHOTO

"Traditionalist" Archbishop Marcel Lefebvre's consecration of four bishops, including Bernard Tissier de Mallerais (centre foreground) and Alfonso de Galarreta (right), resulted in the excommunication of all five.

little more than a few changes of name and a redistribution of tasks. Significantly, the Secretariat for Christian Unity, which had hitherto taken the lead in ecumenical work, was now downgraded to a "Council"—a "promotional agency" performing no "acts of government." This confirmed the tendency to make the Congregation for the Doctrine of Faith, responsible for orthodoxy, the supreme body in the Curia.

Other moves were designed to strengthen the Curia against the local churches. A private study document argued that episcopal conferences (regional or national teams of bishops) were merely a practical arrangement of no theological significance. Their "right to teach" on their own initiative was also questioned. The U.S. bishops felt this was directed against their pastoral letters on nuclear weapons and economic justice. In April they released the first draft of their pastoral letter on women, which denounced "sexism" but still excluded women from priestly ordination. (See *Introduction,* above.) In November they rejected the Vatican document by a vote of 205–59.

The ordination of women in some provinces of the Anglican Communion affected ecumenical relations. Pope John Paul sent a message to the Lambeth Conference, meeting in Canterbury in August, saying that the ordination of women was a "new ecumenical obstacle." (See *Anglican Communion,* above.) Although Lambeth accepted the reports of the Anglican Roman Catholic International Commission (ARCIC) on Authority, Eucharist, and Ministry, ecumenism made little real progress. Once again, it looked as though the Vatican were turning away from the churches that issued from the 16th-century Reformation and counting on better relations with the Orthodox churches who were firmly opposed to women's ordination. In the encyclical *Redemptoria Mater* written for the Marian Year, which ended on August 15, Pope John Paul claimed that devotion to Mary "cast light on ecumenism"—true of the Orthodox, doubtfully so in the West.

If old schisms could not be healed, a new one came into being June 30 when Archbishop Marcel Lefebvre (*see* BIOGRAPHIES) ordained four bishops at Econe, Switz. This led to automatic excommunication. Lefebvre's defiance of the pope was all the more surprising because in May a formula of reconciliation had been worked out that gave him most of what he wanted, including the right to use the Latin Tridentine Mass. Lefebvre accepted this plan May 5 but reneged on it when he returned to Switzerland.

There were papal journeys to Latin America in May, to Austria in June, to southern Africa in September, and to France in October. Having denounced apartheid as a "moral evil" in Harare, Zimbabwe, and refused to include South Africa on his itinerary, the pope was forced by bad weather to land in Johannesburg and go overland to Lesotho. He did not kiss the ground on alighting.

On August 20 Laszlo Cardinal Paskai, primate of Hungary, in a rare televised Mass on the feast of St. Stephen, the first Hungarian king, announced that he had invited the pope to Hungary. There were difficulties ahead, but this was further ev-

Orthodox bishops fill the Soviet Union's Trinity-St. Sergius Monastery to commemorate the 1,000th anniversary of Christianity in that country.
AFP PHOTO

idence that the pope was determined to exploit to the full, while it lasted, the new atmosphere of *glasnost.*

(*See* WORLD AFFAIRS [Western Europe]: *Vatican City State.*)

(PETER HEBBLETHWAITE)

THE ORTHODOX CHURCH

The millennium of the baptism of Vladimir, prince of Kiev, in 988 was the occasion of spectacular celebrations in Moscow, Kiev, Vladimir, and Leningrad. The event of 988 was seen by all Christians of Russia, the Ukraine, and other parts of Eastern Europe as the official beginning of Christianity in their lands. The millennium was also marked by academic and ecclesiastical celebrations elsewhere.

The celebrations coincided in the U.S.S.R. with Gorbachev's policy of *glasnost,* and for the first time since the 1917 Revolution, church events were covered prominently in the media. The Soviet press and television featured candid discussions of the role of religion in society and bitter criticism of the antireligious persecutions of the past. On April 9, the eve of Orthodox Easter, the newspaper *Izvestiya* published a picture of Patriarch Pimen and an interview in which the patriarch not only treated the usual themes of world peace and the church's loyalty to the state but also criticized the authorities for preventing the opening of new churches and forbidding participation of the church in welfare and other social activities. In addition to the impressive monastery of St. Daniel in Moscow, rebuilt for the occasion and destined to become the administrative headquarters of the patriarchate, a few other institutions, formerly secularized, were returned to the church.

The celebrations themselves took place on June 3–14 and were attended by the leaders of religious groups, both Orthodox and non-Orthodox, including the Vatican's secretary of state, Cardinal Casaroli. During those days, a council (or *sobor*), technically the highest canonical and administrative body of the church, was held in Zagorsk. It proclaimed the canonization of nine saints and approved the text

of a new "statute" restoring the authority of the priest in the parish and promoting catechization of the laity. The government made public its intention to publish a new, more liberal law on the practice of religion.

Western observers and independent (or "dissident") sources varied in their appreciation of these developments. Optimists and skeptics agreed, however, that after so much public discussion on the abuses of the past, it would be difficult for the state to return soon to direct repression of religious practice.

Other notable events within the Orthodox world included the travels of the ecumenical patriarch Dimitrios of Constantinople (Istanbul) to the Vatican, Canterbury, and Geneva in December 1987 as well as to the Orthodox churches in Poland, Czechoslovakia, and Finland (June–July 1988). As on previous occasions, the patriarch's ecumenical activities, particularly with Rome, were criticized by the monastic communities of Mt. Athos and other Greek conservative circles. In Romania drastic antireligious measures continued as part of the increasingly dictatorial policies of the Ceaucescu government. St. Gorazd, a bishop shot by the Nazis in 1942, was canonized by the Orthodox Church of Czechoslovakia.   (JOHN MEYENDORFF)

EASTERN NON-CHALCEDONIAN CHURCHES

Late in 1987 the Coptic pope Shenuda III, leader of the most numerous Christian community in the Middle East, organized a meeting of ecclesiastical heads belonging to both the Chalcedonian (Orthodox) and non-Chalcedonian churches. The meeting was held at the monastery of Amba-Bishoi in the Egyptian desert and was attended by the Greek patriarch of Alexandria, Parthenios, by Ignatius, patriarch of Antioch (living in Damascus, Syria), and by the non-Chalcedonian patriarch Zakka I (Syrian Jacobite) and Armenian catholicos Karekin II (Antelyas, Lebanon). The prelates affirmed that "fundamentally and essentially" they all confessed the same faith in Christ, in spite of the diversity of historical formulations since the Council

of Chalcedon (AD 451). This significant meeting, the first of its kind, might represent an important step toward restoration of communion between the churches.

On June 5 Patriarch Tekle Haimanot of Ethiopia died in Addis Ababa. A simple monk, he had been imposed upon the Ethiopian church by the Marxist government in 1976.   (JOHN MEYENDORFF)

JUDAISM

In a year of strife and contention, the headlines of 1988 did not always highlight the developments that would make their mark beyond the year's end. Though not nearly so widely noted as the disorders in the West Bank/Judea and Samaria, which soured the celebration of the State of Israel's 40th birthday, planning for New York City's projected Museum of Jewish Heritage, "a living memorial to the Holocaust," would certainly highlight the year in the perspective of time.

The tragic events of 1933–45, when most of the Jews in continental Europe were killed in Nazi death factories, remained a formative event for contemporary Judaism. At issue in the memorialization of what was called "the Holocaust" was whether and how Judaism as a living religion had been changed because of the European catastrophe. Writing in the *Jewish Advocate* (April 14, 1988), Sholom Stern pointed out that the exemplars of Judaic learning who survived the war "directed their energies at having their students learn Talmudic methodology." The Holocaust as such was rarely mentioned. "My teachers," Stern wrote, "never permitted the Holocaust to become a substitute for" the study of the Torah, because "the challenge of Jewish survival was best met by the study of Judaism." In that same spirit, New York's "living memorial to the Holocaust" would be called the Museum of Jewish Heritage. In the words of the director, David Altshuler, the new museum was "about life and the values of human life and the continuities of Jewish traditions and faith."

The headlines emanating from the State of Israel, nonetheless, registered political and military events bearing religious meaning. The latest chapter in the long Arab-Israeli war, Leon Wieseltier wrote in the *Baltimore Jewish Times* (March 11, 1988), precipitated "Israel's moment of truth" and stirred debate within Jewish communities throughout the world. Wieseltier referred to "an experience of moral dissonance" involved in fighting against what the Palestinians called "the awakening." Whether Israeli policy in the West Bank/Judea and Samaria was expedient politically did not form a moral or religious concern. Whether it was right did. (*See* WORLD AFFAIRS [Middle East and North Africa]: *Israel.*)

Yet another political controversy bearing religious meaning in Judaism swirled around the candidacy of Jesse Jackson for the Democratic nomination for the U.S. presidency. On the one hand a candidate from a long-oppressed minority, on the other, a man widely held in Jewry to be an anti-Semite and unfriendly to the State of Israel, Jackson elicited mixed feelings. New York Mayor Edward Koch's statement that any Jew who would vote for Jackson was "crazy" provoked the novelist Norman Mailer to reply (*New York Times,*

A group of Hasidic Jews rejoice over gains made by right-wing religious parties in Israel's November elections. It appeared for a time that the religious parties might hold the balance of power in the Knesset (parliament), but Labour and Likud formed a coalition in December.

AP/WIDE WORLD

April 18, 1988) in language reminiscent of the prophetic tradition: "What made us great as a people is that we, of all ethnic groups, were the most concerned with the world's problems. . . . The imperative to survive at all costs . . . left us smaller, greedier, narrower, preternaturally touchy, and self-seeking. . . . 'Is this good for the Jews?' became, for all too many of us, all of our politics."

Controversy from without did not preempt discussion of the inner life of the community of Judaism. Yehoshafat Harkabi of Hebrew University raised the issue of the divisive power of the Jewish religion within the Jewish people itself. Suggesting that "the Jewish religion that hitherto has bolstered Jewish existence might become detrimental to it," he pointed to manifestations of hostility against Gentiles, formerly repressed, but ascendant in the past decade, notably in the State of Israel. Thus a scholar who had received the Israel Prize in Judaic Studies, Rabbi Eliezer Waldernberg, declared that a Gentile should not be permitted to live in Jerusalem. Explaining these and other expressions of anti-Gentile prejudice, Harkabi pointed to the belief of what he called "religious radicals" in the imminent coming of the Messiah. He called for "discarding those elements" of Judaism that instill or express hostility to outsiders.

Rabbi Harold M. Schulweis of California addressed the character of Jewish law, which many within the faith perceive to be mechanical and legalistic, and called for expanding the sense of the law to deal with personal, emotional connections as well. His "expanded notion of law" (in Hebrew, Halakhah) not only would involve going through the forms of the law, for instance, the preparation of a writ of divorce in accord with Jewish law, but would also require concern for "the pained and confused parents and children whose need is for spiritual guidance and direction." Writing in the *Baltimore Jewish Times* (Jan. 29, 1988), Schulweis argues, "We have conceded too much to the secular world and narrowed too much of the halakhic arena. The halakhic process must regain its holistic approach." (JACOB NEUSNER)

BUDDHISM

The year 1988 brought renewed hope to the persecuted Buddhists of Indochina. As the spirit of reform spread in the Commu-

nist world, Vietnamese and Laotian leaders began to soften their stance against the religion. With record numbers of Buddhist monks and nuns graduating from state-controlled institutions, Buddhism slowly regained its vitality in Laos, Vietnam, and Hanoi-dominated Kampuchea. In December 1987 the Vietnamese National Assembly passed a land-use law that promised to restore some of the temple lands confiscated during the Vietnam war, while Laotian officials began appearing at religious rites and loosened their prohibition on almsgiving.

The shattered hopes of Tibetan Buddhists for restoration of their spiritual-political nation under the leadership of the Dalai Lama erupted in violence in October 1987 and March 1988. Despite an eight-year campaign by Beijing to pacify nationalist sentiment among the Tibetans with ever greater leniency toward the religion, paralleling the restoration of Buddhism in China itself, Tibetan Buddhists demonstrated against the Chinese occupation. Although the suppression of the October riots was reportedly characterized by beatings, killings, and arrests, 200 to 300 Buddhist monks broke up a religious festival in March at Lhasa's Jokhang Temple, site of the October riots, by chanting pro-independence slogans. As many as 10,000 of the assembled pilgrims joined in, and Chinese forces stormed the city to put down the rioting, leaving at least 18 dead and hundreds more injured or arrested. The Dalai Lama denounced the demonstrators' use of violence, while the pro-Chinese Panchen Lama called the revolt itself "an un-Buddhist crime."

In July Buddhism emerged as a factor in the antigovernment riots that exploded in Burma. Early that month Buddhist-Muslim rioting broke out in Prome following an incident between a Muslim betel-nut seller and his Buddhist customer. At the end of July students shouted antigovernment slogans at the country's most important Buddhist shrine, the Shwedagon Pagoda. In August the government asked the Buddhist *bhikkhus* to assist in restoring law and order. (See WORLD AFFAIRS [Southeast Asia]: *Burma.*)

In December 1987 the world's only reigning Buddhist king, Thailand's King Rama IX (Bhumibol Adulyadej), celebrated his auspicious 60th birthday with splendour reminiscent of the Buddhist

kingships of old. The growing importance of Buddhism in American society was confirmed by the U.S. Army's decision to recognize Buddhist chaplains certified by the Buddhist Churches of America. Catharine Burroughs of Brooklyn, N.Y., became the first Western woman recognized as an incarnate lama.   (FRANK E. REYNOLDS; JONATHAN S. WALTERS)

HINDUISM

In India the continuing conflict between Hindus and Sikhs and violence by Sikh extremists in their efforts to establish a separate nation (Khalistan, "Land of the Pure") led Prime Minister Rajiv Gandhi to use military force against the insurgents. In May 1988 nearly 4,000 troops laid siege to the most sacred Sikh shrine, the Golden Temple in Amritsar. Sikh terrorists stepped up guerrilla attacks to drive Hindus from the Punjab. The brutal assaults inflamed the already existent antipathy of Hindus toward Sikhs and raised fears of Hindu retribution. (*See* WORLD AFFAIRS [South Asia]: *India.*)

Another secessionist movement ironically had some beneficial effects. Because of the violence associated with the Gurkha demand for an autonomous "Gurkhaland" in West Bengal, the popular hill area of Darjeeling had been closed to tourists for over two years. As a result, the state government undertook in 1988 to develop other tourist spots, including the Bankura district with its splendid but long-neglected 17th- and 18th-century temples. In July the Karnataka Directorate of Archaeology and Museums published a collection of 60 photographs taken in 1856 by a British army officer, Alexander J. Greenlaw, of monuments of the great Vijayanagara Hindu empire in South India. They show the major temples of the Vijayanagara capital at present-day Hampi in a relatively unspoiled condition, thus providing an excellent guide for restoration.

The February suicide of three sisters in Kanpur whose father was unable to provide them with dowries dramatized the state of Hindu women and intensified the efforts of Hindu feminist groups. Of particular concern to these groups had been the recurring practice of *sati,* the self-immolation of women on the funeral pyres of their husbands. Though outlawed, there had been 40 reported cases of *sati* since India's independence in 1947. In demonstrations throughout the year, Sahali, an organization for abused women, called for more aggressive action by the government. Counterdemonstrations were organized by the Dharma Raksha Samiti (Society for the Protection of Religion), which proclaimed that *sati* is one of the most virtuous and holy acts a Hindu woman can perform. Over 100,000 people attended a pro-*sati* rally sponsored by Samiti in Jaipur in January, and more than half a million "pilgrims" reportedly visited the site of the 1987 *sati* of an 18-year-old woman in Deorala, suggesting the great tenacity of traditional Hindu attitudes toward women.

Over 1,000 devotees attended the Sri Rama Navami (birthday of the god Rama) festival in March at the Sri Venkatesvara temple in Malibu, Calif. Designed in the 10th-century Chola style, the temple was the largest of its kind outside India.

(H. PATRICK SULLIVAN)

ISLAM

Violence again afflicted many Muslims in 1988, but in at least two areas hopes were raised for the cessation of conflict. In the spring the U.S.S.R. announced it was withdrawing its troops from Afghanistan, and in the summer Iraq and Iran announced a cease-fire, giving rise to hopes that their long war was ending. (*See* WORLD AFFAIRS [South Asia]: *Afghanistan;* [Middle East and North Africa]: *Middle Eastern and North African Affairs.*) These developments had religious as well as political consequences. Iran supported Shi'ite Afghanis who had taken refuge there, while in Pakistan the presence of refugees (largely Sunnites) created political tensions. As Soviet troops withdrew, fighting broke out among rival Afghani groups, representing various Islamic religious as well as political interests.

Disorders erupted in the Caucasus region of the U.S.S.R., where Armenians in the Nagorno-Karabakh Autonomous Region wished to secede from predominantly Muslim Azerbaijan. Current estimates were that 45 million persons, or 16% of the U.S.S.R.'s population, were Muslim.

At the end of March the yearly Islamic Conference denounced Iran for its part in instigating the previous year's riots during the annual Pilgrimage rites in Mecca and approved Saudi Arabia's decision to limit the number of pilgrims. Iran urged Muslims to rally against the limitations. However, the Pilgrimage, in July, was carried out without serious incident.

Islamic fundamentalist activities continued, with effects felt throughout the Muslim world. Amnesty International and other groups charged in May that Morocco, Algeria, and Tunisia were forcibly repressing Islamic fundamentalist groups; the three governments denied the allegations. In Egypt 33 Muslims brought to trial in early April for complicity in the attempted assassination of two former interior ministers were said to be associated with the fundamentalist Muslim Brotherhood. Muslim leaders in Indonesia continued their attempt to find a cultural and religious accommodation that would bring together Islamic interests and Indonesian state policy, but fundamentalist Muslims opposed their efforts. In Israel, where Arab-Israeli difficulties were exacerbated by riots and demonstrations in the West Bank and Gaza, a new group, Islamic Resistance Movement (also known as Hamas), composed of radical fundamentalist Muslims, appeared to be wresting political control from the more secular Palestine Liberation Organization. In January Muslims and Israeli police clashed at the al-Aqsa Mosque (the Temple Mount) in Jerusalem.

In June Bangladesh declared Islam to be its state religion. In the U.S. members of the Nation of Islam organized neighbourhood anticrime patrols in Brooklyn, N.Y., and Washington, D.C. Initially of concern to established police authority, which viewed them as possible vigilantes, the patrols were later praised in New York by both residents and police.

The 1988 Templeton Prize for Progress in Religion was awarded to Inamullah Khan of Pakistan, founder of the World Muslim Congress.   (REUBEN W. SMITH)

WORLD RELIGIOUS STATISTICS

The global religious situation can be portrayed at one point in time by the kind of geographico-religious statistical table given below. To many casual readers, such a table suggests inactivity, sluggishness, or absence of change, but this is completely untrue. The table is simply a black-and-white photograph taken with a high-speed lens and an ultrafast shutter. It freezes the action. It hides enormous, seething religious activity, religious upheaval, religious migration, religious change, religious revolution. Thus during 1988 some 25 million more Christians appeared on the face of the Earth; Islam increased by 20 million; tribal religions decreased by nearly 3 million adherents; and so on.

All of this growth or decline, for every religious bloc and any geographic area, can be analyzed and explained in terms of three basic varieties of change: demographic increase (births minus deaths among that religion's adherents), conversion increase (converts minus defectors from that religion), and transfer increase (immigrant adherents minus emigrant adherents). For the world as a whole, this last, third category is, of course, zero.

One notable indicator of regular change concerns pilgrimages. Some 100 million Muslims and Hindus and 95 million Christians are on the move as pilgrims every year, in most countries, visiting large numbers of local, national, and international pilgrimage centres and shrines. This is mass religion on the march.

(DAVID B. BARRETT)

This article updates the *Macropædia* articles The Buddha and BUDDHISM; CHRISTIANITY; EASTERN ORTHODOXY; HINDUISM; Muhammad and the Religion of ISLAM; JUDAISM; PROTESTANTISM; The Study and Classification of RELIGIONS; ROMAN CATHOLICISM; and *Micropædia* entries on the various denominations.

Adherents of All Religions by Eight Continental Areas, 1988

	Africa	East Asia	Europe	Latin America	Northern America	Oceania	South Asia	U.S.S.R.	World	%	Countries
Christians	282,526,720	81,585,730	412,312,390	402,245,550	232,557,080	21,431,200	132,198,760	104,663,010	1,669,520,440	32.9	254
Roman Catholics	106,487,220	9,503,860	260,457,890	377,753,520	94,274,950	7,557,820	90,524,300	5,283,800	951,843,360	18.8	242
Protestants	74,678,880	35,328,490	73,330,350	14,502,350	93,637,200	7,570,210	29,234,900	9,198,600	337,480,980	6.6	230
Orthodox	25,363,450	87,810	35,861,140	718,760	5,871,470	508,670	3,198,740	90,164,310	161,774,350	3.2	98
Anglicans	23,282,850	341,230	32,696,030	1,228,900	7,262,000	5,236,620	293,010	300	70,340,940	1.4	148
Other Christians	52,714,320	36,324,340	9,966,980	8,042,020	31,511,460	557,880	8,947,810	16,000	148,080,810	2.9	110
Muslims	253,153,340	23,446,260	8,760,660	664,820	2,689,480	98,480	559,621,790	32,120,380	880,555,210	17.4	172
Nonreligious	1,556,150	664,128,370	53,058,980	13,772,620	22,785,380	2,909,630	22,916,140	85,682,390	866,759,660	17.1	220
Hindus	1,424,610	10,460	594,460	683,660	855,800	305,920	659,619,440	1,100	663,495,450	13.1	88
Buddhists	11,750	154,432,950	222,400	483,020	186,560	15,120	156,194,080	290,290	311,836,170	6.1	86
Atheists	245,530	140,189,970	18,452,730	2,687,590	1,116,880	516,080	5,515,660	60,986,970	229,711,410	4.5	130
Chinese folk religionists	8,780	164,156,970	47,650	51,540	103,840	12,830	7,896,520	100	172,278,230	3.4	56
New-Religionists	13,920	43,145,100	34,530	382,170	1,126,150	7,290	67,202,200	200	111,911,560	2.2	25
Tribal religionists	66,268,630	687,230	150	1,151,840	54,790	77,270	23,800,660	0	92,040,570	1.8	98
Jews	237,610	1,650	1,447,140	1,003,770	8,117,900	86,460	4,206,190	3,068,620	18,169,340	0.3	125
Sikhs	22,890	920	217,760	6,050	150,340	6,670	16,782,710	50	17,187,390	0.3	20
Shamanists	900	12,171,470	500	300	110	110	8,000	200,250	12,381,640	0.2	10
Confucians	450	6,164,410	1,010	500	18,980	110	2,371,740	200	6,188,160	0.1	3
Baha'is	1,210,650	52,600	73,910	596,540	319,890	61,460	2,371,740	5,100	4,691,890	0.1	205
Jains	45,020	570	9,930	2,020	1,960	820	3,495,350	20	3,555,690	0.1	10
Shintoists	50	3,376,040	330	610	1,290	410	200	100	3,379,030	0.1	3
Other religionists	66,600	65,500	323,860	6,812,590	674,950	26,730	244,250	7,000	8,221,480	0.2	170
Total Population	**606,793,600**	**1,293,616,200**	**495,558,390**	**430,495,190**	**270,761,380**	**25,556,590**	**1,622,076,190**	**287,025,780**	**5,071,883,320**	**100.0**	**254**

NOTES:
Continents. UN demographic practice divides the world into eight continental areas as shown above (see United Nations, *World Population Prospects*, New York, 1986, with populations of all countries covering the period 1950–2025).
Countries. The last column enumerates sovereign and nonsovereign countries in which each religion has a significant following.
Rows. The list of religions is arranged by descending order of magnitude of global adherents in 1988 (last two columns but one).
Adherents. As defined and enumerated for each of the world's countries in *World Christian Encyclopedia* (1982), projected to mid-1988.
Christians. Followers of Jesus Christ affiliated to churches (church members, including children), plus persons professing in censuses or polls though not so affiliated.
Other Christians. Catholics (non-Roman), marginal Protestants, crypto-Christians, and adherents of African, Asian, Black, and Latin-American indigenous churches.
Muslims. 83% Sunnite, 16% Shi'ites, 1% other schools.
Nonreligious. Persons professing no religion, nonbelievers, agnostics, freethinkers, dereligionized secularists indifferent to all religion.
Hindus. 70% Vaishnavites, 25% Shaivites, 2% neo-Hindus and reform Hindus.
Buddhists. 56% Mahayana, 38% Theravada, 6% Tantrism.
Atheists. Persons professing atheism, skepticism, disbelief, or irreligion, including antireligious (opposed to all religion).
Chinese folk religionists. Followers of traditional Chinese religion (local deities, ancestor veneration, Confucian ethics, Taoism, universism, divination, some Buddhist elements).
New-Religionists. Followers of Asiatic 20th-century New Religions, New Religious movements, radical new crisis religions, and non-Christian syncretistic mass religions, all founded since 1800 and mostly since 1945.
Jews. 84% Ashkenazim, 10% Orientals, 4% Sephardim.
Confucians. Non-Chinese followers of Confucius and Confucianism, mostly Koreans in Korea.
Other religionists. Including 50 minor world religions and a large number of spiritist religions, New Age religions, quasi religions, pseudoreligions, parareligions, religious systems, mystic systems, religious and semireligious brotherhoods of numerous varieties.
Total Population. UN medium variant figures for mid-1988, as given in *World Population Prospects* (1986), pages 72–77.

(DAVID B. BARRETT)

Social Security and Welfare Services

Reform of social security was still high on the agenda of many governments in 1988. Some of the most interesting developments during the year concerned assistance to families, through both universal and means-tested benefits.

National Developments in Social Security. A major reform of the health insurance system was under consideration in West Germany. The government's proposals had four components: (1) increasing emphasis on preventive measures; (2) cost containment through higher copayments from insured persons, for example, for drugs and dentures; (3) various measures to promote fair competition between the different sickness funds (there were approximately 1,300 throughout the country); and (4) improving long-term care benefits, with emphasis on additional services when care is provided by a family member in the home.

In South Korea a national pension program came into effect in January. The new system provided old-age, invalidity, and survivor benefits. Coverage was compulsory in enterprises with more than ten employees, and since others could enter the system voluntarily, all citizens between the ages of 18 and 60 residing in the country were entitled to coverage. The basic old-age pension was payable at age 60, with 20 years of contributions required. The invalidity pension was proportional to the degree of disability. Benefits would be financed from contributions, set at 3% of the monthly standard remuneration for 1988–92, shared equally between employees and employers. A subsidy from the government would cover administrative costs.

The social security review conducted in France during 1987 resulted in several legislative measures in 1988. A partial pension program, similar to those in several Scandinavian countries, came into effect on July 1. Under this program, employees who were at least 60 years of age and had the required contributions for a full retirement pension could work part-time and receive a pension that was proportional to the reduction in hours, which had to be at least 20%. Another requirement was that an employee had to work exclusively for a single employer. The legislation also provided that older workers in danger of being laid off could receive special benefits from the national employment fund if they agreed to work part-time.

Agreement could not be reached on a proposal for overall reform of social security in Italy, but the 1988 budget law contained a major technical change in the way old-age, disability, survivor, and seniority benefits administered by the National Social Insurance Institute were calculated. Previously benefits were based on earnings up to a ceiling, although no ceiling existed for earnings subject to contributions. Under the new formula, earnings for benefit computation were divided into four bands, each subject to a different accrual rate. The result would be to increase benefits for higher-income employees. The relationship between contributions paid and benefits received had deteriorated for this group.

Social security coverage in Colombia was extended to domestic workers. New legislation signed by the president in January provided that domestic workers would be covered for cash benefits as well as medical care. Contributions were paid on actual earnings, even when earnings were down to half the minimum wage (the minimum for benefits and contributions for other employees). Benefits, however, would be based on an amount not lower than the minimum wage. The government would make up the difference between contributions and benefits in an annual subsidy to the Colombian Social Insurance Institute.

Also effective from January, in Kenya the qualifying age for receipt of old-age benefits from the provident fund was reduced from 60 to 55 years. In Switzerland in June, voters rejected a popular initiative to lower the retirement age from 65 to 62 years for men and from 62 to 60 years for women on the grounds that the financial stability of the pension system would be jeopardized. Nonetheless, in the review of the old-age pension scheme currently being conducted by the government, there was a proposal to introduce flexible retirement from age 62 for men, with reduced benefits.

Hungary and Poland put new measures for financing social security into effect in 1988. In Hungary the variable contribution rates paid by insured persons, ranging from 3 to 15% according to income, were replaced by a uniform rate of 10%. In addition, the employer's contribution was raised to 10, 30, or 40% of payroll, according to the economic sector. In Poland employers' contributions were reduced (there was no contribution from insured persons) from 43 to 38% (20% for scientific and other nonpublic institutes and 5% for pensioners and the disabled), but the payroll base on which contributions were paid was enlarged to include both cash and in-kind payments.

In the U.K. implementation of the Social Security Act 1986 was completed in April with the introduction of new means-tested benefits. In reforming its social assistance (welfare) system, the government sought to simplify the benefits available to those with low incomes, to target assistance to those most in need, and to bolster incentives for working. For those who did not work full-time (defined as working less than 24 hours per week), a new benefit, Income Support, replaced the previous Supplementary Benefit and many additional weekly payments. The new benefit retained the requirement that claimants register at an unemployment office as available for work, with certain exclusions. Income Support payments consisted of three parts: personal allowances, which varied in amount by age; premium payments for those with special needs, such as families with children and the disabled; and, in some cases, housing-cost payments.

For low-income families with children and with at least one member working full-time, Family Credit replaced Family Income Supplement. Benefit was related to income and the number and ages of children in the family. Unlike the previous system, the new benefits were related to net earnings (after deductions for taxes and social security contributions). The object was to eliminate the so-called poverty trap, in which an increase in earnings from work leaves people worse off because benefits are reduced and earnings are subject to tax and contributions.

A new family allowance program was established in Cyprus in 1988. A cash payment, called Child Benefit, was made to families with at least four dependent children, at the rate of £7 monthly for the third and each succeeding child. Benefits were financed from general revenues. A reform of the Italian family allowance program also occurred during the year. The previous flat-rate family allowances for children, including income-tested supplements and benefits for dependent parents and other family members, were replaced by a new single allowance for the entire family unit. The new allowance was calculated in relation to the number of eligible members: children under 18, disabled children of any age, and a spouse in the same household. The amount of the allowance decreased as family income rose, with no benefits payable to high-income families.

(continued on page 303)

Children at Risk

BY MARIAN WRIGHT EDELMAN

The past decade has not been good for millions of children in the United States. There were relatively more poor children than there were poor people in any other age group, and the plight of very young children was worse still. According to the U.S. Bureau of the Census, some 13 million children—more than one in five youngsters under the age of 18—were poor in 1987; among children under three years old, nearly one in four was poor. Children were more likely to be poor if they belonged to a minority group, were very young, or had very young parents.

Growth in Poverty. The steepest growth in child poverty occurred between 1979, when 9.9 million children were poor, and 1983, when some 3.5 million more children had joined the ranks of the poor in the U.S. The economic recovery that began in 1983 slightly reversed that trend, but the main beneficiaries were the same white adults who had been hardest hit by the recession. Fewer than one-third of the children who had become trapped in poverty during that five-year period had escaped its clutches by 1987.

Minorities, children, and especially minority children continued to constitute a disproportionate percentage of the poor in the U.S. In 1987, 45.8% of all black children and 39.8% of all Hispanic children were poor. Children also made up a large percentage, perhaps half, of America's homeless.

Poor children became poorer, too. The 1987 federal definition of poverty was set at an annual income of $9,056 for a family of three. A total of 5.4 million children lived in families of all sizes with incomes below half the poverty line. The numbers of children in such families were 50% higher than in 1978.

Obstacles Facing Families. There were four major reasons why so many children in the U.S. were mired in poverty. First, children—especially younger children— tended to live in younger families (those headed by persons under age 30), and young workers were particularly hard hit by declining wages. Between 1973 and 1986 the average inflation-adjusted earnings of males aged 20 to 24 fell by more than 25%. The poverty rate for young families with children nearly doubled in that period, from 16 to 30%. One-third of all poor children in the U.S. lived in young families. Among the youngest families— those headed by persons under the age of 25—54% of all children were poor.

Structural changes in the economy, which accelerated the shift toward low-wage employment, affected young workers the most. Since 1979 more than three-quarters of all new jobs were created in wholesale or retail trade, or in the service sector, while the nation lost two million manufacturing jobs. Many newly created jobs paid the minimum wage, which had lost one-fourth of its real value to inflation since it was last raised in 1981.

A second factor contributing to the large number of

Marian Wright Edelman is president of the Children's Defense Fund, Washington, D.C.

poor children was unemployment. Despite the economic recovery, many fathers and mothers remained unemployed or underemployed (employed part-time because full-time work was not available). Of poor family householders, only 47% worked at all during 1987; only 15% worked year-round, full-time.

Female-Headed Households. Third, the number of female-headed households grew dramatically, owing in significant measure to the fact that young men with low earnings were less likely to marry than were their better-off peers, and more young men had low earnings. One in every five children lived in a female-headed household in 1987, up from one in eight in 1970. Because women's earnings remained substantially lower than men's, children living in those families were almost three times as likely to be poor as children generally. In 1987, 54.7% of children in female-headed households were poor.

Again, the youngest suffered disproportionately; more than eight out of ten children under the age of three who were living with very young (under 22 years old) single mothers were poor in 1986. The plight of minorities was particularly disturbing. In 1987, 68.3% of black children and 70.1% of Hispanic children in female-headed households were poor.

Child-care costs, burdensome for most families, were prohibitive for many single-parent families. High child-care expenses kept some mothers who would otherwise have sought employment out of the work force, while others were forced to accept makeshift and often unsafe day-care arrangements. The need for affordable, quality day care was recognized in 1988 by both political parties. Congress considered passage of the Act for Better Child Care Services, which would help the lowest-income families pay the full cost of child care.

Single mothers, who tended to depend heavily on support payments from their children's fathers, often found such payments elusive. In 1985, 25% of women who were owed payments received only partial payments, and another 25% received nothing at all. Although the federal government had sought to remedy this situation in

MARY ELLEN MARK

Two small children sit with their parents in the family car, where the four sometimes live. In the U.S. more than one-third of the homeless were families with children.

A woman waits with her children before being evicted from their welfare motel, a building that had earlier been condemned by the state Board of Health.
EUGENE RICHARDS—MAGNUM

1984 with the Child Support Enforcement Amendments, many states failed to comply fully with the measure. Even when mothers received payment, the money was often insufficient to rescue them and their children from poverty.

Federal Programs Slashed. A fourth reason so many children sank into poverty in the 1980s was that the federal safety net—the tissue of programs designed to keep the poor from disaster—was in shreds, in large measure because of cuts and changes imposed in the early 1980s. In 1979 nearly one of every five families with children that otherwise would have been poor was lifted out of poverty by such government cash-benefit programs as Aid to Families with Dependent Children (AFDC), unemployment insurance, and Social Security. By 1987, however, these programs were able to rescue from poverty only one in every ten such families with children.

Because each state mandated its own AFDC eligibility and benefit levels, those levels did not have to be adjusted for inflation. As a result, the real value of the median state AFDC monthly benefit for a family of four fell more than one-third between 1970 and 1987. In July 1987 AFDC payments for a family of three were less than one-half the federal poverty level in 28 states. Single women headed nearly 90% of all AFDC households, and fully three-fifths of those households included children younger than six years.

Arbitrary restrictions on eligibility denied several large groups of the very poor even basic AFDC support. The federal government allowed, but did not require, states to provide AFDC to two-parent families that were needy because the principal wage earner was either unemployed or underemployed. In January 1988, 23 states were failing to extend AFDC to that category.

Restrictions on Medicaid, imposed in 1981, led to the exclusion of hundreds of thousands of children in poor working families. The Title V Maternal and Child Health Block Grant, the Family Planning, and the Migrant Health Center programs were all operating at funding levels below the amounts needed to maintain their services at 1981 levels.

Children in poor working families were increasingly likely to be without any form of health coverage. While one-third of all poor children were uninsured, 43% of poor children in families headed by a full-time worker lacked coverage in 1986. Gaps in employer-based private coverage and high deductibles tended to deter poor families from seeking medical care even if they had insurance. A privately insured poor child was 1.5 times less likely than a poor child covered by Medicaid to receive preventive health care. Health professionals working with low-income children estimated that as many as 80% were suffering from one or more untreated medical conditions.

Prenatal Care Neglected. Studies have also established that poor women are significantly less likely to receive early prenatal care and that babies born to mothers who receive no maternity care are three times more likely to die in the first year of life than babies whose mothers receive early and adequate care. In the 1980s, by one index, only seven in ten women—and only one of every two nonwhite women—received adequate prenatal care. In 1985 the incidence of low-birthweight deliveries rose nationally for the first time since 1961, and the rate of premature births also increased.

Immunizations Decline. Despite the U.S. surgeon general's stated goal of achieving 90% immunization against polio, measles, rubella, mumps, and DPT (diphtheria, pertussis, and tetanus) by 1990, the percentage of preschool children adequately immunized against the seven major childhood diseases actually declined after 1980, and the dropoff was steepest among nonwhites.

Children were stunted academically, too, by poverty. Lower-income children usually lived in communities that had fewer resources to invest in public schools. Poor children were likelier to be channeled out of academic tracks and into vocational programs. They often saw little to gain by staying in school or delaying parenthood.

More than half of the 15- to 18-year-olds from families with incomes below the poverty level had basic reading and math skills that placed them in the bottom 20% of all teens. More than three-quarters of all poor youths were below average in reading and math, the key determinant of whether they would succeed in school and after graduation.

While Hispanics and blacks made up a disproportionate number of teens with poor basic skills, poor teens, regardless of race, were about three times more likely to drop out of school than were nonpoor teens. Regardless of race, one in five young women with below-average skills who came from a poor family became a parent while still a teenager. Thus the cycle was perpetuated, with another generation of children being born into poverty.

(continued from page 300)
However, the income limits were increased in the case of single-parent families and the disabled.

The French social security law of January 5 contained several measures to ensure that women who stayed home to raise children were given adequate social protection. In particular, the law provided that in the event of divorce or the death of a spouse, single parents age 45 or over who had at least three dependent children would be covered by the national health insurance without charge. In addition, voluntary coverage for invalidity was established for any parent with a dependent child residing in France who was not in paid employment. Contributions, which would be based on the minimum wage, could be deducted from family allowance payments. In October the National Assembly passed a bill to establish a "minimum integration income" for the poorest and most disadvantaged members of society. It would guarantee a certain level of income to everyone over age 25 and those under 25 with families. Recipients would be helped to improve their social and vocational skills.

In another approach to the problem of low-income families, a new child-support program was introduced in Australia to ensure that noncustodial parents contributed more to the financial well-being of their children. It had been estimated that fewer than one-third of such parents were paying regular maintenance. In the first stage of the scheme, implemented in 1988, a Child Support Agency was established in the Taxation Office. The agency would collect maintenance payments, through salary deductions where possible, and child-support payments would be distributed to custodial parents through the Department of Social Security. (LYNN VILLACORTA)

A comprehensive reform of the U.S. welfare system—the first since its creation in 1935—was enacted into law in 1988. Its goal was to move people from welfare to work through education, training, and job assistance. In addition, the measure tightened child-support enforcement and provided child care, health insurance, and other services to welfare families while they made the transition to work. Entitled the Family Support Act of 1988, the new program would gradually replace Aid to Families with Dependent Children (AFDC).

When the 100th Congress convened in 1987, hopes were high that welfare reform could finally be achieved. Pres. Ronald Reagan had supported it in his 1986 state of the union address; the National Governors' Association had urged change; and there was bipartisan support for using education and training to get people off welfare. (Although most recipients stayed on the rolls only briefly, at any given time more than half had been getting benefits for ten years or longer.) In 1987 House Democrats pushed through a bill that would have expanded benefits and cost about $7 billion over five years. The Senate passed a more modest $2.8 billion version in June 1988. Ten weeks of conference committee struggles produced a compromise that would cost an estimated $3,340,000,000 over the next five years.

Major provisions of the reform were: All states would have to establish a Job Opportunities and Basic Skills Training Program (JOBS), which would provide welfare families with a broad range of education, job-skills training, job-search assistance, and work experience. To the extent that resources were available, all able-bodied welfare recipients would be required to take part, with some exceptions, such as parents whose youngest child was under three (or, at state option, under one). States would be required to enroll at least 7% of their eligible welfare caseload in a JOBS program by 1990, increasing to 20% by 1995.

Starting on Oct. 1, 1990, states would have to provide welfare benefits for at least six months a year to impoverished two-parent families in which the principal wage earner was unemployed. In return, at least one parent would be required to spend a minimum of 16 hours a week in some kind of unpaid community service or other type of work experience. Currently, under an optional AFDC program, 27 states provided benefits for two-parent families in which the breadwinner was out of work. Some 238,000 such families took part. The new law was expected to add 65,000 families.

States would have to provide improved "transition" benefits, including Medicaid health insurance coverage and child care assistance, for most recipients who left the welfare rolls for jobs. Current regulations discouraged parents from going off welfare because they could lose those benefits.

Procedures would be strengthened for collecting child-support payments for welfare families. States would be required to withhold legally due child-support payments automatically from an absent parent's paycheck and, if appropriate, to conduct periodic reviews and adjustments of child-support orders for welfare recipients. Currently, automatic withholding began only when a parent was behind by 30 days' worth of payments.

One provision of the House welfare bill that was dropped by the conference committee would have offered states financial incentives to raise welfare-payment levels. Because of inflation, the real value of benefits shrank by 26% between 1975 and 1988, according to a study by the Center on Social Welfare Policy and Law. The study found that no state provided combined AFDC and food stamp payments that equaled 100% of the poverty level. In March 1988 AFDC benefits ranged from highs of $779 a month in Alaska and $633 in California to lows of $118 in Alabama and $120 in Mississippi. The median was $356.

The Census Bureau in 1988 reported that 32.5 million Americans, or 13.5% of the population, were living in poverty in 1987, a statistically insignificant decrease from 13.6% in 1986. (The poverty level for a family of four was $11,611 cash income.) The poverty rate for whites declined between 1986 and 1987, from 11 to 10.5%, but rose 2 percentage points for blacks, to 33.1%, and 0.9 of a point for Hispanics, to 28.2%. Forty percent of the poor were children under 18, and 21% of children were poor. (See Special Report.)

Besides reforming the welfare system, Congress in 1988 enacted a catastrophic health insurance plan for the 33 million elderly Medicare recipients. It was the largest expansion of Medicare since the program's inception in 1965 and would be financed by gradual increases in premiums. The lawmakers also reauthorized a two-year, $1.3 billion package of housing, health, job, and food assistance for the homeless and voted the largest expansion of the food stamp program since 1977, increasing it to $288 million in 1989 and $590 million in 1991.

Because of increases in the Consumer Price Index, benefits for the nation's 38.5 million Social Security recipients would go up 4% in 1989, bringing the maximum payment for a worker retiring at age 65 to $899 a month. The Social Security payroll tax rate would remain at 7.51% for both workers and employers and 13.02% for self-employed persons, but the amount of an employee's annual earnings subject to the Social Security tax would rise from $45,000 to $48,000. (DAVID M. MAZIE)

See also Education; Health and Disease; Industrial Review: Insurance.

This article updates the Macropædia article SOCIAL WELFARE.

Space Exploration

The return of the U.S. space shuttle to flight status, along with the launching by the Soviet Union of twin probes to Mars and the unveiling of their version of the space shuttle, highlighted 1988.

Policy and Politics. Reaffirming directions for the future in space, the U.S. government on February 11 released a new "Space Policy and Commercial Space Initiative to Begin the Next Century." Its major components were meant to establish "human presence and activity beyond Earth orbit into the solar system," create opportunities for U.S. commerce in space, and continue the national commitment to the space station. James C. Fletcher, administrator of the National Aeronautics and Space Administration (NASA), said the policy "stresses that civilian space activities contribute significantly to enhancing America's world leadership" and "lays the necessary groundwork for the decisions of the next century."

Where space science should be going at that time was outlined by the National Research Council (NRC) in its long-awaited *Space Science in the Twenty-First Century— Imperatives for the Decades 1995 to 2015.* In it the NRC requested that the "present ordering of priorities in the national space program be changed" from manned and large engineering projects "for their own sake." The NRC recommended instead that "the advance of science and its applications to human welfare be adopted and implemented as an objective no less central to the space program."

The battle over the space station budget led to strong warnings from NASA administrator Fletcher. Of particular concern was a $1 billion difference between House and Senate budget bills for NASA. Fletcher threatened that if the lower bill was passed, he would recommend terminating the space station program lest it suffer from inadequate funding. Congress restored a "bare minimum" amount, $900 million, with $515 million held until May 15, 1989, when the new president was to decide his priorities in space. The total NASA appropriation for fiscal 1989 was $10.7 billion.

At a summit between the two superpowers on May 31, U.S. Pres. Ronald Reagan and Soviet leader Mikhail Gorbachev signed an expansion of the 1987 U.S.-Soviet Cooperative Agreement on the Exploration and Use of Outer Space for Peaceful Purposes. It endorsed exchanging flight opportunities, including the placement of instruments on another nation's spacecraft, and sharing data on missions to the planets.

Space Shuttles. The U.S. space shuttle made its first flight in almost three years when *Discovery* was launched on September 29 with five astronauts aboard. The near-perfect mission reflected hundreds of design changes totaling $2.4 billion since the 1986 *Challenger* accident, which killed seven astronauts and grounded the program.

Most of NASA's redesign effort focused on the shuttle's solid-propellant rocket boosters, which give it the thrust to climb through the atmosphere for the first two minutes of flight. A leak in a joint between the segments of one of the boosters led to the destruction of *Challenger.*

Tests went well until a demonstration firing on Dec. 23, 1987, when a portion of the boot assembly in the exhaust nozzle collapsed. NASA decided to proceed with an older boot design, which had been successfully tested, but this delayed the shuttle launch from June 2 to between July 15 and August 15.

Three more solid-rocket motor (SRM) firings in 1988 cleared the way for the shuttle to return to flight. Qual-

A group of photographers snap pictures of the space shuttle *Discovery* during lift-off from Cape Canaveral, Florida. The *Discovery* was the first U.S. space shuttle to be launched since the 1986 tragedy of the space shuttle *Challenger*, which exploded, killing all who were on board.
UPI/BETTMANN NEWSPHOTOS

ification motor firings (QM-6 and -7) on April 20 and June 14 were followed by a production-verification motor (PVM-1) firing on August 18. The QM-7 firing was the most demanding because it took place in a new test stand equipped with hydraulics that simulated flight loads during the most demanding portion of ascent. PVM-1 was the ultimate test of the SRM since it incorporated the largest number yet of deliberate flaws.

Dozens of modifications were also made to the shuttle's main engines, external tank, and winged orbiter. In March NASA concluded testing on an escape-pole system for the shuttle crew. The escape pole, like a fire fighter's pole, would help the crew slide clear of the shuttle when bailing out during level flight between 3,000 and 6,000 m (10,000 and 20,000 ft). The orbiter was not expected to survive a crash landing or ditching. Tests were conducted by navy parachutists aboard a military cargo jet. It replaced a rocket extraction system that was considered in 1987.

Discovery was finally taken to the launch pad on July 4. The shuttle had been scheduled to be launched August 22, but a number of minor problems caused a series of small delays that pushed launch to September 4. Yet another launch delay was threatened by a leak in a relief valve for one of two main maneuvering rockets. Facing a delay of months if they had to send *Discovery* back to the hangar for repairs, engineers devised a way to cut a hole in the aft cargo bulkhead and clamp a seal around the leak without taking the spaceship off the launch pad.

The shuttle was finally launched on September 29, 32 months after the *Challenger* disaster. Ironically, it was delayed for another hour and 38 minutes because of good weather; winds aloft were lighter than expected and in the wrong direction, which meant that flight loads might have pushed structures too far. The countdown was resumed when the winds appeared to become more favourable. Lift-off, at 11:37 AM Eastern Daylight Time, was perfect; a brief flash of light, which appeared to mimic those preceding the *Challenger* accident, was believed to have been caused by exhaust gas recirculating below the external tank. The flight was manned by five veteran astronauts: Comdr. Frederick Hauck, Pilot Richard Covey, and Mission Specialists George Nelson, David Hilmers, and John Lounge.

Six hours after launch they deployed a tracking and data relay satellite (TDRS-C) identical to the one lost aboard *Challenger*. The remainder of the mission was spent performing various mid-deck experiments and testing the im-

proved systems aboard *Discovery.* Reentry took place on October 3, with touchdown occurring at 9:37 AM Pacific Daylight Time. Postflight analyses showed that *Discovery* performed almost perfectly, although a small crack developed in a main engine as it cooled down after cutoff. Examination of the booster rockets also revealed a flawless performance.

On December 2 another shuttle, *Atlantis,* was launched. Although details of the four-day flight were not released by the government, it was widely believed that *Atlantis* carried a radar spy satellite dubbed La Crosse. The crew comprised Comdr. Robert Gibson, Pilot Guy Gardner, and Mission Specialists Richard M. Mullane, Jerry Ross, and William M. Shepherd. Nine flights were to follow in 1989 as NASA gradually built the flight rate to 14 a year. Many would carry science payloads.

Assembly of a replacement for *Challenger* continued with the wings and other major sections being mated to the fuselage during the year. NASA also announced that it would hold a contest for U.S. schoolchildren to name the replacement orbiter, now known only as OV-105, and that it would resume biennial selection of astronauts starting in 1990 with applications submitted by July 1, 1989.

The Soviet space shuttle, *Buran* ("blizzard"), was unveiled in October and launched on November 15. The 60-m (200-ft)-tall vehicle was remarkably similar to the U.S. shuttle in shape and size, even down to the pattern of heat-shield tiles on the winged orbiter. There were marked differences, though, including the placement of all the main rocket engines in the launch vehicle (the *Energia*). The unmanned first flight completed two orbits of the Earth and landed 3 hours 25 minutes after lift-off.

Space Stations. Soviet cosmonaut Yury Romanenko set a space duration record of 326 days (breaking the previous record of 237 days) when he returned to the Earth on Dec. 29, 1987, from the *Mir* space station. He and Aleksandr Aleksandrov were joined on Dec. 21, 1987, by Vladimir Titov, Musa Manarov, and Anatoly Levchenko, who were launched aboard Soyuz TM-3. Levchenko, one of two test pilots in training for the *Buran* shuttle, returned with Romanenko and died at age 47 on August 9 of a brain tumour. Titov and Manarov broke the endurance record by spending a full year in space, returning to the Earth on December 21.

The Soyuz TM-4 flight on June 7–17 carried Viktor Savinykh and Anatoly Solovyov of the U.S.S.R. and Alexander Alexandrov of Bulgaria on a visit to *Mir* before returning to Earth. It was the second manned flight for Bulgaria.

That space travel is risky at any phase of a mission was made apparent when the crew of Soyuz TM-5, returning from *Mir,* was almost marooned in orbit by equipment and crew errors. Vladimir Lyakhov and Valery Polyakov of the U.S.S.R. and Abdul Ahad Mohmand of Afghanistan were launched on August 29 and spent the next eight days aboard *Mir.* Polyakov, a physician, stayed aboard *Mir* to monitor the health of cosmonauts Titov and Manarov, who had been aboard since December 1987. On September 6 Lyakhov and Mohmand left *Mir* aboard their Soyuz spacecraft. The first attempted retro-rocket firing was aborted when a piece of attitude-control equipment malfunctioned. The crew attempted a second firing three hours later, but it lasted only 6 seconds instead of the necessary 230 because the onboard computer had not been properly reset. Lyakhov briefly refired the engine manually, a move that he later admitted was an error and that complicated reentry calculations because of changes in the orbit. A third firing was postponed a day to let ground controllers analyze the

problem. The crew had only 48 hours of air and water when they left *Mir,* but they were in only modest danger since they could have made a manually controlled reentry almost anywhere, if necessary.

Agreements to develop a U.S. space station, now named *Freedom,* were completed during the year. International agreements were finally signed in October by the U.S., the European Space Agency, Canada, and Japan to formalize those nations' commitments to the space station. About the same time, final contracts were signed with Boeing Aerospace, McDonnell Douglas, General Electric, and Rocketdyne to build major components of *Freedom.*

Satellites. The International Ultraviolet Explorer (IUE) marked its tenth anniversary in space on January 26. The IUE had discovered galactic halos of hot hydrogen gas, monitored volcanic eruptions on Jupiter's moon Io, and observed Halley's Comet and Supernova 1987A. More than 1,400 professional papers had resulted from IUE investigations, far more than from any other telescope in the same period.

On March 25 the San Marco D/L satellite was launched by the U.S. and Italy from the San Marco platform in the Indian Ocean off the coast of Kenya. The satellite contained instruments from the U.S., Italy, and West Germany that were designed to study the region where the atmosphere and space meet.

The Solar Maximum Mission satellite discovered two Sun-grazing comets, SMM-1 and -2, which were apparently consumed by their close brush with the Sun. Repairing Solar Max yet again (it was first done in orbit in 1984) was being considered by NASA to upgrade the satellite's instruments and systems and boost its orbit so it could stay in flight a few years longer. NASA started redesign work on an orbiting solar laboratory (OSL) that would carry instruments for observing the Sun's surface at unprecedented resolution in white and ultraviolet light and in X-rays.

The fourth major ground system test was conducted during the year on the Hubble Space Telescope to determine its readiness for flight after major components were reinstalled following extensive tests and reevaluation. The Hubble, the first of NASA's Great Observatories for

AP/WIDE WORLD

Soviet Cosmonaut Vladimir Lyakhov (right) and crewmate Abdul Ahad Mohmand from Afghanistan talk cheerfully after their return voyage, which had been plagued by equipment troubles.

Astrophysics, was to carry a 2.4-m (8-ft)-wide reflector telescope that was expected to revolutionize astrophysics in the 1990s.

Major elements of the Gamma-Ray Observatory started coming together as the spacecraft, the second Great Observatory, was assembled for a launch in 1990. NASA selected TRW and Eastman Kodak to build the third Great Observatory, the Advanced X-ray Astrophysics Facility (AXAF). AXAF was to have the largest X-ray telescope ever flown, double the diameter of the one flown on the Einstein Observatory in 1978. The European Space Agency started the advanced design and development of the Infrared Space Observatory (ISO), a satellite designed to continue the work begun by the Infrared Astronomy Satellite (IRAS) several years earlier.

A U.S. polar orbit weather satellite was launched on September 24 by an Atlas E rocket. In addition to mapping equipment, it carried instruments for locating downed air crews and for monitoring the Earth's ozone layer by observing solar ultraviolet light scattered back into space.

Launchers. Israel joined the space age on September 19 when, using a Shavitt (Comet) booster rocket believed to have been derived from the Jericho ballistic missile, it launched a satellite from a secret base near the Mediterranean Sea. Although Offeq 1 gathered geophysical data, it was to be a forerunner of Israeli spy satellites that would relieve Israel of dependence on U.S. sources.

India's sole launch attempt for the year failed on July 13 as its satellite and booster rocket fell into the Bay of Bengal. In March the U.S.S.R. launched a remote sensing satellite, IRS-1, for India. Indian officials reported that by October it had already showed the location of a fault line believed to hold lead and zinc ores.

The Ariane launch vehicle of the European Space Agency (ESA) had a busy year. On March 11 an Ariane 3 launched two telecommunications satellites, Telecom 1C for France and Spacenet IIIR for GTE of the U.S. On May 17 an Ariane 2 placed in orbit an Intelsat V communications satellite. On June 15 ESA launched its first Ariane 4, the latest and most powerful member of the Ariane stable, capable of boosting up to 4,200 kg (9,300 lb) into geostationary transfer orbit or 7,000 kg (15,400 lb) into low Earth orbit. Its first flight carried a European Meteosat P2 weather satellite, a Pan American Satellite 1 for telecommunications, and the Amsat IIIC ham radio satellite. On July 21 an Ariane 3 launched the ECS-3 European communications satellite and India's Insat 1C communications and weather satellite.

China's new Long March 4 vehicle on September 7 launched a weather satellite that soon was returning high-quality images. Japan launched its CS-3A and -3B communications satellites with H-1 booster rockets in February and September.

Planetary Missions. Launch of the U.S.S.R.'s two Phobos probes to Mars and the loss of one a few weeks later were the year's outstanding events in planetary exploration. The two craft were launched on July 7 and 12 and were scheduled to arrive in Mars orbit on January 29 and February 5, 1989, respectively. Both were to rendezvous with and study Phobos, the larger of Mars's two asteroid-like moons. In September, however, a "suicide" order accidentally was sent to Phobos 1, commanding its solar cells to stare away from the Sun. Within hours its batteries were depleted, and the spacecraft froze before the error was realized. Phobos 1 carried a complement of space science instruments, including solar telescopes, and Phobos 2 carried a "hopper" that would touch down on the moon.

The Pioneer Venus Orbiter completed its tenth year in space on May 20. Another record setter was Pioneer 10, the most distant man-made object (6.8 billion km [4.2 billion mi] from the Sun on June 14) after 14 years in space.

A new flight plan for the Galileo Jupiter orbiter/probe mission was announced in February. Galileo now would have to take a six-year journey through the inner solar system to reach its goal because only midsize upper stages are allowed aboard the shuttle. The spacecraft was to be launched in 1989 and would make a flyby of Venus followed by two flybys of Earth, each designed to use the planet's gravity to move Galileo's trajectory into the outer solar system.   (DAVE DOOLING)

See also Astronomy; Earth Sciences; Industrial Review: *Aerospace; Telecommunications;* Military Affairs; Television and Radio.

This article updates the *Macropædia* article EXPLORATION: *Space Exploration.*

Sports and Games

AERIAL SPORTS

The "repeat" of a mythical feat some 35 centuries old—the flight of Daedalus from the isle of Crete to Greece—was the major aerial sports event of 1988. According to legend, the ancient Greek hero Daedalus escaped the labyrinth of Crete and, fashioning wings of feathers and wax, flew with his son, Icarus, across the Sea of Crete to freedom. His son perished when he flew too close to the Sun and the wax of his wings melted.

On April 23, flying a bicycle-chain-driven propeller aircraft made of superlight man-made materials rather than wax and feathers, Greek cycling champion Kanellos Kanellopoulos completed a man-powered flight of 123 km (74 mi) from Crete's Heraklion military airfield to the Greek island of Thera in 3 hours 54 minutes. In the process, Kanellopoulos set a new world distance record for human-powered flight, nearly doubling the 62-km (37.2-mi) record set by Glenn Tremml of the U.S. in 1987 over a desert course at Edwards Air Force Base, California.

On June 6 British balloonist Per Lindstrand set a new world altitude record for hot-air balloons by ascending 18,062 m (58,700 ft) into the stratosphere over Laredo, Texas, in a 12-story-tall, 16,800-cu m (600,000-cu ft) balloon named "Stratoquest." The Swedish-born Lindstrand already held distance, duration, and speed records for hot-air balloons.

Christopher Lee Marshall, 11, of the U.S. became the youngest pilot ever to cross the Atlantic, touching down at Paris's Le Bourget Airport on Bastille Day, July 14, after a 5,933-km (3,560-mi) flight from New York City emulating the epochal 1927 crossing of his hero, Charles Lindbergh.

Unlike Lindbergh, Marshall encountered engine trouble and was also compelled by bad visibility to set his single-engine Mooney 252 down on an island near Greenland before continuing on his journey. Marshall also had an adult copilot, Randy Cunningham, 47, a retired U.S. Navy pilot, who temporarily took over the controls during the Greenland incident.

Another boy to be honoured was Erik Fiederer of the U.S. In January the U.S. National Aeronautic Association confirmed that in November 1987 the ten-year-old became the youngest pilot to complete a U.S. transcontinental flight.

The Fédération Aéronautique Internationale (FAI) confirmed the July 11, 1987, world record for largest freefall formation, set by a Belgian team of Marcel Aeby and 125 other jumpers over Koksijde, Belgium. Also confirmed

were the Sept. 16, 1987, world record for largest canopy formation, achieved by Patrice Barazzutti and 31 other persons at Lapalisse, France, and the world women's record for largest canopy formation, set by Schantz Basir and a U.S. team of 10 other jumpers at Davis, Calif., on Aug. 29, 1987.

Coy Foster of the U.S. set a world distance record for Class A balloons of 47.44 km (29.48 mi). His flight was in a Colt N-BMAM on February 7.

A new world multiplace gliding record for speed around a 750-km (450-mi) triangular course was set on January 8 at Kimberly, South Africa, by Klaus Holihaus and R. Van Tonder of West Germany. In a Nimbus 3D (T) they achieved a speed of 147.9 km/h (86.4 mph). On the same day, they also set a 1,000-km (600-mi) triangular course speed record of 138.1 km/h (85.8 mph) in the same aircraft.

The motor gliding world record for single-seater speed over a 100-km (60-mi) triangular course of 191.2 km/h (118 mph), set by Beat Bunzli of Switzerland on Dec. 29, 1987, in a DG-400 at Bitterwasser, Namibia, was confirmed by the FAI. Also at Bitterwasser, on Jan. 9, 1988, Bunzli set a 500-km (300-mi) single-place motor gliding speed record of 170.1 km/h (105.7 mph) in a DG-400.

On January 9 at Tempe, South Africa, Otto Wegscheider and Otmar Roder of West Germany set a world out-and-return distance mark for two-seater motor gliders of 1,017.2 km (611 mi) in an ASH 25 BM. On the same day at Tempe, West Germany's Otto Schauble continued his country's success with a single-seater motor glider out-and-return distance record of 1,084 km (651 mi) in an ASW 22 BE.

A fixed-wing mono hang glider distance-to-a-goal world record of 79.3 km (47.4 mi) was achieved by Randy Bergum of the U.S. in an Easy Rider from Big Pine, Calif., on July 12. From the same place on June 27, William Reynolds of the U.S. in a Wills Wing set a world record of 223.7 km (134.4 mi) for fixed-wing mono hang glider distance in a straight line. Flying from Lone Pine, Calif., Britain's Geoffrey Lyons set a world flex-wing mono hang gliding out-and-return distance record of 308.8 km (185.4 mi) in an Enterprise Wings aircraft.

A flex-wing mono hang glider world distance-in-a-straight-line record of 360.5 km (216.6 mi) was achieved by Kevin Christopherson of the U.S. in a Mystic flying out of Whiskey Peak, Wyo., on June 5. On January 6 at Corridsery, Australia, Stephen Blenkinsop of Australia, flying a Moyes GTR Racer, set a world flex-wing, single-place general hang gliding mark of 112.9 km (70.2 mi) for distance over a triangular course. Thomas Pratt of the U.S., flying a Mitchell Silver Eagle out of Avon Lake, Ohio, set a world microlight record for distance in a straight line of 1,065 km (639.3 mph). (MICHAEL D. KILIAN)

AUTOMOBILE RACING

Grand Prix Racing. International Formula One automobile racing was as intense in 1988 as in previous years, and the changed regulations, reducing the boost pressure and the fuel allowance on $1\frac{1}{2}$-litre turbocharged engines in an effort to reduce top speed and to even up competition between such cars and the nonboosted $3\frac{1}{2}$-litre entries, had no great effect. The season was notable for the domination of Japanese engine technicians, who monitored the behaviour of the Honda V6 turbocharged power units in the McLaren and Lotus cars from the pits. One of the two McLaren-Honda cars won all but one of the 16 Formula One Grands Prix. In 1989, with turbochargers barred, Formula One racing would enter a fresh phase.

The season began as usual in Brazil, where Alain Prost

Ayrton Senna of Brazil exults in his victory in the British Grand Prix. Senna clinched the 1988 world drivers' championship with a winning performance in Japan, becoming the world's top Formula One racer.
AFP PHOTO

(France) in a McLaren-Honda MP 4/4 won from Gerhard Berger (Austria) in a Ferrari. Former world champion Nelson Piquet (Brazil) finished third in a Lotus-Honda 100T. The pattern for the remainder of the year was shown at San Marino, where the two McLaren-Hondas annihilated every other car. Ayrton Senna (Brazil) won from Prost, and Piquet was third. At Monaco Prost took the race for McLaren. Senna did not finish, and Berger and Michele Alboreto (Italy) placed second and third for Ferrari.

At the Mexican Grand Prix, Prost and Senna finished first and second ahead of the two Ferraris. In Canada the position was reversed, with Senna leading Prost home. Thierry Boutsen (Belgium) finished third in a Benetton-Ford. Senna then dominated the U.S. Grand Prix on the streets of Detroit, followed closely by Prost; Boutsen was again third for Benetton. Prost won the French Grand Prix ahead of Senna. Alboreto finished third for Ferrari.

Senna was by now proving himself the outstanding driver. He won the German Grand Prix at Hockenheim. Prost was second, and the two Ferraris of Berger and Alboreto were third and fourth.

The 1988 world drivers' championship became exciting after the result of the Hungarian Grand Prix, where Prost's starting-line strategy failed to pay off and Senna won by the narrowest of margins, both drivers thus having 66 points toward the championship. Yet again it was Boutsen in the Benetton who was third. The British Grand Prix was won by Senna as Prost did not finish; Nigel Mansell (U.K.) in a

Formula One Grand Prix Race Results, 1988		
Race	Driver	Car
Brazilian	A. Prost	McLaren-Honda
San Marino	A. Senna	McLaren-Honda
Belgian	A. Senna	McLaren-Honda
Monaco	A. Prost	McLaren-Honda
U.S.	A. Senna	McLaren-Honda
French	A. Prost	McLaren-Honda
British	A. Senna	McLaren-Honda
German	A. Senna	McLaren-Honda
Hungarian	A. Senna	McLaren-Honda
Canadian	A. Senna	McLaren-Honda
Italian	G. Berger	Ferrari
Portuguese	A. Prost	McLaren-Honda
Spanish	A. Prost	McLaren-Honda
Mexican	A. Prost	McLaren-Honda
Japanese	A. Senna	McLaren-Honda
Australian	A. Prost	McLaren-Honda

WORLD DRIVERS' CHAMPIONSHIP: Senna 90 pt, Prost 87 pt Berger 41 pt.
CONSTRUCTORS' WORLD CHAMPIONSHIP: McLaren-Honda 199 pt, Ferrari 65 pt, Benetton-Ford 46 pt.

Williams-Judd was second, and Alessandro Nannini (Italy) in a Benetton-Ford finished third.

At the quick and demanding Spa circuit in Belgium, Senna led Prost home by some 31 seconds, Boutsen finishing third. At the Italian Grand Prix at Monza, however, there was a most unexpected development when both McLaren-Hondas developed troubles that caused their retirement, Senna on lap 50 and Prost on lap 35 of the 51-lap contest. Senna collided with a curb and damaged the car. The Ferraris of Berger and Alboreto sailed into the first two places. Two Arrows with BMW power, driven by Eddie Cheever (U.S.) and Derek Warwick (U.K.), finished third and fourth, respectively. Prost took the Portuguese Grand Prix after Senna had fallen back, allowing Ivan Capelli (Italy) in a March-Judd V8 to take second spot and Boutsen a third place in the Benetton-Ford. Prost also won the Spanish Grand Prix, with Mansell finishing second and Nannini third.

The drivers' championship was decided before the last race because in Japan Prost's engine was not at its best and Senna won, clinching the championship; Prost finished second and Boutsen was third. In Australia for the last race of the 1988 season and the end of the turbocharger era, Prost showed his old form and finished first, ahead of Senna. Piquet was third. Senna thus won the championship with 90 points to Prost's 87 and Berger's 41. The constructors' world championship was an easy victory for McLaren-Honda, which scored 199 points to 65 by Ferrari and 46 by Benetton-Ford.

Rallies and Other Races. In long-distance sports-car racing, Jaguar made a comeback in 1988 by winning at Le Mans, where in the famous 24-hour event a Silk Cut Jaguar XJR-9 driven by Jan Lammers, Johnny (the earl of) Dumfries, and Andy Wallace just beat a Porsche 926C. In the 800-km Jerez race (1 km = 0.62 mi) a Sauber-Mercedes C9 led a Jaguar home, and at the Silverstone 1,000-km event Jaguar was again marginally superior. Mercedes then beat Jaguar at Brno, Czech., but in the British Brands Hatch 1,000-km race a Jaguar led a Porsche and a Sauber-Mercedes. At the Nurburgring 1,000-km contest it was Sauber-Mercedes, Jaguar, and Porsche in that order.

Rallying remained a popular sport. Lancia won in Sweden and Portugal with a 4WD Delta, and a Ford Sierra Cosworth was first in Ireland and in the Tour de Corse. Lancia dominated in the Acropolis and finished first and second ahead of Ford in the 1,000 Lakes Rally. The arduous East African Safari Rally was a victory for Miki Biasion and Tiziano Siviero in a Lancia Delta Integrale, and the Monte Carlo Rally went to a 4WD Lancia Delta. Biasion won the 1988 World Rally Championship, the first Italian to do so. The manufacturers' championship was easily won by Lancia.   (WILLIAM C. BODDY)

U.S. Racing. Rick Mears won the most important battle, but Danny Sullivan won the Championship Auto Racing Teams' war, the 1988 CART season championship. Mears annexed his third Indianapolis 500-mi race victory (1 mi = 1.61 km), collecting $804,000 of a $5,016,000 purse, both money records. He had placed his Penske PC-17 turbocharged Chevrolet on the pole with a record ten-mile qualifying run of 219.198 mph (including a record 220.453-mph single lap). That led to an all-Roger Penske team front row of Mears, Sullivan, and Al Unser, Sr., unprecedented in the world's oldest and richest race. Sullivan led the first 30 laps until he experienced handling problems (a broken front wing adjustment), leading ultimately to a crash.

Finishing second was former world champion Emerson Fittipaldi of Brazil driving a March 88C Chevrolet. The only driver in the same lap as Mears, he appealed a two-lap penalty for illegal passing and won. Third was Al Unser, Sr. Mears won at Milwaukee, Wis., the next race on the CART schedule, but then Sullivan took command, eventually edging out Al Unser, Jr., for the $300,000 CART championship.

In the Winston Cup series of the U.S. National Association for Stock Car Auto Racing (NASCAR), Bill Elliott in a Ford and Rusty Wallace in a Pontiac dueled throughout the year for the championship. Wallace won four of the final five races in an attempt to overcome Elliott but ended 24 points behind, even though he won the season-ending Atlanta Journal 500. The manufacturers' title went to Ford. Ironically, the two men did not fare well in NASCAR's classic, the Daytona 500, although Wallace did lead four early laps. The stars there were the Allison family. Bobby won in a Buick, and son Davey in a Ford Thunderbird finished second.

The Electramotive Nissan GT Prototype dominated the International Motor Sports Association season and earned Geoff Brabham the drivers' crown. The Nissan team began its ascendancy at Road Atlanta after the endurance classics and then won almost every other race, including the Del Mar, Calif., finale. The main challenge was mounted by Jaguar, which won the classic Sunbank 24 Hours of Daytona and at Road America.

In Sports Car Club of America's Trans-Am series, a surprise season champion was the Audi Quattro Turbo driven by Hans Stuck and veteran Hurley Haywood. Toyota dominated SCCA's series for compact trucks, and New Zealander Rod Millen in a Mazda four-wheel-drive turbo 323 GTX won the class A rally crown.

(ROBERT J. FENDELL)

BADMINTON

China remained on top of the badminton world in 1988 by capturing the Thomas Cup for men and the Uber Cup for women. Negara Stadium in Kuala Lumpur, Malaysia, was the site of the competition, which took place from May 23 to June 4.

In the semifinals of the Thomas Cup, China defeated Denmark 5-0, and Malaysia beat Indonesia 3-2. In the finals China defeated Malaysia 4-1 to retain its hold on the top rung of the badminton ladder. The only bright spot for Malaysia was the doubles win by Razif Sidek and Jalani Sidek over Li Yongbo and Tian Bingyi 15-12, 15-1. In the singles competition Yang Yang beat Misbun Sidek 15-2, 15-2; Xiong Guobao beat Foo Kok Keong 15-2, 15-11; and Zhao Jianhua defeated Rashid Sidek 15-12, 15-9. In the other doubles match, China's Chen Kang and Chen Hongyong beat the Malaysian pair of Ong Beng Teong and Cheah Soon Kit 15-12, 15-12.

In the Uber Cup semifinals, China defeated Indonesia 5-0, and South Korea beat Japan 5-0. In the finals China completed its domination of the tournament by disposing of South Korea 5-0. Li Lingwei of China needed three games in singles to subdue South Korea's Hye Young Hwang 10-12, 11-1, 11-3. In doubles both matches required three games to determine the winners. Lin Ying and Guan Weizhen beat Yun Ja Kim and So Young Chung 5-15, 18-13, 15-7, while Han Aiping and Zheng Yuli defeated Hye Young Hwang and Myung Hee Chung 9-15, 15-10, 15-9. In the other singles matches, Han Aiping beat Young Suk Lee 11-7, 11-4, and Gu Jiaming beat Heung Soon Lee 11-7, 11-5.

At the summer Olympic Games in Seoul, South Korea, badminton was introduced as an exhibition sport. It was scheduled to become a full medal sport at the Olympics in Barcelona, Spain, in 1992.   (C. R. ELI)

BASEBALL

For the fourth consecutive season—and the sixth time in the last seven—major league baseball established an attendance record in 1988. The 26 teams in the American and National leagues attracted 52,957,752 spectators, bettering the 1987 mark of 52,011,506.

With a season attendance of 3,030,672, the defending world champion Minnesota Twins became the first American League franchise to draw more than three million fans in one year. This figure helped the American League reach a single-season record of 28,497,310.

Six franchises—Boston, Minnesota, New York, and Oakland in the American League and New York and Pittsburgh in the National League—broke franchise attendance records. New York's National League team, the Mets, exceeded the three million barrier for a second time.

World Series. The Los Angeles Dodgers, though beset by injuries, defeated the Oakland Athletics four games to one in the best-of-seven series to win the World Series. The Dodgers thus became the seventh different champion in as many seasons but the first team to win twice during the 1980s, having downed the New York Yankees in 1981.

The Dodgers rallied to win the series opener at Dodger Stadium on October 15, and the stirring conquest seemed to set a tone for subsequent events. The powerful Athletics had achieved a 4–3 lead on the strength of a grand-slam home run by slugger Jose Canseco. The A's then entrusted the narrow margin to Dennis Eckersley, arguably the best relief pitcher in either league during the season.

After Eckersley walked Mike Davis, a .196 hitter, the crowd was surprised to witness the appearance of Kirk Gibson as a ninth-inning pinch batter. Gibson, hobbled by leg injuries, was thought to be unavailable. However, he responded by driving a 3–2 pitch into the right-field seats for a two-out, two-run homer that afforded the Dodgers a 5–4 triumph. Gibson's blast was considered one of the most dramatic in World Series history.

In game two at Dodger Stadium the next evening, Oakland managed only three hits off Orel Hershiser (*see* BIOGRAPHIES), the outstanding Los Angeles right-hander who struck out eight men en route to a 6–0 victory. The Dodgers built a 5–0 lead in the third inning against Oakland starter Storm Davis and thus took a commanding 2–0 lead in the fall classic.

The Athletics, heavily favoured to defeat the Dodgers, hoped to activate their estimable offense upon resuming the series at Oakland Coliseum October 18. They finally did prevail, 2–1, but not until Mark McGwire swatted a home run in the bottom of the ninth inning.

The next evening the Dodgers hung on with the excellent relief pitching of Jay Howell to defeat the Athletics 4–3. The winning pitcher was Tim Belcher; the loser was Dave Stewart, who had started the first game for Oakland. Once again, the Dodgers survived with a depleted lineup. Gibson, who was to make only that one crucial appearance during the entire series, was again on the bench. He was joined at game's end by Mike Scioscia, the Dodgers' regular catcher, and Mike Marshall, a power hitter who departed because of an ailing back.

The Dodgers persevered, however. In game five on October 20, journeyman Mickey Hatcher, who had hit only one home run in 191 at bats during the regular season, clubbed a two-run shot to left for a 2–0 Los Angeles margin. In the fourth inning Davis, another unlikely source, smashed a 3–0 pitch to right field for another two-run homer and a 4–1 lead. That was all that Hershiser needed. He struck out nine, surrendered just four hits, and pitched

Chicago's Wrigley Field comes to life on August 8 under the bright lights of its first night game, which was subsequently postponed because of rain. The Cubs ballpark officially broke with its 74-year tradition of day-only games on August 9 in a game against the New York Mets.
AP/WIDE WORLD

a complete game in the Dodgers' clinching 5–2 conquest. With half the Dodger victories, Hershiser was voted most valuable player of the World Series.

Oddly enough, with his two doubles and one single in game two, Hershiser wound up with more hits than Canseco and McGwire—Oakland's feared one-two punch. Aside from his grand slam homer, Canseco was ineffective. He finished with just that one hit in 19 at bats. McGwire was one for 17. The Athletics managed only 11 runs in five games against Dodger pitching, batting a paltry .177.

Championship Series. The Dodgers did it the hard way in the National League championship series. In the opener at Dodger Stadium October 4, Hershiser had a 2–0 lead entering the ninth inning, but the New York Mets arose to win 3–2. The Dodgers rebounded the next night 6–3 but lost game three in New York 8–4. In that contest Howell was ejected (and eventually suspended) after being found with pine tar in his glove while on the mound. The Dodgers, however, used this incident as another rallying point the next night, when they shocked the Mets with a 5–4 triumph in 12 innings. Scioscia tied the game with a two-run homer in the ninth off New York ace Dwight Gooden. The redoubtable Gibson then won the game with a home run in the 12th. Hershiser, pressed into relief duty, saved the game by recording the last out for the Dodgers.

Final Major League Standings, 1988

AMERICAN LEAGUE East Division					NATIONAL LEAGUE East Division				
Club	W.	L.	Pct.	G.B.	Club	W.	L.	Pct.	G.B.
Boston	89	73	.549	–	New York	100	60	.625	–
Detroit	88	74	.543	1	Pittsburgh	85	75	.531	15
Milwaukee	87	75	.537	2	Montreal	81	81	.500	20
Toronto	87	75	.537	2	Chicago	77	85	.475	24
New York	85	76	.528	3½	St. Louis	76	86	.469	25
Cleveland	78	84	.481	11	Philadelphia	65	96	.404	35½
Baltimore	54	107	.335	34½					

West Division					West Division				
Club	W.	L.	Pct.	G.B.	Club	W.	L.	Pct.	G.B.
Oakland	104	58	.642	–	Los Angeles	94	67	.584	–
Minnesota	91	71	.562	13	Cincinnati	87	74	.540	7
Kansas City	84	77	.522	19½	San Diego	83	78	.516	11
California	75	87	.463	29	San Francisco	83	79	.512	11½
Chicago	71	90	.441	32½	Houston	82	80	.506	12½
Texas	70	91	.435	33½	Atlanta	54	106	.338	39½
Seattle	68	93	.422	35½					

The teams split the next two games. Then on October 12 in Los Angeles, Hershiser worked another masterpiece, yielding only five hits in a 6–0 decision. The Dodgers won the cross-country play-off by four games to three and thus won the National League pennant.

Oakland, meanwhile, dispatched the Boston Red Sox, four games to none, for the American League pennant. Eckersley, who recorded 45 saves during the regular season, saved all four postseason victories over Boston. The league championship for the Athletics was their first since 1974, and most experts had considered them destined to defeat the Dodgers in the World Series.

Regular Season. Though dismissed as a fourth- or fifth-place team, the Dodgers seized first place in the National League West Division on May 26 and remained there. They won 94 games—21 more than in each of their previous two seasons—and finished 7 games ahead of the Cincinnati Reds. In the National League East, the Mets enjoyed an exceptional season, finishing with a record of 100–60 and a 15-game bulge over second-place Pittsburgh.

The Athletics were the most dominant team in either league. They took first place in the American League West on April 21 and spent 165 days there, easing to a 13-game margin over Minnesota. The Red Sox were nine games out of first place in the American League East at the mid-July All-Star break, but they surged in the second half under new manager Joe Morgan and won by one game over the Detroit Tigers. The Red Sox also broke the American League record for most consecutive victories at home, 23. At the opposite end of the spectrum were the Baltimore Orioles, who opened their season with a record 21 losses.

The Chicago Cubs also made history by staging the first night game in the annals of Wrigley Field on August 8. Actually, the scheduled contest was postponed because of rain after a long delay. Thus, the first official Cubs' home game under the lights occurred the next evening, August 9, against the New York Mets.

The annual All-Star game was won by the American League 2–1. Although the National League had won 22 of the last 25 midsummer classics, it was Whitey Herzog's third loss as National League manager. Most valuable player of the game was Terry Steinbach, catcher of the Athletics, who drove in both American League runs.

Individual Accomplishments. Hershiser, who achieved a splendid 23–8 record for Los Angeles, put together a late-season streak of 59 scoreless innings (August 30–September 28), breaking the previous mark of former Dodger Don Drysdale. Hershiser and Cincinnati's Danny Jackson tied at 23 for most victories in the National League; New York's David Cone had 20. Hershiser won the Cy Young Award as the league's outstanding pitcher in a unanimous vote.

Darryl Strawberry of the Mets led the National League in home runs with 39, while Will Clark of the San Francisco Giants paced runs-batted-in leaders with 109. The best average was .313, posted by Tony Gwynn of the San Diego Padres. Gibson was voted the league's most valuable player. National League rookie of the year was Chris Sabo of Cincinnati.

In the American League, Oakland's Canseco became the first player in history to hit at least 40 home runs (he had 42) and steal 40 bases in one season. Canseco led the league in home runs and in runs batted in (124) and was the unanimous choice for the league's most valuable player. Wade Boggs, Boston's outstanding third baseman, paced all batters with a .366 mark. Walt Weiss became the third Oakland player in a row to be named rookie of the year.

Frank Viola of the Twins had the best pitching record,

24–7, and later won the American League's Cy Young Award. Stewart of the Athletics was the second best pitcher at 21–12, and Mark Gubicza of the Kansas City Royals was the only other 20-game winner (20–8). Rickey Henderson of the New York Yankees led the major leagues in stolen bases with 93.

At season's end both World Series managers—Tommy Lasorda of the Dodgers in the National and Tony LaRussa of the Athletics in the American—were honoured as the best in their respective leagues. In other developments, A. Bartlett Giamatti, the president of the National League, was voted in as the next commissioner of baseball, succeeding Peter Ueberroth.   (ROBERT WILLIAM VERDI)

Japan. Tokorozawa's Seibu Lions of the Pacific League became Japan's number one baseball team when they defeated Nagoya's Chunichi Dragons of the Central League four games to one in the best-of-seven Japan Series. This was the third championship in a row for the Lions. Hiromichi Ishige of the Lions, who batted .389 with three home runs and six runs batted in, was voted the most valuable player of the series.

For the Lions the 1988 season was not an easy one. Not until the runner-up Kintetsu Buffaloes lost their final game of the season did the Lions clinch the Pacific League pennant. Hiromitsu Kadota of the Nankai Hawks was voted the most valuable player of the year in the Pacific League. Kadota hit 44 home runs, batted in 125 runs, and won the batting championship. Pitcher Ryoji Moriyama of the Seibu Lions, who won ten games, was the rookie of the year.

In the Central League, the defending champions, the Yomiuri Giants, were the preseason favourites. However, injury took Warren Cromarty (who was batting third) and Masaaki Yoshimura (who was batting fifth) out of the lineup in the middle of the season, and thereafter the Giants fell far behind the Chunichi Dragons, the 1987 runner-up.

Kuo Yuan-tzu, who won 8 and saved 37 games for the Dragons, was voted the most valuable player of the Central League. The rookie of the year was Dragon shortstop Kazuyoshi Tatsunami.   (TOSHIHIKO SUZUKI)

Latin America. For the second year in a row, a Dominican Republic team took baseball's top winter tournament in 1988. The Escogido Lions, who had defeated the former Caribbean champions, the Cibao Eagles, in the Dominican baseball league, went on to win the 18th Caribbean Series in February.

The Lions enjoyed solid home crowd support, as the series was held in Santo Domingo, but they did not have as easy a time as the undefeated Eagles had in 1987. In the six-game round-robin format (reintroduced after a one-year experiment with another system), Escogido dropped two games. Four wins, though, were sufficient for the crown. The Tijuana (Mexico) Colts and the Mayagüez (Puerto Rico) Indians tied for second place with even 3–3 records. The Caracas (Venezuela) Lions were last, even though they had two victories.

The Mexico City Red Devils won the summer's Mexican League. Their superiority was indicated by the fact that, in three consecutive play-off series, a total of 14 games, the Devils dropped only 2.

The Cuban national baseball team, reputed to be the best in Latin America in spite of its nominal amateur status, missed the year's most important nonprofessional meet, as Cuba stayed away from the Olympic Games in Seoul, South Korea. The U.S., narrowly defeated by Cuba in the 1987 Pan American Games, took the Olympic gold medal.   (SERGIO SARMIENTO)

BASKETBALL

United States. *College.* Very few college basketball experts thought Kansas had a chance to win the 1988 National Collegiate Athletic Association (NCAA) championship. The Jayhawks' coach, Larry Brown, fretted during a midseason slump that his team probably would not even receive an invitation to the tournament.

Yet Brown's team was there when the NCAA meet began and—remarkably—still there when it ended, alone at the top. Shaking off a string of injuries, internal problems, and tough defeats, the Jayhawks won 15 of their last 18 games, capping the comeback with a stunning 83–79 upset over top-ranked Oklahoma in the final. Knocking off Oklahoma to nail down the crown was all the sweeter because Coach Billy Tubbs's Sooners had beaten Kansas twice in regular-season meetings between these Big Eight Conference rivals.

Even though Brown's underdogs had been written off as serious contenders in the 64-team NCAA field, they had two trump cards to play, both aces. Kansas parlayed the coach's burning will to win with the superb talent of 6-ft 8-in forward Danny Manning to produce an irresistible force at the right time.

The Jayhawks earned a semifinal berth by ousting another Big Eight foe, Kansas State, in the Midwest Regional final. Kansas State had forged the shocker of the tournament by eliminating consensus favourite Purdue but could not sustain that magic against Manning and his supporting cast in the semifinals. Oklahoma defeated Arizona 86–78, and Kansas topped Duke 66–59, setting up only the third championship clash between members of the same conference in NCAA history. Manning's brilliance and Oklahoma's fondness for rolling up the score against outclassed opponents inclined most of the nationwide television audience to root for the giant-killer Jayhawks.

Brown gave a masterful performance as coach, both on and off the court. His bench coaching was superb, taking some of the burden off Manning with artful substitutions that enabled Kansas reserves to make vital contributions. Somehow, Brown also managed to keep the spotlight off his own coaching future, despite recurrent rumours that he planned to go elsewhere after the season.

Perhaps the most stunning aspect of this surprising night was Kansas's ability to match the Sooners' blistering pace in the early going. Attempting to play run-and-shoot with Tubbs's speedsters had proved an exercise in futility for other coaches all season, but not this time. The Jayhawks went stride-for-stride with the high-powered offense that had vaulted Oklahoma to the top of the college basketball rankings, pulling into a 50–50 tie at halftime. Then Brown calmly eased back on the throttle, turning the closing 20 minutes into a slowdown duel that conserved Manning's energy for the frantic finish.

Members of the U.S. women's basketball team are clearly moved by the rendition of the U.S. national anthem. They retained their Olympic title by defeating the team from Yugoslavia to take the gold.
AFP PHOTO

With its victory Kansas (27–11) became the only team to capture an NCAA basketball title with more than ten defeats on its record. Manning, voted an All-American and the most valuable player of the tournament, was the driving force, adding 18 rebounds, 5 steals, and a pair of blocked shots to his game-high 31 points.

After the celebrations died down on the Kansas campus, the well-traveled Brown moved on, as expected. Most fans anticipated that he would return for his second coaching stint at UCLA, but there was a surprise in store for them; Brown took another fling at the professional ranks, signing a lucrative contract as head coach of the San Antonio Spurs in the professional National Basketball Association (NBA).

In women's collegiate basketball Louisiana Tech staged a whirlwind comeback, erasing a 14-point second-half deficit to nip Auburn 56–54 and capture the NCAA championship. The Lady Techsters had been humiliated by Texas 67–44 in the finals of the 1987 tournament, and they were determined not to let history repeat itself.

Coach Leon Barmore refused to let his team get downhearted, despite trailing upstart Auburn 31–19 at the half. "We thought about last year's game quite a bit," admitted Teresa Weatherspoon, the Lady Techsters' playmaker. The gap grew to 33–19 before Weatherspoon triggered the resurgence by putting a defensive stranglehold on Auburn's Ruthie Bolton, who had scored 16 points in the opening half. Bolton was blanked the rest of the way, and Weatherspoon also dished out seven assists.

Erica Westbrooks tallied 25 points for the winners, to be named outstanding player of the four teams to make the semifinals. After struggling all afternoon, Angela Lawson hit a 16-ft jumper with 39 seconds left to win it for Louisiana Tech.

Professional. The Los Angeles Lakers finally beat the NBA jinx, but it was not easy. The Lakers fought back to eliminate the Detroit Pistons in the final play-off, becoming the first repeat NBA champion since the Boston Celtics racked up back-to-back titles in the 1967–68 and 1968–69 seasons.

Compared with their easy victory a year earlier, the Lakers did it the hard way in 1988. All three of their best-of-seven play-off series went to the full seven games, and

NBA Final Standings, 1987–88

EASTERN CONFERENCE			WESTERN CONFERENCE		
Team	Won	Lost	Team	Won	Lost
Boston	57	25	L.A. Lakers	62	20
Detroit	54	28	Denver	54	28
Atlanta	50	32	Dallas	53	29
Chicago	50	32	Portland	53	29
Cleveland	42	40	Utah	47	35
Milwaukee	42	40	Houston	46	36
New York	38	44	Seattle	44	38
Washington	38	44	San Antonio	31	51
Indiana	38	44	Phoenix	28	54
Philadelphia	36	46	Sacramento	24	58
New Jersey	19	63	Golden State	20	62
			L.A. Clippers	17	65

Kareem Abdul-Jabbar of the Los Angeles Lakers (33) reaches to block a shot by Detroit Piston Rick Mahorn (44) during the NBA championship play-offs. The Lakers won the series, 4–3.

ALLSPORT USA

they had to overcome a 3–2 deficit in games against the Pistons in the championship round. Fortunately for them, the sixth and seventh games were played on the home-court setting of the Forum in Inglewood, Calif.

Even at that, the Pistons might have pulled off an upset had it not been for an injury to their playmaker and floor leader, Isiah Thomas. The sensational guard, who had carried Bobby Knight and the Indiana Hoosiers to an NCAA title as a sophomore, suffered a severe right ankle sprain that snuffed out his hopes of wearing an NBA championship ring.

The Pistons came within one game of their goal by taking two straight in Detroit to seize momentum. They almost closed out the series in game six, but Los Angeles prevailed 103–102 to set up the dramatic climax. With a capacity crowd of 17,505 cheering them on, the Lakers broke open the decisive contest by outscoring Detroit 36–21 in the third quarter. Even with Thomas on the sidelines, helplessly hobbling on crutches, the Pistons refused to concede. They stormed back to trail 98–96 with only 2:50 remaining.

While their fans screamed "Repeat! Repeat!," the Lakers almost let it slip away when Detroit's Bill Laimbeer hit a three-point basket, cutting the gap to 106–105 just six seconds before the end. Unheralded A. C. Green then broke free for the clinching lay-up, and the fans swarmed onto the court to celebrate the Lakers' 108–105 triumph.

"We kept coming back," summed up Earvin "Magic" Johnson, pointing to the Lakers' seventh-game decisions over Utah and Dallas in preliminary play-off rounds. "This was the hardest championship of them all."

The Hollywood ending saved Lakers' coach Pat Riley from having to swallow his "guarantee" that the Lakers would win the championship again. At the age of 41, centre Kareem Abdul-Jabbar was ineffective in the finals, but Laker teammate James Worthy came to the rescue with 36 points on 15-for-22 shooting in the decisive game. Worthy was named most valuable player of the series.

(ROBERT G. LOGAN)

World Basketball. The outstanding event in world basketball in 1988 was the competition for gold medals in the Olympic Games at Seoul, South Korea, in September. The United States men's team failed in its effort to gain revenge

for its defeat by the Soviet Union in the 1972 Olympics, as the Soviets, inspired by 2.2-m (7-ft 3-in) centre Arvydas Sabonis, gained an 82–76 victory in the semifinals. Rimas Kurtinaitis led the victors with 28 points, and the Soviets then went on to win the gold medal 76–63 over Yugoslavia. The U.S. gained the bronze medal by defeating Australia 78–49.

In the women's competition, the U.S. won the gold medal by beating the Soviet squad 102–88 in the semifinals and then winning the final 77–70 over Yugoslavia. The Soviet Union won the bronze medal by defeating Australia 68–53. Teresa Edwards and Katrina McClain were outstanding for the U.S.

In other competition Tracer Milan of Italy retained the European Champions' Cup with a 90–84 victory over Maccabi Tel Aviv of Israel at Ghent, Belgium, in April. Primigi Vicenza of Italy won the women's European Champions' Cup with a 70–64 triumph over Dinamo Novosibirsk of the Soviet Union. At the Central American championships, held at San José, Costa Rica, in January, El Salvador defeated Costa Rica 83–82 for the men's title and Honduras won the women's crown with a 71–67 triumph over Costa Rica.

The International Basketball Federation during the year continued to move toward integration with the professional National Basketball Association by calling a special congress for April 1989 to abolish the distinction between professional and amateur players and also by encouraging and supporting several open tournaments for the first time. The first open event, held in October 1987 in Milwaukee, Wis., under the title McDonald's Basketball Open, involved the Milwaukee Bucks of the NBA, the national team of the Soviet Union, and Tracer Milan of Italy. Although the Bucks won comfortably, the tournament provided valuable experience for the European teams. In August 1988 the Atlanta Hawks of the NBA traveled to the U.S.S.R. to play three games with the Soviet team. After two narrow defeats the Soviets came from behind to win the third game 132–123.

(MELVIN D. WELCH)

BILLIARD GAMES

Billiards. Three-cushion billiards, the most popular and widely played discipline of the cue sports worldwide, suffered in recent years as two sanctioning organizations with greatly differing views and objectives sought to govern international competition. In mid-1988, to the relief of fans and players alike, the groups announced an agreement to conduct a program that should prove acceptable to the vast majority of the world's top competitors. The Union Mondial de Billiard (UMB), which for decades conducted amateur world tournaments, and the Billiard World Cup Association (BWA), which began a $200,000 professional tour in late 1986, would jointly produce a traditional 12-player annual world championship event. The BWA professional tour would employ a point system to qualify ten of the players, and a UMB tournament of national billiard federation amateur representatives would produce the other two.

The absence of an amateur world meet in 1987 failed to dull the skills of reigning UMB world champion Torbjorn Blomdahl of Sweden. He won his third European championship in four years in Vejle, Denmark, besting a field of 20 with a 1.506 (caroms per inning) scoring average. He had a high run of 14-and-out, no small feat given that the format was 15-point games with the best three games out of five constituting a match. He also teamed with his father, Lennart, to capture the biannual World Three-Cushion National Teams championship in Madrid,

edging out Allen Gilbert and Frank Torres of the U.S. The German Open 3-Cushion championship also went to Blomdahl (3–2, 15-point games) over 19-time UMB world titlist Raymond Ceulemans.

The BWA professional tour's first three events were dominated by Ceulemans and Blomdahl. In Paris Ceulemans won the first over Marco Zanetti of Italy; in the second in Deurne, Belgium, it was Blomdahl defeating Ceulemans; and in the third tournament, at West Berlin, Ceulemans triumphed over Blomdahl. Ceulemans also competed in the Belgium Three-Cushion open in Antwerp, where he topped a field of 23 and averaged 1.414. Gilbert of the U.S. finished second. Belgium was also the host nation for the Balkline Cup, won by native Fredric Caudren with a 32.63 scoring average. The Netherlands was the site of two major three-cushion tests: the Oosterhout Invitational, won by Junichi Komori of Japan (high run, 13), and The Netherlands three-cushion championships, won for the third time by Christ van der Smissen of the host nation (new Dutch record average of 1.500).

In the U.S. the National Amateur Three-Cushion Billiards Association tournament took place in Louisville, Ky. Joe Brisson of the Denver Athletic Club was the winner. The U.S. professional and semiprofessional three-cushion scene was almost a mirror image of the international one, with the long-running struggle for power between the Billiard Federation of the U.S.A. (BFUSA) and the American Billiard Association (ABA) finally ending. The groups merged into the United States Billiard Association (USBA) and would begin competition in early 1989.

Pocket Billiards. The traditional start of the U.S. winter tournament circuit for the world's top pool players set the tone for the remainder of the year, as the winners of the prestigious U.S. Nineball Open in Norfolk, Va., went on to sweep unanimous honours as players of the year in both men's and women's competition. Earl Strickland of Richmond, Ky., won $7,000 in the 52-player Professional Billiards Association-sanctioned event and was later named player of the year by the PBA, *Billiards Digest,* and *Pool & Billiard Magazine.* An elite field of 14 fell to the talents of Jean Balukas in the Women's Professional Billiard Association-sanctioned event at Norfolk. The WPBA joined both major billiard publications in naming her woman player of the year.

The Open victory was an astounding 14th consecutive one for Balukas since her return to competition (following a softball injury) in August 1986. She added a 15th straight title a week later at the Fall Classic in Charlotte, N.C. The 28-year-old Brooklyn native then signed a promotional contract and began competing regularly on the PBA ("men's") tour, becoming the first woman to do so. In July she also resumed women's competition in the Brunswick World Open Nine-Ball championship in Las Vegas, Nev. Her incredible string was extended to 16 with her $3,000 victory there.

Mary Kenniston (Las Vegas) won the ninth WPBA Nationals in Sandusky, Ohio, besting a record field of 35 to win $2,000. Loree Jon Jones (Hillsborough, N.J.) topped 12 invitees to nab $2,400 and the Women's World Nine-Ball title in Cleveland, Ohio.

Strickland's successes on the men's circuit were far-flung. He was victorious in the Joe Farhat Nine-Ball Open (in Lansing, Mich., field of 64, prize of $4,500), the Fall Classic (Charlotte, N.C., 31, $5,000), the sixth Akron Open (Ohio, 88, $4,500), the Tara Open (College Park, Ga., 51, $5,300), and the Brunswick World Open Nine-Ball (Las Vegas, 64, $15,000). He also was runner-up in four other major events.

Mike Sigel of Towson, Md., struck for some of the tour's biggest prizes with wins at the second RAKM Up Classic (Columbia, S.C., 64, $10,000), the Governor's Cup Nine-Ball (Columbus, Ohio, 58, $6,000), and the Sands/Regent Open VI (Reno, Nev., 94, $10,000). The 35-year-old Sigel also won the $7,500 top prize in one of the two major 14.1 Continuous tournaments, the World 14.1 Championship in Cleveland. Steve Mizerak of Edison, N.J., took the other straight pool title and $6,000 first-place check at the U.S. Invitational 14.1 tournament in Eastlake, Ohio.

(BRUCE H. YENZKE)

Snooker. Steve Davis of England won the world professional championship for the fifth time after defeating Terry Griffiths of Wales by 18 frames to 11 in the final at Sheffield, England, in May 1988. The first prize of £95,-000 brought his earnings for the season to £425,612 and enabled him to retain first position in world rankings. He won five of the seven events, Stephen Hendry of Scotland taking the remaining two. Hendry was ranked fourth in the world, with Jimmy White and Neil Foulds, both of England, taking second and third place, respectively. Davis won the first two tournaments of the 1988–89 season but lost the third to White. (SYDNEY E. FRISKIN)

BOWLING

World Tenpins. Worldwide elimination tournaments—for Europe in Barcelona, Spain; North and South America in Caracas, Venezuela; and Asia-Australia in Hong Kong—preceded the final pre-Olympic eliminations in Apopka, Fla., to determine the 12 women and men eligible for the bowling exhibition in the Olympic Games at Seoul, South Korea, on Sept. 18, 1988. This was the first time tenpin bowling had been included in Olympic competition, though it was not a medal sport.

In Seoul the participants bowled a round-robin of one-game matches, after which the three top women and men rolled a stepladder play-off: the third-place finisher in the round-robin against the person placing second, and the winner of that one-game match in a two-game contest against the champion after the round-robin. In the men's play-offs Keon Jong Yul of South Korea defeated Tapani Peltola of Finland 177–163 in the first round and then won the championship by beating Wong Loke Chin Jack of Singapore 236–194 and 254–223. In the women's competition Atsuko Asai of Japan defeated Annikki Maattola of Finland 209–187 but then lost in the final to Arianne Cerdena of the Philippines, winning the first game 197–180 but losing the second 249–211.

Another major tournament of the year was the first International Youth Bowling Championships, held in Manila July 1–7. Twenty-two countries from throughout the world were represented. Bowlers from China made their debut in international championship competition, and Qatar won its first international title in bowling. The winners in the boys' competition were: singles, Peer Jensen of Denmark, 1,212; doubles, U.S., 2,390; teams of four, Qatar, 4,779; all-events, Cliff Dew of the U.K.; and masters finals, Carl Bottomley of Australia, 356–354 over Salem Monsouri of Qatar. In girls' play the champions were: singles, Lisa Kwan of Malaysia, 1,250; doubles, U.S., 2,288; teams of four, Philippines, 4,466; all-events, Kim Terrell of the U.S., 3,467; and masters finals, Karen Shafer-Wakefield of the U.S., 357–324 over Marika Felipe of Philippines.

(YRJÖ SARAHETE)

U.S. Tenpins. Professional bowling continued to be lucrative for its participants in 1988, but it was a 19-year-old amateur who took home the most prize money. In the High Roller tournament at Las Vegas, Nev., which barred

current or recent members of the Professional Bowlers Association (PBA), Larry Lichstein, Jr., of West Suffield, Conn., defeated Harry Mickelson of Kodiak, Alaska, 231–171, to win $200,000. Mickelson received $100,000.

The most prestigious PBA meet, the Firestone Tournament of Champions at Fairlawn, Ohio, was won for the second time by Mark Williams of Beaumont, Texas, who topped Tony Westlake of Edmond, Okla., 237–214, in the title match and won $50,000. Finishing third was Brian Voss of Tacoma, Wash., who also won tournaments in Peoria, Ill., and Toledo, Ohio.

In the 85th annual American Bowling Congress tournament for male nonprofessionals, held over a 103-day period in Jacksonville, Fla., the Regular Division winners were: team, Minnesota Loons "B," St. Paul, Minn., 3,152; singles, Steve Hutkowski, Hershey, Pa., 774; doubles, Mark Lewis and Mark Jensen, Wichita, Kan., 1,450; all-events, Rick Steelsmith, Wichita, 2,053.

A record 77,735 bowlers competed in the 69th annual Women's International Bowling Congress (WIBC) tournament in Reno/Carson City, Nev. The Open Division singles title was won by Michelle Meyer-Welty of Vacaville, Calif., two days before the 96-day meet ended on July 4. Meyer-Welty started her series with a 156 game, but then rolled 299 and 235 for a 690 total. Other Open Division winners included: team, Cook County Sales of Chicago, 3,027; doubles, Dee Alvarez of Tampa, Fla., and Pat Costello of Merritt Island, Fla., 1,216; all-events, Lisa Wagner of Palmetto, Fla., 1,988. Two 20-year-olds met in the championship game of the WIBC Queens tournament, with Wendy Macpherson of San Diego, Calif., defeating Leanne Barrette of Oklahoma City, Okla., 213–199, to win the $10,000 top prize.   (JOHN J. ARCHIBALD)

BOXING

Professional Competition. Mike Tyson (U.S.) continued to dominate the world heavyweight scene. The youngest fighter ever to be crowned heavyweight champion remained undefeated throughout 1988, bringing his record to 35 wins with 31 knockouts. First he crushed Larry Holmes (U.S.) in four rounds. Holmes, 38 years old and unbeaten in 48 contests, including 24 title bouts, was attempting to regain the championship he had never lost in the ring. Tyson next flattened Tony Tubbs (U.S.) in two rounds in Tokyo. Several days before his 22nd birthday, he knocked

out Michael Spinks (U.S.), another former and undefeated champion, in 91 seconds. Tyson collected more than $20 million and Spinks $13 million for the fight—a record for any sporting event. Like Holmes, Spinks then announced his retirement.

As sensational as Tyson had been inside the ring, he attracted even more worldwide attention outside with lurid headlines related to his traumatic marriage to TV actress Robin Givens, which ended after eight months with both parties seeking divorce. At one point the emotional upset threatened Tyson's future career, and he announced his retirement, only to change his mind later. His defense of his title against Frank Bruno (England) was postponed three times and eventually rescheduled for 1989. The champion fractured his right hand in an early morning street brawl in Harlem, drove his wife's car into a tree in the Catskills, and reinjured his damaged hand punching a heavy bag in the gym.

The internal and political disputes within boxing continued, with three bodies controlling their own world championships. The International Boxing Federation (IBF), based in Newark, N.J., established a firmer footing by reluctantly going along with the World Boxing Council (WBC), headquartered in Mexico, and the World Boxing Association (WBA), run from Venezuela, in reducing all major contests from 15 rounds to 12. This decision allowed the IBF to stage its world championships in Europe and Britain, appointing its own officials.

The European Boxing Union (EBU) and the British Boxing Board of Control (BBBC) still declined to become affiliated with the IBF, which then aggravated the situation by announcing its intention to hold IBF European and British championships. The EBU and BBBC warned all members that they faced suspension if they took part in such contests.

As Tyson unified the heavyweight championship, so Evander Holyfield (U.S.) became undisputed cruiserweight champion. Already recognized by the WBC and the IBF, he stopped WBA champion Carlos de León (P.R.). Holyfield then began to concentrate on heavyweight competition, with hopes of a match against Tyson in 1989.

When making his third comeback at 32, Sugar Ray Leonard (U.S.) was featured in the most extraordinary contest of the year. By knocking out Donny Lalonde (Canada) in nine rounds at Las Vegas, Nev., in November to cap-

JOHN IACONO—SPORTS ILLUSTRATED

U.S. light middleweight Roy Jones looks on in frustration as Park Si Hun of South Korea is declared the winner in a controversial decision. Many who saw the fight felt Jones had won by a wide margin.

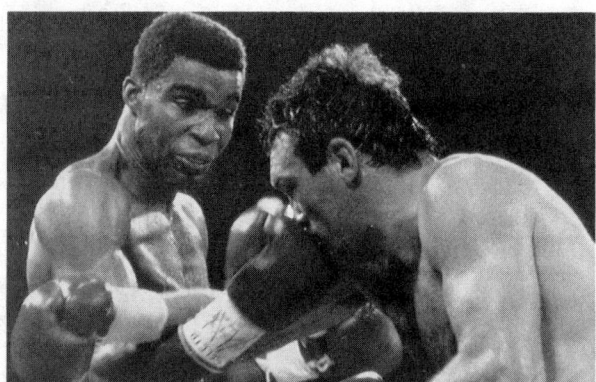

Michael Nunn (left) of the U.S. catches Argentina's Juan Roldan with a quick right to the face. Nunn won the IBF middleweight title fight by knocking out Roldan in the eighth round.

AP/WIDE WORLD

ture the Canadian's WBC light heavyweight crown plus the WBC's newly created super middleweight championship, he became the first boxer to win world titles at five different weights. Though Leonard was knocked down in the fourth round for only the second count against him in a professional career spanning 11 years, he came back to defeat the Canadian. It was only Leonard's third ring appearance in nearly seven years. Having won welterweight and junior middleweight titles, he first retired in 1982 following two operations for a detached retina. He returned in 1984 to win a nontitle contest and again retired, but he came back in 1987 to score a controversial victory and capture the middleweight crown from Marvin Hagler (U.S.). He retired once more, only to be tempted back to take on Lalonde for two titles and a reported $15 million payday. Within two weeks of winning the light-heavyweight and super middleweight crowns, Leonard informed the WBC that he was relinquishing both titles. He made no statement about yet another retirement, however, and the WBC persuaded him to retain the super middleweight championship.

Thomas Hearns (U.S.) had hoped that he could beat Leonard in the race for five titles. Having won championships at the welterweight, junior middleweight, middleweight, and light heavyweight levels, he was matched to challenge for the super middleweight crown held by Fulgencio Obelmejias (Venezuela) three days before the Leonard-Lalonde event; the Venezuelan was injured, however, and the fight was canceled. The promoter substituted James Kinchen (U.S.), the North American super middleweight champion, and almost overnight a new body, the World Boxing Organization, was formed following a walkout of many delegates at the WBA annual conference in Venezuela. After Hearns had gained a disputed decision on points, he claimed to have won five world titles, and it suited the promoter to recognize Hearns as the WBO super middleweight champion.

Hearns had earlier taken part in the biggest upset of 1988 when Iran Barkley (U.S.) stopped him in three rounds to capture the WBC middleweight championship. Michael Nunn (U.S.) also caused some surprise by lifting the IBF version from Frank Tate (U.S.). Sumbu Kalambay (Italy) remained WBA champion, outpointing Mike McCallum (Jamaica) and Robbie Sims (U.S.) and knocking out Doug DeWitt (U.S.). Don Curry (U.S.), former welterweight champion, made a comeback by winning the junior middleweight title from Gianfranco Rosi (Italy).

The WBC and WBA welterweight championships were contested on the same bill at Atlantic City, N.J., and both fights ended in controversy. Lloyd Honeyghan (England),

having regained the WBC crown from Jorge Vaca (Mexico), defended it against Chung Young Kil (South Korea). The latter was unable to continue after being hit low in the fifth round. He was allowed five minutes in which to recover but after three minutes indicated he could not do so, and the official verdict was a win for Honeyghan on a technical knockout. Honeyghan then returned to the ringside to watch his main rival, Marlon Starling (U.S.), defend the WBA title against Tomas Molinares (Colombia). As the sixth round ended, Molinares, given little chance of victory, swung a heavy right that completely flattened the champion. The referee ruled that the punch had been thrown before the bell. Television replays, however, gave the impression that the punch began after the bell, and Starling protested that Molinares should have been disqualified. The New Jersey Boxing Commission declared the decision void, but the WBA upheld it and Molinares kept the title.

Julio César Chávez (Mexico) settled an all-Mexican dispute when he added the WBC lightweight title to his WBA crown by stopping José Luis Ramírez. Though the IBF lightweight championship was held by Greg Haugen (U.S.), there was little doubt that the 26-year-old Chávez, with 62 consecutive wins, was the world's best in that division.

Azumah Nelson (Ghana), who had dominated the WBC featherweight division for some years, relinquished his crown but went on to gain the vacant WBC super featherweight (junior lightweight) championship by beating Mario Martínez (Mexico). He then retained the title by defeating Lupe Suárez (U.S.).

The WBA junior lightweight title remained in the firm grip of Brian Mitchell (South Africa). Because of apartheid, no citizen of South Africa was permitted to fight for either the WBA or the WBC championship. The WBA, however, decided not to strip Mitchell of his crown, and in 1988 he retained it by defeating Joe Rivera (P.R.) in Madrid and Jim McDonnell (England) in London. Jeff Fenech (Australia) took over the WBC featherweight crown by stopping Victor Callejas (P.R.) and retained it by halting Tyrone Downes (Barbados) and Georgie Navarro (U.S.).

Miguel Lora (Colombia) survived a drug inquiry after retaining the WBC bantamweight championship for the seventh time by beating Alberto Davila (U.S.) but was fined $1,000. Lora later lost the championship when outpointed by Raul Pérez (Mexico). It was Lora's first defeat since he began his career in 1979 at the age of 18.

Gilberto Román (Mexico) was fined $15,000 following a drug test after regaining the WBC super flyweight crown from Jesús Rojas (Colombia). He was allowed to keep the title, which he later retained against Yoshiyuki Uchida (Japan). Sot Chitalada (Thailand), holder of the WBC flyweight championship since 1984, lost it to Kim Young Kang (South Korea). Sot immediately announced his retirement. Fidel Bassa (Colombia) continued to control the WBA flyweight title, outpointing Dave McAuley (Northern Ireland) and Ray Medel (U.S.). Samuth Sithnarvelpol (Thailand) retained the IBF miniflyweight title, beating Inkyu Hwang (South Korea) at Bangkok in August in the last 15-round contest. All championships following this bout were limited to 12 rounds.

While the WBA, WBC, and IBF recognized 17 weight divisions, there was confusion over the names given to various divisions. WBC and IBF cruiserweights were labeled as junior heavyweights by the WBA. The WBC's straw weights were named miniflyweights by the other two bodies. While all three accepted the latest super middleweight division, the "junior" weights of the WBA and IBF were listed by the WBC as "super" attached to the weight division below.

World, European, and Commonwealth Boxing Champions
as of Dec. 31, 1988

Division	WBC[1]	WBA[2]	IBF[3]	Europe	Commonwealth
Heavyweight	M. Tyson (U.S.)	M. Tyson (U.S.)	M. Tyson (U.S.)	F. Damiani (Italy)	D. Williams (England)
Cruiserweight	vacant	vacant	vacant	vacant	G. McCrory (England)
Light heavyweight	vacant	V. Hill (U.S.)	C. Williams (U.S.)	J. Lefeber (The Netherlands)	W. Featherstone (Canada)
Super middleweight	R. Leonard (U.S.)	F. Obelmejias (Venezuela)	C. Rocchigiani (West Germany)	—	—
Middleweight	I. Barkley (U.S.)	S. Kalambay (Italy)	M. Nunn (U.S.)	C. Tiozzo (France)	N. Benn (England)
Junior middleweight	D. Curry (U.S.)	J. Jackson (Virgin I.)	R. Hines (U.S.)	R. Jacquot (France)	T. Waters (Australia)
Welterweight	L. Honeyghan (England)	T. Molinares (Colombia)	S. Brown (U.S.)	vacant	G. Jacobs (Scotland)
Junior welterweight	R. Mayweather (U.S.)	J. Coggi (Argentina)	M. Taylor (U.S.)	T. N'Kalankete (France)	L. Ellis (Australia)
Lightweight	J.C. Chávez (Mexico)	J.C. Chávez (Mexico)	G. Haugen (U.S.)	P. Diaz (Spain)	M. Hussein (England)
Junior lightweight	A. Nelson (Ghana)	B. Mitchell (South Africa)	T. López (U.S.)	R. Lawal (Denmark)	J. Sichula (Zambia)
Featherweight	J. Fenech (Australia)	A. Esparragoza (Venezuela)	J. Paez (Mexico)	J.-M. Renard (Belgium)	vacant
Junior featherweight	D. Zaragoza (Mexico)	J.J. Estrada (Mexico)	J. Sanabria (U.S.)	—	—
Bantamweight	R. Pérez (Mexico)	Moon Sung Kil (South Korea)	O. Canizales (U.S.)	V. Belcastro (Italy)	R. Minus (The Bahamas)
Super flyweight	G. Román (Mexico)	K. Galaxy (Thailand)	E. Pical (Indonesia)	—	—
Flyweight	Kim Young Kang (South Korea)	F. Bassa (Colombia)	D. McKenzie (England)	vacant	N.Y. Konadu (Ghana)
Junior flyweight	G. Torres (Mexico)	Yuh Myung Woo (South Korea)	T. Macalos (Philippines)	—	—
Straw weight	N. Kiatwanchai (Thailand)	R. Gamez (Venezuela)	S. Sithnarvelpol (Thailand)	—	—

[1]World Boxing Council.   [2]World Boxing Association.   [3]International Boxing Federation.

For example, the WBA and IBF junior middleweight was the same as the WBC super welterweight.

Olympic Games. Following the most controversial boxing events in the history of the Olympic Games—at Seoul, South Korea, in September—the future of the sport in the Olympics was in some doubt. Prior to the Games some members of the International Olympic Committee (IOC) were not in favour of including boxing. Though it was in other sports such as track and field, weight lifting, and judo that the use of drugs brought shame, boxing was disgraced by a riot inside the ring and some controversial decisions that led to accusations of bias and incompetence by officials. The worst incident occurred when a South Korean official physically attacked the New Zealand referee for penalizing a South Korean boxer who subsequently lost the decision. Many other South Koreans then entered the ring, causing a riot. The losing boxer staged a sitdown strike, refusing to leave the ring for more than an hour until the lights in the arena were turned off and the tournament was postponed for that day.

With Cuba, generally regarded as having the world's strongest amateur boxing team, boycotting the Games, the tournament became the most open in years; 8 countries shared 12 gold medals, and 25 countries collected at least one medal. (For a list of the champions, *see* Special Report.)   (FRANK BUTLER)

CHESS

The year 1988 began with the traditional Foreign and Colonial International Tournament at Hastings, England. A new format pitted eight leading players against one another in a double-round event. Britain's top-ranked competitor, grand master Nigel Short, won first prize ahead of his compatriot Jon Speelman.

In the second half of January, Short and Speelman became the first two British players ever to qualify for the quarterfinal of the World Championship Candidates' Tournament, held in the Canadian town of Saint John, N.B. Short defeated the Hungarian grand master Gyula Sax, while Speelman overcame the U.S. champion, Yasser Seirawan. The remaining quarterfinalists were Anatoly Karpov (U.S.S.R.), Johann Hjartarson (Iceland), Jan Timman (Neth.), Lajos Portisch (Hung.), Artur Yusupov (U.S.S.R.), and Kevin Spraggett (Canada).

The Grand Master Association, headed by world champion Garry Kasparov, took an increasingly critical view throughout the year of the official world body, the Fédération Internationale des Échecs (FIDE). Consequently, FIDE found itself in competition with a series of World Cup Tournaments organized by the Grand Master Association, each with a prize fund of $200,000. At Brussels in the first World Cup Tournament, Karpov emerged the winner, while in the next two events, at Belfort, France, and Reykjavík, Iceland, Kasparov dominated the field.

In the early spring Short won the Euwe Memorial Tournament in Amsterdam ahead of Karpov. Chess life in Amsterdam continued on an exceptionally active scale with the Optiebeurs Tournament there in April. This resulted in a tremendous triumph for Kasparov, who won the tournament with 9 points out of a possible 12, inflicting a 3-1 defeat on Karpov in the process.

In June 14-year-old Matthew Sadler created a sensation in London when he achieved second prize in the Watson Farley and Williams Grand Master Tournament organized by the English Chess Association. As a result of his success, a London-based company, Craton Lodge and Knight, offered Sadler a £20,000 grant spread over four years to further his chess career. Sadler became the youngest male international master in the world when he achieved his third IM result (a score no lower than a predetermined minimum for that ranking) at the Lloyds Bank Tournament in London in August.

Other important events in the United Kingdom included Jonathan Mestel's victory in the 1988 British championship and grand master results for David Norwood and 16-year-old Michael Adams in the National Westminster Bank International Tournament. Adams thus became the youngest player in the world to achieve a grand master result. In November the James Capel Speed Chess Challenge in London was screened in seven episodes by Thames Television. All the top British players took part, and the first prize of £3,000 was won by Short. Adams took second prize, beating Britain's world championship candidate, Speelman, in the process. Earlier, Speelman had become Britain's first world championship semifinalist when he

Final Game of Chess Olympics

White G. Kasparov	Black N. Short	White G. Kasparov	Black N. Short
1 c4	e6	13 Nge2	Nbd7
2 Nc3	d5	14 Bg2	Nb6
3 d4	Be7	15 b3	Rc8
4 c×d5	e×d5	16 0-0	Rc6
5 Bf4	c6	17 h3	Nfd7
6 Qc2	g6	18 Nd1	Rg8
7 e3	Bf5	19 Nf2	f5
8 Qd2	Nf6	20 Rae1	g5
9 f3	c5	21 g×f5	Bf7
10 Bh6	c×d4	22 Ng4	Bh5
11 e×d4	a6	23 Ng3	Black resigned
12 g4	Be6		

surprisingly crushed Short in a quarterfinal match in London in August. Short repaired his reputation significantly when soon afterward he took second prize to Karpov in the strong annual tournament in Tilberg, Neth. Short was also selected to play on top board for England in the Chess Olympics in Greece.

Michael Wilder won the 1988 U.S. championship, while Kasparov and Karpov shared first prize in the Soviet championship, an exceptionally powerful event. Both Kasparov and Karpov were in top form for the Soviet team in the Chess Olympics held at Salonika, Greece, in November. Kasparov, who made the outstanding personal score of 85%, led his team to the gold medal. England finished second for the third Olympics in a row, and The Netherlands placed third without the presence of its usual top player, grand master Timman.

In the women's Olympics the gold medal was won by Hungary, with the U.S.S.R. finishing second. The outstanding Hungarian player was 12-year-old Judit Polgar, whom many experts considered to be a potential future rival to Kasparov. Not even Kasparov or Bobby Fischer could rival her achievement of gaining the international master title before becoming a teenager.

Tremendous international interest greeted the remarkable elopement at the Olympic tournament of John Donaldson (captain of the U.S. men's team) and Yelena Akhmilovskaya, the board two of the Soviet women's team. The two married in Greece before the Olympics had concluded and left immediately in secret for Seattle, Wash. Akhmilovskaya, in spite of leaving the Olympics before they were over, still won the individual silver medal.

In the U.S. the computer Deep Thought achieved a breakthrough when it tied for first place in a tournament with grand master Tony Miles. En route to this remarkable accomplishment, Deep Thought inflicted defeat on three-time world championship semifinalist Bent Larsen (Den.). Larsen was the strongest player ever to have been beaten by a computer in a tournament game.

In the area of chess publication, *The Times* (London) inaugurated a daily chess puzzle for the first time in its history, while Pergamon Press revitalized *Chess* magazine, putting it under the editorship of Paul Lamford, the former Welsh champion.   (RAYMOND KEENE)

CONTRACT BRIDGE

The growing interest in tournament bridge was reflected in a record entry for the eighth World Team Olympiad, held in Venice, Italy, in October 1988. Fifty-eight nations competed, 56 in the Open Series and 37 in the Women's. Most impressive of the newcomers were the Bulgarian women, who surprised most people when they qualified for the quarterfinals in this, their first appearance, and astounded them when they eliminated a strong favourite, the U.S.

The U.S. went to Venice as holders of every world championship title with the exception of the Open Series of the World Team Olympiad. The team seemed destined for a further disappointment when they trailed Denmark by 19 points with 16 boards to play in the quarterfinals. They reached top form in the closing boards to win that match, however, and went on to defeat India and Austria in the semifinals and final, respectively, thus winning their first Open Olympic Team title. Bob Wolff and Bob Hamman, Jim Jacoby and Seymon Deutsch, Jeff Meckstroth and Eric Rodwell, and nonplaying captain Dan Morse took the gold medal. Silver medalist Austria was represented by Heinrich Berger and Wolfgang Meinl, Jan Fucik and Friedrich Kubac, Alfred Kadlec and Franz Terraneo, and nonplaying captain Franz Baratta. Sweden and India,

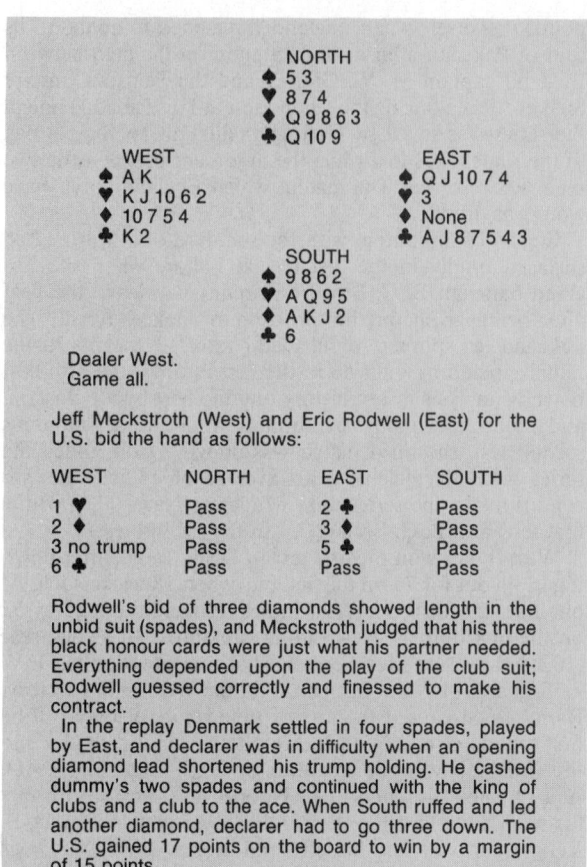

Dealer West.
Game all.

Jeff Meckstroth (West) and Eric Rodwell (East) for the U.S. bid the hand as follows:

WEST	NORTH	EAST	SOUTH
1 ♥	Pass	2 ♣	Pass
2 ♦	Pass	3 ♦	Pass
3 no trump	Pass	5 ♣	Pass
6 ♣	Pass	Pass	Pass

Rodwell's bid of three diamonds showed length in the unbid suit (spades), and Meckstroth judged that his three black honour cards were just what his partner needed. Everything depended upon the play of the club suit; Rodwell guessed correctly and finessed to make his contract.

In the replay Denmark settled in four spades, played by East, and declarer was in difficulty when an opening diamond lead shortened his trump holding. He cashed dummy's two spades and continued with the king of clubs and a club to the ace. When South ruffed and led another diamond, declarer had to go three down. The U.S. gained 17 points on the board to win by a margin of 15 points.

defeated semifinalists, took the bronze medal. For Wolff and Hamman, the world's top-ranking pair, this was their eighth world championship title; for Jacoby, Meckstroth, and Rodwell, their third; and for Deutsch, a newcomer to championship bridge, his first.

In the Women's Series Denmark became the first Scandinavian winner of an Olympic title by defeating Great Britain, 1984 silver medalist, in a nail-biting finish. With 16 boards to play, Denmark had a comfortable lead of 29. With two boards to play, they led by only four, but they then finished in style to win 178–157, adding this title to the Nordic Championship, which they had won earlier in the year. The new champions Judy Norris and Dorthe Schaltz, Charlotte Palmund and Bettina Kalkerup, Trine Dahl and Kirsten Steen Moller, led by nonplaying captain Inger Lindegaard, were in excellent form throughout.

The main subject of discussion at the championships was the growth of "Strong Pass" systems. In such bidding systems, a Pass would indicate a normal opening bid, and some opening bids would show a Pass; an opening bid of One in a suit might indicate strength and length in a different suit, and an opening bid of Two in a suit might show two different suits. There were many variations on these themes.   (HAROLD FRANKLIN)

CRICKET

In a year marred by controversy and bad weather, Pakistan and the West Indies emerged as the top teams. The highlight of the year's international cricket was Australia's victory in the World Cup, held in India and Pakistan for the first time, and the thrilling drawn series between West Indies and Pakistan, which was decided late on the final day of the last test. Cricket reached one of its lowest

points, however, when England threatened to abandon its tour of Pakistan after a confrontation on the field between England captain M. W. Gatting and the Pakistan umpire Shakoor Rana during the second test at Faisalabad. Though the series was saved by Gatting's reluctant apology, a day of the match was lost while the argument between the two men was resolved. The match, which England could have won, was drawn.

England's discontent with the standard of umpiring had surfaced briefly in the first test at Lahore when the England batsman B. C. Broad had refused to leave the field after being given out by the umpire Shakeel Khan. The Pakistan leg spinner Abdul Qadir took 13 wickets in the match, including 9 for 56 in the first innings, the fifth best bowling analysis in test history and the best by a Pakistani, and Pakistan won by an innings. After the acrimonious second test, the third match was drawn. Qadir ended the series with 30 wickets at an average of 14.56. The two centurions in the series were Mudassar Nazar (120 in the first test) and B. C. Broad (116 in the second test).

West Indies won the first test in Delhi, India, after bowling India out for 75 on the first day when 18 wickets fell. At one time 29 for 6, the West Indies recovered to lead by 52 on the first innings. New Indian captain D. B. Vengsarkar (102) led his side's recovery, but his opposite number, I. V. A. Richards (109 not out), brought the West Indies victory. Rain, which caused the loss of nine hours of play on the first two days, cost West Indies another win in the second test in Bombay, while centuries by C. G. Greenidge (141), A. L. Logie (101), and C. L. Hooper (100 not out in only his second test) for the West Indies were matched by D. B. Vengsarkar, who had his left hand broken by W. W. Davis and had to retire hurt after scoring 102 in the drawn third test. India squared the series, however, with a crushing victory in the final match in Madras, in which Narendra Hirwani, a 19-year-old leg spinner, took a remarkable 16 for 136 on his test debut. Hirwani's figures were the best by a bowler in his first test and the third best in test history. For the West Indies C. A. Walsh took 26 wickets in the series and B. P. Patterson took 17.

Australia's good form in the one-day World Cup continued in the test series against New Zealand. Led by a century by D. C. Boon (143), Australia won the first test in Brisbane, Australia. Centuries by A. N. Jones (150 in only his third test) and M. D. Crowe (137) for New Zealand and Australian A. R. Border's highest test score (205) ensured a draw in Adelaide, but the series reached a dramatic climax on the final day of the last test in Melbourne when Australia needed 247 to win. It reached 147 for 3 but collapsed to 227 for 9 before the last pair, C. J. McDermott and M. R. Whitney, survived the last five overs to draw the match and give Australia its first win in a series since 1983–84. R. J. Hadlee took 5 for 109 and 5 for 67 for New Zealand, while McDermott took 5 for 97 and A. I. C. Dodemaide 6 for 58 for Australia.

The bicentennial test in Sydney, Australia, was a disappointing draw. B. C. Broad (139) set up England's large first innings total but, after following on, Australia survived, thanks to D. C. Boon (184 not out). Sri Lanka's first test in Australia ended in defeat in Perth. Australia won by an innings and 108 runs, with D. M. Jones (102) and M. G. Hughes (5 for 67 in the second innings) rounding off a highly successful international season for the Australians.

England, on the third leg of its winter tour, played a tired and dull series in New Zealand, all three tests being drawn. B. C. Broad (114 in the first test at Christchurch) scored England's only century of the series, while J. G. Wright (103) and M. J. Greatbatch (107 not out on his test debut) in the second test in Auckland and M. D. Crowe (143) and K. R. Rutherford (107 not out) in the third at Wellington were the home side's centurions. England's G. R. Dilley took 15 wickets at 14.00 but, fittingly after such a tedious series, the final two days' play was lost to rain.

England began its home series against the West Indies with high hopes but, after the drawn first test at Nottingham, it was proved short-lived. The West Indies, led by M. D. Marshall, who took a series record 35 wickets, won the next four tests by margins of 134 runs (at Lord's), an innings and 156 runs (Manchester), 10 wickets (Leeds), and 8 wickets (The Oval). Only G. A. Gooch, who scored 459 runs at 45.90, matched the skill and speed of Marshall and C. E. L. Ambrose, who took 22 test wickets on his first tour. With this victory the West Indians had won 14 of the last 15 tests against England.

England used four different captains in the series, the original choice, M. W. Gatting, having been dropped as a

Test Series Results, September 1987–September 1988

Test	Host country and its scores		Visiting country and its scores		Result
1st	Pakistan	392	England	175 and 130	Pakistan won by an innings and 87 runs
2nd	Pakistan	191 and 51 for 1 wkt	England	292 and 137 for 6 wkt dec	Match drawn
3rd	Pakistan	353	England	294 and 258 for 9 wkt	Match drawn
1st	India	75 and 327	West Indies	127 and 276 for 5 wkt	West Indies won by 5 wkt
2nd	India	281 and 173	West Indies	337 and 4 for 1 wkt	Match drawn
3rd	India	565	West Indies	530 for 5 wkt dec and 157 for 2 wkt	Match drawn
4th	India	382 and 217 for 8 wkt dec	West Indies	184 and 160	India won by 255 runs
1st	Australia	305 and 97 for 1 wkt	New Zealand	186 and 212	Australia won by 9 wkt
2nd	Australia	496	New Zealand	485 and 182 for 7 wkt	Match drawn
3rd	Australia	357 and 230 for 9	New Zealand	317 and 286	Match drawn
Bicentenary test					
	Australia	214 and 328 for 2 wkt	England	425	Match drawn
Only test	Australia	455	Sri Lanka	194 and 153	Australia won by an innings and 108 runs
1st	New Zealand	168 and 130 for 4 wkt	England	319 and 152	Match drawn
2nd	New Zealand	301 and 350 for 7 wkt	England	323	Match drawn
3rd	New Zealand	512 for 6 wkt dec	England	183 for 2 wkt	Match drawn
1st	West Indies	292 and 172	Pakistan	435 and 32 for 1 wkt	Pakistan won by 9 wkt
2nd	West Indies	174 and 391	Pakistan	194 and 341 for 9 wkt	Match drawn
3rd	West Indies	306 and 268 for 8 wkt	Pakistan	309 and 262	West Indies won by 2 wkt
1st	England	245 and 301 for 3 wkt	West Indies	448 for 9 wkt dec	Match drawn
2nd	England	165 and 307	West Indies	209 and 397	West Indies won by 134 runs
3rd	England	135 and 93	West Indies	384 for 7 wkt dec	West Indies won by an innings and 156 runs
4th	England	201 and 138	West Indies	275 and 67 for 0 wkt	West Indies won by 10 wkt
5th	England	205 and 202	West Indies	183 and 226 for 2 wkt	West Indies won by 8 wkt
Only test	England	429 and 100 for 3 wkt	Sri Lanka	194 and 331	England won by 7 wkt

disciplinary measure in response to newspaper allegations about his conduct off the field during the first test. J. E. Emburey took over the next two tests before giving way to C. S. Cowdrey and, when Cowdrey was injured before the final test, to G. A. Gooch. Gooch led England to victory against Sri Lanka at Lord's, breaking a record sequence of 18 tests without a win.

In one-day cricket Australia beat England by just 7 runs in Calcutta to win the Reliance World Cup for the first time after a highly successful tournament. In the English season Worcestershire was the dominant team, winning the Britannic Assurance Championship by 1 point from Kent, taking the Refuge Assurance Sunday League for the second year, and narrowly losing in the NatWest Cup final to Middlesex. Much of Worcestershire's success was due to batsman Graeme Hick (*see* BIOGRAPHIES), who scored a remarkable quadruple century (405 not out) against Somerset in May and finished the season with 2,713 runs. Hampshire won the Benson & Hedges Cup; Western Australia beat Queensland in the final of the Sheffield Shield; Transvaal beat Orange Free State to win the Currie Cup; and Jamaica won the Red Stripe Cup.

(ANDREW LONGMORE)

CYCLING

Eastern European cyclists dominated the Olympic Games competition in Seoul, South Korea, in September, winning seven of the nine titles. The Soviet Union recorded a world

Francesco Moser of Italy grits his teeth as he maintains a record pace in Stuttgart, West Germany. Moser set a new world indoor cycling record of 50.644 kilometres (about 31.5 miles) per hour.
AFP PHOTO

outdoor record of 4 min 13.3 sec on the way to a gold medal in the 4,000-m team pursuit, and Lutz Hesslich of East Germany recaptured the men's sprint title that he had won in 1980 but was prevented from defending four years later by the Eastern European boycott of the Olympics. In a new event, the women's sprint, Erika Salumyae of the Soviet Union beat Christa Luding-Rothenburger in the final to deny the East German, a gold medalist in speed skating at the 1988 Winter Olympic Games, a unique double. (For other winners, *see* Special Report.)

The 1988 world championships, excluding Olympic events, were held in Belgium. There was a controversial ending to the professional road race in Ronse (Renaix) when Steve Bauer of Canada, who crossed the line in second place behind Italy's Maurizio Fondriest, was disqualified for dangerous riding. Claude Criquielion of Belgium, the 1984 champion, was challenging Bauer and Fondriest for the lead but crashed 60 m (197 ft) from the finish when Bauer apparently forced him into the spectator barriers. In the track program at Ghent, Lech Piasecki of Poland became the first Eastern European to gain a professional title by winning the individual pursuit.

Pedro Delgado became the first Spanish winner since 1973 of professional cycling's most important race, the Tour de France, which covered 3,300 km (2,051 mi) in three weeks. Delgado beat his nearest challenger by more than seven minutes, but a shadow was cast over the Tour when a compulsory drug test following stage 13 indicated that Delgado had taken probenecid, a drug that helps the kidneys eliminate uric acid from the system. Delgado was not penalized for this, however, because the drug, which had been banned by the International Olympic Committee, was not scheduled to be added to the list of substances forbidden by cycling's governing body, the Union Cycliste Internationale (UCI), until eight days after the end of the Tour.

Francesco Moser of Italy, already the holder of the world outdoor altitude (over 600 m) and sea-level records, set a new world indoor one-hour record of 50.644 km (about 31.5 mi) in Stuttgart, West Germany, in May. He rode a bicycle with an experimental oversized back wheel 1.03 m (40.55 in) in diameter, prompting the UCI to again consider design limitations.

(JOHN R. WILKINSON)

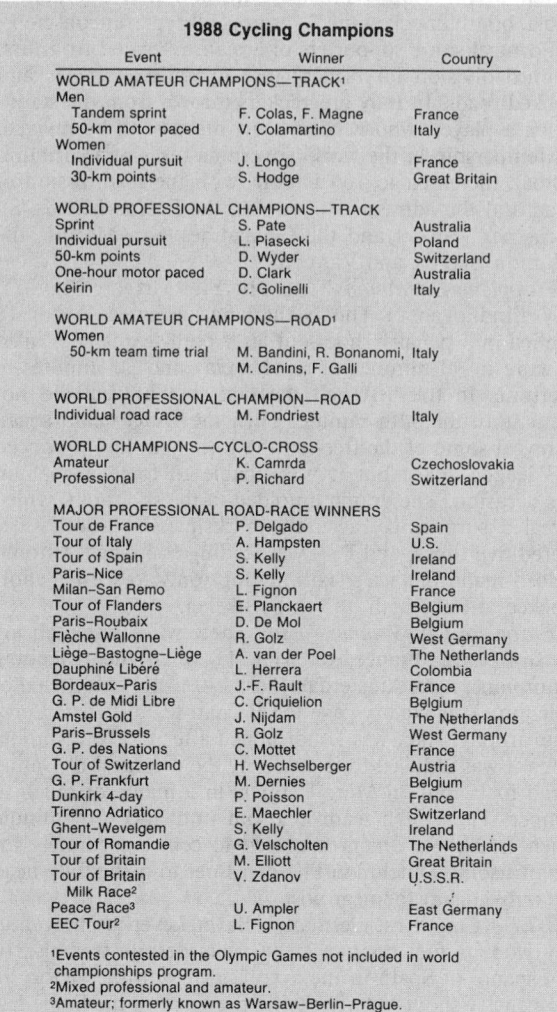

Event	Winner	Country
1988 Cycling Champions		
WORLD AMATEUR CHAMPIONS—TRACK[1]		
Men		
Tandem sprint	F. Colas, F. Magne	France
50-km motor paced	V. Colamartino	Italy
Women		
Individual pursuit	J. Longo	France
30-km points	S. Hodge	Great Britain
WORLD PROFESSIONAL CHAMPIONS—TRACK		
Sprint	S. Pate	Australia
Individual pursuit	L. Piasecki	Poland
50-km points	D. Wyder	Switzerland
One-hour motor paced	D. Clark	Australia
Keirin	C. Golinelli	Italy
WORLD AMATEUR CHAMPIONS—ROAD[1]		
Women		
50-km team time trial	M. Bandini, R. Bonanomi,	Italy
	M. Canins, F. Galli	
WORLD PROFESSIONAL CHAMPION—ROAD		
Individual road race	M. Fondriest	Italy
WORLD CHAMPIONS—CYCLO-CROSS		
Amateur	K. Camrda	Czechoslovakia
Professional	P. Richard	Switzerland
MAJOR PROFESSIONAL ROAD-RACE WINNERS		
Tour de France	P. Delgado	Spain
Tour of Italy	A. Hampsten	U.S.
Tour of Spain	S. Kelly	Ireland
Paris–Nice	S. Kelly	Ireland
Milan–San Remo	L. Fignon	France
Tour of Flanders	E. Planckaert	Belgium
Paris–Roubaix	D. De Mol	Belgium
Flèche Wallonne	R. Golz	West Germany
Liège–Bastogne–Liège	A. van der Poel	The Netherlands
Dauphiné Libéré	L. Herrera	Colombia
Bordeaux–Paris	J.-F. Rault	France
G. P. de Midi Libre	C. Criquielion	Belgium
Amstel Gold	J. Nijdam	The Netherlands
Paris–Brussels	R. Golz	West Germany
G. P. des Nations	C. Mottet	France
Tour of Switzerland	H. Wechselberger	Austria
G. P. Frankfurt	M. Dernies	Belgium
Dunkirk 4-day	P. Poisson	France
Tirenno Adriatico	E. Maechler	Switzerland
Ghent–Wevelgem	S. Kelly	Ireland
Tour of Romandie	G. Velscholten	The Netherlands
Tour of Britain	M. Elliott	Great Britain
Tour of Britain	V. Zdanov	U.S.S.R.
Milk Race[2]		
Peace Race[2]	U. Ampler	East Germany
EEC Tour[2]	L. Fignon	France

[1]Events contested in the Olympic Games not included in world championships program.
[2]Mixed professional and amateur.
[3]Amateur; formerly known as Warsaw–Berlin–Prague.

FIELD HOCKEY

At the Olympic Games in Seoul, South Korea, in September 1988, Great Britain won the gold medal in field hockey, West Germany the silver, and The Netherlands the bronze. Australia was fourth, followed by Pakistan, India, the Soviet Union, Argentina, Spain, South Korea, Canada, and Kenya. In tournaments preceding the Games, Pakistan won the Indira Gandhi Gold Cup at Lucknow, India, in January by defeating the Soviet Union 3–0 in the final. South Korea finished third and New Zealand fourth. At Lahore, Pak., in April, West Germany retained the Champions Trophy. Pakistan finished second, Australia third, and the Soviet Union fourth. In June Britain won a tournament at Ipoh, Malaysia, with a 4–0 victory over South Korea in the final. Pakistan finished third, and the Soviet Union fourth. In Nairobi, Kenya, India defeated Pakistan in the final in a penalty stroke competition after the score was tied at 2–2 at the end of regulation time. The remaining places were taken by the Soviet Union, Kenya, Canada, and Kenya B. Pakistan and India tied a six-match series at various sites, winning two matches each and leaving two tied.

In January at Vienna, West Germany became European indoor champion again. France finished second, followed by Austria, Scotland, and Poland. At Perth, Scotland, England won the Home Countries title. Scotland was second, Wales third, and Ireland fourth.

In women's hockey Australia won the Olympic gold medal, South Korea the silver, and The Netherlands the bronze. Great Britain was fourth, followed by West Germany, Canada, Argentina, and the United States. In earlier events Australia defeated The Netherlands 2–1 at Perth, Australia; South Korea took third place and Britain was fourth. Great Britain won at Essen, West Germany, in June, finishing ahead of Australia, West Germany, and Canada. In August The Netherlands prevailed in Amsterdam, where Britain was second, the Soviet Union third, and Spain fourth. England won the Home Countries championship from Ireland, Scotland, and Wales. Indoors the order was England, Scotland, Ireland, and Wales.

(SYDNEY E. FRISKIN)

FOOTBALL

Association Football (Soccer). The tactical stalemate that had characterized recent European competition was refreshingly relieved by the manner in which The Netherlands won the 1988 European championship, beating the U.S.S.R. 2–0 in West Germany in June. It revived aspects of the Dutch concept of "total" football from the 1970s, embracing all-out attack and reinforced defense. The final games to select the eight qualifiers were played on a league basis. The first two teams in each of the two groups of four—the U.S.S.R. and The Netherlands in one section, Italy and West Germany in the other—then proceeded to a single-game elimination semifinal round.

By far the most gifted, resourceful, and enterprising team, The Netherlands also had an element of luck in each of its matches. Its shrewd coach, Rinus Michels, who had been the architect of Ajax Amsterdam's 1971 European Champions' Cup victory, fashioned a side of superior technique, balancing patient possession football with swift penetrating attacks.

Success was achieved despite the loss of 1–0 to the U.S.S.R. in the opening group match. In addition, before emerging as 3–1 winners over England, The Netherlands was twice saved from conceding goals when England struck their shots against the goalposts. A fortunate header from Wim Kieft, one of two substitute strikers, won the game for the Dutch against Ireland. This was the prelude to a 2–1 semifinal win over hosts West Germany in Hamburg on June 21, though for just a few minutes the Dutch team lost its composure and conceded a penalty, only to be awarded one itself after a controversial decision, to tie the score at 1–1. It snatched victory in the last minute with the winning goal scored by Marco van Basten, the outstanding player of the tournament.

Van Basten had scored all three goals against England but reserved his best strike for the final at the Olympic Stadium in Munich on June 25 against the U.S.S.R., which had beaten Italy 2–0 in Stuttgart on June 22 in torrential rain. After heading the ball across the goal area for Ruud Gullit to head the opening goal after 33 minutes, Van Basten responded to Arnold Muhren's long, speculative cross from the left wing, spectacularly volleying a goal at an angle some eight yards from the goal line on the far side of the penalty area in the 54th minute. The U.S.S.R. later had a penalty kick, but Hans van Breukelen saved Igor Belanov's shot.

During the tournament violent clashes between hooligan elements among visiting supporters of England and local troublemakers in West German city centres forced the Football Association to withdraw England's application for reinstatement in European club football. Heavy policing and undercover operations were still needed to control unruly factions, and most European countries experienced trouble. Dutch fans rioted in Amsterdam after Ajax was beaten in the Cup Winners' Cup, and in Rotterdam a smoke bomb knocked the Cypriot goalkeeper unconscious. In Portugal some supporters of a team relegated from first to third division for bribery tore up railroad tracks and blocked roads. In Italy firecrackers thrown from the stands struck a player, who needed heart massage to be revived.

Membership in the world governing body of association football increased to 166 nations with the readmission of Chad and the admission of Aruba, the Faeroe Islands, St. Lucia, St. Vincent and the Grenadines, San Marino, the Solomon Islands, and Vanuatu.

European Champions' Cup. In Stuttgart on May 25, PSV Eindhoven of The Netherlands defeated Portugal's Benfica in a penalty shoot-out after both teams had failed to score in 90 minutes of regular play and 30 minutes of overtime. In the first half the first shot at goal did not occur until the 34th minute. Then the Dutch team began to reveal some of the free-scoring form that had produced 117 league goals, but it was unable to force a goal on this occasion. The drama unfolded in the shoot-out, which revealed surprisingly accurate marksmanship. Both sides scored five times, and PSV was leading 6–5 when Antonio Veloso made Benfica's sixth attempt only to see his effort blocked at full length by van Breukelen.

European Cup-Winners' Cup. There was less Dutch joy in Strasbourg, France, on May 11 when the defending champions, Ajax Amsterdam, lost 1–0 to KV Mechelen of Belgium. This victory gave the Belgian team its first European trophy. Ajax was handicapped after the 16th minute when it was reduced to ten men by the dismissal of Danny Blind for a foul on Marc Emmers in a match of much ill temper. The Dutch team held out until the 53rd minute when Israeli Eli Ohana managed to centre accurately for the inrushing Dutchman Piet den Boer to powerfully head the only goal at the near post.

UEFA Cup. West Germany's Bayer Leverkusen eventually won its first honour in 84 years despite trailing 3–0 to Español of Spain in the away leg. It won the victory in the penalty shoot-out after tying the score in the home leg. In the Sarria stadium at Barcelona, Spain, on May 4, the

Table I. Association Football National Champions

Nation	League winners	Cup winners
Albania	17 Nentori	Flamurtari
Argentina	Newell's Old Boys	
Austria	Rapid Vienna	Kremser
Belgium	FC Brugge	Anderlecht
Bolivia	Bolívar	
Brazil	Sport Recife	
Bulgaria	Vitosha	Sredets
Chile	Universidad Católica	
Colombia	Millonarios	
Costa Rica	Liga Deportiva Alajuelense	
Cyprus	Pezoporikos	Omonia
Czechoslovakia	Sparta Prague	Sparta Prague
Denmark	Brondby	Arhus
Ecuador	Barcelona	
El Salvador	Aguilar	
England	Liverpool	Wimbledon
Finland	HJK Helsinki	Kuusysi
France	Monaco	Metz
Germany, East	Dynamo Berlin	Dynamo Berlin
Germany, West	Werder Bremen	Eintracht Frankfurt
Greece	Larissa	Panathinaikos
Guatemala	Aurora	
Honduras	Olimpia	
Hungary	Honved	Bekescsaba
Iceland	Valur	Fram
Ireland	Dundalk	Dundalk
Italy	AC Milan	Sampdoria
Luxembourg	Jeuness d'Esch	Jeuness d'Esch
Malta	Hamrun Spartans	Hamrun Spartans
Mexico	América	
Netherlands, The	PSV Eindhoven	PSV Eindhoven
Northern Ireland	Glentoran	Glentoran
Norway	Moss	Bryne
Paraguay	Cerro Porteño	
Peru	Universitario de Deportes	
Poland	Gornik Zabrze	Lech Poznan
Portugal	FC Porto	FC Porto
Romania	Steaua Bucharest	Steaua Bucharest
Scotland	Celtic	Celtic
Spain	Real Madrid	Barcelona
Sweden	IFK Göteborg	Norrköping
Switzerland	Neuchatel	Grasshoppers
Turkey	Galatasaray	Sakaryaspor
U.S.S.R.	Spartak Moscow	Metallist
U.S.	San Diego	
Uruguay	Defensor	
Venezuela	Maritimo	
Wales	—	Cardiff City
Yugoslavia	Red Star Belgrade	Borac Banjaluka

West Germans failed to press home territorial advantage and suffered for it when Español took the lead a minute before halftime. Miguel Soler crossed for Sebastian Losada to head in.

Soler added a second goal three minutes after the match resumed, and Losada again scored after 57 minutes with a header from Ernesto Valverde's cross. Leverkusen did not allow the initiative to be taken away from it in the return match on May 18 and opened the scoring with a goal by Tita of Brazil after 56 minutes following a mix-up in the Español defense. East German exile Faklo Götz added a second score seven minutes later with a spectacular diving header, and nine minutes before the end of the game, Bum Kun Cha of South Korea tied the aggregate scores at 3–3. Overtime failed to break the deadlock, and in the penalty shoot-out West German goalkeeper Rüdjer Vollborn's gamesmanship tactics of arm waving proved a distraction to the Spanish penalty takers and, cruelly, it was Losada's miss that gave the cup to Leverkusen 3–2 on penalties.

World Club Championship. Nacional of Uruguay defeated PSV Eindhoven in a match in Tokyo. The game finished in an overtime 2–2 tie, but the Uruguayans beat their Dutch rivals after a series of penalty kicks for a final score of 9–8.

North America. Although the Major Indoor Soccer League, won by San Diego over Cleveland in the final playoffs, faced financial crisis, two semiprofessional leagues were formed, the American Soccer League for ten teams on the eastern seaboard and a revival of the Western Soccer Alliance for six west coast teams. The U.S. was named as host nation for the 1994 World Cup.   (JACK ROLLIN)

Latin America. For the second year in a row, a team from the city of Rosario, the Newell's Old Boys, won Argentina's national league championship, beating the powerful Buenos Aires squads. Newell's Old Boys, for decades a second-rate team, outdistanced its nearest competitor, San Lorenzo de Almagro, by six points at the end of the championship. In Brazil's national championship there was also a surprise winner, Sport Recife, a team from the country's underdeveloped northeast. In the national championship final it edged Guaraní of São Paulo 1–0. More predictable was the result of the new Copa União, dubbed as the Super League, in which 16 nationally ranked teams competed. Flamengo of Rio de Janeiro beat Internacional of Belo Horizonte in the two-game final. In the country's two most important state tournaments, the Liga Paulista (São Paulo) and the Liga Carioca (Rio de Janeiro), the respective winners were Corinthians and Vasco da Gama over Guaraní and Flamengo.

Bolívar of La Paz won the Bolivian league championship, and Universidad Católica triumphed in Chile. Millonarios of Bogotá finally ended the long reign of América of Cali in the Colombian league. Barcelona was the Ecuadorean champion. There were two league champions in Uruguay in 1988. The 1987–88 pennant was won by Defensor. The 1988 season was played entirely within the calendar year, and the winner was Danubio. A special tournament was held to select the country's representative in the Libertadores de América Cup, South America's team championship. In Venezuela Marítimo won the league title, followed by Táchira. The Paraguayan league was conquered by Cerro Porteño, with Olympia finishing second. Two championships were held again in Peru; Alianza of Lima took the Descentralizado and Universitario de Deportes the Regional. The two teams met to determine a national champion, and Universitario edged Alianza 1–0.

Nacional of Uruguay conquered the Libertadores de América Cup after beating Newell's Old Boys. The coveted cup had been won by another Montevideo team, Peñarol, in 1987.

América of Mexico City again won the Mexican league after a one-year hiatus. In Central America the champions were Aurora in Guatemala, Aguilar in El Salvador, Olimpia in Honduras, and Liga Deportiva Alajuelense in Costa Rica.   (SERGIO SARMIENTO)

Rugby. *Rugby Union.* Having won the inaugural World Cup in June 1987, New Zealand showed its continuing power by destroying Wales twice when the Welsh made an eight-match tour of New Zealand in May and June 1988. The All Blacks won the first match of their two-test series 52–3 in Christchurch and the second 54–9 in Auckland.

The Southern Hemisphere also came out on top when England made an eight-match tour of Australia during the same time. In another two-test series England was defeated 22–16 at Brisbane and 28–8 in Sydney. This tour was followed by a visit to Australia by New Zealand during which three tests were played. The New Zealanders won the first test 32–7 in Sydney and, although the second test, at Brisbane, was tied 19–19, New Zealand ran away with the third by a score of 30–9 in Sydney.

Argentina flourished remarkably in 1987–88. In October and November 1987 they received a visit by Australia and, after drawing the first of their two tests 19–19, went on to beat the Wallabies 27–19 in the second, both tests being played in Buenos Aires. Then, in June 1988, France toured Argentina. The French, finalists in the World Cup the previous year, won the first test 18–15, but the Pumas came back to win the second 18–6, all 24 points coming from penalty goals; both contests took place at Buenos Aires.

In October and November 1987 the U.S. team made a six-match tour of Wales. They achieved a notable victory, 15–6, over the Neath club but were beaten 46–0 in their one international match, at Cardiff.

The Five Nations Championship, in the first three months of 1988, was shared by Wales and France, which, in a fitting climax, met at Cardiff on the last day of the tournament. At that point Wales had beaten England, Scotland, and Ireland, thus gaining the Triple Crown, while France had beaten England and Ireland and lost only to Scotland, by 12–23 at Murrayfield. At Cardiff, France frustrated Welsh hopes of a first Grand Slam in ten years by winning 10–9.

Rugby League. Australia maintained its dominance in rugby league competition when Great Britain toured there in June and July 1988. The British, who began their tour with a pioneering visit to Papua-New Guinea, played a three-test series against the Australians, being beaten 17–6 in the first test, at Sydney, and 34–14 in the second, at Brisbane. There was some consolation for the British, however, when they won the third test 26–12 in Sydney. The British team then went on to New Zealand, and in the only test of that visit they were defeated 12–10 at Christchurch.

The traditional home and away tests between France and Great Britain were played in January and February. For the first test the British traveled to Avignon and beat France 28–14, and in the return match the French were defeated 30–12 at Headingley, Leeds.   (DAVID FROST)

U.S. Football. *College.* Notre Dame won its eighth national championship of college football by defeating West Virginia 34–21 in the Fiesta Bowl at Tempe, Ariz., Jan. 2, 1989. The Fighting Irish finished the 1988 season with the only unblemished won–lost record among major colleges, 12–0, and victories over four other teams that ranked among the top seven in the national polls. It was their first championship since 1977.

Notre Dame finished third in regular-season scoring defense, allowing 12.3 points per game, and first in kickoff returns behind Raghib Ismail's top individual average of 36.1 yd. West Virginia (11–1) had the second best scoring offense, with 42.9 points per game.

Second-ranked Miami of Florida finished 11–1 by beating Big Eight champion Nebraska 23–3 in the Orange Bowl. Miami ranked second in points and yards allowed, third in rushing defense, and fifth in passing offense, in which quarterback Steve Walsh tied for first with 29 touchdown passes.

Florida State (11–1) ranked third after defeating Southeastern Conference champion Auburn 13–7 in the Sugar Bowl. Big Ten champion Michigan ranked fourth and fifth in different polls and finished 9–2–1 by beating seventh-ranked Pacific Ten champion Southern California (10–2) 22–14 in the Rose Bowl. The other top-seven teams in different polls were West Virginia and UCLA (10–2), the latter of which won the Cotton Bowl 17–3 against Southwest Conference champion Arkansas.

Other teams to receive top 12 recognition were Nebraska, Auburn, Atlantic Coast Conference champion Clemson, Oklahoma State, Arkansas, and Syracuse. They all were 10–2 except Nebraska, which was 11–2.

Oklahoma State junior halfback Barry Sanders was honoured as the country's best college player with both the Heisman Trophy and the Maxwell Award. Sanders finished the regular season with 26 Division I-A (major-college) records, many by wide margins. His 2,553 yd rushing for the season broke the old record by 211 yd and beat runner-up Darren Lewis of Texas A&M by 861 yd. His 39 touchdowns broke the record by 10 and beat runner-up Anthony Thompson of Indiana by 15. His 3,250 all-purpose yards broke the record by 617. Sanders had three games with at least 300 yd rushing, a figure no major-college back had exceeded more than once in a career. His 342 rushing attempts and 7.5 yd per attempt also were national highs.

Oklahoma State led the country with 47.5 points per game. Its quarterback, Mike Gundy, led Division I-A passers with 9.4 yd per pass attempt and finished 1.6 points behind Washington State quarterback Timm Rosenbach's top efficiency rating of 162.0. Rosenbach's 65.9 completion percentage also was the best, and UCLA's Troy Aikman had the lowest interception percentage, 2.45.

Utah had the country's top passing and total offense, gaining 395.9 and 526.8 yd per game, respectively. Utah quarterback Scott Mitchell led individual passers with a record of 392.9 passing yards per game, ranked first in total offense with 390.8 yd per game, and tied Walsh in touchdown passes. Nebraska's number one rushing offense gained 382.3 yd per game.

Houston wide receivers Jason Phillips and James Dixon became the first teammates to rank 1–2 in receptions, the first to exceed 100 catches, and the first to exceed 1,000

PHOTOS, AP/WIDE WORLD

Joe Montana of the San Francisco 49ers (far left) and Boomer Esiason of the Cincinnati Bengals (left) were quarterbacks of two of the four teams heading for the NFL play-offs to see which two teams would make it to the Super Bowl. The 49ers, the NFC West Division champs, were to go against the Central Division champs, the Chicago Bears; Cincinnati, winner of AFC Central, was to go against the East Division champs, Buffalo.

Notre Dame quarterback Tony Rice clutches the ball during the Fiesta Bowl game against West Virginia in Tempe, Arizona. Notre Dame's victory brought them their record eighth national championship and left them the only undefeated major college team of the 1988 season.
FOCUS ON SPORTS

yd receiving. Phillips led with 108 catches, 1,444 yd, and 15 touchdown catches. Dixon's 102 catches were the fifth most in Division I-A history. Houston led the country with 38 touchdown passes.

The top defense, Auburn, allowed 7.2 points per game. Auburn also ranked first by allowing only an average of 63.2 rushing yards and 218.1 total yards per game. Baylor gave up a national low of 117.8 passing yards per game. Auburn defensive tackle Tracy Rocker won the Lombardi and Outland awards given to the best lineman. His 354 tackles were a career record at Auburn. The Butkus Award for the top linebacker went to Alabama's Derrick Thomas, who had 27 quarterback sacks.

Other Division I-A regular-season leaders in individual categories were Kendall Trainor of Arkansas with 2.18 field goals per game; Texas-El Paso's Chris Jacke with 25 field goals—a 92.6 percentage on 27 attempts—and 123 points kicking; Colorado's Keith English with a 45-yd punting average; and Florida State's Deion Sanders with a 15.2-yd punt-return average.

In other Division I-A and I-AA conferences, the champions were Fresno State (9–2) of the Big West, Western Michigan (9–2) of the Mid-American, and Wyoming (11–1) of the Western Athletic. In Division I-AA, Towson (Md.) State halfback David Meggett won the Walter Payton Award as player of the year. Bill Russo of Colonial Conference champion Lafayette (8–2–1) won the Eddie Robinson Award as coach of the year.

Furman (13–2) won the Division I-AA championship with a 17–12 victory over Georgia Southern (12–2), which had won the previous two in a row. North Dakota State (14–0) won its fourth Division II title in six years with a 35–21 victory over Portland (Ore.) State (11–3–1). Division III champion Ithaca of New York (13–1) won its title game 39–24 over Central College of Iowa (11–2).

Boston College defeated Army 38–24 at Dublin, in the first major college football game in Europe. Army's third straight victory over Navy, 20–15, tied that traditional series at 41–41 with 7 ties. Columbia's 16–13 victory over Princeton October 8 ended the longest losing streak ever in Division I, 44 games over nearly five years.

Professional. For the first time in the game's 22 years, neither team in a January Super Bowl qualified for the National Football League (NFL) play-offs the following December. The defending champion Washington Redskins had a 1988 won–lost record of only 7–9, and the team they beat in the January 1988 Super Bowl, the Denver Broncos, finished 8–8.

The only two teams to repeat as division champions were Chicago, with its fifth consecutive title in the National Football Conference (NFC) Central Division, and San Francisco, which won the NFC West a third straight time. Those teams also played for the NFC championship Jan. 8, 1989. The American Football Conference (AFC) championship game was between AFC Central winner Cincinnati and AFC East winner Buffalo, two of the four play-off teams that had finished below .500 in 1987.

The other teams that rebounded from losing seasons into the play-offs were the NFC wild-card Los Angeles Rams and NFC East champion Philadelphia, which reached the play-offs for the first time since 1981. Minnesota was the other NFC wild card. Seattle won the AFC West for the first time in its 13 years of existence. The AFC wild cards were Houston and Cleveland, with its fourth consecutive play-off berth.

Cincinnati's improvement from 4–11 to 12–4 was the third-biggest jump in one season since the American Football League (AFL) merged into the NFL in 1970. Offensive player of the year Norman ("Boomer") Esiason helped the Bengals make their first play-offs in six years with a 97.4 passer rating and 9.21 yd per pass attempt, both league highs. Rookie fullback Elbert ("Ickey") Woods led the AFC with 15 rushing touchdowns. The Bengals led the NFL with 44.2% success on third downs, 448 points, and per-game averages of 378.6 yd and 169.4 yd rushing. Their coach, Sam Wyche, was named AFC coach of the year.

Buffalo, in its first play-off season in seven years, set a league attendance record with 622,793 in eight games and led AFC defenses by allowing 237 points and 286.1 yd per game. Scott Norwood's 129 points and 86.5 field-goal percentage (32 for 37) for Buffalo led the league.

For Chicago, Mike Ditka (*see* BIOGRAPHIES) was the NFL's coach of the year and middle linebacker Mike Singletary the defensive player of the year. The Bears' defense led the league in allowing 215 points and 82.9 yd rushing per game.

San Francisco led the NFC offensively with 368.8 yd and 157.7 yd rushing per game. John Taylor had the league's best punt-return average, 12.6 yd, and Roger Craig tied Indianapolis's Eric Dickerson with 2,036 yd from scrim-

mage. Dickerson, with 1,659 yd, led NFL rushers for the fourth time in his six seasons.

Minnesota's defense allowed the NFL's fewest yards, 255.7 per game. Its 36 interceptions, 53 turnovers defensively, and plus-23 turnover difference were NFL highs. Wade Wilson's 91.5 passer rating led the NFC, and his 61.4 completion percentage led the league.

The Rams' 407 points were the most in the NFC, and they had three individual NFL leaders: Jim Everett with 31 touchdown passes, Henry Ellard with 1,414 yd on pass receptions, and Greg Bell with 18 touchdowns and 16 by rushing. Ellard's 86 catches led the NFC. Other individual statistical leaders were Philadelphia's Reggie White with 18 sacks, Atlanta's Scott Case with 10 interceptions, the Los Angeles Raiders' Tim Brown with a 26.8-yd kickoff-return average, the New York Jets' Al Toon with 93 catches and Ken O'Brien with a 1.7 interception percentage, and Miami's Mark Clayton with 14 touchdown catches and Dan Marino with 4,434 yd passing, which tied him for second on the all-time list with five 3,000-yd seasons.

Miami led the league with 282.3 yd passing per game, 23.8 yd ahead of NFC leader Washington. Kansas City allowed the NFL's fewest passing yards per game, 152.1. Indianapolis's 8 fumbles lost were the league's fewest; Green Bay's 26 fumbles lost and Detroit's 21 recovered were the most.

Mervyn Fernandez's 26 yd per catch was the highest average for anyone with at least 30 catches. Pittsburgh's league-leading punter, Harry Newsome, averaged 45.4 yd but had six punts blocked, a league record. Denver's Mike Horan had the highest net punting average, 37.8 yd. Dallas's Herschel Walker led NFC rushers with 1,514 yd. Tampa Bay's Vinnie Testaverde threw 35 interceptions, the second most by anyone in a season.

Indianapolis kicker Dean Biasucci's six field goals of at least 50 yd set an NFL record. Seattle's Steve Largent reached 12,686 yd on receptions for his career, a new NFL record. Tony Dorsett went to Denver after 11 years at Dallas and passed Jim Brown for second on the all-time rushing list with 12,739 yd. Atlanta's John Settle became the first undrafted player in 23 years to run for 1,000 yd in a season, clearing the mark by 24. Philadelphia tight end Keith Jackson and New England running back John

Stephens were rookies of the year in the NFC and AFC, respectively.

Arthur J. Rooney, Sr. (see OBITUARIES), the last of the league's original owners, died at 87 more than 55 years after founding the Pittsburgh Steelers. The oldest continually run professional football team became the Phoenix Cardinals by moving from St. Louis 28 years after moving there from Chicago.

The Arena Indoor Football League finished its second season July 30 when the Detroit Drive defeated the Chicago Bruisers 24–13 in the Arena Bowl before a sellout crowd of 15,018 in Chicago. The Bruisers, behind coach of the year Perry Moss and most valuable player Ben Bennett, led the league during the regular season at 10–1–1, with the second-place Drive at 9–3.

Canadian Football. The Winnipeg Blue Bombers won the Grey Cup championship game in the Canadian Football League 22–21 over the British Columbia Lions Nov. 27, 1988, at Ottawa. Winnipeg wide receiver James Murphy, voted the game's outstanding player, scored his team's only touchdown with five catches for 165 yd. The game's outstanding Canadian, punter Bob Cameron, scored two points on singles, and Trevor Kennard kicked four field goals.

Both finalists won play-off upsets against the regular-season winners of the league's two divisions. Winnipeg (9–9) defeated Toronto (14–4) in the Eastern Division, and British Columbia (10–8) triumphed over Edmonton (11–7) in the Western Division.

British Columbia wide receiver David Williams won the Schenley Award as the league's most outstanding player after leading it with 83 catches, 1,468 yd and 18 touchdowns, and 1,472 yd from scrimmage. His 18 touchdowns tied a league record. Ottawa running back Orville Lee, the most outstanding rookie, ranked first with 1,075 yd rushing. League-leading passers were British Columbia's Matt Dunnigan with 26 touchdowns and Toronto's Gilbert Renfro with 4,113 yd, 527 attempts, and 290 completions.

(KEVIN M. LAMB)

GOLF

Though Europe and the United States shared the honours in golf's major championships in 1988, the Europeans, as in 1987, had the better of the year as a whole. Not only did Sandy Lyle of Scotland become the first British golfer to win the Masters at Augusta (Ga.) National and Severiano Ballesteros of Spain win the British Open championship at Royal Lytham and St. Anne's, Lancashire, but further distinction was provided in other quarters. Ireland won the international team competition for the Dunhill Cup at St. Andrews in Scotland; Great Britain and Ireland's men took the world amateur team championship for the Eisenhower Trophy at Lake Ullna, Sweden; the British and Irish women retained the Curtis Cup at Royal St. George's, Sandwich, Kent; and Liselotte Neumann of Sweden followed Laura Davies of Britain as the new U.S. Women's Open champion at Baltimore (Md.) Country Club.

Against that, U.S. success was limited to Curtis Strange, who won the U.S. Open championship at the Country Club, Brookline, Mass.; Jeff Sluman, who took the PGA (Professional Golfers' Association) championship at the Oak Tree Golf Club in Edmond, Okla.; and the U.S. women's team, which regained the Espirito Santo trophy at Drottningholm, Sweden.

The male golfer of the year was probably Lyle. He became a double "Master" by also winning the Dunhill Masters at Woburn in Bedfordshire, England, took the Suntory world match-play title at Wentworth, Surrey, England, and

Table II. NFL Final Standings and Play-offs, 1988

AMERICAN CONFERENCE	W	L	T	NATIONAL CONFERENCE	W	L	T
Eastern Division				**Eastern Division**			
*Buffalo	12	4	0	*Philadelphia	10	6	0
Indianapolis	9	7	0	New York Giants	10	6	0
New England	9	7	0	Washington	7	9	0
New York Jets	8	7	1	Phoenix	7	9	0
Miami	6	10	0	Dallas	3	13	0
Central Division				**Central Division**			
*Cincinnati	12	4	0	*Chicago	12	4	0
*Cleveland	10	6	0	*Minnesota	11	5	0
*Houston	10	6	0	Tampa Bay	5	11	0
Pittsburgh	5	11	0	Detroit	4	12	0
				Green Bay	4	12	0
Western Division				**Western Division**			
*Seattle	9	7	0	*San Francisco	10	6	0
Denver	8	8	0	*Los Angeles Rams	10	6	0
Los Angeles Raiders	7	9	0	New Orleans	10	6	0
San Diego	6	10	0	Atlanta	5	11	0
Kansas City	4	11	1				

*Qualified for play-offs.

Play-offs

Wild-card round
Houston 24, Cleveland 23
Minnesota 28, Los Angeles Rams 17

American semifinals	National semifinals
Buffalo 17, Houston 10	Chicago 20, Philadelphia 12
Cincinnati 21, Seattle 13	San Francisco 34, Minnesota 9

Sandy Lyle raises his club in victory after becoming the first British golfer to win the Masters at Augusta (Georgia) National Golf Club in April.
DAVE CANNON—ALLSPORT USA

had two other successes in the U.S., triumphing in both the Phoenix (Ariz.) Open and the Greater Greensboro (N.C.) Open.

For some time Lyle was the leading money winner in the U.S. However, this distinction and the U.S. player of the year award went to Strange. By winning the Nabisco Championship, Pebble Beach, Calif., the season's last event, he became the first person to earn more than $1 million on the tour in a single year.

Lyle's victory in the Masters transcended all his other achievements, and he became only the fourth non-U.S. golfer with the privilege of wearing the green jacket. The others were Gary Player (South Africa), Ballesteros (Spain), and Bernhard Langer (West Germany).

The Masters also featured one of its most dramatic conclusions as Lyle, who had led through the second and third rounds, was slowly overtaken by Mark Calcavecchia (U.S.). The birdie two that Lyle made at the 16th hole restored his flagging morale, but it still left him needing another birdie at the 18th to win.

The chances of that seemed slim indeed when Lyle drove into the fairway bunker, but he played a wonderful shot with a seven iron, picking the ball clean off the top of the sand, and then capped it by holing a slippery putt down the slope of the green. Lyle had rounds of 71, 67, 72, 71 for a total of 281, seven under par.

There was the possibility of further British glory in the U.S. Open as Strange, the ultimate winner, was taken into a play-off by Nick Faldo. If he had won the play-off, Faldo would have become the first British holder of the title since Tony Jacklin in 1970. The two had tied at 278, Strange with rounds of 70, 67, 69, 72 and Faldo with 72, 67, 68, 71. In the play-off, however, Strange scored a 71 to 75 for Faldo.

The British Open at Royal Lytham also finished on a Monday, though for a different reason. Inhospitable July weather led to the third round's being washed out and postponed until Sunday, but it did not thwart Ballesteros, who now probably ranked this course among his favourites. It was there that he won his first British Open in 1979, and from the moment he began his opening round with four consecutive birdies, he always was the man to beat. Even so, he needed a supreme effort, because Nick Price of Zimbabwe, joint runner-up to Tom Watson at Royal Troon in 1982, again came close.

Indeed, with 18 holes to play, Price led by two strokes,

and he continued to play brilliantly on the last afternoon with a final round of 69. However, Ballesteros was a man inspired, shooting a 65, which equaled the course record by an Open champion in the last round. Ballesteros's scores were 67, 71, 70, 65 for 273 against the 70, 67, 69, 69 (275) by Price. Faldo finished third with 279.

Faldo was also very much involved in the PGA at Oak Tree, again playing admirably between tee and green and at one point making par at 24 consecutive holes. However, Sluman, at 1.7 m (5 ft 7 in) one of the smallest men on the U.S. circuit, shot a 65 on his last round, the turning point of which came at the par-five fifth, where he sank a full sand wedge from 105 m (115 yd) for an eagle three. Sluman's rounds of 69, 70, 68, 65 for a total of 272 gave him a three-stroke advantage over Paul Azinger (U.S.), who scored 67, 66, 71, 71.

Faldo tied for fourth, and that, along with his earlier 30th place in the Masters, second in the U.S. Open, and third in the British Open, left him with the best record in the major championships. His playing was generally consistent, and altogether he was runner-up eight times, seven of them in Europe. He did win twice, in the French Open at Chantilly and then in the European tour's concluding tournament of the season, the Volvo Masters at Valderrama, Spain.

For all that, the dominant player in Europe was Ballesteros. He emerged from one of his leaner spells with seven victories to equal his record of 1978. His prize money of £451,559 set a record for the European tour.

No one won as many tournaments on the U.S. circuit. Strange won four titles, Lyle three, and Chip Beck and Ken Green two each. Indeed, the days of dominant golfers, particularly in the U.S., appeared to be over. There were no fewer than 12 first-time winners and, though Ballesteros, Lyle, Faldo, and Ian Woosnam of Wales continued to rule the roost in Europe, there was still room for eight players to record their first victories.

Though there was still not a recognized fifth major championship, the two that came closest to it were the U.S. Tournament Players' Championship at the Players' Club at Sawgrass, Fla., and the Suntory world match-play championship at Wentworth, England. Mark McCumber, very much the local man and indeed living so close to the course that he could go home for lunch, won the former comfortably, by four strokes from Mike Reid, with rounds of 65, 72, 67, 69 (273).

However, McCumber did not last long in his first appearance in the world match-play tournament, and for the second year in succession there was an all-British final, Lyle defeating Faldo by two and one over 36 holes. As in the British Open, bad weather led to a Monday finish, but Lyle was a popular winner, not least because he had previously been beaten in the final on four occasions, once by Ballesteros, twice by Greg Norman, and in 1987 by Woosnam.

Yet the event that captured the imagination of the British public was Ireland's success in the Dunhill Cup at St. Andrews. This was a three-man match-play team competition, and in succession the Irish trio of Eamonn Darcy, Des Smyth, and Ronan Rafferty defeated Canada, the U.S., England, and Australia, all by scores of 2–1.

The Great Britain and Ireland's men's amateur team gained its third success in the Eisenhower Trophy, principally because of the playing of Peter McEvoy. On a tricky course and in persistent wind, McEvoy had rounds of 72, 71, 70, 71 for 284, which was by six strokes the best individual performance. The U.S. finished second and Australia was third.

Eric Meeks defeated Danny Yates by seven and six in the all-U.S. final of the U.S. Amateur Championship at Hot Springs, Va. For the first time, the British Amateur Championship, played at Royal Porthcawl, Wales, was won by a Swede, Christian Hardin, who defeated Ben Fouchee of South Africa by one hole.

After the victory of Liselotte Neumann in the U.S. Women's Open Championship at the Baltimore Country Club, Katherine Graham, chairman of the U.S. Golf Association's women's committee, remarked: "We're going to have to buy pontoons to transport the trophy back and forth across the Atlantic Ocean." This alluded to the victory of Laura Davies of Britain the year before. Neumann had the further distinction of becoming champion in her first full year on the U.S. Ladies Professional Golf Association (LPGA) tour. She was also, at 22, the second youngest winner, by a matter of weeks, to Catherine Lacoste, a French amateur player who won in 1967.

Having begun with a 67, Neumann followed with rounds of 72, 69, 69 for a total of 277 and had three strokes to spare from Patty Sheehan of the U.S. If this was something of a blow to U.S. morale, it was partially restored by Sherri Turner when she became the leading money winner on the tour.

The Woolmark British Women's Open at Lindrick, Yorkshire, was won by Corinne Dibnah of Australia after a play-off with Sally Little (U.S.), both having scored 295 on their four rounds. The outstanding performance on the Women's Professional Golfers' European tour, however, was that of Marie-Laure de Lorenzi de Taya of France. She won no fewer than a record seven tournaments in only her second year on the circuit, and her official winnings were only a few hundred pounds short of £100,000.

Great Britain and Ireland retained the women's Curtis Cup in great style, always having the edge over the U.S. women at Royal St. George's and finally triumphing 11–7. A week later Joanne Furby, who was not on the successful team, won the British Women's Amateur Championship at Royal Cinque Ports, Deal, Kent, beating Julie Wade by four and three. The U.S. Amateur was taken by Pearl Sinn, the winner by six and five against Karen Noble at Minikahda Golf Club in Minneapolis, Minn. Sinn was also on the U.S. team that took the Espirito Santo at Drottningholm, Ann Sander and Carol Thompson assisting in a team total of 587, one stroke better than that of Sweden.

(MICHAEL WILLIAMS)

GYMNASTICS

In the 1988 Olympic Games gymnasts from the Soviet Union dominated men's competition and shared honours with Romania in the women's events. The Soviet men won eight gold medals, three silvers, and one bronze out of a total of 26 medals, and the Soviet women took four gold medals, two silvers, and three bronzes out of a total of 22. The Romanian women won three gold medals, three silvers, and two bronzes.

In men's competition a triple tie on the pommel horse involved Dmitry Bilozerchev of the U.S.S.R., Zsolt Borkai of Hungary, and Lyubomir Gueraskov of Bulgaria. It was the first triple tie in the Olympics since 1948. The all-around men's champion, Vladimir Artyomov of the U.S.S.R., was also a member of the Soviet championship team, won the gold medal on the parallel bars, tied for the gold on the horizontal bar, and placed second in the floor exercise. Bilozerchev was a member of the winning team, tied for first on the pommel horse and the rings, and gained a third in the all-around. The other gold medalists were Holger Behrendt of East Germany, who tied for first on the rings, Lou Yun of China in the vault, Valery Lyukin, who tied for first on the horizontal bar, and Sergey Kharkov of the U.S.S.R. in the floor exercise.

Competition among the women was a dual meet be-

AFP PHOTO

Romanian gymnast Daniela Silivas is strong and steady on the balance beam in the Olympic finals. Silivas scored seven perfect tens and won gold medals in three of the four individual gymnastic events.

tween the Soviet Union and Romania. The Soviets won the team competition 395.475 to 394.125. East Germany and the U.S. trailed in that order. Yelena Shushunova of the U.S.S.R. won the all-around competition by defeating Romania's Daniela Silivas. However, Silivas had to be ranked as the best women's gymnast in the world. This 18-year-old scored seven perfect tens to equal the mark set by her Romanian compatriot Nadia Comaneci in 1976. She earned gold medals in three of the four individual events—balance beam, floor exercise, and the uneven bars. She placed second in both the all-around and the team competition and finished third in the vault. The only U.S. medalist was Phoebe Mills, who tied for the bronze on the balance beam. The other gold medalist was Svetlana Boginskaya of the U.S.S.R. in the vault.

In women's rhythmic gymnastics the Eastern European countries dominated. The Soviets took first and third with Marina Lobach and Alexandra Timoshenko. The silver medalist was Adriana Dunavska of Bulgaria.

The scores during the men's and women's competitions were the highest of any Olympic Games or world championships. They were directly attributable to the "risk, originality and virtuosity" displayed by these top world-class gymnasts. (CHARLES ROBERT PAUL, JR.)

HORSE RACING

Thoroughbred Racing and Steeplechasing. *United States and Canada.* Alysheba and Personal Ensign, acclaimed the champion older male and the champion older female, respectively, in 1988, completed their racing careers in dramatic fashion on Breeders' Cup day at Churchill Downs in Louisville, Ky. Alysheba, which powered to victory in the Breeders' Cup Classic as a curtain of darkness descended on the cool November afternoon, set world records for single-season earnings and career earnings to gain his second straight Eclipse Award. Personal Ensign, which defeated 1988 Kentucky Derby winner Winning Colors by a nose in the final strides in the Breeders' Cup Distaff, completed her career undefeated in 13 starts to become the first major horse in 80 years to retire with an unblemished record.

Alysheba and Personal Ensign, both of which built strong cases for horse of the year honours, were the unanimous choices for their Eclipse Awards along with the eight other divisional winners. For the fifth successive year, five winners of Breeders' Cup races were voted Eclipse Awards. In addition to Alysheba and Personal Ensign, they were Open Mind, two-year-old filly; Miesque, female turf horse; and Gulch, sprinter. Both Alysheba and Miesque repeated as award winners. The other Eclipse Awards went to Easy Goer, two-year-old colt; Risen Star, three-year-old colt; Winning Colors, three-year-old filly; Sunshine Forever, male turf horse; and Jimmy Lorenzo, steeplechaser.

Personal Ensign and Easy Goer were bred and owned by 80-year-old Ogden Phipps, a former chairman of the Jockey Club. Phipps was honoured with Eclipse Awards as outstanding breeder and outstanding owner. His horses won 35 of 87 starts for record earnings of $5,858,168.

All of the Phipps horses were trained by Claude ("Shug") McGaughey III, who was voted champion trainer for the first time. Horses trained by McGaughey won 15 Grade I stakes races and more than $7.1 million in purses in 1988. In addition to Personal Ensign and Easy Goer, his major winners included Seeking the Gold and Personal Flag.

José Santos, who led all riders in earnings for the third straight year, was honoured with his first Eclipse Award for outstanding jockey. He rode day and night the last several months of the season, and his mounts earned $14,877,298

Major Thoroughbred Race Winners, 1988

Race	Won by	Jockey
United States		
Acorn	Aptostar	R. Davis
Arkansas Derby	Proper Reality	J. Bailey
Arlington Million	Mill Native	C. Asmussen
Belmont	Risen Star	E. Delahoussaye
Blue Grass	Granacus	J. Vásquez
Breeders' Cup Juvenile	Is It True	L. Pincay, Jr.
Breeders' Cup Juvenile Fillies	Open Mind	A. Cordero, Jr.
Breeders' Cup Sprint	Gulch	A. Cordero, Jr.
Breeders' Cup Mile	Miesque	F. Head
Breeders' Cup Distaff	Personal Ensign	R. Romero
Breeders' Cup Turf	Great Communicator	R. Sibille
Breeders' Cup Classic	Alysheba	C. McCarron
Brooklyn	Waquoit	J. Santos
Champagne	Easy Goer	P. Day
Charles H. Strub Stakes	Alysheba	C. McCarron
Coaching Club American Oaks	Goodbye Halo	J. Velásquez
Flamingo	Cherokee Colony	J. Velásquez
Florida Derby	Brian's Time	R. Romero
Futurity	Trapp Mountain	A. Cordero, Jr.
Gulfstream Park Handicap	Jade Hunter	J. Bailey
Haskell Invitational	Forty Niner	L. Pincay, Jr.
Hialeah Turf Cup	Double Bed	G. Mosse
Hollywood Derby	Silver Circus	G. Stevens
Hollywood Futurity	King Glorious	C. McCarron
Hollywood Gold Cup	Cutlass Reality	G. Stevens
Hollywood Invitational	Political Ambition	E. Delahoussaye
Hollywood Turf Cup	Great Communicator	R. Sibille
Jockey Club Gold Cup	Waquoit	J. Santos
Kentucky Derby	Winning Colors	G. Stevens
Kentucky Oaks	Goodbye Halo	P. Day
Man o' War	Sunshine Forever	A. Cordero, Jr.
Meadowlands Cup	Alysheba	C. McCarron
Metropolitan	Gulch	J. Santos
Preakness	Risen Star	E. Delahoussaye
Santa Anita Derby	Winning Colors	G. Stevens
Santa Anita Handicap	Alysheba	C. McCarron
Suburban	Personal Flag	P. Day
Super Derby Invitational	Seeking the Gold	P. Day
Travers	Forty Niner	C. McCarron
Turf Classic	Sunshine Forever	A. Cordero, Jr.
United Nations	Equalize	R. Romero
Washington (D.C) International	Sunshine Forever	A. Cordero, Jr.
Whitney	Personal Ensign	R. Romero
Wood Memorial Invitational	Private Terms	C. Antley
Woodward	Alysheba	C. McCarron
Young America	Irish Actor	E. Maple
England		
One Thousand Guineas	Ravinella	G. Moore
Two Thousand Guineas	Doyoun	W. Swinburn
Derby	Kahyasi	R. Cochrane
Oaks	Diminuendo	S. Cauthen
St. Leger	Minster Son	W. Carson
Coronation Cup	Triptych	S. Cauthen
Ascot Gold Cup	Sadeem	G. Starkey
Eclipse Stakes	Mtoto	M. Roberts
King George VI and Queen Elizabeth Diamond Stakes	Mtoto	M. Roberts
Sussex Stakes	Warning	P. Eddery
International Stakes	Shady Heights	W. Carson
Dubai Champion Stakes	Indian Skimmer	M. Roberts
France		
Poule d'Essai des Poulains	Blushing John	F. Head
Poule d'Essai des Pouliches	Ravinella	G. Moore
Prix du Jockey-Club	Hours After	P. Eddery
Prix de Diane	Resless Kara	G. Mosse
Prix Royal-Oak	Star Lift	C. Asmussen
Prix Ganay	Saint Andrews	A. Badel
Prix Lupin	Exactly Sharp	E. Legrix
Grand Prix de Paris	Fijar Tango	A. Cruz
Grand Prix de Saint-Cloud	Village Star	C. Asmussen
Prix Vermeille	Indian Rose	A. Cruz
Prix de l'Arc de Triomphe	Tony Bin	J. Reid
Grand Critérium	Kendor	M. Philipperon
Ireland		
Irish Two Thousand Guineas	Prince of Birds	D. Gillespie
Irish One Thousand Guineas	Trusted Partner	M. Kinane
Irish Derby	Kahyasi	R. Cochrane
Irish Oaks*	Diminuendo	S. Cauthen
	Melodist	W. Swinburn
Irish St. Leger	Dark Lomond	D. Gillespie
Phoenix Champion Stakes	Indian Skimmer	M. Roberts
*Dead heat		
Italy		
Derby Italiano	Tisserand	V. Mezzatesta
Gran Premio del Jockey-Club	Roakarad	J. Heloury
West Germany		
Deutsches Derby	Luigi	W. Swinburn
Grosser Preis von Baden	Carroll House	B. Raymond
Grosser Preis der Berliner Bank	Helikon	L. Mader
Puma Europa Preis	Kondor	P. Remmert

to top the previous record of $13,415,049, set by Laffit Pincay, Jr., in 1985. Steve Capanas was voted the Eclipse Award for outstanding apprentice jockey. The 21-year-old was the nation's leading apprentice in both races won (300) and earnings ($2,423,808). Kent Desormeaux, the Eclipse Award-winning apprentice of 1987, led the nation's jockeys in races won for the second straight year with 474 victories, while D. Wayne Lukas was the leading trainer with 318 wins.

Lukas, who was dethroned as the Eclipse Award trainer after winning the title for three straight years, had another outstanding season. He set his sixth consecutive record for earnings by a trainer with $17,842,358, topping his 1987 mark of $17,502,206.

Alysheba, which won the Kentucky Derby and the Eclipse Award as a three-year-old in 1987, developed into one of the finest handicap horses of the last quarter century in 1988. He earned a record $3,808,600 to surpass Spend a Buck (1985) as the single-season leader. It gave him a career total of $6,679,242, a world record that topped the previous mark set by John Henry.

Trained by Jack Van Berg, Alysheba scored six wins and a second in eight starts, including six Grade I victories, to close out his career. He competed at seven tracks in five states during an 11-month coast-to-coast campaign.

Personal Ensign won all seven of her 1988 starts to retire with a perfect 13-for-13 record, the first prominent horse to go undefeated since Colin went 15-for-15 in 1907 and 1908. Personal Ensign won six Grade I stakes in 1988, including a decision over colts in the Whitney. She earned $1,679,880.

Risen Star won the Preakness and Belmont after finishing third in the Kentucky Derby. The son of 1973 Triple Crown champion Secretariat won the Belmont by 14¾ lengths, the largest winning margin in the race since his sire's stunning 31-length victory. The colt was retired shortly after his Belmont victory with 8 wins in 11 career starts and earnings of $2,029,845. Winning Colors, which earned $1,379,146 in 1987 and 1988, led all the way in the Kentucky Derby to join Regret (1915) and Genuine Risk (1980) as the only fillies to win the 1¼-mi classic.

Miesque was voted the Eclipse Award as champion female turf horse for the second straight year. Although she was raced primarily in France, the Kentucky-bred horse won consecutive runnings of the Breeders' Cup Mile, her only two U.S. appearances in two years. Jimmy Lorenzo, bred in Great Britain, scored victories in the Breeders' Cup Steeplechase and the Colonial Cup to clinch his Eclipse Award as champion steeplechaser.

Kinghaven Farms homebreds Play the King and Carotene were voted Sovereign Awards in five of the nine divisions honouring the champions of Canadian racing. Play the King was named Canada's horse of the year, the fifth Sovereign Award the five-year-old gelding had won. He was also voted champion sprinter and champion older male for the second straight year. Carotene was honoured as champion turf horse for the third consecutive year and champion older female for the second straight year.

Other Sovereign Award winners were Mercedes Won, two-year-old colt; Legarto, two-year-old filly; Tilt My Halo, three-year-old filly; Regal Intention, three-year-old colt; Sam-Son Farms, owner and breeder; Jim Day, trainer; Sandy Hawley, jockey; and Jim McAleney, apprentice jockey.

Regal Intention, which won 7 of 12 starts and $608,039 in 1988, triumphed in the Queen's Plate, Canada's premier event for three-year-olds, but lost by a nose to Regal Classic in the Prince of Wales Stakes.   (JOHN G. BROKOPP)

Europe and Australia. Three-year-olds, usually central to the success of horse racing, had an undistinguished year in Europe in 1988. Only Warning, which won both the Sussex and Queen Elizabeth II stakes, was able to beat older rivals in a British Grade I race. In France the British-trained Salse, which had finished five lengths behind Warning in the Queen Elizabeth II, became the only three-year-old ever to win the Prix de la Foret. Sickness prevented both Warning and the St. James's Palace Stakes winner, Persian Heights, from contesting the 2,000 Guineas, in which Doyoun won a substandard contest. Warning returned in top form in midsummer but found Miesque too speedy for him in the Prix Jacques le Marois at Deauville in August.

Miesque was Europe's champion miler in 1987, but her four-year-old season was designed to bring her, at her peak, to the U.S. for her second triumph in the Breeders' Cup Mile. She ran only three times before that race. Britain's best sprinter, Handsome Sailor, added the Prix de l'Abbaye de Longchamp to his successes at home when the three-year-old Cadeaux Genereux, also British-trained, was disqualified for causing interference at the start.

Disqualifications were an important factor during the year, and Handsome Sailor was not the only lucky winner. Shady Heights was given the International Stakes at York when Persian Heights was disqualified for hampering Indian Skimmer, which finished third. Helikon was awarded the Grosser Preis der Berliner Bank on the disqualification of the British-trained Carroll House in similar circumstances. Most controversial of all was the disqualification of the French-trained Royal Gait after he had won the Ascot Gold Cup by five lengths from Sadeem and cut more than three seconds off the course record. Royal Gait was judged to have caused the fall of jockey Tony Clark, riding the exhausted El Conquistador, whose strong pace was the principal reason for the fast time.

Tony Bin, the best horse trained in Italy in more than a decade, found Mtoto and Unfuwain too good for him in the King George VI and Queen Elizabeth Diamond Stakes in July. He gained his revenge at Longchamp on October 2, though, when he beat Mtoto by a neck in the CIGA Prix de l'Arc de Triomphe. However, Tony Bin suffered a surprising one-length defeat by Roakarad in front of his home crowd in the Gran Premio del Jockey Club two weeks later.

Unfuwain, which finished fourth in the Arc, just ahead of the Epsom and Irish Derby winner, Kahyasi, was among the most consistent three-year-olds in Europe. His jockey, Willie Carson, however, chose to ride Unfuwain's stable companion, the St. Leger winner, Minster Son, in the Epsom Derby, in which both ran below form. Diminuendo was an easy winner of the Epsom and Yorkshire Oaks and tied with the Oaks d'Italia winner, Melodist, in the Irish Oaks, but she was beaten by one length by Minster Son in the St. Leger and finished tenth in the Arc.

The three-year-olds in France were even more disappointing than those in Britain. The two older champions, Miesque and Soviet Star, were retired. Soviet Star dealt Miesque her only defeat of the year, in the Prix du Moulin de Longchamp, run on soft ground in September. He won two of his four visits to England and was most impressive when switching from one mile to sprinting for the July Cup.

André Fabre, Soviet Star's trainer, set a new French record for trainer's earnings, while his jockey, Cash Asmussen, surpassed the record of 184 winners, set by Yves Saint-Martin in 1964, by riding 200. Pat Eddery won his sixth British championship and was already in the lead when his principal rival, Steve Cauthen, was injured in

Winning Colors and Forty Niner run neck and neck toward the finish at the Kentucky Derby. After managing a four-length lead coming into the homestretch, Winning Colors held off a late challenge by Forty Niner to win the roses.

MIKE POWELL—ALLSPORT USA

a fall at Goodwood on August 26. Cauthen missed the remainder of the year but was expected to return in 1989.

For the first time in many years, a French-trained horse won an important jumping event in Britain when Nupsala took the King George VI Chase. Celtic Shot won the Champion Hurdle and Charter Party the Cheltenham Gold Cup, in which Nupsala was fourth. Rhyme 'n Reason, which fell in the Cup, went on to gain a last-gasp success in the Grand National 23 days later.

Empire Rose, second in 1987, won the Melbourne Cup, defeating Natski by a short head. Beau Zam, the best three-year-old of the 1987–88 season, easily won the first running of the H. E. Tancred Stakes as an international event in March. Seven days later the New Zealand-bred colt was an equally comfortable winner of the A. J. C. Derby.

(ROBERT W. CARTER)

Harness Racing. At Lexington, Ky., in September, three-year-old pacer Matt's Scooter time-trialed a mile in 1 min 48.4 sec, smashing the world record of 1 min 49.2 sec set under similar conditions in 1980 by the three-year-old Niatross. In July Matt's Scooter had won the $1,039,000 Meadowlands (N.J.) Pace, and two weeks after his epic time trial, he won the $461,404 Messenger Stakes at Yonkers (N.Y.) Raceway in 1 min 56.6 sec. Four-year-old Call For Rain at Lexington won in 1 min 49.6 sec, matching the fastest race win in the history of the sport, first set by Nihilator in 1985.

Four-year-old U.S. trotter Mack Lobell set a European record of 1 min 54.7 sec and became the sixth U.S. Standardbred and first U.S. trotter to surpass $2 million in earnings, taking the $336,400 Elitlopp in Sweden in May. At home Mack Lobell in June set a world record for 1 1/8 mi of 2 min 9.8 sec at the Meadowlands and then in August won the $200,000 International Trot at Yonkers. In an epic race billed as the "clash of the century," U.S.-bred Norwegian-owned Sugarcane Hanover shaded French champion Ourasi and Mack Lobell to win the $600,000 March of Dimes International Trot at Garden State Park in New Jersey in November.

The coveted $1.1 million Hambletonian for trotters was won at the Meadowlands in heats of 1 min 54.6 sec and 1 min 55.2 sec by Armbro Goal. Kassa Branca became the fastest race-winning two-year-old of all time by winning the $1,041,000 final of the Woodrow Wilson Pace at the Meadowlands in July in 1 min 52.6 sec. The $863,250 Sweetheart at the Meadowlands went to Concertina; the

$581,540 Cane Pace at Yonkers was won by Runnymede Lobell.

Breeders' Crown winners included Call For Rain (aged pacers), Anniecrombie (aged pacing mares, in a world mark of 1 min 52.6 sec), Kentucky Spur (juvenile pacing colts in a world-record 1 min 53.4 sec), and Central Park West (juvenile fillies in a world-record 1 min 53.6 sec).

In New Zealand Luxury Liner, winner of the $400,000 Auckland Cup the previous December, triumphed in the $375,000 New Zealand Cup at Christchurch in November. The seven-year-old paced the 3,200 m in 4 min 0.4 sec, a 2-min 0.9-sec-per-mi rate and easily a world record for the distance from a standing start, to become the first $1 million earner in his homeland. New Zealand-bred, Australian-trained Our Maestro, runner-up to Luxury Liner in the New Zealand Cup, turned the tables by beating him in the $250,000 Miracle Mile at Sydney's Harold Park less than three weeks later.

In the United Kingdom, Whiz On Ted won the National Pacing Derby at York. The Prakas Championship Trot was won by Chandy's Chance narrowly from 1987 winner Buck Fizz in a new British record for a mile trot, 2 min 6.1 sec. The Prakas Trotting Championship for three-year-olds at York was won by Madonna. The National Pacing Futurity for two-year-olds at York was won by Laurie's Com, and Point Blank won the prestigious Famous Musselburgh Pace on the grass.

In Europe during April, Grades Singing won the final of the $540,000 Gran Premio della Lotteria at the Agnano Racetrack outside Naples, Italy, in a 1-min 57.1-sec-per-mi rate for 1,600 m. U.S.-bred but Danish-owned Meadow Roland won the Copenhagen Cup at Denmark's Charlottenlund. Sugarcane Hanover won the SAS Oslo Grand Prix in a world record 1 min 56.3-sec-per-mi rate for 2,100 m over a 5/8-mi track. French trotting star Ourasi posted an all-time French race record mile of 1 min 57 sec, winning (for the third time) the Grand Criterium de Vitesse at the Cagnes-sur-Mer racecourse near Nice in March.

In Australia the brilliant New Zealand-bred West Australian pacer Village Kid was named 1988 Australian harness racing horse of the year. In December 1987 he had become the first horse to win the Sydney Miracle Mile twice. Victoria's True Roman was named Australian trotter of the year, his wins including the Inter-Dominion Trotting Championship and South Australian Trotters Cup.

(RONALD W. BISMAN)

ICE HOCKEY

North America. In a 1987–88 National Hockey League (NHL) season filled with odd happenings, there was one constant. The Edmonton Oilers won the Stanley Cup play-offs for the fourth time in five years, defeating the Boston Bruins, 4 games to 0, in the finals.

The Oilers and the Bruins were involved in the oddities. Wayne Gretzky, the Oilers' centre, failed to win the Hart Trophy as the NHL's most valuable player for the first time in his nine NHL seasons and the Art Ross Trophy as the scoring champion for the first time in eight seasons. The New Jersey Devils, upset when Coach Jim Schoenfeld was suspended for one play-off game, obtained a temporary reprieve in court, leading to a one-game strike by NHL game officials and their replacement by amateur officials. Finally the potentially last game of the play-offs was suspended when the power failed at the 59-year-old Boston Garden.

Following the season, in August, the Oilers traded Gretzky to the Los Angeles Kings along with Mike Krushelnyski and Marty McSorley in return for $15 million in cash, three first-round draft choices, left-wing Martin Gelinas, and centre Jimmy Carson. The trade created a furor in Canada, where Gretzky was a national hero. Apparently, however, it had been made at Gretzky's request so he could be near his wife, a Hollywood actress.

Regular Season. The NHL's 21 teams played 80 games each from October 1987 to April 1988. The division winners were the Calgary Flames with 105 points, the Montreal Canadiens with 103, the Detroit Red Wings with 93, and the New York Islanders with 88. Edmonton finished second to Calgary in the Smythe Division with 44 victories, 25 defeats, and 11 ties for 99 points.

Sixteen teams qualified for the play-offs. New Jersey won its last five games and reached the play-offs for the first time ever. The Toronto Maple Leafs reached the play-offs with the worst record (21–49–10) ever to qualify.

Play-offs. New Jersey was the surprise team in the play-offs, upsetting the Islanders and the Washington Capitols, each 4 games to 2. On May 6, in the conference finals against Boston, Schoenfeld was angered by the officiating. As referee Don Koharski walked off the ice after a Boston victory, Schoenfeld intercepted him. Koharski said that Schoenfeld shoved him although the coach denied that. On the afternoon of the next game Brian O'Neill, the NHL's executive vice president, suspended Schoenfeld for that game. The Devils went to a New Jersey court and obtained a temporary restraining order to allow Schoenfeld to coach that night. The game officials then refused to work, and the game was delayed an hour until three amateur officials, wearing Devils' warm-up pants, could replace them. Other NHL teams were furious that a league matter had been taken to court. John Ziegler, the NHL president, suspended Schoenfeld for the next game and fined him $1,000 and the Devils $10,000.

Boston, which had eliminated Buffalo in six games and defending champion Montreal in five, defeated New Jersey in seven games. Edmonton breezed to the final by beating Winnipeg in five games, Calgary in four, and Detroit in five.

The finals were easy for Edmonton except for the power blackout on May 24, during the fourth game. Boston had just tied the score at 3–3 late in the second period when a 4,000-volt switch outside the arena became overloaded. Power was restored a half hour later, and both teams wanted to resume the game. However, Ziegler feared a further breakdown, and, citing the NHL bylaws, he suspended the game. He said that it would be replayed at the end of the series only if Boston won the next three games and tied the score at 3–3. The series then moved to Edmonton, and the Oilers immediately ended it May 26 with a 6–3 victory that gave them a four-game sweep and the Stanley Cup.

Honours. Gretzky won the Conn Smythe Trophy as the most valuable player in the play-offs. Mario Lemieux, the Pittsburgh Penguins' centre, became the first player from a nonplay-off team to be named the regular season's most valuable player since Andy Bathgate of the New York Rangers in the 1958–59 season. Lemieux was the regular-season scoring champion with 168 points to 149 for Gretzky, the runner-up. Because of a knee injury on December 30 Gretzky missed 13 games, during which Edmonton struggled to a 5–4–4 record.

The 22-year-old Lemieux was playing his fourth NHL season. He led the league with 70 goals, and he also scored three goals for the Wales Conference in its 6–5 victory over the Campbell Conference in the all-star game February 9 in St. Louis, Mo.

Ray Bourque of Boston won the Norris Trophy as the league's outstanding defenseman, Guy Carbonneau of Montreal the Selke Trophy as the best defensive forward, Grant Fuhr of Edmonton the Vezina Trophy for goaltending, Mats Naslund of Montreal the Lady Byng Trophy for sportsmanship and skillful play, Joe Nieuwendyk of Calgary the Calder Trophy as rookie of the year, and Jacques Demers of Detroit the Jack Adams Trophy as coach of the year. The all-star team comprised Fuhr in goal, Bourque and Scott Stevens of Washington on defense, Lemieux at centre, and Luc Robitaille of the Los Angeles Kings and Hakan Loob of Calgary at wing.   (FRANK LITSKY)

European and International. With no separate world championships in 1988, international ice hockey was dominated by the Winter Olympic Games tournament in Calgary, Alta., February 13–28. When the competition ended, the Soviet Union had gained its seventh gold medal since entering the tournament in 1956, having failed only in 1960 and 1980. Finland was runner-up, and Sweden took the bronze medal.

The spacious Saddledome Arena in Calgary was packed to its 19,600 capacity for all the major matches. The tournament comprised 42 games, including preliminary-round matches between the 12 contenders and play-offs for those ranking below the top six.

The Finns looked stronger each time they played and achieved the first of only two medal-round shutouts by humiliating West Germany 8–0. On that same day the U.S.S.R. took a major step toward retaining its title with a 5–0 win over Canada in a bruising match. The defeat all but put the Canadians out of contention for a medal.

Canada kept alive a slim chance to win the bronze with an emphatic 8–1 success against the West Germans, despite being outshot 17–7 in the first period. Later that day Czechoslovakia gained a surprising 5–2 win over Finland.

The most eagerly awaited game was that between the U.S.S.R. and the world champion, Sweden. This, it seemed, would be the Soviets' biggest test, but they proceeded to demolish the Swedes in an explosive three-goal blitz during the opening two minutes; after that they were content to show off their free-wheeling skating and silky passing skills. The Soviets outshot their opponents 44–11 in a 7–1 victory that clinched the gold medal with three matches still left in the schedule.

In the competition for the silver and bronze medals the Canadians beat the Czechs 6–3, but their revived hopes were dashed when Sweden recovered from a 2–0 deficit to defeat West Germany 3–2. This left an anticlimactic Finland versus U.S.S.R. finale to decide whether the Finns

or the Swedes would win the silver. In the contest the eager Finns defeated a sleepwalking Soviet Union 2–1 to gain second place, denying the silver medal to Scandinavian archrival Sweden, which was forced to settle for the bronze. It was the first Olympic ice hockey medal in Finnish history and also Finland's first victory over the U.S.S.R. in either an Olympic or world championship game.

Jukka Tammi in the Finland net turned aside 31 Soviet shots. Erkki Lehtonen scored the winner with just 100 seconds left, when Soviet goaltender Sergey Mylnikov was caught out of position. Janne Ojanen had scored the first Finnish goal, and Aleksandr Mogilny tallied for the Soviets.

Luckily for the Soviets, Mylnikov's faux pas was the only time during the tournament when goaltending—their self-acknowledged Achilles' heel—meant the difference between victory and defeat. After losing the world championship the previous season and being beaten by Canada in the Izvestia Cup and the Canada Cup, the Soviets were regarded as vulnerable by many, but their performance in Calgary suggested otherwise. In particular, Mylnikov proved less weak than some had anticipated, conceding only 11 goals in seven matches—five of them to the U.S. in one game.

Leading point scorers in the tournament were Vladimir Krutov (15 from 6 goals and 9 assists) and Igor Larionov and Viacheslav Fetisov (both 13, 4, 9). All three were Soviets, but the top goal-getter was Serge Boisvert of Canada with seven.

Swedish defenseman Anders Eldebrink said afterward that although his team held the world title, "the Russians

are the best in the world. They just killed us with those three quick goals in the first period and whenever you get a lead like that, it's impossible to catch up." Soviet coach Viktor Tikhonov, with a rare smile on his face, countered rumours that he was on the way out by saying that he expected to coach at the 1989 world championships in Stockholm and would like to remain national coach for the 1992 Winter Olympics. (HOWARD BASS)

ICE SKATING

Competition in 1988 marked the end of an era in women's figure skating that was dominated by the charismatic East German Katarina Witt (see BIOGRAPHIES) and the beginning of a new men's age of quadruple jumps. Compulsory figures were abolished by an overwhelming majority vote at the International Skating Union's biennial congress in June at Davos, Switz. This would take effect from July 1, 1990. In the meantime the number of figures was reduced from three to two, to allow time for competitors to readjust to the new format. New rinks continued to be built throughout the world and, with the first Olympic speed championships to be held indoors and a wider recognition of short-track racing, the year was among the most revolutionary for ice skating in the 20th century.

Figure Skating. The season was dominated by the Winter Olympic competitions in February at Calgary, Alta., and the world championships at Budapest, Hung., in March. Brian Boitano of the U.S. won the closest possible duel with Brian Orser of Canada to gain the men's Olympic title, the judges splitting 5–4 in the American's favour. Viktor Petrenko from the U.S.S.R. finished third.

Witt, master manipulator of the big occasion, became the first to defend the women's crown successfully since Sonja Henie of Norway in the 1930s. A duel for the other medals produced an unexpected outcome, Elizabeth Manley of Canada defeating Debi Thomas of the U.S. for the silver. There were no surprises in the pairs event, Ekaterina Gordeeva and Sergey Grinkov outpointing their Soviet compatriots, Elena Valova and Oleg Vasiliev, with Jill Watson and Peter Oppegard third for the U.S. In ice dancing Natalia Bestemianova and Andrey Bukin defeated their fellow Soviets, Marina Klimova and Sergey Ponomarenko, with Tracy Wilson and Rob McCall finishing third for Canada.

Only three weeks later Witt sealed an exceptional championship career with her fourth world title in five years. The menace of an apparently powerful challenger fell apart when Thomas again did not perform as well as expected and Manley once more passed her for second place.

Boitano recaptured the men's title with a worthy swan-song performance. Orser, the deposed champion, outpointed his great rival in the free skating, receiving three maximum sixes for presentation, but the Canadian's earlier points deficit meant that he had to settle for the silver medal with Petrenko taking the bronze. Kurt Browning of Canada, although seventh, upstaged Boitano by achieving the first correctly landed quadruple jump in competition, a tremendous toe-loop leap with four midair rotations.

Valova and Vasiliev gained their third pairs title in six years by dethroning the defending champions, Gordeeva and Grinkov. Larisa Selezneva and Oleg Makarov placed third to complete a Soviet clean sweep. Bestemianova and Bukin accomplished their fourth successive ice dance victory. As at Calgary, Klimova and Ponomarenko gained the silver ahead of Wilson and McCall.

Speed Skating. Yvonne van Gennip of The Netherlands was queen of the Winter Olympic speed skaters at Calgary, taking three gold medals over the longest distances—1,500,

Table I. NHL Final Standings, 1988

	Won	Lost	Tied	Points
Prince of Wales Conference				
PATRICK DIVISION				
*New York Islanders	39	31	10	88
*Washington	38	33	9	85
*Philadelphia	38	33	9	85
*New Jersey Devils	38	36	6	82
New York Rangers	36	34	10	82
Pittsburgh	36	35	9	81
ADAMS DIVISION				
*Montreal	45	22	13	103
*Boston	44	30	6	94
*Buffalo	37	32	11	87
*Hartford	35	38	7	77
Quebec	32	43	5	69
Clarence Campbell Conference				
NORRIS DIVISION				
*Detroit	41	28	10	93
*St. Louis	34	38	8	76
*Chicago	30	40	9	69
*Toronto	21	49	10	52
Minnesota	19	48	13	51
SMYTHE DIVISION				
*Calgary	48	23	9	105
*Edmonton	44	25	11	99
*Winnipeg	33	36	11	77
*Los Angeles	30	42	8	68
Vancouver	25	46	9	59

*Clinched play-off berth.

Table II. Olympic Games Ice Hockey Tournament, 1988
Final Medal Round Standings

Country	Won	Lost	Tied	Goals	Goals against	Points
U.S.S.R.	4	1	0	25	7	8
Finland	3	1	1	18	10	7
Sweden	2	1	2	15	16	6
Canada	2	2	1	17	14	5
Czechoslovakia	1	4	0	12	22	2
West Germany	1	4	0	8	26	2

Play-offs involving the six nations eliminated after the preliminary round determined their ranking below the top six as follows: 7. U.S., 8. Switzerland, 9. Austria, 10. Poland, 11. France, 12. Norway. Thus, the U.S. and Switzerland earned the right to join the six medal-round nations in the 1989 world championships Pool A tournament in Stockholm.

East German figure skater Katarina Witt combined her acting and skating skills during her winning performance as Carmen. She dominated the competition at the Winter Olympics and became the first woman to win consecutive Olympic figure-skating titles since Sonja Henie in the 1930s.

NEIL LEIFER/TIME MAGAZINE

3,000, and 5,000 m—each of the latter two in world record time. Bonnie Blair of the U.S. won the 500-m sprint, and the 1,000 m went to Christa Rothenburger of East Germany. Tomas Gustafson from Sweden was the most successful in the men's events, winning both the 5,000 m and the stamina-sapping 10,000 m. Two East Germans, Jens-Uwe Mey and Andre Hoffmann, took the 500 m and 1,500 m, respectively, and the 1,000 m went to Nikolay Gulyaev of the Soviet Union. The new indoor track proved exceptionally fast, with new world records established in seven of the ten events.

Eric Flaim of the U.S. captured the overall title in the men's world championships, in March at Medeo, U.S.S.R., without finishing first in any of the four distances. Leo Visser of The Netherlands was runner-up, and Dave Silk of the U.S. placed third. A week later Karin Kania won her third consecutive crown in the women's world championships, at Skien, Norway, with van Gennip runner-up and Erwina Rys-Ferens of Poland third. In the separate world sprint championships, in February at West Allis, Wis., Dan Jansen outpaced Mey and Flaim to gain the men's title for the U.S. and Rothenburger took the women's crown ahead of Kania and Blair.

Speed skating's second World Cup series ended in men's triumphs for Mey (500 m), Jansen (1,000 m), Hoffmann (1,500 m), and Gustafson (5,000 and 10,000 m). The successful women were Rothenburger (500 and 1,000 m), Blair (1,500 m), and Gabi Zange of East Germany (3,000 and 5,000 m).

At the eighth world short-track championships, in February at St. Louis, Mo., Peter van der Velde of The Netherlands took the men's title, with his compatriot Richard Suyten runner-up and Tatsuyoshi Ishihara of Japan third. Sylvie Daigle captured the women's crown for Canada, ahead of two Japanese, Yumiko Yamada and the deposed champion, Eiko Shishii.   (HOWARD BASS)

LAWN BOWLS

At the sixth world championships, held at Auckland, N.Z., in February, David Bryant of England won the singles title to crown an outstanding career. The 56-year-old Bryant had also won the singles gold medal in 1966 and 1980. (The championships are held every fourth year.)

Twenty-three national associations took part in the competition, and many of the larger countries had comparatively little success. Australia, the world's leading bowling country with half a million players, failed to win a medal, as did teams from the U.S., Canada, Japan, and Argentina. The team championship went to England, which finished just ahead of New Zealand; Scotland, the winner in 1984, placed third.

In New Zealand bowls is played on lawns of closely mown cotula weed, which produces an extremely fast surface, especially under sunny conditions. It took players from other countries some time to adjust to the fast surface at Auckland, and New Zealand dominated the first week's play. Rowan Brassey and Peter Belliss won gold medals in the pairs, and Ian Dickison, Morgan Moffat, and Phil Skoglund triumphed in the triples.

There was a different story in the second week. Bryant won all 11 games in his round-robin section, in which Belliss, the world champion in 1984, could only finish fifth. The other section was won by Scotland's Willie Wood, who had lost the world title in 1984 to Belliss in a close contest. Wood was to suffer bitter disappointment again. He led Bryant by 21–12 in the final, but Bryant rallied to tie the score at 21 all; at 22 all, a downpour flooded the green, deferring play. When play resumed, Wood bowled accurately, but his opponent's freak shot, which cannoned the Scot's bowls off the green, left Bryant with the three shots he needed and victory. Ireland won the fours title with Rod McCutcheon, John McLoughlin, Sammy Allen, and Jim Baker outplaying a New Zealand team in the final.

A few weeks later Hugh Duff of Scotland won the annual world indoor singles title, beating England's Wynne Richards over a nine-set final by five sets to one at London's Alexandra Palace. The world indoor pairs championship was won by Australians Jim Yates and Ian Schuback, neither of whom had been selected to play for their country in the world outdoor events.   (DONALD J. NEWBY)

MOTORBOATING

Serving as direct testimony to the fact that a race is not really over until it is over, the 1988 season of the American Power Boat Association (APBA) came to a close with more than its fair share of down-to-the-wire victories. With only a handful of points separating the top boats in four of the five national Offshore classes prior to the final race of 1988, the eventual winners were anybody's guess. In the Superboat class Al Copeland, Sr., wrapped up his fifth consecutive national championship with four first-place finishes out of the eight races. The 1987 Modified class champion, John D'Elia, emerged from the final race a winner again, but this time it was in the Open class, and he took the 1988 national crown with almost 200 points to spare. Not every championship in the Offshore competition was decided at the last minute, however, as Joe Mach had won the Modified class title even before the final race was run.

For those involved in APBA's Unlimited hydroplane racing, 1988 read somewhat like a repeat performance of the year before with only a few minor exceptions. The *Miss Budweiser* entry once again took the national championship, but this time it was with driver Tom D'Eath, who took over behind the wheel after a rough-water mishap early in the season sidelined regular driver Jim Kropfeld. Turning in one other repeat win for the Unlimiteds, Chip Hanauer raised his APBA Gold Cup mark one more notch in 1988 by claiming the coveted prize for the seventh year in a row.

On the 1988 APBA International Outboard Grand Prix (IOGP) circuit, consistency was the key that opened the door for Don Johnston to win his first North American Champ boat class title; he finished no lower than fifth in

all eight races of the season. Locking up their IOGP victories in advance of the season's last race, Kevin Miller took the world championship in the SST-140 class, and Rusty Campbell successfully defended his Mod VP class title for the second consecutive year.   (RENEE J. MAHN)

POLO

At the international level one of the most exciting matches in 1988 was the overtime contest between Australia and England, held as part of Australia's bicentennial celebrations. Australia (P. White, J. McGinley, R. Walker, and S. Gilmore) scored the sudden-death goal to gain an 11–10 victory over England (W. Lucas, A. Kent, H. Hipwood, and J. Horswell). As part of the same celebrations, Argentina (under the "Buenos Aires" name) soundly trounced Australia 13–7. The Buenos Aires team consisted of G. Tanoira, G. Cassett, J. Lagos, and P. Llorente.

On England's International Day in the Coronation Cup tournament, England (A. Seavill, J. Hipwood, J. Horswell, and Lord C. Beresford) scored a memorable victory by 8–7 over North America (M. Egloff, M. Azzarro, R. Walton, and D. Smicklas). North America led throughout the match, and it was only an inspired hat trick by Hipwood in the last period that gave the victory to England. For the Silver Jubilee Cup the prince of Wales's select team (G. Kent, O. Ellis, C. Forsyth, and the prince of Wales) could not provide a double home victory, losing 4½–4 to France (A. Bernard, B. Tari, L. Macaire, and S. Macaire).

In the annual Ladies International held in England, the Rest of the World team (Lesley-Ann Masterton [Jamaica], Alina Carter [U.S.], Susan Stovall [U.S.], and Roweena Murray [Kenya]) narrowly won 3–2 against Europe (Stefanie Powers [U.K.], Caroline Anier [France], Claire Tomlinson [U.K.], and Lavinia Black [U.K.]). (COLIN J. CROSS)

RODEO

The Professional Rodeo Cowboys Association (PRCA) looked back on a successful year in 1988, capped by the National Finals Rodeo in Las Vegas, Nev., December 3–11. The finals were the last of the 707 PRCA rodeos that had been held during the year, and prize money at this "Super Bowl of Rodeo" alone was in excess of $2 million. Professional rodeo's world champions—determined on the basis of total money won throughout the year, including the finals—were named at the conclusion of the finals.

The prestigious world all-around championship, won by the highest money winner in two or more events, went to a transplanted Australian, Dave Appleton, currently of Arlington, Texas, who won $121,546 in bareback and saddle bronc riding. Lewis Feild of Elk Ridge, Utah, world all-around champion for the previous three years, finished second, just $643 behind Appleton.

Ironically, Appleton was not the biggest winner in pro rodeo. Charmayne James Rodman of Galt, Calif., and her remarkable horse, Scamper, continued their domination of barrel racing that began in 1984, when Charmayne was 14 years old. In 1988 she won her fifth straight world barrel racing title with $130,540. National Finals barrel racing also included the youngest-ever competitor at the rodeo—Rachael Myllymaki of Arlee, Mont., who celebrated her 12th birthday during the competition and finished the year in ninth place with $33,443 in winnings.

PRCA event champions for 1988 included Marvin Garrett, Gillette, Wyo., $100,803 in bareback riding; Clint Johnson, Spearfish, S.D., $82,660 in saddle bronc riding; Jim Sharp, Kermit, Texas, $102,588 in bull riding; Joe Beaver, Victoria, Texas, $91,213 in calf roping; John W. Jones, Jr., Morro Bay, Calif., $82,815 in steer wrestling;

Jake Barnes, Bloomfield, N.M., and Clay O'Brien Cooper, Gilbert, Ariz., $84,578 each in team roping; and Shaun Burchett, Pryor, Okla., $33,197 in single steer roping (at the conclusion of the National Finals Steer Roping competition, held in Guthrie, Okla., in November).

In the Canadian Professional Rodeo Association (CPRA), Mel Coleman of Lloydminster, Sask., won his fourth all-around championship. He had gained his earlier titles in 1978, 1982, and 1984. Members of the Women's Professional Rodeo Association, the CPRA, and the PRCA also fielded their own U.S. and Canadian Olympic teams for a seven-performance competition held in February at Calgary, Alta., in conjunction with the winter Olympic Games. The event presented rodeo to an international audience, paid nearly $100,000 in prize money, and awarded gold, silver, and bronze medals in each event. The U.S. team won the largest number of medals.

In the International Professional Rodeo Association (IPRA), which held its International Finals Rodeo each January in Tulsa, Okla., Dan Dailey of Peaster, Texas, won the all-around title for 1987. This was Dailey's 16th championship in the association; ten were all-arounds, one title was in steer wrestling, and five were in saddle bronc riding. The 1988 champions of the IPRA would be determined at the conclusion of the International Finals, Jan. 12–15, 1989. All-around champions in the National Intercollegiate Rodeo Association were Ken Lensegrav, Montana State University at Bozeman, and Cathy Cagliari, West Hills College, Coalinga, Calif.   (RANDALL E. WITTE)

ROWING

Italy displaced East Germany as the top nation in men's rowing in Olympic and world class events in 1988. The Italians won two Olympic, three world lightweight, and three world junior titles, while East Germany won three Olympic championships and two world junior events. However, East Germany continued to dominate women's rowing with five Olympic and four junior titles. Other nations to earn distinction in men's rowing were West Germany, Great Britain, and the Soviet Union.

There were 182 entries from 39 nations at the Olympic Games in Seoul, South Korea, in September. The eight men's events attracted 123 entries from 38 nations, while 20 nations entered 59 contestants in the six women's events. A dozen nations shared the men's Olympic medals, with East Germany winning coxed and coxless fours by more than 2 sec and its single sculler outclassing his rivals by 4.91 sec. The other men's finals were more closely fought, with Italy defeating East Germany in coxed pairs by 1.84 sec and triumphing over Norway in quadruple sculls by 1.71 sec. In coxless pairs Great Britain finished 1.22 sec ahead of Romania in the closest final of the regatta, and The Netherlands denied Switzerland in double sculls by 1.46 sec. West Germany defeated the Soviet Union by 1.96 sec in eights, with the United States 0.25 sec farther behind in third.

In the women's Olympic events the East Germans had the closest race of their five victories against Romania in eights. They won by 2.27 sec, with China earning distinction in third place ahead of the Soviet Union, Bulgaria, and the United States. In coxed fours China took the silver medal, finishing 2.78 sec behind East Germany to attain its highest placing in Olympic rowing. The East Germans were given a good race by the Soviet Union and Romania before winning the quadruple sculls by 2.41 sec, but they won the single and double sculls more comfortably. The only other country to win a women's title was Romania, in coxless pairs.

The world lightweight and junior championships were contested in Milan, Italy, where 10 nations shared the lightweight medals and 14 nations gained junior prizes. Italy dominated the men's lightweight events with three winners, leaving the fourth to West Germany. The women's titles were more evenly distributed between China—with its first world title—The Netherlands, and the United States. In junior events Italy won three championships and East Germany won two, while the Soviet Union, Great Britain, and Romania gained one apiece. East Germany took four of the women's titles but lost to Bulgaria and Romania in the two other events.

In England entries for the Henley Royal Regatta reached an all-time record of 386. Australia won three events. Mercantile Rowing Club became the first Australian winner of the Ladies Plate (eights); the universities of Melbourne and Queensland captured the Queen Mother Cup (quadruple sculls); and Melbourne University student Hamish McGlashan took the Diamond Sculls. Great Britain's prospective Olympic eight denied Australia a fourth success by one foot in the Grand Challenge Cup. Penn Athletic Rowing Association took the Silver Goblets (coxless pairs) for the 75th United States win at Henley since 1892, and the fifth overseas winner was Vancouver (Can.) Rowing Club in the Prince Philip Cup (coxed fours). In the 134th University Boat Race, Oxford won by 5½ lengths to reduce the Cambridge lead in the series to 69–64 with one dead heat.

(KEITH OSBORNE)

SAILING

The America's Cup competition continued to make headlines in 1988 only one year after the triumph over an Australian boat by Dennis Conner of the U.S. In July 1987, only five months after the U.S. victory, Michael Fay (*see* BIOGRAPHIES) of New Zealand challenged the San Diego Yacht Club, Conner's home base, with a yacht that measured 40 m (132 ft) overall. By contrast, the competing yachts in the 1987 race measured about 20 m overall. The Americans, and in particular the San Diego Yacht Club, did not want a challenge from such a large yacht at such short notice. After months of wrangling, the Americans agreed to a three-race series but stated that they would defend the Cup in an 18-m (60-ft) catamaran. Fay went to court to challenge the use of the multihulled catamaran but was told to go ahead and race the series. In the meantime, other challenges by Britain's Peter De Savary and Australia's Alan Bond were rejected by the San Diego Yacht Club.

Stars & Stripes, the U.S. catamaran, with an unusual rigid sail and a crew of nine, was expected to be considerably faster than the giant New Zealand boat (with a crew of

some 40). The series started on schedule in early September 1988. Conner in *Stars & Stripes* was master from the start, demolishing the New Zealand challenge with consecutive victories by margins of 18 min 15 sec and 21 min 10 sec.

Although Fay said that he was returning to the courts on the matter, the future of the America's Cup appeared to have taken a turn for the better. An America's Cup Trustees Committee, including one member each from the New York and Perth (Australia) yacht clubs, was established in order that future challenges might be conducted with less dispute. The committee suggested that the next event be contested by several yachts as challengers in 1991. Uprated 12-m boats (larger sail areas being permitted) would compete so that existing craft could be used as trial horses.

Transatlantic racing, featuring a new breed of multihulled craft manned by professional sailors, continued to increase. The new 18–27-m (60–90-ft) boats were capable of incredible speeds even when sailed single-handedly. In June the Carlsberg Single-handed Race (Ex Ostar) from Plymouth (U.K.) to Newport (U.S.) took place. Philippe Poupon of France, sailing his new Nigel Irens-designed trimaran, *Fleury Michon,* won in the amazing record time of ten days, nine hours, and nine seconds, beating the previous best by six days. However, Mike Birch of Canada, in a similar craft and only 32 km (20 mi) astern at the time, hit a whale, badly damaging the boat and forcing his retirement from the race. Second to finish was Olivier Moussey of France in *Laiterie Mont St. Michel,* a trimaran with an Irens design identical to that of *Fleury Michon.*

In late August the Carlsberg Quebec (Canada) to Saint-Malo (France) fully crewed, 4,700-km (2,900-mi) transatlantic race took place. Serge Madec of France, sailing his new catamaran *Jet Services,* made it a one-man show. He drew away from the fleet and crossed the finish line with the second boat 1,770 km (1,100 mi) astern. For many of the pursuing crews, disasters and mishaps wrecked their chances of any success. Sadly, Moussey was lost overboard while repairing some damaged rigging on *Laiterie Mont St. Michel.*

In September at the Olympic Games in Seoul, South Korea, competition took place in the 470, Finn, Flying Dutchman, Soling, Star, Tornado, and Division II sailboard classes. (For results, *see* Special Report.)

(ADRIAN JARDINE)

SKIING

The spread of skiing throughout the world to some of the least likely areas was demonstrated by the admission of Fiji, Guatemala, India, Puerto Rico, Virgin Islands, and Zimbabwe to the International Ski Federation, bringing the organization's total of member nations to 61. More floodlit runs helped satisfy the still-mushrooming demand for recreational skiing. Plastic slopes and roller skis were increasingly used for training between seasons.

Alpine Racing. The 15th Winter Olympics in February at Calgary, Alta., was the sport's big "shop window" of 1988, thanks to comprehensive worldwide media coverage. Swiss world champion Pirmin Zurbriggen (*see* BIOGRAPHIES) stole victory from the grasp of teammate Peter Müller to capture the men's downhill gold, with Franck Piccard of France third. Zurbriggen's hopes of other wins were thwarted by two Austrians, Hubert Strolz and Bernhard Gstrein, who gained the first two places in the alpine combination, with Paul Accola of Switzerland third.

France claimed its first alpine victory in 20 years when Piccard won the supergiant slalom. Helmut Mayer of Austria was runner-up, with Lars-Börje Eriksson third for

World Class Boat Champions

Class	Winner	Class	Winner
8 Metre	Philip Crebbin (United Kingdom)	H-Boat	Jesper Bank (Denmark)
Enterprise	Ian Barker (United Kingdom)	J24	John Kosteki (United States)
Etchells 22	John Savage (Australia)	Laser	Glen Bourke (Australia)
Finn	Tomas Schmidt (West Germany)	Optimist	Ugo Venelo (Italy)
Fireball	Jim Clifton (Australia)	Soling	John Kosteki (United States)
505	Krister Bergstrom (Sweden)	Star	Paul Cayard (United States)
Flying Dutchman	Jorgen Bojsen-moller (Denmark)	Topper	Andy Carter (United Kingdom)
Flying Fifteen	Nigel Buckley (United Kingdom)	Tornado	Yury Konovalov (Soviet Union)
470	Nigel Buckley (United Kingdom)	12 Metre	Peter Gilmour (Australia)
GP14	Simon Relph (United Kingdom)		

Alberto Tomba of Italy charges down the giant slalom run. "La Bomba" rode his aggressive, sometimes risky style to gold medals in both the slalom and the giant slalom Olympic skiing events.
DAVID CANNON—ALLSPORT

Sweden. Two gold medals went to Alberto Tomba of Italy, who proved too good in the giant slalom for runner-up Strolz; Zurbriggen finished third. Tomba's second triumph came in the slalom; Frank Wörndl of West Germany finished close behind, and Paul Frommelt of Liechtenstein was third. Marina Kiehl captured West Germany's first alpine ski medal since 1976 when she won the women's downhill. Swiss runner-up Brigitte Oertli denied Karen Percy of Canada the silver by 0.01 sec. Anita Wachter took the alpine combination for Austria, with Oertli gaining her second silver ahead of the Swiss world champion, Maria Walliser. Austria's Sigrid Wolf sped through the supergiant slalom in front of Michela Figini of Switzerland, with Percy gaining her second bronze medal. Vreni Schneider of Switzerland won the giant slalom, outpacing Christa Kinshofer of West Germany, the 1980 slalom runner-up; Walliser took her second bronze. Schneider went on to win her second gold medal, defeating Mateja Svet of Yugoslavia in the slalom. Kinshofer took third place. The distribution of medals among many nations was a feature of these Games, with Switzerland winning fewer than had generally been anticipated.

In the 22nd Alpine World Cup series, Zurbriggen, the top scorer in both the downhill and supergiant slalom, retained the men's overall title after an always menacing challenge from Tomba, who was outstanding in the slalom and giant slalom but crashed in the final event when attempting a tenth race victory that would have clinched the cup. Figini won the women's crown by dominating competition in the downhill and supergiant slalom; Oertli was her closest rival.

Nordic Events. In the cross-country racing highlight of the Olympic Nordic events in Calgary, Sweden defeated the powerful Soviet Union by 13 seconds in the team relay. Mikhail Deviatiarov and Aleksey Prokurorov, both of the U.S.S.R., won the 15 km and 30 km, respectively, while the grueling 50 km went to Sweden's Gunde Svan. In the women's events the 5 km was won by Marjo Matikainen of Finland and the 10 km by Vida Ventsene of the Soviet Union. Tamara Tikhonova led her Soviet compatriots to a medal sweep in the 20 km. The team relay also went to the Soviets, who took 8 of the 12 possible medals in the cross-country events. Matti Nykänen became the first ski jumper to win three gold medals in the same Olympics by taking the 90 m, 70 m, and, as a member of Finland's

successful entry, the team event. Hippolyt Kempf won the individual Nordic combination jumping and cross-country event for Switzerland, and West Germany gained the team award. Both the individual biathlon ski-shooting contests were won by East Germany's Frank-Peter Rötsch, while the U.S.S.R. clinched the biathlon team relay.

In the ninth Nordic World Cup series for cross-country racing, Matikainen gained the women's title for a record third consecutive time. Svan captured the men's cup and also played a prominent role in Sweden's team triumph. Nykänen was a convincing victor in the Jumping World Cup series. World records for speed skiing were shattered in April at Les Arcs, France, when Michael Prufer from Monaco set a new men's best time of 223.741 km/h (139.056 mph) over a steep and straight "flying kilometre" course. This was more than double the top speed achieved in any Olympic downhill race. The women's world record was also lowered on the same day by Tarja Mulari of Finland; her 214.413 km/h (133.258 mph) bettered the old time by 13.5 km/h.   (HOWARD BASS)

SQUASH RACKETS

Jahangir Khan returned to the forefront of world squash competition in 1988, overcoming the temporary eclipse created by his Pakistani compatriot Jansher Khan. In March Jahangir ended a sequence of seven consecutive defeats at the hands of 18-year-old Jansher to win the French Open in Paris before going on to triumph at the British Open a month later. In the latter tournament Jansher was beaten in five games in the quarterfinals by Rodney Martin of Australia. Martin then lost to Jahangir in the final, becoming the seventh different opponent that Jahangir had faced in his record seven consecutive British Open final victories. At the world open championship in May at Amsterdam, Jahangir trounced Jansher 3–0 in a final that was marked by a first rally that lasted seven minutes. Following Jahangir's victories over Jansher in the Pakistan Open in September and over Chris Dittmar in the Canadian Open in November, he was again officially ranked number one.

In April at the world junior team championship in Edinburgh, Scotland, Pakistan lost to Australia 2–1 in the final, though Jansher, who led the Pakistani team, won his final match over Australia's Anthony Hill. Jansher did not enter the individual event, however, in which Del Harris of the U.K. beat Anthony Hill three games to two in the final.

In women's competition Susan Devoy of New Zealand continued to dominate the British Open, which she won for a fifth consecutive time. In the final she defeated Liz Irving of Australia 3–0. Illness and injury caused Devoy to be less than the firm favourite that she had been in previous years.   (ANDREW SHELLEY)

SWIMMING

The Games of the XXIV Olympiad in Seoul, South Korea, brought together for the first time since 1972 all the major nations that are members of the International Olympic Committee. At the Olympic Park's indoor pool, the Olympic Games attracted 671 swimmers from 71 nations, the largest entry ever to compete.

In the 1988 gold medal count, East Germany won 11, the United States 8, and Hungary 4. U.S. male swimmers won 5 of 16 events, and U.S. women won 3 of 15. The East German men won one gold and the women ten. A record 22 nations earned medals. The East German medal count in both men's and women's events was 11 gold, 8 silver, and 9 bronze; the U.S., 8 gold, 6 silver, and 4 bronze.

For the year 17 world records were set by men, 8 at the Olympic Games. Six world records were set by women, two at the Games. The first world record for 1988 by women was set by Janet Evans, a 17-year-old from Placentia, Calif. On March 22 at the U.S. indoor championships, Evans sliced 2.41 sec from the 800-m freestyle record with a time of 8 min 17.12 sec. Four days later she lowered her world record by 8.63 sec in the 1,500-m freestyle, a non-Olympic event, with a time of 15 min 52.10 sec.

On September 22 at the Olympic Games, Evans won the 400-m freestyle in 4 min 3.85 sec, taking 1.60 sec off her previous world record. She thus became the first woman since 1976 to hold three swimming world records simultaneously. On September 19 the U.S. star was timed in 4 min 37.76 sec to win the 400-m individual medley title. On September 24 Evans's third gold of the Games came in the 800-m freestyle. Her time of 8 min 20.2 sec set an Olympic record.

Silke Hörner of East Germany on September 21 lowered by 0.69 sec her world record in the 200-m breaststroke with a time of 2 min 26.71 sec. On April 11 Yang Wenyi took 0.3 sec off the 50-m freestyle to give China its first women's world record. She was timed in 24.98 sec.

The first world record of 1988 for men was set on March 15 by Igor Polyansky of the Soviet Union in the 100-m backstroke. He was clocked in 55.17 sec, a time 0.02 sec faster than the previous record by Rick Carey of the U.S. in 1983. The following day Polyansky again lowered the standard, to 55.16 sec, and four months later he further reduced it to 55.00 sec. David Berkoff of Willow Grove, Pa., then continued the onslaught on backstroke records. On August 12 at the U.S. Olympic trials, he was timed at 54.95 sec in the preliminaries and eight hours later lowered the record to 54.91 sec, slicing 0.09 sec off Polyansky's time. In the preliminaries at the Olympic Games, on September 24, Berkoff was timed in 54.51 sec to clip 0.40 sec off his recently established mark. He placed second in the final, losing the gold medal to Daichi Suzuki of Japan, who was timed in 55.05 sec.

On March 25 at the U.S. indoor championship, two world records were set by men. Thomas Jager of Collinsville, Ill., sprinted the 50-m freestyle in 22.23 sec, taking 0.09 sec off his record set in 1987. In the 400-m freestyle Artur Wojdat of Poland was timed in 3 min 47.38 sec to erase by 0.42 sec the record set by Michael Gross of West Germany in the 1984 Olympic Games. On September 23 Uwe Dassler of East Germany won the gold medal in the event in the world record time of 3 min 46.95 sec, taking 0.43 sec off Wojdat's mark.

On August 10 Matt Biondi, at the U.S. Olympic trials, won the 100-m freestyle in a world record of 48.42 sec, lowering by 0.32 sec his mark set in 1986. At the Olympic Games Biondi, from Moraga, Calif., won seven medals—five gold, one silver, and one bronze. His first effort, on September 19, ended with a bronze medal as Duncan Armstrong of Australia took 0.19 sec off the 200-m freestyle world mark of 1 min 47.44 sec set in 1984 by Gross. Biondi won his silver medal on September 21 when he lost the 100-m butterfly by 0.01 sec to Anthony Nesty of Suriname, whose time of 53.00 sec set an Olympic record and who also became the first athlete from his country to win an Olympic medal. Biondi then won the 100-m freestyle in an Olympic record time of 48.63 sec. Two days later he upset Jager for the gold medal in the 50-m freestyle, setting a new world record of 22.14 sec; Jager won the silver.

The U.S quartet of Troy Dalbey, Matt Cetlinski, Douglas Gjertsen, and Biondi was timed in 7 min 12.51 sec in the 4 × 200-m freestyle relay, bettering by 0.59 sec the old mark set in 1987 by West Germany. On September 23 the U.S. team of Chris Jacobs, Dalbey, Jager, and Biondi took 0.55 sec off the 4 × 100-m freestyle relay world record with a time of 3 min 16.53 sec. The previous record was set in 1985 by a U.S. team. On September 25 the 4 × 100 medley relay team of Berkoff, Richard Schroeder, Biondi, and Jacobs took 1.35 sec off the world record set by a U.S. team in 1985 with a time of 3 min 36.93 sec.

On September 21 at the Olympics, Tamas Darnyi of Hungary laid claim to being the world's greatest all-around swimmer, setting a world record in the 400-m individual medley with a time of 4 min 14.75 sec to erase by 0.67 sec his world mark set in 1987. He won his second gold medal in the 200-m individual medley in a world record time of 2 min 00.17 sec, bettering by 0.39 sec his mark set in 1987.

For six days Kristin Otto (see BIOGRAPHIES) of East Germany mounted the victory stand to receive an Olympic

World Swimming Records Set in 1988

Event	Name	Country	Time
MEN			
50-m freestyle	Thomas Jager	U.S.	22.23 sec
50-m freestyle	Matt Biondi	U.S.	22.14 sec
100-m freestyle	Matt Biondi	U.S.	48.42 sec
200-m freestyle	Duncan Armstrong	Australia	1 min 47.25 sec
400-m freestyle	Artur Wojdat	Poland	3 min 47.38 sec
400-m freestyle	Uwe Dassler	E Ger.	3 min 46.95 sec
100-m backstroke	Igor Polyansky	U.S.S.R.	55.17 sec
100-m backstroke	Igor Polyansky	U.S.S.R.	55.16 sec
100-m backstroke	Igor Polyansky	U.S.S.R.	55.00 sec
100-m backstroke	David Berkoff	U.S.	54.95 sec
100-m backstroke	David Berkoff	U.S.	54.91 sec
100-m backstroke	David Berkoff	U.S.	54.51 sec
200-m individual medley	Tamas Darnyi	Hungary	2 min 00.17 sec
400-m individual medley	Tamas Darnyi	Hungary	4 min 14.75 sec
4 × 100-m freestyle relay	U.S. national team (Chris Jacobs, Troy Dalbey, Thomas Jager, Matt Biondi)	U.S.	3 min 16.53 sec
4 × 200-m freestyle relay	U.S. national team (Troy Dalbey, Matt Cetlinski, Douglas Gjertsen, Matt Biondi)	U.S.	7 min 12.51 sec
4 × 100-m medley relay	U.S. national team (David Berkoff, Richard Schroeder, Matt Biondi, Chris Jacobs)	U.S.	3 min 36.93 sec
WOMEN			
50-m freestyle	Yang Wenyi	China	24.98 sec
400-m freestyle	Janet Evans	U.S.	4 min 03.85 sec
800-m freestyle	Janet Evans	U.S.	8 min 17.12 sec
1,500-m freestyle	Janet Evans	U.S.	15 min 52.10 sec
200-m breaststroke	Allison Higson	Canada	2 min 27.27 sec
200-m breaststroke	Silke Hörner	E. Ger.	2 min 26.71 sec

Proudly taking the Olympic gold medal in springboard diving, American Greg Louganis overcame not only other divers but also fear. He had hit his head badly on the board during the preliminaries.
NEIL LEIFER/TIME MAGAZINE

gold medal. She began with a win in the 100-m freestyle on September 19. On September 22 she won the gold medal in the 100-m backstroke and led off East Germany's triumphant 4 × 100-m freestyle relay team. The following day Otto came from behind to win the 100-m butterfly, and on September 24 she led off the winning 4 × 100-m medley relay. In her final event, the 50-m freestyle, she defeated the world record holder, Yang Wenyi of China, by 0.15 sec. Otto's feat broke the record for most gold medals won by a woman in any sport at one Olympic Games (four), which had been shared by seven athletes.

Diving. At Chamsil Swimming Pool Greg Louganis (*see* BIOGRAPHIES) of Boca Raton, Fla., became the first man to sweep gold medals in springboard and platform in back-to-back Olympic Games when on September 27 he came from behind on the 10-m platform to defeat 14-year-old Xiong Ni of China. Louganis, at 28 years of age, hit the most difficult and dangerous dive a person can attempt from the platform—a reverse 3½ somersault tuck with a difficulty rating of 3.4—to win his second gold medal of the 1988 Games. Louganis needed more than 85.56 points to beat Ni in the closest international competition he had ever won. He averaged 8.5s to score 86.70 points, finishing with 638.61 points. Ni, with 637.47 points, took the silver; and Jésus Mena of Mexico gained the bronze with 594.39 points. On September 20 in the Olympic 3-m springboard preliminaries, Louganis hit his head on the springboard on his ninth dive, a reverse dive with 2½ somersaults in the pike position. The head wound required five stitches.

The following day he performed with ballet skill to win the springboard title. Louganis opened a 19.71-point lead after eight dives over Tan Liangde of China. On Louganis's ninth dive, a reverse 2½, he scored between 8.0 and 9.0 to finish with 730.80 to Liangde's 704.88. Li Deliang, the bronze medalist, was far back with 665.28. After the Olympics, Louganis announced his retirement from world-class competitive diving.

In the women's 10-m platform, China won the gold medal for the second consecutive Olympic Games competition. Xu Yanmei, a 17-year-old, scored 8s on her last dive, a back 2½ somersault pike, to hold on to first place. Michele Mitchell of Boca Raton, the silver medalist in the 1984 Games, again finished second, followed by teammate Wendy Williams of Bridgeton, Mo.

In the 3-m springboard China's divers won the gold and silver medals. The winner, Gao Min, showed flawless style to score 580.23 points. Li Qing, Gao's 15-year-old teammate, scored 534.33 points. Kelly McCormick of Columbus, Ohio, the silver medalist in the 1984 Games, scored 8s on her last dive, a reverse 1½ somersault with 2½ twists, to move up from fourth to third with 533.19 points.

Synchronized Swimming. Women from 18 countries competed in synchronized swimming in the Olympic Games. World champion Carolyn Waldo of Canada gained a commanding lead in the compulsory figures over defending Olympic champion Tracie Ruiz-Conforto of Bothell, Wash. Waldo compiled 101.15 points for the six figures, putting her virtually out of reach of Ruiz-Conforto, who had 98.633 points. Waldo scored 99.00 points in the choreographed routine to win the gold medal. Ruiz-Conforto also scored 99.00 points but could not overcome Waldo's lead. Mikako Kotani, Japan, took the bronze.

Waldo and Michelle Cameron won the duet championship for Canada with 197.717 points. A U.S. pair, Karen and Sarah Josephson, twins from Bristol, Conn., scored perfect 10s in the duet and had a final score of 197.284 but were not able to overcome the lead established by the Canadians in the compulsory figures. Kotani and Miyako Tanaka won the bronze for Japan with 190.159 points.

(ALBERT SCHOENFIELD)

TABLE TENNIS

For the first time, international stars of table tennis vied for Olympic medals during the Summer Games held in Seoul, South Korea. Yoo Nam Kyu (South Korea) delighted the home crowd by winning the gold medal in the men's singles. Hyun Jung Hwa and Yang Young Ja (South Korea) won gold medals in the women's doubles. Chen Jing (China) swept to victory in the women's singles, and the team of Chen Longcan and Wei Qingguang (China) captured the men's doubles. China also won two silver medals and one bronze. South Korea and Yugoslavia each won one silver and one bronze. The final bronze was awarded to Sweden. During the European championships

1988 Table Tennis World Rankings	
MEN	WOMEN
1. Jiang Jialiang (China)	1. He Zhili (China)
2. Jan-Ove Waldner (Sweden)	2. Jiao Zhimin (China)
3. Chen Longcan (China)	3. Dai Lili (China)
4. Teng Yi (China)	4. Yang Young Ja (South Korea)
5. Andrzej Grubba (Poland)	5. Li Bun Hui (North Korea)
6. Jorgen Persson (Sweden)	6. Chen Jing (China)
7. Chen Xinhua (China)	7. Li Huifen (China)
8. Wang Hao (China)	8. Hyung Jun Hwa (South Korea)
9. Mikael Appelgren (Sweden)	9. Geng Lijuan (China)
10. Erik Lindh (Sweden)	10. Fliura Bulatova (U.S.S.R.)

held in Paris in March, Mikael Appelgren (Sweden) and Fliura Bulatova (U.S.S.R.) won the singles titles. They also helped their respective teams finish first in the final standings. The World Cup was contested in Wuhan, China, in June. In the men's competition, Andrzej Grubba (Poland) finished in first place. He was followed, in order, by Chen Longcan, Jiang Jialiang, and Xu Zengcai, all representing China.   (ARTHUR KINGSLEY VINT)

TENNIS

A significant event of 1988 was the inclusion of tennis in the Olympic Games at Seoul, South Korea. It had been featured in every Olympics from 1896 to 1924 but was dropped in 1928. It was a demonstration sport in Mexico City in 1968 and an under-21 event in Los Angeles in 1984. The advantage to tennis was less the addition of a tournament to an already rich field of international events than the benefit to nations where Olympic status resulted in increased government support.

The growth of tennis as a spectator sport was maintained; as a participant sport it increased. Member nations of the International Tennis Federation (ITF) numbered 103 in 1978 and 147 in 1988. A record 74 nations competed in the Davis Cup tournament, during which Ghana and Cameroon played for the first time in the African Zone created in 1985. Competing in international tournaments were players of world standard from Nigeria, Senegal, and Haiti.

National associations undertook more promotional activity. For example, the Lawn Tennis Association of Australia changed its name to Tennis Australia and built a tennis complex at Flinders Park in Melbourne for the Australian championships. Grass was replaced by a synthetic playing surface, and the main court was protected from rain by a sliding roof. The change of court surface left Wimbledon as the only major grass court tournament. The British Lawn Tennis Association restructured its organization to be more tax-efficient by providing separate control of junior development and for building indoor facilities.

Commercial sponsorship continued on an ever larger scale. Prize money increased, rising to $4,371,500 in the U.S. Open in 1988. Ivan Lendl of Czechoslovakia won $583,200 in an exhibition event in West Palm Springs, Fla., in November 1987. By October 1988 his career prize money exceeded $12.9 million.

Men's Competition. Lendl was judged "world champion" by the ITF at the end of 1987. At Madison Square Garden in New York City in December 1987, he won the Grand Prix Masters' Tournament for the third successive year. In the final he beat Mats Wilander of Sweden 6–2, 6–2, 6–3.

Wilander made an auspicious start to 1988 by winning the first of the four Grand Slam tournaments, the Australian championship, in Melbourne. He beat his compatriot Stefan Edberg 6–0, 6–7, 6–3, 3–6, 6–1 in the semifinals and Pat Cash of Australia 6–3, 6–7, 3–6, 6–1, 8–6 in the final. Cash had defeated Lendl 6–4, 2–6, 6–2, 4–6, 6–2 in the semifinals.

Wilander won his second Grand Slam tournament of the year in the French championships in Paris. Lendl lost to Jonas Svensson of Sweden in the quarterfinals. Edberg was beaten in the fourth round by Guillermo Pérez-Roldan of Argentina. Wilander won his semifinal against a promising U.S. newcomer, Andre Agassi, 4–6, 6–2, 7–5, 5–7, 6–0 and then triumphed in the final over Henri Leconte of France 7–5, 6–2, 6–1.

At Wimbledon in London Wilander lost his bid for all four Grand Slam titles when he was defeated by Miloslav Mecir of Czechoslovakia in the quarterfinals. In the same

Mats Wilander hammers a return during the finals of the U.S. Open. Wilander broke the three-year reign of Ivan Lendl in the marathon match and became the first Swedish player to win the tournament.
FOCUS ON SPORT

round, Cash, the defending champion, lost to Boris Becker of West Germany, the champion of the two preceding years. In the semifinals Becker beat Lendl 6–4, 6–3, 6–7, 6–4, and Edberg defeated Mecir 4–6, 2–6, 6–4, 6–3, 6–4. In the final Edberg beat Becker 4–6, 7–6, 6–4, 6–2.

Wilander won the U.S. Open in New York City for the first time to take his third Grand Slam title of the year and complete a sweep of the four championships by Swedes. In the semifinals Lendl beat Agassi 4–6, 6–2, 6–3, 6–4, and Wilander topped the unseeded Darren Cahill of Australia 6–4, 6–4, 6–2. In the final Wilander defeated Lendl 6–4, 4–6, 6–3, 5–7, 6–4 after 4 hours 54 minutes.

In the Olympic Games Mecir beat Tim Mayotte of the U.S. 3–6, 6–2, 6–4, 6–2 in the singles final to take the gold medal. He beat the top-seeded Edberg 3–6, 6–0, 1–6, 6–4, 6–2 in the semifinals.

In doubles the only common factor among winners of the Grand Slam tournaments was Emilio Sánchez of Spain, who won the French title with Andre Gómez of Ecuador and the U.S. with his compatriot Sergio Casal.

Rick Leach and Jim Pugh of the U.S. won the Australian Open but had to withdraw from the U.S. final because Leach became ill. Ken Flach and Robert Seguso of the U.S. retained their Wimbledon title. They also won the gold medal in the Olympics with a win in the final against Casal and Sánchez.

In Davis Cup competition the format was amended for 1989 so that the eight first-round losers in the World Group would be required to play a qualifying round against the eight semifinalists from the four zones–Euro-African "A," Euro-African "B," American, and Asian-Oceanian. This gave four more nations a chance to qualify for the championship group.

The tie-break scoring system was instituted, with all sets except the one that would decide the match to be settled by the best of 12 points at six games all. The Davis Cup was the last major event to adopt this system.

In 1988 the U.S., demoted from the World Group in 1987, regained its place there with a 3–2 win against Peru and a 4–1 win against Argentina. Agassi played for the U.S. for the first time and won three singles. Austria, the U.S.S.R., and Indonesia were the other zone winners. Play-off winners in the World Group were Paraguay, Mexico, Spain, and Israel.

In the World Group Sweden beat New Zealand 5–0,

then Czechoslovakia 3–2. France beat Australia 5–0 in the same round at Clermont-Ferrand. Cash was unable to play for Australia. In the semifinals Sweden lost only the doubles in defeating France. West Germany beat Brazil, Denmark, and Yugoslavia by 5–0 to reach the final for the third time. Becker did not lose a set in any of five singles.

Sweden was a finalist for the sixth time in as many years, losing only to Australia in 1983 and 1986. In 1985 it defeated West Germany 3–2 in Munich when Becker beat both Edberg and Wilander. However, West Germany gained revenge in 1988 by defeating Sweden 4–1 at Göteborg, Sweden, in December to win its first Davis Cup. The West Germans took a 2–0 lead when Carl-Uwe Steeb upset Wilander 8–10, 1–6, 6–2, 6–4, 8–6, and Becker trounced Edberg 6–3, 6–1, 6–4. They then clinched the title as Becker and Eric Jelen outlasted Edberg and Anders Jarryd 3–6, 2–6, 7–5, 6–3, 6–2. Edberg gained Sweden's only triumph with a 6–4, 8–6 victory over Steeb. The Swedes defaulted the final match.

Women's Competition. The outstanding player of 1988 was Steffi Graf of West Germany, whose 19th birthday was June 14, 1988. She took the place of Martina Navratilova of the U.S., who was 32 on October 18. For the first time since 1980, Navratilova failed to win any of the four Grand Slam singles titles. She challenged in all, and her best achievement was as losing finalist at Wimbledon, where she had been unbeaten since 1981. Graf, whose game was built on ground power, won the four major singles to become the fourth woman to win the Grand Slam. She joined Navratilova (1983 and 1984), Margaret Court of Australia (1970), and Maureen Connolly of the U.S. (1953).

In the Australian championships at Melbourne, Chris Evert (U.S.) beat Navratilova 6–2, 7–5 in the semifinals. Graf then defeated Evert 6–1, 7–6 in the final, having lost no set in seven rounds. In the spring, however, Graf twice suffered defeat from Gabriela Sabatini of Argentina in Florida tournaments.

In the French championships at Paris, Graf beat Sabatini 6–3, 7–6 in the semifinals. Natalia Zvereva (U.S.S.R.) beat Navratilova 6–3, 7–6 in the fourth round and reached the final. There Graf beat her 6–0, 6–0, the most one-sided final in a major singles event since Wimbledon in 1911. Again Graf lost no set in the event.

Wimbledon brought continued triumph to Graf, and she lost no more than three games in any set in six rounds to the final. She beat Pam Shriver of the U.S. 6–1, 6–2 in one semifinal, while in the other Navratilova defeated Evert 6–1, 4–6, 7–5 to reach the final for the seventh year in a row. In the final she began strongly, but Graf won 5–7, 6–

2, 6–1 to become the second German winner since Cilly Aussem in 1931 and the youngest since Connolly in 1953.

Graf also dominated the U.S. Open. She lost no set in five rounds and then walked over Evert, who was ill, in the semifinals. Zina Garrison of the U.S. beat Navratilova 6–4, 6–7, 7–5 in the quarterfinals. Sabatini defeated Larissa Savchenko of the U.S.S.R. 4–6, 6–4, 6–1 at the same stage and then won the semifinal against Garrison 6–4, 7–5. Graf's victory over Sabatini in the final was 6–3, 3–6, 6–1. Graf also won the gold medal in the Olympics, defeating Sabatini 6–3, 6–3 in the final.

In doubles Navratilova and Shriver successfully defended their Australian and French championships. At Wimbledon they lost to the Soviet pair of Savchenko and Zvereva, who then lost in the final to Graf and Sabatini. Gigi Fernandez and Robin White of the U.S. beat Navratilova and Shriver in the U.S. Open semifinals and won the final against Jill Hetherington of Canada and Patty Fendick of the U.S. Olympic winners were Shriver and Garrison, with Jana Novotna and Helena Sukova of Czechoslovakia the losing finalists.

In the Wightman Cup the U.S. (Garrison, Lori McNeil, Fendick, Betsy Nagelsen, and Fernandez) beat Great Britain (Jo Durie, Sarah Gomer, Monique Javer, Julie Salmon, and Clare Wood) at the Royal Albert Hall, London, to win for the 50th time in 60 contests.

(LANCE TINGAY)

TRACK AND FIELD SPORTS

For the first time since 1972, the Olympic Games in 1988 brought together nearly all of the nations competing in track and field sports. Politics had kept most of the black African nations out of the 1976 Olympics, the United States and many of its allies out of the 1980 Games, and the Eastern European bloc away in 1984. At Seoul, South Korea, in 1988, however, every nation that expected to do well participated, with two exceptions. Ethiopia, with the world's fastest marathoner, and Cuba, with several world-class athletes, did not enter the competition. North Korea also stayed home, having been rejected in its bid to be a cosponsor of the Games of the XXIV Olympiad.

Men's International Competition. There was much competition throughout the world before the athletes gathered in Seoul in September. Three soon-to-be Olympians accounted for four world records. The double record breaker was the Soviet Union's Sergey Bubka (*see* BIOGRAPHIES). The world's best pole vaulter since 1983, he vaulted 6.05 m (19 ft 10¼ in) in Bratislava, Czech., on June 9 and

(continued on page 342)

RONALD C. MODRA/SPORTS ILLUSTRATED

Ben Johnson pushes through a crowd of reporters at the airport in Seoul, South Korea. Johnson left the Olympics after being stripped of his gold medal and world-record time in the 100-metre race when a routine drug test revealed traces of an anabolic steroid.

The Games of the XXIV Olympiad

Winter Games. The Canadian city of Calgary, Alta., played host to nearly 1,800 athletes from 57 nations during the February 1988 winter Olympic Games. Despite severe weather that forced the postponement of six events, there were 1.5 million paid admissions. The $25 million profit would be used to support Canadian sports programs. Katarina Witt (East Germany; *see* BIOGRAPHIES) provided one of the most memorable moments of the Games when she became the first woman in half a century to win back-to-back gold medals in figure skating. Eddie Edwards, a nearsighted British athlete, was nearly banned by apprehensive officials who feared his lack of experience as a ski jumper posed a real danger to his life. Edwards competed and finished last in a field of 58. In the process, he became an international folk hero. After a poor but successful first jump, one newspaper headline proclaimed the joyous news: "The eagle has landed!"

Summer Games. Seoul, the capital of South Korea, was the site of the Summer Games. With athletes from 160 nations participating, it was the largest sports event in history. This occurred because, for the first time since 1972, there was no major political boycott of the Games.

Long before the Games got under way in mid-September, there were fears that the Olympics might be disrupted by North Korea or by internal dissent. Extraordinarily tight security measures helped prevent such problems. A disruption of another sort stunned the sports world, however, when officials announced that Ben Johnson, a Jamaican-born Canadian sprinter, had tested positive for banned drugs and would be stripped of the gold medal he had won in the 100-m dash. His victory over rival Carl Lewis (U.S.) had been heralded as one of the greatest contests between two superior athletes in modern track history. When nine other athletes were also found guilty of drug abuse, officials and the public at large began to wonder whether the determination "to win at any price" had inflicted permanent, and perhaps fatal, damage on the Olympics. The root of the problem, many seemed to agree, was the incredibly lucrative endorsements awaiting superstars who returned home with gold medals.

Among those athletes who would be long remembered for extraordinary performances were Greg Louganis (U.S.; *see* BIOGRAPHIES), who once again won both the platform and springboard diving titles; Vladimir Artemov (U.S.S.R.) and Daniela Silivas (Romania) in gymnastics; Matt Biondi (U.S.), Kristin Otto (East Germany; *see* BIOGRAPHIES), and Janet Evans (U.S.) in swimming; and two sisters-in-law, Florence Griffith Joyner (*see* BIOGRAPHIES) and Jackie Joyner-Kersee, in track and field. As host country, South Korea was especially proud of the fact that its athletes won twice as many gold medals as in 1984 and placed sixth in overall number of medals.

Olympic Champions, 1988 Winter Games, Calgary

Alpine Skiing
Men

Downhill	P. Zurbriggen (Switz.)	1 min 59.63 sec
Slalom	A. Tomba (Italy)	1 min 39.47 sec
Giant slalom	A. Tomba (Italy)	2 min 6.37 sec
Supergiant slalom	F. Piccard (France)	1 min 39.66 sec
Combined event	H. Strolz (Austria)	36.55 pt

Women

Downhill	M. Kiehl (W.Ger.)	1 min 25.86 sec
Slalom	V. Schneider (Switz.)	1 min 36.69 sec
Giant slalom	V. Schneider (Switz.)	2 min 6.49 sec
Supergiant slalom	S. Wolf (Austria)	1 min 19.03 sec
Combined event	A. Wachter (Austria)	29.25 pt

Nordic Skiing
Men

15-km cross-country	M. Deviatiarov (U.S.S.R.)	41 min 18.9 sec
30-km cross-country	A. Prokurorov (U.S.S.R.)	1 hr 24 min 26.3 sec
50-km cross-country	G. Svan (Sweden)	2 hr 4 min 30.9 sec
40-km ski relay	Sweden	1 hr 43 min 58.6 sec
70-m ski jump	M. Nykänen (Fin.)	229.1 pt
90-m ski jump	M. Nykänen (Fin.)	224.0 pt
90-m team ski jump	Finland	634.4 pt
Nordic combined	H. Kempf (Switz.)	217.9 pt
Nordic team combined	West Germany	629.8 pt

Women

5-km cross-country	M. Matikainen (Fin.)	15 min 4.0 sec
10-km cross-country	V. Ventsene (U.S.S.R.)	30 min 8.3 sec
20-km cross-country	T. Tikhonova (U.S.S.R.)	55 min 53.6 sec
20-km ski relay	U.S.S.R.	59 min 51.1 sec

Biathlon

10 km	F. Rötsch (E.Ger.)	25 min 8.1 sec[2]
20 km	F. Rötsch (E.Ger.)	56 min 33.3 sec
30-km relay	U.S.S.R.	1 hr 22 min 30.0 sec

Figure Skating

Men	B. Boitano (U.S.)	3.0 pt
Women	K. Witt (E.Ger.)	4.2 pt
Pairs	E. Gordeeva and S. Grinkov (U.S.S.R.)	1.4 pt
Ice dancing	N. Bestemianova and A. Bukin (U.S.S.R.)	2.0 pt

Speed Skating
Men

500 m	J. Mey (E. Ger.)	36.45 sec[1]
1,000 m	N. Gulyaev (U.S.S.R.)	1 min 13.03 sec[2]
1,500 m	A. Hoffmann (E.Ger.)	1 min 52.06 sec[1]
5,000 m	T. Gustafson (Sweden)	6 min 44.63 sec[1]
10,000 m	T. Gustafson (Sweden)	13 min 48.20 sec[1]

Women

500 m	B. Blair (U.S.)	39.10 sec[1]
1,000 m	C. Rothenburger (E.Ger.)	1 min 17.65 sec[1]
1,500 m	Y. van Gennip (Neth.)	2 min 0.68 sec[2]
3,000 m	Y. van Gennip (Neth.)	4 min 11.94 sec[1]
5,000 m	Y. van Gennip (Neth.)	7 min 14.13 sec[1]

Ice Hockey

Winning team	U.S.S.R. (7–1–0)	

Bobsledding

Two man	U.S.S.R.	3 min 53.48 sec
Four man	Switzerland	3 min 47.51 sec

Tobogganing (Luge)

Men (single)	J. Müller (E.Ger.)	3 min 5.548 sec
Men (double)	J. Hoffmann and J. Pietzsch (E.Ger.)	1 min 31.940 sec
Women (single)	S. Walter (E.Ger.)	3 min 3.973 sec

[1]World record. [2]Olympic record.

Olympic Champions, 1988 Summer Games, Seoul

Archery

	Men			Women	
Individual	J. Barrs (U.S.)	338 pt	Kim Su Nyung (S. Korea)	344[1] pt
Team	South Korea	986 pt	South Korea	982 pt

Basketball

Men	U.S.S.R.	Women	U.S.

Boxing

48-kg class	I. Hristov (Bulg.)	67-kg class	R. Wangila (Kenya)
51-kg class	Kim Kwang Sun (S.Korea)	71-kg class	Park Si Hun (S.Korea)
54-kg class	K. McKinney (U.S.)	75-kg class	H. Maske (E.Ger.)
57-kg class	G. Parisi (Italy)	81-kg class	A. Maynard (U.S.)
60-kg class	A. Zuelow (E.Ger.)	91.5-kg class	R. Mercer (U.S.)
63.5-kg class	V. Yanovsky (U.S.S.R.)	91.5-kg+ class	L. Lewis (Canada)

Canoeing
Men

500-m kayak singles	Z. Gyulay (Hung.)	1 min 44.82 sec
1,000-m kayak singles	G. Barton (U.S.)	3 min 55.27 sec
500-m kayak pairs	P. MacDonald/I. Ferguson (N.Z.)	1 min 33.98 sec
1,000-m kayak pairs	G. Barton/N. Bellingham (U.S.)	3 min 32.42 sec
1,000-m kayak fours	Hungary	3 min 00.20 sec
500-m Canadian singles	O. Heukrodt (E.Ger.)	1 min 56.42 sec
1,000-m Canadian singles	I. Klementev (U.S.S.R.)	4 min 12.78 sec
500-m Canadian pairs	V. Reneysky N. Zhuravsky (U.S.S.R.)	1 min 41.77 sec
1,000-m Canadian pairs	V. Reneysky N. Zhuravsky (U.S.S.R.)	3 min 48.36 sec

Women

500-m kayak singles	V. Guecheva (Bulg.)	1 min 55.19 sec
500-m kayak pairs	B. Schmidt/A. Nothnagel (E.Ger.)	1 min 43.46 sec
500-m kayak fours	E. Germany	1 min 40.78 sec

Cycling

Men

Road race	O. Ludwig (E.Ger.)	4 hr 32 min 22 sec
Team time trial	E. Germany	1 hr 57 min 47.7 sec
(1-km) time trial	A. Kirichenko (U.S.S.R.)	1 min 04.499 sec
4,000-m indiv. pursuit	G. Umaras (U.S.S.R.)	4 min 32.00 sec
4,000-m team pursuit	U.S.S.R.	4 min 13.31 sec[1]
Sprint	L. Hesslich (E.Ger.)	
50-km points race	D. Frost (Den.)	38 pt.

Women

Road race	M. Knol (Neth.)	2 hr 00.52 sec
Sprint	E. Salumyae (U.S.S.R.)	

Diving

	Men		Women	
Springboard	G. Louganis (U.S.)	730.80 pt	Gao Min (China)	580.23 pt
Platform	G. Louganis (U.S.)	638.61 pt	Xu Yanmei (China)	445.20 pt

Equestrian

	Individual	Team
3-day event	Mark Todd (N.Z.)	W.Germany
Dressage	Nicole Uphoff (W.Ger.)	W.Germany
Jumping	Pierre Durand (France)	W.Germany

Fencing

	Individual	Team
Men's foil	S. Cerioni (Italy)	U.S.S.R.
Women's foil	A. Fichtel (W.Ger.)	W.Germany
Épée	A. Schmitt (W.Ger.)	France
Sabre	J.-F. Lamour (France)	Hungary

Field Hockey

Men	U.K.	Women	Australia

Gymnastics

Men

Team	U.S.S.R.	593.350 pt
All-around	V. Artyomov (U.S.S.R.)	119.125 pt
Floor exercise	S. Kharkov (U.S.S.R.)	19.925 pt
Vault	Lou Yun (China)	19.875 pt
	Z. Borkai (Hung.)	19.950 pt
Pommel horse	D. Bilozerchev (U.S.S.R.)	19.950 pt
	L. Gueraskov (Bulg.)	19.950 pt
Rings	D. Bilozerchev (U.S.S.R.)	19.925 pt
	H. Behrendt (E.Ger.)	19.925 pt
Parallel bars	V. Artyomov (U.S.S.R.)	19.925 pt
Horizontal bar	V. Lyukin (U.S.S.R.)	19.900 pt
	V. Artyomov (U.S.S.R.)	19.900 pt

Women

Team	U.S.S.R.	395.475 pt
All-around	Y. Shushunova (U.S.S.R.)	79.662 pt
Floor exercise	D. Silivas (Rom.)	19.937 pt
Vault	S. Boginskaya (U.S.S.R.)	19.905 pt
Uneven bars	D. Silivas (Rom.)	20.000 pt
Balance beam	D. Silivas (Rom.)	19.924 pt
Rhythmic competition	M. Lobach (U.S.S.R.)	60.000 pt

Handball

Men	U.S.S.R.	Women	S. Korea

Modern Pentathlon

Individual	J. Martinek (Hung.)	5,404 pt
Team	Hungary	15,886 pt

Judo

60-kg class	Kim Jae Yup (S. Korea)	86-kg class	P. Seisenbacher (Austria)
65-kg class	Lee Kyung Keun (S. Korea)	95-kg class	A. Miguel (Brazil)
71-kg class	M. Alexandre (France)	95-kg+ class	Hitoshi Saito (Japan)
78-kg class	W. Legien (Poland)		

Rowing

Men

Single sculls	T. Lange (E.Ger.)	6 min 49.86 sec
Double sculls	Netherlands	6 min 21.13 sec
Quadruple sculls	Italy	5 min 53.37 sec
Coxed pairs	Italy	6 min 58.79 sec
Coxless pairs	U.K.	6 min 36.84 sec
Coxed fours	E.Germany	6 min 10.74 sec
Coxless fours	E.Germany	6 min 03.11 sec
Eights	W.Germany	5 min 46.05 sec

Women

Single sculls	J. Behrendt (E.Ger.)	7 min 47.19 sec
Double sculls	E.Germany	7 min 00.48 sec
Quadruple sculls	E.Germany	6 min 21.06 sec
Coxless pairs	Romania	7 min 28.13 sec
Coxed fours	E.Germany	6 min 56.00 sec
Eights	E.Germany	6 min 15.17 sec

Shooting

Men

Rapid-fire pistol	A. Kuzmin (U.S.S.R.)	698 pt[1]
Free pistol	S. Babii (Rom.)	660 pt
Air pistol	T. Kiryakov (Bulg.)	687.9 pt
Running game target	T. Heiestad (Norway)	689 pt
Small-bore rifle, 3 pos.	M. Cooper (U.K.)	1,279.3 pt
Small-bore rifle, prone	M. Varga (Czech.)	703.9 pt
Air rifle	G. Maksimovich (Yugos.)	695.6 pt
Trap (open event)	D. Monakov (U.S.S.R.)	222 pt
Skeet (open event)	A. Wegner (E.Ger.)	222 pt

Women

Air pistol	J. Sekaric (Yugos.)	489.5 pt[1]
Small-bore rifle, 3 pos.	S. Sperber (W.Ger.)	685.6 pt
Air rifle	I. Shilova (U.S.S.R.)	498.5 pt
Sport pistol	N. Salukvadze (U.S.S.R.)	690 pt

Soccer

U.S.S.R.

Swimming

Men

50-m freestyle	M. Biondi (U.S.)	22.14 sec[1]
100-m freestyle	M. Biondi (U.S.)	48.63 sec[2]
200-m freestyle	D. Armstrong (Australia)	1 min 47.25 sec[1]
400-m freestyle	U. Dassler (E.Ger.)	3 min 46.95 sec[1]
1,500-m freestyle	V. Salnikov (U.S.S.R.)	15 min 0.40 sec
100-m backstroke	D. Suzuki (Japan)	55.05 sec
200-m backstroke	I. Polyansky (U.S.S.R.)	1 min 59.37 sec
100-m breaststroke	A. Moorhouse (U.K.)	1 min 2.04 sec
200-m breaststroke	J. Szabo (Hung.)	2 min 13.52 sec
100-m butterfly	A. Nesty (Suriname)	53.00 sec[2]
200-m butterfly	M. Gross (W.Ger.)	1 min 56.94 sec[2]
200-m individual medley	T. Darnyi (Hung.)	2 min 0.17 sec
400-m individual medley	T. Darnyi (Hung.)	4 min 14.75 sec[1]
4 × 100-m freestyle relay	U.S.	3 min 16.53 sec[1]
4 × 200-m freestyle relay	U.S.	7 min 12.51 sec[1]
4 × 100-m medley relay	U.S.	3 min 36.93 sec[1]

Women

50-m freestyle	K. Otto (E.Ger.)	25.49 sec[2]
100-m freestyle	K. Otto (E.Ger.)	54.93 sec[1]
200-m freestyle	H. Friedrich (E.Ger.)	1 min 57.65 sec[2]
400-m freestyle	J. Evans (U.S.)	4 min 3.85 sec[1]
800-m freestyle	J. Evans (U.S.)	8 min 20.20 sec[2]
100-m backstroke	K. Otto (E.Ger.)	1 min 0.89 sec
200-m backstroke	K. Egerszegi (Hung.)	2 min 9.29 sec[2]
100-m breaststroke	T. Dangalakova (Bulg.)	1 min 7.95 sec[2]
200-m breaststroke	S. Hörner (E.Ger.)	2 min 26.71 sec[1]
100-m butterfly	K. Otto (E.Ger.)	59.00 sec[2]
200-m butterfly	K. Nord (E.Ger.)	2 min 9.51 sec
200-m individual medley	D. Hunger (E.Ger.)	2 min 12.59 sec[2]
400-m individual medley	J. Evans (U.S.)	4 min 37.76 sec[2]
4 × 100-m freestyle relay	E.Germany	3 min 40.63 sec[2]
4 × 100-m medley relay	E.Germany	4 min 3.74 sec[2]
Synchronized swimming-solo	C. Waldo (Canada)	200.150 pt
-duet	C. Waldo/M. Cameron (Canada)	197.717 pt

Table Tennis

Men's singles	Yoo Nam Kyu (S.Korea)
Men's doubles	Chen Longcan/Wei Qingguang (China)
Women's singles	Chen Jing (China)
Women's doubles	Hyun Jung Hwa/Yang Young Ja (S.Korea)

Tennis

Men's singles	M. Mecir (Czech.)
Men's doubles	K. Flach/R. Seguso (U.S.)
Women's singles	S. Graf (W.Ger.)
Women's doubles	P. Shriver/Z. Garrison (U.S.)

Track and Field

Men

100 m	C. Lewis (U.S.)	9.92 sec[2]
200 m	J. DeLoach (U.S.)	19.75 sec[2]
400 m	S. Lewis (U.S.)	43.87 sec
4 × 100-m relay	U.S.S.R.	38.19 sec
4 × 400-m relay	U.S.	2 min 56.16 sec[2]
800 m	P. Ereng (Kenya)	1 min 43.45 sec
1,500 m	P. Rono (Kenya)	3 min 35.96 sec
5,000 m	J. Ngugi (Kenya)	13 min 11.70 sec
10,000 m	B. Boutayeb (Morocco)	27 min 21.46 sec[2]
Marathon	G. Bordin (Italy)	2 hr 10 min 32 sec
110-m hurdles	R. Kingdom (U.S.)	12.98 sec[2]
400-m hurdles	A. Phillips (U.S.)	47.19 sec[2]
Steeplechase	J. Kariuki (Kenya)	8 min 5.51 sec[2]
20-km walk	J. Pribilinec (Czech.)	1 hr 19 min 57 sec[2]
50-km walk	V. Ivanenko (U.S.S.R.)	3 hr 38 min 29 sec[2]
High jump	G. Avdeyenko (U.S.S.R.)	2.38 m[2]
Long jump	C. Lewis (U.S.)	8.72 m
Triple jump	K. Markov (Bulg.)	17.61 m[2]
Pole vault	S. Bubka (U.S.S.R.)	5.90 m[2]
Shot put	U. Timmermann (E.Ger.)	22.47 m[2]
Discus throw	J. Schult (E.Ger.)	68.82 m[2]
Javelin throw	T. Korjus (Fin.)	84.28 m
Hammer throw	S. Litvinov (U.S.S.R.)	84.80 m[2]
Decathlon	C. Schenk (E.Ger.)	8,488 pt

Women

100 m	F. Griffith Joyner (U.S.)	10.54 sec
200 m	F. Griffith Joyner (U.S.)	21.34 sec[1]
400 m	O. Bruzgina (U.S.S.R.)	48.65 sec[2]
4 × 100-m relay	U.S.	41.98 sec
4 × 400-m relay	U.S.S.R.	3 min 15.18 sec[1]
800 m	S. Wodars (E.Ger.)	1 min 56.10 sec
1,500 m	P. Ivan (Rom.)	3 min 53.96 sec[2]
3,000 m	T. Samolenko (U.S.S.R.)	8 min 26.53 sec
10,000 m	O. Bondarenko (U.S.S.R.)	31 min 5.21 sec[2]
Marathon	R. Mota (Port.)	2 hr 25 min 40 sec
100-m hurdles	Y. Donkova (Bulg.)	12.38 sec[2]
400-m hurdles	D. Flintoff-King (Australia)	53.17 sec
High jump	L. Ritter (U.S.)	2.03 m[2]
Long jump	J. Joyner-Kersee (U.S.)	7.40 m
Shot put	N. Lisovskaya (U.S.S.R.)	22.24 m
Discus throw	M. Hellmann (E.Ger.)	72.30 m[2]
Javelin throw	P. Felke (E.Ger.)	74.68 m[2]
Heptathlon	J. Joyner-Kersee (U.S.)	7,291 pt[1]

Volleyball

Men	U.S.	Women	U.S.S.R.

Water Polo

Yugoslavia

Weightlifting

52-kg class	S. Marinov (Bulg.)	270 kg[1]
56-kg class	O. Mirzoyan (U.S.S.R.)	292.5 kg[2]
60-kg class	N. Suleymanoglu (Turkey)	342.5 kg[1]
67.5-kg class	J. Kunz (E.Ger.)	340.0 kg
75-kg class	B. Guidikov (Bulg.)	375.0 kg[2]
82.5-kg class	I. Arsamakov (U.S.S.R.)	377.5 kg
90-kg class	A. Khrapaty (U.S.S.R.)	412.5 kg[2]
100-kg class	P. Kuznetsov (U.S.S.R.)	425.0 kg[2]
110-kg class	Y. Zakharevich (U.S.S.R.)	455.0 kg[1]
110-kg+ class	A. Kurlovich (U.S.S.R.)	462.5 kg[2]

Wrestling

	Freestyle	Greco-Roman
48-kg class	T. Kobayashi (Japan)	V. Maenza (Italy)
52-kg class	M. Sato (Japan)	J. Ronningen (Norway)
57-kg class	S. Beloglazov (U.S.S.R.)	A. Sike (Hung.)
62-kg class	J. Smith (U.S.)	K. Madzhidov (U.S.S.R.)
68-kg class	A. Fadzaev (U.S.S.R.)	L. Dzhulfalakyan (U.S.S.R.)
74-kg class	K. Monday (U.S.)	Kim Young Nam (S.Korea)
82-kg class	Han Myang Woo (S.Korea)	M. Mamiashvili (U.S.S.R.)
90-kg class	M. Khadartsev (U.S.S.R.)	A. Komchev (Bulg.)
100-kg class	V. Puscasu (Rom.)	A. Wronski (Poland)
130-kg class	D. Gobedzhishvili (U.S.S.R.)	A. Karelin (U.S.S.R.)

Yachting

Men's 470 class	France	Flying Dutchman (open)	Denmark
Women's 470 class	U.S.	Star (open)	U.K.
Boardsailing (open)	B. Kendall (N.Z.)	Tornado (open)	France
Finn (open)	J. Doreste (Spain)	Soling (open)	E.Germany

[1]World record. [2]Olympic record.

(continued from page 339)

6.06 m (19 ft 10½ in) at Nice, France, on July 10. The shot-put record was advanced to 23.06 m (75 ft 8 in) by Ulf Timmermann of East Germany at Khania, Greece, on May 22. And the next-to-oldest world record fell to Butch Reynolds of the United States when he covered 400 m in 43.29 sec at Zürich, Switz., on August 17. The previous mark, by Lee Evans of the U.S., was 43.86 sec and had lasted 20 years.

Two more global bests were established by athletes who did not participate in the Olympics. Belaine Densimo of Ethiopia ran the marathon in 2 hr 6 min 50 sec at Rotterdam, Neth., on April 17, and Javier Sotomayor of Cuba came within a half inch of breaking the 8-ft barrier in the high jump when he leaped 2.43 m (7 ft 11½ in) on September 8 at Salamanca, Spain. Earlier, Carlo Thranhardt of West Germany had jumped a record-tying 2.42 m (7 ft 11¼ in). It was both an indoor and an outdoor record because an indoor mark made under the proper conditions is also recognized as an outdoor mark.

While no man broke a world record in the Olympics, four of them combined to equal a long-standing relay mark. The U.S., with Evans anchoring, was timed in 2 min 56.16 sec in the 4 × 400-m relay in the 1968 Olympics, and it had proved to be a difficult performance to better. The high altitude of Mexico City had helped create long-standing global marks, two of which were still in the record books— the above-mentioned relay and Bob Beamon's long jump of 8.90 m (29 ft 2½ in). The quartet of record equalers in 1988 included the three men who had taken the three medals in the 400 m. Danny Everett ran first, passing to UCLA teammate Steve Lewis. The third baton carrier was Kevin Robinzine, and he handed to recent world record breaker Reynolds. The time was shown on the scoreboard as just 0.01 sec slower than the 1968 mark, but scrutiny of the photo revealed the tying time.

The 400-m race was one of the most thrilling of the Olympics. Reynolds, the world's best for two years and new record holder, was expected to challenge his own mark. He ran well, but Lewis, a 19-year-old college sophomore, charged to the front and held his lead to the tape, winning in 43.87 sec, just 0.01 sec behind Evans's Olympic record and the third-fastest 400 m ever run. Reynolds dashed 43.93 for second, and Everett won the bronze medal with his 44.09 sec.

The race that attracted the most attention, however— before, while, and after it was run—was the 100 m. Ben Johnson, world record holder from Canada, and Carl Lewis of the U.S., winner of four gold medals in the 1984 Games, renewed their fierce rivalry. Lewis broke the U.S. record with his 9.92-sec achievement but found himself outsprinted by Johnson, who was clocked in 9.79 sec for a new international record.

Johnson's world fell apart the next day. Compulsory blood testing of all medal winners revealed that he had used a banned steroid. Johnson's victory and record were declared nonvalid, and his medal was taken from him. The International Olympic Committee barred Johnson for life, and the international track federation, the IAAF, banned him from international competition for two years. Trailing athletes moved up, Lewis gaining the gold medal and Olympic record. No other track and field athlete tested positive for banned substances.

The third sprint, the 200 m, was also fast. Joe DeLoach of the U.S. defeated his friend and training partner, Lewis, in 19.75 sec, equaling the second-fastest 200 m ever run and the fastest at low altitude. Not so swift was the 4 × 100-m relay, which was considered a certain victory for the U.S. team. In a qualifying heat, however, the U.S. runners passed the baton out of the allowed zone and were disqualified. The Soviet Union then won its first sprint relay in the Olympics in 38.19 sec.

Lewis was the most prolific medal winner in men's competition, with two gold medals and a silver. He became the first man to repeat as 100-m champion and also the first to repeat in the long jump, which he won at 8.72 m (28 ft 7½ in). He was followed in the long jump by Mike Powell and Larry Myricks, both of the U.S.

Another repeater and the second man to become so was Roger Kingdom, who won the 110-m high hurdles in 12.98 sec, just 0.05 sec off the world mark. The 400-m hurdles also was won by the U.S. but not by the expected two-time winner Edwin Moses. He finished third behind teammate Andre Phillips (47.19 sec) and the surprise silver medalist, Amadou Ba of Senegal.

All but one of the 17 men's track and field medals won by the U.S. was earned on the track. The lone exception was shot-putter Randy Barnes, who finished second when the final throw of the competition put Timmermann on the top step of the victory stand. Timmermann's mark was 22.47 m (73 ft 8¾ in).

The Soviet Union finished second behind the U.S. in the medal count in men's competition with five firsts, four seconds, and four thirds. The Soviet hammer throwers, led by Sergey Litvinov (84.80 m [278 ft 2 in]), swept all three medals. Another sweep for the Soviets came in the pole vault, with world record holder Bubka leading the way with 5.90 m (19 ft 4¼ in).

Third in the men's medals division was East Germany, which scored three golds, three silvers, and two bronzes. Timmermann was joined as a gold-medal winner by Christian Schenk, who won the decathlon over teammate Torsten Voss with 8,488 points, and by discus thrower Jurgen Schult, 68.82 m (225 ft 9 in). Schenk helped push two-time decathlon winner Daley Thompson of Great Britain into fourth place.

Perhaps the biggest surprise was the unexpected strength of Kenya, which won seven medals. They all were gained in the middle- and long-distance runs, with wins at 800 m, 1,500 m, 3,000-m steeplechase, and 5,000 m. Kenya's strongest event was the steeplechase, where Julius Kariuki and Peter Koech finished first and second. Kariuki barely missed the world record, achieving a time of 8 min 5.51 sec, compared with the existing record of 8 min 5.4 sec. Paul Ereng won the 800 m in a fast 1 min 43.45 sec. The

Table I. World 1988 Outdoor Records—Men

Event	Competitor and country	Performance
400 m	Butch Reynolds (U.S.)	43.29 sec
4 × 400-m relay	United States	2 min 55.16 sec
High jump	Carlo Thranhardt (West Germany)	2.42 m (7 ft 11¼ in)
	Javier Sotomayor (Cuba)	2.43 m (7 ft 11½ in)
Pole vault	Sergey Bubka (U.S.S.R.)	6.05 m (19 ft 10¼ in)
	Sergey Bubka (U.S.S.R.)	6.06 m (19 ft 10½ in)
Shot put	Ulf Timmermann (East Germany)	23.06 m (75 ft 8 in)

Table II. World 1988 Outdoor Records—Women

Event	Competitor and country	Performance
100-m	Florence Griffith Joyner (U.S.)	10.49 sec
200 m	Florence Griffith Joyner (U.S.)	21.56 sec
	Florence Griffith Joyner (U.S.)	21.34 sec
5,000-m walk	Kerry Saxby (Australia)	20 min 45.32 sec
10,000-m walk	Elena Nikolayeva (U.S.S.R.)	43 min 36.5 sec
4 × 400-m relay	U.S.S.R.	3 min 15.18 sec
100-m hurdles	Yordanka Donkova (Bulg.)	12.21 sec
Long jump	Galina Chistyakova (U.S.S.R.)	7.52 m (24 ft 8½ in)
Discus throw	Gabriele Reinsch (East Germany)	76.80 m (252 ft)
Heptathlon	Jackie Joyner-Kersee (U.S.)	7,215 points
	Jackie Joyner-Kersee (U.S.)	7,291 points
Javelin throw	Petra Felke (East Germany)	80 m (262 ft 5 in)

1,500 went to Peter Rono in 3 min 35.96 sec, while John Ngugi took the 5,000 m in 13 min 11.70 sec. Kenyans also finished second in the marathon and third in the 10,000 m. The latter event was won by another African, Brahim Boutayeb of Morocco, with a time of 27 min 21.46 sec.

Women's International Competition. In pre-Olympic activities world records were set at distances ranging from 100 m to the marathon. No official records are kept for the marathon because the courses vary so greatly, but Lisa Martin of Australia turned in the fastest time ever for a loop course, running 2 hr 23 min 51 sec. She went on to finish a close second in the Olympic race to Rosa Mota of Portugal.

The most excitement of the year, however, was produced by two U.S. sisters-in-law, Jackie Joyner-Kersee and Florence Griffith Joyner. Each accounted for a world record in the Olympics and one in the U.S. Olympic trials. They also accounted for six Olympic medals, five of gold and one silver. In the trials Joyner-Kersee raised her own world heptathlon record to 7,215 points. It was her third global record, and she remained the only woman to have earned 7,000 or more points in the event. She also made the team in the long jump, where she once was record holder. Meanwhile, Griffith Joyner (*see* BIOGRAPHIES), who was married to Jackie's brother and 1984 Olympic triple jumper Al, was astounding the world with her 100-m sprinting. At the trials she lowered the record of 10.76 sec by an unparalleled 0.27 sec. The improvement was so great that fans and officials were inclined to doubt the mark, but careful consideration of all factors led to official approval. Griffith Joyner also set a U.S. record of 21.77 sec in the 200 m.

Moving on to Seoul, the two women were even better. Once again Joyner-Kersee raised the heptathlon mark, this time to 7,291 points. Then she jumped 7.40 m (24 ft 3½ in) in the long jump. In her wake were world record holder Galina Chistyakova of the Soviet Union, third, and former world champion Heike Drechsler of East Germany, second. Griffith Joyner was even more active. She opened by winning the 100 m in a wind-aided 10.54 sec. Then once again she mastered a world record so thoroughly that it was hard to believe. In the semifinal she lowered the 21.71-sec 200-m record to 21.56 and about two hours later knocked down the new mark, clocking 21.34 sec. Her two sprint medals became four when she ran on the victorious 4 × 100-m relay team and on the second-place 4 × 400-m relay.

In earlier competition Chistyakova accounted for two long-jump marks. She equaled the 7.45 m (24 ft 5½ in) mark shared by Joyner-Kersee and Drechsler and went on to take sole possession of the record with a leap of 7.52 m (24 ft 8¼ in). Yordanka Donkova of Bulgaria lowered the 100-m hurdle mark to 12.21 sec, and Gabriele Reinsch of East Germany threw the discus an amazing 76.80 m (252 ft). The last world record before the Olympics was set by Petra Felke of East Germany, who added to her own javelin mark for the third time, reaching 80 m (262 ft 5 in). The 5,000-m-walk standard was lowered by Kerry Saxby of Australia to 20 min 45.32 sec. The Soviet Union's 4 × 400-m relay team wrapped up the year's record-setting activities by winning the Olympics with a world mark of 3 min 15.18 sec.

Indoor Competition. Only three men's world indoor records were established, as most athletes decided not to reach peak conditioning until the Olympic Games. The most significant was Thranhardt's indoor and outdoor best in the high jump. Thomas Schonlebe of East Germany reduced the 400-m best to 45.05 sec, and Rob Druppers of The Netherlands ran 1,000 m in 2 min 16.62 sec.

Florence Griffith Joyner exults in her victory in the 100-metre track finals in Seoul, South Korea. Griffith Joyner had set a new world record of 10:49 for the distance during the Olympic trials.
RICH CLARKSON/TIME MAGAZINE

Women athletes produced ten world and three U.S. bests. Christine Wachtel of East Germany improved the 800-m mark twice, her best being 1 min 56.40 sec, while Doina Melinte of Romania covered the mile in 4 min 18.86 sec. The busiest athletes were the 50-m hurdlers. Gloria Siebert and Cornelia Oschkenat, both of East Germany, took turns reducing the record, the latter ending up with the new mark of 6.58 sec. Stefka Kostadinova of Bulgaria upped the high-jump best to 2.06 (6 ft 9 in), while Drechsler long jumped 7.37 m (24 ft 2¼ in). Brenda Webb of the United States bettered the record for the seldom-run 5,000 m, timed in 15 min 25.02 sec.

Marathon Running and Cross Country. The premier prize of the year went to Gelindo Bordin of Italy, the surprise winner of the marathon at the Olympic Games in Seoul, South Korea. He ran the course in 2 hr 10 min 32 sec. The women's Olympic race was won by Mota in 2 hr 25 min 40 sec. She already had won the Boston marathon in 2 hr 24 min 30 sec. The men's victor in Boston was Ibrahim Hussein of Kenya in 2 hr 8 min 43 sec. Winners at Chicago were Alejandro Cruz of Mexico, 2 hr 8 min 57 sec, and Lisa Weidenbach of the U.S., 2 hr 29 min 17 sec. Champions in New York City were Steve Jones of Wales with a time of 2 hr 8 min 20 sec and Grete Waitz of Norway, for the ninth time, in 2 hr 28 min 7 sec.

Led by Ngugi, Kenya dominated the annual world cross country title meet, with eight among the first nine finishers. It was the third straight win for Ngugi. Kenya also was unbeatable in the junior men's run, Wilfred Kirochi taking his second title as Kenya had six of the first seven finishers. Norway's Ingrid Christiansen captured the women's crown. (BERT NELSON)

VOLLEYBALL

The Olympic Games in Seoul, South Korea, were the focal point of 1988 for international volleyball competition. The United States men successfully defended their 1984 gold medal with a victory in the championship match over the Soviet Union 3–1 (13–15, 15–10, 15–4, 15–8). Argentina took home its first Olympic volleyball medal with a 3–2 victory over Brazil (15–10, 15–17, 15–8, 12–15, 15–9) for third place.

In women's Olympic competition the Soviet Union won the gold medal with a 3–2 championship match victory over Peru (10–15, 12–15, 15–13, 15–7, 17–15). Defending champion China gained the third-place bronze medal with a 3–0 victory over Japan (15–13, 15–6, 15–6).

Both the men's and women's competitions were probably affected to some degree by Cuba's withdrawal from the Games. The Cuban women probably would have been favoured for the gold medal if they had participated. They finished second to the Chinese at the 1986 world championships and during 1987 and early 1988 had gained some impressive victories over all of the Olympic contestants, including the Chinese. The Cuban men had posted impressive results in all major competitions during the past ten years and would have been expected to challenge strongly for a medal in Seoul.

The results of the men's Olympic competition probably reflected accurately the comparative strengths of the teams involved. The relative decline of the Asian and Eastern European nations, with the exception of the Soviet Union and occasionally Bulgaria, the continued dominance of the U.S., the increasing strength in South America, and the great advancement by the countries of Western Europe seemed to be an accurate portrayal of men's volleyball strength. On the other hand, the results in the women's Olympic tournament were a bit confusing when compared with other results during the previous four to eight years. The Olympic scores suggested a rather close balance among all of the participating teams, with no nation clearly superior to the others. For example, in women's preliminary play the Japanese defeated the Soviets 3–2, South Korea beat East Germany 3–1, the U.S. defeated Brazil 3–2, and Peru barely escaped the U.S. 3–2. By contrast, in semifinal play Peru narrowly defeated Japan 3–2, and Brazil slipped past South Korea by the same score.

(ALBERT M. MONACO, JR.)

WEIGHT LIFTING

The Soviet Union dominated the Olympic weight-lifting competition by winning six gold medals and a pair of silvers in the ten weight classes. The Bulgarian team, previously ranked first in the world, went home with two gold medals, two disqualified champions, a silver medal, and a bronze medal in the first five classes to be contested. The Bulgarian National Olympic Committee sent its team home after two of its lifters were disqualified for the use of the drug furosemide. Late in the competition Hungary also withdrew after one of its lifters had been disqualified for testing positive. Naim Suleymanoglu (*see* BIOGRAPHIES) of Turkey, repatriated from Bulgaria upon the payment of $1 million to the Bulgarian government two years earlier, set three world records, including total lift, as he won the 60-kg (132-lb) title.

The lifters vigorously attacked world and Olympic records. World records for total lifts were set in two other classes. Sevdalin Marinov, Bulgaria's two-time world champion, won the 52-kg (114.4-lb) class with a total lift of 270 kg (594 lb). The third world record was claimed by

Naim Suleymanoglu of Turkey is elated after setting a new world record during the Olympics weight-lifting competition.
AFP PHOTO

the Soviet Union's Yury Zakharevich with a total lift of 455 kg (1,001 lb) in the 110-kg (242-lb) class. Soviet super-heavyweight Aleksandr Kurlovich unofficially became the "world's strongest man" after his Olympic-record total lift of 462.5 kg (1,017.5 lb) in the over 110-kg (over 242-lb) class.

(CHARLES ROBERT PAUL, JR.)

WRESTLING

Despite a strong showing in freestyle wrestling by the United States, the battle for medals at the Olympic Games in September in Seoul, South Korea, left the Soviet dynasty unchallenged. Placing nine of their ten wrestlers, the Soviets earned four gold, three silver, and two bronze medals to claim the unofficial world championship. (No team titles are awarded at the Olympic Games in wrestling.) The U.S. placed second with two gold, one silver, and two bronze medals. South Korea finished third with one gold, one silver, and two bronze medals.

In Greco-Roman wrestling the Soviet Union continued its domination, winning four gold medals, one silver medal, and one bronze medal and thus far outdistancing second-place Bulgaria, which finished with one gold medal, three silver medals, and one bronze medal. Third-place South Korea received one gold medal, one silver medal, and three bronze medals.

At the National Collegiate Athletic Association tournament March 17–19 in Ames, Iowa, Arizona State University surprised the field by winning the championship with 93 points—the first university from the western United States to hold this distinction. The University of Iowa finished second with 85.5 points, and Iowa State University, the host school and defending champion, placed third with 83.75 points.

(MARVIN G. HESS)

Olympic Games Wrestling Champions, 1988		
Weight class	Freestyle	Greco-Roman
48 kg (105.5 lb)	T. Kobayashi (Japan)	V. Maenza (Italy)
52 kg (114.5 lb)	M. Sato (Japan)	J. Ronningen (Norway)
57 kg (125.5 lb)	S. Beloglazov (U.S.S.R.)	A. Sike (Hung.)
62 kg (136.5 lb)	J. Smith (U.S.)	K. Madzhidov (U.S.S.R.)
68 kg (149.5 lb)	A. Fadzaev (U.S.S.R.)	L. Dzhulfalakyan (U.S.S.R.)
74 kg (163 lb)	K. Monday (U.S.)	Kim Young Nam (S.Korea)
82 kg (180.5 lb)	Han Myeng Woo (S.Korea)	M. Mamiashvili (U.S.S.R.)
90 kg (198 lb)	M. Khadartsev (U.S.S.R.)	A. Komchev (Bulg.)
100 kg (220 lb)	V. Puscasu (Rom.)	A. Wronski (Poland)
130 kg (286 lb)	D. Gobedzhishvili (U.S.S.R.)	A. Karelin (U.S.S.R.)

Sporting Record

ARCHERY

FITA Outdoor World Target Archery Championships

year	men's individual		men's team		women's individual		women's team	
	winner	points	winner	points	winner	points	winner	points
1979	D. Pace (U.S.)	2,474	United States	7,409	Kim Jin Ho (S.Kor.)	2,507	South Korea	7,341
1981	K. Laasonen (Fin.)	2,541	United States	7,547	N. Butuzova (U.S.S.R.)	2,514	U.S.S.R.	7,455
1983	R. McKinney (U.S.)	2,617	United States	7,812	Kim Jin Ho (S.Kor.)	2,616	South Korea	7,704
1985	R. McKinney (U.S.)	2,601	South Korea	7,660	I. Soldatova (U.S.S.R.)	2,595	U.S.S.R.	7,721
1987	V. Esheyev (U.S.S.R.)	329	West Germany	891	Ma Xiangjun (China)	330	U.S.S.R.	884

ATHLETICS

World Cup Championship—men

	100 metre	200 metre	400 metre	800 metre	1,500 metre
1979	J. Sanford (U.S.)	S. Leonard (Americas)	K. Hassan (Africa)	J. Maina (Africa)	T. Wessinghage (Europe)
1981	A. Wells (Europe)	M. Lattany (U.S.)	C. Wiley (U.S.)	S. Coe (Europe)	S. Ovett (Europe)
1985	B. Johnson (Americas)	R. Caetano da Silva (Americas)	M. Franks (U.S.)	S. Koskei (Africa)	O. Khalifa (Africa)

	5,000 metre	10,000 metre	Steeplechase	110-m hurdles	400-m hurdles
1979	M. Yifter (Africa)	M. Yifter (Africa)	K. Rono (Africa)	R. Nehemiah (U.S.)	E. Moses (U.S.)
1981	E. Coghlan (Europe)	W. Schildhauer (E.Ger.)	B. Maminski (Europe)	G. Foster (U.S.)	E. Moses (U.S.)
1985	D. Padilla (U.S.)	W. Bulti (Africa)	J. Kariuki (Africa)	T. Campbell (U.S.)	A. Phillips (U.S.)

	4 × 100 relays	4 × 400 relays	Triple jump	High jump	Pole vault
1979	Americas	United States	J. de Oliveira (Americas)	F. Jacobs (U.S.)	M. Tully (U.S.)
1981	Europe	United States	J. de Oliveira (Americas)	T. Peacock (U.S.)	K. Volkov (U.S.S.R.)
1985	United States	United States	W. Banks (U.S.)	P. Sjoberg (Europe)	S. Bubka (U.S.S.R.)

	Long jump	Shot put	Discus throw	Hammer throw	Javelin throw
1979	L. Myricks (U.S.)	U. Beyer (E.Ger.)	W. Schmidt (E.Ger.)	S. Litvinov (U.S.S.R.)	W. Hanisch (W.Ger.)
1981	C. Lewis (U.S.)	U. Beyer (E.Ger.)	A. Lemme (E.Ger.)	Yu. Sedykh (U.S.S.R.)	D. Kula (U.S.S.R.)
1985	M. Conley (U.S.)	U. Timmerman (E.Ger.)	G. Kolnootchenko (U.S.S.R.)	Yu. Tamm (U.S.S.R.)	U. Hohn (E.Ger.)

	Team		Marathon		
1979	United States		1985 A. Salah (Djibouti)		
1981	Europe		1987 A. Salah (Djibouti)		
1985	United States				

World Cup Championship—women

	100 metre	200 metre	400 metre	800 metre	1,500 metre
1979	E. Ashford (U.S.)	E. Ashford (U.S.)	M. Koch (E.Ger.)	N. Shtereva (Europe)	C. Wartenburg (E.Ger.)
1981	E. Ashford (U.S.)	E. Ashford (U.S.)	J. Kratochvílová (Europe)	L. Veselkova (U.S.S.R.)	T. Sorokina (U.S.S.R.)
1985	M. Göhr (E.Ger.)	M. Koch (E.Ger.)	M. Koch (E.Ger.)	C. Wachtel (E.Ger.)	H. Korner (E.Ger.)

	3,000 metre	10,000 metre	100-m hurdles	400-m hurdles	4 × 100 relays
1979	S. Ulmasova (U.S.S.R.)	—	G. Rabsztyn (Europe)	B. Klepp (E.Ger.)	Europe Select
1981	A. Zauber (E.Ger.)		T. Anisimova (U.S.S.R.)	E. Neumann (E.Ger.)	East Germany
1985	U. Bruns (E.Ger.)	A. Cunha (Europe)	C. Oschkenat (E.Ger.)	S. Busch (E.Ger.)	East Germany

	4 × 400 relays	High jump	Long jump	Shot put	Discus throw
1979	East Germany	D. Brill (Americas)	A. Stukane (U.S.S.R.)	I. Slupianek (E.Ger.)	E. Jahl (E.Ger.)
1981	East Germany	U. Meyfarth (Europe)	S. Ulbricht (E.Ger.)	I. Slupianek (E.Ger.)	E. Jahl (E.Ger.)
1985	East Germany	S. Kostadinova (U.S.S.R.)	H. Daute Drechsler (E.Ger.)	N. Lisovskaya (U.S.S.R.)	M. Optiz (E.Ger.)

	Javelin throw	Team	Marathon		
1979	R. Fuchs (E.Ger.)	East Germany	1985 K. Dörre (E.Ger.)		
1981	A. Todorova (Europe)	East Germany	1987 Z. Ivanova (U.S.S.R.)		
1985	O. Gavrilova (U.S.S.R.)	East Germany			

East Germany (no. 521): 4 × 400-m relay World Cup
championship—women (1985)

MARK SHEARMAN

For records of previous years, *see* the entry SPORTING RECORD in the Micropædia.

World Track-and-Field Championships—men

event	1983	1987
100 m	C. Lewis (U.S.)	B. Johnson (Can.)
200 m	C. Smith (U.S.)	C. Smith (U.S.)
400 m	B. Cameron (Jam.)	T. Schoenlebe (E.Ger.)
800 m	W. Wülbeck (W.Ger.)	B. Konchellah (Kenya)
1,500 m	S. Cram (U.K.)	A. Bile (Som.)
5,000 m	E. Coghlan (Ire.)	S. Aouita (Mor.)
10,000 m	A. Cova (Italy)	P. Kipkoech (Kenya)
steeplechase	P. Ilg (W.Ger.)	F. Panetta (Italy)
110-m hurdles	G. Foster (U.S.)	G. Foster (U.S.)
400-m hurdles	E. Moses (U.S.)	E. Moses (U.S.)
marathon	R. de Castella (Australia)	D. Wakihuru (Kenya)
20-km walk	E. Canto (Mex.)	M. Damilano (Italy)
50-km walk	R. Weigel (E.Ger.)	H. Gauder (E.Ger.)
4 × 100 m relay	United States (E. King, W. Gault, C. Smith, C. Lewis)	United States (L. McRae, L. McNeil, H. Glance, C. Lewis)
4 × 400 m relay	U.S.S.R. (S. Lovachev, A. Troschilo, N. Chernetsky, V. Markin)	United States (D. Everett, R. Haley, A. McKay, H. Reynolds)
high jump	G. Avdeyenko (U.S.S.R.)	P. Sjöberg (Swed.)
pole vault	S. Bubka (U.S.S.R.)	S. Bubka (U.S.S.R.)
long jump	C. Lewis (U.S.)	C. Lewis (U.S.)
triple jump	Z. Hoffman (Pol.)	C. Markov (Bulg.)
shot put	E. Sarul (Pol.)	W. Guenther (Switz.)
discus throw	I. Bugár (Czech.)	J. Schult (E.Ger.)
hammer throw	S. Litvinov (U.S.S.R.)	S. Litvinov (U.S.S.R.)
javelin throw	D. Michel (E.Ger.)	S. Raty (Fin.)
decathlon	D. Thompson (U.K.)	T. Voss (E.Ger.)

United States: 4 × 100-m relay world track and field championships—men (1987)

GRAY MORTIMORE—ALLSPORT USA

World Track-and-Field Championships—women

event	1983	1987
100 m	M. Göhr (E.Ger.)	S. Gladisch (E.Ger.)
200 m	M. Koch (E.Ger.)	S. Gladisch (E.Ger.)
400 m	J. Kratochvílová (Czech.)	O. Bryzgina (U.S.S.R.)
800 m	J. Kratochvílová (Czech.)	S. Wodars (E.Ger.)
1,500 m	M. Decker (U.S.)	T. Samolenko (U.S.S.R.)
3,000 m	M. Decker (U.S.)	T. Samolenko (U.S.S.R.)
10,000 m*		I. Kristiansen (Nor.)
100-m hurdles	B. Jahn (E.Ger.)	G. Zagorcheva (Bulg.)
400-m hurdles	Ye. Fesenko (U.S.S.R.)	S. Busch (E.Ger.)
marathon	G. Waitz (Nor.)	R. Mota (Port.)
10-km walk*		I. Strakhova (U.S.S.R.)
4 × 100 m relay	East Germany (S. Gladisch, M. Koch, M. Göhr, I. Auerswald)	United States (A. Brown, D. Williams, F. Griffith, P. Marshall)
4 × 400 m relay	East Germany (K. Walther, D. Rubsam, M. Koch, S. Busch)	East Germany (D. Neubauer, K. Emmelmann, P. Mueller, S. Busch)
high jump	T. Bykova (U.S.S.R.)	S. Kostadinova (Bulg.)
long jump	H. Daute (E.Ger.)	J. Joyner-Kersee (U.S.)
shot put	H. Fibingerová (Czech.)	N. Lisovskaya (U.S.S.R.)
discus throw	M. Opitz (E.Ger.)	M. Hellmann (E.Ger.)
javelin throw	T. Lillak (Fin.)	F. Whitbread (U.K.)
heptathlon	R. Neubert (E.Ger.)	J. Joyner-Kersee (U.S.)

*Event added in 1987.

Boston Marathon

year	men	h:min:s	women	h:min:s
1984	G. Smith (Eng.)	2:10:34	L. Moller (N.Z.)	2:29:28
1985	G. Smith (Eng.)	2:14:05	L. Larsen (U.S.)	2:34:06
1986	R. de Castella (Australia)	2:07:51	I. Kristiansen (Nor.)	2:24:55
1987	T. Seko (Japan)	2:11:50	R. Mota (Port.)	2:25:21
1988	I. Hussein (Kenya)	2:08:43	R. Mota (Port.)	2:24:30

New York Marathon

year	men	h:min:s	women	h:min:s
1984	O. Pizzolato (U.S.)	2:14:53	G. Waitz (Nor.)	2:29:30
1985	O. Pizzolato (U.S.)	2:11:34	G. Waitz (Nor.)	2:28:34
1986	G. Poli (Italy)	2:11:06	G. Waitz (Nor.)	2:28:06
1987	I. Hussein (Kenya)	2:11:01	P. Welch (U.K.)	2:30:17
1988	S. Jones (Wales)	2:08:20	G. Waitz (Nor.)	2:28:07

America's Marathon/Chicago

year	men	h:min:s	women	h:min:s
1984	S. Jones (U.K.)	2:08:05	R. Mota (Port.)	2:26:01
1985	S. Jones (U.K.)	2:07:13	J. Benoit Samuelson (U.S.)	2:21:21
1986	T. Seko (Japan)	2:08:27	I. Kristiansen (Nor.)	2:27:08
1987	not held			
1988	A. Cruz (Mexico)	2:08:57	L. Weidenbach (U.S.)	2:29:17

World Cross-Country Championship—men (12,000 m)

year	individual	team
1983	B. Debele (Eth.)	Ethiopia
1984	C. Lopes (Port.)	Ethiopia
1985	C. Lopes (Port.)	Ethiopia
1986	J. Ngugi (Kenya)	Kenya
1987	J. Ngugi (Kenya)	Kenya
1988	J. Ngugi (Kenya)	Kenya

World Cross-Country Championship—women (5,000 m)

year	individual	team
1983	G. Waitz (Nor.)	United States
1984	M. Puica (Rom.)	United States
1985	Z. Budd (U.K.)	United States
1986	Z. Budd (U.K.)	England
1987	A. Sergent (Fr.)	United States
1988	I. Christiansen (Nor.)	

R. Mota: Boston Marathon (1988)

FOCUS ON SPORTS

AUTOMOBILE RACING

United States Auto Club Champions	
year	driver
1982/83	T. Sneva
1983/84	R. Mears
1984/85	D. Sullivan
1985/86	B. Rahal
1986/87	A. Unser

Indianapolis 500		
year	winner	avg. speed in mph
1984	R. Mears	163.612
1985	D. Sullivan	152.982
1986	B. Rahal	170.722
1987	A. Unser	162.175
1988	R. Mears	144.809

International Cup for Formula One Manufacturers			
year	car	year	car
1983	Ferrari	1986	Williams/Honda
1984	McLaren/Porsche-TAG	1987	Williams/Honda
1985	McLaren/Ferrari	1988	McLaren/Honda

World Championship of Drivers		
year	winner	car
1984	N. Lauda (Austria)	McLaren/Porsche-TAG
1985	A. Prost (Fr.)	McLaren/Porsche-TAG
1986	A. Prost (Fr.)	McLaren/Porsche-TAG
1987	N. Piquet (Braz.)	Williams/Honda
1988	A. Senna (Braz.)	McLaren/Honda

Le Mans 24-hour Grand Prix d'Endurance		
year	car	drivers
1984	Porsche	H. Pescarolo, K. Ludwig
1985	Porsche	K. Ludwig, J. Winter, P. Barilla
1986	Porsche	D. Bell, H. Stuck, A. Holbert
1987	Porsche	H. Stuck, D. Bell, A. Holbert
1988	Jaguar	J. Lammers, J. Dumfries, A. Wallace

Monte-Carlo Rally		
year	car	driver, codriver
1984	Audi Quattro	Röhrl, Geistdorfer
1985	Peugeot 205 Turbo	Vatanen, Harryman
1986	Lancia Martini Delta	Toivonen, Cresto
1987	Lancia Delta HF	Biasion, Siviero
1988	Lancia Delta 4WD	

National Association for Stock Car Auto Racing (NASCAR) Winston Cup Champions			
year	winner	year	winner
1983	B. Allison	1986	D. Earnhardt
1984	T. Labonte	1987	D. Earnhardt
1985	D. Waltrip	1988	B. Elliott

R. Mears: Indianapolis 500 (1988)
FOCUS ON SPORTS

Jaguar—J. Lammers, J. Dumfries, A. Wallace: Le Mans 24-hour race (1988)
BERNARD ASSET—ALLSPORT

BADMINTON

World Badminton Championships			
year	men's singles	women's singles	men's doubles	women's doubles
1977	F. Delfs (Den.)	L. Köppen (Den.)	T. Tjun, J. Wahjudi (Indon.)	E. Toganu, E. Ueno (Japan)
1980	R. Hartono (Indon.)	W. Verawaty (Indon.)	A. Chandra, C. Hadinata (Indon.)	N. Perry, J. Webster (U.K.)
1983	I. Sugiarto (Indon.)	Li Lingwei (China)	S. Fladberg, J. Helledie (Den.)	Lin Ying, Wu Dixi (China)
1985	Han Jian (China)	Han Aiping (China)	Park Joo Bong, Kim Moon Soo (S.Kor.)	Han Aiping, Li Lingwei (China)
1987	Yang Yang (China)	Han Aiping (China)	Li Yongbo, Tian Bingyi (China)	Lin Ying, Guan Weizhen (China)

All-England Championships—singles		
year	men	women
1984	M. Frost (Den.)	Li Lingwei (China)
1985	Zhao Jianhua (China)	Han Aiping (China)
1986	M. Frost (Den.)	Kim Yun Ja (S.Kor.)
1987	M. Frost (Den.)	K. Larsen (Den.)
1988	I. Frederiksen (Den.)	Gu Jiaming (China)

Uber Cup (women)		
year	winner	runner-up
1977–78	Japan	Indonesia
1980–81	Japan	Indonesia
1983–84	China	England
1985–86	China	Indonesia
1987–88	China	S.Korea

Thomas Cup (men)		
year	winner	runner-up
1978–79	Indonesia	Denmark
1981–82	China	Indonesia
1983–84	Indonesia	China
1985–86	China	Indonesia
1987–88	China	Malaysia

BASEBALL

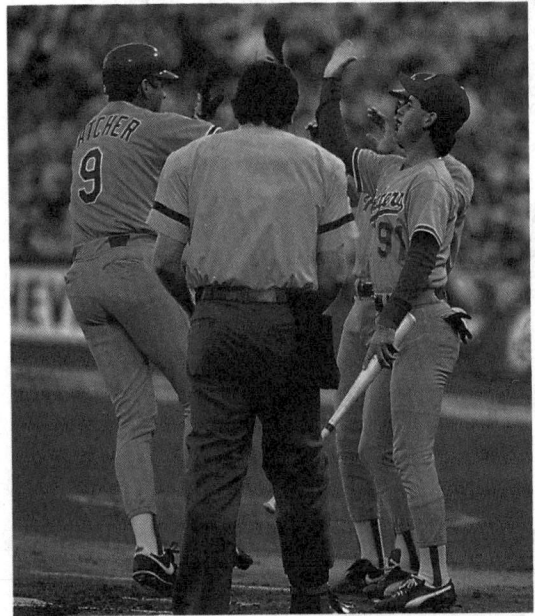

Los Angeles Dodgers: World Series (1988)
FOCUS ON SPORTS

Baseball Hall of Fame

year elected	members
1984	R. Ferrell, Pee Wee Reese, H. Killebrew, L. Aparicio, D. Drysdale
1985	Hoyt Wilhelm, Enos Slaughter, Lou Brock, Joseph Floyd (Arky) Vaughan
1986	Willie McCovey, Bobby Doerr, Ernie Lombardi
1987	Billy Williams, Jim (Catfish) Hunter, Ray Dandridge
1988	Willie Stargell

World Series*

year	winning team	losing team	results
1984	Detroit Tigers (AL)	San Diego Padres (NL)	4–1
1985	Kansas City Royals (AL)	St. Louis Cardinals (NL)	4–3
1986	New York Mets (NL)	Boston Red Sox (AL)	4–3
1987	Minnesota Twins (AL)	St. Louis Cardinals (NL)	4–3
1988	Los Angeles Dodgers (NL)	Oakland Athletics (AL)	4–1

*AL—American League; NL—National League.

Japan Series*

year	winning team	losing team	results
1984	Hiroshima Tōyō Carp (CL)	Hankyū Braves (PL)	4–3
1985	Hanshin Tigers (CL)	Seibu Lions (PL)	4–2
1986	Seibu Lions (PL)	Hiroshima Tōyō Carp (CL)	4–3
1987	Seibu Lions (PL)	Yomiuri Giants (CL)	4–2
1988	Seibu Lions (PL)	Chunichi Dragons (CL)	4–1

*CL—Central League; PL—Pacific League.

BASKETBALL

National Basketball Association (NBA) Championship

season	winner	runner-up	results
1983–84	Boston Celtics	Los Angeles Lakers	4–3
1984–85	Los Angeles Lakers	Boston Celtics	4–2
1985–86	Boston Celtics	Houston Rockets	4–2
1986–87	Los Angeles Lakers	Boston Celtics	4–2
1987–88	Los Angeles Lakers	Detroit Pistons	4–3

World Amateur Basketball Championship—men

year	winner	runner-up
1980	Yugoslavia	Italy
1982	U.S.S.R.	United States
1984	United States	Spain
1986	United States	U.S.S.R.
1988	U.S.S.R.	Yugoslavia

World Amateur Basketball Championship—women

year	winner	runner-up
1980	U.S.S.R.	Bulgaria
1983	U.S.S.R.	United States
1984	United States	South Korea
1986	United States	U.S.S.R.
1988	United States	Yugoslavia

Division I National Collegiate Athletic Association (NCAA) Championship—men

year	winner	runner-up	score
1984	Georgetown	Houston	84–75
1985	Villanova	Georgetown	66–64
1986	Louisville	Duke	72–69
1987	Indiana	Syracuse	74–73
1988	Kansas	Oklahoma	83–79

Division I National Collegiate Athletic Association (NCAA) Championship—women

year	winner	runner-up	score
1984	Southern California	Tennessee	72–61
1985	Old Dominion	Georgia	70–65
1986	Texas	Southern California	97–81
1987	Tennessee	Louisiana Tech	67–44
1988	Louisiana Tech	Auburn	56–54

National Invitation Tournament (NIT) Championship

year	winner	runner-up	score
1984	Michigan	Notre Dame	83–63
1985	UCLA	Indiana	65–62
1986	Ohio State	Wyoming	73–63
1987	Southern Mississippi	LaSalle	84–80
1988	Connecticut	Ohio St.	72–67

Kansas: NCAA championship (1988)
FOCUS ON SPORTS

BILLIARDS

World Amateur Three-Cushion Championship

year	winner
1984	N. Kobayashi (Japan)
1985	R. Ceulemans (Belg.)
1986	A. Rico (Spain)
1987	T. Blomdahl (Swed.)
1988	T. Blomdahl (Swed.)

World Professional (English) Billiards Champions

year	winner
1983	R. Williams
1984	M. Wildman
1985	R. Edmonds
1986	R. Foldvari
1987	N. Dagley

BOWLING

ABC Bowling Championships—Regular Division

year	singles	score	all-events	score
1985	G. Harbison	774	B. Asher	2,033
1986	J. Mackey	774	E. Marzka	2,116
1987	T. Taylor	749	R. Shafer	2,044
1988	S. Hutkowski	774	R. Steelsmith	2,053

WIBC Bowling Championship—Open Division

year	singles	score	all-events	score
1984	F. Gate	712	S. Saitō (Japan)	1,921
1985	P. Schwarzel	694	A. Rzepecki Sill	1,900
1986	D. Stewart	698	Romeo, Lewis (tie)	1,877
1987	R. Jonak	728	L. Barrette	1,972
1988	M. Meyer-Welty	690	L. Wagner	1,988

FIQ World Bowling Championship—men

year	singles	pairs	triples	fives	eights
1975	M. Stoudt (U.S.)	United Kingdom		Finland	West Germany
1979*	G. Bugden (U.K.)	Australia	Malaysia	Australia	
1983	T. Cariello (U.S.)	Australia	Sweden	Finland	
1987	P. Rolland (Fr.)	Sweden	United States	Sweden	

*In 1979 eights were discontinued and triples were introduced.

Professional Bowlers Association (PBA) Firestone Tournament of Champions

year	champion	runner-up
1984	M. Durbin	M. Aulby
1985	M. Williams	B. Handley
1986	M. Holman	M. Baker
1987	P. Weber	J. Murtishaw
1988	M. Williams	T. Westlake

FIQ World Bowling Championship—women

year	singles	pairs	triples	fours	fives
1975	A. Haefker (W.Ger.)	Sweden		Japan	Japan
1979*	L. de la Rosa (Phil.)	Philippines	United States		United States
1983	L. Sulkanen (Swed.)	Denmark	West Germany		Sweden
1987	E. Piccini (Mex.)	United States	United States		United States

*In 1979 fours were discontinued and triples were introduced.

BOWLS

World Lawn Bowls Championships

year	singles	pairs	triples	fours	team
1972	M. Evans (Wales)	Hong Kong	United States	England	Scotland
1976	D. Watson (S.Af.)	South Africa	South Africa	South Africa	South Africa
1980	D. Bryant (Eng.)	Australia	England	Hong Kong	—
1984	P. Bellis (N.Z.)	United States	Ireland	England	Scotland
1988	D. Bryant (Eng.)	New Zealand	New Zealand	Ireland	England

BOXING

World heavyweight champions—no weight limit

WBA	WBC
Greg Page (U.S.; 12/1/84)	Tim Witherspoon (U.S.; 3/9/84)
Tony Tubbs (U.S.; 4/29/85)	Pinklon Thomas (U.S.; 8/31/84)
Tim Witherspoon (U.S.; 1/17/86)	Trevor Berbick (Can.; 3/22/86)
James Smith (U.S.; 12/12/86)	Mike Tyson (U.S.; 11/22/86)
Mike Tyson (U.S.; 3/7/87)	

M. Tyson (left): WBA and WBC heavyweight champion (1988)
FOCUS ON SPORTS

World cruiserweight champions—top weight 195 pounds

WBA	WBC
Ossie Ocasio (P.R.; 2/13/82)	Alfonso Ratliff (U.S.; 6/6/85)
Piet Crous (S.Af.; 12/1/84)	Bernard Benton (U.S.; 9/21/85)
Dwight Muhammad Qawi (U.S.; 7/27/85)	Carlos de León (P.R.; 3/22/86)
Evander Holyfield (U.S.; 7/12/86)	Evander Holyfield (U.S.; 4/9/88)
gave up title in 1988	gave up title in 1988

World junior middleweight champions—top weight 154 pounds (also called super welterweight)

WBA	WBC
Roberto Durán (Pan.; 6/16/83)	Duane Thomas (U.S.; 12/5/86)
gave up title in 1984	Lupe Aquino (Mex.; 7/12/87)
Mike McCallum (Jam.; 10/19/84) vacant	Gianfranco Rosi (Italy; 10/2/87)
Julian Jackson (Virgin Is. U.S.; 11/21/87)	Donald Curry (U.S.; 7/8/88)

World light heavyweight champions—top weight 175 pounds

WBA	WBC
Marvin Johnson (U.S.; 2/9/86)	Thomas Hearns (U.S.; 3/7/87)
Leslie Stewart (Trinidad and Tobago; 5/23/87)	gave up title in 1987
	Don Lalonde (Can.; 11/27/87)
Virgil Hill (U.S.; 9/5/87)	Sugar Ray Leonard (U.S.; 11/7/88)
	gave up title in 1988

World welterweight champions—top weight 147 pounds

WBA	WBC
Lloyd Honeyghan (U.K.; 9/27/86)	Milton McCrory (U.S.; 8/13/83)
gave up title in 1986	Donald Curry (U.S.; 12/6/85)
Mark Breland (U.S.; 2/6/87)	Lloyd Honeyghan (U.K.; 9/27/86)
Marlon Starling (U.S.; 8/22/87)	Jorge Vaca (Mex.; 10/28/87)
Tomas Molinares (Colom.; 7/29/88)	Lloyd Honeyghan (U.K.; 3/29/88)

World middleweight champions—top weight 160 pounds

WBA	WBC
Alan Minter (U.K.; 3/16/80)	Marvin Hagler (U.S.; 9/27/80)
Marvin Hagler (U.S.; 9/27/80)	Sugar Ray Leonard (U.S.; 4/6/87)
stripped of title in 1987	retired
Sumbu Kalambay (Italy; 10/23/87)	Thomas Hearns (U.S.; 10/29/87)
	Iran Barkley (U.S.; 6/6/88)

World junior welterweight champions—top weight 140 pounds (also called super lightweight)

WBA	WBC
Gene Hatcher (U.S.; 6/1/84)	René Arredondo (Mex.; 5/6/86)
Ubaldo Sacco (Arg.; 7/21/85)	Tsuyoshi Hamada (Japan; 7/24/86)
Patrizio Oliva (Italy; 3/15/86)	René Arredondo (Mex.; 7/22/87)
Juan Martin Coggi (Arg.; 7/4/87)	Roger Mayweather (U.S.; 11/12/87)

World lightweight champions—top weight 135 pounds	
WBA	**WBC**
Ray Mancini (U.S.; 5/8/82) Livingstone Bramble (Vir.Is.; 6/1/84) Edwin Rosario (P.R.; 9/26/86) Julio César Chávez 　(Mex.; 11/21/87)	José Luis Ramírez (Mex.; 11/3/84) Hector Camacho (P.R.; 8/10/85) 　stripped of title in 1987 José Luis Ramírez (Mex.; 7/19/87) Julio Cesar Chávez (Mex.; 10/29/88)

World junior lightweight champions—top weight 130 pounds (also called super featherweight)	
WBA	**WBC**
Rocky Lockridge (U.S.; 2/26/84) Wilfredo Gómez (P.R.; 5/19/85) Alfredo Layne (Pan.; 5/24/86) Brian Mitchell (S.Af.; 9/27/86)	Julio César Chavez (Mex.; 9/13/84) 　gave up title Azumah Nelson (Ghana; 2/29/88)

World featherweight champions—top weight 126 pounds	
WBA	**WBC**
Cecilio Lastra (Spain; 12/17/77) Eusebio Pedroza (Pan.; 4/15/78) Barry McGuigan (N.Ire.; 6/8/85) Steve Cruz (U.S.; 6/23/86) Antonio Esparragoza (Venez.; 3/6/87)	Juan LaPorte (P.R.; 9/15/82) Wilfredo Gómez (P.R.; 3/31/84) Azumah Nelson (Ghana; 12/8/84) 　gave up title in 1988 Jeff Fenech (Australia; 3/7/88)

World junior featherweight champions (also called super bantamweight)—top weight 122 pounds	
WBA	**WBC**
Julio Gervacio (Dom.Rep.; 11/28/87) Bernardo Pinango (Venez.; 3/5/88) Juan José Estrada (Mex.; 5/28/88)	Samart Payakaroon (Thai.; 1/18/86) Jeff Fenech (Australia; 5/8/87) 　gave up title in 1988 Daniel Zaragoza (Mex.; 2/29/88)

Sugar Ray Leonard (right): winner of the WBC light heavyweight and WBC super middleweight titles (1988)

ANTHONY NESTE/SPORTS ILLUSTRATED

World bantamweight champions—top weight 118 pounds	
WBA	**WBC**
Takuyama Muguruma (Japan; 3/29/87) Park Chang Young (S.Kor.; 5/24/87) Wilfredo Vásquez (P.R.; 10/4/87) Khaokor Galaxy (Thai.; 5/9/88) Moon Sung Kil (S.Kor.; 8/14/88)	Alberto Davila (U.S.; 9/1/83) 　stripped of title in 1985 Daniel Zaragoza (Mex.; 5/4/85) Miguel Lora (Colom.; 8/9/85) Raul Pérez (Mex.; 10/29/88)

World flyweight champions—top weight 112 pounds	
WBA	**WBC**
Juan Herrera (Mex.; 9/26/81) Santos Laciar (Arg.; 5/1/82) 　gave up title in 1985 Hilario Zapata (Pan.; 10/5/85) Fidel Bassa (Colom.; 2/13/87)	Frank Cedeno (Phil.; 9/27/83) Kobayashi Koji (Japan; 1/18/84) Gabriel Bernal (Mex.; 4/9/84) Sot Chitalada (Thai.; 10/8/84) Kim Young Kang (S.Kor.; 7/24/88)

World junior bantamweight champions (also called super flyweight)—top weight 115 pounds	
WBA	**WBC**
Gustavo Ballas (Arg.; 9/12/1981) Rafael Pedroza (Pan.; 12/5/81) Watanabe Jiro (Japan; 4/8/82) 　stripped of title in 1984 Khaosai Galaxy (Thai.; 11/21/84)	Watanabe Jiro (Japan; 7/5/84) Gilberto Román (Mex.; 3/30/86) Santos Laciar (Arg.; 5/16/87) Jesús Rojas (Colom.; 8/9/87) Gilberto Román (Mex.; 4/8/88)

World junior flyweight champions—top weight 108 pounds	
WBA	**WBC**
Tokashiki Katsuo (Japan; 12/16/81) Lupe Madera (Mex.; 7/10/83) Francisco Quiroz (Dom.Rep.; 5/19/84) Joey Olivo (U.S.; 3/29/85) Yuh Myung Woo (S.Kor.; 12/8/85)	Amado Ursua (Mex.; 2/6/82) Tomori Tadashi (Japan; 4/13/82) Hilario Zapata (Pan.; 7/20/82) Chang Jung Koo (S.Kor.; 3/26/83) German Torres (Mex.)

CHESS

World Chess Championships—men

year	winner	runner-up
1975	A. Karpov (U.S.S.R.)*	*
1978	A. Karpov (U.S.S.R.)	V. Korchnoy (U.S.S.R.)
1981	A. Karpov (U.S.S.R.)	V. Korchnoy (U.S.S.R.)
1984–85	G. Kasparov (U.S.S.R.)	A. Karpov (U.S.S.R.)
1986	G. Kasparov (U.S.S.R.)	A. Karpov (U.S.S.R.)
1987	G. Kasparov (U.S.S.R.)	A. Karpov (U.S.S.R.)

*By default. R. Fischer (U.S.) was stripped of the title for failure to comply with an FIDE ruling, and Karpov was declared the new world champion.

World Chess Championships—women

year	winner	runner-up
1976	N. Gaprindashvili (U.S.S.R.)	N. Aleksandriya (U.S.S.R.)
1978	M. Chiburdanidze (U.S.S.R.)	N. Gaprindashvili (U.S.S.R.)
1981	M. Chiburdanidze (U.S.S.R.)	N. Aleksandriya (U.S.S.R.)
1984	M. Chiburdanidze (U.S.S.R.)	I. Levitina (U.S.S.R.)
1986	M. Chiburdanidze (U.S.S.R.)	E. Akhmilovskaya (U.S.S.R.)

International Team Chess Championships—men

year	winner	runner-up
1980	U.S.S.R.	Hungary
1982	U.S.S.R.	Czechoslovakia
1984	U.S.S.R.	United Kingdom
1986	U.S.S.R.	United Kingdom
1988	U.S.S.R.	United Kingdom

International Team Chess Championships—women

year	winner	runner-up
1980	U.S.S.R.	Hungary
1982	U.S.S.R.	Romania
1984	U.S.S.R.	Bulgaria
1986	U.S.S.R.	Hungary
1988	Hungary	U.S.S.R.

CONTRACT BRIDGE

Bermuda Bowl

year	winner	runner-up
1983	United States	Italy
1985	United States	Austria
1987	United States	United Kingdom

World Contract Bridge Pair Championship

year	open winner	women's winner	mixed winner
1978	Brazil	United States	United States
1982	United States	United States	Canada
1986	United States	United States	United States

World Team Olympiad

year	open winner	open runner-up	women's winner	women's runner-up
1984	Poland	France	United States	United Kingdom
1988	United States	Austria	Denmark	United Kingdom

CRICKET

All-time First-class Test Cricket Standings (as of August 31, 1988)

	England wins draws losses			Australia w d l			South Africa w d l			West Indies w d l			New Zealand w d l			India w d l			Pakistan w d l			Sri Lanka w d l		
England v.	—	—	—	88	77	97	46	38	18	21	35	39	30	32	4	29	34	11	13	29	5	2	1	0
Australia v.	97	77	88	—	—	—	29	13	11	27	16*	19	10	9	5	20	17*	8	11	9	8	2	0	0
South Africa v.	18	38	46	11	13	29	—	—	—	†			19	6	2	†			†			†		
West Indies v.	39	35	21	19	16*	27	†			—	—	—	8	12	4	23	29	6	9	10	6	†		
New Zealand v.	4	32	30	5	9	10	2	6	19	4	12	8	—	—	—	4	11	10	3	14	10	4	2	0
India v.	11	34	29	8	17*	20	†			6	29	23	10	11	4	—	—	—	4	29	7	3	3	1
Pakistan v.	5	29	13	8	9	11	†			6	10	9	10	14	3	7	29	4	—	—	—	5	3	1
Sri Lanka v.	0	1	2	0	0	2	†			†			0	2	4	1	3	3	1	3	5	—	—	—

*Including one tie.   †No matches.

CURLING

International Olympic Committee President's Cup

year	winner	runner-up
1983	Canada	West Germany
1984	Norway	Switzerland
1985	Canada	Sweden
1986	Canada	Scotland
1987	Canada	West Germany

World Curling Championship—women

year	winner	runner-up
1983	Switzerland	Norway
1984	Canada	Switzerland
1985	Canada	Scotland
1986	Canada	West Germany
1987	Canada	West Germany

CYCLING

Tour de France

year	winner	km
1984	L. Fignon (Fr.)	3,880
1985	B. Hinault (Fr.)	4,100
1986	G. LeMond (U.S.)	4,091
1987	S. Roche (Ire.)	4,100
1988	P. Delgado (Spain)	3,300

Cycling World Track Championships—women (amateur)

year	sprint	3-km pursuit
1984	C. Paraskevin (U.S.)	R. Twigg (U.S.)
1985	I. Nicoloso (Fr.)	R. Twigg (U.S.)
1986	C. Rothenburger (E.Ger.)	J. Longo (Fr.)
1987	E. Salumyae (U.S.S.R.)	R. Twigg-Whitehead (U.S.)
1988	E. Salumyae (U.S.S.R.)	J. Longo (Fr.)

Cycling World Road-Racing Championships

year	men (amateur)	men (professional)	women (amateur)
1984	A. Grewa (U.S.)	C. Criquelion (Belg.)	C. Carpenter-Phinney (U.S.)
1985	L. Piasecki (Pol.)	J. Zoetemelk (Neth.)	J. Longo (Fr.)
1986	U. Ampler (E.Ger.)	M. Argentin (Italy)	J. Longo (Fr.)
1987	R. Vivien (Fr.)	S. Roche (Ireland)	J. Longo (Fr.)
1988	O. Ludwig (E.Ger.)	M. Fondriest (Italy)	M. Knol (Neth.)

P. Delgado: Tour de France (1988)
WINNING—ALLSPORT USA

Cycling World Track Championships—men

year	sprint (amateur)	sprint (professional)	pursuit (amateur)	pursuit (professional)	motor-paced (amateur)	motor-paced (professional)
1984	M. Gorski (U.S.)	Nakano K. (Japan)	S. Hegg (U.S.)	H.-H. Oersted (Den.)	J. de Nijs (Neth.)	H. Schütz (W.Ger.)
1985	L. Hesslich (E.Ger.)	Nakano K. (Japan)	V. Ekimov (U.S.S.R.)	H.-H. Oersted (Den.)	R. Dotti (Italy)	B. Vicino (Italy)
1986	M. Hübner (E.Ger.)	Nakano K. (Japan)	V. Ekimov (U.S.S.R.)	T. Doyle (U.K.)	M. Gentili (Italy)	B. Vicino (Italy)
1987	L. Hesslich (E.Ger.)	Tawara N. (Japan)	G. Umaras (U.S.S.R.)	H.-H. Oersted (Den.)	M. Gentili (Italy)	M. Huerzeler (Switz.)
1988	L. Hesslich (E.Ger.)	S. Pate (Australia)	G. Umaras (U.S.S.R.)	L. Piasecki (Pol.)	V. Colamartino (Italy)	D. Clark (Australia)

FENCING

World Fencing Championships—men

year	individual			team		
	foil	épée	sabre	foil	épée	sabre
1984	M. Numa (Italy)	P. Boisse (Fr.)	J.F. Lamour (Fr.)	Italy	West Germany	Italy
1985	M. Numa (Italy)	P. Boisse (Fr.)	G. Nebald (Hung.)	Italy	West Germany	U.S.S.R.
1986	A. Borella (Italy)	P. Riboud (Fr.)	S. Mindirgasov (U.S.S.R.)	Italy	West Germany	U.S.S.R.
1987	M. Gey (W.Ger.)	V. Fischer (W.Ger.)	J.-F. Lamour (Fr.)	West Germany	U.S.S.R.	U.S.S.R.
1988	S. Cerioni (Italy)	A. Schmitt (W.Ger.)	J.-F. Lamour (Fr.)	U.S.S.R.	France	Hungary

World Fencing Championships—women

year	individual foil	team foil
1984	Luan Jujie (China)	West Germany
1985	C. Hanisch (W.Ger.)	West Germany
1986	A. Fichtel (W.Ger.)	U.S.S.R.
1987	E. Tufan (Rom.)	Hungary
1988	A. Fichtel (W.Ger.)	West Germany

West Germany: world fencing championships—women's foil (1988)

AFP PHOTO

The European Cup of Champion Clubs

season	result			
1984–85	Juventus (Italy)	1	Liverpool	0
1985–86	Steaua Bucharest*	0	Barcelona	0
1986–87	Porto (Port.)	2	Bayern Munich	1
1987–88	PSV Eindhoven (Neth.)*	0	Benfica (Port.)	0

*Won on penalty kicks.

FIELD HOCKEY

World Cup Field Hockey Championships—men

year	winner	runner-up
1982	Pakistan	West Germany
1986	Australia	England

World Cup Field Hockey Championships—women

year	winner	runner-up
1983	The Netherlands	Canada
1986	The Netherlands	West Germany

FOOTBALL

FIFA World Cup

year	result			
1982	Italy	3	West Germany	1
1986	Argentina	3	West Germany	2

European Cup-Winners' Cup

season	result			
1983–84	Juventus (Italy)	2	Porto (Port.)	1
1984–85	Everton (Eng.)	3	Rapid Vienna	1
1985–86	Dinamo Kiev	3	Atlético Madrid	0
1986–87	Ajax Amsterdam	1	Lokomotiv Leipzig	0
1987–88	KV Mechelen (Belg.)	1	Ajax Amsterdam	0

Libertadores de América Cup

year	winner (country)	runner-up (country)	scores
1984	Independiente (Arg.)	Grêmio (Braz.)	1–0, 0–0
1985	Argentinos Juniors (Arg.)	América (Colom.)	1–0, 0–1, 1–1*
1986	River Plate (Arg.)	América de Cali (Colom.)	2–1, 1–0
1987	Peñarol (Uruguay)	América de Cali (Colom.)	0–2, 2–1, 1–0

*Winner determined in penalty shootout after tiebreaking game.

U.S. Football—professional

Super Bowl

	season	result			
XIX	1984–85	San Francisco 49ers (NFC)	38	Miami Dolphins (AFC)	16
XX	1985–86	Chicago Bears (NFC)	46	New England Patriots (AFC)	10
XXI	1986–87	New York Giants (NFC)	39	Denver Broncos (AFC)	20
XXII	1987–88	Washington Redskins (NFC)	42	Denver Broncos (AFC)	10

U.S. Football—college

U.S. College Football National Champion

season	champion
1985	Oklahoma
1986	Penn State
1987	Miami (Fla.)
1988	Notre Dame

Heisman Memorial Trophy winner

year	player	school
1984	Doug Flutie	Boston College
1985	Bo Jackson	Auburn
1986	Vinnie Testaverde	Miami (Fla.)
1987	Tim Brown	Notre Dame
1988	B. Sanders	Oklahoma State

B. Sanders: Heisman Memorial Trophy winner (1988)

DAMIAN STROHMEYER/SPORTS ILLUSTRATED

Rose Bowl				
season	result			
1984–85	Southern California	20	Ohio State	17
1985–86	UCLA	45	Iowa	28
1986–87	Arizona State	22	Michigan	15
1987–88	Michigan St.	20	Southern California	17
1988–89	Michigan	22	Southern California	14

Orange Bowl				
season	result			
1984–85	Washington	28	Oklahoma	17
1985–86	Oklahoma	25	Penn State	10
1986–87	Oklahoma	42	Arkansas	8
1987–88	Miami (Fla.)	20	Oklahoma	14
1988–89	Miami (Fla.)	23	Nebraska	3

Sugar Bowl				
season	result			
1984–85	Nebraska	28	Louisiana State	10
1985–86	Tennessee	35	Miami (Fla.)	7
1986–87	Nebraska	30	Louisiana State	15
1987–88	Auburn	16	Syracuse	16
1988–89	Florida St.	13	Auburn	7

Cotton Bowl				
season	result			
1984–85	Boston College	45	Houston	28
1985–86	Texas A&M	36	Auburn	16
1986–87	Ohio State	28	Texas A&M	12
1987–88	Texas A&M	35	Notre Dame	10
1988–89	UCLA	17	Arkansas	3

Canadian football—professional

Grey Cup				
year	result			
1984	Winnipeg Blue Bombers (WFC)	47	Hamilton Tiger-Cats (EFC)	17
1985	British Columbia Lions (WFC)	37	Hamilton Tiger-Cats (EFC)	24
1986	Hamilton Tiger-Cats (EFC)	39	Edmonton Eskimos (WFC)	15
1987	Edmonton Eskimos (WFC)	38	Toronto Argonauts (EFC)	36
1988	Winnipeg Blue Bombers (EFC)	22	British Columbia Lions (WFC)	21

Rugby Union football

Record of International Test matches 1871 to September 30, 1988

	England wins	draws	losses	Scotland wins	draws	losses	Ireland wins	draws	losses	Wales wins	draws	losses	British Isles wins	draws	losses
England v.	—			50	16	38	56	8	36	36	12	46	—		
Scotland v.	38	16	50	—			49	4	45	38	2	52	—		
Ireland v.	36	8	56	45	4	49	—			30	5	56	—		
Wales v.	46	12	36	52	2	38	56	5	30	—			—		
British Isles* v.	—			—			—			—			—		
South Africa v.	6	1	2	5	0	3	8	1	1	6	1	0	20	6	14
New Zealand v.	12	0	3	11	2	0	8	1	0	11	0	3	24	3	5
Australia v.	10	0	5	4	0	7	6	0	6	5	0	8	2	0	12
France v.	24	7	32	28	3	28	31	5	25	22	3	36			

	South Africa wins	draws	losses	New Zealand wins	draws	losses	Australia wins	draws	losses	France wins	draws	losses
England v.	2	1	6	3	0	12	5	0	10	32	7	24
Scotland v.	3	0	5	0	2	11	7	0	4	28	3	28
Ireland v.	1	1	8	0	1	8	6	0	6	25	5	31
Wales v.	0	1	6	3	0	11	8	0	5	36	3	22
British Isles* v.	14	6	20	5	3	24	12	0	2			
South Africa v.	—			20	2	15	21	0	7	12	4	3
New Zealand v.	15	2	20	—			60	5	21	19	0	5
Australia v.	7	0	21	21	5	60	—			6	2	10
France v.	3	4	12	5	0	19	10	2	6	—		

*The British Isles ("British Lions") is a combined team from the four "Home Unions" (England, Ireland, Scotland, and Wales).

Five Nations Championship	
year	result
1984	Scotland†
1985	Ireland†
1986	France, Scotland*
1987	France‡
1988	Wales†

*Tied. †Triple Crown (all three matches, excluding France) and Grand Slam (all four matches) winner. ‡Grand Slam winner.

Rugby League football

Record of Test matches from January 25, 1908, to September 30, 1988

	Great Britain wins	draws	losses	Australia wins	draws	losses	New Zealand wins	draws	losses	France wins	draws	losses
Great Britain v.	—			50	4	46	48	3	25	30	3	13
Australia v.	48	4	50	—			38	0	22	24	3	12
New Zealand v.	25	3	45	22	0	38	—			15	3	11
France* v.	13	3	30	12	3	24	11	3	15	—		

*France began playing in this series of matches in 1954.

GOLF

British Open Golf Tournament—men	
year	winner
1985	S. Lyle (Scot.)
1986	G. Norman (Australia)
1987	N. Faldo (U.K.)
1988	S. Ballesteros (Spain)

United States Open Golf Championship—men	
year	winner
1985	A. North (U.S.)
1986	R. Floyd (U.S.)
1987	S. Simpson (U.S.)
1988	C. Strange (U.S.)

Masters Tournament	
year	winner
1984	B. Crenshaw (U.S.)
1985	B. Langer (W.Ger.)
1986	J. Nicklaus (U.S.)
1987	L. Mize (U.S.)
1988	S. Lyle (Scot.)

U.S. Professional Golfers' Association (PGA) championship	
year	winner
1985	H. Green (U.S.)
1986	B. Tway (U.S.)
1987	L. Nelson (U.S.)
1988	J. Sluman (U.S.)

L. Neumann: U.S. Women's Open (1988)
FRED VUICH—ALLSPORT

S. Ballesteros: British Open golf tournament—men (1988)
DAVE CANNON—ALLSPORT

British Amateur Golf Championship—men

year	winner
1984	J.-M. Olazabal (Spain)
1985	G. McGimpsey (Ire.)
1986	D. Curry (U.K.)
1987	P. Mayo (U.K.)
1988	C. Hardin (Swed.)

United States Amateur Golf Championship—men

year	winner
1984	S. Verplank (U.S.)
1985	S. Randolph (U.S.)
1986	B. Alexander (U.S.)
1987	B. Mayfair (U.S.)
1988	E. Meeks (U.S.)

Ladies' British Open Golf Championship

year	winner
1984	Okamoto A. (Japan)
1985	B. King (U.S.)
1986	L. Davies (U.K.)
1987	A. Nicholas (U.K.)
1988	C. Dibnah (Australia)

British Ladies Amateur Golf Championship

year	winner
1984	J. Rosenthal (U.S.)
1985	L. Behan (Ire.)
1986	J. Thornhill (U.K.)
1987	J. Collingham (U.K.)
1988	J. Furby (U.S.)

United States Women's Open champions

year	winner
1984	H. Stacy (U.S.)
1985	K. Baker (U.S.)
1986	J. Geddes (U.S.)
1987	L. Davies (U.K.)
1988	L. Neumann (Swed.)

United States Women's Amateur Golf Championship

year	winner
1984	D. Richard (U.S.)
1985	Hattori M. (Japan)
1986	K. Cockerill (U.S.)
1987	K. Cockerill (U.S.)
1988	P. Sinn (U.S.)

Ladies' Professional Golf Association (LPGA) champions

year	winner
1984	P. Sheehan (U.S.)
1985	N. Lopez (U.S.)
1986	P. Bradley (U.S.)
1987	J. Geddes (U.S.)
1988	S. Turner (U.S.)

Team events

Walker Cup—men (amateur)

year	result	tied	place
1979	United States 14, Britain and Ireland 7	3	Muirfield, East Lothian, Scot.
1981	United States 15, Britain and Ireland 9	0	Monterey, Calif., U.S.
1983	United States 13, Britain and Ireland 10	1	Hoylake, Cheshire, Eng.
1985	United States 13, Britain and Ireland 11	2	Pine Valley, N.J., U.S.
1987	United States 16, Britain and Ireland 7	1	Sunningdale, Berkshire, Eng.

World Cup—men (professional)

year	winner
1984	Spain (J. Cañizares and J. Rivero)
1985	Canada (D. Halldorson and D. Barr)
1986	not held
1987	Wales (I. Woosnam and D. Llewellyn)

Ryder Cup—men (professional)

year	result	tied	place
1979	United States 16, Great Britain 10	2	White Sulphur Springs, W.Va., U.S.
1981	United States 18, Great Britain 9	1	Walton Heath, Surrey, Eng.
1983	United States 13, Great Britain 12	3	Palm Beach Gardens, Fla., U.S.
1985	Europe 16, United States 11	1	Belfry, West Midlands, Eng.
1987	Europe 13, United States 11	4	Dublin, Ohio, U.S.

Curtis Cup—women (amateur)

year	result	tied	place
1980	United States 11, Britain and Ireland 3	4	Chepstow, Gwent, Wales
1982	United States 14, Britain and Ireland 3	1	Denver, Colo., U.S.
1984	United States 9, Britain and Ireland 8	1	Muirfield, East Lothian, Scot.
1986	Britain and Ireland 11, United States 3	4	Hutchinson, Kan., U.S.
1988	Britain and Ireland 11, United States 7	0	Sandwich, Kent, U.K.

GREYHOUND RACING

British Greyhound Derby

year	winning dog	time (s)	year	winning dog	time (s)
1980	Indian Joe	29.69	1984	Whisper Wishes	29.43
1981	Parkdown Jet	29.57	1985	Pagan Swallow	29.04*
1982	Laurie's Panther	29.60	1986	Tico	28.69
1983	I'm Slippy	29.40	1987	Signal Spark	28.83

*In 1985 the distance was lowered from 500 m to 480 m.

GYMNASTICS

World Gymnastics Championships—men

year	all-around team	all-around individual	horizontal bar	parallel bars
1984	United States	K. Gushiken (Japan)	S. Morisue (Japan)	B. Conner (U.S.)
1985	U.S.S.R.	Y. Korolyov (U.S.S.R.)	Tong Fei (China)	S. Kroll (E.Ger.)* V. Mogilny (U.S.S.R.)*
1987	U.S.S.R.	D. Bilozerchev (U.S.S.R.)	D. Bilozerchev (U.S.S.R.)	V. Artyomov (U.S.S.R.)
1988	U.S.S.R.	V. Artyomov (U.S.S.R.)	V. Artyomov (U.S.S.R.)* V. Lyukin (U.S.S.R.)*	V. Artyomov (U.S.S.R.)

year	pommel horse	rings	vault	floor exercise
1985	V. Mogilny (U.S.S.R.)	Li Ning (China)* Y. Korolyov (U.S.S.R.)*	Y. Korolyov (U.S.S.R.)	Tong Fei (China)
1987	D. Bilozerchev (U.S.S.R.)* Z. Borkai (Hung.)*	Y. Korolyov (U.S.S.R.)	S. Kroll (E.Ger.)* Lou Yun (China)*	Lou Yun (China)
1988	D. Bilozerchev (U.S.S.R.)* Z. Borkai (Hung.)* L. Gueraskov (Bulg.)*	H. Behrendt (E.Ger.)* D. Bilozerchev (U.S.S.R.)*	Lou Yun (China)	S. Kharkov (U.S.S.R.)

*Tied.

D. Bilozerchev: pommel horse world gymnastics championships (1988)
FOCUS ON SPORTS

E. Shushunova: all-around individual world gymnastics championships (1988)
FOCUS ON SPORTS

World Gymnastics Championships—women

year	all-around team	all-around individual	balance beam
1984	Romania	M.L. Retton (U.S.)	E. Szabo (Rom.)* S. Pauca (Rom.)*
1985	U.S.S.R.	Y. Shushunova (U.S.S.R.)* O. Omelyanchik (U.S.S.R.)*	D. Silivas (Rom.)
1987	Romania	A. Dobre (Rom.)	A. Dobre (Rom.)
1988	U.S.S.R.	Y. Shushunova (U.S.S.R.)	D. Silivas (Rom.)

year	uneven parallel bars	vault	floor exercise	rhythmic
1984	J. McNamara (U.S.)* Ma Yanhong (China)*	E. Szabo (Rom.)	E. Szabo (Rom.)	
1985	G. Fahnrich (E.Ger.)	Y. Shushunova (U.S.S.R.)	O. Omelyanchik (U.S.S.R.)	
1987	D. Silivas (Rom.) E. Thuemmler (E.Ger.)	Y. Shushunova (U.S.S.R.)	Y. Shushunova (U.S.S.R.) D. Silivas (Rom.)	
1988	D. Silivas (Rom.)	S. Boginskaya (U.S.S.R.)	D. Silivas (Rom.)	M. Lobach (U.S.S.R.)

*Tied.

HORSE RACING

The Derby

year	horse	jockey	owner	trainer
1984*	Secreto	C. Roche	L. Miglitti	D. O'Brian
1985	Slip Anchor	S. Cauthen	Lord H. de Walden	H. Cecil
1986	Shahrastani	W.R. Swinburn	Aga Khan IV	M.R. Stoute
1987	Reference Point	S. Cauthen	L. Freedman	H. Cecil
1988	Kahyasi	R. Cochrane		

*Record time—2 min 12 s.

The St. Leger

year	horse	jockey	owner	trainer
1984	Comanche Run	L. Piggott	I. Allen	L. Cumani
1985	Oh So Sharp	S. Cauthen	Sheikh Mohammed	H. Cecil
1986	Moon Madness	P. Eddery	Duchess of Norfolk	J. Dunlop
1987	Reference Point	S. Cauthen	L. Freedman	H. Cecil
1988	Minster Son	W. Carson		

Triple Crown champions—British

year	winner
1915	Pommern
1917	Gay Crusader
1918	Gainsborough
1935	Bahram
1970	Nijinsky

2,000 Guineas

year	horse	jockey	owner	trainer
1984	El Gran Señor	P. Eddery	R. Sangster	V. O'Brien
1985	Shadeed	L. Piggott	M. al-Maktoum	M. Stoute
1986	Dancing Brave	G. Starkey	K. Abdullah	G. Harwood
1987	Don't Forget Me	W. Carson	J. Horgan	R. Hannon
1988	Doyoun	W. Swinburn	Aga Khan IV	

The American Thoroughbred classics

The Kentucky Derby

year	horse	jockey	owner	trainer
1984	Swale	L. Pincay	Claiborne Farm	W. Stephens
1985	Spend a Buck	A. Cordero, Jr.	D. Diaz	C. Gambolati
1986	Ferdinand	W. Shoemaker	E. Keck	C. Whittingham
1987	Alysheba	C. McCarron	D. & P. Scharbauer	J. Van Berg
1988	Winning Colors	G. Stevens	E. Klein	D.W. Lukas

The Preakness Stakes

year	horse	jockey	owner	trainer
1985	Tank's Prospect	P. Day	E.V. Klein	D.W. Lukas
1986	Snow Chief	A. Solis	C. Grinsted, B. Rochelle	M. Stute
1987	Alysheba	C. McCarron	D. & P. Scharbauer	J. Van Berg
1988	Risen Star	E. Delahoussaye	R. Lamarque, L. Roussel	L. Roussel

The Belmont Stakes

year	horse	jockey	owner	trainer
1985	Creme Fraiche	E. Maple	E. Moran	W. Stephens
1986	Danzig Connection	C. McCarren	H. de Kwiatkowski	W. Stephens
1987	Bet Twice	C. Perret	Cisley Stable	J. Croll
1988	Risen Star	E. Delahoussaye	R. Lamarque, L. Roussel	L. Roussel

Triple Crown champions—U.S.

year	horse
1946	Assault
1948	Citation
1973	Secretariat
1977	Seattle Slew
1978	Affirmed

Risen Star: Belmont Stakes (1988)
FOCUS ON SPORTS

Harness racing

The Hambletonian Trot

year	horse	driver
1984	Historic Freight	B. Webster
1985	Prakas	B. O'Donnell
1986	Nuclear Kosmos	U. Thoresen
1987	Mack Lobell	J. Campbell
1988	Armbro Goal	J. Campbell

Australian Thoroughbred racing

Melbourne Cup

year	horse	jockey	owner	trainer
1984	Black Knight	P. Cook	R. Holmes A'Court	G.M. Hanlon
1985	What a Nuisance	P. Hyland	Mr. & Mrs. L.J. Williams	J.F. Meagher
1986	At Talaq	M. Clarke	Sheikh al-Maktoum	C. Hayes
1987	Kensei	L. Olsen	Six-man syndicate	L. Bridge
1988	Empire Rose			

Edmonton Oilers: Stanley Cup (1988)
DAVID KLUTHO—ALLSPORT USA

ICE HOCKEY

The Stanley Cup

season	winner	runner-up	games
1983–84	Edmonton Oilers	New York Islanders	4–1
1984–85	Edmonton Oilers	Philadelphia Flyers	4–1
1985–86	Montreal Canadiens	Calgary Flames	4–1
1986–87	Edmonton Oilers	Philadelphia Flyers	4–3
1987–88	Edmonton Oilers	Boston Bruins	4–0

World Amateur Hockey Championships

year	winner
1984	U.S.S.R.
1985	Czechoslovakia
1986	U.S.S.R.
1987	Sweden
1988	U.S.S.R.

ICE SKATING

World figure skating champions—women	
year	winner
1984	K. Witt (E.Ger.)
1985	K. Witt (E.Ger.)
1986	D. Thomas (U.S.)
1987	K. Witt (E.Ger.)
1988	K. Witt (E.Ger.)

World figure skating champions—pairs	
year	winners
1984	B. Underhill, P. Martini (Can.)
1985	E. Valova, O. Vasilev (U.S.S.R.)
1986	Ye. Gordeyeva, S. Grinkov (U.S.S.R.)
1987	Ye. Gordeyeva, S. Grinkov (U.S.S.R.)
1988	E. Valova, O. Vasilyev (U.S.S.R.)

D. Jansen: sprint championship (1988)
AP/WIDE WORLD

World figure skating champions—men	
year	winner
1984	S. Hamilton (U.S.)
1985	A. Fadeyev (U.S.S.R.)
1986	B. Boitano (U.S.)
1987	B. Orser (Can.)
1988	B. Boitano (U.S.)

World ice dancing champions	
year	winners
1984	J. Torvill, C. Dean (U.K.)
1985	N. Bestemyanova, A. Bukin (U.S.S.R.)
1986	N. Bestemyanova, A. Bukin (U.S.S.R.)
1987	N. Bestemyanova, A. Bukin (U.S.S.R.)
1988	N. Bestemyanova, A. Bukin (U.S.S.R.)

E. Valova, O. Vasilyev: world figure skating champions—pairs (1988)
GERARD VANDYSTADT—ALLSPORT USA

B. Boitano: world figure skating champion—men (1988)
GERARD VANDYSTADT—ALLSPORT

World all-around speed skating champions—men	
year	winner
1984	O. Bozhiev (U.S.S.R.)
1985	H. Vergeer (Neth.)
1986	D. Jansen (U.S.)
1987	N. Gulyaev (U.S.S.R.)
1988	E. Flaim (U.S.)

World all-around speed skating champions—women	
year	winner
1984	K. Enke (E.Ger.)
1985	A. Schöne (E.Ger.)
1986	K. Kania (E.Ger.)
1987	K. Kania (E.Ger.)
1988	K. Kania (E.Ger.)

World Speed Skating Sprint Championships		
year	men	women
1984	G. Boucher (Can.)	K. Enke (E.Ger.)
1985	I. Zhelezovsky (U.S.S.R.)	C. Rothenburger (E.Ger.)
1986	I. Zhelezovsky (U.S.S.R.)	K. Kania (E.Ger.)
1987	A. Kuroiwa (Japan)	K. Kania (E.Ger.)
1988	D. Jansen (U.S.)	C. Rothenburger (E.Ger.)

JUDO

World Judo Championships				
year	open weights	60 kg	65 kg	71 kg
1979	S. Endo (Japan)	T. Rey (Fr.)	N. Solodukhin (U.S.S.R.)	K. Katsuki (Japan)
1981	Y. Yamashita (Japan)	Y. Moriwaki (Japan)	K. Kashiwazaki (Japan)	Park Chong Hak (S.Kor.)
1983	H. Saito (Japan)	K. Tletseri (U.S.S.R.)	N. Solodukhin (U.S.S.R.)	H. Nakanishi (Japan)
1985	Y. Masaki (Japan)	S. Hosokawa (Japan)	Y. Sololov (U.S.S.R.)	Keun Ahn Byung (S. Kor.)
1987	N. Ogawa (Japan)	Kim Jae Yup (S.Kor.)	Y. Yamamoto (Japan)	M. Swain (U.S.)

year	78 kg	86 kg	95 kg	+ 95 kg
1979	S. Fujii (Japan)	D. Ultsch (E.Ger.)	T. Khubuluri (U.S.S.R.)	Y. Yamashita (Japan)
1981	N. Adams (U.K.)	B. Tchoullouyan (Fr.)	T. Khubuluri (U.S.S.R.)	Y. Yamashita (Japan)
1983	N. Hikage (Japan)	D. Ultsch (E.Ger.)	A. Preschel (E.Ger.)	Y. Yamashita (Japan)
1985	N. Hikage (Japan)	P. Seisenbacher (Austria)	H. Sugai (Japan)	Chul Cho Yong (S.Kor.)
1987	H. Okada (Japan)	F. Canu (France)	H. Sugai (Japan)	G. Veritchev (U.S.S.R.)

West Germany: world rowing championship—eights (1988)
SIMON BRUTY—ALLSPORT

MOTORBOAT RACING

Gold Cup Championship

year	boat	driver
1984	Atlas Van Lines	C. Hanauer
1985	Miller American	C. Hanauer
1986	Miller American	C. Hanauer
1987	Miller American	C. Hanauer
1988	Miller American	C. Hanauer

POLO

Coronation Cup

year	result			
1984	Rest of the World	8	England	7
1985	Mexico	8	England I	6
1986	Mexico	8	England	4
1987	United States	8	England	5
1988	England	8	North America	7

Copa de las Americas

year	winner
1936	Argentina
1950	Argentina
1966	Argentina
1969	Argentina
1980	Argentina

RODEO

Men's World All-Around Rodeo Championship

year	winner
1984	D. Pickett
1985	L. Feild
1986	L. Feild
1987	L. Feild
1988	D. Appleton

ROWING

World Rowing Championship—men

year	single sculls	min:s	double sculls	min:s	coxed pairs	min:s
1984	P. Karppinen (Fin.)	7:00.24	B. Lewis, P. Enquist (U.S.)	6:36.87	G. Abbagnale, C. Abbagnale (Italy)	7:05.99
1985	P. Karppinen (Fin.)	6:48.08	U. Heppner, T. Lange (E.Ger.)	6:15.49	G. Abbagnale, C. Abbagnale (Italy)	6:53.40
1986	P.-M. Kolbe (W.Ger.)	6:54.09	A. Belgeri, I. Pescialli (Italy)	6:33.64	A. Holmes, S. Redgrave (U.K.)	6:51.66
1987	T. Lange (E.Ger.)	7:36.41	D. Yorddanov, V. Dadev (Bulg.)	7:03.33	G. Abbagnale, C. Abbagnale (Italy)	7:40.81
1988	T. Lange (E.Ger.)	6:49.86	R. Florijan, N. Rienks (Neth.)	6:21.13	G. Abbagnale, C. Abbagnale (Italy)	6:58.79

year	coxless pairs	min:s	coxed fours	min:s	coxless fours	min:s	eights	min:s
1984	P. Iosub, V. Toma (Rom.)	6:45.39	Great Britain	6:18.64	New Zealand	6:03.48	Canada	5:41.32
1985	N. Pimenov, Yu. Pimenov (U.S.S.R.)	6:38.39	U.S.S.R.	6:07.23	West Germany	6:00.19	U.S.S.R.	5:33.71
1986	Yu. Pimenov, N. Pimenov (U.S.S.R.)	6:42.37	East Germany	6:03.81	United States	6:03.53	Australia	5:33.54
1987	S. Redgrave, A. Holmes (U.K.)	7:11.20	East Germany	6:41.74	East Germany	6:39.70	United States	5:58.83
1988	S. Redgrave, A. Holmes (U.K.)	6:36.84	East Germany	6:10.74	East Germany	6:03.11	West Germany	5:46.05

World Rowing Championships—women

year	single sculls	min:s	double sculls	min:s	quadruple sculls	min:s
1984	V. Racila (Rom.)	3:40.68	M. Popescu, E. Oleniuc (Rom.)	3:26.75	Romania	3:14.11
1985	C. Linse (E.Ger.)	7:40.37	S. Schwabe, M. Schröter (E.Ger.)	6:58.80	East Germany	6:22.47
1986	J. Hampe (E.Ger.)	7:29.60	S. Schwabe, B. Schramm (E.Ger.)	6:57.71	East Germany	6:13.91
1987	M. Georgieva (Bulg.)	8:59.26	S. Madina, V. Ninova (Bulg.)	7:47.89	East Germany	6:58.42
1988	J. Behrendt (E.Ger.)	7:47.19	B. Peter, M. Schröter (E.Ger.)	7:00.48	East Germany	6:21.06

year	coxless pairs	min:s	coxed fours	min:s	eights	min:s
1984	R. Arba, E. Horvat (Rom.)	3:32.60	Romania	3:19.30	United States	2:59.80
1985	R. Arba, E. Florea (Rom.)	7:25.08	East Germany	6:50.08	U.S.S.R.	6:14.00
1986	R. Arba, O. Homeghi (Rom.)	7:12.20	Romania	6:43.86	U.S.S.R.	6:08.76
1987	R. Arba, O. Homeghi (Rom.)	8:00.73	Romania	7:30.12	Romania	6:55.61
1988	R. Arba, O. Homeghi (Rom.)	7:28.13	East Germany	6:56.00	East Germany	6:15.17

The Diamond Challenge Sculls

year	winner	min:s
1984	C.L. Baillieu (Leander Club)	7:57
1985	S. Redgrave (Marlow R.C.)	8:28
1986	B. Eltang (Den.)	*
1987	P.-M. Kolbe (Ruder-Club Hamburg)	7:52
1988	H. McGlashan (Melbourne Univ.)	

*Not rowed out.

Grand Challenge Cup

year	winner	min:s
1984	Leander Club and London R.C.	6:22
1985	Harvard University, U.S.	6:27
1986	Nautilus R.C.	6:18
1987	Soviet Army	6:11
1988	Great Britain Olympic team	

SKIING

World Nordic Skiing Championships—men

year	15-km cross-country	30-km cross-country	50-km cross-country	relay
1982	O. Braa (Nor.)	T. Eriksson (Swed.)	T. Wassberg (Swed.)	Norway; U.S.S.R. (tied)
1984	G. Svan (Swed.)	N. Zimyatov (U.S.S.R.)	T. Wassberg (Swed.)	Sweden
1985	K. Haerhoenen (Fin.)	G. Svan (Swed.)	G. Svan (Swed.)	Norway
1987	M. Albarello (Italy)	T. Wassberg (Swed.)	M. De Zoll (Italy)	Sweden
1988	M. Deviatiarov (U.S.S.R.)	A. Prokurorov (U.S.S.R.)	G. Svan (Swed.)	Sweden

World Nordic Skiing Championships—women

year	5-km cross-country	10-km cross-country	20-km cross-country	relay
1982	B. Aunli (Nor.)	B. Aunli (Nor.)	R. Smetanina (U.S.S.R.)	Norway
1984	M.-L. Hämälainen (Fin.)	M.-L. Hämälainen (Fin.)	M.-L. Hämälainen (Fin.)	Norway
1985	A. Boe (Nor.)	A. Boe (Nor.)	G. Nykelmo (Nor.)	U.S.S.R.
1987	M. Matikainen (Fin.)	A. Jahren (Nor.)	M.-H. Westin (Swed.)	U.S.S.R.
1988	M. Matikainen (Fin.)	V. Ventsene (U.S.S.R.)	T. Tikhonova (U.S.S.R.)	U.S.S.R.

World Nordic Skiing Championships—ski jump

year	jump (70 m)	special jump (90 m)	combined
1982	A. Kogler (Austria)	M. Nykänen (Fin.)	T. Sandberg (Nor.)
1984	J. Weissflog (E.Ger.)	M. Nykänen (Fin.)	T. Sandberg (Nor.)
1985	J. Weissflog (E.Ger.)	P. Bergerud (Nor.)	H. Weinbach (W.Ger.)
1987	J. Parma (Czech.)	A. Felder (Austria)	T. Loekken (Nor.)
1988	M. Nykänen (Fin.)	M. Nykänen (Fin.)	H. Kempf (Switz.)

M. Nykänen: world Nordic skiing
championships—ski jump (1988)
DAVID CANNON—ALLSPORT

World Alpine Skiing Championships—slalom

year	men's slalom	men's giant slalom	women's slalom	women's giant slalom
1982	I. Stenmark (Swed.)	S. Mahre (U.S.)	E. Hess (Switz.)	E. Hess (Switz.)
1984	P. Mahre (U.S.)	M. Julen (Switz.)	P. Magoni (Italy)	D. Armstrong (U.S.)
1985	J. Nilsson (Swed.)	M. Wasmaier (W.Ger.)	P. Pelen (Fr.)	D. Roffe (U.S.)
1987	F. Woerndl (W.Ger.)	P. Zurbriggen (Switz.)	E. Hess (Switz.)	V. Schneider (Switz.)
1988	A. Tomba (Italy)	A. Tomba (Italy)	V. Schneider (Switz.)	V. Schneider (Switz.)

World Alpine Skiing Championships—downhill

year	men	women
1982	H. Weirather (Austria)	G. Sorensen (Can.)
1984	B. Johnson (U.S.)	M. Figini (Switz.)
1985	P. Zurbriggen (Switz.)	M. Figini (Switz.)
1987	P. Müller (Switz.)	M. Walliser (Switz.)
1988	P. Zurbriggen (Switz.)	M. Kichl (W.Ger.)

World Alpine Skiing Championships—combined

year	men	women
1976	G. Thoeni (Italy)	R. Mittermaier (W.Ger.)
1978	A. Wenzel (Liech.)	A. Moser-Proell (Austria)
1982	M. Vion (Fr.)	E. Hess (Switz.)
1987	M. Girardelli (Lux.)	E. Hess (Switz.)
1988	H. Strolz (Austria)	A. Wachter (Austria)

V. Schneider: alpine skiing—slalom and giant slalom (1988)
GUIDO BENETTON—ALLSPORT USA

Alpine World Cup

year	men	women
1984	P. Zurbriggen (Switz.)	E. Hess (Switz.)
1985	M. Girardelli (Lux.)	M. Figini (Switz.)
1986	M. Girardelli (Lux.)	M. Walliser (Switz.)
1987	P. Zurbriggen (Switz.)	M. Walliser (Switz.)
1988	P. Zurbriggen (Switz.)	M. Figini (Switz.)

Nordic World Cup

year	men	women
1984	G. Svan (Swed.)	M.-L. Hämälainen (Fin.)
1985	G. Svan (Swed.)	A. Boe (Nor.)
1986	G. Svan (Swed.)	M. Matikainen (Fin.)
1987	T. Mogren (Swed.)	M. Matikainen (Fin.)
1988	G. Svan (Swed.)	M. Matikainen (Fin.)

SQUASH RACKETS

British Open Championships—men

year	winner
1983–84	Jah. Khan (Pak.)
1984–85	Jah. Khan (Pak.)
1985–86	Jah. Khan (Pak.)
1986–87	Jah. Khan (Pak.)
1987–88	Jah. Khan (Pak.)

British Open Championships—women

year	winner
1983–84	S. Devoy (N.Z.)
1984–85	S. Devoy (N.Z.)
1985–86	S. Devoy (N.Z.)
1986–87	S. Devoy (N.Z.)
1987–88	S. Devoy (N.Z.)

World Open Championships—men

year	winner
1984–85	Jah. Khan (Pak.)
1985–86	Jah. Khan (Pak.)
1986–87	R. Norman (N.Z.)
1987–88	Jan. Khan (Pak.)
1988–89	Jah. Khan (Pak.)

World Open Championships—women

year	winner
1979–80	H. McKay (Australia)
1981–82	R. Thorne (Australia)
1983–84	V. Cardwell (Australia)
1985–86	S. Devoy (N.Z.)
1987–88	S. Devoy (N.Z.)

SWIMMING

World Swimming Championships—men					
freestyle				**backstroke**	
year	100 m	200 m	400 m	1,500 m	100 m	200 m

year	100 m	200 m	400 m	1,500 m	100 m	200 m
1975	A. Coan (U.S.)	T. Shaw (U.S.)	T. Shaw (U.S.)	T. Shaw (U.S.)	R. Matthes (E.Ger.)	Z. Verraszto (Hung.)
1978	D. McCagg (U.S.)	B. Forrester (U.S.)	V. Salnikov (U.S.S.R.)	V. Salnikov (U.S.S.R.)	B. Jackson (U.S.)	J. Vassallo (U.S.)
1982	J. Woithe (E.Ger.)	M. Gross (W.Ger.)	V. Salnikov (U.S.S.R.)	V. Salnikov (U.S.S.R.)	D. Richter (E.Ger.)	R. Carey (U.S.)
1986	M. Biondi (U.S.)	M. Gross (W.Ger.)	R. Henkel (W.Ger.)	R. Henkel (W.Ger.)	I. Polyansky (U.S.S.R.)	I. Polyansky (U.S.S.R.)

	breaststroke		**butterfly**		**individual medley**	
	100 m	200 m	100 m	200 m	200 m	400 m
1975	D. Wilkie (U.K.)	D. Wilkie (U.K.)	G. Jagenburg (U.S.)	B. Forrester (U.S.)	A. Hargitay (Hung.)	A. Hargitay (Hung.)
1978	W. Kusch (W.Ger.)	N. Nevid (U.S.)	J. Bottom (U.S.)	M. Bruner (U.S.)	G. Smith (Can.)	J. Vassallo (U.S.)
1982	S. Lundquist (U.S.)	V. Davis (Can.)	M. Gribble (U.S.)	M. Gross (W.Ger.)	A. Sidorenko (U.S.S.R.)	R. Prado (Braz.)
1986	V. Davis (Can.)	J. Szabo (Hung.)	P. Morales (U.S.)	M. Gross (W.Ger.)	T. Darnyi (Hung.)	T. Darnyi (Hung.)

	team relays			**diving**	
	4 × 100-m freestyle	4 × 200-m freestyle	4 × 100-m medley	springboard	platform
1975	United States	West Germany	United States	P. Boggs (U.S.)	K. Dibiasi (Italy)
1978	United States	United States	United States	P. Boggs (U.S.)	G. Louganis (U.S.)
1982	United States	United States	United States	G. Louganis (U.S.)	G. Louganis (U.S.)
1986	United States	East Germany	United States	G. Louganis (U.S.)	G. Louganis (U.S.)

World Swimming Championships—women					
freestyle				**backstroke**	

year	100 m	200 m	400 m	800 m	100 m	200 m
1975	K. Ender (E.Ger.)	S. Babashoff (U.S.)	S. Babashoff (U.S.)	J. Turrall (Australia)	U. Richter (E.Ger.)	B. Treiber (E.Ger.)
1978	B. Krause (E.Ger.)	C. Woodhead (U.S.)	T. Wickham (Australia)	T. Wickham (Australia)	L. Jezek (U.S.)	L. Jezek (U.S.)
1982	B. Meineke (E.Ger.)	A. Verstappen (Neth.)	C. Schmidt (E.Ger.)	K. Linehan (U.S.)	K. Otto (E.Ger.)	C. Sirch (E.Ger.)
1986	K. Otto (E.Ger.)	H. Friedrich (E.Ger.)	H. Friedrich (E.Ger.)	A. Strauss (E.Ger.)	B. Mitchell (U.S.)	C. Sirch (E.Ger.)

	breaststroke		**butterfly**		**individual medley**	
	100 m	200 m	100 m	200 m	200 m	400 m
1975	H. Anke (E.Ger.)	H. Anke (E.Ger.)	K. Ender (E.Ger.)	R. Kother (E.Ger.)	K. Heddy (U.S.)	U. Tauber (E.Ger.)
1978	J. Bogdanova (U.S.S.R.)	L. Kachushite (U.S.S.R.)	J. Pennington (U.S.)	T. Caulkins (U.S.)	T. Caulkins (U.S.)	T. Caulkins (U.S.)
1982	U. Geweniger (E.Ger.)	S. Varganova (U.S.S.R.)	M.T. Meagher (U.S.)	I. Geissler (E.Ger.)	P. Schneider (E.Ger.)	P. Schneider (E.Ger.)
1986	S. Gerasch (E.Ger.)	S. Hörner (E.Ger.)	K. Gressler (E.Ger.)	M. Meagher (U.S.)	K. Otto (E.Ger.)	K. Nord (E.Ger.)

	team relays			**diving**	
	4 × 100-m freestyle	4 × 200-m freestyle	4 × 100-m medley	springboard	platform
1975	East Germany		East Germany	I. Kalinina (U.S.S.R.)	J. Ely (U.S.)
1978	United States		United States	I. Kalinina (U.S.S.R.)	I. Kalinina (U.S.S.R.)
1982	East Germany		East Germany	M. Neyer (U.S.)	W. Wyland (U.S.)
1986	East Germany	East Germany	East Germany	Gao Min (China)	Chen Lin (China)

R. Henkel: world swimming championships—400 m and 1,500 m (1986)

TONY DUFFY—ALLSPORT

TABLE TENNIS

World Table Tennis Championships—men			
year	St. Bride's Vase (singles)	Iran Cup (doubles)	Swaythling Cup (team)
1981	Guo Yuehua (China)	Cai Zhenhua, Li Zhenshi (China)	China
1983	Guo Yuehua (China)	D. Surbek, Z. Kalinic (Yugos.)	China
1985	Jiang Jialiang (China)	M. Appelgren, U. Carlsson (Swed.)	China
1987	Jiang Jialiang (China)	Chen Longcan, Wei Qingguang (China)	China

World Table Tennis Championships—women			
year	G. Geist Prize (singles)	W.J. Pope Trophy (doubles)	Corbillon Cup (team)
1981	Tong Ling (China)	Cao Yanhua, Zhang Deying (China)	China
1983	Cao Yanhua (China)	Shen Jianping, Dai Lili (China)	China
1985	Cao Yanhua (China)	Dai Lili, Geng Lijuan (China)	China
1987	He Zhili (China)	Hyun Jung Hwa, Yang Young Ja (S.Kor.)	China

World Table Tennis Championships—mixed	
year	Heydusek Prize
1979	Liang Geliang, Ge Xinai (China)
1981	Xie Saike, Huang Junqun (China)
1983	Guo Yuehua, Ni Xialian (China)
1985	Cai Zhenhua, Cao Yanhua (China)
1987	Hui Jun, Geng Lijuan (China)

Table Tennis World Cup	
year	winner
1983	M. Appelgren (Swed.)
1984	Jiang Jialiang (China)
1985	Chen Xinhua (China)
1986	Chen Longcan (China)
1987	Teng Yi (China)

TENNIS

S. Edberg (far left), S. Graf (left): All-England (Wimbledon) tennis championships—singles (1988)

PHOTOGRAPHS, BOB MARTIN—ALLSPORT

All-England (Wimbledon) Tennis Championships—singles

year	men	women
1984	J. McEnroe (U.S.)	M. Navratilova (U.S.)
1985	B. Becker (W.Ger.)	M. Navratilova (U.S.)
1986	B. Becker (W.Ger.)	M. Navratilova (U.S.)
1987	P. Cash (Australia)	M. Navratilova (U.S.)
1988	S. Edberg (Swed.)	S. Graf (W.Ger.)

French Open Tennis Championships—singles

year	men	women
1984	I. Lendl (Czech.)	M. Navratilova (U.S.)
1985	M. Wilander (Swed.)	C. Evert Lloyd (U.S.)
1986	I. Lendl (Czech.)	C. Evert Lloyd (U.S.)
1987	I. Lendl (Czech.)	S. Graf (W.Ger.)
1988	M. Wilander (Swed.)	S. Graf (W.Ger.)

All-England (Wimbledon) Tennis Championships—doubles

year	men	women
1984	J. McEnroe/P. Fleming	M. Navratilova/P. Shriver
1985	H. Gunthardt/B. Taroczy	K. Jordan/E. Smylie
1986	J. Nystrom/M. Wilander	M. Navratilova/P. Shriver
1987	R. Seguso/K. Flach	C. Kohde-Kilsche/H. Sukova
1988	R. Seguso/K. Flach	S. Graf/G. Sabatini

French Open Tennis Championships—doubles

year	men	women
1984	H. Leconte/Y. Noah	M. Navratilova/P. Shriver
1985	M. Edmondson/K. Warwick	M. Navratilova/P. Shriver
1986	J. Fitzgerald/T. Smid	M. Navratilova/A. Temesvari
1987	R. Seguso/A. Jarryd	M. Navratilova/P. Shriver
1988	E. Sánchez/A. Gomez	M. Navratilova/P. Shriver

United States Open Tennis Championships—singles

year	men	women
1984	J. McEnroe (U.S.)	M. Navratilova (U.S.)
1985	I. Lendl (Czech.)	H. Mandlikova (Czech.)
1986	I. Lendl (Czech.)	M. Navratilova (U.S.)
1987	I. Lendl (Czech.)	M. Navratilova (U.S.)
1988	M. Wilander (Swed.)	S. Graf (W.Ger.)

Australian Open Tennis Championships—singles

year	men	women
1984	M. Wilander (Swed.)	M. Navratilova (U.S.)
1985	M. Wilander (Swed.)	C. Evert Lloyd (U.S.)
1986	S. Edberg (Swed.)	M. Navratilova (U.S.)
1987	S. Edberg (Swed.)	H. Mandlikova (Czech.)
1988	M. Wilander (Swed.)	S. Graf (W.Ger.)

United States Open Tennis Championships—doubles

year	men	women
1984	J. Fitzgerald/T. Smid	M. Navratilova/P. Shriver
1985	K. Flach/R. Seguso	C. Kohde-Kilsche/H. Sukova
1986	A. Gómez/S. Zivojinovic	M. Navratilova/P. Shriver
1987	S. Edberg/A. Jarryd	M. Navratilova/P. Shriver
1988	S. Casal/E. Sánchez	G. Fernandez/R. White

Australian Open Tennis Championships—doubles

year	men	women
1984	M. Edmondson/P. McNamee	M. Navratilova/P. Shriver
1985	M. Edmondson/S. Stewart	M. Navratilova/P. Shriver
1986	P. Annacone/C. van Rensburg	M. Navratilova/P. Shriver
1987	S. Edberg/A. Jarryd	M. Navratilova/P. Shriver
1988	R. Leach/J. Pugh	M. Navratilova/P. Shriver

Davis Cup

year	winner
1984	Sweden
1985	Sweden
1986	Australia
1987	Sweden
1988	West Germany

Wightman Cup

year	winner
1984	United States
1985	United States
1986	United States
1987	United States
1988	United States

Federation Cup

year	winner	runner-up	results
1983	Czechoslovakia	West Germany	2–1
1984	Czechoslovakia	Australia	2–1
1985	Czechoslovakia	United States	2–1
1986	United States	Czechoslovakia	3–0
1987	West Germany	United States	2–1

VOLLEYBALL

World Volleyball Championships

year	men	women	year	men	women
1978	U.S.S.R.	Cuba	1984	United States	China
1980	U.S.S.R.	U.S.S.R.	1986	United States	China
1982	U.S.S.R.	China	1988	United States	U.S.S.R.

WRESTLING

World Wrestling Championships—Freestyle

year	48 kg	52 kg	57 kg	62 kg	68 kg
1983	Kim Hwan Cher (N.Kor.)	V. Iordanov (Bulg.)	S. Beloglazov (U.S.S.R.)	V. Alekseev (U.S.S.R.)	A. Fadzaev (U.S.S.R.)
1984	R. Weaver (U.S.)	S. Trstena (Yugos.)	H. Tomiyama (Japan)	R. Lewis (U.S.)	You I.T. (S.Kor.)
1985	Kim Chol Hwan (N.Kor.)	V. Iordanov (Bulg.)	S. Beloglazov (U.S.S.R.)	V. Alekseev (U.S.S.R.)	A. Fadzaev (U.S.S.R.)
1986	Y. Li (N.Kor.)	K. Sik (N.Kor.)	S. Beloglazov (U.S.S.R.)	K. Isaev (U.S.S.R.)	A. Fadzaev (U.S.S.R.)
1987	Li Jae Sik (N.Kor.)	V. Iordanov (Bulg.)	S. Beloglazov (U.S.S.R.)	J. Smith (U.S.)	A. Fadzaev (U.S.S.R.)
1988	T. Kobayashi (Japan)	M. Sato (Japan)	S. Beloglazov (U.S.S.R.)	J. Smith (U.S.)	A. Fadzaev (U.S.S.R.)

year	74 kg	82 kg	90 kg	100 kg	130 kg
1983	D. Schultz (U.S.)	T. Dzgoev (U.S.S.R.)	P. Naniev (U.S.S.R.)	A. Khadartzev (U.S.S.R.)	S. Khasimikov (U.S.S.R.)
1984	D. Schultz (U.S.)	M. Schultz (U.S.)	E. Banach (U.S.)	L. Banach (U.S.)	B. Baumgartner (U.S.)
1985	R. Cascaret (Cuba)	M. Schultz (U.S.)	B. Scherr (U.S.)	L. Khabelov (U.S.S.R.)	D. Gobedzhishvili (U.S.S.R.)
1986	R. Cascaret (Cuba)	V. Modozyan (U.S.S.R.)	M. Khadartsev (U.S.S.R.)	A. Khadartsev (U.S.S.R.)	B. Baumgartner (U.S.)
1987	A. Varaev (U.S.S.R.)	M. Schultz (U.S.)	M. Khadartsev (U.S.S.R.)	L. Khabelov (U.S.S.R.)	A. Khadartsev (U.S.S.R.)
1988	K. Monday (U.S.)	Han Myang Woo (S. Kor.)	M. Khadartsev (U.S.S.R.)	V. Puscasu (Rom.)	D. Gobedzhishvili (U.S.S.R.)

World Wrestling Championships—Greco-Roman style

year	48 kg	52 kg	57 kg	62 kg	68 kg
1983	B. Tsenov (Bulg.)	B. Pashayan (U.S.S.R.)	M. Ito (Japan)	H. Lahtinen (Fin.)	T. Sipila (Fin.)
1984	V. Maenza (Italy)	A. Miyahara (Japan)	P. Passarelli (W.Ger.)	Kim W.K. (S.Kor.)	V. Lisjak (Yugos.)
1985	M. Allakhverdiev (U.S.S.R.)	J. Ronningen (Nor.)	S. Balov (Bulg.)	J. Vangelov (Bulg.)	S. Negrisan (Rom.)
1986	M. Allakhverdiev (U.S.S.R.)	S. Dudyaev (U.S.S.R.)	E. Ivanov (Bulg.)	K. Madzhidov (U.S.S.R.)	L. Dzhulfalakyan (U.S.S.R.)
1987	M. Allakhverdiev (U.S.S.R.)	P. Roque (Cuba)	P. Mourier (France)	J. Vanguelov (Bulg.)	A. Abaev (U.S.S.R.)
1988	V. Maenza (Italy)	J. Ronningen (Nor.)	A. Sike (Hung.)	K. Madzhidov (U.S.S.R.)	L. Dzhulfalakyan (U.S.S.R.)

year	74 kg	82 kg	90 kg	100 kg	130 kg
1983	M. Mamiashvili (U.S.S.R.)	T. Abkhasava (U.S.S.R.)	I. Kanygin (U.S.S.R.)	A. Dimitrov (Bulg.)	E. Arthuine (U.S.S.R.)
1984	J. Salomaki (Fin.)	I. Draica (Rom.)	S. Fraser (U.S.)	V. Andrei (Rom.)	J. Blatnick (U.S.)
1985	M. Mamiashvili (U.S.S.R.)	B. Daras (Pol.)	M. Houck (U.S.)	A. Dimitrov (Bulg.)	I. Rostotsky (U.S.S.R.)
1986	M. Mamiashvili (U.S.S.R.)	not awarded	A. Malina (Poland)	T. Gaspar (Hung.)	T. Johansson (Swed.)
1987	J. Salomaki (Fin.)	T. Komaromi (Hung.)	V. Popov (U.S.S.R.)	G. Guedekhaorui (U.S.S.R.)	I. Rostorotski (U.S.S.R.)
1988	Kim Young Nam (S.Kor.)	M. Mamiashvili (U.S.S.R.)	A. Komchev (Bulg.)	A. Wronski (Pol.)	A. Karelin (U.S.S.R.)

YACHTING

America's Cup

year	winning yacht	owner	skipper	losing yacht	owner
1974	*Courageous* (U.S.)	Courageous syndicate	T. Hood	*Southern Cross* (Australia)	A. Bond
1977	*Courageous* (U.S.)	Courageous syndicate	T. Turner	*Australia* (Australia)	A. Bond and syndicate
1980	*Freedom* (U.S.)	Maritime College at Fort Schuyler Foundation, Inc.	D. Conner	*Australia* (Australia)	A. Bond and syndicate
1983	*Australia II* (Australia)	A. Bond and syndicate	J. Bertrand	*Liberty* (U.S.)	Maritime College at Fort Schuyler Foundation, Inc.
1987	*Stars & Stripes* (U.S.)	Sail America syndicate	D. Conner	*Kookaburra III* (Australia)	K. Parry and syndicate
1988	*Stars & Stripes* (U.S.)	Sail America syndicate	D. Conner	*New Zealand* (New Zealand)	M. Fay

Stars & Stripes (left): America's Cup (1988)

KIRK SCHLEA—ALLSPORT USA

Bermuda Race

year	winning yacht	owner
1978	*Babe*	A. Gay
1980	*Holger Danske*	R. Wilson
1982	*Brigadoon III*	B. Morton
1984	*Pamir*	F. Curren, Jr.
1986	*Silver Star* and *Puritan*	D. Clarke D. Robinson

Transpacific Race

year	winning yacht	owner
1979	*Arriba*	D. Choate
1981	*Sweet Okole*	D. Treadway
1983	*Bravura*	I. Loube
1985	*Montgomery Street*	D. Denning
1987	*Merlin*	D. Campion

Fastnet Cup

year	winning yacht	owner
1981	*Mordicus*	G. Taylor, C. Volters (Belg.)
1983	*Condor*	B. Bell (U.K.)
1985	*Panda*	P. Whipp (U.K.)
1987	*Irish Independent Pelt*	S. Fein (Ire.)

Television and Radio

The dominance of radio and television as the major sources of the world's news and entertainment could be demonstrated by the number of radio and TV sets in use. According to the latest statistics provided by Unesco, 1,598,000,000 radio sets and 735,441,200 television receivers were providing access to news, information, and entertainment around the world as of 1985. About one-third of the radio sets—500 million—were in the U.S., and more than 220 million were in the U.S.S.R. The U.S. and U.S.S.R. also ranked one and two in the number of television sets in use—190 million in the U.S. and 100 million in the Soviet Union. Japan was third (70 million), followed by the United Kingdom (24.5 million), West Germany (22.7 million), and France (21.5 million).

Organization of Services. In the U.S. in 1988, it seemed that technology would influence the television business in the future to an even greater degree than it had in the past. Increasing attention was being paid—by industry and government alike—to high-definition television (HDTV), which permitted television pictures of much greater clarity than the present technology could provide. There was also the growing concern that many in broadcasting and cable television were feeling about the possible invasion of those businesses by telephone companies, an invasion seen as being made likely, if not inevitable, by the development of fibre-optic cable. The technology would enable telephone companies to transmit not only telephone calls but television signals and other services into the home.

The U.S. appeared to be trailing the Japanese and Europeans in the development of HDTV. Indeed, according to many observers, the U.S. had been asleep while Japan and Europe were forging ahead in the potentially lucrative field. However, the Federal Communications Commission (FCC) in September took an initial step in the development of HDTV policy. Its proposal was to employ standards that would require HDTV broadcasts to be compatible with conventional television receivers in the same way that colour broadcasts were compatible with black-and-white sets.

As for the telephone companies' entry into television, as of 1988 such a move was barred by law. Nevertheless, the possibility appeared to concern the leaders of the broadcasting and cable television businesses, whose views on other issues were seldom in accord. Edward Fritts, president of the National Association of Broadcasters, warned that the telephone industry intended to provide "state-of-the-art television over fibre-optic cable." He also believed that telephone companies would produce or package some of the programming and then charge television stations for carrying this material.

Telephone company executives were not hiding their interest in getting into the television business. They made it clear that they would be spending a considerable amount of time and effort lobbying members of Congress and the FCC to seek removal of the regulations that prevent telephone companies from owning cable television systems in the areas where they already operate. Even if successful on those fronts, however, the telephone companies would still be barred from entering the television business by a consent decree approved by the U.S. District Court in Washington, D.C.

In another controversial action bearing on cable television, the FCC reopened a proceeding aimed at repealing a rule that prohibited the networks from owning cable television systems. The networks and their affiliates were on opposite sides of that issue.

Congress, in the final hours before adjourning, approved copyright legislation designed to strengthen the struggling television receive-only—or home satellite-dish—industry, as well as to assure dish owners access to network and independent broadcast signals. It created a six-year compulsory license for the satellite distribution of broadcast signals to dish owners.

Congress during the year passed a law requiring the FCC to write an anti-indecency rule that would apply throughout the broadcast day. U.S. Pres. Ronald Reagan signed the measure into law. However, opponents said that they would challenge the constitutionality of the law on the grounds that it violated the First Amendment.

Cable television continued to expand in 1988. The A. C. Nielsen Co., the leading TV audience measurement service, estimated in July that the number of cable-equipped homes in the U.S. had increased to slightly more than 47 million, or 52.8% of the total number of homes equipped to receive television. In July 1987 the number of cable-equipped homes had been estimated at 43,260,000, or 49.5% of the television households.

The popularity in the U.S. of videocassette recorders (VCRs), which record and play back television programs

STEVEN FERRY—GAMMA/LIAISON

Members of the Writers Guild of America picket in front of New York City's Columbia and Orion studios. The writers, dissatisfied with their residual payments for syndicated shows, went on a lengthy strike that delayed the release of new fall programs.

as well as playing prerecorded movies and other programming, continued to grow. The Electronic Industries Association reported that as of June, 56% of all households—about 49,840,000—had VCR units, compared with 45% a year earlier.

Radical measures to change the structure of British broadcasting were being prepared by the government, which was intent on deregulation and increased commercial competition. The proposals were expected to announce a new fifth channel, an end to the long-established Independent Broadcasting Authority in order to make way for a new commercial TV authority that would provide light regulation for all commercial services including cable, and a more competitive bidding system for allocating independent television (ITV) franchises. Radio was included in the new prescription with proposals for a radio authority, together with two national commercial networks and a chain of low-power local community stations.

In France, however, where deregulation and privatization had been most drastic, a change of government toward the left resulted in proposals to impose advertising limits and programming quotas on commercial broadcasters. Legislation was prepared to replace the CNCL (Commission Nationale des Communications et de la Liberté) with a tough new regulatory council. While Canal Plus, the subscription channel, proved to be Europe's television success story, recording F 407 million pretax profits and with more than 2.3 million subscribers, accounting for 90% of Europe's pay-TV homes, other commercial channels fared less profitably. Both the LA 5 and M6 commercial networks suffered heavy losses and were unable to rise above their respective 13 and 5% audience shares.

In Spain controversy raged around a leading lady of the media, Pilar Miro, who was under pressure to resign as director general of the national radio and TV network RTVE after allegations of mismanagement and political manipulation. Spain passed legislation to permit three national private channels despite opposition from both left and right and attempts to have the proposals declared unconstitutional. Canal 10, a subscription service, closed in August after financial difficulties, but authorities hoped to relaunch it early in 1989. In Portugal the government seemed likely to reduce its planned two national commercial channels to only one because of the uncertainty of obtaining sufficient advertising revenue.

In Italy a new broadcast bill legalized commercial TV. This was expected to allow media owner Silvio Berlusconi to retain control of his three national commercial channels, Canale 5, Rete 4, and Italia Uno.

Elsewhere in Europe the move toward deregulation and competition continued. There were proposals for third networks in Austria, Greece, and The Netherlands. In Ireland a third channel was to operate from 1989 using a combination of cable and MMDS (multichannel microwave distribution systems), and a new regulatory body, the Independent Radio and TV Commission (IRTC), was set up to control commercial broadcasting.

In Norway it appeared likely that advertising would be allowed on the state channel NRK (Norsk Rikringskasting) to finance a second independent TV channel. The launch in Denmark of the new competitive channel TV2, financed by both advertising and license fees, was marred by arguments over program policy, the departure of John Ranelagh as director of programs, and the early resignation of his successor, Erik Crone. Meanwhile, only Sweden seemed to remain immune from the pressures of commercialism, continuing to retain its state monopoly channel free from advertising.

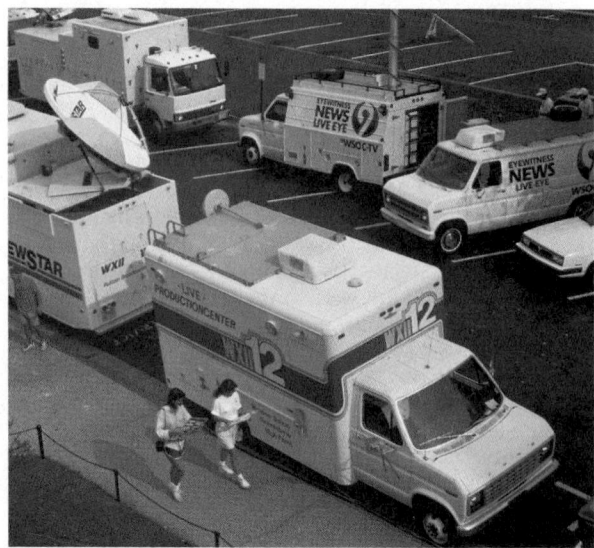

Satellite vans from local news stations are crowded together to provide live coverage of the 1988 presidential campaign. The rise of satellite technology enabled local news stations to cover national and international news events once covered solely by the networks.
ROB NELSON—PICTURE GROUP

Deep concern was growing with regard to the effect marketplace broadcasting was having on European programming. A report by the influential European TV Task Force headed by former French president Valéry Giscard d'Estaing revealed that while broadcasting hours had increased by as much as 30% during the past ten years, the amount of original production had dropped by an average of 40%. Giscard declared, "Television is too important to be left entirely to the marketplace"; he recommended a system of European program quotas and financial incentives for investors in productions. However, efforts by the European Communities to create conditions for an internal European broadcast market met sharp resistance from national broadcasting organizations. A majority of members of the European Broadcasting Union opposed proposals that a minimum quota of all air time be set aside for European-produced programming. Attempts to impose Europe-wide regulations on screen advertising also aroused opposition, particularly in the U.K.

The dream of pan-European satellite broadcasting fared little better. All satellite channels intended for European reception either operated at a loss or were dependent on subsidies. The most dramatic setback involved Super Channel, a transnational service that sought to transmit the "Best of British" English-language programming. Within 22 months of its launch, losses had reached £55 million, and most of the original shareholders had forsaken the project.

Programming. NBC continued to dominate the ratings in the contest for U.S. viewers. For the fourth year in a row, it finished first in the 52-week season, which ended Sept. 17, 1988, easily topping its two rivals. CBS, once the perennial winner in the contest for viewers, finished second again, and ABC was third. The top five programs during the year were all from the NBC lineup: "The Cosby Show," "A Different World," "Cheers," "The Golden Girls," and "Night Court." If that was the good news for NBC, however, the bad news for all three networks was that the audience for network programs in prime time continued to decline as cable television, videocassettes, and independent television stations drained off viewers. The three-network

prime time viewing level fell 8%, to a combined rating of 41.3, for the first six weeks of the new season compared with the same period a year earlier. The networks' share of those actually watching television in prime time fell 6%, to a combined figure of 68% over the same period.

Despite such figures, overall network earnings appeared to increase in the first half of 1988 by 9.2%—to $4.7 billion—over the same period in 1987. Most of the network growth was enjoyed by ABC, whose advertising revenues jumped 31.5%, to $1.6 billion.

One of the top programming stories of the year did not involve new programming but, rather, the industry's inability to produce it. Members of the Writers Guild of America went on strike early in March in a dispute with the Alliance of Motion Picture and Television Producers over residual payments for syndicated programming and creative control; they remained on strike until early August. As a result, the new network season was delayed beyond the usual early September start, except for NBC. It selected September 19 as the start of its season, but that was because it was broadcasting the Olympic Games and the World Series in the early fall. It did not have most of its new and returning programming ready for broadcast until the first week of November. ABC and CBS chose October 24 as the start of their seasons.

ABC expected its lengthy miniseries "War and Remembrance" to be a major factor in the battle for ratings in the fall. Eighteen hours of the series, a sequel to the popular 1983 production "Winds of War," was to air in seven parts between November 13 and November 23. The remainder of the proposed 32-hour series was to be broadcast in 1989.

NBC had hoped that its coverage of the summer Olympic Games would boost its ratings and profits; it did neither. The ratings were 20% lower than the figure the network had guaranteed sponsors. As a result, NBC was obliged to provide advertisers with some $70 million worth of additional "makegood" (or replacement) ads. NBC was said to have achieved a profit of $500 million for the coverage of the Games but only if the revenues from the seven television stations it owned were included with that earned by the network.

It was not only the major commercial networks that were struggling in an effort to find and hold an audience. The Public Broadcasting System included eight new series during the summer, to take advantage of the major networks' practice of relying on reruns, but the strategy failed. PBS ratings, as measured by Nielsen, were down by 11% compared with the three summer months of 1987, with the new series doing particularly badly. The premiere episodes of "P.O.V." and "Struggles for Poland," for instance, earned 1.2 and 1.3 cumulative ratings, respectively, in contrast to the 3.6 PBS average in prime time. Also, a new commercial network, Fox Broadcasting Co., canceled its late-night offering, "The Late Show," after two years because of poor ratings.

Politics loomed large in programming in the presidential election year of 1988. Because of the emergence of satellite technology, stations and ad hoc networks, as well as the major networks, covered the primary campaigns of Republican and Democratic hopefuls intensively. The Democratic and Republican national conventions drew thousands of reporters, television and radio correspondents, and technicians from around the world.

The viewers at home were not as interested as the media, however. Network ratings were poor. The reason generally given was that, with the candidates preselected—because of the primary system—conventions held little drama and suspense for the viewer. As a result, even though the net-

works reduced their live coverage to the evening hours, there was increasing talk of cutting back even further in 1992. Those sharing that view argued that Cable News Network and C-SPAN, the cable public service network, routinely offered gavel-to-gavel live coverage for those who were interested.

The election itself was another major media event. The networks, as was their custom, spent six hours or more on election night reporting the results of the presidential, congressional, and gubernatorial races and offering analyses. As in the past, the networks, basing projections of results on exit polling at voting areas throughout the U.S., were able to announce winners in a state as soon as the polls there had closed. They were also able to call the winner of the presidency on the basis of results from states with a majority of electoral college votes—270—long before all polls had closed. CBS was the first to call a victory for George Bush—at 9:17 PM Eastern Standard Time, before the polls in some western states had closed. Congress in the past had considered but failed to pass legislation designed to prevent such early projections of results. The next Congress was expected to consider the matter again.

Sports events continued to loom large on broadcasting's agenda, and they were expensive. According to a survey by *Broadcasting* magazine, broadcasters paid some $616 million for the rights to college and professional football games in the 1988–89 season. That was some $46 million more than was paid in the previous year. Most of the money—$470 million—was being paid by the three major networks for rights to professional games.

Major league baseball was also enriched by broadcasters and cable operators seeking exhibition rights. A *Broadcasting* magazine survey indicated that the major leagues were paid $366 million for those rights, an increase of $16 million over the amount paid in 1987. ABC-TV and NBC-TV were in the fifth year of a six-year, $1.2 billion contract with the leagues that was said to have cost the networks $200 million in 1988. The fees paid by stations and cable operators for rights to cover local teams increased 3.2%, to $158 million.

Basketball was also generating revenue for professional and college teams. A *Broadcasting* survey indicated that payments to the National Basketball Association for the 1988–89 season would approach, if not top, $130 million. For college basketball CBS signed an agreement that cost the network $55 million, including $4 million for exclusive national rights to the Big East Conference.

As for radio programming, the adult contemporary format, comprising a wide spectrum of music, much of it of the "soft rock" variety, remained the most popular choice of programming among the top ten stations in the top 50 markets in 1988. The second most popular format was contemporary hits, followed by country music.

However, radio programming was not limited to music. Radio network news programs, for instance, continued to attract substantial audiences, none more than ABC Radio's Paul Harvey. His weekday morning show topped the list with an average of 6,033,000 listeners daily, according to a report of Statistical Research Inc.

NBC's success in the ratings war did not translate into success in the contest for Emmy awards in 1988 as well as it had in 1987 and 1986. Its shows and people had been nominated 114 times, compared with 87 for CBS's and 75 for ABC's. Nevertheless, ABC walked off with the most statuettes, 21, followed by CBS with 20. NBC won 19. ABC's Emmys included two for surprise winners: "thirtysomething," which won for outstanding drama series, and "The Wonder Years," a midseason replacement in the

French television star Stephane Collaro poses with his political puppets on Channel 5, a privately owned station in France once owned by the state. Until 1986 France had only three television channels—all state owned—but in 1988 there were six, four of which were privately owned.
AFP PHOTO

1987–88 season, which won for best comedy series. CBS's awards included one for outstanding variety, music, or comedy program for "Irving Berlin's 100th Birthday Celebration," and NBC's included one for outstanding drama/comedy special for "Inherit the Wind."

In the Soviet Union the new era of liberal reform opened up remarkable opportunities for program makers. The most popular program on Soviet television was "Vzglyad" ("Outlook"), made by the youth section of Gostelradio, the state broadcasting monopoly. It regularly showed exposés of corruption and mismanagement interspersed with what used to be the forbidden fruit of Western rock music videos. The program, broadcast in six separate 90-minute transmissions to cover the entire range of time zones in the Soviet Union, attracted audiences of 120 million.

Other new Soviet programs that attracted wide attention were "Twelfth Story," a phone-in series in which government and party officials took live questions from viewers, and a late-night talk show, "To Midnight and After." The latter showed a controversial documentary, "Is It Easy to Be Young?" In that show embittered veterans of the Afghan war spoke frankly to the cameras about their experiences of drug addiction while serving in the Soviet Army.

The popular youth magazine program "Do 16 i Starshe" ("To 16 and Older") provided a diet of Western rock music along with interviews with Soviet youth. It caused a sensation when it revealed interviews with the neo-Nazi punk street gangs of Moscow, the *Liuberi*.

On the opposite side of the world and political spectrum, in Chile, a series of 30 nightly 15-minute programs on the national network was credited with capturing the imagination of the electorate and contributing to the vote against Augusto Pinochet Ugarte in the presidential plebiscite. The programs, made by Francisco Varvas, a commercials director at the Santiago production studios Film Centro, made effective use of screen advertising techniques to create a sense of freedom and reconciliation.

Ironically, while TV made a dash for freedom in the dictatorships, back in the United Kingdom, the traditional home and guardian of independent-minded, pluralistic public service broadcasting, program makers were faced with increasing restriction and the threat of censorship. The home secretary used his reserve powers to "deny the oxygen of publicity" to supporters of political violence in Northern Ireland, banning interviews on radio or TV and thereby arousing vigorous protests from broadcasters.

Another controversy that overshadowed program making in the U.K. concerned what Prime Minister Margaret Thatcher called "trial by TV." It was brought to a head by a documentary from Thames, the London ITV company, entitled "Death on the Rock," which made serious allegations against the security services in the shooting of three members of the Irish Republican Army in Gibraltar. The program went ahead despite government pleas that it be withheld until after an inquest into the incident. Some 39 errors were allegedly made in the program, and Thames appointed a former minister, Lord Windlesham, to conduct its own inquiry into claims that the program team used fabricated evidence.

Additional controversy raged over a Thames drama, "Jack The Ripper," which claimed that the fabled killer was Sir William Gull, personal physician to Queen Victoria. Experts said that the program named the wrong man. Then Central, a Midland regional ITV company, asserted in a documentary, "The Men Who Killed Kennedy," that the assassination of John F. Kennedy was the work not of Lee Harvey Oswald but of three French criminals. French authorities dismissed the claims as "pure fantasy," and the sole surviving member of the trio threatened legal proceedings against the program makers.

One of the most distinguished BBC drama productions, "Tumbledown," was also among the most controversial; it was based on the personal experiences of a Scots Guard officer seriously wounded in the Falklands campaign. Allegations that he had been neglected by his regiment after he was injured were denied by the Ministry of Defence, which demanded cuts in the script. "Tumbledown" went on to win the Prix Italia drama award.

In France the highlight of the year was a six-hour documentary series, "De Gaulle—The Eternal Challenge," based on the monumental biography by Jean Lacouture and produced for the TF1 channel by an independent company, Kuiv Productions. Using an unusual biographical technique of following a series of themes rather than a chronological order, the production included interviews with some 80 international figures, including former U.S. president Richard Nixon, Henry Kissinger, and former West German chancellor Willy Brandt. Because the recently commercialized TF1 transmitted the series in an off-peak late-evening time slot, it attracted only 16% of the possible audience.   (MARTIN JACKSON; LAWRENCE B. TAISHOFF; LEONARD ZEIDENBERG)

Amateur Radio. Ham radio operators over the years have put their hobby to good use during emergencies. In 1988, for instance, they provided communications services in areas of the western U.S. ravaged by forest fires. In one case reported by the American Radio Relay League, more than a score of amateurs maintained an amateur radio emergency service over five days at an evacuation centre near Grants Pass, Ore., in an area threatened by two fires. During Hurricane Gilbert in September, amateurs activated the Hurricane Watchnet, relaying information on the weather to areas in the path of the storm.

The FCC reported 436,963 licensed amateur radio operators in the U.S. as of Oct. 30, 1988, some 6,000 more than in 1987. Officials at the American Radio Relay League said that, excluding the U.S.S.R., for which no estimates were available, there were some two million operators worldwide, about the same number they reported in 1987.

(LAWRENCE B. TAISHOFF; LEONARD ZEIDENBERG)

See also Industrial Review: *Advertising; Telecommunications;* Motion Pictures; Music.

This article updates the *Macropædia* article BROADCASTING.

Theatre

Great Britain and Ireland. Arts Minister Richard Luce, head of the Office of Arts and Libraries (OAL), came in for much criticism but also for some praise during the year. His failure to provide subsidies that kept pace with inflation provoked angry comment from such critics of "market forces" as Sir Peter Hall, even though Sir Peter, before resigning in June as head of the National Theatre (NT), had already formed his own private company and become a partner in an Anglo-American producing management.

Qualified approval was later given to such OAL decisions as a grant to the city of Glasgow, Scotland, of £500,000, appointing the millionaire property developer and art collector Peter Palumbo to succeed Lord Rees-Mogg in March 1989 as ninth chairman of the Arts Council of Great Britain (ACGB), launching the first issue of *The Arts in Britain,* the OAL's new sumptuously produced "Flagship

publication on British Artistic Achievement," and instituting an inquiry into the workings of the ACGB. As a first step, British theatre, due to receive £170 million as its part of £400 million for arts, libraries, and museums in 1991— the last year of the current three-year funding period— would benefit from its extension into a fourth year and a final increase of 6% in 1991–92.

As in 1987, the latest ACGB figures for theatre grants revealed a cut (of about 2.5%) in real terms and reallocations that had spelled death to some smaller companies, while yet others had been taken on as clients for the first time. Fortunately, attendance figures at the NT and the Royal Shakespeare Company (RSC) increased, previous deficits were largely wiped out, and the RSC was given a three-year ACGB incentive grant of £250,000.

Eight of the awards given by the *Evening Standard* (ES), *Plays and Players* (PP), *Drama Magazine* (DM), and *Time Out* (TO) went to the NT. Michael Bryant, winner of the Society of West End Theatre's 1987 Laurence Olivier (LO) award as best supporting actor, made a memorable Prospero in *The Tempest,* one of Sir Peter Hall's swan song productions of Shakespeare's last three plays at the Cottesloe. Michael Gambon, winner of the 1987 LO best actor award, played the sadistic prison guard in Harold Pinter's production of his own *Mountain Language* at the Lyttelton. Thelma Holt, winner of the 1987 LO special award as organizer of the NT's international season, who had left to join Sir Peter's new company, was asked by Richard Eyre, Sir Peter's successor at the NT, to stage a new foreign season in 1989. The PP best supporting actor award for 1988 went to Tony Haygarth for his Caliban in Sir Peter's *The Tempest.*

The PP best director award was won by Howard Davies for *Cat on a Hot Tin Roof* and for *The Secret Rapture,* David Hare's PP- and DM-prizewinning best play. Eric Porter and Lindsay Duncan were named ES best actor and actress in *Cat on a Hot Tin Roof.* Two more PP awards were given, one to William Dudley for the designs for Howard Davies's production of *The Shaughraun* and a special one to the NT for its splendid 25-year achievements. Eyre and Dudley staged and designed *Bartholomew*

CLIVE BARDA, LONDON

Michael Crawford and Sarah Brightman starred in Andrew Lloyd Webber's *The Phantom of the Opera.* A combination of elaborate staging, masterful directing, and fine special effects made it Broadway's biggest hit of 1988.

B. D. Wong (left) beckons to John Lithgow in *M. Butterfly*, a startling play by David Henry Hwang. Based on an actual event, *M. Butterfly* is about a French diplomat and his Chinese mistress, who is, in fact, a man using the diplomat to gain information for the Communist Party of China.
MARTHA SWOPE

Fair and *The Changeling,* while with *'Tis Pity She's a Whore* Alan Ayckbourn directed his first NT classic.

At the Cottesloe, where Athol Fugard (*see* BIOGRAPHIES) staged his own drama of a Soviet Army deserter, *A Place with the Pigs,* David Leveaux had a notable directing debut with *The Father,* and Peter Gill's subtle staging of Nicholas Wright's Freudian drama *Mrs. Klein* helped to ensure its success. Simon Curtis's handling of Brian Friel's seven-year-old *Making History,* in which Stephen Rea brilliantly impersonated the 16th-century earl of Tyrone (alias Hugh O'Neill), confirmed Friel's reputation as Ireland's leading dramatist.

The RSC's awards went to Deborah Warner (best director, ES) for *Titus Andronicus,* Doug Lucie for his satirical *Fashion* (TO), and Donald Sumpter (best actor, TO) for his Iachimo in *Cymbeline,* all at the Pit, and to Peter Brook (best director, DM) for his *Mahabharata,* partly funded by the RSC, on its visit to the Glasgow Mayfest. The ACGB's John Whiting Award was won by Nick Dear, author of 1987's *The Art of Success.* Also at the Pit, Warner staged *Electra,* and Di Trevis revised her *The Revenger's Tragedy,* a transfer from Stratford. Besides the Stratford transfers of James Shirley's *Hyde Park,* the Gulag tragedy *A Question of Geography* by John Berger and Nella Bielski, and Vaclav Havel's *Temptation,* the new works at the Pit included Howard Barker's challenging *The Bite of the Night* and Stephen Lowe's black comedy *Divine Gossip.* The main theatre presented new productions of *Three Sisters* and Howard Brenton's prophetic *The Churchill Play,* newly updated. Lucy Gannon won the PP promising new playwright title for *Keeping Tom Nice,* seen at the RSC season at the Almeida, and *Raping the Gold,* premiered at the Bush.

At the Hampstead Theatre, with its sprightly revival of *Hedda Gabler,* Friel's *Aristocrats* picked up the ES new play award. The two parts of *Faust,* in David Freeman's dazzling staging of Goethe's verse-drama at the Lyric Hammersmith, won for Peter Lindford, ably playing Mephistopheles to Simon Callow's Faust, the DM supporting role citation. Timberlake Wertenbaker's *Our Country's Good,* about Australian convicts rehearsing Farquhar's *The Recruiting Officer*—with which it played in repertory at the Royal Court—was named most promising new play by the ES. Upstairs a revival of Howard Brenton's scathing

Sore Throats won for Nancy Diuguid the TO director award, which she shared with Garry Hynes, Irish director of Frank McGuinness's *Factory Girls* at the Riverside. The TO designer award went to Kate Barnett for *Dr. Faustus* at the Young Vic, where Tom Wilkinson, as Dr. Stockman in *An Enemy of The People,* won half of the DM best actor award, the other half-share going to Alex Jennings, the Glumov of Ostrovsky's *Too Clever by Half* at the Old Vic and PP actor of the year prizewinner. For her Nora Melody in the Young Vic's *A Touch of the Poet,* Vanessa Redgrave was named the DM best supporting actress.

In the West End (London commercial theatre), Pauline Collins in William Russell's monodrama of a rebel Liverpool housewife, *Shirley Valentine,* directed by Callow, won both the DM and PP best actress awards. Imelda Staunton was named PP best supporting actress for her heartbreaking Sonia in *Uncle Vanya.* Renaissance Theatre, besides taking *Hamlet* to Elsinore, won special DM and TO awards, which also singled their founders out "for revitalizing the actor-manager." Other TO awards went to three actresses, two actors, and an artistic director and to Ian McKellen

T. COOKE—CAMERA PRESS/GLOBE PHOTOS

Maggie Smith (left) plays opposite Margaret Tyzack in Peter Shaffer's new play, *Lettice and Lovage.* Although presented as a comedy, Shaffer's prize-winning play addresses such issues as modern architecture and its scorn for the past.

for his "fight against censorship." Sir Michael Hordern was rewarded by the DM for "50 years' service to the theatre."

Several Dublin "Millennium" Festival programs won major Harvey's Irish Theatre (HIT) awards. At the Abbey Jude Kelly staged Jean Binney's *Colours, Jane Barry Esq.*, with Veronica Quilligan as the 1813 miss who spent her life as an army surgeon. After Aodham Madden's monodrama *Josephine in the Night* at the Peacock came Frank McGuinness's *The Carthaginians*, in which six mourners in the doomed city of Derry gathered in a graveyard to await the Resurrection, among them Rosaleen Linehan (best actress) as the skeptical Malea and David Herlihy (best supporting actor) as Bido, their gay servant. For McGuinness's three-part Irish revision of *Peer Gynt* at the 60-year-old Gate, Patrick Mason won the director and Joe Vaneck the designer awards. Best supporting actress Doreen Hepburn and Olwen Fouere were Peer's Mother and Solveig, respectively, and Barry Lynch (best actor), Garrett Keogh, and Joe Dowling shared the roles of the young, mature, and elderly Peer among them. Though no prizewinner, *Torchlight and Laser Beams*, which Michael Scott built around the works of the crippled Christopher Nolan (*see* BIOGRAPHIES), received many critical accolades in the press. The HIT "Special Critics" award went to Brendan Kennelly's *Medea*, starring Susan Carrow. Friel's *Making History* was the HIT best play.

France, Italy, Spain, Low Countries, Greece. After the death of Jean Le Poulain, Claude Winter (Brigadier Prizewinner) acted as part-time head of the Comédie Française (CF) until Antoine Vitez became "administrateur général"; Winter then left to play Linda in a tour of *Death of a Salesman* that won Jean-Claude Grumberg a Molière prize for his new translation. François Périer, Winter's Willy Loman, won a Molière for his 50 years' service in the theatre. Other Molières went to Jacques Dufilho (*I'm Not Rappaport*); Jeanne Moreau for her acclaimed one-woman show; Loleh Bellon's penultimate drama, *The Distancing;* Laurent Terzieff, a double Molière as actor-director of James Saunders's *Fall;* Ezio Frigerio for his decor for the Théâtre National Populaire's (TNP) *Georges Dandin;* Thierry Forinau in his one-man show (Georges Bernanos's *Diary of a Country Curate*); *The School for Wives* at Marseilles (which also won for Nicola Sire a Critics' Union [CU] designer award); and Vitez's *The Satin Slipper,* his last production at the Chaillot, which won him the CU "Grand Prize."

Other CU awards went to Jean-Pierre Vincent, director

of *Der Theatermacher,* and André Marcon in *Baal,* both at the TNP; Copi's posthumous *An Untimely Visit,* a drama about AIDS, the disease that caused his death in 1987; designers Richard Peduzzi and Nicola Sire and Spanish-born actress Maria Casarès, as Hecuba, all at Gennevilliers; and playwright Cathérine Anne. Society of Authors' awards went to playwrights Roland Dubillard and French-African Sony Labu Tansi, director Antoine Bourseiller, and Marianne Basler, the Chimène of *The Cid* at Bobigny. The City of Paris Prize was won by Daniel Auteuil in *La Double Inconstance,* and the "Plaisir du Théâtre" went to Ariane Mnouchkine.

Three new Italian plays were seen in Rome, one by Gigi Lunari in Milan, and another, by Mario Missiroli, in Turin. Giorgio Strehler's major new production at the Milan Piccolo was *As You Desire Me,* with Andrea Jonasson, his wife, in the lead. Foreign imports included Sardou's *Tosca,* staged by Aldo Trionfo, and *Carmelite Dialogues,* staged by Luca Ronconi, who also put on a revival of Alfieri's *Mirra.*

The Madrid National Theatre's *El Publico,* by Federico García Lorca, also visited Strehler's European Theatre in Paris. Dirk Tanghe's updated version of *Romeo and Juliet,* at the Royal Flemish Theatre in Brussels, won a prize at the Rotterdam Festival. The new director at the Hague Comedy Theatre, now renamed the National, Hans Croiset, announced an international repertoire for his first season, including the 350-year-old *Cijsbrecht van Aemstel,* by Joost van den Vondel. London's NT made history by performing its Shakespearean trilogy at the 15,000-seat Greek Theatre of Epidaurus.

Switzerland, West and East Germany, Austria. Important productions at the Zürich Schauspielhaus were *Uncle Vanya* and *Man Is Man,* staged by its new manager, Achim Benning, and by guest director Benno Besson. Stormy debates followed the visit to the midyear "Theatre Meeting" in West Berlin, Europe's Cultural Capital '88, of two anti-Nazi plays from the Vienna Burg Theatre, Brecht's *Arturo Ui* and George Tabori's *My Struggle,* which won the Festival prize. Highlight of the autumn Festival Weeks was an extended version of Pirandello's *Six Characters in Search of an Author,* made and directed by Anatoly Vasilyev of the Moscow School of Dramatic Art.

Interesting firsts elsewhere were Tankred Dorst's *Mr. Korbes* at the Hamburg Schauspielhaus, where Michael Bogdanov was to succeed Peter Zadek as manager in 1989, Anthony Burgess's own adaptation of *A Clockwork Orange*

Two Hundred Years of "Dramaten"

The bicentennial of the Royal Dramatic Theatre, popularly known as "Dramaten," founded as Sweden's national theatre by King Gustav III on May 17, 1788, was launched on Aug. 10, 1987, with a performance in the historic Gripsholm Theatre of *Christina,* one of several plays written by Gustav III before his untimely death from an assassin's bullet in 1792. *Christina* had, in the role of the abdicating queen, the veteran Dramaten actress Anita Björk, star of Alf Sjöberg's film of *Miss Julie,* and, as the king, Jarl Kulle, recently seen in Ingmar Bergman's (*see* BIOGRAPHIES) production of *King Lear.*

In choosing the repertoire for the celebration year, which began officially on Sept. 4, 1987, and continued over the ensuing 12 months, Lars Löfgren, head

of Dramaten since 1985, placed the emphasis on Swedish drama, ancient and modern. Also included was a revival of Eugene O'Neill's *Long Day's Journey into Night,* staged by Bergman. It had Kulle as James Tyrone, Sr., and Bibi Andersson as his drug-addicted wife. The other main productions ranged from a revival of C. J. L. Almqvist's 19th-century melodrama *The Queen's Jewels,* which had been inspired by the assassination of Gustav, to one of Vilhelm Moberg's *Your Hour on Earth,* which deals with the story of a Swedish immigrant to the U.S. Another highlight was the prose version of *Mäster Olof,* Strindberg's first historical verse-drama, with which Dramaten had welcomed its first audiences into its present home in 1908. (OSSIA TRILLING)

Madonna, Joe Mantegna (centre), and Ron Silver wheel and deal in David Mamet's *Speed-the-Plow*, a scathing play about Hollywood's movie industry.
BRIGITTE LACOMBE

in Bonn, and the "Moscow Theatre Festival" in Munich, at which four companies presented ten Soviet plays. Ulrich Mühe won two top prizes as best actor at the Deutsches in East Berlin, where Volker Braun's prizewinning *The Interim Society* was also staged. Events at the Vienna Festival included performances by troupes from Hungary and the U.S.S.R. and Tabori's production of the world premiere of West German Thomas Brasch's latest antiwar drama.

Eastern Europe, Israel, Scandinavia. Events in the Soviet Union included Shatrov's anti-Stalinist *Onward, Onward, Onward,* Gennadi Bortnikov in *Krapp's Last Tape,* and Mark Lamos's production of *Desire Under the Elms* in Moscow. Nagle Jackson produced *The Glass Menagerie* in Leningrad.

At the Warsaw Theatre Meetings the Krakow Stary Theatre received the cherished prize of the International Theatre Institute. The Witkiewicz Prize for popularizing Polish theatre abroad went to London-based émigré Boleslaw Taborski. Two first productions were Jerzy Jarocki's of Erdman's *The Suicide* and Maciej Englert's of Bulgakov's *The Master and Margarita.* In Hungary the first stage version of Pasternak's *Doctor Zhivago* was put on in Szolnok. An acclaimed entry at the Belgrade "bitef" festival was the Vilnius State Theatre's prizewinning *Uncle Vanya.*

In Haifa, Israel, Yehoshua Sobol's antifundamentalist *Jerusalem Syndrome* was roundly condemned by Israel's religious right wing. In Tel-Aviv–Yafo, Andrzej Wajda revived the Habima's 66-year-old classic *The Dybbuk,* and the first permanent Yiddish Theatre was opened in March with *It's Hard to Be a Jew* by Sholem Aleichem.

Denmark's Royal Theatre celebrated 400 years since Christian IV's accession to the throne with Sven Holm's costume-drama of *Your Majesty,* starring John Hahn-Petersen in the lead. Rodil Kjer's popular one-woman version of the Oscar-winning *Babette's Feast* delighted Norwegian audiences at the Bergen Festival, where Tormod Skagestad's critical drama about Norway's disgraced Nobel Prize winner Knut Hamsun was also seen. Stockholm's Royal Dramatic Theatre's bicentennial was cause for a yearlong celebration. (*See* Sidebar.) New plays from Scandinavia were staged at the 60th Theatre Festival in Helsinki.   (OSSIA TRILLING)

United States and Canada. Although theatre activity on Broadway declined again in 1988, amounting to some 15 shows specifically created for production there, the ones that did succeed were so successful and so striking that they proved that whatever was wrong with Broadway was

wrong financially rather than artistically. The notion of a commercial stage remained valid. That was as plain as the mask on the face of *The Phantom of the Opera.*

The achievements of Andrew Lloyd Webber had certainly been great in recent years. Even with *Cats* already the most profitable show in history and still running alongside the composer's *Starlight Express,* however, nothing was to compare with his *Phantom of the Opera,* which in 1988 became the hit of hits and, in effect, the only show in town.

Webber's love of opera, which had led to such "rock operas" as *Evita* and *Cats,* could in this show be exploited in legitimate operatic forms. The composer took the opportunity to compose parodies ranging from the banality of *La Gioconda* to the heavenliness of *The Marriage of Figaro* and to such modern-day experiments as 12-tone music. His gift for melody soared above these musical jokes, carried by the fundamental theatrics of this story and its setting. As directed by Harold Prince and starring Michael Crawford (*see* BIOGRAPHIES), *Phantom* was a spectacle of unprecedented brilliance (and expense).

Broadway's dramatic success story for 1988 was similarly spectacular. David Henry Hwang based his play *M. Butterfly* on a true story but one so bizarre that, by his own admission, no writer would ever have dared dream it up. A transvestite Chinese is enlisted by the Communists to romance a French diplomat in order to learn military secrets about France's struggle with the North Vietnamese. The espionage leads to a 20-year "affair," during which the Frenchman admits (or claims) that he never knew his lover was a man. By drawing a parallel between these strange (to say the least) goings-on and Puccini's opera *Madame Butterfly,* Hwang makes observations on how Western misconceptions about the Far East affect international politics, how there is a sexual aspect to East-West relations, and how men create the idea of female sexuality in their own image.

The play became Broadway's first outright dramatic hit in many years and, ironically, it did so during a year that was unusually strong in drama. Strongest, perhaps, of all was a new play by Chicago's redoubtable David Mamet. Called, to the bewilderment of most, *Speed-the-Plow,* it is set in a nearly bare and almost abstract Hollywood movie office in which two executives are gleefully celebrating a surefire movie deal until they are interrupted by a secretary who is sexually liberated but a social reformer. Seducing one of the producers, she nearly persuades him to replace

Ron Richardson (right) plays opposite Hiroyuki Sanada in the Tokyo production of *Big River,* a musical based on *The Adventures of Huckleberry Finn.* Richardson, an American actor, delivered his lines in phonetically learned Japanese but sang his songs in English.
THE NEW YORK TIMES

his planned commercial movie with one about the continued existence of mankind.

Other dramas produced on Broadway during the year were Lee Blessing's *A Walk in the Woods,* a two-character piece about the personal side of U.S.-Soviet disarmament talks, and an ambitious but somewhat confusing dream play called *Joe Turner's Come and Gone* by August Wilson (*see* BIOGRAPHIES), author of the previous year's prizewinning *Fences.*

So estimable a level of drama made the June best-of-the-year Tony awards contest particularly competitive (*M. Butterfly* won), and that was true of the contest for musicals as well, even though the competition involved only two shows, *The Phantom of the Opera* and *Into the Woods* by Stephen Sondheim. Sondheim won the prize for music, but Webber's show won almost everything else, including best new musical.

Inevitably, others attempted to copy the formula that Webber had presumably been following. Their attempts only proved that the successful succeed because they are gifted and able, not because they have found a simple formula. One such rock opera, *Chess,* had been written by Webber's former lyricist, Tim Rice, to music by the Swedish rock group ABBA. First produced in London in 1986 and first staged by the late U.S. director Michael Bennett, *Chess* finally arrived on Broadway under the directorship of Trevor Nunn, who had staged both *Cats* and *Starlight Express.* Within weeks, *Carrie,* another rock opera, which also had begun in London, arrived under the direction of Nunn's assistant, Terry Hands. Despite their imitation of all the externals of Webber's shows, both *Chess* and *Carrie* were multimillion-dollar disasters.

As if to demonstrate the continuing unpredictability of theatre, while these modern-day rock operas were vying for audiences, the long-dark Lincoln Center Theatre found

its revival of *Anything Goes* so popular that it canceled the entire season to let the Cole Porter musical run indefinitely. In the smaller theatre downstairs, *Waiting for Godot* was presented with a cast that included Robin Williams and Steve Martin. With such stars, the limited engagement was sold out even before the show opened, and audiences cared little that the comedians were playing slipshod with Samuel Beckett's masterwork.

With such glamour and success at Lincoln Center, New York City's other institutional theatres were left in the background, but they carried on. Joseph Papp's New York Shakespeare Festival, ever true to its original purposes, embarked on an ambitious cycle intended, over the next several years, to present every one of Shakespeare's plays with casts including the likes of Meryl Streep and Christopher Walken. The initial productions were more appealing to the audiences than to the critics until Walken's *Coriolanus,* which proved to be to the taste of all.

Outside of New York, institutional theatres remained torn between their original purpose of presenting either classics or uncommercial plays and finding box-office attractions to replace the government funding lost because of federal government policies. San Diego's Old Globe Theatre, for instance, produced a new Neil Simon play, *Rumors,* in what amounted to a Broadway tryout (it did not fare especially well when it opened on Broadway). On the other hand, Chicago's Goodman Theatre continued as a model of imaginative institutional responsibility, ranging from classic musical comedies such as *Pal Joey* to Shakespeare's *Romeo and Juliet.*

In Canada the prestigious Stratford Festival seemed to have found a way, at last, of keeping the professionalism of an established institution without developing a museum lifelessness. In 1987 the festival presented its first musical, *Cabaret,* and in 1988 it produced *My Fair Lady.* On the Shakespearean front, artistic director John Neville freshened his acting company with bright newcomers while steadying them with a core of such Stratford veterans as Douglas Campbell, William Hutt, and Nicholas Pennell. Their most publicized Shakespeare was a *Taming of the Shrew* reset in pre-rock, teenage America, circa 1950, but there was also a solid set of traditional Shakespearean productions, including *All's Well That Ends Well, The Two Gentlemen of Verona, Twelfth Night, Richard III,* and *King Lear.* There was one sad note to the season, however: the death of Jean Gascon (*see* OBITUARIES), at one time an artistic director at Stratford.   (MARTIN GOTTFRIED)

See also Dance; Music.

This article updates the *Macropædia* article The History of Western THEATRE.

Transportation

The successful privatization of railways and airlines in Japan prompted other countries to take similar steps. Mexico and New Zealand privatized their airlines, although further consolidations within U.S. airlines demonstrated the cyclical nature of such activity. Argentina and Brazil approved plans for the sale of their railway networks, while Malaysia was reconsidering revised plans for rail disposal. The U.K. government received offers for BREL, the railways' engineering division, and for the Settle–Carlisle line, as precursors of more extensive disposals.

Within Europe deregulation issues were given additional momentum by the initiatives to implement a single-market policy within the European Communities (EC) by 1992. In a wider context, environmental issues gained some promi-

Flight paths, weather conditions, and visibility are monitored on a prototype of a system designed for air traffic controllers. Congested airways and anticipated increases in air travel were forcing the U.S. Federal Aviation Administration to upgrade its air traffic control system.
WALTER P. CALAHAN

nence, ranging from emission controls in vehicles to the devastating floods that inundated Bangladesh and seriously damaged its transport networks.   (JOHN H. EARP)

AVIATION

The dominant concern for the air transport industry in 1988 was the increase in airport and airspace congestion, particularly in the U.S. and Western Europe. Only 78% of the departures of major Western European airlines from airports in Europe were within 15 minutes of the scheduled time during June, and there were some delays of 18 hours or more to nonscheduled flights during the peak season.

Approximately 1.1 billion passengers traveled by air in 1988 worldwide. According to industry forecasts, the number was expected to reach two billion by the end of the century. The implications of this growth for airport and air traffic control authorities were serious. In the U.S. the Federal Aviation Administration was taking action to increase airspace capacity, and in August 1988 it awarded a $3.6 billion contract to upgrade the national air traffic control system. Some Western European authorities planned similar action, though progress was slower, partly because of poor international coordination. Airport development in many countries was aimed at increasing capacity, but few entirely new airports were planned. The only large new airports currently under construction were at Osaka, Japan, and Munich, West Germany, and both were intended to replace existing airports.

In its 1988 annual report, the International Civil Aviation Organization (ICAO) said that in 1987, scheduled passenger traffic experienced its highest growth rate since 1979. Passenger-kilometres totaled 1,590,000,000 (1 km = 0.62 mi), 9.7% above 1986, and freight ton-kilometres, at 48,350,000,000, registered a 12% increase. Overall, 1987 scheduled traffic reached 196,640,000,000 ton-kilometres, up 10.1%. The U.S. airline industry accounted for 37% of total world scheduled traffic, and that of the Soviet Union for 11%, according to ICAO data. The highest growth rate in scheduled traffic among major nations in 1987 was in China, with 33%.

Scheduled international traffic for 1988 was about 9% higher than in 1987, according to preliminary estimates by the International Air Transport Association (IATA). The figure related to IATA member airlines, which accounted for two-thirds of world traffic. In the first half of 1988 IATA recorded a 10.5% increase in passenger traffic and an 11.1% increase in freight traffic, compared with the same

period of 1987. IATA member airlines flew 99.8 billion passenger-km on scheduled services in 1987, an increase of 13.9% over 1986. The passenger load factor was 65.7%, substantially better than the 1986 figure of 62.7%. Ton-kilometres flown in 1987 totaled 90.2 billion for passenger traffic, 36.3 billion for freight, and 3.1 billion for mail.

The North Atlantic routes remained the biggest international market. IATA members' total scheduled traffic on these routes grew by 18.1% in 1987, and strong growth continued into 1988. ICAO data on regional activity showed the Asia/Pacific region as the third most important, after North America and Europe, with the fastest growth in total traffic. Major U.S. carriers experienced 22.3% growth in passenger traffic on Pacific routes in the first half of 1988. In domestic operations by U.S. major carriers, the number of passengers carried declined in the first half of 1988 by 2.6%, though traffic (in passenger-kilometres) declined only 0.6%, indicating longer average journeys. The U.S. national carriers, which had approximately an 11% share of domestic passenger traffic (in passenger-kilometres), reported an 18.2% increase in number of passengers.

Overall financial results for the industry, though better than in recent years, still showed low returns. ICAO figures placed world airline revenue at $144.5 billion. This was 16% higher than in 1986, but fluctuations in dollar exchange rates made meaningful year-on-year comparisons difficult. According to IATA, airlines were having problems maintaining revenue yield (the rate of revenue per traffic unit) when traffic was increasing rapidly.

The fatal accident rate on world scheduled services in 1987 was 0.18 per 100,000 landings, according to the ICAO. There were 23 fatal accidents. Though the rate was higher than in 1986 (when it was 0.14), it was about average for the past five years.   (DAVID WOOLLEY)

SHIPPING AND PORTS

One of the most important events affecting shipping was the resolution of a cease-fire between Iraq and Iran. During the protracted Gulf war 400 ships had been attacked and 61, amounting to ten million deadweight tons (dwt), either sunk or written off by insurers. The first results of the cease-fire were a cut in insurance rates and a general easing of shipping problems in the Gulf. Longer-term effects could be the release of as much as three million dwt of tankers to the world freight market. Poor harvests in China and large grain demand from the U.S.S.R. set the scene for a continued dry bulk cargo market during the summer and

autumn. The volume of laid-up tonnage fell to the lowest level in recent history, amounting in August to 458 ships of around 10.2 million dwt.

Optimism was reflected in port infrastructures around the world. The Polish port of Gdansk embarked on a massive investment program to cope with the growth of intermodal business as trans-Europe north–south links developed. In Southeast Asia the Asian Development Bank provided technical assistance to the Philippines for a feeder ports project. Hong Kong International Terminals won the right to build and operate a seventh terminal at Kwai Chun, the world's largest container terminal. The 31.5-ha (78-ac) Hong Kong complex was to be completed in 1991. The Suez Canal Authority commissioned a $2.5 million feasibility study for further deepening and widening of the canal to take ships up to 260,000 dwt.

The phenomenal success of the cruise market continued, with many new cruise ships under construction, including three for Sitmar Cruises, which was taken over by P&O for $210 million. P&O would thus be the largest cruise fleet operator with, eventually, ten ships with 9,770 berths. The Indian shipowner Ravi Tikkoo sought a £70 million U.K. government grant to take over the Harland and Wolff shipyard in Belfast and build the world's largest cruise ship there. Named *Ultimate Dream,* it would be 345 m long (1 m = 3.28 ft), have a gross tonnage of 160,000, and accommodate 3,026 passengers in 1,513 cabins.

At 403.4 million gross tons (gt), the total tonnage of the world fleet remained almost the same as in 1987. At the end of 1988 the principal merchant fleets by flag registry were Liberia 49.7 million gt (down 1.6 million), Panama 44.6 million gt (up 1.3 million), Japan 32 million gt (down 3.8 million), the U.S.S.R. 25.7 million gt (up 500,000), Greece 21.9 million gt (down 1.5 million), and the U.S. 20.8 million gt (up 600,000). Oil tankers accounted for 122.3 million gt of the world fleet and bulk/ore carriers for 109.6 million gt. Other principal ship types were general cargo ships (71.8 million gt), containerships (22.1 million gt), liquefied gas carriers (9.7 million gt), and chemical tankers (8.9 million gt). (EDWARD CROWLEY)

FREIGHT AND PIPELINES

Freight activity continued to focus on the Asia-Pacific Rim. Hong Kong retained its number one position in container handling. With additional midstream activities, total handling was increased to nearly four million TEU per year. Rotterdam, Neth., remained the busiest port in freight tons, including oil. U.S. freight totals were at record levels, with 1,512,000,000 revenue/metric tons in 1988. Growth of containerized freight in the U.S. was helped by the expanded use of piggybacking and double-stacked containers weighing up to 54,400 kg (120,000 lb). Rail haulage of grain and coal in the U.S. grew at the expense of barge traffic as the Mississippi dried up in the worst drought in 50 years.

In Europe container traffic increased 10% to new record levels of 794.3 million TEU/km. The Swiss were negotiating with the EC for a north-south rail link involving increased tunnel width to allow heavy trucks to pass through on railroad cars. The year saw the introduction of 3,800-TEU containerships that were wider than the Panama Canal and a new, nonstandard 53' container. In East Germany record levels of freight were moved in a system wholly comprising 20' boxes. A nonstop Perth–Adelaide container train was introduced in Australia, and first freight services were started between Algeria and Morocco. Mongolia reached an agreement to move its freight through China, thereby reducing its dependence on routing via the Soviet Union.

Barges back up along the Mississippi River after drought conditions lowered its waters to an unnavigable level. As the water level dropped, the amount of freight shipped by rail rose; shippers who normally moved goods on barges had to turn to the railroads.
AP/WIDE WORLD

Despite the continuance of a five-year downward trend in pipeline usage, the planned mileage to be installed in 1988 had increased by 38% to 35,979 km, 10,619 in the U.S. and 25,342 elsewhere. Two more trunk-line systems to bypass the Strait of Hormuz were being developed: from Iraq to Yanbu' in Saudi Arabia and from Taheri/Jask in Iran to the Gulf of Oman. These two pipelines and other new trunk lines from Iraq and Iran through Turkey would reduce the total world movement of oil by sea by up to 5%, with serious implications for tanker replacement in the 1990s.

ROADS AND TRAFFIC

Planning and construction of highway networks continued in the developed countries in 1988, and many major bridges were opened as key links in these networks. The 12-km-long Seto Ohashi bridge chain linking the Japanese islands of Honshu and Shikoku via Kojima and Sokaide was completed after ten years. In Turkey a second Bosporus bridge, linking Asia with Europe, was opened, with a 1,090-m main span length. Also completed was the world's longest single-plane cable-stayed bridge (450 m) over the Chao Phraya River in Thailand. Bids were received for a 2.6-km suspension bridge linking Rion and Antirion in Greece; this would be 300 m longer than the Humber Bridge in the U.K., currently the world's longest suspension bridge.

In less developed countries the emphasis was on maintenance. According to a World Bank report, one-fourth of all paved roads outside urban areas and one-third of all unpaved roads needed to be rebuilt. Poor road conditions increased vehicle operating costs by 50 to 100%. The guidelines "fix it—don't build" were appropriate for Bangladesh, where 80% of the country was flooded and the whole

A magnetic train known as the Transrapid is tested on a track in West Germany. The West Germans were hoping to outmaneuver the Japanese in the race to produce a high-speed magnetic train; at stake were several multimillion-dollar contracts in the United States.
DPA/PHOTOREPORTERS

transport network was seriously damaged. Bangladesh was to be the recipient of a 900-m section of a 2.8-km bridge that was no longer needed after completion of the Eastern Scheldt barrier project in The Netherlands.

In East Africa a start was made on the 1,500-km transportation route from Dar es Salaam, Tanzania, to Malawi, consisting of 750 km of rail, 250 km of road, and 400 km of ship links. When completed, it would provide a secure import-export route for landlocked Malawi.

The first automatic toll system was opened on Norway's west coast using an electric identity plate. A surcharge on gasoline and diesel fuel paid for construction of a 1,600-km road program in Australia, completed for the nation's bicentennial in 1988.

Privately funded BOT (build-operate-transfer) projects were emerging in the highway sector; a north-south artery through Malaysia was being discussed, as were a second tunnel crossing at Hong Kong (linked to the metro [subway] development) and a tunnel crossing of Sydney (Australia) Harbour.

INTERCITY RAIL

Spurred on by the success of the Japanese Shinkansen and the French Train à Grand Vitesse, the number of high-speed 300 km/h rail projects was growing steadily, although there were some difficulties in obtaining financial backing. In the U.S. the most advanced scheme was a 480-km line through Florida. In Australia studies were under way for a 360-km/h Very Fast Train to cut the journey time from Sydney to Melbourne to three hours.

In Japan work was begun on the Fukushima–Yamagata route and on the Hokuriku line on Honshu Island. In Europe the Channel Tunnel was proceeding, although it was behind schedule. With new lines open or under construction in France, Britain, Belgium, The Netherlands, East and West Germany, Austria, Switzerland, Italy, and Spain, a new high-speed rail network was beginning to emerge in Western Europe. New express services opened linking Rome with Milan (576 km in less than four hours) and Moscow with the Black Sea. A new Paris–Kowloon (Hong Kong) through service taking 20 days was opened in September.

In Africa the emphasis was on rehabilitation of lines in Mozambique and Tanzania, the Benguela railway in Angola, and lines in Zaire. The World Bank voted funds for rehabilitation of lines in The Sudan, Ghana, and India. China completed the electrification of its main east-west route, Zhengzhon–Xi'an–Lanzhou (Chengchou–Sian–Lan-

chou). The Dutch introduced a new intercity train, the IC3, not hauled by locomotives but driven by diesel truck engines, which reduced noise and vibration.

The French National Railways had a particularly black year with six accidents that killed 68 persons and injured 192. The most serious incident, at the Gare de Lyon in Paris, involved the malfunction of fail-safe equipment. In Rio de Janeiro, Brazil, a craze for riding on top of railroad cars, called train surfing, killed over 150 youths.

URBAN MASS TRANSIT

Light-rail systems continued their spectacular growth. They were seen both as a cost-effective means of transport and as a catalyst to urban regeneration. New systems were opened in Tuen Mun, Hong Kong; Krivoy Rog near Dnepropetrovsk, U.S.S.R.; Istanbul; and Rochefort, Belgium. Extensions to existing systems were opened in Atlanta, Ga.; San Jose, Calif.; Düsseldorf, West Germany; and Melbourne, Australia. Construction contracts were placed for new systems for Milan; Bangkok, Thailand; St. Louis, Mo.; Córdoba, Spain; Manila; and Goiás, Brazil.

Franchising was a new feature of light-rail systems; for example, in Ankara, Turkey. Use of automated control was also growing. A number of cities authorized the upgrading of trolley systems to light rail, including Lü-ta (Talien) and Tientsin (T'ienchin), China, and Guadalajara, Mexico. In Paris the 9.1-km Ladefense–Isey Plaine line was to be reinstalled. Seattle introduced a dual mode (diesel-electric) bus, the first such vehicle in 40 years. Germany introduced a similar vehicle.

Voters in Dallas, Texas, vetoed the construction of a planned $2.9 billion, 150-km subway, and U.S. subway systems came under federal criticism for being overexpensive and underused. Nevertheless, New York City's system carried a record volume of passengers, and a $177 million rehabilitation program was begun on its 84-year-old Lexington line. Existing lines were extended in Singapore and Brussels, and new lines were planned or under construction in Haifa, Israel; Hong Kong; Tehran, Iran; and Shanghai. Seoul was planning nine more lines. Chiba, Japan, and Sydney, Australia, opened new monorail systems.

South African Transport Services was to be broken into five companies prior to privatization. In the U.K. privatization of the bus companies was followed by a 6% loss in patronage. (JOHN H. EARP)

See also Energy; Engineering Projects; Environment; Industrial Review: *Aerospace; Automobiles.*

This article updates the *Macropædia* article TRANSPORTATION.

World Affairs: Contents

For your convenience this article groups the countries of the world by the geopolitical regions to which they belong. Certain related topics, such as United Nations, Dependent States, and various regional affairs articles (*e.g.*, Latin-American Affairs), are also included. An alphabetical list of these topics appears below, indicating the page where each may be found. Articles on the various countries update the *Macropædia* articles of the same name (except where otherwise noted), as do the more extensive statistical treatments in the *World Data* section.

World Affairs

According to the Western media, 1988 was the year when "peace broke out." Relations between West and East improved; the rapprochement between the Soviet Union and China continued; the Soviet Union announced its willingness, in principle, to withdraw troops from Afghanistan. Iran accepted the UN proposal to end the Gulf war, and Angolan peace accords were signed. The popular conception was, on the whole, correct, even though local conflicts persisted, and civil wars and domestic tension were aggravated in some countries and erupted in others that had been enjoying relative calm (for example, Burma).

When U.S. Pres. Ronald Reagan and Soviet leader Mikhail Gorbachev met in Washington in December 1987 and again in Moscow in late May 1988, the signing of the intermediate-range nuclear forces (INF) treaty had been the high point of the talks. Other strategic arms had been discussed, as well as nuclear and space weapons, nuclear testing, nuclear nonproliferation, and chemical weapons, but it was clear from the outset that further progress, though likely, would be slow. In both countries domestic policies took pride of place during the months that followed. The United States was preoccupied with the presidential election campaign, which resulted, after a bitter fight, in a victory for Vice-Pres. George Bush. In the U.S.S.R. Gorbachev strengthened his position at the 19th (extraordinary) Communist Party conference, which led to the demotion of some of his leading opponents. *Perestroika* (restructuring), according to candid public announcements, proceeded less quickly and smoothly than expected, but Soviet "new thinking" in foreign policy expressed itself in a constant stream of state and diplomatic visits.

One of the main issues discussed in Western capitals and in Tokyo was whether and to what extent the industrialized countries should help Gorbachev's policy (and Eastern Europe) by means of a new Marshall Plan. The phrase had been coined by Ciriaco De Mita, the new Italian prime minister. Such a policy was strongly supported by West Germany, but it was viewed with skepticism by Britain and the United States, in view of the magnitude of the loans and investments that would be involved and the uncertainty of success barring radical reform in the Soviet economic system, and also because of political considerations.

In April 1988 a four-party peace accord (Afghanistan and Pakistan, with the U.S. and the U.S.S.R. as guarantors) was signed in Geneva concerning the withdrawal of Soviet troops from Afghanistan. The conviction that armed intervention had been a mistake had been gaining ground in the Soviet Union for years, but for obvious political reasons the decision to disengage had not come easily. The withdrawal of Soviet troops began in May 1988, but the fighting continued, albeit on a reduced scale.

The war in the Persian Gulf between Iran and Iraq had lasted almost as long as the Afghan civil war, but its end came as a greater surprise. Having rejected many mediation efforts, the Tehran government suddenly announced on July 18 that it accepted the UN Security Council's peace plan; a cease-fire came into force on August 20. Iran's growing international isolation, as well as the weakening of its economy, greatly contributed to this decision; the Iraqi use of long-range missiles, poison gas, and chemical weapons (reportedly also applied by Baghdad against its Kurdish minority) may also have played a role. Elsewhere in the Middle East, Palestinian demonstrations and attacks against Israeli occupation of the West Bank and Gaza continued during 1988. Jordan's King Hussein renounced the

"Jordanian option" and cut his country's legal and administrative ties to the West Bank. The Palestine Liberation Organization declared an independent Palestinian state, but it also recognized Israel's right to exist in language clear enough to convince the U.S. that contacts with the PLO were justified. Meanwhile, no end was in sight for the Lebanese crisis.

At year's end the four-power talks on Angola produced agreements providing for the withdrawal of Cuban troops from that country and independence for South West Africa/ Namibia. South African foreign policy showed considerable initiative on the African continent, in the hope, no doubt, that a normalization of relations with key African countries would lessen internal pressures on the part of the black majority.

European politics were largely dominated by the coming abolition of the last internal economic barriers: by 1992 a European Common Market was to exist in practice as well as in theory. The opposition to a further extension of European supervision and control came, above all, from British Prime Minister Margaret Thatcher's government and probably had to do more with the political than with the economic implications of this development. Western Europe enjoyed a period of relative prosperity and stability; the reelection of Pres. François Mitterrand in France and the coming to power of a Socialist government under Prime Minister Michel Rocard brought no radical domestic changes and even fewer new departures in French foreign policy. Eastern Europe, on the other hand, went through a time of considerable turbulence: galloping inflation and growing national tensions shook Yugoslavia; Romania was in the throes of a general crisis; Poland, Hungary, and Czechoslovakia faced both economic difficulties and domestic dissent. In the Baltic republics of the Soviet Union, a strong movement for greater national independence reemerged. While the European countries felt less afraid of each other (Gorbachev's concept of the "common home"), the differences between them grew no smaller and the specific problems confronting them no less urgent.

Leaders of the major industrial countries expressed broad satisfaction after having discussed the world economy at their annual meeting in Toronto (June 19–21). Such optimism was justified inasmuch as no major shocks occurred in 1988. But the long-range issues and potential sources of economic crisis had not disappeared and were bound to resurface sooner or later.   (WALTER LAQUEUR)

This article updates the *Macropædia* article 20th-Century INTERNATIONAL RELATIONS.

UNITED NATIONS

As the U.S. and the U.S.S.R. achieved something of a rapprochement in 1988, the United Nations began to justify the original assumption underlying its charter—namely, that great-power unity is an essential condition for establishing peace. During the year war weariness and converging great-power interests led to movement on issues that had been stuck for decades on the UN agenda: Soviet troops in Afghanistan, the Iran-Iraq war, independence for South West Africa/Namibia, and conflicts in Angola and in the Western Sahara.

UN achievements received a formal accolade on September 29 when the Nobel Peace Prize Committee awarded $388,000 to UN peacekeeping forces (*see* BIOGRAPHIES), 14 of which had since 1948 monitored trouble spots around the world. The committee hailed them for helping the UN "play a more central part in world affairs" and investing it with "increasing trust." The committee credited the UN with reducing strife even when it could not find polit-

ical solutions and congratulated Secretary-General Javier Pérez de Cuéllar (*see* BIOGRAPHIES) and Ecuadorian Foreign Minister Diego Cordóvez, the former under secretary-general who worked for years on the Afghanistan problem. The award was the fourth Nobel honour for the UN; in 1954 and 1981 prizes went to its High Commissioner for Refugees and in 1965 to the UN International Children's Fund (UNICEF).

At the time of the award, UN forces were stationed along the India-Pakistan border, in the Sinai, on the Golan Heights, in Lebanon, and in Cyprus. During 1988 two new UN forces went to monitor cease-fire agreements in Afghanistan and on the Iran-Iraq border, and another was being organized for Namibia.

Afghanistan. Soviet Foreign Minister Eduard A. Shevardnadze indicated (January 6) that his government hoped to withdraw its 115,000 troops from Afghanistan by the end of 1988. Long, intensive negotiations followed, and by agreement (April 14), the U.S.S.R. began to withdraw (May 15) while 50 UN military observers watched. By August 15 half the Soviet troops had left.

At a Security Council meeting (September 28) each side charged the other with violating the April accords. On November 3 the Assembly called on all parties to respect them and work for a broad-based Afghan government. The next day, however, the U.S.S.R. suspended troop withdrawals, although it said that it still expected to withdraw completely by February 1989. On November 19 Soviet leader Mikhail Gorbachev accused the U.S. and Pakistan of trying, despite "grave consequences," to force Moscow to abandon its commitments; he later said that the UN might have to call an international conference to preserve Afghanistan's "independence, territorial integrity, and nonaligned character."

Iran-Iraq War. Progress toward settling the Iran-Iraq conflict was slow and erratic, but the secretary-general worked at it constantly. He condemned Iraq (March 25) for using poison gas against Kurdish civilians, both on its own territory and in Iran, and agreed to send investigators to Iran. They reported that, while chemical weapons had been used, they could not detect their "nationality." Another UN report (August 1) accused both belligerents of using chemical weapons but called Iraq the major offender.

The Security Council unanimously expressed (July 20) "deep distress" over the shooting down by the U.S. (July 3) of an Iranian airliner, killing all 290 people aboard. In a Council debate (July 14) Vice-Pres. George Bush called the incident a "terrible human tragedy." He maintained, however, that the U.S. had mistaken the airliner for an Iranian fighter jet and insisted that Iran made an "irresponsible" and "tragic error" by allowing a civilian aircraft to pass over a warship engaged in battle.

The Iran-Iraq poison gas inquiry initiated talks between the secretary-general and Iranian authorities to establish a cease-fire in the war with Iraq under Security Council Resolution 598 (1987). On July 18, after eight years of combat and one million deaths on both sides, Iran accepted the idea of a truce; on August 8 both parties pledged to end hostilities on August 20 and to start direct talks five days later, with the secretary-general acting as mediator; and the Security Council unanimously agreed (August 9) to send 350 unarmed UN observers to check on the truce.

Talks between the two belligerents occurred intermittently after that but were complicated by renewed charges that Iraq was using poison gas against the Kurds and by Iranian objections to Iraq's demand that it guarantee unhindered navigation for Iraqi shipping in the Persian Gulf and reopen the Shatt al-Arab, the disputed waterway that

The United Nations General Assembly votes to move its session on the Palestinian question to Geneva in order to allow Palestine Liberation Organization chairman Yasir Arafat to speak. Arafat was unable to address the UN at its New York City headquarters because he was denied a visa to the U.S.

BRIAN F. ALPERT—KEYSTONE

was Iraq's only outlet to the sea. By year's end the only firm agreements achieved were that the talks should continue; that Jan K. Eliasson, Sweden's chief UN delegate, should represent the secretary-general in them; and that the two sides should exchange some sick and wounded POWs, which they began to do November 24 and suspended three days later.

Angola and Namibia. After nine sessions at various locations, Angola, Cuba, and South Africa agreed tentatively in November and finally in December to abide by Security Council Resolution 435 (1978), to withdraw Cuban and South African troops from Angola over 27 months from April 1, 1989, and to pave the way for Namibian independence in 1989. The advance part of a UN Transitional Assistance Group that would supervise elections leading to full independence arrived in Namibia October 2 and, on December 20, the Security Council voted to send to Angola a 70-member "verification mission" to check on Cuban withdrawal.

Morocco. Algeria and Morocco announced (May 16) that they would restore diplomatic relations that were broken in 1976 as a result of the dispute over Western Sahara. They also agreed with the secretary-general's plan to hold a referendum to determine the wishes of the Western Saharans. They consented (August 27) to a cease-fire and to having a UN special representative supervise the peacemaking and help determine who exactly would vote in the referendum.

Israel. When Yasir Arafat, chairman of the Palestine Liberation Organization (PLO), asked to address the General Assembly in New York, the U.S. refused to issue him a visa. The Assembly then decided to meet in Geneva to hear him (December 13). Two days later the Assembly called for an international peace conference to "achieve a just and comprehensive settlement" of the Arab-Israeli conflict with all parties (including the PLO) participating with the five permanent Security Council members. The U.S. and Israel cast the only negative votes, although other states abstained.

On November 15 Arafat had announced in Algiers that the Palestine National Council had declared the establishment of a state of Palestine "with holy Jerusalem as its capital." Even though the Palestine Council's 1968 covenant described the 1947 UN resolution that partitioned Palestine between Arabs and Jews as "null and void," the Algiers declaration envisaged peace talks with Israel based upon it.

It also cited as the basis for an international peace conference Security Council Resolutions 242 (1967), implicitly affirming Israel's right to "secure and recognized" borders, and 338 (1973), calling for negotiations based on the earlier resolution. The document stated that the PLO "rejects terrorism in all its forms" but still tolerated violence in lands controlled by Israel. In a press conference (December 14), Arafat said that the PLO renounced terrorism and accepted the right of all parties in the Middle East to exist in peace and security.

The announcement came after 11 months of Arab insurrection against the Israeli-occupied West Bank and Gaza, the subject of several Security Council resolutions. Two (January 5 and 14) asked Israel not to deport Palestinians arrested in the disturbances. Israel defied the resolutions, calling them "biased and unbalanced" for condoning Palestinian violence while condemning Israeli countermeasures. On November 3 the General Assembly voted 130–2 (Israel and the U.S.) with 16 nations abstaining to condemn Israel for "killing and wounding defenseless Palestinians" and for disregarding Council resolutions.

PLO Office. The U.S. tried to close the PLO mission at UN headquarters in New York because the PLO was "a terrorist organization and a threat to the interests of the United States" that "should not benefit from operating" on U.S. territory. Its efforts foundered, however, after the Assembly (March 2 and 23) opposed the U.S. move, the International Court of Justice (April 26) decided that the U.S. must arbitrate the question, and, finally, a U.S. federal district court (June 29) ruled that, under the 1947 Headquarters Agreement, the U.S. "must allow PLO representatives access to and presence in the vicinity of the United Nations." The U.S. decided (August 29) not to pursue the argument.

Kampuchea. On November 3 the Assembly declared (122–19–13) that Kampuchea must not restore the brutal rule of the Khmer Rouge after Vietnam withdrew its 120,000-man-strong occupation forces. Vietnam said that it planned such a withdrawal in the next two years.

Cyprus. The secretary-general asked Turkey (June 9) to withdraw some of the 29,000 troops it had maintained in northern Cyprus since 1974 and arranged (August 24) the first meeting since 1985 between the president of Cyprus, George Vassiliou, and Rauf Denktash, the Turkish-Cypriot leader. The two agreed to try by June 1, 1989, to achieve "a just and lasting solution," but later talks made no progress.

Budget. The U.S. was legally obligated to pay 25% of the UN budget. (The second largest contributor was Japan [10.84%], followed by the U.S.S.R. [10.2%], West Germany [8.26%], France [6.37%], and the U.K. [4.86%].) The U.S. fell so far behind in its payments in 1988, however, that it was actually in danger of losing its Assembly vote under Charter Article 19, which denies a vote to any member two years in arrears. In September and October the U.S. gave the UN checks totaling about $100 million of the $520 million it owed, but UN officials, while pleased to have the money, warned that the remaining indebtedness continued to handicap them heavily. The U.S. said that it wanted further austerity measures, even though the UN had already met demands to cut its staff by 15% and had arranged for Soviet nationals, previously hired only on fixed-term contracts, to accept career posts in the Secretariat.

Third World Debt. The UN Conference on Trade and Development, meeting in Paris, called (September 1) for commercial banks to forgive at least 30% of the debt of 15 heavily indebted less developed nations. Without such forgiveness, an official said, debtor countries "will simply not be able to grow out of their debt problem." Later in September the World Bank decided to take a larger role in managing the economic problems of debtor countries.

Famine Relief. UN famine relief efforts in Ethiopia and The Sudan were interrupted several times during the year by civil wars that intensified starvation as the government forces and rebels intermittently prevented supplies from reaching people in territories controlled by their opponents.

Officials of the Food and Agriculture Organization reported (April 22) that sub-Saharan Africa faced a resurgence of famine because vast swarms of locusts were moving south from northern Africa and would ravage the crops in their path, destroying from 20 to 30% of the year's food supply in some of the world's poorest nations.

AIDS. High-ranking health officials from 145 countries, determined to mount a major attack on AIDS, met in London for a three-day (January 26–28) international summit meeting. The delegates called AIDS "a global problem that poses a serious threat to humanity" and adopted a strategy for slowing its spread by educating people to understand its modes of transmission. UN agencies were working to mobilize against AIDS the combined resources of national ministries of education, planning, and health, as well as agencies charged with family planning, child care, and urban development.

Human Rights. During this 40th anniversary year of the Universal Declaration of Human Rights (celebrated December 10), the UN Commission on Human Rights received a report (in March) indicating that human rights violations, such as torture and involuntary disappearances, continued in Chile, but that the overall situation had improved since February 1985. Another report (released in November) accused Iran of executing more than 1,000 political prisoners in July, August, and September, after Iran accepted the cease-fire in its war with Iraq. Iran refused to admit a UN team to investigate the charges. The commission accepted an invitation to send a six-person delegation to Cuba to investigate human rights there in September and reported in December that Cuban abuses of human rights had declined, with 121 long-term political prisoners still in jail. (In 1987 the U.S. had charged that Cuba held 15,000 political prisoners.)

The UN announced (April 18) that the U.S. had signed the Convention Against Torture and Other Cruel, Inhuman, or Degrading Treatment or Punishment that the Assembly adopted in 1984. The convention, already signed by 62 countries and ratified by 29, called on nations to punish or extradite torturers, compensate torture victims, and establish a committee to monitor violations.

Forty years after the Assembly framed the treaty outlawing genocide (an attempt to destroy national, ethnic, racial, or religious groups), the U.S. joined 97 other UN members in making it law (October 19). The treaty committed signatories to work to prevent genocide and to punish offenders.

On December 10, in Geneva, negotiators from 80 states completed a treaty on children's rights. It was expected to come before the Assembly in 1989.   (RICHARD N. SWIFT)

This article updates the *Macropædia* article UNITED NATIONS.

COMMONWEALTH OF NATIONS

The main international focus of Commonwealth activity in 1988, as in the previous few years, remained on South Africa. As agreed upon at the Vancouver, B.C., summit of October 1987, a Commonwealth Committee of Foreign Ministers was set up as the heir to the Commonwealth Eminent Persons' Group, which two years earlier had led the major diplomatic effort by the international community to try to bring the South African government toward negotiations with its black majority. The new committee brought together the foreign ministers of Australia, Canada, Guyana, India, Nigeria, Tanzania, Zambia, and Zimbabwe. Their goal was to ensure that the international community continued to focus attention on apartheid and the deepening tragedy in South Africa, South West Africa/Namibia, and the southern African region.

During the year two meetings of the committee were held, one in Zambia and one in Toronto. In the second meeting particularly, Commonwealth Secretary-General Sir Shridath Ramphal emphasized how correct had been the Commonwealth analysis in Vancouver that the situation both internally in South Africa and throughout the region was actually deteriorating because of increased violence by the South African regime. Among the measures taken by the Commonwealth during the year as a result of commitments made at Vancouver were the establishment of the Special Fund for Technical Assistance to Mozambique and work on enhancing the security of the frontline nations.

While work on apartheid dominated the Commonwealth agenda, other efforts continued on a wide front. In August the Commonwealth of Learning network of education over long distances was formally launched. The new institution, which was to be based in Canada, was the first Commonwealth organization to have its headquarters outside Britain. On a very different subject, the Commonwealth set up a study of the impact on small islands and low-lying coastal areas of natural disasters that result from man-made climatic changes. Among the member nations that had been seriously affected by these environmental phenomena were Bangladesh and the Maldives.

At the 1988 finance ministers' meeting in Cyprus in September, a report was presented proposing a Commonwealth Equity Fund. The ministers had become aware that many Commonwealth less developed countries were having difficulty in attracting much-needed new financing because private capital flows and net bank lending had virtually dried up. A Commonwealth Equity Fund was proposed as a vehicle for portfolio investment in those countries.

In all of these initiatives, including those on apartheid, the major split that had developed in Vancouver between Britain and the rest of the Commonwealth did not prevent work from continuing. Thus the fears that the Commonwealth might have been seriously weakened by the difference of opinion on methods of dealing with apartheid, the organization's most important policy plank, did not materialize.   (VICTORIA BRITTAIN)

POLITICAL PARTIES

The following table is a general world guide to the political parties of the world. All countries that were independent on Dec. 31, 1988, are included; there are a number for which no analysis of political activities can be given, such as one-party states. Parties are included in most instances only if represented in parliaments (in the lower house in bicameral legislatures); the figures in the last column indicate the number of seats obtained in the last general election (figures in parentheses are those of the penultimate one) and exclude nonelective seats. The date of the most recent election follows the name of the country.

The code letters in the affiliation column show the relative political positions of the parties within each country; there is, therefore, no entry in this column for single-party nations. There are obvious difficulties involved in labeling parties within the political spectrum of a given country. The key chosen is as follows: F-fascist; ER-extreme right; R-right; CR-centre right; C-centre; L-non-Marxist left; SD-social democratic; S-socialist; EL-extreme left; and K-Communist.

The percentages in the column "Voting strength" indicate proportions of the valid votes cast for the respective parties, or the number of registered voters who went to the polls in single-party states. (K. M. SMOGORZEWSKI)

Political Parties

Country / Name of party	Affiliation	Voting strength (%)	Parliamentary representation
Afghanistan (April 1988)			
National Front of Afghanistan	—	—	184
Albania (February 1987)			
Albanian Labour (Communist)	—	100	250 (250)
Algeria (February 1987)			
National Liberation Front	—	87	295 (281)
Angola (August 1980)			
Movimento Popular de Libertação de Angola (MPLA)	—	—	203
Antigua and Barbuda (April 1984)			
Antigua Labour Party	C	...	16 (13)
Progressive Labour Movement	L	...	0 (3)
Independents	—	...	1 (1)
Argentina (September 1987)			
Movimiento Justicialista Nacional (Peronist)	CR	...	105 (103)
Unión Cívica Radical	C	...	117 (130)
Others	—	...	32 (21)
Australia (July 1987)			
National	R	11.5	19 (21)
Liberal	C	34.3	43 (45)
Labor	L	45.8	86 (82)
Austria (November 1986)			
Freiheitliche Partei Österreichs	R	9.7	18 (12)
Österreichische Volkspartei	C	41.3	77 (81)
Sozialistische Partei Österreichs	SD	43.3	80 (90)
Vereinigte Grüne Österreich (Greens)	—	4.8	8 (0)
Bahamas, The (June 1987)			
Progressive Liberal Party	CR	53	31 (32)
Free National Movement	L	...	16 (8)
Others	—	...	2 (3)
Bahrain			
Emirate, no parties	—	—	—
Bangladesh (March 1988)			
Jatiya Party	—	...	250 (183)
Combined opposition	—	...	18 —
Awami League Party	—	(Boycotted)	(76)
Other parties	—	...	5 (39)
Independents	—	...	25 (32)
Barbados (May 1986)			
Democratic Labour Party	C	59.5	24 (7)
Barbados Labour Party	L	40.4	3 (17)
Belgium (December 1987)			
Vlaams Blok	ER	1.9	2 (1)
Volksunie	R	8.0	16 (16)
Front Démocratique des Francophones	R	1.2	3 (3)
Liberals { Flemish	CR	11.5	25 (22)
Liberals { French	CR	9.4	23 (24)
Social Christians { Flemish	C	19.5	43 (49)
Social Christians { French	C	8.0	19 (20)
Socialists { Flemish	SD	14.9	32 (32)
Socialists { French	SD	8.0	40 (35)
Others	—	7.1	9 (10)
Belize (December 1984)			
United Democratic Party	R	...	21 (5)
People's United Party	C	...	7 (13)
Benin (June 1984)			
People's Revolutionary Party	—	—	196 (336)
Bhutan			
A monarchy without parties	—	—	—
Bolivia (July 1985)			
Acción Democrática Nacionalista	R	37.0	52
Movimiento Nacionalista Revolucionaria	C	42.0	60
Christian Democratic Party	C	2.0	3
Movimiento de la Izquierda Revolucionaria	L	11.0	16
Small left-wing parties	L	15.0	22
Botswana (September 1984)			
Botswana Democratic Party	C	...	29 (29)
Botswana People's Party	L	...	1 (1)
Botswana National Front	EL	...	4 (2)

Country / Name of party	Affiliation	Voting strength (%)	Parliamentary representation
Brazil (November 1986)			
Partido do Movimento Democrático Brasileiro (coalition)	R & L	...	479 (200)
Partido Democrático Social	SD	...	0 —
Partido Comunista Brasileiro	K	...	0 —
37 other parties	—	...	8 (277)
Brunei			
Legislative Council (nonelected)	—	—	—
Bulgaria (June 1986)			
Fatherland Front			⌈276
Bulgarian Communist Party			
Bulgarian Agrarian People's Union	}	99.9 { 99	400 (400)
Independents			⌊25
Burkina Faso			
National Revolutionary Council since August 1983	—	—	—
Burma (October 1985)			
Burma Socialist Program Party	—	...	489 (475)
Burundi			
Military Committee for National Salvation took power September 1987	—	—	—
Cameroon (April 1988)			
Rassemblement Démocratique du Peuple Camerounais	—	90.1	180 (120)
Canada (November 1988)			
Progressive Conservative	CR	43	170 (211)
Liberal	C	32	82 (40)
New Democratic	L	20	43 (30)
Others	—	5	0 (1)
Cape Verde (December 1985)			
African Party for the Independence of Cape Verde and independents	—	94	83 (56)
Central African Republic (August 1987)			
Rassemblement Démocratique Centraficain	—	...	52
Chad			
Military government since 1975	—	—	—
Chile			
Military junta since Sept. 11, 1973	—	—	—
China, People's Republic of (March–April 1988)			
Communist (Kungchantang) National People's Congress	—	...	2,978
Colombia (March 1986)			
Partido Conservador	R	...	82 (84)
Partido Liberal	C	49	100 (114)
Nuevo Liberalismo	C	...	7 —
Unión Patriótica	EL	...	10 —
Comoros (March 1987)			
Federal Assembly	—	65	42 (38)
Congo (August 1984)			
Parti Congolais du Travail	—	—	153 (115)
Costa Rica (February 1986)			
Partido de Liberación Nacional	L	...	29 (33)
Partido Unidad Social Cristiana	CR	...	25 (18)
Others	—	...	3 (6)
Côte d'Ivoire (November 1985)			
Parti Démocratique de la Côte d'Ivoire	—	...	175 (100)
Cuba (December 1986)			
Partido Comunista Cubano	—	...	499 (499)
Cyprus			
Greek Zone (December 1985)			
Democratic Rally	CR	33.56	19 (12)
Democratic Party (DIKO)	C	27.65	16 (8)
Socialist Party (EDEK)	SD	11.07	6 (3)
Communist Party (AKEL)	K	27.43	15 (12)
Turkish Zone (June 1985)			
National Turkish Party	—	...	24
Communal Liberation Party	—	...	10
Turkish Republican Party	—	...	12
New Dawn Party (Renaissance)	—	...	4

Country / Name of party	Affiliation	Voting strength (%)	Parliamentary representation
Czechoslovakia (May 1986)			
National Front	—	99.4	200 (200)
Denmark (May 1988)			
Conservative	R	19.3	35 (38)
Liberal Democratic (Venstre)	CR	11.8	22 (19)
Christian People's	CR	2.0	4 (4)
Progress	C	9.0	16 (9)
Radical Liberal (Radikale Venstre)	C	5.6	10 (11)
Centre Democrats	C	4.7	9 (9)
Social Democrats	SD	29.9	55 (54)
Common Course	L	1.9	0 (4)
Socialist People's	EL	13.0	24 (27)
Left Socialists	EL	0.6	0 (0)
Faeroe Islands and Greenland	—	...	4 (4)
Djibouti (April 1987)			
Rassemblement Populaire pour le Progrès	—	87	65 (65)
Dominica (July 1985)			
Freedom Party	C	59.0	15 (17)
Labour Party	L	...	5 (2)
Independents	—	...	1 (2)
Dominican Republic (May 1986)			
Partido Reformista Social Cristiano	R	...	56
Partido Revolucionario Dominicano	L	...	48
Partido de la Liberación Dominicana	EL	...	16
Ecuador (January 1988)			
Frente de Reconstrucción Nacional			⌈ 7 15
Partido Social Cristiano			1 (1)
Partido Conservador			1 (3)
Partido Liberal Radical			
Concentración de Fuerzas Populares	} R & CR	... 16 {	5 (4)
Frente Radical Alfarista			2 (3)
Others			⌊ 0 (1)
Frente Progresista Democrática			⌈31 (17)
Izquierda Democrática			8 (8)
Democracia Popular			4 6
Partido Socialista Ecuatoriano			
Movimiento Popular Democrático	} L & EL	... 55 {	2 (4)
Frente Amplio de Izquierda			2 (3)
Partido Roldosista Ecuatoriano			⌊ 8 (5)
Others	—	...	0 (1)
Egypt (April 1987)			
New Wafd Party	R	7.8	35 (57)
National Democratic Party	CR	77.2	346 (391)
Socialist Labour Party and allies parties	L	13.4	60 (0)
Independents	—	1.6	7 (0)
El Salvador (March 1988)			
Alianza Republicana Nacionalista	R	55	30 (13)
Partido Auténtico Institucional Salvadoreño	R	...	0 (1)
Partido de Conciliación Nacional	CR	...	7 (12)
Partido Acción Democrática	CR	...	0 (1)
Partido Cristiano Democrático	C	...	23 (33)
Equatorial Guinea (July 1988)			
National Assembly	—	...	41
Ethiopia (June 1987)			
Shengo (National Assembly)	—	85.4	835
Fiji			
Military government suspended constitution May 1987	—	—	—
Finland (March 1987)			
National Coalition Party (Conservative)	R	23.2	53 (44)
Swedish People's	R	5.3	13 (11)
Centre (including former Liberal) Party	C	17.6	40 (38)
Christian Union	C	2.6	5 (3)
Rural Party	C	6.3	9 (17)
Social Democratic	SD	24.3	56 (57)
People's Democratic League (Communist)	K	9.4	16 (17)
Green Party	—	4.0	4 (10)
Democratic Alternative	—	4.2	4 (10)
Others	—	6.1	0 (1)

Political Parties

Country / Name of party	Affili-ation	Voting strength (%)	Parlia-mentary represen-tation
France (June 1988)			
Front National	F	1.1	1 (35)
Rassemblement pour la République	R	23.1	127 (147)
Union pour la Démocratie Française	R	21.1	129 (130)
Diverse right	—	2.6	16 (14)
Parti Socialiste	SD	45.3	260
Mouvement des Radicaux de Gauche	SD	1.3	9 } (207)
Diverse left	—	2.1	7 (9)
Parti Communiste	K	3.4	27 (35)
Other	—	...	1 —
Gabon (February–March 1985)			
Parti Démocratique Gabonais	—	95.44	111 (84)
Gambia, The (March 1987)			
People's Progressive Party	C	59.2	31 (27)
National Convention Party	—	...	5 (4)
German Democratic Republic (June 1986)			
National Front (Sozialistische Einheitspartei and others)	—	99.7	500 (500)
Germany, Federal Republic of (January 1987)			
Christlich-Demokratische Union	R	34.5	174 (191)
Christlich-Soziale Union		9.8	49 (53)
Freie Demokratische Partei	C	9.1	46 (34)
Sozialdemokratische Partei Deutschlands	SD	37.0	186 (193)
The Green (Ecology) Party	—	8.3	42 (27)
Ghana			
Military dictatorship since Dec. 31, 1981	—	—	—
Greece (June 1985)			
New Democracy Party	CR	40.8	126 (115)
Panhellenic Socialist Movement (Pasok)	SD	45.8	161 (172)
Greek Communist Party (KKE)	K	9.4	12 (13)
Eurocommunists	K	1.4	1 (0)
Grenada (December 1984)			
New National Party	C	...	14
Grenada United Labour Party	R	...	1
Guatemala (November 1985)			
Movimiento de Liberación Nacional	ER	6.3	6
Partido Institucional Democrático	R	6.3	6
Central Auténtica Nacionalista	R	6.3	1
Partido Nacionalista Renovador	CR	3.2	1
Partido Democracia Cristiana	C	38.7	51
Unión del Centro Nacional	C	20.2	22
Partido Revolucionario/Partido de Democrático de Conciliación Nacional	C	13.8	11
Partido Socialista Democrático	SD	3.2	2
Guinea			
Military Committee for National Redress in power since April 1984	—	—	—
Guinea-Bissau (March–May 1984)			
African Party for the Independence of Guinea and Cape Verde	—	...	150
Guyana (December 1985)			
People's National Congress	S	77.0	42 (41)
People's Progressive Party	K	11.0	8 (10)
Others	...	0.5	3 (0)
Haiti			
Military government since February 1986	—	—	—
Honduras (November 1985)			
Partido Nacional	R	...	63 (34)
Partido Liberal	CR	...	67 (44)
Others	C	...	4 (4)
Hungary (June 1985)			
Patriotic People's Front	—	...	361
Independents	—	...	25
Iceland (April 1987)			
Independence Party	R	27.2	18 (23)
Citizen's Party	R	10.9	7 —
Progressive (Farmers') Party	C	18.9	13 (14)
Social Democratic Party	SD	15.2	10 (6)
People's Alliance	K	13.3	8 (10)
Women's Alliance	—	10.1	6 (3)
Others	—	...	1 (4)
India (December 1984; figures incomplete)			
Congress (I)	C	...	395 (351)
Communist Party of India (Marxist)	K	...	22 (35)
Communist Party (pro-Soviet)	K	...	6 (10)
Other opposition parties and independents	—	...	121
Indonesia (April 1987)			
Golkar (Functional Groups)	—	73.0	299 (246)
United Development Party	—	16.0	61 (94)
Indonesian Democratic Party (merger of five nationalist and Christian parties)	—	11.0	40 (24)

Country / Name of party	Affili-ation	Voting strength (%)	Parlia-mentary represen-tation
Iran (April–May 1988)			
Consultative Assembly, no parties since 1987	—	...	270
Iraq (October 1984)			
Ba'th Party	—	...	183
Others	—	...	67
Ireland (February 1987)			
Fianna Fail (Sons of Destiny)	C	44.1	81 (75)
Fine Gael (United Ireland)	C	27.1	51 (70)
Progressive Democrats	C	11.9	14 —
Irish Labour Party	L	6.5	12 (16)
Others	—	10.4	8 (5)
Israel (November 1988)			
Tehiya	ER	...	3 (5)
Shas	R	...	6 (4)
Likud	R	...	39 (41)
National Religious	CR	...	5 (4)
Agudat Israel	C	...	5 (2)
Labour Alignment { Labour	SD	...	38 } (44)
Labour Alignment { Mapam	SD	...	3 }
Citizens' Rights	SD	...	5 (3)
Hadash	K	...	5 (4)
Other parties	—	...	11 (13)
Italy (June 1987)			
Movimento Sociale Italiano	F	5.9	35 (42)
Partito Liberale Italiano	CR	2.1	11 (16)
Democrazia Cristiana	C	34.3	234 (225)
Partito Repubblicano Italiano	C	3.7	21 (29)
Partito Social-Democratico Italiano	L	3.4	17 (23)
Partito Socialista Italiano	SD	14.3	94 (73)
Partito Radicale	EL	2.6	13 (11)
Partito Comunista Italiano	K	26.6	177 (198)
Democrazia Proletariana	K	1.7	8 (7)
Greens	—	2.5	13 —
Others	—	...	7 (6)
Jamaica (December 1983)			
Jamaica Labour Party	L	...	60 (51)
People's National Party	SD	(Boycotted)	(9)
Japan (July 1986)			
Liberal-Democratic Party	R	49.6	300 (250)
Komeito (Clean Government)	C	...	57 (58)
Democratic Socialist Party	SD	...	28 (38)
Japan Socialist Party	S	...	87 (112)
Japan Communist Party	K	...	27 (26)
Others	—	...	13 (27)
Jordan			
Royal government, no parties	—	...	142
Kampuchea (May 1981)			
Kampuchean United Front for National Salvation (Vietnamese-backed)	—	99.0	117
Kenya (March 1988)			
Kenya African National Union	—	48.0	188
Kiribati (March 1987)			
House of Assembly, no parties	—	84.0	39 (36)
Korea, North (November 1986)			
Korean Workers' (Communist) Party	—	...	...
Korea, South (April 1988)			
Democratic Justice Party	C	33.9	125
Party for Peace and Democracy	L	19.3	70
Reunification Democratic Party	L	23.8	59
New Democratic Republican Party	L	15.6	35
Others	—	7.4	(10)
Kuwait			
National Assembly abolished July 1986	—	—	—
Laos, People's Democratic Republic of			
Lao People's Revolutionary Party	—	...	...
Lebanon (April 1972)			
Maronites (Roman Catholics)	—	...	30
Sunni Muslims	—	...	20
Shi'ah Muslims	—	...	19
Greek Orthodox	—	...	11
Druzes (Muslim sect)	—	...	6
Melchites (Greek Catholics)	—	...	6
Armenian Orthodox	—	...	4
Other Christian	—	...	2
Armenian Catholics	—	...	1
Lesotho			
Military Council in power from January 1986	—	—	—
Liberia (October 1985)			
National Democratic Party of Liberia	R	...	45
Opposition	L	...	19
Libya			
Military government since Sept. 1, 1969	—	—	—
Liechtenstein (February 1986)			
Vaterländische Union	CR	50.2	8 (8)
Fortschrittliche Bürgerpartei	C	42.7	7 (7)

Country / Name of party	Affili-ation	Voting strength (%)	Parlia-mentary represen-tation
Luxembourg (June 1984)			
Parti Chrétien Social	CR	25	(24)
Parti Libéral	C	14	(15)
Parti Ouvrier Socialiste	SD	21	(14)
Parti Communiste	K	2	(2)
Ecologists	—	2	(0)
Madagascar (August 1983)			
Advance Guard of the Malagasy Revolution (Arema)	C	64.8	117 (112)
Madagascar Independence Congress	L	8.8	9 (16)
Movement for Proletarian Power	L	11.1	3 —
People's Party for National Unity	L	10.6	6 (7)
Madagascar National Independence Movement (Monima)	L	3.7	2 —
Malawi (May 1987)			
Malawi Congress Party	—	...	112 (101)
Malaysia (August 1986)			
National Front (Barisan Nasional) Coalition			
United Malays National Organization		83	
Malaysian Chinese Association		17	
Malaysian Indian Congress		57.4 6 } 148 (133)	
Malaysian People's Movement		5	
Sabah and Sarawak parties		37	
Opposition Parties			
Democratic Action Party		15.6 24	
Pan-Malaysian Islamic Party		... 1 } 29 (21)	
Independents		... 4	
Maldives (December 1984)			
Citizens' Assembly	—	...	40
Mali (June 1988)			
Union Démocratique du Peuple Malien	—	...	82
Malta (May 1987)			
Nationalist Party	R	50.9	35 (31)
Labour Party	SD	48.9	34 (34)
Mauritania			
Military government since April 25, 1981	—	—	—
Mauritius (August 1987)			
Mouvement Socialiste Mauricien		26	
Mauritius Labour Party	C	9	
Parti Mauricien Social Démocrate		4 } (43)	
Org. du Peuple Rodriguais		2	
Mouvement Militant Mauricien			
Mouvement Travailliste Démocrate	L	21 (19)	
Front des Travailleurs Socialiste			
Mexico (July 1988)			
Partido Acción Nacional	CR	...	101
Partido Revolucionario Institucional	CR	...	261
National Democratic Front	L	...	138
Monaco (January 1988)			
Union Nationale et Démocratique	—	...	18 (18)
Mongolia (June 1986)			
Mongolian People's Revolutionary Party	—	99.9	370 (354)
Morocco (September 1984)			
Union Constitutionelle	CR	...	83 —
Rassemblement National des Indépendants	CR	...	61 (141)
Mouvement Populaire	CR	...	47 (44)
Istiqlal (Independence)	C	...	41 (49)
Union Socialiste des Forces Populaires	L	...	36 (16)
Others	—	...	38 (14)
Mozambique (November–December 1986)			
Frente da Libertação de Moçambique (Frelimo)	—	...	250 (210)
Nauru (January 1987)			
Independents	—	...	18 (18)
Nepal (May 1986)			
140-member Parliament, 122 elected and 28 appointed by the king; no parties			
Netherlands, The (May 1986)			
Christen Democratisch Appèl	CR	34.6	54 (45)
Volkspartij voor Vrijheid en Democratie	C	17.4	27 (36)
Democraten 1966	C	6.1	9 (6)
Partij van de Arbeid	SD	33.3	52 (47)
Others	—	...	8 (16)
New Zealand (August 1987)			
National (Conservative) Party	CR	45.0	39 (37)
Democratic Party	C	6.0	0 (2)
Labour Party	L	47.0	58 (56)
Nicaragua (November 1984)			
Democratic Conservative Party	CR	14.0	14
Independent Liberal Party	C	9.6	9
Popular Social Christian Party	L	5.6	6
Sandinista National Liberation Front	L	66.8	61
Socialist Party of Nicaragua	EL	1.4	2
Communist Party of Nicaragua	K	1.5	2
Marxist-Leninist Popular Action Movement	K	1.0	2

Political Parties

Country / Name of party	Affiliation	Voting strength (%)	Parliamentary representation
Niger			
Military government since April 1974	—	—	—
Nigeria			
Military government since December 1983	—	—	—
Norway (September 1985)			
Høyre (Conservative)	R	30.1	50 (53)
Kristelig Folkeparti	CR	8.3	16 (15)
Senterpartiet (Agrarian)	C	6.7	12 (11)
Venstre (Liberal)	C	3.1	0 (2)
Progress Party	C	3.7	2 (4)
Arbeiderpartiet (Labour)	SD	41.2	71 (66)
Sosialistisk Venstreparti (Socialist Left)	S	5.4	6 (4)
Oman			
Independent sultanate, no parties	—	·	—
Pakistan (November 1988)			
Islamic Democratic Alliance	R	...	54
Jamit-i-Ulema-i-Islam	R	...	7
Pakistan People's Party	C	...	93
Mohajir Qaumi Movement	—	...	13
Other parties	—	...	11
Independents	—	...	27
Panama			
Since July 1982 a civilian president under "indirect" military supervision	—	—	—
Papua New Guinea (June–July 1987)			
Pangu Party	—	14.7	26 (51)
People's Democratic Movement	—	10.8	18 —
National Party	—	5.1	12 (13)
Melanesian Alliance	—	5.6	7 (8)
People's Action Party	—	3.2	6 (7)
People's Progress Party	—	6.1	5 (14)
Others	—	...	14 (12)
Independents	—	41.2	21 (4)
Paraguay (February 1988)			
Partido Colorado (A. Stroessner)	R	...	48 (40)
Opposition parties	—	...	24 (20)
Peru (April 1985)			
Convergencia Democrática	R	...	12
Acción Popular	CR	...	10
Alianza Popular Revolucionaria Americana	SD	...	107
Izquierda Unida	L	...	48
Izquierda Nacionalista	L	...	1
Independents	—	...	2
Philippines (May 1987)			
House of Representatives	—	...	200
Poland (October 1985)			
Front of National Unity			
Polish United Workers' Party			245 (261)
United Peasants' party			106 (113)
Democratic Party	—	78.86	35 (37)
Non-party			74 (49)
Portugal (July 1987)			
Social Democratic Centre Party	R	4.4	4 (22)
Democratic Renewal Party	CR	4.9	7 (45)
Social Democratic Party	C	50.2	148 (88)
Socialist Party	SD	22.2	60 (57)
United People's Alliance	K	12.1	31 (38)
Qatar			
Independent emirate, no parties	—	—	—
Romania (March 1985)			
Social Democracy and Unity Front	—	99.99	369 (369)
Rwanda (December 1988)			
National Revolutionary Development Movement	—	...	70
Saint Kitts and Nevis (June 1984)			
People's Action Movement	CR	...	6 (3)
Nevis Reformation Party	CR	...	3 (2)
Labour Party	L	...	2 (4)
Saint Lucia (April 1987)			
United Workers' Party	C	52.7	9 (14)
St. Lucia Labour Party	S	38.1	8 (2)
Progressive Labour Party	EL	9.2	0 (1)
Saint Vincent and the Grenadines (July 1984)			
St. Vincent Labour Party	CR	41.4	4 (11)
New Democratic Party	C	51.4	9 (2)
United People's Movement	L	3.2	0 (0)
San Marino (May 1988)			
Partito Comunista		...	18 (15)
Partito Socialista		...	7 (...)
Partito Socialista Unitario		...	8 (8)
Christian Democrats		...	27 (26)
Social Democratic Party		...	0 (1)
Republican Party		...	0 (1)
São Tomé and Príncipe (August–September 1985)			
Movimento Libertação	—	—	40

Country / Name of party	Affiliation	Voting strength (%)	Parliamentary representation
Saudi Arabia			
Royal government, no parties	—	—	—
Senegal (February 1988)			
Parti Socialiste	CR	71.3	103 (111)
Parti Démocratique Sénégalais	L	24.7	17 (8)
Other parties	—	4.0	0 (1)
Seychelles (December 1987)			
People's Progressive Front	—	...	23 (23)
Sierra Leone (May–June 1986)			
All People's Congress and independents	—	...	105 (85)
Singapore (September 1988)			
People's Action Party	CR	61.8	80 (77)
Workers' Party	L	...	0 (1)
Democratic Party	—	...	1 (1)
Solomon Islands (October 1984)			
National Democratic Party	L	...	1
United Party	—	...	13
People's Alliance Party	—	...	12
Solomone Ano Sagufenua	—	...	4
Independents	—	...	7
Somalia (December 1984)			
Somalian Revolutionary Socialist Party	—	99.86	171 (171)
South Africa (May 1987)			
Herstigte Nasionale Party	ER	3.1	0 (0)
Conservative Party	R	26.4	22 —
National Party	R	52.5	123 (131)
New Republic Party	C	1.9	1 (8)
Progressive Federal Party	L	14.1	19 (26)
Independent		0.04	1 —
Spain (June 1986)			
Alianza Popular	R	26	105 (105)
Centro Democrático y Social	C	9	19 (11)
Convergència (Catalan nationalists)	C	4	18 (12)
Partido Socialista Obrero Español	SD	44.1	184 (202)
Izquierda Unida (Communists)	K	4	7 —
Partido Nacionalista Vasco	—	1.5	6 (8)
Herri Batasuna (Basque radicals)	—	1.1	5 (2)
Others	—	...	6 (10)
Sri Lanka (July 1977)			
United National Party	R	...	140 (19)
Freedom Party	C	...	8 (91)
Tamil United Liberation Front	C	...	18 (12)
Communists and others	—	...	2 (44)
Sudan, The (April 1986)			
National Islamic Front	R	...	51
National Umma Party	C	...	99
Democratic Unionist Party	L	...	63
South Sudan Political Alliance	—	...	9
39 other parties	—	...	42
Suriname (November 1987)			
National Democratic Party	—	...	2
Front for Democracy and Development (three-party coalition)	—	...	42
Others	—	...	7
Swaziland (November 1987)			
House of Assembly, no parties	—	...	40
Sweden (September 1988)			
Conservative	R	18.4	66 (76)
Centre	CR	11.4	42 (44)
Liberal	C	12.2	44 (51)
Social Democrats	SD	43.6	156 (159)
Communists	K	5.9	21 (19)
Greens	—	5.5	20 (0)
Switzerland (October 1987)			
Christian Democrats	R	...	42 (42)
National Campaign	R	...	3 (5)
Evangelical People's	R	...	3 (3)
Swiss People's	CR	...	25 (23)
Radical Democrats	C	...	51 (54)
League of Independents	C	...	8 (8)
Liberal Democrats	L	...	9 (8)
Social Democrats	SD	...	41 (47)
Progressive Organization (Socialists)	EL	...	4 (3)
Communist Party	K	...	1 (1)
Environmentalist Party	—	...	9 (3)
Others	—	...	4 (3)
Syria (February 1986)			
Ba'th Party	—	...	129
National Progressive Front	—	...	57
Communist Party	—	...	9
Taiwan (Republic of China)			
Nationalist (Kuomintang)	—	...	773
Tanzania (October 1985)			
Chama Cha Mapinduzi	—	...	169 (111)
Thailand (July 1988)			
Prachakorn Thai	ER	8.7	31 (24)
Chart Thai Nation	R	24.4	87 (63)
Democratic Party	C	13.4	48 (100)
Social Action Party	C	15.1	54 (51)
United Democratic Party	C	1.4	5 (38)
United Thai Party	—	9.8	35 (19)
Others	—	27.1	97 (52)

Country / Name of party	Affiliation	Voting strength (%)	Parliamentary representation
Togo (March 1985)			
Rassemblement du Peuple Togolais	—	96.0	77 (67)
Tonga (February 1987)			
Legislative Assembly	—	—	9
Trinidad and Tobago (December 1986)			
People's National Movement	C	32	3 (26)
National Alliance for Reconstruction (four parties)	—	66	33 —
Tunisia (November 1986)			
National Front (led by the Parti Socialiste Destourien)	—	...	138 (136)
Turkey (November 1987)			
Right Path	CR	19.2	59 —
Motherland	CR	36.2	292 (212)
Social Democratic Populist	C	24.8	99 —
Democratic Left	L	8.5	0 —
Others	—	10.9	0 (188)
Tuvalu (September 1985)			
House of Assembly, no political parties	—	—	12
Uganda			
Military Council in power since July 1985	—	—	—
Union of Soviet Socialist Republics (November 1984)			
Communist Party of the Soviet Union	—	99.99	1,500 (1,500)
United Arab Emirates			
Federal government of seven emirates	—	—	—
United Kingdom (June 1987)			
Conservative	R	42.3	375 (397)
Alliance			
Liberal	C	12.8	17 (17)
Social Democratic	SD	9.8	5 (6)
Labour	L	30.8	229 (209)
Communist	K	...	0 (0)
Scottish National Party	—	1.3	3 (2)
Plaid Cymru (Welsh Nationalists)	—	0.4	3 (2)
Ulster Unionists (three groups)	—	1.2	13 (15)
Social Democratic and Labour Party	—	...	3 (1)
Sinn Fein (Northern Ireland)	—	...	1 1
Other (speaker)	—	...	1 —
United States (November 1988)			
Republican	CR	...	173 (177)
Democratic	C	...	262 (258)
Uruguay (November 1984)			
Colorado Party (Conservative)	R	38.6	40
Unión Civica	CR	2.3	2
National (Blanco) Party	C	32.9	36
Frente Amplio (Broad Front)	L	20.4	21
Vanuatu (November 1987)			
Union of Moderate Parties	CR	42.0	20 (12)
Vanuaaku Parti	C	47.0	26 (24)
Others	—	11.0	0 (3)
Venezuela (December 1988)			
COPEI (Social Christians)	CR	31.43	67 —
Acción Democrática	L	43.76	98 (118)
Movimiento al Socialismo			
Movimiento de Izquierda Revolucionaria	SD	10.27	19 ...
Other parties	—	14.54	20 ...
Vietnam (April 1987)			
Vietnam Fatherland Front	—	...	496
Yemen, People's Democratic Republic of (October 1986)			
Yemen Socialist Party and independents	—	...	111
Yemen Arab Republic (July 1988)			
Consultative Council	—	...	128
Yugoslavia (May 1986)			
Communist-controlled Federal Chamber	K	...	220 (220)
Zaire (September 1987)			
Mouvement Populaire de la Révolution	—	...	210 (268)
Zambia (October 1988)			
United National Independence Party		67.0	125
Zimbabwe (June–July 1985)			
Zimbabwe African National Union	—	77.0	63 (57)
Zimbabwe African People's Union	—	20.0	15 (20)
United African National Council	—	...	0 (3)
Zimbabwe African National Union (Sithole)	—	...	1 (0)
white roll			
Conservative Alliance of Zimbabwe	—	...	15 (20)
Independent Zimbabwe	—	...	4
Independent	—	...	1 (0)

Africa South of the Sahara

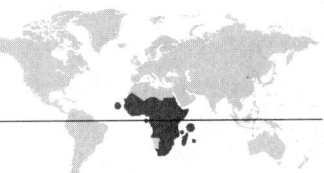

AFRICAN AFFAIRS

Reasonably good climatic conditions over much of the continent except for the Sahel region just south of the Sahara improved the ability of most countries to provide for at least their minimum food requirements in 1988. However, economic recovery in most of sub-Saharan Africa was, at best, marginal, owing to the legacy of almost a decade of deterioration in the agricultural and industrial sectors and also because of reduced exports and the foreign debt burden. AIDS took a heavy toll of life and resources in such countries as Zaire, Zambia, Central African Republic, Uganda, and Tanzania. For the first time in 20 years, there were no successful military coups; however, the wars in Ethiopia and The Sudan and military strife in another half-dozen countries continued. On the positive side were new prospects of peace returning to Angola, South West Africa/Namibia, Chad, and Western Sahara.

Organization of African Unity. The Organization of African Unity (OAU) celebrated the 25th anniversary of its founding in May at a summit meeting in Addis Ababa, Eth. The two items at the top of the agenda were the African Economic Recovery Plan (AERP) and the crisis in southern Africa. Strong misgivings were expressed about AERP's progress; it was decided to try again to persuade the industrialized nations to reduce the burden of foreign indebtedness on many members of the OAU. For the first time in 20 years, the wars in Chad and Western Sahara no longer featured prominently on the OAU agenda.

The OAU encouraged the U.S. initiative to obtain the withdrawal of South African and Cuban troops from Angola and to secure the independence of Namibia. The organization continued to press for comprehensive mandatory sanctions against South Africa, and it backed the Palestinians' right to a state of their own.

Pres. Moussa Traoré of Mali was elected chairman of the OAU for 1988–89. The organization continued to suffer from financial difficulties owing to the failure of many of its members to pay their dues.

Southern Africa. Substantial progress was made toward restoring peace in Angola through tripartite talks among Angola, South Africa, and Cuba, under U.S. chairmanship. In December agreements were signed providing for a phased withdrawal of the approximately 50,000 Cuban troops stationed in Angola and for Namibian independence in accordance with UN Resolution 435. A UN peacekeeping force was to be in Namibia by April 1, 1989, when the first Cuban troops were scheduled to leave. Elections in Namibia were to be held by Nov. 1, 1989, and all Cuban troops were to be out of Angola by July 1, 1991. Thus a dispute that had occupied the international community for more than 40 years seemed to be coming to an end. The success of the talks over Angola and Namibia was facilitated by an agreement between the United States and the Soviet Union reached at the summit meeting between U.S. Pres. Ronald Reagan and Soviet leader Mikhail Gorbachev.

However, the agreement did not touch directly on the civil war in Angola between the government in Luanda and the challenging forces of Jonas Savimbi's National Union for the Total Independence of Angola (UNITA). Nor did it lessen the conflicts inside South Africa itself, where the internal opposition to apartheid and the external challenge by the forces of the African National Congress (ANC) were met with forceful repression under a continuing state of national emergency. Although some discriminatory laws, especially the Group Areas Act, were eased, few substantial reforms were undertaken by the regime of South African Pres. P. W. Botha. Domestic and international concern focused on the release of the charismatic ANC leader Nelson Mandela, who after 25 years in prison became seriously ill in the latter part of the year.

South Africa's destabilization policies in neighbouring countries continued to be a major concern, especially in Mozambique. There the rebel Mozambique National Resistance (MNR or Renamo), allegedly with the backing of South Africa, brought chaos to much of the country, compelling three of its neighbours—Zimbabwe, Tanzania, and Malawi—to commit troops to assist in the fight against the rebels. A new attempt was made to resuscitate the Nkomati Accord, whereby South Africa and Mozambique had agreed in 1984 not to support the armed opponents of their respective regimes. President Botha visited the Mozambican capital, Maputo, to help revivify the agreement.

One major gain in the subcontinent's violent conflicts was registered in Zimbabwe, where the ruling party and the major opposition, Joshua Nkomo's Zimbabwe African People's Union (ZAPU), implemented an agreement to merge and form a unified government.

Horn of Africa. The military conflicts between the government of Ethiopia and its opposition forces intensified. The Eritrean People's Liberation Front (EPLF) crushingly defeated the Ethiopian Army in heavy fighting on the Nakfa front, forcing Pres. Mengistu Haile Mariam to mobilize his supporters behind the slogan of "everything to the war front." Despite substantial new supplies of armaments to Ethiopia by the U.S.S.R., little success was reported in the counteroffensive by the end of the year. The civil war also continued to rage in Tigrai Province, where the Tigrai People's Liberation Front (TPLF) claimed substantial military successes that put them in control of some 90% of the province.The Oromo Liberation Front (OLF) and three other armed movements also kept up their pressures on the Ethiopian government.

Ethiopia and Somalia ended their 28 years of hostility through a treaty restoring good neighbourly relations and an undertaking no longer to support each other's military opponents. As part of this agreement the Ethiopians expelled forces of the Somali National Movement. These had managed for a time to overrun a part of northern Somalia, causing bitter fighting and heavy casualties.

The civil war in The Sudan brought devastation to much of the southern part of the country, where, except for some of the larger towns, the challenging Sudan People's Liberation Army (SPLA) maintained the upper hand. The war, drought, and famine wreaked havoc on the region. A third of the estimated 7.5 million southerners became refugees, either through internal displacement or by fleeing to neighbouring countries. The famine, and later an almost unprecedented flooding of the Nile River, threatened the lives of an estimated five million people. Hopes of a peaceful ending to the war were dashed by a decision of the government to introduce new laws based on the sacred scripture of Islam, the Qur'an. These were denounced by the SPLA as well as by a substantial section of the northern Muslim community.

Inter-African Affairs. The Western Saharan war showed signs of ending when, in August, the Moroccan government and the Popular Front for the Liberation of Saguia el Hamra and Río de Oro (Polisario Front) announced their acceptance of a UN peace plan providing for an in-

Refugees grow crops and raise livestock within a tent city of Western Sahara. Over 100,000 refugees have been forced to live in such makeshift cities after fleeing the regions occupied by Morocco.

PAUL DELANEY—THE NEW YORK TIMES

ternationally supervised referendum to be held among the Western Saharan people. On acceptance of the plan, both sides attached comments reflecting their concerns over conditions of implementation. The level of fighting was substantially reduced while negotiations were under way.

Normal diplomatic relations were established between Chad and Libya after the decisive defeat of the latter's army, which gave cause for optimism that the long military struggle would finally end. However, the Libyans still refused to give up their claims to the Aozou Strip in northern Chad, one of the issues that had precipitated the war.

Relations between the Tutsi-dominated republic of Burundi and the neighbouring Hutu-dominated republic of Rwanda were severely strained in August when members of the Hutu majority in the former country revolted against the Tutsi minority, opening old wounds that had never healed since the two tribes engaged in a genocidal type of killing in the late 1950s. The Hutu revolt was put down with severe force, and hundreds, perhaps thousands, of people were massacred on both sides.

External Relations. The new détente between the U.S. and the U.S.S.R. was widely welcomed by the continent's leaders as presaging the possible ending of superpower rivalry in Africa. The leaders of the nations bordering on South Africa gave their full backing to the U.S. initiative for achieving settlements in Angola and Namibia. They expressed the hope that this would also mean the ending by the U.S. of support for UNITA. Cuba's constructive role in facilitating the Angolan agreement was generally praised.

While the U.S.S.R. continued to give its full support to the ANC, its spokesmen on a number of public occasions expressed the official view that the way to a peaceful settlement in South Africa lay in political negotiations rather than through an armed struggle. However, South Africa continued to be suspicious of Soviet intentions. The U.S.S.R. also showed no sign of suspending its military support for the Ethiopian regime.

The European Communities and the North Americans gave their full support to the Mozambican regime in its fight against the MNR and its resistance to South Africa. All the Western countries contributed substantially to the efforts of the Southern African Development Coordination Conference to lessen the dependency of South Africa's neighbours on trade and communication links with the Botha regime. Britain continued through its military advisory team to train military officers for both Zimbabwe and Mozambique.

Social and Economic Conditions. Reporting on the United Nations Program of Action for African Economic Recovery, UN Secretary-General Javier Pérez de Cuéllar stated that recovery continued to be disappointing. The gross domestic product of sub-Saharan Africa rose by only

1% in 1986 and by 0.8% in 1987, while per capita income fell by 2 and 2.2% during those two years. Nevertheless, he reported that efforts to implement economic reforms had been "impressive," with the majority of countries having adopted policy reforms and structural adjustment measures. The UN Economic Commission for Africa (ECA) reported that the total foreign indebtedness of all OAU member nations had risen by more than $20 billion to a new total of $218 billion. The figure for the sub-Saharan countries was $138 billion. This debt represented three times the export earnings in 1987.

While agricultural production improved by 3.8% in 1986, it rose by only 1.1% in 1987, much lower than the continent's 3% growth in population. In large part, adverse weather conditions caused the slow growth, and better harvests in 1988 gave some promise of improvement. One result of the slow economic recovery was that the share of education and health services fell from 25.2% in 1986 to 23.1% in 1987. Per capita income decreased by about 2% in 1986 and 2.2% in 1987, with a trend suggesting further declines for the rest of the 1980s.

Africa's export earnings fell by almost 24% in 1986 but rose by 13% in 1987; however, this was due mainly to a partial recovery in oil prices. Net resource flows to the continent stagnated. In 1987 they amounted to $22.9 billion, which was 2.3% higher in real terms than in 1986 but 2.2% lower than in 1985. There was a net transfer of financial resources from Africa to the International Monetary Fund (IMF) of almost $1 billion a year for both 1986 and 1987.

(COLIN LEGUM)

See also *Dependent States,* below.

ANGOLA

A people's republic, Angola is located on the Atlantic coast in southwestern Africa. The small exclave of Cabinda is separated from Angola by a strip of Zaire. Area: 1,246,700 sq km (481,350 sq mi). Pop. (1988 est.): 9,386,000. Cap.: Luanda. Monetary unit: kwanza, with (Oct. 10, 1988) a free rate of 29.90 kwanzas to U.S. $1 (51.20 kwanzas = £1 sterling). President in 1988, José Eduardo dos Santos.

Hopes of an end to the war that had lasted 13 years, which had flickered throughout 1988, seemed close to fruition late in the year with the conclusion of an agreement on the withdrawal of Cuban troops from Angola and independence for South West Africa/Namibia. Much of the impetus came from events taking place outside the country or from the activities of external powers acting within Angola itself. The imminent retirement of U.S. Pres. Ronald Reagan and the prospect of his being succeeded by a less supportive candidate gave South Africa pause. Simultaneously, South Africa's powerful assistance to the National Union for the Total Independence of Angola (UNITA) guerrillas fighting

against the government inclined the U.S.S.R. to the view that military victory for the government seemed improbable and a political solution offered the best way out of an involvement that was proving increasingly unprofitable. Better relations between the U.S. and the U.S.S.R. even led the heads of the two countries to propose a deadline of September 29 for a settlement to the Angolan war. Cuba, on the other hand, hoped for some striking military triumph before withdrawing its troops and was prepared, contrary to the Angolan government's wishes, to increase its military contribution.

Under pressure from these various quarters, and subjected to a prolonged attack by South African troops intent upon seizing the important strategic and logistic base of Cuito Cuanavale, the government felt compelled to participate in a series of meetings held mainly on the initiative of the U.S. assistant secretary of state for African affairs, Chester Crocker, and aimed at reaching an accord acceptable to all parties. The series began in London on May 3–4 and continued intermittently in Brazzaville (Congo), Cairo, New York, Sal (Cape Verde), Geneva, and in Brazzaville again in September. Pres. José dos Santos stated firmly that he would accept no settlement that recognized Jonas Savimbi and his UNITA guerrillas. Neither UNITA nor the South West Africa People's Organization was represented.

On August 8, after the Geneva meeting, a cease-fire was agreed to between Angolan and Cuban troops and South African troops. The Angolan government remained alert, however, because South African forces continued to carry out maneuvers along the Angola–Namibia border while, with U.S. assistance, UNITA stepped up its attacks in the north. This latter development made nonsense of an earlier attempt by the government, in June, to improve relations with neighbouring Zaire by signing an agreement

AFP PHOTO

A column of South African troops crosses the bridge connecting South West Africa/Namibia and Angola. The soldiers left Angola after an agreement was reached that would end the civil war in Angola and help lead to Namibian independence.

to strengthen security along their common border. Angola had frequently accused Zaire of allowing the U.S. to send supplies to the guerrillas. After the second Brazzaville meeting early in September, there were hopeful signs, indicating that a settlement might be reached, but the September 29 deadline was not met. Finally, on December 13, Angola, Cuba, and South Africa—again meeting in Brazzaville—reached agreement on timetables for withdrawal of the Cuban troops (to be completed by mid-1991) and for Namibian independence. The accords were formally signed on December 22 at the UN headquarters in New York. They did not provide for an end to the civil war between the Angolan government and UNITA, but Angolan Foreign Minister Afonso Van-Dúnem expressed the hope that they would promote reconciliation.

For Angola the continuing war was an economic disaster. As the year began, its foreign debt stood at $4 billion, two-thirds of which was owed to the U.S.S.R., mainly for arms, and half of which was due to be repaid before the end of 1991. Between 40 and 50% of the budget was earmarked for defense, while the income from oil, the country's largest foreign exchange earner, produced by Americans in the Cabinda exclave, went, ironically, mainly to the U.S.S.R. to pay for military equipment. In a more encouraging development, Italy pledged $300 million in aid—$200 million as a donation and the remaining $100 million as a loan—to be used mainly to assist agriculture but also to help reconstruct the Benguela Railway. In April the African Development Bank also granted a credit of $100 million to be spread over three years.

(KENNETH INGHAM)

This article updates the *Macropædia* article SOUTHERN AFRICA: *Angola.*

BENIN

The people's republic of Benin is on the southern coast of West Africa, on the Gulf of Guinea. Area: 112,600 sq km (43,450 sq mi). Pop. (1988 est.): 4,443,000. Cap.: Porto-Novo (official); Cotonou (de facto). Monetary unit: CFA franc, with (Oct. 10, 1988) a par value of CFAF 50 to the French franc and a free rate of CFAF 316.13 to U.S. $1 (CFAF 541.38 = £1 sterling). President in 1988, Brig. Gen. Mathieu Kérékou.

The year 1988 was an exceptionally difficult one for Pres. Mathieu Kérékou of Benin and his people. The economic situation, which had been deteriorating steadily since the early 1980s, was further undermined by falling world prices for two of the country's main export commodities—cocoa and cotton—and also by the relative strength of the CFA franc against the dollar. At the same time, the economic restructuring needed to end balance of payments and budgetary deficits remained blocked by disagreements with the International Monetary Fund and the World Bank over the conditions attached to new funding and debt rescheduling; as a result, living standards fell further.

The government was dogged, too, by persistent rumours of its own imminent demise. Between 100 and 200 people were reported to have been detained after an unsuccessful coup attempt on March 26, and there were reports of another plot's having been nipped in the bud while President Kérékou was attending a conference in neighbouring Togo in June. No government statement was forthcoming on these events, but on July 29 an extraordinary meeting of the National Assembly was called to endorse a wide-ranging Cabinet reshuffle attributed to the economic situation and defense and security needs. (NIM CASWELL)

This article updates the *Macropædia* article WESTERN AFRICA: *Benin.*

BOTSWANA

A landlocked republic of southern Africa, Botswana is a member of the Commonwealth. Area: 581,730 sq km (224,607 sq mi). Pop. (1988 est.): 1,211,000. Cap.: Gaborone. Monetary unit: pula, with (Oct. 10, 1988) a free rate of 1.98 pula to U.S. $1 (3.39 pula = £1 sterling). President in 1988, Quett Masire.

Botswana made special efforts during 1988 to stimulate the economy and attract foreign investment. Foreign exchange allowances for businessmen were raised, and investment rules were relaxed. Local firms could now invest offshore, while nonresident companies could borrow up to three times their paid-up capital. One effect of these measures would be to make Botswana a conduit for South African funds, and this could be of considerable significance if sanctions were applied to the republic. Diamond and beef exports meant Botswana did not suffer from foreign exchange problems.

There was an easing of relations with Zimbabwe. Zimbabwean exiles in Dukwe camp had returned home (closing a fruitful ground for South African subversive activities), and a joint venture had been announced between Botswana and the Zimbabwe Industrial Development Corporation to explore and develop Botswana's salt resources. During the year a British military team arrived to train the Botswana Defence Force, and Britain also sold Botswana nine secondhand Strikemasters. In June, following a South African raid into Botswana to seek out members of the African National Congress, Pres. Quett Masire accused Pretoria of state terrorism. Three policemen were hurt, while in an earlier (March) raid three women had been killed. A coal utilization project was launched in collaboration with West Germany in order to use part of the country's huge coal resources in place of dwindling wood supplies.

(GUY ARNOLD)

This article updates the *Macropædia* article SOUTHERN AFRICA: *Botswana*.

BURKINA FASO

Burkina Faso is a landlocked country of West Africa. Area: 274,200 sq km (105,869 sq mi). Pop. (1988 est.): 8,530,000. Cap.: Ouagadougou. Monetary unit: CFA franc, with (Oct. 10, 1988) a par value of CFAF 50 to the French franc and a free rate of CFAF 316.13 to U.S. $1 (CFAF 541.38 = £1 sterling). President (chairman) of the Popular Front and head of state and government in 1988, Capt. Blaise Compaoré.

Burkina's Popular Front government, propelled to power by a bloody coup in October 1987, remained very much under the shadow of its predecessor, whose leader, Capt. Thomas Sankara, had won admirers throughout Africa. The PF's statutes, published in March 1988, established a governmental structure consisting of a legislature elected every two years, a coordinating committee, and an executive committee in charge of day-to-day business. However, none of the executive committee members was named, and true mass organizations such as the labour unions maintained a discreet distance from the regime.

A Cabinet reshuffle on August 23 was widely interpreted as a move by the new head of state, Capt. Blaise Compaoré, to consolidate his position. The two other surviving members of the group that had originally brought Sankara to power—Commandant Jean-Baptiste Boukari Lingani and Capt. Henri Zongo—retained their positions, despite rumours of a rift with Compaoré. (NIM CASWELL)

This article updates the *Macropædia* article WESTERN AFRICA: *Burkina Faso*.

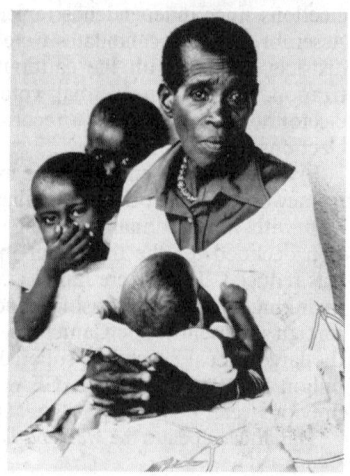

A woman comforts her three grandchildren, whose parents were killed during tribal wars in Burundi. The Hutu and Tutsi people of Burundi brutally attacked each other in continuation of an ancient tribal feud.

AP/WIDE WORLD

BURUNDI

Burundi is a landlocked republic of central Africa. Area: 27,834 sq km (10,747 sq mi). Pop. (1988 est.): 5,131,000. Cap.: Bujumbura. Monetary unit: Burundi franc, with (Oct. 10, 1988) a free rate of FBu 151.85 to U.S. $1 (FBu 260.05 = £1 sterling). President in 1988, Maj. Pierre Buyoya; prime minister from October 19, Adrien Sibomana.

During his first year in power, Pres. Pierre Buyoya gained considerable respect for improving human rights; he curbed repression, released political prisoners, and halted the anti-Roman Catholic policies of former president Jean-Baptiste Bagaza. Then in August 1988—part of a bitter and deep tribal legacy—a new Tutsi-Hutu dispute sparked a series of massacres in which the Tutsi-dominated Army massacred thousands of Hutu in revenge for the earlier killing of Tutsi. Up to 3,000 families were reported to have been slaughtered in and around the capital, Bujumbura, and many more in the rural areas, while tens of thousands of Hutu fled into neighbouring countries. Former president Bagaza was at Masaka in western Uganda near the Burundi border and was reported to be in contact with his supporters. The massacres were the worst since 1972, when an estimated 100,000 Hutu were killed. On October 19, in an effort to restore national unity, Buyoya appointed a new government headed by a Hutu prime minister, Adrien Sibomana.

The 1988 budget raised public spending by 23%. The government was investigating a massive embezzlement of funds, which it claimed took place under Bagaza. Under Buyoya a structural adjustment program had been launched and had had some success. Development priority had been directed to rural activities such as veterinary services.

(GUY ARNOLD)

This article updates the *Macropædia* article CENTRAL AFRICA: *Burundi*.

CAMEROON

A republic of western central Africa, Cameroon lies on the Gulf of Guinea. Area: 465,458 sq km (179,714 sq mi). Pop. (1988 est.): 11,206,000. Cap.: Yaoundé. Monetary unit: CFA franc, with (Oct. 10, 1988) a par value of CFAF 50 to the French franc and a free rate of CFAF 316.13 to U.S. $1 (CFAF 541.38 = £1 sterling). President in 1988, Paul Biya.

Pres. Paul Biya obtained constitutional amendments that allowed him to raise the number of legislators from 120 to 180 and to call elections, which were duly held eight months early on April 24, 1988. These first multicandidate

elections since independence replaced 90% of the National Assembly. Several candidates were allowed to run in some districts, in line with the cautious process of "democratization." Biya's presidential vote fell to 98.75% of the electorate from the 99.98% recorded at the January 1984 elections.

Biya promised Cameroonians more austerity within the framework of an economic stabilization plan under discussion with international financial institutions. Oil production declined for the third year in a row, and the budget was reduced. Taxes were raised and subsidies cut owing to shrinking revenue and rising concern over domestic and foreign payments. The Cameroonian Development Corp., the largest local employer, suffered a net loss of CFAF 4.8 billion in 1986–87 after a CFAF 512 million profit the previous year. (NII K. BENTSI-ENCHILL)

This article updates the *Macropædia* article WESTERN AFRICA: *Cameroon.*

CAPE VERDE

The republic of Cape Verde occupies an island group in the Atlantic Ocean about 620 km (385 mi) off the west coast of Africa. Area: 4,033 sq km (1,557 sq mi). Pop. (1988 est.): 359,000. Cap.: Praia. Monetary unit: Cape Verde escudo, with (Oct. 10, 1988) a free rate of 76.86 escudos to U.S. $1 (131.61 escudos = £1 sterling). President in 1988, Aristides Pereira; prime minister, Pedro Pires.

Early in 1988 Pres. Aristides Pereira said people were free to criticize the country's one-party socialist rule and insisted there were no political prisoners or restrictions on free speech. Cape Verde established a joint commission with Nigeria to strengthen economic and technological cooperation, and Nigeria was to assist Cape Verde in setting up small-scale industries. The prime minister of Mozambique, Mario Machungo, visited Cape Verde in March, and the two countries pledged mutual assistance and friendship. In June Cape Verde signed a two-year cooperation agreement with Portugal covering a wide range of economic, social, and military assistance. It was concluded during the visit to Praia of Portugal's prime minister, Aníbal Cavaço Silva.

In August Cape Verde entered into a maritime agreement with the U.S.S.R., which was to construct Sal-Rei port on Boa Vista Island and provide technical assistance for the Palmeira port in Sal. As part of its telecommunications program, the Economic Community of West African States provided CFAF 34 million for spare parts to rehabilitate the Varzea earth station. A major fisheries project to cost $14.4 million was inaugurated during the year. Its object was to raise the annual fish catch from 4,000 to 13,500 metric tons. (GUY ARNOLD)

This article updates the *Macropædia* article WESTERN AFRICA: *Cape Verde.*

CENTRAL AFRICAN REPUBLIC

The Central African Republic is a landlocked state in central Africa. Area: 622,436 sq km (240,324 sq mi). Pop. (1988 est.): 2,843,000. Cap.: Bangui. Monetary unit: CFA franc, with (Oct. 10, 1988) a par value of CFAF 50 to the French franc and a free rate of CFAF 316.13 to U.S. $1 (CFAF 541.38 = £1 sterling). President in 1988, Gen. André Kolingba.

Pres. André Kolingba in February 1988 commuted the death sentence on former emperor Jean-Bedel Bokassa to life imprisonment with hard labour. During a visit to France in February, Kolingba was thanked by both Pres. François Mitterrand and Prime Minister Jacques Chirac for his support during French military operations in Chad.

More than 1,200 French troops as well as Mirage and Jaguar jets remained in the Central African Republic, but relations between French troops and citizens of the republic were often strained.

Tax reform and import liberalization proceeded despite financial difficulties. The 1988 budget was CFAF 43.4 billion (down CFAF 2.4 billion from 1987), while external debt remained relatively low at $452.7 million. The revenue outlook was gloomy, with coffee export prices lower than domestic producer costs. Smuggling of diamonds through Bangui airport continued to reduce the important financial contribution of that natural resource, worth CFAF 15 billion in 1987 out of CFAF 39 billion total export revenue.

(NII K. BENTSI-ENCHILL)

This article updates the *Macropædia* article CENTRAL AFRICA: *Central African Republic.*

CHAD

Chad is a landlocked republic of central Africa. Area: 1,284,000 sq km (495,755 sq mi). Pop. (1988 est.): 5,395,000. Cap.: N'Djamena. Monetary unit: CFA franc, with (Oct. 10, 1988) a par value of CFAF 50 to the French franc and a free rate of CFAF 316.13 to U.S. $1 (CFAF 541.38 = £1 sterling). President in 1988, Hissen Habré.

Following the heavy fighting of the previous year, a steady improvement in relations between Chad and its northern neighbour, Libya, took place in 1988. The cease-fire of Sept. 11, 1987, held, thanks in part to heavy Libyan fortification of the disputed Aozou Strip and French refusal to provide the air cover necessary for Chadian forces to retake it. Hopes of a longer-term settlement received a setback when Libya's chief of state, Col. Mu'ammar al-Qadhdhafi, failed to attend the summit conference of the Organization of African Unity in Addis Ababa, Eth., at the end of May. The meeting did coincide, however, with a surprise announcement from Libya that it was willing to recognize the government of Pres. Hissen Habré in N'Djamena, free prisoners of war, and launch a "Libyan Marshall Plan" to reconstruct war-torn areas. Observers concluded that Qadhdhafi had given up the attempt to remove Habré from power, at least for the time being.

The resulting loss of interest in Libya among the various Chadian opposition factions brought an easing of domestic pressure on President Habré. A steady trickle of opposition figures continued to announce their conversion to his cause, while a recruitment drive by the ruling Union Nationale pour l'Indépendance et la Révolution brought in large numbers of people dependent on the government for their future employment.

The economy remained devastated by the war; severe flooding and locust infestation caused yet more damage during the 1988 rains. Low world cotton prices and depressed overall economic activity caused government coffers to remain empty, and public employees outside the capital often went months without pay. (NIM CASWELL)

This article updates the *Macropædia* article WESTERN AFRICA: *Chad.*

COMOROS

The republic of Comoros is an island state in the Indian Ocean off the east coast of Africa. Area: 1,862 sq km (719 sq mi), excluding the island of Mayotte, which continued to be a de facto dependency of France. Pop. (1988 est., excluding Mayotte): 433,000. Cap.: Moroni. Monetary unit: Comorian franc, with (Oct. 10, 1988) a par value of CF 50 to the French franc and a free rate of CF 316.13 to U.S. $1 (CF 541.38 = £1 sterling). President in 1988, Ahmed Abdallah.

A coup attempt in December 1987, while Pres. Ahmed Abdallah was attending the Franco-African summit, was defeated. The government said soldiers had attacked the main barracks in Moroni. Comoran security was still handled by the mercenary leader Bob Denard. Opposition groups in Paris said seven people had died from torture in December, not the official toll of three. Comoran refugees from Mohéli Island living in Mayotte circulated tracts in March 1988 attacking government policies. A firm of South African hoteliers, Sun International, would manage two hotels on Grande Comore in equity partnership with the government.

Financial problems overshadowed the 13th anniversary of independence on July 6. Weak prices for exports (principally vanilla) and revenue shortfalls led to serious arrears on the (French) F 1,460,000,000 external debt. Customs receipts were F 62 million for 1987 imports against the projected F 99 million, and F 11.5 million for exports instead of F 38 million. Civil service salaries were three months late. France added F 3 million to its 1988 budgetary aid of F 38 million. Discussions on structural adjustment began in July with the World Bank, the International Monetary Fund, and the African Development Bank.

(NII K. BENTSI-ENCHILL)

This article updates the *Macropædia* article INDIAN OCEAN ISLANDS: *Comoros.*

CONGO

A people's republic, Congo is in central Africa on the Atlantic Ocean. Area: 342,000 sq km (132,047 sq mi). Pop. (1988 est.): 2,266,000. Cap.: Brazzaville. Monetary unit: CFA franc, with (Oct. 10, 1988) a par value of CFAF 50 to the French franc and a free rate of CFAF 316.13 to U.S. $1 (CFAF 541.38 = £1 sterling). President in 1988, Col. Denis Sassou-Nguesso; prime minister, Ange-Édouard Poungui.

Pres. Denis Sassou-Nguesso was embarrassed by Congo's involvement in $300 million contracts to import toxic waste. Both the environment minister and the information minister were dismissed on July 30, 1988, for their role in the affair. This was timely housecleaning, just before the celebrations of the 25th anniversary of the revolution on August 15.

French troops helped government security forces end the ten-month rebellion of Capt. Pierre Anga, who was killed in July near Owando in Cuvette Province. Prominent in the Congolese leadership since 1969, Anga claimed to possess embarrassing secrets about the assassination of Pres. Marien Ngouabi in 1977, from which both the next head of state, Joachim Yhombi-Opango, and Sassou himself benefited.

An estimated budget deficit of $400 million for 1988, a debt-to-exports ratio of 436%, a debt burden of $4.5 billion, and a grain-import requirement of more than 100,000 tons illustrated the nation's economic crisis. Additional austerity and privatization measures were expected.

(NII K. BENTSI-ENCHILL)

This article updates the *Macropædia* article CENTRAL AFRICA: *Congo.*

CÔTE D'IVOIRE

A republic of West Africa, Côte d'Ivoire lies on the Gulf of Guinea. Area: 320,763 sq km (123,847 sq mi). Pop. (1988 est.): 11,634,000. Cap., Abidjan; capital designate, Yamoussoukro. Monetary unit: CFA franc, with (Oct. 10, 1988) a par value of CFAF 50 to the French franc and a free rate of CFAF 316.13 to U.S. $1 (CFAF 541.38 = £1 sterling). President in 1988, Félix Houphouët-Boigny.

The financial problems of the economy dominated 1988. Tumbling cocoa and coffee prices resulted in revenue shortfalls, which caused difficulties in paying external and domestic creditors despite generous rescheduling of some foreign debts. Cocoa production of more than 630,000 tons achieved a record level for the fourth year in a row. Pres. Félix Houphouët-Boigny tried with little success to keep world cocoa prices up by withholding part of Ivorian production. He also resisted World Bank pressure to cut the guaranteed producer price of CFAF 400 per kilogram. The loss of more than CFAF 600 billion in export revenues since 1985 resulted in liquidity problems in the banking sector, and the export produce marketing board was facing its third year of record deficits.

The president maintained absolute political primacy during the year, with a clear successor still to emerge. Henri Konan Bédié retained his National Assembly presidency, and a Cabinet reshuffle in October split up Laurent Dona-Fologo's "superministry" of information, culture, youth, and sports, leaving him the vital information portfolio. A ministry to combat drug abuse and trafficking was created for former internal security minister Gen. Oumar N'Daw.

Laurent Akoun and other dissident members of the secondary school teachers' union were reinstated after months at a military camp in the countryside. Laurent Gbagbo, a prominent opposition figure and historian, returned from six years of self-exile.

(NII K. BENTSI-ENCHILL)

This article updates the *Macropædia* article WESTERN AFRICA: *Ivory Coast.*

DJIBOUTI

The republic of Djibouti is in the Horn of northeastern Africa on the Gulf of Aden. Area: 23,200 sq km (8,950 sq mi). Pop. (1988 est.): 484,000. Cap.: Djibouti. Monetary unit: Djibouti franc, with (Oct. 10, 1988) a pegged rate of DF 177.72 to U.S. $1 (DF 304.38 = £1 sterling) and a free rate of DF 172.85 to U.S. $1 (DF 296 = £1 sterling). President in 1988, Hassan Gouled Aptidon; prime minister, Barkat Gourad Hamadou.

French Pres. François Mitterrand's December 1987 visit, the first by a French president since independence in 1977, and his copious praise for Pres. Hassan Gouled Aptidon underlined Djibouti's strategic value in the Horn of Africa. In July 1988 France replaced its 11 Mirage-111C planes, stationed there since 1978, with modern Mirage F1s to match the MiG-29s of Yemen (Aden) and Ethiopia. France also had 3,600 troops permanently stationed in Djibouti under a mutual defense agreement. It had successfully opposed locating a base there for the U.S. Rapid Deployment Force.

A Somali pilot defected to Djibouti in July. With ethnic Somalis making up nearly one-third of its population, Djibouti occupied a difficult position in relation to the tensions between Ethiopia and Somalia. Interior Minister and Political Bureau member Youssouf Ali Chirdon died in Paris in June.

Foreign aid received in 1988 included F 45 million in French budgetary aid, a DF 1.7 billion loan from the Kuwait fund for port development, and 6,000 metric tons of grain from the European Communities. The $16.6 million preparatory work on a project for geothermal electricity development neared completion, but the $30 million–$40 million construction phase was delayed because of competing options for its financing. A controversial $18 tax was put on imported flour to protect the private Sopinad Milling Co.

(NII K. BENTSI-ENCHILL)

This article updates the *Macropædia* article EASTERN AFRICA: *Djibouti.*

EQUATORIAL GUINEA

The republic of Equatorial Guinea consists of Río Muni, on the Atlantic coast of West Africa, and the offshore islands of Bioko and Annobon. Area: 28,051 sq km (10,831 sq mi). Pop. (1988 est.): 335,000. Cap.: Malabo. Monetary unit: CFA franc, with (Oct. 10, 1988) a par value of CFAF 50 to the French franc and a free rate of CFAF 316.13 to U.S. $1 (CFAF 541.38 = £1 sterling). President in 1988, Col. Teodoro Obiang Nguema Mbasogo; prime minister, Capt. Cristino Seriche Bioko.

Early in 1988 the government of Equatorial Guinea contracted with South Africa for the construction of a satellite-tracking station. All materials and engineering support were to come from the republic, as well as troops to protect the project. The South Africans were also to help extend and revamp Malabo airport. Pres. Teodoro Obiang Nguema stated that all businessmen were welcome in the country, including South Africans, but denied that this meant support by Equatorial Guinea for the Pretoria regime. Later in the year the South Africans were expelled at Nigerian insistence, although five of them reportedly returned in June when Equatorial Guinea braced itself for a Nigerian "invasion." Nigeria had made plain that it would regard a South African presence in Equatorial Guinea as a threat to its security.

During the year Severo Moto, president of the outlawed Progressive Party, claimed that chaos prevailed throughout the country. In late summer a plot to overthrow the government was uncovered. Two of nine plotters were sentenced to be executed, and seven others received long prison terms; later President Obiang Nguema commuted the death sentences to life imprisonment. A number of measures were taken to revive the economy. France replaced Spain as the country's leading aid donor, and ties were being fostered with Washington.   (GUY ARNOLD)

This article updates the *Macropædia* article WESTERN AFRICA: *Equatorial Guinea.*

ETHIOPIA

The people's republic of Ethiopia is in the Horn of northeastern Africa, on the Red Sea. Area: 1,223,500 sq km (472,400 sq mi). Pop. (1988 est.): 47,501,000. Cap.: Addis Ababa. Monetary unit: birr, with (Oct. 10, 1988) a par value of 2.07 birr to U.S. $1 (free rate of 3.54 birr = £1 sterling). President in 1988, Lieut. Col. Mengistu Haile Mariam; prime minister, Fikre Selassie Wogderess.

The political climate in 1988 was defined by the presidential address of September 12, on the 14th anniversary of the revolution and the first anniversary of the founding of the people's democratic republic. Pres. Mengistu Haile Mariam's speech lasted less than 20 minutes and was notable because it was the first time that an address was unencumbered by quantitative data on development issues. Two-thirds of his remarks focused on the war against the dissident separatist groups in the northern provinces of Eritrea and Tigrai. The remainder of the speech was a qualified comment on the limited progress that had been made in implementing the new constitution.

Final agreement on the divisions of the various administrative regions was reached by the national Shengo (assembly) in July. The reorganization defined 25 administrative regions, 5 autonomous regions, and 356 subregions (*awrajas*). Mengistu stated that the program of regional autonomy would begin to be progressively put into practice during the current year, but he acknowledged that progress was "not to the degree we had hoped" and that only 3 autonomous and 11 administrative regions would be established during the year.

In March the Eritrean People's Liberation Front (EPLF) captured a strategic government base at Afabet to the north of Asmara. The rebel group captured or wounded 20,000 government troops, thereby engineering the largest victory ever claimed by a guerrilla force. The Tigrai People's Liberation Front (TPLF) moved dramatically eastward to occupy the major towns in Tigrai and the main road system. These events provoked mobilization of the militia, acceleration of the national military service program for youth, a draft of technicians from various ministries to the north, a compulsory contribution of one month's income from all Ethiopians, and a drastic cutback in budgets for other programs. The government slogan, "Everything to the Warfront," had a negative impact on all development programs because national resources became severely strained.

In November 1987 drought and famine victims were again numbered in the millions. The immediate problem was exacerbated by a growing disruption of the rural economy, threatened by a continuing shortage of draft animals and farm equipment. Invasions of locusts appeared in June and ravaged crops. There were also new waves of refugees from southern Sudan and from northern Somalia.

Ethiopia remained highly dependent on external assistance, which was strained as the result of confrontations

AP/WIDE WORLD

Two women watch as a supply plane departs from a relief station in Ethiopia. The plane, which could carry nearly two tons of cargo and made deliveries to three other Ethiopian relief stations, might make several supply runs a day. Continuing severe drought and shortages of farm animals and equipment forced the Ethiopians to rely more heavily on outside aid.

over the administration of relief supplies and the limited access accorded to relief workers in areas of military activity. External agencies had also been involved in dialogues, often bitter, pertaining to policies for resettlement, grouping of rural people in villages (villagization), and the agricultural economy, particularly with regard to commodity prices. Resettlement, while accepted as a necessary measure in the context of an expanding population and a deteriorating environment, had been criticized on administrative and technical grounds. Villagization, recognized as a component of long-range rural development, had attracted critical comment directed against the priority given to the program, the immediate consequences for agricultural production, and the mandatory rather than participatory nature of the actions.

Ethiopia, which for some time had had an extremely low per capita level of external assistance, was faced during the year with a variety of serious economic problems. Efficient financial management and a large element of "popular sacrifice," however, had saved the country from total financial collapse.

Ethiopian Airlines (EAL) remained one of the strongest elements in the economy. In September 1988, however, one of the worst accidents in EAL's 40-year history resulted when a flock of birds was sucked into an aircraft's engine during takeoff, causing the plane to crash and burst into flames. Thirty-one of the 104 persons aboard died.

External relations improved after Ethiopia signed an accord with Somalia in April, resulting in the resumption of diplomatic relations and the exchange of several thousand prisoners, incarcerated since the 1977–78 Ogaden war. High-level talks continued with The Sudan.

During 1988 Legesse Asfaw, a party strongman, was appointed general administrator of Tigrai region. The patriarch of the Ethiopian Orthodox Church died in June, and the enthronement of his successor took place in September. A senior government official, Amamual AmdeMikael, vice-president of the State Council and a former minister of justice, defected. In early August the country mourned the death of poet Menghistu Lemma (see OBITUARIES).

Though rainfall patterns were more normal in 1988, a serious shortage of food grain by the end of the year was predicted, partly because several areas experienced crop damage caused by excessive rain. In August Asmara received 89.2 mm (3.5 in) of rain during one ten-hour period; it was the heaviest precipitation recorded in 26 years.

(GEOFFREY C. LAST)

This article updates the *Macropædia* article EASTERN AFRICA: *Ethiopia.*

GABON

Gabon is a republic of central Africa, on the Atlantic Ocean. Area: 267,667 sq km (103,347 sq mi). Pop.: in 1988 estimates ranged from 900,000 to 1,490,000 (UN est., 1,219,000). Cap.: Libreville. Monetary unit: CFA franc, with (Oct. 10, 1988) a par value of CFAF 50 to the French franc and a free rate of CFAF 316.13 to U.S. $1 (CFAF 541.38 = £1 sterling). President in 1988, Omar Bongo; prime minister, Léon Mébiame.

The Parti Démocratique Gabonais celebrated its 20th anniversary in March 1988 with Pres. Omar Bongo praising Gabon's progress from "wild capitalism" and claiming that the country had no political prisoners. The presidents of Cameroon, the Central African Republic, Congo, and Zaire attended the celebration.

Bongo mediated with some success in the dispute between Libya and Chad. In January he sent back to France seven Iranians deported to Gabon by the French govern-

ment. Five other Iranians and three Turkish Kurds were deported to Spain. In June the government rounded up over 3,500 African immigrants. Nearly one-third of Libreville's 300,000 people fell into this category. Also in June Mariam Sankara, widow of the late Burkinabe leader, took up Bongo's offer of hospitality.

Gabon still had the second highest gross national product per capita in Africa (over $3,000). However, the oil sector declined by 20% and domestic consumption by 31% in 1987. The Paris Club of Western creditor governments rescheduled bilateral debts in March 1988, and the World Bank approved a $50 million loan in April, with equivalent cofinancing from the African Development Bank.

(NII K. BENTSI-ENCHILL)

This article updates the *Macropædia* article CENTRAL AFRICA: *Gabon.*

GAMBIA, THE

A republic and member of the Commonwealth, The Gambia extends from the Atlantic Ocean along the lower Gambia River in West Africa; it is surrounded by Senegal, with which it has formed an administrative union called Senegambia. Area: 10,689 sq km (4,127 sq mi). Pop. (1988 est.): 811,000. Cap.: Banjul. Monetary unit: dalasi, with (Oct. 10, 1988) a free rate of 7.10 dalasis to U.S. $1 (12.15 dalasis = £1 sterling). President in 1988, Sir Dawda Jawara.

Rumours of a plot to overthrow Pres. Dawda Jawara at the beginning of 1988 led to some 20 arrests. In the subsequent treason trial, which dragged on for the rest of the year, the prosecution alleged that Gambians and Senegalese had been recruited for military training in Libya. The most likely outcome of the trial would be to weaken Gambia-Senegal relations still further; little now remained of the concept of Senegambia.

In July President Jawara became annual chairman of the Economic Community of West African States. The Gambia passed a law against the dumping of industrial waste; like other West African countries, it had been a target for disposal of waste from the developed countries. The World Food Program was to implement a three-year food project to support community-based rural development and food security. Currently, domestic food production met only half of The Gambia's requirements. In presenting his June budget, the minister of finance, Sheriff Sisay, claimed that, for the first time in more than a decade, The Gambia had achieved economic stability and sustained growth. At the beginning of the year, The Gambia signed a $20 million refinancing deal with five banks through the London Club. The Gambia now owed $260 million in external debts, nearly double the country's gross domestic product.

(GUY ARNOLD)

This article updates the *Macropædia* article WESTERN AFRICA: *The Gambia.*

GHANA

A republic of West Africa and member of the Commonwealth, Ghana lies on the Gulf of Guinea. Area: 238,533 sq km (92,098 sq mi). Pop. (1988 est.): 13,754,000. Cap.: Accra. Monetary unit: cedi, with (Oct. 10, 1988) a free rate of 225.85 cedis to U.S. $1 (386.77 cedis = £1 sterling). Chairman of the Provisional National Defense Council in 1988, Jerry John Rawlings.

The year 1988 was the seventh since the Provisional National Defense Council came to power, and in orthodox terms the economy did quite well. In 1987 donors pledged more than $800 million in aid and committed $747 million. The budget stressed better management and showed a

reduction in debt repayment obligations. The government claimed that the economic recovery program had restored the country's international credibility. However, the World Bank report on Ghana said, "The plight of the poor and vulnerable remains desperate with limited access to health, education, or good drinking water."

The country was experiencing a new gold boom. Current gold production was 300,000 oz a year, but this could rise to 2.7 million oz, and it was estimated that 1.8 billion oz could be recovered in two geologic areas. With the fall in cocoa prices, the country had come to rely on gold output for the bulk of its foreign exchange. Currently, gold accounted for 20% of export earnings and employed 24,000. Like many other countries, Ghana had embarked on a privatization program, which would affect as many as 181 state-owned enterprises and another 54 in which the government was the minority shareholder. School dropout figures reached an alarming 40 to 60%, with a corresponding rise in child labour.   (GUY ARNOLD)

This article updates the *Macropædia* article WESTERN AFRICA: *Ghana.*

GUINEA

The republic of Guinea is located in West Africa, on the Atlantic Ocean. Area: 245,857 sq km (94,926 sq mi). Pop. (1988 est.): 6,540,000. Cap.: Conakry. Monetary unit: Guinean franc, with (Oct. 10, 1988) a free rate of GF 299.47 to U.S. $1 (GF 512.85 = £1 sterling). President in 1988, Brig. Gen. Lansana Conté.

The year began in an atmosphere of some political tension following the last-minute cancellation by Pres. Lansana Conté of a planned state visit to France in early December 1987 and reported restiveness among the army troops. Pay raises of 80% were announced for the civil service, Army, and private sector effective Jan. 1, 1988, but the government had to back down on a concurrent 78% increase in the price of fuel when rioting broke out because merchants were passing on the increases in the retail prices of basic necessities. On January 17 there was a wide-ranging Cabinet reshuffle and reorganization of ministerial responsibilities.

Conté's speech to mark the fourth anniversary of the military takeover on April 4 was a catalog of the continuing ills of the economy and public life. There was no prospect, he said, of a new constitution or parliament until the ruling Military Committee for National Recovery (CMRN) had achieved its number one priority of economic recovery. Behind the scenes, however, ethnic tensions and the lack of adequate means of enforcing government decisions resulted in continuing vacillation on the economic program. Privatization of state companies lagged behind schedule, and planned civil service job cuts again failed to materialize. The CMRN was also split over the proposed reestablishment of the Popular Militia (disbanded after the 1984 coup) to fight a rising wave of petty crime.

(NIM CASWELL)

This article updates the *Macropædia* article WESTERN AFRICA: *Guinea.*

GUINEA-BISSAU

A republic of West Africa, Guinea-Bissau lies on the Atlantic Ocean. Area: 36,125 sq km (13,948 sq mi). Pop. (1988 est.): 931,000. Cap.: Bissau. Monetary unit: Guinea-Bissau peso, with (Oct. 10, 1988) a free rate of 649 pesos to U.S. $1 (1,111 pesos = £1 sterling). President in 1988, João Bernardo Vieira.

Pres. João Vieira faced a difficult year in 1988. At home he had to implement changes demanded by the International Monetary Fund, while abroad he was attacked by political opponents more or less openly supported by the Portuguese. Luis Cabral, whom Vieira overthrew in 1980, lived in Lisbon.

The World Bank had urged a series of economic reforms on Guinea-Bissau since the economic recovery program launched in 1983 lost its momentum, and in 1988 the structural adjustment program resulted in a 34% increase in exports, although this was accompanied by a rise in inflation. The main object of the program was to sustain a growth rate in gross domestic product of 3.5% per year and to reduce inflation (45% in 1986) to 8% by 1989.

Early in the year the government agreed to accept toxic waste from Europe, the U.S., and Australia, but it backtracked under fierce criticism both from within the country and from its African neighbours. The contracts would have been worth $600 million over a period of years. Twenty-nine cases of AIDS had been diagnosed since the launching of the anti-AIDS campaign in 1987. In July–August Guinea-Bissau was host to two medical conferences on AIDS for Lusophone (Portuguese-speaking) countries and the World Health Organization. The eighth Lusophone African summit was held in Guinea-Bissau in June.

(GUY ARNOLD)

This article updates the *Macropædia* article WESTERN AFRICA: *Guinea-Bissau.*

KENYA

A republic and member of the Commonwealth, Kenya is in eastern Africa, on the Indian Ocean. Area: 582,646 sq km (224,961 sq mi), including 11,230 sq km of inland water. Pop. (1988 est.): 22,919,000. Cap.: Nairobi. Monetary unit: Kenya shilling, with (Oct. 10, 1988) a free rate of 18.24 shillings to U.S. $1 (31.23 shillings = £1 sterling). President in 1988, Daniel arap Moi.

After the formidable sequence of government attacks on alleged supporters of the so-called MwaKenya movement, on leading Asian businessmen and bankers, on university students, and on U.S. missionaries that took place during the closing months of 1987, the year 1988 began on a more subdued note. Excitement began to build with the approach of the parliamentary elections in February and March. The election to the presidency was a foregone conclusion, with the only political party, the Kenya African National Union (KANU), proposing Pres. Daniel arap Moi as its sole candidate. The preliminary election at which candidates for Parliament were chosen by members of KANU aroused considerable controversy because of a change in procedures; a secret ballot had been replaced by a system under which voters had to line up behind photographs of their candidates. Any candidate who received more than 70% of the votes was then returned unopposed, while in other constituencies as many as three candidates were allowed to run for election.

The government claimed that the new system would prevent any rigging of the elections because it took place in full view of everyone. *Beyond,* a magazine published by the National Council of Churches of Kenya, a body to which most Protestant churches belonged, challenged that claim, offered evidence that rigging had taken place in several constituencies to the disadvantage of candidates known to be critical of the government, and condemned the introduction of queue voting. The magazine was immediately banned, and possession of a copy rendered the person concerned liable to up to three years in prison. Soon afterward, the editor, Bedan Mbugua, was arrested and charged with an offense concerning the nonsubmission of

Masai wait to cast their votes in March in secret-ballot parliamentary elections at a polling station in southern Kenya. In preliminary elections in February the secret ballot had been replaced with a controversial system in which voters lined up behind a picture of their candidate.
AP WIDE WORLD

the magazine's accounts, and in August he was sentenced to nine months in prison.

The parliamentary elections took place in March and produced no surprises because all the candidates had already been approved by the ruling party. In any case, President Moi had already declared that Parliament was subordinate to KANU, and policy decisions on all matters of importance were made neither by Parliament nor by the party but by the president and a close circle of trusted supporters. The power of the president was clearly demonstrated on August 2 when the required three readings of legislation to amend the constitution were waived and Parliament passed the amendments in a single day. Only one member voiced any protest against the waiving of normal procedures, and he was shouted down. The amendments authorized the president to dismiss judges at will and increased—from 24 hours to 14 days—the period during which people suspected of capital offenses could be held without charges.

This new threat to the security of tenure of judges confirmed fears already expressed by Kenyan lawyers that both civil rights and the administration of justice were being steadily eroded. Their fears arose as a result of a series of events, including the death in custody under suspicious circumstances in February 1987 of Peter Karanja, a suspected dissident, and the resignation of Derek Schofield, a judge who had been summarily removed from a case involving the head of the Criminal Investigation Department.

Concern about events in the political and judicial fields had its counterpart in the economic sphere. Unemployment was running at a rate of about 50%, and there was no indication that industrial development was taking place to meet this problem. The continuing rapid growth of the population meant that half of all Kenyans were under 15 years of age, and a foretaste of the problems this would bring was experienced when there were only 67,000 new jobs available for 300,000 school-leavers. In February, however, the International Monetary Fund came to the government's assistance with the offer of a generous standby arrangement aimed at developing rural areas, reviving industry, and reducing the budget deficit.

(KENNETH INGHAM)

This article updates the Macropædia article EASTERN AFRICA: Kenya.

LESOTHO

A monarchy of southern Africa and member of the Commonwealth, Lesotho forms a landlocked enclave within South Africa. Area: 30,355 sq km (11,720 sq mi). Pop. (1988 est.): 1,671,000. Cap.: Maseru. Monetary unit: loti (plural: maloti), at par with the South African rand, with (Oct. 10, 1988) a free rate of 2.49 maloti to U.S. $1 (4.26 maloti = £1 sterling). King, Moshoeshoe II; chairman of the Military Council in 1988, Maj. Gen. Justin Metsino Lekhanya.

The much-heralded visit of Pope John Paul II to Lesotho in September 1988 was a near disaster. The pope's flight was diverted by bad weather to South Africa (providing Pretoria with a propaganda boost). He was then taken by land to Maseru, with a South African escort that ignored the border and accompanied the pope 65 km (40 mi) into Lesotho as though it were less than a Bantustan. A busload of pilgrims was hijacked, and in a drama at the gates of the British High Commission in Maseru, the South African military was called in to deal with the hijackers; three were killed, while the fourth, handed over to the Lesotho authorities, was also killed while in their hands. Two hostages were killed and 20 were hospitalized. Finally, fewer than 10,000 people—far less than the predicted one million—turned up for the papal mass.

Work continued on the first phase of the Lesotho Highlands Water Scheme in the Maluti Mountains. The project was not due for completion until 2020, when it would supply power to South Africa. The huge project was highly technical, and Lesotho would probably benefit only to the extent of 2,000 jobs over the next few years. Meanwhile, the Lesotho National Development Corporation was wooing South African investors.   (GUY ARNOLD)

This article updates the Macropædia article SOUTHERN AFRICA: Lesotho.

AP/WIDE WORLD

Pope John Paul II blesses a Basuto leader during his visit to Lesotho. The Pope traveled to the southern African nation to beatify the Rev. Joseph Gérard, a French missionary who worked among the Zulu and Basuto people.

LIBERIA

The republic of Liberia is located in West Africa, on the Atlantic Ocean. Area: 99,067 sq km (38,250 sq mi). Pop. (1988 est.): 2,427,000. Cap.: Monrovia. Monetary unit: Liberian dollar, at par with the U.S. dollar, with a free rate (Oct. 10, 1988) of L$1.71 to £1 sterling. President in 1988, Gen. Samuel K. Doe.

Early in 1988 Pres. Samuel K. Doe sacked his minister of finance, John Bestman, the man responsible for inviting 17 U.S. financial experts to assist in minimizing "leakages" in the economy, especially in revenue collection. Doe moved David Farhat from commerce to finance and then appointed Wisseh McClain (a nephew of former president William Tolbert, Jr.) minister of commerce in a clear attempt to reconcile those who opposed him in the 1985 elections.

The 1988 budget was approved at $240 million. Efforts to slim down the civil service continued throughout the year. The agency in charge of U.S. aid to Liberia launched a new program designed to encourage the private sector, releasing $5 million to private companies for the importation of machinery, equipment, spare parts, and raw materials. The goods had to originate in the U.S. and be used only by the private sector.

The Liberian Action Party (LAP) called on the government to bring William Gabriel Kpolleh and 13 others held on treason charges to trial speedily, but proceedings were still dragging on late in 1988. They were accused of plotting between 1986 and March 1988 to overthrow the government. In July another plot was alleged to have occurred; Nicholas Podier (former vice-head of state) and others "invaded" Liberia. Four were killed, and others, including two U.S. citizens, were arrested. Podier was later reported killed. James Bush and Curtis Williams, the two U.S. citizens, were released from detention in November.

In June an amendment to the constitution altered clause 93, which had limited the president to two terms. The change allowed the president to serve an unlimited number of times.   (GUY ARNOLD)

This article updates the *Macropædia* article WESTERN AFRICA: *Liberia.*

MADAGASCAR

The republic of Madagascar occupies the island of the same name and minor adjacent islands in the Indian Ocean off the southeast coast of Africa. Area: 587,041 sq km (226,658 sq mi). Pop. (1988 est.): 10,917,000. Cap.: Antananarivo. Monetary unit: Malagasy franc, with (Oct. 10, 1988) a free rate of FMG 1,250 to U.S. $1 (FMG 2,141 = £1 sterling). President in 1988, Didier Ratsiraka; prime ministers, Lieut. Col. Désiré Rakotoari-jaona and, from February 12, Lieut. Col. Victor Ramahatra.

Madagascar's economic recovery program received a boost at the meeting in January 1988 of the World Bank Consultative Group in Paris, when bilateral and multilateral donors pledged a sorely needed $700 million a year for three years. Despite lavish praise from donors, Madagascar's economy grew by just over 2%, thus failing to match the population growth of around 3%. The target for growth of gross domestic product until 1992 was 3.5% a year. The public investment program received an International Development Association loan of $117 million, aimed especially at achieving self-sufficiency in rice by 1990; some 85% of cultivated land was devoted to that crop. Additional balance of payments support amounting to $18.7 million came from the U.S., along with a new International Mone-

tary Fund standby loan of $14.8 million for ten months in expectation of faster currency depreciation. Debt service for 1988 had been projected at $400 million, but in October the Paris Club of Western donor governments rescheduled the external debt, which at the end of 1987 stood at $3.2 billion.

Total liberalization of the economy proceeded with the lifting of all import controls and export duties on all but state-marketed commodities such as coffee and cloves. The three major banks were among the public-sector candidates for foreign participation. The U.S.S.R., which supplied 60% of Madagascar's total petroleum requirements, suspended deliveries in July because of payment errors. Inflation was high at 30%, while civil service salaries rose by only 12%. In February Lieut. Col. Victor Ramahatra replaced Lieut. Col. Désiré Rakotoarijaona as prime minister.

(NII K. BENTSI-ENCHILL)

This article updates the *Macropædia* article INDIAN OCEAN ISLANDS: *Madagascar.*

MALAWI

A republic and member of the Commonwealth, Malawi is a landlocked state in eastern Africa. Area: 118,484 sq km (45,747 sq mi). Pop. (1988 est.): 8,211,000. Cap.: Lilongwe. Monetary unit: Malawi kwacha, with (Oct. 10, 1988) a free rate of 2.66 kwacha to U.S. $1 (4.56 kwacha = £1 sterling). President in 1988, Hastings Kamuzu Banda.

Two heads of neighbouring nations visited Malawi during 1988. The visit of Pres. Joaquim Chissanó of Mozambique in July was intended to strengthen the links between the two countries that had been affirmed by an agreement on security cooperation signed in December 1987. In fulfillment of that agreement, Pres. Hastings Banda had subsequently sent troops to help in the defense of one of Mozambique's main railway lines. Good relations were particularly important because Malawi had suffered an influx of refugees from the fighting in Mozambique, bringing the total of refugees currently in the country to more than half a million. Providing for them placed a heavy burden on the country's limited resources in spite of assistance of $50 million from the UN High Commissioner for Refugees. Cooperation in bringing an end to hostilities in Mozambique was, therefore, vital to both countries, not least to Malawi, whose two outlets to the Indian Ocean, both running through Mozambique, had been severed for four years.

The visit of South Africa's Pres. P. W. Botha in September also had important financial implications. He agreed to the rescheduling of Malawi's debt to South Africa and also offered to provide 3,000 tons of corn (maize) to meet the country's shortfall in the production of that staple food.

(KENNETH INGHAM)

This article updates the *Macropædia* article SOUTHERN AFRICA: *Malawi.*

MALI

Mali is a landlocked republic of West Africa. Area: 1,240,192 sq km (478,841 sq mi). Pop. (1988 est.): 7,778,000. Cap.: Bamako. Monetary unit: CFA franc, with (Oct. 10, 1988) a par value of CFAF 50 to the French franc and a free rate of CFAF 316.13 to U.S. $1 (CFAF 541.38 = £1 sterling). President in 1988, Gen. Moussa Traoré; prime minister until June 6, Mamadou Dembelé.

Malian Finance and Commerce Minister Tienna Coulibaly in October signed an agreement with Western creditor nations that rescheduled the nation's debt at lower inter-

est rates. France, the main creditor, cut the value of the debt that it was owed by one-third. In a major Cabinet reshuffle on June 6, Pres. Moussa Traoré became minister of national defense and the post of prime minister was abolished. The former defense minister, Gen. Sekou Ly, moved to the post of national education—considered sensitive because of the clashes of students and teachers with the authorities in February and March.

Elections to the National Assembly on June 26 resulted in an officially recorded 98.6% endorsement of the candidates of the ruling Union Démocratique du Peuple Malien but were of little importance, given the marginal role of the assembly in political life. The Organization of African Unity recognized Traoré's 20th year in power by electing him chairman at the OAU summit in late May.

(NIM CASWELL)

This article updates the *Macropædia* article WESTERN AFRICA: *Mali*.

MAURITANIA

The republic of Mauritania is on the Atlantic coast of West Africa. Area: 1,030,700 sq km (398,000 sq mi). Pop. (1988 est.): 1,894,000. Cap.: Nouakchott. Monetary unit: ouguiya, with (Oct. 10, 1988) a free rate of 74.14 ouguiya to U.S. $1 (126.97 ouguiya = £1 sterling). President of the Military Committee for National Salvation and prime minister in 1988, Col. Maaouya Ould Sidi Ahmed Taya.

Events in 1988 were overshadowed by the unsuccessful coup attempt against Col. Maaouya Ould Sidi Ahmed Taya in October 1987, in the aftermath of which three black officers were executed. The attempt was the first in Mauritania's history to have been purely ethnically based, exposing latent tensions between the politically dominant white Moors and the black, predominantly Toucouleur, Mauritanians from the Sénégal River Valley.

Rioting was reported to have greeted the three executions, and the abrupt cancellation of a planned trip by Col. Taya to Tunisia at the end of March along with a school strike in April were indicative of continuing tension in the capital. There were two minor Cabinet reshuffles on March 20 and April 11, including the dismissal of the finance minister and his replacement by the former director of the central bank. The trial of 17 people accused of threatening state security began on September 10. Meanwhile, the Senegal-based black opposition group FLAM said that some of those arrested in the wake of the attempted coup of October 1987 had died in the harsh conditions of a desert prison camp. Despite these events, the second stage of local elections—part of a planned gradual return to democracy—passed without incident in January.

(NIM CASWELL)

This article updates the *Macropædia* article WESTERN AFRICA: *Mauritania*.

MAURITIUS

The constitutional monarchy of Mauritius, a member of the Commonwealth, occupies an island in the Indian Ocean about 800 km (500 mi) east of Madagascar and includes the island dependencies of Rodrigues, Agalega, and Cargados Carajos Shoals. Area: 2,040 sq km (788 sq mi). Pop. (1988 est.): 1,049,-000. Cap.: Port Louis. Monetary unit: Mauritian rupee, with (Oct. 10, 1988) a free rate of Mau Rs 14.05 to U.S. $1 (Mau Rs 24.07 = £1 sterling). Queen, Elizabeth II; governor-general in 1988, Sir Veerasamy Ringadoo; prime minister, Aneerood Jugnauth.

In his 1988 budget the minister of finance, Vishnu Lutchmeenaraidoo, forecast continued economic growth and falling unemployment. The growth of Mauritius's manufacturing sector was one of the success stories of the third world. Based mainly on the export processing zones (EPZs), manufacturing accounted for 53% of exports, surpassing sugar. The EPZs contained over 500 companies employing 90,000 people. The high level of education was seen as a key to this success; virtually all primary-age children attended school, and a high proportion of them went on to secondary school. The success of tourism had created its own problems. Sir Gaetan Duval, minister of tourism, suggested that 300,000 arrivals a year were the most the island could accommodate. Sugar still dominated the agricultural sector; the current crop stood at approximately 650,000 metric tons, 540,000 tons of which were exported.

In 1988 Mauritius was establishing its own stock exchange and hoped that the number of publicly owned companies would double over the next five years. The government, which had decided to quit the East and Southern African Preferential Trade Area, changed its mind, although continuing membership would cost it $40 million in lost revenues a year. The decision was political, to maintain solidarity with black Africa. In May the Mauritian delegate had walked out of a meeting of the Organization of African Unity to protest a report that criticized Mauritius's trade and investment ties with South Africa. The first offshore banks opened in Mauritius in October. Curbs on foreign exchange were to be relaxed further, and tax incentives were to be improved with free repatriation of capital and dividends allowed.

(GUY ARNOLD)

This article updates the *Macropædia* article INDIAN OCEAN ISLANDS: *Mauritius*.

MOZAMBIQUE

The people's republic of Mozambique is located in eastern Africa, on the Indian Ocean. Area: 799,380 sq km (308,642 sq mi). Pop. (1988 est.): 14,890,000. Cap.: Maputo. Monetary unit: metical, with (Oct. 10, 1988) a par value of 586 meticais to U.S. $1 (free rate of 1,003 meticais = £1 sterling). President in 1988, Joaquim Chissanó; prime minister, Marío de Graça Machungo.

The guerrilla war carried on by the Mozambique National Resistance (Renamo) rebels remained a constant threat to political stability and economic recovery in 1988. Deliveries of aid from other countries were seriously hampered by Renamo ambushes, while attacks on vital communications and on towns and villages in many parts of the country continued unabated.

It was not guerrilla activity, however, but dissatisfaction with the existing methods of supplying aid that led representatives of several donor countries and private assistance groups to propose in February a new approach to helping Mozambique. Food handouts, it was agreed, worked unevenly and in any case encouraged a spirit of dependence among the recipients. What was needed was greater emphasis on rehabilitation and on developing the country's own resources. The plan was not always easy to put into effect, however. A British-funded scheme to rebuild the railway linking southeastern Zimbabwe with the port of Maputo was constantly sabotaged by Renamo guerrillas, who killed groups of railway workers as well as members of the armed forces posted to guard the railway.

The government believed that the problem resulted from the military assistance given to the guerrillas by South African agencies. There were better prospects for relations with South Africa after April, however, when Jacinto Veloso, minister of international cooperation, flew to Cape Town to meet the South African foreign minister. In the

course of discussions the two agreed to reactivate the Joint Security Commission, established by the Nkomati Accord in 1984; the commission had been allowed to lapse in 1986. Even before the meeting, South Africa had made a grant to upgrade the port of Maputo and later in April had agreed to reschedule Mozambique's debt of more than $11 million. As a further demonstration of its good intentions, South Africa also agreed in May to grant millions of dollars in military aid to help protect the Cabora Bassa hydroelectric project from rebel attacks. At least 1,500 soldiers would be specially trained to guard the dam and the electricity cable to South Africa. In June Mozambique signed an agreement with South Africa and Portugal to reactivate the Cabora Bassa project and to repair the pylons damaged by guerrillas.

During the same month, the government launched an important counteroffensive against the guerrillas, the immediate result of which was a new flood of refugees over the border into neighbouring countries. Pres. Joaquim Chissanó visited Pres. Hastings Banda of Malawi in July and took the opportunity to reaffirm the agreement on security cooperation signed in December 1987, thereby cementing more firmly relations with a neighbouring country that Chissanó had, until recently, openly accused of assisting Renamo.

In September South Africa's Pres. P. W. Botha visited Mozambique and promised Chissanó that his country would not supply the rebels. He also confirmed the agreement to revive the Nkomati Accord and to rebuild and defend the Cabora Bassa project and offered to provide 3,000 tons of corn (maize). South Africa was also to pay more than $85 million a year initially for the electricity supplied by Mozambique and to increase the sum by 25%

AFP PHOTO

A truck is lowered onto a dock in Mozambique as part of an aid shipment from South Africa. South Africa agreed to give Mozambique millions of dollars in military aid to defend the Cabora Bassa hydroelectric project from rebel guerrillas.

in 1994, with a further review at the end of the century.

By entering into these various agreements, Chissanó acknowledged that, for geographic reasons, his country was tied economically to South Africa, but he openly refused to give any support to the racial policies of his powerful neighbour. He did, however, act as a mediator in May between South Africa and Angola to clear the way for discussions leading to the cessation of hostilities between the two countries.   (KENNETH INGHAM)

This article updates the *Macropædia* article SOUTHERN AFRICA: *Mozambique*.

NIGER

Niger is a landlocked republic of West Africa. Area: 1,186,408 sq km (458,075 sq mi). Pop. (1988 est.): 6,937,000. Cap.: Niamey. Monetary unit: CFA franc, with (Oct. 10, 1988) a par value of CFAF 50 to the French franc and a free rate of CFAF 316.13 to U.S. $1 (CFAF 541.38 = £1 sterling). Chief of state and president of the Supreme Military Council in 1988, Gen. Ali Seibou; prime ministers, Ahmid Algabid and, from July 15, Mamane Oumarou.

Niger's new chief of state, Gen. Ali Seibou, who succeeded to the post after the death of Seyni Kountché in November 1987, enjoyed wide popularity during his first year in office. His open and relaxed style of government was demonstrated by an amnesty announced on the 29th anniversary of independence for imprisoned leaders of coup attempts against Kountché in 1976 and 1983, and also by restraint in the face of strikes by students and workers at the Arlit uranium mines. In February 1988 Seibou said that those involved in the amnesty would soon appear before a judicial tribunal. Three reshuffles of central and regional government, in November 1987 and then on March 10 and July 15, 1988, saw Seibou's allies posted to key jobs and his principal rival for the presidency, Col. Moumouni Djermakoye Adamo, put safely out of the way as ambassador to the U.S.

On August 2 Seibou announced the formation of a political party, the Mouvement National de la Société de Développement (MNSD). It was likely to form the core of a one-party state under a new constitution; the National Development Council, presently a consultative body, was to be transformed first into a constituent assembly and later into a full legislature.   (NIM CASWELL)

This article updates the *Macropædia* article WESTERN AFRICA: *Niger*.

NIGERIA

A republic and member of the Commonwealth, Nigeria is located in West Africa, on the Gulf of Guinea. Area: 923,768 sq km (356,669 sq mi). Pop. (1988 est.): 112,258,000. Cap., Lagos; capital designate, Abuja. Monetary unit: naira, with (Oct. 10, 1988) a free rate of 4.63 naira to U.S. $1 (7.92 naira = £1 sterling). President and chairman of the Armed Forces Ruling Council in 1988, Maj. Gen. Ibrahim Babangida.

Nigeria's January 1988 budget, designed to give breathing space in a desperately strained economic situation, was more optimistic than subsequent developments allowed. Total expenditure for the year was set at 24,294,000,000 naira, just over half of which was for recurrent expenditure. In an innovation, 451 million naira was set aside for the maintenance of existing assets. Petroleum subsidies were retained despite International Monetary Fund pressures to reduce them. The five-year wage freeze was lifted, and measures were passed to protect home industries and to restructure the civil service. The fifth development plan

was postponed to January 1989. Like many other African countries, Nigeria had embarked on a program of privatization, details of which were announced at the beginning of the year. The measures covered all commercial and merchant banks. A number of corporations were to remain public, but their operations would be commercialized; these included the Nigerian National Petroleum Corporation, radio, television, and the railways.

Nigeria's first petrochemical plant at Ekpam was commissioned in March; part of the plant was designed to supply Nigeria with half the raw materials required for the plastics industry. Ten years earlier Nigeria had announced plans for the commercial exploitation of its huge natural gas resources, but when oil prices fell these were shelved for lack of development capital. Now, with oil prices still depressed, liquefied natural gas was to be developed as a long-term replacement for the dwindling oil resources. France agreed on new credits to cover the costs of a new water supply service for Lagos. West Germany agreed to resume insurance cover for its exports to Nigeria; this followed the March signing of an agreement to reschedule debts of DM 2.4 billion.

In April the government increased gasoline (petrol) prices by 3%, provoking violent demonstrations and leading to the closure of some 20 institutions of higher education. Nigeria still had very cheap gasoline, but transportation was a major item of individual expenditure, so any change in gasoline prices was felt throughout the economy. The question of whether to abolish gasoline subsidies was central to any restructuring of the economy. Meanwhile, prices continued to rise, and by midyear the January budget proposals had been cut back. Neither oil nor cocoa revenues came up to expectations, and the ending of the Gulf war could mean a greater glut of oil that would depress oil prices still further. Nigeria's economic performance had been so consistently poor in recent years that the country was in danger of being reclassified by the World Bank from a middle-income to a low-income country.

U.K. Prime Minister Margaret Thatcher made a brief visit to Nigeria in January, marking the start of a rapprochement between the two countries after a period of poor relations. The head of state, Maj. Gen. Ibrahim Babangida, reaffirmed the decision to return the country to civilian rule by 1992. In June the 563-member constituent assembly began deliberations on a constitution for the third republic. One proposal being seriously considered was to create three vice-presidents to ensure broad-based representation at the top level of government. A new religious dispute was in the making as the place of Shari'ah (Islamic) law in the new constitution was debated by the country's Muslims. The issue was dividing the constitution makers, as was Nigeria's continued membership in the Islamic Conference Organization. The non-Muslim southern part of the country feared domination by the Muslim north. Abubakar III, the sultan of Sokoto and spiritual leader of Nigeria's Muslims, died on November 1 (see OBITUARIES). Rioting in which more than ten died greeted his government-appointed successor, Ibrahim Dasuki.

(GUY ARNOLD)

This article updates the *Macropædia* article WESTERN AFRICA: *Nigeria.*

RWANDA

The landlocked republic of Rwanda is situated in central Africa. Area: 26,338 sq km (10,169 sq mi). Pop. (1988 est.): 6,709,000. Cap.: Kigali. Monetary unit: Rwanda franc, with (Oct. 10, 1988) a free rate of RF 77.68 to U.S. $1 (RF 133.02 = £1 sterling). President in 1988, Maj. Gen. Juvénal Habyarimana.

In October 1988 bodies from the tribal massacres in Burundi were floating down the Nyabarongo River into Rwanda at the rate of five a day. There were an estimated 63,000 Hutu refugees in camps set up in Rwanda following the August massacres. Rwanda watched the events in Burundi uneasily. The majority Hutu had wielded power in Rwanda ever since they overthrew the monarchy and Tutsi dominance in 1959, but exiled Tutsi periodically attempted a comeback.

During the summer the torrential rains that afflicted much of northern Africa caused flooding and landslides that destroyed over 4,000 dwellings and left 20,000 homeless. Rwanda received emergency relief from the European Communities, which in any case was the country's principal donor. Earlier in the year Rwanda concluded a barter trade agreement with Uganda that permitted the exchange of goods valued at $10 million a year. The 1988 budget increased taxes on fuel, locally made cigarettes, and soft drinks and imposed further cutbacks in government spending. Faced with a CFAF 2.5 billion deficit, the government was reducing its public administration staff, which currently accounted for more than 50% of all state expenditure.

After years of decline, the gorilla population in the Virunga Mountains was increasing again as a result of strict antipoaching measures. There were known to be at least 279 mountain gorillas, and the government opened a clinic for them north of Kigali. (GUY ARNOLD)

This article updates the *Macropædia* article CENTRAL AFRICA: *Rwanda.*

SÃO TOMÉ AND PRÍNCIPE

The republic of São Tomé and Príncipe comprises two main islands and several smaller islets that straddle the Equator in the Gulf of Guinea, off the west coast of Africa. Area: 1,001 sq km (386 sq mi). Pop. (1988 est.): 117,000. Cap.: São Tomé. Monetary unit: dobra, with (Oct. 10, 1988) a free rate of 77.01 dobras to U.S. $1 (131.87 dobras = £1 sterling). President in 1988, Manuel Pinto da Costa; prime minister from January 8, Celestino Rocha da Costa.

In late 1987 the ruling party, the Movimento de Libertaçao de São Tomé e Príncipe, announced constitutional reforms, to include presidential and legislative elections based on the universal right to vote. Pres. Manuel Pinto da Costa then appointed as prime minister (the post had been abolished in 1979) Celestino da Costa (a former minister of state for education, labour, and social security) with instructions to name a Cabinet and present a program of action for the approval of the National Assembly. The Assembly accepted the prime minister's program, in which he called for close cooperation with the European Communities and proposed deregulation of the economy.

A curious coup attempt was mounted in March 1988 when a group landed from canoes and tried to capture São Tomé police headquarters. The government attributed the attempt to the opposition group, the National Resistance Front. Two of the group were killed and about 40 were captured, including 2 U.S. mercenaries. President da Costa described the attempt as the work of adventurers and reaffirmed his commitment to the process of democratization, promising elections for 1990.

Following the coup attempt the U.S. promised to provide the government with two patrol vessels. Portugal agreed to set up a military academy in São Tomé; previously most military assistance had come from the Eastern bloc.

(GUY ARNOLD)

This article updates the *Macropædia* article CENTRAL AFRICA: *São Tomé and Príncipe.*

SENEGAL

The republic of Senegal is located in West Africa, on the Atlantic Ocean; it surrounds the country of The Gambia, with which it has formed an administrative union called Senegambia. Area: 196,722 sq km (75,955 sq mi). Pop. (1988 est.): 7,187,000. Cap.: Dakar. Monetary unit: CFA franc, with (Oct. 10, 1988) a par value of CFAF 50 to the French franc and a free rate of CFAF 316.13 to U.S. $1 (CFAF 541.38 = £1 sterling). President in 1988, Abdou Diouf.

A turbulent year for Pres. Abdou Diouf and his government opened with an increasingly heated campaign for the presidential and legislative elections on Feb. 28, 1988. Six of the 17 registered political parties contested the poll, while four candidates presented themselves for the presidency. The winner was never in serious doubt, with Diouf and his Parti Socialiste reelected for new five-year terms with 71.3% of the vote and 103 of the 120 parliamentary seats, respectively; Abdoulaye Wade's Parti Démocratique Sénégalais (PDS) finished second, with 24.7% and 17 seats. The closing days of the campaign were marked by clashes between government and opposition supporters, and, as the results were declared, gangs of youths took to the streets of the capital, looting and burning to chants of the PDS's campaign cry of "Change!"

A state of emergency was declared, and a number of opposition figures were arrested for complicity in starting the riot. Although order was restored within two days, tension remained high, with continuing strikes in secondary schools and at Cheikh Anta Diop University in Dakar, open divisions between the government and labour unions, three bomb attacks in Dakar, and disturbances and arrests in the southern region of Casamance. The government responded with carefully gauged concessions, announcing a reduction in the retail prices of urban staple foodstuffs on May 1 and subsequently agreeing to talks with the opposition parties. These broke up without agreement in July.

President Diouf pledged that neither Senegal's democratic experiment nor its nine-year-old economic restructuring program would be reversed. Abundant rains from June onward ensured a good harvest with the exception of areas affected by locusts, and this led to a fourth successive year of positive economic growth.   (NIM CASWELL)

This article updates the Macropædia article WESTERN AFRICA: Senegal.

AFP PHOTO

An angry mob hurls rocks at a taxi during riots in protest against the outcome of Senegal's national elections. Six of the nation's 17 registered parties contested the election results.

SEYCHELLES

A republic and member of the Commonwealth, the Seychelles consists of about 100 islands in the Indian Ocean, 1,450 km (900 mi) from the east coast of Africa. Area: 453 sq km (175 sq mi). Pop. (1988 est.): 66,900. Cap.: Victoria. Monetary unit: Seychelles rupee, with (Oct. 10, 1988) a free rate of SR 5.43 to U.S. $1 (SR 9.30 = £1 sterling). President in 1988, France-Albert René.

Pres. France-Albert René held seven portfolios in 1988, including foreign affairs and defense, as well as being the leader of the state's only party, the Seychelles People's Progressive Front. The government emphasized that Seychelles belonged to a "zone of peace," and its nonalignment was accepted by both the U.S. and the U.S.S.R., neither of whom wanted any escalation of tensions in the Indian Ocean. U.S. and Soviet warships visited Seychelles in succession for "rest and recreation."

Nonalignment had meant a widening of the country's sources of international aid, which now included the U.K., the World Bank, the European Communities, India, the Arab states, the U.S.S.R., and China. The economy remained dependent on tourism and fishing. Unfortunately, 60% of the income from tourism went directly to tour operators or to pay for imports of luxury food and drink for the visitors. Even so, net earnings from tourism amounted to about $40 million a year. Despite its narrow economic base, Seychelles had one of the highest per capita incomes in Africa and had been designated a middle-income country.   (GUY ARNOLD)

This article updates the Macropædia article INDIAN OCEAN ISLANDS: Seychelles.

SIERRA LEONE

A republic of West Africa and member of the Commonwealth, Sierra Leone lies on the Atlantic Ocean. Area: 71,740 sq km (27,699 sq mi). Pop. (1988 est.): 3,883,000. Cap.: Freetown. Monetary unit: leone, with (Oct. 10, 1988) an official rate of 37.01 leones to U.S. $1 (63.38 leones = £1 sterling). President in 1988, Maj. Gen. Joseph Saidu Momoh.

In November 1987 Pres. Joseph Momoh had declared a state of economic emergency; measures were passed to prevent hoarding of the national currency and essential commodities, and export licenses for diamonds and gold were suspended. This was the first such emergency in the country's history. In April 1988 the International Monetary Fund (IMF) formally suspended Sierra Leone because of its accumulating arrears with the Fund and the World Bank, a move that provoked anger in Sierra Leone, where President Momoh had inherited a $31.5 million debt to the IMF and a $50 million debt to the World Bank from his predecessor. The general state of the economy remained depressed, although a three-year aid agreement with West Germany and a World Health Organization program to eradicate river blindness were encouraging developments, as was a plan to improve 10,000 km (6,210 mi) of roads.

The civil service was especially affected by an anticorruption drive. As many as 64% of the civil service were "ghost" workers with political connections, not working but drawing pay. In one department it was discovered that 75% of those on the payroll did not exist.

A 15-day period of official mourning was declared following the death of former president Siaka Stevens (see OBITUARIES) on May 29.   (GUY ARNOLD)

This article updates the Macropædia article WESTERN AFRICA: Sierra Leone.

SOMALIA

A republic in the Horn of northeastern Africa, the Somali Democratic Republic, or Somalia, lies on the Gulf of Aden and the Indian Ocean. Area: 637,000 sq km (246,000 sq mi). Pop. (1988 est.): 6,334,000. Cap.: Mogadishu. Monetary unit: Somali shilling, with (Oct. 10, 1988) a free rate of 243.57 Somali shillings to U.S. $1 (417.12 Somali shillings = £1 sterling). President in 1988, Maj. Gen. Muhammad Siyad Barrah; prime minister, Lieut. Gen. Muhammad Ali Samatar.

In 1988 the rebellion in the north of Somalia by the Somali National Movement (SNM), which had smoldered for seven years, flared into a full-scale civil war. The country's economic situation remained precarious, and behind-the-scenes maneuvering continued for the succession to Pres. Muhammad Siyad Barrah, who after 19 years in power was in his 80s and in poor health.

In December 1987 there was a reorganization of government structures in which the previous 25 ministries were reduced to 19. Taking over the Ministry of Finance, Abderrahman Jama Barrah, the president's brother, continued the program of austerity and self-reliance begun the previous year, when Somalia rejected its accommodation with the International Monetary Fund (IMF). In January 1988 price controls were introduced on essential goods, and exchange controls were tightened.

On February 1 six leading politicians, including former vice-president Ismail Ali Abokor, were brought to trial, along with 17 others. The six and two others were found guilty of "engaging in the formation of a group of saboteurs," a reference to the SNM. They were condemned to death, but following protests from abroad, the sentences were commuted to imprisonment and house arrest.

On April 3 the peace talks between Somalia and Ethiopia over the disputed Ogaden region, which had begun in 1986, finally ended in an agreement. Somalia undertook to cease support for Ethiopian antigovernment groups; Ethiopia, in return, undertook to withdraw from a strip of country near the border that it had held since 1983, together with the second Somali antigovernment organization, the Somali Democratic Salvation Front (SDSF), and to withdraw all support from both that organization and the more important SNM.

The reaction of the SNM was to mount a sudden major offensive. At the end of May it captured the town of Burao and several smaller settlements and attacked the northern regional capital, Hargeysa. The strategic port of Berbera, whose air and naval facilities were used by the U.S., was virtually under siege. Reports emerging from the area indicated a disastrous situation, with a large part of Hargeysa and Burao destroyed by government bombing and shelling. The total dead were estimated at 10,000, and 300,000 refugees had crossed into Ethiopia. By November the government appeared to have largely regained control, although fighting continued around Hargeysa.

In October a rapprochement between the Somali government and the IMF opened the way for release of $36 million in U.S. aid, due for 1987–88 but held back because of the government's economic policies. However, there were calls from the U.S. Congress to make this release conditional on the reform of human rights abuses in Somalia.

In early November discontent among the general public erupted in Mogadishu when a march by former prisoners of war to protest living conditions turned into a popular mass demonstration.   (VIRGINIA R. LULING)

This article updates the *Macropædia* article EASTERN AFRICA: *Somalia.*

SOUTH AFRICA

The Republic

South Africa occupies the southern tip of Africa, with the Atlantic Ocean to the west and the Indian Ocean to the east. It partially surrounds the four republics of Bophuthatswana, Ciskei, Transkei, and Venda (whose independence from South Africa is not recognized by the international community). Area: 1,123,226 sq km (433,680 sq mi). Pop. (1988 est.): 29,628,000. (Area and population figures exclude the four republics.) Executive cap., Pretoria; judicial cap., Bloemfontein; legislative cap., Cape Town. Monetary unit: South African rand, with (Oct. 10, 1988) a financial rate of R 4.04 to U.S. $1 (R 6.92 = £1 sterling) and a commercial rate of R 2.49 to U.S. $1 (R 4.26 = £1 sterling). State president in 1988, Pieter Willem Botha.

The Republic. *Domestic Affairs.* South Africa continued to be governed throughout 1988 under the state of emergency declared in June 1986. There was no significant development in the National Party government's program of reform of apartheid, the official policy of racial separation. Pres. P. W. Botha's speech at the opening of Parliament in February concentrated almost exclusively on economic issues.

On February 24 the government announced measures that effectively banned the United Democratic Front (UDF) and 16 other organizations, the main opposition groupings outside of Parliament. Severe restrictions were also imposed on the activities of the Congress of South African Trade Unions (COSATU), whose membership was approximately 800,000.

In March there was an international outcry over the government's intention to hang the "Sharpeville Six," six black youths convicted of murder on the sole grounds that they had been participants in a demonstration in 1984 during which the mayor of the black township complex of Lekoa had been killed. New evidence returned this case to the courts, and in November President Botha commuted the sentences of all six defendants to prison sentences ranging from 18 to 25 years.

Restrictions on the press were tightened during the year, and three newspapers—*New Nation, South,* and the *Weekly Mail*—were prohibited from publication for limited periods. In July a white conscientious objector, David Bruce, was sentenced to six years in prison for refusing to serve in the South African Army because it supported a racist government. Treason trials of black political leaders continued. According to the government, 17% of those arrested under the state of emergency remained in detention. In September three UDF leaders (and then a fourth) escaped from detention and took refuge in the U.S. consulate. The government stated that they would not be rearrested if they left, which they did after several weeks.

Some of these measures were interpreted as attempts by the government to impede the organization of a boycott by blacks of elections for local councils, held on October 26. These, in which, for the first time, white, Indian, Coloured (mixed black and white), and African councils were up for election on the same day, were widely seen as a "referendum" on the government's program, rather than as purely local in character.

In the campaigning before the elections, Khotso House in Johannesburg, headquarters of the South African Council of Churches, as well as Khanya House in Pretoria, headquarters of the South African Catholic Bishops' Conference, were gutted by bombs—as had been the case with COSATU House in 1987. Church leaders such as Anglican Archbishop Desmond Tutu had called for a boycott of the elections.

A man in Soweto casts his ballot during local elections held on October 26. It was the first time that whites, Indians, Coloureds, and Africans had held their separate elections on the same day.
AFP PHOTO

In August African National Congress (ANC) leader Nelson Mandela, imprisoned for 26 years, was transferred from Pollsmoor Prison to Tygerberg Hospital in Cape Town because he was suffering from tuberculosis. He was subsequently moved to Constantiaberg clinic. July 18, his 70th birthday, had been marked by widespread international celebrations, including a concert in Britain watched by an estimated one billion TV viewers throughout the world. In December he was moved again to a house on a prison farm near Cape Town.

Despite the restrictions and repression, the October elections were overwhelmingly boycotted by blacks. The government claimed an overall poll of 25.2% among registered African voters, better than in previous such elections. This meant an actual voting figure of 382,952, however, a tiny proportion of the African population of voting age.

The government's plan—in pursuit of constitutional reform—was that the local councils would elect delegates to the regional service councils ("multiracial" bodies responsible for administration of services at interlocal level). Black councils would also, through an electoral college, elect representatives to the proposed black national council, in which a limited number of nonhomeland Africans would be involved in discussing further constitutional reform.

The elections for white councils registered big gains for the Conservative Party (CP), which stood for a return to old-style apartheid based on racial partition of the country. In the Transvaal the CP gained up to 60 councils and narrowly missed winning control of the administrative capital, Pretoria. The CP threatened to use its position to block the work of the regional service councils and strengthen racial segregation at the local level. In March the CP had also won increased majorities in parliamentary by-elections in Standerton, Schweizer-Reneke, and Randfontein. These results, together with the capture by the National Party (NP) of the Johannesburg and Pietermaritzburg councils, confirmed a drift to the right in white politics. However, the CP gains were not the landslide that some had anticipated. In a move that surprised some observers, Botha in September made a speech calling on CP leader Andries Treurnicht to join in reuniting the Afrikaner people.

' To the left of the NP in white politics, there was continued disarray. Colin Eglin resigned in June as leader of the Progressive Federal Party (PFP) and was replaced by Zach de Beer. The PFP's position was contested by the National Democratic Movement (in which Wynand Malan, a member of Parliament, was a dominant figure) and the In-

dependent Party, launched by former ambassador to Great Britain Denis Worrall. De Beer called for unification of these forces in the face of a likely parliamentary election in 1989.

A drift to the right was also reflected in legislation introduced during the year. Bills were introduced to strengthen the enforcement of residential racial segregation under the Group Areas Act (while also permitting mixed-race areas where local residents agreed) and to strengthen the government's powers to remove squatters forcibly. These provoked a crisis in the tricameral Parliament, marked by walkouts by opposition parties and refusals by the (Coloured) House of Representatives and (Indian) House of Delegates to vote on the measures. In November a presidential council rejected the residential segregation bill.

A stringent Labour Relations Amendment Bill was enacted. It removed a number of the labour union reforms introduced in 1979, including recognition of minority unions. These changes, which were supported by employers' organizations, reflected growing employer concern about union power.

In response to the February restrictions on the UDF and to the labour bill, COSATU called a three-day national stay-away on June 6–8, which was supported by up to three million black workers and two million black youths. This was the biggest and longest such action in the history of South Africa. A one-day general strike also took place on March 21, the anniversary of the 1960 Sharpeville massacre. Industrial strike action declined from the peak it had reached in 1987. Major strikes included those by 30,000 metalworkers for two weeks in August and by up to 25,000 dockworkers during September and October. Coloured women garment workers in the western Cape Province staged their first big strike since 1936.

The climate of repression hampered open activity among blacks. However, it proved unable to break the rent boycott that had continued since 1985–86 in a number of Transvaal townships, notably Soweto, the black urban complex near Johannesburg. The boycott was a protest against rent increases and against the unpopular township councils that enforced them. School youths, particularly hard hit by the post-1986 wave of detentions, again staged sporadic school boycotts in different parts of the country.

The banned ANC continued to be regarded as the most popular organization among the black majority. It maintained its guerrilla actions through its armed wing, Umkhonto We Sizwe. The government claimed 262 "ter-

ror incidents" up to October 20, compared with 230 in 1986 and 235 in 1987. These included bombs or mines placed at restaurants, bus stations, and Ellis Park rugby ground, some admitted to by the ANC. Within the ANC National Executive Committee, there appeared to be division on the acceptability of attacking such "soft targets." Counterattacks were made on ANC targets in Europe and Africa during the year, including the murder of the ANC's representative in France, Dulcie September, in March.

The exiled ANC leadership drew up constitutional proposals for a future nonracial South Africa to supplement the Freedom Charter, which advocated a Bill of Rights and a mixed economy. It also continued discussions with delegations from inside the country on its aims. These included spokesmen for the Indian community, church and labour union leaders, and, in October, Danie Craven, president of the South African Rugby Board (SARB). These latter discussions, in particular, were attacked by the government, and in November the SARB voted to discontinue them.

The violent conflict between vigilante supporters of Chief Buthelezi's Inkatha movement and supporters of the UDF continued in Natal, despite court injunctions and despite talks between Inkatha and COSATU that led to a peace accord in early September. By the end of October, it was estimated that 511 had been killed, as against 497 in the whole of 1987, largely at the hands of Inkatha supporters; 79 of these deaths had followed the peace accord.

Foreign Relations. The limited sanctions agreed upon by Western powers in 1986 remained in force. A bill for far more stringent sanctions measures (the Dellums Bill) was discussed in the U.S. Congress but not passed. West German political leader Franz Josef Strauss (*see* OBITUARIES) visited southern Africa, including South Africa, in January; his funeral in October was attended by Botha on his first visit to Europe since 1984.

In March four people were killed when the South African Defence Force raided Gabarone, capital of Botswana. South African police were also involved in ending the hijack of a bus containing pilgrims by presumed Lesotho Liberation Army guerrillas in September on the occasion of the pope's visit to Lesotho and other southern African countries.

The major foreign policy development of the year was the series of talks among South Africa, the U.S., Angola, and Cuba linking implementation of UN Resolution 435 on independence for South West Africa/Namibia with withdrawal of Cuban troops from Angola. These talks followed a major invasion of Angola by South African forces in late 1987 and early 1988, leading to a battle over the strategic town of Cuito Cuanavale, the biggest land battle in Africa since World War II. The South African forces, reinforcing the National Union for the Total Independence of Angola (UNITA) rebels against the Angolan government, failed to capture the town and suffered losses of at least 61 white conscript troops.

By September 1 South Africa had withdrawn its troops from Angola. Talks continued, though the November 1 deadline for beginning to implement Resolution 435 passed without further agreement. The U.S. government, with the encouragement of the U.S.S.R., continued during November to press the parties toward agreement. There remained considerable skepticism among commentators as to whether the issues could be resolved. However, on December 22 South Africa, Angola, and Cuba signed an accord in which South Africa agreed to grant independence to Namibia provided Cuba withdraw all of its approximately 50,000 troops from Angola by July 1, 1991.

In connection with the talks, Botha for the first time paid visits to Malawi, Zaire, and Côte d'Ivoire. Also during the year, relations between South Africa and Mozambique improved, with a revival of the 1984 Nkomati Accord and a visit by Botha to Mozambique.

Economy. The mild 1986–87 upturn continued into the first part of 1988. For the first time in a number of years, there was a moderate pickup in the rate of fixed investment. However, because it was based upon consumer spending rather than export growth and led to an increase in imports, the upturn rapidly caused balance of trade and payments difficulties. These were compounded by the continued outflow of private capital (R 4.8 billion net in the first three quarters of 1988) and the need for servicing foreign debt obligations. Large surpluses on the current account of the balance of payments in 1986–87 (R 6.2 billion in 1987) had been reduced to a seasonally adjusted annualized R 960 million by the second quarter of 1988. Foreign exchange reserves had declined by October to R 4,610,000,000 ($1,870,000,000, from a peak of $3.4 billion at the end of 1987).

It was estimated that under these conditions, while 5% annual growth of gross domestic product (GDP) was needed for absorbing new entrants to the labour market (in addition to what was needed for reducing existing levels of unemployment, estimated among blacks at between three million and six million), South Africa could not afford more than 3% growth. The 1987 growth had been 2.6%; predictions for growth in 1988 were about the same.

In response to the balance of payments problems, Minister of Finance Barend du Plessis in August introduced a package of measures, including import tariff surcharges of 10–60%. There were expectations that in the period after the elections, with the money supply growing at an annualized rate of 25–29%, further monetary or fiscal measures would have to be taken to curb inflation. The 1988–89 budget in March called for a rise in revenue of 13.3% over 1987–88, a rise in expenditure of 12.6%, and a deficit of 4.9% of estimated GDP.

Bophuthatswana

The republic of Bophuthatswana consists of six discontinuous, landlocked geographic units, entirely surrounded by South Africa except for one unit that borders Botswana on the northwest. Area: 44,000 sq km (16,988 sq mi). Pop. (1988 est.): 2,005,000. Cap.: Mmabatho. Monetary unit: South African rand. President in 1988, Lucas Mangope.

Ciskei

Bordering the Indian Ocean in the south, Ciskei is surrounded on land by South Africa. Area: 7,760 sq km (2,996 sq mi). Pop. (1988 est.): 946,000. Cap.: Bisho. Monetary unit: South African rand. President in 1988, Lennox Sebe.

Transkei

Bordering the Indian Ocean and surrounded on land by South Africa, Transkei comprises three discontinuous geographic units, two of which are landlocked and one of which borders Lesotho. Area: 43,653 sq km (16,855 sq mi). Pop. (1988 est.): 3,714,000. Cap.: Umtata. Monetary unit: South African rand. Head of the Military Council in 1988, Maj. Gen. Bantu Holomisa.

Venda

The landlocked republic of Venda is located in extreme northeastern South Africa. Area: 7,176 sq km (2,771 sq mi). Pop. (1988 est.): 547,000. Cap.: Thohoyandou. Monetary unit: South African rand. Presidents in 1988, Patrick Mphephu and, from April 18, Frank Ravele.

A man in Sudan guides his camel through floodwaters near the city of Khartoum. Extensive rains combined with seasonal shifts of the Nile caused devastating flooding that left at least one million people homeless.
AP/WIDE WORLD

Sections of the Bophuthatswana Defence Force on February 9 attempted to overthrow the government of the homeland, but they were crushed within 24 hours by the South African Defence Force. Subsequently, 195 people were put on trial for treason, and the opposition Peoples' Progressive Party was banned in August. This was the fifth recent attempted coup in the independent homelands, reflecting their increasing instability.

In April Venda President-for-life Patrick Mphephu died in a Pretoria hospital and was succeeded by Minister of Finance Frank Ravele. A school boycott broke out in July in Venda when a schoolteacher was found hanged and ritual murder by government officials was suspected. The incident led to a massive four-day general strike in mid-August, amid allegations of nepotism and corruption. A series of successful court actions against the KwaNdebele government resulted in the dissolution of its assembly and the calling of new elections for December, delaying independence for that homeland.

In all the homelands evidence of massive corruption mounted. Former prime minister George Mantanzima fled the Transkei when a warrant was issued for his arrest on charges of corruption, but he was extradited and brought to trial in September. On the basis of two reports by the Transkei government published in August, the South African government set up a commission to investigate corruption in the Transkei and Ciskei.

In July South African Foreign Affairs Minister Roelof ("Pik") Botha stated in Parliament that the four independent homelands had received R 2,760,000,000 in the 1987–88 financial year: R 1,060,000,000 for Transkei, R 834.1 million for Bophuthatswana, R 323.6 million for Venda, and R 520.5 million for Ciskei. The South African government also guaranteed bank loans to cover budget deficits in 1986–88. The Pretoria-based Africa Institute estimated that a minimum of R 175 million (5% of South African grants) was misappropriated or embezzled in 1987–88.

(MARTIN LEGASSICK)

See also *Dependent States,* below.

SUDAN, THE

A republic of North Africa, The Sudan has a coastline on the Red Sea. Area: 2,503,890 sq km (966,757 sq mi). Pop. (1988 est.): 26,263,000. Cap.: Khartoum. Monetary unit: Sudanese pound, with (Oct. 10, 1988) a par value of LSd 4.50 to U.S. $1 (free rate of LSd 7.69 = £1 sterling). Chairman of the Supreme Council in 1988, Ahmad al-Mirghani; prime minister, Sadiq al-Mahdi.

In April 1988 Sadiq al-Mahdi was reelected prime minister in preparation for the formation of a government of national conciliation. This brought to an end the hiatus that had begun when the ruling coalition was dissolved in August 1987, but it also further emphasized the division between north and south because the latter played no part in the new constitutional arrangements. In addition, the proposal to reintroduce some of the severe punishments approved by Islamic law—suspended since the overthrow of Pres. Gaafar Nimeiry in 1985— did nothing to settle the dispute between the two halves of the country. The inclusion in the government for the first time of members of the fundamentalist National Islamic Front still further alienated the mostly non-Islamic south, and the government's continuing attempts to open negotiations or to destroy southern opposition by force of arms conspicuously failed to produce a solution. By the beginning of the year, the civil war had spread to the Blue Nile Province, a region previously considered to be part of the north. Hundreds of thousands of refugees fled over the Ethiopian border to escape the fighting, and thousands more joined those who had preceded them in settling near Khartoum. The sufferings of the latter group were multiplied in August when torrential rains resulted in serious flooding of the low-lying area in which they had made their temporary homes. Many people were drowned or died from starvation, and an estimated two million were made homeless. Areas in the east and north were similarly affected. In the south the casualties were due less to flooding than to the failure of aid to reach its destination.

On December 21 the government reported that it had thwarted an attempted coup and had arrested 25 civilians and retired soldiers. Demonstrations and a general strike took place in Khartoum in late December in protest against government-imposed price increases, including a 500% rise in sugar. On December 28 the second largest party withdrew from the governing coalition, and on the next day the price increases were rescinded.   (KENNETH INGHAM)

SWAZILAND

Swaziland is a landlocked monarchy of southern Africa and a member of the Commonwealth. Area: 17,364 sq km (6,704 sq mi). Pop. (1988 est.): 716,000. Administrative cap., Mbabane; royal and legislative cap., Lobamba. Monetary unit: lilangeni (plural: emalangeni), at par with the South African rand, with (Oct. 10, 1988) a free rate of 2.49 emalangeni to U.S. $1 (4.26 emalangeni = £1 sterling). King, Mswati III; prime minister, Sotsha Dlamini.

Swaziland's overall economic deficit was expected to reach no more than $4 million (9.5 million emalangeni) in 1988, thanks to strict policies that had brought expenditure under control. Debts were manageable and required only 8% of export earnings to service. The biggest problem concerned unemployment; 18% of those in paid employment (about 17,000) worked in the South African mines. Inflation stood at 15%. Agricultural production was down somewhat, but the manufacturing sector was showing a healthy increase, with an expected growth rate for the year of between 3 and 4%. A shake-up of the public enterprises was aimed at bringing them under more effective public control.

Swaziland remained too dependent for comfort on the South African Customs Union, the terms of which were soon to be renegotiated. The government opposed sanctions against South Africa, since it believed these would hurt it more than the republic. Members of the African National Congress, banned in South Africa, continued to be deported from the country. A new problem concerned the growing number of refugees from Mozambique, amounting to about 25,000 in 1988.   (GUY ARNOLD)

This article updates the *Macropædia* article SOUTHERN AFRICA: *Swaziland*.

TANZANIA

The republic of Tanzania, a member of the Commonwealth, consists of Tanganyika, on the east coast of Africa, and Zanzibar, just off the coast in the Indian Ocean, which includes Zanzibar Island, Pemba Island, and small islets. Area: 945,037 sq km (364,881 sq mi). Pop. (1988 est.): 23,996,000. Seat of government, Dar es Salaam; capital designate, Dodoma. Monetary unit: Tanzania shilling, with (Oct. 10, 1988) a free rate of 106.22 shillings to U.S. $1 (181.90 shillings = £1 sterling). President in 1988, Ali Hassan Mwinyi; prime minister, Joseph Warioba.

With a population growth averaging 3.2% per year, pressure on a weak economy continued to be heavy in Tanzania in 1988. Following International Monetary Fund guidelines, however, the nation slowly increased its gross domestic product in spite of heavy foreign debts, which had to be serviced. A lack of foreign exchange forced the government to keep firm control on the export of profits, and this discouraged foreign investors. Britain, nevertheless, was willing to provide additional financial assistance, guaranteeing $32 million in February to help with the balance of payments deficit. This was in addition to nearly $50 million paid in annual aid for a variety of projects.

Tanzania's relationship with Britain was strengthened further when Pres. Ali Hassan Mwinyi visited London in June. In October the president also visited both Kenya and Uganda, giving rise to hopes that some form of tripartite commission might be set up to encourage cooperation in specific areas. In December Tanzania announced that it had withdrawn its troops from Mozambique, where they had been assisting in the fight against right-wing rebels.

Adverse weather conditions during the year caused a large part of the population in the eastern half of the country to suffer from food shortages. As a result, efforts were made to enlist science and technology in an attempt to reduce Tanzania's reliance upon a regular seasonal rainfall.

The government's determination to deal firmly with anyone who sought to undermine its policies was vividly demonstrated in January when Ali Jusuf Abdurabi, member of Parliament for Songea town, was arrested under the Economic Sabotage Act for being in illegal possession of 105 elephant tusks. Pres. Idris Abdul Wakil of Zanzibar appeared to have encountered even stiffer opposition. On January 12 he announced that he had discovered a plot to

overthrow his government with the help of foreign mercenaries. In consequence he reorganized the Revolutionary Council of Zanzibar, bringing in four new ministers. Particularly significant was the dismissal of the chief minister, Seif Shariff Hamad, and the transfer of control of the Special Zanzibar Revolutionary Government forces from the chief minister's office to that of the president. Hamad had been a longtime opponent of Wakil, having run for the presidency against him at the last election. He was regarded as a keen supporter of Mwinyi's liberalizing policies, which, to the black majority on Zanzibar and Pemba, seemed like an Arab plot to gain control first of the economy and then of political power in the islands.

During a seminar in May organized by the ruling political party, Judge Hamis Msumi drew attention to the ways in which the application of parliamentary, customary, and Islamic law denied women their rights in regard to property, landowning, and many other spheres, even where the law stated that a husband and wife should have equal rights. His statement met with strong support from several women at the conference who claimed that the legal system made it difficult for them to contribute fully to the nation.
                (KENNETH INGHAM)

This article updates the *Macropædia* article EASTERN AFRICA: *Tanzania*.

TOGO

A republic of West Africa, Togo is situated on the Bight of Benin. Area: 56,785 sq km (21,925 sq mi). Pop. (1988 est.): 3,486,000. Cap.: Lomé. Monetary unit: CFA franc, with (Oct. 10, 1988) a par value of CFAF 50 to the French franc and a free rate of CFAF 316.13 to U.S. $1 (CFAF 541.38 = £1 sterling). President in 1988, Gen. Gnassingbe Eyadema.

Pres. Gnassingbe Eyadema's regime—the first in post-independence Africa to be installed by military coup—celebrated its 21st anniversary in power on January 13 with the opposition more fragmented than ever before and the head of state increasingly taking on the role of continental statesman. In June the annual summit of the Economic Community of West African States regional grouping was held in Lomé; shortly before it began, a new Libyan ambassador presented his credentials—an unusual step, given Togo's diplomatic recognition of Israel.

Togo's economic position remained precarious as commodity prices fell and the CFA franc strengthened against the dollar. Cocoa offered particularly poor prospects, while those of Togo's other main export products—coffee, cotton, and phosphates—were no better than mediocre. This affected adversely not only the nation's balance of payments but also its public finances because the policy of guaranteeing crop prices well above world market equivalents required the payment of subsidies to farmers. Togolese phosphates also faced the problem of new health standards in the European Communities governing the cadmium content of fertilizers, which could end exports to one of Togo's traditional markets.   (NIM CASWELL)

This article updates the *Macropædia* article WESTERN AFRICA: *Togo*.

UGANDA

A landlocked republic and member of the Commonwealth, Uganda is located in eastern Africa. Area: 241,040 sq km (93,070 sq mi), including 44,000 sq km of inland water. Pop. (1988 est.): 15,990,000. Cap.: Kampala. Monetary unit: Uganda new shilling, with (Oct. 10, 1988) a par value of 150 new shillings to U.S. $1 (free rate of 257 new shillings = £1 sterling). President in 1988, Yoweri Museveni; prime minister, Samson Kisekka.

At the end of 1987 an accord was reached after a meeting between Presidents Yoweri Museveni of Uganda and Daniel arap Moi of Kenya to put an end to the cross-border shooting that had begun in mid-December. Each country agreed to reduce its security forces along the border in an effort to ease tension. As evidence of the subsequent slight improvement in relations between the two countries, Alice Lakwena, a rebel leader who had been driven by the Uganda Army to take refuge in Kenya, was arrested and jailed for illegally entering the country. Subsequently more than 100 of her followers were arrested by the Kenyan authorities. Lakwena herself was released in March into the hands of the UN High Commissioner for Refugees.

Early in January another rebel group, the Uganda Federal Army, protesting against the Libyan diplomatic presence in Uganda, was responsible for the death of a Libyan diplomat and the injuring of several other persons when a bomb was thrown in Kampala. In an address to mark his second anniversary in office, Museveni urged all rebels to lay down their arms. It appeared to be a vain request, however, for 19 people were killed and 47 seriously wounded in February when rebels ambushed a bus in the northeast. In March, however, after negotiations that took place in Gulu, another rebel group, the Uganda People's Democratic Army, which consisted mainly of Acholi soldiers from the army of the previous regime, was rumoured to be ready to sign a peace agreement. This was strongly denied by the movement's political leader, Otema Allimadi, from his exile in London, and the commander of the UPDA ordered his troops to continue the struggle. In spite of these instructions, however, a peace agreement of sorts was reached; its effect was to reduce guerrilla activities to sporadic clashes with the authorities. In October the government was confident enough to release 950 prisoners who had been captured in the fighting against the rebels in the north and east.

Meanwhile, near the capital itself, mutinous officers and soldiers of the National Resistance Army tried unsuccessfully to assassinate Museveni in June. The mutineers wanted the government to initiate all-party peace talks with all the rebel groups and to expel all Libyan and North Korean military instructors. A month later Paulo Muwanga, who had been vice-president in the government of Milton Obote, was acquitted of charges of kidnapping but was immediately rearrested on similar charges.

In March representatives of the government of Uganda and The Sudan met in Kampala and signed a memorandum that provided for the return of 60,000 Ugandan refugees who had fled over the Sudanese border when the National Resistance Army entered northern Uganda and who now wished to return to their homes. The Sudan could ill afford to maintain them, but their return to Uganda was likely to impose a heavy burden on the government. Indeed, in September the desperate condition of the people in parts of the northern districts was revealed to the outside world by relief workers who were beginning to return to the area as guerrilla warfare died down. The acute cases of malnutrition discovered in the northern town of Lira and elsewhere were not due to the natural hazard of drought, which had caused havoc in other parts of the continent. They were instead the result of the destruction of homes and crops by rebels retreating before the advance of the National Resistance Army, by the Army itself taking reprisals against those whom it regarded as being sympathetic to the rebels, and later by marauding guerrillas.

(KENNETH INGHAM)

This article updates the *Macropædia* article EASTERN AFRICA: *Uganda*.

ZAIRE

The republic of Zaire is located in central Africa with a short coastline on the Atlantic Ocean. Area: 2,344,885 sq km (905,365 sq mi). Pop. (1988 est.): 32,559,000. Cap.: Kinshasa. Monetary unit: zaire, with (Oct. 10, 1988) a free rate of 206.48 zaires to U.S. $1 (353.60 zaires = £1 sterling). President in 1988, Mobutu Sese Seko; first state commissioners (prime ministers), Mabi Mulumba until March 7, Sambwa Pida Nbagui until November 26, and, from November 26, Kengo Wa Dondo.

The Economy. The year 1987 ended with gloomy reports about the rapid rise in the inflation rate, said to have been 60% in the first six months of that year in Kinshasa and higher still in other towns. The government attributed the situation to high transport costs, to shortages of goods caused by the lack of foreign exchange, and to the high cost of maintaining the industrial sector. Assistance provided by the International Monetary Fund had, however, caused some slowing down in the depreciation of the currency during the latter part of the year, and help was forthcoming from a wide range of sources. In January 1988 the International Fund for Agricultural Development agreed to give its support to a development program in the rural areas of southern Shaba that would raise the annual income of farmers holding small amounts of land and improve food supplies through the use of better agricultural techniques. Surprisingly, perhaps, in view of its differing attitude toward affairs in Angola, Cuba expressed its willingness to become involved in the construction of a sugar factory in Bandundu, which was begun in the latter part of the year, and also to give technical assistance in controlling diseases of sugarcane. Japan also offered additional aid and, as in the previous year, half of this took the form of a loan and half was made as a grant.

Substantial assistance was also made available by the African Development Bank, which planned to spend $450 million in Zaire in 1988 to promote a range of projects covering mining, transportation, energy, and agriculture. In its turn the Paris Club of Western creditor nations agreed to study the government's proposals for financing its official debt, while Brazil offered to increase the level of its cooperation by sending technological assistance for both the agricultural and industrial sectors. The Moroccan government awarded 35 scholarships to enable Zairian students to study in that country in 1988–89, and Israel promised to increase the help it had been giving.

Political Affairs. Performance on the diplomatic and political fronts was less uniformly successful. On Dec. 3, 1987, President Mobutu denied charges made by the Angolan minister of external relations that the National Union for the Total Independence of Angola (UNITA) guerrillas were still receiving military supplies sent through Zaire, and he invited observers from the Organization of African Unity to maintain a permanent checkpoint at the Kamina air base. Nevertheless, the charge was repeated by the Angolan defense minister in March, and Angola's confidence was in no way restored when Zaire carried out joint military maneuvers with the U.S. in the vicinity of Kamina, Kolwezi, and Lubumbashi in April.

Plans were announced in January to increase the number of provinces because the existing regions were proving too large to administer effectively. This was an extension of the experiment that had already been tried out with some success in the provinces of Kasai and Leopoldville. At the same time, the number of members of Parliament from Kinshasa was raised from 12 to 24 to ensure that all ethnic groups would be fairly represented.

Pres. Mobutu Sese Seko of Zaire (left) greets Pres. P. W. Botha of South Africa, who made his first visit to Zaire to discuss the Angolan peace settlement. Both countries had supported Angola's antigovernment guerrillas.
AFP PHOTO

In another respect the year began unpromisingly with the arrest of Etienne Tshisekedi wa Mulumba on January 17 while he was addressing a meeting of the opposition Union for Democracy and Social Progress (UDPS). Tshisekedi, a former associate of Mobutu, and the UDPS were working to achieve a multiparty state or at least greater diversity within the ruling party. Largely as a result of Tshisekedi's arrest, 58 U.S. congressmen wrote to Mobutu in April stressing that reform was urgently needed if the U.S. was to continue to supply aid, planned to total some $46 million in the current year. After further pressure, from Amnesty International and other bodies, Tshisekedi was released from prison in March, but a crowd of UDPS supporters that gathered to greet him was fiercely attacked by supporters of the government. Tshisekedi himself was sent to a psychiatric home and later was placed under house arrest. In April, however, he was rearrested after urging voters to boycott the elections in Kinshasa for new members of Parliament. He was released once more in September and announced that he was giving up politics.

Criticism of the use of the Kamina airstrip to assist Angolan guerrillas was also voiced in France, and in February Mobutu visited Paris to try to enlist French sympathy and to seek help in strengthening Zaire's military position. Two months later the former French army chief of staff, Gen. Jeannon Lacaze, was appointed personal adviser to Mobutu with the task of assisting in the restructuring of the armed forces. Meanwhile, in February, violent opponents of Mobutu, the Lumumba Patriotic Army, announced the election of new members to its high command with a view to pursuing more actively its armed struggle to overthrow the government.

The recall of Nguza Karl-I-Bond from his position as ambassador to the U.S. to become foreign minister once again in March was in keeping with Mobutu's practice of transferring officials from one post to another in rapid succession. The move was particularly startling, however, given Nguza's remarkable career both in support of and in opposition to the president. He was replaced as ambassador by Mushobekwa Kalimba Watana, previously ambassador to Belgium. In November Mobutu recalled for-

mer prime minister Kengo Wa Dondo to replace Sambwa Pida Nbagui, who had only held the post since March. Meanwhile, Mobutu himself was elected chairman of the Economic Community of Central African States and immediately called upon members to increase production and to buy within the Community.   (KENNETH INGHAM)

This article updates the *Macropædia* article CENTRAL AFRICA: *Zaire.*

ZAMBIA

A landlocked republic and member of the Commonwealth, Zambia is in eastern Africa. Area: 752,614 sq km (290,586 sq mi). Pop. (1988 est.): 7,384,000. Cap.: Lusaka. Monetary unit: kwacha, with (Oct. 10, 1988) a par value of 8 kwacha to U.S. $1 (a free rate of 13.70 kwacha = £1 sterling). President in 1988, Kenneth Kaunda; secretary-general of the United National Independence Party, Alexander Grey Zulu; prime minister, Kebby Musokotwane.

With the rate of inflation mounting rapidly, Pres. Kenneth Kaunda took stern action in February 1988 against a number of people accused of being involved in the black market. Sixty-six trading licenses were revoked, and several officials were dismissed. In May a rural resettlement project was launched in an attempt to find work for 10,000 youths.

Kaunda, the sole candidate, was elected to a sixth term of office as president in October. His undiminished popularity had been boosted earlier in the year by his decision to restore the subsidy on corn (maize) and to revoke the price increase on fuel. Although the country's debt remained at more than $5 billion, he had been encouraged to take these actions by the rise in the price of copper and by the excellent corn crop. It proved impossible, however, to derive full benefit from the latter because of the lack of transportation to collect the crop.   (KENNETH INGHAM)

This article updates the *Macropædia* article SOUTHERN AFRICA: *Zambia.*

ZIMBABWE

A republic and member of the Commonwealth, Zimbabwe is a landlocked state in eastern Africa. Area: 390,759 sq km (150,873 sq mi). Pop. (1988 est.): 8,878,000. Cap.: Harare. Monetary unit: Zimbabwe dollar, with (Oct. 10, 1988) a free rate of Z$1.88 to U.S. $1 (Z$3.22 = £1 sterling). President in 1988, Robert Mugabe.

The agreement signed on Dec. 22, 1987, by Prime Minister Robert Mugabe and Joshua Nkomo, under the terms of which their two parties were to be united, was confirmed on April 2, 1988, by the last national congress of Nkomo's Zimbabwe African People's Union (ZAPU) and then by Mugabe's Zimbabwe African National Union (Patriotic Front) (ZANU [PF]) a week later. The last obstacle to union, Mugabe's insistence on retaining the name of his own party for the new united party, was at last overcome when Nkomo conceded the point. The agreement also stated that the new party would seek to establish a socialist society in Zimbabwe under the guidance of Marxist-Leninist principles. Both parties committed themselves to taking vigorous steps to eliminate the violence and insecurity in Matabeleland and to establish a one-party state.

Meanwhile, on Dec. 31, 1987, Canaan Banana resigned as president and was succeeded by Mugabe. The formerly ceremonial presidency now incorporated the powers of the office of prime minister, which was abolished, but the change made little difference since Mugabe had been effectively in charge of the government since indepen-

dence. Nkomo was appointed vice-president and second secretary of ZANU (PF). His disappointment at not being appointed state deputy-president—an office awarded to Simon Muzenda, who shared the vice-presidency of the party with Nkomo—was partly assuaged when, in a Cabinet reshuffle announced on January 2, he became one of three senior ministers in the President's Office, with responsibility for overseeing a number of ministries including Local Government and Rural and Urban Development. The other two senior ministers were Bernard Chidzero, responsible for all the economic ministries and for planning, and Maurice Nyagumbo, who was to be in charge of political affairs. The three, together with Mugabe and Muzenda, formed an inner Cabinet, which met weekly.

Mugabe avoided offending some of his old party stalwarts, who feared losing their jobs because of the merger, by enlarging his Cabinet to a total of 27, excluding himself, so as to include a number of ZAPU members proportionate to the number of Matabele in the population as a whole. Witness Mangwende was transferred from the Foreign Office, where his tactlessness was thought to have led to the withdrawal of U.S. aid, and made minister of information. U.S. aid was resumed later in the year. Mangwende's successor was Nathan Shamuyarira. A controversial appointment was that of the outspoken Enos Nkala, an opponent of Nkomo, as defense minister.

On January 11 a car bomb exploded outside a building owned by the African National Congress in Bulawayo, killing two people and injuring three others. The act was believed to have been inspired by the South African government. Six men (five of them white) were arrested; three of them were convicted of murder and sentenced to death in November. Also in January two men accused of spying for South Africa, who had been detained without trial for two years, were unconditionally released, while six others were arrested and held in detention, even after the charges were dropped in August.

On April 19, the same day guerrillas in Matabeleland killed a Roman Catholic missionary in the worst act of violence by dissidents in the area since the signing of the interparty agreement, Mugabe announced an amnesty for political offenders. Almost at once guerrillas began to surrender, and by the deadline at midnight on May 31, more than 100, virtually all of those still active in the bush, had given themselves up. A month later the president ordered the release of 75 members of the security forces and of the ZANU (PF) youth wing who had been convicted of atrocities and abuse of human rights. This was said to have been his response to a demand from senior military officers and members of ZANU (PF) for a quid pro quo for the amnesty offered to the guerrillas.

On May 1 Mugabe announced that a levy of 8% would be imposed on the gross earnings of all employees to provide unemployment and retirement benefits. The serious problem presented by the rapidly rising level of unemployment was revealed in July, when 7,000 prospective recruits offered themselves for service in the armed forces, which had vacancies for only 500. The problem was becoming increasingly acute among young people with secondary or even university education, but the government's immediate concern was with the sheer numbers of students with primary education, products of the rapid expansion in that sector since independence. Mass education and the dissatisfaction felt by school-leavers who could not find what they regarded as suitable work were criticized in Parliament, as was alleged corruption in the Ministry of Transport and the threatening manner adopted by Nkala toward those who leveled charges of corruption. Mugabe's leadership

code, which called for extreme restraint in the standard of living of senior officials, was also attacked. Opposition from those affected by the code had been so consistent that it had never been enforced.

Edgar Tekere, dismissed as secretary-general of ZANU (PF) in 1981 and since then a regular critic of corruption in government and the widening gap between rich and poor, went so far as to denounce the move toward a one-party state. In November his criticisms became so persistent that the party expelled him. His campaign against corruption was taken up by university students, who were confronted by police late in September when they attempted to mount a protest march into Harare, and many were detained. Their actions reflected a measure of disillusionment with the president, who had maintained that he would enforce the leadership code vigorously once the merger between the two parties had been effected.

On the diplomatic front, the government's chief concern was with what was believed to be a growing campaign to destabilize the country orchestrated by South Africa, coupled with South Africa's attempt to establish friendlier relations with some of the other frontline African states. The president continued to urge economic sanctions against his powerful neighbour, although Zimbabwe itself was in no position to participate in any such measures. The route through South Africa was Zimbabwe's main lifeline for exporting and importing goods, and diplomatic links had to be maintained despite a presidential ban on official contacts at the ministerial level.   (KENNETH INGHAM)

This article updates the *Macropædia* article SOUTHERN AFRICA: *Zimbabwe.*

Middle East and North Africa

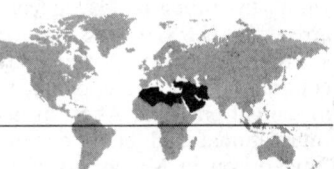

MIDDLE EASTERN AND NORTH AFRICAN AFFAIRS

The Gulf war cease-fire and the historic declaration of statehood by the Palestine National Council (PNC) characterized a year in which violence in the occupied territories and terrorist attacks continued to give rise to international concern. The Arab summit held June 7–9 in Algiers paid homage to the Palestinian uprising, or *intifadeh,* sparked off on Dec. 8, 1987, when an Israeli Army truck killed four Arabs. A year after the uprising began, the stones and bullets were still flying.

The *intifadeh* gave a new political credibility to Palestine Liberation Organization (PLO) chairman Yasir Arafat in the events following the PNC's proclamation of statehood on November 15 in Algiers. On December 6 Arafat received a kiss on both cheeks from the Swedish foreign minister in Stockholm and went on to a hunting lodge for two days of talks with a group of American Jews. On December 13 Arafat attended a UN General Assembly meeting in Geneva and gave members the chance to hear a speech denied to them in New York City after the U.S. government had declined to allow Arafat a visa to enter the country. The international response to Arafat's speech was highly favourable, and two days later, after Arafat had clearly renounced terrorism and recognized Israel, the U.S. ended its 13-year boycott to initiate talks with the PLO.

The Arab World and Arab-Israeli Relations. In the first year of the uprising, more than 300 Palestinians were killed

and thousands more were injured. Ordinary life in the occupied territories collapsed under the weight of strikes and curfews. At the Arab summit in Algiers the PLO asked for $128 million in urgent assistance and $43 million a month to compensate Palestinian police and civil servants who had resigned their jobs with the Israeli administration in the West Bank and Gaza Strip. Among those Palestinian groups opposed to Arafat was the Abu Musa faction, which in July assaulted the Shatila and Burj al-Barajinah camps in Beirut, Lebanon. Abu Musa was one of a handful of Palestinian leaders who did not rally to the PLO mainstream as a result of the uprising.

Additional pressures on the Palestinians were produced when King Hussein of Jordan decided at the end of July to accept the secession from his kingdom of the West Bank, which had been annexed by his grandfather in 1950 and occupied by the Israelis since 1967. In doing this Hussein abandoned his role as an effective representative of the Palestinians. Jordanian policy before the uprising had consisted of trying to persuade influential sections of the Palestinian community in the West Bank and Gaza to work closely with Amman. At the same time, Hussein did his best to promote Middle East peace talks aimed at securing Israel's withdrawal from most of the occupied territories and the establishment of some form of Palestinian-Jordanian federation or confederation.

The problem for King Hussein was that while the leader of Israel's Labour Party, Shimon Peres, was prepared to go some way toward accepting such a framework, he was not able to force the decision on the whole Israeli government. In elections in Israel on November 1, deadlock ensued between the two largest parties. The most notable feature of the poll was the strong showing by the four Orthodox Jewish religious parties; between them they secured 18 of the 120 Knesset (parliament) seats. The Likud bloc, led by the incumbent prime minister, Yitzhak Shamir, emerged with the best chance of forming a government, but extremist demands by Likud's potential allies on the right made compromise with the religious parties difficult. In late December, after seven weeks of intense negotiations, Shamir accepted Peres as finance minister in a Likud-Labour coalition similar to the "national unity government" of the past four years.

The Israeli government claimed the world had been hoodwinked by the PLO declaration in Algiers. The Palestinians claimed to have renounced terrorism and accepted the UN Security Council's Resolution 242, which implied recognition of Israel. The resolution in Algiers, which renounced terrorism in general terms, still sanctioned attacks in Israel and the occupied territories; even as it was being adopted, Palestinian commandos were caught infiltrating Israel from Lebanon. Critics pointed out that the Algiers resolutions were read in front of a map that showed Palestine before Israel was created. There was also much concern over Mahmoud Abul Abbas, a member of the PLO's executive committee, who was responsible for the 1985 *Achille Lauro* hijacking and the murder of Jewish-American Leon Klinghoffer. The Algiers declaration was nevertheless welcomed by more than 50 countries that announced recognition of the Palestinian state. European Communities (EC) foreign ministers meeting in late November stopped short of recognition but welcomed the PNC's decisions.

The U.S. decision on November 26 not to issue Arafat a visa to address the UN drew considerable criticism. At the UN the U.S. and Israel voted no and the U.K. was the only country to abstain on a resolution that passed 151–2 condemning the U.S. for its decision. The U.S. case against Arafat and the PLO was based on the fact that since the

Cairo Declaration of 1985, in which the PLO renounced the use of terrorism outside the occupied territories, the PLO had been involved in "probably more than 30 instances" of terrorist violence.

At a special session of the UN General Assembly in Geneva on December 13, Arafat called for "peace and a just settlement" in the Middle East. He also proposed a three-point plan for a UN-sponsored international peace conference and UN supervision of the occupied territories. The U.S. State Department said that Arafat's statement had not been sufficiently clear and unambiguous on three essential points: recognition of Israel, renunciation of terrorism, and acceptance of UN Resolutions 242 and 338. The next day Arafat clarified his remarks in a press conference, and the U.S. dropped its 13-year ban on formal talks with the PLO. The U.S. ambassador to Tunisia opened the first "substantive dialogue" with PLO representatives on December 15 in Carthage, Tunisia. In Israel, however, both Likud and Labour rejected the possibility of formal talks with the PLO.

More than 500,000 Palestinians turned out to witness the funeral procession and burial of assassinated PLO military commander Khalil al-Wazir (Abu Jihad; *see* OBITUARIES) at the Yarmouk refugee camp south of Damascus, Syria, on April 20. Wazir was killed by unidentified commandos on April 16 in front of his wife and 14-year-old daughter at his home in Tunis . Two bodyguards and a Tunisian driver were also killed. According to a report published by the *Washington Post* on April 21, the operation was directed from an airborne command centre by senior Israeli intelligence officers. The plans had been drawn up immediately after a bus hijacking in March for which Wazir had been held responsible. Tunisia was among the first countries to accuse Israel of organizing the murders. On April 20 a communiqué issued by the 46-member Islamic Conference Organization condemned Israel for the assassination.

The victory of Republican George Bush in the U.S. presidential election in November received a generally favourable reaction in the Arab world. Bush would come to the presidency with more experience of the region than any of his recent predecessors, a professional understanding of the oil industry, and close friendships with several Arab leaders. James Baker, his designated secretary of state, held complex talks with Saudi Arabia on financial issues, and Bush's chief of staff, John Sununu, was an administrator of Lebanese-Palestinian extraction who took pride in his role as the most successful Arab-American to hold public office.

Terrorism. On July 11 a Greek ferry was attacked by extremist Palestinians with machine guns and grenades, killing nine tourists. The alleged reason for the growing number of indiscriminate terrorist attacks was the attackers' desire to put pressure on governments to release jailed convicted terrorists. On April 5 a Kuwaiti airliner was hijacked by eight men demanding the release of 17 convicted guerrillas in Kuwaiti prisons who had been jailed for a bombing campaign in 1983. The hijackers, who were Shi'ite Muslims, killed two Kuwaiti passengers during the course of the hijack. The hijack ended peacefully in Algiers on April 20 without further bloodshed, but the eight hijackers were allowed to go free. Kuwait was praised for its refusal to make concessions despite the presence aboard the airplane of members of the ruling as-Sabah family. The U.S. Airline Pilots Association protested the release of the killers, saying it negated any incentive to stop this type of "guerrilla warfare."

Gulf War. In a separate incident 290 people were killed when a U.S. warship shot down an Iranian airliner over

the Gulf near Dubai, United Arab Emirates, on July 3. U.S. Vice-President Bush defended the shooting down of the aircraft before the UN Security Council on July 14. Prior to the shooting the U.S. ship had been defending a neutral tanker under attack by Iranian gunboats.

A full Gulf war settlement was expected to follow the cease-fire that came into effect between Iran and Iraq on August 20, ending eight years of war. The road to peace began with the surprise acceptance by Iran on July 18 of UN Security Council Resolution 598 of July 20, 1987. Although the cease-fire was at times fragile, the imposition of a monitoring force and ground disengagement was likely to prove easier than resolving the diplomatic arguments over the question of culpability and possible reparations. The initial political gestures were made by Iran, whose leadership, meeting on July 16, agreed to accept Resolution 598—a move ratified by Iran's spiritual leader, Ayatollah Ruhollah Khomeini. The first concrete result of the peace negotiations was the return of wounded prisoners of war, which began on November 24 under the supervision of the International Red Cross. It was hoped that this would soon lead to the repatriation of around 100,000 able-bodied prisoners. The centre of the diplomatic moves shifted to Geneva, where peace talks entered their second round on November 1. UN Secretary-General Javier Pérez de Cuéllar suggested that the question of sovereignty over the Shatt al-Arab waterway, which had blocked progress in the first round, be set aside temporarily. Once the exchange of prisoners was finalized, the UN hoped that talks could move to troop withdrawals. The border situation was described by UN observers in late November as "inherently unstable."

The Gulf war cease-fire exposed internal problems in Iraq and sparked an international row over the use of chemical weapons by Iraq against Kurdish rebels. Large-scale military operations were conducted against the Kurds by Iraqi forces August 27–September 5, during which some 60,000 Kurds fled across the border to Turkey. The allegations centred on an incident on August 29 at Bassat Gorge when 1,500–4,000 people were killed by nerve gas. Iraq's Defense Minister Adnan Khairallah, in a statement in Baghdad on September 15, denied the use of gas, declaring that it was neither logical nor feasible to use poison gas against small groups of Kurds in areas through which government forces had to pass. The U.S. claimed that it had "compelling evidence" that Iraqi forces used chemical weapons. Iraq forced the evacuation of 200 villages in the Kurdish autonomous region near the border with Iran. The Kurds were transferred to a new housing project in Iraq, a policy that had begun several years previously.

Regional Considerations. The Organization of Petroleum Exporting Countries (OPEC) ministerial talks that opened on November 21 offered hope that an oil price rebound to $18 a barrel could be forthcoming. OPEC was aiming for a new deal defining production at between 18 million and 18.5 million bbl a day. This would be within the limit the market could bear without prices falling to below $10 a barrel. To achieve this a difficult balance between Iran and Iraq would be necessary. In separate regional matters the long-moribund Euro-Arab dialogue resumed at a June 24 meeting in Bonn of EC foreign ministers and representatives of Syria, The Sudan, and Somalia. The EC's supportive stance on the Palestinian uprising was expected to allow the talks to focus on economic cooperation, including investment protection.

It was reported at a meeting in Kuwait on February 8 attended by health officials from 21 Middle Eastern countries that the AIDS virus was spreading often unde-

tected in the Middle East. The World Health Organization had been notified of 78 AIDS cases in the region.

North African Affairs. Senior North African politicians met in Fes, Morocco, on October 28–29 to discuss the next phase of the Greater Arab Maghreb initiative, involving Algeria, Libya, Mauritania, Morocco, and Tunisia. The first Arab Maghreb Commission meeting in July followed a June 10 summit of Maghreb heads of state to chart the direction for economic integration and to establish the structures of a future Maghreb Community. At this summit the Libyan leader Col. Mu'ammar al-Qadhdhafi was brought together with King Hassan of Morocco. Also in attendance was Saudi Arabia's King Fahd, who was responsible for reestablishing diplomatic relations between Morocco and Algeria in May. Saudi Arabia and Tunisia had also worked together on a plan to end North Africa's most intractable dispute, over the future of the Western Sahara. On the future agenda would be a single identity card for citizens of the Maghreb and a common currency. A second meeting of the heads of state was, however, delayed until 1989 because of rising tension in Algeria. A Maghreb Community treaty drafted by Tunisia would be presented for approval at that time.

The plague of desert locusts that had begun in late 1987 expanded in 1988 into the worst such infestation since the 1950s. Maghreb countries set aside some political differences to participate in international efforts to control the locusts, but military actions such as those in The Sudan and Ethiopia often interfered. In December the Western Sahara's Popular Front for the Liberation of Saguia el Hamra and Río de Oro (Polisario) mistakenly shot down a U.S. airplane carrying insecticide from Mauritania to Morocco.

The Algerian political crisis in October caused the deaths of at least 500 protesters according to unofficial sources (159 was the official count), but the October "events" failed to split Algeria along the expected lines. Muslim fundamentalists did not make significant political gains; the Berber minority remained silent; and the Army united behind the regime. Pres. Chadli Bendjedid emerged strengthened and was unanimously adopted as the ruling party's candidate for the presidential election on Dec. 22, 1988. On November 3 the electorate voted to make the prime minister more answerable to parliament, thus diminishing the power of the country's single political party, the National Liberation Front.

In an increasingly democratizing Maghreb, Morocco increasingly looked like the exception to the rule. The crown prince, 25-year-old Sidi Muhammad, was neither as strong nor as popular as his father. Morocco could become vulnerable if the economy continued to sag, provoking even more pressure for change elsewhere in the Maghreb. Tunisia, by contrast, appeared secure under its new president, Zine al-Abidine Ben Ali, who wanted to pursue the reforms started too late by his predecessor. All but a handful of Tunisia's imports were to enter duty free by 1992. Some state enterprises were to be privatized, and the liberalization of financial markets was continuing.   (JOHN WHELAN)

ALGERIA

Algeria is a socialist republic of North Africa on the Mediterranean Sea. Area: 2,381,741 sq km (919,595 sq mi). Pop. (1988 census): 23,849,000. Cap.: Algiers. Monetary unit: Algerian dinar, with (Oct. 10, 1988) a free rate of 6.34 dinars to U.S. $1 (10.85 dinars = £1 sterling). President in 1988, Col. Chadli Bendjedid; prime ministers, Abdelhamid Brahimi and, from November 5, Kasdi Merbah.

For the Algerian government 1988 would be marked as the year in which the country faced the worst riots and social unrest since achieving independence in 1962. In early October Algiers and many other towns, including Annaba and Oran, suffered from several days of rioting in which government buildings and state-owned shops were destroyed. The Algerian Army suppressed the rioters at the cost of at least 500 dead, according to unofficial sources (159 officially).

Although the government initially blamed the riots on Islamic fundamentalists, it was evident that the major cause was economic hardship. This was largely engendered by the reduction of consumer imports as a result of the fall in oil prices that began in 1986, coupled with government austerity measures and the 30% devaluation of the Algerian dinar against the U.S. dollar during 1988. In addition, factions within the National Liberation Front (FLN), Algeria's single political party, stimulated popular discontent by their opposition to the government's policies of economic liberalization and encouragement of the private sector.

The government reacted swiftly and, in addition to unleashing the Army to crush the riots, improved consumer supplies. Pres. Chadli Bendjedid also promised constitutional reform by making the government answerable to the directly elected Popular Assembly instead of the FLN. It appeared that these reforms were primarily designed to strengthen the power of the president against the FLN rather than to increase political liberalization inside Algeria. This reflected the determination of both the government and the Army—the ultimate power inside Algeria—to control the FLN's sixth congress in late November. A national referendum on the president's proposed reforms was held on November 3 and received 92% approval from the voters. Bendjedid, armed with this public vote of confidence and backed by a more reform-minded government under the new prime minister, Kasdi Merbah, then dominated the FLN congress. In the presidential election on December 22, Bendjedid was reelected to his third five-year term with 81% of the vote.

The riots interrupted a year that otherwise was marked by significant developments for Algeria. In May the renewal of diplomatic relations with Morocco complemented Algeria's close links with Mauritania, Tunisia, and Libya. The Moroccan monarch, King Hassan II, crowned the new relationship in early June by visiting Algiers to attend both an Arab League meeting and the first joint meeting of all five Maghrebi heads of state.

This new relationship with Morocco—which, like those with Tunisia and Libya, was sealed by closer economic cooperation—was paralleled by changes in Algerian policy concerning Western Sahara. The Algerian government forced the Polisario Front in Western Sahara to accept a UN peace proposal concerning its dispute with Morocco and to reduce its military activities. Algeria also reinforced its image as a mediator in international affairs by successfully resolving the hijacking of a Kuwaiti Airlines airbus by Islamic fundamentalists in April.   (GEORGE JOFFÉ)

This article updates the *Macropædia* article NORTH AFRICA: *Algeria.*

BAHRAIN

The monarchy (emirate) of Bahrain consists of a group of islands in the Persian Gulf between the Qatar Peninsula and Saudi Arabia. Area: 691 sq km (267 sq mi). Pop. (1988 est.): 421,000. Cap.: Manama. Monetary unit: Bahrain dinar, with (Oct. 10, 1988) a free rate of 0.38 dinar to U.S. $1 (0.64 dinar = £1 sterling). Emir in 1988, Isa ibn Sulman al-Khalifah; prime minister, Khalifah ibn Sulman al-Khalifah.

On Feb. 29, 1988, three Bahraini men arrested in December 1987 were charged with spying for Iran. The Interior Ministry said on January 4 that an underground cell "aimed at undermining economic and public installations" had been discovered. In a move to improve security coordination, Maj. Gen. Sheikh Khalifah ibn Ahmad al-Khalifah was appointed defense minister in April, a post formerly held by the heir apparent, Sheikh Hamad ibn Isa al-Khalifah. Security was also uppermost in preparations for the 1988 summit of the Gulf Cooperation Council (GCC) countries, which took place in Manama in December. While Bahrain remained committed to developing as a services centre—with some $3 billion to be spent on expanding oil refining, aluminum, and gas industries in the next two to three years—its minority problem continued to be a cause for concern. Just over 60% of the population was Shi'ite, with a small element opposed to the largely Sunni establishment.

Moving to diversify the financial sector, the government opened a stock exchange in late 1988, listing 28 public companies, with the market capitalized at around $1.8 billion. On the diplomatic front talks were held on June 21 with a Soviet envoy, opening up the possibility of early recognition of Moscow by the GCC's smallest state. In an interview with a Kuwaiti newspaper on April 26, Emir Isa ibn Sulman al-Khalifah warned of a possible severance of diplomatic relations with Iran.   (JOHN WHELAN)

This article updates the *Macropædia* article ARABIA: *Bahrain.*

CYPRUS

An island republic and member of the Commonwealth, Cyprus is in the eastern Mediterranean Sea. Island area: 9,251 sq km (3,572 sq mi). Island pop. (1988 est.): 720,000. Area of the Turkish Republic of Northern Cyprus (TRNC), which has occupied the northern third of the island since 1974: 3,355 sq km (1,295 sq mi); pop. (1988 est.): 167,000. Cap.: Nicosia. Monetary unit: Cyprus pound, with (Oct. 10, 1988) a free rate of £C 0.49 to U.S. $1 (£C 0.83 = £1 sterling). Presidents in 1988, Spyros Kyprianou and, from February 28, George Vassiliou. President of TRNC in 1988, Rauf Denktash.

The year 1988 brought sudden change to Cyprus and the first sign in many years of a possible solution to its 25-year-old problem of Greek and Turkish Cypriot enmity. George Vassiliou (*see* BIOGRAPHIES), a 56-year-old self-made millionaire and political unknown, was elected president. He won the backing of the powerful AKEL (Communist Party), enabling him to sweep Spyros Kyprianou from power in the February election. During his 11 years in office, Kyprianou had failed to reach any accommodation with the Turkish Cypriots in their unrecognized breakaway Turkish Republic of Northern Cyprus (TRNC) in the northern third of the island.

Vassiliou promptly called on Turkish Prime Minister Turgut Ozal to meet him and discuss pulling Ankara's 29,000 troops out of northern Cyprus. He pledged to dismantle all Greek Cypriot military forces if the troops left. Rauf Denktash, the TRNC president, at first eyed the new man with suspicion but later softened his stand. He was prompted in this by Ankara after Ozal and Greek Prime Minister Andreas Papandreou met in Switzerland to begin a historic rapprochement.

Domestically, Vassiliou retained only the highly regarded foreign minister, George Iacovou, from the Kyprianou Cabinet. He promised to remove anomalies from the island's already lively democracy and ordered the secret service to destroy all files on Cypriots' political opinions.

Argentine diplomat Oscar Camilión was appointed to the long-vacant resident post of special UN representative. In Geneva in August to open peace talks in the Gulf war,

George Vassiliou acknowledges his victory after winning the Cyprus presidential election. He defeated incumbent Pres. Spyros Kyprianou, whose 11 years in office were plagued by the unsolved problem of the breakaway Turkish state in northern Cyprus.

AFP PHOTO

UN Secretary-General Javier Pérez de Cuéllar managed to get Vassiliou and Denktash to meet informally. The two men struck up an instant rapport, and in mid-September they met for two sessions in Cyprus, the second held in secret at Camilión's home. In November they again met with Pérez de Cuéllar at UN headquarters in New York City, but little of substance emerged.

Cyprus was again sharply reminded of its proximity to the troubled Middle East. In February three senior Palestinians were killed by a car bomb in Limassol. A day later a ship the Palestinians were planning to use to sail deportees back to Israel was struck by a mine in Limassol Harbour. In April two Kuwaitis were shot dead and dumped from a hijacked Kuwait Airways Boeing 747, which landed at Larnaca and later flew on to Algiers. In the worst act of terrorism, a huge car bomb intended for the Israeli embassy exploded in one of Nicosia's busiest streets, killing 3 people and injuring at least 15. Cyprus reacted angrily by deporting nearly 70 Arabs and refusing entry to another 140.

Economically, the Greek Cypriots continued their 13-year-old success story, and Vassiliou promised more dramatic changes after the first phase of a customs union with the European Communities went into effect in January 1988. However, the isolated TRNC continued to stagnate.

(THOMAS O'DWYER)

EGYPT

A republic of North Africa, Egypt has coastlines on the Mediterranean and Red seas. Area: 997,739 sq km (385,229 sq mi). Pop. (1988 est.): 50,273,000. Cap.: Cairo. Monetary unit: Egyptian pound (LE), with (Oct. 10, 1988) a free rate of LE 2.29 to U.S. $1 (LE 3.93 = £1 sterling). President in 1988, Hosni Mubarak; prime minister, Atef Sedki.

With Egypt's position in the Arab world at its strongest in ten years, Pres. Hosni Mubarak was free in 1988 to concentrate on the domestic economy and on dealing with Egypt's international creditors, whose patience was not inexhaustible. The continuing political trials involving religious extremists and opponents of the regime indicated a background of dissent. Income from tourism and the Suez Canal rose, but this failed to compensate for the weakness in oil prices. Bilateral issues with Israel dragged on, though the dispute over the Taba strip of land in Sinai was decided in Egypt's favour.

Domestic Affairs. Egypt's show trials featured accusations in absentia against Khaled Abdel Nasser, son of the late president and father of Arab nationalism. He was named on February 18 as an alleged member of the Egypt Revolution group, accused of carrying out several guerrilla attacks on foreign targets, including those resulting in the deaths of two Israeli diplomats. Another prominent figure, the late Pres. Anwar as-Sadat's brother Ahmad Esmat as-Sadat, had assets totaling $8 million confiscated by the official prosecutor because of alleged corruption. In June, 19 people were arrested and charged with conspiring with Iran to spread subversion. Members of the group headed by Muhammad Ayman Abdel-Khaleq were alleged to have received terrorist training in Iran.

In April lawyers representing 33 Islamic militants accused of political violence walked out of their trial, demanding more time to read the indictment. The government moved in March to renew, for another three years, the emergency laws imposed in 1981 after the assassination of President Sadat. Leaders of the two opposition groupings—the Wafd and the Socialist Labour-Muslim Brothers-Liberal Alliance—said the proposal showed scorn for principles of parliamentary democracy. Prime Minister Atef Sedki said the extension was needed to combat terrorism and protect freedom.

The government's harsh approach was exemplified by the dragnet policy used by Interior Minister Zaki Badr to arrest hundreds of students and suspected activists following terrorist attacks, especially after the fatal stabbing of a government security agent in December. However, criticism of Badr paled into insignificance compared with the acrimony heaped on the supply and home trade minister, Galal Abul-Dahab, when sweet tea and edible oil were in short supply in the second half of March. The crisis highlighted Egypt's chronic dependence on imported food to feed its 50 million people. The population was increasing at the rate of one million every eight months, although, in a historic ruling in September, the al-Azhar Islamic University's committee on religious edicts said there was no conflict between Islam and birth control.

The Economy. President Mubarak held talks in late September with several Western leaders with a view to pressuring the International Monetary Fund (IMF) to endorse Cairo's own program of economic reforms. He also wanted the current Club of Paris debt-rescheduling agreement extended to the end of 1989. The main areas of disagreement between Egypt and the IMF were energy prices and exchange rates policy. Egypt had resisted the IMF's demands that rapid action be taken to phase out energy subsidies. It also opposed the IMF's view that an overvalued U.S. dollar–Egyptian pound rate be applied to the central bank pool of hard currency. Fearful of social unrest over these unpopular measures, the government was seeking a longer timetable than the IMF required. Egypt was also in trouble over its projected budget deficit for 1988–89 of LE 4.5 billion, almost 50% higher than in the previous year. This failed the IMF criterion that the country should achieve a progressive reduction of the budget deficit as a proportion of gross domestic product. However, total revenues were expected to be up 16%, reflecting a rise in customs revenues, stemming from devaluation, and projected increases in Suez Canal dues and tourism.

A number of developments were under way that would further enhance Egypt's attractiveness as a tourist desti-

Egyptian Pres. Hosni Mubarak (right) greets Palestine Liberation Organization leader Yasir Arafat before a meeting in Cairo. The Egyptian government had formally recognized the Palestinian state proclaimed by the Palestine National Council on Nov. 15, 1988.
AFP PHOTO

nation. These included a scheme for Safaga on the Red Sea by a Swedish entrepreneur and a similar plan by a Kuwaiti group, both targeted at relatively wealthy Europeans, Asians, and Arabs. Tourism and Civil Aviation Minister Fouad Sultan had brought considerable expertise to bear on the problem of restructuring the tourist industry. In the first quarter of 1988 the number of tourists rose 38% to 584,133, with the largest number coming from France and West Germany.

In September it was reported that the Cabinet was to discuss a detailed report about an estimated $700 million plan to widen and deepen the Suez Canal. The canal earned Egypt some $1.2 billion in 1987, with $1.8 billion forecast for 1988.

On January 27 President Mubarak visited Washington, but aid was not on the agenda since it was accepted that U.S. assistance to Egypt was on the order of $2.2 billion–$2.3 billion a year. The U.S. Treasury was working out final details of proposed legislation that would enable debtor nations, such as Egypt and Israel, to raise commercial loans to pay off existing defense-related debt, using the U.S. government as a guarantor for 90% of the new loans. In 1987 oil exports recovered strongly, thanks to increased output and more astute marketing by the Egyptian General Petroleum Corporation. However, Egypt was expected to suffer from the disarray in the Organization of Petroleum Exporting Countries, following the cease-fire in the Gulf war and an increase in output by Iran and Iraq. The surplus on the oil trade account for Egypt in 1987 was $1.5 billion, compared with $697 million in 1986. In February the People's Assembly approved 11 hydrocarbons agreements, 7 of which were in the Western Desert and would result in more exploration. The authorities were pushing increased domestic use of gas in order to boost crude oil exports and reduce home consumption.

A major internal debate took place over the status of Egypt's powerful Islamic investment companies. The People's Assembly passed a law in June providing for a Capital Markets Authority with regulatory powers. Transfers of funds to foreign destinations—a specialty of the companies—was to be controlled. The Islamic companies were the major players in the parallel economy, but any collapse of these investment houses would have severe implications for the economy as a whole. In November the government ordered more than 100 of the companies to comply with strict new regulations or face the prospect of liquidation within two years.

Foreign Affairs. Egypt's improved standing with moderate Arab countries was attributable to its policy of tacit support for the Arab cause in the Iran-Iraq war. Although President Mubarak stepped back from sending troops, Egyptian advisers were present in Iraq and Kuwait during the last year preceding the cease-fire. On January 9 Mubarak made a week-long tour of the six Gulf Cooperation Council countries, and in June he welcomed King Fahd of Saudi Arabia on a visit to Cairo. Diplomatic relations with Saudi Arabia had been restored after the Amman Arab summit in November 1987, and Saudi investment had poured into Egypt, especially into property. Saudi Arabia had also supported Egypt in its struggle with the IMF. The majority of Arab states had restored links with Cairo, broken at the time of the bilateral peace with Israel, and at year's end the only Arab nations that had not done so were Lebanon, Libya, and Syria.

Relations with Israel remained correct but cool. On September 29 an international arbitration panel ruled in favour of Egypt in the six-year dispute over the Taba border strip—640 m (2,100 ft) of Red Sea beach claimed by both countries—although final details of the boundary remained to be worked out. Following the Gulf war cease-fire President Mubarak expressed no objections to restoring relations with Iran but said there was "no hurry" on the matter. According to official reports, several thousand Egyptians seized in the Gulf war fighting were being held by Iran. They were expected to be freed as part of the Baghdad–Tehran prisoner of war exchange.

In August Mubarak called on the Palestine Liberation Organization to adopt a moderate program for its government-in-exile. The appeal was made during a meeting on August 19, after King Hussein of Jordan had announced his decision to cut legal ties with the West Bank. In November Egypt recognized the independent Palestinian state declared that month by the Palestine National Council. In a gesture of reconciliation, Libya withdrew its forces from the Egyptian–Libyan border in March. Telecommunications links were restored, and Egypt silenced Libyan opposition broadcasts from Cairo. The Libyan leader, Col. Mu'ammar al-Qadhdhafi, said that despite these actions he was still politically opposed to the Mubarak regime. In January President Mubarak's planned visit to Tunisia to meet the new Tunisian leader, Pres. Zine al-Abidine Ben Ali, had been canceled because it would have coincided with Qadhdhafi's arrival. On March 1 Mubarak made his first visit in three years to Khartoum, where his talks included conditions in southern Sudan and relations with Ethiopia.

(JOHN WHELAN)

IRAN

The Islamic republic of Iran is in southwestern Asia on the Caspian and Arabian seas and the Persian Gulf. Area: 1,648,-196 sq km (636,372 sq mi). Pop. (1988 est., including some 2.1 million to 2.3 million Afghan and 400,000 Iraqi refugees): 51,225,000. Cap.: Tehran. Monetary unit: Iranian rial, with (Oct. 10, 1988) an official rate of 70.42 rials to U.S. $1 (120.60 rials = £1 sterling). *Valiy-e faqih* (supreme spiritual leader) in 1988, Ayatollah Ruhollah Khomeini; president, Sayyed Ali Khamenei; prime minister, Mir Hossein Moussavi.

On Aug. 20, 1988, a cease-fire came into effect in the eight-year-old Iran-Iraq war following Iran's acceptance of UN Resolution 598. Iran's supreme spiritual leader, Ayatollah Ruhollah Khomeini, declared that taking this decision was "more deadly than taking poison," but he acquiesced in the cease-fire and thus endorsed the move toward a peace settlement. The acceptance of the cease-fire came as a surprise, although the Iranian regime had been facing severe difficulties. On April 17–18 the Iranian military enclave on Iraqi soil at al-Faw (Fao) was overrun with comparative ease by the Iraqi Army. An Iraqi advance on May 25 reclaimed the entire area of the Fish Lake as far as Shalamcheh, northeast of Basra, while the Iranians withdrew from Halabjah on June 14 and on June 25 were driven out of the Majnun oil field area of the important Hawizah marshes. Further losses were incurred at Mehran in June and Dehloran in July.

Iranian losses on the battlefield were aggravated by Iraq's growing dominance in the "war of the cities." Beginning in late February, the Iraqis bombarded Tehran, Qom, and other targets with intermediate-range missiles on a scale that the Iranians could not match. Not only had the Iranians been unable to make good their losses of armour, aircraft, and missiles during the war, but by 1988 they could not even offer dedication, experience, and sacrifice by their troops since losses of battle-hardened troops had been persistently high. Recruitment to the armed forces had fallen off sharply. Iran was also losing the confrontation in the Gulf against the U.S. On April 14 the USS *Samuel B. Roberts* was damaged by a mine while on patrol

AP/WIDE WORLD

Iranians demonstrate their rage and grief at a mass funeral held for some of the 290 people who were killed when the USS *Vincennes* shot down an Iranian passenger plane. The picture some of them hold depicts the incident.

in Gulf waters. In retaliation, the U.S. Navy destroyed Iranian offshore platforms in the Sassan and Sirri oil fields on April 18. That confrontation ended after an engagement in which two Iranian frigates and a number of patrol boats were sunk. Following an incident between Iranian gunboats and U.S. naval vessels off Bandar-e 'Abbas on July 3, the USS *Vincennes* accidentally shot down Iran Air Flight 655, with the loss of 290 lives.

The Iranian economy was crippled by the continuing war. Oil exports had fallen below two million barrels per day during the first quarter of 1988 as a result of Iraqi air attacks on oil facilities and tankers in the Gulf, and the position was exacerbated by falling oil prices. The cease-fire enabled the government to approach the problems of reconstruction in late 1988, though there was no prospect of an immediate cure for Iran's problems of inflation, unemployment, poor productivity, and war damage.

Elections for the 270 seats in the Majlis (parliament) were held in April and May. Some 17 million persons took part, electing more Islamic radicals but fewer clergymen than in the outgoing Majlis. On June 30 Mir Hossein Moussavi was asked to form a new government. He attempted to resign in the wake of the cease-fire but was made to stay on by Khomeini. Hojatolislam Hashemi Rafsanjani, the speaker of the Majlis, increased his authority. The Iranian leadership took a more pragmatic stance toward domestic issues while still ruthlessly removing all sources of opposition. At the year's end there were unconfirmed reports that Moussavi had been arrested.

Negotiations for a permanent peace were slow to develop. The status of the Shatt al-Arab waterway proved a particular problem. Saudi Arabia broke off diplomatic relations with Iran in April, but France restored full relations in June. Iran showed a slightly more amenable face to the outside world once a cease-fire had been arranged. Negotiations on diplomatic and commercial matters with the British and other Western Europeans made some progress, and in December a young Briton was freed after having spent more than two years in an Iranian prison. The U.S.S.R. remained in close touch with Iran in order to ensure the unhindered withdrawal of Soviet troops from Afghanistan. The U.S. made tentative diplomatic gestures and also reduced the level of confrontation in the Gulf area.

(KEITH S. MCLACHLAN)

IRAQ

A republic of southwestern Asia, Iraq has a short coastline on the Persian Gulf. Area: 438,317 sq km (169,235 sq mi). Pop. (1988 est.): 16,630,000. Cap.: Baghdad. Monetary unit: Iraqi dinar, with (Oct. 10, 1988) a par value of 0.31 dinar to U.S. $1 (free rate of 0.53 dinar = £1 sterling). President in 1988, Saddam Hussein at-Takriti.

The Gulf war cease-fire on Aug. 20, 1988, brought the eight-year-old conflict with Iran to a sudden halt. Thousands poured into the streets of Baghdad on August 8 to greet the announcement, which was seen as a victory. Every indication, however, suggested that the UN-sponsored peace negotiations in Geneva would be protracted. The major sticking point was the status of the Shatt al-Arab waterway, which Iran claimed was determined by a 1975 agreement with the former shah. Iraq refused to acknowledge this arrangement, under which sovereignty was to be shared, on the grounds that it was signed under duress. In the immediate aftermath of the cease-fire, both sides repatriated several hundred injured prisoners.

The Iraqis' battlefield successes, notably the recapture of the al-Faw (Fao) Peninsula April 17–18 and the Majnun

A group of Iraqis cheer and dance behind their country's flag to celebrate the cease-fire between Iraq and Iran, which went into effect on August 20. In July Iran had announced a willingness to accept the terms of UN Resolution 598 and had called for a cease-fire in the eight-year-old conflict.
AP/WIDE WORLD

oil fields on June 25, were key factors in bringing about diplomatic capitulation by the Iranian leader Ayatollah Ruhollah Khomeini. Iraq's military triumphs had not been predicted by analysts of the war, in which more than 500,-000 people had died. Pres. Saddam Hussein at-Takriti said Iraq's principles for peace were: a cease-fire and return to international frontiers; the signing of a peace treaty and nonaggression pact; agreement not to interfere in each other's internal affairs; and the commitment of both sides to work for the stability and security of the region.

Iraq would watch with particular concern any Iranian interference in the Kurdish independence struggle. On March 16 Halabjah, a town in Iraqi Kurdistan captured by Iran, was bombed by the Iraqis with chemical weapons. This was followed by an Iraqi offensive against Kurdish rebels in August, during which some 60,000 people fled to southeastern Turkey. Baghdad denied that it had used chemical weapons, but in December a British laboratory found traces of mustard gas in soil samples from Iraqi Kurdistan. In September Iraq announced an amnesty for Kurds who wished to return, and official reports claimed that more than 60,000 accepted the offer, which excluded only the Patriotic Union of Kurdistan leader Jalal Talabani. Kurdish fighters in northern Iraq were unlikely to abandon their struggle for autonomy, but Baghdad now had the military resources to deal them a severe blow.

Oil Minister Issam Abdel-Rahim al-Chalabi indicated in October that Baghdad might revise its demand for an OPEC oil quota equal to Iran's. OPEC allotted Iraq a quota of 1,540,000 bbl a day in late 1987, compared with Iran's 2,369,000 bbl a day. Iraq had been producing up to 2.7 million bbl a day. Iraq's budget deficit for 1988 was projected at $4 billion, compared with about $3 billion in 1987. Excluding military debt to the Eastern bloc and loans from Saudi Arabia and Kuwait, Iraq's international debt amounted to about $25 billion. Because a high proportion was short-term, the country faced a severe debt service burden. Iraq could be expected to try to reschedule trade debts into longer term forms of finance. The introduction of additional competition into the economy was symbolized by the opening on November 1 of the state-owned Rashid Bank to challenge the monopoly held by the Rafidain Bank.

In October the 24-year-old son of Pres. Saddam Hussein was arrested and jailed for killing a presidential bodyguard. He was released from jail late in November but was to go on trial for murder.

An indication of the more promising business climate was the presence of 1,856 foreign companies at the Baghdad International Fair in December. British Airways resumed flights to Baghdad from London on November 2. However, these signs of normality had to be weighed against the possibility that Baghdad would once again aggressively assert itself in the Arab world. Iraq called for the expulsion of Syria from the Arab League because it had backed Iran in the Gulf war, and it formed new links with Samir Geagea, the leader of the Christian Lebanese Forces militia.

(JOHN WHELAN)

ISRAEL

A republic of southwestern Asia, Israel is situated on the Mediterranean Sea. Area: 20,700 sq km (7,992 sq mi), not including territory occupied in the June 1967 war. Pop. (1988 est.): 4,512,000. Cap.: Jerusalem (but *see* Israel table in *World Data* section). Monetary unit: new (Israeli) sheqel, with (Oct. 10, 1988) a free rate of 1.62 sheqalim to U.S. $1 (2.78 sheqalim = £1 sterling). President in 1988, Chaim Herzog; prime minister, Yitzhak Shamir.

It had been intended to be a year of celebration—40 symbolic years since the establishment of a Jewish state out of the ashes of the Holocaust. It was to become a year that lost its way. The celebrations were muted; not so the accumulating problems. It was a year overshadowed by two events: the *intifadeh,* or "uprising," of the West Bank and Gaza Palestinian Arabs, and the pending general election of November 1. Almost everything that happened in Israel during 1988 was somehow related to one or the other or both: all-pervading preoccupations that remained unresolved at the end of the year.

Domestic Affairs. The *intifadeh* dominated Israel's political life rather like a spell of unending rain affects daily life:

Israeli Prime Minister Yitzhak Shamir (left) shakes hands with Rabbi Yitzhak Peretz of the Shas party. Shamir's Likud, which failed to win a majority in the Knesset (parliament), attempted to form an alliance with numerous small religious parties but then reached an agreement in December to form a coalition with Labour.

AP/WIDE WORLD

it does not change anything, but it does create a constant awareness. For one thing, there were few Israeli families where no son, daughter, or husband had been called up for military service in the occupied territories, and the nightly television was a continual reminder. The situation was further complicated for the Israelis by the emergence of a plethora of political "voices" claiming to speak on behalf of the otherwise anonymous "uprising." By late 1988 nine such separate and disparate groups had publicly identified themselves. Only one, the "Unified Council of the National Uprising," identified with the official Palestine Liberation Organization (PLO) led by Yasir Arafat from its base in Baghdad, Iraq. The other eight organizations claiming to speak for the uprising denounced the official PLO and its leader. As the year progressed there emerged a powerful, militant Islamic group based largely on the Gaza Strip, called the Islamic Resistance Movement, or Hamas. Hamas was independent of and hostile to the PLO and radical in its opposition to the Israeli presence.

None of this was evident when the first disorders and riots swept through the Gaza Strip on Dec. 9, 1987. Soon the West Bank and even Jerusalem were engulfed by stone throwing, tire burning, and window smashing. The rioting, mostly by young Palestinians, affected some 50 of the 600 towns and villages of the occupied territories. There were several possible explanations offered for the uprising. Perhaps the most common attributed the violence to a road accident in Gaza on December 8, in which four Arabs were killed by an Israeli driver. Palestinian euphoria had increased after a Palestinian hang-glider "martyr" had successfully jumped the boundary fence on the Lebanon border on November 25 and killed six Israeli soldiers before being shot himself. There was also concern about pent-up Palestinian frustrations over the November Arab summit in neighbouring Amman, Jordan, which had virtually ignored the Palestinian problems. All of these reasons added up to an indication that the Israeli political and military authorities had been surprised by the outbreak and were unable to provide a convincing explanation for it. They also underlined the failure by the government and security agencies to have a proper system of cooperation and coordination, which would have alerted the authorities in time. It was suggested that this had been a spontaneous popular outburst and had taken even the PLO by surprise.

Israeli forces were totally unprepared to deal with the situation, either in terms of training or equipment or in terms of political comprehension. Small units of young and inexperienced soldiers, without adequate personal protec-

tion against stone-throwing rioters, were unable to establish their authority, and this acted as a further incentive to the attacking Palestinians. In the first weeks of the uprising, several rioters were shot and killed, provoking severe international criticism of Israeli actions. By mid-January 1988 Defense Minister Yitzhak Rabin and the army command, under the watchful and critical glare of the world's media, armed with television cameras, had to rethink their tactics and then reequip and reinforce the soldiers dealing with the disturbances. The new tactics, which included beatings, deportations, and enforced curfews, were widely denounced, as was Israeli involvement in the assassination in April of PLO military commander Khalil al-Wazir (Abu Jihad; *see* OBITUARIES). Discipline problems also arose within the armed forces as Israeli conscripts fought to maintain order. In November, 21 soldiers were convicted of using excessive violence against Palestinian protesters and sentenced to short jail terms. All-in-all, it was evident as the disorders continued and the casualties mounted that the Israeli government was at a loss as to how best to deal with this situation, which was largely of its own making.

By the end of 1988, there were more than 300 Palestinians dead, and some 6,000 or more were still in detention camps. On December 9 Palestinians in Israel called a national strike to mark the first anniversary of the *intifadeh.* By that time, however, the uprising had, in effect, been preempted by the decision of the Palestine National Council (PNC) in Algiers on November 15 to proclaim a Palestinian state, but not a Palestinian government—as yet. Israel dismissed the PNC's announcement as irrelevant. In the wake of the Algiers proclamation and Arafat's speech to the UN on December 13, however, attention was focused away from the *intifadeh* and onto the PLO.

The outcome of the voting in the general election on November 1 produced the result feared by most Israelis; neither of the two largest parties was in possession of a majority. The Labour Party had jettisoned some of its best-known faces—especially that of former foreign minister Abba Eban—in its search for a younger and more populist image, but to no avail. In August the Herut and Liberal parties that made up the Likud bloc had formally merged into a single right-wing party, the Likud-National Liberal Movement. Twenty-eight parties had initially entered the election, but one, the Kach Party of Rabbi Meir Kahane, was disqualified for advocating racist measures against the Arab population. The other 27 contested the 120 seats of the Knesset (parliament). Likud polled 709,305 votes and gained 39 seats against the Labour alignment's 685,363

votes and 38 seats. The surprise vote was that of the four ultraorthodox religious parties, which polled 334,422 votes, or 14.6% of the total, and won 18 seats. Prime Minister Yitzhak Shamir of Likud began coalition talks with the far right and ultraorthodox parties. The religious parties, however, demanded new legislation to ban all business activity, public transportation, and organized sports on the Sabbath. They also sought a revision to the Law of Return that would change the legal definition of a Jew and permit only those people born to a Jewish mother or converted by an Orthodox rabbi to immigrate to Israel. Secular Israelis and pro-Israel groups in the U.S., where most Jews were not Orthodox, voiced vehement opposition, and overseas contributions to Israel dropped precipitously. On December 19, after more than seven weeks of often bitter negotiations, Shamir reached accord on a coalition with Labour leader Shimon Peres, similar to the "national unity government" that had led Israel since 1984. Some members of the religious right threatened legal action to prevent the coalition, while a significant minority in the Labour Party argued in favour of forming an official opposition. Shamir and Peres, who would serve as finance minister, promised a stable government that would remain unified against peace talks with the PLO.

Sandwiched between the *intifadeh* and the general election were a series of events that fleetingly engaged the nation. On March 27 Mordechai Vanunu was sentenced to 18 years' imprisonment for selling secrets of Israel's nuclear development at Dimona to *The Sunday Times* in London. On April 18 John Demjanjuk was found guilty of war crimes and crimes against the Jewish people and humanity, and on April 25 he was sentenced to death. An appeal was pending at year's end.

Beyond all the dramatic political events of the year, Israelis began at last to confront the need for fundamental economic reconstruction of the pioneer economy that had prevailed for 40 years and was in seemingly insoluble crisis. In broad terms, the country's economic state was reflected in an almost stagnant growth of the gross national product of 1%. Employment increased by 7%, but there were large pockets of unemployment and of Israelis living beneath the accepted poverty line. Wages for those with work increased by 7% in the private sector and by 10% in the low-paid public sector. It was the fundamental structure of the economy that required serious attention, however, including the kibbutzim (the communal settlements) and the moshavim (the cooperative settlements). The heavy industry Koor complex and the construction industry's giant Solel Boneh were in serious financial straits, as was the entire national health service.

Foreign Affairs. Most of Israel's foreign relations continued to revolve around the occupied territories and the Palestinians. Events that would otherwise have figured prominently in the consciousness of the country provided little more than an ongoing sideshow. Even the peace process so energetically pursued by then foreign minister Peres foundered on the unexpected actions of King Hussein of Jordan. On Jan. 1, 1988, the newspaper *Ma'ariv* published the text of a secret agreement concluded by Peres and Hussein in London in September 1987. The text and intention of the agreement were overtaken on July 31, 1988, when Hussein disengaged from further commitment on the West Bank and in Gaza. In so doing he nullified the "Jordanian option," thereby damaging Peres's challenge to Shamir in the general election and reducing Jordan's role in any future peace process between Israel and the Palestinians.

On December 2 Israel joined the U.S. as the only countries to vote against condemnation of the U.S. for re-

fusing Arafat a visa to address the UN General Assembly. Israel then boycotted Arafat's speech to the UN in Geneva on December 13 and rejected the PLO leader's implied acceptance of Israel as lies and deception. U.S.-Israeli relations were severely strained when the U.S. responded to Arafat's statements by instituting the first "substantive dialogue" with the PLO in 13 years. On December 26 Shamir indicated that Israel might be willing to pursue peace talks with non-PLO Palestinians if Egypt, the U.S., and the Soviet Union participated.

Formal diplomatic relations between Israel and the Soviet Union came a step closer in 1988. Israel sent a delegation to Moscow in July, the first such since relations were severed in 1967. On December 2 Israel acceded to an official request and allowed a hijacked Soviet airliner to land near Tel Aviv; the hijackers were then promptly turned over to Soviet authorities.   (JON KIMCHE)

JORDAN

A constitutional monarchy, Jordan is located in southwestern Asia and has a short coastline on the Gulf of Aqaba. Area: 89,206 sq km (34,443 sq mi). Pop. (1988 est.): 2,965,000. Cap.: Amman. Monetary unit: Jordan dinar, with (Oct. 10, 1988) a free rate of 0.38 dinar to U.S. $1 (0.64 dinar = £1 sterling). King, Hussein I; prime minister in 1988, Zaid ar-Rifai.

King Hussein took a major political step in the summer of 1988 by announcing plans to cut legal and administrative ties with the Israeli-occupied West Bank. In addition, the 60-member lower house of Parliament, where over half the deputies sat from West Bank constituencies, was dissolved. The Palestine Liberation Organization (PLO) responded by calling for an emergency meeting of its 450-member Palestine National Council.

The move marked the Jordanian monarch's acceptance of the de facto separation from his kingdom of the bulge of Palestine on the west bank of the Jordan River, annexed by his grandfather in 1950 and occupied by Israel since 1967. The action was designed to show the Palestinians that Jordan accepted their wish for an independent state in Palestine, but in practice it did little to allay their fears about King Hussein's real motives. The Jordanian government was, however, quite categorical on one point—its desire to abandon its role as spokesman for the Palestinians, in the absence of international recognition of the PLO.

On August 4 Jordan said it would stop paying salaries of about 21,000 civil servants in the West Bank. On August 7 the Jordanian monarch said he now supported the PLO case for a government-in-exile for Palestine. However, PLO chairman Yasir Arafat said he was not given any prior warning of Jordan's move. Three days of talks between Jordanian officials and PLO representatives, August 12–15, went some way toward clarifying the issues. Hussein was reacting to the Palestinian "uprising" in the occupied territories, sparked in part by the cavalier attitude to the Palestinian cause shown at the Amman Arab summit in November 1987. The uprising itself brought into the open the deep resentment of West Bank Palestinians over Hussein's efforts to promote Jordanian influence in the occupied territories at the expense of the PLO. The king's move was seen as an attempt to throw the PLO off balance. The Jordanian authorities had responded to the uprising by clamping down on the Palestinian community within Jordan itself. Surveillance was stepped up, and PLO activists were arrested.

Elsewhere, Jordan improved relations with the U.S. through a top-level trade and investment mission in late May, led by Crown Prince Hassan. The prince told a

meeting in Atlanta, Ga., that Coca-Cola might be removed from the Arab blacklist of firms dealing with Israel. In other respects, Jordan continued to broaden its sources of supply by concluding, on April 22, a contract with France for 18–20 Mirage interceptors. It remained dependent on aid from Saudi Arabia—one of the few countries that had consistently honoured its aid commitment to the Arab countries confronting Israel.

The economy faltered, and pressure on the dinar forced the introduction on June 6 of a fixed exchange rate system. The government blamed delayed Saudi aid and Iraq's failure to make trade debt repayments on time. There was a boost, however, from good winter rains, and the 1987–88 wheat harvest reached 80,000 metric tons. The pace of administrative reforms, announced in 1987, quickened with a minor Cabinet reshuffle on January 9. Tourism was to be encouraged by easing visa fees for groups, while the national carrier, Royal Jordanian airline, signed a contract for five Lockheed TriStars on March 22.

In mid-July Rajiv Gandhi became the first Indian prime minister to visit Jordan. India was Jordan's biggest trading partner, importing mainly phosphates and potash, but India sold little to Jordan in return. During the visit Gandhi said India believed a UN-sponsored international conference attended by all parties, including the PLO, was the best framework for settling the Palestinian problem.

(JOHN WHELAN)

KUWAIT

A constitutional monarchy (emirate), Kuwait is in the northeastern Arabian Peninsula, on the Persian Gulf. Area: 17,818 sq km (6,880 sq mi). Pop. (1988 est.): 1,958,000. Cap.: Kuwait City. Monetary unit: Kuwaiti dinar, with (Oct. 10, 1988) a free rate of 0.29 dinar to U.S. $1 (0.49 dinar = £1 sterling). Emir, Sheikh Jabir al-Ahmad al-Jabir as-Sabah; prime minister in 1988, Crown Prince Sheikh Saad al-Abdullah as-Salim as-Sabah.

The hijacking of a Kuwaiti airliner on April 5, which lasted for 16 days and left two dead, was a sombre reminder of the government's dilemma over security. While Kuwait received international praise for its uncompromising attitude toward the hijackers, attention within the country was drawn to their central demand: the release of 17 men imprisoned for their part in a bombing campaign in December 1983. The mounting tension was also clear from the tough sentence of ten years' imprisonment with hard labour, passed June 28 on a teacher convicted of sabotage and planning assassinations. In April and May three bomb explosions in Kuwait were aimed at civilian targets; two Arabs and an Iranian were arrested. In what was seen as a response to growing criticism of government measures, the Cabinet was reshuffled on January 26. Former defense minister Sheikh Salim Sabah as-Salim as-Sabah took over the Interior Ministry in a bid to improve control over internal security.

The diplomatic highlight of the year was the July 8–14 visit by Prime Minister Sheikh Saad al-Abdullah as-Salim as-Sabah to Washington, where he received a warm welcome from the Reagan administration. On August 27 a $1.9 billion contract for the U.S. to supply 40 F-18 Hornet fighter aircraft and missiles was signed in Kuwait, with deliveries to take place in 1994. However, Kuwait demonstrated its reluctance to depend on the U.S. for weapons by a purchase of armoured personnel carriers from the Soviet Union, agreed on in July, and by discussions with the French defense minister in September. The cease-fire talks in the Gulf war failed to stop the Kuwaiti government

from considering additional defense purchases. Nevertheless, Kuwait continued to maintain its lending program in support of less developed countries, with $380 million disbursed in 1987 by the Kuwait Fund for Arab Economic Development. (JOHN WHELAN)

This article updates the *Macropædia* article ARABIA: *Kuwait.*

LEBANON

A republic of southwestern Asia, Lebanon is situated on the Mediterranean Sea. Area: 10,230 sq km (3,950 sq mi). Pop. (1988 est.): 2,828,000 (including Palestinian refugees estimated to number about 290,000). Cap.: Beirut. Monetary unit: Lebanese pound, with (Oct. 10, 1988) a free rate of LL 429.24 to U.S. $1 (LL 735.08 = £1 sterling). President in 1988, Amin Gemayel until September 23; prime ministers, Selim al-Hoss and, from September 23, Michel Aoun; on September 23 Selim al-Hoss assumed de facto leadership of the civilian government based in West Beirut.

The Lebanese political crisis deepened with the failure to elect a president to succeed Amin Gemayel, whose term ended on September 23. In the absence of elections a military government was announced by the outgoing president. Violence continued to dominate daily life in the principal centres of population. There seemed now to be a real chance that partition would become an established fact.

Army commander Michel Aoun, who headed the military government appointed by Gemayel, pledged that he would work toward convening proper elections. His Cabinet of six officers was quickly cut to three Christian members when two Muslim officers and one Druse refused to serve. The existing civilian government under Prime Minister Selim al-Hoss, who took the precaution of withdrawing his long-standing resignation before Gemayel's six-year term ended, denounced the Aoun regime. This left Lebanon with two governments—Aoun in East Beirut and al-Hoss in the mainly Muslim western half of the city. Aoun also complicated matters by reaching a political accord with Lebanese Forces (LF) militia leader Samir Geagea. However, Aoun's government was completely rejected by Syria, which had played the role of power broker in Lebanese affairs for the past 15 years.

In October the National Assembly was unable to assemble a quorum to renew the term of speaker Hussain al-Hussaini. The only institution retaining its integrity was the Banque du Liban (central bank), which continued to provide finance to both rival governments. There were doubts about how long the bank could continue to fill this void, but in 1988 it was the only institution capable of handling the country's financial management.

AFP PHOTO

Amin Gemayel, outgoing president of Lebanon, named a provisional military government after the Lebanese National Assembly failed to elect a new president.

Syria's Pres. Hafez al-Assad had insisted that the new president be a credible political figure able to push through political reforms that would give the Muslim majority more power. This concern for Arab interests made little impact on Geagea and the LF, which preferred to see the Maronite Christian heartland secede from the rest of Lebanon rather than allow Christian privileges to be taken away. The conflict between the LF and Muslim forces was likely to be a determining factor in the political process. The LF was confident of Israeli backing if Syria were to take military action to enforce its will on Lebanon. Other possible candidates for the presidency had included Syria's candidate, Mikhail Daher, and the Paris-based elder statesman Raymond Edde, while the LF was said to favour Dani Chamoun.

In May more than 250 people were killed in fighting between the two main Shi'ite Muslim groups—Hezbollah and Amal—in the sprawling southern suburbs of Beirut. Fighting stopped only after negotiations by senior Iranian and Syrian officials led to intervention by Syrian troops. On May 2 Israel launched its largest operation in southern Lebanon since the invasion of 1982, with the ostensible purpose of "advising" villagers in the Hasbayya and Rashayya regions not to cooperate with Palestine Liberation Organization (PLO) guerrillas, who had been raiding Israeli territory. On April 23 a car bomb exploded in a crowded marketplace in Tripoli, leaving more than 65 people dead. It was the most serious incident of its kind in three years. Local leaders blamed the incident on the LF.

As part of the general collapse of law and order, there were reports in May that Lebanon had become one of the main centres of the world heroin trade. The U.S. State Department was quoted as saying that most of the local militias were involved in the trade—estimated to be worth $250 million a year and based on cultivation of poppies in the Beqaa Valley.

Syria and Iran continued to be the principal mediators in attempts to release Western hostages, including the archbishop of Canterbury's special envoy, Terry Waite, and two Western newsmen, held in Lebanon by terrorists. In December the International Committee of the Red Cross left Lebanon after its workers received death threats.

In January the Amal movement lifted its three-year blockade of Palestinian refugee camps in Beirut. Amal's leader, Nabih Berri, said that the move was a gesture of solidarity with the Palestinian uprising in the West Bank and Gaza Strip. The siege had failed to achieve its objective of keeping the PLO out of the camps, and its termination may have been a response to a sudden improvement of relations between Syria and the PLO.   (JOHN WHELAN)

LIBYA

A socialist country of North Africa, Libya lies on the Mediterranean Sea. Area: 1,775,500 sq km (685,524 sq mi). Pop. (1988 est.): 4,316,000. Cap.: Tripoli. Monetary unit: Libyan dinar, with (Oct. 10, 1988) a free rate of 0.30 dinar to U.S. $1 (0.51 dinar = £1 sterling). De facto chief of state in 1988, Col. Mu'ammar al-Qadhdhafi; secretary of the General People's Congress (nominal chief of state), Mifta al-Usta Umar; secretary-general of the General People's Committee (premier), Umar Mustafa al-Muntasir.

During 1988 Libya continued the conciliatory policies that were evident in 1987. With no economic surplus to provide international leverage, Libyan leader Col. Mu'ammar al-Qadhdhafi made clear his wish to improve relations with the Maghreb countries and end his country's diplomatic isolation. The accord reached in 1987 with Algeria was followed on Dec. 28, 1987, by a resumption of diplomatic

relations with Tunisia after a break of two years. A visit by the Libyan leader to Tunis was canceled at the last moment in January to indicate disapproval of a meeting between Tunisian Pres. Zine al-Abidine Ben Ali and the commanders of the U.S. and the French fleets, but it went ahead the following month. In March all Libyan barriers at the Libya-Tunisia border were removed, and large numbers of Tunisians entered Libya to work.

In September Colonel Qadhdhafi invited a number of officials on a cruise from Tripoli to the Tunisian coast, where he received President Ben Ali on board. The Libyan leader formally announced that oil resources on the Libyan side of the Tunisia-Libya offshore border would be developed jointly and shared—an option Libya had offered before the start of the protracted case before the International Court of Justice at The Hague. Libya had received a favourable ruling from the court in 1982, but the settlement had not been finally ratified by both sides.

The Libyan leadership was eager to cultivate relations with almost all Arab countries, although there was sensitivity in relating to some, such as Egypt, where the break had been particularly bitter. Qadhdhafi showed no signs of softening his posture toward the U.S. leadership, but at lower levels Libya continued to accommodate to its need for U.S. technology and expertise. Late in the year a conflict developed over a new chemical plant in Libya that the U.S. said would be used to make chemical weapons; Libya denied the charge. The U.K. remained adamant in its isolation of Libya, but other European countries, especially Spain, improved their relations with Tripoli. Libya's failure to pay for arms and other goods and services received in the early 1980s clouded relations with the Soviet Union and other Eastern bloc countries.

At home the economy remained weak, with revenues seriously depressed as a result of low world oil prices. The government maintained its fiercely restrictive controls on imports and again achieved a positive trade balance, but at great cost to the standard of living. Spending on major projects was extremely limited, but the "great man-made river" designed to bring water from the south to the coast was still under construction.

In March Qadhdhafi summoned the resident diplomatic corps to the Furnaj Prison on the outskirts of Tripoli, mounted a bulldozer, and proceeded to breech the wall; 400 prisoners emerged to freedom there and possibly 7,000 from other prisons. The Libyan leader declared that he had been tormented for 18 years by the awareness of those in prison and now recognized the futility of imprisonment. A few days later he visited the emigration office and ceremonially destroyed the lists of those forbidden to leave the country. Overseas visits were being made, and the only restriction seemed to be the understandably limited access to foreign exchange.

In retailing, which since the 1970s had come progressively under public control, licenses for private shops began to be issued. The revolutionary courts were abolished, and welcome changes were made in military conscription, which had come to be viewed as arbitrary and unpredictable. The idea that the country would be defended by a popular militia was reasserted, although the extent to which this would be implemented was not made clear. What did seem to be clear was that a significant proportion of the armed forces were disenchanted after the protracted and unsuccessful conflict with Chad. An agreement with Chad to restore diplomatic relations and to seek a peaceful settlement was announced in October.   (J. A. ALLAN)

This article updates the *Macropædia* article NORTH AFRICA: *Libya.*

MOROCCO

A constitutional monarchy of North Africa, Morocco has coastlines on the Atlantic Ocean and the Mediterranean Sea. Area: 458,730 sq km (177,117 sq mi). Pop. (1988 est.): 23,809,000. (Area and population figures refer to Morocco as constituted prior to the purported division of Western Sahara between Morocco and Mauritania and the subsequent Moroccan occupation of the Mauritanian zone in 1979.) Cap.: Rabat. Monetary unit: dirham, with (Oct. 10, 1988) a selling rate of 8.34 dirhams to U.S. $1 (14.28 dirhams = £1 sterling). King, Hassan II; prime minister in 1988, Azzedine Laraki.

Perhaps for the last time, the Western Sahara issue continued to dominate Moroccan attention throughout the year. The report of a UN mission at the end of 1987 had led the Moroccan government to accept, in August, a UN peace proposal that suggested a referendum over whether the Western Saharans wished to be integrated with Morocco or to seek a separate political existence. Morocco's confidence that it would win the referendum was based on the fact that the UN suggested that the participants in it were to be determined on the basis of a 1974 Spanish census of the territory and that the peace plan did not require Moroccan withdrawal from the territory or direct talks with the Popular Front for the Liberation of Saguia el Hamra and Río de Oro (Polisario Front, the Saharan people's independence movement)—although in late December King Hassan agreed for the first time to talk directly with Polisario representatives. In any case, Morocco's control over the territory, in which it had made more than $2 billion worth of investment, was unaffected by military action. Indeed, the Polisario Front observed a de facto truce during the year, apart from an attack on the defensive wall system in September and the accidental shooting down in December of a U.S. plane spraying locusts.

These developments in the Western Sahara dispute were paralleled by the renewal of diplomatic relations with Algeria in May, for the first time since 1976, and the subsequent opening of the two countries' common border. Immediate results of this were the sudden influx of Algerian tourists to purchase consumer goods in eastern Moroccan towns and the growth of a significant cross-border trade. Morocco also entered into a series of economic agreements with Algeria over joint industrial projects and joined discussions with other North African nations over proposals for regional economic and political unity. This new disposition in Morocco's regional relations was sealed by King Hassan's visit to the Algerian capital, Algiers, in June to attend an Arab League meeting and to consult with other North African leaders.

Domestically, Morocco was able to pursue its economic reform policies against the background of a record harvest estimated at eight million tons of grain. Although external debt rose to $18.5 billion, Morocco was able to convince the International Monetary Fund of its economic progress, as the current account moved into surplus in 1987 and 1988 and the budget deficit for 1988 declined by 9.5% to less than 1.5% of gross domestic product. As a result, a new IMF standby credit facility for 220 million Special Drawing Rights was provided in August.

The government pursued its policies of decentralization during the year, providing financial aid to the 1,500 local government communes. Plans went forward for the construction in Casablanca of the second-largest mosque in the world, paid for by public subscription and due to open in mid-1989.   (GEORGE JOFFÉ)

This article updates the *Macropædia* article NORTH AFRICA: *Morocco*.

OMAN

The sultanate of Oman occupies the southeastern part of the Arabian Peninsula, facing the Persian Gulf, the Gulf of Oman, and the Arabian Sea. A small part of the country lies to the north and is separated from the rest of Oman by the United Arab Emirates. Area: 300,000 sq km (120,000 sq mi). Pop.: in 1988 estimates ranged from 1.2 million to an official 2 million; no census has ever been taken (UN est., 1,372,000). Cap.: Muscat. Monetary unit: rial Omani, with (Oct. 10, 1988) a par value of 0.38 rial to U.S. $1 (free rate of 0.66 rial = £1 sterling). Sultan and prime minister in 1988, Qabus ibn Sa'id.

The Gulf war cease-fire on Aug. 20, 1988, was welcomed by Oman and its Gulf Cooperation Council allies. The minister of state for foreign affairs, Yousef ibn Alawi ibn Abdullah, visited Iran on September 10 for talks with senior officials, but he had also been in Tehran in August in the role of a bridge builder between Iran and the Gulf states. An official visit to Muscat by Pres. Haidar Abu Bakr al-Attas of South Yemen was forecast by Aden sources in Abu Dhabi in September, but no immediate confirmation was available. Eight Yemeni soldiers had been killed in a border incident with South Yemen in 1987.

Several times over the course of the year the sultanate indicated that it was ready to cut oil production to help stabilize prices, as part of a general agreement between OPEC and non-OPEC oil producers. Oman was producing 600,000 bbl a day, 550,000 bbl of which was exported.

The military access agreement with the U.S., particularly regarding the base on Masirah Island, was an important factor in the success of U.S. operations in the Gulf. This support was praised by U.S. Secretary of State George Shultz in March, although Congress cut aid to Oman to $13.5 million from $25.3 million. The Omani government's financial position improved in 1988, however, thanks to a lower-than-expected 1987 budget deficit, and a gift of $5 million was being made to Zanzibar, Oman's former African dependency, to upgrade the airport.

The new Soviet ambassador, Viktor Bosovac, presented his credentials on April 4, marking another step in Muscat's acceptance of the Eastern bloc. A stock exchange was due to open in January 1989.   (JOHN WHELAN)

This article updates the *Macropædia* article ARABIA: *Oman*.

QATAR

A monarchy (emirate) on the Arabian Peninsula, Qatar occupies a desert peninsula on the west coast of the Persian Gulf. Area: 11,400 sq km (4,400 sq mi). Pop. (1988 est.): 420,000. Cap.: Doha. Monetary unit: Qatar riyal, with (Oct. 10, 1988) a free rate of 3.63 riyals to U.S. $1 (6.21 riyals = £1 sterling). Emir and prime minister in 1988, Sheikh Khalifah ibn Hamad ath-Thani.

Qatar agreed to refer its dispute with Bahrain over ownership of disputed islands to the International Court of Justice. The two neighbouring nations remained on friendly terms, however, although Qatar, as a state espousing the Wahhabi interpretation of Islam, appeared to be moving closer to the conservative values and practices of Saudi Arabia. For example, two convicted murderers were publicly beheaded on September 30.

The end of the war between Iran and Iraq was expected to boost the economy, which had already been stimulated by the North Field gas project, on which drilling started in August. In October the Qatar Chamber of Commerce began a campaign to interest local businessmen in trading with Iraq. Oil still accounted for 90% of Qatar's wealth, and within OPEC Qatar produced below its quota, largely

because of marketing problems. Production averaged 300,-000 bbl a day.

On July 9 Qatar established diplomatic relations with China. This was seen as a reaction to U.S. anger over Qatar's purchase of U.S.-made Stinger missiles from the black market. It also could be linked with the ruling ath-Thani family's decision to recognize the Soviet Union, which was announced in August and was to be followed by a visit at minister of state level to Moscow.

The heir apparent to the emir, Sheikh Hamad ibn Khalifah ath-Thani, paid a state visit to London on March 20–23 for talks with U.K. Prime Minister Margaret Thatcher. This meeting affirmed the strong ties that existed between Qatar and the U.K.   (JOHN WHELAN)

This article updates the *Macropædia* article ARABIA: *Qatar*.

SAUDI ARABIA

The kingdom of Saudi Arabia occupies four-fifths of the Arabian Peninsula, with coastlines on the Red Sea and the Persian Gulf. Area: 2,240,000 sq km (865,000 sq mi). Pop. (1988 est.): 12,972,000. Cap.: Riyadh. Monetary unit: Saudi Arabian riyal, with (Oct. 10, 1988) a free rate of 3.75 riyals to U.S. $1 (6.42 riyals = £1 sterling). King and prime minister in 1988, Fahd.

Saudi Arabia's decision to buy ground-to-ground missiles from China provoked a diplomatic rupture with the U.S. in 1988, a year that was also characterized by deteriorating relations with Iran. In October the kingdom exerted pressure within OPEC for a new consensus on oil prices by calling for reduced oil production. By November all 13 member nations of OPEC had agreed to limit total oil production to 18.5 million bbl a day, down from as much as 23 million bbl a day. The accord would take effect Jan. 1, 1989. In 1988 Saudi Arabia expressed its commitment to remaining a major player in the global energy industry by proposing to purchase a 50% stake in Texaco's U.S. East Coast refining operations.

A report published in the *Washington Post* on March 18 revealed that during a visit to China in 1986, Prince Bandar ibn Sultan ibn Abdel-Aziz, the Saudi ambassador to the U.S., had ordered CSS-2 missiles. The announcement soured relations with the U.S. and provoked Israel into threatening a preemptive strike against the al-Kharj base, where the missiles were deployed. U.S. Pres. Ronald Reagan warned Israel against taking any military action. The U.S. recalled its ambassador to the kingdom, Hume Horan, soon after the envoy delivered a protest to King Fahd about the missile sale. Saudi Arabia had no diplomatic links with China because it recognized Taiwan, but China's Foreign Minister Wu Xueqian (Wu Hsüeh-ch'ien) expressed his interest in establishing full diplomatic ties with Saudi Arabia.

Relations with the U.S.S.R., broken off since 1938, remained cool. Moscow's agreement to withdraw troops from Afghanistan was expected to encourage overtures from Riyadh to Moscow. Despite a visit to the kingdom by a senior Soviet diplomat and the Saudi foreign minister's 1987 tour of the Soviet Union, no immediate progress seemed likely. In December, however, Saudi Arabia played host to peace talks between the U.S.S.R. and Afghan guerrillas.

The Saudi government severed diplomatic relations with Iran on April 26, 1988, after imposing a quota on Iranian pilgrims attending the annual hajj (pilgrimage). During the 1987 pilgrimage, some 400 people were killed in riots allegedly started by Iranian agents provocateurs. Iran wanted to send 150,000 pilgrims to Mecca and Medina for the 1988 season, but the Saudi authorities would allow only 45,000. Iranian diplomats left Riyadh peacefully on May

5. King Fahd on May 16 called for the replacement of the Iranian regime by "men of peace." In a more conciliatory speech to the UN in October, Foreign Affairs Minister Prince Saud al-Faisal said the kingdom had no enmity against Iran but relations "would depend on Iran's policy with its neighbours." Four Saudi citizens, accused of complicity with Iran in sabotage of the Jubail plant of the Saudi Petrochemical Company in April, were executed on September 30 in Dammam; Iran denied any involvement. The four were beheaded in accordance with a September ruling by the Council of Grand Ulema, Saudi Arabia's supreme religious body. The council had ruled that the sentence for terrorism and sabotage was death by beheading; drug trafficking had been made subject to the death penalty in 1987. On Oct. 25, 1988, in apparent retaliation for the executions, a Saudi diplomat was killed in Ankara by a group calling itself Islamic Jihad of Hijaz. This hitherto unpublicized group was one of a number of small, externally based Saudi opposition groups. Saudi Arabia embarked on a weapons buildup in response to Iranian aggression against the Saudi regime, including repeated calls on Tehran Radio for the overthrow of the as-Saud family. Fears about internal opposition to the government were not a major factor in defense spending. In Bermuda on July 3 an extension of the existing defense contracts signed in 1985–86 with the U.K. was initialed by Defense and Aviation Minister Prince Sultan ibn Abdel-Aziz and the U.K.'s secretary of state for defense, George Younger. The contract for fighter airplanes, helicopters, minehunters, and minesweepers was criticized in both Israel and the U.S. Even with the new aircraft, however, Saudi Arabia could not equal the leading air forces in the region; Syria, Libya, Egypt, and Israel all boasted more air power than the 400-strong Royal Saudi Air Force at maximum capacity. Iran had fewer than 100 serviceable aircraft. In the first deal to be finalized under the new accord, a U.K. supplier agreed to a $444 million contract in November to supply six minehunters. The next phase included the supply of 88 helicopters. The largest segment in the July memorandum called for the delivery of 48 Tornado jets—including both interdiction strike fighter-bombers and advanced defense versions, around 60 Hawk 100s and 200s, and 15 British Aerospace 125 and 146 jets.

As OPEC ministers wrestled with pricing and quota issues, the Saudi government pushed production up toward seven million barrels a day. Persistent industry reports suggested that average output in early October was at least 6.3 million bbl, or around 2 million bbl more a day than the kingdom's official OPEC quota. Much of this output was being stored. However, later in the month Saudi Arabia spearheaded an initiative for an oil-production cut, and in November the OPEC nations agreed to a production limit.

During 1988 the Saudi oil industry underwent major restructuring. Petroleum Minister Hisham Nazer, who was appointed in 1986, was named on April 5 chairman of Aramco, the state national oil company and the largest oil industry employer in the Middle East. He succeeded 62-year-old John J. Kelberer of the U.S., chairman since 1978. The start-up in July 1988 of methyl tertiary butyl ether (MTBE) production at the Saudi European Petrochemical Company (Ibn Zahr) marked the completion of the first phase of petrochemicals projects undertaken by the Saudi Basic Industries Corporation, the kingdom's main industrial holding group. Its 15 manufacturing affiliates located in the principal industrial cities were producing more than ten million metric tons a year of liquid petrochemicals, plastics, resins, fertilizers, and steel for sale in domestic, regional, and global markets. These plants—most of them

Palestinian mourners in Damascus, Syria, reach toward the coffin of Khalil al-Wazir, better known as Abu Jihad, the Palestine Liberation Organization military chief who had been assassinated by Israeli forces at his home in Tunis, Tunisia.

AP/WIDE WORLD

joint ventures—were largely operating above their design capacities. The Saudi budget, published at the beginning of 1988, contained a controversial decree that introduced an income tax for foreigners. By August 1988 the expatriate population was reported to have reached 3.9 million. After an outcry by senior expatriates, King Fahd revoked the tax proposal on January 5. The government later rescinded plans to introduce tariffs on key imports, including medical supplies, and suspended a proposal to increase the price of utilities. In November King Fahd urged ministers to curb spending. The 1988 budget forecast was for a $9,573,000,-000 deficit, which might be met in part by a treasury bond issue. The pressures on the government to find jobs for the 61,000 Saudis who graduated each year intensified. On September 23 King Fahd urged young men to enlist in the armed forces. Efforts to diversify the economy away from dependence on oil continued. In the 1987–88 winter growing season a total of 2.7 million tons of wheat and 400,000 tons of barley were harvested. On November 25 Prince Muhammad ibn Abdel-Aziz, a brother of King Fahd, died at the age of 80.   (JOHN WHELAN)

This article updates the *Macropædia* article ARABIA: *Saudi Arabia*.

SYRIA

A republic of southwestern Asia, Syria is on the Mediterranean Sea. Area: 185,180 sq km (71,498 sq mi). Pop. (1988 est.): 11,338,000. Cap.: Damascus. Monetary unit: Syrian pound, with (Oct. 10, 1988) a market rate of LS 11.23 to U.S. $1 (LS 19.22 = £1 sterling) and a free rate of LS 20.96 to U.S. $1 (LS 35.90 = £1 sterling). President in 1988, Gen. Hafez al-Assad; prime minister, Mahmoud Zuabi.

Syria's key role in the quest for peace in the Middle East was evident in Pres. Hafez al-Assad's intense efforts to promote dialogue between the Gulf states and Iran during 1988, as well as his influence on the Palestinian question. In Lebanon, long an area of Syrian influence, Syria was frustrated by the growing impetus toward partition when Lebanese leaders failed to agree on a successor for Pres. Amin Gemayel, whose term of office ended in September.

On January 14 the Damascus press reported that a message had been received from Iran's foreign affairs minister, Ali Akbar Velayati, on the Gulf situation. Tehran was asked to give an undertaking that it had no hostile intentions toward noncombatant Gulf states, such as Kuwait and Saudi Arabia. Foreign Affairs Minister Faruq ash-Shara had visited Tehran and Riyadh twice only a few weeks before the announcement. This shuttle diplomacy helped to pave the way toward a settlement of the Iran-Iraq war.

President Assad met Palestine Liberation Organization chairman Yasir Arafat in Damascus on April 25, marking a shift back toward PLO-Syrian cooperation. The atmosphere surrounding the talks was muted, in contrast to the emotional outpourings that accompanied the April 21 funeral in the Syrian capital of Khalil al-Wazir (Abu Jihad; *see* OBITUARIES). Abu Jihad, the PLO military chief, had been assassinated in Tunis by Israeli special forces. When the Palestine National Council in November declared its intention to achieve statehood, Syria did not join its Arab neighbours in supporting the proclamation publicly. There remained disagreement between them on how Palestinian interests should be represented at an international conference to settle the central Middle East dispute. Syria favoured integrating the PLO into an Arab delegation; the PLO wanted to stand independently.

Syria's improved relationship with the U.S. was seen largely as a counterbalance to Soviet pressure on Damascus for a less hostile stand toward Israel. Syria maintained warm links with other left-wing regimes. On October 10–11 President Assad held talks with Ethiopia's Pres. Mengistu Haile Mariam. Links were also being forged with the Iraqi opposition leader Hojatolislam Muhammad Baqr Hakim, who was based in Tehran, and Jalal Talabani, leader of the Patriotic Union of Kurdistan. In Lebanon, Syria and Iran were in direct conflict. While Damascus tried, and failed, to impose a Syrian peace, Tehran was making progress toward its goal of creating a revolutionary Islamic outpost in the heart of the Arab world. One problem not aired publicly but integral to the dialogue between Syria and Iran was the fate of Western hostages held by groups sympathetic to Iran and the extremist Hezbollah faction in Lebanon. Syria had not supported taking hostages, but it was ready to exploit them for diplomatic advantage with the West. The biggest setback for Syria, however, was its inability to supervise the election in September of a new Lebanese president. Its main Lebanese opponents, the

Maronite Christian militias, successfully blocked Syrian nominees for the presidency. Both Samir Geagea, leader of the Christian Lebanese Forces militia, and Gen. Michel Aoun, head of the military government in East Beirut, confidently predicted that Syria would no longer be able to impose its will in Lebanon.

On the economic front there were signs of recovery after a deep recession. In July Finance Minister Khaled Mahayni said the 1987 deficit had been cut, thanks to a drive to collect revenues toward the end of the year. He gave no details, but diplomats said the actual deficit was about LS 2 billion. In past years defense spending accounted for about 55% of current spending. On October 31 talks started with a Soviet delegation, reportedly concerning possible purchases by Syria of the long-range Sukhoi 24 attack bomber. President Assad's expensive commitment to playing a key strategic role in the region started to provoke criticism from a population that had seen living standards drop considerably in recent years. The government was having serious difficulty servicing external debt, and the prolonged imports squeeze had forced many factories to close because they lacked raw materials and spare parts.

(JOHN WHELAN)

TUNISIA

A republic of North Africa, Tunisia lies on the Mediterranean Sea. Area: 154,530 sq km (59,664 sq mi). Pop. (1988 est.): 7,877,000. Cap.: Tunis. Monetary unit: Tunisian dinar, with (Oct. 10, 1988) a selling rate of 0.90 dinar to U.S. $1 (1.55 dinars = £1 sterling). President in 1988, Gen. Zine al-Abidine Ben Ali; prime minister, Hedi Baccouche.

For Tunisia 1988 was a year of reconciliation after the palace coup that removed the president-for-life, Habib Bourguiba, from power on Nov. 7, 1987. His successor, Gen. Zine al-Abidine Ben Ali, released all political prisoners during the year and allowed exiled political opponents of Bourguiba, including the veteran planning minister Ahmed Ben Salah, to return home. The displaced former president, now in his mid-80s, was eventually allowed to retire to his birthplace of Monastir. Two ministerial reshuffles in April and July removed all remaining ministers from the Bourguiba period, and general elections in April 1989—two years before they were due—were announced in November in a move clearly designed to remove the last vestiges of the Bourguiba period. A new law required retirement of an incumbent president at age 70. In another move to improve the political climate, the Destourian Socialist Party was renamed the Constitutional Democratic Gathering and, in its annual congress held at the end of July, came to terms with multiparty democracy. The constitution had been amended to this end in late April, and a press freedom law had been adopted in mid-July.

In the wake of renewed diplomatic relations with Libya at the end of 1987, a similar renewal with Egypt was announced on January 23. President Ben Ali met his Libyan and Algerian counterparts at the Tunisian-Algerian border town of Sakiet Sidi Youssef on February 8 as part of Tunisia's contribution to the development of regional unity. He made official visits to Algiers in February and to Tripoli in mid-August and attended the inaugural celebrations for Libya's new offshore Bouri oil field in September. Libya's decision to remove border controls in March greatly aided the depressed economy of southern Tunisia, and Tunisians began to seek employment in Libya for the first time since 1985. President Ben Ali also visited Saudi Arabia and France during the year.

The economic picture during 1988 was mixed, with gross domestic product growth rates falling from 5.8% in 1987 to around 3%, the result of drought and a major locust infestation that severely damaged agricultural prospects. Thus the 1987 improvement in the trade deficit could not be sustained. Phosphate revenues were depressed by a fall in the world price. Textile exports enjoyed notable growth, but the closing of the Sousse car assembly plant in January led to increased vehicle imports. The government continued its efforts to cut back on public sector expenditure, and its financial management received International Monetary Fund approval in midyear. A value-added tax was introduced on July 1.   (GEORGE JOFFÉ)

This article updates the Macropædia article NORTH AFRICA: Tunisia.

TURKEY

A republic of Asia Minor and southeastern Europe, Turkey has coastlines on the Aegean, Black, and Mediterranean seas. Area: 779,452 sq km (300,948 sq mi), including 23,764 sq km in Europe. Pop. (1988 est.): 54,176,000. Cap.: Ankara. Monetary unit: Turkish lira, with (Oct. 10, 1988) a free rate of 1,698 liras to U.S. $1 (2,908 liras = £1 sterling). President in 1988, Gen. Kenan Evren; prime minister, Turgut Ozal.

Turgut Ozal, the leader of the conservative Motherland Party, began his second term as prime minister with a daring foreign-policy initiative. On Jan. 30–31, 1988, he held discussions with the Greek Socialist prime minister, Andreas Papandreou, in the Swiss mountain resort of Davos. The two prime ministers agreed that the March 1987 crisis in the Aegean Sea, which had brought the two countries to the brink of war, should never be allowed to recur. To this end, they set up committees to resolve problems that had accumulated since the 1950s and agreed to exchange visits. The committees met twice during the year, and Ozal visited Athens in June, but Papandreou's return visit to Ankara was postponed. The diplomatic results of "the spirit of Davos" were meagre. However, personal contacts multiplied, and a record 300,000 Greek tourists visited Turkey during the year. Turkey welcomed the resumption of intercommunal talks in Cyprus. (See Cyprus, above.)

The attempted reconciliation with Greece was part of a wider effort to promote Turkey's integration into the Western community. Countering human rights critics, Turkey signed the European convention banning the use of torture. Pres. Kenan Evren paid his first state visit to a Western country when he went to the U.S. on June 26. The visit was preceded in March by implementation of the decision negotiated in 1987 to extend the U.S.-Turkey Defense and Economic Cooperation Agreement. President Evren also made state visits to the U.K. in July and West Germany in October, while British Prime Minister Margaret Thatcher paid her first visit to Turkey in April. The progress of the Turkish application for full membership in the European Communities was discussed during these visits, but by the end of the year the European Commission had not produced its preliminary report on the subject.

Turkey maintained its neutrality in the Gulf war while continuing to represent Iraqi interests in Tehran and Iranian interests in Baghdad. Despite its own problem with Kurdish secessionist terrorists of the PKK (Kurdish Workers Party), Turkey allowed some 60,000 Iraqi Kurds to enter the country when their homes were overrun by the Iraqi Army. By year's end their number fell to 40,000, as some returned home while others went to Iran. However, the Turkish authorities stated that they could not substantiate the accusation that Iraq had used chemical weapons against the Kurds.

As Soviet natural gas reached Ankara, a crossing was inaugurated on the Turkish frontier with the U.S.S.R. on the Black Sea coast, closed since the 1920s. Turkey took part in the Balkan foreign ministers' conference in Belgrade at the end of February. The Bulgarians allowed the family of the Bulgarian-born weight lifter Naim Suleymanoglu (*see* BIOGRAPHIES), who won a gold medal for Turkey in the Olympics, to immigrate to Turkey in October. However, the problem posed by the attempted forcible assimilation of the million-strong Muslim Turkish minority in Bulgaria remained unresolved.

Turkey's external balance of payments improved, with the current account deficit dropping to $322 million by the end of July. However, this result was achieved only by a steep devaluation of the Turkish lira, which was halved in value during the year. Devaluation coupled with fast economic growth, estimated at some 7%, pushed inflation to above 80%, despite austerity measures, and the prime minister was subjected to constant criticism from both right and left. Ozal's attempt to advance local government elections to November failed when a constitutional amendment to that effect was defeated on September 25. On June 18 Ozal survived an assassination attempt by a right-wing terrorist.

On July 3 Ozal inaugurated a second bridge linking the European and Asian shores of the Bosporus. The bridge was built by a Japanese-Italian-Turkish consortium.

(ANDREW MANGO)

UNITED ARAB EMIRATES

Consisting of Abu Dhabi, Ajman, Dubai, Fujairah, Ras al-Khaimah, Sharjah, and Umm al-Qaiwain, the United Arab Emirates is a federation of seven largely autonomous emirates located on the eastern Arabian Peninsula. Area: 77,700 sq km (30,000 sq mi). Pop. (1988 est.): 1,774,000. Provisional cap.: Abu Dhabi. Monetary unit: United Arab Emirates dirham, with (Oct. 10, 1988) a free rate of 3.67 dirhams to U.S. $1 (6.29 dirhams = £1 sterling). President in 1988, Sheikh Zaid ibn Sultan an-Nahayan; prime minister, Sheikh Rashid ibn Said al-Maktum.

The United Arab Emirates (U.A.E.) continued its economic recovery in 1988 and expected a major boost to its transshipment trade from the cease-fire in the war between Iran and Iraq. Dubai emerged during the last 18 months of the war as a major supply centre for foreign navies, but the revenue lost from this service would be outweighed by the business boom that was expected to result from reconstruction of war-damaged facilities in the northern Gulf. In June the Dubai Business and Tourism Development Board was constituted to help promote and market Dubai as a centre for international business and for winter tourism.

The U.A.E.'s close diplomatic contacts with Iran were enhanced on April 30 by a visit from Mohammad Besharati, the Iranian deputy foreign affairs minister. Only 12 days earlier the Iranians had attacked oil installations offshore from Sharjah, closing the Mubarak field for two months. On other diplomatic fronts, there were suggestions that the U.A.E. would soon recognize East Germany and Poland as part of its détente with the Eastern bloc.

On September 12 Abu Dhabi's Crown Prince Sheikh Khalifah ibn Zayed was quoted as saying that the quota allocated to the U.A.E. by OPEC of 948,000 bbl of petroleum a day was not fair and did not match the large oil potential of his country. He was seeking an OPEC quota that would give the U.A.E. "its natural weight among oil-producing countries."

(JOHN WHELAN)

This article updates the *Macropædia* article ARABIA: *United Arab Emirates.*

YEMEN, PEOPLE'S DEMOCRATIC REPUBLIC OF

The People's Democratic Republic of Yemen (Yemen [Aden]; South Yemen) is located in the southern coastal region of the Arabian Peninsula, on the Gulf of Aden and the Arabian Sea. Area: 336,869 sq km (130,066 sq mi). Pop. (1988 est.): 2,345,000. Cap.: Aden. Monetary unit: Yemeni dinar, with (Oct. 10, 1988) a par value of 0.35 dinar to U.S. $1 (free rate of 0.59 dinar = £1 sterling). President in 1988, Haidar Abu Bakr al-Attas; prime minister, Yasin Said Numan.

A unity accord signed with Yemen (San'a'; North Yemen) on May 4, 1988, provided for wide-scale political and economic cooperation. A joint constitution was to be agreed on, and travel restrictions between the two states were to be eliminated. A joint oil project would be established in a 2,200-sq km (850-sq mi) area between Marib and Shabwa. Tension had been running high in the months before the agreement was reached, but the accord acknowledged only that clashes occurred in January 1985.

In a four-day visit to Oman, which ended on November 1, Pres. Haidar Abu Bakr al-Attas agreed to demarcate formally the Yemeni-Omani border. His visit was the first by a South Yemeni head of state and was significant because of Aden's past support for rebels opposed to Sultan Qabus ibn Sa'id. There were reports in midsummer of border clashes with Saudi security forces, and in mid-October Interior Minister Saleh Monasser as-Siyali made a highly publicized visit to Riyadh in an attempt to smooth out the relationship between the royalist Saudi regime and the Marxist government in South Yemen. After nearly a decade, diplomatic relations with Egypt were restored in February.

(JOHN WHELAN)

This article updates the *Macropædia* article ARABIA: *People's Democratic Republic of Yemen.*

YEMEN ARAB REPUBLIC

The Yemen Arab Republic (Yemen [San'a']; North Yemen) is situated in the southwestern coastal region of the Arabian Peninsula, on the Red Sea. Area: 195,000 sq km (75,300 sq mi). Pop. (1988 est.): 8,614,000. Cap.: San'a'. Monetary unit: Yemen rial, with (Oct. 10, 1988) an official rate of 9.76 rials = U.S. $1 (16.71 rials = £1 sterling). President in 1988, Col. Ali Abdullah Saleh; prime minister, Abdel Aziz Abdel Ghani.

The nation's first exports of oil, in the last week of December 1987, heralded a new era of prosperity for North Yemen. By the third quarter of 1988, production was averaging 175,000 bbl a day, and there were good prospects of additional discoveries.

Pres. Ali Abdullah Saleh was reelected for a third five-year term by the Consultative Council on July 17, with 152 of the 159 members voting for him. Some 25% of the councillors were believed to be Muslim Brothers, a fundamentalist Islamic group also strong in Egypt and The Sudan. All six constituencies in the capital, San'a', were held by fundamentalists. Critics of these Islamic extremists suggested that they would surrender North Yemen's claim to the Asir and Najran provinces of Saudi Arabia, which the Saudis had seized in the 1920s. The majority of the council were tribal supporters of the Saleh regime.

On May 4 a unity accord was signed with South Yemen. (See *Yemen, People's Democratic Republic of,* above.) It provided for comprehensive economic cooperation, abolition of travel restrictions, and the establishment of a joint constitution.

(JOHN WHELAN)

This article updates the *Macropædia* article ARABIA: *Yemen Arab Republic.*

East Asia

CHINA

The People's Republic of China is situated in eastern Asia, with coastlines on the Yellow Sea and the East and South China seas. Area: 9,572,900 sq km (3,696,100 sq mi), including Tibet and excluding Taiwan. (See *Taiwan,* below.) Pop. (1988 est., excluding Taiwan): 1,088,200,000. Cap.: Beijing (Peking). Monetary unit: renminbi yuan, with (Oct. 10, 1988) a free rate of 3.70 yuan to U.S. $1 (6.33 yuan = £1 sterling). General secretary of the Communist Party of China in 1988, Zhao Ziyang (Chao Tzu-yang); presidents, Li Xiannian (Li Hsien-nien) and, from April 8, Yang Shangkun (Yang Shang-k'un); premiers, Zhao and, from April 9, Li Peng (Li P'eng).

For China 1988 was a trying and problem-laden year. Ten years after its leaders initiated far-reaching economic reforms and greatly expanded ties with the outside world, major complications slowed the pace of reform. Efforts to initiate wage and price reforms during the summer led to rapid inflation and the reimposition of stricter central economic controls. Repeated challenges to the authority of the Communist Party of China (CPC)—from dissident intellectuals, university students, and Tibetans—called into question the party's ability to guide the country's political and economic life. Undaunted, China's leaders remained dedicated to reform and expanded foreign commitments. Relations with the U.S.S.R. improved substantially, while those with the U.S. and Japan were generally positive.

Domestic Affairs. The reinvigoration of China's reformist policies of the past decade dominated the agenda during much of the year, but with uneven results. Deng Xiaoping (Teng Hsiao-p'ing), the 84-year old architect of China's shift toward market-oriented socialism and away from ideologically-based politics, continued his effort to ensure the perpetuation of his programs after his death. Zhao Ziyang (Chao Tzu-yang), the 69-year old former premier and, since the fall of 1987, the CPC general secretary, remained the leading exponent of reformist policies. Zhao emphasized labour-intensive industries that were expected to generate increased foreign exchange.

A more cautious approach to change was advocated by 59-year-old Li Peng (Li P'eng; *see* BIOGRAPHIES), a Soviet-trained engineer who succeeded Zhao as premier in April. Li supported reform but was much more circumspect than Zhao in urging change. His chief concern appeared to be stability and continuity under the guidance and direction of the central government. Veteran economic planner Yao Yilin (Yao Yi-lin) also favoured more gradual change. Such disagreements with Zhao, however, did not approximate the bitter, highly factionalized political struggles of earlier decades; instead, they reflected legitimate differences of opinion. Certain officials did not see eye to eye with Zhao when he favoured coastal regions in allocating funds and granting local officials greater authority to make decisions. Some feared these policies would further skew China's pattern of economic development, with interior regions seriously lagging behind coastal provinces in their rates of growth and in their access to imported technology. Some also believed Zhao's assessment of the country's ability to compete in international markets was overly optimistic. Despite the success of the reform program in spurring economic development, many observers concluded that the current economic and administrative

structures were ill-suited to sustaining long-term growth. Zhao therefore urged additional steps to separate party and governmental functions, seeking to remove the CPC more definitively from its past economic management function and further restrict governmental authority over individual enterprises. The promulgation of an enterprise law was deemed crucial to these changes, since the law sought to separate ownership of state-run factories from managerial authority. Otherwise, reform advocates asserted, it would prove impossible to introduce genuine competition among the country's industrial enterprises or to provide meaningful incentives to stimulate productivity.

Zhao's reform strategy also required a stable social and political framework. The policy changes of recent years had unleashed new forces that stimulated certain groups to demand that their grievances be addressed. These groups included intellectuals dissatisfied with their opportunities for free expression, Tibetans resentful of Beijing's (Peking's) control over their political and religious activities, and other social groups, especially in the interior, that benefited less from the economic reforms. The disaffection assumed a variety of forms, some of it violent. In March anti-Chinese riots in Tibet resulted in at least 18 deaths. In June university students in Beijing openly defied the government by marching peacefully to protest the death of a fellow student. There was also a very sharp increase in the crime rate, in riots, and in illegal strikes.

Rectification of the country's irrational price structure had long been one of the most sensitive issues on the reform agenda. The leadership remained very wary of abrupt action, especially after the inflation rate in 1987 approached 20%. Despite reservations and anxieties on the part of top leaders, Deng Xiaoping personally intervened as a forceful advocate of price reform. In May price controls on pork, sugar, eggs, and vegetables were eased, and deregulation of cigarettes and alcohol followed in July. This led to panic buying and the most severe inflation in the regime's 40-year history.

In the wake of these developments, the leadership sharply shifted political course. In August the Political Bureau effectively shelved price and wage reforms for the near-term. Zhao declared that attention would instead focus on a longer-term restructuring of the economy, notably on revamping the enterprise system and on developing the market mechanism. In addition, the State Council announced there would be no additional deregulation during the remainder of 1988 or 1989 and that stricter anti-inflationary policies would be adopted.

Many observers interpreted these changes as a political setback for Zhao and a victory for Li Peng. Zhao's credibility and political position were perhaps somewhat damaged, but rumours that his party post was endangered proved erroneous. When Deng reiterated his desire to scale back his political activities even further, he asserted that Zhao and Li would be jointly responsible for the nation's political fortunes. The leadership as a whole preferred cooperation and positive action to factionalism. The government launched a major new assault on official speculation and corruption, which had grown especially rampant in recent years. It also hoped that the reimposition of greater central control would lead to a restoration of popular support for the reforms and generate confidence in the government's ability to act decisively.

At the same time, Zhao and other leading reformers appealed to intellectuals for understanding and support, knowing many were still suspicious after the 1987 government crackdown on university campuses. Zhao also sought to involve highly educated youth in the reform process,

Chinese Premier
Li Peng (Li P'eng;
left) casts his ballot
during selection
of the new State
Council while Pres.
Yang Shangkun
(Yang Shang-k'un)
waits his turn.
AFP PHOTO

aware that their skills and technical knowledge were crucial to China's long-term prospects for scientific and technical advancement. Astrophysicist Fang Lizhi (Fang Li-chih) and other well-known dissidents, however, continued to air their views publicly, an indication that cynicism about CPC policy ran deep.

The Economy. The problems encountered in price reform reflected the complexity of shifting from a highly planned system toward a more mixed economy. The economy continued to grow at a very rapid pace, with industrial output increasing nearly 18% over 1987. But this rapid growth obscured underlying economic problems, including rapid increases in the money supply, shortages of raw materials and energy, uncontrolled expenditures for construction and consumption (especially at the local level), and an inflationary spiral that in most instances wiped out real growth. The principal goal, therefore, was to cool the overheated economy by curtailing capital construction and reducing the money supply.

Much of the nation's recent economic growth had not involved the central government because localities and enterprises had increasingly made their own financial decisions, sometimes in defiance of the central authorities. Quite apart from measures to curb total demand and reduce the amount of money in circulation, there had already been a major devolution of authority to different regions, with market forces proving increasingly decisive in the overall distribution and control of economic resources. The impact of this decentralization was greatest in China's southern provinces, where links to the outside world were most fully developed. Decisions to curtail excessive investment initially worried foreign investors who feared numerous projects might be canceled, but Beijing's new policies did not appear likely to diminish these activities appreciably.

Economic uncertainties also affected China's foreign trade. Official data indicated that foreign trade would again reach record levels in 1988, with exports increasing nearly 15% over 1987 and imports increasing nearly 25%. By year's end, however, foreign trade officials were conceding that the overheated economy and the high inflation rate had altered plans for reform of the foreign trade system. The objective of the reform had been to increase the power of Chinese manufacturing and marketing organizations, thereby making them more responsive and adaptive in an increasingly competitive trading environment. But efforts to decentralize the foreign trade sector had led to numerous abuses by various local governments and import-export organizations, with profiteering and corruption rampant in many areas.

At the same time, inflation diminished investor confidence in Chinese currency, and the gap between the official and unofficial exchange rates widened. But China continued to resist calls for a devaluation of the renminbi yuan, largely because it would increase the cost of imports. Although some officials claimed that China would enjoy a modest trade surplus for the year, other sources acknowledged a trade deficit of more than $4 billion, with little expectation that the amount would narrow appreciably in the near future.

Some of the most unsettling consequences of recent economic changes occurred in agriculture, which had long been considered one of the principal success stories of the Deng Xiaoping era. However, for four consecutive years grain production had failed to surpass the record of 407 million tons established in 1984. Declining prices for farm products, continued reductions in agricultural investment, fertilizer shortages, and the removal of arable land from crop production (often for new housing and rural industry) had adversely affected agricultural performance at a time when population increases and changing dietary patterns placed new demands on food supplies. As a result, the rationing of pork, eggs, and sugar, reinstated in late 1987, continued into 1988, and China increased its large-scale grain purchases from abroad, acquiring more than 7 million tons from the U.S. alone. Some officials, including Li Peng, called for a much larger infrastructural investment in the agricultural sector, but providing such needed resources was a major problem.

A second long-term problem concerned the growing income disparities between China's interior and coastal provinces, one consequence of giving priority to the coastal areas. Expectations that more prosperous regions would provide economic aid to poorer locales had yet to be met, especially with enhanced local control over economic resources.

Foreign Affairs. China's leaders remained vigorous in pursuing their twin goals of foreign policy independence and diminished regional tensions. Although Beijing's economic and technological links were strongest with the U.S., Japan, and other major developed powers, at a political level Chinese diplomacy was increasingly diversified and adaptable.

Some of the most notable developments during the year occurred in relations with the Soviet Union. Since the accession of Mikhail Gorbachev to top leadership in the Kremlin, both Moscow and Beijing had more actively pursued the possibilities for reduced tensions and expanded contact. The Soviet decision to withdraw its forces from Afghanistan and partially withdraw its troops deployed along the Chinese border, and the heightened diplomatic maneuverings on resolving the Kampuchean conflict, had a significant effect on Chinese thinking. At the same time, Gorbachev's increasing decisiveness helped convince Chinese officials, especially Deng, that the new Soviet leader was sincere in seeking better relations.

The tempo of Sino-Soviet relations increased at all levels. A rapid expansion of trade had catapulted the Soviet Union into the ranks of China's top half dozen trading partners; two-way trade increased by at least one-third in 1988 and seemed likely to surpass $4 billion. Despite infrastructural constraints, both sides appeared intent on enlarging the scope of this cooperation. Conducting trade on a barter basis also proved beneficial, given the foreign exchange limitations encountered by both states.

Movement at the political level attracted the most attention. In August, Moscow and Beijing conducted their first meetings for the explicit purpose of resolving the

Kampuchean conflict, China urging the U.S.S.R. to end its support of the Vietnamese occupation of Kampuchea and to increase pressure on Vietnam to commit itself to an early withdrawal of all its forces. In October Deng Xiaoping voiced his most optimistic assessment to date on the prospects for a full normalization of relations, indicating for the first time that a summit with Gorbachev was increasingly likely during the first half of 1989. With the exception of a hastily arranged meeting of the premiers during border tensions in 1969, no such meeting had been held in 30 years. Thus, a Deng-Gorbachev summit was expected to signify the end of three decades of estrangement between the world's two leading Communist states.

To expedite movement toward a summit, newly appointed Foreign Minister Qian Qichen (Ch'ien Ch'i-ch'en) visited Moscow in December for discussions with his Soviet counterpart, Eduard Shevardnadze, as well as with Gorbachev. It marked the first visit of China's senior diplomat to the Soviet capital since the 1950s. The two sides announced that Shevardnadze would pay a reciprocal visit to Beijing early in 1989.

Despite these developments, Chinese officials repeatedly emphasized they were not pursuing improved Sino-Soviet ties at the expense of existing relationships, especially those with the U.S. Sino-American relations, although encountering difficulties and tensions on political and economic issues, continued to develop. According to U.S. data, two-way trade in 1987 surpassed $10.5 billion, and estimates for 1988 ranged as high as $13.5 billion, second only to that with Japan. U.S. investment in China surpassed $3 billion, more than that of any other country. Approximately 30,000 Chinese students were in the U.S. for advanced training, and increasing numbers of U.S. students and teachers resided in China.

Disagreements in several areas created uncertainties and tensions. China's increasing arms sales in the Middle East and the Persian Gulf caused consternation among senior U.S. officials. Continued Chinese sales of Silkworm anti-ship missiles to Iran had created difficulties in 1987, but even greater concern was expressed by disclosure of Beijing's 1988 sales to Saudi Arabia of intermediate-range ballistic missiles. Although Chinese officials assured the U.S. that there had been no transfer of any nuclear warheads, the proliferation of ballistic missiles into the highly volatile, heavily armed area sent reverberations throughout the region. During separate farewell visits to China, both U.S. Secretary of State George Shultz and Secretary of Defense Frank Carlucci warned the Chinese of the destabilizing consequences of such sales. Especially after Carlucci's October visit, it appeared that the Chinese had given more definitive assurances about future restraints on such transactions.

The Chinese also sought to put relations with Japan on a more solid footing. There had been frequent tensions with Tokyo in recent years, with China voicing rising concern over the growth of the Japanese defense budget and manifestations of what Beijing deemed excessive nationalism. Chinese officials had complained repeatedly about Japan's unwillingness to expedite more fully the transfer of advanced industrial technology to China. They had also voiced concern about trade deficits with Tokyo, which in 1985 had reached $5 billion. However, a major effort by Beijing to curtail imports from Japan had achieved substantial results, with China showing a surplus of approximately $700 million through October 1988. Total trade for ten months was nearly $16 billion, and it seemed likely that the final figure would approach $20 billion, far exceeding any of Beijing's other bilateral trade relationships.

Japan also sought to offer reassurances to China at a political level. In August Noboru Takeshita made his first visit to China as prime minister. Takeshita's visit was a distinct success, in part because Japan extended a major new low-interest loan for the period 1990–95 totaling about $6 billion. But China also continued to press Japan for greater direct investment and additional technology transfer.

Another major diplomatic event was the visit of Indian Prime Minister Rajiv Gandhi in December, the first such visit in nearly 35 years. Sino-Indian relations had been severely estranged since the late 1950s, but especially since 1962, when the two sides fought a border war. Although the visit was more symbolic than substantive, Gandhi's visit was considered a major development by both sides.

Breakthroughs of a different sort were achieved in relations with South Korea. Although the absence of formal diplomatic relations with Seoul placed obvious limits on the scope of these ties, contacts grew appreciably. China sent a large contingent to the Summer Olympics in Seoul, and two-way trade for 1988 was expected to approach $3 billion. At the same time, China indicated its readiness to facilitate South Korean investment in China and expand other forms of direct commercial contacts that were unthinkable only a few years earlier.

(JONATHAN D. POLLACK)

JAPAN

A constitutional monarchy in the northwestern Pacific Ocean, Japan comprises an archipelago with four main islands (Hokkaido, Honshu, Kyushu, and Shikoku), the Ryukyus (including Okinawa), and minor adjacent islands. Area: 377,815 sq km (145,875 sq mi). Pop. (1988 est.): 122,620,000. Cap.: Tokyo. Monetary unit: yen, with (Oct. 10, 1988) a free rate of 132.26 yen to U.S. $1 (226.50 yen = £1 sterling). Emperor, Hirohito; prime minister in 1988, Noboru Takeshita.

Domestic Affairs. In the autumn of 1988 the country's attention was centred on the condition of 87-year-old Emperor Hirohito, who fell seriously ill on September 18. On September 22 the Cabinet asked Crown Prince Akihito (*see* BIOGRAPHIES), the heir to the throne, to assume the emperor's largely ceremonial duties. Akihito had also acted for his father late in 1987, when the emperor underwent intestinal surgery. On September 24 the Japanese press reported that Hirohito was suffering from cancer, thus breaking a national taboo against publicly mentioning the disease. Thousands of Japanese traveled to the gates of the imperial palace to hold a vigil for the emperor's recovery. Hirohito, who took the reign name of Showa or "bright peace" when he ascended the throne in 1926, was the world's longest-reigning chief of state.

In November 1987, after becoming president of the ruling Liberal-Democratic Party (LDP) and prime minister in succession to Yasuhiro Nakasone, Noboru Takeshita had formed a Cabinet in which Kiichi Miyazawa was reappointed finance minister as well as deputy prime minister. Shintaro Abe was named secretary-general of the LDP. Thus Takeshita's two chief rivals (among the so-called three new leaders) were placed in important posts. Sosuke Uno, a former international trade minister, became the foreign minister. The Cabinet remained intact through most of 1988 except for two dramatic changes. On May 13 Seisuke Okuno resigned as head of the National Land Agency in favour of Hideo Utsumi. Okuno, by denying Japanese aggression during the Pacific War (World War II), had triggered strong protests from China and endangered Takeshita's planned visit to Beijing (Peking). In August Tsutomu Kawara, director of the Defense Agency, resigned

週間の休暇を命令。

この夏、年次有給休暇で

"We order you to take one week of vacation" reads a poster created
for the Labor Ministry of Japan. The ministry began a new campaign
that urged the people of Japan, long known for their industriousness
and diligence, to slow down and relax.

LABOR MINISTRY OF JAPAN

to take responsibility for a collision in Tokyo Bay, July 23,
between a Maritime Self-Defense Force submarine and a
fishing boat in which 30 people died. He was replaced by
Kichiro Tazawa, a former agriculture minister.

In December 1987, after Takeshita had taken office,
party strength in the (lower) House of Representatives was
apportioned as follows: LDP 302; Japan Socialist Party
(JSP) 86; Clean Government Party (Komeito) 57; Democratic Socialist Party (DSP) 29; Japan Communist Party
(JCP) 27; independents 5; vacancies 6 (total 512). In the
(upper) House of Councillors the standings were: LDP 143;
JSP 42; Komeito 24; DSP 12; JCP 16; independents 14;
vacancies 1 (total 252).

In his policy speech before a joint session of the Diet,
which reconvened Jan. 25, 1988, the prime minister urged
achievement of "harmony and vitality" by establishment
of a new *furusato* ("native place"). This would involve restructuring of the economy, normalization of land prices,
stabilization of social security, and reform of education.
A radical tax reform, he stated, was one of the most important issues facing Japan. In late January, in a three-
day plenary session of the lower house, Takako Doi, the
leader of the JSP, spearheaded the opposition to the LDP's
plan for a new consumption tax combined with an income tax cut. The JSP was joined by the Komeito, the
DSP, and independent socialists (Shaminren) in urging a
tax cut without an indirect levy. Some 3,500 retailers and
wholesalers also expressed strong opposition to the LDP-
proposed consumption tax. Business and industry organizations, including the Federation of Economic Organizations (Keidanren), the Japanese Association of Executives
(Keizai Doyukai), the Federation of Employers' Associa-

tions (Nikkeiren), and the Japan Chamber of Commerce
and Industry (Nissho), all supported the new tax. The tax
reform was finally passed at the end of a 26-hour parliamentary session on December 24.

In the midst of the turmoil over taxes, public approval
ratings for the Takeshita Cabinet showed a sharp decline,
from 58.6% in November 1987 to 52.5% in March 1988,
according to Kyodo News Service. Indeed, in June an
opposition-backed candidate for governor of Saitama Prefecture who opposed new taxes won handily over his LDP
opponent. In September in Fukushima Prefecture, however, opposition parties failed to arouse antitax sentiment,
and the LDP scored a double victory, in the gubernatorial race and in an upper house by-election. Nevertheless,
parliamentary proceedings became stalled over the tax and
other issues. In July Prime Minister Takeshita ended a
boycott of an extraordinary session of the Diet by the
three opposition parties by agreeing to proceed with a 1.3
trillion yen tax cut before debating the consumption tax.
By August even a few LDP faction leaders were predicting
collapse of the party's tax-reform plan.

The LDP leadership had also been hampered by yet
another scandal affecting the party. In August Diet proceedings were again disrupted by opposition demands for
an investigation of private sales of unlisted stocks of an
advertising agency, the Recruit Cosmos Co. The "Recruit-
gate" incident had netted secretaries—and therefore the
factions of LDP leaders, if not the officials—enormous
profits. Among those mentioned were Hiromasa Ezoe, former chairman of Recruit, Takeshita, Nakasone, Miyazawa,
and Abe. In Diet debate, government spokesmen argued
that security exchange legislation did not apply to the sales.

Miyazawa resigned as finance minister in December,
helping to clear the way for enactment of the tax reform;
following its passage, he was replaced by Tatsuo Murayama,
a taxation specialist who had helped devise the tax overhaul. On December 27 Prime Minister Takeshita reshuffled
his Cabinet, retaining Uno as foreign minister and naming
Tsutomu Hata as minister of agriculture, forestry, and fisheries and Hiroshi Mitsuzaka as minister of international
trade and industry. Takashi Hasegawa, appointed minister
of justice, resigned three days later because of involvement
in the Recruit affair and was replaced by a former Supreme
Court justice, Masami Takatsuji. Another victim of the Recruit scandal was 78-year-old Hisashi Shinto, who stepped
down on December 14 as chairman of Nippon Telegraph
and Telephone Corporation.

In 1988 two land links were completed that would integrate Japan's relatively isolated islands more closely into
the national economy. On March 13, after over 20 years
of construction, the Seikan Tunnel opened for rail service
between Hakodate on Honshu and Aomori on Hokkaido.
At 53.85 km (33.44 mi), it became the world's longest
undersea passage. On April 10 the Seto Ohashi, over the
Inland Sea, the world's longest motor-rail bridge system,
opened, connecting Kojima on Honshu with Sakaide on
Shikoku.

The Economy. Despite delays, the 150-day 112th regular term of the Diet ended on May 25, having passed 75
of 83 bills introduced by the Cabinet. These included a
general account budget with expenditures set at 56,699,-
700,000,000 yen, up 4.8% from the 1987 fiscal year. With
new emphasis being given to domestic demand, outlays
for public works rose 20%. Defense expenditure increased
5.2% to 3.7 trillion yen (just over the politically established
ceiling of 1% of gross national product [GNP]). Issues of
bonds to cover the deficit, however, were reduced toward
the target of zero by fiscal 1990.

Japan ended the 1987 calendar year with a robust 4.2% annual growth in GNP in real terms, to 311,890,000,-000,000 yen, according to the Economic Planning Agency (EPA). In dollar terms, the GNP per capita rose 20.3% to $19,642 (topping the U.S. equivalent of $18,403). Growth represented a 5% rise in domestic demand and a 0.7% drop in external demand. On March 31 the EPA announced that in the first quarter of 1988 Japan's economy grew at the fastest rate in a decade. The 4.9% annualized growth rate, in real terms, was above the government's target (3.7%).

Foreign Affairs. In a New Year's Eve press conference at the end of 1987, Prime Minister Takeshita, who was generally described as a domestically oriented leader, announced a surprising schedule of international travel for 1988. The "cornerstone" of Japan's foreign policy, he reaffirmed, lay in relations with the U.S., which he planned to visit during January 12–15. A stop in Canada would follow. Takeshita was also scheduled to attend the inauguration of South Korean Pres. Roh Tae Woo in Seoul, February 24–25. A swing through Western Europe in May would precede the June summit meeting of Western industrial democracies in Toronto. In July the prime minister was to talk with his counterpart, Prime Minister Robert Hawke, in Australia. A six-day visit to China was planned for August.

In their first official meeting, in Washington, Takeshita assured U.S. Pres. Ronald Reagan that Japan would continue the process of structural adjustment of its economy, boosting domestic demand and opening up markets to foreign competition. As usual, U.S.-Japan trade issues dominated the discussions. As a result of the January summit, Japan agreed, in talks with U.S. trade representative Clayton Yeutter on March 29, to permit U.S. firms to be involved in public works in Japan. On June 20 Cabinet-level talks in Tokyo between Agriculture Minister Takashi Sato and Ambassador Yeutter resulted in agreements calling for Japan to liberalize beef imports. In addition, Japan was required to remove import quotas on fresh oranges in 1991 and on orange juice by 1992. Yeutter praised the results as "a landmark agreement in U.S.-Japan economic relations."

On July 12 the Finance Ministry announced that Japan's trade surplus had fallen 15% in the first six months of 1988. It thus continued a decline from the record $48.5 billion reached in the last six months of 1986. Japanese politicians and business leaders were therefore disappointed in the passage by the U.S. Congress, on August 3, of the Omnibus Trade Bill that provided for retaliation against nations with "unjustifiable" trade practices, a proviso that appeared to be aimed mainly at Japan. President Reagan signed the bill on August 23, though he urged flexibility in enforcing its provisions. In November Japan's trade surplus rose by a surprising 37.9% above a year earlier, while the imbalance with the U.S. increased 5.1% from October.

Early in July the value of the U.S. dollar rose above 135 yen for the first time in eight months. Uncertainty in the financial markets was triggered by the downing of an Iranian airliner by U.S. forces in the Gulf. Finance Minister Miyazawa expressed the opinion that monetary intervention to support the sagging yen was not necessary.

The question of racial prejudice within Japan once again troubled relations with the U.S. In 1986 then prime minister Nakasone had been compelled to apologize for suggesting that the presence of blacks and Puerto Ricans lowered the U.S. intelligence level. In 1988 the offending remark was made by Michio Watanabe, chairman of the LDP's Policy Research Council and a former Cabinet minister. In a speech critical of American spending habits, he intimated that blacks were especially prone to financial irresponsibility. In August Prime Minister Takeshita formally apologized for the comments to the congressional Black Caucus, composed of black members of the U.S. House of Representatives. Another cause of resentment was the sale in Japan of Little Black Sambo dolls, which American blacks saw as offensive caricatures.

In December 1987 Prime Minister Takeshita had welcomed free elections in South Korea and Roh's victory in the presidential contest. During Takeshita's visit to Seoul in February, the two leaders unveiled plans for establishment of a bilateral committee (the "Wisemen Group") to discuss common issues. Japan praised Roh for his call, on July 7, for an end to the bitter confrontation between North and South Korea. Although North Korea was the only country with which Japan had no diplomatic relations, Keizo Obuchi, the chief Cabinet secretary, said that Tokyo was prepared to open talks with Pyongyang. Seoul urged caution, however, asking Japan to heed South Korean efforts to reach a rapprochement with China and the Soviet Union before improving relations with North Korea.

On August 26 in Beijing, Prime Minister Takeshita received a warm welcome from Chinese leader Deng Xiaoping (Teng Hsiao-p'ing). In talks with his counterpart, Chinese Premier Li Peng (Li P'eng), Takeshita pledged 810 billion yen in soft loans for 42 modernization projects during fiscal years 1990–95.

Although Japan had normalized contacts with the U.S.S.R. in 1956, diplomatic relations with Moscow—even a promised visit to Japan by Soviet Pres. Mikhail Gorbachev—remained hampered by Tokyo's insistence on discussion of what Japanese called the "Northern Territories" dispute. The issue involved a small group of islands north of Hokkaido, claimed by the Japanese but occupied since World War II by Soviet forces. On May 6 in Moscow, JSP leader Doi was told that the U.S.S.R. had rejected Japan's territorial claim. When former prime minister Nakasone visited Moscow on July 22, he spent 2 hours and 40 minutes in talks with Gorbachev, chiefly devoted to the "Northern Territories" problem. The Soviet leader argued that in 1956 Japan had rejected the Soviet offer to return two of the four islands. It was the first time Moscow had admitted that there was any legitimacy to Japan's claim. However, no progress toward solving the issue was made during Soviet Foreign Minister Eduard Shevardnadze's visit to Tokyo in December.

In a meeting with Canadian Prime Minister Brian Mulroney June 19, on the eve of the Western summit meeting in Toronto, Prime Minister Takeshita unveiled his debt-relief proposals for the least less developed countries (LLDCs). He offered to recycle $5.5 billion in debts, due to be paid in 1988, into grants and new loans. The Foreign Ministry, meanwhile, had announced that Japan would extend more than $50 billion in official development assistance (ODA) in a new five-year program. In 1987 Japan's ODA as a ratio of GNP came to 0.31%. In late June Foreign Minister Uno visited Jordan, Egypt, Syria, and Israel. In talks with Israeli Prime Minister Yitzhak Shamir, Uno reiterated Japan's position to the effect that Israel should recognize the Palestinians' right to self-determination.

On August 9 in Tokyo, the Ministry of International Trade and Industry announced that Japan stood ready to help Iran and Iraq with yen-denominated loans for reconstruction of their war-ravaged economies. The offer followed the announcement by UN Secretary-General Javier Pérez de Cuéllar of a cease-fire in the eight-year-old Gulf war, to begin August 20. Although it was barred by peace clauses in its constitution from offering patrol forces to the UN peacekeeping team that was to monitor the cease-

fire, Japan could provide civilian personnel. On August 18 the UN accepted the nomination of Jiro Okuyama, 29, of the UN Policy Division of the Foreign Ministry, to be a political officer, and Jiro Mizuno, 42, then assigned to Harvard University's research centre on international affairs, as legal adviser. (ARDATH W. BURKS)

KOREA

A country of northeastern Asia, bordered by the Sea of Japan, the Korea Strait, and the Yellow Sea, Korea is divided into two parts roughly at the 38th parallel.

The Olympic Games, held in Seoul, South Korea, between Sept. 17 and Oct. 2, 1988, proved a triumph for the South while contributing markedly to the further isolation of the North. Feared disruptions of the Games by the latter did not materialize. Apart from controversies that arose during the competition (in particular the banning of some athletes for taking performance-enhancing drugs), the Games were conducted with admirable efficiency. Until just a few weeks before competition was to begin, it was uncertain whether North Korea would accept an offer from the International Olympic Committee to act as host for two sports and part of three others. The North Korean government, which in January had declined to field a joint Korean team, kept demanding additional concessions until it was too late to gain any at all.

The Games were the catalyst for far-reaching realignments of big-power attitudes toward Korea. The presence in Seoul of Soviet and Chinese teams, which the North had been unable to prevent, brought about a thaw in diplomatic relations between South Korea and those nations. China, for example, allowed commercial airliners bound for Seoul to fly over its territory. Trade contacts blossomed and feelings warmed. On the other hand, the United States was surprised by anti-American sentiments among some Korean spectators, who often cheered Soviet athletes. There were calls by mainstream South Korean politicians as well as by radical students for a reevaluation of the need for the U.S. military force of 43,000 troops.

There was a steady erosion during the year of South Ko-

rea's hostile stance toward the Communists, yet 1988 had begun with considerable ill-feeling. On January 15 Kim Hyon Hui, who had been arrested in Bahrain following the Nov. 29, 1987, crash of a South Korean commercial aircraft in the sea off Burma with the loss of 115 lives, admitted on live television that she had helped plant a bomb on the plane on the orders of Kim Jong Il, son and designated successor of North Korean leader Kim Il Sung. Nevertheless, South Korea actively pursued détente with the North. In May a long-standing ban on discussion of reunification was lifted. In June Pres. Roh Tae Woo (see BIOGRAPHIES) proposed sports contests between the two, and early the following month he called for political dialogue, trade relations, and cultural and humanitarian exchanges. He offered to help the North improve its relations with the U.S. and other Western powers and at the same time declared his determination to improve ties with both the Soviet Union and China. In October the government declared trade with the North to be "internal" and duty-free. Though direct exchanges could occur only with mutual cooperation, the government pointed out that deals through third countries would not be impeded.

About the same time, Roh lifted a ban on meetings between students in the two parts of Korea. Earlier the determination of some South Korean students to march to the border 55 km (35 mi) north of Seoul to discuss reunification with students from the North had provoked ugly clashes. The government mobilized 60,000 riot police to prevent the meeting from taking place. On August 15, 3,000 students fought police outside Seoul's Yonsei University. Tens of thousands of students at other colleges rallied in support. Opposition leaders urged the students to abandon the plan, which was effectively stymied. The increasingly leftist, pro-North Korean stance of radical student leaders caught many observers by surprise.

On July 21 North Korea proposed interparliamentary talks. A preliminary meeting in August accomplished nothing, but agreement on a format was reached in November. However, Western observers did not believe that the North, which had suggested in July 1987 that both sides reduce their armed forces to below 100,000 by 1992, was

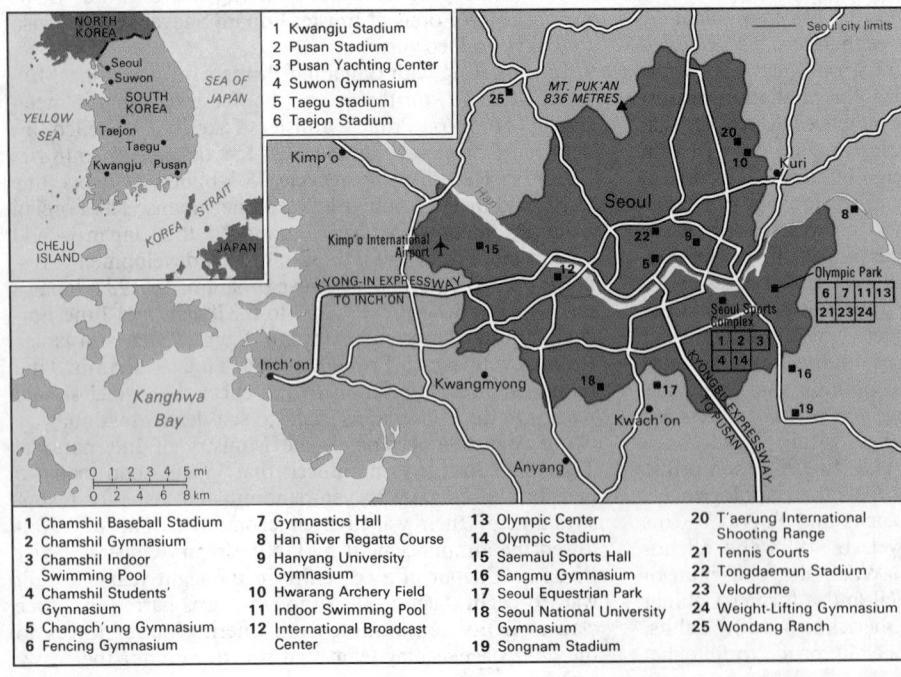

1 Kwangju Stadium			— Seoul city limits
2 Pusan Stadium			
3 Pusan Yachting Center			
4 Suwon Gymnasium			
5 Taegu Stadium			
6 Taejon Stadium			

1 Chamshil Baseball Stadium	7 Gymnastics Hall	13 Olympic Center	20 T'aerung International Shooting Range
2 Chamshil Gymnasium	8 Han River Regatta Course	14 Olympic Stadium	21 Tennis Courts
3 Chamshil Indoor Swimming Pool	9 Hanyang University Gymnasium	15 Saemaul Sports Hall	22 Tongdaemun Stadium
4 Chamshil Students' Gymnasium	10 Hwarang Archery Field	16 Sangmu Gymnasium	23 Velodrome
5 Changch'ung Gymnasium	11 Indoor Swimming Pool	17 Seoul Equestrian Park	24 Weight-Lifting Gymnasium
6 Fencing Gymnasium	12 International Broadcast Center	18 Seoul National University Gymnasium	25 Wondang Ranch
		19 Songnam Stadium	

sincerely proposing deescalation of tension. In the "war of the dams," the South began construction of its "Peace Dam" on the Han River north of Seoul and 20 km (12 mi) south of the border. It was designed to catch the flow from the North's "water bomb," a dam farther upstream that supposedly had the capability of flooding Seoul.

Republic of Korea (South Korea)

Area: 99,173 sq km (38,291 sq mi). Pop. (1988 est.): 42,593,-000. Cap.: Seoul. Monetary unit: won, with (Oct. 10, 1988) a free rate of 710 won to U.S. $1 (1,217 won = £1 sterling). Presidents in 1988, Chun Doo Hwan and, from February 25, Roh Tae Woo; prime ministers, Kim Chung Yul, Lee Hyun Jae from February 25, and, from December 5, Kang Young Hoon.

Pres. Roh Tae Woo, elected on Dec. 16, 1987, to succeed Chun Doo Hwan, was inaugurated on February 25. As he had gained only 35.9% of the vote and had won only because neither of his opponents, Kim Dae Jung (26.5%) and Kim Young Sam (27.5%), had been willing to drop out, he was unable to consider his victory an unconditional mandate. Yet he gained so much goodwill in the early part of the year that his Democratic Justice Party (DJP) was widely predicted to triumph at the April 26 National Assembly elections, especially as the two Kims continued to bicker. Instead of improving on the presidential election, however, the DJP won only 33.9% of the popular vote. Kim Dae Jung's Party for Peace and Democracy (PPD) won 19.3%, and Kim Young Sam's Reunification Democratic Party (RDP) won 23.8%. Unexpected was the 15.6% share for the New Democratic Republican Party (NDRP) led by Kim Jong Pil, who had won only 7.9% in the presidential election. After allocation of seats under a complicated mixed direct and proportional system, the DJP ended up with 125, far short of a majority in the 299-seat Assembly. The PPD had 70 seats and the RDP, though it had received a larger share of the popular vote, had 59. The NDRP gained 35 and others 10. Roh was unable to put together a coalition from his own party, independents, and the NDRP, so the opposition remained in control of the legislature.

Exercising this control, the opposition insisted on an inquiry into the Kwangju riots of 1980, which had led indirectly to the election of Chun Doo Hwan as president. It also forced an investigation of alleged criminal activi-

ties by Chun's family. His brother, Chun Kyong Hwan, was subsequently convicted of misappropriation of funds. Throughout November there were violent demonstrations calling for his arrest and Roh's resignation. On November 23 Chun made a televised address apologizing to the nation for abuses of power that had occurred during his term of office and then retired to a monastery. On December 5 Roh reshuffled his Cabinet, replacing many of the ministers associated with the previous regime. However, the opposition claimed the housecleaning had not gone far enough.

Commerce and industry early in 1988 were badly disrupted by labour disputes. The major industrial conglomerates were severely affected by stoppages that paralyzed industrial activity for a time. However, most strikes had run their course by midyear. Workers gained wage concessions, though fewer than they had demanded.

Despite the industrial unrest, the economy performed remarkably well. Exports remained high, and the trade surplus grew. This led to relaxation of policies dating from the days of foreign-exchange shortages. Overseas tourism was permitted, and restrictions were lifted on investment abroad. Trade with the Communist bloc was encouraged. By October two Soviet trade missions were in Seoul and trade with China grew rapidly, reaching $2 billion by the middle of the year.

Democratic People's Republic of Korea (North Korea)

Area: 122,370 sq km (47,250 sq mi). Pop. (1988 est.): 21,903,-000. Cap.: Pyongyang. Monetary unit: won, with (Oct. 10, 1988) a nominal exchange rate of 0.97 won to U.S. $1 (1.66 won = £1 sterling). General secretary of the Central Committee of the Workers' (Communist) Party of Korea and president in 1988, Marshal Kim Il Sung; chairmen of the Council of Ministers (premiers), Li Gun Mo and, from December 12, Yong Hyong Muk.

Though there was no unequivocal evidence of opposition to the regime of Pres. Kim Il Sung, who celebrated his 76th birthday with the customary extravagant adulation, there appeared to be dissension within the top ranks of the government. It was not known whether there was a power struggle for the succession or whether the abysmal performance of the economy was shaking up the regime. On February 12 Gen. O Guk Ryol, chief of staff of the

AFP PHOTO

Chief delegates Park Joon Kyu (left) of South Korea and Chon Kum Chol of North Korea extend their hands in a gesture of goodwill at Korea's preliminary South-North interparliamentary talks.

armed forces and considered the third most powerful man in the country, after Kim Il Sung and Kim Jong Il, was suddenly replaced by the much older Gen. Choe Kwang. In June and again in October there were reshuffles among government ministers. In December Yong Hyong Muk replaced Li Gun Mo as premier.

In June North Korea gave the two consortia of 140 international banks to which it owed $900 million some $5 million as a "goodwill payment." North Korea had defaulted on the loan in 1987, and the banks were moving toward a settlement that would involve writing off 70% of the debt in exchange for a commitment to pay the rest by 1991. Many creditors, however, complained that this was setting a dangerous precedent. In September North Korea announced a shift in economic emphasis from heavy industry to agriculture, though the government denied that there was a food shortage.   (ROBERT WOODROW)

MONGOLIA

A landlocked people's republic of eastern Asia, Mongolia occupies the geographic area known as Outer Mongolia. Area: 1,566,500 sq km (604,800 sq mi). Pop. (1988 est.): 2,041,000. Cap.: Ulan Bator. Monetary unit: tugrik, with (Oct. 10, 1988) a free rate of 3.35 tugriks to U.S. $1 (5.74 tugriks = £1 sterling). First secretary of the Mongolian People's Revolutionary (Communist) Party and chairman of the Presidium of the Great People's Hural (chief of state) in 1988, Zhambyn Batmunkh; chairman of the Council of Ministers (premier), Dumaagiyn Sodnom.

A far-reaching reorganization of the Mongolian government took place at the end of 1987 and the beginning of 1988, with the formation of new ministries including Light Industry, Agriculture and Food Industry (both headed by vice-premiers), Foreign Economic Relations, and Protection of Nature and the Environment. Supervision of a Soviet-style restructuring of economic management was undertaken by a new State Planning and Economic Committee chaired by another vice-premier.

In the pursuit of "renewal" and "openness," the Mongolian official media began a lively debate over the legacy of economic and social stagnation and bureaucracy left by the country's former leader, Yumzhagiyen Tsedenbal. There was concern about food supplies, since production was not keeping pace with population growth, and the government permitted an increase in private livestock holdings.

The status and prospects of the Asia-Pacific region were debated at the second Mongol-American Bilateral Conference, held in Ulan Bator in June. According to Robert Scalapino of the University of California, the leader of the U.S. delegation, some differences of opinion emerged at the conference, but this was to be expected. "We are just trying to get to know one another." (ALAN J. K. SANDERS)

TAIWAN

Taiwan, which consists of the island of Taiwan and surrounding islands off the coast of China, is the seat of the Republic of China (Nationalist China). Area: 36,000 sq km (13,900 sq mi), including the island of Taiwan and its 85 outlying islands, 21 in the Taiwan group and 64 in the Pescadores group. Pop. (1988 est.): 19,813,000. (Area and population figures exclude the Quemoy and Matsu groups, which are administered as an occupied part of Fujian [Fukien] Province.) Cap.: Taipei. Monetary unit: new Taiwan dollar, with (Oct. 10, 1988) an official rate of NT$28.72 to U.S. $1 (NT$49.18 = £1 sterling). Presidents in 1988, Chiang Ching-kuo and, from January 13, Lee Teng-hui; president of the Executive Yuan (premier), Yu Kuo-hwa.

The year 1988 was marked by extraordinary political change in Taiwan. The death of long-time leader Chiang

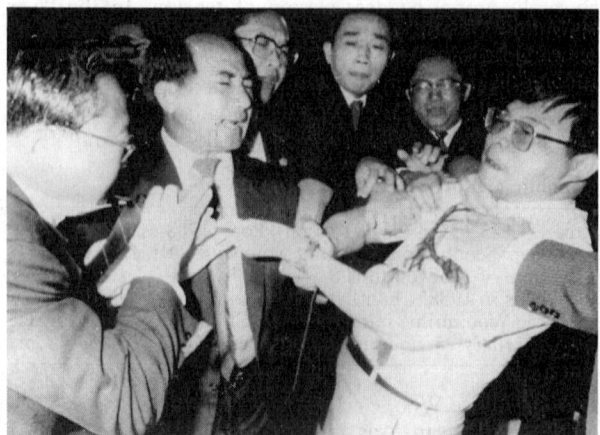

Chu Kao-cheng (right), a legislator from Taiwan's opposition Democratic Progressive Party whose frequent fights earned him the nickname "Rambo," grabs the tie of Chang Hung-hsieh, a Kuomintang (Nationalist Party) legislator, during a meeting of Taiwan's Legislative Yuan.
AP/WIDE WORLD

Ching-kuo (see OBITUARIES) on January 13 had been preceded by fears of a possible power struggle within the Kuomintang (KMT, Nationalist Party). The smooth transition, however, was remarkably uneventful. Vice-Pres. Lee Teng-hui (see BIOGRAPHIES) immediately assumed the presidency, in accord with constitutional law, and was elected chairman of the KMT at the party's 13th congress in July. It was the first time a native of Taiwan had held either office.

Moving with confidence, Lee named 12 newcomers to his Cabinet in July. Although some appointments appeared to be dictated by a desire to give conservatives a continuing voice in government, Lee had clearly favoured reform-minded politicians, many with advanced academic degrees.

During the last years of his life, Chiang had initiated extraordinary changes in Taiwan. Restrictions on political activity (including the sanctioning of a formal political opposition and an increasingly vibrant press) were largely removed. These trends also included radical changes in Taiwan's mainland policy. Although the KMT had repeatedly insisted it would not deal directly with the Communist Party of China (CPC), such a policy did not preclude a range of other dealings. Indirect trade, for example, was expected to exceed $2 billion in 1988; Taiwanese businessmen made direct but limited investments in China's coastal provinces, and citizens of both governments were involved in an ever wider range of contacts. Lee supported these initiatives and encouraged the heavy flow of visitors from Taiwan to the mainland. Since the change in the visitation policy was announced in late 1987, more than 300,000 citizens of Taiwan had visited the mainland.

At the same time, the KMT sought to maintain firm control over any dealings with the CPC, and it continued to reject all appeals from Beijing (Peking) for direct, official contact between the two ruling parties. During a mainland visit in October, senior KMT legislator Hu Ch'iu-yüan held unauthorized meetings with senior Chinese officials, which led to his immediate expulsion from the party. Although the KMT continued to explore other ways of dealing indirectly with Beijing, Lee clearly preferred that these measures be undertaken on a step-by-step basis.

The leadership in Taipei also reiterated its determination to maintain technologically advanced military forces. In December, after years of effort and the expenditure of more than $1 billion, Taiwan unveiled the prototype of its

indigenous defense fighter (IDF), the aircraft intended to replace aging U.S. planes in Taipei's defense arsenal. Plans to build approximately 250 of these aircraft and to upgrade Taiwan's naval capabilities suggested that there would be no weakening of the island's defenses.

Taiwan's long-term viability also continued to rest on its vibrant economy. Over the past several decades, Taiwan had sustained one of the highest economic growth rates in the world. Economic growth for the year was expected to exceed 7%, a decline from the double-digit growth in 1987 but still very robust. Per capita income was expected to surpass $6,000, bespeaking Taiwan's rapid advance to modernity. The steady increase in income, much of it a consequence of export-led growth, was manifested in foreign exchange reserves of approximately $75 billion, an amount exceeded only by Japan's reserves.

Taiwan was also under increasing pressure to reduce its huge trade advantage, especially with the U.S., its leading trading partner. As a result of a number of "buy America" missions and the stimulation of domestic consumption, Taiwan's trade surplus with the U.S. dropped from $19 billion in 1987 to $14 billion in 1988. However, continued pressures from the U.S. to further reduce the deficit and provisions of U.S. trade legislation that Taipei deemed protectionist clouded the longer-term economic picture.

(JONATHAN D. POLLACK)

South Asia

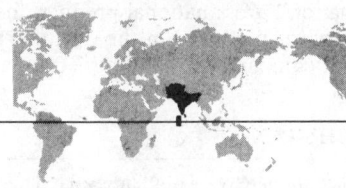

AFGHANISTAN

Afghanistan is a landlocked people's republic in central Asia. Area: 652,225 sq km (251,825 sq mi). Pop. (1988 est.): 14,-481,000 (excluding Afghan refugees estimated to number about 3.2 million in Pakistan and 2.1 million to 2.3 million to Iran). Cap.: Kabul. Monetary unit: afghani, with (Oct. 10, 1988) a free rate of 57.96 afghanis to U.S. $1 (99.25 afghanis = £1 sterling). General secretary of the People's Democratic (Communist) Party and president in 1988, Mohammad Najibullah; prime ministers, Sultan Ali Keshtmand and, from May 26, Mohammad Hassan Sharq.

The withdrawal of an estimated 115,000 Soviet troops, who had entered Afghanistan in December 1979 to prop up a faltering Communist regime, began on May 15, 1988. The United States, the Soviet Union, Pakistan, and Afghanistan had signed an agreement in Geneva on April 14 after years of painstaking efforts by the United Nations to end one of modern history's most bitter conflicts. Under the accord Afghanistan and Pakistan pledged not to intervene in each other's affairs and to work for the safe, voluntary return of refugees. Early in November, however, the Soviets halted the withdrawal of their troops and also began supplying the Afghan Army with powerful weapons. The Soviets said that their action was caused by increased guerrilla activity in Afghanistan, and they accused Pakistan of supporting the rebels.

The redesigned flag of Afghanistan does not have the red star that was present on its previous flag.

The government of Afghanistan revealed on December 3 that high-level negotiations between the Soviet Union and guerrilla leaders were beginning in Saudi Arabia. This was the first publicly announced top-level meeting between the two antagonists since the conflict began. Though it was not represented at the meeting or at a subsequent conference in Pakistan on December 17, the Afghan government was said to support the negotiations.

Even if the troop withdrawal resumed and was completed, it was not expected to bring peace to Afghanistan; as the Soviets left, the division between Afghan Marxists and Muslims became even sharper, and the fear of even bloodier fighting heightened. Leaders of the Pakistan-based Muslim insurgent groups vowed to continue fighting until they toppled the Marxist regime and proclaimed Afghanistan an Islamic republic. The efforts by the government either to form a coalition or to bring King Mohammad Zahir Shah back from his exile in Italy failed.

A UN report released in Geneva on September 22 said that the conflict had "produced unparalleled human sufferings and immeasurable social and economic havoc." The report stated that the war had reduced Afghanistan "to the status of one of the poorest, least developed countries." It also said that the fighting had caused an estimated one million deaths and that hundreds of thousands of widows, orphans, and disabled people would need sustained care for years to come.

The 169-page report cited extensive damage to agriculture, with the wheat-growing area reduced to 70% of its prewar size and one-fifth of the nation's livestock lost. It estimated that 2,000 schools and 130 health centres were damaged and that road transport infrastructure would require intensive repairs. The countryside, it said, was "littered with mines, unexploded bombs, hand grenades, shells and other ordnance [that would] pose a major threat to life and limb for years to come."

For the first time, the Soviet Union admitted that it had suffered almost 50,000 casualties, including 13,310 deaths, in the conflict. A top general said in Moscow on May 25 that 35,478 soldiers were wounded and 311 missing without a trace. Gen. Aleksey D. Lizichev said that the death and injury toll included casualties suffered from Dec. 27, 1979, until May 1, 1988. The figure was slightly higher than some Western analysts had estimated.

The UN Humanitarian and Economic Assistance Program for Afghanistan estimated that rebuilding the war-shattered nation would cost $1,160,000,000 in 1988–89. Another $839 million would be needed for 1990–93, bringing the total cost to more than $2 billion, the agency determined.

In the first phase of the program about one-third of the funds would be devoted to the relief needs and repatriation of the Afghan refugees. Of the remaining funds, about 65% was to go toward reviving agriculture. The remainder would be spent on rural health care facilities, education, basic agriculture industries, and clearing an estimated three million mines sown by the Soviet Army.

(DILIP GANGULY)

BANGLADESH

A republic and member of the Commonwealth, Bangladesh is in the northeastern part of the Indian subcontinent, on the Bay of Bengal. Area: 143,998 sq km (55,598 sq mi). Pop. (1988 est.): 107,756,000. Cap.: Dhaka. Monetary unit: taka, with (Oct. 10, 1988) a free rate of 31.07 taka to U.S. $1 (53.20 taka = £1 sterling). President in 1988, Lieut. Gen. Hossain Mohammad Ershad; prime ministers, Mizanur Rahman Chowdhury and, from March 27, Moudud Ahmed.

As a result of heavy monsoon rains, Bangladesh was battered by floods in 1988 that were the worst in seven decades. An estimated 2,000 people were killed, 30 million people were made homeless, and $2 billion worth of property and crops were lost. Floodwaters entered Dhaka, submerging several low-lying areas and spreading hardship and disease among the city's six million residents.

A seesaw political battle was waged during the year between the opposition and Pres. Hossain Mohammad Ershad's Jatiya Party. It climaxed in the March 3 elections to Parliament during which violence left at least 13 people dead. The balloting was boycotted by the main opposition parties, which contended that no elections could be conducted fairly with Ershad in power.

Beginning Nov. 10, 1987, the opposition sponsored a series of rallies and strikes in an effort to oust Ershad, who had seized power in a bloodless coup in 1982. Ershad went ahead with the elections, however, and his Jatiya Party won 250 of the seats. Twenty-five independent members were elected, and 23 seats were shared by small opposition parties. Opposition leaders claimed that only 4.8 million among 48 million eligible voters exercised their right to vote, but the government said that the turnout was more than 50%.

On March 27 Ershad announced a new 23-member Council of Ministers. He replaced Prime Minister Mizanur Rahman Chowdhury with Deputy Prime Minister Moudud Ahmed, a British-trained lawyer. Foreign Minister Humayun Rasheed Chowdhury retained his portfolio. On April 12 Ershad lifted the state of emergency that he had imposed on Nov. 27, 1987, to counter the opposition threat.

Ershad took steps to strengthen the Islamic orientation of his Muslim-dominated country. Ignoring protests from the opposition, women, and minority groups, Ershad on June 7 amended the country's constitution and made Islam the state religion. He justified this step by saying that it would give due recognition to Islam, the religion of about 85% of the 110 million inhabitants of Bangladesh.

Various women's groups challenged the validity of the amendment, claiming that it was aimed at curbing women's rights. Two women led the main opposition parties. Begum Khaleda Zia, wife of the slain president Zia ur-Rahman, headed the Bangladesh Nationalist Party, and Sheikh Hasina Wajed, eldest daughter of the country's first president, Mujibur Rahman, was the chief of the Awami League Party.

The Parliament in July enacted a law providing the death penalty for drug traffickers and manufacturers. People convicted of trafficking more than 25 g (0.883 oz) of dangerous drugs could be sentenced to death under the new law. Bangladesh was estimated to have nearly 1.2 million drug addicts.

The year was marked by escalating violence by Buddhist Chakma rebels in the Chittagong Hill Tracts, a 13,000-sq km (5,000-sq mi) rugged, hilly region bordering the Indian states of Tripura and Mizoram. The Chakmas had been fighting in the area for 12 years to gain autonomy. More than 200 people were killed in Chakma violence in 1988.

Bangladesh continued to depend on foreign loans and grants for development projects. Defense spending for the 1988–89 fiscal year, which began on July 1, was projected to rise to $298 million from $249 million in 1987–88. The nation's gross national product, the value of all goods and services produced in the country, rose just 2.6% in 1987–88, compared with the projected target of 5.1%.

(DILIP GANGULY)

BHUTAN

The monarchy of Bhutan is a landlocked state situated in the eastern Himalayas between China and India. Area: 47,000 sq km (18,150 sq mi). Pop. (1988 est.): 1,365,000. Cap.: Thimphu. Monetary unit: ngultrum, at par with the Indian rupee (which is also in use), with (Oct. 10, 1988) a free rate of 14.39 ngultrums to U.S. $1 (24.65 ngultrums = £1 sterling). Druk gyalpo (king) in 1988, Jigme Singye Wangchuk.

The tiny Himalayan kingdom closed its doors to individual tourists in 1988 after a government-appointed commission painted a grim picture of tourist-generated destruction. The commission said tourists were desecrating Buddhist monasteries, defiling sacred relics, stealing valuable artifacts, and corrupting the local population; more than 50 monasteries had been robbed since 1974, when foreign tourists were first allowed into the country. The ban did not apply to tourists in groups, but restrictions were imposed on their movements, and hotel prices were raised. The decision was expected to have an adverse effect on the country's foreign exchange earnings from tourism, which had amounted to about $2 million annually.

Relations with China improved during the year. In May the two countries agreed on guiding principles looking toward demarcation of their border and undertook not to use force to resolve the issue. The mountainous 500-km (310-mi) border between Bhutan and China had never been precisely defined. Talks had been held annually since 1984, with the next round expected in the spring of 1989. Relations with India remained warm, with New Delhi providing liberal manpower and financial assistance in setting up hydroelectric units and industries. Bhutan improved communications with the outside world by purchasing its first passenger jet airliner.   (DILIP GANGULY)

This article updates the *Micropædia* article BHUTAN.

AFP PHOTO

Bangladesh Pres. Hossain Mohammad Ershad votes during parliamentary elections in March. The main opposition parties had urged voters to boycott the election, claiming that any election conducted under Ershad's Jatiya Party would be fixed.

INDIA

A federal republic of southern Asia and member of the Commonwealth, India is situated on a peninsula extending into the Indian Ocean with the Arabian Sea to the west and the Bay of Bengal to the east. Area: 3,166,414 sq km (1,222,559 sq mi), including the Indian-administered portion of Jammu and Kashmir. Pop. (1988 est.): 801,806,000, including Indian-administered Jammu and Kashmir. Cap.: New Delhi. Monetary unit: Indian rupee, with (Oct. 10, 1988) a free rate of Rs 14.39 to U.S. $1 (Rs 24.65 = £1 sterling). President in 1988, Ramaswamy Venkataraman; prime minister, Rajiv Gandhi.

Domestic Affairs. In 1988, for the first time in several years, India had a good monsoon, which dispelled anxiety regarding food shortages. The political scene was marked by hectic moves by opposition parties to form an alternative to the Indian National Congress for the elections due in 1989. The efforts were spurred by the belief that Prime Minister Rajiv Gandhi might choose to hold the election on short notice. Leaders of seven parties—the Lok Dal, the Janata, the Assam Gana Parishad, the Congress (S), the Dravida Munnetra Kazhagam, the Telugu Desam, and the Jan Morcha—met in New Delhi in August to form the National Front, which announced a 71-point program. Four of these parties—the Janata, the Lok Dal, Congress (S), and the Jan Morcha—decided in July to unite into the Janata Dal under the chairmanship of Vishwanath Pratap Singh, who had held the portfolios of finance and defense in the Gandhi government. However, many followers of the new organization's constituent units seemed to favour the retention of their parties' identity. The two Communist parties and the Bharatiya Janata Party were lukewarm toward the new group.

There were changes of government in several states. In Tamil Nadu, following the death of Chief Minister M. G. Ramachandran in December 1987, there was a split in his party, the All-India Anna Dravida Munnetra Kazhagam. His widow, Janaki Ramachandran, formed a government in January, but within a month it was dismissed by the union (national) government, and the state was placed under president's rule. The governor had claimed that Tamil Nadu had become impossible to govern. It was announced that elections would be held in the state early in 1989. In January Rajasthan gained a new chief minister, S. C. Mathur, who took the place of Harideo Joshi. In February B. J. Azad became the chief minister of Bihar, and Arjun

Singh went to Madhya Pradesh as chief minister. Also in February, elections were held for the state assemblies of Tripura and Meghalaya. In the former the Congress Party formed a government led by S. R. Majumdar in alliance with the Tripura Upjati Juba Samiti. In Meghalaya P. A. Sangma headed the government. R. K. Jaichandra Singh became chief minister of Manipur in March. In June N. D. Tiwari took over as chief minister of Uttar Pradesh, and Sharad Pawar became the head of the Maharashtra government. In August the Nagaland government fell, and president's rule was proclaimed. The Karnataka chief minister, Ramakrishna Hegde, resigned in favour of S. R. Bommai after a report that telephones had been tapped.

In Punjab the terrorists continued their killing, but the police drive against them gathered strength. The authorities cleared terrorist hideouts in and around the Golden Temple in Amritsar. Nonetheless, four Sikh extremists in early November ordered ten people off a bus in northern Punjab and shot them to death. A solution was found for the discontent of Gurkhas in West Bengal after long-drawn-out negotiations among the union and West Bengal governments and the Gurkha National Liberation Front. A tripartite agreement, signed in August, provided for the establishment of a Gurkha Hill Council in the state. Peace returned to Tripura with an agreement signed with the TNV (Tripura National Volunteers). During the year, pro-Pakistan elements caused riots in Jammu and Kashmir. The Indian government sent troops to Andhra Pradesh in December after more than 25 people were killed in rioting set off by the killing of a legislator.

Late in October thousands of farmers arrived in New Delhi on tractor-driven wagons to stage a protest rally. Believing that agriculture should receive a larger share of the nation's development efforts, they demanded higher prices for their grains and sugarcane, longer hours of electricity for farms, and the writing off of bank loans. Prime Minister Gandhi said that he was willing to listen to the demands but "not under pressure," and after three days the protesters were escorted out of town by the police.

The Union Cabinet underwent two major reshuffles during the year. Victories of opposition parties in by-elections to the House of the People (Lok Sabha) in June (especially that of Vishwanath Pratap Singh) set off a bid by the Congress Party to reorganize itself. Several veteran politicians who had quit or been expelled from the party were readmitted, among them Pranab Mukerji, Nandini

AP/WIDE WORLD

Sikh militants surrender to Indian police after having been barricaded within the Golden Temple in Amritsar. The government had conducted a ten-day blockade of the shrine in an attempt to clear out the extremists.

Satpathy, and Chandrajit Yadav. The government invited opposition parties for discussions on the reform of the electoral system. The executive of the Congress Party in October put forward a recommendation for lowering the voting age from 21 to 18.

The Supreme Court upheld the conviction of Satwant Singh and Kehar Singh for the murder of Indira Gandhi in 1984 but acquitted Balbir Singh. On August 21 Bihar and other eastern states were rocked by the country's worst earthquake in 50 years, which killed at least 450 people. In July 103 persons died when a train fell into a lake in Kerala. Two air crashes on the same day, October 19, in Gujarat and Assam, killed 164 people. The Madhya Pradesh High Court in April ordered Union Carbide to pay Rs 2.5 billion as interim damages to the victims of the Bhopal gas tragedy of 1984. The government expelled Pakistan's military attaché and another Pakistani official in December on charges of spying.

The Navy acquired its first nuclear-powered submarine, the Soviet-built INS *Chakra,* in February. Orders for West German HDW submarines were canceled. A remote-sensing satellite, IRS-IA, was launched from the Soviet Union, and the multiple satellite Insat I-C was placed in orbit in July from Kourou in French Guiana. However, an attempt to launch an augmented satellite launch vehicle, ASLV-D2, from Sriharikota failed. The first Jaguar aircraft to be built in India were introduced into the Indian Air Force. The Army and Air Force gained new chiefs of staff—Gen. V. N. Sharma (succeeding Gen. K. Sundarji) and Air Chief Marshal S. K. Mehra (succeeding Air Chief Marshal D. A. La Fontaine). The death in Pakistan in January of Khan Abdul Ghaffar Khan (*see* OBITUARIES), a major figure of the Indian freedom movement, was widely mourned.

The Economy. Prices during the year increased approximately 6.8%; the wholesale price index on October 23 stood at 439.1, compared with 411 on Sept. 5, 1987. A major achievement during the first half of the year was the avoidance of famine in spite of widespread drought, thanks to an efficient public distribution system. The good rains that followed raised hopes of a record harvest in spite of floods in large areas.

The union budget estimates for 1988–89, presented on February 29, provided Rs 287,150,000,000 for development outlay and Rs 130 billion for defense. Revenue and capital receipts were placed at Rs 427,980,000,000 and Rs 232,780,000,000, respectively, and revenue and capital expenditure at Rs 526.4 billion and Rs 209.2 billion, leaving an overall deficit of Rs 74,840,000,000. New levies that would bring in Rs 6,140,000,000 were proposed. In February proposals were separately announced to increase the income from the railways and telecommunications by Rs 6,220,000,000 and Rs 5 billion, respectively.

The World Bank in April announced credits of $3 billion for 11 projects. The Aid India Consortium in June announced concessional aid of $6.3 billion for the next 12 months. A major hydroelectric project was commissioned at Salal in the state of Jammu and Kashmir in February. In October the Planning Commission set a 6% growth target for the eighth five-year plan.

Foreign Relations. The Indian Peace-Keeping Force continued its operations in Sri Lanka and was subjected to repeated attacks by Tamil activists belonging to the group called Liberation Tigers of Tamil Eelam. A large number of Sri Lankan Tamil refugees in India were sent back to the island. Early in November India sent troops to the Maldives to help put down an attempt by some 150 armed men to overthrow the government of that island nation.

Prime Minister Gandhi in January attended a meeting of the five-continent initiative on disarmament in Stockholm. He also addressed the UN Special Session on Disarmament in June and presented a plan to achieve a world free of nuclear weapons by 2010. Other nations he visited during the year included Japan, Vietnam, Syria, West Germany, Hungary, Jordan, Yugoslavia, Spain, Turkey, and Bhutan. Pres. Ramaswamy Venkataraman went to the Pakistan capital in August to attend the funeral of Pres. Mohammad Zia-ul-Haq. Soviet leader Mikhail Gorbachev visited New Delhi in November to take part in the closing ceremony of the yearlong Soviet festival in India and to receive the Indira Gandhi Prize. He and Prime Minister Gandhi signed five agreements, including a Soviet credit of Rs 53 billion. Among other notable visitors to India were Pres. J. R. Jayawardene of Sri Lanka, Premier Li Gun Mo of North Korea, Prime Minister Lee Kwan Yew of Singapore, and Pres. Mohammad Najibullah of Afghanistan.

(H. Y. SHARADA PRASAD)

MALDIVES

A republic and member of the Commonwealth in the Indian Ocean, the Maldives consists of about 2,000 small islands southwest of the southern tip of India. Area: 298 sq km (115 sq mi). Pop. (1988 est.): 202,000. Cap.: Male. Monetary unit: rufiyaa, with (Oct. 10, 1988) a free rate of 10.08 rufiyaa to U.S. $1 (17.27 rufiyaa = £1 sterling). President in 1988, Maumoon Abdul Gayoom.

Maumoon Abdul Gayoom was returned for a third term as president of Maldives in a referendum on Sept. 23, 1988. He had been selected as the sole candidate by the country's Parliament in August. At the beginning of November, India responded to an urgent request for help when Sri Lankan mercenaries invaded the islands in an attempted

AP/WIDE WORLD

Security forces in Maldives take into custody a mercenary soldier involved in an unsuccessful coup attempt. On November 6 a boatload of Sri Lankan mercenaries had attacked the capital city of Male, but Indian commandos regained control for the president the same day.

coup. Indian troops regained control for President Gayoom and later rounded up the fleeing mercenaries, who were identified as members of a Tamil guerrilla force. At year's end it was not clear who had hired the fighters.

Since 1985 Maldives had enacted a series of economic adjustment measures designed to encourage "market forces." These included the introduction of credit controls and exchange rate depreciations, which between them had led to a drop in excessive bank credit and a reduction of imports over exports, thus substantially lowering the current account deficit. Fishing, which now accounted for 25% of gross domestic product and employed 50% of the labour force, had been undergoing modernization.

According to recent scientific reports on the "greenhouse effect," Maldives was one of six countries that could disappear during the next century if the predicted warming of the Earth caused the Indian Ocean to rise.

(GUY ARNOLD)

This article updates the *Macropædia* article INDIAN OCEAN ISLANDS: *Maldives*.

NEPAL

A constitutional monarchy, Nepal is a landlocked country in the Himalayas between India and the Tibetan Autonomous Region of China. Area: 147,181 sq km (56,827 sq mi). Pop. (1988 est.): 18,004,000. Cap.: Kathmandu. Monetary unit: Nepalese rupee, with (Oct. 10, 1988) a free rate of NRs 22.26 to U.S. $1 (NRs 38.12 = £1 sterling). King, Birendra Bir Bikram Shah Deva; prime minister, Marich Man Singh Shrestha.

A massive earthquake hit Nepal in August, killing more than 700 people by official count; however, witnesses and news reports from the affected areas put the death toll above 1,000. The tremor, registering 6.5 on the Richter scale, caused extensive damage to homes and road communications in the mountainous country and killed or injured a large number of cattle. The devastation would have been severe had the quake occurred in the northern region close to the Himalayas. The epicentre was in the south, however, close to Nepal's border with India.

Two more tragic events took place during the year in the Himalayan kingdom. In March a stampede during a football (soccer) match in Kathmandu left approximately 80 fans dead and more than 100 seriously injured. Panicked by a sudden hailstorm, the crowd surged toward locked doors at the National Stadium. Most of those killed were crushed or trampled. In September a flash flood in the village of Darbang in western Nepal killed at least 87 people and destroyed at least 15 buildings.

On the political front, Prime Minister Marich Man Singh Shrestha in March expanded his Council of Ministers from 17 to 33. Six ministers were dropped and 22 new faces were inducted in an effort to infuse new blood into Nepali politics.

(DILIP GANGULY)

PAKISTAN

A federal republic, Pakistan is in the northwestern part of the Indian subcontinent, on the Arabian Sea. Area: 796,095 sq km (307,374 sq mi), excluding the 83,716-sq km Pakistani-controlled section of Jammu and Kashmir. Pop. (1988 est., including some 3 million Afghan refugees and 3 million residents of Pakistani-controlled Jammu and Kashmir): 109,434,000. Cap.: Islamabad. Monetary unit: Pakistan rupee, with (Oct. 10, 1988) a free rate of PRs 18.10 to U.S. $1 (PRs 31 = £1 sterling). Presidents in 1988, Gen. Mohammad Zia-ul-Haq and, from August 17 (acting to December 12), Ghulam Ishaq Khan; prime ministers, Mohammad Khan Junejo to May 29, Zia from June 9 to August 17, and, from December 2, Benazir Bhutto.

Pakistan in 1988 lost its longest-serving president and ended the year with the first woman prime minister to hold office in a Muslim country. Mohammad Zia-ul-Haq (*see* OBITUARIES), who had ruled the country with an iron hand since 1977, died in a plane crash on August 17. The U.S.-built C-130 transport plane crashed shortly after takeoff from Bahawalpur, 530 km (330 mi) south of Islamabad. All 30 people on board, including the U.S. ambassador, Arnold Raphel, and five Pakistani Army generals, were killed. The cause of the crash remained uncertain. Pakistani officials believed the evidence pointed to sabotage, probably Soviet-backed, while U.S. investigators were inclined to blame mechanical failure.

Contrary to fears that Zia's death would trigger a power struggle within the Army, there was a smooth transfer of power as set forth in the constitution. Ghulam Ishaq Khan, the 73-year-old chairman of the Senate, became acting president and pledged that a parliamentary election would

AFP PHOTO

Pakistan's Benazir Bhutto has her thumb marked to signify that she had voted in National Assembly elections in November. Her Pakistan People's Party won the largest block of seats, and in December Bhutto became the first woman prime minister of a Muslim country.

be held as scheduled on November 16. Earlier, on May 29, Zia had abruptly dismissed the government of Prime Minister Mohammad Khan Junejo for "incompetence, corruption and lack of attention to the Muslim faith" and on June 9 had formed a caretaker Cabinet, headed by himself.

Zia had wanted the election to be partyless, but on October 2 the Supreme Court ruled that Pakistan's constitution provided for elections open to all political parties and not merely to individuals. The principal contenders were the conservative Islamic Democratic Alliance and the Pakistan People's Party. The latter was headed by Benazir Bhutto, daughter of Prime Minister Zulfikar Ali Bhutto, who had been overthrown by Zia in 1977 and executed two years later.

In the election the PPP won the largest block of seats, 105 out of 237. (For tabulated results, see *Political Parties,* above.) After two weeks of political maneuvering, on December 1 President Ishaq Khan named Bhutto as prime minister, and she was sworn in the following day. On December 12, as required by the constitution, Bhutto's government received a vote of confidence, with independents and minor parties joining the PPP to give her a 148–55 majority. On the same day, Ishaq Khan was elected to a five-year term as president by an electoral college composed of both houses of Parliament and the four provincial assemblies.

A presidential decree on June 15 confirmed the introduction of the Shari'ah, or Islamic legal code, and repealed all existing secular civil law. The move was criticized by women's organizations, but it was believed the Bhutto government would move slowly in this area.

Zia's death had no apparent effect on U.S. relations with Islamabad. The U.S. informed the Soviet Union and India on August 22 that its support for Pakistan's security remained strong. Despite the signing in April of the Geneva agreement for the phased withdrawal of Soviet troops from Afghanistan, relations between Islamabad and Kabul remained strained, with each side accusing the other of violating the accords.

The year witnessed the worst ethnic violence in two years in southern Pakistan, where riots in September between the native Sindhis and Muslim immigrants from India known as *muhajirun* left at least 175 dead by official count (hospitals reported 217). In July–September Pakistan was hit by monsoon-triggered floods, which killed at least 31 people and left one million homeless.

Pakistan's economy registered moderate growth in 1988. Gross domestic product rose by 5.8%, a shade better than the 1987 rate of 5.7%. The government reported a 7% inflation rate, but independent economists put it close to 17%. The foreign debt stood at $12,440,000,000, up from $12 billion in 1987.   (DILIP GANGULY)

SRI LANKA

A republic and member of the Commonwealth, Sri Lanka occupies an island in the Indian Ocean off the southeast coast of peninsular India. Area: 65,610 sq km (25,332 sq mi). Pop. (1988 est.): 16,606,000. Legislative and judicial cap., Sri Jayawardenapura; administrative cap., Colombo. Monetary unit: Sri Lanka rupee, with (Oct. 10, 1988) a free rate of SL Rs 32.50 to U.S. $1 (SL Rs 55.65 = £1 sterling). President in 1988, Junius Richard Jayawardene; prime minister, Ranasingne Premadasa.

Pres. Junius Jayawardene announced on Sept. 16, 1988, that he was stepping down after 11 years in office. He named Prime Minister Ranasingne Premadasa to be his successor as candidate for the United National Party in the

next presidential election. The opposition Freedom Party nominated as its candidate former prime minister Sirimavo Bandaranaike.

The election took place on December 20, and Premadasa was declared the winner with 50.4% of the vote to 44.9% for Banadaranaike and 4.5% for the candidate of a leftist alliance. Bandaranaike charged that there had been widespread fraud by the ruling party and the military during the election and said that she would challenge the result in the Sri Lankan Supreme Court. Some 55% of the electorate went to the polls, and only scattered incidents of violence were reported.

Peace continued to elude Sri Lanka, where a five-year-old Tamil separatist war showed no sign of abatement in 1988. In addition, the People's Liberation Front, an organization of radical Sinhalese who were opposed to the Tamils, emerged and helped turn the once idyllic country into a nation where political assassinations, ethnic riots, and intragroup bloodshed occurred with near clockwise regularity.

The Tamils, who made up about 18% of Sri Lanka's approximately 16 million people, were fighting for an independent homeland in the northern and eastern regions of the island. They alleged that they were discriminated against by the Sinhalese, who made up about 74% of the population and controlled the government and the military. The peace plan signed by Sri Lanka and India in July 1987 to end the Tamil ethnic strife crumbled in 1988 with the most important of the Tamil militant groups, the Liberation Tigers of Tamil Eelam, fighting an estimated 50,000 Indian troops. The troops were mobilized after the Tamil Tigers, as the group was popularly known, refused to surrender arms and abide by the accord, which offered limited autonomy to the Tamils. India was involved in the affair because of its own 60 million politically powerful Tamils.

Elections for Parliament were scheduled to take place on Feb. 15, 1989. In December a Tamil party that had not participated in politics in more than ten years announced that it would take part in the elections. This decision by the Tamil United Liberation Front would give Tamil voters a mainstream alternative to the militant Tamil parties.

The Sri Lankan economy showed no improvement in 1988. The country lost $200 million in tourism revenue, $250 million in foreign investment, and another $250 million in agriculture and fishing industries as compared with 1987. The government said that it would need $3.3 billion over the next three years for reconstruction and for its youth employment program.   (DILIP GANGULY)

Southeast Asia

SOUTHEAST ASIAN AFFAIRS

The person who stayed most consistently in the forefront of regional news in 1988 was the unpredictable Prince Norodom Sihanouk, former king and later head of state of Kampuchea, who had not been in a position of real power since 1970. His country, occupied since 1979 by Vietnamese troops (120,000 by U.S. count at the beginning of 1988), remained the dominant focus of diplomatic effort as the major world powers and members of the Association

Vietnamese Lieut. Gen. Le Ngoc Hien waves to Kampucheans during the pullout of Vietnamese soldiers. After ten years of occupation, Vietnam announced in May that it planned to withdraw 50,000 troops from Kampuchea by the end of the year and all remaining troops by early 1990.
AP/WIDE WORLD

of Southeast Asian Nations (ASEAN) struggled to find an acceptable formula to end the civil war. At the end of January, after an inconclusive meeting near Paris with Hun Sen, prime minister of the Vietnamese-supported government, Sihanouk announced his "irrevocable" decision to resign as president of the Coalition Government of Democratic Kampuchea, the grouping of three anti-Vietnamese resistance movements: the Khmer Rouge, the Khmer People's National Liberation Front, and Sihanouk's own military forces led by his son, Prince Norodom Rannariddh.

As the year progressed, it became clear that the U.S. was emerging as Sihanouk's chief supplier of military aid in place of China, which continued to support the Khmer Rouge with arms and money. The Soviet Union, meanwhile, by backing Vietnam, indirectly propped up the Hun Sen government in Phnom Penh. But with détente actively pursued by Soviet leader Mikhail Gorbachev, Moscow grew impatient with Vietnam's intransigence over a settlement. Japan for the first time took an active role, urging the creation of an international peacekeeping force proposed by Sihanouk and expressing willingness to help supervise free elections.

By the end of February Sihanouk had withdrawn his resignation on the grounds that the Vietnamese refused to negotiate with him. He resigned again in July, just before an informal meeting held in Bogor, Indon., on Kampuchea, during which he was "visiting" President Suharto. Present at this meeting were Hun Sen and leaders of the three resistance groups, as well as Vietnamese Foreign Minister Nguyen Co Thach and representatives of Laos and the ASEAN countries (Indonesia, the Philippines, Thailand, Malaysia, Singapore, and Brunei). No breakthrough was achieved, however. In November Hun Sen and Sihanouk again held discussions in France, again inconclusively. On June 30 the Vietnamese high command left Kampuchea as part of a promised withdrawal of 50,000 troops in 1988. At the same time Vietnam revealed that 55,000 of its soldiers had died in action in Kampuchea since 1977.

In the Siberian city of Krasnoyarsk on September 16, Gorbachev made a watershed speech that had a strong bearing on Southeast Asian affairs. He proposed a number of measures to lower military tension in the area, including a mutually balanced reduction of naval forces on the part of the U.S. and the Soviet Union, and called for an international conference to declare the Indian Ocean a zone of peace. Four months earlier, Thai Foreign Minister Siddhi Savetsila had said the Soviet Union had approached him about joining ASEAN's "dialogue partners," the U.S., the European Communities, Japan, Canada, Australia, and New Zealand. In particular, Gorbachev offered to abandon Soviet naval support facilities at Cam Ranh Bay in Vietnam (Moscow consistently denied it was a "base") if the U.S. would simultaneously give up two bases in the Philippines, Subic Bay (Navy) and Clark Air Base (Air Force).

The suggestion was not taken seriously in Washington. The U.S. at the time was in the final stages of protracted negotiations with the Philippine government of Corazon Aquino over the future of those military installations. Philippine Foreign Secretary Raul Manglapus had been pushing for annual "rent" (actually an aid package) of $1.2 billion a year until 1991, when a longer-term agreement was to be signed. U.S. Secretary of State George Shultz warned that the Philippines was "pricing itself out of the market." For a time it appeared that Subic Bay and Clark might be abandoned, but an agreement was signed at the end of October providing for $481 million a year in economic and military aid.

The insurgency situation in the Philippines stabilized. In January armed forces commander Gen. Fidel Ramos, the key figure in the 1986 overthrow of then president Ferdinand Marcos, resigned and joined the Cabinet as defense secretary. Though the guerrillas remained powerful, the advantage appeared to be moving toward the military. This was due in part to a rapidly improving economy, though the gains tended to benefit mainly urban dwellers. On June 10 President Aquino signed the long-debated Comprehensive Agrarian Reform Program, which provided for redistribution of cultivated farmland. It was widely criticized, however, for leaving loopholes that rich landowners could exploit. In New York on October 21, Marcos and his wife, Imelda, were indicted on charges of having used $103 million from the Philippine treasury to purchase real estate in the U.S. for themselves.

While concern about the Philippines was lessening, it was mounting in long-quiescent Burma, which for much of the year dominated regional and international news.

First reports of serious unrest against the 26-year regime of Gen U Ne Win emerged in March. On July 23 Ne Win resigned as chairman of the ruling party and was replaced by the hard-liner Sein Lwin, but in less than three weeks, during which time as many as 3,000 civilians may have been killed, Sein Lwin resigned; he was replaced by the moderate Attorney General Maung Maung on August 19. The revolt continued, however. The Army seized power in a coup on September 18, and Gen. Saw Maung took command under martial law, abolishing the state apparatus. It was widely believed that Ne Win was wielding behind-the-scenes authority.

In March the Spratly Islands, a cluster of widely spaced reefs and atolls in the South China Sea, were the cause of heightened tensions. The uninhabited islands had long been claimed, in whole or in part, by Vietnam, China, Taiwan, the Philippines, and Malaysia. In a clash between Chinese and Vietnamese naval personnel, 3 Vietnamese died and more than 70 were missing. The following month relations between Malaysia and the Philippines were strained over the arrest at sea in the Spratlys of Filipino fishermen in waters claimed by Malaysia. The situation was defused in August when President Aquino telephoned Malaysian Prime Minister Datuk Seri Mahathir bin Mohamad.

Several Southeast Asian leaders were replaced during the year. In March Vietnam's premier, Pham Hung, died and was succeeded briefly by Vice-Premier Vo Van Kiet and then in June by Do Muoi. After an election on July 24, Thailand's Prime Minister Prem Tinsulanond declined overtures to draft him for another term; following much negotiation, Chatichai Choonhavan (*see* BIOGRAPHIES), leader of the Chart Thai party, was installed as prime minister. Powerful army chief Gen. Chaovalit Yongchaiyuth did not, as had been widely expected, move into the political scene. In February Chaovalit had personally negotiated a settlement to a tense situation on the border with Laos. There had been fighting over a disputed border demarcation, but a truce was called and both sides withdrew. President Suharto of Indonesia was reelected unopposed on March 10 to a fifth five-year term by the 1,000-member People's Consultative Assembly. Indonesia was active in diplomacy in the South Pacific.

Both Singapore and Malaysia were criticized by international human rights groups for jailing without trial citizens who were opposed to the government. In April eight of nine detainees who had been released in Singapore were rearrested after issuing a statement saying that they had been both physically and psychologically abused. The next month a former solicitor general was detained, and immediately afterward a U.S. diplomat was ordered to leave for allegedly interfering in domestic affairs, prompting a retaliatory expulsion by Washington. In the general election on September 3, the ruling People's Action Party won 63% of the vote and 80 out of 81 seats. In Malaysia the top judge was dismissed after he complained that politicians were interfering with the judiciary. In October two judges who supported him in a ruling from the bench were also dismissed.

Free-market economies in the region prospered. Thailand and Singapore achieved high growth on top of impressive performances the year before, and Malaysia and the Philippines staged remarkable comebacks after recession. Indonesia did less well but, given low oil prices, showed good resilience. Burma and the Indochina states were economically stagnant. At the ASEAN foreign ministers' conference in Bangkok, Thailand, in July, the Philippines requested "polysectoral" assistance to enable it to reestablish a healthy economy. (ROBERT WOODROW)

BRUNEI

The sultanate of Brunei is located on the northern coast of the island of Borneo, on the South China Sea. Area: 5,765 sq km (2,226 sq mi). Pop. (1988 est.): 250,000. Cap.: Bandar Seri Begawan. Monetary unit: Brunei dollar, with (Oct. 10, 1988) a free rate of Br$2.04 to U.S. $1 (Br$3.49 = £1 sterling). Sultan and prime minister in 1988, Sir Muda Hassanal Bolkiah Mu'izzadin Waddaulah.

Sultan Hassanal Bolkiah underlined his determination not to allow party politics when his government dissolved the reformist Brunei National Democratic Party (BNDP) in January 1988. The authorities reportedly arrested the party's president, Latif Hamid, and its secretary-general, Latif Chuchu, under the sultanate's emergency powers, which permit indefinite detention without trial; the arrests were not confirmed by the government. The BNDP called for the sultan to step down as prime minister, the lifting of the emergency, and the holding of general elections.

On National Day on February 23, the government released four political prisoners, one of whom had been in jail since 1962. The four were members of the banned Brunei People's Party, which staged a failed revolt in 1962. Singapore businessman Khoo Teck Puat, the partner of the royal family in the National Bank of Brunei, sold his Australian hotel chain to help pay off his $225 million debt with the bank, which had been closed after a dispute involving fraud charges.

Brunei experienced a drop in oil revenues resulting from the decline in world prices, but the sultanate was able to fall back on its enormous foreign reserves.

(ZOHER F. ABDOOLCARIM)

This article updates the *Macropædia* article EAST INDIES: *Brunei*.

BURMA

Burma is a people's republic of Southeast Asia with coastlines on the Bay of Bengal and the Andaman Sea. Area: 676,577 sq km (261,228 sq mi). Pop. (1988 est.): 39,952,000. Cap.: Rangoon. Monetary unit: kyat, with (Oct. 10, 1988) a free rate of 6.58 kyats to U.S. $1 (11.28 kyats = £1 sterling). Chairmen of the Burma Socialist Program Party in 1988, U Ne Win to July 25, U Sein Lwin from July 26, and, from August 19 to September 18, Maung Maung; chairman of the National Unity Party from September 29, U Tha Kyaw; presidents, U San Yu to July 25, U Sein Lwin to August 12, Maung Maung from August 19, and, from September 18, Gen. Saw Maung; prime ministers, U Maung Maung Kha to July 26, U Tun Tin to September 18, and, from September 21, Gen. Saw Maung.

Ne Win, who had wielded authoritarian powers over Burma for 26 years, resigned as chairman of the ruling Burma Socialist Program Party (BSPP) on July 23, 1988, after waves of antigovernment demonstrations had led to violent deaths, mass arrests, and closure of the universities. The 77-year-old leader cited old age and indirect responsibility for bloody rioting in March and June. His resignation triggered a power struggle and more street violence by students and others who wanted a return to democracy.

Ne Win was replaced by Sein Lwin, a former military officer accused of having harshly repressed dissent. A series of protests led to Sein Lwin's resignation on August 12. His replacement on August 19 by Maung Maung, a Western-educated lawyer and Burma's first civilian leader since 1962, failed to end the street violence, and on September 18 Saw Maung (*see* BIOGRAPHIES), a four-star general and close associate of Ne Win, toppled the civilian government. Saw Maung cracked down on looters and imposed

Thousands of protesters jam the streets of Rangoon to demand the removal of Burma's new leader, U Sein Lwin. Sein Lwin, who had replaced long-standing leader Ne Win—himself forced to resign after waves of antigovernment riots—was pressured to leave office after a surge of violent antigovernment demonstrations.
ALAIN EVRARD

a strict nighttime curfew in Rangoon. By official count at least 450 people were killed in security force actions and street violence after September 18. Diplomatic sources in Rangoon put the death toll at more than a thousand.

Saw Maung promised elections as soon as peace was restored. On September 10 Article 11 of the constitution, making Burma a one-party state, was dropped. The opposition remained fragmented in 14 parties, but efforts were being made to bring the smaller parties into the National League for Democracy, headed by two former military officers, Aung Gyi and Tin Oo, and Aung San Suu Kyi, daughter of the revolutionary hero Aung San. On September 26 the name of the BSPP was changed to the National Unity Party.

A Japan-led economic boycott by the international community exacerbated Burma's near economic ruin. The political turmoil had crippled an economy already on a rapid downward spiral. Factories halted production, transport was paralyzed, and foreign currency reserves were virtually nil, while foreign debt climbed to more than $4 billion. Burma was ranked as the tenth poorest nation in the world, with a per capita income of $200.   (DILIP GANGULY)

INDONESIA

A republic of Southeast Asia, Indonesia consists of the major islands of Sumatra, Java, Kalimantan (Indonesian Borneo), Celebes, and Irian Jaya (West New Guinea) and approximately 3,000 smaller islands and islets. Area: 1,919,443 sq km (741,101 sq mi). Pop. (1988 est.): 175,904,000. (Area and population figures include East [former Portuguese] Timor.) Cap.: Jakarta. Monetary unit: rupiah, with (Oct. 10, 1988) a free rate of 1,698 rupiah to U.S. $1 (2,907 rupiah = £1 sterling). President in 1988, Suharto.

The early months of 1988 were dominated by the March elections for president and vice-president. Suharto, the sole presidential candidate, was elected to his fifth consecutive five-year term by the 1,000-member People's Consultative Assembly (MPR). The nominees for vice-president included Suharto's personal choice, Sudharmono, a Suharto loyalist and chairman of the dominant Golkar ("functional groups"), the country's most powerful political force, and Jailani Naro, leader of the United Development Party (PPP). The nomination of Naro by the PPP shattered the established tradition of consensus politics in the assembly.

Naro reportedly had some backing from the Indonesian Armed Forces (ABRI). Some elements in ABRI were said to be unhappy with Sudharmono, a retired lieutenant general, because he had reduced the Army's influence in Golkar; there were also unsubstantiated charges that he had had ties to the Communists. Moments after Suharto's election, Brig. Gen. Ibrahim Saleh leaped to the podium to defend the candidacy of Naro. This violation of traditional Indonesian political protocol expressed the unhappiness felt by certain elements within the military over the nomination of Sudharmono. Although Naro had no hope of winning the election, he waited until the last minute to withdraw from the vice-presidential race, thus paving the way for Sudharmono to fill the post vacated by Umar Wirhadikusuma. Gen. Try Sutrisno became commander in chief of ABRI, replacing Gen. Benny Murdani, who became defense minister.

Senior government officials sounded warnings about the possibility of a comeback by the banned Indonesian Communist Party (PKI). At the same time, Beijing (Peking), which had once backed the PKI, seemed to move closer to Jakarta. Chinese Deputy Foreign Minister Liu Shuqing (Liu Shu-ching) visited Indonesia and called for a normalization of bilateral relations, which had been suspended following the bloody abortive Communist coup in 1965. Suharto again declared that improved relations depended in part on China's noninterference in other countries' affairs, but he did not reiterate his demand that Beijing apologize for its involvement in the 1965 coup. There were also moves to allow greater access to the largely isolated province of East Timor, a former Portuguese colony that Indonesia had annexed in 1976.

Indonesia remained Asia's biggest foreign debtor—its total debt was expected to reach $51 billion by March 1989. A large proportion of Indonesia's debt was yen-denominated. To help ease the burden, Japan's Export-Import Bank lent Indonesia U.S. $200 million. The government expected foreign aid to reach $4.3 billion in 1988.

The economy performed better than expected in 1987, with a 3.5% growth in the gross domestic product (GDP), fueled especially by a dramatic increase in manufactured exports. GDP growth was expected to reach 3.8% in 1988. The private sector was given a boost when the government announced a wide range of reforms in its continuing

At a meeting in Bogor, Indonesia, Vietnamese Foreign Minister Nguyen Co Thach talks to members of the media following informal talks with all four Kampuchean factions and representatives from Laos and the Association of Southeast Asian Nations.
AP/WIDE WORLD

efforts to restructure the economy. It abolished a host of import monopolies and licensing requirements, introduced tax incentives in export and tourism industries, and relaxed limits on foreign ownership of joint ventures. Along with the devaluation of the rupiah in 1986, the ongoing liberalization of the economy boosted the nation's non-oil exports to approximately $900 million a month. After three years of decline, foreign investment in 1987 rose 77% over the level of the previous year to $1,460,000,000.

(ZOHER F. ABDOOLCARIM)

This article updates the *Macropædia* article EAST INDIES: *Indonesia.*

KAMPUCHEA

A people's republic of Southeast Asia, Kampuchea occupies the southwestern part of the Indochinese Peninsula, on the Gulf of Thailand. Area: 181,035 sq km (69,898 sq mi). Pop. (1988 est.): 7,876,000. Cap.: Phnom Penh. Monetary unit: riel, with (Oct. 10, 1988) a free rate of 100 riels to U.S. $1 (171.25 riels = £1 sterling). Secretary-general of the People's Revolutionary (Communist) Party of Kampuchea and chairman of the Council of State (president) in 1988, Heng Samrin; chairman of the Council of Ministers (prime minister), Hun Sen.

In 1988 the focus of attention in Kampuchea switched from the battlefield to diplomacy. In January Norodom Sihanouk, who had resigned from his position as leader of the UN-recognized resistance coalition, met Hun Sen, prime minister of the People's Republic of Kampuchea (PRK), for the second time in two months. The dialogue, which took place in Paris, broke off when they failed to agree on conditions for a future government, but in July, when Sihanouk resigned from the coalition presidency, the two scheduled further meetings.

Also in July there was an unprecedented get-together of all the Kampuchean factions and their allies in Indonesia. Hun Sen led a PRK delegation that talked to Sihanouk's group (headed by his son Norodom Rannariddh) and its two allies, the Khmer People's National Liberation Front (KPNLF) and Democratic Kampuchea (better known as the Khmer Rouge). PRK allies Vietnam and Laos sent delegations, and the Association of Southeast Asian Nations (ASEAN), which backed the resistance, sent representatives, the most prominent of whom was Indonesian Foreign Minister Ali Alatas. The talks were cordial but made no material progress beyond the establishment of working groups to continue discussions.

The international atmosphere favoured moves toward resolution of the Kampuchean situation as the Soviet Union increased its efforts to improve relations with ASEAN and China. Beijing (Peking) had told Moscow that better ties depended in large measure on the Soviets pressuring Vietnam to withdraw its Kampuchean occupation force. Whether because of such pressure or not, Hanoi speeded up its pullout, which had been scheduled for the end of 1990. A partial pullout of some 20,000 men in December 1987 was pronounced genuine by U.S. and Thai officials. That left 120,000 (by U.S. calculations) or 90,000–100,000 (according to veiled references from Vietnam). In May Hanoi announced that it would withdraw half of those troops by the end of the year and the rest by early 1990. In a publicized ceremony, it withdrew all its high-ranking officers in June, leaving its forces under Kampuchean command. The prospect of a Vietnamese withdrawal without a political settlement raised fears of an escalation in the conflict and spurred the search for a negotiated solution.

Meanwhile, the fighting continued, particularly along the Thai border in the northwestern and northern provinces of Battambang, Siem Reap, Oddar Meanchey, and Preah Vihear and around the Great Lake. The main resistance force continued to be the Khmer Rouge, whose army, estimated at 35,000, was reportedly trying to take advantage of the Vietnamese withdrawal to reestablish its superiority in the north and west. The KPNLF, headed nominally by Son Sann, still suffered from a leadership split and did little fighting. Sihanouk's smaller army had a better reputation for efficiency.

Splits in the coalition widened. Sihanouk increased his complaints of atrocities by the Khmer Rouge. Human rights violations by Khmer Rouge officials were documented by outside observers, and UN officials cut food aid to some remote Khmer Rouge border camps because they had not been allowed to verify that their supplies were being used for civilians only.

The PRK, in charge of a war-fatigued economy and facing the usual problems of drought and flooding, made moves to show its independence. Reports said that Vietnamese advisers to the ruling party's Central Committee had been sent home. In August the department that oversaw matters of cooperation with socialist countries was dissolved. At the same time, a Cabinet reshuffle moved Communications Minister Tea Banh, who was not one of the group of Kampucheans trained in Vietnam, to the im-

portant defense portfolio and elevated him to deputy prime minister. Ke Kimyan was replaced as army chief of staff, indicating dissatisfaction with the conduct of the fighting.

(JUDITH L. CLARKE)

This article updates the *Macropædia* article Mainland SOUTH-EAST ASIA: *Kampuchea.*

LAOS

A landlocked people's republic, Laos is in the northern part of the Indochinese Peninsula. Area: 236,800 sq km (91,400 sq mi). Pop. (1988 est.): 3,850,000. Cap.: Vientiane. Monetary unit: kip, with (Oct. 10, 1988) a par value of 350 kip to U.S. $1 (free rate of 599.38 kip = £1 sterling). President in 1988 (interim), Phoumi Vongvichit; chairman of the Council of Ministers (prime minister), Kaysone Phomvihan.

Although 1988 opened with a border conflict with Thailand, Laos made marked progress in diplomatic, economic, and political affairs. The clash was the second between the neighbours since the Communist government came to power in Laos in 1975. This time it began over a logging dispute on land claimed by both sides; hostilities broke out in December 1987 and continued until a cease-fire was signed in Bangkok, Thailand, on February 19.

Once the fighting was over, relations with Thailand's military improved dramatically. Chatichai Choonhavan, who became Thai prime minister in August, backed more pragmatic policies toward Indochina. Ties with China also improved. A visit by Laotian Deputy Foreign Minister Khamphai Boupha to Beijing (Peking) at the end of 1987 led to the exchange of ambassadors at midyear, upgrading relations from chargé d'affaires level. There was also talk of opening the Laotian-Chinese border, closed since the 1979 Sino-Vietnamese war. Relations with the U.S. were less consistent. The U.S. government said the Laotian government was involved in drug trafficking, but later U.S. officials resumed a long-delayed search for the remains of servicemen missing in the Vietnam war.

Laos's closest allies were still Kampuchea and Vietnam, but Vientiane showed more independence from them. Some 25,000 of the estimated 40,000–50,000 Vietnamese troops stationed in Laos withdrew during the year. One factor was an assurance from China that it would stop aiding the small but active resistance. Laos also began to go its own way in dealings with Indochina's common ally, the Soviet Union. A visit to Moscow by Prime Minister Kaysone Phomvihan in October 1987 led to a strengthening of economic ties in 1988.

Laos relaxed its rules on production and trade, allowing a greater role for private enterprise. This resulted in a stronger currency, which did away with the entrenched black market, and greater availability of consumer goods. A foreign investment code was planned. The landlocked country still depended mainly on Thailand as a conduit for foreign trade, despite efforts to upgrade roads to Vietnam. The Thai government planned a new border crossing to add to the three already open. Figures published in 1988 showed bilateral trade between Thailand and Laos to have risen from $22 million in 1985 to $46 million in 1987, though it was still in Thailand's favour.

Though still debating a constitution, Laos went ahead with its first elections since 1975. In June Laotians voted for 113 new district assemblies. Candidates were screened, but there were nearly twice as many as there were seats, giving voters a choice. Further elections were planned for provinces and prefectures. (JUDITH L. CLARKE)

This article updates the *Macropædia* article Mainland SOUTH-EAST ASIA: *Laos.*

MALAYSIA

A federal constitutional monarchy of Southeast Asia and member of the Commonwealth, Malaysia consists of the former Federation of Malaya at the southern end of the Malay Peninsula (excluding Singapore) and Sabah and Sarawak on the northern part of the island of Borneo. Area: 330,434 sq km (127,581 sq mi). Pop. (1988 est.): 16,965,000. Cap.: Kuala Lumpur. Monetary unit: ringgit, with (Oct. 10, 1988) a free rate of 2.69 ringgits to U.S. $1 (4.60 ringgits = £1 sterling). Paramount ruler in 1988, with the title of *yang di-pertuan agong,* Tuanku Mahmood Iskandar ibni al-Marhum Sultan Ismail; prime minister, Datuk Seri Mahathir bin Mohamad.

The politically dominant United Malays National Organization (UMNO) was declared an illegal society by the Kuala Lumpur High Court in February 1988. The ruling stemmed from a suit filed by a group of UMNO dissidents challenging the results of party elections in April 1987. Prime Minister Mahathir bin Mohamad, UMNO's incumbent president, had narrowly defeated the then trade and industry minister Razaleigh Hamzah in divisive polling by some 1,500 delegates at the party's triennial congress. The dissidents charged that the voting was invalid because some UMNO branches had not been registered. Under the Societies Act, an entire organization could be illegal if a branch was unregistered. Mahathir then launched a new political party called UMNO Baru (New UMNO). By October, 16 parliamentarians elected on an UMNO ticket had declared themselves independents. They included Razaleigh and the influential former deputy prime minister Musa Hitam.

The government continued to attack the judiciary for allegedly abusing its powers. The feud reached a peak when Lord President Salleh Abas, the head of the Supreme Court, was dismissed by the *yang di-pertuan agong* (paramount ruler), King Mahmood Iskandar, for "misbehaviour." Salleh had been charged with making public statements criticizing the government and for acting improperly by writing letters to the king and to the country's eight other hereditary state rulers in which he defended the judiciary against the government's attacks. Salleh contended, however, that the government moved against him because he was to preside over an appeal to the Supreme Court by the UMNO dissidents, a claim the government denied. A six-man tribunal, consisting of four judges from Malaysia and one each from Singapore and Sri Lanka, heard Salleh's case and recommended he be dismissed. Salleh refused to give evidence at the hearings.

In October the king dismissed another two Supreme Court judges. The two were among five who had ordered that the Salleh tribunal be restrained from submitting any recommendation to the king. The five had been charged with sitting without the approval of the acting lord president, Hamid Omar, who headed the Salleh tribunal. Two had been charged with not hearing scheduled cases elsewhere in the country in favour of the Salleh appeal in Kuala Lumpur the same day. The five contended, however, that they had heard the appeal "in the interest of justice" and "as a matter of urgency" before the tribunal submitted its recommendation. Another tribunal heard their case and recommended that the two judges who were assigned the cases outside Kuala Lumpur be dismissed.

Parliamentary opposition leader Lim Kit Siang remained in detention under the Internal Security Act (ISA), which permitted indefinite detention without trial. Lim had been arrested in October 1987, along with other oppositionists and social activists, for allegedly inciting racial tension.

The political strife was offset somewhat by good news on the economic front. The economy was expected to

grow by 7%, compared with 4.7% in 1987. The growth was fueled by the boom in manufacturing exports, which were forecast to increase 20% from 1987 to some $9.2 billion. Export earnings were also assisted by steady demand and strong prices for primary commodities such as rubber, tin, palm oil, and timber. Both inflation and unemployment, however, were also expected to increase, to 3% and 9.6%, respectively. Moreover, capital flight had reportedly nearly doubled from an average of $1.2 billion a year in 1976–85 to $2.3 billion in 1987. The capital flight was said to be caused in part by ethnic Chinese investors' concern over the New Economic Policy (NEP). The NEP, enacted in 1970, sought to increase ownership of the economy by indigenous Malaysians, mostly Malays, to 30% by 1990.

(ZOHER F. ABDOOLCARIM)

This article updates the *Macropædia* article Mainland SOUTH-EAST ASIA: *Malaysia*.

PHILIPPINES

Situated in the western Pacific Ocean off the southeast coast of Asia, the republic of the Philippines consists of an archipelago of about 7,100 islands. Area: 300,000 sq km (115,800 sq mi). Pop (1988 est.): 58,723,000. Cap.: Manila. Monetary unit: Philippine peso, with (Oct. 10, 1988) a free rate of 20.32 pesos to U.S. $1 (34.80 pesos = £1 sterling). President in 1988, Corazon Aquino.

The first free local elections since 1971 were held Jan. 18, 1988, to fill 16,113 provincial and municipal posts. While 905 persons had died in 1971 election violence, approximately 100 were killed, including 39 candidates, as the 1988 elections took the Philippines another step toward the restoration of democracy. Candidates backed by Pres. Corazon C. Aquino won a majority of contests.

Vice-Pres. Salvador H. Laurel broke politically with Aquino. His influence had waned since they came into office in 1986. In a public letter on August 13, he charged that under her presidency "the nation has gone from bad to worse," with corruption, deteriorating law and order, and unchecked Communist insurgency. On August 27 Laurel joined with former defense minister Juan Ponce Enrile to launch the Union for National Action, but this new opposition party failed to rally much support.

On June 10 Aquino signed into law the Comprehensive Agrarian Reform Program, which set limits on the amount of agricultural land an individual could hold. Excess land would be acquired by the government over a ten-year period, with compensation paid from foreign aid and illegal assets seized from cronies of former president Ferdinand E. Marcos. This land would be distributed to landless labourers on 30-year payment terms. Critics claimed, however, that it would be too easy for landowners to evade the law.

Aquino refused permission for Marcos, living in exile in Hawaii, to go home for the funeral of his mother on the grounds that his presence might cause public disturbances. Marcos's associates denied reports that he had offered to return $5 billion acquired while he was president if he was allowed to live in the Philippines.

Defense Secretary Rafael Ileto resigned January 21. He said that he had not been able to reorganize the armed forces because of "divisive elements and controversial issues." He had taken the job in November 1986, Ileto said, because the Communist insurgency had "grown alarmingly strong because of a regime that had not addressed the welfare of its people." Aquino named the armed forces chief of staff, Gen. Fidel V. Ramos, to succeed him.

In a state of the nation address on July 25, Aquino said 1988 "may be remembered as the year the insurgency was broken." Her statement was partly based on the capture in February and March of eight senior leaders of the Communists' New People's Army. The March arrests yielded information on an extensive network run by the Communist Party of the Philippines that used foreign bank accounts to buy weapons abroad and trained recruits in the use of those weapons. Despite government actions and vigilante organizations' successes against the insurgents, however, a military report prepared in May said that, on the whole, "the enemy gained the tactical initiative in major engagements." The Communists continued to use terror. In Leyte Province, where some 400 persons were missing, authorities found mass graves of those believed killed for refusing to help the insurgents. Several international human rights groups accused both the government and the Communists of atrocities.

Typhoon Ruby struck the nation in October. Some 500 persons were killed, and crop damage totaled $45 million.

AP/WIDE WORLD

Demonstrators, protesting the government's support of continued U.S. military bases in the Philippines, burn an effigy of Philippine Pres. Corazon Aquino wrapped in an American flag.

After months of negotiations, the Philippines and the U.S. signed an agreement on October 17 that would permit the U.S to continue operating Clark Air Base and Subic Bay Naval Base through September 1991. The U.S. agreed to provide $962 million in military and economic aid and to allow aid to be used to help pay the Philippines' foreign debt. The Philippines had sought $2.4 billion in aid, and the agreement was controversial in Manila. Some 42% of the government's budget went to pay debts. Despite overall economic growth of nearly 6% a year, the World Bank found that about 30 million people in the country lived in "absolute poverty." (HENRY S. BRADSHER)

SINGAPORE

Singapore, a republic of Southeast Asia and member of the Commonwealth, occupies a group of islands, the largest of which is Singapore, at the southern extremity of the Malay Peninsula. Area: 622 sq km (240 sq mi). Pop. (1988 est.): 2,641,000. Monetary unit: Singapore dollar, with (Oct. 10, 1988) a free rate of S$2.04 to U.S. $1 (S$3.49 = £1 sterling). President in 1988, Wee Kim Wee; prime minister, Lee Kuan Yew.

Prime Minister Lee Kuan Yew's People's Action Party (PAP) was returned with a near sweep of Parliament in the September 1988 general election. The PAP secured 80 of the 81 seats. The sole opposition winner was Chiam See Tong, who retained a seat won in 1984. The PAP won 63.2% of the 1,342,435 valid votes cast, slightly down from its 64.8% share in the previous general election. The government said Lee would remain prime minister for up to two years before handing the post to First Deputy Prime Minister Goh Chok Tong.

The PAP's campaign platform stressed its record in making Singapore prosperous, backing its claims with impressive figures: 11% economic growth in the first half of 1988 and a projected 9% for the full year. Although the outcome was lopsided, the opposition performed creditably. Much attention centred on Francis Seow, a former solicitor general and former president of the Law Society. Earlier in the year he had been detained for 72 days for allegedly conspiring with U.S. diplomats to build a strong opposition in the republic. One of the diplomats, based in Singapore, was asked to leave.

The general election saw the introduction of the "group representation constituency" (GRC) system. Under this scheme, candidates in 13 of the 55 wards stood in teams of three, at least one of whom had to be from a minority race. The government said this would ensure minority representation in Parliament, but opposition parties attacked it as an attempt to further dilute their already thin electoral ranks. Under Singapore law, the opposition was entitled to a minimum of three parliamentary seats, filled by the closest losers. The two available seats were filled by Seow and one of his running mates. (Nonconstituency MPs may participate in debates but cannot vote on important motions.)

The government continued its crackdown on Singaporeans allegedly involved in a Marxist conspiracy to subvert the state. Of the 22 people arrested in mid-1987 under the Internal Security Act, permitting indefinite detention without trial, all but one had been released by the end of 1987. In April nine of those released issued a statement claiming they had been physically and psychologically abused. Eight were rearrested (the other was overseas). Seven Singaporeans linked to the alleged conspiracy were still in detention by October. (ZOHER F. ABDOOLCARIM)

This article updates the *Macropædia* article Mainland SOUTH-EAST ASIA: *Singapore.*

THAILAND

Thailand is a constitutional monarchy in Southeast Asia, on the Andaman Sea and the Gulf of Thailand. Area: 513,115 sq km (198,115 sq mi). Pop. (1988 est.): 54,862,000. Cap.: Bangkok. Monetary unit: baht, with (Oct. 10, 1988) a free rate of 25.11 baht to U.S. $1 (43 baht = £1 sterling). King, Bhumibol Adulyadej; prime ministers in 1988, Gen. Prem Tinsulanond and, from August 4, Chatichai Choonhavan.

On July 2 King Bhumibol Adulyadej became the country's longest-reigning monarch, having completed 42 years and 23 days on the throne, one day longer than his grandfather King Chulalongkorn. The royal family, government, and people joined in three days of festivities in Bangkok.

On April 29 Prime Minister Prem Tinsulanond dissolved Parliament and called a general election for July 24. A split in the Democrat Party, biggest in the ruling coalition, had led to the resignation of the party's 16 ministers, and a motion of no-confidence in Prem's government had been scheduled for early May. After the election the leading parties were Chart Thai, with 87 of the 357 seats; the Social Action Party, 54; and the Democrats, 48. Prem, prime minister since 1980, had been expected to continue in office, but when the three biggest parties and two others formed a coalition (a sixth joined later) and asked him to become prime minister, he declined. Chart Thai leader Chatichai Choonhavan, formerly one of Prem's deputies, became prime minister, the first elected member of Parliament to hold the post in 12 years.

Declaring that he had shed the playboy life-style for which he had been known, Chatichai instituted policies that would encourage trade and industry with the emphasis on private investment. He clashed with Prem's economic think tank, the National Economic and Social Development Board, and succeeded in reducing its influence. The Eastern Seaboard project, a plan originally made in the late 1970s to upgrade facilities on the coast southeast of Bangkok, was taken up again. Chatichai's government came into conflict with the Army and the popular Bangkok governor, Chamlong Srimuang, over key appointments. The removal of an official in the government's Mass Communications Organization caused controversy. In October the government weathered its first major challenge, a no-

AFP PHOTO

Thailand's newly elected prime minister, Chatichai Choonhaven (left), shakes hands with Vietnam's foreign minister, Nguyen Co Thach, before their meeting in Bangkok. At the meeting they agreed to increase trade between their nations.

confidence vote against a deputy interior minister accused of abusing his position.

Prem had continued to be successful in curbing the role of the Army. Army commander in chief Gen. Chaovalit Yongchaiyuth, widely known to be politically ambitious, offered his resignation on May 2 in keeping with a pledge to retire at 55. Prem, however, rejected the resignation. As an active officer, Chaovalit was not able to run for election or hold office in government. At the annual military reshuffle in September, Chaovalit retained his post.

A border conflict with northern neighbour Laos broke out in December 1987 and ended with a cease-fire signed by the army chiefs of both sides in February. The dispute began over logging rights and became a tussle for 70 sq km (27 sq mi) of territory ill defined by frontier treaties. The armed forces were reported to have boosted their weapons supply with a $76 million deal for equipment from China.

The economy was buoyant. In October the year's economic growth was estimated at 10%. Exports rose; garments were the top earner, rice second, and gems third. Tourism grew. The small Bangkok stock exchange was little affected by the 1987 stock market crash and rose spectacularly. By September it had gone up 280% compared with January, but then it fell sharply.

Relations with Laos improved after the cease-fire. Chatichai's government encouraged joint ventures in Laos and prepared to open more border crossings. Relations with the U.S.S.R. became more friendly after a visit by Prem to Moscow in May. There was also a slight softening of Thailand's stance toward Kampuchea, and the government supported and participated in an informal conference with the Kampuchean factions and other Southeast Asian nations in Indonesia in July.   (JUDITH L. CLARKE)

This article updates the *Macropædia* article Mainland SOUTH-EAST ASIA: *Thailand.*

VIETNAM

The socialist republic of Vietnam occupies the eastern part of the Indochinese Peninsula in Southeast Asia and is bounded on the south and east by the South China Sea. Area: 331,653 sq km (128,052 sq mi). Pop. (1988 est.): 63,807,000. Cap.: Hanoi. Monetary unit: dong, with (Oct. 10, 1988) a par value of 368 dong to U.S. $1 (free rate of 630.20 dong = £1 sterling). General secretary of the Communist Party in 1988, Nguyen Van Linh; chairman of the State Council (president), Vo Chi Cong; chairmen of the Council of Ministers (premiers), Pham Hung to March 10, Vo Van Kiet (acting) from March 10, and, from June 22, Do Muoi.

Vietnam suffered deepening economic problems in 1988. The 1987 winter rice harvest had been 1.6 million tons short as a result of drought and pest infestations. In April the government said that eight million people in the north were seriously lacking food and three million faced famine, and it called for international relief. Small amounts of emergency aid came from the West and the Soviet Union, but officially sanctioned trade and aid from the West, Japan, and the Association of Southeast Asian Nations (ASEAN) remained embargoed because Vietnam still had troops in Kampuchea. A Communist Party resolution in April tried to boost food production by reducing the size of collective and state farms and allowing farmers to sell more produce privately. The June harvest was good, but typhoons in October damaged the next crop.

An 80% devaluation of the dong in December 1987 had failed to halt inflation. In March the issue of new high-denomination bank notes spurred fears of another devaluation, and people rushed to buy U.S. dollars and gold. The black-market value of the dong plunged from 400 to the U.S. dollar to 1,000 within weeks and continued to drop. In November Vice-Premier Vo Van Kiet estimated the year's inflation rate at 800%. In October Premier Do Muoi had announced a budget deficit of 100 billion dong. Hanoi applied to the International Monetary Fund for a new loan of $250 million, promising to repay the $90 million loan it had defaulted on in 1985.

An official report in July noted unemployment at almost 20%. It also said there were 100,000 Vietnamese working abroad. Early in the year the government had increased its 1988 quota for overseas workers from 40,000 to 60,000. Nearly one-third were in the Soviet Union and most of the rest in Eastern Europe. Part of the workers' wages went to pay off Vietnam's debts.

A foreign investment code in December 1987 sanctioned the establishment of export enterprises with up to 100% foreign ownership, joint ventures with up to 99% foreign ownership, and individual contracts with foreigners. It guaranteed that assets would not be nationalized. Many countries showed interest, but the trade embargo prevented most signed deals. In March a new law forced enterprises to make profits and gave them more freedom to plan and produce goods.

The purge of corrupt officials continued. Some 1,500 former officials of the defeated South Vietnam government were released between September 1987 and February 1988, and Interior Minister Mai Chi Tho said in July that only 190 were left in detention.

AFP PHOTO
Vietnamese prisoners at the Nam Ha reeducation camp gather their belongings before being released. The men, former officials of the South Vietnamese government, had been in detention since the fall of Saigon in 1975.

Kampuchea dominated Hanoi's external relations. A pullout of 20,000 of the Vietnamese troops there in late 1987 was judged genuine by the U.S. and Thailand. The U.S. estimate of the total number at the beginning of the year was 120,000. In May Hanoi announced plans to withdraw 50,000 more by the end of the year, and in June it said 3,000 had gone, along with the Vietnamese high command. Departing commanders said they had lost 25,000 men in Kampuchea since 1979, many of them to malaria. Vietnam joined informal talks with the four Kampuchean factions and representatives from Laos and the ASEAN countries in Indonesia in July, but no final agreement was signed. At the UN in November, 122 countries voted in favour of the annual resolution calling for Vietnam's withdrawal. At midyear Vietnam was reported to have pulled out 20,000–25,000 of its troops from Laos. Demobilized soldiers were presenting a growing social problem.

Vietnam clashed with China over the Spratly Islands in the South China Sea. A battle in March left two Vietnamese ships sunk, a third damaged, 3 Vietnamese dead, and more than 70 missing. Demands for talks by Hanoi were rejected by Beijing (Peking), but Vietnam began talks with the Philippines, which also claimed part of the Spratlys.

Relations with the U.S. improved. Early in the year Pres. Ronald Reagan announced that private humanitarian aid would be encouraged despite the embargo, and visits were made by charitable groups. Vietnam handed back some 130 sets of remains that could be those of U.S. servicemen killed during the Vietnam war. A disagreement at the end of July held up joint excavations in search of the 1,757 still listed as missing, but they went ahead in September and October. Vietnam also agreed in principle to allow 11,000 former South Vietnam officials and their families to go to America.

Ties with the U.S.S.R., which supplied Vietnam with some $3 billion in aid annually, became more strained. China asked the Soviets to pressure Vietnam to withdraw from Kampuchea. Although Moscow insisted it could not, there were clearly differences with Hanoi over Kampuchea. There were complaints that Soviet aid was inefficient, and Moscow upset Hanoi when it took a neutral stand on the Spratly Islands dispute.

Refugees continued to pour out of Vietnam. In Hong Kong a public outcry led to a new policy to send them back, and negotiations with Hanoi began in August. After a London meeting in October, Vietnam agreed to take back those who would go voluntarily, and Britain agreed to provide financing. A visit to Hanoi by Malaysian Deputy Prime Minister Ghafar Baba in August opened similar negotiations with Malaysia.

Premier Pham Hung (see OBITUARIES) died of a heart attack on March 10. Vice-Premier Vo Van Kiet became acting premier, dropping his post as head of the State Planning Commission. The Communist Party chose another candidate for the premiership, Do Muoi, as better suited to deal with the economic crisis, but some members of the National Assembly insisted that Vo Van Kiet also be nominated. In Vietnam's first vote for a premier, the National Assembly chose Do Muoi. On September 30 former president and party leader Truong Chinh (see OBITUARIES) died after a fall at his home.

In June the Vatican canonized 117 Catholics martyred in Vietnam between 1740 and 1883. Hanoi urged the country's several million Catholics not to celebrate.

(JUDITH L. CLARKE)

This article updates the Macropædia article Mainland SOUTH-EAST ASIA: Vietnam.

Western Europe

WESTERN EUROPEAN AFFAIRS

For a year that began with an unprecedented internal crisis facing the European Communities (EC, comprising the European Economic Community [EEC], the European Coal and Steel Community [ECSC], and Euratom), 1988 finished on a remarkably optimistic note concerning the prospects for wider European unity. It was a year that saw major progress toward the completion of the single European market, involving the eventual removal of all barriers to free trade and the free movement of capital and people by the end of 1992. At the same time, there was controversy over the extent to which national governments should cede political power and sovereignty to EC decision-making institutions. There was also a growing debate on the speed and direction of future moves toward European monetary union. A number of Western European countries indicated their interest in applying for full membership in the EC. The Community concluded a framework cooperation agreement with the countries of the Council for Mutual Economic Assistance (Comecon), as well as agreements with a number of individual Eastern European states.

At the start of 1988 there was considerable speculation about whether a long-standing and bitter dispute over the EC's internal budget and spending policies might lead to political disarray and paralysis. In December 1987 a meeting of EC heads of government had broken up in bitter recrimination when it failed to agree on measures to bring the Community's soaring budget deficit under control. The West German government, which, under the EC system of rotating presidencies, took over responsibility for Community affairs at the start of 1988, called a further emergency summit in Brussels in mid-February. After more than two days of intense bargaining, the 12 agreed that by 1992 EC budget revenue would be boosted by more than 30% and farm spending brought down to less than 60% of the budget. The agreement cleared the way for a major legislative push to accelerate the single market. About one-third of some 300 pieces of legislation removing obstacles to free trade and the free movement of capital had been passed by mid-1988.

In their efforts to bring EC spending under better discipline, Community agriculture ministers extended the freeze on guaranteed prices paid to farmers for most produce at a series of meetings in the spring. The Community's finances were helped by external developments. The higher exchange rate for the dollar and—later in the summer—the serious drought that hit the U.S. pushed up world food prices, thus reducing the de facto subsidies paid on the exports of EC agricultural produce. By the end of 1988, the European Commission in Brussels, which was responsible for the day-to-day management of EC affairs, reported an effective saving of between $3 billion and $4 billion. This was in spite of a decision, also taken at the February European summit, to double expenditure on aid to the poorer regions and communities in the EC over the period to 1993, in order to help them deal with the problems of economic adjustment that were expected to follow completion of the single market.

In April the European Commission released a special

Leaders of the 12-nation European Communities, including (left to right) British Prime Minister Margaret Thatcher, French Pres. François Mitterrand, EC head Jacques Delors, and West German Chancellor Helmut Kohl, met at an emergency session in Brussels in February.
AP/WIDE WORLD

study on the economic benefits of the single market, which showed that creation of a market of more than 300 million people could be expected to boost growth and job creation, both directly and indirectly. The experts predicted that the improved competitiveness of EC industry would reduce inflation and provide a margin of maneuver for EC governments to expand output, so that a total of some seven million new jobs might be created over the coming four years or so.

In general 1988 was a year of remarkable continued economic growth in Western Europe, although unemployment persisted at worryingly high levels, and there were fears for the world economic outlook because of persisting imbalances in international trade and the U.S. budget. Nevertheless, there was concern that the single market might bring adverse social effects. For this reason, the Commission and the Greek government, which assumed the EC presidency in July, decided to give priority to policies that would create a European "social space." There were some doubts about what such a social space would mean in practice, although the Commission was eager to legislate to help the more vulnerable social groups and regions of the EC, to raise minimum health and safety standards for workers in the EC, to create a new form of European corporation that would give workers a bigger say in the affairs of their companies, and to cooperate with the trade unions in determining broader economic and social objectives.

This approach proved highly controversial with some centre-right EC governments, notably the British. The issue of EC social legislation was one of British Prime Minister Margaret Thatcher's targets in a major speech in Bruges, Belgium, during September, when she assailed the concept of a supranational European state. The notion of a full-scale European federal economic and political union had been hinted at in speeches by other EC leaders. In June, in an address to the directly elected European Parliament in Strasbourg, France, the president of the Commission, Jacques Delors, predicted that by the mid-1990s the EC would develop "an embryo European government." Thatcher referred to these possible developments as "a nightmare" that would create intolerable "bureaucratic centralism" in the EC and made it clear that she would not support moves to create a European central bank and a single EC currency.

At their meeting in Hannover, West Germany, in June, the Community heads of government turned these issues over to a special committee of experts, which was to report back at the summit planned for Madrid in June 1989.

Thatcher's onslaught on the goals of supranational union was in turn attacked by many of her fellow EC leaders in speeches made prior to the EC summit in Rhodes, Greece, in December. At Rhodes the heads of government reiterated their commitment to a unitary Europe, although several serious issues remained unresolved. Among others that surfaced at the summit were the question of border controls on people (which Thatcher considered vital in the fight against terrorism and crime) and a proposed Community-wide tax on investment capital.

Although there was a fairly smooth transition to the new system of majority voting in the EC Council of Ministers, outlined in the Single European Act (SEA), which went into effect in 1987, the European Parliament continued to press for greater policy-making powers. It showed a willingness to use the modest extra power allocated to it under the SEA when it blocked an EC trade agreement with Israel to protest Israeli brutality against Palestinian demonstrators in the occupied territories. In October most parties in the European Parliament declared themselves in favour of even faster and more radical moves toward European union, including Community control of foreign and security policy. Together with the wider debate about democracy and a "social Europe," these issues were expected to feature prominently in the direct elections to the European Parliament to be held in June 1989.

Negotiations continued between the EC and the European Free Trade Association to extend many of the benefits of the EC single market to the six EFTA countries. However, fears that the removal of internal EC frontier controls might be accompanied by greater de facto external trade protection led at least two EFTA governments, Austria and Norway, to indicate informally that they were considering making formal application for Community membership. The response of the EC countries to these developments and similar expressions of interest from Malta and Cyprus was unenthusiastic. The 12 pointed out that their first priority was to complete the single market. The Community's major trading partners, notably the U.S. and Japan, also expressed concern that the EC single market might lead

The Far Right in Western Europe

BY ANDREW GAMBLE

The Far Right in Western Europe has received much more attention than its size and performance in elections would seem to deserve. One reason is that whenever a party of the Far Right enjoys a sudden spurt in its support, fears of a Fascist revival return. The speed with which the Italian Fascists and the German National Socialists advanced from a very low base of support and membership to control of the state has not been forgotten.

What is the Far Right? The Far Right is a broad category that is not easy to define. In organizational terms it signifies the fringe of right-wing parties and groups that are independent of the constitutional mass parties of the Right and Centre Right. In ideological terms its identity is much less clear. It shares many ideas and values with other parts of the Right, and there is no neat dividing line between the Right and the Far Right on attitudes toward race, nation, and social order.

One solution is to reserve the term Far Right for those parties that see themselves as part of a Fascist tradition, such as the Italian Movimento Sociale Italiano (MSI), the West German Nationaldemokratische Partei Deutschlands, and the British National Front. This, however, would mean excluding other parties, such as Jean-Marie Le Pen's National Front in France and the Progress Party in Denmark.

It has also been questioned whether any of the parties of the Far Right in contemporary Europe should be labeled "fascist" on the grounds that true Fascism belonged to a particular phase of European history, which has ended and will not return. Yet because of the attempt by some groups and intellectuals on the Far Right to keep Nazi rituals, symbols, and ideology—in particular anti-Semitism—alive, controversies over the responsibility of the Nazi regime for the Holocaust remain important issues in Europe. Some leaders of the Far Right have seen the Nazi link as a major liability, but they have not always succeeded in suppressing it.

In terms of their political methods and objectives, there is also less difference between the parties of the Far Right and the right-wing groups within the political mainstream than is sometimes supposed. The parties of the Far Right often support constitutional reforms, such as a strengthened executive, but they no longer advocate the overthrow of parliamentary democracy and the founding of a new political and social order. The Far Right's hostility to democracy and pluralism is more muted than in the past.

Parties of the Far Right have often been distinctive for their readiness to use force to achieve their political objectives, particularly through street violence and demonstrations. There are also important links between some of the parties of the Far Right and political terrorism.

This connection has sometimes been difficult to prove, however, even in Italy, where right-wing involvement in outrages such as the Bologna railway station bombing in 1980 has long been suspected.

How Widespread Is Its Support? In terms of electoral support the record of the Far Right is not impressive. Only the Italian MSI has consistently polled a significant percentage of the vote, and then only in a range between 4 and 8%. Most other parties have experienced sudden upsurges in support that has been lost just as quickly. This has been the pattern in France (1956–58 and 1986–88), the U.K. (1973–79), and West Germany (1965–69). In most postwar elections the Far Right parties in those three countries have failed to achieve more than 1% of the vote.

Far Right parties have sometimes succeeded in mobilizing a protest vote, reflecting temporary disaffection with the established parties, but then have been unable to establish a solid social base. Their support has been transient, built around specific issues—particularly unemployment and race—and has been drawn from many groups, including white-collar workers, the self-employed, and sections of the white male working class, such as British football hooligans.

The vote for Far Right parties has sometimes been explained as an expression of "authoritarian personalities" or the status anxieties of lower-middle-class groups, but there are many more authoritarian personalities than there are Far Right voters. Similarly, many groups with status anxieties do not turn to right-wing political extremism.

What Are Its Prospects? All contemporary industrial societies possess a potential for mobilization and recruitment of the Far Right. The question is, under what circumstances is such a potential realized? The existence of a strong, mass democratic party of the Right inhibits the growth of the Far Right. It is when the main party of the Right suddenly weakens or divides that support for the Far Right can surge.

The continuing legitimacy of the political systems of the European states is therefore an important factor in containing the Far Right. Such parties have their best prospects in relatively new democratic systems like that of Spain. The Alianza Popular (AP) has thrived on the collapse of the centrist mass party of the Right, the Unión Centro Democrático, and is able to mobilize a significant base of former supporters of the Franco regime. Even the AP, however, has publicly accepted the legitimacy of the new constitutional order in Spain.

The Far Right in Europe has recently received new impetus from the growth of the New Right in the 1970s and 1980s. The market liberal strand in the New Right is far removed from the traditional attachment to protectionism and nationalism of the Far Right parties. However, these parties have much in common with the conservative strand of the New Right, including the Nouvelle Droite in France, the Nuova Destra in Italy, and the Salisbury Review in the U.K. All seek the restoration of a conservative intellectual and cultural hegemony. The emergence of this powerful and novel right-wing discourse on race, culture, authority, and national identity has already influenced internal political debate in France and the U.K. It may assist the emergence of a much stronger Far Right political presence within the existing democratic parties of the Right and help to make the fringe parties of the Far Right more legitimate. Nevertheless, a major breakthrough for the Far Right is likely to occur only if the political and economic stability of the European states is seriously threatened.

Andrew Gamble is Professor of Politics at the University of Sheffield, England.

to a protectionist "Fortress Europe" in the 1990s. Serious trade frictions persisted with Washington over agriculture and the future of the European Airbus and with Tokyo over Japanese import penetration and the resulting Japanese trade surplus. At year's end an EC ban on beef treated with hormones (mainly from the U.S.) was countered by extra U.S. duties on a range of EC food products.

Relations between the EC and the Comecon countries took a major step forward with the signing of a mutual recognition agreement in June. This was followed by a far-reaching trade and cooperation agreement with Hungary, a more limited trade agreement with Czechoslovakia, and negotiations for similar arrangements with the Soviet Union and other Eastern European countries. The EC viewed with sympathy the Soviet experiment with liberalization. A number of EC countries advanced increased trade credits to the Soviet Union and encouraged joint ventures between Soviet and EC enterprises. However, the desire of some EC governments to export high technology products to the Eastern bloc led to disagreements with the U.S.

During 1988 EC governments discussed ways of stepping up coordination of the industrial and political aspects of security policy, but the goal of creating a stronger "European pillar" for the NATO alliance fell mainly to the seven-nation Western European Union countries. Under the British presidency of the WEU in the second half of the year, Portugal and Spain were admitted to membership, but differences emerged among the core NATO European governments over their approach to arms control and nuclear arms modernization. The Belgian government joined West Germany and others in the ranks of those anxious to defer implementation of the NATO decision taken in Montebello, Quebec, in 1983 to modernize short-range nuclear weapons in Western Europe, a strategy strongly supported by the U.K. At the same time, there were divisions over whether a link should be formed between negotiations with the Warsaw Pact to reduce short-range nuclear forces and progress in the East/West conventional arms reduction talks, which were expected to begin early in 1989. The main WEU countries did succeed in coordinating their naval presence to protect merchant shipping in the Gulf during the Iran-Iraq war. Although this was appreciated by the U.S., the Reagan administration did not disguise its fear that the ever increasing emphasis on European security policy might weaken the NATO alliance itself.

The increased self-confidence of the EC during 1988 was also reflected in the priority given to coordination of its foreign policy. EC governments pressed the U.S. to give stronger backing to a Middle East international peace conference. The European shift of sympathy away from Israel was also reflected in the warm reception given to the leader of the Palestine Liberation Organization, Yasir Arafat, when he visited the European Parliament in September. At Rhodes, however, the EC failed to forge a united response to Arafat's newly conciliatory stance toward Israel. (*See* Middle East and North Africa: *Middle Eastern and North African Affairs,* above.)

Overshadowed somewhat by EC developments and the prospects of closer links between EFTA and the EC was the 21-country Council of Europe. However, the Council did attract attention for its debates on cultural cooperation issues, including measures to encourage greater European self-sufficiency in broadcasting and television. Meanwhile, the European Court of Human Rights, linked to the Council of Europe, handled a record volume of cases involving citizens' complaints against public authorities in their own countries. (JOHN PALMER)

See also Economic Affairs; Military Affairs.

ANDORRA

A landlocked independent coprincipality of Europe, Andorra is in the Pyrenees Mountains between Spain and France. Area: 468 sq km (181 sq mi). Pop. (1988 est.): 51,400. Cap.: Andorra la Vella. Monetary units: French franc and Spanish peseta. Coprinces: the president of the French Republic and the bishop of Urgel, Spain, represented by their *veguers* (provosts) and *batlles* (prosecutors); chief executive in 1988, Josep Pintat-Solans. An elected Council General of 28 members elects the first syndic, in 1988 Francesc Cerqueda Pascuet.

Developments within the European Communities (EC) were the major talking point in Andorra once again in 1988. As a result of the accession of Spain to the EC in January 1986, the coprincipality was now completely surrounded by EC territory. The 1867 agreement between France and Spain, which had exempted Andorra from paying import duties, was likely to be threatened by the prospect of lower value-added-tax rates in Spain and France after 1992, when the unified internal market would come into effect in the EC.

A great amount of Andorra's income was obtained from trading in duty-free goods, and the economy would be adversely affected if developments within the EC brought an end to this trade. According to Gerard Martinez, an economic adviser to the Andorran government, "After 1992 it will become less worthwhile for people to come here solely to shop." Thus, the preoccupation of the Andorran government was to target tourism to a more affluent market and to negotiate a special relationship with the EC. Andorra's status was being reviewed by the Community. As Fernando Galainena, a Spanish diplomat who represented Andorra's interests in Brussels, had said, "The Community doesn't want to hurt Andorra." (ALUN JONES)

This article updates the *Micropædia* article ANDORRA.

AUSTRIA

The republic of Austria is a landlocked state of central Europe. Area: 83,857 sq km (32,377 sq mi). Pop. (1988 est.): 7,577,000. Cap.: Vienna. Monetary unit: Austrian Schilling, with (Oct. 10, 1988) a free rate of 13.04 Schillings to U.S. $1 (22.33 Schillings = £1 sterling). President in 1988, Kurt Waldheim; chancellor, Franz Vranitzky.

The year 1988, the 50th anniversary of the annexation of Austria by Nazi Germany, also marked a low point in the national crisis of conscience brought about by the election of Kurt Waldheim as president in 1986. In February 1988 a commission of international historians released its report on Waldheim's wartime activities. The commission found no proof of Waldheim's personal guilt, but it concluded that he had been fully informed about the Nazi cruelties committed in the Balkans. Waldheim, who refused to step down to avoid a state crisis, was shunned by most Western governments. Chancellor Franz Vranitzky performed many of Waldheim's duties, and it seemed unlikely that the U.S. would revise its watch list of undesirable aliens in Waldheim's favour.

The governing coalition of the Socialist Party of Austria (SPÖ) and the Austrian People's Party (ÖVP) remained intact despite the Waldheim controversy. With two-thirds of its exports going to the European Communities (EC), Austria was forced to seek closer economic ties with the EC to stay competitive after the formation of a single market in 1992. The government confirmed its intention to make a formal application for EC membership, perhaps as early as 1989, if Austrian neutrality could be guaranteed. As a first step toward full participation in the EC, Austria

passed tax-reform legislation (to become effective on Jan. 1, 1989) that would provide greater incentives for domestic industry. The government was also proceeding with plans to restructure deficit-ridden state-owned industries and to partially privatize the public sector. Other programs included a reform of the financially troubled state pension system and a planned reduction in the federal deficit by means of tighter budgets, reduced agricultural subsidies, and increased tariffs and fees. Conditions for the reforms were favourable, with an inflation rate of only 1.5%, unemployment of 5.5%, and a projected annual growth rate of 2–3% between 1988 and 1992. Unemployment was expected to increase slightly, however.

Austria's engagement in UN peacekeeping missions, which had involved 25,000 participants and resulted in 25 deaths, would be continued through new deployments in Afghanistan and the Persian Gulf. The country's liberal refugee program faced a heavy financial burden in 1988, with some 25,000 persons under the care of the state. A new, accelerated procedure would make it possible to reject those seeking asylum on purely economic grounds and would increase the involvement of the countries of origin.

In the spring there was a breakthrough on the question of autonomy for southern Tirol, a German-speaking region in Italy. A report dealing with the conditions of autonomy, which had been requested by the UN, was completed, and Italy was expected to issue a declaration ending the dispute. Meanwhile, Austria continued to be the protective power in southern Tirol.

In the summer, resistance against the construction of the nuclear reprocessing plant in Wackersdorf, Bavaria, reached a new high point, culminating in the collection of

AFP PHOTO

"Never Forget" reads the memorial at the site of the former Gestapo headquarters in Vienna. The year 1988 marked the 50th anniversary of the Anschluss, Nazi Germany's annexation of Austria.

several thousand petitions and the participation of high-ranking public officials.

The movement for greater openness in Eastern Europe helped to improve Austrian relations with the Soviet Union, East Germany, Poland, and Hungary with regard to travel restrictions, industrial cooperation, cultural exchanges, and the protection of the environment. In May Austria and Hungary announced plans for a joint world's fair in 1995.

Several scandals shook Austria in 1988. The former director of Noricum, the state arms manufacturer, admitted in January that Noricum had sold arms to Iran during the Iran-Iraq war in direct contravention of Austrian neutrality. Also in January, the former vice-chancellor Hannes Androsch was convicted of perjury for his testimony in a 1981 parliamentary inquiry and resigned his post as general director of Austria's largest commercial bank. In November Heinrich Keller resigned as general secretary of the SPÖ because of a tax scandal. After a West German newspaper publisher purchased 45% of the shares of Austria's two largest newspapers, the federal government deliberated measures to preserve freedom of the press and diversity of opinion and still avoid foreign control of the Austrian media. (ELFRIEDE DIRNBACHER)

BELGIUM

A constitutional monarchy, the Benelux country of Belgium is situated on the North Sea coast of northwestern Europe. Area: 30,518 sq km (11, 783 sq mi). Pop. (1988 est.) 9,865,000. Cap. Brussels. Monetary unit: Belgian franc, with (Oct. 10, 1988) a commercial rate of BF 38.86 to U.S. $1 (BF 66.55 = £1 pound sterling) and a financial rate of BF 39.36 to U.S. $1 (BF 67.40 = £1 pound sterling). King, Baudouin I; prime minister in 1988, Wilfried Martens.

When Wilfried Martens took the helm of his eighth government early in May 1988, nearly five months had passed since the general elections. After a first round of preliminary contacts, King Baudouin had invited Jean-Luc Dehaene, a Flemish Social Christian, to form a new government. Because the French Social Christians vetoed participation by the Liberals, he turned to the French and Flemish Social Christians and Socialists and the Flemish Nationalists (Volksunie), which together would provide the two-thirds majority in Parliament needed to alter the constitution. Dehaene wanted a solution for the Voeren (Fourons) problem, which had brought down the previous government. José Happart, mayor of the small township officially located in Dutch-speaking Flanders, refused to speak Dutch, and he continued to function as acting mayor despite his removal by the Council of State.

Dehaene convinced the negotiators to seek the answer within the larger framework of a general reform of the state structures, which would give the country a federal type of organization with three regions, Flanders, Wallonia, and Brussels, and two main language communities, Dutch- and French-speaking. This would imply transferring more powers from the national government to the regional and community authorities established in 1980. By simultaneously changing the existing language legislation in a number of communes with a mixed population around Brussels and along the linguistic border, Dehaene hoped to remove the threat of another Happart affair.

The proposals submitted by Dehaene covered transfer of a wide range of powers, one of the most important being national education. They provided for arbitration in case of conflicts between the national and regional community authorities, or between regional community authorities. To placate the Flemish Socialists and Nationalists, he proposed

Turkey's Prime Minister Turgut Ozal (left) talks with Greece's Prime Minister Andreas Papandreou as they leave a bilateral meeting during the NATO summit in Brussels in March.
AFP PHOTO

to reintroduce proportional representation in the slightly enlarged Flemish executive. However, for the Walloon (French-speaking) regional executive and the French community executive, the majority system was maintained. For Brussels, Dehaene proposed a five-member executive, two French- and two Dutch-speaking under a French-speaking chairman. In six communes on the Brussels periphery and a few along the linguistic border, proportional representation was also introduced for the aldermen, ensuring the presence of Flemish-speakers on the local executives. This was intended to thwart further moves by Happart to again become mayor, though it appeared from their statements that Flemish and Walloon politicians had differing views of what the effect on Happart would be. In local elections in October, which generally indicated support for the government, Happart was elected again.

Agreement on these issues was endorsed by the majority parties on May 2, and the new government, under Martens, was sworn in May 9. Martens said the new government would pursue the same objectives as the one which he had previously led with the Liberals: reduction of the budget deficit to 7% of gross national product, requiring cuts of some BF 80 billion in public expenditures or new revenue; and reform of the state structures as outlined by Dehaene. A major reform of the tax system, which would reduce personal income tax but raise corporate taxes, as well as taxes and excises on alcoholic beverages and oil products, would take effect in 1989; also, certain tax deductions would be abolished. The government announced also an end to further privatization of public enterprises. By early August Parliament had approved the first set of constitutional changes.

Financial news in the first half of the year was dominated by the attempt of the Italian financier Carlo De Benedetti (see BIOGRAPHIES) to take over the Société Générale de Belgique, Belgium's largest holding company with interests reaching throughout the country's economy. In a bidding war that at one point quadrupled the price of Générale's stock, a group of French and Belgian investors gained control of the company, but they later agreed to share power with De Benedetti, who was elected to the board in September.

Viscount Gaston Eyskens (see OBITUARIES), former prime minister and a prominent figure in post-World War II Belgian politics, died on January 3.   (JAN R. ENGELS)

This article updates the Macropædia article The Low COUNTRIES: Belgium.

DENMARK

A constitutional monarchy of north central Europe, Denmark lies between the North and Baltic seas. Area: 43,092 sq km (16,638 sq mi), excluding the Faeroe Islands and Greenland. Pop. (1988 est.): 5,130,000. Cap.: Copenhagen. Monetary unit: Danish krone, with (Oct. 10, 1988) a free rate of 7.13 kroner to U.S. $1 (12.21 kroner = £1 sterling). Queen, Margrethe II; prime minister in 1988, Poul Schlüter.

Denmark, the member of the European Communities (EC) with the highest material standard of living and, paradoxically, the greatest foreign debt, faced political and economic instability during 1988. On May 10 the country experienced its second inconclusive general election in eight months. It was fought over the issue of Danish membership in NATO and the question of allowing NATO warships to continue visiting Danish waters without divulging whether they were carrying nuclear weapons on board. The election, which showed a slight shift to the right, produced another centre-right minority coalition under the Conservative prime minister, Poul Schlüter, and included the Liberals and the Radicals. (For tabulated results, see *Political Parties,* above.) In June the new government announced a compromise procedure whereby they would send notice to all countries seeking entry into Danish waters that it was assumed that their ship was in compliance with Danish law but without a specific mention of Denmark's ban on nuclear weapons.

The Organization for Economic Cooperation and Development (OECD) released a report in 1988 that clearly spelled out Denmark's urgent need to curb both government and consumer spending to cut its growing current account deficit and foreign debt. The OECD concluded that Denmark's foreign debt of some $38 billion, or 40% of gross national product, had reached a magnitude that made its reduction of foremost concern. The balance of payments deficit, which had shown a shortfall for 25 consecutive years, was forecast to remain at $2.5 billion in 1988–89.

Denmark's poor export performance was one cause of the deficit. Manufacturing, which was dominated by small companies, exported 60% of its industrial production and provided 70% of the country's exports. In early 1988 legislation worth about $150 million took effect. This was intended to boost Denmark's export competitiveness by up to 10%, create 50,000 jobs, and ease tax regulations for export industries. Most experts, however, felt that the package would be insufficient.

The situation for agriculture looked similarly bleak. Denmark, with two-thirds of its land devoted to farming, was—relative to population—Europe's greatest producer and exporter of farm products. Ultraefficient Danish farmers made up only 6% of the work force yet produced 25% of the country's exports. In the summer, however, the government was forced to take emergency measures to help farmers hit by debt, falling prices, and stagnant exports. The legislative package provided more than $150 million in state aid to ease the $3 billion of debt owed by more than 16,000 of Denmark's 90,000 farmers. The agricultural sector also struggled with ongoing reforms to limit farm production under the EC's common agricultural policy and with the Danish government's ambitious antipollution programs designed to reduce emissions of agricultural fertilizers into inshore and offshore waters.

The government, faced with eight minority parties in the Folketing (parliament), appeared unable to forge consistent policies or find lasting solutions to Denmark's eco-

Western Europe: France 449

nomic woes. Four tough austerity budgets in three years had failed to solve the country's problems or lessen the average Dane's high income tax burden. Most Danes paid 50–68% of their income in direct taxes, the highest in the EC, partly to support the country's streamlined cradle-to-grave welfare system. In October 1988 Schlüter presented to the Folketing a 1989 budget calling for $1.5 billion in fresh public-expenditure cuts to achieve an annual surplus. Despite the fact that state spending had been frozen for five years, with an annual surplus from 1986, the prime minister called for severe wage restraints (a move generally supported by trade unions) and increased charges for such public services as libraries, prescription drugs, and higher education. (CHRISTOPHER FOLLETT)

FINLAND

The republic of Finland is in northern Europe, on the Gulf of Bothnia and the Gulf of Finland. Area: 338,145 sq km (130,559 sq mi). Pop. (1988 est.): 4,952,000. Cap.: Helsinki. Monetary unit: Finnish markka, with (Oct. 10, 1988) a free rate of 4.37 markkaa to U.S. $1 (7.48 markkaa = £1 sterling). President in 1988, Mauno Koivisto; prime minister, Harri Holkeri.

For Finland 1988 was a stable but eventful year. On February 15 the popularly chosen electoral college gave Pres. Mauno Koivisto, then 64, a second six-year term of office. The college was convened because a national poll held January 31–February 1 had failed to give any candidate the 50% necessary for immediate election. Koivisto, however, recorded almost 48%, far outdistancing his four rivals. His reelection was secured in the college by votes from his own Social Democrats and from the Conservatives, the major parties in the government formed in May 1987. The majority government, which also contained members from the Rural and Swedish parties, proceeded with legislation envisaged in its program. This included measures promoting greater job security, advocated by the Conservatives.

Finland announced it would seek full membership in the Council of Europe. It had been an observer at meetings of this largely human rights organization for many years but had refrained from joining because of concern that this might affect relations with the neighbouring Soviet Union. However, Foreign Minister Kalevi Sorsa declared that Finland would be prevented by its geopolitical situation from considering membership in the more highly political European Communities, although it would seek closer economic ties with the integrating Western Europe represented by that organization. Meanwhile, Finland was elected as one of the ten nonpermanent members of the UN Security Council.

A Soviet general working on a biography of Joseph Stalin wrote in a Finnish magazine during the summer that the dead dictator had been responsible for the Russo-Finnish Winter War of 1939–40. This was followed by similar admissions in a Soviet political weekly. The Kremlin neither confirmed nor denied such disclosures of responsibility, the first to come openly from the U.S.S.R. The Finnish Communist Party, steadily in decline for some decades and excluded from coalition governments since the late 1970s, was beset by scandal. Its entire "Politburo" resigned after disclosing that the party had lost sums equivalent to many millions of dollars in the Finnish stock market on investments that included a Helsinki fashion clothing store and a string of harness race horses known as the Hot Trotters.

Prime Minister Harri Holkeri visited Moscow in September, the first Finnish Conservative in that office to do so since World War II. He was received at the top level, and Soviet news media, in previous years antagonistic to his

Finland's Pres. Mauno Koivisto (left) and his wife, Tellervo, raise their glasses to friends and supporters upon his reelection.
AFP PHOTO

party, went so far as to describe him as a possible future president. The year's major visitor to Finland was U.S. Pres. Ronald Reagan, who stopped in Helsinki en route to his summit meeting in Moscow with Soviet party leader Mikhail Gorbachev. His strong appeal for the establishment of greater human rights in the Soviet Union, made on May 27, was well received in the Finnish media, which had previously tended to be highly critical of him.

Trade with other Western countries, with which Finland traditionally does most of its international business, continued to improve. This more than offset a continuing decline in trade with the Soviet Union resulting from the fall in the price of oil, Finland's major import from the U.S.S.R. While overall foreign trade in merchandise remained in surplus, the government expressed concern over the deficit in the current account balance of payments that accompanied heavy borrowing from abroad, where money continued to be cheaper. The gross national product grew an estimated 3% during the year, but a slight downturn was predicted for 1989.

Finland enjoyed its warmest June on record, according to the official weather statistics.

(EDWARD M. SUMMERHILL)

FRANCE

A republic of western Europe, France includes the island of Corsica in the Mediterranean Sea and has coastlines on the English Channel, the Mediterranean, and the Atlantic Ocean. Area: 543,965 sq km (210,026 sq mi). Pop. (1988 est.): 55,860,000. Cap.: Paris. Monetary unit: franc, with (Oct. 10, 1988) a free rate of F 6.32 to U.S. $1 (F 10.83 = £1 sterling). President in 1988, François Mitterrand; prime ministers, Jacques Chirac and, from May 10, Michel Rocard.

Domestic Affairs. The year 1988 was rich with political events: a presidential election, which renewed the mandate for Socialist Pres. François Mitterrand (*see* BIOGRAPHIES) for a second seven-year term, was followed by legislative elections, which gave a relative majority to the leftists. After two years the "cohabitation" between a chief of state of the left, Mitterrand, and a parliamentary majority coalition of the right, presided over by Prime Minister Jacques Chirac, came to an end. Both parties in the right-wing coalition offered candidates for president, Chirac representing the Rassemblement pour la République (RPR) and former prime minister Raymond Barre the Union pour la Démocratie Française (UDF). Chirac faced Mitterrand in

the decisive second round on May 8 and lost badly. (*See* Sidebar.)

On May 10 Chirac submitted his letter of resignation to the president, who chose Michel Rocard (*see* BIOGRAPHIES) as Chirac's replacement. The new prime minister took 48 hours to form an *ouverture* (open) government, in which he sought to include non-Socialist ministers. Among the 26 ministers named were 18 Socialists, two members of the UDF, and several independents. The appointment of Socialist Party (PS) leader Lionel Jospin as education minister created a furor within the party. Jospin left the directorship of the PS, where he was succeeded by former prime minister Pierre Mauroy, after a bitter duel with Laurent Fabius, also a former prime minister, who was later elected president of the National Assembly.

After his failure to convince centrists to enter his government, Rocard, who had hoped to achieve a "stable majority," looked favourably on the rapid dissolution of the National Assembly. Mitterrand agreed and on May 14 announced his decision to dissolve the assembly and call for legislative elections.

The elections were held on June 5 and 12. The first round was marked by a voter turnout of only 66%, much lower than in preceding elections. No bloc for the left or the right held a majority, and France remained divided in two. The Communist Party (PC) improved its showing over past elections, but the National Front declined.

The second round of legislative elections brought no great changes. No force obtained an absolute majority, contrary to the hopes of Mitterrand and Rocard. The PS, the largest party, together with its allied parties, collected only 276 seats, 13 seats short of a majority. The RPR-UDF coalition that had formerly controlled the National Assembly could muster only 258 seats. The National Front, with only one delegate, was the big loser, paying dearly for the return to the two-round system that had been abandoned in 1986. The PS and PC (with a decline to 27 seats) confirmed that there was no question of governing except together, but the right was no more capable of governing alone. (For tabulated results, see *Political Parties,* above.) Comparing the results of the presidential and legislative elections made it apparent that the French, on May 8, voted less for ideology than for a man thought to carry more weight than his opponent.

On June 28 the prime minister announced the formation of his second government, marking a new step in the *ouverture* toward the centre and the *société civil,* civilians without previous government service. To the 26 Socialists on this team, Rocard added 23 ministers and secretaries of state who were not Socialists, as well as 6 centrists. Among the new civilians was the junior minister of health, Léon Schwarzenberg, a cancer specialist who was fired by Rocard a record nine days after his nomination. Schwarzenberg's dismissal over a disagreement on public policy in the fight against drugs was seen as a setback in Rocard's *ouverture* government. The next day Rocard presented to the

---

The 1988 Presidential Election

At the beginning of the year, the politicians from the right announced their candidacies for the presidential election. First was Prime Minister Jacques Chirac of the Rassemblement pour la République, who reported on his "Project for France" entitled "the decade of renewal." He was followed by former prime minister Raymond Barre of the Union pour la Démocratie Française, who began his campaign three weeks later. Jean-Marie Le Pen, leader of the far right-wing National Front, who also had declared his candidacy in January, was acclaimed in Marseille by 20,000 enthusiastic supporters for denouncing immigration and supporting the reestablishment of the death penalty. Finally, Socialist Pres. François Mitterrand, after a long period of suspense, finished up in March by announcing his bid for reelection, presenting himself as the most capable leader to prepare France for the European Communities single market in 1992. He also became only the third president from the Fifth Republic to court a second mandate. Charles de Gaulle was reelected at 75 in 1965, and Valéry Giscard d'Estaing was beaten in 1981. In a "Letter to all the French people" published in several newspapers, Mitterrand explained in seven "grand positions" his conception of France, Europe, and their place in the world and took the offensive against the pugnacious Chirac.

On April 24, leading the field of nine candidates in the first round of the presidential election with 34.09% of the votes cast (10,367,220 votes), Mitterrand immediately issued a call "for the union of all the French." His chief rival, Chirac, had beaten Barre by a little more than three points, with 19.94% (6,063,514 votes) to 16.54% (5,031,849 votes). In keeping with a previous agreement, Barre shifted his support to Chirac for the second round, which was reduced to a simple battle between the incumbent president and his prime minister, a great "first" in the history of the Fifth Republic. Chirac faced a difficult choice with regard to the growing support for the National Front. Le Pen finished close on the heels of the two candidates of the rightist parliamentary majority, with 14.39% (4,375,894 votes), an increase of 5% over 1986. The Communist Party continued to decline with 6.76% (2,055,995 votes), 4% less than in 1986.

On April 28 Mitterrand and Chirac participated in a nationally televised traditional face-to-face debate. This event, which showed the two violently opposed, had above all else signified the brutal end to their two-year period of "cohabitation." In fact, the size of the Mitterrand victory on May 8— 54.02% (16,704,279 votes) to 45.98% (14,218,970 votes) for Chirac—had the effect of a true Socialist "pink tide" crossing all of France and creating the conditions for a remodeling of the political landscape. These results testified above all to Mitterrand's personal success. The margin that separated the two candidates (2.5 million votes) was comparable to that between de Gaulle and Mitterrand in 1965. Although Mitterrand's victory was not a cause for real surprise after his showing in the first round, it was without doubt one of the Socialists' strongest mobilizations ever that had manifestly assisted the president. Above all, the entire left had showed strong voter turnout in the second round, while a significant drop in the votes of the right hurt Chirac.

(JEAN KNECHT)

French Pres. François Mitterrand pauses during a speech at a campaign stop in Rennes. Mitterrand's strong run for reelection ended in an easy defeat of his opponents.
WITT/STEVENS—SIPA

National Assembly his government's programs, contained in his "Letter to all the French people." Rocard stressed reconciliation and solidarity and placed his second government and its actions under the symbol of a "new spirit."

In the meantime, on June 26 Prime Minister Rocard brought back his first personal success from New Caledonia. Rioting among Kanaks—the indigenous Melanesians—in the spring led Rocard to intervene personally on the question of independence for the overseas territory. The accord reached by the Kanak Socialist National Liberation Front (FLNKS) and the Rassemblement pour la Calédonie dans la République, representing the French settlers, specified that the territory would be entrusted to the care of the state for one year. The accord fixed the statute of New Caledonia for a period of ten years, at the end of which, in 1998, a ballot for self-determination would be organized for the territory. Rocard's success paled in November, however, when only 37% of all French voters turned out for the referendum on the accord.

The government was put to the test late in the year when a series of strikes by public-sector employees broke out, including a one-day national strike on October 20. After striking prison guards, railway workers, nurses, and postal workers hardened their positions, some differences appeared within the Socialist Party. Several PS leaders had hoped that Rocard would loosen his austerity policy and authorize contract negotiations in favour of salaried employees. Despite assurances from the prime minister, the tension did not abate. In November maintenance workers on the Paris metro (subway) began a strike that paralyzed public transportation in Paris for six weeks. They returned to work on December 21, having failed to achieve their demand for a pay raise.

The Economy. In 1988 the strong points of the economy were focused on the Paris Bourse, which, in a world economy of rapid growth, had regained and surpassed its levels from before the crash of October 1987. After the presidential election French stock held up well. Apparently investors feared Socialist power less than in 1981, when the stock exchange had fallen some 30% in the first week after Mitterrand's victory. Inflation was also contained in 1988, and stock prices for the year were expected to rise 2.5–3%. Plans to privatize more national industries, however, were delayed.

In the fall the trade deficit showed a slight improvement, but unemployment hit 10% in October, with some 2,556,400 people out of work. Rocard launched a plan

to provide financial aid to small and medium-sized enterprises. Also in October the prime minister reported back-to-back successes when the National Assembly approved a new guaranteed minimum income and reintroduced a tax on personal wealth, half the revenues from which would aid the less fortunate. In the autumn budget Pierre Bérégovoy, the minister of finance, projected increased economic growth in 1989 and proposed lower personal tax rates, a cut in the value-added tax (VAT), and increased public spending.

Foreign Affairs. In keeping with the international atmosphere of détente, France improved its relations with Eastern Europe. In January 1988 East German leader Erich Honecker met with Mitterrand in Paris, the first such visit in 15 years. The visit of Soviet Foreign Minister Eduard Shevardnadze to Paris in early October was fruitful for both countries. In November Mitterrand attended the launch of a Soviet spacecraft for a joint Soviet-French mission, in which French astronaut Jean-Loup Chrétien participated, and met with Soviet leader Mikhail Gorbachev. Gorbachev was expected to visit France in 1989.

In October France released plans for an international conference on chemical weapons, to be held in January 1989 in Paris. Mitterrand also sought closer cooperation between France and NATO in negotiations with the Warsaw Pact countries on conventional disarmament. In November, however, French objections to negotiating procedures delayed the proposed Conventional Stability Talks.

The summit of the European Communities (EC) in February in Brussels concluded with an accord on the reform of EC finances and an increase in aid to poorer regions in preparation for the 1992 single market. In June the 39th European Council of Ministers met in Brussels and created a committee to define the procedure for the monetary integration of Europe. Mitterrand remained a strong supporter of the single market and the proposed European central bank, but in September he joined with British Prime Minister Margaret Thatcher to reject a change in EC VAT policy.

French relations with West Germany were excellent in 1988, and Mitterrand held a series of successful meetings with West German Chancellor Helmut Kohl. In January France and West Germany created a joint military council and an economic advisory council to coordinate economic policies. The two men jointly received the Charlemagne Prize for "services rendered to Europe" before launching a vibrant appeal in favour of a united European culture. In early November Mitterrand and Kohl announced the creation of Franco-German cultural links beginning in 1990.

During his visit to France, Pope John Paul II defined before the European Parliament the church's wishes for the "New Europe": a communal political authority, an extension of European integration to the East, and redoubled generosity toward the third world.

Diplomatic relations between France and Iran were restored in June after the liberation of the last three French hostages held in Lebanon. Later in the summer France announced its intention to ease an embargo on Iranian oil that had been in effect since August 1987, and in September Defense Minister Jean-Pierre Chevènement recalled 4 of the 11 French naval vessels on patrol in the Persian Gulf. Prime Minister Rocard and Foreign Minister Roland Dumas came under sharp criticism in October when they failed to condemn Algeria for violent repressions of protests in the former French colony. Military aid to another former colony, Chad, decreased as Chad normalized relations with Libya.   (JEAN KNECHT)

See also *Dependent States,* below.

GERMANY, FEDERAL REPUBLIC OF

The Federal Republic of Germany (West Germany) is in central Europe, on the North and Baltic seas. Area: 248,709 sq km (96,027 sq mi). Pop. (1988 est., including West Berlin, which is an enclave within East Germany): 60,782,000. Provisional cap.: Bonn. Monetary unit: Deutsche Mark, with (Oct. 10, 1988) a free rate of DM 1.86 to U.S. $1 (DM 3.18 = £1 sterling). President in 1988, Richard von Weizsäcker; chancellor, Helmut Kohl.

Gloomy forecasts of West German economic sclerosis, mostly emanating from abroad, proved to be inaccurate. As the end of 1988 approached, it was clear that growth would be around 3.5%, with domestic consumer spending playing a major role. The rate of inflation scarcely rose above 1%, and the country had a vast and growing balance of payments surplus with the rest of Western Europe, though unemployment remained persistently high at more than two million.

Domestic Affairs. A year after the federal election had confirmed Chancellor Helmut Kohl in power for another term, there was mounting discontent with his leadership and the state of the coalition of the Christian Democratic Union (CDU), its Bavarian wing, the Christian Social Union (CSU), and the Free Democratic Party (FDP). Criticism came to a head at the CDU's annual congress in Wiesbaden in June, when young party members, pensioners, trade unionists, and other speakers expressed bitterness and disappointment over the frequent and confusing disputes between party leaders and over the government's controversial tax, health, and pension reforms. Some delegates questioned the government's commitment to reducing unemployment, and Kohl was accused of standing idly by while the quarrels raged.

The chancellor shrugged off the attacks while acknowledging that "we all know we are going through a bad patch." He said that he, too, frequently became angry over unnecessary internal strife, which he blamed on personal vanities. Nonetheless, he forecast that, just as the government's unpopular policy of allowing the deployment of Pershing and cruise missiles on its soil had been rewarded with the 1987 intermediate-range nuclear forces disarmament agreement, so the domestic reforms would eventually pay off.

At the root of the trouble was Kohl's style of government; he lacked the ability to present his ideas and policies to the public. First the public was told it would pay less in taxes, then unexpected tax increases were announced. Supposedly unforeseen raises in contributions to the European Communities (EC), in aid to farmers, and in expensive projects like the Airbus and the European Fighter Aircraft upset calculations. Kohl was not the only target of criticism, however; there was also strong disappointment with the performance of the finance minister, Gerhard Stoltenberg, in his handling of the tax changes. He had been considered a potential successor to Kohl but appeared to have wrecked his chances.

Lothar Späth, the popular Christian Democrat minister-president (prime minister) of Baden-Württemberg, emerged as the strongest candidate to succeed Kohl after retaining his absolute majority in the state election in March. His victory was a great personal success and was partly attributed to the fact that he had been openly critical of the chancellor's government in Bonn. Späth avoided campaigning on national issues, such as tax reform or nuclear power, let alone on European issues, such as farm spending cuts. However, although he remained the only CDU prime minister with an absolute majority, his share of the vote dropped from 51.9% in the preceding election to 49.1%. Stripped of the Späth factor, the election clearly reflected dissatisfaction with the coalition in Bonn and confirmed a run of CDU local election setbacks in the previous year. Modest losses were also suffered in Baden-Württemberg by the Social Democratic Party (SPD) and the Greens, though surprising gains were made by an assortment of right-wing splinter groups, who cornered about 5% of the vote.

Suggestions that this was the start of a neo-Nazi revival seemed without foundation; the right-wing groups served chiefly as vehicles for the discontents of archconservatives dissatisfied with the CDU, and their outlooks were by no means homogenous. Thus the National Democratic Party, which increased its share of the vote from 0.9 to 2.1%, appealed to the xenophobic feelings of Germans alarmed by the presence of foreign workers, while other groups found their constituencies in nationalists who disapproved of the CDU's good relations with Communist countries, conservative Roman Catholics, discontented farmers, and right-wing environmentalists in areas that had experienced high fallout from the 1986 Chernobyl nuclear accident in the U.S.S.R. Kohl likened the small parties to Poujadism, a populist right-wing protest movement that surfaced briefly in France in the 1950s.

The possibility of a right-wing resurgence was belied by the landslide victory of the Social Democrats in the rural, ultraconservative Land of Schleswig-Holstein, ending 38 years of CDU rule. In large measure, the Social Democrats' victory in the May state election stemmed from a 1987 political scandal involving Uwe Barschel, the former Christian Democratic prime minister. Revelations of his "dirty tricks" campaign against Social Democrat Björn Engholm had led to his resignation in disgrace and subsequent suicide and to the calling of a fresh election only eight months after the previous one. In the May election the Social Democrats increased their share of the vote by 9.6% to 54.8%, while the CDU's vote fell from 42.6 to 33.3%. The election in the previous year had resulted in a stalemate.

Kohl had to make a Cabinet reshuffle in the autumn. Martin Bangemann resigned as economics minister and chairman of the FDP to take up a senior post on the European Commission in Brussels. He was replaced at the Economics Ministry by the former general secretary of the FDP, Helmut Haussmann, and as party chairman by Count Otto Lambsdorff. Lambsdorff was himself a former economics minister and the main representative of the strain of right-wing liberalism in his party. Earlier, Rupert Scholz (CDU), a West Berlin senator, was appointed defense minister to succeed Manfred Wörner (*see* BIOGRAPHIES), who took over from Lord Carrington as secretary-general of NATO.

Franz Josef Strauss (*see* OBITUARIES), minister-president of Bavaria and a towering figure in West German political life for nearly 40 years, died on October 3, aged 73. In the immediate postwar years he had played a decisive role in building up the CSU, becoming its secretary-general in 1949. He entered the Bundestag (parliament) in the same year and four years later was the youngest member of Konrad Adenauer's Cabinet, at first without portfolio and then with responsibility for the new and sensitive field of nuclear affairs. He subsequently served as defense minister, 1956–62, and as finance minister, 1966–69. He unsuccessfully contested the federal chancellorship in the election of 1980. At the time of his death, he had been prime minister of his native Bavaria for ten years, though he always played a significant—and highly controversial—role in federal affairs. Strauss was succeeded as prime minister by Max

Streibl, who had been deputy prime minister and finance minister, and as chairman of the CSU by Theo Waigel. On March 9 Kurt Georg Kiesinger (*see* OBITUARIES), who was federal chancellor in 1966–69, died at the age of 83. He headed the grand coalition government of Christian Democrats and Social Democrats. He remained a member of the Bundestag until 1980.

A disaster in August at an air show at the U.S. Air Force base at Ramstein caused the deaths of 67 spectators and 3 pilots of Italy's Frecce Tricolori aerobatic team. The team was giving a display involving a crossover with close formations when three of the aircraft collided, and one of them plowed into the crowd. An investigation found that human error on the part of one of the pilots was to blame. The West German Defense Ministry canceled further military air shows and ordered a review of whether such events should be allowed in the future. Concern heightened in December, when a U.S. Air Force plane crashed into a residential neighbourhood of Remscheid, killing the pilot and five persons on the ground.

Mathias Rust, the young student who astounded the world in May 1987 by flying a light aircraft to Moscow and landing it in Red Square, was released from prison by the Soviets in August and sent home. He had been sentenced to four years in a labour camp for a variety of offenses. His feat had made him something of a hero in West Germany, but after his return he emerged as a remarkably unimaginative man. Psychiatrists said the young pilot needed treatment.

That Germans had not yet come to terms with the Nazi past seemed apparent from a controversy that erupted in November. In a speech commemorating the 50th anniversary of Kristallnacht, the pogrom that foreshadowed Hitler's "final solution" to the Jewish question, Philipp Jenninger, the speaker of the Bundestag, attempted to explain how Germans of the time felt toward the Nazi regime. Jenninger was regarded as sympathetic to Israel, and he went on to say the German people had been "blinded and seduced" by their leaders. Nevertheless, many listeners interpreted the speech as an attempt at justification, and Jenninger was forced to resign. He was succeeded by Rita Süssmuth.

Plans were announced in February to streamline the Bundeswehr, the federal armed forces, to cope with the consequences of a falling birthrate and mounting pressure to cut government spending. The government gave assurances, however, that the country's contribution to NATO would remain unchanged at 12 divisions, with 495,000 men in peacetime, rising to 1,340,000 when reservists were called up in time of war. The plans involved much juggling of figures, however, with the permanent staff of many units being cut by as much as 50% and the number of reservists doubled. The number of national servicemen—conscripts—would drop from 220,000 to 206,000, and the number of professional soldiers would increase to 250,000, with the total being made up by civilians and the 15,000 reservists who would be in uniform at any given time. The government said the plans would entail no increase in the current defense budget of DM 52 billion. This contradicted West Germany's declared intention, along with other NATO members, of meeting U.S. demands to increase defense spending by 3% annually in real terms.

Foreign Affairs. Kohl, accompanied by 5 members of his Cabinet and a party of 50 leading industrialists and bankers, visited Moscow in October. His mission was seen in Bonn as a fence-mending exercise, an attempt to end a long period of strain between the West German and Soviet governments. Clearly, both sides were in favour of improving relations. Before Kohl's arrival, the Soviet press found complimentary things to say about him. Speaking at a Kremlin banquet in his honour, Kohl characterized the division of Germany as unnatural. Admitting that unity could be achieved only with the approval of the Soviets and the three Western powers that, together, were responsible for post-World War II Germany, he urged that Moscow help bring about circumstances that would make unity possible. Soviet leader Mikhail Gorbachev's response was a reiteration of Moscow's unchanging line that the existing frontiers of Europe were sacrosanct, including the divided status of Berlin. However, discussions between Kohl and Gorbachev were described as friendly, if straightforward and serious. Many business contracts were signed by the German delegation, and a group of West German banks arranged a $1.6 billion credit for the Soviet Union.

Before he left Moscow, Kohl said he had been told by the Soviet authorities that they would release all those whom the West regarded as political prisoners before the end of 1989. The Germans considered that this news, assuming

AP/WIDE WORLD

A large group of people endure a long wait at an unemployment office in Hamburg, West Germany. Despite steady economic growth and low inflation, more than two million people remained unemployed.

it was borne out by deeds, enhanced the prospects of an early conclusion to the Vienna talks on European security and cooperation, as well as the Soviet Union's own hopes of acting as host to a follow-up East-West conference on human rights in Moscow in 1991. Kohl made it clear that his government's own consent to a human rights conference depended on three conditions, of which the release of political prisoners was but one. The others were an end to the jamming of Western radio stations and greater freedom for Soviet citizens to travel abroad and to emigrate.

Foreign policy throughout the year was marked by Bonn's determination to reactivate the *Ostpolitik,* the policy of coming to terms with Eastern Europe that had been somewhat neglected since Kohl came to office in 1982. The Soviet foreign minister, Eduard Shevardnadze, was in Bonn in January, and in that same month the West German foreign minister, Hans-Dietrich Genscher, went to Poland and the chancellor to Prague. Kohl was in Washington in February. During his meeting with Pres. Ronald Reagan he emphasized the need for NATO to work out what he called "an overall arms control concept" that would involve tactical nuclear weapons and conventional forces in Europe, as well as a 50% cut in U.S. and Soviet strategic arsenals and a global ban on chemical weapons.

The 25th anniversary of the Franco-German friendship treaty was celebrated in January—at a time when political friendship and cooperation between the two countries were warmer than ever before. Perhaps the most remarkable development was the formation of a joint army brigade of 4,500 German and French soldiers, demonstrating France's growing involvement in defense east of the Rhine.

An important speech by the chancellor in Brussels in October was widely interpreted as a rebuff to the European policy of the British prime minister, Margaret Thatcher. Kohl called for an eventual European union while denying that this necessarily involved a loss of national identity. He said that no single member state should hold up progress in Europe in order to preserve its own interests. The EC would be condemned to deadlock if that were allowed to happen. Thatcher's attitude to Europe had long irritated the Germans. They were annoyed by her refusal to let Britain join the European Monetary System or to contemplate a European central bank and currency system, which they saw as essential to the internal market due to come into being in 1992. In the German view, Thatcher regarded the EC as little more than a trading organization. The Germans insisted that the creation of a European union would not weaken the Atlantic alliance. Kohl emphasized that Europe would continue to need the presence of powerful U.S. forces on its soil.   (NORMAN CROSSLAND)

This article updates the *Macropædia* article GERMANY: *Federal Republic of Germany.*

GREECE

The republic of Greece occupies the southern part of the Balkan Peninsula and several adjoining island groups in southeastern Europe, in and between the Ionian and Aegean seas. Area: 131,957 sq km (50,949 sq mi). Pop. (1988 est.): 10,055,000. Cap.: Athens. Monetary unit: drachma, with (Oct. 10, 1988) a free rate of 150.26 drachmas to U.S. $1 (257.33 drachmas = £1 sterling). President in 1988, Christos Sartzetakis; prime minister, Andreas Papandreou.

Relations between Greece and Turkey, which had been clouded by territorial disputes in the Aegean Sea and on Cyprus, improved dramatically after a summit meeting in the Swiss Alpine resort of Davos (Jan. 30–31, 1988). The Greek prime minister, Andreas Papandreou, and his Turk-

ish counterpart, Turgut Ozal, agreed to promote peace and to meet at least once a year to discuss mutual concerns.

The breakthrough prompted a flurry of Greek-Turkish political, economic, and cultural exchanges. They culminated in June in an official visit to Athens by the Turkish prime minister—the first in 36 years. Minor problems between the two countries were eliminated; trade was stimulated; and a spirit of goodwill began to emerge. However, the main problem areas continued to cause friction. Turkish aircraft repeatedly challenged Greek sovereignty and jurisdiction in the Aegean airspace, and Greece obstructed Turkey's efforts to achieve closer ties with the European Communities (EC). If the dialogue survived these irritants, it was thanks to the personal commitment of the two prime ministers.

The "spirit of Davos," however, was treated by the Greeks with much skepticism. They remained convinced that Turkey's expansionist designs in the Aegean and Cyprus had not changed. The prime minister himself, who had encouraged their suspicions since he came to power in 1981, failed to explain convincingly his change of heart. Sensing voter doubts, Papandreou postponed his own visit to Turkey, tentatively set for October. He was clearly concerned that this policy could harm him at a sensitive time—a general election was due by June 1989.

Papandreou, on being informed by Greek physicians that he had a serious heart ailment, flew to London on August 25 for treatment; he underwent open heart surgery in mid-September. His ordeal exposed the structural weaknesses of a government that had virtually become a one-man show under his rule. The leader's sudden absence caused dismay and confusion and also encouraged ambitions within the ruling Panhellenic Socialist Movement (Pasok).

Adding to the distress of his party associates was the decision by the 69-year-old Papandreou to be escorted to London not by his wife of 37 years nor by any of their four children but by Dimitra Liani, a 34-year-old former flight attendant with whom he was romantically involved. Later he made it known that he would divorce his wife, presumably to marry Liani. It was hardly a situation to enhance the ailing prime minister's image at home. Worried party associates of Papandreou pressed for early elections to capitalize on voter sympathy for him because of his physical ailments. In fact, they seemed concerned that if elections were left for the following June, either Papandreou's health or the health of the national economy, or both, might have given way. Papandreou himself, heeding medical advice, resisted the pressure. Greece had assumed on July 1 the rotating presidency of the EC, and the prime minister was fully aware of the domestic prestige value of chairing the European summit in Rhodes on December 2–3. By that time, however, the government was enmeshed in a financial scandal that led to the resignation or dismissal of five Cabinet ministers. At its centre was George Koskotas, a banker and publisher who fled Greece in November to escape prosecution for fraud and embezzlement. At year's end the Greek government was attempting to arrange his extradition from the U.S., while a parliamentary investigation indicated that senior government officials had been involved in his dealings.

The Greek economy was hardly in a position to withstand the shock of the largesse customary during Greek election campaigns. Early in 1988 Papandreou was forced to relax a successful austerity program launched in 1986 because its unpopularity was becoming palpable. His flexible incomes policy, however, combined with mismanagement and corruption in the public sector, led to huge deficits. These fueled inflation to levels above 14%, revers-

ing a promising trend achieved through austerity. Thanks to Greece's membership in the EC and the substantial net cash benefits, however, the country remained internationally solvent despite a foreign debt in excess of $20 billion.

Despite efforts to placate workers by relaxing austerity, 1988 was a year of social unrest, strikes, and demonstrations as groups protested against rising prices and demanded higher wages, better education, pollution control, and action against drug trafficking. The Greek police—largely discredited by accusations of unnecessary brutality, gross inefficiency, and protection rackets—reacted with noticeable sluggishness when gangs of anarchists repeatedly went on rampages through central Athens, smashing shop windows and burning cars. It was not surprising, therefore, that terrorism, both the international and the domestic variety, took a heavy toll during the year. The November 17 Revolutionary Organization, an elusive extreme left group, claimed responsibility for the assassination of a Greek industrialist (March 1), an explosion that killed the U.S. defense and naval attaché (June 28), and a humiliating raid against a suburban police station to obtain arms (August 14). In all cases the terrorists escaped.

The worst case of terrorism was a machine-gun and grenade attack aboard the Greek pleasure boat *City of Poros* (July 11) on its return from a day cruise. Nine persons were killed and more than 80 wounded, many of them foreign tourists. In a "safe house" used by the Palestinian group led by Abu Nidal, evidence was later found that linked the group to the shipboard attack as well as to an explosion earlier that day that wrecked a rented car parked near the *City of Poros* landing pier and killed its two occupants.

(MARIO MODIANO)

ICELAND

Iceland is an island republic in the North Atlantic Ocean, near the Arctic Circle. Area: 103,000 sq km (39,769 sq mi). Pop. (1988 est.): 248,000. Cap.: Reykjavík. Monetary unit: Icelandic króna, with (Oct. 10, 1988) a free rate of 47.63 krónur to U.S. $1 (81.57 krónur = £1 sterling). President in 1988, Vigdís Finnbogadóttir; prime ministers, Thorsteinn Pálsson and, from September 28, Steingrímur Hermannsson.

The three-party coalition government that came into office on July 8, 1987, resigned on Sept. 17, 1988, following protracted disagreements over economic policy. No new elections were called; instead, the right-of-centre Independence Party left the government and went into opposition, and its place was taken by the left-wing People's Alliance. Prime Minister Thorsteinn Pálsson left office with his fellow Independence Party ministers, and 60-year-old Steingrímur Hermannsson, chairman of the Progressive Party, became prime minister, a post that he had held a year earlier. His nine-member Cabinet was composed of himself and two other ministers from the Progressive Party and three ministers each from the Social Democrats and the People's Alliance.

The change of government was prompted by disagreements over economic policy to counter a cyclical downturn in the economy after three years of strong expansion. Profits in export industries were declining sharply, while domestic costs were rising with inflation at the same time that foreign prices for fish exports were falling. The currency was devalued twice by a total of 18%. These devaluations did not help much, however, since domestic costs rose so rapidly in their wake that the competitive position of export industries had no chance to improve. The new government decided to halt the process of devaluations with concomitant domestic inflation, and in September it instituted a near-complete wage and price freeze until February 1989. A freeze on wage rates and new wage agreements had been introduced in May. It established a fund to extend loans to export firms in difficulty as a means of counteracting the downturn in foreign markets. The gross domestic product (GDP) in real terms was estimated to decline by 1½% in 1988, following a three-year period in which it rose by an average of 5½% a year. Stagnating exports and rising imports led to an estimated 12 billion krónur current account deficit, equivalent to 4½% of GDP. Moreover, prospects for 1989 were for another year of decline in production and a continuing deficit on the current account of the balance of payments.

The issue of whaling continued to cause difficulty for Iceland abroad. Iceland had decided to ban commercial whaling several years earlier but, at the same time, it embarked on a three-year whaling research program that called for a catch of 120 whales a year, reduced to 78 in 1988. The whale catch program had been strongly opposed by a number of nations as well as by active conservation groups, which had mounted protest boycotts against Icelandic products in foreign markets. By late 1988 this pressure was growing intense, and the government was beginning to doubt the wisdom of continuing its scientific whaling program.

The term of office of Pres. Vigdís Finnbogadóttir was to expire at the end of July. President Vigdís decided to run for another term, her third. She was opposed by Sigrún Thorsteinsdóttir, a 46-year-old housewife from the Westman Islands. The election took place on June 25, and President Vigdís won handsomely with 92.7% of the votes cast. This was the first time in Iceland's 44-year history as a republic that an incumbent president had been opposed for another term of office.

One of the hottest political issues in Iceland in 1988 was the legalization of alcoholic beer. The ban against alcoholic beer, which had been in effect since 1915, was finally repealed in May by the Althing (parliament) after a long and acrimonious debate. Iceland had originally introduced total prohibition but later repealed the ban on wine and hard liquor; however, the ban on beer was never lifted. The temperance movement, long a powerful influence in Iceland, had managed to keep beer out of reach, but it was finally defeated by modern consumer habits and a new generation of voters who no longer believed in old-style temperance.

(BJÖRN MATTHÍASSON)

IRELAND

The republic of Ireland, separated from Great Britain by the North Channel, the Irish Sea, and St. George's Channel, shares its island with Northern Ireland to the northeast. Area: 70,285 sq km (27,137 sq mi). Pop. (1988 est.): 3,553,000. Cap.: Dublin. Monetary unit: Irish pound (punt), with (Oct. 10, 1988) a free rate of Ir£0.69 to U.S. $1 (Ir£1.19 = £1 sterling). President in 1988, Patrick J. Hillery; prime minister, Charles Haughey.

In 1988 Ireland continued to tighten its belt. Charles Haughey's minority Fianna Fail government pursued a policy of economic rectitude, and the support of the opposition parties allowed him to make tough, unpopular decisions and remain in power. The threat of a general election arose spasmodically throughout the year, but it was never very serious. Opinion polls clearly showed that harsh economic realities were apparent to the electorate and that most people approved of and were prepared to follow the government course. Although the polls indicated that Haughey would be assured of a majority if he called

elections, he resisted the temptation to secure his position.

In January the minister for finance introduced a tough deflationary budget, which was seen as a major attempt to restore order to public finances. Exchequer borrowing was reduced by over Ir£300 million, which brought the borrowing requirement down from 10.3% of gross national product to 8.2%. Real tax relief to the PAYE sector was welcomed, as were increased welfare payments. Later in the year the government announced a tax amnesty. Though experts predicted that the total sum collected would amount to Ir£200 million, surprisingly Ir£500 million was collected; this major windfall was expected to further reduce borrowing to 4.5%.

With so much agreement on essential economic objectives between the major parties in the Dail (parliament), 1988 was a dull year politically. Fine Gael, the largest opposition party, was unable to make much impact because the government implemented the very policies they themselves had tried to pursue while in coalition. Not even a front bench reshuffle revived Fine Gael's failing fortunes. The Progressive Democrats (Ireland's newest political party) saw their support drop from 17 to 7%. There was a minor Cabinet reshuffle in November following the appointment of Finance Minister Ray MacSharry to the European Commission.

Unemployment continued to be a major problem, running at 16.6%. There was, however, an employment gain in the private services sector, and total employment figures increased by 6,000. This increase, the first significant jobs gain since 1980, was good news for the government; most independent forecasters had predicted a fall in total employment. With falling interest rates, the prospects for the economy, at least as far as the private sector was concerned, began to improve.

Dublin, the country's capital city, celebrated its millennium in 1988. The actual founding date of the city remained obscure, but the millennium—a promotional idea conceived by the city manager—enhanced civic pride and increased international awareness of Ireland.

The controversial Extradition Act, enacted late in 1987, caused a number of problems during 1988. A six-month deadlock in its operation was caused by the refusal of the British attorney general to adhere to certain safeguards introduced by the Irish government. It was not until May that agreement was reached. The first test case of the new extradition procedures between Ireland and Britain collapsed in June.

Attempts to extradite suspected terrorist Patrick McVeigh failed owing to misunderstandings between the British and Irish governments concerning the necessary identification. This caused a good deal of embarrassment on both sides. An even more emotional case involved Patrick Ryan, a Roman Catholic priest wanted by the British in connection with alleged IRA terrorism. Arrested in Brussels, Ryan was sent to Ireland by Belgian authorities who considered the British charges too vague. The Irish government refused to extradite him on grounds that he could not receive a fair trial in the U.K. Robert Russell was the only person extradited in 1988; he was handed over to the authorities in Northern Ireland in August, amid conditions of unprecedented security.

Other events during the year also placed strains and tensions on the 1985 Anglo-Irish agreement on Northern Ireland. In January 1988 a British court upheld the convictions of six men for the 1974 bombing murder of 21 people in Birmingham. Then a former British policeman, John Stalker, revealed in his memoirs that there was an inclination by police to "shoot to kill" suspects in Northern Ireland without warning or arrest. After the publication of the Sampson Report on the alleged shoot-to-kill policy, the British government announced in January 1988 that it would not prosecute Northern Ireland policemen for their roles in an alleged 1982 shoot-to-kill case. A special meeting of the Anglo-Irish conference was held in March 1988 to help soothe Anglo-Irish relations. A review of the agreement was undertaken in November.

In November the United Kingdom and Ireland ended a 700-year dispute by resolving all territorial issues between the islands with the exceptions of Rockall and Northern Ireland. Sean MacBride (*see* OBITUARIES), one of Ireland's most famous sons and the 1974 Nobel Peace Prize winner, died in January at the age of 83.   (MAVIS ARNOLD)

See also *United Kingdom*, below.

ITALY

A republic of southern Europe, Italy occupies the Apennine Peninsula, Sicily, Sardinia, and a number of smaller islands in the Mediterranean Sea. Area: 301,277 sq km (116,324 sq mi). Pop. (1988 est.): 57,401,000. Cap.: Rome. Monetary unit: Italian lira, with (Oct. 10, 1988) a free rate of 1,383 lire to U.S. $1 (2,368 lire = £1 sterling). President in 1988, Francesco Cossiga; prime ministers, Giovanni Goria and, from April 13, Ciriaco De Mita.

The new man in the prime minister's chair, Giovanni Goria, who had taken over that office in July 1987, submitted his resignation in February 1988. His budget bill had been defeated 17 times in three weeks when about 60 government MPs voted against various clauses. Goria made the mistake of throwing in the towel himself rather than allowing his trainers to make that decision. The timing of his resignation did not suit the Christian Democrat Party (CD), of which he was a member, or the Socialists (PSI). Three days later Goria was advised that his letter of resignation was annulled, and he had to stay on to see the budget bill through. The Christian Democrat "snipers"—those MPs who took advantage of the secret ballot to vote against party instructions—were momentarily chastised and fell into line. One month later the short, unhappy premiership of the youngest man to take that office came to a whimpering end.

Ciriaco De Mita (*see* BIOGRAPHIES), the Christian Democrat leader who had preferred being the party boss to being prime minister and had thus allowed Goria, his one-time protégé, to try his luck, found that there was no way of avoiding the premiership this time and was sworn into office in April. De Mita insisted, however, on retaining his title as the party's secretary-general. The two-hat arrangement displeased those who wanted to take command of the party as his successor. Being head of Italy's largest political party was viewed as more rewarding than being a minister, even the prime minister. That issue, probably of no interest to those outside the CD party, was to be settled early in 1989 at the party conference. Even after six years as party boss, preceded by two terms as a Cabinet minister, De Mita remained something of a nonentity to the general public. He was possibly the most colourless prime minister of the decade. He was also clearly one of the most intelligent and honest in his public utterances. His government was the same coalition of five parties that had served his predecessors through most of the 1980s. Almost everyone seemed to agree that if De Mita should resign, because of some unlikely major gaffe or because of his preference for party administration, the PSI leader, Bettino Craxi, would be waiting in the wings, eager to bound onto the stage again as prime minister and saviour.

Ciriaco De Mita, leader of Italy's Christian Democrat Party, was sworn in as Italy's prime minister but insisted on retaining his position as the party's secretary-general.
LUIGI BALDELLI—CONTRASTO/ PICTURE GROUP

The Social Democrats in 1988 lost not only their founder, former president Giuseppe Saragat (*see* OBITUARIES), but also their then leader, Franco Nicolazzi, who was forced to resign following disclosures of alleged monetary kickbacks he (or his party, as he insisted) received when he was public works minister. He was succeeded by Sen. Antonio Cariglia as party leader. It was thought that the new party leader favoured a merger with the PSI, but when the ailing, 89-year-old Saragat received Cariglia on a courtesy call, he said, "Please let me die a Social Democrat." Saragat had led the split with the Socialists in 1947, when he formed the Social Democrats, because the PSI was then in alliance with the Communists. The Social Democrats received 7% of the national vote in the first postwar elections in 1948, but support was down to 3% in 1987.

Apart from the fleeting glories of sports idols, the Italians had not done well in creating other, more lasting heroes. However, in 1981 they had found, or were told they had found, an Italian who was supremely diabolic. He was Licio Gelli, and the country was advised that a maverick Masonic lodge, called the P2, had been created by Gelli solely to manipulate politicians, bankers, generals and admirals, and, ultimately, the entire country. In 1982 he was arrested in Geneva while trying to withdraw up to $60 million from numbered accounts, but he escaped from a Swiss jail in 1983. When the Italian public first heard of the nefarious P2 lodge, Gelli was already out of the country, probably in South America. In 1987 he surrendered to authorities in Switzerland so that he could obtain treatment for a heart condition. In February 1988 the Swiss agreed to extradite him to Italy, but on the condition that he be tried only for his presumed role in the 1982 collapse of Milan's Banco Ambrosiano. The bank had been found to have $1.2 billion "missing." Since Gelli had been accused in the press of being responsible for or at least involved in many other disasters, including bomb outrages, the Swiss extradition restrictions were frustrating. After his return to Italy, Gelli lived cheerfully in his Tuscan villa, granting interviews that were intended to cloud the already muddy waters swirling around his name. He quickly became a most domesticated devil, one perhaps headed for public oblivion in the media.

Alessandro Natta, who succeeded the late Enrico Berlinguer as Communist Party leader in 1984, resigned because of ill health and a setback in the local elections in May, and the deputy whom he had chosen one year earlier, Achille Occhetto, took over the party in June at the age of 52. A native of Turin, Occhetto had spent all his adult life as a party worker. He could be the Communist leader capable of bringing about a serious and lasting alliance with the Socialists, thus creating a stronger opposition to the Christian Democrats and, at the same time, offering the electorate an alternative that would be light-years away from the old image of the two Marxist parties as satellites of Moscow.

The neo-Fascist Italian Social Movement (MSI) suffered a double loss in May when two party founders, Pino Romualdo and Giorgio Almirante, died within two days of each other. The MSI staged a nationally televised joint funeral, which completely overshadowed the death of Dino Grandi, the former minister of justice who engineered Benito Mussolini's downfall in 1943. (*See* OBITUARIES.)

Municipal and provincial elections in May brought nearly seven million Italians to the polling stations. In the larger centres the Christian Democrats won 29% and the Communists only 22%, while the Socialists gathered in 18%—4% more than in the parliamentary election of one year earlier. The decline of the Communist vote was the most drastic in any election, while the Socialists had much to boast about, even though local elections often are decided by the personalities of local politicians and by local issues.

Italy was the centre of an industrial-waste-disposal scandal in 1988, though one that would probably bring about better management of that problem. An Italian entrepreneur living in Nigeria hired ships to transport, at cheap rates, industrial waste from Italy and other countries to be dumped on land he had rented in Nigeria. The Nigerian government demanded its removal, and Rome moved into the threatening situation by hiring its own ships for the task. Environmental groups in Italy and Britain objected to the importing or reimporting of unlabeled but presumed toxic wastes. Unfortunately, Italian disposal plants were not equipped to cope with the quantity of waste then considered to be Italian. An emergency decree was declared that would eventually oblige each Italian region to handle, at the expense of the industries, its own industrial refuse.

In October the Chamber of Deputies, where the secret vote had always been the rule and the open, or no-secret, vote the exception, finally turned that regulation topsy-turvy. The Communists regarded the secrecy of the ballot as their secret weapon, as did some Christian Democrats who often rebelled against party orders. It had become risky for any Italian government to present a bill to Parliament because the government's own MPs might turn it down under secrecy's mask. That had happened time and again to both the Craxi and Goria governments and led to the latter's resignation. Now that the secret ballot in the chamber would be the exception, the electorate would know how each MP voted, but so would the parties that put him or her in Parliament, thus strengthening the parties' already exaggerated power.

The man considered by many Italians to be their most famous compatriot, Enzo Ferrari, died in August at the age of 90. Almost to the end he had supervised his car plant near Modena, where fewer than 4,000 Ferraris were virtually handcrafted each year for a waiting list of rich clients. In 1969 he had sold 50% of his company to Fiat, which planned to keep the line alive. Marisa Bellisario, Italy's only female "top manager" (as she called her autobiography), died in August of bone cancer. In 1981 she had been put in charge of the faltering state-owned Italtel

company, causing it to blossom anew and to show 1987 profits of 106 billion lire. (*See* OBITUARIES.)

In September a report was released concerning the case of Ciro Cirillo, who was kidnapped by the Red Brigades near Naples in 1981. Cirillo was released three months later upon payment of nearly 5 billion lire. His family said that the ransom had been paid "by friends." Cirillo was at the time in charge of awarding building contracts worth millions of dollars for the vast area around Naples that had been devastated by an earthquake in 1980. The 1,600-page indictment, made public by a Naples investigating magistrate, Carlo Alemi, said that "there are elements which lead us to think that four Christian Democrat leaders were involved in the ransom negotiations" and that they had appealed to Raffaele Cutolo, the then imprisoned boss of the Camorra (the Neapolitan version of the Mafia), to use his good offices in contacting the Red Brigades in Naples. The ransom money then was divided by the terrorists and the Camorra. One of the CD leaders was said to be Antonio Gava, the Catholic Party's boss in Naples. In April he was named De Mita's interior minister, a post that put him in charge of the state police. The Communists—and others—demanded that Gava resign, which he said he had offered to do but had been told by De Mita to remain.

(GEORGE ARMSTRONG)

LIECHTENSTEIN

A landlocked constitutional monarchy of central Europe, Liechtenstein is united with Switzerland by a customs and monetary union. Area: 160 sq km (62 sq mi). Pop. (1988 est.): 27,800. Cap.: Vaduz. Monetary unit: Swiss franc, with (Oct. 10, 1988) a free rate of Sw F 1.58 to U.S. $1 (Sw F 2.70 = £1 sterling). Sovereign prince, Francis Joseph II; deputy head of state in 1988, Prince Hans Adam; head of government, Hans Brunhart.

During 1988 Liechtensteiners monitored with considerable interest the overtures toward the European Communities (EC) made by both its neighbours, Switzerland and Austria. Both countries were currently members of the European Free Trade Association, an economic grouping likely to be severely affected by the emergence of a unified market in the EC in 1992. Any new development in this relationship was apt to have repercussions on the Liechtenstein economy, especially the banking sector. Other issues facing the state were how to continue economic expansion despite the lack of territorial space and the wish to limit the number of foreign nationals (mainly Swiss and Austrian).

July 26 was the 50th anniversary of the accession of Prince Francis Joseph, Europe's longest reigning head of state. In a referendum on the weekend of January 23–24, 69% of the electorate voted by 4,537 votes to 4,234 to increase the number of seats in the Landtag (parliament) from 15 to 25. Free public transport was introduced for a 12-month trial period from January 1, with the aims of discouraging private commuting and thus reducing atmospheric pollution, which was seriously damaging the principality's forests.   (ALUN JONES)

This article updates the *Micropædia* article LIECHTENSTEIN.

LUXEMBOURG

The Benelux country of Luxembourg is a landlocked constitutional monarchy in western Europe. Area: 2,586 sq km (999 sq mi). Pop. (1988 est.): 372,000. Cap.: Luxembourg. Monetary unit: Luxembourg franc, at par with the Belgian franc, with (Oct. 10, 1988) a free rate of Lux F 38.86 to U.S. $1 (Lux F 66.55 = £1 sterling). Grand duke, Jean; prime minister in 1988, Jacques Santer.

From Jan. 1, 1988, Luxembourg prohibited imports of leaded gasoline (petrol), and in July, with existing stocks depleted, the sale of leaded gasoline was also banned. The Luxembourg government's action followed a European Communities (EC) directive that enabled member countries to enact such a ban. The country already had a pricing policy that largely favoured unleaded gasoline. Paul Weber, a government spokesman, declared in July that the reason for the action was that over a quarter of the grand duchy's woodland was affected by pollution.

Although Luxembourg was the only landlocked state in the EC, in 1988 it developed a maritime tradition by finalizing details for the launch of a shipping register, aimed at shipowners in other Community countries. Despite Luxembourg's lack of experience in shipowning, maritime law, and administration, government officials hoped that many would see the register as a respectable alternative to such existing flag-of-convenience registers as Liberia.

Of all the member states of the EC, Luxembourg might be expected to welcome most the prospect of complete freedom of capital movements. On the face of it, the final removal of all exchange controls by the least liberal member states should benefit most those financial centres, like Luxembourg, that were already adapted to the movements of international capital. However, the plans proposed by the EC were regarded with considerable trepidation in the grand duchy. There was a feeling that the raison d'être of the country's success as an international banking centre could be undermined.   (ALUN JONES)

This article updates the *Macropædia* article The Low COUNTRIES: *Luxembourg.*

MALTA

The republic of Malta, a member of the Commonwealth, comprises the islands of Malta, Gozo, and Comino in the Mediterranean Sea between Sicily and Tunisia. Area: 316 sq km (122 sq mi). Pop. (1988 est.): 347,000. Cap.: Valletta. Monetary unit: Maltese lira (formerly Maltese pound), with (Oct. 10, 1988) a free rate of 0.34 lira to U.S. $1 (0.59 lira = £1 sterling). President in 1988, Paul Xuereb (acting); prime minister, Eddie Fenech Adami.

During 1988 Malta strove primarily to reestablish itself as a full and active member of the international community. Prime Minister Eddie Fenech Adami's government continued to work toward full membership in the European Communities and intended to make formal application before 1990. The prime minister was the guest of U.S. Pres. Ronald Reagan in Washington in July and of U.K. Prime Minister Margaret Thatcher in London in September. He also addressed the Congress of Europe at The Hague in May. At the same time, relations with Libya improved; in September the two countries opened a joint radio station and abolished visa requirements for each other's citizens.

UN Secretary-General Javier Pérez de Cuéllar inaugurated the UN Institute on Aging in Valletta in April, as part of his official visit to Malta. In October the secretary-general of the International Maritime Organization, C. P. Srivastava, opened the IMO International Maritime Law Institute at the University of Malta. Malta also signed a number of international human rights conventions.

The visit of the Royal Navy aircraft carrier HMS *Ark Royal* brought violent protests from supporters of the opposition Malta Labour Party over the alleged presence of nuclear weapons on board. Development of the island as a services centre was highlighted by the enactment of legislation on offshore activities. The government reopened applications for oil exploration.   (ALBERT GANADO)

MONACO

A sovereign principality on the northern Mediterranean coast, Monaco is bounded on land by the French département of Alpes-Maritimes. Area: 1.9 sq km (0.73 sq mi). Pop. (1988 est.): 28,900. Monetary unit: French franc, with (Oct. 10, 1988) a free rate of F 6.32 to U.S. $1 (F 10.83 = £1 sterling). Chief of state, Prince Rainier III; minister of state in 1988, Jean Ausseil.

As with other microstates in Europe, the thoughts of Monaco's National Council (parliament) during 1988 turned to the prospect of a single market existing in the European Communities by 1992. The geographic situation of Monaco provided a logical basis for the customs and monetary union with France, which had been in force since 1861. However, Monaco's finances were likely to suffer after 1992, with the loss of a large slice of income from value-added tax because of the parity Monaco was obliged to maintain with France.

Worries were also expressed about Monaco's future as a tax haven. In Monte Carlo people took a more sanguine view of the future. Jean-Charles Rey, the president of the National Council, said, "We've been an independent sovereign state for nearly 800 years, and I don't see why anything should change now." The ruling National and Democratic Union retained all 18 seats in the National Council in the January 24 elections.   (ALUN JONES)

This article updates the *Micropædia* article MONACO.

NETHERLANDS, THE

A constitutional monarchy of northwestern Europe, The Netherlands, a Benelux country, is on the North Sea. Area: 41,863 sq km (16,163 sq mi). Pop. (1988 est.): 14,741,000. Cap., Amsterdam; seat of government, The Hague. Monetary unit: Netherlands guilder, with (Oct. 10, 1988) a free rate of 2.09 guilders to U.S. $1 (3.58 guilders = £1 sterling). Queen, Beatrix; prime minister in 1988, Ruud Lubbers.

On March 8, 1988, a final report was issued in the parliamentary inquiry into the manipulation of building costs by the construction trade in order to obtain higher government subsidies. The inquiry commission, headed by Klaas de Vries of the Labour Party, concluded that there were serious shortcomings in the way the Department for Housebuilding had applied the rules for granting subsidies. As a result, the government had lost billions of guilders over the period 1968–86. Contrary to expectations, however, no evidence was found to indicate actual fraud.

A parliamentary inquiry that caused greater problems for the government of Prime Minister Ruud Lubbers was the investigation into the so-called passport project. This inquiry, which began on May 11, concerned the unsuccessful attempt to introduce a new fraud-resistant passport in The Netherlands. According to the inquiry commission's report, which was released on August 29, the Department of Foreign Affairs had underestimated the complexity of the passport project, and the entire scheme had been grossly mismanaged. The secretary of state for foreign affairs, P. R. H. M. van der Linden, was accused of having given incorrect information to Parliament and was forced to resign on September 9. Three days later the minister of defense, W. F. van Eekelen, who had started the project in the previous Lubbers Cabinet, also resigned. During a 12-hour debate in Parliament on the night of September 22–23, the entire Cabinet seemed for a time to be in danger of falling as Foreign Minister Hans van den Broek and Prime Minister Lubbers refused to accept all aspects of the Parliament's criticism.

Queen Beatrix's traditional speech to open the new parliamentary year was given on September 20. The government budget deficit was decreased as planned, while the economy showed steady growth and the inflation rate was at zero. On the other hand, the unemployment rate was still high; some 670,000 people were unemployed in a working population of about four million. No significant changes in policy were planned by the Lubbers Cabinet.

On May 1, 1988, three British servicemen were killed in the border towns of Roermond and Bergen. The Irish Republican Army (IRA) claimed responsibility for the attack, which it said was in retaliation for the shooting of three IRA members by British agents in Gibraltar in March. A few months later Irish suspects were arrested at the Dutch–German border. During June 17–20 Prime Minister Lubbers and Foreign Minister van den Broek paid a visit to Israel to help celebrate the 40th anniversary of the creation of the Israeli state. The visit took place a month later than had been planned. Officially, the delay was said to have been caused by agenda problems, but in reality it was meant as a protest against Israeli behaviour in the occupied territories. While in Israel, Lubbers and van den Broek held separate meetings with both Israeli and Palestinian leaders. Later in the year van den Broek declared that The Netherlands would officially recognize the Palestine Liberation Organization if the PLO would recognize the state of Israel. During the year van den Broek also paid official visits to Bulgaria (March 8–9), Greece (March 10), and Czechoslovakia (April 21–22). While in Czechoslovakia, he spoke with members of the dissident organization Charter 77.

On June 25 the Dutch national football (soccer) team won the European championship. In the final match they defeated the Soviet national team by a score of 2–0. Spontaneous festivities began throughout the country as news of the victory spread, and a day later millions of people turned out to welcome the team home. On June 27 the players and team officials were received by Queen Beatrix.
          (KLAAS J. HOEKSEMA)

See also *Dependent States,* below.

This article updates the *Macropædia* article The Low COUNTRIES: *The Netherlands.*

NORWAY

A constitutional monarchy of northern Europe, Norway occupies the western part of the Scandinavian Peninsula, with coastlines on the Skagerrak, the North Sea, the Norwegian Sea, and the Arctic Ocean. Area: 323,878 sq km (125,050 sq mi), excluding the Svalbard Archipelago and Jan Mayen Island. Pop. (1988 est.): 4,202,000. Cap.: Oslo. Monetary unit: Norwegian krone, with (Oct. 10, 1988) a free rate of 6.86 kroner to U.S. $1 (11.74 kroner = £1 sterling). King, Olav V; prime minister in 1988, Gro Harlem Brundtland.

A predominantly bleak economic climate prevailed in Norway during 1988. The minority Labour government maintained the austerity policies adopted after it replaced a three-party coalition led by Conservatives in May 1986. Labour's goals were to curb private consumption, stimulate exports, bring down the inflation rate, and reduce dependence on the offshore petroleum industry.

In the autumn Finance Minister Gunnar Berge proclaimed that the cure was working. Strong world demand for some of Norway's traditional exports, such as forest products and metals, combined with shrinking imports, improved the balance of payments.

The draft budget for 1989, introduced on Oct. 4, 1988, envisaged only a small rise in public-sector spending and zero growth in private consumption. Direct and indirect

taxes and charges for public services would be increased overall only enough to keep pace with inflation.

On the political scene, opinion polls showed the two largest parties—Labour and the Conservatives—losing ground to the smaller parties of the centre and to the maverick, right-wing Progress Party. The latter won converts mainly because of its tough line on third world immigration. This was an increasingly sensitive political issue in Norway, which lagged behind other European nations in tightening controls on admission of self-styled "asylum seekers."

Despite Labour's flagging popularity in the polls, Prime Minister Gro Harlem Brundtland's minority government seemed increasingly likely to remain in office at least until the 1989 elections. The three members of the old coalition—Conservatives, Christian Democrats, and Centre (farmers') Party—had drifted apart since losing office. During the spring of 1988, members of Parliament from the Centre Party helped provide a majority to pass a measure crucial to the government's economic policy—a temporary law regulating wages and dividend payments. The measure, valid until the end of March 1989, was credited with slowing the inflation rate in 1988.

Environmental issues often made headlines during the year. A poisonous algae tide hit southern and western Norway in the summer, killing both wild marine life and tens of thousands of farmed fish in pens along the coast. This was followed by an epidemic of seal distemper—believed to be indirectly caused by pollution—that affected all the countries around the North Sea, leaving beaches littered with dead seals. The lucrative, rapidly expanding fish farming industry was also under scrutiny as a possible threat to the environment. Scientists worried about seepage of pollutants from the fish pens—particularly the huge quantities of antibiotics used to keep fish diseases in check.

In August Denmark informed Norway that it had submitted a long-standing boundary dispute between the two countries to the International Court at The Hague for arbitration. The dispute concerned overlapping economic zone claims in the waters between Greenland and Jan Mayen Island, where Norway maintained a weather station. Hearings in the case began on October 12.

In September NATO held its largest ever combined sea, land, and air maneuvers along the coast of northern Norway. The exercise, dubbed "Teamwork," involved 45,000 personnel from the U.S., Canada, West Germany, The Netherlands, Belgium, Denmark, and Norway, as well as 200 ships and 500 aircraft, including carrier-based fighters and helicopters. Critics said it was badly timed, in view of the improved political climate between East and West. Four violations of neutral Sweden's airspace, by U.S. planes, led to official protests from the Stockholm government, followed by a Norwegian order grounding all the allied aircraft taking part in the event. In November Norway announced plans to end exports of heavy water following scandals involving the illegal diversion of earlier shipments.   (FAY GJESTER)

See also *Dependent States*, below.

PORTUGAL

A republic of southwestern Europe, metropolitan Portugal is on the Atlantic coast of the Iberian Peninsula, which it shares with Spain. Area: 92,389 sq km (35,672 sq mi), including the Azores and Madeira island groups/archipelagoes in the Atlantic. Pop. (1988 est.): 10,349,000. Cap.: Lisbon. Monetary unit: Portuguese escudo, with (Oct. 10, 1988) a free rate of 152.85 escudos to U.S. $1 (261.75 escudos = £1 sterling). President in 1988, Mário Soares; prime minister, Aníbal Cavaço Silva.

The convincing victory for Prime Minister Aníbal Cavaço Silva's Social Democratic Party (PSD) in the 1987 elections appeared to end more than a decade of instability based on precarious coalitions and political alliances. Cavaço Silva won the election on a pro-European Communities ticket and with a clear mandate to reform the country's labour laws and slim down the government's role in the economy. Although the PSD claimed that a full frontal assault on the 1975 constitution was not planned, the new government had already initiated privatizations of one of the small banks and of a brewery nationalized after the April 1974 revolution. Nevertheless, wholesale denationalizations seemed as far away as ever, although it was thought that private firms would gradually be allowed to enter the previously reserved oil, steel, gas, electricity, communications, and transport businesses, introducing a much-needed element of competition to the public sector.

New labour legislation introduced to the Assembly on March 3 was intended to liberalize the country's rigid 1975 labour laws, making it possible to dismiss workers for economic and disciplinary reasons. On March 28, in response to the proposed legislation, the Communist CGTP and socialist UGT trade unions cooperated for the first time to stage the biggest general strike in Portuguese history. Nevertheless, the legislation was passed on April 16 by the PSD, with the Communists and Socialists voting against it and the Christian Democrats abstaining. The watchdog Constitutional Tribunal then ruled that the intended changes violated guarantees of job security (Article 53 of the constitution) and the right to work (Article 59). Singled out as being objectionable were the clauses allowing the dismissal of workers judged to be "unsuited" to the conditions of the company and the general authorization given employers to refuse, on the pretext of a deterioration in the social atmosphere in the firm, to reemploy a worker whose dismissal had been judged by a worker tribunal to have been unjustified.

Following this ruling, an intense period of discussions among the parties ensued, which ended with the Socialists accepting the premise that, if Portugal was to be ready for the single European market by 1992, work on a new constitution had to start immediately. To ensure the two-thirds majority needed to change the law, the PSD and the Socialists signed a pact on October 14 allowing Marxist ideology to be eliminated from the constitution on such aspects as the irreversibility of nationalizations (Article 83) and the undoing of farm reforms that collectivized much of the Alentejo in 1975. The new constitution should also permit eventual full privatization of government-owned enterprises, with the proceeds going toward reducing the public debt, which amounted to approximately 80% of gross domestic product.

The economy had surged after investment poured in from Common Market partners and outsiders as the country adapted to its membership in the European Communities (EC). However, the openness of the economy and its propensity to import continued to worry the authorities. The Organization for Economic Cooperation and Development's (OECD's) annual Report on Portugal for 1987–88 commented favourably on the thrust of the PSD's budget and its target of tackling "the rigidities of the economy" through action on controlling expenditure, fiscal reform, and the control of inflation. Nevertheless, the government found inflation slipping out of its control after July, guaranteeing further confrontations with the labour unions, which had withdrawn earlier from an agreement with the government on wage ceilings.

On August 25 a fire in Lisbon destroyed the old Chi-

A thick cloud of smoke hangs above the burning Chiado district of Lisbon. Described as the city's worst disaster in centuries, the fire destroyed the historic shopping district, causing 2,000 people to lose their jobs and leaving some 300 homeless.

FERREIRA—GAMMA/LIAISON

ado district, causing an estimated $350 million worth of damage and the destruction of more than 40 businesses. Although the Rua do Carmo and the Rua Garrett shopping districts were burned, only one person was killed in what was described as the worst disaster since the 1755 earthquake. Concern, especially after the fire, had been growing about the fate of the district and its surrounding area, fed by rumours that redevelopment would change the character of the area for the worse. This concern was felt despite the fact that the district had fallen into disrepair, partly as the result of a 40-year rent freeze, and that much of the property was used commercially rather than for residences. Rebuilding of the Chiado and the restoration of the old city were likely to be major issues in the municipal elections in 1989. Financial support would not be too difficult since the EC's bank had promised help, but it was necessary for the city to develop a comprehensive plan.

(MICHAEL WOOLLER)

See also *Dependent States,* below.

SAN MARINO

The republic of San Marino is a landlocked enclave in northeastern Italy. Area: 61 sq km (24 sq mi). Pop. (1988 est.): 22,800. Cap.: San Marino. Monetary unit: Italian lira, with (Oct. 10, 1988) a free rate of 1,383 lire to U.S. $1 (2,368 lire = £1 sterling). The republic is governed by two *capitani reggenti,* or coregents, appointed every six months by a popularly elected Great and General Council. Executive power rests with the Congress of State, headed by the coregents and composed of three secretaries of state and seven ministers.

San Marino feared the prospect of a unified market in the European Communities (EC) less than Europe's other microstates. By virtue of its customs union with Italy, San Marino's goods already had unrestricted access to EC markets. Only the possibility of stiffer competition in its traditional industries of leather and textile goods seemed to worry the republic's politicians. Following the general election in May, the Christian Democrats (27 of 60 seats) and the Communists (18) formed a coalition. (For tabulated results, see *Political Parties,* above.)

San Marino was the sole European microstate that could

not be counted as a tax haven. However, certain tax advantages existed for those companies that set up business in the republic, though it was likely that these would have to be abolished after the unified European market came into existence in 1992. In addition to the cement, textile, and leather industries, tourism continued to play an important part in the economy. In 1988 some three million people visited the small state, a fact that some claimed had added to the self-confidence exuded by the republic.

(ALUN JONES)

This article updates the *Micropædia* article SAN MARINO.

SPAIN

A constitutional monarchy of southwestern Europe with coastlines on the Bay of Biscay, the Atlantic Ocean, and the Mediterranean Sea, Spain shares the Iberian Peninsula with Portugal; it includes the Balearic and Canary island groups, in the Mediterranean and the Atlantic, respectively, and enclaves in northern Morocco. Area: 504,783 sq km (194,898 sq mi). Pop. (1988 est.): 38,996,000. Cap.: Madrid. Monetary unit: Spanish peseta, with (Oct. 10, 1988) a free rate of 122.13 pesetas to U.S. $1 (209.15 pesetas = £1 sterling). King, Juan Carlos I; prime minister in 1988, Felipe González Márquez.

On July 4, 1988, during a lecture to the Menéndez Pelayo International University at Santander, the minister of the economy announced a series of measures aimed at bringing Spain's antiquated labour laws more into line with European Communities (EC) standards. In response, the socialist and Communist unions decided to cooperate formally for the first time in their negotiations with the government and the employers' federation during the next wage round. Strains appeared in the government between those following a hard reformist line and those wishing to appease the unions and retain their loyalty. On July 8, in Prime Minister Felipe González Márquez's fourth reshuffle since taking power, the ministers of justice, industry, transport, and education were replaced, respectively, by Enrique Mugíca, Claudio Aranzadi, José Barrionuevo, and Javier Solana. Jorge Semprún took over at culture, and the Basque José Luis Corcuera at home affairs. Matilde Fernández at the newly created Ministry of Social Affairs

and Rosa Condé as head of the Cabinet Office were the first women to be included in the Cabinet in 50 years.

Two years earlier Manuel Fraga Iribarne had announced his resignation as leader of the right-wing Alianza Popular (AP) after a series of dismal performances in both local and national elections. He was replaced by Antonio Hernández Mancha, but the fortunes of the party continued to decline. In October Fraga announced that, at the behest of many in his party, he would challenge Hernández for the leadership at the party congress in January 1989. Local elections in May in Catalonia were won by the governing Convergencia i Unio (CiU).

An agreement in principle was reached on withdrawal of the U.S. Tactical Air Wing from the Torrejón air base. A joint declaration was issued stating that the U.S. could still expect to use the base in time of war and that a new eight-year bilateral treaty would be drawn up. The accord cleared the way for the government to tackle the issue of its involvement with NATO, which had been frozen since the government won a referendum allowing Spain to remain a member on the basis of limited participation. Having made progress on the U.S. base question, González felt strong enough to assert that his administration would no longer insist on the withdrawal of nuclear weapons from Europe, nor would it require visiting NATO vessels to declare whether they were carrying such weapons.

To clear the way for further participation in NATO, Spain signed bilateral accords with Portugal and the U.K. Spain agreed that its navy in the Eastern Atlantic could come under Portuguese command, subject to certain conditions. In November the Spanish and Portuguese prime ministers agreed on lowering trade barriers for textiles, as well as increased cooperation in communications, energy, and infrastructural projects. This would serve as a dress rehearsal for the EC single market, scheduled to come into existence in 1992. Skirting the issue of Gibraltar, the U.K. and Spain agreed that rather than dealing directly with each other, both would deal with NATO's Southern Command in Naples. Nevertheless, later in the year there was evidence of a thaw. Queen Elizabeth II and Prime Minister Margaret Thatcher paid official visits to Spain, the first by a reigning British monarch or a prime minister. The Spanish ambassador in London lit the first of the beacons celebrating England's escape from the Spanish Armada in 1588. Both Spain and Portugal were asked to join the Western European Union in November.

Despite the promise of increased French cooperation in the campaign against the Basque separatist group Euzkadi ta Azkatasuna (ETA; Basque Homeland and Liberty), the results were disappointing. The ETA murdered about a dozen people and mounted a bombing campaign in the Basque area, mainly against French targets. French displeasure came to a head after the Spanish government refused to accept the evidence of one of its own judges regarding secret funds allegedly transferred to finance surveillance and police operations in France. It was hoped that a meeting between the two ministers of home affairs in León in October might clear the air, but this was prevented by misunderstandings over the handling of the kidnap and ransom of the businessman Emiliano Revilla. In November the ETA in Algeria released Revilla after collecting a ransom reportedly amounting to 1.2 billion pesetas. A few days later it offered the government a 60-day cease-fire on condition that negotiations be reopened with its exiled leadership in Algeria.

The economy boomed, helped by Spain's entry into the EC and the resulting strong foreign investment inflows. In advance of the 1992 deadline, the government moved to encourage further financial deregulation. Although an attempted merger between the Banco de Bilbao and the Banco Español de Credíto had failed in 1987 on a technicality, both banks found new partners in 1988, reducing the number of leading banks from seven to five. Companies stepped up their investments, and the government was carrying out much-needed investment in the infrastructure and public-sector firms in an effort to modernize the country in time for the single market. Serious problems persisted, however, despite the country's buoyant growth. General unemployment stood at 20% and the rate among youth was 40%. Signs of overheating included surging current account and trade deficits; inflation was rising to over 5%. On December 14 the country was paralyzed by a one-day general strike, but at year's end, following a plea from King Juan Carlos, representatives of the government and the two largest labour unions met in an attempt to resolve their differences.   (MICHAEL WOOLLER)

AFP PHOTO

A technical crew works on an F-16 fighter plane at a U.S. military base in Spain. A new agreement between the U.S. and Spain called for the phased withdrawal over three years of the U.S. Tactical Air Wing from the base.

SWEDEN

A constitutional monarchy of northern Europe, Sweden occupies the eastern side of the Scandinavian Peninsula, with coastlines on the North and Baltic seas and the Gulf of Bothnia. Area: 449,964 sq km (173,732 sq mi). Pop. (1988 est.): 8,415,000. Cap.: Stockholm. Monetary unit: Swedish krona, with (Oct. 10, 1988) a free rate of 6.36 kronor to U.S. $1 (10.89 kronor = £1 sterling). King, Carl XVI Gustaf; prime minister in 1988, Ingvar Carlsson.

A general election in 1988 resulted in victory for the Social Democrats, allowing them to continue as the ruling party in Sweden, but it also introduced a new element into the Riksdag (parliament) in the shape of 20 Greens pledged to campaign for a drastic cleanup of the environment and a shutdown of nuclear power. There had been fears before the election that the Greens might be left holding the balance of power between the socialist and nonsocialist blocs, but these proved groundless.

The voters appeared to pay more attention to the pragmatic economic policies of socialist Finance Minister Kjell-Olof Feldt than to a scandal involving the party's alleged abuse of power in sanctioning a private investigation into the 1986 assassination of Prime Minister Olof Palme, which earlier in the year had led to the resignation of Justice Minister Anna-Greta Leijon. The national characteristic of conformity also played a part; many who had threatened to vote Green after a year of environmental scares switched to traditional allegiances once actually inside the polling booth.

Even though the Social Democrats won the election, they lost three seats. However, this was compensated for by a gain of two seats by the Communists, who traditionally supported socialist administrations. The Social Democrats won 43.6% of the vote, giving them 156 seats in the Riksdag and a four-seat majority over the nonsocialist parties, which all lost seats. Thus, at the end of the day, Prime Minister Ingvar Carlsson had even greater room for maneuverability than he had enjoyed with his first administration, with the Communists' 21 seats assuring him a majority even in the unlikely event that the Greens joined forces with the nonsocialists. The three nonsocialist parties suffered most from the Green revolution, the Conservatives winning only 66 seats, a drop of 10; the Liberals 44, down 7; and the Centre 42, a decline of 2.

The entry of the Greens into the Riksdag—the first new party to gain admission in 70 years—was triggered by a wave of concern over the environment, in particular sea pollution. This was thought to be responsible for a sudden rapid blooming of algae that killed thousands of tons of fish along the west coast in warm spring weather. The algae were believed to have "fed" on nitrogen and phosphorus pouring from the Elbe River into the North Sea. The chemicals were contained in fertilizers washed into the river from surrounding fields by exceptionally heavy winter and spring rains. When the weather changed, the algae began to die and the threat receded. Later in the year, however, a virus killed the greater proportion of Sweden's harbour seal population and spread rapidly along the coasts of Denmark, Germany, and The Netherlands to Britain. This too was blamed ultimately on pollution in Sweden, researchers claiming that the seals' immune defense systems had been so weakened by the polluted water that they could not withstand the virus.

Elsewhere, Sweden began to make cautious overtures to the European Communities as anxiety grew among business leaders that the country could be left behind in 1992

(Left to right) Eva Goes, Per Garthon, and Jill Lindgren, the first Greens to gain entry to Sweden's Riksdag (parliament), pause for photographers on their way into the Riksdag building. Their election was triggered by concern for the environment.
AFP PHOTO

when the EC removed internal trade barriers. Prime Minister Carlsson established a Cabinet committee for European affairs and a Council for European Affairs that comprised leading industrialists and labour union officials. He then appointed Ulf Dinkelspiel, a senior Foreign Ministry official, as chief negotiator for European affairs. In December police in Stockholm arrested Carl Gustav Christer Pettersson and charged him with the assassination of Palme. The 41-year-old Pettersson had a criminal record that included the killing of a youth with a bayonet in 1970.

(CHRIS MOSEY)

SWITZERLAND

A landlocked federal state in west central Europe, Switzerland consists of a confederation of 26 cantons (6 of which are demicantons). Area: 41,293 sq km (15,943 sq mi). Pop. (1988 est.): 6,626,000. Cap.: Bern. Monetary unit: Swiss franc, with (Oct. 10, 1988) a free rate of Sw F 1.58 to U.S. $1 (Sw F 2.70 = £1 sterling). President in 1988, Otto Stich.

If, as researchers at Geneva University's sociology department claimed, the traditional Swiss work ethic was no longer what it had been—though proposals for a 40-hour workweek, longer holidays, and earlier retirement were rejected by a two-thirds majority in recent national referenda—the effects of this changing attitude were not yet detectable in the nation's economic performance in 1988. The country, indeed, sailed on largely unperturbed by repercussions of the October 1987 market crash. While the process of industrial reconstruction, under way for six years, had led to the elimination of many jobs, unemployment remained around the 1% mark.

The year was notable for the rapid emergence of public uncertainty regarding 1992, when the 12-nation European Communities (EC) was due to become an economically integrated entity. The government, while favouring closer collaboration with the EC, firmly reasserted that membership "under present conditions cannot be an objective." Instead, for the time being, the "European consciousness" of the Swiss, especially the young, was to be encouraged. Long before the issue came to public discussion, however, the main Swiss banks and multinational companies had embarked on a preemptive strategy, acquiring subsidiaries within the EC countries. Maintenance of Switzerland's traditional neutrality was unlikely to preclude adaptability.

Another proud tradition appeared to be at risk: the trains were running late, albeit, for the most part, by only five minutes or so. The cause was an increase in the number of trains, made necessary by an increase in passengers. This, in turn, was a result of low incentive fares in conjunction with highway congestion and parking difficulties. Nevertheless, frustrated commuters were not amused by a cheerful railway official's "These delays are really a sign of health." There were no doubts regarding a similar assurance from the watchmaking industry. The universally successful Swatch had stimulated demand for all the industry's products, enabling Swiss manufacturers to regain almost half the world market.

Subjects of controversy as well as compassion were the seekers of political asylum, many of them entering the country clandestinely, aided by professional *passeurs*. The total for the year was around 15,000. Turks were in the majority, a result of the tightening of West German laws on the admission of foreign workers. Consequently, most applicants were judged to be "economic refugees," and no more than 7% could hope to be accepted. However, under the 1951 Convention on Refugees, all were entitled to board and lodging at public expense while awaiting the official decision. The procedures took at least six months, and the backlog, though being steadily reduced, was about 28,000 at year's end. Asylum seekers were thus assured of being in Switzerland for several months at least. After three months they were permitted to find work—a simple matter because of the perennial shortage of unskilled labour for jobs spurned by the Swiss. However, the cost of maintaining mostly able-bodied young male refugees was resented by sections of the population.

The right-wing National Action Party was the chief mover in securing a national referendum vote on "limitation of immigration." Contending that Switzerland was overpopulated, the party proposed that for every three foreign workers returning to their own countries, only two newcomers be admitted. Their initiative was rejected by a two-thirds majority.

Other preoccupations during the year included the continuing rise in the cost of housing, acid rain, drug addiction, and AIDS cases, which now numbered 7.6 per 100,000 population. Elizabeth Kopp, Switzerland's first and only woman Cabinet member, resigned as minister of justice and police on December 12, only six days after Parliament elected her vice-president of the confederation for 1989. Six weeks earlier Kopp's husband had resigned from a Lebanese-owned firm in Zürich being investigated in a case involving money laundering. Relations with Lebanon deteriorated, and Switzerland withdrew its diplomats from that country in December.   (ALAN MCGREGOR)

UNITED KINGDOM

A constitutional monarchy in northwestern Europe and member of the Commonwealth, the United Kingdom comprises the island of Great Britain (England, Scotland, and Wales) and Northern Ireland, together with many small islands. Area: 244,110 sq km (94,251 sq mi), including 3,218 sq km of inland water but excluding the crown dependencies of the Channel Islands and Isle of Man. Pop. (1988 est.): 57,006,000. Cap.: London. Monetary unit: pound sterling, with (Oct. 10, 1988) a free rate of £0.58 to U.S. $1 (U.S. $1.71 = £1 sterling). Queen, Elizabeth II; prime minister in 1988, Margaret Thatcher.

Domestic Affairs. Prime Minister Margaret Thatcher (*see* BIOGRAPHIES) continued to dominate the Conservative Party, and the party continued to dominate British politics. With the government holding a secure 102-seat majority in the House of Commons, obtained at the June 1987

Margaret Thatcher chats with reporters after becoming the U.K.'s longest-serving prime minister of the 20th century.
AP/WIDE WORLD

general election, ministers were able to press ahead with an ambitious legislative program, building upon the work of the previous nine years.

The most controversial new law was the Local Government Finance Act, which received the royal assent in July. This law established a timetable for abolishing the rates, Britain's local property tax, by 1990 and establishing a flat-rate "community charge" in its place, payable by every adult to his or her local authority. According to the government, the new charge would make local councils more responsive to their electors; critics, however, called it a "poll tax" and said it would be costly to administer and unfair in operation because better-off people, currently paying high rates on valuable properties, would save money under the new system, whereas many poorer people, whose rates were more modest, would end up paying more. Politically, the government had less difficulty passing the act into law than seemed likely when the bill was first published. A number of Conservative back-bench MPs and peers opposed it, but their rebellions were too weak to secure any substantial changes in the legislation.

In the event, the opposition Labour Party was more discomforted by the new tax. Earlier legislation meant that it would be introduced in Scotland before the rest of the U.K. Labour had won 50 of the 72 Scottish seats in the 1987 general election and raised the hopes of many Scottish people that it would fight effectively against the government. However, the Labour Party in Scotland was divided between those who wanted to mount a campaign of resistance, including nonpayment of the new tax, and those (including the party leadership) who advocated remaining "inside the law" and working to secure a future Labour government that would repeal the legislation. The Scottish National Party (SNP), which wanted Scotland to secede from the U.K., accused Labour of incompetence in its opposition to the new tax. A by-election in one of Labour's safest Scottish seats, the Glasgow constituency of Govan, on November 10, put this dispute to the test. Labour lost the seat with one of the largest swings ever recorded in a by-election. Labour's support fell from 65 to 37%, while the SNP jumped from 10 to 49% to win the seat with a majority of 3,554.

The most important of the other new laws concerned

education. The Education Reform Act became law after 370 hours of parliamentary debate and 5,000 amendments, setting new records for postwar legislation. The act, steered through Parliament by Kenneth Baker, the education secretary (*see* BIOGRAPHIES), gave parents at individual schools the power to vote to "opt out" of control by the local education authority and make their schools self-governing charitable trusts. It also established a "national core curriculum" and required children to take formal tests at set intervals, thus limiting the power of councils and schools to vary their teaching and assessment methods.

During the year ministers unveiled other policies that they planned to implement into the 1990s. In major speeches in September and October, Thatcher embraced a "green" approach to politics, saying that humankind had "begun a massive experiment with the system of the planet itself," of which two of the most notable features were the holes in the ozone layer over Antarctica and the "greenhouse effect," in which emissions of carbon dioxide into the atmosphere had the effect of increasing the planet's average temperature. Thatcher advocated policies to conserve energy, reduce pollution, and—most controversial of all—to increase reliance on nuclear power, as this emitted less carbon dioxide than fossil fuels. Thatcher's remarks were widely interpreted as a new development in government thinking; however, she did not indicate how this would affect the breakup and privatization of the electricity industry, planned to take place before the next general election, or the privatization of the coal industry, which Cecil Parkinson, the energy secretary, announced in July would take place if the Conservatives won a fourth term in office. Thatcher's new approach was dealt a blow in November when the Department of the Environment's chief pollution inspector resigned, charging the inspectorate with poor organization and insufficient government funding.

Other policies unveiled during 1988 affected the media and the administration of justice. In June the home secretary, Douglas Hurd, issued a White Paper on official secrets. This proposed making it a criminal offense to publish any unauthorized information concerning the security services, telephone tapping, and certain categories of government information concerning international relations. In October Hurd announced that radio and television would be prohibited from broadcasting interviews with members or supporters of Provisional Sinn Fein (PSF) or the Irish Republican Army (IRA). (See *Northern Ireland,* below.) Also in October Hurd and Tom King, the Northern Ireland secretary, announced a curtailment of defendants' right to silence in criminal cases. Under their proposals, to be implemented first in Northern Ireland and then in the rest of the U.K., juries could be invited to take note whenever an accused person remained silent and to decide whether it should be interpreted as a tacit admission of guilt. On November 30 the government published the Official Secrets Bill. The areas outlined in the White Paper remained unchanged in the bill, but Hurd attempted to meet criticism by narrowing the scope of some of the provisions. In particular, the bill made it clear that it would not be an offense, as the White Paper had proposed, simply to disclose information received in confidence from other governments or international organizations.

On all those issues, the government faced criticism from the opposition parties as well as a wide range of lawyers, journalists, and broadcasters. In September the journal *Index on Censorship,* which normally monitored violations of freedom of speech in dictatorships and incomplete democracies, devoted a special issue to freedom of speech in Britain. *Index*'s editorial commented: "If freedom is diminished in the United Kingdom, where historically it has deep roots, it is potentially diminished everywhere." The government's one significant defeat over press freedom occurred on October 13, when five law lords ruled unanimously that the press could report the allegations made in *Spycatcher,* the memoirs of a former secret service officer, Peter Wright. Wright's most serious charges were that he had led a conspiracy to discredit the then prime minister, Harold Wilson, in 1975; that in the 1950s the British security services secretly (and unsuccessfully) planned the assassination of Pres. Gamal Abdel Nasser of Egypt; and that officers in the domestic intelligence agency MI5 had illegally "bugged and burgled" telephones and offices throughout London, monitoring left-wing groups and

AFP PHOTO

Mourners hide behind tombstones and scramble for cover to escape a gunman who opened fire at a funeral in Belfast held for three members of the Irish Republican Army who had been killed in Gibraltar on March 6.

foreign embassies. *Spycatcher* had already been published in other countries, but the government had been trying to prevent publication in the U.K.

The opposition parties had a lean year. Labour, attempting to recover from its third consecutive general election defeat, embarked on a wide-ranging policy review. At its annual conference in October, the party endorsed a new strategy for the economy. In effect, Labour abandoned its theoretical ambition of abolishing capitalism and embraced the market and private ownership for the majority of transactions.

The future of Labour's defense policy was less clear-cut. The party remained committed to continuing membership in NATO; the doubts concerned its policy toward Britain's own nuclear weapons. In both 1983 and 1987 Labour's general election manifesto had promised that these weapons would be scrapped unilaterally; this policy was opposed by a majority of voters and was seen as a factor in Labour's heavy defeats in both elections. In a television interview on June 5, 1988, party leader Neil Kinnock appeared to edge away from this policy when he said, "There is no need now for something-for-nothing unilateralism." His remarks provoked a dispute within the party. Denzil Davies resigned on June 14 as Labour's defense spokesman.

Kinnock was challenged for the leadership of the party by Tony Benn, a left-winger and experienced former member of Labour Cabinets in the 1960s and 1970s. Under Labour's rules, leadership elections were determined by the weighted votes of members of Parliament, trade unions, and local constituency parties. The result of the election, announced on October 2, showed that Kinnock had won decisively in all three groups, winning a total weighted vote of 88.6%, compared with Benn's 11.4%. In a parallel contest, Kinnock's deputy, Roy Hattersley, won 66.8% support, comfortably defeating a challenge to his position from two left-wing candidates.

The centre parties had an even rougher year than Labour. Following the decisions of the Liberals and Social Democrats in the summer of 1987 to negotiate a merger between the two parties, an attempt was made to devise a common statement of principles. This was published on January 13 under the title *Voices and Choices for All* but was immediately withdrawn following opposition from a number of Liberals who considered it too right-wing. A six-member team—three from each party—devised a new statement, *A Democracy of Conscience,* which was published on January 17. Majorities in both parties subsequently ratified the merger, but the near fiasco of *Voices and Choices for All* demoralized many people in the new party before its official launch on March 3 under the name Social and Liberal Democrats.

The SLD's prospects were further diminished by the decision of the SDP's former leader, David Owen, to resume the leadership of the minority of SDP members who opposed the merger. Thus by the spring of 1988 there were, once again, two centre parties—SLD and SDP—but this time working not in alliance but in bitter competition. On July 28 the SLD had a new leader, Paddy Ashdown (*see* BIOGRAPHIES), who won 71.9% of the vote of party members, defeating Alan Beith, who had previously served as deputy to David Steel, the former Liberal Party leader.

On December 21 a Pan American World Airways Boeing 747 jumbo jet en route from London to the U.S. crashed in Scotland, killing all 259 people aboard the plane and apparently 11 more on the ground in the village of Lockerbie. Analysis of the wreckage revealed that the accident was caused by a powerful plastic explosive device in the luggage compartment. At year's end the person or

Britain's foreign secretary, Sir Geoffrey Howe, speaks with members of the press after his meeting with Iranian Foreign Secretary Ali Akbar Velayati on the resumption of full diplomatic ties.
AP/WIDE WORLD

persons responsible for the crash remained unknown.

Princess Beatrice Elizabeth Mary, first child of the duke and duchess of York and fifth in succession to the throne, was born on August 8. Meanwhile, Prince Charles continued to generate controversy with his outspoken criticism of modern urban architecture and his vigorous work on behalf of inner-city youths.

Economic Affairs. During the early months of the year, it looked as if Britain's chancellor of the Exchequer, Nigel Lawson (*see* BIOGRAPHIES), could do little wrong. He was set to preside over steady growth, low inflation, moderate interest rates, declining unemployment, lower taxes, and a surplus of tax revenues over government spending. In his budget on March 15 he reduced the standard rate of income tax from 27 to 25% and the top rate from 60 to 40% as part of a strategy for simplifying as well as reducing personal taxation.

By the summer, however, it was clear that some of Lawson's predictions would be wide of the mark. The economy was growing faster than expected, mainly because of rapidly rising consumption, financed by easy credit and a sharp reduction in savings. This was helping to bring unemployment down, but it also meant higher inflation and a worsening trade balance. By November the Treasury was predicting that the economy would grow overall by 4.5% in 1988 (the prediction in March had been 3%), but that inflation would be running at 6.25% (4%) and that there would be a deficit on the balance of payments current account of £13 billion (£4 billion).

In an attempt to rein in consumer spending, Lawson raised interest rates in a rapid sequence of 0.5% and 1% steps from 7% in May to 13% in November. Lawson told the House of Commons that he expected inflation to fall again in 1989, that the economy would grow at a "sustainable" 3%, and that the balance of payments would begin to improve. At the end of 1988, independent economists agreed that the British economy had overheated during the year; they were, however, divided over whether Lawson would achieve a "soft landing" in 1989, in which the economy settled down as the chancellor predicted, or whether there would be a financial crisis, provoking higher interest rates and a domestic recession.

Foreign Affairs. The government's main foreign policy preoccupations in 1988 concerned the European Communities (EC). At the February EC meeting, Thatcher succeeded in holding the line on agricultural spending and retained Britain's budget rebate. In a speech on September 20 in Bruges, Belgium, Thatcher distanced herself from the notion of European union. She said: "Willing and active cooperation between independent sovereign states is the best way to build a successful European Community. To try to suppress nationhood and concentrate power at the centre of a European conglomerate would be highly damaging and would jeopardize the objectives we seek to achieve. . . . We have not successfully rolled back the frontiers of the state in Britain, only to see them reimposed at a European level, with a European super-state exercising a new dominance from Brussels."

In November Thatcher visited Poland and received a rapturous reception from workers at the Lenin Shipyard in Gdansk, birthplace of the banned labour union Solidarnosc (Solidarity). During her visit Thatcher embraced Solidarity leader Lech Walesa, who called Thatcher "fantastic." In a speech to the Polish government, Thatcher advocated the merits of free enterprise and urged Polish leader Gen. Wojciech Jaruzelski to hold a "real dialogue with representatives of all sections of society, including Solidarity." Thatcher indicated that the West would be willing to help Poland overcome its foreign debt burden, but that this would be dependent on Polish moves toward greater democracy. (*See* Eastern Europe and the U.S.S.R.: *Poland,* below.)

In a farewell visit with U.S. Pres. Ronald Reagan in November, Thatcher urged the U.S. to take a more positive view of recent developments in the Middle East. Also in November, Britain restored diplomatic relations with Iran after an eight-year break, but officials denied that a deal had been made regarding British hostages held in Lebanon.

In December a British government minister met with an official of the Palestine Liberation Organization (PLO) for the first time in more than five years. The meeting, between Foreign Office minister William Waldegrave and Bassam Abu Sharif, a political adviser to PLO chairman Yasir Arafat, was seen as part of a British effort to "encourage and draw out moderate elements" within the PLO. Speaking for the PLO, Sharif said, "The Palestinians are fully for international guarantees for all states in the region to live behind secure borders."

Northern Ireland. On March 6 members of the Special Air Service in Gibraltar shot three IRA terrorists dead, precipitating a series of controversies. According to the British government, the terrorists were members of a team planning to bomb British troops in Gibraltar. The SAS had intended to arrest them but, believing them to be armed and primed to detonate the bomb at any time, opened fire rather than risk either themselves or other troops being killed. Subsequent press and television investigations cast doubt on the SAS actions, but then the quality of some of those investigations became a matter of dispute.

Six months later a lengthy inquest took place in Gibraltar. The SAS officers involved gave evidence, although their names were never disclosed. On September 30, by a majority of nine to two, the jury returned a verdict of lawful killing. However, the government had to continue to defend itself against two persistent charges: that it had issued false statements to the media at the time of the shootings and that it either operated or condoned a "shoot to kill" policy, in which suspected terrorists could be killed rather than prosecuted through the courts.

On October 19 Hurd announced that he was using powers given to him by the BBC's charter and the Broadcasting Act to prohibit radio and television programs from broadcasting interviews with members or supporters of the IRA or the Protestant paramilitary organization, the Ulster Defence Association. The only time this ban would be lifted would be during elections, when candidates could be interviewed. On November 22, however, the government moved to minimize the number of people who came into this category when the queen's speech promised legislation to require candidates for parliamentary or council office to swear an oath dissociating themselves from violence. BBC and Independent Television News criticized the restrictions of their coverage but agreed to implement them.

These measures, together with the qualification of the right to silence of defendants in criminal cases (see *Domestic Affairs,* above), prompted widespread criticism that the government was curbing basic freedoms in Northern Ireland. On November 14, in a speech to the lord mayor's banquet in London, Thatcher responded: "Yes, some of those measures do restrict freedom. But those who choose to live by the bomb and the gun, and those who support them, can't in all circumstances be accorded exactly the same rights as everyone else."   (PETER KELLNER)

See also *Commonwealth of Nations,* above; *Dependent States,* below.

VATICAN CITY STATE

The independent sovereignty of Vatican City State is surrounded by but is not part of Rome. As a state with territorial limits, it is properly distinguished from the Holy See, which constitutes the worldwide administrative and legislative body for the Roman Catholic Church. Area: 44 ha (109 ac). Pop. (1988 est.): 750. As sovereign pontiff, John Paul II is the chief of state. Vatican City is administered by a pontifical commission of five cardinals headed by the secretary of state, in 1988 Agostino Cardinal Casaroli.

During a trip to Moscow in June 1988 for the celebration of the millennium of Christianity in Russia, the secretary of state, Agostino Cardinal Casaroli, met with General Secretary Mikhail Gorbachev, to whom he delivered a papal message. In the same month a schism developed in the church when the traditionalist French archbishop Marcel Lefebvre (*see* BIOGRAPHIES) defied Rome by ordaining four bishops, all of whom were excommunicated. On May 29 the pope named 25 new cardinals, but the Swiss theologian Hans Urs von Balthasar (*see* OBITUARIES) died before his installation. The new cardinals included a Lithuanian, under jurisdiction of the U.S.S.R. The pope approved the election of Andrew Bertie, the first Scot to become grand master of the Order of Malta.

John Paul II visited South America in May and Austria in June. The itinerary of his September trip to southern Africa did not include South Africa, although a communiqué explained that he hoped to meet "the faithful in the Republic of South Africa" on a future visit. However, a storm over Maseru, Lesotho, obliged the papal plane to land in Johannesburg, where the pope was met by the South African minister of foreign affairs, Pik Botha. In October the pope visited the European organizations headquartered in Strasbourg, France.

Visitors to the Vatican included the king and the queen of Spain; King Hussein of Jordan; the presidents of Egypt, West Germany, the Philippines, Nicaragua, Colombia, Venezuela, and Zambia; and U.S. Secretary of State George Shultz.   (MAX BERGERRE)

See also Religion: *Roman Catholic Church.*
This article updates the *Micropædia* article VATICAN CITY STATE.

Eastern Europe and the U.S.S.R

EASTERN EUROPEAN AFFAIRS

Probably the most significant pattern to emerge in Eastern Europe during 1988 was the growing awareness among ever larger sections of the population that qualitative changes in the Soviet-type system were in the air. Very little of this change had actually been put into practice, but the atmosphere of politics was undeniably shifting. Not all of this was positive; in some places, notably Poland, the indicators were pointing downward, as there appeared to be no way of resolving the sterile confrontation between state and society.

The single most important factor that had triggered this change was the mounting realization that the program of reform launched by Mikhail Gorbachev in the Soviet Union was not a nine-day wonder but a longer term project. As the implications of this sank in, those in Eastern Europe who had opted out, who concluded that the political order was unchangeable, began to reconsider and, not necessarily in any conscious or organized way, sought to increase their autonomy and power.

For the better part of two decades, the relationship between the Soviet Union and its Eastern European allies was governed by the Brezhnev Doctrine, by which the Kremlin arrogated to itself the right to determine the acceptable limits of socialism. Under Gorbachev this changed, though it was very far from clear how much. As nearly as could be judged, the terms of what constituted a "socialist" order were now defined as the maintenance of a one-party system that called itself "socialist"; continued adherence to the outward form of a Marxist-Leninist ideology; and loyalty to the Warsaw Pact, the Council for Mutual Economic Assistance (CMEA or Comecon), and broadly to the Soviet alliance system. The Soviet decision to withdraw from Afghanistan was a clear signal that military intervention in Eastern Europe was now far less likely than ever before. It seemed that Eastern European regimes were fairly free to experiment with quite radical new forms of government without incurring the Kremlin's wrath. Nevertheless, the limits were ambiguous, and this ambiguity in itself became a factor that raised popular expectations.

Other factors involved included the parallel recognition on the part of many in Communist elites that the system was, indeed, failing to deliver the goods, that it was unable to satisfy popular aspirations in consumption, let alone politics. For decades, the tacit trade-off between rulers and ruled in the area was that, in exchange for access to a reasonable standard of living, the people would remain out of politics. With the downturn in the Eastern European economies, half of this equation was crumbling.

This had other consequences, notably for the rulers. As their self-confidence ebbed, so did their raison d'être—the question could legitimately be asked, and was being asked with ever greater frequency, why were they still in power if they had failed to deliver on their promises? The only remaining solution was repression, but that was counterproductive, because a repressively run economy is highly inefficient. The combination of a deteriorating politico-economic base and rising popular expectations is very dangerous in one-party, authoritarian systems. Whenever the rulers in such systems are placed under pressure, they

crumble very rapidly, and a major upheaval can ensue. This had been the lesson of Poland in 1980 and Hungary in 1956.

The manifestations of this fragmentation varied in time and place. It was obviously further advanced in, say, Hungary and Poland than in East Germany. The signs included increasingly vocal pressures from articulate minorities for a greater say in how they were governed and a rejection of the tutelage that Communist governments had preferred to exercise. The emphasis was on greater choice, and it was argued in terms of human rights, a set of ideas concerning which official Marxism-Leninism had little to say.

Most outspoken, predictably, were the various democratic opposition groups, which had begun to come into existence a decade earlier. They had the experience of taking on the systems and had reasonably well-constructed platforms. This did not mean, however, that they corresponded to broad popular currents—at best, they were lobbies, pressure groups, or embryo parties. Nevertheless, they were beginning to articulate genuine interests and grievances and to that extent were resolving one of the central problems that had haunted Communist systems, that of representation. Because the Communist Party itself claimed to represent everything and, at the same time, because it could not renew its mandate by elections, it was extremely hard to see what real popular interests were and how the party could connect with them.

The opposition groups, furthermore, were looking more and more toward cross-frontier links. The democratic opposition in Poland, Czechoslovakia, Hungary, and East Germany had embarked on a gradual process of coordination and mutual learning, on the theory that the exchange of experiences could be helpful for all of them, seeing that there were certain basic similarities in all Soviet-type systems. The coordinated protest against the repressive nature of the regime in Romania was an example of this. Others included joint seminars and meetings, exchanges of written material, and the publication of some materials in English, the de facto lingua franca for these groups.

Not all opposition was expressed in this form. Even more striking, and in some ways more alarming, was the growing saliency of nationalism in Eastern Europe. Communist leaders had always encountered a problem with nationalism, inasmuch as it was a complete anomaly in Marxist-Leninist terms. According to Marx, national consciousness disappears once socialism is put into practice. This had not happened. Hence, Communist leaderships had to deal with nationalism, and the closer they came to it, the more problematic they found it. In this way nationalism could become a vehicle for popular autonomy and thereby erode the legitimacy and self-legitimation of Communist rulers. None of this was to suggest that collapse in Eastern Europe was imminent, but there was no doubt that as the 1980s were drawing to a close, the Communist regimes were markedly weaker than they had been when the decade started.   (GEORGE SCHÖPFLIN)

See also Economic Affairs; Military Affairs.

ALBANIA

A socialist republic in the western Balkan Peninsula of southeastern Europe, Albania is situated on the Adriatic Sea. Area: 28,748 sq km (11,100 sq mi). Pop. (1988 est.): 3,149,000. Cap.: Tirane. Monetary unit: lek, with (Oct. 10, 1988) a free rate of 5.95 leks to U.S. $1 (10.19 leks = £1 sterling). First secretary of the Albanian (Communist) Party of Labour and chairman of the Presidium of the People's Assembly (president) in 1988, Ramiz Alia; chairman of the Council of Ministers (premier), Adil Carcani.

Albania's decision to send its foreign minister, Reis Malile, to the conference of Balkan foreign ministers in Belgrade, Yugos., in February 1988 provided the most clear-cut evidence to date of its more pragmatic approach to international relations under party leader Ramiz Alia. Malile stressed that his country wished to play a more active role in Balkan affairs. Although Alia was not proposing an Albanian *glasnost* (openness) or *perestroika* (restructuring), he had been reasonably successful in promoting a more pragmatic approach to the economy, in apparent recognition of the need to boost trade and import much-needed foreign technology. There were further signs that Albania was emerging from its diplomatic isolation. Following the establishment of diplomatic relations at the ambassadorial level with Bulgaria and East Germany, Albania was reported to be considering an exchange of ambassadors with Czechoslovakia, one of its major trading partners.

Improving relations with Yugoslavia, ministerial exchanges with Turkey and Greece, and the strengthening of trade and transport links with Greece and Italy indicated that Alia realized that the aspirations of Albania's young population, increasingly exposed to the sophisticated outside world via Italian and Yugoslav radio and television, could no longer be ignored. (PATRICK ARTISIEN)

BULGARIA

The socialist republic of Bulgaria is on the eastern Balkan Peninsula of southeastern Europe, along the Black Sea. Area: 110,994 sq km (42,855 sq mi). Pop. (1988 est.): 8,978,000. Cap.: Sofia. Monetary unit: lev, with (Oct. 10, 1988) a free rate of 0.84 lev to U.S. $1 (1.45 leva = £1 sterling). General secretary of the Bulgarian Communist Party and chairman of the State Council (president) in 1988, Todor Zhivkov; chairman of the Council of Ministers (premier), Georgy Atanasov.

By January 1988 it had become clear that the need to implement the radical ideas expounded in 1987 had generated a profound political contest in Bulgaria. A national Communist Party conference met on January 28–29, but it failed to produce the practical reforms for which many had hoped. The party newspaper published the speeches of party leader Todor Zhivkov only in condensed form, which was taken as an indication that his star was waning.

In February a new factor emerged in Bulgarian political life. An art exhibition in Ruse focused on the harmful effects of atmospheric pollution in that town, most of it caused by a copper-smelting plant in Romania. This initiated an intense media debate on pollution. In April Zhivkov's "Considerations on 'Restructuring' in the Intellectual Sphere" were published, but they were followed by other official documents that suggested a more liberal approach.

A contest between Zhivkov and the less cautious reformers had clearly developed, but despite the earlier indications of decline, Zhivkov reasserted his supremacy. A Central Committee plenum to discuss the restructuring of intellectual and cultural life met, after some delay, on July 19–20 and ended with the resignation of Chudomir Alexandrov, who was a top reformer, a Politburo member, and head of the Central Committee Secretariat for Party Organization and Cadres. Other political casualties were Stoyan Mihailov, a Central Committee member and critic of Zhivkov's "Considerations"; Svetlin Rusev, chairman of the Artists' Union and an organizer of the Ruse exhibition; and Stanko Todorov, a Politburo member and president of the National Assembly, whose wife had been prominent in the Ruse protest.

The reform movement appeared further weakened by

Todor Zhivkov, general secretary of the Bulgarian Communist Party and president, addresses the national party conference, advocating Soviet-style reforms tempered with caution.
AFP PHOTO

the National Assembly session of July 27–29, which did nothing to implement the relaxation of foreign travel regulations that had been promised in February. Such a relaxation would have eased emigration by Bulgarian Turks and thereby helped to dissipate tensions between Sofia and Ankara. Bulgarian-Turkish relations had improved somewhat as a result of the Belgrade conference of Balkan foreign ministers in February. (RICHARD J. CRAMPTON)

CZECHOSLOVAKIA

The federal socialist republic of Czechoslovakia is a landlocked state of central Europe. Area: 127,900 sq km (49,382 sq mi). Pop. (1988 est.): 15,604,000. Cap.: Prague. Monetary unit: koruna, with (Oct. 10, 1988) a noncommercial rate of 9.40 koruny to U.S. $1 (16.10 koruny = £1 sterling). General secretary of the Communist Party of Czechoslovakia in 1988, Milos Jakes; president, Gustav Husak; federal premier, Lubomir Strougal and, from October 11, Ladislav Adamec.

The 1988 political scene in Czechoslovakia was dominated by the departure of Gustav Husak as leader of the Communist Party and the installation of his successor, Milos Jakes (*see* BIOGRAPHIES), on Dec. 17, 1987. Husak, leader since 1969, had presided over a deeply conservative, anti-reformist system, one that appeared increasingly at odds with the ideas emanating from the Soviet Union. Though Husak had paid lip service to the need for change, no substantive reform was introduced during his tenure.

His resignation and Jakes's succession came at an unusual time. Husak stepped down only a few weeks before his 75th birthday, a move that seemed inconsistent with the Communists' strict adherence to protocol and ceremony. The action also suggested that the Czechoslovak Communist Party was in a hurry to forge greater unity within its leadership before a pro-reformist leadership emerged, backed by Moscow.

There was no evidence to support the proposition that Jakes would do any more than maintain Husak's line. His credentials as a reformer were nonexistent. Jakes oversaw the purge in the early 1970s of the supporters of the short-lived Prague Spring of 1968, the reform movement that was

terminated by the Soviet military in August of that year. Husak presided over the economy at a time when the very word reform was excluded from Czechoslovakia's political vocabulary. Indeed, during 1988 there was no initiative launched by Jakes that could be described as reformist. On the contrary, his pronouncements were more and more at variance with Soviet leader Mikhail Gorbachev's *perestroika* (restructuring).

Jakes revealed his hand in October 1988, when he finally succeeded in removing Premier Lubomir Strougal from office. Strougal was Jakes's main rival and the sole possible leader of the reform faction. Strougal had been premier since 1970 and, while he could hardly have remained in office had he not been a conformist, he was not an "ultrahard" enemy of change; even worse from Jakes's standpoint, Strougal was popular. The fact that the archpriest of the "ultras," the ideologist Vasil Bilak, retained his Politburo position indicated that the antireform coalition of the 1970s was determined to retain power in Prague in the 1990s. The clash between reformists and antireformists ended in a clear victory for the latter.

Evidence was mounting that the Czechoslovak economy was entering a slow but inexorable downward slide. Economic performance indicators remained sluggish at best, and the economy grew by no more than an estimated rate of over 2% in 1987. There was no significant improvement in 1988. In July it was announced that growth targets for the year would be revised downward from 3.5 to 2.3%, a clear admission that the economy was doing badly and that only a cosmetic exercise would permit the leadership to claim that growth targets had been met. In effect, the Czechoslovak economy was no longer being planned in any real sense but was steered by a series of ad hoc adjustments. Five-year planning had been abandoned, except in rhetorical terms.

While the leadership remained obdurately attached to its antireformist positions, Czechoslovak society showed increasing signs of restiveness. Twenty years had passed since the Prague Spring, and an entire generation that had no memory of that reform movement had come to maturity, anxious for greater freedom and stifled by official conformism. At the same time, the breeze of political *glasnost* (openness) blowing from the Soviet Union was a source of encouragement for many. It was much easier to legitimate demands for change by reference to Soviet practice, the supposed model that Czechoslovakia was emulating, than to cite human rights or democracy.

There was some surprise, however, when on August 21, on the 20th anniversary of the Soviet invasion that ended the 1968 reforms, substantial numbers of demonstrators took to the streets of Prague. The size of the crowd was estimated at 10,000 persons, demanding greater freedom and the withdrawal of Soviet troops.

The Charter 77 dissident organization remained active and issued a fair number of documents during the year, notably those dealing with the 20th anniversary of the Soviet invasion, police arbitrariness, the ethnic Hungarian minority, religious freedom, and the victims of Stalinist repression. On October 28, Charter 77 and five other independent groups rallied some 5,000 persons in Prague's Wenceslas Square to demand political change and greater freedom on the 70th anniversary of Czechoslovak independence. It was noteworthy that the demonstrators repeatedly chanted the name of Masaryk, the country's first president and a powerful symbol of democracy. More than 80 dissidents were detained by police, who dispersed the crowd with clubs and water cannons. French Pres. François Mitterrand met with Charter 77 members during a visit to Prague in December.

Religious opposition by the Roman Catholic Church was especially prominent in Slovakia. The funeral of Bishop Julius Gabris was attended by an estimated 15,000 people; a petition supporting religious freedom attracted some 600,000 signatures; a pilgrimage to Levoca, in northern Slovakia, was attended by 280,000 people; and Frantisek Cardinal Tomasek, the archbishop of Prague, defended the rights of the church and of believers in a letter to the premier. The authorities, however, disregarded these initiatives, and by November there was evidence of an intensified crackdown on religious as well as other dissident groups.   (GEORGE SCHÖPFLIN)

GERMAN DEMOCRATIC REPUBLIC

A socialist republic, the German Democratic Republic (East Germany) is in central Europe on the Baltic Sea. Area: 108,333 sq km (41,827 sq mi). Pop. (1988 est.): 16,588,000. Cap.: Berlin (East). Monetary unit: Mark of Deutsche Demokratische Republik, with (Oct. 10, 1988) a free rate of M 1.86 to U.S. $1 (M 3.18 = £1 sterling). General secretary of the Socialist Unity (Communist) Party and chairman of the Council of State (president) in 1988, Erich Honecker; chairman of the Council of Ministers (premier), Willi Stoph.

The East German leadership set itself firmly against the importation of *glasnost* (openness) and *perestroika* (restructuring) from Mikhail Gorbachev's Soviet Union in 1988. "German Communists never aimed at applying the Soviet system in their country," said East German leader Erich Honecker to foreign correspondents in June. Fol-

AP/WIDE WORLD

Thousands of demonstrators march through Prague's Old Town Square on the 20th anniversary of the Soviet invasion of Czechoslovakia.

lowing several leadership changes in the Warsaw Pact states—the fall of Janos Kadar in Hungary, Gustav Husak in Czechoslovakia, and the Polish government—there was much speculation about the future of Honecker, now 76. Soviet representatives were hinting that he might soon be a candidate for retirement. Moscow's dilemma, however, was that there was no one in the East German Communist Party's 22-member ruling Politburo who could even remotely be regarded as a reformer. East German officials argued that their country was on the front line of socialism and warned that reforms in East Germany could lead to an uncontrollable situation, which the Soviet Union would be the first to regret. So Honecker was left alone to advocate even more central planning and tighter ideological control.

Soviet sources considered that Honecker's autocratic rule was wholly out of tune with East Germany's political and economic realities. They suggested that East Germany's economic growth rate in recent years was heavily doctored and that the 1987 growth rate was closer to nil than to the 3.6% officially reported. Nearly 80% of East Germany's giant industrial combines were said to have failed to fulfill their plan. But if the East German leadership professed not to like Gorbachev's policies, many East German citizens clearly did. East Germans of all ages deluged the Soviet embassy with letters calling for *glasnost* to be introduced to East Germany. The House of Soviet Science and Culture was unable to satisfy the demand for publications about the Soviet reforms at a time when the official East German media were refusing to comment on Soviet developments. Outside the party hierarchy there was considerable public criticism. The Protestant church said that only its teaching was aimed at encouraging people to think for themselves; some industrialists called for the breaking of "neo-Stalinist economic taboos"; and many youth groups openly challenged the regime.

The security services responded in March with a crackdown, the second within a few months. More than 80 human rights activists and would-be emigrants were rounded up, and identity checks were carried out on people attending services at the Sophienkirche in East Berlin. Many dissidents were expelled to West Germany, among them songwriter Stephan Krawczyk and his theatre producer wife, Freya Klier. They had been given the choice of emigration or prison. Most of the expellees were arrested when

some 200 young people tried to join an official march commemorating the Communist revolutionaries Rosa Luxemburg and Karl Liebknecht. There was trouble again when thousands of young East Germans gathered near the Berlin Wall in June to eavesdrop on a concert being given on the Western side by pop star Michael Jackson. West German television crews were kicked and punched, and some were poked with cattle prods and chased back to their offices. Despite this harsh attitude, the East German government was at pains to keep on good terms with West Germany. A record number of East Germans were allowed to visit West Germany during the year.

Honecker paid a visit to France in January, his first to any of the three Western powers that governed West Berlin. He saw it as enhancing the international recognition wrung from his visit to West Germany in September 1987. Pres. François Mitterrand did not seem overanxious to flatter him or his country, however. The French president told East German television that the division of Europe—the sole reason for the existence of a German Democratic Republic—"corresponds to nothing, either in geography, or history, or in culture." For his part, Honecker issued a veiled warning against the new Franco-German military cooperation.

Trade between East and West Germany fell by 5% in the first half of 1988, with a particularly sharp drop of 15% in West German exports. This was the third successive year in which trade between the two states declined. East Germany had been running a trade surplus with the countries of the Organization for Economic Cooperation and Development for several years, although it was declining with the fall in the value of its raw material exports. After applying for full diplomatic relations with the European Communities, East Germany surprised EC officials by signaling interest in a trade and economic cooperation pact. Since the creation of the Community, West Germany had been allowed to maintain privileged, and rather private, trade relations with its eastern neighbour, giving East Germany "back-door" access to the EC market. The East German government now said it was interested in a full-fledged trade agreement with all the member states, in addition to the pact with West Germany.

The small East Berlin Jewish community was allowed to have a rabbi for the first time in 20 years, signaling an

AFP PHOTO

"I want to live into the year 2000 without nuclear weapons" say placards held by East Germans awaiting the departure of Soviet soldiers. Soviet SS-12 missiles and equipment based in East Germany were to be transported to the U.S.S.R., where they would be destroyed.

attempt by East Germany to get on better terms with world Jewry after decades of official anti-Zionism and unofficial anti-Semitism. In October the president of the World Jewish Congress, Edgar Bronfman, paid an official visit to East Berlin during which compensation for the Jewish victims of Nazism was discussed. East Germany had never paid such compensation.   (NORMAN CROSSLAND)

This article updates the *Macropædia* article GERMANY: *German Democratic Republic.*

HUNGARY

A socialist republic, Hungary is a landlocked state in central Europe. Area: 93,031 sq km (35,919 sq mi). Pop. (1988 est.): 10,591,000. Cap.: Budapest. Monetary unit: forint, with (Oct. 10, 1988) a free rate of 53.50 forints to U.S. $1 (91.63 forints = £1 sterling). General secretaries of the Hungarian Socialist Workers' (Communist) Party in 1988, Janos Kadar and, from May 22, Karoly Grosz; chairmen of the Presidential Council (chiefs of state), Karoly Nemeth and, from June 29, Bruno Ferenc Straub; chairmen of the Council of Ministers (prime ministers), Grosz and, from November 23, Miklos Nemeth.

The year 1988 was a momentous one for Hungary, possibly the most momentous since the 1956 revolution. Janos Kadar, the country's leader since 1956, disappeared from the political stage and was replaced by Karoly Grosz, prime minister since 1987, while that position was taken over in November by a Harvard-trained economist, Miklos Nemeth. But this was no more than the tip of the iceberg. Barely concealed beneath it was a far-reaching crisis of the system, of public confidence in the authorities, of national identity, and of the economy.

There was little to suggest that the Grosz team, which took over in May, had any intention of launching a thoroughgoing program of reform. The team was a coalition of committed reformers like Imre Pozsgay and Rezso Nyers on the one hand and conservatives like Janos Berecz on the other. Grosz himself lacked the instincts of a reformer but was thought to be prepared to accept even radical measures if they would safeguard his power.

The origins of the crisis lay in the steady deterioration of the economy during the 1980s. Hungary's foreign debt—at $18 billion the highest per capita in the Communist world—was the clearest indication of this. Although the country could maintain its creditworthiness for the next two years, by 1990–91 the debt service ratio would jump from 40% to over 65%. The only way this could be met

was through refinancing, and refinancing was likely only if the leadership had embarked on genuine reform.

Popular restiveness and dissatisfaction, coupled with the voicing of alternatives by widening sections of the intelligentsia, threatened to undermine the self-confidence of the rulers. Large sections of the intelligentsia who had accepted and supported the political order constructed by Kadar had finally concluded in 1987 that it no longer deserved their backing.

By 1988 the atmosphere in Hungary was one of extraordinary political diversity, in which virtually nothing was taboo. Political regrouping led to the emergence or reemergence of de facto political parties. Notably, the Hungarian Democratic Forum, which had recruited a membership of around 10,000 by the autumn of 1988, was beginning to assume the shape of a national-radical party. The unofficial Alliance of Young Democrats (FIDESZ) was moving in a similar direction, though its membership was thought to be smaller and its ideas were liberal democratic. The Democratic Union of Scientific Workers was the first independent trade union to be launched in Eastern Europe since the suppression of Solidarity in Poland. There were also smaller Social Democratic and radical groups, as well as others on the right. The status of these groups was ambiguous. They were tolerated—barely—by the authorities, but they had no clear legal standing. The projected Law on Associations would eventually offer them a chance of registration, though whether the authorities would ultimately accept them was still undecided.

The area most directly affected by the intellectual ferment was that of the press and media, where the spirit of *glasnost* (openness) had taken over with a vengeance. The Hungarian press had been far more open than its Soviet counterpart when the process began. Now virtually no area was exempt from comment, except perhaps the link with the U.S.S.R.

Anxiety over the fate of ethnic Hungarians in Romania had been mounting for years, and when Pres. Nicolae Ceausescu announced his plans to destroy thousands of villages and move their inhabitants—many of them ethnic Hungarians—into housing developments ("systematization"), Hungarians took it as an assault on their cultural heritage. Matters were further complicated by a steady seepage of refugees from Romania to Hungary, and the Hungarian authorities turned a blind eye to an ethnic Romanian emigré group operating in Budapest. The govern-

AFP PHOTO

Delegates of the Hungarian Socialist Workers' (Communist) Party convene at their national conference. The conference, the first in more than 30 years, was held in an attempt to rectify economic and political problems.

ment was officially neutral toward the mass protest against systematization on June 27, involving around 50,000 people. Grosz's tactic was evidently to try to use Hungarian indignation over Transylvania as a source of support. In August, however, he paid a one-day visit to Romania to negotiate with Ceausescu and, in effect, returned empty handed.   (GEORGE SCHÖPFLIN)

POLAND

A socialist republic of eastern Europe, Poland is on the Baltic Sea. Area: 312,683 sq km (120,727 sq mi). Pop. (1988 est.): 37,864,000. Cap.: Warsaw. Monetary unit: zloty, with (Oct. 10, 1988) an official rate of 474.55 zlotys to U.S. $1 (812.66 zlotys = £1 sterling). First secretary of the Polish United Workers' (Communist) Party and chairman of the Council of State (chief of state) in 1988, Gen. Wojciech Jaruzelski; chairmen of the Council of Ministers (premiers), Zbigniew Messner and, from September 27, Mieczyslaw Rakowski.

Conflict between workers and the authorities erupted in 1988. There had been no improvement in the standard of living, and salaries in real terms were lower by one-fifth than they had been seven years earlier, during the last outbreak of unrest. In late April and early May, a wave of strikes spread over the country. The steelworks in Nowa Huta and Stalowa Wola were involved, as was the Lenin Shipyard in Gdansk, birthplace of the banned independent trade union movement Solidarity. The strikes were the most serious since 1981, although they were not organized by the Solidarity leadership. They were brutally repressed by the police, but in mid-August new strikes broke out as industrial unrest spread from coal mines in Jastrzebie (Upper Silesia) to other mines, to the Baltic port of Szczecin, and to the shipyard in Gdansk. By the end of the month, workers in about 20 large industrial units were on strike, demanding not only higher wages but also recognition of Solidarity. The government responded by authorizing curfew orders for three strike-ridden districts and reinforcing police detachments in the affected areas.

However, as the economic situation worsened, on August 31 Lech Walesa, Solidarity's founder, was invited for talks by Gen. Czeslaw Kiszczak, the minister of the interior. As the official communiqué stated, the discussions included "crucial problems" of trade union pluralism and "the role of Solidarity." It was agreed that talks between Solidarity leaders and representatives of government and other areas of Polish public life, including the Roman Catholic Church, should start in October, but they were later postponed. On November 30 Walesa appeared on television in a live debate with the head of the official union.

On September 19, during a daylong debate on the economy in the Sejm (parliament), Premier Zbigniew Messner offered his resignation, which was accepted by an overwhelming majority. A week later Mieczyslaw Rakowski (see BIOGRAPHIES) was elected as the new premier, and within ten days he presented his new Cabinet with four places reserved for representatives of "the constructive opposition." An advocate of economic reforms but a committed opponent of Solidarity, Rakowski told the Sejm in his inauguration speech that the aim of his government was to build a "democratic, legally governed and modern Poland." As his first move, he announced that the Lenin Shipyard was an unprofitable enterprise and would be closed. This met with strong opposition from the workers, who viewed the decision as more political than economic. A few hundred workers, mostly young, declared a strike, but it was not supported by the Solidarity leadership and collapsed in a day. At a Central Committee meeting in December there was a reshuffle of the party leadership,

Solidarity leader Lech Walesa addresses strikers at the Lenin Shipyard in Gdansk, Poland. Despite an agreement for peaceful negotiations, neither the government nor the strikers eased up on demands.
RYSZARD WESOLOWSKI—SYGMA

with six officials, including Messner, dismissed from the Politburo and eight new, predominantly younger men promoted to membership.

In February the Sejm accepted a new adjusted plan for the so-called second stage of the reform started six years earlier. The main aim of the plan was to reinforce the free market sector of the economy by expanding the share of private enterprises, breaking the state monopoly in purchasing agricultural commodities, and reducing subsidies on food and other products (in 1988 subsidies made up about one-third of the country's budget). This should strengthen the value of the zloty. However, as of late October there were no signs that the economic situation was improving.

In February and April prices of basic food products, services, coal, gas, and electricity rose substantially, and salaries in the public sector increased. Retail prices of consumer goods rose by over 50%, and there were acute shortages of a large number of products. It was expected that in 1988 national income would rise by more than 4.5% over 1987, but its total value would still be about 1.5% lower than in 1978. In August 1988 Polish debts owed to Western countries reached $36.4 billion, as against $25.5 billion at the end of 1981, largely because of accrued interest and changes in the value of the U.S. dollar. Over the same period, debt owed to socialist countries rose to 6.9 billion rubles from 3.1 billion rubles. Despite a rising trend, the total net value of industrial production in 1988 was more than 3% lower than in 1978, and the quality of products deteriorated. Agriculture, based on private farms, had been more resilient than other sectors, and in 1987 it reached the 1978 level. However, a decline was expected in 1988 since the grain harvest, at 24.5 million tons, was 1.5 million tons lower than a year earlier. Imports of grain and protein-rich compounds were expected to reach about four million tons, placing a heavy burden on the Treasury.

British Prime Minister Margaret Thatcher visited Poland November 2–4. Her reception reflected the division in Polish society: businesslike meetings with the authorities and warm encounters with the Polish people and representatives of Solidarity. Her program included talks with the head of state, Gen. Wojciech Jaruzelski, Prime Minister Rakowski, and the primate of Poland, Jozef Cardinal Glemp, as well

as Walesa and other Solidarity activists. Thatcher turned a deaf ear to Rakowski's appeal for her help in debt negotiations with the Paris Club of Western creditor governments and the International Monetary Fund, making clear that any future assistance would depend on political and economic reforms. She visited the grave of Jerzy Popieluszko, the Solidarity priest murdered by secret police in 1984, and in Gdansk she laid a wreath at the Three Crosses Monument to the memory of workers shot by security forces in 1970. Despite her bluntness, British-Polish relations remained good, and General Jaruzelski came to the airport unexpectedly to see her off.

In sharp contrast, Soviet leader Mikhail Gorbachev, visiting in July, was received enthusiastically by Jaruzelski and other officials but cooly by the Polish people. It was widely expected that in his speech in the Sejm Gorbachev would admit that 14,000 Polish army officers had been murdered by the Soviets in 1940, but this did not happen. He mentioned only that there were "white spots" in the history of Polish-Soviet relations that needed to be cleared up. Visiting the Szczecin shipyard, one of the strongholds of Solidarity, Gorbachev told a selected audience that Solidarity was a mistake and the U.S.S.R. believed it would never be repeated. Gorbachev and Jaruzelski signed a declaration stating that Polish-Soviet relations were based on mutual respect for each country's right to choose its own methods of building socialism.   (K. M. SMOGORZEWSKI)

ROMANIA

A socialist republic on the Balkan Peninsula in southeastern Europe, Romania has a coastline on the Black Sea. Area: 237,500 sq km (91,699 sq mi). Pop. (1988 est.): 23,014,000. Cap.: Bucharest. Monetary unit: leu, with (Oct. 10, 1988) a noncommercial rate of 8.63 lei to U.S. $1 (14.78 lei = £1 sterling). General secretary of the Romanian Communist Party, president of the republic, and president of the State Council in 1988, Nicolae Ceausescu; chairman of the Council of Ministers (prime minister), Constantin Dascalescu.

During 1988 Romania's self-imposed isolation accelerated owing to mounting international criticism of Pres. Nicolae Ceausescu's internal policies. Relations with Hungary and West Germany deteriorated over what they perceived as insensitive treatment of their respective ethnic minorities, while the Soviet leadership expressed disappointment over Ceausescu's failure to adopt Gorbachev-style reforms. Bulgaria voiced concern about pollution emanating from Romanian chemical plants.

The record 1987 trade surplus showed signs of being equaled in 1988, thus enabling the country to reduce its foreign debts more rapidly than expected. Net debt in the third quarter of 1988 was estimated at $4 billion. It seemed likely that Romania would pay off its debts by the middle of 1990. Living standards, however, had dropped sharply during the last decade following the country's incurrence of large foreign debts—they reached a peak of $10.2 billion in 1981—in order to industrialize. It was agriculture, however, largely neglected at the expense of industry, that was expected to increase exports in order to pay off the debt. The export of foodstuffs exacerbated food shortages and prolonged the rationing of bread, flour, and sugar.

On March 3, 1988, Ceausescu announced plans to complete by the year 2000 the urbanization or "systematization" of about half of Romania's 13,000 villages by moving the country's peasants into "agro-industrial" complexes consisting of small blocks of apartments and communal civic amenities. The application of this policy led to the bulldozing of the villagers' private houses and the destruction of their plots of land, which provided the main source

of private-sector food for urban dwellers. The chronic shortages of food that characterized urban existence in every major town outside the capital were likely to become commonplace in the villages as well.

Ceausescu's urbanization drive had significant international repercussions. Neighbouring Hungary was particularly alarmed because members of Romania's two million-strong Hungarian minority, most of whom lived in Transylvania, believed that the program was part of a plan to assimilate them by destroying their cultural identity and heritage. Leading members of the Hungarian Communist Party publicly criticized Ceausescu's plan, and on June 27, 1988, a protest rally was staged in Budapest, Hung., involving around 50,000 demonstrators. Ceausescu responded by closing the Hungarian consulate in Cluj-Napoca in Transylvania. In an effort to bridge the rift between the two countries, Hungarian Prime Minister Karoly Grosz met Ceausescu in the Romanian border town of Arad at the end of August. The meeting was followed by the visit of a senior Hungarian party official to Transylvania in September, but relations between the two countries remained severely strained. Each country expelled one of the other's diplomats in November.

In February Ceausescu declared that he would not seek renewal of Romania's most-favoured-nation status with the U.S. when it expired in July. An official Romanian communiqué issued on February 27 stated that the U.S. government had made "the annual granting of the clause dependent upon a number of political demands which represented an inadmissible interference in Romania's domestic affairs."

In July Ceausescu rejected proposals to establish an integrated market at the 44th Comecon (Council for Mutual Economic Assistance) session held in Prague. The Romanian delegation's refusal to sign such an accord, which had the backing of Soviet leader Mikhail Gorbachev, was a further illustration of the differences between Ceausescu and Gorbachev on economic planning. Despite the strain in relations with the Soviet Union, trade between the two countries grew by 4% in the first quarter of 1988.

Ceausescu and his wife, Elena, made official visits to five Asian countries: China, North Korea, Vietnam, Mongolia, and Indonesia; and to four African countries: Liberia, Guinea, Mauritania, and Tanzania. They also visited Australia.   (DENNIS J. DELETANT)

UNION OF SOVIET SOCIALIST REPUBLICS

The Union of Soviet Socialist Republics is a federal state covering parts of eastern Europe and northern Asia. Area: 22,403,000 sq km (8,649,800 sq mi). Pop (1988 est.): 285,796,000. Cap.: Moscow. Monetary unit: ruble, with (Oct. 10, 1988) a free rate of 0.62 ruble to U.S. $1 (1.06 rubles = £1 sterling). General secretary of the Communist Party of the Soviet Union in 1988, Mikhail S. Gorbachev; chairmen of the Presidium of the Supreme Soviet (presidents), Andrey A. Gromyko to September 30 and, from October 1, Gorbachev; chairman of the Council of Ministers (premier), Nikolay I. Ryzhkov.

In a year of whirlwind activity, Mikhail Gorbachev (see BIOGRAPHIES) consolidated his power. He welcomed U.S. Pres. Ronald Reagan to Moscow, convened a party conference and Central Committee (CC) plenums, traveled regularly abroad, announced a new disarmament initiative before the UN, played host to a stream of foreign leaders, and indefatigably toured the country, all to promote *perestroika* (restructuring), *glasnost* (openness), and democratization. Following in the footsteps of Leonid Brezhnev, Yury Andropov, and Konstantin Chernenko, he was elected Soviet president in October.

On balance, personnel changes in the party Politburo and Secretariat favoured the general secretary. At the CC plenum in February, as expected, Boris Yeltsin, who had been unceremoniously sacked as Moscow city party leader the previous November, lost his candidate membership in the Politburo, but he was appointed to a post in the construction industry that carried ministerial status. Nikolay Talyzin, who had lost his position as chairman of the U.S.S.R. State Planning Committee (Gosplan)—becoming, instead, chairman of the U.S.S.R. Council of Ministers' Bureau for Social Development—held onto his candidate Politburo membership. He was later made Soviet permanent representative to the Council for Mutual Economic Assistance (Comecon). His replacement as Gosplan chief was Yury Maslyukov, formerly chairman of the Military-Industrial Commission and one of the most senior officials ever to be transferred from the military to the civilian sector. Maslyukov was later named first deputy premier and made a candidate member of the Politburo. Georgy Razumovsky, CC secretary for party cadres, also joined the ranks of Politburo candidate members. The U.S.S.R. minister of general machine building (responsible for missile production), Oleg Baklanov, was elected a CC secretary, presumably to cover defense.

At a CC plenum on September 30–October 1, there were even more dramatic developments. Andrey Gromyko, Soviet president since July 1985, and Mikhail Solomentsev, both full Politburo members, were dropped; Petr Demichev and Vladimir Dolgikh, both candidate members, departed the scene, as did Anatoly Dobrynin, adviser on U.S.S.R.-U.S. relations and former longtime ambassador to Washington. Only one new name was added to the elite; Aleksandr Vlasov, formerly minister of internal affairs, was promoted to candidate membership in the Politburo and became chairman of the Council of Ministers (premier) of the Russian Soviet Federated Socialist Republic. Vitaly Vorotnikov, the previous premier and a full member of the Politburo, in due course was elected president of the R.S.F.S.R. Supreme Soviet. In hindsight it was clear that this was not a demotion, as was first thought, since Vorotnikov was to play the role of an executive president of the largest republic. The only new full member of the Politburo was Vadim Medvedev, formerly CC secretary for relations with ruling Communist parties. Aleksandra Biryukova, CC secretary for consumer goods, food, and light industry, became the first woman in the Politburo, albeit a candidate member, since Ekaterina Furtseva under Nikita Khrushchev. Anatoly Lukyanov, CC secretary, also joined the Politburo as a candidate member. Gen. Viktor Chebrikov lost the post of KGB chairman but was made a CC secretary.

Six CC Secretariat commissions were set up: legal policy, agrarian policy, ideology, party and cadre policy, socioeconomic policy, and international policy. The new commissions were to take over the work of some of the CC departments, but the exact working relationship between the commissions and the departments was unclear, indicating that the plenum and the changes announced had been put together hastily. The timing of the plenum was apparently due to the fact that Egor Ligachev (*see* BIOGRAPHIES), Gorbachev's main rival, and three other members of the Politburo were away on holiday and had to return to Moscow quickly and thus did not have much time to launch a counterargument to Gorbachev's plans.

The new Politburo appeared to guarantee Gorbachev a majority. One of the most interesting moves was the transfer of Chebrikov from head of the KGB to CC secretary. In the past he had embarrassed Gorbachev internationally

U.S. Pres. Ronald Reagan and Soviet leader Mikhail Gorbachev enjoy a fine photo opportunity during a friendly stroll in Red Square. Although the Moscow summit broke no new ground in arms control, it did much to promote goodwill.
AP/WIDE WORLD

on more than one occasion, so his replacement by Gen. Vladimir Kryuchkov, promoted over the heads of some more senior colleagues, could be seen as a net gain for Gorbachev. However, Chebrikov's new brief in the Secretariat was to oversee legal reform, which went to the heart of *glasnost* and democratization, since new laws on the press, public assembly, and freedom of conscience, for example, were planned. Ligachev also suffered some loss of prestige, but as head of the commission on agrarian policy, he headed the most sensitive policy area. Unless more food appeared on the tables of the Soviet working man and woman, there was little likelihood of *perestroika* taking off. Of the top 21 party officeholders, 18 were Russian and the other 3 were Ukrainian, Belorussian, and Georgian. The Baltic states and Central Asia were not represented.

Gorbachev had more time to organize the 19th party conference, which met between June 28 and July 2. Almost 5,000 delegates engaged in vigorous and open debate, unprecedented since the 1920s. There were, in reality, two parallel conferences—one visible to television viewers and the other, at which the key decisions were taken, behind the scenes, in the committees drafting the six conference resolutions. In his speech Gorbachev called for radical political reform—previously only radical economic reform had been mentioned—and sprang two surprises. He proposed setting up what could be called a Soviet parliament; the party was to disengage gradually from the economy, and its powers were to pass to local soviets. His proposal that the local party secretary be nominated as chairman of the local soviet met with some resistance from party secretaries who were aware of the risk of not being elected.

Neither proposal had been included in the theses published before the conference. At the head of the revitalized soviets would stand an executive president, and it was plain that Gorbachev himself expected to be elected to the post.

The conference voted to limit tenure of elected party posts to two terms or ten years. This was to affect all levels of the party apparatus and to take effect from the next party congress. It was also agreed to hold party conferences between congresses and to renew up to 20% of the members of party committees—presumably to include the CC. One of Gorbachev's failures at the 19th conference was his inability to achieve a partial or complete reelection of the CC. Since the tradition had been that new members could be elected only at a party congress, the anomalous situation existed in late 1988 of at least five republican first secretaries not being CC members.

Since many of the members of the new Soviet parliament would come from the ranks of the conference delegates, it was instructive to examine which issues caused the most controversy and which received the most applause. Most criticized were the behaviour of some members of "informal groups"—referred to as "demagogues"—and the freedom of the media to criticize the power and privileges of party officials. There were many heated exchanges, with demands that the media be made more "accountable." All this did not augur well for free speech and open debate in the coming parliament.

Draft changes to the Soviet Union's constitution and the new electoral law were adopted by the U.S.S.R. Supreme Soviet in December. In March 1989 elections were to take place to a Congress of Soviets, to consist of 750 delegates each from the Soviet of the Union, from the Soviet of Nationalities, and from social organizations, making 2,250 in all. All elections could be contested by more candidates than there were seats. Among those who could put up candidates were religious organizations—probably the first time that this had happened since 1917. The Congress of Soviets was to elect 422 of its number as members of parliament. Certain categories of officials were ineligible—for instance, government ministers. Parliament was to convene for up to two four-month sessions each year, with the first session planned for April 1989. The relationship between this parliament and the U.S.S.R. Supreme Soviet was not clear, but it appeared that the latter would meet twice a year for a day or so, as it did at present. Parliament was to elect an executive-style president with much greater power than the present Soviet president. Republics

and autonomous republics would also have executive-style presidents.

In a remarkable year this was the most astonishing governmental innovation. However, it was clear that the power and prerogatives of the new parliament, its debating procedures, access by citizens to their MP, and a host of other questions still had to be worked out. An indication of what the parliament might bring was provided by the October meeting of the U.S.S.R. Supreme Soviet. Thirty-one deputies voted against and 24 abstained when a decree, empowering a special paramilitary police force to keep order at demonstrations, was presented for approval, and 13 voted against and 4 abstained in the vote on a decree requiring advance permission for demonstrations and setting penalties for offenders. It was the first time in decades that deputies had voted against legislation. In the December session 5 deputies voted against some part of the constitutional changes and 27 abstained; all were from the Baltic republics.

Domestic Affairs. No less remarkable were developments in nationality affairs, which now, according to Gorbachev, constituted the "most fundamental, vital issue of our society." In February riots in the Azerbaijani city of Sumgait and elsewhere left many Armenians and some Azerbaijanis dead. The toll in this and other incidents was at least 34 dead and over 200 injured, and thousands became refugees, with Armenians suffering most. Armenians in Nagorno-Karabakh, a mountainous region of Azerbaijan, led by the party first secretary, demanded that the territory be transferred to Armenia. This was seconded by the Armenian Supreme Soviet and the Communist Party but opposed by the Azerbaijani Supreme Soviet and Communist Party. Such a constitutional conflict between two republics, one mainly Muslim and the other Christian, was unprecedented. Prolonged strikes in Armenia and Nagorno-Karabakh backed the demand that the problem be resolved in the Armenians' favour. Some concessions, such as more investment and more Armenian schools, churches, and newspapers, did not satisfy the Armenians. De facto the region came under Moscow rule when Arkady Volsky, head of the machine-building department of the CC Secretariat, was dispatched to sort out the mess. The problem proved intractable for Gorbachev, who could not afford to alienate either Armenians or Azerbaijanis.

Armenia's problems were compounded on December 7, when an earthquake measuring 6.9 on the Richter scale struck the northern part of the republic. Leninakhan, the

BORIS YURCHENKO—AP/WIDE WORLD

Meron Gordon (front right), a Soviet-born diplomat from Israel, arrives with a group of colleagues at Moscow's Sheremetyevo Airport. The diplomats, who opened an office in the Dutch embassy, were the first Israeli officials to enter the Soviet Union since relations were broken off in 1967.

The largely Armenian autonomous region of Nagorno-Karabakh lies within the Azerbaijan S.S.R. In 1988 the age-old enmity between Armenians and Azerbaijanis erupted into violence as the Armenians demanded that Nagorno-Karabakh be annexed to the Armenian republic. A severe earthquake decimated much of Armenia on December 7.

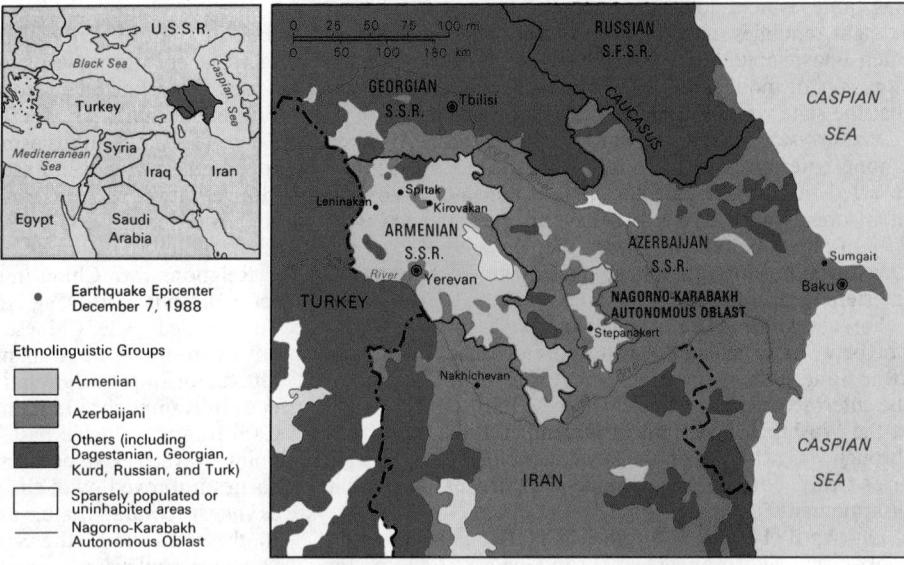

• Earthquake Epicenter
December 7, 1988

Ethnolinguistic Groups

Armenian

Azerbaijani

Others (including Dagestanian, Georgian, Kurd, Russian, and Turk)

Sparsely populated or uninhabited areas
Nagorno-Karabakh Autonomous Oblast

republic's second largest city, Kirovakan, and Stepanavan suffered extensive damage, and Spitak, with a population of some 16,000, was leveled. The death toll was set at 25,000, while thousands were injured and an estimated half a million were homeless. An international relief effort was mounted, including the first large-scale U.S. aid to be accepted by the Soviet government since World War II. The Soviet press noted that concrete buildings constructed during the "years of stagnation" under Brezhnev had collapsed almost instantly while many older buildings remained standing.

The potent mix of nationalism and religion surfaced in the Baltic states. The region was the most developed in the Soviet Union, and traditionally Estonia had been used as a laboratory for economic experiments. Estonia, Latvia, and Lithuania all elected new party first secretaries, who immediately spearheaded national demands. These demands were articulated through Popular Fronts set up in Estonia in September and in Latvia in October and the Movement for Perestroika in Lithuania, also established in October. In Estonia the Popular Front called for the introduction of Estonian citizenship, for Estonian to be the republic's official language, and for sharp restrictions on Russian immigration. Economic autonomy, more links between Estonia and the outside world, and a separate time zone for the Baltic states were also desired. In Latvia the demand for the use of the national language was made more significant by the fact that only about half the population of the republic was Latvian. Most immigrants were Russian. There were calls for Lithuanian autonomy, and some demanded outright independence. In all three republics pre-1940 flags were again permitted, and pent-up frustration was defused by concessions on religious freedom and limited autonomy. Riga cathedral was handed back to the Lutherans, and in Vilnius mass was celebrated in the Roman Catholic cathedral after it had been returned to the church. Greater democracy, especially in cultural and economic affairs, was being conceded. Moscow appeared to have decided that the best way to contain the national movements was to join them.

Gorbachev met Patriarch Pimen and members of the Synod of the Orthodox Church on April 29. The historic meeting was given full coverage on Soviet television and in the press and was an indication that the state wished to improve relations with believers. This was significant in

the year that marked the millennium of Russian Christianity. Many world church leaders visited the Soviet Union to help celebrate the event, although Pope John Paul II was not among them. Jewish emigration from the Soviet Union in October was 2,473, the highest monthly figure since 1980. This made a total of 14,288 for the first ten months of the year, 1,232 of whom had gone to Israel. The teaching of Hebrew was to be legalized, and Soviet Jews were to be permitted to participate in the World Jewish Congress. Some 45,000 Soviet Germans were expected to leave in 1988, compared with 14,700 in 1987. Of the 1988 total, only one in 13 was of pensionable age. Many were skilled workers, precisely those whom Gorbachev needed to win over to *perestroika*.

The Economy. During the first nine months of 1988, industrial production was up 4.3%, but no republic or industrial branch fulfilled its plan. In the important machine-building sector, 47% of enterprises did not meet their contractual obligations, and in the chemical industry, 42%. Labour productivity rose 5.4%, compared with 2.5% in 1987. The grain harvest was smaller than in 1987, necessitating more grain imports at a time when Soviet revenues from oil, gas, and war matériel exports were falling. The minister of finance stated in October that the 1986 Chernobyl nuclear accident had cost the country over 8 billion rubles so far. Reconstruction of the earthquake-damaged areas of Armenia would be an even greater burden.

For the first time, the minister admitted a budget deficit. It would rise to 36.3 billion rubles or 7.3% of expenditure in 1989. Food subsidies—the difference between what the state pays farms for produce and what it gets back from consumers—came to 91.5 billion rubles and would climb to 103 billion in 1989. About 20% of budget expenditure covered various subsidies, with food accounting for approximately 90%. Gorbachev wanted to cut subsidies, but the issue was so sensitive that nothing had been done. It was especially important to those workers whose incomes declined because more production was being rejected by government inspectors. Some 6,500 farms were losing money, and they had accumulated debts amounting to 63 billion rubles. In a bid to increase agricultural efficiency, land was leased to families for up to 50 years, and it was planned to extend this system to other sectors of the economy. An Academy of Sciences economist admitted that living standards had not risen over the last two years, something that

was quite evident to the population. Meat was rationed in eight republics, and sugar and other staple goods were often unavailable. Sugar was bought up by those brewing *samogon,* or moonshine. It became evident during the year that the state was losing the battle against alcoholism.

Perestroika spluttered forward during the year. A survey among enterprises in the Urals, published in September, revealed that 68% of directors judged that higher government organs were trying to behave in the same old way; 77% of directors thought powers they possessed under the Law on State Enterprise were inadequate for fending off interference from above.

Foreign Affairs. The highlight of the year was the summit between President Reagan and Gorbachev held May 28 to June 1. Its main achievement was the ratification of the intermediate-range nuclear forces (INF) treaty, signed at the Washington summit in December 1987. No breakthrough was achieved on the key issues blocking a strategic arms treaty, but Gorbachev spoke of a "new era of nuclear disarmament."

On April 14 the U.S., the U.S.S.R., Pakistan, and Afghanistan signed an agreement in Geneva providing for the almost 115,000 Soviet troops in Afghanistan to begin leaving the country by May 15 and to be out nine months later. The Afghan withdrawal was only one tangible aspect of the "new political thinking" in foreign policy. Gorbachev's aim was to reduce tension worldwide and to gain support for the view that the U.S.S.R. was a normal, civilized state. He spoke of Europeans living in a "common house" and called on all powers to help eliminate nuclear weapons by the year 2000. Relations with the U.S. improved—a key part of his strategy since reduced Soviet military expenditure was vital to the success of *perestroika.*

In December Gorbachev visited the UN in New York City, where he made a major address, the highlight of which was the announcement of a unilateral reduction in the Soviet armed forces of 500,000 troops, plus a "substantial" amount of conventional armament, and removal of about 5,000 tanks from Eastern Europe. The visit, which included talks with Reagan and President-elect George Bush, was a public relations success, but it was cut short—and trips to Cuba and the U.K. were postponed—when Gorbachev returned home because of the Armenian earthquake.

Western European leaders were often enthusiastic in their support for *perestroika,* and the Italian and West German leaders, during visits to Moscow in October, called for a new "Marshall Plan" to promote it. However, Britain's Prime Minister Margaret Thatcher was not of like mind. There was little enthusiasm for *perestroika* in Eastern Europe. Indeed, trends in East Germany, Czechoslovakia, and Hungary favoured conservatives. Gorbachev's most ardent supporter remained Gen. Wojciech Jaruzelski, but the Polish economy was not an advertisement for restructuring.

Relations with China improved, but Gorbachev's desire for a summit with Deng Xiaoping (Teng Hsiao-p'ing) was not fulfilled. The Chinese welcomed the withdrawal of Soviet troops from Afghanistan—one of their three conditions for improving relations—but the Vietnamese presence in Kampuchea remained a problem. Soviet use of the Cam Ranh Bay naval base in Vietnam was also a sticking point. Nevertheless, contacts between the two Communist parties improved, with the Chinese addressing the Soviets as *tongzi* (comrade) after a break of almost three decades. In the third world the Soviets counseled their allies involved in civil wars to negotiate settlements. Moves toward a renewal of diplomatic relations with Israel formed part of a pattern of seeking a settlement in the Middle East. The Soviets adopted a much more constructive stance in the UN Security Council and had clearly upgraded the UN as an instrument of foreign policy.   (MARTIN MCCAULEY)

YUGOSLAVIA

A federal socialist republic, Yugoslavia is in southern Europe on the Adriatic Sea. Area: 255,804 sq km (98,766 sq mi). Pop. (1988 est.): 23,591,000. Cap.: Belgrade. Monetary unit: Yugoslav dinar, with (Oct. 10, 1988) a free rate of 3,397 dinars to U.S. $1 (5,818 dinars = £1 sterling). Presidents of the Presidium of the League of Communists in 1988, Bosko Krunic and, from June 30, Stipe Suvar; presidents of the Collective Presidency, Lazar Mojsov and, from May 15, Raif Dizarevic; president of the Federal Executive Council (premier), Branko Mikulic.

Yugoslavia's economic and social situation deteriorated dramatically in 1988 against the background of a deepening conflict among the leaders of the country's six federal republics and two autonomous provinces. Slobodan

HORVAT—PICTURE GROUP

Steelworkers on strike at a mill in Niksic, Montenegro, protest police violence against demonstrators. The weak government and ailing economy of Yugoslavia caused public unrest and stirred up ethnic rivalries.

Milosevic, the Communist party leader in Serbia, Yugoslavia's largest republic, campaigned for reintegration of the provinces of Kosovo and Vojvodina into Serbia proper. The two provinces (Kosovo with a nearly 90% Albanian ethnic majority and Vojvodina with just over 50% Serbs and a large Hungarian group, as well as other minorities) had been given virtually republican status under the 1974 constitution, including responsibility for the police, the judiciary, and territorial defense. Some 40 rallies backing the Milosevic campaign were held between July and November, and more than a million people attended a meeting in Belgrade on November 19. The campaign's biggest success was the collective resignation on October 6, after a mass meeting in Novi Sad, Vojvodina's capital, of the entire party and government leadership of that province. In Kosovo, however, the Milosevic campaign met strong resistance from the local (chiefly Albanian) party apparatus. A rally in Titograd, the capital of Montenegro, on October 7 and 8, at which resignation of the republic's leadership was demanded, did not go well for Milosevic. It was dispersed by police, and in non-Serb parts of Yugoslavia it was condemned as an attempt to overturn Yugoslavia's federal system and bring Montenegro into Serbia.

The leadership of Slovenia, Yugoslavia's westernmost republic, came under attack in March by the Military Council, a senior army body, for its political liberalism. *Mladina*, the outspoken youth magazine, accused the Army in May of preparing a plot to overthrow Slovenia's leadership. This was denied, but on July 27 a military court in Ljubljana, Slovenia's capital, sentenced a Slovene sergeant major and three *Mladina* journalists to prison for allegedly divulging military secrets. The sentences provoked strong criticism, and the authorities postponed the start of the sentences. Meanwhile, Adm. Branko Mamula, Yugoslavia's defense minister, whom *Mladina* had attacked for, among other things, using army conscripts in the building of his villa, resigned on May 15. Political and cultural associations were allowed to function with increasing freedom in Slovenia, and in June Milovan Djilas, Yugoslavia's most famous dissident, gave his first public lecture in 35 years in Maribor.

Premier Branko Mikulic's "intervention program"—a combination of a partial liberalization of prices and wages frozen in November 1987 and measures to stimulate productivity and exports—was adopted by the Federal Assembly in July. On November 29 the Federal Assembly adopted 39 constitutional amendments, chiefly designed to prepare the way for a series of new laws aimed at revitalizing the economy by encouraging market forces. Yugoslavia managed to raise a $1.4 billion standby credit from the International Monetary Fund (IMF), as well as $500 million worth of credits from Western banks, enabling it to put some reform measures into effect. On December 30, however, Mikulic and his Cabinet resigned when the Federal Assembly refused to pass budgetary measures needed to ensure continued IMF support. He would remain in a caretaker capacity until a new premier was named.

The holding of the first Balkan conference since before World War II in Belgrade, February 23–26, was a considerable success for Yugoslavia's diplomacy. Even hitherto isolated Albania attended. Yugoslavia's relations with Albania improved despite the Kosovo crisis, and in February the two countries signed an agreement on cultural cooperation. Mikhail Gorbachev, the Soviet party leader, visited Yugoslavia in March. An economic agreement was signed aimed at reducing Yugoslavia's $1.7 billion trade surplus with the Soviet Union. The nonaligned movement, meeting in Nicosia, Cyprus, in September, elected Yugoslavia as its next chairman. (K. F. CVIIC)

North America

CANADA

Canada is a federal parliamentary state and member of the Commonwealth covering North America north of conterminous United States and east of Alaska. Area: 9,970,610 sq km (3,849,675 sq mi). Pop (1988 est.): 25,880,000. Cap.: Ottawa. Monetary unit: Canadian dollar, with (Oct. 10, 1988) a free rate of Can$1.21 to U.S. $1 (Can$2.07 = £1 sterling). Queen, Elizabeth II; governor-general in 1988, Jeanne Sauvé; prime minister, Brian Mulroney.

Domestic Affairs. Canada held one of the most important elections in its history on Nov. 21, 1988. One issue dominated the election: whether Canada should enter into a comprehensive free-trade arrangement with the U.S. A commercial agreement, signed by Prime Minister Brian Mulroney of Canada and U.S. Pres. Ronald Reagan on January 2, had already been accepted by the U.S. Senate on September 19. It had also been approved by the elected House of Commons in Ottawa but had been stalled by the Liberal majority in the appointed Senate, which demanded that Mulroney's Progressive Conservative (PC) government first hold a national election on the issue. Mulroney's government, which had come to power in September 1984, called an election for November 21. At the polls the PCs won a decisive victory, obtaining 170 seats in a 295-seat House of Commons. The opposition Liberals elected 82 members, the socialist New Democratic Party (NDP) 43. (A PC member died later, leaving 169 PC members and one vacancy at year's end.) The Mulroney government was now free to press ahead with ratification of the free-trade pact with the object of bringing it into effect on or about Jan. 1, 1989. Parliament was recalled during the week of December 12 for this purpose. The legislation implementing the agreement was duly passed by both houses and received the royal assent on December 30.

The election campaign, which began on October 1 with Mulroney's request to Gov.-Gen. Jeanne Sauvé to dissolve Parliament, was one of the most emotional in recent memory. At the start of the campaign Mulroney assumed a lofty stance, asking for reelection on the basis of a booming economy, competent economic management, and the promise of continued prosperity with the implementation of free trade. Liberal leader John Turner concentrated on portraying the free-trade pact as injurious to Canada's long-term interests. He claimed that it offered no real security of access to the U.S. market for Canadian exports and would result in the loss of jobs. It would also produce an irresistible pressure to harmonize Canadian and U.S. social policies, leading to dismemberment of Canada's unemployment insurance, health insurance, and regional support programs. A safer course would be to negotiate trade concessions with a number of countries, including the U.S., through the General Agreement on Tariffs and Trade (GATT). Edward Broadbent, leader of the NDP, took the same line, although he claimed that Turner and the Liberals were as friendly to business interests as Mulroney's Conservatives. Turner's strong showing in a national television debate on October 25, when he accused Mulroney of "selling out" Canada, worked in his favour. As the campaign progressed, support for the NDP began to fall away.

The campaign was the subject of more electoral surveys than any other political contest in Canadian history. Their varying results reflected the volatility of the Canadian electorate regarding such a complex issue as bilateral free trade, but they also confused the voter. The electorate was also assaulted by expensive advertising, some of it misleading. The PC's defense of the agreement was probably less successful in persuading the electorate than the attacks upon it. Support for free trade across the country dropped from a majority to less than 50% as the campaign progressed.

In the voting, the country gave the Mulroney government a solid endorsement, trusting it to safeguard Canada's economic and social interests within a free-trade arrangement with the U.S. Confidence in the government, expressed in electoral results, varied, however, from region to region. The four provinces of Atlantic Canada went against the trend to the PCs. Of the 32 seats in the region, 20 were taken by the Liberals. Mulroney had cultivated Quebec through generous regional support programs and through his leadership in securing the 1987 Meech Lake accord, spelling out terms under which Quebec would accept the 1982 Canadian constitution. The PCs won 63 of Quebec's 75 seats, more than they had secured in 1984. The free-trade cause in Quebec was aided by the strong support of a well-established Liberal premier, Robert Bourassa, who saw free trade as vital for Quebec's continued economic advancement.

Ontario gave a solid block of representatives to the PCs: 47, compared with 42 for the Liberals and 10 for the NDP. This result surprised many observers, since Ontario's popular Liberal premier, David Peterson, was one of only two provincial premiers to oppose free trade. The Canadian Auto Workers Union, with thousands of members in Ontario, church organizations, and many of Canada's writers and artists also opposed free trade, while manufacturing, business, and financial interests, heavily concentrated in the central province, supported the trade pact. Rural Ontario went largely to the PCs, while the Liberals made their gains in the cities, winning 12 of the 23 seats in Metropolitan Toronto and 12 of the 14 ridings (electoral districts) in and around Ottawa. In the prairie provinces, a PC bastion in the 1984 election, the Liberals captured 5 seats in Winnipeg and the NDP won 10 in Saskatchewan, although all but one of the 26 seats in Alberta returned PC candidates. In British Columbia the NDP, traditionally strong, won 19 seats, the PCs captured 12, and Turner retained his seat in Vancouver. The Northwest Territories returned 2 Liberals and Yukon an NDP member to complete the 295-seat House of Commons. (*See* TABLE; the Commons had been increased by 13 members since the 1984 election, so the boundaries of most constituencies had been changed.)

Six members of Mulroney's Cabinet lost their seats in the election. The most prominent were Ramon Hnatyshyn, minister of justice; Flora MacDonald, minister of communications; and Thomas McMillan, minister of the environment. Another senior minister, Patricia Carney, did not run again because of ill health. Turner also lost a senior colleague, Raymond Garneau, his chief lieutenant in Quebec.

The popular vote went 43% to the PCs, 32% to the Liberals, and 20% to the NDP. Five percent of the vote went to other parties, including a new Reform Party organized to defend the interests of western Canada. Thus more Canadians supported parties opposed to free trade than supported the PCs. However, under the Canadian system, the party that wins a majority of seats in the Commons forms the government. Both opposition leaders had announced during the campaign that they would not obstruct the implementation of free trade if the PCs were returned to power. The Senate had taken the same position.

The PC party, out of office for much of the present century, was restored as a "governing party." No party had won two successive elections with majority results in Canada since 1953. The PCs had also changed the political map of Canada by displacing the Liberals as the dominant party in Quebec. The election result was a great personal triumph for Mulroney. His personal standing and that of his party had been catastrophically low two years after he came to power, but he had dramatically reversed that opinion by his determination, his policies, his management style, and the team of ministers he had gathered around him. His party was now well represented in every region of the country, and he possessed a firm mandate to lead Canada into a challenging and more intimate economic relationship with the U.S.

Late in the year the country was rocked by a language controversy. On December 15 the Supreme Court of Canada ruled that Quebec's language law, which prohibited the use of any language but French on exterior commercial signs in the province, violated both the federal Charter of Rights and Freedoms and Quebec's own human rights charter. The Quebec law was held to violate freedom of expression, particularly for Quebec's Anglophone population, representing 12% of the people of the province. Premier Bourassa was under great pressure from the Francophone majority, which saw in French-only signs a symbol of their distinctive culture. On December 17 he announced that his government would use the "notwithstanding clause" of

AP/WIDE WORLD

Canadian Prime Minister Brian Mulroney (right) argues with Liberal Party leader John Turner during a television debate. Turner and many other Canadians objected strongly to Mulroney's commitment to a free-trade agreement with the United States, fearing that the arrangement would undermine the Canadian economy.

the federal charter to exempt his language law from the rights guaranteed in the two charters. He thus confirmed the position of the majority at the expense of minority groups. His legislative solution to the dilemma caused three English-speaking members of his Cabinet to resign, angered by what they considered a betrayal of the rights of the English community in Quebec. Bourassa's decision also called into question the future of the Meech Lake accord, which needed the approval of all ten provinces by June 1990 to go into effect. By the end of 1988 two provinces, New Brunswick and Manitoba, had not yet ratified it. Following Bourassa's decision, the new premier of Manitoba, Gary Filmon (*see* BIOGRAPHIES), announced that he would not introduce the document for discussion in his province until a constitutional conference was held to discuss possible changes to the accord.

Controversy between the House of Commons and the Senate dominated legislative proceedings during 1988. Besides the free-trade agreement, other pieces of Conservative legislation were delayed or amended in the Senate. The Meech Lake accord was approved by the Commons in October 1987 but substantially amended in the Senate. The Mulroney government refused to accept the changes, and the accord was endorsed again by the Commons before the election call dissolved Parliament. Under the constitution, the second Commons endorsement did not require Senate approval. The government's Child Care Act, providing funds to create 200,000 day-care spaces over the next seven years, was under study in the Senate when Parliament was dissolved. Under legislative rules, it would have to be introduced again in the new Parliament. After long study, which the Mulroney government characterized as obstructionism, the Senate accepted two 1987 government measures dealing with immigration: one bill was designed to streamline the assessment of refugee claimants; the other imposed penalties on those who arranged entry of bogus refugees into Canada.

Two provinces held elections in 1988. In Manitoba the governing NDP, hurt by allegations of mismanagement and unpopular taxes, fell from power on April 26. The PCs formed a minority government under Filmon, who became premier on May 9. The Liberal Party showed a dramatic resurgence, increasing its representation in the legislature from one to 20 seats. The PCs narrowly retained office in an election in Nova Scotia on September 6. Premier John Buchanan's personal popularity helped win the party 28 seats in a 52-seat legislature despite a number of ministerial scandals. The Liberals took 21 seats to continue as the official opposition.

Election Results, Nov. 21, 1988
(1984 results in parentheses)

Area	Progressive Conservatives	Liberals	New Democratic Party
Atlantic Provinces (Newfoundland, Nova Scotia, New Brunswick, Prince Edward Island)			
32 (32)	12 (25)	20 (7)	0 (0)
Quebec			
75 (75)	63 (58)	12 (17)	0 (0)
Ontario			
99 (95)	47 (67)	42 (14)	10 (13)
Prairie Provinces (Manitoba, Saskatchewan, Alberta)			
54 (49)	36 (39)	5 (1)	13 (9)
British Columbia			
32 (28)	12 (19)	1 (1)	19 (8)
North (Yukon, Northwest Territories)			
3 (3)	0 (3)	2 (0)	1 (0)
Total			
295 (282)	170 (211)	82 (40)	43 (30)

There was also one independent elected in Ontario in 1984.

The Economy. The Canadian economy grew impressively in 1988. Its estimated 4% growth rate was second only to Japan's among the leading industrial nations. It was the sixth straight year of expansion for the economy. Real gross domestic product (GDP), on an annual basis, was recorded at $590.9 billion at the end of the second quarter. Unemployment fell to its lowest rate in seven years in June but increased marginally to 7.9% in October. Job prospects were especially good in southern Ontario, the centre of Canada's manufacturing. There was concern about inflationary pressures in prices and wages, but the high interest rate policy of the Bank of Canada imposed a curb on spending. The Bank of Canada rate, which controls commercial lending, rose steadily to 10.63% in early November. The cost of living, on a year-by-year basis, stood at 4.2% in October. The soundness of the economy contributed to a strengthening of the Canadian dollar against its U.S. counterpart. It reached a six-year high at 83.6 U.S. cents in October but had fallen to 81–82 cents by November.

A severe drought in the spring and early summer reduced grain and livestock production in the three prairie provinces. The federal and provincial governments were forced to provide relief assistance on a large scale. Ottawa, concerned about the long-term decline in oil production from conventional sources, moved to support three energy megaprojects in 1988. The most ambitious was the development of the offshore Hibernia oil field, lying in the North Atlantic 315 km (195 mi) southeast of Newfoundland. Two other projects were located in the West. One, at Fort McMurray in northern Alberta, was to increase the production of synthetic crude oil from the area's vast oil sands deposits. The other involved construction of an upgrader at Lloydminster, on the Alberta-Saskatchewan border, to produce light crude oil from the pools of heavy oil found in the district. All the projects assumed a world price of at least U.S. $25 a barrel by the mid-1990s.

Finance Minister Michael Wilson presented his fourth budget on February 10. Aside from a tax increase on gasoline and aviation fuel, it was a "standstill budget." Higher revenues from economic growth allowed Wilson to reduce the deficit for the third year in a row. In June he was able to announce that the deficit on the year's operations had fallen to $28.3 billion, representing a smaller proportion of GDP than had been the case when Wilson assumed the finance portfolio in 1984. Total spending for 1988–89 was predicted at $132.3 billion, an increase of 5.5% over the previous year. The largest increase (6.1%) was for defense. Government revenues were predicted to grow to $103.3 billion. Wilson made no changes in the new personal and corporate income tax structure, which went into effect in January 1988.

Foreign Affairs. The 14th annual summit meeting of the leaders of the Group of Seven industrialized countries was held in Toronto on June 19–21. The leaders welcomed recent progress on disarmament and the Soviet Union's decision to withdraw from Afghanistan but made little progress in resolving the meeting's principal economic issue of farm subsidies. They agreed only that the problem should be taken up through the current round of GATT talks.

Peacekeeping figured prominently in Canada's diplomacy during 1988. On May 2 the country sent five officers to observe the Soviet withdrawal from Afghanistan on behalf of the UN. On August 10 about 500 Canadian troops began taking up positions along the frontier between Iran and Iraq in the former Persian Gulf war zone. Canada took special pleasure in the award of the Nobel Peace Prize for 1988 to the UN peacekeeping forces (*see* BIOGRAPHIES).

Canadian troops had taken part in more peacekeeping operations in more locations than those of any other state.

Canada's dispute with France over maritime boundaries in the Gulf of St. Lawrence escalated in 1988. The dispute arose from France's claim that it possessed a 200-mi maritime boundary around its tiny possession, the islands of St. Pierre and Miquelon. Canada recognized only the standard 12-mi territorial sea around the islands, which lie just off the southern coast of Newfoundland. Canada also claimed that the French were seriously overfishing the waters of the disputed zone. On April 15, 21 St. Pierre fishermen, including four local politicians, were arrested and charged with illegal fishing in Canadian waters, and on May 5 a Canadian fishing vessel was seized off St. Pierre and charged with the same offense. All the sailors were released on bail, and negotiations were suspended most of the summer. On September 21 Canada called for nonbinding mediation. In the background of the dispute was Canada's belief that fishermen of the European Communities countries, operating beyond Canada's 200-mi limit of fisheries jurisdiction, were depleting its inshore fish stocks.

A series of expulsions of Canadian and Soviet diplomats disturbed relations between the two countries in June. Canada initially ordered eight Soviet representatives to leave the country on the grounds they were attempting to collect sensitive military and industrial information. Moscow responded by expelling two Canadian diplomats and by forbidding 25 Soviet nationals to continue to work at the Canadian embassy. These diplomatic exchanges contrasted with the cooperation of Canadian and Soviet adventurers in a joint exercise to ski across the frozen Arctic from the Soviet Union to the North Pole and on to one of Canada's Arctic islands. The Transpolar Ski Expedition, composed of four Canadians and nine Soviets, made the 1,730-km (1,070-mi) journey in 91 days.   (D. M. L. FARR)

UNITED STATES

The United States of America is a federal republic composed of 50 states, 49 of which are in North America and one of which consists of the Hawaiian Islands. Area: 9,372,571 sq km (3,618,770 sq mi), including 205,856 sq km of inland water but excluding the 156,492 sq km of the Great Lakes that lie within U.S. boundaries. Pop. (1988 est.): 246,113,000. Cap.: Washington, D.C. Monetary unit: U.S. dollar, with (Oct. 10, 1988) a free rate of U.S. $1.71 to £1 sterling. President in 1988, Ronald Reagan.

After more than seven years of the presidency of Ronald Reagan (*see* BIOGRAPHIES), the U.S. seemed on the surface to be in fine shape. The economy was in the midst of a long and steady expansion. According to the University of Michigan's Survey Research Center, more Americans felt good about economic conditions than at any other time since the late 1960s. Though U.S. troops had occasionally been dispatched to foreign trouble spots during the Reagan years, the U.S. in 1988 was remarkably unentangled overseas. As the 1988 presidential election campaign got seriously under way early in the year, it appeared that prosperity and peace would not be major issues.

Contributing importantly to the sense that times were good was the apparent improvement in relations with the Soviet Union. Two meetings between President Reagan and Soviet leader Mikhail Gorbachev (*see* BIOGRAPHIES) took place in an atmosphere of cordiality and a willingness to negotiate. In late May and early June the two leaders met in Moscow, where Reagan supported Gorbachev's efforts to achieve economic and social changes in the U.S.S.R. but where little progress was made on issues related to arms control. In December Gorbachev traveled to New

U.S. President-elect George Bush (left), Pres. Ronald Reagan (centre), and visiting Soviet leader Mikhail Gorbachev held a meeting on Governors Island in New York Harbor in December.
PAUL HOSEFROS/THE NEW YORK TIMES

York City, where he addressed the United Nations and also met with Reagan and President-elect George Bush (*see* BIOGRAPHIES), but his visit was cut short by a disastrous earthquake in Soviet Armenia.

Nevertheless, beneath that blanket of apparent well-being, Americans in 1988 could not help feeling a bit anxious. Times had been good, but there was a gnawing expectation that the bills piling up during the Reagan years would eventually have to be paid. In a 1988 *New York Times*/CBS News poll, more than half of respondents believed that the next generation of Americans would be bogged down by problems left behind for them.

The Economy. Though the stock market recovered somewhat after its sharp drop on Oct. 19, 1987, Black Monday—as that chilling day was known—had sent a shiver through the economy. The crash had reminded Americans that they had been living beyond their means. Under the Reagan administration the national debt had nearly tripled, reaching $2.6 trillion. The federal budget deficit for fiscal 1988 widened to $155 billion.

That deficit would be a major problem for the next president. It presented a particularly difficult challenge because more than 80% of the federal budget consisted of such hard-to-cut items as defense, interest on the national debt, and entitlement programs such as Social Security and

(continued on page 485)

U.S. Election

BY DONALD MORRISON

In *The American Commonwealth,* a perceptive look at the U.S. political system published exactly 100 years before the presidential election of 1988, Lord Bryce, a British scholar and politician, devoted an entire chapter to the question of "Why Great Men Are Not Chosen President." Given a choice between a safe candidate and a brilliant candidate, Bryce said, Americans tend to play it safe. So it seemed early in 1988, when voters surveyed the field of candidates at the start of the primary season. Commentators referred derisively to the Democratic Party's contenders as "The Seven Dwarfs." They included former Arizona governor Bruce Babbitt, Delaware Sen. Joseph Biden, Massachusetts Gov. Michael Dukakis, Missouri Rep. Richard Gephardt, Tennessee Sen. Albert Gore, civil rights leader Jesse Jackson, and Illinois Sen. Paul Simon. Three candidates who were somewhat more inspiring had decided not to run: former senator Gary Hart of Colorado, who dropped out because of a sex scandal, reentered the race and then dropped out for good; New Jersey Sen. Bill Bradley; and New York Gov. Mario Cuomo, who simply declined to run.

The Republicans, seeking a candidate who could match the stature and electability of Ronald Reagan, were similarly at a loss. The nominal front-runner, George Bush (*see* BIOGRAPHIES), suffered from a reputation as a "wimp" who in 22 years of public life—as a former representative, U.S. ambassador to the United Nations, director of the Central Intelligence Agency, and, for more than seven years, Reagan's vice-president—had failed to distinguish himself as anything more than a docile instrument of someone else's policy. There were three interesting Republican alternatives: Robert Dole of Kansas, the Senate minority leader, who was respected for his wit and intelligence though considered by some to be overly acerbic; former New York representative Jack Kemp, revered among conservative Republicans as Reagan's true ideological heir; and the Rev. Pat Robertson, a popular

Donald Morrison is the Special Projects Editor of Time *magazine.*

television evangelist. None of the three, however, made it through the primary season.

The peculiar U.S. nominating system, though it had changed much since the smoke-filled rooms of Bryce's day, nonetheless militated against brilliance. Each of the two major parties held a series of primary elections and caucuses in many of the states early in the election year to choose delegates to the party convention. In 1988 there were a record 32 such primaries, and a successful candidate could win enough delegates to capture the nomination well before the nominating convention met. In addition, media attention focused on the first primaries, so a candidate who triumphed in such early-choosing states as Iowa and New Hampshire had a great chance of gaining momentum to go on to other victories. The entire process was so long and arduous that generally only the candidates with the most money and the strongest campaign organizations triumphed. In the end, that is pretty much what happened in 1988.

Biden retired from the race after he was caught quoting, without credit, from the speeches of Neil Kinnock, the British Labour Party leader. Among the other Democrats, Babbitt, Simon, and Gephardt all dropped out along the way after failing to string together enough primary victories—or raise enough money—to continue. Babbitt, though he gained attention with a courageous promise to raise taxes to help reduce the swollen U.S. budget deficit, did not come across well on television. Simon's old-fashioned, big-government approach to domestic problems failed to attract enough support. Gephardt managed to win the crucial Iowa caucuses, but his basic theme—trade protectionism—did not play well outside the Midwest.

That left Gore, Jackson, and Dukakis. Young, attractive, and southern, Gore appeared to have momentum after he won five southern primaries on a single day, "Super Tuesday," March 8. Yet his campaign fizzled in New York, where he had unwisely accepted the backing of New York City's controversial mayor, Edward Koch. When the votes were counted for the April 19 New York primary, Dukakis had finished first, providing a major impetus to his campaign. Dukakis (*see* BIOGRAPHIES), who was born and raised in Brookline, Mass., the son of Greek immigrants, went on to become the first Greek-American to be nominated for the presidency. Jackson, who by then had the second-highest delegate count and was the first black American to mount a serious presidential campaign, decided to continue running through the final four primaries, California, Montana, New Mexico, and New Jersey, on June 7.

When the Democrats convened in Atlanta, Ga., in July

TRIPPETT-SIPA

During a record number of primaries, Richard Gephardt, Michael Dukakis, Joseph Biden, Albert Gore, Jesse Jackson, Paul Simon, and Bruce Babbitt (from left to right) vied for the Democratic presidential nomination. Governor Dukakis of Massachusetts became the Democratic presidential candidate.

George Bush and some family members celebrate his victory in the presidential election. Bush carried 54% of the popular vote and swept past Democratic candidate Michael Dukakis with 426 of the 538 votes in the electoral college.

J. L. ATLAN—SYGMA

to crown Dukakis as their nominee, Jackson made a behind-the-scenes effort to claim the vice-presidency but soon relented, fearful of splitting the party along racial lines, and contented himself with winning a few planks favourable to minorities in the party platform. Dukakis instead chose Texas Sen. Lloyd Bentsen (*see* BIOGRAPHIES) to be his running mate. The convention ended on a note of uncharacteristic harmony for the Democrats, whose ticket was soon as far as 17 percentage points ahead of the Republicans in opinion polls.

That lead did not last long. Bush, who had gotten off to a poor start in the primaries, finishing third in Iowa behind Robertson and Dole, made an impressive comeback. He outpolled Dole and Kemp in the February 16 New Hampshire vote and did well on Super Tuesday. On March 29, after Bush won the Illinois primary with 55% of the vote (Kemp had by then dropped out), Dole withdrew from the race, and Bush became the Republicans' de facto nominee. That role was made official in August at the party's convention in New Orleans, La., where Bush surprised many politicians by picking J. Danforth Quayle (*see* BIOGRAPHIES), a young and relatively undistinguished Indiana senator, as his running mate.

Bush's success in winning the nomination was due more to the strength of his organization than to his ability to project a clear vision of what a Bush presidency would be like—a deficiency that the candidate himself referred to as "the vision thing." Trailing his Democratic opponent in the polls late in the summer, the vice-president made a risky decision; instead of stressing his qualifications for the job and his plans for the country, Bush would campaign against his opponent's weaknesses. Accordingly, Bush's speeches and campaign advertising focused on such ostensibly trivial issues as a Massachusetts prison furlough plan, Dukakis's veto of a state law requiring public school students to recite the Pledge of Allegiance, and Dukakis's alleged failure to deal with pollution in Boston Harbor. More pressing national concerns—the federal deficit and a host of domestic and foreign policy questions—went largely unaddressed.

Though many commentators criticized the Bush approach as negative and trivial, it worked. By mid-August, Bush had taken the lead in opinion polls. He never lost it, though Dukakis enjoyed a minor rebound after his vigor-

ous performance in the first of two televised presidential debates. Much of Bush's ultimate success could be traced to the relatively inept performance of the Dukakis camp, which was slow to respond to Bush's attacks. As a result, the vice-president was able to depict his opponent as a dangerous liberal. That was an unaccustomed accusation for Dukakis, whose three terms as governor had marked him as a moderate. Dukakis himself proved to be a passionless campaigner at crucial points in the race. One such moment came in the second debate, when he was asked whether he would still oppose capital punishment if his wife were raped and murdered. Instead of responding to that provocative question with outrage or earnestness, Dukakis delivered a cool, academic brief against the death penalty without once mentioning his wife's name. A few days later the governor was as far as 17 points behind in one opinion poll.

The Dukakis effort finally caught fire in the last two weeks of the campaign. Embracing the "liberal" label and making a fiercely populist appeal, the governor began drawing huge, enthusiastic crowds. He even edged closer to Bush in the polls. By then, however, it was too late. On election day, November 8, Bush won 54% of the vote to Dukakis's 46%. The vice-president carried all but ten states and the District of Columbia. That gave him a 426–112 margin in the electoral college, the body that, under the U.S. Constitution, was the official arbiter of victory. When the electoral college met in December, however, Dukakis received only 111 votes. Apparently in protest against the electoral college system, an elector from West Virginia, a state that Dukakis had won, chose Bentsen for president and Dukakis for vice-president.

"The people have spoken," Bush said shortly after learning he had won. Nevertheless, in the minds of many Americans—and especially the Democrats, who retained control of Congress—Bush's negative campaign had left a sour impression. Perhaps sensing those doubts, he attempted in his victory address to deal with "the vision thing" and reach out to those who had voted against him. "When I said I wanted a kinder and gentler nation, I meant it—and I mean it," he said. "My hand is out to you, and I want to be your president, too." George Herbert Walker Bush, 64, was scheduled to take office as the 41st president of the United States on Jan. 20, 1989.

(continued from page 482)

Medicare. Even without any policy changes, federal spending would rise by 24% in the next five years because of various provisions for automatic increases. No matter who was in the White House, a top priority would be to hold down such increases through further unpleasant spending cuts and to help attack the budget deficits by raising taxes (a step Bush had ruled out during the campaign).

Perhaps even more distressing, the U.S. had lost its competitive edge in the world. In the first eight months of 1988, it imported $92 billion more in goods than it exported. At that rate the 1988 trade deficit was expected to reach $138 billion. The figure was less than that of the previous year, but by all rights the decline should have been steeper; the value of the dollar had fallen sharply, making U.S. goods comparatively cheap. (The dollar's drop, meanwhile, had prompted foreigners to buy up large amounts of U.S. companies and real estate.) The inability to meet foreign competition had virtually wiped out some U.S. industries. For example, the share of the domestic consumer electronics market held by U.S. companies plunged from almost 100% in 1970 to less than 5% in 1988.

While the U.S. was losing its position as the world's leading economic power, voices could be heard warning of a larger decline. In *The Rise and Fall of the Great Powers,* a book that aroused considerable debate among policymakers in 1988, historian Paul M. Kennedy argued that great military powers tended to decline once their overseas commitments became too taxing, as was allegedly the case with the U.S. In another much-discussed book, *The Birth Dearth,* demographer Ben J. Wattenberg warned that a declining birthrate was undermining the country's global eminence and that the free Western nations would soon account for only a tiny fraction of the world's people.

Drugs and Scandals. Doubts about the nation's economy and global power were not the only ones nibbling at the corner of the electorate's consciousness. Many Americans in 1988 were beginning to worry that the very fabric of the nation was unraveling. Drugs had become a problem of frightening proportions, especially with the emergence of crack, a potent, cheap, and highly addictive derivative of cocaine. In 1981 the U.S. Customs Service confiscated 1,872 kg (4,118 lb) of cocaine; by the beginning of 1988

UPI/BETTMANN NEWSPHOTOS

William Rehnquist (right), chief justice of the United States, swears in Judge Anthony Kennedy as a new Supreme Court justice. Kennedy's wife, Mary, looks on.

Sen. George Mitchell of Maine (left) is congratulated by his opponent Sen. J. Bennett Johnston of Louisiana (right) on becoming the new Senate majority leader. Alan Cranston (centre) was reelected majority whip.

PAUL HOSEFROS/THE NEW YORK TIMES

it was seizing cocaine at a rate nearly 20 times higher. In addition, confiscations were estimated by some authorities to equal only one-third the amount consumed in the U.S. In 1988 Princeton University professor Ethan Nadelmann estimated that federal, state, and local governments were spending $8 billion a year on drug-enforcement activities. The cost to society, however, was incalculable. (*See* CRIME, LAW ENFORCEMENT, AND PENOLOGY: *Special Report.*)

Government corruption flourished at high levels, and a number of Reagan administration officials left office under a cloud in 1988. Chief among them was Attorney General Edwin Meese, who resigned amid charges of questionable conduct. An independent counsel who investigated the charges found no grounds for indicting Meese but cited cases in which the attorney general may have violated federal ethics rules. Among those examples were Meese's relationship with E. Robert Wallach, a San Francisco lawyer indicted on influence-peddling charges; assistance Meese gave to Wedtech Corp., a New York City-based defense contractor; and the attorney general's connection with a plan to make secret payments to Israeli officials in return for their promise not to disrupt a proposed Iraqi oil pipeline.

The so-called Iran-*contra* arms scandal rolled toward a conclusion in 1988. Independent counsel Lawrence Walsh announced a 23-count indictment that contained sweeping charges of criminal dealings at the White House. Most prominent among those indicted was former National Security Council aide Lieut. Col. Oliver North. He and three codefendants were charged with conspiring to defraud the U.S. by establishing and concealing a plan for illegally supporting the U.S.-backed *contras,* a guerrilla force fighting to overthrow the leftist government of Nicaragua.

Some almost comical difficulties beset the lame-duck Reagan administration. Donald Regan, who had resigned in 1987 as White House chief of staff, revealed in a best-selling memoir, *For the Record,* that Nancy Reagan had relied on a San Francisco astrologer to determine the timing of her husband's activities. For the president's late-1987 Washington summit meeting with Gorbachev, for instance, she had cast the charts of both men and determined that 2 PM on December 8 would be the most propitious moment

for signing the intermediate-range nuclear forces treaty. At Mrs. Reagan's behest, the entire summit was built around that hour. The Reagans never convincingly refuted Regan's charges, though they denied his implication that astrological considerations interfered with affairs of state.

Legislation. Though Reagan was perhaps the most conservative president since Herbert Hoover, he made little progress in advancing the conservative agenda in 1988. That was partly because of the lethargy that seemed to envelop the White House as his presidency wound down and partly a result of the Republican Party's minority position in the national legislature. By the time the Democratic-controlled 100th Congress adjourned in October, it had passed—occasionally over Reagan's veto—considerable progressive legislation. The measures included a clean-water bill that Reagan had vetoed in the previous session and a requirement that companies give workers 60-day notification of plant closings and layoffs. Also passed were expensive measures to aid the homeless, provide protection against catastrophic illness, and improve highways, mass transit, and education. "There were pent-up needs too long deferred," said House Speaker Jim Wright by way of explanation.

Many needs went unmet in 1988. The spectre of AIDS continued to haunt the U.S. By October at least 75,000 Americans had contracted the disease, which so far had no cure. The coastlines and waterways of the U.S. were increasingly polluted; in the summer of 1988 beaches in the Northeast were closed to bathers when medical wastes began washing ashore. Accidents and radiation leaks at nuclear-weapons plants, covered up for decades by the government, were brought into the public eye in 1988, amid charges that many people may have developed cancer as a result.

An old problem gained new urgency in 1988: the homeless. On any given night, an estimated 735,000 people in the U.S. did not have a home. During the year as many as two million people were without shelter for one night or more. Many were mentally ill and were on the streets because many states had a long-standing policy of deinstitutionalization. Many were drug or alcohol abusers. A growing number, however, were the working poor, often entire families, who could not afford the price of housing. About 2.5 million units of low-income housing had disappeared since 1980, partly because of cutbacks in government spending, while prices of existing housing had zoomed by double-digit percentages in many parts of the country.

Income and Employment. For that reason, among others, many younger Americans were beginning to wonder if they would ever enjoy a living standard as high as that of their parents. College tuitions were soaring, but federally subsidized tuition-loan programs were being slashed. Though inflation had largely been tamed, real hourly wages had declined by 2.6% since 1981, and nearly one million factory jobs had disappeared. Real per capita income had risen by over $1,500, to $12,287 a year, but median incomes for younger and less experienced workers had fallen substantially. More women were working than ever before. There were also more two-paycheck families, and the median income for those households reached $40,422. In many families, however, both parents had to work just to stay

Church Membership in the United States

Religious body	Total clergy	Inclusive membership	Religious body	Total clergy	Inclusive membership
Baptist bodies			Independent Fundamental Churches of America	1,366	120,446
American Baptist Association	1,760	250,000	Jehovah's Witnesses	None	773,219
American Baptist Churches in the U.S.A.	7,872	1,568,778	Jews	6,500	5,943,700
Baptist Bible Fellowship, International	4,500	1,405,900	Latter Day Saints (Mormons)		
Baptist General Conference	1,700	131,480	Church of Jesus Christ of Latter-day Saints	28,598	3,860,000
Baptist Missionary Association of America	2,720	227,638	Reorganized Church of Jesus Christ of L.D.S.	16,929	191,618
Conservative Baptist Association of America	...	225,000	Lutherans		
Free Will Baptists	2,895	200,387	Evangelical Lutheran Church in America	17,052	5,288,230
General Baptists (General Association of)	1,527	73,515	Lutheran Church—Missouri Synod	8,139	2,614,375
Liberty Baptist Fellowship	...	200,000	Wisconsin Evangelical Lutheran Synod	1,525	418,791
National Baptist Convention of America	28,574	2,668,799	Mennonites		
National Baptist Convention, U.S.A., Inc.	27,500	5,500,000	Mennonite Church	2,553	92,902
National Primitive Baptist Convention	636	250,000	Old Order Amish Church	2,910	64,980
Primitive Baptists	...	72,000	Methodists		
Progressive National Baptist Convention	863	521,692	African Methodist Episcopal Church	6,550	2,210,000
Regular Baptist Churches, General Association of	2,045	300,839	African Methodist Episcopal Zion Church	6,696	1,220,260
Southern Baptist Convention	63,400	14,722,617	Christian Methodist Episcopal Church	2,650	718,922
Buddhist Churches of America	115	100,000	Free Methodist Church of North America	1,786	73,225
Christian and Missionary Alliance	2,189	244,296	United Methodist Church	37,999	9,124,575
Christian Brethren	500	98,000	Wesleyan Church	3,783	185,641
Christian Congregation	1,461	106,831	North American Old Roman Catholic Church	150	62,611
Church of God (Anderson, Ind.)	3,238	198,552	Pentecostals		
Church of the Brethren	1,972	154,067	Assemblies of God	27,264	2,160,667
Church of the Nazarene	8,811	543,762	Church of God	2,737	75,890
Churches of Christ—Christian Churches			Church of God (Cleveland, Tenn.)	9,638	505,775
Christian Church (Disciples of Christ)	6,802	1,086,668	Church of God in Christ	10,426	3,709,661
Christian Churches and Churches of Christ	7,041	1,071,995	Church of God in Christ, International	1,600	200,000
Churches of Christ	...	1,623,754	Church of God of Prophecy	7,573	74,588
Community Churches, International Council of	350	200,000	Full Gospel Fellowship of Churches and Ministers, Intl.	850	65,000
Congregational Christian Churches, Natl. Assn. of	826	108,115	International Church of the Foursquare Gospel	5,050	192,237
Eastern Churches			Pentecostal Church of God	1,565	88,616
American Carpatho-Russian Orthodox Greek Catholic Ch.	66	100,000	Pentecostal Holiness Church, International	3,422	113,000
Antiochian Orthodox Christian Archdiocese of N. Am.	275	280,000	United Pentecostal Church, International	6,984	500,000
Apostolic Catholic Assyrian Ch. of the East, N. Am. Dioc.	57	80,000	Polish National Catholic Church of America	141	282,411
Armenian Church of America, Diocese of the	61	450,000	Presbyterians		
Bulgarian Eastern Orthodox Church	11	86,000	Cumberland Presbyterian Church	734	91,646
Coptic Orthodox Church	28	115,000	Presbyterian Church in America	1,722	190,960
Greek Orthodox Archdiocese of N. and S. America	655	1,950,000	Presbyterian Church (U.S.A.)	19,840	2,967,781
Orthodox Church in America	531	1,000,000	Reformed bodies		
Romanian Orthodox Episcopate of America	67	60,000	Christian Reformed Church in North America	1,000	225,951
Russian Orthodox Church Outside of Russia	168	55,000	Reformed Church in America	1,621	338,348
Serbian Eastern Orth. Ch. in the U.S.A. and Canada	82	67,000	United Church of Christ	10,080	1,662,568
Ukrainian Orthodox Church in the U.S.A.	131	87,745	Roman Catholic Church	53,522	53,496,862
Episcopal Church	14,355	2,462,300	Salvation Army	5,174	434,002
Evangelical Covenant Church of America	973	86,741	Seventh-day Adventist Church	4,512	675,702
Evangelical Free Church of America	1,484	95,722	Triumph the Church and Kingdom of God in Christ	1,375	54,307
Friends United Meeting	600	55,616	Unitarian Universalist Association	1,069	173,167

Table includes churches reporting a membership of 50,000 or more and represents the latest information available.
Source: National Council of the Churches of Christ in the U.S.A.

(CONSTANT H. JACQUET)

even. Nearly 57% of all mothers with preschool children had joined the work force, though surveys indicated that most of them would have preferred to stay at home.

On balance, women had made some impressive gains by 1988. The gap between women's and men's salaries had narrowed five percentage points since 1980, to 65%. Meanwhile, the number of women employed in management jobs had increased about 48%. More new businesses were being launched by women in 1988 than by men. Female equality was marching forward on many fronts, from children's athletic teams to the U.S. Supreme Court, where Sandra Day O'Connor had become the first female justice in 1981.

Economically, however, it appeared that the U.S. was becoming a nation divided. The top fifth of the population received nearly 44% of all income in 1988, and the bottom fifth less than 5%. That gap had been widening since 1969. The rich were getting richer, and the poor were growing more numerous. At the beginning of the year, 13.5% of Americans were living below the federally defined poverty line ($11,611 for a family of four), up from 13% in 1980. Almost one-third of blacks were poor, as were more than one-third of single-parent families headed by women. Between 1980 and 1987 the proportion of Hispanic poor increased from 25.7 to 28.2%. Among whites the figure rose from 10.2 to 10.5%.

For blacks, who made up roughly 12% of the population in 1988, the picture was in some ways better and in other ways worse at the end of the Reagan era. Unemployment among black teenagers was down sharply, and the black middle class had gained ground; median incomes among black couples working full time rose a real 10%, to almost $40,000. Still, of the many black families headed by single women, more than half were poor, versus just over a quarter of single-parent families headed by white women. Other problems also ravaged the black community in 1988; the leading cause of death among young black men was murder by another young black man, and in the inner cities drug use and its attendant problems had grown to tragic proportions.

Many Americans were ambivalent about the poor. In the self-absorbed era of the late 1980s, with its emphasis on entrepreneurial vigour and market solutions to problems of all sorts, few citizens could be expected to stay awake nights worrying about income distribution. In the earnest 1960s poverty and its attendant ills were considered a responsibility of society as a whole, but by 1988 it was important to be rich. In a poll taken the previous year by the American Council on Education and the Cooperative Institutional Research Program, 76% of college freshmen said that one of their most important goals in life was to "be very well off financially," up from only 41% in a similar poll two decades earlier.

Role of Government. Poverty was increasingly blamed on the system of government support designed to ameliorate it. Welfare programs survived in the 1980s, of course, but there was growing concern that they tended to create dependency. Such conservative theorists as Charles Murray contended that Aid to Families with Dependent Children, a major federal program, provided an economic incentive for women to have babies out of wedlock and for men to avoid supporting their children. Though this argument was perhaps an exaggeration, it was persuasive enough to help frame the debate on government social spending for the 1988 election campaign. Before adjourning in the fall, Congress passed a major overhaul of the welfare system that stressed getting recipients into jobs. (*See* SOCIAL SECURITY AND WELFARE SERVICES.)

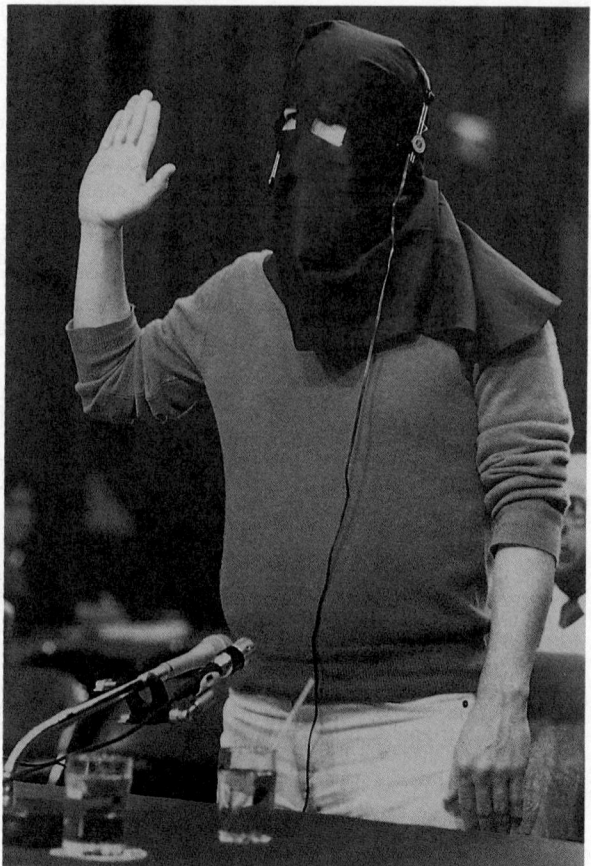

A hooded witness is sworn in before a Senate foreign relations subcommittee before beginning his testimony on Gen. Manuel Noriega of Panama and his involvement in drug and arms trafficking.
AFP PHOTO

Yet voters in 1988 seemed ambivalent about what their government should be doing. In a poll by the Gallup Organization for the Times Mirror Co., more than three-quarters of respondents agreed that the federal government should run only those things that could not be run at the local level, but in a *Time*/Yankelovich poll only a year earlier, some three-quarters of respondents believed that federal spending should be increased on such items as health care for the elderly, cleaning up the environment, and aid to the homeless. Americans evidently wanted things to stay the way they were, but they also wanted them to change. Thus when the electorate trooped to the polls on November 8, they chose George Bush, a man who had promised to preserve the accomplishments of the Reagan era—but who also talked of a "kinder, gentler nation" than the one shaped by his predecessor. (*See* Special Report.)

In his first appointments Bush appeared to be stressing continuity with the Reagan administration. William Webster was retained as director of central intelligence, Richard Thornburgh as attorney general, Nicholas Brady as secretary of the treasury, and Lauro Cavazos as secretary of education. James Baker, Reagan's White House chief of staff and later secretary of the treasury, was named secretary of state. Other early appointments included former Texas senator John Tower, secretary of defense; Jack Kemp, secretary of housing and urban development; former transportation secretary Elizabeth Dole, secretary of labour, and Gov. John Sununu of New Hampshire, White House chief of staff.   (DONALD MORRISON)

See also *Dependent States,* below.

Developments in the States in 1988

The beginnings of a consumer revolt over escalating insurance costs, particularly for automobile liability coverage, were felt in state capitals during 1988. The development produced bitterly contested voter initiatives in California, and by the year's end the backlash against insurers had reached New Jersey and Massachusetts, promising future problems for legislators and lobbyists alike.

Arizona's Evan Mecham in 1988 became the first governor in 60 years to be impeached and removed from office. Even so, it was a generally uneventful year for states fiscally and politically, with both tax increases and legislative seat turnovers at recent low points. The popularity of voter-sponsored ballot initiatives continued to soar, with California setting a new record for the number of propositions in a single year. State prison populations also set new records, but the number of executions dropped sharply.

Federalism continued to thrive during the year with the election of George Bush, who praised states for innovation in several fields and appointed a leading governor as his top aide. Stepping into a void created by a federal pullback, state attorneys general became increasingly aggressive in pursuing consumer and antitrust complaints.

Forty-four states staged regular legislative sessions during the year, and 11 called special sessions.

Party Strengths. Voters ordered virtually no changes in political party lineups during state elections in 1988. Of the 6,000 state legislative seats contested in the fall balloting, Democrats picked up a net total of nine, the fewest seats changing hands in history. Prior to the elections Democrats enjoyed total control of 28 state legislatures, while Republicans dominated 9 and 12 were split or tied. The postelection lineup was 28 Democratic control, 8 Republican, and 13 split or tied.

For 1989 Democrats would control legislatures in all states except Arizona, Colorado, Idaho, Kansas, New Hampshire, South Dakota, Utah, and Wyoming (where Republicans had control in both houses); Alaska, Michigan, Montana, Nevada, New York, Ohio, Pennsylvania, and Washington (where Republicans controlled the state senate and Democrats organized the lower chamber); Delaware, New Jersey, North Dakota, and Vermont (where Democrats controlled the Senate and Republicans the lower house); Indiana (Senate Republican and House tied); and Nebraska (a nonpartisan, one-house legislature).

Democrats made a net gain of two governorships during the year. When Arizona's Republican governor was impeached, he was replaced by a Democratic secretary of state. During the elections Democrats captured GOP-held statehouses in Indiana and West Virginia but lost the Montana gubernatorial chair to the Republicans. That left the 1989 gubernatorial lineup at 28 Democrats and 22 Republicans. Thus Democrats would control the governorship and both legislative chambers in 14 states, while Republicans enjoyed overall control in only 4.

Government Structures, Powers. The popularity of citizen-driven ballot initiatives continued to grow in 1988, with Cal-

ifornia voters deciding a record number of 18 such measures in two statewide elections during the year. The state legislature also submitted nine bond issues and eight constitutional amendments to the voters, prompting some critics to call the process "democracy run wild." In spring balloting California voters approved two initiatives with contradictory provisions—one mandated public financing of election campaigns, and the other made public financing impossible—and some scholars called for restrictions on ballot measures to avoid future instances of voter confusion.

New Mexico legislators and voters approved a measure providing for effective merit selection of state judges, who were previously elected. Alabama lawmakers overrode a gubernatorial veto and repealed their previous call for a national constitutional convention to require a balanced federal budget. During a fiscal crisis sparked by declining energy prices, Louisiana legislators relinquished broad constitutional powers to allow the governor a free hand in closing a $1 billion budget deficit.

The California legislature designated the banana slug (*Ariolimax dilichophallus*) as the official state mollusk.

Government Relations. As the deficit-plagued federal government continued to cut financial assistance, reduce regulation, and soft-pedal antitrust enforcement, state government continued to gain credibility as the nation's new source of creativity and problem solving in regard to domestic affairs. Relations between the federal government and the nation's governors, though sometimes bumpy and contentious, improved steadily during the year. President-elect Bush named the chairman of the National Governors' Association, New Hampshire Gov. John Sununu, as his White House chief of staff and scheduled three meetings with governors in the two months following the election.

Sununu had earlier advocated an initiative to "restore balance to the state-federal relationship," usually by giving states more power over their own affairs. In his first official trip as president-elect, Bush told governors meeting in Charlottesville, Va., that they were "on the cutting edge" in many policy areas and sought their advice on environmental and educational problems. He applauded the governors for submitting lists of more than 240 proposals to eliminate, trim, or consolidate federal regulations deemed burdensome.

State attorneys general continued their recent activism during 1988, particularly in consumer matters as federal regulatory and antitrust enforcement waned. Also, states accelerated a trend toward regional cooperation for economic and environmental purposes. Arkansas, Louisiana, and Mississippi began planning jointly on foreign investment, rural development, highway construction, and federal assistance matters. Ohio, Michigan, Wisconsin, Illinois, Indiana, and Minnesota signed a Great Lakes compact to jointly promote economic development.

Several adverse U.S. Supreme Court decisions failed to slow the general trend toward revitalization of federalism. The high court ruled in January that state court judges could be sued for employment discrimination, a setback to the concept of judicial immunity. Of potentially greater

importance was a 7–1 Supreme Court decision in April holding that Congress could end the 93-year exemption of state and local bond interest from income tax reporting requirements. State lobbyists reacted vigorously to the decision, and by the year's end Congress had made no serious move to begin taxing the interest earned on local government bonds.

State officials again failed to persuade Congress to close a tax loophole that allowed most mail-order firms to avoid paying state sales taxes. State officials estimated the revenue loss to state treasuries at $2.5 billion annually.

Finances. Following an extremely heavy round of tax increases in 1987, states enjoyed a tranquil fiscal year in 1988 as the national economy continued to grow. The National Conference of State Legislatures reported that 13 states raised taxes and 15 lowered them during the year, for a net increase in revenue of only $600 million.

Eleven states were forced to cut their budgets at midyear, often because of sluggish local economies, poor forecasting, or misjudgment of capital gains tax declines resulting from federal tax reform. A U.S. Census Bureau study revealed that the sales tax, at 49%, was still the largest source of state revenue but that state income taxes, at 38%, were gaining in importance.

Most state tax changes during the year involved relatively small amounts of money. Personal income taxes were increased slightly in Arizona and Massachusetts and lowered in Delaware, Hawaii, Kansas, Minnesota, Nebraska, North Dakota, Oklahoma, Utah, Vermont, and Virginia. Personal income taxes were reformed, usually conforming to federal changes, in Iowa, Kansas, and Maine.

Sales taxes were raised significantly in Louisiana and West Virginia and increased slightly in Arizona, Illinois, and Massachusetts. Kansas, Minnesota, and South Dakota nudged sales tax coverage down. While no state altered its corporate income tax rate, Arizona and Kansas increased business tax coverage, and Minnesota, New Hampshire, North Carolina, and Rhode Island lowered it.

Cigarette taxes were boosted in Iowa and Rhode Island. Motor fuel taxes were increased in Arizona, Idaho, Indiana, Iowa, Kentucky, Maine, Minnesota, South Dakota, and Tennessee. Arizona and Washington increased hotel taxes; Kentucky raised its coal severance tax; Vermont added to its real estate transfer levy; and Arizona increased state property taxes.

Figures compiled in 1988 revealed that state revenue from all sources totaled $517 billion in the 1987 fiscal year, an increase of 7.4% over the preceding 12 months. General revenue (excluding state liquor and state insurance trust revenue) was $419.5 billion, up 6.6% from the previous year. Total state expenditures rose 7.4% to $455.8 billion, creating a technical surplus of $61.2 billion.

General expenditures, not including outlays of the liquor stores and insurance trust systems, amounted to $403.9 billion, up 7.3% for the year. Of general revenue 58.8% came from state taxes and licenses, 16.8% from charges and miscellaneous revenue, including educational tuition, and 24.4% from intergovernmental revenue, mostly from the federal government.

The largest state outlay was $149.9 billion for education, of which $50.7 billion went to state colleges and universities and $88.3 billion to local public schools. Other major outlays included $78.5 billion for public welfare, $38.3 billion for highways, and $32.1 billion for health and public hospitals.

During the year, Louisiana became the first state to rebate sales taxes to foreign visitors. The move was seen as a boost to tourism. South Dakota and Wyoming signed the International Fuel Tax Agreement, bringing to eight the number of states cooperating to simplify reporting for interstate bus and trucking concerns. South Dakota voters rejected a tax-limitation ballot measure, but Californians narrowly rejected an initiative to relax previously imposed limits on state and local spending.

Ethics. Arizona Governor Mecham, a Republican, was impeached and then removed from office by the state Senate on April 4. Mecham was convicted on two impeachment articles voted by the state House but acquitted on a third, which would have barred him from ever holding state office again. After the legislative action the state Supreme Court canceled a recall election scheduled for May 17 that was aimed at removing Mecham from office. Mecham was later acquitted by a criminal trial jury on charges similar to the third count, which alleged that he concealed a $350,000 campaign loan from a local developer.

The impeachment highlighted a tumultuous year in Arizona politics. In February the state House of Representatives, like the Senate controlled by Republicans, voted three impeachment charges against Mecham. The most serious accused him of loaning $80,000 from the state protocol fund to his car dealership. Mecham was also accused of trying to block an investigation into an alleged death threat made by a campaign fund-raiser and concealing the developer's loan. As the Senate trial got under way, Mecham supporters mounted recall efforts against 18 legislative critics of the governor, and several legislators reported death threats. The Senate vote to convict Mecham was 21–9 on the investigation-blocking charge and 26–4 on misusing the protocol fund.

Mecham enjoyed a measure of revenge later in the year. In the fall elections 11 Republican legislators who had voted to impeach or convict the governor were themselves cast out of office, including Carl Kunasek, the Senate president, and Joe Lane, the speaker of the House. Republicans managed to maintain control of both legislative chambers by narrow margins, but both GOP delegations were almost evenly split between pro- and anti-Mecham factions.

Voters in California and New York showed little concern over reports of corruption in their state legislatures, returning most affected incumbents to office. In New York nine state senators had been indicted on a variety of charges, including payroll abuse, but only one, Republican Richard Schermerhorn, was defeated for reelection. Schermerhorn was indicted twice on charges of tax and mail fraud and for taking money from a former mobster. Three California state Assembly members named in an FBI corruption investigation were also reelected, but one, GOP Assembly leader Patrick Nolan, resigned his leadership post two days after the election.

California voters approved two contradictory initiatives touted as campaign-reform proposals. Proposition 68, which provided for public financing of state election campaigns, was approved 52–48%. However, voters simultaneously gave a 58% margin to Proposition 73, which specifically declined to limit campaign spending and thus ruled out public financing. An attorney general's opinion held that since Proposition 73 got more votes, its provisions would be controlling. Both initiatives imposed contribution limits for state and local office campaigns and prohibited the transfer of funds from one candidate to another.

Alabama state Rep. Thomas Reed, also president of the state chapter of the National Association for the Advancement of Colored People (NAACP), was convicted of extortion after being charged with accepting $10,000 to get a murderer out of prison early. Former New Jersey senator David Fried, who staged his own death and then led authorities on a two-year worldwide manhunt, pleaded guilty to charges that he attempted to defraud a union insurance-pension fund of $20 million.

Education. States continued to experiment with innovative programs to improve teaching and learning standards during the year. Tennessee initiated an intensive drive to counter dropouts, and Wisconsin designed a plan to reduce welfare benefits to families in which children miss excessive days of school. Michigan expanded its preschool program to include every "at risk" four-year-old.

Georgia became the first state to use standardized tests to determine whether kindergarten students should be promoted to first grade. New Jersey became the first state to take over a local school district, Jersey City, as "academically bankrupt" under a new law. Forty states moved to establish or strengthen assessment programs for college freshmen, establishing levels of skills and matching them with future job market needs.

Nine western states agreed to lower public college tuition for residents of cooperating jurisdictions. A 1982 Michigan law, the first in the nation to require public colleges to sell stock in companies doing business in South Africa, was overturned by a federal appeals court.

Health, Welfare. State innovation in welfare reform was recognized yet again when Congress approved a national workfare-oriented bill patterned after state initiatives. The new legislation, like its state predecessors, was designed to promote independence through work, education, and training and to strengthen youth health care and collection of child-support payments. It also required work for unemployed welfare parents and required states to set up job-opportunity and basic-skill programs toward that end.

Massachusetts became the first state to establish comprehensive health insurance for all citizens, phased in over a four-year period. The program was a plus in the presidential campaign of Gov. Michael Dukakis, though some businesses objected to its cost. Wisconsin became the fifth state to approve a parental leave bill. It allowed workers to take six-week unpaid leave for birth or adoption and also guaranteed a two-week unpaid leave for care of a seriously ill relative.

Illinois mandated immediate income withholding for child-support payments. Maine joined California and Delaware in accelerating training and reemployment for the unemployed and those facing economic dislocation. Maine and Illinois became the first states to allow families and businesses to provide long-term care for the handicapped without jeopardizing basic government support.

California voters approved a controversial toxins measure requiring all businesses to post warning signs near hazardous substances. In confusion following the vote, several grocery chains pulled pipe tobacco, cigars, and chewing tobacco from their shelves rather than post the signs. California voters rejected a controversial AIDS measure backed by Lyndon LaRouche. The measure would have required doctors to report names of persons with AIDS, made willful transmission of the disease a criminal offense, and mandated disclosure of all sex partners by persons with AIDS or others "reasonably believed" to have been afflicted with the AIDS virus.

Virginia and Florida adopted a no-fault liability approach for newborn birth-related neurological injuries. The new law removed many severe injuries from the tort system, paying their claims in a scheme similar to workers' compensation. Missouri agreed to indemnify physicians working for local hospitals against malpractice claims.

Massachusetts became the first state to prohibit new police and fire recruits from smoking, either on or off the job. Violators could be fired. The public interest goal of the legislation, which did not apply to incumbent public service employees, was reduction of disability costs. Oregon became the first state to ask physicians to comment—while filling out death certificate papers—on the role, if any, that smoking had played in the death.

Antiabortion forces won two ballot battles during the year. Michigan voters made abortion procedures ineligible for Medicaid reimbursement, and Colorado voters defeated a measure that could have cleared the way for public funding of abortions. The U.S. Supreme Court voided an Illinois law requiring minors to wait 24 hours before an abortion so that their parents could be notified.

Drugs. States enacted a wide variety of measures designed to combat drug use during the year, attempting with varying degrees of success to discourage abuse, especially among young people. South Carolina established an antidrug police unit to coordinate drug raids. Alabama troopers stepped up drug flow patrol efforts. Illinois set up a multijurisdictional prosecution program. Michigan stressed education programs, and Colorado encouraged widespread community involvement. A Kansas program aimed at reducing drug use among college students, and South Dakota improved treatment facilities.

Illinois joined five other states in attempting to tax illegal drug dealers. New legislation required a tax stamp to be affixed to drug packages; violators were subject to a three-year prison term in addition to drug-conviction penalties.

Law, Justice. Controversy continued to swirl over legal issues surrounding surrogate motherhood. Michigan and Florida became the first states to criminalize the making of a surrogate motherhood contract for pay. Louisiana, Nebraska, Indiana, and Kentucky had previously declared such contracts unenforceable.

Idaho, Iowa, Kansas, Maryland, Michigan, and Ohio joined California, Oregon, Texas, and Washington in allowing judges to require that breath-operated locking devices be installed in the autos of convicted drunk drivers. Georgia became the first state to ban the execution of mentally retarded murderers.

Maryland dealt two rare defeats to the National Rifle Association (NRA). The legislature approved a bill banning the sale of "Saturday night specials," joining Hawaii, Illinois, Minnesota, and South Carolina in regulating these small, inexpensive handguns. The NRA mounted a campaign to overturn the law in the November election, but the voters endorsed it. Idaho banned paramilitary training exercises. Voters in Michigan approved a victims' rights referendum.

After a full year of charges and countercharges, a state grand jury in Poughkeepsie, N.Y., concluded that black teenager Tawana Brawley had lied in 1987 when she claimed to have been kidnapped and raped by a gang of white men. State Attorney General Robert Abrams, who acted as special prosecutor in the case, subsequently asked for a disciplinary investigation of two Brawley lawyers and launched an inquiry into the handling of funds by a third Brawley adviser.

Seeking to uphold good taste without running afoul of First Amendment protections, the Louisiana legislature prohibited the display of bumper stickers with certain four-letter words printed more than ⅛ in high or wide. The fine for the first violation was $200.

Prisons. Populations of state prisons continued to set new records during 1988. A survey by the Bureau of Justice Statistics found a record 555,666 inmates in state prisons at midyear, a 6.2% increase over a year earlier. Colorado's penal population jumped by more than 27% in a year, to 5,105, while California's fast-growing inmate total rose by 7,500 to 72,121. Women prisoner counts grew at a rapid pace, up 8.6% in a year, compared with 5.8% for men.

States continued to experiment with alternatives to expensive prison construction. Texas contracted with a private firm to build four prerelease camps for 2,000 inmates. Arizona, Georgia, and Tennessee tried providing a "boot camp" experience, including shock incarceration, for youthful offenders. Ohio stepped up the awarding of prison "good time" to speed parole eligibility. Alabama started a community diversion project for low-risk offenders. Eleven states attempted electronic monitoring of work-release prisoners, and New Mexico, Michigan, Georgia, and South Dakota joined Illinois in trying intensive probation as an alternative to incarceration.

The NAACP Legal Defense Fund announced that 2,151 prisoners awaited execution in late 1988, up from 1,977 a year earlier. A trend toward increased executions was reversed during the year, as legal appeals caused postponement of numerous death sentences. Only 11 inmates were executed in 1988, compared with 25 a year earlier, bringing to 105 the number of prisoners put to death since the U.S. Supreme Court reinstated capital punishment in 1976.

Gambling. North Dakota voters turned down a state lottery proposal early in the year. Citizens in Indiana, Kentucky, and Minnesota, however, gave the green light to new state-sponsored games of chance in fall elections, bringing to 32 the number of jurisdictions with government lottery operations. South Dakota voters also okayed slot machine and card gambling in the tourist town of Deadwood.

Environment. Referenda supporting environmental projects continued to enjoy widespread public support during the year. In fall balloting California voters authorized $776 million in bonds to acquire parkland and wildlife habitat, Michigan voters approved $660 million in toxic-waste cleanup and environmental bonds, and Minnesota voters established an environmental trust fund. South Dakota voters turned down a measure that would have allowed corporations to reclaim major strip-mine sites in return for restoring them to pre-mining condition.

In an extraordinary confrontation with the federal government, governors of Colorado, Idaho, and New Mexico demanded an expensive environmental cleanup effort as their price for allowing a key nuclear weapons plant to stay open. Waste was piling up at the Rocky Flats plutonium-processing plant near Denver at the year's end; a boxcar of waste was refused by Idaho, and an alternative storage site in New Mexico was unable to open.

Maine and Minnesota banned the sale of polystyrene foam packing products often used as clamshell containers by fast-food outlets. Florida required local governments to reduce the amount of trash they dumped by 30% within five years.

Energy. Two days after the presidential election, the U.S. Department of Energy chose Texas as the site of the Superconducting Super Collider, billed as the largest single construction project ever envisioned. Twenty-five states had attempted to land the project, estimated to cost up to $6 billion. Energy officials admitted that politics influenced the timing of the announcement but denied that President-elect Bush, a resident of Texas, had influenced the choice.

By a 2–1 margin, Massachusetts voters turned down a proposal to prohibit plants that generate nuclear waste. The referendum would have closed the state's two existing nuclear power plants. A New Jersey judge declared unconstitutional the state's law against self-service gasoline stations. That left Oregon as the sole state banning pump-your-own gas.

Equal Rights. Wyoming belatedly raised its drinking age to 21 during the year, becoming the 50th state to bow to federal highway safety pressure and the threat of a cutoff of road funds. Earlier in 1988 the U.S. Supreme Court rejected a suit brought by South Dakota challenging the highway fund cutoff as "federal blackmail."

Voters in Arizona, Colorado, and Florida approved ballot measures making English the official state language. Opponents said that the measures could rekindle ethnic bigotry. The National Governors' Association announced that all states were now honouring plates and tags for handicapped persons issued by other states.

South Dakota voters approved an initiative prohibiting any corporation except a family farm company from engaging in hog farming. Also in South Dakota, Melvin Hansen, a state truck-weight inspector who weighed 210 kg (463 lb) when he was fired for obesity in 1987, was reinstated during the year. The state personnel board ruled he was a victim of discrimination.

Consumer Protection. A revolt over spiraling auto insurance rates ignited in California, birthplace of American trends, generating four ballot initiatives, hotly contested campaigns, and complicated legal action. At the year's end insurers' fear that the ratepayer revolt would spread quickly to other states prompted hasty compromise in at least two states, and some insurance firms threatened to stop writing automobile liability policies.

Faced with rates topping $2,000 per year even for good drivers, California motorists approved an initiative requiring an immediate 20% cut in virtually all insurance rates, with no increase possible for two years. The initiative called for an additional 20% cut for good drivers.

Insurance firms filed four lawsuits attempting to block the new law as unconstitutional, and several firms threatened to quit business in California. Nonetheless, the revolt threatened to spread. New Jersey approved a bill boosting rates for bad drivers, limiting lawsuit awards, and cutting insurance company profits. In Massachusetts insurers agreed to cut rates by 16% in an attempt to head off a California-style insurance revolt there. At the year's end the California Supreme Court said that it would hear the insurance industry's lawsuits.

As federal consumer protection and antitrust enforcement continued to be soft-pedaled by the Reagan administration, state attorneys general moved into the void. Eight states filed suit against major liability insurance companies, charging that "back-room deals, secret communications, and thinly-veiled threats" by insurers fueled the liability insurance crisis of the mid-1980s. Twenty-five states also sued the U.S. Department of Transportation for allowing airlines to omit fare surcharges in advertising. Attorneys general had earlier, in the absence of federal regulation, adopted standards defining deceptive airline advertising.

Florida joined Pennsylvania in requiring disclosures by individuals collecting funds for others. The move followed reports that Maria DeSillers had purchased jewelry, clothes, and a BMW with part of $689,000 raised for her son Ronnie's liver-transplant operation.

A trend toward requiring seat-belt usage slowed during 1988. Georgia approved a new seat-belt law, bringing to 33 the number of jurisdictions requiring front-seat usage. Oregon voters bucked a trend toward repeal and mandated helmet usage by motorcycle operators and passengers. Twelve states joined the Federal Trade Commission in establishing a computer data bank on telemarketing swindlers.

(DAVID C. BECKWITH)

Latin America and the Caribbean

LATIN-AMERICAN AFFAIRS

Only minimal progress was made toward solving Latin America's economic problems in 1988, and the region's foreign debt continued to give grounds for concern. The principal political events were presidential and congressional elections in Mexico, Ecuador, and Venezuela, the promulgation of a new constitution in Brazil, a presidential plebiscite in Chile, and the likely demise of the Central American peace agreement.

In Mexico, Carlos Salinas de Gortari (*see* BIOGRAPHIES) of the ruling Partido Revolucionario Institucional (PRI) took office as president on December 1. The election on July 6 was strongly contested, and Salinas obtained just over 50% of the votes, against Cuauhtémoc Cárdenas (*see* BIOGRAPHIES), representing a left-wing coalition, 31%, and Manuel Clouthier, of the right-wing Partido Acción Nacional (PAN), 17%. The PRI was compelled to recognize its loss of omnipotence after 71 years in power. Salinas's victory was confirmed by Congress in September, when the PRI won only 260 of the 500 seats.

A new Brazilian constitution, the eighth in the country's history, entered into force on October 5 after 20 months of debate in Congress. Presidential elections were to be held in November 1989, with a new president taking office in March 1990. A presidential system of government was maintained, but the powers of the office were curtailed; decree-laws would be subject to congressional approval. Gen. Augusto Pinochet Ugarte was the sole candidate in a presidential plebiscite in Chile on October 5. A unified campaign by 16 opposition parties resulted in a vote of 55% against allowing him an eight-year term from March 1990 and 43% in favour. Under the 1980 constitution Pinochet could stay in office until March 1990, when a new president was to take over following direct elections in December 1989.

In Ecuador Rodrigo Borja Cevallos (*see* BIOGRAPHIES) of Izquierda Democrática (ID) won 46.3% of the valid votes in the second round of presidential elections on May 8 and took office on August 10. In congressional elections held in January, ID emerged as the largest single party with 31 of the 71 seats. On December 4 former Venezuelan president Carlos Andrés Pérez of the Acción Democrática (AD) defeated the Social Christian candidate, Eduardo Fernández, by a vote of 54.6 to 41.7%. The AD retained a congressional majority, with 98 of the 204 seats. In congressional and mayoral elections in El Salvador on March 20, the right-wing Nationalist Republican Alliance won a convincing victory over the ruling Christian Democrats. The elected president of Haiti, Leslie Manigat, was displaced by an army coup in June, and another coup installed Lieut. Gen. Prosper Avril as president in September.

Central America remained bedeviled by social and economic difficulties, and guerrilla activity continued in El Salvador, Guatemala, and Nicaragua. The peace accord signed in August 1987 by the presidents of these countries, Costa Rica, and Honduras, at the instigation of Pres. Oscar Arias Sánchez of Costa Rica, made no headway. The *contra* rebels opposing the Nicaraguan government were still in place in Honduras, despite the refusal of the U.S. Congress in February to renew military funding for them. In Nicaragua a partial cease-fire with the *contras* agreed to in March remained extant, but a state of emergency was reintroduced after Hurricane Joan devastated the country on October 20–22. The presidents of the five countries met in San Salvador November 12–15 to assess prospects for peace, but no formal decisions were taken apart from a reaffirmation of support for a Central American parliament. Tensions in the region increased in December when the World Court agreed to hear a case brought by Nicaragua against Honduras. U.S. Secretary of State George Shultz visited Guatemala, Honduras, and Costa Rica June 29–July 1 to assess U.S. policy in the region, which had suffered a serious reverse following the failure to dislodge the Panamanian strongman Gen. Manuel Noriega by economic sanctions and other means. Noriega gained support from Latin-American governments and seemed to be firmly installed, with Pres. Manuel Solís Palma acting as his nominee.

The Central American Common Market (CACM), comprising Costa Rica, El Salvador, Guatemala, Honduras, and Nicaragua, remained in the doldrums despite an increase in intraregional trade from $411 million in 1986 to $483 million in 1987, mainly attributable to an increased volume of Guatemalan exports. The San José Pact, whereby

AP/WIDE WORLD

The presidents of seven Latin-American countries convene at the Group of Eight regional forum. They include (left to right) Alan García of Peru, Virgilio Barco of Colombia, Raúl Alfonsín of Argentina, Julio Sanguinetti of Uruguay, José Sarney of Brazil, Miguel de la Madrid of Mexico, and Jaime Lusinchi of Venezuela. Panama was suspended from the meeting to protest Gen. Manuel Noriega's removal of Panama's president, Eric Arturo Delvalle.

Venezuela and Mexico supplied up to 130,000 bbl of oil a day on concessional terms to the CACM, Panama, Barbados, Jamaica, and the Dominican Republic, was renewed for a year in August.

Neither the Latin American Integration Association (LAIA: Argentina, Bolivia, Brazil, Chile, Colombia, Ecuador, Mexico, Paraguay, Peru, Uruguay, Venezuela) nor the Andean Group (Bolivia, Colombia, Ecuador, Peru, Venezuela) made notable progress during the year. Bilateral trade remained the most prominent trend, as exemplified in the growing ties between Brazil and Argentina. Since 1985 Presidents José Sarney of Brazil and Raúl Alfonsín of Argentina had exchanged six state visits and signed 22 commercial and technological accords. The only significant event under the LAIA was the conclusion in July of an agreement among all members providing for duty reductions of up to 88% for certain goods traded among themselves. However, the presidents of Argentina, Brazil, Colombia, Mexico, Peru, Venezuela, and Uruguay, meeting at Punta del Este, Uruguay, at the end of October, decided to expand the LAIA's role in promoting regional integration. No major resolutions furthering integration in the Andean Group were forthcoming, but intraregional trade rose from $1.3 billion in 1983 to $2 billion in 1987.

Uruguay's foreign minister, Enrique Iglesias, was elected president of the Inter-American Development Bank (IDB) in February in succession to Antonio Ortiz Mena, who resigned in December after 17 years in the post. At the IDB conference in Caracas, Venezuela, in March, the U.S. restated its refusal to contribute to a capital replenishment unless broad reforms were undertaken. In December Iglesias announced a staff cut as the first step in a major restructuring of the bank.

Many barriers to trade between the 13 members of the Caribbean Economic Community (Caricom) were dismantled on October 1. (At the insistence of the governments of St. Lucia, Grenada, Dominica, St. Vincent, Montserrat, St. Kitts, Antigua, and Belize, trade barriers on 17 products were to remain in force for three years.) The move was expected to improve trade within Caricom, which had declined from $598 million in 1981 to $317 million in 1987. In July the Caricom heads of state, at a meeting in Antigua, shelved plans to create a Caribbean Export Bank, deciding instead to seek the establishment of an export credit facility through the Caribbean Development Bank. Members of the U.S. Congress tried during the year to change the Caribbean Basin Initiative, an integrated program of trade and tax incentives giving duty-free access to the U.S. market for 12 years (from 1984) to a wide range of Caribbean and Central American products, mainly manufactured goods. The proposals included an extension of the program for another 12 years and the elimination of all duties and quotas on original products assembled from 100% U.S.-made components. A summit meeting of the Organization of Eastern Caribbean States in June declined to set a date for a referendum on political unification, although it was agreed that citizens of member countries could travel within the grouping without passports from October 1 and that regulations for the acquisition of property would be liberalized.

During 1987 economic growth within the region reached 2.4%. The recovery of 1984–86, when growth averaged 3.6% a year, was not maintained. The four largest economies (Argentina, Brazil, Mexico, and Venezuela) had growth rates of 3% or less. All these countries had to adapt economic policies to cope with accelerating inflation, which averaged 134% throughout the region in 1987, against 90% in 1986. There was little investment, and growth originated

mainly from the use of idle productive capacity. Overall, the level of investment in 1987 was one-fourth lower than that of 1980, in real terms. Per capita income was $2,223, 5% below 1980. The external accounts showed some improvement. Exports from Latin America reached $91.3 billion, 13% higher than in 1986, despite worsening terms of trade. The trade surplus rose by 18% to $20.2 billion, and the current account deficit fell from $15.2 billion to $8.8 billion. Total external debt (excluding the International Monetary Fund [IMF]) rose by 5% to $414.6 billion at the end of 1987. Estimates of gross domestic product for 1988 envisaged a further slowdown in growth to 1%.

Brazil and Mexico remained the world's most indebted less developed countries. In October Brazil formally ended its moratorium on interest payments on commercial bank medium- and long-term debt of $68 billion introduced in February 1987. A commercial bank financing package was completed in November involving $5.2 billion in new money, rescheduling of $62 billion in external debt principal, and renewal of $14.8 billion in short-term trade and interbank credits for 2½ years. In October Mexico secured a $3.5 billion bridge loan from the U.S. government, and it was expected to seek funds from the IMF and the World Bank to cope with economic difficulties caused by the fall in oil prices and high interest rates. Earlier in the year it had offered to convert public-sector debt held by banks into 20-year bonds backed by zero coupon bonds issued by the U.S. Treasury. For $3.7 billion of debt, bonds were issued for $2.6 billion, and therefore $1.1 billion of debt was canceled with an average discount of 30%. This was a prime example of the greater flexibility and innovation in debt financing schemes that were features of the year.

(ROBIN CHAPMAN)

ANTIGUA AND BARBUDA

A constitutional monarchy and member of the Commonwealth, Antigua and Barbuda comprises the islands of Antigua, Barbuda, and Redonda in the eastern Caribbean Sea. Area: 442 sq km (171 sq mi). Pop. (1988 est.): 83,000. Cap.: Saint John's. Monetary unit: Eastern Caribbean dollar, with (Oct. 10, 1988) a par value of EC$2.70 to U.S. $1 (free rate of EC$4.62 = £1 sterling). Queen, Elizabeth II; governor-general in 1988, Sir Wilfred E. Jacobs; prime minister, Vere Cornwall Bird.

Contending factions within the governing Antigua Labour Party (ALP) curbed their public dispute early in 1988 after Prime Minister Vere Bird declared a "year of peace." In April the party executive endorsed the 16 sitting Antigua members of Parliament as candidates for the general election due by April 1989, rejecting challenges to some members by supporters of the widely criticized public works minister, Vere Bird, Jr. The ALP's electoral chances were improved by differences between the opposition United National Democratic Party and the Antigua-Caribbean Liberation Movement.

The ambassador to the UN, Lloydstone Jacobs, was dismissed in April after the U.S. government revealed that he was under investigation for the alleged sale of passports.

Following an 8.7% rise in gross domestic product in 1987, growth of 8% was forecast for 1988, based on continuing expansion in the tourism sector; however, arrivals from the U.S. slackened in the first four months. The rapid economic growth produced an increase in the trade deficit and the public debt; Finance Minister John St. Luce announced in March that the external debt stood at $240 million.

(ROD PRINCE)

This article updates the *Macropædia* article The West Indies: *Antigua and Barbuda*.

ARGENTINA

The federal republic of Argentina occupies the eastern section of the Southern Cone of South America, along the Atlantic Ocean. Area: 2,780,092 sq km (1,073,399 sq mi). Pop. (1988 est.): 31,963,000. Cap.: Buenos Aires. Monetary unit: austral, with (Oct. 10, 1988) a free rate of 12.12 australes to U.S. $1 (20.76 australes = £1 sterling). President in 1988, Raúl Alfonsín.

Domestic Affairs. The political calendar in 1988 was dominated by party nominations for the presidential elections to be held on May 14, 1989. In July Eduardo Angeloz was nominated by the ruling Unión Cívica Radical (UCR) as its candidate to succeed Pres. Raúl Alfonsín, who was constitutionally debarred from seeking a second consecutive term of office. As governor of Córdoba Province, Angeloz was widely respected as an efficient local administrator and enjoyed the support of the business community and UCR moderates. It was hoped that such a candidate would help to restore the ruling party's credibility; public faith in the government's economic policies, in particular its ability to stem inflation, was at a low ebb in 1988.

The selection of Carlos Saul Menem as presidential candidate for the main opposition party, the Partido Justicialista (Peronists), aroused considerable controversy. For the first time in the Peronists' 40-year history, the candidate was chosen by free internal elections, and the narrowess of Menem's victory reflected deep divisions within the party. The favourite to win had been Antonio Cafiero, governor of the province of Buenos Aires and leader of the *renovador* faction, which favoured distancing the party from the influence of Argentina's powerful labour unions. In contrast, Menem was a populist who had strong blue-collar support and, as governor of the impoverished province of La Rioja, had stirred traditional provincial resentment against the country's domination by cosmopolitan Buenos Aires. Notwithstanding widespread fears of Menem's fundamentalism, he maintained a strong lead in opinion polls, with a popularity rating of 31% in November, compared with 17% for Angeloz.

One of the intriguing controversies of the campaign's early stages was sparked in October by the unexpected return to Argentina from exile in Spain of María Estela Martínez de Perón (Isabelita), widow of the Peronists' founder, Gen. Juan Perón, and president of Argentina in 1974–76. Her visit, described as purely personal in nature, evoked painful memories of the political chaos that characterized her presidency and led to a military takeover in 1976. Thus Isabelita's presence embarrassed many Peronists and fueled speculation that she may have been invited by Alfonsín to damage the Peronists' electoral prospects.

The government faced considerable pressure from labour unions in 1988, mainly for wage concessions. There were many work stoppages, the most prolonged being a six-week strike by teachers in March–April, while most public services suffered severe and frequent disruption during the year. The labour union federation, the Confederación General de Trabajo (CGT), called a one-day general strike on September 9 to protest the government's economic policies. A mass rally in the Plaza de Mayo in central Buenos Aires coincided with the strike. Although it attracted only 12,000 participants, it erupted into violent clashes between riot police and demonstrators in which 113 people were injured. The CGT blamed the confrontation on brutal police repression, while the government blamed clashes between the Peronists' left- and right-wing factions for the riots. A second general strike on September 12 brought the public sector to a halt for 24 hours but passed without violence.

Discontent by middle-ranking officers over both the military's high command and the state trials of officers accused of human rights violations during the 1976–83 period of military rule continued to plague President Alfonsín in 1988. In January Lieut. Col. Aldo Rico, leader of the so-called Easter rebellion in April 1987, escaped from house arrest to stage a second revolt. However, forces loyal to the government were able to crush the three-day uprising without the need for direct intervention by the president. A second military putsch, staged in early December by Col. Mohamed Ali Seineldín, proved more difficult to resolve. The mutineers demanded an amnesty for all members of the military arrested or under trial for human rights violations, greater official control over attacks by the media on the armed forces, the resignation of the Army's chief of staff, Gen. José Segundo Dante Caridi, and substantial increases in the defense budget and military salaries. Most sections of the military were believed to have offered at least moral support to the uprising, and soon after the rebels' surrender on December 6 it became clear that the government had conceded substantial pay raises and the resignation of General Caridi. President Alfonsín refused to countenance an amnesty for jailed officers, however. On December 26 Gen. Francisco Gassino was sworn in as the new chief of staff.

AFP PHOTO

Rebel troops under Lieut. Col. Aldo Rico prepare to meet troops loyal to Pres. Raúl Alfonsín. The rebels were demanding amnesty for officials of previous governments accused of violating human rights.

Foreign Relations. Little progress was made in resolving the dispute between Argentina and the U.K. over sovereignty of the Falkland Islands/Islas Malvinas, although the election of Argentina's foreign minister, Dante Caputo, as president of the General Assembly of the United Nations raised hopes of a thaw in relations between the two countries. In December Caputo met with the U.K.'s permanent representative to the UN, Sir Crispin Tickell, reportedly to consider ways of breaking the deadlock over restoring normal diplomatic and commercial ties.

In 1988 Argentina and Brazil moved closer to establishing a bilateral common market. In April agreements were signed to add 524 products to the list of manufactured goods eligible for tariff exemption. In November Pres. José Sarney of Brazil paid an official visit to Argentina and signed further accords to remove all tariff and nontariff barriers to trade by 1998, to set up a government committee to coordinate economic policies, and to build a pipeline to carry Argentine natural gas to Brazil.

President Alfonsín made a state visit to Western European capitals in November to seal agreements on foreign investments in Argentina. He secured promises of $9 billion in investment credits, including a five-year accord with Italy involving projects with a total value of $5 billion, of which Argentina was committed to providing 40%. West Germany pledged investment finance of $1.1 billion but only after its government and business representatives had pressed Pres. Alfonsín on the need to develop coherent economic policies to generate confidence and a sound climate for foreign investment.

The Economy. Rising inflation depressed real incomes in 1988, while investment suffered from political uncertainties and lack of confidence in the government's economic policies. As a result, most sectors of the economy contracted, although agriculture benefited from a fortuitous combination of optimum weather conditions for Argentina's main crops and high world grain prices because of the U.S. drought. The overall rise in gross domestic product (GDP) was, therefore, unlikely to have significantly exceeded the 1.6% recorded in 1987, when poor harvests constrained growth. The 1988 trade surplus was expected to quadruple, to $3 billion, because of the windfall gains from agricultural exports, a more competitive exchange rate in the first half of the year, and weak domestic demand for imports. In turn, the current account deficit was expected to improve from $4.3 billion in 1987 to about $2 billion.

Despite a package of wage and price controls introduced in October 1987, annual inflation reached 175% at the end of 1987 and rose to 207% in March. In April the government lifted most price controls and restored labour's collective bargaining rights. Monthly inflation immediately began to accelerate, reaching 26% in July to give an annual rate of 381%. With its mind turning to the 1989 election campaign, and partly in the hope of appeasing the International Monetary Fund, the government introduced a package of measures designed to avert the threat of hyperinflation. A voluntary pact to restrain price and wage increases was agreed upon with major private-sector industrialists, and public-sector wages and prices were frozen until the end of September after a 25% rise. The exchange rate against the U.S. dollar was devalued by 11%, frozen until the end of September, and adjusted by 4% a month later. In order to reduce the public-sector deficit, limits were placed on the transfer of funds to provincial governments and public companies. A trade-liberalization program was also announced, including the reduction of tariffs and other restrictions on imports, while certain subsidies to nontraditional exports were eliminated. The prefreeze

hikes in public-sector wages and prices pushed August inflation to 28%, but monthly rates fell to 12% in September, 9% in October, and 6% in November. December inflation was expected to be higher, however, partly because of the increase in military expenditure agreed upon by the government early in the month. A new World Bank loan of $1,250,000 would enable Argentina to pay some overdue interest on old debts.   (JANET KRENGEL)

BAHAMAS, THE

A constitutional monarchy and member of the Commonwealth, The Bahamas comprises an archipelago of about 700 islands in the North Atlantic Ocean just southeast of the United States. Area: 13,939 sq km (5,382 sq mi). Pop. (1988 est.): 245,000. Cap.: Nassau. Monetary unit: Bahamian dollar, with (Oct. 10, 1988) a par value of B$1 to U.S. $1 (free rate of B$1.71 = £1 sterling). Queen, Elizabeth II; governors-general in 1988, Sir Gerald Cash and, from June 25, Sir Henry Taylor; prime minister, Sir Lynden O. Pindling.

Further allegations of involvement in drug trafficking against the prime minister, Sir Lynden Pindling, and other government ministers were made during the trial in the U.S. of Carlos Lehder Rivas, a Colombian accused of managing a cocaine smuggling operation. The government, which strongly denied the allegations, called on the U.S. to provide more assistance for its drug interception program, including ships, helicopters, and personnel. In July the Supreme Court granted an order prohibiting any dealings with property belonging to Lehder and another convicted smuggler, Dennis Record.

After a record tourist year in 1987, during which there were 1,480,000 stay-over visitors and some 1.6 million cruise ship passengers, a more modest result was forecast for 1988. As of the end of April stay-over arrivals had declined by 2.5%, with the U.S. market showing the main fall; cruise ship arrivals were up by 3.5%. For the overall economy a growth rate of 5% was recorded in 1987, and the external debt decreased by 17% to $102 million.

(ROD PRINCE)

This article updates the *Macropædia* article The WEST INDIES: *The Bahamas*.

BARBADOS

The constitutional monarchy of Barbados, a member of the Commonwealth, occupies the most easterly island in the southern Caribbean Sea. Area: 430 sq km (166 sq mi). Pop. (1988 est.): 254,000. Cap.: Bridgetown. Monetary unit: Barbados dollar, with (Oct. 10, 1988) a par value of BDS$2.01 to U.S. $1 (free rate of BDS$3.44 = £1 sterling). Queen, Elizabeth II; governor-general in 1988, Sir Hugh Springer; prime minister, Erskine Sandiford.

Political debate during 1988 centred on economic policy, with the former finance minister, Richie Haynes, emerging as a frequent critic of government policies. Haynes singled out for criticism a rise in interest rates announced in January and a package of tax increases in the budget presented in May. He was one of three members of Parliament belonging to the governing Democratic Labour Party who spoke against the budget and abstained from voting for it, on the grounds that the increases were a betrayal of party election pledges and that they would reduce investment and growth prospects. The tax changes, which were expected to produce BDS$55.6 million in revenue, aimed at overcoming a BDS$48.6 million fiscal deficit.

Real growth of gross domestic product for 1988 was forecast at 2–3%, similar to the 1987 figure of 2%. Tourism and construction were again expected to be the leading sec-

tors. First-quarter results showed a decline in arrivals from the U.S. but a strong increase in the European market. Unemployment at the end of June was 17.3%, down from 18.8% a year earlier. The trade deficit for the first quarter rose to BDS$203 million, compared with BDS$722.4 million for all of 1987. (ROD PRINCE)

This article updates the *Macropædia* article The WEST INDIES: *Barbados*.

BELIZE

A constitutional monarchy and member of the Commonwealth, Belize is on the Caribbean coast of Central America. Area: 22,965 sq km (8,867 sq mi). Pop. (1988 est.): 178,000. Cap.: Belmopan. Monetary unit: Belize dollar, with (Oct. 10, 1988) a par value of BZ$2 to U.S. $1 (free rate of BZ$3.42 = £1 sterling). Queen, Elizabeth II; governor-general in 1988, Dame Minita Gordon; prime minister, Manuel Esquivel.

Prime Minister Manuel Esquivel, presenting his 1988–89 budget in mid-March, predicted further growth in all sectors of the economy except sugar. International reserves, the central bank's gross foreign assets, and exports of citrus concentrate and bananas were all on the increase. Current expenditures were budgeted at BZ$132 million and capital expenditures at BZ$47 million. In a revised budget on September 2, total expenditure was budgeted at BZ$244.2 million. Because of U.S. budget cuts, Belize would receive less assistance.

Bad weather and disease took a heavy toll on crops. Sugar production dropped to 700,000 tons, deepening concerns about the future of the industry. Belize and the Caribbean Agricultural Research and Development Institute (CARDI) began studying the feasibility of growing soybeans and sesame, mustard, and sunflower seeds.

The opposition People's United Party (PUP) improved its position by winning four of the seven seats on the town boards. This was the first victory for the PUP since the United Democratic Party won the 1985 general election. Guatemala and Britain established a joint commission to draft a treaty resolving Guatemala's territorial claims against Belize. (INES T. BAPTIST)

This article updates the *Macropædia* article CENTRAL AMERICA: *Belize*.

BOLIVIA

Bolivia is a landlocked republic in central South America. Area: 1,098,581 sq km (424,164 sq mi). Pop. (1988 est.): 6,993,000. Judicial cap., Sucre; administrative cap., La Paz. Monetary unit: boliviano, with (Oct. 10, 1988) an official rate of 2.57 bolivianos to U.S. $1 (4.39 bolivianos = £1 sterling). President in 1988, Víctor Paz Estenssoro.

In 1988 Pres. Víctor Paz Estenssoro's resolution to reverse Bolivia's declining economic fortunes through austerity and movement away from state control remained firm. The political cost of his determination had been made clear in the December 1987 municipal elections when the ruling Movimiento Nacionalista Revolucionario (MNR) lost heavily to opposition parties from both the left and right; the MNR's popularity continued to plummet in 1988. Labour unions registered their protest against government policies with a series of strikes between January and April, culminating in a hunger strike joined by thousands. The political conflict was temporarily defused by the visit of Pope John Paul II in May. However, local bishops used the occasion to express their fears that the social and moral fabric of the country was crumbling under the strain of the economic crisis and the power of Bolivia's cocaine barons.

The government's campaign to reduce the country's output of coca, the raw material for cocaine, met with violent opposition from peasant farmers whose livelihoods were threatened at a time when alternative employment opportunities were scarce. In June more than 4,000 coca growers seized police barracks in Villa Tunari, Chaparé Province, where much of the Bolivian crop was grown. Five farmers were killed in the ensuing battle with police, who were assisted by agents from the U.S. Drug Enforcement Agency. Later that month miners and factory workers staged a two-day strike to protest against the U.S agents' presence in the country. In July the Bolivian Congress passed a law that restricted national coca cultivation to 12,000 ha (30,000 ac); this rendered production on an additional 48,000 ha (119,000 ac) illegal. Opposition leaders were incensed and accused the government of slavishly following U.S. dictates. Drug traffickers were blamed for a bomb attack on the U.S. secretary of state, George Shultz, when he visited La Paz in August. Although Shultz and his party were unhurt, the incident highlighted the strength of anti-American feeling in Bolivia and the local hostility toward the anticocaine drive. In October five army officers were dismissed for allowing cocaine to be smuggled out of the country. (*See* CRIME, LAW ENFORCEMENT, AND PENOLOGY: *Special Report.*)

Notwithstanding the country's efforts to reduce its own output, the supply of Latin-American cocaine to the U.S. market reached a saturation point. Inevitably, the price of coca leaves declined dramatically in 1988, reducing the supply of dollars on the Bolivian market and exacerbating an already chronic shortage of funds for sorely needed investment projects. In addition Bolivia faced delays in payments for its major export, natural gas, from Argentina (its only customer for the commodity) because of the latter's own financial difficulties. As a result a $1.6 billion, three-year economic reactivation program unveiled in 1987 got off to a slow start in 1988, and growth in the gross domestic product was unlikely to have reached the hoped-for 2.5%. Meanwhile, a 35% rise in fuel prices together with a 20% increase in public-sector wages pushed up the annual inflation rate to 21% by August, compared with 11% for the 12 months ended in December 1987.

(JANET KRENGEL)

BRAZIL

Brazil is a federal republic in eastern South America on the Atlantic Ocean. Area: 8,511,965 sq km (3,286,488 sq mi). Pop. (1988 est.): 144,262,000. Cap.: Brasília. Monetary unit: cruzado, with (Oct. 10, 1988) a free rate of 383.74 cruzados to U.S. $1 (657.15 cruzados = £1 sterling). President in 1988, José Sarney.

Domestic Affairs. During 1988 the political scene was dominated by the drafting of a new constitution, the eighth in Brazilian history, replacing that of 1969. It was promulgated on October 5, 20 months after the 559-member Constituent Assembly (congress) was convened under the chairmanship of Ulysses Guimarães, president of the Brazilian Democratic Movement Party (PMDB). The final document resulted from the work of three dozen subcommittees whose drafts were put together by committees and finally joined together in a comprehensive first draft; this latter was taken to the floor of the Assembly earlier in the year, where it was submitted to two rounds of votes, the last of which was taken on September 2. A presidential election was to be held in November 1989, with a new president taking office in March 1990. Presidential powers were curtailed with the abolition of laws by decree. A presidential form of government was maintained, with a

Brazil's Constituent Assembly celebrates completion of a draft of the new constitution. It included liberalized social and labour laws, Amazon rain forest protection, and other popular provisions.
AFP PHOTO

plebiscite to be held in 1993 on whether to establish that system or a parliamentary form of government or to revert to a monarchy, abolished in 1880. For the first time, 16-year-olds would be allowed to vote. The military retained powers to intervene in government, and there was no extension of land reform.

The constitution contained liberal social and labour provisions. A 44-hour workweek was provided for (previously 48), along with 120 days of maternity and 5 of paternity leave, and state pensions were to be based on earnings during the last three years of employment. An unlimited right to strike was granted. The most important economic provisions were the transfer of 23% of federal revenues to states and municipalities by 1992 and the establishment of a 12% limit on bank interest rates. Also, foreign companies were banned from oil and mineral exploration and could operate in the mining sector only as minority shareholders. Brazilian companies were given "protection and incentives" to develop sectors deemed to be essential to the national interest.

On June 20 the Assembly decided to extend Pres. José Sarney's mandate to five years. For 18 months he had concentrated primarily on prolonging his term beyond the four years that he had endorsed when taking office in March 1985.

Political parties in Congress were in disarray, particularly the majority PMDB. In June 38 deputies mainly from the PMDB formed a new party, the Brazilian Social Democratic Party. The governing coalition between the PMDB and the Liberal Front Party (PFL) had broken down in October 1987.

There was considerable labour unrest throughout the year because of declining wages. Several strikes were staged, the most prolonged by federal civil servants and bank employees.

The Economy. The economic slowdown that had begun in June 1987 continued during the year, and growth was estimated at 1%, compared with 2.9% in 1987. Industrial production during the first half of the year was 5% below the level of January–June 1987, and services activity also declined. However, the agricultural sector performed quite well, with gains in soybeans and livestock. Export-oriented industries expanded output, and the volume of exports was substantially higher than during 1987. The rate of inflation reached 599% in the 12 months ended in September and was officially forecast at 930% for the whole year. The principal causes of inflation were widespread indexation and a lack of meaningful reductions in fiscal and monetary imbalances. (Indexation is a system of economic control in which such variables as wages and interest are tied to a cost-of-living index so that all rise or fall at the same rate.) Weak domestic demand was the main cause of a trade surplus of $14.5 billion in January–September, and a surplus of at least $18 billion was expected for the whole year. A medium-term trade liberalization program was begun during the year, with an import tariff reform becoming effective in July.

A sharp turn in economic policy in December 1987 aimed at correcting domestic financial imbalances and reestablishing normal relations with the international financial community. An 18-month program was agreed upon with the International Monetary Fund in July, and the Fund provided a standby credit of $1.4 billion. The program's main goals were operational public sector deficits of 4% of the gross domestic product in 1988 and 2% in 1989, inflation of 600% in 1988, and a trade surplus of $13 billion in 1988. A number of measures were adopted, including a freeze on the indexed portion of public servants' pay in May and June and the maintenance of the real price of public sector services and products. It had become clear by October that the first three targets would not be met; a new anti-inflationary pact adopted in November was also unsuccessful.

The interest payments moratorium imposed in February 1987 was ended in October. A commercial bank financing package was also completed in that month. New money amounting to $5.2 billion included parallel and cofinancing with the World Bank, a trade deposit facility, and bonds. A total of $62.1 billion of external debt principal was to be rescheduled over 20 years from 1995 except for a down payment of $1.7 billion from 1991–93 maturities. Trade and interbank loans totaling $14.5 billion were renewed for 2½ years. There were also provisions for relending and exit bonds. In addition, the Paris Club, an informal group of official creditors, agreed to reschedule $5 billion of 1987–90 debt and refinance 100% of interest to be paid in 1990 and 1991. (ROBIN CHAPMAN)

CHILE

The republic of Chile extends along the Pacific coast of the Southern Cone of South America. Area: 756,626 sq km (292,135 sq mi), not including Chile's Antarctic claim. Pop. (1988 est.): 12,750,000. Cap.: Santiago. Monetary unit: Chilean peso, with (Oct. 10, 1988) a free rate of 245.63 pesos to U.S. $1 (420.64 pesos = £1 sterling). President in 1988, Maj. Gen. Augusto Pinochet Ugarte.

The holding of a plebiscite on October 5 dominated political events in 1988. As dictated by the 1980 constitution, Chileans were called upon to vote on the military junta's choice of a presidential candidate, who, if elected, would govern the country until 1997. As long expected, the junta nominated Gen. Augusto Pinochet Ugarte on August 30. The voters, however, turned him down in the plebiscite by a margin of 55 to 43%. General Pinochet accepted the rejection of his rule but made it clear that he intended to remain firmly in charge of the government for the rest of his term. Constitutionally allowed to continue in the presidency until March 1990, he planned to call for presidential and congressional elections in December 1989.

Headlines in two Chilean newspapers reflect the voter decision on whether to extend Gen. Augusto Pinochet's term of office. Pinochet was soundly defeated in the yes-no plebiscite, in which more than seven million voters took part.
AFP PHOTO

The opposition assumed the task of conquering voters' apathy, which was generated partly by a disbelief that the referendum was going to be free and fair and partly by the continued infighting among the emerging political coalitions. Increased violence by extremist organizations of both the right and left, particularly since late 1987, was another factor. Having failed to alter the constitution to introduce free presidential elections in 1988, the Committee for Free Elections, led by Sergio Molina, pressed the government to guarantee fairness in the referendum results by establishing an independent count. In February the political opposition, with the exception of the Communist Party and other smaller Marxist parties, succeeded in establishing a common platform for launching the campaign for the vote against Pinochet. Thirteen centre-left parties, including the Partido Demócrata Cristiano (PDC), the Partido por la Democracia (PPD), and the Partido Humanista, formed the Comando por el No (COPEN), and Patricio Aylwin, leader of the PDC, the largest political party in the country, became their coordinator. Three more political groups joined the COPEN later. Other nonpolitical organizations, such as the Acuerdo Nacional por el No (ACUSO) and Independientes por el No, were also set up. Meanwhile, efforts to register people to vote continued, bringing the number of registered voters by the time of the plebiscite to 7.4 million out of an estimated total of 8 million.

Some right-wing political groups showed signs of adopting an independent stance, generally favouring a civilian candidate rather than Pinochet. This position had occasionally been voiced in the past by the nonarmy members of the junta but was dropped at the time of the nomination, allegedly to avoid a rift in the armed forces. Pressures to register as political parties, however, forced groups into coalitions, with the resulting loss of ideological autonomy. In February Renovación Nacional (RN) was set up as a national political party formed by the fusion of the Unión Nacional, Unión Demócrata Independiente, and the Frente Nacional del Trabajo. The traditional Partido Nacional failed to qualify as a national party and later split over Pinochet's candidacy. The Avanzada Nacional, though regional in status, gave Pinochet unconditional support.

Well before his nomination, Pinochet started to campaign for the continuation of his rule. Economic measures were announced, aimed generally at increasing people's purchasing power and in particular at winning over the still-undecided middle-class voters. Social spending was increased, especially on housing. As polls began to show the government trailing behind the opposition, Pinochet swapped his army uniform for civilian clothes and adopted a more conciliatory campaign posture. Also, in mid-August the state of emergency was lifted, and in early September the remaining exiles were allowed to return to Chile. Although television time continued to be dominated by the regime, the opposition was allowed limited guaranteed access to the screen in the month before the plebiscite. The government's campaign was largely defensive, reminding people of the chaos that prevailed during the Salvador Allende administration; the opposition's campaign centred on the building of a new, democratic nation.

Latin-American leaders hailed the defeat of Pinochet as a triumph for democracy in the region. The U.S. Department of State congratulated the Chilean people for having given the world such an impressive demonstration of the power of the ballot box and pledged U.S. support for the evolution of democracy in Chile. The vote was fundamentally against the person and style of the 72-year-old general. The campaign exposed him as aging and vituperative—an unlikely figure to lead the nation to the end of the century. The margin by which he was defeated, however, was sufficient to be convincing yet narrow enough to engender a sense of national reconciliation.

Having initially rejected the resignation of his 18-member government the day after the plebiscite, Pinochet proceeded to make nine Cabinet changes two weeks later. He named Carlos Cáceres, former finance minister, as the new minister of the interior and head of the Cabinet, replacing Sergio Fernández, a controversial figure who became a symbol of the regime's intransigence after the defeat. The economic team headed by Hernán Büchi, the finance minister, was retained. Also, with some delay in its announcement, the traditional list of promotions and retirements in the Army hinted at some shake-up in the institution's high command. Thirteen generals were retired, and ten brigadier generals were promoted, reducing the number of army generals from 53 to 49. Of significance was the promotion of Brig. Gen. Jorge Zincke Quiroz to deputy commander in chief, taking over from Gen. Santiago Sinclair, who in turn was appointed as the Army's representative on the junta.

The opposition's joint statements on the economy revealed that there would be no reversal of the economic course, though attempts would be made to spread the country's new wealth more equitably. Having grown at an annual average rate of 5% since the 1982–83 recession, the economy was expected to expand by an additional 5.5% in 1988.   (ALEXANDER JOHNS CAMPBELL)

COLOMBIA

A republic in northwestern South America, Colombia has coastlines on the Caribbean Sea and the Pacific Ocean. Area: 1,141,748 sq km (440,831 sq mi). Pop. (1988 est.): 30,661,000. Cap.: Bogotá. Monetary unit: Colombian peso, with (Oct. 10, 1988) a free rate of 318.03 pesos to U.S. $1 (544.63 pesos = £1 sterling). President in 1988, Virgilio Barco Vargas.

Pressure on the administration of Pres. Virgilio Barco Vargas to come to grips with the country's increasing violence mounted in 1988. Public protests were organized throughout the country to give the government a vote of no confidence in its ability to guarantee the people's right to live. For a country that had experienced decades of violence, this unprecedented outcry was prompted partly

by ineffectual government action to restore law and order and partly by the costs that the security crisis imposed on the economy.

As the mid-March date set for mayoral elections drew closer, political violence surged. Although continuing to operate largely independently, the guerrilla groups sought maximum economic havoc and media coverage. On May 29 guerrillas abducted Alvaro Gómez Hurtado, the former presidential candidate for the Partido Conservador. He was released on July 20, the insurgents having drawn attention during that time to the dirty war waged by the security forces and also having gathered support for a national dialogue for peace. Under the auspices of the Roman Catholic Church a commission was created to identify points on which the government and guerrillas could reach agreement.

The New Statute for the Defense of Democracy, a 50-article decree issued early in the year, sought to strengthen the powers of the security forces. However, rather than helping bring drug traffickers to heel for the murder of Attorney General Carlos Mauro Hoyos on January 25, the decree appeared to fuel partisan violence in rural areas. Peasant massacres in the banana region of Urabá and the Eastern Plains were reported, together with a growing number of "disappeared people." In April Amnesty International reported that the Colombian armed forces had adopted a policy of terror designed to intimidate and eliminate opposition without recourse to law. Also of concern were the intensified operations of death squads long believed to have close links with security forces.

The presence of a powerful drug cartel unquestionably contributed to lawlessness, not only because of the criminal activities of the trade itself and the growing rivalries between the Medellín and Cali cabals, but also because of its connections with paramilitary death squads. The administration came close to acknowledging the futility of fighting the cartel alone and called for more concerted international action against it. (*See* CRIME, LAW ENFORCEMENT, AND PENOLOGY: *Special Report.*)

Undoubtedly, the most significant political development was the holding, for the first time, of mayoral elections on March 13. This posed a direct threat to the time-honoured system of patronage. Paradoxically, the elections were held in relative calm. The Liberals, including the Nuevo Liber-

alismo faction, won in 429 cities, while the Partido Conservadors took 415, including Bogotá and Medellín. The Unión Patriótica won only 14, but it was part of a great many more victorious coalitions.

Violence continued to take an ever heavier toll on the economy. In the first half of the year losses from the bombings of the Caño Limón–Coveñas oil pipeline totaled $235 million, of which $138 million amounted to foregone export receipts. Some $12 million in export revenue losses resulted from lost banana production and flower shipments subject to long delays by U.S. customs in retaliation for Colombia's failure to extradite drug traffickers.

Economic management during the year largely concentrated on the control of inflation by means of tight monetary and fiscal policies. Following a record growth of 5.4% in 1987, the economy was expected to expand by an additional 5% in 1988, largely on the strength of investment.

(ALEXANDER JOHNS CAMPBELL)

COSTA RICA

The Central American republic of Costa Rica has coastlines on the Caribbean Sea and the Pacific Ocean. Area: 51,100 sq km (19,730 sq mi). Pop. (1988 est.): 2,672,000. Cap.: San José. Monetary unit: Costa Rican colón, with (Oct. 10, 1988) a free rate of 77.76 colones to U.S. $1 (133.17 colones = £1 sterling). President in 1988, Oscar Arias Sánchez.

In early January the International Verification and Monitoring Commission visited Costa Rica to verify fulfillment of the Esquipulas II peace agreement. The commission found that Costa Rica had breached the neutrality portion of the agreement and heard testimony from the Costa Rican Human Rights Commission (CODEHU), which claimed that rights abuses such as arbitrary detentions and abuse of prisoners persisted. Pres. Oscar Arias Sánchez remained active in his work to achieve peace in Central America. In his midterm report to Congress, he emphasized his efforts on behalf of peace and Costa Rica's responsibility in contributing to the peace process. However, the opposition criticized the speech on the grounds that it concentrated too much on international problems and gave little heed to internal matters, especially agriculture. The year was marked by agrarian conflicts, including land invasions and blocked highways. Small- and medium-sized farmers ob-

ROSS—PICTURE GROUP

Police conduct random drug searches in the Colombian city of Medellín. Medellín had become the world centre for the cocaine business and was plagued with violence and corruption.

The five Central American presidents (from left to right), José Azcona of Honduras, José Napoleón Duarte of El Salvador, Oscar Arias of Costa Rica, Vinicio Cerezo of Guatemala, and Daniel Ortega of Nicaragua, attend a meeting in Costa Rica, where they signed a peace accord calling for direct talks between the Nicaraguan Sandinista government and *contra* rebels.

GREGORY KEARNEY—GAMMA/LIAISON

jected to the government's agriculture policies, which had led to increased production of nontraditional export crops and the reduction of grain output, with a consequent rise in food imports to meet local demand.

Amid vociferous opposition and several strikes, the government continued to implement policies designed to open the economy to outside market forces. Changes were made in the country's tariff structure in order to promote foreign trade and to reduce the trade deficit.   (SARAH CAMERON)

This article updates the *Macropædia* article CENTRAL AMERICA: *Costa Rica.*

CUBA

The socialist republic of Cuba comprises the island of Cuba and several thousand smaller islands and cays in the Caribbean Sea. Area: 110,861 sq km (42,804 sq mi). Pop. (1988 est.): 10,421,000. Cap.: Havana. Monetary unit: Cuban peso, with (Oct. 10, 1988) a free rate of 0.76 peso to U.S. $1 (1.30 pesos = £1 sterling). President of the Councils of State and Ministers in 1988, Fidel Castro Ruz.

Cuba enjoyed relative political stability in 1988, and Pres. Fidel Castro Ruz remained firmly in charge. However, a siege mentality developed during the year because of a depressed economy. In his annual state of the nation speech on July 26, the president proposed to maintain a tight, centrally planned economy, emphasizing moral rather than material incentives.

Efforts were made to impress international opinion with an improved human rights record. On May 26 Cuba was elected to the UN Human Rights Commission despite U.S. pressure to prevent it. A six-member delegation from the commission visited Havana in August, and a Red Cross mission visited there in late May–early June. The government announced in June that hundreds of political prisoners would be released, and between May and June a number of prisoners and their relatives were flown to the U.S.

Relations with the U.S. remained strained despite the resumption in November 1987 of the agreement signed in December 1984 and suspended by Cuba in May 1985 when the Voice of America's Radio Martí began transmission. The agreement provided for 20,000 Cubans to immigrate to the U.S. each year. Also, Cuba was to take back at the rate of 100 a month 2,545 of 2,746 persons jailed in the U.S. since 1980 when 125,000 Cubans arrived in the U.S.

following the Mariel boat lift; the other 201 had returned in 1985.

Relations with Latin America continued to improve. In August President Castro paid his first known visit to the South American mainland in 17 years to attend the inauguration in Quito of Rodrigo Borja Cevallos as president of Ecuador. While there, he had talks with four Latin-American heads of state. The foreign minister, Isidoro Malmierca, visited Panama, Brazil, Uruguay, and Mexico in January. While in Brazil, he announced that Brazilian Pres. José Sarney had been invited to visit Havana. In 1988 Cuba had resumed diplomatic links with all South American countries except Colombia, Chile, and Paraguay, and there was an exchange of missions with Venezuela. Close ties with Nicaragua were cemented in July when Cuba agreed to provide an emergency aid package of $150 million in 1988–91 and 270,000 metric tons of oil. Cuba also wrote off $50 million of Nicaraguan debt.

Negotiations began in May between Cuba, Angola, and South Africa, with U.S. mediation, on a peace settlement in Angola and Namibia that would involve the withdrawal of an estimated 50,000 Cuban troops from Angola. A cease-fire was agreed upon in Angola on August 8. On December 22 a peace accord was signed in New York City. Cuba agreed to withdraw all of its troops from Angola by July 1, 1991, with at least half of the forces to be pulled out by Nov. 1, 1989.

Cuba continued to rely heavily on Soviet economic and financial aid, which amounted to about $5 billion in 1987. The level of aid was reduced in 1987 and 1988 because of a 7% cut in the 1986–90 subsidized sugar price. A protocol on economic and technical cooperation between the two countries was signed on May 20. Designed to provide the framework of Soviet aid for the next 15–20 years, the agreement put aid on a project basis, with heavy industry given priority. Increased emphasis was to be placed on the efficient completion of projects and their utilization.

The slowdown in economic activity that began in 1986 continued during 1988. Growth was expected to fall by 1%, compared with declines of 3.2% in 1987 and 7.6% in 1986. Economic difficulties stemmed mainly from weakness in sugar prices and an acute shortage of foreign exchange. The major source of the latter, oil reexports, fell to an estimated $100 million in 1988 from $400 million in 1987 because of low prices. Austerity measures begun in December 1986 depressed living standards; they included cuts

Fireworks light the sky above Cuba's Moncado army barracks in celebration of the 35th anniversary of Pres. Fidel Castro's rise to power.
AP/WIDE WORLD

in subsidies on consumer goods, measures to restrain energy consumption, and tightened controls on wages. Heavy rains early in June caused the worst flooding in nearly 30 years and widespread damage to crops and infrastructure. The 1987–88 sugar crop totaled 7.4 million tons, against 7.7 million in 1986–87. However, the floods ended a four-year drought, and a 1988–89 sugar crop of eight million tons was expected, as well as substantially increased citrus production.

Cuba's convertible currency debt rose to an estimated $6 billion at the end of March 1988, against $5.7 billion in December 1987 and $5 billion in December 1986. (Convertible currency is that which can be exchanged without restrictions for currency of another kind.) Debt service payments remained suspended throughout the year. Official and private creditors were reluctant to conclude a rescheduling agreement until some arrears were settled. Early in the year the Soviet Union was asked to cancel Cuba's debt to it, estimated at $9 billion for repayment from 1990.

A program begun in 1987 to develop the tourism industry, the second largest foreign exchange earner, was continued. Cuba was expecting 193,000 visitors from market-oriented countries in 1988 and 600,000 in 1991, against 207,000 in 1987. The number of hotel rooms was to be doubled to 3,700 by 1991, and the José Martí International Airport in Havana was being expanded. In June a Cuban-Spanish company was set up to build two hotels in Havana with a total of 900 rooms and to participate in a tourism development program on the north coast.

(ROBIN CHAPMAN)

This article updates the *Macropædia* article The WEST INDIES: *Cuba.*

DOMINICA

An island republic within the Commonwealth, Dominica is in the eastern Caribbean Sea. Area: 750 sq km (290 sq mi). Pop. (1988 est.): 79,300. Cap.: Roseau. Monetary unit: Eastern Caribbean dollar, with (Oct. 10, 1988) a par value of EC$2.70 to U.S. $1 (free rate of EC$4.62 = £1 sterling). President in 1988, Clarence Augustus Seignoret; prime minister, Eugenia Charles.

To mark the tenth anniversary of independence in 1988, the government organized an extensive program of events including visits from heads of other Caribbean Community (Caricom) countries. The year was politically uneventful; a new political party, the Dominica United Workers' Party, was launched in July, apparently as a rival to the existing opposition Labour Party.

Further growth in gross domestic product of about 4% was expected, following 4.6% growth in 1987. Agriculture, tourism, construction, and transport were the main growth sectors. The 1988–89 budget, which provided for an increase of 18% in recurrent expenditure and a fiscal surplus of EC$4.5 million, imposed no new taxes and included some tax concessions. However, Prime Minister Eugenia Charles revealed that the public external debt at the end of July was $69.3 million, more than double the last quoted figure. She said the government would attempt to slow down the growth of the debt by seeking a higher proportion of grant financing for capital projects. Public sector salaries were to be frozen in 1988–89. Another successful year was expected for the banana industry, which exported 60,640 metric tons in 1987 and earned EC$85.3 million.

(ROD PRINCE)

This article updates the *Macropædia* article The WEST INDIES: *Dominica.*

DOMINICAN REPUBLIC

The Dominican Republic covers the eastern two-thirds of the Caribbean island of Hispaniola, which it shares with Haiti. Area: 48,443 sq km (18,704 sq mi). Pop. (1988 est.): 6,850,000. Cap.: Santo Domingo. Monetary unit: Dominican peso, with (Oct. 10, 1988) a free rate of 4.99 pesos to U.S. $1 (8.55 pesos = £1 sterling). President in 1988, Joaquín Balaguer.

Pres. Joaquín Balaguer remained firmly in charge in 1988, although his health gave grounds for concern. He strengthened his control of the Cabinet in June and August. The interior minister, Gen. Elías Wessín y Wessín, was appointed armed forces minister in June, and other supporters were named as ministers of interior and of industry and commerce. In August new ministers of agriculture, labour, and foreign affairs were appointed. A wave of demonstrations and strikes, sparked by sharp increases in food prices, took place over one-third of the country—including the capital, Santo Domingo—between mid-February and mid-March; at least six people were killed and hundreds arrested. The government reduced some food prices and raised public-

sector wages by one-third in April. Reforms to the labour code and an extension of social security benefits were promised. In November former president Salvador Jorge Blanco, who was undergoing medical treatment in exile in the U.S., was convicted in absentia of corruption and sentenced to 20 years' imprisonment.

There was little economic progress. Growth of gross domestic product was expected to fall to 2% in 1988 from 8% in 1987, despite the continuing strength of tourism and construction. A freeze was imposed on new public works projects in June to help reduce the public deficit—the prime cause of inflation, which reached 29.4% in January–July. In April President Balaguer announced that the International Monetary Fund would be approached for a structural adjustment loan.　　　　　(ROBIN CHAPMAN)

This article updates the *Macropædia* article The WEST INDIES: *Dominican Republic.*

ECUADOR

The republic of Ecuador is in western South America, on the Pacific Ocean. Area: 269,178 sq km (103,930 sq mi), including the Galápagos Islands. Pop. (1988 est.): 10,203,000. Cap.: Quito. Monetary unit: sucre, with (Oct. 10, 1988) a free market rate of 519.15 sucres to U.S. $1 (889.05 sucres = £1 sterling). Presidents in 1988, León Febres Cordero Rivadeneira and, from August 10, Rodrigo Borja Cevallos.

Presidential and congressional elections were held in Ecuador on Jan. 31, 1988. None of the ten presidential candidates nor any of the 17 parties contesting the congressional elections won an overall majority. The centre-left Izquierda Democrática (ID) maintained its position as the largest of the 11 parties represented in the 71-seat Congress by winning 31 seats, compared with the 17 it held under the previous government. By contrast, incumbent Pres. León Febres Cordero's centre-right Partido Social Cristiano (PSC) saw its share of seats fall from 15 to 7. The two leading presidential candidates contested a run-off election on May 8. The ID's Rodrigo Borja Cevallos (*see* BIOGRAPHIES) took 46.3% of the vote, while the populist Partido Roldosista Ecuatoriano's Abdalá Bucaram Ortiz took 41.3% (12.4% were annulled or blank).

President Borja, inaugurated at the start of the congressional year on August 10, promised a government of national consensus. By forming a 42-seat alliance among the ID, the centre-left Democracia Popular (8 seats), the Frente Amplio de la Izquierda (2 seats), and the Partido Liberal Radical (1 seat), he ensured that Ecuador's legislative process would be calmer than it had been under the outgoing government, which had faced an opposition majority. Immediately after his inauguration, President Borja reestablished diplomatic relations with the Sandinista government of Nicaragua.

The economy deteriorated, and inflation soared. Servicing of the $11 billion foreign debt was suspended in February, and arrears to all creditors mounted. The new government introduced an economic austerity program prior to opening negotiations with the International Monetary Fund.　　　　　(JANET KRENGEL)

EL SALVADOR

The republic of El Salvador is situated on the Pacific coast of Central America. Area: 21,041 sq km (8,124 sq mi). Pop. (1988 est.): 5,083,000. Cap.: San Salvador. Monetary unit: Salvadoran colón, with (Oct. 10, 1988) a par value of 5 colones to U.S. $1 (free rate of 8.57 colones = £1 sterling). President in 1988, José Napoleón Duarte.

El Salvador's right-wing death-squad activity intensified at the beginning of 1988, and a new guerrilla offensive was launched in protest against the Legislative Assembly and mayoral elections set for March 20. Political assassinations in the first half of 1988 exceeded the total for 1987, and they accelerated in the second half. The elections were held against a background of unrest as sabotage attacks by the left-wing Farabundo Martí National Liberation Front kept private traffic off the roads and left most of the country without electricity. The voting results were a resounding defeat for the ruling Christian Democratic Party and led to the far right Nationalist Republican Alliance (ARENA) becoming the dominant party in Congress. ARENA disputed the final results, which gave it 30 seats in the 60-seat Legislative Assembly, against 23 seats for the Christian Democrats and 7 for the National Conciliation Party.

AP/WIDE WORLD

An immense mural hangs on the wall of the Ecuadorian Congress meeting hall. The mural bears anti-American symbols and proclaims the resurrection of the homeland.

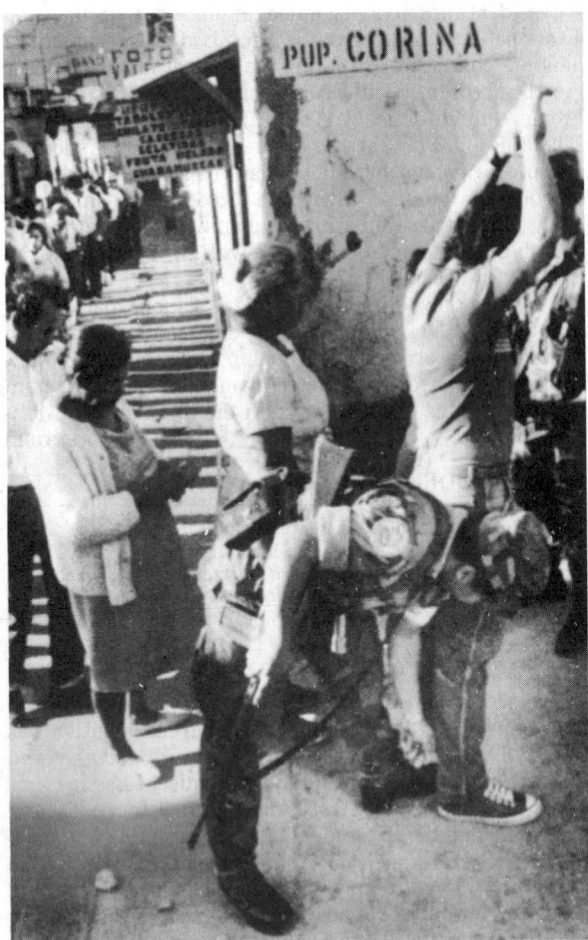

A soldier searches a man waiting to vote in El Salvador's national elections. Although the elections were marred by guerrilla attacks and bombings, the Nationalist Republican Alliance (Arena) was able to defeat the ruling Christian Democratic Party.

REUTERS/BETTMANN NEWSPHOTOS

ARENA's appeal to the Supreme Court delayed the seating of the new Assembly for many weeks and led to warnings from the Army that feuding between the parties was leading the country into anarchy.

The political chaos was intensified with the news that Pres. José Napoleón Duarte was suffering from terminal cancer of the stomach and was not expected to live long. Treatment for his illness debilitated him, the power vacuum grew, and corruption scandals proliferated. His Christian Democratic Party was already divided over the choice of a candidate for the 1989 presidential elections, and infighting grew more bitter. The two main contestants were Julio Rey Prendes, an old friend and confidante of the president, and Fidel Chávez Mena, a former foreign minister. Although the former was nominated as candidate at a party convention in April, the latter refused to accept the decision and, with the help of the U.S., received the nomination himself at an extraordinary convention in June. Meanwhile, Arena chose as its candidate Alfredo Cristiani, the party's secretary-general.

The nation's political future might also be influenced by a shake-up in the Army that occurred during the year. It increased the power of the Tandona, a group of officers critical of the civilian government's war against the guerrillas. (SARAH CAMERON)

This article updates the *Macropædia* article CENTRAL AMERICA: *El Salvador*.

GRENADA

A constitutional monarchy within the Commonwealth, Grenada (with its dependency, the Southern Grenadines) is in the eastern Caribbean Sea. Area: 345 sq km (133 sq mi). Pop. (1988 est.): 106,000. Cap.: Saint George's. Monetary unit: Eastern Caribbean dollar, with (Oct. 10, 1988) a par value of EC$2.70 to U.S. $1 (free rate of EC$4.62 = £1 sterling). Queen, Elizabeth II; governor-general in 1988, Sir Paul Scoon; prime minister, Herbert A. Blaize.

Renewed criticism of the leadership of Prime Minister Herbert Blaize surfaced within the governing New National Party in the third quarter of 1988. A challenge to the elderly and infirm Blaize for the party leadership appeared likely before the next general election, due at the end of 1989. The minister of communications and works, Keith Mitchell, was reported to be seeking the leadership.

At a hearing of the appeal in the Maurice Bishop murder case in June, it was revealed that the government had applied to rejoin the Eastern Caribbean court system, but that the application had been shelved until the end of the judicial proceedings. Hearings were continuing at the end of the year in the appeal of 14 people convicted of the murder of Bishop and others in October 1983, together with 3 convicted of manslaughter.

The 1988–89 budget provided for only a slight increase in recurrent expenditure, with the aim of reducing the fiscal deficit to EC$6.8 million, compared with EC$55.2 million in 1987. A growth rate of 5% was forecast for 1988, against 6% in 1987, with tourism, manufacturing, and construction the main growth sectors. (ROD PRINCE)

This article updates the *Macropædia* article The WEST INDIES: *Grenada*.

GUATEMALA

A republic of Central America, Guatemala has coastlines on the Caribbean Sea and the Pacific Ocean. Area: 108,889 sq km (42,042 sq mi). Pop. (1988 est.): 8,681,000. Cap.: Guatemala City. Monetary unit: quetzal, at par with the U.S. dollar, with (Oct. 10, 1988) an official market rate of 1 quetzal to U.S. $1 (1.71 quetzals = £1 sterling) and a free market rate of 2.76 quetzals to U.S. $1 (4.73 quetzals = £1 sterling). President in 1988, Marco Vinicio Cerezo Arévalo.

Several coup attempts were staged in Guatemala in 1988, the first and most serious on May 11. None succeeded in removing Pres. Marco Cerezo Arévalo from power, but they did impose limits on his efforts to end the guerrilla war, improve social conditions, and raise taxes. The coups were inspired by a combination of military dissatisfaction with Defense Minister Gen. Héctor Gramajo's anti-insurgency campaign and right-wing business opposition to Cerezo's economic policy.

Dialogue between the national reconciliation commission, which included a government representative, and the Guatemalan National Revolutionary Unity guerrillas was postponed from May until August, and the president approved new purchases of arms and helicopters. Government claims that there were fewer active members of the three guerrilla movements did not tally with the Army's inability to bring about a military solution to the conflict. At the same time, the first coup attempt was followed by an increase in right-wing death squad activity and in unauthorized repression against the unions and the press.

On March 8 the government and trade unions agreed to a package of price controls, salary increases, and social program improvements; however, the "Guatemala 2000" plan,

drawn up in June, abandoned most of the March accord. It was accompanied by the lifting of price restrictions on many basic items, increased fuel prices, and a devaluation of the quetzal. Also, previous commitments to raise taxes on the wealthy were dropped. In July labour groups began a series of demonstrations and strikes against these changes in economic policy, and in late August Cerezo called for a meeting to discuss a new "social pact." Also in August, the International Monetary Fund approved a standby loan and compensatory finance worth $126 million, the first granted to Guatemala since 1984. (BEN BOX)

This article updates the *Macropædia* article CENTRAL AMERICA: *Guatemala.*

GUYANA

A republic and member of the Commonwealth, Guyana is situated in northeastern South America, on the Atlantic Ocean. Area: 215,000 sq km (83,000 sq mi). Pop. (1988 est.): 757,000. Cap.: Georgetown. Monetary unit: Guyana dollar, with (Oct. 10, 1988) a par value of G$10 to U.S. $1 (free rate of G$17.13 = £1 sterling). President in 1988, Desmond Hoyte; prime minister, Hamilton Green.

The government's efforts to open the economy to domestic and foreign capital investment intensified during 1988. Negotiations with the International Monetary Fund (IMF) and the World Bank opened in April with a view to obtaining a financial package that Pres. Desmond Hoyte said would require $1.7 billion in refinancing and fresh capital. It was forecast that an IMF agreement would be in place by September, but at the year's end negotiations between the parties were still under way. The delay appeared to have been caused by difficulty in raising a bridging loan to pay $70 million in arrears to the Fund.

In July the government published a proposed investment policy, providing for unrestricted foreign private ownership of Guyanese enterprises, with a range of fiscal incentives and guarantees of profit and capital repatriation. During visits to the U.S., Britain, and Europe, Hoyte assured potential investors that the era of nationalization was at an end.

The government also announced that it was seeking a three-year moratorium on debt repayments. Expectations that an IMF package would involve a fresh devaluation

put pressure on the exchange rate; by mid-September the commercial bank rate was G$21.75 = U.S. $1, while the illegal street rate reached G$42. (ROD PRINCE)

This article updates the *Macropædia* article The GUIANAS: *Guyana.*

HAITI

The republic of Haiti occupies the western one-third of the Caribbean island of Hispaniola, which it shares with the Dominican Republic. Area: 27,400 sq km (10,579 sq mi). Pop. (1988 est.): 5,451,000. Cap.: Port-au-Prince. Monetary unit: gourde, with (Oct. 10, 1988) a par value of 5 gourdes to U.S. $1 (free rate of 8.56 gourdes = £1 sterling). President of the interim governing council in 1988, Lieut. Gen. Henri Namphy until February 7; presidents, Leslie Manigat, from February 7 until June 20; Namphy, from June 20 to September 17; and Lieut. Gen. Prosper Avril, from September 17; prime minister from February 9 to June 20, Martial Célestin.

In 1988 Haiti experienced three elections and sporadic violence. On January 24, with the Army's support, Leslie Manigat, a centre-right professor, was elected president, receiving 50.38% of the votes; he took office on February 7. The election was held after a presidential poll in November 1987 was canceled because of widespread violence. Approximately one million of the three million eligible voters went to the polls, and of them only about half voted for Manigat. The election was declared invalid by opposition leaders.

On June 20 the army commander, Lieut. Gen. Henri Namphy, seized power. He announced a Cabinet containing only one civilian, dissolved the legislature, and stated that the 1987 constitution would be rewritten. The coup followed a power struggle in which President Manigat had dismissed Namphy and placed him under house arrest for alleged insubordination. As president, however, Namphy lacked widespread support in the Army and was forced to provide jobs in the administration to supporters of former president Jean-Claude Duvalier, who still wielded considerable economic and financial power. On September 17 Namphy was deposed by a group of young officers and noncommissioned officers, led by Sgt. Joseph Hébreux, who installed Lieut. Gen. Prosper Avril as president. Avril had difficulty in asserting his authority in the face of army mutinies in October. None of the three gov-

AFP PHOTO

Haiti's newly appointed president, Lieut. Gen. Prosper Avril (left), stands beside Sgt. Joseph Hébreux, leader of the September 1988 coup. Although Hébreux effected the overthrow of the Henri Namphy regime, he chose to install Avril as president and serve as an adviser.

Flames leap from a burning truck in the midst of an anti-American riot outside the U.S. embassy in Honduras. Student rioters had marched on the embassy to protest the abduction of alleged drug trafficker Juan Ramón Matta Ballesteros to the U.S.
SYGMA

ernments pursued coherent economic policies, and Haiti in 1988 experienced its sixth year of economic decline.

(ROBIN CHAPMAN)

This article updates the *Macropædia* article The WEST INDIES: *Haiti.*

HONDURAS

A republic of Central America, Honduras has coastlines on the Caribbean Sea and the Pacific Ocean. Area: 112,088 sq km (43,277 sq mi). Pop (1988 est.): 4,803,000. Cap.: Tegucigalpa. Monetary unit: lempira, with (Oct. 10, 1988) a par value of 2 lempiras to U.S. $1 (free rate of 3.43 lempiras = £1 sterling). President in 1988, José Azcona Hoyo.

Relations with the U.S. continued to dominate Honduran affairs in 1988, particularly U.S. support for the anti-Sandinista *contra* forces operating out of Honduras. Government officials expressed concern over future responsibility for the *contras* if the Nicaraguan conflict should end. In March the U.S. government, claiming that Nicaraguan troops had entered Honduran territory in pursuit of *contras* and that Pres. José Azcona Hoyo had requested U.S. military assistance, sent 3,200 combat troops to Honduras. Renegotiation in September of the 1954 U.S.-Honduras military assistance agreement raised doubts about Honduras's commitment to the 1987 Central American peace treaty, which called for the limitation of foreign military presence in the region.

Popular resentment against the U.S. was fueled by the abduction to the U.S. in April of the Honduran millionaire Juan Ramón Matta Ballesteros, a suspected drug trafficker. Since Honduras had no extradition treaty with the U.S., the arrest was seen as foreign intervention. During a demonstration the U.S. embassy annex in Tegucigalpa was set on fire and five people were killed by police. A state of emergency was declared in the capital and in San Pedro Sula, the second largest city, for five days.

The Inter-American Court of Human Rights in San José, Costa Rica, returned a guilty verdict against Honduras in the 1981 disappearance of a student leader at the hands of government-maintained death squads; the cases of three other disappearances were also being considered. Although the government stated that the charges pertained to a past era, it accepted the verdict.

The total foreign debt was $3,140,000,000, 90% of which was owed to multilateral agencies. Disbursement of loans from both the U.S. Agency for International Development and the World Bank was stopped temporarily, either because Honduras had fallen behind on repayments or because the government failed to introduce austerity measures or devalue the lempira.

(BEN BOX)

This article updates the *Macropædia* article CENTRAL AMERICA: *Honduras.*

JAMAICA

A constitutional monarchy within the Commonwealth, Jamaica occupies an island in the Caribbean Sea. Area: 10,991 sq km (4,244 sq mi). Pop. (1988 est.): 2,407,000. Cap.: Kingston. Monetary unit: Jamaica dollar, with (Oct. 10, 1988) a free rate of J$5.40 to U.S. $1 (J$9.25 = £1 sterling). Queen, Elizabeth II; governor-general in 1988, Sir Florizel Glasspole; prime minister, Edward Seaga.

Jamaica's recovery from the economic depression of the early 1980s received a severe setback when Hurricane Gilbert hit the island on Sept. 12, 1988, killing some 45 people and causing extensive damage. An early assessment of the devastation could not be made, but losses in agriculture alone were put at J$2.4 billion. The hurricane destroyed or damaged half the nation's houses, making thousands of people homeless; the banana crop was completely destroyed, and coffee exports were expected to be only a third of the previous target. Electric power, water supplies, and telecommunications were seriously disrupted. Immediate aid requirements were put at $500 million in hard currency, $200 million of which was pledged within two weeks. The government, which had reached agreement with the International Monetary Fund in August for an additional $114 million standby credit, said it would apply for changes in the conditions of the arrangement.

During the year agreements were reached with the Alcoa and Alcan bauxite companies on a new tax arrangement and increased production. In August the two main political parties signed an agreement aimed at avoiding violence in the general election, due to be held by April 10, 1989.

(ROD PRINCE)

This article updates the *Macropædia* article The WEST INDIES: *Jamaica.*

A plane from Jamaica's Kingston airport is wedged in a group of trees after being tossed about by Hurricane Gilbert. The storm tore through Jamaica with heavy rain and 320-kilometre (200-mile)-per-hour winds that caused billions of dollars in damages and left some 45 dead.
C. W. GRIFFIN—THE MIAMI HERALD/MATRIX

MEXICO

A federal republic of North America, Mexico has coastlines on the Pacific Ocean, the Gulf of Mexico, and the Caribbean Sea. Area: 1,958,201 sq km (756,066 sq mi). Pop. (1988 est.): 82,659,000. Cap.: Mexico City. Monetary unit: Mexican peso, with (Oct. 10, 1988) a free rate of 2,289 pesos to U.S. $1 (3,919 pesos = £1 sterling) and a controlled rate of 2,253 pesos to U.S. $1 (3,858 pesos = £1 sterling). Presidents in 1988, Miguel de la Madrid Hurtado and, from December 1, Carlos Salinas de Gortari.

The Mexican political scene was dominated in 1988 by the presidential election in July. In 1987 the ruling Partido Revolucionario Institucional (PRI; Institutional Revolutionary Party) had chosen as its candidate Carlos Salinas de Gortari (*see* BIOGRAPHIES), formerly minister of budget and planning. During the 1988 election campaign it became clear that, contrary to previous elections, the PRI candidate was unlikely to win easily. Harvard-educated Salinas, who had never previously run for any elected office, found it difficult to gather popular support. He was opposed by five candidates, two of whom were capable of mobilizing massive support from their constituencies

and of garnering votes from PRI members disillusioned by years of economic decline.

The right-wing Partido Acción Nacional (PAN; National Action Party) chose Manuel Clouthier as its presidential candidate. PAN's support came mostly from the prosperous northern region, but Clouthier also expected to win substantial numbers of votes from the business classes in Mexico City. On the left was Cuauhtémoc Cárdenas (*see* BIOGRAPHIES), a former state governor and the son of Gen. Lázaro Cárdenas, the Mexican president (1934–40) who nationalized the oil industry in 1938. Cuauhtémoc Cárdenas led a breakaway movement from the PRI as a protest against the lack of democracy and openness in choosing its candidate, and he soon became the figurehead for an alliance of left-wing groups.

In response to growing pressure for more democracy within the Mexican political system, Salinas called for clean elections that could produce a viable opposition and an effective legislature. The opposition largely disbelieved his pleas, pointing to his privileged access to broadcasting and the press and the use of public funds to finance his campaign. Nevertheless, it was clear that Salinas was prepared to accept a much lower majority than the more than

SERGIO DURANTES/TIME MAGAZINE

Cuauhtémoc Cárdenas (centre) stands amid supporters during his presidential campaign. Cárdenas's policies on land reform, wages, and foreign debt earned him a strong following, thus dealing a powerful blow to the ruling Partido Revolucionario Institucional (PRI).

70% vote received by his predecessor, Pres. Miguel de la Madrid, and that there would be opposition members in the Senate for the first time ever. Meanwhile, the Cárdenas campaign gathered massive support with huge crowds turning out to endorse his policies for land reform, real wage increases, and a suspension of foreign debt servicing. In recognition of his growing popularity, the Mexican Socialist Party (PMS) withdrew its candidate for the presidency and committed its forces to the Cardenista movement; the National Democratic Front (FDN) thus presented the PRI with a united left-wing opposition.

The election was held on July 6 and was marked by bitter allegations of electoral fraud. The PRI immediately claimed victory for its candidate, although no official results were known for several days because of the inexplicable and suspicious collapse of the Federal Electoral Commission's (CFE's) computer. Salinas's aides released preliminary figures based on a count of 4.4 million votes showing Salinas leading with 47.4% against 26.7% for Cárdenas and 20.7% for Clouthier. These were contradicted by a Cárdenas tally, based on 6.7 million votes counted, showing Cárdenas winning with 38.8% over Salinas with 32.3% and Clouthier with 29.2%. When results were finally issued by the CFE on July 13, Salinas emerged the official winner with 50.4%, compared with 31.1% for Cárdenas and 17.1% for Clouthier. Clouthier conceded defeat, but both he and Cárdenas refused to accept the results and initiated a campaign of nationwide protests, calling for a poll rerun. Salinas accepted the outcome as a "mandate for change," but it clearly came as a blow to the leaders of the PRI, and the small size of the majority begged questions of its honesty.

In the months that followed the election, the PRI was forced to come to terms with the loss of its omnipotence after 59 years in power and the realization that there were now a right, a left, and a centre in Mexican politics. Powerful labour groups had switched their allegiance to Cárdenas, as had millions of peasants and bureaucrats. Salinas aides attributed the delay in releasing the results in part to the difficulty in persuading PRI congressional candidates that they had to accept losses.

The first session of Congress, in August, when the deputies had to ratify their own elections through the Federal Electoral Commission and allocate the 200 remaining seats by a method of proportional representation, degenerated into chaos as the opposition rained insults on the PRI members, tore up ballot papers, and protested loudly and violently at the way the commission was overwhelmingly

weighted toward the PRI. Salinas's election was finally ratified by the electoral college when 263 votes were cast for him to 85 votes against by the PAN. The FDN walked out before the vote, having failed to force a recount. Salinas faced the prospect of a vociferous opposition and the loss of a rubber-stamp Congress, with the PRI controlling only 260 of the 500 seats.

At the end of 1987 the government introduced a gradualist anti-inflation plan called the Economic Solidarity Pact designed to reduce the public sector borrowing requirement and bring down triple-digit inflation rates before the July election. It achieved a dramatic reduction in the rate of inflation, partly by freezing the peso in March, and the annual rate was expected to be down to 50% for the year. However, the cost of cutting inflation with a peso freeze was a steadily deteriorating trade surplus, worsened by falling oil prices. In December President Salinas ended the freeze in favour of a slow devaluation of the peso and "moderate adjustments in wages." The president also asked Congress for approval to seek $6 billion in foreign credits in 1989 and called for a renegotiation of Mexico's $104 billion foreign debt.

Hurricane Gilbert, one of the most violent storms of the century, struck Mexico in September. Extensive damage was reported at the popular resorts Cancun and Cozumel, and an estimated 200 died when flash floods swept four buses away in Monterrey.   (SARAH CAMERON)

NICARAGUA

A republic of Central America, Nicaragua has coastlines on the Caribbean Sea and the Pacific Ocean. Area: 127,849 sq km (49,363 sq mi). Pop. (1988 est.): 3,622,000. Cap.: Managua. Monetary unit: new córdoba, with (Oct. 10, 1988) an official rate of 320 new córdobas to U.S. $1 (547.20 new córdobas = £1 sterling). President in 1988, Daniel Ortega Saavedra.

In a reversal of policy, Pres. Daniel Ortega Saavedra agreed at a Central American presidential summit in January to hold direct cease-fire talks with the U.S.-backed *contra* rebels. He also lifted the six-year-old state of emergency, activated a previously promulgated amnesty law, and pledged to hold municipal elections before 1990 and a vote for members of a Central American parliament later in the year.

The first direct talks between the Sandinista government and the *contras* were held in late January under the threat of a renewal of U.S. congressional funding for the rebels. Both sides put forward widely varying negotiating posi-

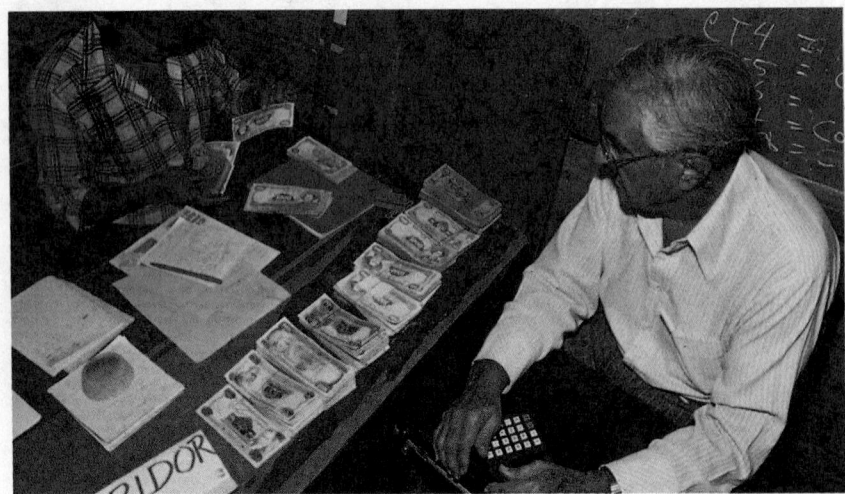

AFP PHOTO

A man in Managua, Nicaragua, converts his córdobas into new córdobas. The currency was revalued in an attempt to stabilize the economy and arrest runaway inflation.

At a rally, Panama's Gen. Manuel Antonio Noriega (centre) shows his support for acting president Manuel Solís Palma. Noriega, despite intense pressure from the U.S., refused to relinquish his control and in February replaced Pres. Eric Arturo Delvalle, favoured by the U.S., with Solís Palma.

BILL GENTILE—PICTURE GROUP

tions and proposals, with the *contras* insisting that cease-fire talks could not be separated from negotiations for "full democratization." Mediator Miguel Cardinal Obando y Bravo broke off the second set of negotiations after only two days. President Ortega dismissed the cardinal because the Sandinistas doubted his neutrality. Defense Minister Humberto Ortega announced that talks with the *contras* would resume, on Nicaraguan soil for the first time.

After clashes in March between Sandinista forces and the *contras,* allegedly on Honduran territory, the U.S dispatched 3,200 troops to Honduras. The move provoked both sides to agree to a cease-fire during the peace talks, and the venue for the talks was moved from the border region to Managua. Despite initial rejoicing at the signing of the truce, peace negotiations continued to stall amid doubts about the *contras'* commitment to a negotiated settlement. Further talks proved inconclusive.

After Sandinista concessions on several *contra* proposals, talks failed in June when the *contras* delivered an ultimatum on the release of political prisoners and on sweeping political reforms. Deteriorating relations between the two sides coincided with the expulsion in July of U.S. Ambassador Richard Melton and seven other U.S. diplomats from Nicaragua, on the grounds that they had incited revolt against the government, after their alleged involvement in an opposition demonstration. Washington retaliated with the expulsion of Nicaraguan Ambassador Carlos Tunnermann and seven other officials. At the year's end negotiations remained deadlocked. Hurricane Joan crossed Nicaragua in October. With winds as high as 200 km/h (125 mph), it killed at least 50 people and left 300,000 homeless.   (SARAH CAMERON)

This article updates the *Macropædia* article CENTRAL AMERICA: *Nicaragua.*

PANAMA

A republic of Central America, Panama lies between the Caribbean Sea and the Pacific Ocean on the Isthmus of Panama. Area: 77,082 sq km (29,762 sq mi). Pop. (1988 est.): 2,322,000. Cap.: Panama City. Monetary unit: balboa, at par with the U.S. dollar, with a free rate (Oct. 10, 1988) of 1.71 balboas to £1 sterling. Commander of the National Defense Forces (de facto ruler) in 1988, Gen. Manuel Antonio Noriega Morena; presidents, Eric Arturo Delvalle and, from February 26, Manuel Solís Palma.

Early in 1988 the country's lingering political crisis was brought to a boil when the U.S. administration became openly involved in the local opposition's attempt to depose the commander in chief of Panama's Defense Forces and the country's de facto ruler, Gen. Manuel Antonio Noriega. On February 5 two U.S. federal grand juries indicted Noriega for drug trafficking and racketeering. Panama's president, Eric Arturo Delvalle, asked for the general's resignation while the charges were being investigated, but Noriega refused. Delvalle publicly announced the dismissal on February 25; on the following day the National Assembly, at the instigation of the general, decreed that Delvalle was no longer president and appointed Manuel Solís Palma as his successor. At this point the U.S., having previously questioned the legitimacy of the Delvalle government, was only too eager to recognize Delvalle as president. On March 4 the U.S. agreed to freeze Panama's financial assets that had been deposited in U.S. banks, totaling about $50 million, and later it instructed U.S. companies and citizens working in Panama to withhold any payments to the local authorities. On March 11 the U.S. readily acceded to Delvalle's request to withhold indefinitely payments due to the Panamanian government from the operations of the Panama Canal and the transisthmian oil pipeline, totaling about $15 million a month.

Despite the social unrest and the economic hardships brought about by the U.S. measures, the fall of Noriega did not occur. He survived an attempted coup in mid-March, and the initial tightening of the economic sanctions was more detrimental to U.S. business interests in Panama than to the military regime. The U.S. interference with Panama's domestic affairs actually seemed to strengthen Noriega's hold on the country and raise his stature both domestically and regionally. The militarization of Panama increased, and the local political opposition lapsed almost into insignificance as the crisis became more one between Noriega and the administration of U.S. Pres. Ronald Reagan. Also, Noriega succeeded in giving the affair an international dimension by bringing the 1977 Panama Canal treaties to the fore. Although the regional forum of the Group of Eight suspended Panama from its deliberations in protest against the ousting of Delvalle, Latin-American governments generally disapproved of the U.S. tactics and failed to support the Reagan administration's attempt to bring regional pressure to bear upon the general.

Arnulfo Arias Madrid (*see* OBITUARIES), leader of the Partido Panameñista Auténtico, the largest opposition party, died in Miami, Fla., on August 10. His funeral in Panama turned into a massive outpouring of sentiment against Noriega's rule. Arias thus achieved in death what the opposition had been unable to do in the last 14 months of his life. Although his death was unlikely to be the catalyst that would bring the political opposition together, it was expected to facilitate negotiations with the government.

(ALEXANDER JOHNS CAMPBELL)

This article updates the *Macropædia* article CENTRAL AMER-ICA: *Panama.*

PARAGUAY

Paraguay is a landlocked republic of central South America. Area: 406,752 sq km (157,048 sq mi). Pop. (1988 est.): 4,007,-000. Cap.: Asunción. Monetary unit: guaraní, with (Oct. 10, 1988) an official rate of 400 guaraníes to U.S. $1 (685 guaraníes = £1 sterling) and a free market rate of 958 guaraníes to U.S. $1 (1,641 guaraníes = £1 sterling). President in 1988, Gen. Alfredo Stroessner.

In February 1988 Gen. Alfredo Stroessner, Paraguay's ruler since 1954, was reelected as president for another five years over two token opponents. Official figures gave him 89% of the vote; however, opposition leaders charged widespread fraud. While the majority of the population appeared sub-jugated and indifferent, the campaign was marked by an unusual level of antigovernment protests.

In May Pope John Paul II visited Paraguay as part of his Latin-American tour. The government tried to prevent him from meeting with members of opposition parties and independent trade unions but had to back down when the Vatican threatened to cancel the entire visit. In a speech critical of Stroessner, the pope called for the "moral cleansing" of Paraguay and said that "liberty, justice and participation" were essential requirements for building an "authentic democracy." Nevertheless, many opponents of the regime were arrested before the pope had even left the country, and repression against the church and dissident leaders intensified after his departure.

In an attempt to improve his image abroad, Stroessner visited the U.S. in June. Fewer than half the delegates attended his address before the plenary session of the United Nations, and he was denied a meeting at the White House.

(SARAH CAMERON)

PERU

The republic of Peru is located in western South America, on the Pacific Ocean. Area: 1,285,216 sq km (496,225 sq mi). Pop. (1988 est.): 21,256,000. Cap.: Lima. Monetary unit: inti, with (Oct. 10, 1988) an official rate of 250 intis to U.S. $1 (428.13 intis = £1 sterling) and a free rate of 435.13 intis to U.S. $1 (745.16 intis = £1 sterling). President in 1988, Alan García Pérez; prime ministers, Guillermo Larco Cox and, from May 13, Armando Villanueva del Campo.

The year 1988 was dominated by a precipitous decline into economic chaos, marking the end of Pres. Alan García Pérez's controversial experiment with financial autarchy. Confidence in the government collapsed, and it was feared that Peru's still fragile democracy would not survive.

On January 28 the country was paralyzed by a general strike called by the main trade union federation and backed by the largest opposition party, the Marxist Izquierda Unida (IU). Workers were protesting a wave of price in-creases that followed a 39% devaluation of the inti in mid-December 1987. The strike was notable for its backing by the Sendero Luminoso (Shining Path) guerrillas, who, notwithstanding this new focus on above-ground activity, remained committed to acts of violence against civilian, political, and economic targets. As a result, 37 of Peru's 172 provinces remained under emergency military control throughout the year.

At the start of 1988 it was clear that the economy was dangerously overheated; industrial capacity was almost fully utilized and exports were contracting, while rising im-ports were eating into rapidly diminishing foreign exchange reserves. The government was printing money to meet its burgeoning expenditure deficit, and inflation was inevitably accelerating. In March an economic package was unveiled that caused inflation to soar. On May 9 García's entire 15-member Cabinet resigned. Prime Minister Guillermo Larco Cox and Finance Minister Gustavo Saberbein were succeeded by Armando Villanueva del Campo and César Robles Freyre, respectively. Robles, who held the post for less than four months, introduced another series of eco-nomic measures, which caused inflation of 30.9% in July and 21.4% in August. A second general strike was held on July 19–20 to protest deteriorating economic conditions.

By early September foreign exchange reserves had dwin-dled to zero, and even the most essential food imports

AP/WIDE WORLD

A group of Peruvian union leaders and others march in support of the general strike called by the General Confederation of Peruvian Workers in July to protest deteriorating economic conditions.

were held up for lack of hard currency. On September 6 the country's third finance minister in 1988, Abel Salinas, announced a harsh austerity program. Subsidies and price controls were lifted, fuel prices were increased by 300%, and the inti was devalued by 87%. Many basic goods became unaffordable; inflation in September soared to 114%, and annual inflation reached a record-high 1,722%. Salinas resigned as finance minister in November.

A third nationwide strike on October 13 was declared illegal by the government, and bonuses were offered to those attending work. In mid-July metal production came to a standstill for 29 days when miners went on strike to support a national negotiating board, earlier retirement, and wage increases. The strike, which cost the country an estimated $140 million, ended when the government compromised on most of the miners' demands. However, the measures were never implemented, and on October 10 miners began a second stoppage. The government declared a state of emergency in the mining industry, which gave companies the right to fire striking workers.

President García's popularity rating plunged to 16% in 1988, compared with the 96% support he enjoyed when he took office in 1985. He came under mounting pressure from the political right and centre in 1988 to abandon the anti-International Monetary Fund (IMF) rhetoric that had been the hallmark of his national popularity. In late October he announced that he was prepared to hold talks with the IMF, and teams from the Fund and the World Bank visited Peru. García suffered another blow in late December when his own party, the Alianza Popular Revolucionaria Americana (APRA), abolished the position of party president that he had held and elected as its leader and secretary-general his archrival, former prime minister Luis Alva Castro.   (JANET KRENGEL)

SAINT KITTS AND NEVIS

A constitutional monarchy and member of the Commonwealth, St. Kitts and Nevis comprises the islands of St. Kitts and Nevis in the eastern Caribbean Sea. Area: 267 sq km (103 sq mi). Pop. (1988 est.): 43,200. Cap.: Basseterre. Monetary unit: Eastern Caribbean dollar, with (Oct. 10, 1988) a par value of EC$2.70 to U.S. $1 (free rate of EC$4.62 = £1 sterling). Queen, Elizabeth II; governor-general in 1988, Sir Clement Arrindell; prime minister, Kennedy A. Simmonds.

Another year of economic growth was expected in 1988, with early data showing a modest increase in tourist arrivals by air and an 81% rise in cruise-ship arrivals for the first quarter. The start of work on the new road opening up the southeast peninsula of St. Kitts gave a boost to the already growing construction industry. Work continued on two major hotel projects in Nevis, but financing difficulties delayed the start of a 200-room hotel in St. Kitts, to be managed by Ramada International. A report from the Caribbean Development Bank warned in mid-1988 that a serious shortage of skilled and technical labour was being experienced as a result of the growth of the manufacturing, construction, and service industries.

Sugar production from the 1988 harvest was estimated at about 30,000 tons, as compared with 25,256 in 1987. Two mechanical harvesters were used for the first time, to overcome a shortage of cane cutters.

In Nevis the Nevis Reformation Party won a second term in elections for the island assembly held in December 1987. However, the party lost one of its five seats to the Concerned Citizens' Movement.   (ROD PRINCE)

This article updates the *Macropædia* article The WEST INDIES: *Saint Christopher and Nevis.*

SAINT LUCIA

A constitutional monarchy and member of the Commonwealth, St. Lucia is the second largest of the Windward Islands in the eastern Caribbean Sea. Area: 617 sq km (238 sq mi). Pop. (1988 est.): 145,000. Cap.: Castries. Monetary unit: Eastern Caribbean dollar, with (Oct. 10, 1988) a par value of EC$2.70 to U.S. $1 (free rate of EC$4.62 = £1 sterling). Queen, Elizabeth II; governor-general in 1988, Sir Vincent Floissac; prime minister, John Compton.

The economy was expected to recover in 1988 from the previous year's slow growth, caused principally by adverse weather conditions that reduced banana production to 87,-000 tons. As a result, the gross domestic product rose only 2.1% over 1986. In September 1988 Hurricane Gilbert caused damage of EC$2 million to roads and EC$1 million to the banana industry.

Growth was expected to result from an increase in tourism, with the first four months of 1988 showing a 6.4% gain in travelers arriving by air. Other developments included construction of a dam in the Roseau Valley to provide a large reservoir; a new power station to be built at Cul-de-Sac, south of Castries; new roads and factory space; and improved telecommunications. Exploratory drilling in the Soufrière area in February located a reservoir of high-pressure steam estimated to be capable of generating five megawatts of electricity. The government announced in February that it was to allow casino gambling in tourist hotels, a proposal that had been vigorously opposed by the Roman Catholic Church.   (ROD PRINCE)

This article updates the *Macropædia* article The WEST INDIES: *Saint Lucia.*

SAINT VINCENT AND THE GRENADINES

A constitutional monarchy within the Commonwealth, St. Vincent and the Grenadines comprises the islands of St. Vincent and the northern Grenadines in the eastern Caribbean Sea. Area: 389 sq km (150 sq mi). Pop. (1988 est.): 113,000. Cap.: Kingstown. Monetary unit: Eastern Caribbean dollar, with (Oct. 10, 1988) a par value of EC$2.70 to U.S. $1 (free rate of EC$4.62 = £1 sterling). Queen, Elizabeth II; governors-general in 1988, Joseph Lambert Eustace and, from February 29, Henry Harvey Williams; prime minister, James Fitz-Allen Mitchell.

Infrastructural development aimed at enabling economic diversification to take place continued to occupy the centre of attention in government planning during 1988. Capital expenditure for the year was budgeted to increase by 43% to EC$100 million, and the government obtained financing pledges from a wide range of sources for its land-reform, forestry, and airport-development programs. Despite growth of 3.2% in the gross domestic product during 1987, unemployment was expected to remain a major problem, and the trade deficit in 1987 almost doubled, to EC$63 million.

For the second year in a row, a dispute over editorial independence at the state radio station occurred when, in May, a senior news editor was suspended and then transferred to the sales department for allegedly having failed to give sufficient priority to government press releases. Human rights organizations also protested against a government proposal to introduce flogging, at the beginning and end of a 20-year jail sentence, for those convicted of vandalizing the Soufrière volcano monitoring equipment.   (ROD PRINCE)

This article updates the *Macropædia* article The WEST INDIES: *Saint Vincent and the Grenadines.*

SURINAME

The republic of Suriname is in northeastern South America, on the Atlantic Ocean. Area: 163,820 sq km (63,251 sq mi), not including a 17,635-sq km area disputed with Guyana. Pop. (1988 est.): 425,000. Cap.: Paramaribo. Monetary unit: Suriname guilder, with (Oct. 10, 1988) a par value of 1.75 Suriname guilders to U.S. $1 (free rate of 3.05 Suriname guilders = £1 sterling). Chairman of the National Military Council in 1988, Dési Bouterse; presidents, L. F. Ramdat Misier (acting) and, from January 25, Ramsewak Shankar; prime ministers, Jules Wijdenbosch (temporary) and, from January 26, Henck Arron.

On Jan. 25, 1988, Ramsewak Shankar of the Indian Progressive Reform Party (VHP) was sworn in as president of Suriname, and Henck Arron, leader of the Creole Party (NPS), was installed as vice-president, thus ending eight years of military rule. The following day Arron was also named prime minister of the new Cabinet. The first official government statement on March 14 made no conciliatory gestures toward the guerrilla movement led by Ronnie Brunswijk. Peace talks, which started on June 27 in neighbouring French Guiana between the government and representatives of the guerrilla movement, were stalemated.

After the democratic government was installed, financial aid was promised by the U.S., Brazil, and Venezuela. The Dutch government, which had withheld 1.6 billion guilders of vital aid funds during Suriname's military rule, again denied aid until political stability could be guaranteed and agreements on investments could be reached.

(KLAAS J. HOEKSEMA)

This article updates the Macropædia article The GUIANAS: Suriname.

TRINIDAD AND TOBAGO

A republic and member of the Commonwealth, Trinidad and Tobago consists of two islands in the Caribbean Sea off the coast of Venezuela. Area: 5,124 sq km (1,978 sq mi). Pop. (1988 est.): 1,258,000. Cap.: Port-of-Spain. Monetary unit: Trinidad and Tobago dollar, with (Oct. 10, 1988) a par value of TT$4.25 to U.S. $1 (free rate of TT$7.28 = £1 sterling). President in 1988, Noor Mohammad Hassanali; prime minister, A. N. R. Robinson.

A worsening financial situation, marked by a 25% shortfall in government revenue and a continuing decline in foreign exchange reserves, prompted a series of emergency measures in August 1988, including a 15.3% currency devaluation. The new exchange rate was fixed at TT$4.25 = U.S. $1, as compared with a previous rate of TT$3.60. In November the International Monetary Fund approved a loan of $109 million.

The shortfall in revenue resulted in late payment of salaries to civil servants and public sector workers in August and September, leading to protest demonstrations. In September 1988 unemployment was estimated at 25%, against 17.8% at the end of 1986; inflation had risen to more than its 1987 average of 10.8%.

However, the first half year's trade surplus showed a 30% increase over the first half of 1987. The government continued its efforts to reduce the losses of state-owned companies, announcing the divestment of some shareholdings. A seven-year plan published at the end of July set ambitious targets for economic recovery, involving a resumption of real growth of the gross domestic product by 1990 and the creation of 100,000 new jobs by 1995.

Divisions within the governing National Alliance for Reconstruction (NAR) led to the dismissal of three gov-

Presidents Julio Sanguinetti of Uruguay (left), Raúl Alfonsín of Argentina (centre), and José Sarney of Brazil greet reporters after a meeting on their countries' economic integration.
AFP PHOTO

ernment ministers in February, including External Affairs Minister Basdeo Panday. In September the three were expelled from the NAR.   (ROD PRINCE)

This article updates the Macropædia article The WEST INDIES: Trinidad and Tobago.

URUGUAY

A republic of eastern South America, Uruguay lies on the Atlantic Ocean. Area: 176,215 sq km (68,037 sq mi). Pop. (1988 est.): 2,981,000. Cap.: Montevideo. Monetary unit: Uruguayan new peso, with (Oct. 10, 1988) a free rate of 401.12 new pesos to U.S. $1 (686.91 new pesos = £1 sterling). President in 1988, Julio María Sanguinetti Cairolo.

Uruguay was politically stable in 1988 and made modest economic progress. An accord reached in April among the four main political parties to cooperate in facilitating passage of government measures through Congress worked fitfully, following the death in March of Wilson Ferreira Aldunate (see OBITUARIES), the president of the principal opposition party, the National Party. The campaign by a centre-left coalition to overthrow a law passed by Congress in December 1986 granting an amnesty to members of the armed forces accused of human rights violations during the period of military rule, 1973–85, succeeded in forcing a national referendum on the issue in early 1989. There was an upsurge of labour unrest as pay fell behind inflation. Government proposals in May for 18-month pay agreements based on productivity and past and forecast inflation gained limited acceptance.

In March Uruguay signed a new multiyear debt-rescheduling agreement that added amortizations due in 1990–91 to the amount rescheduled in 1986. It rescheduled $1,779,000,000 of principal repayments due between January 1985 and December 1991. Growth was expected to fall from 4.9% in 1987 to 2.5% in 1988, mainly because of high real interest rates and moderate external demand.

(ROBIN CHAPMAN)

VENEZUELA

A republic of northern South America, Venezuela lies on the Caribbean Sea. Area: 912,050 sq km (352,144 sq mi). Pop. (1988 est.): 18,757,000. Cap.: Caracas. Monetary unit: bolívar, with (Oct. 10, 1988) a "free market" rate of 37.31 bolívares to U.S. $1 (63.90 bolívares = £1 sterling), a "preferential" rate of 7.50 bolívares to U.S. $1 (12.82 bolívares = £1 sterling), and an "official" rate of 14.50 bolívares to U.S. $1 (24.79 bolívares = £1 sterling). President in 1988, Jaime Lusinchi.

Although campaigning for the presidential election on Dec. 4, 1988, officially began in May, the choice of candidates and probable outcome were known from the beginning of the year. Opinion polls consistently gave former president Carlos Andrés Pérez of the ruling Acción Democrática (AD) a large lead over his Social Christian (COPEI) opponent, Eduardo Fernández. Pérez received 3,884,202 valid votes, or 54.6% of the total, while Fernández obtained only 2,971,677 votes, or 41.7%. The strength of Pérez's popularity was such that his personal majority was greater than that of his own party in the House of Representatives. In the congressional elections the AD received only 43.8% of the vote and held a small majority, with 98 of the 204 seats, down from 118. COPEI gained 67 seats (31.4%), and the leftist coalition of the Movement to Socialism (MAS) and the Revolutionary Left Movement (MIR) won 19 (10.3%). Eight smaller parties divided the remaining seats. The decrease in the AD majority served to highlight the split between factions within AD.

Rivalries within AD surfaced most visibly during the year over the application for inclusion on the party's electoral slate by Blanca Ibáñez, the companion of Pres. Jaime Lusinchi. Senorita Ibáñez, who played a leading role in President Lusinchi's divorce proceedings against his wife, was vehemently opposed by another AD aspirant, Luis Piñerua Ordaz. In the end, the party decided not to choose either candidate, but President Lusinchi's standing within AD was diminished, leaving Pérez even more in command.

During the period just before the election, the AD administration determined not to introduce any major new measures. Therefore, discussions on a social pact between government, labour unions, and business were terminated. Labour demands for wage increases and better working conditions were held over until the new administration, as were private sector concerns over prices and the release of preferential dollars to purchase vital imports. Consequently, there was much debate but little action domestically except in the case of university teachers, whose strike for higher wages caused the loss of the entire first semester. Violent protests broke out in cities around the country in early November after an army patrol mistakenly shot and killed 14 civilians who were on a picnic near the Colombian border.

The government's unwillingness to act before the election had serious repercussions for the external economy because a slump in oil revenue led to a sharp decline in international reserves. Oil exports in 1988 were forecast to total only $7.2 billion–$7.5 billion (compared with $9.1 billion in 1987) as a result of low world prices and poor sales of Venezuela's higher priced petroleum products. The resulting fall in reserves jeopardized Venezuela's ability to service its $35 billion external debt.

The shortage of reserves also exacerbated the government deficit, which was expected to be similar to 1987's 6% of gross domestic product. The failure to cut public spending, largely because of the pressures of the election year, fueled inflation. In 1987 the cost-of-living index rose by a record 40.3%. Government measures in the first five months successfully held inflation to under 2% a month, but agricultural shortages in the middle of the year forced prices up again, contributing to a forecast annual rate of about 30%.

The government pressed ahead with the development of nonpetroleum sources of foreign exchange. Moves were made to formalize the exploitation of the large gold deposits in the Guayana region; also, expansion plans were approved for the aluminum and steel industries.

(BEN BOX)

Oceania

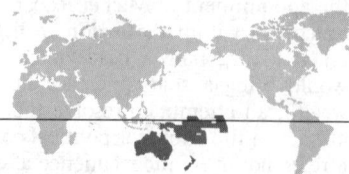

OCEANIAN AFFAIRS

In 1988 two major factors affected relationships within Oceania. They were the continuing aftershocks from the Fiji coups of May and September 1987 and the need for the governments of the region to adjust to the implications first of the "Ouvéa Massacre" in New Caledonia in May and then, within a matter of weeks, to the election in France of a moderate Socialist government committed to a policy of securing political and economic development in New Caledonia.

Relations with Fiji. While some island governments expressed concern about the military takeover in Fiji, there was a degree of sympathy with ethnic Fijians in the shared cause of "indigenous rights" and an emphatic view that other nations should not criticize or interfere in Fiji's internal affairs. The appointment of a civilian government in December 1987, even without any timetable for elections or a return to constitutional government, provided most governments of the region with the opportunity to resume formal relationships with the Fiji regime. Some, like Australia and Kiribati, adopted the stance of recognizing the country rather than the government, while others formally recognized the new regime. Even New Zealand, which had remained critical of the Fiji situation, made a new diplomatic appointment, albeit at a subambassadorial level, and resumed its aid program.

One important consideration for Fiji's traditional aid donors—notably Australia, the United Kingdom, and New Zealand—was the opportunity provided by the suspension of their programs for the expansion of French influence; France demonstrated its interest in Fiji with a naval visit and the initiation of a major aid program.

Conflicts with France. Governments in the region continued to protest France's nuclear testing at Mururoa Atoll, and the announcement that testing would also resume at the nearby Fangataufa site fueled speculation that the change amounted to a concession that the volcanic and coral substructure at Mururoa was being compromised by repeated testing and that there was a possibility of leakage of radioactive material into the lagoon and surrounding ocean. Following the earlier release from Hao Atoll by *Rainbow Warrior* saboteur Alain Mafart on supposed health grounds, the repatriation of his fellow agent Dominique Prieur on the eve of the French presidential election caused a further deterioration of relations between France and New Zealand. (In 1985 the *Rainbow Warrior,* flagship of the Greenpeace environmental organization, was bombed and sunk in the harbour at Auckland, N.Z., by French military agents Mafart and Prieur.)

Events that caused more serious damage to France's reputation in Oceania occurred in New Caledonia in April and May when militant separatist Melanesian Kanaks kidnapped 27 gendarmes on the island of Ouvéa and held most of them hostage against political demands. The subsequent assault on the remote Kanak position by French security forces was seen as a bid by the Chirac government for conservative support in the upcoming French elections. (See *Dependent States,* below.) The confrontation exacerbated already deep divisions within New Caledonian society and further isolated France within Oceania. The reelection of François Mitterrand as president of France in May and

the appointment of Michel Rocard as prime minister were welcomed within the region in light of the positive steps taken to negotiate a peace plan for New Caledonia that would bring a sharp increase in aid, a redistribution of wealth, an attempt to resolve the land issue, and the creation of a timetable for political change that would lead to a referendum on independence after ten years.

South Pacific Forum. At the 1988 meeting of the South Pacific Forum in Tonga in September, island leaders gave their endorsement to France's plan for New Caledonia. They also considered the possibility of further expansion of the South Pacific Regional Trade and Economic Cooperation Agreement (Sparteca), under which island goods enjoy preferential entry to the markets of Australia and New Zealand. It was agreed that the South Pacific Bureau for Economic Cooperation in Suva should be expanded and that it should formally become the secretariat of the Forum, a role that it had performed informally since its creation some 15 years earlier. At its formal sessions the Forum refused to discuss the political situation in Fiji, regarding this as an internal matter for Fiji alone. However, the presence of the acting Fijian prime minister, Ratu Sir Kamisese Mara, marked the reentry of Fiji into the regional politics of Oceania.

The South Pacific Forum also directed the Forum Fisheries Agency based in the Solomon Islands to investigate the possibility of negotiating a general agreement with Japan in regard to the exclusive economic zones of the Forum countries. This followed the successful conclusion of a multilateral fisheries agreement between the Forum and the U.S. after several years of negotiation. The agreement, which was finalized in negotiations early in 1987, was given unanimous approval by the U.S. Senate in November 1987 and passed by the U.S. House of Representatives and signed by Pres. Ronald Reagan in June. Under this agreement the U.S. government and the American Tuna Boat Association would pay island governments some $60 million over five years for the right to fish in their combined exclusive economic zones, covering some 26 million sq km (10 million sq mi) of the Pacific. The agreement resolved a long-standing disagreement over the "ownership" of tuna and other highly migratory species of fish.

In March the governments of Papua New Guinea, the Solomon Islands, and Vanuatu formalized their collective commitment to the "Melanesian Spearhead" group—an initiative that recognized the factors of size and culture that set the Melanesian countries apart from the smaller nations of Polynesia and Micronesia. Through their collective action in the Spearhead group, the Melanesian nations adopted an aggressively anticolonial stance and expressed their strong commitment to self-determination in the region and to the cause of Melanesian militants in New Caledonia.   (BARRIE MACDONALD)

AUSTRALIA

A federal parliamentary state (formally a constitutional monarchy) and member of the Commonwealth, Australia occupies the smallest continent and includes the island state of Tasmania. Area: 7,682,300 sq km (2,966,200 sq mi). Pop. (1988 est.): 16,470,000. Cap.: Canberra. Monetary unit: Australian dollar, with (Oct. 10, 1988) a free rate of $A 1.24 to U.S. $1 ($A 2.13 = £1 sterling). Queen, Elizabeth II; governor-general in 1988, Sir Ninian Martin Stephen; prime minister, Robert J. Hawke.

Domestic Affairs. Australia celebrated its bicentennial in 1988. Prime Minister Robert ("Bob") Hawke (*see* BIOGRAPHIES) began the celebrations with a speech at the Sydney Opera House on Australia Day, January 26, in which he said that as a nation of immigrants from 130 countries, Australia had created a nation without privilege of origin. As part of the celebration of the nation, Australia's federal politicians moved into a new, enlarged Parliament House in June 1988, the first move since 1927. Hawke made a powerful speech, in which he said the Parliament moved forward, not just to a new home but to an era of achievement in the service of democracy and in one of the great parliaments of the world. Public opinion was less enthusiastic, however, and the new building was regarded as an extravagant monument to political egotism and a colossal waste of taxpayers' money.

As part of the new-broom syndrome accompanying the beginning of a third century of European occupation of the continent, the majority Australian Labor Party (ALP) held a referendum on September 3 to enable Australian electors to vote yes or no to four changes to the constitution. The proposed laws were designed to establish a four-year maximum term for members of both houses of the Commonwealth Parliament, to provide for fair and demo-

AFP PHOTO

Boats and ships assembled in Sydney Harbour for Australia's "Parade of Sail." The tall ships reenacted the arrival in 1788 of Capt. Arthur Philip and his fleet, which transported the passengers—among them about 730 convicts—who began the colonization of the country.

cratic parliamentary elections, to recognize the status of local government, and to extend certain rights concerning trial by jury, freedom of religion, and just-compensation laws. All the referendum proposals were overwhelmingly defeated.

Despite its referendum defeats, the Hawke Labor government itself made a strong recovery during 1988 after reaching low levels of popularity early in the year following the resignation of several high-ranking Labor ministers. One of the first to go was the minister for education, Susan Ryan, who resigned in December 1987 to take up a career in publishing. In late 1987 the ALP also lost the minister for tourism, John Brown, who left office after mishandling his portfolio. To make matters worse, in February 1988 the ALP suffered a by-election shock in the seat of Adelaide, which the Liberal Party won when there was a swing against the government following the resignation of the minister for immigration, Chris Hurford, who took up a diplomatic posting in the U.S. The by-election loss at Adelaide was the first such defeat since the loss of the Tasmanian seat of Bass in 1975. Hawke recognized the danger signs and moved quickly to turn defeat into victory, taking some share of the blame and acknowledging the protest vote. Hawke admitted that he had received a clear message from the Adelaide outcome and as a result would modify his policies so as not to appear the friend of wealthy beer barons rather than of the party's traditional poorer working-class supporters.

Compared with these larger reverses, Hawke faced only minor problems with the Tasmanian state government, with Aborigines, and with his most accident-prone minister, Michael ("Mick") Young. Young resigned in February following the misdirection of a donation of $A 10,000 to the ALP. Young was not responsible for the misdirection of funds, and the prime minister felt that the press had unjustly forced the resignation. Hawke made some effort to reconcile Aboriginal and non-Aboriginal Australians in the bicentennial year, but without convincing the most politically active people of his sincerity. Similarly, the Commonwealth and Tasmanian governments remained at an impasse in the quarrel over the competing claims of environmentalists and industrialists in Tasmania's wilderness areas. To try to resolve the problems, Hawke commissioned the Helsham Report on the Tasmanian Lemonthyme and Southern forests, but following a battle between the minister for the environment, Graham Richardson, and the minister for resources, Peter Cook, a compromise was reached, and the report was largely ignored. Under the compromise, logging was to be carried out in 20%

of the Lemonthyme and Southern forests. In return for conserving 80% of the area, the Tasmanian government was offered $A 40 million as compensation. The Tasmanian premier, R. T. Gray, attacked the compromise, but Richardson defended it, pointing out that it was necessary to protect Australia's longest and deepest caves and some of the oldest rock art sites in the world, dating from the last ice age.

An era ended in August 1988 when the foreign minister, William ("Bill") Hayden, announced that he would leave the ALP and the government in order to succeed Sir Ninian Stephen as governor-general in February 1989. The announcement ended months of speculation on the pros and cons of having Hayden as governor-general. Critics of the appointment centred on Hayden's atheism and republicanism, qualities they said ill-fitted the representative of Queen Elizabeth II in Australia.

To make matters worse, Hayden's private papers, amounting to 10,000 documents, were leaked to the press, and some of them were published. The documents were an acute embarrassment to the government, which took court action to seize them and prevent further damaging disclosures. The excerpts that were published, however, showed that Hayden privately thought that the Papua New Guinea government was immature, that the Indonesian people were erratic and hostile, and that the Japanese were hypocritical. He also described the Malaysian foreign minister as "oafish" and revealed that in 1983 Australia bowed to direct U.S. pressure to allow docking rights to foreign warships possibly carrying nuclear arms.

Foreign Affairs. Australia's foreign policy relations with its nearest Asian neighbours and most important trading partners were affected less by Hayden's ruminations than by public debates within Australia concerning immigration. The Hawke government commissioned an inquiry from a former ambassador to China, Stephen Fitzgerald, hoping that Fitzgerald's close association with Asian interests would defuse any unfavourable comment should Fitzgerald recommend changes to Australia's immigration policy. In his report Fitzgerald called for an increase in the immigration intake to 150,000 a year for two years. He also recommended a boost in family migration numbers from 33,000 to 40,000 over the same period and, more controversially, called for an increasing emphasis on English as well as skills in languages of national importance, such as those of Australia's major trading partners. His most important recommendation, however, was that the government "disengage" itself from Indochinese resettlement in line with the diminishing number of refugees from

JAMES POZARIK/TIME MAGAZINE

Vacationers enjoy the surf, sand, and sun of Surfers Paradise beach in Queensland. The area's attractive coastline had lured many Japanese investors, enabling them to control about 70% of the property that was destined for development.

that area. Within months of Fitzgerald's report, the opposition leader, John Howard, declared that he hoped a new immigration policy, based on the slogan "One Australia," would abandon multiculturalism because of its divisive nature. Howard added that, if elected, a new Liberal-National coalition government would reserve the right to maintain social harmony by slowing the rate of Asian immigration. He was enthusiastically supported by National Party leaders Ian Sinclair and John Stone. Some Liberals, fearing an electoral backlash by migrant groups, encouraged him to stop provocative comments on migration, and for a time a shaky unanimity of silence followed. Shortly afterward, Hawke took the moral high ground and declared that he was prepared to lose the next election if necessary rather than be labeled a racist bigot. When Howard attempted to back away from the racist implications of his "One Australia" policy, he ordered his shadow cabinet to remain silent on the issue. However, Stone continued to repeat his view that a reduction in Asian migration was a possible policy for any new government, and Howard was forced to dismiss him from the shadow cabinet. A new immigration policy package approved by the Cabinet in December cut the number of parents allowed to join their immigrant children in Australia by 40%. The Cabinet rejected many of Fitzgerald's recommendations, most notably by keeping immigration intake at 140,000 per year.

Changing attitudes toward Japan combined to provide difficulties for both governments. Following what local Australians took to be unacceptable levels of Japanese investment in real estate in Queensland, public meetings canvassed the view that foreign ownership of Australian land should be reduced if not denied. This cut against government policy to encourage Japanese investment but was sufficiently disturbing to cause the Japanese government to caution potential investors in Australia to be less visible and less aggressive in their entrepreneurship. The Japanese, disturbed to find that the Japanese militarism of the World War II era was returning to the Australian mind as the dominant image, tried to reassure Australia that militarism was a thing of the past and that trade, tourism, and the exchange of information should increase.

Relations with Fiji proved troublesome for Australian diplomats following the 1987 military coup d'état. The ousted Fijian prime minister, Timoci Bavandra, bitterly criticized Australia for deserting him, but the ALP government replied that its decision to normalize relations with Fiji was the best policy in the long run for all concerned. Within Australia a "Movement for Democracy in Fiji" was founded, under the influential chairmanship of Don Dunstan, who, as a former South Australian ALP premier, used his influence to publicize human rights and civil liberties violations. Dunstan criticized the Fijian government as a racist regime, imposed at the point of a gun, where Indians lived in fear, and he called upon his former colleagues in the party to impose on Fiji the same sanctions that were imposed on South Africa. Relations with Fiji deteriorated further when Hayden's successor as foreign minister, Gareth Evans, tried unsuccessfully to place more emphasis on Pacific affairs than had his predecessor and made visits to the Pacific nations as a first priority for his term of office. However, he immediately caused a diplomatic row when Fiji refused him permission to visit Bavandra. Hawke threatened to withhold vital Australian aid unless Fiji permitted the meeting to go ahead, and the Fijian government backed down, but relations remained tense.

The relationship between the queen and the prime minister of Australia was damaged in 1988 when Hawke permitted the foreign minister to receive a diplomatic service merit medal from South Korea. Queen Elizabeth II was annoyed to be consulted only after the event and said it was a pity that the rule which forbade her ministers—even in Australia—from accepting awards from foreign nations should be honoured in the breach. Australia, anxious to promote its regional political and economic interests in the Pacific Rim, had put its relationship with South Korea before that of the crown and had sought the queen's acceptance of a fait accompli in full knowledge of the convention precluding it.

Australia's relationship with the Soviet Union improved in 1988 to the extent that the government agreed to begin negotiations on the use of Australian ports as bases for the Soviet fishing fleet and on landing rights for the Soviet airline Aeroflot in Australia. The deputy Soviet prime minister, Vladimir M. Kamentsev, went so far as to reassure worried Australians that no spies would be aboard Soviet trawlers or aircraft, a guarantee accepted by Foreign Minister Hayden, although not by the shadow minister or the opposition.

The Economy. The Australian economy performed strongly in 1988, aided by two major adjustments from the treasurer, Paul Keating. Keating's first adjustment was in May, when he brought a minibudget into Parliament and his second in August when the budget proper was delivered. Keating set out to make a series of far-reaching economic reforms that were designed to carry Australia into the 21st century. He said that the government was committed to getting all aspects of the economy right by adopting a complete and comprehensive strategy and that he was making "big brush economic changes reinforced by sweeping strokes going to the micro or industry level." He made cuts in industry tariffs, equal to a 20% reduction phased in over four years. The government introduced a tax-file number system, which would be used to identify taxpayers earning wages, salaries, and other incomes by making it compulsory for all employers, banks, and other financial institutions to establish and verify tax-file numbers before processing any financial transactions. The new tax-file number, which was accompanied by a short-term amnesty for those who had neglected to put in recent tax returns, was expected to raise $A 1.8 billion in ten years from funds that would otherwise circulate in an undeclared black economy.

In two other important announcements, Keating cut the corporate tax rate by 20% from 49 cents to 39 cents on the dollar and made sweeping reforms in Australia's pension laws. These involved a tax of 15% on pension fund earnings, the taxation of employer contributions, and the reduction of concessional benefits to lump-sum recipients. The Australian Taxpayers Association described the May minibudget as "a tax massacre," and the influential national director, Eric Risstrom, said that the new tax was a mathematical nightmare that few would properly understand.

The opposition ignored Keating's May minibudget strategy and called for a more generous treatment of the budget surplus, claiming that instead of reducing foreign debt, the government should reduce the taxation burden faced by ordinary wage and salary earners, a point of view they repeated when the treasurer introduced the August budget. On that occasion, making his first major formal speech in the new Parliament House, Keating claimed that Australia was back on its way to prosperity. The major improvements were in the giant $A 5.5 billion surplus and the decision of the government to make no new borrowing whatsoever. This achievement, he said, was without precedent in Australia's history. Keating announced that the

government's strategy for the coming year was to reduce the balance of payments deficit (which, however, reached a near-record $A 1.7 billion in October) and to cut inflation. His hope was that inflation would be reduced to 4.5% by June 1989 and to 3% in 1990. The public response to the budget was disappointment that no tax cuts would be forthcoming until the eve of the next election and that then the size of the tax cuts would be related to the degree of wage restraint shown by the workers. Bankers were happier than most with the decision by Keating to remove the distinction between trading and savings banks and to phase out a regulation requiring banks to deposit money with the Commonwealth Reserve Bank at low interest rates as a guarantee of their solvency. In an unexpected move, taxes on beer were reduced, with greater cuts for low-alcohol beer, and in a less popular move the treasurer announced that most postsecondary school students entering universities or their equivalents would have to pay an education tax. The government expected the new tax to help them provide 40,000 new student places in postsecondary institutions over three years and pointed out that the tax would be due only when graduate students were earning incomes equal to the national average. The tax also could be paid "up front" at a 15% discount.

The government continued to rely on the Arbitration and Conciliation Commission to adjust the economy through imposing wage restraints on workers. In August 1988 the commission made its annual decision on pay increases for Australia's seven million workers. In a break with traditional across-the-board increases, the commission decided that a 3% raise could be paid in cases where unions could agree with employers on improvements to efficiency and productivity. Unions seeking the 3% raise had to agree to a review of the award covering their conditions of employment. This pay increase was available from Sept. 1, 1988. However, the commission did not expect all employers and employees to agree to award changes and so, in addition to providing their own officers to decide in cases of unresolvable disagreement, laid down that, whatever happened, all the work force was to receive a flat increase of $A 10 a week no less than six months after September 1. The government welcomed the bench's introduction of a new structural efficiency principle. The clear message was that Australian workers would receive either wage raises or tax cuts but not both.   (A. R. G. GRIFFITHS)

FIJI

The republic of Fiji occupies an island group in the South Pacific Ocean. Area: 18,274 sq km (7,056 sq mi). Pop. (1988 est.): 742,000. Cap.: Suva. Monetary unit: Fiji dollar, with (Oct. 10, 1988) a free rate of F$1.46 to U.S. $1 (F$2.50 = £1 sterling). President in 1988, Ratu Sir Penaia Ganilau; prime minister, Ratu Sir Kamisese Mara.

The appointment of a civilian government in December 1987, following the coups of May and September, saw former governor-general Ratu Sir Penaia` Ganilau return as president and former prime minister Ratu Sir Kamisese Mara again serving in that office. Brig. Gen. Sitiveni Rabuka, leader of the coups, became minister of home affairs. Decrees that gave preference to ethnic Fijians in the public service and bestowed immunity from civil and criminal proceedings on military personnel involved in the 1987 coups caused controversy at home and abroad.

There was some cause for optimism in the economy. Sugar exports were the highest since 1980; China provided assistance with medical services and rural electrification; closer ties with France brought F$14 million in aid; and re-

sumption of aid was announced by the U.S. in December. Overall, however, the economy remained in decline, with the 34% devaluation of the Fijian dollar in 1987 raising export receipts but also fueling inflation. The government was forced to borrow F$37 million to cover a record budget deficit of F$120 million.

In September the Cabinet gave its approval to a proposed constitution that would reserve a majority of parliamentary seats, and key positions in government, for ethnic Fijians, and a meeting of 270 chiefs approved it in principle in November. No date was given for elections or the introduction of the new structure.   (BARRIE MACDONALD)

This article updates the *Macropædia* article PACIFIC ISLANDS: *Fiji*.

KIRIBATI

A republic in the western Pacific Ocean and member of the Commonwealth, Kiribati comprises the former Gilbert Islands, Banaba (Ocean Island), the Line Islands, and the Phoenix Islands. Area: 849 sq km (328 sq mi). Pop. (1988 est.): 68,200. Cap.: Bairiki. Monetary unit: Australian dollar, with (Oct. 10, 1988) a free rate of $A 1.24 to U.S. $1 ($A 2.13 = £1 sterling). President (*berititenti*) in 1988, Ieremia Tabai.

After gaining a new aid relationship with the United Kingdom, in which the end of aid for recurrent expenditure was offset by the opportunity to maximize returns on invested income from phosphate mining in the years before independence, Kiribati embarked on a new five-year plan aimed at achieving economic self-sufficiency. The plan called for maximizing returns from agriculture and offering incentives for a range of small industries.

The United Kingdom, Australia, and New Zealand remained major aid donors, together with the European Communities' Stabex Fund, which provided Kiribati with about $A 1 million a year to compensate for fluctuating copra prices; a renewed fishing agreement with South Korea secured $A 420,000 as an annual rental for access to Kiribati's exclusive economic zone. The government was considering plans to reopen the phosphate industry at Banaba and use a new suction technique. It was estimated that as many as one million tons of phosphate could be recovered by this method. A project to produce salt at Kiritimati (Christmas) Island was foundering for want of a secure market.   (BARRIE MACDONALD)

This article updates the *Macropædia* article PACIFIC ISLANDS: *Kiribati*.

NAURU

An island republic within the Commonwealth, Nauru lies in the Pacific Ocean about 1,900 km (1,200 mi) east of New Guinea. Area: 21 sq km (8 sq mi). Pop. (1988 est.): 8,100. Cap.: Yaren. Monetary unit: Australian dollar, with (Oct. 10, 1988) a free rate of $A 1.24 to U.S. $1 ($A 2.13 = £1 sterling). President in 1988, Hammer DeRoburt.

In an effort to improve Nauru's relationship with Australia, Pres. Hammer DeRoburt paid a goodwill visit to that country on the occasion of Australia's bicentennial celebrations. Relations had deteriorated when the Australian Council of Trade Unions considered banning all Air Nauru flights to Australia after the Nauru government sacked 27 pilots who had been on strike. All commercial flights in and out of Nauru were grounded by the strike for over three weeks.

Nauru was extremely critical of Australia in February during an inquiry into repairing the damage done to the Pacific island by more than 60 years of phosphate mining. Nauru argued that the British Phosphate Commission, in

which Australia, New Zealand, and the United Kingdom were partners, ought to be at least partly responsible for any expenses involved. Peter Macsporran, counsel for the Nauru government, called for the partner governments, particularly Australia, to stop their "ridiculous posturing" and start negotiating to see what they could do to make good past mistakes.   (A. R. G. GRIFFITHS)

This article updates the *Micropædia* article NAURU.

NEW ZEALAND

New Zealand, a constitutional monarchy and member of the Commonwealth in the South Pacific Ocean, consists of North and South islands and Stewart, Chatham, and other minor islands. Area: 267,515 sq km (103,288 sq mi). Pop. (1988 est.): 3,354,000. Cap.: Wellington. Monetary unit: New Zealand dollar, with (Oct. 10, 1988) a free rate of $NZ 1.60 to U.S. $1 ($NZ 2.74 = £1 sterling). Queen, Elizabeth II; governor-general in 1987, Sir Paul Reeves; prime minister, David Russell Lange.

In the second year of its second term, New Zealand's fourth Labour government increased its reliance on privatization and sales of assets to balance its books. It continued to deregulate industry, and reduction of the inflation rate remained its first priority. This provoked resentment and some retaliation from its trade union base, though it had not deregulated the labour market. The unions and much of the community were concerned that unemployment by the end of November was running at an unprecedented 8% of the work force. In December the government introduced a program to reduce unemployment called Restart.

Seven months before the introduction of his budget, Finance Minister Roger Douglas had signaled the possibility of a single income tax rate, amounting to around 25%, and a rise in the goods and services tax (GST; a value-added tax) from 10 to 12.5%. Within two months, however, this plan had lost out in the Cabinet to a two-tier personal-tax scale of 24 and 33% (previous top rate, 48%) and a company tax rate (for resident companies) of 28% (previous rate, 48%). Up to budget night (July 28), Prime Minister David Lange seemed doubtful that the plan to lower income tax rates and hold GST steady could be sustained. As it turned out, however, the projected sale of assets (including the Bank of New Zealand) totaling some $NZ 2 billion grabbed the headlines. Without this revenue, it was estimated that the deficit would reach $NZ 1.4 billion (2.2% of gross domestic product, the same as in the previous year). Douglas

was more successful in his fight against inflation, and the 0.8% rise posted for the June quarter was the best quarterly result since 1969. The annual rate to June 30 was 6.3% (9.6% for calendar 1987).

Ten months after the August 1987 general elections, the government lost a seat when the courts disqualified the successful candidate, following a recount and examination of his campaign expenses. This changed the standing in Parliament to 57 for the government and 40 for the National Party opposition. Prime Minister Lange returned from hospital treatment for angina with plans for some reshuffling of ministerial responsibilities, and on September 7, in a move that was seen as reining in Douglas's reforms, he flanked the finance minister with deputy finance ministers Michael Moore (who continued to specialize in overseas trade) and David Caygill (also in charge of health). Richard Prebble, the minister responsible for the privatization program and a supporter of Douglas, was sacked in November after Prebble called Lange dictatorial and irrational.

After his illness, the prime minister arranged for Justice Minister Geoffrey Palmer to represent him at the meeting in Tonga of the South Pacific Forum. However, he went to Canberra himself for talks at a time of increasingly close commercial and social ties with Australia. The two countries had agreed to lift their last trade barriers by July 1990 and to end restrictions on companies providing banking and insurance services by January 1989. Lange addressed the UN in New York in September.

The latest export statistics showed that in the half year to December 1987 Japan nudged out Australia as New Zealand's largest market. Trade with the U.S. was down 12.3%. Migration loss in the year to January 1988 totaled 12,140, mostly to Australia, a situation acknowledged in a government agreement to reimburse that country for national pension payments made to New Zealanders.

The governor-general, Sir Paul Reeves, who was part Maori, included states outside his jurisdiction on his itinerary when he made an extensive and successful tour of the Pacific islands. Race relations in New Zealand were tested by a government proposal to disband the Maori Affairs Department and turn over related responsibilities to regional tribes. Also leading to strain was the decision of an enlarged Waitangi Tribunal, set up to reinterpret the 1840 Treaty of Waitangi between Maori chiefs and white settlers, to grant special fishing rights to Northland Maoris.

(JOHN A. KELLEHER)

AP/WIDE WORLD

A houseboat sinks into the waters of New Zealand's Bay of Islands. When Cyclone Bola hit the east cape of northern New Zealand, wind and massive flooding forced more than 1,000 people to evacuate the area.

PAPUA NEW GUINEA

A constitutional monarchy and member of the Commonwealth, Papua New Guinea is situated in the southwestern Pacific Ocean and comprises the eastern part of the island of New Guinea, the islands of the Bismarck, Trobriand, Woodlark, Louisiade, and D'Entrecasteaux groups, and parts of the Solomon Islands, including Bougainville. Area: 462,840 sq km (178,704 sq mi). Pop. (1988 est.): 3,562,000. Cap.: Port Moresby. Monetary unit: kina, with (Oct. 10, 1988) a free rate of 0.87 kina to U.S. $1 (1.49 kinas = £1 sterling). Queen, Elizabeth II; governor-general in 1988, Sir Kingsford Dibela; prime ministers, Paias Wingti to July 4 and Rabbie Namaliu.

Rabbie Namaliu (*see* BIOGRAPHIES) became Papua New Guinea's fourth prime minister in July 1988, following a vote of no confidence in Paias Wingti. Namaliu, who represented an electorate on East New Britain, took over leadership of the Pangu Pati from the elder statesman Michael Somare on the eve of the no-confidence motion. After the vote, which Namaliu won 58–50, the new prime minister formed a coalition government comprising his own Pangu Pati, the Melanesian Alliance of Father John Momis, and the People's Action Party of Ted Diro, as well as the Papua Party, the League for National Advancement, and elements of the National Party. Wingti, who left Parliament, attributed his defeat to opposition to his tough stand against corruption in government.

Strikes at the Ok Tedi mines in 1988 were marked by violence. The dispute was resolved when the mine owners agreed to build 200 houses for workers during the next 18 months. (A. R. G. GRIFFITHS)

This article updates the *Macropædia* article EAST INDIES: *Papua New Guinea.*

SOLOMON ISLANDS

A parliamentary state and member of the Commonwealth, the Solomon Islands comprises a 1,450-km (900-mi) chain of islands and atolls in the western Pacific Ocean. Area: 28,370 sq km (10,954 sq mi). Pop. (1988 est.): 301,000. Cap.: Honiara. Monetary unit: Solomon Islands dollar, with (Oct. 10, 1988) a free rate of SI$2.15 to U.S. $1 (SI$3.68 = £1 sterling). Queen, Elizabeth II; governor-general in 1988, Sir Baddeley Devesi; prime minister, Ezekiel Alebua.

The government of Prime Minister Ezekiel Alebua survived the year despite an attempted parliamentary vote of no confidence in April. In response to political pressure, the prime minister appointed a commission of inquiry into alleged misuse and mismanagement of funds that had been allocated by the World Bank for the development of primary schools.

Following a visit by its minister for defense, Australia pledged funds for a maritime surveillance centre, which would provide base facilities for the new fisheries patrol vessel presented by Australia in midyear. Following negotiations, the Solomon Islands and Papua New Guinea signed a border agreement; one of its major concerns was protection of the traditional rights of those who inhabit the islands close to and on both sides of the border.

The 1988 budget provided for expenditure of SI$170 million. The government announced plans to concentrate development funds on farming and food-production projects. An agreement was reached on plans for a new fish cannery to be built with Japanese assistance on New Georgia. A new minimum wage was fixed at SI$141 per month, or 74 cents an hour. (BARRIE MACDONALD)

This article updates the *Macropædia* article PACIFIC ISLANDS: *Solomon Islands.*

TONGA

A constitutional monarchy and member of the Commonwealth, Tonga is an island group in the Pacific Ocean east of Fiji. Area: 780 sq km (301 sq mi). Pop. (1988 est.): 95,300. Cap.: Nuku'alofa. Monetary unit: pa'anga, with (Oct. 10, 1988) a free rate of 1.24 pa'anga to U.S. $1 (2.13 pa'anga = £1 sterling). King, Taufa'ahau Tupou IV; prime minister in 1988, Prince Fatafehi Tu'ipelehake.

On July 4, 1988, Tonga celebrated the 70th birthday of Taufa'ahau Tupou IV; visiting dignitaries attended a prayer breakfast. Also, in the centennial year of the first treaty between the United States and Tonga, a new Treaty of Amity, Commerce, and Navigation was signed under which Tonga guaranteed the transit of U.S. nuclear-armed vessels through Tongan waters.

In its 1988–89 budget Tonga proposed to increase expenditure by 23% to 75 million pa'anga, with most of this (42 million pa'anga) being for development projects. Work neared completion on the 3.5 million pa'anga project (paid from Australian aid) to upgrade the country's main airport so that it could accommodate Boeing 747s.

Major political controversy surrounded a successful action for wrongful dismissal brought by 'Akilisi Pohiva, a former broadcaster; the action followed 1985 broadcasts critical of the government. In 1987 Pohiva was elected to Parliament, where he embarrassed the government with revelations of misuse of funds by politicians. There was further controversy when it was discovered that a member of the royal family was involved in a venture to build a local incineration plant for toxic waste exported from the U.S. The scheme was dropped as a result of public opposition. (BARRIE MACDONALD)

This article updates the *Macropædia* article PACIFIC ISLANDS: *Tonga.*

TUVALU

A constitutional monarchy within the Commonwealth, Tuvalu comprises nine main islands and their associated islets and reefs in the western Pacific Ocean. Area: 24 sq km (9 sq mi). Pop. (1988): 8,700. Cap.: Fongafale. Monetary unit: Tuvalu dollar, at par with the Australian dollar ($A, also a legal currency), with (Oct. 10, 1988) a free rate of $T 1.24 to U.S. $1 ($T 2.13 = £1 sterling). Queen, Elizabeth II; governor-general in 1988, Tupua Leupena; prime minister, Tomasi Puapua.

The stock market crash of October 1987 caused a loss of $A 2 million of the $A 27 million trust fund provided by the United Kingdom, Australia, and New Zealand to generate recurrent revenue and reduce Tuvalu's level of dependence on foreign aid; the high proportion of investments held in government bonds protected the fund from further losses. Tuvalu's 1988 budget provided for recurrent income of $A 4.7 million, including $A 1 million from U.K. budgetary assistance, $A 800,000 from the investment trust, and $A 262,000 from fishing license fees from Asian countries and the U.S. Development expenditure showed a sharp increase to $A 9 million because of the once-only cost of replacing the *Nivanga,* the government's interisland freight and passenger vessel.

There were widespread celebrations in the islands when four men who had been blown out to sea in a storm while fishing in a small dinghy safely reached land at Futuna Island, more than 600 km (400 mi) away. They had been drifting for nearly two months. (BARRIE MACDONALD)

This article updates the *Macropædia* article PACIFIC ISLANDS: *Tuvalu.*

VANUATU

The republic of Vanuatu, a member of the Commonwealth, comprises 12 main islands and some 60 smaller ones in the southwestern Pacific Ocean. Area: 12,190 sq km (4,707 sq mi). Pop. (1988 est.): 149,000. Cap.: Vila. Monetary unit: vatu, with (Oct. 10, 1988) a free rate of 106.48 vatu to U.S. $1 (182.35 vatu = £1 sterling). President in 1988, George Sokomanu; prime minister, the Rev. Walter Lini.

In the general election of November 1987, the Vanuaaku Party, which had dominated politics since independence, saw its support drop to 47% as it won 26 of the 46 seats in Parliament. The following month Barak Sope, a left-wing militant who was secretary-general of the Vanuaaku Party, unsuccessfully challenged the leadership of the prime minister, the Rev. Walter Lini, whose health was still in question following a stroke several months earlier. In May a major land rights demonstration organized by Sope erupted into violence that resulted in one death. The political crisis worsened in July when, after a boycott, 18 opposition members of Parliament were dismissed for having failed to attend three consecutive sessions of the House. At about the same time, Sope and four supporters were dismissed after Lini argued that under 1983 legislation they had vacated their seats by resigning from the party that sponsored their election. In October the Court of Appeal ruled that by-elections for the 18 opposition seats could take place in December, and that Sope and his followers remained members of the House. Sope boycotted the by-elections, and on December 16 Pres. George Sokomanu dissolved Parliament, later swearing in an interim government headed by Sope. Lini ignored the dissolution and ordered the arrest of the president, Sope, and the other four members of the new government, who at year's end were in detention.   (BARRIE MACDONALD)

This article updates the *Macropædia* article PACIFIC ISLANDS: *Vanuatu*.

WESTERN SAMOA

A constitutional monarchy and member of the Commonwealth, Western Samoa occupies an island group in the South Pacific Ocean. Area: 2,831 sq km (1,093 sq mi). Pop. (1988 est.): 162,-000. Cap.: Apia. Monetary unit: Western Samoa tala, with (Oct. 10, 1988) a free rate of 2.13 tala to U.S. $1 (3.65 tala = £1 sterling). Head of state (*O le Ao o le Malo*) in 1988, Malietoa Tanumafili II; prime ministers, Va'ai Kolone and, from April 8, Tofilau Eti Alesana.

After elections on February 26 for Western Samoa's 47-seat Legislative Assembly, it seemed that the ruling coalition would retain power by a single seat. However, after election results had been recounted and one member of the coalition had defected, the opposition Human Rights Protection Party, led by Tofilau Eti Alesana, was able to form a government. Tofilau Eti, 64, the son of a Congregational pastor, had served an earlier term as prime minister from 1983 to 1985.

In its 1988 budget the government provided for recurrent expenditure of 95 million tala (up from 84 million tala in 1987) and a 38.5 million tala development budget; 21 million tala were required for meeting loan repayments for 1988. In January, in an effort to encourage foreign investment, the Legislative Assembly approved legislation to provide an offshore banking facility.

                      (BARRIE MACDONALD)

This article updates the *Macropædia* article PACIFIC ISLANDS: *Samoa*.

Dependent States

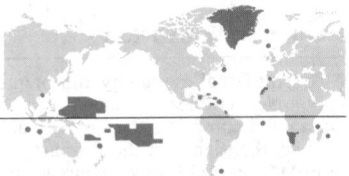

Europe and the Atlantic. In Gibraltar on March 6, 1988, British commandos in the Special Air Service shot and killed three unarmed Irish Republican Army terrorists. (*See* CRIME, LAW ENFORCEMENT, AND PENOLOGY.) A Gibraltarian jury ruled on September 30 that the soldiers had acted in "a lawful manner." In elections held less than three weeks after the shooting incident, the Gibraltar Socialist Labour Party was swept into power by a margin of 58 to 29%, ending 16 years of rule by the Labour Party-Association for the Advancement of Civil Rights. Socialist leader Joe Bossano promised that his government would seek friendly relations with Spain but would reject the 1987 agreement between Spain and the U.K. for joint operation of the Gibraltar airport.

A long-standing territorial dispute around St. Pierre and Miquelon islands led to a diplomatic crisis between France and Canada in April 1988, when a Canadian Coast Guard vessel arrested 17 islanders and four French politicians for fishing in disputed waters. France recalled its ambassador to Ottawa and in May arrested a Canadian fishing trawler in the same waters. The territorial dispute over the Falkland Islands/Islas Malvinas continued in 1988, with Argentina filing a formal protest to the UN in March over British naval maneuvers in the area. In the Faeroe Islands the Social Democrat-led coalition lost its parliamentary majority in a voter swing to the right in elections in November.

REUTERS/BETTMANN NEWSPHOTOS

Protesters burn copies of the British White Paper outlining measures for Hong Kong's government. The document was viewed by many as timid because it postponed major changes until 1991, when a Chinese territorial law would come into effect.

Caribbean. Constitutional government was restored to the Turks and Caicos Islands in a general election on March 3, which brought the People's Democratic Movement (PDM) led by Oswald Skippings to power. The PDM won 11 of the 13 Legislative Council seats and four of the five constituencies. As chief minister, Skippings led a delegation to London in April that agreed on a three-year aid program of £15 million.

The deputy chief minister of the British Virgin Islands, Omar Hodge, was dismissed in March after he had obtained a court order blocking publication of the report of an official inquiry into alleged financial wrongdoing on his part. He was replaced by the former leader of the opposition United Party, Ralph O'Neal, who joined the governing Virgin Islands Party. Hodge subsequently joined the VIP.

In the French elections held in the spring, the three overseas départements of Guadeloupe, Martinique, and French Guiana gave substantial majorities to Pres. François Mitterrand, while the left-wing parties increased their hold in the National Assembly, winning eight of the ten seats. This shift to the left was also evident in council elections in the fall. In Guadeloupe the Communist Party, which was in alliance with the dominant Socialist Party, announced in April that it would henceforth support independence for the island; both parties had previously supported limited autonomy.

The Netherlands Antilles government headed by Premier Don Martina resigned on March 22 following the withdrawal of one of its supporting coalition members. A new government headed by Maria Liberia-Peters of the Partido Nashonal di Pueblo was formed on May 17 with the support of 13 of the 22 assembly members. The Netherlands agreed to provide 170 million guilders in aid over four years, half the amount requested by Liberia-Peters.

Puerto Rico's governor, Rafael Hernández Colón of the Popular Democratic Party, was narrowly reelected in November. Hernández Colón, who supported Puerto Rico's commonwealth status, won 48.7% of the vote, while Baltasar Corrada del Rio of the pro-statehood New Progressive Party received 45.8%. The island's economy registered strong growth in the fiscal year ended June 30, but growth of gross domestic product was expected to slow to about 2–3% in 1988–89. Unemployment fell to 14.8% in June 1988, and for the first time in two decades, the island registered net inward migration of almost 48,000 people.

Africa. In July South Africa, Cuba, Angola, and the U.S. agreed to principles for a peace settlement for South West Africa/Namibia linking implementation of UN Resolution 435 on Namibian independence with agreement on a timetable for withdrawal of Cuban troops from Angola. Subsequently, it appeared that the negotiations were stalled, but on December 13 agreement was reached among the parties, and the accords were formally signed at the UN on December 22. The agreement consisted of a U.S.-mediated pact, signed by South Africa, Angola, and Cuba, setting out a timetable for Namibian independence, and a second accord, signed by Cuba and Angola, providing for a phased withdrawal of Cuban troops from Angola, to be completed by July 1, 1991. It was envisaged that Namibia would hold elections by November 1989. Peace talks continued in Western Sahara, where Morocco and the Popular Front for the Liberation of Saguia el Hamra and Río de Oro (Polisario) agreed to a cease-fire and a UN-sponsored referendum on independence.

Pacific. In November 1987 Bernard Pons, France's minister for the overseas départements and territories, announced a constitutional plan for New Caledonia that would have restructured regional political boundaries to reduce the influence of Kanaks—the indigenous Melanesians—who were outnumbered by French settlers and migrants from other Pacific countries. The plan was denounced locally by Kanaks and in Paris by President Mitterrand, who condemned the scheme as "unjust and divisive." The scene was set for violent confrontation when 100 Kanak separatists in the northeastern part of the island attacked gendarmes with clubs and stones. On April 22, on the island of Ouvéa, Kanak separatists attacked a police station, hacking 4 gendarmes to death and capturing 27 hostages, most of whom they held in a remote limestone cave. Later, the commander of the antiterrorist forces sent to the area was also captured. On May 5, while negotiations for the release of the hostages were proceeding, the security forces launched an assault that left 2 soldiers and 19 Kanaks dead. Alphonse Dianoud, leader of the Kanaks, was wounded and, it was alleged, subsequently killed by French soldiers. In a disappointing turnout of only 37%, French voters in November overwhelmingly approved a referendum that would permit New Caledonia to vote on self-determination in 1998. The low turnout was seen as a setback for Prime Minister Michel Rocard, who had negotiated the settlement, and President Mitterrand, who, in a televised address just before the election, had urged voters to go to the polls.

In October 1987 rioting by striking dockworkers in Tahiti brought on the declaration of a state of emergency and the dispatch of additional police and security forces to the island by the French government. French Polynesian workers at Mururoa also went on strike to protest the advantages enjoyed by workers from metropolitan France. In the political instability that followed, Alexandre Léontieff assumed the presidency of the Council of Ministers, effectively becoming the leader of French Polynesia. This meant a major defeat for Gaston Flosse, for many years the dominant figure in local politics as leader of the Tahoeraa Party and, more recently, as secretary of state for the South Pacific in the government of French Prime Minister Jacques Chirac. In May the French government announced that it would reopen its nuclear testing site at Fangataufa Atoll. This was interpreted in the region as an admission that repeated blasts at Mururoa had destabilized the substructure of the island.

The difficulty in securing legal endorsement of the Compact of Free Association between the U.S. and Palau

AFP PHOTO

Pro-independence leader Jean-Marie Tjibaou casts his ballot in a referendum that might ultimately lead to independence for New Caledonia. Although many French settlers were against the statute, the voters approved the referendum by an overwhelming 80%.

continued in 1988. The U.S. Senate endorsed the compact subject to the outcome of legal challenges, and at midyear the Trusteeship Council of the UN gave its approval, despite opposition from the U.S.S.R., leaving unresolved differences to negotiation between the two governments. Palauans had voted ten times on the compact but were unable to reach the required 75% majority for approval. An attempt in 1987 to overcome the impasse by amending the constitution itself was ruled unconstitutional in 1988. Palauans had been deeply divided over the issue, and there had been several incidents of intimidation, violence, and firebombing. On August 20 Pres. Lazarus Salii apparently committed suicide. Some commentators linked his death to frustration and tension over the compact, others to allegations of misuse of funds that were currently under investigation by the U.S. government. A new president was elected on November 2.

In the Marshall Islands the U.S. Department of Energy embarked on a $100 million campaign to make Bikini Island, the site of nuclear tests in the 1950s, safe for habitation and food production. In American Samoa, after Rep. Fofo Sunia was charged with conspiracy to defraud the government, he announced that he would not seek reelection to Congress. "Ghost" employees on his payroll apparently had received more than $130,000.

During a year of comparative political stability, the Cook Islands placed major emphasis on broadening the base of economic development and reducing aid from New Zealand, which covered most development costs and 20% of recurrent expenditure in a budget of about $NZ 55 million. It issued a license to the Taiwan Tuna Boat Association to cover the presence of 40 fishing boats within the Cook Islands' exclusive economic zone. In Niue a large majority in Parliament was opposed to the idea of recognizing an official parliamentary opposition. Members argued that the move, proposed by the People's Action Party, which won four seats in the 1987 elections, was contrary to the consensus basis of traditional politics.

East Asia. Vietnamese "boat people," undeterred by the closed camps that awaited them, continued to arrive in Hong Kong. By June 16, 1988, when the government began a "screening" process to separate "genuine refugees" from "economic emigrants," 15,866 were in the prison-

like camps. By late October another 10,000 had landed.

Elections in September, in which fewer than 2% of Hong Kong's citizens were eligible to vote, returned conservative members to the Legislative Council. These members were selected by voters through the "functional constituencies" of professional persons and an electoral college made up of partly appointed district boards. A government proposal that 10 of 56 councillors be elected by universal suffrage in 1991 was coolly received in Beijing (Peking). There was heated debate in the council and the media over a plan to hold a grand international exposition in 1997 to coincide with the transfer of sovereignty to China. A draft of the Basic Law, a miniconstitution designed to preserve a large measure of post-1997 autonomy, was heavily criticized when it was released in April for being too vague on the rights of Beijing to intervene in local affairs.

In January Portugal and China exchanged documents formalizing the arrangement whereby Macau would become, two years after Hong Kong, a "special administrative region" of China. In May China asked Portugal not to implement major political changes before the changeover. An election in October for 6 of 12 Legislative Assembly seats (the governor appoints 5 others) resulted in the return of 3 liberals.

(MARTIN LEGASSICK; BARRIE McDONALD; ROD PRINCE; MELINDA SHEPHERD; ROBERT WOODROW)

This article updates the *Macropædia* articles HONG KONG; INDIAN OCEAN ISLANDS; PACIFIC ISLANDS; SOUTHERN AFRICA: *South West Africa/Namibia;* THE WEST INDIES.

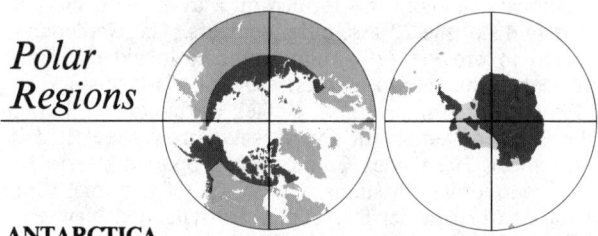

Polar Regions

ANTARCTICA

On June 2, 1988, nations party to the Antarctic Treaty signed a convention to regulate Antarctic mineral resource activities, including prospecting, exploration, and development. Negotiations had been under way since 1982. The agreement was significant because neither the 1961 Antarctic Treaty, which reserves the region for peace and defers issues of territorial ownership, nor any other instrument provided for commercial use of Antarctic minerals. While Antarctica had never had a minerals industry, in 1975 nations agreed to refrain from commercial exploration and exploitation pending completion of a regime to govern such activity.

The new convention would be open for ratification at Wellington, N.Z., where the signing took place, for a year beginning Nov. 25, 1988. It would enter into force after 16 of the 20 Antarctic Treaty consultative parties that signed it had deposited their ratifications. Any nation could accede to the convention after it entered into force.

Antarctica has no known deposits of minerals that would be worth extracting at current prices. The most likely mineral resource is offshore oil, but the deep continental shelf, large icebergs, and harsh climate led experts to suggest that only a giant or supergiant oil field would attract interest, and even a price of $40 a barrel would not lead to development in the next few decades. Under these circumstances, it might be asked why a minerals agreement should be negotiated now. Many observers presumed that negotiation of the new convention, made particularly difficult by the

Dependent States*

Australia	**South Africa**
Christmas Island	South West Africa/Namibia
Cocos (Keeling) Islands	**United Kingdom**
Norfolk Island	Anguilla
Denmark	Bermuda
Faeroe Islands	British Virgin Islands
Greenland	Cayman Islands
France	Falkland Islands
French Guiana	Gibraltar
French Polynesia	Guernsey
Guadeloupe	Hong Kong
Martinique	Isle of Man
Mayotte	Jersey
New Caledonia	Montserrat
Réunion	Pitcairn Island
Saint Pierre and Miquelon	Saint Helena
Wallis and Futuna	Turks and Caicos Islands
Netherlands, The	**United States**
Aruba	American Samoa
Netherlands Antilles	Guam
New Zealand	Puerto Rico
Cook Islands	Trust Territory of the Pacific Islands
Niue	Marshall Islands
Tokelau	Federated States of Micronesia
Norway	Northern Marianas
Jan Mayen	Palau
Svalbard	Virgin Islands (of the U.S.)
Portugal	
Macau	

*Excludes territories (1) to which Antarctic Treaty is applicable in whole or in part, (2) without permanent civilian population, (3) without internationally recognized civilian government (Western Sahara, Gaza Strip), or (4) representing unadjudicated unilateral or multilateral territorial claims.

A geologist perches on a ledge in Antarctica while taking rock samples. In June 1988 a pact was signed that would regulate exploration and development of Antarctica's mineral resources.

LYNN JOHNSON—BLACK STAR

existence of Antarctic territorial claims asserted by seven nations and recognized by no others, was easier in the absence of immediate pressure from developers. The time pressure was less intense, and the negotiating countries were not driven to action by the known presence of a deposit in any of the claimed sectors of Antarctica. In addition, the successful momentum of the Antarctic Treaty system as the world's management structure for Antarctic affairs was sustained.

Another reason for negotiating a regime before development became imminent was to maintain the strong tradition of environmental preservation that was encouraged by the Antarctic Treaty. Representatives of environmental groups stated that the convention signed in Wellington might be the most environmentally sound international treaty negotiated to date. The convention, however, disappointed those who argued for a total ban on minerals development in Antarctica. The convention on the regulation of Antarctic mineral resource activities was the third major regime negotiated within the Antarctic Treaty system, following a 1972 convention for the preservation of Antarctic seals and a 1980 convention on the conservation of Antarctic marine living resources.

The Antarctic Treaty itself continued to grow in 1988. With the accession of its 38th member (Canada), the treaty now represented two-thirds of the world's population. The treaty's consultative nations—the original 12 signatories plus those conducting substantial scientific research in Antarctica—grew to 22 with the addition of Sweden and Spain. Consultative nations have a vote at the biennial treaty meetings (the most recent one took place in Brazil, Oct. 5–16, 1987; the next would be in Paris in 1989). The other acceding states agree to abide by the treaty, and they participate in the meetings as observers.

Stratospheric Ozone. Unpopulated and without an economic base, Antarctica since the 1950s had had as its main "industry" research into its characteristics and its relationship to global environmental change. Scientists had long postulated, for example, that global warming as a result of the concentration of carbon dioxide in the upper atmosphere—the so-called greenhouse effect—would be seen first in Antarctica, where changes in temperature over

the centuries had exceeded those in mid-latitudes several times over. In the 1987–88 Antarctic summer, 20 nations supported some 3,000 investigators throughout the region; they performed research in astronomy; atmospheric, Earth, and ocean sciences; glaciology; biology; and the medical sciences. In the 1988 winter the human presence dropped to about a thousand at 36 year-round stations.

Unlike the temperature modelers, no one foresaw the dramatic springtime depletions of stratospheric ozone over Antarctica, first observed in 1979 and reported in 1985. Springtime Antarctic ozone in 1987 dropped further (to half of normal), and the hole got bigger and stayed longer than in any earlier season. In 1988 scientists reported a smaller but still serious global decrease than had been predicted. During the 1987–88 austral summer, intensive study of the Antarctic loss was made by satellite observation, aircraft sensing flights, and ground-based and balloon-borne observations from McMurdo Station. This work, together with experiments in laboratories, established beyond reasonable doubt that man-made chlorofluorocarbons (CFCs) are the cause of stratospheric ozone loss. In Antarctica special atmospheric conditions, particularly the presence of polar stratospheric clouds whose particles support reactions between chlorine and ozone, exacerbate the effect of the CFCs and produce large losses of ozone. Scientists from several nations continued their scrutiny of the Antarctic ozone hole during the year, broadening their research to four areas: continuing to document the areal extent and the intensity of the ozone depletions; studying chemical mechanisms of the depletions; installing sensors to monitor the increase in ultraviolet radiation (UV) reaching the Earth's surface as a result of the depletions; and beginning observations of the effect of increased UV on Antarctic life forms.

Calculations indicated that, because of Antarctica's low sun angles, levels of harmful wavelengths of UV reaching Antarctica when the ozone hole formed had not exceeded those in the U.S. Antarctic personnel could protect themselves by wearing proper sunglasses and applying UV-blocking skin cream. Native Antarctic species were not so lucky. In the U.S. research program marine phytoplankton, at the base of the Antarctic food chain, were given high priority in 1988 for study of UV-induced change. U.S. investigators in 1988 also installed UV monitors at three Antarctic stations and at the tip of South America. Working along the Antarctic Peninsula, a team evaluated the DNA repair capabilities of Antarctic species. (*See* EARTH SCIENCES: *Meteorology:* Sidebar.)

Tourism. Tourists in Antarctica reached record levels in the 1987–88 season; their numbers exceeded 2,000 and approached the number of scientists and support personnel in government programs. Most of the commercial tours were shipborne, and their destinations were the islands, shores, and research stations near the west side of the Antarctic Peninsula. But tourists also managed to reach the South Pole, traveling on a wheeled DC-4 to a blue (hard) ice runway at 80° S latitude, just south of the Ronne Ice Shelf, and transferring there to ski-equipped Twin Otters for the final 1,000-km (670-mi) flight to the U.S. station at the Pole, which they visited for a few minutes.

The response to tourism varied among the Antarctic Treaty nations. Chile, for example, with a gravel runway on King George Island at 62° S, had been receptive, installing a hotel and providing air access from Tierra del Fuego. In accordance with U.S. government policy prohibiting taxpayer-supported assistance to private expeditions except to extend humanitarian assistance in an emergency, the U.S. Antarctic Program tolerated tourism at its coastal Palmer

Station for years as a pleasant diversion until 1987, when the growing number of visits began to interfere seriously with research projects. Following an acrimonious one-season experiment in which the U.S. program forced tour operators to restrict the number of tourists visiting the station, the arrangement for 1988–89 was to accept those responsible tour groups requesting visits in advance.

Tourism could be the harbinger of a variety of future commercial uses of Antarctica. Optimal management of Antarctic tourism seemed certain in the future, resolving the current unsettled balance between the public's wish to observe Antarctic research and governments' missions to move research forward without undue interruption. Both the Antarctic Treaty system and a new international group—Managers of National Antarctic Programs—were considering ways to accommodate such new activities.

(GUY G. GUTHRIDGE)

This article updates the *Macropædia* article ANTARCTICA.

ARCTIC REGIONS

Oil and Natural Gas. Despite the overproduction of oil throughout the world and the consequent decline in crude oil prices, good news was reported from the Alaskan North Slope during 1988. *Alaska Construction and Oil* reported in April that North Slope oil producers could drill more than 1,000 new wells, adding an extra 40,000 bbl per day of production from existing fields over the next decade. It also was forecast that Alaskan revenues from oil production would reach $2,080,000,000 in fiscal 1988.

After a 15-year hiatus there was again speculation that pipelines might be built from Alaska and the Canadian Arctic to southern markets—the visionary projects of the 1970s that were postponed by aboriginal land claims, environmental concerns, and staggering costs. In midyear the sponsors of the Alaska Highway natural gas pipeline suggested that the long-delayed project might, at last, get on track. The huge development, which was put on hold in 1982, would transport natural gas from the Alaskan North Slope through the Yukon and Alberta to the lower 48 states of the U.S. It was the favoured route of Justice Thomas Berger, whose controversial royal commission effectively killed an alternative route down the Mackenzie River Valley.

The line's sponsors said the delay in building the 3,400-km (2,113-mi) pipeline had reduced the estimated construction costs from $34.9 billion to $19.5 billion in 1988 dollars, a saving of 44%. The lower costs were attributed to inflation and interest rates that were lower than had been forecast in 1982, as well as to innovations in pipeline design and construction. In June Esso Resources Canada and Shell Canada announced plans to begin the regulatory process for establishing a pipeline from the Mackenzie Delta and Beaufort Sea to the United States. Such a move was a sign that energy companies were planning multibillion-dollar projects for a market that was expected to open up only in the mid-1990s.

In May a report by the U.S. Fish and Wildlife Service indicated that oil development in northern Alaska had caused more environmental damage than envisioned in environmental impact statements prepared before the projects had begun. The report concluded that the projects had created substantially more air and water pollution and had destroyed significantly greater amounts of wildlife habitat than had been expected. The release of the report was expected to have a significant impact on the debate over whether to open Alaska's Arctic National Wildlife Refuge to development.

In October Canada substantially reduced its estimates of northern oil and gas reserves. Oil reserves under the Beaufort Sea and inland along the Mackenzie River were rated at 7.1 billion bbl, 26% less than the 9.6 billion estimated earlier. Natural gas expectations were about 68 trillion cu ft, down about 9% from the 75 trillion previously anticipated. Nevertheless, northern oil reserves were still estimated to be double the reserves in western Canada, although development of northern oil faced severe economic handicaps because of the distance from markets and the high cost of technology for finding and transporting the resource. For purposes of comparison, it was estimated that western Canadian oil could be found and brought to market if the world oil price were in the range of $16.50 per barrel, while prices would have to rise to $25 per barrel for northern oil to be profitable. Predictions were made that northern oil production would eventually peak at 200,000 bbl a day, or about 10% of overall Canadian production.

Land Claims. On September 5 a historic agreement in principle to settle the land claim of the Dene Indians and Métis peoples, descendants of Indians and early French and Scottish settlers, was signed by the Canadian prime minister and the presidents of the Dene Nation and the Métis

CHARLES MASON—BLACK STAR

Two Eskimo women give a friendly pat to one of three California gray whales trapped by Arctic ice. The whales' plight drew worldwide attention. One died, but the other two were eventually freed with the aid of Soviet icebreakers.

Adm. Robert Peary poses with his dog team during his famous trek to the North Pole in 1909. Recent studies of his diary and related sources indicated that Peary may not have reached the Pole.
THE BETTMANN ARCHIVE

Association of the Northwest Territories. After 13 years of negotiations, a final agreement was to be signed within two years. Among the major provisions of the agreement would be that the 13,000 Dene and Métis cede their aboriginal claims to lands and waters in return for the largest such land transfer in Canadian history—surface and subsurface rights to about 180,000 sq km (70,000 sq mi)—Can$500 million in cash over the next 20 years, and limited rights to harvest wildlife. Among the most contentious issues standing in the way of a final agreement were guarantees of native self-government and the actual boundaries of the 180,000 sq km to be selected.

Toward the end of the year, the Canadian government was also involved in negotiating two other large land claims, one with the Council of Yukon Indians and the other with the Tungavik Federation of Nunavut in the central and eastern Arctic. The tentative agreement with the approximately 6,000 Yukon Indians involved title to about 41,500 sq km (16,000 sq mi) of land and a cash settlement of Can$243 million. The Nunavut negotiations were expected to produce by far the largest comprehensive land-claims settlement ever to be reached with aboriginal people in northern Canada, affecting as many as 18,000 Inuit who lived across a vast area. It was anticipated that their settlement would amount to about 352,000 sq km (136,000 sq mi) of land and Can$650 million.

International Developments. Late in the year the first real test of the Canada-U.S. Arctic cooperation agreement occurred when the U.S. requested permission for one of its icebreakers, the *Polar Star*, to enter Arctic waters. The agreement obliged the U.S. to seek permission for entry into Canada-claimed waters and required compliance with Canadian pollution laws. This was a change from the contentious 1985 voyage of the U.S. icebreaker *Polar Sea* through the Northwest Passage.

In February it was reported in the *Toronto Globe and Mail* that the Soviet Union had offered to discuss joint Arctic interests with Canada as a way of accelerating the process of demilitarization of the northern regions. The initial Canadian reaction was that the Soviet proposal to demilitarize the Arctic regions of northern Europe and North America was meaningless unless it specifically included demilitarization of the adjacent Kola Peninsula in the U.S.S.R., an area of concentrated Soviet military installations around Murmansk. In a related matter, it was indicated that Sweden, Finland, and Norway already had expressed interest in Soviet offers to share information on scientific, cultural, environmental, and energy matters in the Arctic.

According to the *Arctic News Record & Polar Bulletin,* the Norwegian government stated that it had no intention of building its own icebreaker despite the embarrassment suffered in 1987 when a Norwegian Coast Guard vessel went to the rescue of some fishing vessels off Spitsbergen and got stuck itself. Private shipowners and businesses with Arctic experience and research institutions contended that it was time for Norway, with possessions in both the Arctic and Antarctica, to build icebreaking ships on a large scale for research and expeditions.

Research. In May the Associated Press reported that U.S. and Canadian researchers had discovered that an ozone hole, similar to the one being created over the South Pole, might be developing in the stratosphere near the North Pole. Ozone losses at the North Pole could have serious implications for the ozone layer, which screens out harmful ultraviolet radiation.

In August a study supported by *National Geographic* magazine raised strong doubts about the credibility of Robert Peary's claim that on April 6, 1909, he became the first man to reach the North Pole. The new assessment of information and data in Peary's diary focused on navigational errors, doubtful distance records, and inexplicable blank pages in the explorer's diary. In October the *Washington Post* reported that a Baltimore astronomer and historian had recently claimed that his analysis of Peary's navigational notes revealed that Peary came no closer than about 195 km (120 mi) to the Pole. Should Peary's claim be disproved, the first people to reach the Pole by land would be a four-man team headed by Ralph Plaisted, who arrived there by snowmobile in 1968.

(KENNETH DE LA BARRE)

This article updates the *Macropædia* article The ARCTIC.

CONTRIBUTORS

Abdoolcarim, Zoher F. Senior Editor, *Asiaweek,* Hong Kong.
WORLD AFFAIRS: *Brunei; Indonesia; Malaysia; Singapore*

Aers, Vivianne L. Editor and Publisher. Editor, *World Fishing.*
AGRICULTURE AND FOOD SUPPLIES: *Fisheries*

Allaby, Michael. Free-lance Writer and Lecturer. Author of *Ecology Facts; Who Will Eat?*
ENVIRONMENT *(in part)*

Allan, J. A. Reader in Geography, School of Oriental and African Studies, University of London.
WORLD AFFAIRS: *Libya*

Aloff, Mindy. Dance Critic, *The Nation;* Senior Critic, *Dance Magazine.*
DANCE *(in part)*

Amedeo, Michael. Writer, Encyclopædia Britannica Educational Corp.; Film Critic, *New City.*
BIOGRAPHIES *(in part)*

Archibald, John J. Feature Writer, *St. Louis Post-Dispatch;* Adjunct Professor, Washington University, St. Louis, Mo.
SPORTS AND GAMES: *Bowling (in part)*

Armstrong, George. Rome Correspondent, *The Guardian.*
BIOGRAPHIES *(in part);* WORLD AFFAIRS: *Italy*

Arnold, Guy. Free-lance Writer. Author of *Modern Nigeria; Aid in Africa.*
WORLD AFFAIRS: *Botswana; Burundi; Cape Verde; Equatorial Guinea; Gambia, The; Ghana; Guinea-Bissau; Lesotho; Liberia; Maldives; Mauritius; Nigeria; Rwanda; São Tomé and Príncipe; Seychelles; Sierra Leone; Swaziland*

Arnold, Mavis. Free-lance Journalist, Dublin.
WORLD AFFAIRS: *Ireland*

Arrington, Leonard J. Formerly Church Historian, Church of Jesus Christ of Latter-day Saints.
RELIGION: *Church of Jesus Christ of Latter-day Saints*

Artisien, Patrick. Lecturer in Business and Economics, Univeristy of Wales, Cardiff. Author of *Joint Ventures in Yugoslav Industry; North-South Direct Investment in the European Communities.*
WORLD AFFAIRS: *Albania*

Baptist, Ines T. Free-lance Writer.
WORLD AFFAIRS: *Belize*

Barford, Michael F. Editor and Director, *Tabacosmos,* London.
INDUSTRIAL REVIEW: *Tobacco*

Bargad, Warren. Samuel M. Melton Professor of Jewish Studies and Director, Center for Jewish Studies, University of Florida.
LITERATURE: *Hebrew*

Barrett, David B. Missions Researcher, Foreign Mission Board, U.S. Southern Baptist Convention.
RELIGION: *World Religious Statistics*

Barrett, John C. A. Headmaster, Kent College, Pembury, England; Secretary, British Committee, World Methodist Council. Author of *Family Worship in Theory and Practice.*
RELIGION: *Methodist Churches*

Bass, Howard. Journalist and Broadcaster. Editor, *Winter Sports,* 1948–69; author of 15 books on winter sports.
BIOGRAPHIES *(in part);* SPORTS AND GAMES: *Ice Hockey (in part); Ice Skating; Skiing*

Beckwith, David C. White House Correspondent, *Time* magazine, Washington, D.C.
WORLD AFFAIRS: *United States:* Developments in the States in 1988

Bentsi-Enchill, Nii K. Assistant Editor, *West Africa* magazine.
WORLD AFFAIRS: *Cameroon; Central African Republic; Comoros; Congo; Côte d'Ivoire; Djibouti; Gabon; Madagascar*

Bergerre, Max. Vatican Affairs Correspondent, *La Vie,* Paris.
WORLD AFFAIRS: *Vatican City State*

Beyer, Reginald Ian. Deputy Curator, Royal Botanic Gardens, Kew, England.
BOTANICAL GARDENS AND ZOOS *(in part)*

Bickelhaupt, David L. Professor Emeritus, Faculty of Finance, College of Business, Ohio State University, Columbus.
INDUSTRIAL REVIEW: *Insurance*

Bigger, Frank C. Special Assistant for Public Relations, American Chemical Society, Washington, D.C. Author of *DNA: Master Molecule of Life.*
CHEMISTRY

Bird, Thomas E. Director, Council for the Study of Ethics and Public Policy, Queens College, City University of New York.
LITERATURE: *Yiddish*

Bisman, Ronald W. North Island Editor, *New Zealand Harness Racing Weekly.* Author of *Cardigan Bay; Salute to Trotting; Globetrotting Simpson.*
SPORTS AND GAMES: *Horse Racing (in part)*

Bleibtreu, Hermann K. Professor of Anthropology, University of Arizona.
ANTHROPOLOGY

Boddy, William C. Editor, *Motor Sport.* Full Member, Guild of Motoring Writers.
SPORTS AND GAMES: *Automobile Racing (in part)*

Boden, Edward. Editor, *Veterinary Record.*
HEALTH AND DISEASE: *Veterinary Medicine*

Booth, John Nicholls. Lecturer and Writer. Author of *The Quest for Preaching Power.*
RELIGION: *Unitarian (Universalist) Churches*

Boswall, Jeffery. Head of Film and Video, Royal Society for the Protection of Birds, Bedfordshire, England.
LIFE SCIENCES: *Ornithology*

Box, Ben. Free-lance Writer and Researcher.
WORLD AFFAIRS: *Honduras; Guatemala; Venezuela*

Boye, Roger. Coin columnist, *Chicago Tribune.*
PHILATELY AND NUMISMATICS: *Coins and Paper Money*

Bradsher, Henry S. Foreign Affairs Writer.
WORLD AFFAIRS: *Philippines*

Braidwood, Robert J. Professor Emeritus of Old World Prehistory, Oriental Institute and Department of Anthropology, University of Chicago. Author of *Prehistoric Men.*
ARCHAEOLOGY: *Eastern Hemisphere*

Brazee, Rutlage J. Geophysical Consultant.
EARTH SCIENCES: *Geophysics*

Brecher, Kenneth. Professor of Astronomy and Physics, Boston University. Coauthor and coeditor of *Astronomy of the Ancients.*
ASTRONOMY

Brittain, Victoria. Third World Report Editor, *The Guardian,* London. Coeditor of *Voices from the South; Children of Resistance;* Author of *Hidden Lives, Hidden Deaths.*
WORLD AFFAIRS: *Commonwealth of Nations*

Brokopp, John G. Specialist in publicity, public relations, and free-lance writing involving the sport of horse racing.
SPORTS AND GAMES: *Horse Racing (in part)*

Burdin, Joel L. Professor of Educational Administration, City College of the City University of New York.
EDUCATION *(in part)*

Burks, Ardath W. Emeritus Professor of Asian Studies, Rutgers University, New Brunswick, N.J.
WORLD AFFAIRS: *Japan*

Bush-Brown, Albert. Chancellor, Long Island University, Greenvale, N.Y. Author of *Louis Sullivan;* coauthor of *The Architecture of America.*
Macropædia: ARCHITECTURE, THE HISTORY OF WESTERN *(in part)*

Bushnell, Geoffrey H. S. (d. 1978). Reader in New World Archaeology, University of Cambridge, 1966–70; Fellow of Corpus Christi College, Cambridge; Curator, Museum of Archaeology and Ethnology, 1948–70. Author of *Peru* and others.
Macropædia: PRE-COLUMBIAN CIVILIZATIONS *(in part)*

Butler, Frank. Former Sports Editor, *News of the World,* London. Author of *The Good, the Bad and the Ugly: A Story of Boxing.*
SPORTS AND GAMES: *Boxing*

Byrd, Ty. Managing Editor, *New Civil Engineer* magazine.
ENGINEERING PROJECTS: *Bridges*

Cameron, Sarah. Economic Advisor, Latin America and the Caribbean, Economics Department, Lloyds Bank PLC, London.
BIOGRAPHIES *(in part);* WORLD AFFAIRS: *Costa Rica; El Salvador; Mexico; Nicaragua; Paraguay*

Campbell, Alexander Johns. Lloyds Bank PLC, London.
WORLD AFFAIRS: *Chile; Colombia; Panama*

Carter, Robert W. Journalist, London.
SPORTS AND GAMES: *Horse Racing (in part)*

Caswell, Nim. Subeditor, *Financial Times,* international edition, London.
WORLD AFFAIRS: *Benin; Burkina Faso; Chad; Guinea; Mali; Mauritania; Niger; Senegal; Togo*

Chapman, Kenneth F. Former Editor, *Stamp Collecting* and *Philatelic Magazine.*
PHILATELY AND NUMISMATICS: *Stamps*

Chapman, Robin. Senior Economist, Economics Department, Lloyds Bank PLC, London.
WORLD AFFAIRS: *Brazil; Cuba; Dominican Republic; Haiti; Latin-American Affairs; Uruguay*

Chappell, Duncan. Director, Australian Institute of Criminology.
CRIME, LAW ENFORCEMENT, AND PENOLOGY: *Crime; Law Enforcement*

Chapple, Abby. Writer and Consumer Consultant, Consumer Communications, Annapolis, Md.
INDUSTRIAL REVIEW: *Furniture*

Cheuse, Alan. Writing Faculty, English Department, George Mason University, Fairfax, Va. Author of *The Grandmothers' Club; Candace; Fall Out of Heaven; The Bohemians.*
LITERATURE: *English (in part)*

Clarke, Judith L. Senior Editor, *Asiaweek,* Hong Kong.
WORLD AFFAIRS: *Kampuchea; Laos; Thailand; Vietnam*

Clarke, R. O. University of Western Australia.
BIOGRAPHIES *(in part);* LABOUR–MANAGEMENT RELATIONS

Cleveland, William A. Editor, Britannica World Data and Britannica Atlas.
MINING

Coe, Michael D. Professor of Anthropology, Yale University. Author of *The Maya.*
Macropædia: PRE-COLUMBIAN CIVILIZATIONS *(in part)*

Cogle, T. C. J. Editor, *Electrical Review,* London.
INDUSTRIAL REVIEW: *Electrical*

Costin, Stanley H. British Correspondent, Nykytekstiili, Finland, and others.
FASHION AND DRESS *(in part)*

Crampton, Richard J. Professor of East Euro-

pean History, University of Kent at Canterbury. Author of *A Short History of Modern Bulgaria; Bulgaria 1878–1918: A History.*
WORLD AFFAIRS: Bulgaria
Cromie, William J. Editor, *The MIT Report,* Massachusetts Institute of Technology; Executive Director, Council for the Advancement of Science Writing.
INDUSTRIAL REVIEW: *Microelectronics; Telecommunications*
Cross, Colin J. Chairman, European Polo Academy.
SPORTS AND GAMES: *Polo*
Crossland, Norman. Former Bonn Correspondent, *The Economist,* London.
WORLD AFFAIRS: *German Democratic Republic; Germany, Federal Republic of*
Crowley, Edward. Editor, *100A1* magazine and Annual Report, Lloyd's Register of Shipping.
INDUSTRIAL REVIEW: *Shipbuilding;* TRANSPORTATION *(in part)*
Cviic, K. F. East European Specialist, *The Economist,* London.
WORLD AFFAIRS: *Yugoslavia*
Czerwinski, Edward J. Chairman, Germanic and Slavic Languages and Literature, State University of New York at Stony Brook.
LITERATURE: *Eastern European (in part); Russian (in part)*
David, Tudor. Education Journalist; former Managing Editor, *Education,* London.
EDUCATION *(in part)*
Davies, C. R. M. Research Lecturer in Criminology and Penology, University of Liverpool, England.
CRIME, LAW ENFORCEMENT, AND PENOLOGY: *Prisons and Penology*
Davis, Donald A. Editor, *Drug & Cosmetic Industry* and *Cosmetic Insider's Report.*
INDUSTRIAL REVIEW: *Pharmaceuticals*
Deam, John B. Technical Director, National Machine Tool Builders Association, McLean, Va.
INDUSTRIAL REVIEW: *Machinery and Machine Tools*
de la Barre, Kenneth. Director, Katimavik, Montreal.
WORLD AFFAIRS: *Arctic Regions*
Deletant, Dennis J. Senior Lecturer in Romanian Studies, University of London. Author of *Colloquial Romanian; Romania* (World Bibliographical Series).
WORLD AFFAIRS: *Romania*
Denselow, Robin. Rock Music Critic, *The Guardian,* London; Current Affairs Reporter, BBC Television.
MUSIC: *Popular*
De Puy, Norman R. Minister, First Baptist Church, Newton Centre, Mass.; Editor and Publisher, *Cabbages and Kings* newsletter.
RELIGION: *Baptist Churches*
Deshayes, Marie-Jose. Head of Documentation Service, International Vine and Wine Office, Paris.
INDUSTRIAL REVIEW: *Beverages (in part)*
Dicks, Geoffrey R. Senior Research Fellow, London Business School. Author of *Sources of World Financial and Banking Information.*
INDUSTRIAL REVIEW: *Introduction*
Dirnbacher, Elfriede. Austrian Civil Servant.
WORLD AFFAIRS: *Austria*
Dixon, Bernard. Science Writer and Consultant. European Editor, *The Scientist.* Author of *Magnificent Microbes; Health and the Human Body.*
HEALTH AND DISEASE: *Mental Health; Overview (in part)*
Dooling, Dave. Manager, Program Development, Alabama Space and Rocket Center, Huntsville.
SPACE EXPLORATION
Dorris, Thomas Hartley. Editor, Ecumenical Press Service, Geneva.
RELIGION: *Lutheran Communion*

Doyle, Peter J. Information Officer, British Glass. Author of *Glass Making Today.*
INDUSTRIAL REVIEW: *Glass*
Earp, John H. Associate Director, London Transport International.
TRANSPORTATION *(in part)*
Edelman, Marian Wright. President, Children's Defense Fund. Author of *Families in Peril.*
SOCIAL SECURITY AND WELFARE SERVICES: Special Report
Eli, C. R. Former Executive Director, U.S. Badminton Association.
SPORTS AND GAMES: *Badminton*
Elliot, Betsy R. Assistant Geography Editor, *Compton's Encyclopedia.*
BIOGRAPHIES *(in part)*
Engels, Jan R. Director, Centre Paul Hymans; Editor, *Vooruitgang-Progrès* magazine.
WORLD AFFAIRS: *Belgium*
Ewing, John. Professor and Chairman, Department of Mathematics, Indiana University. Author of *Puzzle It Out.*
MATHEMATICS
Farr, D. M. L. Professor of History, Carleton University, Ottawa.
WORLD AFFAIRS: *Canada*
Faust, Joan Lee. Garden Editor, *New York Times.*
GARDENING *(in part)*
Fendell, Robert J. Author of *The New Era Car Book and Auto Survival Guide; Encyclopedia of Auto Racing Greats; How to Make Your Car Last.*
SPORTS AND GAMES: *Automobile Racing (in part)*
Fiddick, Peter. Media Editor, *The Guardian,* London.
BIOGRAPHIES *(in part);* PUBLISHING: *Newspapers (in part); Magazines (in part)*
Finkelstein, Ellen. Copy Editor, Encyclopædia Britannica, Inc.
BIOGRAPHIES *(in part)*
Firth, David. Editor, *The Friend,* London; formerly Editor, *Quaker Monthly,* London.
RELIGION: *Religious Society of Friends*
Follett, Christopher. Denmark Correspondent, *The Times,* London; Newscaster, Radio Denmark, English service. Author of *Fodspor paa Cypern.*
WORLD AFFAIRS: *Denmark*
Franklin, Harold. Bridge Correspondent, *Yorkshire Post.*
SPORTS AND GAMES: *Contract Bridge*
Franz, Frederick W. President, Watch Tower Bible and Tract Society of Pennsylvania.
RELIGION: *Jehovah's Witnesses*
Friday, Elbert W., Jr. Assistant Administrator for Weather Services, National Oceanic and Atmospheric Administration.
EARTH SCIENCES: *Meteorology;* METEOROLOGY: Sidebar
Fridovich, Irwin. James B. Duke Professor of Biochemistry, Duke University Medical Center, Durham, N.C.
LIFE SCIENCES: *Molecular Biology (in part)*
Fridovich-Keil, Judith L. Postdoctoral Fellow, Department of Pharmacology, Harvard Medical School, Dana Farber Cancer Institute.
LIFE SCIENCES: *Molecular Biology (in part);* MOLECULAR BIOLOGY: Sidebar
Friskin, Sydney E. Hockey Correspondent, *The Times,* London.
SPORTS AND GAMES: *Billiard Games (in part); Field Hockey*
Frost, David. Rugby Union Writer, *The Guardian,* London.
SPORTS AND GAMES: *Football (in part)*
Gaddum, Anthony H. Chairman, H. T. Gaddum and Company Ltd., Silk Merchants, Macclesfield, Cheshire, England.
INDUSTRIAL REVIEW: *Textiles (in part)*
Gamble, Andrew. Professor of Politics, University of Sheffield, England. Author of *Britain*

in Decline; The Free Economy and the Strong State.
WORLD AFFAIRS: *Western European Affairs:* Special Report
Ganado, Albert. Lawyer, Malta.
WORLD AFFAIRS: *Malta*
Ganguly, Dilip. Senior Correspondent, Associated Press (USA), South Asia Bureau, New Delhi, India.
WORLD AFFAIRS: *Afghanistan; Bangladesh; Bhutan; Burma; Nepal; Pakistan; Sri Lanka*
Gibbons, Anne R. Free-lance Writer.
LIFE SCIENCES: *Entomology*
Gibbons, J. Whitfield. Senior Research Ecologist, Savannah River Ecology Laboratory, Aiken, S.C.
LIFE SCIENCES: *Zoology*
Gillespie, Hugh M. Director of Communications, International Road Federation, Washington, D.C.
ENGINEERING PROJECTS: *Roads*
Gjester, Fay. Free-lance Journalist and Editor; formerly Oslo Correspondent, *Financial Times,* London.
WORLD AFFAIRS: *Norway*
Goldsmith, Arthur. Editor-at-Large, *Popular Photography,* New York City.
PHOTOGRAPHY
Goldstein, William W. Trade News Editor, *Publishers Weekly.*
PUBLISHING: *Books (in part)*
Goodwin, Noël. Free-lance Writer and Broadcaster. Associate Editor and Music Editor, *Dance & Dancers.*
DANCE *(in part)*
Gottfried, Martin. Drama Critic, New York City. Author of *Opening Nights; Broadway Musicals; Jed Harris: The Curse of Genius.*
THEATRE *(in part)*
Green, Anthony L. Copy Editor, Encyclopædia Britannica, Inc.
BIOGRAPHIES *(in part)*
Griffin, Ernst C. Professor and Chairman, Department of Geography, San Diego State University, California.
Macropædia: MEXICO
Griffiths, A. R. G. Senior Lecturer in History, Flinders University of South Australia. Author of *Contemporary Australia.*
BIOGRAPHIES *(in part);* WORLD AFFAIRS: *Australia; Nauru; Papua New Guinea*
Grossman, Joel W. Archaeologist.
ARCHAEOLOGY: *Western Hemisphere*
Guthridge, Guy G. Manager, Polar Information Program, U.S. National Science Foundation. Editor, *Antarctic Journal of the United States,* 1972–80.
WORLD AFFAIRS: *Antarctica*
Harper, Nicholas. Music Writer; Foreign Correspondent, *Fanfare,* Tenafly, N.J.
MUSIC: *Classical*
Havard-Williams, P. Professor of Library and Information Studies, University of Botswana. Emeritus Professor, Loughborough University, Leicestershire, England.
LIBRARIES *(in part)*
Hawkland, William D. Chancellor and Professor of Law, Louisiana State University.
LAW: *Court Decisions*
Hebblethwaite, Peter. Vatican Affairs Writer, *National Catholic Reporter,* Kansas City, Mo.
BIOGRAPHIES *(in part);* RELIGION: *Roman Catholic Church*
Hébert, Pierre. Associate Professor, University of Toronto.
LITERATURE: *French (in part)*
Hendershott, Myrl C. Professor of Oceanography, Scripps Institution of Oceanography, La Jolla, Calif.
EARTH SCIENCES: *Oceanography*
Hess, Marvin G. Executive Vice-President, National Wrestling Coaches Association.
SPORTS AND GAMES: *Wrestling (in part)*
Hoeksema, Klaas J. Assistant Professor, De-

partment of Political Science, Free University, Amsterdam.
WORLD AFFAIRS: *Netherlands, The; Suriname*
Hogg, Sarah. Business and Finance Editor, *The Independent,* London.
ECONOMIC AFFAIRS: Special Report
Hope, Thomas W. Chairman, Hope Reports, Inc., Rochester, N.Y.
MOTION PICTURES *(in part)*
Hunnings, Neville March. Editorial Director, European Law Centre, London. Editor, *Common Market Law Reports.*
LAW: *International Law*
IEIS. International Economic Information Services, London.
ECONOMIC AFFAIRS: *World Economy; Stock Exchanges (in part)*
Ingham, Kenneth. Emeritus Professor of History, University of Bristol, England. Author of *Jan Christian Smuts: The Conscience of a South African.*
WORLD AFFAIRS: *Angola; Kenya; Malawi; Mozambique; Sudan, The; Tanzania; Uganda; Zaire; Zambia; Zimbabwe*
Jackson, Martin. Editor in Chief, *Broadcast* magazine, London.
TELEVISION AND RADIO *(in part)*
Jacquet, Constant H. Staff Associate, Office of Research and Evaluation, National Council of Churches. Editor of *Yearbook of American and Canadian Churches.*
WORLD AFFAIRS: *United States (table)*
Jardine, Adrian. Company Director. Member, Guild of Yachting Writers.
SPORTS AND GAMES: *Sailing*
Jaspert, W. Pincus. Technical and Editorial Consultant. International Editor, *American Printer* and *World-Wide Printer.* Author of *Encyclopaedia of Typefaces.*
INDUSTRIAL REVIEW: *Printing*
Joffé, George. Journalist and Writer on North African and Middle Eastern Affairs.
WORLD AFFAIRS: *Algeria; Morocco; Tunisia*
Jones, Alun. University Lecturer.
WORLD AFFAIRS: *Andorra; Liechtenstein; Luxembourg; Monaco; San Marino*
Jones, D. A. N. Novelist and Critic. Author of *Parade in Pairs; Never Had It So Good.*
LITERATURE: *Introduction; United Kingdom*
Jones, W. Glyn. Professor of European Literature, University of East Anglia, Norwich, England.
LITERATURE: *Danish*
Joseph, Lou. Senior Science Writer, Hill and Knowlton, Chicago.
HEALTH AND DISEASE: *Dentistry*
Jotischky, Helma. Principal Research Officer, Paint Research Association, London.
INDUSTRIAL REVIEW: *Paints and Varnishes*
Kase, Hideaki. Writer. Author of *Han no Kankokujun kashikomaru Nihonjin.*
BIOGRAPHIES *(in part)*
Katz, William A. Professor, School of Library Science, State University of New York, Albany.
PUBLISHING: *Magazines (in part)*
Keene, Raymond. Chess Correspondent, *The Times,* London; International Chess Grandmaster.
SPORTS AND GAMES: *Chess*
Kelleher, John A. New Zealand Journalist. Former Editor, *The Dominion* and *Dominion Sunday Times,* Wellington, N.Z. President, National Press Club of New Zealand.
WORLD AFFAIRS: *New Zealand*
Kellner, Peter. Political Columnist, *The Independent,* London. Author of *The Civil Servants: An Inquiry into Britain's Ruling Class; Callaghan: The Road to Number Ten.*
BIOGRAPHIES *(in part)*; WORLD AFFAIRS: *United Kingdom*
Kennedy, Richard M. Agricultural Economist, Agriculture and Trade Analysis Division of the Economic Research Service, U.S. Department of Agriculture.
AGRICULTURE AND FOOD SUPPLIES *(in part)*
Kilian, Michael D. Washington Columnist, *Chicago Tribune.* Author of *Flying Can Be Fun.*
SPORTS AND GAMES: *Aerial Sports*
Kimche, Jon. Formerly Editor, *New Middle East; Afro-Asian Affairs,* London. Author of *Second Arab Awakening; Palestine or Israel.*
WORLD AFFAIRS: *Israel*
Kind, Joshua B. Professor of Art History, Northern Illinois University, De Kalb. Author of *Rouault; Geometry as Abstract Art.*
MUSEUMS *(in part)*
King, Charles. Press Officer, International Headquarters, Salvation Army.
RELIGION: *Salvation Army*
Kloos, Jean Clark Cameron. Editor, *Timber Trades Journal.*
INDUSTRIAL REVIEW: *Wood Products*
Knecht, Jean. Formerly Assistant Foreign Editor, *Le Monde,* Paris.
BIOGRAPHIES *(in part)*; WORLD AFFAIRS: *France;* FRANCE*: Sidebar*
Knox, Richard A. Managing Editor, *Power Technology International.* Author of *Power Production International* (forthcoming).
INDUSTRIAL REVIEW: *Nuclear Industry*
Krengel, Janet. Economist, Economics Department, Lloyds Bank PLC, London.
BIOGRAPHIES *(in part)*; WORLD AFFAIRS: *Argentina; Bolivia; Ecuador; Peru*
Kushnick, Louis. Lecturer, Department of American Studies, University of Manchester, England.
POPULATIONS AND POPULATION MOVEMENTS: *International Migration;* RACE RELATIONS
Kuznetsov, Felix. Literary Historian and Book Reviewer; Corresponding Member, U.S.S.R. Academy of Sciences.
LITERATURE: *Russian (in part)*
Lamb, Kevin M. Sportswriter, *Chicago Sun-Times.* Author of *Quarterbacks, Nickelbacks & Other Loose Change.*
BIOGRAPHIES *(in part)*; SPORTS AND GAMES: *Football (in part)*
Laqueur, Walter. Codirector, Institute of Contemporary History and Wiener Library, London. Author of *Europe Since Hitler.*
WORLD AFFAIRS: *Introduction*
Laskey, Elizabeth. Copy Editor, Encyclopædia Britannica, Inc.
BIOGRAPHIES *(in part)*
Last, Geoffrey C. Adviser, Ministry of Education, Ethiopia.
WORLD AFFAIRS: *Ethiopia*
Lee, Audrey Bertina. Director of News and Information, Office of Communication, Christian Church (Disciples of Christ).
RELIGION: *Christian Church (Disciples of Christ)*
Legassick, Martin. Coordinator (honorary), Southern Africa Labour Education Project; formerly Senior Lecturer in Sociology, University of Warwick, Coventry, England.
WORLD AFFAIRS: *Dependent States (in part); South Africa*
Legum, Colin. Associate Editor (1947–81), *The Observer;* Editor, *Africa Contemporary Record* and *Third World Reports,* London.
BIOGRAPHIES *(in part)*; WORLD AFFAIRS: *African Affairs*
Lennox-Kerr, Peter. Editor, *High Performance Textiles* and *OE Report;* European Editor, *Textile World.* Author of *The World Fibres Book.*
INDUSTRIAL REVIEW: *Textiles (in part)*
Litsky, Frank. Sportswriter, *New York Times.*
SPORTS AND GAMES: *Ice Hockey (in part)*
Logan, Robert G. Sportswriter, *Chicago Tribune.* Author of *Cubs Win!; So You Think You're a Diehard Cub Fan.*
SPORTS AND GAMES: *Basketball (in part)*

Longmore, Andrew. Free-lance Sportswriter, *The Times;* former Assistant Editor, *The Cricketer.*
BIOGRAPHIES *(in part)*; SPORTS AND GAMES: *Cricket*
Luling, Virginia R. Social Anthropologist.
WORLD AFFAIRS: *Somalia*
Lyles, Jean Caffey. Senior News Editor, *The Lutheran.* Author of *A Practical Vision of Christian Unity.*
RELIGION: *Introduction*
McBride, Gail W. Free-lance Medical Writer and Editor; formerly Medical News Editor, *Journal of the American Medical Association.*
HEALTH AND DISEASE: *Overview (in part)*
McCauley, Martin. Senior Lecturer in Soviet and East European Studies, School of Slavonic and East European Studies, University of London.
BIOGRAPHIES *(in part)*; WORLD AFFAIRS: *Union of Soviet Socialist Republics*
Macdonald, Barrie. Reader in History, Massey University, Palmerston North, N.Z.
BIOGRAPHIES *(in part)*; WORLD AFFAIRS: *Dependent States (in part); Fiji; Kiribati; Oceanian Affairs; Solomon Islands; Tonga; Tuvalu; Vanuatu; Western Samoa*
McGregor, Alan. Geneva Correspondent, *The Times,* London; Swiss Radio International, Bern; ABC, Australia; and RNZ, New Zealand.
WORLD AFFAIRS: *Switzerland*
McLachlan, Keith S. Senior Lecturer, School of Oriental and African Studies, University of London.
WORLD AFFAIRS: *Iran*
Mahn, Renee J. Publications Editor, American Power Boat Association.
SPORTS AND GAMES: *Motorboating*
Mallett, H. M. F. Editor, *Wool Record Weekly Market Report,* Bradford, England.
INDUSTRIAL REVIEW: *Textiles (in part)*
Mango, Andrew. Orientalist and Broadcaster.
WORLD AFFAIRS: *Turkey*
Marty, Martin E. Fairfax M. Cone Distinguished Service Professor of the History of Modern Christianity, University of Chicago.
RELIGION: Special Report
Mateja, James L. Auto Editor, Columnist, and Financial Reporter, *Chicago Tribune.* Author of *Used Cars: Finding the Best Buy.*
INDUSTRIAL REVIEW: *Automobiles (in part)*
Matthews, Ian D. Manager, International Affairs, British Steel Corp.
INDUSTRIAL REVIEW: *Iron and Steel*
Matthíasson, Björn. Economist, Ministry of Finance, Iceland.
WORLD AFFAIRS: *Iceland*
Mazie, David M. Associate of Carl T. Rowan, syndicated columnist. Free-lance Writer.
SOCIAL SECURITY AND WELFARE SERVICES *(in part)*
Mazze, Edward Mark. Professor of Marketing, School of Business Administration, Temple University, Philadelphia.
CONSUMER AFFAIRS *(in part)*; INDUSTRIAL REVIEW: *Advertising*
Mermel, T. W. Consultant; formerly Chairman, Committee on World Register of Dams of the International Commission on Large Dams.
ENGINEERING PROJECTS: *Dams; Dams table*
Meyendorff, John. Professor, Dean of St. Vladimir's Orthodox Theological Seminary; Professor of History, Fordham University, New York City.
RELIGION: *The Orthodox Church; Eastern Non-Chalcedonian Churches*
Millikin, Sandra. Architectural Historian.
ARCHITECTURE; ART EXHIBITIONS AND ART SALES: *Art Exhibitions;* BIOGRAPHIES *(in part)*; MUSEUMS *(in part)*
Miyahara, Masato. Free-lance Industrial Reporter and Technical Writer. Author of *The*

Recent Trends in the American Specialty Steel Industry.
INDUSTRIAL REVIEW: *Automobiles (in part);* INFORMATION PROCESSING AND INFORMATION SYSTEMS *(in part)*
Modiano, Mario. Athens Correspondent, *The Times,* London.
WORLD AFFAIRS: *Greece*
Monaco, Albert M., Jr. Executive Director, United States Volleyball Association.
SPORTS AND GAMES: *Volleyball*
Moragne, Edward P. Index Editor, Encyclopædia Britannica, Inc.
BIOGRAPHIES *(in part)*
Morgenstern, Dan M. Director, Institute of Jazz Studies, Rutgers, The State University of New Jersey. Author of *Jazz People.*
MUSIC: *Jazz*
Morris, Jacqui M. Editor, *Oryx* magazine.
ENVIRONMENT *(in part)*
Morrison, Donald. Special Projects Editor, *Time* magazine.
PUBLISHING: *Newspapers (in part);* WORLD AFFAIRS: *United States;* UNITED STATES: Special Report
Mosey, Chris. Associate Editor, *Sweden Now,* Stockholm; Nordic Correspondent, *The Observer;* Swedish Correspondent, *The Times* and *Daily Mail.*
WORLD AFFAIRS: *Sweden*
Murra, John V. President, Institute of Andean Research, New York City. Emeritus Professor of Anthropology, Cornell University, Ithaca, N.Y. Author of *The Economic Organization of the Inka State* and others.
Macropædia: PRE-COLUMBIAN CIVILIZATIONS *(in part)*
Myers, Susan Marts. Index Editor, Encyclopædia Britannica, Inc.
BIOGRAPHIES *(in part)*
Nadelmann, Ethan A. Assistant Professor of Politics and Public Affairs, Woodrow Wilson School of Public and International Affairs, Princeton University.
CRIME, LAW ENFORCEMENT, AND PENOLOGY: Special Report
Napier, Elspeth. Editor of publications of the Royal Horticultural Society.
GARDENING *(in part)*
Naylor, Ernest. Lloyd Roberts Professor of Marine Zoology, University College of North Wales.
LIFE SCIENCES: *Marine Biology*
Nelson, Bert. Editor, *Track and Field News.* Author of *Olympic Track and Field.*
SPORTS AND GAMES: *Track and Field Sports*
Netschert, Bruce C. Vice-President, National Economic Research Associates, Inc., Washington, D.C.
ENERGY
Neusner, Jacob. University Professor, Brown University, Providence, R.I. Author of *Judaism, The Evidence of the Mishnah.*
RELIGION: *Judaism*
Newby, Donald J. Bowls Correspondent, *Daily Telegraph,* London; former Editor, *World Bowls.*
SPORTS AND GAMES: *Lawn Bowls*
Newton, Carolyn D. Associate Science Editor, *Compton's Encyclopedia.*
BIOGRAPHIES *(in part)*
Niesz, Dale E. Director, Center for Ceramic Research, Rutgers, The State University of New Jersey.
INDUSTRIAL REVIEW: *Ceramics*
Nixon, Robert W. Director, Communication Department, General Conference of Seventh-day Adventists, Washington, D.C.
RELIGION: *Seventh-day Adventist Church*
Noblett, Geoffrey J. Night Operations Manager, Channel Tunnel Project Transmanche Link Joint Venture, London.
ENGINEERING PROJECTS: *Tunnels*
Norman, Geraldine. Art Market Correspon-

dent, *The Independent,* London. Author of *The Sale of Works of Art; Nineteenth Century Painters and Painting; Biedermeier Painting;* Coauthor of *The Fake's Progress.*
ART EXHIBITIONS AND ART SALES: *Art Sales*
Oberman, Bonnie. Writer and Editor.
BIOGRAPHIES *(in part)*
O'Donoghue, Michael. Curator, Science Reference Library, London; Lecturer in Gemmology, City of London Polytechnic.
INDUSTRIAL REVIEW: *Gemstones*
O'Dwyer, Thomas. Director, Levant Bureau; Formerly Reuters Bureau Chief, Cyprus; Writer on East Mediterranean and Arab Affairs, Nicosia, Cyprus.
BIOGRAPHIES *(in part);* WORLD AFFAIRS: *Cyprus*
Olney, P. J. Curator of Birds and Reptiles, Zoological Society of London. Editor, *International Zoo Yearbook.*
BOTANICAL GARDENS AND ZOOS *(in part)*
Osborne, Keith. Editor, *British Rowing Almanack.* Author of *Boat Racing in Britain, 1715–1975.*
SPORTS AND GAMES: *Rowing*
Osterbind, Carter C. Associate, Gerontology Center, and Professor Emeritus of Economics, University of Florida.
INDUSTRIAL REVIEW: *Building and Construction*
O'Toole, James. University Associates' Chair, Graduate School of Business, University of Southern California. Author of *Vanguard Management.*
Feature Article: FROM MARX TO MADISON: SOCIALISM'S CULTURAL CONTRADICTIONS
Palmer, John. European Editor, *The Guardian,* London.
WORLD AFFAIRS: *Western European Affairs*
Palmer, S. B. Professor of Experimental Physics, Department of Physics, University of Warwick, England.
PHYSICS
Parker, Sandy. Publisher of weekly international newsletter on fur industry; Copublisher, *Fur World.*
INDUSTRIAL REVIEW: *Furs*
Paul, Charles Robert, Jr. Special Assistant to the Secretary-General, U.S. Olympic Committee, Colorado Springs.
SPORTS AND GAMES: *Gymnastics; Weight Lifting*
Penfold, Robin C. Free-lance Writer on industrial topics. Formerly Editor, *Shell Petrochemicals.* Author of *A Journalist's Guide to Plastics.*
INDUSTRIAL REVIEW: *Plastics*
Perlinska, Agnieszka K. Graduate Research Assistant, Germanic and Slavic Languages and Literatures, State University of New York at Stony Brook.
LITERATURE: *Eastern European (in part); Russian (in part)*
Pertile, Lino. Professor of Italian, University of Edinburgh, Scotland.
LITERATURE: *Italian*
Petherick, Karin. Reader in Swedish, University of London.
LITERATURE: *Swedish*
Pfeffer, Irving. Attorney. Author of *The Financing of Small Business.*
ECONOMIC AFFAIRS: *Stock Exchanges (in part)*
Pinfold, Geoffrey M. Director, NCL Stewart Scott Ltd., London. Author of *Reinforced Concrete Chimneys and Towers.*
ENGINEERING PROJECTS: *Buildings*
Plotnik, Arthur. Editor, *American Libraries* magazine, American Library Association.
LIBRARIES *(in part)*
Poirié, François. Writer and Critic. Author of *La Passade légendaire.*
LITERATURE: *French (in part)*
Pollack, Jonathan D. Department Head, Po-

litical Science Department, Rand Corp., Santa Monica, Calif.
WORLD AFFAIRS: *China; Taiwan*
Post, Avery D. President, United Church of Christ, New York City.
RELIGION: *United Church of Christ*
Prasad, H. Y. Sharada. Secretary, Indira Gandhi Memorial Trust, New Delhi, India.
WORLD AFFAIRS: *India*
Prince, Rod. Journalist specializing in Caribbean matters. Editor, *Caribbean Insight.*
WORLD AFFAIRS: *Antigua and Barbuda; Bahamas, The; Barbados; Dependent States (in part); Dominica; Grenada; Guyana; Jamaica; Saint Kitts and Nevis; Saint Lucia; Saint Vincent and the Grenadines; Trinidad and Tobago*
Ranger, Robin. Peace Fellow, U.S. Institute of Peace, Washington, D.C. Author of *Arms and Politics 1958–1978; Arms Control in a Changing Political Context.*
MILITARY AFFAIRS
Read, Anthony A. Director, Book Development Council, London.
PUBLISHING: *Books (in part)*
Rebelo, L. S. Reader Emeritus, Department of Portuguese Studies, King's College, University of London.
LITERATURE: *Portuguese (in part)*
Reed, Dwight C. President, National Soft Drink Association, Washington, D.C.
INDUSTRIAL REVIEW: *Beverages (in part)*
Reid, J. H. Reader in German, University of Nottingham, England. Author of *Heinrich Böll: Withdrawal and Re-emergence; Heinrich Böll: A German for His Time.*
LITERATURE: *German*
Reid, Philip D. Professor of Biological Sciences, Smith College, Northampton, Mass.
LIFE SCIENCES: *Botany*
Reynolds, Frank E. Professor of the History of Religions and Buddhist Studies, Divinity School, University of Chicago.
RELIGION: *Buddhism (in part)*
Ripley, Michael D. Senior Public Relations Officer, Brewers' Society, U.K.
INDUSTRIAL REVIEW: *Beverages (in part)*
Robinson, David. Film Critic, *The Times,* London. Author of *A History of World Cinema; Chaplin: His Life and Art.*
MOTION PICTURES *(in part)*
Rollin, Jack. Association Football Columnist, *Sunday Telegraph,* London. Editor, *Rothmans Football Yearbook.* Author of *England's World Cup Triumph; Guinness Book of Soccer Facts and Feats.*
SPORTS AND GAMES: *Football (in part)*
Saeki, Shoichi. Professor of Literature, Chuo University, Tokyo. Author of *In Search of Japanese Ego.*
BIOGRAPHIES *(in part);* LITERATURE: *Japanese*
Sanders, Alan J. K. Editor, U.S.S.R. edition, *Summary of World Broadcasts,* BBC. Author of *Mongolia: Politics, Economics and Society.*
WORLD AFFAIRS: *Mongolia*
Sarahete, Yrjö. General Secretary, Fédération Internationale des Quilleurs, Helsinki.
SPORTS AND GAMES: *Bowling (in part)*
Sarmiento, Sergio. Editor in Chief, Spanish-language publications, Encyclopædia Britannica Publishers, Inc.
SPORTS AND GAMES: *Baseball (in part); Football (in part)*
Schaeffer, Reverend Jill. Secretary, Department of Cooperation and Witness, World Alliance of Reformed Churches, Geneva.
RELIGION: *Reformed, Presbyterian, and Congregational Churches*
Schoenfield, Albert. Formerly Publisher, *Swimming World;* Vice-Chairman, U.S. Olympic Swimming Committee; Honoree, International Swimming Hall of Fame.
SPORTS AND GAMES: *Swimming*
Schöpflin, George. Lecturer in East European Political Institutions, London School of Eco-

nomics and School of Slavonic and East European Studies, University of London.
WORLD AFFAIRS: *Czechoslovakia; Eastern European Affairs; Hungary*
Shackleford, Peter. Chief of Research, World Tourism Organization, Madrid.
INDUSTRIAL REVIEW: *Tourism*
Shelley, Andrew. Squash Manager, Squash Rackets Association, England.
SPORTS AND GAMES: *Squash Rackets*
Shepherd, Melinda. Associate Editor, Encyclopædia Britannica Yearbooks.
BIOGRAPHIES *(in part)*; WORLD AFFAIRS: *Dependent States (in part)*
Sherman, Francine Shonfeld. Assistant Editor Trainee, Compton's Encyclopedia.
BIOGRAPHIES *(in part)*
Smith, Donald. Editor, *Rubber World* magazine, Akron, Ohio.
INDUSTRIAL REVIEW: *Rubber*
Smith, Reuben W. Dean, Graduate School, and Professor of History, University of the Pacific, Stockton, Calif.
RELIGION: *Islam*
Smogorzewski, K. M. Writer on contemporary history. Founder and Editor, *Free Europe,* London.
BIOGRAPHIES *(in part)*; WORLD AFFAIRS: *Poland; Political Parties (in part)*
Snijder, Suzanne Lark. Publications, Central Office, International Organization of Consumers Unions.
CONSUMER AFFAIRS *(in part)*
Soustelle, Jacques. Professor of Social Anthropology, School of Advanced Studies in the Social Sciences, Paris. Author of *La Vie quotidienne des Aztèques* and others.
Macropædia: PRE-COLUMBIAN CIVILIZATIONS *(in part)*
Stern, Irwin. Assistant Professor of Portuguese, Columbia University, New York City.
LITERATURE: *Portuguese (in part)*
Stevens, Kate. Director, Gameway Ltd.; former Assistant Editor, *British Toys and Hobbies Briefing.*
INDUSTRIAL REVIEW: *Games and Toys*
Støverud, Torbjørn. Honorary Research Fellow, University College, London.
LITERATURE: *Norwegian*
Sullivan, H. Patrick. Dean of the College and Professor of Religion, Vassar College, Poughkeepsie, N.Y.
RELIGION: *Hinduism*
Summerhill, Edward M. Staff Member, Reuters; Free-lance Writer, Finnish News Agency.
WORLD AFFAIRS: *Finland*
Sumner, David E. Ph.D. Candidate and Journalism Instructor, College of Communications, University of Tennessee, Knoxville. Author of *The Episcopal Church's History: 1945–1985.*
RELIGION: *Anglican Communion*
Suzuki, Toshihiko. Associate Editor, *Newsweek Japan,* TBS-Britannica Co., Ltd., Tokyo.
SPORTS AND GAMES: *Baseball (in part)*
Sweetinburgh, Thelma. Fashion Writer, Paris.
FASHION AND DRESS *(in part)*
Swift, Richard N. Professor Emeritus of Politics, New York University, New York City.
WORLD AFFAIRS: *United Nations*
Synan, Vinson. Chairman, North American Renewal Service Committee. Author of *The Holiness-Pentecostal Movement.*
RELIGION: *Pentecostal Churches*

Taggart, Charles Johnson. Free-lance Writer.
BIOGRAPHIES *(in part)*
Taishoff, Lawrence B. President, Broadcasting Publications, Inc., and Publisher, *Broadcasting* magazine and others.
TELEVISION AND RADIO *(in part)*
Tak, Jean van der. Formerly Senior Editor, Population Reference Bureau, Inc.
POPULATIONS AND POPULATION MOVEMENTS: *Demography*
Talbot, Nathan A. Manager, Committees on Publication, The First Church of Christ, Scientist, Boston.
RELIGION: *Church of Christ, Scientist*
Tateishi, Kay K. Free-lance Writer and Translator.
BIOGRAPHIES *(in part)*
Tingay, Lance. Former Tennis Correspondent, *Daily Telegraph,* London. Author of *100 Years of Wimbledon; Tennis Facts and Feats.*
SPORTS AND GAMES: *Tennis*
Trilling, Ossia. Coeditor and Contributor, *International Theatre.* Contributor, BBC, *The Times,* London, and other media.
BIOGRAPHIES *(in part)*; THEATRE *(in part)*; THEATRE: Sidebar
UNHCR. The Office of the United Nations High Commissioner for Refugees.
POPULATIONS AND POPULATION MOVEMENTS: *Refugees*
Utt, Roger L. Editor, *Puerta del Sol;* formerly Assistant Professor of Spanish, Department of Romance Languages and Literatures, University of Chicago.
LITERATURE: *Spanish (in part)*
Vale, Norman K. Retired Director of News Services, The United Church of Canada.
RELIGION: *The United Church of Canada*
Van Haveren, Bruce P. Adjunct Professor, Department of Environmental Sciences, Colorado School of Mines, Golden. Author of *Water Resource Measurements: A Handbook.*
EARTH SCIENCES: *Hydrology*
Venzke, Bruce H. Associate Editor, *Pool & Billiard Magazine;* Member, Statistics and Records Committee, Billiard Congress of America; President, Billiard Congress of Wisconsin.
SPORTS AND GAMES: *Billiard Games (in part)*
Verdi, Robert William. Sports Columnist, *Chicago Tribune.*
SPORTS AND GAMES: *Baseball (in part)*
Villacorta, Lynn. Social Security Specialist, International Labour Office, Geneva.
SOCIAL SECURITY AND WELFARE SERVICES *(in part)*
Vint, Arthur Kingsley. Counselor, International Table Tennis Federation.
SPORTS AND GAMES: *Table Tennis*
Walters, Jonathan S. Ph.D. Candidate, Divinity School, University of Chicago.
RELIGION: *Buddhism (in part)*
Warner, Antony C. Managing Director, Warner, Robinson and Associates, London.
INDUSTRIAL REVIEW: *Beverages (in part)*
Warner, Edward S. Associate Managing Editor, *High Technology Business* magazine.
INFORMATION PROCESSING AND INFORMATION SYSTEMS *(in part)*; INFORMATION PROCESSING AND INFORMATION SYSTEMS: Sidebar
Watkin, David J. Lecturer in the History of Art, University of Cambridge. Author of *Thomas Hope 1769–1831 and the Neo-Classical Idea* and others.
Macropædia: ARCHITECTURE, THE HISTORY OF WESTERN *(in part)*

Way, Diane Lois. Historical Researcher.
BIOGRAPHIES *(in part)*
Weinthal, John R. Writer on the automotive industry.
INDUSTRIAL REVIEW: *Automobiles (in part)*
Welch, Melvin D. Secretary, English Basket Ball Association; Editor (1971–78), *Basketball Magazine.*
SPORTS AND GAMES: *Basketball (in part)*
Whelan, John. Publishing Director, *Middle East Economic Digest.*
WORLD AFFAIRS: *Bahrain; Egypt; Iraq; Jordan; Kuwait; Lebanon; Middle Eastern and North African Affairs; Oman; Qatar; Saudi Arabia; Syria; United Arab Emirates; Yemen, People's Democratic Republic of; Yemen Arab Republic*
Wilkinson, John R. Sportswriter, East Midland Provincial Newspapers Ltd., U.K.
SPORTS AND GAMES: *Cycling*
Willey, Gordon R. Bowditch Professor Emeritus of Mexican and Central American Archaeology, Harvard University. Author of *An Introduction to American Archaeology.*
Macropædia: PRE-COLUMBIAN CIVILIZATIONS *(in part)*
Williams, Michael. Golf Correspondent, *Daily Telegraph,* London.
SPORTS AND GAMES: *Golf*
Williams, Raymond Leslie. Professor of Spanish, University of Colorado, Boulder.
LITERATURE: *Spanish (in part)*
Wilson, Michael. Free-lance Aviation Writer and Consultant.
INDUSTRIAL REVIEW: *Aerospace*
Winton, John M. Senior Editor, McGraw-Hill, Inc., New York City.
INDUSTRIAL REVIEW: *Chemicals*
Witte, Randall E. Editor, *The Western Horseman* magazine, Colorado Springs, Colo.
SPORTS AND GAMES: *Rodeo*
Woodrow, Robert. Assistant Managing Editor, *Asiaweek,* Hong Kong.
BIOGRAPHIES *(in part)*; WORLD AFFAIRS: *Dependent States (in part); Korea; Southeast Asian Affairs*
Woods, Elizabeth. Writer. Author of *The Yellow Volkswagen; Gone; Men; The Amateur.*
LITERATURE: *English (in part)*
Woollen, Anthony. Editor (1959–79), *Food Manufacture,* London. Editor, *Food Industries Manual* (20th ed.).
AGRICULTURE AND FOOD SUPPLIES: *Food Processing*
Wooller, Michael. Economist, Economics Dept., Lloyds Bank PLC, London.
WORLD AFFAIRS: *Portugal; Spain*
Woolley, David. International Editor, *Airline Executive;* Contributing Editor, *Airport Forum.*
TRANSPORTATION *(in part)*
Wyllie, Peter John. Division of Geological and Planetary Sciences, California Institute of Technology.
EARTH SCIENCES: *Geology and Geochemistry*
Yang, Winston L. Y. Chairman, Department of Asian Studies, Seton Hall University, South Orange, N.J.
BIOGRAPHIES *(in part)*; LITERATURE: *Chinese*
Young, M. Norvel. Chancellor Emeritus, Pepperdine University, Malibu, Calif. Author of *Preachers of Today.*
RELIGION: *Churches of Christ*
Zeidenberg, Leonard. Chief Correspondent, *Broadcasting* magazine, Washington, D.C.
TELEVISION AND RADIO *(in part)*

1989
Britannica
World Data

Encyclopædia Britannica, Inc.
Chicago
Auckland/Geneva/London/Madrid/Manila/Paris/Rome
Seoul/Sydney/Tokyo/Toronto

Editor	William A. Cleveland
Associate Editors	Marino P. PeBenito, Joseph R. Sturgis
Research Editors	Rosaline Keys, W. Peter Kindel, Stephen Neher, Lyudmila Skoropistsev
Editorial Assistant	Elizabeth B. Luft
Consultant	M. C. MacDonald, Director World Economics, Ltd., London
Director, Yearbook Production and Control	J. Thomas Beatty
Manager, Copy Department	Anita Wolff
Copy Coordinator	Dennis Skord
Copy Staff	Carol Smith, Judith West
Manager, Production Control	Mary C. Srodon
Production Control Staff	Marilyn L. Barton, Vernetta McCoy, Yvonne G. Pua
Manager, Composition and Page Makeup	Melvin Stagner
Coordinator, Composition and Page Makeup	Philip Rehmer
Composition Staff	Duangnetra Debhavalya, Morna Freund, John Krom, Jr., Thomas Mulligan, Gwen E. Rosenberg, Tammy Tsou
Page Makeup Staff	Michael Born, Jr., Griselda Cháidez, Arnell Reed, Danette Wetterer
Director, Editorial Computer Services	Michelle J. Brandhorst
Art Director	Cynthia Peterson
Manager, Map Group	Gerzilla Leszczynski
Cartography Staff	Steven Bogdan
Typographic Designer	Harvey Retzloff
Manager, Index Department	Frances E. Latham
Librarian	Terry Miller
Associate Librarian	Shantha Uddin
Curator/Geography	David W. Foster
Assistant Librarian	Robert M. Lewis

Editorial Administration
Editor in Chief, Philip W. Goetz
Managing Editor, Michael Reed
Executive Director of Editorial Production, Karen M. Barch
Director of Budgets and Controller, Carl Holzman

Encyclopædia Britannica, Inc.
Chairman of the Board, Robert P. Gwinn
President, Peter B. Norton

© 1989

BY ENCYCLOPÆDIA BRITANNICA, INC.

Copyright Under International Copyright Union
All Rights Reserved Under International and Universal Copyright Conventions
by Encyclopædia Britannica, Inc.

No part of this work may be reproduced or utilized in any form or by
any means, electronic or mechanical, including photocopying, recording,
or by any information storage and retrieval system, without permission in writing from the publisher.

CONTENTS

INTRODUCTION

Britannica World Data provides a statistical portrait of some 220 countries and dependencies of the world, at a level appropriate to the size and importance of each. It contains 186 country statements, ranging in length from one to four pages, for the largest and most significant of these, and permits, in the development of more than a score of major thematic subject areas (employment, agriculture, trade), simultaneous comparison among all of these larger countries and 34 additional smaller dependent states.

Updated annually, *Britannica World Data* can be consulted as a separate work of reference developing a particular body of subject matter, but it is particularly intended as direct, structured support for many of Britannica's other reference works—encyclopedias, yearbooks, atlases—at a level of detail that their editorial style or space requirements do not permit.

Like the textual, graphic, or cartographic modes of expression of these other products, statistics possess their own inherent editorial virtues and weaknesses. Two principal goals in the creation of *Britannica World Data* were up-to-dateness and comparability, each possible separately, but not always possible to combine. If, for example, research on some subject (say, registered motor vehicles) is completed during a particular year (x), figures may be available for 100 countries for the preceding year ($x - 1$), for 140 countries for the year before that ($x - 2$), and for 180 countries for the year before that ($x - 3$).

Which year should be the basis of a thematic compilation for 220 countries so as to give the best combination of up-to-dateness and comparability? And, should $x - 1$ be adopted for the thematic table, ought up-to-dateness in the country table (for which year x is already available) be sacrificed for agreement with the thematic table? In general, the editors have opted for maximum up-to-dateness in the country statistical boxes and maximum comparability in the thematic tables, so as to take the best advantage of late information, published and unpublished.

Comparability, however, also resides in the meaning of the numbers compiled, which may differ greatly from country to country. The headnotes to the thematic tables explain many of these definitional problems; the Glossary serves the same purpose for the country statistical pages. Since the researcher or editor does not always find a neat, unambiguous choice between a datum compiled on two different bases (say, railroad track length, or route length), one of which is wanted and the other not, a choice must be made between the latest official national data (which may be incomplete, published only after a delay of several years, politically suspect, compiled on the wrong basis [for international comparability], or may refer to some time period other than a standard Gregorian calendar year) and some external figure, often only an estimate, compiled by an international organization (such as the

UN, FAO, or IMF), on the desired basis, but often at a considerable remove from the country's own most recent data, both in time and distance. Every effort has been made to obtain the best combination of comparability and up-to-dateness from available sources, and, when the completeness of a country's published data permitted, to analyze it further for better agreement in coverage, scope, and datedness, For certain subjects, especially population, the editors have prepared their own estimates.

The published basis of the information compiled is the statistical collections of Encyclopædia Britannica, Inc., some of the principal elements of which are enumerated in the Bibliography. All of these sources are held, and updated continuously for editorial use, in Britannica's editorial offices. The publications themselves are issued in some 75 languages in common use among the countries of the world; the information contained in them is supplemented by unpublished data received in correspondence from the countries concerned. Usual holdings for a country with a well-developed statistical and publishing program may include any of the following kinds of documents: the national statistical abstract; the most recent censuses of population; periodic or occasional reports on vital statistics, social indicators, agriculture, mining, labour, manufacturing, wholesale and retail trade, finance and banking, development planning, foreign trade, transportation, and communication. These primarily statistical sources are supplemented by other kinds of national reference works, such as gazetteers (of place names), national atlases, constitutions, and monographs by domestic or external analysts.

No reference work on the countries of the world can, or should, be used in isolation. To say that the population density of Hungary is about 300 persons per square mile will not be misleading, because the population is rather evenly distributed across the landscape outside the cities. To give a density for Greenland calculated on the same basis (total population ÷ total area) *would* be misleading (and would amount to only 0.06 person per square mile) because much of Greenland is uninhabitable ice cap. Similarly, the great majority of the social, economic, and financial data contained in this work should not be interpreted in isolation. Interpretive text of long perspective, such as that of the *Encyclopædia Britannica* itself; political, geographic, and topical maps; and recent analysis of political events and economic trends, such as that contained in the articles of the *Book of the Year,* will all help to supply balance, physical framework, and analytical focus that numbers alone cannot provide. By the same token, study of those sources will be amplified and made more concrete by use of the *Britannica World Data* to supply up-to-date geographic, demographic, economic, and financial data to illuminate the generalized and more impressionistic methodology of those works.

GLOSSARY

A number of terms that are used to classify and report data in the "Nations of the World" section require some explanation.

Those italicized terms that are used regularly in the country compilations to introduce specific categories of information (*e.g., birth rate, budget*) appear in this glossary in italic boldface type, followed by a description of the precise kind of information being offered and how it has been edited and presented.

All other terms are printed here in roman boldface type. Many terms have quite specific meanings in statistical reporting, and they are so defined here. Other terms have less specific application as they are used by different countries or organizations. Data in the country compilations based on definitions markedly different from those below will usually be footnoted.

Terms that appear in small capitals in certain definitions are themselves defined at their respective alphabetical locations.

Terms whose definitions are marked by an asterisk (*) refer to data supplied only in the larger two- to four-page country compilations.

access to services, a group of measures indicating the general population's level of access to public services, including electrical power, treated public drinking water, sewage removal, and fire protection.*

activity rate, *see* participation rate.

age breakdown, the distribution of a given population by age, usually reported here as percentages of total population in each of six 15-year age brackets. When substantial numbers of persons do not know, or state, their exact age, distributions may not total 100.0%.

area, the total surface area of a country or its administrative subdivisions, including both land and inland (nontidal) water area. Land area is usually calculated from "mean low water" on a "plane table," or "flat," basis.

area and population, a tabulation usually including the first-order administrative subdivisions of the country (such as the states of the United States), with capital or administrative seat, area, and population. When these subdivisions are especially numerous or, occasionally, nonexistent, a regional, electoral, census, or other nonadministrative scheme of subdivisions has been substituted.

associated state, *see* (free) association; *see* state.

atheist, in statements of religious affiliation, one who professes active opposition to religion; "nonreligious" refers to those professing only no religion, nonbelief, or doubt.

balance of payments, a financial statement for a country for a given period showing the balance among: (1) transactions in goods, services, and income between that country and the rest of the world, (2) changes in ownership or valuation of that country's monetary gold, SPECIAL DRAWING RIGHTS, and claims on and liabilities to the rest of the world, and (3) unrequited transfers and counterpart entries needed (in an accounting sense) to balance transactions and changes among any of the foregoing types of exchange that are not mutually offsetting. The United Nations *System of National Accounts* (SNA) provides a framework for international comparability in classifying such transactions, but detail of local law as to what constitutes a transaction, the basis of its valuation, and the size of a transaction visible to fiscal authorities all result in differences in the meaning of a particular national statement.*

balance of trade, the net value of all international-goods trade of a country, usually excluding reexports (goods received only for transshipment), and the percentage that this net represents of total trade.

Balance of trade refers only to the "visible" international trade of goods as recorded by customs authorities and is thus a segment of a country's BALANCE OF PAYMENTS, which takes all visible and invisible trade with other countries into account. (Invisible trade refers to imports and exports of money, financial instruments, and services such as transport, tourism, and insurance.) A country has a favourable balance of trade when the value of exports exceeds that of imports.

barrel (bbl), a unit of liquid measure. The barrel conventionally used for reporting crude petroleum and petroleum products is equal to 42 U.S. gallons, or 159 litres. The number of barrels of crude petroleum per metric ton, ranging typically from 6.45 to 8.13, depends upon the specific gravity of the petroleum. The world average is roughly 7.33 barrels per ton.

birth rate, the number of live births annually per 1,000 of midyear population. Birth rates for individual countries may be compared with the world annual average of 29 births per 1,000 population between 1980 and 1985.

budget, the annual receipts and expenditures of the central government for its activities only; does not include state, provincial, or local governments or semipublic (parastatal, quasi-nongovernmental) corporations unless otherwise specified. Figures for budgets are limited to ordinary (recurrent) receipts and expenditures, wherever possible, and exclude capital expenditures, *i.e.,* funds for development and other special projects originating as foreign-aid grants or loans.

When both a recurrent and a capital budget exist for a single country, the former is the budget funded entirely from national resources (taxes, duties, excises, etc.) that would recur year by year as would be generated by economic activity every year. It funds the most basic governmental services, those least able to stand interruption. The capital budget is usually funded by exter-

Abbreviations

Measurements

cu m	cubic metre(s)
kg	kilogram(s)
km	kilometre(s)
kW	kilowatt(s)
kW-hr	kilowatt-hour(s)
metric ton-km	metric ton-kilometre(s)
mi	mile(s)
passenger-km	passenger-kilometre(s)
passenger-mi	passenger-mile(s)
short ton-mi	short ton-mile(s)
sq km	square kilometre(s)
sq m	square metre(s)
sq mi	square mile(s)
troy oz	troy ounce(s)
yr	year(s)

Political Units and International Organizations

CARICOM	Caribbean Community and Common Market
CUSA	Customs Union of Southern Africa
E.Ger.	East Germany
EEC	European Economic Community
FAO	United Nations Food and Agriculture Organization
IMF	International Monetary Fund
OECS	Organization of Eastern Caribbean States
U.A.E.	United Arab Emirates
U.K.	United Kingdom
U.S.	United States
U.S.S.R.	Union of Soviet Socialist Republics
W.Ger.	West Germany

Months

Jan.	January	Oct.	October
Feb.	February	Nov.	November
Aug.	August	Dec.	December
Sept.	September		

Miscellaneous

avg.	average
c.i.f.	cost, insurance, and freight
commun.	communications
est.	estimate(d)
excl.	excluding
f.o.b.	free on board
GDP	gross domestic product
GNP	gross national product
govt.	government
incl.	including
mo.	month(s)
n.a.	not available (in text)
n.e.s.	not elsewhere specified
NMP	net material product
no.	number
pl.	plural
pos.	position
pub. admin.	public administration
SDR	Special Drawing Right
SITC	Standard International Trade Classification
svcs.	services
teacher tr.	teacher training
transp.	transportation
voc.	vocational
$	dollar (of any currency area)
£	pound (of any currency area)
...	not available (in tables)
—	none, less than half the smallest unit shown, or not applicable (in tables)

nal aid and may change its size considerably from year to year.

capital, usually, the actual seat of administration and government of a state. When more than one capital exists, each is identified by kind; when interim arrangements exist during the creation or movement of a national capital, the de facto situation is described.

Anomalous cases are footnoted, such as those in which (1) the de jure designation under the country's laws differs from actual local practice (*e.g.,* Benin's designation of one capital in constitutional law, but another in actual practice), (2) international recognition does not support a country's claim (as with the proclamation by Israel of a capital on territory not fully recognized as part of Israel), or (3) both a state and a capital have been proclaimed on territory recognized as part of another state (as with the Turkish Republic of Northern Cyprus).

capital budget, *see* budget.

causes of death, as defined by the World Health Organization, "the disease or injury which initiated the train of morbid events leading directly to death, or the circumstances of accident or violence which produced the fatal injury." This principle, the "underlying cause of death," is the basis of the medical judgment as to cause; the statistical classification system according to which these causes are grouped and named is the *International List of Causes of Death,* the latest revision of which is the Ninth. Reporting is usually in terms of events per 100,000 population. When data on actual causes of death are unavailable, information on morbidity, or illness rate, usually given as reported cases per 100,000 of infectious diseases (notifiable to WHO as a matter of international agreement), may be substituted.

chief of state/head of government, paramount national governmental officer(s) exercising the highest executive and/or ceremonial roles of a country's government. In general usage, the chief of state is the formal head of a national state. The primary responsibilities of the chief of state may range from the purely ceremonial—convening legislatures and greeting foreign officials—to the exercise of complete national executive authority. The head of government, when this function exists separately, is the officer nominally charged (by the constitution) with the majority of actual executive powers, though they may not in practice be exercised, especially in military or single-party regimes in which effective power may reside entirely outside the executive governmental machinery provided by the constitution. A prime minister, for example, usually understood to be the head of government, may in practice exercise only cabinet-level authority. The head of government of a dependent political unit is the chief executive officer, either appointive or elective, who wields the most local executive prerogatives, regardless of administrative prerogatives reserved elsewhere.

In communist countries the official identified as the chief of state is the chairman of the policy-making organ, and the official given as the head of government is the chairman of the nominal administrative/executive organ.

c.i.f. (trade valuation): *see* imports.

colony, an area annexed to, or controlled by, an independent state but not an integral part of it; a non-self-governing territory. A colony has a charter and may have a degree of self-government. A crown colony is a colony originally chartered by the British government.

commonwealth (U.S.), a self-governing political entity associated with the United States; examples are Puerto Rico since 1952, or the Northern Marianas since 1979.

communications, collectively, the means available for the public transmission of information within a country. Data are provided for daily newspapers, their number and total cir-

culation, and the per capita rate of circulation implied by that total; for radio, television, and telephone receivers, total numbers and rates of availability are supplied.

constant prices, an adjustment to the members of a time series (of values) to eliminate the effect of inflation year by year. It consists of referring all data in the series to a single year so that "real" change may be seen.

constitutional monarchy, *see* monarchy.

consumer price index, also known as the retail price index, or the cost-of-living index, a series of index numbers assigned to the price of a selected "basket," or assortment, of basic consumer goods and services in a country or region to measure changes over time in prices paid by a typical household for those goods and services. Items included in the consumer price index are ordinarily determined by governmental surveys of typical household expenditures and are assigned weights relative to their proportion of those expenditures. Index values are period averages unless otherwise noted.

coprincipality, *see* monarchy.

current prices, the valuation of a financial aggregate as of the year reported, without adjustment for inflation.

daily per capita caloric intake (supply), the calories equivalent to the known average daily supply of foodstuffs for human consumption in a given country divided by the population of the country (and the proportion of that supply provided, respectively, by vegetable and animal sources). This measure may differ from actual daily per capita consumption of food as a result of waste, inefficient distribution, and exploitation of sources of food not included in the known supply of foodstuffs. The daily per capita caloric intake of a country may be compared with the corresponding recommended daily per capita caloric requirement. The latter is calculated by the Food and Agriculture Organization of the United Nations from the age and sex distributions, average body weights, and environmental temperatures in a given region to determine the calories needed to sustain a person there at normal levels of activity

and health. The daily per capita caloric requirement ranges from 2,200 to 2,500.

de facto population, for a given area, the population composed of those actually present at a particular time, including temporary residents and visitors (such as immigrants not yet granted permanent status, "guest" or expatriate workers, refugees, or tourists), but excluding legal residents temporarily absent.

de jure population, for a given area, the population composed only of those legally resident at a particular time, excluding temporary residents and visitors (such as "guest" or expatriate workers, refugees, or tourists), but including legal residents temporarily absent.

deadweight tonnage, the maximum weight of cargo, fuel, fresh water, stores, and persons that may safely be carried by a ship. It is customarily measured in long tons of 2,240 pounds each, equivalent to 1.016 metric tons. Deadweight tonnage is the difference between the tonnage of a fully loaded ship and the fully unloaded tonnage of that ship.

death rate, the number of deaths annually per 1,000 of midyear population. Death rates for individual countries may be compared with the world annual average of 11 deaths per 1,000 population between 1980 and 1985.

density (of population), usually, the DE FACTO POPULATION of a country divided by its total area. Special adjustment is made for inland water or other uninhabitable areas, *e.g.,* excluding the lake area of Finland.

department, a first-order civil administrative subdivision. The *overseas department* (France) is an overseas subdivision of the French Republic, almost equivalent to a department of metropolitan France, with elected representation in the French Parliament.

dependency, any area outside of and under the jurisdiction of an independent state but not formally annexed to it.

direct taxes, taxes levied directly on firms and individuals, such as taxes on income, profits, and capital gains. The immediate incidence, or burden, of direct taxes is on the firms and individuals thus taxed; direct taxes on firms may, however, be passed on to consumers and

---

Dependent states[1]

Australia	**South Africa**
Christmas Island	South West Africa/Namibia
Cocos (Keeling) Islands	**United Kingdom**
Norfolk Island	Anguilla
Denmark	Bermuda
Faeroe Islands	British Virgin Islands
Greenland	Cayman Islands
France	Falkland Islands
French Guiana	Gibraltar
French Polynesia	Guernsey
Guadeloupe	Hong Kong
Martinique	Isle of Man
Mayotte	Jersey
New Caledonia	Montserrat
Réunion	Pitcairn Island
Saint Pierre and Miquelon	Saint Helena and Dependencies
Wallis and Futuna	Turks and Caicos Islands
Netherlands, The	**United States**
Aruba	American Samoa
Netherlands Antilles	Guam
New Zealand	Puerto Rico
Cook Islands	Trust Territory of the Pacific Islands
Niue	Marshall Islands
Tokelau	Federated States of Micronesia
Norway	Northern Mariana Islands
Jan Mayen	Palau
Svalbard	Virgin Islands (of the U.S.)
Portugal	
Macau	

[1]Excludes territories (1) to which Antarctic Treaty is applicable in whole or in part, (2) without permanent civilian population, (3) without internationally recognized civilian government (Western Sahara, Gaza Strip), or (4) representing unadjudicated unilateral or multilateral territorial claims.

other economic units in the form of higher prices for goods and services, with the result that the distinction between direct and indirect taxation may be unclear.

distribution of income/wealth, the portion of personal income or wealth accruing to households or individuals comprising each respective decile (tenth) or quintile (fifth) of a country's households or individuals.*

divorce rate, the number of legal, civilly recognized divorces annually per 1,000 population.

doubling time, the number of complete years required for a country to double its population at its current rate of natural increase; it does not take into account expected demographic change during the period, such as changes in birth rate, death rate, or population migration.

earnings index, a series of index numbers comparing average wages in a collective industrial sample for a country or region with the same industries at a previous period to measure changes over time in those wages. It is most commonly reported for wages paid on a daily, weekly, or monthly basis; annual figures represent averages of these shorter periods. The scope of the earnings index varies from country to country; the index is often limited to earnings in manufacturing industries. The index for each country applies to all wage earners in a designated group and ordinarily takes into account basic wages (overtime is normally distinguished), bonuses, cost-of-living allowances, and contributions toward social security. Some countries include payments in kind. Contributions toward social security by employers are usually excluded, as are social security benefits received by wage earners.

economically active population, *see* population economically active.

education, tabulation of the principal elements of the country's educational establishment, classified as far as possible according to the country's own system of primary, secondary, and higher levels (the usual age limits for these levels being identified in parentheses), with total number of schools (physical facilities) and of teachers and students (whether full- or part-time). The student–teacher ratio is calculated whenever available data permit.

educational attainment, the distribution of the population age 25 and over with completed educations by the highest level of formal education attained or completed; it is often reported, however, for age groups still in school or for the economically active only.

emirate, *see* monarchy.

enterprise, a legal entity formed to conduct a business, which it may do from more than one establishment (place of business or service point).

ethnic/linguistic composition, ethnic, racial, or linguistic composition of a national population, reported here according to the most reliable breakdown available, whether published in official sources (such as a census) or in external analysis (when the subject is not addressed in national sources [usually because of social or political sensitivities]).

exchange rate, the value of one currency compared with another, or with a standardized value such as the SPECIAL DRAWING RIGHT, or as mandated by local statute when one currency is "tied" by a par value to another. Rates given usually refer to market values when the currency itself is traded or to the value of trade transactions either averaged over the period of a year or as of a single date during the year.

exports, material goods legally leaving a country (or customs area) and subject to customs regulations. The total value and distribution by percentage of the major items (in preference to groups of goods) exported are given, together with the distribution of trade among major trading partners (usually single countries or trading blocs). Figures given for goods exported are free on board (f.o.b.) unless otherwise specified. The value of goods exported and imported f.o.b. is calculated from the cost of production and excludes the cost of transport.

external debt, public and publicly guaranteed debt with a maturity of more than one year owed to nonnationals of a country and repayable in foreign currency, goods, or services. The debt may be an obligation of a national or subnational governmental body (or an agency of either), of an autonomous public body, or of a private debtor that is guaranteed by a public entity. The debt is usually either outstanding (contracted) or disbursed (drawn).

external territory (Australia), *see* territory.

farm, economic unit comprising an operator and the land on which agricultural operations are conducted. The legal tenure of the farm may be under the control of a person, partnership, or corporation.

federal, consisting of first-order political subdivisions that are prior to and independent of the central government in certain functions.

federal republic, *see* republic.

federation, a union of coequal political entities that retain some degree of autonomy within the union.

fertility rate, *see* total fertility rate.

financial aggregates, tabulation of seven-year time series, providing principal measures of the financial condition of a country, including: (1) the exchange rate of the national currency against the U.S. dollar, the pound sterling, and the International Monetary Fund's SPECIAL DRAWING RIGHT (SDR); (2) the amount and kind of international reserves (holdings of SDRs, gold, and foreign currencies) and reserve position of the country in the IMF; and (3) principal economic rates and prices (central bank discount rate, government bond yields, and industrial stock [share] prices). For BALANCE OF PAYMENTS, the origin in terms of component balance of trade items and balance of invisibles (net) is given.*

fish catch, the live-weight equivalent of the aquatic animals (including fish, crustaceans, mollusks, etc., but excluding whales, seals, and other aquatic mammals) caught in freshwater or marine areas by national fleets and landed in domestic or foreign harbours for commercial, industrial, or subsistence purposes.

f.o.b. (trade valuation): *see* exports.

food, *see* daily per capita caloric intake.

form of government/political status, the structure of a country's administration provided for in normal constitutional operation—whether or not suspended by extralegal military or civil action, although such de facto administrations are identified—together with the number of members (elected, appointed, and ex officio) for each legislative house, named according to its English rendering. Dependent states (*see* Table) are classified according to the status of their political association with the administering country.

(free) association, late stage in the process by which U.K. and U.S. dependencies achieve independence; it usually implies a relation between a largely self-governing dependency and its administering power that is capable of termination in full independence at the instance of the dependent state, though always in consultation with the administering power.

global social product, *see* material product.

gross domestic product (GDP), the total value of the final goods and services produced by residents and nonresidents within a given country during a given year. The GDP excludes the value of net income earned abroad, which is included in the GROSS NATIONAL PRODUCT (GNP). Unless otherwise noted, the value is given in current prices of the year indicated.

gross national product (GNP), the total value of final goods and services produced both from within a given country *and* from external

(foreign) transactions in a given year. Unless otherwise noted, the value is given in current prices of the year indicated. GNP is equal to GROSS DOMESTIC PRODUCT adjusted by net factor income from abroad, which is the income residents receive from abroad for factor services (labour, investment, and interest) less similar payments made to nonresidents who contribute to the domestic economy.

gross (register) ton, unit of measure of the permanently enclosed volume of a ship, less certain exempted spaces such as those devoted to machinery, bunkers, crew accommodations, and so on; the gross register tonnage of a ship is thus a rough estimation of its volumetric cargo capacity. The gross register ton is equivalent to 100 cubic feet, or 2.83 cubic metres.

head of government, *see* chief of state/head of government.

health, a group of measures including number of accredited physicians (according to World Health Organization criteria) and their ratio to the total population; total hospital beds and their ratio; and INFANT MORTALITY RATE.

household income and expenditure, data for average household size (by number of individuals) and average household income. Sources of income and expenditures for major items of consumption are reported as percentages.

In general, household income is the amount of funds, usually measured in monetary units, received by the members (generally those 14 years old and over) of a HOUSEHOLD in a given time period. The income can be derived from (1) wages or salaries, (2) nonfarm or farm SELF-EMPLOYMENT, (3) transfer payments, such as pensions, public assistance, unemployment benefits, etc., and (4) other income, including interest and dividends, rent, royalties, etc. The income of a household is expressed as a gross amount before deductions for taxes. Data on expenditure refer to consumption of personal or household goods and services; they normally exclude savings, taxes, and insurance; practice with regard to inclusion of credit purchases differs markedly.

households, groups of related or unrelated individuals living in the same housing unit, distributed by size of household. A family household is one composed principally of individuals related by blood or marriage.*

immigration, usually, the number and origin of those immigrants admitted to a nation in a legal status that would eventually permit the granting of the right to settle permanently or to acquire citizenship.*

imports, material goods legally entering a country (or customs area) and subject to customs regulations; excludes financial movements. The total value and distribution by percentage of the major items (in preference to groups of goods) imported are given, together with the direction of trade among major trading partners (usually single countries), trading blocs (such as the European Economic Community), or customs areas (such as Belgium–Luxembourg). The value of goods imported is given free on board (f.o.b.) unless otherwise specified; f.o.b. is defined above under EXPORTS.

The principal alternate basis for reporting valuation of goods in international trade is that of cost, insurance, and freight (c.i.f.); its use is restricted to imports, as it comprises the principal charges needed to bring the goods to the customs house in the country of destination. Because it inflates the value of imports relative to exports, more countries have, latterly, been providing estimates of imports on an f.o.b. basis as well.

incorporated territory (U.S.), *see* territory.

independent, of a state, autonomous and controlling both its internal and external affairs.

indirect taxes, taxes levied on sales or transfers of selected intermediate goods and services, including excises, value-added taxes, and tariffs,

that are ordinarily passed on to the ultimate consumers of the goods and services. Figures given for individual countries are limited to indirect taxes levied by their respective central governments unless otherwise specified.

infant mortality rate, the number of children per 1,000 live births who die before their first birthday. Total infant mortality includes neonatal mortality, which is deaths of children within one month of birth.

invisibles (invisible trade), *see* balance of trade.

kingdom, *see* monarchy.

labour force, portion of the POPULATION ECONOMICALLY ACTIVE comprising those most fully employed or attached to the labour market (the unemployed are considered to be "attached" in that they usually represent persons previously employed seeking to be reemployed), particularly as viewed from a short-term perspective. It normally includes those who are self-employed, employed by others (whether full-time, part-time, seasonally, or on some other less than full-time basis), and, as noted above, the unemployed (both those previously employed and those seeking work for the first time). In the "gross domestic product and labour force" table, the majority of the labour data provided refer to population economically active, since PEA represents the longer-term view of working population and, thus, subsumes more of the marginal workers who are often missed by shorter-term surveys.

land use, distribution by classes of vegetational cover or economic use of the land area only (excluding inland water, for example, but not marshland), reported as percentages.

leisure, the principal uses or reported preferences in the use of the individual's free time for recreation, rest, or self-improvement.*

life expectancy, the number of years a person born within a particular population group (age cohort) would be expected to live, based on actuarial calculations.

literacy, the ability to read and write a language with some degree of competence; the precise degree constituting the basis of a particular national statement is usually defined by the national census and is often tested by the census enumerator. Elsewhere, particularly where much adult literacy may be the result of literacy campaigns rather than passage through a formal educational system, definition and testing of literacy may be better standardized.

major cities, usually the five largest cities proper whose population is at least one-tenth that of the primate (largest) city; fewer will be listed if the size disparity is very great or there are fewer urban localities in the country. For multipage tables, ten or more will be listed without regard for the size of the primate city.* All populations will refer to the most specific administrative or demographically defined city proper, unless a municipality or METROPOLITAN AREA is specified.

manufacturing, mining, and construction enterprises/retail sales and service enterprises, a detailed tabulation of the principal industries in these sectors, showing for each industry the number of enterprises and employees, wages in that industry as a percentage of the general average wage, and the value of that industry's output in terms of value added or turnover.*

marriage rate, the number of legal, civilly recognized marriages annually per 1,000 population.

material (or social) product, in the national accounting systems of the socialist countries, the aggregate (sometimes "global") value of all "productive" services, generally omitting personal (nonpublic) services, financial activities, and the like that in conventional Western national accounts would contribute to the GROSS DOMESTIC PRODUCT, a more comprehensive

measure that includes not only material output but also every identifiable service element of a national economy. Socialist countries that are members of the International Monetary Fund have begun, however, to report gross domestic, and national, product according to the *System of National Accounts* that forms the basis of international reporting of national accounts.

material well-being, a group of measures indicating the percentage of households or dwellings possessing certain goods or appliances, including automobiles, telephones, television receivers, refrigerators, air conditioners, and washing machines.*

merchant marine, the privately or publicly owned ships of a nation (limited to those in Lloyd's of London statistical reporting of 100 or more GROSS REGISTER TONS) that are employed in commerce.

metropolitan area, a city and the region of dense, predominantly urban, settlement around the city; the population of the whole is usually economically dependent upon the central city for employment, shopping, transportation services, and the like. Such areas are usually compact and contiguous, containing no physically discontinuous elements.

military expenditure, the apparent value of all identifiable military expenditure by the central government on hardware, personnel, pensions, research and development, etc., reported here both as a percentage of the GNP, with a comparison to the world average, and as a per capita value in U.S. dollars.

military personnel, *see* total active duty personnel.

mobility, the rate at which individuals or households change dwellings, usually measured between censuses and including international as well as domestic migration.*

monarchy, a government in which the CHIEF OF STATE holds office, usually hereditarily, but sometimes electively, and for life (sometimes electively for a term). The state may be a co-principality, emirate, empire, kingdom, principality, sheikhdom, or sultanate. The powers of the monarch may range from absolute, *i.e.,* he or she both reigns and rules; through various degrees of limitation of authority; to merely nominal, as in a constitutional monarchy, in which the titular monarch reigns but others, as elected officials, participate in the ruling.

monetary unit, currency of issue, or that in official use in a given country; name, spelling, and abbreviation in English according to International Monetary Fund recommendations or local practice; name of the lesser, usually decimal, monetary unit comprising the main currency; and valuation in U.S. dollars and U.K. pound sterling, usually according to market or commercial rates.

See also exchange rate.

natural increase, also called natural growth, or the balance of births and deaths, the excess of births over deaths in a population; the rate of natural increase is the difference between the BIRTH RATE and the DEATH RATE of a given population. Natural increase is added to the balance of migration to calculate the total growth of that population.

net material product, *see* material product.

nonreligious, *see* atheist.

official language(s), that (or those) prescribed for actual day-to-day conduct and publication of a country's official business. Other languages may have local protection, may be permitted in legal action (such as a trial), or may be "national languages," for the protection of which special provisions have been made, but these are not deemed official.

official name, the local official form(s), short or long, of a country's legal name(s) taken from the country's constitution or from other official documents. The English-language form is usually the protocol form in use by the

country, the U.S. Department of State, and the United Nations.

official religion, generally, any religion prescribed or given special protection by the constitution or legal system of a given country.

organized territory (U.S.), *see* territory.

overseas department (France), *see* department.

overseas territory (France), *see* territory.

parliamentary state, *see* state.

part of a realm, a dependent political entity with some degree of self-government and having a special status above that of a colony (*e.g.,* the prerogative of rejecting for local application any law enacted by the motherland).

participation/activity rates, measures defining differential rates of economic activity within a population. Participation rate refers to the percentage of those employed or economically active who possess a particular characteristic (sex, age, etc.); activity rate refers to the fraction of the total population who *are* economically active.

passenger-miles, or **passenger-kilometres,** aggregate measure of passenger carriage by a specified means of transportation, equal to the number of passengers carried multiplied by the number of kilometres each is transported. Figures given for countries are often calculated from ticket sales and ordinarily exclude passengers carried free of charge.

people's republic, *see* republic.

place of birth/national origin, if the former, numbers of native- and foreign-born population of a country by actual place of birth; if the latter, any of several classifications, including those based on origin of passport at original admission to country, on cultural heritage of family name, on self-designated (often multiple) origin of (some) ancestors, and on other systems for assigning national origin.*

political status, *see* form of government/political status.

population, the number of persons actually present within the borders of a country, state, or other civil entity at the date of a census of population, survey, cumulation of a civil register, or other estimate. Unless otherwise specified, populations given are DE FACTO, referring to those actually present, rather than DE JURE, those legally resident but not necessarily present on the referent date. If a time series, noncensus year, or per capita ratio referring to a country's total population is cited, it will usually refer to midyear of the calendar year indicated. Populations for cities will usually refer to the city proper, *i.e.,* the legally bounded corporate entity, or the most compact, contiguous, demographically urban portion of the entity as defined by the local authorities. Occasionally it has been necessary to provide city figures for METROPOLITAN AREAS when the relevant civil entity at the core of a major agglomeration had an unrepresentatively small population.

population economically active, the total number of persons (above a set age for economic labour, usually 10–15 years) in all employment statuses—self-employed, wage- or salary-earning, part-time, seasonal, unemployed, etc. The International Labour Organisation's *Yearbook of Labour Statistics* defines the economically active as "all persons of either sex who furnish the supply of labour for the production of economic goods and services." National practices vary as regards the treatment of such groups as armed forces, inmates of institutions, persons seeking their first job, seasonal workers and persons engaged in part-time economic activities. In some countries, all or part of these groups may be included among the economically active, while in other countries the same groups may be treated as inactive. In general, however, the data on economically active population do not include

students, women occupied solely in domestic duties, retired persons, persons living entirely on their own means, and persons wholly dependent upon others.

See also labour force.

population projection, the expected population in 1990 and 2000, embodying the country's own projections wherever possible. Estimates of the future size of a population are usually based on assumed future levels of fertility, mortality, and migration. Projections in the tables, unless otherwise specified, are medium (*i.e.,* most likely) variants, whether based on external estimates by the United Nations, World Bank, or U.S. Department of Commerce or on those of the country itself.

price and earnings indexes, tabulation comparing the change in the CONSUMER PRICE INDEX over a period of seven years with the change in the general labour force's EARNINGS INDEX for the same period.

principality, see monarchy.

production, the physical quantity or monetary value of the output of an industry, usually tabulated here as the most important items or groups of items (depending on the available detail) of primary (extractive) and secondary (manufactured) production. When a single consistent measure of value, such as "value added," can be obtained, this is given, ranked by value; otherwise, and usually, quantity of production is given.

public debt, the current outstanding debt of all periods of maturity for which the central government and its organs are obligated. Publicly guaranteed private debt is excluded. For many developing countries, only figures for long-term EXTERNAL DEBT are available.

quality of working life, a group of measures including weekly hours of work (including overtime); rates per 100,000 for job-connected injury, illness, and mortality; coverage of labour force by insurance for injury, permanent disability, and death; workdays lost to labour strikes and stoppages; and commuting patterns (length of journey to work in minutes and usual method of transportation).*

railroads, mode of transportation by self-driven or locomotive-drawn cars over fixed rails. Length-of-track figures given for individual countries ordinarily include the total length of all mainline and spurline running track and exclude switching sidings and yard track. Route length, when given, does not compound multiple running tracks laid on the same trackbed.

recurrent budget, see budget.

religious affiliation, distribution of practicing or nominal religionists, as a percentage of total population. This usually assigns to children the religion of their parents.

republic, a state with elected leaders and a centralized presidential form of government, local subdivisions being subordinate to the national government. A *federal republic* (as distinguished from a unitary republic) is a republic in which power is divided between the central government and the constituent subnational administrative divisions (*e.g.,* states, provinces, or cantons) in whom the central government itself is held to originate, the division of power being defined in a written constitution and jurisdictional disputes usually being settled in a court; sovereignty usually rests with the authority that has the power to amend the constitution. A *people's republic,* in the dialectics of Communism, is the first stage of development toward a communist state, the second stage being a *socialist republic.* A *soviet republic* is a republic governed by an elected soviet (council). A *unitary republic* (as distinguished from a federal republic) is a republic in which power is held by a central authority and not derived from constituent subdivisions.

retail price index, see consumer price index.

retail sales and service enterprises, see manufacturing, mining, and construction enterprises/retail sales and service enterprises.

roundwood, wood obtained from removals from forests, felled or harvested (with or without bark), in all forms.

rural, see urban–rural.

self-employment, work in which income derives from direct employment in one's own business, trade, or profession, as opposed to work in which salary or wages are earned from an employer.

self-governing, of a state, in control of its internal affairs in degrees ranging from control of most internal affairs (though perhaps not of public order or of internal security) to complete control of all internal affairs (*i.e.,* the state is autonomous) but having no control of external affairs or defense. In this work the term self-governing refers to the final state in the successive stages of increasing self-government, generally followed by independence.

service/trade enterprises, see manufacturing, mining, and construction enterprises/retail sales and service enterprises.

sex distribution, ratios, calculated as percentages, of male and female population to total population.

sheikhdom, see monarchy.

social deviance, a group of measures, usually reported as rates per 100,000, for principal categories of socially deviant behaviour, including specified crimes, alcoholism, drug abuse, and suicide.*

social participation, a group of measures indicative of the degree of social engagement possessed by a particular population, including rates of participation or membership in public activities such as elections, voluntary work (or non-job-connected organizational memberships), trade unions, and religion.*

social security, public programs designed to protect individuals and families from loss of income owing to unemployment, old age, sickness or disability, or death and to provide other services such as medical care, health and welfare programs, or income maintenance programs.

socialist republic, see republic.

soviet republic, see republic.

Special Drawing Right (SDR), a unit of account utilized by the International Monetary Fund (IMF) to denominate monetary reserves available under a quota system to IMF members to maintain the value of their national currency unit in international transactions.

state, an autonomous political entity; also, a first-order civil administrative subdivision, especially of a federated union. An *associated state* is an autonomous state in free association with another that conducts its external affairs and defense. A *parliamentary state* is an independent state in the Commonwealth that is governed by a parliament and that may recognize the British monarch as its titular head.

structure of gross domestic product and labour force, tabulation of the principal elements of the national economy, according to standard industrial categories, together with the distribution of the labour force (when possible POPULATION ECONOMICALLY ACTIVE) that generates the GROSS DOMESTIC PRODUCT.

sultanate, see monarchy.

territory, a noncategorized political dependency; a first-order administrative subdivision; a dependent political entity with some degree of self-government, but with fewer rights and less autonomy than a colony since there is no charter. An *external territory* (Australia) is a territory situated outside the area of the country. An *incorporated territory* (U.S.) is a part of the United States with nonvoting representation in the Congress but with most constitutional provisions extended to its inhabitants (*e.g.,* Alaska until 1959). An *organized territory*

(U.S.) is a territory for which a system of laws and a settled government have been provided by an act of the United States Congress. An *overseas territory* (France) is an overseas subdivision of the French Republic with elected representation in the French Parliament, having individual statutes, laws, and internal organization adapted to local conditions. A *trust territory* is a non-self-governing former mandate of the League of Nations, administered by an independent state under trust arrangements with the United Nations, with the goal of eventual self-government. An *unincorporated territory* (U.S.) is a dependency of the United States with limited self-government, whose inhabitants can claim the fundamental but not all of the procedural rights (*e.g.,* trial by jury) guaranteed by the United States Constitution.

theocracy, a state governed by hierarchs, *i.e.,* by religious leaders.

ton-miles, or *ton-kilometres,* aggregate measure of freight hauled by a specified means of transportation, equal to tons of freight multiplied by the miles (or kilometres) each ton is transported. Figures are compiled from waybills (nationally) and ordinarily exclude mail, specie, passengers' baggage, the fuel and stores of the conveyance in question, and goods carried free of charge.

total active duty personnel, full-time active duty military personnel (excluding militias and part-time, informal, or other paramilitary elements), with their distribution by percentages among the major services.

See also military expenditure.

total fertility rate, the sum of the current age-specific birth rates for each of the childbearing years (usually 15–49). It is the probable number of births, given present fertility data, that would occur during the lifetime of each woman should she live to the end of her childbearing years.

tourism, service industry comprising activities connected with domestic and international travel for pleasure or recreation; confined here to international travel and reported as expenditures in U.S.$ by tourists of all nationalities visiting a particular country and, conversely, the estimated expenditures of that country's nationals in all countries of destination.

transport, all mechanical methods of moving persons or goods. Data reported for national establishments include: for railroads, length of track and volume of traffic for passengers and cargo (but excluding mail, etc.); for roads, length of network and numbers of passenger cars and of commercial vehicles, *i.e.,* trucks and buses; for merchant marine, the number of vessels of more than 100 gross tons and their total deadweight tonnage; for air transport, traffic data for passengers and cargo, and the number of airports with scheduled flights.

trust territory, see territory.

unincorporated territory (U.S.), *see* territory.

unitary republic, see republic.

urban–rural, social characteristic of local or national populations, defined by predominant economic activities, "urban" referring to a group of largely nonagricultural pursuits, "rural" to agriculturally oriented employment patterns. The distinction is usually based on the country's own definition of urban, which may depend only upon the size (population) of a place or upon factors like employment, administrative status, density of housing, etc.

value added, also called value added by manufacture, the GROSS OUTPUT VALUE of a firm or industry minus the cost of inputs—raw materials, supplies, and payments to other firms—required to produce it. Value added is the portion of the sales value or gross output value that is actually created by the firm or industry. Value added generally includes labour costs, administrative costs, and operating profits.

The Nations of the World

Afghanistan

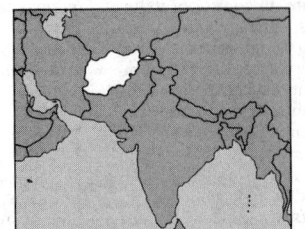

Official name: Da Afghānestān Jamhawrīyat (Pashto); Jomhūrī-ye Afghānestān (Dari) (Republic of Afghanistan).
Form of government: unitary single-party people's republic with two legislative houses (Council of Representatives [234]; Council of Elders [128[1]]).
Chief of state: President.
Head of government: Prime Minister.
Capital: Kābul.
Official languages: Pashto; Dari Persian.
Official religion: Islam.
Monetary unit: 1 afghani (AF) = 100 puls (puli); valuation (Oct. 10, 1988) 1 U.S.$ = AF 57.96; 1 £ = AF 99.25.

Area and population	area		population
Regions	sq mi	sq km	1984 estimate
Eastern	28,664	74,240	1,923,081
North-central	20,461	52,994	2,062,677
North-east	29,911	77,468	1,442,099
North-west	50,581	131,005	2,368,323
South-central	32,963	85,375	1,140,390
South-east	12,546	32,494	3,875,364
Western	76,699	198,649	1,554,500
TOTAL	251,825	652,225	14,366,434[2]

Demography

Population (1988): 14,481,000[2].
Density (1987): persons per sq mi 57.5, persons per sq km 22.2.
Urban–rural (1987): urban 18.1%; rural 81.9%.
Sex distribution[3] (1985): male 51.04%; female 48.96%.
Age breakdown[3] (1985): under 15, 45.4%; 15–29, 26.7%; 30–44, 15.6%; 45–59, 8.4%; 60–74, 3.4%; 75 and over, 0.5%.
Population projection: (1990) 14,805,000; (2000) 17,081,000.
Doubling time: 32 years.
Ethnic composition (1983): Pashtun 52.3%; Tadzhik 20.3%; Uzbek 8.7%; Hazāra 8.7%; Chahar Aimak 2.9%; Turkmen 2.0%; Baluchi 1.0%; other 4.1%.
Religious affiliation (1986): Sunnī Muslim 74%; Shīʿī Muslim 25%; other 1%.
Major cities (1987): Kābul 1,297,000; Qandahār 213,900; Herāt 168,200; Mazār-e Sharīf 123,900.

Vital statistics

Birth rate per 1,000 population (1987): 47.5 (world avg. 26.0).
Death rate per 1,000 population (1987): 22.5 (world avg. 9.9).
Natural increase rate per 1,000 population (1987): 25.0 (world avg. 16.1).
Total fertility rate (avg. births per childbearing woman; 1987): 6.7.
Life expectancy at birth (1987): male 40.6 years; female 41.6 years.
Major reported illness (1981–82): tuberculosis 17,499 cases.

National economy

Budget (1984–85). Revenue: AF 37,615,000,000 (tax revenue 45.4%, nontax revenue 54.6%). Expenditures: AF 51,177,000,000 (1981–82; governmental ministries 50.0%, developmental budget 31.9%, foreign debt service 13.9%, surplus 1.6%).
Public debt (external, outstanding; 1985)[4]: U.S.$1,424,000,000.
Tourism (1986): receipts from visitors U.S.$1,000,000.
Production (metric tons except as noted). Agriculture, forestry, fishing (1986): wheat 2,500,000, corn (maize) 750,000, grapes 500,000, rice 454,000, barley 300,000; livestock (number of live animals) 20,000,000 sheep, 3,750,000 cattle, 3,000,000 goats, 1,250,000 asses, 410,000 horses, 270,000 camels; roundwood 6,730,000 cu m; fish catch 1,500. Mining and quarrying (1986): copper 20,000; salt 10,000; gypsum 3,000; barite 2,000. Manufacturing (by production value in afghanis; 1981–82): food products 3,762,000,000; textiles (all forms) 2,770,000,000; industrial chemicals (including fertilizers) 751,000,000; printing and publishing 539,000,000; cement (1986) 77,000. Construction (AF '000,000; 1985): 1,094. Energy production (consumption): electricity (kW-hr; 1986) 1,171,000,000 (1,171,000,000); coal (metric tons; 1986) 160,000 (160,000); petroleum products (metric tons; 1986) 7,000 (398,000); natural gas (cu m; 1986) 2,856,198,000 (626,475,000).
Household size. Average household size[3] (1979): 6.2.
Population economically active[3] (1981–82): total 3,828,820; activity rate of total population 27.8% (participation rates: ages 10–59, 43.8%; female 12.8%; unemployed 5.5%).

Price indexes (1980 = 100)

	1980	1981	1982	1983	1984	1985	1986
Consumer price index	100.0	104.9	111.0	107.7	116.0	126.6	134.6

Gross national product (1985): U.S.$3,520,000,000 (U.S.$230 per capita).

Structure of net material product and labour force

	1985–86		1981–82	
	in value AF '000,000[5]	% of total value	labour force[4]	% of labour force
Agriculture	65,100	64.8	2,194,770	57.3
Manufacturing, mining, and public utilities	16,300	16.2	466,860	12.2
Construction	4,000	4.0	48,880	1.3
Transp. and commun.	3,100	3.1	65,650	1.7
Trade	10,200	10.2	126,100	3.3
Public administration			79,260	2.1
Public services	1,700	1.7	204,940	5.3
Other			642,360	16.8
TOTAL	100,400	100.0	3,828,820	100.0

Land use (1985): forested 2.9%; meadows and pastures 46.3%; agricultural and under permanent cultivation 12.4%; other 38.4%.

Foreign trade

Balance of trade (current prices)

	1981	1982	1983	1984	1985	1986
AF '000,000	3,555	629	−5,941	−4,569	−32,252	−29,998
% of total	5.5%	0.9%	7.5%	5.4%	36.4%	30.8%

Imports (1986): U.S.$1,043,500,000 (1981–82; vehicles 22.7%, petroleum products 18.0%, sugar 8.1%, woven fabrics of flax or ramie 7.9%, processed animal and vegetable oils 4.2%, tea 4.0%). *Major import sources:* U.S.S.R. 30.0%; Japan 9.3%; China 7.2%; South Korea 6.8%; Pakistan 2.8%; Hong Kong 2.4%; W.Ger. 1.8%; U.K. 1.3%.
Exports (1986): U.S.$551,900,000 (natural gas 47.0%, dried fruit and nuts 24.4%, carpets and rugs 7.2%, wool and hides 2.6%, cotton 1.8%). *Major export destinations:* U.S.S.R. 86.1%; India 9.0%; W.Ger. 5.1%; U.K. 2.9%; Pakistan 2.6%.

Transport and communications

Transport. Railroads (1984): length 6 mi, 10 km. Roads (1981–82): total length 11,789 mi, 18,974 km (paved 42%). Vehicles (1981–82): passenger cars 31,754; trucks and buses 30,997. Merchant marine: none. Air transport (1987): passenger-mi 108,538,000, passenger-km 174,676,000; short ton-mi cargo 5,543,000, metric ton-km cargo 8,093,000; airports (1988) 2.
Communications. Daily newspapers (1987): total number 14; total circulation 108,400; circulation per 1,000 population 7.6. Radio (1986): 135,000 receivers (1 per 102 persons). Television (1986): 12,800 receivers (1 per 1,079 persons). Telephones (1984): 31,200 (1 per 443 persons).

Education and health

Education (1985)

	schools	teachers	students	student/ teacher ratio
Primary	792	15,581	580,499	37.3
Secondary	332	5,715	105,032	18.4
Voc., teacher tr.[6, 7]	16	666	7,360	11.1
Higher[6]	5	1,283	13,450	10.5

Educational attainment (1980). Percent of population age 25 and over having: no formal schooling 88.5%; some primary education 6.8%; complete primary 0.3%; some secondary 1.2%; postsecondary 3.2%. *Literacy* (1980): total population age 15 and over literate 1,436,000 (20.0%); males 33.2%; females 5.8%.
Health: physicians (1982–83) 1,160 (1 per 12,172 persons); hospital beds (1981–82) 6,875 (1 per 2,054 persons); infant mortality rate per 1,000 live births (1987) 175.
Food (1979–81): daily per capita caloric intake 2,055 (vegetable products 90%, animal products 10%); 84% of FAO recommended minimum.

Military

Total active duty personnel (1988): 50,000 (army 90.0%, air force 10.0%).
Military expenditure as percent of GNP (1984): 7.7% (world 6.0%); per capita expenditure U.S.$21.

[1]Includes 45 nonelective seats. [2]Total includes 2,615,000 nomads not distributed by region. Afghan refugees in Pakistan and Iran numbered more than 5.6 million in 1988. [3]Based on settled population only. [4]Includes external long-term private debt not guaranteed by the government. [5]At prices of 1978. [6]1985. [7]Includes technical institutes.

Albania

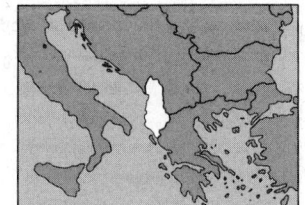

Official name: Republika Popullore Socialiste e Shqipërisë (People's Socialist Republic of Albania).
Form of government: unitary single-party socialist republic with one legislative house (People's Assembly [250]).
Chief of state: President (Chairman of the Presidium of the People's Assembly).
Head of government: Premier (Chairman of the Council of Ministers).
Capital: Tiranë.
Official language: Albanian.
Official religion: none.
Monetary unit: 1 lek = 100 qindars; valuation (Oct. 10, 1988) 1 U.S.$ = 5.95 leks; 1 £ = 10.19 leks.

Area and population		area		population
				1983
Provinces	Capitals	sq mi	sq km	estimate
Berat	Berat	396	1,027	157,300
Dibër	Peshkopi	605	1,568	137,800
Durrës	Durrës	327	848	220,600
Elbasan	Elbasan	572	1,481	213,200
Fier	Fier	454	1,175	216,400
Gjirokastër	Gjirokastër	439	1,137	61,200
Gramsh	Gramsh	268	695	39,300
Kolonjë	Ersekë	311	805	22,500
Korçë	Korçë	842	2,181	201,300
Krujë	Krujë	234	607	94,600
Kukës	Kukës	514	1,330	88,400
Lezhë	Lezhë	185	479	54,200
Librazhd	Librazhd	391	1,013	64,100
Lushnjë	Lushnjë	275	712	117,800
Mat	Burrel	397	1,028	68,700
Mirditë	Rrëshen	335	867	45,800
Përmet	Përmet	359	929	37,100
Pogradec	Pogradec	280	725	62,700
Pukë	Pukë	399	1,034	46,100
Sarandë	Sarandë	424	1,097	78,200
Shkodër	Shkodër	976	2,528	210,200
Skrapar	Çorovoda	299	775	42,500
Tepelenë	Tepelenë	315	817	46,100
Tiranë	Tiranë	478	1,238	316,100
Tropojë	Bajram	403	1,043	40,900
Vlorë	Vlorë	621	1,609	158,200
TOTAL		11,100[1]	28,748	2,841,300

Demography

Population (1988): 3,149,000.
Density (1988): persons per sq mi 283.7, persons per sq km 109.5.
Urban–rural (1985): urban 34.0%; rural 66.0%.
Sex distribution (1984): male 51.58%; female 48.42%.
Age breakdown (1985): under 15, 35.8%; 15–29, 29.3%; 30–44, 17.0%; 45–59, 11.1%; 60–74, 5.3%; 75 and over, 1.5%.
Population projection: (1990) 3,281,000; (2000) 4,030,000.
Doubling time: 34 years.
Ethnic composition (1983): Albanian 96.7%; Greek 2.0%; Romanian 0.5%; Macedonian 0.4%; Montenegrin 0.2%; Gypsy 0.2%.
Religious affiliation (1980): nonreligious 55.4%; Muslim 20.5%; atheist 18.7%; Christian 5.4%.
Major cities (1985): Tiranë 215,900; Durrës 75,300; Elbasan 74,300; Shkodër 73,600; Vlorë 64,100.

Vital statistics

Birth rate per 1,000 population (1985): 26.2 (world avg. 29.0).
Death rate per 1,000 population (1985): 5.8 (world avg. 11.0).
Natural increase rate per 1,000 population (1985): 20.4 (world avg. 18.0).
Total fertility rate (avg. births per childbearing woman; 1980): 3.6.
Marriage rate per 1,000 population (1985): 8.5.
Divorce rate per 1,000 population (1982): 0.8.
Life expectancy at birth (1982–83): male 67.9 years; female 72.9 years.
Major causes of death per 100,000 population: n.a.; however, major health problems include tuberculosis, hypertension, liver and stomach disorders; malaria and syphilis, formerly widespread, are now practically nonexistent.

National economy

Budget (1987). Revenue: 9,350,000,000 leks (surplus from state enterprises 96.3%, other 3.7%). Expenditures: 9,300,000,000 leks (national economy 54.3%, social and cultural services 28.7%, defense 11.3%, administration 1.6%).
Public debt (1985): U.S.$5,600,000,000[2].
Tourism (1986): number of tourists 8,000; receipts from visitors, n.a.; expenditures by nationals abroad, n.a.
Production (metric tons except as noted). Agriculture, forestry, fishing (1986): wheat 540,000, corn (maize) 410,000, vegetables and fruit except grapes 354,000, sugar beets 320,000, potatoes 136,000, grapes 83,000, sunflower seeds 55,000, barley 36,000, oats 30,000, olives 30,000, tobacco 20,000; livestock (number of live animals) 1,230,000 sheep, 700,000 goats, 610,000 cattle, 220,000 pigs, 74,000 mules and asses, 42,000 horses; roundwood

(1985) 2,330,000 cu m; fish catch (1985) 4,000. Mining and quarrying (1986): ferronickel ores 1,200,000; chromite ore 1,200,000; salt 70,000; copper (metal content) 17,600; nickel 9,700. Manufacturing (1984): bitumen (asphalt) 1,800,000; cement 860,000; distillate fuel oils 270,000; nitrogenous and phosphate fertilizers 104,000; raw sugar 37,000; paper and paperboard 21,200; olive oil 5,000; wine 230,000 hectolitres; beer 140,000 hectolitres; cigarettes 6,200,000,000 units; cotton and woolen fabrics 60,900,000 m[3]. Construction (1981–83): 1,706,000,000 leks. Energy production (consumption): electricity (kW-hr; 1986) 3,880,000,000 (3,230,000,000); coal (metric tons; 1986) 2,300,000 (2,530,000); crude petroleum (barrels; 1986) 19,800,000 (19,800,000); petroleum products (metric tons; 1986) 1,205,000 (1,205,000); natural gas (cu m; 1986) 440,000,000 (440,000,000).
Gross national product (at current market prices; 1986): U.S.$2,800,000,000 (U.S.$880 per capita).

Structure of net material product and labour force				
	1983			
	value	% of total value	labour force[4]	% of labour force
Agriculture	...	34.1	152,400	21.8
Manufacturing, mining, public utilities	...	43.3	252,700	36.2
Construction	...	7.8	80,700	11.6
Transportation and communications			33,400	4.8
Trade	...	14.8	53,900	7.7
Pub. admin., defense			87,200	12.5
Other			37,500	5.4
TOTAL	...	100.0	697,800	100.0

Population economically active (1985): total 1,398,000; activity rate of total population 45.8% (participation rates: ages 15–64, 74.5%; female 41.0%; unemployed, n.a.).
Price and earnings indexes: n.a.
Household income and expenditure. Average household size (1984) 5.5; income per household: n.a.; sources of income: n.a.; expenditure: n.a.
Land use (1985): forested 37.9%; meadows and pastures 14.6%; agricultural and under permanent cultivation 26.0%; other 21.5%.

Foreign trade

Balance of trade (current prices)						
	1978	1979	1980	1981	1982	1983
'000,000 leks	...	100	...	...	...	...
% of total	...	5.3	...	...	...	...

Imports (1982): U.S.$373,500,000 (mineral fuels and lubricants 33.3%, machinery and transport equipment 22.2%, chemicals and related products 16.6%, food and live animals 16.6%, consumer goods 5.9%). *Major import sources:* U.S.S.R. and Eastern European countries 35.6%; European Economic Community countries 28.7%; United States 4.6%; Japan 2.8%.
Exports (1982): U.S.$350,700,000 (mineral fuels 27.1%, crude minerals and metalliferous ores 26.2%, electricity 13.2%, food and food preparations 13.2%, consumer products 9.8%). *Major export destinations:* U.S.S.R. and Eastern European countries 35.7%; European Economic Community countries 31.2%; United States 3.8%; Japan 1.1%.

Transport and communications

Transport. Railroads (1985): length 277 mi, 445 km; passenger-mi 181,000,-000[3], passenger-km 291,000,000[3]; short ton-mi cargo 87,000,000[3], metric ton-km cargo 127,000,000[3]. Roads (1985): total length 7,456 mi, 12,000 km (paved 40%). Vehicles (1970): passenger cars 3,500; trucks and buses 11,200. Merchant marine (1987): vessels (100 gross tons and over) 20; total deadweight tonnage 79,940. Air transport: passengers, n.a.; cargo, n.a.; airports (1988) with scheduled flights 1.
Communications. Daily newspapers (1985): total number 2; total circulation 145,000[3]; circulation per 1,000 population 52.0[3]. Radio (1986): total number of receivers 210,000 (1 per 14 persons). Television (1985): total number of receivers 52,000 (1 per 59 persons). Telephones, n.a.

Education and health

Education (1984)	schools	teachers	students	student/teacher ratio
Primary (age 6–13)	1,631	27,387	540,332	19.7
Secondary (age 14–17)	205	1,552	35,643	23.0
Voc., teacher tr.	313[5]	5,405	123,797	22.9
Higher	8[5]	1,502	21,285	14.2

Educational attainment (1979). Percent of population age 25 and over having: primary education 74.7%; secondary 20.9%; higher 4.4%. *Literacy* (1970): total population age 15 and over literate 1,234,376 (75.0%).
Health (1983): physicians 4,957[6] (1 per 609 persons); hospital beds 17,600 (1 per 161 persons); infant mortality rate per 1,000 live births (1982) 44.0.
Food (1980–82): daily per capita caloric intake 3,060 (vegetable products 87%, animal products 13%); 127% of FAO recommended minimum requirement.

Military

Total active duty personnel (1987): 42,000 (army 75.0%, navy 7.9%, air force 17.1%). *Military expenditure as percent of GNP* (1985): 5.3% (world 6.1%); per capita expenditure U.S.$48.

[1]Detail does not add to total given because of rounding. [2]Estimated total since 1949. [3]1981. [4]State sector only. [5]1983. [6]Includes dentists.

Algeria

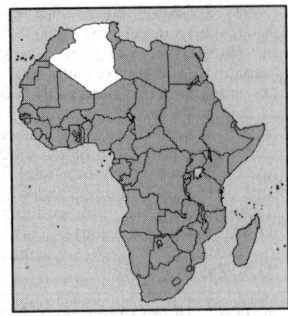

Official name: al-Jumhūrīyah al-Jazā'irīyah ad-Dīmuqrāṭīyah ash-Sha'bīyah (Arabic) (Democratic and Popular Republic of Algeria).
Form of government: socialist republic with one legislative house (The National People's Assembly [295]).
Head of state and government: President.
Capital: Algiers.
Official language: Arabic.
Official religion: Islam.
Monetary unit: 1 Algerian dinar (DA) = 100 centimes; valuation (Oct. 10, 1988) 1 U.S.$ = DA 6.34; 1 £ = DA 10.85.

Population (1987 Census[1])

Wilāyat	population	Wilāyat	population
Adrar	216,931	Médéa	650,623
Ain Defla	536,205	Mila	511,047
Ain Temouchent	271,454	Mostaganem	504,124
Alger	1,687,579	M'Sila	605,578
Annaba	453,951	Naâma	112,858
Batna	757,059	Oran	916,578
el-Bayadh	155,494	Ouargla	286,696
Béchar	183,896	el-Oued	379,512
Bejaia	697,669	Oum el-Bouaghi	402,683
Biskra	429,217	Relizane	545,061
Blida	704,462	Saïda	235,240
Bordj Bou Arreridj	429,094	Sétif	997,482
Bouira	525,460	Sidi bel-Abbès	444,047
Boumerdes	646,870	Skikda	619,094
ech-Chlef	679,717	Souk Ahras	298,236
Constantine	662,330	Tamanrasset	94,219
Djelfa	490,240	el-Tarf	276,836
Guelma	353,329	Tébessa	409,317
Ghardaïa	215,955	Tiaret	574,786
Illizi	19,698	Tindouf	16,339
Jijel	471,319	Tipaza	615,140
Khenchela	243,733	Tissemsilt	227,542
Laghouat	215,183	Tizi Ouzou	931,501
Mascara	562,806	Tlemcen	707,453
		TOTAL	22,971,558

Demography

Area: 919,595 sq mi, 2,381,741 sq km.
Population (1988): 23,849,000.
Density (1987): persons per sq mi 25.9, persons per sq km 10.0.
Urban–rural (1987): urban 49%; rural 51%.
Sex distribution (1986): male 49.64%; female 50.36%.
Age breakdown (1987): under 15, 43.9%; 15–29, 28.0%; 30–44, 13.9%; 45–59, 8.4%; 60–74, 4.2%; 75 and over, 1.6%.
Population projection: (1990) 25,350,000; (2000) 34,400,000.
Doubling time: 23 years.
Ethnic composition (1983): Arab 82.6%; Berber 17.0%; French 0.1%; other 0.3%.
Religious affiliation (1980): Sunnī Muslim 99.1%; Roman Catholic 0.5%; other 0.4%.
Major cities (1987): Algiers 1,483,000; Oran 590,000; Constantine 438,000; Annaba 310,000; Batna 182,000.

Vital statistics

Birth rate per 1,000 population (1987): 34.6 (world avg. 26.0); legitimacy rate, n.a.; marriage, however, is nearly universal.
Death rate per 1,000 population (1987): 7.0 (world avg. 9.9).
Natural increase rate per 1,000 population (1987): 27.6 (world avg. 16.1).
Total fertility rate (avg. births per childbearing woman; 1987): 5.9.
Marriage rate per 1,000 population (1985): 5.7[2].
Divorce rate per 1,000 population (1985): 2.1[2].
Life expectancy at birth (1983): male 61.6 years; female 63.3 years.
Notified cases of infectious diseases per 100,000 population (1986): measles 15.2; typhoid fever 12.5; dysentery 11.8.

National economy

Budget (1987–88). Revenue: DA 103,000,000,000 (ordinary receipts 76.5%, hydrocarbons 23.5%). Expenditures: DA 113,000,000,000 (current expenditures 58%, investment 42%).
Production (metric tons except as noted). Agriculture, forestry, fishing (1986): wheat 1,445,000, barley 1,100,000, potatoes 850,000, grapes 465,000, tomatoes 275,000, oranges 220,000, dates 190,000; livestock (number of live animals) 14,795,000 sheep, 3,090,000 goats, 1,557,000 cattle; round-wood 1,944,000 cu m; fish catch 90,000. Mining and quarrying (1987): iron ore 3,382,000; phosphates 1,209,000; gypsum (1986) 303,000; barite (1986) 66,000; silver (1986) 120,000 troy oz. Manufacturing (1987): cement 7,541,000; flour and semolina 2,487,000; bricks 1,701,000; pig iron and ferroalloys 1,677,000; crude steel 1,477,000; edible oils 304,000; sugar 205,200; trucks 5,785 units. Construction (1981): residential 28,000 units. Energy production (consumption): electricity (kW-hr; 1986) 12,746,000,000 (12,830,000,000); coal (metric tons; 1986) 9,000 (1,109,000); crude petroleum (barrels; 1987) 241,318,000 ([1986] 174,592,000); petroleum products (metric tons; 1986) 36,303,000 (5,819,000); natural gas (cu m; 1986) 33,894,000,-000 (13,851,000,000).
Gross national product (1986): U.S.$58,040,000,000 (U.S.$2,570 per capita).

Structure of gross domestic product and labour force

	1986		1985	
	in value DA '000,000	% of total value	labour force[3]	% of labour force
Agriculture	33,270	13.9	999,000	25.7
Crude pet., nat. gas	40,890	17.0		
Other mining	1,020	0.4		
Manufacturing	34,770	14.5	595,000	15.3
Public utilities	3,260	1.4		
Construction	41,225	17.2	670,000	17.3
Transp. and commun.	12,465	5.2	202,000	5.2
Trade	37,615	15.7	311,000	8.0
Services	11,570	4.8	1,107,000[4]	28.5[4]
Customs duties, production taxes	23,750	9.9	—	—
TOTAL	239,835	100.0	3,884,000	100.0

Public debt (external, outstanding; 1986): U.S.$14,770,000,000.
Tourism (1986): receipts from visitors U.S.$137,000,000; expenditures by nationals abroad U.S.$446,000,000.
Population economically active (1987): total 4,204,460[3]; activity rate of population 18.3%[3] (participation rates [1985]: ages 15–64, 40.0%; female 11.6%).

Price and earnings indexes (1980 = 100)

	1981	1982	1983	1984	1985	1986	1987
Consumer price index	114.6	122.3	127.9	136.3	156.4	173.9	186.9
Earnings index	...	...	...	...	...	...	...

Household income and expenditure. Average household size (1987) 6.9; income per household: n.a.; sources of income: n.a.; expenditure (1979–80): food and beverages 55.7%, housing and household durable goods 10.8%, clothing and footwear 9.2%, transport and communications 6.7%, recreation 3.4%, medical care and health 3.1%.
Land use (1985): forested 1.8%; meadows and pastures 13.5%; agricultural and under permanent cultivation 3.2%; other (mostly desert) 81.5%.

Foreign trade

Balance of trade (current prices)

	1982	1983	1984	1985	1986	1987
DA '000,000	+11,151	+14,686	+18,672	+15,073	−6,567	+4,959
% of total	10.1%	13.9%	17.2%	13.9%	8.2%	6.8%

Imports (1986): DA 47,782,500,000 (1985; raw materials for industry 37.4%; machinery and transport equipment 35.8%, of which transport equipment 10.6%; food and beverages 19.7%; consumer products 5.5%). *Major import sources:* European Economic Community 63.9%; North America 9.3%; Japan 4.3%; Eastern Europe 4.0%; Arab countries 3.0%.
Exports (1986): DA 37,033,400,000 (1985; mineral fuels and lubricants 98.0%, crude materials 1.3%). *Major export destinations:* European Economic Community 73.6%; North America 16.4%; Eastern Europe 4.0%; Japan 1.3%; Arab countries 0.8%.

Transport and communications

Transport. Railroads (1987): route length 2,337 mi, 3,761 km; passenger-mi 1,225,000,000, passenger-km 1,972,000,000; short ton-mi cargo 2,012,-000,000, metric ton-km cargo 2,937,000,000. Roads (1986): total length 50,734 mi, 81,648 km (paved 59%). Vehicles (1985): passenger cars 712,-700; trucks and buses 471,500. Merchant marine (1987): vessels (100 gross tons and over) 148; total deadweight tonnage 1,043,030. Air transport[5] (1987): passenger-mi 1,397,000,000, passenger-km 2,248,000,000; short ton-mi cargo 7,275,000, metric ton-km cargo 10,622,000; airports (1988) with scheduled flights 22.
Communications. Daily newspapers (1986): total number 4; total circulation 480,000; circulation per 1,000 population 23. Radio (1986): 3,250,000 receivers (1 per 6.9 persons). Television (1987): 1,550,000 receivers (1 per 15 persons). Telephones (1986): 819,722 (1 per 28 persons).

Education and health

Education (1987–88)

	schools	teachers	students	student/ teacher ratio
Primary (age 6–11)	11,843	139,875	3,801,651	27.2
Secondary (age 12–18)	2,479	110,738	2,082,646	18.8
Voc., teacher tr.[6]	717	2,528	98,000	38.8
Higher	15[8]	17,581	160,195	12.3

Educational attainment (1971). Percent of population age 25 and over having: no formal schooling 84.4%; primary education 13.0%; secondary education 2.2%; higher 0.3%; unknown 0.4%. *Literacy* (1982): total population age 15 and over literate 4,753,000 (44.7%); males literate 3,087,400 (57.3%); females literate 1,666,000 (31.7%).
Health (1987): physicians 17,760 (1 per 1,302 persons); hospital beds 63,000 (1 per 367 persons); infant mortality rate (1985) 64.1.
Food (1984–86): daily per capita caloric intake 2,688 (vegetable products 88%, animal products 12%); (1983) 115% of FAO recommended minimum requirement.

Military

Total active duty personnel (1988): 139,000 (army 86.0%, navy 5.0%, air force 9.0%). *Military expenditure as percent of GNP* (1985): 2.5% (world 6.1%); per capita expenditure U.S.$62.

---

[1]March 20. [2]Algerian population only. [3]Employed persons only. [4]Excludes military. [5]Air Algérie international traffic only. [6]1986–87. [7]1980–81. [8]1981–82.

Andorra

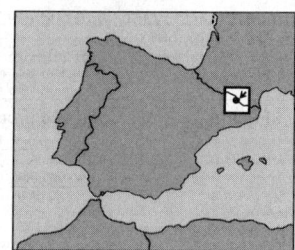

Official name: Principat (Co-Principat) or Senyoriu (Co-Senyoriu) d'Andorra; les Valls d'Andorra (Principality [or Co-Principality] of Andorra; the Valleys of Andorra).
Form of government: co-principality with one nonpartisan legislative house (General Council of the Valleys [28]).
Chiefs of state: President of France; Bishop of Urgel, Spain.
Head of government: Chief executive.
Capital: Andorra la Vella.
Official language: Catalan.
Official religion: Roman Catholicism.
Monetary unit: There is no local currency of issue; the French franc and Spanish peseta are both in circulation. 1 franc (F) = 100 centimes; 1 peseta (Pta) = 100 céntimos. Valuation (Oct. 10, 1988) 1 U.S.$ = F 6.32, 1 £ = F 10.83; 1 U.S.$ = Ptas 122.13, 1 £ = Ptas 209.15.

Area and population		area		population
Parishes	Capitals	sq mi	sq km	1986 census
Andorra la Vella	Andorra la Vella	49[1]	127[1]	18,463
Canillo	Canillo ⎫	74	191	1,153
Encamp	Encamp ⎬			5,766
La Massana	La Massana	25	65	3,229
Les Escaldes–Engordany	—	1	1	11,734
Ordino	Ordino	33	85	1,096
Sant Julià de Lòria	Sant Julià de Lòria	1	1	5,535
TOTAL		181	468	46,976

Demography

Population (1988): 51,400.
Density (1988): persons per sq mi 284.0, persons per sq km 109.8.
Urban–rural (1986): urban 64.7%; rural 35.3%.
Sex distribution (1986): male 53.12%; female 46.88%.
Age breakdown (1986): under 15, 19.0%; 15–29, 27.3%; 30–44, 26.4%; 45–59, 14.8%; 60–74, 9.4%; 75 and over, 3.1%.
Population projection[2]: (1990) 57,100; (2000) 96,300.
Doubling time: 97 years.
Ethnic composition (1986): Spanish 55.1%; Andorran 27.5%; French 7.4%; Portuguese 4.1%; British 1.5%; other 4.4%.
Religious affiliation (1980): Roman Catholic 94.2%; Jewish 0.4%; Jehovah's Witnesses 0.3%; Protestant 0.2%; other 4.9%.
Major cities (1986): Andorra la Vella 15,639; Les Escaldes 11,955; Encamp 3,535.

Vital statistics

Birth rate per 1,000 population (1987): 11.1 (world avg. 26.0).
Death rate per 1,000 population (1987): 3.7 (world avg. 9.9).
Natural increase rate per 1,000 population (1987): 7.4 (world avg. 16.1).
Total fertility rate (avg. births per childbearing woman): n.a.
Marriage rate per 1,000 population (1986): 2.8.
Divorce rate per 1,000 population: n.a.
Life expectancy at birth: (1980; both sexes) 70 years.
Major causes of death per 100,000 population: n.a.; however, health problems are those of a developed country—cardiovascular disease, hypertension, malignant neoplasms (cancers).

National economy

Budget (1986). Revenue: Ptas 6,655,098,711 (1983; excise taxes on imported consumer goods and gasoline 93.9%; additional revenue is derived from a 3% tax on alcoholic beverages). Expenditures: Ptas 6,655,098,711 (primarily administrative services and education; Andorra has virtually no military expenditures).
Public debt: n.a.
Production. Agriculture, forestry, fishing (1981): potatoes 472 metric tons, tobacco 264 metric tons, and unknown amounts of hay, rye, buckwheat, olives, and grapes; livestock (number of live animals; 1982) 9,000 sheep, 1,115 cattle, 217 horses. Mining and quarrying: building stone, alum, iron, and lead. Manufacturing: ceramics, cigars and cigarettes, alcoholic beverages (including anisette and brandy), clothing, jewelry, textiles (including woolen blankets and scarves), and wooden furniture. Construction (1984): 90 buildings totaling 83,834 sq m were authorized for construction. Energy production (consumption): electricity (kW-hr; 1986) 132,470,000 (166,675,-000[3,4]); coal, none (n.a.); crude petroleum, none (n.a.); petroleum products (metric tons; 1986) none (95,349); natural gas, none (n.a.).
Population economically active (1986): total 21,484; activity rate of total population 46.8% (participation rates: ages 15–64, n.a.; female, n.a.; unemployed, n.a.).

Price and earnings indexes (1980 = 100)[5]							
	1982	1983	1984	1985	1986	1987	1988
Consumer price index	131.0	147.0	163.6	178.0	193.6	203.8	210.1[6]
Earnings index	...	...	...	...	...	...	...

Gross national product (at current market prices; 1982): U.S.$340,000,000 (U.S.$9,000 per capita)[7].

Structure of labour force		
	1986	
	labour force	% of labour force
Agriculture and forestry	132	0.6
Mining	571	2.7
Manufacturing	957	4.5
Construction	1,754	8.2
Public utilities	1,266	5.9
Transportation and communications	1,832	8.5
Trade	5,777	26.9
Finance	1,281	6.0
Pub. admin., defense	650	3.0
Services and hotel	5,209	24.3
Other	2,025	9.4
TOTAL	21,454	100.0

Household income and expenditure. Average household size: n.a.; income per household: n.a.; sources of income: n.a.; expenditure: n.a.
Land use (1985): forested 23.7%; meadows and pastures 44.2%; agricultural and under permanent cultivation 4.0%; other 28.1%.
Tourism (1983): receipts from tourist arrivals, n.a.; expenditures by nationals abroad, n.a.; number of tourist arrivals, approximately 10,000,000 annually, most of whom do not stay overnight; number of hotels 235; number of hotel rooms (1987) 35,000.

Foreign trade

Balance of trade (current prices)						
	1981	1982	1983	1984	1985	1986
Ptas '000,000	−28,090	−30,197	−32,011	−35,795	...	−71,871
% of total	94.8%	91.5%	91.6%	92.1%	...	96.9%

Imports (1986): Ptas 74,312,755,085, of which from France Ptas 31,525,-222,000, from Spain Ptas 20,036,199,000 (includes fuels, food, perfumes, clothing, and radio and television sets)[8].
Exports (1986): Ptas 2,325,252,000, of which to France Ptas 1,261,917,000, to Spain Ptas 762,196,000 (includes wooden furniture, handicrafts, cigarettes, cigars, leather goods, and electricity).

Transport and communications

Transport. Railroads: none; however, both French and Spanish railways stop near the border. Roads (1981): total length 138 mi, 220 km (paved 55%). Vehicles (1986): passenger cars 25,000; trucks and buses 6,250. Merchant marine: vessels (100 gross tons and over) none. Airports with scheduled flights: none; the airport at nearby Seo de Urgel, Spain, has scheduled daily flights to Barcelona and Palma (on Majorca).
Communications. Weekly newspapers (1986): total number 1; circulation 4,000; circulation per 1,000 population 86.4. Radio (1986): total number of receivers 8,000 (1 per 5.8 persons). Television (1986): total number of receivers 4,000 (1 per 12 persons). Telephones (1982): 17,719 (1 per 2.1 persons).

Education and health

Education (1986–87)	schools	teachers[9]	students	student/ teacher ratio
Primary (age 6–12)	13	214	5,344	...
Secondary (age 12–18)	10	53	2,253	...
Voc., teacher tr.	5	37	1,248	...
Higher	...	...	...	...

Educational attainment, n.a.; education is compulsory to age 16, however.
Literacy (1987): total population literate (virtually 100%).
Health: physicians (1984) 53 (1 per 784 persons); hospital beds (1981) 113 (1 per 316 persons); infant mortality rate per 1,000 live births (1987) 13.3.
Food (1984–86)[10]: daily per capita caloric intake 3,320 (vegetable products 67%, animal products 33%); (1983) 135% of FAO recommended minimum requirement.

Military

Total active duty personnel (1982): none. France and Spain are responsible for Andorra's external security; a 100-man police force maintains domestic security. *Military expenditure as a percent of central government expenditure* (1981): 0.0001% (world 19.0%).

---

[1]Andorra la Vella includes Les Escaldes-Engordany and Sant Julià de Lòria. [2]Includes substantial in-migration. [3]1984. [4]Most of the consumption is produced within Andorra; the remainder is imported from Spain. [5]In Spanish pesetas. [6]May. [7]Trade, tourism (including winter-season sports, fairs, and festivals), and the banking system (of some importance as a tax haven for foreign financial investment and transactions) are the primary sources of GNP. [8]Imported manufactured items are less expensive in Andorra than in neighbouring countries because they are duty free. As a result, smuggling remains a profitable sideline for some. [9]1985–86. [10]Composite values derived from Spanish and French food data.

Angola

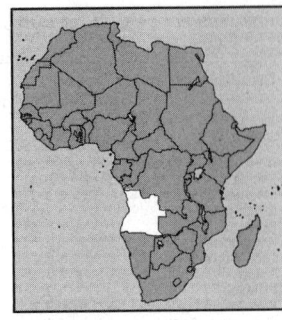

Official name: República Popular de Angola (People's Republic of Angola).
Form of government: people's republic with one legislative house (People's Assembly [290]).
Head of state and government: President.
Capital: Luanda.
Official language: Portuguese.
Official religion: none.
Monetary unit: 1 kwanza (Kw) = 100 lwei; valuation (Oct. 10, 1988) 1 U.S.$ = Kw 29.90; 1 £ = Kw 51.20.

Area and population

Provinces	Capitals	area sq mi	area sq km	population 1988 estimate[1]
Bengo	Caxito	12,112	31,371	154,000
Benguela	Benguela	12,273	31,788	717,000
Bié	Kuito	27,148	70,314	962,000
Cabinda	Cabinda	2,807	7,270	114,000
Cunene	N'Giva	34,495	89,342	251,000
Huambo	Huambo	13,233	34,274	1,300,000
Huíla	Lubango	28,958	75,002	836,000
Kuando Kubango	Menongue	76,853	199,049	174,000
Kuanza Norte	N'Dalatando	9,340	24,190	475,000
Kuanza Sul	Sumbe	21,490	55,660	710,000
Luanda	Luanda	934	2,418	1,192,000
Lunda Norte	Lucapa	39,685	102,783	311,000
Lunda Sul	Saurimo	17,625	45,649	149,000
Malanje	Malanje	37,684	97,602	851,000
Moxico	Lwena	86,110	223,023	284,000
Namibe	Namibe	22,447	58,137	79,000
Uíge	Uíge	22,663	58,698	604,000
Zaire	M'Banza Kongo	15,494	40,130	224,000
TOTAL		481,353[2]	1,246,700	9,386,000[2]

Demography

Population (1988): 9,386,000.
Density (1988): persons per sq mi 19.5, persons per sq km 7.5.
Urban-rural (1986): urban 30.8%; rural 69.2%.
Sex distribution (1988): male 51.11%; female 48.89%.
Age breakdown (1988): under 15, 42.2%; 15–29, 27.5%; 30–44, 16.4%; 45–59, 9.5%; 60 and over, 4.4%.
Population projection: (1990) 9,978,000; (2000) 13,151,000.
Doubling time: 28 years.
Ethnic composition (1983): Ovimbundu 37.2%; Mbundu 22.8%; Kongo 13.2%; Luimbe 5.4%; Humbe and Nyaneka 5.4%; Chokwe 4.2%; Luena 3.4%; Luchasi 2.4%; Ambo 2.4%; Lunda 1.2%; MBundu 1.2%; Portuguese 0.5%; mulatto 0.5%; other 0.2%.
Religious affiliation (1980): affiliated Christian 65.7%, of which Roman Catholic 55.1%, Protestant 9.2%; nominal Christian 24.3%; traditional beliefs 9.5%; other 0.5%.
Major cities (1988)[3]: Luanda 1,134,000; Lubango 105,000[4]; Namibe 77,000.

Vital statistics

Birth rate per 1,000 population (1985–86): 47.3 (world avg. 26.0).
Death rate per 1,000 population (1985–86): 21.9 (world avg. 9.9).
Natural increase rate per 1,000 population (1985–86): 25.4 (world avg. 16.1).
Total fertility rate (avg. births per childbearing woman; 1984): 6.4.
Marriage rate per 1,000 population (1972): 4.5.
Divorce rate per 1,000 population: n.a.
Life expectancy at birth (1987): male 41.0 years; female 44.0 years.
Major causes of death per 100,000 population (1973): accidents, poisonings, and violence 89.0; infectious and parasitic diseases 73.2; diseases of the respiratory system 24.6; diseases of the circulatory system 19.2; neoplasms 6.5.

National economy

Budget (1986). Revenue: Kw 86,205,000,000 (taxes 41.2%, revenues from mixed enterprises 21.3%, loans 17.4%, other 20.1%). Expenditures: Kw 86,205,000,000 (defense[5] and social welfare 37.9%, social services 24.9%, economic and social development 15.9%, administration 12.5%, other 8.8%).
Public debt (external, outstanding; 1985): U.S.$1,106,000,000.
Tourism: receipts from visitors, n.a.; expenditures by nationals abroad, n.a.
Price and earnings indexes: n.a.
Production (metric tons except as noted). Agriculture, forestry, fishing (1986): cassava 1,970,000, bananas 280,000, sugarcane 250,000, corn (maize) 230,000, sweet potatoes 180,000, pulses 40,000, palm oil 40,000, coffee 35,000, peanuts (groundnuts) 20,000; livestock (number of live animals) 3,380,000 cattle, 965,000 goats, 470,000 pigs, 255,000 sheep, 6,000,000 poultry; roundwood 5,009,000 cu m; fish catch 58,442. Mining and quarrying (1986): diamonds 250,000 carats, of which gem quality 240,000 carats, industrial quality 10,000 carats; cement 350,000; salt 10,000. Manufacturing (1986): bricks 297,700; bread 52,500; corn flour 41,700; wheat flour 25,200; refined sugar 20,300; soaps 11,000; molasses 11,000; crude steel 7,000; leather shoes 295,000 pairs; beer 5,830,000 hectolitres; matches 28,000,000 boxes. Construction (value in '000,000 Kw; 1986): residential 608; nonresidential 1,977. Energy production (consumption): electricity (kW-hr; 1986) 1,790,000,000 (1,790,000,000); coal (metric tons; 1986) none (negligible); crude petroleum (barrels; 1986) 103,178,000 (11,010,000); petroleum products

(metric tons; 1986) 1,270,000 (398,000); natural gas (cu m; 1986) 128,136,000 (128,136,000).
Gross national product (at current market prices; 1984): U.S.$6,930,000,000 (U.S. $830 per capita).

Structure of gross domestic product and labour force

	1986 in value Kw '000,000	1986 % of total value	1985 labour force	1985 % of labour force
Agriculture	16,408.2	13.9	2,672,000	71.8
Mining Manufacturing	36,933.7	31.2		
Construction	4,979.1	4.2		
Trade, finance	15,022.4	12.7	361,000	9.7
Public utilities	685.1	0.6		
Transportation and communications	8,546.8	7.2		
Pub. admin., defense Services	37,292.0	31.5	686,000	18.5
Other	−1,588.8[6]	−1.3[6]		
TOTAL	118,278.5	100.0	3,719,000	100.0

Population economically active (1985): total 3,719,000; activity rate of total population 42.5% (participation rates: ages 15–64, 71.8%; female 39.7%; unemployed, n.a.).
Household income and expenditure. Average household size (1980) 4.8; annual income per household: n.a.; sources of income: n.a.; expenditure: n.a.
Land use (1985): forested 42.8%; meadows and pastures 23.3%; agricultural and under permanent cultivation 2.8%; other 31.1%.

Foreign trade

Balance of trade (current prices)

	1981	1982	1983	1984	1985	1986
Kw '000,000	+5,807	+22,217	+34,007	+39,453	+47,274	+23,265
% of total	5.5%	29.5%	45.3%	48.0%	54.5%	42.5%

Imports (1986): Kw 15,708,000,000 (electrical machinery and equipment 25.6%, transport equipment 16.6%, industrial chemicals 8.0%, vegetable products 7.4%, food and beverages 7.0%). *Major import sources:* France 12.1%; Brazil 11.5%; Portugal 9.9%; United States 9.2%; West Germany 7.8%; The Netherlands 7.6%.
Exports (1986): Kw 38,973,000,000 (mineral fuels 93.4%, vegetable products 4.0%, animal products 1.7%). *Major export destinations:* United States 38.3%; Spain 10.9%; Brazil 8.1%; The Netherlands 5.8%; Portugal 4.1%; United Kingdom 2.7%.

Transport and communications

Transport. Railroads (1987): route length 1,739 mi, 2,798 km; passengers carried 7,980,000[7]; cargo transported 456,000 metric tons[7]. Roads (1986): total length 45,877 mi, 73,830 km (paved 51%). Vehicles (1984): passenger cars 56,625; trucks and buses 29,000. Merchant marine (1987): vessels (100 gross tons and over) 108; total deadweight tonnage 125,292. Air transport (1985)[8]: passenger-mi 606,000,000, passenger-km 975,000,000; short ton-mi cargo 23,200,000, metric ton-km cargo 33,900,000; airports (1988) with scheduled flights 18.
Communications. Daily newspapers (1984): total number 4; total circulation 111,500; circulation per 1,000 population 13.5. Radio (1986): total number of receivers 400,000 (1 per 22 persons). Television (1987): total number of receivers 33,000 (1 per 280 persons). Telephones (1987): 40,300 (1 per 226 persons).

Education and health

Education (1984)

	schools[9]	teachers[9]	students	student/ teacher ratio
Primary (age 7–10)	6,308	32,004	870,410	...
Secondary (age 11–16)	...	3,870[10]	151,759	...
Voc., teacher tr.	...	530	7,147	13.5
Higher	1	316	4,493	...

Educational attainment, n.a. *Literacy* (1980): total population over age 15 literate 1,196,000 (about 28%); males literate 771,000 (36.2%); females literate 425,000 (19.3%).
Health (1986): physicians 655 (1 per 13,489 persons); hospital beds 13,145 (1 per 672 persons); infant mortality rate per 1,000 live births (1986) 200.0.
Food (1979–81): daily per capita caloric intake 2,353 (vegetable products 92%, animal products 8%); 100% of FAO recommended minimum requirement.

Military

Total active duty personnel (1988): 100,000[11] (army 91.5%, navy 1.5%, air force 7.0%). *Military expenditure as percent of GNP* (1984): 14.3% (world 5.9%); per capita expenditure U.S.$119.

---

[1]Unified national estimates and projections based on sample surveys, partial censuses, and analysis of provincial vital statistics. [2]Detail does not add to total given because of rounding. [3]Populations (1970 census) of other important towns were: Huambo 61,885; Lobito 59,258; and Benguela 40,996. [4]1984. [5]According to unofficial estimates, defense consumed more than 60% of the budget in 1983. [6]Net subsidies. [7]1986. [8]TAAG airline only. [9]1982–83. [10]1981–82. [11]In 1988, about 52,000 Cuban troops and other Soviet-bloc advisers and technicians were assisting government forces. On July 20, 1988, an agreement was reached between South Africa, Cuba, Angola, and the United States calling for the withdrawal of all foreign troops over a period of 27 months.

Antigua and Barbuda

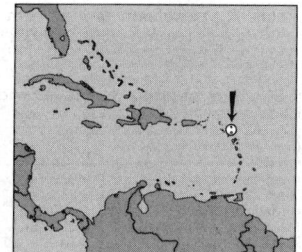

Official name: Antigua and Barbuda.
Form of government: constitutional
monarchy with two legislative houses
(Senate [17]; House of Representatives
[17]).
Chief of state: British Monarch
represented by governor-general.
Head of government: Prime Minister.
Capital: Saint John's.
Official language: English.
Official religion: none.
Monetary unit: 1 East Caribbean dollar
(EC$) = 100 cents; valuation (Oct. 10,
1988) 1 U.S.$ = EC$2.70;
1 £ = EC$4.62.

Area and population

Parishes[1]	area sq mi	area sq km	population 1986 estimate
Saint George	10.2	26.4	
Saint John's	26.2	67.9	
Saint Mary	25.1	65.0	80,000
Saint Paul	17.7	45.8	
Saint Peter	12.8	33.2	
Saint Phillip	16.0	41.4	
Islands[1]			
Barbuda	62.0	160.6	1,500
Redonda	0.5	1.3	2
TOTAL	170.5	441.6	81,500[3]

Demography

Population (1988): 77,400.
Density (1988): persons per sq mi 486.8, persons per sq km 188.0.
Urban–rural (1985): urban 30.8%; rural 69.2%.
Sex distribution (1985): male 48.00%; female 52.00%.
Age breakdown (1985): under 15, 37.2%; 15–29, 30.8%; 30–44, 12.8%; 45–59
11.5%; 60–74, 6.4%; 75 and over, 1.3%.
Population projection: (1990) 79,000; (2000) 85,000.
Doubling time: 58 years.
Ethnic composition (1980): black 94.4%; mulatto 3.5%; white 1.3%; other
0.8%.
Religious affiliation (1980): Anglican 44.5%; other Protestant (largely Mora-
vian, Methodist, and Seventh-day Adventist) 42.2%; Roman Catholic
10.2%; Rastafarian 0.7%; other 2.4%.
Major cities (1982): Saint John's 30,000; Codrington 1,200.

Vital statistics

Birth rate per 1,000 population (1986): 14.8 (world avg. 26.0); legitimate
21.2%; illegitimate 78.8%.
Death rate per 1,000 population (1986): 5.0 (world avg. 9.9).
Natural increase rate per 1,000 population (1986): 9.8 (world avg. 16.1).
Total fertility rate (avg. births per childbearing woman; 1987): 1.7.
Marriage rate per 1,000 population (1986): 4.1.
Divorce rate per 1,000 population (1986): 0.3.
Life expectancy at birth (1987): male 70.0 years; female 74.0 years.
Major causes of death per 100,000 population (1985): malignant neoplasms
(cancers) 83.3; hypertensive disease 68.8; acute myocardial infarction 38.3;
diabetes mellitus 27.8; pneumonia 26.4; diseases of pulmonary circulation
and other forms of heart disease 22.5.

National economy

Budget (1987)[4]. Revenue: EC$165,900,000 (tax revenue 85.0%, of which
consumer taxes 28.0%, import duties 21.0%, income taxes 11.9%, hotel
taxes 6.9%; nontax revenue 15.0%). Expenditure: EC$160,900,000 (personal
emoluments 24.9%, public debt charges 20.2%; wages 18.3%).
Public debt (external, outstanding; 1985): U.S.$64,900,000.
Production (metric tons except as noted). Agriculture, forestry, fishing
(1986): cucumbers 329, limes 189, eggplant 186, pumpkins 177, sweet
potatoes 166, carrots 135, ginger 32, sea island cotton lint 30; livestock
(number of live animals; 1986): 18,000 cattle, 13,000 sheep; roundwood,
n.a.; fish catch (1985) 2,407, of which lobsters 117. Mining and quarrying
(1985): crushed stone 82,500. Manufacturing (value of production in EC$;
1983): clothing 24,000,000; mattresses 4,500,000; stoves 3,300,000; refrigerators 1,700,000; rum 1,200,000; electronic components are assembled for
reexport. Construction (1986): total building applications 879; gross value
EC$80,700,000. Energy production (consumption): electricity (kW-hr; 1986)
86,400,000 (72,400,000); coal, none (none); crude petroleum (barrels; 1986)
none (none); petroleum products (metric tons; 1986) negligible (48,000);
natural gas, none (none).
Tourism (1987): receipts from visitors U.S.$142,600,000; expenditures by
nationals abroad U.S.$14,800,000.
Population economically active (1983): total 30,843; activity rate of total
population 39.4% (participation rates: age 16 and over 56.2%; female 39.6%;
unemployed [1985] 21.1%).

Price and earnings indexes (1982 = 100)

	1980	1981	1982	1983	1984	1985	1986
Consumer price index	86.1	96.0	100.0	102.3	106.3	107.4	109.6
Weekly earnings index[5]	...	...	100.0	115.7	123.6	131.5	140.9

Household income and expenditure. Average household size (1970) 4.2;
income per household: n.a.; sources of income: n.a.; expenditure (1974)[6]:
food and nonalcoholic beverages 42.9%, housing 23.3%, transportation
10.0%, clothing and footwear 7.5%, energy 5.5%, alcoholic beverages and
tobacco 3.6%, other 7.2%.
Gross national product (at current market prices; 1986): U.S.$190,000,000
(U.S.$2,380 per capita).

Structure of gross domestic product and labour force

	1986[7] in value EC$'000,000	1986[7] % of total value	1982 labour force[8]	1982 % of labour force
Agriculture, fishing	24.6	4.6	2,090	9.0
Quarrying	9.9	1.8	60	0.3
Manufacturing	21.5	4.0	1,718	7.4
Construction	50.6	9.4	2,577	11.1
Public utilities	19.9	3.7	340	1.5
Transp. and commun.	88.4	16.5	2,575	11.1
Trade, restaurants, and hotels	133.6	24.9	5,201	22.4
Finance, real estate	85.0	15.8	778	3.3
Pub. admin., defense	89.7	16.7	7,883	33.9
Services	43.9	8.2		
Other	−29.9[9]	−5.6[9]	—	—
TOTAL	537.2	100.0	23,222	100.0

Land use (1985): forested 11.0%; meadows and pastures 9.0%; agricultural
and under permanent cultivation 18.0%; other 62.0%.

Foreign trade[10]

Balance of trade (current prices)

	1982	1983	1984	1985	1986	1987
EC$'000,000	−318	−241	−309	−351	−690	−573
% of total	73.5%	69.3%	76.5%	70.8%	82.0%	77.5%

Imports (1984): EC$356,100,000 (crude petroleum and petroleum products
24.1%, of which petroleum spirits and kerosene 11.8%; machinery and
transport equipment 21.8%, of which motor vehicle parts 6.0%; food and
live animals 19.1%, of which meat 5.4%; chemical products 6.4%). *Major
import sources:* United States 37.8%; United Kingdom 10.6%; Caricom
7.4%; Yugoslavia 3.9%; Canada 3.4%.
Exports (1984): EC$47,500,000 (miscellaneous manufactured articles 37.8%;
machinery and transport equipment 30.1%; mineral fuels 11.5%; chemical
products 7.5%). *Major export destinations:* Caricom 38.2%; United States
17.9%; United Kingdom 3.4%; other Western Hemisphere 22.7%.

Transport and communications

Transport. Railroads[11]. Roads (1984): total length 341 mi, 548 km (paved
44%). Vehicles (1986): passenger cars 11,188; trucks and buses 3,321. Merchant marine (1987): vessels (100 gross tons and over) 55; total deadweight
tonnage 102,701. Air transport (1986)[12]: passenger arrivals 276,568, passenger departures 267,406; short ton-mi cargo, n.a., metric ton-km cargo, n.a.;
airports (1988) with scheduled flights 2.
Communications. Daily newspapers (1988): total number 1; total circulation
5,500; circulation per 1,000 population 66. Radio (1986): total number of
receivers 35,000 (1 per 2.3 persons). Television (1987): total number of
receivers 27,000 (1 per 3.0 persons). Telephones (1984): 11,000 (1 per 7.2
persons).

Education and health

Education (1983)

	schools	teachers	students	student/ teacher ratio
Primary (age 5–10)	48	426	9,933	23.3
Secondary (age 11–16)	16	331	4,197	12.7
Voc., teacher tr.[13]	2	...	631	...
Higher	...	...	...	...

Educational attainment (1970). Percent of total population having: no
schooling 15.0%; primary education 79.2%; secondary 4.5%; higher 1.3%.
Literacy (1985): total population age 15 and over literate 45,000 (90.0%).
Health: physicians (1986) 45 (1 per 1,695 persons); hospital beds (1984) 415
(1 per 190 persons); infant mortality rate per 1,000 live births (1985) 24.4.
Food (1984–86): daily per capita caloric intake 2,089 (vegetable products
75%, animal products 25%); (1983) 81% of FAO recommended minimum
requirement.

Military

Total active duty personnel (1986): 700-member defense and police force.
Military expenditure as percent of central government expenditure: 1.7%[14].

[1]Community councils are the actual organs of local governments. [2]Uninhabited.
[3]Unofficial estimate. 1986 official estimate (without separate island populations)
totals 76,296. [4]Current revenue and current expenditures only. 1984 budget: current
revenue EC$96,400,000; current expenditures EC$103,000,000, development expenditures EC$104,000,000 (mostly financed by grants). [5]Employees of deluxe hotels
only. [6]Weights of consumer price index components. [7]At factor cost. [8]Wage earners
and self-employed only. [9]Less imputed bank service charges. [10]Imports c.i.f.; exports
f.o.b. [11]48 mi (78 km) of privately owned track are mostly nonoperative. [12]Vere
Bird Airport. [13]1986. [14]May not agree with military expenditure as percent of GNP
because of different bases used.

Argentina

Official name: República Argentina (Argentine Republic).
Form of government: federal republic with two legislative houses (Senate [46]; Chamber of Deputies [254]).
Head of state and government: President.
Capital: Buenos Aires[1].
Official language: Spanish.
Official religion: Roman Catholicism.
Monetary unit: 1 austral (pl. australes)[2] (₳) = 1,000 pesos ($a 1,000); valuation (Oct. 10, 1988) 1 U.S.$ = ₳12.12; 1 £ = ₳20.76.

Area and population		area		population
				1986
Provinces	Capitals	sq mi	sq km	estimate
Buenos Aires	La Plata	118,754	307,571	12,226,000
Catamarca	San Fernando del Valle de Catamarca	38,984	100,967	230,000
Chaco	Resistencia	38,469	99,633	791,000
Chubut	Rawson	86,752	224,686	316,000
Córdoba	Córdoba	65,161	168,766	2,629,000
Corrientes	Corrientes	34,054	88,199	724,000
Entre Ríos	Paraná	30,418	78,781	968,000
Formosa	Formosa	27,825	72,066	338,000
Jujuy	San Salvador de Jujuy	20,548	53,219	487,000
La Pampa	Santa Rosa	55,382	143,440	231,000
La Rioja	La Rioja	34,626	89,680	183,000
Mendoza	Mendoza	57,462	148,827	1,344,000
Misiones	Posadas	11,506	29,801	690,000
Neuquén	Neuquén	36,324	94,078	315,000
Río Negro	Viedma	78,384	203,013	477,000
Salta	Salta	59,759	154,775	768,000
San Juan	San Juan	34,614	89,651	520,000
San Luis	San Luis	29,633	76,748	234,000
Santa Cruz	Río Gallegos	94,187	243,943	138,000
Santa Fe	Santa Fe	51,354	133,007	2,675,000
Santiago del Estero	Santiago del Estero	52,222	135,254	660,000
Tucumán	San Miguel de Tucumán	8,697	22,524	1,112,000
Other federal entities				
Distrito Federal	Buenos Aires	77	200	2,924,000
Tierra del Fuego	Ushuaia	8,210	21,263	50,000
TOTAL		1,073,399[3]	2,780,092	31,030,000

Demography

Population (1988): 31,963,000.
Density (1988): persons per sq mi 29.8, persons per sq km 11.5.
Urban–rural (1987): urban 85.3%; rural 14.7%.
Sex distribution (1985): male 49.61%; female 50.39%.
Age breakdown (1985): under 15, 31.1%; 15–29, 23.0%; 30–44, 19.1%; 45–59, 14.5%; 60–74, 9.5%; 75 and over, 2.8%.
Population projection: (1990) 32,880,000; (2000) 37,197,000.
Doubling time: 48 years.
Ethnic composition (1986): European 85%; mestizo, Amerindian, and other 15%.
Religious affiliation (1984): Roman Catholic 92.8%; other 7.2%.
Major cities (1980): Buenos Aires 2,922,829 (Greater Buenos Aires 9,967,826); Córdoba 968,829; Rosario 875,664; La Plata 454,884.

Vital statistics

Birth rate per 1,000 population (1987): 20.7 (world avg. 26.0); (1982) legitimate 67.5%; illegitimate 29.8%; unknown 2.7%.
Death rate per 1,000 population (1987): 8.6 (world avg. 9.9).
Natural increase rate per 1,000 population (1987): 12.1 (world avg. 16.1).
Total fertility rate (avg. births per childbearing woman; 1987): 2.9.
Marriage rate per 1,000 population (1983): 6.0.
Life expectancy at birth (1981): male 68.6 years; female 73.3 years.
Major causes of death per 100,000 population (1982): circulatory diseases 361.4; cancers 141.2; respiratory diseases 43.7; accidents 38.2.

National economy

Budget (1985). Revenue: ₳8,284,989,000 (social security taxes 27.1%, excise taxes 22.3%, general sales tax 13.8%, export duties 7.3%, income taxes 4.9%, property tax 4.9%, import duties 4.0%). Expenditures: ₳9,381,019,000 (social security and welfare 32.6%, economic service 18.4%, debt service 11.5%, education 6.0%, defense 5.2%, health 1.3%).
Public debt (external, outstanding; 1986): U.S.$38,453,200,000.
Tourism (1986): receipts from visitors U.S.$545,000,000; expenditures by nationals abroad U.S.$853,000,000.
Production (metric tons except as noted). Agriculture, forestry, fishing (1987): sugarcane 14,465,000[4], wheat 10,030,000, corn (maize) 9,250,000, soybeans 7,000,000, sunflower seeds 4,100,000[4], sorghum 3,000,000, grapes 2,750,000[4], potatoes 2,100,000[4], tomatoes 824,400[4]; livestock (number of live animals; 1986) 53,000,000 cattle, 29,243,000 sheep; roundwood (1986) 12,562,000 cu m; fish catch (1986) 420,306. Mining and quarrying (1986): uranium 101; silver 2,283,000 troy oz; gold 28,936 troy oz. Manufacturing (by value of production in ₳'000; 1986): motor vehicles 1,783,321; paper and paper products 672,396; refined sugar 466,481; iron and steel 452,429; iron and steel pipes and tubes 377,523; beer 134,924. Construction (authorized; 1984): 10,606,800 sq m. Energy production (consumption): electricity (kW-hr; 1986) 48,984,000,000 (48,978,000,000); coal (metric tons; 1986) 365,000 (1,525,000); crude petroleum (barrels; 1986) 159,300,000 (157,-

570,000); petroleum products (metric tons; 1986) 20,634,000 (19,061,000); natural gas (cu m; 1986) 15,903,290,000 (18,114,200,000).
Gross national product (1986): U.S.$72,920,000,000 (U.S.$2,350 per capita).

Structure of gross domestic product and labour force				
	1986[5]		1980	
	in value ₳'000,000	% of total value	labour force	% of labour force
Agriculture	1,379	14.6	1,200,992	12.0
Mining	240	2.5	47,171	0.5
Manufacturing	2,297	24.3	1,985,995	19.9
Construction	309	3.3	1,003,175	10.1
Public utilities	449	4.8	103,256	1.0
Transp. and commun.	1,082	11.5	460,476	4.6
Trade	1,370	14.5	1,702,080	17.0
Finance	741	7.8	395,704	4.0
Pub. admin., defense	} 1,575	16.7	2,399,039	24.0
Services				
Other	...	...	691,302	6.9
TOTAL	9,444[3]	100.0	9,989,190	100.0

Population economically active (1985): total 11,452,444; activity rate of total population 37.5% (participation rates: ages 15–64, 59.2%; female 26.8%; unemployed 5.7%).

Price and earnings indexes (1981 = 100)							
	1981	1982	1983	1984	1985	1986	1987
Consumer price index	100.0	265.2	1,177.9	8,559.8	66,094.6	138,990.3	309,772.8
Monthly earnings index[6]	100.0	236.9	1,362	12,033	75,667	...	...

Land use (1985): forested 21.8%; meadows and pastures 52.1%; agricultural and under permanent cultivation 13.2%; other 12.9%.

Foreign trade

Balance of trade (current prices)						
	1982	1983	1984	1985	1986	1987
U.S.$'000,000	+2,764	+3,716	+3,982	+4,878	+2,446	+1,000
% of total	22.1%	34.5%	32.6%	29.5%	21.7%	8.5%

Imports (1986)[7]: ₳4,531,315,000 (machinery and transport equipment 35.7%, of which electrical machinery 13.6%, transport equipment 7.4%; chemicals 21.9%; petroleum and products 10.6%; iron and steel products 5.3%; plastics 3.3%). *Major import sources:* U.S. 18.2%; Brazil 16.0%; W.Ger. 10.6%; Japan 7.0%.
Exports (1986)[7]: ₳6,403,225,000 (cereals 27.3%; vegetable oils 11.8%; petroleum and petroleum products 9.2%; animal feed 6.2%; iron and steel products 5.0%; meat 4.6%; hides and skins 4.2%). *Major export destinations:* U.S.S.R. 14.4%; U.S. 12.2%; The Netherlands 10.2%; Brazil 5.9%; Japan 4.3%; Italy 3.4%; West Germany 3.4%.

Transport and communications

Transport. Railroads (1986): route length 21,233 mi, 34,172 km; passenger-km 12,456,000,000; metric ton-km cargo 8,760,000,000. Roads (1986): total length 131,338 mi, 211,369 km (paved 27%). Vehicles (1986): passenger cars 3,898,000; commercial vehicles and buses 1,434,700. Merchant marine (1987): vessels (100 gross tons and over) 434; total deadweight tonnage 2,853,308. Air transport (1986): passenger-km 8,721,997,000; metric ton-km cargo 984,000,000; airports (1988) 63.
Communications. Daily newspapers (1986): total number 227; total circulation 2,748,400[8]; circulation per 1,000 population 88[8]. Radio (1985): 19,-866,000 receivers (1 per 1.5 persons). Television (1986): 5,950,000 receivers (1 per 5.2 persons). Telephones (1986): 3,206,298 (1 per 9.8 persons).

Education and health

Education (1985)				
	schools	teachers	students	student/ teacher ratio
Primary (age 6–12)	20,700	229,715	4,589,291	20.0
Secondary (age 13–17)[9]	1,987[10]	93,675	715,518	7.6
Vocational	3,117[10]	136,418	1,084,531	8.0
Higher	1,251[10]	70,699	846,145	12.0

Educational attainment (1980). Percent of population age 25 and over having: no formal schooling 6.0%; less than primary education 32.0%; primary 34.6%; secondary 20.5%; higher 6.9%. *Literacy* (1980): total population age 15 and over literate 94.9%; males literate 95.5%; females literate 94.4%.
Health (1984): physicians 81,260 (1 per 370 persons); hospital beds (1980) 151,568 (1 per 186 persons); infant mortality rate per 1,000 live births (1988) 35.3.
Food (1984–86): daily per capita caloric intake 3,191 (vegetable products 68%; animal products 32%); (1983) 119% of FAO recommended minimum requirement.

Military

Total active duty personnel (1987): 78,000 (army 57.7%, navy 25.6%, air force 16.7%). *Military expenditure as percent of GNP* (1985): 3.3% (world 6.1%); per capita expenditure: U.S.$76.

[1]Legislation has been enacted to move the capital from Buenos Aires to Viedma in northern Patagonia by 1989. [2]Introduced June 14, 1985, at the rate of 1 austral (₳) = 1,000 pesos ($a). [3]Detail does not add to total given because of rounding. [4]1986. [5]At 1970 prices. [6]Skilled workers in manufacturing only. [7]Commodities breakdown is for 1985. [8]For 109 newspapers only. [9]Teacher training included with secondary. [10]1984.

Aruba

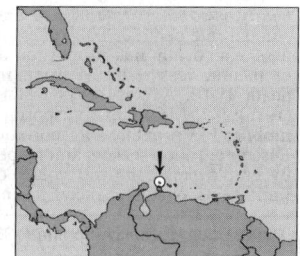

Official name: Aruba.
Political status: nonmetropolitan part of The Netherlands realm with one legislative house (States of Aruba [21])[1].
Chief of state: Dutch Monarch represented by governor.
Head of government: Prime Minister.
Capital: Oranjestad.
Official language: Dutch.
Official religion: none.
Monetary unit: 1 Aruban florin[2] (Afl.) = 100 cents; valuation (Oct. 10, 1988) 1 U.S.$ = Afl. 1.79; 1 £ = Afl. 3.06.

Area and population

Island	Capital	area sq mi	area sq km	population 1981 census
Aruba	Oranjestad	75	193	60,312
TOTAL		75	193	60,312

Demography

Population (1988): 65,500.
Density (1988): persons per sq mi 873.3, persons per sq km 339.4.
Urban–rural: n.a..
Sex distribution (1981): male 48.64%; female 51.36%.
Age breakdown (1981): under 15, 25.9%; 15–29, 30.6%; 30–44, 21.3%; 45–59, 12.7%; 60–74, 7.4%; 75 and over, 2.1%.
Population projection: (1990) 66,000; (2000) 67,000.
Doubling time: 59 years.
Ethnic composition (1980): mostly Netherlands Antillean (Dutch/Spanish/black/Amerindian) creole[3].
Religious affiliation (1981): Roman Catholic 88.5%; Protestant 7.4%, of which Lutheran/Reformed tradition 2.5%, Methodist 2.4%; other Christian (Jehovah's Witness) 1.1%; Jewish 0.2%; nonreligious 1.6%; other 1.2%.
Major cities (1986): Oranjestad 19,800; San Nicolas 17,000.

Vital statistics

Birth rate per 1,000 population (1983): 16.9 (world avg. 29.0); (1982) legitimate 41.3%; illegitimate 58.7%.
Death rate per 1,000 population (1983): 5.1 (world avg. 11.0).
Natural increase rate per 1,000 population (1983): 11.8 (world avg. 18.0).
Total fertility rate (avg. births per childbearing woman; 1987): 1.8.
Marriage rate per 1,000 population (1983): 7.5.
Divorce rate per 1,000 population (1982): 2.0.
Life expectancy at birth (1981): male 71.6 years; female 76.8 years.
Major causes of death per 100,000 population: n.a.

National economy

Budget (1985)[4]. Revenue: NA f. 144,000,000 (taxes on wages 55.7%, taxes on profits 18.1%, taxes on goods and services 8.4%). Expenditures: NA f. 220,100,000 (current expenditures 89.6%, transfers to central government 8.3%, development expenditures 2.1%).
Public debt (funded debt to The Netherlands; end of 1986): U.S.$92,000,000.
Tourism (1987): receipts from visitors U.S.$202,500,000; expenditures by nationals abroad U.S.$16,500,000.
Production (metric tons except as noted). Agriculture, forestry, fishing (1986): aloes are cultivated for export; small amounts of tomatoes, beans, cucumbers, gherkins, watermelons, and lettuce are grown on hydroponic farms; divi-divi pods, sour orange fruit, sorghum, and peanuts (groundnuts) are nonhydroponic crops of limited value; livestock (number of live animals; 1986[5]) 23,000 goats, 9,000 cattle, 9,000 sheep, 8,000 pigs; roundwood, n.a.; fish catch 1,060. Mining and quarrying: excavation of sand for local use. Manufacturing: rum, cigarettes, paints, pharmaceuticals, motor vehicle parts, furniture, and soft drinks[6]. Construction: n.a. Energy production (consumption): electricity (kW-hr; 1986[5]) 1,485,000,000 (1,485,000,000); coal, none (none); crude petroleum (barrels; 1986[5, 7]) none (60,800,000); petroleum products (metric tons; 1986[5, 7]) 7,800,000 (1,391,000); natural gas, none (none).
Gross national product (at current market prices; 1985[5]): U.S.$1,610,000,000 (U.S.$6,810 per capita).

Structure of gross domestic product and labour force

	1987 in value U.S.$'000,000	1987 % of total value	1981[8] labour force	1981[8] % of labour force
Agriculture	...	...	40	0.2
Mining	...	...	4	—
Manufacturing	...	...	2,020	8.6
Construction	...	...	1,882	8.0
Public utilities	...	...	484	2.1
Transportation and communications	...	...	1,277	5.4
Trade, restaurants, hotels	...	...	7,720	32.7
Finance	...	...	1,045	4.4
Pub. admin., defense	...	... }	9,082	38.5
Services	...	...		
Other	...	...	22	0.1
TOTAL	440	100.0	23,576	100.0

Population economically active (1981): total 26,031; activity rate of total population 43.2% (participation rates: ages 15–64, 62.0%; female 36.7%; unemployed [1986] 22.0%).

Price and earnings indexes (1980 = 100)

	1985	1986	1987	1988
Consumer price index	...	131.0	135.8	138.8[9]
Monthly earnings index	...	...	...	...

Household income and expenditure (1981): average household size 3.6; income per household: n.a.; sources of income: n.a.; expenditure: food 24.5%, housing 18.4%, transportation and communications 17.4%, household furnishings 9.1%, clothing and footwear 8.4%, recreation and education 5.0%, health 2.9%, beverages and tobacco 2.9%, other 11.4%.
Land use (1985): forested, negligible; meadows and pastures, negligible; agricultural and under permanent cultivation 5.0%; other (dry savanna and built-up) 95.0%.

Foreign trade[7, 10]

Balance of trade (current prices)

	1982	1983	1984	1985	1986	1987[11]
NA f. '000,000	+91	−33	−68	...	−301	−257
% of total	0.9%	0.4%	0.9%	...	78.0%	78.0%

Imports (1984): NA f. 3,827,000,000 (crude petroleum and petroleum products 88.1%, machinery and transport equipment 2.8%, food 2.6%, chemicals 2.3%, basic and miscellaneous manufactures 1.8%). *Major import sources* (1983): Venezuela 83.0%; United States 9.4%; Saudi Arabia 2.2%; The Netherlands 1.5%.
Exports (1984): NA f. 3,759,000,000 (crude petroleum and petroleum products 98.9%, crude materials including sulfur pyrite 0.7%). *Major export destinations* (1983): United States 55.5%; Puerto Rico 9.7%; United Kingdom 4.5%; Chile 2.7%; Colombia 2.6%.

Transport and communications

Transport. Railroads: none. Roads (1984): total length 236 mi, 380 km (paved 100%). Vehicles (1984): passenger cars 23,409; trucks and buses 582. Merchant marine: vessels (100 gross tons and over) n.a. Air transport (1985): passenger arrivals 329,061, passenger departures 333,261; cargo unloaded 2,056 metric tons, cargo loaded 893 metric tons; airports (1988) with scheduled flights 1.
Communications. Daily newspapers (1987): total number 2; total circulation 8,591; circulation per 1,000 population 131. Radio: (1986): total number of receivers 12,000 (1 per 5.1 persons). Television (1987): total number of receivers 19,000 (1 per 3.4 persons). Telephones (1986): 21,679 (1 per 3.0 persons).

Education and health

Education (1987–88)

	schools	teachers	students	student/teacher ratio
Primary (age 6–12)	31	327	6,341	19.4
Secondary (age 12–17)	11	173	3,011	17.4
Voc., teacher tr.	15	225	2,807	12.5
Higher	...	...	...	...

Educational attainment (1981). Percent of population age 25 and over having: no formal schooling or incomplete primary education 34.9%; completed primary 28.6%; completed secondary/vocational 36.1%; completed higher 0.4%. *Literacy* (1985): total population age 15 and over literate 95.0%.
Health (1985): physicians 59 (1 per 1,043 persons); hospital beds 279 (1 per 221 persons); infant mortality rate per 1,000 live births (1987) 10.0.
Food (1984–86)[5]: daily per capita caloric intake 2,922 (vegetable products 66%; animal products 34%); (1983) 116% of FAO recommended minimum requirement.

Military

Total active duty personnel (1987): A small Dutch naval contingent is stationed permanently in the Netherlands Antilles and Aruba.

[1]Aruba withdrew from the Netherlands Antilles on Jan. 1, 1986, becoming an autonomous member of the Kingdom of The Netherlands, the same status as that of the whole of the Netherlands Antilles. [2]The Aruban florin (Afl.), introduced Jan. 1, 1986, is pegged to the U.S. dollar at a fixed rate of Afl. 1.79 = 1 U.S.$ and is at near parity with the Netherlands Antillean guilder (NA f., Aruba's currency until 1986), which has had an official exchange rate of NA f. 1.80 = 1 U.S.$ since 1971. [3]Nationality (1981): Dutch 93.8%, of which born in Aruba or the Netherlands Antilles 88.3%, born in The Netherlands 2.3%, born elsewhere 3.2%; citizen of the United Kingdom 1.3%; Colombian 0.8%; Venezuelan 0.7%; citizen of the Dominican Republic 0.7%; citizen of the United States 0.6%; other 2.1%. [4]Island government of Aruba prior to withdrawal from the Netherlands Antilles. [5]Includes the Netherlands Antilles. [6]Servicing facilities, including a petroleum transshipment terminal and two ship repair and bunkering facilities, are underutilized. [7]Aruba's oil refinery was closed in March 1985. [8]Employed persons only. [9]March. [10]Imports c.i.f.; exports f.o.b. [11]First three quarters only.

Australia

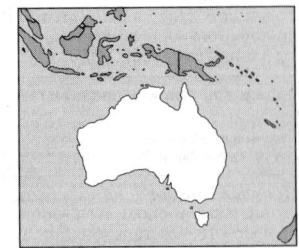

Official name: Commonwealth of
Australia.
Form of government: federal
parliamentary state (formally a
constitutional monarchy) with two
legislative houses (Senate [76]; House
of Representatives [148]).
Chief of state: British Monarch
represented by governor-general.
Head of government: Prime Minister.
Capital: Canberra.
Official language: English.
Official religion: none.
Monetary unit: 1 Australian dollar
($A) = 100 cents; valuation (Oct. 10,
1988) 1 U.S.$ = $A 1.24;
1 £ = $A 2.13.

Area and population

		area		population
States	**Capitals**	sq mi	sq km	1988 estimate
New South Wales	Sydney	309,500	801,600	5,681,200
Queensland	Brisbane	666,900	1,727,200	2,726,300
South Australia	Adelaide	379,900	984,000	1,404,900
Tasmania	Hobart	26,200	67,800	448,100
Victoria	Melbourne	87,900	227,600	4,247,300
Western Australia	Perth	975,100	2,525,500	1,532,700
Territories				
Australian Capital Territory	Canberra	900	2,400	271,900
Northern Territory	Darwin	519,800	1,346,200	156,100
TOTAL		2,966,200	7,682,300	16,468,600

Demography

Population (1988): 16,470,000.
Density (1988): persons per sq mi 5.6, persons per sq km 2.1.
Urban-rural (1981): urban 85.7%; rural 14.3%.
Sex distribution (1987): male 49.93%; female 50.07%.
Age breakdown (1987): under 15, 22.6%; 15-29, 25.1%; 30-44, 22.5%; 45-59, 14.6%; 60-74, 11.1%; 75 and over, 4.1%.
Population projection: (1990) 16,921,000; (2000) 19,371,000.
Doubling time: 91 years.
Ethnic composition (1983): white 94.4%; Asian 2.1%; aboriginal 1.1%; other 2.4%.
Religious affiliation (1981): Christian 76.4%, of which Anglican Church of Australia 26.1%, Roman Catholic 26.0%, other Protestant 20.8% (Uniting Church 4.9%, Presbyterian 4.4%, Methodist 3.4%), Orthodox 2.9%; Muslim 0.5%; Jewish 0.4%; Buddhist 0.2%; no religion 10.8%; other 11.7%.
Major cities (1986): Sydney 3,472,700; Melbourne 2,931,900; Brisbane 1,196,-000; Adelaide 1,003,800; Perth 1,050,400; Newcastle 416,100; Canberra 281,000[1]; Gold Coast 233,900[2]; Wollongong 232,500; Hobart 178,900.
Place of birth (1986): 77.6% native-born; 22.4% foreign-born, of which Europe 14.2% (United Kingdom 7.2%[3], Italy 1.7%, Yugoslavia 1.0%, Greece 0.9%, East and West Germany 0.7%, other Europe 2.7%); Asia 3.4%; New Zealand 1.4%; Africa 0.7%; the Americas 0.7%; other 2.0%.
Mobility (1986). Population age 15 and over living in the same residence as in 1985: 84.2%; different residence, same state 14.2%; different state or territory 1.6%.
Households (1986). Total number of households 5,713,000. Average household size 2.9; (1981) 1 person 18.0%, 2 persons 29.2%, 3 persons 16.9%, 4 persons 19.1%, 5 persons 10.5%, 6 persons 4.1%, 7 or more persons 2.2%. Family households (1986): 4,087,100 (71.5%), nonfamily 1,625,900 (28.5%).
Immigration (1986): permanent immigrants admitted 103,330, from United Kingdom and Ireland 20.0%[3], New Zealand 13.7%, Vietnam 7.1%, Philippines 4.7%, South Africa 4.0%, Hong Kong 3.1%, Lebanon 2.7%, Malaysia 2.7%, China 2.6%, India 2.1%, Yugoslavia 2.0%, Chile 1.8%, United States 1.7%, East and West Germany 1.2%. Refugee arrivals (1986-87) 12,000.

Vital statistics

Birth rate per 1,000 population (1987): 15.2 (world avg. 26.0); (1986) legitimate 83.2%; illegitimate 16.8%.
Death rate per 1,000 population (1987): 7.5 (world avg. 9.9).
Natural increase rate per 1,000 population (1987): 7.7 (world avg. 16.1).
Total fertility rate (avg. births per childbearing woman; 1986): 1.9.
Marriage rate per 1,000 population (1987): 7.0.
Divorce rate per 1,000 population (1987): 2.4.
Life expectancy at birth (1986): male 72.8 years; female 79.1 years.
Major causes of death per 100,000 population (1986): diseases of the circulatory system 345; malignant neoplasms (cancers) 174; diseases of the respiratory system 49; accidents, poisonings, and violence 34; diseases of the digestive system 25; endocrine, nutritional, and metabolic diseases and immunity disorders 14; chronic liver diseases 7; nephritis and nephrosis 7.

Social indicators

Educational attainment (1986). Percent of population age 15 and over having: no formal schooling 0.4%; primary and secondary education 64.8%, of which completed secondary 11.4%; postsecondary, technical, or other certificate/diploma 27.7%; university 7.1%.
Leisure, n.a.

Quality of working life (1987). Average workweek: 35.6 hours (19% overtime). Annual rate per 100,000 workers for: injury or accident, n.a.; industrial illness, n.a.; death, n.a. Proportion of employed persons insured for damages or income loss resulting from: injury 100%; permanent disability 100%; death 100%. Average days lost to labour stoppages per 1,000 workdays (1986): 0.7. Means of transportation to work (1981): 62.2% private automobile; 13.9% public transportation; 1.3% bicycle; 5.4% foot; 17.2% other. Discouraged job seekers among persons not in the labour force (considered by employers to be too young or too old, having language or training limitations, or no vacancies in line of work; 1984): 1.3% of labour force.

Distribution of family income (1985-86)

percent of family income by quintile

1	2	3	4	5 (highest)
4.7%	9.5%	15.8%	24.6%	45.4%

Access to services (1976). Proportion of dwellings having access to: electricity 99.5%; bathroom 96.0%; flush toilet 92.2%; kitchen 97.9%; public sewer 73.4%.
Social participation. Eligible voters participating in last national election (1987): 88.0%. Population age 16 and over participating in voluntary work (1982): 4.2%. Trade union membership in total work force (1986): 55%. Practicing religious population in total affiliated population: n.a.
Social deviance (1984). Offense rate per 100,000 population for: murder 3.4; rape 13.8; serious assault 58.6; auto theft 584.7; burglary and housebreaking 1,754.3; fraud and forgery 473.8. Incidence per 100,000 in general population of (1984): alcoholism, n.a.; drug and substance abuse (charges) 360.8; suicide (1986) 12.4.
Material well-being (1983). Households possessing: automobile 86%; telephone 85%; refrigerator 99.6%; air conditioner 32.3%; washing machine 91.7%; hot water 98.7%; central heating 3.9%; swimming pool 10.1%.

National economy

Gross national product (at current market prices; 1986): U.S.$190,470,000,-000 (U.S.$11,910 per capita).

Structure of gross domestic product and labour force

	1985-86		1986	
	in value $A '000,000	% of total value	labour force	% of labour force
Agriculture	9,609	4.0	414,800	5.5
Mining	15,275	6.4	95,900	1.3
Manufacturing	40,063	16.8	1,126,700	15.1
Construction	16,473	6.9	491,000	6.6
Public utilities	8,386	3.5	137,000	1.8
Transportation and communications	17,162	7.2	542,400	7.2
Trade	37,475	15.7	1,383,600	18.5
Finance	48,794	20.4	699,200	9.3
Pub. admin., defense	10,400	4.3	324,000	4.3
Services	37,076	15.5	1,671,000	22.3
Other	-1,774[4]	-0.7[4]	595,800[5]	8.0[5]
TOTAL	238,939	100.0	7,481,400	100.0[6]

Budget (1986-87). Revenue: $A 71,261,000,000 (income tax 62.9%, of which individual 51.6%, corporate 11.3%; excise duties and sales tax 27.1%). Expenditures: $A 74,764,000,000 (1985-86; social security and welfare 27.6%; transfers to state governments 19.6%; health 9.7%; interest on public debt 9.7%; defense 9.5%; education 7.2%; general public services 6.9%; economic services 6.3%; housing 2.0%; culture and recreation 1.2%).
Public debt (1988): $A 55,095,000,000[7].
Tourism (1986): receipts from visitors U.S.$1,371,000,000; expenditures by nationals abroad U.S.$1,932,000,000.

Manufacturing, mining, and construction enterprises (1986-87)[8]

	no. of establishments	no. of employees	Avg. annual wages[9] as a % of all wages	annual value added ($A '000,000)
Manufacturing				
Food, beverages, and tobacco	3,598	167,700	96.3	8,511
Paper, printing, and publishing	3,111	104,900	106.7	5,102
Basic metal products	572	75,200	128.9	4,498
Chemical, petroleum, and coal products	865	52,600	124.2	4,140
Transport equipment	1,381	108,900	103.6	3,975
Fabricated metal products	4,396	93,300	95.0	3,431
Wood, wood products, and furniture	4,331	72,000	81.8	2,402
Nonmetallic mineral products	1,797	38,700	112.2	2,314
Clothing and footwear	2,121	72,400	72.0	2,006
Textiles	664	34,300	93.2	1,503
Mining[10]				
Coal, oil, and gas	127	38,924 }	150.5	8,646
Metallic minerals	272	30,977 }		3,657
Nonmetallic minerals	1,087	8,859	...	716
Construction[11]	51,351	246,510	104.0	3,925

Production (gross value in $A '000 except as noted). Agriculture, forestry, fishing (1986-87): livestock slaughtered—cattle 2,819,100, sheep and lambs 728,300, pigs 457,500; wool 3,330,300, wheat 2,570,300, sugarcane 585,500, barley 428,300, cotton 358,300, grapes 274,800, potatoes 264,200, apples 184,000, oats 163,900, sorghum 137,800, oranges 120,300, bananas 105,-600, rice 80,400, pears 75,800, pineapples 40,400, sunflower seeds 39,600, peanuts (groundnuts) 39,000, peaches 37,900; livestock (number of live animals; 1987) 154,471,000 sheep, 21,976,000 cattle, 2,450,000 pigs, 52,000,000 poultry; roundwood 1,999,000 cu m; fish catch 156,600 metric tons. Mining and quarrying (metric tons; 1986-87): iron ore 96,770,000; bauxite 33,216,-

000; refined metals—aluminum 921,000, zinc 300,411, copper 170,858, lead 142,432, tin 784, gold 81,856 kg. Manufacturing (metric tons; 1986–87): raw steel 6,387,000; cement 5,902,000; pig iron 5,783,000; iron and steel slabs 3,670,000; superphosphate 2,434,000; sulfuric acid 1,678,000; beef and veal 1,508,000; wheat flour 1,217,000; refined sugar 725,400; newsprint 386,320; lamb 296,900; mutton 285,900; pork 282,300; plaster sheets 71,511,000 sq m; textile floor coverings 41,468,000 sq m; woven cotton cloth 38,327,000 sq m; woven woolen cloth 11,242,000 sq m; concrete roofing tiles 14,391,000 cu m; automotive gasoline 152,960,000 hectolitres; furnace fuel 22,740,000 hectolitres; beer 18,610,000 hectolitres; finished and partly finished motor vehicles 322,451 units. Construction (buildings completed by value in $A '000; 1986–87): new dwellings 6,929,400,000; alterations and additions to dwellings 1,112,800,000; nonresidential 8,456,100.

Retail sales and service enterprises (1979–80)

	no. of estab-lishments	no. of employees	total wages and salaries ($A '000,000)	annual turnover ($A '000,000)
Motor vehicle dealers, gasoline and tire dealers	26,516	175,995	1,319	18,203
Food stores	39,416	260,266	1,131	12,747
Department and general stores	857	99,569	717	4,254
Clothing, fabrics, and furniture stores	17,908	81,797	519	4,143
Household appliances and hardware stores	8,196	43,542	320	2,966
Restaurants, hotels and accommodations	17,702	183,310	1,022	4,670
Licensed clubs	3,243	52,297	697	1,515
Laundries and dry cleaners	1,365	12,106	91	224
Motion picture theatres	577	6,777	45	178
Hairdressers and beauty salons	2,265	12,282	78	173

Energy production (consumption): electricity (kW-hr; 1986–87) 130,190,000,000 (130,190,000,000); coal (metric tons; 1986–87) 182,255,000 (76,743,000[12]); crude petroleum (barrels; 1986) 187,000,000 (219,000,000); petroleum products (metric tons; 1986) 27,037,000 (27,645,000); natural gas (cu m; 1986) 14,748,000 (15,332,000).
Population economically active (1986): total 7,481,400; activity rate of total population 46.8% (participation rates: ages 15–64, 70.2%; female 39.5%; unemployed 8.0%).

Price and earnings indexes (1980 = 100)

	1982	1983	1984	1985	1986	1987	1988
Consumer price index	121.9	134.3	139.6	149.0	162.0	176.0	187.0
Weekly earnings index	124.5	133.3	146.0	153.4	165.3	174.3	184.5

Household income and expenditure. Average household size (1986): 2.8; average annual income per household (1985–86) $A 21,390 (U.S.$14,219); sources of income (1985–86): wages and salaries 60.3%, transfer payments 25.7%, self-employment 7.4%, other 6.6%; expenditure (1985–86): housing 21.9%, food and nonalcoholic beverages 20.8%, transportation and communications 13.4%, household durable goods 6.7%, health 6.4%, clothing and footwear 6.2%, recreation 3.9%, energy 2.4%.
Land use (1985): meadows and pastures 59.0%; agricultural and under permanent cultivation 4.3%; other 36.7%[13].

Financial aggregates

	1982	1983	1984	1985	1986	1987	1988 (10 mo.)
Exchange Rate, $A 1.00 per:							
U.S. Dollar	1.02	0.90	0.88	0.70	0.67	0.70	0.81
£	0.50	0.59	0.64	0.54	0.46	0.43	0.47
SDR	0.89	0.86	0.84	0.62	0.54	0.51	0.61
International reserves (U.S.$)							
Total (excl. gold; '000,000)	6,371	8,962	7,441	5,768	7,246	8,744	13,386
SDRs ('000,000)	86	81	209	310	332	369	339
Reserve pos. in IMF ('000,000)	...	114	183	207	231	268	274
Foreign exchange ('000,000)	6,285	8,768	7,049	5,250	6,684	8,107	12,773
Gold ('000,000 fine troy oz)	7.93	7.93	7.93	7.93	7.93	7.93	7.93
% world reserves	0.8	0.8	0.8	0.8	0.8	0.8	0.8
Interest and prices							
Central bank discount (%)	15.76	12.14	12.03	15.98	16.93	14.95	13.20
Gov't. Bond yield (%)	15.2	12.8	12.2	14.0	14.0	13.17	12.90
Industrial share prices (1980 = 100)	79.5	100.4	117.0	143.5	193.4	277.6	259.7
Balance of payments (U.S.$'000,000)							
Balance of visible trade	−2,613	30	−884	−1,284	−2,103	−511	...
Imports, f.o.b.	23,406	19,470	23,653	23,559	24,292	26,827	...
Exports, f.o.b.	20,793	19,500	22,769	22,275	22,189	26,316	...
Balance of invisibles	−5,810	−6,057	−7,751	−7,952	−8,379	−9,207	...
Balance of payments, current account	−8,514	−5,951	−8,518	−8,704	−9,810	−8,676	...

Foreign trade

Balance of trade (current prices)

	1981–82	1982–83	1983–84	1984–85	1985–86	1986–87
$A '000,000	−2,099	+1,331	+720	+614	−1,872	−1,239
% of total	4.6%	3.0%	1.5%	1.0%	2.8%	1.7%

Imports (1986–87): $A 37,021,910,000 (machinery 29.9%, of which office machines and automatic data-processing equipment 6.9%; basic manufactures 16.4%, of which textile yarn and fabrics 4.9%, nonferrous metals 2.7%, paper and paperboard 2.7%; transport equipment 11.0%, of which road motor vehicles 7.3%; chemicals and related products 9.2%; mineral fuels and lubricants 4.6%; food and live animals 4.3%; crude materials [inedible] excluding fuels 2.9%; beverages and tobacco 0.9%). Major import sources: United States 22.4%; Japan 20.9%; United Kingdom 7.3%; West Germany 7.2%; New Zealand 3.9%; Italy 3.0%; Saudi Arabia 2.4%; Hong Kong 2.2%; France 2.2%; Singapore 2.0%.

Exports (1986–87): $A 35,782,583,000 (crude materials excluding fuels 27.7%, of which metalliferous ores and metal scrap 13.6%; food and live animals 22.3%, of which cereals 7.8%, meat 6.3%; mineral fuels and lubricants 20.4%, of which coal, coke, and briquettes 15.2%; textile fibres and their waste 10.8%; petroleum, petroleum gases, and petroleum products 5.2%; machinery and transport equipment 7.3%). Major export destinations: Japan 25.4%; United States 12.3%; New Zealand 5.0%; China 4.4%; South Korea 4.2%; United Kingdom 3.8%; Taiwan 3.4%; West Germany 3.1%; Hong Kong 3.0%; U.S.S.R. 1.9%; Papua New Guinea 1.9%.

Trade by commodity group (1986–87)

SITC Group	imports $A '000,000	imports %	exports $A '000,000	exports %
00 Food and live animals	1,612.0	4.3	7,993.5	22.3
01 Beverages and tobacco	326.8	0.9	151.6	0.4
02 Crude materials, excluding fuels	1,083.3	2.9	9,904.0	27.7
03 Mineral fuels, lubricants, and related materials	1,749.2	4.6	7,309.1	20.4
04 Animal and vegetable oils, fat and waxes	91.4	0.2	123.3	0.3
05 Chemicals and related products, n.e.s.	3,472.0	9.2	663.4	1.9
06 Basic manufactures	6,185.8	16.4	3,834.7	10.7
07 Machinery and transport equipment	15,422.6	40.9	2,612.2	7.3
08 Miscellaneous manufactured articles	5,184.8	13.8	853.7	2.4
09 Goods not classified by kind	2,563.3	6.8	2,337.1	6.5
TOTAL	37,691.2	100.0	35,782.6	100.0[6]

Direction of trade (1987–88)

	imports $A '000,000	imports %	exports $A '000,000	exports %
Africa	369.0	0.9	609.5	1.5
Asia	16,282.5	40.1	22,689.5	55.6
Japan	7,816.6	19.3	10,644.1	26.1
South America	416.8	1.0	254.3	0.6
North and Central America	9,460.1	23.3	5,391.7	13.2
United States	8,529.9	21.0	4,631.2	11.3
Europe	11,920.3	29.4	8,298.8	20.3
EEC	9,745.7	24.0	6,406.4	15.7
U.S.S.R.	21.7	0.1	631.8	1.5
Other Europe	2,152.9	5.3	1,260.6	3.1
Oceania	1,983.8	4.9	3,408.9	8.4
New Zealand	1,732.7	4.3	2,408.9	5.9
Other countries, including destinations unknown	158.8	0.4	172.7	0.4
TOTAL	40,591.3	100.0	40,825.4	100.0

Transport and communications

Transport. Railroads[14] (1986): route length 24,084 mi, 38,760 km; passenger-mi 1,359,051,000[15], passenger-km 2,187,120,000[15]; short ton-mi cargo 33,120,000,000, metric ton-km cargo 48,357,000,000. Roads (1986): total length 530,020 mi, 852,986 km (paved 50%). Vehicles (1986): passenger cars 8,770,899; trucks and buses 1,231,359. Merchant marine (1987): vessels (100 gross tons and over) 690; total deadweight tonnage 3,701,273. Air transport (1987): passenger-mi 14,111,070,000, passenger-km 22,709,609,000; short ton-mi cargo 2,076,979,000, metric ton-km cargo 3,032,334,000; airports (1988) with scheduled flights 441.
Communications. Daily newspapers (1983): total number 61; total circulation 4,739,500; circulation per 1,000 population 308. Radio (1985): total number of receivers 20,000,000 (1 per 0.8 person). Television (1985): total number of receivers 6,500,000 (1 per 2.3 persons). Telephones (1985): 8,727,000 (1 per 1.8 persons).

Education and health

Education (1986)

	schools	teachers	students	student/teacher ratio
Primary (age 6–12)	8,466	95,606	1,711,932	17.9
Secondary (age 13–17)	1,619	101,115	1,289,457	12.8
Vocational[16]	234	52,587	859,195	16.3
Higher	95	26,036	390,706	15.0

Literacy (1980): total population age 15 and over literate 99.5%.
Health (1986): physicians (1982) 27,500 (1 per 552 persons); hospital beds 87,586 (1 per 185 persons); infant mortality rate per 1,000 live births (1987) 8.7.
Food (1984–86): daily per capita caloric intake 3,326 (vegetable products 65%, animal products 35%); (1983) 115% of FAO recommended minimum requirement.

Military

Total active duty personnel (1988): 70,500 (army 45.4%, navy 22.4%, air force 32.2%). Military expenditure as percent of GNP (1985): 2.9% (world 6.1%); per capita expenditure U.S.$323.

[1]Includes Queanbeyan. [2]Includes part of Tweed Shire. [3]Includes both Northern Ireland and Republic of Ireland. [4]Less imputed bank service charges. [5]Unemployed. [6]Detail does not add to total given because of rounding. [7]First quarter. [8]Excludes operations of single-establishment enterprises employing fewer than four persons. [9]Excludes the drawings of working proprietors. [10]1985–86. [11]1985. [12]1986. [13]Urban areas, state forests and mining leases, unoccupied land (mainly desert). [14]Government railways only. [15]1978–79. [16]Includes special education.

Austria

Official name: Republik Österreich
  (Republic of Austria).
Form of government: federal multi-
  party republic with two legislative
  houses (Federal Council [63]; National
  Council [183]).
Chief of state: President.
Head of government: Chancellor.
Capital: Vienna.
Official language: German.
Official religion: none.
Monetary unit: 1 Schilling (S) = 100
  Groschen; valuation (Oct. 10, 1988)
  1 U.S.$ = S 13.04; 1 £ = S 22.33.

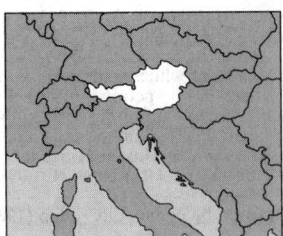

Area and population

States	Capitals	area		population
		sq mi	sq km	1986 estimate
Burgenland	Eisenstadt	1,531	3,966	267,279
Kärnten	Klagenfurt	3,681	9,533	541,526
Niederösterreich	Sankt Pölten	7,403	19,174	1,424,911
Oberösterreich	Linz	4,626	11,980	1,290,497
Salzburg	Salzburg	2,762	7,154	459,886
Steiermark	Graz	6,327	16,387	1,182,599
Tirol	Innsbruck	4,883	12,647	605,774
Vorarlberg	Bregenz	1,004	2,601	311,732
Wien	—	160	415	1,481,399
TOTAL		32,377	83,857	7,565,603

Demography

Population (1988): 7,557,000.
Density (1988): persons per sq mi 233.4, persons per sq km 90.1.
Urban-rural (1981): urban 55.0%; rural 45.0%.
Sex distribution (1987): male 47.47%; female 52.53%.
Age breakdown (1987): under 15, 17.7%; 15–29, 24.6%; 30–44, 20.0%; 45–59,
  17.5%; 60–74, 13.3%; 75 and over, 6.9%.
Population projection: (1990) 7,857,000; (2000) 7,628,000.
Doubling time: not applicable; population is stable.
Ethnic composition (national origin; 1981): Austrian 96.1%; Yugoslavian
  1.7%; Turkish 0.8%; German 0.5%; other 0.9%.
Religious affiliation (1981): Roman Catholic 84.3%; Protestant 5.6%; non-
  religious and atheist 6.0%; other 4.1%.
Major cities (1981): Vienna 1,481,399[1]; Graz 243,166; Linz 199,910; Salzburg
  139,426; Innsbruck 117,287.

Vital statistics

Birth rate per 1,000 population (1986): 11.5 (world avg. 26.0); legitimate
  76.7%; illegitimate 23.3%.
Death rate per 1,000 population (1986): 11.5 (world avg. 9.9).
Natural increase rate per 1,000 population (1986): 0.0 (world avg. 16.1).
Total fertility rate (avg. births per childbearing woman; 1986): 1.4.
Marriage rate per 1,000 population (1986): 6.1.
Divorce rate per 1,000 population (1986): 1.9.
Life expectancy at birth (1980–82): male 69.2 years; female 76.4 years.
Major causes of death per 100,000 population (1986): diseases of the cir-
  culatory system 617.9, of which ischemic heart disease 205.6; malignant
  neoplasms (cancers) 247.1; diseases of the respiratory system 57.7; acci-
  dents 51.4.

National economy

Budget (1986). Revenue: S 343,600,000,000 (taxes 90.5%, of which indirect
  income 47.6%, direct income 31.5%, corporate 6.1%, property income and
  entrepreneurship 5.3%). Expenditures: S 361,100,000,000 (transfer payments
  41.5%, of which to public authorities 23.8%, to private households 17.4%;
  goods and services 28.0%; interest on public debt 11.2%; subsidies 9.1%).
Production (metric tons except as noted). Agriculture, forestry, fishing
  (1986): sugar beets 2,041,818, corn (maize) 1,739,740, wheat 1,414,599, barley 1,292,450, potatoes 982,405, apples 368,585, rye 286,601, milk 3,776,500;
  livestock (number of live animals) 3,800,513 pigs, 2,637,224 cattle, 14,197,-
  751 chickens; roundwood 12,131,000. Mining and quarrying (metal content
  of ore; 1986): iron 970,000; zinc 17,880; lead 5,640; magnesite (ore) 1,084,-
  360. Manufacturing (value added in S '000,000; 1984): machinery 64,912, of
  which electrical 26,631; transport 15,813; metal products (including steel)
  22,629; beverages and tobacco 21,303; textiles and apparel 20,478; chemical
  products 18,795; food products 15,616. Construction (dwellings completed;
  1986): residential 3,790,000 sq m; nonresidential, n.a. Energy production
  (consumption): electricity (kW-hr; 1986) 44,134,000,000 (42,670,000,000);
  coal (metric tons; 1986) 2,969,000 (7,850,000); crude petroleum (barrels;
  1986) 7,904,000 (53,531,000); petroleum products (metric tons; 1986) 7,764,-
  000 (10,216,000); natural gas (cu m; 1986) 1,114,660,000 (4,795,000,000).
Population economically active (1986): total 3,388,100; activity rate of total
  population 44.8% (participation rates: ages 15–64, 65.9%; female 39.6%;
  unemployed 5.2%).

Price and earnings indexes (1980 = 100)

	1981	1982	1983	1984	1985	1986	1987
Consumer price index	106.8	112.6	116.3	122.9	126.9	129.0	130.8
Monthly earnings index	106.1	112.7	117.8	123.7	131.2	137.0	141.3

Gross national product (at current market prices; 1986): U.S.$75,540,000,000
  (U.S.$10,000 per capita).

Structure of gross domestic product and labour force

	1986			
	in value S '000,000	% of total value	labour force	% of labour force
Agriculture	47,000	3.3	285,200	8.4
Mining			14,300	0.4
Manufacturing }	394,820	27.6	956,100	28.2
Construction	94,820	6.6	284,000	8.4
Public utilities	44,500	3.1	40,700	1.2
Transportation and communications	83,390	5.8	222,700	6.6
Trade	225,110	15.7	624,400	18.4
Finance	221,580	15.5	190,400	5.6
Pub. admin., defense	207,690	14.5 }	753,600	22.2
Services	49,970	3.5 }		
Other	63,650	4.4	16,400	0.5
TOTAL	1,432,530	100.0	3,388,100	100.0

Household income and expenditure. Average household size (1986) 2.6;
  income per household[2] (1985) S 179,000 (U.S.$8,665); sources of income
  (1984): wages and salaries 56.1%, social security benefits and social assistance grants 24.3%, other 19.6%; expenditure (1984): food 23.1%, housing
  and utilities 18.1%, clothing and footwear 10.7%.
Land use (1985): forested 38.9%; meadows and pastures 24.0%; agricultural
  and under permanent cultivation 18.4%; other 18.7%.
Tourism (1986): receipts from visitors U.S.$6,076,000,000; expenditures by
  nationals abroad U.S.$3,257,000,000.

Foreign trade

Balance of trade (current prices)

	1981	1982	1983	1984	1985	1986
S '000,000	−69,520	−53,460	−55,940	−55,950	−57,570	−47,480
% of total	12.1%	9.1%	9.2%	8.7%	7.5%	6.5%

Imports (1986): S 407,954,099,000 (machinery and transport equipment
  33.8%, of which road vehicles 10.2%; manufactured goods 19.2%, of which
  textile yarn 4.6%, iron and steel 3.0%; chemicals and related products
  10.1%; clothing and wearing apparel 6.0%). *Major import sources:* West
  Germany 44.0%; Italy 9.0%; Switzerland 4.8%; Japan 4.4%; France 3.9%;
  United States 3.2%.
Exports (1986): S 342,478,717,000 (machinery and transport equipment
  33.2%, of which electrical equipment 6.5%; manufactured goods 32.8%, of
  which iron and steel 7.7%, paper and paper products 5.6%; chemicals 8.6%).
  Major export destinations: West Germany 32.7%; Italy 9.3%; Switzerland
  7.8%; United Kingdom 4.5%; France 4.3%; United States 4.0%.

Transport and communications

Transport. Railroads (1986): length 4,128 mi, 6,643 km; passenger-mi 4,555,-
  800,000, passenger-km 7,331,900,000; short ton-mi cargo 7,718,000,000[3],
  metric ton-km cargo 11,268,000,000[3]. Roads (1986): total length 67,791 mi,
  109,100 km (paved 100%). Vehicles (1986): passenger cars 2,609,390; trucks
  and buses 221,672. Merchant marine (1987): vessels (100 gross tons and
  over) 29; total deadweight tonnage 337,855. Air transport (1986): passenger-
  mi 857,300,000, passenger-km 1,380,000,000; short ton-mi cargo 16,100,000,
  metric ton-km cargo 23,500,000; airports (1988) with scheduled flights 6.
Communications. Daily newspapers (1986): total number 33; total circulation, 2,574,000[4]; circulation per 1,000 population, n.a. Radio (1986): total
  number of receivers 2,639,497 (1 per 2.9 persons). Television (1987): total number of receivers 2,660,160 (1 per 2.8 persons). Telephones (1986):
  3,843,000 (1 per 2.0 persons).

Education and health

Education (1986–87)

	schools	teachers	students	student/ teacher ratio
Primary (age 6–9)	3,395	28,454	342,378	12.0
Secondary (age 10–18)	2,067	57,177	483,167	8.5
Voc., teacher tr.	1,392	22,662	364,264	16.1
Higher	18	10,352	175,924	16.4

Educational attainment (1986). Percent of population age 25 and over having: primary education 43.3%; lower secondary 32.7%; higher secondary
  15.1%; postsecondary 4.0%; university 4.9%. *Literacy* (1986): virtually 100%.
Health (1987): physicians 20,228 (1 per 374 persons); hospital beds 83,341
  (1 per 91 persons); infant mortality rate per 1,000 live births 10.3.
Food (1984–86): daily per capita caloric intake 3,416 (vegetable products
  62%, animal products 38%); (1983) 126% of FAO recommended minimum requirement.

Military

Total active duty personnel (1987): 54,700 (army 91.4%; navy, none; air force
  8.6%). *Military expenditure as percent of GNP* (1984): 1.3% (world 6.0%);
  per capita expenditure U.S.$112.

---

[1]1986. [2]Median net household or disposable income. [3]Federal railways only. [4]For 28
newspapers only.

Bahamas, The

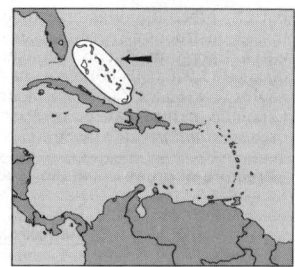

Official name: The Commonwealth of
  The Bahamas.
Form of government: constitutional
  monarchy with two legislative houses
  (Senate [16]; House of Assembly [49]).
Chief of state: British Monarch
  represented by governor-general.
Head of government: Prime Minister.
Capital: Nassau.
Official language: English.
Official religion: none.
Monetary unit: 1 Bahamian dollar
  (B$) = 100 cents; valuation
  (Oct. 10, 1988) 1 Bahamian
  dollar = U.S.$1.00 = £1.71.

Area and population

Islands and Island Groups[2]	Residence of Commissioner[2]	area[1] sq mi	area[1] sq km	population 1980 census[3]
Abaco, Great and Little, and Mores Island and cays	Marsh Harbour	649	1,681	7,324
Acklins Island	Pompey Bay	192	497	616
Andros Island	Kemps Bay	2,300	5,957	8,397
Berry Islands	Nicolls Town	12	31	509
Biminis, North and South, Cay Lobos, and Cay Sal	Alice Town	11	28	1,432
Cat Island	Arthur's Town	150	388	2,143
Crooked Island	Colonel Hill	84	218	517
Eleuthera, Harbour Island, and Spanish Wells	Rock Sound	200	518	10,600
Exuma, Great and Little, and cays	George Town	112	290	3,672
Grand Bahama	Freeport	530	1,373	33,102
Inagua, Great and Little	Matthew Town	599	1,551	939
Long Cay	...	9	23	33
Long Island	Clarence Town	230	596	3,358
Mayaguana	Abraham's Bay	110	285	476
New Providence	Nassau	80	207	135,437
Ragged Island and cays	Duncan Town	14	36	146
San Salvador and Rum Cay	Cockburn Town	90	233	804
TOTAL		5,382[4]	13,939[4]	209,505

Demography

Population (1988)[3]: 245,000.
Density (1988): persons per sq mi 45.7, persons per sq km 17.6.
Urban–rural (1986): urban 54.1%; rural 45.9%.
Sex distribution (1985): male 49.80%; female 50.20%.
Age breakdown (1985): under 15, 38.0%; 15–29, 27.9%; 30–44, 17.9%; 45–59, 10.5%; 60–74, 4.8%; 75 and over, 0.9%.
Population projection: (1990) 253,000; (2000) 302,000.
Doubling time: 60 years.
Ethnic composition (1980): black 72.3%; mixed 14.2%; white 12.9%; other 0.6%.
Religious affiliation (1980): non-Anglican Protestant (mostly Baptist and Church of God [Anderson Ind.]) 48.4%; Roman Catholic 25.5%; Anglican 20.7%; other 5.4%.
Major cities (1980): Nassau 110,000; Freeport 25,423.

Vital statistics

Birth rate per 1,000 population (1987): 16.7 (world avg. 26.0); (1986) legitimate 42.4%, illegitimate 57.6%.
Death rate per 1,000 population (1987): 5.0 (world avg. 9.9).
Natural increase rate per 1,000 population (1987): 11.7 (world avg. 16.1).
Total fertility rate (avg. births per childbearing woman; 1987): 2.6.
Marriage rate per 1,000 population (1987): 7.6.
Divorce rate per 1,000 population (1986): 1.6.
Life expectancy at birth (1980–85): male 66.9 years; female 70.9 years.
Major causes of death per 100,000 population (1986): diseases of the circulatory system 166.4; malignant neoplasms (cancers) 120.7; diabetes mellitus 29.2%; homicide and violence 26.3.

National economy

Budget (1987). Revenue: B$404,245,000 (customs receipts 60.9%, stamp taxes 7.6%, fines and forfeits 6.9%, departure taxes 3.9%, business and professional licenses 3.6%). Expenditures: B$435,980,000 (education 22.1%, health 17.1%, general administration 10.8%, public order 9.5%, interest on the public debt 9.3%, public works 8.3%, defense 3.0%).
Public debt (external, outstanding; 1986): U.S.$199,100,000.
Production (value of production in B$'000 except as noted). Agriculture, forestry, fishing (1987): poultry products 21,400; marine products landed at Nassau (mostly crayfish, groupers, conchs) 20,400; fruits and vegetables 11,000; beef and mutton 400; roundwood (1985) 115,000 cu m. Mining and quarrying (1987): salt 9,400; aragonite 1,800. Manufacturing (1987): pharmaceuticals 124,700; rum 15,800. Construction (gross value of buildings completed in B$'000,000; 1987)[5]: residential 81; nonresidential 32. Energy production (consumption): electricity (kW-hr; 1986) 865,000,000 (865,000,-000); coal, none (none); crude petroleum, none (negligible); petroleum products (metric tons; 1986) negligible (387,000); natural gas, none (none).
Gross national product (at current market prices; 1986): U.S.$1,700,000,000 (U.S.$7,190 per capita).

Structure of gross domestic product and labour force

	1986 in value B$'000,000	1986 % of total value	1980 labour force	1980 % of labour force
Agriculture	90	4.5	4,554	5.2
Mining			346	0.4
Manufacturing	206	10.3	4,957	5.7
Public utilities			1,271	1.5
Construction	61	3.1	6,675	7.7
Transp. and commun.	219	10.9	6,176	7.1
Trade	524	26.2	24,474	28.1
Finance	245	12.2	6,441	7.4
Pub. admin., defense	342	17.1	32,158[6]	36.9[6]
Services	315	15.7		
TOTAL	2,003[7]	100.0	87,052	100.0

Population economically active (1980): total 87,052; activity rate of total population 41.6% (participation rates: ages 15–64, 70.5%; female 44.5%; unemployed [1987] 18.0%).

Price and earnings indexes (1980 = 100)

	1981	1982	1983	1984	1985	1986	1987
Consumer price index	111.1	117.8	122.6	127.4	133.2	140.5	146.6[8]
Annual earnings index	...	...	...	...	...	...	...

Household income and expenditure. Average household size (1980) 4.3; income per household (1979) B$13,537 (U.S.$13,537)[5]; sources of income: n.a.; expenditure (1982)[9]: food and beverages 20.5%, expenditures in restaurants and hotels 16.1%, transport and communications 15.1%, housing 14.1%, recreation 6.5%, household furnishings 6.0%, clothing and footwear 4.0%.
Tourism: receipts from visitors (1987) U.S.$1,092,000,000; expenditures by nationals abroad (1986) U.S.$131,000,000.
Land use (1985): forested 32.2%; meadows and pastures 0.2%; agricultural and under permanent cultivation 0.9%; other 66.7%.

Foreign trade

Balance of trade (current prices)

	1981	1982	1983	1984	1985	1986
B$'000,000	−1,095	−1,814	−646	−705	−349	−591
% of total	8.1%	16.7%	7.5%	9.4%	6.0%	9.9%

Imports (1986): B$3,293,000,000 (petroleum [all forms] 73.8%, machinery and transport equipment 6.1%, food 5.0%). *Major import sources* (1985): Nigeria 33.9%; United States 27.3%; Mexico 7.7%; Angola 4.8%; United Kingdom 4.3%.
Exports (1986): B$2,702,000,000 (petroleum [all forms] 87.5%, chemicals 8.4%, nonpetroleum reexports 1.3%, hormones 0.9%, crayfish 0.7%, rum 0.4%). *Major export destinations* (1985): United States 82.9%; Puerto Rico 4.9%; United Kingdom 3.3%; Japan 2.0%.

Transport and communications

Transport. Railroads: none. Roads (1984): total length 2,548 mi, 4,100 km (paved 40%). Vehicles (1984): passenger cars 88,000; trucks and buses 5,600. Merchant marine (1987): vessels (100 gross tons and over) 469; total deadweight tonnage 15,695,840. Air transport (1985)[10]: passenger-mi 135,200,000, passenger-km 217,600,000; short ton-mi cargo 148,600, metric ton-km cargo 217,000; airports (1988) with scheduled flights 21.
Communications. Daily newspapers (1986): total number 3; total circulation 28,000; circulation per 1,000 population 118. Radio (1986): total receivers 120,000 (1 per 2.0 persons). Television (1987): total receivers 50,000 (1 per 4.8 persons). Telephones (1986): 108,054 (1 per 2.2 persons).

Education and health

Education (1985)

	schools	teachers	students	student/teacher ratio
Primary (age 5–11)	183	1,757	37,181	21.2
Secondary (age 11–17)	38	1,472	23,563	16.0
Higher	1	135	2,000	14.8

Educational attainment (1970). Percent of population age 25 and over having: no formal schooling 6.7%; primary education only 15.4%; secondary 63.0%; postsecondary or higher 14.9%. *Literacy* (1984): total population age 15 and over literate 125,000 (89.0%).
Health (1985): physicians 218 (1 per 1,031 persons); hospital beds 999[11] (1 per 235 persons); infant mortality rate per 1,000 live births (1985–87 avg.) 29.8.
Food (1984–86): daily per capita caloric intake 2,699 (vegetable products 69%, animal products 31%); (1983) 94% of FAO recommended minimum requirement.

Military

Total active duty personnel (1987): 496[12]. *Military expenditure as percent of GNP* (1984): 0.5% (world 6.1%); per capita expenditure U.S.$40.

---

[1]Land area only of individual islands or island groups. [2]Out Islands (all islands and island groups other than New Providence) are governed by commissioners assigned by the central government. [3]De jure. [4]Total includes 10 sq mi (27 sq km) unaccounted for in breakdown. [5]New Providence and Grand Bahama islands only. [6]Includes 1,705 not adequately defined and 6,359 unemployed persons not previously employed. [7]Detail does not add to total given because of rounding. [8]Average of first quarter. [9]Excludes significant volume of direct purchases abroad. [10]Bahamasair only. [11]Excludes two private hospitals. [12]All paramilitary (coast guard) personnel.

Bahrain

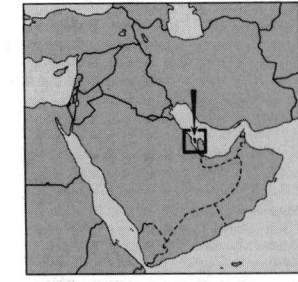

Official name: Dawlat al-Baḥrayn (State of Bahrain).
Form of government: monarchy (emirate) with a cabinet appointed by the Emir.
Chief of state: Emir.
Head of government: Prime Minister.
Capital: Manama.
Official language: Arabic.
Official religion: Islam.
Monetary unit: 1 Bahrain dinar (BD) = 1,000 fils; valuation (Oct. 10, 1988) 1 BD = U.S.$2.66 = £1.56.

Area and population

Regions	area[1]		population
	sq mi	sq km	1981 census
Central	13.6	35.2	16,776
al-Ḥadd	1.9	5.0	7,111
Judd Ḥafṣ	8.3	21.6	33,693
al-Manāmah	9.8	25.4	121,986
al-Muḥarraq	5.9	15.2	61,853
Northern	14.2	36.8	22,117
Rifāʿ	112.6	291.6	28,150
Sitrah	11.0	28.6	22,993
Western	60.2	156.0	14,503
Towns with special status			
Ḥammād	5.1	13.1	...
Madīnat ʿĪsā	4.8	12.4	21,275
Islands			
Ḥawār and other	19.3	50.0	341
TOTAL	266.7	690.9	350,798

Demography

Population (1988): 421,000.
Density (1988): persons per sq mi 1,578.5, persons per sq km 609.4.
Urban–rural (1986): urban 82.7%; rural 17.3%.
Sex distribution (1987): male 58.42%; female 41.58%.
Age breakdown (1987): under 15, 33.4%; 15–29, 33.9%; 30–44, 20.2%; 45–59, 8.7%; 60 and over, 3.8%.
Population projection: (1990) 431,000; (2000) 471,900.
Doubling time: 23 years.
Ethnic composition (1981): Bahraini Arab 68.0%; Persian, Indian, and Pakistani 24.7%; other Arab 4.1%; European 2.5%; other 0.7%.
Religious affiliation (1981): Muslim 85.0%; (Shīʿī 60.0% and Sunnī 40.0%); Christian 7.3%; other 7.7%.
Major cities (1987): Manama 146,994; al-Muḥarraq 75,579; Judd Ḥafṣ 46,741; ar-Rifāʿ 45,530; Madīnat ʿĪsā 39.783.

Vital statistics

Birth rate per 1,000 population (1986): 36.8 (world avg. 26.0); legitimate, n.a.; illegitimate, n.a.
Death rate per 1,000 population (1986): 5.8 (world avg. 9.9).
Natural increase rate per 1,000 population (1986): 31.0 (world avg. 16.1).
Total fertility rate (avg. births per childbearing woman; 1986): 5.2.
Marriage rate per 1,000 population (1985): 6.6.
Divorce rate per 1,000 population (1985): 1.1.
Life expectancy at birth (1986): male 65.0 years; female 68.4 years.
Major causes of death per 100,000 population (1985): diseases of the circulatory system 102.1; certain conditions originating in the perinatal period 46.3; malignant neoplasms (cancers) 35.0; injuries and poisonings 31.3; ill-defined conditions 20.5; congenital anomalies 9.5; respiratory diseases 19.5; diseases of the genito-urinary system 9.5; endocrine, nutritional, and metabolic diseases 9.3; diseases of the digestive system 7.5; infectious and parasitic diseases 6.5.

National economy

Budget (1986)[2]. Revenue: BD 560,000,000 (petroleum company dividends and oil field receipts 64.4%; tax revenue 20.8%, of which taxes on international trade 9.9%; social security contributions 3.9%). Expenditures: BD 560,000,000 (public utilities 12.9%; defense 10.2%; education 10.2%; health 6.4%; roads 6.3%; social security and welfare 2.3%).
Population economically active (1986): total 183,179; activity rate of total population 42.1% (participation rates: ages 15–64, 65.3%; female 14.2%; unemployed [1987] 10.0%).

Price and earnings indexes (1980 = 100)

	1981	1982	1983	1984	1985	1986	1987[3]
Consumer price index	111.3	121.2	124.8	125.2	121.9	119.1	116.4
Monthly earnings index	...	...	...	...	...	...	...

Production (metric tons except as noted). Agriculture, forestry, fishing (1986): fruit excluding melons 45,000, dates 40,000[4], tomatoes 13,000, cow's milk 6,000, eggplants 3,000, onions 3,000, hen's eggs 2,400, cucumbers 2,000, melons 1,000; livestock (number of live animals) 15,000 goats, 7,000 sheep, 6,000 cattle, 1,000,000 chickens; fish catch 8,299. Manufacturing (1986): fuel oil 22,611,000; gasoline 21,207,000; naphtha 13,383,000; kerosene 2,924,000; heavy lubricant distillate 1,091,000; petroleum bitumen 1,085,000; aluminum metal 178,000; manufactured gases 3,000,000

barrels; other manufactures include methanol, plastics, and paper products. Construction (permits issued; 1985): residential 6,820; nonresidential 2,012. Energy production (consumption): electricity (kW-hr; 1986) 2,970,-000,000 (2,970,000,000); coal, none (n.a.); crude petroleum (barrels; 1986) 15,484,000 (86,890,000); petroleum products (metric tons; 1986) 8,814,000 (572,000); natural gas (cu m; 1986) 4,312,000,000 (4,312,000,000).
Gross national product (1986): U.S.$3,670,000,000 (U.S.$8,530 per capita).

Structure of gross domestic product and labour force

	1984		1986	
	value in BD '000,000	% of total value	labour force	% of labour force
Agriculture	19.4	1.0	3,654	2.0
Mining	356.1	19.0	6,374	3.5
Manufacturing	206.3	11.0	14,364	7.8
Construction	185.4	9.9	38,444	21.0
Public utilities	24.5	1.3	3,869	2.1
Transp. and commun.	197.5	10.5	17,236	9.4
Trade	187.0	10.0	24,634	13.5
Finance	277.3	14.8	7,693	4.2
Pub. admin., defense	240.6	12.8	...	...
Services	183.4	9.7	66,911	36.5
Other			...	...
TOTAL	1,877.5	100.0	183,179	100.0

Households. Average household size (1986) 6.5; income per household: n.a.; sources of income: n.a.; expenditure: n.a.
Land use (1985): meadows and pastures 6.5%; agricultural and under permanent cultivation 3.2%; built-on and wasteland (mostly sand plains and salt marshes) 90.3%.
Public debt (external, outstanding; 1985): U.S.$330,000,000.
Tourism[5]: receipts from visitors (1986) U.S.$100,000,000; expenditures by nationals abroad U.S.$112,000,000.

Foreign trade[6]

Balance of trade (current prices)

	1981	1982	1983	1984	1985	1986
BD '000,000	+238	+201	+71	−16	−129	+59.3
% of total	7.9%	7.6%	3.0%	0.7%	5.8%	3.5%

Imports (1986): BD 912,400,000 (nonpetroleum products 59.3%, petroleum products 40.7%). *Major import sources* (1985): Saudi Arabia 50.3%; United Kingdom 7.8%; Japan 7.1%; United States 4.0%; West Germany 3.7%.
Exports (1986): BD 881,300,000 (petroleum products 83.6%, nonpetroleum products [mostly aluminum products] 16.4%). *Major export destinations* (1985): United Arab Emirates 18.9%; India 12.6%; Japan 10.5%; United States 3.2%; country not specified 17.6%.

Transport and communications

Transport. Railroads: none. Roads (1984): total length 155 km (paved 100.0%). Vehicles (1986): passenger cars 81,872; trucks and buses 24,720. Merchant marine (1987): vessels (100 gross tons and over) 94; total deadweight tonnage 51,975. Air transport (1986)[7]: passenger-mi 721,000,000, passenger-km 1,160,000,000; short ton-mi cargo 21,500,000, metric ton-km cargo 31,400,000; airports (1988) with scheduled flights 1.
Communications. Daily newspapers (1987): total number 5; total circulation 21,000[8]; circulation per 1,000 population 50[8]. Radio (1986): total number of receivers 142,000 (1 per 2.9 persons). Television (1987): total number of receivers 135,000 (1 per 3.1 persons). Telephones (1986): 119,077 (1 per 3.5 persons).

Education and health

Education (1984–85)

	schools	teachers	students	student/ teacher ratio
Primary (age 6–11)	114	2,963	49,644	16.8
Secondary (age 12–17)	21	951	32,927	34.6
Voc., teacher tr.	5	233	2,846	12.2
Higher	2	159	3,650	22.9

Educational attainment (1981). Percent of population age 10 and over having: no formal education 27.2%; knowledge of reading and writing 26.3%; primary education 24.9%; secondary 13.3%; higher 8.3%.
Literacy (1986): total population age 15 and over literate 213,693 (75.1%); males literate 145,761 (82.0%); females literate 67,932 (63.5%).
Health (1985): physicians 518 (1 per 839 persons); hospital beds 1,481 (1 per 294 persons); infant mortality rate per 1,000 live births (1986) 50.0.

Military

Total active duty personnel (1987): 2,800 (army 82.1%, navy 10.7%, air force 7.2%). *Military expenditure as percent of GNP* (1985): 4.0% (world 6.1%); per capita expenditure U.S.$378.

---

[1]Total area includes numerous small uninhabited islands and dependencies of Bahrain. [2]Revenue and expenditures detail is given for 1984. [3]November. [4]1984. [5]*Tourism* (1986–87): number of tourist arrivals (1986) 260,000; number of tourist arrivals in first 6 months of 1987 after completion of causeway with Saudi Arabia 1,400,000. [6]Import figures are f.o.b. in balance of trade and c.i.f. for commodities and trading partners. [7]One-fourth apportionment of international flights of Gulf Air (jointly administered by the governments of Bahrain, Oman, Qatar, and the United Arab Emirates). [8]Circulation based on three dailies only.

Bangladesh

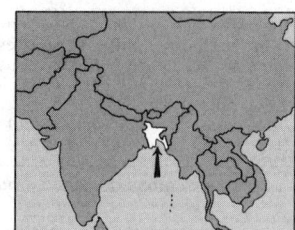

Official name: Gana Prajātantrī Bangladesh (People's Republic of Bangladesh).
Form of government: unitary multiparty republic with one legislative house (Parliament [330[1]]).
Head of state and government: President.
Capital: Dhākā (formerly Dacca).
Official language: Bengali.
Official religion: Islam.
Monetary unit: 1 Bangladesh taka (Tk) = 100 paisa; valuation (Oct. 10, 1988) 1 U.S.$ = Tk 31.07; 1 £ = Tk 53.20.

Area and population

Divisions[2]	Administrative centres	area sq mi	area sq km	population 1986 estimate
Chittagong	Chittagong	17,535	45,415	26,682,000
Dhākā	Dhākā	11,881	30,772	29,737,000
Khulna	Khulna	12,963	33,574	20,242,000
Rājshāhi	Rājshāhi	13,219	34,237	26,200,000
TOTAL		55,598	143,998	102,861,000

Demography

Population (1988): 107,756,000.
Density (1988): persons per sq mi 1,938.1, persons per sq km 748.3.
Urban–rural (1985): urban 20.3%; rural 79.7%.
Sex distribution (1985): male 51.51%; female 48.49%.
Age breakdown (1985): under 15, 44.3%; 15–29, 26.6%; 30–44, 15.2%; 45–59, 8.6%; 60 and over, 5.3%.
Population projection: (1990) 113,005,000; (2000) 139,693,000.
Doubling time: 27 years.
Ethnic composition (1983): Bengali 97.7%; Bihārī 1.3%; tribal (Chakmā, Gāro, Khāsi, Santāl, etc.) 1.0%.
Religious affiliation (1981): Muslim 86.6%; Hindu 12.1%; Buddhist 0.6%; Christian 0.3%; other 0.4%.
Major cities (1986): Dhākā 4,470,000; Chittagong 1,750,000; Khulna 820,000; Rājshāhi 380,000, Mymensingh 191,000.

Vital statistics

Birth rate per 1,000 population (1987): 42.1 (world avg. 26.0).
Death rate per 1,000 population (1987): 15.9 (world avg. 9.9).
Natural increase rate per 1,000 population (1987): 26.2 (world avg. 16.1).
Total fertility rate (avg. births per childbearing woman; 1987): 5.6.
Marriage rate per 1,000 population (1986): 15.9.
Divorce rate per 1,000 population: n.a.
Life expectancy at birth (1987): male 50.5 years; female 49.6 years.
Major causes of death per 100 deaths (1976): diseases of the respiratory system 25.7, of which tuberculosis 4.8; malignant neoplasms (cancers) 19.8; infectious intestinal diseases 15.5; diseases of the liver and kidney 11.4; diseases of the circulatory system 5.9; virus fevers 4.5; childbirth related causes 4.4.; diabetes 3.6.

National economy

Budget (1985–86). Revenue: Tk 37,540,000,000 (tax receipts 79.8%, of which customs duties 30.9%, excise duties 22.0%, sales tax 12.3%, income taxes 11.5%, stamps [nonjudicial] 3.1%; dividends and profits from public enterprises 5.4%; interest receipts 4.5%). Expenditures: Tk 33,130,000,000 (defense 15.1%; education 14.7%; debt service 11.8%; subsidy and grants-in-aid 11.6%; social and community services 5.1%; justice and police 4.1%; health and population control 3.9%; unexpected expenditures 11.8%).
Production (metric tons except as noted). Agriculture, forestry, fishing (1986–87): paddy rice 15,406,000, sugarcane 6,896,000, jute 1,206,000, wheat 1,091,000, potatoes 1,069,000, bananas 795,000, sweet potatoes 548,000, jackfruit 235,000, pineapples 133,000, tobacco leaf 40,000, tea 38,000, peanuts (groundnuts) 22,000; livestock (number of live animals; 1986) 23,200,000 cattle, 10,722,000 goats, 1,860,000 buffalo, 1,110,000 sheep, 71,000,000 chickens, 20,000,000 ducks; roundwood (1985–86) 27,144,000 cu m; fish catch (1986) 793,982. Mining and quarrying (1986): marine salt 500,000; industrial limestone 22,082. Manufacturing (1986–87): chemical fertilizers 981,490; jute manufactures 540,000; iron and steel 212,067; sugar 181,925; cotton yarn 164,620; newsprint 46,643; tea 39,337; chemicals 24,877; glass sheet 1,120,000 sq m; matches 14,894,000 gross boxes; television sets 75,071. Construction: n.a. Energy production (consumption): electricity (kW-hr; 1986) 5,125,000,000 (5,125,000,000); coal (metric tons; 1986) none (148,000); crude petroleum (barrels; 1986) 169,000 (7,462,000); petroleum products (metric tons; 1986) 800,000 (1,558,000); natural gas (cu m; 1986) 3,324,549,000 (3,324,549,000).
Land use (1985): forested 16.0%; meadows and pastures 4.5%; agricultural and under permanent cultivation 68.2%; other 11.3%.
Household income. Average household size (1983–84) 5.6; average annual income per household (1981–82) Tk 13,254 (U.S.$668); sources of income (1981–82): wages and salaries 19.6%, self-employment 60.6%, transfer payments 1.2%, other 18.6%; expenditure (1981–82): food and drink 66.1%, housing and rent 8.9%, clothing and footwear 7.9%, fuel and light 6.9%, education 1.2%.

Gross national product (at current market prices; 1986): U.S.$16,070,000,000 (U.S.$160 per capita).

Structure of gross domestic product and labour force

	1986–87 in value Tk '000,000	1986–87 % of total value	1984–85 labour force	1984–85 % of labour force
Agriculture	238,295	45.7	16,706,000	56.4
Mining			3,000	
Manufacturing }	40,590	7.8	2,688,000	9.1
Construction	29,818	5.7	553,000	1.9
Public utilities	3,532	0.7	91,000	0.3
Transp. and commun.	35,493	6.8	1,170,000	4.0
Trade	44,448	8.5	3,610,000	12.2
Finance	10,299	2.0	199,000	0.7
Public admin., defense	24,683	4.7	2,552,000	8.6
Services and other	94,481	18.1	2,028,000	6.9
TOTAL	521,639	100.0	29,600,000	100.0[3]

Population economically active (1984–85): total 29,600,000; activity rate of total population 30.2% (participation rates: over age 10, 48.9%; female 8.2%; unemployed 2.1%).

Price and earnings indexes (1980 = 100)

	1982	1983	1984	1985	1986	1987	1988[4]
Consumer price index	130.7	143.0	158.1	175.0	194.3	212.7	228.4
Hourly earnings index[5]	106.3	106.4	106.8	...	...	...	...

Public debt (external, outstanding; 1986): U.S.$7,281,700,000.
Tourism (1986): receipts from visitors U.S.$14,682,000; expenditures by nationals abroad U.S.$50,000,000.

Foreign trade

Balance of trade (current prices)

Tk '000,000	1982	1983	1984	1985	1986	1987
	−28,508	−30,138	−40,882	−41,543	−47,222	−47,948
% of total	45.5%	45.8%	46.4%	42.6%	46.9%	46.6%

Imports (1986–87): Tk 67,641,482,000 (crude oil 7.8%; wheat 7.1%; refined petroleum 6.2%; vegetable oils 5.7%; iron plates and sheets 3.5%; textile yarn 3.3%; synthetic fabrics 2.9%; cement 2.8%; kerosene 1.9%). *Major import sources:* Japan 13.3%; United States 13.0%; United Arab Emirates 9.1%; Singapore 8.3%; India 5.4%; West Germany 5.0%; South Korea 5.0%.
Exports (1986–87): Tk 33,682,131,000 (finished outer garments 16.5%; finished undergarments 13.5%; jute fabrics 12.9%; jute bags 10.7%; frozen shrimps 10.0%; raw jute 8.2%; cowhides 4.5%). *Major export destinations:* United States 31.1%; Italy 8.6%; Japan 6.4%; United Kingdom 5.7%; Singapore 4.7%; West Germany 4.2%; Belgium 3.7%.

Transport and communications

Transport. Railroads (1985–86): route length 1,797 mi, 2,892 km; passenger-mi 3,731,000,000, passenger-km 6,005,000,000; short ton-mi cargo 419,000,000, metric ton-km cargo 612,000,000. Roads (1982): total length 98,522 mi, 158,551 km (paved 12%). Vehicles (1986): passenger cars 40,776; trucks and buses 24,525. Merchant marine (1987): vessels (100 gross tons and over) 283; total deadweight tonnage 574,558. Air transport (1985)[6]: passenger-mi 1,021,845,000, passenger-km 1,643,924,000; short ton-mi cargo 151,174,000, metric ton-km cargo 220,711,000; airports with scheduled flights (1988) 8.
Communications. Daily newspapers (1985): total number 54; total circulation 554,000; circulation per 1,000 population 5.5. Radio (1985): 775,000 receivers (1 per 130 persons). Television (1985–86): 368,647 receivers (1 per 276 persons). Telephones (1986): 163,959 (1 per 627 persons).

Education and health

Education (1985–86)

	schools	teachers	students	student/teacher ratio
Primary (age 5–9)	43,712	184,668	10,776,000	58.4
Secondary (age 10–14)	8,793	99,016	2,745,000	27.7
Voc., teacher tr.	157	2,151	34,840	16.2
Higher	43	3,774	44,464	11.8

Educational attainment (1981). Percent of population age 25 and over having: no formal schooling 70.4%; primary education 24.1%; secondary 4.2%; postsecondary 1.3%. *Literacy* (1985): total population age 15 and over literate 18,166,000 (33.1%); males literate 12,272,000 (43.3%); females literate 5,894,000 (22.2%).
Health (1985): physicians 16,294 (1 per 6,166 persons); hospital beds 31,987 (1 per 3,141 persons); infant mortality rate (1987) 120.0.
Food (1984–86): daily per capita caloric intake 1,922 (vegetable products 96%, animal products 4%); (1983) 84% of FAO recommended minimum.

Military

Total active duty personnel (1987): 101,500 (army 88.7%, navy 7.4%, air force 3.9%). *Military expenditure as percent of GNP* (1985): 1.7% (world 6.1%); per capita expenditure U.S.$3.

---

[1]Includes 30 seats reserved for women. [2]Geographic reorganization at the district level took place in 1984; each division is now divided into the following number of new districts: Chittagong 15, Dhākā 17, Khulna 16, and Rājshāhi 16. [3]Detail does not add to total given because of rounding. [4]May. [5]Skilled wage earnings in manufacturing. [6]Bangladesh Biman only.

Barbados

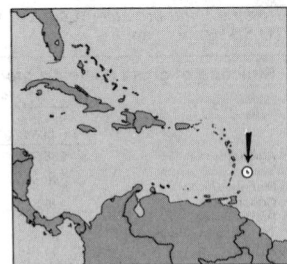

Official name: Barbados.
Form of government: constitutional monarchy with two legislative houses (Senate [21]; House of Assembly [27]).
Chief of state: British Monarch represented by governor-general.
Head of government: Prime Minister.
Capital: Bridgetown.
Official language: English.
Official religion: none.
Monetary unit: 1 Barbados dollar (BDS$) = 100 cents; valuation (Oct. 10, 1988) 1 U.S.$ = BDS$2.01; 1 £ = BDS$3.44.

Area and population

Parishes[1]	area		population
	sq mi	sq km	1980 census
Christ Church	22	57	40,790
St. Andrew	14	36	6,731
St. George	17	44	17,361
St. James	12	31	17,255
St. John	13	34	10,330
St. Joseph	10	26	7,211
St. Lucy	14	36	9,264
St. Michael[2]	15	39	99,953
St. Peter	13	34	10,717
St. Philip	23	60	18,662
St. Thomas	13	34	10,709
TOTAL	166	430[3]	248,983

Demography

Population (1988): 254,000.
Density (1988): persons per sq mi 1,530, persons per sq km 591.
Urban–rural (1985): urban 42.3%; rural 57.7%.
Sex distribution (1987): male 47.85%; female 52.15%.
Age breakdown (1985): under 15, 27.3%; 15–29, 30.5%; 30–44, 17.2%; 45–59, 12.1%; 60–74, 9.4%; 75 and over, 3.5%.
Population projection: (1990) 255,000; (2000) 261,000.
Doubling time: 99 years.
Ethnic composition (1980): black 91.9%; white 3.3%; mulatto 2.6%; East Indian 0.5%; other 1.7%.
Religious affiliation (1980): Anglican 39.7%; other Protestant 25.6%, of which Pentecostal 7.6%, Methodist 7.1%; nonreligious 17.5%; Roman Catholic 4.4%; not stated 2.7%; other 10.1%.
Major cities (1980): Bridgetown 7,552 (urban area [1986] 102,000); other cities cannot be identified because no other bounded localities exist.

Vital statistics

Birth rate per 1,000 population (1987): 15.1 (world avg. 26.0); (1979) legitimate 26.9%; illegitimate 73.1%.
Death rate per 1,000 population (1987): 8.1 (world avg. 9.9).
Natural increase rate per 1,000 population (1987): 7.0 (world avg. 16.1).
Total fertility rate (avg. births per childbearing woman; 1987): 2.0.
Marriage rate per 1,000 population (1984): 4.6.
Divorce rate per 1,000 population (1984): 1.2.
Life expectancy at birth (1980–85): male 70.0 years; female 75.4 years.
Major causes of death per 100,000 population (1984): diseases of the circulatory system 364.7, of which cerebrovascular disease 129.0, diseases of pulmonary circulation and other forms of heart disease 101.2; malignant neoplasms (cancers) 142.1; diabetes mellitus 51.2.

National economy

Budget (1987). Revenue: BDS$702,881,000 (tax revenue 85.3%, of which taxes on goods and services 30.8%, taxes on income and profit 18.8%, taxes on international trade 16.8%; nontax revenue 8.3%). Expenditures: BDS$941,870,000 (current expenditure 80.4%, of which education 16.3%, economic services 13.2%, general public services 12.8%, health 12.6%, defense 0.5%; development expenditure 19.6%).
Production (metric tons except as noted). Agriculture, forestry, fishing (1986): sugarcane 788,000, sweet potatoes 2,192, yams 1,989, carrots 985, cabbages 944, beans 409, cotton lint 161[4]; livestock (number of live animals) 54,000 sheep, 49,000 pigs, 32,000 goats, 18,000 cattle; roundwood, n.a.; fish catch (1986) 2,956, of which flying fishes 1,907. Manufacturing (value added in U.S.$'000; 1985): food, beverages, and tobacco (mostly sugar, molasses, rum, cigarettes, and beer) 77,900; metal products and assembly-type goods (mostly electronic components) 66,000; textiles and wearing apparel 36,-800; paper products, printing, and publishing 20,400. Construction, n.a. Energy production (consumption): electricity (kW-hr; 1987) 425,000,000 (356,000,000[5]); coal, none (none); crude petroleum (barrels; 1987) 496,000 (1,819,000[5]); petroleum products (metric tons; 1986) 228,000 (222,000); natural gas (cu m; 1987) 22,200,000 (26,300,000[5]).
Population economically active (1987): total 119,300; activity rate of total population 47.1% (participation rates: ages 15–64, 75.4%[5]; female 47.2%; unemployed 17.1%).

Price and earnings indexes (1980 = 100)

	1981	1982	1983	1984	1985	1986	1987
Consumer price index	114.6	126.4	133.0	139.2	144.7	146.6	151.5
Annual earnings index	110.5	123.0	130.1	142.0	148.9	155.9	...

Household income and expenditure. Average household size (1980) 3.7; income per household: n.a.; sources of income: n.a.; expenditure (1978–79): food 43.2%, housing 13.1%, household operations 9.6%, alcohol and tobacco 8.4%, fuel and light 6.2%, clothing and footwear 5.1%, transportation 4.6%, other 9.8%.
Gross national product (at current market prices; 1986): U.S.$1,310,000,000 (U.S.$5,140 per capita).

Structure of gross domestic product and labour force

	1986			
	in value BDS$'000	% of total value	labour force	% of labour force
Agriculture, fishing	149,450	5.6	9,000	7.7
Mining	31,170	1.2		
Manufacturing	229,262	8.6	24,500	20.9
Construction	131,354	4.9		
Public utilities	71,736	2.7	2,300	2.0
Transportation and communications	211,475	7.9	6,000	5.1
Trade	719,579	26.9	25,300	21.7
Finance	311,045	11.6	3,400	2.9
Pub. admin., defense	379,043	14.1	41,200	35.3
Services	94,065	3.5		
Other	348,735[6]	13.0[6]	5,200	4.4
TOTAL	2,676,914	100.0	116,900	100.0

Public debt (external, outstanding; 1986): U.S.$453,800,000.
Tourism: receipts from visitors (1986) U.S.$336,900,000; expenditures by nationals abroad U.S.$28,900,000.
Land use (1985): forested, negligible; meadows and pastures 9.0%; agricultural and under permanent cultivation 77.0%; other 14.0%.

Foreign trade[7]

Balance of trade (current prices)

	1982	1983	1984	1985	1986	1987
BDS$'000,000	−498.6	−499.0	−431.3	−402.7	−521.0	−628.2
% of total	32.5%	27.9%	21.5%	22.1%	32.0%	50.0%

Imports (1987): BDS$1,035,900,000 (machinery, transport equipment, and electrical goods 24.2%, food and beverages 18.4%, mineral fuels and lubricants 10.8%, chemicals and related products 10.4%). *Major import sources:* United States 32.1%; United Kingdom 11.7%; Trinidad and Tobago 9.1%; other EEC 8.4%.
Exports (1987): BDS$313,531,000 (domestic exports 68.4%, of which sugar 18.1%, electrical components 16.7%, clothing 7.6%, chemicals 7.0%; reexports 31.6%). *Major export destinations:* CARICOM 29.6%; United States 26.8%; United Kingdom 22.1%.

Transport and communications

Transport. Railroads: none. Roads (1986): total length 1,020 mi, 1,642 km (paved 79%). Vehicles (1986): passenger cars 34,850; trucks and buses 5,282. Merchant marine (1987): vessels (100 gross tons and over) 37; total deadweight tonnage 8,639. Air transport (1987): passenger arrivals 599,900, passenger departures 601,000; cargo unloaded 7,741 metric tons, cargo loaded 4,055 metric tons; airports (1988) with scheduled flights 1.
Communications. Daily newspapers (1987): total number 2; total circulation 41,000; circulation per 1,000 population 162. Radio (1986): total number of receivers 335,000 (1 per 0.8 persons). Television (1987): total number of receivers 62,000 (1 per 4.1 persons). Telephones (1986): 90,708 (1 per 2.8 persons).

Education and health

Education (1984–85)

	schools	teachers	students	student/ teacher ratio
Primary (age 5–11)	130	1,464	30,792	21.0
Secondary (age 12–16)	36	1,449	28,815	19.9
Vocational	3	154	3,592	23.3
Higher	1	108	1,617	15.0

Educational attainment (1980). Percent of population age 25 and over having: no formal schooling 0.8%; primary education 63.5%; secondary 32.3%; higher 3.3%. *Literacy* (1980): total population age 15 and over literate[8] 169,894 (98.0%); males literate 78,022 (98.3%); females literate 91,872 (97.7%).
Health (1984): physicians 213 (1 per 1,183 persons); hospital beds 2,143 (1 per 118 persons); infant mortality rate per 1,000 live births (1985–87) 12.7.
Food (1983–85): daily per capita caloric intake 3,129 (vegetable products 74%, animal products 26%); (1983) 132% of FAO recommended minimum requirement.

Military

Total active duty personnel (1987): 154 (paramilitary marine and coast guard components only). *Military expenditure as percent of GNP* (1985): 0.9% (world 6.1%); per capita expenditure U.S.$40.

[1]Parishes have no local administrative function. [2]Includes Bridgetown. [3]Detail does not add to total given because of rounding. [4]1986–87. [5]1986. [6]Net indirect taxes. [7]Import figures are f.o.b. in balance of trade and c.i.f. in commodities and trading partners. [8]National literacy standard based solely on school attendance. Functional literacy may be appreciably lower.

Belgium

Official name: Koninkrijk België
(Dutch); Royaume de Belgique
(French) (Kingdom of Belgium).
Form of government: constitutional
monarchy with two legislative
houses (Senate [183]; House of
Representatives [212]).
Chief of state: Monarch.
Head of government: Prime Minister.
Capital: Brussels.
Official languages: Dutch; French;
German.
Official religion: none.
Monetary unit: 1 Belgian franc
(BF) = 100 centimes; valuation (Oct.
10, 1988) 1 U.S.$ = BF 38.86;
1 £ = BF 66.55.

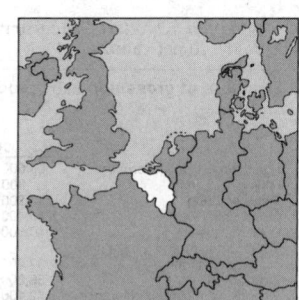

Area and population		area		population
Provinces	Capitals	sq mi	sq km	1987 estimate[1]
Antwerp	Antwerp	1,107	2,867	1,585,163
Brabant	Brussels	1,297	3,358	2,219,272
East Flanders	Ghent	1,151	2,982	1,328,931
Hainaut	Mons	1,462	3,787	1,274,034
Liège	Liège	1,491	3,862	991,089
Limburg	Hasselt	935	2,422	734,382
Luxembourg	Arlon	1,715	4,441	225,563
Namur	Namur	1,415	3,665	413,621
West Flanders	Brugge	1,210	3,134	1,092,696
TOTAL		11,783	30,518	9,864,751

Demography

Population (1988): 9,865,000.
Density (1988): persons per sq mi 837.2, persons per sq km 323.3.
Urban–rural (1980): urban 72.4%; rural 27.6%.
Sex distribution (1987): male 48.82%; female 51.18%.
Age breakdown (1984): under 15, 19.3%; 15–29, 23.5%; 30–44, 19.8%; 45–59, 18.2%; 60–74, 13.1%; 75 and over, 6.1%.
Population projection: (1990) 9,867,000; (2000) 9,881,000.
Doubling time: n.a.; doubling time exceeds 100 years.
Nationality (1981): Belgian 91.1%; Italian 2.8%; Moroccan 1.1%; French 1.1%; Dutch 0.7%; Turkish 0.6%; other 2.6%.
Religious affiliation (1980): Roman Catholic 90.0%; Muslim 1.1%; Protestant 0.4%; nonreligious and atheist 7.5%; other 1.0%.
Major cities (1987[1]): Brussels 136,920 (973,499[2]); Antwerp 479,748; Ghent 233,856; Charleroi 209,395; Liège 200,891.

Vital statistics

Birth rate per 1,000 population (1987): 11.9 (world avg. 26.0); (1983) legitimate 94.3%; illegitimate 5.7%.
Death rate per 1,000 population (1987): 11.3 (world avg. 9.9).
Natural increase rate per 1,000 population (1987): 0.6 (world avg. 16.1).
Total fertility rate (avg. births per childbearing woman; 1985): 1.6.
Marriage rate per 1,000 population (1987): 5.8.
Divorce rate per 1,000 population (1987): 1.9.
Life expectancy at birth (1979–82): male 70.0 years; female 76.8 years.
Major causes of death per 100,000 population (1984): heart and circulatory diseases 480.0, of which cerebrovascular disease 124.8; malignant neoplasms (cancers) 273.5.

National economy

Budget (1987). Revenue: BF 1,452,591,000,000 (direct taxes 62.1%; value-added, stamp, and similar duties 26.7%; customs and excise duties 7.1%). Expenditures: BF 1,855,148,000,000 (government departments 40.4%; public debt 21.7%; education and culture 15.2%; pension 9.8%; defense 5.7%).
Tourism (1986): receipts from visitors U.S.$2,271,000,000; expenditures by nationals abroad U.S.$2,889,000,000.
Production (metric tons except as noted). Agriculture, forestry, fishing (1986): sugar beets 5,886,200, potatoes 2,055,400, wheat 1,256,900, barley 793,100, apples 243,000[3], tomatoes 171,000[3], oats 59,300, corn (maize) 56,900, milk 3,918,000; livestock (number of live animals) 5,762,700 pigs, 2,967,400 cattle, 128,000 sheep, 24,400 horses; roundwood (1985) 3,086,000 cu m; fish catch 39,540, of which European plaice (flounder) 9,773, Atlantic cod 8,221, common sole 4,776. Mining and quarrying (1985): quartz 300,000; barite 40,000. Manufacturing (value added in BF '000,000; 1986): metal products and machinery 316,700; food, beverages, and tobacco 235,800; chemicals and chemical products 137,400; pig iron, steel, and nonferrous metals 64,800; paper, printing, and publishing 59,200; furniture and fixtures 50,200; textiles 46,000; building materials 40,800; clothing and footwear 34,400. Construction (1985): residential 17,776,000 cu m; nonresidential 22,422,000 cu m. Energy production (consumption): electricity (kW-hr; 1986) 57,621,000,000 (57,408,000,000); coal (metric tons; 1986) 5,625,000 (13,165,000); petroleum (barrels; 1986) none (170,225,000); natural gas (cu m; 1986) 24,090,000 (7,023,570,000).
Household income and expenditure. Average household size (1981) 2.7; sources of income (1986): wages and salaries 51.9%, transfer payments 20.7%, property income 17.0%, self-employment 10.4%; expenditure (1986): food 23.5%, housing 16.7%, transportation and communications 12.8%, personal care and health 11.6%, recreation 9.8%, household durable goods 9.3%, clothing and footwear 8.4%, energy 6.3%, other 1.6%.

Gross national product (at current market prices; 1986): U.S.$91,010,000,000 (U.S.$9,230 per capita).

Structure of gross domestic product and labour force				
	1986			
	in value BF '000,000	% of total value	labour force	% of labour force
Agriculture	114,200	2.2	103,200	2.4
Mining	22,400	0.4	22,600	0.5
Manufacturing	1,164,500	22.7	799,100	19.0
Construction	260,400	5.1	204,600	4.9
Public utilities	190,800	3.7	31,700	0.8
Transportation and communications	381,900	7.5	260,500	6.2
Trade	1,066,800	20.8	712,700	16.9
Finance	318,000	6.2	301,500	7.1
Pub. admin., defense } Services	1,798,800	35.0	1,262,000	30.0
Other	−184,500[4]	−3.6	513,700[5]	12.2
TOTAL	5,133,300	100.0	4,211,600	100.0

Population economically active (1986): total 4,211,600; activity rate of total population 42.7% (participation rates: ages 15–64, n.a.; female 40.3%; unemployed 11.3%).

Price and earnings indexes (1980 = 100)							
	1981	1982	1983	1984	1985	1986	1987
Consumer price index	107.6	117.0	126.0	134.0	141.8	142.3	144.5
Hourly earnings index	110.1	116.9	122.0	128.0	136.4	136.3	139.0

Public debt (1987): U.S.$170,431,000,000.
Land use[3] (1985): forested 21.2%; meadows and pastures 21.5%; agricultural and under permanent cultivation 24.6%; other 32.7%.

Foreign trade[3]

Balance of trade (current prices)					
	1982	1983	1984	1985	1986	1987
BF '000,000	−180,400	−84,800	−107,600	−50,300	+96,800	+124,300
% of total	3.6%	1.6%	1.8%	0.8%	1.6%	2.0%

Imports (1986): BF 3,061,850,000,000 (machinery and transport equipment 27.9%, of which road vehicles and parts 12.4%; mineral fuels and lubricants 10.6%, of which petroleum and petroleum products 7.1%, natural gas 2.4%; chemicals and chemical products 10.4%; food and live animals 9.1%; nonindustrial [gem] diamonds 5.6%). *Major import sources:* West Germany 23.1%; The Netherlands 17.9%; France 15.8%; U.K. 8.4%; U.S. 5.0%.
Exports (1986): BF 3,066,578,000,000 (machinery and transport equipment 25.8%, of which passenger cars 10.7%; chemicals and chemical products 12.5%, of which plastics 4.5%; food and live animals 8.9%; iron and steel 7.7%; nonindustrial [gem] diamonds 5.7%; textile yarns and fabrics 5.7%; petroleum and petroleum products 4.4%). *Major export destinations:* France 20.0%; West Germany 19.7%; The Netherlands 15.0%; U.K. 8.7%; Italy 5.8%; U.S. 5.3%.

Transport and communications

Transport. Railroads (1987): route length[6] 2,248 mi, 3,618 km; passenger-mi 3,788,000,000, passenger-km 6,096,000,000; short ton-mi cargo 4,981,-000,000, metric ton-km cargo 7,272,000,000. Roads (1986): total length 79,600 mi, 128,100 km (paved [1985] 96%). Vehicles (1986): passenger cars 3,379,180; trucks and buses 326,879. Merchant marine (1987): vessels (100 gross tons and over) 350; total deadweight tonnage 3,653,840. Air transport (1986): passenger-mi 3,452,000,000, passenger-km 5,556,000,000; short ton-mi cargo 406,872,000; metric ton-km cargo 594,024,000; airports (1988) with scheduled flights 3.
Communications. Daily newspapers (1986): total number 37; total circulation c. 2,500,000; circulation per 1,000 population c. 250. Radio (1986): 4,515,973 receivers (1 per 2.2 persons). Television (1986): 2,984,119 receivers (1 per 3.3 persons). Telephones (1986): 4,555,955 (1 per 2.2 persons).

Education and health

Education (1985–86)				
	schools	teachers	students	student/ teacher ratio
Primary (age 6–12)	4,790[7]	45,261[8]	758,260	...
Secondary (age 12–18)	2,272[7]	56,719[9]	855,704	...
Voc., teacher tr.	209[9]	6,864[9]	218,813	...
Higher	17[7]	...	103,598	...

Educational attainment (1977). Percent of population age 25 and over having: less than secondary education 64.4%; lower secondary 16.0%; upper secondary 10.0%; vocational 3.7%; teacher's college 2.1%; university 3.8%.
Literacy (1987): virtually 100% literate.
Health (1986): physicians 29,776 (1 per 331 persons); hospital beds (1984) 91,638 (1 per 105 persons); infant mortality rate per 1,000 live births (1985) 9.4.
Food[3] (1984–86): daily per capita caloric intake 3,950 (vegetable products 56%, animal products 44%); (1983) 139% of FAO recommended minimum.

Military

Total active duty personnel (1987): 90,800 (army 74.3%, navy 5.0%, air force 20.7%). *Military expenditure as percent of GNP* (1985): 3.0% (world 6.1%); per capita expenditure U.S.$237.

[1]January 1. [2]Région Bruxelloise. [3]Includes Luxembourg. [4]Includes imputed bank service charges. [5]Includes 477,900 unemployed. [6]1986. [7]1984–85. [8]1983–84. [9]1982–83.

Belize

Official name: Belize.
Form of government: constitutional
  monarchy with two legislative houses ·
  (Senate [8][1]; House of Representatives
  [28][2]).
Chief of state: British Monarch
  represented by governor-general.
Head of government: Prime Minister.
Capital: Belmopan.
Official language: English.
Official religion: none.
Monetary unit: 1 Belize dollar
  (BZ$) = 100 cents; valuation (Oct. 10,
  1988) 1 U.S.$ = BZ$2.00[3];
  1 £ = BZ$3.42.

Area and population		area		population
Districts	**Capitals**	sq mi	sq km	1986 estimate
Belize	Belize City	1,624	4,206	56,600
Cayo	San Ignacio	2,061	5,338	28,000
Corozal	Corozal	718	1,860	28,300
Orange Walk	Orange Walk	1,829	4,737	27,300
Stann Creek	Dangriga	840	2,176	16,800
Toledo	Punta Gorda	1,795	4,649	14,000
TOTAL		8,867	22,965[4]	171,000[5]

Demography

Population (1988): 178,000.
Density (1988): persons per sq mi 20.1, persons per sq km 7.8.
Urban–rural (1985): urban 50.0%; rural 50.0%.
Sex distribution (1986): male 50.58%; female 49.42%.
Age breakdown (1985): under 15, 44.9%; 15–29, 28.0%; 30–44, 12.0%; 45–59, 7.8%; 60–74, 5.0%; 75 and over, 2.3%.
Population projection: (1990) 187,000; (2000) 240,000.
Doubling time: 22 years.
Ethnic composition (1980): Creole (predominantly black) 39.7%; mestizo (Spanish-Indian) 33.1%; Mayan Indian 9.5%, of which Kekchi 2.7%; Garifuna (black-Carib Indian) 7.6%; white 4.2%; East Indian 2.1%; other 3.8%.
Religious affiliation (1980): Roman Catholic 61.7%; Protestant 28.9%, of which Anglican 11.8%, Methodist 6.0%, Mennonite 3.9%, Seventh-day Adventist 3.0%; Bahā'ī 2.5%; Jewish 1.2%; other Christian 1.0%; other 4.7%.
Major cities (1986): Belize City 47,000; Orange Walk 9,900; Corozal 8,100; Dangriga 7,700; Belmopan 3,500.

Vital statistics

Birth rate per 1,000 population (1986): 36.1 (world avg. 26.0); (1985) legitimate 45.1%; illegitimate 54.9%.
Death rate per 1,000 population (1986): 4.1 (world avg. 9.9).
Natural increase rate per 1,000 population (1986): 32.0 (world avg. 16.1).
Total fertility rate (avg. births per childbearing woman; 1985): 4.9.
Marriage rate per 1,000 population (1986): 6.0.
Divorce rate per 1,000 population (1985): 0.4.
Life expectancy at birth (1987): male 66.0 years; female 71.0 years.
Major causes of death per 100,000 population (1985): malignant neoplasms (cancers) 40.9; pneumonia 39.1; perinatal mortality 37.3; heart diseases 33.1; accidents 33.1; cerebrovascular disease 29.4; diabetes mellitus 23.4.

National economy

Budget (1986–87). Revenue: BZ$213,800,000 (local revenue sources 65.8%, foreign sources 34.2%). Expenditures: BZ$213,800,000 (capital projects 45.8%, administration 11.9%, public debt payment 11.5%, education 9.0%, security 5.0%, health 4.9%).
Public debt (external, outstanding; 1986): U.S.$96,600,000.
Tourism (1986): receipts from visitors U.S.$11,700,000; expenditures by nationals abroad, n.a.
Production (metric tons except as noted). Agriculture, forestry, fishing (1986): sugarcane 738,000[6], oranges 51,600, grapefruits 23,600, bananas 22,900[6], corn (maize) 18,500, rice 4,400, coconuts 3,000, red kidney beans 1,630[6], honey 280, cocoa 66[6]; livestock (number of live animals) 49,000 cattle, 25,000 pigs, 350,000 chickens[7]; roundwood (1985) 164,000 cu m; fish catch 1,434, of which marine fishes 525, spiny lobster 520, shrimps 250, conchs 135. Mining and quarrying (1986): limestone 600,000; sand and gravel 500,000. Manufacturing (1986): sugar 83,300[6]; molasses 25,400; fertilizer 3,620; orange and grapefruit concentrate 72,000 hectolitres[6]; beer 24,600 hectolitres; cigarettes 76,000,000 units; garments 2,800,000 units. Construction (1984): residential 6,185 sq m; nonresidential, n.a. Energy production (consumption): electricity (kW-hr; 1986) 62,000,000 (62,000,-000); coal, none (none); crude petroleum, none (none); petroleum products (metric tons; 1986) none (62,000); natural gas, none (none).
Population economically active (1983–84): total 47,325; activity rate of total population 29.6% (participation rates: ages 15–64 [1980] 63.0%; female 32.5%; unemployed [1987] 14.0%).

Price and earnings indexes (1980 = 100)							
	1981	1982	1983	1984	1985	1986	1987
Consumer price index	111.2	118.8	124.8	129.4	134.1	135.4	138.6
Earnings index	...	...	...	...	...	...	...

Gross national product (at current market prices; 1986): U.S.$200,000,000 (U.S.$1,170 per capita).

Structure of gross domestic product and labour force				
	1986		1983–84	
	in value BZ$'000[8]	% of total value	labour force	% of labour force
Agriculture, fishing, forestry	69,600	20.4	13,065	27.6
Mining	800	0.2	81	0.2
Manufacturing	37,200	10.9	4,192	8.9
Construction	18,400	5.4	1,994	4.2
Public utilities	10,800	3.2	611	1.3
Transportation and communications	32,200	9.4	2,035	4.3
Trade	56,800	16.7	4,558	9.6
Finance, real estate, insurance	42,100	12.3	570	1.2
Pub. admin., defense	43,800	12.9	6,268	13.2
Services	41,600	12.2	7,326	15.5
Other	−12,400	−3.6	6,625[9]	14.0[9]
TOTAL	340,900	100.0	47,325	100.0

Household income and expenditure. Average household size (1986) 5.2; income per household: n.a.; sources of income: n.a.; expenditure (1980): food and beverages 51.5%, clothing and footwear 11.1%, household furnishings 10.1%, transportation and communications 6.5%, energy and water 6.0%, health care 3.4%, housing 2.3%, other 9.1%.
Land use (1985): forested 44.4%; meadows and pastures 2.1%; agricultural and under permanent cultivation 2.3%; other 51.2%.

Foreign trade[10]

Balance of trade (current prices)					
	1982	1983	1984	1985	1986	1987
BZ$'000,000	−50.6	−47.8	−50.2	−51.8	−37.5	−62.3
% of total	12.2%	13.3%	11.9%	11.9%	9.2%	13.6%

Imports (1986): BZ$243,930,000 (manufactured goods 31.4%; food 23.8%; machinery and transport 18.0%; fuels 13.9%; chemicals and chemical products 8.4%). *Major import sources* (1987): United States 58.2%; Mexico 8.9%; United Kingdom 8.2%; The Netherlands 4.4%; Canada 3.9%.
Exports (1986): BZ$185,250,000 (domestic exports 80.0%, of which sugar 34.6%, garments 17.8%, citrus concentrate 12.8%, fish, crustaceans, and mollusks 6.0%, bananas 4.8%; reexports 20.0%). *Major export destinations* (1987): United States 46.7%; United Kingdom 31.5%; Mexico 9.7%; Canada 3.5%; Jamaica 3.3%.

Transport and communications

Transport. Railroads: none. Roads (1984): total length 1,639 mi, 2,637 km (paved 16%). Vehicles (1984): passenger cars 3,707; trucks and buses 1,855. Merchant marine (1987): vessels (100 gross tons and over) 3; total deadweight tonnage 805. Air transport (1986)[11]: passenger arrivals 56,829, passenger departures 60,417; cargo loaded 752 metric tons, cargo unloaded 908 metric tons. Airports (1988) with scheduled flights 8.
Communications. Daily newspapers: none. Radio (1986): total number of receivers 88,000 (1 per 1.9 persons). Television (1987): total number of receivers, 12,000 (1 per 15 persons). Telephones (1985): 9,740 receivers (1 per 17 persons).

Education and health

Education (1986)	schools	teachers	students	student/teacher ratio
Primary (age 5–14)	225	1,582[12]	39,190	24.3[12]
Secondary (age, n.a.)	24	504[12]	6,853	13.2[12]
Voc., teacher tr. } Higher	5	62[12]	834	12.3[12]

Educational attainment (1980). Percent of population age 25 and over having: no formal schooling 10.7%; primary education 75.3%; secondary 11.7%; higher 2.3%. *Literacy* (1985): total population age 15 and over literate 85,000 (93%).
Health (1986): physicians 75 (1 per 2,260 persons); hospital beds 583 (1 per 291 persons); infant mortality rate per 1,000 live births (1984–86 avg.) 22.0.
Food (1984–86): daily per capita caloric intake 2,585 (vegetable products 74%, animal products 26%); (1983) 117% of FAO recommended minimum requirement.

Military

Total active duty personnel (1987): 600 (army 90.8%, maritime wing 6.7%, air wing 2.5%); British troops 1,400. *Military expenditure as percent of GNP* (1986): 1.8% (world, n.a.); per capita expenditure U.S.$21.

[1]Excludes president of the Senate, who *may* be elected by the Senate from outside its appointive membership. [2]Excludes speaker of House of Representatives, who *may* be elected by the House from outside its elected membership. [3]The Belize dollar is officially pegged to the U.S. dollar. [4]Detail does not add to total given because of rounding. [5]Preliminary estimate; total revised downward to 169,500. [6]1987. [7]1984. [8]At prices of 1984. [9]Unemployed. [10]Imports are f.o.b. in balance of trade and c.i.f. in commodities and trading partners. [11]Belize International Airport only. [12]1985.

Benin

Official name: République Populaire du Bénin (People's Republic of Benin).
Form of government: unitary single-party people's republic with one legislative house (National Revolutionary Assembly [196]).
Head of state and government: President.
Capitals[1]: Porto-Novo (official); Cotonou (de facto).
Official language: French.
Official religion: none.
Monetary unit: 1 CFA franc (CFAF) = 100 centimes; valuation (Oct. 10, 1988) 1 U.S.$ = CFAF 316.13; 1 £ = CFAF 541.38.

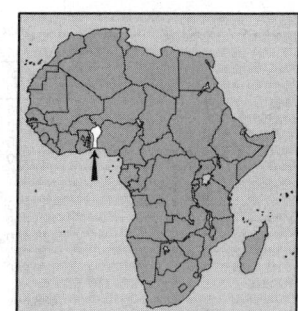

Area and population

Provinces	Capitals	area sq mi	area sq km	population 1985 estimate
Atacora	Natitingou	12,050	31,200	568,000
Atlantique	Cotonou	1,250	3,200	824,000
Borgou	Parakou	19,700	51,000	577,000
Mono	Lokossa	1,450	3,800	560,000
Ouémé	Porto-Novo	1,800	4,700	738,000
Zou	Abomey	7,200	18,700	670,000
TOTAL		43,450	112,600	3,937,000

Demography

Population (1988): 4,443,000.
Density (1987): persons per sq mi 102.3, persons per sq km 39.5.
Urban–rural (1985): urban 19.0%; rural 81.0%.
Sex distribution (1985): male 49.11%; female 50.89%.
Age breakdown (1985): under 15, 46.5%; 15–29, 25.7%; 30–44, 14.8%; 45–59, 8.5%; 60 and over, 4.5%.
Population projection: (1990) 4,733,000; (2000) 6,532,000.
Doubling time: 22 years.
Ethnic composition (1983): Fon 65.6%; Bariba 9.7%; Yoruba 8.9%; Somba 5.4%; Fulani 4.0%; other 6.4%.
Religious affiliation (1980): traditional beliefs 61.4%; Christian 23.1%, of which Roman Catholic 18.5%, Protestant 2.8%; Muslim 15.2%; other 0.3%.
Major cities (1982): Cotonou 487,000; Porto-Novo 208,000; Parakou 66,000; Abomey 54,000; Kandi 53,000.

Vital statistics

Birth rate per 1,000 population (1984): 49.0 (world avg. 29.0).
Death rate per 1,000 population (1984): 17.0 (world avg. 11.0).
Natural increase rate per 1,000 population (1984): 32.0 (world avg. 18.0).
Total fertility rate (avg. births per childbearing woman; 1985): 6.5.
Marriage rate per 1,000 population (1980–85): 12.8.
Divorce rate per 1,000 population (1980–85): 0.8.
Life expectancy at birth (1984): male 47.0 years; female 51.0 years.
Major causes of death per 100,000 population (1977): malaria 227.7; diseases of the respiratory system 206.5; diseases of the digestive system 200.7.

National economy

Budget (1987). Revenue: CFAF 47,800,000,000 (indirect taxes 58.6%, direct taxes 27.0%, other 14.4%). Expenditures: CFAF 47,800,000,000 (administration and services 81.8%, economic development 9.0%).
Production (metric tons except as noted). Agriculture, forestry, fishing (1986–87): yams 874,500, cassava 725,300, corn (maize) 375,600, seed cotton 110,000, millet and sorghum 106,300, tomatoes 73,000, palm kernels 67,398, peanuts (groundnuts) 67,000, dry beans 40,300, sweet potatoes 35,900, coconuts 20,000, oranges 13,000, bananas 13,000, mango 12,000, paddy rice 8,500, coffee beans 4,000, pineapples 3,000, cacao beans 1,000, tobacco 300; livestock (number of live animals; 1986) 1,160,000 sheep, 1,110,000 goats, 930,000 cattle, 470,000 pigs, 22,000,000 chickens; roundwood 4,538,000 cu m; fish catch 23,500. Mining and quarrying (1986): marine salt 100. Manufacturing (1986): cement 321,000; meat 58,000; sugar 52,000; cotton fibre 37,456[2]; palm oil and palm kernel oil 7,850[2]. Construction: n.a. Energy production (consumption): electricity (kW-hr; 1986) 5,000,000 (195,000,000); coal, none (n.a.); crude petroleum (barrels; 1986) 2,665,000 (none); petroleum products (metric tons; 1986) none (125,000).
Gross national product (at current market prices; 1986): U.S.$1,140,000,000 (U.S.$270 per capita).

Structure of gross domestic product and labour force

	1985 in value CFAF '000,000	1985 % of total value	1980 labour force	1980 % of labour force
Agriculture	179,571	35.9	1,246,000	70.2
Mining and manufacturing	46,699	9.3		
Public utilities	3,556	0.7	118,000	6.7
Construction	23,423	4.7		
Trade	96,500	19.3		
Transportation and communications	46,014	9.2	410,000	23.1
Finance	38,293	7.7		
Pub. admin., defense	38,841	7.8		
Other	26,951	5.4		
TOTAL	499,848	100.0	1,774,000	100.0

Tourism: receipts from visitors (1986) U.S.$10,000,000; expenditures by nationals abroad (1985) U.S.$4,000,000.
Population economically active (1985): total 1,964,000; activity rate of total population 48.5% (participation rates: ages 15–64, 86.6%; female 48.3%; unemployed, n.a.).

Price and earnings indexes (1980 = 100)

	1981	1982	1983	1984	1985	1986	1987
Consumer price index	113.1	...	...	...	...	...	...
Hourly earnings index	100.0	100.0	156.9	156.9	156.9	156.9	156.9[3]

Land use (1985): forested 34.5%; meadows and pastures 4.0%; agricultural and under permanent cultivation 16.3%; other 45.2%.
Public debt (external, outstanding; 1986): U.S.$780,600,000.
Household income and expenditure. Average household size (1979) 5.4; income per household (1983): U.S.$240; sources of income: n.a.; expenditure: n.a.

Foreign trade[4]

Balance of trade (current prices)

	1981	1982	1983	1984	1985	1986
CFAF '000,000	−138,358	−144,716	−86,681	−81,830	−100.47	−98.23
% of total	88.3%	90.2%	63.1%	46.2%	42.9%	55.5%

Imports (1983): CFAF 112,032,000,000 (manufactured goods 38.7%, of which cotton yarn and fabric 12.6%, chemical products 7.0%; machinery and transport equipment 22.6%, of which nonelectrical equipment 8.0%, electrical equipment 7.4%, transport equipment 7.3%; food products 16.7%, of which cereals 7.6%). *Major import sources* (1985): France 19.0%; United States 15.1%; The Netherlands 6.9%; Japan 5.8%; Austria 5.5%; Italy 4.7%; India 4.6%; Brazil 4.1%; West Germany 2.5%; United Kingdom 2.5%; Spain 2.3%; China 2.0%.
Exports (1983): CFAF 25,351,000,000 (energy 53.6%; cotton 18.4%; food products 12.6%, of which cocoa beans 6.9%, coffee 2.6%; palm kernel oil and palm oil 6.7%; machinery and transport equipment 0.4%; cement 0.3%). *Major export destinations* (1985): Spain 27.1%; West Germany 21.9%; France 10.4%; Portugal 10.1%; Italy 7.3%; The Netherlands 5.9%; United Kingdom 5.0%.

Transport and communications

Transport. Railroads (1985): length 360 mi, 580 km; passenger-mi 85,500,000[5], passenger-km 137,600,000[5]; short ton-mi cargo 121,100,000[5], metric ton-km cargo 176,800,000[5]. Roads (1986): total length 4,626 mi, 7,445 km (paved 11%). Vehicles (1985): passenger cars 2,740; trucks and buses 567. Merchant marine (1987): vessels (100 gross tons and over) 13; total deadweight tonnage 4,760. Air transport[6] (1985): passenger-mi 144,226,000, passenger-km 232,109,000; short ton-mi cargo 27,420,000, metric ton-km cargo 40,035,000; airports (1988) with scheduled flights 5.
Communications. Daily newspapers (1986): total number 1; total circulation 12,000; circulation per 1,000 population 3.1. Radio (1986): total number of receivers 300,000 (1 per 14 persons). Television (1984): total number of receivers 15,600 (1 per 276 persons). Telephones (1986): 15,492 (1 per 274 persons).

Education and health

Education (1985)

	schools	teachers	students	student/ teacher ratio
Primary	2,715	13,452	444,163	33.1
Secondary	133[7]	2,409[8]	112,267[8]	46.6[8]
Voc., teacher tr.	30[7]	609[9]	6,784[8]	...
Higher[9]	1	803	6,818	8.4

Educational attainment (1979): Percent of population age 25 and over having: no formal schooling 89.2%; primary education 8.3%; some secondary 1.4%; secondary 0.8%; postsecondary 0.3%. *Literacy* (1980): total population age 15 and over literate 530,000 (27.9%); males literate 368,000 (39.8%); females literate 162,000 (16.6%).
Health (1982): physicians 270 (1 per 13,570 persons); hospital beds 4,902 (1 per 749 persons); infant mortality rate per 1,000 live births (1984) 116.0.
Food (1984–86): daily per capita caloric intake 2,188 (vegetable products 95%, animal products 5%); (1983) 83% of FAO recommended minimum requirement.

Military

Total active duty personnel (1987): 4,350 (army 87.4%, navy 4.6%, air force 8.0%). *Military expenditure as percent of GNP* (1984): 2.6% (world 5.9%); per capita expenditure U.S.$7.

[1]Porto-Novo is the official capital established under the constitution, but Cotonou, where the president and most government ministers reside, is de facto capital. [2]Export figures. [3]January. [4]Figures do not include unaccountable reexports of black market goods, which originate mainly in Nigeria and amounted to an estimated 90% of Benin's actual exports in 1981. [5]1984–85. [6]Cotonou airport only. [7]1982. [8]1984. [9]1983.

Bermuda

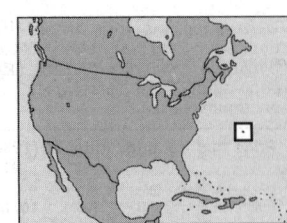

Official name: Bermuda.
Political status: colony (United Kingdom) with two legislative houses (Senate [11]; House of Assembly [40]).
Chief of state: British Monarch, represented by Governor.
Head of government: Premier.
Capital: Hamilton.
Official language: English.
Official religion: none.
Monetary unit: 1 Bermuda dollar (Ber$) = 100 cents; valuation (Oct. 10, 1988) 1 U.S.$ = Ber$1.00[1]; 1 £ = Ber$1.71.

Area and population	area		population
	sq mi	sq km	1980 census
Municipalities			
Hamilton	0.3	0.8	1,617
St. George	0.5	1.3	1,647
Parishes			
Devonshire	1.9	4.9	6,843
Hamilton	2.0	5.2	3,784
Paget	2.0	5.2	4,497
Pembroke[2]	1.8	4.7	10,443
St. George's[3]	1.7	4.4	2,940
Sandys	1.9	4.9	6,255
Smith's	1.9	4.9	4,463
Southampton	2.2	5.7	4,613
Warwick	2.2	5.7	6,948
TOTAL	21.0[4, 5]	54.0[4, 5]	54,050[6]

Demography

Population (1988): 58,300.
Density (1988): persons per sq mi 2,776, persons per sq km 1,080.
Urban–rural (1987): urban 100.0%; rural, none.
Sex distribution (1985): male 48.81%; female 51.19%.
Age breakdown (1985): under 15, 21.3%; 15–29, 24.6%; 30–44, 25.0%; 45–59, 16.1%; 60–74, 9.7%; 75 and over, 3.3%.
Population projection: (1990) 59,300; (2000) 64,500.
Doubling time: 87 years.
Ethnic composition (1980): black 61.3%; white 37.3%; other 1.4%.
Religious affiliation (1980): Protestant 72.5%, of which Anglican 37.3%, Methodist 16.3%; Roman Catholic 13.8%; nonreligious 7.8%; other 5.9%.
Major cities (1985): St. George 1,707; Hamilton 1,676.

Vital statistics

Birth rate per 1,000 population (1987): 15.5 (world avg. 26.0); legitimate 67.8%; illegitimate 32.2%.
Death rate per 1,000 population (1987): 7.5 (world avg. 9.9).
Natural increase rate per 1,000 population (1987): 8.0 (world avg. 16.1).
Total fertility rate (avg. births per childbearing woman; 1980): 1.7.
Marriage rate per 1,000 population (1987): 13.4.
Divorce rate per 1,000 population (1985): 3.7.
Life expectancy at birth (1980): male 68.8 years; female 76.3 years.
Major causes of death per 100,000 population (1985): diseases of the circulatory system 397.0; malignant neoplasms (cancers) 185.0; accidents and violence 54.0; diseases of the respiratory system 26.0.

National economy

Budget (1987). Revenue: Ber$258,300,000 (customs duty 41.2%, hospital levy 10.6%, employment tax 8.2%, land tax 4.3%, hotel occupancy tax 4.3%). Expenditures: Ber$263,100,000 (public works and agriculture[7] 24.8%, education 16.9%, health and social services 15.1%, police 8.2%, tourism 8.0%).
Public debt (external, outstanding; 1986–87): none.
Tourism (1987): receipts from visitors U.S.$475,000,000; expenditures by nationals abroad, n.a.
Production (value in Ber$ except as noted). Agriculture, forestry, fishing (1986): fish 5,230,000, vegetables 3,700,000, milk 1,121,000, spiny lobsters 550,000, fruits 450,000, eggs 360,000, meat 166,000, flowers 55,000[8]; livestock (number of live animals) 3,000 pigs, 1,000 cattle, 1,000 horses; roundwood, n.a. Mining and quarrying: limestone quarried for construction material. Manufacturing: major industries include pharmaceuticals, electronics wares, fish processing, handicrafts, woodworking, small boat building, and textiles. Construction (value in Ber$; 1987)[9]: residential 13,300,000; nonresidential 62,700,000. Energy production (consumption): electricity (kW-hr; 1986) 400,000,000 (400,000,000); coal, none (none); crude petroleum, none (none); petroleum products (metric tons; 1986) none (135,000); natural gas, none (none).
Population economically active (1986): total 33,445; activity rate of total population 58.3% (participation rates: ages 16–64 [1980] 82.1%; female 46.8%; registered unemployed [1986] 0.1%).

Price and earnings indexes (1985 = 100)							
	1981	1982	1983	1984	1985	1986	1987
Consumer price index	80.4	86.6	91.8	96.6	100.0	104.1	108.7
Weekly earnings index	66.6	77.0	86.2	92.9	100.0	106.2	...

Gross national product (at current market prices; 1985–86): U.S.$1,184,000,-000 (U.S.$20,700 per capita).

Structure of gross domestic product and labour force

	1978–79		1986	
	in value Ber$'000	% of total value	labour force	% of labour force
Agriculture, fishing	2,900	0.7 ⎫	383	1.1
Quarrying	1,300	0.3 ⎬		
Manufacturing	19,500	4.4	1,112	3.3
Construction	21,400	4.9	2,095	6.3
Public utilities	7,400	1.7	491	1.5
Transportation and communications	30,500	6.9	2,375	7.1
Trade	143,900	32.8	11,872	35.5
Finance	96,600	22.0	4,337	13.0
Pub. admin., defense	35,800	8.2	4,109	12.3
Services	79,200	18.1	3,985	11.9
Other	...	...	2,686[10]	8.0
TOTAL	438,500	100.0	33,445	100.0

Household income and expenditure. Average household size (1982) 2.7; income per household Ber$34,944 (U.S.$34,944); sources of income (1982): wages and salaries 72.2%, imputed income from owner occupancy 9.7%, investments including rents 8.0%, self-employment 6.7%; expenditure (1982): housing 20.8%, food and nonalcoholic beverages 17.3%, household furnishings 11.9%, transportation 10.6%, gifts, contributions, and life insurance 8.2%, foreign travel 6.4%, recreation 5.4%, clothing and footwear 5.3%.
Land use (1986): forested 20.0%; meadows and pastures, 0.8%; agricultural and under permanent cultivation, 4.2%; built-on, wasteland, and other 75.0%.

Foreign trade

Balance of trade (current prices)						
	1980	1981	1982	1983	1984	1985
Ber$'000,000	−274.7	−293.4	−334.1	−355.0	−373.5	−379.4
% of total	78.9%	83.3%	90.8%	88.6%	80.4%	89.2%

Imports (1985): Ber$402,491,000 (food 16.0%, of which meat and meat preparations 4.9%; petroleum and petroleum products 14.1%; electrical machinery, including apparatus and appliances 8.4%; clothing 7.4%; transport equipment 6.0%; nonelectrical machinery 4.7%; pharmaceutical products 4.4%). *Major import sources:* United States 60.1%; United Kingdom 10.1%; Canada 6.3%; Netherlands Antilles 5.8%.
Exports (1985): Ber$23,054,000 (reexports 98.4%, of which drugs and medicine 57.1%, personal effects 8.0%, electrical supplies 5.2%, books and papers 4.6%, electronic supplies 4.0%; Bermuda-originated exports 1.6%). *Major export destinations:* United States 22.7%; Italy 22.0%; Canada 9.5%; United Kingdom 6.9%; Hong Kong 6.4%.

Transport and communications

Transport. Railroads: none. Roads (1986): total length 150 mi, 240 km (paved 100%). Vehicles (1986): passenger cars and buses 17,852; trucks 2,768. Merchant marine (1987): vessels (100 gross tons and over) 105; total deadweight tonnage 3,131,539. Air transport (passengers; 1986): arrivals 558,993, departures 559,782; metric tons cargo unloaded 7,614, metric tons cargo loaded 590; airports (1988) with scheduled flights 1.
Communications. Daily newspapers (1986): total number 1; total circulation 18,000; circulation per 1,000 population 314. Radio (1986): total number of receivers 100,000 (1 per 0.6 person). Television (1987): total number of receivers 67,000 (1 per 0.9 person). Telephones (1984): 52,067 (1 per 1.1 persons).

Education and health

Education (1986–87)	schools	teachers	students	student/ teacher ratio
Primary (age 5–11)	22	314	5,258	16.7
Secondary (age 11–16)	12	337	4,005	11.9
Vocational ⎫ Higher ⎬	1	68[11]	638	...

Educational attainment (1980). Percent of total population age 25 and over having: no formal schooling, primary education, or incomplete secondary 57.4%; completed secondary 19.5%; completed higher 18.5%; other 4.6%.
Literacy (1980): total population age 15 and over literate 39,577 (96.9%); males literate 19,026 (96.7%); females literate 20,551 (97.0%).
Health (1986): physicians 75 (1 per 765 persons); hospital beds 261 (1 per 222 persons); infant mortality rate per 1,000 live births (1984–86 avg.) 10.6.
Food (1983–85): daily per capita caloric intake 2,530 (vegetable products 59%, animal products 41%); (1983) 107% of FAO recommended minimum requirement.

Military

Total active duty personnel: British (1985) 700; U.S. (1987) 1,600.

[1]The Bermuda dollar is at par with the U.S. dollar. [2]Excludes the area and population of the city of Hamilton. [3]Excludes the area and population of the town of St. George. [4]Grand total includes 2.3 sq mi (5.4 sq km) leased to the United States for military bases. [5]Detail does not add to total given (less area for the military bases) because of rounding. [6]Excludes 10,918 short-term visitors, 2,173 on-base military personnel, 620 institutionalized persons, and Bermudians residing abroad. [7]Breakdown based on first 6 months only. [8]1982. [9]Excludes residential developments valued below Ber$500,000. [10]Includes 1,970 employees of international companies. [11]1985–86.

Bhutan

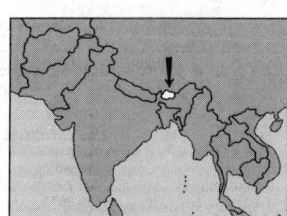

Official name: Druk-Yul (Kingdom of Bhutan).
Form of government: constitutional[1] monarchy with one legislative house (National Assembly [151][2]).
Head of state and government: Monarch (*druk gyalpo*).
Capital: Thimphu.
Official language: Dzongkha (a Tibetan dialect).
Official religion: Mahāyāna Buddhism.
Monetary unit: 1 Ngultrum[3] (Nu) = 100 chetrum; valuation (Oct. 10, 1988) 1 U.S.$ = Nu 14.39; 1 £ = Nu 24.65.

Area and population

Districts	Capitals	area[4] sq mi	area[4] sq km	population[5] 1985 estimate
Bumthang	Jakar	1,150	2,990	23,900
Chirang	Damphu	310	800	108,800
Dagana	Dagana	540	1,400	28,400
Gasa	Gasa	2,000	5,180	16,900
Gaylegphug	Gaylegphug	1,020	2,640	111,300
Haa	Paro	830	2,140	16,700
Lhuntsi	Lhuntshi	1,120	2,910	39,600
Mongar	Mongar	710	1,830	73,200
Paro	Paro	580	1,500	45,600
Pema Gatsel	Pema Gatsel	150	380	37,100
Punakha	Punakha	330	860	16,700
Samchi	Samchi	830	2,140	172,100
Samdrup Jongkhar	Samdrup Jongkhar	900	2,340	73,100
Shemgang	Shemgang	980	2,540	44,500
Tashigang	Tashigang	1,640	4,260	177,700
Thimphu	Thimphu	630	1,620	58,700
Tongsa	Tongsa	570	1,470	26,000
Wangdi Phodrang	Wangdi Phodrang	1,160	3,000	47,200
TOTAL		18,150	47,000	1,285,300[6]

Demography

Population (1988): 1,365,000.
Density (1988): persons per sq mi 75.2, persons per sq km 29.0.
Urban-rural (1985): urban 13.1%; rural 86.9%.
Sex distribution (1986): male 51.00%; female 49.00%.
Age breakdown (1986): under 15, 39.8%; 15–29, 26.7%; 30–44, 16.5%; 45–59, 10.6%; 60–74, 5.2%; 75 and over, 1.2%.
Population projection: (1990) 1,420,000; (2000) 1,731,000.
Doubling time: 35 years.
Ethnic composition (1983): Bhutia 62.5%; Gurung 15.5%; Assamese 13.2%; other 8.8%.
Religious affiliation (1980): Buddhist 69.6%; Hindu 24.6%; Muslim 5.0%; other 0.8%.
Major cities (1985): Thimphu 20,000; Phuntsholing 10,000[7].

Vital statistics

Birth rate per 1,000 population (1987): 37.5 (world avg. 26.0); legitimate, n.a.; illegitimate, n.a.
Death rate per 1,000 population (1987): 17.0 (world avg. 9.9).
Natural increase rate per 1,000 population (1987): 20.5 (world avg. 16.1).
Total fertility rate (avg. births per childbearing woman; 1987): 5.4.
Marital status of population 15 years and over (1985): married 71.2%; single 19.7%; widowed 7.5%; divorced 1.6%.
Divorce rate per 1,000 population: n.a.
Life expectancy at birth (1987): male 48.1 years; female 46.8 years.
Major causes of death per 100,000 population (1986): n.a.; however, major health problems include diarrhea and dysentery, respiratory tract infections, parasitic worms, skin infections, malaria, and nutritional deficiencies.

National economy

Budget (1987–88). Revenue: Nu 1,698,113,000 (grants from government of India 49.3%, internal revenue 24.2%, grants from UN and other international agencies 20.0%, internal borrowing 5.9%). Expenditures: Nu 2,019,-567,000 (industries and mines 16.5%, public works 13.9%, power 13.5%, education 9.1%, agriculture 6.1%, finance 5.4%, post and telecommunications 4.0%, health 3.9%).
Tourism (1986): receipts from visitors U.S.$2,200,000; expenditures by nationals abroad, n.a.
Production (metric tons except as noted). Agriculture, forestry, fishing (1986): corn (maize) 88,000, rice 63,000, potatoes 28,000, oranges 27,000, wheat 11,000, millet 8,000, barley 5,000, jute 4,000, apples 4,000; livestock (number of live animals) 339,000 cattle, 89,000 pigs, 44,000 sheep, 39,000 goats, 36,000 yaks, 29,000 buffalo, 211,000 poultry; roundwood 3,224,000 cu m; fish catch 1,000. Mining and quarrying (1986): dolomite 217,400; limestone 172,000; gypsum 24,800; slate 57,100 sq m. Manufacturing (value in Nu; 1980–81): distillery products 47,000,000; cement 36,000,000; chemical products 19,000,000; processed food 14,000,000; forest products 3,000,000. Construction (number of buildings completed; 1977–78): residential 10; nonresidential (guest house) 1. Energy production (consumption): electricity (kW-hr; 1986) 21,000,000 (31,000,000); coal (metric tons; 1986), none (1,000); crude petroleum, none (n.a.); petroleum products (metric tons; 1986) none (10,000); natural gas, none (n.a.).
Household income and expenditure. Average household size (1980): 5.4; income per household: n.a.; sources of income: n.a.; expenditure (1979):

food 72.3%, clothing 21.2%, energy 3.7%, household durable goods 0.7%, personal effects and other 2.1%.
Gross national product (at current market prices; 1986): U.S.$200,000,000 (U.S.$160 per capita).

Structure of gross domestic product and labour force

	1986 in value Nu '000,000	1986 % of total value	1984 labour force	1984 % of labour force
Agriculture	1,373.8	51.3	580,000[8]	87.2
Mining	14.8	0.5		
Manufacturing	96.0	3.6		
Construction	234.4	8.7		
Trade	290.1	10.8		
Public utilities	96.0	3.6	6,000[8]	0.9
Transportation and communications	68.8	2.6		
Finance	192.6	7.2		
Pub. admin., defense	355.1	13.3	23,000[8]	3.4
Other	–43.3[9]	–1.6[9]	56,000[8]	8.5[10]
TOTAL	2,678.3	100.0	664,000	100.0

Public debt (external, outstanding): n.a.
Population economically active (1984): total 664,000; activity rate of total population 52.7% (participation rates: ages 15–64, 94.8; female 55.0; unemployed 6.5).

Price and earnings indexes (1980 = 100)

	1981	1982	1983	1984	1985	1986	1987
Consumer price index	114.3	129.9	150.2	159.3	160.4	176.5	185.0
Earnings index	...	...	...	...	...	...	...

Land use (1985): forested 70.0%; meadows and pastures 4.6%; agricultural and under permanent cultivation 2.2%; other 23.2%.

Foreign trade

Balance of trade (current prices)

	1981–82	1982–83	1983–84	1984–85	1985–86	1986–87
Nu '000,000	–414.2	–487.1	–662.6	–644.8	–654.9	–802.5
% of total	54.7%	60.4%	67.3%	64.1%	54.6%	55.4%

Imports (1983): Nu 394,017,158 (aircraft 10.7%, diesel fuel 10.2%, rice 4.4%, electricity 4.0%, gasoline 3.4%, bulk tank containers 2.4%, automobiles 2.1%, industrial tractors 1.7%, sugar 1.7%, power generators 1.6%). *Major import source* (1984–85): India 87.9%.
Exports (1983): Nu 140,368,445 (cement 25.0%, talcum powder 10.2%, fruit products 7.8%, rosin 5.8%, cardamon 5.7%, sawn timber 4.2%, potatoes 3.6%, alcoholic beverages 3.2%, oranges 2.6%, veneer 2.1%). *Major export destination* (1984–85): India 95.9%.

Transport and communications

Transport. Railroads: none. Roads (1987): total length 1,345 mi, 2,165 km (paved about 79%). Vehicles (1986): passenger cars 1,587; trucks and buses 916. Merchant marine: none. Air transport (1986): passenger-mi 2,722,000, passenger-km 4,381,000; metric ton-km cargo, n.a.; airports (1988) with scheduled flights, none[11].
Communications. Daily newspapers: none[12]. Radio (1987): total number of receivers 12,800 (1 per 104 persons). Television (1983): total number of receivers 200 (1 per 6,180 persons). Telephones (1985): 1,880 (1 per 684 persons).

Education and health

Education (1986)

	schools	teachers	students	student/ teacher ratio
Primary (age 7–11)	147	1,321	36,998	28.0
Secondary (age 12–16)	30	613	15,454	25.2
Voc., teacher tr.[13]	8	103	688	6.7
Higher	2	18[14]	422	...

Educational attainment, n.a. *Literacy* (1977): total population age 15 and over literate 124,000 (18.0%); males literate 98,000 (31.0%); females literate 26,000 (9.0%).
Health (1986): physicians 134 (1 per 9,791 persons); hospital beds 915 (1 per 1,434 persons); infant mortality rate per 1,000 live births (1987) 135.0.
Food (1975–77): daily per capita caloric intake 2,058 (vegetable products 98%, animal products 2%); 89% of FAO recommended minimum requirement.

Military

Total active duty personnel (1987): about 4,000 (army 100%).

[1]There is no formal constitution, but a form of constitutional monarchy is in place. [2]Includes 46 nonelective seats. [3]Indian currency is also accepted legal tender; the Ngultrum is at par with the Indian rupee. [4]2,700 sq mi (7,000 sq km) are not included in the district area totals. [5]Rural only. [6]Includes urban population. [7]1982. [8]Derived value. [9]Imputed bank service charges. [10]Includes 6.5% with no occupation. [11]An airport at Paro receives unscheduled air service from Calcutta. [12]A government weekly is published from Thimphu in Dzongkha, Nepalese, and English, circulation (1988) 8,500. [13]1985. [14]1983.

Bolivia

Official name: República de Bolivia (Republic of Bolivia).
Form of government: unitary, multiparty republic with two legislative houses (Chamber of Senators [27]; Chamber of Deputies [130]).
Head of state and government: President.
Capital: La Paz (administrative); Sucre (judicial).
Official languages: Spanish, Aymara, Quechua.
Official religion: Roman Catholicism.
Monetary unit: 1 boliviano[1] (Bs) = 100 centavos; valuation (Oct. 10, 1988) 1 U.S.$ = Bs 2.57; 1 £ = Bs 4.39.

Area and population		area		population
Departments	**Capitals**	sq mi	sq km	1987 estimate
Beni	Trinidad	82,458	213,564	256,260
Chuquisaca	Sucre	19,893	51,524	479,990
Cochabamba	Cochabamba	21,479	55,631	1,029,730
La Paz	La Paz	51,732	133,985	2,221,922
Oruro	Oruro	20,690	53,588	432,301
Pando	Cobija	24,644	63,827	49,615
Potosí	Potosí	45,644	118,218	916,329
Santa Cruz	Santa Cruz	143,098	370,621	1,124,383
Tarija	Tarija	14,526	37,623	286,829
TOTAL		424,164	1,098,581	6,797,359

Demography

Population (1988): 6,993,000.
Density (1988): persons per sq mi 16.5, persons per sq km 6.4.
Urban–rural (1987): urban 49.0%; rural 51.0%.
Sex distribution (1985): male 49.25%; female 50.75%.
Age breakdown (1985): under 15, 43.4%; 15–29, 26.4%; 30–44, 15.7%; 45–59, 9.3%; 60–74, 4.4%; 75 and over, 0.8%.
Population projection: (1990) 7,400,000; (2000) 9,837,000.
Doubling time: 25 years.
Ethnic composition (1982): mestizo 31.2%; Quechua 25.4%; Aymara 16.9%; white 14.5%; other 12.0%.
Religious affiliation (1981): Roman Catholic 94.0%; Bahā'ī 2.6%; other 3.4%.
Major cities (1985): La Paz 992,592; Santa Cruz 441,717; Cochabamba 317,251; Oruro 178,393; Sucre 86,609.

Vital statistics

Birth rate per 1,000 population (1980–85): 44.0 (world avg. 29.0).
Death rate per 1,000 population (1980–85): 15.9 (world avg. 11.0).
Natural increase rate per 1,000 population (1980–85): 28.1 (world avg. 18.0).
Total fertility rate (avg. births per childbearing woman; 1980–85): 6.3.
Marriage rate per 1,000 population (1980): 4.8.
Divorce rate per 1,000 population: n.a.
Life expectancy at birth (1980–85): male 48.6 years; female 53.0 years.
Major causes of death per 100,000 population: n.a.; however, major health problems include diseases of the respiratory system, gastrointestinal infections, measles, diphtheria, malaria, and tetanus.

National economy

Budget (1986). Revenue: $b 844,537,338,600,000 (royalties on petroleum 56.3%, internal taxes 16.2%, customs duties 12.0%, consular fees 1.0%). Expenditures: $b 786,432,056,400,000 (public services 41.4%, public debt service 14.3%, materials and equipment 12.7%, currency adjustment 12.5%, transfers and contributions 8.1%).
Production (metric tons except as noted). Agriculture, forestry, fishing (1986): sugarcane 1,850,000, potatoes 697,000, corn (maize) 457,000, cassava 420,000, bananas and plantains 399,000, rice 137,000, wheat 81,000, soybeans 81,000, barley 78,000, sorghum 59,000; livestock (number of live animals) 9,500,000 sheep, 6,000,000 cattle, 1,200,000 goats, 1,100,000 pigs, 600,000 asses, 311,000 horses; roundwood (1985) 1,317,000 cu m; fish catch 4,800. Mining and quarrying (metric tons of pure metal; 1986): zinc 33,472; tin 10,479; antimony 10,248; lead 3,121; tungsten 1,198; silver 95,115 kilograms; gold 763 kilograms. Manufacturing[2] (value added in $b '000,000; 1984): food products 997,100; nonferrous metals 472,100; beverages 268,300; textiles 131,900; chemicals 120,000; petroleum refining 105,700; footwear 67,900; printing and publishing 45,900. Construction[3] (1983): residential dwellings 323. Energy production (consumption): electricity (kW-hr; 1986) 1,625,000,000 (1,627,000,000); coal (metric tons; 1986) none (1,000); crude petroleum (barrels; 1986) 8,039,000 (8,433,000); petroleum products (metric tons; 1986) 1,152,000 (1,137,000); natural gas (cu m; 1986) 2,335,600,000 (238,200,000).
Population economically active (1986): total 2,076,782; activity rate of total population 31.4% (participation rates: ages 15–64, 54.0%; female 23.4%; unemployed 20.0%).

Price and earnings indexes (1980 = 100)							
	1979	1980	1981	1982	1983	1984	1985
Consumer price index	50.0	100.0	204.0	541.0	2,403	17,462	134,833
Monthly earnings index	71.8	100.0	120.6	265.6	1,102.7	9,060.7	...

Gross national product (1986): U.S.$3,540,000,000 (U.S.$540 per capita).

Structure of gross domestic product and labour force				
	1986		1982	
	in value $b '000,000	% of total value	labour force[4]	% of labour force
Agriculture	2,918,649	27.6	792,600	46.4
Mining	514,245	4.9	76,200	4.5
Manufacturing	1,300,795	12.3	155,500	9.1
Construction	530,967	5.0	56,500	3.3
Public utilities	42,496	0.4	7,200	0.4
Transp. and commun.	869,679	8.2	94,700	5.5
Trade	2,152,144	20.4	128,800	7.5
Finance	1,246,210	11.8	13,300	0.8
Pub. admin., defense	681,168	6.5	} 382,600	22.4
Services	271,035	2.6		
Other	31,625[5]	0.3[5]		
TOTAL	10,559,013	100.0	1,707,400	100.0[6]

Household income and expenditure. Average household size: n.a.; average annual income per household: n.a.; sources of income: n.a.; expenditure (1979): food 41.7%, housing 12.6%, transportation and communications 12.6%, clothing and footwear 9.8%, household durable goods 8.9%, health 4.6%, recreation 3.1%, education 1.2%.
Public debt (external, outstanding; 1986): U.S.$3,522,600,000.
Tourism (1985): receipts from visitors U.S.$36,000,000; expenditures by nationals abroad U.S.$38,000,000.
Land use (1985): forested 51.5%; meadows and pastures 24.8%; agricultural and under permanent cultivation 3.1%; other 20.6%.

Foreign trade[7]

Balance of trade (current prices)						
	1982	1983	1984	1985	1986	1987
U.S.$'000,000	+399.0	+282.0	+311.9	+160.6	−36.9	−85.4
% of total	31.8%	23.0%	27.4%	14.8%	3.2%	7.0%

Imports (1986): U.S.$711,500,000 (capital goods 39.8%, of which capital goods for industry 20.0%, transport equipment 11.9%; raw materials 35.0%, of which raw materials for industry 31.7%; consumer goods 24.5%, of which durable consumer goods 15.0%, nondurable consumer goods 9.5%). *Major import sources* (1985): United States 22.0%; Brazil 21.0%; Argentina 15.0%; West Germany 7.2%; Japan 7.0%; Chile 5.0%; Peru 5.0%; United Kingdom 2.0%; France 1.8%; The Netherlands 1.7%.
Exports (1986): U.S.$632,500,000 (natural gas 52.0%; tin 16.5%; zinc 4.4%; silver 4.3%; lumber 3.4%; coffee 2.1%). *Major export destinations:* Argentina 53.8%; United States 14.6%; United Kingdom 7.9%; West Germany 5.5%; Chile 3.5%; Brazil 3.3%; Peru 3.0%; Belgium 1.7%; Switzerland 1.1%.

Transport and communications

Transport. Railroads: route length (1987) 2,263 mi, 3,642 km; (1986) passenger-mi 491,122,000, passenger-km 790,386,000; (1986) short ton-mi cargo 364,221,000, metric ton-km cargo 531,754,000. Roads (1984): total length 25,468 mi, 40,987 km (paved 4%). Vehicles (1986): passenger cars 69,836; trucks and buses 130,796. Merchant marine (1987): vessels (100 gross tons and over) 2; total deadweight tonnage 22,155. Air transport (1987): passenger-mi 567,000,000, passenger-km 912,000,000; short ton-mi cargo 18,428,000, metric ton-km cargo 26,904,000; airports (1988) with scheduled flights 22.
Communications. Daily newspapers (1984): total number 13; total circulation 311,000; circulation per 1,000 population 50. Radio (1985): total number of receivers 3,700,000 (1 per 1.7 persons). Television (1987): total number of receivers 390,000 (1 per 17 persons). Telephones (1986): 182,433 (1 per 37 persons).

Education and health

Education (1984)	schools	teachers	students	student/ teacher ratio
Primary (age 6–13)	8,038	47,224	1,181,246	25.0
Secondary (age 14–17)	845[8]	8,091[8]	199,944	...
Higher	25[8]	1,487[8]	79,836	...

Educational attainment (1976). Percent of population age 25 and over having: no formal schooling 48.6%; primary education 28.5%; secondary 17.9%; higher 5.0%. *Literacy* (1976): total population age 15 and over literate 1,706,718 (63.2%); males literate 990,408 (75.8%); females literate 716,310 (51.4%).
Health: physicians (1984) 4,032 (1 per 1,551 persons); hospital beds (1983) 10,789 (1 per 564 persons); infant mortality rate per 1,000 live births (1985) 110.0.
Food (1984–86): daily per capita caloric intake 2,128 (vegetable products 84%, animal products 16%); (1983) 82% of FAO recommended minimum requirement.

Military

Total active duty personnel (1987): 27,600 (army 72.5%, navy 13.0%, air force 14.5%). *Military expenditure as percent of GNP* (1984): 2.2% (world 6.0%); per capita expenditure U.S.$19.

[1]Effective Jan. 1, 1987, a new currency, the boliviano, was introduced at a rate of one boliviano = 1,000,000 old Bolivian pesos ($b). [2]Establishments with 20 or more employees. [3]National government sponsored only. [4]Employed persons only. [5]Includes imputed bank service charges. [6]Detail does not add to total given because of rounding. [7]Import figures are f.o.b. (free on board) in balance of trade and c.i.f. (cost, insurance, and freight) for commodities and trading partners. [8]1983.

Botswana

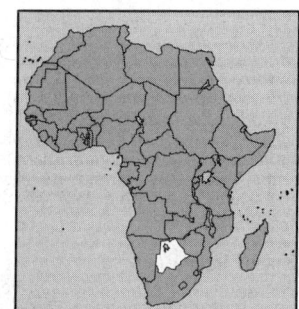

Official name: Botswana (Tswana),
Republic of Botswana. (English).
Form of government: multiparty
republic with one legislative body
(National Assembly [39]).
Head of state and government:
President.
Capital: Gaborone.
Official languages: Tswana; English.
Official religion: none.
Monetary unit: 1 pula (P) = 100 thebe;
valuation (Oct. 10, 1988)
1 U.S.$ = P 1.98; 1 £ = P 3.39.

Area and population

Districts	Capitals	area sq mi	area sq km	population 1986 estimate
Barolong	...	425	1,100	18,004
Central	Serowe	57,039	147,730	350,168
Ghanzi	Ghanzi	45,525	117,910	22,468
Kgalagadi	Tsabong	41,290	106,940	28,498
Kgatleng	Mochudi	3,073	7,960	49,427
Kweneng	Molepolole	13,857	35,890	139,249
North East	Masunga	1,977	5,120	41,946
North West				
Chobe	Kasane	8,031	20,800	9,574
Ngamiland	Maun	42,135	109,130	76,320
Ngwaketse	Kanye	10,568	27,370	117,967
South East	Ramotswa	687	1,780	28,970
Towns[1]				
Francistown	—	31	79	43,837
Gaborone	—	37	97	95,163
Jwaneng	—	39	100	10,308
Lobatse	—	12	30	23,829
Orapa	—	4	10	7,389
Palapye	—	10	26	13,814
Selebi-Pikwe	—	19	50	41,382
Tlokweng	—	8	21	9,574
TOTAL		224,607	581,730	1,127,888[2]

Demography

Population (1988): 1,211,000.
Density (1988): persons per sq mi 5.4, persons per sq km 2.1.
Urban–rural (1986): urban 21.7%; rural 78.3%.
Sex distribution (1986): male 47.60%; female 52.40%.
Age breakdown (1986): under 15, 48.2%; 15–29, 25.9%; 30–44, 13.2%; 45–59, 7.4%; 60–74, 4.0%; 75 and over, 1.3%.
Population projection: (1990) 1,302,600; (2000) 1,817,400.
Doubling time: 21 years.
Ethnic composition (1983): Tswana 75.5%; Shona 12.4%; San (Bushman) 3.4%; Khoikhoin (Hottentot) 2.5%; Ndebele 1.3%; other 4.9%.
Religious affiliation (1980): traditional beliefs 49.2%; Protestant 29.0%; African Christian 11.8%; Roman Catholic 9.4%; other 0.6%.
Major cities (1986): Gaborone 95,163; Francistown 43,837; Selebi-Pikwe 41,-382; Lobatse 23,829; Palapye 13,814.

Vital statistics

Birth rate per 1,000 population (1986): 45.6 (world avg. 26.0); legitimate, n.a.; illegitimate, n.a.
Death rate per 1,000 population (1986): 11.1 (world avg. 9.9).
Natural increase rate per 1,000 population (1986): 34.5 (world avg. 16.1).
Total fertility rate (avg. births per childbearing woman; 1986): 6.7.
Life expectancy at birth (1986): male 54.7 years; female 61.4 years.
Major causes of death (as percent of total deaths; 1977): measles 16.3%; heart disease 8.4%; influenza and pneumonia 7.6%; diarrheal diseases 7.5%; malignant neoplasms (cancers) 6.0%.

National economy

Budget (1986–87). Revenue: P 1,547,530,000 (mineral royalties and dividends 54.6%; nontax revenue 19.6%; customs and excise taxes 12.4%; other income taxes 7.8%; foreign aid grants 4.4%). Expenditures: P 980,870,000 (recurrent expenditure 59.2%; development expenditure 41.3%, of which economic services 22.2%, general services including defense 20.3%, social services 13.4%).
Population economically active (1984–85): total 367,949; activity rate of total population 37.0% (participation rates: ages 15–64, 72.7%; female 54.6%; unemployed [1981] 12.2%).

Price and earnings indexes (1980 = 100)

	1981	1982	1983	1984	1985	1986	1987
Consumer price index	90.0	100.0	110.5	119.9	129.7	142.7	156.6
Earnings index[3]	...	100.0	109.1	120.4	127.3	145.5	...

Production (metric tons except as noted). Agriculture, forestry, fishing (1985–86): cereals 20,800 (of which sorghum 16,000, corn [maize] 3,200, millet 1,600), vegetables and melons 17,000, pulses 17,000, fruit 11,000, roots and tubers 9,000, seed cotton 3,000, cotton seed 2,000, peanuts (groundnuts) 1,000; livestock (number of live animals; 1986) 2,720,000 cattle, 1,000,000 goats, 210,000 sheep, 143,000 mules and asses, 24,000 horses; roundwood 1,225,000 cu m; fish catch 1,900. Mining and quarrying (1986): diamonds 13,100,000 carats; nickel–copper matte 41,263, of which copper 21,703, nickel 19,560; cobalt 162. Manufacturing (1984): beer 155,000 hectolitres.

Construction (1985): residential 70,200 sq m; nonresidential 80,700 sq m.
Energy production (consumption): electricity (kW-hr; 1986) 725,000,000 (621,000,000[4]); coal (metric tons; 1985) 437,000 (n.a.); crude petroleum, none (n.a.); petroleum products, n.a. (n.a.); natural gas, none (n.a.).
Public debt (external, outstanding; 1986): U.S.$355,100,000.
Tourism (1986): receipts from visitors U.S.$28,000,000; expenditures by nationals abroad U.S.$21,000,000.
Gross national product (1986): U.S.$930,000,000 (U.S.$840 per capita).

Structure of gross domestic product and labour force

	1986–87 in value P '000,000	1986–87 % of total value	1984–85 labour force	1984–85 % of labour force
Agriculture	87.4	3.2	159,134	43.2
Mining	1,211.1	44.1	8,999[5]	2.5
Manufacturing	169.2	6.2	8,954	2.4
Construction	108.3	3.9	9,280	2.5
Public utilities	70.9	2.6	1,988	0.5
Transp. and commun.	59.3	2.2	2,573	0.7
Trade	459.9	16.7	15,670	4.3
Finance	164.2	6.0	3,038	0.8
Pub. admin., defense	393.7	14.3 }	65,153	17.7
Services	71.8	2.6 }		
Other	−48.4	−1.8	93,160[6]	25.3[6]
TOTAL	2,747.4	100.0	367,949	100.0[2]

Household income and expenditure. Average household size (1981) 5.7; average annual income per household, n.a.; sources of income (1981): wages and salaries 65.6%, transfers 19.6%, self-employment 14.8%; expenditure (1985)[7]: food, beverages, and tobacco 40.1%, rent and services 13.6%, clothing 10.8%, transportation 10.5%, health 1.3%.
Land use (1985): forested 1.6%; meadows and pastures 75.2%; agricultural and under permanent cultivation 2.3%; other 20.9%.

Foreign trade[8]

Balance of trade (current prices)

	1982	1983	1984	1985	1986	1987
P '000,000	−122.7	27.5	122.4	444.9	510.9	840.0
% of total	11.5%	2.0%	7.5%	19.1%	19.3%	20.4%

Imports (1986): P 1,325,600,000 (machinery and electrical goods 17.9%; food, beverages, and tobacco 16.9%; vehicles and transport equipment 14.0%; mineral fuels 10.3%; metal and metal products 10.0%; chemical and rubber products 9.2%; textiles and footwear 7.1%; wood and paper 3.4%). *Major import sources:* CUSA (Customs Union of Southern Africa, which includes Botswana, Lesotho, South West Africa/Namibia, South Africa, and Swaziland) 77.7%; European countries 8.9%, of which United Kingdom 2.8%; United States 3.7%.
Exports (1986): P 1,449,600,000 (diamonds 77.8%; meat and meat products 8.0%; copper–nickel matte 6.3%; textiles 2.6%). *Major export destinations:* European countries 87.7%, of which United Kingdom 4.6%; African countries 11.6%, of which CUSA 5.6%; United States 0.2%.

Transport and communications

Transport. Railroads (1986): length 442 mi, 712 km; number of passengers 542,692[4]; short ton-mi cargo 888,133[4], metric ton-km cargo 1,296,735[4]. Roads (1986): total length 8,388 mi, 13,500 km (paved 15%). Vehicles (1986): passenger cars 16,426; trucks and buses 24,786. Merchant marine: none. Air transport (1986)[9]: passenger-mi 13,953,000, passenger-km 22,-456,000; short ton-mi cargo 100,000, metric ton-km cargo 146,000; airports (1988) with scheduled flights 8.
Communications. Daily newspapers (1986): total number 1; total circulation 30,000; circulation per 1,000 population 22. Radio (1985): total number of receivers 140,000 (1 per 7.8 persons). Television (1986): none. Telephones (1985): 19,109 (1 per 57 persons).

Education and health

Education (1986)

	schools	teachers	students	student/ teacher ratio
Primary (age 7–13)	537	7,324	235,941	32.2
Secondary (age 14–19)	73	1,619	35,966	22.2
Voc., teacher tr.	22	317	3,217	10.1
Higher	1	249	1,700	6.8

Educational attainment (1981). Percent of population age 25 and over having: no formal schooling 54.7%; some primary education 31.0%; complete primary 9.4%; some secondary 3.1%; complete secondary 1.3%; postsecondary 0.5%. *Literacy* (1985): total population over age 15 literate 385,000 (70.8%); males literate 179,000 (72.6%); females literate 206,000 (69.5%).
Health (1984): physicians 155 (1 per 6,748 persons); hospital beds 2,367 (1 per 442 persons); infant mortality rate per 1,000 live births (1981) 68.4.
Food (1984–86): daily per capita caloric intake 2,230 (vegetable products 85%, animal products 15%); (1983) 93% of FAO recommended minimum.

Military

Total active duty personnel (1987): 3,250 (army 95.4%; navy, none; air force 4.6%). *Military expenditure as percent of GNP* (1985): 2.7% (world 6.1%); per capita expenditure U.S.$23.

[1]Areas included with respective district area totals. [2]Detail does not add to total given because of rounding. [3]Excludes government sector. [4]1985. [5]16,397 Batswana were employed in South African mines in 1985. [6]Mostly unemployed. [7]Weights of consumer price index components. [8]Import figures are f.o.b. in balance of trade and c.i.f. in commodities and trading partners. [9]Air Botswana only.

Brazil

Official name: República Federativa do Brasil (Federative Republic of Brazil).
Form of government: multiparty federal republic with 2 legislative houses (Federal Senate [72]; Chamber of Deputies [487]).
Chief of state and government: President.
Capital: Brasília.
Official language: Portuguese.
Official religion: none.
Monetary unit: 1 cruzado (Cz$) = 100 centavos; valuation (Oct. 10, 1988) 1 U.S.$ = 383.74 cruzados; 1 £ = 657.15 cruzados.

Area and population		area		population
				1988
States	Capitals	sq mi	sq km	estimate
Acre	Rio Branco	58,915	152,589	385,000
Alagoas	Maceió	10,707	27,731	2,381,000
Amapá	Macapá	54,161	140,276	234,000
Amazonas	Manaus	604,036	1,564,445	1,887,000
Bahia	Salvador	216,613	561,026	11,396,000
Ceará	Fortaleza	57,150	148,016	6,207,000
Espírito Santo	Vitória	17,605	45,597	2,429,000
Goiás[1]	Goiânia	137,215	355,386	3,665,000
Maranhão	São Luís	126,897	328,663	4,978,000
Mato Grosso	Cuiabá	340,156	881,001	1,660,000
Mato Grosso do Sul	Campo Grande	135,347	350,548	1,729,000
Minas Gerais	Belo Horizonte	226,708	587,172	15,239,000
Pará	Belém	481,871	1,248,042	4,617,000
Paraíba	João Pessoa	21,765	56,372	3,146,000
Paraná	Curitiba	77,048	199,554	8,308,000
Pernambuco[2]	Recife	37,957	98,307	7,106,000
Piauí	Teresina	96,886	250,934	2,584,000
Rio Grande do Norte	Natal	20,469	53,015	2,244,000
Rio Grande do Sul	Pôrto Alegre	108,952	282,184	8,859,000
Rio de Janeiro	Rio de Janeiro	17,092	44,268	13,541,000
Rondônia	Pôrto Velho	93,840	243,044	862,000
Roraima	Boa Vista	88,844	230,104	116,000
Santa Catarina	Florianópolis	37,060	95,985	4,339,000
São Paulo	São Paulo	95,714	247,898	32,091,000
Sergipe	Aracaju	8,492	21,994	1,366,000
Tocantins[1]	...	110,698	286,706	1,100,000
Federal District				
Distrito Federal	Brasília	2,245	5,814	1,793,000
Disputed areas[3]		2,044	5,294	—
TOTAL		3,286,488[4,5]	8,511,965[5]	144,262,000

Demography

Population (1988): 144,262,000.
Density (1988): persons per sq mi 43.9, persons per sq km 16.9.
Urban–rural (1987): urban 74.2%; rural 25.8%.
Sex distribution (1987): male 49.90%; female 50.10%.
Age breakdown (1985): under 15, 36.4%; 15–29, 28.9%; 30–44, 17.8%; 45–59, 10.3%; 60–74, 5.2%; 75 and over, 1.4%.
Population projection: (1990) 150,368,000; (2000) 179,487,000.
Doubling time: 34 years.
Ethnic composition (1980): Brazilian white 53.0%, of which Portuguese 15.0%, Italian 11.0%, Spanish 10.0%, German 3.0%; mulatto 22.0%; mestizo 12.0%; black 11.0%; Japanese 0.8%; indigenous Indian 0.1%; other 1.1%.
Religious affiliation (1980): Roman Catholic 87.8%, of which Spiritist Catholic 15.7%[6], Evangelical Catholic 9.0%[7]; Protestant (mostly Assemblies of God, other Pentecostal, and Baptist) 6.1%; Afro-American Spiritist 2.0%[8]; Spiritist 1.7%[9]; nonreligious 1.0%; atheist 0.4%; Buddhist 0.3%; Jewish 0.2%; other 0.5%.
Major cities (*município;* 1985)[10]: São Paulo 10,099,086 (15,280,375); Rio de Janeiro 5,615,149 (10,217,269); Belo Horizonte 2,122,073 (3,059,727); Salvador 1,811,367 (2,125,792); Fortaleza 1,588,709; Brasília 1,576,657; Nova Iguaçu[11] 1,324,639; Recife 1,289,627; Curitiba 1,285,027; Porto Alegre 1,275,483.

Other principal *municipios* (1985)

	population		population		population
Belém	1,120,777	Maceió	484,094	São Bernardo	
Campinas	845,057	Manaus	834,541	do Campo	565,620
Duque de Caxias[11]	666,128	Natal	512,241	São Gonçalo	731,061
Goiânia	928,046	Niterói[11]	442,706	São João de	
Guarulhos[12]	717,723	Osasco[12]	594,249	Meriti[11]	459,103
Jaboatão	411,341	Santo André[12]	637,010	São Luís	564,434
João Pessoa	397,715	Santos	461,096	Teresina	476,102

Place of birth/national origin (1980): 99.07% native-born; 0.93% foreign-born, of which Portugal 0.33%, Japan 0.12%, Italy 0.09%, Spain 0.08%.
Mobility (1980). Population living in same residence: less than 1 year 19.3%; 1–3 years 19.5%; 3–6 years 22.1%.
Families (1985). Average family size 4.2; 1–2 persons 24.6%, 3 persons 20.0%, 4 persons 20.1%, 5–6 persons 23.0%, 7 or more persons 12.3%.
Immigration (1982–84): permanent immigrants admitted 7,673, from Portugal 28.4%, Uruguay 8.7%, Argentina 8.2%.

Vital statistics

Birth rate per 1,000 population (1985–90): 28.6 (world avg. 26.0).
Death rate per 1,000 population (1985–90): 7.9 (world avg. 9.9).

Natural increase rate per 1,000 population (1985–90): 20.7 (world avg. 16.1).
Total fertility rate (avg. births per childbearing woman; 1985–90): 3.5.
Marriage rate per 1,000 population (1985): 7.0.
Divorce rate per 1,000 population (1985): 0.3.
Life expectancy at birth (1985–90): male 62.3 years; female 67.6 years.
Major causes of death per 100,000 population (1983): diseases of the circulatory system 155.0, of which cerebrovascular disease 51.9, acute myocardial infarction 31.5; malignant neoplasms (cancers) 61.8; infectious and parasitic diseases 44.0; accidents 34.5; diseases of the respiratory system 32.0, of which pneumonia 25.3; homicide and other violence 22.0; ill-defined conditions 126.1.

Social indicators

Educational attainment (1980). Percent of population age 25 and over having: no formal schooling 32.9%; some primary education 50.3%; complete primary 4.9%; secondary 6.9%; higher 5.0%.

Distribution of income (1985)[13]

			percent of national income by decile						
1	2	3	4	5	6	7	8	9	10 (highest)
0.9	1.8	2.5	3.5	4.3	5.0	7.3	10.5	16.5	47.7

Quality of working life. Average workweek (1980): 80.6% of the labour force works 40 or more hours per week. Annual estimated rate per 100,000 insured urban workers (1982) for: injury or accident 5,500; industrial illness, n.a.; death 21. Proportion of labour force participating in national social insurance system: 51.8%. Proportion of employed population receiving minimum wage (1987): 52.0%.
Access to services (1985). Proportion of households having access to: electricity 81.2%, of which urban households having access 94.9%, rural households having access 38.6%; safe public (piped) water supply 67.9%, of which urban households having access 87.0%, rural households having access 8.9%; public sewage collection 30.8%[14], of which urban households having access 40.5%, rural households having access 1.3%; public fire protection, n.a.
Social participation. Eligible voters participating in last (November 1986) national election: 85.0%. Trade union membership in total work force (1980): 10–15%. Practicing religious population in total affiliated population: most men, and in particular Portuguese-Brazilian men, attend Mass only on special occasions. They believe religion is the domain and duty of women.
Social deviance: The incidence of crime is not accurately reported. Crimes resulting in imprisonment (1984): 258,505, of which murder 4.3%, rape 0.9%, other assault 17.7%, burglary and housebreaking 23.6%, armed robbery 0.3%, narcotics trafficking 3.8%, narcotics usage 4.9%. Suicides (1984): 4,432.
Leisure. Favourite leisure activities: n.a.
Material well-being (1980). Households possessing: automobile 22.4% (urban 28.3%, rural 9.5%); telephone 12.4% (urban 17.5%, rural 0.9%); television receiver 56.1% (urban 73.0%, rural 15.7%); refrigerator 63.1%[15] (urban 75.4%, rural 25.1%); air conditioner, n.a.; washing machine, n.a.

National economy

Gross national product (at current market prices; 1986): U.S.$250,520,000,-000 (U.S.$1,810 per capita).

Structure of gross domestic product and labour force

	1986		1985	
	in value U.S.$'000,000[16]	% of total value	labour force[13,17]	% of labour force
Agriculture	31,793	9.3	15,190,393	28.5
Mining	2,846	0.8	8,686,592	16.3
Manufacturing	90,355	26.5		
Construction	20,032	5.9	3,097,386	5.8
Public utilities	8,164	2.4	...	...
Transportation and communications	17,504	5.1	1,916,009	3.6
Trade	47,132	13.8	5,814,660	10.9
Pub. admin., defense	21,084	6.2	2,346,736	4.4
Finance, real estate	56,563	16.6	14,438,558	27.1
Services	45,125	13.2		
Other	—	—	1,746,602	3.3
TOTAL	340,598	100.0[4]	53,236,936	100.0[4]

Budget (1987). Revenue: Cz$591,845,000,000 (current revenue 69.8%, of which property taxes 26.2%, taxes on goods and services 18.4%, social security contributions 7.1%, customs duties 3.0%; development revenue 24.3%). Expenditures: Cz$591,845,000,000[18] (administration and planning 16.8%; transportation 14.2%; agriculture and water supply 13.7%; regional development 12.1%; education and culture 11.5%; social welfare 8.0%; national defense and public security 7.5%; health and sanitation 3.5%; industry and commerce 3.5%).
Public debt (external, outstanding; 1986): U.S.$82,522,800,000.
Population economically active (1985)[13]: total 55,098,494; activity rate of total population 41.9% (participation rates: ages 15–59, 66.8%; female 33.5%; unemployed [1987] 9.7%[19]).

Price and earnings indexes (1980 = 100)

	1981	1982	1983	1984	1985	1986	1987
Consumer price index	206	407	984	2,924	9,556	23,436	77,258
Earnings index[20]	203	403	865	2,374	8,018	...	...

Land use (1985): forested 66.6%; meadows and pastures 19.6%; agricultural and under permanent cultivation 9.0%; other 4.8%.
Tourism (1986): receipts from visitors U.S.$1,527,000,000; expenditures by nationals abroad U.S.$1,464,000,000.

Manufacturing enterprises (1980)

	no. of enterprises	number of labourers	wages of labourers as a % of avg. of all wages	value added in producer's prices (in '000s of cruzados)
Chemicals	3,419	163,227	169.9	577,003
Metallurgy	14,407	531,729	116.5	452,469
Mechanical products	9,748	538,146	161.5	398,678
Food products	49,366	622,062	62.2	394,759
Transportation equipment	3,983	281,272	141.2	297,171
Textiles	6,062	377,600	80.6	251,520
Electric and communications equipment	3,337	243,494	121.3	249,754
Mineral products (not metals)	43,170	437,405	67.7	228,555
Clothing and footwear	15,338	459,869	59.5	190,255
Paper and paper products	1,704	107,433	109.1	118,980
Lumber	21,018	263,004	57.7	105,715
Publishing and printing	8,328	142,078	118.8	102,055
Plastics	2,651	118,852	90.2	95,711
Furniture	12,667	174,685	69.1	70,200
Pharmaceutical products	492	34,008	128.5	64,516

Production. Agriculture, forestry, fishing ('000 metric tons; 1986) sugarcane 249,277, cassava 25,542, corn (maize) 20,510, soybeans 13,335, oranges 13,321, bananas 7,563, wheat 5,433, seed cotton 2,314, dry beans 2,221, tomatoes 1,838, potatoes 1,834, pineapples 1,258, coffee 1,004, papayas 658, onions 635, grapes 590, cocoa 459, cashews 95; livestock (number of live animals) 128,918,000 cattle, 33,000,000 pigs, 18,473,000 sheep, 5,500,000 horses, 2,000,000 mules; roundwood (1985) 225,905,000 cu m; fish catch 847, of which crustaceans 112. Mining and quarrying (value of production in '000,000s of cruzados; 1985): iron ore 5,784; tin 3,199; granite 2,380; gold 2,211[21]; limestone 2,088; clay 1,192; bauxite 996; phosphate fertilizers 923; manganese 473; copper 353. Manufacturing (value of production in '000,000s of cruzados; 1980): chemicals 1,850; food products 1,333; iron and steel and other worked metals 1,318; transport equipment 753; electric and nonelectric machinery 729; textiles 616; electrical goods (including computers, televisions, and radios) 498; cement and other worked nonmetals 403; clothing and footwear 370; paper and paper products 258; lumber 195; plastic products 194; tires and other rubber products 144. Construction (new buildings completed; 1984) residential 14,304,000 sq m; nonresidential 3,698,000 sq m.

Retail trade enterprises (1980)

	no. of enterprises	total no. of employees	annual wage as a % of all wages	annual value of sales (in '000s of cruzados)
General merchandise stores (including food products)	16,186	274,379	145.5	658,096
Gasoline stations	21,588	140,865	127.6	594,063
Food, beverages, and tobacco stores	538,638	963,106	16.5	586,249
Automobile dealers and auto parts stores	25,284	157,285	205.4	581,354
Stores selling clothing, fabrics, and textiles	117,595	452,641	102.3	434,793
Hardware stores	37,396	208,783	134.5	407,266
Stores selling radios, televisions, and related electronic goods	26,114	168,431	180.1	353,169
Drugstores	33,631	142,030	118.0	217,781
Agricultural machinery and heavy equipment dealers	6,565	59,244	329.5	204,332
General merchandise stores (excluding food products)	3,367	58,729	239.9	124,359
Book, magazine, and office supply stores	20,192	63,529	123.1	60,327

Energy production (consumption): electricity (kW-hr; 1986) 211,779,000,000 (188,085,000,000); coal (metric tons; 1986) 7,391,000 (17,131,000); crude petroleum (barrels; 1987) 206,720,000 (396,893,000); petroleum products (metric tons; 1986) 49,404,000 (44,173,000); natural gas (cu m; 1986) 2,671,000,000 (2,671,000,000); alcohol[22] (hectolitres; 1986) 102,000,000 (84,600,000).

Household income and expenditure. Average household size (1985) 4.3; income per household of families having income (1985)[13,23,24] 21,802 cruzados (U.S.$2,922); sources of income: n.a.; expenditure (1971)[25]: food 43.6%, energy and water 11.8%, housing 8.6%, clothing and footwear 6.4%, transportation 6.3%, beverages and tobacco 5.4%, health care 5.3%, other 12.6%.

Financial aggregates[26]

	1982	1983	1984	1985	1986	1987
Exchange rate, cruzados per:						
U.S. dollar	0.253	0.984	3.184	10.490	14.895	72.251
£	0.408	1.427	3.682	15.153	21.963	132.328
SDR	0.279	1.030	3.121	11.522	18.219	102.500
International reserves (U.S.$)						
Total (excl. gold; '000,000)	3,928	4,355	11,508	10,605	5,803	6,299
SDRs ('000,000)	—	—	1	1	—	—
Reserve pos. in IMF ('000,000)	287	—	—	—	—	—
Foreign exchange ('000,000)	3,641	4,355	11,507	10,604	5,803	6,299
Gold ('000,000 fine troy oz)	0.15	0.54	1.47	3.10	2.43	2.43
% world reserves	0.02	0.06	0.16	0.33	0.26	0.26
Interest and prices						
Central bank discount (%)	49.0	156.6	215.3	219.4	50.7	391.5
Gov't. bond yield (%)	...	...	...	...	...	...
Industrial share prices	...	...	...	...	...	...
Balance of payments (U.S.$'000,000)						
Balance of visible trade	+780	+6,470	+13,089	+12,486	+8,348	...
Imports, f.o.b.	19,395	15,429	13,916	13,153	14,044	...
Exports, f.o.b.	20,173	21,898	27,002	25,639	22,392	...
Balance of invisibles	−17,082	−13,414	−13,215	−12,894	−12,911	...
Balance of payments, current account	−16,312	−6,837	+42	−273	−4,477	...

Foreign trade[27]

Balance of trade (current prices)

	1982	1983	1984	1985	1986	1987
U.S.$'000,000	+780	+6,470	+13,089	+12,486	+8,349	+11,161
% of total	2.0%	17.3%	32.0%	32.2%	22.9%	27.0%

Imports (1985): U.S.$14,332,000,000 (crude petroleum and petroleum products 47.2%; chemicals 11.3%, of which organic chemicals 5.3%, fertilizers 1.9%; nonelectrical machinery 9.1%; food products 7.4%, of which cereals 5.7%; electrical and electronic goods 5.6%; transport equipment 3.7%, of which road vehicles 2.1%, airplanes 1.4%; metals [all forms] 3.2%, of which iron and steel 1.4%; photographic, surgical, and scientific instruments and apparatus 1.7%; plastics 1.3%; natural and synthetic rubber materials 1.3%). *Major import sources:* United States 21.2%; Iraq 12.7%; Nigeria 9.5%; Saudi Arabia 7.2%; West Germany 5.9%; Japan 4.4%; Canada 3.6%; China 3.6%; Argentina 3.4%; Mexico 2.9%.
Exports (1985): U.S.$25,639,000,000 (metals [all forms] 11.3%, of which iron and steel 8.9%; coffee 9.7%; crude petroleum and petroleum products 6.4%; nonelectrical machinery 6.2%; road vehicles 5.3%; animal feedstuffs 5.1%; textiles 3.9%; footwear 3.8%; animal and vegetable fats and oils 3.3%; cocoa beans and cocoa 3.2%; processed vegetables and fruits 3.2%; seeds, juice, and industrial products of diverse fruits 3.1%; organic chemicals 2.5%; electrical and electronic goods 2.3%; fresh and frozen meat 2.2%; paper and paper products 2.2%). *Major export destinations:* United States 26.6%; The Netherlands 6.1%; Japan 5.4%; West Germany 5.0%; Italy 4.4%; Nigeria 3.3%; China 3.2%; France 3.0%; United Kingdom 2.6%; Iraq 2.5%.

Transport and communications

Transport. Railroads (1985): route length 18,503 mi, 29,777 km; passenger-mi 10,167,000,000, passenger-km 16,362,000,000; short ton-mi cargo 68,-401,000,000, metric ton-km cargo 99,863,000,000. Roads (1986): total length 881,349 mi, 1,418,396 km (paved 9%). Vehicles (1986): passenger cars 10,516,000; trucks and buses 1,067,000. Merchant marine (1987): vessels (100 gross tons and over) 718; total deadweight tonnage 10,437,858. Air transport (1986): passenger-km 24,423,000,000; metric ton-km cargo 1,226,-000,000; airports (1988) with scheduled flights 110.
Communications. Daily newspapers (1986): total number 279; total circulation 8,528,000; circulation per 1,000 population 62. Radio (1986): total number of receivers 50,540,000 (1 per 2.7 persons). Television (1987): total number of receivers 36,000,000 (1 per 4.0 persons). Telephones (1986): 12,580,408 (1 per 11 persons).

Education and health

Education (1985)

	schools	teachers	students	student/ teacher ratio
Primary (age 7–14)	187,274	1,040,566	24,769,736	23.8
Secondary (age 15–17)	9,260	206,111	3,016,138	14.6
Higher	859	122,486	1,367,609	11.2

Literacy (1985)[13,28]: total population age 15 and over literate 66,255,-000 (79.3%); males literate 32,757,000 (80.4%); females literate 33,498,000 (78.3%).
Health: physicians (1981) 103,000 (1 per 1,200 persons); hospital beds (1986) 492,519 (1 per 287 persons); infant mortality rate per 1,000 live births (1985–90) 63.2.
Food (1984–86): daily per capita caloric intake 2,644 (vegetable products 86%, animal products 14%); (1983) 106% of FAO recommended minimum requirement.

Military

Total active duty personnel (1987): 295,700 (army 66.6%, navy 16.2%, air force 17.2%). *Military expenditure as percent of GNP* (1985): 1.0% (world 6.1%); per capita expenditure U.S.$17.

[1]Tocantins was created from northern Goiás as of promulgation of new national constitution on Oct. 5, 1988. [2]Includes former federal territory of Fernando de Noronha. [3]Includes 1,035 sq mi (2,680 sq km) in dispute between Amazonas and Pará and 1,009 sq mi (2,614 sq km) in dispute between Ceará and Piauí. [4]Detail does not add to total given because of rounding. [5]Land area excluding inland water is 3,265,076 sq mi (8,456,508 sq km). [6]Spiritist Catholics are actively and regularly involved in the practice of medium religions; about 60,000,000 Roman Catholics defer to spiritist dogma and participate in organized spiritism occasionally. [7]Evangelical Catholics are persons who are officially regarded as Roman Catholic but who are affiliated to Protestant churches. [8]Non-Christian followers of Afro-Brazilian syncretistic religions ("low spiritism"). [9]Non-Christian followers of Kardecism ("high spiritism"). [10]First population cited refers to the *municipio,* an officially delimited area including a central city and adjacent urban and rural districts; second (parenthetical) figure refers to the metropolitan area, defined as the adjoining predominantly urban *municipios* that are economically dependent on the central city. [11]*Municipio* within Rio de Janeiro metropolitan area. [12]*Municipio* within São Paulo metropolitan area. [13]Excludes rural population of Acre, Amazonas, Pará, Rondônia, Amapá, and Roraima. [14]1984. [15]1985. [16]At factor cost. [17]Excludes persons not employed regularly on a weekly basis. [18]Development expenditure equals 27.5% of total. [19]Metropolitan São Paulo only. [20]Minimum wages paid in the *municipio* of São Paulo. [21]Official sources estimate 65% of all locally mined gold and 97% of all locally mined precious stones were smuggled out of the country in 1987. [22]Fuel produced from sugarcane used in the operation of locally produced automobiles as either hydrous alcohol or gasohol. [23]Prices of September 1985. [24]Excludes pensioners, domestic servants, and relatives of domestic servants. [25]Weights of CPI components for middle-income families in São Paulo. [26]End-of-year figures. [27]Import figures are f.o.b. in balance of trade and c.i.f. in commodities and trading partners. [28]Per official estimate, 1986 functional literacy may be as low as 42.0% of total population over age 15.

Brunei

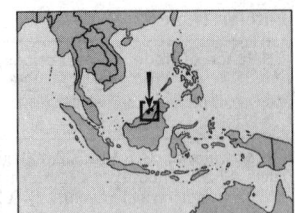

Official name: Negara Brunei
Darussalam (State of Brunei, Abode
of Peace).
Form of government: monarchy
(sultanate).
Head of state and government: Sultan.
Capital: Bandar Seri Begawan.
Official language: Malay.
Official religion: Islam.
Monetary unit: 1 Brunei dollar
(Br$) = 100 cents; valuation (Oct. 10,
1988) 1 U.S.$ = Br$2.04;
1 £ = Br$3.49.

Area and population

Districts	Capitals	area sq mi	area sq km	population 1986 estimate
Belait	Kuala Belait	1,052	2,724	53,600
Brunei and Muara	Bandar Seri Begawan	220	571	136,100
Temburong	Bangar	504	1,304	8,500
Tutong	Tutong	450	1,166	28,100
TOTAL		2,226	5,765	226,300

Demography

Population (1988): 250,000.
Density (1988): persons per sq mi 112.3, persons per sq km 43.4.
Urban–rural (1981): urban 59.4%; rural 40.6%.
Sex distribution (1986): male 51.61% female 48.39%.
Age breakdown (1986): under 15, 36.7%; 15–29, 33.3%; 30–44, 18.3%; 45–59, 7.4%; 60–69, 2.3%; 70 and over, 2.0%.
Population projection: (1990) 269,000; (2000) 388,000.
Doubling time: 26 years.
Ethnic composition (1986): Malay 68.8%; Chinese 18.3%; other indigenous 5.0%; Indian and other 7.9%.
Religious affiliation (1982): Muslim 63.4%; Buddhist 14.0%; Christian 9.7%; other 12.9%.
Major cities (1981): Bandar Seri Begawan 55,000[1]; Seria 23,511; Kuala Belait 19,281; Tutong 6,161.

Vital statistics

Birth rate per 1,000 population (1986): 30.6 (world avg. 26.0); (1982) legitimate 99.6%; illegitimate 0.4%.
Death rate per 1,000 population (1986): 3.2 (world avg. 9.9).
Natural increase rate per 1,000 population (1986): 27.4 (world avg. 16.1).
Total fertility rate (avg. births per childbearing woman): n.a.
Marriage rate per 1,000 population (1986): 7.4.
Divorce rate per 1,000 population (1985): 0.7[2].
Life expectancy at birth (1986): male 70.1 years; female 72.7 years.
Major causes of death per 100,000 population (1986): cardiovascular disease 32.7; malignant neoplasms (cancers) 27.0; cerebrovascular disease 19.4; conditions originating from perinatal period 15.9; pneumonia 12.4; bronchitis, emphysema, and asthma 11.0; motor vehicle accidents 11.0; tuberculosis 4.9; signs, symptoms, and other ill-defined conditions 99.4.

National economy

Budget (1986). Revenue: Br$3,331,530,000 (indirect taxes 59.4%, government property 36.7%[3]). Expenditures: Br$2,720,370,000 (development expenditure 13.9%, defense 8.8%, education 7.6%, public works 5.7%, health 3.4%).
Public debt (external, outstanding; 1987): none.
Tourism (1985): number of tourist arrivals 6,418.
Production (metric tons except as noted). Agriculture, forestry, fishing (1986): 1,045,000 coconuts[4], vegetables and melons 9,000, fruits excluding melons 6,000, rice 3,000, eggs 1,900, cassava 1,000, roots and tubers 1,000, pineapples 1,000; livestock (number of live animals) 14,000 pigs, 12,000 buffalo, 4,000 cattle, 1,000 goats, 2,000,000 chickens; roundwood 293,000 cu m; fish catch 2,758. Mining and quarrying (1986): other than petroleum and natural gas (see below), none except sand and gravel for construction. Manufacturing (1986): gasoline 125,000; diesel oils 58,000; liquid petroleum gas 40,000; jet fuels 18,000; naphtha 4,000; kerosene 3,000. Construction (number of buildings completed; 1984): residential 195; nonresidential 5. Energy production (consumption): electricity (kW-hr; 1986) 958,000,000 (958,000,000); coal, none (none); crude petroleum (barrels; 1986) 60,555,000 (n.a.); petroleum products (metric tons; 1986) 988,000 (715,000); natural gas (cu m; 1986) 8,055,300,000 (342,800,000).
Population economically active (1981): total 70,690; activity rate of total population 36.4% (participation rates: ages 15–64, 61.1%; female 23.8%; unemployed [1984] 3.4%).

Price and earnings indexes (1980 = 100)

	1980	1981	1982	1983	1984	1985	1986
Consumer price index	100.0	109.1	116.1	117.4	121.1	123.9	126.1
Monthly earnings index[5]	100.0	107.5	111.7	139.3	127.9	129.0	113.4

Household income and expenditure. Average household size (1981) 5.8.; income per household: n.a.; sources of income: n.a.; expenditure (1977): food 45.1%; transportation and communications 17.2%; recreation, education, and cultural services 8.9%; household furnishings 8.3%; clothing and footwear 6.1%; rent and utilities 5.0%.

Gross national product (at current market prices; 1986): U.S.$3,570,000,000[6] (U.S.$15,400 per capita).

Structure of gross domestic product and labour force

	1986 in value Br$'000,000	1986 % of total value	1981 labour force	1981 % of labour force
Agriculture	107.7	1.9	3,440	4.9
Mining	2,920.2	50.6	3,860	5.5
Manufacturing			2,780	3.9
Construction	233.5	4.0	12,650	17.9
Public utilities	17.7	0.3	1,960	2.8
Transportation and communications	139.0	2.4	4,530	6.4
Trade	666.8	11.5	7,360	10.4
Finance	379.5	6.6	2,010	2.8
Services	1,451.7	25.1	29,280	41.4
Other	−142.7[7]	−2.57	2,820[8]	4.0[8]
TOTAL	5,773.3[9]	100.0[9]	70,690	100.0

Land use (1985): forested 52.2%; meadows and pastures 1.1%; agricultural and under permanent cultivation 1.3%; other 45.4%.

Foreign trade

Balance of trade (current prices)

	1981	1982	1983	1984	1985	1986
Br$'000,000	+7,327	+6,582	+5,629	+5,482	+5,184	+2,540
% of total	74.3%	67.7%	64.6%	67.3%	65.8%	46.7%

Imports (1986): Br$1,450,410,000 (machinery and transport equipment 38.0%, manufactured goods 21.1%, food and live animals 14.4%, miscellaneous manufactured articles 10.6%, chemicals 7.0%, beverages and tobacco 5.9%, crude materials 1.2%, mineral fuels 1.0%). *Major import sources:* Singapore 25.7%; Japan 17.7%; United States 12.2%; United Kingdom 7.9%; West Germany 6.0%; Malaysia 5.2%[10]; The Netherlands 3.3%; Thailand 3.1%; Australia 2.6%.
Exports (1986): Br$3,990,100,000 (natural gas 52.9%, crude oil 40.6%, petroleum products 3.7%, other 2.8%). *Major export destinations:* Japan 66.9%; Thailand 8.1%; South Korea 7.4%; Singapore 6.7%; United States 6.1%; Taiwan 1.7%.

Transport and communications

Transport. Railroads[11] (1987): length 12 mi, 19 km. Roads (1986): total length 1,156 mi, 1,860 km (paved 50%). Vehicles (1986): passenger cars 84,527; trucks and buses 11,051. Merchant marine (1987): vessels (100 gross tons and over) 24; total deadweight tonnage 343,647. Marine transport (1986): cargo loaded 18,627,000 metric tons, cargo unloaded 671,700 metric tons. Air transport (1985): passenger-mi 153,500,000, passenger-km 247,000,000; short ton-mi cargo 3,014,000, metric ton-km cargo 4,400,000; airports (1988) with scheduled flights 1.
Communications. Daily newspapers (1987): none. Radio (1986): total number of receivers 78,000 (1 per 3.0 persons). Television (1986): total number of receivers 49,500[12] (1 per 4.7 persons). Telephones (1986): 35,636 (1 per 6.6 persons).

Education and health

Education (1986)

	schools	teachers	students	student/ teacher ratio
Primary (age 5–11)	146	2,225	36,983	16.6
Secondary (age 12–20)	29	1,636	18,714	11.4
Voc., teacher tr.	8	414[13]	1,688	4.1
Higher	1	33	176	5.3

Educational attainment (1981). Percent of population age 25 and over having: no formal schooling 32.1%; primary education 28.3%; secondary 30.1%; postsecondary and higher 9.4%. *Literacy* (1984): total population age 15 and over literate 108,900 (80.3%); males literate 64,300 (86.5%); females literate 44,600 (72.8%).
Health (1986): physicians 171 (1 per 1,323 persons); hospital beds 876 (1 per 258 persons); infant mortality rate per 1,000 live births 10.0.
Food (1984–86): daily per capita caloric intake 2,850 (vegetable products 80%, animal products 20%); (1983) 139% of FAO recommended minimum requirement.

Military

Total active duty personnel (1987): 4,050[14] (army 83.5%, navy 11.6%, air force 4.9%). *Military expenditure as percent of GNP* (1983): 5.8% (world 6.1%); per capita expenditure U.S.$1,200.

[1]1985 estimate. [2]For Muslim population only. [3]In 1983 more than 98% of state revenue was derived from exports of oil and gas. [4]1985. [5]Nonagricultural sectors only. [6]GDP data. [7]Imputed bank service charge. [8]Includes unemployed. [9]Detail does not add to total given because of rounding. [10]Peninsular Malaysia only. [11]Privately owned. [12]Colour receivers only. [13]Vocational and teacher training includes higher. [14]All services form part of the army.

Bulgaria

Official name: Narodna Republika Bŭlgaria (People's Republic of Bulgaria).
Form of government: unitary single-party socialist republic with one legislative house (National Assembly [400]).
Chief of state: Chairman of the State Council (president).
Head of government: Chairman of the Council of Ministers (premier).
Capital: Sofia.
Official language: Bulgarian.
Official religion: none.
Monetary unit: 1 lev (leva) = 100 stotinki; valuation (Oct. 10, 1988) 1 lev = U.S.$0.84; 1 £ = 1.45 leva.

Area and population		area		population
				1987
Provinces[1]	Capitals	sq mi	sq km	estimate[2]
Blagoevgrad	Blagoevgrad	2,503	6,484	349,546
Burgas	Burgas	2,974	7,702	450,516
Gabrovo	Gabrovo	785	2,034	174,066
Khaskovo	Khaskovo	1,547	4,008	303,064
Kŭrdzhali	Kŭrdzhali	1,555	4,027	303,877
Kyustendil	Kyustendil	1,180	3,055	189,327
Lovech	Lovech	1,597	4,135	200,939
Mikhaylovgrad	Mikhaylovgrad	1,399	3,623	222,553
Pazardzhik	Pazardzhik	1,721	4,457	328,755
Pernik	Pernik	923	2,391	175,469
Pleven	Pleven	1,674	4,335	361,218
Plovdiv	Plovdiv	2,178	5,642	759,114
Razgrad	Razgrad	1,025	2,654	199,196
Ruse	Ruse	1,011	2,618	304,965
Shumen	Shumen	1,309	3,390	255,945
Silistra	Silistra	1,102	2,854	174,066
Sliven	Sliven	1,398	3,620	240,012
Smolyan	Smolyan	1,346	3,487	165,566
Sofiya	Sofia (Sofiya)	2,738	7,091	304,123
Stara Zagora	Stara Zagora	1,960	5,077	413,519
Tolbukhin	Tolbukhin	1,817	4,707	257,544
Tŭrgovishte	Tŭrgovishte	1,049	2,717	170,207
Varna	Varna	1,480	3,832	464,946
Veliko Tŭrnovo	Veliko Tŭrnovo	1,794	4,646	338,073
Vidin	Vidin	1,174	3,041	164,848
Vratsa	Vratsa	1,522	3,943	286,740
Yambol	Yambol	1,588	4,113	203,910
City Commune				
Sofiya	Sofia (Sofiya)	506	1,311	1,203,553
TOTAL		42,855	110,994	8,965,657

Demography

Population (1988): 8,978,000.
Density (1988): persons per sq mi 209.6, persons per sq km 80.9.
Urban–rural (1987): urban 65.5%; rural 34.5%.
Sex distribution (1987): male 49.70%; female 50.30%.
Age breakdown (1987): under 15, 20.8%; 15–29, 19.8%; 30–44, 21.1%; 45–59, 20.0%; 60–74, 13.7%; 75 and over, 4.5%[3].
Population projection: (1990) 8,998,000; (2000) 9,099,000.
Doubling time: not applicable; population stable.
Ethnic composition (1986): Bulgarian 85.3%; Turkish 8.5%, Gypsy 2.5%; other 3.7%.
Religious affiliation (1982): atheist 64.5%; Eastern Orthodox 26.7%; Muslim 7.5%; Protestant 0.7%; Roman Catholic 0.5%; other 0.1%.
Major cities (1987): Sofia 1,119,152; Plovdiv 349,148; Varna 303,071; Ruse 186,428; Burgas 186,369.

Vital statistics

Birth rate per 1,000 population (1986): 13.4 (world avg. 26.0); (1984) legitimate 88.6%; illegitimate 11.4%.
Death rate per 1,000 population (1986): 11.6 (world avg. 9.9).
Natural increase rate per 1,000 population (1986): 1.8 (world avg. 16.1).
Total fertility rate (avg. births per childbearing woman; 1985): 2.0.
Marriage rate per 1,000 population (1986): 7.3.
Divorce rate per 1,000 population (1986): 1.1.
Life expectancy at birth (1978–80): male 68.4 years; female 73.6 years.
Major causes of death per 100,000 population (1985): diseases of the circulatory system 721.1; malignant neoplasms (cancers) 163.8.

National economy

Budget (1987). Revenue: 20,672,800,000 leva (national economy 92.0%, other 8.0%). Expenditures: 20,662,800,000 leva (economy 46.4%, education and health 18.8%, social security 18.0%, administration 15.1%).
Public debt (external, outstanding; 1986): U.S.$1,300,000,000.
Tourism (1986): number of tourist arrivals 7,567,000; receipts from visitors U.S.$345,000,000; expenditures by nationals abroad, n.a.
Production (metric tons except as noted). Agriculture, forestry, fishing (1986): wheat 4,326,600, corn (maize) 2,848,000, barley 1,144,200, sugar beets 869,500; livestock (number of live animals; 1987) 9,563,298 sheep, 4,050,255 pigs, 1,704,696 cattle; roundwood 4,263,000 cu m; fish catch 138,000. Mining and quarrying (1986): iron ore 2,179,000; lead 95,000; copper 75,000; zinc 68,000; manganese 45,000. Manufacturing (1986): cement 5,702,000; crude steel 2,800,000; pig iron 1,651,000; fertilizers 837,800; wood pulp and paper 544,700; cigarettes 90,000; cotton fabrics 371,800,000 m. Construction (1986): residential 3,669,223 sq m. Energy production (consumption): electricity (kW-hr; 1986) 41,817,000,000 (45,774,000,000); coal (metric tons; 1986) 35,222,000 (42,190,000); crude petroleum (barrels; 1986) 2,200,000 (93,800,000); petroleum products (metric tons; 1986) 11,392,000 (12,975,-000); natural gas (cu m; 1985) 127,872,000 (5,533,000,000).
Gross national product (1986): U.S.$60,618,000,000 (U.S.$6,766 per capita).

Structure of net material product and labour force				
	1986			
	in value '000,000 leva	% of total value	labour force[4]	% of labour force
Agriculture	3,957.2	14.7	848,088	20.8
Mining	104.9	0.4	24,261	0.6
Manufacturing	16,676.8	62.1	1,403,013	34.4
Public utilities			56,748	1.4
Construction	2,564.3	9.5	359,212	8.8
Transp. and commun.	1,752.2	6.5	306,332	7.5
Trade	1,227.0	4.6	360,704	8.8
Finance	—	—	22,350	0.5
Pub. admin., defense	—	—	54,296	1.3
Services	—	—	602,020	14.8
Other	569.0[5]	2.1[5]	39,457	1.0
TOTAL	26,851.4	100.0[3]	4,076,481	100.0[3]

Population economically active (1985): total 4,802,000; activity rate of total population 53.7% (participation rates: ages 15–64, n.a.; female 47.6%).

Price and earnings indexes (1980 = 100)							
	1980	1981	1982	1983	1984	1985	1986
Consumer price index	100.0	100.5	100.8	102.2	102.9	104.6	108.3
Monthly earnings index	100.0	105.2	108.1	109.5	113.9	117.3	123.4

Household income and expenditure. Average household size (1982) 3.3; income per household (1986) 7,149 leva (U.S.$8,410); sources of income (1986): wages and salaries 53.8%, transfer payments 18.8%; self-employment 11.0%; expenditure (1986): food 44.3%, clothing 10.1%, housing 7.1%.
Land use (1985): forested 34.9%; meadows and pastures 18.4%; agricultural and under permanent cultivation 37.5%; other 9.2%.

Foreign trade

Balance of trade (current prices)						
	1981	1982	1983	1984	1985	1986
'000,000 leva	−97.6	+95.9	−148.5	−145.0	−327.1	−1,022.6
% of total	0.5%	0.4%	0.6%	0.6%	1.2%	3.6%

Imports (1986): 14,353,300,000 leva (fuels, mineral raw materials, and metals 43.9%; machinery and equipment 37.4%; food and consumer goods 7.3%; chemical fertilizers and rubber 4.5%). *Major import sources:* U.S.S.R. 56.4%; East Germany 5.2%; West Germany 4.8%; Czechoslovakia 4.6%; Poland 4.1%; Libya 3.6%; Cuba 1.4%; United States 0.9%.
Exports (1986): 13,350,500,000 leva (machinery and equipment 56.0%; food and beverages 12.3%; consumer goods 10.8%; tobacco 6.9%; fuels, mineral raw materials, and metals 9.9%; chemicals 3.9%). *Major export destinations:* U.S.S.R. 61.1%; East Germany 5.6%; Czechoslovakia 4.6%; Poland 4.1%.

Transport and communications

Transport. Railroads (1986): length 2,668 mi, 4,294 km; passenger-km 8,004,000,000; metric ton-km cargo 18,327,000,000. Roads (1986): total length 23,237 mi, 37,397 km (paved 91%). Vehicles (1985): passenger cars 1,030,090; trucks and buses 587,400. Merchant marine (1987): vessels (100 gross tons and over) 205; total deadweight tonnage 2,302,919. Air transport (1986): passenger-km 2,960,700,000; metric ton-km cargo 43,148,000; airports (1988) 13.
Communications. Daily newspapers (1986): total number 17; total circulation 2,834,000; circulation per 1,000 population 316. Radio (1986): 1,997,-355 receivers (1 per 4.5 persons). Television (1986): 1,692,744 receivers (1 per 5.3 persons). Telephones (1986): 1,876,317 (1 per 4.8 persons).

Education and health

Education (1986–87)	schools	teachers	students	student/ teacher ratio
Primary (age 6–14)	3,501	62,188	1,097,437	17.6
Secondary (age 15–17)		9,637	164,107	17.0
Voc., teacher tr.	528	18,692	228,620	12.2
Higher	30	16,453	109,291	6.6

Educational attainment (1983): Percent of employed population having: postsecondary vocational certificate 15.6%; 4-year college 7.5%. *Literacy* (1980): total population age 15 and over literate 95.5%.
Health (1986): physicians 26,451 (1 per 337 persons); hospital beds 87,085 (1 per 103 persons); infant mortality rate per 1,000 live births 15.4.
Food (1984–86): daily per capita caloric intake 3,634 (vegetable products 76%, animal products 24%); (1983) 146% of FAO minimum requirement.

Military

Total active duty personnel (1987): 152,800 (army 72.0%, navy 5.7%, air force 22.3%). *Military expenditure as percent of GNP* (1985): 8.0% (world 6.1%); per capita expenditure U.S.$517.

[1]On Aug. 26, 1987, Bulgaria's 28 administrative districts were reorganized into nine regions: Burgas, Khaskovo, Lovech, Mikhaylovgrad, Plovdiv, Razgrad, Sofiya, Sofiya city, and Varna. [2]January 1. [3]Detail does not add to total given because of rounding. [4]Socialized sector only. [5]Includes other material activities.

Burkina Faso[1]

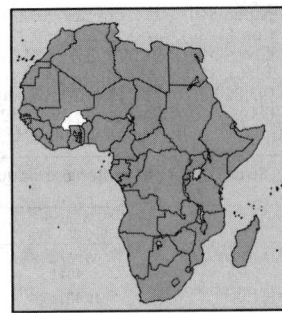

Official name: Burkina Faso
(Burkina Faso).
Form of government: military
regime.
Head of state and government:
Chairman of the Popular Front[2].
Capital: Ouagadougou.
Official language: French.
Official religion: none.
Monetary unit: 1 CFA franc
(CFAF) = 100 centimes; valuation
(Oct. 10, 1988) 1 U.S.$ = CFAF
316.13; 1 £ = CFAF 541.38.

Area and population		area		population
				1985
Provinces	Capitals	sq mi	sq km	census
Bam	Kongoussi	1,551	4,017	164,263
Bazéga	Kombissiri	2,051	5,313	306,976
Bougouriba	Diébougou	2,736	7,087	221,522
Boulgou	Tenkodogo	3,488	9,033	403,358
Boulkiemde	Koudougou	1,598	4,138	363,594
Comoé	Banfora	7,102	18,393	250,510
Ganzourgou	Zorgho	1,578	4,087	196,006
Gnagna	Bogandé	3,320	8,600	229,249
Gourma	Fada N'Gourma	10,275	26,613	294,123
Houet	Bobo-Dioulasso	6,360	16,472	585,031
Kadiogo	Ouagadougou	451	1,169	459,138
Kénédougou	Orodara	3,207	8,307	139,722
Kossi	Nouna	5,088	13,177	330,413
Kouritenga	Koupéla	628	1,627	197,027
Mouhoun	Dédougou	4,032	10,442	289,213
Nahouri	Pô	1,484	3,843	105,273
Namentenga	Boulsa	2,994	7,755	198,798
Oubritenga	Ziniaré	1,812	4,693	303,229
Oudalan	Gorom Gorom	3,879	10,046	105,715
Passoré	Yako	1,575	4,078	225,115
Poni	Gaoua	4,000	10,361	234,501
Sanguie	Réo	1,994	5,165	218,289
Sanmatenga	Kaya	3,557	9,213	368,365
Sèno	Dori	5,202	13,473	230,043
Sissili	Léo	5,303	13,736	246,844
Soum	Djibo	5,154	13,350	190,464
Sourou	Tougan	3,663	9,487	267,770
Tapoa	Diapaga	5,707	14,780	159,121
Yatenga	Ouahigouya	4,746	12,292	537,205
Zoundwéogo	Manga	1,333	3,453	155,142
TOTAL		105,869[3]	274,200	7,967,019

Demography

Population (1988): 8,530,000.
Density (1988): persons per sq mi 80.6, persons per sq km 31.1.
Urban-rural (1986): urban 8.1%; rural 91.9%.
Sex distribution (1985): male 48.23%; female 51.77%.
Age breakdown (1985): under 15, 44.5%; 15–29, 26.2%; 30–44, 14.4%; 45–59, 9.4%; 60–74, 4.5%; 75 and over, 1.0%.
Population projection: (1990) 8,994,000; (2000) 11,716,000.
Doubling time: 24 years.
Ethnic composition (1983): Mossi 47.9%; Mande 8.8%; Fulani 8.3%; Lobi 6.9%; Bobo 6.8%; Senufo 5.3%; Grosi 5.1%; Gurma 4.8%; Tuareg 3.3%; other 2.8%.
Religious affiliation (1980): traditional beliefs 44.8%; Muslim 43.0%; Christian 12.2%, of which Roman Catholic 9.8%, Protestant 2.4%.
Major cities (1985): Ouagadougou 442,223; Bobo-Dioulasso 231,162; Koudougou 59,644; Ouahigouya 41,595; Banfora 16,843.

Vital statistics

Birth rate per 1,000 population (1980–85): 47.8 (world avg. 29.0).
Death rate per 1,000 population (1980–85): 20.1 (world avg. 11.0).
Natural increase rate per 1,000 population (1980–85): 27.7 (world avg. 18.0).
Total fertility rate (avg. births per childbearing woman; 1980–85): 6.5.
Marriage rate per 1,000 population (1975): 9.4.
Divorce rate per 1,000 population (1975): 1.3.
Life expectancy at birth (1980–85): male 43.7 years; female 46.8 years.
Morbidity (percent of reported cases of illness; 1984): measles 39.6%; malaria 12.4%; tetanus 5.7%; diarrheal diseases 5.3%.

National economy

Budget (1988). Revenue: CFAF 90,295,000,000 (1987; taxes 88.6%, of which indirect 63.1%; direct 22.6%; other 1.1%). *Expenditures:* CFAF 96,287,000,-000 (1987; administration 45.0%; debt payment 18.8%; capital equipment 12.6%; material purchases 8.2%).
Public debt (external, outstanding; 1986): U.S.$615,700,000.
Tourism: receipts from visitors (1986) U.S.$7,300,000; expenditures by nationals abroad U.S.$30,000,000.
Production (metric tons except as noted). Agriculture, forestry, fishing (1986): sorghum 1,012,000, millet 687,000, sugarcane 345,000, pulses 177,000, corn (maize) 158,000, peanuts (groundnuts) 152,000, seed cotton 142,000, cassava 33,000, rice 28,000, sweet potatoes 16,000, sesame 16,000; livestock (number of live animals; 1987) 3,057,000 cattle, 3,268,000 goats, 2,169,000 sheep, 21,000,000 chickens; roundwood 6,931,000 cu m; fish catch 7,000. Mining and quarrying (1986): phosphates 3,000. Manufacturing (1986): flour 25,518; soap 13,835; cotton yarn 238; bicycle and motorcycle tires 526,100 units; motorcycles and scooters 52,800 units; footwear 890,000 pairs; beer 389,269 hectolitres; soft drinks 128,644 hectolitres. Construction

(value added in CFAF; 1983): 7,749,300,000. Energy production (consumption): electricity (kW-hr; 1986) 123,000,000 (123,000,000); coal, none (n.a.); crude petroleum, none (n.a.); petroleum products (metric tons; 1986) none (140,000); natural gas, none (n.a.).
Gross national product (1986): U.S.$1,240,000,000 (U.S.$150 per capita).

Structure of gross domestic product and labour force				
	1984		1985	
	in value CFAF '000,000	% of total value	labour force	% of labour force
Agriculture	157,843.8	43.4	3,398,000	91.8
Mining	303.8	0.1		
Manufacturing	50,860.6	13.9	148,000	4.0
Construction	4,933.7	1.4		
Public utilities	4,246.2	1.2		
Transp. and commun.	23,554.0	6.5		
Trade	42,186.8	11.6	155,000	4.2
Pub. admin., defense	63,652.4	17.5		
Services				
Other	16,219.3[4]	4.4[4]	...	...
TOTAL	363,800.6	100.0	3,701,000	100.0

Population economically active: total (1985) 3,701,000; activity rate 47.1% (participation rates: over age 15 85.4%; female 40.9%; unemployed, n.a.).

Price and earnings indexes (1980 = 100)						
	1983	1984	1985	1986	1987	1988[5]
Consumer price index	130.6	133.4	146.3	142.5	138.7	142.2
Hourly earnings index	126.7	126.7	126.7	126.7	145.2	...

Household income and expenditure. Average household size (1984) 4.9; average annual income per household CFAF 303,000 (U.S.$640); sources of income: n.a.; expenditure (1985)[6]: food 38.7%; transportation 18.6%; electricity and fuel 13.7%; beverages 9.0%; health 5.2%; housing 5.1%.
Land use (1985): forested 25.2%; meadows and pastures 36.5%; agricultural and under permanent cultivation 9.6%; other 28.7%.

Foreign trade

Balance of trade (current prices)						
	1981	1982	1983	1984	1985	1986
CFAF '000,000	−51.41	−70.82	−63.76	−51.92	−82.91	−80.25
% of total	56.3%	66.2%	59.5%	42.7%	57.1%	58.3%

Imports (1986): CFAF 139,640,000,000 (machinery and transport equipment 28.0%, of which road transport equipment 12.7%, nonelectrical machinery 10.8%; manufactured goods 24.0%; chemicals 11.2%; petroleum products 11.0%; cereals 5.5%; dairy products 3.8%; raw materials 2.7%; grease and lubricants 2.3%). *Major import sources:* France 29.4%; Côte d'Ivoire 21.4%; U.S. 9.0%; The Netherlands 5.0%; Italy 4.9%; Japan 4.3%.
Exports (1986): CFAF 28,665,000,000 (raw cotton 37.1%; manufactured goods 32.1%; live animals 9.5%; machinery and transport equipment 5.8%; vegetable food products 3.3%). *Major export destinations:* France 26.4%; Taiwan 25.0%; Côte d'Ivoire 15.1%; Switzerland 7.6%; Spain 3.2%; Italy 3.1%; United Kingdom 2.4%; West Germany 2.1%.

Transport and communications

Transport. Railroads (1984)[7]: length 342 mi, 550 km; passenger-km 679,790,-000; metric ton-km cargo 469,675,000. Roads (1986): total length 6,979 mi, 11,231 km (paved 12.0%). Vehicles (1983): passenger cars 21,182; trucks and buses 5,729. Merchant marine: none. Air transport (1986): passenger-km 237,571,000; metric ton-mi cargo 38,455,000; airports (1988) with scheduled flights 3.
Communications. Daily newspapers (1987): total number 2; total circulation 6,500; circulation per 1,000 population 0.8. Radio (1986): 311,000 receivers (1 per 26 persons). Television (1987): 41,500 receivers (1 per 198 persons). Telephones (1986): 16,769 (1 per 482 persons).

Education and health

Education (1986)	schools	teachers	students	student/ teacher ratio
Primary	1,758	6,091	351,807	57.8
Secondary	107	1,519	48,875	32.2
Vocational	18	421	4,808	11.4
Higher	1	325	3,869	11.9

Educational attainment, n.a. *Literacy* (1985): total population age 15 and over literate 509,700 (13.2%); males 392,100 (20.7%); females 119,900 (6.1%).
Health (1984): physicians 180 (1 per 42,128 persons); hospital beds 5,580 (1 per 1,359 persons); infant mortality rate per 1,000 live births (1985) 137.0.
Food (1984–86): daily per capita caloric intake 2,049 (vegetable products 95%, animal products 5%); (1983) 85% of FAO recommended minimum.

Military

Total active duty personnel (1988): 7,200 (army 97.2%; navy, none; air force 2.8%). *Military expenditure as percent of GNP* (1984): 2.7% (world 6.0%); per capita expenditure U.S.$4.

[1]Known as Upper Volta before Aug. 4, 1984. [2]On Oct. 15, 1987, a coup took place changing the leadership of the country from the President and the National Recovery Council, to the Chairman of the Popular Front and the Military Council (formed later in the month). [3]Detail does not add to total given because of rounding. [4]Import duties. [5]April. [6]Weights of consumer price index components; Ouagadougou only. [7]Passenger-mi and short ton-mi cargo figures are based on traffic between Abidjan, Côte d'Ivoire, and Ouagadougou.

Burma

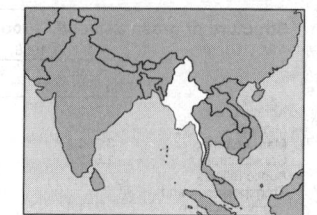

Official name: Pyeidaungzu Myanma Naingngandaw (Union of Burma).
Form of government: multiparty republic with one legislative house (People's Assembly [489[1]]) under interim military emergency rule.
Chief of state: President (Chairman).
Head of government: Prime Minister.
Capital: Rangoon.
Official language: Burmese.
Official religion: none.
Monetary unit: 1 Burmese kyat (K) = 100 pyas; valuation (Oct. 10, 1988) 1 U.S.$ = K 6.58; 1 £ = K 11.28.

Area and population		area		population
				1983
Divisions	Capitals	sq mi	sq km	census
Irrawaddy	Bassein	13,567	35,138	4,994,061
Magwe	Magwe	17,305	44,820	3,243,166
Mandalay	Mandalay	14,295	37,024	4,577,762
Pegu	Pegu	15,214	39,404	3,799,791
Rangoon	Rangoon	3,927	10,171	3,965,916
Sagaing	Sagaing	36,535	94,625	3,862,172
Tenasserim	Tavoy	16,735	43,343	917,247
States				
Chin	Falam	13,907	36,019	368,949
Kachin	Myitkyinä	34,379	89,041	904,794
Karen	Pa-an	11,731	30,383	1,055,359
Kayah	Loi-kaw	4,530	11,733	168,429
Mon	Moulmein	4,748	12,297	1,680,157
Rakhine (Arakan)	Sittwe (Akyab)	14,200	36,778	2,045,559
Shan	Taunggyi	60,155	155,801	3,716,841
TOTAL		261,228	676,577	35,307,913[2]

Demography

Population (1988): 39,952,000.
Density (1988): persons per sq mi 152.9, persons per sq km 59.1.
Urban–rural (1985): urban 23.9%; rural 76.1%.
Sex distribution (1987–88): male 49.59%; female 50.41%.
Age breakdown (1985): under 15, 41.2%; 15–29, 27.2%; 30–44, 15.3%; 45–59, 10.3%; 60–74, 5.0%; 75 and over, 1.0%.
Population projection: (1990) 41,186,000; (2000) 48,596,000.
Doubling time: 36 years.
Ethnic composition (1983): Burman 69.0%; Shan 8.5%; Karen 6.2%; Rakhine 4.5%; Mon 2.4%; Chin 2.2%; Kachin 1.4%; other 5.8%.
Religious affiliation (1983): Buddhist 89.4%; Christian 4.9%; Muslim 3.8%; tribal religions 1.1%; Hindu 0.5%; other 0.3%.
Major cities (1983): Rangoon 2,458,712; Mandalay 532,895; Moulmein 219,991; Pegu 150,447; Bassein 144,092.

Vital statistics

Birth rate per 1,000 population (1987): 32.6 (world avg. 26.0).
Death rate per 1,000 population (1987): 13.2 (world avg. 9.9).
Natural increase rate per 1,000 population (1987): 19.4 (world avg. 16.1).
Total fertility rate (avg. births per childbearing woman; 1987): 4.3.
Marriage rate per 1,000 population, n.a.
Divorce rate per 1,000 population, n.a.
Life expectancy at birth (1987): male 51.9 years; female 55.0 years.
Major causes of death per 100,000 population (1978): pneumonia 16.1; heart diseases 10.5; enteritis and other diarrheal diseases 10.0; tuberculosis 9.4; malignant neoplasms (cancers) 6.5; cerebrovascular disease 4.1; malaria 3.5.

National economy

Budget (1988–89). Revenue: K 7,331,400,000 (commodities and services tax 34.0%, receipts from state economic enterprises 24.6%, customs duties 13.6%, taxes on income and property 6.3%, taxes on the use of state properties 6.1%, interest income 3.8%). Expenditures: K 6,461,800,000 (manufacturing 19.8%, transport and communications 17.0%, agriculture 16.9%, mining 13.7%, power 10.9%, administration 7.0%, social services 6.6%).
Public debt (external, outstanding; 1986): U.S.$3,664,500,000.
Tourism (1986): receipts from visitors U.S.$14,000,000; expenditures by nationals abroad U.S.$400,000.
Land use (1985): forested 49.0%; meadows and pastures 0.5%; agricultural and under permanent cultivation 15.3%; other 35.2%.
Production (metric tons except as noted). Agriculture, forestry, fishing (1987–88): rice 13,722,000, sugarcane 3,072,000, pulses 756,000, peanuts (groundnuts) 559,000, corn (maize) 278,000, sunflower seeds 274,000, wheat 241,000, sorghum 200,000, onions 192,000, sesame seeds 190,000, potatoes 133,000, tobacco leaves 90,000, seed cotton 82,000, garlic 42,000, jute 41,000, chillies 35,000, natural rubber 15,000; livestock (number of live animals) 9,919,000 cattle, 3,059,000 pigs, 2,189,000 buffalo, 1,458,000 sheep and goats, 6,032,000 ducks, 33,483,000 chickens; roundwood 19,096,000 cu m; fish catch 643,750, of which marine fishing areas 496,950. Mining and quarrying (1987–88): copper concentrates 50,800; gypsum 22,700; barites 17,000; jade 13,500; zinc concentrates 10,160; refined lead 6,000; tin concentrates 868; tungsten concentrates 496; refined silver 450,000 troy oz. Manufacturing (value of production in '000,000 kyats; 1987–88): food and beverages 23,549.8; clothing and wearing apparel 1,606.6; industrial raw materials 1,468.9; construction materials 1,120.9; transport vehicles 719.0; personal goods 327.8. Construction[3] (units; 1987–88): residential 1,193; nonresidential 1,483. Energy production (consumption): electricity

(kW-hr; 1987–88) 2,279,000,000 (1,664,000,000); coal (metric tons; 1986) 98,000 (278,000); crude petroleum (barrels; 1986) 10,130,000 (10,130,000); petroleum products (metric tons; 1986) 959,000 (959,000); natural gas (cu m; 1986) 1,084,300,000 (1,084,300,000).
Gross national product (1986): U.S.$7,450,000,000 (U.S.$200 per capita).

Structure of gross domestic product and labour force				
	1987–88			
	in value K '000,000	% of total value	labour force	% of labour force
Agriculture	30,668.6	50.5	10,289,000	65.1
Mining	532.7	0.9	91,000	0.6
Manufacturing	5,597.2	9.2	1,369,000	8.7
Construction	977.2	1.6	265,000	1.7
Public utilities	281.6	0.5	20,000	0.1
Transp. and commun.	2,438.7	4.0	518,000	3.3
Trade	13,468.6	22.2	1,556,000	9.8
Finance	1,499.3	2.5 }	1,047,000	6.6
Public admin., services	5,196.4	8.6 }		
Other			658,000	4.1
TOTAL	60,660.3	100.0	15,813,000	100.0

Population economically active (1987–88): total 15,813,000; activity rate of total population 41.0% (participation rates [1983]: ages 15–64, 64.2%; female 35.3%; unemployed 4.3%).

Price and earnings indexes (1980 = 100)						
	1981	1982	1983	1984	1985	1986	1987[4]
Consumer price index	100.3	105.6	111.6	117.0	125.0	136.5	168.5
Monthly earnings index[5]	101.9	105.1	111.7	108.5	...	...	...

Household income and expenditure. Average household size (1983) 5.2; average annual income per household: n.a.; sources of income: n.a.; expenditure (1978)[6]: food and beverages 64.4%, clothing and footwear 8.0%, fuel and light 7.8%, household rent and repairs 3.8%, tobacco 3.7%, other 12.3%.

Foreign trade[7]

Balance of trade (current prices)						
	1982	1983	1984	1985	1986	1987
K '000,000	+172.9	+1,084.1	+1,338.1	+393.2	+160.0	−173.5
% of total	2.9%	21.7%	26.7%	8.3%	3.8%	5.6%

Imports (1987–88): K 3,936,100,000 (industrial raw materials 45.8%, machinery and equipment 37.7%, construction materials 14.8%, tools and spare parts 13.1%, transport equipment 8.5%, consumer goods 5.9%). Major import sources: Japan 50.4%; EEC 19.5%; Southeast Asian countries 8.0%; eastern European countries 6.8%; China 2.4%.
Exports (1987–88): K 2,528,200,000 (forest products 43.2%, agricultural products 31.8%, minerals and gems 11.2%, animal and marine products 5.0%). Major export destinations: Southeast Asian countries 29.6%; EEC 12.4%; Japan 10.6%; India 6.8%; African countries 5.7%; China 4.8%.

Transport and communications

Transport. Railroads (1987): route length 1,949 mi, 3,137 km; passenger-mi 2,707,000,000, passenger-km 4,356,000,000; short ton-mi cargo 378,000,000, metric ton-km cargo 552,000,000. Roads (1985–86): total length 14,416 mi, 23,200 km (paved 17%). Vehicles (1980): passenger cars 43,300; trucks and buses 44,700. Merchant marine (1987): vessels (100 gross tons and over) 117; total deadweight tonnage 363,286. Air transport (1987–88): passenger-mi 133,270,000, passenger-km 214,471,000; short ton-mi cargo 1,470,000, metric ton-km cargo 2,146,000; airports (1988) with scheduled flights 21.
Communications. Daily newspapers (1987): total number 6; total circulation 533,000; circulation per 1,000 population 14. Radio (1986): total receivers 800,000 (1 per 48 persons). Television (1987): total receivers 67,500 (1 per 581 persons). Telephones (1987–88): 61,872 (1 per 624 persons).

Education and health

Education (1987–88)				
	schools	teachers	students	student/ teacher ratio
Primary (age 5–9)	31,499	188,417	5,369,641	28.5
Secondary (age 10–15)	2,429	61,556	1,591,927	25.9
Voc., teacher tr.	146	1,536	17,000	11.1
Higher	35	7,191	255,866	35.6

Educational attainment (1983). Percent of population age 25 and over having: no formal schooling 55.8%; primary education 39.4%; secondary 4.6%; religious 0.1%; postsecondary 0.1%. *Literacy* (1983): total population age 15 and over literate 16,472,494 (78.5%); males literate 8,816,031 (85.8%); females literate 7,656,463 (71.6%).
Health (1987–88): physicians 11,076 (1 per 3,485 persons); hospital beds 25,759 (1 per 1,498 persons); infant mortality rate per 1,000 live births (1987) 102.
Food (1984–86): daily per capita caloric intake 2,592 (vegetable products 95%, animal products 5%); (1983) 114% of FAO recommended minimum.

Military

Total active duty personnel (1988): 186,000 (army 91.4%, navy 3.8%, air force 4.8%). *Military expenditure as percent of GNP* (1985): 3.0% (world 6.1%); per capita expenditure U.S.$6.

---

[1]Includes 14 nonelective seats. [2]Includes 7,710 persons not distributed by area. [3]Construction Corporation activity only. [4]December. [5]Males in manufacturing only. [6]Based on 24 rural townships. [7]Import figures are f.o.b. in balance of trade and c.i.f. in commodities and trading partners.

Burundi

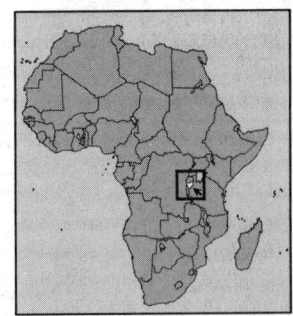

Official name: Republika y'u Burundi
(Rundi); République du Burundi
(French) (Republic of Burundi).
Form of government: military regime[1].
Head of state and government:
President.
Capital: Bujumbura.
Official languages: Rundi; French.
Official religion: none.
Monetary unit: 1 Burundi franc
(FBu) = 100 centimes; valuation (Oct.
10, 1988) 1 U.S.$ = FBu 151.85;
1 £ = FBu 260.05.

Area and population

		area		population
Provinces	Capitals	sq mi	sq km	1987 estimate[2]
Bubanza	Bubanza	422	1,093	200,420
Bujumbura	Bujumbura	515	1,334	584,812
Bururi	Bururi	971	2,515	374,660
Cankuzo	Cankuzo	749	1,940	129,275
Cibitoke	Cibitoke	633	1,639	235,279
Gitega	Gitega	768	1,989	561,950
Karuzi	Karuzi	563	1,459	258,811
Kayanza	Kayanza	475	1,229	446,219
Kirundo	Kirundo	661	1,711	359,485
Makamba	Makamba	761	1,972	155,676
Muramvya	Muramvya	591	1,530	437,846
Muyinga	Muyinga	705	1,825	315,008
Ngozi	Ngozi	567	1,468	476,408
Rutana	Rutana	733	1,898	179,302
Ruyigi	Ruyigi	913	2,365	206,933
TOTAL LAND AREA		10,026[3]	25,967	4,922,084
INLAND WATER		721	1,867	
TOTAL AREA		10,747	27,834	

Demography

Population (1988): 5,131,000.
Density[4] (1988): persons per sq mi 511.8, persons per sq km 197.6.
Urban–rural (1986): urban 7.5%; rural 92.5%.
Sex distribution (1986): male 48.60%; female 51.40%.
Age breakdown (1986): under 15, 44.3%; 15–29, 28.2%; 30–44, 14.5%; 45–59, 7.9%; 60–74, 4.0%; 75 and over, 1.1%.
Population projection: (1990) 5,425,000; (2000) 7,170,000.
Doubling time: 25 years.
Ethnic composition (1983): Rundi 97.4%, of which Hutu 81.9%, Tutsi 13.5%; Twa Pygmy 1.0%; other 1.6%.
Religious affiliation (1980): Christian 85.5%, of which Roman Catholic 78.3%, Protestant 7.1%; traditional beliefs 13.5%; Muslim 0.9%; other 0.1%.
Major cities (1986): Bujumbura 272,600; Gitega 95,300; Ngozi 20,000[5].

Vital statistics

Birth rate per 1,000 population (1986–87): 45.7 (world avg. 26.0).
Death rate per 1,000 population (1986–87): 17.4 (world avg. 9.9).
Natural increase rate per 1,000 population (1986–87): 28.4 (world avg. 16.1).
Total fertility rate (avg. births per childbearing woman; 1986–87): 6.3.
Marriage rate per 1,000 population: n.a.
Divorce rate per 1,000 population: n.a.
Life expectancy at birth (1986–87): male 46.9 years; female 50.2 years.
Major causes of death per 100,000 population (1983)[6]: measles 45.1; bacillary dysentery 26.2; other diarrheal diseases 7.9; malaria 7.4; pulmonary tuberculosis 2.6.

National economy

Budget (1986). Revenue: FBu 20,000,000,000 (1984; customs duties 31.7%, income tax 25.9%, other indirect taxes 22.6%, excise duties 14.9%, administrative receipts 4.3%, property tax 0.6%). Expenditures: FBu 20,000,000,000 (1984; goods and services 57.4%, subsidies and transfers 17.6%, loans 0.5%, other 24.5%).
Public debt (external, outstanding; 1986): U.S.$527,700,000.
Tourism: receipts from visitors (1986) U.S.$35,000,000; expenditures by nationals abroad (1986) U.S.$18,000,000.
Production (metric tons except as noted). Agriculture, forestry, fishing (1986): bananas 1,260,000, sweet potatoes 550,000, cassava 520,000, pulses 332,000, sorghum 220,000, corn (maize) 160,000, yams and taros 112,000, peanuts (groundnuts) 80,000, millet 50,000, coffee 30,000, rice 20,000, wheat 14,000, sugarcane 7,000, palm kernels 2,400, cotton lint 2,000; livestock (number of live animals) 820,000 goats, 415,000 cattle, 370,000 sheep, 4,000,000 chickens; roundwood (1986) 3,635,000 cu m; fish catch (1985) 14,900. Mining and quarrying (1986): peat 12,455; kaolin clay 5,113; lime 160; gold 980 troy oz. Manufacturing (1986): beer 132,912,000 bottles; carbonated beverages 1,870,900 cases; cigarettes 29,900 cartons; blankets 402,400 units; footwear 364,500 pairs. Construction: n.a. Energy production (consumption): electricity (kW-hr; 1986) 2,000,000 (74,000,000); coal, none (n.a.); crude petroleum, none (n.a.); petroleum products (metric tons; 1986) none (48,000); natural gas, none (n.a.); peat (metric tons; 1985) 10,000 (10,000).
Land use (1985): forested 2.5%; meadows and pastures 35.5%; agricultural and under permanent cultivation 51.6%; other 10.4%.
Gross national product (at current market prices; 1986): U.S.$1,140,000,000 (U.S.$240 per capita).

Structure of gross domestic product and labour force

	1986		1979	
	in value FBu '000,000[7]	% of total value	labour force	% of labour force
Agriculture	19,761.2	63.1	2,246,200	93.1
Mining	142.6	0.5	1,400	0.1
Manufacturing	3,200.4	10.2	36,700	1.5
Construction	1,675.0	5.3	14,700	0.6
Public utilities	...	...	1,700	0.1
Transportation and communication	774.4	2.5	6,400	0.2
Trade	2,217.0	7.1	20,900	0.9
Finance	...	...	1,300	0.1
Pub. admin., defense	3,129.0	10.0	5,700	0.2
Services	418.1	1.3	75,000	3.1
Other	...	...	3,100	0.1
TOTAL	31,317.7	100.0	2,413,100	100.0

Population economically active (1986): total 2,653,951; activity rate of total population 55.5% (participation rates: ages 15–64, 88.7%; female 52.7%; unemployed, n.a.).

Price and earnings indexes (1980 = 100)

	1981	1982	1983	1984	1985	1986	1987
Consumer price index	112.0	118.4	128.3	146.7	152.1	154.9	166.2
Monthly earnings index[8]	110.0	103.0	143.4	170.0			

Household income and expenditure. Average household size (1980) 4.9; income per household: n.a.; sources of income: n.a.; expenditure[9]: food 59.6%, clothing and footwear 11.1%, furniture and household goods 6.0%, energy and water 5.8%, housing 4.4%, other 13.1%.

Foreign trade[10]

Balance of trade (current prices)

	1982	1983	1984	1985	1986	1987
FBu '000,000	−8,864	−7,326	−5,930	−6,001	−864	−12,273
% of total	35.9%	32.7%	18.0%	18.0%	2.2%	37.0%

Imports (1986): FBu 23,195,000,000 (intermediate goods 39.2%, consumer goods 32.8%, capital goods 28.0%). *Major import sources:* Belgium–Luxembourg 20.4%; West Germany 11.8%; France 9.8%; Japan 6.7%; Italy 5.0%; The Netherlands 4.3%.
Exports (1986): FBu 19,306,200,000 (coffee 90.7%; tea 2.7%; animal hides and skins 0.8%; raw cotton 0.1%). *Major export destinations:* West Germany 54.6%; Belgium–Luxembourg 10.9%; The Netherlands 7.2%; United States 6.8%; United Kingdom 2.9%; Italy 2.4%; France 1.8%.

Transport and communications

Transport. Railroads: none. Roads (1988): total length 3,666 mi, 5,900 km (paved 7%). Vehicles (1986): passenger cars 8,977; trucks and other vehicles 7,342. Merchant marine (1979): vessels (100 gross tons and over) 1; total gross tonnage 385. Air transport (1985): passenger arrivals 20,202, departures 20,379; cargo loaded 4,007 short tons (3,643 metric tons), unloaded 5,944 short tons (5,404 metric tons); airports (1988) with scheduled flights 2.
Communications. Daily newspapers (1988): total number 1; total circulation 20,000; circulation per 1,000 population 3.9. Radio (1986): total number of receivers 230,000 (1 per 21 persons). Television (1987): total number of receivers 4,500 (1 per 1,110 persons). Telephones (1986): 7,910 (1 per 622 persons).

Education and health

Education (1985–86)

	schools	teachers	students	student/ teacher ratio
Primary (age 6–11)	1,023	7,245	387,710	53.5
Secondary (age 12–18)	62	795	13,037	16.4
Voc., teacher tr.	47	1,064	12,902	12.1
Higher	8	468	2,783	5.9

Educational attainment, n.a. *Literacy* (1982): total population age 10 and over literate 991,600 (33.8%); males literate 601,500 (42.8%); females literate 390,100 (25.7%).
Health (1985): physicians 178 (1 per 20,942 persons); hospital beds 5,506 (1 per 792 persons); infant mortality rate per 1,000 live births (1986–87) 114.
Food (1984–86): daily per capita caloric intake 2,270 (vegetable products 98%, animal products 2%); (1983) 102% of FAO recommended minimum requirement.

Military

Total active duty personnel (1987): 5,700 (army 96.5%, navy 0.9%, air force 2.6%). *Military expenditure as percent of GNP* (1985): 3.2% (world 6.1%); per capita expenditure U.S.$7.

[1]Constitution suspended on Sept. 3, 1987. [2]January 1. [3]Detail does not add to total given because of rounding. [4]Based on land area. [5]1982. [6]Data shown is for four provinces only. [7]At prices of 1970. [8]Nonagricultural activities in Bujumbura only; includes family allowances. [9]Weights of consumer price index components. [10]Import figures are f.o.b. in balance of trade and c.i.f. in commodities and trading partners.

Cameroon

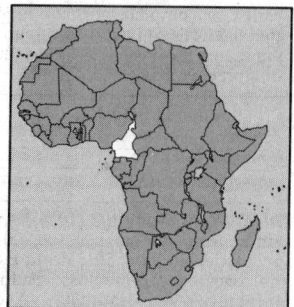

Official name: République du Cameroun (French); Republic of Cameroon (English).
Form of government: republic with one legislative house (National Assembly [180]).
Head of state and government: President.
Capital: Yaoundé.
Official languages: French; English.
Official religion: none.
Monetary unit: 1 CFA franc (CFAF) = 100 centimes; valuation (Oct. 10, 1988) 1 U.S.$ = CFAF 316.13; 1 £ = CFAF 541.38.

Area and population

Provinces	Capitals	area sq mi	area sq km	population 1984 estimate
Adamoua	Ngaoundéré	23,979	62,105	355,800
Centre	Yaoundé	26,655	69,035	1,764,400
Est	Bertoua	42,086	109,002	420,000
Extrême-Nord	Maroua	12,477	32,316	1,400,000
Littoral	Douala	7,810	20,229	1,829,900
Nord	Garoua	26,134	67,686	508,200
Nord-Ouest	Bamenda	6,722	17,409	1,009,100
Ouest	Bafoussam	5,360	13,883	1,197,700
Sud	Ebolowa	18,200	47,137	356,400
Sud-Ouest	Buea	9,540	24,709	700,900
LAND AREA		178,963	463,511	9,542,400
INLAND WATER		751	1,947	
TOTAL AREA		179,714	465,458	

Demography

Population (1988): 11,206,000.
Density (1988)[1]: persons per sq mi 62.6, persons per sq km 24.2.
Urban–rural (1985): urban 43.8%; rural 56.2%.
Sex distribution (1985): male 49.26%; female 50.74%.
Age breakdown (1984): under 15, 44.6%; 15–29, 25.2%; 30–44, 15.6%; 45–59, 9.0%; 60 and over, 5.6%.
Population projection: (1990) 11,935,000; (2000) 16,360,000.
Doubling time: 26 years.
Ethnic composition (1983): Fang 19.6%; Bamileke and Bamum 18.5%; Duala, Luanda, and Basa 14.7%; Fulani 9.6%; Tikar 7.4%; Mandara 5.7%; Maka 4.9%; Chamba 2.4%; Mbum 1.3%; Hausa 1.2%; French 0.2%; other 14.5%.
Religious affiliation (1980): Roman Catholic 35%; Protestant 18%; animist 25%; Muslim 22%.
Major cities (1985): Douala 852,700; Yaoundé 583,500; Nkongsamba 105,200; Maroua 100,200; Garoua 96,200.

Vital statistics

Birth rate per 1,000 population (1985–86): 42.8 (world avg. 26.0).
Death rate per 1,000 population 15.5 (world avg. 9.9).
Natural increase rate per 1,000 population (1980–85): 27.3 (world avg. 16.1).
Total fertility rate (avg. births per childbearing woman; 1987): 5.9.
Life expectancy at birth (1987): male 49.0 years; female 52.0 years.
Major causes of death per 100,000 population: n.a.; however, major health problems include measles, malaria, tuberculosis of respiratory system, anemias, meningitis, intestinal obstruction and hernia, avitaminoses and other nutritional deficiency diseases.

National economy

Budget (1987–88). Revenue: CFAF 650,000,000,000 (1986–87; indirect taxes 36.0%; customs duties and taxes 30.6%; petroleum royalties 18.8%; receipts for services 7.3%; registration and stamp duties 4.6%). Expenditures: CFAF 650,000,000,000 (1986–87; current expenditure 57.5%, of which education 8.8%, defense 6.5%, health 3.5%, administration 2.1%, agriculture 2.0%).
Gross national product (1986): U.S.$9,580,000,000 (U.S.$910 per capita).

Structure of gross domestic product and labour force

	1984–85 in value CFAF '000,000,000	1984–85 % of total value	1982 labour force	1982 % of labour force
Agriculture	790.4	20.6	2,594,800	73.2
Mining	629.7	16.4	1,580	0.1
Manufacturing	422.4	11.0	159,560	4.5
Construction	227.6	5.9	62,860	1.8
Public utilities	37.7	1.0	3,230	0.1
Transp. and commun.	230.7	6.0	47,400	1.3
Trade	564.6	14.7	141,300	4.0
Finance	455.3	11.9	7,900	0.2
Public admin., defense,	248.8	6.5	271,100	7.7
Services	89.6	2.3		
Other	142.1[2]	3.7[2]	253,270[3]	7.1[3]
TOTAL	3,838.9	100.0	3,543,000	100.0

Household income and expenditure. Average household size (1980) 5.2; average annual income per household[4] (1983): U.S.$420; sources of income: n.a.; expenditure[4] (1983): food 33.6%, clothing and footwear 16.3%, housing 14.6%, transportation and communications 10.5%, recreation 5.1%, health 5.0%.
Tourism (1986): receipts from visitors U.S.$47,000,000; expenditures by nationals abroad U.S.$130,000,000.

Population economically active (1985): total 3,958,000; activity rate of total population 40.1% (participation rates: ages 15–64, 59.5%; female 20.5%; unemployed, n.a.).

Price and earnings indexes (1980 = 100)

	1980	1981	1982	1983	1984	1985	1986
Consumer price index	100.0	110.7	125.4	146.3	162.9	165.0	170.2
Earnings index	...	...	...	...	...	...	...

Public debt (external, outstanding; 1986): U.S.$2,267,300,000.
Production (metric tons except as noted). Agriculture, forestry, fishing (1986): sugarcane 1,250,000, plantains 986,000, cassava 690,000, millet 430,000, vegetables and melons 429,000, yams 400,000, corn (maize) 350,000, potatoes 200,000, peanuts (groundnuts) 150,000, sweet potatoes 150,000, cocoa 120,000, dry beans 113,000, rice 113,000, palm oil 85,000, bananas 67,000, palm kernels 52,300; livestock (number of live animals) 4,361,000 cattle, 2,600,000 goats, 2,500,000 sheep, 1,180,000 pigs; roundwood 12,166,000 cu m; fish catch 83,980. Mining and quarrying (1986): marble 331,000; pozzolana 168,435; aluminum 83,810; limestone 78,260; tin ore and concentrate 13.0. Manufacturing (1985): cement 785,000; aluminum 81,800; palm oil 73,000; sugar 70,000; rubber 16,233[5]; fish products 8,331[5]; cigarettes 2,795[5]; footwear 3,964,000 pairs; sawnwood 565,000 cu m; beer 4,904,000 hectolitres. Construction (1983): residential 230,400 sq m; nonresidential 51,100 sq m. Energy production (consumption): electricity (kW-hr; 1986) 2,385,000,000 (2,385,000,000); coal (metric tons; 1985) 1,000 (1,000); petroleum (barrels; 1986) 64,672,000 (15,923,000); petroleum products (metric tons; 1986) 1,956,000 (1,877,000); natural gas, none (n.a.).
Land use (1986): forested 52.8%; meadows and pastures 17.5%; agricultural and under permanent cultivation 14.6%; other 15.1%.

Foreign trade[6]

Balance of trade (current prices)

	1981	1982	1983	1984	1985	1986
CFAF '000,000,000	−89.3	−65.7	−94.8	−44.2	−140.8	−265.1
% of total	13.0%	9.2%	11.3%	4.8%	17.9%	32.8%

Imports (1986): CFAF 590,439,000,000 (machinery and transport equipment 32.8%, of which road transport equipment and parts 13.5%; iron and steel 6.0%; chemical and pharmaceutical products 4.1%; textile yarn 3.5%; malt 2.5%; cement 0.9%). *Major import sources:* France 42.2%; West Germany 9.1%; Japan 7.6%; United States 4.9%; Italy 4.7%; United Kingdom 3.7%; Belgium–Luxembourg 3.4%; The Netherlands 2.7%.
Exports (1986): CFAF 541,728,000,000 (crude petroleum 35.6%; coffee 21.5%; cacao 16.1%; aluminum and aluminum products 4.1%; sawnwood and logs 3.4%; cotton yarn and fabrics 3.0%; cocoa pulp and butter 2.6%; rubber 1.1%; bananas 1.0%). *Major export destinations:* The Netherlands 27.5%; France 20.6%; United States 16.4%; West Germany 7.3%; Italy 5.7%; Nigeria 2.6%; Belgium–Luxembourg 2.2%; Japan 0.9%; United Kingdom 0.8%.

Transport and communications

Transport. Railroads (1986): route length 729 mi, 1,173 km; passenger-mi 268,000,000, passenger-km 432,000,000; short ton-mi cargo 518,000,000, metric ton-km cargo 756,000,000. Roads (1986): total length 32,408 mi, 52,157 km (paved 5%). Vehicles (1985): passenger cars 72,449; trucks and buses 41,301. Merchant marine (1985): vessels (100 gross tons and over) 47; total deadweight tonnage 71,802. Air transport (1985): passenger-mi 360,000,000, passenger-km 580,000,000; short ton-mi cargo 76,000,000, metric ton-km cargo 111,000,000; airports (1988) with scheduled flights 9.
Communications. Daily newspapers (1986): 1; total circulation 66,000; circulation per 1,000 population 6.3. Radio (1986): total number of receivers 800,000 (1 per 12 persons). Television (1987): total number of receivers 5,000 (1 per 2,172 persons). Telephones (1984): 49,180 (1 per 210 persons).

Education and health

Education (1986–87)

	schools	teachers	students	student/ teacher ratio
Primary (age 6–14)	5,920	35,431	1,723,024	48.6
Secondary (age 15–24)	388	9,289	288,515	31.1
Voc., teacher tr.	220	4,449	93,857	21.1
Higher	5	975	19,586	20.1

Educational attainment (1976). Percent of population age 15 and over having: no schooling 51.1%; primary education 41.7%; some postprimary 0.2%; secondary 5.7%; some postsecondary 0.3%; higher 0.2%; other 0.8%.
Literacy (1980): total population age 15 and over literate 2,344,100 (55.2%); males literate 1,453,200 (70.2%); females literate 890,900 (41.0%).
Health: physicians (1982) 604 (1 per 14,800 persons); hospital beds (1984–85) 26,832 (1 per 377 persons); infant mortality rate per 1,000 births (1985–86) 94.0.
Food (1984–86): daily per capita caloric intake 2,040 (vegetable products 95%, animal products 5%); (1983) 88% of FAO recommended minimum.

Military

Total active duty personnel (1988): 7,600 (army 86.8%, navy 9.2%, air force 4.0%). *Military expenditure as percent of GNP* (1985): 2.0% (world 6.1%); per capita expenditure U.S.$15.

---

[1]Based on land area. [2]Includes import duties less imputed bank service charges. [3]Includes 161,270 unemployed not previously employed. [4]Capital city only. [5]1983–84. [6]Import figures are f.o.b. in balance of trade and c.i.f. for commodities and trading partners.

Canada

Official name: Canada.
Form of government: federal multiparty parliamentary state with two legislative houses (Senate [104]; House of Commons [295]).
Chief of state: British Monarch represented by governor-general.
Head of government: Prime Minister.
Capital: Ottawa.
Official languages: English; French.
Official religion: none.
Monetary unit: 1 Canadian dollar (Can$) = 100 cents; valuation (Oct. 10, 1988) 1 U.S.$ = Can$1.21; 1 £ = Can$2.07.

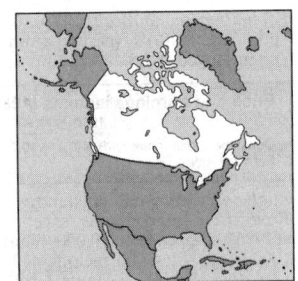

Area and population		area		population
		sq mi	sq km	1988 estimate[1]
Provinces	**Capitals**			
Alberta	Edmonton	248,800	644,390	2,393,300
British Columbia	Victoria	358,971	929,730	2,973,000
Manitoba	Winnipeg	211,723	548,360	1,083,600
New Brunswick	Fredericton	27,834	72,090	713,500
Newfoundland	Saint John's	143,510	371,690	567,600
Nova Scotia	Halifax	20,402	52,840	882,600
Ontario	Toronto	344,090	891,190	9,399,300
Prince Edward Island	Charlottetown	2,185	5,660	128,500
Quebec	Quebec	523,859	1,356,790	6,628,100
Saskatchewan	Regina	220,348	570,700	1,011,000
Territories				
Northwest Territories	Yellowknife	1,271,442	3,293,020	51,800
Yukon Territory	Whitehorse	184,931	478,970	25,100
TOTAL LAND AREA		3,558,096	9,215,430	25,857,400
INLAND WATER		291,579	755,180	
TOTAL AREA		3,849,675	9,970,610	

Demography

Population (1988): 25,880,000.
Density[2] (1988): persons per sq mi 7.3, persons per sq km 2.8.
Urban–rural (1985): urban 75.9%; rural 24.1%.
Sex distribution[3] (1986): male 49.14%; female 50.86%.
Age breakdown[3] (1986): under 15, 21.4%; 15–29, 25.8%; 30–44, 22.9%; 45–59, 14.9%; 60–74, 10.9%; 75 and over, 4.1%.
Population projection: (1990) 26,343,000; (2000) 28,785,000.
Doubling time: 77 years.
Ethnic origin (1981): British 40.2%; French 26.7%; German 4.1%; Italian 3.1%; Ukrainian 2.2%; Dutch 1.7%; other European 8.5%; Asiatic 2.1%; Amerindian and Inuktitut (Eskimo) 1.7%; multiple origin and other 9.7%.
Religious affiliation (1981): Roman Catholic 46.5%; Protestant 41.2%; Eastern Orthodox 1.5%; Jewish 1.2%; Muslim 0.4%; Hindu 0.3%; Sikh 0.3%; nonreligious 7.4%; other 1.2%.
Major metropolitan areas (1986): Toronto 3,427,168; Montreal 2,921,357; Vancouver 1,380,729; Ottawa–Hull 819,263; Edmonton 785,465; Calgary 671,326; Winnipeg 625,304; Quebec 603,267; Hamilton 557,029; Saint Catharines–Niagara 343,258.

Other metropolitan areas (1986)					
	population		population		population
Chicoutimi-Jonquière	158,458	London	342,302	Sherbrooke	129,960
Halifax	295,990	Oshawa	203,543	Sudbury	148,877
Kingston	122,350	Regina	186,521	Trois Rivières	128,888
Kitchener	311,195	Saint John's	161,901	Victoria	255,547
		Saskatoon	200,665	Windsor	253,988

Place of birth (1986): 84.2% native-born; 15.8% foreign-born, of which United Kingdom 3.2%, other European 6.6%, Asian countries 3.2%, other 2.8%.
Mobility (1986). Population living in the same residence as in 1981: 56.3%; different residence, same municipality 24.2%; same province, different municipality 13.5%; different province 4.0%.
Households (1986). Total number of households 8,991,670. Average household size 2.8; (1985) 1 person 20.5%, 2 persons 30.8%, 3 persons 18.0%, 4 persons 18.8%, 5 persons 8.1%, 6 or more persons 3.8%. Family households: 6,635,000 (73.8%), nonfamily 2,356,670 (26.2%, of which 1 person 21.5%).
Immigration (1987): permanent immigrants admitted 149,384, from Asia 43.5%, Europe 24.8%, Central and South America 18.9%, Africa 5.4%, United States 5.2%, other 2.2%; refugee arrivals (1986) 18,282.

Vital statistics

Birth rate per 1,000 population (1986): 14.8 (world avg. 26.0); (1985) legitimate 83.8%; illegitimate 16.2%[4].
Death rate per 1,000 population (1986): 7.3 (world avg. 9.9).
Natural increase rate per 1,000 population (1986): 7.5 (world avg. 16.1).
Total fertility rate (avg. births per childbearing woman; 1985): 1.7.
Marriage rate per 1,000 population (1986): 7.4.
Divorce rate per 1,000 population (1985): 2.4.
Life expectancy at birth (1983–85): male 72.9 years; female 79.8 years.
Major causes of death per 100,000 population (1985): diseases of the circulatory system 309.6; malignant neoplasms (cancers) 182.7; diseases of the respiratory system 55.4; accidents and violence 52.9.

Social indicators

Educational attainment (1986). Percent of population age 25 and over having: no formal schooling, negligible; less than complete primary education or complete primary 20.6%; secondary 35.0%; postsecondary vocational 25.1%; university without degree 8.3%; completed university 11.0%; graduates by level (1987): 4-year higher degree 101,960, master's 15,790, doctorate 2,385.

Distribution of income (1985)				
percent of national income by quintile				
1	2	3	4	5 (highest)
4.7%	10.4%	17.0%	25.0%	43.0%

Quality of working life (1986). Average workweek: 38.8 hours (3.1% overtime). Annual rate per 100,000 workers for (1985): injury, accident, or industrial illness 4,501; death 6.8. Proportion of labour force insured for damages or income loss resulting from (1984): injury 99%; permanent disability 99%; death 99%. Average days lost to labour stoppages per 1,000 employee-workdays (1986): 1.2. Average duration of journey to work (1983): 23 minutes[5] (17.3% public transportation, 72.8% automobile, 9.9% other). Rate per 1,000 workers of discouraged (unemployed no longer seeking work; 1983): 10.5.
Access to services (1985). Proportion of households having access to: electricity 100.0%; public water supply 99.7%; public sewage collection 99.3%; public fire protection (1978) 90.4%.
Social participation. Eligible voters participating in last national election (1988): *c.* 77%. Population over 18 years of age participating in voluntary work (1980): 15.0%. Trade union membership in total work force (1986): 29.7%. Practicing religious population in total affiliated population: 92.7%.
Social deviance (1985). Offense rate per 100,000 population for: violent crime 749; property crime 5,555, of which auto theft 324, burglary and housebreaking 1,407. Incidence per 100,000 in general population of: alcoholism (1981) 2,405; drug and substance abuse 322.4; suicide (1985) 13.6.
Leisure (1985). Favourite leisure activities (hours weekly): television 23.5; social time 10.7[6]; reading 3.5[6]; recreation and culture 2.7[6].
Material well-being (1986). Households possessing: automobile 81.9%; telephone 98.1%; radio 99.1%; television receiver 98.6%; refrigerator 99.2%; central air conditioner 17.8%; automatic washing machine 77.4%; cable television 62.4%[7]; videocassette recorders 35.1%.

National economy

Gross national product (1986): U.S.$361,720,000,000 (U.S.$14,100 per capita).

Structure of gross domestic product and labour force				
	1987		1986	
	in value Can$'000,000	% of total value	labour force	% of labour force
Agriculture	15,301	4.0	590,000	4.6
Mining	21,883	5.8	185,000	1.4
Manufacturing	74,575	19.6	2,015,000	15.7
Construction	27,050	7.1	627,000	4.9
Public utilities	11,828	3.1	121,000	0.9
Transportation and communications	30,557	8.0	777,000	6.0
Trade	45,794	12.0	2,082,000	16.2
Finance	54,352	14.3	654,000	5.1
Pub. admin., defense	23,659	6.2	800,000	6.2
Services	75,474	19.8	3,783,000	29.4
Other	—	—	1,236,000[8]	9.6[8]
TOTAL	380,473[9]	100.0[10]	12,870,000	100.0

Budget (1987–88). Revenue: Can$93,220,000,000 (personal income tax 46.4%; sales tax 12.8%; corporation income tax 10.5%; excise taxes and import duties 8.6%). Expenditures: Can$122,550,000,000 (education, health, and welfare 46.7%; public debt interest 23.0%; economic development 9.8%; defense 8.3%).
National debt (1988): Can$245,608,000,000[11].
Tourism (1986): receipts from visitors U.S.$3,860,000,000; expenditures by nationals abroad U.S.$4,294,000,000.

Manufacturing, mining, and construction enterprises (1986)			
	no. of enterprises[7]	no. of employees	hourly wages as a % of avg. of all wages	annual shipments (Can$'000,000)
Manufacturing			
Transport equipment	1,471	187,088	119.4	43,150.4
Food and beverages	3,532	220,168	90.3	38,118.3
Paper and related products	688	121,426	125.3	19,145.9
Chemicals and related products	1,256	92,048	114.8	18,166.8
Primary metals	435	99,667	127.1	16,596.0
Metal fabricating	5,537	149,490	96.5	14,428.4
Electrical and electronics products	1,471	112,564	105.0	12,765.4
Wood	3,476	95,822	93.8	11,853.4
Printing, publishing, and related products	5,443	179,480	105.4	9,483.1
Machinery	1,815	81,749	101.3	7,598.8
Rubber and plastic	1,239	66,761	91.8	7,348.1
Clothing	2,497	88,840	56.5	6,153.4
Nonmetallic mineral products	1,532	38,763[7]	...	5,879.1[7]
Furniture and fixtures	1,727	57,960	73.5	3,472.6
Textile	1,017	62,330	82.3	2,983.4
Tobacco products industries	25	8,711	90.5	1,645.1
Leather industries	384	20,632	58.4	1,374.0
Mining	121	145,994	149.3	20,545.0
Construction	...	395,676	112.3	21,428.0

Production (farm cash receipts in Can$'000 except as noted). Agriculture, forestry, fishing (1986): wheat 2,452,100, barley 741,300, rapeseed 681,-500, vegetables 566,300, tobacco 447,900, corn (maize) 444,200, floriculture 401,300, potatoes 285,400, fruits 266,900, soybeans 240,300; livestock (number of live animals) 11,465,000 cattle, 10,708,000 pigs, 722,000 sheep, 96,300,000 poultry; roundwood (1985) 171,305,000 cu m; pelts 4,143,414 units; fish catch 1,399,027 metric tons. Mining and quarrying (metric tons;

1987): iron ore 37,553,000; zinc 1,329,408; copper 767,000; lead 390,503; nickel 187,505; uranium 13,202; molybdenum 11,581; silver 1,250; gold 118. Manufacturing (metric tons; 1987): wood pulp 24,935,000; crude steel 14,737,000; cement 11,880,000; newsprint 9,673,000; pig iron 9,672,000; sulfuric acid 3,898,000[12]; caustic soda 1,769,000[12]; synthetic rubber 179,-800; road motor vehicles 1,635,014 units, of which passenger cars 809,887 units, truck and buses 825,127 units; washing machines and dryers 830,-520 units[12]; refrigerators 568,960 units[12]; footwear 38,774,000 pairs; beer 235,470,000 hectolitres[12]. Construction (building permits; 1987): residential Can$18,647,000,000; nonresidential Can$11,899,000,000.

Service enterprises (1987)

	no. of enter-prises	no. of employees[13]	weekly wages as a % of all wages	annual sales (Can$'000,000)
Retail trade				
Food stores	...	213,400	...	37,272
Motor vehicle dealers	...	79,800	...	32,248
Service stations	...	63,700	...	13,976
Department stores	...	14	...	12,906
Clothing stores	...	50,200	...	7,083
Pharmacies	...	52,400	...	6,691
Furniture and appliance stores	...	62,100	...	4,198
Automotive stores	...	31,500	...	3,440
General merchandise	...	231,700[14]	...	3,064
Sporting goods	...	...	...	2,342
General stores	...	14	...	2,263
Shoe stores	...	18,400	...	1,496
Variety stores	...	45,100	...	1,074
Hardware stores	...	17,300	...	1,610
Jewelry stores	...	14,000	...	1,137

Energy production (consumption): electricity (kW-hr; 1986) 468,571,000,000 (434,594,000,000); coal (metric tons; 1986) 57,047,000,000 (44,854,000,000); crude petroleum (barrels; 1986) 537,137,000 (455,676,000); petroleum products (metric tons; 1986) 74,794,000 (67,157,000); natural gas (cu m; 1986) 78,601,400,000 (56,670,000,000).

Population economically active (1986): total 12,870,000; activity rate of total population 50.9% (participation rates: ages 15–64, 74.3%; female 42.9%; unemployed 9.6%).

Price and earnings indexes (1981 = 100)

	1982	1983	1984	1985	1986	1987	1988
Consumer price index	110.8	117.2	122.3	127.2	132.4	138.2	142.1[15]
Monthly earnings index	111.8	118.1	123.3	127.6	131.4	139.1	...

Household income and expenditure. Average household size (1986) 2.8; average annual income per family (1985) Can$38,100 (U.S.$27,400); sources of income (1984): wages and salaries 65.4%, transfer payments 15.3%, self-employment 6.9%, other 12.4%; expenditure (1984): housing 24.0%, food 19.8%, transportation and communications 16.0%, clothing 8.6%, recreation 7.2%, energy 5.7%, household durable goods 4.7%, health 2.6%, education 1.1%.

Financial aggregates

	1982	1983	1984	1985	1986	1987	1988 9 mos.
Exchange rate, Can$ per:							
U.S. dollar	1.23	1.23	1.29	1.37	1.39	1.33	1.22
£	2.15	1.88	1.50	1.78	2.04	2.18	2.07
SDR	1.36	1.30	1.30	1.54	1.69	1.84	1.57
International reserves (U.S.$)							
Total (excl. gold; '000,000)	3,000	3,465	2,491	2,503	3,251	7,277	13,915
SDRs ('000,000)	71	21	72	218	247	399	820
Reserve pos. in IMF ('000,000)	365	703	678	711	686	661	492
Foreign exchange ('000,000)	2,564	2,741	1,741	1,574	2,318	6,218	12,603
Gold ('000,000 fine troy oz)	20.26	20.17	20.14	20.11	19.72	18.52	18.05
% world reserves	2.14	2.13	2.13	2.13	2.12	2.12	2.12[16]
Interest and prices							
Central bank discount (%)	10.26	10.04	10.16	9.49	8.49	8.66	9.53[16]
Gov't. bond yield (%)	14.26	11.79	12.75	11.04	9.52	9.95	10.42
Industrial share prices (1980 = 100)	76.8	111.4	110.2	130.5	143.9	168.0	151.9[16]
Balance of payments (U.S.$'000,000)							
Balance of visible trade,	14,955	14,959	16,558	13,287	8,078	8,755	1,030[17]
of which:							
Imports, f.o.b.	55,491	60,672	72,328	79,917	81,079	88,854	25,912[17]
Exports, f.o.b.	70,446	75,631	88,986	90,204	89,157	97,609	26,942[17]
Balance of invisibles	−13,813	−13,429	−14,768	−14,033	−15,800	−17,555	−5,301[17]
Balance of payments, current account	2,231	2,487	2,569	−877	−6,657	−7,235	−3,776[17]

Land use (1985): forested 35.4%; meadows and pastures 2.6%; agricultural and under permanent cultivation 5.0%; built-on, wasteland, and other 57.0%.

Foreign trade

Balance of trade (current prices)

	1981	1982	1983	1984	1985	1986	1987
Can$'000,000,000	4.5	15.8	19.4	16.6	14.3	7.8	10.1
% of total	2.8%	9.9%	11.8%	8.0%	6.4%	3.3%	4.1%

Imports (1986): Can$112,678,000,000 (machinery and transport equipment 49.3%, of which road motor vehicles and parts 29.6%, electrical equipment 10.4%, nonelectrical machinery 9.3%; food, feed, beverages, and tobacco 5.7%; chemicals 5.2%; mineral fuels 4.5%, of which crude petroleum 2.8%; nonferrous metals 2.3%; iron and steel 1.7%). Major import sources: United States 68.6%; Japan 6.8%; United Kingdom 3.3%; West Germany 3.1%; South Korea 1.6%; Taiwan 1.5%; France 1.4%; Hong Kong 0.9%.

Exports (1986): Can$120,494,900,000[18] (transportation and communications equipment 33.7%, of which road motor vehicles and parts 28.4%; crude materials 12.7%, of which crude petroleum 3.1%, natural gas 2.1%; food 7.9%, of which wheat 2.4%; newsprint 4.7%; lumber 4.1%; wood pulp 3.4%; machinery 3.2%; chemicals 2.2%; iron and steel 2.1%; aluminum 1.9%). Major export destinations: United States 77.3%; Japan 4.9%; United Kingdom 2.3%; West Germany 1.1%; U.S.S.R. 1.0%; China 0.9%; The Netherlands 0.8%; South Korea 0.8%; Belgium–Luxembourg 0.7%; France 0.7%; Brazil 0.7%.

Trade by commodities (1986)

		imports		exports	
SITC Group		Can$'000,000	%	Can$'000,000	%
00	Food and live animals	5,841.8	5.2	9,188.6	7.9
01	Beverages and tobacco	517.7	0.5	322.0	0.3
02	Crude materials, excluding fuels	2,011.6	1.8	8,353.2	7.2
03	Mineral fuels, lubricants, and related materials	5,125.4	4.5	6,256.9	5.4
04	Animal and vegetable oils, fat, and waxes	708.0	0.6	718.1	0.6
05	Chemicals and related products, n.e.s.	5,840.0	5.2	5,078.4	4.3
06	Basic manufactures	41,015.0	36.4	33,287.9	28.5
07	Machinery and transport equipment	42,977.6	38.1	44,459.0	38.1
08	Miscellaneous manufactured articles	7,436.7	6.6	4,271.3	3.7
09	Goods not classified by kind	1,204.2	1.1	4,626.3	4.0
TOTAL		112,678.0	100.0	116,561.7[19]	100.0

Direction of trade (1986)

	imports		exports	
	Can$'000,000	%	Can$'000,000	%
Africa	1,009.9	0.9	886.7	0.7
Asia	14,463.8	12.8	10,162.8	8.4
Americas	81,316.4	72.2	96,555.8	80.1
United States	77,337.0	68.6	93,182.3	77.3
South America	1,894.7	1.7	1,782.0	1.5
Central America	2,084.7	1.9	1,558.9	1.3
Europe	15,201.8	13.5	12,056.3	10.0
EEC	12,811.7	11.4	8,161.0	6.8
U.S.S.R. and Eastern Europe	360.7	0.3	2,823.2	2.3
Other Europe	2,029.4	1.8	1,072.1	0.9
Oceania	686.1	0.6	833.3	0.7
TOTAL	112,678.0	100.0	120,494.9	100.0[10]

Transport and communications

Transport. Railroads (1986): length 74,564 mi, 120,000 km; passenger-mi 1,297,000,000, passenger-km 2,088,000,000; short ton-mi cargo 161,856,-000,000, metric ton-km cargo 236,320,000,000. Roads (1984): total length 549,445 mi, 884,249 km (paved 81%). Vehicles (1986): passenger cars 11,118,071; trucks and buses 3,095,243. Merchant marine (1987): vessels (100 gross tons and over) 1,238; total deadweight tonnage 3,502,916. Air transport (1987): passenger-mi 29,963,000,000, passenger-km 48,222,000,-000; short ton-mi cargo 859,545,000, metric ton-km cargo 1,254,993,000; airports (1988) with scheduled flights 61.
Communications. Daily newspapers (1986): total number 110; total circulation 5,700,000; circulation per 1,000 population 225. Radio (1985): total number of receivers 28,800,000 (1 per 0.9 person). Television (1987): total number of receivers 15,709,000 (1 per 1.6 persons). Telephones (1987): 19,598,000 (1 per 1.3 persons).

Education and health

Education (1987–88)

	schools	teachers	students	student/teacher ratio
Primary (age 6–14)	15,512	273,190	3,017,900	18.1
Secondary (age 14–18)			1,501,900	
Postsecondary and higher	266	59,300	795,730	13.4

Literacy (1975): total population age 14 and over literate 16,185,000 (95.6%); males literate 8,003,000 (95.6%); females literate 8,182,000 (95.7%).
Health (1985): physicians 51,966 (1 per 491 persons); hospital beds 170,721[20] (1 per 147 persons); infant mortality rate per 1,000 live births (1985) 7.9.
Food (1984–86): daily per capita caloric intake 3,425 (vegetable products 66%, animal products 34%); (1983) 130% of FAO recommended minimum requirement.

Military

Total active duty personnel (1988): 84,600 (army 26.6%, navy 11.8%, air force 27.2%, not identified by service 34.4%). Military expenditure as percent of GNP (1985): 2.3% (world 6.1%); per capita expenditure U.S.$314.

[1]April. [2]Based on land area. [3]Excludes 45,000 population in Indian reserves and settlements. [4]Births to single mothers. [5]Urban areas. [6]1981. [7]1985. [8]Unemployed. [9]At factor cost in 1981 prices; GDP at current market prices is Can$493,012,000,000. [10]Detail does not add to total given because of rounding. [11]February. [12]1986. [13]1984. [14]Department and general stores included with general merchandise. [15]March. [16]July. [17]First quarter. [18]Includes reexports of Can$3,933,200,000. [19]Excludes reexports. [20]Excludes federal and private hospitals.

Cape Verde

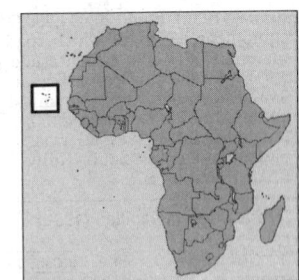

Official name: República de Cabo
Verde (Republic of Cape Verde).
Form of government: unitary
single-party republic with one
legislative house (People's National
Assembly [83]).
Chief of state: President.
Head of government: Prime Minister.
Capital: Praia.
Official language: Portuguese.
Official religion: none.
Monetary unit: 1 escudo (C.V.
Esc) = 100 centavos; valuation (Oct.
10, 1988) 1 U.S.$ = C.V. Esc 76.86;
1 £ = C.V. Esc 131.61.

Area and population

Islands Counties	Capitals	area sq mi	area sq km	population 1980 census
Boa Vista		239	620	3,372
Boa Vista	Sal Rei			
Brava		26	67	6,985
Brava	Nova Sintra			
Fogo		184	476	30,978
Fogo	São Filipe			
Maio		104	269	4,098
Maio	Porto Inglês			
Sal		83	216	5,826
Sal	Santa Maria			
Santiago		383	991	145,957
Praia	Praia			57,748
Santa Catarina	Assomada			41,012
Santa Cruz	Pedra Badejo			22,995
Tarrafal	Tarrafal			24,202
Santo Antão		301	779	43,321
Paúl	Pombas			7,983
Porto Novo	Porto Novo			13,236
Ribeira Grande	Ponta Sol			22,102
São Nicolau		150	388	13,572
São Nicolau	Ribeira Brava			
São Vicente		88	227	41,594
São Vicente	Mindelo			
TOTAL		1,557[1]	4,033	295,703

Demography

Population (1988): 359,000.
Density (1988): persons per sq mi 230.6, persons per sq km 89.0.
Urban–rural (1980): urban 35.1%; rural 64.9%.
Sex distribution (1985): male 46.32%; female 53.68%.
Age breakdown (1985): under 15, 45.6%; 15–29, 31.8%; 30–44, 7.9%; 45–59, 8.0%; 60–74, 4.6%; 75 and over, 2.1%.
Population projection: (1990) 376,600; (2000) 478,800.
Doubling time: 29 years.
Ethnic composition (1986): mixed 71%; black 28%; white 1%.
Religious affiliation (1985): Roman Catholic 97.8%; Protestant and other 2.2%.
Major cities (1980): Praia 49,500[2]; Mindelo 36,746; São Filipe 4,370.

Vital statistics

Birth rate per 1,000 population (1987): 32.1 (world avg. 26.0); (1975) legitimate 55.2%; illegitimate 44.8%.
Death rate per 1,000 population (1987): 7.7 (world avg. 9.9).
Natural increase rate per 1,000 population (1987): 24.4 (world avg. 16.1).
Total fertility rate (avg. births per childbearing woman; 1980–85): 2.6.
Marriage rate per 1,000 population (1975): 5.4.
Divorce rate per 1,000 population: n.a.
Life expectancy at birth (1980–85): male 60.3 years; female 64.0 years.
Major causes of death per 100,000 population (1980): enteritis and other diarrheal diseases 85.5; heart disease 51.9; cerebrovascular disease 45.7; malignant neoplasms (cancers) 43.8; measles and other infectious and parasitic diseases 34.6; pneumonia 27.2; bronchitis, emphysema, and asthma 20.4; avitaminoses and other nutritional deficiencies 14.5.

National economy

Budget. Revenue (1987): C.V. Esc 3,428,939,000 (indirect taxes 38.2%, of which import duties 15.4%; direct taxes 21.2%, of which taxes from industry 7.2%; receipts from petroleum 3.1%). Expenditures (1984): C.V. Esc 2,134,500,000 (no breakdown available).
Public debt (external, outstanding; 1986): U.S.$107,400,000.
Tourism: n.a.
Production (metric tons except as noted). Agriculture, forestry, fishing (1986): corn (maize) 12,000; coconuts 10,000, sugarcane 10,000, fruit except melons 10,000, sweet potatoes 7,000, pulses 6,000, vegetables 6,000, bananas 4,000, cassava 4,000, potatoes 3,000, dates 2,000; livestock (number of live animals) 66,000 goats, 54,000 pigs, 13,000 cattle, 8,000 asses and mules, 1,000 horses, 1,000 sheep; roundwood, n.a.; fish catch 10,180, of which tuna 4,043 (39.7%), other marine fishes 6,137 (60.3%). Mining and quarrying (1986): salt C.V. Esc 9,710,000. Manufacturing (C.V. Esc; 1987): cigars 232,253,000; flour 176,677,000; cacao powder 94,439,000[3]; canned fish 78,401,000; bread 35,530,000[3]; alcoholic beverages 25,972,000; soft drinks 7,419,000 litres. Construction (1982): residential C.V. Esc 365,800,-000; nonresidential C.V. Esc 1,700,000. Energy production (consumption):

electricity (kW-hr; 1987) 30,890,482 (30,876,142); coal, none (none); crude petroleum, n.a. (n.a.); petroleum products (metric tons; 1986) n.a. (9,000); natural gas, n.a. (n.a.).
Gross national product (at current market prices; 1986): U.S.$150,000,000 (U.S.$460 per capita).

Structure of gross domestic product and labour force

	1981 in value C.V. Esc '000,000	1981 % of total value	1980 labour force	1980 % of labour force
Agriculture	560.0	17.6	20,925	33.1
Manufacturing and } Public utilities	125.0	3.9	1,854	2.9
			330	0.5
Mining	9.0	0.3	524	0.8
Construction	645.0	20.3	17,825	28.2
Transportation and communications	...	...	3,299	5.2
Pub. admin., defense	550.0	17.3	2,128	3.4
Trade			3,851	6.1
Finance }	1,290	40.6	224	0.4
Other			4,911	7.8
TOTAL	3,179	100.0	63,192[1]	100.0[1]

Population economically active (1980): total 63,192; activity rate of total population 21.9% (participation rates: ages 15–64, 60.6%[2]; female 29.9%; unemployed, n.a.).

Price and earnings indexes (1975 = 100)

	1976	1977	1978	1979	1980	1981
Consumer price index	101.2	108.3	122.7	131.2	150.4	167.7
Monthly earnings index	...	...	...	...	...	...

Household income and expenditure. Average household size (1980) 4.3; income per household: n.a.; sources of income: n.a.; expenditure (1986)[4]: food 63.4%, clothing and footwear 9.2%, beverages and tobacco 6.7%, other 20.7%.
Land use (1985): forested 0.2%; meadows and pastures 6.2%; agricultural and under permanent cultivation 9.9%; other 83.7%.

Foreign trade

Balance of trade (current prices)

	1982	1983	1984	1985	1986	1987
C.V. Esc '000,000	−3,978	−5,482	−5,766	−6,983	−6,129	−6,715
% of total	89.8%	92.0%	92.9%	88.3%	90.4%	85.6%

Imports (1987): C.V. Esc 7,281,471,000 (foodstuffs and beverages 32.8%; machinery and transport equipment 22.7%, of which transport equipment 14.6%; mineral products 15.8%; metals 6.4%; chemical products 5.1%; textiles and textile products 3.6%; plastics and resins 3.5%). *Major import sources:* Portugal 33.2%; The Netherlands 12.1%; Hungary 11.4%; Spain 7.7%; France 5.2%; Denmark 4.7%; West Germany 4.2%.
Exports (1987): C.V. Esc 566,861,000 ([5]foodstuffs and beverages 68.4%; textiles and textile products 28.5%). *Major export destinations:* Portugal 31.5%; Angola 21.4%; Algeria 14.6%; Belgium–Luxembourg 14.6%; France 6.7%; Italy 5.6%; United Kingdom 4.5%.

Transport and communications

Transport. Railroads: none. Roads (1984): total length 1,398 mi, 2,250 km (paved 29%). Vehicles (1981): passenger cars 3,000[6], trucks and buses 1,343. Merchant marine (1987): vessels (100 gross tons and over) 29; total deadweight tonnage 22,092. Air transport (1985): passenger-mi 16,148,000, passenger-km 25,987,000; short ton-mi cargo 1,606,000, metric ton-km cargo 2,345,000; airports (1988) with scheduled flights 8.
Communications. Daily newspapers: none. Radio (1986): total number of receivers 50,000 (1 per 6.8 persons). Television (1985): total number of receivers 500 (1 per 668 persons). Telephones (1985): 4,379 (1 per 76 persons).

Education and health

Education (1986–87)

	schools	teachers	students	student/ teacher ratio
Primary (age 7–10)	347	1,464	49,703	34.0
Secondary (age 10–17)	16	321	10,304	32.1
Voc., teacher tr.	3	53	211	4.0
Higher	...	...	...	...

Educational attainment (1980). Percent of population age 25 and over having: no formal schooling 89.4%; primary education 9.2%; completed primary education 0.1%; secondary education 1.3%. *Literacy* (1981): total population age 15 and over literate 78,839 (49.3%); males literate 43,814 (55.3%); females literate 35,025 (43.4%).
Health (1980): physicians 51 (1 per 5,820 persons); hospital beds 632 (1 per 470 persons); infant mortality rate per 1,000 live births (1985) 76.5.
Food (1984–86): daily per capita caloric intake 2,729 (vegetable products 88%, animal products 12%); (1983) 100% of FAO recommended minimum requirement.

Military

Total active duty personnel (1987): 1,185 (army 84.4%, navy 13.5%, air force 2.1%). *Military expenditure as percent of GNP* (1982): 2.2% (world 6.0%); per capita expenditure U.S.$7.

[1]Detail does not add to total given because of rounding. [2]1985. [3]1986. [4]Praia only. [5]Distribution based on tonnage rather than value. [6]1984.

Central African Republic

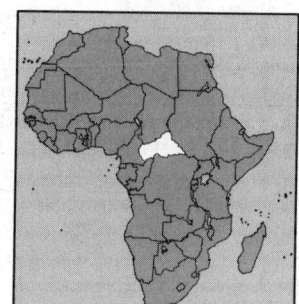

Official name: République Centrafricaine (Central African Republic).
Form of government: unitary single-party republic with one legislative house (National Assembly [52]).
Head of state and government: President.
Capital: Bangui.
Official language: French.
Official religion: none.
Monetary unit: 1 CFA franc (CFAF) = 100 centimes; valuation (Oct. 10, 1988) 1 U.S.$ = CFAF 316.13; 1 £ = CFAF 541.38.

Area and population

Prefectures	Capitals	area sq mi	area sq km	population 1985[1] estimate
Bamingui-Bangoran	Ndélé	22,471	58,200	29,400
Bangui	Bangui	26	67	473,800
Basse-Kotto	Mobaye	6,797	17,604	187,200
Gribingui-Économique	Kaga-Bandoro	7,720	19,996	85,700
Haut-Mbomou	Obo	21,440	55,530	52,200
Haute-Kotto	Bria	33,456	86,650	233,100
Haute-Sangha	Berbérati	11,661	30,203	37,400
Kemo-Gribingui	Sibut	6,642	17,204	78,300
Lobaye	Mbaiki	7,427	19,235	160,700
Mbomou	Bangassou	23,610	61,150	132,900
Nana-Mambere	Bouar	10,270	26,600	197,600
Ombella-Mpoko	Bimbo	12,292	31,835	127,900
Ouaka	Bambari	19,266	49,900	216,200
Ouham	Bossangoa	19,402	50,250	269,300
Ouham-Pendé	Bozoum	12,394	32,100	242,100
Sangha-Économique	Nola	7,495	19,412	59,600
Vakaga	Birao	17,954	46,500	24,200
TOTAL		240,324[2]	622,436	2,607,600

Demography

Population (1988): 2,843,000.
Density (1988): persons per sq mi 11.8, persons per sq km 4.6.
Urban–rural (1986): urban 43.3%; rural 56.7%.
Sex distribution (1985): male 48.42%; female 51.58%.
Age breakdown (1985): under 15, 42.5%; 15–59, 25.5%; 30–44, 15.9%; 45–59, 10.1%; 60 and over, 6.0%.
Population projection: (1990) 2,987,000; (2000) 3,824,000.
Doubling time: 30 years.
Ethnic composition (1983): Banda 28.6%; Baya (Gbaya) 24.5%; Ngbandi 10.6%; Azande 9.8%; Sara 6.9%; Mbaka 4.3%; Mbum 4.1%; Kare 2.4%; French 0.1%; other 8.7%.
Religious affiliation (1980): Protestant 50.0%; Roman Catholic 33.1%; traditional 12.0%; Muslim 3.2%; Bahá'í 0.3%; other 1.4%.
Major cities (1985): Bangui 473,800; Bambari 44,500; Bouar 42,000; Berberati 38,000; Bossangoa 35,800.

Vital statistics

Birth rate per 1,000 population (1980–85): 44.6 (world avg. 29.0); legitimate, n.a.; illegitimate, n.a.
Death rate per 1,000 population (1980–85): 21.8 (world avg. 11.0).
Natural increase rate per 1,000 population (1980–85): 22.8 (world avg. 18.0).
Total fertility rate (avg. births per childbearing woman; 1985–86): 5.9.
Marriage rate per 1,000 population: n.a.
Divorce rate per 1,000 population: n.a.
Life expectancy at birth (1980–85): male 41.4 years; female 44.6 years.
Morbidity (as percent of reported cases of illness; 1984): malaria 13.3%; dysentery, enteritis, and other intestinal diseases 12.5%; respiratory diseases 9.9%, of which pneumonia 2.7%.

National economy

Budget (1988). Revenue: CFAF 43,400,000,000 (1982; indirect taxes 52.4%, nonfiscal receipts 21.1%, direct taxes 20.3%). Expenditures: CFAF 58,150,-000,000 (1982; education and culture 13.9%, defense 8.3%, repayment of public debt 8.1%).
Public debt (external, outstanding; 1986): U.S.$392,600,000.
Tourism (1986): receipts from visitors U.S.$3,000,000; expenditures by nationals abroad U.S.$33,000,000.
Production (metric tons except as noted). Agriculture, forestry, fishing (1986): cassava 708,000, yams 198,000, peanuts (groundnuts) in shell 142,-000, cocoa beans 120,000, bananas 83,000, plantains 65,000, seed cotton 63,000, taro 59,000, corn (maize) 53,000, millet 40,000, cotton seed 32,000, coffee 18,000, rice 16,000, cotton lint 13,000, pulses 6,000; livestock (number of live animals) 2,135,000 cattle, 1,100,000 goats, 360,000 pigs, 112,000 sheep, 2,000,000 chickens; roundwood 3,417,000 cu m; fish catch 13,000. Mining and quarrying (1986): diamonds 357,379 carats, of which 258,701 gem quality and 98,678 industrial; gold 212 kg. Manufacturing (1986): beauty products 87,119; ice cream 2,753; paints 541; leather goods 452; household aluminum articles 348; coffee 233; printed cloth 5,515,000 m; footwear 321,209 pairs; cigarettes and cigars 252,339,000 units; motorcycles 3,167 units; bicycles 2,924 units; assembled vehicles 72 units; beer 318,706

hectolitres; soft drinks 61,248 hectolitres. Construction (1984): residential 6,500 sq m; nonresidential 16 units. Energy production (consumption): electricity (kW-hr; 1986) 93,000,000 (93,000,000); coal, none (n.a.); crude petroleum, none (n.a.); petroleum products (metric tons; 1986) none (51,-000); natural gas, none (n.a.).
Land use (1985): forested 57.5%; meadows and pastures 4.8%; agricultural and under permanent cultivation 3.2%; other 34.5%.
Gross national product (1986): U.S.$770,000,000 (U.S.$290 per capita).

Structure of gross domestic product and labour force

	1985 in value CFAF '000,000	1985 % of total value	1985 labour force	1985 % of labour force
Agriculture	130,297	40.9	869,000	67.8
Mining	7,822	2.5		
Manufacturing	23,149	7.3		
Construction	7,946	2.5	54,000	4.2
Public utilities	2,557	0.8		
Transportation and communications	12,982	4.1		
Trade	68,015	21.3	359,000	28.0
Finance				
Pub. admin., defense	65,278	20.5		
Services				
TOTAL	318,676[2]	100.0[2]	1,282,000	100.0

Population economically active (1985): total 1,282,000; activity rate of total population 49.8% (participation rates: over ages 15–64, 81.6%; female 47.0%; unemployed, n.a.).

Price and earnings indexes (1980 = 100)

	1981	1982	1983	1984	1985	1986	1987
Consumer price index	112.6	127.5	144.5	151.1	171.3	184.3	199.1
Earnings index	...	...	...	...	...	...	...

Household income and expenditure. Average household size (1980) 4.3; average annual income per household CFAF 91,985 (U.S.$435); sources of income: n.a.; expenditure[3] (1983): food 70.5%, clothing 9.5%, energy 6.5%, transportation and communications 4.1%, recreation 1.3%, health 1.0%, housing 0.6%.

Foreign trade

Balance of trade (current prices)

	1982	1983	1984	1985	1986	1987
U.S.$'000,000	−16.1	−11.9	−9.4	−41.7	−40.4	−31.9
% of total	7.0%	6.2%	4.9%	31.4%	25.6%	14.7%

Imports (1986): CFAF 80,064,000,000 (1980; machinery and equipment 33.9%, food 20.9%, chemicals and plastics 12.2%, textiles 8.4%, fuels and lubricants 1.8%). Major import sources (1987): France 52.4%; West Germany 6.9%; Japan 3.4%; Zaire 2.8%; Italy 2.0%; The Netherlands 2.0%.
Exports (1986): CFAF 45,480,000,000 (diamonds 27.0%, coffee 23.3%, wood 17.7%, cotton 9.7%). Major export destinations (1987): Belgium–Luxembourg 42.3%; France 16.8%; Spain 7.5%; Italy 6.5%; West Germany 4.3%; United States 4.8%; Zaire 1.9%.

Transport and communications

Transport. Railroads: none. Roads (1986): total length 12,600 mi, 20,278 km (paved 2%). Vehicles (1984): passenger cars 43,321; trucks and buses 3,861. Merchant marine: vessels (100 gross tons and over) none. Air transport (1987)[4]: passenger-mi 132,791,000, passenger-km 213,706,000; short ton-mi cargo 24,739,000, metric ton-km cargo 36,119,000; airports (1988) with scheduled flights 1.
Communications. Daily newspapers (1987): total number 1; total circulation 200; circulation per 1,000 population 0.1. Radio (1986): total number of receivers 125,000 (1 per 22 persons). Television (1983): total number of receivers 1,400 (1 per 1,817 persons). Telephones (1985): 6,952 (1 per 380 persons).

Education and health

Education (1985)

	schools	teachers	students	student/ teacher ratio
Primary (age 6–11)	986	4,502	294,312	65.4
Secondary (age 12–18)	41	914	45,166	49.4
Voc., teacher tr.	4	127	2,233	17.6
Higher[5]	...	105	2,133	20.3

Educational attainment (1975). Percent of population age 15 and over having: no formal schooling 73.5%; primary education 22.8%; lower secondary 3.0%; upper secondary 0.6%; higher 0.1%. Literacy (1985): total population age 15 and over literate 40.0%; males literate 53.0%; females literate 29.0%.
Health (1984): physicians 112 (1 per 22,997 persons); hospital beds 3,774 (1 per 682 persons); infant mortality rate per 1,000 live births (1980–85) 142.0.
Food (1984–86): daily per capita caloric intake 1,940 (vegetable products 90%, animal products 10%); (1983) 91% of FAO recommended minimum requirement.

Military

Total active duty personnel (1988): 3,800 (army 92.1%; navy, none; air force 7.9%). Military expenditure as percent of GNP (1983): 2.0% (world 6.2%); per capita expenditure U.S.$5.

[1]Beginning of year. [2]Detail does not add to total given because of rounding. [3]Capital city only. [4]Air Afrique only. [5]1983–84.

Chad

Official name: République du Tchad (Republic of Chad).
Form of government: pending adoption of a constitution, republican in form with one political party and a single advisory organ (National Consultative Assembly [30]).
Head of state and government: President.
Capital: N'Djamena.
Official languages: Arabic; French.
Official religion: none.
Monetary unit: 1 CFA franc (CFAF) = 100 centimes; valuation (Oct. 10, 1988) 1 U.S.$ = CFAF 316.13; 1 £ = CFAF 541.38.

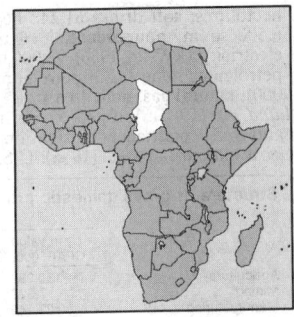

Area and population		area		population
		sq mi	sq km	1984 estimate
Préfectures	Capitals			
Batha	Ati	34,285	88,800	410,000
Biltine	Biltine	18,090	46,850	200,000
Borkou-Ennedi-Tibesti	Faya	231,795	600,350	103,000
Chari-Baguirmi	N'Djamena	32,010	82,910	719,000
Guéra	Mongo	22,760	58,950	234,000
Kanem	Mao	44,215	114,520	234,000
Lac	Bol	8,620	22,320	158,000
Logone Occidental	Moundou	3,355	8,695	324,000
Logone Oriental	Doba	10,825	28,035	350,000
Mayo-Kebbi	Bongor	11,625	30,105	757,000
Moyen-Chari	Sarh	17,445	45,180	582,000
Ouaddai	Abéché	29,435	76,240	411,000
Salamat	Am Timan	24,325	63,000	121,000
Tandjilé	Lai	6,965	18,045	341,000
TOTAL		495,755[1]	1,284,000	4,944,000

Demography

Population (1988): 5,395,000.
Density (1987): persons per sq mi 10.9, persons per sq km 4.2.
Urban–rural (1986): urban 23.9%; rural 76.1%.
Sex distribution (1985): male 49.24%; female 50.76%.
Age breakdown (1985): under 15, 42.5%; 15–29, 26.0%; 30–44, 15.8%; 45–59, 9.9%; 60–74, 4.9%; 75 and over, 0.9%.
Population projection: (1990) 5,668,000; (2000) 7,308,000.
Doubling time: 29 years.
Ethnic composition (1983): Bagirmi, Sara, and Kreish 30.5%; Sudanic Arab 26.1%; Teda (Tubu) 7.3%; Mbum 6.5%; Masalit, Maba, and Mimi 6.3%; Mubi 4.2%; Tama 6.3%; Kanuri 2.3%; Hausa 2.3%; Masa 2.3%; Kotoko 2.1%; other 3.8%.
Religious affiliation (1980): Muslim 44.0%; Christian 33.0%, of which Roman Catholic 21.0%, Protestant 11.6%; traditional beliefs 22.8%; other 0.2%.
Major cities (1986): N'Djamena 511,700; Sarh 100,000; Moundou 90,000; Abéché 71,000; Kélo 27,000[2].

Vital statistics

Birth rate per 1,000 population (1985): 44.2 (world avg. 29.0); legitimate, n.a.; illegitimate, n.a.
Death rate per 1,000 population (1985): 19.9 (world avg. 11.0).
Natural increase rate per 1,000 population (1985): 24.3 (world avg. 18.0).
Total fertility rate (avg. births per childbearing woman; 1985): 5.9.
Marriage rate per 1,000 population: n.a.
Divorce rate per 1,000 population: n.a.
Life expectancy at birth (1985): male 43.4 years; female 46.6 years.
Major causes of death per 100,000 population: n.a.; however, major diseases include malaria, sleeping sickness, leprosy, venereal diseases, and tuberculosis.

National economy

Budget (1988). Revenue: CFAF 17,900,000,000 (1984; indirect taxes 73.2%, of which customs receipts 60.1%; direct taxes 21.7%). Expenditures: CFAF 25,600,000,000 (1984; defense 46.5%; education 10.9%; community projects 9.1%; health 3.8%).
Public debt (external, outstanding; 1987): U.S.$498,500,000.
Tourism (1986): receipts from visitors U.S.$12,000,000; expenditures by nationals abroad U.S.$20,000,000.
Production (metric tons except as noted). Agriculture, forestry, fishing (1986): millet 624,000, cassava 306,000, sugarcane 290,000, yams 219,000, peanuts (groundnuts) 90,000, seed cotton 70,000, pulses 60,000, corn (maize) 53,000, sweet potatoes 41,000, dates 33,000, mangoes 32,000, lint cotton 27,000, rice 25,000, onions 14,000, potatoes 14,000, sesame seed 11,000; livestock (number of live animals) 5,017,000 cattle, 2,620,000 sheep, 2,620,000 goats, 4,000,000 chickens; roundwood 3,654,000 cu m; fish catch 110,000. Mining and quarrying: clay, natron, tungsten, bauxite, and gold. Manufacturing (1985): beef and veal 48,000; refined sugar 23,000; salted, dried, or smoked fish 20,000[3]; mutton and lamb 9,000; goat meat 7,000; wheat flour 1,000[3]; woven cotton fabrics 13,075,000 metres[3]; beer 130,000 hectolitres[3]; cigarettes 259,000,000 units[3]. Construction: n.a. Energy production (consumption): electricity (kW-hr; 1986) 51,000,000 (51,000,000); coal, none (n.a.); crude petroleum, none (n.a.); petroleum products (metric tons; 1986) none (68,000); natural gas, none (n.a.).
Household income and expenditure. Average household size (1980) 3.9; average annual income per household CFAF 96,806 (U.S.$458); sources

of income: n.a.; expenditure[4] (1983): food 45.3%, health 11.9%, energy 5.8%, clothing 3.3%.
Gross domestic product (at current market prices; 1986): U.S.$817,000,000 (U.S.$160 per capita).

Structure of gross domestic product and labour force				
	1985			
	in value U.S.$'000,000	% of total value	labour force	% of labour force
Agriculture	272.0	46.7	1,454,000	81.2
Mining	3.0	0.5		
Manufacturing	50.0	8.6		
Construction	10.0	1.7	93,000	5.2
Public utilities	3.0	0.5		
Transportation and communications	11.0	1.9		
Trade	155.0	26.6		
Pub. admin., defense	74.0	12.7	243,000	13.6
Finance	5.0	0.8		
Services				
TOTAL	583.0[5]	100.0	1,790,000	100.0

Population economically active (1985): total 1,790,000; activity rate of total population 35.7% (participation rates: ages 15–64, 57.4%; female 21.7%; unemployed, n.a.).

Price and earnings indexes (1980 = 100)							
	1982	1983	1984	1985	1986	1987	1988
Consumer price index	...	111.6	134.2	141.0	122.7	119.3	129.8[6]
Earnings index	...	...	...	...	...	...	...

Land use (1985): forested 10.5%; meadows and pastures 35.7%; agricultural and under permanent cultivation 2.5%; built-on, wasteland, and other 51.3%.

Foreign trade[7]

Balance of trade (current prices)						
	1979	1980	1981	1982	1983	1984
CFAF '000,000	+644	−534	−6,684	−19,255	−31,793	−26,239
% of total	1.7%	1.7%	12.9%	36.1%	36.1%	21.3%

Imports (1983): CFAF 74,802,000,000 (petroleum products 16.8%; cereal products 16.8%; pharmaceutical products and chemicals 11.5%; machinery and transport equipment 8.5%, of which transport equipment 7.3%; electrical equipment 5.7%; textiles 2.9%; raw and refined sugar 2.3%). Major import sources: France 16.6%; Cameroon 9.2%; United States 8.9%; Italy 4.5%; West Germany 3.2%; United Kingdom 2.4%; The Netherlands 1.9%.
Exports (1983): CFAF 48,563,000,000 (raw cotton 91.1%; live cattle and frozen bovine meat 1.8%). Major export destinations: United States 36.6%; West Germany 8.0%; Portugal 8.0%; Cameroon 4.0%; France 3.1%; Italy 1.6%; Spain 1.3%; Japan 1.2%.

Transport and communications

Transport. Railroads: none. Roads (1983): total length 24,855 mi, 40,000 km (paved 1%). Vehicles (1982): passenger cars 7,000; trucks and buses 5,000. Merchant marine vessels (100 gross tons and over) none. Air transport[8] (1987): passenger-mi 132,791,000, passenger-km 213,706,000; short ton-mi cargo 24,739,000, metric ton-km cargo 36,119,000; airports (1988) with scheduled flights 1.
Communications. Daily newspapers (1987): total number 1; total circulation 1,500; circulation per 1,000 population 0.3. Radio (1986): total number of receivers 100,000 (1 per 51 persons). Television: none. Telephones (1987): 4,668 (1 per 1,114 persons).

Education and health

Education (1984)	schools	teachers	students	student/ teacher ratio
Primary (age 6–12)	1,231	4,494	288,479	64.2
Secondary (age 13–19)	...	590[9]	43,053	...
Voc., teacher tr.	...	...	2,559	...
Higher	1	141	1,643	11.6

Educational attainment, n.a. Literacy (1980): total population age 15 and over literate 466,500 (17.8%); males literate 459,700 (35.6%); females literate 6,800 (0.5%).
Health: physicians (1980) 94 (1 per 47,640 persons); hospital beds (1978) 3,553 (1 per 1,190 persons); infant mortality rate per 1,000 live births (1984) 139.
Food (1980–82): daily per capita caloric intake 1,821 (vegetable products 92%, animal products 8%); 77% of FAO recommended minimum requirement.

Military

Total active duty personnel (1988): 17,000 (army 98.8%; navy, none; air force 1.2%). Military expenditure as percent of GNP (1985): 1.9% (world 6.1%); per capita expenditure U.S.$2.

[1]Detail does not add to total given because of rounding. [2]1979. [3]1983. [4]Capital city only. [5]At current factor cost. [6]First quarter. [7]Imports c.i.f. (cost, insurance, and freight); exports f.o.b. (free on board). [8]The airport at N'Djamena is underutilized because of the political and military unrest in Chad. [9]1976–77.

Chile

Official name: República de Chile (Republic of Chile).
Form of government: military regime.
Head of state and government: President (general) assisted by a four-member junta.
Capital: Santiago.
Official language: Spanish.
Official religion: none.
Monetary unit: 1 peso (Ch$) = 100 centavos; valuation (Oct. 10, 1988) 1 U.S.$ = Ch$245.63; 1 £ = Ch$420.64.

Area and population

Regions	Capitals	area[1] sq mi	sq km	population 1987 estimate
Aisén del General Carlos				
Ibáñez del Campo	Coihaique	42,095	109,025	74,500
Antofagasta	Antofagasta	48,820	126,444	370,600
Araucania	Temuco	12,300	31,858	755,100
Atacama	Copiapó	29,179	75,573	196,000
Bío-Bío	Concepción	14,258	36,929	1,625,800
Coquimbo	La Serena	15,697	40,656	459,400
Libertador General				
Bernardo O'Higgins	Rancagua	6,319	16,365	627,700
Los Lagos	Puerto Montt	25,868	66,997	903,400
Magallanes y de la				
Antártica Chilena	Punta Arenas	50,932	131,914	145,500
Maule	Talca	11,700	30,302	805,100
Santiago,				
Región Metropolitana de	Santiago	5,926	15,349	4,913,100
Tarapacá	Iquique	22,663	58,698	324,100
Valparaíso	Valparaiso	6,331	16,396	1,336,100
TOTAL		292,135[2]	756,626[2]	12,536,400

Demography

Population (1988): 12,750,000.
Density (1988): persons per sq mi 43.6, persons per sq km 16.9.
Urban–rural (1987)[3]: urban 80.8%; rural 19.2%.
Sex distribution (1988)[4]: male 49.55%; female 50.45%.
Age breakdown (1986): under 15, 31.1%; 15–29, 28.6%; 30–44, 19.9%; 45–59, 12.1%; 60–74, 6.4%; 75 and over, 2.0%[2].
Population projection: (1990) 13,188,000; (2000) 15,617,000.
Doubling time: 44 years.
Ethnic composition (1983): mestizo 91.6%; Indian (mostly Araucanian) 6.8%; others (mainly European) 1.6%.
Religious affiliation (1982): Roman Catholic 79.2%; Protestant 6.0%; atheist and nonreligious 2.0%; other 12.8%.
Major cities (1987): Greater Santiago 4,858,300; Viña del Mar 297,300; Concepción 294,400; Valparaíso 278,800; Talcahuano 231,400.

Vital statistics

Birth rate per 1,000 population (1986): 22.1 (world avg. 26.0); (1985) legitimate 68.2%; illegitimate 31.8%.
Death rate per 1,000 population (1986): 5.9 (world avg. 9.9).
Natural increase rate per 1,000 population (1986): 16.2 (world avg. 16.1).
Total fertility rate (avg. births per childbearing woman; 1981): 3.0.
Marriage rate per 1,000 population (1985): 7.5.
Divorce rate per 1,000 population (1985): 0.4.
Life expectancy at birth (1985–90): male 68.1 years; female 75.1 years.
Major causes of death per 100,000 population (1985): diseases of the circulatory system 168.5; malignant neoplasms (cancers) 104.4; diseases of the respiratory system 66.6; accidents and adverse effects 24.3.

National economy

Budget (1986)[4]. Revenue: Ch$929,960,000,000 (excise taxes 43.3%, nontax revenue 20.6%, income taxes 11.6%, import and export duties 8.8%, social security contributions 7.5%, stamp taxes 4.6%). Expenditures: Ch$969,300,000,000 (social security and welfare 38.0%, education 12.5%, public services 12.5%, defense 10.7%, economic services 9.2%, health 6.0%).
Public debt (external, outstanding; 1986): U.S.$15,108,700,000.
Tourism (1986): receipts from visitors U.S.$172,000,000; expenditures by nationals abroad U.S.$319,000,000.
Production (metric tons except as noted). Agriculture, forestry, fishing (1986–87): sugar beets 2,649,500, wheat 1,874,100, potatoes 726,900, corn (maize) 617,200, rice 147,000, oats 127,500, rapeseed 95,100, barley 48,300; livestock (number of live animals; 1986) 1,063,800 pigs, 796,400 sheep, 707,200 cattle; roundwood (1985) 15,493,000 cu m; fish catch (1986) 5,696,000. Mining (1987): iron ore 6,822,536; copper 1,418,000; manganese 31,800; zinc 19,500; molybdenum 16,900; silver 448,500 kilograms; gold 18,100 kilograms. Manufacturing (1987): cement 1,500,300; cellulose 673,100; fish meal 469,400; iron or steel plates 259,100; newsprint 184,500; carbonated drinks 3,954,000 hectolitres; tires 1,222,800 units; pressed fibre panels 14,578,500 sq m; flat glass 2,310,500 sq m. Construction[5] (1985) residential 29,900 sq m; nonresidential 93,800 sq m. Energy production (consumption): electricity (kW-hr; 1987) 14,821,400,000 (14,821,400,000); coal (metric tons; 1986) 1,633,000 (1,858,000); crude petroleum (barrels; 1986) 11,146,000 (30,639,000); petroleum products (metric tons; 1986) 4,228,000 (4,648,000); natural gas (cu m; 1986) 878,980,000 (878,980,000).
Land use (1985): forested 20.7%; meadows and pastures 15.9%; agricultural and under permanent cultivation 7.4%; other 56.0%.

Gross national product (1986): U.S.$16,200,000,000 (U.S.$1,320 per capita).

Structure of gross domestic product and labour force

	1986 in value Ch$'000,000[6]	% of total value	labour force	% of labour force
Agriculture	37,107	9.9	825,500	19.4
Mining	31,523	8.4	88,200	2.1
Manufacturing	78,507	20.8	581,500	13.6
Construction	20,852	5.5	226,600	5.3
Public utilities	9,744	2.6	26,100	0.6
Transp. and commun.	21,571	5.7	245,500	5.7
Trade[7]	62,919	16.7	707,500	16.6
Finance			164,900	3.9
Pub. admin., defense				
Services[7]	114,404	30.4	1,320,600	31.0
Other			77,700[8]	1.8[8]
TOTAL	376,627	100.0	4,264,100	100.0

Population economically active (1986): total 4,269,000; activity rate of total population 35.1% (participation rates: ages 15–64, 54.8%; female 30.0%; unemployed 8.7%[9]).

Price and earnings indexes (1980 = 100)

	1981	1982	1983	1984	1985	1986	1987
Consumer price index	119.7	131.6	167.5	200.7	262.3	313.4	375.7
Monthly earnings index	130.3	142.9	162.5	195.0	243.6	298.4	...

Household income and expenditure. Average household size (1982) 4.5; average annual income per family (household) (1985)[10] Ch$440,738 at June prices (U.S.$2,840); sources of income, n.a.; expenditure (1978): food 41.9%, housing 13.3%, transportation and communications 11.8%, recreation and education 8.2%, household goods 7.8%, clothing and footwear 7.6%.

Foreign trade[11]

Balance of trade (current prices)

	1981	1982	1983	1984	1985	1986	1987
U.S.$'000,000	−1,487	+720	+1,320	+953	+1,473	+1,620	+1,704
% of total	16.0%	10.7%	20.8%	15.0%	24.1%	23.7%	20.1%

Imports (1987): U.S.$4,023,300,000 (intermediate goods 55.4%; capital goods 24.4%; consumer goods 14.5%). *Major import sources* (1987): U.S. 19.2%; Japan 9.6%; Brazil 9.4%; West Germany 8.3%; Argentina 4.0%; Venezuela 3.6%; U.K. 3.2%; Spain 2.9%.
Exports (1987): U.S.$5,101,900,000 (mining 53.8%, of which copper 41.2%; industrial products 31.6%; fruits and vegetables 11.8%; paper and paper products 7.2%; chemical and petroleum products 2.0%). *Major export destinations* (1987): U.S. 22.4%; Japan 11.0%; West Germany 9.5%; Brazil 6.8%; U.K. 6.2%; Italy 5.4%; France 3.5%; Argentina 3.4%.

Transport and communications

Transport. Railroads (1986): route length 5,037 mi, 8,107 km; passenger-mi 790,000,000, passenger-km 1,272,000,000; short ton-mi cargo 1,701,000,000, metric ton-km cargo 2,484,000,000. Roads (1986): total length 49,144 mi, 79,089 km (paved 12%). Vehicles (1986) passenger cars 638,000; trucks and buses 263,000. Merchant marine (1987): vessels (100 gross tons and over) 264; total deadweight tonnage 824,869. Air transport (1986): passenger-mi 1,218,000,000, passenger-km 1,960,000,000; short ton-mi cargo 93,982,000, metric ton-km cargo 137,212,000; airports (1988) with scheduled flights 17.
Communications. Daily newspapers (1987): total number 33[12]; total circulation 1,145,000; circulation per 1,000 population 91. Radio (1986): 14,000,000 receivers (1 per 1.1 persons). Television (1987): 2,330,500 receivers (1 per 5.4 persons). Telephones (1986): 795,854 (1 per 16 persons).

Education and health

Education (1984)

	schools	teachers	students[13]	student/ teacher ratio
Primary (age 6–13)	8,862	62,746[14]	2,099,413	...
Secondary (age 14–17)	1,401	...	588,123	...
Vocational	369	...	143,788	...
Higher	24	15,131	197,437	...

Educational attainment (1982). Percent of population age 25 and over having: no formal schooling 9.4%; primary education 56.6%; secondary 26.9%; higher 7.1%. *Literacy* (1983): total population age 12 and over literate 8,301,000 (95.6%); males 4,100,000 (95.0%)[15]; females 4,201,000 (93.8%)[15].
Health: physicians (1985) 12,334 (1 per 983 persons); hospital beds (1986) 33,136 (1 per 372 persons); infant mortality rate (1987) 18.7.
Food (1984–86): daily per capita caloric intake 2,573 (vegetable products 85%, animal products 15%); (1983) 105% of FAO recommended minimum requirement.

Military

Total active duty personnel (1987): 97,500 (army 58.5%, navy 26.1%, air force 15.4%). *Military expenditure as percent of GNP* (1985): 4.1% (world 6.1%); per capita expenditure: U.S.$63.

[1]Excludes the territory of Antártica Chilena and "inland" (actually tidal) water areas. [2]Detail does not add to total given because of rounding. [3]September. [4]Preliminary. [5]Private new construction only. [6]In constant 1977 pesos. [7]Services includes restaurants and hotels. [8]Includes 76,300 unemployed persons not previously employed. [9]Fourth quarter. [10]Greater Santiago area. [11]Import figures are f.o.b. (free on board) in balance of trade and c.i.f. (cost, insurance, and freight) for commodities and trading partners. [12]In September 1986 several opposition publications were banned by the government. [13]1985. [14]1982. [15]Calculated from the 1981 literacy rate of 94.4%.

China

Official name: Chung-hua Jen-min
 Kung-ho-kuo (People's Republic
 of China).
Form of government: single-party
 people's republic with one legislative
 house (National People's Congress
 [2,978]).
Chief of state: President.
Head of government: Premier.
Capital: Peking (Beijing).
Official language: Mandarin Chinese.
Official religion: none.
Monetary unit: 1 Renminbi (yuan)
 (Y) = 10 jiao = 100 fen; valuation
 (Oct. 10, 1988) 1 U.S.$ = Y 3.70;
 1 £ = Y 6.33.

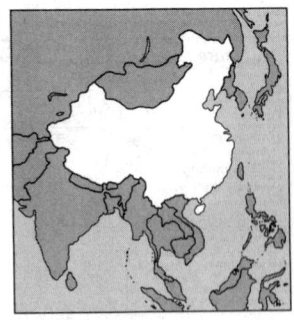

Area and population[1,2]

Provinces	Capitals	area sq mi	area sq km	population 1987[3] estimate
Anhwei (Anhui)	Ho-fei (Hefei)	54,000	139,900	52,170,000
Chekiang (Zhejiang)	Hangchow (Hangzhou)	39,300	101,800	40,700,000
Fukien (Fujian)	Foochow (Fuzhou)	47,500	123,100	27,490,000
Heilungkiang (Heilongjiang)	Harbin (Harbin)	179,000	463,600	33,320,000
Honan (Henan)	Cheng-chou (Zhengzhou)	64,500	167,000	78,080,000
Hopeh (Hebei)	Shih-chia-chuang (Shijiazhuang)	78,200	202,700	56,170,000
Hunan (Hunan)	Ch'ang-sha (Changsha)	81,300	210,500	56,960,000
Hupeh (Hubei)	Wu-han (Wuhan)	72,400	187,500	49,890,000
Kansu (Gansu)	Lan-chou (Lanzhou)	141,500	366,500	20,710,000
Kiangsi (Jiangxi)	Nan-ch'ang (Nanchang)	63,600	164,800	35,090,000
Kiangsu (Jiangsu)	Nanking (Nanjing)	39,600	102,600	62,700,000
Kirin (Jilin)	Ch'ang-ch'un (Changchun)	72,200	187,000	23,150,000
Kwangtung (Guangdong)	Canton (Guangzhou)	89,300	231,400	63,460,000
Kweichow (Guizhou)	Kuei-yang (Guiyang)	67,200	174,000	30,080,000
Liaoning (Liaoning)	Shen-yang (Shenyang)	58,300	151,000	37,260,000
Shansi (Shanxi)	T'ai-yüan (Taiyuan)	60,700	157,100	26,550,000
Shantung (Shandong)	Tsinan (Jinan)	59,200	153,300	77,760,000
Shensi (Shaanxi)	Sian (Xi'an)	75,600	195,800	30,430,000
Szechwan (Sichuan)	Ch'eng-tu (Chengdu)	219,700	569,000	103,200,000
Tsinghai (Qinghai)	Hsi-ning (Xining)	278,400	721,000	4,120,000
Yunnan (Yunnan)	K'un-ming (Kunming)	168,400	436,200	34,560,000
Autonomous regions				
Inner Mongolia (Nei Monggol)	Hu-ho-hao-t'e (Hohhot)	454,600	1,177,500	20,290,000
Kwangsi Chuang (Guangxi Zhuang)	Nan-ning (Nanning)	85,100	220,400	39,460,000
Ningsia Hui (Ningxia Hui)	Yin-ch'uan (Yinchuan)	25,600	66,400	4,240,000
Sinkiang Uighur (Xinjiang Uygur)	Urumchi (Urumqi)	635,900	1,646,900	13,840,000
Tibet (Xizang)	Lhasa (Lhasa)	471,700	1,221,600	2,030,000
Municipalities				
Peking (Beijing)	—	6,500	16,800	9,750,000
Shanghai (Shanghai)	—	2,400	6,200	12,320,000
Tientsin (Tianjin)	—	4,400	11,300	8,190,000
TOTAL		3,696,100[4]	9,572,900[4]	1,057,210,000[5]

Demography

Population (1988): 1,088,200,000.
Density (1988): persons per sq mi 294.4, persons per sq km 113.7.
Urban–rural (1987): urban 46.6%; rural 53.4%.
Sex distribution (1987): male 51.50%; female 48.50%.
Age breakdown (1982): under 15, 33.6%; 15–29, 29.1%; 30–44, 17.5%; 45–59, 12.2%; 60–74, 6.3%; 75 and over, 1.3%.
Population projection: (1990) 1,112,000,000; (2000) 1,253,000,000.
Doubling time: 50 years.
Ethnic composition (1982): Han (Chinese) 93.30%; Chuang 1.33%; Hui 0.72%; Uighur 0.59%; Yi 0.54%; Miao 0.50%; Manchu 0.43%; Tibetan 0.39%; Mongolian 0.34%; Tuchia 0.28%; Puyi 0.21%; Korean 0.18%; Tung 0.14%; Yao 0.14%; Pai 0.11%; Hani 0.11%; Kazakh 0.09%; Tai 0.08%; Li 0.08%; other 0.44%.
Religious affiliation (1980): nonreligious 59.2%; Chinese folk-religionist 20.1%; atheist 12.0%; Buddhist 6.0%; Muslim 2.4%; Christian 0.2%; other 0.1%.
Major cities (1987)[3]: Shanghai 7,100,000; Peking 5,970,000; Tientsin 5,460,-000; Shen-yang 4,290,000; Wu-han 3,490,000; Canton 3,360,000; Chungking (Chongqing) 2,830,000; Harbin 2,670,000; Ch'eng-tu 2,640,000; Sian 2,390,-000; Nanking 2,290,000; T'ai-yüan 1,930,000; Ch'ang-ch'un 1,910,000; Ta-lien (Dalian) 1,680,000; Cheng-chou 1,610,000; K'un-ming 1,590,000; Tsi-nan 1,460,000; Lan-chou 1,390,000; An-shan (Anshan) 1,270,000; Ch'ing-tao (Qingdao) 1,270,000; Hangchow 1,270,000.
Households (1986). Average rural household size 5.1; urban household size 3.8. Family households (1982): 220,100,755 (99.5%); collective 1,073,010 (0.5%).

Vital statistics

Birth rate per 1,000 population (1987): 21.0 (world avg. 26.0).
Death rate per 1,000 population (1987): 6.6 (world avg. 9.9).
Natural increase rate per 1,000 population (1987): 14.4 (world avg. 16.1).
Total fertility rate (avg. births per childbearing woman; 1987): 2.4.
Marriage rate per 1,000 population (1986): 8.3.
Divorce rate per 1,000 population (1986): 0.5.
Life expectancy at birth (1987): male 67.8 years; female 70.7 years.

Major causes of death per 100,000 population (percent distribution; 1986)[6]: diseases of the heart 24.5%; diseases of the circulatory system 15.7%; malignant neoplasms (cancers) 15.2%; diseases of the respiratory system 12.6%; digestive diseases 5.5%; poisonings 3.9%; trauma 3.6%; tuberculosis 3.5%.

Social indicators

Educational attainment (1982). Percent of population age 25 and over having: no schooling and incomplete primary 44.5%; completed primary 32.7%; completed junior secondary 16.1%; completed senior secondary 5.6%; postsecondary 1.1%.

Distribution of rural household income (1986)

by per capita income group (avg. Y 424)

Y 150 and under	Y 151–Y 300	Y 301–Y 500	over Y 500
4.3%	28.8%	38.2%	28.7%

Quality of working life (1986). Average workweek: 48 hours. Annual rate per 100,000 workers for: injury or accident, n.a.; industrial illness, n.a.; death, n.a. Expenditure on pensions and social welfare relief (1983): Y 2,404,000,-000. Average days lost to labour stoppages per 1,000 workdays: n.a. Average duration of journey to work: n.a. Method of transport: n.a. Rate per 1,000 workers of discouraged (unemployed no longer seeking work): n.a.
Access to services. Proportion of communes having access to electricity (1979) 87.1%. Percent of urban population with: safe public water supply (1986) 87.2%; public sewage collection, n.a.; public fire protection, n.a.
Social participation. Eligible voters participating in last national election: n.a. Population participating in voluntary work: n.a. Trade union membership in total labour force (1986): 18.0%. Practicing religious population in total affiliated population: n.a.
Social deviance. Annual reported arrest rate per 100,000 population (1986) for: property violation 20.7; infringing personal rights 7.2; disruption of social administration 3.3; endangering public security[7] 1.0.
Leisure. Favourite leisure activities: n.a.
Material well-being (1987). Urban families possessing (number per family): wristwatches 3.1; bicycles 1.8; sewing machines 0.7; radios 0.7; televisions 0.9. Rural families possessing (number per family): wristwatches 1.6; bicycles 1.0; sewing machines 0.5; radios 0.5; televisions 0.2.

National economy

Gross national product (at current market prices; 1986): U.S.$314,800,000,-000 (U.S.$300 per capita).

Structure of national income[8] and labour force

	1986 in value Y '000,000,000	1986 % of total value	1988[3] labour force ('000)[9]	1988[3] % of labour force
Agriculture	317.8	40.8	317,200	60.1
Mining	...	...	1,070	0.2
Manufacturing	309.3	39.7	93,420	17.7
Construction	48.9	6.3	24,190	4.6
Public utilities	...	...	5,400	1.0
Transp. and commun.	28.3	3.6	13,730	2.6
Trade	74.8	9.6	26,560	5.0
Finance	—	—	1,700	0.3
Pub. admin.	—	—	9,250	1.8
Services	—	—	20,290	3.8
Other	—	—	15,020	2.8
TOTAL	779.0[10]	100.0	527,830	100.0[10]

Budget (1987). Revenue: Y 237,930,000,000 (taxes 92.2%; funds collected for energy and transport projects 7.4%). Expenditures: Y 245,950,000,000 (capital construction 26.7%; culture, education, public health 15.8%; defense 8.3%).
Public debt (external, outstanding; 1986): U.S.$16,313,300,000.
Tourism: receipts from visitors (1987) U.S.$1,844,000,000; expenditures by nationals abroad (1986) U.S.$314,000,000.

Retail and service enterprises (1986)

	no. of enterprises	no. of employees	annual wage as a % of all wages	annual gross output value (Y '000,000)
Retail trade	7,967,000	18,430,000	...	...
Grocery stores	165,000	1,157,000	...	...
Department stores	155,000	1,523,000	...	...
Other food shops	115,000	755,000	...	...
Agricultural supplies stores	75,000	344,000	...	...
Household supplies stores	66,000	352,000	...	...
Grain and oil shops	51,000	509,000	...	...
Electrical appliances stores	50,000	511,000	...	...
Textile stores	36,000	213,000	...	...
Drug stores	24,000	181,000	...	...
Book stores	23,000	105,000	...	...
Coal stores	13,000	149,000	...	...
Service trade	1,609,000	3,699,000	...	...
Repair shops	730,000	1,083,000	...	...
Barber shops	231,000	445,000	...	...
Hotels	137,000	914,000	...	...
Photo studios	85,000	202,000	...	...

Production (metric tons except as noted). Agriculture, forestry, fishing (1986): grains—rice 177,000,000, wheat 89,002,000, corn (maize) 65,560,000, sorghum 6,538,000, millet 6,102,000, barley 2,701,000; oilseeds—peanuts (groundnuts) 5,995,000, rapeseed 5,871,000, sunflower seed 1,700,000; fruits and nuts—watermelons 5,419,000, apples 4,015,000, pears 2,434,000, cantaloupes 2,224,000, oranges 2,111,000; others—sweet potatoes 88,869,000, sugarcane 57,103,000, potatoes 45,028,000, soybeans 11,010,000, seed cotton 10,620,000, sugar beets 8,310,000, cabbage 7,219,000, pulses 5,640,000, tomatoes 5,266,000, cucumbers 3,586,000, tobacco leaves 1,728,000, tea

486,000; livestock (number of live animals) 338,074,000 pigs, 94,210,000 sheep, 66,925,000 cattle, 61,901,000 goats, 20,038,000 water buffalo, 11,-000,000 horses, 10,415,000 asses, 10,000,000 ducks, 1,459,000,000 chickens; roundwood 268,385,000 cu m; fish catch 8,000,063, of which 3,363,502 freshwater fish, 2,013,495 marine fish, 669,139 clams, 428,410 marine crabs. Mining and quarrying (1986): metals (metal content of ores)—zinc 200,000, copper 185,000, lead 160,000, tin 15,000, tungsten 15,000, molybdenum 2,000; other metals—iron ore 90,000,000, bauxite 1,650,000, manganese 1,600,000, silver 3,000,000 troy oz, gold 2,100,000 troy oz; nonmetals—salt 17,300,000, gypsum 6,500,000, phosphates 2,000,000, barite 1,000,000, talc 1,000,000, fluorspar 650,000, graphite 185,000, asbestos 150,000. Manufacturing (1987): cement 180,000,000; steel 56,020,000; chemical fertilizer 17,030,000; paper and paperboard 10,080,000; sulfuric acid 9,620,000; sugar 5,110,000; cotton yarn 4,320,000; woolen fabrics 260,000,000 metres; bicycles 40,910,000 units; television sets 19,380,000 units; household washing machines 9,920,000 units; household refrigerators 3,980,000 units; motor vehicles 472,000 units. Construction (1986): residential 945,183,000 sq m; nonresidential 246,473,300 sq m. Distribution of industrial production (percent of total value of output by sector; 1978 [1986]): state-operated enterprises 80.6% (68.7%); collectives 19.2% (29.2%); privately operated enterprises 0.2% (2.1%). Retail sales (percent of total sales by sector; 1978 [1987]): state-operated enterprises 90.5% (42.0%); collectives 7.4% (38.8%); privately operated enterprises 2.1% (19.2%).

Manufacturing and mining enterprises (1986)

	no. of enterprises	no. of employees[11]	annual wages as a % of avg. of all wages[12]	annual gross output value (Y '000,000)[13]
Manufacturing				
Machinery, transport equipment, and basic manufactures,	115,621	10,751,000	96.7	172,986
of which,				
Industrial equipment	5,695	...	...	18,431
Transport equipment	11,786	...	...	32,539
Electronic goods	4,330	1,043,000[14]	...	30,437
Metalware for daily use	7,884	...	...	16,580
Textiles,	23,306	4,500,000	95.5	123,072
of which,				
Cotton	6,931	...	...	69,754
Foodstuffs,	65,556	3,262,000	87.5	69,950
of which,				
Grains and edible oils	22,793	...	...	22,304
Processed meat	...	...	...	12,337
Tobacco manufactures	407	...	...	17,195
Chemicals,	38,208	4,008,000	92.1	121,633
of which,				
Organic chemicals	5,093	...	...	12,856
Plastics	14,487	191,000	...	17,831
Building materials,	63,543	2,643,000	93.0	36,315
of which,				
Brick, tile, other	...	...	...	12,777
Cement (all forms)	5,427	856,000[14]	...	9,104
Secondary forest products (including paper and stationery)	38,584	959,000	96.1	28,015
Primary forest products	2,457	1,075,000	114.3	4,453
Mining				
Nonferrous and ferrous metals	3,817	797,000	107.6	5,331
Crude petroleum	32	526,000	...	17,153
Coal	10,962	4,325,000	119.8	20,055

Energy production (consumption): electricity (kW-hr; 1986) 444,130,000,000 (445,296,000,000); coal (metric tons; 1987) 898,669,000 (915,120,000,000); crude petroleum (barrels; 1987) 980,797,000 (748,088,000); petroleum products (metric tons; 1986) 75,405,000 (70,772,000); natural gas (cu m; 1987) 14,-071,263,000 (13,872,353,000).

Financial aggregates[15]

	1982	1983	1984	1985	1986	1987	June 1988[16]
Exchange rate, Y per:							
U.S. dollar	1.92	1.98	2.80	3.20	3.72	3.72	3.72
£	3.10	2.87	3.23	4.62	5.49	6.96	6.36
SDR	2.12	2.07	2.74	3.52	4.55	5.28	4.88
International reserves (U.S.$)							
Total (excl. gold; '000,000)	11,339	14,853	15,081	12,728	11,453	16,305	19,056
SDRs ('000,000)	214	335	406	483	569	640	582
Reserve pos. in IMF ('000,000)	—	176	223	332	370	429	397
Foreign exchange	11,125	14,342	14,420	11,913	10,514	15,236	18,078
Gold ('000,000 fine troy oz)	12.7	12.7	12.7	12.7	12.7	12.7	12.7
% world reserves	1.3	1.3	1.3	1.3	1.3	1.3	1.3
Interest and prices							
Central bank discount (%)	...	...	...	...	...	...	...
Gov't bond yield (%)	...	...	...	...	...	...	...
Industrial share prices	...	...	...	...	...	...	...
Balance of payments (Y '000,000)							
Balance of visible trade,	8,610	5,130	1,590	−54,310	−28,930	−990	700[17]
of which:							
Imports, f.o.b.	32,820	38,700	56,370	176,820	137,510	148,170	32,540[17]
Exports, f.o.b.	41,430	43,830	57,960	122,510	108,580	147,180	33,240[17]
Balance of invisibles							
Balance of payments, current account							

Household income and expenditure. Average household size (1987) 4.3; rural household 5.0, urban household 3.7. Average annual income per household, Y 3,002; rural household Y 2,317, urban household Y 3,786. Sources of income (1987): rural household—income from the collective[18] and nonproductive sources 9.1%, sideline production 82.9%, of which farming 48.2%, livestock raising 11.2%, labour service 6.7%; urban household[11]—time wages 56.5%, subsidies 15.5%, bonuses 15.4%, piece-rate wages 9.6%. Expenditure (1987): rural household—food 55.2%, housing 14.5%, personal effects 11.8%, clothing 8.6%, fuel 4.8%, cultural activities 5.2%; urban

household—food 53.5%, clothing 13.7%, personal effects 11.4%, cultural activities 6.8%, fuel 2.7%, housing 2.6%, transportation and communications 1.1%, other 8.2%.
Population economically active (1982): total 521,506,000; activity rate of total population 52.3% (participation rates: ages 15–64, 83.7%; female 43.7%; unemployed [1987] 2.0%[19]). Urban work force by sector of employment, 1978 (1987): state-run enterprises 74,500,000 (96,540,000); collectives 20,-000,000 (34,880,000); self-employment or privately run enterprises 150,000 (5,690,000).

Price and earnings indexes (1980 = 100)

	1981	1982	1983	1984	1985	1986	1987
Consumer price index	102.5	104.6	106.7	109.6	122.2	129.5	139.0
Earnings index[20]	101.1	104.1	107.7	128.8	151.1	176.0	192.5

Land use (1985): forested 14.8%; meadows and pastures 30.6%; agricultural and under permanent cultivation 10.8%; other 43.8%.

Foreign trade[21]

Balance of trade (current prices)

	1982	1983	1984	1985	1986	1987
Y '000,000	+5,660	+1,650	−3,480	−45,050	−41,310	−14,330
% of total	7.3%	1.9%	2.9%	21.8%	16.0%	4.6%

Imports (1987): U.S.$43,240,000,000 (machinery and transportation equipment 33.8%; products of textile industries, rubber and metal products 22.5%; chemical and related products 11.6%; inedible raw materials 7.7%; food and live animals 5.6%; light industrial products 4.3%). *Major import sources* (1985): Japan 35.6%; United States 12.0%; Hong Kong 11.4%; West Germany 5.7%; Canada 2.7%; Australia 2.7%; Brazil 2.3%; U.S.S.R. 2.3%; Italy 2.2%; United Kingdom 1.8%; France 1.7%.
Exports (1987): U.S.$39,486,000,000 (products of textile industries, rubber and metal products 21.7%; light industrial products 15.9%; food and live animals 12.1%; mineral fuels and lubricants 11.5%; inedible raw materials 9.2%; chemical and related products 5.7%). *Major export destinations* (1985): Hong Kong 26.3%; Japan 22.3%; United States 8.6%; Singapore 7.6%; Jordan 3.6%; U.S.S.R. 3.6%; West Germany 3.1%; Brazil 1.6%; United Kingdom 1.3%; The Netherlands 1.2%; Philippines 1.2%.

Transport and communications

Transport. Railroads (1987): length 39,845 mi, 64,125 km; passenger-mi 176,-700,000,000, passenger-km 284,300,000,000; short ton-mi cargo 648,700,-000,000, metric ton-km cargo 974,100,000,000. Roads (1987): total length 609,750 mi, 981,300 km (paved [1986] 81%). Vehicles (1986): passenger cars and buses 966,149; trucks 2,465,689. Merchant marine (1987): vessels (100 gross tons and over) 1,773; total deadweight tonnage 18,484,230. Air transport (1987): passenger-mi 11,600,000,000, passenger-km 18,600,000,-000; short ton-mi cargo 450,000,000, metric ton-km cargo 660,000,000; airports (1988) with scheduled flights 80.
Communications. Daily newspapers (1986)[3]: total number 222; total circulation, n.a.; circulation per 1,000 population 50. Radio (1987)[3]: total number of receivers 253,900,000 (1 per 4.2 persons). Television (1987)[3]: total number of receivers 92,140,000 (1 per 12 persons). Telephones (1986): 7,059,000 (1 per 149 persons).

Education and health

Education (1986)

	schools	teachers	students	student/teacher ratio
Primary (age 7–13)	820,846	5,414,000	131,825,000	24.3
Secondary (age 13–17)	92,967	2,758,000	48,899,000	17.7
Secondary specialized	15,751	550,000	6,074,000	11.0
Higher	1,054	372,000	1,880,000	5.1

Literacy (1982): total population age 15 and over literate 609,283,011 (72.6%); males literate 358,744,834 (83.5%); females literate 250,538,177 (61.2%).
Health (1987): physicians 1,482,000 (1 per 724 persons); hospital beds 2,685,-000 (1 per 399 persons); infant mortality rate per 1,000 live births 33.0.
Food (1984–86): daily per capita caloric intake 2,628 (vegetable products 91%, animal products 9%); (1983) 133% of FAO recommended minimum requirement.

Military

Total active duty personnel (1987): 3,200,000 (army 71.9%, navy 10.6%, air force 17.5%). *Military expenditure as percent of GNP* (1985): 6.7% (world 6.1%); per capita expenditure U.S.$24.

---

[1]Names of the provinces, autonomous regions, and municipalities are stated in conventional form, followed by Pinyin transliteration; names of capitals are stated in conventional form or Wade–Giles transliteration, followed by Pinyin transliteration. [2]Data for Taiwan, Quemoy, and Matsu are excluded. [3]January 1. [4]Includes 4,600 sq mi (11,900 sq km) not shown separately. [5]Total includes servicemen not assigned to any political division. [6]Based on rural sample population. [7]Excludes arrests for anti-Communist activities. [8]Application of term differs from functional definition in a market economy. [9]Employed only. [10]Detail does not add to total given because of rounding. [11]In state-owned industries only. [12]1979. [13]In constant 1980 prices. [14]1984. [15]Exchange rates and international reserves are based on end-of-year figures. [16]End-of-month figures for exchange rates and international reserves. [17]January to March total. [18]Breakdown of sideline production is for 1985. [19]Rate of waiting for employment in cities and towns. [20]Average annual wage of staff and workers in state-owned enterprises. [21]Imports, c.i.f. (cost, insurance, and freight); exports, f.o.b. (free on board).

Colombia

Official name: República de Colombia (Republic of Colombia).
Form of government: unitary, multiparty republic with two legislative houses (Senate [114]; House of Representatives [199]).
Head of state and government: President.
Capital: Bogotá.
Official language: Spanish.
Official religion: none.
Monetary unit: 1 peso (Col$) = 100 centavos; valuation (Oct. 10, 1988) 1 U.S.$ = Col$318.03; 1 £ = Col$544.63.

Area and population

Commissariats	Capitals	area sq mi	area sq km	population 1985 census
Amazonas	Leticia	42,342	109,665	30,327
Guainía	San Felipe (Obando)	27,891	72,238	9,214
Guaviare	Guaviare	16,342	42,327	35,305
Vaupés	Mitú	25,200	65,268	18,935
Vichada	Puerto Carreño	38,703	100,242	13,770
Departments				
Antioquia	Medellín	24,561	63,612	3,888,067
Atlántico	Barranquilla	1,308	3,388	1,428,601
Bolívar	Cartagena	10,030	25,978	1,197,623
Boyacá	Tunja	8,953	23,189	1,097,618
Caldas	Manizales	3,046	7,888	838,094
Caquetá	Florencia	34,349	88,965	214,473
Cauca	Popayán	11,316	29,308	795,838
Cesar	Valledupar	8,844	22,905	584,631
Chocó	Quibdó	17,965	46,530	242,768
Córdoba	Montería	9,660	25,020	913,636
Cundinamarca	Bogotá	8,735	22,623	1,382,360
Huila	Neiva	7,680	19,890	647,756
La Guajira	Riohacha	8,049	20,848	255,310
Magdalena	Santa Marta	8,953	23,188	769,141
Meta	Villavicencio	33,064	85,635	412,312
Nariño	Pasto	12,845	33,268	1,019,098
Norte de Santander	Cúcuta	8,362	21,658	883,884
Quindío	Armenia	712	1,845	377,860
Risaralda	Pereira	1,598	4,140	625,451
Santander	Bucaramanga	11,790	30,537	1,438,226
Sucre	Sincelejo	4,215	10,917	529,059
Tolima	Ibagué	9,097	23,562	1,051,852
Valle	Cali	8,548	22,140	2,847,087
Intendancies				
Arauca	Arauca	9,196	23,818	70,085
Casanare	Yopal	17,236	44,640	110,253
Putumayo	Mocoa	9,608	24,885	119,815
San Andrés y Providencia	San Andrés	17	44	35,936
Special District				
Bogotá		613	1,587	3,982,941
TOTAL		440,831[1]	1,141,748	27,867,326[2]

Demography

Population (1988): 30,661,000.
Density (1988): persons per sq mi 69.6, persons per sq km 26.9.
Urban–rural (1985): urban 67.2%; rural 32.8%.
Sex distribution (1985): male 49.49%; female 50.51%.
Age breakdown (1985): under 15, 36.1%; 15–29, 31.2%; 30–44, 17.2%; 45–59, 9.5%; 60–74, 4.6%; 75 and over, 1.4%.
Population projection: (1990) 31,686,000; (2000) 36,313,000.
Doubling time: 34 years.
Ethnic composition (1985): mestizo 58.0%; white 20.0%; mulatto 14.0%; black 4.0%; mixed black-Indian 3.0%; Amerindian 1.0%.
Religious affiliation (1984): Roman Catholic 94.8%; other 5.2%.
Major cities (1985): Bogotá 3,974,813; Medellín 1,418,554; Cali 1,323,944; Barranquilla 896,649; Cartagena 491,368.

Vital statistics

Birth rate per 1,000 population (1983–88): 27.9 (world avg. 26.0); (1982) legitimate 75.2%; illegitimate 24.8%.
Death rate per 1,000 population (1983–88): 7.4 (world avg. 9.9).
Natural increase rate per 1,000 population (1983–88): 20.5 (world avg. 16.1).
Total fertility rate (avg. births per childbearing woman; 1981–86): 3.4.
Marriage rate per 1,000 population (1977): 3.5.
Life expectancy at birth (1980–85): male 63.4 years; female 69.2 years.
Major causes of death per 100,000 population (1984): ischemic heart disease 47.7; cerebrovascular disease 37.7; diseases of pulmonary circulation 36.9; homicide 32.7.

National economy

Budget (1986). Revenue: Col$974,699,000,000 (indirect taxes 43.2%, credit resources 23.8%, direct taxes 19.0%). Expenditures: Col$954,176,000,000 (transfer payments 35.3%, capital investments 27.0%, debt service 20.9%).
Public debt (external, outstanding; 1986): U.S.$11,436,900,000.
Tourism (1986): receipts from visitors U.S.$220,000,000; expenditures by nationals abroad U.S.$340,000,000.
Production (metric tons except as noted). Agriculture (1987): sugarcane 2,513,000, plantains 2,473,300, potatoes 2,432,500, rice 1,970,500, cassava 1,285,300, bananas 1,178,800, corn (maize) 1,000,800, coffee (green) 778,440; roundwood (1985) 17,224,000 cu m; fish catch 80,445; livestock (number of live animals; 1986) 23,590,000 cattle, 2,440,000 pigs, 1,959,000 sheep. Mining and quarrying (1987): iron ore 606,764; gold 853,968 troy oz;

silver 168,897 troy oz. Manufacturing (value added in Col$'000,000; 1985): processed food 165,933; beverages 146,848; textiles 137,903; paper products 38,987; pharmaceuticals 31,889; transport equipment 31,420; basic steel 29,201; plastic products 24,086. Construction (1987)[3]: residential 7,552,361 sq m; nonresidential 1,854,604 sq m. Energy production (consumption): electricity (kW-hr; 1985) 27,000,000,000 (26,998,000,000); coal (metric tons; 1986) 10,700,000 (4,800,000); crude petroleum (barrels; 1986) 110,978,000 (76,734,000); petroleum products (metric tons; 1986) 9,100,000 (6,827,000); natural gas (cu m; 1986) 4,275,216,000 (4,275,216,000).
Gross national product (1986): U.S.$35,530,000,000 (U.S.$1,230 per capita).

Structure of gross domestic product and labour force

	1986 in value U.S.$'000,000	1986 % of total value	1980 labour force	1980 % of labour force
Agriculture	8,136	21.1	2,412,413	28.5
Mining	1,008	2.6	49,740	0.6
Manufacturing	8,398	21.7	1,136,735	13.4
Construction	1,448	3.7	242,191	2.9
Public utilities	400	1.0	44,233	0.5
Transp. and commun.	3,734	9.7	352,623	4.2
Trade	4,805	12.4	1,261,633	14.9
Finance	2,739	7.1	278,210	3.2
Pub. admin., defense	3,079	8.0	1,998,460	23.6
Services	4,887	12.7	690,762[4]	8.2[4]
Other				
TOTAL	38,634	100.0	8,467,000	100.0

Population economically active (1985): total 9,558,000; activity rate 34.3% (participation rates: over age 12, 49.4%; female 32.8%; unemployed 4.3%).

Price and earnings indexes (1980 = 100)

	1981	1982	1983	1984	1985	1986	1987
Consumer price index	127.5	158.8	190.2	220.8	273.9	325.7	401.5
Monthly earnings index[5]	102.4	106.2	112.2	119.3	116.7	121.4	...

Household income and expenditure. Average household size (1985) 4.7; sources of income: wages 49.3%, self-employment 36.6%, transfer payments 6.2%; expenditure: food 35.7%, transportation 14.1%, housing 11.5%, health 6.1%.
Land use (1985): forested 47.2%; pastures 28.9%; agricultural 5.5%.

Foreign trade

Balance of trade (current prices)

	1981	1982	1983	1984	1985	1986
U.S.$'000,000	−1,729.0	−1,841.8	−1,390.7	−590.4	−179.9	+1,537.6
% of total	22.6%	22.9%	18.4%	7.9%	2.5%	17.7%

Imports (1986): U.S.$3,852,085,000 (machinery 24.9%, chemicals 10.4%, transport equipment 9.2%, steel products 7.5%, plastic products 4.0%, crude petroleum 3.9%). *Major import sources:* U.S. 36.1%; W.Ger. 6.6%; Venezuela, 4.9%; Spain 4.3%; France 4.0%; Brazil 3.6%.
Exports (1986): U.S.$5,107,936,000 (coffee 58.5%, petroleum and petroleum products 13.0%, fruits 3.9%, flowers 2.9%, cotton 1.7%, textile apparel 1.3%). *Major export destinations:* U.S. 30.0%; W.Ger. 20.6%; The Netherlands 5.2%; Venezuela 2.9%; U.K. 2.6%; France 2.6%.

Transport and communications

Transport. Railroads (1986): route length 3,255 km; passenger-km 180,000,000; metric ton-km cargo 696,000,000. Roads (1986): total length 106,218 km (paved 10%). Vehicles (1986): cars 840,776; trucks and buses 391,433. Merchant marine (1987): vessels (100 gross tons and over) 93; deadweight tonnage 597,376. Air transport (1986): passenger-km 1,974,658,000; metric ton-km cargo 252,042,000; airports (1988) 101.
Communications. Daily newspapers (1987): 30; circulation 1,861,500; circulation per 1,000 population 61. Radio (1986): 7,980,000 receivers (1 per 3.5 persons). Television (1987): 5,500,000 receivers (1 per 5.5 persons). Telephones (1986): 2,289,087 (1 per 13 persons).

Education and health

Education (1986)

	schools	teachers	students	student/ teacher ratio
Primary	36,979	135,924	4,002,543	29.4
Secondary[6]	6,336	107,084	2,136,239	19.9
Higher	231	43,447	402,438	9.3

Educational attainment (1985). Percent of population age 25 and over having: no schooling 15.3%; primary education 50.1%; secondary 25.4%; higher 6.8%; not stated 2.4%. *Literacy* (1985): population age 18 and over literate 10,714,936 (69.1%).
Health (1983): physicians 21,778 (1 per 1,969 persons); hospital beds (1982) 28,880 (1 per 586 persons); infant mortality rate 40.0.
Food (1984–86): daily per capita caloric intake 2,550 (vegetable products 85%, animal products 15%); (1983) 111% of FAO minimum requirement.

Military

Total active duty personnel (1987): 70,200 (army 81.2%, navy 12.8%, air force 6.0%). *Military expenditure as percent of GNP* (1985): 1.2% (world 6.1%); per capita expenditure U.S.$15.

---

[1]Detail does not add to total given because of rounding. [2]Census total adjusted for underenumeration is 29,265,499. [3]Includes 11 urban centres. [4]Includes unemployed not previously employed. [5]Real wages in the industrial sector. [6]Secondary includes vocational and teacher training.

Comoros[1]

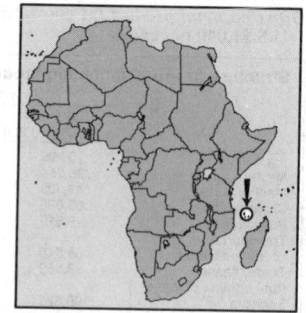

Official name: Jumhurīyat al-Qumur al-Ittihādīyah al-Islāmīyah (Arabic); République Fédéral Islamique des Comores (French) (Federal Islamic Republic of the Comoros).
Form of government: federal Islamic republic with one legislative house (Federal Assembly [42]).
Head of state and government: President.
Capital: Moroni.
Official languages: Arabic; French.
Official religion: Islam.
Monetary unit: 1 Comorian franc (CF) = 100 centimes; valuation (Oct. 10, 1988) 1 U.S.$ = CF 316.13; 1 £ = CF 541.38.

Area and population

Governorates/Islands[3]	Capitals	area sq mi	area sq km	population 1988 estimate[2]
Moili (Mohéli)	Fomboni	112	290	22,676
Ngazidja (Grande Comore)	Moroni	443	1,148	233,955
Ndzouani (Anjouan)	Mutsamudu	164	424	179,600
TOTAL		719	1,862	436,231

Demography

Population (1988): 433,000.
Density (1988): persons per sq mi 602.2, persons per sq km 232.5.
Urban–rural (1985): urban 25.2%; rural 74.8%.
Sex distribution (1985): male 49.72%; female 50.28%.
Age breakdown (1985): under 15, 48.3%; 15–29, 24.8%; 30–44, 13.6%; 45–59, 8.1%; 60–74, 4.1%; 75 and over, 1.1%.
Population projection: (1990) 463,000; (2000) 644,000.
Doubling time: 21 years.
Ethnic composition (1980): Comorian (a mixture of Bantu, Arab, and Malagasy peoples) 96.9%; Makua (a Bantu people from East Africa) 1.6%; French 0.4%; other 1.1%.
Religious affiliation (1980): Sunnī Muslim 99.7%; Christian 0.2%; Bahā'ī 0.1%.
Major cities (1980): Moroni 21,000[4]; Mutsamudu 16,883; Domoni 7,147; Ouani 6,936; Tsembehou 6,578.

Vital statistics

Birth rate per 1,000 population (1987): 47.0 (world avg. 26.0).
Death rate per 1,000 population (1987): 14.0 (world avg. 9.9).
Natural increase rate per 1,000 population (1987): 33.0 (world avg. 16.1).
Total fertility rate (avg. births per childbearing woman; 1987): 7.0.
Marriage rate per 1,000 population: n.a.
Divorce rate per 1,000 population: n.a.
Life expectancy at birth (1987): male 53.0 years; female 57.0 years.
Major causes of death per 100,000 population: n.a.; however, major diseases (1980) include malaria (afflicts 80% of the adult population), tuberculosis, leprosy, and kwashiorkor (a nutritional deficiency disease).

National economy

Budget (1986). Revenue: CF 18,509,000,000 (tax revenue 41.2%, of which consumption tax on imported items 17.5%, export duties 6.6%; external grants applied to development 36.7%; external grants applied to current revenue 14.6%; nontax revenue 7.3%). Expenditures: CF 27,752,000,000 (development expenditures 62.6%; current expenditures 37.4%, of which public debt 10.2%, education, youth, and sports 8.9%, defense 3.1%, health 2.3%).
Public debt (external, outstanding; 1986): U.S.$156,000,000.
Tourism (1986)[5]: receipts from visitors U.S.$2,000,000; expenditures by nationals abroad U.S.$13,000,000.
Production (metric tons except as noted). Agriculture, forestry, fishing (1986)[5]: cassava 93,000, coconuts 47,000, bananas 36,000, sweet potatoes 18,000, rice 16,000, corn (maize) 6,000, copra 3,000, pulses 3,000, cloves 788[6,7], vanilla 258[6,7], ylang-ylang 60[6,7]; livestock (number of live animals) 95,000 goats, 86,000 cattle, 9,000 sheep, 4,000 asses; roundwood, n.a.; fish catch (1985) 5,200. Mining and quarrying: sand and gravel for local construction. Manufacturing (1987): products include processed vanilla and ylang-ylang, cement, handicrafts, soaps, soft drinks, aluminum kitchen utensils, and clothing. Construction: n.a. Energy production (consumption): electricity (kW-hr; 1986) 12,000,000 (12,000,000); coal, none (none); crude petroleum, none (none); petroleum products (metric tons; 1986) none (13,000); natural gas, none (none).
Population economically active (1985): total 117,216; activity rate of total population 29.6% (participation rates: ages 15–64, 53.1%; female 26.2%; unemployed [1985] 13.3%).

Price and earnings indexes (1979 = 100)

	1977	1978	1979	1980	1981	1982	1983
Consumer price index	75.5	87.9	100.0	111.2	131.9	177.2	188.5
Daily earnings index[8]	...	...	100.0	...	...	...	133.3

Household income and expenditure. Average household size (1985) 5.6; income per household: n.a.; sources of income: n.a.; expenditure (1983)[9]:

food and beverages 56.0%, energy 14.4%, clothing and footwear 10.0%, transportation and communication 6.6%, health care 5.0%, recreation 3.0%, tobacco 3.0%, other 2.0%.
Gross national product (at current market prices; 1986): U.S.$130,000,000 (U.S.$280 per capita).

Structure of gross domestic product and labour force

	1986 in value CF '000,000	1986 % of total value	1980 labour force	1980 % of labour force
Agriculture	19,053	37.0	53,063	53.3
Mining	...	...	62	0.1
Manufacturing	2,060	4.0	3,946	4.0
Construction			3,267	3.3
Public utilities }	5,149	10.0	129	0.1
Transportation and communications	2,060	4.0	2,118	2.1
Trade, restaurants, hotels	12,873	25.0	1,873	1.9
Finance, insurance	...	...	237	0.2
Public admin., defense }	8,239	16.0	2,435	2.5
Services			4,646	4.7
Other	2,060	4.0	27,687[10]	27.8[10]
TOTAL	51,494	100.0	99,463	100.0

Land use (1985)[5]: forested 16.0%; meadows and pastures 7.0%; agricultural and under permanent cultivation 45.0%; other 32.0%.

Foreign trade[11]

Balance of trade (current prices)

	1981	1982	1983	1984	1985	1986
CF '000,000	−4,330	−4,291	−5,680	−15,700	−9,433	−5,796
% of total	32.5%	25.0%	27.7%	71.7%	40.1%	29.1%

Imports (1986): CF 12,849,000,000 (rice 14.0%, petroleum products 8.0%, vehicles 7.0%, cement 5.0%, unspecified commodities 66.0%). *Major import sources* (1985): France 41.4%; Madagascar 19.9%; Pakistan 9.4%; Kenya and Tanzania 8.4%; China 4.0%.
Exports (1986): CF 7,053,000,000 (vanilla 77.0%, cloves 11.6%, ylang-ylang 9.0%). *Major export destinations* (1985): France 65.5%; United States 21.4%; Madagascar 5.0%; West Germany 3.4%.

Transport and communications

Transport. Railroads: none. Roads (1985): total length 466 mi, 750 km (paved 53%). Vehicles (1983): passenger cars, 3,600; trucks and buses, 2,000. Merchant marine (1987): vessels (100 gross tons and over) 5; total deadweight tonnage 2,814. Air transport (1983)[12]: passenger arrivals and departures 30,537; cargo loaded and unloaded 172 metric tons; airports (1988) with scheduled flights 3.
Communications. Daily newspapers: none. Radio (1987): total number of receivers 100,000 (1 per 4.2 persons). Television: total number of receivers, none. Telephones (1983): 496 (1 per 740 persons).

Education and health

Education (1980–81)

	schools	teachers	students	student/teacher ratio
Primary (age 7–13)	236	1,617[13]	61,469[13]	38.0[13]
Secondary	32	432	13,528	31.3
Voc., teacher tr.	4	17	270	15.9

Educational attainment (1980). Percent of population age 25 and over having: no formal schooling 56.7%; Qur'anic school education 8.3%; primary 3.6%; secondary 2.0%; higher 0.2%; not specified 29.2%. *Literacy* (1980): total population age 15 and over literate 82,053 (46.3%); males literate 46,586 (54.2%); females literate 35,467 (39.0%).
Health (1982): physicians 20 (1 per 17,300 persons); hospital beds 813 (1 per 439 persons); infant mortality rate per 1,000 live births (1987) 96.0.
Food (1984–86)[5]: daily per capita caloric intake 2,110 (vegetable products 95%, animal products 5%); (1983) 91% of FAO recommended minimum requirement.

Military[14]

Total active duty personnel (1987): 700–800 (army 100%). *Military expenditure as percent of GNP* (1983): 1.9% (world 6.1%); per capita expenditure U.S.$6.

[1]Excludes Mayotte, a *collectivité territoriale* ("territorial collectivity") of France, unless otherwise indicated. [2]Mid-September. [3]Island names in Comorian Swahili and French, respectively. [4]1986. [5]Includes Mayotte. [6]Excludes Mayotte. [7]Export only. [8]Construction sector only. [9]Weights of consumer price index components. [10]Not adequately defined. [11]Import figures c.i.f.; export figures f.o.b. [12]Air Comores only. [13]1982–83. [14]In 1983 France assumed sole responsibility for the defense of the Comoros.

Congo

Official name: République Populaire du Congo (People's Republic of the Congo).
Form of government: people's republic with one legislative body (People's National Assembly [153]).
Head of state and government: President (Chairman of the Central Committee).
Capital: Brazzaville.
Official language: French.
Official religion: none.
Monetary unit: 1 CFA franc (CFAF) = 100 centimes; valuation (Oct. 10, 1988) 1 U.S.$ = CFAF 316.13; 1 £ = CFAF 541.38.

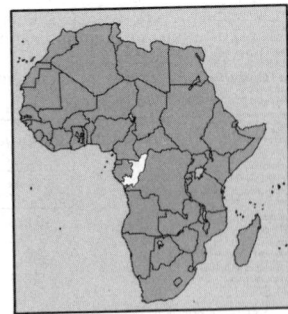

Area and population

| | | area | | population |
| | | | | 1984 |
Regions	Capitals	sq mi	sq km	census
Bouenza	Madingou	4,734	12,260	150,603
Cuvette	Owando	28,900	74,850	135,744
Kouilou	Pointe-Noire	5,274	13,660	74,870
Lékoumou	Sibiti	8,089	20,950	68,287
Likouala	Impfondo	25,500	66,044	49,505
Niari	Loubomo	10,011[1]	25,930[1]	110,003
Plateaux	Djambala	14,826	38,400	109,663
Pool	Kinkala	13,124	33,990	184,263
Sangha	Ouesso	21,544[2]	55,800[2]	34,213
Communes				
Brazzaville	—	25	65	585,812
Loubomo	—	5	12	49,134
Mossendjo	—	1	1	14,469
Nkayi	—	2	5	36,540
Ouesso	—	2	2	11,939
Pointe-Noire	—	13	34	294,203
TOTAL		132,047	342,000	1,909,248

Demography

Population (1988): 2,266,000.
Density (1987): persons per sq mi 17.2, persons per sq km 6.6.
Urban–rural (1984): urban 51.1%; rural 48.9%.
Sex distribution (1985): male 49.31%; female 50.69%.
Age breakdown (1985): under 15, 43.6%; 15–29, 25.8%; 30–44, 15.6%; 45–59, 9.5%; 60–74, 4.6%; 75 and over, 0.9%.
Population projection: (1990) 2,447,000; (2000) 3,600,000.
Doubling time: 27 years.
Ethnic composition (1983): Kongo 51.5%; Teke 17.3%; Mboshi 11.5%; Mbete 4.8%; Punu 3.0%; Sanga 2.7%; Maka 1.8%; Pygmy 1.5%; other 5.9%.
Religious affiliation (1980): Roman Catholic 53.9%; Protestant 24.9%; African Christian 14.2%; traditional beliefs 4.8%; other 2.2%.
Major cities (1984): Brazzaville 585,812; Pointe-Noire 294,203; Loubomo 49,134; Nkayi 36,540; Owando 16,021.

Vital statistics

Birth rate per 1,000 population (1980–85): 44.5 (world avg. 29.0); legitimate, n.a.; illegitimate, n.a.
Death rate per 1,000 population (1980–85): 18.6 (world avg. 11.0).
Natural increase rate per 1,000 population (1980–85): 25.9 (world avg. 18.0).
Total fertility rate (avg. births per childbearing woman; 1980–85): 6.0.
Marriage rate per 1,000 population: n.a.
Divorce rate per 1,000 population: n.a.
Life expectancy at birth (1980–85): male 44.9 years; female 48.1 years.
Morbidity (reported cases per 100,000 population; 1985): malaria 2,306.0; diarrhea 845.6; measles 491.2; gonorrhea 300.9; tuberculosis 36.3.

National economy

Budget (1988). Revenue: CFAF 284,000,000,000 (external financing 44.7%, petroleum revenue 24.7%, taxes and duties 16.4%, customs duties 12.0%). Expenditures: CFAF 284,000,000,000 (public debt 44.7%, administrative staff 27.6%, transfers 13.2%, investment 11.3%).
Public debt (external, outstanding; 1986): U.S.$2,860,700,000.
Tourism (1986): receipts from visitors U.S.$7,000,000; expenditures by nationals abroad U.S.$67,000,000.
Production (metric tons except as noted). Agriculture, forestry, fishing (1986): cassava 620,000, sugarcane 510,000, pineapples 110,000, bananas 34,000, palm oil 16,000, peanuts (groundnuts) 16,000, yams 14,000, sweet potatoes 14,000, corn (maize) 8,000, rice 3,000, coffee 2,000, cacao beans 2,000; livestock (number of live animals) 184,000 goats, 71,000 cattle, 63,000 sheep; roundwood 2,574,000 cu m; fish catch 29,994. Mining and quarrying (1986): lead 7,000; copper 250; gold 7,041 troy oz. Manufacturing (1985): raw sugar 51,010; cement 50,895; soap 2,146; wheat flour 1,048; cigarettes 1,027; peanut oil 1,000; beer 881,667 hectolitres; soft drinks 279,000 hectolitres; wine 58,150 hectolitres; veneer sheets 61,807 cu m; footwear 1,121,000 pairs. Construction: n.a. Energy production (consumption): electricity (kW-hr; 1986) 235,000,000 (292,000,000); coal, none (n.a.); crude petroleum (barrels; 1986) 43,910,000 (3,933,000); petroleum products (metric tons; 1986) 508,000 (525,000); natural gas (cu m; 1986) 34,000,000 (n.a.).
Land use (1985): forested 62.2%; meadows and pastures 29.3%; agricultural and under permanent cultivation 2.0%; other 6.5%.

Gross national product (at current market prices; 1986): U.S.$2,020,000,000 (U.S.$1,040 per capita).

Structure of gross domestic product and labour force

| | 1984 | | 1985 | |
	in value CFAF '000,000	% of total value	labour force	% of labour force
Agriculture	70,299	7.7	434,000	61.2
Mining	395,854	43.0		
Manufacturing	42,509	4.6		
Construction	65,096	7.1		
Public utilities	9,510	1.0	86,000	12.1
Transportation and communications	68,576	7.5		
Trade, finance	98,659	10.7		
Pub. admin., defense				
Services	169,625	18.4	190,000	26.7
Other				
TOTAL	920,128	100.0	710,000	100.0

Population economically active (1985): total 710,000; activity rate of total population 40.8% (participation rates: ages 15–64, 69.4%; female 39.3%; unemployed, n.a.).

Price and earnings indexes (1980 = 100)

	1981	1982	1983	1984	1985	1986	1987[3]
Consumer price index	117.0	132.0	142.3	160.3	170.1	174.3	174.8
Earnings index	...	...	...	...	...	...	...

Household income and expenditure. Average household size (1980) 4.7; income per household, n.a.; sources of income: n.a.; expenditure: n.a.

Foreign trade[4]

Balance of trade (current prices)

	1980	1981	1982	1983	1984	1985
CFAF '000,000,000	92.1	121.5	120.4	194.9	297.2	182.2
% of total	31.5%	38.0%	22.6%	31.8%	40.4%	22.9%

Imports (1985): CFAF 306,198,400,000 (machinery and transport equipment 29.6%, of which transport equipment 9.2%; food and beverages 15.4%; iron and steel 11.8%; chemicals and related products 6.7%; textiles 2.8%; petroleum products 2.7%; plastic and rubber goods 2.3%; precision instruments 2.1%). *Major import sources:* France 38.8%; Italy 7.0%; United States 5.6%; West Germany 4.0%; Japan 2.9%; The Netherlands 2.3%; Belgium–Luxembourg 2.0%.
Exports (1985): CFAF 488,365,700,000 (crude petroleum 93.3%; wood and wood products 2.5%; pearls and precious stones 1.0%; coffee, cocoa, and tobacco 0.2%). *Major export destinations:* United States 60.0%; Spain 13.9%; France 10.9%; The Netherlands 6.0%; Italy 1.8%; Belgium–Luxembourg 1.0%.

Transport and communications

Transport. Railroads (1985): length 498 mi, 802 km; passenger-mi 268,000,000, passenger-km 432,000,000; short ton-mi cargo 353,000,000, metric ton-km cargo 516,000,000. Roads (1985): total length 6,835 mi, 11,000 km (paved 5%). Vehicles (1982): passenger cars 30,500; trucks and buses 78,600. Merchant marine (1987): vessels (100 gross tons and over) 21; total deadweight tonnage 10,840. Air transport[5] (1986): passenger-mi 147,619,000, passenger-km 237,571,000; short ton-mi cargo 26,339,000, metric ton-km cargo 38,455,000; airports (1988) with scheduled flights 14.
Communications. Daily newspapers (1986): total number 3; total circulation 24,000; circulation per 1,000 population 11. Radio (1986): total number of receivers 200,000 (1 per 10 persons). Television (1987): total number of receivers 5,500 (1 per 396 persons). Telephones (1986): 18,541 (1 per 115 persons).

Education and health

Education (1984–85)

	schools	teachers	students	student/ teacher ratio
Primary (age 6–13)	1,522	7,612	458,338	60.2
Secondary (age 14–18)	247	5,188	199,073	38.4
Voc., teacher tr.	19	1,073	5,477	22.2
Higher	1	...	9,385	...

Educational attainment[6] (1974). Percent of population age 15 and over having: secondary education 30%, of which males 37%, females 23%. *Literacy* (1985): total population age 15 and over literate 620,000 (62.9%); males literate 332,000 (71.4%); females literate 288,000 (55.4%).
Health: physicians (1980) 278 (1 per 5,986 persons); hospital beds (1978) 6,876 (1 per 224 persons); infant mortality rate per 1,000 live births (1980–85) 81.0.
Food (1984–86): daily per capita caloric intake 2,599 (vegetable products 93%, animal products 7%); (1983) 109% of FAO recommended minimum requirement.

Military

Total active duty personnel (1988): 8,800 (army 90.9%, navy 3.4%, air force 5.7%). *Military expenditure as percent of GNP* (1985): 3.4% (world 6.1%); per capita expenditure U.S.$34.

---

[1]Mossendjo is included with Niari. [2]Ouesso is included with Sangha. [3]First quarter. [4]Import figures are c.i.f. [5]Air Afrique only. [6]For the Commune of Brazzaville only.

Costa Rica

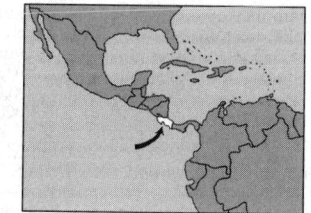

Official name: República de Costa Rica (Republic of Costa Rica).
Form of government: unitary multiparty republic with one legislative house (Legislative Assembly [57]).
Head of state and government: President.
Capital: San José.
Official language: Spanish.
Official religion: Roman Catholicism.
Monetary unit: 1 Costa Rican colón (₡) = 100 céntimos; valuation (Oct. 10, 1988) 1 U.S.$ = ₡77.76; 1 £ = ₡133.17.

Area and population

Provinces	Capitals	area sq mi	area sq km	population 1984 census
Alajuela	Alajuela	3,766	9,753	427,962
Cartago	Cartago	1,206	3,125	271,671
Guanacaste	Liberia	3,915	10,141	195,208
Heredia	Heredia	1,026	2,656	197,575
Limón	Limón	3,548	9,188	168,076
Puntarenas	Puntarenas	4,354	11,277	265,883
San José	San José	1,915	4,960	890,434
TOTAL		19,730	51,100	2,416,809

Demography

Population (1988): 2,672,000.
Density (1988): persons per sq mi 135.4, persons per sq km 52.3.
Urban–rural (1986): urban 50.3%; rural 49.7%.
Sex distribution (1984): male 49.99%; female 50.01%.
Age breakdown (1984): under 15, 36.6%; 15–29, 31.1%; 30–44, 16.7%; 45–59, 9.1%; 60–74, 4.9%; 75 and over, 1.6%.
Population projection: (1990) 2,804,000; (2000) 3,572,000.
Doubling time: 24 years.
Ethnic composition (1980): European 86.8%; mestizo 7.0%; black/mulatto 2.0%; Chinese 1.9%; Amerindian 0.5%; other 1.8%.
Religious affiliation (1984): Roman Catholic 92.4%; other (mostly Protestant) 7.6%.
Major cities (1984): San José 241,464; Limón 33,925; Alajuela 29,273; Puntarenas 28,390; Cartago 23,928.

Vital statistics

Birth rate per 1,000 population (1985): 33.3 (world avg. 29.0); (1984) legitimate 62.8%; illegitimate 37.2%.
Death rate per 1,000 population (1985): 4.3 (world avg. 11.0).
Natural increase rate per 1,000 population (1985): 29.0 (world avg. 18.0).
Total fertility rate (avg. births per childbearing woman; 1984): 3.3.
Marriage rate per 1,000 population (1985): 7.8.
Divorce rate per 1,000 population (1983): 1.0.
Life expectancy at birth (1980–85): male 70.5 years; female 75.7 years.
Major causes of death per 100,000 population (1984): diseases of the circulatory system 117.7, of which ischemic heart disease 58.6, cerebrovascular disease 29.7; malignant neoplasms (cancers) 81.0, of which stomach cancer 20.9; diseases of the respiratory system 38.6; accidents 33.2.

National economy

Budget (1986). Revenue: ₡54,563,700,000 (tax revenue 84.5%, of which taxes on goods and services 28.2%, social security contributions 24.7%, taxes on foreign trade 21.1%; nontax revenue 15.5%). Expenditures: ₡65,126,600,000 (health 19.3%; social security and welfare 19.2%; education 16.2%; economic services 12.3%; defense 2.8%).
Public debt (external, outstanding; 1986): U.S.$3,582,200,000.
Gross national product (at current market prices; 1986): U.S.$3,790,000,000 (U.S.$1,420 per capita).

Structure of gross domestic product and labour force

	1986 in value U.S.$'000,000	1986 % of total value	labour force[1]	% of labour force
Agriculture	955	19.1	229,832	26.9
Mining	} 1,099	22.0	146,283	17.1
Manufacturing				
Construction	228	4.6	49,393	5.8
Public utilities	152	3.0	} 48,629	5.7
Transp. and commun.	368	7.4		
Trade	836	16.8	} 162,877	19.1
Finance	658	13.2		
Public admin. and defense	483	9.7	} 209,319	24.5
Services	208	4.2		
Other			7,885[2]	0.9
TOTAL	4,987	100.0	854,218	100.0

Production (metric tons except as noted). Agriculture, forestry, fishing (1986): sugarcane 2,650,000, bananas 1,000,000, rice 186,000, coffee 128,000, corn (maize) 104,000, oranges 81,000, palm oil 40,000, dry beans 31,000, sorghum 31,000, cocoa beans 5,000, other products include cut flowers and ornamental plants grown for export; livestock (number of live animals): 2,415,000 cattle, 222,000 pigs, 4,000,000 chickens; roundwood (1985) 3,055,000 cu m; fish catch 20,899, of which shrimps 8,710. Mining

and quarrying (1985): gold 35,000 troy oz. Manufacturing (value added in ₡'000,000; 1984): food products 9,836; alcoholic and nonalcoholic beverages 3,734; petroleum products 1,622; wearing apparel 1,418; drugs and medicines 1,225; textiles 1,129; wood products 1,075. Construction (gross value of buildings authorized in ₡'000,000; 1984): residential 1,559; nonresidential 413. Energy production (consumption): electricity (kW-hr; 1986) 2,918,000,000 (2,995,000,000); coal, none (none); crude petroleum (barrels; 1986) none (3,299,000); petroleum products (metric tons; 1986) 387,000 (610,000); natural gas, none (none).
Population economically active (1985): total 887,456; activity rate of total population 35.7% (participation rates: ages 15–69, 55.8%; female 26.1%; unemployed [1987] 5.5%).

Price index (1980 = 100)

	1981	1982	1983	1984	1985	1986	1987
Consumer price index	137.1	260.6	345.6	386.9	445.1	497.8	581.6
Earnings index[3]	120.7	183.1	269.0	323.1	406.5	...	...

Tourism: receipts from visitors (1986) U.S.$133,000,000; expenditures by nationals abroad (1983) U.S.$36,000,000.
Family income and expenditure: average household size (1984) 4.84; income per urban family (1983) ₡181,416 (U.S.$4,415), income per rural family ₡98,328 (U.S.$2,393); sources of income: n.a.; expenditure (1974)[5]: food 40.8%, housing 12.3%, clothing and footwear 10.0%, education and recreation 9.2%, household furnishings 8.2%, energy 6.6%, transportation 6.5%, other 6.4%.
Land use (1985): forested 32.4%; meadows and pastures 45.0%; agricultural and under permanent cultivation 11.9%; other 10.7%.

Foreign trade[6]

Balance of trade (current prices)

	1980	1981	1982	1983	1984	1985	1986
₡'000,000	−3,297	−1,728	+2,628	−411	+814	−810	+5,041
% of total	16.1%	3.8%	4.2%	0.6%	0.9%	0.8%	4.2%

Imports (1985): ₡55,408,000,000 (primary and intermediate goods 43.8%, consumer goods 22.3%, capital goods 21.0%, fuels and lubricants 8.2%). *Major import sources:* United States 37.1%; Venezuela 9.8%; Japan 8.7%; Guatemala 5.1%; West Germany 5.0%.
Exports (1985): ₡49,242,000,000 (coffee 32.4%, nonagricultural manufactured products 30.6%, bananas 21.3%, cattle and meat 5.5%, other agricultural products 9.5%). *Major export destinations:* United States 41.4%; West Germany 9.1%; Guatemala 5.9%; El Salvador 4.6%; Honduras 4.0%.

Transport and communications

Transport. Railroads (1987): route length 435 mi, 700 km; passenger-mi 56,000,000, passenger-km 90,000,000; short ton-mi cargo 102,700,000, metric ton-km cargo 150,000,000. Roads (1986): total length 21,942 mi, 35,313 km (paved 14%). Vehicles (1986): passenger cars 119,067; trucks and buses 76,287. Merchant marine (1987): vessels (100 gross tons and over) 24; total deadweight tonnage 13,636. Air transport (1986)[7]: passenger-mi 347,000,000, passenger-km 558,000,000; short-ton mi cargo 20,163,000, metric ton-km cargo 29,437,000; airports (1988) with scheduled flights 6.
Communications. Daily newspapers (1986): total number 5; total circulation 200,500; circulation per 1,000 population 78. Radio (1986): total number of receivers 200,000 (1 per 13 persons). Television (1987): total number of receivers 470,000 (1 per 5.5 persons). Telephones (1986): 343,530 (1 per 7.5 persons).

Education and health

Education (1985)

	schools	teachers	students	student/ teacher ratio
Primary (age 5–11)	3,091	11,526	362,877	31.5
Secondary (age 12–17)	...	...	87,038	
Vocational	...	...	25,493	
Higher	14[8]	...	63,771	

Educational attainment (1984). Percent of economically active population age 25 and over having: no formal schooling 8.3%; incomplete primary education 28.6%; complete primary 26.3%; secondary 22.6%; postsecondary and higher 14.2%. *Literacy* (1984): total population age 15 and over literate 1,419,365 (92.6%); males literate 702,045 (92.6%); females literate 717,320 (92.6%).
Health: physicians (1982) 1,929 (1 per 1,198 persons); hospital beds (1986) 7,382 (1 per 345 persons); infant mortality per 1,000 live births (1984) 18.9.
Food (1983–85): daily per capita caloric intake 2,772 (vegetable products 85%, animal products 15%); (1983) 114% of FAO recommended minimum requirement.

Military

Military expenditure as percent of GNP (1985): 1.0% (world 6.1%); per capita expenditure U.S.$12. The army was officially abolished in 1948. About 9,500 long-term volunteers made up of 6,000 civil guards and 3,500 rural guards conduct both police and paramilitary activities.

[1]Employed labour force. [2]Undefined activities. [3]Wages of insured persons in nonagricultural activities. [4]Average urban household size (1984) 4.5, rural 5.1. [5]Based on survey of selected low- and middle-income families in San José only. [6]Import figures are f.o.b. in balance of trade and c.i.f. for commodities and trading partners. [7]LACSA (Costa Rican Airlines) only. [8]1983.

Côte d'Ivoire

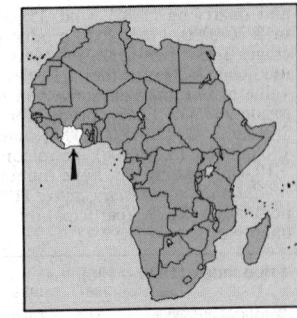

Official name: République de Côte d'Ivoire (Republic of Côte d'Ivoire [Ivory Coast][1]).
Form of government: single-party republic with one legislative house (National Assembly [175]).
Head of state and government: President.
Capital[2]: Abidjan (de facto; legislative).
  Capital designate: Yamoussoukro (de jure; administrative).
Official language: French.
Official religion: none.
Monetary unit: 1 CFA franc (CFAF) = 100 centimes; valuation (Oct. 10, 1988) 1 U.S.$ = CFAF 316.13; 1 £ = CFAF 541.38.

Area and population		area		population
		sq mi	sq km	1975 census
Departments[3]	Capitals			
Abengourou	Abengourou	2,664	6,900	177,692
Abidjan	Abidjan	5,483	14,200	1,389,141
Aboisso	Aboisso	2,413	6,250	148,823
Adzopé	Adzopé	2,019	5,230	162,837
Agboville	Agboville	1,486	3,850	141,970
Biankouma	Biankouma	1,911	4,950	75,711
Bondoukou	Bondoukou	6,382	16,530	296,551
Bongouanou	Bongouanou	2,151	5,570	216,907
Bouaflé	Bouaflé	2,189	5,670	164,817
Bouaké	Bouaké	9,189	23,800	808,048
Bouna	Bouna	8,290	21,470	84,290
Boundiali	Boundiali	3,048	7,895	96,449
Dabakala	Dabakala	3,734	9,670	56,230
Daloa	Daloa	4,483	11,610	265,529
Danané	Danané	1,776	4,600	170,249
Dimbokro	Dimbokro	3,293	8,530	258,116
Divo	Divo	3,058	7,920	202,511
Ferkessedougou	Ferkessedougou	6,845	17,728	90,423
Gagnoa	Gagnoa	1,737	4,500	174,018
Guiglo	Guiglo	5,463	14,150	137,672
Issia	Issia	1,386	3,590	104,081
Katiola	Katiola	3,637	9,420	77,875
Korhogo	Korhogo	4,826	12,500	276,816
Lakota	Lakota	1,054	2,730	76,105
Man	Man	2,722	7,050	278,659
Mankono	Mankono	4,116	10,660	82,358
Odienné	Odienné	7,954	20,600	124,010
Oumé	Oumé	927	2,400	85,486
Sassandra	Sassandra	6,768	17,530	116,644
Séguéla	Séguéla	4,340	11,240	75,181
Soubré	Soubré	3,193	8,270	75,350
Tingréla	Tingréla	849	2,200	35,829
Touba	Touba	3,367	8,720	77,786
Zuénoula	Zuénoula	1,093	2,830	98,792
TOTAL		123,847[4]	320,763	6,702,866

Demography

Population (1988): 11,634,000.
Density (1987): persons per sq mi 93.9, persons per sq km 36.3.
Urban–rural (1986): urban 47.0%; rural 53.0%.
Sex distribution (1985): male 51.09%; female 48.91%.
Age breakdown (1985): under 15, 45.1%; 15–29, 25.4%; 30–44, 15.6%; 45–59, 9.2%; 60–74, 4.0%; 75 and over 0.7%.
Population projection: (1990) 12,657,000; (2000) 19,290,000.
Doubling time: 23 years.
Ethnic composition (1975): Akan 41.4%; Kru 16.7%; Voltaic 15.7%; Malinke 14.9%; Southern Mande 10.2%; other 1.1%.
Religious affiliation (1980): folk religionist 43.8%; Christian 32.0%; Muslim 24.0%; other 0.2%.
Major cities (1984): Abidjan 1,850,000; Bouaké 220,000; Yamoussoukro 120,000; Gagnoa 93,500[5]; Daloa 59,500.

Vital statistics

Birth rate per 1,000 population (1985–86): 45.5 (world avg. 26.0).
Death rate per 1,000 population (1985–86): 15.3 (world avg. 9.9).
Natural increase rate per 1,000 population (1985–86): 30.2 (world avg. 16.1).
Total fertility rate (avg. births per childbearing woman; 1985–86): 6.6.
Life expectancy at birth (1984): male 51.0 years; female 54.0 years.
Major causes of death per 100,000 population: n.a.; however, the major infectious diseases include malaria, dysentery, yaws, pneumonia, leprosy.

National economy

Budget (1988). Revenue: CFAF 493,500,000,000 (import taxes and duties 37.2%, income taxes 23.3%, indirect taxes 19.0%, export taxes and duties 16.1%). Expenditures: 493,500,000,000 (personnel 61.0%, administration 15.2%, equipment 0.4%).
Public debt (external, outstanding; 1986): U.S.$6,500,200,000.
Tourism (1986): receipts from visitors U.S.$70,000,000; expenditures by nationals abroad U.S.$96,000,000.
Production (metric tons except as noted). Agriculture (1986): yams 2,996,000, cassava 1,500,000, sugarcane 1,500,000, plantains 1,400,000, corn (maize) 550,000, cacao beans 520,000, rice 460,000, coconuts 323,000, pineapples 300,000, coffee 280,000, cotton 206,000, palm oil 180,000; livestock (number of live animals) 1,502,000 sheep, 1,496,000 goats, 881,000 cattle; roundwood (1985) 12,486,000 cu m; fish catch 97,174. Mining and quarrying (1987): di-

amonds 600,000 carats. Manufacturing (1986): cement 770,000; beer 1,300,000 hectolitres; carbonated beverages 495,000 hectolitres; synthetic fibres 5,000,000 metres; other principal industries include food processing, cotton fibre and textiles, and chemicals (fertilizers, insecticides, paints). Construction (in CFAF; 1984): 62,000,000,000. Energy production (consumption): electricity (kW-hr; 1986) 1,817,000,000 (1,817,000,000); coal, none (n.a.); crude petroleum (barrels; 1986) 7,336,000 (12,931,000); petroleum products (metric tons; 1986) 1,694,000 (1,368,000).
Gross national product (1986): U.S.$7,730,000,000 (U.S.$740 per capita).

Structure of gross domestic product and labour force				
	1987		1985	
	in value CFAF '000,000,000	% of total value	labour force	% of labour force
Agriculture	890[6]	28.8	2,452,000	60.5
Manufacturing, construction, mining, and public utilities	640[6]	20.6	409,000	10.1
Trade, finance, transp. and commun., pub. admin., defense, and services	1,570[6]	50.6	1,192,000	29.4
TOTAL	3,100	100.0	4,053,000	100.0

Population economically active (1985): total 4,053,000; activity rate of total population 41.3% (participation rates: ages 15–64 71.4%; female 34.7%).

Price and earnings indexes (1980 = 100)							
	1981	1982	1983	1984	1985	1986	1987
Consumer price index	108.8	116.8	123.5	129.0	131.4	140.1	147.5
Annual wage index	107.0	117.4	117.4	117.4	117.4	117.4	117.4

Household income and expenditure. Average household size (1980) 4.5; average annual income per household CFAF 500,000; sources of income: self-employment 49.9%, wages 44.9%, transfers and other resources 5.2%; expenditure (1979): food 51.1%, housing 11.6%, clothing 8.4%.
Land use (1985): forested 23.2%; meadows and pastures 9.4%; agricultural and under permanent cultivation 12.9%; other 54.5%.

Foreign trade[7]

Balance of trade (current prices)						
	1981	1982	1983	1984	1985	1986
CFAF '000,000,000	+7.8	+36.8	+92.5	+525.8	+545.0	+451.4
% of total	0.6%	2.0%	6.2%	28.5%	26.1%	24.1%

Imports (1986): CFAF 709,044,000,000 (machinery and transport equipment 22.7%, of which nonelectrical machinery 9.8%, transport equipment 8.8%, electrical machinery 4.1%; food products 17.8%; crude petroleum 14.7%; chemicals 14.2%). *Major import sources:* France 31.0%; Nigeria 9.9%; Japan 6.2%; W.Ger. 5.7%; U.S. 4.1%.
Exports (1986): CFAF 1,160,441,000,000 (cacao beans 33.9%; coffee 20.1%; energy products 8.1%; wood 6.6%; cacao butter 5.6%; chemicals 2.6%; cotton 2.4%; pineapples 2.2%). *Major export destinations:* The Netherlands 18.7%; France 14.2%; U.S. 10.5%; Italy 7.8%; W.Ger. 5.5%; U.S.S.R. 5.1%.

Transport and communications

Transport. Railroads (1987): length 549 km; passenger-km 857,800,000[8]; metric ton-km cargo 530,200,000[8]. Roads (1986): total length 55,000 km (paved 9%). Vehicles (1984): passenger cars 182,956; trucks and buses 52,491. Merchant marine (1987): vessels (100 gross tons and over) 56; total deadweight tonnage 149,337. Air transport[9] (1986): passenger-km 320,124,000; metric ton-km cargo 52,237,000; airports (1988) with scheduled flights 15.
Communications. Daily newspapers (1987): total number 2; total circulation 130,000; circulation per 1,000 population 12. Radio (1986): 1,210,000 receivers (1 per 8.8 persons). Television (1987): 625,000 receivers (1 per 18 persons). Telephones (1980): 88,000 (1 per 97 persons).

Education and health

Education (1984)	schools	teachers	students	student/ teacher ratio
Primary (age 7–12)	5,976	28,561	1,179,456	41.3
Secondary (age 13–19)	218[10]	4,569[10]	245,043	...
Voc., teacher tr.	38[10]	1,947[11]	21,758	...
Higher	1[10]	1,204[12]	19,660	...

Educational attainment (1975). Percent of population age 6 and over having: no formal schooling 75.3%; primary education 17.3%; secondary 5.1%; higher 0.5%. *Literacy* (1985): population age 15 and over literate 57.3%.
Health (1982): physicians 502 (1 per 17,847 persons); hospital beds 10,062 (1 per 891 persons); infant mortality rate per 1,000 live births (1985–86) 100.
Food (1984–86): daily per capita caloric intake 2,550 (vegetable products 94%, animal products 6%); (1983) 112% of FAO recommended minimum.

Military

Total active duty personnel (1988): 7,100 (army 77.5%, navy 9.8%, air force 12.7%). *Military expenditure as percent of GNP* (1984): 1.3% (world 6.0%); per capita expenditure U.S.$8.

[1]From 1986, Côte d'Ivoire has requested that the French version of the country's name be utilized as the official protocol version in all languages. [2]Yamoussoukro officially named capital in 1983, but transfer of government functions remains incomplete. [3]Fifteen additional departments were created in 1985, for which separate data are not available. [4]Detail does not add to total given because of rounding. [5]1986. [6]Value is derived from given GDP total and corresponding percentage. [7]Imports c.i.f.; exports f.o.b. [8]1984; traffic includes Burkina Faso. [9]Air Afrique only. [10]1979–80. [11]1981. [12]1982.

Cuba

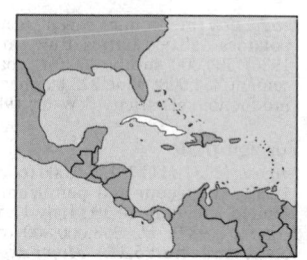

Official name: República de Cuba
(Republic of Cuba).
Form of government: unitary socialist
republic with one legislative house
(National Assembly of the People's
Power [510]).
Head of state and government:
President.
Capital: Havana.
Official language: Spanish.
Official religion: none.
Monetary unit: 1 peso = 100 centavos;
valuation (Oct. 10, 1988)
1 peso = U.S.$1.30 = £0.76.

Area and population

Provinces	Capitals	area sq mi	area sq km	population 1987 estimate[1]
Camagüey	Camagüey	6,174	15,990	715,115
Ciego de Avila	Ciego de Avila	2,668	6,910	347,086
Cienfuegos	Cienfuegos	1,613	4,178	348,676
Ciudad de la Habana[2]	—	281	727	2,036,799
Granma	Bayamo	3,232	8,372	767,563
Guantánamo	Guantánamo	2,388	6,186	479,212
Holguín	Holguín	3,591	9,301	962,236
La Habana[3]	Havana	2,213	5,731	621,780
Las Tunas	Las Tunas	2,544	6,589	470,846
Matanzas	Matanzas	4,625	11,978	589,041
Pinar del Río	Pinar del Río	4,218	10,925	671,987
Sancti Spíritus	Sancti Spíritus	2,604	6,744	416,988
Santiago de Cuba	Santiago de Cuba	2,382	6,170	957,627
Villa Clara	Santa Clara	3,345	8,662	791,123
Special municipality				
Isla de la Juventud	Nueva Gerona	926	2,398	69,834
TOTAL		42,804	110,861	10,245,913

Demography

Population (1988): 10,421,000.
Density (1988): persons per sq mi 243.5, persons per sq km 94.0.
Urban–rural (1987): urban 71.9%; rural 28.1%.
Sex distribution (1987): male 50.37%; female 49.63%.
Age breakdown (1987): under 15, 24.8%; 15–29, 30.7%; 30–44, 19.7%; 45–59, 13.2%; 60 and over, 11.6%.
Population projection: (1990) 10,683,000; (2000) 11,844,000.
Doubling time: 63 years.
Ethnic composition (1981): white 66.0%; mulatto 21.9%; black 12.0%.
Religious affiliation (1980): nonreligious 48.7%; Roman Catholic 39.6%; atheist 6.4%; Protestant 3.3%; Afro-American Spiritist 1.6%; other 0.4%.
Major cities (1987): Havana 2,036,799; Santiago de Cuba 364,554; Camagüey 265,588; Holguín 199,861; Santa Clara 182,349.

Vital statistics

Birth rate per 1,000 population (1987): 17.4 (world avg. 26.0).
Death rate per 1,000 population (1987): 6.3 (world avg. 9.9).
Natural increase rate per 1,000 population (1987): 11.1 (world avg. 16.1).
Total fertility rate (avg. births per childbearing woman; 1987): 1.8.
Marriage rate per 1,000 population (1987): 7.6.
Divorce rate per 1,000 population (1987): 3.1.
Life expectancy at birth (1983–84): male 72.6 years; female 76.1 years.
Major causes of death per 100,000 population (1985): diseases of the circulatory system 277.8, of which ischemic heart diseases 151.6, cerebrovascular disease 62.0; malignant neoplasms (cancers) 116.9; diseases of the respiratory system 65.8.

National economy

Budget (1987). Revenue: 11,574,600,000 pesos. Expenditures: 11,689,600,000 pesos (production capital 32.0%; education and public health 23.6%; social, cultural, and scientific activities 15.7%; defense, internal security 11.1%; housing, community services 7.5%).
Public debt (external, outstanding; 1985)[4]: U.S.$5,937,000,000.
Production (metric tons except as noted). Agriculture, forestry, fishing (1986): sugarcane 67,000,000, roots and tubers 675,000, rice 571,000, oranges 390,-000, tomatoes 254,000, grapefruit 240,000, bananas 205,000, tobacco 46,000, jute 27,000, coffee 21,000; livestock (number of live animals): 6,400,000 cattle, 2,400,000 pigs, 718,000 horses; roundwood (1985) 3,344,000 cu m; fish catch 244,600, of which spiny lobster 11,800. Mining and quarrying (1986): chromite 40,000[5]; nickel and cobalt (metal content) 35,102. Manufacturing (value of production in '000,000 pesos; 1986): processed food (excluding fish and refined sugar) 1,988; refined sugar 1,628; nonelectrical machinery 890; fuels 548; chemicals and chemical products 527; beverages and tobacco products 508; construction materials 427; processed fish, crustaceans, and mollusks 337. Construction (1984): residential 989,000 sq m; nonresidential 1,145,000 sq m. Energy production (consumption): electricity (kW-hr; 1986) 13,167,000,000 (13,167,000,000); coal (metric tons; 1986) none (100,000); crude petroleum (barrels; 1987) 5,954,000 (46,817,000[6]); petroleum products (metric tons; 1986) 6,111,000 (9,886,000); natural gas (cu m; 1987) 26,191,000 (26,191,000).
Household income and expenditure. Average household size (1981) 4.2; average annual income per household (1982) 3,680 pesos (U.S.$4,330); sources of income (1982): wages and salaries 57.3%, bonuses and other payments 42.7%; personal consumption (1986): purchases of food 25.4%, other pur-chases 63.2%, imputed value of provided goods and services 9.9%, imputed value of self-produced and consumed food 1.5%.
Population economically active (1981): total 3,540,692; activity rate of total population 36.4% (participation rates: ages 15–64, 57.2%; female 31.3%; unemployed [1983] 4.4%).

Price and earnings indexes (1980 = 100)

	1980	1981	1982	1983	1984	1985	1986
Consumer implicit deflator index	100.0	106.4	114.1	120.1	124.2	126.6	128.4
Annual earnings index	100.0	114.7	119.1	121.7	125.7	126.9	127.1

Tourism (1986): receipts from visitors U.S.$136,500,000; expenditures by nationals abroad, n.a.
Gross national product (at current market prices; 1984): U.S.$26,920,000,000 (U.S.$2,690 per capita).

Structure of global social product and labour force

	1986 in value '000,000 pesos	1986 % of total value	1986 labour force[7]	1986 % of labour force
Agriculture	3,906	14.8	601,700	18.4
Mining } Manufacturing } Public utilities	9,812	37.1	725,900	22.2
Construction	2,317	8.7	322,000	9.9
Transp. and commun.	2,019	7.6	224,200	6.9
Finance	—	—	20,500	0.6
Trade	8,190	30.9	371,400	11.4
Public administration	—	—	168,700	5.2
Services	—	—	776,500	23.8
Other	230	0.9	51,800	1.6
TOTAL	26,473	100.0	3,262,700	100.0

Land use (1985): forested 24.6%; meadows and pastures 23.9%; agricultural and under permanent cultivation 29.3%; other 22.2%.

Foreign trade[8]

Balance of trade (current prices)

	1981	1982	1983	1984	1985	1986
'000,000 pesos	−890	−597	−687	−1,751	−2,043	−2,244
% of total	9.5%	5.7%	5.9%	13.8%	14.6%	17.4%

Imports (1986): 7,569,000,000 pesos (mineral fuels and lubricants 33.5%, nonelectrical machinery and apparatuses 19.3%, transport equipment 7.0%, electrical machinery and apparatuses 4.4%, cereals 3.8%). *Major import sources:* U.S.S.R. 70.2%; E.Ger. 4.0%; Japan 3.5%; Bulgaria 2.5%; Czech. 2.4%.
Exports (1986): 5,325,000,000 pesos (sugar 76.4%, petroleum products 6.5%, nickel ore 5.7%, citrus fruits 2.8%, fish products 2.3%). *Major export destinations:* U.S.S.R. 73.9%; E.Ger. 4.8%; Bulgaria 2.8%; Czech. 2.3%.

Transport and communications

Transport. Railroads (1986): route length[9] 3,033 mi, 4,881 km; passenger-km 2,212,000,000; metric ton-km cargo 2,472,000,000. Roads (1984): total length 21,000 mi, 34,000 km (paved 30%). Vehicles (1984): passenger cars 200,100; trucks and buses 164,500. Merchant marine (1987): vessels (100 gross tons and over) 422, total deadweight tonnage 1,291,122. Air transport (1986): passenger-km 2,637,000,000; metric ton-km cargo 34,800,000; airports with scheduled flights (1988) 12.
Communications. Daily newspapers (1986): total number 17; total circulation 1,290,000; circulation per 1,000 population 126. Radio (1986): 3,232,-000 receivers (1 per 3.2 persons). Television (1987): 2,000,000 receivers (1 per 5.2 persons). Telephones (1986): 543,200 (1 per 19 persons).

Education and health

Education (1986–87)

	schools	teachers	students	student/ teacher ratio
Primary (age 6–11)	9,837	61,490	1,000,971	16.3
Secondary (age 12–17)	1,275	64,859	800,732	12.3
Voc., teacher tr.	798	33,246	352,927	10.6
Higher	35	21,573	256,619	11.9

Educational attainment (1981). Percent of population age 25 and over having: no formal schooling or some primary education 39.6%; completed primary 26.6%; secondary 29.6%; higher 4.2%. *Literacy* (1980): total population age 15 and over literate 6,087,000 (91.1%); males literate 3,101,000 (91.1%); females literate 2,986,000 (91.1%).
Health (1986): physicians 25,567 (1 per 399 persons); hospital beds 54,028 (1 per 189 persons); infant mortality rate per 1,000 live births (1987) 13.3.
Food (1984–86): daily per capita caloric intake 3,107 (vegetable products 78%, animal products 22%); (1986) 128% of FAO recommended minimum requirement.

Military

Total active duty personnel (1987): 175,500 (army 82.6%, navy 6.8%, air force 10.6%)[10]. *Military expenditure as percent of GNP* (1985): 5.4% (world 6.1%); per capita expenditure: U.S.$158.

[1]January 1. [2]Province coextensive with the city of Havana. [3]Province bordering the city of Havana on the east, south, and west. [4]Includes external long-term private debt not guaranteed by the government. [5]1985. [6]1986. [7]State sector only; excludes military and unemployed. [8]Imports c.i.f.; exports f.o.b. [9]Figures exclude 4,830 mi (7,773 km) of nonpublic railways serving mostly sugar plantations or sugar factories. [10]Additional Soviet forces total 8,000.

Cyprus

Island of Cyprus

Area: 3,572 sq mi, 9,251 sq km.
Population (1988): 720,000.

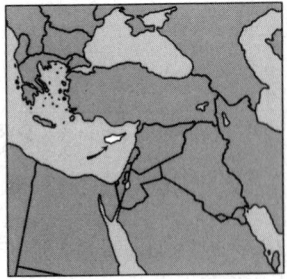

Two states currently exist de facto on the island of Cyprus: the Republic of Cyprus, predominantly Greek in character, occupying the southern two-thirds of the island, which is the original and still the internationally recognized de jure government of the whole island; and the Turkish Republic of Northern Cyprus (TRNC), proclaimed unilaterally Nov. 15, 1983, on territory originally secured for the Turkish Cypriot population by the July 20, 1974, intervention of Turkey, one of the guarantor powers entitled by Cyprus' 1960 independence treaties to act unilaterally "with the sole aim of reestablishing the state of affairs created by the ... treaty." The TRNC has received no international recognition and the two ethnic communities have been unable to negotiate the reestablishment of a single state. Provision of separate data below is necessitated by the decade-long lack of unified data.

Republic of Cyprus

Official name: Kipriakí Demokratía (Greek); Kıbrıs Cumhuriyeti (Turkish) (Republic of Cyprus).
Form of government: unitary multiparty republic with a unicameral legislature (House of Representatives [80]).
Head of state and government: President.
Capital: Nicosia.
Official languages: Greek; Turkish.
Monetary unit: 1 Cyprus pound (£C) = 1,000 mils; valuation (Oct. 10, 1988) 1£C = U.S.$2.04 = £1.20.

Area and population[1]

Districts	Capitals	area		population
		sq mi	sq km	1982 census
Famagusta	Famagusta	...	...	24,187
Larnaca	Larnaca	433	1,121	83,151
Limassol	Limassol	538	1,393	143,847
Nicosia	Nicosia	...	...	207,290
Paphos	Paphos	539	1,396	45,023
TOTAL		2,276	5,896	503,498

Demography

Population (1988): 553,000.
Urban-rural (1982): urban 63.6%; rural 36.4%.
Age breakdown (1986): under 15, 25.4%; 15–29, 25.3%; 30–44, 20.8%; 45–59, 14.3%; 60–69, 7.0%; 70 and over, 7.2%.
Ethnic composition (1982): Greek 99.2%; other 0.8%.
Religious affiliation (1988): predominantly Greek Orthodox.
Major cities (1982): Nicosia 123,298; Limassol 100,254; Larnaca 35,823.

Vital statistics

Birth rate per 1,000 population (1987): 18.5[2] (world avg. 26.0).
Death rate per 1,000 population (1987): 8.9[2] (world avg. 9.9).
Natural increase rate per 1,000 population (1987): 9.6[2] (world avg. 16.1).
Life expectancy at birth (1987): male 72.3 years; female 77.0 years.

National economy

Budget (1988): Revenue: £C 386,800,000 (indirect taxes 41.5%, direct taxes 32.1%). Expenditures: £C 582,500,000 (ordinary 83.1%, development 11.7%).
Tourism (1987): receipts U.S.$666,500,000; expenditures U.S.$66,500,000.
Household expenditure (1984): food and beverages 25.1%, transportation and communications 16.8%, clothing and footwear 12.3%, household goods 11.8%, housing 6.8%.
Gross national product (1986): U.S.$2,920,000,000 (U.S.$4,360 per capita).

Structure of gross domestic product and labour force

	1987			
	in value £C '000,000	% of total value	labour force	% of labour force
Agriculture	135.2	7.5	35,700	13.9
Mining	7.5	0.4	900	0.4
Manufacturing	269.2	15.0	45,500	17.8
Construction	168.4	9.4	22,100	8.6
Public utilities	33.5	1.9	1,300	0.5
Transp. and commun.	172.0	9.6	13,500	5.3
Trade	361.1	20.2	50,300	19.6
Finance	248.4	13.9	12,400	4.8
Pub. admin., defense	133.6	7.5 }	44,000	17.2
Services	178.2	9.9 }		
Other	84.5[3]	4.7[3]	30,500[4]	11.9[4]
TOTAL	1,791.6	100.0	256,300	100.0

Production (metric tons except as noted). Agriculture (1987): grapes 173,000, potatoes 150,000, citrus fruit (mainly oranges) 147,300; livestock (head; 1986) 500,000 sheep, 360,000 goats, 221,000 pigs. Manufacturing (1987): cement 854,000; wine 223,000 hectolitres; footwear 7,800,000 pairs. Energy production: electricity (kW-hr; 1987) 1,512,000,000.

Foreign trade

Imports (1987): £C 711,400,000 (consumer goods 21.7%, transport equipment 10.4%, petroleum and petroleum products 6.1%). *Major import sources:* United Kingdom 14.3%; Italy 11.5%; Japan 10.2%.
Exports (1987): £C 298,000,000 (clothing 23.0%, potatoes 7.4%, footwear 5.4%, citrus fruit 5.2%). *Major export destinations:* United Kingdom 21.5%; Libya 8.0%; Saudi Arabia 5.3%.

Transport and communications

Transport. Roads (1986): total length 13,784 km. Vehicles (1986): passenger cars 127,400; trucks and buses 54,600. Merchant marine (1987): vessels (100 gross tons and over) 1,341; total deadweight tonnage 27,322,868. Air transport (1987): passenger-km 2,150,607,000; metric ton-km cargo 225,981,000; airports (1988) 3.
Communications. Daily newspapers (1987): 10; total circulation 85,550; circulation per 1,000 population 157. Radio (1986): 171,500 receivers (1 per 3.2 persons). Television (1987): 88,800 receivers (1 per 6.0 persons). Telephones (1986): 153,300 (1 per 3.5 persons).

Education and health

Education (1986–87)

	schools	teachers	students	student/ teacher ratio
Primary (age 5–12)	373	2,225[5]	54,254	
Secondary (age 12–18)	94	2,639	40,627	15.4
Vocational	10	458	4,094	8.9
Higher	15	282	3,006	10.7

Literacy (1980): population age 15 and over literate 93.1%.
Health (1987): physicians 1,195 (1 per 570 persons); hospital beds 4,256 (1 per 160 persons); infant mortality rate per 1,000 live births 12.0.

Turkish Republic of Northern Cyprus

Official name: Kuzey Kıbrıs Türk Cumhuriyeti (Turkish) (Turkish Republic of Northern Cyprus).
Capital: Lefkoşe (Nicosia).
Official language: Turkish.
Monetary unit: 1 Turkish lira (LT) = 100 kurush; valuation (Oct. 10, 1988) 1 U.S.$ = LT 1,698; 1£ = LT 2,908.

Area and population

Provinces	Administrative centres	area		population
		sq mi	sq km	1978 estimate
Lefkoşe (Nicosia)	Lefkoşe	...	...	68,286
Gazimagosa (Famagusta)	Gazimagosa	...	...	55,647
Girne (Kyrenia)	Girne	247	640	22,807
TOTAL		1,295	3,355	146,740

Population (1988): 167,000.
Ethnic composition (1985): Turkish 98.7%, other 1.3%.

Structure of gross domestic product and labour force

	1986		1985	
	in value LT '000,000	% of total value	labour force	% of labour force
Agriculture	28,016	14.6	20,595	33.6
Manufacturing	20,513	10.7	6,213	10.1
Construction	15,892	8.3	4,454	7.3
Transp. and commun.	13,408	7.0	4,004	6.5
Trade	44,011	23.0	5,386	8.8
Finance	8,512	4.4	1,531	2.5
Real estate	5,407	2.8	...	...
Pub. admin.	34,108	17.8	14,475	23.6
Services	10,444	5.4	4,641	7.6
Other (customs duties)	11,465	6.0	—	—
TOTAL	191,776	100.0	61,299[6]	100.0

Budget (1987). Revenue: LT 103,079,616,000 (1985; indirect taxes 19.6%, direct taxes 18.8%, grants 53.1%). Expenditures: LT 45,788,700,000 (current expenditures 78.1%, defense 7.8%).
Imports (1986): U.S.$153,169,500 (machinery and transport equipment 24.6%). *Major import sources:* Turkey 45.8%; United Kingdom 14.8%; Italy 7.2%.
Exports (1986): U.S.$52,007,823 (food and live animals 74%). *Major export destinations:* United Kingdom 63.1%; Turkey 14.8%.

Education (1986–87)

	schools	teachers	students	student/ teacher ratio
Primary (age 7–12)	161	751	20,781	27.7
Secondary (age 13–18)	35	706	11,103	15.7
Vocational	10	192	1,748	9.1
Higher	4	84	1,649	19.6

Health (1986): physicians 118 (1 per 1,379 persons); hospital beds 755 (1 per 215 persons); infant mortality rate per 1,000 live births 19.0.

[1]Areas under government control; includes UN Buffer Zone and U.K. Sovereign Base Areas. [2]Includes imputed adjustment for de jure population of Turkish sector. [3]Bank service charges. [4]Includes 8,700 unemployed. [5]1985–86. [6]Total of available detail.

Czechoslovakia

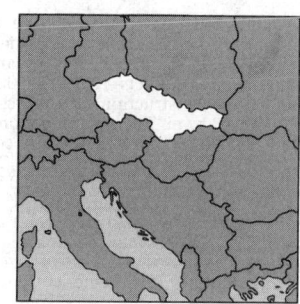

Official name: Československá Socialistická Republika (Czechoslovak Socialist Republic).
Form of government: federal socialist republic with two legislative houses (Chamber of Nations [150]; Chamber of the People [200]).
Chief of state: President.
Head of government: Premier.
Capital: Prague.
Official languages: Czech; Slovak.
Official religion: none.
Monetary unit: 1 koruna (Kčs) = 100 halura; valuation (Oct. 10, 1988) 1 U.S.$ = Kčs 5.43; 1 £ = Kčs 9.30.

Area and population

Republics Regions	Capitals	area sq mi	area sq km	population 1986 estimate
Czech Socialist Republic	Prague			
Jihočeský	České Budějovice	4,380	11,345	695,095
Jihomoravský	Brno	5,802	15,028	2,056,733
Severočeský	Ústí nad Labem	3,019	7,819	1,184,132
Severomoravský	Ostrava	4,273	11,067	1,960,788
Středočeský	Prague	4,245	10,994	1,134,537
Východočeský	Hradec Králové	4,340	11,240	1,243,316
Západočeský	Plzeň	4,199	10,875	872,341
Slovak Socialist Republic	Bratislava			
Středoslovenský	Banská Bystrica	6,944	17,986	1,585,574
Východoslovenský	Košice	6,251	16,191	1,468,975
Západoslovenský	Bratislava	5,595	14,492	1,717,115
Capital Cities				
Prague	—	192	496	1,194,873
Bratislava	—	142	367	420,901
TOTAL		49,382	127,900	15,534,380

Demography

Population (1988): 15,604,000.
Density (1988): persons per sq mi 316.0, persons per sq km 122.0.
Urban–rural (1985): urban 74.1%; rural 25.9%.
Sex distribution (1987): male 48.71%; female 51.29%.
Age breakdown (1987): under 15, 24.2%; 15–29, 21.0%; 30–44, 22.6%; 45–59, 15.7%; 60–74, 11.7%; 75 and over, 4.8%.
Population projection: (1990) 15,664,000; (2000) 16,086,000.
Doubling time: n.a.; population growth is negligible.
Ethnic composition (1986): Czech 63.2%; Slovak 31.5%; Hungarian 3.8%; Polish 0.5%; German 0.4%; Ukrainian 0.3%; other 0.3%.
Religious affiliation (1980): Roman Catholic 65.6%; atheist 20.1%; Czechoslovak Church 4.4%; Evangelist Church of Czech Brethren 1.4%; other 8.5%.
Major cities (1987): Prague 1,203,700; Bratislava 427,500; Brno 387,400; Ostrava 329,500; Košice 227,600.

Vital statistics

Birth rate per 1,000 population (1986): 14.2 (world avg. 26.0); legitimate 93.0%; illegitimate 7.0%.
Death rate per 1,000 population (1986): 11.9 (world avg. 9.9).
Natural increase rate per 1,000 population (1986): 2.2 (world avg. 16.1).
Total fertility rate (avg. births per childbearing woman; 1986): 2.0.
Marriage rate per 1,000 population (1986): 7.7.
Divorce rate per 1,000 population (1986): 2.4.
Life expectancy at birth (1985): male 67.3 years; female 74.7 years.
Major causes of death per 100,000 population (1986): diseases of the circulatory system 651.4; malignant neoplasms (cancers) 238.8; bronchitis, emphysema, and asthma 86.7; accidents, poisoning, and violence 78.0, of which suicides 18.8; diseases of the digestive system 47.0.

National economy

Budget (1986). Revenue: Kčs 368,696,000,000 (receipts from enterprises 72.1%; taxes 9.2%). Expenditures: Kčs 365,949,000,000 (education, health, social welfare, and culture 26.9%; national economy 24.2%; defense 7.7%).
Tourism: receipts from visitors (1985) U.S.$307,000,000; expenditures by nationals abroad (1983) U.S.$229,000,000.
Production (metric tons except as noted). Agriculture, forestry, fishing (1986): sugar beets 7,134,000, wheat 5,585,000, potatoes 3,545,000, barley 3,535,000, corn (maize) 942,000; livestock (number of live animals; 1987) 6,651,000 pigs, 5,073,000 cattle, 1,104,000 sheep, 48,726,000 chickens; roundwood 18,803,000 cu m; fish catch 20,723. Mining and quarrying (1986): iron ore 1,784,000; copper 26,182; lead 19,800; zinc 8,300. Manufacturing (1986): crude steel 15,112,000; rolled steel 11,180,000; cement 10,298,000; sulfuric acid 1,292,000; plastic and resins 1,140,000; chemical fertilizers 921,361; cotton fabrics 606,457,000 m; beer 22,789,000 hectolitres; other alcoholic beverages 1,224,000 hectolitres; road motor vehicles 245,229 units. Construction (1985): 5,498,000 sq m. Energy production (consumption): electricity (kW-hr; 1986) 84,775,000,000 (86,232,000,000); coal (metric tons; 1986) 126,429,000 (126,870,000); crude petroleum (barrels; 1986) 970,000 (116,500,000); petroleum products (metric tons; 1986) 13,153,000 (12,536,000); natural gas (cu m; 1986) 638,000,000 (17,080,000,000).
Land use (1986): agricultural 40.4%; forested 35.8%; meadows and pastures 13.0%; other 10.8%.
Gross national product (at current market prices; 1986): U.S.$142,550,000,000 (U.S.$9,175 per capita).

Structure of net material product and labour force

	1986 in value Kčs '000,000	% of total value	labour force[1]	% of labour force[1]
Agriculture	45,608	8.0	989,419	12.8
Mining and manufacturing	340,920	59.8	2,889,471	37.3
Construction	61,000	10.7	780,559	10.1
Public utilities	—	—	137,190	1.8
Transportation and communications	29,075	5.1	516,332	6.7
Trade	89,506	15.7	867,041	11.2
Finance	—	—	[2]	[2]
Pub. admin., defense	—	—	174,071	2.2
Services	—	—	1,396,251[2]	18.0[2]
Other	3,991[3]	0.7[3]	...	...
TOTAL	570,100	100.0	7,750,334	100.0[4]

Public debt (external, outstanding, to the West; 1985): U.S.$2,800,000,000.
Population economically active[1, 5] (1986): total 7,750,334; activity rate of total population 49.8% (participation rates: working age 88.2%; female 46.0%; unemployed, n.a.).

Price and earnings indexes (1977 = 100)

	1979	1980	1981	1982	1983	1984	1985
Consumer price index	106.4	109.5	110.4	116.0	117.1	118.2	120.9
Monthly earnings index	105.5	107.9	109.5	112.0	114.1	116.1	118.1

Household income and expenditure. Average household size (1986) 2.9; income per household (1985) Kčs 77,970 (U.S.$12,100); sources of income: wages and salaries 62.8%, transfer payments 20.1%, other 17.1%; expenditure (1986): food 26.4%, services 12.0%, clothing and footwear 8.5%.

Foreign trade

Balance of trade (current prices)

	1980	1981	1982	1983	1984	1985	1986
Kčs '000,000	−1,377	+1,413	+1,345	+826	+493	−505	−3,672
% of total	0.9%	0.8%	0.7%	0.4%	0.2%	0.2%	1.5%

Imports (1986): Kčs 125,449,000,000 (machinery and transport equipment 35.7%, of which industrial machinery 9.4%, agricultural and construction machinery 8.4%, transport equipment 7.4%; fuels and other energy 31.2%; consumer goods 9.1%; mineral ores 8.1%; food 7.2%; chemicals 6.7%).
Major import sources: U.S.S.R. 44.1%; East Germany 9.6%; Poland 8.7%; Hungary 5.5%; West Germany 4.9%.
Exports (1986): Kčs 121,777,000,000 (machinery and transport equipment 57.4%, of which industrial machinery 12.9%, road vehicles and parts 8.2%; consumer goods 16.2%; chemicals 5.4%; mineral fuels and lubricants 3.5%).
Major export destinations: U.S.S.R. 43.5%; East Germany 8.9%; Poland 8.7%; Hungary 5.1%; West Germany 4.6%; Bulgaria 3.2%; Yugoslavia 2.8%; Austria 2.4%; Romania 2.1%.

Transport and communications

Transport. Railroads (1986): length 8,150 mi, 13,116 km; passenger-mi 12,387,000,000, passenger-km 19,935,000,000; short ton-mi cargo 47,536,000,000, metric ton-km cargo 69,401,000,000. Roads (1987): total length 45,556 mi, 73,316 km (paved 100%). Vehicles (1985): passenger cars 2,694,994; trucks and buses 425,174. Merchant marine (1987): vessels (100 gross tons and over) 18; total deadweight tonnage 220,363. Air transport (1986): passenger-mi 1,368,900,000, passenger-km 2,203,057,000; short ton-mi cargo 39,937,000, metric ton-km cargo 58,307,000; airports (1988) 14.
Communications. Daily newspapers (1986): total number 30; total circulation 4,372,000; circulation per 1,000 population 280. Radio (1985): 4,208,538 receivers (1 per 3.7 persons). Television (1986): 4,368,000 receivers (1 per 3.5 persons). Telephones (1986): 3,707,000 (1 per 4.2 persons).

Education and health

Education (1986–87)

	schools	teachers	students	student/teacher ratio
Primary (age 6–14)	6,274	97,385	2,088,750	21.4
Secondary (age 15–18)	343	9,723	134,103	13.8
Voc., teacher tr.	561	17,044	257,968	15.1
Higher	36	19,459	169,011	8.7

Educational attainment (1980). Percent of adult population having: less than full primary education 1.2%; primary and less than full secondary 52.6%; full secondary 41.2%; higher 5.0%. Literacy (1985): total population age 15 and over literate 11,739,911 (100%); males literate 5,626,006 (100%); females literate 6,113,905 (100%).
Health (1987): physicians 48,414 (1 per 321 persons); hospital beds 122,842 (1 per 124 persons); infant mortality rate per 1,000 live births (1986) 13.9.
Food (1984–86): daily per capita caloric intake 3,473 (vegetable products 66%, animal products 34%); (1983) 145% of FAO recommended minimum requirement.

Military

Total active duty personnel (1987): 201,000 (army 72.1%; navy, none; air force 27.9%). Military expenditure as percent of GNP (1985): 5.8% (world 6.1%); per capita expenditure U.S.$511.

[1]End of 1986. [2]Services include finance. [3]Includes other activities of the material sphere. [4]Detail does not add to total given because of rounding. [5]Excludes women on maternity leave and includes workers of working age, which is 15–59 for men and 15–54 for women.

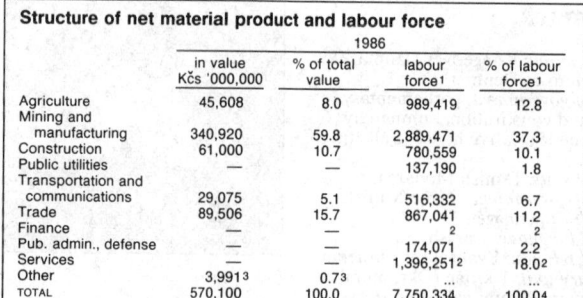

Denmark

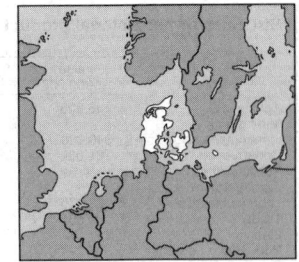

Official name: Kongeriget Danmark
(Kingdom of Denmark).
Form of government: parliamentary
state and constitutional monarchy
with one legislative house (Folketing
[179]).
Chief of state: Danish Monarch.
Head of government: Prime Minister.
Capital: Copenhagen.
Official language: Danish.
Official religion: Evangelical Lutheran.
Monetary unit: 1 krone (Dkr; plural
kroner) = 100 øre; valuation (Oct. 10,
1988) 1 U.S.$ = Dkr 7.13;
1 £ = Dkr 12.21.

Area and population[1]		area		population
		sq mi	sq km	1988 estimate[2]
Counties	Capitals			
Århus	Århus	1,761	4,561	591,993
Bornholm	Rønne	227	588	46,642
Frederiksborg	Hillerød	520	1,347	339,914
Fyn	Odense	1,346	3,486	457,070
København	—	203	526	605,127
Nordjylland	Ålborg	2,383	6,173	483,675
Ribe	Ribe	1,209	3,131	217,973
Ringkøbing	Ringkøbing	1,874	4,853	266,554
Roskilde	Roskilde	344	891	215,164
Sønderjylland	Åbenrå	1,520	3,938	250,132
Storstrøm	Nykøbing	1,312	3,398	257,161
Vejle	Vejle	1,157	2,997	329,590
Vestsjælland	Sorø	1,152	2,984	282,775
Viborg	Viborg	1,592	4,122	230,966
Cities				
Copenhagen (København)	—	34	88	468,704
Frederiksberg	—	3	9	85,814
TOTAL		16,638[3]	43,092	5,129,254

Demography

Population (1988): 5,130,000.
Density (1988): persons per sq mi 308.3, persons per sq km 119.1.
Urban–rural (1986): urban 84.4%; rural 15.6%.
Sex distribution (1988): male 49.29%; female 50.71%.
Age breakdown (1988): under 15, 17.6%; 15–29, 22.8%; 30–44, 22.8%; 45–59, 16.4%; 60–74, 13.7%; 75 and over, 6.7%.
Population projection: (1990) 5,135,000; (2000) 5,146,000.
Doubling time: n.a.; doubling time exceeds 100 years.
Ethnic composition (1988): Danish 97.3%; Turkish 0.5%; other Scandinavian 0.4%; Yugoslavian 0.2%; other 1.6%.
Religious affiliation (1987): Evangelical Lutheran 90.6%; Roman Catholic 0.5%; Baptist 0.1%; Jewish 0.1%; other 8.7%.
Major cities (1986): Greater Copenhagen 1,351,999; Århus 195,152; Odense 137,286; Ålborg 113,650.

Vital statistics

Birth rate per 1,000 population (1987): 11.0 (world avg. 26.0); (1986) legitimate 56.1%; illegitimate 43.9%.
Death rate per 1,000 population (1987): 11.3 (world avg. 9.9).
Natural increase rate per 1,000 population (1986): −0.3 (world avg. 16.1).
Total fertility rate (avg. births per childbearing woman; 1986): 1.5.
Marriage rate per 1,000 population (1986): 6.0.
Divorce rate per 1,000 population (1986): 2.8.
Life expectancy at birth (1985–86): male 71.6 years; female 77.5 years.
Major causes of death per 100,000 population (1986): ischemic heart disease 321.6; malignant neoplasms (cancers) 285.7; cerebrovascular disease 102.0.

National economy

Budget (1988). Revenue: Dkr 258,113,000,000 (customs and excise taxes 47.4%, income and property taxes 41.3%, other 11.3%). Expenditures: Dkr 257,596,000,000 (social services 26.3%, interest payments 18.9%, education 7.5%, defense 5.2%, other 42.1%).
Public debt (1986): Dkr 101,464,000,000.
Tourism (1986): receipts from visitors U.S.$1,759,000,000; expenditures by nationals abroad U.S.$2,119,000,000.
Population economically active (1985): total 2,752,961; activity rate of total population 53.8% (participation rates: ages 15–64, 79.6%; female 45.6%; unemployed 9.0%).

Price and earnings indexes (1980 = 100)							
	1982	1983	1984	1985	1986	1987	1988[4]
Consumer price index	123.0	131.5	139.8	146.4	151.7	157.8	165.2
Monthly earnings index	120.6	128.5	134.6	141.1	149.2	...	...

Household income and expenditure. Average household size (1987) 2.3; income per household (1985) Dkr 124,800 (U.S.$11,780); principal sources of income (1982): wages and salaries 65.5%, transfers 12.4%, self-employment 8.8%, other 13.3%; expenditure (1984): food and beverages 21.3%, housing 19.3%, transportation and communications 16.5%, education, recreation, and culture 9.4%, clothing and footwear 5.8%.
Production (metric tons except as noted). Agriculture, forestry, fishing (1987): barley 4,355,000, sugar beets 2,681,000, wheat 2,311,000, potatoes 942,000; livestock (number of live animals) 9,266,418 pigs, 2,350,833 cattle;

roundwood (1986) 2,191,000 cu m; fish catch 1,593,578. Manufacturing (value added in kroner; 1985): fabricated metal products and machinery 35,810,000,000; food, beverages, and tobacco 25,450,000,000; chemicals and petroleum products 12,080,000,000; paper and printed products 10,670,-000,000. Construction (1985): residential 3,176,200 sq m; nonresidential 5,058,900 sq m. Energy production (consumption): electricity (kW-hr; 1986) 30,720,000,000 (30,802,000,000); coal (metric tons; 1986) none (11,721,000); crude petroleum (barrels; 1986) 27,849,000 (53,730,000); petroleum products (metric tons; 1986) 7,309,000 (9,662,000); natural gas (cu m; 1986) 2,087,037,000 (1,282,862,000).
Gross national product (at current market prices; 1986): U.S.$64,610,000,000 (U.S.$12,640 per capita).

Structure of gross domestic product and labour force				
	1987		1985	
	in value Dkr '000,000	% of total value	labour force	% of labour force
Agriculture	28,276	4.9	176,399	6.4
Mining	5,053	0.9	4,794	0.2
Manufacturing	115,006	19.8	550,158	20.0
Construction	40,405	7.0	188,677	6.8
Public utilities	6,992	1.2	19,030	0.7
Transp. and commun.	48,146	8.3	188,021	6.8
Trade	77,002	13.3	418,676	15.2
Finance	24,711	4.2	198,816	7.2
Pub. admin., defense	131,916	22.7 }	968,068	35.2
Services	124,051	21.4 }		
Other	−21,402[5]	−3.7[5]	40,322	1.5
TOTAL	580,156	100.0	2,752,961	100.0

Land use (1985): forested 11.6%; meadows and pastures 5.2%; agricultural and under permanent cultivation 61.8%; other 21.4%.

Foreign trade

Balance of trade (current prices)						
	1982	1983	1984	1985	1986	1987
Dkr '000,000	−4,696	−4,371	+1,076	−3,560	−4,830	+8,677
% of total	1.8%	1.5%	0.3%	1.0%	1.4%	2.5%

Imports (1987): Dkr 173,918,000,000 (machinery and transportation equipment 29.8%, of which road vehicles 6.6% [of which passenger cars 3.0%, trucks and buses 2.2%]; manufactured goods 16.2%, of which iron and steel 3.4%; food and live animals 10.5%; chemicals and related products 9.5%; mineral fuels 7.7%, of which crude petroleum and petroleum products 5.6%). *Major import sources:* West Germany 23.5%; Sweden 12.2%; U.K. 7.6%; U.S. 5.3%; The Netherlands 5.3%; France 5.3%.
Exports (1987): Dkr 175,097,000,000 (food and live animals 26.4%, of which meat and meat preparations 8.1%, fish and shellfish 6.4%, dairy products 6.2%; machinery and transport equipment 24.0%; chemicals and related products 8.2%; furniture 3.7%). *Major export destinations:* West Germany 16.9%; U.K. 11.5%; Sweden 11.5%; Norway 7.4%; U.S. 7.1%.

Transport and communications

Transport. Railroads (1986): length 1,535 mi, 2,471 km; passenger-mi 2,818,-000,000, passenger-km 4,535,000,000; short ton-mi cargo 1,227,000,000, metric ton-km cargo 1,791,000,000. Roads (1986): total length 43,614 mi, 70,190 km (paved 100%). Vehicles (1986): passenger cars 1,557,880; trucks and buses 282,050. Merchant marine (1987): vessels (100 gross tons and over) 983; total deadweight tonnage 6,961,068[6]. Air transport (1987): passenger-mi 4,596,204,000, passenger-km 7,396,888,000; short ton-mi cargo 565,951,000, metric ton-km cargo 826,274,000; airports (1988) with scheduled flights 13.
Communications. Daily newspapers (1986): total number 47; total circulation 1,880,000; circulation per 1,000 population 367. Radio (1986): total number of receivers 2,052,467 (1 per 2.5 persons). Television (1987): total number of receivers 1,953,732 (1 per 2.6 persons). Telephones (1986): 4,195,000 (1 per 1.2 persons).

Education and health

Education (1985–86)				
	schools	teachers	students	student/ teacher ratio
Primary (age 7–12)	2,556	34,541[7]	402,707	12.0[7]
Secondary (age 13–18)	3,251	36,105[7]	336,754	9.4[7]
Vocational	288	...	150,772	...
Higher	96[8]	10,411[8]	116,319	...

Educational attainment (1985). Percent of population age 25–64 having: primary education 2.9%; lower secondary 30.8%; upper secondary 48.7%; some postsecondary 13.5%; graduated from university 4.1%. *Literacy* (1986): virtually 100%.
Health (1986): physicians 13,144 (1 per 390 persons); hospital beds 35,606 (1 per 144 persons); infant mortality rate per 1,000 live births 8.2.
Food (1984–86): daily per capita caloric intake 3,512 (vegetable products 56%, animal products 44%); (1983) 128% of FAO recommended minimum requirement.

Military

Total active duty personnel (1987): 29,300 (army 58.0%, navy 18.4%, air force 23.6%). *Military expenditure as percent of GNP* (1985): 2.3% (world 6.1%); per capita expenditure U.S.$241.

[1]Excludes Greenland and the Faeroe Islands. [2]January 1. [3]Detail does not add to total given because of rounding. [4]May. [5]Includes imputed bank service charges. [6]Includes Greenland and Faeroe Islands. [7]1984–85. [8]1982–83.

Djibouti

Official name: Jumhūrīyah Jībūtī
(Arabic); République de Djibouti
(French) (Republic of Djibouti).
Form of government: unitary
single-party republic with one
legislative house (National Assembly
[65]).
Chief of state: President.
Head of government: Prime Minister.
Capital: Djibouti.
Official languages: Arabic; French.
Official religion: none.
Monetary unit: 1 Djibouti franc
(DF) = 100 centimes; valuation (Oct.
10, 1988) 1 U.S.$ = DF 172.85;
1 £ = DF 296.00.

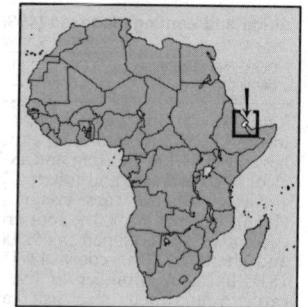

Area and population

Districts	Capitals	area[1] sq mi	sq km	population 1982 estimate
'Alī Sabīḥ (Ali-Sabieh)	'Alī Sabīḥ	925	2,400	15,000
Dikhil	Dikhil	2,775	7,200	30,000
Djibouti	Djibouti	225	600	200,000
Obock	Obock	2,200	5,700	15,000
Tadjoura (Tadjourah)	Tadjoura	2,825	7,300	30,000
TOTAL		8,950	23,200	335,000[2]

Demography

Population (1988): 484,000.
Density (1988): persons per sq mi 54.1, persons per sq km 20.9.
Urban–rural (1985): urban 75.0%; rural 25.0%.
Sex distribution (1985): male 50.28%; female 49.72%.
Age breakdown (1983): under 15, 38.0%; 15–29, 34.0%; 30–44, 17.0%; 45–50, 3.0%; 51 and over, 8.0%.
Population projection: (1990) 513,000; (2000) 690,000.
Doubling time: 22 years.
Ethnic composition (1984): Issa 47%; Afar 38%; Arab (mostly Yemeni) 6%; other 9%.
Religious affiliation (1983): Sunnī Muslim 94%; Christian 6%, of which Roman Catholic 4%, Protestant 1%, Orthodox 1%.
Major city and towns (1982): Djibouti 200,000[3]; 'Alī Sabīḥ 4,000; Tadjoura 3,500; Dikhil 3,000.

Vital statistics

Birth rate per 1,000 population (1980–85): 49.2 (world avg. 29.0).
Death rate per 1,000 population (1980–85): 18.3 (world avg. 11.0).
Natural increase rate per 1,000 population (1980–85): 30.9 (world avg. 18.0).
Total fertility rate (avg. births per childbearing woman; 1980–85): 6.8.
Marriage rate per 1,000 population (1982): 6.7.
Divorce rate per 1,000 population (1982): 1.9.
Life expectancy at birth (1985): 45 years.
Major causes of death[4] (percentage of total deaths; 1984): diarrhea and acute dehydration 16.0%; malnutrition 16.0%; poisonings 11.0%; tuberculosis 6.0%; acute respiratory disease 6.0%; malaria 6.0%; anemia 6.0%; heart disease 2.0%; kidney disease 1.0%; other ailments 19.0%; no diagnosis 11.0%.

National economy

Budget (1985). Revenue: DF 22,585,800,000 (customs duties 47.4%; direct taxes 29.2%, of which licenses and patent fees 7.1%, income tax 6.6%; foreign aid grants 6.6%; excises and stamps 4.1%). Expenditures: DF 22,585,800,000 (general administration 41.7%; defense 21.0%; education 6.8%; economic development 6.1%; debt payment 3.4%).
Public debt (external, outstanding; 1986): U.S.$119,100,000.
Tourism: receipts from visitors (1986) U.S.$6,400,000; expenditures by nationals abroad, n.a.
Production (metric tons except as noted). Agriculture, forestry, fishing (1986): vegetables and melons 13,000; livestock (number of live animals) 545,000 goats, 500,000 sheep, 410,000 camels, 47,000 cattle, 8,000 asses; fish catch 385. Mining and quarrying: mineral production limited to locally used construction material and evaporated salt. Manufacturing (1984): detail n.a.; main items produced are furniture, nonalcoholic beverages, light electromechanical goods, and mineral water. Construction (1985): residential 32,214 sq m; nonresidential 21,722 sq m. Energy production (consumption): electricity (kW-hr; 1986) 165,000,000 (165,000,000); coal, none (n.a.); crude petroleum, none (n.a.); petroleum products (metric tons; 1986) none (72,000); natural gas, none (n.a.).
Population economically active (1985): total 161,000; activity rate of total population 44.5% (participation rates: over age 10, 65.2%; female 39.1%; unemployed [1985] c. 60%).

Price and earnings indexes (1975 = 100)

	1977	1978	1979	1980	1981	1982	1983
Consumer price index	136.6	163.4	187.6	210.5	222.2	217.0	...
Monthly earnings index	...	...	...	...	...	...	...

Household income and expenditure. Average household size[5] (1982) 5.6; income per household: n.a.; sources of income (1976): wages and salaries 51.6%, self-employment 36.0%, transfer payments 10.5%, other 1.9%; expenditure (expatriate households; 1984): food 50.3%, energy 13.1%, recreation

10.4%, housing 6.4%, clothing 1.7%, personal effects 1.4%, health care 1.0%, household goods 0.3%, other 15.4%.
Gross national product (at current market prices; 1984): U.S.$301,540,000 (U.S.$740 per capita).

Structure of gross domestic product and labour force

	1984 in value DF '000,000	% of total value	1985 labour force	% of labour force
Agriculture	2,690	4.5	125,000	77.5
Mining				
Manufacturing	4,920	8.2		
Construction	4,490	7.5	12,000	7.3
Public utilities	1,942	3.2		
Transportation and communications	6,010	10.0		
Trade	9,400	15.6		
Finance	6,530	10.8	24,000	15.2
Pub. admin., defense	16,170	26.8		
Services	950	1.6		
Other	7,132[6]	11.8[6]		
TOTAL	60,234	100.0	161,000	100.0

Land use (1985): forested 0.3%; meadows and pastures 9.1%; agricultural and under permanent cultivation[7]; built-on, wasteland, and other 90.6%.

Foreign trade[8]

Balance of trade (current prices)

	1977	1978	1979	1980	1981	1982	1983
DF '000,000	−15,585	−25,963	−31,431	−35,699	−28,311	−37,965	−12,599
% of total	69.8%	80.4%	88.7%	88.9%	90.1%	89.5%	24.7%

Imports (1983): DF 39,307,000,000 (machinery and transport equipment 23.0%, of which electrical machinery and appliances 10.9%; food and live animals 19.1%; textiles and clothing 12.0%; petroleum products 9.4%; kat [a narcotic leaf] 9.0%; special transactions, including importation of gold coins, personal effects, and military goods, 4.8%; tobacco and tobacco products 4.3%). *Major import sources:* France 35.4%; Ethiopia 9.7%; Japan 7.6%; The Netherlands 5.3%; Italy 4.3%; United Kingdom 3.8%.
Exports (1983): DF 1,919,000,000 (unspecified special transactions 89.6%, of which live animals [including camels] 30.8%, food and food products 18.6%). *Major export destinations* (1981): France 31.0%; Yemen (San'ā') 29.8%; Somalia 9.1%; Ethiopia 7.7%; The Netherlands 6.6%; United States 5.9%.

Transport and communications

Transport. Railroads (1984): length 66 mi, 106 km; short ton-mile cargo 90,140,000, metric ton-km cargo 131,600,000[9]. Roads (1986): total length 1,799 mi, 2,895 km (paved 7%). Vehicles (1985): passenger cars 12,049; trucks and buses 951. Merchant marine (1987): vessels (100 gross tons and over) 7; total deadweight tonnage 2,650. Air transport[10] (1985): passenger arrivals 55,023, passenger departures 48,256; cargo loaded 1,655 metric tons, cargo unloaded 6,627 metric tons; airports (1988) with scheduled flights 3.
Communications. Weekly newspapers (1987): total number 1; total circulation 4,000; circulation per 1,000 population 8.5. Radio (1986): total number of receivers 32,000 (1 per 14 persons). Television (1987): total number of receivers 14,000 (1 per 34 persons). Telephone subscribers (1986): 8,250 (1 per 56 persons).

Education and health

Education (1986–87)

	schools	teachers	students	student/ teacher ratio
Primary (age 6–14)	59	559	27,136	48.5
Secondary (age 12–20) Voc., teacher tr.	21	302	8,003	26.5
Higher[11]	—	—	161	—

Educational attainment, n.a. *Literacy* (c. 1980): population age 14 and over literate 11.9% (8.8% if expatriate population is discounted).
Health (1985): physicians 68 (1 per 6,323 persons); hospital beds 1,283 (1 per 335 persons); infant mortality rate per 1,000 live births 200.
Food: n.a.

Military

Total active duty personnel (1988): 3,030 (army 94.7%, navy 2.0%, air force 3.3%). *Military expenditure as percent of GNP* (1984): 9.0% (world 6.0%); per capita expenditure U.S.$67.

[1]Original figures are those given in sq km; sq mi equivalent is rounded to appropriate level of generality. [2]Including 45,000 not distributed by district. [3]District population. [4]Infants and children to age 10, district of Djibouti only. [5]City of Djibouti only. [6]Import duties, less imputed bank service charge. [7]In 1985 only 900 acres (400 hectares) of land were cultivated. [8]The value of imports includes merchandise destined for Ethiopia and northern Somalia; that of exports excludes reexports coming from those areas. In 1980 the value of reexports from Ethiopia and northern Somalia was approximately five times greater than the value of domestic exports. [9]Based on total weight of Ethiopian exports and imports transported to and from the port of Djibouti. [10]Djibouti International Airport only. [11]1983–84.

Dominica

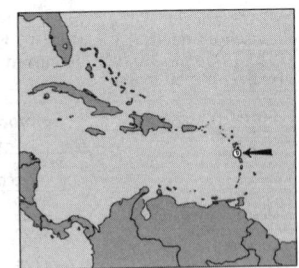

Official name: Commonwealth of Dominica.
Form of government: multiparty republic with one legislative house (House of Assembly [31][1]).
Chief of state: President.
Head of government: Prime Minister.
Capital: Roseau.
Official language: English.
Official religion: none.
Monetary unit: 1 East Caribbean dollar (EC$) = 100 cents; valuation (Oct. 10, 1988) 1 U.S.$ = EC$2.70; 1 £ = EC$4.62.

Area and population

Parishes[2]	area		population 1981 census
	sq mi	sq km	
St. Andrew	69	179	12,748
St. David	49	127	7,337
St. George	21	54	20,501
St. John	23	60	5,412
St. Joseph	46	119	6,606
St. Luke	4	10	1,503
St. Mark	4	10	1,921
St. Patrick	32	83	9,780
St. Paul	26	67	6,386
St. Peter	11	29	1,601
TOTAL	290[3,4]	750[4]	73,795[5,6]

Demography

Population (1988): 79,300.
Density (1988): persons per sq mi 273.4, persons per sq km 105.7.
Urban–rural: n.a.
Sex distribution (1981)[5]: male 49.81%; female 50.19%.
Age breakdown (1981)[5]: under 15, 39.8%; 15–29, 28.6%; 30–44, 11.9%; 45–59, 9.2%; 60–74, 7.4%; 75 and over, 3.1%.
Population projection: (1990) 80,500; (2000) 87,000.
Doubling time: 45 years.
Ethnic composition (1981): black 91.2%; mixed race 6.0%; Amerindian 1.5%; white 0.5%; not stated 0.6%; other 0.2%.
Religious affiliation (1981): Roman Catholic 76.9%; Protestant 15.5%, of which Methodist 5.0%, Seventh-day Adventist 3.2%, Pentecostal 2.9%; other 7.6%.
Major towns (1981): Roseau 8,346; Marigot 3,554; St. Joseph 2,665; Portsmouth 2,220.

Vital statistics

Birth rate per 1,000 population (1984): 20.8 (world avg. 29.0); (1980) legitimate 35.0%; illegitimate 65.0%.
Death rate per 1,000 population (1984): 5.2 (world avg. 11.0).
Natural increase rate per 1,000 population (1984): 15.6 (world avg. 18.0).
Total fertility rate (avg. births per childbearing woman; 1987): 3.2.
Marriage rate per 1,000 population: n.a.
Divorce rate per 1,000 population: n.a.
Life expectancy at birth (1987): male 73.0 years; female 79.0 years.
Major causes of death per 100,000 population (1984): diseases of the circulatory system 197.8; malignant neoplasms (cancers) 88.6; diseases of the respiratory system 27.9; endocrine and metabolic disorders 26.7; ill-defined conditions 44.9.

National economy

Budget (1985–86). Revenue: EC$124,100,000 (tax revenues 61.5%, of which taxes on international trade 35.0%, income tax 20.8%, consumption tax 5.7%; foreign grants 32.0%; nontax revenue 6.5%). Expenditures: EC$125,500,000 (wages and salaries 37.5%; development expenditure 35.4%; goods and services 11.4%; interest on public debt 6.1%; transfer payments 5.7%).
Gross national product (1986): U.S.$100,000,000 (U.S.$1,210 per capita).

Structure of gross domestic product and labour force

	1986		1981	
	in value EC$'000,000[7]	% of total value	labour force	% of labour force
Agriculture	34.0	29.5	7,843[8]	31.0[8]
Mining	0.9[8]	0.8[8]	8	—
Manufacturing	10.2	8.8	1,417	5.6
Construction	8.6	7.4	2,306	9.1
Public utilities	2.3	2.0	245	1.0
Transportation and communications	10.0	8.7	914	3.6
Trade, hotels, restaurants	15.6	13.5	1,613	6.3
Finance, real estate, insurance	13.7[9]	11.9[9]	257	1.0
Pub. admin., defense	24.2	21.0	4,980	19.7
Services	9	9	5,750[11]	22.7
Other	-4.1[10]	-3.6[10]		
TOTAL	115.4	100.0	25,333	100.0

Public debt (external, outstanding; 1985): U.S.$45,000,000.
Population economically active (1981): total 25,333; activity rate of total population 34.3% (participation rates: ages 15–64, 61.7%; female 34.1%; unemployed [1986] 13.0%).

Price and earnings indexes (1980 = 100)

	1981	1982	1983	1984	1985	1986	1987
Consumer price index	113.3	118.4	123.2	125.9	128.5	132.3	139.2[12]
Earnings index							

Household income and expenditure. Average household size (1981) 4.3; income per household: n.a.; expenditure (1984)[13]: food and nonalcoholic beverages 43.1%, housing and utilities 16.1%, clothing and footwear 6.5%, alcoholic beverages and tobacco 2.0%, other 32.3%.
Production (metric tons except as noted). Agriculture, forestry, fishing (1986): bananas 67,000[14], root crops (mostly dasheens and tanias) 26,000, coconuts 13,000, grapefruits 9,700, limes 6,000, oranges 3,000, cucumbers and gherkins 3,000, cocoa 429[15], coffee 366[15], cut flowers 20[15], bay oil 18[15]; livestock (number of live animals) 9,000 pigs, 6,000 goats, 4,000 cattle; roundwood, n.a.; fish catch (1985) 446. Mining and quarrying (1985): pumice and volcanic ash 110,000. Manufacturing (1984)[16]: galvanized sheets 2,739; laundry soap 2,424; toilet soap 1,644; coconut meal 789; edible coconut oil 6,600 hectolitres; other products include paint and bottled spring water. Construction: n.a. Energy production (consumption): electricity (kW-hr; 1986) 18,000,000 (18,000,000); coal, none (none); crude petroleum, none (none); petroleum products (metric tons; 1986) none (12,000); natural gas, none (none).
Tourism: receipts from visitors (1986) U.S.$10,600,000; expenditures by nationals abroad (1983) U.S.$700,000.
Land use (1985): forested 41.0%; meadows and pastures 3.0%; agricultural and under permanent cultivation 23.0%; other 33.0%.

Foreign trade

Balance of trade (current prices)[17]

	1981	1982	1983	1984	1985	1986
EC$'000,000	-82.3	-62.2	-53.5	-81.6	-72.6	-36.1
% of total	44.3%	32.0%	28.2%	37.1%	32.1%	13.6%

Imports (1984): EC$156,100,000[18] (food 16.1%, of which meat 5.0%, flour 3.3%; electric and nonelectric machinery 13.9%; transport equipment 11.1%; metals and their manufactures 9.4%; petroleum products 6.1%; cardboard boxes 4.2%). *Major import sources:* United States 26.7%; United Kingdom 12.8%; Trinidad and Tobago 7.7%; Canada 7.7%; St. Lucia 5.5%.
Exports (1984): EC$69,200,000[18] ([19]bananas 44.6%; toilet soap 13.5%; galvanized sheets 9.8%; household soap 8.6%; refined coconut oil 4.3%; crude coconut oil 2.4%; grapefruit 2.3%). *Major export destinations:* United Kingdom 45.7%; Jamaica 15.6%; Trinidad and Tobago 14.1%; Antigua and Barbuda 4.3%; Barbados 3.0%.

Transport and communications

Transport. Railroads: none. Roads (1984): total length 489 mi, 787 km (paved 60%). Vehicles (1983): passenger cars 2,713; trucks and buses 1,250. Merchant marine (1987): vessels (100 gross tons and over) 6; total deadweight tonnage 2,475. Air transport (1984): passenger arrivals 33,954, passenger departures 34,381; cargo unloaded 196 metric tons, cargo loaded 271 metric tons; airports (1988) with scheduled flights 2.
Communications. Daily newspapers: none. Radio (1986): total number of receivers 35,000 (1 per 2.5 persons). Television: total number of receivers, n.a. Telephones (1985): 6,882 (1 per 12 persons).

Education and health

Education (1985–86)

	schools	teachers	students	student/teacher ratio
Primary	66	642	12,340	30.3
Secondary	...		7,111	
Voc., teacher tr.[20]	...	35	436	12.5
Higher[21]	...	17	60	3.5

Educational attainment (1981). Percent of population age 25 and over having: no formal schooling 6.6%; primary education 80.6%; secondary 11.1%; higher 1.7%. *Literacy* (1981): total population age 15 and over literate 42,100 (94.9%).
Health (1986): physicians 27 (1 per 2,893 persons); hospital beds 312 (1 per 250 persons); infant mortality rate per 1,000 live births (1982–84 avg.) 16.3.
Food (1984–86): daily per capita caloric intake 2,649 (vegetable products 84%, animal products 16%); (1983) 100% of FAO recommended minimum requirement.

Military

Total active duty personnel (1987): none[22].

[1]Includes 10 nonelective seats. [2]Dominica is divided into 10 parishes for administrative purposes only. Local government is based on village or town councils. [3]Includes inland water area. [4]Detail does not add to total given because of rounding. [5]Excludes institutionalized population. [6]Total population including institutionalized residents equals 74,785. [7]In prices of 1977. [8]Includes fishing and forestry. [9]Finance, real estate, insurance includes Services. [10]Less imputed service charges. [11]Includes 4,746 unemployed. [12]Average of second and third quarters. [13]Weights of consumer price index components. [14]1987. [15]1984. [16]Coconut-based soap products accounted for 75% of total value added of manufacturing sector in 1986. [17]Imports c.i.f.; exports f.o.b. Exports include reexports. [18]Preliminary figure. [19]Breakdown based on domestic exports only, totaling EC$67,307,000. [20]1983–84. [21]1984–85. [22]300-member police force has residual responsibilities for defense.

Dominican Republic

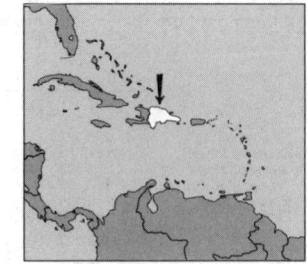

Official name: República Dominicana (Dominican Republic).
Form of government: multiparty republic with two legislative houses (Senate [30]; Chamber of Deputies [120]).
Head of state and government: President.
Capital: Santo Domingo.
Official language: Spanish.
Official religion: none.
Monetary unit: 1 Dominican peso (RD$) = 100 centavos; valuation (Oct. 10, 1988) 1 U.S.$ = RD$4.99; 1 £ = RD$8.55.

Area and population		area		population
		sq mi	sq km	1987 estimate
Provinces	**Capitals**			
Azua	Azua	938	2,430	178,877
Bahoruco (Baoruco)	Neiba	531	1,376	85,356
Barahona	Barahona	976	2,528	148,881
Dajabón	Dajabón	344	890	62,640
Duarte	San Francisco de Macorís	499	1,292	255,672
El Seibo	El Seibo	641	1,659	95,333
Espaillat	Moca	386	1,000	178,033
Hato Mayor	Hato Mayor	514	1,330	76,023
Independencia	Jimaní	719	1,861	42,081
La Altagracia	Higüey	1,191	3,084	108,667
La Estrelleta	Elías Piña	690	1,788	70,971
La Romana	La Romana	209	541	149,652
La Vega	La Vega	916	2,373	296,039
María Trinidad Sánchez	Nagua	506	1,310	122,253
Monseñor Nouel	Bonao	388	1,004	121,906
Monte Cristi	Monte Cristi	768	1,989	90,534
Monte Plata	Monte Plata	841	2,179	170,758
Pedernales	Pedernales	373	967	18,459
Peravia	Baní	626	1,622	182,489
Puerto Plata	Puerto Plata	726	1,881	224,425
Salcedo	Salcedo	206	533	107,667
Samaná	Samaná	382	989	71,313
San Cristóbal	San Cristóbal	604	1,564	313,497
San Juan	San Juan	1,375	3,561	260,462
San Pedro de Macorís	San Pedro de Macorís	450	1,166	184,078
Sánchez Ramírez	Cotuí	453	1,174	137,382
Santiago	Santiago de los Caballeros	1,205	3,122	657,729
Santiago Rodríguez	Sabaneta	394	1,020	60,146
Santo Domingo[1]	—	570	1,477	2,127,496
Valverde	Mao	220	570	108,891
TOTAL		18,704[2]	48,443[2]	6,707,710

Demography

Population (1988): 6,850,000.
Density (1988): persons per sq mi 366.2, persons per sq km 141.4.
Urban–rural (1986): urban 54.6%; rural 45.4%.
Sex distribution (1985): male 50.31%; female 49.69%.
Age breakdown (1985): under 15, 40.7%; 15–29, 30.7%; 30–44, 15.4%; 45–59, 8.5%; 60–74, 3.7%; 75 and over, 1.0%.
Population projection: (1990) 7,144,000; (2000) 8,816,000.
Doubling time: 28 years.
Ethnic composition (1983): mulatto 73%; white 16%; black 11%.
Religious affiliation (1983): Roman Catholic 93.7%; other 6.3%.
Major cities (1983): Santo Domingo 1,410,000; Santiago de los Caballeros 285,000; La Romana 101,000; San Pedro de Macorís 81,000.

Vital statistics

Birth rate per 1,000 population (1985): 34.0 (world avg. 29.0); (1976) legitimate 32.8%; illegitimate 67.2%.
Death rate per 1,000 population (1985): 9.0 (world avg. 11.0).
Natural increase rate per 1,000 population (1985): 25.0 (world avg. 18.0).
Total fertility rate (avg. births per childbearing woman; 1984): 4.0.
Marriage rate per 1,000 population (1985): 3.4.
Divorce rate per 1,000 population (1985): 1.2.
Life expectancy at birth (1980–85): male 60.7 years; female 64.6 years.
Major causes of death per 100,000 population (1982): infectious and parasitic diseases 47.0; diseases of pulmonary circulation 31.6%; diseases of the respiratory system 29.4; ill-defined conditions 96.3.

National economy

Budget (1987). Revenue: RD$3,085,400,000 (tax revenue 82.8%, of which import duties 34.5%, excise taxes 23.9%, taxes on income and profits 19.2%; nontax revenue 9.6%). Expenditures: RD$3,287,900,000 (administration 53.7%; education 7.8%; agriculture 7.2%; defense 6.7%).
Public debt (external, outstanding; 1986): U.S.$2,609,200,000.
Tourism: receipts from visitors (1986) U.S.$463,900,000; expenditures by nationals abroad (1983) U.S.$87,000,000.
Production (metric tons except as noted). Agriculture (1987): sugarcane 8,772,000, unhusked rice 514,700, bananas 320,000[3], tomatoes 173,100, coffee cherries 134,300, beans 52,200, cacao 38,700, raw tobacco 28,700, raw cotton 7,400; livestock (number of live animals; 1986) 2,500,000 pigs; 2,055,000 cattle; roundwood (1985) 982,000 cu m; fish catch (1986) 17,182. Mining (value of production in RD$'000,000; 1985): ferronickel 123; gold 104. Manufacturing (value of production in RD$'000,000; 1984): food products 2,007; refined petroleum 469; all beverages 452; cement and fertilizers 165; cigarettes 157. Construction (buildings authorized[4]; 1985): residential

641,000 sq m; nonresidential 229,000 sq m. Energy production (consumption): electricity (kW-hr; 1987) 3,711,000,000 (2,713,000,000); coal, none (none); crude petroleum (barrels; 1986) none (10,990,000); petroleum products (metric tons; 1986) 1,434,000 (1,899,000).
Gross national product (1986): U.S.$4,680,000,000 (U.S.$710 per capita).

Structure of gross domestic product and labour force				
	1986		1981	
	in value U.S.$'000,000[5]	% of total value	labour force	% of labour force
Agriculture	513.4	16.0	420,463	22.0
Mining	119.8	3.7	4,743	0.2
Manufacturing	544.3	16.9	224,437	11.7
Construction	221.8	6.9	80,850	4.3
Public utilities	62.1	1.9	13,891	0.7
Transp. and commun.	257.4	8.0	40,470	2.1
Trade	497.1	15.5	192,181	10.0
Finance, real estate	351.2	10.9	22,369	1.2
Pub. admin., defense	335.3	10.4 }	363,125	18.9
Services	313.9	9.8 }		
Other	—	—	552,859[6]	28.9
TOTAL	3,216.3	100.0	1,915,388	100.0

Population economically active (1981): total 1,915,388; activity rate of total population 33.9% (participation rates: ages 15–64, 53.6%; female 28.9%; unemployed [1986] 28.0%).

Price and earnings indexes (1980 = 100)							
	1982	1983	1984	1985	1986	1987	1988[7]
Consumer price index	15.8	121.3	154.0	211.8	232.5	269.4	398.4
Monthly earnings index[8]	119.4	122.6	133.7	...	...	...	...

Household income and expenditure. Average household size (1981) 5.1; average annual income per family (1975) urban family RD$2,299, rural family RD$654; sources of income: n.a.; expenditure (1976–77)[9]: food, beverages, and tobacco 51.7%, housing 23.9%, clothing and footwear 6.0%.
Land use (1985): forested 12.9%; meadows and pastures 43.2%; agricultural and under permanent cultivation 30.4%; other 13.5%.

Foreign trade

Balance of trade (current prices)						
	1981	1982	1983	1984	1985	1986
RD$'000,000	−262.8	−491.3	−493.8	−389.0	−557.8	−528.2
% of total	9.9%	24.1%	23.9%	18.3%	27.5%	26.9%

Imports (1985): RD$1,293,000,000 (crude petroleum and petroleum products 33.2%, foodstuffs 13.4%, machinery 9.3%). *Major import sources:* U.S. 35.2%; Venezuela 25.8%; Mexico 7.9%; Japan 6.1%.
Exports (1985): RD$735,200,000 (raw sugar 21.5%, ferronickel 16.3%, gold alloy 15.4%, coffee 11.7%, cacao 7.9%, raw tobacco 2.4%). *Major export destinations:* U.S. 68.9%; The Netherlands 7.2%; Puerto Rico 7.1%.

Transport and communications

Transport. Railroads (1987)[10]: length 1,654 km. Roads (1982): total length 17,362 km (paved 29%). Vehicles (1984): passenger cars 101,979; trucks and buses 61,307. Merchant marine (1987): vessels (100 gross tons and over) 37; total deadweight tonnage 70,825. Air transport (1986)[11]: passenger-km 633,800,000; metric ton-km cargo 62,700,000; airports (1988) 5.
Communications. Daily newspapers (1987): total number 8; total circulation 294,000; circulation per 1,000 population 44. Radio (1986): 800,000 receivers (1 per 8.2 persons). Television (1987): 425,000 receivers (1 per 16 persons). Telephones (1984): 185,537 (1 per 34 persons).

Education and health

Education (1986–87)				
	schools	teachers	students	student/ teacher ratio
Primary (age 7–12)	6,299	31,275	1,296,366	41.5
Secondary (age 13–18)	...	9,963	426,962	42.9
Vocational, teacher tr.	...	...	24,758	...
Higher[12]	...	6,539	123,748	18.9

Educational attainment (1970). Percent of population age 25 and over having: no formal schooling 40.1%; primary education 45.9%; secondary 12.1%; higher 1.9%. *Literacy* (1985): total population age 15 and over literate 2,860,000 (77.3%); males literate 1,447,000 (77.7%); females literate 1,413,000 (76.8%).
Health: physicians (1984) 3,555 (1 per 1,817 persons); hospital beds (1980)[13] 8,953 (1 per 620 persons); infant mortality rate per 1,000 live births (1985) 74.0.
Food (1983–85): daily per capita caloric intake 2,468 (vegetable products 87%, animal products 13%); (1983) 105% of FAO recommended minimum.

Military

Total active duty personnel (1988): 20,800 (army 62.5%, navy 19.2%, air force 18.3%). *Military expenditure as percent of GNP* (1985): 1.4% (world 6.1%); per capita expenditure U.S.$22.

[1]National district. [2]Total includes 63 sq mi (163 sq km) of offshore islands not shown separately. [3]1986. [4]Excludes work under contract to Instituto Nacional de la Vivienda. [5]At 1970 prices. [6]Not adequately defined (421,628); and those seeking work for first time (131,231). [7]July. [8]Manufacturing only. [9]Weights of consumer price index components. [10]Most track serves the sugar industry only except for 88 mi (142 km) for public transport. [11]CDA (Dominicana) airlines only. [12]1985–86. [13]Institute of Social Security hospitals only.

Ecuador

Official name: República del Ecuador
(Republic of Ecuador).
Form of government: unitary multiparty
republic with one legislative house
(National Congress [71]).
Head of state and government:
President.
Capital: Quito.
Official language: Spanish.
Official religion: none.
Monetary unit: 1 Sucre (S/.) = 100
centavos; valuation (Oct. 10, 1988)
1 U.S.$ = S/. 389.61; 1 £ = S/. 667.21.

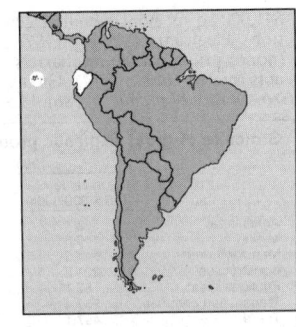

Area and population

Regions Provinces	Capitals	area sq mi	area sq km	population 1987 estimate
Coastal				
El Oro	Machala	2,281	5,908	421,000
Esmeraldas	Esmeraldas	5,854	15,162	306,600
Guayas	Guayaquil	8,256	21,382	2,573,700
Los Rios	Babahoyo	2,459	6,370	547,700
Manabí	Portoviejo	6,990	18,105	1,060,700
Eastern				
Morona-Santiago	Macas	10,200	26,418	88,900
Napo	Tena	20,200	52,318	161,000
Pastaza	Puyo	11,687	30,269	39,900
Zamora-Chinchipe	Zamora	7,102	18,394	62,000
Sierra				
Azuay	Cuenca	3,124	8,092	525,500
Bolívar	Guaranda	1,599	4,142	165,600
Cañar	Azogues	1,344	3,481	202,000
Carchi	Tulcan	1,446	3,744	145,200
Chimborazo	Riobamba	2,338	6,056	372,900
Cotopaxi	Latacunga	2,007	5,198	317,600
Imbabura	Ibarra	1,921	4,976	285,900
Loja	Loja	4,429	11,472	409,700
Pichincha	Quito	6,404	16,587	1,774,900
Tungurahua	Ambato	1,201	3,110	381,600
Island territory				
Galápagos Islands	Puerto Baquerizo Moreno	3,086	7,994	8,400
TOTAL		103,930[1]	269,178	9,850,700[1, 2]

Demography

Population (1988): 10,203,000.
Density (1988): persons per sq mi 98.2, persons per sq km 37.9.
Urban–rural (1987): urban 53.5%; rural 46.5%.
Sex distribution (1987): male 50.30%; female 49.70%.
Age breakdown (1987): under 15, 41.3%; 15–29, 28.3%; 30–44, 16.2%; 45–64, 10.5%; 65 and over, 3.7%.
Population projection: (1990) 10,782,000; (2000) 13,939,000.
Doubling time: 22 years.
Ethnic composition (1980): Quechua 49.9%; mestizo 40.0%; white 8.5%; Amerindian 1.6%.
Religious affiliation (1984): Roman Catholic 92.1%; other 7.9%.
Major cities (1987): Guayaquil 1,572,615; Quito 1,137,705; Cuenca 201,490; Machala 144,396; Portoviejo 141,568.

Vital statistics

Birth rate per 1,000 population: (1986) 36.8[3] (world avg. 26.0); (1982) legitimate 67.9%; illegitimate 32.1%.
Death rate per 1,000 population (1986): 5.3[3] (world avg. 9.9).
Natural increase rate per 1,000 population (1986): 31.5[3] (world avg. 16.1).
Total fertility rate (avg. births per childbearing woman; 1985): 4.8.
Marriage rate per 1,000 population (1986): 6.2[3, 4].
Divorce rate per 1,000 population (1984): 0.4.
Life expectancy at birth (1981): male 59.8 years; female 63.6 years.
Major causes of death per 100,000 population (1984): infectious and parasitic diseases 87.5; circulatory diseases 85.6; respiratory diseases 71.0; accidents poisonings, and violence 66.8; neoplasms (cancers) 45.9.

National economy

Budget (1987). Revenue: S/. 236,761,600,000 (income from petroleum 37.9%, production and sales tax 19.7%, import duties 17.6%, income taxes 10.7%). Expenditures: S/. 368,703,500,000 (debt service 34.5%, education 19.1%, public services 18.2%, transport and communications 7.6%).
Public debt (external, outstanding; 1986): U.S.$7,918,600,000.
Production (metric tons except as noted). Agriculture, forestry, fishing (1986): sugarcane 2,749,516, bananas 2,316,437, palm nut 657,740, rice 575,868, coffee 483,755, corn (maize) 416,215, potatoes 388,660, cacao 89,913; livestock (number of live animals) 4,986,000 pigs, 3,727,000 cattle, 1,959,000 sheep, 45,000,000 chickens; roundwood (1985) 8,571,000 cu m; fish catch (1985) 901,059. Mining and quarrying (1986): limestone 4,200,000; gold 319,000 troy oz. Manufacturing (value added in S/. '000,000; 1986): food products 147,915, of which beverages (including liquors) 23,427; petroleum products 138,081; textiles and clothing 44,895. Construction (in S/.[5]; 1984): residential 17,268,900,000; nonresidential 2,910,100,000. Energy production (consumption): electricity (kW-hr; 1986) 5,301,000,000 (5,311,000,000); crude petroleum (barrels; 1986) 103,749,000 (34,481,000); petroleum products (metric tons; 1986) 4,541,000 (3,855,000); natural gas (cu m; 1986) 87,405,000 (87,405,000).
Gross national product (1986): U.S.$11,200,000,000 (U.S.$1,160 per capita).

Structure of gross domestic product and labour force

	1986 in value S/. '000,000	1986 % of total value	1982 labour force	1982 % of labour force
Agriculture	205,641	15.0	786,972	33.5
Mining	148,149	10.8	7,406	0.4
Manufacturing	275,327	20.2	286,530	12.2
Construction	62,385	4.6	158,009	6.8
Public utilities	4,592	0.3	13,183	0.5
Transp. and commun.	127,112	9.3	101,321	4.3
Trade	240,436	17.6	271,914	11.6
Finance	58,590	4.3	44,116	1.9
Pub. admin., defense	104,825	7.7 }	554,915	23.6
Services	102,346	7.5 }		
Other	36,901	2.7	121,697[6]	5.2[6]
TOTAL	1,366,304	100.0	2,346,063	100.0

Tourism (1986): receipts from visitors U.S.$135,000,000; expenditures by nationals abroad U.S.$210,000,000.
Population economically active (1985): total 2,713,000; activity rate of total population 28.9% (participation rates: ages 15–64, 43.3%; female 8.5%; unemployed [1982] 4.6%).

Price and earnings indexes (1980 = 100)

	1981	1982	1983	1984	1985	1986	1987
Consumer price index	116.4	135.3	200.8	263.6	337.3	415.0	537.5
Monthly earnings index[7]	111.5	120.4	154.7	201.1	...	...	...

Household income and expenditure. Average household size (1982) 5.1; average annual income per household (1982) S/. 28,747 (U.S.$956); sources of income (1982): self-employment 53.6%, wages and salaries 38.0%, interest, dividends, and rent 2.9%, social security 2.9%; expenditure (1986): food, beverages, and tobacco 37.6%, transportation and communications 12.0%, clothing 11.1%, household furnishings 7.1%, energy/water 6.7%.
Land use (1985): forested 44.8%; meadows and pastures 17.3%; agricultural and under permanent cultivation 9.2%; other 28.7%.

Foreign trade[8]

Balance of trade (current prices)

	1982	1983	1984	1985	1986	1987
U.S.$'000,000	+425.8	+971.6	+1,124.3	+1,285.9	+603.4	+232.2
% of total	11.0%	28.0%	27.8%	30.4%	16.0%	6.1%

Imports (1987): U.S.$2,232,517,000 (industrial raw materials 35.5%, industrial capital goods 22.4%, fuels and lubricants 16.5%, transport equipment 9.1%, consumer goods 9.3%). *Major import sources* (1986): United States 29.2%; Japan 11.2%; West Germany 9.5%; Brazil 6.7%; Italy 6.0%.
Exports (1987): U.S.$2,021,327,000 (crude petroleum 36.6%, shrimp 19.0%, bananas 13.2%, coffee 9.5%, cacao 4.1%, petroleum products 3.9%). *Major export destinations* (1986): United States 60.5%; West Germany 3.6%; Panama 2.7%; Japan 2.6%; Chile 2.2%; Taiwan 1.7%; Colombia 1.4%.

Transport and communications

Transport. Railroads (1986): route length 600 mi, 965 km; passenger-mi 17,800,000, passenger-km 28,600,000; short ton-mi cargo 5,100,000, metric ton-km cargo 7,400,000. Roads (1986): total length 22,486 mi, 36,187 km (paved 16%). Vehicles (1986): passenger cars 256,812; trucks and buses 36,691. Merchant marine (1987): vessels (100 gross tons and over) 156; total deadweight tonnage 588,224. Air transport (1984): passenger-mi 555,000,000, passenger-km 893,000,000; short ton-mi cargo 29,200,000, metric ton-km cargo 42,600,000; airports (1988) 14.
Communications. Daily newspapers (1985): total number 7; total circulation 538,000; circulation per 1,000 population 57. Radio (1985): 2,750,000 receivers (1 per 3.4 persons). Television (1987): 600,000 receivers (1 per 17 persons). Telephones (1986): 351,886 (1 per 28 persons).

Education and health

Education (1985–86)

	schools	teachers	students	student/ teacher ratio
Primary (age 4–12)	15,969	58,584	1,973,445	33.7
Secondary (age 12–18) Vocational[9] }	2,056	49,641	860,419	17.3
Higher	21	11,186	172,649	15.4

Educational attainment (1982). Percent of population age 25 and over having: no schooling 25.4%; incomplete primary 17.0%; complete primary 34.1%; some secondary 8.1%; secondary 7.9%; postsecondary 7.6%[1]. *Literacy* (1982): total population age 15 and over literate 3,914,694 (69.1%); males 2,005,455 (86.8%); females 1,909,239 (56.9%).
Health (1984): physicians 11,000 (1 per 829 persons); hospital beds 15,455 (1 per 590 persons); infant mortality rate per 1,000 live births (1985) 50.6.
Food (1984–86): daily per capita caloric intake 2,058 (vegetable products 82%, animal products 18%); (1983) 89% of FAO minimum requirement.

Military

Total active duty personnel (1987): 37,000 (army 78.4%, navy 10.8%, air force 10.8%). *Military expenditure as percent of GNP* (1984): 1.6% (world 5.9%); per capita expenditure U.S.$22.

[1]Detail does not add to total given because of rounding. [2]Total includes 71,800 persons not shown separately. [3]Excluding nomadic Indian tribes. [4]Based on incomplete registration. [5]Authorized construction. [6]Includes 83,103 unemployed persons not previously employed. [7]Wages in manufacturing. [8]Import figures are f.o.b. in balance of trade and c.i.f. for commodities and trading partners. [9]Includes teacher training.

Egypt

Official name: Jumhūrīyah Miṣr al-'Arabīyah (Arab Republic of Egypt).
Form of government: republic with one legislative house (People's Assembly [458])[1].
Chief of state: President.
Head of government: Prime Minister.
Capital: Cairo.
Official language: Arabic.
Official religion: Islam.
Monetary unit: 1 Egyptian pound (LE) = 100 piastres = 1,000 millièmes; valuation (Oct. 10, 1988)
1 U.S.$ = LE 2.29;
1 £ = LE 3.93.

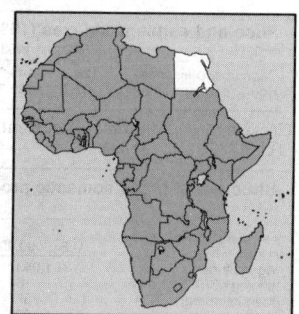

Area and population		area		population
Regions				1986
Governorates	Capitals	sq mi	sq km	census
Desert				
al-Baḥr al-Aḥmar	al-Ghurdaqah	78,643	203,685	90,491
Maṭrūḥ	Marsá Maṭrūḥ	81,897	212,112	160,567
Sīnā' al-Janūbīyah	aṭ-Ṭūr	12,796	33,140	28,988
Sīnā' ash-Shamālīyah	al-'Arīsh	10,646	27,574	171,505
al-Wādī al-Jadīd	al-Khārijah	145,369	376,505	113,838
Lower Egypt				
al-Buḥayrah	Damanhūr	3,911	10,130	3,257,168
ad-Daqahlīyah	al-Manṣūrah	1,340	3,471	3,500,470
Dumyāṭ	Dumyāṭ	227	589	741,264
al-Gharbīyah	Ṭanṭā	750	1,942	2,870,960
al-Ismā'īlīyah (Ismailia)		557	1,442	544,427
Kafr ash-Shaykh	Kafr ash-Shaykh	1,327	3,437	1,800,129
al-Minūfīyah	Shibīn al-Kawm	592	1,532	2,227,087
al-Qalyūbīyah	Banhā	387	1,001	2,514,244
ash-Sharqīyah	az-Zaqāzīq	1,614	4,180	3,420,119
Upper Egypt				
Aswān	Aswān	262	679	801,408
Asyūṭ	Asyūṭ	600	1,553	2,223,034
Banī Suwayf	Banī Suwayf	510	1,322	1,442,981
al-Fayyūm	al-Fayyūm	705	1,827	1,544,047
al-Jīzah	al-Jīzah	32,878	85,153	3,700,054
al-Minyā	al-Minyā	873	2,262	2,648,043
Qinā	Qinā	715	1,851	2,252,315
Sawhāj	Sawhāj	597	1,547	2,455,134
Urban				
Būr Sa'īd (Port Said)	—	28	72	399,793
al-Iskandarīyah (Alexandria)	—	1,034	2,679	2,917,327
al-Qāhirah (Cairo)	—	83	214	6,052,836
as-Suways (Suez)	—	6,888	17,840	326,820
TOTAL		385,229	997,739	48,205,049

Demography

Population (1988): 50,273,000.
Density (1988): persons per sq mi 127.6, persons per sq km 49.3.
Urban–rural (1986): urban 43.9%; rural 56.1%.
Sex distribution (1986): male 51.15%; female 48.85%.
Age breakdown (1986): under 15, 41.8%; 15–29, 26.1%; 30–44, 16.2%; 45–59, 10.4%; 60–74, 4.7%; 75 and over, 0.8%.
Population projection: (1990) 52,536,000; (2000) 63,941,000.
Doubling time: 25 years.
Ethnic composition (1983): Egyptian 99.8%; other 0.2%.
Religious affiliation (1986): Sunnī Muslim 94.1%; Christian 5.9%.
Major cities (1986): Cairo 6,052,836; Alexandria 2,917,327; al-Jīzah 1,670,800; Shubrā al-Khaymah 533,300; al-Maḥallah al-Kubrā 385,300.

Vital statistics

Birth rate per 1,000 population (1985): 37.5 (world avg. 29.0).
Death rate per 1,000 population (1985): 9.1 (world avg. 11.0).
Natural increase rate per 1,000 population (1985): 28.4 (world avg. 18.0).
Total fertility rate (avg. births per childbearing woman; 1986): 5.3.
Marriage rate per 1,000 population (1985): 9.1.
Divorce rate per 1,000 population (1981): 1.6.
Life expectancy at birth (1986): male 59.0 years; female 62.1 years.
Major causes of death per 100,000 population (1982): diseases of the circulatory system 186.3; infectious and parasitic diseases 168.9; diseases of the respiratory system 106.3; malignant neoplasms (cancers) 21.8.

National economy

Budget (1987–88). Revenue: LE 18,113,200,000 (1986–87; sovereign tax 66.3%, oil revenue 5.3%, Suez Canal revenue 1.6%). Expenditures: LE 23,058,900,000 (1986–87; debt servicing 13.5%, subsidies 8.7%, increase in the wages in the civil service and the state sector 5.9%).
Public debt (external, outstanding; 1986): U.S.$22,788,200,000.
Tourism: receipts from visitors (1985) U.S.$990,000,000; expenditures by nationals abroad (1984) U.S.$146,000,000.
Production (metric tons except as noted). Agriculture, forestry, fishing (1986): corn (maize) 3,801,000, tomatoes 2,840,000, rice 2,450,000, wheat 1,929,000, watermelons 1,350,000, potatoes 1,275,000, dry onions 877,000, millet 600,000, dates 460,000, cotton (lint) 434,000; livestock (number of live animals) 2,750,000 cattle, 2,700,000 goats, 2,600,000 buffalo, 2,550,000 sheep, 1,900,000 asses, 170,000 camels, 51,000,000 chickens; roundwood 2,057,000 cu m; fish catch 138,782. Mining and quarrying (1986): iron ore 2,135,000; phosphate rock 1,038,000; sodium carbonate 50,000. Manufacturing (1984–85): cement 4,893,000; nitrate fertilizers 4,038,000; phosphate fertilizers 900,000; sugar 764,000; steel 281,000; aluminum 175,000; cotton

yarn 243,000; pig iron 121,000; jute yarn and fabrics 50,000. Construction (1985): urban residential units 148,266. Energy production (consumption): electricity (kW-hr; 1986) 25,100,000,000 (25,100,000,000); coal (metric tons; 1986) n.a. (1,200,000); crude petroleum (barrels; 1986) 292,000,000 (153,000,000); petroleum products (metric tons; 1986) 19,782,000 (17,824,000); natural gas (cu m; 1986) 4,192,000,000 (4,192,000,000).
Gross national product (1986): U.S.$37,700,000,000 (U.S.$760 per capita).

Structure of gross domestic product and labour force				
	1986–87		1986	
	in value LE '000,000	% of total value	labour force	% of labour force
Agriculture	4,660.0	16.1	5,160,500	42.7
Mining	} 9,598.3	33.2	37,000	0.3
Manufacturing			1,872,400	15.5
Construction	1,384.0	4.8	571,200	4.7
Public utilities	266.9	0.9	92,400	0.8
Transp. and commun.	2,262.3	7.8	595,900	4.9
Trade	3,811.3	13.2	1,027,300	8.5
Finance	1,524.0	5.3	121,900	1.0
Pub. admin., defense	4,286.4	14.8	} 2,616,000	21.6
Services	1,126.8	3.9		
Other	...	...	...	...
TOTAL	28,920.0	100.0	12,094,600	100.0

Population economically active (1986): total 12,094,600; activity rate of total population 25.3% (participation rates: ages 15–64, 45.1%; female 14.6%).

Price and earnings indexes (1980 = 100)							
	1982	1983	1984	1985	1986	1987	1988[2]
Consumer price index	126.8	147.2	172.3	195.2	239.3	286.4	299.4
Earnings index	...	...	...	...	...	...	...

Household income and expenditure. Average household size (1986): 4.9; income per household: n.a.; sources of income: n.a.; expenditure[3] (1974–75): food 49.7%, clothing and footwear 14.2%, housing 12.4%, transportation 5.2%, tobacco 4.9%, recreation 1.3%.
Land use (1985): meadows and pastures 0.6%; agricultural and under permanent cultivation 2.5%; built-on, wasteland, and other 96.9%.

Foreign trade

Balance of trade (current prices)					
	1981	1982	1983	1984	1985	1986
LE '000,000	−3,924.5	−4,170.4	−4,982.0	−5,338.1	−4,373.1	−4,261.8
% of total	46.4%	48.8%	52.3%	54.8%	45.7%	45.2%

Imports (1985–86): LE 6,845,100,000 (foodstuffs 25.6%; machinery and transport equipment 24.2%; chemical products 10.7%; lubricants, fuel, and minerals 9.3%). *Major import sources* (1984): U.S. 11.4%; W.Ger. 10.2%; Italy 8.5%; France 7.8%; Japan 6.3%.
Exports (1985–86): LE 2,583,300,000 (petroleum and petroleum products 64.5%; raw cotton 9.6%; cotton yarn, textiles, and fabrics 8.8%). *Major export destinations* (1984): Italy 17.2%; Romania 8.4%; France 6.6%; U.S. 5.5%; U.S.S.R. 5.3%; The Netherlands 5.2%.

Transport and communications

Transport. Railroads (1984–85): length 3,335 mi, 5,367 km; passenger-mi 16,300,000,000, passenger-km 26,232,000,000; short ton-mi cargo 1,912,000,000, metric ton-km cargo 2,792,000,000. Roads (1986): total length 19,661 mi, 31,641 km (paved 16%). Vehicles (1986): passenger cars 757,925; trucks and buses 354,139. Merchant marine (1987): vessels (100 gross tons and over) 428; total deadweight tonnage 1,515,156. Inland water (1987): Suez Canal, number of transits 17,541; metric ton cargo 347,038,000. Air transport (1986): passenger-km 4,023,130,000; metric ton-km cargo 111,516,000; airports (1988) 11.
Communications. Daily newspapers (1986): total number 17; total circulation 4,216,268[4]; circulation per 1,000 population 88[4]. Radio (1986): 12,000,000 receivers (1 per 3.9 persons). Television (1987): 3,860,000 receivers (1 per 13 persons). Telephones (1986): 1,393,630 (1 per 35 persons).

Education and health

Education (1985)				
	schools	teachers	students	student/ teacher ratio
Primary (age 6–11)	13,233	194,929	6,002,850	30.8
Secondary (age 12–17)	20,106	128,616	2,704,371	21.0
Voc., teacher tr.[5]	519	48,605	765,057	15.7
Higher	12	33,200[5]	739,017	...

Educational attainment (1986). Percent of population age 10 and over having: no formal education 73.8%; primary and secondary 21.8%; higher 4.4%. *Literacy* (1986): total population age 15 and over literate 12,447,057 (44.9%); males 8,101,831 (57.6%); females 4,345,226 (31.8%).
Health (1984): physicians 73,300 (1 per 635 persons); hospital beds 85,350 (1 per 545 persons); infant mortality rate per 1,000 live births (1985) 70.5.
Food (1984–86): daily per capita caloric intake 3,313 (vegetable products 92%, animal products 8%); (1983) 126% of FAO recommended minimum.

Military

Total active duty personnel (1987): 445,000 (army 71.9%, navy 4.5%, air force 23.6%). *Military expenditure as percent of GNP* (1985): 14.2% (world 6.1%); per capita expenditure U.S.$135.

[1]Includes 10 nonelective seats. [2]February. [3]Urban only. [4]Based on 12 dailies only. [5]1983.

El Salvador

Official name: República de El
Salvador (Republic of El Salvador).
Form of government: republic with
one legislative house (Legislative
Assembly [60]).
Chief of state and government:
President.
Capital: San Salvador.
Official language: Spanish.
Official religion: none[1].
Monetary unit: 1 colón (ϕ) = 100
centavos; valuation (Oct. 10, 1988)
1 U.S.$ = ϕ5.00[2]; 1 £ = ϕ8.57.

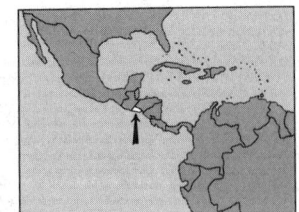

Area and population

Departments	Capitals	area sq mi	area sq km	population 1985 estimate
Ahuachapán	Ahuachapán	479	1,240	271,990
Cabañas	Sensuntepeque	426	1,104	199,229
Chalatenango	Chalatenango	779	2,017	256,688
Cuscatlán	Cojutepeque	292	756	222,389
La Libertad	Nueva San Salvador	638	1,653	440,030
La Paz	Zacatecoluca	473	1,224	278,719
La Unión	La Unión	801	2,074	346,087
Morazán	San Francisco (Gotera)	559	1,447	235,632
San Miguel	San Miguel	802	2,077	480,486
San Salvador	San Salvador	342	886	1,094,249
Santa Ana	Santa Ana	781	2,023	490,367
San Vicente	San Vicente	457	1,184	220,630
Sonsonate	Sonsonate	473	1,226	364,075
Usulután	Usulután	822	2,130	437,325
TOTAL		8,124	21,041	5,337,896[3]

Demography

Population (1988): 5,083,000.
Density (1988): persons per sq mi 625.7, persons per sq km 241.6.
Urban–rural (1986): urban 42.8%; rural 57.2%.
Sex distribution (1985): male 50.01%; female 49.99%.
Age breakdown (1985): under 15, 45.3%; 15–29, 27.8%; 30–44, 14.4%; 45–59,
7.8%; 60–74, 3.7%; 75 and over, 1.0%.
Population projection: (1990) 5,234,000; (2000) 6,996,000.
Doubling time: 26 years.
Ethnic composition (1980): mestizo (white and Indian) 93.7%; Indian 5.3%;
white 1.0%.
Religious affiliation (1984): Roman Catholic 91.7%; other 8.3%.
Major cities (1985): San Salvador 459,902; Santa Ana 137,879; Mejicanos
91,465; San Miguel 88,520; Delgado 67,684.

Vital statistics

Birth rate per 1,000 population (1987): 37.0 (world avg. 26.0); (1984) legiti-
mate 32.6%; illegitimate 67.4%.
Death rate per 1,000 population (1987): 10.0 (world avg. 9.9).
Natural increase rate per 1,000 population (1987): 27.0 (world avg. 16.1).
Total fertility rate (avg. births per childbearing woman; 1987): 4.9.
Marriage rate per 1,000 population (1984): 3.5.
Divorce rate per 1,000 population (1984): 0.3.
Life expectancy at birth (1981): male 61.7 years; female 65.3 years.
Major causes of death per 100,000 population (1984): homicide and other
violence 67.3; diseases of the circulatory system 63.9; infectious and para-
sitic diseases 60.0; accidents 45.0; ill-defined conditions 115.9.

National economy

Budget (1986)[4]. Revenue: ϕ3,508,000,000 (indirect taxes 58.6%, of which
taxes on coffee exports 27.2%; direct taxes 18.4%; development income
14.3%). Expenditures: ϕ3,480,000,000 (current expenditure 73.0%; debt
amortization 13.7%; development expenditure 13.3%).
Public debt (external, outstanding; 1986): U.S.$1,463,300,000.
Tourism: receipts from visitors (1986) U.S.$22,000,000; expenditures by na-
tionals abroad (1983) U.S.$74,000,000.
Production (value added in ϕ'000,000 except as noted). Agriculture, forestry,
fishing (1986): coffee 2,528, corn (maize) 226, sugarcane 121, aviculture 144,
maicillo (variety of millet) 50, beans 48, cotton 38, rice 32, bananas 55,000
metric tons; livestock (number of live animals) 1,010,000 cattle, 400,000
pigs, 4,000,000 chickens; forestry 56; fishing 90. Mining and quarrying
(1987): very limited amounts of gold, silver, and limestone. Manufacturing
(1986): food products 1,123; beverages 469; petroleum products 236; textiles 189; chemical products 173; nonmetallic products 155; tobacco 133;
clothing and footwear 116. Construction: residential 537; nonresidential
122. Energy production (consumption): electricity (kW-hr; 1986) 1,750,-
000,000 (1,675,000,000); coal, none (none); petroleum (barrels; 1986) none
(4,581,000); petroleum products (metric tons; 1986) 549,000 (510,000); natural gas, none (none).
Household income and expenditure. Average household size (1978) 5.1;
income per household ϕ8,650 (U.S.$3,460); sources of income: n.a.; ex-
penditure (1978): food and beverages 42.7%, household furnishings 13.2%,
transportation 11.2%, clothing and footwear 9.8%.
Population economically active (1980): total 1,593,353; activity rate of total
population 35.4% (participation rates: ages 15–64, 62.4%; female 34.8%;
unemployed [1987] 33%).

Price and earnings indexes (1980 = 100)

	1982	1983	1984	1985	1986	1987	1988
Consumer price index	128.3	145.3	162.1	198.2	261.6	326.6	361.1[5]
Hourly earnings index[6]	107.7	125.3	126.8	136.4	...	...	...

Gross national product (at current market prices; 1986): U.S.$4,000,000,000
(U.S.$820 per capita).

Structure of gross domestic product and labour force

	1986 in value U.S.$'000,000	1986 % of total value	1980 labour force	1980 % of labour force
Agriculture	1,043	24.0	636,617	40.0
Mining	6	0.1	4,394	0.3
Manufacturing	757	17.4	247,621	15.5
Construction	136	3.1	80,089	5.0
Public utilities	165	3.8	9,681	0.6
Transportation and communications	262	6.1	65,593	4.1
Trade	709	16.3	256,086	16.1
Finance	364	8.4	15,863	1.0
Public admin., defense	616	14.2 }	250,158	15.7
Services	285	6.6 }		
Other	—	—	27,251[7]	1.7[7]
TOTAL	4,343	100.0	1,593,353	100.0

Land use (1985): forested 5.3%; meadows and pastures 29.5%; agricultural
and under permanent cultivation 35.3%; other 29.9%.

Foreign trade[8]

Balance of trade (current prices)

	1981	1982	1983	1984	1985	1986
ϕ'000,000	−224.9	−181.0	−169.5	−387.9	−467.7	−296.5
% of total	5.3%	4.9%	4.4%	9.7%	12.1%	4.0%

Imports (1986): ϕ4,284,000,000 (basic and miscellaneous manufactures
34.6%; consumer goods 24.3%, of which nondurable goods 21.4%; machinery and transport equipment 17.5%; crude petroleum 9.7%; fertilizers
3.8%). *Major import sources:* United States 39.8%; Guatemala 12.3%; Mexico 6.9%; Venezuela 6.5%; West Germany 4.8%.
Exports (1986): ϕ3,563,000,000 (coffee 70.9%; other exports include unrefined sugar, chemical products, raw cotton, petroleum products). *Major
export destinations:* United States 49.2%; West Germany 24.1%; Guatemala
6.7%; Japan 3.8%; Costa Rica 3.7%.

Transport and communications

Transport. Railroads (1986): route length 374 mi, 602 km; passenger-mi
3,104,000, passenger-km 4,996,000; short ton-mi cargo 16,701,500, metric
ton-km cargo 24,385,300. Roads (1985): total length 7,558 mi, 12,164 km
(paved 14%). Vehicles (1985): passenger cars 136,163; trucks and buses
19,461. Merchant marine (1987): vessels (100 gross tons and over) 14; total
deadweight tonnage 3,318. Air transport (1986)[9]: passenger-mi 238,689,000,
passenger-km 384,133,000; short ton-mi cargo 1,240,000, metric ton-km
cargo 1,810,000; airports (1988) with scheduled flights 1.
Communications. Daily newspapers (1986): total number 5; total circulation
253,200; circulation per 1,000 population 52. Radio (1986): total number
of receivers 1,200,000 (1 per 4.1 persons). Television (1987): total number
of receivers 425,000 (1 per 12 persons). Telephones (1986): 128,795 (1
per 39 persons).

Education and health

Education (1985)

	schools	teachers	students	student/ teacher ratio
Primary (7–15)	2,883	24,295	940,963	38.7
Secondary (16–18)	285	3,880	90,288	23.3
Vocational	17[10]	667[10]	9,505	...
Higher	34	3,404	60,994	17.9

Educational attainment (1980). Percent of population over age 10 having:
no formal schooling 30.2%; primary education 60.7%; secondary 6.9%;
higher 2.3%. *Literacy* (1980): total population over age 15 literate 1,771,431
(69.0%); males literate 880,908 (73.2%); females literate 890,523 (65.3%).
Health (1984): physicians 1,592[11] (1 per 3,002 persons); hospital beds 6,525[11]
(1 per 732 persons); infant mortality rate per 1,000 live births (1987) 88.0.
Food (1979–81): daily per capita caloric intake 2,155 (vegetable products
88%, animal products 12%); (1983) 91% of FAO recommended minimum
requirement.

Military

Total active duty personnel (1988): 47,000 (army 91.5%, navy 5.3%, air force
3.2%). *Military expenditure as percent of GNP* (1985): 5.5% (world 6.1%);
per capita expenditure U.S.$53.

[1]Roman Catholicism, although not official, enjoys special recognition per constitution. [2]Official buying rate. [3]De jure population. [4]Excludes U.S. foreign aid.
[5]February. [6]Wages in manufacturing for males in San Salvador department. [7]Mostly
unemployed not previously employed. [8]Import figures are f.o.b. in balance of trade
and c.i.f. for commodities and trading partners. [9]TACA airlines; data for January–
September only. [10]1983. [11]Public sector only.

Equatorial Guinea

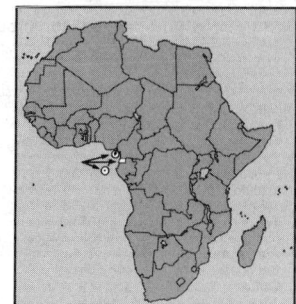

Official name: República de Guinea
Ecuatorial (Republic of Equatorial
Guinea).
Form of government: unitary
single-party republic with one
legislative house (House of
Representatives of the People [41]).
Head of state and government:
President.
Capital: Malabo.
Official language: Spanish.
Official religion: none.
Monetary unit[1]: 1 CFA franc
(CFAF) = 100 centimes; valuation
(Oct. 10, 1988) 1 U.S.$ = CFAF
316.13; 1 £ = CFAF 541.38.

Area and population

Regions	area		population
Provinces	sq mi	sq km	1983 census
Insular	785[2]	2,034	59,196
Annobón	7	17	2,006
Bioko Norte	300	776	46,221
Bioko Sur	479	1,241	10,969
Continental	10,045[2]	26,017	240,804
Centro-Sur	3,834	9,931	52,393
Kie-Ntem	1,522	3,943	70,202
Litoral	2,573	6,665	66,370
Wele-Nzas	2,115	5,478	51,839
TOTAL	10,830	28,051	300,000

Demography

Population (1988): 335,000.
Density (1988): persons per sq mi 30.9, persons per sq km 11.9.
Urban–rural (1986): urban 60.7%; rural 39.3%.
Sex distribution (1985): male 49.00%; female 51.00%.
Age breakdown (1985): under 15, 38.1%; 15–29, 26.0%; 30–44, 17.7%; 45–59, 11.5%; 60–74, 5.6%; 75 and over, 1.1%.
Population projection: (1990) 351,000; (2000) 445,000.
Doubling time: 32 years.
Ethnic composition (1983): Fang 72.0%; Bubi 14.7%; Duala 2.7%; Ibibio 1.3%; Maka 1.3%; other 8.0%.
Religious affiliation (1980): Christian (mostly Roman Catholic) 88.8%; traditional beliefs 4.6%; atheist 1.4%; Muslim 0.5%; other 0.2%; none 4.5%.
Major cities (1983): Malabo 37,500; Ela-Nguema 6,179; Bata 5,633; Campo Yaunde 5,199; Los Angeles 4,079.

Vital statistics

Birth rate per 1,000 population (1980–85): 42.5 (world avg. 29.0); legitimate, n.a.; illegitimate, n.a.
Death rate per 1,000 population (1980–85): 21.0 (world avg. 11.0).
Natural increase rate per 1,000 population (1980–85): 21.5 (world avg. 18.0).
Total fertility rate (avg. births per childbearing woman; 1985–86): 5.7.
Marriage rate per 1,000 population: n.a.
Divorce rate per 1,000 population: n.a.
Life expectancy at birth (1988): male 44.0 years; female 48.0 years.
Major causes of death per 100,000 population: n.a.; however, major diseases include malaria (affecting about 60% of the population), cholera, leprosy, trypanosomiasis (sleeping sickness), and waterborne (especially gastrointestinal) diseases.

National economy

Budget (1987). Revenue: CFA 7,170,000,000 (indirect taxes 70.0%, of which customs duties 65.0%; public revenue 17.7%; direct taxes 4.0%; other fiscal receipts 1.7%). Expenditures: CFA 8,900,000,000 (goods and services 21.6%; debt service 21.5%; administration 16.3%; capital expenditure 9.3%; transfer payments 6.2%).
Public debt (external, outstanding; 1986): U.S.$141,000,000.
Household income and expenditure. Average household size (1980) 4.5; income per household: n.a.; sources of income: n.a.; expenditure: n.a.
Gross domestic product (at current market prices; 1986): U.S.$107,000,000 (U.S.$330 per capita).

Structure of gross domestic product and labour force

	1986		1983	
	in value CFAF '000,000	% of total value	labour force	% of labour force
Agriculture, forestry	20,548	59.5	86,500	85.7
Manufacturing	326	0.9	900	0.9
Construction	3,126	9.1	1,000	1.0
Public utilities	728	2.1	...	...
Transportation and communications	897	2.6	...	...
Trade	1,740	5.0	2,600	2.6
Finance				
Pub. admin., defense	} 7,175	20.8	7,400	7.3
Services			2,500	2.5
Other			...	...
TOTAL	34,540	100.0	100,900	100.0

Production (metric tons except as noted). Agriculture, forestry, fishing (1986): roots and tubers 91,000 (of which cassava 55,000, sweet potatoes 35,000),
bananas 19,000, fruit excluding melons 19,000, coconuts 8,000, coffee 7,000, cacao beans 5,500, palm oil 5,100, palm kernels 2,900; livestock (number of live animals) 35,000 sheep, 8,000 goats, 5,000 pigs, 4,000 cattle, 160,000 chickens; roundwood 607,000 cu m; fish catch 4,400. Mining and quarrying: details n.a.; however, in addition to quarrying for construction materials, unexploited deposits of iron ore, lead, zinc, manganese, and molybdenum are present; traces of gold, diamonds, and radioactive ores have also been located. Manufacturing (1986): palm oil 5,100. Construction: n.a. Energy production (consumption): electricity (kW-hr; 1986) 16,000,000 (16,000,-000); coal, none (n.a.); crude petroleum[3], none (n.a.); petroleum products (metric tons; 1985) none (26,000); natural gas, none (n.a.).
Population economically active (1983): total 100,900; activity rate of total population 34.0% (participation rates: ages 15–64 n.a.; female, n.a.; unemployed, n.a.).

Price and earnings indexes (1984 = 100)

	1984	1985	1986	1987
Consumer price index	100.0	185.0	152.0	121.0[4]
Earnings index	...	...	...	...

Tourism (1987): Tourism remains undeveloped.
Land use (1985): forested 46.2%; meadows and pastures 3.7%; agricultural and under permanent cultivation 8.2%; built-on, wasteland, and other 41.9%.

Foreign trade

Balance of trade (current prices)

	1978	1979	1980	1981	1982	1983
EK '000,000	+547.6	+351.9	−4,704.0	−5,400.0	−6,657.0	−9,326.0
% of total	18.6%	9.8%	54.8%	51.1%	27.5%	29.3%

Imports (1981): EK 7,982,000,000 (food, beverages, and tobacco 24.9%; petroleum and petroleum products 22.4%; motor vehicles and machinery 17.4%; iron and steel products 12.4%; clothing 6.0%). *Major import sources* (1985): Spain 30.2%; France 23.6%; Italy 14.6%; The Netherlands 4.8%; West Germany 4.1%; Belgium–Luxembourg 3.0%; China 2.4%; United States 1.9%; Japan 1.7%; Norway 1.5%; United Kingdom 1.1%; Switzerland 0.9%.
Exports (1981): EK 2,582,000,000 (cacao 71.5%; timber 24.4%; coffee 2.8%). *Major export destinations* (1985): The Netherlands 37.6%; Spain 31.5%; West Germany 16.4%; Italy 5.0%; France 2.2%; Switzerland 1.4%; Portugal 1.3%; Belgium–Luxembourg 0.7%; Greece 0.3%.

Transport and communications

Transport. Railroads: none. Roads (1982): total length 1,715 mi, 2,760 km (paved 12%). Vehicles (1979): passenger cars 4,000; trucks and buses 3,000. Merchant marine (1987): vessels (100 gross tons and over) 2; total deadweight tonnage 6,700. Air transport (1985): passenger-mi 4,000,000, passenger-km 7,000,000; short ton-mi cargo 700,000, metric ton-km cargo 1,000,000; airports (1988) with scheduled flights 2.
Communications. Daily newspapers (1986): total number 2; total circulation 1,000; circulation per 1,000 population 3.1. Radio (1986): total number of receivers 35,000 (1 per 9.1 persons). Television (1987): total number of receivers 2,500 (1 per 131 persons). Telephones (1982): 1,366 (1 per 209 persons).

Education and health

Education (1980–81)[5]

	schools	teachers	students	student/ teacher ratio
Primary (age 6–11)	511	647	40,110	62.0
Secondary (age 12–17)	14	288	3,013	10.5
Voc., teacher tr.[6]	...	...	...	...

Educational attainment, n.a. *Literacy* (c. 1985): total population literate, about 31%; males literate 46%; females literate 17%.
Health: physicians (mid-1980s) 5 (1 per 61,000 persons); hospital beds (1982) 3,200 (1 per 95 persons); infant mortality rate per 1,000 live births (1983) 137.
Food (latest): daily per capita caloric intake 2,230; 68% of FAO recommended minimum requirement.

Military

Total active duty personnel (1988): 1,400 (army 78.6%, navy 14.3%, air force 7.1%). *Military expenditure as percent of GNP* (1981): 1.8% (world 5.8%); per capita expenditure U.S.$9.

---

[1]As of Jan. 1, 1985, Equatorial Guinea became a member of the franc zone, substituting the CFA franc for the previous monetary unit, the ekwele (EK, plural bipkwele), effectively devaluing the latter by 82%. [2]Detail does not add to total given because of rounding. [3]Equatorial Guinea's offshore potential oil areas totaled about 13,450 sq km. [4]September 1987. [5]In 1982–83 there were 52,021 students in primary; and in 1980–81 there were 175 students in higher education studying abroad. [6]Efforts are being undertaken to provide the training necessary to qualify nondegree teachers for service. Also, teacher training schools are to be expanded in order to increase the number of primary-school teachers.

Ethiopia

Official name[1]: YeĒtiyop'iya Hezbawi Dimokrasīyawī Republēk (People's Democratic Republic of Ethiopia).
Form of government: unitary single-party people's republic with one legislative house (Shengo [835]).
Chief of state and government: President.
Capital: Addis Ababa.
Official language: Amharic.
Official religion: none.
Monetary unit: 1 Ethiopian Birr (Br) = 100 cents; valuation (Oct. 10, 1988) 1 U.S.$ = Br 2.07; 1 £ = Br 3.54.

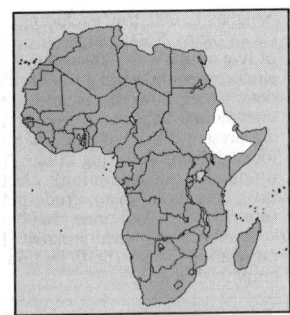

Area and population

Regions	Capitals	area sq mi	area sq km	population 1988 estimate
Arsi	Asela	9,500	24,600	1,860,606
Bale	Goba	49,500	128,300	1,126,697
Eritrea[2]	Asmera	45,300	117,400	3,039,465
Gemu Gofa	Arba Minch	15,400	40,100	1,395,331
Gojam	Debre Markos	24,900	64,400	3,632,276
Gonder	Gonder	28,300	73,400	3,270,440
Hararge	Harer	98,400	254,800	4,657,859
Ilubabor	Metu	19,600	50,800	1,078,308
Kefa	Jima	20,500	53,000	2,740,773
Shewa[2]	Addis Ababa	33,000	85,500	10,714,244
Sidamo	Awasa	45,100	116,700	4,241,527
Tigray	Mekele	25,400	65,700	2,700,921
Welega	Nekemte	27,000	69,800	2,770,598
Welo	Dese	30,500	79,000	4,075,959
TOTAL		472,400	1,223,500	47,305,304[3]

Demography

Population (1988): 47,501,000.
Density (1988): persons per sq mi 100.6, persons per sq km 38.8.
Urban–rural (1988): urban 10.6%; rural 89.4%.
Sex distribution (1988): male 49.95%; female 50.05%.
Age breakdown (1988): under 15, 46.5%; 15–29, 22.8%; 30–44, 15.6%; 45–59, 8.9%; 60–74, 4.5%; 75 and over, 1.7%.
Population projection: (1990) 50,341,000; (2000) 67,523,000.
Doubling time: 26 years.
Ethnolinguistic composition (1983): Amhara 37.7%; Galla 35.3%; Tigrinya 8.6%; Gurage 3.3%; Ometo (Omotic) 2.7%; Sidamo 2.4%; Tigre 1.9%; Afar 1.8%; Somali 1.7%; other 4.6%.
Religious affiliation (1980): Ethiopian Orthodox 52.5%; Muslim 31.4%; traditional beliefs 11.4%; other Christian 4.5%; other 0.2%.
Major cities (1984): Addis Ababa 1,423,111; Asmera 275,385; Dire Dawa 98,104; Gonder 68,958; Dese 68,848.

Vital statistics

Birth rate per 1,000 population (1985): 49.7 (world avg. 29.0).
Death rate per 1,000 population (1985): 23.1 (world avg. 11.0).
Natural increase rate per 1,000 population (1985): 26.6 (world avg. 18.0).
Total fertility rate (avg. births per childbearing woman; 1985): 6.7.
Life expectancy at birth (1985): male 39.5 years; female 42.6 years.
Major causes of death (1977–78)[4]: infectious and parasitic diseases 24.0%; digestive system diseases 17.6%; allergy, endocrine, metabolic, nutritional, and circulatory diseases 14.9%; respiratory diseases 9.9%.

National economy

Budget (1986–87). Revenue: Br 2,800,000,000 (1984–85; taxes 71.3%, of which income and profit tax 27.3%, excise tax 14.6%, import duties 12.2%, export duties 7.4%; nontax revenue 28.7%). Expenditures: Br 5,390,000,000 (1984–85; general services 35.9%; economic development 31.3%, of which agriculture and settlement 11.8%; social services 15.6%, of which education 8.5%, public health 3.1%; debt service 5.6%).
Tourism: receipts from visitors (1986) U.S.$5,000,000; expenditures by nationals abroad (1986) U.S.$4,000,000.
Production (metric tons except as noted). Agriculture, forestry, fishing (1986): sugarcane 1,725,000, corn (maize) 1,500,000, barley 1,000,000, pulses 945,000, wheat 700,000, coffee 225,000, yams 215,000, potatoes 210,000, millet 200,000, seed cotton 73,000; livestock (number of live animals) 26,300,000 cattle, 23,550,000 sheep, 17,280,000 goats, 6,990,000 horses, mules, and asses, 1,040,000 camels; roundwood (1985) 37,896,000 cu m; fish catch 4,100. Mining and quarrying (1986): cement 250,000; salt 135,000; limestone 5,000; gold 15,000 troy oz; platinum 150 troy oz. Manufacturing (gross value in Br '000[5]; 1985–86): food and beverages 796,300; textiles 376,200; leather and shoes 181,200; metal products 120,200; cigarettes 107,800; chemicals 103,700; paper and printing 91,600; nonmetallic mineral products 69,400. Construction (authorized; 1981): residential 162,000 sq m; nonresidential 32,300 sq m, of which commercial 24,800 sq m. Energy production (consumption): electricity (kW-hr; 1986) 802,000,000 (802,000,000); coal, none (n.a.); crude petroleum (barrels; 1986) n.a. (6,003,000); petroleum products (metric tons; 1986) 689,000 (524,000); natural gas, n.a. (n.a.).
Land use (1985): forested 25.1%; meadows and pastures 41.0%; agricultural and under permanent cultivation 12.6%; other 21.3%.
Gross national product (at current market prices; 1986): U.S.$5,400,000,000 (U.S.$120 per capita).

Structure of gross domestic product and labour force

	1985–86 in value Br '000,000	1985–86 % of total value	1985 labour force	1985 % of labour force
Agriculture	4,354.5	44.8	14,982,000	78.1
Mining	15.3	0.2		
Manufacturing	1,072.9	11.1		
Construction	387.6	4.0	1,630,000	8.5
Public utilities	109.9	1.1		
Transportation and communications	718.1	7.4		
Trade	1,036.3	10.7		
Finance	339.2	3.5	2,570,000	13.4
Pub. admin., defense	781.6	8.0		
Services	687.3	7.1		
Other	205.1	2.1		
TOTAL	9,707.6[3]	100.0	19,182,000	100.0

Public debt (external, outstanding; 1986): U.S.$1,989,100,000.
Population economically active (1987): total 19,814,900; activity rate of total population 43.1% (participation rates: ages 15–64 [1985] 73.5%; female 35.2%; unemployed, n.a.).

Price and earnings indexes (1980 = 100)

	1981	1982	1983	1984	1985	1986	1987
Consumer price index	106.1	112.4	111.6	121.0	144.1	130.0	126.8
Monthly earnings index	...	...	...	...	...	...	...

Household income and expenditure. Average household size (1984) 4.5; income per household c. U.S.$600; sources of income: n.a.; expenditure[6] (1963): food 49.0%, energy and household utilities 14.6%, clothing and footwear 6.7%, miscellaneous goods and services 5.4%, transportation 4.5%, recreation and reading 2.6%, medical care 1.8%, personal care 0.8%.

Foreign trade

Balance of trade (current prices)

	1981	1982	1983	1984	1985	1986
Br '000,000	−723.8	−775.6	−980.4	−1,086.7	−1,367.0	−981.2
% of total	31.0%	31.7%	37.0%	38.6%	49.8%	34.3%

Imports (1985): Br 2,061,900,000 (food and beverages 26.8%, industrial supplies 21.3%, transport equipment 15.7%, petroleum and petroleum products 14.7%, machinery 14.4%, consumer goods 7.0%). *Major import sources:* U.S.S.R. 17.4%; United States 16.1%; West Germany 10.0%; United Kingdom 8.7%; Italy 8.0%; Japan 6.0%.
Exports (1985): Br 688,400,000 (coffee 61.9%, hides 15.9%, petroleum products 9.8%, vegetables and fruits 2.6%, refined sugar 1.0%). *Major export destinations:* West Germany 18.5%; The Netherlands 13.2%; United States 10.5%; Japan 10.3%; South Yemen 8.1%; Italy 7.7%; U.S.S.R. 5.2%.

Transport and communications

Transport. Railroads[7] (1986): length 485 mi, 781 km; passenger-mi 217,000,000, passenger-km 350,000,000; short ton-mi cargo 86,000,000, metric ton-km cargo 125,000,000. Roads (1985): total length 23,532 mi, 37,871 km (paved 34%). Vehicles (1985–86): passenger cars 41,161; trucks and buses 19,986. Merchant marine (1987): vessels (100 gross tons and over) 25; total deadweight tonnage 94,142. Air transport (1987): passenger-mi 346,931,000, passenger-km 558,333,000; short ton-mi cargo 71,130,000, metric ton-km cargo 103,848,000; airports (1988) with scheduled flights 37.
Communications. Daily newspapers (1987): total number 3; total circulation 47,000; circulation per 1,000 population 1.0. Radio (1986): 2,000,000 receivers (1 per 22 persons). Television (1987): 70,000 receivers (1 per 659 persons). Telephones (1986): 132,209 (1 per 344 persons).

Education and health

Education (1985–86)

	schools	teachers	students	student/ teacher ratio
Primary (age 7–12)	7,900	50,922	2,448,778	48.1
Secondary (age 13–18)	1,209	15,218	655,517	43.1
Voc., teacher tr.[8]	...	390	4,969	12.7
Higher	11[9]	1,314[8]	18,436	...

Educational attainment, n.a. *Literacy* (1980)[10]: total population age 15 and over literate 1,000,000 (4.8%); males (9.3%); females (0.5%).
Health (1983–84): physicians 539 (1 per 78,740 persons); hospital beds 11,307 (1 per 3,754 persons); infant mortality rate (1980–85) 155.0.
Food (1979–81): daily per capita caloric intake 2,149 (vegetable products 93%, animal products 7%); (1983) 84% of FAO recommended minimum requirement.

Military

Total active duty personnel (1988): 315,800[11] (army 98.1%, navy 0.6%, air force 1.3%). *Military expenditure as percent of GNP* (1985): 9.1% (world 6.1%); per capita expenditure U.S.$9.

[1]On Feb. 1, 1987, a referendum approved a constitution providing for civilian rule. A National Assembly (Shengo) was elected on June 14, 1987. [2]Eritrea includes Aseb Administration, and Shewa includes Addis Ababa region. [3]Detail does not add to total given because of rounding. [4]Percentage of deaths in a sample population of hospital inpatients. [5]At constant prices of 1978–79. [6]Weights of consumer price index components; excludes rent. Addis Ababa only. [7]Includes 62 mi (100 km) of the Chemin de Fer Djibouti–Ethiopien (CDE) in Djibouti; excludes 190 mi (306 km) of Northern Ethiopia Railway, not in use since 1978. [8]1985. [9]1983–84. [10]Adult illiteracy is reported to have been reduced to about 37% in 1987. [11]About 2,200 Cuban and other Soviet-bloc advisers were assisting government forces.

Faeroe Islands

Official name: Faerøerne (Danish);
Føroyar (Faeroese) (Faeroe Islands).
Political status: self-governing region
of the Danish realm with a single
legislative body (Lagting [32]).
Chief of state: Danish Monarch
represented by state commissioner.
Head of home government: chairman
of Landsstyre (executive body), also
formally titled Head of the Home
Government.
Capital: Tórshavn (Thorshavn).
Official languages: Faeroese; Danish.
Official religion: Evangelical Lutheran.
Monetary unit: 1 Faeroese krone (FKr)
= 100 øre; valuation (Oct. 10, 1988)
1 U.S.$ = Fkr 7.13; 1£ = FKr 12.21.

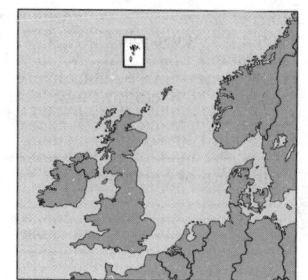

Area and population

Districts	Capitals	area		population
		sq mi	sq km	1987 estimate
Eysturoyar (Østerø)	—	110	286	10,196
Nordhoya (Norderøernes)	—	93	241	6,016
Sandoyar (Sandø)	—	48	125	1,745
Streymoyar (Strømø)	—	151	392	19,521
Sudhuroyar Nordhara (Suderø Nordre)	—	38	97	3,112
Sudhuroyar Sunnara (Suderø Søndre)	—	27	70	2,778
Vága (Vågø)	—	73	188	2,944
TOTAL		540	1,399	46,312

Demography

Population (1988): 46,986.
Density (1988): persons per sq mi 33.6, persons per sq km 87.0.
Urban-rural (1987): urban (Tórshavn only) 30.0%; rural 70.0%.
Sex distribution (1987): male 52.40%; female 47.60%.
Age breakdown (1986): under 15, 25.0%; 15–29, 25.1%; 30–44, 20.5%; 45–59, 13.7%; 60–74, 11.5%; 75 and over, 4.3%.
Population projection: (1990) 47,900; (2000) 53,000.
Doubling time: 99 years.
Ethnic composition (by place of birth; 1970): born in Faeroe Islands 95.3%; born elsewhere 4.7%.
Religious affiliation (1980): Evangelical Lutheran Church of Denmark 74.4%; Plymouth Brethren 19.8%; Roman Catholic 0.1%; other 5.2%.
Major cities (1987): Tórshavn 13,905.

Vital statistics

Birth rate per 1,000 population (1986): 15.0 (world avg. 26.0); legitimate 60.0%; illegitimate 40.0%.
Death rate per 1,000 population (1986): 8.0 (world avg. 9.9).
Natural increase rate per 1,000 population (1986): 7.0 (world avg. 16.1).
Total fertility rate (avg. births per childbearing woman; 1986): 2.4.
Marriage rate per 1,000 population (1986): 4.8.
Divorce rate per 1,000 population (1983): 0.5.
Life expectancy at birth (1981–85): male 73.3 years; female 79.6 years.
Major causes of death per 100,000 population (1986): diseases of the circulatory system 332.2, of which ischemic heart disease 284.4, cerebrovascular disease 93.4; malignant neoplasms (cancers) 162.9; diseases of the respiratory system 41.3, of which pneumonia 21.7, bronchitis, emphysema, and asthma 17.4; automobile accidents 26.1; suicides 10.9.

National economy

Budget (1988). Revenue: FKr 2,859,135,000 (customs and excise duties 38.5%; taxes 36.9%; payments from the Danish government 23.2%). Expenditures: FKR 2,859,135,000 (social welfare 26.7%; agriculture, fishing, and commerce 17.1%; medical services 13.1%; education 13.0%; roads and bridges 9.8%; administration 5.7%).
Public debt: n.a.
Gross national product (at current market prices; 1986): U.S.$550,000,000 (U.S.$11,940 per capita).

Structure of gross domestic product and labour force

	1987		1977	
	in value FKr '000,000	% of total value	labour force	% of labour force
Agriculture	61	1.2	282	1.6
Fishing	728	13.9	3,032	17.2
Manufacturing and mining	1,198	22.8	3,854	21.9
Construction	447	8.5	1,952	11.1
Public utilities	122	2.3	1	1
Transportation and communications	546	10.4	1,944	11.1
Trade	809	15.4	2,237[1]	12.7[1]
Finance and real estate	525	10.0	1	1
Pub. admin.	1,047	19.9	2,927	16.6
Services	220	4.2	796	4.5
Other[2]	−452	−8.6	561	3.2
TOTAL	5,250	100.0	17,585	100.0[3]

Production (metric tons except as noted). Agriculture, forestry, fishing (1984): potatoes 1,282, vegetables and grass are also produced; livestock (number of live animals) 65,029 sheep, 2,255 cattle; fish catch (1987) 373,000, of which industrial fish (not for human consumption) 206,000, fish for human consumption 167,000 (of which cod 50,000, saithe 40,000, haddock 16,000, rose fish 14,000, prawn, shrimp, and other crustaceans 11,000). Mining and quarrying: coal. Manufacturing (1986): frozen fish 92,560; salted and smoked fish 30,978; mutton and lamb 4844; other important products include handicrafts and woolen textiles and clothing. Construction: n.a. Energy production (consumption): electricity (kW-hr; 1985–86) 187,500,000 (187,500,000); coal, n.a. (n.a.); crude petroleum, none (n.a.); petroleum products (metric tons; 1977) none (129,000); natural gas, none (none).
Tourism (1986): receipts from visitors U.S.$5,000,000; expenditures by nationals abroad U.S.$24,000,000.
Population economically active (1977): total 17,585; activity rate of total population 41.9% (participation rates: age 14–64, 64.2%; female 27.2%; unemployed, n.a.).

Price and earnings indexes (Jan. 1, 1980 = 100)

	1982	1983	1984	1985	1986	1987	1988
Consumer price index	132.0	145.9	153.8	164.6	171.6	164.0	170.8
Earnings index	...	...	...	...	...	...	...

Household income and expenditure. Average household size (1977) 3.7; average annual income per household: n.a.; sources of income[5]: self-employment 11.7%, wages and salaries 88.3%; expenditure (1980): food and beverages 40.9%, fuel and energy 18.9%, housing 17.5%, clothing and footwear 11.3%, other 11.4%.
Land use (1983): agricultural and under permanent cultivation 2.1%; other 97.9%.

Foreign trade

Balance of trade (current prices)

	1981	1982	1983	1984	1985	1986	1987
FKr '000,000	−309	−414	−587	−1,039	−688	−838	−838
% of total	11.3%	14.0%	15.5%	23.6%	15.0%	17.1%	14.9%

Imports (1987): FKr 3,513,096,000 (machinery and transport equipment 50.9%, of which transport equipment 31.1% [including road vehicles 3.1%]; chemicals and chemical products 14.3%; food and live animals 9.1%; petroleum products 6.3%). *Major import sources:* Denmark 32.7%; Norway 32.6%; Sweden 7.3%; West Germany 7.0%; United Kingdom 3.3%; The Netherlands 1.7%; United States 1.5%; France 1.3%.
Exports (1987): FKr 2,359,000,000 (1986; fishery products 94.0%, of which frozen fish fillets and filleted fish 46.8%, salted, dried, and smoked fish 21.5%, crustaceans and mollusks 10.1%, fresh or chilled fish 5.8%, fish meal for animal feed 4.8%). *Major export destinations:* Denmark 16.2%; The Netherlands 13.6%; West Germany 11.1%; United States 10.2%; France 8.5%; United Kingdom 7.6%; Italy 7.1%; Spain 4.5%; Portugal 4.1%.

Transport and communications

Transport. Railroads: none. Roads (1986): total length 269 mi, 433 km (paved 36%). Vehicles (1986): passenger cars 13,211; trucks and buses 3,041. Merchant marine (1986): vessels (20 gross tons and over) 339; total deadweight tonnage 120,254. Air transport (1988): airports with scheduled flights 1.
Communications. Daily newspapers: none. Radio (1986): total number of receivers 18,000 (1 per 2.6 persons). Television (1987): total number of receivers 10,000 (1 per 4.6 persons). Telephones (1986): 18,033 (1 per 2.6 persons).

Education and health

Education (1986–87)

	schools	teachers	students	student/ teacher ratio
Primary (first 7 grades)	71	573	5,550	14.8
Secondary (8th through 10 grades)			2,904	
Vocational, teacher training	10		1,422	...
Higher	1		94	...

Educational attainment (1977). Percent of population age 14–49 having: primary education 45.2%; secondary education 34.2%. *Literacy* (1984): 99%.
Health (1986): physicians 79 (1 per 583 persons); hospital beds 370 (1 per 124 persons); infant mortality rate per 1,000 live births (1981–85) 10.6.
Food (1979–81): daily per capita caloric intake 3,195 (vegetable products 68%, animal products 32%); 120% of FAO recommended minimum requirement.

Military

Defense responsibility lies with Denmark.

[1]Trade includes Public untilities and Finance and real estate. [2]Imputed bank service charges and nature of employment not stated, respectively. [3]Detail does not add to total given because of rounding. [4]1984–85. [5]Percentages refer to principal sources of income of economically active population.

Fiji

Official name: Republic of Fiji.
Form of government: republic[1].
Chief of state: President[2].
Head of government: Prime Minister[2].
Capital: Suva.
Official language: English.
Official religion: none.
Monetary unit: 1 Fiji dollar
  (F$) = 100 cents; valuation (Oct. 10,
  1988) 1 U.S.$ = F$1.46; 1£ = F$2.50.

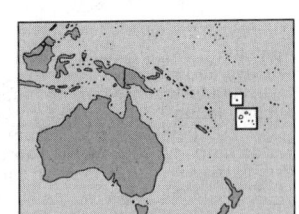

Area and population

Divisions Provinces[3]	Capitals	area sq mi	area sq km	population 1986 census
Central	Suva			
Naitasiri		643	1,666	100,227
Namosi		220	570	4,836
Rewa		105	272	97,442
Serua		320	830	13,356
Tailevu		369	955	44,249
Eastern	Levuka			
Kandavu		185	478	9,805
Lau		188	487	14,203
Lomaiviti		159	411	16,066
Rotuma		18	46	2,688
Northern	Labasa			
Mathuata		774	2,004	74,735
Mbua		532	1,379	13,986
Thakaundrove		1,087	2,816	40,433
Western	Lautoka			
Mba		1,017	2,634	197,633
Nandronga-Navosa		921	2,385	54,431
Ra		518	1,341	31,285
TOTAL		7,056	18,274	715,375

Demography

Population (1988): 742,000.
Density (1988): persons per sq mi 105.2, persons per sq km 40.6.
Urban-rural (1986): urban 38.7%; rural 61.3%.
Sex distribution (1986): male 50.68%; female 49.32%.
Age breakdown (1986): under 15, 38.2%; 15–29, 29.5%; 30–44, 17.8%; 45–59, 9.6%; 60–74, 3.8%; 75 and over, 1.1%.
Population projection: (1990) 771,000; (2000) 939,000.
Doubling time: 30 years.
Ethnic composition (1986): Indian 48.6%; Fijian 46.3%; other 5.1%.
Religious affiliation (1986): Christian 52.9%; Hindu 38.1%; Muslim 7.8%; Sikh 0.7%; other 0.5%.
Major cities (1986): Suva 69,665; Lautoka 28,728; Lami 8,601; Nadi 7,679; Ba 6,518.

Vital statistics

Birth rate per 1,000 population (1987): 28.0 (world avg. 26.0); (1978) legitimate 82.7%; illegitimate 17.3%.
Death rate per 1,000 population (1987): 5.2 (world avg. 9.9).
Natural increase rate per 1,000 population (1987): 22.8 (world avg. 16.1).
Total fertility rate (avg. births per childbearing woman; 1987): 3.2.
Marriage rate per 1,000 population (1985): 9.4.
Divorce rate per 1,000 population (1979): 0.7.
Life expectancy at birth (1987): male 68.0 years; female 72.4 years.
Major causes of death per 100,000 population (1985): diseases of the circulatory system 190.8; birth trauma 169.5; malignant neoplasms (cancers) 53.3; accidents, poisonings, and violence 48.5; diseases of the respiratory system 43.1; infectious and parasitic diseases 31.3; diabetes mellitus 29.1; diseases of the digestive system 13.3.

National economy

Budget (1986). Revenue: F$360,811,000 (income taxes, estate taxes, and gift duties 39.8%; customs duties and port dues 35.0%). Expenditures: F$370,-983,000 (departmental expenditure 65.2%, of which education 19.4%; public debt charges 20.1%; pensions and gratuities 4.0%).
Public debt (external, outstanding; 1986): U.S.$293,100,000.
Production (metric tons except as noted). Agriculture, forestry, fishing (1987): sugarcane 2,960,000, paddy rice 23,900, copra 12,999, ginger 4,500; livestock (number of live animals; 1986) 159,000 cattle, 56,000 goats, 31,-000 pigs; roundwood (1986) 188,000 cu m; fish catch 10,325. Mining and quarrying (1987): gold 2,647 kilograms; silver (1986) 774 kilograms. Manufacturing (1987): refined sugar 401,000; cement 58,700; flour 25,720; stock feed 16,145; coconut oil 8,417; soap 7,406; beer 147,400 hectolitres; paint 16,430 hectolitres. Construction (1987): residential 60,000 sq m; nonresidential 60,000 sq m. Energy production (consumption): electricity (kW-hr; 1987) 394,000,000 (310,503,000); coal (metric tons; 1986) none (15,000); crude petroleum, none (n.a.); petroleum products (metric tons; 1986) none (147,000); natural gas, none (n.a.).
Population economically active (1986): total 241,160; activity rate of total population 33.7% (participation rates: over age 15, 54.6%; female 21.2%; unemployed 7.5%).

Price and earnings indexes (1980 = 100)

	1981	1982	1983	1984	1985	1986	1987
Consumer price index	111.2	119.0	127.0	133.7	139.6	142.1	150.2
Hourly earnings index	109.5	118.1	125.9	127.6	129.3	129.3	...

Household income and expenditure. Average household size (1986) 5.7; income per household (1980) F$2,837 (U.S.$3,546); sources of income (1973): wages and salaries 81.5%, self-employment 9.1%, other 9.4%; expenditure (1985): food 33.9%, housing 18.6%, transportation 11.3%, household furnishings 7.6%, clothing and footwear 6.3%, energy 4.9%.
Gross national product (at current market prices; 1986): U.S.$1,280,000,000 (U.S.$1,810 per capita).

Structure of gross domestic product and labour force

	1986 in value F$'000	% of total value	labour force	% of labour force
Agriculture	276,055	20.9	106,305	44.1
Mining	11,910	0.9	1,345	0.5
Manufacturing	148,645	11.3	18,106	7.5
Construction	70,471	5.3	11,786	4.9
Public utilities	46,202	3.5	2,154	0.9
Transportation and communications	128,498	9.7	13,151	5.4
Trade	221,950	16.8	26,010	10.8
Finance	176,008	13.3	6,016	2.5
Pub. admin., defense, services	282,719	21.4	36,619	15.2
Other	−41,862[4]	−3.1[4]	19,668[5]	8.2[5]
TOTAL	1,320,596	100.0	241,160	100.0

Land use (1985): forested 64.9%; agricultural and under permanent cultivation 13.1%; meadows and pastures 3.3%; other 18.7%.
Tourism: receipts from visitors (1987) U.S.$145,700,000; expenditures by nationals abroad (1986) U.S.$24,000,000.

Foreign trade

Balance of trade (current prices)

	1982	1983	1984	1985	1986	1987
F$'000,000	−151.0	−189.0	−148.4	−183.2	−124.7	−131.4
% of total	22.0%	27.8%	20.9%	25.8%	16.6%	16.4%

Imports (1987): F$465,583,000 (machinery and transport equipment 19.4%; food, beverages, and tobacco 18.6%; mineral fuels and related materials 16.2%; miscellaneous manufactured consumer articles 8.8%; chemicals 8.6%). *Major import sources:* Australia 28.7%; New Zealand 16.9%; Japan 12.1%; Singapore 11.1%; United States 5.2%; United Kingdom 4.7%; Taiwan 3.9%; China 2.6%.
Exports (1987)[6]: F$334,173,000 (sugar 55.8%; gold 15.1%; fish 7.5%; molasses 3.2%; wood and by-products 3.2%; veneer sheets 0.9%; coconut oil 0.9%). *Major export destinations*[7]: United Kingdom 41.4%; Australia 20.3%; United States 5.3%; New Zealand 4.9%; China 3.9%; Japan 3.5%; Taiwan 3.1%; Canada 1.6%.

Transport and communications

Transport. Railroads[8] (1986): length 660 mi, 1,062 km. Roads (1986): total length 2,564 mi, 4,127 km (paved 13%). Vehicles (1987): passenger cars 34,380; trucks and buses 24,318. Merchant marine (1987): vessels (100 gross tons and over) 60; total deadweight tonnage 32,398. Air transport (1986)[9]: passenger-mi 316,538,000, passenger-km 509,420,000; short ton-mi cargo 4,393,000, metric ton-km cargo 6,414,000; airports (1988) with scheduled flights 17.
Communications. Daily newspapers (1985): total number 2; total circulation 53,000; circulation per 1,000 population 74. Radio (1986): total number of receivers 400,000 (1 per 1.8 persons). Television: n.a. Telephones (1986): 58,382 (1 per 12 persons).

Education and health

Education (1986)

	schools	teachers	students	student/ teacher ratio
Primary (age 5–15)	672	4,315	131,221	30.4
Secondary (age 16–19)	140	2,551	42,200	16.5
Voc., teacher tr.	44	257	3,793	14.8
Higher	5[10]	...	1,877	...

Educational attainment (1986). Percent of population age 25 and over having: no formal schooling 28.3%; primary only 19.1%; some secondary 44.1%; secondary 4.1%; postsecondary 3.3%; other 1.1%. *Literacy* (1985): total population age 15 and over literate 374,300 (85.5%); males literate 197,300 (90.2%); females literate 177,000 (80.9%).
Health (1986): physicians 385 (1 per 1,859 persons); hospital beds 1,743 (1 per 410 persons); infant mortality rate per 1,000 live births (1987) 19.0.
Food (1984–86): daily per capita caloric intake 2,901 (vegetable products 87%, animal products 13%); (1983) 105% of FAO recommended minimum requirement.

Military

Total active duty personnel (1987): 2,600 (army 96.2%; navy 3.8%; air force, none). *Military expenditure as percent of GNP* (1984): 1.4% (world 6.0%); per capita expenditure: U.S.$23.

[1]After eight months of military rule which resulted in the revocation of the 1970 constitution, Fiji was declared a republic on Oct. 7, 1987. No legislative body existed in late 1988, as a new constitution that was to define it was being drafted. [2]Fiji's first civilian president was appointed Dec. 5, 1987, as was the prime minister, formally returning the nation to civilian rule. [3]The provinces are autonomous only with respect to local affairs. [4]Other activities less imputed bank service charges. [5]Not stated and unemployed. [6]Excludes reexports, valued at F$74,642,000. [7]Based on exports of local products only. [8]Owned by the Fiji Sugar Corporation. [9]Domestic airlines only, including South Pacific service. [10]1983.

Finland

Official name: Suomen Tasavalta
(Finnish); Republiken Finland
(Swedish) (Republic of Finland).
Form of government: multiparty
parliamentary republic with one
legislative house (Eduskunta [200]).
Chief of state: President.
Head of government: Prime Minister.
Capital: Helsinki.
Official languages: Finnish; Swedish.
Official religion: none.
Monetary unit: 1 markka (Fmk) = 100
pennia; valuation (Oct. 10, 1988)
1 U.S.$ = Fmk 4.37; 1 £ = Fmk 7.48.

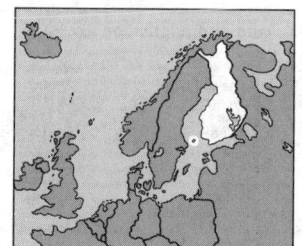

Area and population		land area		population
Provinces	Capitals	sq mi	sq km	1988 estimate[1]
Åland (Ahvenanmaa)[2]	Mariehamn (Maarianhamina)	590	1,527	23,706
Häme	Hämeenlinna	6,568	17,010	681,525
Keski-Suomi	Jyväskylä	6,266	16,230	248,432
Kuopio	Kuopio	6,375	16,511	255,593
Kymi	Kouvola	4,163	10,783	337,339
Lappi	Rovaniemi	35,930	93,057	200,075
Mikkeli	Mikkeli	6,310	16,342	207,974
Oulu	Oulu	21,956	56,866	433,585
Pohjois-Karjala	Joensuu	6,866	17,782	176,721
Turku ja Pori	Turku	8,559	22,170	714,340
Uusimaa	Helsinki	3,822	9,898	1,217,427
Vaasa	Vaasa	10,211	26,447	444,497
TOTAL LAND AREA		117,616	304,623	4,941,214
INLAND WATER		12,943	33,522	
TOTAL AREA		130,559	338,145	

Demography

Population (1988): 4,952,000.
Density[3] (1987): persons per sq mi 42.1, persons per sq km 16.3.
Urban-rural (1988): urban 61.8%; rural 38.2%.
Sex distribution (1987): male 48.43%; female 51.57%.
Age breakdown (1987): under 15, 19.3%; 15–29, 22.0%; 30–44, 24.1%; 45–59, 16.8%; 60–74, 12.5%; 75 and over, 5.3%.
Population projection: (1990) 4,992,000; (2000) 5,192,000.
Doubling time: n.a.; doubling time exceeds 100 years.
Ethnolinguistic composition (1986): Finnish 93.6%; Swedish 6.1%; other 0.3%[4].
Religious affiliation (1986): Lutheran 89.2%; Greek Orthodox 1.1%; nonaffiliated 8.9%; other 0.8%.
Major cities (1988)[1]: Helsinki 490,478; Tampere 170,073; Espoo 166,925; Turku 160,486; Vantaa 148,728.

Vital statistics

Birth rate per 1,000 population (1986): 12.3 (world avg. 26.0); legitimate 82.0%; illegitimate 18.0%.
Death rate per 1,000 population (1986): 9.6 (world avg. 9.9).
Natural increase rate per 1,000 population (1986): 2.7 (world avg. 16.1).
Total fertility rate (avg. births per childbearing woman; 1986): 1.6.
Marriage rate per 1,000 population (1986): 5.3.
Divorce rate per 1,000 population (1986): 2.0.
Life expectancy at birth (1986): male 70.5 years; female 78.7 years.
Major causes of death per 100,000 population (1986): ischemic heart disease 285.5; malignant neoplasms (cancers) 193.9; cerebrovascular diseases 116.8; accidents 47.0; pneumonia 36.9; suicide and self-inflicted injuries 26.6.

National economy

Budget (1987). Revenue: Fmk 109,524,000,000 (tax revenue 75.3%, of which sales tax 29.3%, income and property taxes 26.5%, excise duties 10.5%, vehicle taxes 3.1%, stamp duties 2.8%). Expenditures: Fmk 109,524,000,000 (social security 17.1%; education 16.0%; transportation 8.4%; agriculture and forestry 8.3%; health 8.0%; administration 6.1%; defense 5.2%).
Public debt (1988)[5]: U.S.$15,193,000,000.
Tourism (1985): receipts from visitors U.S.$501,000,000; expenditures by nationals abroad U.S.$776,000,000.
Production (metric tons except as noted). Agriculture, forestry, fishing (1986): barley 1,713,800, oats 1,174,500, sugar beets 792,200, potatoes 773,200, wheat 529,100; livestock (number of live animals; 1987) 1,497,900 cattle, 1,341,900 pigs, 366,000 reindeer; roundwood 38,800,000 cu m; fish catch 158,600. Mining and quarrying (1986)[6]: iron ore 483,000[7]; zinc 60,300; copper 24,100. Manufacturing (value added in Fmk; 1985): machinery 19,987,000,000, of which transport equipment 5,035,000,000, electrical equipment 4,947,000,000; paper and paper products 10,996,000,000; processed food 10,670,000,000; chemical products 5,683,000,000. Construction (1986): residential 15,290,000 cu m; nonresidential 25,060,000 cu m. Energy production (consumption): electricity (kW-hr; 1986) 46,855,000,000 (52,575,000,000); coal (metric tons; 1986) none (5,002,000); crude petroleum (barrels; 1986) none (71,562,000); petroleum products (metric tons; 1986) 8,104,000 (9,892,000); natural gas (cu m; 1986) none (1,086,713,000).
Household income and expenditure. Average household size (1983) 2.5; income per household Fmk 87,668 (U.S.$15,740); sources of income (1987): wages and salaries 68.1%, self-employment 15.0%, transfer payments 14.4%, income from property 2.5%; expenditure (1986): food and beverages 23.7%, housing 14.5%, transportation and communications 17.3%, recreation and education 9.9%, household durable goods 7.3%, clothing 5.6%, energy 4.1%.

Gross national product (at current market prices; 1986): U.S.$60,040,000,000 (U.S.$12,180 per capita).

Structure of gross domestic product and labour force				
	1986[8]		1987	
	in value Fmk '000,000	% of total value	labour force	% of labour force
Agriculture	23,264	6.7	252,000	9.9
Mining	1,210	0.4 }	569,000	22.3
Manufacturing	75,391	21.9 }		
Public utilities	8,785	2.5	...	...
Construction	22,913	6.6	181,000	7.1
Transp. and commun.	24,032	7.0	182,000	7.1
Trade	36,469	10.6	348,000	13.6
Finance	52,273	15.2	177,000	6.9
Pub. admin., defense	51,092	14.8 }	710,000	27.8
Services	11,814	3.4 }		
Other	37,732[9]	10.9[9]	133,000[10]	5.2[10]
TOTAL	344,975	100.0	2,553,000[11]	100.0[11]

Population economically active (1987): total 2,553,000; activity rate of total population 51.8% (participation rates [1986]: ages 15–64, 76.9%; female 47.1%; unemployed 5.1%).

Price and earnings indexes (1980 = 100)							
	1981	1982	1983	1984	1985	1986	1987
Consumer price index	112.0	122.7	133.0	142.4	150.7	156.1	161.9
Hourly earnings index	113.0	124.8	137.8	150.8	163.5	174.9	182.0[12]

Land use (1985): forested 76.0%; meadows and pastures 0.4%; agricultural and under permanent cultivation 7.9%; other 15.7%.

Foreign trade

Balance of trade (current prices)						
	1982	1983	1984	1985	1986	1987
Fmk '000,000	+1,351	+1,667	+9,498	+6,160	+10,735	+4,857
% of total	1.1%	1.2%	6.2%	3.8%	6.9%	2.8%

Imports (1987): Fmk 82,797,000,000 (raw materials and producer goods 61.2%, of which crude petroleum, fuels and lubricants 11.6%; consumer goods 21.0%; machinery and transport equipment 17.0%). Major import sources: West Germany 17.5%; U.S.S.R. 14.4%; Sweden 12.9%; United Kingdom 7.1%; Japan 7.1%.
Exports (1987): Fmk 85,315,000,000 (forestry products 40.0%, of which paper and paper products 31.3%, wood products 8.7%; metal products and machines 30.9%; chemical products 9.2%; other finished goods 19.9%). Major export destinations: U.S.S.R. 15.4%; Sweden 14.9%; United Kingdom 11.4%; West Germany 10.9%; France 5.3%; United States 5.2%; Norway 4.7%.

Transport and communications

Transport. Railroads (1987): length (1986) 5,544 mi, 8,923 km; passenger-mi 1,931,000,000, passenger-km 3,108,000,000; short ton-mi cargo 5,071,000,000, metric ton-km cargo 7,404,000,000. Roads (1987): total length 47,362 mi, 76,223 km (paved 57%). Vehicles (1987): passenger cars 1,619,848; trucks and buses 196,631. Merchant marine (1987): vessels (100 gross tons and over) 257; total deadweight tonnage 1,400,594. Air transport (1986): passenger-mi 1,812,000,000, passenger-km 2,916,000,000; short ton-mi cargo 63,609,000, metric ton-km cargo 92,868,000; airports (1988) 21.
Communications. Daily newspapers (1986): total number 66; total circulation 2,665,000; circulation per 1,000 population 542. Radio (1986): total number of receivers 2,515,000 (1 per 2.0 persons). Television (1987): total number of receivers 1,822,372 (1 per 2.7 persons). Telephones (1985): 3,028,000 (1 per 1.6 persons).

Education and health

Education (1985–86)	schools	teachers	students	student/ teacher ratio
Primary (age 7–12)	4,233	25,140	380,509	15.1
Secondary (age 13–19)	1,093	22,360	300,748	13.4
Voc., teacher tr.	593[13]	22,869[13]	114,183	...
Higher	13	13	127,976	...

Educational attainment (1983). Percent of population age 15 and over having: lower secondary education 51.5%; higher secondary 28.4%; some postsecondary 8.8%; undergraduate 4.3%; graduate 6.1%; postgraduate 0.6%; other 0.3%. Literacy (1987): virtually 100% literate.
Health (1986): physicians 10,556 (1 per 481 persons); hospital beds (1985) 60,598 (1 per 81 persons); infant mortality rate per 1,000 live births 5.8.
Food (1984–86): daily per capita caloric intake 3,080 (vegetable products 57%, animal products 43%); (1983) 111% of FAO recommended minimum requirement.

Military

Total active duty personnel (1987): 34,400 (army 87.2%, navy 5.5%, air force 7.3%). Military expenditure as percent of GNP (1984): 1.4% (world 6.0%); per capita expenditure U.S.$158.

[1]April 1. [2]The predominantly Swedish-speaking Åland Islands (Ahvenanmaa) were granted internal legislative and economic autonomy by the Autonomy Act of Dec. 28, 1951. [3]Based on land area only. [4]Includes Russian 0.05%; English 0.04%; German 0.04%; Lappish 0.03%. [5]April. [6]Metal content of ores. [7]1985. [8]At prices of 1985. [9]Includes imputed bank service charges, net commodity taxes and other corrections. [10]Includes 130,000 unemployed. [11]Detail does not add to total given because of rounding. [12]March. [13]Voc., teacher tr. includes higher.

France

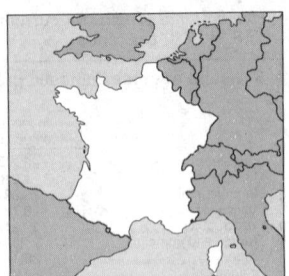

Official name: République Française
(French Republic).
Form of government: republic with
two legislative houses (Parliament;
Senate [319], National Assembly
[577]).
Chief of state: President.
Head of government: Prime Minister.
Capital: Paris.
Official language: French.
Official religion: none.
Monetary unit: 1 Franc (F) = 100
centimes; valuation (Oct. 10, 1988)
1 U.S.$ = F 6.32; 1 £ = F 10.83.

Area and population

Regions Departments	Capitals	area sq mi	area sq km	population 1987 estimate[1]
Alsace				
Bas-Rhin	Strasbourg	1,836	4,755	941,400
Haut-Rhin	Colmar	1,361	3,525	663,600
Aquitaine				
Dordogne	Périgueux	3,498	9,060	379,100
Gironde	Bordeaux	3,861	10,000	1,146,800
Landes	Mont-de-Marsan	3,569	9,243	308,500
Lot-et-Garonne	Agen	2,070	5,361	304,200
Pyrénées-Atlantiques	Pau	2,952	7,645	569,700
Auvergne				
Allier	Moulins	2,834	7,340	364,400
Cantal	Aurillac	2,211	5,726	159,600
Haute-Loire	Le Puy	1,922	4,977	209,100
Puy-de-Dôme	Clermont-Ferrand	3,077	7,970	596,200
Basse Normandie				
Calvados	Caen	2,142	5,548	602,900
Manche	Saint-Lô	2,293	5,938	476,900
Orne	Alençon	2,356	6,103	294,100
Bretagne				
Côtes-du-Nord	Saint-Brieuc	2,656	6,878	542,600
Finistère	Quimper	2,600	6,733	836,300
Ille-et-Vilaine	Rennes	2,616	6,775	778,600
Morbihan	Vannes	2,634	6,823	609,800
Bourgogne				
Côte-d'Or	Dijon	3,383	8,763	478,000
Nièvre	Nevers	2,632	6,817	238,800
Saône-et-Loire	Mâcon	3,311	8,575	572,700
Yonne	Auxerre	2,868	7,427	314,900
Centre				
Cher	Bourges	2,793	7,235	322,600
Eure-et-Loire	Chartres	2,270	5,880	378,700
Indre	Châteauroux	2,622	6,791	238,200
Indre-et-Loire	Tours	2,366	6,127	524,500
Loiret	Orléans	2,616	6,775	568,800
Loir-et-Cher	Blois	2,449	6,343	300,500
Champagne-Ardenne				
Ardennes	Charleville-Mézières	2,019	5,229	298,500
Aube	Troyes	2,318	6,004	294,900
Haute-Marne	Chaumont	2,398	6,211	204,700
Marne	Châlons-sur-Marne	3,151	8,162	560,900
Corse				
Corse-du-Sud	Ajaccio	1,550	4,014	107,800
Haute-Corse	Bastia	1,802	4,666	134,900
Franche-Comté				
Doubs	Besançon	2,021	5,234	486,500
Haute-Saône	Vesoul	2,070	5,360	234,200
Jura	Lons-le-Saunier	1,930	4,999	247,400
Territoire de Belfort	Belfort	235	609	131,000
Haute-Normandie				
Eure	Évreux	2,332	6,040	490,100
Seine-Maritime	Rouen	2,424	6,278	1,195,000
Île-de-France				
Essonne	Évry	696	1,804	1,044,400
Hauts-de-Seine	Nanterre	68	176	1,377,100
Paris	Paris	40	105	2,085,500
Seine-et-Marne	Melun	2,284	5,915	978,300
Seine-Saint-Denis	Bobigny	91	236	1,347,900
Val-de-Marne	Créteil	95	245	1,204,900
Val-d'Oise	Pontoise	481	1,246	986,700
Yvelines	Versailles	882	2,284	1,265,200
Languedoc-Roussillon				
Aude	Carcassonne	2,370	6,139	289,300
Gard	Nîmes	2,260	5,853	569,800
Hérault	Montpellier	2,356	6,101	778,500
Lozère	Mende	1,995	5,167	72,600
Pyrénées-Orientales	Perpignan	1,589	4,116	361,700
Limousin				
Corrèze	Tulle	2,261	5,857	238,900
Creuse	Guéret	2,149	5,565	135,700
Haute-Vienne	Limoges	2,131	5,520	360,000
Lorraine				
Meurthe-et-Moselle	Nancy	2,024	5,241	709,700
Meuse	Bar-le-Duc	2,400	6,216	197,100
Moselle	Metz	2,400	6,216	1,020,300
Vosges	Épinal	2,268	5,874	392,800
Midi-Pyrénées				
Ariège	Foix	1,888	4,890	136,100
Aveyron	Rodez	3,373	8,736	276,100
Gers	Auch	2,416	6,257	175,100
Haute-Garonne	Toulouse	2,436	6,309	859,500
Hautes-Pyrénées	Tarbes	1,724	4,464	232,200
Lot	Cahors	2,014	5,217	154,600
Tarn	Albi	2,223	5,758	341,400
Tarn-et-Garonne	Montauban	1,435	3,718	194,800
Nord-Pas-de-Calais				
Nord	Lille	2,217	5,742	2,506,100
Pas-de-Calais	Arras	2,576	6,671	1,417,300

Area and population (continued)

		area sq mi	area sq km	population
Pays de la Loire				
Loire-Atlantique	Nantes	2,631	6,815	1,015,700
Maine-et Loire	Angers	2,767	7,166	705,900
Mayenne	Laval	1,998	5,175	276,200
Sarthe	Le Mans	2,396	6,206	518,500
Vendée	La Roche-sur-Yon	2,595	6,720	496,300
Picardie				
Aisne	Laon	2,845	7,369	535,500
Oise	Beauvais	2,263	5,860	700,300
Somme	Amiens	2,382	6,170	551,200
Poitou-Charentes				
Charente	Angoulême	2,300	5,956	346,600
Charente-Maritime	La Rochelle	2,650	6,864	528,000
Deux-Sèvres	Niort	2,316	5,999	344,700
Vienne	Poitiers	2,699	6,990	381,700
Provence-Côte d'Azur				
Alpes-Maritimes	Nice	1,660	4,299	908,300
Alpes-de-Haute-Provence	Digne	2,674	6,925	125,900
Bouches-du-Rhône	Marseille	1,964	5,087	1,755,900
Hautes-Alpes	Gap	2,142	5,549	108,700
Var	Toulon	2,306	5,973	755,300
Vaucluse	Avignon	1,377	3,567	461,300
Rhône-Alpes				
Ain	Bourg-en-Bresse	2,225	5,762	453,200
Ardèche	Privas	2,135	5,529	274,400
Drôme	Valence	2,521	6,530	412,100
Haute-Savoie	Annecy	1,694	4,388	535,100
Isère	Grenoble	2,869	7,431	983,100
Loire	Saint-Étienne	1,846	4,781	739,600
Rhône	Lyon	1,254	3,249	1,445,200
Savoie	Chambéry	2,327	6,028	334,100
TOTAL		210,026	543,965	55,510,000[2]

Demography

Population (1988): 55,860,000.
Density (1988): persons per sq mi 266.0, persons per sq km 102.7.
Urban–rural (1985): urban 73.4%; rural 26.6%.
Sex distribution (1988): male 48.72%; female 51.28%.
Age breakdown (1988): under 15, 20.5%; 15–29, 23.0%; 30–44, 21.8%; 45–59, 16.0%; 60–74, 12.1%; 75 and over, 6.6%.
Population projection: (1990) 56,320,000; (2000) 58,673,000.
Doubling time: n.a.; doubling time exceeds 100 years.
Ethnolinguistic composition (1982): French (mother tongue) 93.2%, of which fully or substantially bilingual in Occitan 2.7%, German (mostly Alsatian) 2.3%, Breton 1.0%, Catalan 0.4%; Arabic 2.6%; other 4.2%.
Religious affiliation (1980): Roman Catholic 76.4%; other Christian 3.7%; atheist 3.4%; Muslim 3.0%; other 13.5%.
Major cities (1982): Paris 2,165,892 (metropolitan area 10,210,059); Marseille 868,435 (1,227,901); Lyon 410,455 (1,533,305); Toulouse 344,917 (648,267); Nice 331,165 (865,492); Strasbourg 247,068 (613,380); Nantes 237,789 (558,-814); Bordeaux 201,965 (843,411); Saint-Étienne 193,938 (547,729).
National origin (1982): French 90.6%; Algerian 1.5%; Portuguese 1.4%; Moroccan 0.8%; Spanish 0.6%; Italian 0.6%; other 4.5%[3].
Mobility (1982). Population living in same residence as in 1975: n.a.; same region 91.7%; different region 5.8%; different country 2.5%.
Households (1982). Average household size 2.7; 1 person 24.6%, 2 persons 28.5%, 3 persons 18.8%, 4 persons 16.1%, 5 persons 7.4%, 6 persons or more 4.6%. Family households: 14,118,940 (72.1%); nonfamily 5,471,460 (27.9%, of which 1-person 24.6%).
Immigration (1987): permanent immigrants admitted 39,000, from Morocco 21.9%, Turkey 11.9%, Tunisia 6.6%, Italy 3.0%, West Germany 2.7%.

Vital statistics

Birth rate per 1,000 population (1987): 13.8 (world avg. 26.0); (1986) legitimate 78.1%; illegitimate 21.9%.
Death rate per 1,000 population (1987): 9.5 (world avg. 9.9).
Natural increase rate per 1,000 population (1987): 4.3 (world avg. 16.1).
Total fertility rate (avg. births per childbearing woman; 1987): 1.8.
Marriage rate per 1,000 population (1987): 4.8.
Divorce rate per 1,000 population (1986): 2.0.
Life expectancy at birth (1984–86): male 71.3 years; female 79.5 years.
Major causes of death per 100,000 population (1986): malignant neoplasms (cancers) 239.8; heart disease 203.7; other circulatory diseases 148.0.

Social indicators

Educational attainment (1974). Percent of adult employed population having: less than full primary education 36.2%; primary 30.4%; secondary 21.0%; some postsecondary 7.0%; 4-year degree 2.4%; postgraduate 2.8%.

Distribution of income (1975)

percent of household income by quintile

1	2	3	4	5 (highest)
5.5%	11.5%	17.1%	23.7%	42.2%.

Quality of working life. Average workweek (1988): 38.9 hours. Annual rate per 100,000 workers (1986) for: injury or accident 2,907; industrial illness 15.9; death 4.1. Proportion of labour force insured for damages or income loss resulting from: injury, permanent disability, or death, n.a. Average days lost to labour stoppages per 1,000 workers (1986): 26.0. Average duration of journey to work (1974): 53 minutes.
Access to services (1982). Proportion of dwellings having: central heating 67.5%; piped water 99.2%; indoor plumbing 85.0%; natural gas 48.9%.
Social participation. Eligible voters participating in last national election: 78.0%. Population over 15 years of age participating in voluntary associations: 28.0%.

Social deviance. Offense rate per 100,000 population (1987) for: murder 3.9; rape 5.7; other assault 64.3; theft, including burglary and housebreaking 3,650.9. Incidence per 100,000 in general population of: alcoholism[4] (late 1970s) 3,500–4,000; drug and substance abuse, n.a.; suicide (1986) 22.5.
Leisure (1974–75). Favourite leisure activities: television 34%; reading 14%; knitting 10%; conversation 10%; games 8%; walking 4%; radio 4%.
Material well-being (1987). Households possessing: automobile 74.6%; television receiver 94.0%, of which colour 78.1%; refrigerator 97.0%; washing machine 86.2%.

National economy

Gross national product (at current market prices; 1986): U.S.$595,180,000,-000 (U.S.$10,740 per capita).

Structure of gross domestic product and labour force

| | 1987 | | | |
	in value F '000,000	% of total value	labour force	% of labour force
Agriculture	332,441	6.3	1,650,900	6.8
Mining	} 915,831	} 17.3	68,300	0.3
Manufacturing			4,420,200	18.4
Construction	287,096	5.4	1,521,900	6.3
Public utilities	245,586	4.7	210,000	0.9
Transp. and commun.	315,948	6.0	1,371,200	5.7
Trade	567,976	10.7	3,691,100	15.3
Finance	260,643	4.9	673,100	2.8
Pub. admin., defense	873,588	16.5	4,228,700	17.6
Services	1,258,149	23.8	3,394,800	14.1
Other	231,441[5]	4.4[5]	2,854,100[6]	11.8[6]
TOTAL	5,288,699[7]	100.0	24,084,300	100.0

Budget (1986). Revenue: F 997,000,000,000 (value-added taxes 47.2%, income tax 23.2%, customs taxes 10.3%). Expenditure: F 1,030,819,000,000 (educ. 23.4%, health and soc. services 18.9%, defense 15.9%, admin. 12.2%).

Manufacturing and mining enterprises (1985)

	no. of enterprises	no. of employees	hourly wages as a % of avg. of all wages[8]	annual value added (F '000,000)
Food products	...	548,000	100	160,500
Transport equipment	671	560,000	115	141,200
Electrical machinery	704	479,000	101	89,300
Petroleum refineries	49	26,000	...	89,100
Industrial chemicals	291	126,000	117	66,100
Iron and steel	134	206,000	...	56,800
Metal products	3,284	234,000	109	52,100
Textiles	1,877	237,000	83	39,100
Printing, publishing	1,779	214,000	117	31,600
Paper and products	638	106,000	109	31,200
Beverages	...	52,000	100	31,200
Wearing apparel	2,464	217,000	79	26,400
Rubber products	169	89,000	97	16,800
Tobacco	...	8,000	100	14,700
Glass products	144	58,000	112	12,000

Production (metric tons except as noted). Agriculture, forestry, fishing (1987): wheat 27,415,000, sugar beets 25,739,000, corn (maize) 12,040,000, barley 10,849,000, grapes 8,950,000, potatoes 6,720,000, rapeseed 2,651,000, sunflower seeds 2,651,000, apples 1,920,000, oats 1,117,000, tomatoes 685,-000, cauliflower 541,000, carrots 528,000, pears 420,000, peaches 324,000, rye 299,000; livestock (number of live animals) 22,339,000 cattle, 12,577,-000 pigs, 12,091,000 sheep, 1,115,000 goats; roundwood (1986) 39,115,000 cu m; fish catch (1986) 850,000. Mining and quarrying (1987): iron ore 3,260,000[9]; potash salts 1,620,000[10]; bauxite 1,270,000; zinc 55,920[9]; lead 1,800[9, 10]; gold 90,021 troy oz[9, 11]. Manufacturing (1987): cement 23,544,-000; crude steel 17,724,000; pig iron 14,052,000[10]; sulfuric acid 3,957,600; rubber products 540,840[10], of which tires 51,576,000 units[10]; aluminum 511,200; automobiles 2,631,500 units[10]. Construction (dwelling units completed; 1987) 254,000.

Retail trade enterprises (1986)

	no. of enterprises	no. of employees	weekly wages as a % of all wages	annual turnover (F '000,000)
Large food stores	3,263	335,478	...	397,744
Small food stores	125,102	335,252	...	176,024
butcher shops	47,494	145,121	...	66,955
Clothing stores	70,854	188,174	...	82,463
Pharmacies	21,661	116,195	...	68,542
Department stores	2,454	66,075	...	48,005
Furniture stores	7,029	48,011	...	39,393
Electrical and electronics stores	10,266	47,641	...	29,693
Gas, coal, and other energy products	4,769	18,550	...	28,152
Publishing and paper	19,544	52,169	...	21,680

Energy production (consumption)[12]: electricity (kW-hr; 1986) 343,045,000,-000 (317,845,000,000); coal (metric tons; 1986) 18,451,000 (32,900,000); crude petroleum (barrels; 1986) 21,615,000 (509,354,000); petroleum products (metric tons; 1986) 66,981,000 (73,695,000); natural gas (cu m; 1986) 4,388,300,000 (44,185,000,000).
Household income and expenditure. Average household size (1987) 2.7; average annual income per household (1985) F 165,200 (U.S.$18,385). Sources of income (1985): wages and salaries 52.2%, social security 26.3%, self-employment 21.5%; expenditure (1985): housing 28.6%, food 19.7%, health 10.9%, transportation 10.4%, clothing 7.4%, recreation 6.8%.
Tourism (1986): receipts from visitors U.S.$9,704,000,000; expenditures by nationals abroad U.S.$6,504,000,000.
Population economically active (1987): total 24,084,300; activity rate of total population 43.3% (participation rates: ages 15–64, 65.4%[10]; female 42.4%; unemployed 10.6%).

Price and earnings indexes (1980 = 100)

	1982	1983	1984	1985	1986	1987	1988[13]
Consumer price index	126.8	139.0	149.3	157.9	161.9	167.3	173.1
Hourly earnings index	137.5	155.1	168.2	178.4	186.4	195.2	...

Public debt (1987): F 988,800,000,000.

Financial aggregates

	1983	1984	1985	1986	1987	1988[14]
Exchange rate, F per:						
U.S. dollar	8.35	9.59	7.56	6.46	5.34	6.36
£	12.11	11.09	10.92	9.52	9.99	10.70
SDR	8.74	9.40	8.30	7.90	7.58	8.20
International reserves (U.S.$)						
Total (excl. gold; '000,000)	19,851	20,940	26,589	31,454	33,049	29,328
SDRs ('000,000)	442	572	900	1,290	1,502	1,407
Reserve pos. in IMF ('000,000)	1,352	1,265	1,370	1,736	1,914	1,601
Foreign exchange	18,057	19,102	24,319	28,428	29,634	26,320
Gold ('000,000 fine troy oz)	81.85	81.85	81.85	81.85	81.85	81.85
% world reserves	8.7	8.6	8.6	8.6	8.7	8.6
Interest and prices						
Central bank discount (%)	9.50	9.50	9.50	9.50	9.50	9.50
Gov't. bond yield (%)	13.61	12.41	10.94	8.44	9.43	9.21
Industrial share prices (1980 = 100)	115.8	155.8	182.0	280.6	320.9	305.6
Balance of payments (U.S.$'000,000)						
Balance of visible trade	−8,754	−4,651	−5,276	−2,354	−9,821	...
Imports, f.o.b.	98,460	96,865	101,203	120,343	148,713	...
Exports, f.o.b.	89,706	92,214	95,927	117,988	138,893	...
Balance of invisibles	7,403	6,673	7,868	9,671	9,558	...
Balance of payments, current account	−5,166	−876	−35	3,002	−5,091	...

Land use (1985): forested 26.8%; meadows and pastures 22.4%; agricultural and under permanent cultivation 34.7%; other 16.1%.

Foreign trade

Balance of trade (current prices)

	1982	1983	1984	1985	1986	1987
F '000,000,000	−71.9	−34.5	−19.7	−24.2	−3.0	−30.7
% of total	5.4%	2.3%	3.0%	1.3%	0.2%	1.7%

Imports (1987): F 949,810,000,000 (machinery 24.8%; chemicals and chemical products 15.6%; agricultural products 12.4%; fuels 10.6%, of which crude petroleum 5.3%; transport equipment 9.6%, of which automobiles 5.2%). *Major import sources:* West Germany 19.7%; Italy 11.7%; Belgium-Luxembourg 9.3%; U.S. 7.1%; U.K. 7.0%; The Netherlands 5.6%.
Exports (1987): F 889,830,000,000 (machinery 28.1%; agricultural products 16.7%; chemicals 15.7%; transport equipment 12.7%, of which automobiles 6.1%). *Major export destinations:* West Germany 16.0%; Italy 11.7%; Belgium-Luxembourg 9.0%; U.K. 8.5%; U.S. 7.0%; The Netherlands 4.9%.

Transport and communications

Transport. Railroads (1987): route length 21,528 mi, 34,647 km; passenger-mi 37,155,000,000, passenger-km 59,796,000,000; short ton-mi cargo 35,-154,000,000, metric ton-km cargo 51,324,000,000. Roads (1986): total length 500,055 mi, 804,765 km (paved [1985] 92%). Vehicles (1986): passenger cars 21,250,000; trucks and buses 3,406,000. Merchant marine (1987): vessels (100 gross tons and over) 954; total deadweight tonnage 8,406,743. Air transport[15] (1987): passenger-mi 27,380,000,000, passenger-km 44,064,000,-000; short ton-mi cargo 2,395,536,000, metric ton-km cargo 3,497,424,000; airports (1988) with scheduled flights 67.
Communications. Daily newspapers (1986): number 95; circulation 11,-369,000; circulation per 1,000 population 205. Radio (1987): 58,000,000 receivers (1 per 1.0 persons). Television (1987): 18,168,330 receivers (1 per 3.1 persons). Telephones (1987): 33,357,900[16] (1 per 1.7 persons).

Education and health

Education (1986–87)

	schools	teachers[17]	students	student/teacher ratio[17]
Primary (age 6–10)	41,045	221,439[18]	4,355,660	16.4[18]
Secondary (age 11–18) Voc., teacher tr. }	11,207	323,969[18]	5,390,023	13.0[18]
Higher	1,062	47,221	1,208,783	25.3

Literacy (1980): total population literate 41,112,000 (98.8%); males literate 19,933,000 (98.9%); females literate 21,179,000 (98.7%).
Health (1986): physicians 138,825 (1 per 417 persons); hospital beds 722,378 (1 per 80 persons); infant mortality rate per 1,000 live births (1987) 7.6.
Food (1984–86): daily per capita caloric intake 3,273 (vegetable products 63%, animal products 37%); (1983) 138% of FAO recommended minimum requirement.

Military

Total active duty personnel (1988): 456,900 (army 61.5%, navy 16.5%, air force 20.8%, other 1.2%). *Military expenditure as percent of GNP* (1985): 4.1% (world 6.1%); per capita expenditure U.S.$365.

[1]January 1. [2]Detail does not add to total given because of rounding. [3]Includes 2.6% naturalized citizens not identified by national origin. [4]Estimated according to a narrow definition of alcoholism. [5]Includes value-added taxes, customs duties, and imputed bank service charges. [6]Includes 2,545,800 unemployed persons and 250,-800 members of the armed forces. [7]At 1980 prices. [8]1982. [9]Metal content of ores. [10]1986. [11]1985. [12]All energy statistics include Monaco. [13]September. [14]August. [15]Air France, UTA, and Air Inter only. [16]Does not include public telephones. [17]1985–86. [18]Public schools only; representing 83.6% and 78.6% of all primary and secondary pupils, respectively.

French Guiana

Official name: Département de la Guyane française (Department of French Guiana).
Political status: overseas department of France with two legislative houses (General Council [19]; Regional Council [31]).
Chief of state: President of France.
Heads of government: Commissioner of the Republic (for France); President of the General Council (for French Guiana); President of the Regional Council (for French Guiana).
Capital: Cayenne.
Official language: French.
Official religion: none.
Monetary unit: 1 franc (F) = 100 centimes; valuation (Oct. 10, 1988) 1 U.S.$ = F 6.32; 1 £ = F 10.83.

Area and population		area		population
				1982
Arrondissements	**Capitals**	sq mi	sq km	census
Cayenne	Cayenne	17,590	45,559	61,587
Saint-Laurent-du-Maroni	Saint-Laurent-du-Maroni	15,809	40,945	11,435
TOTAL		33,399	86,504	73,022

Demography

Population (1988): 92,100.
Density (1988): persons per sq mi 2.8, persons per sq km 1.1.
Urban–rural (1982): urban 73.4%; rural 26.6%.
Sex distribution (1982): male 52.66%; female 47.34%.
Age breakdown (1982): under 15, 34.2%; 15–29, 29.2%; 30–44, 19.9%; 45–59, 9.8%; 60–74, 5.1%; 75 and over, 1.8%.
Population projection: (1990) 99,000; (2000) 142,000.
Doubling time: 29 years.
Ethnic composition (1982): Guianese (mixed) Creole 42.6%; Guiana Chinese 14.0%; French (metropolitan) 10.7%; Haitian 7.5%; French West Indian 6.6%; Bush Negro 4.7%; Brazilian 4.6%; Amerindian 4.1%; other (other West Indian, Surinamese, Hmong, and other Southeast Asian) 5.2%.
Religious affiliation (1980)[1]: Roman Catholic 87.0%; Protestant 3.9%; nonreligious 2.5%; Afro-American spiritist 2.0%; traditional beliefs 1.5%; Chinese folk-religionist 1.3%; Muslim 1.0%; Baha'i 0.7%; other 0.1%.
Major cities (1982): Cayenne 37,097; Kourou 6,465; Rémire-Montjoly 5,921; Saint-Laurent-du-Maroni 5,042.

Vital statistics

Birth rate per 1,000 population (1987): 30.4 (world avg. 26.0); legitimate 19.8%; illegitimate 80.2%.
Death rate per 1,000 population (1987): 6.3 (world avg. 9.9).
Natural increase rate per 1,000 population (1987): 24.1 (world avg. 16.1).
Total fertility rate (avg. births per childbearing woman; 1975–79): 3.1.
Marriage rate per 1,000 population (1987): 4.1.
Divorce rate per 1,000 population (1987): 0.3.
Life expectancy at birth (1975–79): male 63.4 years; female 69.7 years.
Major causes of death per 100,000 population (1984): diseases of the circulatory system 152.9, of which hypertensive disease 51.4, cerebrovascular disease 40.1; accidents 76.5; malignant neoplasms (cancers) 62.7; infectious and parasitic diseases 55.2.

National economy

Budget (1987). Revenue: F 847,000,000 (internal loans and ordered advancements 47.9%, receipts from French central government 18.5%). Expenditures: F 847,000,000 (health and social services 27.2%, public works 12.5%, debt payments 1.7%, unspecified services 47.9%).
Production. Agriculture, forestry, fishing (value of production in F '000 except as noted; 1986): market-garden vegetables 103,800, roots and tubers 46,600, cereals (mostly rice) 20,900, pork 19,500, beef 10,000, poultry 9,900, fruits (mostly limes, other citrus, and bananas) 9,800, eggs 4,700, milk 2,700, sugarcane 667; roundwood (1985) 254,000 cu m; fish catch (metric tons; 1987)—shrimps and prawns caught by foreign vessels 1,621, local catch of shrimps and prawns 2,755, local fish catch 543. Mining and quarrying (1986): gold 326 kg; stone, sand, and gravel 312,000 metric tons. Manufacturing (1987): yogurt 1,820,000 cups[3]; flans 295,000 units[3]; sawnwood and veneer sheets 39,900 cu m; finished wood products 2,300 cu m; rum 907 hectolitres; other products include leather goods, clothing, rosewood essence, and beer. Construction (1987): residential 20,956 sq m; nonresidential authorized 25,207 sq m. Energy production (consumption): electricity (kW-hr; 1987) 249,200,000 (189,400,000[3]); coal, none (none); crude petroleum, none (none); petroleum products (metric tons; 1986) none (90,000); natural gas, none (none).
Household income and expenditure. Average household size (1982) 3.3; income per household (1980) F 75,762 (U.S.$16,776); sources of income (1980): wages and salaries 76.4%, industrial and commercial profits 12.3%, pensions and rents 3.8%, noncommercial profits 2.5%, income from stocks and bonds 1.6%, other 3.4%; expenditure (1969)[4]: food and beverages 50.0%, clothing and footwear 10.4%, transportation and communications 7.5%, housing 7.3%, household furnishings 6.7%, recreation and education 4.9%, energy 4.1%, health 2.2%, other 6.9%.

Gross national product (at current market prices; 1985): U.S.$176,000,000 (U.S.$2,130 per capita).

Structure of gross domestic product and labour force				
	1979		1982	
	in value F 000,000	% of total value	labour force	% of labour force
Agriculture, forestry fishing	53.4	5.3	3,706	11.4
Mining	...	...	163	0.6
Manufacturing	36.6	3.7	1,359	4.1
Construction	82.5	8.2	2,837	8.8
Public utilities	−6.4	−0.6	380	1.2
Transp. and commun.	65.1	6.5	1,347	4.2
Trade	123.2	12.3	2,025	6.2
Finance, real estate	89.5	8.9	3,662	11.3
Pub. admin., defense, services	557.1	55.7	10,123	31.3
Other	—	—	6,773[5]	20.9
TOTAL	1,001.0	100.0	32,375	100.0

Public debt (external, outstanding; 1985)[2]: U.S.$18,000,000.
Population economically active (1982): total 32,375; activity rate of total population 44.3% (participation rates: ages 15–64, 69.8%; female 35.8%; unemployed [1987] more than 15.0%).

Price and earnings indexes (December 1980 = 100)[6]							
	1981	1982	1983	1984	1985	1986	1987
Consumer price index	116.5	130.3	151.5	163.0	172.8	176.4	183.0
Monthly earnings index[7]	113.5	137.0	147.9	168.0	178.9	180.6	185.5

Tourism: (1986): number of tourist arrivals 10,237.
Land use (1985): forested 81.9%; meadows and pastures 0.05%; agricultural and under permanent cultivation 0.05%; other 18.0%.

Foreign trade

Balance of trade (current prices)					
	1982	1983	1984	1985	1986	1987
F '000,000	−1,431	−1,843	−1,831	−1,956	−1,801	−2,048
% of total	77.1%	75.8%	73.7%	74.7%	77.9%	76.0%

Imports (1987): F 2,372,000,000 (food products 22.3%; electrical and non-electrical machinery 20.9%; consumer goods 15.8%; mineral fuels 10.1%; metals and metal products 8.1%; chemicals and chemical products 8.0%). *Major import sources:* France 62.1%; other EEC 11.6%; Trinidad and Tobago 9.3%; United States 4.3%; Japan 3.2%.
Exports (1987): F 323,735,000 (agricultural products [mostly shrimps, prawns, and rice] 70.2%; consumer goods [mostly wood and wood products] 12.7%; professional and scientific goods 8.3%; base-metal products 7.7%). *Major export destinations:* France 38.4%; United States 21.9%; Guadeloupe 14.2%; Japan 10.7%; Martinique 10.3%.

Transport and communications

Transport. Railroads (1986): none. Roads (1984): total length 691 mi, 1,112 km (paved 65%). Vehicles (1987): passenger cars 27,010; trucks and buses 1,120. Merchant marine: n.a. Air transport (1987): passenger arrivals 101,564; passenger departures 103,077; cargo unloaded 2,934 metric tons, cargo loaded 1,484 metric tons; airports (1988): with scheduled flights 7.
Communications. Daily newspapers (1987): total number 2; total circulation 17,000; circulation per 1,000 population 191. Radio (1986): 44,000 receivers (1 per 1.9 persons). Television (1987): 6,500 receivers (1 per 14 persons). Telephones (1986): 28,209 (1 per 3.1 persons).

Education and health

Education (1983)	schools	teachers	students	student/ teacher ratio
Primary (age 6–11)	51	409	9,780	23.9
Secondary (age 12–18)	11[8]	470[8]	6,468[9]	...
Vocational	...	177[8]	2,623	...
Higher	...	...	...	...

Educational attainment (1982). Percent of population age 25 and over having: no formal schooling 20.8%; some primary education 40.4%; some secondary 32.4%; completed secondary and higher 6.4%. *Literacy* (1982): total population age 16 and over literate 38,964 (82.0%); males literate 21,021 (82.5%); females literate 17,943 (81.3%).
Health: physicians (1986) 149 (1 per 574 persons); hospital beds (1984) 1,001 (1 per 80 persons); infant mortality rate per 1,000 live births (1985–87 avg.) 22.2.
Food (1983–85): daily per capita caloric intake 2,783 (vegetable products 71%, animal products 29%); (1983) 111% of FAO recommended minimum requirement.

Military

Total active duty personnel (1984): 2,700[10].

[1]*Religious affiliation* (1984): Roman Catholic 77.6%; other 22.4%. [2]Includes external long-term private debt not guaranteed by the government. [3]1986. [4]Weights of consumer price index components based on lower income households in Cayenne. [5]Includes 2,013 in categories not clearly defined and 4,760 unemployed. [6]Indexes based on end-of-year figures. [7]Based on minimum-level wage in public administration. [8]1984–85. [9]1985–86. [10]Includes French Foreign Legion troops assigned to guard the Kourou Space Centre.

French Polynesia

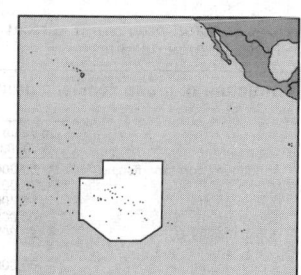

Official name: Territoire de la
Polynésie française (French);
Polynesia Farani (Tahitian) (Territory
of French Polynesia).
Political status: overseas territory
(France) with one legislative house
(Territorial Assembly [41]).
Chief of state: President of France.
Head of government: High
Commissioner (for France); President
of the Territorial Assembly (for
French Polynesia).
Capital: Papeete.
Official languages: French; Tahitian.
Official religion: none.
Monetary unit: 1 Franc de la Comptoirs
française du pacifique (CFPF) = 100
centimes; valuation (Oct. 10,
1988) 1 U.S.$ = CFPF 110.95;
1 £ = CFPF 190.00.

Area and population

Circumscriptions	Capitals	area sq mi	area sq km	population 1983 census
Îles Australes	Mataura	57	148	6,283
Îles Marquises	Taiohae	405	1,049	6,548
Îles sous le Vent	Uturoa	156	404	19,060
Îles Tuamotu et Gambier	Papeete	280	726	11,793
Îles du Vent	Papeete	461	1,194	123,069
TOTAL		1,550[1]	4,000[1]	166,753

Demography

Population (1988): 188,000.
Density (1988)[2]: persons per sq mi 138.3, persons per sq km 53.4.
Urban–rural (1985): urban 62.2%; rural 37.8%.
Sex distribution (1983): male 52.12%; female 47.88%.
Age breakdown (1985): under 15, 37.9%; 15–29, 30.0%; 30–44, 16.5%; 45–59,
10.5%; 60–74, 4.3%; 75 and over, 0.8%.
Population projection: (1990) 197,000; (2000) 254,000.
Doubling time: 30 years.
Ethnic composition (1983): Polynesian 68.5%; mixed 14.5%, of which Poly-
nesian-European 9.5%, Polynesian-Chinese 3.8%, European-Chinese 0.3%;
European (mostly French) 11.6%; Chinese 4.5%; other 0.9%.
Religious affiliation (1980): Protestant 46.6%, of which Evangelical Church
of French Polynesia 32.8%; Roman Catholic 39.4%; other Christian 8.2%,
of which Mormon 3.5%; nonreligious 5.0%; other 0.8%.
Major cities (1983)[3]: Papeete 23,496 (urban agglomeration 78,814); Faaa
21,927[4]; Punaauia 12,414[4].

Vital statistics

Birth rate per 1,000 population (1987): 28.0 (world avg. 26.0); (1983) legiti-
mate 41.1%; illegitimate 58.9%.
Death rate per 1,000 population (1987): 5.1 (world avg. 9.9).
Natural increase rate per 1,000 population (1987): 22.9 (world avg. 16.1).
Total fertility rate (avg. births per childbearing woman; 1987): 3.5.
Marriage rate per 1,000 population (1987): 5.3.
Divorce rate per 1,000 population (1983): 0.8.
Life expectancy at birth (1987): male 70.0 years; female 74.0 years.
Major causes of death per 100,000 population (1984): diseases of the circula-
tory system 120.1; malignant neoplasms (cancers) 67.7; accidents, suicide,
and violence 58.9; ill-defined conditions 94.2.

National economy

Budget (1987). Revenue: CFPF 67,510,000,000 (indirect taxes 62.3%, of
which entry fee 30.1%, social protection tax 11.7%, tax on hydrocarbons
6.4%; loans and grants for investment 22.8%; direct taxes 11.3%). Expenditures: CFPF 67,510,000,000 (investments 18.7%; public debt service 6.6%;
unspecified 74.7%).
Public debt (external, outstanding; 1985)[5]: U.S.$126,000,000.
Tourism (1987): receipts from visitors U.S.$151,000,000; expenditures by
nationals abroad, n.a.
Production (metric tons except as noted). Agriculture, forestry, fishing[6]
(1987): coconuts 150,000[7], cassava 5,000[7], pineapples 3,000[7], watermelon
1,820[8], potatoes 1,800, taros 464, tomatoes 457[8], cucumbers 409[8], lemons
300, bananas 291[8], carrots 250[8], *fei* (wild bananas) 243[9], vanilla 23, flowers (value of production; 1984) CFPF 655,000,000[10]; livestock (number of
live animals; 1986) 48,000 pigs, 7,000 cattle; roundwood, n.a.; fish catch
2,084[8], of which skipjack tuna 523[8], black cultured pearls (1986) c. 350 kg.
Mining and quarrying: none. Manufacturing (1987): copra 14,988; refined
coconut oil 191; other manufactures include *monoï* oil (primarily refined
coconut and sandalwood oils), beer, printed cloth, and sandals. Construction (buildings completed; 1986): 101,100 sq m. Energy production (consumption): electricity (kW-hr; 1987) 244,700,000 (221,500,000); coal, none
(none); crude petroleum, none (none); petroleum products (metric tons;
1986) none (194,000); natural gas, none (none).
Household income and expenditure. Average household size (1983) 5.0; average annual income per household (1977) CFPF 2,118,161 (U.S.$23,624);
sources of income (1982): salaries 48.0%, self-employment 40.9%, transfer payments 9.4%, other 1.7%; expenditure (1979)[11]: food and beverages

36.5%, household furnishings 14.4%, transportation 13.1%, clothing 9.0%,
recreation and education 8.7%, energy 8.6%, other 9.7%.
Gross domestic product (at current market prices; 1985): U.S.$1,370,000,000
(U.S.$7,830 per capita).

Structure of gross domestic product and labour force

	1984 in value CFPF '000,000	1984 % of total value	1983 labour force	1983 % of labour force
Agriculture	8,142	4.6	8,014	12.8
Manufacturing[12]	16,779	9.5	4,164	6.7
Construction	20,222	11.5	6,231	10.0
Public utilities	1,544	0.9	384	0.6
Transp. and commun.	11,729	6.7	3,410	5.5
Trade	24,585	14.0	9,688	15.5
Finance, real estate	} 92,883[13]	52.8	2,582	4.1
Pub. admin., defense, and services			23,375	37.4
Other	—	—	4,597[14]	7.4
TOTAL	175,884	100.0	62,445	100.0

Population economically active (1983): total 62,445; activity rate of total
population 37.4% (participation rates: ages 14–59, 60.8%; female 32.0%;
unemployed [1987] 10.0%).

Price and earnings indexes (1981 = 100)[15]

	1981	1982	1983	1984	1985	1986	1987
Consumer price index	100.0	114.5	130.2	144.0	155.2	154.2	157.3
Monthly earnings index[16]	100.0	129.9	155.2	176.1	197.6	199.8	208.8

Land use (1985): forested 31.4%; meadows and pastures 5.5%; agricultural
and under permanent cultivation 20.5%; other 42.6%.

Foreign trade[17]

Balance of trade (current prices)

	1982	1983	1984	1985	1986	1987
CFPF '000,000	−58,957	−69,399	−80,392	−82,300	−87,555	−81,493
% of total	90.0%	87.0%	88.1%	85.7%	89.0%	81.8%

Imports (1987): CFPF 90,587,000,000 (machinery and appliances 20.9%; food
products 17.8%; transport equipment 15.0%; metal manufactures 8.3%;
petroleum products 7.0%; industrial chemical products 5.7%). *Major import
sources:* France 52.1%; other EEC 12.9%; United States 10.3%; Australia
5.5%; New Zealand 5.0%.
Exports (1987): CFPF 9,094,000,000 (reexports 69.2%, of which petroleum
products 36.1%, fish 4.6%; black cultured pearls 24.8%; coconut oil 3.6%;
mother-of-pearl 0.6%; vanilla 0.5%). *Major export destinations*[9]: France
43.7%; United States 20.9%; Japan 11.8%; New Caledonia 10.4%.

Transport and communications

Transport. Railroads: none. Roads (1984): total length 495 mi, 797 km
(paved 33%). Motor vehicles (1985): 44,000. Merchant marine: vessels (100
gross tons and over), n.a. Air transport (1987): passenger arrivals 379,400,
passenger departures 396,700; cargo unloaded 7,919 metric tons[18], cargo
loaded 616 metric tons[18]; airports (1988) with scheduled flights 32.
Communications. Daily newspapers (1987): total number 3; total circulation
23,000; circulation per 1,000 population 126. Radio (1986): total number
of receivers 84,000 (1 per 2.1 persons). Television (1987): total number of
receivers 26,500 (1 per 6.9 persons). Telephones (1986): 41,210 (1 per 4.4
persons).

Education and health

Education (1984–85)

	schools	teachers	students	student/ teacher ratio
Primary (age 6–10)	198	1,337	27,401	20.5
Secondary (age 11–17)	24	804	13,611	16.9
Vocational	17	362	3,441	9.5
Higher[19]	...	...	180	...

Educational attainment (1983): Percent of population age 25 and over having: no formal schooling 9.3%; primary education 58.7%; secondary 25.7%;
higher 6.3%. *Literacy* (1983): total population age 15 and over literate 98,-
314 (95.0%); males literate 51,910 (94.9%); females literate 46,404 (95.0%).
Health: physicians (1983) 174 (1 per 950 persons); hospital beds (1980) 982
(1 per 154 persons); infant mortality rate per 1,000 live births (1985–87
avg.) 20.2.
Food (1984–86): daily per capita caloric intake 2,896 (vegetable products
78%, animal products 22%); (1983) 105% of FAO recommended minimum requirement.

Military

Total active duty personnel (1987): 5,400 French military personnel. *Military
expenditure as percent of GNP:* n.a.

[1]Approximate total area including inland water; total land area is 1,359 sq mi (3,521
sq km). [2]Based on land area. [3]Populations cited are for communes unless otherwise
noted. [4]Part of Papeete urban agglomeration. [5]Includes external long-term private
debt not guaranteed by the government. [6]Includes marine-produced commodities,
e.g., pearls. [7]1986. [8]Commercial production only. [9]1985. [10]Excludes flowers processed for perfume. [11]Weights of consumer price index components. [12]Includes mining. [13]Includes nonmarket services with an imputed value of CFPF 56,479,000,000.
[14]Includes 1,339 not adequately defined and 3,258 unemployed. [15]All end-of-year.
[16]Manufacturing sector. [17]Imports c.i.f.; exports f.o.b. [18]Excludes local interisland
traffic. [19]1983–84.

Gabon

Official name: République Gabonaise
  (Gabonese Republic).
Form of government: unitary
  single-party republic with one
  legislative house (National Assembly
  [120[1]]).
Chief of state: President.
Head of government: Prime Minister.
Capital: Libreville.
Official language: French.
Official religion: none.
Monetary unit: 1 CFA franc
  (CFAF) = 100 centimes; valuation
  (Oct. 10, 1988) 1 U.S.$ = CFAF
  316.13; 1 £ = CFAF 541.38.

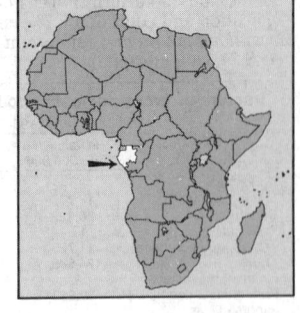

Area and population

		area		population
				1978
Provinces	Capitals	sq mi	sq km	estimate[2]
Estuaire	Libreville	8,008	20,740	359,000
Haut-Ogooué	Franceville	14,111	36,547	213,000
Moyen-Ogooué	Lambaréné	7,156	18,535	49,000
Ngounié	Mouila	14,575	37,750	118,000
Nyanga	Tchibanga	8,218	21,285	98,000
Ogooué-Ivindo	Makokou	17,790	46,075	53,000
Ogooué-Lolo	Koulamoutou	9,799	25,380	49,000
Ogooué-Maritime	Port-Gentil	8,838	22,890	194,000
Woleu-Ntem	Oyem	14,851	38,465	166,000
TOTAL		103,347[3]	267,667	1,300,000[3]

Demography

Population (1988)[2]: 1,219,000.
Density (1988): persons per sq mi 11.8, persons per sq km 4.6.
Urban–rural (1985): urban 40.9%; rural 59.1%.
Sex distribution (1985): male 49.14%; female 50.86%.
Age breakdown (1985): under 15, 34.6%; 15–29, 24.4%; 30–44, 18.3%; 45–59, 13.3%; 60–74, 7.6%; 75 and over, 1.8%.
Population projection: (1990) 1,273,000; (2000) 1,603,000.
Doubling time: 44 years.
Ethnic composition (1983): Fang 35.5%; Mpongwe 15.1%; Mbete 14.2%; Punu 11.5%; other 23.7%.
Religious affiliation (1980): Christian 96.2%, of which Roman Catholic 65.2%, Protestant 18.8%, African indigenous 12.1%; traditional religion 2.9%; Muslim 0.8%; other 0.1%.
Major cities (1987): Libreville 352,000; Port-Gentil 164,000; Franceville 75,000.

Vital statistics

Birth rate per 1,000 population (1980–85): 33.8 (world avg. 29.0).
Death rate per 1,000 population (1980–85): 18.1 (world avg. 11.0).
Natural increase rate per 1,000 population (1980–85): 15.7 (world avg. 18.0).
Total fertility rate (avg. births per childbearing woman; 1985): 5.0.
Marriage rate per 1,000 population: n.a.
Divorce rate per 1,000 population: n.a.
Life expectancy at birth (1980–85): male 48.0 years; female 51.4 years.
Major causes of death per 100,000 population: n.a.; however, major diseases include malaria, measles, shigellosis (infection with dysentery), trypanosomiasis, and tuberculosis.

National economy

Budget (1987). Revenue: CFAF 460,000,000,000 (loans 37.8%; taxes on petroleum organizations and petroleum fees 13.0%). Expenditures: CFAF 450,000,000,000 (current expenditure 59.1%; development expenditure 40.9%, of which infrastructure 22.2%; public debt 18.7%).
Public debt (external, outstanding; 1986): U.S.$1,094,700,000.
Tourism (1986): receipts from visitors U.S.$4,000,000; expenditures by nationals abroad U.S.$83,000,000.
Production (metric tons except as noted). Agriculture, forestry, fishing (1986): roots and tubers 396,000, cassava 255,000, plantains 170,000, sugarcane 130,000, corn (maize) 11,000, peanuts (groundnuts) 8,000, bananas 8,000, palm oil 3,600, cacao beans 2,000, coffee 1,000; livestock (number of live animals) 152,000 pigs, 82,000 sheep, 70,000 goats, 8,000 cattle, 2,000,000 chickens; roundwood (1985) 1,382,000 cu m; fish catch 20,400. Mining and quarrying (1986): manganese 3,000,000; uranium 917. Manufacturing (1986): cement 210,000; flour 28,240; raw sugar 18,000; beer 820,000 hectolitres; soft drinks 480,000 hectolitres; cigarettes 17,800,000 packs[4]; textiles CFAF 2,420,000,000[4]. Construction: n.a. Energy production (consumption): electricity (kW-hr; 1986) 867,000,000 (867,000,000); crude petroleum (barrels; 1986) 58,100,000 (9,100,000); petroleum products (metric tons; 1986) 1,052,000 (627,000); natural gas (cu m; 1986) 203,400,000 (203,400,000); fuelwood and bagasse (cu m; 1985) 1,310,000 (1,310,000).
Population economically active (1985): total 518,000; activity rate of total population 45.0% (participation rates: ages 15–64, 68.2%; female 38.4%; unemployed, n.a.).

Price and earnings indexes (1980 = 100)

	1981	1982	1983	1984	1985	1986	1987[5]
Consumer price index	108.7	126.8	137.0	148.2	159.1	169.1	170.0
Earnings index	101.1	126.6	156.3	...	...	...	...

Gross national product (at current market prices; 1986): U.S.$3,150,000,000 (U.S.$3,020 per capita).

Structure of gross domestic product and labour force

	1986		1983	
	in value CFAF '000,000	% of total value	labour force[6]	% of labour force[6]
Agriculture, forestry, fishing	80,000	7.0	14,118	10.2
Mining	276,000	24.0	3,919	2.9
Manufacturing	55,700	4.9	4,123	3.0
Construction	103,000	9.0	13,154	9.5
Public utilities	26,200	2.3	[7]	[7]
Transportation and communications	60,000	5.2	[7]	[7]
Trade	154,000	13.4	3,732	2.7
Finance	12,800	1.1	[7]	[7]
Pub. admin., defense	157,300	13.7	42,678	31.0
Services	131,000	11.4	[7]	[7]
Other, including taxes on imports	92,000	8.0	56,143[7]	40.7[7]
TOTAL	1,148,000	100.0	137,867	100.0

Household income and expenditure. Average household size (1980) 4.0; income per household: n.a.; sources of income (1983): private sector 73.4%, public sector 26.6%; expenditure[8] (1983): food and tobacco 54.7%, clothing and footwear 17.5%, housing 13.0%, transportation and communications 6.3%.
Land use (1985): forested 77.6%; meadows and pastures 18.2%; agricultural and under permanent cultivation 1.8%; other 2.4%.

Foreign trade

Balance of trade (current prices)

	1981	1982	1983	1984	1985	1986
CFAF '000,000	+371,100	+252,100	+421,700	+492,600	+500,000	+140,000
% of total	45.0%	32.4%	39.4%	40.8%	39.2%	18.9%

Imports (1985): CFAF 387,000,000,000 (machinery and mechanical equipment 20.9%; transport equipment and parts 16.3%; food, beverages, and tobacco products 12.9%; metal and metal products 11.5%; chemical products 3.9%; textiles 3.9%; precision instruments 3.5%; hygiene and cleaning products 3.3%; mineral products 2.2%). *Major import sources:* France 45.5%; United States 10.0%; Japan 6.3%; West Germany 5.8%; United Kingdom 4.2%; Italy 4.0%; Belgium–Luxembourg 3.9%; The Netherlands 2.3%; Spain 1.6%.
Exports (1985): CFAF 887,000,000,000 (crude petroleum and petroleum products 82.9%; wood 6.2%, of which okoumé and ozigo 4.5%; manganese ore and concentrate 6.0%; uranium ore and concentrate 3.0%). *Major export destinations:* France 33.3%; United States 18.6%; Spain 7.1%; United Kingdom 4.2%; The Netherlands 3.4%; Italy 2.3%.

Transport and communications

Transport. Railroads (1987): length 416 mi, 670 km; passenger-mi 12,000,-000[9], passenger-km 19,000,000[9]; short ton-mi cargo 71,000,000[9], metric ton-km cargo 103,000,000[9]. Roads (1986): total length 4,682 mi, 7,535 km (paved 8%). Vehicles (1985): passenger cars 16,093; trucks and buses 10,503. Merchant marine (1987): vessels (100 gross tons and over) 22; total deadweight tonnage 29,276. Air transport (1986): passengers carried 905,072; cargo carried 43,246 short tons (39,351 metric tons); airports (1988) with scheduled flights 25[10].
Communications. Daily newspapers (1984): total number 2; total circulation 33,000; circulation per 1,000 population 35. Radio (1986): total number of receivers 145,000 (1 per 8.1 persons). Television (1987): total number of receivers 37,200 (1 per 32 persons). Telephones (1984): 13,800 (1 per 81 persons).

Education and health

Education (1984–85)

	schools	teachers	students	student/teacher ratio
Primary	940	3,837	178,811	46.6
Secondary	51	1,894	25,815	13.6
Voc., teacher tr.	29	720	13,529	18.8
Higher[11]	1	616	3,228	5.2

Educational attainment, n.a. *Literacy* (1978): total population age 15 and over literate 800,000 (77%); males literate, n.a.; females literate, n.a.
Health (1984): physicians 565 (1 per 2,000 persons); hospital beds 10,980 (1 per 103 persons); infant mortality rate per 1,000 live births (1980–85) 121.6.
Food (1984–86): daily per capita caloric intake 2,700 (vegetable products 88%, animal products 12%); (1983) 102% of FAO recommended minimum requirement.

Military

Total active duty personnel (1987): 2,850 (army 66.7%, navy 12.3%, air force 21.0%), not including 600 French troops. *Military expenditure as percent of GNP* (1985): 2.0% (world 6.1%); per capita expenditure U.S.$69.

---

[1]Including 9 nonelective seats. [2]Population distribution is based on country estimate, which is substantially higher than estimates from external sources (such as the United Nations and the World Bank), which form the basis of the 1988 estimate. [3]Detail does not add to total given because of rounding. [4]1984. [5]First quarter. [6]Official government figures for salaried workers only, not including traditional agricultural workers; agricultural workers (FAO estimate, 1986) totaled 370,000 (71.0% of the labour force). [7]Public utilities, transportation and communication, finance, and service employees included with other. [8]Libreville only. [9]1986. [10]Includes airfields. [11]1983–84.

Gambia, The

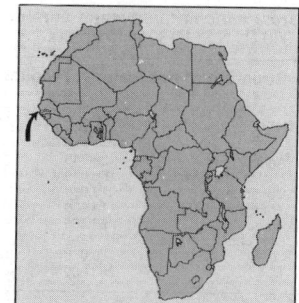

Official name: Republic of The Gambia.
Form of government: multiparty republic with one legislative house (House of Representatives [50])[1].
Head of state and government: President.
Capital: Banjul.
Official language: English.
Official religion: none.
Monetary unit: 1 dalasi (D) = 100 butut; valuation (Oct. 10, 1988) 1 U.S.$ = D 7.10; 1 £ = D 12.15.

Area and population

Divisions	Capitals	area sq mi	area sq km	population 1983 census[2]
Kombo Saint Mary	Kanifing	29	76	101,504
Lower River	Mansakonko	625	1,618	55,263
MacCarthy Island	Kuntaur/Georgetown	1,117	2,894	126,004
North Bank	Kerewan	871	2,256	112,225
Upper River	Basse	799	2,069	111,388
Western	Brikama	681	1,764	137,245
City				
Banjul	—	5	12	44,188
TOTAL		4,127	10,689	687,817

Demography

Population (1988): 811,000.
Density[3] (1988): persons per sq mi 243.9, persons per sq km 94.2.
Urban–rural (1984): urban 21.2%; rural 78.8%.
Sex distribution (1983): male 49.74%; female 50.26%.
Age breakdown (1983): under 15, 43.8%; 15–29, 26.5%; 30–44, 15.7%; 45–59, 9.4%; 60–74, 4.0%; 75 and over, 0.6%.
Population projection: (1990) 860,000; (2000) 1,156,000.
Doubling time: 33 years.
Ethnic composition (1983): Malinke 40.4%; Fulani 18.7%; Wolof 14.6%; Dyola 10.3%; Soninke 8.2%; other 7.8%.
Religious affiliation (1983): Muslim 95.4%; Christian 3.7%; traditional beliefs and other 0.9%.
Major cities (1986): Serekunda 102,600; Banjul 44,188[4]; Brikama 24,300; Bakau 23,600; Basse 5,612.

Vital statistics

Birth rate per 1,000 population (1980–85): 48.4 (world avg. 29.0); legitimate, n.a.; illegitimate, n.a.
Death rate per 1,000 population (1980–85): 29.0 (world avg. 11.0).
Natural increase rate per 1,000 population (1980–85): 19.4 (world avg. 18.0).
Total fertility rate (avg. births per childbearing woman; 1985): 6.5.
Marriage rate per 1,000 population: n.a.
Divorce rate per 1,000 population: n.a.
Life expectancy at birth (1980–85): male 40.9 years; female 44.1 years.
Major causes of death per 100,000 population: n.a.; however, major infectious diseases include malaria, gonococcal infections and syphilis, leprosy (Hansen's disease), chicken pox, schistosomiasis, tetanus, tuberculosis, and trypanosomiasis (sleeping sickness).

National economy

Budget (1986–87). Revenue: D 498,017,000 (recurrent revenue 296,780,000, of which import and excise duties 67.5%; income tax 11.9%; export duties 2.7%). Expenditures: D 463,864,000 (current expenditure D 262,627,000, of which education, sports, and culture 9.4%; health, labour, and social welfare 6.6%; public works, transport, and communications 4.8%; agriculture, forestry, fisheries, and mineral resources 4.6%).
Public debt (external, outstanding; 1986): U.S.$228,000,000.
Production (metric tons except as noted). Agriculture, forestry, fishing (1986): peanuts (groundnuts) in shell 100,000, millet and sorghum 56,000, paddy rice 45,000, corn (maize) 31,000, cassava 6,000, palm oil 2,500, palm kernels 2,000; livestock (number of live animals) 290,000 cattle, 200,000 goats, 191,000 sheep, 12,000 pigs, 4,000 asses, 310,000 chickens; roundwood (1985) 783,000 cu m, of which fuel wood 528,000 cu m, sawn logs, veneer logs and logs for sleepers 21,000 cu m, industrial wood 7,000 cu m; fish catch 10,712, of which inland water 2,712, Atlantic Ocean 8,000. Mining and quarrying: n.a.; however, deposits of kaolin, tin, ilmenite, zircon, and rutile are significant locally. Manufacturing (value of production in D '000; 1982): processed food, including peanut and palm kernel oil 62,878; beverages 10,546; textiles 3,253; chemicals and related products 1,031; nonmetals 922; printing and publishing 358; leather 150. Construction: n.a. Energy production (consumption): electricity (kW-hr; 1986) 42,000,000 (42,000,000); coal, none (n.a.); crude petroleum, none (n.a.); petroleum products (metric tons; 1986) none (51,000); natural gas, none (n.a.).
Population economically active (1983): total 325,600; activity rate of total population 47.3% (participation rates: ages 15–64 78.2%; female 46.3%; unemployed, n.a.).

Price and earnings indexes (1980 = 100)

	1982	1983	1984	1985	1986	1987	1988[5]
Consumer price index	117.6	130.1	158.9	188.0	294.3	363.5	383.6
Earnings index	...	...	...	...	...	...	...

Household income and expenditure. Average household size (1980) 4.9; income per household: n.a., sources of income: n.a., expenditure[6] (1986): food, beverages, and tobacco 58.0%, clothing and footwear 17.5%, energy and water 5.4%, housing 5.1%, education, health, transportation and communications, recreation, and other 14.0%.
Gross national product (at current prices; 1986): U.S.$180,000,000 (U.S.$230 per capita).

Structure of gross domestic product and labour force

	1986–87 in value D'000,000	1986–87 % of total value	1983 labour force	1983 % of labour force
Agriculture	113.3	26.0	239,940	73.7
Mining	—	—	66	0.0
Manufacturing	20.3	4.6	8,144	2.5
Construction	17.0	3.9	4,373	1.3
Public utilities	3.5	0.8	1,233	0.4
Transportation and communications	37.2	8.5	8,014	2.5
Trade	124.8	28.6	16,551	5.1
Finance	27.3	6.3	4,577	1.4
Public administration	48.5	11.1	8,295	2.5
Services	7.1	1.6	9,381	2.9
Other	37.4[7]	8.6[7]	25,049	7.7
TOTAL	436.4[8]	100.0	325,623	100.0

Tourism (1986): receipts from visitors U.S.$21,807,000; expenditures by nationals abroad U.S.$11,000,000.
Land use (1985): forested 19.2%; meadows and pastures 9.0%; agricultural and under permanent cultivation 16.5%; built-on area, wasteland, and other 55.3%.

Foreign trade

Balance of trade (current prices)

	1981	1982	1983	1984	1985	1986
D '000,000	−157.4	−91.0	−134.1	−140.9	−137.3	−363.4
% of total	60.5%	31.6%	34.6%	30.2%	28.4%	43.5%

Imports (1986): D 567,631,000 (food, beverages, and tobacco 35.8%; basic manufactured goods 20.1%; machinery and transport equipment 17.2%; mineral fuels and lubricants 10.0%; chemicals and related products 6.0%; animal and vegetable oils and fats 1.4%). *Major import sources:* France 14.4%; United Kingdom 11.3%; Thailand 5.7%; China 5.4%; The Netherlands 5.3%; West Germany 5.1%; United States 4.7%.
Exports (1986): D 204,195,000[9] (peanut oil 28.1%; shelled peanuts 24.5%; peanut meal and cake 2.4%; fish and fish preparations 2.3%). *Major export destinations:* Switzerland 22.9%; The Netherlands 14.8%; Guinea-Bissau 8.3%; United Kingdom 6.7%; Mali 4.3%; France 4.0%; Guinea 2.3%.

Transport and communications

Transport. Railroads: none. Roads (1986): total length 1,484 mi, 2,388 km (paved 21%). Vehicles (1986): passenger cars 5,200; trucks and buses 720. Merchant marine (1987): vessels (100 gross tons and over) 8; total deadweight tonnage 5,098. Air transport (1986): passenger arrivals and departures 905,072; cargo 39,351 metric tons; airports (1988) with scheduled flights 1.
Communications. Daily newspapers (1984): total number 1; total circulation 2,000; circulation per 1,000 population 2.8. Radio (1986): total number of receivers 110,000 (1 per 7.0 persons). Television: none. Telephones (1985): 3,500 (1 per 215 persons).

Education and health

Education (1984–85)

	schools	teachers	students	student/ teacher ratio
Primary (age 8–14)	189	2,640	66,257	25.1
Secondary (age 15–21)	8	235	4,348	18.5
Secondary vocational	16	502	10,102	20.1
Postsecondary	9	177	1,489	8.4

Educational attainment (1973). Percent of population age 20 and over having: no formal schooling 90.8%; primary education 6.2%; secondary 2.6%; higher 0.4%. *Literacy* (1985): total population age 15 and over literate 74.9%; males literate 35.6%; females literate 15.1%.
Health (1981): physicians 66 (1 per 9,900 persons); hospital beds 756 (1 per 865 persons); infant mortality rate per 1,000 live births (1980–85) 174.0.
Food (1984–86): daily per capita caloric intake 2,367 (vegetable products 93%, animal products 7%); (1983) 95% of FAO recommended minimum requirement.

Military

Total active duty personnel (1987): 600 (army 87.5%, navy 8.3%, air force 4.2%). *Military expenditure as percent of GNP* (1985): n.a. (world 6.1%).

[1]Includes 14 nonelective seats. [2]Preliminary. [3]Based on land area, which is 8,613 sq km (3,325 sq mi). [4]1983. [5]February. [6]Low-income population in Banjul and Kombo St. Mary only; weights of consumer price index components. [7]Direct taxes less imputed bank charges. [8]At constant market prices. [9]Includes reexports of D 136,938,000.

German Democratic Republic

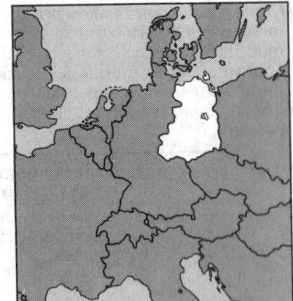

Official name: Deutsche Demokratische Republik (German Democratic Republic).
Form of government: unitary single-party republic with one legislative house (People's Chamber [500]).
Chief of state: Chairman, Council of State.
Head of government: Chairman, Council of Ministers (Premier).
Capital: Berlin.
Official language: German.
Official religion: none.
Monetary unit: 1 Mark of Deutsche Demokratische Republik (M) = 100 Pfennige; valuation (Oct. 10, 1988) 1 U.S.$ = M 1.86; 1 £ = M 3.18.

Area and population		area		population
		sq mi	sq km	1987 estimate[1]
Districts	**Capitals**			
Berlin, capital city	—	156	403	1,236,248
Cottbus	Cottbus	3,190	8,262	883,591
Dresden	Dresden	2,602	6,738	1,768,990
Erfurt	Erfurt	2,837	7,349	1,235,785
Frankfurt	Frankfurt	2,774	7,186	710,634
Gera	Gera	1,546	4,004	739,856
Halle	Halle	3,386	8,771	1,783,987
Karl-Marx-Stadt	Karl-Marx-Stadt	2,320	6,009	1,866,321
Leipzig	Leipzig	1,917	4,966	1,371,427
Magdeburg	Magdeburg	4,450	11,526	1,249,636
Neubrandenburg	Neubrandenburg	4,227	10,948	620,057
Potsdam	Potsdam	4,853	12,568	1,121,640
Rostock	Rostock	2,732	7,075	909,550
Schwerin	Schwerin	3,348	8,672	592,519
Suhl	Suhl	1,489	3,856	549,636
TOTAL		41,827	108,333	16,639,877

Demography

Population (1988): 16,588,000.
Density (1988): persons per sq mi 396.6, persons per sq km 153.1.
Urban–rural (1986): urban 76.6%; rural 23.4%.
Sex distribution (1986): male 47.50%; female 52.50%.
Age breakdown (1986): under 15, 19.2%; 15–29, 22.0%; 30–44, 19.6%; 45–59, 19.9%; 60–74, 11.0%; 75 and over, 8.3%.
Population projection: (1990) 16,551,000; (2000) 16,371,000.
Doubling time: not applicable; population is declining.
Ethnic composition (1986): German 99.7%; other 0.3%.
Religious affiliation (1986): Protestant 47.0%; Roman Catholic 7.0%; unaffiliated and other 46.0%.
Major cities (1987): Berlin (East) 1,236,248; Leipzig 550,641; Dresden 519,810; Karl-Marx-Stadt 313,799; Magdeburg 288,975; Rostock 249,349.

Vital statistics

Birth rate per 1,000 population (1986): 13.4 (world avg. 26.0); (1985) legitimate 66.2%; illegitimate 33.8%.
Death rate per 1,000 population (1986): 13.4 (world avg. 9.9).
Natural increase rate per 1,000 population (1986): 0.0 (world avg. 16.1).
Total fertility rate (avg. births per childbearing woman; 1985): 1.6.
Marriage rate per 1,000 population (1986): 8.3.
Divorce rate per 1,000 population (1986): 3.2.
Life expectancy at birth (1985): male 69.5 years; female 75.4 years.
Major causes of death per 100,000 population (1985): circulatory diseases 797.0; malignant neoplasms (cancers) 212.0; accidents 42.0; pneumonia 26.0; stomach and intestinal diseases 8.0; tuberculosis 3.0.

National economy

Budget (1988). Revenue: M 291,180,400,000 (revenue from state-owned enterprises 69.0%, taxes and dues 7.1%, social insurance contributions 6.4%, health care contributions 3.2%). Expenditures: M 291,005,400,000 (economic development 33.8%, social welfare and health 18.2%, economic subsidies and price supports 17.0%, housing construction 5.6%, defense 5.4%, education 3.6%).
Production (metric tons except as noted). Agriculture, forestry, fishing (1986): potatoes 9,996,578, sugar beets 7,746,988, barley 4,293,337, wheat 4,195,095, rye 2,406,057, oats 666,476; livestock (number of live animals; 1987) 12,840,200 pigs, 5,804,200 cattle, 2,647,200 sheep, 50,216,400 chickens; commercial timber 10,825,000 cu m; fish catch 247,700. Mining and quarrying (1986) potash (K$_2$O content) 3,485,000; copper ore 10,000; tin 2,500; silver 1,200,000 troy oz. Manufacturing (1986): cement 11,988,000; steel 7,967,200; fertilizer 5,046,300; pig iron 2,737,600; plastics and synthetic resins 1,045,400; sulfuric acid 883,300; paper 891,400; sugar 834,800; caustic soda 638,060; consumer goods (1985): 1,267,000 vacuum cleaners; 1,132,400 radios; 829,900 refrigerators; 668,100 television receivers; 503,000 washing machines. Construction (sq m; 1986): residential 7,202,000; non-residential, n.a. Energy production (consumption): electricity (kW-hr; 1986) 115,291,000,000 (116,290,000); coal (metric tons; 1986) 311,260,000 (317,995,000); crude petroleum (barrels; 1986) 284,000 (163,000,000); petroleum products (metric tons; 1986) 20,525,000 (15,096,000); natural gas (cu m; 1986) 7,958,000,000 (10,600,000,000).

Gross national product (at current market prices; 1986): U.S.$185,751,000,000 (U.S.$11,180 per capita).

Structure of net material product and labour force				
	1986			
	in value M '000,000	% of total value	labour force[2]	% of labour force
Agriculture	29,845	11.3	926,500	10.8
Mining, manufacturing	168,040[3]	63.9[3]	3,472,900	40.6
Construction	18,920	7.2	574,100	6.7
Transp. and commun.	14,320	5.4	627,400	7.3
Trade	22,805	8.7	877,800	10.3
Services	—		2,068,900[4]	24.2[4]
Other	9,070[5]	3.4[5]		
TOTAL	263,000[6]	100.0[7]	8,547,600	100.0[7]

Public debt (external, outstanding; 1986): U.S.$10,900,000,000.
Population economically active (1986): total 8,547,600[2]; activity rate of total population 51.4% (participation rates: ages 15–64, n.a.; female 49.1%).

Price and earnings indexes (1980 = 100)							
	1980	1981	1982	1983	1984	1985	1986
Consumer price index	100.0	100.3	100.3	100.3	100.3	100.3	100.3
Monthly earnings index	100.0	102.4	105.2	106.6	107.4	...	...

Household income and expenditure. Average household size (1986) 2.9; average annual income per household (1985) M 21,000 (U.S.$10,340); sources of income: wages and salaries 68.3%, social welfare 31.7%; expenditure (1986): food and beverages 41.1%, clothing and footwear 15.4%, education 4.3%, household durable goods 4.1%, housing 3.2%, energy 2.0%.
Tourism (1986): total tourist arrivals 1,038,866.
Land use (1985): forested 27.3%; meadows and pastures 11.8%; agricultural and under permanent cultivation 47.3%; other 13.6%.

Foreign trade

Balance of trade (current prices)							
	1980	1981	1982	1983	1984	1985	1986
M '000,000	−5,840	−1,073	+5,353	+8,031	+6,901	+6,789	+1,040
% of total	4.9%	0.8%	3.7%	5.0%	4.0%	3.8%	0.6%

Imports (1986): M 90,465,100,000 (fuels, minerals, and unfabricated metals 39.8%; machinery, equipment, and transportation equipment 29.5%; fabricated and partially fabricated industrial materials 15.6%; chemicals and related products 8.6%; consumer goods 6.5%).
Exports (1986): M 91,505,100,000 (machinery, equipment, and transportation equipment 46.7%; consumer goods 16.4%; fuels, minerals, and unfabricated metals 15.9%; chemical products 13.2%; fabricated industrial materials 7.8%). *Direction of total trade*[8]: U.S.S.R. 38.8%; Czechoslovakia 7.4%; West Germany 6.0%; Poland 6.0%; Hungary 5.1%; Bulgaria 3.1%; Romania 2.9%.

Transport and communications

Transport. Railroads (1986): length 8,702 mi, 14,005 km; passenger-mi 13,920,000,000, passenger-km 22,402,000,000; short ton-mi cargo 40,328,000,000, metric ton-km cargo 58,881,000,000. Roads (1985): total length 77,434 mi, 124,615 km (paved n.a.). Vehicles (1986): passenger cars 3,462,184; trucks and buses 425,049. Merchant marine (1987): vessels (100 gross tons and over) 377; total deadweight tonnage 1,880,002. Air transport (1986): passenger-mi 1,646,000,000, passenger-km 2,649,000,000; short ton-mi cargo 48,400,000, metric ton-km cargo 70,700,000; airports (1988) with scheduled flights 4.
Communications. Daily newspapers (1986): total number 39; total circulation 9,300,000; circulation per 1,000 population 559. Radio (1987): 6,698,695 receivers (1 per 2.5 persons). Television (1987): 6,181,860 receivers (1 per 2.7 persons). Telephones (1986): 3,755,000 (1 per 4.4 persons).

Education and health

Education (1985)	schools	teachers	students	student/ teacher ratio
Primary (age 6–10)	5,649	58,406	859,830	14.7
Secondary (age 10–18)	5,711	112,076	1,140,391	10.2
Vocational	4,500	55,234	378,761	6.9
Higher	54	42,336	432,672	10.2

Educational attainment (1986). Percent of employed population age 20 and over having: primary education, virtually 100%; academic secondary 15.9%; vocational 75.2%; higher 8.9%. *Literacy* (1987): total population age 15 and over literate, virtually 100%.
Health (1987): physicians 39,157 (1 per 424 persons); hospital beds 169,179 (1 per 98 persons); infant mortality rate per 1,000 live births (1986) 9.2.
Food (1984–86): daily per capita caloric intake 3,800 (vegetable products 64%, animal products 36%); (1983) 142% of FAO recommended minimum requirement.

Military

Total active duty personnel (1987): 176,000 (army 68.2%, navy 9.1%, air force 22.7%). *Military expenditure as percent of GNP* (1985): 6.4% (world 6.1%); per capita expenditure U.S.$678.

[1]January 1. [2]Employed only. [3]Includes public utilities. [4]Includes finance, public administration, and defense. [5]Other material activities. [6]At 1985 prices. [7]Detail does not add to total given because of rounding. [8]Separate figures are not available for import sources and export destinations.

Germany, Federal Republic of

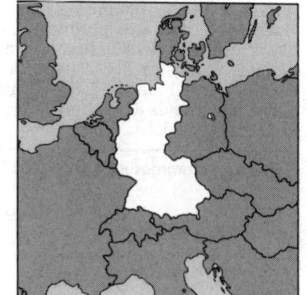

Official name: Bundesrepublik Deutschland (Federal Republic of Germany).
Form of government: federal multiparty republic with two legislative houses (Federal Council [45]; Federal Diet [519]).
Chief of state: President.
Head of government: Chancellor.
Capital: Bonn (provisional).
Official language: German.
Official religion: none.
Monetary unit: 1 Deutsche Mark (DM) = 100 Pfennige; valuation (Oct. 10, 1988) 1 U.S.$ = DM 1.86; 1 £ = DM 3.18.

Area and population		area		population
States	Capitals	sq mi	sq km	1987 estimate[1]
Baden–Württemberg	Stuttgart	13,804	35,751	9,326,800
Bayern	Munich	27,241	70,553	11,026,500
Bremen	Bremen	156	404	654,200
Hamburg	Hamburg	292	755	1,571,300
Hessen	Wiesbaden	8,152	21,114	5,543,700
Niedersachsen	Hannover	18,316	47,439	7,196,100
Nordrhein–Westfalen	Düsseldorf	13,153	34,068	16,676,500
Rheinland–Pfalz	Mainz	7,663	19,848	3,611,400
Saarland	Saarbrücken	992	2,569	1,042,100
Schleswig–Holstein	Kiel	6,073	15,729	2,612,700
Berlin (West)[2]	Berlin (West)	185	480	1,879,200
TOTAL		96,027	248,709[3]	61,140,500

Demography

Population (1988): 60,782,000.
Density (1988): persons per sq mi 633.0, persons per sq km 244.4.
Urban–rural (1985): urban 85.5%; rural 14.5%.
Sex distribution (1987): male 47.92%; female 52.08%.
Age breakdown (1987): under 15, 14.7%; 15–29, 24.3%; 30–44, 20.1%; 45–59, 20.3%; 60–74, 13.5%; 75 and over, 7.1%.
Population projection: (1990) 60,500,000; (2000) 59,107,000.
Doubling time: not applicable; population has been in approximate balance since about 1980.
Ethnic composition (1987): German 92.6%; Turk 2.3%; Yugoslav 1.0%; Italian 0.9%; Greek 0.5%; Austrian 0.3%; Spanish 0.3%; Dutch 0.2%; other 1.9%.
Religious affiliation (1980): Christian 92.8%, of which Protestant 47.3% (including Lutheran-Reformed tradition 23.5%, Lutheran tradition 21.7%, Reformed tradition 0.7%, other 1.4%), Roman Catholic 43.8%, New Apostolic (non-Roman) Catholic 0.6%, Orthodox 1.0%, other Christian 0.1%; nonreligious 3.7%; Muslim 2.4%; atheist 0.9%; other 0.1%.
Major cities (1987): Berlin (West) 1,879,200; Hamburg 1,571,300; Munich 1,274,700; Cologne 914,300; Essen 615,400; Frankfurt am Main 592,400; Dortmund 568,200; Stuttgart 565,500; Düsseldorf 560,600; Bonn 291,400.
Place of birth: n.a.
Mobility: n.a.
Households (1986). Number of households 26,739,000; average household size 2.2; 1 person 34.3%, 2 persons 29.5%, 3 persons 17.1%, 4 persons 13.1%, 5 or more persons 6.0%. Family households: 17,562,000 (66.4%); nonfamily 9,177,000.
Immigration (1986): immigrants admitted 598,479, from Poland 17.6%, Turkey 10.5%, Italy 8.2%, Iran 5.8%, German Democratic Republic 4.9%, United States 4.6%, Yugoslavia 4.5%, Romania 2.7%, Austria 2.7%, United Kingdom 2.6%, France 2.5%.

Vital statistics

Birth rate per 1,000 population (1987): 10.5 (world avg. 26.0); legitimate (1986) 90.4%; illegitimate 9.6%.
Death rate per 1,000 population (1987): 11.2 (world avg. 9.9).
Natural increase rate per 1,000 population (1987): −0.7 (world avg. 16.1).
Total fertility rate (avg. births per childbearing woman; 1986): 1.3.
Marriage rate per 1,000 population (1987): 6.2.
Divorce rate per 1,000 population (1986): 2.0.
Life expectancy at birth (1984–86): male 71.5 years; female 78.1 years.
Major causes of death per 100,000 population (1986): diseases of the circulatory system 575.7, of which cerebrovascular disease 148.4, acute myocardial infarction 131.5; malignant neoplasms (cancers) 267.0, of which stomach, colon, and rectum 63.0, bronchial, lung, and tracheal 43.1, breast 23.2; pulmonary diseases 76.5, of which chronic bronchitis 36.9, pneumonia 28.7; chronic liver disease and cirrhosis 22.3; suicide 19.0.

Social indicators

Educational attainment (1985). Percent of population age 25 and over having: less than full primary education, virtually nil; primary and secondary 26.5%, of which primary with general secondary 15.7%; some postsecondary in preparation for higher education 11.5%; advanced postsecondary vocational education 62.0%, of which trade school graduates with apprenticeship 48.2%, skilled technicians or craftsmen 6.1%, engineers 2.8%, university graduates (all levels) 4.9%.

Quality of working life (1986). Average workweek: 40.5 hours. Annual rate per 100,000 workers[4] for: injury or accident at work 6,193; injury or accident on way to work 617; industrial illness 128; death 9.5. Proportion of labour force insured for damages or income loss resulting from: injury, virtually 100%; permanent disability, virtually 100%; death, virtually 100%. Average days lost to labour stoppages per 1,000 workers (1985): 1.2. Principal means of journey to work: private automobile 32.4%; public transportation 19.2%; bicycle 6.2%; foot 37.5%; other 4.7%. Percentage of unemployed workers not eligible for unemployment benefits (1986): 31.9%.

Distribution of income (1978)				
percent of household income by quintile				
1	2	3	4	5 (highest)
6.9	11.0	15.9	21.9	44.8

Access to services. Proportion of dwellings having: electricity 99.7%; piped water supply 99.2%; flush sewage disposal 94.2%; public fire protection, virtually 100%.
Social participation. Eligible voters participating in last (January 1987) national election 84.3%. Population participating in voluntary work: n.a. Trade union membership in total work force (1987): 36.9%. Practicing religious population in total affiliated population: n.a.
Social deviance (1986). Offense rate per 100,000 population for: murder and manslaughter 4.4; sexual abuse 63.4, of which child molestation 17.3, rape 15.4; assault and battery 105.0; larceny 4,455.7, of which burglary 242.0, auto theft 115.1. Incidence per 100,000 in general population (late 1970s) of: alcoholism 2,500 to 3,000; drug and substance abuse 650; suicide 19.0[5].
Leisure (1981). Favourite leisure activities: hiking and walking 27%; reading 27%; yard work 16%; swimming 14%; watching television 14%.
Material well-being (1984). Households possessing: automobile 64%; telephone 81%; colour television receiver 82%; refrigerator 82%; washing machine 87%; home freezer 40%.

National economy

Gross national product (at current market prices; 1986): U.S.$735,940,000,-000 (U.S.$12,080 per capita).

Structure of gross domestic product and labour force				
	1987		1986	
	in value DM '000,000	% of total value	labour force	% of labour force
Agriculture	29,360	1.6	1,369,000	4.6
Mining	62,270	3.1	329,000	1.1
Manufacturing	664,700	33.0	8,547,000	28.8
Construction	101,640	5.0	1,805,000	6.1
Public utilities	...	...	238,000	0.8
Transportation and communications	110,170	5.5	1,573,000	5.3
Trade	174,180	8.6	4,153,000[6]	14.1[6]
Finance	108,140	5.4	1,740,000	5.9
Services	299,630	14.9 }	7,433,000	25.1
Pub. admin., defense	226,470	11.2 }		
Other	236,060[7]	11.7[7]	2,436,000[8]	8.2[8]
TOTAL	2,012,620	100.0	29,623,000	100.0

Budget (1986). Revenue: DM 574,910,000,000 (tax revenue 86.5%, of which social security contributions from employers 25.3%, from employees 21.5%, taxes on individual wages 13.5%, value added tax on goods and services 12.6%, taxes paid by self-employed or nonemployed 6.2%, mineral oil tax 4.5%, tobacco tax 2.5%; nontax revenue 7.2%). Expenditures[9]: DM 582,-830,000,000 (social security and welfare 50.2%; health 18.7%; defense 9.2%; economic services 7.1%, of which transportation and communication 3.0%; education 0.7%).
Total national debt (1988[10]) DM 457,960,000,000.
Tourism (1986)[11]: receipts from visitors U.S.$7,826,000,000; expenditures by nationals abroad U.S.$20,664,000,000.

Manufacturing, mining, and construction enterprises (1986)			
	no. of enterprises	no. of tradesmen and professionals	wages as a % of avg. of all wages	annual gross production value (DM '000,000)
Road motor vehicle	1,728	829,000	111.8	196,371
Chemical	1,159	587,000	124.4	170,467
Machinery (nonelectric)	4,643	999,000	107.1	169,439
Machinery and appliances (electric)	2,444	1,018,000	102.9	163,143
Food and beverage	3,726	447,000	85.9	154,496
Petroleum and natural gas	49	32,000	162.6	79,315
Iron and steel	104	223,000	101.6	48,944
Calculator, computer	2,031	286,000	90.4	43,916
Plastics	1,731	210,000	88.2	37,181
Textile	1,328	228,000	77.1	35,699
Mining	83	214,000	109.6	31,937
Cement, sand, and gravel	1,982	148,000	100.7	29,477
Wood and wood products	2,048	186,000	86.9	26,874
Metalware	1,255	148,000	105.4	24,168
Construction	14,558	929,000	82.5	...

Production (metric tons except as noted). Agriculture, forestry, fishing (1986): sugar beets 20,260,000, wheat 10,406,000, barley 9,377,000, potatoes 8,700,000, oats 2,687,000, rye 1,818,000; livestock (number of live animals) 24,282,000 pigs, 15,627,000 cattle, 1,296,000 sheep; roundwood 29,177,000 cu m; fish catch 202,366, of which Atlantic cod 47,941, blue mussel 29,939, Atlantic redfish 15,276. Mining and quarrying (metal content of ore; 1987): iron ore 80,640; zinc 80,500; lead 18,900; copper 1,500. Manufacturing (value added at factor cost in DM; 1986): machinery and transport equipment 219,842,000,000, of which electrical equipment 63,626,000,000, transport equipment 56,296,000,000; chemicals (including medicinal products) 50,104,000,000; food and beverages 25,421,000,000; calculators and com-

puters 16,034,000,000; semiprocessed iron and steel 12,370,000,000; plastics and other synthetic products 12,143,000,000; textiles 10,797,000,000; furniture and other wood products 9,270,000,000; metalware 9,111,000,000; printed matter 8,839,000,000; office machines 8,227,000,000; clocks and other precision products 7,668,000,000; clothing 6,597,000,000; cast metals 5,757,000,000. Construction (1985): residential 154,283,000 cu m; nonresidential 123,491,000 cu m; restoration and conversion 2,590,000 cu m.

Service enterprises (1986)

	no. of enterprises	no. of employees	weekly wage as a % of all wages	annual turnover (DM '000,000)
Gas	119	24,000	...	32,300
Water	161	18,000	...	3,873
Electrical power	475	236,000	...	119,468
Transport				
air	177	41,803	...	12,944
buses, trains	5,651	140,459	...	11,732
shipping	1,835	10,707	...	...
Communications				
press	2,223	213,193	...	28,575
film[12]	615	3,000	...	836
Mail	17,719	510,082	...	49,641
Hotels and restaurants	114,167	651,600	...	42,736
Wholesale trade[4]	41,215	965,800	...	846,585
Retail trade[4]	142,184	1,931,500	...	433,689
Health services[13]	88,000	318,000	...	...
Financial services[13]	36,000	427,000	...	...

Energy production (consumption): electricity (kW-hr; 1986) 406,386,000,000 (411,517,000,000); hard coal (metric tons; 1986) 87,125,000 (89,442,000); lignite-brown coal (metric tons; 1986) 311,260,000 (311,260,000); crude petroleum (barrels; 1986) 40,721,000 (519,558,000); petroleum products (metric tons; 1986) 72,409,000 (106,851,000); natural gas (cu m; 1986) 15,-311,000,000 (49,995,000,000).

Population economically active (1986): total 29,623,000; activity rate of total population 48.5% (participation rates: ages 15–64, 67.2%[4]; female 39.7%; unemployed 6.9%).

Price and earnings indexes (1980 = 100)

	1982	1983	1984	1985	1986	1987	1988[14]
Consumer price index	111.9	115.6	118.4	121.0	120.7	121.0	122.6
Hourly earnings index	110.5	114.1	116.8	121.3	125.5	130.5	132.9[15]

Household income and expenditure. Average household size (1986) 2.2; average annual income per household (1986) DM 45,330 (U.S.$20,875); sources of take home income (1986): wages 83.8%, self-employment 7.9%, transfer payments 8.3%; expenditure (1986): food 24.1%, rent 19.0%, transportation 15.8%, entertainment and education 9.9%, clothing and footwear 8.8%, household expenses 8.7%, electricity and gas 6.9%, other 6.8%.

Financial aggregates

	1982	1983	1984	1985	1986	1987	1988[16]
Exchange rate, DM per:							
U.S. dollar	2.3765	2.7238	3.1480	2.9440	2.1715	1.7974	1.8440
£	3.8369	3.9511	3.6407	3.8163	3.1856	2.9458	3.1446
SDR	2.6215	2.8517	3.0857	2.7035	2.3740	2.2436	2.4387
International reserves (U.S.$)							
Total (excl. gold; '000,000)	44,762	42,674	40,141	44,380	51,734	78,756	61,343
SDRs ('000,000)	2,054	1,613	1,362	1,547	2,020	1,964	1,831
Reserve pos. in IMF ('000,000)	3,088	3,748	3,750	3,808	3,848	3,900	3,468
Foreign exchange	39,620	37,313	35,028	39,025	45,866	72,893	56,044
Gold ('000,000 fine troy oz)	95.18	95.18	95.18	95.18	95.18	95.18	95.18
% world reserves	10.05	10.06	10.06	10.03	10.03	10.07	10.09
Interest and prices							
Central bank discount (%)	5.0	4.0	4.5	4.0	3.5	2.5	3.0
Gov't. bond yield (%)	9.1	8.0	7.8	6.9	5.9	5.8	6.4
Industrial share prices							
(1980 = 100)	99.0	133.5	150.4	199.9	270.4	249.0	212.2
Balance of payments							
(U.S.$ '000,000)							
Balance of visible trade	24.72	21.42	22.19	28.54	55.71	70.16	...
Imports, f.o.b.	141.10	138.48	139.20	145.12	175.32	208.59	...
Exports, f.o.b.	165.82	159.90	161.38	173.66	231.03	278.75	...
Balance of invisibles	–9.06	–6.15	–2.15	–1.61	–3.49	–9.04	...
Balance of payments, current account	4.96	5.40	9.65	17.03	39.75	45.23	...

Land use (1985): forested 30.0%; meadows and pastures 18.7%; agricultural and under permanent cultivation 30.5%; other 20.8%.

Foreign trade

Balance of trade (current prices)

	1982	1983	1984	1985	1986	1987
DM '000,000	+23,500	+19,840	+20,340	+26,950	+53,630	+70,160
% of total	7.7%	6.7%	6.8%	8.5%	13.3%	14.4%

Imports (1987): DM 409,641,300,000 (machinery and transport equipment 27.9%, of which transport equipment 7.0%, electrical machinery 4.8%, office equipment 4.0%; food and beverages 10.3%, of which fruits and vegetables 3.4%, coffee, tea, and spices 1.4%, meat and meat products 1.4%; chemicals and chemical products 9.4%, of which plastics and synthetics 2.6%, medicinal products 1.0%; mineral fuels 9.3%, of which crude petroleum and petroleum products 7.4%, natural gas 1.7%; clothing and wearing apparel 7.5%; iron and steel 3.3%; textiles and yarn 3.6%; paper and paper products 2.3%; metallic ores and scrap metal 1.8%). *Major import sources:* France 11.6%; The Netherlands 11.0%; Italy 9.6%; United Kingdom 7.2%; Belgium–Luxembourg 7.1%; United States 6.6%; Japan 6.2%.
Exports (1987): DM 527,376,700,000 (machinery and transport equipment 48.4%, of which transport equipment 17.6%, specialized equipment for specific industries 6.5%, electrical machinery 6.1%; chemicals and chemical

products 13.0%, of which plastics and synthetics 3.5%, medicinal products 1.4%, dyes and dye products 1.4%; food and beverages 4.2%, of which dairy products 1.1%, meat and meat products 0.6%; iron and steel 4.0%; textiles and yarn 3.3%; paper and paper products 2.0%). *Major export destinations:* France 12.1%; United States 9.5%; United Kingdom 8.8%; The Netherlands 8.7%; Italy 8.7%; Belgium–Luxembourg 7.4%; Switzerland 6.1%; Austria 5.4%.

Trade by commodity group (1987)

SITC Group	imports DM '000,000	imports %	exports DM '000,000	exports %
00 Food and live animals	40,147	9.8	21,103	4.0
01 Beverages and tobacco	4,472	1.1	3,096	0.6
02 Crude materials, excluding fuels	25,112	6.1	9,241	1.8
03 Mineral fuels, lubricants, and related materials	39,508	9.6	7,104	1.3
04 Animal and vegetable oils, fat, and waxes	1,173	0.3	1,322	0.3
05 Chemicals and related products, n.e.s.	38,512	9.4	68,485	13.0
06 Basic manufactures	71,643	17.5	93,344	17.7
07 Machinery and transport equipment	114,475	27.9	255,132	48.4
08 Miscellaneous manufactured articles	61,538	15.0	56,837	10.8
09 Goods not classified by kind	13,060	3.2	11,712	2.2
TOTAL	409,641[3]	100.0[3]	527,377[3]	100.0[3]

Direction of trade (1987)[17]

	imports U.S.$'000,000	imports %	exports U.S.$'000,000	exports %
Africa	7,533	3.3	7,775	2.6
Asia	30,759	13.5	27,566	9.4[3]
Middle East	2,722	1.2	7,127	2.4
Japan	14,100	6.2	5,903	2.0
other Asia	13,937	6.1	14,536	4.9
South America	5,204	2.3	4,658	1.6
North and Central America	17,339	7.6	32,141	10.9
United States	14,282	6.3	27,877	9.5
other North and Central Am.	3,057	1.3	4,264	1.4
Europe	163,399	71.5	217,763	74.0
EEC	120,224	52.6	155,070	52.7
U.S.S.R.	4,045	1.8	4,379	1.5
other Europe	39,130	17.1	58,314	19.8
Oceania	1,578	0.7	2,305	0.8
TOTAL	228,339[3]	100.0[3]	294,165[3]	100.0[3]

Transport and communications

Transport. Railroads (1987): length 41,965 mi[5], 67,536 km[5]; passenger-mi 28,973,000,000, passenger-km 46,672,000,000; short ton-mi cargo 41,254,-000,000, metric ton-km cargo 60,231,000,000. Roads (1987): total length 305,242 mi, 491,240 km (paved 99%). Vehicles (1987): passenger cars 27,908,200; trucks and buses 1,375,500. Merchant marine (1987): vessels (100 gross tons and over) 1,414; total deadweight tonnage 5,659,148. Air transport (1987): passenger-mi 19,370,000,000, passenger-km 31,752,000,-000; short ton-mi cargo 2,319,729,000, metric ton-km cargo 3,386,748,000; airports (1988) with scheduled flights 27.
Communications. Daily newspapers (1987): total number 356; total circulation 25,255,000; circulation per 1,000 population 413. Radio (1987): total number of receivers 26,391,000 (1 per 2.4 persons). Television (1987): total number of receivers 23,378,000 (1 per 2.6 persons). Telephones (1987): 40,288,000 (1 per 1.5 persons).

Education and health

Education (1986–87)

	schools	teachers	students	student/ teacher ratio
Primary (age 6–10)	24,282	302,097	4,221,948	14.0
Secondary (age 10–19)	5,312	188,541	2,670,458	14.2
Voc., teacher tr.	7,568	89,829	2,600,822	30.0
Higher	110	336,996	1,366,057	4.0

Literacy (1987): virtually 100%.
Health (1987): physicians 165,015 (1 per 370 persons); hospital beds 674,384 (1 per 91 persons); infant mortality rate per 1,000 live births (1986) 8.6.
Food (1984–86): daily per capita caloric intake 3,475 (vegetable products 62%, animal products 38%); (1983) 129% of FAO recommended minimum requirement.

Military

Total active duty personnel (1987): 488,400 (army 70.3%, navy 7.4%, air force 22.3%). *Military expenditure as percent of GNP* (1985): 3.2% (world 6.1%); per capita expenditure U.S.$330.

[1]January 1. [2]Berlin (West) is under tripartite (France, United Kingdom, United States) jurisdiction and is only administratively a part of West Germany. [3]Detail does not add to total given because of rounding. [4]1985. [5]1986. [6]Includes hotels. [7]Includes import duties, value added taxes, less imputed bank service charge. [8]Includes 2,046,000 unemployed. [9]Percentage breakdown for expenditures is for 1984. [10]May. [11]Includes West Berlin. [12]1984. [13]1970. [14]June. [15]First quarter. [16]July. [17]Totals include $2,527,000,000 in imports and $1,957,000,000 in exports (0.8% of all foreign trade; mostly special transactions) not distributable by region.

Ghana

Official name: Republic of Ghana.
Form of government: military regime.
Head of state and government: Chairman of the Provisional National Defense Council.
Capital: Accra.
Official language: English.
Official religion: none.
Monetary unit: 1 cedi (₵) = 100 pesewas; valuation (Oct. 10, 1988) 1 U.S.$ = ₵225.85; 1 £ = ₵386.77.

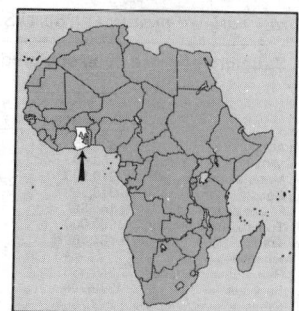

Area and population

Regions	Capitals	area sq mi	area sq km	population 1988 estimate[1]
Ashanti	Kumasi	9,417	24,389	2,308,100
Brong-Ahafo	Sunyani	15,273	39,557	1,332,200
Central	Cape Coast	3,794	9,826	1,262,200
Eastern	Koforidua	7,461	19,323	1,855,800
Greater Accra	Accra	1,253	3,245	1,580,000
Northern	Tamale	27,175	70,384	1,285,900
Upper East	Bolgatanga	3,414	8,842	853,200
Upper West	Wa	7,134	18,476	483,600
Volta	Ho	7,942	20,570	1,338,200
Western	Sekondi-Takoradi	9,236	23,921	1,278,300
TOTAL		92,098[2]	238,533	13,577,500

Demography

Population (1988): 13,754,000.
Density (1988): persons per sq mi 149.3, persons per sq km 57.7.
Urban-rural (1984): urban 32.0%; rural 68.0%.
Sex distribution (1984): male 49.32%; female 50.68%.
Age breakdown (1984): under 15, 45.0%; 15–29, 26.4%; 30–44, 14.6%; 45–59, 8.1%; 60–74, 4.1%; 75 and over, 1.8%.
Population projection: (1990) 14,500,000; (2000) 18,800,000.
Doubling time: 22 years.
Ethno-linguistic composition (1983): Akan 52.4%; Mossi 15.8%; Ewe 11.9%; Ga-Adangme 7.8%; Gurma 3.3%; Yoruba 1.3%; other 7.5%.
Religious affiliation (1980): Christian 62.6%, of which Protestant 27.9%, Roman Catholic 18.7%, African indigenous 16.0%; traditional beliefs 21.4%; Muslim 15.7%, of which Aḥmadīyah 7.9%; other 0.3%.
Major cities (1988): Accra 949,100; Kumasi 385,200; Tamale 151,100; Tema 110,000; Sekondi-Takoradi 103,600.

Vital statistics

Birth rate per 1,000 population (1980–85): 46.9 (world avg. 29.0); legitimate, n.a.; illegitimate, n.a.
Death rate per 1,000 population (1980–85): 14.6 (world avg. 11.0).
Natural increase rate per 1,000 population (1980–85): 32.3 (world avg. 18.0).
Total fertility rate (avg. births per childbearing woman; 1980–85): 6.5.
Life expectancy at birth (1980–85): male 50.3 years; female 53.8 years.
Major causes of death per 100,000 population: n.a.; however, major infectious diseases include malaria, tuberculosis, leprosy, trypanosomiasis (sleeping sickness), and onchocerciasis (river blindness).

National economy

Budget[3] (1986–87). Revenue: ₵109,711,000,000 (taxes on international trade 40%; domestic taxes 60%). Expenditures: ₵104,207,000,000 (recurrent expenditures 70.0%; development 29.0%, of which roads and highways 3.2%; health 0.7%; education 0.6%).
Tourism: receipts from visitors (1984) U.S.$2,000,000; expenditures by nationals abroad (1983) U.S.$25,000,000.
Production (metric tons except as noted). Agriculture, forestry, fishing (1986): roots and tubers 5,279,000 (of which cassava 3,692,000, yams 937,000, taro 650,000), cereals 906,000 (of which corn [maize] 471,000, sorghum 210,000, millet 130,000, rice 95,000), bananas and plantains 700,000, cocoa 240,000, peanuts (groundnuts) 129,000, sugarcane 110,000, coconuts 108,000, oranges 37,000, lemons and limes 30,000, palm kernels 30,000, pulses 11,000; livestock (number of live animals) 2,400,000 goats, 2,175,000 sheep, 1,188,000 cattle, 586,000 pigs, 10,000,000 chickens; roundwood (1985) 8,459,000 cu m; fish catch (1985) 254,171 (of which anchovies 43,073). Mining and quarrying (1986): manganese ore 338,979; bauxite 226,461; gold 8,931 kg; diamonds 557,301 carats. Manufacturing (1986): kerosene, gasoline, and diesel 587,000; cement 219,000; wheat flour 62,800; cocoa cake, cocoa butter, and cocoa liquor 19,852[4]; soap 12,406; iron rods 3,360[4]; margarine 941[4]; toothpaste 122[4]; textiles 12,600,000 metres[4]; soft drinks 658,000 hectolitres; beer 546,000 hectolitres; evaporated milk 146,000 hectolitres[4]; ice cream 1,152 hectolitres[4]; cigarettes 1,826,000,000 units. Construction (value added in ₵'000; 1983): 2,796,100. Energy production (consumption): electricity (kW-hr; 1986) 3,749,000,000 (3,474,000,000); coal (metric tons; 1986) none (2,000); crude petroleum (barrels; 1986) 182,000 (8,210,000); petroleum products (metric tons; 1986) 884,000 (631,000); natural gas, none (n.a.).
Household income and expenditure. Average household size (1983) 4.9; average annual income per household (1978) ₵9,600 (U.S.$[5]); sources of income: n.a.; expenditure (1978): food and beverages 57.4%, housing and energy 11.5%, clothing and footwear 14.3%, transport and communications 3.3%, health care 1.3%.

Gross national product (at current market prices; 1986): U.S.$5,130,000,000 (U.S.$390 per capita).

Structure of gross domestic product and labour force

	1985 in value ₵'000,000	1985 % of total value	1984 labour force	1984 % of labour force
Agriculture	153,373	41.1	3,310,967	59.4
Mining	3,739	1.0	26,828	0.5
Manufacturing	40,087	10.8	588,418	10.5
Construction	9,780	2.6	64,686	1.2
Public utilities	4,045	1.1	15,437	0.3
Transportation and communications	27,031	7.2	122,806	2.2
Trade	105,944	28.4	792,147	14.2
Finance			27,475	0.5
Pub. admin., defense	28,983	7.8	97,548	1.7
Services			376,168	6.7
Other			157,624[6]	2.8[6]
TOTAL	372,982	100.00	5,580,104	100.0

Public debt (external, outstanding; 1986): U.S.$1,412,900,000.
Population economically active (1984): total 5,580,104; activity rate of total population 45.4% (participation rates: over age 15, 82.5%; female 51.2%; unemployed 2.8%).

Price and earnings indexes (1981 = 100)

	1981	1982	1983	1984	1985	1986	1987
Consumer price index	100.0	122.3	272.6	380.6	419.9	523.0	713.3
Earnings index	100.0	78.4	187.2	385.7	564.4	...	...

Land use (1985): forested 36.6%; meadows and pastures 14.9%; agricultural and under permanent cultivation 12.3%; other 36.2%.

Foreign trade

Balance of trade (current prices)

	1981	1982	1983	1984	1985	1986
₵'000,000	+79.0	+588.0	−85.0	+637.1	−4,070.0	+11,578.0
% of total	1.4%	13.9%	0.4%	1.6%	5.8%	8.1%

Imports (1983): ₵11,021,818,000 (machinery and transport equipment 32.5%, food and live animals 11.1%, chemicals 10.3%, basic manufactures 10.1%, petroleum products 10.1%, beverages and tobacco 2.5%). *Major import sources:* United Kingdom 23.4%; West Germany 13.2%; United States 9.1%; Italy 5.1%; Nigeria 4.8%; Japan 4.3%.
Exports (1983): ₵8,851,000,000 (cocoa beans 45.1%[7], gold 23.9%, logs and timber 2.4%, manganese ore 1.4%, industrial diamonds 0.7%). *Major export destinations:* Japan 79.0%; United Kingdom 11.4%; The Netherlands 10.5%; U.S.S.R. 9.2%; West Germany 7.8%; United States 7.1%.

Transport and communications

Transport. Railroads (1985): length[8] 592 mi, 947 km; passenger-mi 125,958,000, passenger-km 201,101,000; short ton-mi cargo 50,500,000, metric ton-km cargo 73,800,000. Roads (1985): total length 17,600 mi, 28,300 km (paved 20%). Vehicles (1984): passenger cars 52,864; trucks and buses 23,375. Merchant marine (1987): vessels (100 gross tons and over) 138; total deadweight tonnage 143,029. Air transport (1986): passenger-mi 168,404,000, passenger-km 271,021,000; short ton-mi cargo 23,084,000, metric ton-km cargo 33,703,000; airports (1988) with scheduled flights 4.
Communications. Daily newspapers (1986): total number 4; total circulation 460,000; circulation per 1,000 population 35. Radio (1986): 3,000,000 receivers (1 per 4.4 persons). Television (1987): 175,000 receivers (1 per 77 persons). Telephones (1986): 72,662 (1 per 182 persons).

Education and health

Education (1985–86)

	schools	teachers	students	student/ teacher ratio
Primary (6–12)	9,180	67,261	1,567,778	23.3
Secondary (13–20)	5,702	44,578	768,347	17.2
Voc., teacher tr.	137	2,887	40,485	14.0
Higher	9	1,316	10,225	7.8

Educational attainment (1984). Percent of population age 25 and over having: no formal schooling 60.4%; primary education 7.1%; middle school 25.4%; secondary 3.5%; vocational and other postsecondary 2.9%; higher 0.6%. *Literacy* (1985): total population age 15 and over literate 3,835,000 (53.2%); males literate 2,261,000 (64.1%); females literate 1,574,000 (42.8%).
Health: physicians (1984) 1,900 (1 per 6,640 persons); hospital beds (1981) 20,582 (1 per 563 persons); infant mortality rate per 1,000 live births (1980–85) 98.
Food (1984–86): daily per capita caloric intake 1,733 (vegetable products 95%, animal products 5%); (1983) 66% of FAO minimum recommended requirement.

Military

Total active duty personnel (1987): 10,600 (army 84.9%, navy 7.5%, air force 7.6%). *Military expenditure as percent of GNP* (1985): 0.9% (world 6.1%); per capita expenditure U.S.$6.

---

[1]Jan. 1. [2]Detail does not add to total given because of rounding. [3]Budget detail is for 1985–86. [4]1985. [5]Unofficial exchange rate (7.5 to 9.9 times the official rate) does not permit meaningful conversion into other currencies. [6]Unemployed only. [7]In 1984, 1985, and 1986, cocoa beans averaged more than 65% of export earnings. [8]1986.

Greece

Official name: Ellinikí Dimokratía
(Hellenic Republic).
Form of government: unitary multiparty
republic with one legislative house
(Greek Chamber of Deputies [300]).
Chief of state: President.
Head of government: Prime Minister.
Capital: Athens.
Official language: Greek.
Official religion: Eastern Orthodox.
Monetary unit: 1 drachma (Dr) = 100
lepta; valuation (Oct. 10, 1988)
1 U.S.$ = Dr 150.26; 1 £ = Dr 257.33.

Area and population

Regions[1]		area sq mi	area sq km	population 1981 census
Anatolikí Makedhonía kaí Thráki	(Eastern Macedonia and Thrace)	5,466	14,157	575,210
Attikí	(Attica)	1,470	3,808	3,369,424
Dhytikí Ellás	(Western Greece)	4,382	11,350	655,262
Dhytikí Makedhonía	(Western Macedonia)	3,649	9,451	289,071
Iónioi Nisoí	(Ionian Islands)	891	2,307	182,651
Ípiros	(Epirus)	3,553	9,203	324,541
Kedrikí Makedhonía	(Central Macedonia)	7,393	19,147	1,602,892
Kríti	(Crete)	3,218	8,336	502,165
Nótion Aiyaíon	(Southern Aegean)	2,041	5,286	233,529
Pelopónnisos	(Peloponnesos)	5,981	15,490	577,030
Stereá Ellás	(Central Greece)	6,004	15,549	537,984
Thessalía	(Thessaly)	5,420	14,037	695,654
Vóreion Aiyaíon	(Northern Aegean)	1,481	3,836	195,004
TOTAL		50,949	131,957	9,740,417

Demography

Population (1988): 10,055,000.
Density (1988): persons per sq mi 197.4, persons per sq km 76.2.
Urban–rural (1985): urban 57.7%; rural 42.3%.
Sex distribution (1986): male 49.20%; female 50.80%.
Age breakdown (1986): under 15, 20.5%; 15–29, 22.1%; 30–44, 19.3%; 45–59, 19.7%; 60–74, 12.7%; 75 and over, 5.7%.
Population projection: (1990) 10,145,000; (2000) 10,608,000.
Doubling time: n.a.; doubling time exceeds 100 years.
Ethnic composition (1983): Greek 95.5%; Macedonian 1.5%; Turkish 0.9%; Albanian 0.6%; other 1.5%.
Religious affiliation (1980): Christian 98.1%, of which Greek Orthodox 97.6%, Roman Catholic 0.4%, Protestant 0.1%; Muslim 1.5%; other 0.4%.
Major cities (1981): Athens 885,737; Thessaloníki 406,413; Piraiévs 196,389; Pátrai 142,163; Peristérion 140,858.

Vital statistics

Birth rate per 1,000 population (1987): 10.6 (world avg. 26.0); legitimate 97.9%; illegitimate 2.1%.
Death rate per 1,000 population (1987): 9.5 (world avg. 9.9).
Natural increase rate per 1,000 population (1987): 1.1 (world avg. 16.1).
Total fertility rate (avg. births per childbearing woman; 1986): 2.2.
Marriage rate per 1,000 population (1987): 6.3.
Divorce rate per 1,000 population (1985): 0.8.
Life expectancy at birth (1980): male 72.2 years; female 76.4 years.
Major causes of death per 100,000 population (1987): malignant neoplasms (cancers) 185.1; cerebrovascular disease 177.6; diseases of pulmonary circulation and other forms of heart disease 176.4; ischemic heart disease 108.9.

National economy

Budget (1987). Revenue: Dr 1,840,000,000,000 (indirect and excise taxes 65.0%; direct taxes 26.8%; European Community 2.9%). Expenditures: Dr 2,209,000,000,000 (government ministries 79.2%; defense 12.6%; European Community 3.2%; police and other sectors 2.8%).
Tourism (1986): receipts from visitors U.S.$1,834,000,000; expenditures by nationals abroad U.S.$494,000,000.
Production (metric tons except as noted). Agriculture, forestry, fishing (1986): sugarbeets 2,700,000, wheat 2,200,000, corn (maize) 2,070,000, tomatoes 1,864,000, grapes 1,712,000, olives 1,205,000, potatoes 939,000, barley 750,000, oranges 610,000, cotton 176,000, tobacco 153,000, onions 150,000, rice 102,000; livestock (number of live animals) 10,122,000 sheep, 5,600,000 goats, 1,095,000 pigs, 740,000 cattle, 200,000 asses, 31,000,000 chickens; roundwood (1985) 2,683,000 cu m; fish catch 112,714. Mining and quarrying (1986): bauxite 2,476,800[3]; iron ore 900,000; zinc ore 22,500; lead ore 21,000; nickel 9,200[3]. Manufacturing (value added in Dr; 1985): food, beverages, and tobacco 159,759,000,000; textiles 124,694,000,000; chemicals 95,449,000,000; clothing and footwear 54,475,000,000; paper and printing 49,085,000,000; transport equipment 46,323,000,000. Construction (cu m authorized; 1987): residential 44,423,000; nonresidential 68,349,000. Energy production (consumption): electricity (kW-hr; 1986) 28,237,000,000 (29,523,000,000); coal (metric tons; 1986) 38,096,000 (39,835,000); crude petroleum (barrels; 1986) 9,184,000 (108,938,000); petroleum products (metric tons; 1986) 14,732,000 (10,067,000); natural gas (cu m; 1986) 116,-705,000 (116,705,000).
Household income and expenditure. Average household size (1982) 3.3; income per household (1982) Dr 252,300 (U.S.$3,777); sources of income (1984): wages and salaries 42.3%, transfer payments 17.3%, other 39.9%; expenditure (1984): food, beverages, and tobacco 41.4%, housing 8.9%, clothing and footwear 8.4%, other 41.3%.

Gross national product (1986): U.S.$36,690,000,000 (U.S.$3,680 per capita).

Structure of gross domestic product and labour force

	1986 in value Dr '000,000	1986 % of total value	1986 labour force	1986 % of labour force
Agriculture	831,350	16.9	1,030,800	25.5
Mining	80,000	1.6	24,600	0.6
Manufacturing	910,500	18.5	749,200	18.5
Construction	313,500	6.4	252,100	6.2
Public utilities	145,800	3.0	36,000	0.9
Transp. and commun.	380,000	7.7	255,400	6.3
Trade	784,100[4]	15.9[4]	580,100	14.3
Finance	[4]	[4]	143,100	3.5
Pub. admin., defense	849,150	17.2 }	636,900	15.7
Services	379,900	7.7 }		
Other	253,700[5]	5.1[5]	340,000[6]	8.4[6]
TOTAL	4,928,000	100.0	4,048,200	100.0[7]

Public debt (1985): U.S.$14,632,600,000.
Population economically active (1986): total 4,048,200; activity rate of total population 40.6% (participation rates: ages [1985] 15–64, 57.5%; female 36.0%; unemployed 7.1%).

Price and earnings indexes (1980 = 100)

	1982	1983	1984	1985	1986	1987	1988
Consumer price index	150.6	181.1	214.5	255.9	314.8	366.3	426.9[8]
Hourly earnings index	169.8	202.7	256.0	306.8	345.7	379.0	...

Land use (1985): forested 20.0%; meadows and pastures 40.3%; agricultural and under permanent cultivation 30.1%; other 9.6%.

Foreign trade

Balance of trade (current prices)

	1981	1982	1983	1984	1985	1986	1987
Dr '000,000	−199.1	−303.0	−356.6	−416.6	−621.2	−614.8	−688.4
% of total	29.5%	34.6%	31.2%	27.7%	33.0%	28.0%	28.1%

Imports (1987): Dr 1,758,951,400,000 (machinery and transport equipment 24.4%, of which passenger cars 3.0%; food, beverages, and tobacco 17.7%, of which meat products 5.7%, milk and cream 1.8%, coffee 1.0%; crude petroleum 11.6%; chemical products 11.0%, of which plastics and resins 2.7%, medicinal and pharmaceutical products 1.4%). *Major import sources:* West Germany 22.2%; Italy 12.3%; France 7.8%; The Netherlands 7.0%; United Kingdom 4.9%; Japan 4.2%; Saudi Arabia 3.8%.
Exports (1987): Dr 880,985,200,000 (food, beverages, and tobacco 26.4%, of which tobacco 4.2%, olive oil 3.0%, concentrated tomato puree 1.9%; clothing 22.1%; textile yarn 5.8%; petroleum products 5.4%). *Major export destinations:* West Germany 24.3%; Italy 16.2%; France 8.6%; United Kingdom 8.2%; United States 6.8%; The Netherlands 3.8%.

Transport and communications

Transport. Railroads (1986): route length 1,540 mi, 2,479 km; passenger-mi 1,184,000,000, passenger-km 1,905,000,000; short ton-mi cargo 481,100,000, metric ton-km cargo 702,366,000. Roads (1985): total length 64,191 mi, 103,306 km (paved 83%). Vehicles (1987): passenger cars 1,444,850; trucks and buses 680,762. Merchant marine (1987): vessels (100 gross tons and over) 1,948; total deadweight tonnage 42,775,945. Air transport (1986): passenger-mi 3,967,000,000, passenger-km 6,384,000,000; short ton-mi cargo 69,400,000, metric ton-km cargo 101,352,000; airports (1988) with scheduled flights 29.
Communications. Daily newspapers (1986): total number 130; total circulation 932,000[9]; circulation per 1,000 population, n.a. Radio (1986): 4,000,000 receivers (1 per 2.5 persons). Television (1986): 1,750,000 receivers (1 per 5.7 persons). Telephones (1987): 3,597,000 (1 per 2.8 persons).

Education and health

Education (1984–85)

	schools	teachers	students	student/teacher ratio
Primary (age 6–12)	9,229	36,093	904,426	25.1
Secondary (age 12–18)	2,613	36,851	701,711	19.0
Voc., teacher tr.	601	8,427	101,558	12.0
Higher	102	11,735	167,957	14.3

Educational attainment (1981). Percent of population age 25 and over having: no formal schooling (illiterate) 11.4%; some primary education 16.8%; completed primary 44.1%; lower secondary 6.0%; higher secondary 13.5%; some postsecondary 2.5%; a degree from institution of higher education 4.9%. *Literacy* (1985): total population age 14 and over literate 7,209,500 (93.8%); males literate 3,555,000 (97.3%); females literate 3,654,500 (90.6%).
Health (1986): physicians (1985) 29,103 (1 per 341 persons); hospital beds 52,864 (1 per 188 persons); infant mortality rate per 1,000 live births 12.2.
Food (1984–86): daily per capita caloric intake 3,686 (vegetable products 75%, animal products 25%); (1983) 143% of FAO minimum.

Military

Total active duty personnel (1988): 214,000 (army 79.7%, navy 9.1%, air force 11.2%). *Military expenditure as percent of GNP* (1985): 7.2% (world 6.1%); per capita expenditure U.S.$244.

---

[1]New administrative regions approved by the Greek Cabinet on Jan. 19, 1987. [2]Metal content of ore. [3]1987. [4]Trade includes finance. [5]Income from ownership of buildings. [6]Includes 286,900 unemployed. [7]Detail does not add to total given because of rounding. [8]September. [9]For 21 dailies only.

Greenland

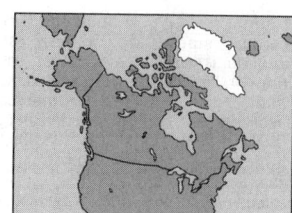

Official name: Kalaallit Nunaat
(Greenlandic); Grønland (Danish)
(Greenland).
Political status: integral part of the
Danish realm with a local legislative
house (Landsting [27]).
Chief of state: Danish Monarch.
Heads of government: High Commis-
sioner (for Denmark); Prime Minister
(for Greenland).
Capital: Nuuk (Godthåb).
Official languages: Greenlandic;
Danish.
Official religion: Lutheran Church of
Greenland (Evangelical Lutheran).
Monetary unit: 1 Danish krone
(DKr) = 100 øre; valuation (Oct. 10,
1988) 1 U.S.$ = DKr 7.13;
1 £ = DKr 12.21.

Area and population

Counties / Communes	area sq mi	area sq km	population 1988 estimate[1]
Avanersuaq (Nordgrønland)	41,200	106,700	
Qaanaaq (Thule)	...	...	823
Kitaa (Vestgrønland)	46,000	119,100	
Aasiaat (Egedesminde)	...	...	3,617
Ilulissat (Jakobshavn)	...	...	4,575
Ivittuut (Ivigtut)	...	...	20
Kangaatsiaq (Kangåtsiaq)	...	...	1,254
Maniitsoq (Sukkertoppen)	...	...	3,974
Nanortalik	...	...	2,692
Narsaq (Narssaq)	...	...	2,148
Nuuk (Godthåb)	...	...	12,071
Paamiut (Frederikshåb)	...	...	2,564
Qaqortoq (Julianehåb)	...	...	3,482
Qasigianguit (Christianshåb)	...	...	1,750
Qeqertarsuaq (Godhavn)	...	...	1,133
Sisimiut (Holsteinsborg)	...	...	5,042
Upernavik	...	...	2,281
Uummannaq (Umanaq)	...	...	2,581
Tunu (Østgrønland)	44,800	115,900	
Illoqqortoormiut (Scoresbysund)	...	...	545
Tasiilaq (Angmagssalik)	...	...	2,836
TOTAL (ICE-FREE)	131,900	341,700	54,524[2]
Permanent ice[3]	708,100	1,833,300	
TOTAL	840,000	2,175,000	

Demography

Population (1988): 54,600.
Density[3] (1988): persons per sq mi 0.41, persons per sq km 0.16.
Urban–rural (1988): urban (town) 79.3%; rural (settlement) 20.7%.
Sex distribution (1988): male 54.43%; female 45.57%.
Age breakdown (1988): under 15, 24.6%; 15–29, 32.3%; 30–44, 23.7%; 45–59,
13.4%; 60–74, 4.9%; 75 and over, 1.1%.
Population projection: (1990) 56,000; (2000) 61,000.
Doubling time: 60 years.
Ethnic composition (by place of birth; 1988): born in Greenland 82.4%; born
elsewhere 17.6%.
Religious affiliation (1980): Protestant 97.8%; other 2.2%.
Major towns (1986): Nuuk (Godthåb) 11,209[4]; Sisimiut (Holsteinsborg)
4,583; Ilulissat (Jakobshavn) 4,043; Aasiaat (Egedesminde) 3,200; Maniit-
soq (Sukkertoppen) 3,055.

Vital statistics

Birth rate per 1,000 population (1987): 20.4 (world avg. 26.0); (1986) legiti-
mate 26.8%; illegitimate 73.2%.
Death rate per 1,000 population (1987): 8.3 (world avg. 9.9).
Natural increase rate per 1,000 population (1987): 12.1 (world avg. 16.1).
Total fertility rate (avg. births per childbearing woman; 1986): 2.1.
Marriage rate per 1,000 population (1986): 6.4.
Divorce rate per 1,000 population (1985): 2.7.
Life expectancy at birth (1981–85): male 60.4 years; female 66.3 years.
Major causes of death per 100,000 population (1986): malignant neoplasms
(cancers) 140.0; heart disease 121.3; suicide 104.5; accidents 97.1%.

National economy

Budget (1986). Revenue: DKr 2,125,100,000 (contributions from Danish
government 42.4%, taxes and royalties 13.9%, customs duties 11.9%, fishing
licenses 10.0%). Expenditures: DKr 1,403,500,000 (contributions to municipalities 42.4%, education 22.6%, administration 11.2%, social welfare 7.1%).
Public debt (external, outstanding): n.a.
Tourism: receipts from visitors, n.a.; expenditures by nationals abroad, n.a.
Production (metric tons except as noted). Agriculture, forestry, hunting,
fishing (1985): fish catch 149,424; livestock (number of live animals) 21,443
sheep, 5,980 reindeer; hunting (number of animals killed; 1983) 92,794 seals,
2,308 whales, of which 601 white whales, 492 narwhals; hunting products
(number) 50,526 seal skins, 1,182 fox skins, 24 polar bear skins. Mining
and quarrying (1986): cryolite 70,343; zinc concentrates 62,100; lead concentrates 16,500; silver 385,000 troy oz. Manufacturing (1985): principally
handicrafts and food processing. Construction (1985): residential 33,100 sq
m; nonresidential 12,300 sq m. Energy production (consumption): electricity (kW-hr; 1987) 172,000,000 (172,000,000); coal (1983) none (1,000); crude
petroleum, none (n.a.); petroleum products (cu m; 1986) none (182,500);
natural gas, none (n.a.).
Gross national product (at current market prices; 1986): U.S.$470,000,000
(U.S.$8,790 per capita).

Structure of gross domestic product and labour force

	1979 in value DKr '000,000	1979 % of total value	1976 labour force	1976 % of labour force
Agriculture, fishing, hunting, and sheep breeding	335.3	16.0	3,222	15.1
Mining	661.2	31.6	318	1.5
Manufacturing			2,887	13.5
Construction	574.9	27.4	3,112	14.5
Transportation and communication	100.4	4.8	1,842	8.6
Trade	167.8	8.0	2,153	10.1
Public utilities			293	1.4
Public administration				
Social, health, and education services	255.0	12.2	1,519	7.1
			5,444	25.5
Other			588	2.7
TOTAL	2,094.6	100.0	21,378	100.0

Population economically active (1976): total 21,378; activity rate of total
population 43.1% (participation rates: ages 15–64, n.a.; female 33.4%; unemployed, n.a.).

Price and earnings indexes (January 1980 = 100)

	1981	1982	1983	1984	1985	1986	1987
Consumer price index[5]	113.3	129.9	145.7	157.4	172.2	181.5	186.4
Monthly earnings index[5]	110.9	128.4	141.2	155.8	169.7	177.6	...

Household income and expenditure. Average household size (1976) 3.9;
taxable income per taxpayer (1980) DKr 84,160 (U.S.$9,200); sources of in-
come: n.a.; expenditure (1987): food 30.1%, housing 10.0%, transportation
and communications 8.1%, clothing 7.8%, fuel and light 5.4%.
Land use (1985): forested 0.1%; meadows and pastures 0.7%; agricultural
and under permanent cultivation, none; other (principally ice cap) 99.3%.

Foreign trade

Balance of trade (current prices)

	1982	1983	1984	1985	1986	1987
DKr '000,000	−875	−779	−1,085	−1,303	−834	−1,101
% of total	23.4%	19.2%	23.6%	26.3%	16.7%	18.8%

Imports (1987): DKr 3,470,676,000 (machinery and transport equipment
32.7%, of which ships and aircraft 9.3%, automobiles 1.0%; food 20.2%;
metal products and semimanufactures 18.8%; mineral fuels 3.7%). *Major
import sources:* Denmark 67.0%; Sweden 4.6%; Norway 4.6%; West Germany 4.0%; Japan 3.9%.
Exports (1987): DKr 2,369,475,000 (shrimps, prawns, and mollusks 71.6%;
fish and fish products 21.9%; zinc 8.5%; lead 3.0%). *Major export destinations:* Denmark 84.8%; France 5.1%; West Germany 4.0%; Canada 2.7%;
Finland 1.0%; Norway 0.8%.

Transport and communications

Transport. Railroads: none. Roads (1970): total length 93 mi, 150 km (paved
40%). Vehicles (1986): passenger cars 2,037; trucks and buses 1,320. Merchant marine (1986): vessels (100 gross tons and over) 50; total deadweight
tonnage, n.a. Air transport (1983): passenger-mi 8,664,000, passenger-km
13,944,000; short ton-mi cargo 162,000, metric ton-km cargo 236,000. Passenger conveyance within Greenland (1985): by ship 31,522[6]; by aircraft
88,688. Airports (1988) with scheduled flights 21.
Communications. Daily newspapers: none. Radio (1985): total number of
receivers 13,600 (1 per 3.9 persons). Television (1987): total number of
receivers 12,000 (1 per 4.5 persons). Telephone subscribers (1987): 17,900
(1 per 3.0 persons).

Education and health

Education (1987–88)

	schools	teachers	students	student/ teacher ratio
Primary (age 6–15)	90		7,259	...
Secondary (age 15–19)	37[7]	1,131	1,740	...
Voc., teacher tr.	5[7]		1,469[8]	...

Educational attainment (1970). Percent of adult population ages 14 through
39 having: primary education 61.7%; secondary 25.9%. *Literacy* (1986);
total population age 15 and over literate 40,218 (virtually 100%).
Health (1986): physicians 61 (1 per 878 persons); hospital beds 570 (1 per 94
persons); infant mortality rate per 1,000 live births 23.4.
Food: daily per capita caloric intake, n.a.

Military

Total active duty personnel[9] (1980): 320.

---

[1]January 1. [2]Includes 1,136 people not distributed by county. [3]Area of permanent ice
not distributable by county; population density calculated with reference to ice-free
area only. [4]1987. [5]Based on January only. [6]For Western Greenland only. [7]1979–80.
[8]1985–86. [9]Foreign troops only. Mostly air force personnel from the United States.

Grenada

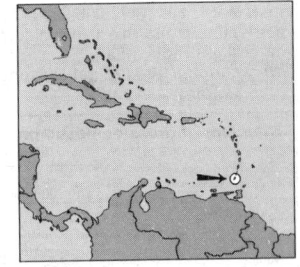

Official name: Grenada.
Form of government: constitutional monarchy with two legislative houses (Senate [13]; House of Representatives [15]).
Chief of state: British Monarch represented by governor-general.
Head of government: Prime Minister.
Capital: St. George's.
Official language: English.
Official religion: none.
Monetary unit: 1 East Caribbean dollar (EC$) = 100 cents; valuation (Oct. 10, 1988) 1 U.S.$ = EC$2.70; 1 £ = EC$4.62.

Area and population[1]

Parishes	Capitals	area sq mi	area sq km	population 1981 census
Carriacou	—	13	34	4,671
St. Andrew	—	35	91	22,425
St. David	—	18	47	10,195
St. George's	—	26	67	29,369
St. John	—	15	39	8,328
St. Mark	—	9	23	3,968
St. Patrick	—	17	44	10,132
TOTAL		133	345	89,088

Demography

Population (1988): 106,000.
Density (1988): persons per sq mi 797.0, persons per sq km 307.2.
Urban–rural: n.a.
Sex distribution (1981): male 48.20%; female 51.80%.
Age breakdown (1985): under 15, 35.1%; 15–29, 35.1%; 30–44, 12.4%; 45–59, 9.3%; 60–74, 6.2%; 75 and over, 2.1%.
Population projection: (1990) 110,000; (2000) 133,000.
Doubling time: 28 years.
Ethnic composition (1983): black 84%; mixed 12%; East Indian 3%; white 1%.
Religious affiliation (1980): Roman Catholic 64.4%; Protestant 34.5%, of which Anglican 20.7%, Seventh-day Adventist 3.1%, Methodist 2.1%; other 1.1%.
Major localities (1986): St. George's 7,500; Gouyave 2,980[2]; Grenville 2,100[2]; Victoria 2,000[2].

Vital statistics

Birth rate per 1,000 population (1986): 32.5 (world avg. 26.0); (1979) legitimate 22.5%; illegitimate 77.5%.
Death rate per 1,000 population (1986): 7.2 (world avg. 9.9).
Natural increase rate per 1,000 population (1986): 25.3 (world avg. 16.1).
Total fertility rate (avg. births per childbearing woman; 1987): 3.1.
Marriage rate per 1,000 population (1979): 3.9.
Divorce rate per 1,000 population (1979): 0.2.
Life expectancy at birth (1980–85): male 65.4 years; female 69.4 years.
Major causes of death per 100,000 population (1981): diseases of the circulatory system 186.3; malignant neoplasms (cancers) 90.9; endocrine, nutritional, and metabolic diseases 48.3; diseases of the respiratory system 41.5; diseases of the digestive system 31.4; ill-defined conditions 158.3.

National economy

Budget (1987). Revenue: EC$226,300,000 (internal sources 56.2%; external loans and grants 43.8%). Expenditures: EC$226,300,000 (current expenditure 64.6%, of which debt service 15.1%, education 9.5%, health and housing 7.4%; development expenditure 35.4%, of which road and bridge improvement 10.5%).
Public debt (external, outstanding; 1986): U.S.$52,800,000.
Tourism: receipts from visitors (1987) U.S.$27,000,000; expenditures by nationals abroad (1985) U.S.$3,000,000.
Gross national product (at current market prices; 1986): U.S.$120,000,000 (U.S.$1,240 per capita).

Structure of gross domestic product and labour force

	1986[3] in value EC$'000,000	1986[3] % of total value	1981[4] labour force	1981[4] % of labour force
Agriculture	41.8	16.9	7,987	28.7
Quarrying	0.9	0.4	75	0.3
Manufacturing	11.8	4.8	1,566	5.6
Construction	22.2	9.0	2,863	10.3
Public utilities	5.3	2.1	371	1.3
Transportation and communications	33.4	13.5	1,689	6.1
Trade	49.2	19.9	3,902	14.0
Finance, real estate	40.7	16.5	367	1.3
Pub. admin., defense	54.0	21.8	1,682	6.0
Services	...	...	2,566	9.2
Other	−12.0[5]	−4.9[5]	4,779	17.2
TOTAL	247.3	100.0	27,847	100.0

Production (metric tons except as noted). Agriculture, forestry, fishing (1985): bananas 8,700[6], coconuts 8,000, sugarcane 6,000, citrus fruits 4,000, roots and tubers 4,000, nutmeg 2,800[6], mangoes 2,000, avocados 2,000, cacao 1,800[6], soursop 709[7], sapodilla plums 456[7], mace 243[6,8]; livestock

(number of live animals) 17,000 sheep, 14,000 goats, 11,000 pigs, 4,000 cattle; roundwood, n.a.; fish catch 2,328[6], of which tuna 771. Mining and quarrying: excavation of gravel for local use. Manufacturing (1984): flour 4,770; clothing EC$1,400,000 in export sales; beer 9,400 hectolitres; malt 2,500 hectolitres; edible coconut oil 5,000 hectolitres; rum 1,900 hectolitres. Construction:[9]. Energy production (consumption): electricity (kW-hr; 1986) 25,000,000 (25,000,000); coal, none (none); crude petroleum, none (none); petroleum products (metric tons; 1986) none (20,000); natural gas, none (none).
Household income and expenditure. Average household size (1970) 4.7; income per household: n.a.; sources of income: n.a.; expenditure (weights of current price index components): food 59.0%, clothing and footwear 8.0%, housing 6.5%, household furnishings 6.5%, fuel and light 6.0%, transportation 4.0%, alcohol and tobacco 2.5%, other 7.5%.
Population economically active (1984): total 46,000; activity rate of total population *c.* 48.0% (participation rates: ages 15–64, n.a.; female, n.a.; unemployed [1987] 20–30%).

Price and earnings indexes (1980 = 100)

	1982	1983	1984	1985	1986	1987
Consumer price index	128.0	135.9	143.5	147.2	148.0	146.7
Earnings index[10]	...	...	...	...	...	...

Land use (1985): forested 9.0%; meadows and pastures 3.0%; agricultural and under permanent cultivation 41.0%; other 47.0%.

Foreign trade[11]

Balance of trade (current prices)

	1982	1983	1984	1985	1986	1987
U.S.$'000,000	−32.7	−32.3	−31.9	−39.7	−46.2	−44.1
% of total	46.8%	46.1%	46.7%	47.0%	44.6%	38.7%

Imports (1983): U.S.$55,600,000 (basic manufactures 25.4%; food 22.9%; machinery and transportation equipment 11.1%; mineral fuels 11.1%; chemicals 7.8%). *Major import sources* (1984): United States 24.1%; United Kingdom 17.9%; Trinidad and Tobago 14.6%; Japan 6.7%; Hong Kong 3.8%.
Exports (1983): U.S.$18,920,000[12] (domestic exports 97.4%, of which fresh fruit 21.9%, cocoa beans 21.4%, nutmeg 17.2%, bananas 17.1%, clothing 9.4%, mace 4.0%; reexports 2.6%). *Major export destinations* (1984): Trinidad and Tobago 36.3%; United Kingdom 33.9%; West Germany 9.8%; The Netherlands 7.6%; United States 5.2%.

Transport and communications

Transport. Railroads: none. Roads (1986): total length 621 mi, 1,000 km (paved 66%). Vehicles (1981): passenger cars 4,784; trucks and buses 981. Merchant marine (1987): vessels (100 gross tons and over) 3; total deadweight tonnage 829. Air transport (1982): passenger arrivals and departures, n.a.; cargo loaded 59 metric tons, cargo unloaded 116 metric tons; airports (1988) with scheduled flights 2.
Communications. Daily newspapers: none. Radio (1986): total number of receivers 50,000 (1 per 2.0 persons). Television: total number of receivers, n.a. Telephones (1987): 6,645 (1 per 16 persons).

Education and health

Education (1986–87)

	schools	teachers	students	student/ teacher ratio
Primary (age 5–11)	59	...	19,984	...
Secondary (age 12–18)	20	...	6,462	...
Vocational	...	...	...	...
Higher	2	195	850	4.4

Educational attainment (1981). Percent of population age 25 and over having: no formal schooling 2.2%; primary education 87.8%; secondary 8.5%; higher 1.5%. *Literacy* (1981): total population age 15 and over literate 46,000 (85.0%).
Health (1986): physicians 38 (1 per 2,687 persons); hospital beds 340 (1 per 300 persons); infant mortality rate per 1,000 live births (1983) 21.2[13].
Food (1984–86): daily per capita caloric intake 2,409 (vegetable products 81%, animal products 19%); (1983) 93% of FAO recommended minimum requirement.

Military

Total active duty personnel (1987):[14]. *Military expenditure as percent of GNP:* n.a.; per capita expenditure, n.a.

[1]Grenada is divided into seven parishes for statistical purposes only. [2]1979. [3]At prices of 1984. [4]Employed labour force only, including 5,932 self-employed. [5]Less imputed bank charges. [6]1986. [7]1984. [8]Export only. [9]Only 260 houses were built by public authorities between 1978 and 1987. [10]Grenada does not have a systematically computed index of wage rates. [11]Import figures are f.o.b. in balance of trade and c.i.f. in commodities and trading partners. [12]*Exports* (1987): U.S.$34,940,000 (nutmeg 41.7%, bananas 11.7%, cacao beans 11.4%, mace 7.7%). [13]Registered data. 1987 unofficial estimate is 48.0. [14]The police force includes an 80-member paramilitary unit.

Guadeloupe

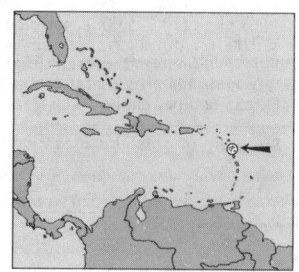

Official name: Département de
la Guadeloupe (Department of
Guadeloupe).
Political status: overseas department
(France) with two legislative houses
(General Council [43]; Regional
Council [41]).
Chief of state: President of France.
Heads of government: Commissioner of
the Republic (for France); President of
the General Council (for Guadeloupe);
President of the Regional Council (for
Guadeloupe).
Capital: Basse-Terre.
Official language: French.
Official religion: none.
Monetary unit: 1 Franc (F) = 100
centimes; valuation (Oct. 10, 1988)
1 U.S.$ = F 6.32; 1 £ = F 10.83.

Area and population

Arrondissements	Capitals	area sq mi	area sq km	population 1982 census
Basse-Terre[1]	Basse-Terre	332	861	138,242
Pointe-à-Pitre[2]	Pointe-à-Pitre	297	769	179,027
Saint-Martin–Saint-Barthélemy[3]	Marigot	29	75	11,131
TOTAL		687[4]	1,780[4]	328,400

Demography

Population (1988): 340,000.
Density (1988): persons per sq mi 494.9, persons per sq km 191.0.
Urban–rural (1985): urban 45.6%; rural 54.4%.
Sex distribution (1982): male 49.10%; female 50.90%.
Age breakdown (1982): under 15, 31.1%; 15–29, 29.2%; 30–44, 16.6%; 45–59,
12.0%; 60–74, 7.8%; 75 and over, 2.8%; not specified 0.5%.
Population projection: (1990) 343,000; (2000) 361,000.
Doubling time: 50 years[5].
Ethnic composition (1980): Creole (mulatto) 77.0%; black 10.0%; Guadeloupe
mestizo (French–Amerindian) 10.0%; white 2.0%; other 1.0%.
Religious affiliation (1984): Roman Catholic 81.2%; other 18.8%.
Major cities (1982): Les Abymes 51,837 (agglomeration 121,157[6]); Pointe-à-
Pitre 25,151; Le Gosier 13,741; Basse-Terre 13,397.

Vital statistics

Birth rate per 1,000 population (1987): 20.3 (world avg. 26.0); (1985) legiti-
mate 43.4%; illegitimate 56.6%.
Death rate per 1,000 population (1987): 6.6 (world avg. 9.9).
Natural increase rate per 1,000 population (1987): 13.9 (world avg. 16.1).
Total fertility rate (avg. births per childbearing woman; 1987): 2.4.
Marriage rate per 1,000 population (1986): 5.1.
Divorce rate per 1,000 population (1986): 1.5.
Life expectancy at birth (1987): male 69.0 years; female 76.0 years.
Major causes of death per 100,000 population (1983): diseases of the cir-
culatory system 243.0, of which cerebrovascular diseases 97.0; malignant
neoplasms (cancers) 105.8; accidents 59.7; diseases of the digestive system
33.9; endocrine and metabolic disorders 31.2.

National economy

Budget (1988). Revenue: F 1,630,000,000 (receipts from French central
government and local administrative bodies 43.4%, new loans 17.1%, investments 9.2%, taxes on motor fuels 8.0%). Expenditures: F 1,630,000,000
(health and social services 32.6%, capital investments and works 31.4%,
debt payments 5.4%).
Public debt (external, outstanding; 1985[7]): U.S.$62,000,000.
Tourism (1986): receipts from visitors U.S.$97,800,000; expenditures by na-
tionals abroad, n.a.
Production. Agriculture, forestry, fishing (value of production in F '000,000;
1985): bananas for export 339, fresh vegetables 208, sugarcane 178, roots
and tubers 126, other fruits (mostly locally consumed bananas, pineapples,
coconuts, and mangoes) 46, fresh-cut flowers and plants 26; livestock
(number of live animals; 1987) 73,000 cattle, 39,000 pigs; roundwood
17,000 cu m; fish catch (1986) 8,500 metric tons. Mining and quarrying
(1986): pozzolan, sand, and gravel for local use. Manufacturing (1987):
cement 169,600[8]; raw sugar 63,200; rum 66,800 hectolitres; other products
include clothing, wooden furniture and posts, and metalware. Construction (buildings authorized): residential (1984) 250,000 sq m; nonresidential
(1987) 105,000 sq m. Energy production (consumption): electricity (kW-hr;
1987) 592,000,000 (514,000,000); coal, none (none); crude petroleum, none
(none); petroleum products (metric tons; 1986) none (214,000); natural
gas, none (none).
Household income and expenditure. Average household size (1982) 3.7;
income per household (1980) F 72,898 (U.S.$16,142); sources of income
(1980): wages and salaries 76.8%, rent 4.0%, other 19.2%; expenditure[9]: food
and beverages 36.7%, transportation 16.4%, housing 13.0%, clothing and
footwear 7.7%, household furnishings 6.5%, recreation 5.2%, other 14.5%.
Gross national product (at current market prices; 1985): U.S.$1,170,000,000
(U.S.$3,490 per capita).

Structure of gross domestic product and labour force

	1980 in value F '000,000	1980 % of total value	1982 labour force	1982 % of labour force
Agriculture	449	7.7	12,997	10.5
Mining and Manufacturing	372	6.3	6,643	5.4
Construction	259	4.4	9,997	8.1
Public utilities	12	0.2	703	0.6
Transportation and communications	267	4.6	4,819	3.9
Trade	1,071	18.3	10,062	8.1
Finance and insurance	1,560	26.6	15,109	12.2
Pub. admin., defense, services, and other	1,870	31.9	34,131[10]	27.5
Unemployed	—	—	29,427	23.7
TOTAL	5,860	100.0	123,888	100.0

Population economically active (1982): total 123,888; activity rate of total
population 37.9% (participation rates: ages 15–64, 63.7%; female 42.5%;
unemployed [end of 1987] 24.0%).

Price and earnings indexes (1981 = 100)[11]

	1981	1982	1983	1984	1985	1986	1987
Consumer price index	100.0	110.2	121.2	130.6	137.4	139.3	144.2
Earnings index[12]	100.0	120.6	130.3	135.6	144.4	144.9	147.3

Land use (1985): forested 40.0%; meadows and pastures 15.0%; agricultural
and under permanent cultivation 23.0%; other 22.0%.

Foreign trade

Balance of trade (current prices)

	1982	1983	1984	1985	1986	1987
F '000,000	−3,569	−4,412	−4,480	−5,076	−4,709	−5,665
% of total	76.5%	77.9%	74.9%	79.1%	75.9%	83.4%

Imports (1987): F 6,229,000,000 (food 22.8%, electrical machinery and apparatuses 14.7%, transport vehicles 14.2%, chemical products 8.9%, metal
manufactures 7.0%, petroleum products 5.7%). *Major import sources:*
France 76.9%; Martinique 6.8%; Italy 3.1%; Netherlands Antilles 2.8%.
Exports (1987): F 564,000,000 (bananas 50.2%, wheat flour 8.2%, rum 7.8%,
sugar 3.3%). *Major export destinations:* France 82.4%; Martinique 10.3%;
Dominica 1.7%.

Transport and communications

Transport. Railroads: none. Roads (1986): total length 1,297 mi, 2,087 km
(paved 80%). Vehicles (1985): passenger cars 95,962; trucks and buses
28,134. Merchant marine: n.a. Air transport (1987)[13]: passenger arrivals
527,301, passenger departures 528,176; cargo loaded 3,811 metric tons,
cargo unloaded 6,907 metric tons; airports (1988) with scheduled flights 7.
Communications. Daily newspapers (1986): total number 1; total circulation
25,000; circulation per 1,000 population 75. Radio (1987): total number
of receivers 100,000 (1 per 3.4 persons). Television (1987): total number
of receivers 70,000 (1 per 4.8 persons). Telephones (1986): 106,744 (1
per 3.1 persons).

Education and health

Education (1985–86)

	schools	teachers	students	student/ teacher ratio
Primary (age 6–10)	230	1,927	42,734	22.2
Secondary (age 11–17)	...	...	38,510	...
Vocational	...	...	13,124	...
Higher	1	92	5,212	56.7

Educational attainment (1982). Percent of population age 25 and over
having: no formal schooling 10.7%; primary education 54.6%; secondary
29.5%; higher 5.2%. *Literacy* (1982): total population age 15 and over
literate 225,400 (90.1%); males literate 108,700 (89.7%); females literate
116,700 (90.5%).
Health (1985): physicians 416 (1 per 800 persons); hospital beds 4,147 (1 per
80 persons); infant mortality rate per 1,000 live births (1986)15.2.
Food (1984–86): daily per capita caloric intake 2,674 (vegetable products
73%, animal products 27%); (1983) 107% of FAO recommended minimum requirement.

Military

Total active duty personnel (1987): 7,900[14].

[1]Comprises Basse-Terre 327 sq mi (848 sq km) and Îles des Saintes 5 sq mi (13 sq
km), pop. 2,901. [2]Comprises Grande-Terre 228 sq mi (590 sq km); Marie-Galante 61
sq mi (158 sq km), pop. 13,757; La Désirade 8 sq mi (20 sq km), pop. 1,602; and
the small, uninhabited Îles de la Petite-Terre. [3]Comprises the French part of Saint-
Martin 20 sq mi (52 sq km), pop. 8,072; Saint-Barthélemy 8 sq mi (21 sq km), pop.
3,059; and the small, uninhabited island of Tintamarre. [4]Total area includes 29 sq mi
(75 sq km) not allocated by arrondissement. [5]Net migration to metropolitan France
nearly outweighs natural increase rate. [6]Includes Pointe-à-Pitre. [7]Includes external
long-term private debt not guaranteed by the government. [8]1986. [9]Weights of current
consumer price index components in Basse-Terre and Pointe-à-Pitre. [10]Includes 5,963
not adequately defined. [11]Base and indexes are end of year. [12]Based on minimum-
level wage in public administration. [13]Raizet international airport only. [14]Includes
Martinique and French Guiana.

Guam

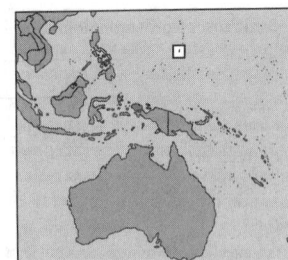

Official name: Guam.
Political Status: self-governing organized unincorporated territory of the United States with one legislative house (21).
Chief of state: President of the United States.
Head of government: Governor.
Capital: Agana.
Official language: English.
Official religion: none.
Monetary unit: 1 United States dollar (U.S.$) = 100 cents; valuation (Oct. 10, 1988) 1 U.S.$ = £0.58.

Area and population	area		population[1]
Election Districts	sq mi	sq km	1988 estimate
Agana	1	3	1,100
Agana Heights	1	3	3,900
Agat	10	26	4,800
Asan	6	16	2,400
Barrigada	9	23	9,300
Chalan Pago-Ordot	6	16	3,700
Dededo	30	78	28,200
Inarajan	19	49	2,500
Mangilao	10	26	8,200
Merizo	6	16	2,000
Mongmong-Toto-Maite	2	5	6,300
Piti	7	18	3,400
Santa Rita	17	44	11,000
Sinajana	1	3	3,000
Talofofo	17	44	2,400
Tamuning	6	16	16,200
Umatac	6	16	900
Yigo	35	91	12,400
Yona	20	52	5,000
TOTAL	209	541[2]	126,400[2]

Demography

Population (1988): 126,000.
Density (1988): persons per sq mi 602.9, persons per sq km 232.9.
Urban–rural (1980): urban[3] 39.5%; rural 60.5%.
Sex distribution (1985): male 54.31%; female 45.69%.
Age breakdown (1980): under 15, 34.9%; 15–29, 30.6%; 30–44, 19.4%; 45–59, 10.5%; 60–74, 3.9%; 75 and over, 0.7%.
Population projection: (1990) 132,000; (2000) 165,000.
Doubling time: 29 years.
Ethnic composition (1980): Chamorro 41.8%; Filipino 21.2%; German 2.1%; Korean 1.8%; Japanese 1.8%; other[4] 31.3%.
Religious affiliation (1980): Roman Catholic 79.5%; Protestant 17.3%; other 3.2%.
Major populated places (1980): Tamuning 8,862; Apra Harbor 5,633; Andersen Air Force Base 4,892; Mangilao 4,029.

Vital statistics

Birth rate per 1,000 population (1986): 27.4 (world avg. 26.0); legitimate 68.6%; illegitimate 31.4%.
Death rate per 1,000 population (1986): 3.7 (world avg. 9.9).
Natural increase rate per 1,000 population (1986): 23.7 (world avg. 16.1).
Total fertility rate (avg. births per childbearing woman; 1980): 3.2.
Marriage rate per 1,000 population (1986): 12.6.
Divorce rate per 1,000 population (1986): 8.5.
Life expectancy at birth (1980–82): male 69.6 years; female 74.5 years.
Major causes of death per 100,000 population (1985): heart disease 93.0; malignant neoplasms (cancers) 55.8; cerebrovascular diseases 26.2; diabetes mellitus 18.6; motor vehicle accidents 17.7; pneumonia 16.1; other diseases of the central nervous system 14.4; congenital abnormalities 10.1.

National economy

Budget (1985). Revenue: U.S.$190,828,130 (local income taxes 43.6%, gross business receipts taxes 22.4%, revenues from United States agencies[5] 13.6%, special revenue fund 5.8%, capital projects funds 5.5%). Expenditures: U.S.$162,863,053 (public education 38.0%, general government operations 28.5%, law and public safety 15.0%, public health and community services 12.9%, economic development 2.4%).
Tourism (1986): receipts from visitors U.S.$308,000,000; expenditures by nationals abroad, U.S.$303,900,000.
Land use (1985): forested 18.2%; meadows and pastures 14.5%; agricultural and under permanent cultivation 21.8%; other 45.5%.
Production. Agriculture, forestry, fishing (value of production in U.S.$ except as noted; 1985): watermelons 1,039,500, cucumbers 381,889, pineapples 321,840, cantaloupes 236,250, tomatoes 184,585, bananas 166,042, long beans 155,496, pepino melons 149,400, bitter melon 145,152, eggs 937,860; livestock (number of live animals) 4,750 pigs, 1,420 goats, 410 cattle, 85 carabaos; fish catch (metric tons; 1986) 650. Mining and quarrying (1983): sand and gravel. Manufacturing (value of gross business receipts in U.S.$; 1980): petroleum refining and related products 322,083,000; food processing 11,742,000; printing and publishing 6,039,000; industrial and medical goods and materials 412,000. Construction (gross value of building and construction permits in U.S.$; 1987): residential 108,956,000; nonresidential 38,329,000. Energy production (consumption): electricity (kW-hr; 1986) 1,100,000,000 (1,100,000,000); coal, none (n.a.); crude petroleum (barrels;

1986) none (10,995,000); petroleum products (metric tons; 1986) 1,400,000 (820,000); natural gas, none (n.a.).
Public debt (external, outstanding): n.a.
Gross national product (at current market prices; 1985): U.S.$670,000,000 (U.S.$5,660 per capita).

Structure of gross business income and labour force				
	1982		1987	
	in value U.S.$'000,000	% of total value	labour force[6]	% of labour force
Agriculture	1.4	0.2	260	0.6
Manufacturing	107.3	13.1	1,920	4.4
Construction	64.6	7.9	4,170	9.5
Trade	422.3	51.5	8,520	19.4
Transp. and commun.	45.3	5.5	2,400[7]	5.5
Finance	80.8	9.9	2,020	4.6
Pub. admin., defense	...	...	16,430	37.3
Services	99.6	12.2	8,260	18.8
TOTAL	819.2[2]	100.0[2]	43,980	100.0[2]

Population economically active (1987): total 36,540[8]; activity rate of total population 29.5% (participation rates: over age 16, 61.0%; female 41.7%; unemployed 3.7%).

Price and earnings indexes (1980 = 100)						
	1981	1982	1983	1984	1985	1986	1987
Consumer price index	114.0	128.1	132.6	144.2	149.8	153.4	160.6
Hourly earnings index	...	...	112.8	109.3	115.2	123.2	118.7

Household income and expenditure. Average household size (1980) 3.7; median annual income per household (1979) U.S.$16,203; sources of income: n.a.; expenditure (1978): housing 28.6%, food 24.1%, transportation 18.0%, clothing 10.6%, entertainment 5.1%, medical care 4.7%.

Foreign trade

Balance of trade (current prices)						
	1978	1979	1980	1981	1982	1983
U.S.$'000	−236,227	−403,144	−483,141	...	...	−571,519
% of total	76.7%	82.5%	79.8%	...	...	87.9%

Imports (1983): U.S.$610,743,985 (mineral fuels 46.9%, of which crude petroleum 28.8%; machinery and transport equipment 19.1%, of which passenger cars 12.4%; food and live animals 12.0%, of which beef and veal 1.5%; beverages and tobacco 4.5%, of which cigarettes 1.3%; manufactured goods 4.4%; chemicals 2.3%). *Major import sources* (1984): United States 37.5%; Japan 24.7%; Hong Kong 4.6%; Taiwan 1.9%; Philippines 1.4%.
Exports (1983): U.S.$39,224,728 (clothing 16.9%; beverages and tobacco 12.0%, of which alcoholic beverages 4.4%, cigarettes 3.5%, nonalcoholic beverages 1.9%; machinery and transport equipment 11.4%; travel goods 3.0%; lubricating oils and greases 2.7%; fish and fish products 2.6%; cosmetics 2.6%; watches and watch cases 1.5%; cement 1.5%). *Major export destinations* (1984): Micronesia[9] 79.2%; Japan 9.9%; United States 7.2%.

Transport and communications

Transport. Railroads: none. Roads (1986): total length 419 mi, 674 km (paved 100%). Vehicles[10] (1985): passenger cars 60,804; trucks and buses 17,569. Merchant marine (1987): vessels (100 gross tons and over) 5, total deadweight tonnage, n.a.; surface cargo loaded, unloaded, or transshipped (1985) 1,041,800 metric tons. Air transport (1985): passenger arrivals 364,-938; passenger departures, n.a.; cargo loaded 3,837 metric tons; cargo unloaded 5,136 metric tons; airports (1988) with scheduled flights 1.
Communications. Daily newspapers (1986): total number 1; total circulation 18,076; circulation per 1,000 population 149. Radio (1986): total receivers 102,000 (1 per 1.2 persons). Television (1987): total receivers 83,000 (1 per 1.5 persons). Telephones (1985): 23,724[11] (1 per 5.0 persons).

Education and health

Education (1986–87)	schools	teachers	students	student/ teacher ratio
Primary (age 5–10)	31	822	14,471	17.6
Secondary (age 11–18)	24	944	15,281	16.2
Vocational	3	117	2,410	20.6
Higher	1	206	2,208	10.7

Educational attainment (1980). Percent of population age 25 and over having: primary education 21.3%; some secondary 13.1%; secondary 31.2%; college 34.4%. *Literacy* (1980): total population age 15 and over literate 66,-537 (96.4%); males literate 35,091 (96.4%); females literate 31,446 (96.5%).
Health: physicians (1982) 83 (1 per 1,334 persons); hospital beds (1979) 223 (1 per 470 persons); infant mortality rate per 1,000 live births (1985) 12.2.
Food: daily per capita caloric intake, n.a.

Military

Total active duty U.S. personnel (1986): 11,800 (navy 61.3%, air force 34.2%, other 4.5%).

[1]Includes active-duty military personnel, U.S. Department of Defense employees, and dependents. [2]Detail does not add to total given because of rounding. [3]Places of 2,500 or more. [4]Includes various Pacific Island groups (mostly Micronesian) and persons of multiple ethnic origin. [5]Consists largely of federal income tax. [6]Employed persons only. [7]Includes public utilities. [8]Excludes nonimmigrant aliens and civilians living on military reservations. [9]Includes Commonwealth of Northern Marianas Islands, Federated States of Micronesia, Republic of Palau, and Marshall Islands. [10]Excludes military vehicles. [11]Number of lines.

Guatemala

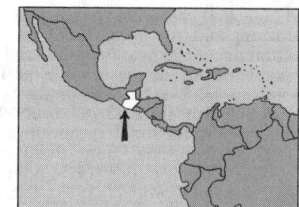

Official name: República de Guatemala (Republic of Guatemala).
Form of government: republic with one legislative house (Congress of the Republic [100]).
Head of state and government: President.
Capital: Guatemala City.
Official language: Spanish.
Official religion: none.
Monetary unit: 1 Guatemalan quetzal (Q) = 100 centavos; valuation (Oct. 10, 1988) 1 U.S.$ = Q 1.00[1]; 1 £ = Q 1.71.

Area and population		area		population
		sq mi	sq km	1987 estimate
Departments	**Capitals**			
Alta Verapaz	Cobán	3,354	8,686	530,746
Baja Verapaz	Salamá	1,206	3,124	168,001
Chimaltenango	Chimaltenango	764	1,979	311,282
Chiquimula	Chiquimula	917	2,376	234,867
El Progreso	Progreso	742	1,922	101,165
Escuintla	Escuintla	1,693	4,384	488,755
Guatemala	Guatemala City	821	2,126	1,825,709
Huehuetenango	Huehuetenango	2,857	7,400	640,316
Izabal	Puerto Barrios	3,490	9,038	292,179
Jalapa	Jalapa	797	2,063	175,066
Jutiapa	Jutiapa	1,243	3,219	329,300
Petén	Ciudad Flores	13,843	35,854	209,419
Quetzaltenango	Quetzaltenango	753	1,951	506,439
Quiché	Santa Cruz	3,235	8,378	515,612
Retalhuleu	Retalhuleu	717	1,856	215,532
Sacatepéquez	Antigua Guatemala	180	465	162,517
San Marcos	San Marcos	1,464	3,791	636,274
Santa Rosa	Cuilapa	1,141	2,955	249,575
Sololá	Sololá	410	1,061	217,286
Suchitepéquez	Mazatenango	969	2,510	329,086
Totonicapán	Totonicapán	410	1,061	269,390
Zacapa	Zacapa	1,039	2,690	151,562
TOTAL		42,042[2]	108,889	8,560,078

Demography

Population (1988): 8,681,000.
Density (1988): persons per sq mi 206.5, persons per sq km 79.7.
Urban–rural (1987): urban 36.4%; rural 63.6%.
Sex distribution (1985): male 50.56%; female 49.44%.
Age breakdown (1985): under 15, 45.9%; 15–29, 26.5%; 30–44, 14.3%; 45–59, 8.6%; 60–74, 3.8%; 75 and over, 0.9%.
Population projection: (1990) 9,197,000; (2000) 12,222,000.
Doubling time: 26 years.
Ethnic composition (1983): Amerindian 55%; Ladino (Hispanic/Amerindian) 42%; white or black 3%.
Religious affiliation (1985): Roman Catholic *c.* 75%; Protestant (mostly evangelical churches) *c.* 25%.
Major cities (1981): Guatemala City 754,243; Quetzaltenango 62,719; Escuintla 36,931; Puerto Barrios 24,235; Retalhuleu 22,001.

Vital statistics

Birth rate per 1,000 population (1987): 36.5 (world avg. 26.0).
Death rate per 1,000 population (1987): 9.5 (world avg. 9.9).
Natural increase rate per 1,000 population (1987): 27.0 (world avg. 16.1).
Total fertility rate (avg. births per childbearing woman; 1987): 5.1.
Marriage rate per 1,000 population (1985): 4.8.
Divorce rate per 1,000 population (1983): 0.2.
Life expectancy at birth (1987): male 58.0 years; female 62.0 years.
Major causes of death per 100,000 population (1984): infectious and parasitic diseases 211.5; diseases of the respiratory system 145.7, of which pneumonia 112.4; diseases of the circulatory system 57.2; malnutrition 45.3; homicide and other violence 35.1; ill-defined conditions 72.6.

National economy

Budget (1986). Revenue: Q 1,466,900,000 (tax revenue 76.7%, of which taxes on goods and services 31.4%, taxes on international transactions 27.3%; nontax revenue 19.2%; grants 4.1%). Expenditures: Q 1,663,600,000 (current expenditures 82.8%; development expenditures 17.2%).
Public debt (external, outstanding; 1986): U.S.$2,186,900,000.
Tourism (1986): receipts from visitors U.S.$77,000,000; expenditures by nationals abroad U.S.$24,000,000.
Production (metric tons except as noted). Agriculture, forestry, fishing (1986): sugarcane 7,000,000, corn (maize) 1,106,000, bananas 690,000, coffee 156,000, seed cotton 120,000, dry beans 113,000, tomatoes 95,000, cardamom, n.a.; livestock (number of live animals) 2,284,000 cattle, 862,000 pigs, 680,000 sheep; roundwood (1985) 6,869,000 cu m; fish catch (1985) 2,707, of which shrimps 1,918. Mining and quarrying (1986): limestone 1,000,000; gypsum 16,800[3]; antimony (metal content) 1,057[3]. Manufacturing (1985): raw sugar 616,000[4]; cement 526,000; beer 645,000 hectolitres[5]; cigarettes 1,936,000,000 units, essential oils 2,770 hectolitres[6]. Construction (1984)[7]: residential 128,700 sq m; nonresidential 98,800 sq m. Energy production (consumption): electricity (kW-hr; 1986) 1,760,000,000 (1,760,000,000); coal, none (none); crude petroleum (barrels; 1986) 2,118,000 (5,600,000); petroleum products (metric tons; 1986) 646,000 (928,000); natural gas, none (none).

Gross national product (1986): U.S.$7,640,000,000 (U.S.$930 per capita).

Structure of gross domestic product and labour force				
	1986		1985	
	in value[8] U.S.$'000,000	% of total value	labour force	% of labour force
Agriculture	748.6	25.6	1,422,580	58.1
Mining	8.4	0.3	2,449	0.1
Manufacturing	468.5	16.0	332,996	13.6
Construction	50.3	1.7	100,388	4.1
Public utilities	62.2	2.1	7,345	0.3
Transp. and commun.	206.1	7.0	61,213	2.5
Trade	727.3	24.9	178,741	7.3
Finance	268.6	9.2 }		
Pub. admin., defense	198.6	6.8 }	293,820	12.0
Services	187.7	6.4 }		
Other	—	—	48,970	2.0
TOTAL	2,926.3	100.0	2,448,502	100.0

Population economically active (1981): total 1,696,464; activity rate of total population 28.0% (participation rates: age 15–64, 49.1%; female 14.6%; unemployed [1986] 14.5%).

Price and earnings indexes (1980 = 100)							
	1981	1982	1983	1984	1985	1986	1987
Consumer price index	111.4	111.8	116.8	120.8	143.4	196.4	220.6
Annual earnings index[9]	131.2	139.3	135.2	138.9	148.6	...	...

Household income and expenditure. Average household size (1981) 5.5[10]; income per household: n.a.; sources of income: n.a.; expenditure (1979–81)[11]: food 57.3%, housing and energy 12.7%, clothing and footwear 10.4%, household furnishings 6.0%, transportation 5.8%, other 7.8%.
Land use (1985): forested 38.3%; meadows and pastures 12.3%; agricultural and under permanent cultivation 16.9%; other 32.5%.

Foreign trade[12]

Balance of trade (current prices)						
	1981	1982	1983	1984	1985	1986
Q '000,000	−286.3	−164.5	+102.7	−59.9	−56.2	+185.2
% of total	10.2%	6.8%	4.7%	2.6%	2.7%	9.6%

Imports (1985): Q 1,174,800,000 (mineral fuels and lubricants 23.1%, chemical products 23.0%, machinery and transport equipment 19.0%, food 7.0%). *Major import sources* (1986): U.S. 43.2%; W.Ger. 7.3%; Mexico 6.3%; Japan 5.6%; Venezuela 5.6%.
Exports (1985): Q 1,020,600,000 (coffee 40.3%, bananas 6.1%, cotton 5.9%, cardamom 5.8%, sugar 4.3%). *Major export destinations* (1986): U.S. 45.5%; El Salvador 9.5%; W.Ger. 8.2%; Costa Rica 5.0%; Japan 3.9%.

Transport and communications

Transport. Railroads (1987): route length 467 mi, 751 km; number of passengers transported (1983) 995,000. Roads (1985): total length 11,200 mi, 18,000 km (paved 16%). Vehicles (1983): passenger cars 188,100; trucks and buses 58,500. Merchant marine (1987): vessels (100 gross tons and over) 5; total deadweight tonnage 6,450. Air transport (1986): passenger-mi 84,500,000, passenger-km 136,000,000; short ton-mi cargo 4,910,000, metric ton-km cargo 7,169,000; airports (1988) with scheduled flights 2.
Communications. Daily newspapers (1986): total number 9; total circulation 225,500[13]; circulation per 1,000 population 28. Radio (1986): 500,000 receivers (1 per 16 persons). Television (1987): 475,000 receivers (1 per 18 persons). Telephones (1985): 128,179 (1 per 63 persons).

Education and health

Education (1984)	schools	teachers	students	student/ teacher ratio
Primary (age 7–12)	7,820	26,963	979,888	36.3
Secondary (age 13–18) }	...	12,023	174,653	14.5
Voc., teacher tr. }				
Higher[14]	1	3,043	45,552	15.0

Educational attainment (1981). Percent of population age 25 and over having: no formal schooling 52.9%; primary education 34.5%; incomplete secondary 7.1%; complete secondary and higher 2.1%; unknown 3.4%. *Literacy* (1981): total population age 15 and over literate 1,835,379 (55.0%); males literate 1,029,174 (62.8%); females literate 806,205 (47.4%).
Health: physicians (1984) 3,544 (1 per 2,256 persons); hospital beds (1982) 9,881 (1 per 740 persons); infant mortality rate per 1,000 live births (1987) 66.0.
Food (1984–86): daily per capita caloric intake 2,297 (vegetable products 92%, animal products 8%); (1983) 95% of FAO recommended minimum.

Military

Total active duty personnel (1987): 40,200 (army 94.5%, navy 3.7%, air force 1.8%). *Military expenditure as percent of GNP* (1985): 1.8% (world 6.1%); per capita expenditure U.S.$22.

[1]The official market value of the quetzal is fixed at par with that of the U.S.$; the free market rate is Q 2.76 per U.S.$. [2]Detail does not add to total given because of rounding. [3]Includes data available through July 1986. [4]1987. [5]1983. [6]1982. [7]Authorized construction in Guatemala City metropolitan area. [8]At 1958 prices. [9]Based on employees entitled to social security. [10]Excludes vacant households. [11]Weights of consumer price index components; urban areas only. [12]Import figures are f.o.b. in balance of trade and c.i.f. for commodities and trading partners. [13]Five newspapers only. [14]University of San Carlos only.

Guinea

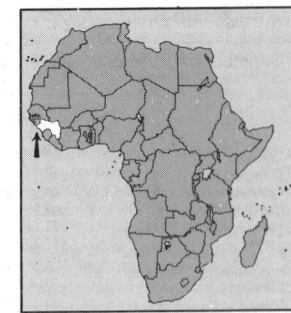

Official name: République de Guinée (Republic of Guinea).
Form of government: interim military regime ruling through the Military Committee for National Recovery (CMRN [20]).
Head of state and government: President (and Head of Military Committee for National Recovery).
Capital: Conakry.
Official language: French.
Official religion: none.
Monetary unit: 1 Guinean franc[1] (GF) = 100 cauris; valuation (Oct. 10, 1988) 1 U.S.$ = GF 299.47; 1 £ = GF 512.85.

Area and population

Regions	Capitals	area sq mi	area sq km	population 1983 census
Beyla	Beyla	6,738	17,452	161,347
Boffa	Boffa	1,932	5,003	141,719
Boké[2]	Boké	3,881	10,053	225,207
Conakry	Conakry	119	308	705,280
Coyah (Dubréka)	Coyah	2,153	5,576	134,190
Dabola	Dabola	2,317	6,000	97,986
Dalaba	Dalaba	1,313	3,400	132,802
Dinguiraye	Dinguiraye	4,247	11,000	133,502
Faranah[2]	Faranah	4,788	12,400	142,923
Forécariah	Forécariah	1,647	4,265	116,464
Fria	Fria	840	2,175	70,413
Gaoual	Gaoual	4,440	11,500	135,657
Guéckédou	Guéckédou	1,605	4,157	204,757
Kankan	Kankan	7,104	18,400	229,861
Kérouané	Kérouané	3,070	7,950	106,872
Kindia	Kindia	3,409	8,828	216,052
Kissidougou	Kissidougou	3,425	8,872	183,236
Koubia	Koubia	571	1,480	98,053
Koundara	Koundara	2,124	5,500	94,216
Kouroussa	Kouroussa	4,647	12,035	136,926
Labé	Labé	973	2,520	253,214
Lélouma	Lélouma	830	2,150	138,467
Lola	Lola	1,629	4,219	106,654
Macenta	Macenta	3,363	8,710	193,109
Mali	Mali	3,398	8,800	210,889
Mamou	Mamou	2,378	6,160	190,525
Mandiana	Mandiana	5,000	12,950	136,317
Nzérékoré	Nzérékoré	1,460	3,781	216,355
Pita	Pita	1,544	4,000	227,912
Siguiri	Siguiri	7,626	19,750	209,164
Télimélé	Télimélé	3,119	8,080	243,256
Tougué	Tougué	2,394	6,200	113,272
Yomou	Yomou	843	2,183	74,417
TOTAL		94,926[3]	245,857	5,781,014

Demography

Population (1988): 6,540,000.
Density (1988): persons per sq mi 68.9, persons per sq km 26.6.
Urban-rural (1985): urban 26.0%; rural 74.0%.
Sex distribution (1985): male 48.63%; female 51.37%.
Age breakdown (1985): under 15, 43.1%; 15–29, 26.2%; 30–44, 16.2%; 45–59, 9.6%; 60–74, 4.2%; 75 and over, 0.7%.
Population projection: (1990) 6,876,000; (2000) 8,879,000.
Doubling time: 30 years.
Ethnic composition (1983): Fulani 38.6%; Malinke 23.2%; Susu 11.0%; Kissi 6.0%; Kpelle 4.6%; other 16.6%.
Religious affiliation (1980): Muslim 69.0%; traditional beliefs 29.5%; Christian 1.4%, of which Roman Catholic 1.2%; other 0.1%.
Major cities (1983): Conakry 705,280; Kankan 88,760; Labé 65,439; Kindia 55,904.

Vital statistics

Birth rate per 1,000 population (1980–85): 46.8 (world avg. 29.0).
Death rate per 1,000 population (1980–85): 23.5 (world avg. 11.0).
Natural increase rate per 1,000 population (1980–85): 23.3 (world avg. 18.0).
Total fertility rate (avg. births per childbearing woman; 1980–85): 6.2.
Life expectancy at birth (1980–85): male 38.7 years; female 41.8 years.
Major causes of death per 100,000 population: n.a.; however, major diseases include malaria, venereal disease, tuberculosis, intestinal infections, measles, and schistosomiasis.

National economy

Budget (1986). Revenue: GF 109,602,000,000 (customs duties 42.2%, income tax 14.1%, excise tax 3.1%). Expenditures: GF 136,999,000,000 (material expenses 24.1%, wages 22.1%, debt service 17.1%, infrastructure 14.3%, rural development 7.6%, industry and mining development 7.5%).
Public debt (external, outstanding; 1986): U.S.$1,421,100,000.
Tourism: n.a.
Production (metric tons except as noted). Agriculture, forestry, fishing (1986): roots and tubers 663,000 (of which cassava 500,000, yams 61,000), rice 480,000, vegetables and melons 420,000, plantains 350,000, sugarcane 200,000, citrus fruit 161,000, bananas 105,000, peanuts (groundnuts) 75,-000, pulses 50,000, corn (maize) 50,000, palm kernels 40,000, pineapples 20,000, coconuts 15,000, coffee 15,000, eggs 12,180; livestock (number of live animals) 1,838,000 cattle, 470,000 goats, 465,000 sheep, 49,000 pigs,

12,000,000 chickens; roundwood (1985) 3,689,000 cu m; fish catch 30,000. Mining and quarrying (1986): bauxite 14,780,000; alumina 556,000; gem diamonds 190,000 carats; industrial diamonds 14,000 carats. Manufacturing (value of production in GS '000; 1985): corrugated and sheet iron 571,081; plastics 462,242; tobacco products 375,154; cement 326,138; printed matter 216,511; fruit juice 75,763; beer 69,934; matches 22,449. Construction: n.a. Energy production (consumption): electricity (kW-hr; 1986) 497,000,000 (497,000,000); coal, none (n.a.); crude petroleum, none (n.a.); petroleum products (metric tons; 1986) none (318,000); natural gas, none (n.a.).
Gross national product (1985): U.S.$1,950,000,000 (U.S.$320 per capita).

Structure of gross domestic product and labour force

	1985 in value GS '000,000[4]	1985 % of total value	labour force	% of labour force
Agriculture	16,195	40.0	2,236,000	78.6
Mining	5,420	13.4		
Manufacturing	724	1.8	268,000	9.4
Construction	2,593	6.4		
Public utilities	133	0.3		
Transp. and commun.	531	1.3		
Trade	8,697	21.5		
Finance	1,295	3.2	342,000	12.0
Pub. admin., defense	4,765	11.8		
Services				
Other	127	0.3	...	...
TOTAL	40,480	100.0	2,846,000	100.0

Population economically active (1985): total 2,846,000; activity rate of total population 46.8% (participation rates: ages 15–64, 76.2%; female 40.8%; unemployed, n.a.).
Household income and expenditure. Average household size (1980) 4.7; average annual income per capita (1984) GS 7,660 (U.S.$305); sources of income: n.a.; expenditure (1985): food 61.5%, health care 11.2%, clothing and footwear 7.9%, housing and energy 7.3%, transportation 5.1%, recreation 4.2%, durable goods 2.9%.
Land use (1985): forested 41.3%; meadows and pastures 12.2%; agricultural and under permanent cultivation 6.4%; other 40.1%.

Foreign trade[5]

Balance of trade (current prices)

	1979	1980	1981	1982	1983	1984
GS '000,000	−400	+1,000	+1,611	+2,511	+2,617	+3,467
% of total	2.7%	4.8%	9.9%	16.3%	16.6%	18.7%

Imports (1984): GS 7,542,000,000 (food, machinery and transport equipment, petroleum products, building materials, textiles). *Major import sources:* France 31.9%; Brazil 12.3%; U.S. 11.6%; W.Ger. 6.9%; Belgium 6.4%; Spain 5.3%.
Exports (1984): GS 11,009,000,000 (bauxite and alumina 90–95%; coffee, pineapples, bananas, palm kernels). *Major export destinations:* U.S. 27.5%; W.Ger. 18.9%; Spain 16.3%; Ireland 10.1%; Italy 5.8%.

Transport and communications

Transport. Railroads (1986): route length 584 mi, 940 km. Roads (1984): total length 17,600 mi, 28,400 km (paved 4%). Vehicles (1982): passenger cars 9,948; trucks and buses 9,992. Merchant marine (1987): vessels (100 gross tons and over) 19; total deadweight tonnage 2,927. Air transport (1986): passenger-mi 17,873,000, passenger-km 28,764,000; short ton-mi cargo 1,684,000, metric ton-km cargo 2,458,000; airports (1988) with scheduled flights 2.
Communications. Daily newspapers (1987): none. Radio (1986): 200,000 receivers (1 per 31 persons). Television (1987): 12,000 receivers (1 per 532 persons). Telephones (1981): 15,800 (1 per 310 persons).

Education and health

Education (1986–87)

	schools	teachers	students	student/ teacher ratio
Primary (age 7–12)	2,204	7,493	270,140	36.0
Secondary (age 13–18)	225	3,577	76,493	21.4
Voc., teacher tr.	31	758	4,929	6.5
Higher	23	946	7,470	7.9

Educational attainment, n.a. *Literacy* (1985): total population age 15 and over literate 874,000 (28.3%); males literate 603,000 (39.7%); females literate 271,000 (17.2%).
Health: physicians (1980) 301 (1 per 17,000 persons); hospital beds[6] (1976) 7,650 (1 per 579 persons); infant mortality rate per 1,000 live births (1980–85) 159.
Food (1984–86): daily per capita caloric intake 1,782 (vegetable products 96%, animal products 4%); (1983) 84% of FAO recommended minimum.

Military

Total active duty personnel (1987): 9,900 (army 85.8%, navy 6.1%, air force 8.1%). *Military expenditure as percent of GNP* (1984): 3.2% (world 6.0%); per capita expenditure U.S.$10.

---

[1]In January 1986 the Guinean syli (GS) was replaced at par by the Guinean franc (GF), and its value was depreciated by 92.5% in terms of foreign currency. [2]The provinces of Boké and Faranah were abolished by presidential decree in January 1988. [3]Detail does not add to total given because of rounding. [4]In constant prices of 1981. [5]Trade with the Socialist bloc is not included in major import sources and major export destinations; the U.S.S.R., however, is a major trading partner. [6]Government hospitals only.

Guinea-Bissau

Official name: Rêpublica da Guiné-Bissau (Republic of Guinea-Bissau).
Form of government: single-party republic with one legislative house (National People's Assembly [150]).
Head of state and government: President.
Capital: Bissau.
Official language: Portuguese.
Official religion: none.
Monetary unit: 1 peso (PG) = 100 centavos; valuation (Oct. 10, 1988) 1 U.S.$ = PG 649; 1 £ = PG 1,111.

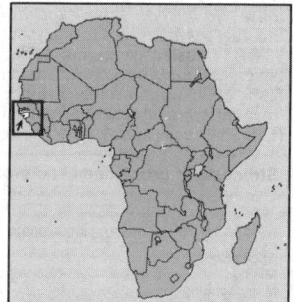

Area and population

Regions	Capitals	area sq mi	area sq km	population 1979 census[1]
Bafatá	Bafatá	2,309	5,981	115,656
Biombo[2]	Bissau	324	840	51,796
Bolama	Bolama	1,013	2,624	25,449
Cacheu	Cacheu	1,998	5,175	127,514
Gabú	Gabú	3,533	9,150	103,683
Oio	Farim	2,086	5,403	131,271
Quinara	Fulacunda	1,212	3,138	35,567
Tombali	Catió	1,443	3,736	55,088
Autonomous Sector				
Bissau	—	30	78	107,281
TOTAL		13,948	36,125	753,305

Demography

Population (1988): 931,000.
Density (1988): persons per sq mi 66.7, persons per sq km 25.8.
Urban–rural (1985): urban 27.0%; rural 73.0%.
Sex distribution (1985): male 48.42%; female 51.58%.
Age breakdown (1985): under 15, 42.9%; 15–29, 25.6%; 30–44, 15.7%; 45–59, 10.2%; 60–74, 4.7%; 75 and over, 0.9%.
Population projection: (1990) 971,000; (2000) 1,200,000.
Doubling time: 37 years.
Ethnic composition (1979): Balante 27.2%; Fulani 22.9%; Malinke 12.2%; Mandyako 10.6%; Pepel 10.0%; other 17.1%.
Religious affiliation (1986): traditional beliefs 65%; Muslim 30%; Christian 5%.
Major cities (1979): Bissau 109,214; Bafatá 13,429; Gabú 7,803; Mansôa 5,390; Catió 5,179.

Vital statistics

Birth rate per 1,000 population (1980–85): 40.7 (world avg. 29.0); legitimate, n.a.; illegitimate, n.a.
Death rate per 1,000 population (1980–85): 21.7 (world avg. 11.0).
Natural increase rate per 1,000 population (1980–85): 19.0 (world avg. 18.0).
Total fertility rate (avg. births per childbearing woman; 1985): 6.0.
Marriage rate per 1,000 population: n.a.
Divorce rate per 1,000 population: n.a.
Life expectancy at birth (1980–85): male 41.4 years; female 44.6 years.
Major causes of death per 100,000 population: n.a.; however, major diseases include tuberculosis of the respiratory system, whooping cough, typhoid fever, bacillary dysentery and amebiasis, malaria, pneumonia, and meningococcal infections.

National economy

Budget (1985). Revenue: PG 1,000,000,000 (1981; indirect taxes 49.6%; direct taxes 25.8%; duties, fines, and other penalties 3.0%). Expenditures: PG 1,000,000,000 (1979; finance 16.3%; defense 15.6%; education 13.3%; economic affairs 11.6%; health and social welfare 9.5%; rural development 5.0%; public works 3.0%).
Public debt (external, outstanding; 1986): U.S.$293,800,000.
Tourism: n.a.; however, the island of Bubaque is being developed as a tourist resort, with 110 rooms in 1979; work began in 1985 on a 180-room hotel in Bissau.
Production (metric tons except as noted). Agriculture, forestry, fishing (1986): rice 125,000, roots and tubers (sweet potatoes and cassava) 40,000, fruit 40,000, sorghum 33,000, peanuts (groundnuts) 29,000, coconuts 25,000, plantains 25,000, vegetables 20,000, millet 18,000, corn (maize) 18,000, palm kernels 14,000, cashews 10,000, copra 5,000, sugarcane 5,000, papayas 2,000, pulses 2,000; livestock (number of live animals) 333,000 cattle, 286,000 pigs, 205,000 goats, 200,000 sheep, 1,000,000 chickens[3]; roundwood (1985) 559,000 cu m; fish catch 3,620. Mining and quarrying: n.a.; however, prospecting for bauxite, petroleum, and phosphates was being carried out in the mid-1980s. Manufacturing (in PG '000,000; 1982): beverages 143.7, of which beer 122.3, orangeade and lemonade 16.5; clothing 14.0[4]; peanut oil 7.0; palm oil 2.4. Construction (in PG '000,000; 1982): total buildings 2.5. Energy production (consumption): electricity (kW-hr; 1986) 14,000,000 (14,000,000); coal, none (n.a.); crude petroleum (barrels; 1981) none (210,000); petroleum products (metric tons; 1986) none (27,000); natural gas, none (n.a.).
Population economically active (1979): total 213,010; activity rate of total population 38.7% (participation rates: ages 15–64, 41.0%; female 3.6%; unemployed 0.5%).

Price and earnings indexes (1975 = 100)

	1975	1976	1977	1978	1979	1980	1981
Consumer price index	100.0	101.5	104.5	114.1	136.6	147.4	147.4
Monthly earnings index	...	...	...	...	...	...	...

Land use (1985): forested 38.2%; meadows and pastures 45.7%; agricultural and under permanent cultivation 10.3%; other 5.8%.
Gross national product (1986): U.S.$150,000,000 (U.S.$170 per capita).

Structure of gross domestic product and labour force

	1985 in value PG '000,000	1985 % of total value	1979 labour force	1979 % of labour force
Agriculture	12,250	57.8	153,069	71.9
Mining and manufacturing	900	4.2	3,067	1.4
Construction	650	3.1	1,667	0.8
Public utilities	}		162	0.1
Transportation and communications	} 3,000	14.2	2,372	1.1
Trade			5,085	2.4
Finance			162	0.1
Pub. admin., defense	3,950	18.6	26,194	12.3
Services	450	2.1 }		
Other	...	...	21,232	10.0
TOTAL	21,200[5]	100.0	213,010	100.0[6]

Household income and expenditure. Average household size (1981) 4.1; income per household: n.a.; sources of income: n.a.; expenditure: n.a.

Foreign trade

Balance of trade (current prices)

	1980	1981	1982	1983	1984	1985
US$'000,000	−49.8	−38.1	−57.6	−49.8	−42.7	−51.4
% of total	68.8%	57.8%	79.9%	74.0%	55.1%	68.9%

Imports (1985): US$63,000,000 (food, beverages, and tobacco 23.3%; oil and petroleum products 12.5%; other 64.2%). *Major import sources:* Portugal 20.1%; Italy 14.7%; Belgium–Luxembourg 10.9%; France 6.0%; West Germany 5.8%; The Netherlands 5.5%; Burma 3.3%; Senegal 2.8%; U.S.S.R. 2.3%; China 2.3%; Eastern European countries 1.5%.
Exports (1985): PG 11,600,000 (vegetables and fruits, including peanuts and cashew nuts 53.1%; fish, including shrimp 11.4%; cork and wood 10.4%; palm kernels 10.4%; groundnuts 7.3%; cotton 5.2%). *Major export destinations:* Romania 44.6%; France 16.1%; Portugal 12.5%; China 12.5%; Spain 4.5%; Senegal 3.7%; Belgium–Luxembourg 3.5%.

Transport and communications

Transport. Railroads: none. Roads (1983): total length 3,143 mi, 5,058 km (paved, 8.0%). Vehicles (1982): private motor vehicles 4,100. Merchant marine (1987): vessels (100 gross tons and over) 17; total deadweight tonnage 2,846. Air transport (1985): passenger-mi 6,000,000, passenger-km 9,000,000; short ton-mi cargo 700,000, metric ton-km cargo 1,000,000; airports (1988) with scheduled flights 1.
Communications. Daily newspapers (1984): total number 1; total circulation 6,000; circulation per 1,000 population 7.0. Radio (1986): total number of receivers 26,000 (1 per 34 persons). Television: none. Telephones (1986): 3,000 (1 per 297 persons).

Education and health

Education (1984–85)

	schools	teachers	students	student/ teacher ratio
Primary (age 7–13)	668	3,153	81,444	25.8
Secondary (age 13–18)	12	650	11,710	18.0
Voc., teacher tr.	4	107	1,027	9.6

Educational attainment (1979). Percent of population age 7 and over having: no formal schooling or knowledge of reading and writing 90.4%; primary education 7.9%; secondary 1.0%; technical 0.5%; higher 0.2%. *Literacy* (1985): total population age 15 and over literate 31.4%; males literate 46.2%; females literate 17.3%.
Health: physicians (1980) 108 (1 per 7,287 persons); hospital beds (1983) 1,593 (1 per 526 persons); infant mortality rate per 1,000 live births (1980–85) 143.0.
Food (1984–86): daily per capita caloric intake 2,278 (vegetable products 93%, animal products 7%); (1983) 82% of FAO recommended minimum requirement.

Military

Total active duty personnel (1987): 8,550[7] (army 95.9%, navy 3.2%, air force 0.9%). *Military expenditure as percent of GNP* (1983): 8.4% (world 6.1%); per capita expenditure U.S.$11.

[1]Preliminary. [2]Biombo region excludes Bissau city. [3]1985. [4]Production figure for first three quarters only. [5]At current factor cost. [6]Detail does not add to total given because of rounding. [7]Includes Gendarmerie.

Guyana

Official name: Co-operative Republic of Guyana.
Form of government: unitary multiparty republic with one legislative house (National Assembly [65[1]]).
Head of state and government: President assisted by Prime Minister.
Capital: Georgetown.
Official language: English.
Official religion: none.
Monetary unit: 1 Guyana dollar (G$) = 100 cents; valuation (Oct. 10, 1988) 1 U.S.$ = G$10.00; 1 £ = G$17.13.

Area and population

Administrative Regions	area sq mi	area sq km	population 1980 census
Region 1 (Barima/Waini)	...	...	18,297
Region 2 (Pomeroon/Supenaam)	...	...	42,268
Region 3 (Essequibo Islands/West Demerara)	...	...	104,747
Region 4 (Demerara/Mahaica)	...	...	318,952
Region 5 (Mahaica/Berbice)	...	...	53,862
Region 6 (East Berbice/Corentyne)	...	...	152,517
Region 7 (Cuyuni/Mazaruni)	...	...	14,142
Region 8 (Potaro/Siparuni)	...	...	4,265
Region 9 (Upper Takutu/Upper Essequibo)	...	...	13,051
Region 10 (Upper Demerara/Berbice)	...	...	36,518
TOTAL	83,000[2]	215,000[2]	758,619

Demography

Population (1988): 757,000.
Density (1988): persons per sq mi 9.1, persons per sq km 3.5.
Urban-rural (1986): urban 32.1%; rural 67.9%.
Sex distribution (1985): male 50.16%; female 49.84%.
Age breakdown (1985): under 15, 37.5%; 15–29, 31.9%; 30–44, 15.8%; 45–59, 8.8%; 60–74, 4.8%; 75 and over, 1.2%.
Population projection: (1990) 765,000; (2000) 821,000.
Doubling time: 39 years.
Ethnic composition (1983): East Indian 51.2%; black (African Negro and Bush Negro) 29.4%; mulatto 13.1%; Amerindian 4.0%, of which Carib 2.8%, Arawak 1.1%; Portuguese 0.8%; Chinese 0.5%; other 1.0%.
Religious affiliation (1980): Christian 52.0%, of which Protestant 34.0% (including Anglican 16.0%), Roman Catholic 18.0%; Hindu 34.4%; Muslim 9.0%; traditional beliefs 2.2%; other 2.4%.
Major cities (1985): Georgetown 200,000; Linden 35,000; New Amsterdam 25,000; Corriverton 13,718[3]; Rose Hall 5,311[3].

Vital statistics

Birth rate per 1,000 population (1985): 25.5 (world avg. 29.0); legitimate, n.a.; illegitimate, n.a.
Death rate per 1,000 population (1985): 7.6 (world avg. 11.0).
Natural increase rate per 1,000 population (1985): 17.9 (world avg. 18.0).
Total fertility rate (avg. births per childbearing woman; 1987): 2.9.
Marriage rate per 1,000 population: n.a.
Divorce rate per 1,000 population: n.a.
Life expectancy at birth (1980–85): male 66.9 years; female 70.9 years.
Major causes of death per 100,000 population (1977): diseases of the circulatory system 236.2; infectious and parasitic diseases 88.1; diseases of the respiratory system 69.3; accidents, poisonings, and violence 67.3; ill-defined conditions 95.9.

National economy

Budget (1986). Revenue: G$842,000,000 (current revenue 93.0%, of which income taxes 35.5%, consumption taxes 25.6%, excise duties 5.5%; development revenue 7.0%). Expenditures: G$1,947,200,000 (current expenditure 64.3%, of which debt charges 23.2%, general public services 16.0%, defense 8.1%, education 4.1%, health 3.1%; development expenditure 35.7%).
Production (metric tons except as noted). Agriculture, forestry, fishing (1986): sugarcane 3,365,000, rice 357,000, coconuts 41,000, roots and tubers 30,000, plantains 18,000, oranges 11,000, pineapples 2,000; livestock (number of live animals) 200,000 cattle, 180,000 pigs, 120,000 sheep, 15,000,000 chickens; roundwood 192,000 cu m[4]; fish catch 42,095[4], of which shrimps and prawns 3,410[4]. Mining and quarrying (1987): bauxite 1,500,000[5], of which calcined bauxite 492,000[5]; gold 21,400 troy oz; diamonds 7,000 carats. Manufacturing (1985): refined sugar 221,000[6]; stock feeds 25,500; rum 179,000 hectolitres; beer 80,000 hectolitres; cigarettes 467,000,000 units. Construction: n.a. Energy production (consumption): electricity (kW-hr; 1986) 390,000,000 (390,000,000); coal, none (none); crude petroleum, none (none); petroleum products (metric tons; 1986) none (439,000); natural gas, none (none).
Population economically active (1980)[7]: total 239,331; activity rate of total population 31.5% (participation rates: ages 15–64, 57.3%; female 24.8%; unemployed [1985] c. 30.0%).

Price and earnings indexes (1980 = 100)

	1981	1982	1983	1984	1985	1986	1987
Consumer price index	124.7	150.0	169.9	212.7	244.7	263.9	313.9
Weekly earnings index[8]	110.0	168.9	160.7	...	...	...	...

Household income and expenditure. Average household size (1980) 5.0; income per household: n.a.; sources of income (1974): wages and salaries 73.0%, transfer payments 6.3%, other 20.7%; expenditure (1970)[9]: food, beverages, and tobacco 42.5%, rent and water 21.5%, clothing and footwear 8.6%, education and recreation 6.4%, fuel and light 5.2%, other 15.8%.
Gross national product (at current market prices; 1986): U.S.$400,000,000 (U.S.$500 per capita).

Structure of gross domestic product and labour force

	1986 in value U.S.$'000,000[10]	1986 % of total value	1980 labour force[7]	1980 % of labour force
Agriculture	151	26.5	48,603	20.3
Mining	45	7.9	9,389	3.9
Manufacturing	60	10.5	27,939	11.7
Construction	40	7.0	6,574	2.8
Public utilities	11	11	2,772	1.2
Transportation and communications	42	7.4	9,160	3.8
Trade	39	6.9	14,690	6.1
Finance	39	6.9	2,878	1.2
Pub. admin., defense	125[11]	22.0[11] }	57,416	24.0
Services	13	2.3		
Other	15	2.6	59,910[12]	25.0
TOTAL	569	100.0	239,331	100.0

Public debt (external, outstanding; 1986): U.S.$772,000,000.
Tourism: receipts from visitors (1986) U.S.$4,000,000; expenditures by nationals abroad (1983) U.S.$11,000,000.
Land use (1985): forested 83.2%; meadows and pastures 6.2%; agricultural and under permanent cultivation 2.5%; other 8.1%.

Foreign trade[13]

Balance of trade (current prices)

	1980	1981	1982	1983	1984	1985
G$'000,000	+74.6	−124.3	−45.4	−103.7	+61.1	−82.3
% of total	3.9%	6.0%	3.0%	8.4%	3.9%	4.9%

Imports (1985): G$1,053,500,000 (fuels and lubricants 44.3%, capital goods 17.8%, consumer goods 10.3%). *Major import sources:* Trinidad and Tobago 26.8%; United States 17.6%; Barbados 14.4%; Venezuela 13.3%; United Kingdom 9.8%.
Exports (1985): G$875,400,000 (calcined bauxite 34.4%, sugar 31.2%, dried bauxite 11.6%, rice 6.3%, rum 3.2%, shrimps 2.0%, timber 2.0%). *Major export destinations:* United Kingdom 26.7%; United States 21.1%; West Germany 7.6%; Canada 7.4%; Trinidad and Tobago 6.8%.

Transport and communications

Transport. Railroads: length (1985) 65 mi, 109 km; passenger-mi; none; short ton-mi cargo, n.a. Roads (1985): total length 5,524 mi, 8,890 km (paved 9%). Vehicles (1985): passenger cars 25,541; trucks and buses 7,648. Merchant marine (1987): vessels (100 gross tons and over) 100; total deadweight tonnage 20,406. Air transport (1985): passenger-mi 104,000,000, passenger-km 168,000,000; short ton-mi cargo 12,000,000, metric ton-km cargo 18,000,000; airports (1988) with scheduled flights 18.
Communications. Daily newspapers (1986): total number 2; total circulation 78,000; circulation per 1,000 population 98. Radio (1986): total number of receivers 350,000 (1 per 2.3 persons). Television (1987): n.a.[14]. Telephones (1986): 33,000 (1 per 24 persons).

Education and health

Education (1983)

	schools	teachers	students	student/ teacher ratio
Primary (age 6–11)	423[15]	3,257	121,869	37.4
Secondary (age 12–17)	88	3,334	64,518	19.4
Voc., teacher tr.[16]	15	348	4,647	13.4
Higher[5]	1	258	1,626	6.3

Educational attainment (1980). Percent of population age 25 and over having: no formal schooling 8.1%; primary education 72.8%; secondary 17.3%; higher 1.8%. *Literacy* (1980): total population age 15 and over literate 505,-300 (95.5%); males literate 255,200 (97.1%); females literate 250,100 (94.0%).
Health: physicians (1982) 270 (1 per 2,860 persons); hospital beds (1979) 4,002 (1 per 188 persons); infant mortality rate per 1,000 live births (1985) 41.0.
Food (1984–86): daily per capita caloric intake 2,456 (vegetable products 89%, animal products 11%); (1983) 104% of FAO recommended minimum requirement.

Military

Total active duty personnel (1987): 5,425[17] (army 92.2%, navy 4.1%, air force 3.7%). *Military expenditure as percent of GNP* (1985): 8.9% (world 6.1%); per capita expenditure U.S.$43.

[1]Includes 12 seats not popularly elected. [2]Estimated; no dated survey available. [3]1980. [4]1985. [5]1986. [6]1987. [7]Ages 15–64 only. [8]Wages in nonagricultural activities excluding public utilities, finance and real estate, and services. [9]Weights of consumer price index components for Georgetown, New Amsterdam, and Linden only. [10]At factor cost. [11]Public administration, defense includes Public utilities. [12]Includes 15,-260 persons in activities not adequately defined and 44,650 unemployed. [13]Import figures are f.o.b. in balance of trade and c.i.f. in commodities and trading partners. [14]No television service within Guyana. [15]1981. [16]1979–80. [17]All services are part of the army.

Haiti

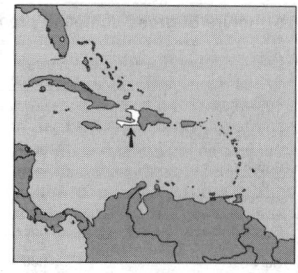

Official name: Repiblik Dayti (Haitian Creole): République d'Haïti (French) (Republic of Haiti).
Form of government: military regime.
Head of state and government:
 President.
Capital: Port-au-Prince.
Official languages: Haitian Creole; French.
Official religion: none.
Monetary unit: 1 gourde (G) = 100 centimes; valuation (Oct. 10, 1988) 1 U.S.$ = G 5.00; 1 £ = G 8.56.

Area and population		area		population
Departements	Capitals	sq mi	sq km	1987 estimate
Artibonite	Gonaïves	1,750	4,532	789,019
Centre	Hinche	1,429	3,700	393,217
Grande Anse	Jérémie	1,268	3,284	514,962
Nord	Cap-Haïtien	790	2,045	602,336
Nord-Est	Fort-Liberté	676	1,752	197,669
Nord-Ouest	Port-de-Paix	899	2,330	320,632
Ouest	Port-au-Prince	1,795	4,649	1,808,274
Sud	Les Cayes	1,117	2,894	526,420
Sud-Est	Jacmel	855	2,215	379,273
TOTAL		10,579	27,400[1]	5,531,802[2]

Demography

Population (1988): 5,451,000.
Density (1988): persons per sq mi 515.3, persons per sq km 198.9.
Urban–rural (1987): urban 26.0%; rural 74.0%.
Sex distribution (1982): male 48.48%; female 51.52%.
Age breakdown (1982): under 15, 39.2%; 15–29, 26.9%; 30–44, 15.6%; 45–59, 10.0%; 60–74, 5.4%; 75 and over, 2.9%.
Population projection: (1990) 5,590,000; (2000) 6,338,000.
Doubling time: 30 years.
Ethnic composition (1985): black 95.0%; mulatto 5.0%.
Religious affiliation (1982): Roman Catholic 80.3%[3]; Protestant 15.8%, of which Baptist 9.7%, Pentecostal 3.6%; other 3.9%.
Major cities (1987): Port-au-Prince 472,895; Cap-Haïtien 72,161; Gonaïves 37,034; Les Cayes 35,829; Pétionville 35,333[4].

Vital statistics

Birth rate per 1,000 population (1985): 36.0 (world avg. 29.0).
Death rate per 1,000 population (1985): 13.0 (world avg. 11.0).
Natural increase rate per 1,000 population (1985): 23.0 (world avg. 18.0).
Total fertility rate (avg. births per childbearing woman; 1984): 4.5.
Marriage rate per 1,000 population (1980): 0.7[5].
Divorce rate per 1,000 population (1980): 0.1[5].
Life expectancy at birth (1980–85): male 51.2 years; female 54.4 years.
Major causes of death per 100,000 population (1982)[6]: infectious and parasitic diseases 46.0, of which tuberculosis 13.1; diseases of the circulatory system 11.9; diseases associated with malnutrition 8.5; diseases of the respiratory system 8.3; endocrine and metabolic disorders 8.0; ill-defined conditions 115.2.

National economy

Budget (1986). Revenue: G 1,596,800,000 (tax revenue 64.1%, of which excises 18.4%, import duties 16.0%, general sales taxes 11.1%; nontax revenue and foreign grants 35.9%). Expenditures: G 1,780,400,000[7] (goods and services 53.8%; interest payments 7.1%).
Production (metric tons except as noted). Agriculture, forestry, fishing (1986–87): sugarcane 4,543,000, sweet potatoes 360,000[8], mangoes 350,000[8], plantains 275,000[8], bananas 235,000[8], corn (maize) 206,000, rice 135,000, sorghum 124,000, dry beans 49,000, oranges 32,000[8], coffee 30,000, cacao 5,200; livestock (number of live animals; 1986) 1,400,000 cattle, 1,100,000 goats, 700,000 pigs; roundwood (1985) 5,902,000 cu m; fish catch (1985) 4,400. Mining and quarrying (1986–87): limestone 246,000. Manufacturing (value of production in G '000,000; 1986–87): articles assembled for reexport 1,559 (including garments 688, transformers and switches 315, sports equipment and toys 238, jewelry, optical goods, and recording discs 151); cement 253,000 metric tons; flour 91,800 metric tons; essential oils (mostly amyris, neroli, and vetiver) 167 metric tons; cigarettes 888,000,000 units. Construction: n.a. Energy production (consumption): electricity (kW-hr; 1986) 438,000,000 (438,000,000); coal, none (none); crude petroleum, none (none); petroleum products (metric tons; 1986) none (200,000); natural gas, none (none).
Household income and expenditure. Average household size (1982) 4.4; sources of income: n.a.; expenditure (1976): food and beverages 77.9%[9], housing 8.3%, household furnishings 4.0%, clothing and footwear 3.2%, other 6.6%.
Population economically active (1983): total 2,263,832; activity rate of total population 44.2% (participation rates: ages 15–64, 69.1%; female 42.9% (unemployed [1987] unofficially 60.0%).

Price and earnings indexes (1980 = 100)							
	1982	1983	1984	1985	1986	1987	1988[10]
Consumer price index	119.0	131.2	139.6	154.5	159.5	141.3	144.8
Daily earnings index[11]	118.2	120.0	120.0	136.4	...	...	...

Public debt (external, outstanding; 1986): U.S.$584,700,000.
Gross national product (at current market prices; 1985): U.S.$1,900,000,000 (U.S.$360 per capita).

Structure of gross domestic product and labour force				
	1986		1983	
	in value U.S.$'000,000	% of total value	labour force	% of labour force
Agriculture	602	32.4	1,299,440	57.4
Mining	2	0.1	20,374	0.9
Manufacturing	280	15.1	129,038	5.7
Construction	112	6.0	22,638	1.0
Public utilities	17	0.9	2,264	0.1
Transp. and commun.	42	2.3	18,111	0.8
Trade	328	17.7	303,353	13.4
Finance	103	5.5	4,528	0.2
Pub. admin., defense	138	7.4	...	...
Services	232	12.5	133,566	5.9
Other	—	—	330,520[12]	14.6[12]
TOTAL	1,856	100.0[1]	2,263,832	100.0

Tourism (1986): receipts from visitors U.S.$58,000,000; expenditures by nationals abroad U.S.$38,000,000.
Land use (1985): forested 1.9%; meadows and pastures 18.1%; agricultural and under permanent cultivation 32.8%; other 47.2%.

Foreign trade[13,14]

Balance of trade (current prices)						
	1981–82	1982–83	1983–84	1984–85	1985–86	1986–87
G '000,000	−623.9	−696.5	−616.4	−608.5	−562.3	−570.0
% of total	26.0%	27.2%	22.3%	21.4%	22.8%	22.4%

Imports (1986–87): G 1,884,300,000 (food and live animals 18.6%; machinery and transport equipment 17.4%; basic manufactures 15.8%; petroleum products 13.4%; chemical products 10.2%). *Major import sources:* United States 45.6%; Caribbean area 13.6%; Japan 6.9%; Canada 6.0%; France 4.9%.
Exports (1986–87): G 1,001,800,000 (assembled manufactured goods for reexport 51.9%; coffee 17.5%; leather, wood, and other local handicrafts 13.4%; cocoa 2.3%; essential oils 1.8%). *Major export destinations:* United States 52.7%; Italy 12.2%; France 11.0%; Belgium 8.1%; Caribbean area 5.0%.

Transport and communications

Transport. Railroads (1986)[15]. Roads (1985): total length 2,299 mi, 3,700 km (paved 17%). Vehicles (1985): passenger cars 34,669; trucks and buses 11,658. Merchant marine (1987): vessels (100 gross tons and over) 2; total deadweight tonnage 170. Air transport (1986)[16]: passenger arrivals 248,676, passenger departures 238,582; cargo unloaded 14,740 metric tons, cargo loaded 14,901 metric tons; airports (1988) with scheduled flights 2.
Communications. Daily newspapers (1985): total number 6; total circulation 21,500; circulation per 1,000 population 4.0. Radio (1986): total number of receivers 200,000 (1 per 27 persons). Television (1987): total number of receivers 25,000 (1 per 215 persons). Telephones (1986): 82,000 (1 per 65 persons).

Education and health

Education (1984–85)				
	schools	teachers	students	student/ teacher ratio
Primary (age 6–12)	3,677	20,311	819,565	40.4
Secondary (age 13–18)	314[17]	6,106	154,271	25.3
Voc., teacher tr.	...	...	3,210	...
Higher[17]	...	818	5,492	6.7

Educational attainment (1982). Percent of population age 25 and over having: no formal schooling 76.9%; primary education 15.2%; secondary 7.2%; higher 0.7%. *Literacy* (1982): total population age 15 and over literate 1,066,966 (34.7%); males literate 547,318 (37.1%); females literate 519,648 (32.5%).
Health (1985): physicians 803 (1 per 6,539 persons); hospital beds (1982) 3,608 (1 per 1,397 persons); infant mortality rate per 1,000 live births 107.0.
Food (1983–85): daily per capita caloric intake 1,843 (vegetable products 95%, animal products 5%); (1983) 83% of FAO recommended minimum requirement.

Military

Total active duty personnel (1988): 7,600 (army 92.1%, navy 4.0%, air force 3.9%). *Military expenditure as percent of GNP* (1985): 1.6% (world 6.1%); per capita expenditure U.S.$6.

---

[1]Detail does not add to total given because of rounding. [2]Preliminary estimate; total revised downward to 5,382,800. [3]About 90% of all Roman Catholics also practice Voodoo. [4]1982 preliminary census figure. [5]Registered only. [6]Public health facilities only. [7]Current expenditure only; data for negligible development expenditure not available. [8]1986. [9]Excludes alcoholic beverages. [10]June. [11]Minimum wage in industrial enterprises. [12]Includes 54,332 not adequately defined and 276,188 unemployed persons not previously employed. [13]Import figures are f.o.b. in balance of trade and c.i.f. in commodities and trading partners. [14]Figures exclude large-scale smuggling from the United States and the Dominican Republic. [15]The only railway is privately owned and used to transport sugarcane. [16]Port-au-Prince airport only. [17]1983–84.

Honduras

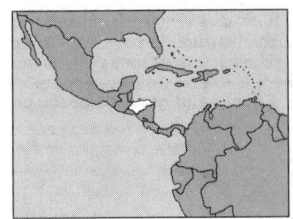

Official name: República de Honduras (Republic of Honduras).
Form of government: multiparty republic with one legislative house (Congress [134]).
Head of state and government: President.
Capital: Tegucigalpa[1].
Official language: Spanish.
Official religion: none.
Monetary unit: 1 Honduran lempira (L) = 100 centavos; valuation (Oct. 10, 1988) 1 U.S.$ = L 2.00; 1 £ = L 3.43.

Area and population

Departments	Administrative centres	area sq mi	area sq km	population 1985 estimate
Atlántida	La Ceiba	1,641	4,251	262,227
Choluteca	Choluteca	1,626	4,211	306,939
Colón	Trujillo	3,427	8,875	138,473
Comayagua	Comayagua	2,006	5,196	226,259
Copán	Santa Rosa de Copán	1,237	3,203	227,997
Cortés	San Pedro Sula	1,527	3,954	683,025
El Paraíso	Yuscarán	2,787	7,218	218,296
Francisco Morazán	Tegucigalpa	3,068	7,946	792,227
Gracias a Dios	Puerto Lempira	6,421	16,630	38,681
Intibucá	La Esperanza	1,186	3,072	115,677
Islas de la Bahía	Roatán	100	261	19,674
La Paz	La Paz	900	2,331	89,089
Lempira	Gracias	1,656	4,290	181,849
Ocotepeque	Nueva Ocotepeque	649	1,680	65,418
Olancho	Juticalpa	9,402	24,351	242,880
Santa Bárbara	Santa Bárbara	1,975	5,115	305,461
Valle	Nacaome	604	1,565	130,795
Yoro	Yoro	3,065	7,939	327,520
TOTAL		43,277	112,088	4,372,487

Demography

Population (1988): 4,803,000.
Density (1988): persons per sq mi 111.0, persons per sq km 42.9.
Urban–rural (1986): urban 40.7%; rural 59.3%.
Sex distribution (1985): male 50.14%; female 49.86%.
Age breakdown (1985): under 15, 46.9%; 15–29, 26.9%; 30–44, 13.8%; 45–59, 7.9%; 60–74, 3.7%; 75 and over 0.8%.
Population projection: (1990) 5,105,000; (2000) 6,978,000.
Doubling time: 21 years.
Ethnic composition (1982): mestizo 90.0%; black (including Black Carib) 5.0%; Indian 4.0%; white 1.0%.
Religious affiliation (1984): Roman Catholic 96.1%; other 3.9%.
Major cities (1986): Tegucigalpa 604,600[2]; San Pedro Sula 399,700; La Ceiba 63,800; Choluteca 60,700; El Progreso 58,300.

Vital statistics

Birth rate per 1,000 population (1985): 41.0 (world avg. 29.0); legitimate, n.a.; illegitimate, n.a.
Death rate per 1,000 population (1985): 8.0 (world avg. 11.0).
Natural increase rate per 1,000 population (1985): 33.0 (world avg. 18.0).
Total fertility rate (avg. births per childbearing woman; 1984): 6.2.
Marriage rate per 1,000 population (1983): 4.9.
Divorce rate per 1,000 population (1983): 0.4.
Life expectancy at birth (1983): male 60.2 years; female 63.9 years.
Major causes of death per 100,000 population (1981): infectious and parasitic diseases 80.9; accidents and violence 53.9; diseases of the circulatory system 53.1; diseases of the respiratory system 31.9; ill-defined conditions 160.2.

National economy

Budget (1986). Revenue: L 3,041,000,000 (current revenue 63.7%, of which nontax revenue 21.1%, tax on production and internal trade 11.7%, import duties 9.9%, individual income tax 8.3%; development revenue 36.3%). Expenditures: L 3,192,000,000 (current expenditure 60.9%, of which wages and salaries 31.6%; development expenditure 19.7%; debt servicing 17.0%).
Tourism (1986): receipts from visitors U.S.$26,000,000; expenditures by nationals abroad U.S.$30,000,000.
Production. Agriculture, forestry, fishing (gross value added in L '000,000 except as noted; 1985): bananas 366; coffee 244; wood 227; livestock 218; corn (maize) 120; sugarcane 54; apicultural, wild game, and fish products 49; beans 48; poultry products 45; rice 30; tobacco 24; cotton 24; plantains 20; African palm oil 18. Mining and quarrying (metric tons; 1986): limestone 500,000; zinc (metal content) 40,000; lead 19,000; silver 2,700,000 troy oz; gold 5,000 troy oz. Manufacturing (metric tons; 1986): cement 360,000; raw sugar 227,200; beef and veal 66,000; steel rods 11,800; beer 514,000 hectolitres; hard liquor 17,000 hectolitres; cigarettes 2,134,000,000 units. Construction (1986)[3]: residential 214,000 sq m; nonresidential 98,000 sq m. Energy production (consumption): electricity (kW-hr; 1986) 1,456,900,000 (1,216,900,000); coal, none (none); crude petroleum (barrels; 1986) none (2,016,000); petroleum products (metric tons; 1986) 251,000 (544,000); natural gas, none (none).
Land use (1985): forested 32.7%; meadows and pastures 30.4%; agricultural and under permanent cultivation 15.9%; other 21.0%.
Gross national product (at current market prices; 1986): U.S.$3,360,000,000 (U.S.$740 per capita).

Structure of gross domestic product and labour force

	1987 in value L '000,000	1987 % of total value	1984 labour force	1984 % of labour force
Agriculture	1,529	19.1	718,505	57.2
Mining	118	1.5	3,895	0.3
Manufacturing	1,015	12.7	167,597	13.3
Construction	383	4.8	43,470	3.5
Public utilities	133	1.7	5,151	0.4
Transportation and communications	483	6.0	37,565	3.0
Trade	957	11.9	107,292	8.5
Finance, real estate	1,056[4]	13.2	12,438	1.0
Public admin., defense	433	5.4	} 160,436	} 12.8
Services	930	11.6		
Other	983[5]	12.3		
TOTAL	8,020	100.0[6]	1,256,349	100.0

Public debt (external, outstanding; 1986): U.S.$2,341,700,000.
Population economically active (1984): total 1,256,349; activity rate of total population 29.7% (participation rates: ages 15–64, 53.6%; female 16.7%; unemployed [1987] 27.0%).

Price and earnings indexes (1980 = 100)

	1981	1982	1983	1984	1985	1986	1987
Consumer price index	109.4	119.2	129.1	135.2	139.7	145.8	149.4
Annual earnings index[7]	114.8	124.4	124.4	124.4	124.4	...	...

Household income and expenditure (1983): Average household size 5.7; income per household: n.a.; sources of income: wages and salaries 52.7%, transfer payments 1.7%, other 45.6%; expenditure: food 44.4%, utilities and housing 22.3%, clothing and footwear 9.1%, household furnishings 8.3%, health care 6.9%, other 9.0%.

Foreign trade[8]

Balance of trade (current prices)

	1981	1982	1983	1984	1985	1986
L '000,000	−256.8	+77.8	−140.1	−239.5	−80.9	+124.7
% of total	8.1%	3.0%	5.0%	7.4%	2.6%	3.8%

Imports (1986): L 1,750,100,000 (machinery and transport equipment 25.1%, basic manufactures 23.4%, chemical products 21.6%, mineral fuels 10.4%, food products 9.9%). *Major import sources:* U.S. 38.0%; Japan 8.7%; Venezuela 6.5%; Mexico 5.4%; Guatemala 4.2%.
Exports (1986): L 1,708,500,000 (coffee 37.3%, bananas 29.5%, shrimp and lobsters 5.2%, wood 3.7%, lead and zinc 2.4%). *Major export destinations:* U.S. 50.0%; West Germany 13.0%; Japan 11.0%; Italy 7.5%; Belgium 4.1%.

Transport and communications

Transport. Railroads (1986): route length 571 mi, 919 km; passengers, n.a.; cargo, n.a. Roads (1986): total length 10,831 mi, 17,431 km (paved 12%). Vehicles (1985): passenger cars 66,666; trucks and buses 18,759. Merchant marine (1987): vessels (100 gross tons and over) 503; total deadweight tonnage 741,691. Air transport (1985)[9]: passenger-mi 242,600,000, passenger-km 390,500,000; short ton-mi cargo 9,784,000, metric ton-km cargo 14,285,000; airports (1988) with scheduled flights 5.
Communications. Daily newspapers (1986): total number 7; total circulation 293,000; circulation per 1,000 population 65. Radio (1986): total number of receivers 300,000 (1 per 15 persons). Television (1987): total number of receivers 140,000 (1 per 33 persons). Telephones (1986): 49,659 (1 per 91 persons).

Education and health

Education (1986)

	schools	teachers	students	student/ teacher ratio
Primary (age 7–13)	6,710	20,732	805,504	38.9
Secondary (age 14–19)	428	6,945	130,247	18.8
Voc., teacher tr.	...	...	81,920	...
Higher[10]	7	2,692	34,478	14.0

Educational attainment (1983). Percentage of population age 25 and over having: no formal schooling 33.5%; incomplete primary education 51.3%; incomplete secondary 4.3%; complete secondary 7.6%; higher 3.3%. *Literacy* (1985): total population age 15 and over literate 1,381,000 (59.5%); males literate 706,000 (60.7%); females literate 675,000 (58.4%).
Health (1986): physicians 2,087 (1 per 2,163 persons); hospital beds 5,601 (1 per 703 persons); infant mortality rate per 1,000 live births (1985) 73.0.
Food (1983–85): daily per capita caloric intake 2,208 (vegetable products 89%, animal products 11%); (1983) 94% of FAO recommended minimum.

Military

Total active duty personnel (1987): 16,950 (army 86.1%, navy 5.0%, air force 8.9%). *Military expenditure as percent of GNP* (1985): 3.8% (world 6.1%); per capita expenditure U.S.$27.

[1]Tegucigalpa and adjacent city of Comayagüela jointly form the capital according to the constitution. [2]Population cited is for Central District (Tegucigalpa and Comayagüela). [3]Tegucigalpa, San Pedro Sula, and La Ceiba only. [4]Includes rent. [5]Includes net indirect taxes. [6]Detail does not add to total given because of rounding. [7]Average minimum wage paid in manufacturing and mining in Central District and San Pedro Sula only. [8]Import figures are f.o.b. in balance of trade and c.i.f. for commodities and trading partners. [9]TAN and SAHSA airlines only. [10]1985.

Hong Kong

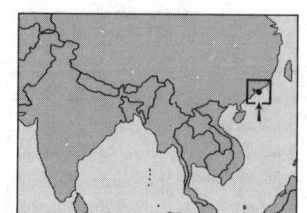

Official name: Hsiang Kang (Chinese); Hong Kong (English).
Political status: colony (United Kingdom) with three nominated advisory councils (Executive Council [15]; Legislative Council [57]; Urban Council [30]).
Chief of state: British Monarch.
Head of government: Governor.
Capital: none[1].
Official languages: Chinese; English.
Official religion: none.
Monetary unit: 1 HK dollar (HK$) = 100 cents; valuation (Oct. 10, 1988) 1 U.S.$ = HK$7.82; 1 £ = HK$13.39.

Area and population	area[2]		population[3]
Area	sq mi	sq km	1986 census
Hong Kong Island	30.4	78.7	1,175,860
Kowloon	16.3	42.2	2,301,691
New Territories	356.6	923.7	1,881,166
Marine	—	—	37,280
TOTAL	403.3	1,044.6	5,395,997

Demography

Population (1988): 5,683,000.
Density[4] (1987): persons per sq mi 14,091.2, persons per sq km 5,440.4.
Urban–rural (1987): urban 100.0%.
Sex distribution (1987): male 51.42%; female 48.58%.
Age breakdown[2] (1986): under 15, 23.1%; 15–29, 29.9%; 30–44, 21.2%; 45–59, 14.3%; 60–74, 9.1%; 75 and over, 2.4%.
Population projection: (1990) 5,823,000; (2000) 6,582,000.
Doubling time: 91 years.
Ethnic composition (1987): Chinese 97.0%; Filipino 0.7%; British 0.3%; other 2.0%.
Religious affiliation (1988): predominantly Buddhist and Taoist; however, there are about 500,000 Christians, 50,000 Muslims, and 12,000 Hindus.
Major cities: no bounded localities exist within Hong Kong.

Vital statistics

Birth rate per 1,000 population (1987): 12.5 (world avg. 26.0); legitimate (1985) 94.5%; illegitimate 5.5%.
Death rate per 1,000 population (1987): 4.8 (world avg. 9.9).
Natural increase rate per 1,000 population (1987): 7.7 (world avg. 16.1).
Total fertility rate (avg. births per childbearing woman; 1987): 1.4.
Marriage rate per 1,000 population (1987): 9.0.
Divorce rate per 1,000 population (1987): 1.0.
Life expectancy at birth (1987): male 73.0 years; female 78.5 years.
Major causes of death per 100,000 population (1987): malignant neoplasms (cancers) 150.2; diseases of circulatory system 139.1; diseases of respiratory system 77.5; accidents and poisoning 27.9; diseases of the genitourinary system 21.8; diseases of digestive system 19.9.

National economy

Budget (1987–88 est.). Revenue: HK$50,905,000,000 (earnings and profit taxes 43.3%; indirect taxes 26.1%, of which entertainment and stamp duties 13.1%, duties 7.3%; capital revenue 10.0%). Expenditures: HK$53,435,200,000 (education 18.3%; housing 11.9%; medical 9.7%; law and order 8.8%; general services support 8.2%; culture and recreation 6.2%; social welfare 5.8%).
Public debt: n.a.
Gross domestic product (at current market prices; 1986): U.S.$37,360,000,000 (U.S.$6,720 per capita).

Structure of gross domestic product and labour force				
	1986			
	in value HK$'000,000	%,of total value	labour force	% of labour force
Agriculture	1,333	0.5	48,748	1.8
Mining	342	0.1	882	—
Manufacturing	62,252	21.9	985,517	35.8
Construction	12,758	4.5	173,172	6.3
Public utilities	8,385	3.0	18,053	0.7
Transp. and commun.	24,011	8.4	218,592	7.9
Trade	62,266	21.9	617,008	22.4
Finance	78,281	27.5	174,776	6.3
Pub. admin., defense, and services	47,926	16.8	498,039	18.1
Other	−12,971[5]	−4.6[5]	19,061	0.7
TOTAL	284,583	100.0	2,753,848	100.0

Production (metric tons except as noted). Agriculture, forestry, fishing (1987): vegetables 141,000, fruits and nuts 2,350, field crops 1,540, milk 2,200, eggs 194,400,000 units; livestock (number of live animals) 660,000[6] pigs, 790 cattle, 17,000,000 chickens; roundwood (1985) 180,000 cu m; fish catch 206,740, of which marine 164,220. Mining and quarrying (1987): clay and kaolin 92,504; feldspar 22,853. Manufacturing (value added in HK$; 1985): wearing apparel 12,416,000,000; textile 7,509,000,000; plastic products 4,769,000,000; consumer electrical appliances and products 3,917,000,000; fabricated metal products 3,585,000,000; publishing and printed material 2,730,000,000; electrical and electronic machinery 2,572,000,000. Construction (value in HK$; 1985): residential 6,622,000,000; nonresidential 12,536,000,000. Energy production (consumption): electricity (kW-hr; 1986) 21,412,000,000 (20,204,000,000); coal (metric tons; 1986) none (6,393,000); petroleum products (metric tons; 1986) none (3,614,000); natural gas (cu m; 1986) none (271,239,000).
Population economically active (1987): total 2,736,000; activity rate of total population 48.7% (participation rates: over age 15, 64.8%; female 48.6%; unemployed 1.7%).

Price and earnings indexes (1980 = 100)							
	1981	1982	1983	1984	1985	1986	1987
Consumer price index	114.2	126.2	138.6	150.0	154.7	159.2	168.0
Daily earnings index[7]	116.5	157.0	174.2	195.7	210.8	232.3	260.3

Household income and expenditure. Average household size (1986) 3.7; income per household (1983) HK$92,000 (U.S.$11,800); sources of income: n.a.; expenditure (1984–85): food 38.0%, housing 21.0%, clothing and footwear 7.0%, transportation and vehicles 7.0%, durable goods 4.0%, fuel and light 3.0%.
Tourism (1987): receipts from visitors U.S.$3,200,662,000; expenditures by nationals abroad, n.a.
Land use (1987): forested 20.5%; agricultural and under permanent cultivation 6.7%; fish ponds 2.0%; built-on, scrublands, and other 70.8%.

Foreign trade

Balance of trade (current prices)						
	1982	1983	1984	1985	1986	1987
HK$'000,000	−15,508	−14,743	−1,929	+3,733	+575	+86
% of total	5.7%	4.4%	0.4%	0.8%	0.1%	—

Imports (1987): HK$377,948,000,000 (machinery and transport equipment 26.0%, of which electrical machinery 9.3%, telecommunications equipment 5.7%; textile yarn and fabrics 15.2%; chemicals and related products 8.1%; apparel and accessories 6.9%; food and live animals 6.8%; photographic apparatus, watches, and clocks 5.5%). *Major import sources:* China 31.1%; Japan 19.0%; Taiwan 8.8%; United States 8.5%; South Korea 4.5%; Singapore 3.8%; United Kingdom 3.1%; West Germany 2.7%.
Exports (1987): HK$195,254,000,000[8] (clothing accessories and apparel 33.5%; machinery and transport equipment 22.1%, of which telecommunications equipment 7.6%, electrical machinery 7.4%; textile yarn and fabrics 8.2%; photographic apparatus, watches, and clocks 8.0%). *Major export destinations:* United States 37.3%; China 14.3%; West Germany 7.6%; United Kingdom 6.6%; Japan 4.9%; Canada 2.9%; The Netherlands 2.1%.

Transport and communications

Transport. Railroads (1987): length 21 mi, 34 km; passenger-mi 1,327,000,000, passenger-km 2,136,000,000; short ton-mi cargo 49,000,000, metric ton-km cargo 72,000,000. Roads (1987): total length 867 mi, 1,395 km (paved 100%). Vehicles (1987): passenger cars 183,787; trucks and buses 115,320. Merchant marine (1987): vessels (100 gross tons and over) 409; total deadweight tonnage 13,470,976. Air transport (1987): passenger arrivals 5,497,000, passenger departures 5,663,000; airports (1988) with scheduled flights 1.
Communications. Daily newspapers (1984): total number 68[9]; total circulation 3,189,000[10]; circulation per 1,000 population 602[10]. Radio (1986): total number of receivers 2,740,000 (1 per 2.0 persons). Television (1987): total number of receivers 1,357,000 (1 per 4.1 persons). Telephones (1987): 2,654,000 (1 per 2.1 persons).

Education and health

Education (1986–87)	schools	teachers	students	student/ teacher ratio
Primary (age 6–11)	714	19,368	531,993	27.5
Secondary (age 12–18)	397	18,323	434,145	23.7
Vocational	27	1,174	21,593	18.4
Higher	11	3,530	34,434	9.8

Educational attainment (1986). Percent of population age 25 and over having: no formal schooling 18.4%; primary education 35.6%; lower secondary 15.5%; upper secondary 18.4%; matriculation 4.4%; nondegree tertiary 2.7%, degreed tertiary 5.0%. *Literacy* (1985): total population age 15 and over literate 3,668,000 (88.1%); males literate 2,040,000 (94.7%); females literate 1,628,000 (80.9%).
Health (1987): physicians 5,484 (1 per 1,024 persons); hospital beds 25,004 (1 per 225 persons); infant mortality rate per 1,000 live births 7.5.
Food (1984–86): daily per capita caloric intake 2,779 (vegetable products 70%, animal products 30%); (1983) 117% of FAO recommended minimum requirement.

Military

Total active duty personnel (1987): 6,729[11] (army 86.1%; navy 9.9%; air force 4.0%). *Military expenditure as percent of GNP* (1984): 0.6% (world 5.9%); per capita expenditure U.S.$39.

[1]Victoria, for some time, had been regarded as the capital because it is the seat of the British administration of the Crown Colony. [2]Excludes the surface areas of reservoirs. [3]Excludes 26,100 transients and 9,100 Vietnamese refugees. [4]Density based on land area. [5]Less imputed bank service charges. [6]Excludes local pigs not slaughtered in abattoirs. [7]In manufacturing. [8]Excludes reexports valued at HK$182,780,000,000. [9]1987. [10]Thirty-five newspapers only. [11]British forces with a few locally enlisted personnel.

Hungary

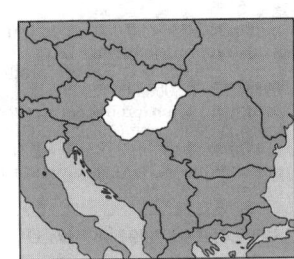

Official name: Magyar Népköztársaság
(Hungarian People's Republic).
Form of government: unitary single-
party republic with one legislative
house (National Assembly [387]).
Chief of State: President.
Head of government: Prime Minister.
Capital: Budapest.
Official language: Hungarian.
Official religion: none.
Monetary unit: 1 forint (Ft) = 100
filler; valuation (Oct. 10, 1988)
1 U.S.$ = Ft 53.50; 1 £ = Ft 91.63.

Area and population		area		population
		sq mi	sq km	1988 estimate[1]
Counties	Capitals			
Baranya	Pécs	1,732	4,487	433,188
Bács-Kiskun	Kecskemét	3,229	8,362	553,444
Békés	Békéscsaba	2,175	5,632	415,463
Borsod-Abaúj-Zemplén	Miskolc	2,798	7,246	778,659
Csongrád	Szeged	1,646	4,263	456,507
Fejér	Székesfehérvár	1,688	4,373	425,964
Győr-Sopron	Győr	1,549	4,013	426,277
Hajdú-Bihar	Debrecen	2,398	6,211	549,479
Heves	Eger	1,404	3,637	337,648
Komárom	Tatabánya	869	2,251	320,277
Nógrád	Salgótarján	982	2,544	228,817
Pest	Budapest[2]	2,469	6,394	987,899
Somogy	Kaposvár	2,331	6,036	349,437
Szabolcs-Szatmár	Nyíregyháza	2,292	5,937	569,729
Szolnok	Szolnok	2,165	5,607	428,762
Tolna	Szekszárd	1,430	3,703	263,201
Vas	Szombathely	1,288	3,337	276,957
Veszprém	Veszprém	1,810	4,689	387,106
Zala	Zalaegerszeg	1,461	3,784	310,846
Capital City				
Budapest[2]		203	525	2,104,700
TOTAL		35,919	93,031	10,604,360

Demography

Population (1988): 10,591,000.
Density (1988): persons per sq mi 294.8, persons per sq km 113.8.
Urban-rural (1988): urban 59.2%; rural 40.8%.
Sex distribution (1988): male 48.25%; female 51.75%.
Age breakdown (1988): under 15, 21.1%; 15–29, 19.5%; 30–49, 29.1%; 50–59, 11.8%; 60 and over, 18.5%.
Population projection: (1990) 10,554,000; (2000) 10,370,000.
During the intercensal period 1970–80, the average annual growth rate was 0.2%; since 1980, however, the population has been decreasing.
Ethnic composition (nationality; 1987): Magyar 96.6%; German 1.6%; Slovak 1.1%; other 0.7%.
Religious affiliation (1980): Christian 83.2%, of which Roman Catholic 53.9%, Protestant 21.6%; Jewish 0.9%; nonreligious 8.7%; atheist 7.2%.
Major cities (1988)[1]: Budapest 2,104,700; Debrecen 217,364; Miskolc 209,807; Szeged 187,800; Pécs 181,356.

Vital statistics

Birth rate per 1,000 population (1987): 11.8 (world avg. 26.0); (1985) legitimate 90.8%, illegitimate 9.2%.
Death rate per 1,000 population (1987): 13.4 (world avg. 9.9).
Natural increase rate per 1,000 population (1987): −1.6 (world avg. 16.1).
Total fertility rate (avg. births per childbearing woman; 1985): 1.7.
Marriage rate per 1,000 population (1987): 6.2.
Divorce rate per 1,000 population (1987): 2.9.
Life expectancy at birth (1987): male 65.3 years; female 73.2 years.
Major causes of death per 100,000 population (1987): diseases of the circulatory system 739.3; malignant neoplasms (cancers) 276.0.

National economy

Budget (1986). Revenue: Ft 682,000,000,000 (payments by enterprises 63.7%, turnover tax 15.1%, personal income tax 10.7%). Expenditures: Ft 727,300,-000,000 (expenditure of budgetary organs 30.1%, social welfare and health 19.5%, economic tasks 19.4%).
Public debt (external, outstanding; 1986): U.S.$13,567,100,000.
Tourism (1987): receipts from visitors U.S.$831,000,000; expenditures by nationals abroad U.S.$278,000,000.
Production (metric tons except as noted). Agriculture, forestry, fishing (1986): corn (maize) 7,024,000, wheat 5,744,000, sugar beets 3,764,000, barley 845,000, potatoes 812,000, sunflower seeds 810,000, rye 169,000; livestock (number of live animals; 1987) 8,216,000 pigs, 2,336,000 sheep, 1,664,000 cattle, 64,000,000 poultry; roundwood 6,929,000 cu m; fish catch 36,062. Mining and quarrying (1987): bauxite 3,101,142; dolomite 1,200,-000; iron ore 119,000. Manufacturing (1987): cement 4,153,000; crude steel 3,622,000; rolled steel 2,825,000; pig iron 2,109,000; chemical fertilizers 1,247,000; aluminum 183,000; cotton fabrics 311,000,000 sq m; leather footwear 38,613,000 pairs; buses and trucks 13,537 units. Construction (1986): residential 4,633,000 sq m. Energy production (consumption): electricity (kW-hr; 1986) 28,042,000,000 (32,519,000,000); coal (metric tons; 1986) 23,128,000 (25,348,000); crude petroleum (barrels; 1986) 13,593,000 (59,006,000); petroleum products (metric tons; 1986) 8,227,000 (8,307,000); natural gas (cu m; 1986) 6,422,000,000 (10,808,000,000).
Gross national product (1986): U.S.$83,806,000,000 (U.S.$7,890 per capita).

Structure of net material product and labour force

	1986			
	in value Ft '000,000,000	% of total value	labour force	% of labour force
Agriculture	156.1	17.9	986,200	20.2
Mining and manufacturing	411.6	47.2	1,536,500	31.4
Construction	89.8	10.3	347,500	7.1
Public utilities	5.2	0.6	78,700	1.6
Transp. and commun.	79.3	9.1	400,500	8.2
Trade	119.5	13.7	508,800	10.4
Services	—	—	985,700	20.1
Other	10.5[3]	1.2[3]	48,600[4]	1.0[4]
TOTAL	872.0	100.0	4,892,500	100.0

Population economically active (1986): total 4,892,500; activity rate of total population 46.0% (participation rates: working age 78.4%; female 46.0%; unemployed, n.a.).

Price and earnings indexes (1980 = 100)						
	1981	1982	1983	1984	1985	1986	1987[5]
Consumer price index	104.6	111.8	120.0	129.9	138.9	146.4	163.0
Monthly earnings index	107.2	114.0	119.7	127.5	141.0	151.4	172.4

Household income and expenditure. Average household size (1986) 2.7; income per household Ft 194,700 (U.S.$4,200); sources of income: (1987): wages 65.9%, social income 34.1%; expenditure (1985): food 31.4%, clothing and footwear 10.5%, transportation 10.3%, housing 8.7%, beverages and tobacco 8.1%, culture and recreation 8.0%.
Land use (1987): forested 17.9%; meadows and pastures 13.9%; agricultural and under permanent cultivation 56.8%; other 11.4%.

Foreign trade

Balance of trade (current prices)						
	1981	1982	1983	1984	1985	1986	1987
Ft '000,000,000	−8.4	+5.5	+15.0	+30.0	+14.5	−19.4	−11.8
% of total	1.2%	0.8%	2.0%	3.8%	1.7%	2.3%	1.2%

Imports (1987): Ft 505,860,000,000 (machinery and transport equipment 26.7%; semifinished products 21.9%; fuel and electric energy 19.4%; raw and basic materials 12.8%; industrial consumer goods 11.7%; agricultural and food products 7.4%). *Major import sources:* U.S.S.R. 28.5%; West Germany 13.9%; East Germany 6.4%; Austria 6.4%; Czechoslovakia 5.4%; Poland 4.0%; Italy 2.7%; Yugoslavia 2.1%.
Exports (1987): Ft 494,110,000,000 (machinery and transport equipment 36.9%, of which road vehicles and parts 6.8%; food and agricultural products 20.0%; semifinished products 17.5%; industrial consumer goods 16.2%). *Major export destinations:* U.S.S.R. 32.7%; West Germany 9.8%; East Germany 5.6%; Austria 5.6%; Czechoslovakia 5.0%; Italy 3.6%; Poland 3.4%; United States 3.0%; Yugoslavia 2.5%.

Transport and communications

Transport. Railroads (1986): length 8,160 mi, 13,133 km; passenger-mi 6,974,000,000, passenger-km 11,224,000,000; short ton-mi cargo 15,131,-000,000, metric ton-km cargo 22,092,000,000. Roads (1986): total length 18,514 mi, 29,796 km (paved 98.0%). Vehicles (1987): passenger cars 1,660,300; trucks and buses 201,890. Merchant marine (1987): vessels (100 gross tons and over) 16; total deadweight tonnage 109,444. Air transport[6] (1987): passenger-mi 799,080,000, passenger-km 1,286,000,000; short ton-mi cargo 10,876,000, metric ton-km cargo 15,879,000; airports (1988) with scheduled flights 4.
Communications. Daily newspapers (1986): total number 29; total circulation 2,569,900; circulation per 1,000 population 242. Radio (1985): 5,500,-000 (1 per 2.0 persons). Television (1986): 2,958,000 (1 per 3.5 persons). Telephones (1987): 1,609,400 (1 per 6.6 persons).

Education and health

Education (1987–88)	schools	teachers	students	student/ teacher ratio
Primary (age 6–13)	3,540	90,925	1,277,300	14.0
Secondary (age 14–18)	186	8,368	125,811	15.0
Vocational	758	22,467	373,187	16.6
Higher	54	15,302	99,025	6.5

Educational attainment (1984). Percent of population age 7 and over having: no formal schooling 1.3%; primary education 65.5%; secondary 27.1%; higher 6.1%. *Literacy* (1984): total population age 15 and over literate 8,269,850 (98.9%); males literate 3,934,250 (99.2%); females literate 4,335,600 (98.6%).
Health (1987): physicians 30,924 (1 per 343 persons); hospital beds 104,581 (1 per 101 persons); infant mortality rate per 1,000 live births (1987) 17.4.
Food (1984–86): daily per capita caloric intake 3,540 (vegetable products 64%; animal products 36%); (1983) 135% of FAO recommended minimum.

Military

Total active duty personnel (1987): 106,000 (army 79.2%, air force 20.8%). *Military expenditure as percent of GNP* (1985): 4.4% (world 6.1%); per capita expenditure U.S.$332.

[1]January 1. [2]Budapest has separate county status. The area and population of the city are excluded from the larger county (Pest), which it administers. [3]Includes other material activities, balance of taxes on products and value differences, and cost of nonmaterial services. [4]Other material activities. [5]September. [6]Malev airline only.

Iceland

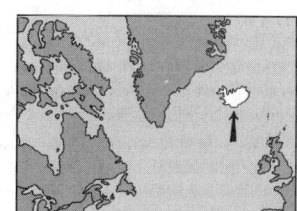

Official name: Lýdhveldidh Ísland (Republic of Iceland).
Form of government: unitary multiparty republic with two legislative houses (Upper House [21]; Lower House [42]).
Chief of state: President.
Head of government: Prime minister.
Capital: Reykjavík.
Official language: Icelandic.
Official religion: Evangelical Lutheran.
Monetary unit: 1 króna (ISK) = 100 aurar; valuation (Oct. 10, 1988) 1 U.S.$ = ISK 47.63; 1 £ = ISK 81.57.

Area and population

Regions Counties[1]	Administrative centres	area sq mi	area sq km	population 1987 estimate[2]
Austurland		8,683	22,490	13,096
Austur-Skaftafellssýsla	Höfn	2,347	6,080	2,173
Nordhur-Múlasýsla	Seydhisfjördhur	4,799	12,430	3,280
Sudhur-Múlasýsla	Eskifjördhur	1,537	3,980	7,643
Nordhurland eystra		8,370	21,680	25,925
Eyjafjardharsýsla	Akureyri	1,602	4,150	19,060
Nordhur-Thingeyjarsýsla	Húsavik	2,077	5,380	1,574
Sudhur-Thingeyjarsýsla	Húsavik	4,691	12,150	5,291
Nordhurland vestra		4,973	12,880	10,646
Austur-Húnavatnssýsla	Blönduós	1,900	4,920	2,622
Skagafjardharsýsla	Saudhárkrókur	2,077	5,380	6,516
Vestur-Húnavatnssýsla	Blönduós	996	2,580	1,508
Rekjavikursvaedhi og Reykjanessvaedhi		741	1,920	152,544
Gullbringusýsla	Keflavík	405	1,050	35,950
Kjósarsýsla	Hafnarfjördhur	336	870	116,594
Sudhurland		9,649	24,990	19,993
Árnessýsla	Selfoss	3,401	8,810	10,623
Rangárvallasýsla	Hvolsvöllur	3,197	8,280	8,082
Vestur-Skaftafellssýsla	Vík	3,050	7,900	1,288
Vestfirdhir		3,676	9,520	10,217
Austur-Bardhastran- darsýsla	Patreksfjördhur	444	1,150	374
Nordhur-Isafjardharsýsla	Ísafjördhur	1,181	3,060	5,110
Strandasýsla	Hólmavik	1,015	2,630	1,128
Vestur-Bardhastran- darsýsla	Patreksfjördhur	598	1,550	2,030
Vestur-Isafjardharsýsla	Ísafjördhur	436	1,130	1,575
Vesturland		3,676	9,520	14,936
Borgarfjardharsýsla	Borgarnes	753	1,950	6,811
Dalasýsla	Budhardalur	815	2,110	1,016
Mýrasýsla	Borgarnes	1,262	3,270	2,545
Snaefellsnessýsla	Stykkishólmur	846	2,190	4,564
TOTAL		39,768	103,000	247,357

Demography

Population (1988): 248,000.
Density (1988): persons per sq mi 6.2, persons per sq km 2.4.
Urban–rural (1987): urban 90.0%; rural 10.0%.
Sex distribution (1987): male 50.22%; female 49.78%.
Age breakdown (1987): under 15, 25.8%; 15–29, 26.1%; 30–44, 20.9%; 45–59, 13.2%; 60–74, 9.9%; 75 and over, 4.1%.
Population projection: (1990) 252,000; (2000) 276,000.
Doubling time: 72 years.
Ethnic composition (1986): native Icelander 96.9%; other European 2.4%; other 0.7%.
Religious affiliation (1986): Lutheran 96.7%; Roman Catholic 0.7%; other 2.6%.
Major cities (1987): Reykjavík 93,425; Kópavogur 15,037; Akureyri 13,856; Hafnarfjördhur 13,780; Keflavík 7,113.

Vital statistics

Birth rate per 1,000 population (1987): 16.9 (world avg. 26.0); legitimate (1986) 49.4%; illegitimate 50.6%.
Death rate per 1,000 population (1987): 6.9 (world avg. 9.9).
Natural increase rate per 1,000 population (1987): 10.0 (world avg. 16.1).
Total fertility rate (avg. births per childbearing woman; 1986): 1.9.
Marriage rate per 1,000 population (1986): 5.0.
Divorce rate per 1,000 population (1986): 2.0.
Life expectancy at birth (1985–86): male 75.0 years; female 80.4 years.
Major causes of death per 100,000 population (1985): heart and circulatory diseases 326.3; malignant neoplasms (cancers) 161.3; respiratory diseases 83.3; accidents, suicide, etc. 47.3.

National economy

Budget (1987). Revenue: ISK 48,963,000,000 (indirect taxes 81.3%, of which sales tax 52.9%, import duties 13.6%; income taxes 9.4%). Expenditures: ISK 51,688,000,000 (social services 61.1%, of which social security and welfare 24.0%, education 16.6%, health 16.0%; industrial services 18.3%; housing and community amenities 4.5%).
Public debt (1986): U.S.$867,920,000.
Tourism (1987): receipts from visitors U.S.$139,075,000; expenditures by nationals abroad U.S.$186,829,000.
Production (metric tons except as noted). Agriculture, forestry, fishing (1986): fodder crops 3,499,000, milk 119,000, potatoes 17,000; livestock (number of live animals; 1987) 624,300 sheep, 69,000 cattle, 59,200 horses; fish catch (1987) capelin 803,500, cod 389,800, herring 75,400, lobster, shrimp, and shellfish 41,400. Mining and quarrying (1986): diatomite 22,-

897. Manufacturing (1985): frozen fish 122,000; cement 117,000; salted fish 75,000; aluminum, refined 73,400; ferrosilicon 57,700. Construction (1985): residential 756,000 cu m, nonresidential 926,500[3] cu m. Energy production (consumption): electricity (kW-hr; 1986) 4,098,000,000 (4,098,000,000); coal (1986) none (74,000); petroleum, none (none); petroleum products (1986) none (468,000); natural gas, none (none).
Gross national product (1986): U.S.$3,260,000,000 (U.S.$13,370 per capita).

Structure of gross domestic product and labour force

	1987 in value ISK '000,000	1987 % of total value[4]	1984 labour force	1984 % of labour force
Agriculture	...	5.8 ⎫	23,726	20.3
Fishing and processing	...	16.9 ⎭		
Manufacturing	...	12.1	27,813	23.9
Construction	...	7.5	11,614	10.0
Public utilities	...	6.3		
Transp. and commun.	...	8.5	...	...
Trade	...	13.6	16,866	14.5
Pub. admin., defense, services, and other	...	29.4	36,540[5]	31.3
TOTAL	206,346	100.0[6]	116,559	100.0

Population economically active (1984): total 116,559; activity rate of total population 48.7% (participation rates: 15–64, n.a.; female 39.5%; unemployed 1.3%).

Price and earnings indexes (1980 = 100)

	1982	1983	1984	1985	1986	1987	1988[7]
Consumer price index	227.5	422.6	550.7	730.5	880.9	1,047.5	1,377.7
Hourly wages index	239.1	363.5	444.2	595.5	789.1	1,121.2	...

Household income and expenditure. Average household size: n.a.; disposable income per person (1982) ISK 82,240 (U.S.$6,660); sources of income (1983): wages and salaries 52.7%, self-employment 45.6%, transfer payments 1.7%; expenditure (1984): food 25.3%, housing 25.3%, transportation and communications 18.8%, education and recreation 10.1%, clothing and footwear 8.8%, health 1.7%, other 9.4%.
Land use (1985): forested 1.2%; meadows and pastures 22.7%; agricultural and under permanent cultivation 0.1%; other 76.0%[8].

Foreign trade

Balance of trade (current prices)

	1982	1983	1984	1985	1986	1987
ISK '000,000	−2,109	−90	−789	−356	+3,356	−2,617
% of total	11.1%	0.2%	1.6%	0.5%	3.9%	2.4%

Imports (1987): ISK 61,237,000,000 (machinery and transport equipment 26.8%, of which ships and aircraft 6.3%; fuels and lubricants 6.7%, of which gasoline 1.4%; construction materials 5.1%). *Major import sources:* West Germany 15.2%; Denmark 9.2%; U.K. 8.2%; Sweden 8.2%; Japan 8.2%; The Netherlands 8.1%; Norway 5.2%.
Exports (1987): ISK 53,053,000,000 (fish and fish products 76.0%, of which white fish 56.3%, lobster, shrimp, and scallops 8.9%; aluminum, refined 9.6%; agricultural products 1.3%). *Major export destinations:* U.K. 19.4%; U.S. 18.3%; West Germany 10.0%; Portugal 9.4%; Japan 7.8%.

Transport and communications

Transport. Railroads: none. Roads (1986): total length 7,068 mi, 11,376 km (paved 12%). Vehicles (1986): passenger cars 112,760; trucks and buses 13,-366. Merchant marine (1987): vessels (100 gross tons and over) 396; total deadweight tonnage 150,987. Air transport (1987): passenger-mi 1,719,356,-000, passenger-km 2,767,041,000; short ton-mi cargo 193,076,000, metric ton-km cargo 281,887,000; airports (1988) with scheduled flights 31.
Communications. Daily newspapers (1986): total number 6; total circulation c. 100,000; circulation per 1,000 population c. 412. Radio (1986): 79,000 receivers (1 per 3.1 persons). Television (1987): 71,143 receivers (1 per 3.4 persons). Telephones (1986): 102,657 (1 per 2.4 persons).

Education and health

Education (1982–83)

	schools	teachers	students	student/ teacher ratio
Primary (age 7–12)	187	2,600	25,000	9.6
Secondary (age 12–19)	157	...	21,800	...
Voc., teacher tr.	44	...	4,280	...
Higher	4	280	4,780	17.1

Educational attainment, n.a. *Literacy* (1984): total population age 15 and over literate 175,029 (100.0%).
Health (1985): physicians 626 (1 per 385 persons); hospital beds 2,677 (1 per 90 persons); infant mortality rate per 1,000 live births (1987) 3.4.
Food (1984–86): daily per capita caloric intake 3,146 (vegetable products 54%, animal products 46%); (1983) 113% of FAO recommended minimum.

Military

Iceland maintains no domestic military forces; external security is guaranteed by the NATO-sponsored U.S.-manned Iceland Defense Force, numbering no more than 2,900 (mostly air force). In 1986 a domestic coast guard consisted of about 125 officers and men.

[1]Counties include county cities and towns, which are within, but administratively independent of, the counties. [2]Dec. 1, 1986. [3]1984. [4]Percent of contribution to gross national product. [5]Includes 1,480 unemployed. [6]Detail does not add to total given because of rounding. [7]August. [8]Glaciated, covered with peat bogs, or lava desert.

India

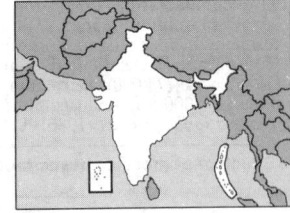

Official name: Bhārat (Hindī); Republic of India (English).
Form of government: multiparty federal republic with two legislative houses (Council of States [244][1], House of the People [546][2]).
Chief of state: President.
Head of government: Prime Minister.
Capital: New Delhi.
Official languages: Hindī; English.
Official religion: none.
Monetary unit: 1 Indian rupee (Rs) = 100 paisa; valuation (Oct. 10, 1988) 1 U.S.$ = Rs 14.39; 1 £ = Rs 24.65.

Area and population

States	Capitals	area sq mi	area sq km	population 1981 census
Andhra Pradesh	Hyderābād	106,204	275,068	53,549,673
Arunāchal Pradesh	Itanagar	32,333	83,743	631,839
Assam	Prāgjyotiṣapura	30,285	78,438	19,896,843[3]
Bihār	Patna	67,134	173,877	69,914,734
Goa	Panaji	1,430	3,702	1,007,749
Gujarāt	Gāndhinagar	75,685	196,024	34,085,799
Haryāna	Chandīgarh	17,070	44,212	12,922,618
Himāchal Pradesh	Simla	21,495	55,673	4,280,818
Jammu and Kashmir	Srinagar	39,145[4]	101,387[4]	5,987,389
Karnātaka	Bangalore	74,051	191,791	37,135,714
Kerala	Trivandrum	15,005	38,863	25,453,680
Madhya Pradesh	Bhopāl	171,215	443,446	52,178,844
Mahārāshtra	Bombay	118,800	307,690	62,784,171
Manipur	Imphāl	8,621	22,327	1,420,953
Meghālaya	Shillong	8,660	22,429	1,335,819
Mizorām	Aizawl	8,140	21,081	493,757
Nāgāland	Kohīma	6,401	16,579	774,930
Orissa	Bhubaneswar	60,119	155,707	26,370,271
Punjab	Chandīgarh	19,445	50,362	16,788,915
Rājasthān	Jaipur	132,140	342,239	34,261,862
Sikkim	Gangtok	2,740	7,096	316,385
Tamil Nādu	Madras	50,216	130,058	48,408,077
Tripura	Agartala	4,049	10,486	2,053,058
Uttar Pradesh	Lucknow	113,673	294,411	110,862,013
West Bengal	Calcutta	34,267	88,752	54,580,647
Union Territories				
Andaman and Nicobar Islands	Port Blair	3,185	8,249	188,741
Chandigarh	Chandigarh	44	114	451,610
Dādra and Nagar Haveli	Silvassa	190	491	103,676
Daman and Diu	...	43	112	78,981
Delhi	Delhi	572	1,483	6,220,406
Lakshadweep	Kavaratti	12	32	40,249
Pondicherry	Pondicherry	190	492	604,471
TOTAL		**1,222,559[4]**	**3,166,414[4]**	**685,184,692**

Demography

Population (1988): 801,806,000.
Density (1988)[4]: persons per sq mi 655.8, persons per sq km 253.2.
Urban–rural (1985): urban 25.5%; rural 74.5%.
Sex distribution (1985): male 51.74%; female 48.26%.
Age breakdown (1985): under 15, 36.8%; 15–29, 27.8%; 30–44, 17.2%; 45–59, 11.4%; 60–74, 5.7%; 75 and over, 1.1%.
Population projection: (1990) 825,000,000; (2000) 972,000,000.
Doubling time: 33 years.
Linguistic composition (1971): Hindī 28.1%; Telugu 8.2%; Bengali 8.1%; Marāṭhī 7.6%; Tamil 6.9%; Urdū 5.2%; Gujarātī 4.7%; Malayālam 4.0%; Kannada 3.9%; Oriyā 3.6%; Bhojpurī 2.6%; Punjābī 2.5%; Assamese 1.6%; Chhattisgarhī 1.2%; Magadhī 1.2%; Maithilī 1.1%; other 9.5%.
Religious affiliation (1981)[5]: Hindu 82.64%; Muslim 11.35%; Christian 2.43%; Sikh 1.97%; Buddhist 0.71%; Jain 0.48%; Zoroastrian 0.01%; other 0.41%.
Major cities (1981): Greater Bombay 8,243,405 (10,137,000[6]); Delhi 4,884,234 (6,993,000[6]); Calcutta 3,305,006 (10,462,000[6]); Madras 3,276,622 (4,983,-000[6]); Bangalore 2,476,355 (3,685,000[6]); Hyderābād 2,150,580 (3,022,000[6]); Ahmadābād 2,059,725 (3,037,000[6]); Kānpur 1,481,789; Nāgpur 1,219,461; Pune 1,203,351; New Delhi 273,036.

Other principal cities (1981)

	population		population		population
Āgra	694,191	Jaipur	977,165	Rānchi	489,626
Ajmer	375,593	Jalapur	614,162	Sholāpur	
Allahābād	616,051	Jamshedpur	438,385	(Solapur)	511,103
Amritsar	594,844	Jodhpur	506,345	South Suburban	378,765
Bareilly	386,734	Jullundur	408,196	Srinagar	586,038
Bhopāl	671,018	Kozhidkode		Surat	776,583
Chandigarh	373,789	(Calicut)	394,447	Tiruchchirāppalli	362,045
Cochin	513,249	Lucknow	895,721	Trivandrum	483,086
Coimbatore	704,514	Ludhiāna	607,052	Vadodara	
Dhārwār-Hubli	527,108	Madurai	820,891	(Baroda)	734,473
Guntūr	367,699	Meerut	417,395	Vārānasi	
Gwalior	539,015	Mysore	441,754	(Benares)	708,647
Howrah (Haora)	744,429	Patna	776,371	Vijayawāda	454,577
Indore	829,327	Rājkot	445,076	Vishākhapatnam	565,321

Place of birth (foreign born; 1981): other Asia 7,875,399, of which Bangladesh 4,170,524, Pakistan 2,736,038, Nepal 501,292, Sri Lanka 211,514, Burma 134,783; Africa 42,726; Europe 13,046; United States and Canada 5,923.

Mobility (1981). Population living in same district but at different residence as in 1971: 47,604,000; different district, same state 22,557,000; different state 10,860,000; moved outside the country 1,179,000.
Households[5] (1981). Total households 119,230,710. Average household size 5.6; 1 person 5.6%, 2 persons 8.3%, 3 persons 11.0%, 4 persons 14.6%, 5 persons 15.9%, 6 or more persons 44.6%. Average number of rooms per household 2.0; no exclusive room 0.6%, 1 room 44.7%, 2 rooms 28.6%, 3 rooms 12.2%, 4 rooms 6.3%, 5 rooms 2.7%, 6 or more rooms 3.1%, unspecified number of rooms 1.8%. Average number of persons per room 2.8. Homeless population (1987) estimated at more than 100,000,000.
Emigration (1984): persons living abroad 11,644,000 (accepting foreign citizenship, 7,394,000), of which in Nepal 3,800,000 (2,388,000); Malaysia 1,170,000 (1,030,000); Sri Lanka 1,028,000 (426,000); Middle Eastern countries 949,000 (112,000); United Kingdom 719,000 (359,000); Mauritius 697,000 (696,000); Guyana 500,000 (500,000); United States 440,000 (320,-000); Trinidad and Tobago 421,000 (420,000); Burma 350,000 (50,000).

Vital statistics

Birth rate per 1,000 population (1986): 32.4 (world avg. 26.0); legitimate, n.a.; illegitimate, n.a.
Death rate per 1,000 population (1986): 11.1 (world avg. 9.9).
Natural increase rate per 1,000 population (1986): 21.3 (world avg. 16.1).
Total fertility rate (avg. births per childbearing woman; 1987): 4.1.
Marriage rate per 1,000 population: n.a.
Divorce rate per 1,000 population: n.a.
Life expectancy at birth (1987): male 56.7 years; female 57.6 years.
Major causes of death (rural areas only; 1986)[7]: senility 22.4%; infectious and parasitic diseases 15.8%, of which tuberculosis 5.3%; diseases of the respiratory system 14.3%, of which bronchitis and asthma 8.5%; all causes peculiar to infancy 10.5%; diseases of the circulatory system 9.0%; diseases of the digestive system 7.7%; accidents, violence, and suicide 7.0%; diseases of the nervous system 3.7%.

Social indicators

Educational attainment (1981). Percent of population age 25 and over having: no formal schooling (illiterate) 64.8%; literate population with no formal schooling 0.9%; some primary education only 11.2%; some secondary only 6.2%; completed secondary 7.1%; higher 2.5%; other 7.3%.

Distribution of income (1975–76)

percent of household income by quintile:

1	2	3	4	5 (highest)
7.0%	9.2%	13.9%	20.5%	49.4%

Quality of working life (1981). Average workweek: 45 hours. Rate of fatal (nonfatal) injuries per 100,000 workers (1981–82): industrial workers 16 (7,657); miners 34 (371); railway workers 20 (1,531). Employees covered under Employee's State Insurance Scheme (1984–85) 7,011,500, number of beneficiaries 27,204,600. Average days lost to labour stoppages per 1,000 workdays (1986–87): 0.4. Average duration of journey to work: n.a. Rate per 1,000 workers of discouraged (unemployed no longer seeking work): n.a.
Access to services. Proportion of villages having access to electricity (1987–88) 73.6%; proportion of population having access to safe water supply (1984) 54.0%.
Social participation. Eligible voters participating in last (December 1984) national election: 64.0%. Verified trade union membership in total workforce (1986): less than 5% (about 10,000,000 workers). Practicing religious population in total affiliated population: n.a.
Social deviance (1984). Offense rate per 100,000 population for: murder 3.4; dacoity (gang robbery) 1.4; theft and housebreaking 43.7; rape 0.8. Incidence in general population of: alcoholism, n.a.; drug and substance abuse, n.a. Rate per 100,000 population of suicide (1983): 6.4.
Leisure (1987). Favourite leisure activities in urban areas: listening to the radio, watching television, reading periodicals, and attending the cinema.
Material well-being (1983). Households possessing: automobile 0.8%; telephone 2.3%; television receiver 1.6%; radio receiver 17.2%.

National economy

Gross national product (at current market prices; 1986): U.S.$213,440,000,-000 (U.S.$270 per capita).

Structure of gross domestic product and labour force

	1985–86 in value Rs '000,000,000	1985–86 % of total value	1981[5] labour force	1981[5] % of labour force
Agriculture	675.6	31.4	153,015,000	62.5
Mining	64.8	3.0	1,264,000	0.5
Manufacturing	358.0	16.7	25,143,000	10.3
Construction	116.3	5.4	3,565,000	1.5
Public utilities	47.2	2.2	974,000	0.4
Transp. and commun.	149.2	6.9	6,069,000	2.5
Trade	318.5	14.8	12,165,000	5.0
Finance, real estate	172.4	8.0	1,764,000	0.7
Pub. admin., defense	117.9	5.5	...	...
Services	130.3	6.1	18,557,000	7.6
Other	—	—	22,089,000[8]	9.0
TOTAL	2,150.2	100.0	244,605,000	100.0

Budget (1987–88). Revenue: Rs 562,468,400,000 (tax revenue 61.4%, of which excise taxes 29.6%, customs duties 22.9%, taxes on corporations 6.3%; nontax revenue 38.6%, of which interest receipts 11.1%). Expenditures: Rs 629,893,000,000 (transfers to local government 24.9%; interest payments 16.9%; defense 14.1%; transportation 14.1%; industry and minerals 4.4%; agriculture 4.3%; social services 3.3%).

Public debt (external, outstanding; 1986): U.S.$31,913,400,000.
Production (gross value of production in Rs '000,000 except as noted). Agriculture, forestry, fishing (1984–85): grains 281,180, of which rice 162,030, wheat 72,280, jowar (variety of sorghum) 17,780, bajra (variety of millet) 8,430; oilseeds 71,670, of which peanuts (groundnuts) 28,540, rapeseed and mustard 13,070; fruits and vegetables 70,370; pulses 46,260, of which gram (mostly chick-peas) 19,090; sugarcane 41,080; cotton 24,400; condiments and spices 21,700; tea 8,590; jute 6,890; tobacco 4,770; coffee 3,190; rubber 2,140; livestock (number of live animals; 1986) 200,000,000 cattle, 102,870,000 goats, 75,010,000 water buffalo, 54,460,000 sheep, 1,100,000 camels; roundwood (1985) 245,029,000 cu m; fish catch (metric tons; 1986–87) 2,920,000, of which freshwater fishes 1,200,000. Mining and quarrying (1986): crude petroleum 44,467; hard coal 33,318; iron ore 2,790; limestone 1,901; lignite 1,359; copper 886; chromite 500; gold 447; zinc 410[9]; manganese 340; lead 230[9]; bauxite 176; natural gas 140[9]; mica 24; diamonds 16,000 carats. Manufacturing (metric tons; 1987): cement 37,011,000; steel ingots 12,003,-000; finished steel 8,662,000; refined sugar 8,537,000; nitrogenous fertilizers 5,693,000; paper and paperboard 1,653,000; jute manufactures 1,236,000; vanaspati (hydrogenated vegetable fat) 947,100; soda ash 969,600; soap 475,000; hessian cloth (burlap) 295,000; copper cathodes 28,400; raw silk 7,897[10]; bicycles 6,544,000 units; electric motors 4,177,000 units; motorcycles and scooters 1,480,000 units; power-driven pumps 500,500 units; sewing machines 368,000 units; passenger cars and jeeps 123,900 units; tractors 78,500 units; cotton cloth 9,617,000,000 metres. Construction (value in Rs; 1984) residential 87,010,000,000; nonresidential 40,730,000,000.

Manufacturing enterprises (1983–84)

	no. of factories	no. of employees	annual wages as a % of avg. of all wages	annual value added (Rs '000,000)
Chemicals and chemical products	5,824	516,051	101.3	25,543
Food products	17,523	1,047,488	42.5	16,521
Cotton textiles	6,371	1,042,302	92.0	14,978
Nonelectrical machinery	7,138	454,051	110.6	14,023
Transport equipment	2,815	504,423	110.8	13,905
Electrical machinery	3,661	340,061	95.9	12,960
Nonmetallic mineral products	7,618	435,337	75.5	8,350
Wool, silk, and synthetic textiles	3,532	278,720	103.6	6,282
Rubber, plastic, petroleum, and coal products	3,778	199,775	58.0	6,177
Paper, paper products, printing, publishing, etc.	4,710	303,091	62.2	5,538
Beverages and tobacco products	8,188	446,643	51.0	5,340
Metal products	6,054	192,409	92.1	4,498
Jute, hemp, mesta textiles	236	222,274	86.9	2,104
Basic metals and alloys	5,888	638,508	101.1	2,043
Textile products, apparel	2,621	109,878	64.8	1,761
Leather products	942	64,158	61.6	1,129
Wood and wood products	3,599	80,160	64.4	1,070

Energy production (consumption): electricity (kW-hr; 1987) 198,101,000,-000 (202,489,000,000[10]); coal (metric tons; 1986) 174,124,000 (176,374,000); crude petroleum (barrels; 1987) 224,324,000 (334,428,000[10]); petroleum products (metric tons; 1986) 34,358,000 (36,591,000); natural gas (cu m; 1987) 7,055,000,000 (5,566,000,000[10]).

Financial aggregates[11]

	1982	1983	1984	1985	1986	1987	1988
Exchange rate, Rs per:							
U.S. dollar	9.63	10.49	12.45	12.17	13.12	12.88	14.73
£	15.55	15.22	14.40	17.59	19.35	24.10	25.57
SDR	10.63	10.99	12.20	13.36	16.05	18.27	19.96
International reserves (U.S.$)							
Total excl. gold; '000,000)	4,315	4,937	5,842	6,420	6,396	6,454	4,877[12]
SDRs ('000,000)	374	110	331	336	356	159	138
Reserve pos. in IMF ('000,000)	402	510	477	535	596	691	656[12]
Foreign exchange ('000,000)	3,539	4,318	5,034	5,549	5,444	5,603	4,132
Gold ('000,000 fine troy oz)	8.594	8.594	8.737	9.397	10.449	10.449	10.449[12]
% world reserves	0.9	0.9	0.9	0.9	1.1	1.1	1.1
Interest and prices							
Central bank discount (%)	10.0	10.0	10.0	10.0	10.0	10.0	10.0[13]
Gov't. bond yield (%)	7.6	8.0	8.7	9.0	10.0	10.0	16.50[13]
Industrial share prices (1980 = 100)	120.1	126.2	134.8	200.0	244.3	219.4	219.9[13]
Balance of payments (U.S.$'000,000)							
Balance of visible trade	−4,820	−4,098	−4,024	−5,616	−5,438	...	...
Imports, f.o.b.	14,046	13,868	14,216	15,081	15,686	...	...
Exports, f.o.b.	9,226	9,770	10,192	9,465	10,248	...	...
Balance of invisibles	−621	−979	−1,089	−1,337	−1,780	...	...
Balance of payments, current account	−2,524	−1,932	−2,343	−4,214	−4,627	...	...

Population economically active (1981)[5]: total 244,605,000; activity rate of total population 36.8% (participation rates: over age 15, 57.4%; female 26.0%; unemployed [1985] 4.6%).

Price and earnings indexes (1980 = 100)

	1982	1983	1984	1985	1986	1987	1988
Consumer price index	121.9	136.3	147.7	155.9	169.5	184.4	174.3[12]
Daily earnings index[14]	113.5	127.8	...	...	...	...	...

Household income and expenditure. Average household size[5] (1981) 5.6; income per household: n.a.; sources of income (1984–85): salaries and wages 42.2%, self-employed 39.7%, interest 8.6%, profits and dividends 6.0%, rent 3.5%; expenditure (1984): food and beverages 56.8%, transportation and communications 11.0%, clothing and footwear 10.8%, energy 4.8%, household furnishings 4.5%, housing 2.7%, education 2.2%, other 7.2%.

Service enterprises (1980)

	no. of enterprises	no. of employees	annual wage as a % of all wages	annual value added (Rs '000,000)[15]
Wholesale and retail trade	6,046,200	10,228,700	...	262,270
Transportation	307,400	1,194,300	...	110,246
Community and personal services	3,177,700	13,128,800	...	108,670
Construction	152,000	451,200	...	96,290
Finance and insurance	273,500	1,570,800	...	73,970
Real estate and business services			86.4[16]	71,180
Electricity, gas, and steam	33,700	363,500	...	35,580
Restaurants and hotels	807,000	2,080,500	...	19,120
Communications	98,900	530,900	...	14,580
Storage and warehousing	122,400	356,900	...	34
Water works and supply	208[17]	14,607[17]	108.7[16]	1,840

Tourism (1986): receipts from visitors U.S.$1,400,000,000; expenditures by nationals abroad U.S.$354,000,000.
Land use (1985): forested 22.6%; meadows and pastures 4.0%; agricultural and under permanent cultivation 56.8%; other 16.6%.

Foreign trade[18]

Balance of trade (current prices)

	1982	1983	1984	1985	1986	1987
Rs '000,000	−36,641	−34,733	−33,214	−63,688	−54,153	−46,641
% of total	17.2%	15.8%	12.8%	21.8%	18.4%	13.7%

Imports (1986–87): Rs 200,063,000,000 (nonelectrical machinery 18.5%; crude petroleum and petroleum products 13.3%; pearls, precious and semiprecious stones [mostly diamonds] 7.4%; iron and steel 7.2%; chemical elements and compounds 5.2%; electrical machinery 4.3%; manufactured fertilizers 3.9%). *Major import sources:* Japan 12.7%; United States 9.8%; West Germany 9.7%; United Kingdom 8.1%; Belgium 5.4%; U.S.S.R. 5.3%; Saudi Arabia 3.4%; France 3.3%.
Exports (1986–87): Rs 125,550,000,000 (pearls, precious and semiprecious stones [mostly diamonds], and jewelry 16.5%; ready-made garments 9.7%; machinery, transport equipment, and nonferrous metal manufactures 7.0%; leather and leather manufactures 6.3%; cotton fabrics 4.5%; tea and maté 4.4%; iron ore 4.3%). *Major export destinations:* United States 18.8%; U.S.S.R. 14.9%; Japan 10.7%; United Kingdom 5.9%; West Germany 5.9%; Belgium 2.8%; France 2.2%; The Netherlands 1.8%.

Transport and communications

Transport. Railroads (1987): route length 38,407 mi, 61,810 km; passenger-mi 160,621,000,000, passenger-km 258,495,000,000; short ton-mi cargo 148,-846,000,000, metric ton-km cargo 217,312,000,000. Roads (1984–85): total length 1,101,000 mi, 1,772,000 km (paved 47%). Vehicles (1984–85): passenger cars 1,517,000; trucks and buses 952,000. Merchant marine (1987): vessels (100 gross tons and over) 803; total deadweight tonnage 10,890,782. Air transport (1987): passenger-mi 10,655,000,000, passenger-km 17,148,-000,000; short ton-mi cargo 459,756,000, metric ton-km cargo 671,232,000; airports (1988) with scheduled flights 95.
Communications. Daily newspapers (1986): total number 1,802; total circulation 12,895,680[19]; circulation per 1,000 population 26[19]. Radio (1986): total number of receivers 50,000,000 (1 per 15 persons). Television (1987): total number of receivers 9,300,000 (1 per 84 persons). Telephones (1986): 4,057,000 (1 per 192 persons).

Education and health

Education (1985–86)

	schools	teachers	students	student/ teacher ratio
Primary (age 6–10)	528,079	...	86,465,189	c. 42.0
Secondary (age 11–17)	195,388	...	43,230,690	
Voc., Teacher tr. } Higher	5,494	...	3,196,963	...

Literacy (1981): total population age 15 and over literate 168,900,000 (40.8%); males literate 117,600,000 (54.8%); females literate 51,300,000 (25.7%).
Health: physicians (1984–85) 297,200 (1 per 2,522 persons); hospital beds (1985–86) 645,000 (1 per 1,184 persons); infant mortality rate per 1,000 live births (1987) 96.0.
Food (1984–86): daily per capita caloric intake 2,204 (vegetable products 94%, animal products 6%); (1983) 96% of FAO recommended minimum requirement.

Military

Total active duty personnel (1988): 1,362,000 (army 88.1%, navy 3.8%, air force 8.1%). *Military expenditure as percent of GNP* (1985): 3.8% (world 6.1%); per capita expenditure U.S.$10.

[1]Includes 13 nonelective seats. [2]Includes 2 nonelective seats. [3]Estimate; state not censused. [4]Excludes 46,660 sq mi (120,849 sq km) of territory claimed by India as part of Jammu and Kashmir but occupied by Pakistan or China. Final status of these claims is not determined. [5]Excludes Assam. [6]Population of urban agglomeration; 1985 est. [7]Percentage breakdown based on 18,262 deaths recorded at 1,160 nationally dispersed, primary health centre villages. [8]Includes not adequately defined and unemployed. [9]1985. [10]1986. [11]End of period. [12]June. [13]August. [14]Male agricultural workers. [15]1984. [16]1983. [17]1983–84. [18]Import figures are f.o.b. in balance of trade and c.i.f. in commodities and trading partners. [19]Circulation of 238 main dailies only.

Indonesia

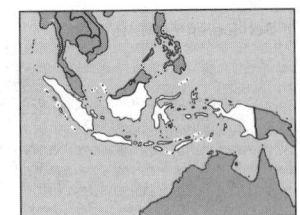

Official name: Republik Indonesia (Republic of Indonesia).
Form of government: unitary multiparty republic with two legislative houses (House of People's Representatives [500[1]]; People's Consultative Assembly [1,000[2]]).
Head of state and government: President.
Capital: Jakarta.
Official language: Bahasa Indonesia.
Official religion: monotheism.
Monetary unit: 1 Indonesian rupiah (Rp) = 100 sen; valuation (Oct. 10, 1988) 1 U.S.$ = Rp 1,698; 1 £ = Rp 2,907.

Area and population		area		population
		sq mi	sq km	1987 estimate
Metropolitan district	**Capitals**			
Jakarta Raya	Jakarta	228	590	8,465,400
Provinces				
Bali	Denpasar	2,147	5,561	2,746,700
Bengkulu	Bengkulu	8,173	21,168	1,025,700
Irian Jaya	Jayapura	162,928	421,981	1,395,600
Jambi	Jambi	17,345	44,924	1,889,400
Jawa Barat	Bandung	17,877	46,300	32,624,700
Jawa Tengah	Semarang	13,207	34,206	28,126,700
Jawa Timur	Surabaya	18,503	47,922	32,013,200
Kalimantan Barat	Pontianak	56,664	146,760	2,883,400
Kalimantan Selatan	Banjarmasin	14,541	37,660	2,371,100
Kalimantan Tengah	Palangkaraya	58,919	152,600	1,195,200
Kalimantan Timur	Samarinda	78,162	202,440	1,782,200
Lampung	Tanjung Karang	12,860	33,307	6,771,600
Maluku	Ambon	28,767	74,505	1,701,600
Nusa Tenggara Barat	Mataram	7,790	20,177	3,171,200
Nusa Tenggara Timur	Kupang	18,485	47,876	3,099,000
Riau	Pakanbaru	36,511	94,562	2,655,900
Sulawesi Selatan	Ujung Pandang	28,101	72,781	6,765,100
Sulawesi Tengah	Palu	26,921	69,726	1,661,500
Sulawesi Tenggara	Kendari	10,690	27,686	1,153,800
Sulawesi Utara	Menado	7,345	19,023	2,453,600
Sumatera Barat	Padang	19,219	49,778	3,924,500
Sumatera Selatan	Palembang	40,034	103,688	5,754,700
Sumatera Utara	Medan	27,331	70,787	9,887,900
Timor Timur	Dili	5,743	14,874	628,600
Special autonomous districts				
Aceh	Banda Aceh	21,387	55,392	3,158,700
Yogyakarta	Yogyakarta	1,224	3,169	2,937,800
TOTAL		741,101[3]	1,919,443	172,244,800

Demography

Population (1988): 175,904,000.
Density (1988): persons per sq mi 237.4, persons per sq km 91.6.
Urban-rural (1985): urban 26.2%; rural 73.8%.
Sex distribution (1985): male 49.77%; female 50.23%.
Age breakdown (1985): under 15, 39.4%; 15–29, 27.2%; 30–44, 16.9%; 45–59, 10.8%; 60–74, 4.7%; 75 and over, 1.0%.
Population projection: (1990) 183,457,000; (2000) 222,753,000.
Doubling time: 39 years.
Ethnolinguistic composition (1980): Javanese 40.1%; Sundanese 15.3%; Bahasa Indonesian 12.0%; Madurese 4.8%; other 27.8%.
Religious affiliation (1985): Muslim 86.9%; Christian 9.6%, of which Roman Catholic 3.1%; Hindu 1.9%; Buddhist 1.0%; other 0.6%.
Major cities (1985): Jakarta 7,829,000; Surabaya 2,345,000; Medan 2,110,000; Bandung 1,633,000; Semarang (1984) 1,077,000.

Vital statistics

Birth rate per 1,000 population (1987): 29.3 (world avg. 26.0).
Death rate per 1,000 population (1987): 11.4 (world avg. 9.9).
Natural increase rate per 1,000 population (1987): 17.9 (world avg. 16.1).
Total fertility rate (avg. births per childbearing woman; 1987): 3.6.
Marriage rate per 1,000 population (1984–85): 6.8.
Divorce rate per 1,000 population (1984–85): 1.0.
Life expectancy at birth (1987): male 54.4 years; female 57.2 years.
Major causes of death: n.a.; however, major diseases include tuberculosis, malaria, dysentery, cholera, and plague.

National economy

Budget (1988–89 est.). Revenue: Rp 28,963,600,000,000 (royalties from energy production 30.6%, aid for development 24.7%, value added tax 16.5%, income tax 13.0%, excise tax 4.6%, nontax revenues 4.3%). Expenditures: Rp 28,963,600,000,000 (debt service 36.8%, development 30.7%, civil service 16.6%, subsidies for autonomous regions 10.0%).
Public debt (external, outstanding; 1986): U.S.$31,901,200,000.
Tourism (1986): receipts from visitors: U.S.$590,500,000; expenditures by nationals abroad U.S.$699,000,000.
Production (metric tons except as noted). Agriculture, forestry, fishing (1986): rice 39,275,000, sugarcane 25,500,000, cassava 13,329,000, corn 5,767,000, sweet potatoes 2,287,000, copra 1,300,000, palm oil 1,298,000, rubber 1,016,000; livestock (number of live animals) 12,289,000 goats, 6,465,000 cattle, 5,193,000 sheep, 2,936,000 buffalo; roundwood 157,768,000 cu m; fish catch 2,498,000. Mining and quarrying (1986): nickel ore 1,533,094; bauxite 648,815; copper ore[4] 251,229; iron ore[4] 152,271; tin ore[4] 24,049;

silver 2,529,993 kg. Manufacturing (1986): cement 11,316,282; fertilizer 5,726,000; paper 110,542; cotton yarn 117,750 bales; beer 639,650 hectolitres; cigarettes 16,761,101,000 units. Energy production (consumption): electricity (kW-hr; 1986) 29,850,000,000 (29,850,000,000); coal (metric tons; 1986) 1,725,000 (2,221,000); crude petroleum (barrels; 1986) 536,709,000 (243,065,000); petroleum products (metric tons; 1986) 28,375,000 (24,014,-000); natural gas (cu m; 1986) 28,693,700,000 (7,086,500,000).
Gross national product (1986): U.S.$82,110,000,000 (U.S.$500 per capita).

Structure of gross domestic product and labour force				
	1986		**1985**	
	in value Rp '000,000	% of total value	labour force	% of labour force
Agriculture	24,921.6	25.8	34,141,809	53.5
Mining	10,740.9	11.1	415,512	0.7
Manufacturing	13,899.9	14.4	5,795,919	9.1
Construction	5,242.6	5.4	2,095,577	3.3
Public utilities	858.0	0.9	69,715	0.1
Transp. and commun.	6,392.0	6.6	1,958,333	3.1
Trade	16,081.2	16.7	9,345,210	14.6
Finance, real estate	5,911.0	6.1	250,481	0.4
Pub. admin., defense	8,307.3	8.6 }	8,317,285	13.0
Services	4,134.8	4.3 }		
Other	...	...	1,435,774[5]	2.2[5]
TOTAL	96,489.3	100.0[3]	63,825,615	100.0

Population economically active: total (1985) 63,825,615; activity rate 38.6% (participation rates: over age 15, 62.1%; female 36.0%; unemployed 2.1%).

Price and earnings indexes (1980 = 100)							
	1981	1982	1983	1984	1985	1986	1987
Consumer price index	112.2	122.9	137.4	151.7	158.9	168.2	183.8
Monthly earnings index[6]	127.6	152.0	168.9	191.3	210.8	...	...

Household income and expenditure. Average household size (1985) 4.6; income per household: n.a.; sources of income (1976): wages 42.1%, self-employment 41.5%, transfer payments 2.5%; expenditure (1984): food 63.3%, housing and utilities 17.4%, clothing 4.6%, durable goods 3.1%.
Land use (1985): forested 67.1%; meadows and pastures 6.5%; agricultural and under permanent cultivation 11.5%; other 14.9%.

Foreign trade

Balance of trade (current prices)						
	1982	1983	1984	1985	1986	1987
U.S.$'000,000	+7,240	+6,545	+9,508	+9,430	+5,249	+5,625
% of total	19.4%	18.3%	27.7%	34.0%	21.5%	19.6%

Imports (1986): U.S.$10,718,400,000 (machinery 26.7%, chemicals 14.0%, mineral products 12.0%, transport equipment 11.3%, base metals 11.1%). *Major import sources:* Japan 29.2%; U.S. 13.8%; Singapore 9.0%.
Exports (1986): U.S.$14,805,000,000 (crude petroleum 31.0%, natural gas 18.7%, plywood 6.8%, petroleum products 6.1%, coffee 5.5%). *Major export destinations:* Japan 44.9%; U.S. 19.6%; Singapore 8.4%.

Transport and communications

Transport. Railroads: (1987) length 6,536 km; (1986) passenger-km 7,332,-000,000; (1986) metric ton-km cargo 1,452,000,000. Roads (1986): length 219,791 km (paved 39%). Vehicles (1986): passenger cars 1,059,851; trucks and buses 1,132,658. Merchant marine (1987): vessels (100 gross tons and over) 1,734; deadweight tonnage 2,963,181. Air transport (1986): passenger-km 9,180,000,000; metric ton-km cargo 226,236,000; airports (1988) 130.
Communications. Daily newspapers (1986): total number 97; total circulation 3,048,635; circulation per 1,000 population 18. Radio (1985): 32,800,-000 receivers (1 per 5.1 persons). Television (1986): 8,948,195[7] receivers (1 per 19 persons). Telephones (1986): 763,567[8] (1 per 221 persons).

Education and health

Education (1985–86)[9]				
	schools	teachers	students	student/teacher ratio
Primary (age 7–12)	139,511	1,037,174	26,550,015	25.6
Secondary (age 13–18)	22,086	480,464	7,680,417	16.0
Voc., teacher tr.	2,774	75,158	1,106,106	14.7
Higher[10]	478	74,044	806,470	10.9

Educational attainment (1985). Percent of population age 25 and over having: no schooling 30.3%; less than complete primary 32.2%; primary 22.8%; some secondary 6.4%; secondary 7.1%; higher 1.2%. *Literacy* (1985): total population over age 15 and over literate 79,197,000 (74.1%); males literate 41,450,000 (83.0%); females literate 33,708,000 (65.4%).
Health (1985): physicians 18,947 (1 per 8,717 persons); hospital beds 110,426 (1 per 1,496 persons); infant mortality rate per 1,000 live births (1987) 75.0.
Food (1983–85): daily per capita caloric intake 2,504 (vegetable products 98%, animal products 2%); (1983) 110% of FAO recommended minimum.

Military

Total active duty personnel (1987): 284,000 (army 76.1%, navy 14.8%, air force 9.1%). *Military expenditure as percent of GNP* (1985): 2.5%; (world 6.1%); per capita expenditure U.S.$13.

[1]Includes 100 nonelective seats reserved for the military. [2]Includes the 500 members of the House of People's Representatives plus 500 other delegates. [3]Detail does not add to total given because of rounding. [4]Concentrates. [5]Includes unemployed. [6]Based on daily average wages of agricultural estate workers. [7]Registered. [8]Licensed. [9]Refers to schools under the Department of Education and Culture only. [10]1983–84; includes private schools.

Iran

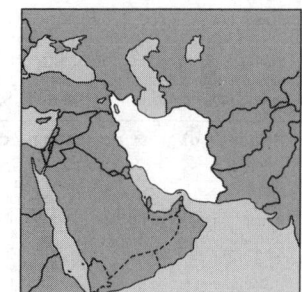

Official name: Jomhūrī-ye Eslamī-ye Īrān (Islamic Republic of Iran).
Form of government: unitary Islamic republic with a single legislative house (Islamic Consultative Assembly [270]).
Chief of state: Velayat Faghih (religious leader).
Head of state: President.
Head of government: Prime Minister.
Capital: Tehrān.
Official language: Farsī (Persian).
Official religion: Islam.
Monetary unit: 1 rial (Rls) = 100 dinars; valuation (Oct. 10, 1988)
1 U.S.$ = Rls 70.42; 1£ = Rls 120.60.

Area and population		area[1]		population
				1986
Provinces	Capitals	sq mi	sq km	census
Azārbāijān-e Gharbi	Orūmiyeh	15,000	38,850	1,989,935
Azārbāijān-e Sharqi	Tabriz	25,908	67,102	4,180,376
Bakhtarān	Bakhtarān	9,138	23,667	1,471,224
Boyer Aḥmad-e Kohkilūyeh	Yāsūj	5,506	14,261	413,096
Būshehr	Būshehr	10,677	27,653	578,556
Chahār Maḥāl-e Bakhtiāri	Shahr Kord	5,741	14,870	637,167
Eṣfahān	Eṣfahān	40,405	104,650	3,317,081
Fārs	Shirāz	51,467	133,298	3,229,226
Gilān	Rasht	5,677	14,704	2,086,659
Hamadān	Hamadān	7,639	19,784	1,533,885
Hormozgān	Bandar 'Abbās	25,819	66,870	760,014
Īlām	Īlām	7,353	19,044	384,417
Kermān	Kermān	69,466	179,916	1,639,031
Khorāsān	Mashhad	120,980	313,337	5,312,991
Khūzestān	Ahvāz	25,978	67,282	2,702,533
Kordestān	Sanandaj	9,652	24,998	1,091,064
Lorestān	Khorramābād	11,121	28,803	1,369,897
Markazi	Arāk	15,403	39,895	1,092,214
Māzandarān	Sari	18,292	47,375	3,449,359
Semnān	Semnān	34,764	90,039	418,152
Sistān-e Balūchestān	Zāhedān	70,108	181,578	1,205,980
Tehrān	Tehrān	7,381	19,118	8,719,480
Yazd	Yazd	27,031	70,011	582,300
Zanjān	Zanjān	14,053	36,398	1,600,237
TOTAL		634,559	1,643,503	49,764,874

Demography

Population (1988): 51,225,000.
Density (1988): persons per sq mi 80.7, persons per sq km 31.2.
Urban–rural (1984–85): urban 51.4%; rural 48.6%.
Sex distribution (1984–85): male 51.65%; female 48.6%.
Age breakdown (1984–85): under 15, 43.4%; 15–29, 26.0%; 30–44, 16.0%; 45–59, 9.3%; 60–74, 1.9%; 75 and over, 3.4%.
Population projection: (1990) 52,997,000; (2000) 64,976,000.
Doubling time: 25 years.
Ethnic composition (1983): Persian 45.6%; Azerbaijani 16.8%; Kurdish 9.1%; Gīlakī 5.3%; Luri 4.3%; Māzandarānī 3.6%; Baluchi 2.3%; Arab 2.2%; Bakhtiari 1.7%; Turkmen 1.5%; Armenian 0.5%; other 7.1%.
Religious affiliation (1985): Muslim 98% (Shī'ī 93%, Sunnī 5%); other 2%.
Major cities (1985): Tehrān 6,022,078; Mashhad 1,466,018; Eṣfahān 1,001,248; Shīrāz 848,011; Ahvaz 589,529.

Vital statistics

Birth rate per 1,000 population (1985–90): 38.5 (world avg. 26.0).
Death rate per 1,000 population (1985–90): 10.8 (world avg. 9.9).
Natural increase rate per 1,000 population (1985–90): 27.7 (world avg. 16.1).
Total fertility rate (avg. births per childbearing woman; 1987): 5.2.
Marriage rate per 1,000 population (1984–85): 8.9.
Divorce rate per 1,000 population (1984–85): 0.8.
Life expectancy at birth (1985): male 58.0 years; female 58.3 years.
Major causes of death per 100,000 population (1984–85)[2]: diseases of the circulatory system 52.7; accidents, poisonings, and suicides 29.7; diseases of early infancy 15.2; malignant neoplasms (cancers) 14.0; diseases of the respiratory system 13.1; diseases of the nervous system 5.9.

National economy

Budget (1986–87). Revenue: Rls 3,574,700,000,000 (oil and gas 44.8%, taxes 32.7%). Expenditures: Rls 3,780,000,000,000 (current expenditure 61.9%, economic affairs 25.1%, national defense 11.4%).
Tourism (1985): receipts from visitors U.S.$27,500,000; expenditures by nationals abroad U.S.$488,000,000.
Production (metric tons except as noted). Agriculture, forestry, fishing (1986): wheat 7,128,000, barley 2,500,000, potatoes 1,600,000, rice (paddy) 1,569,000, grapes 1,350,000, sugarcane 1,100,000, watermelons 960,000; livestock (number of live animals) 34,500,000 sheep, 13,600,000 goats, 8,350,000 cattle, 1,800,000 asses, 316,000 horses, 100,000,000 chickens; roundwood 6,757,000 cu m; fish catch 152,065. Mining and quarrying (1986): iron ore 2,800,000; kaolin 429,000; barite 90,000; chromium ore (oxide content) 56,000; copper ore 48,000; zinc ore 36,000; lead 21,600. Manufacturing (value in Rls; 1983–84): machinery 513,148,000,000; textiles 388,755,000,000; chemicals 226,085,000,000; iron and steel 135,688,000,000. Construction (1984): residential 20,991,000 sq m; nonresidential 1,830,000 sq m. Energy production (consumption): electricity (kW-hr; 1986) 36,800,000,000 (36,800,000,000); coal (metric tons; 1986) 800,000 (950,000); crude petroleum (barrels; 1986) 682,141,000 (211,845,000); petroleum products

(metric tons; 1986) 25,830,000 (27,265,000); natural gas (cu m; 1986) 8,537,424,000 (8,537,424,000).
Gross national product (at current market prices; 1985–86): U.S.$188,200,000,000 (U.S.$4,170 per capita).

Structure of gross domestic product and labour force				
	1984–85		1980	
	in value Rls '000,000,000	% of total value	labour force	% of labour force
Agriculture	446.7	13.1	4,026,000	36.4
Mining	480.6	14.0		
Manufacturing	491.6	14.4	3,635,000	32.8
Construction	118.7	3.5		
Public utilities	66.7	2.0		
Transp. and commun.	203.0	5.9		
Trade	747.4	21.8	3,411,000	30.8
Finance	445.5	13.0		
Services	475.9	13.9		
Pub. admin., defense				
Other	−54.8[3]	−1.6[3]		
TOTAL	3,421.3	100.0	11,072,000	100.0

Population economically active (1985): total 13,023,000; activity rate of total population 29.2% (participation rates: ages 15–64, 50.1%; female 16.7%; unemployed [1983–84] 13.9%).

Price and earnings indexes (1980 = 100)							
	1980	1981	1982	1983	1984	1985	1986[4]
Consumer price index[2]	100.0	124.2	147.4	176.5	198.6	207.4	227.2
Monthly earnings index[5]	100.0	108.9	19.7	138.1	158.8	180.3	...

Household income and expenditure. Average household size (1984–85) 5.0; income per household (1975) Rls 298,761 (U.S.$4,235); sources of income: wages 40.8%, self-employment 28.2%, assistance 4.5%; expenditure (1984): food and tobacco 43.3%, housing and energy 22.8%, clothing and footwear 9.6%, furniture and household equipment 6.3%, transportation 6.0%, health care 4.6%, recreation 1.0%.
Land use (1985): forested 10.9%; meadows and pastures 26.9%; agricultural and under permanent cultivation 9.4%; other 52.8%.

Foreign trade

Balance of trade (current prices)[6]						
	1980	1981	1982	1983	1984	1985
Rls '000,000	+228,200	+119,200	+587,500	+275,800	−65.1	+303.5
% of total	12.9%	6.5%	27.0%	8.9%	2.8%	14.2%

Imports (1984–85): Rls 1,312,301,000,000 (machinery and transport equipment 37.6%, food and live animals 14.3%, chemicals 12.2%). *Major import sources* (1985): West Germany 16.3%; Japan 13.4%; United Kingdom 6.7%; Italy 6.0%; Singapore 3.9%; Australia 2.1%.
Exports (1985): Rls 1,218,600,000,000 (petroleum and petroleum products 98.0%). *Major export destinations:* Japan 16.5%; Italy 9.8%; Spain 5.8%; France 5.2%; United States 5.0%; West Germany 4.2%.

Transport and communications

Transport. Railroads (1984–85): route length 2,837 mi, 4,567 km; passenger-mi 1,570,000,000, passenger-km 2,526,000,000; short ton-mi cargo 2,645,000,000, metric ton-km cargo 3,861,000,000. Roads (1984): total length 84,740 mi, 136,380 km (paved 41%). Vehicles (1984): passenger cars 2,246,143; trucks and buses 434,944. Merchant marine (1987): vessels (100 gross tons and over) 370; total deadweight tonnage 7,222,831. Air transport (1986): passenger-mi 3,362,646,000, passenger-km 5,411,666,000; short ton-mi cargo 469,776,000, metric ton-km cargo 685,860,000; airports (1988) 13.
Communications. Daily newspapers (1987): 13; circulation 640,000[7]; circulation per 1,000 population 12.5[7]. Radio (1986): 10,000,000 receivers (1 per 4.8 persons). Television (1986): 2,100,000 receivers (1 per 23 persons). Telephones (1986): 1,883,570 (1 per 26 persons).

Education and health

Education (1985–86)	schools	teachers	students	student/ teacher ratio
Primary (age 7–11)	48,982	268,606	6,343,300	23.6
Secondary (age 12–18)	13,818	167,769	2,922,576	17.4
Voc., teacher tr.	1,325	20,683	277,609	13.4
Higher	114[8]	13,698	145,809	10.6

Educational attainment (1976). Percent of population age 10 and over having: no formal schooling 16.1%; Qur'anic education 10.7%; primary education 43.0%; secondary 23.7%; higher 6.4%; certificate not reported 0.1%. *Literacy* (1980): total population age 15 and over literate 10,980,000 (42.8%); males literate 7,163,000 (55.4%); females literate 3,817,000 (30.1%).
Health: physicians (1982–83) 15,945 (1 per 2,582 persons); hospital beds (1984–85) 70,152 (1 per 616 persons); infant mortality rate (1987) 109.
Food (1978–80): daily per capita caloric intake 2,912 (vegetable products 90%, animal products 10%); 121% of FAO recommended minimum requirement.

Military

Total active duty personnel (1988): 604,500 (revolutionary guard corps 41.3%, army 50.5%, navy 2.4%, air force 5.8%). *Military expenditure as percent of GNP* (1984): 7.2% (world 5.9%); per capita expenditure U.S.$252.

[1]Total area excludes the area of Lake Orumiyeh (4,686 sq km [1,809 sq mi]). [2]For urban areas only. [3]Imputed bank service charge. [4]April. [5]Compensation paid to employees in large manufacturing establishments. [6]Imports derived from the Direction of Trade Statistics (DOTS). [7]Circulation based on three dailies only. [8]1982–83.

Iraq

Official name: al-Jumhūrīyah al-ʿIrāqīyah (Republic of Iraq).
Form of government: unitary single-party republic with one legislative house (National Assembly [250]).
Head of state and government: President.
Capital: Baghdād.
Official language: Arabic.
Official religion: Islam.
Monetary unit: 1 Iraqi dinar (ID) = 20 dirhams = 1,000 fils; valuation (Oct. 10, 1988) 1 ID = U.S.$3.22; 1 ID = £1.89.

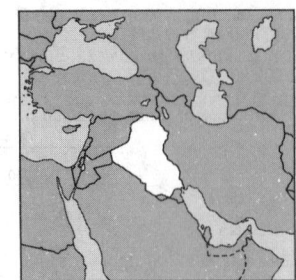

Area and population		area[1]		population
				1986
Governorates	Capitals	sq mi	sq km	estimate
al-Anbār	ar-Ramādī	53,175	137,723	598,000
Bābil	al-Ḥillah	2,030	5,258	759,000
Baghdād	Baghdād	1,992	5,159	4,868,000
al-Baṣrah	Basra	7,363	19,070	1,346,000
Dhī Qār	an-Nāṣirīyah	5,261	13,626	741,000
Diyālā	Baʿqūbah	7,449	19,292	706,000
Karbalāʾ	Karbalāʾ	1,944	5,034	337,000
Maysān	al-ʿAmārah	5,445	14,103	417,000
al-Muthannā	as-Samāwah	19,702	51,029	259,000
an-Najaf	an-Najaf	10,751	27,844	484,000
Ninawā	Mosul	14,555	37,698	1,393,000
al-Qādisiyah	ad-Dīwānīyah	3,285	8,507	524,000
Ṣalāḥ ad-Dīn	Sāmarrāʾ	11,198	29,004	454,000
at-Taʾmīm	Kirkūk	4,012	10,391	674,000
Wāsiṭ	al-Kūt	6,683	17,308	494,000
Kurdish Autonomous Region				
Dahūk	Dahūk	2,363	6,120	343,000
Irbil	Irbil	5,587	14,471	774,000
as-Sulaymānīyah	as-Sulaymānīyah	6,083	15,756	939,000
LAND AREA		168,878	437,393	16,110,000
INLAND WATER		357	924	
TOTAL AREA		169,235	438,317	

Demography

Population (1988): 16,630,000.
Density[2] (1988): persons per sq mi 98.5, persons per sq km 38.0.
Urban–rural (1986): urban 72.2%; rural 27.8%.
Sex distribution (1987): male 51.39%; female 48.61%.
Age breakdown (1986): under 15, 45.3%; 15–29, 28.4%; 30–44, 13.6%; 45–59, 7.6%; 60–74, 3.8%; 75 and over, 1.3%.
Population projection: (1990) 17,676,000; (2000) 23,801,000.
Doubling time: 23 years.
Ethnic composition (1983): Arab 77.1%; Kurd 19.0%; Turkmen 1.4%; Persian 0.8%; Assyrian 0.8%; other 0.9%.
Religious affiliation (1980): Muslim 95.8% (of which Shīʿī 53.5%, Sunnī 42.3%); Christian 3.5%; other 0.7%.
Major cities (1985): Baghdād 4,648,609; Basra 616,700; Mosul 570,926; Irbil 333,903; as-Sulaymānīyah 279,424.

Vital statistics

Birth rate per 1,000 population (1986): 45.1 (world avg. 26.0).
Death rate per 1,000 population (1986): 8.6 (world avg. 9.9).
Natural increase rate per 1,000 population (1986): 36.5 (world avg. 16.1).
Total fertility rate (avg. births per childbearing woman; 1986): 7.1.
Marriage rate per 1,000 population (1982): 4.0.
Divorce rate per 1,000 population (1981): 0.1.
Life expectancy at birth (1986): male 61.0 years; female 64.5 years.
Major causes of death per 100,000 population (1975): heart disease (except ischemic) 69.9; accidents (all types) 27.6; pneumonia 27.2; malignant neoplasms (cancers) 19.6; during the 1980s, however, there were high war casualties and high incidence of trachoma, influenza, measles, whooping cough, and tuberculosis.

National economy

Budget (1982). Revenue: ID 8,740,000,000 (1981; revenue from oil and public enterprises 88.5%, sales tax 7.7%, income tax 1.3%). Expenditures: ID 8,740,000,000 (1981; economic services 44.9%, defense 24.0%, local government 8.3%, internal security 5.2%, health 4.6%, education 2.9%).
Public debt (external, outstanding; 1986): U.S.$50,500,000,000.
Production (metric tons except as noted). Agriculture, forestry, fishing (1986): barley 1,046,000, wheat 1,036,000, watermelons 551,000, tomatoes 523,000, grapes 440,000, dates 434,000, cucumbers and gherkins 368,000, melons 356,000, green beans 236,000, oranges 160,000, eggplants 150,000, potatoes 120,000; livestock (number of live animals) 8,800,000 sheep, 2,400,000 goats, 1,573,000 cattle, 900,000 mules and asses, 150,000 buffalo, 60,000 camels, 75,000,000 chickens; roundwood 143,000 cu m; fish catch 20,564. Mining and quarrying (1986): elemental sulfur 600,000; gypsum 300,000. Manufacturing (1981): cement 8,000,000[3]; vegetable oil 109,230; toilet soap 7,062; woolen cloth 2,906 m; beer 6,693,900 hectolitres; shoes 7,334,000 pairs; matches 540,720,000 units; cigarettes 7,700,000 units. Construction (1985): authorized residential 11,521,000 sq m; authorized nonresidential 1,176,000 sq m. Energy production (consumption): electricity (kW-hr; 1986) 18,850,000,000 (18,850,000,000); coal, none (n.a.); crude petroleum (barrels;

1986) 603,352,000 (109,500,000); petroleum products (metric tons; 1986) 12,045,000 (7,025,000); natural gas (cu m; 1986) 565,844,000 (565,844,000).
Tourism (1986): receipts from visitors U.S.$100,000,000; expenditures by nationals abroad, n.a.
Gross national product (1985): U.S.$37,930,000,000 (U.S.$2,330 per capita).

Structure of gross domestic product and labour force				
	1985		1986	
	in value ID '000,000	% of total value	labour force	% of labour force
Agriculture	2,265.8	15.6	1,193,170	27.7
Mining	3,596.4	24.7	62,096	1.4
Manufacturing	1,416.2	9.7	386,809	9.0
Construction	1,094.6	7.5	521,013	12.1
Public utilities	172.4	1.2	34,179	0.8
Transp. and commun.	783.0	5.4	260,237	6.0
Trade	1,597.6	11.0	329,704	7.7
Finance			50,043	1.2
Pub. admin., defense	} 3,620.8	} 24.9	1,470,090	34.1
Services				
Other			—	—
TOTAL	14,546.8	100.0	4,307,341	100.0

Population economically active (1986): total 4,307,341; activity rate of total population 26.9% (participation rates: over age 15, 50.6%; female 18.2%; unemployed [1984] 0.9%).

Price and earnings indexes (1980 = 100)					
	1980	1981	1982	1983	1984
Consumer price index	100.0	110.6	135.2	151.4	168.5
Earnings index	...	...	...	...	...

Household income and expenditure. Average household size (1986) 7.8; income per household: n.a.; sources of income: n.a.; expenditure (1971–72): food 55.4%, clothing 10.3%, housing 7.9%, household goods 6.2%, transp. and commun. 5.3%, energy 4.1%, medical care 2.4%, recreation 1.2%.
Land use (1985): forested 4.4%; meadows and pastures 9.2%; agricultural and under permanent cultivation 12.5%; built-on, wasteland, and other 73.9%.

Foreign trade[4]

Balance of trade (current prices)						
	1982	1983	1984	1985	1986	1987
ID '000,000	−11,304	−2,381	+282	+966	−1,124	+2,006
% of total	35.6%	10.8%	1.3%	4.4%	6.9%	12.5%

Imports (1985): U.S.$10,534,000,000 (machinery and transport equipment 30.6%; food and agricultural raw materials 24.3%; chemical and pharmaceutical products 7.2%). *Major import sources* (1987): Turkey 14.8%; United States 10.7%; West Germany 7.3%; U.K. 7.0%; Japan 6.2%; France 5.8%; Brazil 5.2%; Yugoslavia 4.6%; Romania 4.6%; Italy 4.1%.
Exports (1985): U.S.$11,500,000,000 (fuels and other energy 99.6%; food and agricultural raw materials 0.4%). *Major export destinations* (1987): Brazil 16.5%; Italy 12.2%; France 10.2%; Turkey 7.5%; Japan 6.9%; Spain 6.7%; Yugoslavia 6.4%; United States 5.3%; West Germany 4.1%.

Transport and communications

Transport. Railroads (1986): route length (1987) 1,516 mi, 2,439 km; passenger-mi 624,000,000, passenger-km 1,005,000,000; short ton-mi cargo 886,000,000, metric ton-km cargo 1,294,000,000. Roads (1986): total length 20,653 mi, 33,238 km (paved 72%). Vehicles (1986): passenger cars 491,800; trucks and buses 246,700. Merchant marine (1987): vessels (100 gross tons and over) 142; total deadweight tonnage 1,683,083. Air transport (1984): passenger-mi 746,000,000, passenger-km 1,200,000,000; short ton-mi cargo 36,000,000, metric ton-km cargo 52,000,000; airports (1988) with scheduled flights 3.
Communications. Daily newspapers (1987): total number 6; total circulation 328,000; circulation per 1,000 population 21. Radio (1986): 2,800,000 receivers (1 per 5.6 persons). Television (1986): 605,000 receivers (1 per 26 persons). Telephones (1985): 886,133 (1 per 17 persons).

Education and health

Education (1986–87)	schools	teachers	students	student/ teacher ratio
Primary (age 6–11)	8,210	123,310	2,920,959	23.7
Secondary (age 12–17)	2,315	39,261	1,012,426	25.8
Voc., teacher tr.	228	9,198	166,335	18.1
Higher	25	8,327	142,495	17.1

Educational attainment, n.a. *Literacy* (1984): total population age 15 and over literate 2,815,895 (45.9%); males literate 2,034,011 (65.9%); females literate 781,884 (26.5%).
Health (1984): physicians 4,428 (1 per 3,324 persons); hospital beds 26,657 (1 per 552 persons); infant mortality rate per 1,000 live births (1986) 63.3.
Food (1983–85): daily per capita caloric intake 2,901 (vegetable products 88%, animal products 12%); (1983) 121% of FAO recommended minimum.

Military

Total active duty personnel (1988): 1,000,000 (army 95.5%, navy 0.5%, air force 4.0%). *Military expenditure as percent of GNP* (1984): 42.5% (world 5.9%); per capita expenditure U.S.$1,080.

[1]Excluding Iraq–Saudi Arabia Neutral Zone. [2]Based on land area only. [3]1986. [4]Balance of trade is based on f.o.b. valuation of imports and exports; however, commodities traded and trade partners information are based on c.i.f.

Ireland

Official name: Éire (Irish); Ireland[1] (English).
Form of government: unitary multi-party republic with two legislative houses (Senate [60]; House of Representatives [166]).
Chief of state: President.
Head of government: Prime Minister.
Capital: Dublin.
Official languages: Irish; English.
Official religion: Roman Catholic.
Monetary unit: 1 Irish pound (I£) = 100 new pence; valuation (Oct. 10, 1988) 1 I£ = U.S.$1.45 = £0.84.

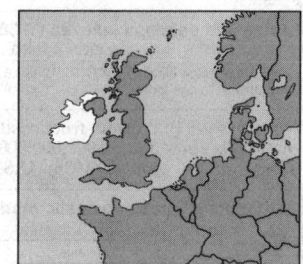

Area and population	area		population
			1986
Provinces Counties	sq mi	sq km	census
Connacht	6,611	17,122	431,409
Galway[2]	2,293	5,940	178,552
Leitrim	581	1,525	27,035
Mayo	2,084	5,398	115,184
Roscommon	951	2,463	54,592
Sligo	693	1,796	56,046
Leinster	7,580	19,633	1,852,649
Carlow	346	896	40,988
Dublin[2]	356	922	1,021,449
Kildare	654	1,694	116,247
Kilkenny	796	2,062	73,186
Laoighis	664	1,719	53,284
Longford	403	1,044	31,496
Louth	318	823	91,810
Meath	902	2,336	103,881
Offaly	771	1,998	59,835
Westmeath	681	1,763	63,379
Wexford	908	2,351	102,552
Wicklow	782	2,025	94,542
Munster	9,315	24,127	1,020,577
Clare	1,231	3,188	91,344
Cork[2]	2,880	7,460	412,735
Kerry	1,815	4,701	124,159
Limerick[2]	1,037	2,686	164,569
Tipperary North Riding	771	1,996	59,522
Tipperary South Riding	872	2,258	77,097
Waterford[2]	710	1,838	91,151
Ulster	3,093	8,012	236,008
Cavan	730	1,891	53,965
Donegal	1,865	4,830	129,664
Monaghan	498	1,291	52,379
TOTAL LAND AREA	26,600	68,895[3]	3,540,643
INLAND WATER	537	1,390	
TOTAL AREA	27,137	70,285	

Demography

Population (1988): 3,553,000.
Density (1988): persons per sq mi 133.6, persons per sq km 51.6.
Urban–rural (1985): urban 57.0%; rural 43.0%.
Sex distribution (1986): male 49.97%; female 50.03%.
Age breakdown (1985): under 15, 30.5%; 15–29, 24.4%; 30–44, 17.4%; 45–59, 12.7%; 60–74, 10.8%; 75 and over, 4.2%.
Population projection: (1990) 3,572,000; (2000) 3,673,000.
Doubling time: 92 years.
Ethnic composition (1981): more than 94% Irish nationality.
Religious affiliation (1981): Roman Catholic 93.1%; Church of Ireland (Anglican) 2.8%; Presbyterian 0.4%; other 3.7%.
Major cities[4] (1986): Dublin 502,749; Cork 133,271; Limerick 56,279; Galway 47,104; Waterford 39,529.

Vital statistics

Birth rate per 1,000 population (1987): 16.6 (world avg. 26.0); (1984) legitimate 92.2%; illegitimate 7.8%.
Death rate per 1,000 population (1987): 8.8 (world avg. 9.9).
Natural increase rate per 1,000 population (1987): 7.8 (world avg. 16.1).
Total fertility rate (avg. births per childbearing woman; 1980–85): 3.2.
Marriage rate per 1,000 population (1987): 5.1.
Life expectancy at birth (1980–82): male 70.1 years; female 75.6 years.
Major causes of death per 100,000 population (1984): heart and circulatory diseases 451.0; malignant neoplasms (cancers) 188.9; pneumonia 57.0.

National economy

Budget (1987). Revenue: I£7,216,900,000 (income taxes 37.7%, value-added tax 22.6%, excise taxes 20.1%). Expenditures: I£8,437,000,000 (debt service 25.4%, social welfare 19.7%, education 12.6%, health 12.4%, defense 3.5%).
Public debt (Dec. 31, 1987): U.S.$24,446,900,000.
Tourism (1986): receipts from visitors U.S.$634,000,000; expenditures by nationals abroad U.S.$472,000,000.
Production (metric tons except as noted). Agriculture, forestry, fishing (1987): sugar beets 1,623,000, barley 974,000, potatoes 424,000, wheat 266,000, oats 45,000, milk 53,620,000 hectolitres; livestock (number of live animals; 1986) 6,718,000 cattle, 4,234,000 sheep, 1,003,000 pigs; roundwood (1986) 1,245,000 cu m; fish catch (1986) 228,910. Mining and quarrying (1987): gypsum 284,200; zinc ore 177,000[5]; lead ore 33,800[5]. Manufacturing (value added in I£; 1984): food, beverages, and tobacco 1,450,400,000; metals and engineering goods 1,381,700,000; chemical products 805,900,000; nonmetallic mineral products 302,300,000; paper and paper products, printing, and publishing 190,400,000; textiles 135,800,000. Construction (1985): residen-

tial 2,265,000 sq m. Energy production (consumption): electricity (kW-hr; 1986) 12,307,000,000 (12,307,000,000); coal (metric tons; 1986) 54,000 (2,307,000); crude petroleum (barrels; 1986) none (10,880,000); petroleum products (metric tons; 1986) 1,431,000 (4,325,000); natural gas (cu m; 1986) 1,590,600,000 (1,589,600,000).
Gross national product (1986): U.S.$18,190,000,000 (U.S.$5,080 per capita).

Structure of gross domestic product and labour force				
	1986			
	in value I£'000,000	% of total value	labour force	% of labour force
Agriculture	1,622	10.0	168,000	12.8
Mining			8,000	0.6
Manufacturing	6,105	37.5	206,000	15.8
Construction			72,000	5.5
Public utilities			15,000	1.2
Transp. and commun.	2,971	18.2	65,000	5.0
Trade			212,000[6]	16.2
Pub. admin., defense	1,106	6.8	71,000	5.4
Services			...[7]	...
Finance	4,476	27.5	...[6]	...
Other			491,000[7, 8]	37.6
TOTAL	16,280	100.0	1,307,000[3]	100.0[3]

Population economically active (1986): total 1,307,000; activity rate of total population 36.9% (participation rates [1985]: ages 15–64, 59.8%; female 29.0%; unemployed [1986] 17.8%).

Price and earnings indexes (1980 = 100)						
	1981	1982	1983	1984	1985	1986	1987
Consumer price index	120.4	141.0	155.8	169.2	178.4	185.2	191.0
Weekly earnings index	116.7	131.7	147.1	165.1	178.2	191.5	202.4[9]

Household income and expenditure. Average household size (1983) 3.9; income per household: n.a.; sources of income (1985): wages and salaries 60.3%, self-employment 14.4%, interest and dividends 5.1%; expenditure (1985): food 38.1%, rent and household goods 18.9%, transportation 13.0%.
Land use (1985): forest 4.8%; pasture 71.2%; agricultural 11.6%; other 12.4%.

Foreign trade

Balance of trade (current prices)						
	1982	1983	1984	1985	1986	1987
I£'000,000	−1,120	−420	−15.3	+312	1,164	2,004
% of total	9.1%	2.9%	0.1%	1.6%	6.6%	10.6%

Imports (1986): I£8,629,706,000 (mach. and transp. equip. 31.4%; chemicals 12.1%; petroleum and petroleum products 8.5%; food 4.3%; textiles 3.9%; paper 3.1%; iron and steel 1.8%). *Major import sources:* U.K. 41.6%; U.S. 15.8%; W.Ger. 8.9%; France 5.1%; The Netherlands 3.8%; Japan 3.8%.
Exports (1986): I£9,388,206,000 (mach. and transp. equip. 30.5% of which office machinery 19.8%, electrical machinery 4.3%; food 14.1%, of which meat 7.0%, dairy products 5.0%). *Major export destinations:* U.K. 34.1%; W.Ger. 10.9%; France 9.4%; U.S. 8.7%.

Transport and communications

Transport. Railroads (1986): length (1985) 2,975 km; passenger-km 1,085,-600,000; metric ton-km cargo 574,400,000. Roads (1987): length 92,303 km (paved 94%). Vehicles (1986): passenger cars 711,087; trucks and buses 106,285. Merchant marine (1987): vessels (100 gross tons and over) 153; total deadweight tonnage 162,870. Air transport (1986): passenger-km 2,496,000,000; metric ton-km cargo 79,020,000; airports (1988) 5.
Communications. Daily newspapers (1986): 7; circulation 708,682; circulation per 1,000 population 200. Radio (1985): total number of receivers 2,050,000 (1 per 1.7 persons). Television (1987): total number of receivers 795,000 (1 per 4.5 persons). Telephones (1985): 942,000 (1 per 3.8 persons).

Education and health

Education (1985–86)	schools	teachers	students	student/ teacher ratio
Primary (age 6–14)	3,384	21,144	567,086	26.8
Secondary (age 12–18)	563	14,284	252,896	17.7
Voc., teacher tr.	256	5,173	83,938	16.2
Higher	25	3,690[10]	51,341	...

Educational attainment (1981). Percent of population age 25 and over having: primary education 52.3%; secondary 23.3%; some postsecondary 16.5%; university or like institution 7.9%. *Literacy* (1987): virtually 100% literate.
Health (1984): physicians 4,250 (1 per 830 persons); hospital beds (1982) 32,468[11] (1 per 181 persons); infant mortality rate per 1,000 live births (1986) 8.7.
Food (1984–86): daily per capita caloric intake 3,689 (vegetable products 62%, animal products 38%); (1983) 143% of FAO recommended minimum.

Military

Total active duty personnel (1987): 13,600 (army 87.5%, navy 6.6%, air force 5.9%). *Military expenditure as percent of GNP* (1985): 1.9% (world 6.1%); per capita expenditure U.S.$84.

[1]As provided by the constitution; the 1948 Republic of Ireland Act provides precedent for this longer formulation of the official name but, per official sources, "has not changed the usage *Ireland* as the name of the state in the English language." [2]Includes county borough(s). [3]Detail does not add to total given because of rounding. [4]County boroughs. [5]Metal content of ores. [6]Trade includes Finance. [7]Other includes Services. [8]Includes unemployed. [9]Third quarter. [10]1983–84. [11]Includes an attribution of 13,-321 beds based on the average number of long-term resident psychiatric patients.

Israel

Official name: Medinat Yisra'el
(Hebrew); Isrā'īl (Arabic) (State
of Israel).
Form of government: multiparty
republic with one legislative house
(Knesset [120]).
Chief of state: President.
Head of government: Prime Minister.
Capital: Jerusalem is the proclaimed
capital of Israel (from Jan. 23, 1950)
and the actual seat of government,
but recognition of its status as capital
by the international community has
largely been withheld pending final
settlement of territorial and other
issues through peace talks between
Israel and the Arab parties concerned.
Official languages: Hebrew; Arabic.
Official religion: none.
Monetary unit: 1 New (Israeli) sheqel
(NIS) = 100 agorot; valuation (Oct. 10,
1988) 1 U.S.$ = NIS 1.62;
1 £ = NIS 2.78.

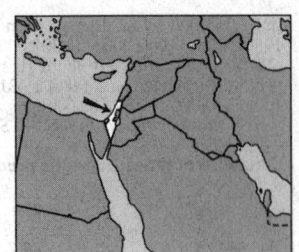

Area and population		area[1]		population
				1987
Districts	Capitals	sq mi	sq km	estimate
Central (Ha Merkaz)	Ramla	479	1,242	907,700
Haifa (Ḥefa)	Haifa	330	854	596,100
Jerusalem (Yerushalayim)	Jerusalem	215	557	518,200
Northern (Ha Ẓafon)	Tiberias	1,347	3,490	718,900
Southern (Ha Darom)	Beersheba	5,555	14,387	518,100
Tel Aviv	Tel Aviv–Yafo	66	170	1,018,800
TOTAL		7,992	20,700	4,277,800

Demography[2]

Population (1988): 4,512,000.
Density[1] (1988): persons per sq mi 564.6, persons per sq km 218.0.
Urban–rural (1986): urban 89.4%; rural 10.6%.
Sex distribution (1986): male 49.89%; female 50.11%.
Age breakdown (1986): under 15, 32.4%; 15–29, 24.6%; 30–44, 19.1%; 45–59, 11.6%; 60–74, 8.9%; 75 and over, 3.4%.
Population projection: (1990) 4,614,000; (2000) 5,490,000.
Doubling time: 43 years.
Ethnic composition (1983): Jewish 83.0%; Arab 16.8%; other 0.2%.
Religious affiliation (1987): Jewish 82.2%; Muslim (mostly Sunnī) 13.7%; Christian 2.3%; Druze and other 1.8%.
Major cities (1986): Jerusalem 457,700; Tel Aviv–Yafo 322,800; Haifa 224,600; Ḥolon 138,800; Bat Yam 131,200.

Vital statistics[2]

Birth rate per 1,000 population (1987): 22.7 (world avg. 26.0); (1984) legitimate 99.0%; illegitimate 1.0%.
Death rate per 1,000 population (1987): 6.7 (world avg. 9.9).
Natural increase rate per 1,000 population (1987): 16.0 (world avg. 16.1).
Total fertility rate (avg. births per childbearing woman; 1986): 3.1.
Marriage rate per 1,000 population (1987): 6.9.
Divorce rate per 1,000 population (1987): 1.2.
Life expectancy at birth (1985): male 73.5 years; female 77.0 years.
Major causes of death per 100,000 population (1985): diseases of the circulatory system 273.5; malignant neoplasms (cancers) 118.5; diseases of the respiratory system 46.2.

National economy

Budget (1987–88). Revenue: NIS 39,294,000,000 (internal loans 25.1%, income tax and property tax 22.7%, foreign loans 18.0%, value-added tax 13.1%, sales tax 5.3%). Expenditures: NIS 39,294,000,000 (debt repayment 27.8%, defense 20.9%, interest on loans 16.6%, health 13.7%).
Public debt (external, outstanding; 1986): U.S.$15,937,600,000.
Production (metric tons except as noted). Agriculture, forestry, fishing (value of production in NIS '000; 1986): fruit excluding citrus 534,299 (of which apples 109,202, avocados 89,157, grapes 65,132, bananas 56,097, peaches 43,324, olives 32,606), citrus fruits 446,428, vegetables 287,587 (of which tomatoes 63,564, potatoes 88,041), cotton lint 118,502, wheat 48,015; livestock (number of live animals) 318,600 cattle, 281,300 sheep, 127,500 goats, 30,250,000 chickens; roundwood 118,000 cu m; fish catch 22,000. Mining and quarrying (1986–87): phosphate rock 2,731,000; potash 2,100,000; phosphoric acid 190,000; bromine compounds 162,000; periclase 38,000. Manufacturing (1987): cement 2,226,000; wheat flour 529,000; polyethylene 90,323; paper 65,119; cardboard 61,636; ammonium sulfate 40,843. Construction (1987): residential 2,676,000 sq m; nonresidential 1,240,000 sq m. Energy production (consumption): electricity (kW-hr; 1986) 16,277,000,000 (15,908,100,000); coal (metric tons; 1986) none (3,222,000); crude petroleum (barrels; 1986) 89,862 (53,336,000); petroleum products (metric tons; 1986) 5,880,000 (5,373,000); natural gas (cu m; 1986) 39,571,000 (39,571,000).
Land use (1985): forested 5.7%; meadows and pastures 40.2%; agricultural and under permanent cultivation 21.5%, other 32.6%.
Population economically active (1987)[3]: total 1,494,000; activity rate of total population 33.5% (participation rates: over age 15, 50.4%; female (1986) 19.6%; unemployed 6.1%).

Price and earnings indexes (1980 = 100)

	1982	1983	1984	1985	1986	1987	1988[4]
Consumer price index	477.8	1,173.5	5,560.4	22,498	33,330	39,937	44,374
Monthly earnings index	553.8	1,414.8	7,028.0	24,789	39,977	52,598	61,140

Tourism (1987): receipts from visitors U.S.$1,347,000,000; expenditures by nationals abroad U.S.$998,000,000.
Gross national product (1986): U.S.$26,730,000,000 (U.S.$4,300 per capita).

Structure of gross domestic product and labour force

	1986		1987	
	in value NIS '000,000	% of total value	labour force	% of labour force
Agriculture	1,581.0	5.2	72,000	4.8
Manufacturing, mining	6,705.0	22.3	328,400	22.0
Construction	1,159.0	3.8	67,700	4.5
Public utilities	666.0	2.2	13,600	0.9
Transp. and commun.	2,451.0	8.1	91,600	6.1
Trade	4,241.0	14.1	193,400	12.9
Finance			134,300	9.0
Public and community services	13,328.0	44.2	404,300	27.1
Services			89,100	6.0
Other			99,600[5]	6.7[5]
TOTAL	30,131.0	100.0[6]	1,494,000	100.0

Household income and expenditure (1986). Average urban household size 3.6; monthly income per household NIS 1,667 (U.S.$1,120); sources of income (1984): wages 90.8%, transfer payments and other 8.4%, self-employment 0.8%; expenditure (1986): food 30.3%, housing 21.3%, transportation 12.4%, education 9.1%, household durable goods 7.2%, health 6.8%, clothing 5.6%, energy 2.2%.

Foreign trade

Balance of trade (current prices)

	1982	1983	1984	1985	1986	1987
U.S.$'000,000	−3,242	−3,210	−2,600	−2,426	−1,939	−3,441
% of total	22.6%	22.5%	17.4%	15.5%	11.2%	16.9%

Imports (1987): US$11,916,400,000 (investment goods 18.0%; diamonds 17.8%; fuel and lubricants 9.6%; consumer goods 11.2%, of which durable goods 5.2%, foodstuffs 3.1%). *Major import sources:* U.S. 16.2%; Belgium and Luxembourg 14.2%; W.Ger. 12.9%; U.K. 9.4%; Switzerland 7.4%; France 4.6%.
Exports (1987): US$8,475,400,000 (machinery and electronics 28.7%; diamonds 27.2%; agricultural products 7.2%; textiles, clothing, and leather 7.0%; food, beverages, and tobacco 5.1%). *Major export destinations:* U.S. 32.5%; U.K. 7.7%; Japan 5.8%; W.Ger. 5.6%; France 4.6%; The Netherlands 4.5%; Hong Kong 4.5%; Belgium and Luxembourg 3.3%.

Transport and communications

Transport. Railroads (1986–87): route length 328 mi, 528 km; passenger-mi 107,700,000, passenger-km 173,400,000; short ton-mi cargo 673,700,000, metric ton-km cargo 983,600,000. Roads (1986): total length 7,968 mi, 12,823 km (paved 100%). Vehicles (1986): passenger cars 648,847; trucks and buses 129,033. Merchant marine (1987): vessels (100 gross tons and over) 62; total deadweight tonnage 612,579. Air transport[7] (1987): passenger-mi 4,526,000,000, passenger-km 7,284,000,000; short ton-mi cargo 443,900,000, metric ton-km cargo 648,000,000; airports (1988) with scheduled flights 5.
Communications. Daily newspapers (1986): total number 25; total circulation 1,148,000; circulation per 1,000 population 263. Radio (1986): 700,000 receivers (1 per 6.2 persons). Television (1986): 620,000 receivers (1 per 7.0 persons). Telephones (1986–87): 1,935,000 (1 per 2.3 persons).

Education and health

Education (1986–87)

	schools	teachers	students	student/ teacher ratio
Primary (age 6–13)	1,832	44,409	621,393	14.0
Secondary (age 14–17)[8]	572	39,242	249,040	6.3
Vocational	373	...	102,739	...
Higher	7[9]	8,112[10]	98,821[11]	...

Educational attainment (1982). Percent of population age 25 and over having: no formal schooling 9.7%; primary education 30.6%; secondary 36.6%; postsecondary, vocational, and higher 23.1%. *Literacy* (1983): total population age 15 and over literate 2,542,403 (91.8%); males literate 1,312,258 (95.0%); females literate 1,230,145 (88.7%).
Health (1986): physicians (1983) 11,895 (1 per 345 persons); hospital beds 27,399 (1 per 159 persons); infant mortality rate per 1,000 live births 11.2.
Food (1984–86): daily per capita caloric intake 3,037 (vegetable products 79%, animal products 21%); (1983) 121% of FAO recommended minimum.

Military

Total active duty personnel (1987): 141,000 (army 73.7%, navy 6.4%, air force 19.9%). *Military expenditure as percent of GNP* (1985): 13.9% (world 6.1%); per capita expenditure U.S.$854.

[1]Excluding West Bank, Gaza Strip, Golan Heights, and East Jerusalem. [2]De jure; includes population of East Jerusalem and about 25,000 Israeli residents living in occupied territories. [3]Excludes armed forces; includes Israelis in occupied territories. [4]May. [5]Mostly unemployed. [6]Detail does not add to total given because of rounding. [7]El Al only. [8]Includes intermediate education age 12–14. [9]Universities only. [10]1985–86. [11]Includes post-secondary teacher training.

Italy

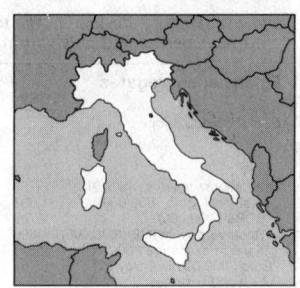

Official name: Repubblica Italiana (Italian Republic).
Form of government: republic with two legislative houses (Senate [323]; Chamber of Deputies [630]).
Chief of state: President.
Head of government: Prime Minister.
Capital: Rome.
Official language: Italian.
Official religion: none.
Monetary unit: 1 lira (Lit, plural lire) = 100 centesimi; valuation (Oct. 10, 1988) 1 U.S.$ = Lit 1,383; 1 £ = Lit 2,368.

Area and population

Regions Provinces	Capitals	area sq mi	area sq km	population 1987[1] estimate
Abruzzi	L'Aquila	4,168	10,794	1,254,129
Chieti	Chieti	999	2,587	382,765
L'Aquila	L'Aquila	1,944	5,034	298,299
Pescara	Pescara	473	1,225	293,669
Teramo	Teramo	752	1,948	279,396
Basilicata	Potenza	3,858	9,992	620,260
Matera	Matera	1,331	3,447	207,899
Potenza	Potenza	2,527	6,545	412,361
Calabria	Catanzaro	5,823	15,080	2,139,301
Catanzaro	Catanzaro	2,026	5,247	771,585
Cosenza	Cosenza	2,568	6,650	777,000
Reggio di Calabria	Reggio di Calabria	1,229	3,183	590,716
Campania	Naples	5,249	13,595	5,690,431
Avellino	Avellino	1,078	2,792	447,822
Benevento	Benevento	800	2,071	298,159
Caserta	Caserta	1,019	2,639	803,438
Napoli	Naples	452	1,171	3,087,246
Salerno	Salerno	1,900	4,922	1,053,766
Emilia-Romagna	Bologna	8,542	22,123	3,931,014
Bologna	Bologna	1,429	3,702	917,016
Ferrara	Ferrara	1,016	2,632	372,240
Forlì	Forlì	1,123	2,910	608,159
Modena	Modena	1,039	2,690	595,610
Parma	Parma	1,332	3,449	396,491
Piacenza	Piacenza	1,000	2,589	273,606
Ravenna	Ravenna	718	1,859	353,375
Reggio nell'Emilia	Reggio nell'Emilia	885	2,292	414,517
Friuli-Venezia Giulia	Trieste	3,029	7,845	1,214,557
Gorizia	Gorizia	180	467	141,215
Pordenone	Pordenone	878	2,273	276,102
Trieste	Trieste	82	212	269,878
Udine	Udine	1,889	4,893	527,362
Lazio	Rome	6,642	17,203	5,116,125
Frosinone	Frosinone	1,251	3,239	478,931
Latina	Latina	869	2,251	463,141
Rieti	Rieti	1,061	2,749	145,475
Roma	Rome	2,066	5,352	3,752,360
Viterbo	Viterbo	1,395	3,612	276,218
Liguria	Genoa	2,092	5,418	1,758,961
Genova	Genoa	709	1,836	1,006,711
Imperia	Imperia	446	1,155	222,067
La Spezia	La Spezia	341	882	236,625
Savona	Savona	596	1,545	293,558
Lombardia	Milan	9,211	23,857	8,876,787
Bergamo	Bergamo	1,066	2,760	912,688
Brescia	Brescia	1,846	4,782	1,030,360
Como	Como	798	2,067	783,881
Cremona	Cremona	684	1,771	328,613
Mantova	Mantova	903	2,339	372,802
Milano	Milan	1,066	2,762	3,978,658
Pavia	Pavia	1,145	2,965	501,470
Sondrio	Sondrio	1,240	3,212	176,120
Varese	Varese	463	1,199	792,195
Marche	Ancona	3,743	9,693	1,426,965
Ancona	Ancona	749	1,940	438,045
Ascoli Piceno	Ascoli Piceno	806	2,087	358,827
Macerata	Macerata	1,071	2,774	294,759
Pesaro e Urbino	Pesaro	1,117	2,892	335,334
Molise	Campobasso	1,713	4,438	334,195
Campobasso	Campobasso	1,123	2,909	240,753
Isernia	Isernia	590	1,529	93,442
Piemonte	Turin	9,807	25,399	4,389,430
Alessandria	Alessandria	1,375	3,560	452,493
Asti	Asti	583	1,511	211,041
Cuneo	Cuneo	2,665	6,903	547,116
Novara	Novara	1,388	3,594	501,706
Torino	Turin	2,637	6,830	2,292,068
Vercelli	Vercelli	1,159	3,001	385,006
Puglia	Bari	7,470	19,348	4,026,151
Bari	Bari	1,980	5,129	1,515,742
Brindisi	Brindisi	710	1,838	406,162
Foggia	Foggia	2,774	7,185	699,624
Lecce	Lecce	1,065	2,759	808,294
Taranto	Taranto	941	2,437	596,329
Sardegna	Cagliari	9,301	24,090	1,643,789
Cagliari	Cagliari	2,662	6,895	759,076
Nuoro	Nuoro	2,720	7,044	277,107
Oristano	Oristano	1,016	2,631	159,551
Sassari	Sassari	2,903	7,520	448,055
Sicilia (Sicily)	Palermo	9,926	25,709	5,112,073
Agrigento	Agrigento	1,175	3,042	488,768
Caltanissetta	Caltanissetta	822	2,128	294,247
Catania	Catania	1,371	3,552	1,060,527
Enna	Enna	989	2,562	197,701
Messina	Messina	1,254	3,248	687,776
Palermo	Palermo	1,927	4,992	1,249,005
Ragusa	Ragusa	623	1,614	287,927
Siracusa	Siracusa	814	2,109	409,509
Trapani	Trapani	951	2,462	436,613

Area and population (continued)

Regions Provinces	Capitals	area sq mi	area sq km	population 1987[1] estimate
Toscana	Florence	8,877	22,992	3,571,538
Arezzo	Arezzo	1,248	3,232	313,396
Firenze	Florence	1,498	3,879	1,197,310
Grosseto	Grosseto	1,739	4,504	220,170
Livorno	Livorno	468	1,213	345,175
Lucca	Lucca	684	1,773	382,882
Massa-Carrara	Massa-Carrara	447	1,157	205,001
Pisa	Pisa	945	2,448	388,620
Pistoia	Pistoia	373	965	265,509
Siena	Siena	1,475	3,821	253,475
Trentino-Alto Adige	Bolzano	5,258	13,618	880,237
Bolzano-Bozen	Bolzano	2,857	7,400	435,377
Trento	Trento	2,401	6,218	444,860
Umbria	Perugia	3,265	8,456	817,852
Perugia	Perugia	2,446	6,334	591,166
Terni	Terni	819	2,122	226,686
Valle d'Aosta	Aosta	1,259	3,262	113,855
Veneto	Venice	7,090	18,364	4,372,869
Belluno	Belluno	1,420	3,678	216,763
Padova	Padova	827	2,142	816,226
Rovigo	Rovigo	691	1,789	250,734
Treviso	Treviso	956	2,477	731,893
Venezia	Venice	950	2,460	837,170
Verona	Verona	1,195	3,096	782,754
Vicenza	Vicenza	1,051	2,722	737,329
TOTAL		116,324	301,277	57,290,519

Demography

Population (1988): 57,401,000.
Density (1988): persons per sq mi 492.6, persons per sq km 190.2.
Urban–rural (1987): urban 67.0%; rural 33.0%.
Sex distribution (1987): male 48.58%; female 51.42%.
Age breakdown (1985): under 15, 19.9%; 15–29, 22.8%; 30–44, 19.8%; 45–59, 18.7%; 60–74, 13.2%; 75 and over 5.6%.
Population projection: (1990) 57,408,000; (2000) 57,117,000.
Doubling time: n.a.; population stable.
Ethnolinguistic composition (1983): Italian 94.1%; Sardinian 2.6%; Rhaetian 1.3%; other 2.0%.
Religious affiliation (1980): Roman Catholic 83.2%; nonreligious 13.6%; atheist 2.6%; other 0.6%.
Major cities (1987): Rome 2,815,457; Milan 1,495,260; Naples 1,204,211; Turin 1,035,565; Genoa 727,427; Palermo 723,732; Bologna 432,406; Florence 425,835; Catania 372,486; Bari 362,524; Venice 331,454.
National origin (1980): Italian 98.8%; foreign-born 1.2%, of which Austrian 0.4%, French 0.2%, Slovene 0.2%, Albanian 0.1%, other 0.3%.
Mobility (1981). Population living in the same residence as in 1976: 92.4%.
Households. Average household size (1986) 2.9; composition of households (1981) 1 person 17.9%, 2 persons 23.6%, 3 persons 22.1%, 4 persons 21.5%, 5 persons 9.5%, 6 or more persons 5.4%. Family households (1983): 15,-205,000 (85.3%); nonfamily 2,617,000 (14.7%), of which 1-person 13.0%.
Immigration (1985): immigrants admitted 66,737, from Europe 75.8%, of which W.Ger. 31.6%, Switzerland 25.6%, France 6.1%; Africa 6.5%; U.S. 5.3%; Asia 3.0%.

Vital statistics

Birth rate per 1,000 population (1986): 9.7 (world avg. 26.0); legitimate 94.4%; illegitimate 5.6%.
Death rate per 1,000 population (1986): 9.2 (world avg. 9.9).
Natural increase rate per 1,000 population (1986): 0.5 (world avg. 16.1).
Total fertility rate (avg. births per childbearing woman; 1980–85): 1.6.
Marriage rate per 1,000 population (1986): 5.2.
Divorce rate per 1,000 population: (1986): 0.3.
Life expectancy at birth (1983): male 71.4 years; female 78.1 years.
Major causes of death per 100,000 population (1984): diseases of the circulatory system 429.7; malignant neoplasms (cancers) 226.0; diseases of the respiratory system 60.5; diseases of the digestive system 54.7.

Social indicators

Educational attainment (1981). Percent of population age 25 and over having: no formal schooling 19.3%[2]; primary education 47.4%; lower secondary 18.0%; upper secondary 11.2%; higher 4.1%.

Distribution of income (1980)

percent of household income by quintile

1	2	3	4	5 (highest)
7.0	11.0	16.0	22.0	45.0

Quality of working life. Average workweek (1985): 36.6 hours. Annual rate per 100,000 workers (1984) for: injury or accident 3,702; industrial illness 405[3]; death 6.7. Proportion of labour force insured for damages or income loss (1982) resulting from: injury 100%; permanent disability 100%; death 100%. Number of working days lost to labour stoppages (1986): 5,643,700[4]. Average duration of journey to work: n.a. Rate per 1,000 workers of discouraged (unemployed no longer seeking work; 1982): 0.9.
Material well-being. Rate per 1,000 of population possessing (1985): telephone 469[5]; automobile 391; television 254 (colour 128). Households possessing (1979): television 72%; refrigerator 91%; washing machine 88%.
Social participation. Eligible voters participating in last national election (1987): 88.5%. Population participating in voluntary work: n.a. Trade union membership in total workforce (1984): c. 70%. Practicing religious population in total affiliated population (1980): 65.7%, of which weekly 28.0%.
Social deviance (1986). Offense rate per 100,000 population for: murder 12.1; rape 71.8; other assault 48.8; theft, including burglary and housebreaking 2,088. Incidence per 100,000 in general population of: alcoholism (1978) 2.0; drug and substance abuse (1978) 25.1; suicide (1986) 4.6.

Access to services (1981). Proportion of dwellings having access to: electricity 99.5%; safe water supply 98.7%; toilet facilities 98.5%; bath facilities 86.4%.
Leisure (1985). Favourite leisure activities (as percent of public spending on culture): cinema 24.4%; sporting events 18.9%; theatre 11.3%.

National economy

Gross national product (1986): U.S.$489,880,000,000 (U.S.$8,570 per capita).

Structure of gross domestic product and labour force

	1986			
	in value 000,000,000 lire	% of total value	labour force	% of labour force
Agriculture	38,841	4.3	2,241,000	9.5
Mining	23,563	2.6	220,000	0.9
Manufacturing	186,004	20.8	4,719,000	20.0
Construction	50,179	5.6	1,882,000	8.0
Public utilities	47,730	5.4	...	...
Transp. and commun.	51,138	5.7	1,120,000	4.7
Trade	171,955	19.2	4,407,000	18.7
Finance	105,439	11.8	749,000	3.2
Pub. admin., defense	104,512	11.7 }	5,668,000	24.0
Services	106,448	11.9 }		
Other	8,553[6]	1.0[6]	2,611,000[7]	11.0[7]
TOTAL	894,362	100.0	23,617,000	100.0

Budget (1986). Revenue: Lit 258,355,000,000,000 (property and income taxes 46.2%, business taxes 22.6%, customs duties and value added taxes 8.3%). Expenditures: Lit 326,731,000,000,000 (social services 29.8%, education and culture 10.1%, transportation and communications 8.6%, national defense 4.5%, general administration 3.5%).
Public debt (1986): U.S.$460,000,000,000.
Tourism (1985): receipts from visitors U.S.$8,758,000,000; expenditures by nationals abroad U.S.$2,283,000,000.

Manufacturing, mining, and construction enterprises (1984)

	no. of enter- prises[8]	no. of employees[9]	hourly wages as a % of avg. of all wages[10]	annual value added (Lit '000,000,000)
Manufacturing				
Transport equipment	924	354,161	117.7	11,839
Industrial chemicals	1,184	205,789	119.7	11,570
Electrical machinery	1,559	296,320	112.1	10,483
Metal products	4,232	280,627	86.7	9,553
Machinery, nonelectrical	3,043	252,798	98.0	9,531
Textiles	3,393	253,598	84.4	8,360
Iron and steel	409	143,115	122.6	4,938
Food products	1,631	112,780	92.2	4,655
Printing, publishing	1,022	92,031	103.2	4,017
Wearing apparel	2,475	162,991	75.0	3,849
Pottery, ceramics, and glass	950	98,964	...	3,502
Plastic products	1,236	81,796	84.4	3,159
Paper and paper products	689	65,519	102.2	2,830
Petroleum and gas	17	6,590	138.6	2,702
Mining and quarrying	...	206,000	...	20,060
Construction	326,000[11]	1,645,000	...	46,686

Production (metric tons except as noted). Agriculture, forestry, fishing (1986): sugar beets 13,100,000, grapes 11,950,000, wheat 9,070,000, corn (maize) 6,560,000, tomatoes 5,280,000, potatoes 2,640,000, oranges 2,190,000, apples 2,080,000, olives 2,050,000, barley 1,548,000, peaches and nectarines 1,434,000, rice 1,082,000; livestock (number of live animals) 8,910,000 cattle, 9,718,000 sheep, 9,120,000 pigs, 111,000,000 chickens; roundwood (1985) 80,444,000 cu m; fish catch 414,203. Mining and quarrying (1986): rock salt 3,432,600; potash 1,260,600; feldspar 1,141,500; asbestos 115,200; barite 112,500; magnesium 82,200; zinc 50,500; lead 21,700. Manufacturing (1986): cement 36,396,000; crude steel 22,740,000; pig iron 11,839,000; chemical fertilizers 6,726,000; sulfuric acid 4,172,000; olive oil 3,900,000[12]; plastics and resins 2,662,000; caustic soda 1,043,000; textiles and cloth 253,400[13]; wine 76,987,000 hectolitres; beer 11,372,000 hectolitres; 2,650,-853 motorized road vehicles, of which 1,652,827 automobiles, 819,026 motorcycles, scooters, and mopeds, 179,000 trucks and buses; 3,991,000 washing machines; 3,589,671 refrigerators; 1,847,429 television receivers, of which 1,647,488 colour. Construction (1986): residential 64,068,212 cu m; commercial, industrial, and other 58,809,987 cu m.

Service enterprises (1986)

	no. of enter- prises[10]	no. of employees	hourly wage as a % of all wages	annual value added (Lit '000,000,000)
Public utilities	1,398	...	...	47,730
Transportation	132,164	1,120,000	...	51,138
Communications }				5,842
Finance	89,092	749,000	...	105,439
Wholesale and retail trade	1,495,702	4,407,000	...	171,955
Pub. admin., services	...	5,668,000	...	210,960

Energy production (consumption): electricity (kW-hr; 1986) 188,989,000,000 (211,103,000,000); coal (metric tons; 1986) 1,554,000 (22,111,000); crude petroleum (barrels; 1986) 17,331,000 (547,690,000); petroleum products (metric tons; 1986) 74,712,000 (78,496,000); natural gas (cu m; 1986) 14,-209,100,000 (30,987,400,000).
Population economically active (1986): total 23,617,000; activity rate of total population 41.5% (participation rates: ages 14–64, 58.5%; female 35.9%; unemployed 11.0%).

Price and earnings indexes (1980 = 100)

	1981	1982	1983	1984	1985	1986	1987
Consumer price index	119.5	139.2	159.5	176.8	193.0	204.3	214.0
Monthly earnings index	123.9	145.7	167.9	186.7	207.5	217.5	...

Land use (1985): forested 21.8%; meadows and pastures 17.1%; agricultural and under permanent cultivation 41.5%; other 19.6%.

Financial aggregates

	1982	1983	1984	1985	1986	1987
Exchange rate, Lit per:						
U.S. dollar	1,352.5	1,518.8	1,757.0	1,909.4	1,490.8	1,296.1
£	2,367.6	2,304.0	2,347.9	2,759.1	2,187.0	2,124.2
SDR	1,511.3	1,737.4	1,897.6	1,843.7	1,661.3	1,658.8
International reserves (U.S.$)						
Total (excl. gold; '000,000)	14,091	20,105	20,795	15,595	19,987	30,214
SDRs ('000,000)	785	591	633	326	587	948
Reserve pos. in IMF ('000,000)	696	990	1,074	1,160	1,268	1,447
Foreign exchange ('000,000)	12,610	18,259	19,089	14,029	18,116	27,765
Gold ('000,000 fine troy oz)	66.67	66.67	66.67	66.67	66.67	66.67
% world reserves	7.0	7.1	7.1	7.0	7.0	7.1
Interest and prices						
Central bank discount (%)	18.00	17.00	16.50	15.00	12.00	12.00
Gov't. bond yield (%)	20.90	18.02	14.95	13.00	10.52	9.65
Industrial share prices (1980 = 100)	123.1	153.1	171.9	286.7	667.4	641.2[14]
Balance of payments (U.S.$'000,000)						
Balance of visible trade	−8,130	−4,390	−5,994	−6,853	+5,005	...
Imports, f.o.b.	−80,678	−75,215	−78,976	−85,145	−91,973	...
Exports, f.o.b.	72,810	72,070	74,022	75,992	97,088	...
Balance of invisibles	1,553	2,609	1,921	1,569	682	...
Balance of payments, current account	−6,394	+1,367	−2,284	−3,490	+4,263	...

Household income and expenditure (1984). Average household size (1986) 2.9; average annual income per household Lit 19,692,000 (U.S.$11,208); sources of income: salaries and wages 49.5%, transfer payments 20.6%, self-employment 19.9%; expenditure (1986): food and beverages 27.0%, transport and communications 15.7%, housing 13.7%, recreation and education 6.0%.

Foreign trade

Balance of trade (current prices)

	1981	1982	1983	1984	1985	1986
Lit '000,000,000	−13,713	−10,951	−2,689	−10,807	−6,614	+6,592
% of total	7.4%	5.2%	2.4%	4.0%	2.2%	2.3%

Imports (1986): Lit 149,044,966,000,000 (machinery and transport equipment 26.5%, of which transport equipment 10.0%, precision machinery 5.7%; chemicals and chemical products 16.0%; food and live animals 9.0%; metal and semiprocessed metal 8.4%; crude petroleum 8.4%; refined petroleum products 3.4%). *Major import sources:* W.Ger. 20.4%; France 14.6%; The Netherlands 5.9%; U.S. 5.7%; U.K. 5.1%; Switzerland 4.4%.
Exports (1986): Lit 145,322,982,000,000 (nontransport machinery 28.0%; chemicals and chemical products 11.0%; transport equipment 10.4%, of which automobiles 4.0%, tractors and construction equipment 0.7%; textiles 9.7%; wearing apparel 9.2%, of which shoes 4.3%; metal and processed metal 7.4%; petroleum products 3.0%). *Major export destinations:* W.Ger. 18.1%; France 15.6%; U.S. 10.8%; U.K. 7.1%; Switzerland 4.5%.

Transport and communications

Transport. Railroads (1986): length 12,257 mi, 19,726 km; passenger-mi 25,165,000,000, passenger-km 40,500,000,000; short ton-mi cargo 11,967,-000,000, metric ton-km cargo 17,472,000,000. Roads (1984): total length 187,223 mi, 301,307 km (paved 100%). Vehicles (1985): passenger cars 22,398,000; trucks and buses 1,863,250. Merchant marine (1987): vessels (100 gross tons and over) 1,571; total deadweight tonnage 12,178,324. Air transport (1986)[15]: passenger-mi 8,694,000,000, passenger-km 13,992,000,-000; short ton-mi cargo 589,282,000, metric ton-km cargo 859,000,000; airports (1988) 30.
Communications. Daily newspapers (1986): total number 99; total circulation 6,805,300[16]; circulation per 1,000 population, n.a. Radio (1986): 14,817,162 receivers (1 per 3.9 persons). Television (1986): 14,605,448 receivers (1 per 3.9 persons). Telephones (1986): 26,873,730 (1 per 2.1 persons).

Education and health

Education (1986–87)

	schools	teachers	students	student/ teacher ratio
Primary (age 6–10)	27,188	222,160	3,530,825	15.9
Secondary	10,031	128,210	2,714,038	21.2
Voc., teacher tr.	7,624	116,119	2,658,588	22.9
Higher[17]	...	...	1,179,851	...

Literacy (1985): total population age 15 and over literate 38,421,342 (97.0%); males literate 18,767,897 (97.9%); females literate 19,653,445 (96.3%).
Health (1985): physicians 109,199 (1 per 523.3 persons); hospital beds 470,579 (1 per 121.4 persons); infant mortality rate per 1,000 live births (1985) 10.9.
Food (1983–85): daily per capita caloric intake 3,486 (vegetable products 72%, animal products 28%); (1983) 140% of FAO recommended minimum requirement.

Military

Total active duty personnel (1987): 388,300 (army 68.2%, navy 13.0%, air force 18.8%). *Military expenditure as percent of GNP* (1985): 2.7% (world 6.1%); per capita expenditure U.S.$170.

[1]January 1. [2]More than two-thirds are age 55 and over. [3]1978. [4]Calculated in terms of a seven-hour day. [5]1986. [6]Imputed bank charges less duties on imports. [7]Unemployed. [8]Enterprises with 20 or more persons engaged. [9]Total number of persons engaged. [10]1981. [11]All enterprises (1982). [12]1984. [13]1983. [14]Eleven-month average. [15]Alitalia only. [16]For 66 newspapers only. [17]1985–86.

Jamaica

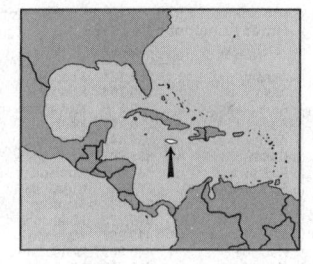

Official name: Jamaica.
Form of government: constitutional monarchy with two legislative houses (Senate [21]; House of Representatives [60]).
Chief of state: British Monarch represented by governor-general.
Head of government: Prime Minister.
Capital: Kingston.
Official language: English.
Official religion: none.
Monetary unit: 1 Jamaica dollar (J$) = 100 cents; valuation (Oct. 10, 1988) 1 U.S.$ = J$5.40; 1 £ = J$9.25.

Area and population

Parishes	Capitals	area sq mi	area sq km	population 1985 estimate
Clarendon	May Pen	462	1,196	212,100
Hanover	Lucea	174	450	64,000
Kingston	1	8	22	2
Manchester	Mandeville	321	830	153,800
Portland	Port Antonio	314	814	76,200
Saint Andrew	1	166	431	625,8002
Saint Ann	Saint Ann's Bay	468	1,213	144,600
Saint Catherine	Spanish Town	460	1,192	388,000
Saint Elizabeth	Black River	468	1,212	142,400
Saint James	Montego Bay	230	595	145,300
Saint Mary	Port Maria	236	611	109,900
Saint Thomas	Morant Bay	287	743	83,800
Trelawny	Falmouth	338	875	72,200
Westmorland	Savanna-la-Mar	312	807	125,600
TOTAL		4,244	10,991	2,343,7003

Demography

Population (1988): 2,407,000.
Density (1988): persons per sq mi 567.2, persons per sq km 219.0.
Urban–rural (1986): urban 49.1%; rural 50.9%.
Sex distribution (1985): male 49.54%; female 50.46%.
Age breakdown (1985): under 15, 37.2%; 15–29, 30.6%; 30–44, 14.4%; 45–59, 9.1%; 60–74, 6.3%; 75 and over, 2.4%.
Population projection: (1990) 2,481,000; (2000) 2,882,000.
Doubling time: 41 years.
Ethnic composition (1983): black 76.3%; Afro-European 15.1%; East Indian and Afro-East Indian 3.4%; white 3.2%; other 2.0%.
Religious affiliation (1982): Church of God 18.4%; Baptist 10.0%; Anglican 7.1%; Seventh-day Adventist 6.9%; Pentecostal 5.2%; Roman Catholic 5.0%; Methodist 3.1%; other (mostly other Protestant, indigenous Christian, Rastafarian, and not stated) 44.3%.
Major cities (1982): Kingston 104,0414 (metropolitan area 524,638); Spanish Town 89,097; Portmore 73,400; Montego Bay 70,265.

Vital statistics

Birth rate per 1,000 population (1987): 22.2 (world avg. 26.0); (1983) legitimate 15.7%, illegitimate 84.3%.
Death rate per 1,000 population (1987): 5.3 (world avg. 9.9).
Natural increase rate per 1,000 population (1987): 16.9 (world avg. 16.1).
Total fertility rate (avg. births per childbearing woman; 1987): 3.1.
Marriage rate per 1,000 population (1985): 5.1.
Divorce rate per 1,000 population (1985): 0.4.
Life expectancy at birth (1985): male 68.1 years; female 72.6 years.
Major causes of death per 100,000 population (1982): cerebrovascular disease 80.5; ischemic heart diseases 77.4; malignant neoplasms (cancers) 75.3; hypertensive disease 29.7; diabetes mellitus 23.5.

National economy

Budget (1987–88). Revenue: J$7,190,500,000 (tax revenue 59.9%, foreign loans 16.3%, treasury bills 7.4%, nontax revenue 2.8%). Expenditures: J$6,580,400,000 (public debt and fiscal services 42.1%, education 12.9%, health 6.4%, police 4.4%, agriculture 4.4%, defense 2.1%).
Public debt (external, outstanding; 1986): U.S.$2,993,200,000.
Tourism: receipts from visitors (1987) U.S.$551,000,000; expenditures by nationals abroad (1986) U.S.$32,000,000.
Production (metric tons except as noted). Agriculture, forestry, fishing (1986): sugarcane 2,083,000, yams 160,000, bananas 160,000, coconuts 120,000, oranges 33,000, plantains 31,000, tomatoes 20,000, pimientos 2,500, cocoa 2,400, coffee 2,000, tobacco 2,000; livestock (number of live animals) 430,000 goats, 290,000 cattle, 245,000 pigs; roundwood (1985) 93,000 cu m; fish catch 10,496. Mining and quarrying (1987): bauxite 7,543,000; alumina 1,613,000; gypsum 117,0005. Manufacturing (1987): cement 308,000; sugar 175,000; stout and beer 466,000 hectolitres5; rum 140,000 hectolitres5; cigarettes 1,132,000,000 units5; garments, U.S.$101,300,0006. Construction (private sector only): residential completions (1986) 54,500 sq m; non-residential starts (1986) 16,300 sq m. Energy production (consumption): electricity (kW-hr; 1986) 2,400,000,000 (2,400,000,000); coal, none (none); crude petroleum (barrels; 1986) none (7,330,000); petroleum products (metric tons) 859,000 (1,791,000); natural gas, none (none).
Land use (1985): forested 17.6%; meadows and pastures 18.0%; agricultural and under permanent cultivation 24.8%; other 39.6%.
Gross national product (at current market prices; 1986): U.S.$1,980,000,000 (U.S.$880 per capita).

Structure of gross domestic product and labour force

	1987 in value J$'000,000	1987 % of total value	1986 labour force	1986 % of labour force
Agriculture	956.8	6.1	267,200	25.3
Mining	1,145.4	7.3	6,300	0.6
Manufacturing	3,505.9	22.3	115,300	10.9
Construction	1,315.6	8.3	35,400	3.4
Public utilities	455.3	2.9 }	38,300	3.6
Transp. and commun.	1,323.1	8.4 }		
Trade	3,391.8	21.6	125,100	11.9
Pub. admin., defense	1,415.0	9.0	79,900	7.6
Finance, real estate	2,337.7	14.9 }	150,100	14.2
Services	704.3	4.5 }		
Other	−833.77	−5.3	237,9008	22.5
TOTAL	15,717.2	100.0	1,055,500	100.0

Population economically active (1987): total 1,079,200; activity rate of total population 45.8% (participation rates: ages 14–64 [1982] 78.0%; female 45.3%; unemployed 20.8%).

Price and earnings indexes (1980 = 100)

	1982	1983	1984	1985	1986	1987	1988
Consumer price index	120.1	134.0	171.3	215.3	247.8	264.3	278.09
Monthly earnings index	...	...	...	...	...	...	...

Household income and expenditure. Average household size (1982) 4.3; income per household, n.a.; sources of income (1982): wages and salaries 70.9%, self-employment 27.3%, transfers 1.8%; expenditure (1986): food and beverages 34.7%, transportation and communications 13.1%, energy and water 6.1%, rent 6.1%, household durable goods 5.2%, tobacco 4.2%, clothing and footwear 3.9%, personal effects 3.5%, health care 2.4%, recreation 2.1%, education 0.2%, other 18.5%.

Foreign trade10

Balance of trade (current prices)

	1982	1983	1984	1985	1986	1987
J$'000,000	−841.2	−1,071.2	−1,103.8	−2,417.5	−1,370.6	−2,254.2
% of total	24.5%	27.8%	16.5%	28.4%	17.3%	24.0%

Imports (1987): J$6,623,400,000 (raw materials 52.1%, of which fuels 17.9%; capital goods 28.7%, of which construction materials 6.6%, transport equipment 5.0%; food 7.8%). *Major import sources:* United States 45.7%; United Kingdom 7.2%; Canada 5.7%; Japan 4.1%; Trinidad and Tobago 3.1%.
Exports (1987): J$3,560,900,000 (alumina 29.8%; bauxite 16.8%; garments 15.0%; raw sugar 9.1%; bananas 3.0%; rum 1.6%; coffee 1.4%). *Major export destinations:* United States 32.8%; United Kingdom 17.3%; Canada 11.6%; U.S.S.R. 3.0%; Trinidad and Tobago 2.5%; Japan 1.3%.

Transport and communications

Transport. Railroads (1985): length 215 mi, 346 km; passenger-mi 24,887,000, passenger-km 40,052,000; short ton-mi cargo 88,514,00011, metric ton-km cargo 129,228,00011. Roads (1985): total length 7,680 mi, 12,360 km (paved 39%). Vehicles (1987): passenger cars 44,457; trucks and buses 20,737. Merchant marine (1987): vessels (100 gross tons and over) 14; total deadweight tonnage 18,540. Air transport (1987): passenger-mi 1,316,000,000, passenger-km 2,118,000,000; short ton-mi cargo 18,297,000, metric ton-km cargo 26,713,000; airports (1988) with scheduled flights 6.
Communications. Daily newspapers (1987): total number 2; total circulation 90,000; circulation per 1,000 population 38. Radio (1986): 910,000 receivers (1 per 2.6 persons). Television (1987): 387,000 receivers (1 per 6.1 persons). Telephones (1987): 160,918 (1 per 15 persons).

Education and health

Education (1986–87)12

	schools	teachers	students	student/teacher ratio
Primary (age 6–11)	787	9,419	332,636	35.3
Secondary (age 12–16)	131	7,447	226,288	30.4
Voc., teacher tr.	10	501	8,778	17.5
Higher	17	...	17,791	...

Educational attainment (1982). Percent of population age 25 and over having: no formal schooling 3.2%; some primary education 79.8%; some secondary 15.0%; complete secondary and higher 2.0%. *Literacy* (1980): total population age 14 and over literate 1,100,600 (88.6%); males literate 542,600 (88.2%); females literate 558,000 (89.1%).
Health (1987): physicians 33013 (1 per 7,186 persons); hospital beds 5,463 (1 per 434 persons); infant mortality rate per 1,000 live births 18.0.
Food (1984–86): daily per capita caloric intake 2,581 (vegetable products 86%, animal products 14%); (1983) 111% of FAO recommended minimum requirement.

Military

Total active duty personnel (1987): 2,520 (army 87.3%; navy 6.0%; air force 6.7%). *Military expenditure as percent of GNP* (1985): 0.9% (world 6.1%); per capita expenditure U.S.$8.

1The parishes of Kingston and Saint Andrew are jointly administered from the Half Way Tree section of Saint Andrew. 2Kingston included with Saint Andrew. 3Preliminary estimate; total revised downward to 2,311,000. 4City of Kingston is coextensive with Kingston parish. 51986. 6Value of exports. 7Less imputed service charges. 8Includes 234,900 unemployed. 9March. 10Import figures are f.o.b. in balance of trade and c.i.f. in commodities and trading partners. 111981. 12Public schools only. 13Government-employed only.

Japan

Official name: Nihon (Japan).
Form of government: constitutional monarchy with a National Diet consisting of two legislative houses (House of Councillors [252]; House of Representatives [512]).
Chief of state: Emperor.
Head of government: Prime Minister.
Capital: Tōkyō.
Official language: Japanese.
Official religion: none.
Monetary unit: 1 yen (¥) = 100 sen; valuation (Oct. 10, 1988)
1 U.S.$ = ¥132.26;
1 £ = ¥226.50.

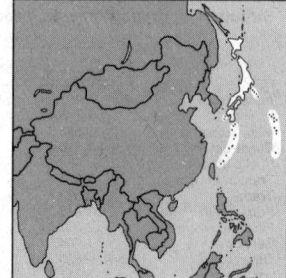

Area and population

Regions Prefectures	Capitals	area sq mi	area sq km	population 1987 estimate[1]
Chūbu				
Aichi	Nagoya	1,984	5,138	6,555,000
Fukui	Fukui	1,619	4,192	822,000
Gifu	Gifu	4,091	10,596	2,045,000
Ishikawa	Kanazawa	1,620	4,197	1,157,000
Nagano	Nagano	5,245	13,585	2,149,000
Niigata	Niigata	4,857	12,579	2,479,000
Shizuoka	Shizuoka	3,001	7,773	3,617,000
Toyama	Toyama	1,642	4,252	1,121,000
Yamanashi	Kōfu	1,723	4,463	842,000
Chūgoku				
Hiroshima	Hiroshima	3,269	8,467	2,839,000
Okayama	Okayama	2,737	7,090	1,927,000
Shimane	Matsue	2,559[2]	6,628[2]	793,000
Tottori	Tottori	1,349[2]	3,494[2]	617,000
Yamaguchi	Yamaguchi	2,358	6,106	1,596,000
Hokkaidō				
Hokkaidō (Territory)	Sapporo	32,247	83,519	5,671,000
Kantō				
Chiba	Chiba	1,988	5,150	5,299,000
Gumma	Maebashi	2,454	6,356	1,939,000
Ibaraki	Mito	2,353	6,094	2,769,000
Kanagawa	Yokohama	927	2,402	7,661,000
Saitama	Urawa	1,467	3,799	6,063,000
Tochigi	Utsunomiya	2,476	6,414	1,892,000
Kinki				
Hyōgo	Kōbe	3,236	8,381	5,323,000
Mie	Tsu	2,231	5,778	1,766,000
Nara	Nara	1,425	3,692	1,336,000
Shiga	Ōtsu	1,551	4,016	1,179,000
Wakayama	Wakayama	1,824	4,725	1,082,000
Kyūshū				
Fukuoka	Fukuoka	1,915	4,961	4,755,000
Kagoshima	Kagoshima	3,539	9,166	1,818,000
Kumamoto	Kumamoto	2,860	7,408	1,846,000
Miyazaki	Miyazaki	2,986	7,735	1,176,000
Nagasaki	Nagasaki	1,588	4,112	1,587,000
Ōita	Ōita	2,447	6,338	1,248,000
Saga	Saga	939	2,433	881,000
Ryukyu				
Okinawa	Naha	871	2,255	1,202,000
Shikoku				
Ehime	Matsuyama	2,190	5,672	1,528,000
Kagawa	Takamatsu	727	1,882	1,026,000
Kōchi	Kōchi	2,744	7,107	837,000
Tokushima	Tokushima	1,600	4,145	836,000
Tohoku				
Akita	Akita	4,483[3]	11,612[3]	1,245,000
Aomori	Aomori	3,714[3]	9,619[3]	1,516,000
Fukushima	Fukushima	5,322	13,784	2,091,000
Iwate	Morioka	5,898	15,277	1,426,000
Miyagi	Sendai	2,815	7,292	2,206,000
Yamagata	Yamagata	3,601	9,327	1,262,000
Metropolis				
Tōkyō[4]	Tōkyō	836	2,164	11,898,000
Urban prefectures				
Kyōto[5]	Kyōto	1,781	4,613	2,602,000
Ōsaka[5]	Ōsaka	721	1,868	8,739,000
TOTAL		145,875[6,7]	377,815[6,7]	122,264,000

Demography

Population (1988): 122,620,000.
Density (1988): persons per sq mi 840.6, persons per sq km 324.6.
Urban–rural (1985): urban 76.7%; rural 23.3%.
Sex distribution (1988): male 49.15%; female 50.85%.
Age breakdown (1988): under 15, 20.0%; 15–29, 21.3%; 30–44, 22.9%; 45–59, 19.8%; 60–69, 8.7%; 70 and over, 7.3%.
Population projection: (1990) 123,942,000; (2000) 130,771,000.
Doubling time: n.a.; doubling time exceeds 100 years.
Composition by nationality (1986): Japanese 99.4%; Korean 0.5%; Chinese and other 0.1%.
Place of birth (1987): 99.4% native-born; 0.6% foreign-born (mainly Korean).
Religious affiliation (1986): most Japanese consider themselves to be adherents of both Shintō (93.1%), a body of indigenous beliefs and practices, and Buddhism (73.9%). A small proportion of the population is Christian (1.4%). Most of the others are members of the "new religions," which incorporate to varying degrees Shintō, Buddhist, Taoist, and Christian beliefs.
Major cities (1987): Tōkyō 8,354,459; Yokohama 3,110,273; Ōsaka 2,648,-621; Nagoya 2,142,896; Sapporo 1,594,914; Kyōto 1,479,386; Kōbe 1,432,-462; Fukuoka 1,190,551; Kawasaki 1,126,485; Hiroshima 1,065,201; Kita-Kyūshū 1,045,560.

Other principal cities (1987)

	population		population		population
Akashi	263,124	Kasugai	262,168	Otsu	242,296
Akita	298,794	Kawagoe	294,658	Sagamihara	501,126
Amagasaki	505,618	Kawaguchi	416,808	Sakai	817,512
Aomori	293,712	Kōchi	314,924	Sasebo	249,403
Asahikawa	365,441	Koriyama	307,023	Sendai	700,790
Chiba	805,607	Koshigaya	269,705	Shimizu	241,479
Fujisawa	337,084	Kumamoto	565,685	Shimonoseki	267,047
Fukushima	273,515	Kurashiki	415,058	Shizuoka	471,792
Fukuyama	363,432	Machida	336,194	Suita	352,706
Funabashi	519,772	Maebashi	281,804	Takamatsu	329,316
Gifu	410,367	Matsudo	440,155	Takatsuki	355,623
Hachiōji	440,907	Matsuyama	433,968	Tokorozawa	289,762
Hakodate	315,579	Miyazaki	283,541	Tokushima	260,576
Hamamatsu	523,292	Nagano	341,296	Toyama	317,177
Higashi–Ōsaka	522,787	Nagasaki	449,149	Toyohashi	328,394
Himeji	453,974	Naha	306,430	Toyonaka	417,182
Hirakata	388,766	Nara	339,809	Toyota	318,611
Ibaraki	254,574	Neyagawa	258,896	Urawa	390,872
Ichikawa	415,073	Niigata	479,803	Utsunomiya	415,355
Ichinomiya	260,391	Nishinomiya	424,798	Wakayama	400,143
Iwaki	352,347	Ōita	398,573	Yamagata	247,284
Kagoshima	533,592	Okayama	582,924	Yao	276,721
Kanazawa	434,708	Okazaki	293,949	Yokkaichi	268,077
Kashiwa	289,734	Ōmiya	383,452	Yokosuka	428,646

Mobility (1980). Population living in same residence as in October 1975: 77.6%; different residence, same prefecture 17.3%; different prefecture 5.1%.
Households (1987). Total households 39,536,000; average household size 3.1; composition of households (1985) 1 person 20.8%, 2 persons 18.4%, 3 persons 17.9%, 4 persons 23.6%, 5 persons 11.0%, 6 persons 5.2%, 7 or more persons 2.9%. Family households (1985) 30,021,000 (79.0%); nonfamily 7,967,000 (21.0%), of which 1-person 7,900,000 (20.8%).

Type of household (1983)

Total number of dwelling units: 34,704,500

	number of dwellings	percent of total
by kind of dwelling		
exclusive entry (do not share bathroom or kitchen)	31,935,000	92.0
combined with nondwelling	2,770,000	8.0
detached house	22,306,000	64.3
apartment building	9,329,000	26.9
tenement (substandard or overcrowded building)	2,882,000	8.3
other	188,000	0.5
by legal tenure of householder		
owned	21,649,600	62.4
rented	12,951,000	37.3
other	103,900	0.3
by kind of amenities		
running water	32,637,000	94.0
flush toilet	20,197,900	58.2
bathroom	30,633,000	88.3
by year of construction		
prior to 1950	5,184,300	14.9
1951–60	3,471,500	10.0
1961–70	8,870,100	25.6
1971–80	14,473,200	41.7
1981–83	2,705,400	7.8

Immigration (1986): permanent immigrants/registered aliens admitted 867,-200, from South Korea 78.2%, Taiwan 9.7%, United States 3.5%, Philippines 2.2%, United Kingdom 0.9%, West Germany 0.4%, Canada 0.3%, France 0.3%.

Vital statistics

Birth rate per 1,000 population (1987): 11.2 (world avg. 26.0); (1985) legitimate 99.0%; illegitimate 1.0%.
Death rate per 1,000 population (1987): 6.1 (world avg. 9.9).
Natural increase rate per 1,000 population (1987): 5.1 (world avg. 16.1).
Total fertility rate (avg. births per childbearing woman; 1986): 1.8.
Marriage rate per 1,000 population[8] (1987): 5.7; median age at first marriage, men 28.3 years, women 25.6 years.
Divorce rate per 1,000 population[8] (1987): 1.3.
Life expectancy at birth (1987): male 75.2 years; female 80.9 years.
Major causes of death per 100,000 population (1986): malignant neoplasms (cancers) 157.8; heart diseases 117.1; cerebrovascular diseases 106.2; pneumonia and bronchitis 43.6; accidents and adverse effects 23.3; senility without mention of psychosis 22.0; suicide 21.1; cirrhosis of the liver 13.9; nephritis, nephrotic syndrome, and nephrosis 11.5; hypertensive diseases 9.6.

Social indicators

Educational attainment (1980). Percent of population aged 15 years and over having: no schooling 0.3%; primary and lower secondary education 38.5%; higher secondary 38.0%; junior college and technical college 5.7%; university and postgraduate 8.0%; still in school 9.5%.

Distribution of income (1986)

percent of average household income by decile

1	2	3	4	5	6	7	8	9	10 (highest)
33.0	49.8	61.1	71.6	81.8	92.8	105.8	122.6	148.2	232.9

Quality of working life. Average workweek (1987): 46.8 hours (11.9% overtime). Annual rate of industrial deaths per 100,000 workers (1986): 3.1. Proportion of labour force insured for damages or income loss resulting from injury, permanent disability, and death (1988): 47.7%. Average mandays lost to labour stoppages per 1,000 workdays (1986): 0.1. Average du-

ration of journey to work[9] (1983): 32 minutes (26.7% private automobile, 67.4% public transportation, 5.5% taxi, 0.4% other). Rate per 1,000 workers of discouraged (unemployed no longer seeking work; 1982): 69.7.

Access to services (1983). Proportion of households having access to: gas supply (1980) 63.0%; safe public water supply 93.7%; public sewage collection 89.4%.

Social participation. Eligible voters participating in last national election (1986): 69.9%. Population 15 years and over participating in social service activities on a voluntary basis (1986): 25.2%. Trade union membership in total work force (1986): 28.2%.

Social deviance (1986). Offense rate per 100,000 population for: homicide 1.5; rape 1.5; robbery 1.5; larceny and theft 1,130.1. Incidence in general population of: alcoholism, n.a.; drug and substance abuse, n.a. Rate of suicide per 100,000 population (1986) 21.1.

Leisure/use of personal time
Discretionary daily activities (1986)
(Population age 15 years and over)

	weekly average hrs./min.
Total discretionary daily time	5:47
of which	
Hobbies and amusements	0:31
Sports	0:10
Learning (except schoolwork)	0:12
Social service	0:02
Voluntary social organizations and associations	0:28
Radio, television, newspapers, and magazines	2:18
Rest and relaxation	1:21
Other activities	0:45

Major leisure activities (1986)
(Population age 15 years and over)

	Percentage of participation		
	Male	Female	Total
Hobbies and amusements	89.4	86.8	88.0
Sports	84.0	69.1	76.3
Light exercises	30.4	32.9	31.6
Swimming	31.5	21.0	26.1
Bowling	29.6	18.8	24.0
Learning (except schoolwork)	37.0	34.1	35.5
Travel			
Domestic	76.1	70.4	73.1
Foreign	5.8	3.7	4.7

Material well-being (1987). Households possessing: automobile 70.6%; telephone, virtually 100%; colour television receiver 98.7%; refrigerator 97.9%; air conditioner 57.0%; washing machine 99.2%; vacuum cleaner 98.1%; videocassette recorder 43.0%; camera 83.8%; microwave oven 52.2%.

National economy
Gross national product (at current market prices; 1986): U.S.$1,559,720,000,-000 (U.S.$12,850 per capita).

Structure of gross domestic product and labour force

	1986		1987	
	in value ¥'000,000,000	% of total value	labour force	% of labour force
Agriculture, fishing	8,870.7	3.0	4,890,000	8.0
Mining	1,325.0	0.4	80,000	0.1
Manufacturing	100,723.4	33.8	14,250,000	23.4
Construction	20,059.4	6.7	5,330,000	8.8
Public utilities	10,105.7	3.4	310,000	0.5
Transportation and communications	17,816.0	6.0	3,480,000	5.7
Trade	43,434.1	14.6	13,660,000	22.4
Finance	46,597.2	15.7	2,340,000	3.8
Pub. admin., defense	12,652.5	4.2	1,980,000	3.3
Services	52,157.4	17.5	12,550,000	20.6
Other	−16,005.9[10]	−5.4[10]	1,970,000[11]	3.2[11]
TOTAL	297,735.5	100.0[7]	60,840,000	100.0[7]

Budget (1988)[12]. Revenue: ¥56,700,000,000,000 (income tax 30.8%; corporation tax 24.6%; public bonds 15.6%; liquor tax 3.6%; stamp duties 3.6%; custom duties 1.1%). Expenditures: ¥56,700,000,000,000 (national debt 20.3%; transfers to local governments 19.2%; social security 18.3%; public works 10.7%; culture, education, and science promotion 8.6%; national defense 6.5%; pensions 3.3%; economic cooperation 1.2%; foodstuff control 0.8%; measures for energy 0.8%; small enterprises 0.3%).

Public debt (1987): U.S.$1,054,342,000,000.

Population economically active (1987): total 60,840,000; activity rate of total population 49.8% (participation rates: ages 15–64, 68.7%; female 39.9%; unemployed 2.8%).

Price and earnings indexes (1980 = 100)

	1982	1983	1984	1985	1986	1987	1988
Consumer price index	107.8	109.9	112.3	114.6	115.3	115.4	115.3[13]
Monthly earnings index	110.6	115.0	119.8	124.6	129.2	128.1[14]	....

Household income and expenditure[15] (1987). Average household size 3.8; average annual income per household ¥5,527,400 (U.S.$38,200); sources of income: wages and salaries 93.7%, of which regular income of household head 64.4%, temporary income and bonuses of household head 17.3%, income of other household members 12.0%; expenditure: food 24.8%, transportation 10.2%, reading and recreation 8.8%, clothing and footwear 7.0%, fuel, light, and water charges 5.3%, housing 5.1%, education 4.6%, furniture and household utensils 4.3%, medical care 2.5%.

Tourism (1986): receipts from visitors U.S.$1,463,000,000; expenditures by nationals abroad U.S.$7,229,000,000.

Manufacturing and mining enterprises (1985)

	no. of establishments	avg. no. of persons engaged	monthly as a % of avg. of all contract wages[16]	annual value added (¥'000,000,000)
Electrical machinery	34,193	1,826,000	96.3	14,880
Nonelectrical machinery	43,876	1,126,000	113.6	10,003
Transport equipment	15,518	962,000	118.0	9,723
Food, beverages, and tobacco	52,347	1,156,000	85.1	8,560
Chemical products	5,350	395,000	136.6	7,917
Fabricated metal products	50,312	787,000	101.4	5,522
Iron and steel	6,852	388,000	132.9	5,181
Printing and publishing	29,543	515,000	141.0	4,552
Ceramic, stone, and clay	21,191	465,000	101.4	3,934
Textiles	35,410	609,000	73.6	3,010
Plastic products	18,128	382,000	92.2	2,844
Paper and paper products	11,898	275,000	109.2	2,285
Precision instruments	7,906	262,000	98.0	1,837
Nonferrous metal products	4,337	163,000	117.0	1,556
Apparel products	30,760	540,000	56.3	1,702
Lumber and wood products	22,762	276,000	82.0	1,364
Petroleum and coal products	1,010	38,000	155.9	1,251
Furniture and fixtures	17,376	222,000	87.8	1,205
Rubber products	5,699	166,000	102.4	1,202
Leather products	5,650	77,000	78.6	391
Mining	879	46,977	115.6	329

Energy production (consumption): electricity (kW-hr; 1986) 601,520,000,000 (537,740,000,000); coal (metric tons; 1986) 16,012,000 (106,404,000); crude petroleum (barrels; 1986) 3,849,000 (3,987,000,000); petroleum products (metric tons; 1986) 141,816,000, of which (by volume) heavy fuel oil 38.7%, gasoline 21.7%, kerosene and jet fuel 16.6%, diesel 14.5%, naphtha 5.9% (169,441,000, of which [by volume] heavy fuel oil 36.2%, gasoline 20.2%, kerosene and jet fuel 15.2%, diesel 14.7%, naphtha 13.8%); natural gas (cu m; 1986) 2,105,000,000 (2,208,000,000). Composition of energy supply by source (1986): crude oil and petroleum products 55.2%, coal 19.1%, nuclear power 10.3%, natural gas 9.6%, hydroelectric power 5.3%, other 0.5%. Domestic energy demand by end use (1986): mining and manufacturing 37.3%, residential and commercial 27.9%, transportation 15.6%, agriculture, forestry, and fisheries 2.5%, other 16.7%.

Financial aggregates

	1981	1982	1983	1984	1985	1986	1987
Exchange rate[17] ¥ per:							
U.S. dollar	220.54	249.08	237.51	237.52	238.54	168.52	144.64
£	419.57	379.41	336.83	290.40	289.62	247.2	237.0
SDR	255.95	259.23	243.10	246.13	220.23	194.61	175.2
International reserves (U.S.$)[17]							
Total (excl. gold; '000,000)	28,208	23,334	24,602	26,429	26,719	42,257	80,973
SDRs ('000,000)	1,934	2,091	1,935	1,927	2,116	2,218	2,463
Reserve pos. in IMF ('000,000)	1,558	2,071	2,303	2,219	2,275	2,382	2,853
Foreign exchange ('000,000)	24,716	19,172	20,364	22,283	22,328	37,657	75,657
Gold ('000,000 fine troy oz)	24.23	24.23	24.23	24.23	24.23	24.23	24.23
% world reserves	2.5	2.6	2.6	2.6	2.6	2.6	2.6
Interest and prices							
Central bank discount (%)	5.50	5.50	5.00	5.00	5.00	3.00	3.30
Gov't. bond yield (%)	8.66	8.06	7.42	6.81	6.34	4.94	4.94
Industrial share prices (1980 = 100)	116.3	115.8	136.5	172.1	210.2	279.2	412.9
Balance of payments (U.S.$'000,000,000)							
Balance of visible trade	19.9	18.1	31.5	44.3	56.0	92.8	...
Imports, f.o.b.	129.6	119.6	114.0	124.0	118.0	112.8	...
Exports, f.o.b.	149.5	137.7	145.5	168.3	174.0	205.6	...
Balance of invisibles	−13.6	−9.9	−9.1	−7.8	−5.2	−4.9	...
Balance of payments, current account	4.8	6.9	20.8	35.0	49.2	85.8	...

Production (metric tons except as noted). Agriculture, forestry, fishing (1986): rice 11,647,000, potatoes 4,073,000, radishes 2,655,000, mandarin oranges 2,168,000, cabbages 1,666,000, sweet potatoes 1,507,000, Chinese cabbages 1,503,000, onions 1,252,000, cucumbers 1,040,000, apples 986,100, wheat 876,000, watermelons 840,400, tomatoes 816,200, carrots 670,400, Welsh onions 574,200, lettuce 500,900, Japanese pears 480,600, spinach 385,-400, taro 384,900, grapes 301,300, persimmons 290,500, summer oranges 287,800, pumpkins 277,700, burdocks 268,800, peaches 219,200, turnips 211,500, strawberries 200,500, Spanish paprika 177,800, cauliflowers 140,-600, soybeans 113,600, string peas 99,300, string beans 65,700, cow's milk 7,457,000 (of which marketed as fluid milk 4,324,000), hen's eggs 2,225,-000; livestock (number of live animals) 11,061,000 pigs, 4,742,000 cattle (of which 2,103,000 dairy cows), 48,000 goats, 23,000 horses, 180,947,000 hens, 155,647,000 broiler chickens; roundwood 64,490,000 cu m, of which coniferous species 20,244,000 cu m, broadleaved species 11,276,000 cu m; fish catch 12,677,000, of which sardines 4,215,000, mackerel 1,067,000 (jack mackerel 10.5%), bonito 408,000, tuna 335,000, sauries 211,000, salmon and trout 168,000, squid 87,000, yellowtails 33,000. Mining and quarrying (1986): limestone 162,368,000; quicklime 6,617,000; gypsum 6,400,000; dolomite 3,953,000; fire clay 1,004,150; pyrophyllite clay 307,810; iron ore 290,573; zinc 222,071; talc 84,522; barite 66,018; lead 48,374; copper 34,934; chromium 7,420; silver 339,659 kg; gold 3,100 kg. Manufacturing (1986): crude steel 98,275,000; semifinished steel 91,508,000; hot-rolled steel products 78,136,000; pig iron 74,651,000; cement 71,264,000; cold-rolled steel strips 20,706,000; tubes and pipes 12,046,000; paper pulp 9,067,600; sulfuric acid 6,562,400; plastic products 4,494,900, of which film 1,257,400; compound fertilizers 3,545,600; spun yarn 1,136,200; raw silk 833,600; finished products (in number of units) 311,468,000 fluorescent lamps, 200,819,000 watches, 147,517,000 motor vehicle tires, 64,211,000 electronic desk calculators, 31,272,000 videocassette recorders, 17,738,000 35-mm cameras, 12,-958,000 colour television receivers, 8,441,000 microwave ovens, 7,809,700 passenger cars, 7,293,900 trucks and buses, 4,697,000 electric refrigerators, 4,661,000 automatic washing machines, 4,173,000 typewriters, 3,396,000 copying machines, 2,627,900 motorcycles. Construction (floor area started;

1987): residential 123,703,000 sq m; nonresidential 237,226,000 sq m, of which government and public owned 21,040,000 sq m, private owned 216,186,000 sq m.

Retail and wholesale trade and services (1985)

	no. of establish-ments	avg. no. of em-ployees	annual sales (¥'000,000,000)
Retail trade	1,628,644	6,329,000	101,719
Food and beverages	671,190	2,351,000	31,818
Grocery	92,602	622,000	12,846
Liquors	106,693	294,000	5,045
General merchandise	3,531	389,000	13,855
Department stores	1,827	381,000	13,694
Gasoline service stations	74,470	357,000	11,109
Apparel and accessories	229,634	755,000	10,721
Motor vehicles and bicycles	83,931	464,000	10,271
Furniture and home furnishings	172,686	586,000	8,767
Eating and drinking places	838,449	1,965,000	8,686
Wholesale trade	413,016	3,998,000	428,291
General merchandise	985	58,000	84,080
Machinery and equipment	85,072	960,000	76,666
General machinery except electrical	40,389	393,000	23,836
Motor vehicles and parts	13,745	195,000	19,575
Minerals and metals	21,017	245,000	59,775
Farm, livestock, and fishery products	39,193	380,000	53,359
Food and beverages	54,082	496,000	34,866
Textiles, apparel, and accessories	41,004	461,000	30,781
Building materials	56,029	355,000	20,534
Chemicals	15,546	149,000	17,742
Drugs and toilet goods	16,809	238,000	12,665
Medical services	171,986	2,026,000	...
Educational services	84,512	2,065,000	...

Land use (1985): forested 67.0%; meadows and pastures 1.7%; agricultural and under permanent cultivation 12.9%; other 18.4%.

Foreign trade[18]

Balance of trade (current prices)

	1982	1983	1984	1985	1986	1987
¥'000,000,000	+4,473	+7,373	+10,674	+13,238	+15,519	+12,174
% of total	6.9%	11.8%	20.9%	18.7%	28.2%	22.4%

Imports (1987): ¥21,736,900,000,000 (food 15.0%, of which fish 5.3%; crude petroleum 13.9%; machinery and equipment 12.8%; chemicals 7.9%; petroleum products 4.5%; wood 4.2%; metal ores and scrap 4.1%, of which iron ore 1.8%; nonferrous metal ores 3.8%; coal 3.1%; textiles 2.9%). *Major import sources:* United States 21.1%; Indonesia 5.6%; South Korea 5.4%; Australia 5.3%; China 4.9%; Saudia Arabia 4.9%; Taiwan 4.7%; West Germany 4.1%; Canada 4.1%; Malaysia 3.2%; U.S.S.R. 1.6%.
Exports (1987): ¥33,315,200,000,000 (motor vehicles 19.6%; office machinery 6.3%; iron and steel 5.5%; tape recorders 3.7%; chemicals 5.1%, of which plastic materials 1.5%; scientific and optical equipment 4.1%; textiles and allied products 3.7%; electron tubes 3.6%; power-generating machinery 2.6%; metalworking machinery 1.5%; radio receivers 1.1%; television receivers 0.6%). *Major export destinations:* United States 36.5%; South Korea 5.8%; West Germany 5.6%; Taiwan 4.9%; Hong Kong 3.9%; China 3.6%; United Kingdom 3.6%; Canada 2.5%; Australia 2.2%.

Trade by commodity group (1987)

SITC group	imports U.S.$'000,000	%	exports U.S.$'000,000	%
00 Food and live animals	22,395	15.0	1,546	0.7
01 Beverages and tobacco				
02 Crude materials, excluding fuels	22,022[19]	14.7[19]	1,575[19]	0.7[19]
03 Mineral fuels, lubricants, and related materials	39,137	26.2	782	0.3
04 Animal and vegetable oils, fats, and waxes	19	19	19	19
05 Chemicals and related products, n.e.s.				
06 Basic manufactures				
07 Machinery and transport equipment	60,560	40.5	222,950	97.3
08 Miscellaneous manufactured articles				
09 Goods not classified by kind	5,401	3.6	2,368	1.0
TOTAL	149,515	100.0	229,221	100.0

Direction of trade (1987)

	imports U.S.$'000,000	%	exports U.S.$'000,000	%
Africa	4,002	2.7	5,822	2.5
Asia	66,313	44.3	69,569	30.4
South America	4,019	2.7	3,183	1.4
North America and Central America	40,005	26.8	94,771	41.3
United States	31,490	21.1	83,580	36.5
other North and Central Am.	8,513	5.7	11,191	4.8
Europe	25,579	17.1	49,003	21.4
EEC	17,596	11.7	39,219	17.1
U.S.S.R.	2,352	1.6	2,563	1.1
other Europe	5,631	3.8	7,221	3.2
Oceania	9,597	6.4	6,873	3.0
TOTAL	149,515	100.0	229,221	100.0

Transport and communications

Transport. Railroads (1986): length 16,016 mi, 25,776 km; rolling stock (1985) locomotives 3,177, passenger cars 46,192, freight cars 40,951; passen-

gers carried 19,414,000,000; passenger-mi 208,032,000,000, passenger-km 334,796,000,000; short ton-mi cargo 14,121,000,000, metric ton-km cargo 20,617,000,000. Roads (1987): total length 700,600 mi, 1,127,500 km (paved 58%). Vehicles (1987): passenger cars 28,653,692; trucks 19,091,587; buses 232,516. Merchant marine (1987): vessels (100 gross tons and over) 9,822; total deadweight tonnage 54,669,378. Air transport (1986): passengers carried 53,640,000; passenger-mi 44,076,000,000, passenger-km 70,934,000,000; short ton-mi cargo 2,450,000,000, metric ton-km cargo 3,650,000,000; airports (1988) with scheduled flights 65. Shares of domestic passenger traffic by mode of transportation (1986): automobiles 45.5%; railway 38.2%; buses 11.6%; airplanes 4.0%; ships 0.6%.

Distribution of traffic (1986)

	cargo carried ('000,000 tons)	% of nat'l total	passengers carried ('000,000)	% of nat'l total
Road	4,969.0	90.3	34,943.0	47.7
Rail (intercity)	90.0	1.6	19,234.0	26.3
Urban transport	—	—	18,875.0	25.8
road	—	—	7,900.0	10.8
rail	—	—	10,975.0	15.0
Inland water	441.0	8.0	154.0	0.2
Air	0.6	0.0	46.4	0.1
TOTAL	5,500.6	100.0[7]	73,252.4	100.0[7]

Communications. Daily newspapers (1987): total number 124; total circulation 70,669,000; circulation per 1,000 population 578. Radio (1986): 94,700,000 receivers (1 per 1.3 persons). Television (1987): 31,595,000 receivers (1 per 3.9 persons). Telephones (1985): 66,636,000 (1 per 1.8 persons).

Other communication media (1986)

Print	titles	Electronic	traffic ('000)
Books (new)	37,016	Telegram	41,231
of which		Domestic	40,050
Social sciences	8,996	International	1,181
Fiction	6,610	Telex	50,000[20]
Engineering	3,459		
Art	3,170		
Natural sciences	3,078		
History	2,283	**Post**	
Philosophy	1,825	Mail	18,109,400
Magazines/journals	3,777	Domestic	17,871,000
Weekly	105	International	238,400
Monthly	2,503	Parcels	163,049
		Domestic	163,045
Cinema		International	4,000
Feature films (greater than 1,600 m)	311		

Radio and television broadcasting (1987): total radio stations 1,152, of which commercial 834; total television stations 13,322, of which commercial 6,914. Commercial broadcasters' broadcasting hours (by percentage of programs; 1986): reports—radio 12.6%, television 17.2%; education—radio 5.7%, television 11.9%; culture—radio 17.5%, television 23.9%; entertainment—radio 29.6%, television 42.1%; music—radio 28.6%, television 0%; sports—radio 4.8%, television 3.4%; other—radio 1.1%, television 1.6%. Advertisements (daily avg.; 1986): radio 156, television 254.

Education and health

Education (1987)

	schools	teachers	students	student/teacher ratio
Primary (age 6–11)	24,933	448,978	10,226,325	22.8
Secondary (age 12–17)	16,738	566,976	11,456,437	20.2
Higher	1,097	138,587	2,597,073	18.7

Literacy (1987): total population age 15 and over literate 97,150,000 (100%); males literate 47,230,000 (100%); females literate 49,920,000 (100%).
Health (1987): physicians 183,129 (1 per 668 persons); dentists 66,797 (1 per 1,830 persons); nurses[21] 333,040 (1 per 367 persons); pharmacists 135,990 (1 per 899 persons); midwives 24,056 (1 per 5,082 persons); hospital beds 1,533,887 (1 per 80.0 persons), of which general 72.9%, mental 22.2%, tuberculosis 3.3%, other 1.6%; infant mortality rate per 1,000 live births 4.9.
Food (1984–86): daily per capita caloric intake 2,858 (vegetable products 79%, animal products 21%); (1983) 119% of FAO recommended minimum.

Military

Total active duty personnel (1987): 246,000 (army 63.4%, navy 18.3%, air force 18.3%). *Military expenditure as percent of GNP* (1985): 1.0% (world 6.1%); per capita expenditure U.S.$112.

---

[1]Oct. 1, 1987. [2]Excludes Lake Naka (38 sq mi [98 sq km]), which is part of both Tottori and Shimane prefectures. [3]Excludes Lake Towada (23 sq mi [60 sq km]), which is part of both Akita and Aomori prefectures. [4]Part of Kanto geographical region. [5]Part of Kinki geographical region. [6]1987 survey; includes Lake Naka and Lake Towada. [7]Detail does not add to total given because of rounding. [8]Figures relate only to Japanese nationals in Japan. [9]Applies to passengers carried within the metropolitan areas of Tōkyō, Ōsaka, and Nagoya only. [10]Import duties and statistical discrepancy less imputed bank service charge. [11]Includes 1,730,000 unemployed. [12]Initial budget. [13]February. [14]First quarter. [15]Worker's household. [16]1986. [17]End of period. [18]Import figures are f.o.b. in balance of trade and c.i.f. in commodities and trading partners. [19]Crude materials includes animal and vegetable oils, fats, and waxes. [20]1985. [21]Clinical nurses only.

Jordan

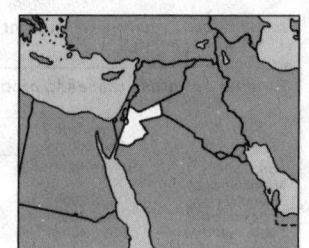

Official name: al-Mamlakah al-Urdunnīyah al-Hāshimīyah (al-Urdun) (Hashemite Kingdom of Jordan).
Form of government: constitutional monarchy with two legislative houses (Senate [30 appointed by king]; House of Deputies [142][1]).
Chief of state: Monarch.
Head of government: Prime Minister (on King's authority).
Capital: Amman.
Official language: Arabic.
Official religion: Islam.
Monetary unit: 1 Jordan Dinar (JD) = 1,000 fils; valuation (Oct. 10, 1988) JD 1.00 = U.S.$2.63 = £1.56.

Area and population

Governorates	Capitals	area sq mi	area sq km	population 1986 estimate[2]
'Ammān	Amman	...	...	1,160,000
al-Balqā'	aṣ-Ṣalt	...	...	193,800
Irbid	Irbid	...	...	680,200
al-Karak	al-Karak	...	...	120,100
Ma'ān	Ma'ān	...	...	97,500
al-Mafraq	al-Mafraq	...	...	98,600
aṭ-Ṭafilah	aṭ-Ṭafilah	...	...	41,400
az-Zarqā'	az-Zarqā'	...	...	404,500
TOTAL		34,443	89,206	2,796,100

Demography

Population (1988): 2,965,000.
Density (1988): persons per sq mi 86.1, persons per sq km 33.2.
Urban–rural (1986): urban 69.6%; rural 30.4%.
Sex distribution (1986): male 52.31%; female 47.69%.
Age breakdown (1986): under 15, 48.1%; 15–29, 27.4%; 30–44, 12.5%; 45–59, 8.0%; 60–74, 3.1%; 75 and over, 0.9%.
Population projection: (1990) 3,202,000; (2000) 4,705,000.
Doubling time: 19 years.
Ethnic composition (1983): Arab 99.2%; Circassian 0.5%; Armenian 0.1%; Turk 0.1%; Kurd 0.1%.
Religious affiliation (1980): Sunnī Muslim 93.0%; Christian 4.9%; other 2.1%.
Major cities (1986): Amman 833,500; az-Zarqā' 285,000; Irbid 150,000; ar-Ruṣayfah 65,560; aṣ-Ṣalt 42,690.

Vital statistics

Birth rate per 1,000 population (1986): 34.7 (world avg. 26.0).
Death rate per 1,000 population (1986): 5.8 (world avg. 9.9).
Natural increase rate per 1,000 population (1986): 28.9 (world avg. 16.1).
Total fertility rate (avg. births per childbearing woman; 1986): 7.4.
Marriage rate per 1,000 population (1986): 6.9.
Divorce rate per 1,000 population (1986): 1.2.
Life expectancy at birth (1986): male 65.0 years; female 68.8 years.
Major causes of death per 100,000 population: n.a.; however, major diseases include tuberculosis, typhoid, and paratyphoid fevers, salmonella, hepatitis, and dysentery; nonvenereal syphilis is widespread in the southern desert region.

National economy

Budget (1988). Revenue: JD 1,008,500,000 (1986; foreign grants and loans 37.0%; indirect taxes 31.2%, of which import duties 13.8%, excise taxes 6.6%, fees 5.3%; direct taxes 7.2%). Expenditures: JD 1,075,300,000 (1986; finance administration 26.6%; defense 20.8%; economic development 19.8%; social welfare 11.3%; internal security 5.5%; communications and transport 2.3%).
Public debt (external, outstanding; 1986): U.S.$3,078,600,000.
Production (metric tons except as noted). Agriculture, forestry, fishing (1986): tomatoes 220,565, citrus fruit 87,358, cucumbers 64,263, watermelons 51,292, eggplants 50,568, squash 36,850, olives 31,781, wheat 30,842, cauliflower 24,553, grapes 23,186, green peppers 11,221, barley 9,004; livestock (number of live animals) 930,000 sheep, 439,200 goats, 31,100 cattle, 14,300 camels; roundwood 9,000 cu m; fish catch 65. Mining and quarrying (1986): phosphate ore 6,249,200; potash 1,103,700. Manufacturing (1986): cement 1,837,100; chemical acids 1,024,800; fertilizer 551,100; steel 209,600; fodder 44,600; detergents 27,600; metallic pipes 12,500; cigarettes 3,327,700,000 units; liquid batteries 55,400 units; alcoholic beverages 5,322,-600 litres. Construction (1986): residential 1,709,300 sq m; nonresidential 557,300 sq m. Energy production (consumption): electricity (kW-hr; 1986) 2,955,000,000 (2,722,000,000); coal, none (n.a.); crude petroleum (barrels; 1986) 107,000 (16,921,000); petroleum products (metric tons; 1986) 2,162,-000 (2,535,000,000); natural gas, none (n.a.).
Population economically active (1986): total 535,440; activity rate of total population 19.5% (participation rates: over age 15, 39.0%; female 10.9%; unemployed 4.5%).

Price and earnings indexes (1980 = 100)

	1982	1983	1984	1985	1986	1987	1988[3]
Consumer price index	115.7	121.5	126.2	130.0	130.0	129.6	129.5
Daily earnings index	...	...	...	...	...	...	...

Household income and expenditure. Average household size (1984) 6.9; income per household (1979)[4] JD 1,820 (U.S.$6,055); sources of income: n.a.; expenditure (1985): food and beverages 37.5%; housing 6.3%; transportation 5.8%; clothing and footwear 5.5%; household durable goods 4.7%; health care 4.0%; education 3.3%; other goods and services 32.9%.
Gross national product (at current market prices; 1986): U.S.$4,220,000,000 (U.S.$3,630 per capita).

Structure of gross domestic product and labour force

	1986 in value JD '000,000	% of total value	labour force	% of labour force
Agriculture	116.2	7.2	37,436	7.0
Mining	53.0	3.3 }	52,706	9.8
Manufacturing	193.9	12.0 }		
Construction	112.5	7.0	54,183	10.1
Public utilities	37.7	2.3	5,418	1.0
Transportation and communications	161.6	10.0	46,302	8.6
Trade	243.1	15.1	49,258	9.2
Finance	164.6	10.2	16,748	3.1
Pub. admin., defense	281.9	17.5 }	230,525	43.1
Services	70.7	4.4 }		
Other	178.4[5]	11.0[5]	42,864[6]	8.0[6]
TOTAL	1,613.6	100.0	535,440	100.0[7]

Land use (1985): forested 0.4%; meadows and pastures 1.0%; agricultural and under permanent cultivation 4.2%; wasteland (mostly desert), built-on, and other 94.4%.
Tourism (1986): receipts from visitors U.S.$534,000,000; expenditures by nationals abroad U.S.$433,000,000.

Foreign trade

Balance of trade (current prices)[8]

	1982	1983	1984	1985	1986	1987
JD '000,000	−878	−893	−781	−763	−594	−530
% of total	52.9%	61.0%	45.7%	55.1%	53.7%	51.5%

Imports (1986): JD 850,199,200 (electrical and nonelectrical machinery 12.1%; crude petroleum 10.9%; transport equipment and spare parts 8.6%; iron and steel 4.9%; wheat, wheat flour, and rice 3.0%; fruits, vegetables, and nuts 3.0%; meat 2.9%; clothing and footwear 2.6%). *Major import sources:* Iraq 9.1%; United States 8.9%; United Kingdom 8.1%; Japan 7.8%; West Germany 7.7%; Italy 5.9%; Saudi Arabia 5.8%.
Exports (1986)[9]: JD 225,615,100 (natural phosphate fertilizer 29.3%; food [mostly assorted vegetables, tomatoes, olives, citrus fruit, and spices] and live animals 18.6%; chemical fertilizer 12.9%; pharmaceuticals 6.8%). *Major export destinations:* Iraq 18.8%; India 15.1%; Saudi Arabia 12.3%; Kuwait 3.9%; Yugoslavia 3.4%; Indonesia 3.4%; China 3.4%; Romania 3.3%.

Transport and communications

Transport. Railroads (1986): route length 385 mi, 619 km; passengers, 31,304; short ton-mi cargo 864,000,000[10], metric ton-km cargo 1,262,000,000[10]. Roads (1984): total length 3,934 mi, 6,332 km (paved 74.4%). Vehicles (1986): passenger cars 158,892; trucks and buses 73,469. Merchant marine (1987): vessels (100 gross tons and over) 4; total deadweight tonnage 47,710. Air transport (1987): passenger-mi 2,230,000,000, passenger-km 3,589,000,-000; short ton-mi cargo 113,600,000, metric ton-km cargo 165,900,000; airports (1988) with scheduled flights 2.
Communications. Daily newspapers (1987): total number 5; total circulation 185,000; circulation per 1,000 population 65.0. Radio (1986): total number of receivers 700,000 (1 per 4.3 persons). Television (1986): total number of receivers 240,000 (1 per 12 persons). Telephones (1986): 177,894[11] (1 per 15 persons).

Education and health

Education (1985–86)

	schools	teachers	students	student/ teacher ratio
Primary (age 6–11)	1,239	16,979	530,906	31.3
Secondary (age 12–17)	1,671	17,074	305,046	17.9
Voc., teacher tr.	52	1,012	27,042	26.7
Higher	3	1,295	26,711	20.6

Educational attainment (1979). Percent of population age 14 and over having: no formal schooling 47.9%; primary education 19.8%; secondary 26.4%; higher 5.9%. *Literacy* (1986): total population age 15 and over literate 1,451,100 (79.4%); males literate 761,900 (81.7%); females literate 689,200 (73.9%).
Health (1986): physicians 3,114 (1 per 881 persons); hospital beds 5,246 (1 per 523 persons); infant mortality rate per 1,000 live births (1985) 49.
Food (1984–86): daily per capita caloric intake 2,498 (vegetable products 89%, animal products 11%); 102% of FAO recommended minimum requirement.

Military

Total active duty personnel (1988): 82,250 (army 86.8%, navy 0.3%, air force 12.9%). *Military expenditure as percent of GNP* (1985): 17.4% (world 6.1%); per capita expenditure U.S.$272.

---

[1]House of Deputies, the membership of which included representatives from the Israeli-occupied West Bank, was dissolved July 30, 1988, pending elections to be held in 1989. [2]End of year. [3]July. [4]Households involved in nonagricultural activities only. [5]Includes indirect taxes less imputed bank charges. [6]Includes unemployed. [7]Detail does not add to total given because of rounding. [8]Includes reexports. [9]Domestic exports only. [10]1985. [11]Subscribers.

Kampuchea

Official name: Sathearanakrath
Pracheachon Kampuchea (People's
Republic of Kampuchea)[1].
Form of government: single-party
people's republic with one legislative
house (National Assembly [123]).
Chief of state: President, Council
of State.
Head of government: Chairman,
Council of Ministers (Prime Minister).
Capital: Phnom Penh.
Official language: Khmer.
Official religion: none.
Monetary unit: 1 riel = 100 sen;
valuation (Oct. 10, 1988)
1 U.S.$ = 100 riels; 1 £ = 171.25 riels.

Area and population

Provinces	Capitals	area sq mi	area sq km	population 1981 census
Bătdâmbâng	Bătdâmbâng	7,407	19,184	719,000
Kâmpóng Cham	Kâmpóng Cham	3,783	9,799	1,070,000
Kâmpóng Chhnăng	Kâmpóng Chhnăng	2,132	5,521	221,000
Kâmpóng Saôm	Kâmpóng Saôm	26	68	53,000
Kâmpóng Spoe	Kâmpóng Spoe	2,709	7,017	340,000
Kâmpóng Thum	Kâmpóng Thum	10,657[2]	27,602[2]	379,000
Kâmpôt	Kâmpôt	2,320	6,008	354,000
Kândal	...	1,472	3,812	720,000
Kaôh Kŏng	Krŏng Kaôh Kŏng	4,309	11,161	25,000
Krâchéh	Krâchéh	4,283	11,094	157,000
Môndól Kiri	Senmonorom	5,517	14,288	16,000
Phnom Penh	Phnom Penh	18	46	329,000
Poŭthĭsăt	Poŭthĭsăt	4,900	12,692	175,000
Preăh Vihéar	Phnum Tbĕng Meanchey	2	2	70,000
Prey Vêng	Prey Vêng	1,885	4,883	672,000
Rôtânôkiri	Lumphăt	4,163	10,782	45,000
Siĕmréab	Siĕmréab	6,354	16,457	477,000
Stœ̆ng Trêng	Stœ̆ng Trêng	4,283	11,092	39,000
Svay Riĕng	Svay Riĕng	1,145	2,966	292,000
Takêv	Takêv	1,376	3,563	531,000
TOTAL LAND AREA		68,721	177,987	6,684,000
INLAND WATER		1,177	3,048	
TOTAL AREA		69,898	181,035	

Demography

Population (1988): 7,876,000.
Density[3] (1988): persons per sq mi 114.6, persons per sq km 44.3.
Urban–rural (1985): urban 10.8%; rural 89.2%.
Sex distribution (1985): male 49.73%; female 50.27%.
Age breakdown (1985): under 15, 32.5%; 15–29, 33.5%; 30–44, 19.6%; 45–59, 9.8%; 60–74, 4.0%; 75 and over 0.6%.
Population projection: (1990) 8,246,000; (2000) 9,772,000.
Doubling time: 28 years.
Ethnic composition (1983): Khmer 88.1%; Chinese 4.6%; Vietnamese 4.6%; (although recent Vietnamese immigration may have raised their proportion to as much as 8%); other 2.7%.
Religious affiliation (1980): Buddhist 88.4%; Muslim 2.4%; other 9.2%.
Major cities (1971): Phnom Penh 750,000[4]; Kâmpóng Cham 34,706; Kâmpóng Chhnăng 15,813; Kratié 14,765; Pursat 14,736; Svay Riĕng 13,766.

Vital statistics

Birth rate per 1,000 population (1987): 41.8 (world avg. 26.0); legitimate, n.a.; illegitimate, n.a.
Death rate per 1,000 population (1987): 16.9 (world avg. 9.9).
Natural increase rate per 1,000 population (1987): 24.9 (world avg. 16.1).
Total fertility rate (avg. births per childbearing woman; 1987): 4.8.
Marriage rate per 1,000 population: n.a.
Divorce rate per 1,000 population: n.a.
Life expectancy at birth (1987): male 46.5 years; female 49.4 years.
Major causes of death per 100,000 population (registered deaths only; 1966): tuberculosis of the respiratory system 154; all accidents other than vehicle accidents 111; malaria 55; pneumonia 51.

National economy

Budget. The lack, since the mid-1970s, of a taxable domestic economic base or of much income-earning exports has left Kampuchea without a central governmental budget other than the dispersal of foreign aid and the management of development grants.
Production (metric tons except as noted). Agriculture, forestry, fishing (1986): rice 2,000,000; roots and tubers 143,000, of which cassava 100,000, sweet potatoes 34,000; corn (maize) 92,000; beans 37,000; rubber 24,500; tobacco 9,000; livestock (number of live animals) 1,571,000 cattle, 1,299,000 pigs, 705,000 buffalo, 6,000,000 chickens; roundwood (1985) 5,303,000 cu m; fish catch 70,000. Mining and quarrying (1986): salt 40,000. Manufacturing (1986): cement 50,000[4]; pork 24,000; beef and veal 16,000; sawn wood 43,000 cu m[5]; plywood 2,000 cu m[5]; cigarettes 4,100,000,000 units[4]. Construction: n.a. Energy production (consumption): electricity (kW-hr; 1986) 155,000,000 (155,000,000); coal, n.a. (n.a.); crude petroleum, n.a. (n.a.); petroleum products (metric tons; 1986), none (150,000); natural gas, n.a. (n.a.).
Household income and expenditure. Average household size (1980) 5.6; income per household: n.a.; sources of income: n.a.; expenditure: n.a.

Gross national product (at current market prices; 1981): U.S.$600,000,000 (U.S.$90 per capita).

Structure of gross domestic product and labour force

	1966 in value '000,000 riels	1966 % of total value	1980 labour force	1980 % of labour force
Agriculture	13,100	40.9	2,454,000	74.4
Mining and manufacturing	3,300	10.3		
Construction	1,700	5.3		
Public utilities	400	1.3	220,000	6.7
Transportation and communications	700	2.2		
Trade	7,300	22.8		
Public admin., defense	3,900	12.2	625,000	18.9
Services	1,600	5.0		
TOTAL	32,000	100.0	3,299,000	100.0

Public debt: (1985): U.S.$508,000,000.
Population economically active (1985): total 3,602,000; activity rate of total population 49.5% (participation rates: ages 15–64, 71.4%; female 40.5%; unemployed, n.a.).

Price and earnings indexes (1970 = 100)

	1967	1968	1969	1970	1971	1972	1973
Consumer price index[6]	79.5	84.1	89.4	100.0	172.0	215.2	556.1
Earnings index	...	...	...	...	...	...	...

Land use (1985): forested 75.8%; meadows and pastures 3.3%; agricultural and under permanent cultivation 17.2%; other 3.7%.
Tourism: none.

Foreign trade

Balance of trade (current prices)

	1978	1979	1980	1981	1982	1983
U.S.$'000,000	...	...	...	−60	...	−20
% of total	...	...	...	41.1%	...	67.0%

Imports (1983): U.S.$30,000,000 (major imports include machinery, fuel, consumer goods, raw materials, fertilizers, and insecticide). *Major import sources* (1985): Vietnam; U.S.S.R.; Eastern European countries; Japan; India.
Exports (1983): U.S.$10,000,000 (important exports include rubber, pepper, sandalwood, resin, tobacco, soybeans, handicrafts). *Major export destinations* (1985): Vietnam; U.S.S.R.; Eastern European countries; Japan; India.

Transport and communications

Transport. Railroads (1986): length 380 mi, 612 km; passenger-mi 33,554,-000[7], passenger-km 54,000,000[7]; short ton-mi cargo 6,850,000[7], metric ton-km cargo 10,000,000[7]. Roads (1986): total length 8,296 mi, 13,351 km (paved 20%). Vehicles (1981): passenger cars 700; trucks 1,800. Merchant marine (1987): vessels (100 gross tons and over) 3; total deadweight tonnage 3,839. Air transport (1977): passenger-mi 26,098,800, passenger-km 42,000,000; short ton-mi cargo 274,000, metric ton-km cargo 400,000; airports (1988) with scheduled flights 1.
Communications. Daily newspapers (1984): total number 10; total circulation, n.a. Radio (1986): total number of receivers 200,000 (1 per 37 persons). Television (1987): total number of receivers 30,000 (1 per 256 persons). Telephones (1981): 7,315 (1 per 790 persons).

Education and health

Education (1983–84)

	schools	teachers	students	student/ teacher ratio
Primary (age 6–11)	3,629[8]	36,520	1,504,840	41.2
Secondary	207	4,494	145,730	32.4
Voc., teacher tr.	13	278	7,334	26.4
Higher	2[9]	...	586[9]	...

Educational attainment, n.a. *Literacy* (1980): total population age 15 and over literate 48.0%.
Health (1984): physicians 200 (1 per 36,000 persons); hospital beds 16,200 (1 per 441 persons); infant mortality rate per 1,000 live births (1987) 133.0.
Food (1984–86): daily per capita caloric intake 2,170 (vegetable products 95%, animal products 5%); (1983) 85% of FAO recommended minimum requirement.

Military

Total active duty personnel (1986): 50,000[10]. *Military expenditure as percent of GNP:* n.a.; per capita expenditure, n.a.

[1]The UN continues to seat Democratic Kampuchea (DK), whose present leadership calls itself the Coalition Government of Democratic Kampuchea and is composed of Khmer People's National Liberation Front, the DK (Khmer Rouge), and the organization of Norodom Sihanouk. [2]Area of Preăh Vihéar included with Kâmpóng Thum. [3]Based on land area. [4]1987. [5]1984. [6]Phnom Penh only. [7]1981. [8]1981–82. [9]1982–83. [10]Excludes about 120,000 Vietnamese troops and about 40,000 opposition forces of Democratic Kampuchea.

Kenya

Official name: Jamhuri ya Kenya (Swahili); Republic of Kenya (English).
Form of government: unitary single-party republic with one legislative house (National Assembly [202[1]]).
Head of state and government: President.
Capital: Nairobi.
Official languages: Swahili; English.
Official religion: none.
Monetary unit: 1 Kenyan shilling (K Sh) = 100 cents; valuation (Oct. 10, 1988) 1 U.S.$ = K Sh 18.24; 1 £ = K Sh 31.23.

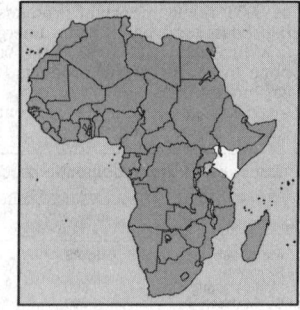

Area and population

		area		population
Provinces	**Provincial headquarters**	sq mi	sq km	1984 estimate
Central	Nyeri	5,087	13,176	2,926,200
Coast	Mombasa	32,279	83,603	1,688,000
Eastern	Embu	61,734	159,891	3,423,500
Nairobi	Nairobi	264	684	1,103,600
North Eastern	Garissa	48,997	126,902	484,700
Nyanza	Kisumu	6,240	16,162	3,508,500
Rift Valley	Nakuru	67,131	173,868	4,132,400
Western	Kakamega	3,228	8,360	2,269,400
TOTAL LAND AREA		220,625	571,416	19,536,300
INLAND WATER		4,336	11,230	
TOTAL AREA		224,961	582,646	

Demography

Population (1988): 22,919,000.
Density[2] (1988): persons per sq mi 103.9, persons per sq km 40.1.
Urban-rural (1985): urban 19.7%; rural 80.3%.
Sex distribution (1985): male 49.77%; female 50.23%.
Age breakdown (1984): under 15, 52.0%; 15–29, 22.7%; 30–44, 12.6%; 45–59, 7.9%; 60–74, 3.6%; 75 and over, 0.9%.
Population projection: (1990) 24,821,000; (2000) 36,977,000.
Doubling time: 17 years.
Ethnic composition (1979): Kenyan 98.8% (Kikuyu 20.9%, Luhya 13.8%, Luo 12.8%, Kamba 11.3%, Kalenjin 10.8%, other Kenyan 29.2%); other 1.2%.
Religious affiliation (1980): Christian 73.0%, of which Protestant 26.5%, Roman Catholic 26.4%; African Indigenous 17.6%, Orthodox 2.5%; traditional beliefs 18.9%; Muslim 6.0%; other 2.1%.
Major cities (1984): Nairobi 1,162,000[3]; Mombasa 425,600; Kisumu 167,100; Nakuru 101,700; Machakos 92,300[4].

Vital statistics

Birth rate per 1,000 population (1980–85): 55.1 (world avg. 29.0).
Death rate per 1,000 population (1980–85): 14.0 (world avg. 11.0).
Natural increase rate per 1,000 population (1980–85): 41.1 (world avg. 18.0).
Total fertility rate (avg. births per childbearing woman; 1984): 7.7.
Life expectancy at birth (1980–85): male 51.2 years; female 54.7 years.
Major causes of death per 100,000 population: n.a.; however, major infectious diseases include malaria, gastroenteritis, venereal diseases, diarrhea and dysentery, trachoma, amebiasis, and schistosomiasis.

National economy

Budget (1987–88). Revenue: K Sh 42,497,000,000 (indirect taxes 48.8%, of which sales tax 25.6%, custom and excise duties 20.2%; direct taxes 24.0%; grants 12.9%; nontax revenue 9.9%). Expenditures: K Sh 42,497,000,000 (recurrent expenditure 72.6%; development expenditure 27.4%).
Production (metric tons except as noted). Agriculture, forestry, fishing (1986): sugarcane 3,887,000, corn (maize) 2,650,000, potatoes 720,000, pulses 518,000, cassava 518,000, sweet potatoes 350,000, wheat 270,000, plantains 265,000, pineapples 160,000, bananas 145,000, tea 140,000, sorghum 130,000, coffee 125,000, coconuts 71,000, millet 65,000, sisal 50,000, seed cotton 27,000, tomatoes 20,000, cottonseed 18,000, barley 15,000, cashew nuts 12,000, copra 10,000, sunflower seeds 5,000; livestock (number of live animals) 9,000,000 cattle, 8,500,000 goats, 7,100,000 sheep; roundwood (1985) 32,409,000 cu m; total fish catch 102,471, of which freshwater fish 94.2%. Mining and quarrying (1986): limestone 2,069,020; soda ash 237,650; salt 100,379; fluorspar 50,851; corundum (ruby) 66 kilograms. Manufacturing (1985): wheat flour 292,600; corn meal 242,300; canned fruits 156,000; pyrethrum extract 120; rubber sandals 6,000,000 pairs; textbooks 3,500,000 units; floor and wall tiles 1,600,000 units; leather shoes 1,300,000 pairs; wheel barrows 15,000 units; assembled vehicles 8,860 units, of which coaches and buses 401 units; water meters 5,374 units. Construction (1984): residential 118,000 sq m; nonresidential 37,000 sq m. Energy production (consumption): electricity (kW-hr; 1986) 2,500,000,000 (2,720,000,000); coal (metric tons; 1986) none (85,000); crude petroleum (barrels; 1986) none (14,660,000); petroleum products (metric tons; 1986) 1,790,000 (902,000).
Public debt (external, outstanding; 1986): U.S.$3,437,900,000.
Household income and expenditure. Average household size (1980) 6.2; average annual income per household: n.a.; sources of income: n.a.; expenditure (1980): food 46.5%, housing 10.0%, furniture and utensils 9.4%, transportation 8.4%, clothing and footwear 7.7%, health 2.2%, education 1.0%.
Population economically active (1985): total 8,389,000; activity rate of total population 40.7% (participation rates: ages 15–64, 76.2%; female 40.9%; unemployed, n.a.).

Price and earnings indexes (1980 = 100)

	1982	1983	1984	1985	1986	1987	1988[5]
Consumer price index	134.7	150.2	165.4	187.0	194.4	204.5	221.9
Annual earnings index	124.5	132.7	145.3	157.4	...	...	...

Gross national product (at current market prices; 1986): U.S.$6,470,000,000 (U.S.$300 per capita).

Structure of gross domestic product and labour force

	1986		1985	
	in value K Sh '000,000	% of total value	labour force[6]	% of labour force
Agriculture	28,723.4	25.6	240,900	20.5
Mining	229.0	0.2	4,800	0.4
Manufacturing	11,527.4	10.3	158,800	13.5
Construction	5,805.0	5.2	49,900	4.3
Public utilities	1,866.6	1.6	17,700	1.5
Transp. and commun.	6,106.0	5.4	55,700	4.7
Trade	12,671.8	11.3	89,700	7.6
Finance	14,109.6	12.6	53,400	4.6
Pub. admin., defense	15,147.8	13.5	158,600	13.5
Services	3,598.4	3.2	344,900	29.4
Other	12,519.2[7]	11.1[7]	—	—
TOTAL	112,304.2	100.0	1,174,400	100.0

Tourism: receipts from visitors (1987) U.S.$355,000,000; expenditures by nationals abroad (1986) U.S.$21,000,000.
Land use (1985): forested 6.5%; meadows and pastures 6.6%; agricultural and under permanent cultivation 4.2%; other 82.7%.

Foreign trade[8]

Balance of trade (current prices)

	1982	1983	1984	1985	1986	1987
K Sh '000,000	−4,383	−2,514	−3,511	−4,609	−3,271	−9,063
% of total	16.2%	8.8%	10.2%	12.6%	7.7%	22.3%

Imports (1986): K Sh 26,711,310,000 (crude petroleum 17.9%, chemicals 16.6%, manufactured goods 12.7%, food and live animals 5.7%, machinery and transport equipment 3.8%). *Major import sources:* U.K. 15.8%; France 11.6%; Japan 11.0%; W.Ger. 10.9%; U.S. 4.8%; Italy 3.7%; The Netherlands 2.6%; Iran 1.5%.
Exports (1986): K Sh 19,633,950,000[9] (coffee [not roasted] 40.8%, tea 18.1%, petroleum products 10.8%, vegetables and fruit 6.9%, soda ash 1.7%, corn [maize] 1.5%, cement 1.4%). *Major export destinations:* U.K. 14.1%; W.Ger. 13.9%; The Netherlands 9.4%; U.S. 8.7%; Uganda 7.4%.

Transport and communications

Transport. Railroads (1986): route length 1,649 mi, 2,654 km; passenger-mi 422,507,000, passenger-km 679,960,000; short ton-mi cargo 1,252,007,000, metric ton-km cargo 1,827,900,000. Roads (1985): total length 33,700 mi, 54,200 km (paved 12%). Vehicles (1985): passenger cars 126,188; trucks and buses 103,844. Merchant marine (1987): vessels (100 gross tons and over) 28; total deadweight tonnage 4,841. Air transport[10] (1987): passenger-mi 652,461,000, passenger-km 1,050,037,000; short ton-mi cargo 93,685,000, metric ton-km cargo 136,778,000; airports (1988) with scheduled flights 16.
Communications. Daily newspapers: total number (1985) 5; total circulation 268,600; circulation per 1,000 population 13. Radio (1986): 2,100,000 receivers (1 per 10 persons). Television (1987): 192,000 receivers (1 per 117 persons). Telephones (1986): 291,627 (1 per 74 persons).

Education and health

Education (1985–86)

	schools	teachers	students	student/ teacher ratio
Primary (age 5–11)	12,936	138,374	4,702,414	34.0
Secondary (age 12–17)	2,396[11]	21,966	437,207	19.9
Voc., teacher tr.	40[11]	1,343	20,560	15.3
Higher	4[11]	...	21,756	...

Educational attainment (1979). Percent of population over age 25 having: no formal schooling 58.6%; primary education 32.2%; some secondary 7.9%; complete secondary and higher 1.3%. *Literacy* (1985): total population over age 15 literate 5,758,000 (59.2%); males literate 3,311,000 (69.6%); females literate 2,447,000 (49.2%).
Health (1985): physicians 2,752 (1 per 7,387 persons); hospital beds 30,936 (1 per 657 persons); infant mortality rate per 1,000 live births (1984) 92.
Food (1984–86): daily per capita caloric intake 2,140 (vegetable products 92%, animal products 8%); (1983) 87% of FAO recommended minimum requirement.

Military

Total active duty personnel (1988): 23,000 (army 82.6%; navy 4.3%; air force 13.1%). *Military expenditure as percent of GNP* (1985): 3.6% (world 6.1%); per capita expenditure U.S.$11.

[1]Includes 14 nonelective seats. [2]Land area only. [3]1985. [4]1983. [5]July. [6]Employed persons only. [7]Indirect taxes less subsidies and imputed bank service charges. [8]Import figures are f.o.b. in balance of trade and c.i.f. in commodities and trading partners. [9]Includes K Sh 578,440,000 reexports. [10]Kenya Airways only. [11]1984–85.

Kiribati

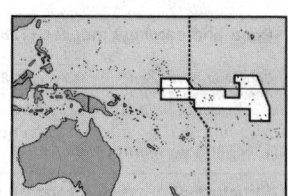

Official name: Republic of Kiribati.
Form of government: unitary republic with one legislature (House of Assembly [40[1]]).
Head of state and government: President.
Capital: Bairiki, on Tarawa Atoll.
Official language: English.
Official religion: none.
Monetary unit: 1 Australian Dollar ($A) = 100 cents; valuation (Oct. 10, 1988) 1 U.S.$ = $A 1.24; 1 £ = $A 2.13.

Area and population

Island Groups Islands	Capitals	area[2] sq mi	area[2] sq km	population 1985 census
Gilberts Group	Bairiki Islet	110	285	61,226
Abaiang	Tuarabu	7	17	4,386
Abemama	Kariatebike	11	27	2,966
Aranuka	Takaeang	4	12	984
Arorae	Roreti	4	9	1,470
Banaba	Anteeren	2	6	189
Beru	Taubukinberu	7	18	2,702
Butaritari	Butaritari	5	13	3,622
Kuria	Tabontebike	6	15	1,052
Maiana	Tebangetua	6	17	2,141
Makin	Makin	3	8	1,777
Marakei	Rawannawi	5	14	2,693
Nikunau	Rungata	7	19	2,061
Nonouti	Teuabu	8	20	2,930
Onotoa	Buariki	6	16	1,927
Tabiteuea North	Utiroa	10	26	3,171
Tabiteuea South	Buariki	5	12	1,322
Tamana	Bakaka	2	5	1,378
Tarawa North	Abaokoro	6	15	3,205
Tarawa South	Bairiki	6	16	21,393
Line Group	Kiritimati	207	535	2,633
Northern		167	432	2,633
Kiritimati (Christmas)	London	150	388	1,737
Tabuaeran (Fanning)	Paelau	13	34	445
Teraina (Washington)	Washington	4	10	451
Southern		40	103	—
(Caroline, Flint, Malden, Starbuck, Vostok)				
Phoenix Group	Kanton	11	29	24
(Birnie, Enderbury, Kanton [Canton], McKean, Manra [Sydney], Nikumaroro [Gardner], Orona [Hull], Rawaki [Phoenix])				
TOTAL		328	849	64,026

Demography

Population (1988): 68,200.
Density[3] (1988): persons per sq mi 243.6, persons per sq km 93.9.
Urban–rural (1985): urban 33.4%; rural 66.6%.
Sex distribution (1985): male 49.56%; female 50.44%.
Age breakdown (1985)[4]: under 15, 38.9%; 15–29, 29.9%; 30–44, 16.1%; 45–59, 9.3%; 60–74, 4.9%; 75 and over, 0.9%.
Population projection: (1990) 71,000; (2000) 87,000.
Doubling time: 33 years.
Ethnic composition (1985): I-Kiribati 96.1%; mixed (part I-Kiribati and other) 2.6%; Tuvaluan 0.7%; European 0.4%; other 0.2%.
Religious affiliation (1985)[4]: Roman Catholic 52.6%; Kiribati Protestant (Congregational) 40.9%; Baha'i 2.4%; Seventh-day Adventist 1.4%; other 2.7%.
Major cities (1985): Urban Tarawa 21,393.

Vital statistics

Birth rate per 1,000 population (1981–85): 37.5 (world avg. 29.0); legitimate, n.a.; illegitimate, n.a.
Death rate per 1,000 population (1981–85): 23.6 (world avg. 11.0).
Natural increase rate per 1,000 population (1981–85): 23.6 (world avg. 18.0).
Total fertility rate (avg. births per childbearing woman; 1981–85): 4.9.
Marriage rate per 1,000 population (1973): 4.5.
Divorce rate per 1,000 population: n.a.
Life expectancy at birth (1981–85): male 50.6 years; female 55.6 years.
Major causes of death per 100,000 population: n.a.; however, the major causes include tuberculosis, diarrheal and respiratory diseases, and nutritional disorders.

National economy

Budget (1985). Revenue: $A 14,747,000 (nontax revenue 66.5%, of which reserve fund income 35.1%, fish royalties 20.4%; tax revenue 33.5%, of which import duties 25.4%, income tax 7.0%). Expenditures: $A 16,807,000 (economy 38.1%; public service 25.7%; education 17.8%; health 10.0%; police 8.3%).
Public debt: n.a.
Tourism (1977): visitors 796.
Production (metric tons except as noted). Agriculture, forestry, fishing (1986): coconuts 90,000, roots and tubers 13,000 (of which taro 3,000), copra 12,000, fruit 5,000, vegetables and melons 5,000, bananas 4,000; livestock (number of live animals) 10,000 pigs, 191,000 chickens[5]; fish catch 33,585. Mining and quarrying: none[6]. Manufacturing (1986): copra $A

459,000; other important products are processed fish, baked goods, clothing, boats, and handicrafts. Energy production (consumption): electricity (kW-hr; 1986) 6,000,000 (6,000,000) coal: none (n.a.); crude petroleum: none (n.a.); petroleum products (metric tons; 1986) none (6,000); natural gas: none (n.a.).
Gross national product (at current market prices; 1986): U.S.$21,421,000 (U.S.$327 per capita).

Structure of gross domestic product and labour force

	1986 in value $A '000	1986 % of total value	1985 labour force	1985 % of labour force
Agriculture, fishing	8,528	29.2	19,200[7]	72.9
Mining	—	—	14	0.1
Manufacturing	600	2.1	132	0.5
Construction	1,500	5.1	440	1.7
Public utilities	900	3.1	232	0.9
Transportation and communications	4,500	15.4	1,050	4.0
Trade	3,600	12.3	1,127	4.3
Finance	1,950	6.7	93	0.4
Pub. admin., defense	8,100	27.7	1,601	6.1
Services	750	2.6	1,802	6.8
Other	−1,200	−4.1	646[8]	2.5
TOTAL	29,228[9]	100.0[10]	26,337	100.0[10]

Population economically active (1985): total 26,337; activity rate of total population 41.2% (participation rates: over age 15, 67.8%; female 36.1%, unemployed 2.4%).

Price and earnings indexes (1980 = 100)

	1980	1981	1982	1983	1984	1985	1986
Consumer price index	100.0	107.7	113.7	120.8	128.1	134.6	133.1
Monthly earnings index	...	...	...	...	...	...	...

Household income and expenditure. Average household size (1985) 6.1; income per household: n.a.; sources of income (1978): agriculture 35.9%, wages only 27.5%, wages and other 19.3%, agriculture and other 12.6%, other 4.7%; expenditure (1982): food 50.0%, tobacco and alcohol 14.0%, clothing 8.0%, transportation 8.0%, housing, energy, and household operation 7.5%.
Land use (1985): forested 2.8%; agricultural and under permanent cultivation 50.7%; other 46.5%.

Foreign trade

Balance of trade (current prices)

	1980	1981	1982	1983	1984	1985	1986
$A '000	−14,422	−16,312	−15,681	−15,900	−10,381	−15,525	−19,082
% of total	74.8%	−71.2%	77.2%	65.4%	28.5%	56.2%	79.4%

Imports (1986): $A 21,554,000 (food 26.4%, manufactured goods 20.5%, machinery and transport equipment 20.2%, mineral fuels 10.4%, beverages and tobacco 5.7%, chemicals 5.3%, crude materials 1.6%). *Major import sources:* Australia 40.3%; Japan 19.4%; Fiji 11.8%; New Zealand 4.9%; United States 3.6%; China 2.7%; United Kingdom 2.6%.
Exports (1986): $A 2,472,000 (fish and fish preparations 70.8%, copra 18.6%). *Major export destinations:* Fiji 46.1%; United States 18.7%; The Netherlands 6.5%; American Samoa 5.7%.

Transport and communications

Transport. Roads (1986): total length 398 mi, 640 km (paved, n.a.). Vehicles (1978): passenger cars and trucks 163; motorcycles 2,822. Merchant marine (1987): vessels (100 gross tons and over) 7; total deadweight tonnage 2,841. Air transport (1986): passenger-mi 6,184,000, passenger-km 9,953,000; short ton-mi cargo 32,000, metric ton-km cargo 47,000; airports (1988) with scheduled flights 18.
Communications. Daily newspapers: none. Radio (1986): total number of receivers 10,000 (1 per 6.6 persons). Television: none. Telephones (1986): 1,130 (1 per 57 persons).

Education and health

Education (1986)

	schools	teachers	students	student/ teacher ratio
Primary (age 6–13)	112	457	13,331	29.2
Secondary (age 14–18)	8	128	2,167	16.9
Voc., teacher tr.	3	43	534	12.4
Higher[11]	—	—	—	—

Educational attainment (1985)[4]. Percent of population age 25 and over having: no schooling 5.8%; less than full primary education 56.1%; primary 22.3%; some secondary 15.3%; secondary 0.5%. *Literacy* (1985): total population age 15 and over literate 90%.
Health (1982): physicians 19 (1 per 3,210 persons); hospital beds 283 (1 per 215 persons); infant mortality rate per 1,000 live births 82.
Food (1984–86): daily per capita caloric intake 2,936 (vegetable products 91%, animal products 9%); (1983) 117% of FAO recommended minimum requirement.

---

[1]Includes 1 nonelective member. [2]Includes uninhabited islands. [3]Density based on inhabited island areas (280 sq mi, 726 sq km) only. [4]Indigenous population only, who constitute 98.7% of the total population. [5]1982. [6]Mining of phosphates on Banaba (Ocean Island) ceased in 1979. [7]Includes 18,719 persons engaged in "village work" (subsistence agriculture or fishing). [8]Includes 627 unemployed. [9]At factor cost. [10]Detail does not add to total given because of rounding. [11]185 students overseas.

Korea, North

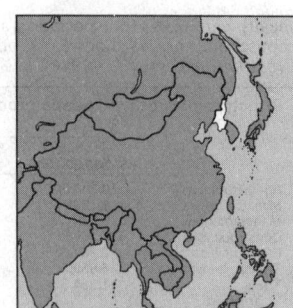

Official name: Chosŏn Minjujuŭi In'min Konghwaguk (Democratic People's Republic of Korea).
Form of government: unitary single-party republic with one legislative house (Supreme People's Assembly [655]).
Chief of state: President.
Head of government: Premier.
Capital: P'yŏngyang.
Official language: Korean.
Official religion: none.
Monetary unit: 1 won = 100 chon; valuation (Oct. 10, 1988) 1 U.S.$ = 0.97 won; 1 £ = 1.66 won.

Area and population

Provinces	Capitals	area[1] sq mi	area[1] sq km	population 1968 estimate
Chagang-do	Kanggye	6,300	16,200	780,000
Hamgyŏng-namdo	Hamhŭng	7,400	19,200	1,315,000
Hamgyŏng-pukto	Ch'ŏngjin	6,100	15,900	1,110,000
Hwanghae-namdo	Haeju	2,900	7,600	1,340,000
Hwanghae-pukto	Sariwŏn	3,300	8,600	1,060,000
Kangwŏn-do	Wŏnsan	4,100	10,700	1,030,000
P'yŏngan-namdo	P'yŏngsan	4,700	12,300	2,250,000
P'yŏngan-pukto	Sinŭiju	4,600	12,000	1,760,000
Yanggang-do	Hyesan	5,400	14,100	435,000
Special cities				
Ch'ŏngjin-si	—	700	1,900	385,000
Hamhŭng-si	—	300	800	530,000
P'yŏngyang-si	P'yŏngyang	700	1,800	1,275,000
Special district				
Kaesŏng-chigu	Kaesŏng	500	1,200	289,000
TOTAL		47,300[2]	122,400[2]	13,559,000

Demography

Population (1988): 21,903,000.
Density (1988): persons per sq mi 463.1, persons per sq km 178.9.
Urban–rural (1985): urban 63.8%; rural 36.2%.
Sex distribution (1985): male 49.55%; female 50.45%.
Age breakdown (1985): under 15, 38.7%; 15–29, 29.2%; 30–44, 16.6%; 45–59, 9.8%; 60–74, 4.7%; 75 and over, 1.0%.
Population projection: (1990) 22,939,000; (2000) 28,166,000.
Doubling time: 28 years.
Ethnic composition (1983): Korean 99.8%; Chinese 0.2%.
Religious affiliation (1980): atheist or nonreligious 67.9%; traditional beliefs 15.6%; Ch'ŏndogyo 13.9%; Buddhist 1.7%; Christian 0.9%.
Major cities (1981): P'yŏngyang 1,283,000; Hamhŭng-Hŭngnam 775,000; Ch'ŏngjin 490,000; Kaesŏng 240,000; Wŏnsan 240,000.

Vital statistics

Birth rate per 1,000 population (1980–85): 30.5 (world avg. 29.0).
Death rate per 1,000 population (1980–85): 6.0 (world avg. 11.0).
Natural increase rate per 1,000 population (1980–85): 24.5 (world avg. 18.0).
Total fertility rate (avg. births per childbearing woman; 1985): 3.8.
Marriage rate per 1,000 population: n.a.
Divorce rate per 1,000 population: n.a.
Life expectancy at birth (1984): male 65 years; female 72 years.
Major causes of death: n.a.; however, major diseases include endemic diseases (typhoid fever, dysentery, clonorchiasis [liver fluke], paragonimiasis [lung fluke], encephalitis, poliomyelitis, diphtheria, measles, tuberculosis of respiratory system, bronchitis, malignant neoplasms (cancers), hypertensive and ischemic heart diseases, and intestinal obstruction and hernia.

National economy

Budget (1987). Revenue: 30,308,000,000 won (1984; turnover tax 55.0%, payments by state enterprises 30%). Expenditures: 30,308,000,000 won (1984; national economy 63.3%, social and cultural affairs 20.0%, defense 14.6%, other 2.1%).
Production (metric tons except as noted). Agriculture, forestry, fishing (1986): rice 6,000,000, vegetables 2,825,000, corn (maize) 2,700,000, potatoes 1,895,-000, wheat 710,000, barley 568,000, millet 545,000, sweet potatoes 482,000, soybeans 438,000, pulses 291,000, sugarcane 190,000, sorghum 187,000, pears 103,000, peaches 89,000, tobacco 58,000, dry onions 39,000, seed cotton 16,000; livestock (number of live animals) 2,920,000 pigs, 1,122,-000 cattle, 359,000 sheep, 272,000 goats, 19,000,000 chickens; roundwood 4,627,000 cu m; fish catch 1,700,000. Mining and quarrying (1986): iron ore 8,500,000; magnesite (metal content) 882,000; phosphate rock 500,000; sulfur 230,000; zinc 180,000; lead (metal content) 110,000; gypsum 82,000; fluorspar 40,000; graphite 25,000; silver 1,600,000 troy oz; gold 160,000 troy oz. Manufacturing (1986): cement 7,600,000; pig iron 5,750,000; crude steel 4,500,000; chemical fertilizers 4,000,000; steel semimanufactures 3,400,-000[3]; meat 235,000; television sets 200,000 units[3]; machine tools 29,000 units[3]; tractors 24,000 units; cars 18,000 units[3]; textile fabrics 535,000,-000 m. Construction: n.a. Energy production (consumption): electricity (kW-hr; 1986) 50,000,000 (50,000,000); coal (metric tons; 1986) 52,000,000 (54,450,000); crude petroleum (barrels; 1986) none (19,700,000); petroleum products (metric tons; 1986) 2,650,000 (3,140,000); natural gas, none (n.a.).

Population economically active (1985): total 9,084,000; activity rate of total population 44.6% (participation rates: ages 15–64, 75.3%; female 46.0%; unemployed, n.a.).
Price and earnings indexes: n.a.
Public debt (external, outstanding; 1985): U.S.$4,000,000,000.
Household income and expenditure. Average household size (1980) 5.7; average annual income per household 3,677 won (U.S.$4,275); sources of income: n.a.; expenditure[4] (1984): food 46.5%; clothing 29.9%; furniture 3.8%; energy 3.3%; housing 0.6%.
Gross national product (1986): U.S.$17,400,000,000 (U.S.$860 per capita).

Structure of gross domestic product and labour force

	1982 in value '000,000 won	1982 % of total value	1982 labour force	1982 % of labour force
Agriculture	...	...	3,276,000	44.1
Mining and manufacturing	...	...		
Construction	...	...	2,790,000	33.0
Public utilities	...	...		
Transp. and commun.	...	...	418,000	4.9
Trade	...	...		
Finance	...	...		
Pub. admin., defense	...	...	1,521,000	18.0
Services	...	...		
Other	...	...		
TOTAL	11,800	100.0	8,455,000	100.0

Land use (1985): forested 74.5%; meadows and pastures 0.4%; agricultural and under permanent cultivation 19.2%; other 5.9%.
Tourism: n.a.

Foreign trade

Balance of trade (current prices)

	1974	1976	1978	1979	1980	1981
'000,000 won	−601	−176	−53	+165	−256	−285
% of total	31.6%	11.5%	3.3%	6.3%	9.4%	10.3%

Imports (1986): U.S.$2,000,000,000[5] (crude petroleum, coal and coke, industrial machinery and transport equipment [including trucks], industrial chemicals, textile yarn and fabrics, and grain are among the major imports). *Major import sources* (1985): U.S.S.R. 36.1%; China 18.8%; Japan 13.2%; West European countries 4.0%; Hong Kong 3.5%.
Exports (1985): U.S.$1,700,000,000[5] (minerals [including lead, magnesite, and zinc], metallurgical products [iron and steel, nonferrous metals], cement, agricultural products [including fish, grain, fruit and vegetables, tobacco], and manufactured goods [textile fabrics, clothing], are among the major exports). *Major export destinations* (1985): U.S.S.R. 43.6%; Japan 15.1%; China 13.4%; West European countries 4.3%; Australia 3.3%; Hong Kong 3.1%.

Transport and communications

Transport. Railroads (1985): length 2,779 mi, 4,473 km; passengers, n.a.; cargo, n.a. Roads (1985): total length 13,670 mi, 22,000 km (paved 2%). Vehicles (1982): passenger cars 180,000. Merchant marine (1987): vessels (100 gross tons and over) 73; total deadweight tonnage 603,049. Air transport (1979): passenger-mi 52,200,000, passenger-km 84,000,000; short ton-mi cargo 1,370,000, metric ton-km cargo 2,000,000; airports (1988) with scheduled flights 3.
Communications. Daily newspapers (1984): total number 11; total circulation 1,000,000[6]; circulation per 1,000 population 50[6]. Radio (1984): total number of receivers 4,100,000 (1 per 5 persons). Television (1984): total number of receivers 1,050,000 (1 per 19 persons). Telephones (1983): 10,000 (1 per 2,000 persons).

Education and health

Education (1982)

	schools	teachers	students	student/ teacher ratio
Primary (age 5–9)	4,700[7]		c. 2,500,000	...
Secondary (age 10–15)	...	c. 100,000	c. 2,500,000[8]	...
Voc., teacher tr.	...		...	...
Higher	175	9,244	200,000	21.6

Educational attainment, n.a. *Literacy* (1979): 90%.
Health (1982): physicians 45,000 (1 per 417 persons); hospital beds 244,000 (1 per 77 persons); infant mortality rate per 1,000 live births (1980–85) 29.7.
Food (1984–86): daily per capita caloric intake 3,199 (vegetable products 92%, animal products 8%); (1983) 127% of FAO recommended minimum requirement.

Military

Total active duty personnel (1987): 838,000 (army 89.5%, navy 4.2%, air force 6.3%). *Military expenditure as percent of GNP* (1985): 22.2% (world 6.1%); per capita expenditure U.S.$265.

[1]Areas approximate. [2]Detail does not add to total given because of rounding. [3]1984. [4]Workers and clerical workers only. [5]Estimate based on trading partners' information. [6]One daily only. [7]1976. [8]Includes vocational students.

Korea, South

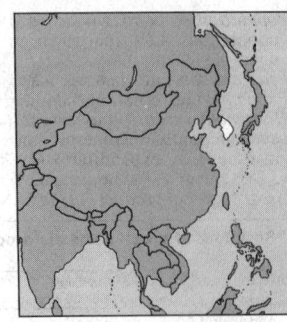

Official name: Taehan Min'guk
(Republic of Korea).
Form of government: unitary multiparty
republic with a National Assembly
(299 members).
Chief of state: President.
Head of government: Prime Minister.
Capital: Seoul.
Official language: Korean.
Official religion: none.
Monetary unit: 1 won (W) = 100 chon;
valuation (Oct. 10, 1988)
1 U.S.$ = W 710; 1 £ = W 1,217.

Area and population

Provinces	Capitals	area sq mi	area sq km	population 1985 census
Cheju-do	Cheju	705	1,825	488,576
Chŏlla-namdo	Kwangju	4,649	12,040	2,842,532
Chŏlla-pukto	Chŏnju	3,109	8,051	2,202,078
Ch'ungch'ŏng-namdo	Taejŏn	3,416	8,848	3,001,179
Ch'ungch'ŏng-pukto	Ch'ŏngju	2,871	7,436	1,391,004
Kangwŏn-do	Ch'unch'ŏn'	6,524	16,896	1,724,809
Kyŏngi-do	Inch'ŏn[1]	4,194	10,863	4,794,135
Kyŏngsang-namdo	Masan	4,578	11,856	3,010,945
Kyŏngsang-pukto	Taegu[1]	7,506	19,441	3,516,660
Special cities				
Inch'ŏn-si	Inch'ŏn	80	207	1,386,911
Kwangju-si	Kwangju	83	215	905,896
Pusan-si	Pusan	168	435	3,514,798
Sŏul-t'ŭkpyŏlsi	Seoul	234	605	9,639,110
Taegu-si	Taegu	176	455	2,029,853
TOTAL		38,291[2]	99,173	40,448,486

Demography

Population (1988): 42,593,000.
Density (1988): persons per sq mi 1,112.7, persons per sq km 429.6.
Urban–rural (1985): urban 65.4%; rural 34.6%.
Sex distribution (1987): male 50.42%; female 49.58%.
Age breakdown (1985): under 15, 29.9%; 15–29, 31.3%; 30–44, 19.5%; 45–59, 12.5%; 60–74, 5.5%; 75 and over, 1.3%.
Population projection: (1990) 43,773,000; (2000) 49,914,000.
Doubling time: 53 years.
Ethnic composition (1985): Korean 99.9%; other 0.1%.
Religious affiliation (1985)[3]: Buddhist 19.9%; Protestant 16.1%; Roman Catholic 4.6%; Confucian 1.2%; Wonbulgyo 0.2%; Ch'ondogyo 0.1%; other 0.5%; none 57.4%.
Major cities (1985): Seoul 9,639,110; Pusan 3,514,798; Taegu 2,029,853; Inch'ŏn 1,386,911; Kwangju 905,896.

Vital statistics

Birth rate per 1,000 population (1987): 19.4 (world avg. 26.0).
Death rate per 1,000 population (1987): 6.1 (world avg. 9.9).
Natural increase rate per 1,000 population (1987): 13.3 (world avg. 16.1).
Total fertility rate (avg. births per childbearing woman; 1987): 2.1.
Marriage rate per 1,000 population (1982): 8.3.
Divorce rate per 1,000 population (1982): 0.6.
Life expectancy at birth (1987): male 65.6 years; female 71.8 years.
Major causes of death per 100,000 population: (1985): diseases of the circulatory system 155.0; malignant neoplasms (cancers) 73.5; accidents, poisonings, and violence 56.5; diseases of the digestive system 43.9; diseases of the respiratory system 22.6.

National economy

Budget (1988). Revenue: W 17,541,900,000,000 (internal tax 61.7%, defense surtax 13.9%, customs duties 12.4%, monopoly profits 4.2%). Expenditures: W 17,541,900,000,000 (defense 32.8%, education 20.6%, economic development 14.4%, administration 10.2%, supports to provinces 8.7%).
Tourism (1986): receipts from visitors U.S.$1,550,000,000; expenditures by nationals abroad U.S.$613,000,000.
Production (metric tons except as noted). Agriculture, forestry, fishing (1986): rice 5,607,000, cabbages 3,409,000, radishes (1985) 1,586,000, sweet potatoes 684,000, potatoes 566,000, apples (1985) 533,000, barley 453,000, dry onions 379,000, garlic 370,000, tangerines 340,000, soybeans 199,000, chilies and peppers 198,000; livestock (number of live animals) 3,347,000 pigs, 2,807,000 cattle, 217,000 goats, 56,095,000 chickens; roundwood 8,564,000 cu m; fish catch 3,660,000. Mining and quarrying (1986): iron ore 528,000; zinc ore 77,366; lead ore 20,061; tungsten ore 4,081; refined silver 51,581 kg. Manufacturing (1986): cement 23,403,000; pig iron 9,017,000; crude steel 4,081,000; chemical fertilizers 2,859,000; man-made fabrics 1,116,200,000 sq m; steel cargo ships 1,835,587 gross tons; television receivers 11,268,823 units; passenger cars 456,994 units. Construction (1986): residential 22,518,000 sq m; nonresidential 21,024,000 sq m. Energy production (consumption): electricity (kW-hr; 1986) 69,763,000,000 (69,763,000,000); coal (metric tons; 1986) 24,253,000 (41,153,000); crude petroleum (barrels; 1986) none (210,019,000); petroleum products (metric tons; 1986) 24,313,000 (22,800,000).
Household income and expenditure (1986)[4]. Average household size 4.2; income per household W 5,772,200 (U.S.$6,550); sources of income: wages and salaries 62.2%, other 37.8%; expenditure: food and beverages 36.1%, education and recreation 12.3%, energy 7.6%, clothing and footwear 7.5%,

health care 6.5%, transportation and communications 6.2%, housing 5.2%, household durable goods 5.0%, other 13.6%.
Gross national product (1986): U.S.$98,370,000,000 (U.S.$2,370 per capita).

Structure of gross domestic product and labour force

	1986 in value W '000,000,000	% of total value	1986 labour force	% of labour force
Agriculture	10,648.5	12.3	3,662,000	22.7
Mining	1,158.7	1.3	187,000	1.2
Manufacturing	25,965.5	30.0	3,826,000	23.7
Construction	6,769.0	7.8	889,000	5.5
Public utilities	2,737.6	3.2	40,000	0.2
Transp. and commun.	6,965.5	8.1	733,000	4.6
Trade	11,294.9	13.1	3,480,000	21.6
Finance			614,000	3.8
Pub. admin., defense	20,970.2	24.2	2,074,000	12.9
Services				
Other			611,000[5]	3.8[5]
TOTAL	86,509.9	100.0	16,116,000	100.0

Population economically active (1986): total 16,116,000; activity rate 38.8% (participation rates: ages 15–64, 57.3%; female 39.1%; unemployed 3.8%).

Price and earnings indexes (1980 = 100)

	1981	1982	1983	1984	1985	1986	1987
Consumer price index	121.3	130.1	134.5	137.6	141.0	145.0	149.3
Monthly earnings index	120.0	137.7	154.4	167.3	186.9	200.6	223.9

Public debt (external, outstanding; 1986): U.S.$29,107,600,000.
Land use (1985): forested 66.8%; meadows and pastureland 0.8%; agricultural and under permanent cultivation 21.8%; other 10.6%.

Foreign trade

Balance of trade (current prices)

	1982	1983	1984	1985	1986	1987
US$'000,000	−2,400	−1,970	−1,386	−853	4,236	−6,940
% of total	5.4%	3.9%	2.3%	1.4%	7.4%	9.8%

Imports (1986): U.S.$31,583,900,000 (machinery and transport equipment 33.7%, mineral fuels and related products 16.0%, crude materials except fuels 13.6%, chemicals and chemical products 11.1%). *Major import sources:* Japan 34.4%; United States 20.7%; West Germany 3.8%; Australia 3.4%; Malaysia 2.9%; Canada 2.2%; France 2.2%; Saudi Arabia 2.0%; United Kingdom 1.4%; China 1.4%; Indonesia 1.4%.
Exports (1986): U.S.$34,714,500,000 (manufactured goods 55.5%, machinery and transport equipment 33.6%, food and live animals 4.5%, chemicals and chemical products 3.1%). *Major export destinations:* United States 40.0%; Japan 15.6%; Hong Kong 4.9%; Canada 3.6%; West Germany 3.6%; United Kingdom 3.0%; Saudi Arabia 2.5%; France 1.6%.

Transport and communications

Transport. Railroads (1986): length 3,914 mi, 6,299 km; passenger-km 23,563,000,000; metric ton-km cargo 12,831,000,000. Roads (1986): total length 32,475 mi, 52,264 km (paved 50%). Vehicles (1986): passenger cars 664,226; trucks and buses 627,228. Merchant marine (1987): vessels (100 gross tons and over) 1,899; total deadweight tonnage 11,452,759. Air transport (1986): passenger-km 13,404,000,000; metric ton-km cargo 1,467,528,000; airports (1988) with scheduled flights 5.
Communications. Daily newspapers (1986): total number 26; total circulation 11,000,000; circulation per 1,000 population 265. Radio (1985): 38,605,000 receivers (1 per 1.1 persons). Television (1987): 8,643,235 receivers (1 per 4.9 persons). Telephones (1987): 9,288,000 (1 per 4.5 persons).

Education and health

Education (1986–87)

	schools	teachers	students	student/ teacher ratio
Primary (age 6–13)	6,535	126,677	4,798,323	37.9
Secondary (age 14–19)	3,408	114,658	4,111,043	35.9
Vocational	736	34,189	1,007,272	29.5
Higher	459	35,573	1,332,455	37.5

Educational attainment (1985). Percent of population age 25 and over having: no formal schooling 14.3%; primary education 46.2%; some secondary 3.8%; secondary 24.8%; postsecondary 10.9%. *Literacy* (1981): total population age 15 and over literate 13,191,432 (92.7%); males literate 6,937,242 (97.5%); females literate 6,254,190 (87.9%).
Health (1986): physicians 31,616 (1 per 1,315 persons); hospital beds 79,935 (1 per 520 persons); infant mortality rate per 1,000 live births (1987): 25.0.
Food (1984–86): daily per capita caloric intake 2,876 (vegetable products 88%, animal products 12%); (1983) 118% of FAO recommended minimum requirement.

Military

Total active duty personnel (1987): 629,000 (army 86.2%, navy 8.6%, air force 5.2%). *Military expenditure as percent of GNP* (1986): 5.5% (world 6.1%); per capita expenditure: U.S.$107.

[1]During the 1980s Inch'ŏn, Taegu, and Kwangju also became special cities. [2]Detail does not add to total given because of rounding. [3]Refers to persons who have received commandments, accepted baptism, or entered a faith and who participate in a religious function regularly or put the religious idea into practice. [4]Excludes farm households. [5]Unemployed.

Kuwait

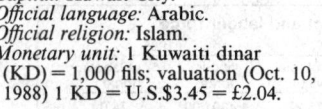
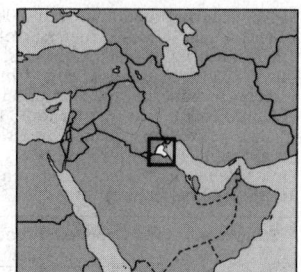

Official name: Dawlat al-Kuwayt (State of Kuwait).
Form of government: Constitutional monarchy with a single parliamentary house (National Assembly [64])[1].
Chief of state: Emir.
Head of government: Prime Minister.
Capital: Kuwait City.
Official language: Arabic.
Official religion: Islam.
Monetary unit: 1 Kuwaiti dinar (KD) = 1,000 fils; valuation (Oct. 10, 1988) 1 KD = U.S.$3.45 = £2.04.

Area and population

Governorates	Capitals	area sq mi	area sq km	population 1987 estimate
al-Aḥmadī	al-Aḥmadī	1,984	5,138	345,783
al-Jahrā'	al-Jahrā'	4,372	11,324	329,588
Capital	Kuwait City	38	98	160,860
Ḥawallī	Ḥawallī	138	358	1,036,337
Islands[2]	—	348	900	...
TOTAL		6,880	17,818	1,872,568

Demography

Population (1988): 1,958,000.
Density (1988): persons per sq mi 284.6, persons per sq km 109.9.
Urban–rural (1986): urban 90.1%; rural 9.9%.
Sex distribution (1987): male 56.77%; female 43.23%.
Age breakdown (1986): under 15, 37.4%; 15–29, 27.9%; 30–44, 23.9%; 45–59, 8.6%; 60–74, 1.8%; 75 and over, 0.4%.
Population projection: (1990) 2,143,000; (2000) 2,877,000.
Doubling time: 26 years.
Ethnic composition (1985): Kuwaiti Arab 40.1%; non-Kuwaiti Arab 37.9%; Asian 21.0%; European 0.7%; other 0.3%.
Religious affiliation (1980): Muslim 91.5% (Sunnī about 80%, Shī‘ah about 20%); Christian 6.4%; other 2.1%.
Major cities (1985): as-Sālimīyah 153,220; Ḥawallī 145,215; al-Jahrā' 111,165; al-Farwānīyah 68,665; Kuwait City 44,224.

Vital statistics

Birth rate per 1,000 population (1986): 29.5 (world avg. 26.0); legitimate, n.a.; illegitimate, n.a.
Death rate per 1,000 population (1986): 2.4 (world avg. 9.9).
Natural increase rate per 1,000 population (1986): 27.1 (world avg. 16.1).
Total fertility rate (avg. births per childbearing woman; 1986): 5.1.
Marriage rate per 1,000 population (1987): 5.2.
Divorce rate per 1,000 population (1987): 1.5.
Life expectancy at birth (1986): male 70.3 years; female 73.0 years.
Major causes of death per 100,000 population (1986): circulatory diseases 75.7; accidents, poisonings, and violence 37.8; malignant neoplasms (cancers) 29.5%; respiratory diseases 13.7; infectious and parasitic diseases 8.8; endocrine, nutritional, and metabolic diseases 8.5; diseases of the nervous system 6.3; diseases of the digestive system 5.1

National economy

Budget (1987–88). Revenue: KD 1,979,400,000 (oil revenue 87.2%). Expenditures: KD 3,355,900,000 (wages and salaries 24.9%, construction and expropriations 22.3%, goods and services 7.9%, reserve fund for future generations 5.9%, transport equipment 0.7%).
Public debt: none.
Tourism (1986): receipts from visitors U.S.$86,000,000; expenditures by nationals abroad U.S.$1,222,000,000.
Gross national product (at current market prices; 1986): U.S.$24,650,000,000 (U.S.$13,890 per capita).

Structure of gross domestic product and labour force

	1986 in value KD '000,000	% of total value	labour force	% of labour force
Agriculture	51.9	1.0	13,718	1.9
Mining (oil sector)	1,841.8	36.9	7,544	1.1
Manufacturing	556.3	11.1	53,613	7.5
Construction	156.0	3.1	130,471	18.3
Public utilities	−94.1	−1.9	7,819	1.1
Transportation and communications	269.7	5.4	39,401	5.5
Trade	470.1	9.4	80,141	11.3
Finance	233.5	4.7	22,252	3.1
Pub. admin., defense, services	1,512.8	30.3	356,640	50.1
Other				
TOTAL	4,998.0	100.0	711,599	100.0[3]

Production (metric tons except as noted). Agriculture, forestry, fishing (1986): tomatoes 15,000, melons 2,000, dates 2,000, onions 2,000, pumpkins and squash 1,000, cucumbers and gherkins 1,000, garlic 1,000; livestock (number of live animals) 265,000 sheep, 34,000 goats, 21,000 cattle, 7,000 camels, 8,000,000 chickens; fish catch 7,013. Mining and quarrying (1985): sulfur 202,377; asphalt 945,000 barrels. Manufacturing (1987): urea 857,000; flour

139,493; bread 73,850; bran 36,448; salt 35,279; cattle feed 17,500; liquefied caustic soda 16,110; chlorine gas 11,593; fats and oil 11,195; asbestos pipes 7,482; biscuits 2,107; detergents 1,550; hydrochloric acid 742,000 gallons; hydrogen gas 4,518,000 cu m; concrete 70,448 cu m; sodium hydrochloride 25,325 cu m; standard accumulators (batteries) 4,794 units. Construction (1987): residential 3,262,000 sq m; nonresidential 177,000 sq m. Energy production (consumption): electricity (kW-hr; 1986) 17,216,000,000 (17,216,000,000); coal, none (none); crude petroleum (barrels; 1986) 518,100,000 (216,600,000); petroleum products (metric tons; 1986) 27,434,000 (4,000,000); natural gas (cu m; 1986) 5,417,600,000 (6,699,000,000).
Population economically active (1986): total 711,600; activity rate of total population 39.0% (participation rates: ages 15–64, 63.5%; female 20.6%; unemployed [1985] 0.1%.

Price and earnings indexes (1980 = 100)

	1981	1982	1983	1984	1985	1986	1987[4]
Consumer price index	107.4	115.7	121.2	122.6	124.4	125.6	125.6
Monthly earnings index	...	...	...	...	...	...	...

Household income and expenditure. Average household size (1986) 7.4; annual income per household (1973)[5] KD 4,246 (U.S.$12,907); sources of income: wages and salaries 53.8%, self-employment 20.8%, other 25.4%; expenditure (1986–87): housing and energy 27.2%; food, beverages, and tobacco 26.5%; transportation 13.0%, household appliances 10.5%, clothing and footwear 7.7%, education and recreation 4.9%, health 0.7%.
Land use (1985): forested 0.1%; meadows and pastures 7.5%; agricultural and under permanent cultivation 0.1%; other, built-up, and wasteland 92.3%.

Foreign trade

Balance of trade (current prices)

	1982	1983	1984	1985	1986	1987
KD '000,000	+771.8	+1,224.5	+1,590.7	+1,367.2	+389.9	+854.0
% of total	13.9%	22.2%	28.0%	27.7%	10.2%	22.4%

Imports (1987): KD 1,476,000,000 (1984: machinery and transport equipment 43.6%, manufactured goods 22.1%, miscellaneous manufactured articles 15.3%, food and live animals 12.3%, chemicals 3.6%). *Major import sources* (1986): Japan 21.1%; United States 11.2%; West Germany 7.9%; United Kingdom 7.5%; Italy 5.8%; France 5.0%.
Exports (1987): KD 2,330,000,000 (crude petroleum and petroleum products 90.0%). *Major export destinations* (1986): Japan 15.9%; Italy 11.2%; United States 3.6%; West Germany 2.3%; France 2.1%; United Kingdom 1.2%.

Transport and communications

Transport. Railroads: none. Roads (1984): total length 1,208 mi, 1,944 km (paved 100%). Vehicles (1987): passenger cars 420,643; trucks and buses 114,607. Merchant marine (1987): vessels (100 gross tons and over) 236; total deadweight tonnage 3,183,610. Air transport (1986): passenger-mi 2,304,410,000, passenger-km 3,708,595,000; short ton-mi cargo 235,040,000, metric ton-km cargo 343,152,000; airports (1988) with scheduled flights 1.
Communications. Daily newspapers (1986): total number 7; total circulation 453,000; circulation per 1,000 population 253. Radio (1986): total number of receivers 500,000 (1 per 3.6 persons). Television (1987): total number of receivers 700,000 (1 per 2.7 persons). Telephones (1986): 310,132 (1 per 5.9 persons).

Education and health

Education (1986–87)

	schools	teachers	students	student/ teacher ratio
Primary (age 6–10)	282	9,704	175,767	18.1
Secondary (age 11–18)	401	19,158	245,865	12.8
Voc., teacher tr.[6]	6	788	12,272	15.6
Higher	1	887	17,414	19.6

Educational attainment (1985). Percent of population age 15 and over having: no formal schooling 44.4%; primary education 9.2%; some secondary 19.6%; complete secondary 18.2%; higher 8.6%. *Literacy* (1986): total population age 15 and over literate 856,146 (75.1%); males literate 539,058 (78.7%); females literate 317,088 (69.6%).
Health (1986): physicians 2,803 (1 per 553 persons); hospital beds 5,521[7] (1 per 295 persons); infant mortality rate per 1,000 live births (1986) 34.2.
Food (1984–86): daily per capita caloric intake 3,076 (vegetable products 75%, animal products 25%); (1983) 142% of FAO recommended minimum requirement.

Military

Total active duty personnel (1987): 16,100 (army 80.7%, navy 6.9%, air force 12.4%). *Military expenditure as percent of GNP* (1985): 6.3% (world 6.1%); per capita expenditure U.S.$884.

[1]Parliament was suspended on July 3, 1986; its membership includes 50 elected and (at its most recent sitting) 14 ex officio members of the Cabinet. [2]Bubian Island and Warba Island. [3]Detail does not add to total given because of rounding. [4]October. [5]Kuwaiti households only. [6]1985–86. [7]Government hospitals only.

Laos

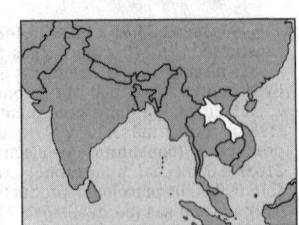

Official name: Sathalanalat Paxathipatai Paxaxôn Lao (Lao People's Democratic Republic).
Form of government: unitary single-party people's republic with one legislative house (Supreme People's Council [45])[1].
Chief of state: President.
Head of government: Prime Minister.
Capital: Vientiane.
Official language: Lao.
Official religion: none.
Monetary unit: 1 new kip (KN) = 100 at; valuation (Oct. 10, 1988)
1 U.S.$ = KN 350.00;
1 £ = KN 599.38.

Area and population

		area		population
				1985
Provinces	Capitals	sq mi	sq km	census
Attapu	Attapu	...	...	69,631
Bokeo	Houayxay	...	...	54,925
Bolikhamxay	Pakxan	...	...	122,300
Champasak	Pakxé	...	...	403,041
Houaphan	Xam Nua	...	...	209,921
Khammouan	Thakhek	...	...	213,462
Louang Namtha	Louang Namtha	...	...	97,028
Louangphrabang	Louangphrabang	...	...	295,475
Oudomxay	Xay	...	...	187,115
Phôngsali	Phôngsali	...	...	122,984
Saravan	Saravan	...	...	187,515
Savannakhét	Savannakhét	...	...	543,611
Vientiane	Vientiane	...	...	264,277
Xaignabouri	Xaignabouri	...	...	223,611
Xékong	Thong	...	...	50,909
Xiangkhoang	Phônsavan	...	...	161,589
Municipalities				
Vientiane	—	...	...	377,409
TOTAL		91,400	236,800	3,584,803

Demography

Population (1988): 3,850,000.
Density (1988): persons per sq mi 42.1, persons per sq km 16.3.
Urban–rural (1987): urban 16.0%; rural 84.0%.
Sex distribution (1985): male 49.02%; female 50.98%.
Age breakdown (1985): under 15, 42.5%; 15–29, 26.6%; 30–44, 16.2%; 45–59, 9.7%; 60–74, 4.3%; 75 and over, 0.7%.
Population projection: (1990) 4,024,000; (2000) 4,964,000.
Doubling time: 24 years.
Ethnic composition (1983): Lao 67.1%; Palaung-Wa 11.9%; Tai 7.9%; Miao (Hmong) and Man (Yao) 5.2%; Mon-Khmer 4.6%; other 3.3%.
Religious affiliation (1980): Buddhist 57.8%; tribal religionist 33.6%; Christian 1.8%, of which Roman Catholic 0.8%, Protestant 0.2%; Muslim 1.0%; atheist 1.0%; Chinese folk-religionist 0.9%; none 3.8%; other 0.1%.
Major cities (1975): Vientiane 379,400[2]; Savannakhét 53,000; Pakxé 47,000; Louangphrabang 46,000.

Vital statistics

Birth rate per 1,000 population (1987): 42.7 (world avg. 26.0).
Death rate per 1,000 population (1987): 14.1 (world avg. 9.9).
Natural increase rate per 1,000 population (1987): 28.6 (world avg. 16.1).
Total fertility rate (avg. births per childbearing woman; 1987): 6.0.
Marriage rate per 1,000 population: n.a.
Divorce rate per 1,000 population: n.a.
Life expectancy at birth (1987): male 50.3 years; female 53.3 years.
Major causes of death per 100,000 population: n.a; however, during the 1970s malaria, influenza, dysentery, and pneumonia were among the country's major health problems.

National economy

Budget (1985). Revenue: KN 6,142,800,000 (state enterprises 80.8%, private sector taxes 19.2%). Expenditures: KN 10,473,400,000 (current expenditure 51.9%, capital expenditure 48.1%).
Public debt (external, outstanding; 1987): U.S.$528,000,000.
Tourism (1982): total number of tourist arrivals 29,000.
Population economically active (1985): total 2,014,000; activity rate of total population 48.9% (participation rates: ages 15–64, 84.2%; female 45.3%; unemployed, n.a.).

Price and earnings indexes (1979 = 100)

	1980	1981	1982	1983	1984	1985
Consumer price index	170	209	296	467	594	982
Monthly earnings index	...	...	...	...	...	...

Production (metric tons except as noted). Agriculture, forestry, fishing (1986): rice 1,490,000, sweet potatoes 115,000, sugarcane 102,000, cassava 84,000, potatoes 52,000, pineapples 42,000, onions 40,000, melons 36,000, oranges 29,000; livestock (number of live animals) 1,516,000 pigs, 1,017,000 water buffalo, 593,000 cattle, 71,000 goats, 6,000,000 chickens; roundwood (1985) 4,051,000 cu m; fish catch 20,000. Mining and quarrying (1986): gypsum 100,000; rock salt 10,000; tin (metal content) 520. Manufacturing

(1983): domestic animal feed 3,000; washing powder 970; plastic products 185; textiles 1,451,400 metres; clothing 474,900 pieces; cigarettes 12,000,000 packets; bricks 10,900,000 units; rubber tires and tubes 1,000,000 units; beer 13,000 hectolitres; soft drinks 12,370 hectolitres. Construction: n.a. Energy production (consumption): electricity (kW-hr; 1986) 1,050,000,000 (311,000,000); coal (metric tons; 1981) 1,000 (1,000); crude petroleum, n.a. (n.a.); petroleum products (metric tons; 1986) none (67,000); natural gas, n.a. (n.a.).
Gross domestic product (at current market prices; 1987): U.S.$500,000,000 (U.S.$130 per capita).

Structure of gross domestic product and labour force

	1984		1985	
	in value KN '000,000[3]	% of total value	labour force	% of labour force
Agriculture	9,105	75.2	1,490,000	74.0
Manufacturing }	553[4]	4.6[4]		
Mining				
Construction	620	5.1		
Public utilities	4	4		
Transportation and communications	178	1.5	524,000	26.0
Trade	1,470	12.1		
Finance				
Pub. admin., defense }	180	1.5		
Services				
TOTAL	12,106	100.0	2,014,000	100.0

Household income and expenditure. Average household size (1980) 5.3; average annual income per household KN 3,710 (U.S.$371); sources of income: n.a.; expenditure: n.a.
Land use (1985): forested 55.0%; meadows and pastures 3.5%; agricultural and under permanent cultivation 3.9%; other 37.6%.

Foreign trade

Balance of trade (current prices)

	1981	1982	1983	1984	1985	1986
U.S.$'000,000	−68.1	−61.9	−66.8	−36.7	−115.7	−147.0
% of total	66.8%	54.7%	56.7%	61.9%	54.9%	55.9%

Imports (1986): U.S.$205,000,000 (important imports include cereals, other food products, petroleum products, and agricultural and general machinery). *Major import sources* (1985): Thailand 34.2%; Japan 20.4%; Singapore 17.2%; France 2.4%; Sweden 1.5%; Vietnam 1.3%; United Kingdom 1.2%; unspecified countries 21.8%.
Exports (1986): U.S.$58,000,000 (electricity 50.1%; wood 29.3%; coffee 17.2%; tin 3.4%). *Major export destinations* (1985): China 45.6%; Singapore 8.3%; Japan 6.5%; Thailand 4.9%; Australia 4.8%; United States 4.8%; Belgium–Luxembourg 3.3%; Iran 2.7%; unspecified countries 19.1%.

Transport and communications

Transport. Railroads: none. Roads (1987): total length 17,105 mi, 27,527 km (paved 34%). Vehicles: passenger cars (1987) 15,800; trucks and buses (1982) 3,000. Merchant marine: none. Air transport (1985): passenger-mi 6,000,000, passenger-km 9,000,000; short ton-mi cargo 685,000, metric ton-km cargo 1,000,000; airports (1988) with scheduled flights 7.
Communications. Daily newspapers (1985): total number 3; total circulation (1983) 12,500; circulation per 1,000 population (1983) 3.6. Radio (1987): total number of receivers 367,000 (1 per 10 persons). Television (1987): total number of receivers 32,000 (1 per 118 persons). Telephones (1985): 8,136 (1 per 450 persons).

Education and health

Education (1984)

	schools	teachers	students	student/teacher ratio
Primary (age 6–10)	7,470	18,070	495,375	27.4
Secondary (age 11–16)	419[5]	5,815	91,356	15.7
Voc., teacher tr.	117[6]	2,326	19,358	8.3
Higher	8	452[5]	6,400[6]	...

Educational attainment, n.a. *Literacy* (1980): total population age 15 and over literate 997,600 (45.2%); males literate 586,600 (52.8%); females literate 412,500 (37.6%).
Health (1985): physicians 558 (1 per 6,495 persons); hospital beds 9,815 (1 per 369 persons); infant mortality rate per 1,000 live births (1987) 111.0.
Food (1981–83): daily per capita caloric intake 2,185 (vegetable products 90%, animal products 10%); (1983) 88% of FAO recommended minimum requirement.

Military

Total active duty personnel (1987): 55,500 (army 94.6%, navy 1.8%, air force 3.6%). *Military expenditure as percent of GNP* (1984): 10.5% (world 5.9%); per capita expenditure U.S.$16.

[1]An interim legislative body established in 1975 pending election of a National Assembly; it continues to serve, since no election had taken place by late 1988. [2]1985. [3]At constant prices of 1982. [4]Manufacturing includes public utilities. [5]1983–84. [6]1986.

Lebanon

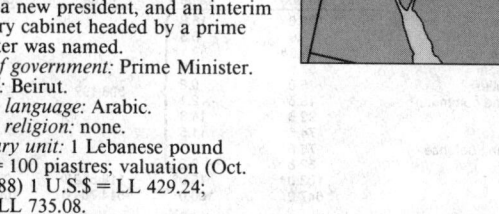

Official name: al-Jumhūrīyah
al-Lubnānīyah (Republic of Lebanon).
Form of government: nominally,
a multiparty republic with one
legislative house (National Assembly
[99]). On Sept. 23, 1988, however,
the Assembly failed to meet a
constitutionally required deadline to
name a new president, and an interim
military cabinet headed by a prime
minister was named.
Head of government: Prime Minister.
Capital: Beirut.
Official language: Arabic.
Official religion: none.
Monetary unit: 1 Lebanese pound
(LL) = 100 piastres; valuation (Oct.
10, 1988) 1 U.S.$ = LL 429.24;
1 £ = LL 735.08.

Area and population		area		population
				1970
Governorates	Capitals	sq mi	sq km	estimate
Bayrūt	Beirut (Bayrūt)	7	18	474,870
al-Biqā'	Zahlah	1,653	4,280	203,520
Jabal Lubnān	B'abdā	753	1,950	833,055
al-Janūb	Sidon (Ṣaydā)	364	943	249,945
an-Nabaṭīyah	an-Nabaṭīyah	408	1,058	...
ash-Shamāl	Tripoli (Ṭarābulus)	765	1,981	364,935
TOTAL		3,950	10,230	2,126,325

Demography

Population (1988): 2,828,000.
Density (1988): persons per sq mi 716.0, persons per sq km 276.4.
Urban–rural (1986): urban 80.8%; rural 19.2%.
Sex distribution (1986): male 48.36%; female 51.64%.
Age breakdown (1986): under 15, 37.0%; 15–29, 29.5%; 30–44, 14.7%; 45–59, 10.9%; 60–74, 6.1%; 75 and over, 1.8%.
Population projection: (1990) 2,967,000; (2000) 3,617,000.
Doubling time: during the 1970–75 prewar period the average growth rate was 2.6%; however, since 1976 continuing dislocation of the population by the civil war has rendered both the absolute size and principal components of population change (births, deaths, migration) highly problematic.
Ethnic composition (1983): Lebanese 82.6%; Palestinian 9.6%; Armenian 4.9%; Syrian, Kurd, and other 2.9%.
Religious affiliation: no official data exist subsequent to the 1932 census, when Christians (predominantly Maronite Roman Catholic) were a slight majority; it is thought that Muslims today constitute the majority but by what margin is highly uncertain. An unofficial estimate (1984) indicated that the main religious groups were distributed as follows: Shī'ī Muslim 32%; Maronite Christian 24.5%; Sunnī Muslim 21%; Druze 7%; Greek Orthodox 6.5%; Greek Catholic 4%; Armenian Christian 4%; other 1.0%.
Major cities (1985): Beirut 1,500,000; Tripoli 500,000; Zahlah 200,000; Sidon (Ṣaydā) 100,000; an-Nabaṭīyah 100,000.

Vital statistics

Birth rate per 1,000 population (1986): 30.4 (world avg. 26.0); legitimate, n.a.; illegitimate, n.a.
Death rate per 1,000 population (1986): 7.7 (world avg. 9.9).
Natural increase rate per 1,000 population (1986): 22.7 (world avg. 16.1).
Total fertility rate (avg. births per childbearing woman; 1986): 3.8.
Life expectancy at birth (1986): male 64.7 years; female 68.8 years.
Major causes of death: normally, heart ailments and gastrointestinal diseases, including typhoid fever and dysentery; but, with the continuing civil war, violence and acts of war are now among the principal causes of mortality.

National economy

Budget (1989). Revenue: LL 130,000,000,000 (1986; income taxes 49.6%, customs duties 31.5%). Expenditure: LL 219,500,000,000 (1986; internal debt service 30.2%, defense 20.7%).
Public debt (external, outstanding; 1986): U.S.$211,000,000.
Production (metric tons except as noted). Agriculture, forestry, fishing (1986): fruits and vegetables 1,193,000 (of which oranges 250,000, grapes 158,000, apples 133,000, tomatoes 130,000, cucumbers 73,000, lemons and limes 42,000, watermelons 31,000, cabbages 21,000, bananas 19,000, eggplants 19,000, cantaloupes 14,000, green beans 10,000, carrots 9,000, cauliflowers 7,000, onions 7,000), potatoes 230,000, sugar beets 80,000, wheat 13,000; livestock (number of live animals) 460,000 goats, 137,000 sheep, 50,000 cattle, 11,000,000 chickens; roundwood 486,000 cu m; fish catch 1,600. Mining and quarrying (1985): salt 6,000; gypsum 3,000. Manufacturing (1984): cement 800,000; wheat flour 190,000[1]; paper and paperboard 45,000; quicklime 20,000. Construction (1981): 5,863,000 sq m. Energy production (consumption): electricity (kW-hr; 1986) 1,370,000,000 (1,400,000,000); coal, n.a. (none); crude petroleum (barrels; 1986) n.a. (8,136,000); petroleum products (metric tons; 1986) 1,030,000 (1,871,000); natural gas, none (n.a.).
Household income and expenditure. Average household size (1980) 5.3; income per household: n.a.; sources of income (1974): wages and salaries 27.9%, transfers 3.0%, other 69.1%; expenditure[2, 3]: food 42.8%, housing 16.8%, clothing 8.6%, health care 7.2%.
Tourism (1980): number of tourist arrivals 135,548[4].

Population economically active

Population economically active (1986): total 693,812; activity rate of total population 25.1% (participation rates: ages 15–60, 45.6%; female 18.7%; unemployed [1987] 25–50%).

Price and earnings indexes (1980 = 100)							
	1981	1982	1983	1984	1985	1986	1987
Consumer price index	119.4	141.5	149.9	c. 172	c. 266	c. 518	c. 2,700
Monthly earnings index[5]	118.5	137.0	...	...	...	...	...

Gross national product (at current market prices; 1983): U.S.$4,600,000,000–$5,500,000,000 (U.S.$1,636–$1,956 per capita).

Structure of gross domestic product and labour force				
	1984		1986	
	in value LL '000,000	% of total value	labour force	% of labour force
Agriculture	814.0	8.4	132,211	18.9
Mining	...	...	694	0.1
Manufacturing	1,277.0	13.2	123,647	17.8
Construction	331.2	3.4	43,357	6.2
Public utilities	516.4	5.3	6,668	1.0
Transp. and commun.	741.4	7.6	48,242	7.0
Finance	1,218.0	12.5	24,224	3.5
Trade	2,722.6	28.0	114,706	16.5
Pub. admin., defense	1,060.2	10.9	200,063	28.8
Services	1,036.5	10.7 }		
TOTAL	9,717.3	100.0	693,812	100.0[6]

Land use (1985): forested 7.8%; meadows and pastures 1.0%; agricultural and under permanent cultivation 29.3%; wasteland and other areas 61.9%.

Foreign trade

Balance of trade (current prices)						
	1982	1983	1984	1985	1986	1987
LL '000,000	−9,890	−12,461	−13,987	−25,581	−59,090	−269,311
% of total	48.5%	69.0%	64.9%	61.8%	60.6%	50.4%

Imports (1987): LL 402,027,000,000 (1982; consumer goods 40%, machinery and transport equipment 35%, petroleum products 20%). *Major import sources:* Italy 10.7%; Turkey 8.5%; France 8.1%; West Germany 5.9%; United States 5.5%; Romania 4.7%; Saudi Arabia 4.5%.
Exports (1987): LL 132,716,000,000 (1985; jewelry 10.2%, clothing 5.2%, pharmaceutical products 4.9%, metal products 4.8%). *Major export destinations:* Saudi Arabia 8.7%; Switzerland 7.6%; Jordan 6.0%; Kuwait 5.4%; United States 5.2%.

Transport and communications

Transport. Railroads (1982): length (1986) 259 mi[7], 417 km[7]; passenger-mi 5,325,000, passenger-km 8,570,000; short ton-mi cargo 28,770,000, metric ton-km cargo 42,010,000. Roads (1987): total length 4,580 mi, 7,370 km (paved 85%). Vehicles (1982): passenger cars 473,372; trucks and buses 49,560. Merchant marine (1987): vessels (100 gross tons and over) 214; total deadweight tonnage 729,538. Air transport[8] (1987): passenger-mi 399,029,000, passenger-km 642,157,000; short ton-mi cargo 12,422,000, metric ton-km cargo 18,135,000; airports (1988) with scheduled flights 1.
Communications. Daily newspapers (1986): total number 39; total circulation 572,734[9]; circulation per 1,000 population 211.6[9]. Radio (1987): 2,000,000 receivers (1 per 1.4 persons). Television (1987): 500,000 receivers (1 per 5.4 persons). Telephones (1987): 150,400 (1 per 18.4 persons).

Education and health

Education (1984–85)				
	schools[10]	teachers	students	student/ teacher ratio
Primary (age 5–9)	1,116 }	53,450[10]	329,340	...
Secondary (age 10–16)	1,405 }		230,934	...
Voc., teacher tr.	181	3,506	37,036	10.6
Higher	18	7,460	70,510	9.4

Educational attainment (1970). Percent of population age 25 and over having: no formal schooling 45.6%; ability to read and write 35.6%; primary education 10.8%; secondary 4.9%; higher 3.1%. *Literacy* (1985): total population age 15 and over literate, c. 1,325,000 (77.0%); males literate, c. 715,000 (85.7%); females literate, c. 610,000 (68.9%).
Health (1986): physicians 3,509 (1.3 per 1,000 persons); hospital beds (1982) 11,400 (1 per 263 persons); infant mortality rate per 1,000 live births 49.2.
Food (1979–81): daily per capita caloric intake 2,995 (vegetable products 84%, animal products 16%); (1983) 120% of FAO recommended minimum.

Military

Total active duty personnel (1988): Lebanese national armed forces 16,300 (army 92.0%, navy 3.1%, air force 4.9%); external regular military forces include: UN peacekeeping force in Lebanon 5,500; Syrian army 30,000. Principal armed civilian factions include[11]: Maronite Christian (Lebanese Forces [Phalange]) 20,000; Shī'ī Muslim (pro-Syrian Amal) 10,000; Druze (Progressive Socialist Party) 9,000–10,000; Palestine Liberation Organization 7,500–10,000; Shī'ī Muslim (pro-Iran Hezbollah [Party of God]) 5,000. *Military expenditure as percent of GNP* (1983): 8.2% (world 6.2%); per capita expenditure: U.S.$201.

---

[1]1983. [2]Weights based on consumer price index components. [3]For capital city only. [4]Approximately one-fourth the annual prewar rates of the early 1970s. [5]Excludes banking sector. [6]Detail does not add to total given because of rounding. [7]Only 138 mi (222 km) is currently in use. [8]MEA-Airliban international flights only. [9]For 20 newspapers only. [10]1981–82. [11]Active-duty personnel only.

Lesotho

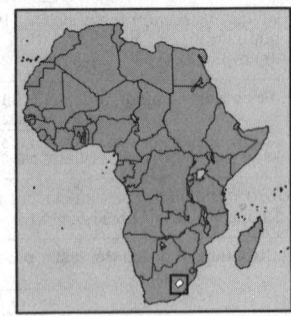

Official name: Lesotho (Sotho); King-dom of Lesotho (English).
Form of government: monarchy with two legislative houses (National Assembly [80]; Senate [30])[1].
Chief of state: King[1].
Head of government: Chairman of the Military Council[1].
Capital: Maseru.
Official languages: Sotho; English.
Official religion: Christianity.
Monetary unit: 1 loti (plural maloti [M]) = 100 lisente; valuation (Oct. 10, 1988) 1 U.S.$ = M 2.49; 1 £ = M 4.26.

Area and population

Districts	Capitals	area sq mi	area sq km	population 1986 census
Berea	Teyateyaneng	858	2,222	194,631
Butha-Buthe	Butha-Buthe	682	1,767	100,644
Leribe	Leribe	1,092	2,828	257,988
Mafeteng	Mafeteng	818	2,119	195,591
Maseru	Maseru	1,652	4,279	311,159
Mohale's Hoek	Mohale's Hoek	1,363	3,530	164,392
Mokhotlong	Mokhotlong	1,573	4,075	74,676
Qacha's Nek	Qacha's Nek	907	2,349	63,984
Quthing	Quthing	1,126	2,916	110,376
Thaba-Tseka	Thaba-Tseka	1,649	4,270	104,095
TOTAL		11,720	30,355	1,577,536

Demography

Population (1988): 1,671,000.
Density (1988): persons per sq mi 142.6, persons per sq km 55.0.
Urban–rural (1985): urban 16.7%; rural 83.3%.
Sex distribution (1986): male 48.21%; female 51.79%.
Age breakdown (1985): under 15, 42.3%; 15–29, 25.9%; 30–44, 16.2%; 45–59, 9.9%; 60–74, 4.7%; 75 and over, 1.0%.
Population projection: (1990) 1,760,000; (2000) 2,281,800.
Doubling time: 27 years.
Ethnic composition (1983): Sotho 99.7%; other 0.3%.
Religious affiliation (1980): Roman Catholic 43.5%; Protestant (mostly Lesotho Evangelical) 29.8%; Anglican 11.5%; other Christian 8.0%; tribal 6.2%; other 1.0%.
Major urban centres (1976): Maseru 55,031 (Maseru-Roma-Morija metropolitan area [1986] 109,382); Maputsoe 15,823; Teyateyaneng 8,589.

Vital statistics

Birth rate per 1,000 population (1980–85): 41.8 (world avg. 29.0); legitimate, n.a.; illegitimate, n.a.
Death rate per 1,000 population (1980–85): 16.5 (world avg. 11.0).
Natural increase rate per 1,000 population (1980–85): 25.3 (world avg. 18.0).
Total fertility rate (avg. births per childbearing woman; 1980–85): 5.8.
Life expectancy at birth (1980–85): male 46.3 years; female 52.3 years.
Major causes of death per 100,000 population: n.a.; however, major diseases include malaria, typhoid fever, and infectious and parasitic diseases.

National economy

Budget (1987–88). Revenue: M 294,600,000 (tax revenue 83.3%, of which customs receipts 53.4%, sales tax 18.0%, income tax 6.4%, company tax 3.5%; nontax revenue 12.4%; grants 4.3%). Expenditures: M 414,200,000 (recurrent expenditure 68.1%, of which personal emoluments 28.2%, interest payments 6.6%, subsidies and transfers 5.8%, other goods and services 27.6%; capital expenditure 31.9%).
Production (metric tons except as noted). Agriculture, forestry, fishing (1986): corn (maize) 86,488, sorghum 33,458, vegetables and melons 29,000, fruit 18,000, wheat 11,000, pulses 6,000, roots and tubers 6,000, peas 3,779, beans 1,502; livestock (number of live animals) 1,420,000 sheep, 1,010,000 goats, 520,000 cattle, 108,000 horses, 108,000 mules and asses, 65,000 pigs, 1,000,000 chickens; roundwood (1985) 293,000 cu m; fish catch 22. Mining and quarrying (1986): diamonds M 2,100,000[3]. Manufacturing (total value added; 1986): M 59,200,000; food and beverages 60.7%; textiles, apparel, and leather 14.7%; iron and steel products 5.3%; chemical products 4.8%; printing and publishing 4.5%; furniture and fixtures 3.4%. Construction (total value added; 1986): M 57,500,000. Energy production (consumption): electricity (kW-hr; 1986) 1,000,000 (n.a.); coal, none (n.a.); petroleum, none (n.a.); natural gas, none (n.a.).
Public debt (external, outstanding; 1986): U.S.$182,100,000.
Tourism (1986): receipts from visitors U.S.$7,000,000; expenditures by nationals abroad U.S.$5,000,000.
Population economically active (1985): total 514,704[4]; activity rate of total population 33.3% (participation rates: age 12 and over, 55.8%; female 34.9%; unemployed 23%).

Price and earnings indexes (1980 = 100)

	1982	1983	1984	1985	1986	1987	1988
Consumer price index	125.9	147.1	164.0	188.2	220.5	275.9	285.8[5]
Annual earnings index[6]	311.2	441.8	518.8	577.6	597.8	...	...

Household income and expenditure. Average household size (1980) 4.4; average annual income per household (1985–86) M 3,110 (U.S.$1,400);

sources of income (1978–79): self-employment 51.6%, wages and salaries 42.0% (of which migrant workers' remittances 32.4%), transfer payments and other 6.4%; expenditure (1975)[7]: food 34.0%, clothing 19.3%, housing 16.7%, transportation 9.5%, education 4.1%, health 1.8%.
Gross national product (at current market prices; 1986): U.S.$660,000,000 (U.S.$410 per capita).

Structure of gross domestic product and labour force

	1986 in value M '000,000	1986 % of total value	1985 labour force	1985 % of labour force
Agriculture	108.6	16.8		
Mining	1.9	0.3		
Manufacturing	59.2[8]	9.1[8]		
Construction	57.5	8.9		
Public utilities	5.0	0.8		
Transp. and commun.	13.5	2.1	396,192	77.0
Trade	92.5	14.3		
Finance	74.6	11.5		
Pub. admin., defense	78.6	12.1		
Services	52.8	8.2		
Other	103.0[9]	15.9[9]	118,512[10]	23.0[10]
TOTAL	647.2	100.0	514,704[11]	100.0

Land use (1985): meadows and pastures 65.9%; agricultural and under permanent cultivation 9.9%; other 24.2%.

Foreign trade[12]

Balance of trade (current prices)

	1980	1981	1982	1983	1984	1985	1986
M '000,000	−327.0	−405.9	−528.1	−594.0	−684.5	−746.9	−834.6
% of total	78.3%	82.5%	87.1%	89.9%	89.5%	88.2%	87.8%

Imports (1981): M 449,060,000 (manufactured goods [excluding chemicals, machinery, and transport equipment] 37.4%, of which clothing 8.4%, blankets and traveling rugs 3.6%, footwear 3.3%; food and live animals 18.9%, of which cereals [all forms] 5.9%, sugar [all forms] 2.6%; machinery and transport equipment 17.0%, of which trucks and vans 3.5%; petroleum products 8.6%). *Major import sources:* Customs Union of Southern Africa 97.1%; European Economic Community 1.5%.
Exports (1981): M 43,124,000 (diamonds 42.1%; food and live animals 10.3%; umbrellas, brooms, brushes, and basketwork 8.1%; mohair 8.0%; road vehicles 3.1%; footwear 3.0%). *Major export destinations:* Customs Union of Southern Africa 46.7%; Switzerland 41.8%; West Germany 7.0%.

Transport and communications

Transport. Railroads (1985): length 1 mi, 2 km. Roads (1986): total length 2,640 mi, 4,250 km (paved 12%). Vehicles (1982): passenger cars 5,129; trucks and buses 11,962. Merchant marine: vessels (100 gross tons and over) none. Air transport (1987): passenger-mi 6,810,000, passenger-km 10,960,000; short ton-mi cargo 860,000, metric ton-km cargo 1,255,000; airports (1987) with scheduled flights 14.
Communications. Daily newspapers (1985): total number 3; total circulation 44,000; circulation per 1,000 population 28. Radio (1986): total number of receivers 100,000 (1 per 16 persons). Television (1987): total number of receivers 1,500 (1 per 1,085 persons). Telephones (1986): 13,738 (1 per 112 persons).

Education and health

Education (1984–85)[13]

	schools	teachers	students	student/teacher ratio
Primary (age 6–12)	1,141	5,663	314,003	55.4
Secondary (age 13–17)	143	1,676	35,423	21.1
Voc., teacher tr.	9	221	2,221	10.0
Higher	1	146	1,119	7.7

Educational attainment (1976). Percent of population age 10 and over having: no formal education 28.8%; primary 64.6%; secondary 2.3%; higher 0.6%. *Literacy* (1985): total population age 15 and over literate 655,400 (73.6%); males literate 273,800 (62.4%); females literate 381,600 (84.5%).
Health (1982): physicians 114 (1 per 12,265 persons); hospital beds 2,300 (1 per 608 persons); infant mortality rate per 1,000 live births (1983) 109.
Food (1984–86): daily per capita caloric intake 2,296 (vegetable products 93%, animal products 7%); (1983) 104% of FAO recommended minimum requirement.

Military

Total active duty personnel (1986): 1,500[14]. *Military expenditure as percent of GNP* (1984): 6.5% (world 5.9%); per capita expenditure U.S.$37.

[1]Following a military coup in January 1986, executive and legislative powers were nominally vested in the King, though effectively exercised by a six-member Military Council and a Council of Ministers. The 1966 independence constitution, suspended in 1970 and reinstated in 1983, was again suspended in 1986 following the coup, dissolving Lesotho's legislative organs. [2]Estimate. [3]Individual diamond diggers. [4]Age 12 and over. [5]First quarter; urban households only. [6]Based on Basotho miners working in South Africa. [7]Weights of consumer price index components. [8]Includes handicrafts. [9]Indirect taxes less imputed bank service charges. [10]Unemployed. [11]In 1986, 140,950 workers, or 19% of the total labour force, were employed in South Africa, mostly as gold miners. [12]Import figures are f.o.b. in balance of trade and c.i.f. in commodities and trading partners. [13]Excludes private schools. [14]Royal Lesotho Defence Force.

Liberia

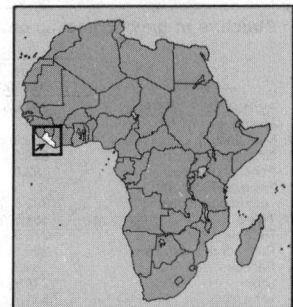

Official name: Republic of Liberia.
Form of government: multiparty republic with two legislative houses (Senate [26]; House of Representatives [64]).
Head of state and government: President.
Capital: Monrovia.
Official language: English.
Official religion: none.
Monetary unit: 1 Liberian dollar (L$) = 100 cents; valuation (Oct. 10, 1988) 1 U.S.$ = L$1.00; 1 £ = L$1.71.

Area and population

Counties	Capitals	area sq mi	area sq km	population 1986 estimate
Bong	Gbarnga	3,127	8,099	268,100
Grand Bassa	Buchanan	3,382	8,759	166,900
Grand Cape Mount	Robertsport	2,250	5,827	83,900
Grand Gedeh	Zwedru	6,575	17,029	109,000
Grand Kru[1]	Barclayville	[2]	[2]	[2]
Lofa	Voinjama	7,475	19,360	261,000
Margibi[3]	Kakata	1,260	3,263	104,000
Maryland	Harper	2,066[2]	5,351[2]	137,700[2]
Montserrado	Bensonville	1,058	2,740	582,400
Nimba	Sanniquellie	4,650	12,043	325,700
Sinoe	Greenville	3,959	10,254	65,400
Territories				
Bomi	Tubmanburg	755	1,955	67,300
Rivercess	Rivercess City	1,693	4,385	39,900
TOTAL		38,250	99,067[4]	2,221,300[5]

Demography

Population (1988): 2,436,000.
Density (1988): persons per sq mi 63.7, persons per sq km 24.6.
Urban–rural (1984): urban 38.8%; rural 61.2%.
Sex distribution (1984): male 50.59%; female 49.41%.
Age breakdown (1984): under 15, 43.2%; 15–29, 28.2%; 30–44, 14.7%; 45–59, 7.7%; 60–74, 4.4%; 75 and over, 1.8%.
Population projection: (1990) 2,605,000; (2000) 3,641,000.
Doubling time: 21 years.
Ethnic composition (1984): Kpelle 19.4%; Bassa 13.8%; Grebo 9.0%; Gio 7.8%; Kru 7.3%; Mano 7.1%; other 35.6%.
Religious affiliation (1984): Christian 67.7%; Muslim 13.8%[6]; traditional beliefs and other 18.5%.
Major cities (1974): Monrovia 425,000[7]; Buchanan 23,999; Congo Town 21,495; Yekepa 14,189; Tubmanburg 14,089; Harbel 11,445.

Vital statistics

Birth rate per 1,000 population (1984–89): 46.8 (world avg. 26.0).
Death rate per 1,000 population (1984–89): 12.6 (world avg. 9.9).
Natural increase rate per 1,000 population (1984–89): 34.2 (world avg. 16.1).
Total fertility rate (avg. births per childbearing woman; 1984–89): 6.9.
Marriage rate per 1,000 population: n.a.
Divorce rate per 1,000 population: n.a.
Life expectancy at birth (1984–89): male 53.9 years; female 56.3 years.
Major causes of death per 100,000 population[8] (1985): complications during pregnancy 632.6[7]; malaria 79.8; pneumonia 64.2; anemia 50.2; malnutrition 23.4; measles 12.7.

National economy

Budget (1987). Revenue: L$184,300,000 (import duties and consular fees 28.0%; income and profits taxes 25.3%; excise tax 15.8%; nontax revenue 13.7%). Expenditures: L$290,500,000 (current expenditure 85.6%, of which wages and salaries 37.2%, interest on public debt 19.7%, goods and services 8.1%, subsidies and grants 1.9%; development expenditure 14.4%).
Public debt (external, outstanding; 1986): U.S.$1,001,800,000.
Tourism: receipts from visitors (1986) U.S.$6,000,000; expenditures by nationals abroad, n.a.
Population economically active (1984): total 669,330; activity rate of total population 31.8% (participation rates: ages 15–59, 64.7%[9]; female 31.2%[9]; unemployed 12.5%).

Price and earnings indexes (1980 = 100)

	1980	1981	1982	1983	1984	1985	1986
Consumer price index	100.0	107.6	114.0	117.2	118.6	117.9	122.1
Monthly earnings index	...	...	...	...	...	...	...

Production (metric tons except as noted). Agriculture, forestry, fishing (1986): cassava 326,000, rice 295,000, sugarcane 159,000, natural rubber 90,000, bananas 81,000, plantains 33,000, sweet potatoes 18,000, yams 18,000, green coffee 9,000, oranges 7,000, pineapples 7,000, cocoa beans 5,000; livestock (number of live animals) 246,000 sheep, 243,000 goats, 131,000 pigs, 43,000 cattle, 4,000,000 chickens; roundwood (1985) 4,262,000 cu m; fish catch (1985) 11,478. Mining and quarrying (1986): iron ore 14,233,000; diamonds 229,500 carats; gold 20,229 troy oz. Manufacturing (1986): cement 96,350; palm oil 35,000; cigarettes 91,235,200 units; soft drinks 115,092 hectolitres; beer 105,547 hectolitres. Construction: n.a. Energy production (consumption): electricity (kW-hr; 1986) 819,000,000 (819,000,000); coal, none (n.a.);

crude petroleum (barrels; 1985) none (4,764,000); petroleum products (metric tons; 1986) 632,000[9] (201,000); natural gas, none (n.a.).
Household income and expenditure. Average household size (1983) 4.3; income per household: n.a.; sources of income: n.a.; expenditure (1963)[10]: food 34.4%, rent 14.9%, clothing and footwear 13.8%, household goods and services 6.1%, beverages and tobacco 5.7%, fuel and light 5.0%.
Gross national product (at current market prices; 1986): U.S.$1,030,000,000 (U.S.$450 per capita).

Structure of gross domestic product and labour force

	1985 in value L$'000,000[11]	1985 % of total value	1984 labour force	1984 % of labour force
Agriculture	138.9	19.4	481,177	71.9
Mining	137.0	19.2	17,500	2.6
Manufacturing	58.7	8.2	10,699	1.6
Construction	26.9	3.8	4,072	0.6
Public utilities	16.5	2.3	2,878	0.4
Transportation and communications	50.9	7.1	13,986	2.1
Trade	51.4	7.2	46,850	7.0
Finance	105.9	14.8	2,117	0.3
Pub. admin., defense	115.3	16.1 }	61,168	9.2
Services	34.0	4.7 }		
Other	−20.3[12]	−2.8[12]	28,883	4.3
TOTAL	715.2	100.0	669,330	100.0

Land use (1985): forested 39.0%; meadows and pastures 2.5%; agricultural and under permanent cultivation 3.9%; other 54.6%.

Foreign trade

Balance of trade (current prices)

	1981	1982	1983	1984	1985	1986
L$'000,000	+146.5	+107.4	+73.8	+137.6	+189.4	+201.1
% of total	16.1%	12.7%	9.4%	17.1%	27.8%	33.1

Imports (1986): L$259,000,000 (machinery and transportation equipment 22.8%, food and live animals 20.7%, petroleum and petroleum products 20.5%, basic manufactures 13.9%, miscellaneous manufactured articles 7.1%, beverages and tobacco 1.5%, animal and vegetable oils 1.2%, chemicals 1.0%). *Major import sources* (1985): United States 25.9%; West Germany 9.8%; Japan 8.4%; United Kingdom 7.4%; The Netherlands 6.5%; Spain 2.5%; Belgium–Luxembourg 2.5%; China 2.3%; Denmark 2.1%.
Exports (1986): L$408,400,000 (iron ore 60.8%, rubber 19.8%, logs and timber 8.1%, coffee 4.0%, cocoa 2.2%, diamonds 1.6%). *Major export destinations* (1985): West Germany 32.3%; United States 19.2%; Italy 15.8%; France 8.9%; Belgium–Luxembourg 5.9%; The Netherlands 4.4%; Spain 4.0%; United Kingdom 1.0%; Japan 0.5%.

Transport and communications

Transport. Railroads[13] (1986): route length 304 mi, 490 km; short ton-mi cargo 2,154,000,000[14], metric ton-mi cargo 3,145,000,000[14]. Roads (1985): total length 4,138 mi, 6,659 km (paved 7%). Vehicles (1984): passenger cars 12,747; trucks and buses 8,288. Merchant marine (1987): vessels (100 gross tons and over) 1,574; total deadweight tonnage 97,957,869. Air transport (1980): passenger-mi 10,600,000, passenger-km 17,000,000; short ton-mi cargo 68,000, metric ton-km cargo 100,000; airports (1988) with scheduled flights 1.
Communications. Daily newspapers (1986): total number 5; total circulation, n.a.; circulation per 1,000 population, n.a. Radio (1986): total number of receivers 500,000 (1 per 4.6 persons). Television (1987): total number of receivers 43,000 (1 per 55 persons). Telephones (1985): 1,023[15] (1 per 2,150 persons).

Education and health

Education (1980)

	schools	teachers	students	student/ teacher ratio
Primary (age 6–12)	1,232	9,099	208,045[9]	...
Secondary (age 13–18)	419	1,129	52,514[9]	...
Voc., teacher tr.	6	63	2,322	36.9
Higher	3	190	3,955[9]	...

Educational attainment (1974). Percent of population age 25 and over having: no grade completed 87.1%; some primary education 4.8%; complete primary 1.5%; some secondary 5.1%; higher 1.5%. *Literacy* (1984): total population age 15 and over literate 273,670 (22.4%); males literate 164,059 (27.4%); females literate 109,611 (18.4%).
Health (1981): physicians 236 (1 per 8,305 persons); hospital beds 3,000 (1 per 653 persons); infant mortality rate per 1,000 live births (1984–89) 122.0.
Food (1984–86): daily per capita caloric intake 2,358 (vegetable products 95%, animal products 5%); (1983) 102% of FAO recommended minimum.

Military

Total active duty personnel (1987): 5,750 (army 92.2%[16], navy 7.8%). *Military expenditure as percent of GNP* (1985): 2.7% (world 6.1%); per capita expenditure U.S.$12.

---

[1]New county created from Kru Coast and Sasstown territories and part of Maryland County. [2]Figures for Grand Kru included in Maryland. [3]New county created from Marshall and Gibi territories. [4]Detail does not add to total given because of rounding. [5]Includes 10,000 persons not accounted for. [6]Some external sources estimate the Muslim population to exceed 30%. [7]1984. [8]Hospital inpatient morbidity rates. [9]1985. [10]Monrovia only. [11]At current factor cost. [12]Imputed bank service charges. [13]For iron-ore transport only. [14]Lamco and Bong Mining Company railroads only. [15]Number of subscribers. [16]Army includes air force personnel.

Libya

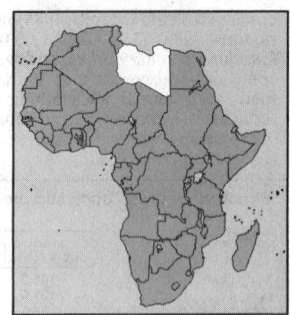

Official name: al-Jamāhīrīyah al-'Arabīyah al-Lībīyah ash-Sha'bīyah al-Ishtirākīyah (Socialist People's Libyan Arab Jamahiriya).
Form of government: socialist state with one policy-making body (General People's Congress [1,112]).
Chief of state[1]: Mu'ammar al-Qadhdhafī.
Head of government: Secretary of the General People's Committee (prime minister).
Capital: Tripoli[2].
Official language: Arabic.
Official religion: Islam.
Monetary unit: 1 Libyan dinar (LD) = 1,000 dirhams; valuation (Oct. 10, 1988) 1 Libyan dinar = U.S.$3.33 = £1.96.

Area and population

Baladiyāt	Capitals	area sq mi	area sq km	population 1984 census
Ajdābiyā	Ajdābiyā	...	...	100,547
Awbāri	Awbāri	...	...	48,701
al-'Azīzīyah	al-'Azīzīyah	...	...	85,068
Banghāzī	Banghāzī	...	...	485,386
Darnah	Darnah	...	...	105,031
al-Fatah	al-Marj	...	...	102,763
Ghadāmis	Ghadāmis	...	...	52,247
Gharyān	Gharyān	...	...	117,073
al-Jabal al-Akhḍar	al-Bayḍā'	...	...	120,662
al-Khums	al-Khums	...	...	149,642
al-Kufrah	al-Kufrah	...	...	25,139
Marzuq	Marzuq	...	...	42,294
Miṣrātah	Miṣrātah	...	...	178,295
Niqāṭ al-Khums	Zuwārah	...	...	181,584
Sabhā	Sabhā	...	...	76,171
Sawfajjīn	Banī Walīd	...	...	45,195
ash-Shāṭi	Birāk	...	...	46,749
Surt	Surt	...	...	110,996
Ṭarābulus	Tripoli (Ṭarābulus)	...	...	990,697
Tarhunah	Tarhunah	...	...	84,640
Ṭubruq	Ṭubruq	...	...	94,006
Yafran	Yafran	...	...	73,420
az-Zāwiyah	az-Zāwiyah	...	...	220,075
Zlīṭan	Zlīṭan	...	...	101,107
TOTAL		685,524	1,775,500	3,637,488

Demography

Population (1988): 4,316,000.
Density (1988): persons per sq mi 6.3, persons per sq km 2.4.
Urban–rural (1985): urban 64.5%; rural 35.5%.
Sex distribution (1984): male 53.61%; female 46.39%.
Age breakdown (1985): under 15, 45.0%; 15–29, 25.6%; 30–44, 17.2%; 45–59, 8.4%; 60–74, 3.2%; 75 and over, 0.6%.
Population projection: (1990) 4,710,000; (2000) 7,292,000.
Doubling time: 20 years.
Ethnic composition (1984): Libyan Arab and Berber 89.0%; other 11.0%.
Religious affiliation (1982): Sunnī Muslim 97.0%; other 3.0%.
Major cities (1979): Tripoli 587,400; Banghāzī 267,700; Miṣrātah 52,200.

Vital statistics

Birth rate per 1,000 population (1980–85): 47.3 (world avg. 29.0).
Death rate per 1,000 population (1980–85): 12.7 (world avg. 11.0).
Natural increase rate per 1,000 population (1980–85): 34.6 (world avg. 18.0).
Total fertility rate (avg. births per childbearing woman; 1980–85): 7.4.
Marriage rate per 1,000 population (1981): 4.3[3].
Divorce rate per 1,000 population (1981): 1.1[3].
Life expectancy at birth (1980–85): male 56.6 years; female 60.0 years.
Major causes of death per 100,000 population: n.a.; however, major diseases include trachoma, tuberculosis, malaria, and dysentery.

National economy

Budget (1987). Revenue and expenditure: LD 4,060,000,000 (development expenditures 34.5%, trade 33.7%, current spending 30.5%).
Production (metric tons except as noted). Agriculture, forestry, fishing (1986): tomatoes 205,000, wheat 190,000, watermelons 142,000, olives 120,000, potatoes 112,000, dates 105,000, barley 90,000, onions 88,000, oranges 75,000, grapes 21,000, pulses 11,000; livestock (number of live animals) 5,550,000 sheep, 950,000 goats, 210,000 cattle, 180,000 camels, 61,000 asses; roundwood (1986) 635,000 cu m; fish catch 7,800. Mining and quarrying (1986): gypsum 180,000; salt 12,000. Manufacturing (1985): lime 270,000,000; cement 4,600,000; urea 668,300; ammonia 495,000; methanol 495,000; ethylene 247,500; asphalt 150,000; crude steel 10,000. Construction (gross value in LD; 1982): residential 127,051,000; nonresidential 200,877,000. Energy production (consumption): electricity (kW-hr; 1986) 9,000,000,000 (9,000,000,000); coal (metric tons; 1986) none (2,000); crude petroleum (barrels; 1986) 376,674,000 (65,903,000); petroleum products (metric tons; 1986) 7,380,000 (6,502,000); natural gas (cu m; 1985) 3,989,213,000 (2,998,262,000).
Gross national product (at current market prices; 1986): U.S.$20,000,000,000 (U.S.$5,410 per capita).

Structure of gross domestic product and labour force

	1984 in value LD '000,000	1984 % of total value	1985 labour force	1985 % of labour force
Agriculture	266.4	3.6	178,000	16.8
Mining	3,039.1	40.4	24,500	2.3
Manufacturing	359.9	4.8	112,000	10.5
Construction	819.5	10.9	256,500	24.2
Public utilities	92.0	1.2	25,500	2.4
Transportation and communications	392.5	5.2	93,000	8.7
Trade	554.5	7.4	41,000	3.9
Finance	273.5	3.6	13,000	1.2
Pub. admin., defense	1,395.5	18.6	69,000	6.5
Services	84.7	1.1	183,500	17.3
Other	244.1	3.2	66,000	6.2
TOTAL	7,521.7	100.0	1,062,000	100.0

Public debt (external, outstanding; 1985): U.S.$1,177,000,000.
Tourism (1984): receipts from visitors U.S.$2,000,000; expenditures by nationals abroad U.S.$494,000,000.
Population economically active (1985): total 1,062,000; activity rate of total population 29.3% (participation rates: ages 15–64, 47.6%; female 8.1%; unemployed, n.a.).

Price and earnings indexes (1975 = 100)

	1973	1974	1975	1976	1977	1978	1979
Consumer price index	85.3	91.6	100.0	105.4	112.1	145.0	137.1
Monthly earnings index	...	...	...	...	...	...	...

Household income and expenditure. Average household size (1980) 5.1; income per household: n.a.; sources of income: n.a.; expenditure (1977): food 37.2%, housing 32.2%, transportation 9.4%, education and recreation 8.5%, clothing 6.9%, medical care 3.3%.
Land use (1985): forested 0.4%; meadows and pastures 7.6%; agricultural and under permanent cultivation 1.2%; desert and built-up areas 90.8%.

Foreign trade

Balance of trade (current prices)

	1980	1981	1982	1983	1984	1985
LD '000,000	+4,674	+2,238	+1,894	+1,348	+1,486.2	+1,790.5
% of total	56.3%	32.0%	29.8%	25.9%	69.4%	38.3%

Imports (1982): LD 2,124,323,000 (machinery and transport equipment 36.8%, consumer goods 27.1%, food and live animals 14.2%, chemicals 3.9%, animal and vegetable oil and fats 1.3%). *Major import sources* (1984): Italy 26.6%; West Germany 12.9%; Japan 6.6%; United Kingdom 5.3%; Austria 1.6%.
Exports (1982): LD 4,131,000,000 (crude petroleum 99.9%). *Major export destinations* (1984): Italy 24.0%; West Germany 19.0%; Spain 9.2%; Switzerland 3.8%; The Netherlands 3.5%; United Kingdom 1.8%.

Transport and communications

Transport. Railroads: none. Roads (1987): total length 11,992 mi, 19,300 km (paved 56%). Vehicles (1982): passenger cars 415.509; trucks and buses 334,405. Merchant marine (1987): vessels (100 gross tons and over) 102; total deadweight tonnage 1,447,491. Air transport[4] (1987): passenger-mi 900,000,000, passenger-km 1,447,000,000; short ton-mi cargo 2,398,000, metric ton-km cargo 3,501,000; airports (1988) with scheduled flights 12.
Communications. Daily newspapers (1987): total number 1; circulation 40,000; circulation per 1,000 population 9.7. Radio (1986): total number of receivers 500,000 (1 per 7.9 persons). Television (1987): total number of receivers 235,500 (1 per 18 persons). Telephones (1982): 102,000 (1 per 33 persons).

Education and health

Education (1982–83)

	schools	teachers	students	student/ teacher ratio
Primary (age 6–12)	2,744	42,202	741,502	17.6
Secondary (age 13–18)	1,555	25,044	301,415	12.0
Voc., teacher tr.	195	3,883	50,363	12.9
Higher[5]	8	1,340[6]	25,700	...

Educational attainment (1973). Percent of population age 25 and over having: no formal schooling (illiterate) 72.7%; ability to read and write 18.8%; primary education 3.5%; secondary 4.0%; higher 1.0%. *Literacy* (1985): total population age 10 and over literate 2,701,446 (74.4%); males literate 1,666,170 (85.0%); females literate 1,035,276 (62.0%).
Health (1982): physicians 5,210[7] (1 per 637 persons); hospital beds 16,051 (1 per 207 persons); infant mortality rate per 1,000 live births (1980–85) 107.0.
Food (1984–86): daily per capita caloric intake 3,611 (vegetable products 83%, animal products 17%); (1983) 155% of FAO recommended minimum requirement.

Military

Total active duty personnel (1988): 71,500 (army 76.9%, navy 9.1%, air force 14.0%). *Military expenditure as percent of GNP* (1984): 17.8% (world 5.9%); per capita expenditure U.S.$1,408.

---

[1]No formal titled office exists. [2]Al-Jufur, designated new capital on Jan. 1, 1986, is located 650 km south of Tripoli. Actual effective date of transfer is not clear yet. [3]Incomplete. [4]International scheduled flights only. [5]1981–82. [6]1979–80. [7]Personnel in government services only.

Liechtenstein

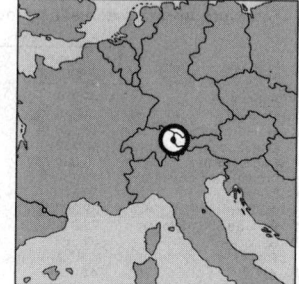

Official name: Fürstentum Liechtenstein (Principality of Liechtenstein).
Form of government: constitutional monarchy with one legislative house (Diet [15]).
Chief of state: Prince.
Head of government: Head of the Government.
Capital: Vaduz.
Official language: German.
Official religion: none.
Monetary unit: 1 Swiss franc (Sw F) = 100 centimes; valuation (Oct. 10, 1988) 1 U.S.$ = Sw F 1.58; 1 £ = Sw F 2.70.

Area and population

Communes	area sq mi	area sq km	population 1988 estimate[1]
Balzers	7.6	19.6	3,509
Eschen	4.0	10.3	2,867
Gamprin	2.4	6.1	927
Mauren	2.9	7.5	2,706
Planken	2.0	5.3	299
Ruggell	2.9	7.4	1,387
Schaan	10.4	26.8	4,836
Schellenberg	1.4	3.5	731
Triesen	10.2	26.4	3,248
Triesenberg	11.5	29.8	2,313
Vaduz	6.7	17.3	4,891
TOTAL	61.8[2]	160.0	27,714

Demography

Population (1988): 27,840.
Density (1988): persons per sq mi 450.5, persons per sq km 174.0.
Urban–rural: n.a.
Sex distribution (1988): male 48.81%; female 51.19%.
Age breakdown (1988): under 15, 19.8%; 15–29, 24.6%; 30–44, 25.6%; 45–59, 15.6%; 60–74, 10.0%; 75 and over, 4.4%.
Population projection: (1990) 28,400; (2000) 31,500.
Doubling time: not applicable; doubling time exceeds 100 years.
Ethnic composition (1988): Liechtensteiner 64.2%; Swiss 15.9%; Austrian 7.8%; German 3.7%; other 8.4%.
Religious affiliation (1988): Roman Catholic 87.4%; Protestant 8.3%; other 4.3%.
Major cities (1987): Vaduz 4,891; Schaan 4,836.

Vital statistics

Birth rate per 1,000 population (1987): 13.2 (world avg. 26.0); legitimate 94.8%; illegitimate 5.2%.
Death rate per 1,000 population (1987): 6.5 (world avg. 9.9).
Natural increase rate per 1,000 population (1987): 6.7 (world avg. 16.1).
Total fertility rate: n.a.
Marriage rate per 1,000 population (1987): 6.0.
Divorce rate per 1,000 population (1984): 7.3.
Life expectancy at birth (1980–84): male 77.6 years; female 82.6 years.
Major causes of death per 100,000 population (1987): diseases of the circulatory system 221.4, of which heart disease 174.2 (including ischemic heart disease 65.3); malignant neoplasms (cancers) 152.4; accidents, poisonings, and acts of violence 40.0 (including suicide 18.1); diseases of the respiratory system 18.1.

National economy

Budget (1986). Revenue: Sw F 337,257,584 (taxes and interest 69.6%; post, telephone, and telegraph 17.6%; other revenue sources include real estate capital-gains taxes and death and estate taxes). Expenditures: Sw F 311,604,845 (financial affairs 45.0%; education 13.7%; post, telephone, and telegraph 13.4%; social affairs 9.8%).
Public debt: none.
Tourism (1987): 75,682 tourist arrivals; receipts from visitors, n.a.; expenditures by nationals abroad, n.a.
Population economically active (1987[3]): total 13,337; activity rate of total population 48.1% (participation rates: ages 15–64, 67.9%; female 35.9%; unemployed 0.3%).

Price and earnings indexes (December 1982 = 100)

	1981	1982	1983	1984	1985	1986	1987[4]
Consumer price index[5]	92.8	98.0	100.9	103.8	107.4	108.2	109.7
Monthly earnings index	...	...	...	...	...	...	...

Household income and expenditure. Average household size (1980) 3.0; income per household: n.a.; sources of earned income (1986): wages and salaries 92.9%, self-employment 7.1%; expenditure (1986)[6]: food 21.3%, rent 18.0%, education and self-improvement 16.3%, transportation 13.3%, health 7.7%, clothing 6.6%.
Production (metric tons except as noted). Agriculture, forestry, fishing (1986): silo corn (maize) 29,400, milk 13,339, potatoes 1,194, barley 480, wheat 360; livestock (number of live animals; 1987) 6,487 cattle, 2,606 pigs, 2,337 sheep; commercial timber (1986) 10,104 cu m. Mining and

quarrying: n.a. Manufacturing (1986): whipped cream 1,449; yogurt 56; cheese 8; wine 100,242 kilograms; small-scale precision manufacturing includes optical lenses, electron microscopes, electronic equipment, and high-vacuum pumps; metal manufacturing is also important. Construction (1986): residential 197,046 cu m; nonresidential 282,504 cu m. Energy production (consumption): electricity (kW-hr; 1986) 43,371,000 (182,414,000); coal (metric tons; 1986) none (86); petroleum products (metric tons; 1986) none (51,457); natural gas (metric tons; 1986) none (2,493).
Gross national product (at current market prices; 1985): c. U.S.$450,000,000 (c. U.S.$16,500 per capita).

Structure of gross domestic product and labour force

	1980 in value Sw F '000	1980 % of total value	1987[3] labour force	1987[3] % of labour force
Agriculture	...	...	380	2.8
Mining	...	...	65	0.5
Manufacturing	...	...	4,540	34.0
Construction	...	...	1,076	8.1
Public utilities	...	...	142	1.1
Transportation and communications	...	...	395	3.0
Trade	...	...	1,604	12.0
Finance	...	...	866	6.5
Pub. admin., defense	...	...	625	4.7
Services	...	...	3,373	25.3
Other	...	...	271[7]	2.0[7]
TOTAL	876,000	100.0	13,337	100.0

Land use (1987): forested 34.8%; meadows and pastures 15.7%; agricultural and under permanent cultivation 24.3%; other 25.2%.

Foreign trade

Balance of trade (current prices)

	1981	1982	1983	1984	1985	1986
Sw F '000,000	+531.9	+523.5	+560.7	+625.4	+755.6	+761.6
% of total	38.6%	39.3%	41.6%	41.8%	46.4%	44.4%

Imports (1986): Sw F 477,479,000 (machinery and transport equipment 32.1%; hardware 13.2%; limestone, cement, and other building materials 9.1%; unrefined and semifabricated metal 6.7%; chemical products 4.9%; food, beverages, and tobacco 2.0%, of which fruits and vegetables 0.6%; wood and cork 1.3%). *Major import sources:* n.a.
Exports (1986): Sw F 1,239,130,000 (machinery and transport equipment 46.5%; other finished goods 23.3%; hardware 19.1%; chemical products 5.7%; limestone, cement, and other building materials 3.8%). *Major export destinations:* European Economic Community countries 40.0%; Switzerland 19.2%; other European Free Trade Association countries 6.6%.

Transport and communications

Transport. Railroads (1987): length 11.5 mi, 18.5 km; passenger and cargo traffic, n.a. Roads (1986): total length 201 mi, 323 km. Vehicles (1987): passenger cars 15,229; trucks and buses 1,651. Merchant marine: none. Air transport: none.
Communications. Daily newspapers (1987): total number 2; total circulation 15,000; circulation per 1,000 population 546. Radio (1986): total number of receivers 9,218 (1 per 3.0 persons). Television (1986): total number of receivers 8,674 (1 per 3.1 persons). Telephones (1986): 26,529 (1 per 1.0 persons).

Education and health

Education (1987–88)

	schools	teachers	students	student/teacher ratio
Primary (age 7–12)	14	102	1,754	17.2
Secondary (age 13–19)	9	98	1,707	17.4
Vocational[8]	1	30[9]	117[9]	...

Educational attainment (1980). Percent of population age 25 and over having: no formal schooling 0.2%; primary and lower secondary education 47.6%; higher secondary and vocational 41.0%; some postsecondary 6.6%; university 4.6%. *Literacy:* virtually 100%.
Health (1986): physicians 26 (1 per 1,048 persons); hospital beds (1985) 100 (1 per 269 persons); infant mortality rate per 1,000 live births (1982–86) 15.4.
Food (1984–86)[10]: daily per capita caloric intake 3,425 (vegetable products 61%, animal products 39%); (1983) 129% of FAO recommended minimum requirement.

Military

Total active duty personnel: none. *Military expenditure as percent of GNP:* none.

---

[1]January 1. [2]Detail does not add to total given because of rounding. [3]December 31. [4]September. [5]The index is for Switzerland, which is united with Liechtenstein in a customs and monetary union. [6]Household expenditures are taken from a 1986 Swiss sample survey; a similarity of consumption patterns is assumed. [7]Includes 36 unemployed persons. [8]One evening school with part-time teachers. [9]1986–87. [10]Figures are derived from statistics for Switzerland and Austria.

Luxembourg

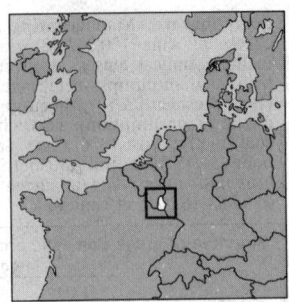

Official name: Grand-Duché de Luxembourg (French); Grossherzogtum Luxemburg (German) (Grand Duchy of Luxembourg).
Form of government: constitutional monarchy with two legislative houses (Council of State [21]; Chamber of Deputies [64]).
Chief of state: Grand Duke.
Head of government: Prime Minister.
Capital: Luxembourg.
Official languages: French; German.
Official religion: none.
Monetary unit: 1 Luxembourg franc (Lux F) = 100 centimes; valuation (Oct. 10, 1988) 1 U.S.$ = Lux F 38.86; 1 £ = Lux F 66.55.

Area and population

Districts Cantons	area sq mi	area sq km	population 1986 estimate[1]
Diekirch	447	1,157	54,420
Clervaux	128	332	9,710
Diekirch	92	239	22,390
Redange	103	267	10,500
Vianden	21	54	2,790
Wiltz	102	265	9,030
Grevenmacher	203	525	40,030
Echternach	72	186	10,990
Grevenmacher	82	211	16,910
Remich	49	128	12,130
Luxembourg	349	904	272,250
Capellen	77	199	28,790
Esch	94	243	112,250
Luxembourg (Ville et Campagne)	92	238	113,570
Mersch	86	224	17,640
TOTAL	999	2,586	366,700

Demography

Population (1988): 372,000.
Density (1988): persons per sq mi 372.4, persons per sq km 143.8.
Urban–rural (1985): urban 77.6%; rural 22.4%.
Sex distribution (1987): male 48.61%; female 51.39%.
Age breakdown (1985): under 15, 17.3%; 15–29, 23.6%; 30–44, 21.9%; 45–59, 19.0%; 60–74, 12.6%; 75 and over, 5.6%.
Population projection: (1990) 375,000; (2000) 388,000.
Doubling time: n.a.; doubling time exceeds 100 years.
Ethnic composition (nationality; 1986): Luxemburger 70.3%; Portuguese 8.6%; Italian 5.9%; French 4.0%; German 2.8%; other 8.4%.
Religious affiliation (1980): Roman Catholic 93.0%; Protestant 1.3%; other 5.7%.
Major cities[2] (1986): Luxembourg 86,200; Esch-sur-Alzette 24,900; Differdange 16,450; Dudelange 14,080.

Vital statistics

Birth rate per 1,000 population (1987): 11.4 (world avg. 26.0); legitimate 89.2%; illegitimate 10.8%.
Death rate per 1,000 population (1987): 10.8 (world avg. 9.9).
Natural increase rate per 1,000 population (1987): 0.6 (world avg. 16.1).
Total fertility rate (avg. births per childbearing woman; 1987): 1.4.
Marriage rate per 1,000 population (1987): 5.3.
Divorce rate per 1,000 population (1987): 2.0.
Life expectancy at birth (1985–87): male 70.6 years; female 77.9 years.
Major causes of death per 100,000 population (1986): circulatory diseases 521.2, of which cerebrovascular disease 189.8, ischemic heart disease 161.5; malignant neoplasms (cancers) 254.6; accidents and suicides 68.4, of which suicide 13.8.

National economy

Budget (1986). Revenue: Lux F 78,625,858,000 (income and excise taxes 51.7%, customs taxes 11.6%). Expenditures[3]: Lux F 78,280,400,000 (social security 24.8%, transport and power 20.2%, education and arts 12.8%, debt service 12.2%, administration 7.7%, defense 2.8%).
Public debt (1987): U.S.$508,000,000.
Tourism: (1986): Number of tourist arrivals 711,000[4].
Production (metric tons except as noted). Agriculture, forestry, fishing (1986): barley 64,561, wheat 29,516, potatoes 25,452, oats 21,934; livestock (number of live animals) 222,864 cattle, 75,609 pigs; roundwood (1985) 465,650 cu m. Mining and quarrying (1986): metal ores, none; sand and gravel 677,058, crushed stone 546,670, gypsum 420,000. Manufacturing (1986): finished rolled steel products 3,770,978; steel ingots and castings 3,705,300; pig iron 2,649,700; meat products 21,879, of which beef and veal 14,779, pork 7,100; wine 159,660 hectolitres. Construction (1985): residential and semiresidential 309,979 sq m; nonresidential 234,554 sq m. Energy production (consumption): electricity (kW-hr; 1986) 1,020,386,000 (3,884,-437,000); coal (metric tons; 1986) none (135,900); crude petroleum, none (n.a.); petroleum products (metric tons; 1986) none (1,160,769); natural gas (cu m; 1986) none (356,600,000).
Gross national product (at current market prices; 1986): U.S.$5,830,000,000 (U.S.$15,920 per capita).

Structure of gross domestic product and labour force

	1985 in value Lux F '000,000	1985 % of total value	1987 labour force	1987 % of labour force
Agriculture	6,270	2.6	5,100	3.2
Mining	240	0.1	32,500	20.5
Manufacturing	71,600	29.7 }		
Construction	12,780	5.3	13,900	8.8
Public utilities	6,030	2.5	900	0.6
Transp. and commun.	13,500	5.6	10,500	6.6
Trade	38,570	16.0	32,700	20.6
Finance	32,300	13.4	16,000	10.1
Pub. admin., defense	28,210	11.7	14,800	9.3
Services	31,580	13.1	27,500	17.4
Other	...	...	4,500[5]	2.9[5]
TOTAL	241,075[6]	100.0	158,400	100.0

Population economically active (1987): total 158,400; activity rate of total population 42.6% (participation rates: ages 15–64 [1981] 61.3%; female 35.3%; unemployed 2.5%).

Price and earnings indexes (1980 = 100)

	1981	1982	1983	1984	1985	1986	1987
Consumer price index	109.3	118.2	128.4	135.7	141.2	141.6	141.5
Hourly earnings index[7]	104.6	116.9	127.6	137.6	...	...	...

Household income and expenditure. Average household size (1982) 2.8; income per household Lux F 751,800 (U.S.$16,455); sources of income (1985): wages and salaries 88.1%, self-employment 9.4%, transfer payments 2.5%; expenditure (1985): food and beverages 16.9%, transportation and communications 16.9%, housing 12.4%, household goods and furniture 9.2%, health 6.7%, clothing and footwear 6.6%.
Land use (1985): forested 34.2%; meadows and pastures 27.1%; agricultural and under permanent cultivation 21.7%; other 17.0%.

Foreign trade

Balance of trade (current prices)

	1981	1982	1983	1984	1985	1986
Lux F '000,000	−17,192	−15,868	−16,492	−14,503	−9,093	−13,390
% of total	8.8%	7.2%	6.9%	4.7%	2.6%	3.9%

Imports (1986): Lux F 179,591,000,000 (metal products, machinery, and transport equipment 41.6%, of which electrical machinery 14.7%, transport equipment 9.8%; mineral products 13.4%; chemical products 8.5%; food, beverages, and tobacco 6.2%). *Major import sources:* Belgium 37.6%; West Germany 30.7%; France 12.2%; The Netherlands 5.1%; Italy 2.5%; United States 2.2%.
Exports (1986): Lux F 166,201,000,000 (metal products, machinery, and transport equipment 60.3%, of which electrical machinery 9.0%; plastic materials and rubber manufactures 13.5%; textile yarn, fabrics, and related products 5.2%; chemical products 4.7%; food, beverages, and tobacco 2.3%). *Major export destinations:* West Germany 29.1%; Belgium 16.7%; France 15.3%; The Netherlands 6.1%; United States 5.2%; United Kingdom 4.6%; Italy 4.4%.

Transport and communications

Transport. Railroads (1986): route length 168 mi, 270 km; passenger-mi 171,000,000, passenger-km 276,000,000; short ton-mi cargo 414,000,000, metric ton-km cargo 604,000,000. Roads (1986): total length 3,244 mi, 5,220 km (paved 99%). Vehicles (1986): passenger cars 162,481; trucks and buses 14,869. Merchant marine: vessels (100 gross tons and over) n.a.; total deadweight tonnage, n.a. Air transport (1986): passenger arrivals 422,598, departures 431,023; cargo loaded and unloaded 77,911 metric tons; airports (1988) with scheduled flights 1.
Communications. Daily newspapers (1986): total number 6; total circulation 130,000; circulation per 1,000 population 365. Radio (1986): 228,000 receivers (1 per 1.6 persons). Television (1987): 91,500 receivers (1 per 4.0 persons). Telephones (1986): 157,112 (1 per 2.3 persons).

Education and health

Education (1985–86)

	schools	teachers	students	student/ teacher ratio
Primary (age 6–15)	...	1,745	24,424	14.0
Secondary (age 12–18)	...		7,951	...
Voc., teacher tr.	... }	3,482[8,9]	15,785	...
Higher	...		934[10]	...

Educational attainment, n.a. *Literacy* (1988): virtually 100% literate.
Health (1986): physicians 686 (1 per 537 persons); hospital beds (1985) 4,587 (1 per 80 persons); infant mortality rate per 1,000 live births (1987) 9.3.
Food (1984–86): daily per capita caloric intake[11] 3,850; (vegetable products 56%, animal products 44%); (1983) 139% of FAO recommended minimum requirement.

Military

Total active duty personnel (1987): 690 (army 100.0%). *Military expenditure as percent of GNP* (1985): 0.8% (world 6.1%); per capita expenditure U.S.$102.

[1]January 1. [2]From country register. [3]Percentage breakdown is for 1984 expenditure of Lux F 73,607,500,000. [4]Hotel, camping, and free lodging arrivals. [5]Includes 3,900 unemployed. [6]Detail does not add to total given because of rounding. [7]Manufacturing only. [8]1982–83. [9]Includes part-time teachers. [10]1984–85. [11]Figures for Belgium–Luxembourg.

Macau

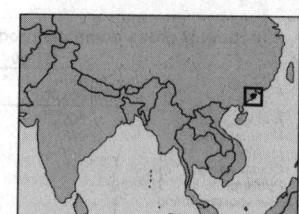

Official name: Macau.
Political status: overseas territory
  (Portugal) with one legislative house
  (Legislative Assembly [17])[1].
Head of state and government:
  Governor.
Capital: Macau.
Official language: Portuguese.
Official religion: Roman Catholicism.
Monetary unit: 1 pataca[2] = 100 avos;
  valuation (Oct. 10, 1988)
  1 U.S.$ = 8.04 patacas; 1 £ = 13.76
  patacas.

Area and population

Districts Parishes	Capital	area sq mi	area sq km	population 1986 estimate
Islands		4.2	10.9	10,200
Nossa Senhora Carmo (Taipa)	—	1.5	3.8	6,500
São Francisco Xavier (Coloane)	—	2.7	7.1	3,700
Macau	Macau	2.4	6.1	416,200
Nossa Senhora Fátima	—	...	...	...
Santo António	—	...	...	...
São Lázaro	—	...	...	...
São Lourenço	—	...	...	...
Sé	—	...	...	...
Marine Area	—	...	...	...
TOTAL		6.5[3]	16.9[3]	426,400

Demography

Population (1988): 479,000.
Density (1988): persons per sq mi 73,692, persons per sq km 28,343.
Urban–rural (1981): urban 94.9%[4].
Sex distribution (1986): male 51.74%; female 48.26%.
Age breakdown (1986): under 15, 24.7%; 15–29, 32.2%; 30–44, 24.8%; 45–59, 9.7%; 60 and over, 8.6%.
Population projection: (1990) 539,000; (2000) 837,000.
Doubling time: 49 years.
Nationality (1981): Chinese 73.5%; Portuguese 20.3%; English 0.9%; other 5.3%.
Religious affiliation (1981): Buddhist 45.1%; Christian 8.7%, of which Roman Catholic 7.4%, Protestant 1.3%; nonreligious 45.8%; other 0.4%.
Major city (1986): Macau 416,200.

Vital statistics

Birth rate per 1,000 population (1986): 17.5 (world avg. 26.0); legitimate, n.a.; illegitimate, n.a.
Death rate per 1,000 population (1986): 3.1 (world avg. 9.9).
Natural increase rate per 1,000 population (1986): 14.4 (world avg. 11.1).
Total fertility rate (avg. births per childbearing woman; 1980–85): 3.8.
Marriage rate per 1,000 population (1986): 6.7.
Divorce rate per 1,000 population (1986): 0.1.
Life expectancy at birth (1979): male 68.0 years; female 73.0 years.
Major causes of death per 100,000 population (1986): diseases of the circulatory system 113.3; malignant neoplasms (cancers) 65.4; diseases of the respiratory system 36.8; injuries and poisonings 22.3; diseases of the digestive system 15.5; infectious and parasitic diseases 11.3; diseases of the genito-urinary system 10.3.

National economy

Budget (1986). Revenue: 2,237,090,000 patacas (gambling revenue 41.1%, direct taxes 12.9%, indirect taxes 9.7%). Expenditures: 2,063,500,000 patacas (1983; security forces 14.1%, health and social welfare 4.6%, education 4.0%).
Gross domestic product (at current market prices; 1986): U.S.$1,648,000,000 (U.S.$3,860 per capita).

Structure of labour force

	1981 labour force	1981 % of labour force
Agriculture	7,551	5.9
Mining	71	0.1
Manufacturing	56,304	44.2
Construction	9,937	7.8
Public utilities	876	0.7
Transportation and communications	5,776	4.5
Trade	23,102	18.1
Finance	2,191	1.7
Public administration	4,056	3.2
Services	15,190	11.9
Other	2,305[5]	1.8[5]
TOTAL	127,359	100.0[3]

Production (metric tons except as noted). Agriculture, forestry, and fishing (1986): grapes 5,000, eggs 635; livestock (number of live animals) 9,000 cattle, 6,000 pigs, 1,000,000 chickens[6]; fish catch 8,042. Mining and quarrying (1982): granite 656,920. Manufacturing (1983): clothing 27,184; knitwear 13,230; meat 9,021; furniture 2,335; wine 796; explosive and pyrotechnic

products 586; footwear 376; optical materials 312. Construction (1986): residential 294,300 sq m; nonresidential 375,000 sq m. Energy production (consumption): electricity (kW-hr; 1986) 513,000,000 (555,000,000); coal (metric tons; 1986) none (none); petroleum (barrels; 1981) none (2,559); petroleum products (metric tons; 1986) none (285,000); natural gas, none (n.a.).
Population economically active (1981): total 127,359; activity rate of total population 48.6% (participation rates: over age 10, 61.5%; female 37.1%; unemployed 3.9%).

Price and earnings indexes (Oct. 1982–Sept. 1983 = 100)

	1983[7]	1984[7]	1985[7]	1986
Consumer price index	100	112.2	115.9	118.5
Earnings index	...	...	...	...

Public debt (long-term, external, 1985): U.S.$91,000,000.
Tourism (1986): number of tourist arrivals 4,238,300.
Household income and expenditure. Average household size (1980): 4.8; income per household: n.a.; sources of income: n.a.; expenditure (1981–82): food 42.0%, housing 22.8%, education, health, and other services 8.1%, clothing and footwear 7.3%, transportation 4.9%, energy 4.9%, household durable goods 2.9%.
Land use (1979): forested 50.0%; agricultural and under permanent cultivation 4.0%; built-on area, wasteland, and other 46.0%.

Foreign trade

Balance of trade (current prices)

	1981	1982	1983	1984	1985	1986
'000,000 patacas	−112.2	+38.5	+250.3	+919.4	+1,002	+1,312
% of total	−1.4%	0.4%	2.3%	6.7%	7.5%	8.2%

Imports (1986): 7,318,100,000 patacas (industrial raw materials 62.8%, nonedible consumer goods 11.8%, food and beverages 9.2%, capital goods 8.4%, fuels and lubricants 5.2%, transport equipment and parts 2.5%). *Major import sources:* Hong Kong 45.9%; China 19.7%; Japan 9.9%; European Economic Community 6.6%; United States 6.1%.
Exports (1986): 8,630,100,000 patacas (textiles and garments 69.7%, toys 11.8%, electronics 4.1%, artificial flowers 2.8%, leather articles 2.0%, ceramics 0.8%, optical products 0.8%). *Major export destinations:* United States 33.3%; Hong Kong 15.6%; France 11.9%; West Germany 11.4%; United Kingdom 7.2%; China 3.8%; Australia 2.4%; Japan 1.5%.

Transport and communications

Transport. Railroads: none. Roads (1984): total length 56 mi, 90 km (paved 100%). Vehicles (1986): passenger cars 19,513; trucks and buses 4,773. Merchant marine (1986): vessels 581[8]; total gross tonnage 22,689. Air transport: none.
Communications. Daily newspapers (1986): total number 14; total circulation 242,000; circulation per 1,000 population 568. Radio (1986): total number of receivers 84,000 (1 per 5.0 persons). Television (1987): total number of receivers 70,000 (1 per 6.3 persons). Telephones (1987): 60,533 (1 per 7.1 persons).

Education and health

Education (1985–86)

	schools	teachers	students	student/ teacher ratio
Primary (age 6–11)	74	1,080	31,669	29.3
Secondary (age 12–18)	31	769	13,849	18.0
Teacher tr.	2	13	52	4.0
Higher	5	75	5,840	77.9

Educational attainment (1981). Percent of economically active population age 10 and over having: no formal schooling 13.8%; primary education 22.6%; some secondary 27.2%; complete secondary 20.5%; some postsecondary 13.0%; higher 2.9%. *Literacy* (1981): total population age 10 and over literate 127,359 (61.3%); males literate 80,102 (76.4%); females literate 47,257 (46.2%).
Health (1986): physicians 697 (1 per 612 persons); hospital beds 1,258 (1 per 339 persons); infant mortality rate per 1,000 live births 6.0.
Food (1984–86): daily per capita caloric intake 2,205 (vegetable products 73%, animal products 27%); (1983) 107% of FAO recommended minimum requirement.

Military

Total active duty personnel (1987): the Portuguese garrison has been replaced by a paramilitary force of 1,800 men drawn from the Chinese residents only.

---

[1]Includes six directly elected; six indirectly elected by social, cultural, and economic functional constituencies; and five appointed by the governor. [2]The pataca free floats with the Hong Kong dollar and has a parity of 1.03 patacas = HK$1.00. [3]Detail does not add to total given because of rounding. [4]5.1% of Macau's population live on sampans and other vessels. [5]Mostly unemployed not previously employed. [6]1985. [7]March. [8]All registered vessels including barges, tugboats, floating casinos, sampans, dredgers, but excluding barges used for restaurants and recreation.

Madagascar

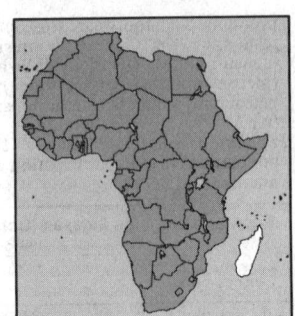

Official name: Repoblika Demokratika Malagasy (Malagasy); République Démocratique de Madagascar (French) (Democratic Republic of Madagascar).
Form of government: single party republic with one legislative house (National People's Assembly [137]).
Chief of state: President.
Head of government: Prime Minister.
Capital: Antananarivo.
Official languages: Malagasy; French.
Official religion: none.
Monetary unit: 1 franc (FMG) = 100 centimes; valuation (Oct. 10, 1988) 1 U.S.$ = FMG 1,250; 1 £ = FMG 2,141.

Area and population

Provinces	Capitals	area sq mi	area sq km	population 1985 estimate
Antananarivo	Antananarivo	22,503	58,283	3,195,800
Antsiranana	Antsiranana	16,620	43,046	689,800
Fianarantsoa	Fianarantsoa	39,526	102,373	2,209,700
Mahajanga	Mahajanga	57,924	150,023	1,075,300
Toamasina	Toamasina	27,765	71,911	1,444,700
Toliara	Toliara	62,319	161,405	1,396,700
TOTAL		226,658	587,041	10,012,000

Demography

Population (1988): 10,917,000.
Density (1988): persons per sq mi 48.2, persons per sq km 18.6.
Urban–rural (1985): urban 21.8%; rural 78.2%.
Sex distribution (1985): male 49.61%; female 50.39%.
Age breakdown (1985): under 15, 44.2%; 15–29, 25.3%; 30–44, 15.5%; 45–59, 9.5%; 60–74, 4.6%; 75 and over, 0.9%.
Population projection: (1990) 11,575,000; (2000) 15,550,000.
Doubling time: 25 years.
Ethnic composition (1983): Malagasy 98.9%, of which Merina 26.6%, Betsimisaraka 14.9%, Betsileo 11.7%, Tsimihety 7.4%, Sakalava 6.4%; Antandroy 5.3%; Comorian 0.3%; Indian and Pakistani 0.2%; French 0.2%; Chinese 0.1%; other 0.3%.
Religious affiliation (1980): Christian 51.0%, of which Roman Catholic 26.0%, Protestant 22.8%; traditional beliefs 47.0%; Muslim 1.7%; other 0.3%.
Major cities (1980): Antananarivo 662,600[1]; Toamasina 95,505; Fianarantsoa 83,250; Mahajanga 80,881.

Vital statistics

Birth rate per 1,000 population (1985–90): 44.1 (world avg. 26.0); legitimate, n.a.; illegitimate, n.a.
Death rate per 1,000 population (1985–90): 15.2 (world avg. 9.9).
Natural increase rate per 1,000 population (1985–90): 28.9 (world avg. 16.1).
Total fertility rate (avg. births per childbearing woman; 1985): 6.5.
Marriage rate per 1,000 population: n.a.
Divorce rate per 1,000 population: n.a.
Life expectancy at birth (1980–85): male 48.9 years; female 50.4 years.
Major causes of death per 100,000 population: n.a.; however, major diseases include malaria, leprosy, and tuberculosis.

National economy

Budget (1987). Revenue: FMG 331,627,000,000 (taxes 80.2%, of which import duties 14.9%, excises 14.8%, income tax 12.5%; other receipts 19.8%). Expenditures: FMG 521,137,000,000 (current expenditure 77.3%, of which education 12.3%, defense 7.5%, health 4.2%, agriculture 1.8%, public works 0.7%).
Tourism: receipts from visitors (1986) U.S.$5,600,000; expenditures by nationals abroad (1983) U.S.$38,000,000.
Production (metric tons except as noted). Agriculture, forestry, fishing (1986): roots and tubers 3,246,000 (of which cassava 2,421,000, sweet potatoes 467,000, potatoes 264,000), rice 2,138,000, sugarcane 1,700,000, vegetables and melons 300,000, bananas 225,000, mangoes 174,000, corn (maize) 153,000, coffee 85,000, oranges 82,000, pineapples 51,000, peanuts (groundnuts) 33,000, sisal 20,000, cloves 12,500[2], tobacco 5,000; livestock (number of live animals) 10,485,000 cattle, 1,350,000 pigs, 1,225,000 goats, 604,000 sheep; roundwood (1985) 6,262,000 cu m; fish catch 63,589. Mining and quarrying (1986): chromite concentrate 82,900; graphite 16,188; industrial calcite 2,000; mica 1,775; beryl 50,000 kg; celestite 30,000 kg; jasper 16,000 kg; agate 8,000 kg; gold 130 kg. Manufacturing (1986): raw sugar 98,462; fuel oils 63,025; cement 50,502; gasoline 15,178; soap 10,419; vegetable oils 4,520; cigarettes 2,188; chewing tobacco 1,225; beer 255,268 hectolitres. Construction (1985): residential 15,600 sq m; nonresidential 9,700 sq m. Energy production (consumption): electricity (kW-hr; 1986) 500,000,000 (500,000,000); coal (metric tons; 1986) none (9,000); crude petroleum (barrels; 1986) none (1,533,000); petroleum products (metric tons; 1986) 208,000 (237,000); natural gas, none (n.a.).
Land use (1985): forested 26.2%; meadows and pastures 58.5%; agricultural and under permanent cultivation 5.2%; other 10.1%.
Gross national product (at current market prices; 1986): U.S.$2,390,000,000 (U.S.$230 per capita).

Structure of gross domestic product and labour force

	1986 in value U.S.$'000,000	1986 % of total value	1985 labour force	1985 % of labour force
Agriculture	966	42.3	3,590,000	79.6
Manufacturing	278	12.2		
Mining			284,000	6.3
Construction	117	5.1		
Public utilities				
Transportation and communications				
Trade	922	40.4	636,000	14.1
Finance				
Services				
Pub. admin., defense				
TOTAL	2,283[3]	100.0	4,510,000	100.0

Public debt (external, outstanding; 1986): U.S.$2,634,500,000.
Population economically active: total (1985) 4,510,000; activity rate of total population 45.1% (participation rates: ages 15–64, 74.9%; female 40.4%; unemployed [1982] 0.6%).

Price and earnings indexes (1980 = 100)

	1982	1983	1984	1985	1986	1987	1988[4]
Consumer price index	172.0	205.3	225.5	249.3	285.5	328.3	406.3
Earnings index	...	...	...	...	...	...	...

Household income and expenditure. Average household size (1980) 4.7; average annual income per household (1981) FMG 4,485 (U.S.$1,650); sources of income[5] (1975): wages and salaries 58.8%, self-employment 14.1%, other 27.1%; expenditure[6]: food 60.4%, fuel and light 9.1%, clothing and footwear 8.6%, household goods and utensils 2.4%.

Foreign trade[7]

Balance of trade

	1981	1982	1983	1984	1985	1986
FMG '000,000,000	−37.8	−19.3	−25.0	+15.1	−39.1	+26.7
% of total	18.1%	8.2%	9.9%	4.1%	9.7	6.7

Imports (1986): FMG 276,983,200,000[8] (mineral products 14.8%, of which crude petroleum 6.4%; chemical products 12.0%; machinery 11.2%; vehicles and parts 9.5%; metal products 7.1%; electrical equipment 4.4%; textiles 1.5%). *Major import sources:* France 29.5%; United States 15.3%; Japan 10.1%; West Germany 5.9%; United Kingdom 2.9%; Italy 2.6%.
Exports (1986): FMG 205,875,700,000 (coffee 44.7%; vanilla 14.5%; cloves and clove oil 8.5%; petroleum products 1.1%). *Major export destinations:* France 34.1%; United States 14.5%; Japan 11.3%; West Germany 6.9%; The Netherlands 6.4%; Italy 4.5%; Réunion 3.2%; United Kingdom 2.4%.

Transport and communications

Transport. Railroads (1986): route length 580 mi, 933 km; passenger-mi 129,000,000, passenger-km 208,000,000; short ton-mi cargo 129,000,000, metric ton-km cargo 188,000,000. Roads (1987): total length 11,560 mi, 18,610 km (paved 30%). Vehicles (1986): passenger cars 21,860; trucks and buses 14,542. Merchant marine (1987): vessels (100 gross tons and over) 72; total deadweight tonnage 82,242. Air transport (1987): passenger-mi 262,570,000, passenger-km 422,566,000; short ton-mi cargo 26,049,000, metric ton-km cargo 38,031,000; airports (1988) with scheduled flights 35.
Communications. Daily newspapers (1987): total number 5; total circulation 115,500; circulation per 1,000 population 11. Radio (1986): total number of receivers 2,020,000 (1 per 5.1 persons). Television (1987): total number of receivers 100,000 (1 per 106 persons). Telephones (1987): 43,600 (1 per 240 persons).

Education and health

Education (1984)

	schools	teachers	students	student/ teacher ratio
Primary (age 6–13)	13,973	42,462	1,625,216	38.3
Secondary (14–18)	104[9]	10,383	288,543	27.8
Voc., teacher tr.[10]	126	1,302	11,041	8.5
Higher	3[11]	1,059	37,746	35.6

Educational attainment, n.a. *Literacy* (1985): total population age 15 and over literate 3,778,000 (67.5%); males literate 2,004,000 (73.7%); females literate 1,774,000 (61.6%).
Health (1982): physicians 940 (1 per 9,851 persons); hospital beds 20,800 (1 per 442 persons); infant mortality rate per 1,000 live births (1980–85) 67.0.
Food (1984–86): daily per capita caloric intake 2,413 (vegetable products 92%, animal products 8%); (1983) 112% of FAO recommended minimum requirement.

Military

Total active duty personnel (1987): 21,000 (army 95.2%, navy 2.6%, air force 2.2%). *Military expenditure as percent of GNP* (1985): 2.4% (world 6.1%); per capita expenditure U.S.$6.

---

[1]1985. [2]1981–82. [3]At factor cost. [4]January. [5]Malagasy households only. [6]Weights of consumer price index components in Antananarivo only; housing not included. [7]Import figures are f.o.b. in balance of trade and c.i.f. in commodities and trading partners. [8]Excludes gold and military equipment. [9]1971–72. [10]1984. [11]Two colleges and one university with six regional centres.

Malaŵi

Official name: Republic of Malaŵi
(English).
Form of government: single-party
republic with one legislative house
(National Assembly [118[1]]).
Head of state and government:
President.
Capital: Lilongwe.
Official language: English.
Official religion: none.
Monetary unit: 1 Malaŵi kwacha
(MK) = 100 Tambala; valuation
(Oct. 10, 1988) 1 U.S.$ = MK 2.66;
1 £ = MK 4.56.

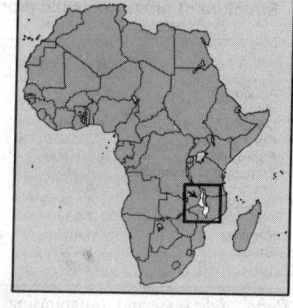

Area and population		area		population
Regions				1987
Districts	Capitals	sq mi	sq km	census[2]
Central	Lilongwe	13,742	35,592	3,116,038
Dedza	Dedza	1,399	3,624	410,847
Dowa	Dowa	1,174	3,041	322,112
Kasungu	Kasungu	3,042	7,878	322,854
Lilongwe	Lilongwe	2,378	6,159	986,411
Mchinji	Mchinji	1,296	3,356	248,161
Nkhotakota	Nkhotakota	1,644	4,259	157,083
Ntcheu	Ntcheu	1,322	3,424	359,618
Ntchisi	Ntchisi	639	1,655	120,697
Salima	Salima	848	2,196	188,255
Northern	Mzuzu	10,398	26,931	907,121
Chitipa	Chitipa	1,353	3,504	96,842
Karonga	Karonga	1,141	2,955	147,096
Mzimba	Mzimba	4,027	10,430	432,437
Nkhata Bay	Nkhata Bay	1,579	4,090	136,044
Rumphi	Rumphi	2,298	5,952	94,702
Southern	Blantyre	12,260	31,753	3,959,448
Blantyre	Blantyre	777	2,012	587,893
Chikwawa	Chikwawa	1,836	4,755	319,781
Chiradzulu	Chiradzulu	296	767	210,736
Machinga	Machinga	2,303	5,964	514,569
Mangochi	Mangochi	2,422	6,272	495,876
Mulanje	Mulanje	1,332	3,450	638,326
Mwanza	Mwanza	886	2,295	121,267
Nsanje	Nsanje	750	1,942	201,311
Thyolo	Thyolo	662	1,715	431,539
Zomba	Zomba	996	2,580	438,150
TOTAL LAND AREA		36,400	94,276[3]	
INLAND WATER		9,347	24,208	
TOTAL		45,747	118,484	7,982,607

Demography

Population (1988): 8,211,000.
Density[4] (1988): persons per sq mi 225.6, persons per sq km 87.1.
Urban–rural (1987): urban 11.0%; rural 89.0%.
Sex distribution (1987): male 48.61%; female 51.39%.
Age breakdown (1987): under 15, 47.8%; 15–29, 25.6%; 30–44, 14.4%; 45–59,
8.1%; 60–74, 3.5%; 75 and over, 0.6%.
Population projection: (1990) 8,831,000; (2000) 12,201,000.
Doubling time: 23 years.
Ethnic composition (1983): Maravi (including Nyanja, Chewa, Tonga, and
Tumbuka) 58.3%; Lomwe 18.4%; Yao 13.2%; Ngoni 6.7%; other 3.4%.
Religious affiliation (1980): Christian 64.5%, of which Protestant 33.7%, Ro-
man Catholic 27.6%; traditional beliefs 19.0%; Muslim 16.2%; other 0.3%.
Major cities (1987): Blantyre 402,500; Lilongwe 220,300; Mzuzu 115,000.

Vital statistics

Birth rate per 1,000 population (1984): 54.0 (world avg. 29.0).
Death rate per 1,000 population (1984): 22.0 (world avg. 11.0).
Natural increase rate per 1,000 population (1984): 32.0 (world avg. 18.0).
Total fertility rate (avg. births per childbearing woman; 1985): 7.6.
Marriage rate per 1,000 population (1977): 7.8.
Divorce rate per 1,000 population (1977): 1.4.
Life expectancy at birth (1984): male 44.0 years; female 46.0 years.
Major causes of death per 100,000 population[5] (1983): infectious and para-
sitic diseases 56.0, of which measles 17.4, malaria 13.7, diarrheal diseases
11.4; pneumonia 17.5; malnutrition 15.9; anemia 12.1.

National economy

Budget (1987–88). Revenue: MK 696,400,000 (recurrent revenue 7.3%, of
which income tax 23.9%, surtax 23.1%, import duties 11.3%; nontax revenue 13.6%). Expenditures: MK 855,800,000 (recurrent expenditures 76.0%,
of which debt payment 28.0%, goods and other services 16.4%, wages and
salaries 15.1%; development expenditure 24.0%).
Public debt (external, outstanding; 1986): U.S.$909,700,000.
Tourism (1986): receipts from visitors U.S.$7,682,000; expenditures by na-
tionals abroad U.S.$7,000,000.
Production (metric tons except as noted). Agriculture (1986): sugarcane
1,600,000, corn (maize) 1,374,000, potatoes 275,000, cassava 184,000,
peanuts (groundnuts) 180,000, sorghum 152,000, plantains 112,000, bananas
79,000, dry beans 72,000, tobacco 71,000, tea 42,000; livestock (number
of live animals) 930,000 cattle, 690,000 goats, 240,000 pigs, 180,000 sheep;
roundwood (1985) 6,588,000 cu m; fish catch 72,852. Mining and quarrying (1986): limestone 110,000; cement 69,000. Manufacturing (1986): raw
sugar 163,800; tea 31,900; beer 627,000 hectolitres; cigarettes 874,000,000
units; blankets 616,000 units. Construction (value in MK; 1986): 5,463,400.
Energy production (consumption): electricity (kW-hr; 1986) 528,000,000

(527,000,000); coal (metric tons; 1986) none (29,000); petroleum products
(metric tons; 1986) none (138,000).
Gross national product (1986): U.S.$1,180,000,000 (U.S.$160 per capita).

Structure of gross domestic product and labour force				
	1987		1985	
	in value MK '000,000	% of total value	labour force	% of labour force
Agriculture	310.9	36.3	2,502,000	81.4
Mining	...	...		0.1
Manufacturing	103.7	12.1		
Construction	36.1	4.2	206,000	6.7
Public utilities	17.9	2.1		
Transp. and commun.	53.1	6.2		
Trade	113.3	13.2		
Finance	93.4	10.9		
Public administration	113.6	13.2	366,000	11.9
Services	37.4	4.4		
Other	−22.4[6]	−2.6[6]		
TOTAL	857.0[7]	100.0	3,074,000	100.0

Population economically active (1985): total 3,074,000; activity rate of total
population 44.3% (participation rates: ages 15–64, 74.3%; female 42.6%;
unemployed 1.0%[8]).

Price and earnings indexes (1980 = 100)							
	1980	1981	1982	1983	1984	1985	1986
Consumer price index	100.0	111.8	122.8	139.4	167.3	184.9	210.8
Monthly earnings index	100.0	112.9	131.9	124.3	125.1	...	...

Household income and expenditure (1979–80). Average household size[9] 4.5;
income per household MK 1,934 (U.S.$2,419); sources of income: wages
83.3%, household enterprise 6.0%; expenditure (1985)[10]: food 32.9%, transportation 17.6%, housing 13.3%, clothing and footwear 10.7%.
Land use (1985): forested 49.2%; meadows and pastures 19.6%; agricultural
and under permanent cultivation 24.9%; other 6.3%.

Foreign trade[11]

Balance of trade (current prices)						
	1981	1982	1983	1984	1985	1986
MK '000,000	−69.7	−65.5	−93.1	+64.7	−62.8	−15.2
% of total	12.5%	11.3%	14.7%	7.8%	6.8%	1.6%

Imports (1986): MK 477,990,000 (basic manufactures 33.2%; transport equipment 14.9%; machinery and equipment 13.9%; consumer goods 13.6%;
mineral fuels and lubricants 12.3%). *Major import sources:* South Africa
29.0%; U.K. 24.7%; Japan 9.2%; West Germany 6.3%; Zimbabwe 4.7%.
Exports (1986): MK 448,747,000 (tobacco 52.8%; tea 14.8%; sugar 8.6%;
peanuts [groundnuts] 3.4%). *Major export destinations:* U.K. 26.4%; U.S.
9.0%; West Germany 9.9%; South Africa 7.4%.

Transport and communications

Transport. Railroads (1987): route length 515 mi, 829 km; passenger-mi
63,963,000, passenger-km 102,939,000; short ton-mi cargo 67,441,000, metric ton-km cargo 98,469,000. Roads (1985): total length 7,590 mi, 12,215
km (paved 21%). Vehicles (1986): passenger cars 15,339; trucks and buses
15,755. Merchant marine (1987): vessels (100 gross tons and over) 1; total
deadweight tonnage 300. Air transport (1986): passenger-mi 74,123,000,
passenger-km 119,289,000; short ton-mi cargo 720,500, metric ton-km cargo
1,052,000; airports (1988) with scheduled flights 5.
Communications. Daily newspapers (1985): total number 2; total circulation
32,000; circulation per 1,000 population 4.5. Radio (1986): total number of
receivers 1,060,000 (1 per 7.2 persons). Television (1985): total number of
receivers, n.a. Telephones (1986): 44,694 (1 per 174 persons).

Education and health

Education (1985–86)				
	schools	teachers	students	student/ teacher ratio
Primary (age 6–13)	2,520	15,440	942,539	61.0
Secondary (age 14–18)	75	1,141	24,894	22.8
Teacher tr., voc.	7	314	2,441	7.8
Higher	4	278	1,974	7.1

Educational attainment (1987). Percent of population age 5 and over having no formal education 54.9%; primary education 41.7%; secondary and
higher 3.4%. *Literacy* (1985): total population age 15 and over literate
1,555,000 (41.2%).
Health: physicians (1983) 161 (1 per 41,108 persons); hospital beds (1986)
12,119 (1 per 600 persons); infant mortality rate (1985) 152.0.
Food (1984–86): daily per capita caloric intake 2,372 (vegetable products
96%, animal products 4%); (1983) 104% of FAO recommended minimum.

Military

Total active duty personnel (1987): 5,250 (army 95.2%, navy 1.9%, air force
2.9%). *Military expenditure as percent of GNP* (1984): 1.7% (world 5.9%);
per capita expenditure U.S.$3.

[1]Includes 6 nonelective members. [2]Preliminary. [3]Detail does not add to total given
because of rounding. [4]Based on land area. [5]Reported inpatient deaths in hospitals.
[6]Less imputed bank service charges. [7]At constant prices of 1978. [8]Registered. [9]Based
on sample survey of the city of Blantyre. [10]Weights of consumer price index components, cities of Blantyre and Lilongwe only. [11]Import figures are f.o.b. in balance of
trade and c.i.f. in commodities and trading partners. Reexports included in balance
of trade, excluded from commodities and trading partners.

Malaysia

Official name: Malaysia.
Form of government: federal
constitutional monarchy with two
legislative houses (Senate [69[1]]; House
of Representatives [177]).
Chief of state: Yang di-Pertuan Agong
(Paramount Ruler).
Head of government: Prime Minister.
Capital: Kuala Lumpur.
Official language: Malay.
Official religion: Islam.
Monetary unit: 1 ringgit, or Malaysian
dollar (M$) = 100 cents; valuation
(Oct. 10, 1988) 1 U.S.$ = M$2.69;
1 £ = M$4.60.

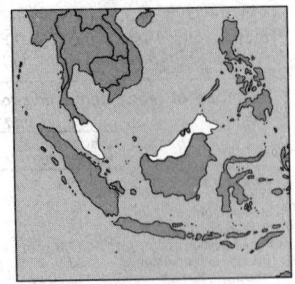

Area and population

Regions States	Capitals	area sq mi	area sq km	population 1987 estimate
East Malaysia				
Sabah	Kota Kinabalu	28,425	73,620	1,322,900[2]
Sarawak	Kuching	48,050	124,449	1,550,000
West Malaysia				
Johor	Johor Baharu	7,331	18,986	1,963,600
Kedah	Alor Setar	3,639	9,426	1,325,700
Kelantan	Kota Baharu	5,769	14,943	1,116,400
Melaka	Melaka	637	1,650	548,800
Negeri Sembilan	Seremban	2,565	6,643	679,000
Pahang Darul Makmur	Kuantan	13,886	35,965	978,100
Perak	Ipoh	8,110	21,005	2,107,800
Perlis	Kangar	307	795	175,600
Pulau Pinang	Pinang	398	1,031	1,087,000
Selangor Darul Ehsan	Shah Alam	3,072	7,956	1,830,800
Terengganu	Kuala Terengganu	5,002	12,955	683,900
Federal Territories				
Kuala Lumpur	—	94	243	1,158,200
Labuan	—	35	91	2
TOTAL LAND AREA		127,320	329,758	16,527,800
INLAND WATER		264	684	
TOTAL AREA		127,584	330,442	

Demography

Population (1988): 16,965,000.
Density (1988): persons per sq mi 133.3, persons per sq km 51.4.
Urban–rural (1985): urban 38.2%; rural 61.8%.
Sex distribution (1987): male 50.39%; female 49.61%.
Age breakdown (1986): under 15, 37.8%; 15–29, 29.2%; 30–44, 17.5%; 45–59, 9.8%; 60–74, 4.5%; 75 and over, 1.2%.
Population projection: (1990) 17,875,000; (2000) 23,212,000.
Doubling time: 28 years.
Ethnic composition (1987): Malay and other indigenous (Orang Asli, or Bumiputera) 60.9%; Chinese 30.4%; Indian 8.2%; other nonindigenous 0.5%.
Religious affiliation (1980): Muslim 52.9%; Buddhist 17.3%; Chinese folk-religionist 11.6%; Hindu 7.0%; Christian 6.4%; other 4.8%.
Major cities (1980): Kuala Lumpur 1,103,200[3]; Ipoh 293,849; Pinang 248,241; Johor Baharu 246,395; Petaling Jaya 207,805.

Vital statistics

Birth rate per 1,000 population (1987): 29.5 (world avg. 26.0).
Death rate per 1,000 population (1987): 5.0 (world avg. 9.9).
Natural increase rate per 1,000 population (1987): 24.5 (world avg. 16.1).
Total fertility rate (avg. births per childbearing woman; 1987): 3.6.
Marriage rate per 1,000 population (1979): 1.7.
Divorce rate per 1,000 population (1979): 0.02.
Life expectancy at birth (1987): male 68.0 years; female 72.7 years.
Major causes of death per 100,000 population (1981)[4]: heart disease 29.1; infectious and parasitic diseases 19.2; malignant neoplasms (cancers) 18.6; cerebrovascular diseases 14.4; pneumonia 10.6.

National economy

Budget (1988). Revenue: M$20,834,000,000 (nontax revenues 34.7%, income tax 30.7%, import duties 11.4%, excise taxes 7.4%). Expenditures: M$21,236,000,000 (debt service 28.1%, social services 28.1%, security 16.0%, administration 10.1%, economic services 9.3%, transfer payments 8.4%).
Tourism (1986): receipts from visitors U.S.$612,000,000; expenditures by nationals abroad U.S.$1,192,000,000.
Production (metric tons except as noted). Agriculture (1987): palm oil 4,400,000, rice 1,642,000, rubber 1,600,000, palm kernels 1,174,000, cacao 150,000, pineapples 131,900, peppers 15,100; livestock (number of live animals; 1986) 2,150,000 pigs, 620,000 cattle, 347,000 goats, 250,000 buffalo, 69,000 sheep, 56,000,000 chickens; roundwood 30,700,000 cu m; fish catch 571,580. Mining and quarrying (1987): bauxite 482,100; iron ore 161,300; copper 120,200; tin concentrates 30,400. Manufacturing (1986): cement 3,176,000; processed palm oil 2,255,000; iron and steel products 362,000; paints 37,062,000 litres; plywood 503,000 cu m; tires 3,846,000 units; television receivers 863,000 units; air conditioners 337,000 units; road motor vehicles 153,000 units. Construction (buildings completed; 1986)[5]: residential 8,809,100 sq m; nonresidential 959,900 sq m. Energy production (consumption): electricity (kW-hr; 1987) 16,633,500,000 (13,936,300,000); coal (metric tons; 1986) none (390,000); petroleum (barrels; 1986) 187,120,000 (55,535,000); petroleum products (metric tons; 1986) 6,998,000 (8,925,000); natural gas (cu m; 1986) 9,469,000,000 (2,096,000,000).
Gross national product (1986): U.S.$29,500,000,000 (U.S.$1,850 per capita).

Structure of gross domestic product and labour force

	1987 in value[6] M$'000,000	% of total value	labour force[7]	% of labour force
Agriculture	12,476	21.1	2,055,600	35.3
Mining	6,439	10.9	56,000	1.0
Manufacturing	13,080	22.2	845,100	14.5
Construction	2,202	3.7	355,800	6.1
Public utilities	1,109	1.9	8	8
Transp. and commun.	4,063	6.9	279,200	4.8
Trade	6,265	10.6	8	8
Finance	5,164	8.8	109,500	1.9
Pub. admin., defense	7,289	12.3	852,300	14.6
Services	1,407	2.4	1,266,000[8]	21.8[8]
Other	−467[9]	−0.8[9]	...	...
TOTAL	59,027	100.0	5,819,500	100.0

Public debt (external, outstanding; 1986): U.S.$16,758,800,000.
Population economically active (1985): total 5,575,900; activity rate of total population 35.6% (participation rates: over age 15, 58.8%; female [1980] 33.6%; unemployed [1987] 8.7%).

Price index (1980 = 100)

	1981	1982	1983	1984	1985	1986	1987
Consumer price index	109.7	116.1	120.4	125.1	125.5	126.4	127.8

Household income and expenditure. Average household size (1980) 5.2; annual income per household (1984): M$13,140; sources of income: n.a.; expenditure (1978): food 37.1%, transportation 18.0%, housing 10.6%, household durable goods 7.7%, recreation 6.0%, clothing and footwear 5.7%, health 2.2%.
Land use (1985): forested 61.1%; meadows and pastures 0.1%; agricultural and under permanent cultivation 13.3%; other 25.5%.

Foreign trade[10]

Balance of trade (current prices)

	1982	1983	1984	1985	1986	1987
M$'000,000	+1,961	+5,028	+8,954	+10,664	+10,480	+11,864
% of total	3.6%	8.3%	13.1%	16.2%	17.1%	17.1%

Imports (1987): M$31,983,000,000 (thermionic valves and tubes 17.8%, petroleum products 5.0%, steel plates and sheets 2.4%, grain 2.1%, crude petroleum 1.5%, raw beet and cane sugar 1.0%). *Major import sources:* Japan 21.7%; U.S. 18.7%; Singapore 14.8%; U.K. 4.3%; West Germany 4.2%; Australia 4.1%.
Exports (1987): M$45,176,000,000 (thermionic valves and tubes 15.3%, crude petroleum 13.9%, sawn logs and timber 13.0%, natural rubber 8.7%, palm oil 7.2%, liquefied natural gas 3.9%). *Major export destinations:* Japan 19.5%; Singapore 18.2%; U.S. 16.6%; South Korea 5.3%; The Netherlands 3.5%; West Germany 3.4%.

Transport and communications

Transport. Railroads (1986): track length 1,381 mi, 2,222 km; passenger-mi 850,363,000[11], passenger-km 1,368,530,000[11]; short ton-mi cargo 714,000,000[11], metric ton-km cargo 1,042,000,000[11]. Roads (1986): total length 24,276 mi, 39,069 km (paved 65%). Vehicles (1986): passenger cars 1,453,561; trucks and buses 330,087. Merchant marine (1987): vessels (100 gross tons and over) 498; total deadweight tonnage 2,388,253. Air transport (1987): passenger-km 7,604,000,000; metric ton-km cargo 354,720,000; airports (1988) with scheduled flights 35.
Communications. Daily newspapers (1985): total number 42; circulation 1,670,000[12]; circulation per 1,000 population 109[12]. Radio (1985): 6,600,000 receivers (1 per 2.4 persons). Television (1987): 1,658,566 receivers[13] (1 per 10 persons). Telephones (1987): 1,380,957 (1 per 12 persons).

Education and health

Education (1987)

	schools	teachers	students	student/ teacher ratio
Primary (age 7–12)	6,691	102,356	2,274,452	22.2
Secondary (age 13–19)	1,165	60,390	1,302,048	21.6
Voc., teacher tr.	54	1,969	23,145	11.8
Higher[14]	42	10,347	109,545	10.6

Educational attainment (1980). Percent of population age 25 and over having: no formal schooling 36.6%; primary education 42.1%; secondary 19.4%; higher 1.9%. *Literacy* (1980): total population age 15 and over literate 5,719,358 (72.6%); males 3,195,031 (82.2%); females 2,524,327 (63.2%).
Health (1986): physicians 5,394 (1 per 2,986 persons); hospital beds 32,960 (1 per 489 persons); infant mortality rate (1987) live births 14.6.
Food (1984–86): daily per capita caloric intake 2,723 (vegetable products 84%, animal products 16%); (1983) 111% of FAO minimum.

Military

Total active duty personnel (1987): 113,000 (army 79.7%, navy 9.7%, air force 10.6%). *Military expenditure as percent of GNP* (1985): 3.8% (world 6.1%); per capita expenditure U.S.$78.

[1]Includes 43 nonelective seats. [2]Includes Labuan federal territory. [3]1985. [4]Medically certified deaths only. [5]Results of the Central Bank Survey of four major towns: Kuala Lumpur, Shah Alam, Kelang, and Seberang Prai. [6]At constant prices of 1978. [7]Employed only. [8]Services includes public utilities and trade. [9]Includes import duties and bank service charges. [10]Import figures are f.o.b. in balance of trade and c.i.f. for commodities and trading partners. [11]Peninsular Malaysia and Singapore; 1985. [12]1984. [13]Licenses. [14]1986.

Maldives

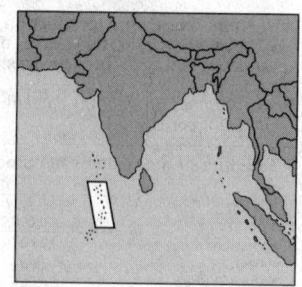

Official name: Divehi Jumhuriyya (Republic of Maldives).
Form of government: republic with one legislative house (People's Council [48[1]]).
Head of state and government: President.
Capital: Male.
Official language: Divehi.
Official religion: Islam.
Monetary unit: 1 Maldivian Rufiyaa (Rf) = 100 laaris; valuation (Oct. 10, 1988) 1 U.S.$ = Rf 10.08; 1 £ = Rf 17.27.

Structure of gross domestic product and labour force

	1986 in value Rf '000[3]	1986 % of total value	1985 labour force	1985 % of labour force
Agriculture[4]	175,500	27.1	36,000	45.5
Mining	7,100	1.1	...	...
Manufacturing }	28,600	4.4	19,400	24.5
Public utilities }			400	0.5
Construction	52,600	8.1	4,700	5.9
Transportation and communications	37,000	5.7	4,800	6.1
Trade	58,100	9.0	2,500	3.2
Pub. admin., defense	125,300	19.3 }		
Finance	29,100	4.5 }	11,300	14.3
Services }	134,700	20.8 }		
Other }				
TOTAL	648,000	100.0	79,100	100.0

Population economically active (1985): total 79,100; activity rate of total population 43.2% (participation rates [1980]: ages 15–59, 79.8%; female 38.8%; unemployed, n.a.).
Land use (1985): forested 3.3%; meadows and pastures 3.3%; agricultural and under permanent cultivation 10.0%; built-on, wasteland, and other 83.4%.

Area and population[2]

Administrative atolls	Capitals	area sq mi	area sq km	population 1985 census
Haa-Alifu	Dhidhdhoo	...	...	9,891
Haa-Dhaalu	Nolhivaranfaru	...	...	10,848
Shaviyani	Farukolhu Funadhoo	...	...	7,529
Noonu	Manadhoo	...	...	6,874
Raa	Ugoofaaru	...	...	9,516
Baa	Eydhafushi	...	...	6,945
Lhaviyani	Naifaru	...	...	6,402
Kaafu	Male	...	...	54,908
Alifu	Mahibadhoo	...	...	7,695
Vaavu	Felidhoo	...	...	1,423
Meemu	Muli	...	...	3,493
Faafu	Magoodhoo	...	...	2,148
Dhaalu	Kudahuvadhoo	...	...	3,576
Thaa	Veymandhoo	...	...	6,942
Laamu	Hithadhoo	...	...	7,158
Gaafu-Alifu	Viligili	...	...	6,081
Gaafu-Dhaalu	Thinadhoo	...	...	8,870
Gnyaviyani	Foah Mulah	...	...	6,189
Seenu	Hithadhoo	...	...	14,965
TOTAL		115	298	181,453

Demography

Population (1988): 202,000.
Density (1988): persons per sq mi 1,756.5, persons per sq km 677.9.
Urban–rural (1985): urban 25.5%; rural 74.5%.
Sex distribution (1986): male 51.84%; female 48.16%.
Age breakdown (1985): under 15, 44.4%; 15–29, 27.0%; 30–44, 13.5%; 45–59, 11.2%; 60 and over, 3.9%.
Population projection: (1990) 216,000; (2000) 300,000.
Doubling time: 22 years.
Ethnic composition: the majority is principally of Sinhalese and Dravidian extraction; Arab, African, and Negrito influences are also present.
Religious affiliation: virtually 100% Sunnī Muslim.
Major cities (1985): Male 46,334.

Vital statistics

Birth rate per 1,000 population (1987): 42.8 (world avg. 26.0); legitimate, n.a.; illegitimate, n.a.
Death rate per 1,000 population (1987): 10.4 (world avg. 9.9).
Natural increase rate per 1,000 population (1987): 32.4 (world avg. 16.1).
Total fertility rate (avg. births per childbearing woman; 1987): 6.4.
Marriage rate per 1,000 population: n.a.
Divorce rate per 1,000 population: n.a.
Life expectancy at birth (1987): male 58.0 years; female 59.0 years.
Major causes of death per 100,000 population: n.a.; however, waterborne diseases (including gastroenteritis, cholera, and typhoid fever) are principal health problems, as are malaria, shigellosis, filariasis, leprosy, and tuberculosis.

National economy

Budget (1985). Revenue: Rf 177,318,000 (import duties 29.4%, tourism 21.7%, civil aviation 9.9%, state trading organization profits 6.8%, foreign aid 5.4%). Expenditures: Rf 199,340,000 (main airport 16.2%, education 11.2%, defense 9.9%, home office and social services 6.9%, health 6.7%, finance 4.7%, atolls administration 4.6%, Islamic centre 4.6%, reclamation 4.3%).
Public debt (external, outstanding; 1986) U.S.$59,800,000.
Production (metric tons except as noted). Agriculture, forestry, fishing (1986): vegetables and melons 18,000, coconuts 12,000, roots and tubers 9,000 (including cassava, sweet potatoes, and yams), fruits excluding melons 8,000, copra 2,000; fish catch 45,816, of which skipjack tuna 32,000, yellow-fin tuna 5,321. Mining and quarrying: coral for construction materials. Manufacturing: details n.a.; however, major industries include boat building and repairing, coir yarn and mat weaving, coconut and fish processing, lacquer work, garment manufacturing, and handicrafts. Construction: n.a. Energy production (consumption): electricity (kW-hr; 1986) 13,000,000 (13,000,000); coal, none (n.a.); petroleum products (metric tons; 1986) none (26,000); natural gas, none (n.a.).
Tourism: receipts from visitors (1986) U.S.$42,000,000; expenditures by nationals abroad (1983) U.S.$3,000,000.
Household income and expenditure. Average household size (1985) 6.1; income per household: n.a.; sources of income: n.a.; expenditure: n.a.
Gross national product (at current market prices; 1986): U.S.$60,000,000 (U.S.$310 per capita).

Foreign trade[5]

Balance of trade (current prices)

	1981	1982	1983	1984	1985	1986
Rf '000,000	−35.6	−91.2	−269.9	−217.5	−177.5	−239.3
% of total	21.4%	39.4%	58.7%	46.7%	35.3%	40.5%

Imports (1985): U.S.$47,891,000 (food, beverages, and tobacco 28.6%, of which tobacco and beverages 6.4%, rice 3.3%, sugar and sugar products 1.9%; machinery and transport equipment 17.8%; petroleum products 15.5%; textiles 12.8%; chemicals 6.2%; iron and steel 3.4%; wood and wood products 2.6%). *Major import sources* (1983): Singapore 62.1%; Japan 11.4%; Sri Lanka 7.9%; India 4.5%; Hong Kong 3.1%; United Kingdom 1.9%.
Exports (1985): U.S.$23,027,000 (fresh skipjack tuna 38.2%; clothing and wearing apparel 32.5%; dried skipjack 13.3%; canned fish 10.0%; salted reef fish [including grouper, perch, and snapper] 9.3%; dried shark fins 1.3%). *Major export destinations:* Thailand 29.4%; United States 24.3%; Sri Lanka 20.3%; Japan 10.1%; Canada 7.9%; West Germany 3.2%.

Transport and communications

Transport. Railroads: none. Roads: total length, n.a. Vehicles (1985): passenger cars 336; trucks 338. Merchant marine (1987): vessels (100 gross tons and over) 38; total deadweight tonnage 159,852. Air transport (1985): passenger arrivals 123,609, passenger departures 122,315; cargo loaded 343 metric tons, cargo unloaded 2,391 metric tons; airports (1988) with scheduled flights 2.
Communications. Daily newspapers (1987): total number 2; total circulation 1,500[6]; circulation per 1,000 population 7.7[6]. Radio (1987): total number of receivers 21,198 (1 per 9.2 persons). Television (1987): total number of receivers 3,828 (1 per 51 persons). Telephones (1985): 2,485 (1 per 75 persons).

Education and health

Education (1986)

	schools	teachers	students	student/teacher ratio
Primary (age 6–11)	243	1,138	41,812	36.7
Secondary (age 11–18)	9	291	3,581	12.3
Voc., teacher tr.	10	52	462	8.9
Higher	—	—	—	—

Educational attainment (1977). Percent of population age 25 and over having: no formal schooling or no standard passed 80.2%; primary standard 15.1%; secondary standard 3.9%; postsecondary 0.1%; higher 0.1%; not stated 0.6%. *Literacy* (1982): total population age 15 and over literate 62,365 (81.1%); males literate 31,896 (80.2%); females literate 30,469 (82.0%).
Health (1985): physicians 23 (1 per 7,957 persons); hospital beds[7] 121 (1 per 1,512 persons); infant mortality rate per 1,000 live births (1987) 77.0.
Food (1979–81): daily per capita caloric intake 1,983 (vegetable products 91%, animal products 9%); 90% of FAO recommended minimum requirement.

Military

Total active duty personnel: Maldives maintains a single security force numbering about 700–1,000; it performs both army and police functions.

[1]Includes eight nonelective seats. [2]Maldives is divided into 19 administrative districts corresponding to atoll groups; arrangement shown here is from north to south; total area excludes 34,634 sq mi (89,702 sq km) of tidal waters. [3]At 1984 prices. [4]Primarily fishing. [5]Import figures are f.o.b. (free on board) in balance of trade and c.i.f. (cost, insurance, and freight) for commodities and trading partners. [6]For one daily newspaper only. [7]In government establishments only.

Mali

Official name: République du Mali
(Republic of Mali).
Form of government: unitary
single-party republic with one
legislative house (National Assembly
[82]).
Head of state and government:
President.
Capital: Bamako.
Official language: French.
Official religion: none.
Monetary unit: 1 CFA franc
(CFAF)[1] = 100 centimes; valuation
(Oct. 10, 1988) 1 U.S.$ = CFAF
316.13; 1 £ = CFAF 541.38.

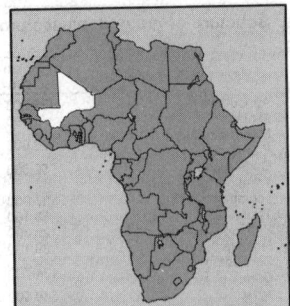

Area and population

		area		population
Regions	Capitals	sq mi	sq km	1987 census
Gao	Gao	124,323	321,996	383,734
Kayes	Kayes	76,356	197,760	1,058,575
Koulikoro	Koulikoro	34,685	89,833	1,180,260
Mopti	Mopti	34,257	88,752	1,261,383
Ségou	Ségou	21,671	56,127	1,328,250
Sikasso	Sikasso	29,529	76,480	1,308,828
Tombouctou[2]	Tombouctou	157,907	408,977	453,032
District				
Bamako	Bamako	103	267	646,163
TOTAL		478,841	1,240,192	7,620,225

Demography

Population (1988): 7,778,000.
Density (1988): persons per sq mi 16.2, persons per sq km 6.3.
Urban–rural (1983): urban 17.3%; rural 82.7%.
Sex distribution (1987): male 48.9%; female 51.1%.
Age breakdown (1983): under 15, 42.7%; 15–29, 26.1%; 30–44, 16.1%; 45–59, 9.4%; 60–74, 4.6%; 75 and over, 1.1%.
Population projection: (1990) 8,047,000; (2000) 9,535,000.
Doubling time: 25 years.
Ethnic composition (1983): Bambara 31.9%; Fulani 13.9%; Senufo 12.0%; Soninke 8.8%; Tuareg 7.3%; Songhai 7.2%; Malinke 6.6%; Dogon 4.0%; Dyula 2.9%; Bobo 2.4%; Arab 1.2%; other 1.8%.
Religious affiliation (1983): Muslim 90%; traditional beliefs 9%; Christian 1%.
Major cities (1976): Bamako 646,163[3]; Ségou 65,400; Mopti 53,300; Sikasso 46,500; Kayes 49,400.

Vital statistics

Birth rate per 1,000 population (1985–86): 50.5 (world avg. 26.0); legitimate, n.a.; illegitimate, n.a.
Death rate per 1,000 population (1985–86): 22.2 (world avg. 9.9).
Natural increase rate per 1,000 population (1985–86): 28.3 (world avg. 16.1).
Total fertility rate (avg. births per childbearing woman; 1985–86): 6.7.
Marriage rate per 1,000 population (1983): 2.8.
Divorce rate per 1,000 population: n.a.
Life expectancy at birth (1985–90): male 42.4 years; female 45.6 years.
Major causes of death per 100,000 population: n.a.; morbidity ([notified cases of illness] percent of all reported illness; 1983): malaria 66.5%; syphilis and gonococcal infections 8.7%; amebiasis and schistosomiasis 8.3%; measles 5.1%; influenza 3.8%.

National economy

Budget (1988). Revenue: CFAF 112,100,000,000 (1986; indirect taxes 35.8%, of which customs duties 15.4%; direct taxes 16.3%; carryover revenue from previous fiscal years 9.7%). Expenditures: CFAF 146,500,000,000 (1986; defense 18.7%, education 12.6%, foreign affairs 3.3%, commerce and finance 2.9%).
Tourism (1986): receipts from visitors U.S.$16,000,000; expenditures by nationals abroad U.S.$25,000,000.
Population economically active (1985): total 2,598,000; activity rate of total population 32.1% (participation rates: ages 15–64, 42.6%; female 16.8%; unemployed 1.3%[4]).

Price and earnings indexes (1980 = 100)

	1981	1982	1983	1984	1985	1986	1987
Consumer price index[5]	112.2	114.8	126.1	141.7	152.7	146.8	125.9
Hourly earnings index[6]	100.0	113.1	113.1	113.1	113.1	152.2	...

Production (metric tons except as noted). Agriculture, forestry, fishing (1986): millet 1,284,000, vegetables (including melons) 252,000, rice 249,000, sugarcane 210,000, corn (maize) 200,000, seed cotton 195,000, cottonseed 122,000, peanuts (groundnuts) in shell 120,000, cassava 76,000, cotton lint 70,000, pulses 60,000, sweet potatoes 57,000, yams 12,000, fruit (excluding melons) 12,000, wheat 2,000, tobacco 1,000; livestock (number of live animals) 5,500,000 sheep, 5,500,000 goats, 4,676,000 cattle, 550,000 asses, 241,000 camels, 60,000 horses, 58,000 pigs, 15,000,000 chickens; roundwood 5,051,000 cu m; fish catch 61,000. Mining and quarrying (1986): gold 16,100 troy oz, salt 4,500. Manufacturing (1986): cotton fibre 70,000; beef and veal 58,000; goat, mutton, and lamb meat 43,000; soft drinks 43,700[7]; cement 26,000; sugar 21,000; molasses 8,400[7]; beer 9,500 hectolitres[8]. Con-

struction: n.a. Energy production (consumption): electricity (kW-hr; 1986) 172,000,000 (172,000,000); coal, none (n.a.); crude petroleum, none (n.a.); petroleum products (metric tons; 1986) none (123,000); natural gas, none (n.a.).
Gross national product (at current market prices; 1986): U.S.$1,330,000,000 (U.S.$170 per capita).

Structure of gross domestic product and labour force

	1985		1982	
	in value CFAF '000,000,000	% of total value	labour force	% of labour force
Agriculture	226.0	47.6	3,355,300	85.9
Mining	48.0	10.1	195,300	5.0
Manufacturing }				
Construction	22.0	4.6		
Public utilities	9	9		
Transp. and commun.	24.0	5.1		
Trade	74.0	15.6	355,400	9.1
Finance	9	9		
Pub. admin., defense	42.0	8.8		
Services	24.0	5.1		
Other	15.0[9]	3.1[9]		
TOTAL	475.0	100.0	3,906,000	100.0

Public debt (external, outstanding; 1986): U.S.$1,565,700,000.
Household income and expenditure. Average household size (1980) 5; average annual income per household: n.a.; sources of income: n.a.; expenditure: n.a.
Land use (1985): forested 7.1%; meadows and pastures 24.6%; agricultural and under permanent cultivation 1.7%; other 66.6%.

Foreign trade

Balance of trade (current prices)

	1982	1983	1984	1985	1986	1987
CFAF '000,000,000	−33.0	−36.9	−35.3	−43.8	−43.1	−21.4
% of total	25.6%	22.7%	17.4%	22.1%	23.9%	12.2%

Imports (1983): U.S.$254,900,000 (machinery, appliances, and transportation equipment 35.5%; petroleum products 19.1%; construction materials 11.8%; food products 10.5%; chemicals and pharmaceutical products 10.5%). *Major import sources* (1985): France 34.3%; Côte d'Ivoire 19.2%; United States 9.1%; West Germany 8.1%; Italy 6.5%; Senegal 4.7%; Spain 3.1%; United Kingdom 2.8%; The Netherlands 2.8%; Belgium–Luxembourg 2.8%; China 2.6%; Hong Kong 1.9%; Japan 1.5%; Pakistan 1.2%; Switzerland 0.5%.
Exports (1983): U.S.$166,800,000 (raw cotton and cotton products 40.9%; live animals 30.4%; salted, dried, or smoked fish 1.2%; peanuts 1.0%). *Major export destinations* (1985): France 18.2%; West Germany 15.3%; Belgium–Luxembourg 12.3%; United Kingdom 6.8%; Portugal 6.5%; Côte d'Ivoire 4.5%; Italy 4.3%; The Netherlands 3.2%; Niger 1.5%.

Transport and communications

Transport. Railroads (1987): route length 401 mi, 646 km; passenger-mi 480,173,000, passenger-km 772,765,000; short ton-mi cargo 213,293,000, metric ton-km cargo 429,334,000. Roads (1987): total length 11,185 mi, 18,000 km (paved 8%). Vehicles (1987): passenger cars 29,436; trucks and buses 7,556. Merchant marine: vessels (100 gross tons and over) none. Air transport (1983): passenger-mi 68,000,000; passenger-km 110,000,000; short ton-mi cargo 411,000, metric ton-km cargo 600,000; airports (1988) with scheduled flights 9.
Communications. Daily newspapers (1985): total number 1; total circulation 40,000; circulation per 1,000 population 4.9. Radio (1986): total number of receivers 300,000 (1 per 25 persons). Television (1987): total number of receivers 900 (1 per 8,497 persons). Telephones (1984): 9,537 (1 per 760 persons).

Education and health

Education (1982–83)

	schools	teachers	students	student/ teacher ratio
Primary (age 6–14)	1,558	10,912	348,373	31.9
Secondary (age 15–17)	20	3,870	64,148	16.6
Voc., teacher tr.	11	890	12,612	14.2
Higher	7	499	5,792	11.6

Educational attainment (1976). Percent of adult population age 25 and over having: no formal schooling 95.4%; primary education 3.8%; secondary 0.6%; postsecondary and higher 0.2%. *Literacy* (1980): total population age 15 and over literate 361,800 (10.1%); males literate 329,200 (18.6%); females literate 32,600 (1.8%).
Health (1983): physicians 283 (1 per 26,879 persons); hospital beds 4,215 (1 per 1,805 persons); infant mortality rate per 1,000 live births (1985–86) 169.
Food (1984–86): daily per capita caloric intake 2,021 (vegetable products 93%, animal products 7%); (1983) 68% of FAO recommended minimum.

Military

Total active duty personnel (1987): 7,350 (army 93.9%, navy 1.0%, air force 5.1%). *Military expenditure as percent of GNP* (1985): 2.5% (world 6.1%); per capita expenditure U.S.$4.

[1]In June 1984, the Mali franc (MF) was replaced by the CFA franc at the rate of 1 CFA franc = 2 Mali francs; older data may be reported in Mali francs. [2]Area for Tombouctou region is estimated as a residue between total reported area and the remainder of the regions. [3]1987 census. [4]Urban areas, estimated. [5]Food index for Bamako only. [6]Minimum hourly wages of industrial workers. [7]1985. [8]1983. [9]Other includes Finance and Public utilities.

Malta

Official name: Repubblika ta' Malta (Maltese); Republic of Malta (English).
Form of government: unitary multiparty republic with one legislative house (House of Representatives [69[1]]).
Chief of state: President.
Head of government: Prime Minister.
Capital: Valletta.
Official languages: Maltese; English.
Official religion: Roman Catholicism.
Monetary unit: 1 Maltese lira (Lm) = 100 cents = 1,000 mils; valuation[2] (Oct. 10, 1988) 1 Lm = U.S.$2.94 = £1.69.

Area and population

Census regions[3]	area		population
	sq mi	sq km	1988 estimate[4]
Gozo and Comino	27	70	25,162
Inner Harbour	6	15	101,043
Northern	30	78	32,083
Outer Harbour	12	32	99,320
South Eastern	20	53	43,179
Western	27	69	44,849
TOTAL	122	316[5]	345,636

Demography

Population (1988): 347,000.
Density (1988): persons per sq mi 2,844.3, persons per sq km 1,098.1.
Urban–rural (1985): urban 85.3%; rural 14.7%.
Sex distribution (1988): male 49.29%; female 50.71%.
Age breakdown (1988): under 15, 23.9%; 15–29, 22.5%; 30–44, 24.2%; 45–59, 14.9%; 60–74, 10.6%; 75 and over, 3.9%.
Population projection: (1990) 351,000; (2000) 368,000.
Doubling time: 98 years.
Ethnic composition (1980): Maltese 95.7%; British 2.1%; other 2.2%.
Religious affiliation (1980): Roman Catholic 97.3%; Anglican 1.2%; other 1.5%.
Major cities (1988): Birkirkara 20,490; Qormi 18,586; Hamrun 13,632; Sliema 13,604; Valletta 9,239.

Vital statistics

Birth rate per 1,000 population (1987): 15.4 (world avg. 26.0); legitimate 98.8%; illegitimate 1.2%.
Death rate per 1,000 population (1987): 8.4 (world avg. 9.9).
Natural increase rate per 1,000 population (1987): 7.0 (world avg. 16.1).
Total fertility rate (avg. births per childbearing woman; 1980–85): 2.0.
Marriage rate per 1,000 population (1987): 7.1.
Divorce rate per 1,000 population: n.a.
Life expectancy at birth (1987): male 72.5 years; female 77.0 years.
Major causes of death per 100,000 population (1987): diseases of the circulatory system 533.2; malignant neoplasms (cancers) 155.8; diseases of the respiratory system 46.8%; endocrine, nutritional, and metabolic diseases of the blood and blood-forming organs 21.5; accidents, poisonings, and violence 18.0; diseases of the digestive system 16.8.

National economy

Budget (1987). Revenue: Lm 221,160,000 (national insurance and Central Bank contributions 52.8%, customs and excise taxes 21.2%, income tax 19.4%, licenses and fees 4.3%). Expenditures[6]: Lm 208,739,000 (national insurance benefits 27.1%, health 11.3%, education 8.8%).
Public debt (1986): U.S.$33,357,000.
Production (value added in Lm except where noted). Agriculture, forestry, fishing (1983): vegetables 7,912,000 (of which tomatoes 2,751,000, melons 387,000, onions 223,000), cereals 2,417,000 (of which wheat 929,000, barley 333,000), fruits 1,900,000 (of which citrus fruits 731,000, strawberries 553,-000), potatoes 1,617,000; livestock (number of live animals; 1983) 53,366 pigs, 12,794 cattle, 3,395 sheep, 1,062,900 chickens; fish catch (metric tons; 1986) 1,067. Mining and quarrying (1985): quarrying 714,000. Manufacturing (1985): textiles and wearing apparel 38,138,000, of which clothing 30,193,000, footwear 4,061,000, textiles 3,884,000; machinery and transport equipment 23,409,000; food and beverages 22,184,000; printing and publishing 9,333,000; wood, cork, and furniture 4,574,000; chemicals 3,756,000; tobacco and tobacco products 3,524,000; plastics 2,085,000. Construction (1985): 17,055,000. Energy production (consumption): electricity (kW-hr; 1986) 850,000,000 (850,000,000); coal (metric tons; 1986) none (146,000); crude petroleum, none (n.a.); petroleum products (metric tons; 1986) none (318,000); natural gas, none (n.a.).
Population economically active (1986): total 123,608; activity rate of total population 36.0% (participation rates: ages 15–64, n.a.; female 24.4%; unemployed 6.9%).

Price and earnings indexes (1980 = 100)

	1981	1982	1983	1984	1985	1986	1987
Consumer price index	111.5	118.0	117.0	116.5	116.2	118.5	119.0
Annual earnings index	108.7	120.2	...	...	...	...	...

Household income and expenditure. Average household size (1982) 3.6; average annual income per household Lm 4,736 (U.S.$11,399); sources of income (1986): wages and salaries 51.4%, professional and unincorpo-

rated enterprises 18.7%, transfer payments 14.7%, property income 12.1%; expenditure (1986): food and beverages 32.0%, transportation and communications 15.0%, clothing and footwear 9.1%, household furnishings and operations 8.8%, recreation, entertainment, and education 6.2%, housing 6.0%, health 3.6%, tobacco 3.3%.
Tourism (1986): receipts from visitors U.S.$150,000,000; expenditures by nationals abroad U.S.$33,000,000.
Gross national product (1986): U.S.$1,240,000,000 (U.S.$3,470 per capita).

Structure of gross domestic product and labour force

	1986			
	in value Lm '000	% of total value	labour force	% of labour force
Agriculture	20,419	4.4	3,291	2.7
Manufacturing	134,676	29.3	34,708	28.1
Mining	18,869	4.1	1,046	0.8
Construction			5,600	4.5
Public utilities	7	7	1,575	1.3
Transportation and communications	26,240	5.7	8,193	6.6
Trade	66,147	14.4	11,936	9.7
Finance	61,255[8]	13.3[8]	3,603	2.9
Pub. admin., defense	97,021[7]	21.1[7]	31,279	25.3
Services	35,639	7.7	13,878	11.2
Other	...	...	8,499[9]	6.9[9]
TOTAL	460,266	100.0	123,608	100.0

Land use (1983): agricultural and under permanent cultivation 41.2%; other (infertile clay soil with underlying limestone) 58.8%.

Foreign trade

Balance of trade (current prices)

	1982	1983	1984	1985	1986	1987
Lm '000,000	−123.8	−128.1	−149.1	−114.1	−167.6	−184.3
% of total	26.8%	28.9%	29.1%	21.8%	31.7%	30.6%

Imports (1987): Lm 392,876,000 (manufactured articles, machinery, and transport equipment 41.2%, of which machinery and transport equipment 32.6%; semimanufactured goods 26.7%; food and live animals 10.6%; chemicals and chemical products 7.8%; mineral fuels 6.6%; beverages and tobacco 2.2%; nonfuel materials 1.9%). *Major import sources:* Italy 19.0%; West Germany 17.4%; United Kingdom 17.2%; United States 10.7%; France 3.5%; The Netherlands 3.2%; Australia 0.4%.
Exports (1987): Lm 208,589,000 (manufactured articles, machinery, and transport equipment 80.9%, of which machinery and transport equipment 28.8%; semimanufactured goods 12.1%; beverages and tobacco 2.4%; food and live animals 2.2%; chemicals and chemical products 1.5%; nonfuel materials 0.8%). *Major export destinations:* West Germany 33.8%; Italy 15.8%; United Kingdom 14.9%; Libya 9.7%; United States 8.4%; Belgium–Luxembourg 1.8%.

Transport and communications

Transport. Railroads: none. Roads (1986): total length 909 mi, 1,463 km (paved 93%). Vehicles (1986): passenger cars 85,598; trucks and buses 17,-824. Merchant marine (1987): vessels (100 gross tons and over) 271; total deadweight tonnage 2,852,641. Air transport (1986): passenger-mi 462,000,-000, passenger-km 744,000,000; short ton-mi cargo 3,049,000, metric ton-km cargo 4,452,000; airports (1988) with scheduled flights 1.
Communications. Daily newspapers (1986): total number 4; total circulation 81,000; circulation per 1,000 population 235. Radio (1985): 92,363 receivers (1 per 3.6 persons). Television (1986): 127,633 receivers (1 per 2.7 persons). Telephones (1986): 140,424 (1 per 2.4 persons).

Education and health

Education (1986–87)

	schools	teachers	students	student/ teacher ratio
Primary (age 5–13)	210[10]	3,776[10]	36,322	...
Secondary (age 11–20)	10	10	21,248	...
Voc., teacher tr.	26	661	6,610	10.0
Higher	1	142	1,449	10.2

Educational attainment (1967). Percent of economically active population having: no formal schooling 10.8%; primary education 60.4%; lower secondary 3.4%; upper secondary 17.6%; technical secondary 3.9%; postsecondary and higher 3.9%. *Literacy* (1985): total population age 15 and over literate 250,419 (96.0%); males literate 121,899 (96.2%); females literate 128,520 (95.9%).
Health (1982): physicians 413 (1 per 799 persons); hospital beds 3,142 (1 per 105 persons); infant mortality rate per 1,000 live births (1987) 7.3.
Food (1984–86): daily per capita caloric intake 2,878 (vegetable products 72%, animal products 28%); 108% of FAO recommended minimum requirement.

Military

Total active duty personnel (1987): 910 (army 100%). *Military expenditure as percent of GNP* (1984): 1.0% (world 5.9%); per capita expenditure U.S.$32.

[1]Normally a 65-member body; however, in the elections of May 9, 1987, 4 additional seats were awarded to the minority party (by seats won), which had obtained a majority of the popular vote. [2]The Maltese lira is tied to the currencies of several principal trading partners. [3]Malta has no first-order administrative subdivisions; data are reported according to census regions. [4]January 1. [5]Detail does not add to total given because of rounding. [6]Breakdown for expenditures is for 1986. [7]Pub. admin., defense includes public utilities. [8]Finance includes income from property. [9]Unemployed only. [10]Multilevel primary and secondary schools include some nursery (preschool) classrooms.

Martinique

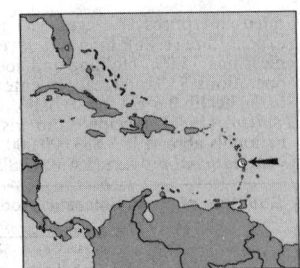

Official name: Département de la Martinique (Department of Martinique).
Political status: overseas department (France) with two legislative houses (General Council [44]; Regional Council [41]).
Chief of state: President of France.
Heads of government: Commissioner of the Republic (for France); President of the General Council (for Martinique); President of the Regional Council (for Martinique).
Capital: Fort-de-France.
Official language: French.
Official religion: none.
Monetary unit: 1 Franc (F) = 100 centimes; valuation (Oct. 10, 1988) 1 U.S.$ = F 6.32; 1 £ = F 10.83.

Area and population		area		population
		sq mi	sq km	1982 census
Arrondissements	**Capitals**			
Fort-de-France	Fort-de-France	141	365	176,749
Le Marin	Le Marin	154	399	78,329
La Trinité	La Trinité	126	327	73,488
TOTAL		421	1,091	328,566[1]

Demography

Population (1988): 336,000.
Density (1988): persons per sq mi 798.1, persons per sq km 308.0.
Urban–rural (1982): urban 57.1%; rural 42.9%.
Sex distribution (1982): male 48.49%; female 51.51%.
Age breakdown (1982): under 15, 28.3%; 15–29, 30.3%; 30–44, 16.2%; 45–59, 13.2%; 60–74, 8.5%; 75 and over, 3.3%; not specified, 0.2%.
Population projection: (1990) 339,000; (2000) 355,000.
Doubling time: 56 years.
Ethnic composition (1983): mulatto 93.7%; French (metropolitan and Martinique white) 2.6%; East Indian 1.7%; other 2.0%.
Religious affiliation (1980): Roman Catholic 91.4%; Protestant (mostly Seventh-day Adventist) 4.7%; syncretist 1.6%; nonreligious 1.2%; other 1.1%.
Major cities (1982): Fort-de-France 96,649; Schoelcher 16,412; Le Lamentin 6,872; Saint-Pierre 4,923.

Vital statistics

Birth rate per 1,000 population (1987): 19.0 (world avg. 26.0); legitimate 34.6%; illegitimate 65.4%.
Death rate per 1,000 population (1987): 6.4 (world avg. 9.9).
Natural increase rate per 1,000 population (1987): 12.6 (world avg. 16.1).
Total fertility rate (avg. births per childbearing woman; 1987): 2.0.
Marriage rate per 1,000 population (1987): 4.6.
Divorce rate per 1,000 population (1987): 1.1.
Life expectancy at birth (1987): male 71.0 years; female 77.0 years.
Major causes of death per 100,000 population (1985): diseases of the circulatory system 234.8, of which cerebrovascular disease 110.4, diseases of pulmonary circulation and other forms of heart disease 74.7; malignant neoplasms (cancers) 129.6; diseases of the digestive system 36.3; diseases of the respiratory system 35.1

National economy

Budget (1988). Revenue: F 1,424,000,000 (general receipts from French central government and local administrative bodies 46.9%, public works subsidies 11.8%, new loans 7.2%, particular health and social service receipts from local administrative bodies 3.2%). Expenditures: F 1,424,000,000 (health and social assistance 41.6%, improvements to public works and property 28.4%, other administrative services 12.4%, debt payments 4.1%).
Public debt (external, outstanding; 1985[2]): U.S.$28,000,000.
Production (metric tons except as noted). Agriculture, forestry, fishing (1987): sugarcane 220,400, bananas 210,200, pineapples 22,500[3], yams 14,000[3], sweet potatoes 8,000[3], plantains 8,000[3], tomatoes 5,000[3], cucumbers 4,000[3], avocados 1,182[4], limes 454[4], pimientos 114[4], flowers and foliage 99[4]; livestock (number of live animals; 1986) 87,000 sheep, 45,000 pigs, 45,000 goats, 41,000 cattle; roundwood 11,000 cu m[5]; fish catch (1986) 4,038. Mining and quarrying (1985): pumice 165,000; sand and gravel for local construction. Manufacturing (1987): petroleum products 438,000[3]; cement 215,000; sugar 6,400; pineapple compote 1,740; pineapple juice 1,430; rum 99,700 hectolitres; other products include clothing, fabricated metals, and yawls and sails. Construction (buildings authorized; 1987): residential, n.a.; nonresidential 115,000 sq m. Energy production (consumption): electricity (kW-hr; 1987) 536,000,000 (461,000,000); coal, none (none); crude petroleum (barrels; 1986) none (3,298,000); petroleum products (metric tons; 1986) 438,000 (213,000); natural gas, none (none).
Household income and expenditure. Average household size (1982) 3.8; income per household (1979) F 70,009 (U.S.$17,415); sources of income (1979): wages and salaries 74.2%, rent 4.8%, other 21.0%; expenditure (1979): food and beverages 34.8%, of which food away from home 8.6%; health 16.1%; clothing and footwear 10.2%; transportation and communications 9.7%; household furnishings 8.1%; housing 5.3%; other 15.8%.

Gross domestic product (at current market prices; 1985): U.S.$1,400,000,000 (U.S.$4,280 per capita).

Structure of gross domestic product and labour force				
	1982			
	in value F '000,000	% of total value	labour force	% of labour force
Agriculture	720	8.1	9,844	7.5
Mining	552	6.2	1,853	1.4
Manufacturing			4,001	3.1
Construction	324	3.6	7,832	6.0
Public utilities	96	1.1	1,006	0.8
Transportation and communications	390	4.4	5,197	4.0
Trade, restaurants, hotels	1,541	17.4	9,864	7.6
Finance, real estate	630	7.1	17,878	13.7
Pub. admin., defense, services	4,267	48.1	29,382	22.5
Other	354	4.0	43,643[6]	33.4
TOTAL	8,874	100.0	130,500	100.0

Population economically active (1982): total 130,500; activity rate of total population 39.9% (participation rates: ages 15–64, 62.5%; female 44.7%; unemployed [1985] 28.0%).

Price and earnings indexes (1980 = 100)[7]							
	1981	1982	1983	1984	1985	1986	1987
Consumer price index	115.4	126.9	140.6	151.6	161.0	165.2	169.6
Monthly earnings index[8]	113.5	137.0	147.9	168.0	178.9	180.6	184.4

Land use (1985): forested 26.0%; meadows and pastures 31.0%; agricultural and under permanent cultivation 19.0%; other 24.0%.
Tourism (1986): receipts from visitors U.S.$92,000,000; expenditures by nationals abroad, n.a.

Foreign trade

Balance of trade (current prices)						
	1982	1983	1984	1985	1986	1987
F '000,000	–3,819	–4,359	–4,632	–4,593	–4,569	–5,544
% of total	65.3%	62.4%	63.2%	61.2%	60.4%	70.4%

Imports (1987): F 6,707,700,000 (transport equipment 22.2%, food products 19.0%, electrical machinery and equipment 13.4%, mineral fuels 9.4%, chemical products 8.3%, metal manufactures 5.6%). *Major import sources:* France 65.2%; other EEC countries 16.4%; Guadeloupe 2.1%; United States 1.6%.
Exports (1987): F 1,163,300,000 (bananas 48.0%, petroleum products 14.0%, rum 13.4%, fertilizer 2.1%). *Major export destinations:* France 64.6%; Guadeloupe 24.1%; other EEC countries 5.7%.

Transport and communications

Transport. Railroads: none. Roads (1987): total length 1,185 mi, 1,907 km (paved [1985] 85%). Vehicles (1985): passenger cars 135,269; trucks and buses 7,328. Fishing fleet (1985): vessels (100 gross tons and over) 2. Air transport (1987): passenger arrivals 496,846, passenger departures 479,628; cargo unloaded 7,330 metric tons, cargo loaded 5,321 metric tons; airports (1988) with scheduled flights 1.
Communications. Daily newspapers (1986): total number 1; total circulation 30,000; circulation per 1,000 population 90. Radio (1986): total number of receivers 55,000 (1 per 6.0 persons). Television (1987): total number of receivers 45,000 (1 per 7.4 persons). Telephones (1986): 120,200 (1 per 2.8 persons).

Education and health

Education (1983–84)	schools	teachers	students	student/ teacher ratio
Primary (age 6–11)	224	2,024	39,050	19.3
Secondary (age 12–18)	...	2,416	31,912	13.2
Vocational[9]	...	653	15,410	23.6
Higher	1	40	1,220	30

Educational attainment (1982). Percent of population age 25 and over having: no formal schooling 9.8%; primary education 62.7%; secondary 21.2%; higher 6.3%. *Literacy* (1982): total population age 15 and over literate 206,807 (92.5%); males literate 97,538 (91.8%); females literate 109,269 (93.2%).
Health (1985): physicians 472 (1 per 701 persons); hospital beds 4,038 (1 per 82 persons); infant mortality rate per 1,000 live births (1985–87) 11.9.
Food (1984–86): daily per capita caloric intake 2,780 (vegetable products 80%, animal products 20%); 110% of FAO recommended minimum requirement.

Military

Total active duty personnel (1984): 2,800[10].

---

[1]De jure (legally resident, but not necessarily present) census result 326,717. [2]Includes external long-term private debt not guaranteed by the government. [3]1986. [4]Production for export only. [5]1985. [6]Includes 35,936 unemployed. [7]All figures are end of year. [8]Based on minimum-level wage in public administration. [9]1982–83. [10]Includes police.

Mauritania

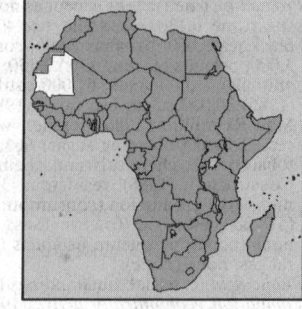

Official name: al-Jumhūrīyah al-Islāmīyah al-Mūrītānīyah (Arabic), République Islamique de Mauritanie (French) (Islamic Republic of Mauritania).
Form of government: military regime.
Head of state and government:
   President heads Military Committee for National Salvation (24).
Capital: Nouakchott.
Official languages: Arabic; French.
Official religion: Islam.
Monetary unit: 1 Mauritanian Ouguiya (UM) = 5 khoums; valuation (Oct. 10, 1988) 1 U.S.\$ = UM 74.14; 1 £ = UM 126.97.

Area and population

		area		population
		sq mi	sq km	1987 estimate[1]
Regions	Capitals			
el-'Açâba	Kiffa	13,900	36,000	160,000
Adrar	Atar	83,100	215,300	70,000
Brakna	Aleg	14,000	37,100	169,000
Dakhlet Nouadhibou	Nouadhibou	11,600	30,000	33,000
Gorgol	Kaédi	5,400	14,000	188,000
Guidimaka	Sélibaby	4,000	10,000	115,000
Hodh ech-Chargui	Néma	64,000	166,000	267,000
Hodh el-Gharbi	'Ayoûn el-'Atroûs	22,000	57,000	140,000
Inchiri	Akjoujt	19,000	49,000	26,000
Tagant	Tidjikdja	36,000	93,000	80,000
Tiris Zemmour	Fdérik	98,600	255,300	37,000
Trarza	Rosso	26,000	67,000	249,000
District				
Nouakchott	Nouakchott	400	1,000	285,000
TOTAL		398,000	1,030,700	1,819,000

Demography

Population (1988): 1,894,000.
Density (1987): persons per sq mi 4.8, persons per sq km 1.8.
Urban–rural (1986): urban 36.1%; rural 63.9%.
Sex distribution (1985): male 49.48%; female 50.52%.
Age breakdown (1985): under 15, 46.4%; 15–29, 26.0%; 30–44, 14.6%; 45–59, 8.4%; 60–74, 3.9%; 75 and over, 0.7%.
Population projection: (1990) 1,999,000; (2000) 2,673,000.
Doubling time: 23 years.
Ethnic composition (1983): Moor 81.5% (about half Arab–Berber and half African Sudanic); Wolof 6.8%; Tukulor 5.3%; Soninke 2.8%; Fulani 1.1%; other 2.5%.
Religious affiliation (1980): Muslim 99.4%; Christian 0.4%; other 0.2%.
Major cities (1987): Nouakchott 600,000; Kaédi 32,000; Nouadhibou 30,000; Zouérate (Zouîrât) 17,500[3].

Vital statistics

Birth rate per 1,000 population (1985–90): 50.0 (world avg. 26.0); legitimate, n.a.; illegitimate, n.a.
Death rate per 1,000 population (1985–90): 19.2 (world avg. 9.9).
Natural increase rate per 1,000 population (1985–90): 30.8 (world avg. 16.1).
Total fertility rate (avg. births per childbearing woman; 1985–90): 6.9.
Marriage rate per 1,000 population (1984)[4]: 1.1.
Divorce rate per 1,000 population (1984)[4]: 0.1.
Life expectancy at birth (1987): male 44.0 years; female 47.0 years.
Morbidity (notified cases of infectious disease per 100,000 population; 1984): enteritis and diarrhea 10,566; conjunctivitis 7,080; malaria 2,897; scarlet fever 2,476; measles 714.0; chicken pox 306.4.

National economy

Budget (1988). Revenue: UM 20,504,000,000 (1984; tax revenue 63.4%). Expenditures: UM 20,504,000,000 (rural development 38.0%, industrial development and fishing 25.0%, infrastructure 21.5%).
Public debt (external, outstanding; 1986): U.S.\$1,637,000,000.
Tourism: receipts from visitors (1986) U.S.\$7,000,000; expenditures by nationals abroad (1983) U.S.\$22,000,000.
Land use (1985): forested 14.6%; meadows and pastures 38.1%; agricultural and under permanent cultivation 0.2%; desert 47.1%.
Production (metric tons except as noted). Agriculture, forestry, fishing (1986): millet 94,000, pulses 24,000, rice 16,000, dates 12,000, vegetables (including melons) 8,000, roots and tubers 6,000 (of which sweet potatoes 2,000, peanuts [groundnuts] 2,000), corn (maize) 1,000; livestock (number of live animals) 3,950,000 goats, 3,000,000 sheep, 1,000,000 cattle, 787,000 camels, 165,000 horses and asses, 4,000,000 chickens; roundwood (1985) 12,000 cu m; fish catch (1985) 57,000. Mining and quarrying (1987): iron ore (gross weight) 9,110,000. Manufacturing (1986): milk 93,000; meat 39,000, of which fresh beef and veal 13,000, fresh mutton and lamb 6,000, goat meat 5,000; hides and skins 4,200; cheese 1,800; butter 700. Construction (1984): 42,478 sq m. Energy production (consumption): electricity (kW-hr; 1986) 92,000,000 (92,000,000); coal (metric tons; 1986) none (5,000); crude petroleum, none (n.a.); petroleum products (metric tons; 1986) none (197,000); natural gas (n.a.).
Gross national product (at current market prices; 1986): U.S.\$760,000,000 (U.S.\$440 per capita).

Structure of gross domestic product and labour force

	1985			
	in value UM '000,000	% of total value	labour force	% of labour force
Agriculture	16,338	30.7	389,000	66.0
Mining	5,975	11.2		
Manufacturing	2,727	5.1		
Public utilities	3,376	6.3	59,000	10.0
Construction				
Transportation and communications	3,881	7.3		
Trade and finance	7,755	14.6	142,000	24.0
Services				
Pub. admin., defense	5,965	11.2		
Other (indirect taxes net of subsidies)	7,213	13.6	...	...
TOTAL	53,230	100.0	590,000	100.0

Population economically active (1985): total 590,000; activity rate of total population 31.2% (participation rates: ages 15–64, 55.7%; female 21.0%; unemployed, n.a.).

Price and earnings indexes (1980 = 100)

	1980	1981	1982	1983	1984	1985	1986
Consumer price index	100.0	119.1	134.1	135.3	144.9	164.6	177.4
Earnings index	...	...	...	...	...	...	...

Household income and expenditure. Average household size (1980) 5.0; income per household: n.a.; sources of income: n.a.; expenditure[4] (1983): food and beverages 61.0%; housing 24.0%; clothing and footwear 5.2%.

Foreign trade

Balance of trade (current prices)

	1981	1982	1983	1984	1985	1986
UM '000,000	+1,178	−530	+4,969	+7,877	+13,129	+10,122
% of total	4.9%	2.1%	18.4%	27.0%	29.4%	24.2%

Imports (1984): UM 10,620,000,000[5] (1983: machinery and transport equipment 40.0%, food 25.0%, crude petroleum and petroleum products 18.6%). *Major import sources:* France 21.9%; Spain 19.8%; West Germany 9.6%; United States 7.6%; Senegal 6.9%; Algeria 6.0%; Thailand 5.7%; China 3.0%; Egypt 3.0%; Italy 2.7%; Belgium–Luxembourg 2.6%; The Netherlands 2.5%; Japan 1.4%; Denmark 1.3%; United Kingdom 1.1%; Canada 0.9%; Côte d'Ivoire 0.8%; India 0.8%; South Korea 0.4%.
Exports (1984): UM 15,982,000,000[5] (fish 50.3%, iron ore 49.7%). *Major export destinations:* Italy 23.9%; Japan 22.1%; Belgium 17.9%; France 15.1%; Spain 7.3%; United Kingdom 5.0%; West Germany 3.2%; Algeria 1.5%; Portugal 1.0%; Senegal 0.9%; Greece 0.9%; Turkey 0.6%; United States 0.4%.

Transport and communications

Transport. Railroads (1984): route length 428 mi, 689 km; passenger-mi 4,350,000, passenger-km 7,000,000; short ton-mi cargo 4,207,000,000, metric ton-km cargo 6,142,000,000. Roads (1985): total length 4,557 mi, 7,335 km (paved 22%). Vehicles (1985): passenger cars 15,017; trucks and buses 2,188. Merchant marine (1987): vessels (100 gross tons and over) 94; total deadweight tonnage 13,878. Air transport[6] (1986): passenger-mi 147,619,000, passenger-km 237,571,000; short ton-mi cargo 26,340,000, metric ton-km cargo 38,455,000; airports (1988) with scheduled flights 9.
Communications. Daily newspapers (1986): total number 1; total circulation, n.a. Radio (1986): total number of receivers 200,000 (1 per 8.5 persons). Television (1987): total number of receivers 1,100 (1 per 1,676 persons). Telephones (1984): 4,827 (1 per 350 persons).

Education and health

Education (1985–86)

	schools	teachers[7]	students	student/ teacher ratio[7]
Primary (age 6–11)	878	2,629	140,871	45.4
Secondary (age 12–17)	44	1,013	34,674	27.6
Voc., teacher tr.	6	372	4,336	9.6
Higher[7]	7	25[8]	4,340	...

Educational attainment, n.a. *Literacy* (1985): total population age 15 and over literate 28.0%; males literate 38.0%; females literate 17.0%.
Health (1984): physicians 170 (1 per 9,547 persons); hospital beds 1,325 (1 per 1,225 persons); infant mortality rate per 1,000 live births 133.0.
Food (1984–86): daily per capita caloric intake 2,283 (vegetable products 68%, animal products 32%); (1983) 92% of FAO recommended minimum requirement.

Military

Total active duty personnel (1987–88): 14,870 (army 96.8%, navy 2.2%, air force 1.0%). *Military expenditure as percent of GNP* (1985): 6.6% (world 6.1%); per capita expenditure U.S.\$25.

[1]January 1. [2]1984. [3]1977. [4]Nouakchott only. [5]1986 Import total UM 14,009,000; Export total UM 25,950,000,000. [6]Includes part of Air Afrique traffic. [7]1983–84. [8]1980–81.

Mauritius

Official name: Mauritius.
Form of government: constitutional monarchy with one legislative house (Legislative Assembly [70[1]]).
Chief of state: British Monarch represented by governor-general.
Head of government: Prime Minister.
Capital: Port Louis.
Official language: English.
Official religion: none.
Monetary unit: 1 Mauritian Rupee (Mau Re; plural Mau Rs) = 100 cents; valuation (Oct. 10, 1988) 1 U.S.$ = Mau Rs 14.05; 1 £ = Mau Rs 24.07.

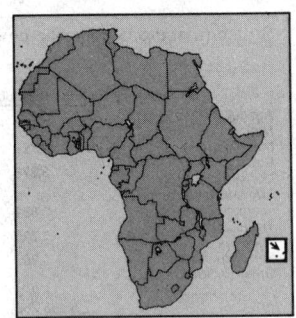

Area and population	area		population
Islands Districts	sq mi	sq km	1987 estimate[2]
Mauritius	720	1,865	1,008,864
Black River	100	259	39,456
Flacq	115	298	113,985
Grand Port	101	262	97,613
Moka	89	230	63,874
Pamplemousses	69	179	95,420
Plaines Wilhems	78	202	312,779
Port Louis	17	44	138,482
Rivière du Rampart	57	148	85,546
Savanne	94	243	61,709
Rodrigues	40	104	36,115
Agalega Saint Brandon	27	71	500
TOTAL	788[3]	2,040	1,045,479

Demography

Population (1988): 1,049,000.
Density (1987): persons per sq mi 1,331.2, persons per sq km 514.2.
Urban–rural (1987)[4]: urban 41.0%; rural 59.0%.
Sex distribution (1987)[4]: male 50.00%; female 50.00%.
Age breakdown (1986)[4]: under 15, 31.3%; 15–29, 31.4%; 30–44, 19.0%; 45–59, 10.8%; 60–74, 6.1%; 75 and over, 1.4%.
Population projection: (1990) 1,068,000; (2000) 1,170,000.
Doubling time: 61 years.
Ethnolinguistic composition (1983): Creole 55.5%; Indian 39.6%; European 3.8%; Chinese 0.6%; other 0.5%.
Religious affiliation (1983)[4]: Hindu 52.5%; Roman Catholic 25.7%; Muslim 12.9%; Protestant 4.4%; Buddhist 0.4%; other 4.1%.
Major cities (1983): Port Louis 148,040; Beau Bassin–Rose Hill 87,520; Quatre Bornes 56,676; Vacoas–Phoenix 56,011; Curepipe 57,613.

Vital statistics

Birth rate per 1,000 population (1986): 18.0 (world avg. 26.0); (1985) legitimate 72.8%, illegitimate 27.2%.
Death rate per 1,000 population (1986): 6.6 (world avg. 9.9).
Natural increase rate per 1,000 population (1986): 11.4 (world avg. 16.1).
Total fertility rate (avg. births per childbearing woman; 1986)[4]: 1.9.
Marriage rate per 1,000 population (1986): 10.3.
Divorce rate per 1,000 population (1986)[4]: 0.6.
Life expectancy at birth (1982–84): male 64.4 years; female 71.2 years.
Major causes of death per 100,000 population (1986): diseases of the circulatory system 286.1; diseases of the respiratory system 61.2; malignant neoplasms (cancers) 51.6; endocrine and metabolic disorders 45.0.

National economy

Budget (1987–88). Revenue: Mau Rs 6,324,000,000 (tax revenue 79.1%, of which import and stamp duties 38.7%, personal and corporate taxes 9.6%; nontax revenue and grants 20.9%). Expenditures: Mau Rs 8,005,000,000 (current expenditure 73.8%, of which debt servicing 25.2%, education 9.0%, social security 6.8%, health 5.2%, police 3.8%; development expenditure 26.2%).
Tourism (1986): receipts from visitors U.S.$88,370,700; expenditures by nationals abroad U.S.$18,900,000[5].
Land use (1985): forested 31.2%; meadows and pastures 3.8%; agricultural and under permanent cultivation 51.5%; other 7.5%.
Gross national product (1986): U.S.$1,240,000,000 (U.S.$1,200 per capita).

Structure of gross domestic product and labour force				
	1987			
	in value Mau Rs '000,000[6]	% of total value	labour force[7]	% of labour force
Agriculture	2,495	13.8	46,200	19.0
Mining	25	0.1	200	0.1
Manufacturing	4,530	25.1	91,800	37.8
Construction	1,015	5.6	6,900	2.8
Public utilities	510	2.8	3,700	1.5
Transportation and communications	1,875	10.5	9,800	4.0
Trade	2,420	13.4	10,500	4.3
Finance	2,435	13.6		
Pub. admin., defense	1,885	10.5	54,700	22.5
Services	830	4.6		
Other	...	...	18,900	7.8
TOTAL	18,020	100.0	242,700	100.0[3]

Production (metric tons except as noted). Agriculture, forestry, fishing (1986): sugarcane 6,130,000, green tea 40,267, potatoes 25,000, tomatoes 9,000, black tea 8,000, bananas 7,000, corn (maize) 5,000, onions 3,000, cabbages 3,000, peanuts (groundnuts) 2,250, tobacco 1,000; livestock (number of live animals) 71,000 goats, 61,000 cattle, 12,000 pigs, 4,000 sheep; roundwood (1985) 30,000 cu m; fish catch (1985) 12,512. Manufacturing (value added, Mau Rs million; 1986): textiles, wearing apparel and footwear 1,241; processed food (including sugar) 665; alcoholic, non-alcoholic beverages and tobacco 162; chemicals and chemical products 144; metal products 109. Construction (1986): residential 357,000 sq m; nonresidential 159,000 sq m. Energy production (consumption): electricity (kW-hr; 1986) 518,000,000 (518,000,000); coal (metric tons; 1986) none (56,000); crude petroleum, none (none); petroleum products (metric tons; 1986) none (232,000); natural gas, none (none).
Public debt (external, outstanding; 1986): U.S.$426,800,000.
Population economically active (1984): total 367,000; activity rate of total population 38.0% (participation rates: over age 15, 58.5%; female 25.9%[8]; unemployed 19.1%).

Price and earnings indexes (1980 = 100)							
	1981	1982	1983	1984	1985	1986	1987
Consumer price index	111.9	124.7	132.9	142.6	152.2	155.0	156.3[9]
Monthly earnings index	114.3	130.5	143.8	153.6	157.0	160.0	166.1[10]

Household income and expenditure. Average household size (1983)[4] 4.7; income per household (1979) Mau Rs 15,540 (U.S.$2,430); sources of income (1984): salaries and wages 53.1%, entrepreneurial income 32.4%, transfer payments 7.3%, interest and dividends 4.3%, other 2.9%; expenditure (1980–81)[11]: food, beverages, and tobacco 50.4, clothing and footwear 10.5%, housing 10.4%, transportation 10.0%, energy 6.4%, health care 3.0%, other 9.3%.

Foreign trade[12]

Balance of trade (current prices)						
	1981	1982	1983	1984	1985	1986
Mau Rs '000,000	−1,260.9	−330.0	−161.6	−482.8	−1,101.8	+310.5
% of total	17.4%	4.0%	1.8%	4.5%	7.3%	1.7%

Imports (1986): Mau Rs 9,090,000,000 (manufactured goods classified chiefly by material 41.8%, machinery and transport equipment 16.8%, food 12.9%, mineral fuels and lubricants 7.9%, chemicals 6.6%, inedible crude materials excluding fuels 4.0%, animal and vegetable oils and fats 1.5%). *Major import sources:* France 13.7%; South Africa 10.0%; United Kingdom 7.5%; Japan 7.0%; China 4.9%; Bahrain 3.5%; Kuwait 3.1%.
Exports (1985): Mau Rs 9,052,000,000 (sugar 39.2%, clothing 44.8%, watches and clocks 2.7%, processed diamonds and synthetic stones 1.9%, fish and fish preparations 1.5%, tea 1.1%, textile yarn and fabric 1.1%). *Major export destinations:* United Kingdom 37.7%; France 23.3%; United States 16.1%; West Germany 7.3%; Italy 2.3%; Réunion 2.3%; Belgium 2.0%.

Transport and communications

Transport. Railroads: none. Roads (1986): total length 1,108 mi, 1,783 km (paved 92%). Vehicles (1986): passenger cars 33,607; trucks and buses 11,433. Merchant marine (1987): vessels (100 gross tons and over) 33; total deadweight tonnage 240,721. Air transport (1986)[13]: passenger-mi 472,591,700, passenger-km 760,564,000; short ton-mi cargo 61,678,000, metric ton-km cargo 90,049,000; airports (1988) with scheduled flights 2.
Communications. Daily newspapers (1987): total number 8; total circulation 77,000; circulation per 1,000 population 74. Radio (1986): 200,000 receivers (1 per 5.2 persons). Television (1987): 128,111 receivers (1 per 8.1 persons). Telephones (1986): 61,881 (1 per 17 persons).

Education and health

Education (1986)	schools	teachers	students	student/ teacher ratio
Primary (age 5–12)	273	6,161	138,765	22.5
Secondary (age 12–20)	125	3,572	68,604	19.2
Voc., teacher tr.[14]	7	69[15]	444	...
Higher[14]	2	184[15]	344	...

Educational attainment (1983). Percent of population age 25 and over having: no formal education 24.2%, incomplete primary 28.1%, primary 23.2%, incomplete secondary 13.1%; secondary 7.7%, higher 3.6%, other 0.1%.
Literacy (1983)[4]: total population age 15 and over literate 501,262 (81.8%); males literate 267,835 (89.0%); females literate 233,427 (74.8%).
Health (1986): physicians 760 (1 per 1,327 persons)[4]; hospital beds 2,825 (1 per 357 persons)[4]; infant mortality rate per 1,000 live births 26.3.
Food (1984–86): daily per capita caloric intake 2,736 (vegetable products 89%, animal products 11%); (1983) 118% of FAO recommended minimum requirement.

Military

Total active duty personnel: none; however, a special 800-man police mobile unit ensures internal security. *Military expenditure as percent of GNP* (1984): 0.3% (world 5.9%); per capita expenditure U.S.$3.

[1]Includes 8 nonelective seats. [2]January 1. [3]Detail does not add to total given because of rounding. [4]Island of Mauritius only. [5]1985. [6]At factor cost. [7]Employed persons in establishments employing 10 or more persons. [8]1983. [9]June. [10]March. [11]Current weights of CPI components; Island of Mauritius only. [12]Import figures are f.o.b. (free on board) in balance of trade and c.i.f. (cost, insurance, and freight) for commodities and trading partners. [13]Air Mauritius only. [14]1984. [15]1982.

Mayotte

Official name: Collectivité Territoriale de Mayotte (Territorial Collectivity of Mayotte).
Political status: overseas dependency of France[1] with one legislative house (General Council [17]).
Chief of state: President of France.
Head of government: Commissioner of the Republic (for France); President of the General Council (for Mayotte).
Capital: Dzaoudzi (Capital designate, Mamoudzou).
Official language: French.
Official religion: none.
Monetary unit: 1 French (metropolitan) franc (F) = 100 centimes; valuation (Oct. 10, 1988) 1 U.S.$ = F 6.32; 1 £ = F 10.83.

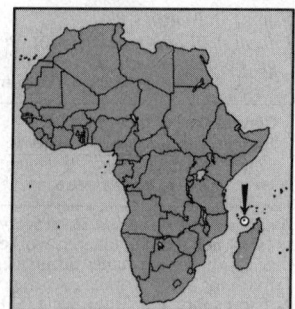

Area and population

Islands Communes	Capitals	area sq mi	area sq km	population 1985 census
Grande Terre				
Acoua	Acoua	4.9	12.6	2,708
Bandraboua	Bandraboua	12.5	32.4	3,533
Bandrele	Bandrele	14.1	36.5	2,974
Boueni	Boueni	5.4	14.1	3,004
Chiconi	Chiconi	3.2	8.3	4,025
Chirongui	Chirongui	10.9	28.3	3,387
Dembeni	Dembeni	15.0	38.8	2,322
Kani-Keli	Kani-Keli	7.9	20.5	2,792
Koungou	Koungou	11.0	28.4	3,479
Mamoudzou	Mamoudzou	16.2	41.9	12,086
Mtsamboro	Mtsamboro	5.3	13.7	3,918
M'tsangamouji	M'tsangamouji	8.4	21.8	3,249
Ouangani	Ouangani	7.3	19.0	2,575
Sada	Sada	4.3	11.2	4,137
Tsingoni	Tsingoni	13.4	34.8	3,007
Petite Terre				
Dzaoudzi-Labattoir	Dzaoudzi	2.6	6.7	5,865
Pamandzi	Pamandzi	1.7	4.3	4,106
TOTAL		144.1	373.2[2]	67,167

Demography

Population (1988): 77,600.
Density (1988): persons per sq mi 538.5, persons per sq km 207.9.
Urban–rural (1978): urban 53.3%; rural 46.7%.
Sex distribution (1985): male 51.26%; female 48.74%.
Age breakdown (1985): under 15, 50.2%; 15–29, 24.7%; 30–44, 13.4%; 45–59, 6.9%; 60–74, 3.4%; 75 and over, 1.4%.
Population projection: (1990) 85,600; (2000) 112,000.
Doubling time: 20 years.
Ethnic composition (1985): Comorian (a mixture of Bantu, Arab, and Malagasy peoples) 96.9%; Europeans 2.5%; other 0.5%.
Religious affiliation (1985): Sunnī Muslim 96.9%; Christian, principally Roman Catholic, 3.0%; other 0.1%.
Major towns (1985): Mamoudzou 7,325; Dzaoudzi 5,425; Pamandzi 4,106; Sada 3,718; Chiconi 3,152.

Vital statistics

Birth rate per 1,000 population (1985): 42.3 (world avg. 29.0); (1978) legitimate (monogamous marriage) 70.8%, legitimate (polygamous marriage) 18.4%, illegitimate 10.8%.
Death rate per 1,000 population (1985): 6.2 (world avg. 11.0).
Natural increase rate per 1,000 population (1985): 36.1 (world avg. 18.0).
Total fertility rate (avg. births per childbearing woman; 1985): 6.7.
Marriage rate per 1,000 population: n.a.; *marital status of adult population* (1985): monogamous marriage 49.1%; unmarried 32.9%; polygamous marriage 10.3%; divorced 4.4%; widowed 3.3%.
Divorce rate per 1,000 population: n.a.
Life expectancy at birth (1987): male 53.0; female 57.0.
Morbidity (percent of reported cases of notifiable infectious disease; 1985): malaria 29.4%; syphilis 25.0%; gonorrhea 24.2%; tuberculosis 5.6%; typhoid 5.6%; leprosy 4.8%.

National economy

Budget (1988). Revenue: F 301,725,000 (subsidies 50.1%, indirect taxes 15.0%, loans 8.3%, direct taxes 3.9%). Expenditures: F 301,725,000 (investments 42.4%, general administrative services 35.4%, debt service 1.6%).
Public debt: n.a.
Tourism: n.a.; estimated arrivals number some 14,000 annually, however.
Production (metric tons except as noted). Agriculture, forestry, fishing (1987): rice 2,300, mangoes 1,500[3], bananas 1,300[3], breadfruit 700[3], citrus fruit 600[3], cassava 500[3], pineapples 200[3], corn (maize) 173, ylang-ylang 22,300 kilograms[4], copra 6,600 kilograms[4,5] vanilla 5,900 kilograms[4], pepper and pimento 1,093 kilograms[4], cloves 1,050 kilograms[4,5], cinnamon 750 kilograms[4]; coconut palm trees (number of producing trees) 350,000; livestock (number of live animals; 1985) 15,000 goats, 3,000 cattle, 1,200 sheep; roundwood, n.a.; fish catch 1,200. Mining and quarrying: negligible. Manufacturing (1987): mostly involves processing of agricultural products for export. Construction (public works authorized in F '000; 1987): res-

idential 51,400; nonresidential 91,300. Energy production (consumption): electricity (installed capacity; 1987) 7,500 kilowatts; coal, none (none); crude petroleum, none (none); petroleum products, none (n.a.); natural gas, none (none).
Gross national product (at current market prices): n.a.

Structure of gross domestic product and labour force

	1985 in value	% of total value	labour force	% of labour force
Agriculture, forestry, and fishing	...	...	12,285	55.0
Mining	...	...	...	...
Manufacturing	...	...	713	3.2
Construction	...	...	1,982	8.9
Public utilities	...	...	137	0.6
Transportation and communications	...	...	570	2.6
Trade	...	...	597	2.7
Finance, insurance, real estate	...	...	895	4.0
Nonmarket services	...	...	2,900	13.0
Other	...	...	2,251[6]	10.1
TOTAL	...	...	22,330	100.0[2]

Population economically active (1985): total 22,330; activity rate of total population 33.4% (participation rates: ages 15–64, 68.9%; female 40.1%; unemployed 8.8%).

Price and earnings indexes (1982 = 100[7,8])

	1982	1983	1984	1985	1986	1987
Consumer price index	108.9	116.6	123.2	132.3	136.0	137.2
Monthly earnings index[9]	106.0	116.9	130.0	140.8	162.7	170.3

Household income and expenditure. Average household size (1985) 5.1; income per household: n.a.; sources of income: n.a.; expenditure (weights of current consumer price index components): food 79.5%, other 20.5%.
Land use (1985): agricultural and under permanent cultivation 64.0%; other 36.0%.

Foreign trade

Balance of trade (current prices)

	1982	1983	1984	1985	1986	1987
F '000,000	−110	−140	−173	−185	−188	−233
% of total	91.1%	90.1%	89.6%	89.1%	85.5%	86.7%

Imports (1987): F 251,003,000 (machinery and apparatus 22.1%; food products 21.2%; mineral fuels 11.3%; transport equipment 9.1%; metals and metal products 9.0%; chemical products 7.2%; wood and wood products 4.1%). *Major import sources:* France 63.0%; South Africa 13.0%; Thailand 5.0%; Bahrain 4.0%; Réunion 3.0%.
Exports (1987): F 17,811,000 (reexports [including rice products, clothing, cigarettes, and chemical products] 67.1%; domestic exports 32.9%, of which ylang-ylang 20.3%, vanilla 12.2%). *Major export destinations:* (domestic exports only)[10]: France 99.0%.

Transport and communications

Transport. Railroads: none. Roads (1984): total length 143 mi, 230 km (paved 49%). Vehicles (1984): 1,528. Merchant marine: n.a. Air transport (1987): passenger arrivals 14,945, passenger departures 14,934; cargo unloaded 483 metric tons, cargo loaded 313 metric tons; airports (1988) with scheduled flights 1.
Communications. Daily newspapers (1986): total number 1; total circulation, n.a. Radio (1986): total number of receivers 30,000 (1 per 2.3 persons). Television: total number of receivers, n.a.[11]. Telephones: (1986)[12]: 1,333 (1 per 54 persons).

Education and health

Education (1984–85)

	schools	teachers	students	student/teacher ratio
Primary (age 6–11)	72	429[13]	15,625[13]	36.4[13]
Secondary (age 12–18) Voc., teacher tr.	3	66	1,374	20.0
Higher	—	—	—	—

Educational attainment (1985). Percent of population age 20 and over having: no formal education 77.3%; some primary 13.3%; lower secondary 5.7%; higher secondary 2.7%; postsecondary and higher 1.0%. *Literacy* (1985): total population age 15 and over literate 10,542 (31.8%).
Health: physicians (1980) 9 (1 per 5,797 persons); hospital beds (1981) 86 (1 per 637 persons); infant mortality rate per 1,000 live births (1984–85) 81.0.
Food: daily per capita caloric intake, n.a.

Military

Total active duty personnel (1985): 300 French troops.

[1]Final status of Mayotte is not yet determined; it is claimed by the Comoros as an integral part of that country. [2]Detail does not add to total given because of rounding. [3]1983. [4]Export production only. [5]1986. [6]Includes 1,966 unemployed. [7]Base period is January 1982. [8]All indexes are for December. [9]Skilled workers. [10]Most reexports are sent to the Comoros. [11]Television transmission began in 1986. [12]Number of telephone lines. [13]1985–86.

Mexico

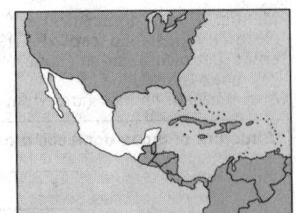

Official name: Estados Unidos Mexicanos (United Mexican States).
Form of government: federal republic with two legislative houses (Senate [64]; Chamber of Deputies [500]).
Chief of state and head of government: President.
Capital: Mexico City.
Official language: Spanish.
Official religion: none.
Monetary unit: 1 peso (Mex$) = 100 centavos; valuation (Oct. 10, 1988)
1 U.S.$ = Mex$2,289;
1 £ = Mex$3,919.

Area and population

States	Capitals	area sq mi	area sq km	population 1988 estimate
Aguascalientes	Aguascalientes	2,112	5,471	684,100
Baja California Norte	Mexicali	26,997	69,921	1,388,300
Baja California Sur	La Paz	28,369	73,475	315,100
Campeche	Campeche	19,619	50,812	592,900
Chiapas	Tuxtla Gutiérrez	28,653	74,211	2,518,500
Chihuahua	Chihuahua	94,571	244,938	2,238,300
Coahuila	Saltillo	57,908	149,982	1,905,900
Colima	Colima	2,004	5,191	419,300
Durango	Durango	47,560	123,181	1,384,400
Guanajuato	Guanajuato	11,773	30,491	3,541,600
Guerrero	Chilpancingo	24,819	64,281	2,559,800
Hidalgo	Pachuca	8,036	20,813	1,822,000
Jalisco	Guadalajara	31,211	80,836	5,198,000
México	Toluca	8,245	21,355	11,565,100
Michoacán	Morelia	23,138	59,928	3,377,500
Morelos	Cuernavaca	1,911	4,950	1,258,200
Nayarit	Tepic	10,417	26,979	846,100
Nuevo León	Monterrey	25,067	64,924	3,148,500
Oaxaca	Oaxaca	36,275	93,952	2,650,100
Puebla	Puebla	13,090	33,902	4,067,400
Querétaro	Querétaro	4,420	11,449	952,600
Quintana Roo	Chetumal	19,387	50,212	393,200
San Luis Potosí	San Luis Potosí	24,351	63,068	2,020,500
Sinaloa	Culiacán	22,521	58,328	2,367,300
Sonora	Hermosillo	70,291	182,052	1,799,300
Tabasco	Villahermosa	9,756	25,267	1,299,300
Tamaulipas	Ciudad Victoria	30,650	79,384	2,266,500
Tlaxcala	Tlaxcala	1,551	4,016	665,500
Veracruz	Jalapa	27,683	71,699	6,658,500
Yucatán	Mérida	14,827	38,402	1,302,500
Zacatecas	Zacatecas	28,283	73,252	1,251,300
Federal District				
Distrito Federal	—	571	1,479	10,263,600
TOTAL		756,066	1,958,201	82,721,200

Demography

Population (1988): 82,721,000.
Density (1988): persons per sq mi 109.4; persons per sq km 42.2.
Urban–rural (1986): urban 69.7%; rural 30.3%.
Sex distribution (1988): male 50.15%; female 49.85%.
Age breakdown (1988): under 15, 37.5%; 15–29, 31.1%; 30–44, 16.9%; 45–59, 9.0%; 60–74, 4.3%; 75 and over, 1.2%.
Population projection: (1990) 85,784,000; (2000) 100,039,000.
Doubling time: 26 years.
Ethnic composition (1981): mestizo 55.0%; Amerindian 29.0%; Caucasian 15.0%; black 0.5%; other 0.5%.
Religious affiliation (1980): Roman Catholic 92.6%; Protestant (including Evangelical) 3.3%; Jewish 0.1%; other 0.9%; none 3.1%.
Major cities (1980): Mexico City 8,831,079; Guadalajara 1,626,152; Ciudad Netzahualcóyotl 1,341,230; Monterrey 1,090,009; Puebla 835,759; León 593,002; Juárez 544,496; Tijuana 429,500; Mérida 400,142; Chihuahua 385,603.
Place of birth (1980): 98.4% native-born; 1.6% foreign-born and unknown.
Mobility (1970). Population living in the same state as in 1960: 87.2%; different state 12.8%.
Households. Total households (1983) 14,795,600; distribution by size (1980): 1 person 5.4%, 2 persons 10.2%, 3 persons 12.4%, 4 persons 14.3%, 5 persons 13.5%, 6 persons 11.7%, 7 or more persons 32.5%. Family households (1983): 13,996,700 (94.6%); nonfamily 798,900 (5.4%).
Immigration (1985): permanent immigrants admitted 66,842.
Emigration (1987): legal immigrants to the United States 72,351.

Vital statistics

Birth rate per 1,000 population (1987): 32.0 (world avg. 26.0); (1983) legitimate 72.5%, illegitimate 27.5%.
Death rate per 1,000 population (1987): 5.1 (world avg. 9.9).
Natural increase rate per 1,000 population (1987): 26.9 (world avg. 16.1).
Total fertility rate (avg. births per childbearing woman; 1986): 3.4.
Marriage rate per 1,000 population (1985): 7.1.
Divorce rate per 1,000 population (1982): 0.4.
Life expectancy at birth (1988): male 65.9 years; female 72.3 years.
Major causes of death per 100,000 population (1983): diseases of the circulatory system 96.0; accidents 81.2; infectious and parasitic diseases 71.5; diseases of the respiratory system 65.8; diseases of the digestive system 45.2; malignant neoplasms (cancers) and nonmalignant tumours 43.4; conditions originating in the perinatal period 32.0; ill-defined conditions 30.0.

Social indicators

Educational attainment (1980). Percent of population age 25 and over having: no primary education 38.0%; some primary 31.7%; completed primary 17.3%; some secondary 8.1%; some postsecondary 4.9%.

Distribution of income (1983)

percent of household income by quintile

1	2	3	4	5 (highest)
4.0	8.8	14.2	22.4	50.6

Quality of working life. Average workweek (1984): 45.8 hours. Annual rate (1984) per 100,000 insured workers for: temporary disability 8,791; indemnification for permanent injury 250; death 19. Labour stoppages (1987): 68, involving 4,750 workers. Average duration of journey to work: n.a. Method of transport: n.a. Rate per 1,000 workers of discouraged (unemployed no longer seeking work): n.a.
Access to services (1980). Proportion of dwellings having access to: electricity 74.6%; safe public water supply 71.2%; public sewage collection 49.2%.
Social participation. Eligible voters participating in national election (1988): c. 50%. Population participating in voluntary work: n.a. Trade union membership in total work force: n.a. Practicing religious population in total affiliated population (1970): weekly 10% of urban dwellers, 25% of rural dwellers; yearly 55% of urban dwellers, 73% of rural dwellers.
Social deviance (1983). Criminal cases tried by local authorities per 100,000 population for: murder 8.4; rape 1.9; other assault 76.9; theft 31.2. Incidence per 100,000 in general population of: alcoholism, n.a.; drug and substance abuse, n.a.[1]; suicide 1.47[2].
Leisure (1984). Favourite leisure activities (average daily paid attendance): cinema 691,047; sporting events 37,238; live theatre 18,825; museums and archaeological sites 8,772; bullfights 2,175.
Material well-being (1985). Households possessing: radio 96%; television 73%; washing machine 33%; automobile 29%; telephone 27%; refrigerator 23%.

National economy

Gross national product (1986): U.S.$149,110,000,000 (U.S.$1,850 per capita).

Structure of gross domestic product and labour force

	1986 in value Mex$'000,000,000	1986 % of total value	1984 labour force	1984 % of labour force
Agriculture	7,015.1	9.0	5,342,000	24.0
Mining	5,571.3	7.2	271,000	1.2
Manufacturing	19,852.4	25.5	2,361,000	10.6
Construction	3,692.1	4.8	1,468,000	6.6
Public utilities	912.1	1.2	68,000	0.3
Transp. and commun.	5,657.8	7.3	1,023,000	4.6
Trade	18,499.6	23.8	2,744,000	12.3
Finance	5,395.3	6.9	480,000	2.2
Pub. admin., defense	12,401.3	15.9	1,121,000	5.0
Services			6,335,000	28.5
Other	−1,218.9	−1.6	1,039,000[3]	4.7[3]
TOTAL	77,778.1	100.0	22,252,000	100.0

Budget (1988). Revenue: Mex$71,878,084,000,000 (revenue from state petroleum company 42.3%, income taxes 25.6%, value-added taxes 17.4%, excise taxes 5.1%, import duties 3.0%). Expenditures: Mex$153,150,780,-000,000 (interest on public debt 63.6%, public education 5.2%, natural resource management and development 2.6%).
Public debt (external, outstanding; 1986): U.S.$74,961,800,000.
Tourism (1986): receipts from visitors U.S.$2,984,000,000; expenditures by nationals abroad U.S.$2,132,000,000.

Manufacturing, mining, and construction enterprises (1985)

	no. of enterprises	no. of employees ('000)	yearly wages as a % of avg. of all wages[2]	annual income (Mex$'000,000)
Manufacturing	127,539	2,303.6	166.2	16,492,900
Food, beverages, and tobacco	46,260	476.2	130.0	4,281,300
Chemicals	4,476	264.8	...	2,777,800
Nonelectrical machinery and transport equipment	6,879	264.9	...	2,456,200
Textiles and apparel	15,753	399.9	122.8	1,462,700
Iron and steel	1,013	113.0	...	1,364,200
Electrical machinery	2,084	220.3	...	1,066,600
Nonmetallic mineral products	9,173	127.7	...	903,000
Paper and printing	6,750	118.7	...	871,100
Metal products	18,750	173.5	...	830,800
Wood and wood products	14,852	108.6	...	297,800
Other manufactures	1,549	36.0	...	181,400
Mining	466	59.5	198.2	374,700
Construction	4,648	336.4	131.8	1,449,100

Production (metric tons except as noted). Agriculture, forestry, fishing (1986): sugarcane 38,900,000, corn (maize) 14,100,000[4], sorghum 5,861,000, wheat 4,009,000[4], bananas and plantains 2,500,000, oranges 2,495,000, tomatoes 1,665,000, dry beans 1,194,000[4], mangoes 1,014,000[4], potatoes 950,000, coconuts 700,000, lemons 675,000, pineapples 649,000[4], grapes 642,000[4], soybeans 633,000, barley 580,000, chillies and green peppers 550,000, apples 530,000[4], rice 523,000, watermelons 450,000, avocados 416,000, cantaloupes 350,000, safflower seed 322,000[4], cottonseed 300,000, coffee 278,-000, cucumbers 250,000, chick peas 180,000, cotton lint 152,000, pumpkins 130,000; livestock (number of live animals) 31,123,000 cattle, 18,631,000 pigs, 10,500,000 goats, 8,419,000 sheep, 6,135,000 horses, 3,183,000 asses, 3,130,000 mules, 220,000,000 chickens; roundwood 21,228,000 cu m; fish catch 1,303,720, of which sardines 466,799, anchovies 116,906. Mining and quarrying (metal content of ores; 1987): iron ore 4,965,130; zinc 274,480; copper 230,570; lead 177,160; manganese 146,410; silver 2,415; gold 8.09;

(nonmetals; 1987) salt 6,393,220; gypsum 2,457,810; sulfur 2,303,750; fluorite 723,590; phosphorite (phosphate rock) 633,200. Manufacturing (value added Mex$'000,000; 1986): machinery and transport equipment 952,700, of which transport equipment 396,600, electrical machinery 334,600; food and beverages 838,000; chemical products 538,200; printed and published materials 274,000; textiles 268,400; metal products 251,500; iron and steel products 228,400; paper and paper products 210,100; wearing apparel and footwear 151,000; rubber products 67,500. Construction (gross value of new construction in Mex$'000,000; 1985): residential 154,835; nonresidential 168,096.

Trade and service enterprises (1985)

	no. of establishments	no. of employees	yearly wage as a % of avg. of all wages[2]	annual income (Mex$'000,000)
Trade	618,059	1,780,700	...	14,348,200
Wholesale	30,264	329,100	...	5,205,700
Retail	587,795	1,451,600	...	9,142,500
Boutiques (excluding food products)	223,601	600,200	...	3,022,900
Food and tobacco speciality stores	339,736	588,500	...	2,050,800
Automobile, tire, and auto parts dealers	16,768	104,400	...	1,737,600
Small supermarkets and grocery stores	4,512	96,400	...	1,227,300
Gasoline stations	2,395	23,900	...	708,700
Other	783	38,200	...	395,200
Services	341,436	1,401,500	85.2	3,476,900
Professional services	21,040	193,000	77.9	645,700
Food and beverages services	109,108	341,400	...	620,600
Transp. and travel agencies	3,058	41,000	133.4	353,400
Lodging	7,819	111,500	...	283,900
Automotive repair	55,850	148,500	...	209,800
Educational services (private)	8,227	124,200	134.3	166,000
Medical and social assistance	38,606	101,000	206.4	151,700
Amusement services (cinemas and theatres)	2,915	29,500	148.9	144,500
Recreation	8,323	41,000	...	139,500
Other repair	36,031	64,200	...	86,500
Commercial and professional organizations	3,209	41,900	77.9	67,400
Other	47,250	164,300	49.9	607,900

Energy production (consumption): electricity (kW-hr; 1986) 97,518,000,-000 (96,176,000,000); coal (metric tons; 1986) 8,450,000 (8,800,000); crude petroleum (barrels; 1986) 879,200,000 (412,100,000); petroleum products (metric tons; 1986) 70,139,000 (67,290,000); natural gas (cu m; 1986) 16,-469,000,000 (16,469,000,000).

Population economically active (1984): total 22,252,000; activity rate of total population 29.2% (participation rates: ages 15–64, 57.2%[5]; female 27.8%[5]; unemployed 9.7%.)

Price and earnings indexes (1980 = 100)

	1982	1983	1984	1985	1986	1987	1988
Consumer price index	203.3	410.2	679.0	1,071.2	1,994.9	4,625.0	10,372.0[6]
Daily earnings index[7]	226.6	326.2	511.0	787.2	1,594.7	4,170.0	5,154.9

Household income and expenditure. Average household size (1986) 5.3; income per household (1983) Mex$442,000 (U.S.$3,680); sources of income (1983): wages and salaries 52.4%, property and entrepreneurship 23.6%, transfer payments 5.6%, other 18.4%; expenditure (1984): food, beverages, and tobacco 35.8%, housing (includes household furnishings) 20.2%, transportation and communications 12.4%, clothing and footwear 10.3%, recreation and entertainment 4.9%, health and medical services 5.0%.

Land use (1985): forested 23.5%; meadows and pastures 38.7%; agricultural and under permanent cultivation 12.9%; other 24.9%.

Financial aggregates[8]

	1983	1984	1985	1986	1987	1988 (7 mo.)
Exchange Rate, Mex$ per:						
U.S. Dollar	120.1	167.8	256.9	611.8	1,378.2	2,281.0
£	182.2	224.9	333.0	897.5	2,258.7	3,889.8
SDR	150.7	188.7	408.3	1,129.6	3,134.8	2,957.3
International reserves (U.S.$)						
Total (excl. gold; '000,000)	3,913	7,272	4,906	5,607	12,464	10,474
SDRs ('000,000)	22	3	—	7	498	532
Reserve pos. in IMF ('000,000)	91	—	—	—	—	—
Foreign exchange	3,795	7,269	4,906	5,661	11,758	9,942
Gold ('000,000 fine troy oz)	2.31	2.42	2.36	2.57	2.28	2.67
% world reserves	0.24	0.26	0.25	0.33	0.24	0.28
Interest and prices						
Treasury bill rate	59.19	49.47	63.36	88.57	103.07	32.48
Balance of payments (U.S.$'000,000)						
Balance of visible trade, of which:	+13,762	+12,941	+8,451	+4,599	+8,433	+2,390[9]
Imports, f.o.b.	8,550	11,255	13,212	11,432	12,222	8,323[9]
Exports, f.o.b.	22,312	24,196	21,663	16,031	20,655	10,713[9]
Balance of invisibles	−9,654	−9,112	−8,317	−6,359	−5,218	...
Balance of payments, current account	+5,208	+4,240	+540	−1,270	+3,883	+168[9]

Foreign trade

Balance of trade (current prices)

	1981	1982	1983	1984	1985	1986	1987
Mex$'000,000,000	−82.8	+489.0	+1,708.6	+2,162.2	+2,249.1	+3,177.8	+11,794.1
% of total	9.3%	19.3%	44.6%	36.5%	24.2%	16.7%	25.2%

Imports (1987): Mex$12,223,000,000 (machinery and transport equipment 47.4%, of which specialized industrial equipment 19.9%, transport equipment 13.9%; industrial chemicals 11.3%; unprocessed agricultural products 9.1%; newsprint 5.0%; petrochemicals 4.4%). *Major import sources:* United States 64.4%; West Germany 6.8%; Japan 6.5%; Canada 2.9%; France 2.8%; United Kingdom 1.8%; Brazil 1.4%.

Exports (1987): Mex$20,656,000,000 (crude petroleum 38.1%; machinery and transport equipment 22.3%; unprocessed agricultural products 7.5%; processed food, beverages, and tobacco 6.4%; industrial chemicals 5.3%; petroleum products 3.1%). *Major export destinations:* United States 64.5%; Japan 6.5%; France 2.8%; West Germany 1.6%; Canada 1.5%; United Kingdom 1.5%; Israel 1.1%.

Trade by commodity group (1985)

SITC group	imports U.S.$'000,000	%	exports U.S.$'000,000	%
00 Food and live animals	1,619	12.0	1,323	6.2
01 Beverages and tobacco	—	—	747	3.5
02 Crude materials, excluding fuels	209	1.6	514	2.4
03 Mineral fuels, lubricants, and related materials	1,341	10.0	15,281	71.7
04 Animal and vegetable oils, fats, and waxes	—	—	—	—
05 Chemicals and related products, n.e.s.	1,373	10.2	676	3.2
06 Basic manufactures	4,726	35.4	1,118	5.2
07 Machinery and transport equipment	1,404	10.5	1,564	7.3
08 Miscellaneous manufactured articles	2,581	19.2	91	0.4
09 Goods not classified by kind	151	1.1	6	0.1
TOTAL[10]	13,440	100.0	21,320	100.0

Direction of trade (1985)

	imports U.S.$'000,000	%	exports U.S.$'000,000	%
Africa	66	0.4	84	0.4
Asia	1,066	6.6	2,155	9.0
South America	470	2.9	619	2.6
North and Central America	11,440	70.4	16,355	68.1
United States	11,132	68.5	15,029	62.6
other North and Central Am.	308	1.9	1,326	5.5
Europe	2,295	14.1	4,049	16.8
EEC	1,851	11.4	3,869	16.1
U.S.S.R.	7	—	6	—
other Europe	437	2.7	174	0.7
Oceania	105	0.6	32	0.1
unknown	810	5.0	725	3.0
freight and insurance charges			—	—
TOTAL	16,252	100.0	24,019	100.0

Transport and communications

Transport. Railroads (1988): route length 16,366 mi, 26,339 km; passenger-mi 4,082,000,000, passenger-km 6,569,000,000; short ton-mi cargo 28,011,-000,000, metric ton-km cargo 40,895,000,000. Roads (1988): total length 145,222 mi, 233,712 km (paved[11] 45.2%). Vehicles (1985): passenger cars 5,195,273; trucks and buses 2,167,000. Merchant marine (1987): vessels (100 gross tons and over) 651; total deadweight tonnage 2,204,977. Air transport[12] (1986): passenger-mi 10,491,000,000, passenger-km 16,884,000,-000; short ton-mi cargo 109,458,000, metric ton-km cargo 159,816,000; airports (1988) 78.

Communications. Daily newspapers (1986): total number 392; total circulation 11,256,000; circulation per 1,000 population 142. Radio (1986): 25,-278,000 receivers (1 per 3.2 persons). Television (1987): 9,500,000 receivers (1 per 8.5 persons). Telephones (1988): 8,816,000 (1 per 9.4 persons).

Education and health

Education (1987–88)

	schools	teachers	students	student/ teacher ratio
Primary (age 6–12)	80,518	455,693	14,875,000	32.6
Secondary (age 12–18)	16,999	224,732[13]	4,401,000	...
Voc., teacher tr.[13]	5,811	139,391	2,088,292	15.0
Higher[13]	1,347	98,061	1,072,764	13.7

Literacy (1988): total population age 15 and over literate 49,221,570 (95.1%); males literate[14] 20,400,000 (92.3%); females literate[14] 20,400,000 (88.3%).

Health: physicians (1982) 66,373 (1 per 1,100 persons); hospital beds (1984) 72,000 (1 per 1,070 persons); infant mortality rate per 1,000 live births (1985) 53.0.

Food (1984–86): daily per capita caloric intake 3,148 (vegetable products 83%, animal products 17%); (1983) 124% of FAO recommended minimum.

Military

Total active duty personnel (1988): 138,000 (army 76.5%, navy 18.8%, air force 4.7%). *Military expenditure as percent of GNP* (1985): 0.6% (world 6.1%); per capita expenditure U.S.$13.

[1]Through 1982, cannabis remained the most abused drug. [2]1984. [3]Includes unemployed. [4]1987. [5]1980. [6]September. [7]December 31, except 1988, March 1. [8]Exchange rates and treasury bill rates are expressed in period averages; international reserves are expressed in end-of-period rates. [9]First 6 months only. [10]Totals include adjustments of unspecified nature. [11]1986. [12]All scheduled traffic of Mexicana and AeroMexico airlines. [13]1985–86. [14]1985.

Micronesia, Federated States of

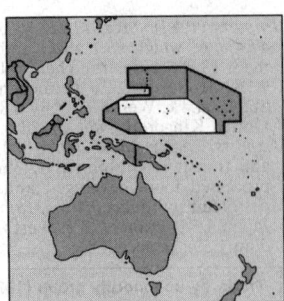

Official name: Federated States of Micronesia.
Political status: federal republic in free association with the United States with one legislative house (National Congress [14])[1].
Head of state and government: President.
Capital: Kolonia.
Official language: none.
Official religion: none.
Monetary unit: 1 U.S. dollar (U.S.$) = 100 cents; valuation (Oct. 10, 1988) 1£ = U.S.$1.71.

Area and population

States Major Islands	area sq mi	area sq km	population 1985 estimate
Kosrae	42.3	109.6	6,462
Kosrae Island	42.3	109.6	6,462
Pohnpei	133.3	345.2	27,871
Pohnpei Island	129.0	334.1	24,788
Truk	49.1	127.2	46,159
Moen Islands	7.0	18.1	14,218
Yap	45.9	118.9	10,948
Yap Island	38.7	100.2	6,951
TOTAL	270.8[2]	701.4[2]	91,440

Demography

Population (1988): 101,000.
Density (1988): persons per sq mi 373.0, persons per sq km 144.0.
Urban–rural (1980): urban 19.4%; rural 80.6%.
Sex distribution (1980): male 51.12%; female 48.88%.
Age breakdown (1980): under 15, 46.4%; 15–29, 26.8%; 30–44, 12.6%; 45–59, 8.5%; 60–74, 4.5%; 75 and over, 1.2%.
Population projection: (1990) 109,000; (2000) 153,000.
Doubling time: 26 years.
Ethnic composition (1980): Trukese 41.1%; Pohnpeian 25.9%; Mortlockese 8.3%; Kosraean 7.4%; Yapese 6.0%; Ulithian, or Woleaian, 4.0%; Pingelapese, or Mokilese, 1.2%; Western Trukese 1.0%; Palauan 0.4%; Filipino 0.2%; other 4.5%.
Religious affiliation: Christianity is the predominant religious tradition, with the Kosraeans, Pohnpeians, and Trukese being mostly Protestant and the Yapese mostly Roman Catholic.
Major cities (1980): Moen 10,351; Tol 6,705; Kolonia 6,306[3].

Vital statistics

Birth rate per 1,000 population (1985): 30.6 (world avg. 29.0); legitimate, n.a.; illegitimate, n.a.
Death rate per 1,000 population (1985)[4]: 3.6 (world avg. 11.0).
Natural increase rate per 1,000 population (1985): 27 (world avg. 18.0).
Total fertility rate (avg. births per childbearing woman; 1985)[5]: 5.3.
Marriage rate per 1,000 population: n.a.
Divorce rate per 1,000 population: n.a.
Life expectancy at birth (1985)[4]: male 64.0 years; female 68.1 years.
Major causes of death per 100,000 population (1985)[4]: diseases of the cerebrovascular system 85.7; major infectious diseases 39.6, of which intestinal diseases 14.3, septicemia 8.9; pneumonia, influenza, and tuberculosis 29.7; malignant and benign neoplasms (cancers) 23.1; homicide, suicide, and accidents 22.0.

National economy

Budget (1986). Revenue: U.S.$51,189,000 (U.S. Department of the Interior 75.7%, domestic taxes and other local revenue sources 19.5%, other U.S. government grants and federal program funds 4.8%). Expenditures: U.S. $13,208,000.
Public debt (external, outstanding): n.a.
Tourism (1986): number of visitors 6,538.
Production (metric tons except as noted). Agriculture, forestry, fishing (1986): n.a.; however, Micronesia's major crops include coconuts (from which more than 4,000 tons of copra is produced), breadfruit, cassava, sweet potatoes, and a variety of tropical fruits (including bananas); livestock comprises mostly pigs and poultry; fish catch, n.a., however, shipjack tuna is one of the major natural resources of Micronesia. Mining and quarrying: quarrying of sand and aggregate for local construction only. Manufacturing: n.a.; however, copra is the most important product, and the manufacture of handicrafts and personal items (clothing, mats, boats, etc.) by individuals is also important. Construction: n.a. Energy production (consumption): electricity[6] (kW-hr; 1984) 150,000,000 (150,000,000); coal, none (n.a.); crude petroleum, none (n.a.); petroleum products (metric tons; 1984) none (50,000[6]); natural gas, none (n.a.).
Price and earnings indexes: n.a.
Household income and expenditure: average household size (1980) 7.0; average annual income per household, n.a.; sources of income (as percent of workers over age 16): wage and salary workers (private) 22.8%, wage and salary workers (government) 51.5%, self-employed persons 2.7%, primarily subsistence workers 5.7%; expenditure (1985): food and beverages 73.5%.

Land use (1984)[6]: forested 22.5%; meadows and pastures 13.5%; agricultural and under permanent cultivation 33.5%; other 30.5%.
Gross domestic product (at current market prices; 1986): U.S.$106,510,000 (U.S.$1,127 per capita).

Structure of gross domestic product and labour force

	1983 in value U.S.$'000,000	1983 % of total value	1980 labour force	1980 % of labour force
Agriculture and Fishing	44.9	42.2	197	2.0
Trade	12.7	11.9	864	8.8
Public administration	31.5	29.6	1,765	18.0
Manufacturing			115	1.2
Construction			945	9.6
Transportation, communications, and public utilities	17.4	16.3	472	4.8
Finance			121	1.2
Services			3,086	31.5
Other			2,233[7]	22.8[7]
TOTAL	106.5	100.0	9,798	100.0[2]

Population economically active (1982): total 9,798; activity rate of total population 13.4% (participation rates: over age 16, 26.1%; female 29.8%; unemployed 17.1%).

Foreign trade

Balance of trade (current prices)

	1979	1980	1981	1982	1983	1984[8]
U.S.$'000,000	...	...	...	...	−54.94	−26.9
% of total	...	...	...	...	88.4%	85.4%

Imports (1984): U.S.$29,223,700[8] (food, beverages, and tobacco 47.5%, manufactured goods 20.1%, machinery and transport equipment 15.3%, petroleum products 8.8%, chemicals 4.2%). *Major import sources:* United States; Japan; Guam; Australia.
Exports (1984): U.S.$2,308,500[8] (primarily from copra, but black pepper, handicrafts, and a few marine products are also exported). *Major export destinations:* United States; Japan.

Transport and communications

Transport. Railroads: none. Roads (1986): total length 19 mi[9], 31 km[9]. Vehicles: passenger cars, trucks, and buses, n.a. Merchant marine: n.a. Air transport: n.a.; airports (1988) with scheduled flights 4.
Communications. Daily newspapers (1985): there are no private newspapers. Radios (1984): total number of receivers 15,800 (1 per 5.6 persons). Television (1987): total number of receivers 1,125 (1 per 84 persons). Telephones: (1986): 1,556 (1 per 61 persons).

Education and health

Education (1983–84)

	schools	teachers	students	student/ teacher ratio
Elementary (age 6–13)	151	1,051	23,345	22.2
Secondary (age 12–18)	14	314	4,159	13.2
College[10]	...	...	920	...

Educational attainment (1980). Percent of population age 25 and over having: no formal schooling 24.8%; some primary education 38.2%; primary 11.7%; some secondary 7.7%; secondary 9.6%; higher 8.0%. *Literacy* (1980): total population age 15 and over literate 30,074 (76.7%); males literate 13,710 (67.0%); females literate 16,364 (87.2%).
Health (1985): physicians 36[11] (1 per 2,540 persons); hospital beds 325 (1 per 280 persons); infant mortality rate per 1,000 live births (1987) 23.3[4].
Food: daily per capita caloric intake, n.a.

Military

External security is provided by the United States.

[1]On Nov. 3, 1986, the United States unilaterally terminated the UN trusteeship it held over the Federated States of Micronesia, thus formally initiating their free-association political status. The United Nations Trusteeship Council has recognized the termination of the trusteeship, but the Security Council, which also participated in the creation of the trusteeship, has not. [2]Detail does not add to total given because of rounding. [3]1985. [4]Registered deaths only. [5]Includes other islands in geographic Micronesia. [6]Includes all areas formerly comprising the U.S. Trust Territory of the Pacific Islands. [7]Includes 1,673 unemployed. [8]For Truk and Pohnpei only. [9]Paved road only. [10]In 1985, 1,200 students were enrolled in colleges and universities in the United States. [11]Excludes medical officers.

Mongolia

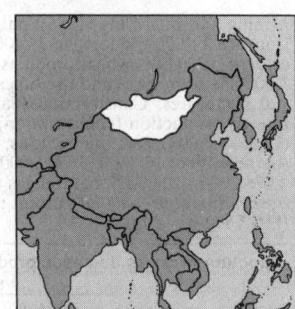

Official name: Bügd Nayramdah
Mongol Ard Uls (Mongolian People's
Republic).
Form of government: unitary
single-party republic with one
legislative house (People's Great
Hural [370]).
Chief of state: Chairman of
the Presidium of the People's
Great Hural.
Head of government: Premier.
Capital: Ulaanbaatar (Ulan Bator).
Official language: Khalkha Mongolian.
Official religion: none.
Monetary unit: 1 tugrik = 100
möngös; valuation (Oct 10, 1988)
1 U.S.$ = 3.35 tugriks; 1 £ = 5.74
tugriks.

Area and population

Provinces	Capitals	area sq mi	area sq km	population 1986 estimate
Arhangay	Tsetserleg	21,000	55,000	85,800
Bayanhongor	Bayanhongor	45,000	116,000	87,900
Bayan-Ölgiy	Ölgiy	18,000	46,000	71,100
Bulgan	Bulgan	19,000	49,000	48,000
Dornod	Choybalsan	47,700	123,500	70,800
Dornogovi	Saynshand	43,000	111,000	49,600
Dundgovi	Mandalgov	30,000	78,000	45,400
Dzavhan	Uliastay	32,000	82,000	91,500
Govi-Altay	Altay	55,000	142,000	64,000
Hentiy	Öndörhaan	32,000	82,000	63,000
Hovd	Hovd	29,000	76,000	76,000
Hövsgöl	Mörön	39,000	101,000	99,900
Ömnögovi	Dalandzadgad	64,000	165,000	36,900
Övörhangay	Arvayheer	24,000	63,000	95,600
Selenge	Sühbaatar	16,000	42,000	81,500
Sühbaatar	Baruun-urt	32,000	82,000	49,300
Töv	Dzuunmod	31,000	81,000	94,700
Uvs	Ulaangom	27,000	69,000	84,100
Autonomous municipalities				
Darhan	—	100	200	74,000
Erdenet	—	300	800	45,400
Ulaanbaatar	—	800	2,000	500,200
TOTAL		604,800[1]	1,566,500	1,914,700

Demography
Population (1988): 2,041,000.
Density (1988): persons per sq mi 3.4, persons per sq km 1.3.
Urban–rural (1986): urban 51.8%; rural 48.2%.
Sex distribution (1986): male 50.10%; female 49.90%.
Age breakdown (1985): under 15, 42.7%; 15–29, 26.2%; 30–44, 16.1%; 45–59, 9.7%; 60–74, 4.4%; 75 and over, 0.9%.
Population projection: (1990) 2,147,000; (2000) 2,766,000.
Doubling time: 26 years.
Ethnic composition (1979): Khalkha Mongol 77.5%; Kazakh 5.3%; Dörbed Mongol 2.8%; Bayad 2.0%; Buryat Mongol 1.9%; Dariganga Mongol 1.5%; other 9.0%.
Religious affiliation: Although formal freedom of worship, or of propagandization against religion, exists, all traditional religious practice (lamaistic Buddhism, shamanism, Islam, and others) has been greatly reduced during the 20th century; reliable data on the current situation do not exist.
Major cities (1986): Ulaanbaatar (Ulan Bator) 500,200; Darhan 74,000; Erdenet 45,400.

Vital statistics
Birth rate per 1,000 population (1985): 36.0 (world avg. 29.0); legitimate, n.a.; illegitimate, n.a.
Death rate per 1,000 population (1985): 9.2 (world avg. 11.0).
Natural increase rate per 1,000 population (1985): 26.8 (world avg. 18.0).
Total fertility rate (avg. births per childbearing woman; 1987): 5.0.
Marriage rate per 1,000 population (1985): 6.3.
Divorce rate per 1,000 population (1985): 0.3.
Life expectancy at birth (1987): male 61.4 years; female 65.5 years.
Major causes of death per 100,000 population: n.a.; however, major diseases include brucellosis, helminthiasis (an infection with worms), bacillary dysentery and amoebiasis, enteritis and other diarrheal diseases, cerebrospinal meningitis, trachoma, and tuberculosis of the respiratory system. Typhus, diphtheria, and acute poliomyelitis, formerly widespread, have reportedly been eliminated.

National economy
Budget (1986). Revenue: 5,743,000,000 tugriks (turnover tax 62.7%, deductions from profits 29.9%, social insurance contributions 3.5%, income tax 0.7%). Expenditures: 5,692,500,000 tugriks (economy 42.6%, social and cultural services 38.7%, defense 13.5%, administration and other 4.1%).
Public debt (1985): U.S.$4,396,000,000.
Tourism (1983): number of tourists 170,000; receipts from visitors, n.a.; expenditures by nationals abroad, n.a.
Production (metric tons except as noted). Agriculture, forestry, fishing (1986): wheat 664,000, potatoes 133,000, barley 114,000, oats 50,000, vegetables 47,000; livestock (number of live animals) 13,248,800 sheep, 4,298,600 goats, 2,408,100 cattle, 1,971,000 horses, 559,000 camels, 56,100 pigs;

roundwood (1985) 1,500,000 cu m; fish catch 380. Mining and quarrying (1985): fluorspar 787,000; copper 120,000. Manufacturing (1985): flour 175,700; cement 150,500; meat 61,600; woolen cloth 2,100,000 sq m; leather shoes 2,900,000 pairs; sheep and goat skins 2,880,000 sq m; beer 88,500,000 hectolitres. Construction (1985): residential 240,000 sq m; nonresidential 169,000 sq m. Energy production (consumption): electricity (kW-hr; 1986) 2,800,000,000 (3,000,000,000); coal (metric tons; 1986) 6,000,000 (5,999,750); crude petroleum, none (n.a.); petroleum products (metric tons; 1986) none (810,000); natural gas, none (n.a.).
Gross national product (1985): U.S.$1,911,000,000 (U.S.$1,010 per capita).

Structure of net material product and labour force

	1985 value	% of total value	labour force	% of labour force
Agriculture	...	18.3	543,900	60.8
Mining and manufacturing	...	32.4	91,000	10.2
Construction	...}	4.9	29,200	3.3
Public utilities	...		17,400	1.9
Transportation and communications	...	11.2	36,400	4.1
Trade	...	31.6	41,600	4.7
Services[2]	...		105,600	11.8
Other	...	1.6	28,900	3.2
TOTAL	...	100.0	894,000	100.0

Population economically active (1985): total 894,000; activity rate of total population 46.9% (participation rates: ages 15–64, 82.2%; female 45.5%; unemployed, n.a.)

Price and earnings indexes (1980 = 100)

	1980	1981	1982	1983	1984	1985
Consumer price index	...	...	...	...	...	...
Monthly earnings index	100	...	...	...	101.4	104.8

Household income and expenditure. Average household size (1980) 5.0; income per household: n.a.; sources of income: n.a.; expenditure: n.a.
Land use (1985): forested 9.7%; meadows and pastures 78.8%; agricultural and under permanent cultivation 0.8%; other 10.7%.

Foreign trade

Balance of trade (current prices)

	1980	1981	1982	1983	1984	1985
U.S.$'000,000	−138.7	−225.7	−220.0	−305.0	−230.0	−388.0
% of total	15.2%	20.1%	17.0%	20.7%	18.1%	22.7%

Imports (1985): U.S.$1,048,000,000 (machinery and equipment 36.3%; fuels, minerals, and metals 28.7%; consumer goods 18.8%; food products 10.5%; chemical products, fertilizers, and rubber 7.3%). *Major import sources:* U.S.S.R. and socialist countries 99.0%; capitalist countries 1.0%.
Exports (1985): U.S.$660,000,000 (minerals and metals 42.0%; raw materials and food products 40.3%; consumer goods 16.8%; chemicals and related products 0.7%). *Major export destinations:* U.S.S.R. and socialist countries 96.1%; capitalist countries 3.9%.

Transport and communications
Transport. Railroads (1985): length 1,086 mi, 1,748 km; passenger-mi 270,900,000, passenger-km 436,000,000; short ton-mi cargo 4,082,000,000, metric ton-km cargo 5,960,000,000. Roads (1986): total length 29,000 mi, 47,600 km (paved 2%). Vehicles: n.a. Merchant marine: vessels (100 gross tons and over) none. Air transport (1985): passenger-mi 183,000,000, passenger-km 295,000,000; short ton-mi cargo 4,500,000, metric ton-km cargo 6,500,000; airports (1988) with scheduled flights 1.
Communications. Daily newspapers (1985): total number 2; total circulation 96,000; circulation per 1,000 population 85.0. Radio (1986): total receivers 194,000 (1 per 9.7 persons). Television (1986): total receivers 88,100 (1 per 21 persons). Telephones (1986): 49,300 (1 per 38 persons).

Education and health

Education (1985–86)

	schools	teachers	students	student/ teacher ratio
Primary and secondary (age 8–18)	678	17,000	428,000	25.2
Voc., teacher tr.	40	1,200	27,700	23.1
Higher	8	1,500	24,500	16.4

Educational attainment (1979). Percent of population age 10 and over having: primary education 48.0%; some secondary 29.7%; complete secondary 9.5%; vocational secondary 7.0%; some higher and complete higher 5.8%.
Literacy (1980): total population age 15 and over literate 849,000 (89.5%); males literate 443,000 (93.4%); females literate 406,000 (85.5%).
Health (1986): physicians 4,400 (1 per 430 persons); hospital beds 21,200 (1 per 89 persons); infant mortality rate per 1,000 live births 47.0.
Food (1984–86): daily per capita caloric intake 2,830 (vegetable products 70%, animal products 30%); (1983) 117% of FAO recommended minimum requirement.

Military
Total active duty personnel (1987): 33,500 (army 89.6%; navy, none; air force 10.4%). *Military expenditure as percent of GNP,* n.a.; estimated foreign military assistance (1986) $600,000,000; per capita expenditure, n.a.

[1]Detail does not add to total given because of rounding. [2]Services includes finance, public administration, and defense.

Morocco

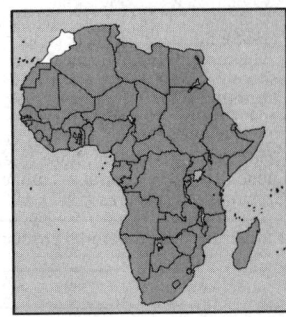

Official name: al-Mamlakah al-Maghribīyah (Kingdom of Morocco).
Form of government: constitutional monarchy with one legislative house (House of Representatives [306]).
Head of state and government: King.
Capital: Rabat.
Official language: Arabic.
Official religion: Islam.
Monetary unit: 1 Moroccan dirham (DH) = 100 Moroccan francs; valuation (Oct. 10, 1988) 1 U.S.$ = DH 8.34; 1 £ = DH 14.28.

Area and population[1]

Provinces	Capitals	area sq mi	area sq km	population 1986 estimate
Agadir	Agadir	2,282	5,910	672,000
Azilal	Azilal	3,880	10,050	407,000
Béni Mellal	Béni Mellal	2,732	7,075	779,000
Ben Slimane	Ben Slimane	1,066	2,760	189,000
Boulemane	Boulemane	5,558	14,395	142,000
Chaouen (Chefchaouen)	Chaouen (Chefchaouen)	1,680	4,350	335,000
Essaouira	Essaouira	2,446	6,335	415,000
Fès	Fès	2,085	5,400	906,000
Figuig	Figuig	21,618	55,990	107,000
Guelmim	Guelmim	11,100	28,750	146,000
al-Hoceima	al-Hoceima	1,371	3,550	339,000
Ifrane	Ifrane	1,278	3,310	109,000
el-Jadida	el-Jadida	2,317	6,000	839,000
el-Kelaa des Srarhna	el-Kelaa des Srarhna	3,888	10,070	629,000
Kénitra	Kénitra	1,832	4,745	806,000
Khémisset	Khémisset	3,207	8,305	438,000
Khénifra	Khénifra	4,757	12,320	401,000
Khouribga	Khouribga	1,641	4,250	486,000
Marrakech	Marrakech	5,697	14,755	1,390,000
Meknès	Meknès	1,542	3,995	686,000
Nador	Nador	2,367	6,130	679,000
Ouarzazate	Ouarzazate	16,043	41,550	588,000
Oujda	Oujda	7,992	20,700	869,000
er-Rachidia	er-Rachidia	23,006	59,585	460,000
Safi	Safi	2,813	7,285	773,000
Settat	Settat	3,764	9,750	742,000
Sidi Kacem	Sidi Kacem	1,568	4,060	557,000
Tangier	Tangier	461	1,195	492,000
Tan-Tan	Tan-Tan	6,678	17,295	52,000
Taounate	Taounate	2,156	5,585	570,000
Taroudannt	Taroudannt	6,355	16,460	607,000
Tata	Tata	10,010	25,925	106,000
Taza	Taza	5,799	15,020	664,000
Tétouan	Tétouan	2,326	6,025	778,000
Tiznit	Tiznit	2,687	6,960	344,000
Prefectures				
Ain Chok–Hay Hassani	—			356,000
Ain Sebaa–Hay Mohammadi	—			489,000
Ben Msik–Sidi Othmane	—	623	1,615	773,000
Casablanca–Anfa	—			997,000
Mohammadia–Znata	—			180,000
Rabat	—			591,000
Salé	—	492	1,275	483,000
Skhirate-Temara	—			152,000
TOTAL		177,117	458,730	22,523,000

Demography

Population (1988): 23,809,000[1].
Density (1988)[1]: persons per sq mi 134.0, persons per sq km 52.0.
Urban–rural (1986)[1]: urban 44.5%; rural 55.5%.
Sex distribution (1986)[2]: male 50.11%; female 49.89%.
Age breakdown (1985): under 15, 41.6%; 15–29, 28.7%; 30–44, 14.5%; 45–59, 9.3%; 60–74, 4.5%; 75 and over, 1.4%.
Population projection: (1990) 25,168,000; (2000) 33,221,000.
Doubling time: 21 years.
Ethnic composition (1982): Arab-Berber 99.1%; other 0.9%.
Religious affiliation (1982): Muslim (mostly Sunnī) 98.7%; Christian 1.1%.
Major cities (1984): Casablanca 2,600,000; Fès 852,000; Rabat 556,000.

Vital statistics

Birth rate per 1,000 population (1980–85): 44.1 (world avg. 29.0).
Death rate per 1,000 population (1980–85): 11.7 (world avg. 11.0).
Natural increase rate per 1,000 population (1980–85): 32.4 (world avg. 18.0).
Total fertility rate (avg. births per childbearing woman; 1980–85): 6.4.
Life expectancy at birth (1980–85): male 56.1 years; female 59.4 years.
Major causes of death (percentage of total deaths; 1985)[3]: circulatory diseases 16.1%; infectious and parasitic diseases 11.2%; accidents 9.6%; childhood diseases 8.1%; malignant neoplasms 4.8%.

National economy

Budget (1988). Revenue: DH 51,148,000,000 (loans 36.6%, indirect taxes 26.0%, direct taxes 16.6%, customs duties 14.4%). Expenditures: DH 58,486,000,000 (administration 43.0%, debt service 29.6%, investment 27.4%).
Public debt (external, outstanding; 1986): U.S.$14,610,300,000.
Tourism (1986): receipts U.S.$800,000,000; expenditures U.S.$100,000,000.
Production (metric tons except as noted). Agriculture, forestry, fishing (1986): wheat 3,809,000, barley 3,563,000, oranges 841,000, potatoes 56,000; livestock (number of live animals) 12,100,000 sheep, 4,700,000 goats, 2,570,000 cattle; roundwood 2,006,000 cu m; fish catch (1987) 600,000.

Mining and quarrying (1986): phosphate rock 13,696,100; barytes 220,000; iron ore 117,000; fluorspar 76,400; copper 54,400. Manufacturing (1986): cement 3,709,000; wheat products 2,411,300; refined sugar 665,377; carpets 1,503,831 sq m; tires and tire tubes 1,406,988 units; pasteurized milk 2,498,720 hectolitres. Construction (value added in DH; 1986): 5,451,082,000.
Energy production (consumption): electricity (kW-hr; 1986) 7,156,000,000 (7,156,000,000); coal (metric tons; 1986) 800,000 (980,000); crude petroleum (barrels; 1986) 182,400 (35,416,000); petroleum products (metric tons; 1986) 4,076,000 (4,202,000); natural gas (cu m; 1986) 85,850,000 (85,850,000).
Gross national product (at current market prices; 1986): U.S.$13,160,000,000 (U.S.$590 per capita).

Structure of gross domestic product and labour force

	1986 in value DH '000,000	1986 % of total value	1982 labour force	1982 % of labour force
Agriculture	28,589	21.3	2,351,629	39.2
Mining	9,457	7.0	63,360	1.1
Public utilities			22,465	0.4
Manufacturing	23,502	17.5	930,615	15.5
Construction	7,415	5.5	437,464	7.3
Transp. and commun.	6,694	5.0	140,981	2.3
Trade and finance	23,290	17.3	498.130	8.3
Pub. admin., defense	15,857	11.8	532,803	8.9
Services	19,530	14.6	474,109	7.9
Other	...	...	547,704[4]	9.1[4]
TOTAL	134,334	100.0	5,999,260	100.0

Population economically active (1982): total 5,999,260; activity rate 29.3% (participation rates: ages 15–64, 48.9%; female 19.7%; unemployed 10.7%).

Price and earnings indexes (1980 = 100)

	1982	1983	1984	1985	1986	1987	1988[5]
Consumer price index	124.4	132.1	148.5	160.0	174.0	178.7	182.2
Hourly earnings index[6]	132.7	150.3	...	...	...	...	...

Household income and expenditure. Average household size (1982) 5.8; income per household: n.a.; sources of income: n.a.; expenditure (1972–73)[7]: food 54.0%, clothing 8.5%, housing 7.0%, transportation 6.9%.
Land use (1985): forested 11.7%; meadows and pastures 46.8%; agricultural and under permanent cultivation 18.8%; other 22.7%.

Foreign trade[8]

Balance of trade (current prices)

	1982	1983	1984	1985	1986	1987
DH '000,000	−10,405	−8,173	−12,190	−13,454	−9,201	−8,707
% of total	29.5%	22.2%	24.2%	23.6%	17.1%	15.7%

Imports (1986): DH 34,607,900,000 (capital goods 23.8%; crude oil 13.3%; food, beverages, and tobacco 12.5%; consumer goods 10.0%; sulfur 6.5%). *Major import sources:* France 23.1%; U.S. 11.3%; Arab countries 11.2%.
Exports (1986): DH 22,103,500,000 (food, beverages, and tobacco 29.5%; phosphates 17.0%; phosphoric acid 13.7%; clothing 7.7%). *Major export destinations:* France 27.3%; West Germany 6.7%; Spain 6.6%; Italy 5.4%.

Transport and communications

Transport. Railroads (1986): route length 1,779 km; passenger-km 1,958,100,000; metric ton-km cargo 4,952,600,000. Roads (1986): total length 59,198 km (paved 47%). Vehicles (1986): passenger cars 527,437; trucks and buses 247,722. Merchant marine (1987): vessels (100 gross tons and over) 315; total deadweight tonnage 579,852. Air transport (1987): passenger-km 2,218,181,000; metric ton-km cargo 50,931,000; airports (1987) 14.
Communications. Daily newspapers (1986): total number 8; total circulation 282,000; circulation per 1,000 population 12.4. Radio (1986): 3,000,000 receivers (1 per 7.5 persons). Television (1987): 1,206,000 receivers (1 per 19.2 persons). Telephones (1986): 325,278 (1 per 70 persons).

Education and health

Education (1986–87)

	schools	teachers	students	student/ teacher ratio
Primary (age 7–12)	3,703	79,678[9]	2,227,960	28.0
Secondary (age 13–17)	1,239	59,860[9]	1,278,855	21.4
Voc., teacher tr.[10]	17	674	7,432	11.0
Higher	28	5,753	157,374	27.4

Educational attainment (1982). Percent of population age 25 and over having: no formal education 47.8%; some primary education 47.8%; some secondary 3.8%; higher 0.6%; not specified 2.3%. *Literacy* (1980): total population over age 15 literate 70.7%; males 82.4%; females literate 58.7%.
Health (1986): physicians 3,945 (1 per 5,755 persons); hospital beds 25,179[11] (1 per 902 persons); infant mortality rate (1980–85) 97.0.
Food (1984–86): daily per capita caloric intake 2,864 (vegetable products 93%, animal products 7%); (1983) 105% of FAO recommended minimum.

Military

Total active duty personnel (1988): 203,500 (army 88.1%, navy 4.1%, air force 7.8%). *Military expenditure as percent of GNP* (1985): 6.5% (world 6.1%); per capita expenditure U.S.$36.

[1]Excludes Western Sahara. [2]Includes Western Sahara. [3]Urban population only. [4]Unemployed, not previously employed only. [5]First quarter. [6]Minimum wages in nonagricultural activities. [7]Weights of consumer price index components. [8]Import figures are f.o.b. in balance of trade and c.i.f. in commodities and trading partners. [9]Public schools only. [10]Teacher's training establishments. [11]Public sector only.

Mozambique

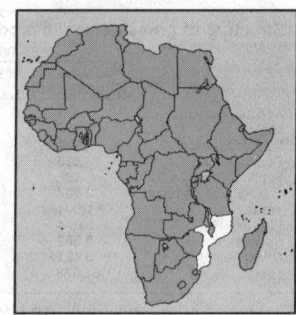

Official name: República Popular de Moçambique (People's Republic of Mozambique).
Form of government: people's republic with a single legislative house (People's Assembly [250]).
Chief of state and head of government: President.
Capital: Maputo.
Official language: Portuguese.
Official religion: none.
Monetary unit: 1 metical (Mt., plural meticais) = 100 centavos; valuation (Oct. 10, 1988) 1 U.S.$ = Mt. 586.00; 1 £ = Mt. 1,003.00.

Area and population

Provinces	Capitals	area[1] sq mi	area[1] sq km	population 1987 estimate[2]
Cabo Delgado	Pemba	31,902	82,625	1,109,900
Gaza	Xai-Xai	29,231	75,709	1,138,700
Inhambane	Inhambane	26,492	68,615	1,167,000
Manica	Chimoio	23,807	61,661	756,900
Maputo	Maputo	9,944	25,756	544,700
Nampula	Nampula	31,508	81,606	2,837,900
Niassa	Lichinga	49,829	129,056	607,700
Sofala	Beira	26,262	68,018	1,257,700
Tete	Tete	38,890	100,724	981,300
Zambézia	Quelimane	40,544	105,008	2,952,200
City				
Maputo	—	232	602	1,006,800
TOTAL LAND AREA		303,623	786,380	14,360,800
INLAND WATER		5,019	13,000	
TOTAL AREA		308,642[3]	799,380	

Demography

Population (1988): 14,890,000.
Density[4] (1988): persons per sq mi 49.0, persons per sq km 18.9.
Urban–rural (1980): urban 13.2%; rural 86.8%.
Sex distribution (1986): male 48.81%; female 51.19%.
Age breakdown (1980): under 15, 44.4%; 15–29, 26.7%; 30–44, 15.9%; 45–59, 8.7%; 60–74, 3.6%; 75 and over, 0.7%.
Population projection: (1990) 15,696,000; (2000) 20,463,000.
Doubling time: 26 years.
Ethnolinguistic composition (1983): Makua 47.3%; Tsonga 23.3%; Malawi 12.0%; Shona 11.3%; Yao 3.8%; Swahili 0.8%; Makonde 0.6%; Portuguese 0.2%; other 0.7%.
Religious affiliation (1980): traditional beliefs 47.8%; Christian 38.9%, of which Roman Catholic 31.4%; Muslim 13.0%; other 0.3%.
Major cities (1986): Maputo 882,800; Beira 269,700; Nampula 182,600.

Vital statistics

Birth rate per 1,000 population (1980–85): 45.1 (world avg. 29.0); (1974) legitimate 73.1%; illegitimate 26.9%.
Death rate per 1,000 population (1980–85): 19.7 (world avg. 11.0).
Natural increase rate per 1,000 population (1980–85): 25.4 (world avg. 18.0).
Total fertility rate (avg. births per childbearing woman; 1980–85): 6.1.
Marriage rate per 1,000 population (1974): 0.7.
Divorce rate per 1,000 population (1973): 0.01.
Life expectancy at birth (1980–85): male 44.4 years; female 46.2 years.
Major infectious diseases (certified cases per 100,000 population; 1980): measles 227.4; pulmonary tuberculosis 55.9; viral hepatitis 19.2; leprosy 13.8; cholera 4.6; tetanus 4.5.

National economy

Budget (1986). Revenue: Mt. 20,300,000,000 (indirect taxes 42.8%, of which excise taxes 27.7%, customs taxes 7.3%; direct taxes 31.0%, of which corporate income tax 22.3%, individual income tax 8.2%; profits from state enterprises 10.8%). Expenditures: Mt. 27,400,000,000 (education 16.8%, health 6.6%).
Production (metric tons except as noted). Agriculture, forestry, fishing (1986): cassava 3,300,000, sugarcane 450,000, coconut 410,000, corn (maize) 350,000, sorghum 190,000, bananas 75,000, peanuts (groundnuts) 65,000; livestock (number of live animals) 1,340,000 cattle, 365,000 goats, 150,000 pigs, 116,000 sheep, 20,000,000 chickens; roundwood (1985) 15,231,000 cu m; fish catch (1985) 37,700. Mining and quarrying (1985): marine salt 28,000; hydraulic lime 10,000; bauxite 5,037; bentonite 361; copper 118[5]; garnet 1,500 kg. Manufacturing (value added in Mt.[6]; 1986): clothing and footwear 2,093,594; processed fish products 1,528,450; alcoholic beverages 1,284,516; flour 1,219,008; textiles 1,110,831; machinery and transport equipment 921,364, of which electrical equipment 410,650; tobacco 788,036; wood 702,419; cotton 520,780; soaps and oils 515,009; cashews 418,624; rubber 411,925; furniture 296,207; dairy products 279,250. Construction (1974): residential 247,000 sq m; nonresidential 121,000. Energy production (consumption): electricity (kW-hr; 1986) 497,000,000 (600,000,000); coal (metric tons; 1986) 4,000 (66,000); crude petroleum (barrels; 1986) none (none[7]); petroleum products (metric tons; 1986) none[7] (251,000); natural gas, none (none).
Population economically active (1980): total 5,671,290; activity rate of total population 48.6% (participation rates: over age 15, 87.3%; female 52.4%; unemployed 1.7%).

Price and earnings indexes (1980 = 100)

	1980	1981	1982	1983	1984	1985	1986
Consumer price index	100	102	120	155	202	261	305
Monthly earnings index	...	...	...	...	...	...	...

Public debt (external, outstanding; 1985)[8]: U.S.$1,224,000,000.
Household income and expenditure. Average household size (1980) 4.2; income per household: n.a.; sources of income: n.a.; expenditure: n.a.
Gross national product (1986): U.S.$3,030,000,000 (U.S.$210 per capita).

Structure of gross domestic product and labour force

	1986[6] in value Mt. '000,000	1986[6] % of total value	1980 labour force	1980 % of labour force
Agriculture	25,000	44.5	4,754,831	83.8
Mining			73,425	1.3
Manufacturing }	14,800	26.3	273,369	4.8
Construction	6,200	11.0	42,121	0.7
Public utilities	...	...	9	9
Transportation and communications	4,600	8.2	77,025	1.4
Trade and finance			112,244	2.0
Pub. admin., defense }	5,600	10.0 }	243,449[9]	4.3[9]
Services				
Other			94,826[10]	1.7[10]
TOTAL	56,200	100.0	5,671,290	100.0

Tourism: n.a.
Land use (1985): forested 19.3%; meadows and pastures 56.1%; agricultural and under permanent cultivation 3.9%; other 20.7%.

Foreign trade

Balance of trade (current prices)

	1981	1982	1983	1984	1985	1986
Mt. '000,000	−18,392	−22,918	−20,286	−18,843	−18,989	−18,739
% of total	48.1%	57.0%	65.7%	70.6%	69.4%	74.6%

Imports (1986): Mt. 21,937,180,000 (foodstuffs 27.5%, capital equipment 16.1%, machinery and spare parts 12.5%, crude petroleum and derivatives 8.8%, chemicals 7.1%, metals 4.0%). *Major import sources:* United States 12.4%; U.S.S.R. 12.1%; South Africa 11.7%; Italy 6.3%; France 6.1%; Portugal 6.1%.
Exports (1986): Mt. 3,198,385,000 (shrimps 48.4%, cashew nuts 21.1%, sugar 10.2%, petroleum products 5.1%, citrus fruit 2.8%, copra 2.6%, tea 1.6%). *Major export destinations:* Japan 22.6%; United States 22.1%; Spain 21.3%; East Germany 7.7%; Portugal 2.9%.

Transport and communications

Transport. Railroads (1986): length 2,182 mi, 3,512 km; passenger-mi 163,793,000, passenger-km 263,600,000; short ton-mi cargo 207,743,000, metric ton-km cargo 303,300,000. Roads (1986): total length 16,215 mi, 26,095 km (paved 20%). Vehicles (1981): passenger cars 99,400; trucks and buses 24,700. Merchant marine (1987): vessels (100 gross tons and over) 105; total deadweight tonnage 28,990. Air transport (1986): passenger-mi 306,000,000, passenger-km 492,000,000; short ton-mi cargo 7,636,000, metric ton-km cargo 11,148,000; airports (1988) with scheduled flights 7.
Communications. Daily newspapers (1987): total number 2; total circulation 81,000; circulation per 1,000 population 5.6. Radio (1986): total number of receivers 500,000 (1 per 28 persons). Television (1987): total number of receivers 10,000 (1 per 1,452 persons). Telephones (1986): 61,847 (1 per 232 persons).

Education and health

Education (1985–86)

	schools	teachers	students	student/ teacher ratio
Primary (age 5–9)[11]	4,382	20,756	1,251,391	60.3
Secondary (age 10–16)	208	3,422	144,012	42.1
Voc., teacher tr.	34	864	10,485	12.2
Higher	2	330	1,569	4.8

Educational attainment (1980). Percent of population age 25 and over having: no formal schooling 80.7%; primary education 18.2%; secondary 0.9%; higher 0.2%. *Literacy* (1985): total population age 15 and over literate 1,270,389 (16.6%); males literate 743,101 (20.0%); females literate 527,288 (13.3%).
Health (1986): physicians 279 (1 per 50,817 persons); hospital beds 12,270 (1 per 1,155 persons); infant mortality rate per 1,000 live births (1980–85) 153.0.
Food (1984–86): daily per capita caloric intake 1,607 (vegetable products 96%, animal products 4%); (1983) 71% of FAO recommended minimum requirement.

Military

Total active duty personnel (1988): 36,700 (army 95.4%, navy 1.9%, air force 2.7%). *Military expenditure as percent of GNP* (1985): 7.4% (world 6.1%); per capita expenditure U.S.$12.

---

[1]Total area is shown for the provinces. [2]January 1. [3]Detail does not add to total given because of rounding. [4]Density is based on land area. [5]Metal content only. [6]At prices of 1980. [7]Internal disorder and a lack of foreign exchange have brought the production of refined petroleum products and importation of crude petroleum practically to a halt. [8]Includes external long-term private debt not guaranteed by the government. [9]Services includes Public utilities. [10]Unemployed. [11]Includes initiation classes in which pupils learn Portuguese.

Nepal

Official name: Nepāl Adhirājya
(Kingdom of Nepal).
Form of government: constitutional
monarchy with one legislative house
(National Panchayat [140[1]]).
Chief of state: King.
Head of government: Prime Minister.
Capital: Kāthmāndu.
Official language: Nepālī.
Official religion: none.
Monetary unit: 1 Nepalese rupee
(NRs) = 100 paisa (pice); valuation
(Oct. 10, 1988) 1 U.S.$ = NRs 22.26;
1 £ = NRs 38.12.

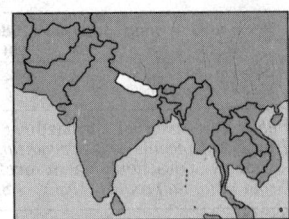

Area and population

Development regions Geographic regions	Capitals	area sq mi	area sq km	population 1981 census
Eastern	Dhankūtā	10,987	28,456	3,708,923
Mountain				338,439
Hill				1,257,042
Tarai				2,113,442
Central	Kāthmāndu	10,583	27,410	4,909,357
Mountain				413,143
Hill				2,108,433
Tarai				2,387,781
Western	Pokharā	11,351	29,398	3,128,859
Mountain				19,951
Hill				2,150,939
Tarai				957,969
Mid-western	Surkhet	16,362	42,378	1,955,611
Mountain				242,486
Hill				1,042,365
Tarai				670,760
Far-western	Dipāyal	7,544	19,539	1,320,089
Mountain				288,877
Hill				604,336
Tarai				426,876
TOTAL		56,827	147,181	15,022,839

Demography

Population (1988): 18,004,000.
Density (1988): persons per sq mi 316.8, persons per sq km 122.3.
Urban–rural (1987): urban 8.3%; rural 91.7%.
Sex distribution (1988): male 51.52%; female 48.48%.
Age breakdown (1986): under 15, 42.2%; 15–29, 25.6%; 30–44, 17.3%; 45–59, 10.0%; 60–74, 4.2%; 75 and over, 0.7%.
Population projection: (1990) 18,910,000; (2000) 23,176,000.
Doubling time: 27 years.
Ethnic composition (1981): Nepalese 58.4%; Bihārī (including Maithilī and Bhojpurī) 18.7%; Tharu 3.6%; Tamang 3.5%; Newār 3.0%; other 12.8%.
Religious affiliation (1981): Hindu 89.5%; Buddhist 5.3%; Muslim 2.7%; Jain 0.1%; other 2.4%.
Major cities (1981): Kāthmāndu 235,160; Birātnagar 93,544; Lalitpur 79,875; Bhaktapur 48,472; Pokhara 46,642.

Vital statistics

Birth rate per 1,000 population (1987): 40.4 (world avg. 26.0).
Death rate per 1,000 population (1987): 14.4 (world avg. 9.9).
Natural increase rate per 1,000 population (1987): 26.0 (world avg. 16.1).
Total fertility rate (avg. births per childbearing woman; 1987): 6.0.
Marriage rate per 1,000 population: n.a.
Divorce rate per 1,000 population: n.a.
Life expectancy at birth (1987): male 53.9 years; female 51.1 years.
Major causes of death per 100,000 population: n.a.; however, major diseases include malaria, tuberculosis, cholera, and typhoid.

National economy

Budget (1987–88). Revenue: NRs 9,848,000,000 (1985–86; taxes on goods and services 38.7%, customs duties 21.0%, income tax 9.9%, interest on loans 9.0%, registration taxes 6.5%, land revenue 6.0%, government services 5.2%). Expenditures: NRs 15,187,700,000 (economic services 47.9%, social services 23.6%, loan repayment 9.9%, defense 5.4%, general administration 4.8%).
Public debt (external, outstanding; 1986): U.S.$711,100,000.
Tourism: receipts from visitors (1987) U.S.$55,956,000; expenditures by nationals abroad (1987) U.S.$29,000,000.
Production (metric tons except as noted). Agriculture, forestry, fishing (1986–87): rice 2,372,000, corn (maize) 868,000, wheat 701,000, sugarcane 616,000, potatoes 395,000, millet 137,000, oil seed 83,000, barley 25,000, jute 23,000, tobacco 5,000; livestock (number of live animals) 6,362,930 cattle, 5,089,933 goats, 2,917,579 buffalo, 836,624 sheep, 476,340 pigs; roundwood (1986) 16,127,000 cu m; fish catch (1986) 9,443. Mining and quarrying (1985–86): limestone 167,789; magnesite 63,190; talc 8,780; garnet (1984–85) 27,300 kg. Manufacturing (1986–87): cement 151,631; sugar 24,565; jute goods 18,239; soap 11,460; tea 1,112; plywood 2,438,000 square feet; cigarettes 5,600,000,000 units; shoes 121,000 pairs. Construction: n.a. Energy production (consumption): electricity (kW-hr; 1986) 427,000,000 (462,000,000); coal (metric tons; 1986) 8,000 (158,000); petroleum products (metric tons; 1986) none (164,000); natural gas, none (none).
Gross national product (at current market prices; 1986): U.S.$2,640,000,000 (U.S.$160 per capita).

Structure of gross domestic product and labour force

	1985–86 in value NRs '000,000	1985–86 % of total value	1981 labour force	1981 % of labour force
Agriculture	29,603	58.0	6,244,289	91.1
Mining	139	0.3	971	[2]
Manufacturing	2,271	4.4	33,029	0.5
Construction	3,223	6.3	2,022	[2]
Public utilities	197	0.4	3,013	[2]
Transp. and commun.	3,087	6.0	7,424	0.1
Trade	1,901	3.7	109,446	1.6
Finance	3,674	7.2	9,850	0.1
Services	3,562	7.0	313,570	4.6
Other	3,421[3]	6.7[3]	127,272[4]	1.9[4]
TOTAL	51,078	100.0	6,850,886	100.0[5]

Population economically active (1986): total 7,760,155; activity rate of total population 45.5% (participation rates: ages 15–64, 82.5%; female 34.7%; unemployed [1980] 5.5%).

Price and earnings indexes (1980 = 100)

	1982	1983	1984	1985	1986	1987	1988[6]
Consumer price index	124.1	139.5	143.4	155.0	184.5	204.3	218.8
Monthly earnings index	...	...	...	...	...	...	...

Household income and expenditure. Average family size (1981) 5.8; income per family (1976–77) NRs 5,914 (U.S.$473); sources of income (1973–74)[7]: wages and salaries 39.2%, self-employment 33.6%, owner-occupied dwellings 17.5%; expenditure (1973–75)[7]: food and beverages 57.4%, housing 11.4%, clothing 10.5%, recreation 7.9%, health care 4.2%, transport and communications 2.1%, personal effects and other 6.5%.
Land use (1985): forested 37.6%; meadows and pastures 13.4%; agricultural and under permanent cultivation 18.0%; other 31.0%.

Foreign trade[8]

Balance of trade (current prices)

	1982	1983	1984	1985	1986	1987
NRs '000,000	–3,827.2	–5,064.2	–4,411.4	–5,048.0	–6,275.7	–7,659.6
% of total	62.2%	65.0%	51.1%	46.3%	51.0%	52.8%

Imports (1986–87): NRs 11,020,300,000 (1985–86; basic manufactured goods 29.5%; machinery and transport equipment 22.9%; chemicals 12.5%; mineral fuels 11.3%; food and live animals, chiefly for food 10.4%; miscellaneous manufactured articles 6.8%; crude materials except fuels 4.2%). *Major import sources* (1985–86): India 42.5%; Japan 16.5%; South Korea 5.1%; Singapore 3.7%; China 3.3%; West Germany 3.0%.
Exports (1986–87): NRs 3,059,700,000 (basic manufactures 34.5%; food and live animals, chiefly for food 22.7%; machinery, transport equipment, and other manufactured articles 22.3%; crude materials except fuels 16.6%; animal and vegetable oils 3.9%). *Major export destinations* (1985–86): India 40.3%; United States 27.3%; West Germany 7.6%; Singapore 7.3%; United Kingdom 3.6%; Soviet Union 2.3%.

Transport and communications

Transport. Railroads (1986–87): route length 33 mi, 53 km; passengers carried 1,673,000; freight handled 19,000 metric tons. Roads (1986–87): total length 3,918 mi, 6,306 km (paved 44%). Vehicles (1978): passenger cars 14,201; trucks and buses 9,988. Merchant marine: none. Air transport[9] (1986): passenger-mi 186,000,000, passenger-km 300,000,000; short ton-mi cargo 4,266,000, metric ton-km cargo 6,228,000; airports (1988) with scheduled flights 5.
Communications. Daily newspapers (1986–87): total number 59; total circulation, n.a.; circulation per 1,000 population, n.a. Radio (1986): 2,012,000 receivers (1 per 8.5 persons). Television (1987): 27,000 receivers (1 per 651 persons). Telephones (1987): 25,606 (1 per 686 persons).

Education and health

Education (1986–87)

	schools	teachers	students	student/ teacher ratio
Primary (age 6–11)	12,186	53,405	1,857,658	34.8
Secondary (age 12–17)	5,140	21,785	540,049	24.8
Vocational[10]	5	117	648	5.5
Higher[10]	116	4,165	67,555	16.2

Educational attainment (1981). Percent of population age 25 and over having: no formal schooling 41.2%; primary education 29.4%; secondary 22.7%; higher 6.8%. *Literacy* (1981): total population age 15 and over literate 1,822,718 (20.7%); males literate 1,425,241 (31.9%); females literate 397,477 (9.2%).
Health (1987): physicians 863 (1 per 20,356 persons); hospital beds 3,842 (1 per 4,572 persons); infant mortality rate per 1,000 live births (1987) 106.
Food (1984–86): daily per capita caloric intake 2,050 (vegetable products 93%, animal products 7%); (1983) 93% of FAO recommended minimum.

Military

Total active duty personnel (1987): 30,000 (army 100.0%). *Military expenditure as percent of GNP* (1985): 1.2% (world 6.1%); per capita expenditure U.S.$2.

[1]Includes 28 members appointed by the King. [2]Less than 0.05%. [3]Includes indirect taxes. [4]Activities not adequately defined. [5]Detail does not add to total given because of rounding. [6]June. [7]For Kāthmāndu only. [8]Import figures are f.o.b. (free on board) in balance of trade and c.i.f. (cost, insurance, and freight) for commodities and trading partners. [9]International flights only. [10]1985–86.

Netherlands, The

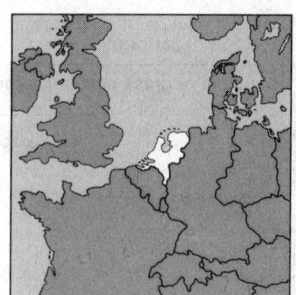

Official name: Koninkrijk der Nederlanden (Kingdom of The Netherlands).
Form of government: constitutional monarchy with two legislative houses (First Chamber [75]; Second Chamber [150]).
Chief of state: Monarch.
Head of government: Prime Minister.
Seat of government: The Hague.
Capital: Amsterdam.
Official language: Dutch.
Official religion: none.
Monetary unit: 1 Netherlands guilder (f.) = 100 cents; valuation (Oct. 10, 1988) 1 U.S.$ = f. 2.09; 1 £ = f. 3.58.

Area and population

Provinces	Capitals	area sq mi	area sq km	population 1987 estimate[1]
Drenthe	Assen	1,025	2,654	434,038
Flevoland	Lelystad	549	1,422	185,365
Friesland	Leeuwarden	1,295	3,353	599,061
Gelderland	Arnhem	1,935	5,011	1,771,972
Groningen	Groningen	906	2,346	558,378
Limburg	Maastricht	838	2,170	1,091,553
Noord-Brabant	's-Hertogenbosch	1,910	4,946	2,139,626
Noord-Holland	Haarlem	1,029	2,665	2,334,209
Overijssel	Zwolle	1,289	3,339	1,003,915
Utrecht	Utrecht	514	1,331	953,957
Zeeland	Middelburg	692	1,792	355,434
Zuid-Holland	The Hague	1,123	2,908	3,186,249
TOTAL LAND AREA		13,103[2]	33,937	14,615,125
INLAND WATER		3,060	7,926	
TOTAL AREA		16,163	41,863	

Demography

Population (1988): 14,741,000.
Density[3] (1988): persons per sq mi 1,125.0, persons per sq km 434.4.
Urban–rural (1987): urban 88.4%; rural 11.6%.
Sex distribution (1987): male 49.43%; female 50.57%.
Age breakdown (1987): under 15, 18.8%; 15–29, 25.5%; 30–44, 23.0%; 45–59, 15.7%; 60–74, 11.8%; 75 and over, 5.2%.
Population projection: (1990) 14,893,000; (2000) 15,679,000.
Doubling time: n.a.; vital rates and net migration in near balance.
Ethnic composition (by nationality; 1987): Netherlander 96.1%; Turkish 1.1%; Moroccan 0.8%; German 0.3%; other 1.7%.
Religious affiliation (1984): Roman Catholic 36.2%; Dutch Reformed Church 18.1%; Reformed Churches 8.3%; other 2.7%; no religion 34.7%.
Major cities (1987): Amsterdam 682,702; Rotterdam 572,642; The Hague 445,127; Utrecht 229,326; Eindhoven 190,962.

Vital statistics

Birth rate per 1,000 population (1986): 12.7 (world avg. 26.0); legitimate 91.2%; illegitimate 8.8%.
Death rate per 1,000 population (1986): 8.6 (world avg. 9.9).
Natural increase rate per 1,000 population (1986): 4.1 (world avg. 16.1).
Total fertility rate (avg. births per childbearing woman; 1986): 1.6.
Marriage rate per 1,000 population (1986): 6.0.
Divorce rate per 1,000 population (1986): 2.0.
Life expectancy at birth (1986): male 73.1 years; female 79.6 years.
Major causes of death per 100,000 population (1985): malignant neoplasms (cancers) 229.2, of which lung cancer 57.2; ischemic heart diseases 177.4; cerebrovascular diseases 81.1; accidents, poisonings, and violence 38.4.

National economy

Budget (1987). Revenue: f. 144,107,000,000 (income and corporate taxes 36.9%, value-added taxes 23.2%, excise and import taxes 7.6%, natural gas royalties 5.4%). Expenditures: f. 172,217,000,000 (education and culture 18.4%, social security and public health 17.3%, debt service 12.7%, defense 7.9%, transportation 6.3%).
Public debt (1986): U.S.$108,912,000,000.
Tourism (1985): receipts from visitors U.S.$1,503,000,000; expenditures by nationals abroad U.S.$3,118,000,000.
Production (metric tons except as noted). Agriculture (1986): sugar beets 7,707,000, potatoes 6,857,000, vegetables and melons 2,887,000, wheat 940,-000; livestock (number of live animals) 12,908,000 pigs, 5,076,000 cattle, 800,000 sheep; roundwood (1985) 1,139,000 cu m; fish catch (1985) 504,181. Manufacturing (value of sales in f. '000,000; 1985): foodstuffs 74,100; synthetic fibres 43,600; petroleum products 29,600; electrical machinery 23,700; transport equipment 12,600. Construction (1982): residential 58,947,000 cu m; nonresidential 51,620,000 cu m. Energy production (consumption): electricity (kW-hr; 1986) 67,123,000,000 (69,494,000,000); coal (metric tons; 1986) none (9,816,000); crude petroleum (barrels; 1986) 31,716,000 (346,-335,000); petroleum products (metric tons; 1986) 55,802,000 (29,616,000); natural gas (cu m; 1986) 80,601,000,000 (47,980,000,000).
Household income and expenditure. Average household size (1985) 2.6; income per household (1985) f. 80,000 (U.S.$24,000); sources of income: wages 40.0%, transfer payments 28.2%, self-employment 19.6%, other 12.2%; expenditure (1986): rent and utilities 19.4%, food, beverages, and tobacco 19.1%, medical care 12.7%, transportation and communications 10.9%, ed-

ucation and recreation 9.5%, household furnishings and appliances 7.5%, clothing and footwear 7.3%, other 13.6%.
Gross national product (at current market prices; 1986): U.S.$146,200,000,-000 (U.S.$10,050 per capita).

Structure of gross domestic product and labour force

	1986 in value f. '000,000	1986 % of total value	1985 labour force	1985 % of labour force
Agriculture	18,590	4.6	268,100	4.6
Mining	23,840	5.9	11,300	0.2
Manufacturing	85,080	21.2	993,400	17.2
Construction	21,640	5.4	385,700	6.7
Public utilities	9,330	2.3	44,200	0.8
Transp. and commun.	27,250	6.8	322,600	5.6
Trade	65,120	16.2	906,500	15.7
Pub. admin., defense			. . .[4]	. . .[4]
Finance	167,810	41.8	457,300	7.9
Services			1,716,100[4]	29.8[4]
Other	−16,880[5]	−4.2[5]	659,900[6]	11.4[6]
TOTAL	401,780	100.0	5,765,000[2]	100.0[2]

Population economically active (1987): total 5,862,400; activity rate of total population 40.2% (participation rates: ages 15–64, 58.1%; female 35.1%; unemployed 12.0%[7]).

Price and earnings indexes (1980 = 100)

	1981	1982	1983	1984	1985	1986	1987
Consumer price index	106.7	113.0	116.2	120.0	122.7	122.9	122.3
Hourly earnings index	103.0	110.0	113.0	115.0	120.0	122.0	124.0

Land use (1985): forested 8.8%; meadows and pastures 33.6%; agricultural and under permanent cultivation 25.8%; other 31.8%.

Foreign trade

Balance of trade (current prices)

	1982	1983	1984	1985	1986	1987
f. '000,000	15,173	16,076	20,978	21,469	20,386	13,201
% of total	4.5%	4.6%	5.3%	5.0%	5.5%	3.6%

Imports (1987): f. 184,477,000,000 (machinery and transport equipment 27.2%, of which transport equipment 9.8%; foodstuffs, beverages, and tobacco 12.3%; mineral fuels 11.2%; chemicals and chemical products 8.6%; metals and metal products 7.6%; textiles 4.9%; plastic, rubber, and synthetic products 4.8%; clothing and footwear 3.4%). *Major import sources* (1986): West Germany 21.0%; Belgium–Luxembourg 10.3%; U.K. 8.3%; U.S. 7.9%; France 6.3%.
Exports (1987): f. 187,574,000,000 (machinery and transport equipment 19.0%, of which transport equipment 4.9%; foodstuffs, beverages, and tobacco 15.6%; chemicals and chemical products 13.2%; mineral fuels 11.0%; plastic, rubber, and synthetic products 7.5%; metals and metal products 7.2%; textiles 3.4%). *Major export destinations* (1986): West Germany 28.4%; Belgium–Luxembourg 13.0%; France 9.6%; U.K. 8.3%; Italy 5.0%.

Transport and communications

Transport. Railroads (1986): length 2,824 km; passenger-km 8,919,000,000; metric ton-km cargo 3,050,000,000. Roads (1986): total length 112,648 km (paved 87%). Vehicles (1986): passenger cars 4,950,000; trucks and buses 408,711. Merchant marine[8] (1987): vessels (100 gross tons and over) 1,307; total deadweight tonnage 5,122,867. Air transport: passenger-km (1987) 27,732,211,000; metric ton-km cargo (1987) 5,078,761,000; airports (1988) 6.
Communications. Daily newspapers (1986): total number 43; total circulation 4,579,000; circulation per 1,000 population 315. Radio (1986): total number of receivers 4,808,728 (1 per 3.0 persons). Television (1987): total number of receivers 4,632,846 (1 per 3.2 persons). Telephones (1986): 9,080,000 (1 per 1.6 persons).

Education and health

Education (1985–86)

	schools	teachers	students	student/ teacher ratio
Primary (age 6–12)	9,388	102,388[9]	1,568,265	15.3[9]
Secondary (age 12–18)	1,382	53,361	803,782	15.1
Voc., teacher tr.	2,002	55,931	635,493	11.4
Higher	453	30,952	307,537	9.9

Educational attainment (1985). Percent of population[10] ages 25–64 having: primary education 16.7%; secondary 61.8%; higher 20.0%; other 1.5%. *Literacy* (1986): virtually 100% literate.
Health (1987): physicians 33,330 (1 per 438 persons); hospital beds 67,545 (1 per 217 persons); infant mortality rate per 1,000 live births (1986) 6.4.
Food (1983–85): daily per capita caloric intake 3,355 (vegetable products 60%, animal products 40%); (1983) 129% of FAO recommended minimum requirement.

Military

Total active duty personnel (1987): 108,100 (army 62.9%, navy 15.8%, air force 16.6%, other[11] 4.7%). *Military expenditure as percent of GNP* (1985): 3.1% (world 6.1%); per capita expenditure U.S.$271.

[1]January 1; includes 1,368 persons having no fixed municipality of residence. [2]Detail does not add to total given because of rounding. [3]Based on land area only. [4]Services include Public administration, defense. [5]Imputed bank service charge. [6]Includes 620,500 unemployed persons. [7]1986. [8]Includes Netherlands Antilles and Aruba. [9]Includes special subject teachers. [10]Economically active population (4,612,000) only. [11]Includes 3,950 military police.

Netherlands Antilles

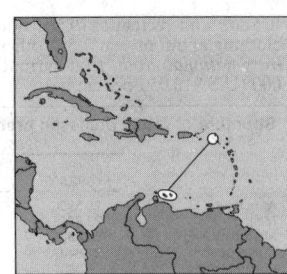

Official name: Nederlandse Antillen (Netherlands Antilles).
Political status: nonmetropolitan territory of The Netherlands with one legislative house (States of the Netherlands Antilles [22])[1].
Chief of state: Dutch Monarch represented by governor.
Head of government: Prime Minister.
Capital: Willemstad.
Official language: Dutch.
Official religion: none.
Monetary unit: 1 Netherlands Antillean guilder (NA f.) = 100 cents; valuation (Oct. 10, 1988) 1 U.S.$ = NA f. 1.80; 1 £ = NA f. 3.08.

Area and population		area		population
				1981
Island councils	Capitals	sq mi	sq km	census
Leeward Islands				
Bonaire	Kralendijk	111	288	8,753
Curaçao	Willemstad	171	444	147,388
Windward Islands				
Saba	The Bottom	5	13	965
Sint Eustatius or Statia	Oranjestad	8	21	1,358
Sint Maarten (Dutch part only)	Philipsburg	13	34	13,156
TOTAL		308	800	171,620

Demography

Population (1988): 177,000.
Density (1988): persons per sq mi 574.7, persons per sq km 221.3.
Urban–rural (1985)[2]: urban 92.4%; rural 7.6%.
Sex distribution (1986): male 48.68%; female 51.32%.
Age breakdown (1981): under 15, 30.0%; 15–29, 29.9%; 30–44, 19.5%; 45–59, 11.3%; 60–74, 6.7%; 75 and over, 2.6%.
Population projection: (1990) 178,000; (2000) 186,000.
Doubling time: 45 years.
Ethnic composition (1980)[2]: Netherlands Antillean (Dutch/Spanish/black/Amerindian) creole 84.0%; white 6.1%; other West Indian 4.9%; Suriname creole 2.9%; other 2.1%.
Religious affiliation (1981): Roman Catholic 83.8%; Protestant 10.2%, of which Lutheran/Reformed tradition 3.3%, Methodist 3.2%, Seventh-day Adventist 1.5%; Jewish 0.3%; nonreligious 2.6%; other 3.1%.
Major cities (1985): Willemstad (urban area) 125,000; Philipsburg 10,000[3].

Vital statistics

Birth rate per 1,000 population (1985)[4]: 21.7 (world avg. 29.0); legitimate 50.7%; illegitimate 49.3%[4].
Death rate per 1,000 population (1985)[4]: 6.2 (world avg. 11.0).
Natural increase rate per 1,000 population (1985)[4]: 15.5 (world avg. 18.0).
Total fertility rate (avg. births per childbearing woman; 1984)[2]: 3.4.
Marriage rate per 1,000 population (1985)[4]: 6.1.
Divorce rate per 1,000 population (1985)[4]: 2.8.
Life expectancy at birth (1981)[5]: male 71.1 years; female 75.7 years.
Major causes of death per 100,000 population (1985): diseases of the circulatory system 247.2; malignant neoplasms (cancers) 113.9; respiratory diseases 45.8; accidents 43.5; conditions originating in the perinatal period 33.8; endocrinal and metabolic diseases 24.6.

National economy

Budget (1987). Revenue: NA f. 979,700,000 (current and development revenue from local sources 82.8%[6], of which profit taxes from offshore sector 27.9%, taxes on wages 17.9%, taxes on goods and services 10.7%; development revenue from The Netherlands 17.2%[7]). Expenditures: NA f. 1,043,100,000 (current expenditures 84.9%[6]; locally funded development expenditures 5.8%[6]; development expenditures from The Netherlands 9.3%[7]).
Public debt (external, outstanding; end of 1987): U.S.$364,000,000.
Tourism: receipts from visitors (1987) U.S.$277,000,000, of which Sint Maarten U.S.$173,000,000, Curaçao U.S.$93,000,000, Bonaire U.S.$11,000,000; expenditures by nationals abroad (1983)[2] U.S.$107,000,000.
Production (metric tons except as noted). Agriculture, forestry, fishing (value of production in NA f. '000; 1982): eggs 3,863, fruits and vegetables 2,850[8], pork 1,250, goat meat 555; livestock (number of live animals; 1986[2]) 23,000 goats, 9,000 cattle, 8,000 sheep, 8,000 pigs; roundwood, n.a.; fish 1,060[2]. Mining and quarrying (1986): unrefined salt 380,000. Manufacturing (1985): residual fuel oil 6,800,000[2, 9]; ship repair NA f. 48,000,000[10]; curaçao liqueur 780 hectolitres; other manufactures include electronic parts, cigarettes, textiles, and rum. Construction (gross value of construction; 1986[5]): NA f. 57,700,000. Energy production (consumption): electricity (kW-hr; 1986[2]) 1,485,000,000 (1,485,000,000); coal, none (none); crude petroleum (barrels; 1986[2, 9]) none (60,800,000); petroleum products (metric tons; 1986[2, 9]) 7,800,000 (1,391,000); natural gas, none (none).
Household income and expenditure. Average household size (1981) 3.7; income per household: n.a.; sources of income: n.a.; expenditure (1984)[11, 12]: food 22.1%, transportation and communications 19.4%, housing 18.8%, household furnishings 10.0%, clothing and footwear 8.7%, recreation and education 5.9%, beverages and tobacco 2.3%, health 2.2%, other 10.6%.

Gross national product (at current market prices; 1985)[2]: U.S.$1,610,000,000 (U.S.$6,810 per capita).

Structure of gross domestic product and labour force				
	1985		1986	
	in value NA f. '000,000	% of total value	labour force	% of labour force
Agriculture	...	0.7	426	0.6
Mining	...	0.4	187	0.2
Manufacturing	...	13.2	5,297	6.9
Construction	...	9.9	5,484	7.1
Public utilities	...	3.1	1,370	1.8
Transportation and communications	...	12.0	3,832	5.0
Trade	...	18.3	16,390	21.2
Finance	...	15.6	5,207	6.7
Pub. admin., defense	...	23.5 }	21,085	27.3
Services	...	6.5 }		
Other	...	−3.2[13]	17,932[14]	23.2[14]
TOTAL		100.0	77,210	100.0

Population economically active (1986): total 77,210; activity rate of total population 44.0% (participation rates [1981]: ages 15–64, 63.5%; female 40.6%; unemployed 23.2%, of which Curaçao 28.9%, Bonaire 15.2%, Windward Islands, negligible).

Price and earnings indexes (1985 = 100)						
	1982	1983	1984	1985	1986	1987
Consumer price index[12]	95.9	98.0	99.7	100.0	103.2	106.0
Monthly earnings index[15]	...	94.5	95.5	100.0	89.3	...

Land use (1985): forested, negligible; meadows and pastures, negligible; agricultural and under permanent cultivation 8.0%; other (dry savanna) 92.0%.

Foreign trade[16]

Balance of trade (current prices)						
	1982	1983	1984	1985	1986	1987
NA f. '000,000	+637	−7	−368	−1,038	−1,206	−1,411
% of total	3.8%	0.1%	2.6%	14.7%	82.5%	83.7%

Imports (1986)[2, 12]: NA f. 2,002,000,000 (crude petroleum and petroleum products 64.7%, other goods 35.3%). *Major import sources* (1984): Venezuela 50.0%; Mexico 15.4%; United States 10.3%; Libya 3.9%; The Netherlands 3.4%.
Exports (1986)[2, 12]: NA f. 1,641,000,000 (crude petroleum and petroleum products 95.2%, other goods 4.8%). *Major export destinations* (1984): United States 17.4%; Jamaica 9.3%; Puerto Rico 8.7%; Cuba 8.4%; The Netherlands 6.0%; Colombia 5.3%.

Transport and communications

Transport. Railroads: none. Roads (1984): total length 510 mi, 820 km (paved, n.a.). Vehicles (1986): passenger cars 54,140; trucks and buses 10,174. Merchant marine (1987): vessels (100 gross tons and over) 79[2]; total deadweight tonnage, n.a. Air transport (1982)[17]: passenger-mi 234,000,000, passenger-km 377,000,000; short ton-mi cargo 1,243,000, metric ton-km cargo 1,815,000; airports (1988) with scheduled flights 5.
Communications. Daily newspapers (1986): total number 5; total circulation 65,700; circulation per 1,000 population 375. Radio (1986): 149,000 receivers (1 per 1.6 persons). Television (1987): 32,000 receivers (1 per 5.5 persons). Telephones (1985)[2]: 49,600 (1 per 4.8 persons).

Education and health

Education (1986)	schools	teachers	students	student/ teacher ratio
Primary (age 6–12)	91	1,145	24,600	21.5
Secondary (age 12–17)	22	630	8,600	13.7
Voc., teacher tr.	3	50	650	13.0
Higher	2	80	700	8.8

Educational attainment (1981). Percent of population age 25 and over having: no formal schooling or some primary education 29.7%; completed primary 31.5%; completed vocational or secondary 37.6%; completed higher 1.2%. *Literacy* (1985): total population age 15 and over literate 95.0%.
Health: physicians (1987) 232 (1 per 760 persons); hospital beds (1985) 1,779 (1 per 98 persons); infant mortality rate per 1,000 live births (1985) 18.2[4].
Food (1984–86)[2]: daily per capita caloric intake 2,850 (vegetable products 66%, animal products 34%); (1983) 116% of FAO recommended minimum requirement.

Military

Total active duty personnel (1986): A small Dutch naval contingent is stationed permanently in the Netherlands Antilles.

[1]Aruba withdrew from the Netherlands Antilles on Jan. 1, 1986, becoming an autonomous member of the Kingdom of The Netherlands, the same status as the whole of the Netherlands Antilles. [2]Includes Aruba. [3]1980. [4]Excludes Sint Eustatius. [5]Curaçao only. [6]For central government and island government of Curaçao. [7]For central government and all island governments. [8]Mostly tomatoes, beans, cucumbers, gherkins, melons, and lettuce grown on hydroponic farms; aloes grown for export, divi-divi pods, and sour orange fruit are non-hydroponic crops. [9]Curaçao's oil refinery was operational in early 1988, but the oil refinery on Aruba was closed in March 1985. [10]Foreign income in 1986. [11]Weights of consumer price index components. [12]Curaçao and Bonaire only. [13]Less imputed bank service charges. [14]Unemployed. [15]Average nonagricultural wage. [16]Imports c.i.f.; exports f.o.b. [17]ALM airlines only.

New Caledonia

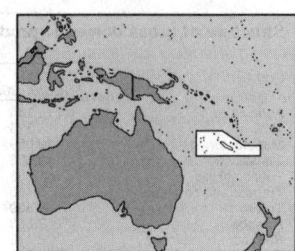

Official name: Territoire de la Nouvelle-Calédonie et Dépendances (Territory of New Caledonia and Dependencies).
Political status: overseas territory (France) under interim direct rule until mid-1989.
Chief of state: President of France.
Head of government: High Commissioner.
Capital: Nouméa.
Official language: French.
Official religion: none.
Monetary unit: 1 franc of the Comptoirs français du Pacifique (CFPF) = 100 centimes; valuation (Oct. 10, 1988) 1 U.S.$ = CFPF 110.95; 1 £ = CFPF 190.00.

Area and population

		area		population
Regions[1]	Capitals	sq mi	sq km	1983 census
Loyauté	...	765	1,981	15,510
Nord	...	2,837	7,348	21,512
Nouméa	Nouméa	637	1,650	85,098
Sud	...	2,995	7,757	23,248
TOTAL		7,233[2,3]	18,734[2,3]	145,368

Demography

Population (1988): 156,000.
Density (1987): persons per sq mi 21.6, persons per sq km 8.3.
Urban–rural (1983): urban 58.5%; rural 41.5%.
Sex distribution (1983): male 51.10%; female 48.90%.
Age breakdown (1983): under 15, 36.2%; 15–29, 26.9%; 30–44, 19.5%; 45–59, 11.2%; 60–74,. 5.1%; 75 and over, 1.1%.
Population projection: (1990) 160,000; (2000) 183,000.
Doubling time: 40 years.
Ethnic composition (1983): Melanesian 43.4%, of which local Melanesian 42.6%; European 37.1%; Polynesian 12.2%, of which Wallisian 8.4%, Tahitian 3.8%; Indonesian 3.7%; Vietnamese 1.6%; other 2.0%.
Religious affiliation (1984): Roman Catholic 62.7%; Sunnī Muslim 4.0%; other (mostly Protestant) 33.3%.
Major cities (1983)[4]: Nouméa 60,112; Mont-Doré 14,614; Dumbéa 5,538.

Vital statistics

Birth rate per 1,000 population (1985): 23.5 (world avg. 29.0); (1983) legitimate 53.0%; illegitimate 47.0%.
Death rate per 1,000 population (1985): 5.7 (world avg. 11.0).
Natural increase rate per 1,000 population (1985): 17.8 (world avg. 18.0).
Total fertility rate (avg. births per childbearing woman; 1984): 3.5.
Marriage rate per 1,000 population (1983): 5.7.
Divorce rate per 1,000 population (1983): 1.1.
Life expectancy at birth (1980–85): male 64.6 years; female 68.5.
Major causes of death per 100,000 population (1981)[5]: diseases of the circulatory system 45.0; traumas 31.6; malignant neoplasms (cancers) 23.5; infectious and parasitic diseases 10.9; ill-defined conditions 94.2.

National economy

Budget (1988). Revenue: CFPF 42,805,000,000 (current revenue 89.2%, of which indirect taxes 36.9%, French government grants 17.8%; direct taxes 15.9%; development revenue 10.8%). Expenditures: CFPF 42,805,000,000 (current expenditure 89.2%, of which contributions to assistance funds 33.4%, social and cultural services 25.5%, public debt 9.3%; development expenditure 10.8%).
Public debt (external, outstanding; 1985[6]): U.S.$126,000,000.
Tourism (1986): receipts from visitors U.S.$40,000,000; expenditures by nationals abroad, n.a.
Production (value of production in CFPF '000,000 except as noted). Agriculture, forestry, fishing (1987): beef 675, vegetables 650, eggs 549, fruits 540, live animals 490, pork 370, forest products 310, chickens 215, frozen deepwater fish 180[7], inshore fish 160[7], coffee 150, potatoes 96, trochas shells 81[7,8], coral 48[7,8]. Mining and quarrying (metric tons; 1987): nickel ore 2,790,000 (ferronickel [metal content] 29,500, nickel matte [metal content] 8,300); chromite ore 153,000 (concentrate 62,000). Manufacturing (metric tons; 1987): cement 58,400; copra 688; soap 373; refined coconut oil 83; beer 64,084 hectolitres. Construction (dwellings authorized; 1984): residential 45,900 sq m; nonresidential, n.a. Energy production (consumption): electricity (kW-hr; 1986) 983,700,000 (977,600,000); coal (metric tons; 1986) none (175,000); crude petroleum, none (none); petroleum products (metric tons; 1986) none (341,000); natural gas, none (none).
Population economically active (1983): total 58,154; activity rate of total population 40.0% (participation rates: ages 15–64, n.a.; female, n.a.; unemployed [1987] 7.0%).

Price and earnings indexes (1980 = 100)[9]

	1981	1982	1983	1984	1985	1986	1987
Consumer price index	115.9	131.3	145.8	156.2	164.3	163.4	165.8
Earnings index[10]	115.9	138.3	153.2	164.2	172.3	173.3	174.8

Land use (1985): forested 37.7%; meadows and pastures 14.7%; agricultural and under permanent cultivation 1.1%; other 46.5%.
Gross national product (at current market prices; 1984): U.S.$920,000,000 (U.S.$6,230 per capita).

Structure of gross domestic product and labour force

	1984		1983	
	in value CFPF '000,000	% of total value	labour force	% of labour force
Agriculture	2,252	1.8	19,700	33.9
Mining	6,396	5.1		
Manufacturing	16,198	12.8	7,272	12.5
Construction	5,301	4.2		
Public utilities	2,491	2.0	565	1.0
Transportation and communications	4,227	3.3	2,659	4.6
Trade	31,274[11]	24.7	4,370[12]	7.5
Finance	20,169[11]	15.9	1,025	1.8
Services }				
Pub. admin., defense	36,852	29.1	18,922[12]	32.5
Other	1,329	1.1	3,641[13]	6.3
TOTAL	126,489	100.0	58,154	100.0[2]

Household income and expenditure. Average household size (1983) 4.1; average annual income per household (1980–81) CFPF 1,627,000 (U.S.$18,598)[14]; sources of income (1980): salaries 71.6%, welfare 5.1%, pensions 4.5%, other 18.8%; expenditure (1981): food 27.5%, transportation 15.1%, housing 13.3%, household furnishings 11.4%, recreation 6.4%, other 26.3%.

Foreign trade

Balance of trade (current prices)

	1982	1983	1984	1985	1986	1987
CFPF '000,000	−16,323	−18,971	−12,902	−11,109	−36,164	−41,391
% of total	22.9%	28.4%	14.9%	11.0%	40.3%	43.3%

Imports (1987): CFPF 68,533,000,000 (transportation equipment 21.3%, food 18.1%, machinery and electrical goods 13.9%, mineral products 9.9%, chemicals and chemical products 6.4%). *Major import sources:* France 53.0%; Australia 7.6%; Japan 4.7%; West Germany 4.0%; United States 3.8%.
Exports (1987): CFPF 27,142,000,000 (ferronickel and nickel matte 64.5%, nickel ore 8.1%, chromite 3.2%). *Major export destinations:* France 44.0%; Japan 19.1%; West Germany 8.6%; United States 7.5%; India 4.5%.

Transport and communications

Transport. Railroads: none. Roads (1985): total length 3,422 mi, 5,507 km (paved 14%). Vehicles (1985): passenger cars 42,000; trucks and buses 2,500. Merchant marine: vessels (100 gross tons and over) n.a. Air transport (1986)[15]: passenger-mi 15,000,000, passenger-km 24,000,000; short ton-mi cargo, n.a.; airports (1988) with scheduled flights 10.
Communications. Daily newspapers (1987): total number 2; total circulation 24,000; circulation per 1,000 population 158. Radio (1986): total number of receivers 85,000 (1 per 1.8 persons). Television (1987): total number of receivers 35,500 (1 per 4.3 persons). Telephones (1984): 32,010 (1 per 4.6 persons).

Education and health

Education (1987)

	schools	teachers	students	student/teacher ratio
Primary (age 6–10)	276	1,564	32,205	20.6
Secondary (age 11–17)	47	1,179	13,540	11.5
Vocational	28	200	5,887	29.4
Higher	6	40	853	21.3

Educational attainment (1983). Percent of population age 20 and over having: no formal schooling 17.4%; primary education 51.8%; secondary 25.9%; higher 4.8%. *Literacy* (1976): total population age 14 and over literate 75,819 (89.4%); males literate 40,296 (90.1%); females literate 35,523 (88.7%).
Health: physicians (1987) 253 (1 per 608 persons); hospital beds (1983) 1,224 (1 per 121 persons); infant mortality rate per 1,000 live births (1985) 13.8.
Food (1983–85): daily per capita caloric intake 2,909 (vegetable products 79%, animal products 21%); (1983) 104% of FAO recommended minimum requirement.

Military

Total active duty personnel (1987): 4,900 French troops. *Military expenditure as percent of GNP:* n.a.

---

[1]Breakdown reflects administrative organization between November 1985 and July 1988. The establishment of 3 new autonomous regions is pending until mid-1989. [2]Detail does not add to total given because of rounding. [3]Total area per new survey equals 7,172 sq mi (18,576 sq km); regional areas are not available. [4]Populations cited are for communes. [5]Public health facilities only. [6]Includes external long-term private debt not guaranteed by the government. [7]1986. [8]Value of sales. [9]All figures are end of year. [10]Based on minimum hourly wage. [11]Finance/Services includes restaurants and hotels. [12]Services/Pub. admin., defense includes restaurants and hotels. [13]Includes 3,500 unemployed. [14]Average European household CFPF 2,243,000 (U.S.$25,640); Melanesian CFPF 777,000 (U.S.$8,882). [15]Air Calédonie only.

New Zealand

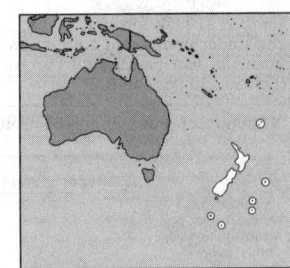

Official name: New Zealand.
Form of government: constitutional
monarchy with one legislative house
(House of Representatives [97]).
Chief of state: British Monarch,
represented by governor-general.
Head of government: Prime Minister.
Capital: Wellington.
Official language: English; Maori.
Official religion: none.
Monetary unit: 1 New Zealand dollar
($NZ) = 100 cents; valuation (Oct.
10, 1988) 1 U.S.$ = $NZ 1.60; 1
£ = $NZ 2.74.

Area and population	area		population
			1986
Statistical areas[1]	sq mi	sq km	census
North Island			
Central Auckland	2,154	5,578	889,225
East Coast	4,212	10,908	48,364
Hawke's Bay	4,356	11,283	150,744
Northland	4,883	12,646	127,558
South Auckland–			
Bay of Plenty	14,240	36,881	518,721
Taranaki	3,754	9,724	108,979
Wellington	10,715	27,751	598,024
South Island			
Canterbury[2]	16,691	43,230	431,421
Marlborough	4,243	10,989	38,087
Nelson	6,768	17,530	81,160
Otago	14,209	36,801	186,142
Southland[3]	11,160	28,905	104,817
Westland	5,903	15,289	23,842
TOTAL	103,288	267,515	3,307,084

Demography

Population (1988): 3,366,000.
Density (1988): persons per sq mi 32.6, persons per sq km 12.6.
Urban–rural (1986): urban 83.8%; rural 16.2%.
Sex distribution (1987): male 49.50%; female 50.50%.
Age breakdown (1987): under 15, 23.7%; 15–29, 26.2%; 30–44, 21.0%; 45–59,
14.2%; 60–74, 10.7%; 75 and over, 4.2%.
Population projection: (1990) 3,422,000; (2000) 3,757,000.
Doubling time: 89 years.
Ethnic composition (1986): European 81.2%; New Zealand Maori 9.0%; Pa-
cific Island Polynesian 2.9%; other and not specified 6.9%.
Religious affiliation (1986): Anglican 24.3%; Presbyterian 18.0%; Roman
Catholic 15.2%; Methodist 4.7%; nonreligious 16.4%; other 21.4%.
Major cities (1987): Manukau 181,000; Christchurch 167,700; Auckland
148,400; Wellington 136,000; Waitemata 98,500.

Vital statistics

Birth rate per 1,000 population (1987): 16.7 (world avg. 26.0); legitimate
71.4%; illegitimate 28.6%.
Death rate per 1,000 population (1987): 8.3 (world avg. 9.9).
Natural increase rate per 1,000 population (1987): 8.4 (world avg. 16.1).
Total fertility rate (avg. births per childbearing woman; 1987): 1.9.
Marriage rate per 1,000 population (1987): 7.4.
Divorce rate per 1,000 population (1986): 0.3.
Life expectancy at birth (1987): male 71.8 years; female 77.8 years.
Major causes of death per 100,000 population (1984): diseases of the cir-
culatory system 368.8, of which ischemic heart diseases 220.8; malignant
neoplasms (cancers) 180.7; accidents 40.7; pneumonia 32.6.

National economy

Budget (1985–86). Revenue: $NZ 15,801,300,000 (income tax 66.9%; cus-
toms, sales tax, and beer duty 16.0%; interest and profits 9.9%; highways
tax 2.7%). Expenditures: $NZ 17,672,300,000 (social services 30.8%; debt
service and investment 18.9%; health 13.1%; education 11.4%; development
of industry 6.9%).
Public debt (external, outstanding; 1986): U.S.$16,700,000,000.
Tourism (1986): receipts from visitors U.S.$286,500,000; expenditures by
nationals abroad U.S.$400,000,000.
Production (metric tons except as noted). Agriculture, forestry, fishing
(1987): fruits 555,000, barley 400,600, wheat 336,800, potatoes 281,000, corn
176,100, oats 78,600; livestock (number of live animals; 1987) 64,244,000
sheep, 8,279,000 cattle, 1,054,000 goats, 426,000 pigs; roundwood 9,902,000
cu m; fish catch (1986) 339,563. Mining and quarrying (1986): limestone
2,422,800; serpentine 22,362; lead 5,000; iron ore and sand concentrate
4,685; gold 1,265. Manufacturing (value added, $NZ '000; 1983–84): food,
beverages, and tobacco 1,919,781, of which meat 764,844, dairy products
242,391, wine 26,883; fabricated metal products, machinery, and equipment
1,772,307; paper and paper products 830,033; textiles, wearing apparel,
and leather 725,006; chemical, petroleum, coal, rubber, and plastic products 669,410; wood and wood products 478,729. Construction ($NZ '000;
1987): residential 1,770,100; nonresidential 1,908,700. Energy production
(consumption): electricity (kW-hr; 1986) 27,017,000,000 (24,275,000,000);
coal (metric tons; 1986) 2,295,000 (1,945,000); petroleum (barrels; 1986)
10,483,800 (21,049,000); petroleum products (metric tons; 1986) 2,414,000
(2,657,000); natural gas (cu m; 1986) 3,288,000,000 (3,288,000,000).
Gross national product (1986): U.S.$23,300,000,000 (U.S.$7,110 per capita).

Structure of gross domestic product and labour force

	1986			
	in value $NZ '000,000	% of total value	labour force[4]	% of labour force[4]
Agriculture	4,165	9.3	164,100	10.4
Mining	513	1.1	5,300	0.3
Manufacturing	10,059	22.4	303,900	19.2
Construction	2,536	5.7	104,900	6.6
Public utilities	1,383	3.1	17,300	1.1
Transp. and commun.	3,463	7.7	112,200	7.1
Trade	8,539	19.0	295,700	18.7
Finance	7,663	17.1	131,600	8.3
Pub. admin., defense	5,113	11.4	} 376,800	23.8
Services	2,065	4.6		
Other	−631[5]	−1.4[5]	69,300[6]	4.4[6]
TOTAL	44,868[7]	100.0	1,581,100	100.0[7]

Population economically active (1986)[8]: total 1,605,030; activity rate 49.2%
(participation rates: ages 15–64, 74.5%; female 41.7%; unemployed 4.2%).

Price and earnings indexes (1980 = 100)

	1981	1982	1983	1984	1985	1986	1987
Consumer price index	115.3	134.0	143.8	152.7	176.2	194.6	231.0
Weekly earnings index	119.0	133.0	134.0	137.0	149.0	171.7	185.2

Household income and expenditure. Average household size (1986) 2.9; income per household $NZ 27,200 (U.S.$14,200); sources of income: wages
and salaries 68.1%, transfer payments 12.7%, self-employment 9.1%; expenditure (1985–86): housing 20.4%, transportation 19.6%, food 16.7%,
household durable goods 10.9%, clothing 5.7%, recreation 5.2%, energy
2.4%, health 1.6%, education 0.5%.
Land use (1985): forested 38.3%; meadows and pastures 52.5%; agricultural
and under permanent cultivation 1.7%; other 7.5%.

Foreign trade

Balance of trade (current prices)

	1982	1983	1984	1985	1986	1987
$NZ '000,000	+351.1	+811.5	+425.9	−868.5	−895.3	−307.0
% of total	2.4%	5.3%	2.5%	3.6%	4.1%	1.3%

Imports (1987): $NZ 11,800,200,000 (machinery and electrical equipment
25.8%; transport equipment 14.5%; chemicals 12.2%; textiles, clothing, and
footwear 7.3%; mineral fuels 6.4%; iron, steel, and nonferrous metals 5.2%;
crude petroleum 3.1%. *Major import sources:* Japan 20.7%; Australia 18.0%;
U.S. 16.1%; U.K. 9.8%; West Germany 5.9%.
Exports (1987): $NZ 12,107,200,000 (food and live animals 46.7%, of which
meat and meat preparations 18.7%, dairy products and eggs 11.6%, wool
12.9%; crude materials except fuels 22.9%, of which forest products 6.2%;
manufactured goods 13.6%; chemicals 4.8%). *Major export destinations:*
U.S. 16.3%; Japan 15.1%; Australia 14.9%; U.K. 9.3%; China 3.5%; U.S.S.R.
1.7%.

Transport and communications

Transport. Railroads (1986): length 2,692 mi, 4,332 km; passenger-mi
(1984) 284,687,000, passenger-km 458,160,000; short ton-mi cargo (1985–
86) 2,186,000,000, metric ton-km cargo 3,192,000,000. Roads (1986): total
length 57,769 mi, 92,971 km (paved 55%). Vehicles (1987): passenger cars
1,552,988; trucks and buses 334,316. Merchant marine (1987): vessels (100
gross tons and over) 124; total deadweight tonnage 371,258. Air transport
(1987): passenger-mi 5,598,000,000, passenger-km 9,009,000,000; short ton-
mi cargo 242,500,000, metric ton-km cargo 354,000,000; airports (1988)
with scheduled flights 36.
Communications. Daily newspapers (1986): total number 32; total circulation 1,055,000; circulation per 1,000 population 324. Radio (1985): 2,800,-
000 receivers (1 per 1.2 persons). Television (1986): 940,190 receivers (1
per 3.5 persons). Telephones (1987): 2,205,825 (1 per 1.5 persons).

Education and health

Education (1986)

	schools	teachers	students	student/ teacher ratio
Primary (age 5–12)	2,408	18,384	441,028	24.0
Secondary (age 13–17)	420	13,310	226,116	17.0
Voc., teacher tr.	28	3,130	131,655	42.1
Higher[9]	7	2,974	35,177	11.8

Educational attainment (1986). Percent of population age 25 and over
having: primary and some secondary education 51.9%; secondary 35.8%;
higher 6.9%; not specified 5.4%. *Literacy* (1986): total population age 15
and over literate (virtually 100.0%).
Health (1986): physicians 8,312 (1 per 398 persons); hospital beds 30,708 (1
per 108 persons); infant mortality rate per 1,000 live births (1987) 10.0.
Food (1984–86): daily per capita caloric intake 3,405 (vegetable products
56%, animal products 44%); (1983) 132% of FAO recommended minimum.

Military

Total active duty personnel (1987): 12,600 (army 46.0%, navy 20.6%, air force
33.4%). *Military expenditure as percent of GNP* (1985): 2.0% (world 6.1%);
per capita expenditure U.S.$136.

[1]The statistical areas listed have no administrative significance; adjacent islands and
land reclamations are included where appropriate. [2]Includes Chatham Island county.
[3]Includes Stewart Island county. [4]December 1986. [5]Includes import duties less imputed bank service charges. [6]Includes 61,500 unemployed. [7]Detail does not add to
total given because of rounding. [8]March 3, 1986, census. [9]Universities only.

Nicaragua

Official name: República de Nicaragua (Republic of Nicaragua).
Form of government: unitary multiparty republic with one legislative house (National Assembly [96]).
Head of state and government: President.
Capital: Managua.
Official language: Spanish.
Official religion: none.
Monetary unit: 1 Nicaraguan new córdoba[1] (C$) = 100 centavos; valuation ([official rate] Oct. 10, 1988) 1 U.S.$ = C$320; 1 £ = C$547.20.

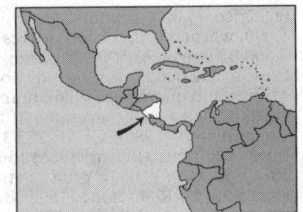

Area and population		area[2]		population
Regions **Departments**	**Capitals**	sq mi	sq km	1985 estimate
Atlantic				
Rio San Juan	San Carlos	2,876	7,448	34,330
Zelaya	Bluefields	22,816	59,094	325,454
North Central				
Boaco	Boaco	1,924	4,982	97,432
Chontales	Juigalpa	1,910	4,947	111,786
Esteli	Esteli	849	2,199	115,333
Jinotega	Jinotega	3,697	9,576	143,264
Madriz	Somoto	756	1,958	80,268
Matagalpa	Matagalpa	2,623	6,794	263,649
Nueva Segovia	Ocotal	1,290	3,341	139,116
Pacific				
Carazo	Jinotepe	398	1,032	97,106
Chinandega	Chinandega	1,800	4,662	285,506
Granada	Granada	372	964	136,068
León	León	2,021	5,234	257,815
Managua	Managua	1,389	3,597	903,998
Masaya	Masaya	224	581	179,114
Rivas	Rivas	830	2,149	101,825
TOTAL LAND AREA		45,775	118,558	3,272,064
INLAND WATER		3,588	9,291	
TOTAL AREA		49,363	127,849	

Demography

Population (1988): 3,622,000.
Density (1988)[3]: persons per sq mi 79.1, persons per sq km 30.6.
Urban–rural (1986): urban 58.0%; rural 42.0%.
Sex distribution (1986): male 50.02%; female 49.98%.
Age breakdown (1986): under 15, 46.6%; 15–29, 27.5%; 30–44, 14.4%; 45–59, 7.4%; 60–74, 3.4%; 75 and over, 0.7%.
Population projection: (1990) 3,871,000; (2000) 5,261,000.
Doubling time: 21 years.
Ethnic composition (1980): mestizo (Spanish/Indian) 68.8%; white 14.0%; black 8.0%; Zambo (black/Indian) 5.0%; Amerindian 4.0%; other 0.2%.
Religious affiliation (1984): Roman Catholic 86.9%; other 13.1%.
Major cities (1985): Managua 682,111; León 100,982; Granada 88,636; Masaya 74,946; Chinandega 67,792.

Vital statistics

Birth rate per 1,000 population (1985): 44.2 (world avg. 29.0).
Death rate per 1,000 population (1985): 9.7 (world avg. 11.0).
Natural increase rate per 1,000 population (1985): 34.5 (world avg. 18.0).
Total fertility rate (avg. births per childbearing woman; 1987): 5.2.
Marriage rate per 1,000 population (1985): 3.6.
Divorce rate per 1,000 population (1985): 0.4.
Life expectancy at birth (1985): male 58.7 years; female 61.0 years.
Major causes of death per 100,000 population (1984): accidents, poisonings, and violence 81.9; diseases of the circulatory system 54.3; infectious and parasitic diseases 43.9; malignant neoplasms (cancers) 28.5.

National economy

Budget (1986). Revenue: C$147,079,000,000 (tax on international transactions 53.1%, income tax 17.5%, import duties 7.6%). Expenditures: C$208,-591,000,000 (current expenditures 88.8%, development expenditures 11.2%).
Public debt (external, outstanding; 1986): U.S.$5,343,100,000.
Tourism: receipts from visitors (1984) U.S.$5,000,000; expenditures by nationals abroad (1983) U.S.$7,000,000.
Land use (1985): forested 33.1%; meadows and pastures 43.4%; agricultural and under permanent cultivation 10.7%; other 12.8%.
Production (metric tons except as noted). Agriculture, forestry, fishing (1986): sugarcane 2,810,000, corn (maize) 264,000, sorghum 184,000, seed cotton 133,000, rice 124,000, bananas 114,000, dry beans 104,000, plantains 85,000, oranges 55,000, coffee 40,900[4]; livestock (number of live animals) 2,100,000 cattle, 750,000 pigs; roundwood 3,674,000 cu m; fish catch 2,421, of which shrimp 1,041. Mining and quarrying (1987): gold 39,600 troy oz. Manufacturing (1987): soap 23,200,000; cement 100,000[5]; bitumen 90; rum 152,420 hectolitres; shirts and trousers 6,058,200 units; footwear 4,234,000 pairs; machetes 547,000 units; mattresses 6,000 units. Construction (buildings authorized[6]; 1985): residential 62,700 sq m; nonresidential 15,300 sq m. Energy production (consumption): electricity (kW-hr; 1986) 1,063,000,-000 (1,253,000,000); coal, none (none); crude petroleum (barrels; 1986) none (3,592,000); petroleum products (metric tons; 1986) 472,000 (651,000); natural gas, none (none).
Gross national product (at current market prices; 1986): U.S.$2,670,000,000 (U.S.$790 per capita).

Structure of gross domestic product and labour force

	1986		1987	
	in value C$'000,000	% of total value	labour force	% of labour force
Agriculture	90,617	20.8	365,200	32.4
Mining	2,428	0.6	3,000	0.3
Manufacturing	120,736	27.7	90,500	8.0
Construction	15,365	3.5	16,800	1.5
Public utilities	7,625	1.8	7,800	0.7
Transportation and communications	18,425	4.2	20,900	1.8
Trade	104,189	23.9	94,600	8.4
Finance, real estate	24,293	5.6	18,700	1.7
Pub. admin., defense	32,011	7.3	77,400	6.9
Services	20,053	4.6	148,500	13.2
Other	—	—	282,900[7]	25.1[7]
TOTAL	435,742	100.0	1,126,300	100.0

Population economically active (1987): total 1,126,300; activity rate of total population 32.2% (participation rates: ages 15–64 [1980] 54.0%; female [1980] 21.6%; unemployed [1985] 30.0%).

Price and earnings indexes (1980 = 100)

	1981	1982	1983	1984	1985	1986	1987
Consumer price index	124	155	203	274	877	7,432	58,238[8]
Monthly earnings index[9]	126	137	157	212	493[10]	...	...

Household income and expenditure. Average household size (1980) 6.9; income per household: n.a.; sources of income: n.a.; expenditure (1986)[6,11]: food, beverages, and tobacco 68.4%, housing, energy, and household furnishings 12.2%, clothing and footwear 11.6%, other 7.8%.

Foreign trade[12]

Balance of trade (current prices)						
	1981	1982	1983	1984	1985	1986
U.S.$'000,000	−491.2	−370.0	−375.1	−439.8	−592.7	−661.4
% of total	32.6%	31.3%	30.3%	36.3%	49.6%	60.2%

Imports (1986): U.S.$880,000,000 (primary industrial materials 26.0%, capital goods 23.6%, consumer goods 20.9%, petroleum products 9.4%). *Major import sources:* Socialist bloc 51.0%; EEC 14.0%; CACM 6.0%; United States 0.6%; not specified 28.4%.
Exports (1986): U.S.$218,600,000 (coffee 43.3%, cotton 17.7%, sugar 7.2%, bananas 6.4%, shrimp and lobster 3.6%). *Major export destinations:* EEC 55.0%; Socialist bloc 13.9%; CACM 5.0%; not specified 26.1%.

Transport and communications

Transport. Railroads (1985): length (1986) 214 mi, 344 km; passenger-mi 15,845,000, passenger-km 25,500,000; short ton-mi cargo 47,000,000, metric ton-km cargo 68,000,000. Roads (1986): total length 9,319 mi, 14,997 km (paved 11%). Vehicles (1986): passenger cars 46,184; trucks and buses 30,535. Merchant marine (1986): vessels (100 gross tons and over) 22; total deadweight tonnage 16,976. Air transport (1985)[6]: passenger arrivals 126,972, passenger departures 134,471; cargo unloaded 3,384, metric tons, cargo loaded 2,595 metric tons; airports (1988) with scheduled flights, n.a.
Communications. Daily newspapers (1987): total number 4; total circulation 218,500; circulation per 1,000 population 62. Radio (1986): 300,000 receivers (1 per 11 persons). Television (1987): 175,000 receivers (1 per 20 persons). Telephones (1984): 50,459 (1 per 64 persons).

Education and health

Education (1986)	schools	teachers	students	student/ teacher ratio
Primary (age 7–12)	4,526	17,199	556,684	32.4
Secondary (age 13–18) Voc., teacher tr.	431[13]	4,037	167,024	41.4
Higher[14]	16	1,410	26,878	19.1

Educational attainment (1971). Percent of population age 25 and over having: no formal schooling 53.9%; some primary and complete primary education 41.7%; some secondary and complete secondary education 4.4%.
Literacy (1983): total population age 15 and over literate 88.0%.
Health (1985): physicians (1984) 2,172 (1 per 1,456 persons); hospital beds 5,083 (1 per 644 persons); infant mortality rate per 1,000 live births 76.4.
Food (1979–81): daily per capita caloric intake 2,188 (vegetable products 84%, animal products 16%); (1983) 102% of FAO recommended minimum requirement.

Military

Total active duty personnel (1988): 77,000 (army 90.9%, navy 5.2%, air force 3.9%). *Military expenditure as percent of GNP* (1985): 16.8% (world 6.1%); per capita expenditure U.S.$215.

[1]Introduced February 1988 at the rate of 1 new córdoba = 1,000 old córdobas. [2]Total land area only is shown for the departments; the total area (both land and water) is shown only in the grand total. [3]Based on land area. [4]1987. [5]1986. [6]Managua only. [7]Mostly underemployed informal workers. [8]Average of second and third quarters. [9]Registrants of Nicaraguan Institute of Social Security and Welfare. [10]January–October only. [11]Weights of consumer price index components. [12]Imports c.i.f.; exports f.o.b. [13]1985. [14]1987.

Niger

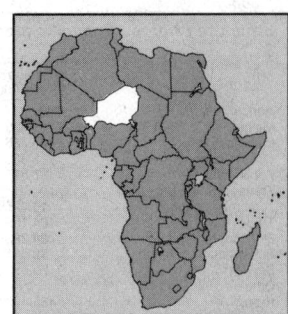

Official name: République du Niger (Republic of Niger).
Form of government: single-party republic with one advisory body (National Development Council [150])[1].
Head of state and government: President of the Supreme Military Council.
Capital: Niamey.
Official language: French.
Official religion: none.
Monetary unit: 1 CFA franc (CFAF) = 100 centimes; valuation (Oct. 10, 1988) 1 U.S.$ = CFAF 316.13; 1 £ = CFAF 541.38.

Area and population

Departments	Capitals	area sq mi	area sq km	population 1988 census[2]
Agadez	Agadez	244,869	634,209	203,959
Diffa	Diffa	54,138	140,216	189,316
Dosso	Dosso	11,970	31,002	1,019,997
Maradi	Maradi	14,896	38,581	1,388,999
Niamey	Niamey	259	670	398,265
Tahoua	Tahoua	41,188	106,677	1,306,652
Tillabéry	Tillabéry	34,604	89,623	1,331,611
Zinder	Zinder	56,151	145,430	1,410,797
TOTAL		458,075	1,186,408	7,249,596

Demography

Population (1988): 6,937,000.
Density (1988): persons per sq mi 15.1, persons per sq km 5.8.
Urban–rural (1988): urban 21.1%; rural 78.9%.
Sex distribution (1985): male 49.53%; female 50.47%.
Age breakdown (1985): under 15, 46.7%; 15–29, 25.6%; 30–44, 14.9%; 45–59, 8.0%; 60–74, 3.9%; 75 and over, 0.9%.
Population projection: (1990) 7,366,000; (2000) 10,083,000.
Doubling time: 26 years.
Ethnic composition (1983): Hausa 52.0%; Zerma 14.7%; Fulani 10.4%; Kanuri 8.7%; Songhai 8.1%; Tuareg 3.0%; French 0.1%; other 3.0%.
Religious affiliation (1983): Sunnī Muslim 97.5%; other 2.5%.
Major cities (1983): Niamey 399,100; Zinder 82,800; Maradi 65,100; Tahoua 41,900.

Vital statistics

Birth rate per 1,000 population (1980–85): 51.0 (world avg. 29.0).
Death rate per 1,000 population (1980–85): 22.9 (world avg. 11.0).
Natural increase rate per 1,000 population (1980–85): 28.1 (world avg. 18.0).
Total fertility rate (avg. births per childbearing woman; 1980–85): 7.1.
Marriage rate per 1,000 population: n.a.
Divorce rate per 1,000 population: n.a.
Life expectancy at birth (1980–85): male 40.9 years; female 44.1 years.
Major causes of death per 100,000 population (1976): malaria 317; measles 229; meningitis 145; other major diseases include bacillary dysentery and amebiasis, typhoid fever, enteritis and other diarrheal diseases, avitaminoses and other nutritional deficiency diseases, tuberculosis of the respiratory system, and bronchitis.

National economy

Budget (1987). Revenue: CFAF 198,073,000,000 (external aid 32.5%; new debt 27.4%; import and export duties 16.6%; excise taxes 9.6%; personal income taxes 7.2%). Expenditures: CFAF 162,400,000,000 (capital expenses 46.7%; administration 33.2%, of which education 10.6%, health 4.8%, defense 2.6%; national debt 20.1%).
Public debt (external, outstanding; 1986): U.S.$1,026,200,000.
Tourism (1986): receipts from visitors U.S.$7,600,000; expenditures by nationals abroad U.S.$13,000,000.
Gross national product (at current market prices; 1986): U.S.$1,690,000,000 (U.S.$260 per capita).

Structure of gross domestic product and labour force

	1987 in value CFAF '000,000	1987 % of total value	1985 labour force	1985 % of labour force
Agriculture	351,100	45.5	2,870,000	89.6
Mining	52,000	6.7		
Manufacturing	31,500	4.1		
Construction	23,500	2.1	64,000	2.0
Public utilities	16,200	3.0		
Transportation and communications	31,800	4.1		
Trade and finance	101,200	13.2	269,000	8.4
Pub. admin., defense	60,900	7.9		
Services	130,000	16.8		
Other	−26,600	−3.4		
TOTAL	771,900[3]	100.0	3,203,000	100.0

Production (metric tons except as noted). Agriculture, forestry, fishing (1986): millet 1,383,000, sorghum 360,000, pulses 313,000, roots and tubers 232,000, vegetables and melons 159,000, sugarcane 110,000, onions 120,-000, rice 75,000, peanuts (groundnuts) 42,000, corn (maize) 6,000, cotton 5,000, wheat 5,000, tobacco leaves 1,000; livestock (number of live animals) 7,500,000 goats, 3,500,000 sheep, 3,300,000 cattle, 507,000 asses, 415,000 camels, 292,000 horses; roundwood (1985) 3,920,000 cu m; fish catch 2,350. Mining and quarrying (1986): uranium 3,108. Manufacturing (1982): cement 16,000; soap 6,600; beverages 101,000 hectolitres; beer 97,000 hectolitres. Construction (1980): CFAF 75,937,000,000. Energy production (consumption): electricity (kW-hr; 1986) 156,000,000 (287,000,000); coal (metric tons; 1986) 50,000 (50,000); crude petroleum, none (n.a.); petroleum products (metric tons; 1986) none (180,000); natural gas, none (n.a.).
Population economically active (1985): total 3,203,000; activity rate of total population 52.4% (participation rates: ages 15–64, 89.7%; female, 47.4%; unemployed, n.a.).

Price and earnings indexes (1980 = 100)

	1981	1982	1983	1984	1985	1986	1987
Consumer price index	122.9	137.2	133.8	145.0	143.7	139.1	129.7
Hourly earnings index[4]	107.3	107.2	107.3	107.3	107.3	107.3	...

Household income and expenditure. Average household size (1980) 5.2; income per household: n.a.; sources of income (1977): self-employment 59.5%, family 30.1%, salary or wages 4.8%, employer 0.7%; (1983): food and beverages 50.5%, household expenses 19.1%, clothing 7.3%.
Land use (1985): forested 2.1%; meadows and pastures 7.3%; agricultural and under permanent cultivation 2.9%; other 87.7%.

Foreign trade[5]

Balance of trade (current prices)

	1980	1981	1982	1983	1984	1985
CFAF '000,000	+18,860	+2,087	−30,161	+1,816	+6,204	−38,057
% of total	8.6%	0.9%	12.1%	0.8%	2.7%	16.8%

Imports (1984): CFAF 124,620,000,000 (food products 28.6%, of which cereals 12.2%, sugar 3.7%; petroleum products 11.0%; chemical products 10.8%; nonelectrical machinery 10.0%; cotton thread and fabrics 3.9%). *Major import sources* (1983): France 32.8%; Nigeria 31.7%; United States 4.6%; Côte d'Ivoire 4.2%; West Germany 3.6%; Japan 2.9%.
Exports (1984): CFAF 119,495,000,000 (uranium 77.8%; foodstuffs 15.3%, of which vegetables 5.2%; live animals 9.2%). *Major export destinations:* France 51.4%; Japan 17.4%; Nigeria 10.6%; West Germany 5.9%; Spain 3.3%.

Transport and communications

Transport. Railroads (1984): none[6]. Roads (1985): total length 11,806 mi, 19,000 km (paved 17%). Vehicles (1984): passenger cars 23,102; trucks and buses 9,052. Air transport (1986)[7]: passenger-mi 147,619,000, passenger-km 237,571,000; short ton-mi cargo 26,340,000, metric ton-km cargo 38,455,-000; airports (1988) with scheduled flights 1.
Communications. Daily newspapers (1987): total number 1; total circulation 5,000; circulation per 1,000 population 0.7. Radio (1986): total number of receivers 300,000 (1 per 22 persons). Television (1987): total number of receivers 25,000 (1 per 280 persons). Telephones (1985): 11,824 (1 per 563 persons).

Education and health

Education (1985)

	schools	teachers	students	student/ teacher ratio
Primary (age 7–12)	1,976	7,690	293,512	38.2
Secondary (age 13–19)	64[8]	1,963	51,448	26.2
Voc., teacher tr.[7]	8	120	2,351	19.6
Higher[9]	1[8]	319[10]	2,863[10]	9.1[10]

Educational attainment (1977). Percent of population age 25 and over having: no formal schooling 91.1%; primary education 8.4%; secondary 0.3%; higher 0.2%. *Literacy* (1980): total population age 15 and over literate 278,-000 (9.8%); males literate 195,000 (14.0%); females literate 83,000 (5.8%).
Health: physicians (1980) 136 (1 per 40,209 persons); hospital beds (1979) 3,261 (1 per 1,633 persons); infant mortality rate per 1,000 live births (1980–85) 146.0.
Food (1984–86): daily per capita caloric intake 2,349 (vegetable products 93%, animal products 7%); (1983) 97% of FAO recommended minimum requirement.

Military

Total active duty personnel (1988): 3,300 (army 97.0%, air force 3.0%). *Military expenditure as percent of GNP* (1985): 0.8% (world 6.1%); per capita expenditure U.S.$2.

[1]The legislature created by Niger's independence (1960) constitution (National Assembly) was suspended in 1974. In 1983 a National Development Council (CND) assumed the transitional role of a constituent assembly and was, ultimately, to be raised to that status. A national charter (statement of intent and transitional governmental forms) restoring some civilian control was approved by referendum June 14, 1987. In late 1988, the CND had been charged with drafting a new constitution. [2]De jure. [3]Detail does not add to total given because of rounding. [4]Guaranteed minimum wage for professionals. [5]Import figures are f.o.b. in balance of trade and c.i.f. for commodities and trading partners. [6]Niger is a cofounder of the Common Benin–Niger Organization for Railroads and Transport, currently maintaining rail operations only in Benin but having the purpose of extending rail services from the sea at Cotonou, Benin, to Dosso and, ultimately, Niamey, Niger. [7]Air Afrique. [8]1980–81. [9]Université de Niamey. [10]1984.

Nigeria

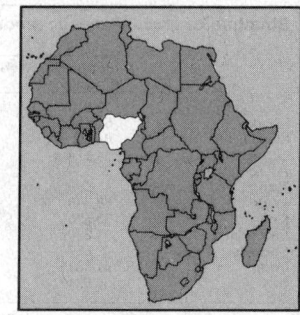

Official name: Federal Republic of Nigeria.
Form of government: federal republic; temporarily governed (pending restoration of civilian governmental apparatus by 1992) under emergency powers by Armed Forces Ruling Council (AFRC).
Head of state and government: President of FRN/Chairman of AFRC.
Capital: Lagos (Capital designate: Abuja[1]).
Official language: English.
Official religion: none.
Monetary unit: 1 Nigerian naira (₦) = 100 kobo; valuation (Oct. 10, 1988) 1 U.S.$ = ₦4.63; 1 £ = ₦7.92.

Area and population		area		population
		sq mi	sq km	1988 estimate
States	**Capitals**			
Akwa Ibom	Uyo	2	2	5,051,000
Anambra	Enugu	6,824	17,675	7,170,600
Bauchi	Bauchi	24,944	64,605	4,847,300
Bendel	Benin City	13,707	35,500	4,906,500
Benue	Makurdi	17,442	45,174	4,838,800
Borno	Maiduguri	44,942	116,400	5,976,200
Cross River	Calabar	10,516[2]	27,237[2]	1,883,500
Gongola	Yola	35,286	91,390	5,194,200
Imo	Owerri	4,575	11,850	7,322,200
Kaduna	Kaduna	27,122[3]	70,245[3]	3,296,200
Kano	Kano	16,712	43,285	11,513,400
Katsina	Katsina	3	3	4,874,600
Kwara	Ilorin	25,818	66,869	3,402,200
Lagos	Ikeja	1,292	3,345	4,145,900
Niger	Minna	25,111	65,037	2,152,700
Ogun	Abeokuta	6,472	16,762	3,092,200
Ondo	Akure	8,092	20,959	5,442,200
Oyo	Ibadan	14,558	37,705	10,385,000
Plateau	Jos	22,405	58,030	4,014,300
Rivers	Port-Harcourt	8,436	21,850	3,429,000
Sokoto	Sokoto	39,589	102,535	9,049,100
Federal Capital Territory		2,824	7,315	271,000
TOTAL		356,669[4]	923,768	112,258,100

Demography

Population (1988): 112,258,000.
Density (1988): persons per sq mi 314.7, persons per sq km 121.5.
Urban–rural (1985): urban 16.1%; rural 83.9%.
Sex distribution (1985): male 49.50%; female 50.50%.
Age breakdown (1985): under 15, 48.3%; 15–29, 25.8%; 30–44, 14.1%; 45–59, 7.8%; 60–74, 3.4%; 75 and over, 0.6%.
Population projection: (1990) 119,812,000; (2000) 166,012,000.
Doubling time: 28 years.
Ethnic composition (1983): Hausa 21.3%; Yoruba 21.3%; Igbo (Ibo) 18.0%; Fulani 11.2%; Ibibio 5.6%; Kanuri 4.2%; Edo 3.4%; Tiv 2.2%; Ijaw 1.8%; Bura 1.7%; Nupe 1.2%; other 8.1%.
Religious affiliation (1980): Muslim 45.0%; Protestant 26.3%; Roman Catholic 12.1%; African indigenous 10.6%; traditional beliefs 5.6%; other 0.4%.
Major cities (1988): Lagos 1,243,000; Ibadan 1,172,000; Ogbomosho 597,500; Kano 551,800; Oshogbo 390,400; Ilorin 389,200.

Vital statistics

Birth rate per 1,000 population (1980–85): 50.4 (world avg. 29.0).
Death rate per 1,000 population (1980–85): 17.1 (world avg. 11.0).
Natural increase rate per 1,000 population (1980–85): 33.3 (world avg. 18.0).
Total fertility rate (avg. births per childbearing woman; 1980–85): 7.1.
Life expectancy at birth (1980–85): male 46.9 years; female 50.2 years.
Major causes of death per 100,000 population: n.a.; major diseases include malaria, tuberculosis, trypanosomiasis, onchocerciasis, and leprosy.

National economy

Budget (1986)[5]. Revenue: ₦14,189,900,000 (petroleum revenues 58.1%; import duties 12.2%; special funds 10.6%). Expenditures: ₦12,524,100,000 (recurrent expenditure 61.0%, of which debt service 40.8%, defense 9.0%, education 7.8%, police 5.4%; health 3.3%; capital expenditure 39.0%).
Public debt (1986): U.S.$21,496,300,000.
Production (metric tons except as noted). Agriculture, forestry, fishing (1987): sorghum 5,182,000, yams 4,951,000, millet 3,905,000, cassava 1,486,000, corn (maize) 1,202,000, plantains 1,071,000, sugarcane 852,000, palm oil 840,000, beans 688,000, palm kernel 353,000, rubber 180,000, melon 145,000, cocoa 141,000, wheat 139,000, soybeans 107,000; livestock (number of live animals) 26,328,000 goats, 13,160,000 sheep, 12,169,000 cattle; roundwood (1987) 95,524,000 cu m; fish catch (1986) 268,482. Mining and quarrying (1986): limestone 1,850,000; marble 1,482,000; tin metal 1,000,000. Manufacturing (value added in producers' prices ₦'000,000; 1983): beverages and tobacco 768.2; transport equipment 754.2, of which motor vehicles 734.4; food products 654.5; textiles 538.6; chemical products 465.0, of which drugs and medicines 95.0; rubber products 62.5. Construction (1980): residential ₦5,964; nonresidential ₦1,592. Energy production (consumption): electricity (kW-hr; 1986) 9,875,000,000 (9,775,000,000); coal (metric tons; 1986) 144,000 (104,000); crude petroleum (barrels; 1986)

532,568,000 (77,590,000); petroleum products (metric tons; 1986) 6,540,000 (8,361,000); natural gas (cu m; 1986) 3,150,000,000 (3,150,000,000).
Tourism (1986): receipts U.S.$125,000,000; expenditures U.S.$109,000,000.
Gross national product (1986): U.S.$66,210,000,000 (U.S.$640 per capita).

Structure of gross domestic product and labour force				
	1985			
	in value ₦'000,000[6]	% of total value	labour force	% of labour force
Agriculture	6,948	26.6	20,866,000	57.8
Mining	5,185	19.8	144,000	0.4
Manufacturing	2,434	9.3	6,570,000	18.2
Construction	1,347	5.1	433,000	1.2
Public utilities	214	0.8	72,000	0.2
Transp. and commun.	746	2.8	217,000	0.6
Trade	5,143	19.7	5,776,000	16.0
Finance	916	3.5		
Pub. admin., defense	2,140	8.2	2,022,000	5.6
Other (including services)	1,086	4.2		
TOTAL	26,159	100.0	36,100,000	100.0

Population economically active (1984): total 33,708,000; activity rate of total population 36.1% (participation rates: ages 15–64, 58.2%; female [1983] 31.9%; unemployed [registered] 0.5%).

Price and earnings indexes (1980 = 100)							
	1981	1982	1983	1984	1985	1986	1987
Consumer price index	120.8	130.1	160.3	223.8	236.1	248.8	274.2
Earnings index	...	...	...	...	...	...	...

Household income and expenditure. Average household size (1983) 5.0; average annual income per household (1981) ₦2,300 (U.S.$3,745)[7]; sources of income (1979): self-employment 49.4%, wages and salaries 36.2%, interest 5.4%, rent 4.7%, transfer payments 4.3%; expenditures (1979): food 53.0%, of which beverages and tobacco 4.9%; fuel and light 11.4%, clothing 6.0%, transportation 4.7%, household goods 3.8%, other 21.1%.
Land use (1985): forested 16.4%; meadows and pastures 23.0%; agricultural and under permanent cultivation 34.1%; other 26.5%.

Foreign trade

Balance of trade (current prices)							
	1981	1982	1983	1984	1985	1986	1987
₦'000,000	−647	−1,523	−540	+2,604	+4,049	+3,043	+15,401
% of total	2.8%	8.5%	3.5%	16.7%	22.0%	21.8%	35.2%

Imports (1986): ₦5,469,700,000 (machinery and transport equipment 46.0%; manufactured goods 19.3% [mostly iron and steel products, textiles, and paper products]; chemicals 13.2%; food 9.8%; mineral fuels 0.6%). *Major import sources* (1984): U.K. 18.1%; France 12.7%; U.S. 12.,7%; West Germany 10.0%; Japan 8.2%; Italy 4.4%.
Exports (1986): ₦8,513,000,000 (crude petroleum 97.2%; other significant exports include cocoa, rubber, and palm kernels). *Major export destinations* (1984): France 20.3%; Italy 15.6%; U.S. 13.7%; The Netherlands 12.7%; West Germany 10.0%; Spain 4.3%.

Transport and communications

Transport. Railroads (1985): length 3,505 km; passenger-km 1,950,000,000[8]; metric ton-km cargo 1,530,000,000[9]. Roads (1984): total length 124,000 km (paved 48%). Vehicles (1981): passenger cars 262,550; trucks 90,731. Merchant marine (1987): vessels (100 gross tons and over) 213; total deadweight tonnage 855,026. Air transport (1986): passenger-km 2,261,000,000; metric ton-km cargo 33,876,000; airports (1988) 16.
Communications. Daily newspapers (1987): total number 26; total circulation 1,345,500[10]; circulation per 1,000 population 12.0[10]. Radio (1986): 15,680,000 receivers (1 per 6.7 persons). Television (1987): 2,000,000 receivers (1 per 54 persons). Telephones (1986): 265,000 (1 per 397 persons).

Education and health

Education (1983–84)				
	schools	teachers	students	student/ teacher ratio
Primary (age 6–12)	38,211	359,701	14,383,487	40.0
Secondary (age 12–17)	5,498[11]	82,749	3,169,624	38.3
Voc., teacher tr.	475[11]	15,738	391,588	24.9
Higher	80[11]	...	101,558	...

Educational attainment, n.a. *Literacy* (1985): total population age 15 and over literate 20,208,000 (42.4%); males literate 12,551,000 (53.8%); females literate 7,657,000 (31.5%).
Health (1983): physicians 11,294 (1 per 8,059 persons); hospital beds 60,840 (1 per 1,496 persons); infant mortality rate (1980–85) 114.0.
Food (1984–86): daily per capita caloric intake 2,115 (vegetable products 97%, animal products 3%); (1983) 86% of FAO recommended minimum.

Military

Total active duty personnel (1988): 94,500 (army 84.7%, navy 5.3%, air force 10.0%). *Military expenditure as percent of GNP* (1985): 1.4% (world 6.1%); per capita expenditure U.S.$10.

[1]It is presently planned to move the capital from Lagos to Abuja in the Federal Capital Territory in 1990. [2]Area of Akwa Ibom is included in Cross River. [3]Area of Katsina is included in Kaduna. [4]Detail does not add to total given because of rounding. [5]Budget (1988). Revenue: ₦25,317,000,000. Expenditures: ₦24,294,000,000 (recurrent expenditure 66.7%; capital expenditure 33.3%). [6]At prices of 1977–78. [7]Urban households only. [8]1984. [9]1983. [10]For 14 newspapers only. [11]1982–83.

Norway

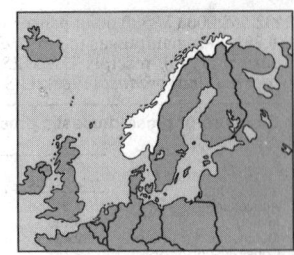

Official name: Kongeriket Norge
(Kingdom of Norway).
Form of government: constitutional
monarchy with one legislative house
(Parliament [157]).
Chief of state: King.
Head of government: Prime Minister.
Capital: Oslo.
Official language: Norwegian.
Official religion: Evangelical Lutheran.
Monetary unit: 1 Norwegian krone
(NKr) = 100 øre; valuation (Oct. 10,
1988) 1 U.S.$ = NKr 6.86;
1 £ = NKr 11.74.

Area and population		area[1]		population
Counties	Capitals	sq mi	sq km	1988 estimate[2]
Akershus	—	1,898	4,917	406,859
Aust-Agder	Arendal	3,557	9,212	96,041
Buskerud	Drammen	5,763	14,927	223,136
Finnmark	Vardø	18,779	48,637	74,271
Hedmark	Hamar	10,575	27,388	186,664
Hordaland	Bergen	6,036	15,634	405,130
Møre og Romsdal	Molde	5,832	15,104	237,873
Nordland	Bodø	14,798	38,327	240,450
Nord-Trøndelag	Steinkjer	8,673	22,463	126,874
Oppland	Lillehammer	9,753	25,260	182,531
Oslo	Oslo	175	454	450,808
Østfold	Moss	1,615	4,183	237,242
Rogaland	Stavanger	3,529	9,141	329,630
Sogn og Fjordane	Leikanger	7,195	18,634	106,192
Sør-Trøndelag	Trondheim	7,271	18,831	248,181
Telemark	Skien	5,913	15,315	163,347
Troms	Tromsø	10,021	25,954	146,608
Vest-Agder	Kristiansand	2,811	7,281	142,181
Vestfold	Tønsberg	856	2,216	194,619
TOTAL		125,050	323,878	4,198,637[3]

Demography

Population (1988): 4,202,000.
Density (1988): persons per sq mi 33.6, persons per sq km 13.0.
Urban–rural (1985): urban 80.3%; rural 19.7%.
Sex distribution (1987): male 49.43%; female 50.57%.
Age breakdown (1987): under 15, 19.4%; 15–29, 23.3%; 30–44, 21.7%; 45–59, 14.3%; 60–74, 14.6%; 75 and over, 6.7%.
Population projection: (1990) 4,232,000; (2000) 4,384,000.
Doubling time: n.a.; doubling time exceeds 100 years.
Ethnic composition (by country of citizenship; 1987): Norway 97.4%; Denmark 0.4%; Sweden 0.3%; United Kingdom 0.3%; United States 0.2%; Pakistan 0.2%; other 1.2%.
Religious affiliation (1980): Lutheran 87.9%; nonreligious 3.2%; other 8.9%.
Major cities (1984[4]): Oslo 450,808; Bergen 209,912; Trondheim 135,542; Stavanger 96,316; Baerum 88,685.

Vital statistics

Birth rate per 1,000 population (1987): 13.0 (world avg. 26.0); (1986) legitimate 72.1%; illegitimate 27.9%.
Death rate per 1,000 population (1987): 10.7 (world avg. 9.9).
Natural increase rate per 1,000 population (1987): 2.3 (world avg. 16.1).
Total fertility rate (avg. births per childbearing woman; 1986): 1.7.
Marriage rate per 1,000 population (1986): 4.9.
Divorce rate per 1,000 population (1986): 1.9.
Life expectancy at birth (1986): male 72.9 years; female 79.7 years.
Major causes of death per 100,000 population (1986): ischemic heart disease 276.3; malignant neoplasms (cancers) 230.2; cerebrovascular disease 127.3.

National economy

Budget (1987). Revenue: NKr 174,186,000,000 (value added taxes 36.4%, taxes on interest and dividends 18.8%, tax on petroleum activity 10.4%, ordinary income tax 9.9%, taxes on petroleum income 5.9%). Expenditures: NKr 146,207,000,000 (social security and welfare 15.9%, defense 13.0%, debt service 12.7%, education 12.4%, health 2.9%).
Public debt (1985): U.S.$15,820,000,000.
Tourism (1987): receipts from visitors U.S.$1,245,000,000; expenditures by nationals abroad U.S.$3,057,000,000.
Production (metric tons except as noted). Agriculture, forestry, fishing (1986): barley 550,000, oats 450,000, potatoes 440,000; livestock (number of live animals) 2,339,100 sheep, 967,500 cattle, 837,800 pigs; roundwood 10,330,-000 cu m; fish catch (1987) 1,867,720, of which herring 337,400, Atlantic cod 202,9495, blue whiting 193,700, capelin 142,600, prawns and shrimp 41,000. Mining and quarrying (1987)[6]: iron ore 2,044,000, titanium 27,000[5], zinc 22,200, copper 21,960. Manufacturing (value added in NKr '000,000; 1986): machinery and equipment 24,539, of which electrical equipment 5,215, transport equipment 4,483; paper and paper products 10,473; food products 9,102; chemical products 7,443; wood and wood products 5,117. Construction (1985): residential 4,634,000 sq m; nonresidential 3,132,000 sq m. Energy production (consumption): electricity (kW-hr; 1986) 96,-359,000,000 (98,402,000,000); coal (metric tons; 1986) 580,000 (1,273,000); crude petroleum (barrels; 1986) 316,516,000 (58,263,000); petroleum products (metric tons; 1986) 7,529,000 (8,351,000); natural gas (cu m; 1986) 27,091,000,000 (611,000,000).
Gross national product (1986): U.S.$64,440,000,000 (U.S.$15,480 per capita).

Structure of gross domestic product and labour force				
	1987			
	in value NKr '000,000	% of total value	labour force	% of labour force
Agriculture	19,348	3.5	139,000	6.4
Mining	51,712	9.3	24,000	1.1
Manufacturing	82,995	14.9	352,000	16.3
Construction	34,574	6.2	166,000	7.7
Public utilities	22,138	4.0	23,000	1.1
Transp. and commun.	47,089	8.5	178,000	8.2
Trade	68,396	12.3	375,000	17.4
Finance	53,596	9.6	155,000	7.2
Pub. admin., defense	85,336	15.3		
Services	49,857	9.0	746,000[7]	34.6[7]
Other	41,882[8]	7.5[8]		
TOTAL	556,924[9]	100.0[9]	2,158,000	100.0

Population economically active (1987): total 2,158,000; activity rate of total population 51.5% (participation rates: ages 15–64 [1986] 77.4%; female [1986] 44.5%; unemployed 1.5%).

Price and earnings indexes (1980 = 100)							
	1982	1983	1984	1985	1986	1987	1988[10]
Consumer price index	126.2	141.1	149.9	154.2	165.2	179.6	191.1
Hourly earnings index	121.0	132.0	143.0	154.0	170.0	197.0	...

Household income and expenditure. Average household size (1982) 2.7; consumption expenditure per household NKr 88,000 (U.S.$13,600); sources of income (1984): wages and salaries 61.8%, social security 19.5%, self-employment and property income 17.5%, other 1.2%; expenditure (1986): food 19.7%, transportation 17.6%, housing 17.1%, recreation 8.7%, clothing 8.2%, household furniture and equipment 8.1%.
Land use (1985): forested 27.1%; meadows and pastures 0.3%; agricultural and under permanent cultivation 2.8%; built-up and other 69.8%.

Foreign trade

Balance of trade (current prices)						
	1982	1983	1984	1985	1986	1987
NKr '000,000	15,486	35,569	43,764	41,498	−12,403	−3,645
% of total	7.3%	15.6%	16.6%	13.8%	4.4%	1.2%

Imports (1987): NKr 152,041,000,000 (machinery and transport equipment 25.8%, of which road vehicles 8.1%; raw materials 11.5%, of which fuels 5.3%; metals and metal products 11.4%, of which iron and steel 3.3%; food products 5.4%, of which fruits and vegetables 1.6%). *Major import sources* (1986): Sweden 18.0%; West Germany 16.9%; U.K. 8.8%; Japan 7.4%.
Exports (1987): NKr 144,543,000,000 (fuels and fuel products 40.6%, of which crude petroleum 25.7%, natural gas 12.1%; metals and metal products 13.8%, of which aluminum 6.5%, iron and steel 3.4%; machinery and transport equipment 7.8%; food products 7.7%, of which fish and fish products 5.5%). *Major export destinations* (1986): U.K. 27.5%; West Germany 18.9%; Sweden 10.0%; The Netherlands 6.1%.

Transport and communications

Transport. Railroads (1986): route length 2,622 mi, 4,219 km; passenger-mi 1,379,000,000, passenger-km 2,220,000,000; short ton-mi cargo 2,065,000,-000, metric ton-km cargo 3,015,000,000. Roads (1986): total length 53,529 mi, 86,147 km (paved 68%). Vehicles (1986): passenger cars 1,592,195; trucks and buses 282,805. Merchant marine (1987): vessels (100 gross tons and over) 1,979; total deadweight tonnage 9,656,349. Air transport (1987): passenger-mi 5,485,359,000, passenger-km 8,827,846,000; short ton-mi cargo 622,351,000, metric ton-km cargo 908,617,000; airports (1988) 48.
Communications. Daily newspapers (1986): total number 84; total circulation 2,209,000; circulation per 1,000 population 530. Radio (1986): 1,510,-000 receivers (1 per 2.8 persons). Television (1987): 1,453,461 receivers (1 per 2.9 persons). Telephones (1984): 2,578,812 (1 per 1.6 persons).

Education and health

Education (1985–86)				
	schools	teachers	students	student/ teacher ratio
Primary (age 7–15)	3,525	31,459	534,000	17.0
Secondary (age 14–18) and vocational	937	18,156	192,000	10.6
Higher	228	7,025	94,503	13.4

Educational attainment (1985). Percent of population age 16 and over having: lower secondary education 49.8%; higher secondary 37.2%; higher 13.0%. *Literacy* (1986): virtually 100% literate.
Health (1986): physicians (1985) 10,110 (1 per 411 persons); hospital beds 24,951 (1 per 167 persons); infant mortality rate per 1,000 live births 7.8.
Food (1984–86): daily per capita caloric intake 3,215 (vegetable products 64%, animal products 36%); (1983) 115% of FAO recommended minimum.

Military

Total active duty personnel (1987): 36,900 (army 53.7%, navy 19.8%, air force 25.7%, joint service personnel 0.8%). *Military expenditure as percent of GNP* (1985): 3.2% (world avg. 6.1%); per capita expenditure U.S.$432.

[1]Excludes Svalbard and Jan Mayen (24,360 sq mi [63,080 sq km]). [2]January 1. [3]Includes the Norwegian population of Svalbard and Jan Mayen registered as residents in municipalities on the mainland. [4]Population of communes. [5]1986. [6]Metal content of ore. [7]Includes 32,391 unemployed. [8]Includes imputed bank service charge and various excise and import taxes. [9]Detail does not add to total given because of rounding. [10]May.

Oman

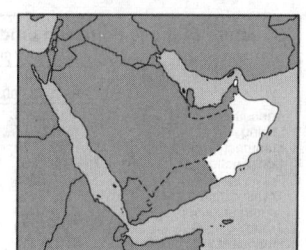

Official name: Salṭanat ʿUmān (Sultanate of Oman).
Form of government: monarchy with a consultative council (55) appointed by the Sultan.
Head of state and government: Sultan.
Capital: Muscat.
Official language: Arabic.
Official religion: Islam.
Monetary unit: 1 rial Omani (RO) = 1,000 baizas; valuation (Oct. 10, 1988) 1 RO = U.S.$2.61 = £1.52.

Area and population	area[1]		population[2]
Region Area	sq mi	sq km	1988 estimate
Dhofar	40,000	100,000	...
Southern	...	...	...
Musandam (Rʾūs al-Jibāl)	800	2,000	13,000
Musandam	...	...	...
Other	79,200	198,000	...
al-Baṭinah	...	...	...
al-Jaww and al-Buraymī	...	...	...
Dhahirah (aẓ-Ẓāhirah)	...	...	...
Capital	...	...	...
Eastern al-Ḥajar	...	...	...
Jaʿlān and Sur (Jaʿlān)	...	...	...
Sharqiyah	...	...	...
ʿUman Interior	...	...	...
Western al-Ḥajar	...	...	...
TOTAL	120,000	300,000	1,372,000

Demography

Population (1988): 1,372,000.
Density (1988): persons per sq mi 11.4, persons per sq km 4.6.
Urban–rural (1986): urban 9.2%; rural 90.8%.
Sex distribution (1986): male 57.31%; female 42.69%.
Age breakdown (1986): under 15, 39.8%; 15–29, 22.2%; 30–44, 25.7%; 45–59, 8.5%; 60–74, 2.9%; 75 and over, 0.9%.
Population projection: (1990) 1,457,000; (2000) 1,973,000.
Doubling time: 33 years.
Ethnic composition (1984): Omani Arab 77%; Indian 15%; Pakistani (mostly Baluchi) 3½%; Bengali 2½%; other 2%.
Religious affiliation (1984): Muslim 86%; Hindu 13%; other 1%.
Major city (1981): Muscat 50,000.

Vital statistics

Birth rate per 1,000 population (1986): 44.2 (world avg. 26.0).
Death rate per 1,000 population (1986): 13.0 (world avg. 9.9).
Natural increase rate per 1,000 population (1986): 31.2 (world avg. 16.1).
Total fertility rate (avg. births per childbearing woman; 1986): 7.0.
Marriage rate per 1,000 population: n.a.
Divorce rate per 1,000 population: n.a.
Life expectancy at birth (1986): male 53.7 years; female 56.0 years.
Morbidity (reported cases of illness per 100,000 population; 1986): influenza 6,281; malaria 6,187; chicken pox 662; mumps 660; dysentery 304; measles 150; tuberculosis 87.

National economy

Budget (1987): Revenue: RO 1,468,100,000 (oil revenue 81.4%, gas revenue 2.7%, interest from investments 2.2%, corporate income tax 1.4%, custom duties 1.7%). Expenditures: RO 1,551,400,000 (defense 36.6%, financing of civil ministries 30.6%, development 20.9%, of which education 3.0%).
Public debt (external, outstanding; 1986): U.S.$2,501,200,000.
Gross national product (at current market prices; 1986): U.S.$6,440,000,000 (U.S.$4,990 per capita).

Structure of gross domestic product and labour force				
	1986			
	in value RO '000,000	% of total value	labour force	% of labour force
Agriculture	89.3	3.2	108,800	23.3
Mining	997.2	35.6	9,700	2.1
Manufacturing	178.3	6.4	5,100	1.1
Construction	220.8	7.9	128,500	27.5
Public utilities	40.4	1.4	500	0.1
Transportation and communications	102.2	3.7	6,300	1.3
Trade	383.2	13.7	123,600	26.4
Finance	286.3	10.2	7,800	1.7
Pub. admin., defense	495.8	17.7 }	77,400	16.5
Services	38.5	1.4 }		
Other	−34.3[3]	−1.2[3]	—	—
TOTAL	2,797.7	100.0	467,700	100.0

Tourism: receipts from visitors, n.a.; expenditures by nationals abroad, n.a.
Household income and expenditure. Average household size (1986) 3.7; income per household: n.a.; sources of income: n.a.; food expenditure (1978): meat and eggs 20.6%, cereals 15.2%, fruits and nuts 12.4%, vegetables 11.9%, dairy products 10.3%, other foods 29.6%.
Production (metric tons except as noted). Agriculture, forestry, fishing (1986): vegetables and melons 159,000, dates 76,000, bananas 38,000, wa-

termelons 11,000, onions 10,000, mangoes 4,000, tobacco leaf 2,000, wheat 1,000, roots and tubers 1,000, potatoes 1,000; livestock (number of live animals) 700,000 goats, 213,000 sheep, 130,000 cattle, 1,000,000 chickens; fish catch 96,339. Mining and quarrying (1986): sand and gravel 7,514,000; stone 2,875,000; marble 44,000; copper 18,000. Manufacturing (1986): major products include cement blocks and floors, furniture, aluminum products, household utensils, fertilizers, and fibreglass products. Construction (1986): number of residential permits 3,091; nonresidential permits 551. Energy production (consumption): electricity (kW-hr; 1986) 2,187,800,000 (2,332,700,000); coal, none (none); crude petroleum (barrels; 1986) 204,300,000 (16,800,000); petroleum products (metric tons; 1986) 6,939,000 (5,461,000); natural gas (cu m; 1986) 4,661,000,000 (4,372,000,000).
Population economically active (1986): total 467,700; activity rate of total population 35.7% (participation rates: ages 15–64, 60.9%; female 7.5%; unemployed, n.a.).

Price and earnings indexes (1978 = 100)						
	1981	1982	1983	1984	1985	1986	1987
Consumer price index[4]	122.7	124.0	118.6	108.8	107.8	118.5	118.6
Annual earnings index	487.7	521.1	788.0	681.8	704.3	...	...

Land use (1985): meadows and pastures 4.7%; agricultural and under permanent cultivation 0.2%; other (mostly desert and developed area) 95.1%.

Foreign trade

Balance of trade (current prices)						
	1981	1982	1983	1984	1985	1986
RO '000,000	+831.6	+600.4	+606.4	+578.3	+628.3	+175.9
% of total	34.5%	24.5%	26.0%	23.3%	22.4%	8.8%

Imports (1986): RO 916,700,000 (machinery and transport equipment 41.2%, manufactured goods 19.2%, food 14.2%, petroleum products 2.9%, beverages and tobacco 1.8%). *Major import sources:* United Arab Emirates 18.7%; United Kingdom 17.9%; Japan 14.4%; West Germany 9.0%; United States 7.6%; The Netherlands 4.0%; France 3.6%; Italy 3.3%; India 2.2%.
Exports (1986): RO 1,092,600,000 (crude petroleum 89.8%, fish 1.8%, copper 0.8%, fruits and vegetables 0.4%). *Major export destinations* (1985): Japan 64.3%; United Arab Emirates 20.5%; Saudi Arabia 7.1%; Jordan 3.5%; Bahrain 2.0%.

Transport and communications

Transport. Railroads: none. Roads (1986): total length 13,781 mi, 22,179 km (paved 15%). Vehicles (1987): private vehicles 120,367, commercial vehicles 106,097. Merchant marine (1987): vessels (100 gross tons and over) 31; total deadweight tonnage 16,399. Air transport (1983)[5]: passenger-mi 553,268,000, passenger-km 890,400,000; short ton-mi cargo 16,313,000, metric ton-km cargo 23,817,000; airports (1987) with scheduled flights 6.
Communications. Daily newspapers (1986): total number 3; total circulation 30,000; circulation per 1,000 population 24. Radio (1986): total number of receivers 500,000 (1 per 2.6 persons). Television (1986): total number of receivers 400,000 (1 per 3.2 persons). Telephones (1986): 74,347 (1 per 18 persons).

Education and health

Education (1986–87)	schools	teachers	students	student/ teacher ratio
Primary (age 6–11)	354	7,517	194,996	25.9
Secondary (age 12–17)	304	3,734	50,749	13.6
Voc., teacher tr.	23	551	2,963	5.4
Higher	1	123	520	4.0

Educational attainment, n.a. *Literacy* (1979): total population age 6 and over literate 38%; males literate 55%; females literate 20%.
Health (1986): physicians 581 (1 per 1,792 persons); hospital beds 2,829 (1 per 470 persons); infant mortality rate per 1,000 live births 110.5.
Food: daily capita caloric intake, n.a.

Military

Total active duty personnel (1987): 21,500 (army 76.7%, navy 9.3%, air force 14.0%); foreign troops 3,700. *Military expenditure as percent of GNP* (1985): 24.4% (world 6.1%); per capita expenditure U.S.$1,737.

[1]Cadastral areas have not been calculated. [2]No census has ever been taken in Oman; the total given is an unofficial estimate. For planning purposes the Omani government uses a 1985 estimate of 2,000,000. [3]Less imputed bank service charges. [4]Applies to food and beverages in the capital area only. [5]International flights only.

Pakistan

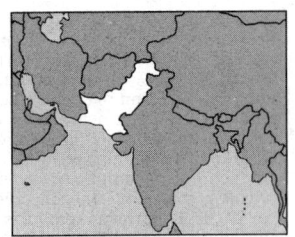

Official name: Islām-ī Jamhūrīya–e Pākistān (Islamic Republic of Pakistan).
Form of government: federal republic with two legislative houses (Senate [87]; National Assembly [237]).
Chief of state: President.
Chief of government: Prime Minister.
Capital: Islāmābād.
Official language: Urdū.
Official religion: Islam.
Monetary unit: 1 Pakistan Rupee (PRs) = 100 paisa; valuation (Oct. 10, 1988) 1 U.S.$ = PRs 18.10; 1 £ = PRs 31.00.

Area and population		area		population
		sq mi	sq km	1983 estimate[1]
Provinces	**Capitals**			
Baluchistān	Quetta	134,050	347,188	4,611,000
North–West Frontier	Peshāwar	28,773	74,522	11,658,000
Punjab	Lahore	79,284	205,345	50,460,000
Sind	Karāchi	54,407	140,913	20,312,000
Federally Administered Tribal Areas	...	10,510	27,221	2,329,000
Federal Capital Area				
Islāmābād	...	350	906	359,000
TOTAL		307,374	796,095	89,729,000

Demography

Population (1988): 109,434,000[1].
Density (1988): persons per sq mi 356.0, persons per sq km 137.5.
Urban–rural (1985): urban 29.8%; rural 70.2%.
Sex distribution (1981): male 52.47%; female 47.53%.
Age breakdown (1981): under 15, 45.2%; 15–29, 23.9%; 30–44, 15.0%; 45–59, 9.2%; 60–74, 5.1%; 75 and over, 1.6%.
Population projection: (1990) 112,236,000; (2000) 137,651,000.
Doubling time: 25 years.
Linguistic composition (1981): Punjābī 48.2%; Pashto 13.1%; Sindhī 11.8%; Saraiki 9.8%; Urdū 7.6%; other 9.5%.
Religious affiliation (1981): Muslim 96.7%; Christian 1.6%; Hindu 1.5%; other 0.2% .
Major cities (1981): Karāchi 5,208,132; Lahore 2,952,689; Faisalābād 1,104,-209; Rāwalpindi 794,843; Islāmābād 204,364.

Vital statistics

Birth rate per 1,000 population (1987): 41.9 (world avg. 26.0).
Death rate per 1,000 population (1987): 14.1 (world avg. 9.9).
Natural increase rate per 1,000 population (1987): 27.8 (world avg. 16.1).
Total fertility rate (avg. births per childbearing woman; 1987): 5.5.
Marriage rate per 1,000 population (1975–80): 10.7.
Divorce rate per 1,000 population (1975–80): 0.3.
Life expectancy at birth (1987): male 53.7 years; female 51.9 years.
Major causes of death per 100,000 population: n.a.; however, major diseases include tuberculosis, cancer, poliomyelitis, typhoid, and dysentery.

National economy

Budget (1987–88). Revenue: PRs 109,086,600,000 (customs duties 31.2%, excise taxes 15.0%, income taxes 11.2%, general sales tax 5.6%). Expenditures: PRs 116,013,100,000 (national defense 38.1%, interest on public debt 30.9%, grants to provinces 9.9%, subsidies 4.9%, general administration 4.5%, education and health 3.8%).
Tourism (1986): receipts from visitors U.S.$180,000,000; expenditures by nationals abroad U.S.$227,900,000.
Production (metric tons except as noted). Agriculture, forestry, fishing (1986–87): sugarcane 29,793,000, wheat 14,251,000, rice 3,520,000, cottonseed (1985–86) 2,434,000, cotton 1,327,000, corn (maize) 1,111,000, tobacco 78,-000; livestock (number of live animals) 31,900,000 goats, 26,600,000 sheep, 16,900,000 cattle, 13,700,000 buffalo, 900,000 camels, 121,700,000 poultry; roundwood (1986) 21,395,000 cu m; fish catch (1986) 390,600. Mining and quarrying (1986–87): limestone 6,885,331; rock salt 502,797; gypsum 411,875; aragonite/marble 203,088; silica sand 126,972; fire clay 100,101; china clay 32,953; barite 20,376; chromite 6,541. Manufacturing (1986–87): cement 5,402,000; chemical fertilizers 2,919,674, of which urea 1,983,712; steel products 2,345,495; refined sugar 1,285,910; chemicals 255,578; jute textiles 113,514; paper and paperboard 63,350; blended tea (1985–86) 44,236; cotton textiles 234,774,000 sq m; beverages 927,076,000 bottles; cigarettes 41,159,000,000 units; bicycles 593,058 units; road motor vehicles (1985–86) 93,070 units. Construction (value in PRs; 1984): residential 8,490,000,000; nonresidential 14,579,000,000. Energy production (consumption): electricity (kW-hr; 1986) 25,768,000,000 (25,768,000,000); coal (metric tons; 1986) 2,086,000 (2,906,000); crude petroleum (barrels; 1986) 14,355,000 (44,355,-000); petroleum products (metric tons; 1986) 5,150,000 (7,360,000); natural gas (cu m; 1986) 8,255,000,000 (8,255,000,000).
Household income and expenditure. Average household size (1981) 6.7; income per household PRs 20,530 (U.S.$2,075); sources of income (1984–85): self-employment 49.1%, wages and salaries 28.9%, transfer payments 1.6%, other 20.4%; expenditure (1984–85): food 48.6%, housing 11.2%, clothing and footwear 7.5%, energy 5.6%, transport 4.5%, other 22.6%.
Gross national product (1986): U.S.$34,690,000,000 (U.S.$350 per capita).

Structure of gross domestic product and labour force				
	1986–87		1984–85	
	in value PRs '000,000	% of total value	labour force	% of labour force
Agriculture	127,473	23.7	14,054,000	48.7
Mining	12,616	2.3	47,000	0.1
Manufacturing	95,079	17.7	3,800,000	13.2
Construction	35,261	6.6	1,556,000	5.4
Public utilities	12,385	2.3	192,000	0.7
Transportation and communication	44,125	8.2	1,445,000	5.0
Trade	89,420	16.7	3,207,000	11.1
Finance	30,613	5.7	245,000	0.8
Pub. admin., defense	47,681	8.9 }	3,077,000	10.7
Services	42,622	7.9 }		
Other	...	...	1,249,000[2]	4.3
TOTAL	537,275[3]	100.0	28,872,000	100.0

Public debt (external, outstanding; 1986): U.S.$11,764,500,000.
Population economically active (1984–85): total 28,872,000; activity rate of total population 29.6% (participation rates: ages 15–64, 50.6%; female 9.4%; unemployed 3.7%).

Price and earnings indexes (1980 = 100)							
	1982	1983	1984	1985	1986	1987	1988[4]
Consumer price index	118.5	126.0	133.7	141.2	146.2	153.0	163.9
Monthly earnings index	...	...	...	...	...	...	...

Land use (1985): forested 4.0%; meadows and pastures 6.4%; agricultural and under permanent cultivation 26.6%; built-on, wasteland, and other 63.0%.

Foreign trade[5]

Balance of trade (current prices)						
	1982	1983	1984	1985	1986	1987
PRs '000,000	−30,823	−23,475	−38,927	−42,029	−25,214	−19,938
% of total	35.3%	22.5%	35.1%	32.5%	18.3%	12.1%

Imports (1986–87): PRs 92,430,800,000 (crude oil 7.7%, gas oils 5.2%, vegetable oils 4.3%, chemical fertilizers 3.5%, refined sugar 3.0%, blended tea 2.9%, passenger motor cars 2.0%, motor trucks 1.9%, insecticides 1.9%). *Major import sources:* Japan 16.4%; United States 11.0%; West Germany 7.5%; Kuwait 7.4%; United Kingdom 6.7%; Saudi Arabia 5.3%; China 3.9%; Malaysia 3.0%.
Exports (1986–87): PRs 63,267,900,000 (cotton yarn 13.9%, raw cotton 12.1%, cotton fabrics 9.4%, rice 8.0%, leather 6.4%, woolen carpets 5.4%, fish and fish preparations 3.1%, sporting goods 1.6%). *Major export destinations:* Japan 10.9%, United States 10.2%; United Kingdom 7.2%; Saudi Arabia 7.1%; West Germany 7.0%; Italy 5.8%; U.A.E (Dubai) 3.4%; France 3.3%.

Transport and communications

Transport. Railroads (1986–87): length 7,842 mi, 12,620 km; passenger-mi 10,513,000,000, passenger-km 16,919,000,000; short ton-mi cargo 5,356,-000,000, metric ton-km cargo 7,819,000,000. Roads (1986–87): total length 67,437 mi, 108,530 km (paved 43%). Vehicles (1986): passenger cars 500,-163; trucks and buses 154,537. Merchant marine (1987): vessels (100 gross tons and over) 74; total deadweight tonnage 565,696. Air transport (1986–87): passenger-km 7,329,477,000; metric ton-km cargo 320,689,000; airports (1988) with scheduled flights 29.
Communications. Daily newspapers (1986): total number 126; total circulation 1,219,589; circulation per 1,000 population 12. Radio (1986): total number of receivers 5,250,000 (1 per 20 persons). Television (1987): total number of receivers 1,436,610 (1 per 74 persons). Telephones (1986): 583,-930 (1 per 177 persons).

Education and health

Education (1986–87)				
	schools	teachers	students	student/ teacher ratio
Primary (age 5–9)	88,734	207,800	8,081,000	38.9
Secondary (age 10–14)	11,436	158,300	2,661,000	16.8
Voc., teacher tr.	296	4,346	61,000	14.0
Higher	595	22,601	550,398	24.4

Educational attainment (1981). Percent of population age 25 and over having: no formal schooling 78.9%; some primary education 8.7%; some secondary 10.5%; postsecondary 1.9%. *Literacy* (1981): total population age 15 and over literate 11,938,790 (25.6%); males literate 8,709,162 (36.0%); females literate 3,229,628 (15.2%).
Health (1987): physicians 51,020 (1 per 2,086 persons); hospital beds 59,903 (1 per 1,777 persons); infant mortality rate per 1,000 live births 120.0.
Food (1983–85): daily per capita caloric intake 2,186 (vegetable products 89%, animal products 11%); (1983) 95% of FAO recommended minimum requirement.

Military

Total active duty personnel (1987): 480,600 (army 93.6%, navy 2.7%, air force 3.7%). *Military expenditure as percent of GNP* (1985): 6.4% (world 6.1%); per capita expenditure U.S.$24.

[1]Provincial estimates exclude and 1988 estimate includes Afghan refugees and residents of Pakistani-occupied Jammu and Kashmir. [2]Includes unemployed. [3]At factor cost. [4]June. [5]Import figures are f.o.b. in balance of trade and c.i.f. for commodities and trading partners.

Panama

Official name: República de Panamá (Republic of Panama).
Form of government: multiparty republic with one legislative house (Legislative Assembly [67]).
Head of state and government: President[1].
Capital: Panama City.
Official language: Spanish.
Official religion: none.
Monetary unit: 1 balboa (B) = 100 cents; valuation (Oct. 10, 1988) 1 U.S.$ = B 1.00; 1 £ = B 1.71.

Area and population		area		population
		sq mi	sq km	1987 estimate
Provinces	**Capitals**			
Bocas del Toro	Bocas del Toro	3,443	8,917	77,500
Chiriquí	David	3,381	8,758	360,300
Coclé	Penonomé	1,944	5,035	164,500
Colón	Colón	1,915	4,961	163,100
Darién	La Palma	6,488	16,803	38,400
Herrera	Chitré	937	2,427	101,300
Los Santos	Las Tablas	1,493	3,867	81,300
Panamá	Panama City	4,642	12,022	1,037,400
Veraguas	Santiago	4,280	11,086	210,000
Special territory				
Comarca de San Blas	El Porvenir	1,238	3,206	40,600
TOTAL AREA		29,762[2]	77,082	2,274,400

Demography

Population (1988): 2,322,000.
Density (1988): persons per sq mi 78.0, persons per sq km 30.1.
Urban–rural (1987): urban 51.9%; rural 48.1%.
Sex distribution (1985): male 50.97%; female 49.03%.
Age breakdown (1986): under 15, 37.0%; 15–29, 29.5%; 30–44, 17.2%; 45–59, 9.6%; 60–74, 5.2%; 75 and over, 1.5%.
Population projection: (1990) 2,418,000; (2000) 2,893,000.
Doubling time: 33 years.
Ethnic composition (1980): mestizo/mulatto 59.5%; black 14.0%; white 12.0%; Amerindian 7.5%; East Indian 4.0%; other 3.0%.
Religious affiliation (1980): Roman Catholic 89.0%; Protestant 5.0%; Muslim 4.5%; Bahá'í 1.0%; Hindu 0.3%; other 0.2%.
Major cities (1987): Panama City 439,996; San Miguelito 231,920; Colón 68,688.

Vital statistics

Birth rate per 1,000 population (1987): 25.7 (world avg. 26.0); (1985) legitimate 28.1%; illegitimate 71.9%.
Death rate per 1,000 population (registered; 1987): 3.8 (world avg. 9.9).
Natural increase rate per 1,000 population (1987): 21.9 (world avg. 16.1).
Total fertility rate (avg. births per childbearing woman; 1984): 3.3.
Marriage rate per 1,000 population (1986): 4.5.
Divorce rate per 1,000 population (1986): 0.5.
Life expectancy at birth (1985–90): male 70.2 years; female 74.1 years.
Major causes of death per 100,000 population (1986)[3]: diseases of the circulatory system 104.1, of which ischemic heart diseases 44.2, cerebrovascular disease 38.3; malignant neoplasms (cancers) 50.0; accidents 32.1; infectious and parasitic diseases 21.3.

National economy

Budget (1987). Revenue: B 1,866,367,000 (loans 40.6%; indirect taxes 20.3%; direct taxes 19.4%; income from state enterprises 6.0%). Expenditures: B 1,866,367,000 (current expenditure 91.4%, of which payments on external debt 36.6%, payments on internal debt 14.6%, education 9.5%, home affairs and justice 6.8%, health 5.1%; development expenditure 8.6%).
Public debt (external, outstanding; 1986): U.S.$3,438,700,000.
Tourism (1986): receipts from visitors U.S.$205,000,000; expenditures by nationals abroad U.S.$73,000,000.
Production (metric tons except as noted). Agriculture, forestry, fishing (1986): sugarcane 1,800,000, bananas 1,100,000, rice 172,000, corn (maize) 75,000, coffee 38,000, oranges 34,000, tomatoes 32,000, mangoes 28,000, cacao 2,000; livestock (number of live animals; 1986) 1,443,000 cattle, 205,000 pigs; roundwood 2,047,000 cu m; fish catch (value of production in B): shrimps 47,895,000, lobster 6,241,000, fish 4,216,000. Mining and quarrying (1987): limestone 294,000[4]; salt 17,100. Manufacturing (value of production in B; 1984): processed food 749,867,000, of which prepared meat 149,387,000, refined sugar and products 80,670,000, milk products 76,830,000, products of grains 67,283,000; garments 54,078,000; plastics 48,393,000. Construction (buildings authorized; 1984): residential 302,000 sq m; nonresidential 76,000 sq m. Energy production (consumption): electricity (kW-hr; 1986) 2,736,000,000 (2,736,000,000); coal (metric tons; 1986) none (5,000); crude petroleum (barrels; 1986) none (9,346,000); petroleum products (metric tons; 1986) 1,150,000 (792,000); natural gas, none (none).
Household income and expenditure. Average household size (1980) 4.8; median income per household (1980) B 2,950 (U.S.$2,950); sources of income (1979): wages and salaries 85.3%, transfers 9.2%, other 5.5%; expenditure (1978): food 47.3%, housing and energy 12.7%, household furnishings 8.5%, transportation 6.8%, health care 4.9%, other 19.8%.
Gross national product (at current market prices; 1986): U.S.$5,190,000,000 (U.S.$2,330 per capita).

Structure of gross domestic product and labour force				
	1986			
	in value B '000,000	% of total value	labour force	% of labour force
Agriculture	478.6	9.3	184,522	25.6
Mining	6.0	0.1	420	0.1
Manufacturing	422.1	8.2	64,173	8.9
Construction	257.0	5.0	34,597	4.8
Public utilities	227.2	4.4	8,687	1.2
Transportation and communications	1,000.9[5]	19.5[5]	37,558	5.2
Trade	701.0	13.7	93,480	13.0
Finance, real estate	958.1	18.7	26,926	3.7
Pub. admin., defense	758.9	14.8 }	179,218	24.9
Services	478.2	9.3 }		
Other	−166.8[6]	−3.2[6]	89,993[7]	12.5[7]
TOTAL	5,121.2	100.0[2]	719,574	100.0[2]

Population economically active (1986)[8]: total 719,574; activity rate of total population 32.1% (participation rates: ages 15–69 [1985] 58.7%; female [1985] 31.8%; unemployed 10.5%).

Price and earnings indexes (1980 = 100)							
	1981	1982	1983	1984	1985	1986	1987
Consumer price index	107.3	111.9	114.2	116.0	117.2	117.2	118.3
Monthly earnings index[9]	104.9	109.8	120.1	124.2	130.3	131.2	...

Land use (1985): forested 52.9%; meadows and pastures 15.3%; agricultural and under permanent cultivation 7.5%; other 24.3%.

Foreign trade[10, 11]

Balance of trade (current prices)						
	1982	1983	1984	1985	1986	1987
B '000,000	−1,031.9	−946.2	−1,000.3	−903.4	−754.2	−784.7
% of total	57.9%	59.6%	64.4%	57.4%	51.9%	53.6%

Imports (1986): B 1,275,247,000 (machinery and transport equipment 25.1%, mineral products 14.0%, chemicals and chemical products 12.1%, metals and metal manufactures 7.8%, textiles 6.9%, food and beverages 5.8%). *Major import sources:* U.S. 34.2%; Colón Free Zone 13.2%; Japan 8.5%; Mexico 5.2%; Ecuador 3.6%; Costa Rica 3.3%.
Exports (1986): B 326,864,000 (bananas 21.4%, shrimps 20.8%, coffee 9.3%, raw sugar 6.1%). *Major export destinations:* U.S. 66.5%; Puerto Rico 13.1%; West Germany 5.8%; Costa Rica 5.3%; Italy 2.3%.

Transport and communications

Transport. Railroads: route length (1987) 354 mi, 569 km; passengers carried 90,576[12]. Roads (1986): total length 6,039 mi, 9,719 km (paved 33%). Vehicles (1984): passenger cars 120,995; trucks and buses 41,753. Merchant marine (1987): vessels (100 gross tons and over) 5,136; total deadweight tonnage 70,435,824. Panama Canal traffic (1987): oceangoing transits 12,313; cargo 148,899,425 metric tons. Air transport (1986)[13]: passenger-mi 313,900,000, passenger-km 505,174,000; short ton-mi cargo 6,343,000, metric ton-km cargo 9,261,000; airports (1988) with scheduled flights 6.
Communications. Daily newspapers (1986): total number 9; total circulation 197,200; circulation per 1,000 population 89. Radio (1986): 900,000 receivers (1 per 2.5 persons). Television (1987): 476,000 receivers (1 per 4.8 persons). Telephones (1986): 231,990 (1 per 9.6 persons).

Education and health

Education (1986)				
	schools	teachers	students	student/ teacher ratio
Primary (age 6–11)	2,574	14,176	341,914	24.1
Secondary (age 12–17)	334	10,113	187,312	18.5
Voc., teacher tr.	70	644	10,548	16.4
Higher	8	4,650	56,227	12.1

Educational attainment (1980). Percent of population age 25 and over having: no formal schooling 17.4%; incomplete primary education 27.3%; complete primary education 23.4%; secondary 23.5%; higher 8.4%. *Literacy* (1985): total population age 15 and over literate 1,204,000 (88.2%); males literate 618,000 (89.0%); females literate 586,000 (87.7%).
Health (1986): physicians 2,596 (1 per 858 persons); hospital beds 7,799 (1 per 286 persons); infant mortality rate per 1,000 live births (1985–90) 22.7.
Food (1984–86): daily per capita caloric intake 2,439 (vegetable products 81%, animal products 19%); (1983) 98% of FAO recommended minimum requirement.

Military

Total active duty personnel (1988): 7,300 (army 82.2%, navy 12.3%, air force 5.5%). *Military expenditure as percent of GNP* (1985): 2.2% (world 6.1%); per capita expenditure U.S.$47.

---

[1]The commander of the National Defense Forces was the de facto executive in late 1988. [2]Detail does not add to total given because of rounding. [3]Registered deaths only. [4]1985. [5]Includes trans-Panamanian oil pipeline, commission of Panama Canal, and all activities of Colón Free Zone. [6]Net of imputed bank service charges and import fees. [7]Includes unemployed. [8]Excludes indigenous areas and former Canal Zone. [9]Median figure of public sector. [10]Import figures are f.o.b. in balance of trade and c.i.f. in commodities and trading partners. [11]Excludes Colón Free Zone (1986 imports c.i.f. B 1,998,700,000; 1986 reexports f.o.b. B 2,198,500,000) and transshipped oil. [12]Chiriquí National Railroad only; 1986. [13]COPA and Air Panama only.

Papua New Guinea

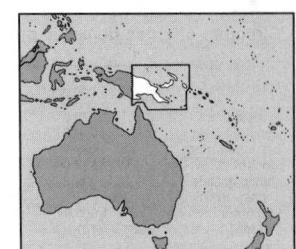

Official name: Papua New Guinea.
Form of government: constitutional
  monarchy with one legislative house
  (National Parliament [109]).
Chief of state: British Monarch
  represented by governor-general.
Head of government: Prime Minister.
Capital: Port Moresby.
Official language: English.
Official religion: none.
Monetary unit: 1 Papua New Guinea
  kina (K) = 100 toea; valuation
  (Oct. 10, 1988) 1 U.S.$ = K 0.87;
  1 £ = K 1.49.

Area and population

Provinces	Administrative centres	area sq mi	area sq km	population 1987 estimate[1]
Central	Port Moresby	11,400	29,500	135,000
Chimbu	Kundiawa	2,350	6,100	186,800
Eastern Highlands	Goroka	4,300	11,200	310,300
East New Britain	Rabaul	6,000	15,500	157,800
East Sepik	Wewak	16,550	42,800	260,000
Enga	Wabag	4,950	12,800	180,100
Gulf	Kerema	13,300	34,500	72,600
Madang	Madang	11,200	29,000	251,100
Manus	Lorengau	800	2,100	30,500
Milne Bay	Alotau	5,400	14,000	153,800
Morobe	Lae	13,300	34,500	364,400
National Capital District	Port Moresby	100	240	145,300
New Ireland	Kavieng	3,700	9,600	78,900
Northern	Popondetta	8,800	22,800	92,200
North Solomons	Kieta	3,600	9,300	159,100
Southern Highlands	Mendi	9,200	23,800	262,400
Western	Daru	38,350	99,300	93,600
Western Highlands	Mount Hagen	3,300	8,500	304,800
West New Britain	Kimbe	8,100	21,000	110,600
West Sepik	Vanimo	14,000	36,300	130,100
TOTAL		178,703[2]	462,840	3,502,400[3]

Demography

Population (1988): 3,562,000.
Density (1988): persons per sq mi 19.9, persons per sq km 7.7.
Urban–rural (1985): urban 14.3%; rural 85.7%.
Sex distribution (1985): male 52.09%; female 47.91%.
Age breakdown (1985): under 15, 41.6%; 15–29, 27.5%; 30–44, 16.0%; 45–59, 9.3%; 60–74, 4.5%; 75 and over, 1.0%[2].
Population projection: (1990) 3,727,000; (2000) 4,706,000.
Doubling time: 31 years.
Ethnic composition (1983): New Guinea Papuan 84.0%; New Guinea Melanesian 15.0%; other 1.0%.
Religious affiliation (1980): Protestant 58.4%; Roman Catholic 32.8%; Anglican 5.4%; traditional beliefs 2.5%; Baha'i 0.6%; other 0.3%.
Major cities (1987): Port Moresby 152,100; Lae 79,600; Madang 24,700; Wewak 23,200; Goroka 21,800.

Vital statistics

Birth rate per 1,000 population (1987): 35.6 (world avg. 26.0); legitimate, n.a.; illegitimate, n.a.
Death rate per 1,000 population (1987): 12.9 (world avg. 9.9).
Natural increase rate per 1,000 population (1987): 22.7 (world avg. 16.1).
Total fertility rate (avg. births per childbearing woman; 1987): 5.2.
Marriage rate per 1,000 population: n.a.
Divorce rate per 1,000 population: n.a.
Life expectancy at birth (1987): male 53.0 years; female 54.6 years.
Major causes of death per 100,000 population: n.a.; however, major infectious diseases include malaria, intestinal infections, and tuberculosis.

National economy

Budget (1988). Revenue: K 883,300,000 (foreign government grants 20.8%, import duties 20.4%, personal income tax 19.8%, business income tax 8.2%, excise duties 7.4%). Expenditures: K 906,100,000 (administrative 42.1%, transfers to provincial governments 25.2%, debt retirement 14.9%).
Public debt (external, outstanding; 1986): U.S.$1,147,000,000.
Tourism: receipts from visitors (1986) U.S.$12,000,000; expenditures by nationals abroad (1986) U.S.$26,000,000.
Land use (1985): forested 84.8%; agricultural and under permanent cultivation 0.8%; meadows and pastures 0.2%; other 14.2%.
Production (metric tons except as noted). Agriculture, forestry, fishing (1986): bananas 960,000, coconuts 820,000, sweet potatoes 470,000, sugarcane 222,000, taro 185,000, yams 175,000, copra 145,000, palm oil 125,000, cassava 105,000, coffee 54,000, palm kernels 51,200, cocoa 30,000, tea 9,000, mangoes 6,000; livestock (number of live animals) 1,489,000 pigs, 123,000 cattle, 16,000 goats, 4,000,000 chickens; roundwood (1985) 7,623,000 cu m; fish catch 6,250. Mining and quarrying (1986): copper 173,903; silver 46,655 kg; gold 35,999 kg. Manufacturing (value added in K; 1985): food, beverages, and tobacco 162,558,000; metals, metal products, machinery, and equipment 47,493,000; wood and wood products 29,807,000. Construction (value[4]; 1986): residential K 19,369,000; nonresidential K 55,675,000. Energy production (consumption): electricity (kW-hr; 1986) 1,575,000,000 (1,575,000,000); coal, none (n.a.); crude petroleum (barrels; 1986) none (n.a.); petroleum products (metric tons; 1986) none (695,000,000); natural gas, none (n.a.).

Gross national product (1986): U.S.$2,470,000,000 (U.S.$690 per capita).

Structure of gross domestic product and labour force

	1983 in value K '000,000	1983 % of total value	1980 labour force[5]	1980 % of labour force[5]
Agriculture	647.8	32.8	564,500	77.0
Mining	210.8	10.7	4,300	0.6
Manufacturing	178.8	9.1	14,000	1.9
Construction	84.7	4.3	21,600	2.9
Public utilities	28.8	1.5	2,800	0.4
Transp. and commun.	68.3	3.5	17,400	2.4
Trade	156.6	7.9	25,100	3.4
Finance	187.4	9.5	4,500	0.6
Pub. admin., defense	147.1	7.5 }	77,100	10.5
Services	225.8	11.4 }		
Other	37.6	1.9	1,500	0.2
TOTAL	1,973.7	100.0[2]	732,800	100.0[2]

Population economically active (1980)[5]: total 732,800; activity rate of total population 24.6% (participation rates: over age 10, 35.2%; female 39.8%; unemployed 12.8%[6]).

Price and earnings indexes (1980 = 100)

	1981	1982	1983	1984	1985	1986	1987[7]
Consumer price index	108.1	114.0	123.0	132.2	137.1	144.6	148.2
Monthly earnings index	...	...	...	...	...	...	...

Household income and expenditure. Average household size (1980) 4.6; income per household (1975–76) K 2,771 (U.S.$3,483); sources of income: n.a.; expenditure (1985)[8]: food, beverages, and tobacco 40.3%, housing 18.6%, transportation and communications 11.3%, durable household goods 7.6%, clothing and footwear 6.3%, heating and lighting 4.9%, services and other 11.0%.

Foreign trade[9]

Balance of trade (current prices)

	1980	1981	1982	1983	1984	1985	1986
K '000,000	+7.5	−173.7	−180.8	−138.0	−64.7	+35.9	−45.0
% of total	0.5%	13.3%	13.7%	9.2%	3.9%	2.0%	2.7%

Imports (1985): K 874,774,000 (machinery and transport equipment 30.0%; mineral fuels, lubricants, and related materials 17.6%; food and live animals 17.6%; manufactured goods 15.4%). *Major import sources:* Australia 40.2%; Japan 17.4%; Singapore 10.2%; United States 9.6%; New Zealand 5.6%; United Kingdom 3.0%; Hong Kong 2.3%.
Exports (1985): K 910,205,000 (copper ore and concentrates 33.2%; gold 19.3%; coffee 12.9%; cocoa beans 6.7%; palm oil 6.7%; timber 6.3%; copra 3.7%; copra oil 2.5%). *Major export destinations:* West Germany 30.0%; Japan 22.5%; Australia 10.4%; United Kingdom 7.5%; Spain 4.7%; The Netherlands 4.3%; United States 3.9%.

Transport and communications

Transport. Railroads: none. Roads (1986): total length 12,263 mi, 19,736 km (paved 6%). Vehicles (1986): passenger cars 18,748; trucks and buses 30,497. Merchant marine (1987): vessels (100 gross tons and over) 92; total deadweight tonnage 44,891. Air transport (1986): passenger-mi 291,000,000, passenger-km 468,000,000; short ton-mi cargo 6,954,000, metric ton-km cargo 10,152,000; airports (1988) with scheduled flights 177.
Communications. Daily newspapers (1986): total number 1; total circulation 28,000; circulation per 1,000 population 8.2. Radio (1986): total number of receivers 225,000 (1 per 15 persons). Television (1985): total number of receivers 230,000 (1 per 14 persons). Telephones (1986): 63,212 (1 per 54 persons).

Education and health

Education (1986)

	schools	teachers	students	student/teacher ratio
Primary (age 7–12)	2,461	12,318	374,950	30.4
Secondary (age 13–16)	122	2,025	49,974	24.7
Voc., teacher tr.	112	745	10,078	13.5
Higher	2	400	3,029	7.6

Educational attainment (1980). Percent of population age 25 and over having: no formal schooling 82.6%; some primary education 8.2%; completed primary 5.0%; some secondary 4.2%. *Literacy* (1980): total population age 15 and over literate 757,500 (42.3%); males literate 490,100 (52.4%); females literate 267,400 (31.3%).
Health (1984): physicians 280 (1 per 11,635 persons); hospital beds 14,661 (1 per 222 persons); infant mortality rate per 1,000 live births (1987) 63.0.
Food (1980–82): daily per capita caloric intake 2,074 (vegetable products 90%, animal products 10%); (1983) 75% of FAO recommended minimum.

Military

Total active duty personnel (1987): 3,530 (army 89.2%, navy 7.1%, air force 3.7%). *Military expenditure as percent of GNP* (1985): 1.5% (world 6.1%); per capita expenditure U.S.$11.

---

[1]De jure. [2]Detail does not add to total given because of rounding. [3]Includes 23,000 noncitizens. [4]Completed new buildings. [5]Citizens of Papua New Guinea over age 10 involved in "money raising activities" only. [6]1977; in six urban centres. [7]Midyear. [8]Weights of consumer price index components. [9]Import figures are f.o.b. (free on board) in balance of trade and c.i.f. (cost, insurance, and freight) for commodities and trading partners.

Paraguay

Official name: República del Paraguay
(Republic of Paraguay).
Form of government: republic with
two legislative houses (Senate [30];
Chamber of Deputies [60]).
Head of state and government:
President.
Capital: Asunción.
Official language: Spanish.
Official religion: Roman Catholicism.
Monetary unit: 1 Paraguayan Guaraní
(₲) = 100 céntimos; valuation[1] (Oct.
10, 1988) 1 U.S.$ = ₲400; 1 £ = ₲685.

Area and population		area		population
Regions Departments	Capitals	sq mi	sq km	1985 estimate
Occidental		95,338	246,925	50,400
Alto Paraguay	Fuerte Olimpio	17,754	45,982	10,100
Boquerón	Dr. Pedro P. Peña	18,034	46,708	12,000
Chaco	Mayor Pablo Lagerenza	14,041	36,367	300
Nueva Asunción	General Eugenio A. Garay	17,359	44,961	200
Presidente Hayes	Pozo Colorado	28,150	72,907	27,800
Oriental		61,710	159,827	3,228,600
Alto Paraná	Puerto Presidente Stroessner	5,751	14,895	255,000
Amambay	Pedro Juan Caballero	4,994	12,933	69,400
Asunción	Asunción	45	117	477,100
Caaguazú	Coronel Oviedo	4,430	11,474	333,000
Caazapá	Caazapá	3,666	9,496	111,400
Canendiyú	Salto del Guairá	5,663	14,667	77,100
Central	Asunción	952	2,465	572,500
Concepción	Concepción	6,970	18,051	143,000
Cordillera	Caacupé	1,910	4,948	194,000
Guairá	Villarrica	1,485	3,846	149,600
Itapúa	Encarnación	6,380	16,525	284,500
Misiones	San Juan Bautista	3,690	9,556	80,100
Ñeembucú	Pilar	4,690	12,147	69,500
Paraguarí	Paraguarí	3,361	8,705	201,900
San Pedro	San Pedro	7,723	20,002	210,500
TOTAL		157,048	406,752	3,279,000

Demography

Population (1988): 4,007,000.
Density (1988): persons per sq mi 25.5, persons per sq km 9.9.
Urban–rural (1986): urban 43.9%; rural 56.1%.
Sex distribution (1984): male 50.20%; female 49.80%.
Age breakdown (1982): under 15, 41.1%; 15–29, 28.1%; 30–44, 15.4%; 45–59,
9.1%; 60–74, 4.8%; 75 and over, 1.5%.
Population projection: (1990) 4,231,000; (2000) 5,405,000.
Doubling time: 25 years.
Ethnic composition (1980): mestizo (Spanish–Guaraní) 90.8%; Amerindian
3.0%; German 1.7%; other 4.5%.
Religious affiliation (1980): Roman Catholic 96.0%; Protestant 2.1%; other
1.9%.
Major cities (1985): Asunción 477,000; Lambaré 84,000; Fernando de la
Mora 80,000; Puerto Presidente Stroessner 64,000.

Vital statistics

Birth rate per 1,000 population (1985–90): 34.9 (world avg. 26.0); (1985)
legitimate 68.7%[2]; illegitimate 31.3%[2].
Death rate per 1,000 population (1985–90): 6.6 (world avg. 9.9).
Natural increase rate per 1,000 population (1985–90): 28.3 (world avg. 16.1).
Total fertility rate (avg. births per childbearing woman; 1985): 4.4.
Marriage rate per 1,000 population (1985): 5.0[2].
Divorce rate per 1,000 population: n.a.
Life expectancy at birth (1985–90): male 63.7 years; female 68.6 years.
Major causes of death per 100,000 population (1984): diseases of the circu-
latory system 95.7; infectious and parasitic diseases 40.5; diseases of the
respiratory system 31.4; malignant neoplasms (cancers) 25.6.

National economy

Budget (1987). Revenue: ₲195,399,100,000 (domestic taxes on goods and
services 35.8%, income tax 17.9%, sales tax 10.4%, customs duties 9.8%,
pension funds 4.7%, alcohol tax 3.9%, real estate taxes 3.6%). Expenditures:
₲189,066,300,000 (public debt 21.7%, defense 14.2%, education 12.6%,
ministry of interior 9.0%, public health 3.6%, public works 3.0%).
Public debt (external, outstanding; 1986): U.S.$1,811,600,000.
Production (metric tons except as noted). Agriculture, forestry, fishing (1986):
cassava 2,875,000, sugarcane 1,296,000, soybeans 662,000, corn (maize)
496,000, seed cotton 375,000, oranges 341,000, bananas 335,000, lint cotton
124,000, sweet potatoes 88,000; livestock (number of live animals) 7,151,-
000 cattle, 1,403,000 pigs, 15,000,000 chickens; roundwood 8,210,000 cu m;
fish catch 13,000. Mining and quarrying (1986): limestone 180,000; kaolin
55,000; gypsum 6,000. Manufacturing (1987): cement 269,200; beef and
veal 118,000[3]; sugar 104,236; hides 13,863; tung oil 8,128; edible coconut
oil 3,619; coconut pulp 2,040; woven cotton fabrics 6,175,000 metres; nonalcoholic beverages 1,292,100 hectolitres; beer 917,980 hectolitres; alcohol
39,410 hectolitres[4]; cigarettes 56,711,000 cases; matches 9,159,000 boxes[4].
Construction (1985): residential 60,800 sq m; nonresidential 163,200 sq m.
Energy production (consumption): electricity (kW-hr; 1986) 1,644,000,000
(1,596,000,000); coal, none (none); crude petroleum (barrels; 1986) none
(1,576,000); petroleum products (metric tons; 1986) 206,000 (518,000); natural gas, none (none).

Tourism (1986): receipts from visitors U.S.$111,000,000; expenditures by
nationals abroad U.S.$49,000,000.
Gross national product (1985): U.S.$3,360,000,000 (U.S.$880 per capita).

Structure of gross domestic product and labour force				
	1986		1982	
	in value ₲'000,000	% of total value	labour force	% of labour force
Agriculture	498,900	27.2	445,518	42.9
Mining	8,300	0.5	1,406	0.1
Manufacturing	296,000	16.1	124,658	12.0
Construction	110,100	6.0	69,900	6.7
Public utilities	44,800	2.4	2,605	0.3
Transp. and commun.	80,100	4.4	30,524	2.9
Trade	489,800	26.7	85,961	8.3
Finance			18,019	1.7
Pub. admin., defense	305,700	16.7	174,228	16.8
Services				
Other			86,444	8.3
TOTAL	1,833,800[5]	100.0	1,039,258[5]	100.0

Population economically active (1982): total 1,039,258; activity rate of total
population 51.5% (participation rates: ages 15–64, 57.5%; female 19.7%;
unemployed 4.6%).

Price and earnings indexes (1980 = 100)							
	1982	1983	1984	1985	1986	1987	1988[6]
Consumer price index	121.7	138.0	166.1	207.9	273.0	333.7	391.1
Monthly earnings index							

Household income and expenditure: average household size (1982) 5.2;
sources of income (1984): wages and salaries 38.1%, transfer payments 2.6%,
other 59.3%; expenditure (1980): food 48.7%, housing 16.4%, clothing 9.7%,
household durable goods 6.2%, transportation and communications 4.5%.
Land use (1985): forested 51.2%; meadows and pastures 38.9%; agricultural
and under permanent cultivation 5.4%; other 4.5%.

Foreign trade

Balance of trade (current prices)						
	1982	1983	1984	1985	1986	1987
₲'000,000	−32,301	−26,519	−42,316	−75,892	−150,210	−115,975
% of total	25.5%	23.5%	21.7%	28.2%	44.9%	21.8%

Imports (1987): U.S.$324,588,000 (machinery and transport equipment
38.6%, of which transport equipment 9.3%; fuels and lubricants 19.9%;
tobacco and beverages 8.0%; chemicals and pharmaceuticals 5.0%; iron
and steel 4.7%). *Major import sources:* Brazil 32.7%; United States 10.7%;
Argentina 8.9%; Algeria 7.4%; United Kingdom 6.7%; West Germany 5.8%.
Exports (1987): U.S.$208,613,000 (soybeans 34.7%; cotton fibres 28.5%; pro-
cessed meat 9.9%; timber 7.6%; tobacco 2.8%; vegetable oil 2.7%, of which
tung oil 2.2%; perfume oils 1.6%). *Major export destinations:* The Netherlands 18.0%; Brazil 17.6%; Argentina 15.2%; Switzerland 6.8%; United
States 3.9%; West Germany 3.8%; Italy 3.4%.

Transport and communications

Transport. Railroads (1980): route length (1987) 274 mi, 441 km; passenger-
mi 13,900,000, passenger-km 22,400,000; short ton-mi cargo 23,600,000,
metric ton-km cargo 34,400,000. Roads (1985): total length 9,186 mi, 14,783
km (paved 13%). Vehicles (1985): passenger cars 84,986; trucks and buses
41,986. Merchant marine (1987): vessels (100 gross tons and over) 40; total
deadweight tonnage 49,224. Air transport (1982): passenger-mi 290,000,000,
passenger-km 466,000,000; short ton-mi cargo 1,400,000, metric ton-km
cargo 2,000,000; airports (1988) with scheduled flights 1.
Communications. Daily newspapers (1987): total number 4; total circulation 123,000; circulation per 1,000 population 32. Radio (1986): 624,000
receivers (1 per 6.1 persons). Television (1986): 350,000 receivers (1 per 11
persons). Telephones (1986): 92,702 (1 per 41 persons).

Education and health

Education (1985)				
	schools	teachers	students	student/ teacher ratio
Primary (age 7–12)	3,993	22,764	570,775	25.1
Secondary (age 13–18)[7]	740	9,044[3,7]	172,132[7]	19.0
Higher	2	2,694	29,154	10.8

Educational attainment (1982). Percent of population age 25 and over having: no formal schooling 13.6%; primary education 64.7%; secondary 15.5%;
higher 3.4%; not stated 2.8%. *Literacy* (1982): total population age 15 and
over literate 1,534,810 (85.7%); males literate 782,560 (88.7%); females literate 752,250 (82.9%).
Health: physicians (1982) 2,201 (1 per 1,379 persons); hospital beds (1985)
3,380 (1 per 1,089 persons); infant mortality rate (1985–90) 48.9.
Food (1984–86): daily per capita caloric intake 2,843 (vegetable products
81%, animal products 19%); (1983) 122% of FAO recommended minimum requirement.

Military

Total active duty personnel (1988): 16,000 (army 78.1%, navy 15.6%, air force
6.3%). *Military expenditure as percent of GNP* (1985): 1.1% (world 6.1%);
per capita expenditure U.S.$17.

[1]Official rate only; free market rate approx. 140% higher. [2]Civil Registry records
only. [3]1986. [4]1984. [5]Detail does not add to total given because of rounding. [6]April.
[7]Includes vocational education and teacher training.

Peru

Official name: República del Perú
(Spanish) (Republic of Peru).
Form of government: unitary multiparty
republic with two legislative
houses (Senate [60]; Chamber of
Deputies [180]).
Head of state and government:
President.
Capital: Lima.
Official languages: Spanish; Quechua.
Official religion: Roman Catholicism.
Monetary unit: 1 Inti (I/.) =
100 céntimos = 1,000 soles;
valuation (Oct. 10, 1988) 1 U.S.$ =
I/. 250.00; 1 £ = I/. 428.13.

Area and population		area		population
		sq mi	sq km	1988 estimate
Departments	**Capitals**			
Amazonas	Chachapoyas	15,945	41,297	319,500
Ancash	Huaraz	14,158	36,669	951,800
Apurímac	Abancay	7,934	20,550	364,800
Arequipa	Arequipa	24,528	63,528	910,500
Ayacucho	Ayacucho	17,058	44,181	557,600
Cajamarca	Cajamarca	13,486	34,930	1,222,600
Cuzco	Cuzco	29,471	76,329	1,000,400
Huancavelica	Huancavelica	8,139	21,079	372,900
Huánuco	Huánuco	13,088	33,897	583,800
Ica	Ica	8,205	21,251	519,500
Junín	Huancayo	15,944	41,296	1,062,600
La Libertad	Trujillo	8,973	23,241	1,180,800
Lambayeque	Chiclayo	5,304	13,737	881,000
Lima	Lima	13,058	33,821	6,313,000
Loreto	Iquitos	146,342	379,025	621,800
Madre de Dios	Puerto Maldonado	30,271	78,403	46,000
Moquegua	Moquegua	6,065	15,709	126,900
Pasco	Cerro de Pasco	9,356	24,233	270,800
Piura	Piura	14,055	36,403	1,413,600
Puno	Puno	27,947	72,382	997,400
San Martín	Moyobamba	20,197	52,309	429,500
Tacna	Tacna	5,881	15,232	195,500
Tumbes	Tumbes	1,827	4,732	135,900
Ucayali	Pucallpa	38,931	100,831	217,700
Constitutional Province				
Callao	Callao	57	148	560,000
TOTAL		496,225[1]	1,285,216[1]	21,255,900

Demography

Population (1988): 21,256,000.
Density (1988): persons per sq mi 42.8, persons per sq km 16.5.
Urban–rural (1987): urban 68.2%; rural 31.8%.
Sex distribution (1988): male 50.37%; female 49.63%.
Age breakdown (1985): under 15, 40.5%; 15–29, 28.2%; 30–44, 16.3%; 45–59, 9.5%; 60–74, 4.5%; 75 and over, 1.0%.
Population projection: (1990) 22,332,000; (2000) 27,952,000.
Doubling time: 28 years.
Ethnic composition (1981): Quechua 47.1%; mestizo 32.0%; white 12.0%; Aymara 5.4%; jungle Amerindian 1.7%; other 1.8%.
Religious affiliation (1984): Roman Catholic 92.4%; other 7.6%.
Major cities (1987): Lima 5,330,800; Arequipa 572,000; Callao 545,000; Trujillo 476,000; Chiclayo 379,000.

Vital statistics

Birth rate per 1,000 population (1988): 34.2 (world avg. 26.0); (1977) legitimate 57.8%; illegitimate 42.2%.
Death rate per 1,000 population (1988): 9.0 (world avg. 9.9).
Natural increase rate per 1,000 population (1988): 25.2 (world avg. 16.1).
Total fertility rate (avg. births per childbearing woman; 1988): 4.4.
Marriage rate per 1,000 population (1982): 6.0[2].
Life expectancy at birth (1988): male 60.1 years; female 64.0 years.
Major causes of death per 100,000 population (1982): respiratory diseases 97.9, of which pneumonia 68.1; infectious and parasitic diseases 88.2; diseases of the circulatory system 58.0; birth trauma and other perinatal causes 42.5; malignant neoplasms (cancers) 33.5.

National economy

Budget (1986). Revenue: I/. 45,331,000,000 (tax on fuel 23.8%; income taxes 21.7%; tax on external trade 20.8%; tax on goods and services 11.5%; property tax 4.6%). Expenditures: I/. 75,995,000,000 (current expenditure 61.8%, of which wages 19.4%, defense 14.1%, transfer payments 12.3%, interest payments 11.5%; public debt amortization 23.6%).
Public debt (external, outstanding; 1986): U.S.$11,048,600,000.
Tourism (1986): receipts from visitors U.S.$247,000,000; expenditures by nationals abroad U.S.$188,000,000.
Production (metric tons except as noted). Agriculture, forestry, fishing (1986): sugarcane 6,272,800, potatoes 1,687,300, corn (maize) 864,300, rice 744,800, plantains 574,700, cassava 340,000, seed cotton 303,800, coffee 97,000; livestock (number of live animals; 1986) 13,500,000 sheep, 3,820,000 cattle, 2,100,000 pigs, 43,000,000 chickens; roundwood 7,735,000 cu m; fish catch 5,610,000. Mining and quarrying (1987): iron ore 3,250,000; zinc 612,477; copper 406,430; lead 203,950; silver 2,054. Manufacturing (1986): cement 2,205,100; wheat flour 874,596; animal feed 628,312; refined sugar 600,209; sulfuric acid 209,424; construction rods 163,000; urea 150,881; motor vehicles 12,691 units. Construction (value added in I/. '000;

1985): buildings 9,753,500[3]. Energy production (consumption): electricity (kW-hr; 1986) 12,818,000,000 (12,818,000,000); coal (metric tons; 1986) 150,000 (105,000); crude petroleum (barrels; 1986) 64,870,500 (60,056,000); petroleum products (metric tons; 1986) 7,772,000 (5,750,000); natural gas (cu m; 1986) 578,267,000 (578,267,000).
Gross national product (1986): U.S.$21,540,000,000 (U.S.$1,130 per capita).

Structure of gross domestic product and labour force				
	1986		1987	
	in value I/. '000[4]	% of total value	labour force	% of labour force
Agriculture	52,084	14.5	2,460,300	35.2
Mining	32,930	9.2	167,700	2.4
Manufacturing	83,969	23.4	719,900	10.3
Construction	16,438	4.6	251,600	3.6
Public utilities			21,000	0.3
Transp. and commun.	145,524	40.6	307,500	4.4
Trade			1,034,400	14.8
Finance			174,700	2.5
Services[5]	27,519	7.7	1,852,400	26.5
TOTAL	358,464	100.0	6,989,500	100.0

Population economically active (1987): total 6,989,500; activity rate of total population 33.7% (participation rates: over age 15, 56.2%; female [1981] 25.4%; unemployed [1985] 11.8%).

Price and earnings indexes (1980 = 100)						
	1982	1983	1984	1985	1986	1987
Consumer price index	288.4	609.0	1,280.2	3,372.0	5,999.5	11,150.0
Monthly earnings index[6]	313.2	542.4	1,041.8	2,403.9	5,410.5	...

Household income and expenditure. Average household size (1981) 4.8; income per household (1971–72) S/.[7] 51,170 (U.S.$1,322); sources of income: n.a.; expenditure (1983)[6]: food, drink, and tobacco 38.1%, rent and utilities 15.6%, transportation 9.8%, recreation and education 7.4%.
Land use (1985): forest 54.4%; pasture 21.2%; agricultural 2.9%; other 21.5%.

Foreign trade

Balance of trade (current prices)						
	1982	1983	1984	1985	1986	1987
I/. '000,000	+457.8	+1,845.0	+5,206.6	+17,914.2	+6,439	+2,161
% of total	11.0%	22.7%	31.2%	37.5%	10.2%	2.5%

Imports (1986): U.S.$2,525,000,000 (raw and intermediate materials 50.7%; capital goods 27.4%, of which private sector 21.1%, public sector 6.3%; consumer goods 13.9%). *Major import sources:* U.S. 26.9%; Japan 8.8%; W.Ger. 8.6%; Argentina 7.7%; Brazil 6.6%; Switzerland 3.8%; U.K. 2.8%.
Exports (1986): U.S.$2,509,000,000 (mineral products 40.8%; agricultural products 16.2%; fish products 12.6%; petroleum and derivatives 9.4%; textiles 9.2%). *Major destinations:* U.S. 30.1%; Japan 10.6%; Belgium–Luxem. 6.7%; W.Ger. 5.6%; U.K. 4.7%; U.S.S.R. 3.8%; Italy 3.2%; Brazil 2.9%.

Transport and communications

Transport. Railroads (1986): route length 2,144 mi, 3,451 km; passenger-km 485,139,000; metric ton-km cargo 1,028,329,000. Roads (1985): total length 42,479 mi, 68,363 km (paved 11%). Vehicles (1986): passenger cars 377,208; trucks and buses 226,533. Merchant marine (1987): vessels (100 gross tons and over) 635; total deadweight tonnage 1,036,162. Air transport (1986): passenger-km 2,114,009,000; metric ton-km cargo 267,407,000[8]; airports (1988) 22.
Communications. Daily newspapers (1985): total number 66; total circulation 1,121,900[9]; circulation per 1,000 population 57[9]. Radio (1986): 3,969,000 receivers (1 per 5.1 persons). Television (1987): 1,600,000 receivers (1 per 13 persons). Telephones (1985): 599,964 (1 per 33 persons).

Education and health

Education (1986)	schools	teachers	students	student/ teacher ratio
Primary (age 6–11)	31,186	123,000	4,060,000	33.0
Secondary (age 12–16)	4,831	74,000	1,676,000	22.6
Voc., teacher tr.	288	7,000	151,000	21.6
Higher	46	22,000	394,000	17.9

Educational attainment (1981). Percent of population age 25 and over having: no formal schooling 20.1%; less than primary education 33.2%; primary 21.1%; secondary 20.8%; higher 4.8%. *Literacy* (1981): total population age 15 and over literate 8,152,451 (81.6%); males 4,440,071 (89.9%); females 3,712,380 (73.5%).
Health: physicians (1986) 19,237 (1 per 1,051 persons); hospital beds (1985) 30,443 (1 per 647 persons); infant mortality rate per 1,000 live births (1988) 85.8.
Food (1983–85): daily per capita caloric intake 2,144 (vegetable products 87%, animal products 13%); (1983) 85% of FAO recommended minimum.

Military

Total active duty personnel (1987): 113,000 (army 66.4%, navy 20.3%, air force 13.3%). *Military expenditure as percent of GNP* (1985): 6.9% (world 6.1%); per capita expenditure U.S.$70.

[1]Detail does not add to total given because of rounding. [2]Excludes Indian jungle population; based on incomplete information. [3]Includes new construction and capital repairs. [4]At prices of 1970. [5]Services includes public administration and defense. [6]Estimate for Lima metropolitan area only. [7]Peruvian sol, the currency prior to 1985. [8]Data for one or more months missing. [9]Partial circulation.

Philippines

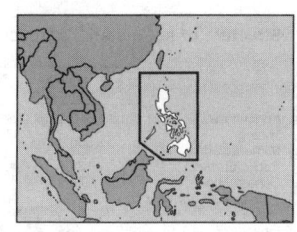

Official name: Republika ñg Pilipinas (Pilipino); Republic of the Philippines (English).
Form of government: unitary republic with two legislative houses (Senate [24]; House of Representatives [250[1]]).
Chief of state and head of government: President.
Capital: Manila.
Official languages: Pilipino; English.
Official religion: none.
Monetary unit: 1 Philippine peso (₱) = 100 centavos; valuation (Oct. 10, 1988) 1 U.S.$ = ₱ 20.32; 1 £ = ₱ 34.80.

Area and population	area		population
Regions	sq mi	sq km	1988 estimate
Bicol	6,808	17,633	4,198,000
Cagayan Valley	14,055	36,403	2,713,000
Central Luzon	7,039	18,231	5,863,000
Central Mindanao	8,994	23,293	2,802,000
Central Visayas	5,773	14,951	4,447,000
Eastern Visayas	8,275	21,432	3,243,000
Ilocos	8,328	21,568	4,134,000
National Capital Region	246	636	7,561,000
Northern Mindanao	10,937	28,328	3,438,000
Southern Mindanao	12,237	31,693	4,132,000
Southern Tagalog	18,117	46,924	7,692,000
Western Mindanao	7,214	18,685	3,061,000
Western Visayas	7,808	20,223	5,439,000
TOTAL	115,800[2]	300,000	58,723,000

Demography

Population (1988): 58,723,000.
Density (1988): persons per sq mi 507.1, persons per sq km 195.7.
Urban–rural (1987): urban 41.0%; rural 59.0%.
Sex distribution (1987): male 50.20%; female 49.80%.
Age breakdown (1984): under 15, 39.0%; 15–29, 30.5%; 30–44, 17.0%; 45–59, 8.7%; 60–74, 4.0%; 75 and over, 0.8%.
Population projection: (1990) 61,483,000; (2000) 74,057,000.
Doubling time: 26 years.
Ethnic composition (by mother tongue of households; 1980): Tagalog 29.7%; Cebuano 24.2%; Ilocano 10.3%; Hiligaynon Ilongo 9.2%; Bicol 5.6%; Samar-Leyte 4.0%; Pampango 2.8%; Pangasinan 1.8%; other 12.5%[2].
Religious affiliation (1980): Roman Catholic 84.1%; Aglipayan (Philippine Independent Church) 6.2%; Muslim 4.3%; Protestant 3.9%; other 1.5%.
Major cities (1984): Manila 1,728,400; Quezon City 1,326,000; Cebu 552,200; Caloocan 524,600; Makati 409,000.

Vital statistics

Birth rate per 1,000 population (1987): 34.6 (world avg. 26.0); (1982) legitimate 93.9%; illegitimate 6.1%.
Death rate per 1,000 population (1987): 7.9 (world avg. 9.9).
Natural increase rate per 1,000 population (1987): 26.7 (world avg. 16.1).
Total fertility rate (avg. births per childbearing woman; 1987): 4.6.
Marriage rate per 1,000 population (1983): 6.8.
Life expectancy at birth (1987): male 61.7 years; female 64.9 years.
Major causes of death per 100,000 population (1984): pneumonia 89.3; heart diseases 61.0; tuberculosis 52.9; vascular diseases 39.6; malignant neoplasms (cancers) 30.2; diarrhea 27.8; accidents 16.8; malnutrition 13.4.

National economy

Budget (1986). Revenue: ₱ 87,500,000,000 (tax revenue 82.9%, of which tax on foreign trade 30.1%, tax on domestic goods and services 28.8%, income tax 19.1%; nontax revenue 9.4%). Expenditures: ₱ 92,888,000,000 (interest on debt 25.3%; education 12.5%; transport and communications 9.4%; defense 8.7%; health 4.4%; agriculture 4.1%; public services 4.1%).
Tourism (1986): receipts from visitors U.S.$647,060,000; expenditures by nationals abroad U.S.$37,000,000.
Production (metric tons except as noted). Agriculture, forestry, fishing (1986): sugarcane 14,600,000, coconuts 10,600,000, rice 9,350,000, corn (maize) 4,155,000, bananas and plantains 3,821,000, copra 2,338,000, cassava 1,727,000, pineapples 1,682,000, centrifugal sugar 1,500,000, sweet potatoes 801,000; livestock (number of live animals) 2,984,000 buffalo, 1,814,000 cattle, 2,177,000 goats, 7,275,000 pigs, 53,000,000 chickens; roundwood (1985) 36,614,000 cu m; fish catch 1,916,347. Mining and quarrying (1986): limestone 4,000,000; copper 222,644; chromite 174,230; silver 52,161 kilograms; gold 40,322 kilograms. Manufacturing (value added in producers' prices ₱ '000,000; 1984): food items 13,056; beverages 8,757; chemicals and chemical products 7,694; electrical machinery 4,894; petroleum products 4,815; iron and steel products 4,621; textiles 4,206; wearing apparel 2,228. Construction[3] (authorized; 1984): residential 3,129,000 sq m; nonresidential 1,912,000 sq m. Energy production (consumption): electricity (kW-hr; 1986) 22,320,000,000 (22,320,000,000); coal (metric tons; 1986) 1,243,000 (1,890,000); petroleum (barrels; 1986) 2,513,000 (57,726,000); petroleum products (metric tons; 1986) 6,653,000 (7,346,000); natural gas, n.a. (n.a.).
Land use (1985): forested 38.1%; meadows and pastures 3.9%; agricultural and under permanent cultivation 26.5%; other 31.5%.
Gross national product (1986): U.S.$31,820,000,000 (U.S.$570 per capita).

Structure of gross domestic product and labour force				
	1986		1985	
	in value ₱ '000,000	% of total value	labour force	% of labour force
Agriculture	163,801	26.1	9,698,000	45.4
Mining	10,198	1.6	127,000	0.6
Manufacturing	154,719	24.7	1,921,000	9.0
Construction	22,685	3.6	691,000	3.2
Public utilities	15,184	2.4	71,000	0.3
Transp. and commun.	39,078	6.2	931,000	4.4
Trade	129,282	20.6	2,611,000	12.2
Finance			342,000	1.6
Services }	91,770	14.7	3,448,000	16.1
Other }			1,517,000[4]	7.1[4]
TOTAL	626,717	100.0[2]	21,357,000	100.0[2]

Population economically active (1985): total 21,357,000; activity rate 39.1% (participation rates: over age 15, 63.5%; female 24.5%; unemployed 7.1%).

Price and earnings indexes (1980 = 100)							
	1982	1983	1984	1985	1986	1987	1988[5]
Consumer price index	124.6	137.1	206.2	253.8	255.7	265.4	285.4

Public debt (external, outstanding; 1986): U.S.$19,827,700,000.
Household income and expenditure. Average household size (1985) 5.7; income per family (1985) ₱ 30,748 (U.S.$1,616); sources of income (1971): wages and salaries 44.8%, self-employment 40.3%, owner-occupied dwellings 7.1%, pensions, social security, and related benefits 2.1%, other 5.7%; expenditure (1984): food, beverages, and tobacco 56.2%, household furnishings and operations 14.0%, clothing 6.2%, fuel and power 4.4%, transport and communications 3.3%.

Foreign trade[6]

Balance of trade (current prices)						
	1982	1983	1984	1985	1986	1987
₱ '000,000	−22,674	−28,566	−10,907	−8,113	−2,974	−22,368
% of total	20.9%	20.7%	5.8%	4.5%	1.5%	8.8%

Imports (1986): U.S.$5,394,295,000 (mineral fuels and lubricants 17.2%; electrical machinery 5.8%; nonelectrical machinery 5.0%; industrial raw materials 4.5%; iron and steel 4.0%; cereals 3.3%; inorganic chemicals 1.9%). *Major import sources:* United States 24.8%; Japan 17.2%; Taiwan 5.5%; Hong Kong 5.1%; West Germany 4.4%; Saudi Arabia 4.3%; South Korea 3.3%; Australia 2.9%.
Exports (1986): U.S.$4,841,780,000 (electrical machinery 7.6%; coconut oil 6.9%; clothing 6.0%; metalliferous ores and scrap metal 5.5%; nonferrous metals 4.2%; cork and wood 2.9%; bananas 2.7%; centrifugal sugar 1.8%; canned pineapples 1.7%). *Major export destinations:* United States 34.1%; Japan 17.6%; The Netherlands 5.1%; West Germany 5.0%; United Kingdom 4.8%; Hong Kong 4.6%; Singapore 3.3%.

Transport and communications

Transport. Railroads (1986): route length (1987) 658 mi, 1,059 km; passenger-mi 104,000,000, passenger-km 168,000,000; short ton-mi cargo 41,000,000, metric ton-km cargo 60,000,000. Roads (1986): total length 101,156 mi, 162,325 km (paved 13%). Vehicles (1986): passenger cars 773,242; trucks and buses 110,192. Merchant marine (1987): vessels (100 gross tons and over) 1,394; total deadweight tonnage 14,827,666. Air transport[7] (1987): passenger-mi 5,734,000,000, passenger-km 9,228,000,000; short ton-mi cargo 168,874,000, metric ton-km cargo 246,552,000; airports (1988) with scheduled flights 42.
Communications. Daily newspapers (1984): total number 25; circulation 2,379,145; circulation per 1,000 population 44. Radio (1986): 7,500,000 receivers (1 per 7.5 persons). Television (1987): 4,114,000 receivers (1 per 14 persons). Telephones (1985): 820,271 (1 per 67 persons).

Education and health

Education (1985–86)	schools	teachers	students	student/ teacher ratio
Primary (age 7–12)	33,104	289,251	8,925,959	30.9
Secondary (age 13–16)	5,388[8]	99,468	3,214,159	32.3
Voc., teacher tr.[8] } Higher[8] }	1,178	33,935	1,127,968	33.2

Educational attainment (1980). Percent of population age 25 and over having: no grade completed 11.7%; elementary education 53.8%; secondary 18.8%; college 15.2%; not stated 0.5%. *Literacy* (1980): total population age 15 and over literate 25,139,700 (88.7%); males literate 12,772,200 (89.9%); females literate 12,367,500 (87.5%).
Health: physicians (1982) 46,579 (1 per 1,090 persons); hospital beds (1985) 79,703 (1 per 756 persons); infant mortality rate (1987) 56.0.
Food (1984–86): daily per capita caloric intake 2,354 (vegetable products 90%, animal products 10%); (1983) 106% of FAO recommended minimum requirement.

Military

Total active duty personnel (1987): 105,000 (army 59.0%, navy 24.8%, air force 16.2%). *Military expenditure as percent of GNP* (1985): 1.3% (world 6.1%); per capita expenditure U.S.$7.

[1]Maximum number. [2]Detail does not add to total given because of rounding. [3]Private only. [4]Includes unemployed. [5]May. [6]Import figures are f.o.b. (free on board) in balance of trade and c.i.f. (cost, insurance, and freight) for commodities and trading partners. [7]Philippines Airlines only. [8]1984–85.

Poland

Official name: Polska Rzeczpospolita
Ludowa (Polish People's Republic).
Form of government: unitary
single-party socialist republic with one
legislative house (Sejm [460]).
Chief of state: President (Chairman).
Head of government: Prime Minister.
Capital: Warsaw.
Official language: Polish.
Official religion: none.
Monetary unit: 1 złoty (Zl) = 100
groszy; valuation (Oct. 10, 1988)
1 U.S.$ = Zl 474.55; 1 £ = Zl 812.66.

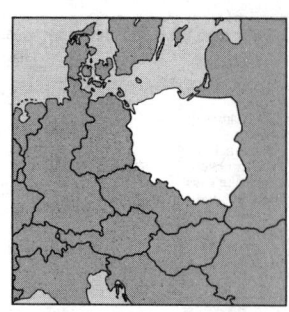

Structure of net material product and labour force

	1986			
	in value Zl '000,000,000	% of total value	labour force	% of labour force
Agriculture	1,650.2	15.4	5,058,900	28.1
Mining			518,700	2.9
Manufacturing }	5,060.9	47.3	4,388,100	24.3
Public utilities	133.8	1.3	216,200	1.2
Construction	1,378.9	12.9	1,316,500	7.3
Transp. and commun.	667.0	6.2	1,023,200	5.7
Trade	1,708.3	16.0	1,476,600	8.2
Finance	—	—	444,400	2.5
Public admin., defense	—	—	275,500	13.4
Services	—	—	2,409,100	1.5
Other	98.0[1]	0.9	877,600[2]	4.9[2]
TOTAL	10,697.1	100.0	18,004,800	100.0

Area and population

Provinces	Capitals	area sq mi	area sq km	population 1987 estimate
Biała Podlaska	Biała Podlaska	2,065	5,348	299,700
Białystok	Białystok	3,882	10,055	676,200
Bielsko	Bielsko Biala	1,430	3,704	878,800
Bydgoszcz	Bydgoszcz	3,996	10,349	1,090,400
Chełm	Chełm	1,493	3,866	242,500
Ciechanów	Ciechanów	2,456	6,362	420,200
Częstochowa	Częstochowa	2,387	6,182	769,500
Elbląg	Elbląg	2,356	6,103	469,600
Gdańsk	Gdańsk	2,855	7,394	1,411,200
Gorzów	Gorzów Wielkopolski	3,276	8,484	486,700
Jelenia Góra	Jelenia Góra	1,690	4,378	512,200
Kalisz	Kalisz	2,514	6,512	700,400
Katowice	Katowice	2,568	6,650	3,946,100
Kielce	Kielce	3,556	9,211	1,112,600
Konin	Konin	1,984	5,139	461,300
Koszalin	Koszalin	3,270	8,470	494,200
Kraków	Kraków	1,256	3,254	1,214,400
Krosno	Krosno	2,202	5,702	479,600
Legnica	Legnica	1,559	4,037	496,600
Leszno	Leszno	1,604	4,154	378,200
Łódź	Łódź	588	1,523	1,149,700
Łomża	Łomża	2,581	6,684	340,600
Lublin	Lublin	2,622	6,792	991,500
Nowy Sącz	Nowy Sącz	2,153	5,576	673,600
Olsztyn	Olsztyn	4,759	12,327	732,600
Opole	Opole	3,295	8,535	1,020,100
Ostrołęka	Ostrołęka	2,509	6,498	387,200
Piła	Piła	3,168	8,205	469,400
Piotrków	Piotrków Trybunalski	2,419	6,266	636,500
Płock	Płock	1,976	5,117	511,400
Poznań	Poznań	3,147	8,151	1,308,300
Przemyśl	Przemyśl	1,713	4,437	398,100
Radom	Radom	2,816	7,294	733,400
Rzeszów	Rzeszów	1,698	4,397	697,500
Siedlce	Siedlce	3,281	8,499	639,800
Sieradz	Sieradz	1,880	4,869	402,600
Skierniewice	Skierniewice	1,529	3,960	411,500
Słupsk	Słupsk	2,878	7,453	400,100
Suwałki	Suwałki	4,050	10,490	454,200
Szczecin	Szczecin	3,854	9,981	951,000
Tarnobrzeg	Tarnobrzeg	2,426	6,283	584,000
Tarnów	Tarnów	1,603	4,151	646,900
Toruń	Toruń	2,065	5,348	645,800
Wałbrzych	Wałbrzych	1,609	4,168	738,100
Warszawa	Warszawa	1,463	3,788	2,422,000
Włocławek	Włocławek	1,700	4,402	427,100
Wrocław	Wrocław	2,427	6,287	1,118,800
Zamość	Zamość	2,695	6,980	489,200
Zielona Góra	Zielona Góra	3,424	8,868	650,400
TOTAL		120,727	312,683	37,571,800

Demography

Population (1988): 37,864,000.
Density (1988): persons per sq mi 313.6, persons per sq km 121.1.
Urban–rural (1987): urban 60.5%; rural 39.5%.
Sex distribution (1987): male 48.77%; female 51.23%.
Age breakdown (1987): under 15, 25.7%; 15–29, 22.1%; 30–44, 22.0%; 45–59, 16.1%; 60–74, 10.1%; 75 and over, 4.0%.
Population projection: (1990) 38,257,000; (2000) 39,866,000.
Ethnic composition (1986): Polish 98.7%; Ukrainian 0.6%; other 0.7%.
Religious affiliation (1986): Roman Catholic 94.2%; other 5.8%.
Major cities (1987): Warsaw 1,664,700; Łódź 847,400; Kraków 744,000.

Vital statistics

Birth rate per 1,000 population (1986): 17.0 (world avg. 26.0); (1985) legitimate 95.0%, illegitimate 5.0%.
Death rate per 1,000 population (1986): 10.1 (world avg. 9.9).
Natural increase rate per 1,000 population (1986): 6.9 (world avg. 16.1).
Total fertility rate (avg. births per childbearing woman; 1986): 2.3.
Marriage rate per 1,000 population (1986): 6.9.
Divorce rate per 1,000 population (1986): 1.4.
Life expectancy at birth (1985): male 66.8 years; female 75.1 years.
Major causes of death per 100,000 population (1986): diseases of the circulatory system 515.4; malignant neoplasms (cancers) 181.8.

National economy

Budget (1986). Revenue: Zl 4,898,600,000,000 (turnover tax 30.8%, tax on state enterprises 30.7%). Expenditures: Zl 4,952,500,000,000 (economy 46.1%, education and culture 13.1%, health 12.2%, defense 9.1%).
Public debt (external, outstanding; 1986): U.S.$35,200,400,000.
Tourism (1986): receipts U.S.$136,000,000; expenditures U.S.$186,000,000.
Gross national product (1986): U.S.$259,524,000,000 (U.S.$6,929 per capita).

Production (metric tons except as noted). Agriculture (value added in Zl '000,000; 1986): potatoes 297,262, wheat 188,673, industrial crops 174,-216, rye 131,647, barley 111,707; livestock (live animals; 1987) 18,949,000 pigs, 10,019,000 cattle; roundwood 24,296,000 cu m; fish catch 645,200. Mining and quarrying (1987): copper 390,000; zinc 177,000; lead 89,000; iron ore 6,300. Manufacturing (value added in Zl '000,000,000; 1986): machinery and transport equipment 1,537.8; textiles 684.3; food 641.9; chemicals 355.1. Construction (1985): 13,182,000 sq m. Energy production (consumption): electricity ('000,000 kW-hr; 1986) 140,294 (148,131); coal ('000 metric tons; 1986) 261,798 (227,483); crude petroleum (barrels; 1986) 1,224,000 (1,327,600); petroleum products (metric tons; 1986) 14,298,000 (17,500,000); natural gas ('000,000 cu m; 1986) 5,436 (12,960).
Population economically active (1987): total 18,004,800; activity rate of total population 47.9% (participation rates: ages 15–64, 82.5%; female 45.7%).

Price and earnings indexes (1980 = 100)

	1981	1982	1983	1984	1985	1986	1987[3]
Consumer price index	121.2	243.4	297.2	341.8	393.4	463.0	577.0
Monthly earnings index	127.4	198.8	253.5	288.2	345.6	418.5	476.2

Household income and expenditure. Average household size (1986) 3.5; average annual income (1986) Zl 638,700 (U.S.$3,004[4]); sources of income: wages 74.8%, other 25.2%; expenditure (1986): food and beverages 44.6%, clothing 12.8%, housing 10.8%.
Land use (1986): forested 27.7%; meadows 13.0%; agricultural and under permanent cultivation 47.3%; other 12.0%.

Foreign trade

Balance of trade (current prices)

	1980	1981	1982	1983	1984	1985	1986
Zl '000,000,000	−6.4	−7.5	+82.2	+90.0	+126.2	+96.1	+151.6
% of total	5.8%	7.7%	4.5%	4.4%	5.0%	2.9%	7.2%

Imports (1986): Zl 1,964,020,000,000 (machinery and transport equipment 34.4%, fuel and power 21.7%, chemicals 12.4%, iron and steel products 8.9%, consumer goods 8.3%). Major import sources: U.S.S.R. 32.5%; W.Ger. 9.8%; Czechoslovakia 6.3%; E.Ger. 5.9%; Yugoslavia 3.7%.
Exports (1986): Zl 2,115,637,000,000 (machinery and transport equipment 42.6%, fuel and power 13.0%, chemicals 10.0%, metals 7.8%, food 7.0%, textiles and clothing 6.4%). Major export destinations: U.S.S.R. 27.6%; W.Ger. 9.4%; Czechoslovakia 6.3%; E.Ger. 4.9%; U.K. 3.5%; Yugoslavia 3.2%.

Transport and communications

Transport. Railroads (1986): length 26,848 km; passenger-km 48,525,500,000; metric ton-km cargo 120,712,000,000. Roads (1986): total length 254,000 km (paved 61%). Vehicles (1986): passenger cars 3,961,953; trucks and buses 912,984. Merchant marine (1987): vessels (100 gross tons and over) 715; total deadweight tonnage 3,452,269. Air transport (1986): passenger-km 2,196,000,000; metric ton-km cargo 12,048,000; airports (1987) 12.
Communications. Daily newspapers (1986): 45; circulation 7,480,000. Radio (1987): 10,512,000 (1 per 3.5 persons). Television (1987): 9,692,000 (1 per 3.9 persons). Telephones (1986): 4,418,000 (1 per 8.5 persons).

Education and health

Education (1986–87)

	schools	teachers	students	student/teacher ratio
Primary (age 7–14)	17,553	262,500	5,007,800	19.1
Secondary (age 15–18)	898	21,100	353,100	16.7
Voc., teacher tr.	6,635	78,500	1,327,300	16.9
Higher	92	57,700	261,100	4.5

Educational attainment (1978). Percent of population age 25 and over having: no formal schooling 2.8%; less than full primary education 12.7%; primary 44.9%; secondary 33.9%; higher 5.7%. Literacy (1983): total population age 15 and over literate 27,352,000 (99.2%).
Health (1987): physicians 75,473 (1 per 498 persons); hospital beds 247,276 (1 per 152 persons); infant mortality rate per 1,000 live births (1986) 17.3.
Food (1984–86): daily per capita caloric intake 3,298 (vegetable products 67%, animal products 33%); (1983) 127% of FAO recommended minimum.

Military

Total active duty personnel (1987): 394,000 (army 74.9%, navy 4.8%, air force 20.3%). Military expenditure as percent of GNP (1985): 6.0% (world 6.1%); per capita expenditure U.S.$393.

[1]Other material activities. [2]Mostly employed abroad. [3]Second quarter average. [4]At official exchange rate; actual purchasing power substantially higher.

Portugal

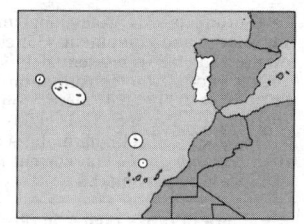

Official name: República Portuguesa (Republic of Portugal).
Form of government: parliamentary state with one legislative house (Assembly of the Republic [250]).
Chief of state: President.
Head of government: Prime Minister.
Capital: Lisbon.
Official language: Portuguese.
Official religion: none.
Monetary unit: 1 Escudo (Esc) = 100 centavos; valuation (Oct. 10, 1988) 1 U.S.$ = Esc 152.85; 1 £ = Esc 261.75.

Area and population

		area		population
				1987
Continental Portugal Districts	Capitals	sq mi	sq km	estimate[1]
Aveiro	Aveiro	1,084	2,808	660,500
Beja	Beja	3,948	10,225	179,900
Braga	Braga	1,032	2,673	763,900
Bragança	Bragança	2,551	6,608	185,600
Castelo Branco	Castelo Branco	2,577	6,675	226,000
Coimbra	Coimbra	1,524	3,947	446,200
Évora	Évora	2,854	7,393	175,600
Faro	Faro	1,915	4,960	339,200
Guarda	Guarda	2,131	5,518	198,300
Leiria	Leiria	1,357	3,515	435,200
Lisboa	Lisbon (Lisboa)	1,066	2,761	2,124,100
Portalegre	Portalegre	2,342	6,065	138,600
Porto	Porto	925	2,395	1,657,700
Santarém	Santarém	2,605	6,747	460,800
Setúbal	Setúbal	1,955	5,064	761,000
Viana do Castelo	Viana do Castelo	871	2,255	265,500
Vila Real	Vila Real	1,671	4,328	264,100
Viseu	Viseu	1,933	5,007	424,800
Azores (Açores) Autonomous Region	Ponta Delgada	868	2,247	253,500
Madeira Autonomous Region	Funchal	306	794	269,500
TOTAL		35,672[2]	92,389[2]	10,230,000

Demography

Population (1988): 10,349,000.
Density (1988): persons per sq mi 290.1, persons per sq km 112.0.
Urban–rural (1981): urban 29.6%; rural 70.4%.
Sex distribution (1987): male 48.28%; female 51.72%.
Age breakdown (1987): under 15, 22.7%; 15–29, 24.6%; 30–44, 18.8%; 45–59, 16.5%; 60–74, 12.6%; 75 and over, 4.8%.
Population projection: (1990) 10,493,000; (2000) 10,838,000.
Nationality (1987): Portuguese 99.1%; Cape Verdean 0.3%; Brazilian 0.1%; Spanish 0.1%; American 0.1%; British 0.1%; other 0.2%.
Religious affiliation (1981): Christian 96.0%, of which Roman Catholic 94.5%, Protestant 0.6%, other Christian (mostly Apostolic Catholic and Jehovah's Witness) 0.9%; nonreligious 3.8%; Jewish 0.1%; Muslim 0.1%.
Major cities (1986): Lisbon 829,600; Porto 347,300; Amadora 95,518[3].

Vital statistics

Birth rate per 1,000 population (1986): 12.4 (world avg. 26.0); legitimate 87.2%; illegitimate 12.8%.
Death rate per 1,000 population (1986): 9.4 (world avg. 9.9).
Natural increase rate per 1,000 population (1986): 3.0 (world avg. 16.1).
Total fertility rate (avg. births per childbearing woman; 1980–85): 2.3.
Marriage rate per 1,000 population (1986): 6.8.
Divorce rate per 1,000 population (1986): 0.8.
Life expectancy at birth (1982–85): male 69.3 years; female 76.2 years.
Major causes of death per 100,000 population (1986): circulatory diseases 411.6, of which cerebrovascular diseases 229.2, ischemic heart disease 80.2; malignant neoplasms (cancers) 161.1; respiratory diseases 64.2.

National economy

Budget (1986). Revenue: Esc 885,021,000,000 (indirect taxes 53.1%; direct taxes 32.8%; property income 8.3%). Expenditures: Esc 1,596,983,000,000 (public debt 25.4%; education 12.5%; health 10.2%; administration 6.3%; defense 5.2%; public works 5.0%).
Public debt (1986): U.S.$16,310,300,000.
Production (metric tons except as noted). Agriculture, forestry, fishing (1986): grapes 1,100,000, potatoes 1,099,000, tomatoes 800,000, corn (maize) 607,000, wheat 463,000, olives 281,000, rice 153,000, oats 137,000, cork 86,299[4]; livestock (number of live animals) 5,100,000 sheep, 3,092,000 pigs, 1,099,000 cattle; roundwood 9,038,000 cu m; fish catch 318,773. Mining and quarrying (1986): copper pyrites 327,966; kaolin 48,821; tungsten 2,756. Manufacturing (value of production in Esc '000,000; 1987): refined petroleum 211,439; cotton and synthetic fibres 210,737; clothing 112,619; knitted fabrics 91,464; motor vehicles 78,860; dairy products 71,716; iron and steel 57,290; cement 44,020; alcoholic beverages 29,383. Construction (1985): residential 5,430,841 sq m; nonresidential 1,349,282 sq m. Energy production (consumption): electricity (kW-hr; 1986) 20,631,000,000 (22,110,000,000); coal (metric tons; 1986) 212,000 (1,963,000); crude petroleum (barrels; 1986) none (62,217,000); petroleum products (metric tons; 1986) 7,236,000 (7,177,000); natural gas, none (n.a.).
Gross national product (1986): U.S.$22,880,000,000 (U.S.$2,230 per capita).

Structure of gross domestic product and labour force

	1986			
	in value Esc '000,000	% of total value	labour force	% of labour force
Agriculture	384,300	8.9	940,100	20.1
Mining			27,400	0.6
Manufacturing	1,330,000	30.7	1,032,100	22.1
Construction	244,500	5.6	352,300	7.5
Public utilities	99,700	2.3	34,300	0.7
Trade	885,900	20.4	630,200	13.5
Pub. admin., defense	479,100	11.1	954,300	20.3
Services				
Transp. and commun.			184,800	4.0
Finance	910,00	21.0	130,800	2.8
Other			394,200[5]	8.4
TOTAL	4,333,500	100.0	4,680,500	100.0

Population economically active (1986): total 4,680,500; activity rate of total population 45.6% (participation rates: ages 15–64, 67.2%; female 41.4%; unemployed 8.4%).

Price and earnings indexes (1980 = 100)

	1981	1982	1983	1984	1985	1986	1987
Consumer price index	120.0	147.3	184.3	237.6	284.2	317.6	347.3
Daily earnings index	121.6	148.0	172.7	203.6	244.2	298.0	...

Household income and expenditure. Average household size (1981) 3.8; income per household: n.a.; sources of income (1986): wages and salaries 42.4%, property and entrepreneurial income 35.8%, transfer payments 21.8%; expenditure (1981): food 34.8%, transportation and communications 14.6%, clothing and footwear 11.2%, cafes and hotels 8.8%, health 4.3%, recreation 3.9%, housing 3.2%, other 9.2%.
Tourism (1986): receipts from visitors U.S.$1,574,000,000; expenditures by nationals abroad U.S.$332,000,000.
Land use (1985): forested 39.7%; meadows and pastures 5.8%; agricultural and under permanent cultivation 30.1%; other 24.4%.

Foreign trade

Balance of trade (current prices)

	1982	1983	1984	1985	1986	1987
Esc '000,000	−351,700	−308,700	−291,700	−213,700	−255,500	−457,800
% of total	34.6%	23.3%	16.1%	9.9%	9.4%	15.2%

Imports (1987): Esc 1,891,257,000,000 (machinery and transport equipment 32.3%, of which road vehicles 12.6%; chemicals 12.8%; crude petroleum 11.6%; textiles and textile products 11.6%). *Major import sources:* W.Ger. 14.7%; Spain 11.8%; France 11.0%; Italy 8.7%; U.K. 8.1%; U.S. 4.9%.
Exports (1987): Esc 1,289,906,000,000 (textiles and textile products 32.2%; machinery and transport equipment 16.2%, of which transport equipment 11.1%; footwear 8.2%; paper and paper products 7.6%; wood and wood products 7.1%[6]; chemicals and chemical products 4.5%). *Major export destinations:* France 15.8%; W.Ger. 15.4%; U.K. 14.0%; Spain 9.0%.

Transport and communications

Transport. Railroads (1986): route length 2,241 mi, 3,607 km; passenger-km 5,802,664,000; metric ton-km cargo 1,448,060,000. Roads (1986): total length 32,282 mi, 51,953 km (paved 86%). Vehicles (1986): passenger cars 1,958,872; trucks and buses 502,267[4]. Merchant marine (1987): vessels (100 gross tons and over) 292; total deadweight tonnage 1,702,913. Air transport (1986)[7]: passenger-km 4,476,000,000; metric ton-km cargo 133,032,000; airports (1988) 18.
Communications. Daily newspapers (1986): total number 30; total circulation 859,315[8]; circulation per 1,000 population 84[8]. Radio (1986): 2,165,000 receivers (1 per 4.7 persons). Television (1987): 1,618,000 receivers (1 per 6.4 persons). Telephones (1986): 1,936,430 (1 per 5.3 persons).

Education and health

Education (1985–86)

	schools	teachers	students	student/teacher ratio
Primary (age 5–11)	12,741	73,343	1,238,112	16.9
Secondary (age 12–19)	1,509	53,881	647,391	12.0
Voc., teacher tr.[9]	345	2,971	27,946	9.4
Higher	51[10]	10,505	107,650	10.2

Educational attainment (1981). Percent of population age 25 and over having: no formal schooling 4.4%; primary education 76.2%; secondary 19.0%; postsecondary 0.1%; higher 0.3%. *Literacy* (1981): total population age 15 and over literate 5,818,135 (79.4%); males literate 2,933,526 (84.8%); females literate 2,884,609 (74.6%).
Health (1987): physicians 25,696 (1 per 400 persons); hospital beds 43,511 (1 per 235 persons); infant mortality rate per 1,000 live births 11.0.
Food (1984–86): daily per capita caloric intake 3,134 (vegetable products 80%, animal products 20%); (1983) 124% of FAO recommended minimum requirement.

Military

Total active duty personnel (1987): 66,500 (army 58.6%, navy 21.3%, air force 20.1%). *Military expenditure as percent of GNP* (1985): 3.3% (world 6.1%); per capita expenditure U.S.$62.

[1]January 1. [2]Includes 156 sq mi (404 sq km) of inland water. [3]1981. [4]1985. [5]Mostly unemployed. [6]Approximately one-half is comprised of cork products. [7]TAP (Air Portugal) only. [8]For 28 newspapers only. [9]1983–84. [10]1984–85.

Puerto Rico

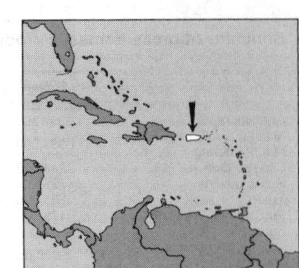

Official name: Estado Libre Asociado de Puerto Rico (Spanish); Commonwealth of Puerto Rico (English).
Political status: self-governing commonwealth associated with the United States, having two legislative houses (Senate [27]; House of Representatives [51]).
Chief of state: President of the United States.
Head of government: Governor.
Capital: San Juan.
Official languages: Spanish; English.
Official religion: none.
Monetary unit: 1 U.S. dollar (U.S.$) = 100 cents; valuation (Oct. 10, 1988) 1 U.S.$ = £0.58.

Population 1984 estimate

Municipio	population	Municipio	population	Municipio	population
Adjuntas	18,900	Fajardo	33,200	Naguabo	21,300
Aguada	32,400	Florida	7,600	Naranjito	25,100
Aguadilla	55,000	Guánica	18,800	Orocovis	20,900
Aguas Buenas	23,000	Guayama	40,300	Patillas	17,900
Aibonito	22,500	Guayanilla	21,000	Peñuelas	20,200
Añasco	24,400	Guaynabo	85,100	Ponce	190,900
Arecibo	87,000	Gurabo	25,000	Quebradillas	19,700
Arroyo	18,200	Hatillo	30,400	Rincón	12,400
Barceloneta	19,600	Hormigueros	15,200	Río Grande	37,700
Barranquitas	22,800	Humacao	52,400	Sabana Grande	21,100
Bayamón	202,500	Isabela	38,200	Salinas	26,600
Cabo Rojo	35,000	Jayuya	15,000	San Germán	34,200
Caguas	121,100	Juana Díaz	43,600	San Juan	428,900
Camuy	26,200	Juncos	27,000	San Lorenzo	33,300
Canóvanas	32,400	Lajas	21,300	San Sebastián	36,100
Carolina	165,700	Lares	28,000	Santa Isabel	19,500
Cataño	25,900	Las Marías	8,600	Toa Alta	33,400
Cayey	43,300	Las Piedras	23,100	Toa Baja	77,700
Ceiba	15,100	Loíza	24,600	Trujillo Alto	50,800
Ciales	17,200	Luquillo	15,400	Utuado	34,600
Cidra	29,600	Manatí	38,000	Vega Alta	30,000
Coamo	32,200	Maricao	6,700	Vega Baja	48,800
Comerio	18,400	Maunabo	11,800	Vieques	7,800
Corozal	29,600	Mayagüez	101,000	Villalba	22,500
Culebra	1,300	Moca	29,900	Yabucoa	31,400
Dorado	26,700	Morovis	21,900	Yauco	39,200
				TOTAL	3,270,000

Demography

Area: 3,515 sq mi, 9,104 sq km.
Population (1988): 3,301,000.
Density (1988): persons per sq mi 939.1, persons per sq km 362.6.
Urban–rural (1985): urban 70.7%; rural 29.3%.
Sex distribution (1980): male 48.70%; female 51.30%.
Age breakdown (1980): under 15, 31.6%; 15–29, 26.5%; 30–44, 18.4%; 45–59, 12.3%; 60–74, 8.3%; 75 and over, 2.9%.
Population projection: (1990) 3,316,000; (2000) 3,389,000.
Doubling time: 57 years.
Ethnic composition (1980): white 80.0%; black 20.0%.
Religious affiliation (1984): Roman Catholic 85.3%; Protestant 4.7%; other 10.0%.
Major cities (municipio; 1984): San Juan 428,900; Bayamón 202,500; Ponce 190,900; Carolina 165,700; Caguas 121,100.

Vital statistics

Birth rate per 1,000 population (1986): 19.4 (world avg. 26.0); (1983) legitimate 75.6%; illegitimate 24.4%.
Death rate per 1,000 population (1986): 7.1 (world avg. 9.9).
Natural increase rate per 1,000 population (1986): 12.3 (world avg. 16.1).
Total fertility rate (avg. births per childbearing woman; 1986): 2.4.
Marriage rate per 1,000 population (1984): 9.0.
Divorce rate per 1,000 population (1984): 4.2.
Life expectancy at birth (1987): male 71.0 years; female 79.0 years.
Major causes of death per 100,000 population (1983): diseases of the circulatory system 260.7, of which ischemic heart diseases 99.0, diseases of pulmonary circulation 60.6; malignant neoplasms (cancers) 105.3; diseases of the respiratory system 72.5.

National economy

Budget (1985–86). Revenue: U.S.$4,624,000,000 (income taxes 34.9%, excise taxes 20.1%, property taxes 3.2%, other receipts 41.8%). Expenditures: U.S.$4,288,000,000 (grants and subsidies 51.0%, personal services 28.3%, debt service 6.4%, other 14.3%).
Public debt (outstanding; 1987): U.S.$10,030,000,000.
Tourism: receipts from visitors (1987) U.S.$896,000,000; expenditures by nationals abroad (1985) U.S.$618,000,000.
Production (in U.S.$'000,000 except as noted). Agriculture, forestry, fishing (gross farm income; 1987): milk 182, poultry 65, coffee 65, starchy vegetables 55, beef 52, pork 47, fruit 38, eggs 25, sugar 23; livestock (number of live animals) 583,000 cattle, 210,000 pigs; roundwood, n.a.; fish catch (1985) 1,496 metric tons. Mining (value of production; 1984): stone 28. Manufacturing (net income in U.S.$'000,000; 1987): chemicals, pharmaceuticals, and allied products 3,758; electrical machinery and equipment 1,330;

food products 981; professional and scientific equipment 670; nonelectrical machinery and equipment 435; clothing 422. Construction (new buildings authorized; 1985): residential 1,798,000 sq m; nonresidential 41,000 sq m.
Energy production (consumption): electricity (kW-hr; 1986) 12,300,000,000 (12,300,000,000); coal (metric tons; 1986) none (40,000); crude petroleum (barrels; 1986) none (32,985,000); petroleum products (metric tons; 1986) 4,715,000 (5,280,000); natural gas, none (none).
Gross national product (at current market prices; 1986): U.S.$17,190,000,000 (U.S.$5,190 per capita).

Structure of gross domestic product and labour force

	1987			
	in value US$'000,000	% of total value	labour force	% of labour force
Agriculture	372.1	1.6	29,000	2.9
Manufacturing	9,388.5	39.7	151,000	15.2
Mining	408.3	1.7 }		
Construction }			41,000	4.2
Public utilities			14,000	1.4
Transp. and commun. }	1,872.4	7.9	38,000	3.8
Trade	3,503.0	14.8	154,000	15.5
Finance, real estate	3,090.6	13.1	32,000	3.2
Pub. admin., defense	2,629.4	11.1 }		
Services	2,154.7	9.1 }	370,000	37.2
Other	226.5	1.0	165,000[1]	16.6[1]
TOTAL	23,645.5	100.0	994,000	100.0

Population economically active (1987): total 993,670; activity rate of total population 30.2% (participation rates: ages 16–64, 48.9%; female 36.1%; unemployed 16.6%).

Price and earnings indexes (1981 = 100)

	1981	1982	1983	1984	1985	1986	1987
Consumer price index	100.0	107.8	109.0	110.6	112.1	111.8	112.8
Hourly earnings index[2]	100.0	107.8	107.1	110.1	113.7	117.7	…

Household income and expenditure. Average family size (1987) 4.1; income per family U.S.$20,016; sources of income (1987): wages and salaries 56.0%, transfers 28.0%, rent 6.6%, self-employment 6.4%, other 3.0%; expenditure (1984): food and beverages 30.2%, transportation 16.2%, housing and energy 16.1%, clothing 9.0%, household furnishings 6.6%, health care 5.1%, recreation 4.7%, education 2.2%, other 9.9%.
Land use (1985): forested 20.1%; meadows and pastures 37.4%; agricultural and under permanent cultivation 14.4%; other 28.1%.

Foreign trade

Balance of trade (current prices)

	1981	1982	1983	1984	1985	1986	1987
U.S.$'000,000	−2,282	+721	−466	−690	+925	+1,472	+1,354
% of total	13.9%	4.2%	2.7%	3.3%	4.4%	6.8%	5.9%

Imports (1986): U.S.$10,099,000,000 (food 18.5%; chemicals [all forms] 14.9%; crude petroleum and petroleum products 14.2%; transportation equipment 12.1%). *Major import sources (1985–86):* United States 60.6%; Japan 8.9%; Ecuador 3.5%; Venezuela 3.2%.
Exports (1986): U.S.$11,571,000,000 (chemicals and chemical products 29.0%, of which drugs and related products 23.8%; food 15.7%; electrical machinery and parts 8.0%; petroleum [all forms] 4.6%). *Major export destinations (1985–86):* United States 87.3%; U.S. Virgin Islands 1.6%; Dominican Republic 1.6%.

Transport and communications

Transport. Railroads (1985)[3]: length 59 mi, 96 km. Roads (1985): total length 5,813 mi, 9,355 km (paved 86%). Vehicles (1985): passenger cars 1,102,155; trucks and buses 197,012. Merchant marine: n.a. Air transport (1985–86): passenger arrivals 2,513,537, passenger departures 2,556,032; cargo loaded and unloaded 128,171 metric tons; airports (1988) with scheduled flights 8.
Communications. Daily newspapers (1986): total number 5; total circulation 599,000; circulation per 1,000 population 183. Radio (1986): 2,000,000 receivers (1 per 1.6 persons). Television (1987): 830,000 receivers (1 per 4.0 persons). Telephones (1985): 772,006 (1 per 4.3 persons).

Education and health

Education (1985–86)

	schools	teachers	students	student/ teacher ratio
Primary (age 5–12)	1,542	18,359	427,582	23.3
Secondary (age 13–18)	395	13,612	334,661	24.6
Voc., teacher tr.	52	…	149,191	…
Higher	45	9,045	156,818	17.3

Educational attainment (1980). Percent of population age 25 and over having: no formal schooling 8.0%; primary education 39.8%; secondary 33.8%; higher 18.4%. *Literacy (1980):* total population age 15 and over literate 1,948,151 (89.1%); males literate 935,553 (89.7%); females literate 1,012,598 (88.5%).
Health (1984): physicians 7,560 (1 per 433 persons); hospital beds 12,493 (1 per 262 persons); infant mortality rate per 1,000 live births (1985) 14.9.
Food: daily per capita caloric intake, n.a.

Military

Total active duty personnel (1986): 3,600 U.S. personnel.

[1]Unemployed. [2]Manufacturing sector only. [3]Privately owned railway for sugarcane transport only.

Qatar

Official name: Dawlat Qaṭar (State of Qatar).
Form of government: constitutional monarchy; Islamic law is the basis of legislation in the state.
Head of state and government: Emir.
Capital: Doha.
Official language: Arabic.
Official religion: Islam.
Monetary unit: 1 riyal (QR) = 100 dirhams; valuation (Oct. 10, 1988) 1 U.S.$ = QR 3.63; 1 £ = QR 6.21.

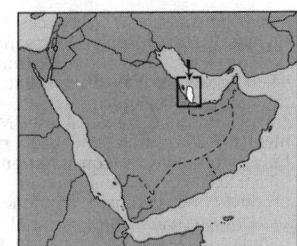

Area and population

Municipalities	area		population[1]
	sq mi	sq km	1986 census
Doha	...	...	217,294
al-Guwayrīyah	...	...	1,629
Jeriān al-Baṭnah	...	...	2,727
al-Jumaylīyah	...	...	7,217
al-Khawr	...	...	8,993
ar-Rayyān	...	...	91,996
ash-Shamāl	...	...	4,380
Umm aṣ-Ṣilāl	...	...	11,161
al-Wakrah	...	...	23,682
TOTAL	4,400	11,400	369,079

Demography

Population (1988): 420,000.
Density (1988): persons per sq mi 95.5, persons per sq km 36.8.
Urban–rural (1986): urban 88.3%; rural 11.7%.
Sex distribution (1986): male 67.15%; female 32.85%.
Age breakdown (1986): under 15, 27.8%; 15–29, 29.3%; 30–44, 32.3%; 45–59, 8.6%; 60 and over, 2.0%.
Population projection: (1990) 467,000; (2000) 640,000.
Doubling time: 29 years.
Ethnic composition (1983): South Asian 34%; Qatari 20%; other Arab 25%; Iranian 16%; other 5%.
Religious affiliation (1980): Muslim 92.4% (mostly Sunnī), Christian 5.9%; Hindu 1.1%; Bahā'ī 0.2%; other 0.4%.
Major cities (1983): Doha 190,000; Musay'īd 40,000.

Vital statistics

Birth rate per 1,000 population (1986): 26.9 (world avg. 26.0); legitimate, n.a.; illegitimate, n.a.
Death rate per 1,000 population (1986): 2.1 (world avg. 9.9).
Natural increase rate per 1,000 population (1986): 24.8 (world avg. 16.1).
Total fertility rate (avg. births per childbearing woman; 1986): 4.9.
Marriage rate per 1,000 population (1986): 3.1.
Divorce rate per 1,000 population (1986): 0.8.
Life expectancy at birth (1986): male 65.2 years; female 67.6 years.
Major causes of death per 100,000 population (1986): diseases of the circulatory system 50.0; injury and poisonings 41.0; neoplasms (including benign neoplasms) 20.4; certain conditions originating in the perinatal period 14.0; diseases of the respiratory system 10.6; endocrine, metabolic, and nutritional diseases and immunity disorders 6.9; diseases of the digestive system 6.1; signs, symptoms, and ill-defined conditions 29.4.

National economy

Budget (1988–89). Revenue: QR 6,335,800,000 (crude oil 85.0%). Expenditures: QR 12,242,500,000 (1987–88; wages and salaries 34.3%; state capital development projects 22.6%, of which electricity and water 4.6%, housing and public buildings 4.4%, education 2.2%, transport and communications 2.1%, social services 0.9%, health 0.8%).
Public debt: none.
Production (metric tons except as noted). Agriculture, forestry, fishing (value of production in QR '000; 1986): vegetables and other crops except cereals 74,237, forage 68,144, fruits and dates 21,116, cereals 1,455; livestock (number of live animals) 118,692 sheep, 68,000 goats, 18,637 camels, 7,713 cattle, 2,415 deer; roundwood, n.a.; fish catch 1,980. Mining and quarrying (1985): limestone 1,300,000; clay, sand, and gypsum are also mined for local use. Manufacturing (1986): urea 746,892; ammonia 658,328; steel reinforcing bars 493,000; cement 324,000; clinker 308,155; ethylene 258,349; sulfur 44,734; organic fertilizers 21,000. Construction (1986): residential 391,400 sq m; nonresidential 167,600 sq m. Energy production (consumption): electricity (kW-hr; 1986) 3,565,000,000 (3,565,000,000); coal, none (n.a.); crude petroleum (barrels; 1986) 115,553,000 (10,094,000); petroleum products (metric tons; 1986) 2,130,000 (609,000); natural gas (cu m; 1986) 3,964,000,000 (3,964,000,000).
Tourism (1986): receipts and expenditures, n.a.; total number of tourists staying in hotels 106,730.
Population economically active (1986): total 201,300; activity rate of total population 54.5% (participation rates: over age 15, 75.5%; female 9.8%; unemployed, 1.0%).

Price and earnings indexes (1981 = 100)

	1981	1982	1983	1984	1985	1986
Consumer price index	100.0	105.7	108.6	109.8	111.9	113.7
Earnings index	...	...	...	...	...	...

Household income and expenditure. Average household size (1986) 6.4; income per household: n.a.; sources of income: n.a.; expenditure (1982–83): food 39.1%, household durable goods 24.4%, recreation and personal effects 15.1%, housing 10.7%, clothing 4.4%, transportation and communications 3.7%, education 1.6%, energy and water 0.8%, health 0.2%.
Gross national product (at current market prices; 1986): U.S.$4,180,000,000 (U.S.$12,520 per capita).

Structure of gross domestic product and labour force

	1987		1986	
	in value QR '000,000	% of total value	labour force	% of labour force
Agriculture	241	1.3	300	0.1
Mining	5,630	30.3	6,600	3.3
Manufacturing	1,847	9.9	27,600	13.7
Construction	1,086	5.9	36,100	17.9
Public utilities	359	1.9	9,100	4.5
Transportation	412	2.2	6,100	3.0
Trade	1,172	6.3	30,800	15.3
Finance	1,958	10.6	7,800	3.9
Pub. admin., defense } Services	5,875	31.6	74,900	37.3
Other	...	...	2,000[2]	1.0[2]
TOTAL	18,580	100.0	201,300	100.0

Land use (1985): meadows and pastures 4.5%; agricultural and under permanent cultivation 0.3%; built-up, desert, and other 95.2%.

Foreign trade

Balance of trade (current prices)

	1982	1983	1984	1985	1986	1987
QR '000,000	+9,307	+6,703	+8,015	+7,130	+2,730	+3,224
% of total	39.6%	38.7%	48.6%	46.2%	25.4%	28.7%

Imports (1987): QR 4,127,900,000 (machinery and transport equipment 40.4%, manufactured goods 17.2%, food and live animals 17.1%, chemicals and chemical products 6.3%, beverages and tobacco 1.9%). *Major import sources:* Japan 16.3%; United Kingdom 16.0%; United States 11.9%; West Germany 7.2%; Italy 4.9%; France 4.3%; Saudi Arabia 2.7%; The Netherlands 2.5%.
Exports (1987): QR 7,224,000,000 (1985; crude petroleum 91.1%, liquefied gas and other nonpetroleum exports 8.9%). *Major export destinations* (1987): Japan 38.5%; Singapore 13.1%; Italy 8.4%; Brazil 4.6%; Australia 2.8%; The Netherlands 2.0%; United Kingdom 1.1%; China 0.9%.

Transport and communications

Transport. Railroads: none. Roads (1986): total length 671 mi, 1,080 km (paved, n.a.). Vehicles (1986): passenger cars 131,044; trucks and buses 3,710. Merchant marine (1987): vessels (100 gross tons and over) 61; total deadweight tonnage 460,938. Air transport[3] (1986): passenger-mi 720,723,-000, passenger-km 1,159,892,000; short ton-mi cargo 21,485,000, metric ton-km cargo 31,368,000; airports (1988) with scheduled flights 1.
Communications. Daily newspapers (1986): total number 5; total circulation 51,500; circulation per 1,000 population 147. Radio (1986): total number of receivers 120,000 (1 per 3.1 persons). Television (1987): total number of receivers 160,000 (1 per 2.5 persons). Telephones (1986): 115,471 (1 per 3.4 persons).

Education and health

Education (1986)

	schools	teachers	students	student/teacher ratio
Primary (age 6–11)	122	3,141	42,502	14.0
Secondary (age 12–17)	68[4]	2,801	21,588	7.7
Vocational	3	113	856	7.6
Higher[5]	1	452	5,281	11.7

Educational attainment (1986). Percent of population age 25 and over having: no formal education 53.2%, of which illiterates 27.9%; primary 9.9%; preparatory (lower secondary) 10.1%; secondary 13.3%; postsecondary 13.3%; other 0.2%. *Literacy* (1986): total population age 15 and over literate 201,734 (74.7%); males literate 149,980 (76.8%); females literate 51,754 (72.5%).
Health (1986): physicians 543 (1 per 679 persons); hospital beds 915 (1 per 403 persons); infant mortality rate per 1,000 live births 37.4.
Food: daily per capita caloric intake, n.a.

Military

Total active duty personnel (1988): 7,000 (army 85.7%, navy 10.0%, air force 4.3%). *Military expenditure as percent of GNP* (1985): 46.9% (world 6.1%); per capita expenditure U.S.$6,700.

[1]Total population excludes 2,784 Qataris residing abroad. [2]Unemployed. [3]Apportionment of one-fourth of international flights of Gulf Air. [4]1985–86. [5]There were also 1,041 Qatari university students studying abroad.

Réunion

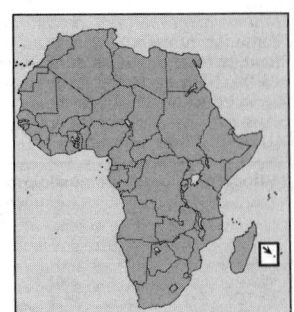

Official name: Département de la Réunion (Department of Reunion).
Political status: overseas department (France) with two legislative houses (General Council [36]; Regional Council [45]).
Chief of state: President of France.
Heads of government: Commissioner of the Republic (for France); President of General Council (for Réunion); President of Regional Council (for Réunion).
Capital: Saint-Denis.
Official language: French.
Official religion: none.
Monetary unit: 1 Franc (F) = 100 centimes; valuation (Oct. 10, 1988) 1 U.S.$ = F 6.32; 1 £ = F 10.83.

Area and population

Arrondissements	Capitals	area sq mi	area sq km	population 1982 census
Saint-Benoît	Saint-Benoît	284	736	74,312
Saint-Denis	Saint-Denis	164	423	180,647
Saint-Paul	Saint-Paul	180	467	94,378
Saint-Pierre	Saint-Pierre	339	878	166,461
TOTAL		969[1,2]	2,510[1,2]	515,798[2]

Demography

Population (1988): 575,000.
Density (1988): persons per sq mi 593.4, persons per sq km 229.1.
Urban–rural (1982): urban 52.8%; rural 47.2%.
Sex distribution (1982): male 49.05%; female 50.95%.
Age breakdown (1982): under 15, 35.6%; 15–29, 29.8%; 30–44, 17.2%; 45–59, 11.1%; 60–74, 4.6%; 75 and over, 1.7%.
Population projection: (1990) 595,000; (2000) 707,000.
Doubling time: 42 years.
Ethnic composition (1983): mixed race 63.5%; East Indian 28.2%; Chinese 2.2%; French 1.9%; East African 1.1%; other 3.1%.
Religious affiliation (1984): Roman Catholic 85.1%; other (includes Muslim, Baha'ï, Hindu, atheist, and other Christian) 14.9%.
Major cities (1982)[3]: Saint-Denis 109,068; Saint-Paul 58,410; Saint-Pierre 50,081; Tampon 40,538; Saint-Louis 31,785.

Vital statistics

Birth rate per 1,000 population (1987): 22.3 (world avg. 26.0); legitimate 49.5%; illegitimate 50.5%.
Death rate per 1,000 population (1987): 5.5 (world avg. 9.9).
Natural increase rate per 1,000 population (1987): 16.8 (world avg. 16.1).
Total fertility rate (avg. births per childbearing woman; 1987): 2.8.
Marriage rate per 1,000 population (1987): 5.3.
Divorce rate per 1,000 population (1987): 1.2.
Life expectancy at birth (1980–85): male 64.6 years; female 68.2 years.
Major causes of death per 100,000 population (1984): diseases of the circulatory system 174.0; accidents, poisonings, violence 71.1; malignant neoplasms (cancers) 46.4; diseases of the respiratory system 38.7; diseases of the digestive system 36.5; endocrine and metabolic disorders 22.4; ill-defined conditions 88.5.

National economy

Budget (1988). Revenue: F 3,207,000,000 (receipts from the French central government and local administrative bodies 59.1%, new loans 10.5%, taxes [including taxes on fuel, motor vehicles, and cigarettes] 9.1%). Expenditures: F 3,784,000,000 (health and social services 38.2%, other administrative and operational services 28.8%, departmental investment programs 10.5%, nondepartmental investment programs 8.6%).
Public debt (external, outstanding; 1985)[4]: U.S.$55,000,000.
Tourism (1987): number of tourist arrivals 135,233.
Gross national product (at current market prices; 1985): U.S.$1,830,000,000 (U.S.$3,350 per capita).

Structure of gross domestic product and labour force

	1983 in value F '000,000	1983 % of total value	1982 labour force	1982 % of labour force
Agriculture	841	6.1	17,390	9.9
Manufacturing	1,247	9.1	7,369	4.2
Construction	699	5.1	11,176	6.4
Public utilities	255	1.9	697	0.4
Transportation and communications	709	5.2	5,871	3.3
Trade	2,135	15.6	14,328	8.1
Finance, real estate, insurance	624	4.6	16,297	9.3
Pub. admin., defense, and services	6,797	49.7	47,343	27.0
Other	368	2.7	55,124[5]	31.4
TOTAL	13,675	100.0	175,595	100.0

Production (metric tons except as noted). Agriculture, forestry, fishing (1987): sugarcane 1,821,000, potatoes 10,824, corn (maize) 10,000, cabbages 6,146, bananas 4,520, mangoes 3,677, pineapples 3,600, tomatoes 2,796, eggplant 2,387, tobacco 209, vanilla 133, geranium extract 15, khuskhus (vetiver) extract 12; livestock (number of live animals; 1985) 72,000 pigs, 44,000 goats, 20,000 cattle; roundwood (1986) 33,000 cu m; fish (value of catch in F '000,000) lobster 46, other 14. Mining and quarrying (1986): gravel and sand for local use. Manufacturing (1987): sugar 225,800; cement 172,800[6]; molasses 74,200; rum 81,700 hectolitres. Construction: n.a. Energy production (consumption): electricity (kW-hr; 1987) 681,900,000 (606,000,000); coal, none (none); crude petroleum, none (none); petroleum products (metric tons; 1986) none (236,000); natural gas, none (none).
Population economically active (1982): total 175,595; activity rate of total population 34.0% (participation rates: ages 16–64, 57.5%; female 35.3%; unemployed [end of 1986] 32.0%).

Price and earnings indexes (December 1980 = 100)[7]

	1982	1983	1984	1985	1986	1987	1988
Consumer price index	124.3	134.4	144.0	152.9	155.8	160.2	160.5[8]
Hourly earnings index[9]	129.8	140.1	145.8	155.2	155.4	158.3	159.9[8]

Household income and expenditure. Average household size (1982) 4.2; income per household (1981) F 82,240 (U.S.$15,133); sources of income (1981): wages and salaries 66.4%, self-employment 17.4%, transfer payments 12.4%, other 3.8%; expenditure (1976–77)[10]: food and beverages 38.8%, clothing and footwear 11.5%, energy 7.4%, transportation 7.2%, housing 7.1%, household furnishings 6.2%, food away from home 2.7%, other 19.1%.
Land use (1985): forested 35.2%; meadows and pastures 4.0%; agricultural and under permanent cultivation 22.0%; other 38.8%.

Foreign trade

Balance of trade (current prices)

	1982	1983	1984	1985	1986	1987
F '000,000	−4,616	−5,748	−6,199	−6,589	−6,930	−7,865
% of total	77.0%	79.3%	79.8%	76.7%	78.8%	81.6%

Imports (1987): F 8,751,200,000 (food and agricultural products 20.7%, electrical and nonelectrical machinery 15.5%, transport equipment 14.0%, metals and metal products 10.5%, chemical products 8.8%). *Major import sources:* France 67.9%; Italy 3.5%; Bahrain 3.0%; West Germany 2.9%.
Exports (1987): F 886,600,000 (sugar 74.9%, rum 3.2%, lobster 2.9%, geranium extract 1.1%, vanilla 0.7%). *Major export destinations:* France 71.4%; Portugal 15.3%; Mayotte 3.1%; Japan 2.7%.

Transport and communications

Transport. Railroads (1984): route length 384 mi, 614 km[11]; traffic, n.a. Roads (1985): total length 1,684 mi, 2,710 km (paved 81%). Vehicles (1985): passenger cars 138,081; trucks and buses 45,017. Merchant marine: n.a. Air transport (1987): passenger arrivals 273,130, passenger departures 275,787; cargo unloaded 9,689 metric tons, cargo loaded 3,222 metric tons; airports (1988) with scheduled flights 1.
Communications. Daily newspapers (1986): total number 3; total circulation 55,000; circulation per 1,000 population 99. Radio (1986): total number of receivers 123,000 (1 per 4.5 persons). Television (1987): total number of receivers 90,000 (1 per 6.3 persons). Telephones (1986): 131,201 (1 per 4.3 persons).

Education and health

Education (1985–86)

	schools	teachers	students	student/ teacher ratio
Primary (age 6–11)	349	3,811	73,985	19.4
Secondary (age 12–18)	85[12]	3,994	46,550	17.5
Voc., teacher tr.			23,313	
Higher[13]	1	90	3,515	39.1

Educational attainment (1974). Percent of population age 20 and over having: no formal schooling 30.1%; primary education 30.2%; secondary 36.5%; higher 2.5%; not specified 0.7%. *Literacy* (1982): total population age 15 and over literate 268,300 (78.6%); males literate 126,500 (76.5%); females literate 141,800 (80.5%).
Health: physicians (1986) 750 (1 per 734 persons); hospital beds (1985) 3,498 (1 per 156 persons); infant mortality rate per 1,000 live births (1987) 9.8.
Food (1984–86): daily per capita caloric intake 3,011 (vegetable products 81%, animal products 19%); (1983) 125% of FAO recommended minimum requirement.

Military

Total active duty personnel (1987): 3,300 French troops[14].

[1]Includes 2 sq mi (6 sq km) not distributed by arrondissement. [2]Indian Ocean islets administered by France from Réunion are excluded from total. Areas of these islets, which have no permanent population, are: Îles Glorieuses 1.7 sq mi (4.3 sq km), Île Juan de Nova 1.9 sq mi (4.8 sq km), Île Tromelin 0.3 sq mi (0.8 sq km), Bassas da India 0.1 sq mi (0.2 sq km), Île Europa 7.8 sq mi (20.2 sq km). [3]Populations cited are for communes. [4]Includes long-term private debt not guaranteed by the government. [5]Includes 54,338 unemployed. [6]1984. [7]Unless footnoted, indexes refer to December. [8]July. [9]Based on minimum-level wage in public administration. [10]Based on urban households whose head is a wage earner. [11]For sugar industry only. [12]1984–85. [13]1986–87. [14]Includes troops stationed on Mayotte.

Romania

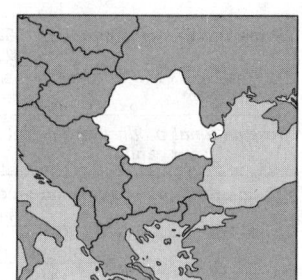

Official name: Republika Socialistă
România (Socialist Republic of
Romania).
Form of government: unitary
single-party socialist republic with
one legislative house (Grand National
Assembly [369]).
Chief of state: President.
Head of government: Prime Minister.
Capital: Bucharest.
Official language: Romanian.
Official religion: none.
Monetary unit: 1 Romanian leu (plural
lei) = 100 bani; valuation (Oct. 10,
1988) 1 U.S.$ = 8.63¹ lei;
1 £ = 14.78¹ lei.

Area and population

Districts	Capitals	area sq mi	area sq km	population 1986 estimate
Alba	Alba Iulia	2,406	6,231	424,700
Arad	Arad	2,954	7,652	504,144
Arges	Pitești	2,626	6,801	669,459
Bacău	Bacău	2,551	6,606	715,054
Bihor	Oradea	2,909	7,535	655,682
Bistrița-Năsăud	Bistrița	2,048	5,305	319,698
Botoșani	Botoșani	1,917	4,965	462,983
Brăila	Brăila	1,824	4,724	398,193
Brașov	Brașov	2,066	5,351	688,151
Buzău	Buzău	2,344	6,072	521,391
Caraș-Severin	Resita	3,283	8,503	403,723
Călărași	Calarași	1,959	5,074	345,936
Cluj	Cluj-Napoka	2,568	6,650	741,096
Constanța	Constanța	2,724	7,055	709,755
Covasna	Sfintu Gheorghe	1,431	3,705	231,531
Dîmbovița	Tîrgoviște	1,559	4,036	561,290
Dolj	Craiova	2,862	7,413	771,406
Galați	Galați	1,708	4,425	632,029
Giurgiu	Giurgiu	1,404	3,636	325,991
Gorj	Tîrgu Tiu	2,178	5,641	376,821
Harghita	Miercurea-Ciuc	2,552	6,610	358,779
Hunedoara	Deva	2,709	7,016	557,396
Ialomița	Slobozia	1,718	4,449	303,914
Iași	Iași	2,112	5,469	787,351
Maramureș	Baia Mare	2,400	6,215	543,261
Mehedinți	Drobeta-Turnu-Severin	1,892	4,900	328,870
Mureș	Tîrgu Mureș	2,585	6,696	614,725
Neamț	Piatra Neamț	2,274	5,890	569,675
Olt	Slatina	2,126	5,507	531,168
Prahova	Ploiești	1,812	4,694	864,274
Sălaj	Zalău	1,486	3,850	410,762
Satu Mare	Satu Mare	1,701	4,405	267,208
Sibiu	Sibiu	2,093	5,422	506,061
Suceava	Suceava	3,303	8,555	679,964
Teleorman	Alexandria	2,224	5,760	506,499
Timiș	Timișoara	3,356	8,692	720,719
Tulcea	Tulcea	3,255	8,430	269,014
Vaslui	Vaslui	2,045	5,297	458,056
Vîlcea	Rîmnicu Vîlcea	2,203	5,705	426,160
Vrancea	Focșani	1,878	4,863	388,064
Muncipality				
Bucharest	Bucharest	654	1,695	2,272,526
TOTAL		91,699	237,500	22,823,479

Demography

Population (1988): 23,014,000.
Density (1988): persons per sq mi 251.0, persons per sq km 96.9.
Urban–rural (1985): urban 50.8%; rural 49.2%.
Sex distribution (1986): male 49.34%; female 50.66%.
Age breakdown (1985): under 15, 24.6%; 15–29, 22.6%; 30–44, 19.6%; 45–59, 18.8%; 60–74, 10.7%; 75 and over, 3.7%.
Population projection: (1990) 23,199,000; (2000) 25,196,000.
Ethnic composition (1983): Romanian 88.4%; Hungarian 7.7%; other 3.9%.
Religious affiliation (1980): Romanian Orthodox 70.0%; Greek Orthodox 10.0%; Muslim 1.0%; atheist 7.0%; other 3.0%; none 9.0%.
Major cities (1986): Bucharest 1,989,800; Brașov 351,500; Constanța 327,700; Timișoara 325,300; Iași 313,000.

Vital statistics

Birth rate per 1,000 population (1985): 15.8 (world avg. 29.0).
Death rate per 1,000 population (1985): 10.9 (world avg. 11.0).
Natural increase rate per 1,000 population (1985): 4.9 (world avg. 18.0).
Total fertility rate (avg. births per childbearing woman; 1985): 2.1.
Marriage rate per 1,000 population (1985): 7.1.
Divorce rate per 1,000 population (1985): 1.4.
Life expectancy at birth (1982–84): male 67.0 years; female 72.6 years.
Major causes of death per 100,000 population (1984): diseases of the circulatory system 603.7; malignant neoplasms (cancers) 128.4.

National economy

Budget (1988). Revenue: 433,093,700,000 lei ([1985] corporate tax 43.0%, turnover tax 28.3%, income tax 15.7%). Expenditures: 433,093,700,000 lei (national economy 41.1%, social services 23.1%, defense 2.7%).
Tourism (1984): receipts from visitors U.S.$230,000,000; expenditures by nationals abroad U.S.$85,000,000.
Production (metric tons except as noted). Agriculture (1986): corn (maize) 20,158,000, potatoes 9,106,100, wheat and rye 7,385,600, sugar beets 7,082,-

100, vegetables 6,907,600; livestock (number of live animals) 18,609,000 sheep, 14,319,000 pigs, 7,077,000 cattle; roundwood (1985) 23,118,000 cu m; fish catch 271,126. Mining and quarrying (1986): iron ore 2,431,000; bauxite 555,000; lead and zinc 74,000. Manufacturing (1986): crude steel 14,276,000; cement 14,216,000; rolled steel 10,207,000; fertilizers 3,164,000; plastics and synthetic rubber 663,954. Construction (1985): 8,591,000 sq m. Energy production (consumption): electricity (kW-hr; 1986) 75,478,-000,000 (74,580,000,000); coal (metric tons; 1986) 47,518,000 (47,518,000); crude petroleum (barrels, 1986) 78,750,000 (187,500,000); petroleum products (metric tons; 1986) 22,797,000 (13,797,000); natural gas (cu m; 1986) 38,600,000,000 (40,680,000,000).
Public debt (external, outstanding; 1986): U.S.$5,345,000,000.
Gross national product (1986): U.S.$137,346,000,000 (U.S.$6,020 per capita).

Structure of net material product and labour force

	1986 in value '000,000 lei	% of total value	labour force	% of labour force
Agriculture	122,700	15.9	3,062,200	28.7
Mining, manufacturing, and public utilities	482,400	62.5	3,979,700	37.3
Construction	58,700	7.6	789,500	7.4
Transp. and commun.	47,800	6.2	736,200	6.9
Trade	2	2	618,800	5.8
Pub. admin., defense	—	—	53,400	0.5
Services	—	—	1,280,300	12.0
Other	60,200²	7.8²	149,400	1.4
TOTAL	771,800	100.0	10,669,500	100.0

Population economically active (1986): total 10,669,500; activity rate of total population 46.7% (participation rates [1985]: over age 15, 61.8%; female 45.9%; unemployed, n.a.).

Price and earnings indexes (1980 = 100)

	1980	1981	1982	1983	1984	1985	1986
Consumer price index	100.0	102.2	119.5	125.7	127.1	126.6	126.5
Monthly earnings index	100.0	103.7	110.8	113.9	122.6	123.3	123.6

Household income and expenditure. Average household size (1984) 3.1; income per household 62,310 lei (U.S.$3,500); sources of income (1982): wages 62.6%, other 37.4%; expenditure (1980): food 62.7%, clothing 13.8%.
Land use (1985): forested 26.7%; meadows and pastures 18.5%; agricultural and under permanent cultivation 43.3%; other 11.5%.

Foreign trade

Balance of trade (current prices)

'000,000 lei	1980	1981	1982	1983	1984	1985	1986
	−8,043	+3,031	+26,987	+34,379	+67,300	+43,934	+31,550
% of total	7.3%	0.9%	9.8%	12.4%	17.3%	12.9%	8.4%

Imports (1986): 171,060,000,000 lei (mineral fuels 34.6%, machinery 29.1%, chemicals 6.1%). *Major import sources* (1985): U.S.S.R. 22.4%; East Germany 5.8%; Poland 5.5%; Iraq 4.7%; China 3.7%; West Germany 3.4%.
Exports (1986): 202,610,000,000 lei (machinery and transport equipment 36.9%, fuels 22.0%, chemicals 8.9%). *Major export destinations* (1985): U.S.S.R. 21.4%; Italy 7.5%; West Germany 7.5%; East Germany 4.2%; China 4.0%.

Transport and communications

Transport. Railroads (1985): length (1986) 6,972 mi, 11,221 km; passenger-km 31,082,000,000; metric ton-km cargo 74,215,000,000. Roads (1986): length 72,799 km (paved 64%). Vehicles (1980): cars 250,000; trucks and buses 130,000. Merchant marine (1987): vessels (100 gross tons and over) 430; total deadweight tonnage 4,893,328. Air transport (1986): passenger-km 3,403,000,000; metric ton-km cargo 73,000,000; airports (1988) 15.
Communications. Daily newspapers (1986): total number 36; total circulation 3,108,900; circulation per 1,000 population 136. Radio (1987): 3,192,-000 (1 per 7.1 persons). Television (1987): 3,856,000 (1 per 5.9 persons). Telephones (1985): 1,962,681 (1 per 11 persons).

Education and health

Education (1986–87)

	schools	teachers	students	student/ teacher ratio
Primary (age 6–13)	14,046	144,878	3,017,339	20.8
Secondary (age 14–17)	981	46,124	1,196,949	25.9
Vocational	747	12,420	257,196	20.7
Higher	44	12,504	157,174	12.6

Educational attainment (1977). Percent of population age 25 and over having: primary education 55.6%; secondary 39.8%; postsecondary 4.6%.
Literacy (1983) 95.8%.
Health (1987): physicians 40,706 (1 per 561 persons); hospital beds 213,560 (1 per 107 persons); infant mortality rate per 1,000 live births (1986) 25.6.
Food (1984–86): daily per capita caloric intake 3,358 (vegetable products 76%, animal products 24%); (1983) 126% of FAO recommended minimum.

Military

Total active duty personnel (1987): 179,500 (army 78.0%, navy 4.2%, air force 17.8%). *Military expenditure as percent of GNP* (1985): 4.3% (world 6.1%); per capita expenditure U.S.$240.

¹Noncommercial rate. ²Includes trade and other material activities.

Rwanda

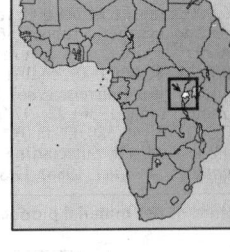

Official name: Repubulika y'u Rwanda (Rwanda); République Rwandaise (French) (Republic of Rwanda).
Form of government: single-party republic with one legislative house (National Development Council [70]).
Head of state and government: President.
Capital: Kigali.
Official languages: Rwanda; French.
Official religion: none.
Monetary unit: 1 Rwanda franc (RF); valuation (Oct. 10, 1988)
1 U.S.$ = RF 77.68; 1 £ = RF 133.02.

Area and population

Prefectures	Capitals	area sq mi	area sq km	population 1983 estimate
Butare	Butare	707	1,830	682,500
Byumba	Byumba	1,925	4,987	623,600
Cyangugu	Cyangugu	859	2,226	343,500
Gikongoro	Gikongoro	846	2,192	401,900
Gisenyi	Gisenyi	925	2,395	566,400
Gitarama	Gitarama	865	2,241	706,200
Kibungo	Kibungo	1,596	4,134	420,200
Kibuye	Kibuye	510	1,320	500,600
Kigali	Kigali	1,255	3,251	835,400
Ruhengeri	Ruhengeri	680	1,762	581,200
TOTAL		10,169[1]	26,338	5,661,400[1]

Demography

Population (1988): 6,709,000.
Density (1988): persons per sq mi 659.8, persons per sq km 254.7.
Urban–rural (1985): urban 6.2%; rural 93.8%.
Sex distribution (1985): male 49.29%; female 50.71%.
Age breakdown (1985): under 15, 48.4%; 15–29, 26.3%; 30–44, 13.6%; 45–59, 8.0%; 60–74, 3.5%; 75 and over, 0.2%.
Population projection: (1990) 7,179,000; (2000) 10,123,000.
Doubling time: 21 years.
Ethnic composition (1983): Hutu 90%; Tutsi 9%; Twa 1%.
Religious affiliation (1986): Roman Catholic 56%; Protestant 12%; Muslim 9%; traditional belief systems 23%.
Major cities (1978): Kigali 156,700[2]; Butare 21,691; Ruhengeri 16,025; Gisenyi 12,436.

Vital statistics

Birth rate per 1,000 population (1985): 52.0 (world avg. 26.0); legitimate (1978) 94.9%; illegitimate 5.1%.
Death rate per 1,000 population (1985): 19.0 (world avg. 9.9).
Natural increase rate per 1,000 population (1985): 33.0 (world avg. 16.1).
Total fertility rate (avg. births per childbearing woman; 1985): 8.0.
Marriage rate per 1,000 population (1984): 2.5[3].
Divorce rate per 1,000 population: n.a.
Life expectancy at birth (1985): male 46.0 years; female 49.0 years.
Major causes of death per 100,000 population[4] (1984): complications of pregnancy, childbirth, and birth injury 192.4; infectious and parasitic diseases (including malaria, typhoid fever, trypanosomiasis [sleeping sickness], pneumonia, tuberculosis of the respiratory system, bacillary dysentery and amoebiasis, diphtheria, meningococcal infection, and acute poliomyelitis) 11.8; diseases of the digestive system 10.3; diseases of the nervous system 10.1; accidents, poisonings, and violence 5.2.

National economy

Budget (1988–89). Revenue: RF 27,500,000,000 (1984; import and export duties 39.6%, taxes on goods and services 25.3%, income tax 18.1%, property taxes 1.9%). Expenditures: RF 27,500,000,000 (1987; education 19.9%, debt repayment 16.6%, defense 9.9%, infrastructure 6.6%, health 4.6%, agriculture 1.1%).
Public debt (external, outstanding; 1985): U.S.$411,900,000.
Production (metric tons except as noted). Agriculture, forestry, fishing (1986): plantains 2,100,000, roots and tubers 2,000,000 (of which sweet potatoes 920,000, cassava 348,000, potatoes 270,000), cereals 317,000 (of which sorghum 184,000, corn [maize] 127,000), coffee 33,000, tea 8,000, tobacco 3,000; livestock (number of live animals) 1,005,000 goats, 670,000 cattle, 343,000 sheep, 104,000 pigs; roundwood 5,842,000 cu m; fish catch 1,485. Mining and quarrying (1986): cassiterite (tin ore) 1,158; wolframite (tungsten ore) 280; gold 220 troy oz. Manufacturing (value added at producers' prices in RF '000,000; 1983): food, beverages, and tobacco products 20,800; textile industry 1,534; building materials 1,168; nonmetal minerals 1,099; wood products 667; industrial chemicals 510; printing and published materials 211. Construction (1981): residential 59,600 sq m; nonresidential 34,400 sq m. Energy production (consumption): electricity (kW-hr; 1986) 170,000,000 (187,000,000); coal, none (n.a.); petroleum products (metric tons; 1986) none (119,000); natural gas (cu m; 1986) 948,000 (948,000).
Tourism: receipts from visitors (1986) U.S.$6,000,000; expenditures by nationals abroad (1981) U.S.$12,000,000.
Land use (1985): forested 10.4%; meadows and pastures 17.6%; agricultural and under permanent cultivation 40.5%; other 31.5%.
Population economically active (1985): total 3,063,000; activity rate of total population 50.5% (participation rates: ages 15–64 89.4%; female 48.6%; unemployed, n.a.).

Price and earnings indexes (1980 = 100)

	1981	1982	1983	1984	1985	1986	1987
Consumer price index	106.6	119.9	127.7	134.6	137.0	135.5	141.0
Earnings index	...	...	...	...	...	...	...

Gross national product (at current market prices; 1986): U.S.$1,820,000,000 (U.S.$290 per capita).

Structure of gross domestic product and labour force

	1984 in value RF '000,000	1984 % of total value	1985 labour force	1985 % of labour force
Agriculture	68,692	43.2	2,827,000	92.3
Mining	572	0.3		
Manufacturing	26,053	16.4	95,000	3.1
Construction	7,885	5.0		
Public utilities	910	0.6		
Transportation and communications	4,425	2.8		
Trade	21,725	13.7		
Finance	7,119	4.5	141,000	4.6
Pub. admin., defense	16,908	10.6		
Services				
Other	4,641	2.9		
TOTAL	158,930	100.0	3,063,000	100.0

Household income and expenditure: Average household size (1983) 5.2; average annual income per household RF 122,870 (U.S.$1,300); sources of income (1977): self-employment (profits, interest, etc.) 71.0%, salaries and wages 16.5%, transfers 9.5%; expenditure: n.a.

Foreign trade

Balance of trade (current prices)

	1982	1983	1984	1985	1986	1987
RF '000,000	−16,650	−17,980	−11,580	−7,840	−4,860	−10,562
% of total	49.7%	55.2%	27.1%	22.9%	12.9%	37.1%

Imports (1986): RF 21,326,000,000 (1984; machinery and transport equipment 25.5%, of which transport equipment 12.7%, electrical equipment 4.2%; mineral fuels and lubricants 12.4%; textiles, clothing, and footwear 11.4%; food 9.6%; construction materials 9.3%). *Major import sources* (1984): Belgium–Luxembourg 14.4%; Kenya 12.7%; Japan 10.1%; France 9.3%; China 8.2%; Iran 6.4%; West Germany 5.6%; United States 2.5%; The Netherlands 2.3%; Italy 2.0%.
Exports (1986): RF 16,466,000,000 (coffee 80.4%; tea 10.4%; tin ores and concentrates 0.6%). *Major export destinations:* Mombasa consignment 82.7%; Belgium–Luxembourg 6.3%; Kenya 4.4%; Italy 2.6%; Spain 0.3%; Uganda 0.3%; West Germany 0.2%.

Transport and communications

Transport. Railroads: none. Roads (1986): total length 7,500 mi, 12,070 km (paved 5%). Vehicles (1986): passenger cars 7,396; trucks and buses 10,357. Merchant marine: none. Air transport (1984): passenger arrivals 46,029, passenger departures 46,586; metric ton cargo loaded 13,120; metric ton cargo unloaded 11,864; airports (1988) with scheduled flights 2.
Communications. Daily newspapers (1984): total number 1; total circulation per 1,000 population, n.a. Radio (1986): total number of receivers 250,000 (1 per 25 persons). Television: none. Telephones (1986): 9,116 (1 per 700 persons).

Education and health

Education (1985)

	schools	teachers	students	student/ teacher ratio
Primary (age 7–15)	1,594	14,896	836,877	56.2
Secondary (age 16–19)	...	1,331[5]	7,252	...
Voc., teacher tr.	...	...	10,881	...
Higher	3	305[6]	1,705[6]	5.6[6]

Educational attainment (1978). Percent of population age 25 and over having: no formal schooling 76.9%; some primary education 16.8%; complete primary education 4.0%; some secondary and complete secondary education 2.0%; some postsecondary vocational and higher education 0.3%.
Literacy (1980): total population age 15 and over literate 1,295,900 (49.4%); males literate 798,800 (62.2%); females literate 497,100 (37.2%).
Health (1984): physicians 177[7] (1 per 33,170 persons); hospital beds 9,046 (1 per 649 persons); infant mortality rate per 1,000 live births (1985) 127.0.
Food (1984–86): daily per capita caloric intake 1,880 (vegetable products 97%, animal products 3%); (1983) 98% of FAO recommended minimum requirement.

Military

Total active duty personnel (1987): 5,150 (army 97.1%; navy, none; air force 2.9%). *Military expenditure as percent of GNP* (1985): 1.7% (world 6.1%); per capita expenditure U.S.$5.

[1]Detail does not add to total given because of rounding. [2]1981. [3]Excludes marriages not registered in court. [4]In hospitals only. [5]Includes vocational and teacher training. [6]1983. [7]Excludes foreign physicians.

Saint Kitts and Nevis

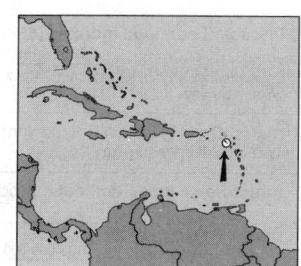

Official name: Federation of Saint Kitts and Nevis[1].
Form of government: constitutional monarchy with one legislative house (National Assembly [15][2]).
Chief of state: British Monarch represented by governor-general.
Head of government: Prime Minister.
Capital: Basseterre.
Official language: English.
Official religion: none.
Monetary unit: 1 Eastern Caribbean dollar (EC$) = 100 cents; valuation (Oct. 10, 1988) 1 U.S.$ = EC$2.70; 1 £ = EC$4.62.

Area and population

Islands[3]	Capitals	area sq mi	area sq km	1986 population estimate
Nevis	Charlestown	36.0	93.2	9,600
St. Kitts	Basseterre	68.0	176.2	34,100
TOTAL		104.0	269.4	43,700

Demography

Population (1988): 43,200.
Density (1988): persons per sq mi 415.4, persons per sq km 160.4.
Urban–rural (1985): urban 45.0%; rural 55.0%.
Sex distribution (1986): male 50.34%; female 49.66%.
Age breakdown (1983): under 15, 34.3%; 15–29, 30.9%; 30–44, 13.2%; 45–59, 9.2%; 60–74, 9.1%; 75 and over, 3.3%.
Population projection: (1990) 43,000; (2000) 40,000.
Doubling time: 56 years.
Ethnic composition (1985): black 90.5%; mixed 5.0%; Indo-Pakistani 3.0%; white 1.5%.
Religious affiliation (1985): Protestant 76.4%, of which Anglican 36.2%, Methodist 32.3%; Roman Catholic 10.7%; other 12.9%.
Major towns (1985): Basseterre 18,500; Charlestown 1,700.

Vital statistics

Birth rate per 1,000 population (1986): 23.0 (world avg. 26.0); (1983) legitimate 19.2%; illegitimate 80.8%.
Death rate per 1,000 population (1986): 10.5 (world avg. 9.9).
Natural increase rate per 1,000 population (1986): 12.5 (world avg. 16.1).
Total fertility rate (avg. births per childbearing woman; 1986): 3.0.
Marriage rate per 1,000 population (1977): 3.5.
Divorce rate per 1,000 population (1977): 0.2.
Life expectancy at birth (1987): male 63.0 years; female 67.0 years.
Major causes of death per 100,000 population (1984): diseases of the circulatory system 462.7, of which cerebrovascular disease 175.4; malignant neoplasms (cancers) 114.0; diseases of the respiratory system 41.7; infectious and parasitic diseases 35.1; ill-defined conditions 142.5.

National economy

Budget (1986). Revenue: EC$77,100,000 (indirect tax revenue 46.2%, nontax revenue 26.5%, loans 12.5%, direct tax revenue 8.2%, development aid 6.6%). Expenditures: EC$75,100,000 (current expenditure 78.4%, development expenditure 21.6%).
Public debt (external, outstanding; 1986): U.S.$22,000,000.
Production (metric tons except as noted). Agriculture, forestry, fishing (1986): sugarcane 262,800[4], coconuts 2,000, fruits 2,000, vegetables 1,000, peanuts (groundnuts) 23[4], cotton 16[4]; livestock (number of live animals) 14,000 sheep, 10,000 pigs, 10,000 goats, 6,000 cattle; roundwood, n.a.; fish catch 1,500. Mining and quarrying: excavation of sand for local use. Manufacturing (1987): sugar 25,700; molasses 8,800; aerated beverages 37,100 hectolitres; alcoholic beverages 13,790 hectolitres; shoes 23,800 pairs[5]; other manufactures include garments and electronic components. Construction: n.a. Energy production (consumption): electricity (kW-hr; 1986) 35,000,000 (35,000,000); coal, none (none); crude petroleum, none (none); petroleum products (metric tons; 1986) none (17,000); natural gas, none (none).
Gross national product (at current market prices; 1986): U.S.$70,000,000 (U.S.$1,700 per capita).

Structure of gross domestic product and labour force

	1986 in value EC$'000,000[6]	1986 % of total value	1984 labour force[7]	1984 % of labour force
Agriculture	11.5	11.0	4,380	29.6
Mining	0.3	0.3	—	—
Manufacturing	13.0	12.3	2,170	14.7
Construction	10.3	9.8	400	2.7
Public utilities	1.3	1.2	1,030	7.0
Transportation and communications	11.9	11.4	450	3.0
Trade	18.8	17.9	940	6.3
Finance, real estate	17.9[8]	17.1[8]	280	1.9
Pub. admin., defense	23.9	22.8 }	4,700	31.7
Services	8	8 }		
Other	−4.0[9]	−3.8[9]	460	3.1
TOTAL	104.9	100.0	14,810	100.0

Household income and expenditure. Average household size (1980) 3.7; income per household: n.a.; sources of income: n.a.; expenditure (1978)[10]: food, beverages, and tobacco 55.6%, household supplies 9.4%, housing 7.6%, clothing and footwear 7.5%, fuel and light 6.6%, transportation 4.3%, other 9.0%.
Population economically active (1980): total 17,125; activity rate of total population 39.5% (participation rates: ages 15–64, 69.5%; female 41.0%; unemployed[11]).

Price and earnings indexes (1980 = 100)

	1980	1981	1982	1983	1984	1985	1986
Consumer price index	100.0	108.0	110.1	112.8	115.8	118.4	118.0
Annual earnings index[12]	100.0	110.0	113.3	115.0	117.3	...	...

Tourism (1986): receipts from visitors U.S.$34,100,000; expenditures by nationals abroad U.S.$3,000,000.
Land use (1985): forested 17.0%; meadows and pastures 3.0%; agricultural and under permanent cultivation 39.0%; other 41.0%.

Foreign trade[13]

Balance of trade (current prices)

	1982	1983	1984	1985	1986	1987
EC$'000,000	−69.0	−88.9	−85.7	−83.6	−102.4	−141.4
% of total	40.4%	47.2%	44.1%	43.2%	41.9%	48.8%

Imports (1983): EC$138,700,000 (manufactured goods 22.7%; food 19.6%; machinery 19.0%; mineral fuels 9.8%; chemicals 8.0%). *Major import sources* (1985): United States 42.3%; CARICOM countries 14.0%; United Kingdom 12.1%.
Exports (1983): EC$49,800,000 (domestic exports 95.0%, of which sugar 55.2%, clothing 9.4%, footwear 8.8%, electronic goods 8.3%, beer and ale 5.5%; reexports 5.0%). *Major export destinations* (1985): United States 31.2%; United Kingdom 25.1%; CARICOM countries 18.9%.

Transport and communications

Transport. Railroads (1987): length 36 mi, 58 km[14]. Roads (1987): total length 190 mi, 305 km (paved 41%). Vehicles (1985): passenger cars 3,540; trucks and buses 690. Merchant marine (1987): vessels (100 gross tons and over) 2; total deadweight tonnage 641. Air transport: passenger arrivals (1985) 66,590, passenger departures (1982) 52,410; cargo handled, n.a.; airports (1988) with scheduled flights 2.
Communications. Daily newspapers (1987): none. Radio (1986): total number of receivers 22,500 (1 per 2.0 persons). Television (1987): total number of receivers 7,000 (1 per 6.6 persons). Telephones (1988): 4,000 (1 per 12 persons).

Education and health

Education (1986–87)

	schools	teachers	students	student/ teacher ratio
Primary (age 5–12)	32	266[15]	7,805	24.7[15]
Secondary (age 13–17)	6	268	4,153	15.5
Voc., teacher tr.	1	18	166	9.2
Higher	1[15]	9[15]	55[15]	6.1[15]

Educational attainment (1980)[16]. Percent of population age 25 and over having: no formal schooling 1.1%; primary education 29.6%; secondary 67.2%; higher 2.1%. *Literacy* (1985): 90.0%.
Health (1987): physicians 22 (1 per 2,090 persons); hospital beds 258 (1 per 178 persons); infant mortality rate per 1,000 live births (1984–86 avg.) 32.6.
Food (1984–86): daily per capita caloric intake 2,349 (vegetable products 75%, animal products 25%); (1983) 93% of FAO recommended minimum requirement.

Military

Total active duty personnel (1987): the country maintains a police force and a small defense force of volunteers.

[1]Saint Christopher and Nevis and Federation of Saint Christopher and Nevis are both officially acceptable, variant, short- and long-form names of the country. [2]Includes 4 nonelective seats. [3]Parish subdivisions of both islands are for statistical purposes only. [4]1987. [5]1986. [6]At prices of 1977. [7]Employed persons only. [8]Finance, real estate includes Services. [9]Less imputed bank service charges. [10]Weights of consumer price index components. [11]Unemployment during tourist and sugarcane-harvesting seasons c. 10.0%; off-season c. 20.0%. [12]Average wages paid sugar industry employees. [13]Imports c.i.f.; exports f.o.b. including reexports. [14]Light railway serving the sugar industry on Saint Kitts. [15]Public institution(s) only. [16]Includes Anguilla.

Saint Lucia

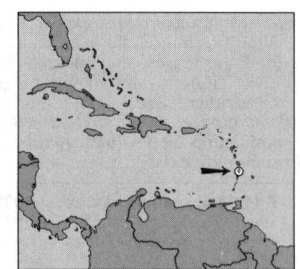

Official name: Saint Lucia.
Form of government: constitutional
monarchy with two legislative houses
(Senate [11]; House of Assembly [17]).
Chief of state: British Monarch
represented by governor-general.
Head of government: Prime Minister.
Capital: Castries.
Official language: English.
Official religion: none.
Monetary unit: 1 Eastern Caribbean
Dollar (EC$) = 100 cents; valuation
(Oct. 10, 1988) 1 U.S.$ = EC$2.70;
1 £ = EC$4.62.

Area and population		area		population
		sq mi	sq km	1986 estimate
Quarters	Capitals			
Anse-la-Raye	Anse-la-Raye	18.1	46.9	6,111
Canaries	Canaries			2,567
Castries	Castries	30.7	79.5	52,868
Choiseul	Choiseul	12.1	31.3	7,995
Dennery	Dennery	26.9	69.7	11,874
Gros Islet	Gros Islet	39.2	101.5	12,502
Laborie	Laborie	14.6	37.8	8,483
Micoud	Micoud	30.9	80.0	14,678
Soufrière	Soufrière	19.5	50.5	8,972
Vieux Fort	Vieux Fort	16.9	43.8	13,479
TOTAL		238.4[1]	617.4[1]	139,529

Demography

Population (1988): 145,000.
Density (1988): persons per sq mi 608.2, persons per sq km 234.9.
Urban–rural (1982): urban 52.1%; rural 47.9%.
Sex distribution (1986): male 48.54%; female 51.46%.
Age breakdown (1986): under 15, 44.5%; 15–29, 27.7%; 30–44, 11.3%; 45–59, 8.5%; 60–74, 5.8%; 75 and over, 2.2%.
Population projection: (1990) 151,000; (2000) 185,000.
Doubling time: 32 years.
Ethnic composition (1982): black 90.3%; mixed 5.5%; East Indian 3.2%; white 0.8%; other 0.2%.
Religious affiliation (1980): Roman Catholic 86.3%; Protestant 11.3%, of which Anglican 3.0%, Seventh-day Adventist 2.5%; Rastafarian 2.2%; other 0.2%.
Major cities (1986)[2]: Castries 52,868; Vieux Fort 13,479.

Vital statistics

Birth rate per 1,000 population (1986): 28.0 (world avg. 26.0); legitimate 15.0%; illegitimate 85.0%.
Death rate per 1,000 population (1986): 6.0 (world avg. 9.9).
Natural increase rate per 1,000 population (1986): 22.0 (world avg. 16.1).
Total fertility rate (avg. births per childbearing woman; 1986): 3.8.
Marriage rate per 1,000 population (1986): 3.1.
Divorce rate per 1,000 population (1986): 0.4.
Life expectancy at birth (1986): male 68.0 years; female 74.8 years.
Major causes of death per 100,000 population (1986): diseases of the circulatory system 203.5, of which ischemic heart diseases 111.1, cerebrovascular diseases 50.9, hypertensive disease 38.0; malignant neoplasms (cancers) 65.2; diseases of the respiratory system 55.9; ill-defined conditions 84.6.

National economy

Budget (1987–88). Revenue: EC$192,800,000 (taxes on international trade 39.1%, taxes on goods and services 25.8%, taxes on income 24.3%, nontax revenue 9.5%). Expenditures: EC$158,000,000 (wages and salaries 53.0%, goods and services 20.9%, transfer payments 13.3%, interest payments 6.9%).
Public debt (external, outstanding; 1985): U.S.$28,700,000[3].
Production (metric tons except as noted). Agriculture, forestry, fishing (1986): bananas 87,000[4], mangoes 46,000, coconuts 31,000, plantains 2,000, sweet potatoes 1,000, tomatoes 305[5], oranges 282[5], cabbages 183[5], ginger 127[5], cocoa beans 52; livestock (number of live animals) 15,000 sheep, 12,000 cattle, 12,000 pigs, 12,000 goats; roundwood, n.a.; fish catch 840. Mining and quarrying: excavation of sand for local construction and pumice. Manufacturing (value of production in EC$'000; 1986): paper products and cardboard boxes 41,210[6]; alcoholic beverages and tobacco 14,483; garments 13,477; nonalcoholic beverages 8,468; electrical components 5,730[6]; copra 5,566; other manufactures include refined coconut oil, scuba-diving suits, and wooden toys. Construction (buildings authorized; 1986): residential 17,300 sq m; nonresidential 10,140 sq m. Energy production (consumption): electricity (kW-hr; 1986) 63,300,000 (53,700,000); coal, none (none); crude petroleum, none (none); petroleum products (metric tons; 1986) none (40,000); natural gas, none (none).
Household income and expenditure. Average household size (1980) 4.6; income per household: n.a.; sources of income: n.a.; expenditure (1984)[7]: food 46.8%, housing 13.5%, clothing and footwear 6.5%, transportation and communications 6.3%, household furnishings 5.8%, fuel and light 4.5%, recreation and education 3.2%, beverages and tobacco 2.8%, health care 2.3%, other 8.3%.
Population economically active (1980): total 49,451; activity rate of total population 41.1% (participation rates: ages 15–64, n.a.; female 55.2%; unemployed [1986] more than 20.0%).

Price and earnings indexes (1980 = 100)

	1982	1983	1984	1985	1986	1987	1988
Consumer price index	120.4	122.2	123.7	125.3	128.1	137.1	137.1[8]
Weekly earnings index[9]	114.9	...	...	162.0	...	...	...

Gross national product (at current market prices; 1985): U.S.$170,000,000 (U.S.$1,240 per capita).

Structure of gross domestic product and labour force

	1986		1983[10]	
	in value EC$'000,000	% of total value	labour force	% of labour force
Agriculture	70.7	16.5	13,000	29.7
Mining	2.5	0.6		
Manufacturing	34.0	8.0	2,600	5.9
Construction	31.9	7.5	1,500	3.4
Public utilities	16.5	3.9		
Transportation and communications	42.2	9.9		
Trade	94.1	22.0	15,800	36.1
Finance	45.2	10.6		
Pub. admin., defense	92.0	21.6		
Services	20.5	4.8		
Other	−23.0[11]	−5.4[11]	10,900[12]	24.9[12]
TOTAL	426.6	100.0	43,800	100.0

Tourism (1986): receipts from visitors U.S.$68,800,000; expenditures by nationals abroad U.S.$52,200,000.
Land use (1985): forested 13.0%; meadows and pastures 5.0%; agricultural and under permanent cultivation 28.0%; other 54.0%.

Foreign trade[13]

Balance of trade (current prices)

	1981	1982	1983	1984	1985	1986
EC$'000,000	203.3	177.0	133.9	161.9	166.3	156.0
% of total	47.5%	44.1%	34.3%	38.5%	37.2%	25.8%

Imports (1986): EC$417,900,000 (food 19.9%, of which meat and meat preparations 5.6%; cereal and cereal preparations 4.6%; machinery and transport equipment 19.8%, of which road vehicles 6.2%; chemicals and chemical products 12.2%; crude petroleum and petroleum products 6.7%; paper and paper products 6.4%; clothing 4.6%; metal manufactures 4.2%). *Major import sources:* United States 34.1%; United Kingdom 15.9%; Trinidad and Tobago 7.8%; Japan 6.9%; Canada 3.1%.
Exports (1986): EC$223,900,000 (bananas 66.9%; clothing 8.4%; cardboard boxes 6.9%; unrefined coconut oil 2.1%; electrical components and parts 2.0%; beer and ale 1.9%). *Major export destinations*[14]: United Kingdom 70.5%; United States 11.3%; Trinidad and Tobago 2.9%; Barbados 2.7%.

Transport and communications

Transport. Railroads: none. Roads (1986): total length 464 mi, 747 km (paved 79%). Vehicles (1984): passenger cars 7,049; trucks and buses 2,084. Merchant marine (1987): vessels (100 gross tons and over) 7; total deadweight tonnage 2,530. Air transport (1986): passenger arrivals 143,571, passenger departures 145,774; cargo unloaded 1,691 metric tons, cargo loaded 2,479 metric tons; airports (1988) with scheduled flights 2.
Communications. Daily newspapers: none. Radio (1986): total number of receivers 92,500 (1 per 1.5 persons). Television (1986): total number of receivers 5,000 (1 per 28 persons). Telephones (1986): 14,104 (1 per 10 persons).

Education and health

Education (1986–87)

	schools	teachers	students	student/teacher ratio
Primary (age 5–11)[15]	78	1,103	32,400	29.4
Secondary (age 12–16)[15]	12	337	5,934	17.6
Voc., teacher tr.	4	...	817	...
Higher	1	16	123	7.7

Educational attainment (1980). Percent of population age 25 and over having: no formal schooling 17.5%; primary education 74.4%; secondary 6.8%; higher 1.3%. *Literacy* (1980): about 75%.
Health: physicians (1985) 43 (1 per 3,185 persons); hospital beds (1986) 501 (1 per 279 persons); infant mortality rate per 1,000 live births (1984–86 avg.) 20.8.
Food (1984–86): daily per capita caloric intake 2,499 (vegetable products 77%, animal products 23%); (1983) 98% of FAO recommended minimum requirement.

Military

Total active duty personnel (1987):[16].

---

[1]Total includes the uninhabited 29.5 sq-mi (76.4-sq-km) Central Forest Reserve. [2]Populations cited are for quarters (first-order administrative subdivisions). [3]Includes external long-term private debt not guaranteed by the government. [4]1987. [5]1983. [6]1985. [7]Weights of consumer price index components. [8]June. [9]Wages in nonagricultural activities excluding mining. [10]Wage earners and self-employed. [11]Less imputed bank service charges. [12]Unemployed. [13]Import figures are f.o.b. in balance of trade and c.i.f. in commodities and trading partners. [14]Based on domestic exports only totaling EC$213,200,000. [15]Public schools only. [16]The 489-member police force includes a specially trained paramilitary unit.

Saint Vincent and the Grenadines

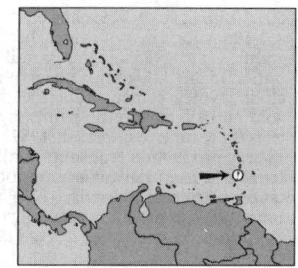

Official name: Saint Vincent and the Grenadines.
Form of government: constitutional monarchy with one legislative house (House of Assembly [19][1]).
Chief of state: British Monarch represented by governor-general.
Head of government: Prime Minister.
Capital: Kingstown.
Official language: English.
Official religion: none.
Monetary unit: 1 Eastern Caribbean Dollar (EC$) = 100 cents; valuation (Oct. 10, 1988) 1 U.S.$ = EC$2.70; 1 £ = EC$4.62.

Area and population

Constituencies[2]	area sq mi	area sq km	population 1987 estimate[3]
Island of Saint Vincent			
Barrouallie	14.2	36.8	5,315
Bridgetown	7.2	18.6	7,699
Calliaqua	11.8	30.6	19,855
Chateaubelair	30.9	80.0	6,953
Colonarie	13.4	34.7	8,211
Georgetown	22.2	57.5	7,398
Kingstown (city)	1.9	4.9	18,830
Kingstown (suburbs)	6.4	16.6	9,805
Layou	11.1	28.7	6,273
Marriaqua	9.4	24.3	9,571
Sandy Bay	5.3	13.7	3,264
Saint Vincent Grenadines			
Northern Grenadines	9.0	23.3	5,393
Southern Grenadines	7.5	19.4	2,852
TOTAL	150.3	389.3[4]	111,419

Demography

Population (1988): 113,000.
Density (1988): persons per sq mi 751.8, persons per sq km 290.3.
Urban–rural[5] (1985): urban 25.7%; rural 74.3%.
Sex distribution (1984): male 48.45%; female 51.55%.
Age breakdown (1985): under 15, 37.4%; 15–29, 32.7%; 30–44, 14.9%; 45–59, 7.5%; 60–74, 5.6%; 75 and over, 1.9%.
Population projection: (1990) 116,000; (2000) 131,000.
Doubling time: 44 years.
Ethnic composition (1983): black 74.0%; mulatto 19.0%; white 3.0%; Amerindian/black 2.0%; East Indian 2.0%.
Religious affiliation (1980): Protestant 77.3%, of which Anglican 36.0%, Methodist 20.4%, Seventh-day Adventist 4.1%, Plymouth Brethren 3.9%; Roman Catholic 19.3%; other 3.4%.
Major city (1987): Kingstown 18,830.

Vital statistics

Birth rate per 1,000 population (1986): 24.5 (world avg. 26.0); legitimate, n.a.; illegitimate, n.a.
Death rate per 1,000 population (1986): 5.9 (world avg. 9.9).
Natural increase rate per 1,000 population (1986): 18.6 (world avg. 16.1).
Total fertility rate (avg. births per childbearing woman; 1984): 3.2.
Marriage rate per 1,000 population (1984): 3.6.
Divorce rate per 1,000 population (1980): 0.2.
Life expectancy at birth (1980–85): male 67.5 years; female 71.4 years.
Major causes of death per 100,000 population (1986): diseases of the circulatory system 118.3, of which hypertensive disease 80.4; malignant neoplasms (cancers) 65.9; endocrine and metabolic disorders 39.7; diseases of the digestive system 27.1; diseases of the respiratory system 27.1.

National economy

Budget (1986). Revenue: EC$105,800,000 (tax revenue 74.9%, of which import duties 38.2%, taxes on income, profits, and capital gains 22.1%; nontax revenue 20.3%; grants 4.7%). Expenditures: EC$101,400,000 (economic services 29.3%; general public services 18.0%; education 17.4%; health 12.7%; police and defense 6.4%).
Public debt (external, outstanding; 1986): U.S.$28,800,000.
Tourism (1986): receipts from visitors U.S.$25,000,000[6]; expenditures by nationals abroad U.S.$8,000,000.
Production (metric tons except as noted). Agriculture, forestry, fishing (1986): bananas 37,100[7], coconuts 22,000, eddoes and dasheens[8] 21,000, sweet potatoes 11,800, tanias[8] 9,700, plantains 4,600, ginger 545, arrowroot 161[7], soursops, guavas, and papaws are other important fruits; livestock (number of live animals) 14,000 sheep, 8,000 cattle, 7,000 pigs; roundwood, n.a.; fish catch (1985) 547. Mining and quarrying: sand and gravel for local use. Manufacturing (1984): flour 24,100; cigarettes 20,000,000 units; rum 4,960 hectolitres[9]; other products include carbonated drinks, beer, garments, yachts, and electronic components. Construction (1986): 1,008,422 sq m. Energy production (consumption): electricity (kW-hr; 1986) 40,400,000 (31,800,000); coal, none (none); crude petroleum, none (none); petroleum products (metric tons; 1986) none (13,000); natural gas, none (none).
Gross national product (1986): U.S.$110,000,000 (U.S.$960 per capita).

Structure of gross domestic product and labour force

	1986[10] in value EC$'000,000	1986[10] % of total value	1970 labour force	1970 % of labour force
Agriculture	22.0	17.1	6,882	29.0
Mining	0.4	0.3	48	0.2
Manufacturing	11.8	9.2	1,851	7.8
Construction	13.7	10.6	2,871	12.1
Public utilities	4.5	3.5	214	0.9
Transportation and communications	27.0	21.0	1,068	4.5
Trade	19.8	15.4	2,871	12.1
Finance	14.0[11]	10.9[11]		
Pub. admin., defense	19.5	15.2	7,190	30.3
Services	11	11		
Other	–4.1[12]	–3.2[12]	736	3.1
TOTAL	128.6	100.0	23,731	100.0

Population economically active (1980)[13]: total 32,617; activity rate of total population 31.7% (participation rates: ages 14–64, 57.2%; female 34.5%; unemployed [1987] 35.0%).

Price and earnings indexes (1980 = 100)

	1980	1981	1982	1983	1984	1985	1986
Consumer price index	100.0	112.7	120.9	127.5	130.9	133.6	135.1[14]
Weekly earnings index[15]	100.0	117.5	143.0	150.1	...	...	...

Household income and expenditure. Average household size (1978) 5.0; income per household: n.a.; sources of income: n.a.; expenditure (1981)[16]: food, beverages, and tobacco 62.6%, clothing 7.7%, household furnishings 6.6%, housing 6.3%, energy 6.2%, other 10.6%.
Land use (1985): forested 41.0%; meadows and pastures 6.0%; agricultural and under permanent cultivation 50.0%; other 3.0%.

Foreign trade[17]

Balance of trade (current prices)

EC$'000,000	1981	1982	1983	1984	1985	1986
	–92.2	–88.8	–79.1	–62.2	–43.1	–63.2
% of total	41.5%	33.8%	26.3%	17.7%	11.2%	15.5%

Imports (1986): EC$235,600,000 (basic and miscellaneous manufactures 34.6%, food 20.8%, machinery and transport equipment 18.1%, chemicals and chemical products 13.3%, mineral fuels 6.6%). *Major import sources:* United States 34.1%; United Kingdom 16.5%; Trinidad and Tobago 10.5%; Canada 7.2%; Japan 4.1%.
Exports (1986): EC$172,400,000 (bananas 30.4%, eddoes and dasheens[8] 18.4%, sweet potatoes 8.9%, flour 8.8%, tanias[8] 8.4%). *Major export destinations:* Trinidad and Tobago 42.9%; United Kingdom 31.2%; United States 9.4%; Saint Lucia 5.1%; Antigua and Barbuda 2.7%.

Transport and communications

Transport. Railroads: none. Roads (1986): total length 463 mi, 745 km (paved 58%). Vehicles (1986): passenger cars 5,069; trucks and buses 2,279. Merchant marine (1987): vessels (100 gross tons and over) 145; total deadweight tonnage 1,132,838. Air transport (1986): passenger arrivals 82,406, passenger departures 81,494; airports (1988) with scheduled flights 4.
Communications. Daily newspapers: none. Radio (1986): total number of receivers 66,000 (1 per 1.7 persons). Television (1987): total number of receivers 10,000 (1 per 11 persons). Telephones (1985): 8,520 (1 per 13 persons).

Education and health

Education (1985–86)

	schools[18]	teachers	students	student/ teacher ratio
Primary (age 5–15)	62	1,263	24,561	19.4
Secondary (age 11–19)	19	368	6,535	17.8
Voc., teacher tr.	5	...	275	...
Higher[18]	1	19	105	5.5

Educational attainment (1980). Percent of population age 25 and over having: no formal schooling 2.4%; primary education 88.0%; secondary 8.2%; higher 1.4%. *Literacy* (1983): total population age 15 and over literate 54,000 (85.0%).
Health: physicians (1986) 25 (1 per 4,400 persons); hospital beds (1984) 350 (1 per 309 persons); infant mortality rate per 1,000 live births (1984–86 avg.) 23.8.
Food (1983–85): daily per capita caloric intake 2,684 (vegetable products 87%, animal products 13%); (1983) 97% of FAO recommended minimum requirement.

Military

Total active duty personnel (1986): part of the 489-member police force is being trained for defense purposes. *Military expenditure as percent of GNP:* n.a.

[1]Includes six nonelective seats. [2]For statistical purposes and the election of legislative representatives; no civil administrative subdivisions exist. [3]January 1. [4]Detail does not add to total given because of rounding. [5]Urban defined as Kingstown and suburbs. [6]Number of the tourist arrivals (1986): St. Vincent 43,301, the Grenadines 53,678. [7]1987. [8]Varieties of taro roots. [9]1986. [10]At prices of 1977; GDP at current prices is EC$255,500,000. [11]Finance includes services. [12]Less imputed service charges. [13]Based on projection of 1970 census except for unemployment rate. [14]Average of second and third quarters. [15]Wages in selected manufacturing and service occupations. [16]Weights of consumer price index components. [17]Imports c.i.f.; exports f.o.b. [18]1982–83.

San Marino

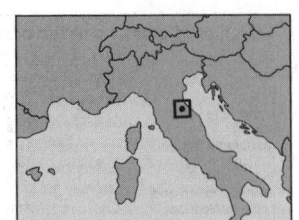

Official name: Serenissima Repubblica di San Marino (Most Serene Republic of San Marino).
Form of government: unitary multiparty republic with one legislative house (Great and General Council [60]).
Head of state and government: Captains-Regent (2).
Capital: San Marino.
Official language: Italian.
Official religion: none.
Monetary unit: 1 Italian lira (Lit; plural lire) = 100 centesimi; valuation (Oct. 10, 1988) 1 U.S.$ = Lit 1,383; 1 £ = Lit 2,368.

Area and population		area		population
				1988
Castles	Capitals	sq mi	sq km	estimate[1]
Acquaviva	Acquaviva	1.88	4.86	1,160
Borgo Maggiore	Borgo	3.48	9.01	4,532
Città	San Marino	2.74	7.09	4,137
Chiesanuova	Chiesanuova	2.11	5.46	732
Domagnano	Domagnano	2.56	6.62	1,877
Faetano	Faetano	2.99	7.75	745
Fiorentino	Fiorentino	2.53	6.56	1,500
Montegiardino	Montegiardino	1.28	3.31	575
Serravalle/Dogano	Serravalle	4.07	10.53	7,046
TOTAL		23.63[2]	61.19	22,304

Demography

Population (1988): 22,830.
Density (1988): persons per sq mi 966.1, persons per sq km 373.1.
Urban–rural (1988): urban 90.0%; rural 10.0%.
Sex distribution (1988): male 49.87%; female 50.13%.
Age breakdown (1988): under 15, 17.5%; 15–29, 25.4%; 30–44, 21.7%; 45–59, 17.2%; 60–74, 12.9%; 75 and over, 5.3%.
Population projection: (1990) 23,126; (2000) 24,662.
Doubling time: not applicable; natural population growth is negligible, averaging only 0.2% during 1983–87.
Ethnic composition (1987): Sammarinesi 87.1%; Italian 12.4%; other 0.4%[2].
Religious affiliation (1980): Roman Catholic 95.2%; no religion 3.0%; other 1.8%.
Major cities (1988): Serravalle/Dogano 4,619; San Marino 2,359; Borgo Maggiore 2,121; Murata 1,325; Domagnano 911.

Vital statistics

Birth rate per 1,000 population (1983–87): 9.6 (world avg. 26.0); (1985) legitimate 95.2%; illegitimate 4.8%.
Death rate per 1,000 population (1983–87): 7.5 (world avg. 9.9).
Natural increase rate per 1,000 population (1983–87): 2.1 (world avg. 16.1).
Total fertility rate (avg. births per childbearing woman; 1984): 1.3.
Marriage rate per 1,000 population (1986): 6.8.
Divorce rate per 1,000 population (1987): 1.0.
Life expectancy at birth (1980–85): male 70.7 years; female 76.2 years.
Major causes of death per 100,000 population (1983–87): diseases of the circulatory system 325.3; malignant neoplasms (cancers) 256.3; accidents, violence, and suicide 54.7.

National economy

Budget (1987). Revenue: Lit 254,670,000,000 (mainly receipts from postage stamp sales, tourism, and customs duties [collected by Italy and paid as a subsidy]). Expenditures: Lit 254,670,000,000 ([3]finance and economic planning 31.0%, internal affairs 11.3%, health and social security 9.0%, education and culture 7.1%, public works 6.3%).
Public debt: n.a.
Tourism: number of tourist arrivals (1987) 2,832,747; receipts from visitors (1983) U.S.$56,454,000; expenditures by nationals abroad, n.a.
Gross national product (at current market prices; 1987): U.S.$188,000,000 (U.S.$8,590 per capita).

Structure of labour force (1988)	labour force	% of labour force
Agriculture	340	2.9
Manufacturing	4,209	35.5
Construction and public utilities	880	7.4
Transportation and communications	146	1.2
Trade	1,704	14.4
Finance and insurance	223	1.9
Services	691	5.8
Public administration and defense	1,920	16.2
Other	1,737[4]	14.7
TOTAL	11,850	100.0

Production (metric tons except as noted). Agriculture, forestry, fishing[3]: wheat *c.* 4,400; grapes *c.* 700; barley *c.* 500; livestock (number of live animals; 1987) 927 cattle, 1,438 pigs, 1,210 sheep, 81 horses[5], 12,045 rabbits[5],

50,040 quails[5], 19,479 chickens[5]. Manufacturing (1987): processed meats 451,726 kilograms, of which beef 239,310 kilograms, swine 171,885 kilograms, veal 16,975 kilograms; milk 1,340,385 litres; cheese 82,022 kilograms; butter 15,507 kilograms; yogurt 9,627 kilograms; other major products include textiles, cement, paper, leather, bricks, pottery, tiles, postage stamps, gold and silver jewelry, paints, synthetic rubber, and furniture. Construction (new units completed; 1987): urban residential 99; nonresidential 55.
Energy production (consumption): all electrical power is imported via electrical grid from Italy, consumption n.a.; coal (metric tons; 1987) none (n.a); crude petroleum (barrels; 1987) none (n.a.); petroleum products (metric tons; 1987) none (n.a.); natural gas (cu m; 1987) none (n.a.).
Population economically active (1988[1]): total 11,850; activity rate of total population 52.1% (participation rates: ages 15–64 [1986] 71.2%; female 41.0%; unemployed 5.7%).

Price and earnings indexes (1980 = 100)							
	1981	1982	1983	1984	1985	1986	1987
Consumer price index	139.2	150.1	165.1	174.9	196.1	204.4	224.7
Monthly earnings index	...	...	...	...	...	...	...

Household income and expenditure. Total number of households (1988): 7,764; average household size (1988) 2.9; income per household: n.a.; sources of income: n.a.; expenditure[6] (1985): food, beverages, and tobacco 30.4%; transportation and communications 14.5%; housing, fuel, and electrical energy 9.7%; clothing and footwear 8.8%; recreation, entertainment, education, and culture 8.1%; furniture, appliances, and goods and services for the home 7.5%; health and sanitary services 5.1%; other goods and services 15.9%.
Land use (1985): agricultural and under permanent cultivation 74%; meadows and pastures 22%; forested, built-on, wasteland, and other 4%.

Foreign trade

Balance of trade: n.a. San Marino and Italy form a single customs area; separate figures for San Marino are not available.
Imports (1987): manufactured goods of all kinds, oil, and gold. *Major import source:* Italy.
Exports (1987): wine, wheat, woolen goods, furniture, wood, ceramics, building stone, dairy products, meat, and postage stamps. *Major export destination:* Italy.

Transport and communications

Transport. Railroads: none (nearest rail terminal is at Rimini, Italy, 17 mi [27 km] northeast). Roads (1980): total length 137 mi, 220 km. Vehicles (1988): passenger cars 17,387; trucks and buses 1,809. Merchant marine: vessels (100 gross tons and over) none. Air transport: airports with scheduled flights, none; however, there is a heliport that provides passenger and cargo service between San Marino and Rimini, Italy, during the summer months.
Communications. Daily newspapers (1985): none; however, there are several journals of lesser frequency; total circulation of the oldest of these, *Il Nuovo Titano,* 1,300; circulation per 1,000 population 58.1. Radio (1983): total number of receivers 11,000 (1 per 2.0 persons). Television (1986): total number of receivers 6,143 (1 per 3.7 persons). Telephones (1986): 13,100 (1 per 1.7 persons).

Education and health

Education (1986–87)	schools	teachers	students	student/ teacher ratio
Primary (age 6–10)	13	171	1,363	8.0
Secondary (age 11–18)	5	179	1,222	6.8
Vocational	...	...	697[7]	...
Teacher tr.	...	...	47[7]	...
Higher	...	...	332[7]	...

Educational attainment (1988). Percent of the adult labour force having: basic literacy or primary education 34.2%; secondary 33.0%; some postsecondary 27.1%; higher degree 5.7%. *Literacy* (1986): total population age 15 and over literate 18,135 (98.0%); males literate 8,957 (98.2%); females literate 9,178 (97.7%).
Health: physicians (1979) 10[8] (1 per 2,115 persons); hospital beds (1980) 61 (1 per 351 persons); infant mortality rate per 1,000 live births (1983–87) 8.4.
Food (1984–86): daily per capita caloric intake 3,494 (vegetable products 73%, animal products 27%); (1983) 140% of FAO recommended minimum requirement.

Military

Total active duty personnel (1984): none[9]. *Military expenditure as a percent of national budget* (1987): 0.9% (world 6.1%); per capita expenditure (1987) U.S.$82.

---

[1]January 1. [2]Detail does not add to total given because of rounding. [3]Early 1980s. [4]Includes 675 unemployed persons. [5]1975. [6]Weighting coefficients for component expenditures are those of the 1985 official Italian consumer price index. [7]In Italy. [8]Panel physicians only. [9]Defense is provided by a public security force of about 50; all fit males 16–55 constitute a militia.

São Tomé and Príncipe

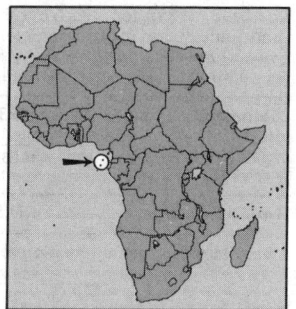

Official name: República democrática de São Tomé e Príncipe (Democratic Republic of São Tomé and Príncipe).
Form of government: single-party republic with one legislative house (National People's Assembly [51]).
Head of state and government:
President assisted by Prime Minister[1].
Capital: São Tomé.
Official language: Portuguese.
Official religion: Roman Catholicism.
Monetary unit: 1 dobra (Db) = 100 cêntimos; valuation (Oct. 10, 1988) 1 U.S.$ = Db 77.01; 1 £ = Db 131.87.

Area and population

Islands Districts	Capitals	area sq mi	area sq km	population 1984 estimate
Príncipe	São António	55	142	5,671
Paguê	Príncipe	55	142	5,671
São Tomé		332	859	98,693
Aqua Grande	São Tomé	7	17	34,997
Cantagalo	Santana	46	119	11,270
Caué	São João Angolares	103	267	4,972
Lemba	Neves	88	229	8,537
Lobata	Guadalupe	41	105	12,717
Mé-zóchi	Trinidade	47	122	26,200
TOTAL		386	1,001	104,364

Demography

Population (1988): 117,000.
Density (1988): persons per sq mi 303.1, persons per sq km 116.9.
Urban–rural (1985): urban 37.6%; rural 62.4%.
Sex distribution (1981): male 49.72%; female 50.28%.
Age breakdown (1981): under 15, 46.3%; 15–29, 25.0%; 30–44, 11.6%; 45–59, 10.0%; 60–74, 5.3%; 75 and over, 1.8%.
Population projection: (1990) 124,000; (2000) 163,000.
Doubling time: 25 years.
Ethnic composition: mestiços, angolares (descendants of Angolan slaves), forros (descendants of freed slaves), serviçais (alien contract labourers), tongas (children of serviçais), and Europeans.
Religious affiliation (1986): Roman Catholic, about 80%; remainder mostly Protestant, predominantly Seventh-day Adventist and an indigenous Evangelical Church.
Major city (1984): São Tomé 34,997.

Vital statistics

Birth rate per 1,000 population (1985): 36.3 (world avg. 29.0); (1977) legitimate 9.8%; illegitimate 90.2%.
Death rate per 1,000 population (1985): 8.8 (world avg. 11.0).
Natural increase rate per 1,000 population (1985): 27.5 (world avg. 18.0).
Total fertility rate (avg. births per childbearing woman; 1985): 5.0.
Marriage rate per 1,000 population: n.a.
Divorce rate per 1,000 population: n.a.
Life expectancy at birth (1980–85): male 41.7 years; female 44.9 years.
Major causes of death per 100,000 population (1972): senility without mention of psychosis, and ill-defined and unknown causes 367.5; gastritis, duodenitis, enteritis, and colitis, except diarrhea of the newborn, 95.5; pneumonia 62.4; heart disease 51.7; malaria 49.1.

National economy

Budget (1986). Revenue: Db 1,092,000,000 (1977; indirect taxes 26.1%, import duties 13.5%, direct taxes 7.5%, export duties 6.3%, other sources 66.4%). Expenditures: Db 1,092,000,000 (1977; services 64.4%, wages and salaries 35.0%, interest on the public debt 0.5%).
Tourism: campaign initiated in 1987 to attract 500 tourists per year to the islands; a 50-room hotel was completed in 1986, and a 175-room hotel will be completed in 1989.
Public debt (external, outstanding; 1986): U.S.$74,200,000.
Production (metric tons except as noted). Agriculture, forestry, fishing (1986): coconuts 35,000, cacao 5,000, palm kernels 5,000, copra 4,000, melons 4,000, bananas 3,000, cassava 3,000, palmetto 3,000, vegetables 3,000, cereals 1,000; livestock (number of live animals) 4,000 goats, 3,000 cattle, 3,000 pigs, 2,000 sheep, 123,000 poultry; roundwood (1985) 6,000 cu m; fish catch 2,833, principally marine fish and shellfish. Mining and quarrying: some quarrying to support local construction industry. Manufacturing (1975): sawn wood 3,000 cu m[2]; bread and biscuits 1,831; soap 470; palm oil 250[3]; ice 191; limes 22; corn (maize) flour 18; other products include soft drinks, beer, clothing, and bricks and clay products. Construction: (1972) buildings authorized 44 (5,561 sq m, of which residential 3,698, mixed residential–commercial 1,361, commercial 502). Energy production (consumption): electricity (kW-hr; 1986) 12,000,000 (12,000,000); coal, none (n.a.); crude petroleum, none (n.a.); petroleum products (metric tons; 1986) none (11,000); natural gas, none (n.a.).
Household income and expenditure: average household size: n.a.; income per household: n.a.; sources of income: n.a.; expenditure: n.a.
Gross national product (at current market prices; 1986): U.S.$40,000,000 (U.S.$340 per capita).

Structure of gross domestic product and labour force

	1984 in value Db '000,000	1984 % of total value	1981 labour force	1981 % of labour force
Agriculture	379	26.1	16,487	53.9
Mining	4	0.3	1,622	5.3
Manufacturing	142	9.8 }		
Construction	137	9.4	1,802	5.9
Public utilities	46	3.2	286	0.9
Transportation and communications	166	11.4	1,030	3.4
Trade	142	9.8	1,994	6.5
Finance	19	1.3	152	0.5
Pub. admin., defense	418	28.8 }	5,814	19.0
Services	11.1	0.6		
Other			1,420[4]	4.6[4]
TOTAL	1,453[5]	100.0[6]	30,607	100.0

Population economically active (1981): total 30,607; activity rate of total population 31.7% (participation rates: ages 15–64, 61.1%; female 32.4%; unemployed 4.6%).

Price and earnings indexes (1974 = 100)

	1974	1975	1976	1977	1978	1979
Consumer price index	100.0	...	...	126.0	139.0	146.7
Earnings index	...	...	...	...	...	...

Land use (1985): meadows and pastures 1.0%; agricultural and under permanent cultivation 37.5%; forest, built-on, wasteland, and other 61.5%.

Foreign trade

Balance of trade (current prices)

	1980	1981	1982	1983	1984	1985
U.S.$'000,000	−11.7	−12.6	−15.9	−3.6	−4.9	−7.6
% of total	22.5%	31.5%	47.7%	23.1%	25.4%	42.7%

Imports (1984): Db 485,900,000 (food and other agricultural products 27.4%, mineral fuels and lubricants 16.3%, consumer goods 14.7%, machinery and transport equipment 12.9%, construction materials 8.6%). *Major import sources* (1985): Portugal 40.9%; Angola 12.6%; United Kingdom 10.2%; France 7.9%; East Germany 6.3%; Spain 6.3%; Belgium–Luxembourg 3.9%; The Netherlands 3.9%; Japan 2.0%; Norway 1.6%.
Exports (1984): Db 539,600,000 (cacao 80.0%, copra 15.0%, coffee 1.0%, palm kernels 0.4%). *Major export destinations* (1985): East Germany 47.0%; The Netherlands, 15.6%; Portugal 15.6%; United Kingdom 5.9%; Italy 5.9%; France 3.9%; Austria 2.0%; Switzerland 2.0%.

Transport and communications

Transport. Railroads: none. Roads (1986): total length 199 mi, 320 km (paved 66%). Vehicles (1975): passenger cars 1,774; trucks and buses 265. Merchant marine (1987): vessels (100 gross tons and over) 3; total deadweight tonnage 1,172. Air transport (1985): passenger-mi 3,800,000, passenger-km 6,100,000; short ton-mi cargo 70,000, short ton-km cargo 100,000; airports (1988) with scheduled flights 1.
Communications. Daily newspapers: none; 3 government weeklies (circulation, n.a.). Radio (1986): total number of receivers 28,000 (1 per 4.0 persons). Television: none. Telephones (1986): 2,200 (1 per 50 persons).

Education and health

Education (1984–85)

	schools	teachers	students	student/ teacher ratio
Primary (age 6–13)	63	517	19,086	36.9
Secondary (age 14–18)	11	300	6,186	20.6
Voc., teacher tr.	2	35	370	10.6
Higher	...	...	700[7]	

Educational attainment (1981). Percent of population age 25 and over having: no formal schooling 56.6%; some primary education 18.0%; primary 19.2%; some secondary 4.6%; secondary 1.3%; postsecondary 0.3%. *Literacy* (1981): total population age 15 and over literate 28,114 (54.2%); males literate 17,689 (70.2%); females literate 10,425 (39.1%).
Health (1985): physicians 53 (1 per 2,016 persons); hospital beds (1978) 665 (1 per 129 persons); infant mortality rate per 1,000 live births 61.7.
Food (1984–86): daily per capita caloric intake 2,385 (vegetable products 93%, animal products 7%); (1983) 97% of FAO recommended minimum requirement.

Military

Total active duty personnel (1987): 600, of which 300 are Angolan troops (distribution by branch of service, n.a.). *Military expenditure as percent of GNP* (1980): 1.6% (world 5.7%); per capita expenditure U.S.$7.

[1]Position of prime minister reintroduced January 1988, but not as effective head of government. [2]1983. [3]1986. [4]Unemployed. [5]At factor cost. [6]Detail does not add to total given because of rounding. [7]Students abroad, 1982–83.

Saudi Arabia

Official name: al-Mamlakah
al-'Arabīyah as-Sa'ūdīyah (Kingdom of
Saudi Arabia).
Form of government: monarchy.
Head of state and government: King.
Capital: Riyadh.
Official language: Arabic.
Official religion: Islam.
Monetary unit: 1 Saudi riyal
(SRls) = 100 halalah; valuation (Oct.
10, 1988) 1 U.S.$ = SRls 3.75;
1 £ = SRls 6.42.

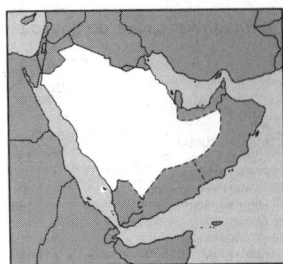

Area and population

Regions	Capitals	area		population 1985
Administrative Districts		sq mi	sq km	estimate
al-Gharbīyah (Western)	—	...	...	3,043,189
al-Bāḥah	al-Bāḥah	...	...	
al-Madīnah	Medina (al-Madīnah)	...	...	
Makkah	Mecca (Makkah)	...	...	
al-Janūbiyah (Southern)	—	...	...	625,017
'Asīr	Abha	...	...	
Jīzān	Jīzān	...	...	
Najrān	Najrān	...	...	
ash-Shamālīyah (Northern)	—	...	...	679,476
al-Ḥudūd ash-Shamālīyah (Northern Borders)	'Ar'ar	...	...	
al-Jawf	Sakākah	...	...	
al-Qurayyāt	an-Nabk	...	...	
Tabūk	Tabūk	...	...	
ash-Sharqiyah (Eastern)	—	...	...	3,030,765
ash-Sharqiyah (Eastern)	ad-Dammām	...	...	
al-Wūsṭā (Central)	—	...	...	3,632,092
Ḥā'il	Ḥā'il	...	...	
al-Qaṣim	Buraydah	...	...	
ar-Riyāḍ	Riyadh (ar-Riyāḍ)	...	...	
TOTAL		865,000	2,240,000	11,010,539

Demography

Population (1988): 12,972,000.
Density (1988): persons per sq mi 15.0, persons per sq km 5.8.
Urban–rural (1986): urban 73.3%; rural 26.7%.
Sex distribution (1986): male 59.71%; female 40.29%.
Age breakdown (1986): under 15, 40.0%; 15–29, 26.2%; 30–44, 19.9%; 45–59,
8.6%; 60–74, 3.9%; 75 and over, 1.4%.
Population projection: (1990) 13,988,000; (2000) 19,824,000.
Doubling time: 21 years.
Ethnic composition (1983): Saudi 82.0%; Yemeni 9.6%; other Arab 3.4%;
other 5.0%.
Religious affiliation (1980): Muslim (mostly Sunnī) 98.8%; Christian 0.8%;
other 0.4%.
Major cities (1980): Riyadh 1,308,000[1]; Jidda (Jiddah) 1,500,000[2]; Mecca
550,000; aṭ-Ṭa'if 300,000.

Vital statistics

Birth rate per 1,000 population (1986): 37.3 (world avg. 26.0).
Death rate per 1,000 population (1986): 12.8 (world avg. 9.9).
Natural increase rate per 1,000 population (1986): 23.5 (world avg. 16.1).
Total fertility rate (avg. births per childbearing woman; 1986): 7.2.
Marriage rate per 1,000 population: n.a.
Divorce rate per 1,000 population: n.a.
Life expectancy at birth (1986): male 54.8 years; female 57.7 years.
Major causes of death per 100,000 population: n.a.; however, major diseases
include cholera, cerebrospinal meningitis, yellow fever, typhoid, tubercu-
losis, lung infections, and asphyxia.

National economy

Budget (1988–89). Revenue: SRls 105,300,000,000 (oil revenues 69.8%).
Expenditures: SRls 141,200,000,000 (defense and security 35.5%, public
administration and other government spending 17.7%, human resources
development 16.6%, health and social development 7.6%, transport and
communications 6.7%).
Public debt: none.
Production (metric tons except as noted). Agriculture, forestry, fishing
(1986): wheat 2,000,000, dates 456,000, watermelons 366,000, tomatoes 330,-
000, grapes 80,000, onions 76,000, pumpkins, squash, and gourds 45,000,
sorghum 43,000, eggplants 37,000, potatoes 30,000, cucumbers and gherkins
15,000, barley 15,000, pulses 7,000, millet 4,000; livestock (number of live
animals), 3,800,000 sheep, 2,350,000 goats, 530,000 cattle, 165,000 camels,
110,000 asses, 36,000,000 poultry; fish catch 45,498. Mining and quarrying
(1986): gypsum 300,000; lime 12,000. Manufacturing (1985): cement 1,-
633,500; methanol 1,287,000; steel rods and bars 948,000; ethylene 927,900;
urea 825,000; ethylene glycol 310,000; industrial ethanol 200,000; ethylene
dichloride 190,000; styrene 125,000; caustic soda 125,000; nitrogen 82,000;
citric acid 75,000; oxygen 55,000; melamine 14,000. Construction (value
added in SRls; 1987): 33,003,000,000. Energy production (consumption):
electricity (kW-hr; 1986) 45,866,000,000 (45,866,000,000); coal, n.a. (n.a.);
crude petroleum (barrels; 1986) 1,829,200,000 (279,091,200); petroleum
products (metric tons; 1986) 42,148,000 (27,480,000); natural gas (cu m;
1986) 7,469,000,000 (7,469,000,000).
Tourism: receipts from visitors (1986) U.S.$2,000,000,000; expenditures by
nationals abroad (1981) U.S.$2,761,000,000.

Land use (1985): forested 0.6%; meadows and pastures 39.5%; agricultural
and under permanent cultivation 0.5%; other, built-on, and waste 59.4%.
Population economically active (1986): total 3,032,000; activity rate of total
population 29.8% (participation rates: over age 15, 51.5%; female 3.2%).

Price and earnings indexes (1980 = 100)

	1982	1983	1984	1985	1986	1987	1988[3]
Consumer price index	102.1	101.5	100.3	97.0	94.1	93.2	94.2
Monthly earnings index	...	...	...	...	...	...	...

Gross national product (1986): U.S.$83,270,000,000 (U.S.$6,930 per capita).

Structure of gross domestic product and labour force

	1986–87		1986	
	in value SRls '000,000	% of total value	labour force	% of labour force
Agriculture	14,352	5.4	432,082	14.3
Mining	1,718	0.6 }	48,514	1.6
Oil sector	77,732	29.0 }		
Manufacturing	17,965	6.7	301,699	9.9
Construction	33,003	12.3	567,619	18.7
Public utilities	−858	−0.3	101,577	3.3
Transp. and commun.	18,992	7.1	210,128	6.9
Trade	22,519	8.4	374,168	12.3
Finance	19,837	7.5	94,300	3.1
Pub. admin., defense	27,661	10.3 }	902,066	29.8
Services and other	35,436	13.2 }		
Other	−714[4]	−0.3[4]	—	—
TOTAL	267,643	100.0[5]	3,032,153	100.0[5]

Pilgrims to Mecca from abroad (1987): 960,386.
Household income and expenditure. Average household size (1986) 6.6;
income per household: n.a.; sources of income: n.a.; expenditure[6] (1980):
food 52.2%, housing 17.2%, clothing 6.6%, furniture and utensils 5.9%,
transport and communications 4.5%, health care 2.1%.

Foreign trade

Balance of trade (current prices)

	1982	1983	1984	1985	1986	1987
SRls '000,000	+131.8	+23.0	+13.6	+14.0	+3.6	+11.6
% of total	32.1%	7.8%	5.4%	7.5%	2.5%	7.1%

Imports (1987): SRls 75,312,600,000 (machinery and appliances 19.1%, foodstuffs and tobacco 16.5%, transport equipment 13.5%, textiles and clothing
13.2%, metals and metal articles 8.4%, chemicals 4.2%, scientific instruments 4.1%). *Major import sources:* Japan 17.3%; U.S. 15.3%; U.K. 7.8%;
W.Ger. 7.7%; Italy 6.8%; France 5.3%; South Korea 4.9%; Taiwan 3.9%;
Switzerland 2.4%; The Netherlands 2.2%; Belgium 1.7%; Spain 1.5%.
Exports (1987): SRls 86,879,000,000 (1986; crude petroleum 89.7%, refined
petroleum 10.3%). *Major export destinations:* Japan 22.1%; U.S. 19.3%;
The Netherlands 6.1%; Bahrain 4.9%; Singapore 4.9%; Taiwan 4.2%; Italy
4.0%; Brazil 3.5%; South Korea 3.1%; France 2.6%; Spain 2.4%; U.K.
1.5%; W.Ger. 1.3%.

Transport and communications

Transport. Railroads (1986–87): route length 544 mi, 875 km; (1986) passenger-mi 43,931,000, passenger-km 70,700,000; short ton-mi cargo 220,-
000,000, metric ton-km cargo 321,190,000. Roads (1987): total length 56,752
mi, 91,350 km (paved 37%). Vehicles (1987): passenger cars 2,245,042;
trucks and buses 2,023,365. Merchant marine (1987): vessels (100 gross tons
and over) 349; total deadweight tonnage 4,588,299. Air transport (1987):
passenger-mi 10,032,000,000, passenger-km 16,145,000,000; short ton-mi
cargo 335,601,000, metric ton-km cargo 490,000,000; airports (1988) 21.
Communications. Daily newspapers (1986): total number 10; total circulation 488,000; circulation per 1,000 population 41.8. Radio (1986): 3,230,000
receivers (1 per 3.7 persons). Television (1986): 3,700,000 receivers (1 per
3.2 persons). Telephones (1986): 980,231 (1 per 11.9 persons).

Education and health

Education (1986–87)

	schools	teachers	students	student/ teacher ratio
Primary (age 6–12)	8,012	90,535	1,460,283	16.0
Secondary (age 13–18)	2,946[7]	43,420	630,251	14.5
Voc., teacher tr.	31	2,378	23,951	10.1
Higher	77	11,694	130,924	11.2

Educational attainment (1986). Percent of population age 25 and over having: no formal schooling 31.8%; primary, secondary, or higher education
68.2%. *Literacy* (1986): total population age 12 and over literate 3,862,439
(57.2%); males literate 3,006,249 (69.7%); females literate 856,190 (35.1%).
Health (1986): physicians 12,707 (1 per 945 persons); hospital beds 28,336
(1 per 424 persons); infant mortality rate per 1,000 live births 108.6.
Food (1984–86): daily per capita caloric intake 3,031 (vegetable products
80%, animal products 20%); (1983) 134% of FAO recommended minimum.

Military

Total active duty personnel (1988): 72,300 (army 52.6%, navy 10.8%, air
force 22.8%, national guard 13.8%). *Military expenditure as percent of GNP*
(1985): 24.4% (world 6.1%); per capita expenditure U.S.$1,984.

[1]1981 estimate. [2]1983 estimate. [3]July. [4]Import duties less imputed bank service
charges. [5]Detail does not add to total given because of rounding. [6]Urban middle-
income households only. [7]1985–86.

Senegal

Official name: République du Sénégal (Republic of Senegal).
Form of government: republic with one legislative house (National Assembly [120]).
Head of state and government: President.
Capital: Dakar.
Official language: French.
Official religion: none.
Monetary unit: 1 CFA franc (CFAF) = 100 centimes; valuation (Oct. 10, 1988) 1 U.S.$ = CFAF 316.13; 1 £ = CFAF 541.38.

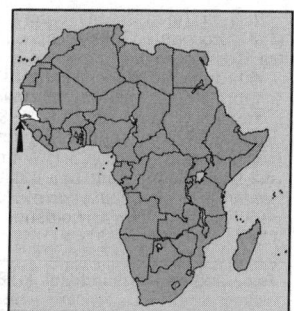

Area and population

Regions	Capitals	area sq mi	area sq km	population 1988 estimate
Dakar	Dakar	212	550	1,608,700
Diourbel	Diourbel	1,683	4,359	558,700
Fatick	Fatick	3,064	7,935	577,600
Kaolack	Kaolack	6,181	16,010	842,100
Kolda	Kolda	8,112	21,011	601,300
Louga	Louga	11,270	29,188	541,900
Saint-Louis	Saint-Louis	17,038	44,127	686,100
Tambacounda	Tambacounda	23,012	59,602	421,800
Thiès	Thiès	2,549	6,601	949,300
Ziguinchor	Ziguinchor	2,834	7,339	399,700
TOTAL		75,955	196,722	7,187,200

Demography

Population (1988): 7,187,000.
Density (1988): persons per sq mi 94.6, persons per sq km 36.5.
Urban–rural (1986): urban 40.0%; rural 60.0%.
Sex distribution (1986): male 49.61%; female 50.39%.
Age breakdown (1986): under 15, 46.5%; 15–29, 25.6%; 30–44, 14.9%; 45–59, 8.4%; 60 and over, 4.6%.
Population projection: (1990) 7,618,000; (2000) 10,193,000.
Doubling time: 23 years.
Ethnic composition (1983): Wolof 36.2%; Fulani (Peul) 17.8%; Serer 17.0%; Tukulor 9.7%; Diola (Jola) 8.1%; Mandingo 6.5%; Soninke 2.1%; Arabs 1.0%; other 1.6%.
Religious affiliation (1980): Sunnī Muslim 91.0%; Roman Catholic 5.6%; traditional beliefs 3.2%; other 0.2%.
Major cities (1985): Dakar 1,382,000; Thiès 156,200; Kaolack 132,400; Ziguinchor 106,500; Saint-Louis 91,500.

Vital statistics

Birth rate per 1,000 population (1984): 48.6 (world avg. 29.0).
Death rate per 1,000 population (1984): 18.5 (world avg. 11.0).
Natural increase rate per 1,000 population (1984): 30.1 (world avg. 18.0).
Total fertility rate (avg. births per childbearing woman; 1984): 7.0.
Marriage rate per 1,000 population: n.a.
Divorce rate per 1,000 population: n.a.
Life expectancy at birth (1984): male 45.0 years; female 48.0 years.
Major causes of death per 100,000 population (officially confirmed transmissible diseases only; 1983): malaria 5.9; meningitis 5.5; tetanus 3.7; tuberculosis of respiratory system 1.9; measles 1.7.

National economy

Budget (1987–88). Revenue: CFAF 488,624,129,000 (indirect taxes 29.4%, direct taxes 10.3%, investment taxes 4.4%, service taxes 1.8%). Expenditures: CFAF 488,624,129,000 (education 12.1%, defense 5.9%, interior 4.4%, health 2.3%, social development 0.6%).
Production (metric tons except as noted). Agriculture, forestry, fishing (1987–88): peanuts (groundnuts) 946,400, millet and sorghum 801,200, sugarcane 725,000, paddy rice 135,800, beans 130,000, corn (maize) 113,600, cotton 36,000, cotton seed 36,000; livestock (number of live animals; 1986) 2,200,000 cattle, 2,202,000 sheep, 1,104,000 goats, 194,000 pigs; roundwood (1985) 4,106,000 cu m; fish catch (1986) 255,381. Mining and quarrying (1987): calcium phosphate 1,874,700; cement 361,800; aluminum phosphate 191,090. Manufacturing (1986): peanut oil 300,000; wheat flour 86,400; nitrogenous fertilizers 62,400; sugar 50,700; soap 29,700; canned fish 26,705; cotton fibres 16,100; carbonated beverages 261,200 hectolitres; beer 197,100 hectolitres; footwear 2,659,900 pairs. Construction (authorized; 1985): residential 228,000 sq m; nonresidential 37,000 sq m. Energy production (consumption): electricity (kW-hr; 1986) 758,000,000 (758,000,000); coal, none (n.a.); crude petroleum (barrels; 1986) none (3,650,000); petroleum products (metric tons; 1986) 476,000 (608,000); natural gas, none (n.a.).
Population economically active (1985): total 3,095,000; activity rate of total population 47.1% (participation rates: ages 15–64, 78.1%; female 41.8%; unemployed [1984] 12.8%[1]).

Price and earnings indexes (1980 = 100)

	1981	1982	1983	1984	1985	1986	1987
Consumer price index	105.9	124.2	138.7	155.1	175.2	186.1	178.4
Hourly earnings index[2]	105.0	105.0	113.6	130.8	137.3	137.3	137.3

Household income and expenditure[3]. Average household size (1980) 4.8; average annual income per household (1975) CFAF 1,105,800 (U.S.$5,160); sources of income: wages and salaries 51.6%, remittances and gifts 17.5%,

pensions, social security, and related benefits 12.5%, other 18.4%; expenditure (1979): food and tobacco 57.5%, housing, maintenance, and utilities 18.4%, clothing 11.9%, transport 5.4%, other 6.8%.
Public debt (external, outstanding; 1986): U.S.$2,456,200,000.
Gross national product (at current market prices; 1986): U.S.$2,840,000,000 (U.S.$420 per capita).

Structure of gross domestic product and labour force

	1985 in value CFAF '000,000,000	1985 % of total value	1982 labour force[4]	1982 % of labour force
Agriculture	218.8	18.4	10,654	9.1
Mining			1,918	1.6
Manufacturing	248.6	20.9	30,736	26.4
Public utilities			3,221	2.8
Construction	81.5	6.9	8,402	7.2
Transportation and communications	87.0	7.3	24,789	21.2
Trade	236.8	20.0	14,648	12.6
Finance	141.2	11.9	7,921	6.8
Services				
Pub. admin., defense	159.1	13.4	14,339	12.3
Other	13.9	1.2	...	...
TOTAL	1,186.9	100.0	116,628	100.0

Tourism (1986): receipts from visitors U.S.$118,000,000; expenditures by nationals abroad U.S.$42,000,000.
Land use (1985): forested 30.9%; meadows and pastures 29.7%; agricultural and under permanent cultivation 27.2%; other 12.2%.

Foreign trade

Balance of trade (current prices)

	1981	1982	1983	1984	1985	1986
CFAF '000,000,000	−156.5	−145.9	−174.4	−203.1	−100.1	−93.0
% of total	36.5%	28.8%	27.5%	30.3%	21.4%	18.7%

Imports (1986): CFAF 295,179,000,000 (crude petroleum and petroleum products 18.1%, agricultural and industrial equipment 16.3%, pharmaceutical and chemical products 4.9%, cereals 4.4%, edible oils 3.3%, milk products 2.9%). *Major import sources:* France 34.2%; Nigeria 9.5%; Italy 6.4%; West Germany 6.2%; United States 4.9%; Côte d'Ivoire 4.9%; The Netherlands 4.2%; Spain 3.9%; Japan 3.4%.
Exports (1986): CFAF 202,166,000,000 (petroleum products 16.8%, crustaceans, mollusks, and shellfish 10.5%, fresh fish 8.9%, phosphates 8.9%, canned fish 7.4%, cotton and cotton fabrics 5.0%, peanut oil cake 2.3%, fresh vegetables 1.4%, fertilizers 0.7%). *Major export destinations:* France 30.8%; The Netherlands 4.5%; Côte d'Ivoire 4.2%; Mauritania 3.7%; Japan 3.1%; Mali 2.9%; Italy 2.9%; United Kingdom 2.7%; Spain 2.5%.

Transport and communications

Transport. Railroads (1984–85): route length (1987–88) 572 mi, 905 km; passenger-mi 18,929,836[5], passenger-km 30,482,827[5]; short ton-mi cargo 316,000,000, metric ton-km cargo 462,000,000. Roads (1987): total length 9,315 mi, 15,000 km (paved 30%). Vehicles (1985): passenger cars 76,142; trucks and buses 37,105. Merchant marine (1987): vessels (100 gross tons and over) 149; total deadweight tonnage 35,991. Air transport[6] (1985): passenger-mi 207,800,000, passenger-km 253,000,000; short ton-mi cargo 12,600,000, metric ton-km cargo 18,400,000; airports (1988) with scheduled flights 12.
Communications. Daily newspapers (1984): total number 1; total circulation 31,000; circulation per 1,000 population 4.9. Radio (1986): total number of receivers 450,000 (1 per 15 persons). Television (1987): total number of receivers 57,000 (1 per 119 persons). Telephones (1985): 33,633 (1 per 192 persons).

Education and health

Education (1985–86)

	schools	teachers	students	student/ teacher ratio
Primary (age 6–11)	2,171	11,513	583,507	41.2
Secondary (age 12–18)	162	2,346[7]	113,653	...
Voc., teacher tr.	5	...	3,515	...
Higher	7	497[7]	13,450	...

Educational attainment (1970). Percent of population age 6 and over having: no formal schooling 95.3%; primary education 3.9%; secondary 0.7%; higher 0.1%. *Literacy* (1980): total population age 15 and over literate 1,274,000 (22.5%); males literate 1,755,000 (31.0%); females literate 804,000 (14.2%).
Health (1982): physicians 470 (1 per 12,987 persons); hospital beds 6,200 (1 per 973 persons); infant mortality rate per 1,000 live births (1986) 110.0.
Food (1984–86): daily per capita caloric intake 2,236 (vegetable products 93%, animal products 7%); (1983) 82% of FAO recommended minimum requirement.

Military

Total active duty personnel (1986–87)[8]: 9,700 (army 87.6%, navy 7.2%, air force 5.2%). *Military expenditure as percent of GNP* (1985): 2.8% (world 6.1%); per capita expenditure U.S.$10.

---

[1]Dakar only. [2]January1; index refers to the *S.M.I.G.* (*salaire minimum interprofessionnel guaranti*), a form of minimum professional wage. [3]Traditional African households in Dakar. [4]Private sector wage earners only. [5]Excludes international travelers. [6]International flights only. [7]1983–84. [8]Confederal armed forces of Senegal and The Gambia.

Seychelles

Official name: Republic of Seychelles (English); République des Seychelles (French); Repiblik Sesel (Creole).
Form of government: unitary single-party republic with one legislative house (People's Assembly [25]).
Head of state and government: President.
Capital: Victoria.
Official languages: English; French; Creole.
Official religion: none.
Monetary unit: 1 Seychelles rupee (SR) = 100 cents; valuation (Oct. 10, 1988) 1 U.S.$ = SR 5.43; 1 £ = SR 9.30.

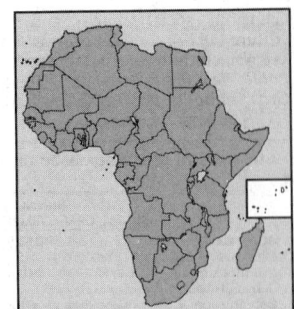

Area and population

Island Groups	Capital	area sq mi	area sq km	population 1984 estimate
Central (Granitic) group				
La Digue and satellites		6	15	2,000
Mahé and satellites	Victoria	61	158	57,400
Praslin and satellites		16	42	4,650
Silhouette		8	20	200
Other islands		2	4	50
Outer (Coralline) islands		83	214	400
TOTAL		175[1]	453	64,700

Demography

Population (1988): 66,900.
Density (1988): persons per sq mi 382.3, persons per sq km 147.7.
Urban–rural (1985): urban 49.6%; rural 50.4%.
Sex distribution (1985): male 49.87%; female 50.13%.
Age breakdown (1985): under 15, 36.5%; 15–29, 32.2%; 30–44, 12.6%; 45–59, 9.7%; 60–74, 6.7%; 75 and over 2.3%.
Population projection: (1990) 67,900; (2000) 73,400.
Doubling time: 39 years.
Ethnic composition (1983): Seychellois Creole (mixture of Asian, African, and European) 89.1%; Indian 4.7%; Malagasy 3.1%; Chinese 1.6%; English 1.5%.
Religious affiliation (1977): Roman Catholic 90.9%; other Christian (mostly Anglican) 7.5%; Hindu 0.7%; other 0.9%.
Major city (1977): Victoria 23,012.

Vital statistics

Birth rate per 1,000 population (1987): 25.4 (world avg. 26.0); (1985) legitimate 29.8%; illegitimate 70.2%.
Death rate per 1,000 population (1987): 7.6 (world avg. 9.9).
Natural increase rate per 1,000 population (1987): 17.8 (world avg. 16.1).
Total fertility rate (avg. births per childbearing woman; 1985): 3.3.
Marriage rate per 1,000 population (1984): 6.0.
Divorce rate per 1,000 population (1985): 0.7.
Life expectancy at birth (1980–85): male 66.2 years; female 73.5 years.
Major causes of death per 100,000 population (1985): diseases of the circulatory system 200.8, of which cerebrovascular disease 69.0; malignant neoplasms (cancers) 115.0; diseases of the respiratory system 64.4, of which pneumonia 42.9; diseases of the digestive system 35.2; accidents and adverse effects 55.2.

National economy

Budget (1987). Revenue: SR 639,300,000 (customs taxes and duties 47.2%; income taxes 21.5%, of which personal 13.0%, companies 8.5%; service on external debt 18.9%; administrative fees 11.2%; dividends and interest 11.8%; rents and royalties 3.3%). Expenditures: SR 641,800,000 (education and information 22.6%; defense 9.9%; health and social services 7.2%; tourism and transport 5.1%; national development 4.5%).
Gross national product (at current market prices; 1986): U.S.$203,800,000 (U.S.$3,100 per capita).

Structure of gross domestic product and labour force

	1986 in value SR '000,000	1986 % of total value	1985 labour force[2]	1985 % of labour force
Agriculture	77.3	5.9	2,282	9.5
Mining and manufacturing	116.3	8.9	1,672	7.0
Construction	76.1	5.8	1,063	4.4
Public utilities	34.7	2.6	633	2.6
Transportation and communications	572.4[3]	43.6[3]	2,256	9.4
Trade	111.0	8.5	3,054	12.8
Finance	105.8	8.1	814	3.4
Public admin., defense	184.0	14.0 }	3,587	15.0
Services	33.8	2.6 }		
Other	...	...	8,582[4]	35.8
TOTAL	1,311.4	100.0	23,943	100.0[1]

Tourism (1986): receipts from visitors U.S.$56,000,000; expenditures by nationals abroad U.S.$10,000,000.
Public debt (external, outstanding; 1986): U.S.$67,300,000.

Production (metric tons except as noted). Agriculture, forestry, fishing (1987): coconuts 17,000[5], copra 2,866, bananas 2,000[5], cinnamon bark 847, tea 109; livestock (number of live animals; 1986) 15,000 pigs, 4,000 goats, 3,000 cattle, 185,200 chickens; fish catch (1986) 4,635, of which jack 1,400, snapper 580, kawakawa 323, mackerel 280. Mining and quarrying (1985): guano 4,500. Manufacturing (1987): beer and stout 46,500 hectolitres; soft drinks 44,120 hectolitres; cigarettes 67,800,000 units. Energy production (consumption): electricity (kW-hr; 1987) 70,400,000 (70,400,000); coal, none (n.a.); petroleum, none (n.a.); natural gas, none (n.a.).
Population economically active (1985): total 27,700; activity rate of total population 42.4% (participation rates: ages 15 and over 66.8%; female 42.4%; unemployed 20.6%).

Price and earnings indexes (1980 = 100)

	1981	1982	1983	1984	1985	1986	1987
Consumer price index	110.6	109.6	116.3	121.0	122.0	122.3	125.4
Monthly earnings index	111.0	120.2	129.5	132.3	134.2	...	...

Household income and expenditure. Average household size (1982) 4.8; average annual income per household (1978) SR 18,480 (U.S.$2,658); sources of income: wages and salaries 77.2%, self-employment 3.8%, transfer payments 3.2%; expenditure (1983–84): food and beverages 53.9%, housing 13.6%, energy and water 9.1%, household and personal goods 6.6%, transportation 6.4%, clothing and footwear 4.2%, recreation 1.4%.
Land use (1985): forested 18.5%; agricultural and under permanent cultivation 22.2%; built-on, wasteland, and other 59.3%.

Foreign trade

Balance of trade (current prices)

	1982	1983	1984	1985	1986	1987
SR '000,000	−457.6	−379.3	−356.6	−422.1	−447.2	−511.6
% of total	69.6%	58.0%	49.6%	52.0%	66.1%	67.3%

Imports (1987): SR 635,806,000 (manufactured goods 31.1%, of which textile yarn, fabrics, and finished articles 3.8%, nonmetallic mineral products 3.6%; machinery and transport equipment 24.6%, of which transport equipment 6.2%, telecommunications equipment 5.1%; food, beverages, and tobacco 21.0%; petroleum and petroleum products 14.6%; chemicals and related products 6.5%). *Major import sources:* United Kingdom 20.2%; France 14.3%; South Africa 13.0%; Yemen (Aden) 12.8%; Singapore 7.5%; Japan 5.5%; The Netherlands 3.3%; United States 2.9%; Hong Kong 2.8%; West Germany 2.5%.
Exports (1987): SR 124,252,000[6] (petroleum products 58.1%[7]; canned tuna 16.7%; fish 6.4%; copra 2.6%; food, beverages, and tobacco 2.6%[7]; cinnamon bark 1.3%). *Major export destinations*[8] (1984): Pakistan 38.6%; Japan 26.1%; Réunion 14.9%; United Kingdom 4.9%; France 2.7%.

Transport and communications

Transport. Railroads: none. Roads (1987): total length 164 mi, 269 km (paved 61%). Vehicles (1985): passenger cars 3,531; trucks and buses 1,277. Merchant marine (1987): vessels (100 gross tons and over) 6; total deadweight tonnage 2,491. Air transport (1987): passenger arrivals 78,000, passenger departures 77,000; metric ton cargo unloaded 1,149, metric ton cargo loaded 417; airports (1988) with scheduled flights 6.
Communications. Daily newspapers (1986): total number 2; total circulation 6,800; circulation per 1,000 population 103.6. Radio (1987): total number of receivers 16,000 (1 per 4.1 persons). Television (1987): total number of receivers 5,000 (1 per 13.1 persons). Telephones (1985): 11,333 (1 per 5.8 persons).

Education and health

Education (1988)

	schools[5]	teachers	students	student/ teacher ratio
Primary (age 6–15)	26	702	14,522	20.7
Secondary (age 16–18)	4	162	2,643	16.3
Voc., teacher tr.	1	147	1,405	9.6

Educational attainment (1977). Percent of population age 15 and over having: no formal schooling 13.7%; primary education 50.1%; some secondary 32.4%; complete secondary 1.4%; postsecondary 1.8%. *Literacy* (1971): total population age 15 and over literate 17,066 (57.3%); males literate 8,103 (54.9%); females literate 8,963 (59.6%).
Health (1987): physicians[9] 37 (1 per 1,794 persons); hospital beds 373 (1 per 178 persons); infant mortality rate per 1,000 live births 18.4.
Food (1981–83): daily per capita caloric intake, 2,324 (vegetable products 84%, animal products 16%); FAO recommended minimum requirement, n.a.

Military

Total active duty personnel (1988): 1,300 (army 76.9%, navy 15.4%, air force 7.7%). *Military expenditure as percent of GNP* (1984): 5.6% (world 5.9%); per capita expenditure U.S.$125.

[1]Detail does not add to total given because of rounding. [2]Excludes self-employed and domestic workers. [3]Includes import duties. [4]Includes 5,713 unemployed. [5]1986. [6]Includes SR 88,494,000 of reexports. [7]Items reexported. [8]Domestic export only. [9]Includes dentists.

Sierra Leone

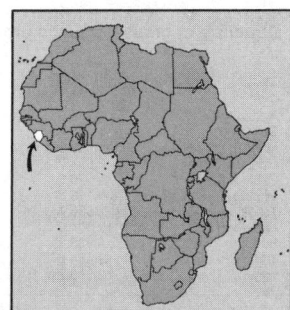

Official name: Republic of
Sierra Leone.
Form of government: a unitary
single-party republic with one
legislative house (House of
Representatives [127[1]]).
Head of state and government:
President.
Capital: Freetown.
Official language: English.
Official religion: none.
Monetary unit: 1 leone (Le) = 100
cents; valuation (Oct. 10, 1988)
1 U.S.$ = Le 37.01; 1 £ = Le 63.38.

Area and population		area		population
Provinces				1985
Districts	**Capitals**	sq mi	sq km	census[2]
Eastern Province	Kenema	6,005	15,553	960,551
Kailahun	Kailahun	1,490	3,859	233,839
Kenema	Kenema	2,337	6,053	337,055
Kono	Sefadu	2,178	5,641	389,657
Northern Province	Makeni	13,875	35,936	1,262,226
Bombali	Makeni	3,083	7,985	315,914
Kambia	Kambia	1,200	3,108	186,231
Koinaduga	Kabala	4,680	12,121	183,286
Port Loko	Port Loko	2,208	5,719	329,344
Tonkolili	Magburaka	2,704	7,003	247,451
Southern Province	Bo	7,604	19,694	740,510
Bo	Bo	2,015	5,219	268,671
Bonthe (incl. Sherbro)	Bonthe	1,339	3,468	105,007
Moyamba	Moyamba	2,665	6,902	250,514
Pujehun	Pujehun	1,585	4,105	116,318
Western Area	Freetown	215	557	554,243
TOTAL		27,699	71,740	3,517,530

Demography

Population (1988): 3,883,000.
Density (1988): persons per sq mi 140.1, persons per sq km 54.1.
Urban–rural (1985): urban 28.3%; rural 71.7%.
Sex distribution (1985): male 49.01%; female 50.99%.
Age breakdown (1985): under 15, 41.4%; 15–29, 26.1%; 30–44, 17.1%; 45–59, 10.3%; 60–74, 4.5%; 75 and over, 0.6%.
Population projection: (1990) 4,033,000; (2000) 4,874,000.
Doubling time: 40 years.
Ethnic composition (1983): Mende 34.6%; Temne 31.7%; Limba 8.4%; Kono 5.2%; Bullom 3.7%; Fulani 3.7%; Koranko 3.5%; Yalunka 3.5%; Kissi 2.3%; other 3.4%.
Religious affiliation (1980): traditional beliefs 51.5%; Sunnī Muslim 39.4%; Protestant 4.7%; Roman Catholic 2.2%; Anglican 1.2%; other 1.0%.
Major cities (1985): Freetown 469,776; Koidu-New Sembehun 80,000; Bo 26,000; Kenema 13,000; Makeni 12,000.

Vital statistics

Birth rate per 1,000 population (1980–85): 47.4 (world avg. 29.0); legitimate, n.a.; illegitimate, n.a.
Death rate per 1,000 population (1980–85): 29.7 (world avg. 11.0).
Natural increase rate per 1,000 population (1980–85): 17.7 (world avg. 18.0).
Total fertility rate (avg. births per childbearing woman; 1980–85): 6.1.
Marriage rate per 1,000 population: n.a.
Divorce rate per 1,000 population: n.a.
Life expectancy at birth (1980–85): male 46.7 years; female 50.0 years.
Major causes of death per 100,000 population: n.a.; however, the major diseases are malaria, tuberculosis, leprosy, whooping cough, measles, tetanus, and diarrhea.

National economy

Budget (1984–85). Revenue: Le 282,935,000 (import duties 36.9%, direct taxes 27.1%, excise taxes 22.0%, export duties 2.2%, other including grants 11.8%). Expenditures: Le 350,795,000 (public debt charges 33.9%, education and social welfare 25.7%, general administration 20.5%, health 8.9%, construction and development 8.4%, defense 7.0%, police and justice 6.9%, agriculture development 4.6%).
Public debt (external, outstanding; 1986): U.S.$459,100,000.
Production (metric tons except as noted). Agriculture, forestry, fishing (1986): rice 525,000, cassava 113,000, sugarcane 70,000, palm oil 44,000, pulses 33,000, palm kernels 30,000, millet 23,000, taros 22,000, sorghum 20,000, peanuts (groundnuts) 18,000, sweet potatoes 13,000, coffee 11,000, corn (maize) 9,000, cocoa beans 9,000; livestock (number of live animals) 333,000 cattle, 332,000 sheep, 175,000 goats, 46,000 pigs, 5,000,000 chickens; roundwood (1985) 7,774,000 cu m; fish catch (1985) 53,000. Mining and quarrying (1986): bauxite 1,242,200; rutile (a titanium ore) 97,101; iron ore 398,000[3]; diamonds 62,453 carats. Manufacturing (1984): salt 19,200; nails 2,300; paint 1,140 hectolitres; beer and stout 35,670 hectolitres; plastic footwear 497,000 pairs[4]; cigarettes 1,346,000 units. Construction (value added in Le; 1981): 56,000,000. Energy production (consumption): electricity (kW-hr; 1986) 184,000,000 (184,000,000); coal, none (n.a.); crude petroleum (barrels; 1986) none (1,759,000); petroleum products (metric tons; 1986) 220,000 (174,000); natural gas, none (n.a.).
Household income and expenditure. Average household size (1983) 4.7; average annual income per household (1984): U.S.$320; sources of income (1984): self-employment 61.6%, wages and salaries 27.9%, other 10.5%; ex-penditure (1984): food, beverages, and tobacco 55.1%, clothing and footwear 12.9%, transport and communications 9.2%, furniture, furnishings, and household durable goods 8.0%, housing 7.4%, recreation, entertainment, and education 3.8%, health 1.3%.
Tourism (1986): receipts from visitors U.S.$3,000,000; expenditures by nationals abroad U.S.$3,000,000.
Gross national product (at current market prices; 1986): U.S.$1,170,000,000 (U.S.$310 per capita).

Structure of gross domestic product and labour force				
	1982–83		1983–84	
	in value Le '000,000	% of total value	labour force[5]	% of labour force
Agriculture	1,062.1	38.9	5,835	7.9
Mining	140.5	5.1	6,075	8.2
Manufacturing	181.9	6.7	8,046	10.9
Construction	71.0	2.6	8,986	12.2
Public utilities	14.4	0.5	2,134	2.9
Transportation and communications	468.9	17.2	7,211	9.8
Trade	295.0	10.8	6,161	8.3
Finance	} 495.7	} 18.2	23,821	32.2
Pub. admin., defense				
Services				
Other			5,639[6]	7.6[6]
TOTAL	2,729.5	100.0	73,908	100.0

Population economically active (1985): total 1,352,000; activity rate of total population 36.9% (participation rates: ages 15–64 62.9%; female 33.7%; unemployed [registered; 1984] 7.6%).

Price index (1980 = 100)							
	1981	1982	1983	1984	1985	1986	1987
Consumer price index	123.3	156.5	263.8	439.4	776.0	1,403.5	3,911.4

Land use (1985): forested 29.2%; meadows and pastures 30.8%; agricultural and under permanent cultivation 24.9%; other 15.1%.

Foreign trade

Balance of trade (current prices)						
	1982	1983	1984	1985	1986	1987
Le '000,000	−231.5	−85.0	−46.7	−249.0	+172.4	+962.5
% of total	45.8%	17.4%	5.9%	18.7%	4.6%	11.5%

Imports (1985): Le 788,654,000 (food and live animals 29.8%; machinery and transport equipment 23.3%; minerals, fuels, and lubricants 21.3%; basic manufactured goods 13.4%; chemicals 4.2%). *Major import sources* (1984): United Kingdom 11.4%; West Germany 11.0%; Japan 6.1%; The Netherlands 5.0%; France 4.9%; United States 4.6%; China 2.3%.
Exports (1985): Le 649,266,000 (rutile 21.8%; coffee 20.3%; diamonds 18.8%[7]; bauxite 17.4%; cacao 15.6%; gold 4.2%). *Major export destinations:* The Netherlands 30.9%; United Kingdom 14.6%; West Germany 11.2%; United States 9.5%.

Transport and communications

Transport. Railroads (1985): length 52 mi, 84 km. Roads (1980): total length 4,635 mi, 7,459 km (paved 16%). Vehicles (1985): passenger cars 23,500; trucks and buses 6,763[3]. Merchant marine (1987): vessels (100 gross tons and over) 34; total deadweight tonnage 3,382. Air transport[8] (1984): passenger-mi 75,698,000, passenger-km 121,825,000; short ton-mi cargo 1,337,000, metric ton-km cargo 1,952,000; airports (1988) with scheduled flights 1.
Communications. Daily newspapers (1986): total number 1; total circulation 10,000; circulation per 1,000 population 2.7. Radio (1986): total number of receivers 225,000 (1 per 17 persons). Television (1987): total number of receivers 25,000 (1 per 152 persons). Telephones (1986): 14,900 (1 per 253 persons).

Education and health

Education (1984–85)				
	schools	teachers	students	student/ teacher ratio
Primary (age 5–11)	1,219	10,451	350,160	33.5
Secondary (age 12–18)	171	3,829	81,879	21.4
Voc., teacher tr.	12	406	4,774	11.8
Higher	2	296	2,445	8.3

Educational attainment (1974). Percent of population age 5 and over having: no formal schooling 81.3%; primary education 12.1%; secondary 5.9%; higher 0.7%. *Literacy* (1980): total population age 15 and over literate 460,300 (23.6%); males literate 294,500 (31.2%); females literate 165,800 (16.5%).
Health: physicians 197 (1 per 17,906 persons); hospital beds 4,754 (1 per 742 persons); infant mortality rate per 1,000 live births (1984) 134.0.
Food (1984–86): daily per capita caloric intake 1,868 (vegetable products 96%, animal products 4%); (1983) 91% of FAO recommended minimum requirement.

Military

Total active duty personnel (1987): 3,100 (army 96.8%, navy 3.2%, air force, none). *Military expenditure as percent of GNP* (1985): 0.9% (world 6.1%); per capita expenditure U.S.$3.

[1]Maximum; includes up to 22 nonelective seats. [2]Preliminary. [3]1984. [4]1983. [5]Registered employment only. [6]Registered unemployed. [7]It is estimated that smuggling accounts for more than 95% of Sierra Leone's diamond exports. [8]International flights only.

Singapore

Official name: Hsin-chia-p'o
Kung-ho-kuo (Mandarin Chinese);
Republik Singapura (Malay);
Singapore Kudiyarasu (Tamil);
Republic of Singapore (English).
Form of government: unitary multiparty
republic with one legislative house
(Parliament [79]).
Chief of state: President.
Head of government: Prime Minister.
Capital: Singapore.
Official languages: Chinese; Malay;
Tamil; English.
Official religion: none.
Monetary unit: 1 Singapore dollar
(S$) = 100 cents; valuation (Oct. 10,
1988) 1 U.S.$ = S$2.04; 1 £ = S$3.49.

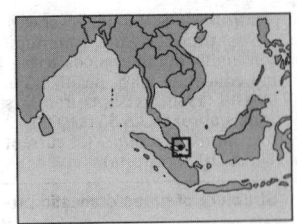

Area and population	area		population
	sq mi	sq km	1984 estimate
Census areas[1]			
Central city area	3	8	157,000
City periphery	17	46	942,800
North	7	19	228,100
Northeast	3	9	301,500
West	7	18	413,200
Suburbs	49	127	754,700
East	7	19	195,000
North	13	34	309,900
West	29	74	249,800
Outlying areas	169	437	674,600
East	46	118	301,100
North	53	137	177,500
West	70	182	196,000
TOTAL	240[2]	622[2]	2,529,100

Demography

Population (1988): 2,641,000.
Density (1988): persons per sq mi 11,004.2, persons per sq km 4,246.0.
Urban–rural (1987): urban 100.0%.
Sex distribution (1987): male 50.91%; female 49.09%.
Age breakdown (1987): under 15, 23.4%; 15–29, 30.3%; 30–44, 25.0%; 45–59, 13.1%; 60 and over, 8.2%.
Population projection: (1990) 2,699,000; (2000) 3,030,000.
Doubling time: 59 years.
Ethnic composition (1987): Chinese 76.1%; Malay 15.1%; Indian[3] 6.5%; other 2.3%.
Religious affiliation (1980): Taoist 29.3%; Buddhist 26.7%; Muslim 16.3%; Christian 10.3%; Hindu 3.6%; nonreligious 13.2%; other 0.6%.
Major cities: Singapore is a unitary city-state having no separately defined cities within its borders.

Vital statistics

Birth rate per 1,000 population (1987): 16.8 (world avg. 26.0).
Death rate per 1,000 population (1987): 5.0 (world avg. 9.9).
Natural increase rate per 1,000 population (1987): 11.8 (world avg. 16.1).
Total fertility rate (avg. births per childbearing woman; 1987): 1.5.
Marriage rate per 1,000 population (1987): 9.0.
Divorce rate per 1,000 population (1985): 0.9.
Life expectancy at birth (1987): male 70.0 years; female 76.3 years.
Major causes of death per 100,000 population (1986): diseases of the circulatory system 173.3, of which acute myocardial infarction 41.5; malignant neoplasms (cancers) 111.6; diseases of the respiratory system 76.3, of which pneumonia 21.9; accidents, poisoning, and violence 39.6.

National economy

Budget (1986–87). Revenue: S$14,552,911,000 (premiums on land sales 44.8%; income tax 17.5%; interest and dividends 12.5%; import and excise duties 6.0%; property tax 5.8%; sales of goods and services 4.3%; motor vehicle taxes 4.0%). Expenditures: S$22,193,618,000 (social welfare and housing 42.4%; defense, justice, and police 12.0%; transport and communication 9.2%; education 8.1%; agricultural, industrial, and commercial development 4.6%; general services 4.0%; health 2.4%).
Tourism (1985): receipts from visitors U.S.$1,754,000,000; expenditures by nationals abroad U.S.$615,000,000.
Production (metric tons except as noted). Agriculture, forestry, fishing (1986): vegetables 21,000, fruits 5,000; livestock (number of live animals) 750,000 pigs, 2,000 goats, 1,000,000 ducks, 9,000,000 chickens; fish catch (1987) 15,096. Mining and quarrying (value added in S$; 1987): granite 63,300,000. Manufacturing (value added in S$; 1987): electronic products and components 4,931,300,000; transport equipment 1,101,000,000; nonelectrical machinery 896,400,000; paints, pharmaceuticals, and chemical products 856,800,000; fabricated metal products except machinery and equipment 781,000,000; petroleum refining and petroleum products 779,100,000; industrial chemicals 709,500,000. Construction (1985): residential 9,222,000 sq m; nonresidential 2,202,000 sq m. Energy production (consumption): electricity (kW-hr; 1987) 11,813,800,000 (10,616,600,000); coal, none (none); crude petroleum (barrels; 1986) none (255,890,000); petroleum products (metric tons; 1986) 27,807,000 (7,469,000); natural gas, none (none).
Land use (1985): forested 5.2%; agricultural and under permanent cultivation 8.8%; built-up area and other 86.0%.
Gross national product (1986): U.S.$19,160,000,000 (U.S.$7,410 per capita).

Structure of gross domestic product and labour force				
	1987			
	in value S$'000,000[4]	% of total value	labour force[5]	% of labour force
Agriculture	234.0	0.5	10,380	0.9
Quarrying	93.4	0.2	634	0.1
Manufacturing	11,650.5	27.0	318,863	26.7
Construction	2,854.2	6.6	91,466	7.7
Public utilities	926.6	2.2	7,208	0.6
Transp. and commun.	6,173.5	14.3	120,957	10.1
Trade	7,336.7	17.0	279,424	23.4
Finance	12,304.9	28.6	105,729	8.9
Services	4,986.1	11.6	256,684	21.5
Other	–3,464.6[6]	–8.0[6]	1,574	0.1
TOTAL	43,095.3	100.0	1,192,919	100.0

Population economically active (1986): total 1,228,570; activity rate of total population 47.5% (participation rates: ages 15–64, 65.9%; female 37.1%; unemployed 4.2%).

Price and earnings indexes (1980 = 100)							
	1981	1982	1983	1984	1985	1986	1987
Consumer price index	108.3	112.4	113.8	116.8	117.3	115.7	116.3
Weekly earnings index	113.8	128.3	137.2	149.0	156.9	...	...

Household income and expenditure. Average household size (1984) 3.9; income per household S$20,800 (U.S.$9,700); sources of income (1977–78): wages and salaries 75.4%, self-employment 18.7%, transfer payments 2.0%, other 3.9%; expenditure (1984): food and tobacco 25.0%, transportation and communications 13.9%, recreation and education 11.0%, housing 9.6%, furniture and household equipment 9.2%, clothing and footwear 8.1%, health 3.1%.
Public debt (external, outstanding; 1986): U.S.$2,120,100,000.

Foreign trade[7]

Balance of trade (current prices)						
	1982	1983	1984	1985	1986	1987
S$'000,000	–12,361	–10,140	–6,497	–4,521	–3,384	–4,265
% of total	12.2%	9.9%	6.0%	4.3%	3.3%	3.4%

Imports (1987): S$68,415,200,000 (crude petroleum 12.5%, petroleum products 5.8%, office machines 4.7%, telecommunications apparatus 4.6%, electric power machinery 3.7%, woven textile fabrics 3.2%, scientific and optical instruments 2.3%, musical instruments 2.2%). *Major import sources:* Japan 20.5%; United States 14.7%; Malaysia 13.9%; Taiwan 4.6%; China 4.3%; Saudi Arabia 4.1%; West Germany 3.4%; United Kingdom 3.2%.
Exports (1987): S$60,265,700,000 (petroleum products 16.0%, office machines 11.7%, telecommunications apparatus 8.6%, clothing 3.5%, crude rubber 2.5%, electrical circuit apparatus 2.3%, scientific and optical instruments 1.7%). *Major export destinations:* United States 24.3%; Malaysia 14.2%; Japan 9.0%; Hong Kong 6.3%; Thailand 4.2%; West Germany 3.2%; United Kingdom 2.8%; Australia 2.7%; Taiwan 2.7%.

Transport and communications

Transport. Railroads (1987): length 16 mi, 26 km. Roads (1987): total length 1,643 mi, 2,644 km (paved 95%). Vehicles (1987): passenger cars 236,120; trucks and buses 113,671. Merchant marine (1987): vessels (100 gross tons and over) 700; total deadweight tonnage 11,924,578. Air transport (1986): passenger-mi 14,212,000,000, passenger-km 22,872,000,000; short ton-mi cargo 791,421,000, metric ton-km cargo 1,155,456,000; airports (1988) 1.
Communications. Daily newspapers (1986): total number 7; total circulation 697,500; circulation per 1,000 population 270. Radio (1986): 593,000 receivers (1 per 4.4 persons). Television (1987): 516,677 receivers (1 per 5.1 persons). Telephones (1987): 1,115,722 (1 per 2.3 persons).

Education and health

Education (1987)	schools	teachers	students	student/ teacher ratio
Primary (age 6–13)	298	11,259	280,889	24.9
Secondary (age 12–18)	157	9,301	201,125	21.6
Voc., teacher tr.	18	2,029	27,001	13.3
Higher	6	3,961	44,746	11.3

Educational attainment (1980). Percent of population age 25 and over having: no schooling and without primary six certificate 43.7%; primary education 38.3%; secondary 14.6%; postsecondary 3.4%. *Literacy* (1980): total population age 15 and over literate 1,459,828 (82.9%); males literate 818,864 (91.6%); females literate 640,964 (74.0%).
Health (1985): physicians 2,631 (1 per 972 persons); hospital beds 9,866 (1 per 259 persons); infant mortality rate per 1,000 live births (1987) 7.4.
Food (1984–86): daily per capita caloric intake 2,854 (vegetable products 73%, animal products 27%); (1983) 115% of FAO recommended minimum requirement.

Military

Total active duty personnel (1987): 55,500 (army 81.1%, navy 8.1%, air force 10.8%). *Military expenditure as percent of GNP* (1985): 6.2% (world 6.1%); per capita expenditure U.S.$468.

[1]The census areas have no administrative function. [2]Includes 2 sq mi (4 sq km) not distributable by census areas. [3]Includes Sri Lankan. [4]At prices of 1985. [5]Employed only. [6]Less imputed bank service charges. [7]Import figures are f.o.b. (free on board) in balance trade and c.i.f. (cost, insurance, and freight) for commodities and trading partners.

Solomon Islands

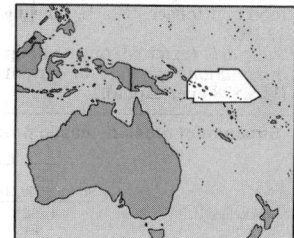

Official name: Solomon Islands.
Form of government: parliamentary state with one legislative house (National Parliament [38]).
Chief of state: British Monarch represented by governor-general.
Head of government: Prime Minister.
Capital: Honiara.
Official language: English.
Official religion: none.
Monetary unit: 1 Solomon Islands dollar (SI$) = 100 cents; valuation (Oct. 10, 1988) 1 U.S.$ = SI$2.15; 1 £ = SI$3.68.

Area and population

Provinces	Capitals	area sq mi	area sq km	population 1986 census
Central Islands	Tulagi	497	1,286	18,457
Guadalcanal	Honiara	2,060	5,336	49,831
Isabel	Buala	1,597	4,136	14,616
Makira	Kira Kira	1,231	3,188	21,796
Malaita	Auki	1,631	4,225	80,032
Temotu	Santa Cruz	334	865	14,781
Western	Gizo	3,595	9,312	55,250
Capital Territory				
Honiara	—	8	22	30,413
TOTAL		10,954[1]	28,370	285,176

Demography

Population (1988): 301,000.
Density (1988): persons per sq mi 27.5, persons per sq km 10.6.
Urban–rural (1986): urban 15.7%; rural 84.3%.
Sex distribution (1986): male 51.76%; female 48.24%.
Age breakdown (1986): under 15, 47.3%; 15–29, 25.7%; 30–44, 13.9%; 45–59, 8.1%; 60 and over, 4.9%[1].
Population projection: (1990) 323,000; (2000) 455,000.
Doubling time: 22 years.
Ethnic composition (1986): Melanesian 94.2%; Polynesian 3.7%; other Pacific Islanders 1.4%; European 0.4%; Asian 0.2%; other 0.1%.
Religious affiliation (1986): Christian 96.7%, of which Protestant 77.5%, Roman Catholic 19.2%; Baha'i 0.4%; traditional beliefs 0.2%; other and no religion 2.7%.
Major cities (1986)[2]: Honiara 30,499; Gizo 3,727; Auki 3,262; Kira Kira 2,585; Buala 1,913.

Vital statistics

Birth rate per 1,000 population (1980–84): 42.0 (world avg. 29.0).
Death rate per 1,000 population (1980–84): 10.0 (world avg. 11.0).
Natural increase rate per 1,000 population (1980–84): 32.0 (world avg. 18.0).
Total fertility rate (avg. births per childbearing woman; 1980–84): 6.4.
Marriage rate per 1,000 population: n.a.
Divorce rate per 1,000 population: n.a.
Life expectancy at birth (1980–84): male 59.9 years; female 61.4 years.
Major causes of death per 100,000 population: n.a.; however, major diseases include malaria, tuberculosis, and leprosy[3].

National economy

Budget (1986). Revenue: SI$82,872,100 (import duties 31.1%; foreign grants 30.6%; income taxes 21.3%; export duties 8.3%; non-tax revenue 6.5%). Expenditures: SI$96,057,000 (transportation and communications 18.1%; agriculture 17.5%; education 15.6%; general public services 14.4%; transfers to provinces 11.4%; health 7.0%; housing and community amenities 2.2%).
Public debt (external, outstanding; 1986): U.S.$68,800,000.
Tourism (1987): tourist arrivals 7,543.
Gross national product (at current market prices; 1986): U.S.$150,000,000 (U.S.$530 per capita).

Structure of gross domestic product and labour force

	1986 in value SI$'000,000	% of total value	labour force[4]	% of labour force
Agriculture	...	5	18,031	46.0
Mining	...	...	703	1.8
Manufacturing	...	...	2,273	5.8
Construction	...	...	2,206	5.6
Public utilities	...	...	426	1.1
Transportation and communications	...	...	2,014	5.1
Trade	...	...	3,300	8.4
Finance	...	...	550	1.4
Pub. admin., defense	...	... }	9,378	23.9
Services	...	...		
Other	...	...	329	0.8
TOTAL	202.2[6]	100.0	39,210	100.0[1]

Household income and expenditure. Average household size (1986) 6.4; average annual income per household (1983) SI$1,010[7] (U.S.$1,160); sources of income (1983): wages and salaries 74.1%, self-employment, remittances, gifts, and other assistance 25.9%; expenditure (1984)[8]: food 47.0%, housing 15.5%, drink and tobacco 9.5%, clothing 5.0%, transportation 1.1%.

Population economically active (1986): total 39,210[4]; activity rate of total population 13.7% (participation rates: over age 14, 24.9%; female 25.6%; unemployed, n.a.).

Price and earnings indexes (1980 = 100)

	1981	1982	1983	1984	1985	1986	1987
Consumer price index	116.4	131.5	140.5	155.9	170.9	193.1	219.3[9]
Annual earnings index[7]	108.0	118.8	133.8	151.9	164.1	174.8	188.2

Production (metric tons except as noted). Agriculture, forestry, fishing (1986): coconuts 253,000, sweet potatoes 51,000, copra 31,700, taro 23,000, yams 19,000, palm oil 14,600, paddy rice 2,400, cocoa 1,900; livestock (number of live animals) 50,000 pigs, 23,000 cattle; roundwood 471,300 cu m; fish catch 44,207. Mining and quarrying (1983): gold 34 kilograms; silver 8 kilograms. Manufacturing (1986): processed fish 44,042; milled rice 2,282; sawn timber 37,400 cu m; other major industries include soap and tobacco manufacturing, weaving, wood carving, fibreglass products, boatbuilding, and leather working. Construction (gross value in SI$; 1980): residential 1,858,000; nonresidential 693,000. Energy production (consumption): electricity (kW-hr; 1986) 30,000,000 (30,000,000); coal, none (n.a.); petroleum products (metric tons; 1986) none (44,000); natural gas, none (n.a.).
Land use (1985): forested 93.0%; meadows and pastures 1.4%; agricultural and under permanent cultivation 2.0%; other 3.6%.

Foreign trade

Balance of trade (current prices)

SI$'000	1982	1983	1984	1985	1986	1987
	−929	+592	+34,725	+1,142	+10,562	−6,646
% of total	0.8%	0.4%	17.2%	0.6%	4.8%	2.5%

Imports (1987): SI$134,944,000 (machinery and transport equipment 29.1%; manufactured goods 20.5%; food 15.0%; mineral fuels and lubricants 14.7%; chemicals 6.7%). *Major import sources:* Australia 41.4%; Japan 19.1%; Singapore 9.2%; New Zealand 7.9%; United Kingdom 4.4%; China 3.5%; United States 2.9%; Hong Kong 2.4%; Papua New Guinea 1.9%.
Exports (1987): SI$128,298,000 (fish products 41.0%; wood products 29.0%; copra 8.0%; cocoa beans 7.4%; palm oil products 5.9%). *Major export destinations:* Japan 35.6%; United Kingdom 13.8%; Thailand 12.2%; South Korea 6.0%; United States 5.3%; West Germany 4.2%; Australia 3.7%; Fiji 2.7%; Belgium 2.2%; The Netherlands 2.0%; Puerto Rico 2.0%.

Transport and communications

Transport. Railroads: none. Roads[10] (1984): total length 1,300 mi, 2,100 km (paved 12%). Vehicles (1986): passenger cars 1,350; trucks and buses 1,708. Merchant marine (1987): vessels (100 gross tons and over) 29; total deadweight tonnage 5,350. Air transport (1984)[11]: passenger-mi 6,852,000, passenger-km 11,027,000; short ton-mi cargo 25,000, metric ton-km cargo 37,000; airports (1988) with scheduled flights 21.
Communications. Daily newspapers[12] (1987): none. Radio (1986): total number of receivers 60,000 (1 per 4.7 persons). Television (1986): none. Telephones (1987): 4,983 (1 per 58 persons).

Education and health

Education (1986)

	schools	teachers	students	student/teacher ratio
Primary (age 7–12)	430	1,849	39,563	21.4
Secondary (age 13–18)	20	276	5,553	20.1
Voc., teacher tr.[13]	2	63	1,142	18.1
Higher	—	—	—	—

Educational attainment (1986)[14]. Percent of population age 25 and over having: no schooling 44.4%; primary education 46.2%; secondary 6.8%; higher 2.6%. *Literacy* (1976): total population age 15 and over literate 55,500 (54.1%); males 33,600 (62.4%); females 21,900 (44.9%).
Health (1986): physicians 38 (1 per 7,418 persons); hospital beds 1,479 (1 per 191 persons); infant mortality rate per 1,000 live births (1982) 46.
Food (1983–85): daily per capita caloric intake 2,085 (vegetable products 90%, animal products 10%); (1983) 80% of FAO recommended minimum requirement.

Military

Total active duty personnel: no military forces are maintained, but a police force of 475 provides internal security.

---

[1]Detail does not add to total given because of rounding. [2]Ward populations. [3]Reported cases of these diseases in 1986 were: malaria 72,108, tuberculosis 337, and leprosy 260. [4]Population working for money only. [5]35–40% of the GDP is generated by subsistence agriculture. [6]Provisional. [7]Public service earnings. [8]Consumer price index components. [9]October. [10]Includes 500 mi (800 km) of privately maintained roads mainly for plantation use. [11]Solair only. [12]In 1985 there were two weekly newspapers with a combined circulation of 6,700. [13]1984. [14]Indigenous population only.

Somalia

Official name: Jamhuuriyadda
Dimuqraadiga Soomaaliya
(Somali); Jumhūrīyah aṣ-Ṣūmāl
ad-Dīmuqrāṭīyah (Arabic) (Somali
Democratic Republic).
Form of government:
military-dominated, single-party
republic with one legislative house
(People's Assembly [177][1]).
Chief of state: President.
Head of government: Prime Minister.
Capital: Mogadishu.
Official languages: Somali; Arabic.
Official religion: Islam.
Monetary unit: 1 Somali shilling
(So.Sh.) = 100 cents; valuation (Oct.
10, 1988) 1 U.S.$ = So.Sh. 243.57;
1 £ = So.Sh. 417.12.

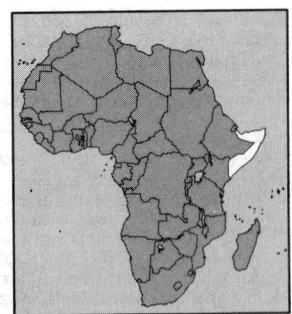

Area and population

Regions	Capitals	area sq mi	area sq km	population 1980 estimate
Bakool	Xuddur	10,000	27,000	148,700
Banaadir	Mogadishu	400	1,000	520,100
Bari	Boosaaso	27,000	70,000	222,300
Bay	Baydhabo	15,000	39,000	451,000
Galguduud	Dhuusa Mareeb	17,000	43,000	255,900
Gedo	Garbahaarrey	12,000	32,000	235,000
Hiiraan	Beled Weyne	13,000	34,000	219,300
Jubbada Dhexe	Bu'aale	9,000	23,000	147,800
Jubbada Hoose	Kismaayo	24,000	61,000	272,400
Mudug	Gaalkacyo	27,000	70,000	311,200
Nugaal	Garoowe	19,000	50,000	112,200
Sanaag	Ceerigaabo	21,000	54,000	216,500
Shabeellaha Dhexe	Towhar	8,000	22,000	352,000
Shabeellaha Hoose	Marca	10,000	25,000	570,700
Togdheer	Burko	16,000	41,000	383,900
Woqooyi Galbeed	Hargeysa	17,000	45,000	655,000
TOTAL		246,000[2]	637,000	5,074,000

Demography

Population (1988): 6,334,000.
Density (1988): persons per sq mi 25.7, persons per sq km 9.9.
Urban-rural (1985): urban 34.1%; rural 65.9%.
Sex distribution (1985): male 45.78%; female 54.22%.
Age breakdown (1985): under 15, 43.7%; 15–29, 25.0%; 30–44, 14.7%; 45–59, 10.1%; 60–74, 5.9%; 75 and over, 0.6%.
Population projection: (1990) 6,695,000; (2000) 8,833,000.
Doubling time: 28 years.
Ethnic composition (1983): Somali 98.3%; Arab 1.2%; Bantu 0.4%; other 0.1%.
Religious affiliation (1980): Sunnī Muslim 99.8%; Christian 0.1%; other 0.1%.
Major cities (1981): Mogadishu 500,000; Hargeysa 70,000; Kismaayo 70,000; Berbera 65,000; Marca 60,000.

Vital statistics

Birth rate per 1,000 population (1985): 47.9 (world avg. 29.0); legitimate, n.a.; illegitimate, n.a.
Death rate per 1,000 population (1985): 23.2 (world avg. 11.0).
Natural increase rate per 1,000 population (1985): 24.7 (world avg. 18.0).
Total fertility rate (avg. births per childbearing woman; 1985–90): 6.6.
Marriage rate per 1,000 population: n.a.
Divorce rate per 1,000 population: n.a.
Life expectancy at birth (1985–90): male 40.3 years; female 43.5 years.
Major causes of death per 100,000 population: n.a.; however, major diseases include leprosy, malaria, tetanus, and tuberculosis.

National economy

Budget (1988). Revenue: So.Sh. 17,807,000,000 (domestic revenue sources, principally indirect taxes and import duties 67.0%; external grants and transfers 33.0%). Expenditures: So.Sh. 17,807,000,000 (equipment and services 67.5%, of which debt service 21.5%; investments 19.3%; wages and salaries 13.2%).
Tourism: receipts from visitors (1986) U.S.$8,000,000; expenditures by nationals abroad (1983) U.S.$13,000,000.
Production (metric tons except as noted). Agriculture, forestry, fishing (1986): corn (maize) 382,000, sugarcane 278,000, sorghum 251,000, bananas 87,000, sesame seed 52,000, roots and tubers 41,000, vegetables 32,000, citrus fruits 22,000, rice 18,000, beans 13,000, dates 10,000, seed cotton 3,000, peanuts (groundnuts) 1,000; livestock (number of live animals) 16,200,000 goats, 10,100,000 sheep, 5,800,000 camels, 3,800,000 cattle; roundwood (1985) 4,435,000 cu m; fish catch 16,500. Mining and quarrying (1986): salt 30,000. Manufacturing (value added in So.Sh. '000,000; 1984): food and beverages 315.2; public utilities 131.8; petroleum products 90.6; printing and publishing 87.5; textiles 53.0; clothing and footwear 36.9. Construction (value added in So.Sh.; 1982): 1,687,200,000. Energy production (consumption): electricity (kW-hr; 1986) 143,000,000 (143,000,000); coal, none (n.a.); crude petroleum (barrels; 1986) n.a. (2,697,000); petroleum products (metric tons; 1986) 352,000 (348,000); natural gas, none (n.a.).
Household income and expenditure. Average household size (1980) 4.9; income per household: n.a.; sources of income: n.a.; expenditure[3] (1983):

food and tobacco 62.3%, housing 15.3%, clothing 5.6%, energy 4.3%, other 12.1%.
Public debt (external, outstanding; 1986): U.S.$1,414,800,000.
Gross national product (at current market prices; 1986): U.S.$1,560,000,000 (U.S.$280 per capita).

Structure of gross domestic product and labour force

	1985 in value So.Sh. '000,000[4]	1985 % of total value	1985 labour force	1985 % of labour force
Agriculture	4,202	57.5	1,475,000	73.8
Mining	21	0.3		
Manufacturing	348	4.8	176,000	8.8
Construction	233	3.2		
Public utilities	8	0.1		
Transportation and communications	472	6.5		
Trade	674	9.2		
Finance	409	5.6	348,000	17.4
Pub. admin., defense	474	6.5		
Services	189	2.6		
Other	273	3.7		
TOTAL	7,303	100.0	1,999,000	100.0

Population economically active (1985): total 1,999,000; activity rate of total population 43.0% (participation rates: ages 15–64, 72.8%; female 39.7%; unemployed, n.a.).

Price and earnings indexes (1980 = 100)

	1981	1982	1983	1984	1985	1986	1987
Consumer price index	144.4	178.5	241.4	464.1	639.5	868.2	1,112.0
Earnings index	...	...	...	...	...	...	...

Land use (1985): forested 14.2%; meadows and pastures 46.0%; agricultural and under permanent cultivation 1.7%; other 38.1%.

Foreign trade

Balance of trade (current prices)

	1980	1981	1982	1983	1984	1985
So.Sh. '000,000	−1,069.9	−1,841.4	−73.5	−1,421.4	−995.3	−275.0
% of total	39.0%	48.9%	1.8%	33.3%	35.8%	3.7%

Imports (1984): So.Sh. 5,135,000,000 (food 25.5%; machinery and transport equipment 22.0%, of which transport equipment 15.1%, electrical equipment 2.5%; construction materials 20.4%; mineral fuels 7.8%; manufacturing raw materials 5.6%; beverages and tobacco 2.0%; chemical products 1.72%; clothing and footwear 1.5%). *Major import sources:* Italy 35.5%; United States 9.1%; West Germany 6.6%; France 6.3%; United Kingdom 4.8%; Kenya 3.2%; Thailand 2.3%; Japan 1.6%; Singapore 1.2%; China 1.0%.
Exports (1984): So.Sh. 1,273,800,000 (live animals 59.6%, of which goats 30.9%, sheep 27.5%; bananas 7.9%; undressed hides, skins, and furs 0.9%). *Major export destinations:* Saudi Arabia 78.7%; Italy 2.9%; China 0.1%.

Transport and communications

Transport. Railroads: none. Roads (1985): total length 10,697 mi, 17,215 km (paved 15%). Vehicles (1985): passenger cars 17,754; trucks and buses 9,533. Merchant marine (1987): vessels (100 gross tons and over) 27; total deadweight tonnage 18,852. Air transport (1987): passenger-mi 181,400,000, passenger-km 291,900,000; short ton-mi cargo 2,700,000, metric ton-km cargo 3,900,000; airports (1988) with scheduled flights 14.
Communications. Daily newspapers (1987): total number 1; total circulation, n.a. Radio (1986): total number of receivers 250,000 (1 per 24 persons). Television[5]: total number of receivers, n.a. Telephones (1985): 6,000 (1 per 971 persons).

Education and health

Education (1984–85)

	schools	teachers	students	student/ teacher ratio
Primary (age 6–14)	1,121	14,521	274,610	18.9
Secondary (age 15–18)	80	2,522	65,186	25.8
Voc., teacher tr.	23	725	10,203	14.1
Higher	1	262[6]	3,405	...

Educational attainment, n.a. *Literacy* (1975): total population age 10 and over literate 54.8%; males literate 60.9%; females literate 47.9%.
Health (1985): physicians 450[7] (1 per 13,315[7] persons); hospital beds 5,536 (1 per 1,053 persons); infant mortality rate per 1,000 live births 152.0.
Food (1984–86): daily per capita caloric intake 2,088 (vegetable products 69%, animal products 31%); (1983) 89% of FAO recommended minimum requirement.

Military

Total active duty personnel (1987): 65,000 (army 94.3%, navy 1.8%, air force 3.9%). *Military expenditure as percent of GNP* (1984): 6.5% (world 5.9%); per capita expenditure U.S.$19.

---

[1]Including 6 nonelective seats. [2]Detail does not add to total given because of rounding. [3]Capital city only. [4]At prices of 1977. [5]Since the end of 1983 television service covers Mogadishu area and Hargeysa. [6]1980–81. [7]1986.

South Africa

Official name: Republiek van Suid-Afrika (Afrikaans); Republic of South Africa (English).
Form of government: multiparty republic with three legislative houses (House of Assembly [178]; House of Representatives [85]; House of Delegates [45][1]).
Head of state and government: State President.
Capitals: Pretoria (executive); Bloemfontein (judicial); Cape Town (legislative).
Official languages: Afrikaans; English.
Official religion: none.
Monetary unit: 1 rand (R) = 100 cents; valuation (Oct. 10, 1988) 1 U.S.$ = R 2.49; 1 £ = R 4.26.

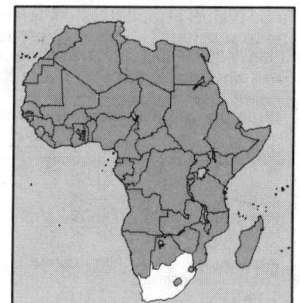

Area and population[2]

Provinces	Capitals	area sq mi	area sq km	population[3] 1983 estimate	population[3] 1985 census
Cape	Cape Town	247,638	641,379	5,374,000	5,041,137
Natal	Pietermaritzburg	23,303	60,355	2,842,000	2,145,018
Orange Free State	Bloemfontein	49,166	127,338	2,080,000	1,776,903
Transvaal	Pretoria	88,556	229,358	8,950,000	7,532,179
National states					
Gazankulu	Giyani	2,535	6,565	585,000	497,213
KaNgwane	Louieville	1,476	3,823	184,000	392,782
KwaNdebele	Siyabuswa	355	920	200,000	235,855
KwaZulu	Ulundi	11,969	31,000	3,792,000	3,747,015
Lebowa	Lebowakgomo	8,430	21,833	1,869,000	1,835,984
Qwaqwa	Phuthaditjhaba	253	655	306,000	181,559
TOTAL		433,680[4]	1,123,226	26,182,000	23,385,645

Demography

Population (1988): 29,628,000[5].
Density (1988): persons per sq mi 68.3, persons per sq km 26.4.
Urban–rural (1985)[6]: urban 55.9%; rural 44.1%.
Sex distribution (1985): male 49.37%; female 50.63%.
Age breakdown (1985)[6]: under 15, 41.0%; 15–29, 26.9%; 30–44, 16.1%; 45–59, 9.8%; 60–74, 5.0%; 75 and over, 1.2%.
Population projection: (1990) 30,872,000; (2000) 37,921,000.
Doubling time: 30 years.
Ethnic composition (1984): black 68.2%, of which Zulu 23.8%, North Sotho 9.8%, Xhosa 9.7%, South Sotho 7.3%, Tswana 5.7%, other 11.9%; white 18.0%; Coloured 10.5%; Asian 3.3%.
Religious affiliation (1980): Christian 78.1%, of which black independent churches 20.8%, Afrikaans Reformed 15.5%, Roman Catholic 9.6%; Hindu 2.1%; Muslim 1.4%; other 18.4%.
Major cities (municipality; 1985): Cape Town 1,911,521; Johannesburg 1,609,408; Durban 982,075; Pretoria 822,925.

Vital statistics

Birth rate per 1,000 population (1985): 33.4 (world avg. 29.0); (1978) legitimate 75.9%[7]; illegitimate 24.1%[7].
Death rate per 1,000 population (1985): 10.4 (world avg. 11.0).
Natural increase rate per 1,000 population (1983): 23.0 (world avg. 18.0).
Total fertility rate (avg. births per childbearing woman; 1980–85)[7]: 5.1.
Life expectancy at birth (1980–85)[6]: male 51.8 years; female 55.2 years.
Major causes of death per 100,000 population (1977)[7]: heart disease 215.3; malignant neoplasms 107.3; cerebrovascular disease 90.2; pneumonia 75.2.

National economy

Budget (1987–88). Revenue: R 38,794,000,000 (income tax 56.4%, sales tax 25.7%, customs duty and excise tax 8.9%). Expenditures: R 46,319,000,000 (education 18.6%, defense 15.2%, debt service 13.2%, health 9.4%, social services 9.2%).
Production (metric tons except as noted). Agriculture, forestry, fishing (1986): sugarcane 20,500,000, corn (maize) 8,077,000, wheat 2,034,000; livestock (number of live animals) 29,481,000 sheep, 11,750,000 cattle; forestry 19,022,000 cu m; fish catch 649,947. Mining and quarrying (1987): iron ore 21,995,510; chrome 3,339,233; manganese ore 2,892,114; gold 604,950 kg; silver 208,120 kg; platinum 115,000 kg[8]; diamonds 9,050,613 carats. Manufacturing (value added in R '000,000; 1985): metal products 5,553, of which iron and steel 2,435; chemicals 5,198; food and beverages 3,770; machinery and transport equipment 3,726, of which electrical machinery 1,461, transport equipment 939; textiles 980; printing and publishing 795; wearing apparel 622. Construction (1987): residential 4,905,088 sq m; non-residential 1,150,496 sq m. Energy production (consumption): electricity[9] (kW-hr; 1986) 130,345,000,000 (130,345,000,000); coal[9] (metric tons; 1986) 175,671,000 (132,671,000); petroleum[9] (barrels; 1986) none (117,000,000); petroleum products[9] (metric tons; 1986) 13,700,000 (10,513,000).
Household income and expenditure. Average household size (1983) 4.5; average annual income per household (1980) R 8,829 (U.S.$11,349); sources of income (1984): wages and salaries 82.9%, transfer payments 4.8%, other 12.3%; expenditure (1984): food and beverages 32.2%, transp. and commun. 17.3%, housing and energy 11.7%; wearing apparel 8.1%, health 4.2%.
Tourism (1986): receipts from visitors U.S.$388,000,000; expenditures by nationals abroad U.S.$543,000,000.
Gross national product (1986): U.S.$59,910,000,000 (U.S.$1,800 per capita).

Structure of gross domestic product and labour force

	1987 in value R '000,000	1987 % of total value	1985 labour force	1985 % of labour force
Agriculture	8,831	5.5	1,179,590	13.6
Mining	21,321	13.2	743,065	8.6
Manufacturing	37,302	23.2	1,379,518	15.8
Construction	4,925	3.0	556,339	6.4
Public utilities	7,152	4.4	92,720	1.1
Transp. and commun.	13,486	8.4	418,156	4.8
Trade	19,270	12.0	941,867	10.8
Finance	24,544	15.2	339,204	3.9
Pub. admin., defense	22,370	13.9	1,965,040	22.6
Services	2,851	1.8	1,076,864	12.4
Other	−1,021[10]	−0.6[10] }		
TOTAL	161,031	100.0	8,692,363	100.0

Population economically active (1985): total 8,692,363; activity rate of total population 37.2% (participation rates: ages 20–64 [1980] 65.4%; female 36.4%; unemployed 8.4%).

Price and earnings indexes (1980 = 100)

	1982	1983	1984	1985	1986	1987	1988[11]
Consumer price index	132.1	148.4	165.7	192.6	228.5	265.3	295.8
Monthly earnings index	149.0	160.5	187.9	210.7	241.6	277.5	...

Total debt (external; 1987): U.S.$772,000,000.
Land use (1985): forested 3.7%; meadows and pastures 66.6%; agricultural and under permanent cultivation 10.8%; other 18.9%.

Foreign trade

Balance of trade (current prices)

	1981	1982	1983	1984	1985	1986
R '000,000	−231	+914	+4,479	+3,705	+13,748	+15,246
% of total	0.6%	2.4%	12.1%	7.9%	23.0%	22.1%

Imports (1986): R 26,863,600,000 (machinery and transport equipment 39.4%, of which motor vehicles 8.1%; chemicals 13.4%; metal products 4.5%; food 3.7%). *Major import sources* (1985): U.S. 16.9%; W.Ger. 16.6%; U.K. 12.0%; Japan 9.9%.
Exports (1986): R 42,011,300,000 (gold 39.8%; metals and metal products 10.8%; diamonds 5.7%; food and tobacco 5.4%; wool 1.4%). *Major export destinations* (1985): U.S. 9.5%; Japan 7.6%; U.K. 5.8%; The Netherlands 3.7%; Switzerland 3.6%; W.Ger. 3.4%.

Transport and communications

Transport. Railroads (1986): routh length (1987) 14,669 mi, 23,607 km; passenger-km 17,826,100,000; metric ton-km cargo 92,859,999,000. Roads (1985): length 114,243 mi, 183,851 km (paved 28%). Vehicles (1986): passenger cars 3,130,288; trucks and buses 1,203,323. Merchant marine (1987): vessels 247; total deadweight tonnage 570,373. Air transport (1985): passenger-km 9,132,000,000; metric ton-km cargo 411,456,000; airports (1988) 37.
Communications. Daily newspapers (1986): total number 21; total circulation 1,162,400; circulation per 1,000 population 40.8. Radio (1986): 10,000,000 receivers (1 per 2.8 persons). Television (1986): 2,629,000 receivers (1 per 11 persons). Telephones (1986): 4,057,683 (1 per 7.0 persons).

Education and health

Education (1987)

	schools	teachers	students	student/ teacher ratio
Primary (age 6–12)	19,310[12]	227,700[12]	5,045,000	29.8[12]
Secondary (age 13–17)	[12]	[12]	1,747,000	...
Voc., teacher tr.	132[13]	18,290	151,131	8.3
Higher	84[13]	27,352	247,694	9.1

Educational attainment (1985). Percent of economically active population having: no formal schooling or incomplete primary 49.4%; complete primary education 9.1%; some secondary 27.5%; complete secondary 12.4%; postsecondary degree 1.6%. *Literacy*[6] (1984): percent of adult population literate 50%; white 93%; Asians 69%; Coloured 62%; black 32%.
Health: physicians (1986) 22,525 (1 per 1,510 persons); hospital beds (1980) 98,308 (1 per 246 persons); infant mortality rate (1985) 59.2.
Food (1984–86): daily per capita caloric intake 2,941 (vegetable products 86%, animal products 14%); (1983) 117% of FAO recommended minimum.

Military

Total active duty personnel (1987): 97,000 (army 77.3%, navy 9.3%, air force 13.4%). *Military expenditure as percent of GNP* (1986): 3.7% (world [1985] 6.1%); per capita expenditure U.S.$69.

---

[1]For representation of whites, Coloureds, and Asians (mainly Indians), respectively. [2]Data exclude Bophuthatswana, Ciskei, Transkei, and Venda, which the South African government recognizes as sovereign nations. Together they had (1986) an area of 39,610 sq mi (102,589 sq km) and a population of 6,724,000. [3]1985 census data represented an estimated undercount of 4,336,455. Some indication of its extent and distribution may be seen by comparing the 1983 estimates (based on the more accurate 1980 census) with the 1985 figures. [4]Detail does not add to total given because of rounding. [5]The 1988 estimate is a continuation of a series incorporating the 1980 census, the 1983 estimates, and the corrected 1985 census. [6]Includes Bophuthatswana, Ciskei, Transkei, and Venda. [7]Whites, Asians, and Coloureds only. [8]1986. [9]Data refer to the Customs Union of Southern Africa, comprising South Africa, Botswana, Lesotho, South West Africa/Namibia, and Swaziland. [10]Includes imputed finance charges. [11]June. [12]Primary includes secondary. [13]1985.

South West Africa/ Namibia

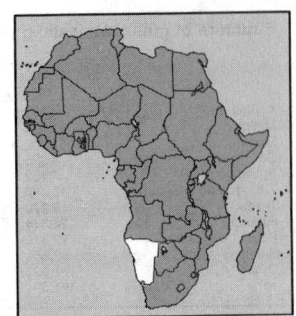

Official name: Suidwes-Afrika/Namibiĕ (Afrikaans); South West Africa/ Namibia (English).
Political status: dependency of South Africa with one legislative house (National Assembly [62]).
Head of state and government: Administrator-General[1].
Capital: Windhoek.
Official languages: Afrikaans; English.
Official religion: none.
Monetary unit: 1 South African rand (R) = 100 cents; valuation (Oct. 10, 1988) 1 U.S.$ = R 2.49; 1 £ = R 4.26.

Area and population[2]

Magisterial Districts	Capitals	area sq mi	area sq km	population 1987 estimate[3]
Bethanien	Bethanien	6,951	18,004	3,000
Boesmanland	Tsumkwe	7,131	18,468	3,000
Caprivi Oos	Katima Mulilo	4,453	11,533	44,000
Damaraland	Khorixas	17,977	46,560	28,000
Gobabis	Gobabis	16,003	41,447	25,000
Grootfontein	Grootfontein	10,239	26,520	25,000
Hereroland-Oos	Otjinene	20,058	51,949	22,000
Hereroland-Wes	Okakarara	6,371	16,500	18,000
Kaokoland	Opuwo	22,467	58,190	20,000
Karasburg	Karasburg	14,717	38,116	11,000
Karibib	Karibib	5,108	13,230	10,000
Kavango	Rundu	19,674	50,955	122,000
Keetmanshoop	Keetmanshoop	14,788	38,302	20,000
Lüderitz	Lüderitz	20,488	53,063	16,000
Maltahöhe	Maltahöhe	9,874	25,573	6,000
Mariental	Mariental	18,413	47,689	24,000
Namaland	Gibeon	8,154	21,120	15,000
Okahandja	Okahandja	6,811	17,640	15,000
Omaruru	Omaruru	3,253	8,425	6,000
Otjiwarongo	Otjiwarongo	7,934	20,550	19,000
Outjo	Outjo	14,951	38,722	10,000
Owambo	Ondangwa	20,000	51,800	520,000
Rehoboth	Rehoboth	5,476	14,182	33,000
Swakopmund	Swakopmund	17,258	44,697	18,000
Tsumeb	Tsumeb	6,340	16,420	22,000
Windhoek	Windhoek	12,930	33,489	129,000
TOTAL		317,818	823,144	1,184,000

Demography

Population (1988): 1,228,000.
Density (1988): persons per sq mi 3.9, persons per sq km 1.5.
Urban–rural (1987): urban *c.* 26%; rural 74%.
Sex distribution (1985): male 49.35%; female 50.65%.
Age breakdown (1985): under 15, 45.1%; 15–29, 25.9%; 30–44, 15.3%; 45–59, 8.7%; 60–74, 4.1%; 75 and over, 0.9%.
Population projection: (1990) 1,288,000; (2000) 1,640,000.
Doubling time: 25 years.
Ethnic composition (1987): Ovambo 49.6%; Kavango 9.3%; Herero 7.5%; Damara 7.5%; white 6.6%; Nama 4.8%; other 14.7%.
Religious affiliation (1981): Lutheran 51.2%; Roman Catholic 19.8%; Dutch Reformed 6.1%; Anglican 5.0%; other 17.9%.
Major cities (1983): Windhoek 105,100; Rundu 15,000; Rehoboth 14,000; Swakopmund 13,500; Keetmanshoop 12,000.

Vital statistics

Birth rate per 1,000 population (1980–85): 45.1 (world avg. 29.0).
Death rate per 1,000 population (1980–85): 17.3 (world avg. 11.0).
Natural increase rate per 1,000 population (1980–85): 27.8 (world avg. 18.0).
Total fertility rate (avg. births per childbearing woman; 1980–85): 6.0.
Marriage rate per 1,000 population: n.a.
Life expectancy at birth (1980–85): male 46.6 years; female 49.9 years.
Major causes of death per 100,000 population: n.a.; however, major diseases include malaria, tuberculosis, and trypanosomiasis (sleeping sickness).

National economy

Budget (1987–88). Revenue: R 1,589,200,000 (customs and excise taxes 22.0%, grants from South Africa 19.4%, general sales tax 11.0%). Expenditures: R 1,896,500,000 (finance 17.2%, national defense 10.1%, transportation 5.4%, education 5.2%, health and welfare 4.2%).
Public debt (external, outstanding; 1984): U.S.$352,000,000.
Tourism (1981): receipts from visitors U.S.$45,960,000; expenditures by nationals abroad, n.a.
Production (metric tons except as noted). Agriculture, forestry, fishing (1986): roots and tubers 235,000, corn [maize] 48,000, millet 42,000, fruit 33,000, vegetables and melons 28,000, sorghum 7,000; pulses 6,000, wool 1,848[4], karakul pelts 556,483 units[5]; livestock (number of live animals; 1987) 2,003,400 cattle, 2,936,700 sheep, 1,603,900 goats; fish catch (1987)[6] 479,360, of which anchovies 376,581, South African pilchard 63,660, mackerel 33,379. Mining and quarrying (1986): diamonds 1,009,520 carats, of which gem quality 960,000 carats; salt 130,000; copper 49,594; lead 37,101; limestone and marble 32,000; zinc 35,371; uranium 4,400; gold 6,400 troy oz; silver 3,148 troy oz. Manufacturing (gross output in R '000,000; 1976): food and beverages 140.8; metal products 34.2; wood products 6.6; chemical products 3.6; printing and publishing 2.4; other 12.4. Construc-

tion (value of buildings completed in R '000,000; 1984): residential 19.4; nonresidential 11.5. Energy production (consumption): electricity (kW-hr; 1986) 692,000,000 (n.a.); coal, none (n.a.); crude petroleum, none (n.a.).
Gross national product (1986): U.S.$1,150,000,000 (U.S.$1,020 per capita).

Structure of gross domestic product and labour force

	1987 in value R '000,000	1987 % of total value	1981 labour force	1981 % of labour force
Agriculture	376.6	12.0	71,402	35.0
Mining	778.7	24.9	15,515	7.6
Manufacturing	157.4	5.0	8,017	3.9
Construction	75.8	2.4	17,654	8.7
Public utilities	53.2	1.7	1,922	0.9
Transp. and commun.	230.3	7.4	9,615	4.7
Trade	384.5	12.3	22,253	10.9
Finance	235.7	7.5	3,764	1.8
Services	63.9	2.0	22,417	11.0
Public admin., defense	680.3	21.7	31,079	15.2
Other	94.2	3.0	360	0.2
TOTAL	3,130.6	100.0[7]	203,998	100.0[7]

Population economically active: total (1985) 477,000; activity rate of total population 40.8% (participation rates: ages 15–64, n.a.; female [1977] 38.8%; unemployed 12.0%).

Price and earnings indexes (1980 = 100)[8]

	1980	1981	1982	1983	1984	1985	1986
Consumer price index	100.0	114.8	132.7	148.5	165.5	182.8	206.5
Earnings index	...	...	...	...	...	...	...

Household income and expenditure. Average household size (1981) 4.8; average annual income per household (1980) R 3,223 (U.S.$4,143); sources of income (1987): wages and salaries 72.8%, income from property 23.9%, transfer payments 3.3%; expenditure: n.a.
Land use (1985): forested 22.4%; meadows and pastures 64.3%; agricultural and under permanent cultivation 0.8%; other 12.5%.

Foreign trade

Balance of trade (current prices)

	1982	1983	1984	1985	1986	1987
R '000,000	−97.4	−68.1	−82.9	324.2	511.7	97.0
% of total	4.6%	3.5%	3.6%	11.3%	14.8%	2.8%

Imports (1986): R 1,479,300,000 (1983 est.; food and other consumer goods 33.5%; fuel 27.5%; transport equipment and other capital goods 25.5%). *Major import sources:* South Africa (75–100%).
Exports (1986): R 1,991,000,000 (minerals 82.6%, of which diamonds 30.9%; agricultural products 7.7%, of which cattle 4.1%, karakul pelts 0.9%). *Major export destinations:* United States 25%; South Africa 19%; Japan 15%.

Transport and communications

Transport. Railroads: length (1987) 1,454 mi, 2,340 km[9]; (1983) metric ton-km cargo 4,900,000,000. Roads (1986): total length 34,230 mi, 55,088 km (paved 9%[10]). Number of registered vehicles (1986): 103,715. Merchant marine: vessels (100 gross tons and over), none. Air transport (1986)[11]: passengers handled 213,514; cargo handled 2,200 metric tons[4]; airports (1988) with scheduled flights 8.
Communications. Daily newspapers (1986): total number 3; total circulation 20,700; circulation per 1,000 population 18.0. Radio (1987): 220,000 receivers (1 per 5.8 persons). Television (1986): 24,582 receivers (1 per 48 persons). Telephones (1986): 69,273 (1 per 17 persons).

Education and health

Education (1986)

	schools	teachers	students	student/ teacher ratio
Primary (age 6–12) } Secondary (age 13–19) }	1,074	11,121	273,500 } 76,580 }	31.5
Voc., teacher tr.	5	81[12]	1,200[12]	14.8[12]
Higher	3	137[12]	537[12]	3.9[12]

Educational attainment (1977). Percent of labour force having: no formal schooling 59.8%; primary education 33.2%; secondary 5.0%; higher 2.0%.
Literacy (1985): total population age 15 and over literate 474,000 (72.5%); males literate 239,000 (74.2%); females literate 235,000 (70.8%).
Health (1986): physicians 317 (1 per 3,780 persons); hospital beds 9,100 (1 per 130 persons); infant mortality rate per 1,000 live births (1985) 110.
Food (1979–81): daily per capita caloric intake 2,197 (vegetable products 77%, animal products 23%); 96% of FAO recommended minimum requirement.

Military

Total active duty personnel[13] (1988): 22,000 (army 100%). *Military expenditure as percent of GNP* (1984): 7.7% (world 5.9%); per capita expenditure U.S.$113.

[1]In June 1985 most executive authority was formally transferred to a cabinet; the role of the South African-appointed administrator-general was nominally downgraded to that of a constitutional figurehead, but the South African State President retains veto power over acts of the Assembly. [2]Excludes area and population of Walvis Bay (part of South Africa), administered as part of South West Africa/Namibia until 1977. [3]January 1. [4]1984. [5]1987. [6]The fishing season concludes in August. [7]Detail does not add to total given because of rounding. [8]Windhoek only. [9]Operated by South African Transport Services (SATS). [10]1985. [11]South West Africa/Namibia's two largest airports only. [12]1982. [13]The South West Africa Territory Force (SWATF), largely controlled by the Republic of South Africa.

Spain

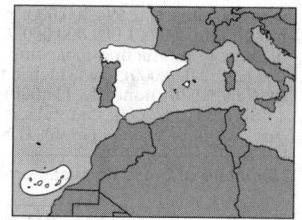

Official name: Reino de España (Kingdom of Spain).
Form of government: constitutional monarchy with two legislative houses (Senate [257]; Congress of Deputies [350]).
Chief of state: King.
Head of government: Prime Minister.
Capital: Madrid.
Official language: Spanish.
Official religion: none.
Monetary unit: 1 peseta (Pta) = 100 céntimos; valuation (Oct. 10, 1988) 1 U.S.$ = Ptas 122.13; 1 £ = Ptas 209.15.

Area and population

Autonomous communities	Capitals	area sq mi	sq km	population 1986 estimate
Andalucía	Seville (Sevilla)	33,694	87,268	6,717,650
Aragón	Zaragoza	18,398	47,650	1,212,362
Asturias	Oviedo	4,079	10,565	1,137,018
Baleares	Palma de Mallorca	1,936	5,014	673,559
Canarias	Santa Cruz de Tenerife	2,796	7,242	1,438,686
Cantabria	Santander	2,042	5,289	526,007
Castilla-La Mancha	Toledo	30,591	79,230	1,665,649
Castilla-León	Valladolid	36,368	94,193	2,595,411
Cataluña	Barcelona	12,328	31,930	6,041,062
Extremadura	Mérida	16,063	41,602	1,081,535
Galicia	Santiago de Compostela	11,365	29,434	2,863,223
La Rioja	Logroño	1,944	5,034	262,380
Madrid	Madrid	3,087	7,995	4,894,015
Murcia	Murcia	4,370	11,317	1,004,783
Navarra	Pamplona	4,023	10,421	521,088
País Vasco	Vitoria	2,803	7,261	2,171,000
Valencia	Valencia	8,998	23,305	3,733,243
TOTAL SPAIN		194,885	504,750	38,538,671
Enclaves in Northern Morocco				
Ceuta	—	7.1	18.5	71,190
Melilla	—	5.4	14.0	58,458
Other enclaves	*(plazas de soberanía)*	.26	.66	...
TOTAL		194,897.79[1]	504,783.16	38,668,319

Demography

Population (1988): 38,996,000.
Density (1988): persons per sq mi 200.1, persons per sq km 77.2.
Urban–rural (1985): urban 75.8%; rural 24.2%.
Sex distribution (1986): male 49.16%; female 50.84%.
Age breakdown (1985): under 15, 24.6%; 15–29, 24.2%; 30–44, 18.5%; 45–59, 16.8%; 60–74, 11.6%; 75 and over, 4.3%.
Population projection: (1990) 39,322,000; (2000) 40,746,000.
Doubling time: n.a.; doubling time exceeds 100 years.
Ethnolinguistic composition (1984): Spanish 72.8%; Catalan 16.4%; Galician 8.2%; Basque 2.3%; other 0.3%.
Religious affiliation (1980): Roman Catholic 97.0%; Protestant 0.4%; nonreligious and atheist 2.6%.
Major cities (1986)[2]: Madrid 3,053,101; Barcelona 1,699,231; Valencia 728,622; Sevilla 651,299; Zaragoza 573,711.

Vital statistics

Birth rate per 1,000 population (1985): 11.7 (world avg. 29.0).
Death rate per 1,000 population (1985): 8.0 (world avg. 11.0).
Natural increase rate per 1,000 population (1985): 3.7 (world avg. 18.0).
Total fertility rate (avg. births per childbearing woman; 1980–85): 2.1.
Marriage rate per 1,000 population (1985): 5.0.
Life expectancy at birth (1980): male 72.5 years; female 78.6 years.
Major causes of death per 100,000 population (1982): circulatory diseases 344.8; malignant neoplasms (cancers) 161.8; respiratory diseases 65.3.

National economy

Budget (1988). Revenue: Ptas 7,296,000,000,000 (indirect taxes 45.2%, personal income taxes 31.7%, direct taxes on enterprises 9.9%). Expenditures: Ptas 7,153,000,000,000 (current transfers 58.2%, wages and salaries 24.2%).
Production (metric tons except as noted). Agriculture, forestry, fishing (1986): sugar beets 7,760,000, barley 7,331,000, grapes 5,788,000, potatoes 4,857,000, wheat 4,292,000, corn (maize) 3,451,000, tomatoes 2,243,000, oranges 2,048,000, onions 1,149,000, apples 850,000, oats 422,000; livestock (number of live animals) 17,735,000 sheep, 10,367,000 pigs, 5,084,000 cattle, 2,282,000 goats; roundwood (1985) 13,696,000 cu m; fish catch 1,303,488. Mining and quarrying (metal content in metric tons; 1986): iron ore 3,042,000, zinc 223,200, lead 79,560, copper 46,920. Manufacturing (value added in Ptas '000,000; 1984): machinery and transport equipment 1,079,033, of which transport equipment 426,509, electrical equipment 124,601; food and beverage products 865,623; chemicals and chemical products 512,375; paper and paper products 322,075; textiles 239,274; clothing and footwear 221,508; wood and cork products 214,344, of which furniture 104,074. Construction (1986): residential dwellings 196,228. Energy production (consumption): electricity (kW-hr; 1986) 127,713,000,000 (126,457,000,000); coal (metric tons; 1986) 38,582,000 (47,308,000); crude petroleum (barrels; 1986) 13,969,000 (354,332,000); petroleum products (metric tons; 1986) 42,958,000 (31,064,000); natural gas (cu m; 1986) 386,993,000 (3,035,000,000).
Gross national product (1986): U.S.$188,030,000,000 (U.S.$4,840 per capita).

Structure of gross domestic product and labour force

	1985 in value Ptas '000,000	1985 % of total value	1986 labour force	1986 % of labour force
Agriculture	1,733,700	6.3	1,996,800	14.5
Mining	} 7,633,500	27.9	100,500	0.7
Manufacturing			2,906,600	21.1
Public utilities	882,200	3.2	87,700	0.6
Construction	1,886,100	6.9	1,194,300	8.7
Transp. and commun.	1,702,200	6.2	672,000	4.9
Trade	5,597,700	20.4	2,374,000	17.2
Finance	1,772,600	6.5	525,700	3.8
Pub. admin., defense	3,222,300	11.8	} 2,695,200	19.6
Services	4,570,400	16.7		
Other	−1,618,800	−5.9	1,228,400[3]	8.9[3]
TOTAL	27,381,900	100.0	13,781,200	100.0

Public debt (1984): Ptas 8,736,600,000,000 (U.S.$50,380,000,000).
Tourism (1986): receipts from visitors U.S.$12,058,000,000; expenditures by nationals abroad U.S.$1,015,000,000.
Population economically active (1986): total 13,781,200; activity rate of total population 35.6% (participation rates: ages 16–64, 56.9%; female 30.8%; unemployed 21.5%).

Price and earnings indexes (1980 = 100)

	1981	1982	1983	1984	1985	1986	1987
Consumer price index	114.5	131.0	147.0	163.6	178.0	193.6	203.8
Monthly earnings index	119.9	138.1	158.8	178.7	197.3	217.3	236.2

Household income and expenditure. Average household size (1983) 2.8; income per household Ptas 1,250,000 (U.S.$8,700); sources of income (1984): wages and salaries 52.3%, profits and self-employment 28.6%, social security 16.8%; expenditure (1982): food 30.2%, housing 12.8%, transportation 11.6%, clothing and footwear 8.9%, health 5.9%, education 2.0%.
Land use (1985): forested 31.3%; meadows and pastures 20.0%; agricultural and under permanent cultivation 40.9%; other 7.8%.

Foreign trade

Balance of trade (current prices)

	1982	1983	1984	1985	1986	1987
Ptas '000,000	−1,031.7	−1,105.5	−588.3	−686.9	−814.5	−1,493.0
% of total	18.6%	16.3%	7.2%	7.7%	9.7%	15.1%

Imports (1986): Ptas 4,890,700,000,000 (petroleum 14.2%; agricultural and food products 13.0%; chemicals, plastics, and rubber 11.6%; transport equipment 6.8%; raw cotton, textiles, and clothing 2.4%). *Major import sources:* West Germany 15.0%; France 11.7%; U.S. 9.9%; U.K. 7.7%.
Exports (1986): Ptas 3,800,100,000,000 (agricultural and food products 16.2%; transport equipment 15.4%; chemicals, plastics, and rubber 8.6%). *Major export destinations:* France 17.9%; West Germany 11.7%; U.K. 9.4%; U.S. 9.2%; Italy 8.0%.

Transport and communications

Transport. Railroads (1987): route length (1986) 7,917 mi, 12,742 km; passenger-km 15,396,000,000; metric ton-km cargo 11,472,000,000. Roads (1987): total length 198,211 mi, 318,991 km (paved 56%). Vehicles (1987): passenger cars 9,761,968; trucks and buses 1,727,172. Merchant marine (1987): vessels (100 gross tons and over) 2,350; total deadweight tonnage 8,387,475. Air transport (1986): passenger-km 19,152,000,000; metric ton-km cargo 568,524,000; airports (1988) with scheduled flights 29.
Communications. Daily newspapers (1984): total number 102; total circulation 3,053,000; circulation per 1,000 population 80. Radio (1986): 10,810,000 receivers (1 per 3.6 persons). Television (1987): 14,870,518 receivers (1 per 2.6 persons). Telephones (1986): 14,747,825 (1 per 2.6 persons).

Education and health

Education (1985–86)

	schools	teachers	students	student/teacher ratio
Primary (age 6–13)	23,105[4]	193,455	5,594,285	28.9
Secondary (age 14–17)	2,635	75,550	1,234,874	16.3
Vocational	2,248	49,408	738,340	14.9
Higher[5]	33	34,378	784,173	22.8

Educational attainment (1981). Percent of population age 25 and over having: less than primary education 46.1%, of which illiterate or no formal schooling 34.5%; primary 34.0%; lower secondary 9.3%; upper secondary 3.3%; higher 7.1%. *Literacy* (1983): total population age 15 and over literate 26,004,225 (92.8%); males literate 12,950,282 (95.9%); females literate 13,053,943 (89.9%).
Health (1986): physicians 131,080 (1 per 295 persons); hospital beds (1986) 181,794 (1 per 213 persons); infant mortality rate per 1,000 live births (1985) 8.5.
Food (1984–86): daily per capita caloric intake 3,365 (vegetable products 72%, animal products 28%); (1983) 132% of FAO recommended minimum.

Military

Total active duty personnel (1987): 325,000 (army 70.8%, navy 19.2%, air force 10.0%). *Military expenditure as percent of GNP* (1985): 2.2% (world 6.1%); per capita expenditure U.S.$94.

[1]Detail does not add to total given because of rounding. [2]For *municipios,* which may contain rural areas as well as the urban city proper. [3]Includes 1,227,200 unemployed persons not previously employed. [4]1982–83. [5]1984–85.

Sri Lanka

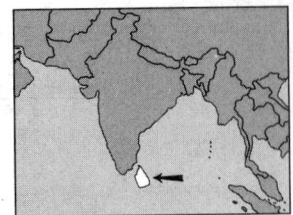

Official name: Sri Lanká Praja-
thanthrika Samajavadi Janarajaya
(Democratic Socialist Republic of
Sri Lanka).
Form of government: unitary multiparty
republic with one legislative house
(Parliament [168]).
Head of state and government:
President.
Capitals: Colombo (administrative),
Sri Jayawardenapura (legislative and
judicial).
Official language: Sinhalese.
Official religion: none.
Monetary unit: 1 Sri Lanka rupee
(SL Rs) = 100 cents; valuation (Oct.
10, 1988) 1 U.S.$ = SL Rs 32.50;
1 £ = SL Rs 55.65.

Area and population

Districts	Capitals	area sq mi	area sq km	population 1986 estimate
Amparai	Amparai	1,778	4,604	439,000
Anuradhapura	Anuradhapura	2,809	7,275	659,000
Badulla	Badulla	1,090	2,822	668,000
Batticaloa	Batticaloa	1,017	2,633	379,000
Colombo	Colombo	268	695	1,836,000
Galle	Galle	652	1,689	881,000
Gampaha	Gampaha	540	1,399	1,466,000
Hambantota	Hambantota	1,013	2,623	477,000
Jaffna	Jaffna	833	2,158	915,000
Kalutara	Kalutara	624	1,615	892,000
Kandy	Kandy	833	2,158	1,188,000
Kegalle	Kegalle	642	1,663	720,000
Kurunegala	Kurunegala	1,844	4,776	1,333,000
Mannar	Mannar	778	2,014	120,000
Matale	Matale	768	1,989	392,000
Matara	Matara	481	1,247	717,000
Monaragala	Monaragala	2,188	5,666	320,000
Mullaitivu	Mullaitivu	798	2,066	86,000
Nuwara Eliya	Nuwara Eliya	555	1,437	514,000
Polonnaruwa	Polonnaruwa	1,332	3,449	294,000
Puttalam	Puttalam	1,172	3,036	552,000
Ratnapura	Ratnapura	1,251	3,239	868,000
Trincomalee	Trincomalee	1,048	2,714	292,000
Vavuniya	Vavuniya	1,021	2,645	108,000
TOTAL		25,332[1]	65,610[1]	16,117,000[1]

Demography

Population (1988): 16,606,000.
Density (1988): persons per sq mi 655.5, persons per sq km 253.1.
Urban-rural (1985): urban 21.1%; rural 78.9%.
Sex distribution (1986): male 50.97%; female 49.03%.
Age breakdown (1986): under 15, 35.3%; 15–24, 21.0%; 25–44, 26.5%; 45–59, 10.6%; 60–69, 4.0%; 70 and over, 2.6%.
Population projection: (1990) 17,108,000; (2000) 19,227,000.
Doubling time: 41 years.
Ethnic composition (1981): Sinhalese 74.0%; Tamil 18.2%; Sri Lankan Moor 7.1%; other 0.7%.
Religious affiliation (1981): Buddhist 69.3%; Hindu 15.5%; Muslim 7.6%; Christian 7.5%; other 0.1%.
Major cities (1985): Colombo 664,000; Dehiwala–Mount Lavinia 188,000; Moratuwa 138,000; Jaffna 138,000; Kandy 125,000; Kotte 102,000.

Vital statistics

Birth rate per 1,000 population (1987): 23.4 (world avg. 26.0); (1982) legitimate 94.6%; illegitimate 5.4%.
Death rate per 1,000 population (1987): 6.1 (world avg. 9.9).
Natural increase rate per 1,000 population (1987): 17.3 (world avg. 16.1).
Total fertility rate (avg. births per childbearing woman; 1987): 2.7.
Marriage rate per 1,000 population (1984): 7.9.
Divorce rate per 1,000 population (1983): 0.1.
Life expectancy at birth (1987): male 68.3 years; female 71.5 years.
Major causes of death per 100,000 population (1982): diseases of the circulatory system 84.7; injury and poisoning 64.9%; infectious and parasitic diseases 50.4; respiratory diseases 43.2[2]; malignant neoplasms (cancers) 24.6.

National economy

Budget (1987). Revenue: SL Rs 44,810,000,000 (import duties 24.9%, general sales and turnover tax 24.4%, income taxes 11.4%, excise taxes 11.3%, nontax revenue 11.1%, grants 9.1%). Expenditures: SL Rs 59,777,000,000 (public debt service 17.1%, general public services 11.6%, economic services 11.4%, social security 10.4%, defense 8.2%, education 8.1%, health 6.1%).
Public debt (external, outstanding; 1986): U.S.$3,448,200,000.
Tourism (1986): receipts from visitors U.S.$75,000,000; expenditures by nationals abroad U.S.$55,000,000.
Production (metric tons except as noted). Agriculture, forestry, fishing (1986): rice 2,594,000, coconuts 2,285,000, sugarcane 793,000, cassava 650,-000, copra 230,000, tea 211,000, cotton lint 189,000, sweet potatoes 147,000; livestock (number of live animals) 1,783,000 cattle, 964,000 buffalo, 534,-000 goats; roundwood 8,687,000 cu m; fish catch 183,065. Mining and quarrying (1985): clays 138,353; ilmenite 114,854; salt 76,858; rutile 8,558; graphite 7,413; gemstones U.S.$20,000,000. Manufacturing (value added in SL Rs; 1985): food, beverages, and tobacco 6,166,000,000; textile and

wearing apparel 2,594,000,000; petrochemicals 1,402,000,000; nonmetallic mineral products 1,089,000,000. Construction (1985): residential 833,200 sq m. Energy production (consumption): electricity (kW-hr; 1986) 2,652,000,-000 (2,652,000,000); coal (metric tons; 1986) none (1,000); crude petroleum (barrels; 1986) none (12,432,000); petroleum products (metric tons; 1986) 1,467,000 (1,082,000); natural gas, none (n.a.).
Gross national product (1986): U.S.$6,460,000,000 (U.S.$400 per capita).

Structure of gross domestic product and labour force

	1986 in value SL Rs '000,000	1986 % of total value	1985 labour force	1985 % of labour force
Agriculture	38,672.7	22.5	2,530,967	42.4
Mining	1,622.0	0.9	66,726	1.1
Manufacturing	28,517.9	16.6	648,469	10.9
Construction	13,369.0	7.8	226,913	3.8
Public utilities	3,073.5	1.8	21,484	0.3
Transp. and commun.	18,982.1	11.0	220,025	3.7
Trade	33,138.8	19.3	513,872	8.6
Finance	10,248.2	6.0	65,094	1.1
Pub. admin., defense	11,610.8	6.8 }	631,408	10.6
Services	4,289.9	2.5 }		
Other	8,286.4	4.8	1,047,043[3]	17.5[3]
TOTAL	171,811.3	100.0	5,972,001	100.0

Population economically active: total (1985) 5,972,001; activity rate 37.7% (participation rates: ages 15–64, 61.0%; female 32.8%; unemployed 14.1%).

Price and earnings indexes (1980 = 100)

	1981	1982	1983	1984	1985	1986	1987
Consumer price index	117.9	130.7	149.0	173.8	176.3	190.4	205.1
Average wage index[4]	100.2	118.0	129.3	162.9	178.0	187.5	196.8

Household income and expenditure. Average household size (1981) 5.2; income per household (1973) SL Rs 3,936 (U.S.$611); sources of income (1984): wages 50.8%, property income 36.4%, government transfers 12.8%; expenditure (1984): food and beverages 54.2%, transportation 16.9%, clothing 6.3%, housing and energy 5.9%, recreation 3.0%, health 1.4%.
Land use (1985): forested 36.8%; meadows and pastures 6.8%; agricultural and under permanent cultivation 34.1%; other 22.3%.

Foreign trade

Balance of trade (current prices)

	1982	1983	1984	1985	1986	1987
SL Rs '000,000	−15,021	−14,519	−3,933	−9,890	−12,773	−13,146
% of total	25.9%	22.4%	5.1%	12.0%	15.8%	13.8%

Imports (1986): SL Rs 51,282,000,000 (machinery and transport equipment 15.1%, petroleum 12.6%, wheat 3.9%, sugar 3.5%, rice 1.9%). *Major import sources:* Japan 17.4%; U.S. 6.4%; U.K. 5.6%; China 4.7%; W.Ger. 4.7%; India 4.3%.
Exports (1986): SL Rs 33,092,000,000 (tea 27.8%, rubber 7.9%, precious and semiprecious stones 5.4%, desiccated coconut 2.6%, coconut oil 2.0%). *Major export destinations:* U.S. 25.6%; W.Ger. 7.0%; U.K. 5.7%; Japan 5.5%; The Netherlands 3.9%.

Transport and communications

Transport. Railroads (1986): length (1985) 1,208 mi, 1,944 km; passenger-km 1,972,000,000; metric ton-km cargo 203,620,000. Roads (1984): total length 53,573 mi, 86,218 km (paved 35%). Vehicles (1986): passenger cars 165,224; trucks and buses 138,253. Merchant marine (1987): vessels (100 gross tons and over) 99; total deadweight tonnage 908,456. Air transport (1986): passenger-km 2,112,000,000; metric ton-km cargo 56,148,000; airports (1988) with scheduled flights 1.
Communications. Daily newspapers (1985): total number 15; total circulation 850,000; circulation per 1,000 population 53. Radio (1986): 2,073,432[5] receivers (1 per 7.8 persons). Television (1987): 500,000 receivers (1 per 33 persons). Telephones (1987): 125,250 (1 per 130 persons).

Education and health

Education (1985)

	schools	teachers	students	student/ teacher ratio
Primary (age 5–10)	9,349	144,707	2,242,645	15.5
Secondary (age 11–17)[6]	5,629	113,148	2,930,070	25.9
Voc., teacher tr.	27	1,101	20,796	18.9
Higher	8[7]	2,792	56,020	20.1

Educational attainment (1981). Percent of population age 25 and over having: no schooling 15.5%; less than complete primary education 12.1%; complete primary 52.3%; postprimary 14.7%; secondary 3.0%; higher 1.1%; unspecified 1.3%. *Literacy* (1981): population age 15 and over literate 86.1%; males literate 90.8%; females literate 81.2%.
Health (1986): physicians 2,222 (1 per 7,253 persons); hospital beds 45,006 (1 per 358 persons); infant mortality rate per 1,000 live births (1987) 29.0.
Food (1983–85): daily per capita caloric intake 2,410 (vegetable products 96%, animal products 4%); (1983) 104% of FAO recommended minimum.

Military

Total active duty personnel (1987): 48,000 (army 83.3%, navy 8.4%, air force 8.3%). *Military expenditure as percent of GNP* (1985): 2.7% (world 6.1%); per capita expenditure U.S.$11.

[1]Detail does not add to total given because of rounding. [2]1981. [3]Includes unemployed. [4]Agricultural minimum rates. [5]Licensed. [6]1983. [7]Universities only.

Sudan, The

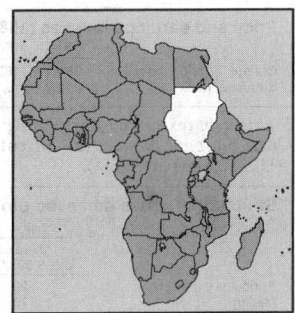

Official name: Jumhūrīyat as-Sūdān (Republic of the Sudan).
Form of government: multiparty republic with one legislative house (Constituent Assembly [301][1]).
Chief of state: Chairman, State Council.
Head of government: Prime Minister.
Capital: Khartoum.
Official language: Arabic.
Official religion: Islam.
Monetary unit: 1 Sudanese pound (LSd) = 100 piastres; valuation (Oct. 10, 1988) 1 U.S.$ = LSd 4.50; 1 £ = LSd 7.69.

Area and population

Regions Provinces	Capitals	area sq mi	area sq km	population 1983 census
A'ālī an-Nīl (Upper Nile)	Malakāl	92,198	238,792	1,599,605
A'ālī an-Nīl (Upper Nile)	Nāṣir	45,231	117,148	802,354
Junqulī (Jongley)	Bor	46,781	121,164	797,251
Baḥr al-Ghazāl (Bahr el-Ghazal)	Wāu	77,566	200,894	2,265,510
Baḥr al-Ghazāl al-Gharbīyah (Western Bahr el-Ghazal)	Raga	51,960	134,576	1,492,597
Baḥr al-Ghazāl ash-Sharqīyah (Eastern Bahr el-Ghazal)	Uwayl			
al-Buḥayrāh (El Buheyrah)	Rumbek	25,606	66,318	772,913
Dārfūr (Darfur)	al-Fāshir	196,404	508,684	3,093,699
Dārfūr al-Janūbīyah (Southern Darfur)	Nyala	62,753	162,529	1,765,752
Dārfūr ash-Shamālīyah (Northern Darfur)	al-Fāshir	133,651	346,155	1,327,947
al-Istiwā'īyah (Equatoria)	Jūbā	76,436	197,969	1,406,181
al-Istiwā'īyah al Gharbīyah (Western Equatoria)	Yambio	30,398	78,732	359,056
al-Istiwā'īyah ash-Sharqiyah (Eastern Equatoria)	Jūbā	46,038	119,237	1,047,125
Kurdufān (Kordofan)	al-Ubayyiḍ	146,817	380,255	3,093,294
Kurdufān al-Janūbīyah (Southern Kordofan)	Kāduqli	61,141	158,355	1,287,525
Kurdufān ash-Shamālīyah (Northern Kordofan)	al-Ubayyiḍ	85,676	221,900	1,805,769
ash-Shamālīyah (Northern)	ad-Dāmir	183,800	476,040	1,083,024
an-Nīl (Nile)	ad-Dāmir	49,167	127,343	649,633
ash-Shamālīyah (Northern)	Dunqulah	134,633	348,697	433,391
ash-Sharqīyah (Eastern)	Kassalā	128,987	334,074	2,208,209
al-Baḥr al-Aḥmar (Red Sea)	Port Sudan	84,912	219,920	695,874
Kassalā (Kassala)	Kassalā	44,075	114,154	1,512,335
al-Wastā (Central)	Wad Madani	53,675	139,017	4,012,543
an-Nīl al-Abyaḍ (White Nile)	ad-Duwaym	16,149	41,825	933,136
al-Jazīrah (El-Gezira)	Wad Madani	13,536	35,057	2,023,094
an-Nīl al-Azraq (Blue Nile)	ad-Damazin	23,990	62,135	1,056,313
National Capital				
Kharṭūm (Khartoum)	Khartoum	10,875	28,165	1,802,299
TOTAL		966,757[2]	2,503,890	20,564,364

Demography

Population (1988): 26,263,000.
Density (1988): persons per sq mi 27.2, persons per sq km 10.5.
Urban–rural (1985): urban 29.4%; rural 70.6%.
Sex distribution (1985): male 50.13%; female 49.87%.
Age breakdown (1985): under 15, 44.6%; 15–29, 26.0%; 30–44, 15.7%; 45–59, 8.9%; 60–74, 4.0%; 75 and over, 0.8%.
Population projection: (1990) 28,311,000; (2000) 37,315,000.
Doubling time: 25 years.
Ethnic composition (1983): Sudanese Arab 49.1%; Dinka 11.5%; Nuba 8.1%; Beja 6.4%; Nuer 4.9%; Azande 2.7%; Bari 2.5%; Fur 2.1%; Shilluk 1.7%; Lotuko 1.5%; other 9.5%.
Religious affiliation (1980): Sunnī Muslim 73.0%; traditional beliefs 16.7%; Roman Catholic 5.6%; Anglican 2.3%; other 2.4%.
Major cities (1983): Omdurman 526,287; Khartoum 476,218; Khartoum North 341,146; Port Sudan 206,727; Wad Madanī 141,065.

Vital statistics

Birth rate per 1,000 population (1980–85): 45.9 (world avg. 29.0).
Death rate per 1,000 population (1980–85): 17.4 (world avg. 11.0).
Natural increase rate per 1,000 population (1980–85): 28.5 (world avg. 18.0).
Total fertility rate (avg. births per childbearing woman; 1980–85): 6.6.
Life expectancy at birth (1980–85): male 46.6 years; female 49.0 years.
Major causes of death per 100,000 population (1979)[3]: pneumonia 26.4; tuberculosis 1.8; meningitis 1.3; infectious hepatitis 1.1.

National economy

Budget (1987–88). Revenue: LSd 3,905,500,000 (tax revenue 60.9%; nontax revenue 34.5%). Expenditures: LSd 6,790,000,000 (current expenditures 77.1%; development budget 22.6%, of which agriculture 6.2%, transport and communications 3.5%, energy and mining 0.5%).
Public debt (external, outstanding; 1986): U.S.$7,057,000,000.
Tourism (1986): receipts from visitors U.S.$30,900,000; expenditures by nationals abroad U.S.$36,900,000.
Production (metric tons except as noted). Agriculture, forestry, fishing (1986): sugarcane 5,200,000, sorghum 3,605,000, millet 544,000, peanuts (groundnuts) 454,000, seed cotton 440,000, sesame seeds 301,000, cotton lint 150,000, cassava 130,000, yams 116,000; livestock (number of live animals) 22,389,000 cattle, 15,581,000 goats, 12,755,000 sheep, 2,800,000 camels; roundwood (1985) 19,524,000 cu m; fish catch 23,942. Mining and quarrying (1986): hydraulic cement 200,000; salt 40,000; chromite concentrate 8,500; gypsum and anhydrite 7,000. Manufacturing (1985–86): refined sugar 451,500; wheat flour 280,300[4]; cement 150,500; textiles 48,200,000 yards; shoes 9,000,000 pairs; cigarettes 2,900,000,000 units; tires and tubes 555,000 units. Construction: n.a. Energy production (consumption): electricity (kW-hr; 1986) 1,052,000,000 (1,052,000,000); crude petroleum (barrels; 1986) none (7,342,000); petroleum products (metric tons; 1986) 845,000 (986,000).
Gross national product (1986): U.S.$7,290,000,000 (U.S.$320 per capita).

Structure of gross domestic product and labour force

	1985–86 in value LSd '000,000	1985–86 % of total value	1985 labour force	1985 % of labour force
Agriculture	4,486	31.8	4,786,000	68.5
Mining	1,392	9.9		
Manufacturing			587,000	8.4
Construction	620	4.4		
Public utilities	356	2.5		
Transp. and commun.	1,466	10.4		
Trade and finance	3,056	21.7		
Pub. admin., defense	1,481	10.5	1,618,000	23.1
Services	1,240	8.8		
TOTAL	14,079	100.0	6,991,000	100.0

Population economically active (1985): total 6,991,000; activity rate of total population 32.4% (participation rates: over age 15–64, 55.6%; female 20.8%; unemployed, n.a.).

Price indexes (1980 = 100)

	1981	1982	1983	1984	1985	1986	1987
Consumer price index	124.6	156.6	204.5	274.3	398.8	492.0	587.9

Household income and expenditure. Average household size (1980) 5.3; income per household: n.a.; sources of income: n.a.; expenditure (1978–80)[5]: food, beverages, and tobacco 66.5%, education, health, transportation, and recreation 15.2%, housing 12.4%, clothing 5.9%.
Land use (1985): forested 19.9%; meadows and pastures 23.6%; agricultural and under permanent cultivation 5.3%; desert and other 51.2%.

Foreign trade

Balance of trade (current prices)

	1981	1982	1983	1984	1985	1986
LSd '000,000	−407.3	−621.3	−791.6	−550.6	−786.5	−1,420.3
% of total	36.3%	36.8%	32.8%	25.2%	31.8%	46.0%

Imports (1986): LSd 2,402,237,000 (machinery and transport equipment 35.0%, of which transport equipment 18.1%; manufactured goods 20.0%; food and tobacco 15.6%; chemicals 14.2%; crude materials 12.2%, of which petroleum products 10.7%; textiles 3.0%). *Major import sources:* Saudi Arabia 14.9%; U.K. 11.8%; West Germany 8.5%; U.S. 7.7%; Japan 5.0%.
Exports (1986): LSd 833,205,000 (cotton 44.0%; gum arabic 14.7%; sheep and lambs 8.0%; sesame seeds 7.0%; hides and skins 4.0%). *Major export destinations:* Saudi Arabia 13.5%; Thailand 12.2%; United Arab Emirates 8.1%; Italy 7.1%; Yugoslavia 6.9%; Japan 6.7%.

Transport and communications

Transport. Railroads (1987–88): route length, 4,786 km; passenger-km 1,149,000[6]; metric ton-km cargo 1,600,000,000[6]. Roads (1985): total length 6,599 km (paved 59%). Vehicles (1985): passenger cars 99,400; trucks and buses 17,211. Merchant marine (1987): vessels (100 gross tons and over) 25; total deadweight tonnage 127,655. Air transport (1987)[7]: passenger-km 470,740,000; metric ton-km cargo 9,305,000; airports (1988) with scheduled flights 10.
Communications. Daily newspapers (1984): total number 6; total circulation 105,000; circulation per 1,000 population 4.6. Radio (1986): 1,500,000 receivers (1 per 16 persons). Television (1987): 240,000 receivers (1 per 105 persons). Telephones (1985): 77,920 (1 per 307 persons).

Education and health

Education (1985)

	schools	teachers	students	student/ teacher ratio
Primary (age 7–12)	6,707	47,750	1,653,491	34.6
Secondary (age 13–18)	2,167	17,591	490,583	27.9
Voc., teacher tr.	98	1,513[8]	30,973	...
Higher	16	1,464[9]	35,648	...

Educational attainment, n.a. *Literacy* (1980): total population age 15 and over literate 2,507,200 (21.6%); males 36.5%; females 6.5%.
Health (1981): physicians[10] 2,169 (1 per 9,369 persons); hospital beds 17,328 (1 per 1,110 persons); infant mortality rate (1980–85) 118.
Food (1984–86): daily per capita caloric intake 2,077 (vegetable products 78%, animal products 22%); (1983) 90% of FAO recommended minimum.

Military

Total active duty personnel (1987): 58,500 (army 92.3%, navy 2.6%, air force 5.1%). *Military expenditure as percent of GNP* (1985): 2.0% (world 6.1%); per capita expenditure U.S.$6.

[1]260 seats are occupied; seats for constituencies in the Southern Region are vacant. [2]Detail does not add to total given because of rounding. [3]Reported by hospitals and dispensaries. [4]1984–85. [5]Low-income households, Khartoum metropolitan area. [6]1981–82. [7]Sudan Airways only. [8]1984. [9]1983. [10]Includes dentists.

Suriname

Official name: Republiek Suriname (Republic of Suriname).
Form of government: multiparty republic with one legislative house (National Assembly [51])[1].
Head of state and government: President[1].
Capital: Paramaribo.
Official language: Dutch.
Official religion: none.
Monetary unit: 1 Suriname guilder (Sf) = 100 cents; valuation (Oct. 10, 1988) 1 U.S.$ = Sf 1.785; 1 £ = Sf 3.05.

Area and population

Districts	Capitals	area[2] sq mi	sq km	population 1980 census[3]
Brokopondo	Brokopondo	8,278	21,440	20,249
Commewijne	Nieuw Amsterdam	1,587	4,110	14,351
Coronie	Tottness	626	1,620	2,777
Marowijne	Albina	17,753	45,980	23,402
Nickerie	Nieuw Nickerie	24,946	64,610	34,480
Para	Onverwacht	378	980	14,867
Saramacca	Groningen	9,042	23,420	10,335
Suriname	...	629	1,628	166,494
Town district				
Paramaribo	Paramaribo	12	32	67,905
TOTAL		63,251	163,820	354,860

Demography

Population (1988): 425,000[4].
Density (1988): persons per sq mi 6.7, persons per sq km 2.6.
Urban-rural (1986): urban 45.3%; rural 54.7%.
Sex distribution (1985): male 49.60%; female 50.40%.
Age breakdown (1985): under 15, 40.2%; 15–29, 36.1%; 30–44, 9.2%; 45–59, 8.4%; 60–74, 4.6%; 75 and over, 1.5%.
Population projection[4]: (1990) 448,000; (2000) 579,000.
Doubling time: 30 years.
Ethnic composition (1983): Indo-Pakistani 37.0%; Suriname Creole 31.3%; Javanese 14.2%; Bush Negro 8.5%; Amerindian 3.1%; Chinese 2.8%; Dutch 1.4%; other 1.7%.
Religious affiliation (1980): Hindu 27.4%; Roman Catholic 22.8%; Muslim 19.6%; Protestant (mostly Moravian) 18.8%; other 11.4%.
Major cities (1980): Paramaribo 67,905[5]; Nieuw Nickerie 6,078; Meerzorg 5,355; Marienburg 3,633.

Vital statistics

Birth rate per 1,000 population (1985): 29.7 (world avg. 29.0); legitimate, n.a.; illegitimate, n.a.
Death rate per 1,000 population (1985): 6.8 (world avg. 11.0).
Natural increase rate per 1,000 population (1985): 22.9 (world avg. 18.0).
Total fertility rate (avg. births per childbearing woman; 1987): 3.2.
Marriage rate per 1,000 population (1985): 6.1.
Divorce rate per 1,000 population (1985): 1.5.
Life expectancy at birth (1987): male 65.0 years; female 70.0 years.
Major causes of death per 100,000 population (1985): diseases of the circulatory system 149.1, of which ischemic heart disease 51.6, diseases of pulmonary circulation and other forms of heart disease 41.9; malignant neoplasms (cancers) 48.0; diseases of the respiratory system 42.2; ill-defined conditions 67.6.

National economy

Budget (1986). Revenue: Sf 497,660,000 (tax revenue 75.4%, of which individual income tax 20.9%, import duties 20.0%, corporate tax 14.4%; nontax revenue 24.0%, of which property income 10.5%). Expenditures: Sf 925,690,000 (general public services 30.6%; economic services 25.2%; education 17.6%; social security 6.2%; defense 4.4%; health 3.7%).
Production (metric tons except as noted). Agriculture, forestry, fishing (1986): rice 300,000, sugarcane 120,000, bananas 40,000, oranges 10,000, palm oil 7,200, coconuts 7,000, plantains 5,000, cassava 3,000, tomatoes 1,000, cucumbers 1,000; livestock (number of live animals) 63,000 cattle, 22,000 pigs; roundwood 196,000 cu m; fish catch 3,116, of which shrimp 850. Mining and quarrying (1986): bauxite 3,731,000[6]; gold 600 troy oz. Manufacturing (1985): alumina 1,471,000[6,7]; cement 79,500; aluminum 28,700[6,7]; sugar 6,700; plywood 13,900 cu m; shoes 253,000 pairs; soft drinks 302,000 hectolitres; beer 140,000 hectolitres; cigarettes 514,000,000 units. Construction (buildings authorized; 1985): residential Sf 46,500,000; nonresidential Sf 8,100,000. Energy production (consumption): electricity (kW-hr; 1985) 1,430,000,000 (1,300,000,000); hard coal (metric tons; 1986) none (1,000); crude petroleum (barrels; 1986) 968,000 (968,000); petroleum products (metric tons; 1986) none (273,000); natural gas, none (none).
Tourism (1986): receipts from visitors U.S.$6,000,000; expenditures by nationals abroad U.S.$11,000,000.
Land use (1985): forested 96.5%; meadows and pastures 0.2%; agricultural and under permanent cultivation 0.4%; other 2.9%.
Population economically active (1984): total 99,240; activity rate of total population 25.9% (participation rates [1980]: ages 10–64, 38.7%; female 27.2%; unemployed [1986] 25.0%).

Price and earnings indexes (1980 = 100)

	1981	1982	1983	1984	1985	1986	1987
Consumer price index[8]	108.7	116.6	121.8	126.2	140.0	166.2	205.4[9]
Earnings index	...	...	...	...	...	...	...

Public debt (external, outstanding; 1985): U.S.$24,000,000.
Gross national product (at current market prices; 1986): U.S.$1,010,000,000 (U.S.$2,510 per capita).

Structure of gross domestic product and labour force

	1986 in value U.S.$'000,000[10]	1986 % of total value	1984 labour force	1984 % of labour force
Agriculture, forestry	99	10.0	16,700	16.8
Mining	73	7.3	4,600	4.7
Manufacturing	149	15.0	10,960	11.1
Construction	62	6.2	2,800	2.8
Public utilities	44	4.4	1,420	1.4
Transportation and communications	78	7.8	3,830	3.9
Trade	142	14.3	12,840	12.9
Finance, real estate	82	8.3	2,100	2.1
Pub. admin., defense	246	24.8	40,190	40.5
Services	19	1.9	3,800	3.8
TOTAL	994	100.0	99,240	100.0

Household income and expenditure. Average household size (1980) 3.9; income per household: n.a.; sources of income (1975): wages and salaries 74.6%, transfer payments 3.2%, other 22.2%; expenditure[8] (1968–69): food and beverages 40.0%, household furnishings 12.3%, clothing and footwear 11.0%, transport and communications 9.5%, recreation and education 8.4%, energy 6.9%, housing 4.4%, other 7.5%.

Foreign trade

Balance of trade (current prices)

	1981	1982	1983	1984	1985	1986
Sf '000,000	−202.0	−217.3	−277.9	−46.6	−19.7	+22.4
% of total	11.1%	13.2%	21.2%	4.2%	1.7%	1.9%

Imports (1985): Sf 603,700,000 (fuels and lubricants 29.1%, food products 5.8%, transport equipment 5.6%, construction materials 4.9%). *Major import sources* (1986): United States 32.1%; The Netherlands 19.4%; Trinidad and Tobago 11.3%; Brazil 7.8%.
Exports (1985): Sf 584,000,000 (alumina 52.7%, rice 14.6%, bauxite 12.0%, aluminum 9.3%, shrimp 6.6%, bananas 3.1%). *Major export destinations* (1986): The Netherlands 22.1%; United States 16.4%; Japan 12.7%; Brazil 8.9%; unspecified 33.1%.

Transport and communications

Transport. Railroads (1987): length[11] 54 mi, 87 km; passengers, n.a.; cargo, n.a. Roads (1985): total length 5,541 mi, 8,917 km (paved 26%). Vehicles (1986): passenger cars 35,052; trucks and buses 14,600. Merchant marine (1987): vessels (100 gross tons and over) 23; total deadweight tonnage 13,706. Air transport (1986)[12]: passenger-mi 248,574,000, passenger-km 400,042,000; short ton-mi cargo 33,881,000, metric ton-km cargo 49,466,000; airports (1988) with scheduled flights 5.
Communications. Daily newspapers (1987): total number 2; total circulation, n.a. Radio (1986): total number of receivers 246,000 (1 per 1.6 persons). Television (1987): total number of receivers 48,000 (1 per 8.6 persons). Telephones (1986): 38,315 (1 per 11 persons).

Education and health

Education (1984–85)

	schools	teachers	students	student/ teacher ratio
Primary (age 6–11)	...	2,809	71,454	25.4
Secondary (age 12–18)	63	1,047	18,612	17.8
Voc., teacher tr.	64	1,283	15,996	12.5
Higher	...	373	2,914	7.8

Educational attainment, n.a. *Literacy* (1980): total population age 15 and over literate 170,817 (79.2%); males literate 88,351 (83.8%); females literate 82,466 (74.8%).
Health (1985): physicians 219 (1 per 1,798 persons); hospital beds 1,964 (1 per 200 persons); infant mortality rate per 1,000 live births 27.6.
Food (1984–86): daily per capita caloric intake 2,713 (vegetable products 86%, animal products 14%); (1983) 108% of FAO recommended minimum requirement.

Military

Total active duty personnel (1987): 2,690[13] (army 91.1%, navy 6.7%, air force 2.2%). *Military expenditure as percent of GNP* (1985): 2.5% (world 6.1%); per capita expenditure U.S.$63.

[1]Balance of power between military and civilian leaders was evolving in late 1988. Military-influenced Council of State has constitutional powers to annul laws passed by National Assembly. [2]Area excludes 6,809 sq mi (17,635 sq km) of territory disputed with Guyana. [3]Preliminary. [4]Based on official estimates. UN estimates are significantly lower: (1988) 392,000; (1990) 403,000; (2000) 469,000. [5]1986 metropolitan area 208,000. [6]Production severely curtailed in 1987 because of civil war. [7]1986. [8]For Paramaribo and environs. [9]February. [10]At factor cost. [11]An additional 44 mi (71 km) of track are inoperative. [12]SLM (Suriname Airways) only. [13]All services are part of the army.

Swaziland

Official name: Umbuso weSwatini (Swazi); Kingdom of Swaziland (English).
Form of government: monarchy with two legislative houses (Senate [20[1]]; House of Assembly [50[1]]).
Chief of state: King.
Head of government: Prime Minister.
Capitals: Mbabane (administrative); Lobamba (royal and legislative).
Official languages: Swazi; English.
Official religion: none.
Monetary unit: 1 lilangeni (plural emalangeni [E]) = 100 cents; valuation (Oct. 10, 1988) 1 U.S.$ = E 2.49[2]; 1 £ = E 4.26.

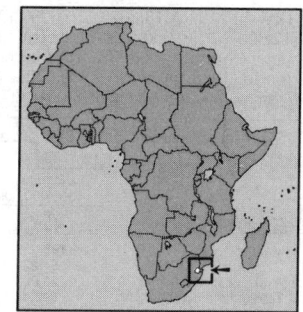

Area and population

Districts	Capitals	area sq mi	area sq km	population 1986 census[3]
Hhohho	Mbabane	1,378	3,569	178,936
Lubombo	Siteki	2,296	5,947	153,958
Manzini	Manzini	1,571	4,068	192,596
Shiselweni	Nhlangano	1,459	3,780	155,569
TOTAL		6,704	17,364	681,059

Demography

Population (1988): 716,000.
Density (1988): persons per sq mi 106.8, persons per sq km 41.2.
Urban–rural (1986): urban 22.8%; rural 77.2%.
Sex distribution (1986): male 47.22%; female 52.78%.
Age breakdown (1986): under 15, 47.3%; 15–29, 26.6%; 30–44, 13.4%; 45–59, 7.4%; 60–74, 3.4%; 75 and over, 1.3%; unknown 0.6%.
Population projection: (1990) 763,000; (2000) 1,042,000.
Doubling time: 23 years.
Ethnic composition (1983): Swazi 84.3%; Zulu 9.9%; Tsonga 2.5%; Indian 0.8%; Pakistani 0.8%; Portuguese 0.2%; other 1.5%.
Religious affiliation (1980): Christian 77.0%, of which Protestant 37.3%, Roman Catholic 10.8%, African indigenous 28.9%; traditional beliefs 20.9%; other 2.1%.
Major cities (1986): Manzini 52,000; Mbabane 38,290; Nhlangano 4,108; Piggs Peak 3,223; Siteki 2,271.

Vital statistics

Birth rate per 1,000 population (1980–85): 47.3 (world avg. 29.0); legitimate, n.a.; illegitimate, n.a.
Death rate per 1,000 population (1980–85): 17.2 (world avg. 11.0).
Natural increase rate per 1,000 population (1980–85): 30.1 (world avg. 18.0).
Total fertility rate (avg. births per childbearing woman; 1985): 7.0.
Marriage rate per 1,000 population: n.a.
Divorce rate per 1,000 population: n.a.
Life expectancy at birth (1980–85): male 45.3 years; female 52.2 years.
Major causes of death (1984)[4]: tuberculosis 11.0%; infectious intestinal diseases 8.5%; nutritional deficiencies 7.6%; diseases of the circulatory system 7.0%; accidents and injuries 7.0%; diseases of the respiratory system 5.7%; diseases of the digestive system 5.6%.

National economy

Budget (1987–88). Revenue: E 290,900,000 (receipts from Customs Union of Southern Africa 46.4%; tax on income and profits 26.1%; sales tax 13.2%; property income 4.6%; foreign aid grants 4.6%; fees, services, and fines 1.3%). Expenditures: E 311,800,000 (recurrent expenditure 75.7%, of which education 20.4%, economic services 12.7%, general administration 11.1%, justice and police 7.9%, health 6.8%, public debt payments 6.8%, defense 5.5%).
Tourism: receipts from visitors (1985) U.S.$12,000,000; expenditures by nationals abroad (1984) U.S.$11,000,000.
Public debt (external, outstanding; 1986): U.S.$207,700,000.
Gross national product (at current market prices; 1986): U.S.$470,000,000 (U.S.$600 per capita).

Structure of gross domestic product and labour force

	1984 in value E '000,000	1984 % of total value	1986 labour force[5]	1986 % of labour force
Agriculture	131.0	20.0	23,072	30.2
Mining	14.3	2.2	2,455	3.2
Manufacturing	108.5	16.6	10,944	14.3
Construction	26.9	4.1	5,210	6.8
Public utilities	10.3	1.6	1,426	1.9
Transp. and commun.	42.1	6.4	5,643	7.4
Trade	68.1	10.4	7,479	9.8
Finance	82.1	12.5	3,469	4.5
Pub. admin., defense	103.7	15.8		
Services	12.5	1.9	16,707	21.9
Other	55.9	8.5		
TOTAL	655.5[6]	100.0	76,405	100.0

Population economically active (1985): total 273,000; activity rate of total population 42.0% (participation rates: ages 15–64, 72.1%; female 39.9%; unemployed [1983] 4.0%).

Price and earnings indexes (1980 = 100)

	1982	1983	1984	1985	1986	1987	1988[7]
Consumer price index	133.9	148.8	168.0	201.2	224.9	252.9	279.1
Monthly earnings index[8]	172.1	181.3	...	...	...	...	...

Production (metric tons except as noted). Agriculture, forestry, fishing (1986): sugarcane 4,085,000, corn (maize) 189,000, citrus fruits 76,000, seed cotton 20,000, roots and tubers 12,000 (of which potatoes 6,000, sweet potatoes 6,000), lint cotton 11,000, pulses 3,000; livestock (number of live animals) 620,000 cattle, 315,000 goats, 37,000 sheep, 20,000 pigs, 1,000,000 chickens; roundwood (1985) 2,223,000 cu m; fish catch 44. Mining and quarrying (1986): asbestos 23,093; diamonds 39,144 carats. Manufacturing (value added in E; 1983): paper products 65,068,000; food products and beverages 57,520,000; industrial chemicals 46,043,000; wood products, furniture, and fixtures 18,477,000; metal products 13,452,000; textiles 10,097,000. Construction (value in E; 1986)[9]: residential 3,400,000; nonresidential 2,400,000. Energy production (consumption): electricity (kW-hr; 1986) 149,300,000 (650,000,000); coal (metric tons; 1986) 172,199 (23,408); crude petroleum, n.a. (n.a.); petroleum products, n.a. (n.a.); natural gas, n.a. (n.a.).
Household income and expenditure. Average household size (1980) 5.0; income per household: n.a.; sources of income: n.a.; expenditure[10]: food, beverages, and tobacco 39.3%, transportation and communications 15.3%, clothing and footwear 10.0%, furniture and utensils 9.0%, health and education 8.0%, energy and water 6.5%.
Land use (1985): forested 5.8%; meadows and pastures 66.9%; agricultural and under permanent cultivation 8.4%; other 18.9%.

Foreign trade[11]

Balance of trade (current prices)

	1981	1982	1983	1984	1985	1986
E '000,000	−102.4	−123.6	−177.4	−205.2	−229.2	−198.3
% of total	13.1%	14.9%	20.7%	23.1%	22.9%	15.5%

Imports (1985): E 706,681,000 (mineral fuels and lubricants 27.1%; machinery and transport equipment 23.3%; manufactured goods 17.4%; food and live animals 7.6%; chemicals 5.1%; beverages and tobacco 2.4%; animal and vegetable oils and fats 0.2%). *Major import sources* (1985–86): South Africa 81.1%; United Kingdom 5.0%; Switzerland 2.6%; The Netherlands 1.6%; France 1.5%.
Exports (1985): E 368,880,000[12] (sugar 37.8%; wood and wood products 27.2%, of which wood pulp 16.9%; canned fruit and juices 7.2%; citrus fruits 6.3%; chrysotile asbestos 6.0%; coal 2.1%; meat and meat products 1.1%; diamonds 1.1%). *Major export destinations* (1983): South Africa 32.4%; United Kingdom 22.1%.

Transport and communications

Transport. Railroads (1987): length 320 mi, 515 km; passengers, n.a.; short ton-mi cargo 73,300,000[13], metric ton-km cargo 107,000,000[13]. Roads (1986): total length 1,773 mi, 2,853 km (paved 18%). Vehicles (1985): passenger cars 18,830; trucks and buses 10,843. Merchant marine: none; landlocked state. Air transport (1984)[14]: passenger-mi 13,977,000, passenger-km 22,494,000; short ton-mi cargo 1,508,000, metric ton-km cargo 2,201,000; airports (1988) with scheduled flights 1.
Communications. Daily newspapers (1986): total number 2; total circulation 16,000; circulation per 1,000 population 24. Radio (1986): total number of receivers 96,000 (1 per 7.0 persons). Television (1987): total number of receivers 12,500 (1 per 56 persons). Telephones (1986): 20,134 (1 per 34 persons).

Education and health

Education (1986–87)

	schools	teachers	students	student/ teacher ratio
Primary (age 6–13)	477	4,462	147,743	33.1
Secondary (age 14–18)	113	1,760	32,942	18.7
Voc., teacher tr.	7	181	1,280	7.1
Higher	1	178	1,270	7.1

Educational attainment (1976). Percent of population age 25 and over having: no formal schooling 53.6%; some primary education 25.4%; complete primary 9.2%; some secondary 7.9%; secondary and higher 3.9%. *Literacy* (1986): total population age 15 and over literate 240,171 (67.0%); males literate 112,578 (69.0%); females literate 127,593 (65.0%).
Health (1984): physicians 80 (1 per 7,971 persons); hospital beds 1,608 (1 per 396 persons); infant mortality rate per 1,000 live births (1980–85) 129.2.
Food (1984–86): daily per capita caloric intake 2,550 (vegetable products 89%, animal products 11%); (1983) 111% of FAO recommended minimum requirement.

Military

Total active duty personnel (1983): 2,657. *Military expenditure as percent of GNP* (1985): 1.5% (world 6.1%); per capita expenditure U.S.$12.

---

[1]Includes 10 nonelective seats. [2]The lilangeni is at par with the South African rand. [3]Preliminary. [4]Percentage of deaths of known cause at government, mission, and private hospitals. [5]Wage earners only. [6]Detail does not add to total given because of rounding. [7]April. [8]Based on earnings of skilled male workers in manufacturing. [9]Urban areas under the jurisdiction of the Manzini and Mbabane town councils only. [10]Weights of consumer price index components. [11]Import figures are f.o.b. in balance of trade and c.i.f. in commodities and trading partners. [12]Reexports accounted for 5.0% of all exports. [13]1984. [14]Royal Swazi National Airways only.

Sweden

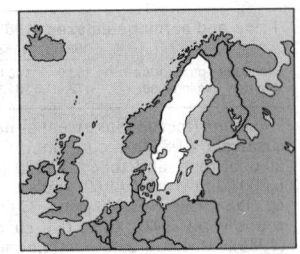

Official name: Konungariket Sverige (Kingdom of Sweden).
Form of government: constitutional monarchy and parliamentary state with one legislative house (Parliament [349]).
Chief of state: King.
Head of government: Prime Minister.
Capital: Stockholm.
Official language: Swedish.
Official religion: Church of Sweden (Lutheran).
Monetary unit: 1 Swedish krona (SKr) = 100 ore; valuation (Oct. 10, 1988) 1 U.S.$ = SKr 6.36; 1 £ = SKr 10.89.

Area and population		area		population
Counties	Capitals	sq mi	sq km	1988 estimate[1]
Älvsborg	Vänersborg	4,400	11,395	430,129
Blekinge	Karlskrona	1,136	2,941	149,600
Gävleborg	Gävle	7,024	18,191	286,907
Göteborg och Bohus	Göteborg	1,985	5,141	726,325
Gotland	Visby	1,212	3,140	56,269
Halland	Halmstad	2,106	5,454	244,377
Jämtland	Östersund	19,090	49,443	133,389
Jönköping	Jönköping	3,839	9,944	302,475
Kalmar	Kalmar	4,313	11,170	237,356
Kopparberg	Falun	10,886	28,194	283,330
Kristianstad	Kristianstad	2,350	6,087	281,907
Kronoberg	Växjö	3,266	8,458	174,116
Malmöhus	Malmö	1,907	4,938	757,643
Norrbotten	Luleå	38,191	98,913	260,833
Örebro	Örebro	3,289	8,519	269,341
Östergötland	Linköping	4,078	10,562	395,580
Skaraborg	Mariestad	3,065	7,937	270,847
Södermanland	Nyköping	2,340	6,060	250,073
Stockholm	Stockholm	2,505	6,488	1,606,157
Uppsala	Uppsala	2,698	6,989	257,739
Värmland	Karlstad	6,789	17,584	279,402
Västerbotten	Umeå	21,390	55,401	245,703
Västernorrland	Härnösand	8,370	21,678	260,332
Västmanland	Västerås	2,433	6,302	254,253
TOTAL LAND AREA		158,661[2]	410,929	8,414,083
INLAND WATER		15,071	39,035	
TOTAL		173,732[2]	449,964	

Demography

Population (1988): 8,415,080.
Density (1988)[3]: persons per sq mi 53.0, persons per sq km 20.5.
Urban–rural (1985): urban 83.4%; rural 16.6%.
Sex distribution (1988): male 49.35%; female 50.65%.
Age breakdown (1987): under 15, 17.9%; 15–29, 20.7%; 30–44, 22.2%; 45–59, 16.1%; 60–74, 15.5%; 75 and over, 7.6%.
Population projection: (1990) 8,450,000; (2000) 8,625,000.
Ethnic composition (1987): Swedish 91.0%; Finnish 3.1%; other 5.9%.
Religious affiliation (1986): Church of Sweden 89.6% (nominally; about 30% nonpracticing); Roman Catholic 1.4%; Pentecostal 1.2%; other 7.8%.
Major cities (1988): Stockholm 666,810; Göteborg 431,521; Malmö 230,838; Uppsala 159,962; Örebro 119,066; Norrköping 119,001.

Vital statistics

Birth rate per 1,000 population (1987): 12.5 (world avg. 26.0); (1986) legitimate 51.6%; illegitimate 48.4%.
Death rate per 1,000 population (1987): 11.1 (world avg. 9.9).
Natural increase rate per 1,000 population (1987): 1.4 (world avg. 16.1).
Total fertility rate (avg. births per childbearing woman; 1986): 1.8.
Marriage rate per 1,000 population (1987): 4.9.
Divorce rate per 1,000 population (1987): 2.2.
Life expectancy at birth (1981–85): male 73.6 years; female 79.5 years.
Major causes of death per 100,000 population (1986): heart disease 429.5; malignant neoplasms (cancers) 255.1; cerebrovascular disease 116.7.

National economy

Budget (1987–88). Revenue: SKr 331,775,000,000 (value-added and excise taxes 40.3%, income and capital gains taxes 25.8%, social security contributions 17.7%, property taxes 4.5%, nontax revenue 11.7%). Expenditures: SKr 341,514,000,000 (health and social affairs 27.2%, interest on national debt 16.7%, education and culture 13.3%, defense 8.3%).
Public debt (1987): U.S.$91,060,000,000.
Tourism (1986): receipts from visitors U.S.$1,540,000,000; expenditures by nationals abroad U.S.$2,811,000,000.
Production (metric tons except as noted). Agriculture, forestry, fishing (1986): barley 2,327,010, sugar beets 2,187,300, wheat 1,730,510, oats 1,486,160, potatoes 1,207,520; livestock (number of live animals) 2,438,-668 pigs, 1,715,539 cattle, 407,112 sheep; roundwood 22,400,000 cu m; fish catch 201,025, of which Baltic herring 153,469. Mining and quarrying (1987): iron ore 12,800,000[4], zinc 393,000[5], copper 359,000[5], lead 133,000[5]. Manufacturing (value added in SKr '000,000; 1985): machinery and transport equipment 93,937, of which automobiles 17,810; food and beverages 20,386, of which meat and dairy products 7,448; paper and paper products 19,186; printing and publishing 13,049. Construction (1986): 28,791 dwellings completed. Energy production (consumption): electricity (kW-hr; 1986) 138,023,000,000 (133,391,000,000); coal (metric tons; 1986) 12,000 (4,230,000); crude petroleum (barrels; 1986) 29,000 (114,400,000); petroleum products (metric tons; 1986) 13,541,000 (14,365,000); natural gas (cu m; 1986) none (215,140,000).
Gross national product (1986): U.S.$109,950,000,000 (U.S.$13,170 per capita).

Structure of gross domestic product and labour force				
	1986			
	in value SKr '000,000	% of total value	labour force	% of labour force
Agriculture	28,090	3.4	179,000	4.1
Mining	3,937	0.5	14,000	0.3
Manufacturing	198,059	24.3	976,000	22.3
Construction	54,229	6.7	257,000	5.9
Public utilities	27,093	3.3	40,000	0.9
Transp. and commun.	59,545	7.3	302,000	6.9
Trade	102,334	12.5	594,000	13.5
Finance	114,218	14.0	328,000	7.5
Pub. admin., defense	190,542	23.4 }	1,575,000	35.9
Services	31,538	3.9 }		
Other	5,829[6]	0.7[6]	120,000[7]	2.7[7]
TOTAL	815,414	100.0	4,385,000	100.0

Population economically active (1986): total 4,385,000; activity rate of total population 52.4% (participation rates: ages 16–64, 83.0%; female 47.6%; unemployed 2.7%).

Price and earnings indexes (1980 = 100)							
	1981	1982	1983	1984	1985	1986	1987
Consumer price index	112.1	121.7	132.6	143.2	153.8	160.3	167.0
Hourly earnings index	110.2	118.2	127.4	141.2	154.1	165.2	...

Household income and expenditure. Average household size (1985) 2.3; income per household (1983) SKr 98,400 (U.S.$15,165); sources of income (1984): wages and salaries 61.5%, transfer payments 21.4% (includes social security 15.0%), self-employment 17.1%; expenditure (1986): housing 25.8%, food 24.0%, transportation 16.4%, education and recreation 9.9%.
Land use (1985): forested 64.2%; meadows and pastures 1.4%; agricultural and under permanent cultivation 7.2%; other 27.2%.

Foreign trade

Balance of trade (current prices)						
	1982	1983	1984	1985	1986	1987
SKr '000,000	−5,800	10,150	24,710	16,080	37,910	29,827
% of total	1.7%	2.5%	5.4%	3.2%	7.7%	5.6%

Imports (1987): SKr 257,365,000,000 (machinery and transport equipment 38.4%, of which transport equipment 12.4%, electrical machinery 8.9%; chemicals 9.6%; food and tobacco products 6.4%; clothing and footwear 6.0%). *Major import sources:* W.Ger. 21.8%; U.K. 9.1%; U.S. 6.9%; Finland 6.9%; Denmark 6.7%; Norway 5.9%.
Exports (1987): SKr 281,406,000,000 (machinery and transport equipment 43.3%, of which transport equipment 17.2%, electrical machinery 7.6%; paper products 10.9%; wood and wood pulp 7.2%; chemicals 6.8%; iron and steel products 5.8%). *Major export destinations:* W.Ger. 11.8%; Norway 10.8%; U.S. 10.7%; U.K. 10.2%; Denmark 7.4%.

Transport and communications

Transport. Railroads (1986): length (1987) 7,279 mi, 11,715 km; passenger-mi 3,825,000,000, passenger-km 6,156,000,000; short ton-mi cargo 12,165,-000,000, metric ton-km cargo 17,760,000,000. Roads (1986): total length 81,296 mi, 130,834 km (paved 74%). Vehicles (1987): passenger cars 3,253,-601; trucks and buses 243,696. Merchant marine (1987): vessels (100 gross tons and over) 642; total deadweight tonnage 2,402,531. Air transport (1986): passenger-mi 3,342,000,000, passenger-km 5,378,000,000; short ton-mi cargo 130,758,000, metric ton-km cargo 190,903,000; airports (1988) 36.
Communications. Daily newspapers (1986): total number 186; total circulation 4,902,000; circulation per 1,000 population 586. Radio (1986): 3,330,-000 receivers (1 per 2.5 persons). Television (1987): 3,282,904 receivers (1 per 2.6 persons). Telephones (1984): 7,410,000 (1 per 1.1 persons).

Education and health

Education (1986–87)				
	schools	teachers	students	student/ teacher ratio
Primary (age 7–9)	4,667	98,920	920,780	9.3
Secondary (age 10–18)	534	28,550	243,971	8.5
Higher	...	24,990	341,712	13.7

Educational attainment (1979). Percent of population age 25 and over having: lower secondary education 7.3%; higher secondary 35.7%; some postsecondary 15.4%. *Literacy* (1988): virtually 100%.
Health (1985): physicians 21,000 (1 per 398 persons); hospital beds 114,202 (1 per 73 persons); infant mortality rate per 1,000 live births (1986) 5.9.
Food (1984–86): daily per capita caloric intake 3,048 (vegetable products 61%, animal products 39%); (1983) 112% of FAO requirement.

Military

Total active duty personnel (1987): 67,000 (army 70.2%, navy 17.9%, air force 11.9%). *Military expenditure as percent of GNP* (1985): 3.0% (world 6.1%); per capita expenditure U.S.$340.

[1]January 1. [2]Detail does not add to total given because of rounding [3]Density based on land area only. [4]Metal content of ore. [5]Ore concentrates. [6]Includes statistical discrepancies and unallocated indirect taxes. [7]Includes 117,000 unemployed.

Switzerland

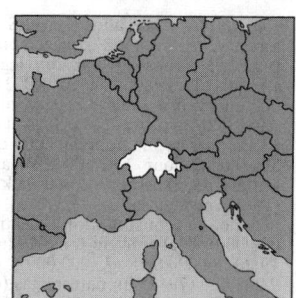

Official name: Confédération Suisse (French); Schweizerische Eidgenossenschaft (German); Confederazione Svizzera (Italian) (Swiss Confederation).
Form of government: federal state with two legislative houses (Council of States [46]; National Council [200]).
Head of state and government: President.
Capital: Bern.
Official languages: French; German; Italian.
Official religion: none.
Monetary unit: 1 Swiss Franc (Sw F) = 100 centimes; valuation (Oct. 10, 1988) 1 U.S.$ = Sw F 1.58; 1 £ = Sw F 2.70.

Area and population

Cantons	Capitals	area sq mi	area sq km	population 1986 estimate
Aargau	Aarau	542	1,405	472,900
Appenzell Ausser-Rhoden[1]	Herisau	94	243	49,700
Appenzell Inner-Rhoden[1]	Appenzell	66	172	13,300
Basel-Landschaft[1]	Liestal	165	428	226,300
Basel-Stadt[1]	Basel	14	37	196,300
Bern	Bern	2,335	6,049	930,600
Fribourg	Fribourg	645	1,670	194,900
Genève	Geneva	109	282	367,900
Glarus	Glarus	264	684	37,000
Graubünden	Chur	2,744	7,106	174,600
Jura	Delémont	323	837	65,200
Luzern	Luzern	576	1,492	307,800
Neuchâtel	Neuchâtel	308	797	156,900
Nidwalden[1]	Stans	107	276	31,300
Obwalden[1]	Sarnen	189	491	28,100
Sankt Gallen	Sankt Gallen	778	2,014	405,900
Schaffhausen	Schaffhausen	115	298	70,100
Schwyz	Schwyz	351	908	103,800
Solothurn	Solothurn	305	791	220,000
Thurgau	Frauenfeld	391	1,013	193,100
Ticino	Bellinzona	1,085	2,811	280,800
Uri	Altdorf	416	1,076	34,000
Valais	Sion	2,018	5,226	238,200
Vaud	Lausanne	1,243	3,219	555,100
Zug	Zug	92	239	81,800
Zürich	Zürich	668	1,729	1,137,300
TOTAL		15,943	41,293	6,572,900[3]

Demography

Population (1988): 6,626,000.
Density (1988): persons per sq mi 415.6, persons per sq km 160.5.
Urban–rural (1985): urban 58.2%; rural 41.8%.
Sex distribution (1986): male 49.09%; female 50.91%.
Age breakdown (1987)[2]: under 15, 17.2%; 15–29, 23.1%; 30–44, 22.8%; 45–59, 17.6%; 60–74, 12.8%; 75 and over, 6.5%.
Population projection: (1990) 6,680,000; (2000) 6,957,000.
Ethnolinguistic composition (1980)[2]: German 65.0%; French 18.4%; Italian 9.8%; Spanish 1.6%; Romansch 0.8%; Turkish 0.6%; other 3.8%.
Religious affiliation (1980): Roman Catholic 47.6%; Protestant 44.3%; Jewish 0.3%; other 7.8%.
Major cities (1987): Zürich 349,549; Basel 173,160; Geneva 160,645; Bern 137,134; Lausanne 124,206.

Vital statistics

Birth rate per 1,000 population (1986): 11.7 (world avg. 26.0); legitimate 94.0%; illegitimate 6.0%.
Death rate per 1,000 population (1986): 9.2 (world avg. 9.9).
Natural increase rate per 1,000 population (1986): 2.5 (world avg. 16.1).
Total fertility rate (avg. births per childbearing woman; 1986): 1.8.
Marriage rate per 1,000 population (1986): 6.1.
Divorce rate per 1,000 population (1986): 1.7.
Life expectancy at birth (1978–83): male 72.4 years; female 79.1 years.
Major causes of death per 100,000 population (1986): circulatory system diseases 414.1; malignant neoplasms (cancers) 239.6.

National economy

Budget (1986). Revenue: Sw F 25,144,000,000 (taxes on income and wealth 45.9%; taxes on consumption 38.1%, of which turnover tax 31.4%; customs duties 16.0%). Expenditures: Sw F 23,176,200,000 (social security 21.8%; defense 19.6%; communications and energy 14.2%; education 8.7%).
Public debt (1987): U.S.$18,556,000,000.
Tourism (1986): receipts from visitors U.S.$4,227,000,000; expenditures by nationals abroad U.S.$3,368,000,000.
Production (metric tons except as noted). Agriculture, forestry, fishing (1986): sugar beets 762,000, potatoes 721,000, wheat 497,000, apples 390,000, barley 232,000, grapes 176,000; livestock (number of live animals) 1,973,000 pigs, 1,902,000 cattle, 365,000 sheep; roundwood (1985) 4,561,000 cu m; fish catch (1985) 4,385. Mining and quarrying (1986): salt 400,000; gypsum 75,000. Manufacturing (1985): cement 4,254,000; refined sugar 142,000; wine 118,000; chocolate 82,563; aluminum 73,000; woolen fabrics 8,696,000 m; 25,137,000 watches; 8,032,000 pairs of shoes. Construction (buildings completed; 1986): residential 17,581; nonresidential 8,109.

Energy production (consumption)[3]: electricity (kW-hr; 1986) 54,857,000,000 (46,271,000,000); coal (metric tons; 1986) none (549,000); crude petroleum (barrels; 1986) none (28,792,000); petroleum products (metric tons; 1986) 4,120,000 (11,808,000); natural gas (cu m; 1986) 15,325,000 (1,547,335,000).
Gross national product (1986): U.S.$115,360,000,000 (U.S.$17,840 per capita).

Structure of gross domestic product and labour force

	1985 in value Sw F '000,000	1985 % of total value	1986 labour force	1986 % of labour force
Agriculture	8,180	3.6	209,200	6.5
Mining	2,573	1.1		
Manufacturing	56,052	24.6 }	966,200	29.8
Construction	17,325	7.6	225,900	7.0
Public utilities	5,023	2.2	29,900	0.9
Transp. and commun.	14,763	6.5	198,500	6.1
Trade	39,742	17.4	603,300	18.6
Finance	23,659	10.4	172,700	5.3
Pub. admin., defense	26,065	11.4	271,400	8.4
Services	31,390	13.8	541,600	16.7
Other	3,178[4]	1.4[4]	22,700[5]	0.7[5]
TOTAL	227,950	100.0	3,241,400	100.0

Population economically active (1986): total 3,241,400; activity rate of total population 49.3% (participation rates: age 15 and over [1984] 58.9%; female 36.9%[6]; unemployed 0.7%).

Price and earnings indexes (1980 = 100)

	1982	1983	1984	1985	1986	1987	1988[7]
Consumer price index	112.5	115.9	119.3	123.4	124.3	126.1	128.6
Annual earnings index	114.0	118.4	121.5	126.3	130.8	...	...

Household income and expenditure. Average household size (1981) 2.5; average income per household (1982) Sw F 61,000 (U.S.$30,045); sources of income (1984): wages 63.9%, self-employment 21.3%, social security 12.0%; expenditure (1986): food and beverages 21.3%, housing 18.0%, education and recreation 16.3%, transportation 13.3%, health 7.7%, utilities 4.4%.
Land use (1985): forested 26.4%; meadows and pastures 40.5%; agricultural and under permanent cultivation 10.4%; other 22.7%.

Foreign trade

Balance of trade (current prices)

	1981	1982	1983	1984	1985	1986	1987
Sw F '000,000	−5,428	−4,583	−6,871	−7,852	−7,359	−5,781	−6,933
% of total	4.9%	4.2%	6.0%	6.1%	5.2%	4.1%	4.9%

Imports (1986): Sw F 73,512,500,000 (machinery and transp. equip. 28.0%, chemical products 11.5%, precious metals and jewelry 10.1%, clothing and textiles 9.6%, mineral fuels 5.2%). *Major import sources:* W.Ger. 33.0%; France 11.5%; Italy 10.2%; U.K. 7.3%; U.S. 5.4%; The Netherlands 4.2%.
Exports (1986): Sw F 67,004,000,000 (nonelectrical machinery 20.3%, electrical machinery 11.6%, pharmaceuticals 7.9%, precious-metal articles and jewelry 7.0%, watches 6.4%). *Major export destinations:* W.Ger. 21.1%; U.S. 9.5%; France 9.0%; U.K. 7.7%; Italy 7.7%.

Transport and communications

Transport. Railroads (1986)[8]: length[9] 3,128 mi, 5,034 km; passenger-km 9,204,000,000; metric ton-km cargo 6,967,000,000. Roads (1985): total length 43,855 mi, 70,578 km. Vehicles (1986): passenger cars 2,678,911; trucks and buses 231,934. Merchant marine (1987): vessels (100 gross tons and over) 30; total deadweight tonnage 579,899. Air transport (1987): passenger-km 13,728,000,000; metric ton-km cargo 784,536,000; airports (1988) 5.
Communications. Daily newspapers (1986): total number 102; total circulation 3,229,158; circulation per 1,000 population 491. Radio (1986): 2,512,012 receivers (1 per 2.6 persons). Television (1987): 2,267,969 receivers (1 per 2.9 persons). Telephones (1986): 5,622,976 (1 per 1.2 persons).

Education and health

Education (1986–87)

	schools	teachers	students	student/teacher ratio
Primary (age 6–11)	...	...	405,800	...
Secondary (age 11–18)	...	...	368,600	...
Voc., teacher tr.	...	...	249,900	...
Higher	...	...	117,000	...

Educational attainment (1970). Percent of population age 25 and over having: no formal schooling 0.4%; primary and lower-secondary education 73.1%; higher-secondary 7.2%; some postsecondary 10.2%; university degree 3.1%. *Literacy:* virtually 100.0%.
Health: physicians (1985) 15,090 (1 per 433 persons); hospital beds (1983) 66,192 (1 per 98 persons); infant mortality rate (1986) 6.8.
Food (1983–85): daily per capita caloric intake 3,440 (vegetable products 60%, animal products 40%); (1983) 129% of FAO recommended minimum.

Military

Total active duty personnel[10] (1987): 625,000 (army 92.8%, air force 7.2%). *Military expenditure as percent of GNP* (1985): 2.2% (world 6.1%); per capita expenditure U.S.$333.

[1]Demicanton; functions as a full canton and has the same legal prerogatives as a full canton. [2]Includes resident aliens but excludes seasonal workers. [3]Figures include Liechtenstein. [4]Includes imputed bank service charges. [5]Unemployed. [6]For employed persons only. [7]Sept. [8]Swiss Federal Railways only. [9]1985. [10]Mobilized personnel.

Syria

Official name: al-Jumhūrīyah al-'Arabīyah as-Sūrīyah (Syrian Arab Republic).
Form of government: unitary multiparty[1] republic with one legislative house (People's Council [195]).
Chief of state: President.
Head of government: Prime Minister.
Capital: Damascus.
Official language: Arabic.
Official religion: none[2].
Monetary unit: 1 Syrian Pound (LS) = 100 piastres; valuation (Oct. 10, 1988) 1 U.S.$ = LS 20.96; 1£ = LS 35.90.

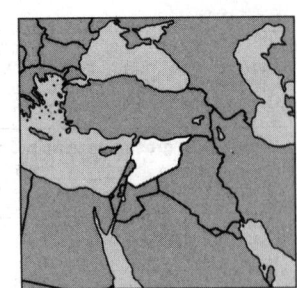

Area and population

Governorates	Capitals	area sq mi	area sq km	population 1988 estimate
Dar'ā	Dar'ā	1,440	3,730	479,000
Dayr az-Zawr	Dayr az-Zawr	12,765	33,060	502,000
Dimashq	al-larmouk	6,962	18,032	1,168,000
Halab	Aleppo	7,143	18,500	2,344,000
Ḥamāh	Ḥamāh	3,430	8,883	919,000
al-Ḥasakah	al-Ḥasakah	9,009	23,334	837,000
Ḥimṣ	Homs	16,302	42,223	1,045,000
Idlib	Idlib	2,354	6,097	748,000
al-Lādhiqīyah	Latakia	887	2,297	690,000
al-Qunayṭirah	al-Qunayṭirah	719[3]	1,861[3]	35,000
ar-Raqqah	ar-Raqqah	7,574	19,616	436,000
as-Suwaydā'	as-Suwaydā'	2,143	5,550	248,000
Ṭarṭūs	Tartous	730	1,892	561,000
Municipality				
Dimashq	Damascus	41	105	1,326,000
TOTAL		71,498[3]	185,180[3]	11,338,000

Demography

Population (1988): 11,338,000.
Density (1988): persons per sq mi 158.6, persons per sq km 61.2.
Urban–rural (1988): urban 50.0%; rural 50.0%.
Sex distribution (1988): male 51.09%; female 48.91%.
Age breakdown (1988): under 15, 49.3%; 15–29, 22.4%; 30–44, 14.3%; 45–59, 7.5%; 60–74, 4.8%; 75 and over, 1.7%.
Population projection: (1990) 12,112,000; (2000) 16,854,000.
Doubling time: 21 years.
Ethnic composition (1981): Arab 88.8%; Kurdish 6.3%; other 4.9%.
Religious affiliation (1980): Muslim (mostly Sunnī) 89.6%; Christian 8.9%; other 1.5%.
Major cities (1987): Damascus 1,292,000; Aleppo 1,216,000; Homs 431,000; Latakia 241,000; Ḥamāh 214,000.

Vital statistics

Birth rate per 1,000 population (1986): 42.4 (world avg. 26.0).
Death rate per 1,000 population (1986): 7.5 (world avg. 9.9).
Natural increase rate per 1,000 population (1986): 34.9 (world avg. 16.1).
Total fertility rate (avg. births per childbearing woman; 1986): 7.1.
Marriage rate per 1,000 population (1987)[4]: 8.0.
Divorce rate per 1,000 population (1987)[4]: 0.7.
Life expectancy at birth (1986): male 64.3 years; female 61.9 years.
Major causes of death per 100,000 population (1981): signs, symptoms, and ill-defined conditions 207.3; diseases of the circulatory system 60.7; infectious and parasitic diseases 15.1.

National economy

Budget (1988). Revenue: LS 51,545,000,000 (taxes and duties 32.6%, of which direct taxes 24.0%; budget surplus carryover 23.4%; loans and assistances 12.1%; special revenues 3.2%). Expenditures: LS 51,545,000,000 (defense 28.2%; administration 14.6%; agriculture 9.0%; education 8.1%; transport and communications 3.3%).
Public debt (external, outstanding; 1986): U.S.$3,060,300,000.
Tourism (1986): receipts from visitors U.S.$395,000,000; expenditures by nationals abroad U.S.$302,000,000.
Gross national product (at current market prices; 1986): U.S.$16,890,000,000 (U.S.$1,560 per capita).

Structure of gross domestic product and labour force

	1987 in value LS '000,000	1987 % of total value	1986 labour force	1986 % of labour force
Agriculture	34,369	27.2	745,550	30.0
Mining	17,099	13.5	3,936	0.2
Manufacturing			330,223	13.3
Construction	6,772	5.3	385,967	15.5
Public utilities	...	...	25,966	1.0
Transportation and communications	11,793	9.3	157,595	6.3
Trade	29,719	23.5	257,887	10.4
Finance	5,545	4.4	22,572	0.9
Pub. admin.	17,808	14.1	558,510	22.4
Services	3,220	2.6		
TOTAL	126,325	100.0[5]	2,488,206	100.0

Production (value added in LS '000,000 except as noted). Agriculture, forestry, fishing (1987): vegetables 8,290.7, fruits 7,625.1, cereals 7,569.0, industrial crops 3,696.0, dry legumes 1,441.8; livestock (number of live animals) 12,669,000 sheep, 1,002,000 goats, 710,000 cattle; roundwood 48,-000 cu m; fish catch 4,850. Mining and quarrying (1987): phosphate rock 1,985,000; gypsum 248,000; salt 81,000; asphalt 54,000; sand and gravel 13,122,000 cu m; stone 608,000 cu m. Manufacturing (tons; 1987): cement 3,870,000; flour 1,016,000; sugar 108,000; fertilizers 101,000; glass and pottery 43,000; soap 41,000; silk and cotton textiles 25,000. Construction (1986): residential 3,993,000 sq m; nonresidential 511,000 sq m. Energy production (consumption): electricity (kW-hr; 1986) 7,032,000,000 (6,902,-000,000); coal (metric tons; 1986) none (2,000); crude petroleum (barrels; 1986) 84,000,000 (75,000,000); petroleum products (metric tons; 1986) 9,208,000 (794,000); natural gas (cu m; 1986) 179,389,000 (179,389,000).
Population economically active (1986): total 2,488,000; activity rate of total population 23.2% (participation rates: over age 15, 46.7%; female 12.8%; unemployed [1987] 13.3%).

Price and earnings indexes (1980 = 100)

	1981	1982	1983	1984	1985	1986	1987
Consumer price index	118.4	135.3	143.4	156.6	183.9	250.3	390.0
Annual earnings index[6]	123.4	153.3	173.2	180.6	203.0	269.4	...

Average household size (1986): 5.7.
Land use (1987): steppe and pasture 44.7%; cultivable 30.4%; forested 2.9%; other 22.0%.

Foreign trade

Balance of trade (current prices)

	1982	1983	1984	1985	1986	1987
LS '000,000	−6,569	−10,281	−8,879	−7,857	−5,510	−12,723
% of total	29.2%	40.5%	37.9%	37.9%	34.6%	29.5%

Imports (1987): LS 27,915,000,000 (machinery and equipment 30.2%; chemicals and chemical products 21.2%; food, beverages, and tobacco 11.5%; basic metals industries 7.9%; textiles 3.2%; paper and paper products 1.9%). *Major import sources:* France 9.8%; U.S.S.R. 8.3%; Iran 8.2%; West Germany 8.2%; Italy 6.7%; Libya 5.6%; United States 5.3%; Switzerland 3.3%.
Exports (1987): LS 15,192,000,000 (crude petroleum and natural gas 33.2%; chemicals and chemical products 29.4%; textiles, wearing apparel, and leather 25.5%; food, beverages, and tobacco 3.6%). *Major export destinations:* Italy 31.1%; U.S.S.R. 20.8%; France 9.9%; Romania 8.6%; Iran 5.0%; West Germany 5.0%; United Kingdom 1.2%.

Transport and communications

Transport. Railroads (1987): route length 1,275 mi, 2,052 km; passenger-mi 559,000,000, passenger-km 900,000,000; short ton-mi cargo 970,000,000, metric ton-km cargo 1,416,000,000. Roads (1987): total length 18,770 mi, 30,208 km (paved 94%). Vehicles (1987): passenger cars 112,595; trucks and buses 127,420. Merchant marine (1987): vessels (100 gross tons and over) 57; total deadweight tonnage 93,205. Air transport (1987): passenger-mi 526,820,000, passenger-km 847,836,000; short ton-mi cargo 61,520,000, metric ton-km cargo 89,817,000; airports (1988) with scheduled flights 5.
Communications. Daily newspapers (1986): total number 9; total circulation 201,400; circulation per 1,000 population 19.0. Radio (1986): total number of receivers 2,000,000 (1 per 5.3 persons). Television (1986): total number of receivers 400,000 (1 per 26.5 persons). Telephones (1986): 637,000 (1 per 16.7 persons).

Education and health

Education (1987)

	schools	teachers	students	student/teacher ratio
Primary (age 6–11)	9,315	85,583	2,158,594	25.2
Secondary (age 12–18)	1,922	52,074	855,453	16.4
Voc., teacher tr.	143	7,245	56,664	7.8
Higher[7]	4	...	138,743	...

Educational attainment (1984). Percent of population having: no schooling 32.0%; knowledge of reading and writing 28.4%; primary education 31.3%; secondary 4.9%; certificate 2.0%; higher 1.9%. *Literacy* (1986): total population age 15 and over literate 3,393,164 (61.1%); males literate 2,144,085 (76.5%); females literate 1,249,079 (45.5%).
Health (1987): physicians 8,146 (1 per 1,347 persons); hospital beds 12,606 (1 per 870 persons); infant mortality rate per 1,000 live births (1986) 48.1.
Food (1984–86): daily per capita caloric intake 3,259 (vegetable products 86%, animal products 14%); (1983) 127% of FAO recommended minimum requirement.

Military

Total active duty personnel (1988): 404,000 (army 74.3%, navy 1.0%, air force 24.7%). *Military expenditure as percent of GNP* (1985): 22.8% (world 6.1%); per capita expenditure U.S.$439.

[1]Parties other than the Communist Party form a coalition (National Progressive Front). [2]Islam is required to be the religion of the head of state and is the basis of the legal system. [3]Includes territory in the Golan Heights recognized internationally as part of Syria (located between the 1949 Israel–Syria Armistice line [west] and the 1974 UN Disengagement of Forces zone [east]) that has been occupied by Israel since 1967. Israel's unilateral annexation of this territory in December 1981 has received no international recognition. [4]Syrian Arabs only. [5]Detail does not add to total given because of rounding. [6]Public sector only. [7]Universities only.

Taiwan

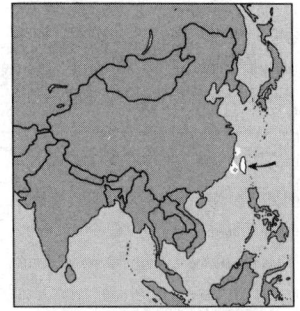

Official name: Chung-hua Min-kuo (Republic of China).
Form of government: unitary republic with a National Assembly (946)[1].
Chief of state: President.
Head of government: Premier.
Capital: Taipei.
Official language: Mandarin Chinese.
Official religion: none.
Monetary unit: 1 New Taiwan dollar (NT$) = 100 cents; valuation (Oct. 10, 1988) 1 U.S.$ = NT$28.72; 1 £ = NT$49.18.

Area and population

Counties	Capitals	area sq mi	area sq km	population 1988 estimate[2,3]
Chang-hua	Chang-hua	415	1,074	1,229,411
Chia-i	Chia-i	734	1,902	558,896
Hsin-chu	Hsin-chu	551	1,428	366,610
Hua-lien	Hua-lien	1,787	4,629	355,383
I-lan	I-lan	825	2,137	447,467
Kao-hsiung	Feng-shan	1,078	2,793	1,083,145
Miao-li	Miao-li	703	1,820	546,004
Nan-t'ou	Nan-t'ou	1,585	4,106	533,601
P'eng-hu	Ma-kung	49	127	99,006
P'ing-tung	P'ing-tung	1,072	2,776	894,652
T'ai-chung	Feng-yuan	792	2,051	1,183,490
T'ai-nan	Hsin-ying	778	2,016	1,006,366
T'ai-pei	Pan-ch'iao	792	2,052	2,800,881
T'ai-tung	T'ai-tung	1,357	3,515	267,363
T'ao-yüan	T'ao-yüan	471	1,221	1,259,503
Yün-lin	Tou-liu	498	1,291	775,588
Municipalities				
Chia-i	—	23	60	254,875
Chi-lung	—	51	133	348,541
Hsin-chu	—	40	104	309,899
Kao-hsiung	—	59	154	1,342,797
T'ai-chung	—	63	163	715,107
T'ai-nan	—	68	176	656,927
Taipei	—	105	272	2,637,100
TOTAL		**13,900[4]**	**36,000**	**19,672,612**

Demography

Population (1988): 19,813,000.
Density (1988): persons per sq mi 1,425.4, persons per sq km 550.3.
Urban–rural[3] (1986): urban 72.5%; rural 27.5%.
Sex distribution[3] (1988): male 51.80%; female 48.20%.
Age breakdown[3] (1986): under 15, 29.3%; 15–29, 29.9%; 30–44, 19.9%; 45–59, 12.6%; 60–74, 6.9%; 75 and over, 1.4%.
Population projection: (1990) 20,476,000; (2000) 23,569,000.
Doubling time: 63 years.
Ethnic composition (1986): Taiwanese 84.0%; mainland Chinese 14.0%; aborigine 2.0%.
Religious affiliation (1980): Chinese folk-religionist 48.5%; Buddhist 43.0%; Christian 7.4%; Muslim 0.5%; other 0.6%.
Major cities (1987): Taipei 2,575,180; Kao-hsiung 1,320,552; T'ai-chung 695,562; T'ai-nan 646,298; Chi-lung 349,616; Hsin-chu 306,088.

Vital statistics

Birth rate per 1,000 population (1987): 16.0 (world avg. 26.0); (1986) legitimate 98.0%; illegitimate 2.0%.
Death rate per 1,000 population (1987): 4.9 (world avg. 9.9).
Natural increase rate per 1,000 population (1987): 11.1 (world avg. 16.1).
Total fertility rate[3] (avg. births per childbearing woman; 1986): 1.7.
Marriage rate per 1,000 population (1987): 7.5.
Divorce rate per 1,000 population (1987): 1.2.
Life expectancy at birth (1986): male 71.0 years; female 75.9 years.
Major causes of death per 100,000 population (1986): malignant neoplasms 85.6; cerebrovascular diseases 76.8; accidents and suicide 63.0; heart disease 51.4; hypertensive disease 17.3; liver diseases 16.6; diabetes 15.3.

National economy

Budget (1986)[5]. Revenue: NT$636,204,000,000 (surplus of public enterprises 15.7%; income taxes 12.5%; customs duties 10.0%; land tax 7.4%; business tax 7.2%). Expenditures: NT$632,661,000,000 (administration and defense 35.3%; education 20.5%; communications 17.1%; social welfare 15.6%).
Public debt (domestic and foreign; 1986): U.S.$1,755,052,000[6].
Production (metric tons except as noted). Agriculture, forestry, fishing (1986): sugarcane 6,001,871, vegetables 3,127,869, rice 1,973,823, citrus fruits 386,819, sweet potatoes 324,042, corn (maize) 271,660, pineapple 157,941, bananas 150,730, peanuts 77,150; livestock (number of live animals) 7,057,039 pigs, 237,252 goats, 214,358 cattle; timber 498,675 cu m; fish catch 1,094,587. Mining and quarrying (1986): silver 12,613 kilograms; gold 910 kilograms. Manufacturing (1987): cement 15,663,437; paperboard 2,020,220; steel ingots 1,851,264; fertilizers 1,324,058; man-made fibre 869,715; PVC plastics 831,527; sulfuric acid 741,829; electronic calculators 62,274,840 units; audio recorders 17,512,245 units; television receivers 5,941,563 units; computer systems 1,465,591 units. Construction (1987): total residential and nonresidential 25,179,000 sq m. Energy production (consumption): electricity (kW-hr; 1987) 65,514,000,000 (41,873,029,000[7]); coal (metric tons; 1987) 1,499,240 (3,202,000[8]); petroleum (barrels; 1986) 704,700 (n.a.); natural gas (cu m; 1987) 1,056,916,000 (n.a.).

Gross national product (1986): U.S.$72,621,000,000 (U.S.$3,750 per capita).

Structure of gross domestic product and labour force[3]

1987	in value NT$'000,000	% of total value	labour force[9]	% of labour force
Agriculture	158,814	5.3	1,226,000	15.3
Mining	15,229	0.5	31,000	0.4
Manufacturing	1,310,506	43.5	2,810,000	35.0
Construction	125,449	4.2	554,000	6.9
Public utilities	115,772	3.8	35,000	0.4
Transp. and commun.	180,851	6.0	429,000	5.3
Trade	429,063	14.2	1,435,000	17.9
Finance	254,911	8.5	229,000	2.9
Pub. admin., defense	268,662	8.9 }	1,275,000	15.9
Services	205,463	6.8 }		
Other	−50,851[10]	−1.7[10]	...	...
TOTAL	3,013,869	100.0	8,024,000	100.0

Tourism (1986): receipts from visitors U.S.$1,333,000,000.
Population economically active (1986): total 9,392,640; activity rate 48.3% (participation rates: age 15–64, 71.0%; female 36.6%; unemployed 2.2%).

Price and earnings indexes (1981 = 100)[3]

	1981	1982	1983	1984	1985	1986	1987
Consumer price index	100.0	103.0	104.4	104.3	104.2	104.9	105.4
Monthly earnings index[11]	100.0	109.7	116.6	134.6	132.2	145.4	159.5

Household income and expenditure (1986). Average household size 4.5; income per household NT$341,728 (U.S.$9,062[6]); sources of income: wages 66.4%, self-employment 5.4%, transfer payments 0.9%, other 27.3%; expenditure: food and tobacco 37.4%, rent, fuel, and power 23.3%, recreation and education 10.0%, transport and communications 8.2%, clothing and footwear 5.8%, health care 5.4%, household furnishings 4.3%.
Land use (1980): forested 55.0%; agricultural and under permanent cultivation 25.2%; other 19.8%.

Foreign trade

Balance of trade (current prices)

	1982	1983	1984	1985	1986	1987
NT$'000,000	128,164	191,518	333,836	421,057	587,927	603,673
% of total	8.0%	10.5%	16.1%	20.8%	24.3%	21.5%

Imports (1987): NT$1,099,495,000,000 (electronic components 8.4%, petroleum and petroleum products 7.8%, nonelectrical machinery 3.4%, iron and steel 2.3%, telecommunication equipment 2.1%, motor vehicle parts 1.7%, raw cotton 1.5%). *Major import sources:* Japan 34.3%; U.S. 22.1%; W.Ger. 4.7%; Saudi Arabia 3.1%; Australia 2.9%; U.K. 2.2%.
Exports (1987): NT$1,703,168,000,000 (electronic products and appliances 8.6%, articles of plastic 8.6%, apparel and clothing 8.0%, textile yarns and fabrics 5.1%, wood, bamboo, and rattan manufactures 2.7%, processed food 2.1%, dolls and toys 1.7%). *Major export destinations:* U.S. 44.2%; Japan 12.9%; Hong Kong 7.7%; W.Ger. 3.7%; Canada 2.9%; U.K. 2.8%.

Transport and communications

Transport. Railroads (1987): track length 4,800 km; passenger-km 8,458,514,-000; metric ton-km cargo 2,490,214,000. Roads (1986): total length 19,885 km (paved 84%). Vehicles (1987): passenger cars 1,254,955; trucks and buses 472,708. Merchant marine (1987): vessels (100 gross tons and over) 594; total deadweight tonnage 6,887,040. Air transport (1987): passenger-km 14,498,202,000; metric ton-km cargo 2,944,571,000; airports (1988) 9.
Communications. Daily newspapers (1987): total number 31; total circulation 3,500,000; circulation per 1,000 population 179. Radio (1985): 13,500,-000 receivers (1 per 1.4 persons). Television (1987): 6,085,000 receivers (1 per 3.2 persons). Telephones (1986): 6,078,000 (1 per 3.2 persons).

Education and health

Education (1986–87)

	schools	teachers	students	student/ teacher ratio
Primary (age 6–12)	2,461	74,433	2,356,304	31.7
Secondary (age 13–18)	839	60,796	1,247,774	20.5
Vocational	203	16,613	436,276	26.3
Higher	105	21,769	442,648	20.3

Educational attainment (1986). Percent of population age 25 and over having: no formal schooling 16.0%; less than complete primary education 7.0%; primary 32.6%; incomplete secondary 16.8%; secondary 17.3%; some college 5.3%; higher 5.0%. *Literacy* (1986): population age 15 and over literate 12,578,401 (90.8%); males 6,898,723 (95.8%); females 5,679,678 (85.4%).
Health (1986): physicians 17,965 (1 per 1,077 persons); hospital beds 81,502 (1 per 237 persons); infant mortality rate per 1,000 live births 6.3.
Food (1983): daily per capita caloric intake (1986) 2,969 (vegetable products 77%, animal products 23%); 118% of FAO recommended minimum.

Military

Total active duty personnel (1987): 424,000 (army 63.7%, navy 18.1%, air force 18.2%). *Military expenditure as percent of GNP* (1985): 7.6% (world 6.1%); per capita expenditure U.S.$248.

[1]As of Sept. 4, 1987. [2]January 1. [3]For Taiwan area only, excluding Quemoy and Matsu. [4]Detail does not add to total given because of rounding. [5]General government. [6]Based on the 1986 average exchange rate of NT$37.71 = U.S.$1.00. [7]By industry only. [8]1986. [9]Civilian employed persons only. [10]Imputed bank service charge. [11]In manufacturing.

Tanzania

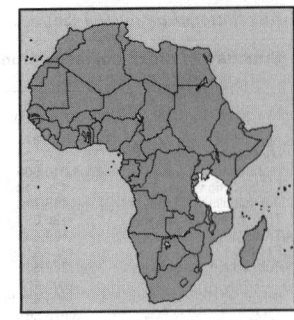

Official name: Jamhuri ya Mwungano wa Tanzania (Swahili); United Republic of Tanzania (English).
Form of government: unitary single-party republic with one legislative house (National Assembly [244[1]]).
Chief of state: President.
Head of government: Prime Minister.
Seat of government: Dar es Salaam (Capital designate, Dodoma).
Official languages: Swahili; English.
Official religion: none.
Monetary unit: 1 Tanzanian shilling (T Sh) = 100 cents; valuation (Oct. 10, 1988) 1 U.S.\$ = T Sh 106.22; 1 £ = T Sh 181.90.

Area and population

Regions	Capitals	area sq mi	area sq km	population 1987 estimate
Arusha	Arusha	31,698	82,098	1,274,000
Bukoba	Bukoba	10,987	28,456	1,397,000
Dar es Salaam	Dar es Salaam	538	1,393	1,605,000
Dodoma	Dodoma	15,950	41,311	1,239,000
Iringa	Iringa	21,950	56,850	1,167,000
Kigoma	Kigoma	14,301	37,040	828,000
Kilimanjaro	Moshi	5,116	13,250	1,159,000
Lindi	Lindi	25,498	66,040	631,000
Mara	Musoma	8,402	21,760	908,000
Mbeya	Mbeya	23,301	60,350	1,421,000
Morogoro	Morogoro	27,268	70,624	1,202,000
Mtwara	Mtwara	6,452	16,710	916,000
Mwanza	Mwanza	7,600	19,683	1,836,000
Pemba North	Wete			
Pemba South	Chake Chake	380	984	[2]
Pwani	Dar es Salaam	12,566	32,547	600,000
Rukwa	Sumbawanga	26,500	68,635	656,000
Ruvuma	Songea	24,583	63,669	725,000
Shinyanga	Shinyanga	19,598	50,760	1,779,000
Singida	Singida	19,050	49,340	770,000
Tabora	Tabora	29,402	76,150	1,185,000
Tanga	Tanga	10,300	26,677	1,305,000
Zanzibar North	Mkokotoni			
Zanzibar South and Central	Koani	641	1,660	605,000[2]
Zanzibar West	Zanzibar			
TOTAL LAND AREA		342,081	885,987	23,208,000
INLAND WATER		22,800	59,050	
TOTAL		364,881	945,037	

Demography

Population (1988): 23,996,000.
Density[3] (1988): persons per sq mi 70.1, persons per sq km 27.1.
Urban–rural (1987): urban 17.9%; rural 82.1%.
Sex distribution (1985): male 49.32%; female 50.68%.
Age breakdown (1985): under 15, 48.8%; 15–29, 25.5%; 30–44, 14.2%; 45–59, 7.7%; 60–74, 3.2%; 75 and over, 0.6%.
Population projection: (1990) 25,635,000; (2000) 36,008,000.
Doubling time: 20 years.
Ethnic composition (1983): Nyamwezi and Sukuma 21.1%; Swahili 8.8%; Hehet and Bena 6.9%; Makonde 5.9%; Haya 5.9%; other 51.4%.
Religious affiliation (1984): Christian 34%; Muslim 33%; traditional beliefs and other 33%.
Major cities (1984): Dar es Salaam 1,400,000; Mwanza 110,553[4].

Vital statistics

Birth rate per 1,000 population (1980–85): 50.3 (world avg. 29.0).
Death rate per 1,000 population (1980–85): 16.8 (world avg. 11.0).
Natural increase rate per 1,000 population (1980–85): 33.5 (world avg. 18.0).
Total fertility rate (avg. births per childbearing woman; 1985): 7.0.
Marriage rate per 1,000 population (1967): 9.8.
Life expectancy at birth (1980–85): male 47.4 years; female 50.7 years.
Major causes of death per 100,000 population: n.a.; however, the major diseases include malaria, bilharziasis, tuberculosis, and sleeping sickness.

National economy

Budget (1986–87). Revenue: T Sh 34,674,000,000 (sales tax 46.4%, income tax 21.2%, customs and excise tax 11.7%). Expenditures: T Sh 46,095,800,000 (public administration 25.5%, defense 20.1%, economic services 16.4%, education 6.4%, health 3.7%).
Public debt (external, outstanding; 1986): U.S.\$3,649,700,000.
Tourism: receipts from visitors (1985) U.S.\$11,446,000; expenditures by nationals abroad (1984) U.S.\$12,000,000.
Production (metric tons except as noted). Agriculture (1986): cassava 5,500,000, corn (maize) 2,210,000, sugarcane 1,130,000, bananas 1,100,000, plantains 1,100,000, sorghum 670,000, sweet potatoes 530,000, rice 527,000, coconuts 330,000, dry beans 282,000, millet 273,000, potatoes 200,000, mangoes 183,000, seed cotton 140,000, cottonseed 87,000, unshelled peanuts (groundnuts) 59,000; livestock (number of live animals) 14,300,000 cattle, 6,500,000 goats, 4,300,000 sheep, 28,000,000 chickens; roundwood (1985) 45,540,000 cu m; fish catch 309,855. Mining and quarrying (1986): phosphate minerals 23,000; diamonds 190,000 carats. Manufacturing (1986): petroleum products 370,000; cement 369,000[5]; meats 229,000; fertilizer 47,-

032; iron sheets 8,557; hides and skins 38,900; aluminum 6,000[5]; textiles 55,770,000 sq m. Construction: n.a. Energy production (consumption): electricity (kW-hr; 1986) 880,000,000 (880,000,000); coal (metric tons; 1986) 1,000 (1,000); crude petroleum (barrels; 1986) none (4,172,000); petroleum products (metric tons; 1986) 503,000 (552,000).
Gross national product (1986): U.S.\$5,370,000,000 (U.S.\$240 per capita).

Structure of gross domestic product and labour force

	1985 in value T SH '000,000	1985 % of total value	1985 labour force	1985 % of labour force
Agriculture	57,180	58.5	9,091,000	83.3
Mining	265	0.3		
Manufacturing	5,112	5.2	469,000	4.3
Construction	1,895	1.9		
Public utilities	878	0.9		
Transportation and communications	6,544	6.7		
Trade	13,088	13.4	1,353,000	12.4
Finance				
Pub. admin., defense	12,805[6]	13.1[6]		
Services				
Other			...	...
TOTAL	97,767[7]	100.0	10,913,000	100.0

Population economically active (1985): total 10,913,000; activity rate of total population 48.5% (participation rates: ages 15–64, 85.7%; female 48.9%; unemployed, n.a.).

Price and earnings indexes (1980 = 100)

	1982	1983	1984	1985	1986	1987
Consumer price index	162.0	205.8	280.2	373.5	495.3	642.7
Monthly earnings index	...	...	...	...	...	...

Household income and expenditure. Average household size (1980) 5.1; income per household: n.a.; sources of income: n.a.; expenditures (1981): food, beverages, and tobacco 54.3%, housing 8.6%, clothing 10.8%, energy 6.6%, transportation 6.4%.
Land use (1985): forested 47.2%; meadows and pastures 39.5%; agricultural and under permanent cultivation 5.9%; other 7.4%.

Foreign trade

Balance of trade (current prices)

	1981	1982	1983	1984	1985	1986
T Sh '000,000	−4,853.0	−4,917.0	−3,384.0	−5,506.0	−10,314	−12,505
% of total	34.1%	36.8%	29.5%	32.3%	51.0%	36.0%

Imports (1986): T Sh 23,621,000,000 (machinery, transport equipment, and industrial goods 73.2%; consumer goods 7.1%; construction materials 6.9%). *Major import sources:* EEC countries 53.5%, of which United Kingdom 11.8%; Japan 10.8%; United States 3.0%; China 1.4%; India 1.3%.
Exports (1986): T Sh 11,116,000,000 (coffee 48.7%; cotton 9.1%; tobacco 4.0%; tea 4.0%; cloves 3.8%; diamonds 3.6%; cashew nuts 3.2%; sisal 1.5%). *Major export destinations:* EEC countries 35.6%, of which United Kingdom 11.7%; Japan 4.0%; India 3.6%; United States 1.7%.

Transport and communications

Transport. Railroads (1985): length 1,615 mi, 2,600 km; passenger-mi 736,900,000[8], passenger-km 1,186,000,000[8]; short ton-mi cargo 527,000,000[8], metric ton-km cargo 770,000,000[8]. Roads (1984): length 50,887 mi, 81,895 km. Vehicles (1984): cars, trucks, and buses 84,190. Merchant marine (1987): vessels (100 gross tons and over) 39; deadweight tonnage 32,888. Air transport (1987): passenger-mi 155,000,000, passenger-km 249,000,000; short ton-mi cargo 1,709,000,000, metric ton-km 2,495,000,000; airports (1988) 19.
Communications. Daily newspapers: total number (1985) 3; total circulation (1984) 101,000; circulation per 1,000 population 5.0. Radio (1986): 2,000,000 receivers (1 per 11 persons). Television (1987): 8,000 receivers (1 per 2,902 persons). Telephones (1986): 117,301 (1 per 195 persons).

Education and health

Education (1986)

	schools	teachers	students	student/ teacher ratio
Primary (age 7–13)	10,147	93,000	3,160,000	34.0
Secondary (age 14–19)[9]	193	4,329	83,098	19.2
Voc., teacher tr.	41	1,277	13,956	10.9
Higher	2	877[9]	3,342	...

Educational attainment (1978). Percent of population age 10 and over having: no schooling 48.6%; some primary education 40.7%; completed primary 8.7%; secondary and higher 1.9%. *Literacy* (1987): 85%.
Health (1984): physicians 1,065 (1 per 19,775 persons); hospital beds 22,800 (1 per 924 persons); infant mortality rate per 1,000 live births 111.
Food (1984–86): daily per capita caloric intake 2,214 (vegetable products 93%, animal products 7%); (1983) 98% of FAO recommended minimum.

Military

Total active duty personnel (1987): 40,050 (army 95.8%, navy 1.7%, air force 2.5%). *Military expenditure as percent of GNP* (1985): 3.4% (world 6.1%); per capita expenditure U.S.\$9.

[1]Includes 40 nonelective seats. [2]Pemba North and Pemba South are included with Zanzibar. [3]Based on land area. [4]1978. [5]1984. [6]Includes indirect taxes, net of subsidies less imputed bank service charges. [7]Excludes Zanzibar. [8]For Tanzania Railways Corporation only. [9]1985.

Thailand

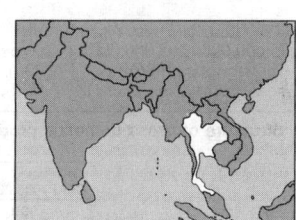

Official name: Muang Thai, or Prathet Thai (Kingdom of Thailand).
Form of government: constitutional monarchy with a multiparty National Assembly (Senate [268]; House of Representatives [357]).
Chief of state: King.
Head of government: Prime Minister.
Capital: Bangkok.
Official language: Thai.
Official religion: Buddhism.
Monetary unit: 1 Thai Baht (B) = 100 stangs; valuation (Oct. 10, 1988) 1 U.S.$ = B 25.11; 1 £ = B 43.00.

Area and population	area		population
Regions	sq mi	sq km	1987 estimate
Bangkok Metropolis	604	1,565	5,972,000
Central[1]	7,236	18,742	5,126,000
Eastern	14,481	37,507	3,232,000
Northeastern	65,195	168,854	18,622,000
Northern	65,500	169,644	10,488,000
Southern	27,303	70,715	6,996,000
Western	17,795	46,088	3,169,000
TOTAL	198,115[2]	513,115	53,605,000

Demography

Population (1988): 54,862,000.
Density (1988): persons per sq mi 276.9, persons per sq km 106.9.
Urban–rural (1985): urban 19.8%; rural 80.2%.
Sex distribution (1988): male 50.06%; female 49.94%.
Age breakdown (1985): under 15, 36.2%; 15–29, 30.7%; 30–44, 17.2%; 45–59, 10.2%; 60–69, 3.5%; 70 and over, 2.2%.
Population projection: (1990) 56,677,000; (2000) 64,348,000.
Doubling time: 40 years.
Ethnic composition (1983): Thai 79.5%, of which Siamese 52.6%, Lao 26.9%; Chinese 12.1%; Malay 3.7%; Khmer 2.7%; other 2.0%.
Religious affiliation (1980): Buddhist 95.0%; Muslim 3.8%; Christian 0.5%; other 0.7%.
Major cities (1983): Bangkok 5,363,378[3]; Chiang Mai 150,499; Hat Yai 113,964; Khon Kaen 115,515; Nakhon Ratchasima 190,692.

Vital statistics

Birth rate per 1,000 population (1987): 24.8 (world avg. 26.0).
Death rate per 1,000 population (1987): 7.3 (world avg. 9.9).
Natural increase rate per 1,000 population (1987): 17.5 (world avg. 16.1).
Total fertility rate (avg. births per childbearing woman; 1987): 2.9.
Marriage rate per 1,000 population (1985): 6.6.
Divorce rate per 1,000 population (1985): 0.6.
Life expectancy at birth (1987): male 61.6 years; female 67.6 years.
Major causes of death per 100,000 population (1985): heart disease 36.4; accidents, poisonings, and violence 28.9; malignant neoplasms (cancers) 27.0; tuberculosis 10.3; pneumonia 7.4; malaria 3.5.

National economy

Budget (1986–87). Revenue: B 227,500,000,000 (taxes 72.6%, of which indirect taxes 55.3%, direct taxes 17.4%; borrowing, state enterprises, and sale of assets and services 27.4%). Expenditures: B 227,500,000,000 (debt service 24.7%; education 18.1%; defense 18.0%; economic services 15.6%; public utilities and health 10.8%; internal security 4.8%; general administration 2.7%).
Tourism (1986): receipts from visitors U.S.$1,421,000,000; expenditures by nationals abroad U.S.$296,000,000.
Production (metric tons except as noted). Agriculture, forestry, fishing (1986): sugarcane 24,093,000, tapioca root 19,263,000, rice 19,100,000, corn (maize) 4,197,000, coconuts 1,278,000, rubber 790,000, cotton 93,000, tobacco 85,000, coffee 26,000; livestock (number of live animals) 6,302,000 buffalo, 4,835,000 cattle, 4,215,000 pigs, 81,000 goats, 79,000,000 chickens; roundwood 36,896,000 cu m; fish catch 2,119,000. Mining and quarrying (1986): limestone 9,604,931; gypsum 1,665,557; fluorite 201,212; barite 142,231; iron ore 37,330; tin 23,298. Manufacturing (1985): cement 7,951,000; refined sugar 2,491,000; galvanized iron sheets 112,169; tin plate 68,200; commercial vehicles 58,244 units. Construction (1985): residential 5,391,000 sq m; nonresidential 4,868,000 sq m. Energy production (consumption): electricity (kW-hr; 1986) 25,932,000,000 (26,671,000,000); coal (metric tons; 1986) 5,476,000 (5,648,000); crude petroleum (barrels; 1986) 7,150,000 (54,821,000); petroleum products (metric tons; 1986) 9,102,000 (10,898,000); natural gas (cu m; 1986) 3,497,772,000 (3,497,772,000).
Land use (1985): forested 29.3%; meadows and pastures 0.6%; agricultural and under permanent cultivation 38.3%; other 31.8%.
Population economically active (1986): total 26,970,100; activity rate of total population 52.1% (participation rates: over age 15, 79.1%; female 45.5%; unemployed 7.8%).

Price and earnings indexes (1980 = 100)							
	1982	1983	1984	1985	1986	1987	1988[4]
Consumer price index	118.6	123.0	124.1	127.1	129.4	132.6	137.4
Monthly earnings index	...	...	...	...	...	...	...

Public debt (external, outstanding; 1986): U.S.$11,022,600,000.
Gross national product (at current market prices; 1986): U.S.$42,440,000,000 (U.S.$810 per capita).

Structure of gross domestic product and labour force				
	1986			
	in value B '000,000	% of total value	labour force[5]	% of labour force
Agriculture	183,037	16.7	14,994,900	55.6
Mining	23,374	2.1	76,600	0.3
Manufacturing	226,571	20.6	2,743,100	10.2
Construction	55,682	5.1	764,300	2.8
Public utilities	28,182	2.5	109,200	0.4
Transportation and communications	101,827	9.3	604,400	2.2
Trade	204,095	18.6	2,808,000	10.4
Finance	102,157	9.3		
Pub. admin., defense	49,139	4.5	2,767,400	10.3
Services	124,325	11.3		
Other	...	...	2,102,200	7.8
TOTAL	1,098,389	100.0	26,970,100	100.0

Household income and expenditure. Average household size (1986) 4.3; average annual income per household (1986) B 44,172 (U.S.$1,680); sources of income (1986): wages and salaries 36.7%, self-employment 29.7%, transfer payments 6.0%, other 27.6%; expenditure (1986): food 37.4%, housing 23.1%, transportation and communications 10.7%, clothing and footwear 6.4%, medical and personal care 5.6%, education and recreation 4.3%, other 12.5%.

Foreign trade[6]

Balance of trade (current prices)						
	1982	1983	1984	1985	1986	1987
B' 000,000	−17,244	−66,497	−45,425	−33,285	−10,133	−1,900
% of total	5.1%	18.5%	11.5%	7.9%	2.1%	0.3%

Imports (1986): B 241,357,737,686 (mineral fuels and oils 13.5%, boiler machinery 12.9%, electrical machinery 11.9%, iron and steel 8.9%, organic chemicals 4.6%, motor vehicles 4.5%). *Major import sources:* Japan 26.4%; United States 14.3%; Singapore 6.6%; West Germany 5.8%; Malaysia 4.2%; Taiwan 3.6%; United Kingdom 3.2%; China 2.9%; South Korea 2.4%; Brunei 2.0%.
Exports (1986): B 231,224,934,193 (rice 8.8%, edible vegetables 8.1%, tapioca products 7.2%, rubber 6.5%, corn 4.0%, canned fish 3.7%, sugar and sugar products 3.6%, unwrought tin 1.4%). *Major export destinations:* United States 17.9%; Japan 14.0%; Singapore 8.9%; The Netherlands 7.3%; West Germany 4.6%; Malaysia 4.3%; Hong Kong 4.0%; United Kingdom 3.2%; China 3.1%; South Korea 2.7%.

Transport and communications

Transport. Railroads (1986)[7]: route length (1987) 2,321 mi, 3,735 km; passenger-mi 5,734,000,000, passenger-km 9,228,000,000; short ton-mi cargo 1,866,000,000, metric ton-km cargo 2,724,000,000. Roads (1986): total length 51,740 mi, 83,268 km (paved 40%). Vehicles (1985): passenger cars 545,479; trucks and buses 856,375. Merchant marine (1987): vessels (100 gross tons and over) 254; total deadweight tonnage 758,442. Air transport (1986): passenger-mi 7,009,000,000, passenger-km 11,280,000,000; short ton-mi cargo 332,812,000, metric ton-km cargo 485,928,000; airports (1988) with scheduled flights 22.
Communications. Daily newspapers (1985): total number 31; total circulation 2,564,500[8]; circulation per 1,000 population 50[8]. Radio (1985): 7,916,000 receivers (1 per 6.5 persons). Television (1985): 4,122,000 receivers (1 per 13 persons). Telephones (1986): 999,678 receivers (1 per 53 persons).

Education and health

Education (1985)	schools	teachers	students	student/ teacher ratio
Primary (age 7–12)	32,359	369,822	7,150,489	19.3
Secondary (age 13–18)	1,437[9]	100,218[10]	1,870,360[10]	18.7
Voc., teacher tr.	1,528[9]	17,893[11]	390,640[11]	21.8
Higher	62[9]	30,905	1,026,952	33.2

Educational attainment (1980). Percent of population age 25 and over having: no formal schooling 20.5%; primary education 67.3%; secondary 9.3%; postsecondary 2.9%. *Literacy* (1985): total population age 15 and over literate 28,451,390 (88.8%); males literate 14,877,240 (93.2%); females literate 13,574,150 (84.5%).
Health (1985): physicians 8,650 (1 per 5,988 persons); hospital beds 81,679 (1 per 634 persons); infant mortality rate per 1,000 live births (1987) 40.0.
Food (1983–85): daily per capita caloric intake 2,440 (vegetable products 94%, animal products 6%); 105% of FAO recommended minimum requirement.

Military

Total active duty personnel (1987): 256,000 (army 64.8%, navy 16.4%, air force 18.8%). *Military expenditure as percent of GNP* (1985): 4.4% (world 6.1%); per capita expenditure U.S.$37.

[1]Excluding Bangkok Metropolis. [2]Detail does not add to total given because of rounding. [3]1986. [4]June. [5]Economically active persons 11 years and over. [6]Import figures are f.o.b. (free on board) in balance of trade and c.i.f. (cost, insurance, and freight) for commodities and trading partners. [7]Traffic data refer to fiscal year ending September 30. [8]Excludes circulation for two dailies. [9]1980. [10]Data refer to public education only. [11]1984.

Togo

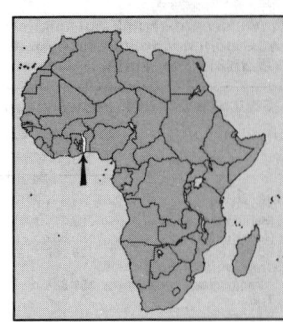

Official name: République Togolaise
(Republic of Togo).
Form of government: single-party
republic with one legislative body
(National Assembly [77]).
Head of state and government:
President.
Capital: Lomé.
Official language: French.
Official religion: none.
Monetary unit: 1 CFA franc
(CFAF) = 100 centimes; valuation
(Oct. 10, 1988) 1 U.S.$ = CFAF
316.13; 1 £ = CFAF 541.38.

Area and population		area		population
Regions				1981
Prefectures	Capitals	sq mi	sq km	census
Centrale	Sokodé			269,174
Sotouboua	Sotouboua	2,892	7,490	128,617
Tchamba	Tchamba	1	1	44,912
Tchaoudjo	Sokodé	2,198[1]	5,692[1]	95,645
De la Kara	Kara			432,626
Assoli	Bafilo	362	938	32,444
Bassar	Bassar	2,444	6,330	118,345
Binah	Pagouda	180	465	50,077
Doufelgou	Niamtougou	432	1,120	66,120
Kéran	Kandé	653	1,692	44,762
Kozah	Kara	419	1,085	120,878
Des Plateaux	Atakpamé			561,656
Amou	Amlamé	1,692[2]	4,382[2]	72,951
Haho	Notsé	1,412	3,658	109,995
Kloto	Kpalimé	1,077	2,790	106,429
Ogou	Atakpamé	2,372	6,145	163,906
Wawa	Badou	2	2	108,375
Des Savanes	Dapaong			326,826
Oti	Sansanné-Mango	1,453	3,762	77,747
Tône	Dapaong	1,869	4,840	249,079
Maritime	Lomé			1,039,700
Golfe	Lomé	133	345	438,110
Lacs	Aného	275	712	140,006
Vo	Vogan	290	750	150,313
Yoto	Tabligbo	483	1,250	100,387
Zio	Tsévié	1,289	3,339	210,884
TOTAL		21,925	56,785	2,700,982[3]

Demography

Population (1988): 3,486,000.
Density (1988): persons per sq mi 159.0, persons per sq km 61.0.
Urban–rural (1981): urban 15.2%; rural 84.8%.
Sex distribution (1981): male 48.20%; female 51.80%.
Age breakdown (1980): under 15, 46.2%; 15–29, 25.8%; 30–44, 14.8%; 45–59, 8.6%; 60–74, 3.9%; 75 and over, 0.7%.
Population projection: (1990) 3,764,000; (2000) 5,113,000.
Doubling time: 24 years.
Ethnic composition (1981): Ewe-Adja 43.1%; Tem-Kabre 26.7%; Gurma 16.1%; Kebu-Akposo 3.8%; Ana-Ife (Yoruba) 3.2%; non-African 0.3%; other 6.8%.
Religious affiliation (1981): traditional beliefs 58.8%; Roman Catholic 21.5%; Muslim 12.1%; Protestant 6.8%; other 0.8%.
Major cities (1983): Lomé 366,476; Sokodé 48,098[4]; Kpalimé 27,669[4].

Vital statistics

Birth rate per 1,000 population (1980–85): 45.2 (world avg. 29.0); legitimate, n.a.; illegitimate, n.a.
Death rate per 1,000 population (1980–85): 15.7 (world avg. 11.0).
Natural increase rate per 1,000 population (1980–85): 29.5 (world avg. 18.0).
Total fertility rate (avg. births per childbearing woman; 1980–85): 6.1.
Marriage rate per 1,000 population (1979): 2.3.
Divorce rate per 1,000 population: n.a.
Life expectancy at birth (1980–85): male 48.8 years; female 52.2 years.
Morbidity (reported cases of illness per 100,000 population; 1978): infectious and parasitic diseases 26,926; diseases of the respiratory system 9,296; diseases of the digestive system 8,007; accidents, poisoning, and traumas 7,172.

National economy

Budget (1988). Revenue: CFAF 89,700,000,000 (indirect taxes 54.8%, direct taxes 33.8%). Expenditures: CFAF 89,700,000,000 (administrative 33.6%, debt service 22.2%, equipment and supplies 16.7%, state enterprises 16.3%).
Public debt (external, outstanding; 1986): U.S.$882,000,000.
Tourism (1986): receipts from visitors U.S.$41,000,000; expenditures by nationals abroad U.S.$28,000,000.
Production (metric tons except as noted). Agriculture, forestry, fishing (1986): roots and tubers 809,000, cassava 442,000, yams 336,000, corn (maize) 133,000, sorghum 90,000, millet 70,000, cottonseed 46,000, pulses 43,000, peanuts (groundnuts) 22,000, bananas 16,000, cacao beans 15,000, rice 15,000, palm kernels 15,000, coconuts 14,000, palm oil 13,800, coffee 10,000, tomatoes 6,000; livestock (number of live animals) 850,000 sheep, 744,000 goats, 288,000 pigs, 276,000 cattle, 4,000,000 chickens; roundwood 789,000 cu m; fish catch 14,823. Mining and quarrying (1986): phosphate rock 2,310,000; salt 600,000[5]; marble 5,000. Manufacturing (1984): cement 284,000[6]; beer 359,000 hectolitres; nonalcoholic beverages 70,000 hectolitres; footwear 485,000 pairs[7]. Construction (value added in CFAF; 1981): 11,-

000,000,000. Energy production (consumption): electricity (kW-hr; 1986) 35,000,000 (265,000,000); crude petroleum, none (n.a.); petroleum products (metric tons; 1986) none (99,000).
Gross national product (1986): U.S.$780,000,000 (U.S.$250 per capita).

Structure of gross domestic product and labour force				
	1983		1985	
	in value CFAF '000,000	% of total value	labour force	% of labour force
Agriculture	90.1	32.0	883,000	71.0
Mining	28.7	10.2		
Manufacturing	20.1	7.1		
Construction	8.1	2.9		
Public utilities	5.7	2.0		
Transp. and commun.	18.1	6.4	361,000	29.0
Trade	61.9	22.0		
Finance	...	...		
Pub. admin., defense	27.8	10.0		
Services	...	...		
Other	20.8	7.4		
TOTAL	281.3	100.0	1,244,000	100.0

Population economically active: total (1985) 1,244,000; activity rate of total population 42.0% (participation rates: ages 15–64, 69.5%; female 37.5%; unemployed [1980] 2.3%).

Price and earnings indexes (1980 = 100)							
	1981	1982	1983	1984	1985	1986	1987
Consumer price index	119.7	133.0	145.5	140.3	137.8	143.5	143.5
Hourly earning index[8]	100.0	110.0	110.0	110.0	110.0	110.0	115.5

Household income and expenditure. Average household size (1980) 5.6; average annual income per household CFAF 102,000 (U.S.$452); sources of income: n.a.; expenditure (1970): food and beverages 60.9%, housing 9.9%, transportation 8.2%, clothing 7.7%, household durable goods 3.9%, other 9.4%.
Land use (1985): forested 26.7%; meadows and pastures 3.7%; agricultural and under permanent cultivation 26.2%; other 43.4%.

Foreign trade

Balance of trade (current prices)						
	1981	1982	1983	1984	1985	1986
CFAF '000,000,000	−60.3	−70.2	−46.2	−34.9	−8.7	−29.7
% of total	34.4%	37.6%	27.2%	17.3%	3.8%	13.2%

Imports (1985): CFAF 129,406,000,000 (food and food products 17.0%, cotton textiles 13.0%, machinery and mechanical equipment 11.1%, transport equipment and parts 7.7%). *Major import sources:* France 31.9%; W.Ger. 11.9%; The Netherlands 10.2%; Japan 6.6%; U.K. 6.3%; Côte d'Ivoire 5.3%.
Exports (1985): CFAF 85,380,000,000 (phosphates 50.2%, coffee 13.9%, raw cotton 13.6%, cacao beans 8.0%, karité nuts 3.9%). *Major export destinations:* France 23.1%; The Netherlands 21.9%; W.Ger. 8.0%; Italy 6.6%; Yugoslavia 6.4%; Poland 3.8%.

Transport and communications

Transport. Railroads (1987): length 250 mi, 403 km; passenger-mi 65,000,-000[5], passenger-km 105,000,000[5]; short ton-mi cargo 11,000,000[5], metric ton-km cargo 16,000,000[5]. Roads (1986): total length 4,349 mi, 7,000 km (paved 24%). Vehicles (1986): passenger cars 41,122; trucks and buses 20,-241. Merchant marine (1987): vessels (100 gross tons and over) 13; total deadweight tonnage 92,082. Air transport (1987): passenger-mi 132,791,000, passenger-km 213,706,000; short ton-mi cargo 24,739,000, metric ton-km cargo 36,119,000; airports (1988) with scheduled flights 1.
Communications. Daily newspapers (1986): total number 2; total circulation 10,000[9]; circulation per 1,000 population 3.3[9]. Radio (1986): 250,000 receivers (1 per 12 persons). Television (1987): 23,000 receivers (1 per 146 persons). Telephones (1983): 11,105 (1 per 255 persons).

Education and health

Education (1986–87)				
	schools	teachers	students	student/ teacher ratio
Primary (age 6–11)	2,345	10,209	474,998	46.5
Secondary (age 12–18)	248[10]	3,985[11]	86,327	...
Voc., teacher tr.	18	198	5,050	25.5
Higher	1	308	4,500	14.6

Educational attainment (1981). Percent of population age 15 and over having: no formal schooling 76.5%; primary education 13.5%; secondary 8.7%; higher 1.3%. *Literacy* (1985): total population age 15 and over literate 631,-700 (39.1%); males literate 401,800 (51.7%); females literate 229,900 (27.5%).
Health: physicians (1985) 230 (1 per 12,992 persons); hospital beds (1982) 3,655 (1 per 752 persons); infant mortality rate (1980–85) 102.0.
Food (1984–86): daily per capita caloric intake 2,224 (vegetable products 96%, animal products 4%); 94% of FAO recommended minimum requirement.

Military

Total active duty personnel (1987): 5,910 (army 93.9%, navy 1.7%, air force 4.4%). *Military expenditure as percent of GNP* (1985): 2.9% (world 6.1%); per capita expenditure U.S.$7.

---

[1]Tchaoudjo includes Tchamba. [2]Amou includes Wawa. [3]Total includes 71,000 persons not counted separately. [4]1981. [5]1982. [6]1985. [7]Excludes rubber. [8]January 1st figures. [9]For one daily only. [10]1981–82. [11]1984.

Tonga

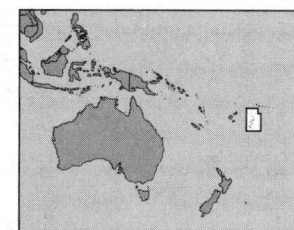

Official name: Pule'anga Fakatu'i 'o Tonga (Tongan); Kingdom of Tonga (English).
Form of government: constitutional monarchy with one legislative house (Legislative Assembly [29][1]).
Head of state and government: King.
Capital: Nuku'alofa.
Official languages: Tongan; English.
Official religion: none.
Monetary unit: 1 pa'anga (T$)[2] = 100 seniti; valuation (Oct. 10, 1988) 1 U.S.$ = T$1.24; 1 £ = T$2.13.

Area and population

Divisions		area		population
Districts	Capitals	sq mi	sq km	1986 census
'Eua	'Ohonua	33.7	87.4	4,393
'Eua Fo'ou		...	...	1,995
'Eua Motu'a		...	...	2,398
Ha'apai	Pangai	42.5	110.0	8,979
Foa		...	...	1,409
Ha'ano		...	...	892
Lulunga		...	...	1,588
Mu'omu'a		...	...	897
Pangai		...	...	2,840
'Uiha		...	...	1,353
Niuas	Hihifo	27.7	71.7	2,379
Niua Fo'ou		...	...	763
Niua Toputapu		...	...	1,616
Tongatapu	Nuku'alofa	100.6	260.5	63,614
Kolofo'ou		...	...	15,782
Kolomotu'a		...	...	13,117
Kolovai		...	...	4,023
Lapaha		...	...	6,992
Nukunuku		...	...	5,790
Tatakamotonga		...	...	6,778
Vaini		...	...	11,132
Vava'u	Neiafu	46.0	119.2	15,170
Hahake		...	...	2,292
Hihifo		...	...	2,095
Leimatu'a		...	...	2,875
Motu		...	...	1,387
Neiafu		...	...	5,273
Pangaimotu		...	...	1,248
TOTAL LAND AREA		289.53	749.93	94,535
INLAND WATER		11.4	29.6	
TOTAL		300.9	779.5	

Demography

Population (1988): 95,300.
Density[4] (1988): persons per sq mi 329.2; persons per sq km 127.1.
Urban–rural (1980): urban 31.8%; rural 68.2%.
Sex distribution (1986): male 50.34%; female 49.66%.
Age breakdown (1985): under 15, 39.6%; 15–29, 31.1%; 30–44, 14.2%; 45–59, 9.4%; 60–74, 4.7%; 75 and over, 1.0%.
Population projection: (1990) 96,200; (2000) 100,900.
Doubling time: 28 years.
Ethnic composition (1976): Tongan 98.3%; other 1.7%.
Religious affiliation (1976): Free Wesleyan 47.4%; Roman Catholic 16.1%; Free Church of Tonga 13.7%; Mormon 9.3%; Church of Tonga 8.9%; Seventh-day Adventist 2.1%; other 2.5%.
Major city (1986): Nuku'alofa 28,899.

Vital statistics

Birth rate per 1,000 population (1985): 28.9 (world avg. 29.0).
Death rate per 1,000 population (1985): 3.5 (world avg. 11.0).
Natural increase rate per 1,000 population (1985) 25.4 (world avg. 18.0).
Total fertility rate (avg. births per childbearing woman; 1980–85): 4.3.
Marriage rate per 1,000 population (1985): 6.6.
Divorce rate per 1,000 population (1985): 0.6.
Life expectancy at birth (1980–85): male 61.0 years; female 64.8 years.
Major causes of death per 100,000 population (1980): diseases of the circulatory system 61.1; infectious and parasitic diseases 53.5; malignant neoplasms (cancers) 46.9; diseases of the respiratory system 41.5; diseases of the digestive system 17.5.

National economy

Budget (1981)[5]. Revenue: T$12,230,000 (import duties 31.4%; income and wealth tax 13.6%; licenses, stamp duties, registration fees 1.3%). Expenditures: T$16,275,000 (investments 37.2%; social services 22.2%; economic services 13.9%; defense 2.7%).
Tourism (1985): receipts from visitors U.S.$7,000,000; expenditures by nationals abroad U.S.$4,000,000.
Production (metric tons except as noted). Agriculture, forestry, fishing (1986): coconuts 52,000, yams 35,000, taro 30,000, sweet potatoes 18,000, cassava 17,000, fruits excluding melons 12,000, vegetables including melons 7,000, copra 6,000; livestock (number of live animals) 65,000 pigs, 11,000 goats, 9,000 horses, 8,000 cattle; roundwood (1985) 3,000 cu m; fish catch 1,993. Mining and quarrying (1982): coral 150,000; sand 25,000. Manufacturing (value added in T$; 1983): food products and beverages 2,623,000; furniture, fixtures, and wood products 328,000; metal products 252,000; glass and china products 203,000; paper and products 26,000. Construction (value in T$; 1984): residential 9,552,300; nonresidential 11,377,100. Energy production (consumption): electricity (kW-hr; 1986) 12,000,000 (12,000,000); coal,

none (n.a.); petroleum, none (n.a.); petroleum products (metric tons; 1986) n.a. (15,000); natural gas, none (n.a.).
Gross national product (1986): U.S.$70,000,000 (U.S.$740 per capita).

Structure of gross domestic product and labour force

	1983		1976	
	in value T$'000	% of total value	labour force	% of labour force
Agriculture	35,790	41.5	9,529	44.5
Mining	394	0.5	16	0.1
Manufacturing	4,271	4.9	386	1.8
Construction	3,354	3.9	1,153	5.4
Public utilities	404	0.5	114	0.5
Transp. and commun.	4,950	5.7	829	3.9
Trade	12,774	14.8	825	3.8
Finance	5,189	6.0	61	0.3
Pub. admin., defense	...	...	1,375	6.4
Services	...	...	2,707	12.6
Other	19,1496	22.26	4,4407	20.77
TOTAL	86,275	100.0	21,435	100.0

Public debt (external, outstanding; 1985): U.S.$24,180,000.
Population economically active (1984): total 30,900; activity rate of total population 32.1% (participation rates [1976]: ages 15–64, 43.7%; female 15.7%; unemployed 4.5%).

Price and earnings indexes (1980 = 100)

	1981	1982	1983	1984	1985	1986	1987
Consumer price index	114.9	127.4	139.8	140.0	167.4	203.9	213.2
Earnings index	120.3	...	...	...	...	...	...

Household income and expenditure. Average household size (1986) 6.3; income per household: n.a.; sources of income: n.a.; expenditure (1983)[8]: food 55.1%, household goods 12.4%, tobacco and beverages 8.5%, clothing and footwear 6.2%, transportation 6.1%, housing 3.8%.
Land use (1985): forested 11.9%; meadows and pastures 6.0%; agricultural and under permanent cultivation 80.6%; other 1.5%.

Foreign trade

Balance of trade (current prices)

	1981	1982	1983	1984	1985	1986
T$'000,000	−27.3	−37.0	−35.2	−36.6	−51.8	−47.7
% of total	63.9%	81.5%	73.2%	64.7%	78.3%	72.7%

Imports (1986): T$56,578,700 (basic manufactures 27.8%, food and live animals 24.0%, machinery and transport equipment 16.8%, mineral fuels 12.9%, chemicals 8.1%, beverages and tobacco 6.0%). *Major import sources:* New Zealand 39.3%; Australia 29.9%; Japan 9.2%; Fiji 5.8%; United States 3.2%; United Kingdom 3.1%.
Exports (1986): T$8,928,200 (coconut oil products 19.9%, bananas 14.3%, desiccated coconut 7.7%). *Major export destinations:* New Zealand 35.3%; Australia 27.4%.

Transport and communications

Transport. Railroads: none. Roads (1987): total length 269 mi, 433 km (paved 65%). Vehicles (1984): passenger cars 1,561, commercial vehicles 3,397. Merchant marine (1987): vessels (100 gross tons and over) 19; total deadweight tonnage 23,429. Air transport (1987): passenger-mi 4,287,000, passenger-km 6,900,000; short ton-mi cargo 8,900, metric ton-km cargo 13,000; airports (1988) with scheduled flights 6.
Communications. Daily newspapers: none. Radio (1986): total number of receivers 50,000 (1 per 1.9 persons). Television: total number of receivers, n.a.[9]. Telephones (1984): 3,996 (1 per 24 persons).

Education and health

Education (1985)

	schools	teachers	students	student/ teacher ratio
Primary (age 6–10)	112	744	17,019	22.9
Secondary (age 13–18)	5010	770	14,641	19.0
Voc., teacher tr.	1210	70	591	8.4
Higher	111	...	705	...

Educational attainment (1976). Percent of population age 25 and over having: no formal schooling 0.4%; incomplete primary education 37.3%; complete primary 12.4%; lower secondary 45.6%; secondary 0.1%; post-secondary 0.1%; higher 0.6%; special education 2.4%; other 1.1%. *Literacy* (1976): total population age 15 and over literate 46,456 (92.8%); males 23,372 (92.9%); females 23,084 (92.8%).
Health (1986): physicians 39 (1 per 2,510 persons); hospital beds 307 (1 per 319 persons); infant mortality rate per 1,000 live births (1983) 26.0.
Food (1984–86): daily per capita caloric intake 2,942 (vegetable products 85%, animal products 15%); (1983) 117% of FAO recommended minimum.

Military

Total active duty personnel: Tonga had a national defense force of about 250 in the early 1980s.

[1]Includes 11 nonelective seats. [2]The pa'anga is at par with the Australian dollar. [3]Also includes 39.0 sq mi (101.1 sq km) of uninhabited islands. [4]Density is based on land area. [5]Estimated budget for 1986–87 was: revenue T$29,353,000; expenditures T$26,113,000. [6]Includes indirect taxes less subsidies. [7]Includes 2,809 persons seeking work for the first time. [8]Current weight of CPI components. [9]Tonga has no authorized television service, but a "pirate" station began transmitting in mid-1984. [10]1984. [11]1982.

Trinidad and Tobago

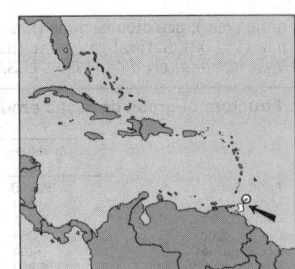

Official name: Republic of Trinidad
and Tobago.
Form of government: multiparty
republic with two legislative houses
(Senate [31]; House of Representatives
[36]).
Chief of state: President.
Head of government: Prime Minister.
Capital: Port-of-Spain.
Official language: English.
Official religion: none.
Monetary unit: 1 Trinidad and Tobago
dollar (TT$) = 100 cents; valuation
(Oct. 10, 1988) 1 U.S.$ = TT$4.25;
1 £ = TT$7.28.

Area and population		area		population
		sq mi	sq km	1987 estimate
Counties	**Capitals**			
Caroni	Chaguanas	213	552	167,300
Nariva/Mayaro	Rio Claro	350	906	33,200
St. Andrew/St. David	Sangre Grande	364	943	57,800
St. George	...	350	907	435,800
St. Patrick	Siparia	255	660	140,100[1]
Tobago	Scarborough	117	303	44,300
Victoria	Princes Town	314	814	218,700
City				
Port-of-Spain	—	4	10	58,300
Boroughs				
Arima	—	3	7	28,500
Point Fortin	—	6	16	[1]
San Fernando	—	2	6	33,100
TOTAL		1,978	5,124	1,217,100

Demography

Population (1988): 1,258,000.
Density (1988): persons per sq mi 636.0, persons per sq km 245.5.
Urban–rural (1986): urban 49.1%; rural 50.9%.
Sex distribution (1986): male 50.05%; female 49.95%.
Age breakdown (1985): under 15, 34.0%; 15–29, 30.2%; 30–44, 17.9%; 45–59,
10.0%; 60–74, 6.1%; 75 and over, 1.8%.
Population projection: (1990) 1,321,000; (2000) 1,608,000.
Doubling time: 34 years.
Ethnic composition (1980): black 40.8%; East Indian 40.7%; mixed 16.3%;
white 0.9%; Chinese 0.5%; Arab 0.1%; other 0.7%.
Religious affiliation (1980): Christian 62.0%, of which Roman Catholic
32.9%, Protestant 28.3% (including Anglican 14.7%, Presbyterian 3.8%, Pentecostal 3.5%, Seventh-day Adventist 2.5%); Hindu 24.9%; Muslim 6.0%;
other (including Rastafarian and Yoruba syncretist) 7.1%.
Major cities (1986): Port-of-Spain 57,400; San Fernando 32,600; Arima 28,-
200; Point Fortin 16,710[2]; Scarborough 6,089[2].

Vital statistics

Birth rate per 1,000 population (1984): 27.0 (world avg. 29.0); (1979) legiti-
mate 56.9%; illegitimate 43.1%.
Death rate per 1,000 population (1984): 6.7 (world avg. 11.0).
Natural increase rate per 1,000 population (1984): 20.3 (world avg. 18.0).
Total fertility rate (avg. births per childbearing woman; 1984): 2.8.
Marriage rate per 1,000 population (1985): 6.6.
Divorce rate per 1,000 population (1985): 0.9.
Life expectancy at birth (1980–85): male 66.2 years; female 71.3 years.
Major causes of death per 100,000 population (1984): diseases of the circula-
tory system 264.5, of which ischemic heart diseases 106.7, cerebrovascular
disease 82.5; malignant neoplasms (cancers) 79.7; diabetes mellitus 67.0.

National economy

Budget (1987): Revenue: TT$6,345,200,000 (current revenue 81.5%, of which
direct taxes 45.8%, indirect taxes 19.8%, property income 13.5%; development revenue 18.5%). Expenditures: TT$7,433,400,000 (current expendi-
tures 76.4%, of which interest payments 6.4%; development expenditures
23.6%).
Tourism (1986): receipts from visitors U.S.$190,000,000; expenditures by
nationals abroad U.S.$165,000,000.
Production (metric tons except as noted). Agriculture, forestry, fishing (1986):
sugarcane 1,062,000, coconuts 62,000, tomatoes 8,000, oranges 7,000, grapefruit 7,000, rice 5,000, coffee 1,842[3], cocoa 1,501[3]; livestock (number of
live animals) 83,000 pigs, 77,000 cattle, 50,000 goats; roundwood 57,000 cu
m; fish catch 3,000. Mining and quarrying (1986): natural asphalt 27,000.
Manufacturing (1987): nitrogenous fertilizers 1,842,000; methanol 358,-
200[4]; cement 326,000; iron and steel billets 166,900[4]; urea 155,000[4]; iron
and steel rods 231,000[5]; sugar 85,500; 9,200 locally assembled television
receivers; 5,900 locally assembled motor vehicles; rum 137,500 hectolitres.
Construction (new building authorized; 1986): residential 344,400 sq m;
nonresidential 39,000 sq m. Energy production (consumption): electricity (kW-hr; 1987) 3,364,000,000 (3,313,000,000[5]); coal, none (none); crude
petroleum (barrels; 1987) 58,100,000 (39,010,000[5]); petroleum products
(metric tons; 1986) 4,948,000 (3,594,000); natural gas (cu m; 1986) 2,974,-
000,000 (2,974,000,000).
Gross national product (at current market prices; 1986): U.S.$6,170,000,000
(U.S.$5,120 per capita).

Structure of gross domestic product and labour force

	1986		1985	
	in value TT$'000,000	% of total value	labour force	% of labour force
Agriculture	592	3.4	44,000	9.5
Mining	3,645[6]	21.0[6]	65,400	14.1
Manufacturing	1,781	10.2		
Construction	1,572[7]	9.0[7]	101,500	21.8
Public utilities	391	2.2		
Transp. and commun.	2,236	12.9	30,400	6.5
Trade	1,184	6.8	105,200	22.6
Finance	2,427	14.0		
Pub. admin., defense	2,881	16.6	107,800	23.2
Services	1,487	8.5		
Other	−804[8]	−4.6[8]	10,700	2.3
TOTAL	17,392	100.0	465,000	100.0

Public debt (external, outstanding; 1986): U.S.$1,154,100,000.
Population economically active (1985): total 465,000; activity rate of total
population 39.4% (participation rates: ages 15–64, 64.5%; female 33.3%;
unemployed [1987] 21.5%).

Price and earnings indexes (1980 = 100)							
	1981	1982	1983	1984	1985	1986	1987
Consumer price index	114.3	127.4	148.7	168.6	181.4	195.4	219.39[9]
Weekly earnings index[10]	118.4	139.8	167.9	192.2	201.7	205.7	...

Household income and expenditure. Average household size (1980) 4.2; income per household: n.a.; sources of income: n.a.; expenditure (1981–82):
food and beverages 27.7%, housing 22.7%, clothing and footwear 15.5%,
transportation 13.2%, household furnishings 8.8%, other 12.1%.
Land use (1985): forested 43.9%; meadows and pastures 2.1%; agricultural
and under permanent cultivation 23.0%; other 31.0%.

Foreign trade[11]

Balance of trade (current prices)						
	1982	1983	1984	1985	1986	1987
TT$'000,000	−694	+77	+1,079	+1,939	+549	+1,439
% of total	4.5%	0.7%	11.5%	22.4%	5.9%	15.9%

Imports (1986): TT$4,877,100,000 (machinery and transport equipment
36.6%, of which mining and industrial machinery 13.7%; food 15.9%;
chemical products 10.6%). *Major import sources:* United States 41.8%;
Japan 10.2%; United Kingdom 10.0%; Canada 6.0%; West Germany 4.6%
Exports (1986): TT$4,962,200,000 (domestic exports 97.8%, of which crude
petroleum 39.9%, petroleum products 30.6%, anhydrous ammonia 9.1%,
iron and steel bar rods 4.8%, manufactured fertilizers 3.4%; reexports 2.2%). *Major export destinations:* United States 61.0%; United
Kingdom 4.8%; French Polynesia 2.9%; Puerto Rico 2.5%.

Transport and communications

Transport. Railroads: none. Roads (1985): total length 4,909 mi, 7,900 km
(paved 46%). Vehicles (1985): passenger cars 241,595; trucks and buses
82,361. Merchant marine (1987): vessels (100 gross tons and over) 50; total
deadweight tonnage 12,491. Air transport (1986)[12]: passenger-mi 1,339,-
000,000, passenger-km 2,155,000,000; short ton-mi cargo 8,605,000, metric
ton-km cargo 12,563,000; airports (1988) with scheduled flights 2.
Communications. Daily newspapers (1986): total number 4; total circulation
175,462; circulation per 1,000 population 146. Radio (1986): 552,000 receivers (1 per 2.2 persons). Television (1987): 345,000 receivers (1 per 3.6
persons). Telephones (1987): 196,203 (1 per 6.3 persons).

Education and health

Education (1984–85)	schools	teachers	students	student/ teacher ratio
Primary (age 5–11)	468	7,627	168,308	22.1
Secondary (age 12–19)	95	4,744	92,595	19.5
Voc., teacher tr.	...	...	3,802	...
Higher	1	...	2,684	...

Educational attainment (1980). Percent of population age 25 and over having: no formal schooling 7.1%; primary education 66.5%; secondary 21.7%;
higher 2.7%; other 2.0%. *Literacy* (1980): total population age 15 and over
literate 653,122 (95.1%); males literate 328,645 (96.7%); females literate
324,477 (93.6%).
Health (1987): physicians 1,164 (1 per 1,055 persons); hospital beds 4,241[13]
(1 per 290 persons); infant mortality rate per 1,000 live births (1983–84
avg.) 13.2.
Food (1983–85): daily per capita caloric intake 2,967 (vegetable products
80%, animal products 20%); (1983) 129% of FAO recommended minimum requirement.

Military

Total active duty personnel (1987): 2,075 (army 100.0%). *Military expenditure as percent of GNP* (1984): 2.7% (world 5.9%); per capita expenditure
U.S.$174.

[1]St. Patrick includes the population of the borough of Point Fortin. [2]1980. [3]1987 production for export. [4]1985. [5]1986. [6]Includes petroleum refining. [7]Includes quarrying.
[8]Less imputed bank service charges. [9]August. [10]Manufacturing sector only. [11]Import
figures are f.o.b. in balance of trade and c.i.f. in commodities and trading partners.
[12]BWIA International airways only. [13]Includes nursing homes.

Tunisia

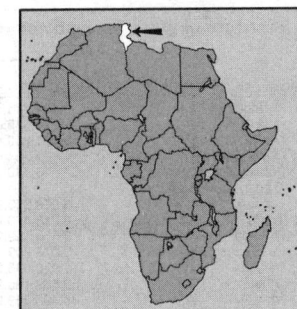

Official name: al-Jumhūrīyah at-Tūnisīyah (Republic of Tunisia).
Form of government: multiparty republic with one legislative house (Chamber of Deputies [125]).
Chief of state: President.
Head of government: Prime minister.
Capital: Tunis.
Official language: Arabic.
Official religion: Islam.
Monetary unit: 1 dinar (D) = 1,000 millimes; valuation (Oct. 10, 1988) D 1.00 = U.S.$1.11 = £0.65.

Area and population

Governorates	Capitals	area sq mi	area sq km	population 1987 estimate
Aryānah	Aryānah	602	1,558	435,200
Bājah	Bājah	1,374	3,558	288,700
Banzart	Banzart	1,423	3,685	420,400
Bin 'Arūs	Bin 'Arūs	294	761	283,200
Jundūbah	Jundūbah	1,198	3,102	386,000
al-Kāf	al-Kāf	1,917	4,965	259,300
Madanīyin	Madanīyin	3,316	8,588	332,800
al-Mahdīyah	al-Mahdīyah	1,145	2,966	296,800
al-Munastir	al-Munastir	393	1,019	304,700
Nābul	Nābul	1,076	2,788	501,000
Qābis	Qābis	2,770	7,175	271,200
Qafşah	Qafşah	3,471	8,990	260,200
al-Qaşrayn	al-Qaşrayn	3,114	8,066	331,200
al-Qayrawān	al-Qayrawān	2,591	6,712	460,800
Qibilī	Qibilī	8,527	22,084	107,200
Şafāqis	Şafāqis	2,913	7,545	640,400
Sīdī Bū Zayd	Sīdī Bū Zayd	2,700	6,994	322,600
Silyānah	Silyānah	1,788	4,631	235,200
Sūsah	Sūsah	1,012	2,621	356,700
Taţāwin	Taţāwin	15,015	38,889	112,600
Tawzar	Tawzar	1,822	4,719	75,800
Tūnis	Tunis (Tūnis)	134	346	828,200
Zaghwān	Zaghwān	1,069	2,768	128,600
TOTAL		59,664	154,530	7,639,000[1]

Demography

Population (1988): 7,877,400.
Density (1988): persons per sq mi 132.0, persons per sq km 51.0.
Urban–rural (1984): urban 52.8%; rural 47.2%.
Sex distribution (1987): male 50.97%; female 49.03%.
Age breakdown (1987): under 15, 39.0%; 15–29, 28.6%; 30–44, 15.2%; 45–59, 10.4%; 60–74, 5.4%; 75 and over, 1.4%.
Population projection: (1990) 8,312,700; (2000) 10,877,500.
Doubling time: 30 years.
Ethnic composition (1983): Arab 98.2%; Berber 1.2%; French 0.2%; Italian 0.1%; other 0.3%.
Religious affiliation (1980): Sunnī Muslim 99.4%; Christian 0.3%; Jewish 0.1%; other 0.2%.
Major cities (commune; 1984): Tunis 596,654; Şafāqis 231,911; Aryānah 98,655; Banzart 94,509; Sūsah 83,509.

Vital statistics

Birth rate per 1,000 population (1987): 29.3 (world avg. 26.0); (1974) legitimate 99.8%; illegitimate 0.2%.
Death rate per 1,000 population (1987): 6.3 (world avg. 9.9).
Natural increase rate per 1,000 population (1987): 23.0 (world avg. 16.1).
Total fertility rate (avg. births per childbearing woman; 1984): 4.3.
Marriage rate per 1,000 population (1987): 6.2.
Divorce rate per 1,000 population (1986): 0.9.
Life expectancy at birth (1980–85): male 60.1 years; female 61.1 years.
Major causes of death per 100,000 population: n.a.; however, of approximately 7,000 deaths[2] for which a cause was reported in 1986, diseases of the circulatory system 20.1%; infectious and parasitic diseases 17.1%; complications of pregnancy and childbirth 14.0%; accidents and poisonings 11.0%.

National economy

Budget (1986). Revenue: D 1,815,888,000 (indirect taxes 51.7%, investment 21.8%, direct taxes 18.0%). Expenditures: D 1,343,807,000 (education 28.6%, finance 17.6%, health 10.7%, interior affairs 8.6%, defense 7.8%, agriculture 6.3%).
Tourism (1986): receipts from visitors U.S.$488,000,000; expenditures by nationals abroad U.S.$107,000,000.
Land use (1985): forested 3.6%; meadows and pastures 19.5%; agricultural and under permanent cultivation 31.7%; other 45.2%.
Production (metric tons except as noted). Agriculture, forestry, fishing (1987): wheat 1,360,000, olives 570,000, barley 569,000, tomatoes 485,000, watermelons and melons 350,000, sugar beets 303,500, potatoes 188,000, oranges 147,000, grapes 118,000, dates 69,000, alfalfa 67,000, almonds 46,000, tobacco 5,400; livestock (number of live animals) 5,707,000 sheep, 1,155,000 goats, 666,000 cattle; roundwood (1986) 2,845,000 cu m; fish catch (1986) 93,000. Mining and quarrying (1987): phosphate rock 6,215,000; iron ore 291,000; zinc 10,700; lead 3,400. Manufacturing (1987): cement 3,215,100; phosphoric acid 593,300; flour 513,400; crude steel 188,200; mineral water 491,300 hectolitres. Construction (1982): residential building authorized 2,679,000 sq m. Energy production (consumption): electricity (kW-hr; 1987) 4,016,200,000 ([1986] 3,302,000,000); coal (metric tons; 1986) none (12,000);

crude petroleum (barrels; 1987) 38,449,613 ([1986] 21,476,915); petroleum products (metric tons; 1987) 1,645,500 (2,184,400); natural gas (cu m; 1987) 318,900,000 ([1986] 373,200,000).
Gross national product (1986): U.S.$8,537,100,000 (U.S.$1,140 per capita).

Structure of gross domestic product and labour force

	1986 in value D '000,000	1986 % of total value	1984 labour force	1984 % of labour force
Agriculture	960.0	13.5	475,370	22.2
Mining	608.0	8.6	22,500	1.1
Manufacturing	924.1	13.0	345,120	16.1
Construction	403.0	5.7	237,490	11.1
Public utilities	115.4	1.6	15,530	0.7
Transp. and commun.	390.5	5.5	86,700	4.1
Trade	1,614.2	22.7	153,860	7.2
Finance	301.4	4.2	13,060	0.6
Pub. admin., defense	865.0	12.2	129,510	6.1
Services	924.4	13.0	212,200	9.9
Other	...	...	445,870[3]	20.9[3]
TOTAL	7,106.8[1]	100.0	2,137,210	100.0

Public debt (external, outstanding; 1986): U.S.$5,001,300,000.
Population economically active (1984): total 2,137,210, activity rate of total population 30.6% (participation rates: age 15 and over 52.9%; female 21.3%; unemployed 16.4%).

Price and earnings indexes (1980 = 100)

	1981	1982	1983	1984	1985	1986	1987
Consumer price index	108.9	123.8	134.9	146.3	158.0	167.1	179.1
Monthly earnings index[4]	123.6	147.2	...	...	...	...	...

Household income and expenditure. Average household size (1984) 5.5; income per household: n.a.; sources of income: n.a.; expenditure (1983): food and beverages 42.8%, clothing and footwear 10.9%, housing 9.3%, transportation 8.0%, recreation 6.1%, household durable goods 5.7%, utilities 5.6%, health care 3.7%, education 1.7%.

Foreign trade

Balance of trade (current prices)

	1982	1983	1984	1985	1986	1987
D '000,000	−735.4	−704.2	−909.6	−690.4	−737.3	−569.9
% of total	24.0%	21.8%	24.6%	19.3%	20.8%	13.9%

Imports (1987): D 2,509,100,000 (textiles 14.9%, wheat 3.4%, plastic materials 3.1%, pharmaceutical products 3.1%, chemical products 3.0%). *Major import sources:* France 27.4%; West Germany 12.6%; Italy 11.4%; United States 5.9%; Spain 4.6%; Belgium–Luxembourg 4.6%; Algeria 3.5%.
Exports (1987): D 1,770,700,000 (petroleum and petroleum products 21.5%, clothing and accessories 20.0%, phosphates 7.8%, phosphoric acid 4.0%, fish and crustaceans 3.8%, olive oil 3.7%). *Major export destinations:* France 21.9%; West Germany 19.7%; Italy 16.6%; Belgium–Luxembourg 6.5%; Greece 6.3%.

Transport and communications

Transport. Railroads (1987): route length 1,314 mi, 2,115 km; passenger-mi 492,000,000, passenger-km 792,000,000; short ton-mi cargo 1,323,000,000, metric ton-km cargo 1,932,000,000. Roads (1986): total length 16,584 mi, 26,689 km (paved 56%). Vehicles (1986): passenger cars 271,133; trucks and buses 182,679. Merchant marine (1987): vessels (100 gross tons and over) 71; total deadweight tonnage 449,685. Air transport (1987): passenger-mi 1,475,493,000, passenger-km 2,374,581,000; short ton-mi cargo 14,757,125, metric ton-km cargo 21,545,010; airports (1988) with scheduled flights 5.
Communications. Daily newspapers (1987): total number 6; total circulation 230,000[5]; circulation per 1,000 population 30[5]. Radio (1986): 1,160,000 receivers (1 per 6.1 persons). Television (1987): 500,000 receivers (1 per 15 persons). Telephones (1986): 291,260 (1 per 26 persons).

Education and health

Education (1987–88)

	schools	teachers	students	student/ teacher ratio
Primary (age 6–11)	3,605	43,189	1,338,905	31.0
Secondary (age 12–18)	428	22,373	480,245	21.5
Voc., teacher tr.	...	...	...	...
Higher	...	5,171[6]	43,797	...

Educational attainment (1984). Percent of population age 25 and over having: no formal schooling 65.8%; Qur'anic education 1.2%; primary 17.5%; secondary 11.2%; vocational 0.8%; higher 1.7%; unspecified 1.8%. *Literacy* (1984): total population age 15 and over literate 2,023,500 (48.2%); males literate 1,282,700 (60.4%); females literate 740,800 (35.7%).
Health (1987): physicians 3,474 (1 per 2,198 persons); hospital beds 15,838 (1 per 482 persons); infant mortality rate per 1,000 live births (1985–90) 71.0.
Food (1984–86): daily per capita caloric intake 2,941 (vegetable products 91%, animal products 9%); (1983) 121% of FAO recommended minimum.

Military

Total active duty personnel (1987): 40,100 (army 77.3%, navy 12.5%, air force 10.2%). *Military expenditure as percent of GNP* (1985): 3.6% (world 6.1%); per capita expenditure U.S.$42.

---

[1]Detail does not add to total given because of rounding. [2]Urban areas only. [3]Includes 95,080 undefined and 350,790 unemployed. [4]Government workers only. [5]Circulation for 4 dailies only. [6]1986–87.

Turkey

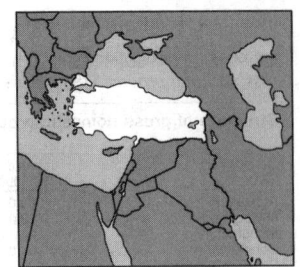

Official name: Türkiye Cumhuriyeti
(Republic of Turkey).
Form of government: multiparty
republic with one legislative house
(Turkish Grand National Assembly
[450]).
Chief of state: President.
Head of government: Prime Minister.
Capital: Ankara.
Official language: Turkish.
Official religion: none.
Monetary unit: 1 Turkish lira
(LT) = 100 kurush; valuation (Oct. 10,
1988) 1 U.S.$ = LT 1,698.00;
1 £ = LT 2,908.00.

Area and population

Geographical regions	area sq mi	area sq km	population 1985 census
Akdeniz kıyısı (Mediterranean Coast)	22,933	59,395	4,653,426
Batı Anadolu (West Anatolia)	29,742	77,031	3,538,252
Doğu Anadolu (East Anatolia)	68,074	176,311	6,290,086
Güneydoğu Anadolu (Southeast Anatolia)	15,347	39,749	2,413,593
İç Anadolu (Central Anatolia)	91,254	236,347	12,193,155
Karadeniz kıyısı (Black Sea Coast)	31,388	81,295	6,652,172
Marmara ve Ege kıyıları (Marmara and Aegean coasts)	33,035	85,560	9,834,576
Trakya (Thrace)	9,175	23,764	5,089,197
TOTAL	300,948	779,452	50,664,458

Demography

Population (1988): 54,176,000.
Density (1988): persons per sq mi 180.0, persons per sq km 69.5.
Urban–rural (1985): urban 45.9%; rural 54.1%.
Sex distribution (1985): male 50.40%; female 49.60%.
Age breakdown (1985): under 15, 37.1%; 15–29, 26.3%; 30–44, 17.1%; 45–59,
12.6%; 60 and over, 6.9%.
Population projection: (1990) 56,941,000; (2000) 73,029,000.
Doubling time: 33 years.
Ethnic composition (1983): Turkish 85.7%; Kurdish 10.6%; Arab 1.6%; other
2.1%.
Religious affiliation (1980): Sunnī Muslim 99.2%; Eastern Orthodox 0.3%;
other 0.5%.
Major cities (1985): Istanbul 5,475,982; Ankara 2,235,000; İzmir 1,489,772;
Adana 777,554; Bursa 612,500.

Vital statistics

Birth rate per 1,000 population (1980–85): 33.6 (world avg. 29.0).
Death rate per 1,000 population (1980–85): 9.3 (world avg. 11.0).
Natural increase rate per 1,000 population (1980–85): 24.3 (world avg. 18.0).
Total fertility rate (avg. births per childbearing woman; 1985): 3.9.
Marriage rate per 1,000 population (1986): 7.5.
Divorce rate per 1,000 population (1986): 1.4.
Life expectancy at birth (1980–85): male 62.5 years; female 65.8 years.
Major causes of death per 100,000 population (1986): heart disease 88.6; ma-
lignant neoplasms (cancers) 23.4; cerebrovascular disease 18.9; infectious
and parasitic diseases 13.8; pneumonia 8.3.

National economy

Budget (1987). Revenue: LT 10,540,497,000,000 (indirect taxes 45.0%, direct
taxes 44.2%, nontax revenue 9.1%). Expenditures: LT 12,696,853,000,000
(personnel 23.7%, investment 18.0%, interest on foreign loans 8.0%).
Tourism (1986): receipts from visitors U.S.$950,000,000; expenditures by
nationals abroad U.S.$313,000,000.
Production (metric tons except as noted). Agriculture, forestry, fishing
(1987): wheat 18,900,000, sugar beets 12,717,000, barley 6,900,000, potatoes
4,300,000, grapes 3,300,000, corn (maize) 2,400,000, apples 1,680,000, dry
onions 1,300,000, sunflower seeds 1,100,000, lentils 925,000, chick-peas
725,000, oranges 700,000, tea leaves 674,000, olives 600,000, rye 380,000,
oats 325,000, rice 168,000; livestock (number of live animals; 1986) 40,400,-
000 sheep, 16,200,000 cattle, 13,100,000 goats; roundwood (1986) 18,446,000
cu m, fuelwood 12,488,000 cu m; fish catch (1986) 579,844. Mining and
quarrying (1987): iron ore 3,300,000; chrome ore 907,000. Manufacturing
(1987): cement 21,980,000; commercial fertilizers 7,691,000; steel ingot
5,771,000; crude iron 4,100,000; rolled steel 2,856,000; iron and steel bars
1,213,000; pig iron 338,000; beer 244,062,000 litres; wine 25,300,000 litres;
cotton fabric 233,847,000 m. Construction (1987): residential 40,857,000
sq m; nonresidential 6,918,000 sq m. Energy production (consumption):
electricity (kW-hr; 1987) 44,331,000,000 (44,905,000,000); coal (metric tons;
1986) 45,464,000 (49,028,000); crude petroleum (barrels; 1986) 17,476,000
(141,562,000); petroleum products (metric tons; 1986) 16,539,000 (15,938,-
000); natural gas (cu m; 1986) 437,935,000 (437,935,000).
Household income and expenditure[1]. Average household size (1980) 5.2;
income per household (1978–79) LT 11,880 (U.S.$471); sources of income:
self-employment 46.8%, wages and salaries 38.9%, transfer grants 9.4%,
other 4.9%; expenditure (1978–79): food 41.2%, housing 25.2%, clothing
14.8%, recreation and entertainment 6.1%, transportation 5.5.%, health
3.3%, other 3.9%.
Gross national product (at current market prices; 1986): U.S.$57,120,000,000
(U.S.$1,110 per capita).

Structure of gross domestic product and labour force

	1986 in value LT '000,000	% of total value	labour force	% of labour force
Agriculture	6,594,615.4	18.6	9,364,000	48.9
Mining	776,019.0	2.2	128,000	0.7
Manufacturing	9,201,240.4	25.9	1,904,000	9.9
Construction	1,451,364.0	4.1	658,000	3.4
Public utilities	1,616,046.7	4.6	143,000	0.7
Transportation and communications	3,678,353.9	10.4	566,000	3.0
Trade	6,216,469.4	17.5	814,000	4.2
Finance	2,564,159.2	7.2	235,000	1.2
Pub. admin., defense	2,073,309.4	5.8 }	2,433,000	12.7
Services	1,912,946.8	5.4 }		
Other	−589,135.2[2]	−1.7[2]	2,920,000[3]	15.2[3]
TOTAL	35,495,389.0	100.0	19,165,000	100.0[4]

Public debt (external, outstanding; 1986): U.S.$23,308,900,000.
Population economically active (1985): total 19,165,000; activity rate of total
population 42.9%[5] (participation rates: over age 15, 68.2%[5]; female 36.1%[5];
unemployed 6.0%).

Price and earnings indexes (1980 = 100)

	1982	1983	1984	1985	1986	1987
Consumer price index	178.7	237.5	352.4	510.9	687.7	954.9
Daily earnings index[6]	161.8	221.2	306.1	418.1	554.7	709.1

Land use (1986): forested 25.9%; meadows and pastures 11.7%; agricultural
and under permanent cultivation 35.3%; other 27.1%.

Foreign trade

Balance of trade (current prices)

	1982	1983	1984	1985	1986	1987
U.S.$'000,000	−3,097	−3,507	−3,624	−3,386	−3,648	−3,973
% of total	21.1%	23.4%	20.3%	17.5%	19.7%	16.3%

Imports (1987): U.S.$14,163,000,000 (fuels 20.5%, machinery 17.3%, chem-
icals 13.7%, iron and steel 10.9%, pharmaceutical products 7.7%). *Major
import sources:* West Germany 14.9%; United States 9.6%; Iraq 8.1%; Italy
7.6%; Japan 6.1%; United Kingdom 4.9%; France 4.3%.
Exports (1987): U.S.$10,190,000,000 (textiles 26.6%, agricultural products
18.2%, iron and nonferrous metals 9.7%, food 8.3%, leather and hides
7.1%, machinery 6.7%, chemical products 5.2%). *Major export destinations:*
West Germany 21.4%; Iraq 9.3%; Italy 8.3%; United States 7.0%; United
Kingdom 5.3%; France 4.9%; Iran 4.3%; Saudi Arabia 4.0%.

Transport and communications

Transport. Railroads (1987): route length 5,076 mi, 8,169 km; passenger-mi
3,797,000,000, passenger-km 6,110,000,000; short ton-mi cargo 4,961,000,-
000, metric ton-km cargo 7,244,000,000. Roads (1986): total length 198,293
mi, 319,133 km (paved 19%). Vehicles (1987): passenger cars 1,193,121;
trucks and buses 559,220. Merchant marine (1987): vessels (100 gross
tons and over) 852; total deadweight tonnage 5,516,139. Air transport
(1986): passenger-mi 1,626,598,000, passenger-km 2,617,761,000; short ton-
mi cargo 31,144,000, metric ton-km cargo 45,469,000; airports (1988) with
scheduled flights 14.
Communications. Daily newspapers (1986)[7]: total number 338; total circulation 4,188,262; circulation per 1,000 population 81.3. Radio (1986):
total number of receivers 8,227,000 (1 per 6.3 persons). Television (1986):
total number of receivers 5,010,000 (1 per 10 persons). Telephones (1987):
3,703,000 (1 per 14 persons).

Education and health

Education (1985–86)

	schools	teachers	students	student/ teacher ratio
Primary (age 5–12)	47,630	212,717	6,635,821	31.2
Secondary (age 13–18)	5,734	93,384	2,282,537	24.4
Voc., teacher tr.	2,075	44,298	635,847	14.3
Higher	310	22,968	449,416	19.6

Educational attainment (1980). Percent of population age 25 and over
having: no formal schooling 52.4%; primary education 35.3%; secondary
8.7%; higher 3.6%. *Literacy* (1980): total population age 15 and over literate 8,561,370 (65.6%); males literate 6,530,035 (81.3%); females literate
2,031,335 (49.8%).
Health (1986): physicians 37,142 (1 per 1,388 persons); hospital beds 107,152
(1 per 481 persons); infant mortality rate per 1,000 live births 84.0.
Food (1984–86): daily per capita caloric intake 3,148 (vegetable products
91%, animal products 9%); (1983) 123% of FAO recommended minimum
requirement.

Military

Total active duty personnel (1988): 635,300 (army 82.3%, navy 8.7%, air force
9.0%). *Military expenditure as percent of GNP* (1985): 4.6% (world 6.1%);
per capita expenditure U.S.$48.

[1]Urban areas only. [2]Imputed bank services. [3]Includes unemployed. [4]Detail does not
add to total given because of rounding. [5]1980. [6]Insured workers only. [7]Principal
daily newspapers only.

Tuvalu

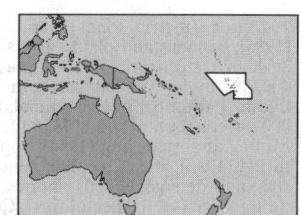

Official name: Tuvalu.
Form of government: constitutional monarchy with one legislative house (Parliament [12]).
Chief of state: British Monarch, represented by governor-general.
Head of government: Prime Minister.
Capital: Fongafale, on Funafuti atoll.
Official language: none.
Official religion: none.
Monetary unit[1]: 1 Tuvalu Dollar = 1 Australian Dollar ($T = $A) = 100 Tuvalu and Australian cents; valuation (Oct. 10, 1988) 1 U.S.$ = $A 1.24; 1 £ = $A 2.13.

Area and population

Islands[2]	area		population
	sq mi	sq km	1985 census
Funafuti	0.91	2.36	2,810
Nanumaga	1.00	2.59	672
Nanumea	1.38	3.57	879
Niulakita	0.16	0.41	74
Niutao	0.82	2.12	904
Nui	1.27	3.29	604
Nukufetau	1.18	3.06	694
Nukulaelae	0.64	1.66	315
Vaitupu	1.89	4.90	1,231
TOTAL	9.25	23.96	8,229[3,4]

Demography

Population (1988): 8,700.
Density (1988): persons per sq mi 940.5, persons per sq km 363.1.
Urban–rural (1985): urban 34.2%; rural 65.8%.
Sex distribution (1985): male 47.42%; female 52.58%.
Age breakdown (1979): under 15, 33.8%; 15–29, 31.0%; 30–44, 14.3%; 45–59, 13.2%; 60–74, 6.1%; 75 and over, 1.6%.
Population projection: (1990) 9,000; (2000) 11,000.
Doubling time: 54 years.
Ethnic composition (1979): Tuvaluan (Polynesian) 91.2%; mixed (Polynesian/Micronesian/other) 7.2%; European 1.0%; other 0.6%.
Religious affiliation (1979): Church of Tuvalu (Congregational) 96.9%; Seventh-day Adventist 1.4%; Baha'i 1.0%; Roman Catholic 0.2%; other 0.5%.
Major locality (1985): Fongafale, on Funafuti atoll 2,810.

Vital statistics

Birth rate per 1,000 population (1985): 23.8 (world avg. 29.0); legitimate 82.2%; illegitimate 17.8%.
Death rate per 1,000 population (1985): 10.7 (world avg. 11.0).
Natural increase rate per 1,000 population (1985): 13.1 (world avg. 18.0).
Total fertility rate (avg. births per childbearing woman; 1985): 2.7.
Marriage rate per 1,000 population: n.a.
Divorce rate per 1,000 population: n.a.
Life expectancy at birth (1987): male 59.0 years; female 62.0 years.
Major causes of death per 100,000 population (1985): diseases of the digestive system 170.0; diseases of the circulatory system 150.0; diseases of the respiratory system 120.0; diseases of the nervous system 120.0; malignant neoplasms (cancers) 70.0; infectious and parasitic diseases 40.0; endocrine and metabolic disorders 20.0; ill-defined conditions 430.0.

National economy

Budget (1987). Revenue: $A 13,498,000 (current revenue 31.1%, of which local sources 25.4%, British grants 5.7%; capital [development] revenue 68.9%, all from foreign grants and loans). Expenditures: $A 13,498,000 (current expenditures 31.1%; capital [development] expenditures 68.9%, of which marine transport 20.7%, education 13.0%, fisheries 5.6%, health 3.1%).
Gross domestic product (at current market prices; 1984): U.S.$4,000,000 (U.S.$450 per capita).

Structure of gross domestic product and labour force

	1979			
	in value $A	% of total value	labour force[5]	% of labour force
Agriculture, fishing	597,100	16.0	38	1.0
Mining	—	—	1	—
Manufacturing	37,300	1.0	62	1.6
Construction	485,200	13.0	224	5.6
Public utilities	...	...	14	0.3
Transportation and communication	149,300	4.0	107	2.7
Trade	1,268,900	34.0	98	2.4
Finance			11	0.3
Pub. admin., defense }	1,194,200	32.0	177	4.4
Services			170	4.2
Unemployed	—	—	162	4.0
Noncash economy	—	—	2,946[6]	73.5
TOTAL	3,732,000	100.0	4,010	100.0

Production (metric tons except as noted). Agriculture[7], forestry, fishing (1986): coconuts 3,000, hens' eggs 13, honey 2, other agricultural products include breadfruit, pulaka (taro), bananas, pandanus fruit, and pawpaws;
livestock (number of live animals) 9,000 pigs[8]; forestry, n.a.; fish catch 793. Mining and quarrying: n.a. Manufacturing (1984): copra 840 metric tons; handicrafts; baked goods. Construction: n.a. Energy production (consumption): electricity (kW-hr; 1987) 3,000,000 (3,000,000); coal, none (none); crude petroleum, none (none); petroleum products, none (n.a.); natural gas, none (none).
Public debt: n.a.
Tourism (1979): number of visitors 474.
Population economically active (1979)[5]: total 4,010; activity rate of total population 55.2% (participation rates: over age 15, 81.1%; female 51.3%; unemployed 4.0%).

Price and earnings indexes (1980 = 100)

	1980	1981	1982	1983	1984	1985	1986
Consumer price index	100.0	109.6	119.8	127.8	132.3	141.7	152.3
Monthly earnings index	...	...	...	...	...	...	...

Household income and expenditure. Average household size (1979) 6.4; average annual income per household: $A 2,575; sources of income: agriculture and other 61.2%, cash economy only 17.9%, agriculture only 14.9%, other 6.0%; expenditure (1983)[9]: food 45.5%, housing and household operations 11.5%, transportation 10.5%, alcohol and tobacco 10.5%, clothing 7.5%, other 14.5%.
Land use (1983): agricultural and under permanent cultivation 75%[10]; other 25%.

Foreign trade

Balance of trade (current prices)

	1979	1980	1981	1982	1983	1984
$A '000	−1,594	−3,061	−2,556	−2,853	−2,877	−3,653
% of total	75.6%	94.7%	98.6%	97.5%	95.0%	85.4%

Imports (1984): $A 3,965,000 (food and live animals 24.8%, manufactured goods 22.0%, machinery and transport equipment 14.8%, petroleum and petroleum products 11.7%, chemicals 5.1%, beverages and tobacco 4.1%, animal and vegetable oils and fats 0.4%). *Major import sources:* Australia 38.9%; New Zealand 17.3%; United Kingdom 7.0%; Japan 4.7%; United States 3.0%.
Exports (1984): $A 312,000 (copra 80.0%, developed cinema film 20.0%). *Major export destinations* (1982): Fiji 47.5%; Australia 39.7%; New Zealand 5.3%.

Transport and communications

Transport. Railroads: none. Roads (1985): total length 5 mi, 8 km (paved, none). Vehicles: passenger cars, n.a.; trucks and buses, n.a.[11]. Merchant marine (1987): vessels (100 gross tons and over) 2; total deadweight tonnage 458. Air transport (1977): passenger arrivals (Funafuti) 1,443; cargo, n.a.; airports (1988) with scheduled flights 1.
Communications. Daily newspapers: none. Radio (1986): total number of receivers 2,200 (1 per 3.7 persons). Television: none. Telephones (1986): 150 (1 per 57 persons).

Education and health

Education (1984)

	schools	teachers	students	student/ teacher ratio
Primary (age 6–14)	11	61	1,349	22.1
Secondary (age 12–18)	1	15[12]	243	...
Vocational[12]	8	16	354	22.1
Higher	—	—	—	—

Educational attainment (1979). Percent of population age 25 and over having: no formal schooling 0.4%; primary education 93.0%; secondary 6.1%; higher 0.5%. *Literacy* (1983): total population literate 5,509 (95.5%); males literate 2,443 (95.5%); females literate 3,066 (95.5%).
Health (1985): physicians 4 (1 per 2,050 persons); hospital beds (1984) 36 (1 per 231 persons); infant mortality rate per 1,000 live births 54.0.
Food: daily per capita caloric intake, n.a.

Military

Total active duty personnel (1987): There is a police force of 32 men.

---

[1]The value of the Tuvalu Dollar is pegged to the value of the Australian Dollar, which is also legal currency in Tuvalu. [2]Local government councils have been established on all islands except Niulakita. [3]Total includes 46 persons unaccounted for in island populations. [4]De facto population; about 1,500 Tuvaluans live abroad, mainly in Nauru or on foreign fishing vessels. [5]Based on indigenous de facto population only. [6]Mostly subsistence fishermen and handicraft workers. [7]Because of poor soil quality, only limited subsistence agriculture is possible on the islands. [8]Other livestock include goats. [9]Weights of consumer price index components. [10]Capable of supporting coconut palms, pandanus, and breadfruit. [11]There are several cars, tractors, trailers, and light trucks on Funafuti; a few motorcycles are in use on most islands. [12]1982–83.

Uganda

Official name: Republic of Uganda.
Form of government: military regime
with one interim legislative body
(National Resistance Council)[1].
Head of state and government:
President.
Capital: Kampala.
Official language: English.
Official religion: none.
Monetary unit: 1 Uganda
new shilling (U Sh) = 100 cents;
valuation (Oct. 10, 1988)
1 U.S.$ = U Sh 150.00[2];
1 £ = U Sh 257.00.

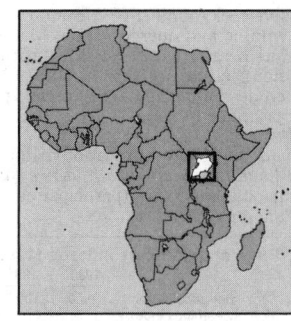

Area and population

Districts	Capitals	area sq mi	area sq km	population 1985 estimate
Apac	Apac	2,510	6,490	369,000
Arua	Olaki	3,020	7,830	543,300
Bundibugyo	Busaru	900	2,340	134,500
Bushenyi	Bumbaire	2,080	5,400	600,300
Gulu	Bungatira	4,530	11,740	305,500
Hoima	Hoima	3,820	9,900	358,400
Iganga	Bulamogi	5,060	13,110	755,100
Jinja	Jinja	280	730	253,400
Kabale	Rubale	960	2,490	503,700
Kabarole	Karambe	3,230	8,360	630,500
Kampala	Kampala	70	180	560,800
Kamuli	Namwendwa	1,680	4,350	400,100
Kapchorwa	Kaptanya	670	1,740	83,100
Kasese	Rukoki	1,240	3,200	342,400
Kitgum	Labongo	6,230	16,140	354,100
Kotido	Kotido	5,100	13,210	194,700
Kumi	Kumi	1,100	2,860	273,100
Lira	Lira	2,800	7,250	430,600
Luwero	Luwero	3,550	9,200	477,800
Masaka	Kaswa Bukoto	6,310	16,330	741,600
Masindi	Nyangeya	3,720	9,640	259,800
Mbale	Bunkoko	980	2,550	647,400
Mbarara	Kakika	4,190	10,840	829,100
Moroto	Katikekile	5,450	14,110	210,900
Moyo	Moyo	1,930	5,010	119,600
Mpigi	Mpigi	2,400	6,220	738,000
Mubende	Bageza	3,980	10,310	616,500
Mukono	Kawuga Mukono	5,500	14,240	708,500
Nebbi	Nebbi	1,120	2,890	258,600
Rakai	Byakabanda	1,920	4,970	329,600
Rukungiri	Kagunga	1,060	2,750	337,400
Soroti	Soroti	3,880	10,060	545,300
Tororo	Sukulu	1,760	4,550	767,100
TOTAL LAND AREA		76,080	197,040	14,679,800
INLAND WATER[3]		16,990	44,000	
TOTAL		93,070[4]	241,040[4]	

Demography

Population (1988): 15,990,000.
Density[5] (1988): persons per sq mi 210.2, persons per sq km 81.2.
Urban–rural (1985): urban 14.4%; rural 85.6%.
Sex distribution (1985): male 49.54%; female 50.46%.
Age breakdown (1985): under 15, 48.5%; 15–29, 25.8%; 30–44, 14.1%; 45–59, 7.4%; 60–74, 3.6%; 75 and over, 0.6%.
Population projection: (1990) 16,928,000; (2000) 22,400,000.
Doubling time: 21 years.
Ethnic composition (1983): Ganda 17.8%; Teso 8.9%; Nkole 8.2%; Soga 8.2%; Gisu 7.2%; Chiga 6.8%; Lango 6.0%; Rwanda 5.8%; Acholi 4.6%; other 26.5%.
Religious affiliation (1980): Roman Catholic 49.6%; Protestant 28.7%; Muslim 6.6%; other 15.1%.
Major cities (1980): Kampala 458,503; Jinja 45,060; Masaka 29,123; Mbale 28,039; Mbarara 23,160.

Vital statistics

Birth rate per 1,000 population (1980–85): 50.3 (world avg. 29.0).
Death rate per 1,000 population (1980–85): 16.8 (world avg. 11.0).
Natural increase rate per 1,000 population (1980–85): 33.5 (world avg. 18.0).
Total fertility rate (avg. births per childbearing woman; 1987): 7.0.
Life expectancy at birth (1984): male 49.0 years; female 53.0 years.
Major causes of death per 100,000 population: n.a.; however, major diseases include malaria, measles, venereal diseases, and dysentery.

National economy

Budget (1987–88). Revenue: U Sh 44,700,000,000 (direct taxes 62.0%, others [mostly loans and grants] 38.0%). Expenditures[6]: U Sh 53,200,000,000 (percentage breakdown not available).
Public debt (external, outstanding; 1986): U.S.$928,800,000.
Tourism (1986): receipts from visitors U.S.$8,000,000; expenditures by nationals abroad U.S.$10,000,000.
Population economically active (1985): total 7,054,000; activity rate of total population 45.6% (participation rates: ages 15–64, 78.9%; female 41.9%).

Price index (1981 = 100)

	1981	1982	1983	1984	1985	1986	1987
Consumer price index	100.0	200.7	248.9	355.3	825.9	2,217.8	7,498.8

Production (metric tons except as noted). Agriculture, forestry, fishing (1986): bananas and plantains 8,440,000; cassava 5,000,000; sweet potatoes 2,540,000; sugarcane 550,000; pulses 528,000; corn (maize) 400,000; beans 400,000; millet 350,000; sorghum 300,000; coffee 195,000; peanuts 115,000; livestock (number of live animals) 5,100,000 cattle, 3,300,000 goats, 1,700,000 sheep; roundwood (1985) 12,488,000 cu m; fish catch (1985) 212,200. Mining and quarrying (1984): copper ore (metal content) 1,100. Manufacturing (1985): meat 166,000; cement 30,000[7]; tea 7,000; raw sugar 6,000; soap and detergents 200[8]; fabrics 14,304,000 sq m[7]; cigarettes 965,000,000 units[7]; beer 148,160 hectolitres[7]. Construction: n.a. Energy production (consumption): electricity (kW-hr; 1986) 656,000,000 (546,000,000); petroleum products (metric tons; 1986) none (251,000).
Gross national product (at current market prices; 1984): U.S.$3,290,000,000 (U.S.$230 per capita).

Structure of gross domestic product and labour force

	1982 in value U Sh '000,000	1982 % of total value	1980 labour force	1980 % of labour force
Agriculture	99,257	75.8	5,940,000	84.2
Manufacturing and mining	5,310	4.2		
Construction	594	0.4	317,000	4.5
Public utilities	451	0.3		
Transp. and commun.	2,353	1.8		
Trade	6,796	5.2		
Finance	7,526	5.7	797,000	11.3
Pub. admin., defense	6,697	5.1		
Services	2,010	1.5		
TOTAL	130,994	100.0	7,054,000	100.0

Household size. Average household size (1983) 4.8; income per household: n.a.; expenditure[9] (1981): food 58.0%, clothing 14.0%, transportation 10.0%, fuel and lighting 6.0%.
Land use (1985): forested 29.1%; meadows and pastures 25.0%; agricultural and under permanent cultivation 33.1%; other 12.8%.

Foreign trade

Balance of trade (current prices)

	1979	1980	1981	1982	1983	1984
U Sh '000,000	+2,068	+818	+3,347	+858	+6,997	+27,245
% of total	46.7%	19.0%	12.1%	1.3%	6.3%	10.9%

Imports (1984): U Sh 111,508,000,000 (sugar 16.0%, motor vehicles 10.8%, clothing and fabrics 9.6%, construction materials 8.0%, food 5.4%). *Major import sources* (1983): Kenya and Tanzania 29.0%; West Germany 8.6%; United Kingdom 8.2%; India 4.7%.
Exports (1984): U Sh 138,753,000,000 (unroasted coffee 91.8%). *Major export destinations* (1983): United States 27.0%; United Kingdom 10.9%; France 9.6%; West Germany 9.3%; Spain 8.8%; Japan 4.4%.

Transport and communications

Transport. Railroads (1986): route length 1,286 km; passengers (1984) 2,100,000; cargo 331,000,000 metric tons. Roads (1986): total length 28,332 km (paved 22%). Vehicles (1986): passenger cars 32,155; trucks and buses 5,646. Merchant marine (1987): vessels (100 gross tons and over) 3; total deadweight tonnage 8,600. Air transport[10] (1986): passenger-km 96,085,000; metric ton-km cargo 23,355,000; airports (1988) 5.
Communications. Daily newspapers (1987): total number 2; total circulation 48,800; circulation per 1,000 population 3.1. Radio (1986): 600,000 receivers (1 per 25 persons). Television (1987): 90,000 receivers (1 per 173 persons). Telephones (1983): 54,439 (1 per 259 persons).

Education and health

Education (1984)

	schools	teachers	students	student/ teacher ratio
Primary (age 5–11)	6,420	58,377	1,908,564	32.7
Secondary (age 12–15)	297	5,603	114,828	20.5
Voc., teacher tr.	118	1,039	23,335	22.5
Higher	14	934	8,216	8.8

Educational attainment (1969). Percent of population age 25 and over having: no formal schooling, or less than one full year 58.2%; primary education 33.9%; lower secondary 5.0%; upper secondary 2.5%; higher 0.4%.
Literacy (1985): population age 15 and over literate 4,822,000 (57.0%); males literate 2,880,000 (69.7%); females literate 1,942,000 (45.3%).
Health: physicians (1984) 700 (1 per 20,300 persons); hospital beds (1983) 20,343 (1 per 683 persons); infant mortality rate (1984) 110.0.
Food (1984–86): daily per capita caloric intake 2,225 (vegetable products 94%, animal products 6%); (1983) 101% of FAO recommended minimum requirement.

Military

Total active duty personnel (1988): 35,000 (army 100%). *Military expenditure as percent of GNP* (1984): 1.1% (world 6.1%); per capita expenditure U.S.$4.

---

[1]Constitution of 1967 suspended July 1985; National Assembly [156 seats] dissolved July 1985. [2]As of Sept. 30, 1988, the Uganda new shilling was fixed at a par value of U Sh 150.00 = 1.00 $US. [3]Includes swamps. [4]Detail does not add to total given because of rounding. [5]Based on land area. [6]Includes U Sh 26,400,000,000 of capital expenditures for development. [7]1984. [8]1982. [9]Middle-income families only. [10]Uganda Airlines only.

Union of Soviet Socialist Republics

Official name: Soyuz Sovetskykh Sotsialisticheskikh Respublik (Sovetsky Soyuz) (Union of Soviet Socialist Republics [Soviet Union]).
Form of government: federal socialist republic with one legislative house (Supreme Soviet) comprising two chambers (Soviet of the Union [750] and Soviet of the Nationalities [750]).
Chief of state: President (Chairman of the Supreme Soviet).
Head of government: Premier (Chairman of the Council of Ministers).
Capital: Moscow.
Official language: Russian.
Official religion: none.
Monetary unit: 1 ruble = 100 kopecks; valuation (Oct. 10, 1988) 1 ruble = U.S.$1.61 = £1.06.

Area and population		area		population
Soviet Federated Socialist Republic	Capitals	sq mi	sq km	1988[1] estimate
Russian S.F.S.R.	Moscow	6,592,800	17,075,400	146,450,000
Soviet Socialist Republics				
Armenian	Yerevan	11,500	29,800	3,459,000
Azerbaijan	Baku	33,400	86,600	6,921,000
Belorussian	Minsk	80,200	207,600	10,141,000
Estonian	Tallinn	17,400	45,100	1,571,000
Georgian	Tbilisi	26,900	69,700	5,297,000
Kazakh	Alma-Ata	1,049,200	2,717,300	16,470,000
Kirgiz	Frunze	76,600	198,500	4,238,000
Latvian	Riga	24,900	64,500	2,673,000
Lithuanian	Vilnius	25,200	65,200	3,682,000
Moldavian	Kishinyov	13,000	33,700	4,224,000
Tadzhik	Dushanbe	55,300	143,100	4,969,000
Turkmen	Ashkhabad	188,500	488,100	3,455,000
Ukrainian	Kiev	233,100	603,700	51,377,000
Uzbek	Tashkent	172,700	447,400	19,569,000
TOTAL LAND AREA		8,600,700	22,275,700	284,496,000
INLAND WATER		49,100	127,300	
TOTAL		8,649,800	22,403,000	

Demography

Population (1988): 285,796,000.
Density (1988): persons per sq mi 33.0, persons per sq km 12.8.
Urban–rural (1988): urban 66.4%; rural 33.6%.
Sex distribution (1988): male 47.10%; female 52.90%.
Age breakdown (1987): under 15, 25.5%; 15–29, 24.0%; 30–44, 18.7%; 45–59, 18.3%; 60–69, 7.1%; 70 and over, 6.4%.
Population projection: (1990) 290,939,000; (2000) 311,637,000.
Doubling time: 70 years.
Ethnic composition (1983): Russian 51.9%; Ukrainian 15.8%; Uzbek 5.1%; Belorussian 3.6%; Kazakh 2.6%; Tatar 2.4%; Azerbaijani 2.2%; Armenian 1.7%; Georgian 1.4%; Tadzhik 1.2%; Moldavian 1.1%; Lithuanian 1.1%; other 9.9%.
Religious affiliation (1987): Christian 36.4%, of which Orthodox 31.5%, Protestant 3.1%, Roman Catholic 1.8%; Muslim 11.2%; Jewish 1.1%; nonreligious 29.7%; atheist 21.4%; other 0.2%.
Major cities (1988): Moscow 8,675,000; Leningrad 4,995,000; Kiev 2,577,000; Tashkent 2,210,000; Baku 1,772,000; Kharkov 1,604,000; Minsk 1,583,000; Novosibirsk 1,440,000; Gorky 1,438,000; Sverdlovsk 1,351,000; Kuybyshev 1,292,000; Tbilisi 1,211,000; Dnepropetrovsk 1,201,000.

Other principal cities (1988)					
	population		population		population
Alma-Ata	1,134,000	Krasnodar	632,000	Saratov	926,000
Barnaul	606,000	Krasnoyarsk	912,000	Tolyatti	643,000
Chelyabinsk	1,134,000	Krivoy Rog	707,000	Tula	541,000
Donetsk	1,099,000	Lvov	780,000	Ufa	1,109,000
Dushanbe	596,000	Novokuznetsk	598,000	Ulyanovsk	613,000
Frunze	646,000	Odessa	1,148,000	Vilnius	579,000
Irkutsk	618,000	Omsk	1,150,000	Vladivostok	627,000
Izhevsk	643,000	Orenburg	544,000	Volgograd	997,000
Karaganda	641,000	Penza	547,000	Voronezh	886,000
Kazan	1,084,000	Perm	1,087,000	Yaroslavl	639,000
Kemerovo	527,000	Riga	913,000	Yerevan	1,186,000
Khabarovsk	600,000	Rostov-na-Donu	1,015,000	Zaporozhye	887,000
Kishinyov	684,000	Samarkand (1987)	588,000	Zhdanov	532,000

Place of birth (1983): 99.9% native-born; 0.1% foreign-born.
Mobility (1985). Population living in the same residence from birth: 57.0%; 15 years and more 20.1%; 14–10 years 5.7%; 9–6 years 5.1%; 5–2 years 7.2%; less than 2 years 4.9%.
Households[2] (1979). Average household size 3.5; 2 persons 29.7%, 3 persons 28.8%, 4 persons 23.0%, 5 persons 9.5%, 6 persons 4.1%, 7 or more persons 4.9%. Family households population: 232,075,245 (86.9%), nonfamily population 30,360,755 (13.1%).
Emigration (1988): 13,000.

Vital statistics

Birth rate per 1,000 population (1987): 19.8 (world avg. 26.0); legitimate, n.a.; illegitimate, n.a.
Death rate per 1,000 population (1987): 9.9 (world avg. 9.9).
Natural increase rate per 1,000 population (1987): 9.9 (world avg. 16.1).
Total fertility rate (avg. births per childbearing woman; 1984): 2.3.
Marriage rate per 1,000 population (1986): 9.8.
Divorce rate per 1,000 population (1986): 3.4.
Life expectancy at birth (1986): male 65.0 years; female 73.6 years.
Major causes of death per 100,000 population (1983): diseases of the circulatory system 554.3, of which cardiovascular atherosclerosis 228.2, cerebrovascular disease 121.6, hypertensive heart disease 82.7, ischemic heart disease 73.0, other diseases of the circulatory system 48.8; malignant neoplasms (cancers) 148.1.

Social indicators

Educational attainment (1984). Percent of population age 10 and over having: less than full primary education 0.2%; primary or secondary 91.0%, of which secondary 60.4%; some postsecondary and higher 8.2%; postgraduate 0.6%.
Distribution of wealth: n.a.
Quality of working life (1986). Average workweek: 39.0 hours (5.0% overtime). Annual rate per 100,000 workers for: injury or accident, n.a.; industrial illness, n.a.; death, n.a. Proportion of labour force insured for damages or income loss resulting from: injury 100.0%; permanent disability 100.0%; death 100.0%. Average days lost to labour stoppages per 1,000 workdays: n.a. Average duration of journey to work: 58–68 minutes (mostly by public transportation and foot). Rate per 1,000 workers of discouraged (unemployed no longer seeking work): n.a.
Access to services[3] (1985). Proportion of dwellings having access to: electricity, virtually 100%; safe public water supply 91.8%; public sewage collection 89.7%; central heating 88.9%; gas 78.3%; hot water 71.2%; bathroom 83.2%.
Social participation. Eligible voters participating in last national election (1984): 99.9%. Population participating in voluntary work (1986): 75.1%. Trade union membership in total work force: 100.0%. Practicing religious population in total affiliated population: n.a; estimated at 10%.
Social deviance. Offense rate per 100,000 population for: murder, n.a.; rape, n.a.; other assault, n.a.; grand and auto theft, n.a.; burglary and housebreaking, n.a. Incidence per 100,000 in general population of: alcoholism, n.a.; drug and substance abuse (1986) 165; suicide, n.a.
Leisure (1986). Favourite leisure activities (annual attendance): movies 3,882,000,000; lectures 302,900,000; museums 195,800,000; concerts 141,200,000; theatre 126,000,000.
Material well-being (1987). Households possessing: automobile 16.0%; telephone 28.5%; television receiver 100%; refrigerator 93.0%; air conditioner, virtually none; washing machine 70.0%; motorcycle 14.0%; bicycle 58.0%; tape recorder 41.0%.

National economy

Gross national product (at current market prices; 1986): U.S.$2,356,700,000,000 (U.S.$8,410 per capita).

Structure of net material product and labour force				
	1986		1987	
	in value '000,000,000 rubles	% of total value	labour force	% of labour force
Agriculture	121.2	20.6	24,835,000	18.9
Mining and manufacturing	258.0	43.9	38,100,000	29.0
Public utilities			5,092,000	3.9
Construction	70.3	12.0	11,965,000	9.1
Transp. and commun.	36.5	6.2	12,170,000	9.3
Trade	101.4	17.3	10,480,000	8.0
Finance	...	...	675,000	0.5
Pub. admin., defense	...	...	1,983,000	1.5
Services	...	...	23,905,000	18.2
Other	...	...	2,095,000[4]	1.6[4]
TOTAL	587.4	100.0	131,300,000	100.0

Public debt (1987): U.S.$39,000,000,000.
Land use (1985): forested 35.7%; meadows and pastures 16.8%; agricultural and under permanent cultivation 10.2%; other 37.3%.

Manufacturing, mining, and construction enterprises (1982)				
	no. of enter-prises	no. of employees	monthly wages as a % of avg. of all wages	annual gross output ('000,000 rubles)
Manufacturing				
Machinery and metal products	8,180	15,011,000	111.2	182,400
Food products	7,538	2,717,000	99.2	104,100
Chemicals and chemical products	1,493	1,148,000	112.8	75,500
Textiles	1,996	2,210,000	88.4	72,700
Clothing	5,118	2,250,000	88.4	30,900
Nonmetallic products	3,200	2,088,000	103.8	24,800
Wood, furniture, and paper	2,275	1,619,000	112.8	22,300
Beverages	1,726	374,000	95.5	7,700
Iron and steel	408	1,044,000	131.1	6,200
Footwear	406	494,000	95.8	5,500
Leather and leather products	266	199,000	95.9	4,200
Tobacco	88	40,000	95.5	3,800
Glass and pottery	333	376,000	99.3	3,300
Building materials	3,938	...	107.1	2,300
Rubber and plastic	...	433,000	103.5	...
Mining				
Petroleum and gas	853	1,105,000	161.1	34,400
Coal			153.9	
Metal ores	1,070	194,000	153.9	15,900
Construction	...	11,299,000	103.3	...

Budget (1989). Revenue: 459,814,445,000 rubles (share in profits of state and cooperative enterprises 91.4%). Expenditures: 494,797,545,000 rubles (national economy 56.4%, social welfare, education, and culture 33.0%, defense 4.1%).

Tourism (1987): tourist arrivals 2,127,000; tourists abroad 920,000.

Production (metric tons except as noted). Agriculture, forestry, fishing (1987): sugar beets 90,400,000, wheat 83,300,000, potatoes 75,900,000, barley 58,400,000, vegetables 28,700,000, oats 18,500,000, rye 18,100,000, corn (maize) 14,800,000, raw cotton 8,090,000, grapes 6,500,000, sunflower seeds 4,830,000, rice 2,680,000, tobacco 480,000; livestock (number of live animals; 1988) 140,500,000 sheep, 120,500,000 cattle, 77,300,000 pigs, 6,700,000 horses, 6,500,000 goats, 1,168,300,000 poultry; roundwood 297,000,000 cu m; fish catch 11,200,000. Mining and quarrying (1987): iron ore 251,000,000; phosphate rock 91,600,000; salt 16,100,000; potash salts 10,400,000; bauxite 4,600,000; chromium ore 3,600,000; manganese (metal content) 2,800,000; magnesite 2,500,000; asbestos 2,400,000; zinc 810,000; copper 630,000; lead 440,000; nickel 185,000; molybdenum 11,500; tungsten 9,200; gold 275; mercury 67,000 flasks; diamonds 10,800,000 carats. Manufacturing (1987): crude steel 162,000,000; cement 137,000,000; pig iron 116,000,000; rolled steel 114,000,000; mineral fertilizers 36,300,000; sulfuric acid 28,500,000; steel pipes 20,300,000; meat 18,600,000; sugar 13,700,000; paper and paperboard 6,200,000; canned fish 5,700,000; resins and plastics 5,500,000; soda ash 4,900,000; caustic soda 3,300,000; vegetable oil 3,000,000; cotton fibre 2,742,000; cotton yarn 1,747,000; man-made fibres 1,957,000[5]; butter 1,700,000; margarine 1,500,000; synthetic detergents 1,200,000[5]; soap 1,100,000; insecticides 600,000[5]; woolen yarn 465,000; woolen fibre 421,000[6]; flax fibre 217,000; leather 123,000; cotton fabrics 7,677,000,000 sq m; silk fabrics 1,936,000,000[5] sq m; linen fabrics 829,000,000 sq m; woolen fabrics 670,000,000 sq m; agricultural equipment 4,000,000,000 rubles[5]; machine tools 2,800,000,000 rubles; food-processing equipment 1,800,000,000 rubles[5]; chemical equipment 966,000,000 rubles[5]; forge press machines 645,000,000 rubles; oil equipment 235,000,000 rubles; leather footwear 805,000,000 pairs; tires 67,800,000 units; television receivers 9,100,000 units; radio receivers 8,100,000 units; refrigerators 6,000,000 units; bicycles 5,300,000 units; washing machines 5,800,000 units; passenger cars 1,300,000 units[5]; motorcycles 960,000 units; buses 85,315 units[5]; railroad freight cars 58,433 units[6]; railroad passenger cars 1,814 units[6]; beer 50,600,000 hectolitres; wine 27,800,000 hectolitres. Construction (1986): residential 118,200,000 sq m, of which urban 115,800,000 sq m, rural 2,400,000 sq m.

Service enterprises (1985)			
	no. of enterprises	no. of employees	monthly wages as a % of all wages
Public utilities	...	3,957,000	77.1
Electrical power	1,517	937,000	116.7
Transport: rail	...	2,639,000	111.1
Transport: road	...	7,788,000	116.1
Transport: water	...	451,000	138.3
Communications	91,600	1,671,000	83.9
Finance	...	679,000	95.2
Wholesale trade	} 709,900	} 7,760,000	78.5
Retail trade			78.5
Tourism	...	...	...
Education	183,000	9,887,000	78.9
Public services and administration	...	2,663,000	87.5
Other services	292,900	13,182,000	...

Energy production (consumption): electricity (kW-hr; 1986) 1,599,000,000,000 (1,570,190,000,000); coal (metric tons; 1986) 751,000,000 (689,391,000,000); crude petroleum (barrels; 1986) 4,616,000,000 (3,659,000,000); petroleum products (metric tons; 1986) 425,734,000 (359,434,000); natural gas (cu m; 1986) 686,000,000,000 (545,000,000,000).

Population economically active (1987): total 131,300,000; activity rate of total population 46.6% (participation rates [1987]: ages [male] 15–60, [female] 15–55, 51.8%; female 45.7%; unemployed, n.a.).

Price and earnings indexes (1980 = 100)							
	1979	1980	1981	1982	1983	1984	1985
Consumer price index	96.9	100.0	101.2	104.5	105.2	104.0	105.0
Monthly earnings index	97.3	100.0	102.3	105.4	107.3	108.8	109.2

Household income and expenditure. Average household size (1985) 3.2; average annual income per household 6,100 rubles (U.S.$8,700); sources of income (1986): wages and salaries 67.1%, transfer payments 22.9%, self-employment 3.0%, other 7.0%; expenditure (1986): food 39.1%, clothing 19.3%, household durable goods 11.0%, recreation and culture 10.8%.

Foreign trade

Balance of trade (current prices)							
	1981	1982	1983	1984	1985	1986	1987
'000,000,000 rubles	4.5	6.7	8.3	9.1	3.4	5.8	7.5
% of total	4.1%	5.6%	6.5%	6.5%	2.4%	4.4%	5.8%

Imports (1987): 60,700,000,000 rubles (machinery and transport equipment 41.4%; cereals and food products 16.1%; consumer goods 13.0%; raw materials 8.1%; mineral fuels and lubricants 5.2%; chemicals and related products 5.3%; textiles and clothing 1.5%). *Major import sources* (1986): East Germany 11.4%; Czechoslovakia 10.5%; Bulgaria 9.9%; Poland 9.8%; Hungary 7.8%; Cuba 6.1%; West Germany 4.6%; Yugoslavia 4.3%; Finland 3.8%; Romania 3.8%; Japan 3.5%; Italy 2.4%; India 2.0%; United States 1.8%; France 1.8%.

Exports (1987): 68,200,000,000 rubles (crude petroleum and petroleum products 35.7%; machinery and transport equipment 15.5%; mineral fuels and

natural gas 10.8%; raw materials 8.5%; chemicals, fertilizers, and resins 3.4%; wood and paper products 3.3%). *Major export destinations* (1986): East Germany 11.5%; Czechoslovakia 10.2%; Poland 10.0%; Bulgaria 9.9%; Hungary 6.8%; Cuba 5.6%; Romania 4.1%; West Germany 4.0%; Yugoslavia 2.6%; Italy 2.3%; Finland 2.3%; France 2.3%; United Kingdom 1.9%; Vietnam 1.9%; Mongolia 1.7%; Japan 1.4%; India 1.4%.

Trade by commodity group (1985)				
	imports		exports	
SITC Group	'000 rubles	%	'000 rubles	%
00 Food and live animals	14,650,000	21.2	1,087,000	1.5
02 Raw materials, excluding fuels	5,804,000	8.4	5,435,000	7.5
03 Mineral fuels, lubricants, and related materials	3,662,000	5.3	38,261,000	52.8
05 Chemicals and related products	3,455,000	5.0	2,826,000	3.9
65 Textile yarn, fabrics and related materials	1,175,000	1.7	942,000	1.3
07 Machinery and transport equipment	25,706,000	37.2	9,855,000	13.6
08 Miscellaneous manufactured articles	8,569,000	12.4	1,449,000	2.0
09 Goods not classified by kind	6,081,000	8.8	12,609,000	17.4
TOTAL	69,102,000	100.0	72,464,000	100.0

Direction of trade (1987)				
	imports		exports	
	'000 rubles	%	'000 rubles	%
Communist				
Comecon	38,900,000	64.1	40,700,000	59.7
Other	3,200,000	5.3	3,500,000	5.1
Market Economy				
Industrial countries	13,900,000	22.9	14,200,000	20.8
Developing countries	4,700,000	7.7	9,800,000	14.4
TOTAL	60,700,000	100.0	68,200,000	100.0

Transport and communications

Transport. Railroads (1987): length 90,471 mi, 145,600 km; passenger-mi 250,000,000,000, passenger-km 402,300,000,000; short ton-mi cargo 2,619,500,000,000, metric ton-km cargo 3,824,700,000,000. Roads (1986): total length 604,000 mi, 971,500 km (paved 84%). Vehicles (1980): passenger cars 8,255,000; trucks and buses 7,254,000. Inland waterways (1987): length 76,550 mi, 123,200 km; passenger-mi 3,480,000,000, passenger-km 5,600,000,000; short ton-mi cargo 172,900,000,000, metric ton-km cargo 252,500,000,000. Merchant marine (1987): vessels (100 gross tons and over) 6,705; total deadweight tonnage 28,555,746. Air transport (1987): passenger-mi 126,900,000,000, passenger-km 204,200,000,000; short ton-mi cargo 2,336,000,000, metric ton-km cargo 3,410,000,000; airports (1988) with scheduled flights 52. Shares of domestic passenger traffic by mode of transportation (1986): buses 43.8%; railway 36.9%; ships and airplanes 18.5%. Oil and gas pipelines (1987): length 165,600 mi, 266,500 km; short ton-mi cargo 1,735,800,000,000; metric ton-km cargo 2,793,500,000,000.

Distribution of traffic (1985)				
	cargo carried ('000,000 tons)	% of nat'l total	passengers carried ('000,000)	% of nat'l total
Road	6,320.0	52.6	47,000.0	43.9
Rail	3,951.2	32.9	4,166.0	3.9
Urban transport	—	—	55,720.0	52.0
road	—	—	32,800.0	30.6
rail	—	—	22,920.0	21.4
Inland water	633.0	5.3	132.0	0.1
Air	3.1	0.0	112.6	0.1
Pipeline	1,113.0	9.2	—	—
TOTAL	12,020.3	100.0	107,130.6	100.0

Communications. Daily newspapers (1986): total number 727; total circulation 96,414,000; circulation per 1,000 population 345. Radio (1986): 182,790,000 receivers (1 per 1.5 persons). Television (1987): 88,000,000 receivers (1 per 3.2 persons). Telephones (1987): 41,800,000 (1 per 6.7 persons).

Education and health

Education (1986–87)				
	schools	teachers	students	student/ teacher ratio
Primary (age 6–13)	65,500 }	2,668,000	36,800,000 }	13.8
Secondary (age 14–17)	62,000		4,600,000	
Vocational	4,506	246,000[7]	2,880,000	...
Higher	896	377,000[7]	2,688,000	...

Literacy (1984): total population age 15 and over literate 99.0%.

Health (1988): physicians 1,232,600[8] (1 per 229 persons); hospital beds 3,720,000 (1 per 80 persons); infant mortality rate per 1,000 live births (1987) 25.2.

Food (1983–85): daily per capita caloric intake 3,403 (vegetable products 74%, animal products 26%); (1983) 132% of FAO recommended minimum.

Military

Total active duty personnel (1988): 5,226,600 (army 38.3%, command and general support troops 29.1%, paramilitary forces 10.9%, navy 9.1%, air force 8.9%, forces abroad 3.7%). *Military expenditure as percent of GNP* (1985): 12.5%[9] (world 6.1%); per capita expenditure U.S.$990.

[1]January 1. [2]Family households only. [3]Urban dwellings only. [4]Other material activities. [5]1986. [6]1985. [7]1985–86. [8]Includes dentists. [9]Estimated by Western sources.

United Arab Emirates

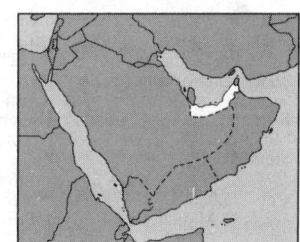

Official name: Ittiḥād al-Imārāt al-'Arabīyah (United Arab Emirates).
Form of government: monarchy; federal union of seven emirates with one appointive advisory body (Federal National Council [40][1]).
Chief of state: President.
Head of government: Prime Minister.
Capital: Abu Dhabi[2].
Official language: Arabic.
Official religion: Islam.
Monetary unit: 1 U.A.E. Dirham (Dh) = 100 fils; valuation (Oct. 10, 1988) 1 U.S.$ = Dh 3.67; 1 £ = Dh 6.29.

Area and population		area		population
				1985
Emirates	Capitals	sq mi	sq km	census
Abu Dhabi (Abū Ẓaby)	Abu Dhabi	26,000	67,350	670,125
Ajman ('Ajmān)	Ajman	100	250	64,318
Dubai (Dubayy)	Dubai	1,510	3,900	419,104
Fujairah (Al-Fujayrah)	Fujairah	440	1,150	54,425
Ras al-Khaimah (Ra's al-Khaymah)	Ras al-Khaimah	660	1,700	116,470
Sharjah (Ash-Shāriqah)	Sharjah	1,000	2,600	268,722
Umm al-Qaiwain (Umm al-Qaywayn)	Umm al-Qaiwain	290	750	29,229
TOTAL		30,000	77,700	1,622,393

Demography

Population (1988): 1,774,000.
Density (1988): persons per sq mi 59.1, persons per sq km 22.8.
Urban–rural (1986): urban 86.6%; rural 13.4%.
Sex distribution (1986): male 68.00%; female 32.00%.
Age breakdown (1986): under 15, 29.8%; 15–29, 25.1%; 30–44, 35.9%; 45–59, 7.6%; 60–74, 1.3%; 75 and over, 0.3%.
Population projection: (1990) 1,881,000; (2000) 2,518,000.
Doubling time: 23 years.
Ethnic composition (1983): Arab 87.1%, of which Arab from United Arab Emirates 30.7%; Pakistani and Indian 9.1%; Persian 1.7%; Baluchi 0.8%; African 0.8%; British 0.2%; American 0.1%; other 0.2%.
Religious affiliation (1980): Muslim 94.9% (Sunnī 80%, Shī'ī 20%); Christian 3.8%; other 1.3%.
Major cities (1980): Dubai 266,000; Abu Dhabi 243,000; Sharjah 125,000; al-'Ayn 102,000; Ras al-Khaimah 42,000.

Vital statistics

Birth rate per 1,000 population (1986): 33.5 (world avg. 26.0); legitimate, n.a.; illegitimate, n.a.
Death rate per 1,000 population (1986): 3.9 (world avg. 9.9).
Natural increase rate per 1,000 population (1986): 29.6 (world avg. 16.1).
Total fertility rate (avg. births per childbearing woman; 1986): 6.0.
Marriage rate per 1,000 population (1986): 2.9[3].
Divorce rate per 1,000 population (1986): 1.3[3].
Life expectancy at birth (1986): male 68.4 years; female 71.7 years.
Major causes of death per 100,000 population (1986)[3]: cardiovascular diseases 68.0; accidents and poisonings 29.1; malignant neoplasms (cancers) 22.5; congenital anomalies 21.5; respiratory diseases 14.6.

National economy

Budget (1987). Revenue: U.S.$7,250,000,000 (oil revenue 85.5%). Expenditures: U.S.$9,000,000,000 (current expenditure 64.4%, development 16.7%).
Gross national product (at current market prices; 1986): U.S.$20,950,000,000 (U.S.$14,410 per capita).

Structure of gross domestic product and labour force				
	1986			
	in value Dh '000,000	% of total value	labour force	% of labour force
Agriculture	1,540	2.0	44,124	5.0
Mining	26,543	33.9	18,100	2.0
Manufacturing	8,405	10.7	57,029	6.4
Construction	8,500	10.8	221,003	24.8
Public utilities	2,308	2.9	17,233	1.9
Transportation and communications	4,138	5.3	65,896	7.4
Trade	8,820	11.2	121,278	13.6
Finance			27,831	3.1
Pub. admin., defense }	18,180	23.2 }	318,447	35.7
Services				
Other	—	—	—	—
TOTAL	78,434	100.0	890,941	100.0[4]

Public debt (external, outstanding; 1982): U.S.$1,117,000,000.
Production (metric tons except as noted). Agriculture, forestry, fishing (1986): watermelons 72,000, tomatoes 70,000, dates 65,000, cantaloupes and other melons 34,000, cabbages 16,000, eggplants 16,000, pumpkins and squash 15,000, cauliflowers 10,000, cucumbers 9,000, lemons and limes 8,000, mangoes 3,000, green peppers 3,000; livestock (number of live animals) 778,000 goats, 382,000 sheep, 115,000 camels, 46,000 cattle, 5,000,000 chickens; fish catch 72,380. Mining and quarrying (1986): lime 45,000; also marble, shale for ceramic applications, and aggregate for cement.

Manufacturing (1986): cement 5,020,000; aluminum 154,000; cow's milk 11,000; mutton and lamb meat 6,000; goat meat 5,000; beef and veal 3,000; sulfur 1,460; butter and ghee 282. Construction (value added in Dh; 1984): 9,860,000,000. Energy production (consumption): electricity (kW-hr; 1986) 6,745,000,000 (6,745,000,000); coal, none (n.a.); crude petroleum (barrels; 1986) 495,460,000 (50,864,000); petroleum products (metric tons; 1986) 11,135,000 (5,850,000); natural gas (cu m; 1986) 3,869,700,000 (858,800,000).
Tourism (1983): 16,351 rooms for tourists.
Population economically active (1986): total 891,000; activity rate of total population 53.2% (participation rates: over age 15, 76.7%; female 6.6%; unemployed, n.a.).
Price and earnings indexes: n.a.
Household income and expenditure: Average household size (1986) 6.8; income per household: n.a.; sources of income: n.a.; expenditure: n.a.
Land use (1985): forested, none; meadows and pastures 2.4%; agricultural and under permanent cultivation 0.2%; built-up, wasteland, and other 97.4%.

Foreign trade

Balance of trade (current prices)						
	1981	1982	1983	1984	1985	1986
Dh '000,000	+14,668	+18,187	+24,430	+27,238	+23,249	+33,286
% of total	26.1%	31.6%	28.5%	36.7%	31.8%	40.1%

Imports (1985): Dh 24,931,000,000 (1984; machinery and transport equipment 32.3%, basic manufactures 22.8%, food and live animals 13.5%, mineral fuels 7.8%, chemicals 5.6%, crude minerals 1.9%). *Major import sources* (1984): Japan 17.8%; United States 12.1%; United Kingdom 9.9%; Italy 7.1%; West Germany 6.7%; Bahrain 5.4%; France 4.6%; The Netherlands 2.8%; Australia 2.3%; Singapore 1.7%; China 1.6%; Belgium–Luxembourg 1.5%; Switzerland 1.4%; Saudi Arabia 0.9%; Thailand 0.9%; Turkey 0.6%.
Exports (1985): Dh 48,180,000,000 (crude petroleum 88.5%, nonpetroleum exports 11.5%). *Major export destinations* (1984): Japan 49.4%; United States 8.2%; France 6.0%; Singapore 4.2%; Oman 3.1%; Italy 2.5%; Pakistan 2.1%; West Germany 1.8%; Australia 1.5%; Saudi Arabia 1.1%; Portugal 1.1%; Bangladesh 0.8%; United Kingdom 0.8%; The Netherlands 0.4%; Belgium–Luxembourg 0.3%; Bahrain 0.2%.

Transport and communications

Transport. Railroads: none. Roads (1984): total length 2,709 mi, 4,360 km (paved [1981] 61%). Vehicles (1984): passenger cars 61,146; trucks and buses 16,618. Merchant marine (1987): vessels (100 gross tons and over) 240; total deadweight tonnage 1,159,928. Air transport (1983): passenger-mi 2,213,000,000, passenger-km 3,562,000,000; short ton-mi cargo 65,300,000, metric ton-km cargo 95,300,000; airports (1988) with scheduled flights 4.
Communications. Daily newspapers (1986): total number 12; total circulation 291,000; circulation per 1,000 population 171. Radio (1986): total number of receivers 434,000 (1 per 3.9 persons). Television (1986): total number of receivers 145,000 (1 per 12 persons). Telephones (1984): 308,793 (1 per 4.6 persons).

Education and health

Education (1985–86)				student/
	schools	teachers	students	teacher ratio
Primary (age 6–11) }	327	6,123[5]	152,125	...
Secondary (age 12–18) }		3,967[5]	61,468	...
Vocational[6]	9	273	2,442	8.9
Higher[7]	...	449	6,326	14.1

Educational attainment (1975). Percent of population age 25 and over having: no formal schooling 72.2%; primary education 5.2%; secondary 16.6%; higher 6.0%. *Literacy* (1986): total population age 15 and over literate 858,149 (73.0%); males literate 657,579 (74.5%); females literate 200,570 (68.4%).
Health (1984): physicians 1,840 (1 per 666 persons); hospital beds 4,853 (1 per 252 persons); infant mortality rate per 1,000 live births (1986) 39.9.
Food (1984–86): daily per capita caloric intake 3,714 (vegetable products 80%, animal products 20%); (1983) 150% of FAO recommended minimum requirement.

Military

Total active duty personnel (1988): 43,000 (army 93.0%, navy 3.5%, air force 3.5%). *Military expenditure as percent of GNP* (1985): 5.7% (world 6.1%); per capita expenditure U.S.$890.

[1]All appointed seats. [2]Provisional. [3]Registered; Abu Dhabi Emirate only. [4]Detail does not add to total given because of rounding. [5]Public schools only. [6]1983–84. [7]1984–85.

United Kingdom

Official name: United Kingdom of
Great Britain and Northern Ireland.
Form of government: constitutional
monarchy with two legislative houses
(House of Lords [1,187]; House of
Commons [650]).
Chief of state: Sovereign.
Head of government: Prime Minister.
Capital: London.
Official language: English.
Official religion: Churches of England
and Scotland "established" (protected
by the state, but not "official") in their
respective countries; no established
church in Northern Ireland or Wales.
Monetary unit: 1 pound sterling
(£) = 100 new pence; valuation (Oct.
10, 1988) 1 £ = U.S.$1.71.

Doubling time: more than 100 years.
Ethnic composition (1986): white 94.2%; Asian Indian 1.4%; West Indian
1.0%; Pakistani 0.8%; African 0.2%; Chinese 0.2%; Bangladeshi 0.2%; Arab
0.1%; other and not stated 1.9%.
Religious affiliation (1980): Christian 86.9%, of which Anglican 56.8%,
Roman Catholic 13.1%, Presbyterian 7.0%, Methodist 4.3%, Baptist 1.4%;
Muslim 1.4%; Jewish 0.8%; Hindu 0.7%; Sikh 0.4%; nonreligious 8.8%;
other 1.0%.
Major cities (1986): Greater London 6,775,000; Birmingham 1,008,000; Glasgow 725,000; Leeds 711,000; Sheffield 534,000; Liverpool 483,000; Bradford
463,000; Manchester 451,000; Edinburgh 438,000; Bristol 391,000.
Place of birth (1985): 93.5% (50,720,000) native-born; 5.9% foreign-born, of
which Ireland 1.0%, India 0.7%, Caribbean 0.5%, Pakistan 0.4%; not stated
0.6%.
Mobility (1981). Population living in the same residence as 1980: 90.9%;
different residence, same country (of the U.K.) 8.2%; different residence,
different country within the U.K. 0.4%; from outside the U.K. 0.5%.
Households[6] (1985). Average household size 2.7 (3.1); 1 person 24% (20%),
2 persons 33% (26%), 3 persons 17% (16%), 4 persons 18% (17%), 5 persons
6% (10%), 6 or more persons 3% (11%). Family households (1984): 16,079,-
300 (74.3%), nonfamily 5,593,100 (25.7%, of which 1-person 22.5%).
Immigration (1986): permanent residents 250,000, from EEC 27.2%, Australia, New Zealand, and Canada 12.0%, United States 10.8%, South Africa
7.2%, Middle East 6.5%, Bangladesh and India 5.6%, Pakistan 4.0%.

Area and population

Countries	Capitals	area sq mi	area sq km	population 1986 estimate
England	London	50,363	130,439	47,254,500
Counties				
Avon		520	1,346	946,600
Bedfordshire		477	1,235	521,000
Berkshire		486	1,259	734,100
Buckinghamshire		727	1,883	612,900
Cambridgeshire		1,316	3,409	635,200
Cheshire		899	2,329	946,500
Cleveland		225	583	557,600
Cornwall[1]		1,376	3,564	448,200
Cumbria		2,629	6,810	486,600
Derbyshire		1,016	2,631	916,800
Devon		2,591	6,711	999,000
Dorset		1,025	2,654	638,200
Durham		941	2,436	599,600
East Sussex		693	1,795	689,700
Essex		1,418	3,672	1,512,100
Gloucestershire		1,020	2,643	517,100
Greater London[2]		610	1,579	6,775,200
Greater Manchester[2]		497	1,287	2,579,500
Hampshire		1,458	3,777	1,527,700
Hereford & Worcester		1,516	3,927	654,500
Hertfordshire		631	1,634	985,700
Humberside		1,356	3,512	848,500
Isle of Wight		147	381	124,600
Kent		1,441	3,731	1,500,900
Lancashire		1,183	3,064	1,380,700
Leicestershire		986	2,553	875,000
Lincolnshire		2,284	5,915	567,300
Merseyside[2]		252	652	1,467,600
Norfolk		2,073	5,368	727,800
Northamptonshire		914	2,367	554,400
Northumberland		1,943	5,032	301,000
North Yorkshire		3,208	8,309	699,800
Nottinghamshire		836	2,164	1,006,400
Oxfordshire		1,007	2,608	574,700
Shropshire		1,347	3,490	392,700
Somerset		1,332	3,451	448,900
South Yorkshire[2]		602	1,560	1,297,900
Staffordshire		1,049	2,716	1,021,000
Suffolk		1,466	3,797	628,600
Surrey		648	1,679	1,011,400
Tyne and Wear[2]		208	540	1,135,500
Warwickshire		765	1,981	480,700
West Midlands[2]		347	899	2,632,300
West Sussex		768	1,989	694,700
West Yorkshire[2]		787	2,039	2,053,100
Wiltshire		1,344	3,480	545,200
Northern Ireland[3]	Belfast	5,452	14,120	1,567,000
Scotland	Edinburgh	30,418[4]	78,783	5,121,000
Regions				
Borders		1,814	4,698	101,800
Central		1,042	2,700	271,800
Dumfries and Galloway		2,481	6,425	146,800
Fife		509	1,319	343,800
Grampian		3,379	8,752	502,800
Highland		10,092	26,137	200,800
Lothian		683	1,770	741,900
Strathclyde		5,318	13,773	2,344,600
Tayside		2,951	7,643	392,400
Island areas[5] (TOTAL)		2,149	5,566	74,300
Wales	Cardiff	8,019	20,768	2,821,000
Counties				
Clwyd		937	2,427	399,600
Dyfed		2,227	5,768	339,000
Gwent		531	1,376	441,800
Gwynedd		1,494	3,869	234,600
Mid Glamorgan		393	1,018	534,500
Powys		1,960	5,077	112,400
South Glamorgan		161	416	395,700
West Glamorgan		316	817	363,400
TOTAL		94,251	244,110	56,763,500

Demography

Population (1988): 57,006,000.
Density (1988): persons per sq mi 604.8, persons per sq km 233.5.
Urban–rural (1985): urban 91.5%; rural 8.5%.
Sex distribution (1988): male 48.77%; female 51.23%.
Age breakdown (1988): under 15, 18.8%; 15–29, 23.6%; 30–44, 20.5%; 45–59,
16.3%; 60–74, 14.0%; 75 and over, 6.8%.
Population projection: (1990) 57,291,000; (2000) 58,859,000.

Vital statistics

Birth rate per 1,000 population (1987): 13.6 (world avg. 26.0); legitimate
(1987) 77.1%; illegitimate 22.9%.
Death rate per 1,000 population (1987): 11.2 (world avg. 9.9).
Natural increase rate per 1,000 population (1987): 1.4 (world avg. 16.1).
Total fertility rate (avg. births per childbearing woman; 1986): 1.8.
Marriage rate per 1,000 population (1986): 6.9.
Divorce rate per 1,000 population (1986): 2.7.
Life expectancy at birth (1983–85): male 71.5 years; female 77.4 years.
Major causes of death per 100,000 population (1986): diseases of the circula-
tory system 560.6, of which ischemic heart disease 319.9, cerebrovascular
disease 144.6; malignant neoplasms (cancers) 277.1; diseases of the respiratory system 128.8, of which pneumonia 59.0; diseases of the digestive
system 35.9; accidents 26.3; diseases of the endocrine system 19.1, of which
diabetes mellitus 15.0; diseases of the genitourinary system 16.0.

Social indicators

Educational attainment (1981): Percent of population age 25 and over having: primary or secondary education only 89.7%; some postsecondary 4.8%;
bachelor's or equivalent degree 4.9%; higher university degree 0.6%.

Distribution of disposable income (1985)

percent of household income by quintile

1	2	3	4	5 (highest)
6.7	11.8	17.4	24.0	40.2

Quality of working life (1986). Average workweek (hours): male 41.8, female
37.3 (overtime male 8.6%, female 2.1%). Annual rate per 100,000 workers
for: injury or accident 63.1; industrial diseases 0.57; death 2.3. Proportion
of labour force (employed persons) insured for damages or income loss resulting from: injury 100%; permanent disability 100%; death 100%. Average
days lost to labour stoppages per 1,000 employee workdays: 0.3. Principal
means of transport to work (1985–86): 67% private automobile, 17% public
transportation, 6% foot, 6% bicycle, 4% other.
Access to services (1982). Proportion of households having access to: bath or
shower 96%; toilet 95%; central heating 63%.
Social participation. Eligible voters participating in last national election:
74.5%. Population age 16 and over participating in voluntary work (1986):
20%. Trade union membership in total work force (1985) 38.6%.
Social deviance (1986). Offense rate per 100,000 population for: theft and
handling stolen goods 3,821.5; burglary 1,938.2; fraud and forgery 278.3;
violence against the person 279.8; robbery 60.1; sexual offense 42.6. Incidence per 100,000 population of: notified drug addicts 9.6[8]; suicide 9.0.
Leisure (1986). Favourite leisure activities (hours weekly): watching television 28.0; listening to radio 8.7; reading 2.6[8]; cultural activities 1.5[8].
Material well-being (1985). Households possessing: automobile 62%, telephone 81%, television receiver 98% (colour 86%), refrigerator 95%, central
heating 69%, washing machine 81%.

National economy

Gross national product (at current market prices; 1986): U.S.$504,850,000,-
000 (U.S.$8,920 per capita).

Structure of gross domestic product and labour force

	1986 in value £'000,000	% of total value	labour force	% of labour force
Agriculture	5,902	1.8	603,000	2.2
Mining	24,445[9]	7.5[9]	243,000	0.9
Manufacturing	79,111	24.2	5,455,000	19.6
Construction	20,061	6.1	1,487,000	5.4
Public utilities	9		293,000	1.1
Transp. and commun.	23,727	7.3	1,454,000	5.2
Trade	45,770	14.0	4,988,000	18.0
Finance	70,386	21.6	2,456,000	8.8
Pub. admin., defense	23,578	7.3	2,309,000	8.3
Services	50,473	15.5	5,257,000	18.9
Other	−17,404[10]	−5.3[10]	3,229,000[11]	11.6[11]
TOTAL	326,049	100.0	27,774,000	100.0

Budget (1987–88). Revenue: £117,500,000,000 (taxes on expenditures 37.3%, income tax 34.0%, corporation tax 12.8%). Expenditures: £109,700,000,-000 (social security benefits 38.6%, defense 17.2%, national health service 14.8%, debt interest 14.5%, education and science 2.4%).
Total national debt (March 1987): £186,000,000,000.

Financial aggregates

	1982	1983	1984	1985	1986	1987	1988[12]
Exchange rate:							
U.S. Dollar per £	1.75	1.52	1.34	1.30	1.47	1.64	1.68
SDRs per £	1.46	1.39	1.18	1.32	1.20	1.32	1.30
International reserves (U.S.$)							
Total (excl. gold; '000,000,000)	12.40	11.34	9.44	12.86	18.42	41.72	41.83
SDRs ('000,000,000)	1.17	0.52	0.50	1.13	1.55	1.38	1.36
Reserve pos. in IMF ('000,000,000)	1.55	2.10	1.97	1.99	1.98	1.78	1.66
Foreign exchange ('000,000,000)	9.67	8.72	6.97	9.74	14.89	38.56	38.81
Gold ('000,000 fine troy oz)	19.01	19.01	19.03	19.03	19.01	19.01	19.01
% world reserves	2.0	2.0	2.0	2.0	2.0	2.0	2.0
Interest and prices							
Central bank discount (%)	...	...	...	...	...	...	...
Gov't. Bond yield (%) long term	12.88	10.81	10.69	10.62	9.87	9.48	9.47
Industrial share prices (1980 = 100)	130.7	164.9	196.2	242.2	300.5	396.8	365.5
Balance of payments (U.S.$'000,000)							
Balance of visible trade.	+3,906	−1,312	−5,851	−2,440	−12,144	−15,800	...
Imports, f.o.b.	93,175	93,391	99,472	103,458	118,887	146,438	...
Exports, f.o.b.	97,081	92,078	93,621	101,017	106,743	130,638	...
Balance of invisibles	8,578	10,043	9,693	12,116	15,323	18,719	...
Balance of payments, current account	6,927	5,177	1,939	4,905	−240	−2,664	...

Tourism (1986): receipts from visitors U.S.$7,921,000,000; expenditures by nationals abroad U.S.$8,686,000,000.

Manufacturing, mining, and construction enterprises (1985)

	no. of enter-prises[8]	no. of employees	annual wages as a % of avg. of all wages[8]	annual value added (£'000,000)
Manufacturing				
Food, beverages, and tobacco	3,282	591,000	103.0	10,175.0
Mechanical engineering	3,023	642,000	108.4	9,533.8
Transport equipment	1,671	570,000		8,397.6
Electrical and electronic engineering	2,412	597,000	96.8	8,066.1
Chemical engineering	1,354	281,000	118.1	7,841.7
Paper and paper products; printing and publishing	3,237	455,000	133.8	7,659.2
Rubber and plastic	1,529	200,000	118.1	2,894.1
Metal manufacturing	901	324,000	102.8	2,810.4
Clothing and footwear	2,727	741,000	85.6	2,541.0
Textiles	1,883	230,000	79.2	2,341.8
Timber and wood products	2,091	194,000	98.1	2,240.1
Mining				
Extraction of coal, mineral oil, and natural gas		206,000	118.1	22,014.8
Extraction of minerals other than fuels	1,649	12,000	103.1	14,778.4
Mineral oil processing		16,000	118.1	1,312.5
Construction	166,184	1,125,000	...	12,093.6

Production (metric tons except as noted). Agriculture, forestry, fishing (1986): wheat 13,911,400, barley 10,013,800, sugar beets 8,118,000, potatoes 6,446,000, turnips and rutabagas 3,855,000, corn (maize) 915,000, oats 505,000; livestock (number of live animals; 1987) 38,788,000 sheep, 12,182,000 cattle, 7,906,000 pigs; roundwood 5,400,000 cu m; fish catch 716,900. Mining (metric tons; 1987): iron ore 262,700; zinc 5,600; tin 3,900; lead 4,300. Manufacturing (total sales in £'000,000; 1987): motor vehicles and parts 13,970; aerospace equipment 8,305; electronic data processing and telecommunications equipment 4,314; radios and electronic goods 3,146; mechanical lifting and handling equipment 1,825; boilers 1,814; constructional steelwork 1,784; telephone and telegraph equipment 1,673; precision instruments 1,578. Construction (value in £; 1987): residential 6,745,000,000; nonresidential 12,321,000,000, of which public 3,870,000,-000, industrial 3,204,000,000, commercial 5,247,000,000.

Retail trade enterprises (1984)

	no. of enter-prises	no. of employees	weekly wage as a % of all wages	annual turnover (£'000,000)[13]
Food and grocery, of which	77,486	850,000	...	31,360
large grocery	100	424,000	...	20,436
other grocery	32,130	137,000	...	3,966
meats	15,573	83,000	...	2,710
Household goods, of which	39,379	282,000	...	12,000
electrical and musical goods	9,606	91,000	...	4,626
furniture	9,447	68,000	...	3,156
Drink, confectionery, and tobacco, of which	41,992	260,000	...	8,686
tobacco and confectionery	37,602	223,000	...	6,575
Clothing and footwear, of which	28,684	285,000	...	7,476
women's, girls', and infants' wear	15,246	107,000	...	2,642
footwear	3,353	84,000	...	1,868
men's and boys' wear	3,443	43,000	...	1,495
Mail order	24	42,000	...	2,737
Pharmaceuticals	8,060	66,000	...	2,458

Energy production (consumption): electricity (kW-hr; 1986) 298,156,000,000 (302,411,000,000); coal (metric tons; 1986) 108,092,000 (112,396,000); crude petroleum (barrels; 1986) 904,600,000 (513,500,000); natural gas (cu m; 1986) 49,527,000,000 (62,525,000,000).

Population economically active (1987): total 28,263,000; activity rate of total population 49.6% (participation rates: ages 15–64, 75.6%; female 52.1%; unemployed 10.3%).

Price and earnings indexes (1980 = 100)

	1982	1983	1984	1985	1986	1987	1988[14]
Consumer price index	121.5	127.1	133.4	141.5	146.3	152.5	159.7
Monthly earnings index	126.3	137.1	144.9	161.1	174.1	188.3	203.5

Household income and expenditure (1986). Average household size 2.6; average annual income per household (1985) £8,133 (U.S.$10,868); sources of income (1986): wages and salaries 64.3%, social security benefits 13.0%, rent, dividends, and interest 9.6%, income from self-employment 7.7%; expenditure (1986): food and beverages 24.6%, housing 16.6%, transport and vehicles 14.7%, services 12.4%, household goods 7.5%, clothing and footwear 7.4%, energy 6.0%.
Land use (1985): forested 9.4%; meadows and pastures 47.9%; agricultural and under permanent cultivation 29.3%; other 13.4%.

Foreign trade

Balance of trade (current prices)

	1981	1982	1983	1984	1985	1986	1987
£'000,000	+3,083	+2,325	−1,076	−4,239	−1,831	−7,999	−13,927
% of total	3.1%	2.1%	0.9%	2.9%	1.2%	5.2%	8.0%

Imports (1987): £94,015,700,000 (machinery and transport equipment 34.9%, of which road vehicles 9.4%, data-processing equipment 5.8%; food and live animals 9.3%, of which vegetables and fruits 2.6%, meat and meat preparations 1.7%; chemicals and chemical products 8.9%, of which organic chemicals 2.2%; petroleum and petroleum products 4.8%; textile yarn and fabrics 3.7%; paper and paperboard 3.4%; iron and steel products 2.1%; nonferrous metals 2.1%). *Major import sources:* West Germany 16.8%; United States 9.7%; France 8.9%; The Netherlands 7.6%; Japan 5.8%; Italy 5.5%; Belgium and Luxembourg 4.6%; Ireland 3.7%; Switzerland 3.5%; Norway 3.5%.
Exports (1987): £79,851,400,000 (machinery and transport equipment 36.1%, of which road vehicles 6.1%, data-processing equipment 5.6%, power generating machinery and equipment 4.1%, machinery specialized for particular industries 4.1%; chemicals and chemical products 13.2%, of which organic chemicals 3.5%; petroleum and petroleum products 10.6%; nonmetallic mineral manufactures 3.3%; professional, scientific, and controlling instruments 2.9%; iron and steel products 2.7%). *Major export destinations:* United States 13.8%; West Germany 11.8%; France 9.7%; The Netherlands 7.3%; Italy 5.2%; Belgium and Luxembourg 4.8%; Ireland 4.8%; Sweden 2.9%; Spain 2.7%; Saudi Arabia 2.5%; Canada 2.4%.

Transport and communications

Transport. Railroads[15] (1987): length (1986) 23,645 mi, 38,053 km; passenger-mi 19,983,000,000, passenger-km 32,160,000,000; short ton-mi cargo 9,912,-000,000, metric ton-km cargo 14,472,000,000. Roads (1986): total length 217,733 mi, 350,407 km (paved 100%). Vehicles (1987): passenger cars 17,421,000; trucks and buses 2,437,000. Merchant marine (1987): vessels (100 gross tons and over) 2,165; total deadweight tonnage 11,676,489. Air transport (1986): passenger-mi 31,697,000,000, passenger-km 51,012,000,-000; short ton-mi cargo 1,286,900,000, metric ton-km cargo 1,878,800,000; airports (1988) with scheduled flights 47.
Communications. Daily newspapers (1986): total number 107; total circulation 25,159,000; circulation per 1,000 population 443. Radio (1986): total number of licenses 63,528,000 (1 per 0.9 person). Television (1987): total number of licenses 18,953,000 (1 per 3.0 persons). Telephones (1984): 29,-518,000 (1 per 1.9 persons).

Education and health

Education (1985–86)[16]

	schools	teachers	students	student/ teacher ratio
Primary (age 5–10)	24,756	205,800	4,520,800	22.0
Secondary (age 11–19)	5,161	260,500	4,080,000	15.7
Voc., teacher tr.[17]	753	93,000[18]	506,600	...
Higher	46[19]	31,412	352,419	11.2

Literacy (1987): total population literate, virtually 100%.
Health (1986): physicians 87,900 (1 per 646 persons); hospital beds 410,000 (1 per 138 persons); infant mortality rate per 1,000 live births (1987) 9.1.
Food (1984–86): daily per capita caloric intake 3,218 (vegetable products 62%, animal products 38%); (1983) 128% of FAO recommended minimum requirement.

Military

Total active duty personnel (1988): 316,700 (army 50.0%, navy 20.5%, air force 29.5%). *Military expenditure as percent of GNP* (1985): 5.3% (world 6.1%); per capita expenditure U.S.$414.

[1]Includes separately administered Isles of Scilly (area 6 sq mi [16 sq km]; pop. 1,900). [2]Geographical entity only; since April 1, 1986, the administrative functions of the former metropolitan county councils have been dispersed among other local authorities. [3]Comprises 26 local government districts not shown separately. [4]Detail does not add to total given because of rounding. [5]Includes three separately administered island groups (Orkney 377 sq mi, pop. 19,400; Shetland 553 sq mi, pop. 23,400; Western Isles 1,119 sq mi, pop. 31,500). [6]Figures in parentheses are for Northern Ireland (1984). [7]1982. [8]1984. [9]Mining includes Public utilities. [10]Less imputed bank service charges. [11]Includes unemployed only. [12]August. [13]Includes value-added taxes. [14]July. [15]British railways only. [16]Public sector only. [17]Third level. [18]1984–85. [19]Universities only.

United States

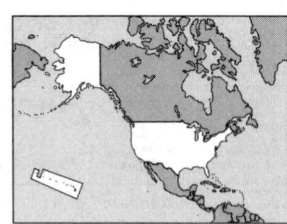

Official name: United States of America.
Form of government: federal republic with two legislative houses (Senate [100]; House of Representatives [435]).
Head of state and government: President.
Capital: Washington, D.C.
Official language: English.
Official religion: none.
Monetary unit: 1 dollar (U.S.$) = 100 cents; valuation (Oct. 10, 1988) 1 U.S.$ = £0.58; 1 £ = U.S.$1.71.

Major cities (1987): New York 7,284,300; Los Angeles 3,341,700; Chicago 3,018,300; Houston 1,740,000; Philadelphia 1,649,400; Detroit 1,091,500; San Diego 1,040,900; Dallas 1,009,900; Phoenix 933,200; San Antonio 920,200.

Other principal cities (1987)

	population		population		population
Akron	227,550	Fort Worth	432,310	Omaha	374,930
Albuquerque	371,760	Fresno	291,900	Pittsburgh	389,020
Anaheim	246,820	Honolulu	832,610	Portland (Ore.)	390,850
Anchorage	231,040	Indianapolis	778,690	Richmond	222,110
Arlington (Tex.)	251,370	Jacksonville	629,890	Rochester (N.Y.)	236,670
Atlanta	429,950	Jersey City	220,980	Sacramento	331,700
Aurora (Colo.)	219,900	Kansas City (Mo.)	444,380	St. Louis	429,410
Austin	469,540	Lexington (Ky.)	212,930	St. Paul	265,550
Baltimore	764,890	Long Beach	406,300	St. Petersburg	246,550
Baton Rouge	242,540	Louisville	286,520	San Francisco	767,900
Birmingham	282,100	Memphis	659,720	San Jose	730,100
Boston	575,880	Mesa	262,430	Santa Ana	242,800
Buffalo	325,790	Miami	385,090	Seattle	494,430
Charlotte	356,600	Milwaukee	607,890	Shreveport	218,410
Cincinnati	371,590	Minneapolis	359,370	Tampa	285,860
Cleveland	548,170	Nashville	487,100	Toledo	344,960
Colorado Springs	275,100	Newark	318,400	Tucson	374,550
Columbus	567,800	New Orleans	549,540	Tulsa	369,960
Corpus Christi	265,590	Norfolk	280,370	Virginia Beach	340,160
Denver	509,520	Oakland	366,000	Washington, D.C.	622,000
El Paso	494,950	Oklahoma City	441,410	Wichita	290,700

Households (1987). Total households 89,479,000 (married-couple families 51,537,000 [57.6%]). Average household size 2.6; 1 person 23.6%, 2 persons 32.0%, 3 persons 18.1%, 4 persons 15.6%, 5 persons 6.9%, 6 persons 2.4%, 7 or more persons 1.4%. Family households: 64,491,000 (72.1%); nonfamily 24,988,000 (27.9%, of which 1-person 23.6%).

Vital statistics

Birth rate per 1,000 population (1988[4]): 15.9 (world avg. 26.0); (1986) legitimate 76.6%; illegitimate 23.4%.
Death rate per 1,000 population (1988[4]): 9.0 (world avg. 9.9).
Natural increase rate per 1,000 population (1988[4]): 6.9 (world avg. 16.1).
Total fertility rate (avg. births per childbearing woman; 1987): 1.8.
Marriage rate per 1,000 population (1988[4]): 9.6; median age at first marriage (1986): men 25.7 years, women 23.1 years.
Divorce rate per 1,000 population (1988[4]): 4.8.
Life expectancy at birth (1986): white male 72.0 years, black male 65.5 years; white female 78.9 years, black female 73.6 years.
Major causes of death per 100,000 population (12 months ending July 1988): cardiovascular diseases 399.0, of which ischemic heart diseases 210.7, other forms of heart disease 87.7, cerebrovascular diseases 61.9, atherosclerosis 9.6, other cardiovascular diseases 9.3; malignant neoplasms (cancers) 196.6; diseases of the respiratory system 64.4, of which pneumonia 30.4; accidents and adverse effects 38.8, of which motor-vehicle accidents 19.7; diabetes mellitus 16.2; suicide 11.8; chronic liver disease and cirrhosis 10.8; nephritis and nephrosis 9.3; homicide 8.5.
Morbidity rates of infectious diseases per 100,000 population (1986): gonorrhea 376.4; chicken pox 122.4; syphilis 28.5; salmonellosis 20.7; hepatitis B (serum) 11.2; hepatitis A (infectious) 10.0; tuberculosis 9.4; shigellosis 7.1; acquired immune deficiency syndrome (AIDS) 5.4 ([1987] 7.2); aseptic meningitis 4.7; mumps 3.4.
Incidence of chronic health conditions per 1,000 population (1985): chronic sinusitis 139.0; arthritis 128.6; hypertension 125.1; deformities or orthopedic impairments 112.6; hearing impairment 90.7; hay fever 84.0; heart conditions 82.6.

Social indicators

Educational attainment (1985). Percent of population age 25 and over having: less than full primary education 7.5%; primary 6.4%; less than full secondary 12.2%; secondary 38.2%; some postsecondary 16.3%; 4-year higher degree and more 19.4%, of which postgraduate 6.9%. Number of earned degrees (1986–87): bachelor's degree 950,000; master's degree 276,000; doctor's degree 33,700; first-professional degrees (in fields such as medicine, theology, and law) 78,000.

Distribution of income (1986)
percent of national household income by quintile

1	2	3	4	5 (highest)
3.7	9.7	16.2	24.3	46.1

Quality of working life (1987). Average workweek: 41.0 hours (8.3% overtime). Annual rate per 100,000 workers for (1986): injury or accident 1,500; death 10.0. Proportion of labour force insured for damages or income loss resulting from: injury, permanent disability, and death (1986) 49.0%. Average days lost to labour stoppages per 1,000 workdays (1987): 0.7. Average duration of journey to work (1979): 22.5 minutes (85.7% private automobile, 5.9% public transportation, 1.3% bicycle or motorcycle, 3.9% foot, 2.3% work at home, 0.9% other). Rate per 1,000 workers of discouraged (unemployed no longer seeking work; 1983): 53.5.
Access to services (1984). Proportion of dwellings having access to: electricity virtually 100.0%; safe public water supply 98.2%; public sewage collection (1983) 98.1%; public fire protection, n.a.
Social participation. Eligible voters participating in last national election (1988): 50.2%. Population age 14 and over participating in voluntary work (1985): 48.0%. Trade union membership in total work force (1986): 17.5%. Practicing religious population in total affiliated population (church attendance; 1987): once a week 47%; once in six months 67%; once a year 74%.
Social deviance (1987). Offense rate per 100,000 population for: murder 8.3; rape 37.4; robbery 212.7; aggravated assault 351.3; motor vehicle theft

Area and population

States	Capitals	area[1] sq mi	area[1] sq km	population 1988 estimate
Alabama	Montgomery	51,705	133,915	4,130,000
Alaska	Juneau	591,004	1,530,693	510,000
Arizona	Phoenix	114,000	295,259	3,470,000
Arkansas	Little Rock	53,187	137,754	2,420,000
California	Sacramento	158,706	411,047	28,170,000
Colorado	Denver	104,091	269,594	3,290,000
Connecticut	Hartford	5,018	12,997	3,240,000
Delaware	Dover	2,044	5,294	660,000
Florida	Tallahassee	58,664	151,939	12,380,000
Georgia	Atlanta	58,910	152,576	6,400,000
Hawaii	Honolulu	6,471	16,760	1,090,000
Idaho	Boise	83,564	216,430	1,000,000
Illinois	Springfield	57,871	149,885	11,540,000
Indiana	Indianapolis	36,413	94,309	5,580,000
Iowa	Des Moines	56,275	145,752	2,830,000
Kansas	Topeka	82,277	213,096	2,490,000
Kentucky	Frankfort	40,409	104,659	3,720,000
Louisiana	Baton Rouge	47,752	123,677	4,420,000
Maine	Augusta	33,265	86,156	1,200,000
Maryland	Annapolis	10,460	27,091	4,640,000
Massachusetts	Boston	8,284	21,455	5,870,000
Michigan	Lansing	97,102	251,493	9,300,000
Minnesota	St. Paul	86,614	224,329	4,310,000
Mississippi	Jackson	47,689	123,514	2,630,000
Missouri	Jefferson City	69,697	180,514	5,140,000
Montana	Helena	147,046	380,847	800,000
Nebraska	Lincoln	77,355	200,349	1,600,000
Nevada	Carson City	110,561	286,352	1,060,000
New Hampshire	Concord	9,279	24,032	1,090,000
New Jersey	Trenton	7,787	20,168	7,720,000
New Mexico	Santa Fe	121,593	314,924	1,510,000
New York	Albany	52,735	136,583	17,900,000
North Carolina	Raleigh	52,669	136,412	6,530,000
North Dakota	Bismarck	70,702	183,117	660,000
Ohio	Columbus	44,787	115,998	10,870,000
Oklahoma	Oklahoma City	69,956	181,185	3,260,000
Oregon	Salem	97,073	251,418	2,740,000
Pennsylvania	Harrisburg	46,043	119,251	12,030,000
Rhode Island	Providence	1,212	3,139	1,000,000
South Carolina	Columbia	31,113	80,582	3,490,000
South Dakota	Pierre	77,116	199,730	720,000
Tennessee	Nashville	42,144	109,152	4,920,000
Texas	Austin	266,807	691,027	16,780,000
Utah	Salt Lake City	84,899	219,887	1,690,000
Vermont	Montpelier	9,614	24,900	560,000
Virginia	Richmond	40,767	105,586	5,990,000
Washington	Olympia	68,139	176,479	4,620,000
West Virginia	Charleston	24,231	62,758	1,880,000
Wisconsin	Madison	66,215	171,496	4,860,000
Wyoming	Cheyenne	97,809	253,324	470,000
District				
Dist. of Columbia	—	69	179	620,000
TOTAL		3,679,192[2]	9,529,063	245,800,000

Demography

Population (1988): 245,800,000.
Density (1988): persons per sq mi 66.8, persons per sq km 25.8.
Urban–rural (1985): urban 73.9%; rural 26.1%.
Sex distribution (1987): male 48.70%; female 51.30%.
Age breakdown (1987): under 15, 21.5%; 15–29, 24.8%; 30–44, 22.9%; 45–59, 14.1%; 60–74, 11.7%; 75 and over, 5.0%.
Population projection: (1990) 250,800,000; (2000) 270,794,000.
Doubling time: 87 years.
Composition by race (1987): white 84.5%; black 12.3%; other races 3.2%.
Religious affiliation (1987): Protestant 55.1%; Roman Catholic 29.7%; Jewish 3.2%; Eastern Orthodox 2.3%; Muslim 1.9%; Hindu 0.2%; nonreligious and atheist 6.8%.
Place of birth (1980): native-born 212,465,899 (93.8%); foreign-born 14,079,906 (6.2%), of which Mexico 2,199,221; Germany (East and West) 849,384; Canada 842,859; Italy 831,922; United Kingdom 669,149; Cuba 607,814; Philippines 501,440; Poland 418,128; U.S.S.R. 406,022; South Korea 289,885; China 286,120; Vietnam (South) 231,120; Japan 221,794; Portugal 211,614; Greece 210,998; India 206,087; others 5,096,349.
Mobility (1986). Population living in the same residence as in 1985: 81.4%; different residence, same county 11.3%; different county, same state 3.7%; different state 3.0%; moved from abroad 0.5%.
Immigration (1987[3]): permanent immigrants admitted 601,516, from Mexico 12.0%, Philippines 8.3%, South Korea 6.0%, Cuba 4.8%, India 4.6%, China 4.3%, Dominican Republic 4.1%, Vietnam 4.0%, Jamaica 3.8%, African countries 2.9%, Haiti 2.5%, Iran 2.4%, United Kingdom 2.2%. Refugee arrivals (1987): 70,000.

529.4; burglary and housebreaking 1,329.6; larceny-theft 3,081.3; drug abuse violation 400.9; drunkenness 346.3. Drug and substance users (population age 26 and over; 1985): alcohol 60.7%; marijuana 6.2%; tranquilizers 1.0%; hallucinogens 0.5%; heroin 0.5%. Rate per 100,000 population of suicide (1987) 12.6.

Crime rates per 100,000 population in metropolitan areas (1987)

| | violent crime | | | | |
	total	murder	rape	robbery	assault
Atlanta	713.3	7.3	64.1	249.5	392.4
Baltimore	992.7	13.0	44.2	412.1	523.4
Boston	677.0	4.0	33.6	259.9	379.5
Chicago	...	12.3	...	526.7	624.6
Dallas	1,048.7	16.7	73.4	448.1	510.5
Detroit	1,023.8	20.2	63.1	466.4	474.1
Houston	764.5	13.8	50.8	353.5	346.3
Los Angeles	1,352.0	16.6	50.3	521.0	764.0
Miami	1,814.2	20.1	50.2	797.7	946.2
Minneapolis	436.2	3.4	45.8	179.4	207.6
New York	1,793.4	20.4	43.2	951.0	778.7
Philadelphia	616.2	9.3	37.9	259.0	310.0
Pittsburgh	355.9	3.1	27.4	172.9	152.4
St. Louis	690.3	10.4	23.3	204.6	452.0
San Francisco	891.7	8.5	42.0	344.2	497.0
Washington, D.C.	616.7	10.2	29.7	255.0	321.8

| | property crime | | | | |
	total	burglary	larceny	auto theft	arson
Atlanta	9,400.8	1,792.0	7,145.0	463.9	65.1
Baltimore	5,270.1	1,304.0	3,344.2	621.9	88.4
Boston	4,456.4	966.9	2,355.9	1,134.4	30.0
Chicago	5,439.9	1,249.1	3,318.6	872.2	92.9
Dallas	10,084.1	2,764.8	6,151.8	1,167.5	93.4
Detroit	6,656.6	1,698.1	3,668.8	1,289.7	143.6
Houston	6,880.7	2,166.9	3,535.8	1,178.0	100.7
Los Angeles	5,432.1	1,432.5	2,753.8	1,245.9	166.8
Miami	10,572.6	2,886.9	5,986.4	1,699.2	49.3
Minneapolis	5,567.3	1,420.6	3,712.6	434.1	73.7
New York	6,516.4	1,567.0	3,763.6	1,185.9	88.5
Philadelphia	3,810.4	920.9	2,303.2	586.3	82.2
Pittsburgh	2,774.8	757.6	1,463.8	553.4	106.7
St. Louis	4,610.7	1,121.7	2,864.2	524.9	131.1
San Francisco	5,224.2	1,034.9	3,523.6	665.7	49.0
Washington, D.C.	4,645.8	1,018.6	2,994.9	632.3	49.4

Leisure (1976). Favourite leisure activities (weekly hours): watching television 9.6; social time 7.6; reading 3.7; cultural activities 1.5; recreation 1.2.
Material well-being (1987). Occupied dwellings with householder possessing: automobile 77.7%[5]; telephone 92.5%; radio receiver 99.0%; television receiver 98.0%; freezer 36.7%[6]; refrigerator 99.7%; air conditioner 59.5%; washing machine 72.8%; videocassette recorder 36.0%.
Recreational expenditures (1986): U.S.$198,000,000,000 (television and radio receivers 20.6%; durable toys and sport equipment 13.6%; nondurable toys and sport supplies 11.0%; golfing, bowling, and other participatory activities 7.9%; magazines and newspapers 6.9%; spectator amusements 5.2%, of which movies 2.0%, theatre and opera 1.7%; books and maps 4.9%; clubs and fraternal organizations 2.7%; spectator sports 1.6%).

National economy

Budget (1988). Revenue: U.S.$909,029,000,000 (individual income tax 43.6%, social insurance taxes and contributions 36.5%, corporation income tax 11.6%, excise taxes 3.6%, customs duties 1.7%). Expenditures: U.S.$1,032,-294,000,000 (defense 28.8%, social security and medicare 28.4%, interest on debt 14.0%, income security 12.1%, health 4.0%, education 3.2%, veteran benefits and services 2.8%).
Total national debt (1988)[7]: U.S.$2,582,150,000,000.

Manufacturing, mining, and construction enterprises (1986)

	no. of enter-prises[6]	no. of employees	weekly wage as a % of all wages	value added (U.S.$'000,000)
Manufacturing				
Transportation equipment	8,466	1,769,000	146.2	125,670.6
Electric and electronic machinery	15,116	1,941,400	110.2	112,322.8
Food and related products	20,208	1,408,900	99.8	112,237.7
Machinery, except electrical	48,947	1,863,000	120.9	108,401.2
Chemical and related products	11,363	801,600	136.8	100,069.3
Fabricated metal products	32,793	1,419,100	112.9	68,675.0
Paper and related products	6,160	602,600	127.6	43,935.9
Instruments and related products	7,661	585,400	108.1	40,000.2
Primary metals	7,048	689,200	135.4	38,159.4
Rubber and plastic products	12,348	741,300	99.7	37,243.5
Stone, clay, and glass products	15,591	514,100	114.7	30,697.6
Apparel and related products	21,367	1,016,500	66.7	28,450.7
Lumber and wood	28,293	619,500	95.1	23,268.1
Textile-mill products	6,192	644,300	79.1	22,225.0
Petroleum and coal products	2,165	124,500	161.9	17,695.9
Furniture and fixtures	9,160	466,700	85.2	17,639.0
Miscellaneous manufacturing industries	14,352	326,100	86.1	14,619.6
Tobacco products	117	46,100	146.7	12,727.9
Leather and leather products	2,558	129,800	67.6	3,593.5
Mining				
Oil and gas extraction	23,577	457,000		
Coal mining	4,133		139.6	122,300[8]
Metal mining	985	326,000		
Nonmetallic, except fuels	5,126			
Construction				
General contractors and operative builders	112,963	1,293,000		
Heavy construction contractors	29,055	1,250,000	155.2	152,500[8]
Special trade contractors	243,729	2,361,000		

Gross national product (at current market prices; 1987): U.S.$4,526,700,000,-000 (U.S.$18,300 per capita).

Gross national product and national income
in U.S.$000,000,000

	1983	1984	1985	1986	1987
Gross national product	3,405.7	3,772.2	4,014.9	4,240.3	4,526.7
By type of expenditure					
Personal consumption expenditures	2,234.5	2,430.5	2,629.4	2,807.5	3,012.1
Durable goods	289.1	335.5	372.2	406.5	421.9
Nondurable goods	816.7	867.3	911.2	943.6	997.9
Services	1,128.7	1,345.6	1,457.3	1,457.3	1,592.3
Gross private domestic investment	502.3	664.8	643.1	665.9	712.9
Fixed investment	509.4	597.1	631.8	650.4	673.7
Changes in business inventories	−7.1	67.7	11.3	15.5	39.2
Net exports of goods and services	−6.1	−58.9	−78.0	−104.4	−123.0
Exports	352.5	383.5	370.9	378.4	428.0
Imports	358.6	442.4	448.9	428.2	551.0
Government purchases of goods and services	675.0	735.9	820.8	871.2	924.7
Federal	283.5	310.5	355.2	366.2	382.0
State and local	391.5	425.4	465.6	505.0	542.8
By major type of product					
Goods output	1,396.1	1,581.4	1,641.2	1,697.9	1,792.5
Durable goods	574.3	681.5	706.6	725.3	776.3
Nondurable goods	821.8	899.9	934.6	972.6	1,016.2
Services	1,682.5	1,813.9	1,968.3	2,118.4	2,295.7
Structures	327.1	377.0	405.4	424.0	438.4
National income	2,719.5	3,028.6	3,234.0	3,437.1	3,678.7
By type of income					
Compensation of employees	2,020.7	2,213.9	2,367.5	2,507.1	2,683.4
Proprietors' income	190.9	234.5	255.9	286.7	312.9
Rental income of persons	55.0	51.9	54.2	57.4	66.2
Corporate profits	213.7	266.9	282.3	298.9	310.4
Net interest	281.0	304.8	319.0	331.9	353.6
By industry division					
Agriculture, forestry, fishing	62.2	79.4	77.0	81.5	88.2
Mining and construction	176.6	198.3	209.1	215.5	196.7
Manufacturing	585.4	660.3	671.2	686.4	727.7
Durable	331.8	392.4	395.8	405.7	419.4
Nondurable	253.6	267.9	275.4	280.7	308.0
Transportation	95.2	106.4	105.9	112.8	120.7
Communications	62.2	65.7	68.9	73.6	76.3
Public utilities	65.9	75.9	77.2	80.2	79.9
Wholesale and retail trade	405.0	455.0	475.0	502.2	529.8
Finance, insurance, real estate	367.0	381.7	425.9	475.5	524.0
Services	463.4	519.6	676.8	639.8	711.6
Government and government enterprise	409.0	436.4	468.9	495.7	529.2
Other	49.9	47.4	40.7	34.9	29.2

Structure of gross domestic product and labour force

| | 1987 | | | |
	in value U.S.$'000,000,000	% of total value	labour force	% of labour force
Agriculture	94.9	2.1	3,208,000	2.6
Mining	85.4	1.9	721,000	0.6
Manufacturing	853.6	18.9	19,065,000	15.7
Construction	218.5	4.9	4,998,000	4.1
Public utilities	136.4	3.0		
Transportation and communication	271.8	6.0	5,385,000[9]	4.4[9]
Trade	740.4	16.5	24,381,000	20.0
Finance	775.4	17.2	6,549,000	5.4
Public administration, defense	535.3	11.9	17,015,000	14.0
Services	793.5	17.6	24,196,000	19.9
Other	−8.0[10]	−0.2[10]	16,084,000[11]	13.2[11]
TOTAL	4,497.2	100.0	121,602,000	100.0[2]

Business activity (1984): number of businesses 16,077,000 (sole proprietorships 70.1%, active corporations 19.7%, active partnerships 10.2%), of which services 4,990,000, wholesaling and retailing 2,381,000; business receipts $7,782,800,000,000 (active corporations 89.3%, sole proprietorships 6.6%, active partnerships 4.1%), of which wholesaling and retailing $2,519,-100,000,000, services $695,600,000,000; net profit $300,200,000,000 (active corporations 77.6%, sole proprietorships 23.6%), of which services $57,900,-000,000, wholesaling and retailing $51,400,000,000. New business concerns and business failures (1987): total number of new incorporations 683,686; total failures 61,235; failure rate per 10,000 concerns 102; current liabilities of failed concerns $33,024,500,000, average liability $539,300. Business expenditures for new plant and equipment (1986): total $395,100,000,000, of which manufacturing businesses $151,800,000,000 (nondurable goods 53.2%, durable 46.8%), trade, services, and communication $161,900,000,-000, public utilities $48,500,000,000, transportation $19,000,000,000, mining $13,900,000,000.
Production (metric tons except as noted). Agriculture, forestry, fishing (1987): corn (maize) 179,437,500, wheat 57,300,000, soybeans 53,600,000, sugarcane 27,032,290, sugar beets 25,400,270, sorghum 18,818,940, potatoes 17,498,-320, barley 11,474,290, oranges 7,018,890, rice 5,793,510, oats 5,425,180, cottonseed 5,263,490, grapes 4,721,260, apples 4,510,680, cotton 3,205,800, grapefruit 2,323,300, peaches and pears 1,946,540, peanuts (groundnuts) 1,626,650, onions 1,541,000, dry beans 1,193,350, sunflower seeds 1,183,030, lemons 986,110, pineapples 627,770, tobacco 556,230, rye 500,860, almonds 285,760, milk 54,500,000,000, cheese 2,405,000,000, butter 496,800,000, eggs 68,520,000,000[12]; livestock (number of live animals) 102,031,000 cattle, 50,-960,000 pigs, 10,580,000 horses, 10,328,000 sheep, 1,550,000 goats, 1,155,-000,000 poultry; roundwood (1986) 451,425,000 cu m; fish catch 3,103,100. Mining and quarrying (1987): iron ore 46,894,000; phosphate rock 40,000,-000; copper 1,255,900; bauxite 560,000; lead 330,000; zinc 213,200; molybdenum 29,000; tin 11,000; uranium 5,900; nickel 2,000[12]; silver 1,200; gold 150. Manufacturing (1987): crude steel 89,151,000; cement 67,380,000; paper and paper products 64,335,000; wood pulp 51,541,000; pig iron 48,326,000; sulfuric acid 38,750,000; nitrogenous and phosphate fertilizers 15,674,000;

gypsum and gypsum products 14,800,000[12]; plastic and resins 14,533,000; caustic soda 11,518,000; newsprint 5,108,400[12]; man-made fibre 3,544,-800[12]; synthetic rubber 2,182,000; aluminum 1,847,000; machine tools U.S.$5,102,000,000[12]; industrial material handling equipment U.S.$4,571,-000,000[12]; cotton fabric 3,248,000[12] sq m; footwear 220,508,000 pairs; motor vehicle tires 202,980,000 units; radio receivers 26,755,000 units; television receivers 23,497,000 units; major household appliances 47,838,-000 units, of which 12,610,000 microwave ovens, 6,972,000 refrigerators, 5,998,000 washing machines, 4,637,000 clothes dryers, 4,032,000 dishwashers, 3,951,000 water heaters, 3,798 air conditioners. Construction (1987): private U.S.$323,800,000,000, of which residential U.S.$194,800,000,000, commercial and industrial U.S.$76,500,000,000, other U.S.$52,500,000,000; federal, state, and local U.S.$75,000,000,000.

Retail and wholesale trade and services (1987)

	no. of establish-ments[5]	no. of employees	weekly wage as a % of all wages	annual sales (U.S.$'000,000)
Retail trade	1,406,800	18,207,000	57.1	1,510,579
Durable goods	...	...	...	559,105
Automotive dealers	95,100	1,943,000	91.1	326,850
Building materials, hardware, garden supply, and mobile home dealers	68,500	743,100	81.7	78,005
Furniture, home furnishings, equipment stores	98,000	789,800	78.3	84,148
Nondurable goods	...	...	...	951,474
Food stores	182,700	2,934,600	66.5	314,287
General merchandise group stores	35,300	2,320,100	58.6	175,885
Eating and drinking places	334,000	6,091,100	...	147,645
Gasoline service stations	105,800	608,600	59.9	103,154
Apparel and accessory stores	139,300	1,083,700	47.4	79,069
Drugstores and proprietary stores	50,700	583,400	52.2	56,000
Liquor stores	32,500	124,500	...	19,506
Wholesale trade[13]	415,829	5,769,000	117.3	1,520,827
Durable goods	256,103	3,403,000	119.9	725,683
Machinery, equipment, and supplies	99,250	1,446,000	128.9	187,737
Motor vehicles, automotive equipment	39,460	433,600	105.5	152,231
Electrical goods	29,170	489,100	124.0	97,686
Metals and minerals, except petroleum	10,121	132,800	133.1	57,756
Lumber and other construction materials	17,041	229,700	116.5	57,286
Hardware, plumbing, heating equipment and supplies	20,815	262,400	113.0	44,225
Furniture and home furnishings	12,498	137,100	78.3	25,187
Sporting, recreational, photographic, and hobby goods	7,266	79,800	112.0	22,135
Miscellaneous durable goods	20,482	192,200	93.5	81,440
Nondurable goods	159,726	2,366,000	113.6	757,292
Groceries and related products	38,516	758,100	115.7	222,377
Farm-products raw materials	13,872	130,200	...	102,200
Apparel and accessories	14,289	191,200	107.5	45,413
Beer, wine, and distilled alcoholic beverages	6,378	153,400	127.4	43,357
Paper and paper products	13,967	192,200	121.3	44,251
Chemicals and allied products	10,724	132,800	149.8	25,198
Drugs, drug proprietaries, and druggists' sundries	3,851	172,600	129.3	32,788
Miscellaneous nondurable goods	39,434	444,600	92.3	106,477
Services[5]	1,711,800	21,543,000	87.3	719,620
Business	258,400	4,272,000	92.1	198,743
Health, except hospitals	390,200	6,337,000	68.6	167,473
Legal	125,700	685,000	129.3	57,143
Engineering, architectural, and surveying	53,200	667,000	162.8	45,397
Hotels, motels, and other lodging places	48,000	1,264,000	60.3	45,952
Amusement and recreation, including motion pictures	60,200	768,000	63.4	18,205
Automotive repair, services, garages	127,600	676,000	92.1	53,563
Personal	175,200	1,069,000	67.9	39,407
Accounting, auditing, and bookkeeping	58,100	400,000	119.7	24,062
Miscellaneous repair services	56,700	327,000	109.0	20,918

Energy production (consumption): electricity (kW-hr; 1987) 2,571,000,000,-000 (2,455,000,000,000); coal (metric tons; 1987) 831,800,000 (758,300,000); crude petroleum (barrels; 1987) 3,613,500,000 (6,059,000,000); petroleum products (metric tons; 1987) 599,400,000 (822,400,000); natural gas (cu m; 1987) 472,300,000,000 (464,400,000,000). Domestic production of energy by source (1987): coal 31.1%, crude oil 27.2%, natural gas 26.0%, nuclear power 7.6%, hydroelectric power 4.0%, other 4.1%.
Energy consumption by end use ('000,000,000 kW-hr; 1987): total 2,455, of which industrial 847, residential 850, commercial 672, other 86; by source: coal 56.9%, nuclear 17.7%, natural gas 10.6%, hydroelectric power 9.7%, crude oil 4.6%.
Household income and expenditure. Average household size (1987) 2.6; average annual income per household U.S.$30,759; sources of income: wages and salaries 59.5%, transfer payments 14.5%, personal interest income 13.9%, proprietors' income 8.2%, other labour income 5.5%; expenditure (1987)[14]: food 17.5%, housing 15.5%, health 13.4%, transportation 12.4%, household durable goods 7.9%, clothing 7.4%, recreation 7.4%, energy 4.2%.
Selected household characteristics (1987). Total number of households 89,-479,000, of which (by race and Spanish origin[15]) white 86.4%, black 11.1%, other 2.5%; Spanish origin 6.1%; (by location) in metropolitan areas 77.5%, outside metropolitan areas 22.5% (farms 1.8%); (by tenure) owned 57,-258,000 (64.0%), rented 32,221,000 (36.0%); family households 64,491,000, of which married couple 79.9%, female head with children under age

18, 11.0%, other 9.1%; nonfamily households 24,998,000, of which female householder 57.4%, male 42.6%. Work disability status of householder (1985): having no work disability 91.9%, having work disability 8.1%; having retirement or disability income 7.9%.

Financial aggregates

	1982	1983	1984	1985	1986	1987	1988[16]
Exchange rate, U.S.$ per:							
£[17]	1.75	1.52	1.34	1.30	1.47	1.63	1.84
SDR[17]	1.10	1.07	1.03	1.02	1.17	1.29	1.37
International reserves (U.S.$)[18]							
Total (excl. gold; '000,000,000)	22.81	22.63	23.84	32.10	37.45	34.72	29.96
SDRs ('000,000,000)	5.25	5.03	5.64	7.29	8.39	10.28	9.18
Reserve pos. in IMF ('000,000,000)	7.35	11.31	11.54	11.95	11.73	11.35	9.99
Foreign exchange ('000,000,000)	10.21	6.29	6.66	12.86	17.33	13.09	10.79
Gold ('000,000 fine troy oz)	264.03	263.39	262.79	262.65	262.04	262.38	262.03
% world reserves	27.83	27.80	27.77	27.68	27.63	27.74	...
Interest and prices							
Central bank discount (%)[18]	8.50	8.50	8.00	7.50	5.5	6.0	6.0
Gov't. bond yield (%)[17]	12.92	10.45	11.89	9.64	7.06	7.67	8.24
Industrial share prices[17] (1980 = 100)	99.3	134.2	134.7	154.5	194.9	246.0	227.3[19]
Balance of payments ($'000,000,000)							
Balance of visible trade[20]	−36.45	−67.08	−112.51	−122.15	−144.54	−160.28	−32.53
Imports, f.o.b.	247.65	268.89	332.41	338.09	368.52	409.85	107.59
Exports, f.o.b.	211.20	201.81	219.90	215.94	223.98	249.57	75.06
Balance of invisibles[20]	36.27	29.88	↓18.19	21.65	21.02	19.74	0.6
Balance of payments, current account	−8.6	−46.28	−107.09	−116.43	−138.84	−153.95	−35.01

Population economically active (1987): total 121,602,000; activity rate of total population 49.9% (participation rates: ages 16 and over 64.7%; female 44.3%; unemployed 6.1%).

Price and earnings indexes (1980 = 100)

	1982	1983	1984	1985	1986	1987	1988[21]
Consumer price index	117.1	120.9	126.1	130.5	133.1	137.9	142.6
Hourly earnings index	116.9	121.5	126.2	131.1	133.7	136.3	139.5

Average employee earnings

	average hourly earnings in U.S.$		average weekly earnings in U.S.$	
	July 1987	June 1988	July 1987	June 1988
Manufacturing				
Durable goods	9.95	10.19	425.58	448.33
Lumber and wood products	8.07	8.20	341.38	351.33
Furniture and fixtures	7.42	7.64	301.04	310.08
Stone, clay, and glass products	9.70	9.86	438.78	448.12
Primary metal industries	11.29	11.43	510.60	531.39
Fabricated metal products	9.52	9.78	405.14	432.37
Machinery, except electrical	10.21	10.40	446.01	464.53
Electrical and electronic equipment	9.54	9.76	397.36	417.17
Transportation equipment	12.26	12.66	525.62	575.34
Instruments and related products	9.41	9.54	396.17	410.85
Miscellaneous manufacturing	7.51	7.69	299.54	312.44
Nondurable goods	8.78	8.99	367.20	377.48
Food and kindred products	8.44	8.67	355.20	368.45
Tobacco manufactures	14.65	15.23	565.84	628.04
Textile mill products	6.78	7.00	296.61	299.80
Apparel and other textile products	5.74	5.94	216.60	226.78
Paper and allied products	10.84	11.01	496.37	500.09
Printing and publishing	9.87	10.08	388.10	392.54
Chemicals and allied products	11.82	12.01	518.30	534.24
Petroleum and coal products	13.71	14.11	651.50	676.80
Rubber and miscellaneous plastics products	8.56	8.62	367.36	377.80
Leather and leather products	5.82	6.10	231.81	237.63
Nonmanufacturing				
Metal mining	13.57	14.00	542.64	560.15
Coal mining	15.36	16.63	614.26	665.18
Oil and gas extraction	12.10	11.96	484.15	478.25
Nonmetallic minerals, except fuels	10.60	10.94	490.78	515.27
Construction	12.60	12.87	486.36	498.07
Transportation and public utilities	12.00	12.29	475.20	485.46
Wholesale trade	9.56	9.85	365.19	376.27
Retail trade	6.07	6.26	182.10	184.04
Finance, insurance, and real estate	8.63	8.96	312.41	321.66
Hotels, motels, and tourist courts	6.01	6.36	186.91	200.34
Health services	8.68	9.16	282.97	296.78
Legal services	11.89	12.61	412.58	438.83
Miscellaneous services	11.99	12.41	459.22	471.58

Tourism (1986): receipts from visitors U.S.$12,913,000,000; expenditures by nationals abroad U.S.$17,627,000,000; number of foreign visitors 8,860,000 (3,722,000 from western Europe, 1,104,000 from Central America and the Caribbean, 944,000 from South America); number of nationals traveling abroad 11,562,000 (5,126,000 to Europe and the Mediterranean, 3,800,000 to Central America and the Caribbean, 616,000 to South America).
Land use (1986): forested 33.1%; meadows and pastures 26.2%; agricultural and under permanent cultivation 20.9%; other 19.8%.

Foreign trade

Balance of trade (current prices)

	1982	1983	1984	1985	1986	1987
U.S.$'000,000,000	−36.5	−67.1	−112.5	−122.1	−144.5	−152.1
% of total	7.9%	14.3%	20.4%	22.0%	24.3%	23.0%

Imports (1987): U.S.$406,241,000,000 (machinery and transport equipment 43.8%, of which new passenger cars 11.8%, telecommunications and sound

recording and reproducing apparatus 5.1%, office machinery and automatic data-processing machines 4.5%, transport-equipment parts 3.4%; basic and miscellaneous manufactures 29.2%, of which clothing 5.0%; mineral fuels and lubricants 10.9%, of which crude petroleum 7.2%, petroleum products 3.0%; food 5.1%). *Major import sources:* Japan 20.8%; Canada 16.9%; West Germany 6.6%; Taiwan 6.2%; Mexico 4.8%; United Kingdom 4.2%; South Korea 4.2%; Italy 2.8%; France 2.6%; Hong Kong 2.5%.
Exports (1987): U.S.$254,121,900,000 (machinery 27.5%, of which office machinery and computers 7.5%, power-generating machinery 4.0%, special-purpose machinery 3.7%; transport equipment 15.4%, of which motor vehicles and parts 8.3%, aircraft and parts 6.7%; basic and miscellaneous manufactures 14.4%, of which professional, scientific, and controlling instruments and apparatus 2.9%; chemicals and related products 10.4%; food 7.6%, of which grain and cereal preparations 3.2%). *Major export destinations:* Canada 23.7%; Japan 11.2%; Mexico 5.8%; United Kingdom 5.6%; West Germany 4.6%; The Netherlands 3.2%; South Korea 3.2%; France 3.1%; Taiwan 2.9%; Belgium–Luxembourg 2.4%.

Trade by commodity group (1987)

	imports (c.i.f.)		exports (f.a.s.)[22]	
SITC Group	U.S.$'000,000	%	U.S.$'000,000	%
00 Food and live animals	20,547.1	5.1	19,178.8	7.8
01 Beverages and tobacco	4,104.9	1.0	3,666.7	1.5
02 Crude materials, excluding fuels	11,525.7	2.8	20,416.3	8.3
03 Mineral fuels, lubricants, and related materials	44,219.5	10.9	7,713.1	3.1
04 Animal and vegetable oils, fat, and waxes	568.1	0.1	981.4	0.4
05 Chemicals and related products, n.e.s.	16,213.4	4.0	26,380.9	10.8
06 Basic manufactures	53,356.3	13.1	17,136.1	7.0
07 Machinery and transport equipment	177,808.7	43.8	108,596.0	44.3
08 Miscellaneous manufactured articles	62,460.1	15.4	41,045.7	16.7
09 Goods not classified by kind	15,437.2	3.8		
TOTAL	406,241.0	100.0	245,115.0	100.0[2]

Direction of trade (1987)

	imports (c.i.f.)		exports (f.a.s.)[23]	
	U.S.$'000,000	%	U.S.$'000,000	%
Africa	11,939.4	2.9	6,283.4	2.5
South Africa	1,345.5	0.3	1,281.2	0.5
Other	10,593.9	2.6	5,002.2	2.0
Americas	117,954.2	29.0	94,795.2	37.3
Canada	71,085.0	17.5	59,814.3	23.5
Caribbean countries and Central America	6,227.1	1.5	7,359.3	2.9
Mexico	20,270.8	5.0	14,582.2	5.7
South America	20,362.8	5.0	13,036.1	5.1
Asia	174,452.3	42.9	73,267.5	28.8
Japan	84,575.0	20.8	28,248.6	11.1
Other Asia	89,877.3	22.1	45,018.9	17.7
Europe	97,418.7	24.0	71,917.2	28.3
EEC	83,181.8	20.5	59,719.3	23.5
Other Western Europe	12,187.2	3.0	9,910.8	3.9
U.S.S.R.	424.7	0.1	1,479.8	0.6
Eastern Europe	1,625.0	0.4	762.4	0.3
Oceania	4,135.9	1.0	6,525.9	2.6
Australia	3,029.5	0.7	5,545.7	2.2
Other Oceania	1,106.4	0.3	980.2	0.4
Other	340.5	...	1,332.7	0.5
TOTAL	406,241.0	100.0	254,121.9	100.0

Transport and communications

Transport. Railroads (1986): length 184,235 mi, 296,497 km; passenger-mi 12,000,000,000, passenger-km 19,200,000,000; short ton-mi cargo 867,-722,000,000, metric ton-km cargo 1,266,852,000,000. Roads (1987): total length 3,879,538 mi, 6,243,340 km (paved 88%). Vehicles (1986): passenger cars 135,431,112; trucks and buses 40,760,227. Merchant marine (1987): vessels (100 gross tons and over) 6,427; total deadweight tonnage 29,111,-255. Air transport (1987)[24]: passenger-mi 381,728,000,000, passenger-km 614,333,000,000; short ton-mi cargo 8,181,200,000, metric ton-km cargo 11,944,300,000; airports (1987) with scheduled flights 824. Certified route passenger/cargo air carriers (1986) 98; operating revenue (U.S. $'000,000; 1986) 49,537, of which domestic 40,921, international 8,616; operating expenses 48,282, of which domestic 39,833, international 8,616; net operating income 1,255, of which domestic 1,088, international 167.

Intercity passenger and freight traffic by mode of transportation (1986)

	cargo traffic ('000,000,000 ton-mi)	% of nat'l total	passenger traffic ('000,000,000 passenger-mi)	% of nat'l total
Rail	896	35.8	12	0.7
Road	627	25.1	1,484	81.7
Inland water	393	15.7	—	—
Air	7.3	0.3	320	17.6
Pipeline	579	23.1	—	—
TOTAL	2,502.3	100.0	1,815	100.0

Communications. Daily newspapers (1987): total number 1,646; total circulation 64,986,148; circulation per 1,000 population 266. Radio (1986): total number of receivers 478,000,000 (1 per 0.5 persons). Television (1987): total number of households having one or more TV sets 87,000,000. Telephones (1986; access lines): 122,203,000 (1 per 2 persons).

Other communication media (1987)

Print	titles		titles
Books (new)	45,401	Home economics	90
of which		Industrial arts	106
Agriculture	470	Journalism and	
Art	1,280	communication	90
Biography	1,818	Labour and industrial	
Business	1,212	relations	70
Education	869	Law	273
Fiction	5,647	Library and information	
General works	2,117	sciences	118
History	2,250	Literature and language	158
Home economics	954	Mathematics and science	238
Juvenile	3,794	Medicine	182
Language	514	Philosophy and religion	130
Law	1,142	Physical education and	
Literature	1,918	recreation	151
Medicine	3,339	Political science	136
Music	271	Psychology	138
Philosophy, psychology	1,515	Sociology and anthropology	149
Poetry, drama	1,011	Zoology	94
Religion	2,303		
Science	2,755	**Cinema**[12]	
Sociology, economics	6,491	Feature films	432
Sports, recreation	1,068		
Technology	2,164		traffic
Travel	496		(units, '000)
Periodicals	3,371	**Electronic**[12]	
of which		Telegrams	53,000
Agriculture	153	Domestic	42,000
Business and economics	262	International	11,000
Chemistry and physics	170	Telex	69,559
Children's periodicals	78		
Education	203		(pieces of mail)
Engineering	265	**Post**[12]	
Fine and applied arts	145	Mail	147,376,000
General interest	181	Domestic	146,578,000
History	151	International	798,000

Education and health

Education (1987–88)

	schools	teachers	students	student/teacher ratio
Primary and preprimary (age 6–13)	101,050	1,517,000	31,704,000	20.9
Secondary and vocational (age 14–17)		1,075,000	13,734,000	12.8
Higher, including teacher-training colleges	3,406	722,000	7,117,000	9.9

Literacy (1980): total population age 15 and over literate 166,497,565 (95.5%); males literate 79,161,126 (95.7%); females literate 87,336,439 (95.3%); other studies indicate adult "functional" literacy may not exceed 85%.
Health: physicians (1986) 576,700 (1 per 419 persons), specialties (1985) internal medicine 16.4%, general practice 12.1%, general surgery 6.9%, pediatrics 6.4%, psychiatry 5.8%, obstetrics and gynecology 5.6%, anesthesiology 4.0%, orthopedics 3.1%, pathology 2.8%, ophthalmology 2.7%, radiology 1.8%, other 32.4%; hospital beds (1985) 1,308,500 (1 per 183 persons), of which nonfederal 91.4% (short-term general and special 76.1%, psychiatric 12.9%, long-term general and special 2.4%, tuberculosis 0.1%), federal 8.6%; infant mortality rate per 1,000 live births (1988[4]) 10.0.
Food (1984–86): daily per capita caloric intake 3,642 (vegetable products 66%, animal products 34%); (1983) 138% of FAO recommended minimum requirement. Per capita consumption of major food groups (pounds annually; 1986): dairy products 594.4; sweeteners 168.2; red meat 150.5; grains 129.6; fresh fruits 91.7; fresh vegetables 79.4; fats and oils 64.2; poultry products 59.1; citrus fruit juices 49.0; fish 14.7.

Military

Total active duty personnel (1988): 2,158,000 (army 35.9%, navy 27.0%, air force 27.9%, marine 9.2%). *Military expenditure as percent of GNP* (1985): 6.6% (world 6.1%); per capita expenditure U.S.$1,110. *Military aid* (1986): total $5,839,000,000 (Middle East and South Asia 75.8%, of which Israel 29.5%, Egypt 21.3%, Turkey 10.6%, Greece 7.4%, Pakistan 5.3%, Jordan 1.4%; Europe 8.5%, of which Spain 6.6%, Portugal 1.9%; East Asia 6.5%, of which South Korea 2.8%, Thailand 1.5%; Africa 3.5%, of which Tunisia 1.1%, Morocco 0.6%; Latin America 4.1%, of which El Salvador 2.1%, Honduras 1.0%; international organizations 1.1%).

[1]Total area excluding U.S. share of Great Lakes is 3,618,770 sq mi (9,372,571 sq km). [2]Detail does not add to total given because of rounding. [3]Fiscal year ending September 30. [4]First eight months only. [5]1985. [6]1984. [7]September 16. [8]Annual value of shipments. [9]Includes public utilities. [10]Statistical discrepancy. [11]Includes 7,425,000 unemployed. [12]1986. [13]Number of establishments is for 1982. [14]Personal consumption expenditure. [15]Persons of Spanish origin may be of any race. [16]Second quarter. [17]Annual average. [18]End of year. [19]April. [20]First quarter. [21]May. [22]Domestic export only; value in f.a.s. (free alongside ship). [23]Includes reexports valued at U.S.$9,006,000. [24]Major carriers only.

Uruguay

Official name: República Oriental del Uruguay (Oriental Republic of Uruguay).
Form of government: republic with two legislative houses (Senate [31]; Chamber of Representatives [99]).
Head of state and government: President.
Capital: Montevideo.
Official language: Spanish.
Official religion: none.
Monetary unit: 1 Uruguayan new peso (NUr$) = 100 centésimos; valuation (Oct. 10, 1988) 1 U.S.$ = NUr$401.12; 1 £ = NUr$686.91.

Area and population		area		population
				1985
Departments	Capitals	sq mi	sq km	census[1]
Artigas	Artigas	4,605	11,928	68,400
Canelones	Canelones	1,751	4,536	359,700
Cerro Largo	Melo	5,270	13,648	78,000
Colonia	Colonia del Sacramento	2,358	6,106	112,100
Durazno	Durazno	4,495	11,643	54,700
Flores	Trinidad	1,986	5,144	24,400
Florida	Florida	4,022	10,417	65,400
Lavalleja	Minas	3,867	10,016	61,700
Maldonado	Maldonado	1,851	4,793	93,000
Montevideo	Montevideo	205	530	1,309,100
Paysandú	Paysandú	5,375	13,922	104,500
Río Negro	Fray Bentos	3,584	9,282	47,500
Rivera	Rivera	3,618	9,370	88,400
Rocha	Rocha	4,074	10,551	68,500
Salto	Salto	5,468	14,163	107,300
San José	San José de Mayo	1,927	4,992	91,900
Soriano	Mercedes	3,478	9,008	77,500
Tacuarembó	Tacuarembó	5,961	15,438	82,600
Treinta y Tres	Trienta y Tres	3,679	9,529	45,500
TOTAL LAND AREA		67,574	175,016	2,940,200
INLAND WATER		463	1,199	
TOTAL AREA		68,037	176,215	

Demography

Population (1988): 2,981,000.
Density (1988): persons per sq mi 43.8, persons per sq km 16.9.
Urban-rural (1985): urban 86.2%; rural 13.8%.
Sex distribution (1985): male 48.68%; female 51.32%.
Age breakdown (1985): under 15, 26.6%; 15–29, 22.9%; 30–44, 18.3%; 45–59, 16.5%; 60–74, 11.4%; 75 and over, 4.3%.
Population projection: (1990) 3,011,000; (2000) 3,168,000.
Doubling time: 83 years.
Ethnic composition (1980): mixed Spanish–Italian 85.9%; mestizo 3.0%; Italian 2.6%; Jewish 1.7%; mulatto 1.2%; other 5.6%.
Religious affiliation (1980): Christian 62.9%, of which Roman Catholic 59.5%; nonreligious and atheist 35.1%; Jewish 1.7%; other 0.3%.
Major cities (1985): Montevideo 1,246,500; Salto 77,400; Paysandú 75,200; Las Piedras 61,300; Rivera 55,400.

Vital statistics

Birth rate per 1,000 population (1986): 18.2 (world avg. 26.0); (1983) legitimate 73.8%; illegitimate 26.2%.
Death rate per 1,000 population (1986): 9.8 (world avg. 9.9).
Natural increase rate per 1,000 population (1986): 8.4 (world avg. 16.1).
Total fertility rate (avg. births per childbearing woman; 1986): 2.7.
Marriage rate per 1,000 population (1986): 8.0.
Divorce rate per 1,000 population (1986): 1.4.
Life expectancy at birth (1981): male 69.1 years; female 73.8 years.
Major causes of death per 100,000 population (1986): diseases of the circulatory system 388.2; malignant neoplasms 224.3; accidents 45.3; respiratory diseases 34.0; infectious and parasitic diseases 21.1; diabetes 20.7.

National economy

Budget (1987). Revenue: NUr$270,939,200,000 (direct taxes 76.9%, receipts from foreign trade 14.7%). Expenditures: NUr$292,987,700,000 (social security and welfare 57.0%, general public services 15.4%, interest on public debt 8.7%, capital investments 7.9%, subsidies 5.7%).
Public debt (external, outstanding; 1986): U.S.$2,759,300,000.
Production (metric tons except as noted). Agriculture, forestry, fishing (1987) sugarcane 599,700, rice 335,500, sugar beets 246,100, wheat 231,700, corn (maize) 103,700, sorghum 90,100; livestock (number of live animals; 1986) 24,526,000 sheep, 9,961,000 cattle, 500,000 horses; roundwood (1986) 2,668,000 cu m; fish catch 134,859. Mining and quarrying (1986): clays 150,000; gypsum 100,000. Manufacturing (value added in NUr$'000,000; 1985): food products excluding beverages 27,008; petroleum products 19,-719; chemicals and chemical products 14,021; textiles (other than clothing, footwear, and leather products) 13,854; beverages 9,282; leather products excluding footwear 7,744; tobacco 6,896; clothing and footwear 5,149; paper and paper products 4,718; transport equipment 3,884. Construction (1985): residential 160,100 sq m; nonresidential 21,400 sq m. Energy production (consumption): electricity (kW-hr; 1986) 7,429,000,000 (4,278,000,000); coal, none (none); crude petroleum (barrels; 1986) none (7,931,000); petroleum products (metric tons; 1986) 965,000 (921,000); natural gas, none (n.a.).
Gross national product (1986): U.S.$5,630,000,000 (U.S.$1,860 per capita).

Structure of gross domestic product and labour force

	1987		1985	
	in value NUr$'000,000	% of total value	labour force	% of labour force
Agriculture	191,929	11.3	179,200	15.3
Mining	[2]	[2]	1,900	0.2
Manufacturing	388,345	22.8	211,600	18.0
Construction	34,751	2.1	63,300	5.4
Public utilities	42,568	2.5	17,100	1.5
Transp. and commun.	92,133	5.4	59,100	5.0
Trade	173,642	10.2	136,800	11.7
Finance	197,844	11.6	42,100	3.6
Pub. admin., defense	152,326	9.0	361,000	30.8
Services	180,807[2]	10.6[2]		
Other	246,214[3]	14.5[3]	99,400[4]	8.5[4]
TOTAL	1,700,559	100.0	1,171,500	100.0

Tourism (1986): receipts from visitors U.S.$259,000,000; expenditures by nationals abroad U.S.$174,000,000.
Population economically active (1985): total 1,171,500; activity rate 39.9% (participation rates: ages 20–64, 71.3%; female 33.1%; unemployed 12.8%).

Price and earnings indexes (1980 = 100)							
	1982	1983	1984	1985	1986	1987	1988[5]
Consumer price index	159.5	238.0	369.6	636.5	1,122.7	1,836.4	2,815.9
Monthly earnings index[6]	169.9	190.1	283.4	474.1	885.0	1,516.3	2,340.4

Household income and expenditure. Average household size (1985) 3.3; average annual income per household (1985): NUr$266,261 (U.S.$2,625); sources of income: wages 53.5%, self-employment 17.0%, pensions, transfer payments, and other 29.5%[7]; expenditure (1982–83)[8]: food 39.9%, housing 17.6%, transport and communications 10.4%, health care 9.3%, clothing 7.0%, household durable goods 6.3%, recreation 3.1%, education 1.3%, personal effects and other 5.1%.
Land use (1985): forested 3.6%; meadows and pastures 78.5%; agricultural and under permanent cultivation 8.3%; other 9.6%.

Foreign trade[9]

Balance of trade (current prices)						
	1982	1983	1984	1985	1986	1987
U.S.$'000,000	−15.3	+305.4	+183.6	+179.1	+305.2	+99.6
% of total	0.7%	17.1%	11.0%	11.7%	16.3%	4.4%

Imports (1987): U.S.$1,141,900,000 (machinery and appliances 19.0%; mineral products 16.5%; chemical products 15.4%; transport equipment 10.8%; synthetic plastic, resins, and rubber 7.9%; base metals and products 6.4%; vegetable products 5.4%). *Major import sources* (1986): Brazil 24.4%; Argentina 14.2%; United States 8.4%; West Germany 7.6%; Mexico 7.4%.
Exports (1987): U.S.$1,189,100,000 (textiles and textile products 32.3%; live animals and live-animal products 21.6%; hides and skins 16.7%; vegetable products 8.4%; food, beverages, and tobacco 2.9%; synthetic plastics, resins, and rubber 2.6%). *Major export destinations* (1986): Brazil 27.2%; United States 11.9%; West Germany 9.1%; Argentina 8.2%; China 5.6%.

Transport and communications

Transport. Railroads (1986): route length (1987) 2,991 km; passenger-km 331,900,000; metric ton-km cargo 204,000,000. Roads (1981): length 49,813 km (paved 20%). Vehicles (1981): passenger cars 281,275; trucks and buses 49,813. Merchant marine (1987): vessels (100 gross tons and over) 90; deadweight tonnage 218,115. Air transport (1985): passenger-km 389,326,-000; metric ton-km cargo 37,037,000; airports (1988) 7.
Communications. Daily newspapers (1985): total number 21; total circulation 556,100[10]; circulation per 1,000 population 185[10]. Radio (1986): total receivers 1,800,000 (1 per 1.6 persons). Television (1987): total receivers 500,000 (1 per 5.9 persons). Telephones (1987): 399,004 (1 per 7.4 persons).

Education and health

Education (1985–86)	schools	teachers	students	student/ teacher ratio
Primary (age 6–12)	2,371	16,212	352,459	21.7
Secondary	268	9,045	169,932	18.8
Vocational	94	...	54,727	...
Higher	1	...	91,580	...

Educational attainment (1985). Percent of population age 25 and over having: no formal schooling 7.5%; less than primary education 26.6%; primary 31.2%; secondary 19.9%; higher 14.8%. *Literacy* (1985): total population age 15 and over literate 95.0%; males 975,200 (94.5%); females 1,074,300 (95.4%).
Health (1986): physicians 6,529 (1 per 397 persons); hospital beds (1983) 23,400 (1 per 127 persons); infant mortality rate per 1,000 live births 27.9.
Food (1984–86): daily per capita caloric intake 2,676 (vegetable products 64%, animal products 36%); (1983) 99% of FAO recommended minimum.

Military

Total active duty personnel (1988): 27,100 (army 69.4%, navy 19.6%, air force 11.0%). *Military expenditure as percent of GNP* (1985): 2.7% (world 6.1%); per capita expenditure U.S.$46.

[1]Preliminary. [2]Mining is included with Services. [3]Includes indirect taxes less subsidies. [4]Includes unemployed not previously employed. [5]June. [6]Salaried employees only. [7]Urban only. [8]Weights of consumer price index components in Montevideo. [9]Import figures are f.o.b. in balance of trade and c.i.f. for commodities and trading partners. [10]Partial circulation only.

Vanuatu

Official name: Ripablik blong Vanuatu (Bislama); République de Vanuatu (French); Republic of Vanuatu (English).
Form of government: republic with a single legislative house (Parliament [46]).
Chief of state: President.
Head of government: Prime Minister.
Capital: Vila.
Official languages: Bislama; French; English.
Official religion: none.
Monetary unit: vatu (VT); valuation (Oct. 10, 1988) 1 U.S.$ = VT 106.48; 1 £ = VT 182.35.

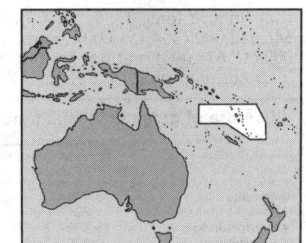

Area and population

Local Government Regions	Capitals	area sq mi	area sq km	population 1987 estimate
Ambrym	Eas	257	666	8,100
Ambae/Maéwo	Longana	270	699	11,780
Banks/Torres	Sola	341	882	6,400
Éfaté	Vila	356	923	28,590
Épi	Ringdove	172	446	3,090
Malekula	Lakatoro	793	2,053	18,850
Paama	Liro	23	60	2,420
Pentecost	Loltong	193	499	11,780
Santo/Malo	Luganville	1,640	4,248	26,310
Shepherd	Morua	33	86	5,160
Taféa	Isangel	629	1,628	22,400
TOTAL		4,707	12,190	144,880

Demography

Population (1988): 149,000.
Density (1988): persons per sq mi 31.7, persons per sq km 12.2.
Urban–rural (1987): urban 14.5%[1]; rural 85.5%.
Sex distribution (1979): male 53.10%; female 46.90%.
Age breakdown (1985): under 15, 45.1%; 15–29, 26.3%; 30–44, 16.5%; 45–59, 8.3%; 60–74, 3.0%; 75 and over, 0.8%.
Population projection: (1990) 159,000; (2000) 215,000.
Doubling time: 21 years.
Ethnic composition (1987): Ni-Vanuatu 96.9%; non-Ni-Vanuatu 3.1%.
Religious affiliation (1979): Christian 81.5%, of which Presbyterian 36.7%, Anglican 15.1%, Roman Catholic 14.8%, Seventh-day Adventist 6.2%; traditional beliefs (mostly followers of cargo cults) 7.6%; nonreligious 1.1%; unknown 9.8%.
Major towns (1987): Vila (Port-Vila) 15,100; Luganville (Santo) 5,900; Port Olry 884[2]; Isangel 752[2].

Vital statistics

Birth rate per 1,000 population (1985): 42.8 (world avg. 29.0).
Death rate per 1,000 population (1985): 9.2 (world avg. 11.0).
Natural increase rate per 1,000 population (1985): 33.6 (world avg. 18.0).
Total fertility rate (avg. births per childbearing woman; 1987): 5.8.
Marriage rate per 1,000 population (1985): c. 7.4.
Divorce rate per 1,000 population (1985): less than 0.7.
Life expectancy at birth (1985): male 61.1 years; female 59.3 years.
Major causes of death per 100,000 population (1985)[3]: infectious and parasitic diseases 69.3; diseases of the respiratory system 60.5; diseases of the circulatory system 37.6; accidents and violence 23.6; malignant neoplasms (cancers) 22.9; ill-defined conditions 117.3.

National economy

Budget (1985). Revenue: VT 5,054,000,000 (local taxes 46.2%, foreign grants 43.7%, local nontax revenue 8.8%). Expenditures: VT 5,054,000,000 (current expenditure 62.9%, development expenditure 37.1%).
Public debt (external, outstanding; 1986): U.S.$8,900,000.
Tourism (1985): receipts from visitors U.S.$19,400,000; expenditures by nationals abroad, n.a.
Production (metric tons except as noted). Agriculture, forestry, fishing (1986): coconuts 327,000, copra 47,000, roots and tubers 30,000, vegetables and melons 7,000, peanuts (groundnuts) 2,000, bananas 1,000, cocoa beans 1,000, corn (maize) 1,000; livestock (number of live animals) 101,000 cattle, 72,000 pigs; roundwood (1985) 38,000 cu m; fish catch 2,920, of which marine mollusks (mostly trochuses) 880, marine crustaceans 490. Mining and quarrying (1985): small quantities of coral reef limestone, crushed stone, sand, and gravel. Manufacturing (value added in '000 VT; 1984): food, beverages, and tobacco 358,000; wood products 96,000; fabricated metal products 60,000; paper products, including printing and publishing 48,800; nonmetallic mineral products 24,600; handicrafts 14,600; textiles, clothing, and leather 12,900. Construction (approvals in Vila and Luganville; 1987): residential 8,550 sq m; nonresidential 17,910 sq m. Energy production (consumption): electricity (kW-hr; 1986) 26,000,000 (26,000,000); coal, none (none); crude petroleum, none (none); petroleum products (metric tons; 1986) none (19,000); natural gas, none (none).
Population economically active (1979): total 51,130; activity rate of total population 46.0% (participation rates: ages 15–64, 84.3%; female 43.4%; unemployed, n.a.).

Price and earnings indexes (1980 = 100)

	1981	1982	1983	1984	1985	1986	1987
Consumer price index	127.5	135.3	137.6	145.2	146.7	153.7	176.4[4]
Monthly earnings index	...	...	...	...	...	...	...

Land use (1985): forested 1.1%; meadows and pastures 1.7%; agricultural 6.4%; limestones, volcanic rock, and other 90.8%.
Gross national product (at current market prices; 1986): n.a.[5]

Structure of gross domestic product and labour force

	1982 in value VT '000,000	1982 % of total value	1979 labour force	1979 % of labour force
Agriculture	1,889	20.0	39,276	76.8
Mining	755[6]	8.0[6]	76	0.1
Manufacturing	472	5.0	990	1.9
Construction	189	2.0	1,103	2.2
Public utilities	6	6	62	0.1
Transportation and communications	283	3.0	1,323	2.6
Trade	944	10.0	2,176	4.3
Finance			326	0.6
Pub. admin., defense	4,910	52.0	5,492	10.8
Services				
Other	—	—	306	0.6
TOTAL	9,442	100.0	51,130	100.0

Household income and expenditure (1985)[1]. Average household size 4.8; income per household: U.S.$11,299; sources of income: wages and salaries 59.0%, self-employment 33.7%; expenditure: food and beverages 36.3%, housing 21.5%, transportation and communications 8.6%, energy 6.8%, household furnishings 5.5%, clothing and footwear 4.8%, other 16.5%.

Foreign trade[7]

Balance of trade (current prices)

	1982	1983	1984	1985	1986	1987
VT '000,000	−3,462	−3,352	−2,416	−4,115	−4,264	−5,696
% of total	44.0%	36.3%	21.6%	38.7%	53.7%	59.5%

Imports (1987): VT 7,639,000,000 (basic and miscellaneous manufactures 34.1%; machinery and transport equipment 25.1%; food and live animals 13.4%; mineral fuels 8.3%; chemical products 5.9%; imports for reexport 2.5%). *Major import sources*[8]: Australia 34.6%; New Zealand 14.0%; Japan 12.8%; Fiji 6.1%; France 4.7%.
Exports (1987): VT 1,942,000,000 (domestic exports 77.3%, of which copra 37.0%, beef and veal 12.9%, cocoa 10.7%, timber 10.7%; reexports 22.7%). *Major export destinations*[9]: The Netherlands 28.0%; Japan 26.9%; France 12.4%; Belgium 6.8%; United Kingdom 6.0%.

Transport and communications

Transport. Railroads: none. Roads (1984): total length 660 mi, 1,062 km; (paved 24%). Vehicles (1984): passenger cars 3,087; trucks and buses, n.a. Merchant marine (1987): vessels (100 gross tons and over) 88; total deadweight tonnage 982,189. Air transport (1986): domestic passenger arrivals 86,940, international passenger arrivals 22,758; international cargo unloaded 357 metric tons, international cargo loaded 88 metric tons; airports (1988) with scheduled flights 24.
Communications. Daily newspapers (1987): none. Radio (1986): total number of receivers 18,000 (1 per 7.8 persons). Television (1987): none. Telephones (1986): 3,240 (1 per 44 persons).

Education and health

Education (1983)

	schools	teachers	students	student/ teacher ratio
Primary (age 6–11)	265[10]	934	23,856[10]	...
Secondary (age 11–18)	9	126[11]	2,186	...
Voc., teacher tr.	2	40[11]	718	...
Higher[12]	—	—	—	

Educational attainment (1979). Percent of population age 25 and over having: no formal schooling 37.2%; some primary education 34.3%, complete primary 6.5%, lower-level secondary 14.7%, upper-level secondary and higher 7.3%. *Literacy* (1979): total population age 15 and over literate 32,120 (52.9%); males 18,550 (57.3%); females 13,570 (47.8%).
Health: physicians (1986) 27 (1 per 5,191 persons); hospital beds (1983) 437 (1 per 294 persons); infant mortality rate per 1,000 live births (1984) 94.
Food (1984–86): daily per capita caloric intake 2,344 (vegetable products 79%, animal products 21%); (1983) 81% of FAO recommended minimum requirement.

Military

Total active duty personnel: Vanuatu has a paramilitary force of about 300.

[1]Vila and Luganville only. [2]1979. [3]Deaths reported to the Ministry of Health only. [4]Average of second and third quarters. [5]GNP per capita estimated to be less than U.S.$425. [6]Mining includes Public utilities. [7]Imports c.i.f.; exports f.o.b. [8]Excludes imports for reexport. [9]Domestic exports only. [10]1986. [11]1982. [12]A centre of the University of the South Pacific in Vila was scheduled for completion in 1988.

Venezuela

Official name: República de Venezuela (Republic of Venezuela).
Form of government: federal multiparty republic with two legislative houses (Senate [47]; Chamber of Deputies [200]).
Head of state and government: President.
Capital: Caracas.
Official language: Spanish.
Official religion: none.
Monetary unit: 1 bolívar (B, plural Bs) = 100 céntimos; valuation[1] (Oct. 10, 1988) 1 U.S.$ = Bs 37.31; 1 £ = Bs 63.90.

Area and population		area		population
				1988
States	Capitals	sq mi	sq km	estimate
Anzoátegui	Barcelona	16,700	43,300	838,714
Apure	San Fernando de Apure	29,500	76,500	243,570
Aragua	Maracay	2,700	7,014	1,241,982
Barinas	Barinas	13,600	35,200	441,437
Bolívar	Ciudad Bolívar	91,900	238,000	932,476
Carabobo	Valencia	1,795	4,650	1,496,710
Cojedes	San Carlos	5,700	14,800	184,586
Falcón	Coro	9,600	24,800	610,749
Guárico	San Juan de Los Morros	25,091	64,986	465,550
Lara	Barquisimeto	7,600	19,800	1,185,014
Mérida	Mérida	4,400	11,300	594,354
Miranda	Los Teques	3,070	7,950	1,901,893
Monagas	Maturín	11,200	28,900	487,264
Nueva Esparta	La Asunción	440	1,150	264,172
Portuguesa	Guanare	5,900	15,200	571,593
Sucre	Cumaná	4,600	11,800	720,293
Táchira	San Cristóbal	4,300	11,100	819,079
Trujillo	Trujillo	2,900	7,400	534,996
Yaracuy	San Felipe	2,700	7,100	364,431
Zulia	Maracaibo	24,400	63,100	2,115,517
Other federal entities				
Amazonas	Puerto Ayacucho	67,900	175,750	80,011
Delta Amacuro	Tucupita	15,500	40,200	92,610
Dependencias Federales	—	50	120	...
Distrito Federal	Caracas	745	1,930	2,570,390
TOTAL		352,144[2]	912,050	18,757,389[2]

Demography

Population (1988): 18,757,000.
Density (1988): persons per sq mi 53.3, persons per sq km 20.6.
Urban–rural (1988): urban 83.2%; rural 16.8%.
Sex distribution (1988): male 50.47%; female 49.53%.
Age breakdown (1988): under 15, 38.8%; 15–29, 28.4%; 30–44, 18.2%; 45–59, 9.1%; 60–74, 4.4%; 75 and over, 1.1%.
Population projection: (1990) 19,735,000; (2000) 24,715,000.
Doubling time: 29 years.
Ethnic composition (1981): mestizo 69%; white 20%; black 9%; Indian 2%.
Religious affiliation (1983): Roman Catholic 90.7%; other 9.3%.
Major cities (1988): Caracas 1,261,116; Maracaibo 1,151,933; Valencia 889,228; Barquisimeto 681,961; Maracay 510,926; Petare 507,260.

Vital statistics

Birth rate per 1,000 population (1986): 28.3 (world avg. 26.0); (1974) legitimate 47.0%; illegitimate 53.0%.
Death rate per 1,000 population (1986): 4.4 (world avg. 9.9).
Natural increase rate per 1,000 population (1986): 23.9 (world avg. 16.1).
Total fertility rate (avg. births per childbearing woman; 1986): 3.4.
Marriage rate per 1,000 population (1986): 5.6.
Divorce rate per 1,000 population (1983): 0.3.
Life expectancy at birth (1985–90): male 66.7 years; female 72.8 years.
Major causes of death per 100,000 population (1986): heart diseases 69.6; malignant neoplasms (cancers) 46.1; accidents 44.8; infectious and parasitic diseases 31.7; conditions originating from perinatal period 31.6; cerebrovascular diseases 26.0.

National economy

Budget (1986). Revenue: Bs 115,925,000,000 (oil revenues 37.0%, indirect taxes 27.1%, direct taxes 12.7%, internal borrowing 12.3%, nontax revenues 10.3%). Expenditures: Bs 124,170,000,000 (goods and services 37.5%, capital investments 28.2%, transfer payments 22.4%, public debt service 11.9%).
Public debt (external, outstanding; 1986): U.S.$24,485,200,000.
Tourism (1986): receipts from visitors U.S.$353,013,168; expenditures by nationals abroad (1984) U.S.$995,000,000.
Production (metric tons except as noted). Agriculture, forestry, fishing (1986): sugarcane 6,535,000, corn (maize) 1,173,000, bananas 1,002,000, sorghum 756,000, oranges 384,000, rice 322,000, sesame seed 65,000, coffee 62,000, cacao 11,000; livestock (number of live animals) 12,371,000 cattle; roundwood 401,372 cu m; fish catch 303,331. Mining and quarrying (1986): iron ore 19,125,000; aluminum ore 382,741; gold 80,152 troy ounces; diamonds 212,000 carats; silica 344,000. Manufacturing (value added in Bs '000; 1986): base metals 13,651,212; food products 13,141,212; chemicals 12,125,445; beverages 7,184,738; nonmetallic minerals 5,405,915; transport equipment 4,989,227; tobacco 4,860,479. Construction (in Bs; 1986): residential 7,671,000,000; nonresidential 29,179,000,000. Energy production (consumption): electricity (kW-hr; 1986) 46,724,000,000 (46,716,000,000);

coal (metric tons; 1986) 57,000 (307,000); crude petroleum (barrels; 1986) 646,582,000 (304,151,000); petroleum products (metric tons; 1986) 43,347,000 (18,671,000); natural gas (cu m; 1986) 19,545,335,000 (19,545,335,000).
Gross national product (1986): U.S.$51,940,000,000 (U.S.$2,930 per capita).

Structure of gross domestic product and labour force				
	1986			
	in value Bs '000,000[3]	% of total value	labour force	% of labour force
Agriculture	5,489	7.3	859,427	14.1
Mining	5,221	7.0	67,464	1.1
Manufacturing	15,300	20.5	1,002,870	16.4
Construction	2,608	3.5	555,018	9.1
Public utilities	2,924	3.9	63,807	1.0
Transp. and commun.	9,649	12.9	374,190	6.1
Trade	6,635	8.9	1,181,317	19.4
Finance	...	...	312,236	5.1
Pub. admin., defense	10,434	13.9 }	1,578,570	25.9
Services }	16,496	22.1 }	112,216[4]	1.8[4]
Other }				
TOTAL	74,756	100.0	6,107,115	100.0

Population economically active (1986): total 6,107,115; activity rate 34.1% (participation rates: ages 15–64, 57.9%; female 27.4%; unemployed 10.3%).

Price and earnings indexes (1980 = 100)							
	1981	1982	1983	1984	1985	1986	1987
Consumer price index	116.2	127.3	135.3	151.8	169.1	188.6	241.6
Monthly earnings index[5]	110.6	...	115.2	130.4	123.4	133.7	...

Household income and expenditure: average household size (1981) 5.3; average annual income per household (1981) Bs 42,492 (U.S.$9,899); sources of income: n.a.; expenditure (1984): food 54.3%, transport and communications 10.8%, rent and utilities 9.3%, education and recreation 5.9%, household furnishings and maintenance 5.1%, medical care 4.4%, clothing 4.1%.
Land use (1985): forested 35.9%; meadows and pastures 19.8%; agricultural and under permanent cultivation 4.3%; other 40.0%.

Foreign trade

Balance of trade (current prices)						
	1981	1982	1983	1984	1985	1986
Bs '000,000	+35,706	+20,765	+31,427	+49,665	+36,786	+11,429
% of total	26.0%	17.2%	31.8%	34.3%	25.0%	7.8%

Imports (1986): Bs 74,651,000,000 (machinery and transport equipment 49.8%; chemicals 14.6%; basic manufactures 11.5%; raw materials 8.3%; food and live animals 4.7%). *Major import sources:* U.S. 45.6%; W.Ger. 7.3%; Japan 6.8%; Italy 4.7%; France 4.4%; Brazil 4.3%; U.K. 4.1%.
Exports (1986): Bs 78,682,000,000 (1981; crude petroleum, petroleum products, and iron ore 88.0%; basic manufactures 7.4%). *Major export destinations:* U.S. 35.8%; Japan 14.6%; Colombia 7.9%; The Netherlands 3.4%; Puerto Rico 2.6%; W.Ger. 2.0%.

Transport and communications

Transport. Railroads (1986): route length 273 mi, 439 km; passenger-km 17,140,000; metric ton-km cargo 11,600,000. Roads (1986): total length 62,492 mi, 100,571 km (paved 33%). Vehicles (1986): passenger cars 2,300,000; trucks and buses 1,248,000. Merchant marine (1987): vessels (100 gross tons and over) 283; total deadweight tonnage 1,418,050. Air transport (1985): passenger-km 2,464,414,000; metric ton-km cargo 215,178,000; airports (1988) with scheduled flights 39.
Communications. Daily newspapers (1982): total number 61; total circulation 2,739,000; circulation per 1,000 population 172. Radio (1986): 6,747,000 receivers (1 per 2.6 persons). Television (1987): 2,760,000 receivers (1 per 6.6 persons). Telephones (1987): 1,581,063 (1 per 11 persons).

Education and health

Education (1985–86)	schools	teachers	students	student/ teacher ratio
Primary (age 7–12)	19,868	130,227	3,332,366	25.6
Secondary (age 13–17)[6]	2,277	60,112	1,037,950	17.3
Higher	82	31,735	444,450	14.0

Educational attainment (1981). Percent of population age 25 and over having: no formal schooling 23.5%; primary education 47.2%; secondary 22.3%; higher 7.0%. *Literacy* (1986): total population age 15 and over literate 10,886,308 (89.0%); males 4,957,087 (90.7%); females 5,420,892 (87.2%).
Health: physicians 24,626 (1 per 722 persons); hospital beds 47,411 (1 per 375 persons); infant mortality rate 25.8.
Food (1983–85): daily per capita caloric intake 2,550 (vegetable products 79%, animal products 21%); (1983) 111% of FAO recommended minimum.

Military

Total active duty personnel (1987): 69,000 (army 78.3%, navy 14.5%, air force 7.2%). *Military expenditure as percent of GNP* (1985): 1.4% (world 6.1%); per capita expenditure U.S.$39.

[1]Free market rate. Venezuela maintains a three-tiered system of official exchange rates, which also includes an "official" rate (Bs 14.50 = U.S.$1.00) and a "preferred" rate (Bs 7.50 = U.S.$1.00) for stimulation of local industry and nonpetroleum exports and for valuation and payment of private external debt and protection of worker's real income. The free-market rate governs, and is sometimes identified as, a luxury goods rate. [2]Detail does not add to total given because of rounding. [3]In prices of 1968. [4]Mostly unemployed persons not previously employed. [5]In nonagricultural activities. [6]Includes vocational and teacher training.

Vietnam

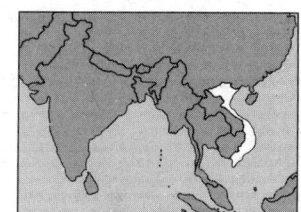

Official name: Cong Hoa Xa Hoi Chu
Nghia Viet Nam (Socialist Republic
of Vietnam).
Form of government: unitary
single-party socialist republic with
one legislative house (National
Assembly [496]).
Chief of state: Chairman of the State
Council (President).
Head of government: Chairman of the
Council of Ministers.
Capital: Hanoi.
Official language: Vietnamese.
Official religion: none.
Monetary unit: 1 dong (D) = 10
hao = 100 xu; valuation (Oct. 10,
1988) 1 U.S.$ = D 368.00;
1 £ = D 630.20.

Area and population		area		population
				1979
Provinces	Capitals	sq mi	sq km	census
An Giang	Long Xuyen	1,349	3,493	1,532,362
Bac Thai	Thai Nguyen	2,521	6,530	815,105
Ben Tre	Ben Tre	859	2,225	1,041,838
Binh Tri Thien	Hue	7,081	18,340	1,901,713
Cao Bang	Cao Bang	3,261	8,445	479,823
Cuu Long	Vinh Long	1,488	3,854	1,504,215
Dac Lac	Buon Me Thuot	7,645	19,800	490,198
Dong Nai	Bien Hoa	2,926	7,578	1,304,799
Dong Thap	Cao Lamh	1,309	3,391	1,182,787
Gia Lai-Kon Tum	Kon Tum	9,860	25,536	595,906
Ha Bac	Bac Giang	1,780	4,609	1,662,671
Ha Nam Ninh	Nam Dinh	1,453	3,763	2,781,409
Ha Son Binh	Hanoi	2,308	5,978	1,537,190
Ha Tuyen	Ha Giang	5,219	13,518	782,453
Hai Hung	Hai Duong	986	2,555	2,145,662
Hau Giang	Can Tho	2,365	6,126	2,232,891
Hoang Lien Son	Lao Cai	5,734	14,852	778,217
Kien Giang	Rach Gia	2,455	6,358	994,673
Lai Chau	Lai Chau	6,586	17,068	322,077
Lam Dong	Da Lat	3,835	9,933	396,657
Lang Son	Lang Son	3,161	8,187	484,657
Long An	Tan An	1,681	4,355	957,264
Minh Hai	Bac Lieu	2,972	7,697	1,219,595
Nghe Tinh	Vinh	8,688	22,502	3,111,989
Nghia Binh	Qui Nhon	4,595	11,900	2,095,354
Phu Khanh	Nha Trang	3,785	9,804	1,188,637
Quang Nam-Da Nang	Da Nang	4,629	11,989	1,529,520
Quang Ninh	Hai Duong	2,293	5,938	750,055
Son La	Son La	5,586	14,468	487,793
Song Be	Thu Dau Mot	3,807	9,859	659,093
Tay Ninh	Ho Chi Minh City	1,556	4,030	684,006
Thai Binh	Thai Binh	577	1,495	1,506,235
Thanh Hoa	Thanh Hoa	4,300	11,138	2,532,261
Thuan Hai	Phan Thiet	4,392	11,374	938,255
Tien Giang	My Tho	918	2,377	1,264,498
Vinh Phu	Viet Tri	1,786	4,626	1,488,348
Municipalities				
Haiphong	—	585	1,515	1,279,067
Hanoi	—	826	2,139	2,570,905
Ho Chi Minh City	—	787	2,029	3,419,978
Special zone				
Vung Tau-Con Dao	—	108	279	91,610
TOTAL		128,052	331,653	52,741,766

Demography

Population (1988): 63,807,000.
Density (1988): persons per sq mi 498.3; persons per sq km 192.4.
Urban–rural (1986): urban 19.0%; rural 81.0%.
Sex distribution (1986): male 48.91%; female 51.09%.
Age breakdown (1985): under 15, 39.3%; 15–29, 31.3%; 30–44, 13.7%; 45–59, 9.4%; 60–74, 5.1%; 75 and over, 1.2%.
Population projection: (1990) 66,573,000; (2000) 82,310,000.
Doubling time: 30 years.
Ethnic composition (1979): Vietnamese 88.0%; Chinese (Hoa) 1.9%; Tai 1.5%; Khmer 1.2%; Muong 1.2%; Thai 1.2%; Nung 0.9%; other 4.1%.
Religious affiliation (1980): Buddhist 55.3%; Roman Catholic 7.0%; Muslim 1.0%; other 36.7%.
Major cities (1979): Ho Chi Minh City 2,441,185; Hanoi 2,961,000[1]; Haiphong 330,755; Da Nang 318,655; Bien Hoa 190,086.

Vital statistics

Birth rate per 1,000 population (1987): 33.1 (world avg. 26.0).
Death rate per 1,000 population (1987): 10.0 (world avg. 9.9).
Natural increase rate per 1,000 population (1987): 23.1 (world avg. 16.1).
Total fertility rate (avg. births per childbearing woman; 1987): 4.3.
Life expectancy at birth (1987): male 58.5 years; female 62.9 years.
Major causes of death per 100,000 population (1979): diseases of the circulatory system 123.8; malignant neoplasms (cancers) 54.0; infectious and parasitic diseases 48.0.

National economy

Budget (1982). Revenue: U.S.$4,120,000,000. Expenditures: U.S.$5,560,000,000.
Gross national product (1986): U.S.$12,400,000,000 (U.S.$200 per capita).

Structure of net material product and labour force				
	1983		1985	
	by value	% of total value	labour force	% of labour force
Agriculture	...	57.6	17,502,000	60.9
Mining and manufacturing	...	23.7[2]	870,000	3.0
Construction	...	3.0	517,000	1.8
Public utilities	...	[2]	37,100	0.1
Transp. and commun.	...	1.9	188,000	0.7
Trade	...	11.7	447,000	1.6
Services	...	...	927,400	3.2
Other	...	2.1[3]	8,266,500[4]	28.7[4]
TOTAL	...	100.0	28,755,000	100.0

Public debt (external, outstanding; 1986): U.S.$5,025,000,000.
Tourism. Receipts from visitors (1987 est.) U.S.$15,000,000; expenditures by nationals abroad, n.a.
Production (metric tons except as noted). Agriculture, forestry, fishing (1986): rice 16,300,000, sugarcane 6,600,000, fruits 3,705,000, vegetables 3,272,000, cassava 3,000,000, sweet potatoes 2,000,000, coconuts 655,000, corn (maize) 600,000, peanuts (groundnuts) 275,000, potatoes 192,000; livestock (number of live animals; 1986) 11,807,000 pigs, 5,188,000 cattle, 403,000 sheep and goats, 91,200,000 poultry; roundwood (1985) 24,872,000 cu m; fish catch 590,000. Mining and quarrying (1986): phosphate rock 530,000; salt 450,000; chromite 15,000; bauxite 6,000; zinc ore 5,000. Manufacturing (1985): cement 1,538,000[5]; fertilizers 516,000; sugar 384,000; paper and paperboard 79,300; crude steel 57,500; soap 52,500; textiles 380,000,000[5] sq m; beer 840,000 hectolitres; leather footwear 210,000 pairs; cigarettes 20,600,000,000 units. Construction: n.a. Energy production (consumption): electricity (kW-hr; 1986) 5,200,000,000 (5,200,000,000); coal (metric tons; 1986) 5,500,000 (5,000,000); crude petroleum, none (n.a.); petroleum products (metric tons; 1986) none (1,405,000); natural gas, none (n.a.).
Population economically active (1985): total 28,755,000; activity rate of total population 48.2% (participation rates: ages 15–64, 80.1%; female 47.2%; unemployed, n.a.).
Land use (1985): forested 40.4%; meadows and pastures 0.8%; agricultural and under permanent cultivation 23.3%; other 35.5%.

Foreign trade

Balance of trade (current prices)						
	1981	1982	1983	1984	1985	1986
U.S.$'000,000	−931	−843	−702	−710	...	−805
% of total	49.9%	41.6%	39.5%	36.4%	...	33.9%

Imports (1986): U.S.$1,590,000,000 (1980; fuel and raw materials 44.7%, machinery 23.2%, wheat flour and food products 17.2%). *Major import sources* (1983): U.S.S.R. 67.0%; Japan 6.6%; Hong Kong 3.0%; Singapore 2.5%; France 1.7%; United States 1.2%.
Exports (1986): U.S.$785,000,000 (1980; manufactured goods 72.8%, handicrafts 18.6%, agricultural products 8.6%). *Major export destinations* (1983): U.S.S.R. 53.2%; Hong Kong 11.7%; Japan 6.3%; Czechoslovakia 5.8%; Singapore 5.5%; Poland 3.1%; Bulgaria 2.1%.

Transport and communications

Transport. Railroads (1986): length 1,829 mi, 2,943 km; passenger-mi 2,087,000,000, passenger-km 3,359,000,000; short ton-mi cargo 595,000,000, metric ton-km cargo 869,000,000. Roads (1987): total length 52,800 mi, 85,000 km (paved 11%). Vehicles (1976): passenger cars 100,000; trucks and buses 200,000. Merchant marine (1987): vessels (100 gross tons and over) 162; total deadweight tonnage 537,838. Air transport (1985): passenger-mi 183,300,000, passenger-km 295,000,000; short ton-mi cargo 4,100,000, metric ton-km cargo 6,000,000; airports (1988) with scheduled flights 3.
Communications. Daily newspapers (1984): 4; total circulation 500,000[6]; circulation per 1,000 population 8.6. Radio (1986): 6,045,000 receivers (1 per 10 persons). Television (1984): 2,250,000 receivers (1 per 27 persons). Telephones (1982): 1,165,000 (1 per 48.1 persons).

Education and health

Education (1980–81)	schools	teachers	students	student/ teacher ratio
Primary and secondary (age 7–18)	13,596	414,000	12,203,000	29.5
Vocational	298	11,400	128,000	11.2
Higher	97	18,800	88,600	4.7

Educational attainment (1983). Percent of state-employed population having[7]: vocational education 12.9%; higher 7.4%. *Literacy* (1979): total population age 15 and over literate 28,903,500 (94.0%).
Health (1986): physicians 19,100[8] (1 per 3,200 persons); hospital beds 216,000 (1 per 283 persons); infant mortality rate per 1,000 live births (1987) 68.
Food (1981–83): daily per capita caloric intake 2,185 (vegetable products 94%, animal products 6%); (1983) 92% of FAO recommended minimum.

Military

Total active duty personnel (1987): 1,260,000 (army 87.3%, navy 3.2%, air force 9.5%). *Military expenditure as percent of GNP* (1984): 7.2% (world 5.9%); per capita expenditure U.S.$22. *Foreign military aid* (1983): U.S.$200,000,000.

[1]1985 estimate. [2]Mining and manufacturing includes public utilities. [3]Other material activities. [4]Includes finance and public administration and defense. [5]1986. [6]One daily only. [7]Total state-employed 3,868,000. [8]Includes dentists.

Virgin Islands (U.S.)

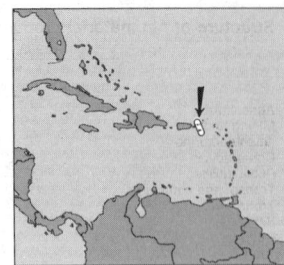

Official name: Virgin Islands of the
United States.
Political status: organized
unincorporated territory
of the United States with
one legislative house (Senate [15]).
Chief of state: President of the
United States.
Head of government: Governor.
Capital: Charlotte Amalie.
Official language: English.
Official religion: none.
Monetary unit: 1 U.S. dollar
(U.S.$) = 100 cents; valuation (Oct.
10, 1988) 1 U.S.$ = £0.58.

Area and population

Municipal Councils	Capitals	area sq mi	area sq km	population 1986 estimate
St. Croix	Christiansted	84	217	54,300
St. Thomas/St. John[1]	Charlotte Amalie	52	135	55,200
TOTAL		136	352	109,500

Demography

Population (1988): 107,000.
Density (1988): persons per sq mi 786.8, persons per sq km 304.0.
Urban–rural (1985): urban 45.2%; rural 54.8%.
Sex distribution (1980): male 47.85%; female 52.15%.
Age breakdown (1980): under 15, 36.0%; 15–29, 24.2%; 30–44, 21.5%; 45–59, 11.1%; 60–74, 5.8%; 75 and over, 1.4%.
Population projection: (1990) 108,000; (2000) 114,000.
Doubling time: 44 years.
Ethnic composition (1980)[2]: black 79.7%, of which Spanish or Hispanic origin 10.3%; white 14.8%, of which Spanish or Hispanic origin 2.3%; other 5.5%, of which Spanish or Hispanic origin 3.7%.
Religious affiliation (1980): Christian 98.0%, of which Protestant 63.2% (Anglican 17.4%, Pentecostal c. 12.0%, Moravian c. 9.0%, Methodist c. 8.0%, Lutheran c. 3.0%), Roman Catholic 33.6%; Bahā'ī 0.5%; Jewish 0.3%; nonreligious 1.2%.
Major cities (1980): Charlotte Amalie 11,842; Christiansted 2,914; Cruz Bay 1,928; Frederiksted 1,046.

Vital statistics

Birth rate per 1,000 population (1986): 20.3 (world avg. 26.0); (1981) legitimate 48.7%; illegitimate 51.3%.
Death rate per 1,000 population (1986): 4.3 (world avg. 9.9).
Natural increase rate per 1,000 population (1986): 16.0 (world avg. 16.1).
Total fertility rate (avg. births per childbearing woman; 1987): 2.6.
Marriage rate per 1,000 population (1984): 13.1.
Divorce rate per 1,000 population (1984): 3.3.
Life expectancy at birth (1980–85): male 66.7 years; female 70.7 years.
Major causes of death per 100,000 population (1986): diseases of the circulatory system 179.9, of which ischemic heart disease 84.9, cerebrovascular diseases 34.7, hypertensive heart disease 22.8; malignant neoplasms (cancers) 74.9; accidents 30.1; diseases of the digestive system 17.4.

National economy

Budget. Revenue (1985): U.S.$263,347,000 (1983; personal income tax 38.6%, gross receipts tax 13.8%, corporate income tax 11.1%, property tax 9.3%, excise tax 3.5%). Expenditures (1983): U.S.$231,000,000 (education 25.4%, health 15.7%, executive branch 12.5%, public works 7.7%, public safety 5.7%, College of the Virgin Islands 3.8%, Territorial Court 2.7%).
Tourism (1986): receipts from visitors U.S.$510,000,000; expenditures by nationals abroad, n.a.
Production (value of sales in U.S.$ except as noted). Agriculture, forestry, fishing (1982): milk 923,000, beef and veal 489,000, poultry and eggs 316,000, ornamental plants and other nursery products 89,700, bananas 63,000, onions 51,000, mangoes 49,000 (other agricultural products include sorghum and bay leaves); livestock (number of live animals; 1986) 11,000 cattle, 4,000 goats, 3,000 sheep; roundwood, n.a.; fish catch (1986) 640 metric tons. Mining and quarrying (1985): sand and crushed stone for local use. Manufacturing (1986): food and related products 28,771,000[3]; watches, clocks, and watchcases 13,845,000[3]; printing, publishing, and allied industries 5,206,000[3]; heavy oils 9,900,000 metric tons; gasoline 1,425,000 metric tons; jet fuel 730,000 metric tons; kerosene 550,000 metric tons; liquefied petroleum gas 40,000 metric tons; rum 88,100 hectolitres[4]. Construction (1982): general building 64,775,000; heavy construction 52,414,000; special trade construction 24,776,000. Energy production (consumption): electricity (kW-hr; 1986) 900,000,000 (900,000,000); coal, none (none); crude petroleum (barrels; 1986) none (114,348,000); petroleum products (metric tons; 1986) 12,685,000 (2,261,000); natural gas, none (none).
Household income and expenditure: average household size (1980) 3.4; average annual income per household (1979) U.S.$14,453; sources of income (1984): wages and salaries 65.7%, transfer payments 13.0%, interest, dividends, and rent 12.7%, self-employment 2.6%; expenditure (1976)[5]: food and beverages 25.3%, housing 24.9%, transportation and communications 11.7%, energy 6.5%, clothing and footwear 5.4%, household furnishings 4.3%, other 21.9%.

Gross domestic product (at current market prices; 1986): U.S.$1,070,000,000 (U.S.$10,050 per capita).

Structure of gross domestic product and labour force

	1986 in value U.S.$'000,000	1986 % of total value	1985 labour force	1985 % of labour force
Agriculture	...	...	522	1.2
Manufacturing	...	...	2,080	4.9
Construction and mining	...	...	2,390	5.7
Transportation and public utilities	...	...	2,310	5.5
Trade, hotels, restaurants	...	...	10,970	26.1
Finance, insurance, real estate	...	...	2,780	6.6
Pub. admin., defense	...	...	12,900	30.6
Services	...	...	3,080	7.3
Other	...	...	5,088[6]	12.1
TOTAL	1,070[7]	100.0	42,120	100.0

Public debt (1985): U.S.$172,000,000.
Population economically active (1980): total 38,082; activity rate of total population 39.4% (participation rates: ages 15–64, 65.1%; female 45.5%; unemployed [1987] 2.8%).

Price and earnings indexes (1980 = 100)

	1982	1983	1984	1985	1986	1987	1988
Consumer price index[8]	117.1	120.9	126.1	130.5	133.1	137.9	143.2[9]
Annual earnings index[10]	118.3	123.0	131.0	137.6	...	...	...

Land use (1985): forested 6.0%; meadows and pastures 26.0%; agricultural and under permanent cultivation 21.0%; other 47.0%.

Foreign trade

Balance of trade (current prices)

	1981	1982	1983	1984	1985	1986
U.S.$'000,000	+54.6	−300.2	−1,019.5	−786.4	−383.5	−523.8
% of total	0.5%	2.9%	12.2%	9.0%	5.4%	11.0%

Imports (1986): U.S.$2,642,800,000 (of which U.S.$1,444,600,000 [crude petroleum 66.8%, food 8.2%, xylenes 4.1%, passenger cars 3.3%]). *Major import sources:* United States 54.7%; other countries 45.3%.
Exports (1986): U.S.$2,119,000,000 (of which U.S.$2,051,800,000 [petroleum products 88.2%, chemical products 8.8%, watches 0.6%, watch movements 0.2%, rum 0.2%]). *Major export destinations:* United States 96.8%; other countries 3.2%.

Transport and communications

Transport. Railroads: none. Roads (1986): total length 660 mi, 1,062 km. Registered motor vehicles (1986): 48,800. Merchant marine, n.a. Air transport (1986)[11]: passenger arrivals 761,672, passenger departures 770,696; cargo unloaded 4,165 metric tons, cargo loaded 703 metric tons; airports (1988) with scheduled flights 6[12].
Communications. Daily newspapers (1987): total number 2; total circulation 19,200; circulation per 1,000 population 181. Radio (1986): total number of receivers 85,000 (1 per 1.3 persons). Television (1987): total number of receivers 31,500 (1 per 3.4 persons). Telephones (1985): 52,314 (1 per 2.1 persons).

Education and health

Education (1986–87)[13]

	schools	teachers	students	student/ teacher ratio
Primary (age 4.5–12)	41	781[14]	14,723	...
Secondary (age 12–18)	10	506[14]	10,903	...
Voc., teacher tr.[15]	3	27	775	28.7
Higher	1	97	757	8.3

Educational attainment (1980): Percent of population age 25 and over having: no formal schooling 1.5%; primary education 34.1%; secondary 40.0%; higher 24.4%. *Literacy* (1982): total population age 15 and over literate 90%.
Health (1985): physicians 167 (1 per 622 persons); hospital beds 507 (1 per 205 persons); infant mortality rate per 1,000 live births (1984–86) 17.8.
Food: daily per capita caloric intake, n.a.

Military

Total active duty personnel: No domestic military force is maintained; the United States is responsible for defense and external security.

[1]Comprises St. Thomas 32 sq mi (83 sq km), pop. 52,260, and St. John 20 sq mi (52 sq km), pop. 2,940. [2]*Place of birth:* U.S. Virgin Islands 44.8%; United States 12.4%; Puerto Rico 5.2%; other West Indies 29.2%, of which St. Kitts and Nevis 6.8%, Antigua and Barbuda 5.1%, British Virgin Islands 3.4%; not reported 5.6%. [3]1982. [4]1984. [5]St. Thomas only. [6]Includes 2,480 self-employed and unpaid family workers and 2,608 unemployed. [7]Tourism accounts for about 70% of GDP. [8]U.S. mainland. [9]June. [10]Annual average gross pay. [11]St. Croix and St. Thomas airports. [12]Scheduled services at 2 airports, 3 seaplane bases, and 1 heliport. [13]Excludes 19 combined primary–secondary schools. [14]Private school teachers not included in total. [15]1983–84.

Western Samoa

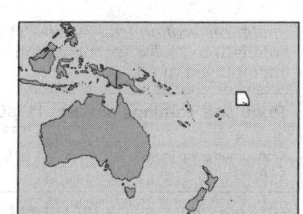

Official name: Malo Sa'oloto
Tuto'atasi o Samoa i Sisifo (Samoan);
Independent State of Western Samoa
(English).
Form of government: constitutional
monarchy[1] with one legislative house
(Legislative Assembly [47]).
Chief of state: Head of State.
Head of government: Prime Minister.
Capital: Apia.
Official languages: Samoan; English.
Official religion: none.
Monetary unit: 1 tala (WS$, plural
tala) = 100 sene; valuation (Oct. 10,
1988) 1 U.S.$ = WS$2.13;
1 £ = WS$3.65.

Area and population	area[2]		population
Islands			1981
Political Districts	sq mi	sq km	census[3]
Savaii	659	1,707	43,150
Fa'aseleleaga			11,876
Gaga'emauga			3,893
Gaga'ifomauga			5,304
Lealataua			1,934
Palauli			9,234
Satupa'itea			5,391
Vaisigano			5,518
Upolu	432	1,119	113,199
A'ana			13,149
A'ana-i-Sisifo			3,363
Aiga-i-le-Tai			3,960
Aleipata			4,236
Anoama'a			7,816
Fagaloa			1,519
Falealili			4,727
Faleata			16,821
Gaga'emauga			2,750
Lefaga			3,776
Lepa and Lotofaga			3,058
Safata			6,711
Sagaga			12,253
Vaimauga			29,060
TOTAL	1,093	2,831	156,349[4]

Demography

Population (1988): 162,000.
Density (1988): persons per sq mi 148.2, persons per sq km 57.2.
Urban–rural (1981): urban 21.2%; rural 78.8%.
Sex distribution (1986): male 52.00%; female 48.00%.
Age breakdown (1981): under 15, 44.3%; 15–29, 29.1%; 30–44, 12.2%; 45–59, 9.0%; 60–74, 3.8%; 75 and over, 1.6%.
Population projection: (1990) 164,000; (2000) 173,000.
Doubling time: 66 years.
Ethnic composition (1982): Samoan (Polynesian) *c.* 88%; Euronesian *c.* 10%; European *c.* 2%.
Religious affiliation (1981): Congregational 47.3%; Roman Catholic 21.7%; Methodist 16.2%; Latter Day Saints 8.3%; other 6.5%.
Major city (1981): Apia 33,170.

Vital statistics

Birth rate per 1,000 population (1985): 12.1[5] (world avg. 29.0); (1978) legitimate 43.5%; illegitimate 56.5%.
Death rate per 1,000 population (1985): 1.5[5] (world avg. 11.0).
Natural increase rate per 1,000 population (1985): 10.6[5] (world avg. 18.0).
Total fertility rate (avg. births per childbearing woman; 1986): 4.4.
Marriage rate per 1,000 population (1985): 5.7[5].
Divorce rate per 1,000 population (1985): 0.3[5].
Life expectancy at birth (1986): male 62.6 years; female 65.6 years.
Major causes of death per 100,000 population[5] (1985): diseases of the circulatory system 42.0; malignant neoplasms (cancers) 18.2; diseases of the respiratory system 13.2; infectious and parasitic diseases 8.8; diabetes mellitus 5.6.

National economy

Budget (1987). Revenue: WS$145,100,000 (current revenue 58.1%, of which taxes 47.4%, nontax revenue 10.7%; foreign aid grants 28.5%; domestic borrowing 13.4%). Expenditures: WS$100,300,000 (capital expenditure 53.3%; current expenditure 46.7%, of which education 9.7%, economic services 9.1%; health 7.1%).
Public debt (external, outstanding; 1986): U.S.$65,400,000.
Tourism (1986): number of visitors 49,280; (1984) number of nationals abroad 27,294.
Land use (1985): forested 47.3%; meadows and pastures 0.4%; agricultural and under permanent cultivation 43.1%; other 9.2%.
Production (metric tons except as noted). Agriculture, forestry, fishing (1986): coconuts 200,000, taro 39,000, copra 24,000, bananas 23,000, papayas 12,-000, mangoes 6,000, pineapples 6,000, avocados 2,000, cacao 2,000, milk 1,000; livestock (number of live animals) 64,000 pigs, 27,000 cattle, 1,000,-000 chickens; roundwood (1985) 131,000 cu m; fish catch 3,700. Mining and quarrying: n.a. Manufacturing (1985): coconut oil 11,766, copra meal 6,098, copra 2,731, sawn wood 21,000 cu m[6], veneer sheets 1,061 cu m[7]; other products include coconut cream, beverages, tobacco products, aluminum products, concrete blocks, handicrafts, and kava. Construction

(permits issued in WS$; 1985): residential 2,114,400; commercial, industrial, and other 5,430,500. Energy production (consumption): electricity (kW-hr; 1986) 45,000,000 (45,000,000); coal, none (n.a.); crude petroleum, none (n.a.); petroleum products (metric tons; 1986) none (37,000).
Gross national product (1986): U.S.$110,000,000 (U.S.$680 per capita).

Structure of gross domestic product and labour force				
	1986[8]		1981	
	in value WS$'000	% of total value	labour force	% of labour force
Agriculture	66,200	31.2	25,050	60.4
Mining	9,400[9]	4.4[9]	9	—
Manufacturing	31,400	14.8	757	1.8
Construction	4,000	1.9	2,279	5.5
Public utilities	3,000	1.4	447	1.1
Transp. and commun.	11,800	5.6	1,353	3.3
Trade	39,000	18.4	1,821	4.4
Finance	20,600	9.7	1,305	3.1
Pub. admin., defense, government services	18,900	8.9	1,842	4.4
Other services }	7,900	3.7	6,374	15.4
Other			269	0.6
TOTAL	212,200	100.0	41,506	100.0

Population economically active (1981): total 41,506; activity rate of total population 26.5% (participation rates: ages 15–64, 48.6%; female 15.0%).

Price and earnings indexes (1980 = 100)							
	1982	1983	1984	1985	1986	1987	1988
Consumer price index	142.6	166.0	185.7	202.2	214.2	224.0	244.0[10]
Monthly earnings index[11]	130.0	146.6	163.0	...	...	...	...

Household income and expenditure. Average household size (1976) 5.9; income per household (1972) WS$1,518 (U.S.$2,200); sources of income (1972): wages 49.4%, self-employment 22.8%, remittances, gifts, and other assistance 18.0%, land rent 8.7%, other 1.1%; expenditure (1976–77)[12]: food 58.8%, transportation 9.0%, housing and furnishings 5.1%, fuel and light 5.0%, clothing 4.2%, other goods and services 1.9%, other 16.0%.

Foreign trade[13]

Balance of trade (current prices)						
	1982	1983	1984	1985	1986	1987
WS$'000	−38,402	−45,719	−48,024	−66,772	−72,388	−94,240
% of total	54.2%	45.5%	39.5%	46.9%	60.6%	65.4%

Imports (1987): WS$131,010,000 (1983; food 21.3%, machinery 21.0%, petroleum products 18.4%, miscellaneous manufactured articles 7.4%, chemicals 5.9%, animal oils and fats 0.5%). *Major import sources* (1985): New Zealand 28.8%; Australia 27.5%; U.S. 11.2%; Japan 11.0%; Singapore 6.0%.
Exports (1987): WS$24,968,000 (1986; coconut oil 29.3%, taro 19.4%, cocoa 14.3%, coconut cream 12.6%, copra and copra meal 7.6%, cigarettes 3.1%, timber 2.7%). *Major export destinations* (1985): U.S. 57.8%; New Zealand 18.7%; Australia 10.3%; West Germany 4.7%; American Samoa 3.7%.

Transport and communications

Transport. Railroads: none. Roads (1983): total length[14] 1,296 mi, 2,085 km (paved 14%). Vehicles (1985): passenger cars 1,757; trucks and buses 2,593. Merchant marine (1987): vessels (100 gross tons and over) 6; total deadweight tonnage 34,751. Air transport: passengers, n.a.; cargo, n.a.; airports (1988) with scheduled flights 3.
Communications. Daily newspapers: none. Radio (1985): 70,000 receivers (1 per 2.3 persons). Television (1985): 5,000 receivers (1 per 32 persons). Telephones (1985): 6,346 (1 per 25 persons).

Education and health

Education (1983)	schools	teachers	students	student/ teacher ratio
Primary (age 5–11)	164	1,502[15]	31,447	20.9
Secondary (age 12–18)	38[8]	520	20,404	39.2
Voc., teacher tr.	4	69	651	9.4
Higher	6	37	562	15.2

Educational attainment (1976). Percent of population age 25 and over having: no formal schooling 60.0%; primary education 31.5%; secondary 6.3%; higher 2.2%. *Literacy* (1971): total population age 15 and over literate 71,206 (97.8%); males 36,447 (97.8%); females 34,759 (97.9%).
Health: physicians (1981) 63 (1 per 2,476 persons); hospital beds (1982) 735 (1 per 215 persons); infant mortality rate per 1,000 live births (1986) 52.0.
Food (1984–86): daily per capita caloric intake 2,463 (vegetable products 81%, animal products 19%); (1980–82) 95% of FAO recommended minimum requirement.

Military

No military forces are maintained; New Zealand is responsible for defense.

[1]According to provisions in the constitution, the current Head of State, paramount chief HH Malietoa Tanumafili II, will hold office for life. Upon his death, the monarchy will functionally cease, and future Heads of State will be elected by the Legislative Assembly. [2]Includes 2 sq mi (5 sq km) of uninhabited islands. [3]Preliminary. [4]The provisional total for the 1986 census is 158,940. [5]Registered only. [6]1984. [7]1982. [8]At prices of 1984. [9]Includes forestry and fishing. [10]July. [11]Government employees only. [12]Consumer price index components. [13]Import figures are f.o.b. in balance of trade and c.i.f. in commodities and trading partners. [14]Total length includes 733 mi (1,180 km) of plantation roads. [15]Includes some secondary teachers.

Yemen (Aden)

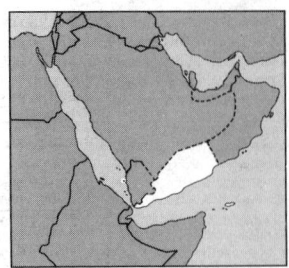

Official name: Jumhūrīyat al-Yaman
ad-Dimuqrāṭīyah ash-Shaʿbīyah
(People's Democratic Republic of
Yemen).
Form of government: single-party
socialist republic with one legislative
house (Supreme People's Council
[111]).
Head of state: Chairman of the
Presidium of the Supreme People's
Council.
Head of government: Prime Minister.
Capital: Aden.
Official language: Arabic.
Official religion: Islam.
Monetary unit: 1 Yemeni dinar
(YD) = 1,000 fils; valuation (Oct. 10,
1988) 1 YD = U.S.$2.86 = £1.69.

Area and population

Governorates	Capitals	area sq mi	area sq km	population 1984 estimate
Abyān	Zinjibār	8,297	21,489	412,574
ʿAdan	Aden	2,695	6,980	386,364
Hadramawt	al-Mukallā	59,991	155,376	651,469
Lahij	Lahij	4,928	12,766	362,809
al-Mahrah	al-Ghaydah	25,618	66,350	80,722
Shabwah	ʿAtāq	28,536	73,908	214,767
TOTAL		130,066[1]	336,869	2,108,705

Demography

Population (1988): 2,345,000.
Density (1988): persons per sq mi 18.0, persons per sq km 7.0.
Urban–rural (1986): urban 40.6%; rural 59.4%.
Sex distribution (1987): male 49.47%; female 50.53%.
Age breakdown (1986): under 15, 47.8%; 15–29, 21.0%; 30–44, 15.9%; 45–59, 8.8%; 60–74, 5.5%; 75 and over, 1.0%.
Population projection: (1990) 2,468,000; (2000) 3,191,000.
Doubling time: 22 years.
Ethnic composition (1983): Arab 95.7%; Indo-Pakistani 1.8%; Somali 1.4%; Amhara and Swahili 0.7%; Jews 0.1%; Persian 0.1%; other 0.2%.
Religious affiliation (1980): predominantly Sunnī Muslim 99.5%; Hindu 0.2%; Christian 0.1%; nonreligious 0.1%; other 0.1%.
Major cities (1984): Aden 318,000; al-Mukallā 59,100; Saywūn 25,400; ash-Shiḥr 23,000; Tarīm 22,500.

Vital statistics

Birth rate per 1,000 population (1986): 49.7 (world avg. 26.0); legitimate, n.a.; illegitimate, n.a.
Death rate per 1,000 population (1986): 17.8 (world avg. 9.9).
Natural increase rate per 1,000 population (1986): 31.9 (world avg. 16.1).
Total fertility rate (avg. births per childbearing woman; 1986): 7.5.
Marriage rate per 1,000 population: n.a.
Divorce rate per 1,000 population: n.a.
Life expectancy at birth (1986): male 47.1 years; female 50.9 years.
Major causes of death per 100,000 population: n.a.; however, major diseases include poliomyelitis, diphtheria, schistosomiasis, typhoid and paratyphoid fevers, yellow fever, hepatitis, asphyxia, trachoma, heart ailments, gastrointestinal diseases, respiratory diseases, salmonella, leprosy, measles, whooping cough, cholera, pulmonary tuberculosis, intestinal bilharzia, influenza, anemia and malnutrition, shigellosis, and malaria.

National economy

Budget (1986). Revenue: YD 7,200,000,000 (custom duties and indirect taxes 83.3%). Expenditures: YD 9,900,000,000 (ordinary expenditures 60.6%, development 39.4%).
Tourism: receipts from visitors (1986) U.S.$7,000,000; expenditures by nationals abroad (1981) U.S.$10,000,000.
Production (metric tons except as noted). Agriculture, forestry, fishing (1986): millet 80,000, watermelons 55,000, pulses 49,000, bananas 23,000, wheat 15,000, seed cotton 15,000, corn (maize) 14,000, tomatoes 13,000, dates 11,000, onions 10,000, potatoes 8,000, lint cotton 5,000, sesame seed 3,000, barley 2,000; livestock (number of live animals) 1,380,000 goats, 930,000 sheep, 170,000 asses, 96,000 cattle, 81,000 camels, 2,000,000 chickens; roundwood 294,000 cu m; fish catch 91,216. Mining and quarrying (1986): salt 75,000. Manufacturing (value added in YD '000; 1984): food, beverages, and tobacco 61,586; electricity 14,100; chemicals, petroleum, coal, rubber, and plastic products 9,469; clothing and apparel industries 5,164; fabricated metal products, machinery, and equipment 5,097; nonmetallic mineral products except petroleum and coal 2,918; paper and paper products, printing, and publishing 2,022; wood and wood products including furniture 1,950. Construction (value of total output; 1984): YD 93,400,000. Energy production (consumption): electricity (kW-hr; 1986) 420,000,000 (420,000,000); coal, none (n.a.); crude petroleum (barrels; 1986) none (24,-189,000); petroleum products (metric tons; 1986) 3,174,000 (1,059,000); natural gas, none (n.a.).
Public debt (external, outstanding; 1986): U.S.$1,927,100,000.
Household income and expenditure. Average household size (1986) 5.6; income per household: n.a.; sources of income: n.a.; expenditure: n.a.

Population economically active (1986): total 550,843; activity rate of total population 24.7% (participation rates: ages 15–64, 50.8%; female 10.9%; unemployed, n.a.).

Price and earnings indexes (1980 = 100)

	1978	1979	1980	1981	1982	1983	1984
Consumer price index	79.8	90.9	100.0	103.8	113.7	125.9	127.8
Earnings index	...	...	...	...	...	...	...

Gross national product (at current market prices; 1986): U.S.$1,030,000,000 (U.S.$480 per capita).

Structure of gross domestic product and labour force

	1983 in value YD '000,000	1983 % of total value	1986 labour force	1986 % of labour force
Agriculture	31.5	8.9	256,693	46.6
Mining	0.5	0.1	10,466	1.9
Manufacturing	43.0	12.2	48,474	8.8
Construction	36.0	10.2	38,614	7.0
Public utilities	4.1	1.3	10,466	1.9
Transportation and communications	33.8	9.6	31,894	5.8
Trade	43.4	12.3	47,373	8.6
Finance	13.7	3.8	551	0.1
Pub. admin., defense	80.0	22.6	...	...
Services	1.7	0.5	106,312	19.3
Other	65.8[2]	18.4[2]	...	...
TOTAL	353.5	100.0[1]	550,843	100.0

Land use (1985): forested 4.7%; meadows and pastures 27.2%; agricultural 0.5%; built-up, wasteland, and other 67.6%.

Foreign trade

Balance of trade (current prices)

	1979	1980	1981	1982	1983	1984
YD '000,000	−123.8	−234.1	−252.9	−248.3	−250.4	−278.7
% of total	27.7%	30.4%	37.6%	31.1%	35.0%	38.5%

Imports (1984): YD 501,600,000 (machinery and transport equipment 30.9%, food and live animals 27.4%, manufactured goods 16.0%, mineral fuels 10.1%, chemicals 4.2%, animal oils and fats 3.1%, crude minerals 2.9%, beverages and tobacco 0.8%). *Major import sources* (1985): Australia 9.2%; United Kingdom 6.5%; Japan 5.7%; The Netherlands 5.2%; France 4.7%; Italy 3.2%; West Germany 3.1%; Denmark 2.8%; Singapore 2.7%; Pakistan 2.6%; United States 1.3%; Thailand 1.2%; Belgium–Luxembourg 1.1%; Norway 0.9%; Spain 0.9%; Sweden 0.7%; Austria 0.4%; Ireland 0.4%; Greece 0.3%; Switzerland 0.3%.
Exports (1984): YD 222,900,000 (petroleum products 95.9%). *Major export destinations* (1984): Italy 33.0%; Japan 11.3%; New Zealand 11.3%; France 10.3%; West Germany 6.0%; Singapore 5.3%; United Kingdom 2.6%; The Netherlands 1.8%.

Transport and communications

Transport. Railroads: none. Roads (1984): total length 6,793 mi, 10,932 km (paved 18%). Vehicles (1984): passenger cars 24,657; commercial vehicles 27,227. Merchant marine (1987): vessels (100 gross tons and over) 26; total deadweight tonnage 13,216. Air transport (1982): passenger-km 100,000,000; metric ton-km cargo 1,700,000; airports (1988) with scheduled flights 7.
Communications. Daily newspapers (1986): total number 2; total circulation 25,000; circulation per 1,000 population 11. Radio (1986): total number of receivers 300,000 (1 per 7.4 persons). Television (1987): total number of receivers 47,000 (1 per 49 persons). Telephones (1984): 16,200 (1 per 131 persons).

Education and health

Education (1983–84)

	schools	teachers	students	student/ teacher ratio
Primary (age 7–12)	924	11,281	294,028	26.1
Secondary (age 13–18)	51	1,493	29,205	19.6
Voc., teacher tr.	29	453	5,602	12.4
Higher	1	486[3]	6,256[4]	...

Educational attainment, n.a. *Literacy* (1980): total population age 15 and over literate 411,900 (38.9%); males literate 354,700 (66.6%); females literate 57,200 (10.9%).
Health (1986): physicians 652 (1 per 3,416 persons); hospital beds 4,499 (1 per 495 persons); infant mortality rate per 1,000 live births 133.3.
Food (1984–86): daily per capita caloric intake 2,331 (vegetable products 88%, animal products 12%); (1983) 94% of FAO recommended minimum requirement.

Military

Total active duty personnel (1988): 27,500 (army 87.3%, navy 3.6%, air force 9.1%). *Military expenditure as percent of GNP* (1985): 17.6% (world 6.1%); per capita expenditure U.S.$89.

---

[1]Detail does not add to total given because of rounding. [2]Import duties. [3]1982–83. [4]1986; excludes 10,403 students studying abroad.

Yemen (Ṣan‘ā’)

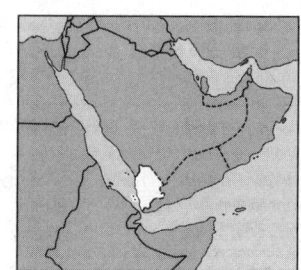

Official name: al-Jumhūrīyah al-‘Arabīyah al-Yamanīyah (Yemen Arab Republic).
Form of government: unitary single-party republic with one legislative house (Consultative Council [159][1]).
Head of state and government: President.
Capital: Ṣan‘ā’.
Official language: Arabic.
Official religion: Islam.
Monetary unit: 1 Yemen Rial (YRl) = 100 fils; valuation (Oct. 10, 1988) 1 U.S.$ = YRls 9.76; 1 £ = YRls 16.71.

Area and population

Governorates	Capitals	area sq mi	area sq km	population 1986 census
al-Bayḍā’	al-Bayḍā’	4,310	11,170	381,249
Dhamār	Dhamār	3,430	8,870	812,981
Ḥajjah	Ḥajjah	3,700	9,590	897,814
al-Ḥudaydah	al-Ḥudaydah	5,240	13,580	1,294,359
Ibb	Ibb	2,480	6,430	1,511,879
al-Jawf	al-Jawf	...	...	87,299
al-Maḥwīt	al-Maḥwīt	830	2,160	322,226
Ma‘rib	Ma‘rib	15,400	39,890	121,437
Ṣa‘dah	Ṣa‘dah	4,950	12,810	344,152
Ṣan‘ā’	Ṣan‘ā’	7,840	20,310	1,856,876
Ta‘izz	Ta‘izz	4,020	10,420	1,643,901
TOTAL		52,210[2,3]	135,230[3]	9,274,173[4]

Demography

Population (1988)[5]: 8,614,000.
Density (1988): persons per sq mi 165.0, persons per sq km 63.7.
Urban–rural (1986): urban 21.0%; rural 79.0%.
Sex distribution (1986): male 50.11%; female 49.89%.
Age breakdown (1986): under 15, 50.4%; 15–29, 20.3%; 30–44, 14.5%; 45–59, 9.1%; 60–74, 4.3%; 75 and over, 1.4%.
Population projection[5]: (1990) 9,060,000; (2000) 11,660,000.
Doubling time: 25 years.
Ethnic composition (1984): predominantly Arab.
Religious affiliation (1980): Shī‘ī Muslim 60%; Sunnī Muslim 40%.
Major cities (1986): Ṣan‘ā’ 427,150; Ta‘izz 178,043; al-Ḥudaydah 155,110.

Vital statistics

Birth rate per 1,000 population (1986): 49.1 (world avg. 26.0); legitimate, n.a.; illegitimate, n.a.
Death rate per 1,000 population (1986): 20.8 (world avg. 9.9).
Natural increase rate per 1,000 population (1986): 28.3 (world avg. 16.1).
Total fertility rate (avg. births per childbearing woman; 1986): 7.5.
Marriage rate per 1,000 population: n.a.
Divorce rate per 1,000 population: n.a.
Life expectancy at birth (1986): male 45.6 years; female 48.9 years.
Major causes of death per 100,000 population: n.a.; however, major infectious diseases include malaria, tuberculosis, intestinal infections, leprosy, schistosomiasis, typhoid and paratyphoid fevers, viral hepatitis, and filarial infections.

National economy

Budget (1986–87). Revenue: YRls 7,179,029,000 (1984; indirect taxes 64.3%, of which import duties 32.8%; nontax revenue 19.1%; direct taxes 16.6%). Expenditures: YRls 9,944,396,000 (1984; defense 26.7%; general public services 19.0%; education 13.2%; health 1.9%).
Public debt (external, outstanding; 1986): U.S.$2,051,600,000.
Production (metric tons except as noted). Agriculture, forestry, fishing (1986): vegetables and melons 432,000, sorghum 391,000, potatoes 208,000, goat's milk 127,000, grapes 85,000, wheat 85,000, pulses 49,000, corn (maize) 49,000, barley 49,000, dates 7,000, coffee 5,000, tobacco 4,000, sesame seed 4,000, cotton lint 2,000, hen's eggs 12,350; livestock (number of live animals) 2,260,000 goats, 1,850,000 sheep, 952,000 cattle, 520,000 asses, 57,000 camels; fish catch 22,341. Mining and quarrying (1986): salt 300,000; gypsum 53,000. Manufacturing (value added in YRls '000,000; 1984): food, beverages, and tobacco 1,218.0; wood and wood products 108.4[6]; textile and wearing apparel 104.0; paper and paper products 48.8[6]. Construction (value added in '000,000 YRls; 1985): 1,550. Energy production (consumption): electricity (kW-hr; 1986) 310,000,000 (310,000,000); coal, none (n.a.); crude petroleum (barrels; 1986) 2,587,000 (2,587,000); petroleum products (metric tons; 1985) 337,000 (823,000); natural gas, none (n.a.).
Population economically active (1986): total 1,492,394; activity rate of total population 18.2% (participation rates: ages 15–64, 38.5%; female 12.5%; unemployed, n.a.).

Price and earnings indexes (1980 = 100)

	1978	1979	1980	1981	1982	1983	1984
Consumer price index	75.0	95.0	100.0	105.0	108.0	114.0	128.0
Earnings index	...	...	...	...	...	...	...

Household income and expenditure. Average household size (1986) 5.6; income per household: n.a.; sources of income: n.a.; expenditure (1972): food, beverages, and tobacco 65.0%, household durable goods 7.8%, energy 7.2%, housing 6.1%, clothing and footwear 5.8%, medical care, health, and hygiene 4.0%, transportation 3.2%, education 0.9%.
Gross national product (1986): U.S.$4,510,000,000 (U.S.$550 per capita).

Structure of gross domestic product and labour force

	1986 in value YRls '000,000	1986 % of total value	1986 labour force	1986 % of labour force
Agriculture	4,126	20.4	894,655	59.9
Mining	397	2.0	1,305	0.1
Manufacturing	2,662	13.1	46,439	3.1
Construction	857	4.2	122,338	8.2
Public utilities	286	1.4	22,386	1.5
Transp. and commun.	2,549	12.6	75,717	5.1
Trade	2,728	13.5	201,606	13.5
Finance	2,597	12.8	8,206	0.5
Pub. admin., defense } Services	2,513	12.4	... 119,742	... 8.0
Other	1,539[7]	7.6	...	...
TOTAL	20,254	100.0	1,492,394	100.0[2]

Land use (1985): forested 8.2%; meadows and pastures 35.9%; agricultural and under permanent cultivation 6.9%; other 49.0%.
Tourism (1986): receipts from visitors U.S.$15,000,000; expenditures by nationals abroad U.S.$23,000,000.

Foreign trade

Balance of trade (current prices)

	1981	1982	1983	1984	1985	1986
YRls '000,000	−7,662	−8,235	−9,439	−8,449	−7,782	−8,466
% of total	82.7%	78.4%	83.1%	79.0%	77.2%	78.4%

Imports (1983): U.S.$1,592,819,000 (machinery and transport equipment 24.9%, food and live animals 22.9%, basic manufactured goods 22.0%, mineral fuels 8.8%, chemical products 8.4%, beverages and tobacco 3.3%). *Major import sources* (1985): Italy 9.7%; Japan 8.7%; United Kingdom 8.3%; The Netherlands 6.2%; West Germany 5.9%; France 5.2%; China 2.7%; United States 2.7%; Belgium–Luxembourg 2.4%; Australia 2.4%; Singapore 2.1%; Austria 1.5%; Sweden 1.4%; Greece 1.3%; Denmark 0.7%.
Exports (1983): U.S.$26,766,000 (cereals and preparation 31.9%, power-generating equipment 12.2%, special industrial machines 7.6%, vegetables and fruits 6.7%, hides and skins 4.5%, vulcanized rubber tubes 3.8%, cotton 3.0%, coffee 2.0%). *Major export destinations* (1985): United States 41.4%; Japan 12.6%; The Netherlands 6.9%; France 3.5%; Italy 3.5%; United Kingdom 2.6%; West Germany 1.7%; Singapore 0.2%.

Transport and communications

Transport. Railroads: none. Roads (1986): total length 23,129 mi, 37,223 km (paved 6%). Vehicles (1986): passenger cars 121,015; trucks and buses 176,203. Merchant marine (1987): vessels (100 gross tons and over) 12; total deadweight tonnage 414,590. Air transport (1987)[8]: passenger-mi 363,167,000, passenger-km 584,461,000; short ton-mi cargo 41,279,000, metric ton-km cargo 60,267,000; airports (1988) with scheduled flights 5.
Communications. Daily newspapers (1986): total number 2; total circulation, n.a.; circulation per 1,000 population, n.a. Radio (1986): total number of receivers 200,000 (1 per 35 persons). Television (1987): total number of receivers 150,000 (1 per 56 persons). Telephones (1984): 63,255 (1 per 104 persons).

Education and health

Education (1985–86)

	schools	teachers	students	student/ teacher ratio
Primary (age 7–12)	5,824	15,092	904,487	59.9
Secondary (age 13–18)	942	5,298	121,922	23.0
Voc., teacher tr.	73	445[9]	11,616	...
Higher[7]	1	245	9,024	36.8

Educational attainment (1975). Percent of population age 10 and over having: no formal schooling, 82.6%; reading ability only 5.3%; reading and writing ability 10.6%; primary education, 0.8%; secondary education 0.2%; higher 0.1%; not specified 0.4%. *Literacy* (1986): total population age 15 and over literate 768,200 (18.9%); males literate 698,021 (38.5%); females literate 70,179 (3.1%).
Health (1986): physicians 1,234 (1 per 6,631 persons); hospital beds 5,986 (1 per 1,367 persons); infant mortality rate per 1,000 live births 164.0.
Food (1984–86): daily per capita caloric intake 2,275 (vegetable products 90%, animal products 10%); (1983) 89% of FAO recommended minimum.

Military

Total active duty personnel (1988): 36,600 (army 95.6%, navy 1.7%, air force 2.7%). *Military expenditure as percent of GNP* (1985): 10.0% (world 6.1%); per capita expenditure U.S.$53.

[1]Includes 31 nonelective members. [2]Detail does not add to total given because of rounding. [3]Area shown is according to the Swiss Technical Co-operation Service. The major part of the eastern boundary with Saudi Arabia and Yemen (Aden) is not officially delimited or demarcated; however, the government of Yemen (Ṣan‘ā’) uses a higher estimate of 77,200 sq mi (200,000 sq km). [4]Includes nationals abroad. [5]Based on reported 1986 census result of 8,105,974 resident population. [6]1983. [7]Includes import duties. [8]Yemen Airways only. [9]1983–84.

Yugoslavia

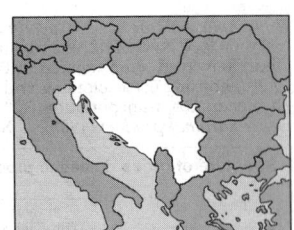

Official name: Socijalistička Federativna Republika Jugoslavija (Macedonian, Serbo-Croatian); Socijalistična Federativna Republika Jugoslavija (Slovenian); (Socialist Federal Republic of Yugoslavia).
Form of government: single-party federal socialist republic with two legislative houses (Chamber of Republics and Provinces [88] and Federal Chamber [220]).
Head of state and government: President.
Capital: Belgrade.
Official languages: Macedonian; Serbo-Croatian; Slovenian.
Official religion: none.
Monetary unit: 1 Yugoslav dinar (Din) = 100 paras; valuation (Oct. 10, 1988) 1 U.S.$ = Din 3,397; 1 £ = Din 5,818.

Area and population		area		population
		sq mi	sq km	1987 estimate
Socialist republics	Capitals			
Bosnia and Hercegovina	Sarajevo	19,741	51,129	4,398,000
Croatia	Zagreb	21,829	56,538	4,672,000
Macedonia	Skopje	9,928	25,713	2,065,000
Montenegro	Titograd	5,333	13,812	625,000
Serbia	Belgrade	21,609	55,968	5,816,000
Slovenia	Ljubljana	7,819	20,251	1,937,000
Autonomous provinces[1]				
Kosovo	Priština	4,203	10,887	1,848,000
Vojvodina	Novi Sad	8,304	21,506	2,050,000
TOTAL		98,766	255,804	23,411,000

Demography

Population (1988): 23,591,000.
Density (1988): persons per sq mi 238.9; persons per sq km 92.2.
Urban–rural (1985): urban 46.5%; rural 53.5%.
Sex distribution (1985): male 49.36%; female 50.64%.
Age breakdown (1985): under 15, 23.5%; 15–29, 23.9%; 30–44, 21.0%; 45–59, 18.8%; 60–74, 9.4%; 75 and over, 3.4%.
Population projection: (1990) 23,915,000; (2000) 25,608,000.
Doubling time: 99 years.
Ethnic composition (1981): Serb 36.3%; Croat 19.7%; Bosnian Muslim 8.9%; Slovenian 7.8%; Albanian 7.7%; Macedonian 6.0%; Montenegrin 2.6%; other 11.0%.
Religious affiliation (1980): Serbian Orthodox 34.6%; Roman Catholic 26.0%; Crypto-Christian 11.3%; Muslim 10.4%; other 17.7%.
Major cities (1981): Belgrade 1,087,915; Zagreb 649,586; Skopje 408,143; Sarajevo 319,017; Ljubljana 224,817.

Vital statistics

Birth rate per 1,000 population (1986): 15.4 (world avg. 26.0); (1982) legitimate 91.6%; illegitimate 8.4%.
Death rate per 1,000 population (1986): 9.1 (world avg. 9.9).
Natural increase rate per 1,000 population (1986): 6.3 (world avg. 16.1).
Total fertility rate (avg. births per childbearing woman; 1984): 2.1.
Marriage rate per 1,000 population (1986): 6.9.
Divorce rate per 1,000 population (1984): 0.9.
Life expectancy at birth (1982–83): male 66.0 years; female 74.0 years.
Major causes of death per 100,000 population (1984): diseases of the circulatory system 470.6; neoplasms 138.0; diseases of the respiratory system 55.7; diseases of the digestive system 40.5.

National economy

Budget (1986). Revenue: Din 1,374,558,400,000 (share in profit of state enterprises 74.5%, import duties 23.6%, other revenue 1.9%). Expenditures: Din 1,374,558,400,000 (national economy 70.4%, social welfare and health 15.6%).
Public debt (external, outstanding; 1986): U.S.$13,173,900,000.
Tourism: receipts from visitors (1985) U.S.$1,050,000,000; expenditures by nationals abroad (1983) U.S.$107,000,000.
Production (metric tons except as noted). Agriculture (1986): corn (maize) 12,502,000, sugar beets 5,615,000, wheat 4,776,000, potatoes 2,519,000, grapes 1,141,000, barley 710,000, plums 708,000, apples 605,000, tomatoes 497,000, melons 451,000, sunflower seeds 449,000, oats 252,000, rye 89,000, tobacco 88,000, rice 36,000; livestock (number of live animals) 7,821,000 pigs, 7,693,000 sheep, 5,034,000 cattle, 78,281,000 poultry; roundwood (1985) 22,428,000 cu m; fish catch 77,453. Mining and quarrying (1987): copper ore 27,745,000; iron ore 6,260,000; lead and zinc ore 3,908,000; bauxite 3,394,000; antimony 48,000; manganese 25,000; silver (refined) 151. Manufacturing (1987): cement 8,963,000; crude steel 4,475,000; rolled steel 4,100,000; pulp and paper 2,803,000; pig iron 2,867,000; sulfuric acid 1,610,000; plastics and resins 644,000[2]; automobile tires 13,723,000 units; radio and television receivers 828,294 units; leather 20,316,000 sq m; cotton fabrics 366,399 sq m. Construction (1985): residential 13,597,000 sq m; industrial 1,664,000 sq m; commercial 798,000 sq m. Energy production (consumption): electricity (kW-hr; 1986) 77,381,000,000 (77,867,000,000);

coal (metric tons; 1986) 68,788,000 (73,274,000); crude petroleum (barrels; 1986) 30,821,000 (111,240,000); petroleum products (metric tons; 1986) 12,589,000 (12,952,000); natural gas (cu m; 1986) 1,833,000,000 (5,091,000,000).
Gross national product (1986): U.S.$144,825,000,000 (U.S.$6,220 per capita).

Structure of gross material product and labour force				
	1986		1981	
	in value Din '000,000	% of total value	labour force	% of labour force
Agriculture	2,924,202	13.2	2,682,828	28.7
Mining and manufacturing	10,339,312	46.7	2,209,693[3]	23.6[3]
Construction	1,525,278	6.9	689,291	7.4
Public utilities	227,775	1.0	[3]	[3]
Transp. and commun.	1,619,525	7.3	445,362	4.8
Trade	4,757,683	21.5	827,575	8.8
Finance	...	...	204,866	2.2
Pub. admin., defense, and services	...	...	1,585,205	16.9
Other	745,187[4]	3.4[4]	713,851[5]	7.6[5]
TOTAL	22,138,962	100.0	9,358,671	100.0

Population economically active (1981): total 9,358,671; activity rate of total population 43.4% (participation rates: ages 20–64, 68.7%; female 38.7%; unemployed [1986] 10.6%).

Price and earnings indexes (1980 = 100)							
	1982	1983	1984	1985	1986	1987	1988[6]
Consumer price index	183.9	257.9	399.0	687.3	1,304.3	2,880.2	5,908.7
Monthly earnings index	175.0	223.0	324.0	574.0	1,176.0	2,077.0	...

Household income and expenditure. Average household size (1983) 3.6; income per household (1986) Din 1,621,374 (U.S.$4,300); sources of income (1985): wages 56.9%, receipts from abroad and interest 12.9%, welfare 11.6%, other 18.6%; expenditure (1986): food 38.3%, transportation 11.8%, beverages and tobacco 11.1%, clothing and footwear 10.2%, housing 8.5%, household utilities 8.2%, recreation 4.0%, health 3.4%.
Land use (1986): forested 36.6%; meadows and pastures 25.0%; agricultural and under permanent cultivation 30.6%; other 7.8%.

Foreign trade

Balance of trade (current prices)						
	1981	1982	1983	1984	1985	1986	1987
Din '000,000,000[7]	−114.4	−747	−564	−437	−407.9	−384	−705
% of total	12.9%	12.5%	9.9%	7.6%	6.8%	6.6%	3.8%

Imports (1987): Din 9,524,073,000,000 (machinery and transport equipment 30.5%, of which nonelectrical machinery 16.5%; mineral fuels 17.4%; chemicals 16.3%; raw materials 9.2%; food and tobacco 5.8%). *Major import sources:* West Germany 18.3%; U.S.S.R. 15.3%; Italy 10.3%; United States 5.7%; Austria 4.5%; France 4.5%; Czechoslovakia 4.3%; Iraq 3.4%.
Exports (1987): Din 8,819,448,000,000 (machinery and transport equipment 30.4%; manufactured goods 26.4%; chemicals 11.3%; food products 8.7%; raw materials 4.9%; mineral fuels 1.9%). *Major export destinations:* U.S.S.R. 19.4%; Italy 13.0%; West Germany 11.6%; Czechoslovakia 3.7%.

Transport and communications

Transport. Railroads (1987): length 5,745 mi, 9,246 km; passenger-km 12,398,000,000; metric ton-km cargo 27,573,000,000. Roads (1987): total length 119,401 km (paved 59%). Vehicles (1987): passenger cars 2,957,116; trucks and buses 283,180. Merchant marine (1987): vessels (100 gross tons and over) 498; total deadweight tonnage 4,939,928. Air transport (1986): passenger-km 7,008,000,000; metric ton-km cargo 110,749,000; airports (1988) 17.
Communications. Daily newspapers (1986): 28; total circulation 2,498,000; circulation per 1,000 population 107. Radio (1986): 4,794,000 receivers (1 per 4.9 persons). Television (1986): 4,126,000 receivers (1 per 5.7 persons). Telephones (1986): 3,598,133 (1 per 6.5 persons).

Education and health

Education (1985–86)	schools	teachers	students	student/ teacher ratio
Primary (age 7–14)	12,148	137,201	2,846,845	20.7
Secondary (age 15–18)	1,212	62,797	952,904	15.2
Higher	103	25,629	349,013	13.6

Educational attainment (1981). Percent of population age 15 and over having: less than full primary education 44.7%; primary 24.2%; secondary 25.5%; higher 5.6%. *Literacy* (1981): total population age 15 and over literate 15,172,877 (89.6%); males 95.5%; females 83.9%.
Health (1986): physicians 40,329 (1 per 577 persons); hospital beds 141,039 (1 per 165 persons); infant mortality rate per 1,000 live births 27.1.
Food (1984–86): daily per capita caloric intake 3,599 (vegetable products 77%, animal products 23%); (1983) 141% of FAO minimum requirement.

Military

Total active duty personnel (1987): 213,500 (army 77.3%, navy 5.8%, air force 16.9%). *Military expenditure as percent of GNP* (1985): 3.7% (world 6.1%); per capita expenditure U.S.$73.

[1]The autonomous provinces are administratively part of the Socialist Republic of Serbia. [2]1986. [3]Public utilities included with mining and manufacturing. [4]Other material activities. [5]Includes unemployed. [6]May. [7]At the parity 1 U.S.$ = Din 451.6.

Zaire

Official name: République du Zaïre (Republic of Zaire).
Form of government: single party republic with one legislative house (Legislative Council [210]).
Head of state and government: President.
Capital: Kinshasa.
Official language: French.
Official religion: none.
Monetary unit: 1 zaïre (Z) = 100 makuta (singular likuta) = 10,000 sengi; valuation (Oct. 10,1988) 1 U.S.\$ = Z 206.48; 1 £ = Z 353.60.

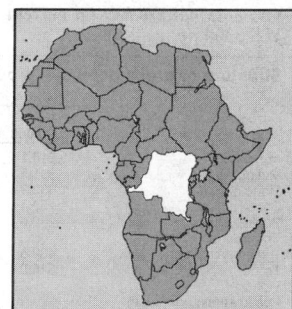

Area and population

Regions	Capitals	area sq mi	area sq km	population 1984 census
Bandundu	Bandundu	114,154	295,658	3,682,845
Bas-Zaire	Matadi	20,819	53,920	1,971,520
Equateur	Mbandaka	155,712	403,293	3,405,512
Haut-Zaire	Kisangani	194,302	503,239	4,206,069
Kasai Occidental	Kananga	60,605	156,967	2,287,416
Kasai Oriental	Mbuji-Mayi	64,949	168,216	2,402,603
Kivu	Bukavu	99,098	256,662	5,187,865
Shaba (Katanga)	Lubumbashi	191,879	496,965	3,874,019
Neutral City				
Kinshasa		3,848	9,965	2,653,558
TOTAL		905,365[1]	2,344,885	29,671,407

Demography

Population (1988): 32,559,000.
Density (1988): persons per sq mi 36.0, persons per sq km 13.9.
Urban–rural (1985): urban 44.2%; rural 55.8%.
Sex distribution (1984): male 49.18%; female 50.82%.
Age breakdown (1985): under 15, 45.2%; 15–29, 26.0%; 30–44, 15.5%; 45–59, 8.7%; 60–74, 3.9%; 75 and over, 0.7%.
Population projection: (1990) 34,138,000; (2000) 42,980,000.
Doubling time: 24 years.
Ethnic composition (1983): Luba 18.0%; Kongo 16.1%; Mongo 13.5%; Rwanda 10.3%; Azande 6.1%; Bangi and Ngale 5.8%; Rundi 3.8%; Teke 2.7%; Boa 2.3%; Chokwe 1.8%; Lugbara 1.6%; Banda 1.4%; Konzo 1.4%; other 15.2%.
Religious affiliation (1980): Roman Catholic 48.4%; Protestant 29.0%; indigenous Christian 17.1%; traditional beliefs 3.4%; Muslim 1.4%; other 0.7%.
Major cities (1984): Kinshasa 2,653,558; Lubumbashi 543,268; Mbuji-Mayi 423,363; Kananga 290,898; Kisangani 282,650.

Vital statistics

Birth rate per 1,000 population (1980–85): 45.1 (world avg. 29.0).
Death rate per 1,000 population (1980–85): 15.8 (world avg. 11.0).
Natural increase rate per 1,000 population (1980–85): 29.3 (world avg. 18.0).
Total fertility rate (avg. births per childbearing woman; 1980–85): 6.1.
Marriage rate per 1,000 population (1977): 0.07[2].
Divorce rate per 1,000 population (1977): 0.02.
Life expectancy at birth (1984): male 49.0 years; female 53.0 years.
Major causes of death per 100,000 population[3] (1977): measles 9.6; meningitis 1.1; influenza 0.4; whooping cough 0.3.

National economy

Budget (1988). Revenue: Z 148,000,000,000 (1986; direct and indirect taxes 91.4%, of which external trade taxes 33.7%, income tax 31.4%, sales tax 22.8%; other revenue 8.6%). Expenditures: Z 153,000,000,000 (1985; service of external debt 33.4%; government salaries 23.5%; service of internal debt 8.8%).
Public debt (external, outstanding; 1986): U.S.\$5,429,900,000.
Tourism (1986): receipts from visitors U.S.\$16,000,000; expenditures by nationals abroad U.S.\$43,000,000.
Production (metric tons except as noted). Agriculture, forestry, fishing (1986): cassava 15,570,000, plantains 1,500,000, sugarcane 1,050,000, corn (maize) 730,000, peanuts (groundnuts) 400,000, sweet potatoes 365,000, bananas 325,000, rice 300,000, yams 220,000, papayas 170,000, pineapples 170,000, mangoes 150,000, oranges 147,000, pulses 127,000, coffee 90,000, seed cotton 74,000, palm kernels 70,000, tomatoes 43,000, natural rubber 23,000; livestock (number of live animals) 2,930,000 goats, 1,400,000 cattle, 780,000 sheep, 770,000 pigs, 18,000,000 chickens; roundwood 31,418,000 cu m; fish catch 101,000. Mining and quarrying (1986): copper 476,600; lime 110,000; zinc 63,930; cobalt 10,677; tin 3,100; silver 38; gold 63,022 troy oz; industrial diamonds 20,400,000 carats; gem diamonds 7,500,000 carats. Manufacturing (1985): cement 480,000; corn flour 119,000; cotton textiles 58,000,000 sq m; cigarettes 4,100,000,000 units; bicycles 13,970 units[4]; trucks 2,335 units[4]; beer 4,222,000 hectolitres; carbonated beverages 880,000 hectolitres; leather shoes 2,600,000 pairs. Construction (1985): residential 20,000 sq m; nonresidential 39,000 sq m. Energy production (consumption): electricity (kW-hr; 1986) 4,619,000,000 (4,521,000,000); coal (metric tons; 1986) 127,000 (167,000); crude petroleum (barrels; 1986) 9,456,000 (2,236,000); petroleum products (metric tons; 1986) 478,000 (422,000); natural gas, none (n.a.).
Household income and expenditure. Average household size (1982) 6.0; average annual income per household Z 1,200 (U.S.\$209); sources of income: wages and salaries, small-scale trading; expenditure (1985): food 61.7%, housing and energy 11.5%, clothing and footwear 9.7%, transportation 5.9%, furniture and utensils 4.9%, medical care 2.6%, recreation and education 2.0%.
Gross national product (1986): U.S.\$5,070,000,000 (U.S.\$160 per capita).

Structure of gross domestic product and labour force

	1984 in value Z '000,000	1984 % of total value	1985 labour force	1985 % of labour force
Agriculture	31,584.7[5]	31.7	8,844,000	68.0
Mining	24,713.4	24.8		
Manufacturing	1,953.2	2.0		
Construction	5,012.4[6]	5.1	1,886,000	14.5
Public utilities	46.7	.7		
Transp. and commun.	999.7	1.0		
Trade	18,523.9	18.6		
Finance				
Pub. admin., defense	15,221.4	15.3	2,276,000	17.5
Services				
Other	1,528.0[8]	1.5[8]		
TOTAL	99,583.4	100.0	13,006,000	100.0

Population economically active (1985): total 13,006,000; activity rate of total population 40.7% (participation rates; age 15–64, 75.1%; female 33.4%; unemployed, n.a.).

Price and earnings indexes (1980 = 100)

	1981	1982	1983	1984	1985	1986	1987
Consumer price index	134.9	183.8	325.5	495.6	613.6	900.3	1,714.0
Annual earnings index	103.1	117.0	298.2	808.1	1,009.9	...	...

Land use (1985): forested 77.7%; meadows and pastures 4.1%; agricultural and under permanent cultivation 2.9%; other 15.3%.

Foreign trade

Balance of trade (current prices)

	1982	1983	1984	1985	1986	1987
Z '000,000	−445.4	+7,102.7	+11,554.3	+13,339.7	+13,228	+36,258
% of total	9.0%	34.2%	18.9%	16.4%	11.3%	19.8%

Imports (1987): Z 73,274,000,000 (1984; machinery and transport equipment 54.0%, of which transport equipment 21.4%, electrical machinery 8.1%; manufactured goods 21.1%; food, beverages, and tobacco 20.7%; chemical products 13.7%; textiles and clothing 4.8%). *Major import sources:* China 37.4%; Belgium–Luxembourg 15.6%; France 7.9%; West Germany 7.2%; U.S. 5.5%; Japan 2.5%.
Exports (1987): Z 109,532,000,000 (1985; minerals 90.1%, of which copper 41.0%; crude petroleum 18.9%; cobalt 13.6%, diamonds 12.3%, zinc 2.9%; coffee 4.8%). *Major export destinations:* Belgium–Luxembourg 35.9%; U.S. 18.4%; West Germany 11.2%; France 7.8%.

Transport and communications

Transport. Railroads (1986)[9]: length 3,180 mi, 5,118 km; passenger-mi 181,150,000, passenger-km 291,534,000; short ton-mi cargo 1,339,047,000, metric ton-km cargo 1,954,976,000. Roads (1981): total length 28,379 mi, 45,671 km (paved 18%). Vehicles (1985): passenger cars 24,253; trucks and buses 60,528. Merchant marine (1987): vessels (100 gross tons and over) 30; total deadweight tonnage 75,932. Air transport (1987)[10]: passenger-mi 302,349,000, passenger-km 486,584,000; short ton-mi cargo 35,975,000, metric ton-km cargo 52,526,000; airports (1988) with scheduled flights 22.
Communications. Daily newspapers (1987): total number 4; total circulation 45,000[11]; circulation per 1,000 population 1.6[11]. Radio (1986): 525,000 receivers (1 per 59 persons). Television (1987): 16,000 receivers (1 per 1,988 persons). Telephones (1986): 38,845 (1 per 800 persons).

Education and health

Education (1985–86)

	schools	teachers	students	student/teacher ratio
Primary (age 6–11)	10,065[11]	112,077[11]	4,993,523	44.6
Secondary (age 12–17)	3,972[11]	43,459[11]	3,198,051	...
Voc., teacher tr.	20[12]		319,805	...
Higher	36	3,072[11]	37,706[11]	12.3

Educational attainment, n.a. *Literacy* (1985): total population age 15 and over literate 11,004,000 (61.2%); males literate 6,872,000 (78.6%); females literate 4,132,000 (44.7%).
Health (1982): physicians 2,000 (1 per 14,092 persons); hospital beds 74,000 (1 per 385 persons); infant mortality rate per 1,000 live births (1983) 106.
Food (1984–86): daily per capita caloric intake 2,160 (vegetable products 97%, animal products 3%); (1983) 96% of FAO recommended minimum.

Military

Total active duty personnel (1988): 26,000 (army 84.6%, navy 5.8%, air force 9.6%). *Military expenditure as percent of GNP* (1985): 1.7% (world 6.1%); per capita expenditure U.S.\$5.

---

[1]Detail does not add to total given because of rounding. [2]Registered marriages only. [3]Infectious diseases only. [4]1984. [5]Includes Z 18,069,500,000 in the subsistence sector. [6]Includes Z 1,670,800,000 in the subsistence sector. [7]Less than 0.1%. [8]Import taxes and duties less imputed bank service charge. [9]Traffic statistics are for 1985 and for services operated by the Zaire National Railways (SNCZ), which controls more than 90% of the country's total rail facility. [10]Air Zaire only. [11]1983–84. [12]1977–78.

Zambia

Official name: Republic of Zambia.
Form of government: republic with
one legislative house (National
Assembly [136]).
Head of state and government:
President.
Capital: Lusaka.
Official language: English.
Official religion: none.
Monetary unit: 1 Zambian kwacha
(K) = 100 ngwee; valuation (Oct.
10, 1988) 1 U.S.$ = K 8.00;
1 £ = K 13.70.

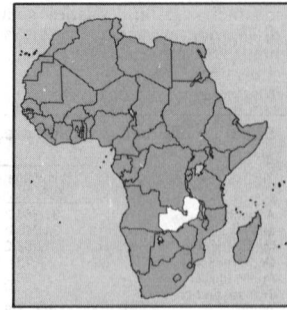

Area and population		area		population
		sq mi	sq km	1987 estimate
Provinces	**Capitals**			
Central	Kabwe	36,446	94,395	669,432
Copperbelt	Ndola	12,096	31,328	1,707,559
Eastern	Chipata	26,682	69,106	783,398
Luapula	Mansa	19,524	50,567	500,833
Lusaka	Lusaka	8,454	21,896	1,030,615
Northern	Kasama	57,076	147,826	795,003
North-Western	Solwezi	48,582	125,827	376,480
Southern	Livingstone	32,928	85,283	849,103
Western	Mongu	48,798	126,386	555,104
TOTAL		290,586	752,614	7,267,527

Demography

Population (1988): 7,384,000.
Density (1988): persons per sq mi 25.4, persons per sq km 9.8.
Urban–rural (1985): urban 49.5%; rural 50.5%.
Sex distribution (1985): male 49.69%; female 50.31%.
Age breakdown (1985): under 15, 47.3%; 15–29, 25.8%; 30–44, 14.4%; 45–59,
8.1%; 60–74, 3.6%; 75 and over, 0.8%.
Population projection: (1990) 7,912,000; (2000) 11,237,000.
Doubling time: 20 years.
Ethnolinguistic composition (1980): Bemba tribes 36.2%; Maravi (Nyanja)
tribes 17.6%; Tonga tribes 15.1%; North-Western tribes 10.1%; Barotze
tribes 8.2%; Mambwe tribes 4.6%; Tumbuka tribes 4.6%; other 3.6%.
Religious affiliation (1980): Christian 72.0%, of whom Protestant 34.2%,
Roman Catholic 26.2%, African Christian 8.3%; traditional beliefs 27.0%;
Muslim 0.3%; other 0.7%.
Major cities (1987): Lusaka 818,994; Kitwe 449,442; Ndola 418,142; Mufulira
192,323.

Vital statistics

Birth rate per 1,000 population (1980–85): 48.1 (world avg. 29.0); legitimate,
n.a.; however, marriage is both early and universal, suggesting that legiti-
mate births are a relatively high proportion of all births.
Death rate per 1,000 population (1980–85): 15.1 (world avg. 11.0).
Natural increase rate per 1,000 population (1980–85): 33.0 (world avg. 18.0).
Total fertility rate (avg. births per childbearing woman; 1980–85): 6.8.
Marriage rate per 1,000 population: n.a.
Divorce rate per 1,000 population: n.a.
Life expectancy at birth (1980–85): male 49.6 years; female 53.1 years.
Major causes of death per 100,000 population: n.a.; however, among the
nearly 7,000,000 visits to outpatient clinics in 1982, nearly two-thirds of
the reported illnesses were related to nutritional deficiencies and infectious
and parasitic diseases.

National economy

Budget (1988). Revenue: K 5,552,000,000 (customs duties and excise taxes
44.5%; income tax 33.1%; mineral revenue 0.2%). Expenditures: K 6,350,-
000,000 (constitutional and statutory expenditures 36.6%; other, including
education, health, land development, and police 63.4%).
Production (metric tons except as noted). Agriculture, forestry, fishing
(1986): sugarcane 1,180,000, corn (maize) 1,112,000, fruits and vegetables
338,000 (of which tomatoes 27,000, onions 25,000, oranges 4,000), cassava
220,000, sorghum 45,000, sunflower seeds 43,000, sweet potatoes 23,000,
peanuts (groundnuts) 15,000, lint cotton 12,000, millet 12,000, pulses 6,000,
tobacco 4,000; livestock (number of live animals) 2,770,000 cattle, 240,000
goats, 207,000 pigs, 46,000 sheep, 14,000,000 chickens; roundwood (1985)
9,891,000; fish catch (1985) 67,731. Mining and quarrying (production year
ending March 31, 1986): copper 543,000; zinc 32,000; lead 15,000; cobalt
4,400; gold 7,903 oz. Manufacturing (1984): sulfuric acid 276,900; raw sugar
141,000; nitrogen fertilizer 86,013[1]; cement 75,000 cu m. Construction
(value in K; 1983): buildings 151,100,000; other construction 43,200,000.
Energy production (consumption): electricity (kW-hr; 1986) 10,100,000,000
(7,020,000,000); coal (metric tons; 1986) 564,000 (554,000); crude petroleum
(barrels; 1986) none (4,178,000); petroleum products (metric tons; 1986)
478,000 (422,000); natural gas, none (n.a.).
Population economically active (1985): total 2,221,000; activity rate of total
population 33.3% (participation rates: ages 15–64, 60.1%; female 28.2%;
unemployed [1982] 0.6%).

Price and earnings indexes (1980 = 100)							
	1981	1982	1983	1984	1985	1986	1987[2]
Consumer price index	114.0	128.2	153.4	184.1	253.0	383.6	636.3
Monthly earnings index	...	...	...	...	...	...	...

Gross national product (at current market prices; 1986): U.S.$2,060,000,000
(U.S.$300 per capita).

Structure of gross domestic product and labour force				
	1985			
	in value K '000,000	% of total value	labour force	% of labour force
Agriculture	916.1	14.5	1,587,000	71.5
Mining	901.5	14.2		
Manufacturing	1,392.9	22.0		
Construction	133.4	2.1	227,000	10.2
Public utilities	72.6	1.2		
Transportation and communications	432.5	6.8		
Trade	816.0	12.9		
Finance	...[3]	...[3]	407,000	18.3
Public admin., defense, and services	...[3]	...[3]		
Other	1,667.1[3]	26.3[3]		
TOTAL	6,332.1	100.0	2,221,000	100.0

Household income and expenditure. Average household size (1981) 5.8; average annual income per household (1981) K 1,041 (U.S.$908); sources of
income (1981): wages and salaries 94.0%, other 6.0%; expenditure (1977):
food 37.7%, housing 11.0%, clothing 8.3%, transportation 4.3%, education
2.1%, health 1.0%.
Public debt (external, outstanding; 1986): U.S.$3,574,700,000.
Tourism: receipts from visitors (1986) U.S.$7,000,000; expenditures by na-
tionals abroad (1983) U.S.$31,000,000.
Land use (1985): forested 39.7%; meadows and pastures 47.2%; agricultural
and under permanent cultivation 7.0%; other 6.1%.

Foreign trade

Balance of trade (current prices)						
	1981	1982	1983	1984	1985	1986
K '000,000	12.1	20.5	154.4	80.4	−124.0	−1,373.3
% of total	0.7%	1.1%	8.0%	3.5%	4.0%	18.2%

Imports (1984): K 1,107,866,000 (machinery and transport equipment 28.7%;
basic manufactures 16.3%; chemicals 14.5%; food 4.6%; mineral fuels, lubricants, and electricity 4.5%). *Major import sources:* South Africa 21.1%;
United Kingdom 12.5%; United States 6.4%; West Germany 5.4%; Japan
3.3%; China 0.2%.
Exports (1984): K 1,188,098,000 (copper 86.8%; zinc 4.3%; cobalt 1.6%;
lead 0.5%; tobacco 0.4%). *Major export destinations:* Japan 23.4%; United
States 9.5%; China 9.4%; United Kingdom 5.8%; West Germany 3.6%;
South Africa 0.8%.

Transport and communications

Transport. Railroads (1985): length[4] 1,340 mi, 2,157 km; passenger-mi
346,834,000, passenger-km 558,176,000; short ton-mi cargo 1,072,208,000,
metric ton-km cargo 1,565,496,000. Roads (1986): total length 23,135 mi,
37,232 km (paved 17%). Vehicles (1982): passenger cars 105,783; trucks and
buses 94,780. Merchant marine: vessels (100 gross tons and over) none.
Air transport (1986): passenger-mi 395,000,000, passenger-km 636,000,000;
short ton-mi cargo 17,244,000, metric ton-km cargo 25,176,000; airports
(1988) with scheduled flights 11.
Communications. Daily newspapers (1987): total number 2; total circulation
105,000; circulation per 1,000 population 15. Radio (1986): total number
of receivers 1,000,000 (1 per 7 persons). Television (1987): total number
of receivers 200,000 (1 per 36 persons). Telephones (1986): 85,385 (1
per 82 persons).

Education and health

Education (1986)	schools	teachers	students	student/ teacher ratio
Primary (age 7–13)	3,164	29,841	1,442,133	48.3
Secondary (age 14–18)	276	5,627	150,298	26.8
Voc., teacher tr.	28	1,055	9,687	9.2
Higher[5]	1	613	4,860	7.9

Educational attainment (1980). Percent of population age 25 and over
having: no formal schooling 54.7%; some primary education 34.4%; some
secondary 10.5%; higher 0.4%. *Literacy* (1980): total population literate
2,128,500 (68.6%); males literate 1,207,300 (79.3%); females literate 921,200
(58.3%).
Health (1984): physicians 798 (1 per 10,008 persons); hospital beds 21,668 (1
per 297 persons); infant mortality rate per 1,000 live births (1980–85) 88.0.
Food (1983–85): daily per capita caloric intake 2,123 (vegetable products
95%, animal products 5%); (1983) 83% of FAO recommended minimum
daily requirement.

Military

Total active duty personnel (1987): 16,200 (army 92.6%; navy, none; air force
7.4%). *Military expenditure as percent of GNP* (1985): 6.8% (world 6.1%);
per capita expenditure U.S.$24.

[1]1983. [2]November. [3]Other includes Finance and Public admin., defense, and services. [4]1986. [5]1985.

Zimbabwe

Official name: Republic of Zimbabwe.
Form of government: unitary
single-party republic with two
legislative houses (Senate [40[1]]; House
of Assembly [100]).
Head of state and government[2]:
President.
Capital: Harare.
Official language: English.
Official religion: none.
Monetary unit: 1 Zimbabwe Dollar
(Z$) = 100 cents; valuation (Oct. 10,
1988) 1 U.S.$ = Z$1.88; 1 £ = Z$3.22.

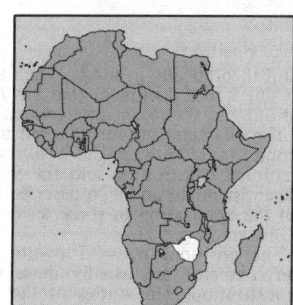

Area and population		area		population
		sq mi	sq km	1982 census
Provinces	Capitals			
Manicaland	Mutare	13,463	34,870	1,099,202
Mashonaland Central	Bindura	10,534	27,284	563,407
Mashonaland East	Harare	9,627	24,934	1,495,984
Mashonaland West	Chinhoyi	23,346	60,467	858,962
Masvingo (Victoria)	Masvingo	17,108	44,310	1,031,697
Matabeleland North	Bulawayo	28,393	73,537	885,339
Matabeleland South	Gwanda	25,633	66,390	519,636
Midlands	Gweru	22,767	58,967	1,091,844
TOTAL		150,873[3]	390,759	7,546,071

Demography

Population (1988): 8,878,000.
Density (1988): persons per sq mi 58.8, persons per sq km 22.7.
Urban–rural (1982): urban 25.7%; rural 74.3%.
Sex distribution (1987): male 49.07%; female 50.93%.
Age breakdown (1987): under 15, 44.9%; 15–29, 29.2%; 30–44, 14.6%; 45–59, 7.3%; 60–74, 3.1%; 75 and over, 0.9%.
Population projection: (1990) 9,369,000; (2000) 11,943,000.
Doubling time: 20 years.
Ethnolinguistic composition (1982): African 97.6%, of which Shona-speaking Bantu 70.8%; Ndebele-speaking Bantu 15.8%; European 2.0%; Asian 0.1%; other 0.3%.
Religious affiliation (1980): Christian 44.8%, of which Protestant (including Anglican) 17.5%, African indigenous 13.6%, Roman Catholic 11.7%; animist 40.4%; other 14.8%.
Major cities (1983): Harare 681,000; Bulawayo 429,000; Chitungwiza 202,000; Gweru 78,900[4]; Mutare 69,600[4].

Vital statistics

Birth rate per 1,000 population (1982–87): 37.9 (world avg. 26.0).
Death rate per 1,000 population (1982–87): 11.2 (world avg. 9.9).
Natural increase rate per 1,000 population (1982–87): 26.7 (world avg. 16.1).
Total fertility rate (avg. births per childbearing woman; 1987): 4.9.
Marriage rate per 1,000 population: n.a.
Divorce rate per 1,000 population: n.a.
Life expectancy at birth (1987): male 57.9 years; female 61.4 years.
Major causes of death per 100,000 population[5] (1982): accidents and violence 46.6; infectious and parasitic diseases 32.2; diseases of the respiratory system 25.4; diseases of the circulatory system 24.5; malnutrition 15.5.

National economy

Budget (1987–88). Revenue: Z$3,661,287,000 (income tax 44.0%, sales tax 14.9%, customs duties 14.0%, excise tax 8.7%, international aid grants 5.7%, revenue from investments and property 5.1%, pension contributions 2.7%). Expenditures: Z$5,206,114,000 (debt service 21.2%, education 15.2%, defense 13.9%, health 5.1%, social security and welfare 1.3%).
Tourism: receipts from visitors (1986) U.S.$45,000,000; expenditures by nationals abroad U.S.$38,000,000.
Population economically active (1982): total 2,484,070; activity rate of total population 33.1% (participation rates: over age 15, 63.5%; female 39.2%; unemployed 19.0%[6]).

Price and earnings indexes (1980 = 100)						
	1982	1983	1984	1985	1986	1987	1988[7]
Consumer price index	125.2	154.1	185.2	200.9	229.7	258.3	266.1
Monthly earnings index	155.1	168.5	168.8	170.0	...	...	...

Production (value of production in Z$ except as noted). Agriculture, forestry, fishing (1986–87): tobacco 365,035,000, corn (maize) 283,586,000, cotton 183,919,000, beef 148,908,000, sugar 146,940,000, milk and dairy products 86,882,000, wheat 74,107,000, coffee 73,890,000, soybeans 28,059,000; livestock (number of live animals; 1986) 5,364,000 cattle, 1,880,000 goats, 457,000 sheep, 194,000 pigs, 9,000,000 chickens; roundwood 7,109,000 cu m; fish catch 17,500 metric tons. Mining and quarrying (1987): gold 349,800,000; coal 103,400,000; asbestos 97,000,000; nickel 73,400,000; copper 45,900,000; chrome 44,100,000; iron ore 27,171,000; silver 10,812,000; tin 10,767,000. Manufacturing (1984–85): foodstuffs 985,300,000; metals and metal products 695,500,000; chemicals and petroleum products 645,800,000; beverages and tobacco 504,700,000; textiles, canvas, and yarns 484,500,000; clothing and footwear 235,700,000; paper, printing, and publishing 215,400,000; transport equipment 161,600,000; wood and furniture 113,500,000; nonmetallic mineral products 108,600,000; other manufactured goods 45,600,000. Construction (Z$; 1986): residential 40,285,000; nonresidential 92,229,000. Energy production (consumption): electricity (kW-hr;

1986) 5,988,000,000 (8,988,000,000); coal (metric tons; 1986) 4,047,000 (4,034,000); crude petroleum, none (none); petroleum products (metric tons; 1986) none (638,000); natural gas, none (none).
Public debt (external, outstanding; 1986): U.S.$1,711,600,000.
Household income and expenditure. Average household size (1980) 5.8; income per household Z$1,689 (U.S.$2,628); sources of income: n.a.; expenditure (1985): food and nonalcoholic beverages 35.3%, clothing, footwear, and textiles 12.2%, household durable goods 9.3%, energy 8.7%, housing 7.3%, transportation 4.0%, education 3.2%, health service 1.6%, recreation 1.4%.
Gross national product (1986): U.S.$5,410,000,000 (U.S.$620 per capita).

Structure of gross domestic product and labour force				
	1986		1985	
	in value Z$'000,000	% of total value	labour force[8]	% of labour force
Agriculture	935	11.4	276,800	26.1
Mining	571	6.9	54,100	5.1
Manufacturing	2,489	30.2	171,400	16.2
Construction	239	2.9	45,700	4.3
Public utilities	463	5.6	7,800	0.7
Transp. and commun.	467	5.7	50,400	4.8
Trade	1,071	13.0	78,800	7.4
Finance	455	5.5	15,500	1.5
Pub. admin., defense	508	6.2	91,800	8.7
Services	1,224	14.9	266,400	25.2
Other	−190[9]	−2.3[9]		
TOTAL	8,232	100.0	1,058,700	100.0

Land use (1985): forested 61.6%; meadows and pastures 12.6%; agricultural and under permanent cultivation 6.9%; other 18.9%.

Foreign trade

Balance of trade (current prices)						
	1981	1982	1983	1984	1985	1986
Z$'000,000	83.0	160.0	84.0	185.0	349.0	529.9
% of total	2.8%	5.7%	3.8%	8.6%	10.8%	13.9%

Imports (1986): Z$1,640,400,000 (machinery and transport equipment 36.9%, of which transport equipment 11.8%; fuels 31.4%, of which petroleum products 25.7%; chemicals 15.9%; basic manufactures 14.5%, of which textile yarns and fabrics 3.6%, iron and steel 2.4%). *Major import sources:* South Africa 21.4%; United Kingdom 10.9%; West Germany 9.9%; United States 8.3%; Botswana 4.7%; Japan 4.3%; Italy 4.3%; France 3.3%; Zambia 2.6%; The Netherlands 1.6%.
Exports (1986): Z$2,170,300,000 (domestic exports 78.3%, of which tobacco 19.4%; gold sales 19.0%; ferroalloys 9.4%; cotton 6.1%; corn [maize] 4.0%; asbestos 3.8%; nickel metal 3.8%; sugar 2.1%; reexports 2.6%). *Major export destinations*[10]: United Kingdom 12.4%; South Africa 12.3%; West Germany 8.6%; The Netherlands 6.1%; Italy 5.9%; Japan 4.6%; Botswana 4.3%; Belgium 3.2%; China 2.8%; Zambia 2.8%.

Transport and communications

Transport. Railroads (1986): route length 2,109 mi, 3,394 km; number of passengers 2,713,000; short ton-mi cargo 9,390,000,000, metric ton-km cargo 13,710,000,000. Roads (1985): total length 48,421 mi, 77,927 km (paved 17%). Vehicles (1985): passenger cars 253,470; trucks and buses 28,839. Merchant marine: none. Air transport (1986): passenger-mi 403,000,000, passenger-km 648,000,000; short ton-mi cargo 8,565,300, metric ton-km cargo 12,505,200; airports (1988) with scheduled flights 8.
Communications. Daily newspapers (1985): total number 3; total circulation 191,000; circulation per 1,000 population 23. Radio (1986): 315,000 receivers (1 per 27 persons). Television (1987): 112,000 receivers (1 per 77 persons). Telephones (1986): 256,369 (1 per 33 persons).

Education and health

Education (1986)				
	schools	teachers	students	student/ teacher ratio
Primary (age 7–13)	4,297	57,823	2,260,367	39.1
Secondary (age 14–19)	1,262[11]	19,560	545,841	27.9
Voc., teacher tr.	14[12]	1,031[12]	30,935	...
Higher	1	431[13]	5,866	...

Educational attainment (1969). Percent of population age 17 and over having: no formal schooling 41.6%; some primary education 36.5%; primary 13.6%; secondary 3.3%; other 5.0%. *Literacy* (1985): total population age 15 and over literate 3,413,000 (76.0%); males literate 1,846,000 (81.5%); females literate 1,567,000 (66.8%).
Health: physicians (1986) 1,257 (1 per 6,687 persons); hospital beds (1984) 19,407 (1 per 433 persons); infant mortality rate per 1,000 live births (1985) 61.0.
Food (1984–86): daily per capita caloric intake 2,120 (vegetable products 93%, animal products 7%); (1983) 82% of FAO minimum requirement.

Military

Total active duty personnel (1987): 47,000 (army 97.9%, air force 2.1%). *Military expenditure as percent of GNP* (1985): 6.3% (world 6.1%); per capita expenditure U.S.$41.

[1]Includes six nonelective seats. [2]In October 1987, Parliament passed a constitutional amendment whereby the presidency became an executive post, incorporating the former post of prime minister. [3]Detail does not add to total given because of rounding. [4]1982. [5]Registered deaths. [6]Excludes communal workers. [7]April. [8]Wage-earning workers only. [9]Imputed bank service charges. [10]Excludes gold sales and reexports. [11]Includes vocational. [12]Teacher training only. [13]1984.

Government and international organizations

This table summarizes principal facts about the governments of the countries of the world, their branches and organs, the topmost layers of local government comprising each country's chief administrative subdivisions, and the participation of their central governments in the principal intergovernmental organizations of the world.

In this table "date of independence" may refer to a variety of circumstances. In the case of the newest countries, those that attained full independence after World War II, the date given is usually just what is implied by the heading—the date when the country, within its present borders, attained full sovereignty over both its internal and external affairs. In the case of longer established countries, the choice of a single date may be somewhat more complicated, and grounds for the use of several different dates often exist. The reader interested in this subject should refer to *Macropædia* and *Micropædia* articles on national histories and relevant historical acts. In cases of territorial annexation or dissolution, the date given here refers either to the final act of union of a state comprised of smaller entities or to the final act of separation from a larger whole (*e.g.*, the separation of Bangladesh from Pakistan in 1971).

The date of the current, or last, constitution is in some ways a less complicated question, but governments sometimes do not, upon taking power, either adhere to existing constitutional forms or trouble to terminate the previous document and legitimize themselves by the installation of new constitutional forms. Often, however, the desire to legitimize extraconstitutional political activity by associating it with existing forms of long precedent leads to partial or incomplete modification, suspension, or abrogation of a constitution, so that the actual day-to-day conduct of government may be largely unrelated to the provisions of a constitution

still theoretically in force. When a date in this column is given in italics, it refers to a document that has been suspended, abolished by extraconstitutional action, or modified extensively.

The characterizations adopted under "type of government" represent a compromise between the ideal forms provided for by the language of the national constitution and the more pragmatic language that a political scientist might adopt to describe these same systems. For an explanation of the application of these terms in the Britannica World Data, *see* the Glossary at p. 533.

The positions denoted by the terms "chief of state" and "head of government" are usually those identified with those functions by the constitution. The duties of the chief of state may range from largely ceremonial responsibilities, with little or no authority over the day-to-day conduct of government, to complete executive authority as the effective head of government. In certain countries, an official of a political party or a revolutionary figure entirely outside the constitutional structure may effectively exercise the powers of both positions.

Membership in the legislative house(s) of each country as given here includes all elected or appointed members, as well as ex officio members (those who by virtue of some other office or title are members of the body), whether voting or nonvoting. The legislature of a country with a unicameral system is shown as the upper house in this table.

The number of administrative subdivisions for each country is listed down to the second level. A single country may, depending on its size, complexity, and historical antecedents, have as many as five levels of administrative subordination (as does the U.S.S.R.) or it may have none at all. Each level of subordination may have several kinds of subdivisions.

Government and international organizations

country	date of independence[a]	date of current or last constitution[b]	type of government	executive branch[c] chief of state	head of government	legislative branch[d] upper house (members)	lower house (members)	admin. subdivisions first-order (number)	second-order (number)	seaward claims territorial (nautical miles)	fishing/economic (nautical miles)
Afghanistan	Aug. 19, 1919	Nov. 30, 1987	people's republic	president		128	234	30	185	—	—
Albania	Nov. 28, 1912	Dec. 27, 1976	socialist republic	chairman PPA	chairman CM	250	—	27	3,315	15	1
Algeria	July 5, 1962	Nov. 19, 1976	socialist republic	president		295	—	48	1,541	12	1
American Samoa	—	July 1, 1967	territory (U.S.)	U.S. president	governor	18	20	3	15	3	200
Andorra	Dec. 6, 1288	—	coprincipality	[3]	chief executive	28	—	7	—	—	—
Angola	Nov. 11, 1975	Nov. 11, 1975	people's republic	president		290	—	18	139	20	200
Anguilla	—	April 1, 1982	territory (U.K.)	British monarch	[4]	11	—	—	—	3	200
Antigua and Barbuda	Nov. 1, 1981	Nov. 1, 1981	constitutional monarchy	British monarch	prime minister	17	17	8	—	12	200
Argentina	July 9, 1816	July 9, 1853	federal republic	president		46	254	24	488	200	1
Aruba	—	Dec. 29, 1954	integral part of Neth.	Dutch monarch	[5]	21	—	...	...	12	200
Australia	Jan. 1, 1901	July 9, 1900	federal parl. state[7]	British monarch	prime minister	76	148	8	866	3	200
Austria	Oct. 30, 1918	Oct. 1, 1920	federal republic	president	chancellor	63	183	9	98	—	—
Bahamas, The	July 10, 1973	July 10, 1973	constitutional monarchy	British monarch	prime minister	16	49	—	17	3	200
Bahrain	Aug. 15, 1971	Dec. 6, 1973	monarchy (emirate)	emir	prime minister	x	—	11	—	3	1
Bangladesh	March 26, 1971	Dec. 16, 1972	republic	president		330	—	4	64	12	200
Barbados	Nov. 30, 1966	Nov. 30, 1966	constitutional monarchy	British monarch	prime minister	21	27	11	—	12	200
Belgium	Oct. 4, 1830	Feb. 7, 1831	constitutional monarchy	monarch	prime minister	183	212	9	—	12	200[8]
Belize	Sept. 21, 1981	Sept. 21, 1981	constitutional monarchy	British monarch	prime minister	8	28	6	—	3	1
Benin	Aug. 1, 1960	Aug. 26, 1977	people's republic	president		196	—	6	84	200	1
Bermuda	—	June 8, 1968	colony (U.K.)	British monarch	[9]	11	40	11	—	3	200
Bhutan	March 24, 1910	—	[10]	king		151	—	18	—	—	—
Bolivia	Aug. 6, 1825	Feb. 2, 1967	republic	president		27	130	9	99	—	—
Botswana	Sept. 30, 1966	March 3, 1965	republic	president		15[11]	40	11	—	—	—
Brazil	Sept. 7, 1822	Oct. 5, 1988	federal republic	president		72	487	27	3,963	200	200
British Virgin Islands	—	June 1, 1977	colony (U.K.)	British monarch	[4]	12	—	—	—	3	200
Brunei	Jan. 1, 1984	*Sept. 29, 1959*	monarchy (sultanate)	sultan		21	—	4	—	12	200
Bulgaria	Oct. 5, 1908	May 18, 1971	socialist republic	chairman SC	chairman CM	400	—	28	4,823	12	12
Burkina Faso	Aug. 5, 1960	*Nov. 27, 1977*	state	chairman PF		x	—	30	300	—	—
Burma	Jan. 4, 1948	*Jan. 4, 1974*	people's republic	prime minister		(489)	—	14	314	12	200
Burundi	July 1, 1962	*Nov. 20, 1981*	republic	president CMSN		(65)	—	15	114	—	—
Cameroon	Jan. 1, 1960	June 2, 1972	republic	president		180	—	10	40	50	1
Canada	July 1, 1867	April 17, 1982	federal parl. state[7]	British monarch	prime minister	104	295	12	4,740	12	200
Cape Verde	July 5, 1975	Feb. 12, 1981	republic	president	prime minister	83	—	14	—	12[12]	200
Cayman Islands	—	Aug. 22, 1972	colony (U.K.)	British monarch	governor	16	—	3	12	3	200
Central African Republic	Aug. 13, 1960	Nov. 21, 1986	republic	president		52	—	17	47	—	—
Chad	Aug. 11, 1960	*April 1962*	republic	president		x	—	14	53	—	—
Chile	Sept. 18, 1810	March 11, 1981[13]	republic	president		—	—	13	51	12	200
China	1523 BC	Dec. 4, 1982	people's republic	president	premier SC	2,978	—	29	327	12	1
Christmas Island	—	Oct. 1, 1958	external territory (Aust.)	Australian GG	administrator	9	—	—	—	3	200
Cocos (Keeling) Islands	—	Nov. 23, 1955	external territory (Aust.)	Australian GG	administrator	7	—	—	—	3	200
Colombia	July 20, 1810	Aug. 5, 1886	republic	president		114	199	33	990	12	200
Comoros	July 6, 1975	Oct. 1, 1978	federal Islamic republic	president		42	—	3	7	12	200
Congo	Aug. 15, 1960	July 8, 1979	people's republic	president		153	—	15	45	200	1
Cook Islands	—	Aug. 4, 1965	territory (N.Z.)[14]	British monarch	prime minister	15[11]	24	14	44	12	200
Costa Rica	Sept. 15, 1821	Nov. 9, 1949	republic	president		57	—	7	80	12	200
Côte d'Ivoire	Aug. 7, 1960	Oct. 31, 1960	republic	president		175	—	34	—	12	200
Cuba	May 20, 1902	Feb. 24, 1976	socialist republic	president		510	—	15	169	12	200
Cyprus[15]	Aug. 16, 1960	Aug. 16, 1960	republic	president		80	—	5	...	12	1
Czechoslovakia	Oct. 28, 1918	July 11, 1960	federal socialist republic	president	premier	150	200	2	12	—	—
Denmark	*c.* 800	June 5, 1953	constitutional monarchy	monarch	prime minister	179	—	16	275	3	200
Djibouti	June 27, 1977	January 1981[16]	republic	president	prime minister	65	—	5	11	12	200
Dominica	Nov. 3, 1978	Nov. 3, 1978	republic	president	prime minister	31	—	10	27	12	200
Dominican Republic	Feb. 27, 1844	Nov. 28, 1966	republic	president		30	120	30	97	6	200
Ecuador	May 24, 1822	Aug. 10, 1979	republic	president		71	—	20	147	200	1
Egypt	Feb. 28, 1922	Sept. 11, 1971	republic	president	prime minister	458	—	26	...	12	200

Finally, in the second half of the table are listed the memberships each country maintains in the principal international intergovernmental organizations of the world. This part of the table may also be utilized to provide a complete membership list for each of these organizations as of Dec. 1, 1988.

Notes for the column headings

a. The date may also be either that of the organization of the present form of government or the inception of the present administrative structure (federation, confederation, union, etc.).
b. Constitutions whose dates are in italic type had been wholly or substantially suspended or abolished as of late 1988.
c. For abbreviations used in this column see the list on the facing page.
d. When a legislative body has been adjourned or otherwise suspended, figures in parentheses indicate the number of members in the legislative body as provided for in constitution or law. If the provision for the legislative body in the constitution has been abrogated then the space has been marked with an "X".
e. Vatican City also a member.
f. States contributing funds to or receiving aid from UNICEF in 1987.
g. Palestine (Liberation Organization) also a member.

International organizations, conventions

ACP	African, Caribbean, and Pacific (Lomé III) convention
ASEAN	Association of South East Asian Nations
COMECON	Council for Mutual Economic Assistance
EC	The European Communities
ECOWAS	Economic Community of West African States
EEC	European Economic Community
FAO	Food and Agriculture Organization
GATT	General Agreement on Tariffs and Trade
I-ADB	Inter-American Development Bank
IAEA	International Atomic Energy Agency
IBRD	International Bank for Reconstruction and Development
ICAO	International Civil Aviation Organization
ICJ	International Court of Justice
IDA	International Development Association
IDB	Islamic Development Bank
IFC	International Finance Corporation
ILO	International Labour Organisation
IMF	International Monetary Fund
IMO	International Maritime Organization
ITU	International Telecommunication Union
LAS	League of Arab States
NATO	North Atlantic Treaty Organization
OAS	Organization of American States
OAU	Organization of African Unity
OPEC	Organization of Petroleum Exporting Countries
SPC	South Pacific Commission
UNCTAD	United Nations Conference on Trade and Development
UNESCO	United Nations Educational Scientific and Cultural Organization
UNICEF	United Nations Children's Fund
UNIDO	United Nations Industrial Development Organization
UPU	Universal Postal Union
WHO	World Health Organization
WIPO	World Intellectual Property Organization
WMO	World Meteorological Organization
WTO	Warsaw Treaty of Friendship, Co-operation and Mutual Assistance (The Warsaw Pact)

Abbreviations used in the executive-branch column

CM	Council of Ministers
CMSN	Military Committee for National Salvation
CP	Collective Presidency
CS	Council of State
FEC	Federal Executive Council
GG	Governor-general
GPC	General People's Committee
MC	Military Council
PC	Presidential Council
PF	Popular Front
PNDC	Provisional National Defense Council
PPA	Presidium, People's Assembly
PPGH	Presidium, People's Great Hural
PSPC	Presidium, Supreme People's Council
PSSU	Presidium, Supreme Soviet of the U.S.S.R.
SC	State Council
SMC	Supreme Military Council
SUC	Supreme Council

---

membership in international organizations

The table below lists, for each country, the date of admission to the United Nations and membership in UN organs★ and affiliated intergovernmental organizations, the Commonwealth of Nations, regional multi-purpose organizations, economic organizations, and military alliances.

Column groups:
- United Nations (date of admission)
- UN organs★ and affiliated intergovernmental organizations: UNCTAD★[c], UNICEF★[f], ICJ★, FAO, GATT, IAEA[e], IBRD, ICAO, IDA, IFC, ILO, IMF, IMO, ITU[e], UNESCO, UNIDO, UPU[e], WHO, WIPO[e], WMO
- Commonwealth of Nations
- regional multi-purpose: ASEAN, EC, LAS[g], OAS, OAU, SPC
- economic: ACP, COMECON, ECOWAS, EEC, I-ADB, IDB[g], OPEC
- military: NATO, WTO

United Nations (date of admission)	country
1946	Afghanistan
1955	Albania
1962	Algeria
—	American Samoa
—	Andorra
1976	Angola
1981	Anguilla
1945	Antigua and Barbuda
	Argentina
	Aruba
1945	Australia
1955	Austria
1973	Bahamas, The
1971	Bahrain
1974	Bangladesh
1966	Barbados
1945	Belgium
1981	Belize
1960	Benin
—	Bermuda
1971	Bhutan
1945	Bolivia
1966	Botswana
1945	Brazil
—	British Virgin Islands
1984	Brunei
1955	Bulgaria
1960	Burkina Faso
1948	Burma
1962	Burundi
1960	Cameroon
1945	Canada
1975	Cape Verde
	Cayman Islands
1960	Central African Republic
1960	Chad
1945	Chile
1945	China
—	Christmas Island
—	Cocos (Keeling) Islands
1945	Colombia
1975	Comoros
1960	Congo
	Cook Islands
1945	Costa Rica
1960	Côte d'Ivoire
1945	Cuba
1960	Cyprus[15]
1945	Czechoslovakia
1945	Denmark
1977	Djibouti
1978	Dominica
1945	Dominican Republic
1945	Ecuador
1945	Egypt

Government and international organizations (continued)

country	date of independence [a]	date of current or last constitution [b]	type of government	executive branch [c] chief of state	executive branch [c] head of government	legislative branch [d] upper house (members)	legislative branch [d] lower house (members)	admin. subdivisions first-order (number)	admin. subdivisions second-order (number)	seaward claims territorial (nautical miles)	seaward claims fishing/economic (nautical miles)
El Salvador	Jan. 30, 1841	Dec. 20, 1983	republic	—president—		60	—	14	261	200	200
Equatorial Guinea	Oct. 12, 1968	Oct. 12, 1982	republic	—president—		41	—	7	—	12	200
Ethiopia	c. 1000 BC	Sept. 12, 1987	people's republic	—president—		835	—	14	103	12	1
Faeroe Islands	—	March 23, 1948	part of Danish realm	Danish monarch [17]		32	—	7	50	3	200
Falkland Islands	—	Oct. 3, 1985	colony (U.K.)	British monarch [4]		10	—	—	—	3	200
Fiji	Oct. 10, 1970	*Oct. 10, 1970*	republic	president	prime minister	(22)	(52)	4	15	12[12]	200
Finland	Dec. 6, 1917	July 17, 1919	republic	president	prime minister	200	—	12	461	4	12
France	August 843	Oct. 4, 1958	republic	president	prime minister	319	577	22	96	12	200
French Guiana	—	March 19, 1946	overseas dept. (Fr.)	French president [18]		19	31	2	20	12	200
French Polynesia	—	Sept. 6, 1984	overseas territory (Fr.)	French president [19]		41	—	5	48	12	200
Gabon	Aug. 17, 1960	May 1975	republic	president	prime minister	120	—	9	37	100	150
Gambia, The	Feb. 18, 1965	April 24, 1970	republic	—president—		50	—	7	35	200	1
Gaza Strip	—	—	Israeli military	— area commander		—	—	3	—	—	—
Germany, East	Oct. 7, 1949	April 9, 1968	socialist republic	chairman CS	chairman CM	500	—	15	227	12	200
Germany, West	May 5, 1955	May 23, 1949	federal republic	president	chancellor	45	519	11	30	3	200
Ghana	March 6, 1957	*Sept. 24, 1979*	republic	—chairman PNDC—		(...)	—	10	154	200	1
Gibraltar	—	Aug. 11, 1969	colony (U.K.)	British monarch	governor	18	—	—	—	3	200
Greece	Feb. 3, 1830	June 11, 1975	republic	president	prime minister	300	—	13	51	6	1
Greenland	—	May 1, 1979	part of Danish realm	Danish monarch [20]		27	—	3	18	3	200
Grenada	Feb. 7, 1974	March 3, 1967	constitutional monarchy	British monarch	prime minister	13	15	7	—	12	200
Guadeloupe	—	March 19, 1946	overseas dept. (Fr.)	French president [18]		43	41	3	34	12	200
Guam	—	Aug. 1, 1950	territory (U.S.)	U.S. president	governor	21	—	19	—	3	200
Guatemala	Sept. 15, 1821	Jan. 14, 1986	republic	—president—		100	—	22	327	12	200
Guernsey	—	Jan. 1, 1949	crown dependency (U.K.)	British monarch[21]	bailiff	60	—	10	—	3	200
Guinea	Oct. 2, 1958	*May 14, 1982*	republic	—president—		x	—	33	...	12	200
Guinea-Bissau	Sept. 10, 1974	May 16, 1984	republic	—president—		150	—	9	37	12	200
Guyana	May 26, 1966	Oct. 6, 1980	cooperative republic	—president[22]—		65	—	10	98	12	200
Haiti	Jan. 1, 1804	*March 29, 1987*[23]	republic	—president—		(27)	(77)	9	41	12	200
Honduras	Nov. 5, 1838	Jan. 20, 1982	republic	—president—		134	—	18	282	12	200
Hong Kong	—	—	colony (U.K.)	British monarch	governor	57	—	4	18	3	1
Hungary	Nov. 16, 1918	Aug. 20, 1949	socialist republic	president PC	prime minister	387	—	25	103	—	—
Iceland	June 17, 1944	June 17, 1944	republic	president	prime minister	21	42	...	...	12	200
India	Aug. 15, 1947	Jan. 26, 1950	federal republic	president	prime minister	244	546	32	386	12	200
Indonesia	Aug. 17, 1945	Aug. 17, 1945	republic	—president—		500	1,000	27	301	12[12]	200
Iran	Oct. 7, 1906	Dec. 2–3, 1979	Islamic republic	president[24]	prime minister[24]	270	—	24	195	12	50[25]
Iraq	Oct. 3, 1932	Sept. 22, 1968[26]	republic	—president—		250	—	18	157	12	1
Ireland	Dec. 6, 1921	Dec. 29, 1937	republic	president	prime minister	60	166	27	49	3	200
Isle of Man	—	1961	crown dependency (U.K.)	British monarch[21]	chief minister	10	24	26	—	3	200
Israel	May 14, 1948	June 1950[27]	republic	president	prime minister	120	—	6	15	6	1
Italy	March 17, 1861	Jan. 1, 1948	republic	president	prime minister	322	630	20	94	12	1
Jamaica	Aug. 6, 1962	Aug. 6, 1962	constitutional monarchy	British monarch	prime minister	21	60	14	—	12	1
Japan	c. 660 BC	May 3, 1947	constitutional monarchy	emperor	prime minister	252	512	47	3,256	12[28]	200
Jersey	—	Jan. 1, 1949	crown dependency (U.K.)	British monarch[21]	bailiff	58	—	12	—	3	200
Jordan	May 25, 1946	Jan. 8, 1952	constitutional monarchy	—king[22]—		30	(142)	8	14	3	1
Kampuchea	Nov. 9, 1953	June 27, 1981	people's republic	chairman CS	chairman CM	117	—	20	...	12	200
Kenya	Dec. 12, 1963	Dec. 12, 1963	republic	—president—		202	—	8	40	12	200
Kiribati	July 12, 1979	July 12, 1979	republic	—president—		41	—	23	—	12	200
Korea, North	Sept. 9, 1948	Dec. 27, 1972	socialist republic	president	premier	655	—	13	152	12	200
Korea, South	Aug. 15, 1948.	Feb. 25, 1988	republic	president	prime minister	299	—	14	97	12[29]	12
Kuwait	June 19, 1961	Nov. 16, 1962	const. mon. (emirate)	—emir[22]—		(64)	—	4	—	12	1
Laos	Oct. 23, 1953	*May 11, 1947*	people's republic	president	chairman CM	45[30]	—	17	...	—	—
Lebanon	Nov. 26, 1941	May 23, 1926	republic[31]	...	...			6	26	12	1
Lesotho	Oct. 4, 1966	*Oct. 4, 1966*	monarchy	king	chairman MC	(33)	(60)	10	22	—	—
Liberia	July 26, 1847	Jan. 6, 1986	republic	—president—		26	64	13	50	200	1
Libya	Dec. 24, 1951	March 2, 1977	socialist state[32]	rev. leader	sec. gen. GPC	1,112	—	24	201	12[33]	1
Liechtenstein	July 12, 1806	Oct. 5, 1921	constitutional monarchy	prince	head of gov't.	15	—	11	—	—	—
Luxembourg	May 10, 1867	Oct. 17, 1868	constitutional monarchy	grand duke	prime minister	21[11]	64	3	12	—	—
Macau	—	August 1976	overseas terr. (Port.)	Port. president	governor	17	—	2	5	6	12
Madagascar	June 26, 1960	Dec. 30, 1975	republic	president	prime minister	137	—	6	18	50	150
Malawi	July 6, 1964	July 6, 1966	republic	—president—		123	—	3	24	—	—
Malaysia	Aug. 31, 1957	Aug. 31, 1957	fed. const. monarchy	paramount ruler	prime minister	69	177	14	126	12	200
Maldives	July 26, 1965	Nov. 11, 1968	republic	—president—		48	—	19	202	12, 34	34
Mali	Sept. 22, 1960	June 19, 1979	republic	—president—		82	—	8	42	—	—
Malta	Sept. 21, 1964	Dec. 13, 1974	republic	president	prime minister	69	—	6	63	12	25
Martinique	—	March 19, 1946	overseas dept. (Fr.)	French president [18]		45	41	3	34	12	200
Mauritania	Nov. 28, 1960	*May 20, 1961*	republic	—president CMSN—		x	—	13	209	70	200
Mauritius	March 12, 1968	March 12, 1968	constitutional monarchy	British monarch	prime minister	70	—	10	...	12	200
Mayotte	—	Dec. 24, 1976	terr. collectivity (Fr.)	French president [35]		17	—	17	—	12	200
Mexico	Sept. 16, 1810	Feb. 5, 1917	federal republic	—president—		64	500	32	2,389	12	200
Monaco	Feb. 2, 1861	Dec. 17, 1962	constitutional monarchy	prince	min. of state	18	—	1	4	12	1
Mongolia	March 13, 1921	July 6, 1960	people's republic	chairman PPGH	premier	370	—	21	331	—	—
Montserrat	—	Jan. 1, 1960	colony (U.K.)	British monarch	governor	12	—	3	—	3	200
Morocco	March 2, 1956	March 10, 1972	constitutional monarchy	—king[22]—		306	—	43	133	12	200
Mozambique	June 25, 1975	June 25, 1975	people's republic	—president—		250	—	11	112	12	200
Nauru	Jan. 31, 1968	Jan. 31, 1968	republic	—president—		18	—	—	—	12	200
Nepal	Nov. 13, 1769	Dec. 16, 1962	constitutional monarchy	king	prime minister	140	—	15	75	—	—
Netherlands, The	March 30, 1814	Feb. 17, 1983	constitutional monarchy	monarch	prime minister	75	150	12	912	12	200
Netherlands Antilles	—	Dec. 29, 1954	integral part of Neth.	Dutch monarch [5]		22	—	5	—	12	1
New Caledonia	—	—	overseas territory (Fr.)[37]	French president	commissioner	—	—	4	—	12	200
New Zealand	Sept. 26, 1907	June 30, 1852[27]	constitutional monarchy	British monarch	prime minister	97	—	...	...	12	200
Nicaragua	April 30, 1838	*Jan. 9, 1987*	republic	—president—		(96)	—	16	136	200	—
Niger	Aug. 3, 1960	*Nov. 8, 1960*[38]	republic	—president SMC—		150[11]	—	8	32	—	—
Nigeria	Oct. 1, 1960	*Oct. 1, 1979*	federal republic	—president—		x	x	22	271	30	200
Niue	—	Oct. 19, 1974	territory (N.Z.)[14]	British monarch	premier	20	—	14	—	12	200
Norfolk Island	—	May 30, 1979	external territory (Aust.)	Australian GG	administrator	9	—	—	—	3	200

membership in international organizations

United Nations (date of admission)	UN organs★ and affiliated intergovernmental organizations																				Commonwealth of Nations	regional multi-purpose						economic							military		country
	UNCTAD★	UNICEF★	ICJ★	FAO	GATT	IAEA	IBRD	ICAO	IDA	IFC	ILO	IMF	IMO	ITU	UNESCO	UNIDO	UPU	WHO	WIPO	WMO		ASEAN	EC	LAS	OAS	OAU	SPC	ACP	COMECON	ECOWAS	EEC	I-ADB	IDB	OPEC	NATO	WTO	
1945	•	•	•	•		•	•	•	•	•	•	•	•	•	•	•	•	•	•	•					•			•				•					El Salvador
1968	•	•	•	•	●2	•	•	•	•	•	•	•	•	•	•	•	•	•	•							•		•									Equatorial Guinea
1945	•	•	•	•		•	•	•	•	•	•	•	•	•	•	•	•	•	•	•						•		•									Ethiopia
—															•		•				•																Faeroe Islands
—																	•																				Falkland Islands
1970	•	•	•	•	●2		•	•	•	•	•	•	•	•	•		•	•	•	•	•						•	•					•				Fiji
1955	•	•	•	•	•	•	•	•	•	•	•	•	•	•	•	•	•	•	•	•			•										•				Finland
1945	•	•	•	•	•	•	•	•	•	•	•	•	•	•	•	•	•	•	•	•			•								•	•			•		France
—																	•																				French Guiana
—																	•			•							•										French Polynesia
1960	•	•	•	•	●2		•	•	•	•	•	•	•	•	•	•	•	•	•	•						•		•				•	•				Gabon
1965	•	•	•	•	•	•	•	•	•	•	•	•	•	•	•	•	•	•	•	•	•					•		•				•					Gambia, The
1973	•	•	•	•		•	•		•	•	•	•	•	•	•	•	•	•		•									•		•	•					Gaza Strip / Germany, East
1973	•	•	•	•	•	•	•	•	•	•	•	•	•	•	•	•	•	•	•	•			•								•	•			•	•	Germany, West
1957	•	•	•	•	•	•	•	•	•	•	•	•	•	•	•	•	•	•	•	•	•					•		•				•					Ghana
—																	•				•										•						Gibraltar
1945	•	•	•	•	•	•	•	•	•	•	•	•	•	•	•	•	•	•	•	•											•	•			•		Greece
—																	•				•																Greenland
1974	•	•	•	•	●2		•	•	•	•	•	•	•	•	•	•	•	•		•	•				•			•				•					Grenada
—																	•																				Guadeloupe
—																	•								•							•					Guam
1945	•	•	•	•	•	•	•	•	•	•	•	•	•	•	•	•	•	•	•	•					•							•					Guatemala
—																	•																				Guernsey
1958	•	•	•	•		•	•	•	•	•	•	•	•	•	•	•	•	•	•	•						•		•				•					Guinea
1974	•	•	•	•	●2		•	•	•	•	•	•	•	•	•	•	•	•		•						•		•		•		•					Guinea-Bissau
1966	•	•	•	•	•	•	•	•	•	•	•	•	•	•	•	•	•	•		•	•				•			•				•					Guyana
1945	•	•	•	•	•	•	•	•	•	•	•	•	•	•	•	•	•	•	•	•					•			•				•					Haiti
1945		•	•	•	•	•	•	•	•	•	•	●6	•	•	•	•	•	•		•					•			•				•					Honduras
—					•						•						•			•	•																Hong Kong
1955	•	•	•	•	•	•	•	•	•	•	•	•	•	•	•	•	•	•	•	•								•	•							•	Hungary
1946	•	•	•	•	•	•	•	•	•	•	•	•	•	•	•	•	•	•	•	•			•												•		Iceland
1945	•	•	•	•	•	•	•	•	•	•	•	•	•	•	•	•	•	•	•	•	•											•	•				India
1950	•	•	•	•	•	•	•	•	•	•	•	•	•	•	•	•	•	•	•	•													•	•			Indonesia
1945	•	•	•	•	•	•	•	•	•	•	•	•	•	•	•	•	•	•	•	•													•	•			Iran
1945	•	•	•	•		•	•	•	•	•	•	•	•	•	•	•	•	•		•				•									•	•			Iraq
1955	•	•	•	•	•	•	•	•	•	•	•	•	•	•	•	•	•	•	•	•	•		•								•						Ireland
—																	•																				Isle of Man
1949	•	•	•	•	•	•	•	•	•	•	•	•	•	•	•	•	•	•	•	•											•	•					Israel
1955	•	•	•	•	•	•	•	•	•	•	•	•	•	•	•	•	•	•	•	•			•								•	•			•		Italy
1962	•	•	•	•	•	•	•	•	•	•	•	•	•	•	•	•	•	•	•	•	•				•			•				•					Jamaica
1956	•	•	•	•	•	•	•	•	•	•	•	•	•	•	•	•	•	•	•	•							•					•					Japan
—																	•																				Jersey
1955	•	•	•	•	●2	•	•	•	•	•	•	•	•	•	•	•	•	•		•				•									•				Jordan
1955	•	•	•	•				•			•	•	•	•	•		•	•		•																	Kampuchea
1963	•	•	•	•	●2	•	•	•	•	•	•	•	•	•	•	•	•	•		•	•					•		•				•					Kenya
—			•														•			•	•						•										Kiribati
—		•		•										•	•		•	•		•																	Korea, North
—	•	•	•	•	●2	•	•	•	•	•	•	•	•	•	•	•	•	•		•												•					Korea, South
1963	•	•	•	•		•	•	•	•	•	•	•	•	•	•	•	•	•		•				•								•	•	•			Kuwait
1955	•	•	•	•				•			•	•		•	•		•	•		•						•											Laos
1945	•	•	•	•		•	•	•	•	•	•	•	•	•	•	•	•	•		•				•									•				Lebanon
1966	•	•	•	•			•	•	•	•	•	•		•	•		•	•		•	•				•			•				•					Lesotho
1945	•	•	•	•		•	•	•	•	•	•	•	•	•	•	•	•	•		•					•	•		•		•		•					Liberia
1955	•	•	•	•		•	•	•	•	•	•	•	•	•	•	•	•	•		•				•		•							•	•			Libya
—			•											•			•	•	•				•														Liechtenstein
1945	•	•	•	•	•	•	•	•	•	•	•	•	•	•	•	•	•	•	•	•			•								•	•			•		Luxembourg
—																	•																				Macau
1960	•	•	•	•	•	•	•	•	•	•	•	•		•	•	•	•	•		•						•		•				•					Madagascar
1964	•	•	•	•	•		•	•	•	•	•	•	•	•	•	•	•	•		•	•					•		•				•					Malawi
1957	•	•	•	•	•	•	•	•	•	•	•	•	•	•	•	•	•	•	•	•	•	•						•				•					Malaysia
1965	•	•	•	•		•	•	•	•	•	•	•	•	•	•	•	•	•		•	•							•				•					Maldives
1960	•	•	•	•	●2		•	•	•	•	•	•	•	•	•	•	•	•		•						•		•		•		•					Mali
1964	•	•	•	•			•	•	•	•	•	•	•	•	•	•	•	•		•	•							•		●6							Malta
—																	•																				Martinique
1961	•	•	•	•		•	•	•	•	•	•	•	•	•	•	•	•	•		•				•		•		•		•		•					Mauritania
1968	•	•	•	•			•	•	•	•	•	•		•	•	•	•	•		•	•					•		•				•					Mauritius
—																	•																				Mayotte
1945	•	•	•	•		•	•	•	•	•	•	•	•	•	•	•	•	•		•					•							•					Mexico
—											•			•			•	•	•	•																	Monaco
1961	•	•	•	•		•					•			•	•	•	•	•		•									•								Mongolia
—																	•				•																Montserrat
1956	•	•	•	•	●2	•	•	•	•	•	•	•	•	•	•	•	•	•		•				•		•		•				•					Morocco
1975	•	•	•	•			•	•	•	•	•	•		•	•	•	•	•		•						•		•									Mozambique
—																	•				●36						•										Nauru
1955	•	•	•	•		•	•	•	•	•	•	•	•	•	•	•	•	•		•												•	•				Nepal
1945	•	•	•	•	•	•	•	•	•	•	•	•	•	•	●6	•	•	•	•	•			•								•	•			•		Netherlands, The
—																	•																				Netherlands Antilles
—																	•				•						•										New Caledonia
1945	•	•	•	•	•	•	•	•	•	•	•	•	•	•	•	•	•	•		•	•						•										New Zealand
1945	•	•	•	•		•	•	•	•	•	•	•		•	•	•	•	•		•					•							•					Nicaragua
1960	•	•	•	•			•	•	•	•	•	•		•	•	•	•	•		•						•		•		•		•					Niger
1960	•	•	•	•		•	•	•	•	•	•	•	•	•	•	•	•	•		•	•					•		•		•		•		•			Nigeria
—		•															•				•																Niue
—																	•																				Norfolk Island

Government and international organizations (continued)

country	date of independence[a]	date of current or last constitution[b]	type of government	executive branch[c] chief of state	head of government	legislative branch[d] upper house (members)	lower house (members)	admin. subdivisions first-order (number)	second-order (number)	seaward claims territorial (nautical miles)	fishing/ economic (nautical miles)
Norway	June 7, 1905	May 17, 1814	constitutional monarchy	king	prime minister	157	—	19	454	4	200
Oman	Dec. 20, 1951		monarchy (sultanate)	—sultan—		55[11]	—	11	41	12	200
Pacific Is., Trust Terr. of											
Marshall Islands	—	May 1, 1979	republic	—president—		12[11]	33	26	—	3	200
Micronesia, F.S. of	—	May 10, 1979	federal republic	—president—		14		4	...	3	200
Northern Mariana Is.	—	Jan. 9, 1978	commonwealth (U.S.)	U.S. president	governor	9	14	4	—	3	200
Palau	—	Jan. 1, 1981		—president—		18	16	16	—	3	200
Pakistan	Aug. 14, 1947	Aug. 14, 1973	federal Islamic republic	president	prime minister	87	237	6	16	12	200
Panama	Nov. 3, 1903	Oct. 11, 1972	republic	—president[39]—		67	—	10	65	200	1
Papua New Guinea	Sept. 16, 1975	Sept. 16, 1975	constitutional monarchy	British monarch	prime minister	109	—	20	86	12[12]	200
Paraguay	May 14, 1811	Aug. 25, 1967	republic	—president—		36	72	20	190	—	—
Peru	July 28, 1821	July 28, 1980	republic	—president—		60	180	25	152	200	1
Philippines	July 4, 1946	Feb. 11, 1987	republic	—president—		24	250	73	1,500	34	200
Pitcairn Island	—	Nov. 30, 1838	colony (U.K.)	British monarch [40]		10	—	—	—	3	200
Poland	Nov. 10, 1918	July 22, 1952	socialist republic	chairman CS	chairman CM	460	—	49	261	12	200
Portugal	c. 1140	April 25, 1976	parliamentary state	president	prime minister	250	—	22	305	12	200
Puerto Rico	—	July 25, 1952	commonwealth (U.S.)	U.S. president	governor	27	51	78	...	3	200
Qatar	Sept. 3, 1971	July 1970[26]	monarchy	—emir—		30[11]	—	—	—	3	41
Réunion	—	March 19, 1946	overseas dept. (Fr.)	French president	[18]	36	45	4	24	12	200
Romania	May 21, 1877	Aug. 21, 1965	socialist republic	president	prime minister	369	—	41	237	12	200
Rwanda	July 1, 1962	Dec. 20, 1978	republic	—president—		70	—	10	143	—	—
St. Helena and Ascension	—	Jan. 1, 1967	colony (U.K.)	British monarch	governor	15	—	3	—	3	200
St. Kitts and Nevis	Sept. 19, 1983	Sept. 19, 1983	constitutional monarchy	British monarch	prime minister	15	—	14	—	12	200
St. Lucia	Feb. 22, 1979	Feb. 22, 1979	constitutional monarchy	British monarch	prime minister	11	17	10	—	3	200
St. Pierre and Miquelon	—	June 1985	terr. collectivity (Fr.)	French president	[35]	14	—	2	—	12	200
St. Vincent	Oct. 27, 1979	Oct. 27, 1979	constitutional monarchy	British monarch	prime minister	19	—	—	—	3	200
San Marino	855	Oct. 8, 1600	republic	—captains-regent (2)—		60	—	9	—	12[8]	200
São Tomé and Principe	July 12, 1975	Dec. 15, 1982	republic	—president[22]—		51	—	2	7	12	—
Saudi Arabia	Sept. 23, 1932		monarchy	—king—		—	—	14	—	12	200
Senegal	Aug. 20, 1960	March 7, 1963	republic	—president—		120	—	10	30	12	200
Seychelles	June 29, 1976	June 5, 1979	republic	—president—		25	—	—	—	12	200
Sierra Leone	April 27, 1961	June 14, 1978	republic	—president—		127	—	4	12	200	1
Singapore	Aug. 9, 1965	June 3, 1959	republic	president	prime minister	84	—	—	—	3	12
Solomon Islands	July 7, 1978	July 7, 1978	constitutional monarchy	British monarch	prime minister	38	—	8	174	12[12]	200
Somalia	July 1, 1960	Aug. 25, 1979	republic	—president—		177	—	16	60	200	1
South Africa	May 31, 1910	Sept. 3, 1984	republic	—state president—		308[42]	—	10	358	12	200
Bophuthatswana	Dec. 6, 1977[43]	Dec. 6, 1977	republic	—president—		108	—	12	76	—	—
Ciskei	Dec. 4, 1981[43]	Dec. 4, 1981	republic	—president—		55	—	7	42	—	—
Transkei	Oct. 26, 1976[43]	Dec. 1963	republic	—head of military council—		(150)	—	28	123	—	—
Venda	Sept. 13, 1979[43]	Sept. 13, 1979	republic	—president—		92	—	4	—	—	—
South West Africa/Namibia	—	—	dependency of S.Af.	state president [44]		62	—	26	—	6	12
Spain	1492	Dec. 29, 1978	constitutional monarchy	king	prime minister	257	350	17	50	12	200
Sri Lanka	Feb. 4, 1948	Sept. 7, 1978	republic	—president—		168	—	24	682	12	200
Sudan, The	Jan. 1, 1956	Oct. 10, 1985[13]	republic	president SUC	prime minister	301	—	8	19	12	1
Suriname	Nov. 25, 1975	Nov. 25, 1987	republic	—president—		51	—	9	—	12	200
Swaziland	Sept. 6, 1968	Sept. 6, 1968	monarchy	—king[22]—		20	50	4	40	—	—
Sweden	before 836	Jan. 1, 1975	constitutional monarchy	king	prime minister	349	—	24	279	12	200
Switzerland	Sept. 22, 1499	May 29, 1874	federal state	—president—		46	200	26	177	—	—
Syria	April 17, 1946	March 14, 1973	republic	—president—		195	—	14	41	35	1
Taiwan	Oct. 25, 1945	Dec. 25, 1947	republic	president	premier	946	—	23	—	12	200
Tanzania	Dec. 9, 1961	April 25, 1977	republic	president	prime minister	244	—	25	105	50	1
Thailand	1350	Dec. 22, 1978	constitutional monarchy	king	prime minister	268	357	72	576	12	200
Togo	April 27, 1960	Dec. 30, 1979	republic	—president—		77	—	5	21	30	200
Tokelau		1948	territory (N.Z.)	New Zealand GG [45]		—	—	3	—	12	200
Tonga	June 4, 1970	Nov. 4, 1875	constitutional monarchy	—monarch[22]—		29	—	3	23	12	200
Trinidad and Tobago	Aug. 31, 1962	July 27, 1976	republic	president	prime minister	31	36	11	30	12	200
Tunisia	March 20, 1956	June 1, 1959	republic	president	prime minister	125	—	23	243	12	1
Turkey	Oct. 29, 1923	Nov. 7, 1982	republic	president	prime minister	450	—	67	580	12[46]	200[46]
Turks and Caicos Islands	—	Aug. 30, 1976	colony (U.K.)	British monarch	governor	16	—	3	—	3	200
Tuvalu	Oct. 1, 1978	Oct. 1, 1978	constitutional monarchy	British monarch	prime minister	12	—	9	—	12	200
Uganda	Oct. 9, 1962	Sept. 8, 1967	republic	—president—		(156)	—	33	—	12	200
U.S.S.R.	c. 900	Oct. 7, 1977	fed. socialist republic	chairman PSSU	chairman CM	750	750	15	167	12	200
United Arab Emirates	Dec. 2, 1971	Dec. 2, 1971[26]	federation of emirates	president	prime minister	40	—	7	—	3	200
United Kingdom	Oct. 14, 1066	[48]	constitutional monarchy	monarch	prime minister	1,187	650	4	...	3	200
United States	July 4, 1776	March 4, 1789	federal republic	—president—		100	435	51	3,137	3	200
Uruguay	Aug. 25, 1828	Feb. 15, 1967	republic	—president—		31	99	19	...	200	1
Vanuatu	July 30, 1980	July 30, 1980	republic	president	prime minister	46	—	4	11	12[12]	200
Venezuela	July 5, 1811	Jan. 23, 1961	federal republic	—president—		47	200	23	156	12	200
Vietnam	Sept. 2, 1954	Dec. 18, 1980	socialist republic	chairman CS	chairman CM	496	—	40	391	12	200
Virgin Islands (U.S.)	—		territory (U.S.)	U.S. president	governor	15	—	2	—	3	200
Wallis and Futuna	—	July 29, 1961	overseas territory (Fr.)	French president [49]		20	—	3	—	12	200
West Bank	—		Israeli military	— area commander		—	—	7	—	—	—
Western Sahara	—		annexture of Morocco			—	—	4	—	12	200
Western Samoa	Jan. 1, 1962	Oct. 28, 1960	[51]	head of state	prime minister	47	—	21	—	12	200
Yemen (Aden)	Nov. 30, 1967	Dec. 27, 1978	socialist republic	chairman PSPC	prime minister	111	—	6	27	12	200
Yemen (Ṣan'ā')	December 1918	June 19, 1974[26]	republic	—president—		159	—	11	41	12	12
Yugoslavia	Dec. 1, 1918	Feb. 21, 1974	federal socialist republic	president CP	president FEC	88	220	8	527	12	12
Zaire	June 30, 1960	Feb. 15, 1978	republic	—president—		210	—	9	41	12	200
Zambia	Oct. 24, 1964	Aug. 25, 1973	republic	—president—		136	—	9	53	—	—
Zimbabwe	April 18, 1980	April 18, 1980	republic	—president—		40	100	8	—	—	—

[1]Territorial sea claim assumed to claim fishing/economic rights within the same zone. [2]Full membership pending. [3]President of France and Bishop of Urgel, Spain. [4]Executive responsibilities divided between (for the U.K.) the governor and (locally) the chief officer of the Executive Council. [5]Executive responsibilities divided between (for The Neth.) the governor and (locally) the prime minister. [6]Associate member. [7]Formally a constitutional monarchy. [8]Defined by equidistant line. [9]Executive responsibilities divided between (for the U.K.) the governor and (locally) the premier of the Cabinet. [10]Resembles a constitutional monarchy without a formal constitution. [11]Body with limited legislative authority. [12]Measured from claimed archipelagic baselines. [13]Transitional constitution. [14]Self-governing state in free association with New Zealand. [15]Republic of Cyprus only. [16]Partial constitution. [17]Executive responsibilities divided between (for Denmark) the state commissioner and (locally) the head of the home government. [18]Executive responsibilities divided among (for France) the commissioner and (locally) the president of the General Council and president of the Regional Council. [19]Executive responsibilities divided between (for France) the high commissioner and (locally) the president of the Council of Ministers. [20]Executive responsibilities divided between (for Denmark) the high commissioner and (locally) the prime minister. [21]Represented by the lieutenant governor. [22]Assisted by the prime minister. [23]Referendum date; constitution pending implementation. [24]Final executive authority with supreme spiritual leader. [25]Sea of Oman only; median line boundaries in the Persian Gulf. [26]Provisional constitution. [27]Evolving body of

membership in international organizations

United Nations (date of admission)	UN organs★ and affiliated intergovernmental organizations																				Commonwealth of Nations	regional multi-purpose						economic							military		country
	UNCTAD★[e]	UNICEF★[f]	ICJ★	FAO	GATT	IAEA[e]	IBRD	ICAO	IDA	IFC	ILO	IMF	IMO	ITU[e]	UNESCO	UNIDO	UPU[e]	WHO	WIPO[e]	WMO		ASEAN	EC	LAS[g]	OAS	OAU	SPC	ACP	COMECON	ECOWAS	EEC	I-ADB	IDB[g]	OPEC	NATO	WTO	
1945	●	●	●	●	●	●	●	●	●	●	●	●	●	●	●	●	●	●	●	●												●			●		Norway
1971	●	●	●	●			●	●	●	●		●	●	●	●	●	●	●		●				●									●				Oman
—																																					Pacific Is., Trust Terr. of
—		●															●										●										Marshall Islands
—		●															●										●										Micronesia, F.S. of
—																	●										●										Northern Mariana Is.
—		●															●										●										Palau
1947	●	●	●	●	●	●	●	●	●	●	●	●	●	●	●	●	●	●	●	●													●				Pakistan
1945	●	●	●	●		●	●	●	●	●	●	●	●	●	●	●	●	●	●	●					●							●					Panama
1975	●	●	●	●	●[2]		●	●	●	●	●	●	●	●	●	●	●	●		●	●						●	●									Papua New Guinea
1945	●	●	●	●		●	●	●	●	●	●	●		●	●	●	●	●		●					●							●					Paraguay
1945	●	●	●	●	●	●	●	●	●	●	●	●	●	●	●	●	●	●	●	●					●							●					Peru
1945	●	●	●	●	●	●	●	●	●	●	●	●	●	●	●	●	●	●	●	●		●															Philippines
—																	●				●						●										Pitcairn Island
1945	●	●	●	●	●	●	●	●			●	●	●	●	●	●	●	●	●	●									●							●	Poland
1955	●		●	●	●	●	●	●		●	●	●	●	●	●	●	●	●	●	●			●								●	●			●		Portugal
—																	●																				Puerto Rico
1971	●		●	●	●[2]	●	●	●			●	●	●	●	●	●	●	●	●	●				●									●	●			Qatar
—																	●																				Réunion
1955	●		●	●	●	●	●	●		●	●	●	●	●	●	●	●	●	●	●									●							●	Romania
1962	●	●	●	●	●		●	●	●	●	●	●		●	●	●	●	●	●	●						●		●									Rwanda
—																	●				●																St. Helena and Ascension
1983	●	●	●	●	●		●					●			●	●	●[2]	●			●				●			●									St. Kitts and Nevis
1979	●	●	●	●	●[2]		●	●	●	●	●	●	●		●	●	●	●		●	●				●			●									St. Lucia
—																	●																				St. Pierre and Miquelon
1980	●	●	●	●	●[2]		●	●	●			●	●	●	●	●	●	●			●				●			●									St. Vincent
—	●	●	●								●			●	●		●	●	●																		San Marino
1975	●	●	●	●	●[2]		●	●	●		●	●		●	●	●	●	●		●						●		●									São Tomé and Príncipe
1945	●	●	●	●		●	●	●	●	●	●	●	●	●	●	●	●	●	●	●				●									●	●			Saudi Arabia
1960	●	●	●	●	●	●	●	●	●	●	●	●	●	●	●	●	●	●	●	●						●		●		●			●				Senegal
1976	●	●	●	●	●[2]		●	●		●	●	●	●		●	●	●	●		●	●					●		●									Seychelles
1961	●	●	●	●	●	●	●	●	●	●	●	●	●	●	●	●	●	●		●	●					●		●		●			●				Sierra Leone
1965	●		●		●	●	●	●		●	●	●	●	●			●	●		●	●	●															Singapore
1978	●	●	●	●	●[2]		●	●	●	●	●	●		●			●	●		●	●						●	●									Solomon Islands
1960	●	●	●	●			●	●	●	●	●	●	●	●	●	●	●	●	●	●				●		●		●					●				Somalia
1945	●		●		●	●	●	●	●	●		●		●				●	●																		South Africa
—																																					Bophuthatswana
—																																					Ciskei
—																																					Transkei
—																																					Venda
—	●			●		●					●			●	●	●		●[6]																			South West Africa/Namibia
1955	●	●	●	●	●	●	●	●	●	●	●	●	●	●	●	●	●	●	●	●			●								●	●			●		Spain
1955	●	●	●	●	●	●	●	●	●	●	●	●	●	●	●	●	●	●	●	●	●																Sri Lanka
1956	●	●	●	●		●	●	●	●	●	●	●	●	●	●	●	●	●	●	●				●		●		●					●				Sudan, The
1975	●		●	●	●		●	●			●	●	●	●	●	●	●	●	●	●					●			●				●					Suriname
1968	●	●	●	●	●[2]		●	●	●	●	●	●		●	●	●	●	●	●	●	●					●		●									Swaziland
1946	●	●	●	●	●	●	●	●	●	●	●	●	●	●	●	●	●	●	●	●												●					Sweden
—	●	●	●	●	●	●		●			●		●	●	●	●	●	●	●	●												●					Switzerland
1945	●	●	●	●		●	●	●	●	●	●	●	●	●	●	●	●	●	●	●				●									●				Syria
—																																					Taiwan
1961	●	●	●	●	●	●	●	●	●	●	●	●	●	●	●	●	●	●	●	●	●					●		●									Tanzania
1946	●	●	●	●	●	●	●	●	●	●	●	●	●	●	●	●	●	●	●	●		●															Thailand
1960	●	●	●	●	●		●	●	●	●	●	●	●	●	●	●	●	●	●	●						●		●		●							Togo
—		●															●				●						●										Tokelau
—	●	●		●	●[2]		●	●	●	●		●		●	●	●	●	●			●						●	●									Tonga
1962	●		●	●	●		●	●	●	●	●	●	●	●	●	●	●	●	●	●	●				●			●				●					Trinidad and Tobago
1956	●	●	●	●	●[2]	●	●	●	●	●	●	●	●	●	●	●	●	●	●	●				●		●							●				Tunisia
1945	●	●	●	●	●	●	●	●	●	●	●	●	●	●	●	●	●	●	●	●											●[6]		●		●		Turkey
—		●															●			●	●																Turks and Caicos Islands
—		●			●[2]												●				●[36]						●	●									Tuvalu
1962	●	●	●	●	●	●	●	●	●	●	●	●		●	●	●	●	●	●	●	●					●		●					●				Uganda
1945[47]	●[47]	●[47]	●[47]			●[47]		●[47]			●[47]		●	●[47]	●[47]	●[47]	●[47]	●[47]	●[47]	●[47]									●							●	U.S.S.R.
1971	●	●	●	●	●[2]	●	●	●	●	●	●	●	●	●	●	●	●	●	●					●									●	●			United Arab Emirates
1945	●	●	●	●	●	●	●	●	●	●	●	●	●	●		●	●	●	●	●	●		●				●				●	●			●		United Kingdom
1945	●	●	●	●	●	●	●	●	●	●	●	●	●	●		●	●	●	●	●					●		●					●			●		United States
1945	●	●	●	●	●	●	●	●		●	●	●	●	●	●	●	●	●	●	●					●							●					Uruguay
1981	●	●	●	●			●	●	●	●		●	●			●	●	●		●	●						●	●									Vanuatu
1945	●	●	●	●		●	●	●		●	●	●	●	●	●	●	●	●	●	●					●							●		●			Venezuela
1977	●		●	●		●	●	●	●	●		●	●	●	●	●	●	●	●	●									●								Vietnam
—																	●																				Virgin Islands (U.S.)
—																	●										●										Wallis and Futuna
—																																					West Bank
—																										●[50]											Western Sahara
1976	●	●	●	●			●		●	●		●			●		●	●			●						●	●									Western Samoa
1967	●	●	●	●	●[2]		●	●	●		●	●	●	●	●	●	●	●		●				●									●				Yemen (Aden)
1947	●	●	●	●			●	●	●	●	●	●	●	●	●	●	●	●	●	●				●									●				Yemen (Şan'ā')
1945	●	●	●	●	●	●	●	●	●	●	●	●	●	●	●	●	●	●	●	●									●[6]								Yugoslavia
1960	●	●	●	●	●	●	●	●	●	●	●	●	●	●	●	●	●	●	●	●						●		●									Zaire
1964	●	●	●	●	●	●	●	●	●	●	●	●		●	●	●	●	●	●	●	●					●		●									Zambia
1980	●	●	●	●	●	●	●	●	●	●	●	●		●	●	●	●	●	●	●	●					●		●									Zimbabwe

constitutional law. [28]3 nm in 5 straits. [29]3 nm in Korean Strait. [30]Interim legislative body. [31]2 interim regimes established after Sept. 22, 1988. [32]Formally a *jamahiriya,* translated as "the masses of people." [33]Based on Gulf of Sidra closing line (32°30'N), in part. [34]Zone defined by geographical coordinates. [35]Executive responsibilities divided between (for France) the commissioner and (locally) the president of the General Council. [36]Special member. [37]Interim direct rule until mid-1989. [38]National charter, antecedent to future constitution approved June 14, 1987. [39]Military commander is de facto executive. [40]Executive responsibilities divided between (for the U.K.) the High Commissioner to N.Z. and (locally) the island magistrate. [41]Limits of continental shelf or median line boundaries. [42]Total of 3 legislative houses. [43]Recognized by South Africa and each other only. [44]Executive responsibilities divided between (for South Africa) the administrator-general and (locally) the Cabinet. [45]Executive responsibilities divided among (for N.Z.) the Deputy Secretary of Foreign Affairs assisted by the Official Secretary based in Western Samoa and (locally) village councils. [46]Black Sea only; complex maritime dispute exists with Greece in Aegean Sea. [47]Belorussian and Ukrainian S.S.R.s are also members. [48]Based on evolving body of statutes and common law. [49]Executive responsibilities divided between (for France) the superior administrator and (locally) the president of the Territorial Assembly. [50]Membership held by the Sahrawi Arab Democratic Republic. [51]Mixed political system approximating a constitutional monarchy.

Area and population

This table provides the area and population for each of the countries of the world and for all political dependencies with a permanent civilian population. Only countries such as the Vatican City State, the British Indian Ocean Territory, and similar anomalous cases are omitted. The data represent the latest published and unpublished data for both the surveyed area of the countries and their populations, the latter both as of a single year (1988) to provide the best comparability and as of the most recent census to provide the fullest comparison of certain demographic measures that are not always available in estimated form between successive national censuses. The 1988 mid-year estimates represent a combination of national, United Nations (UN) or other international organization, and *Encyclopædia Britannica* estimates so as to give the best fit to available published series, to take account of unpublished information received in correspondence, and to incorporate the results of very recent censuses for which published analyses are not yet available.

One principal point to bear in mind when studying these statistics is that all of them, whatever degree of precision may be implied by the exactness of the numbers, are estimates—all of varying, and some of suspect accuracy. Even a country like the United States—which has a long tradition both of census taking and of the use of the most sophisticated analytical tools in processing the data—is unable to determine within 2.5% its total population nationally. And that is an average underenumeration. In larger cities, where enumeration of certain populations, both legal and illegal, is most difficult, the accuracy of the enumerated count may be off considerably more than 5%. When a country like Nigeria, the most populous in Africa, does not know within 20% its real population and is

delayed or prevented from measuring it by political circumstances, both the amount and the margin of error are likely to increase. The editors have tried to take account of the range of variation and accuracy in published data, but it is difficult to establish a value for many sources of inaccuracy unless some country or agency has made a conscientious effort to establish both the relative accuracy (precision) of its estimate and the absolute magnitude of the quantity it is trying to measure—for example, the number of people in Kampuchea (Cambodia) who died at the hands of the Khmer Rouge. Was it 1,000,000, 2,000,000, 3,000,000? If a figure of 1,000,000 is cited, what is its accuracy: ± 1%, 10%, 50%? Is the source of the figure Vietnam (potential bias on the high side to justify its invasion), China (potential bias on the low side because of its political connection with the Khmer Rouge), the United States (habitually unable to obtain or produce by analysis accurate data about Southeast Asia, complicated by political bias)?

Many similar problems exist and in endless variations: What is the extent of southern European immigration to western Europe in search of jobs? How many refugees from Uganda or Afghanistan are there in surrounding countries? How many illegal immigrants are there in the United States? How many Palestinians are there in the Middle East (they are politically inconvenient to enumerate everywhere)? How many Amerindians exist in the countries of South America (any accurate answer to that question raises the question, "Where did they go?")? How many people have died or emigrated as a result of the civil violence in Central America?

Still, much information is accurate, well founded, and updated regularly. The sources of these data are censuses; national population registers (cu-

Area and population

country	area			population (latest estimate)				% annual growth rate 1983–88	population (most recent census)				
	square miles	square kilo- metres	rank	total midyear 1988	rank	density			census year	total	male (%)	female (%)	urban (%)
						per sq mi	per sq km						
Afghanistan	251,825	652,225	40	14,481,000	53	57.5	22.2	1.1	1979	13,051,358[1]	51.4	48.6	15.1
Albania	11,100	28,748	126	3,149,000	109	283.7	109.5	2.1	1982	2,786,100	51.6	48.4	33.6
Algeria	919,595	2,381,741	10	23,849,000	34	25.9	10.0	3.1	1987[3]	22,971,558	49.7[4]	50.3[4]	40.6[5]
American Samoa	77	199	195	37,800	191	490.9	189.9	2.0	1980	32,297	50.7	49.3	17.5
Andorra	181	468	177	51,400	187	284.0	109.8	5.8	1986	45,877	53.1	46.9	64.7
Angola	481,350	1,246,700	21	9,386,000	67	19.5	7.5	3.0	1970	5,673,046	52.1	47.9	14.2
Anguilla	35	91	203	6,700	207	191.4	73.6	0.2	1984	6,987	49.1	50.9	—
Antigua and Barbuda	171	442	179	83,000	176	485.4	187.8	1.2	1970	65,525	47.2[3]	52.8[3]	30.8[4]
Argentina	1,073,399	2,780,092	8	31,963,000	29	29.8	11.5	1.5	1980	27,947,446	49.2	50.8	86.3
Aruba	75	193	196	65,500	182	873.3	339.4	0.1	1981	60,312	48.6	51.4	...
Australia	2,966,200	7,682,300	6	16,470,000	48	5.6	2.1	1.4	1986	16,018,350	49.9	50.1	85.5[4]
Austria	32,377	83,857	109	7,577,000	78	234.0	90.4	0.1	1981	7,555,338	47.4	52.6	55.1
Bahamas, The	5,382	13,939	140	245,000	158	45.5	17.6	1.8	1980	209,505[6]	48.8	51.2	54.4
Bahrain	267	691	169	421,000	146	1,576.8	609.3	2.3	1981	350,798	58.4	41.6	80.7
Bangladesh	55,598	143,998	90	107,756,000	10	1,938.1	748.3	2.4	1981	89,912,000	51.5	48.5	15.7
Barbados	166	430	180	254,000	155	1,530.1	590.7	0.2	1980	248,983	47.6	52.4	40.1[2]
Belgium	11,783	30,518	124	9,865,000	66	837.2	323.3	0.0	1981	9,848,647	48.7	51.3	72.4[2]
Belize	8,867	22,965	133	178,000	162	20.1	7.8	2.5	1980	145,353	50.6	49.4	52.0
Benin	43,450	112,600	96	4,443,000	97	102.3	39.5	3.1	1979	3,331,210	47.9	52.1	38.3
Bermuda	21	54	206	58,300	185	2,776.2	1,079.6	0.8	1980[7]	54,050	48.9	51.1	100.0
Bhutan	18,150	47,000	118	1,365,000	127	75.2	29.0	2.0	1969	931,514	51.4[2]	48.6[2]	3.9
Bolivia	424,164	1,098,581	27	6,993,000	81	16.5	6.4	2.8	1976	4,613,486	49.1	50.9	41.7
Botswana	224,607	581,730	45	1,211,000	131	5.4	2.1	3.7	1981	941,027	47.1	52.9	15.9
Brazil	3,286,488	8,511,965	5	144,262,000	6	43.9	16.9	2.1	1980[3]	119,002,706	49.7	50.3	67.6
British Virgin Islands	59	153	199	12,400	201	210.2	81.0	1.4	1980[9]	10,985	51.1	49.9	12.0
Brunei	2,226	5,765	150	250,000	156	112.3	43.4	3.6	1981	192,832	53.4	46.6	59.4
Bulgaria	42,855	110,994	98	8,978,000	68	209.5	80.9	0.1	1985	8,942,976	49.5	50.5	58.0[10]
Burkina Faso	105,869	274,200	68	8,530,000	72	80.6	31.1	3.1	1985[3]	7,976,019	48.3	51.7	7.0[4]
Burma	261,228	676,577	39	39,952,000	24	152.9	59.1	2.0	1983	35,313,905	49.6	50.4	24.0
Burundi	10,747	27,834	129	5,131,000	91	477.4	184.3	2.8	1979[11]	4,114,135	48.3	51.7	8.2[4]
Cameroon	179,714	465,468	49	11,206,000	59	62.4	24.1	3.2	1976	7,663,246	49.0	51.0	28.5
Canada	3,849,675	9,970,610	2	25,880,000	32	6.7	2.6	0.9	1986	25,354,064	49.3	50.7	75.9[4]
Cape Verde	1,557	4,033	152	359,000	149	230.6	89.0	2.4	1980[3]	295,073	46.3	53.7	35.1
Cayman Islands	102	264	191	23,400	195	229.4	88.6	4.1	1979	16,677[12]	48.6	51.4	100.0
Central African Republic	240,324	622,436	42	2,843,000	112	11.8	4.6	2.5	1975	2,054,610	48.0	52.0	34.6
Chad	495,755	1,284,000	20	5,395,000	90	10.9	4.2	2.4	1975	4,029,917	47.7	52.3	16.0
Chile	292,135	756,626	37	12,750,000	56	43.6	16.9	1.7	1982	11,329,736	49.0	51.0	82.2
China	3,696,100	9,572,900	3	1,088,200,000	1	294.4	113.7	1.3	1982	1,008,175,288	51.5	48.5	21.2
Christmas Island	52	135	200	1,900	212	36.5	14.1	-9.8	1981	2,871	66.8	33.2	—
Cocos (Keeling) Islands	5.6	14.4	211	600	214	107.1	41.7	1.7	1986	616	53.7[13]	46.3[13]	...
Colombia	440,831	1,141,748	26	30,661,000	30	69.6	26.9	1.8	1985	27,867,326	49.5	50.5	63.6[14]
Comoros	719	1,862	158	433,000	144	602.2	232.5	3.4	1980	335,150	49.9	50.1	23.2
Congo	132,047	342,000	57	2,266,000	120	17.2	6.6	3.9	1984	1,912,429	48.5[15]	51.5[15]	51.1
Cook Islands	91	236	194	17,000	198	186.8	72.0	-0.5	1986	19,369	52.2	47.8	...
Costa Rica	19,730	51,100	116	2,672,000	114	135.4	52.3	2.5	1984	2,416,809	50.0	50.0	43.9
Côte d'Ivoire	123,847	320,763	63	11,634,000	57	93.9	36.3	4.3	1975	6,702,866	51.8	48.2	32.0
Cuba	42,804	110,861	99	10,421,000	62	243.5	94.0	1.0	1981	9,723,605	50.6	49.4	69.0
Cyprus	3,572	9,251	147	720,000	138	201.6	77.8	1.3	1982[3]	642,731	49.7	50.3	63.5
Czechoslovakia	49,382	127,900	92	15,604,000	50	316.0	122.0	0.2	1980	15,283,095	48.7	51.3	65.5
Denmark	16,638	43,092	119	5,130,000	92	308.3	119.0	0.1	1988[16]	5,129,254	49.3	50.7	84.4[17]
Djibouti	8,950	23,200	132	484,000	142	54.1	20.9	4.8	1960–61	81,200			75.0[18]
Dominica	290	750	167	79,300	178	273.4	105.7	0.7	1981[7]	73,795	49.8	50.2	...
Dominican Republic	18,704	48,443	117	6,850,000	83	366.2	141.4	2.1	1981	5,647,977	50.1	49.9	52.0
Ecuador	103,930	269,178	69	10,203,000	64	98.2	37.9	2.9	1982	8,060,712	49.9	50.1	49.2
Egypt	385,229	997,739	29	50,273,000	21	130.5	50.4	2.6	1986	48,205,049	51.1	48.9	43.9

mulated periodically); registration of migration, births, and deaths, and so on; sample surveys to establish demographic conditions; and the like.

The statistics provided for area and population by country are ranked, and the population densities based on those values are also provided. The population densities, for purposes of comparison within this table, are calculated on the bases of the 1988 mid-year population estimate as shown and of total area of the country. Elsewhere in individual country presentations the reader may find densities calculated on more specific population figures and more specialized area bases: land area for Finland (because of its many lakes), or ice-free area for Greenland (most of which is ice cap). The data in this section conclude with the estimated growth rate for the country (including both natural growth and net migration) during the five-year period, 1983–88.

In the section containing census data, information supplied includes the census total (usually de facto, the population actually present, rather than de jure, the population legally resident, who might be anywhere); the male–female breakdown; the proportion that is urban (according to the country's own definition of the term "urban," which differs very much from country to country); and finally an analysis of the age structure of the population by 15-year age groups. This last analysis may be particularly useful in distinguishing the general type of population being recorded— young, fast-growing nations show a high proportion of people under 30 (some countries like Jordan or Mayotte have more than 50% of their population under 15 years), while other nations (for example Sweden, which suffered no age-group losses in World War II) exhibit quite uniform proportions among age groups.

Finally, a section is provided giving the population of each country at the end of each decade from 1930 to 2000. The data for years past represent the best available analysis of the published data by the country itself, by the demographers of the United Nations, or by the editors of Britannica. The projections for 1990 and 2000, similarly, represent the best fit of available data through the mid-1980s with projected population structure and growth rates during the next 12 years. The evidence of the last 20 years with respect to similar estimates published around 1970, however, shows how cloudy is the glass through which these numbers are read. In 1970 no respectable Western analyst would have imagined proposing that mainland China could achieve the degree of birth control that it has since then (as evidenced in the 1982 census); on the other hand, even the Chinese admit that their methods have been somewhat Draconian and that they expect some backlash in terms of higher birth-rates among those who have so far postponed larger families. How much is "some" by 2000? Compound that problem with all the social, economic, political, and biological factors that can affect 200 countries' populations, and the difficulty facing the prospective compiler of such projections may be appreciated.

Specific data about the vital rates affecting the data in this table may be found in great detail in both the country statistical boxes in "The Nations of the World" section and in the *Vital statistics, marriage, family* table, beginning at page 764.

Percentages in this table for male and female population will always total 100.0, but percentages by age group may not for reasons such as nonresponse on census forms, "don't know" responses, which are common in countries with poor birth registration systems, and the like.

age distribution (%)						population (by decade, '000s)								country
0–14	15–29	30–44	45–59	60–74	75 and older	1930	1940	1950	1960	1970	1980	1990 projection	2000 projection	
44.5	26.9	15.8	8.6	3.6	0.6	...	...	8,150	9,829	12,431	14,985	15,592	24,501	Afghanistan
37.3[2]	28.9[2]	16.6[2]	10.2[2]	5.5[2]	1.5[2]	1,003	1,088	1,215	1,607	2,136	2,671	3,281	4,030	Albania
46.0[4]	27.2[4]	12.8[4]	8.3[4]	4.4	1.4	6,489	7,628	8,753	10,800	14,330	18,666	25,350	34,000	Algeria
40.9	28.8	16.0	9.4	4.0	0.9	10	13	19	20	27	32	40	48	American Samoa
19.0	27.3	26.4	14.8	9.4	3.1	5	5	6	8	19	33	57	96	Andorra
41.7	23.2	17.0	7.4	3.8	1.0	3,344	3,738	4,145	4,841	5,673	7,426	9,978	13,151	Angola
34.9	28.5	13.6	8.9	10.1	4.0	...	...	...	6	6	7	7	7	Anguilla
44.0	24.2	12.0	11.7	——8.0——		30	34	45	55	66	75	79	85	Antigua and Barbuda
30.4	23.9	18.8	15.1	9.0	2.8	11,896	14,169	17,150	20,611	23,788	28,237	32,880	37,197	Argentina
25.9	30.6	21.3	12.7	7.4	2.1	16	31	51	57	58	60	66	67	Aruba
23.1	25.2	22.1	14.6	11.0	4.0	6,503	7,079	8,219	10,315	12,552	14,741	16,921	19,371	Australia
19.9	23.6	20.1	17.1	13.2	6.1	6,435	6,684	6,935	7,048	7,447	7,549	7,587	7,628	Austria
38.1	27.8	17.9	9.8	5.1	1.3	61	70	79	113	169	210	253	302	Bahamas, The
32.9	34.5	20.0	8.8	3.1	0.7	...	90	127	162	215	337	431	472	Bahrain
46.6	24.6	14.9	8.2	——5.7——		35,353	41,259	45,482	54,699	68,171	88,507	113,005	139,693	Bangladesh
28.9	32.3	14.2	11.2	——13.3——		159	179	209	232	235	249	255	261	Barbados
20.0	23.7	19.1	18.6	12.8	5.8	8,129	8,301	8,639	9,153	9,690	9,859	9,867	9,881	Belgium
46.2	27.1	11.8	8.4	4.7	1.8	51	56	68	90	120	145	187	240	Belize
45.9[2]	25.4[2]	15.1[2]	8.6[2]	3.9[2]	0.9[2]	1,099	1,355	1,538	1,990	2,686	3,494	4,733	6,532	Benin
22.7	27.5	22.2	15.7	9.0	2.9	28	31	37	43	53	55	59	65	Bermuda
39.2[8]	26.5[8]	16.3[8]	10.9[8]	——7.1[8]——		440	500	726	853	1,045	1,165	1,420	1,731	Bhutan
41.5	27.0	15.4	9.8	4.6	1.7	2,153	2,508	2,765	3,405	4,265	5,600	7,400	9,837	Bolivia
56.5	19.9	10.2	6.6	3.4	3.4	212	278	387	522	650	889	1,303	1,817	Botswana
39.1	28.6	16.4	10.0	——5.9——		33,718	41,525	52,901	71,539	93,139	121,286	150,368	179,487	Brazil
34.0	29.0	18.7	9.7	6.3	2.3	5	7	7	7	10	11	13	15	British Virgin Islands
38.5	32.7	16.4	7.9	——4.5——		30	36	48	84	129	187	269	388	Brunei
22.2[4]	20.4[4]	20.4[4]	19.4[4]	13.1[4]	4.5[4]	5,997	6,624	7,273	7,906	8,515	8,862	8,998	9,099	Bulgaria
44.5[4]	26.2[4]	14.4[4]	9.4[4]	4.5[4]	1.0[4]	...	...	3,584	4,350	5,412	6,604	8,994	11,716	Burkina Faso
37.6[4]	28.4[4]	17.6[4]	9.8[4]	5.6[4]	1.1[4]	14,282	16,119	18,489	22,063	26,997	33,938	41,186	48,596	Burma
42.4	29.4	13.4	8.2	4.8	1.8	...	...	2,435	2,908	3,350	4,120	5,425	7,170	Burundi
43.4	24.3	16.6	9.9	4.3	1.5	...	...	4,888	5,609	6,727	8,727	11,935	16,360	Cameroon
21.5[4]	26.5[4]	22.5[4]	14.7[4]	10.7[4]	4.1[4]	10,498	11,693	13,737	17,909	21,324	24,067	26,343	28,785	Canada
46.0	27.6	9.1	9.0	6.3	2.0	146	181	147	200	272	296	377	479	Cape Verde
29.1	25.8	22.1	13.1	7.3	2.6	6	7	7	8	11	17	25	38	Cayman Islands
43.5	23.5	17.1	12.4	2.7	0.8	...	...	1,311	1,500	1,793	2,333	2,987	3,824	Central African Republic
40.6	28.3	17.2	9.5	——4.4——		...	2,351	2,639	3,032	3,643	4,477	5,668	7,308	Chad
31.9	29.1	19.1	11.7	6.3	1.9	4,365	5,063	6,091	7,585	9,368	11,104	13,188	15,617	Chile
33.6	29.1	17.5	12.2	6.3	1.3	500,000	530,000	556,613	682,024	838,396	981,235	1,112,000	1,253,000	China
25.9	26.4	35.8	10.8	——1.1——		...	...	1	1	3	3	2	1	Christmas Island
27.4[13]	28.3[13]	27.2[13]	11.2[13]	——5.9[13]——		...	...	1	1	1	1	1	1	Cocos (Keeling) Islands
36.1	31.2	17.2	9.5	4.6	1.4	7,280	9,097	11,268	15,321	20,884	26,465	31,686	36,313	Colombia
47.2	23.2	14.8	7.6	5.1	1.8	...	...	...	177	245	333	463	644	Comoros
45.6[15]	22.2[15]	15.5[15]	11.3[15]	4.7[15]	0.7[15]	...	...	736	933	1,182	1,664	2,447	3,600	Congo
37.8	29.1	14.1	11.6	5.7	1.5	11	13	15	18	18	18	17	16	Cook Islands
37.9	31.5	15.8	9.2	4.4	1.2	499	619	866	1,250	1,737	2,206	2,804	3,572	Costa Rica
44.5	27.0	16.7	7.8	2.8	1.2	2,075	2,350	2,775	3,865	5,550	8,320	12,657	19,289	Côte d'Ivoire
30.3	27.6	19.1	12.1	8.2	2.7	3,837	4,566	5,752	7,019	8,565	9,724	10,683	11,844	Cuba
25.0	26.6	20.1	13.8	——14.5——		357	413	494	573	615	628	738	834	Cyprus
24.3	22.9	19.8	17.2	11.5	4.3	13,964	14,713	12,389	13,654	14,334	15,265	15,664	16,086	Czechoslovakia
17.6	22.8	22.8	16.4	13.7	6.7	3,542	3,832	4,271	4,581	4,929	5,123	5,135	5,146	Denmark
38.0[18]	34.0[18]	17.0[18]	————11.0[18]————			70	44	60	78	158	355	513	690	Djibouti
39.8	28.6	11.9	9.2	7.4	3.1	41	45	51	60	70	74	81	87	Dominica
43.9[2]	29.3[2]	14.2[2]	8.2[2]	3.5[2]	1.0[2]	1,400	1,759	2,313	3,160	4,343	5,622	7,144	8,823	Dominican Republic
41.9	28.1	15.4	8.6	4.5	1.5	2,102	2,546	3,307	4,421	5,958	8,123	10,782	13,939	Ecuador
39.9[19,20]	26.7[19,20]	16.6[19,20]	10.6[19,20]	5.2[19,20]	1.0[19,20]	14,822	16,942	20,461	26,085	33,329	40,546	52,536	63,941	Egypt

Area and population (continued)

country	area			population (latest estimate)					population (most recent census)				
	square miles	square kilo-metres	rank	total midyear 1988	rank	density per sq mi	per sq km	% annual growth rate 1983–88	census year	total	male (%)	female (%)	urban (%)
El Salvador	8,124	21,041	134	5,083,000	93	625.7	241.6	1.5	1971	3,554,648	49.6	50.4	39.4
Equatorial Guinea	10,831	28,051	128	335,000	153	30.9	11.9	2.2	1983	300,000	48.1	51.9	27.6
Ethiopia	472,400	1,223,500	24	47,501,000	22	100.6	38.8	2.8	1984	42,184,966	49.8	50.2	10.2
Faeroe Islands	540	1,399	160	47,000	188	87.0	33.6	1.1	1987	46,369	52.3	47.7	96.2
Falkland Islands	4,700	12,173	142	1,900	211	0.4	0.2	1.0	1986	1,916	54.7[21]	45.3[21]	56.8[21]
Fiji	7,056	18,274	137	742,000	137	105.2	40.6	2.0	1986	715,375	50.7	49.3	38.7
Finland	130,559	338,145	58	4,952,000	94	37.9	14.6	0.4	1980	4,784,710	48.3	51.7	59.9
France	210,026	543,965	46	55,860,000	17	266.0	102.7	0.4	1982	54,334,871	49.0	51.0	73.2[2]
French Guiana	33,399	86,504	108	92,100	175	2.8	1.1	3.7	1982	73,022	52.7	47.3	73.4
French Polynesia	1,359	3,521	153	188,000	161	138.3	53.4	2.6	1983	166,753	51.1	48.9	39.7
Gabon	103,347	267,667	70	1,219,000	130	11.8	4.6	1.9	1960–61	448,564	49.1[4]	50.9[4]	40.9[4]
Gambia, The	4,127	10,689	145	811,000	135	196.5	75.9	3.0	1983	695,886	50.7[14]	49.3[14]	21.2
Gaza Strip	140	363	184	571,000	141	4,078.6	1,573.0	3.3	1986[16]	527,000	49.9	50.1	...
Germany, East	41,827	108,333	101	16,588,000	47	396.6	153.1	-0.1	1981	16,705,635	47.0	53.0	76.4
Germany, West	96,026	248,709	74	60,782,000	13	633.0	244.4	-0.2	1987[16]	61,140,500	47.9	52.1	85.5[4]
Ghana	92,098	238,533	78	13,754,000	54	149.3	57.7	2.8	1984	12,296,081	49.3	50.7	32.0
Gibraltar	2.3	5.8	213	29,500	192	12,826.1	5,086.2	0.2	1981[22]	26,479	52.2	47.8	...
Greece	50,949	131,957	91	10,055,000	65	197.4	76.2	0.4	1981	9,740,417	49.1	50.9	58.1
Greenland	840,000	2,175,600	13	54,600	186	0.1	0.0	0.9	1988[16]	54,524	54.4	45.6	79.3
Grenada	133	345	186	106,000	172	797.0	307.2	3.1	1981	89,088	47.1[2]	52.9[2]	25.3[24]
Guadeloupe	687	1,780	159	340,000	151	494.9	191.0	0.5	1982[23]	327,002	49.0	51.0	43.5[2]
Guam	209	541	173	126,000	168	602.9	232.9	2.2	1980	105,979	52.2	47.8	39.5
Guatemala	42,042	108,889	100	8,681,000	70	206.5	79.7	2.9	1981[3]	6,043,559	49.8	50.2	34.3
Guernsey	30	78	204	59,300	184	1,976.7	760.3	0.8	1986[25]	55,482[25]	48.3[26]	51.7[26]	...
Guinea	94,926	245,857	75	6,540,000	86	68.9	26.6	2.5	1983	5,781,014	48.6	51.4	26.0
Guinea-Bissau	13,948	36,125	122	931,000	133	66.7	25.8	2.1	1979	767,739	48.2	51.8	14.0
Guyana	83,000	215,000	81	757,000	136	9.1	3.5	0.0	1980	758,619	49.7[24]	50.3[24]	31.9[24]
Haiti	10,579	27,400	130	5,451,000	89	515.3	198.9	1.3	1982	5,053,792	48.5	51.5	20.6
Honduras	43,277	112,088	97	4,803,000	95	111.0	42.9	3.3	1974	2,656,948	49.5	50.5	37.5
Hong Kong	403	1,045	162	5,683,000	88	14,101.7	5,438.3	1.2	1986[27]	5,396,000	51.4	48.6	93.1
Hungary	35,919	93,031	105	10,591,000	61	294.9	113.8	-0.2	1980	10,709,463	48.4	51.6	53.2
Iceland	39,769	103,000	102	248,000	157	6.2	2.4	0.9	1987[16]	247,024	50.2	49.8	90.0
India	1,222,559	3,166,414	7	801,806,000	2	655.8	253.2	1.9	1981	685,184,692	50.3	49.7	23.7
Indonesia	741,101	1,919,443	15	175,904,000	5	237.4	91.6	2.2	1980	147,490,298	49.7	50.3	22.3
Iran	636,372	1,648,196	17	51,225,000	20	80.5	31.1	3.5	1986	49,857,384	51.1	48.9	54.2
Iraq	169,235	438,317	53	16,630,000	45	98.3	37.9	3.1	1977	12,000,497	51.5	48.5	63.7
Ireland	27,137	70,285	113	3,553,000	105	130.9	50.6	0.5	1986	3,540,643	50.0	50.0	55.6[13]
Isle of Man	221	572	172	64,100	183	290.0	112.1	-0.1	1986[3]	64,282	47.9	52.1	51.1
Israel[28]	7,992	20,700	135	4,512,000	96	564.6	218.0	1.9	1983[3, 29]	4,037,620	49.8	50.2	86.9
Italy	116,324	301,277	65	57,401,000	15	493.5	190.5	0.2	1981[3]	56,556,911	48.6	51.4	66.5[2]
Jamaica	4,244	10,991	144	2,407,000	117	567.2	219.0	1.4	1982	2,190,357	49.1	50.9	47.8
Japan	145,875	377,815	56	122,620,000	7	840.6	324.6	0.6	1985	121,047,196	49.2	50.8	76.7
Jersey	45	116	201	82,200	177	1,826.7	708.6	1.1	1986[3]	80,212	48.3	51.7	...
Jordan[30]	34,443	89,206	107	2,965,000	111	86.1	33.2	3.9	1979	2,132,997	52.3	47.7	59.5
Kampuchea	69,898	181,035	85	7,876,000	76	112.7	43.5	2.7	1981	6,684,000	50.0[31]	50.0[31]	10.3[31]
Kenya	224,961	582,646	44	22,919,000	38	101.9	39.3	4.1	1979	15,327,061	49.7	50.3	15.1
Kiribati	328	849	164	68,200	180	207.9	80.3	1.9	1985	64,026	49.6	50.4	33.5
Korea, North	47,250	122,370	94	21,903,000	39	463.6	179.0	2.4	[32]	[32]	49.6[4]	50.4[4]	63.8[4]
Korea, South	38,291	99,173	103	42,593,000	23	1,112.4	429.5	1.3	1985[3]	40,448,486	50.0	50.0	65.4
Kuwait	6,880	17,818	138	1,958,000	122	284.6	109.9	4.6	1985	1,697,301	56.9	43.1	100.0
Laos	91,400	236,800	80	3,850,000	102	42.1	16.3	2.0	1985	3,584,803	50.4[4]	49.6[4]	15.9[4]
Lebanon	3,950	10,230	146	2,828,000	113	715.9	276.4	1.4	1970	2,126,325	50.8	49.2	60.1
Lesotho	11,720	30,355	125	1,671,000	125	142.6	55.0	2.6	1986[3]	1,577,536	48.2	51.8	17.2[20]
Liberia	38,250	99,067	104	2,427,000	116	63.5	24.5	3.3	1984	2,101,628	50.6	49.4	38.8
Libya	685,524	1,775,500	16	4,316,000	98	6.3	2.4	4.5	1984	3,637,488	53.0[14]	47.0[14]	59.8[14]
Liechtenstein	62	160	198	27,800	194	448.4	173.8	1.0	1980	25,215	49.6	50.4	...
Luxembourg	999	2,586	155	372,000	148	372.4	143.9	0.4	1981	364,602	48.8	51.2	77.6[2]
Macau	6.5	16.9	210	466,000	143	71,692.3	27,574.0	7.3	1981[3]	241,729	50.9	49.1	95.4
Madagascar	226,658	587,041	43	10,917,000	60	48.2	18.6	2.9	1974–75	7,603,790	50.0	50.0	16.3
Malawi	45,747	118,484	95	8,211,000	74	179.5	69.3	3.7	1987	7,982,607	48.6	51.4	8.5[5]
Malaysia	127,581	330,434	61	16,965,000	44	133.0	51.3	2.6	1980	13,136,109	50.2	49.8	34.2
Maldives	115	298	188	202,000	159	1,756.5	677.9	3.4	1985	181,453	51.8	48.2	25.5
Mali	478,841	1,240,192	22	7,778,000	77	16.2	6.3	1.7	1987	7,620,225	48.9	51.1	16.8[20]
Malta	122	316	187	347,000	150	2,844.3	1,098.1	0.8	1985	345,418	49.2	50.8	94.3[33]
Martinique	421	1,091	161	336,000	152	798.1	308.0	0.5	1982[3]	326,717	48.5	51.5	57.1
Mauritania	398,000	1,030,700	28	1,894,000	123	4.8	1.8	2.6	1976–77	1,419,939	50.1	49.9	21.9
Mauritius	788	2,040	157	1,049,000	132	1,331.2	514.2	0.9	1983	1,002,178	49.8	50.2	41.7[34]
Mayotte	144	373	183	77,600	179	538.9	208.0	5.1	1985	67,167	49.9[35]	50.1[35]	53.3[35]
Mexico	756,066	1,958,201	14	82,659,000	11	107.6	41.5	2.0	1980	66,846,833	49.4	50.6	66.3
Monaco	0.7	1.9	215	28,900	193	41,285.7	15,210.5	0.9	1982	27,063	46.6	53.4	100.0
Mongolia	604,800	1,566,500	18	2,041,000	121	3.4	1.3	2.6	1979	1,594,800	50.1	49.9	51.2
Montserrat	40	102	202	12,000	202	300.0	117.6	0.5	1980	11,606	48.1	51.9	13.2
Morocco	177,117	458,730	51	23,809,000	35	134.4	51.9	2.8	1982	20,419,555[36]	50.1	49.9	42.7
Mozambique	308,642	799,380	35	14,890,000	51	48.2	18.6	2.6	1980	12,130,000	48.7	51.3	13.2
Nauru	8.2	21.2	209	8,100	205	987.8	382.1	0.0	1983	8,042	52.1[5, 37]	47.9[5, 37]	—
Nepal	56,827	147,181	89	18,004,000	43	316.8	122.3	2.6	1981	15,022,839	51.2	48.8	6.4
Netherlands, The	16,163	41,863	120	14,741,000	52	912.0	352.1	0.5	1987[16]	14,615,125	49.4	50.6	88.4
Netherlands Antilles	308	800	165	177,000	163	574.7	221.3	0.4	1981	171,620	48.3	51.7	...
New Caledonia	7,172	18,576	136	156,000	165	21.8	8.4	1.3	1983	145,368	51.8	48.2	58.5
New Zealand	103,288	267,515	71	3,354,000	107	32.5	12.5	0.6	1986	3,307,084	49.5	50.5	83.8
Nicaragua	49,363	127,849	93	3,622,000	103	73.4	28.3	3.4	1971	1,877,952	48.3	51.7	48.0
Niger	458,075	1,186,408	25	6,937,000	82	15.1	5.8	3.0	1977	5,098,427	49.3	50.7	11.8
Nigeria	356,669	923,768	31	112,258,000	8	314.7	108.9	3.3	1963[38]	55,670,055	50.5	49.5	16.1
Niue	100	258	192	2,400	208	24.0	9.3	-4.8	1984	2,887	51.2	48.8	...
Norfolk Island	14	35	207	2,000	210	142.9	57.1	1.4	1986[3]	1,977	50.7	49.3	—

0–14	15–29	30–44	45–59	60–74	75 and older	1930	1940	1950	1960	1970	1980	1990 projection	2000 projection	country
46.2	25.1	15.2	8.2	4.3	1.0	1,350	1,550	1,931	2,527	3,534	4,508	5,234	6,996	El Salvador
38.1[4]	26.0[4]	17.7[4]	11.5[4]	5.6[4]	1.1[4]	...	...	211	244	291	255	351	445	Equatorial Guinea
46.6	22.7	15.6	8.9	4.5	1.7	...	...	16,675	20,024	24,068	38,426	50,341	67,523	Ethiopia
24.8	—45.7—		13.8	—15.7—		24	27	31	35	39	43	48	53	Faeroe Islands
25.4[21]	22.6[21]	—38.0[21]—		—14.0[21]—		2	2	2	2	2	2	2	2	Falkland Islands
38.2	29.5	17.8	9.6	3.8	0.8	181	218	289	394	520	634	771	939	Fiji
20.2	24.4	22.1	16.8	12.4	4.1	3,449	3,698	4,009	4,430	4,606	4,780	4,992	5,192	Finland
22.0	23.5	19.6	17.3	11.6	6.0	41,150	41,300	41,736	45,684	50,770	53,880	56,319	58,673	France
34.2	29.2	19.9	9.8	5.1	1.8	30	30	27	33	49	69	99	142	French Guiana
38.5	29.7	16.5	10.3	4.2	0.8	39	50	62	84	109	151	197	254	French Polynesia
35.4[4]	24.1[4]	18.1[4]	13.1[4]	7.5[4]	1.8[4]	...	...	...	...	950	1,064	1,273	1,603	Gabon
41.3[14]	26.5[14]	17.6[14]	8.3[14]	4.3[14]	1.7[14]	211	193	232	357	458	632	860	1,156	Gambia, The
49.2	—38.9—			—11.9—		...	...	...	...	370	451	607	807	Gaza Strip
19.4	24.2	20.0	17.3	12.8	6.3	15,400	16,800	18,387	17,240	17,058	16,737	16,552	16,371	Germany, East
14.7	24.3	20.1	20.3	13.5	7.1	37,500	40,600	49,986	55,433	60,714	61,566	60,500	59,107	Germany, West
45.0	26.4	14.6	8.1	4.1	1.8	3,110	3,636	5,297	6,958	8,789	11,133	14,488	18,790	Ghana
21.4	22.2	22.3	17.7	12.6	3.8	16	14	23	24	26	30	30	30	Gibraltar
21.3[23]	22.0[23]	19.1[23]	19.8[23]	12.4[23]	5.4[23]	6,367	7,319	7,566	8,327	8,793	9,643	10,145	10,608	Greece
24.6	32.4	23.7	13.4	4.9	1.1	16	19	23	33	41	50	56	61	Greenland
39.4[2]	31.2[2]	10.1[2]	9.2[2]	7.3[2]	2.8[2]	68	71	76	90	95	91	110	133	Grenada
31.1	29.2	16.6	12.0	7.8	2.8	151	180	206	265	320	327	343	361	Guadeloupe
34.9	30.6	19.4	10.5	3.9	0.5	19	22	59	67	85	107	132	165	Guam
44.9	26.8	14.8	8.5	3.9	1.1	1,771	2,201	3,024	4,005	5,263	6,917	9,197	12,222	Guatemala
21.6[26]	22.2[26]	17.6[26]	17.7[26]	15.2[26]	5.6[26]	40	44	44	45	51	55	60	65	Guernsey
43.1[4]	26.2[4]	16.3[4]	9.6[4]	4.2[4]	0.7[4]	...	...	3,245	3,660	4,388	5,407	6,876	8,879	Guinea
44.3	25.5	15.1	8.2	4.7	2.2	...	341	411	520	653	787	971	1,200	Guinea-Bissau
47.1[24]	25.1[24]	13.4[24]	9.0[24]	4.4[24]	1.0[24]	309	344	423	560	702	759	765	821	Guyana
39.2	26.9	15.6	10.0	5.4	2.9	2,422	2,827	3,097	3,723	4,234	4,922	5,590	6,338	Haiti
48.1	25.8	13.9	7.8	3.6	0.9	948	1,146	1,390	1,873	2,553	3,691	5,105	6,978	Honduras
23.1	29.9	21.2	14.3	9.1	2.4	821	1,786	1,974	3,074	3,942	5,063	5,823	6,582	Hong Kong
21.8	20.7	—40.6—		—16.9—		8,649	9,280	9,338	9,984	10,353	10,708	10,554	10,370	Hungary
25.8	26.1	20.9	13.2	9.9	4.1	107	121	143	176	204	228	252	276	Iceland
39.5	25.9	17.4	10.7	—6.5—		278,000	317,000	352,664	427,802	543,132	687,057	824,885	971,762	India
40.8	27.0	16.4	10.2	4.5	1.1	60,750	70,500	75,449	92,701	119,467	148,040	183,457	222,753	Indonesia
44.5[20]	25.2[20]	14.8[20]	10.1[20]	3.8[20]	1.0[20]	12,400	14,000	16,913	21,554	28,359	38,559	52,997	64,976	Iran
48.9	24.5	12.3	8.2	4.2	1.9	...	3,745	5,180	6,847	9,356	13,031	17,676	23,801	Iraq
30.3[13]	24.6[13]	17.2[13]	13.1[13]	10.9[13]	3.8[13]	2,927	2,958	2,969	2,834	2,954	3,415	3,573	3,673	Ireland
17.6	20.2	19.0	16.0	17.4	9.2	50	52	55	49	52	64	64	63	Isle of Man
32.6	26.4	18.0	12.3	9.4	3.1	...	...	2,114	2,958	3,896	4,614	5,490	5,717	Israel[28]
21.4	22.4	20.0	18.7	12.7	4.7	40,293	43,840	46,769	50,223	53,565	56,434	57,407	57,117	Italy
38.4	28.8	13.8	9.4	6.9	2.6	1,009	1,212	1,403	1,629	1,891	2,133	2,481	2,882	Jamaica
21.5	20.7	23.9	19.2	10.8	3.9	64,450	73,075	83,200	93,419	103,720	116,807	123,942	130,771	Japan
15.3	25.8	22.7	16.9	12.8	6.4	50	51	57	63	68	76	84	94	Jersey
51.6	23.4	13.4	7.4	3.1	1.1	...	...	1,095	1,384	1,795	2,181	3,202	4,705	Jordan[30]
43.8[31]	24.9[31]	16.8[31]	9.8[31]	4.1[31]	0.6[31]	2,800	3,400	4,163	5,364	7,060	6,400	8,246	9,772	Kampuchea
51.4	24.8	13.2	7.0	3.0	0.6	3,400	4,470	6,018	8,115	11,225	16,667	24,821	36,977	Kenya
38.9	29.9	16.1	9.3	4.9	0.9	27	29	33	41	49	59	71	87	Kiribati
38.7[4]	29.2[4]	16.6[4]	9.8[4]	4.7[4]	1.0[4]	...	...	9,740	10,526	13,892	18,025	22,939	28,166	Korea, North
29.9	31.3	19.5	12.5	5.5	1.3	...	...	21,147	25,142	32,976	38,124	43,601	48,017	Korea, South
36.8	28.3	24.1	8.6	1.8	0.4	...	...	145	292	748	1,370	2,143	2,877	Kuwait
42.5[4]	26.6[4]	16.2[4]	9.7[4]	4.3[4]	0.7[4]	930	1,075	1,949	2,382	2,962	3,292	4,024	4,964	Laos
42.6	23.8	16.7	9.1	—7.7—		...	965	1,364	1,786	2,470	2,669	2,967	3,617	Lebanon
39.1[20]	25.5[20]	15.5[20]	10.4[20]	5.2[20]	2.3[20]	537	566	766	885	1,043	1,358	1,760	2,282	Lesotho
43.2	28.2	14.7	7.8	4.4	1.8	...	...	758	1,004	1,393	1,864	2,591	3,596	Liberia
44.3[14]	22.2[14]	15.4[14]	8.2[14]	4.0[14]	1.6[14]	800	900	1,029	1,349	1,982	3,043	4,710	7,292	Libya
23.0	26.5	24.1	14.1	9.2	3.1	10	11	14	16	21	26	28	32	Liechtenstein
18.5	23.7	21.2	18.7	12.8	5.1	297	296	296	314	339	364	375	388	Luxembourg
22.9	36.2	16.7	12.7	8.8	2.6	196	375	188	169	221	270	524	819	Macau
44.4	25.7	14.2	10.0	4.6	1.1	3,722	4,034	4,330	5,370	6,720	8,714	11,575	15,550	Madagascar
44.6[5]	25.7[5]	14.2[5]	9.0[5]	4.3[5]	2.0[5]	1,394	1,696	3,033	3,481	4,511	6,137	8,831	12,201	Malawi
39.5	29.1	16.5	9.2	4.6	1.1	...	...	6,187	7,908	10,466	13,764	17,875	21,147	Malaysia
44.6[5]	24.8[5]	16.4[5]	9.6[5]	3.5[5]	0.6[5]	78	81	82	106	128	155	216	300	Maldives
44.0[20]	24.9[20]	16.1[20]	8.7[20]	4.8[20]	1.5[20]	2,815	3,388	3,426	4,224	5,690	6,791	8,047	9,535	Mali
24.1	23.2	23.0	15.4	10.5	3.8	239	270	308	329	326	324	351	368	Malta
30.5	29.3	15.9	13.0	8.2	3.0	175	200	222	252	287	326	339	355	Martinique
45.7	26.1	14.8[2]	8.7[2]	4.0[2]	0.6[2]	...	...	781	970	1,245	1,548	1,999	2,673	Mauritania
32.6	31.7	17.8	10.9	5.7	1.3	413	428	479	662	824	957	1,068	1,170	Mauritius
50.2[35]	23.4[35]	13.9[35]	7.0[35]	3.8[35]	1.7[35]	...	...	...	...	...	52	86	112	Mayotte
43.0	27.8	14.9	8.4	4.0	1.8	16,589	19,815	26,606	36,369	50,313	69,655	85,784	100,039	Mexico
12.7[10]	17.8[10]	18.6[10]	19.9[10]	20.7[10]	10.0[10]	23	20	22	23	24	27	29	31	Monaco
43.1[2]	26.2[2]	16.3[2]	9.4[2]	4.1[2]	0.9[2]	725	750	747	931	1,248	1,663	2,150	2,778	Mongolia
31.5	27.2	13.8	10.7	11.6	5.3	13	15	14	12	12	12	12	13	Montserrat
42.2	28.3	14.1	9.2	4.8	1.5	6,980	7,750	8,953	11,640	15,126	19,082	25,168	33,221	Morocco
44.4	26.7	15.9	8.7	3.6	0.7	3,890	5,086	5,742	7,046	9,140	12,103	15,696	20,463	Mozambique
44.1[5,37]	33.1[5,37]	11.4[5,37]	8.5[5,37]	1.9[5,37]	1.0[5,37]	3	3	4	5	7	8	8	8	Nauru
41.4	25.5	17.4	10.0	4.7	1.0	6,250	7,000	8,000	9,180	11,232	14,642	18,910	23,176	Nepal
18.8	25.5	23.0	15.7	11.8	5.2	7,936	8,834	10,027	11,417	12,958	14,150	14,893	15,679	Netherlands, The
30.0	29.9	19.5	11.3	6.7	2.6	61	77	112	136	163	171	178	186	Netherlands Antilles
36.2	26.9	19.5	11.2	5.1	1.1	54	53	59	79	110	140	160	183	New Caledonia
24.4	26.0	20.8	14.1	10.7	4.0	1,491	1,636	1,908	2,372	2,820	3,170	3,422	3,757	New Zealand
48.1	25.6	14.1	7.4	3.8	1.1	700	825	1,109	1,472	1,972	2,771	3,871	5,261	Nicaragua
45.9[2]	25.6[2]	14.7[2]	8.2[2]	4.6[2]	1.0[2]	1,490	1,700	2,291	2,913	4,016	5,499	7,366	10,083	Niger
43.0	31.9	16.5	5.1	2.5	1.0	...	...	33,320	42,366	56,346	87,255	119,812	166,012	Nigeria
38.2	26.9	14.4	11.3	6.3	2.8	4	4	4	4	4	3	2	1	Niue
24.2	16.5	22.7	20.0	—16.7—		1	1	1	1	2	2	2	2	Norfolk Island

Area and population (continued)

country	area square miles	area square kilometres	area rank	population total midyear 1988	rank	density per sq mi	density per sq km	% annual growth rate 1983–88	census year	total	male (%)	female (%)	urban (%)
Norway	125,050	323,878	62	4,202,000	99	33.6	13.0	0.4	1987[16]	4,175,521	49.4	50.6	70.3[39]
Oman	120,000	300,000	67	1,372,000	126	11.4	4.6	3.7	[32]	[32]	52.9[4]	47.1[4]	8.8[4]
Pacific Is., Trust Territory of the													
Marshall Islands	70	181	197	42,200	190	602.9	233.1	4.0	1980	30,873	51.3	48.7	47.8
Micronesia, Federated States of	271	702	168	101,000	173	372.7	143.9	3.4	1980	73,160	51.1	48.9	19.4
Northern Mariana Islands	184	477	176	21,900	197	119.0	45.9	2.6	1980	16,780	52.5	47.5	16.0
Palau	188	488	175	14,700	200	78.2	30.1	2.5	1986	13,873	53.3	46.7	51.4[39]
Pakistan	339,697	879,811	33	109,434,000	9	322.2	124.4	3.0	1981[40]	84,253,644	52.5	47.5	28.3
Panama	29,762	77,082	111	2,322,000	119	78.0	30.1	2.1	1980	1,831,399	50.7	49.3	49.7
Papua New Guinea	178,704	462,840	50	3,562,000	104	19.9	7.7	2.3	1980	3,010,727	52.3	47.7	13.1
Paraguay	157,048	406,752	54	4,007,000	100	25.5	9.8	2.9	1982	3,035,360	50.1	49.9	42.8
Peru	496,225	1,285,216	19	21,256,000	40	42.8	16.5	2.6	1981	17,005,210	49.7	50.3	64.9
Philippines	115,800	300,000	66	58,723,000	14	507.1	195.7	2.4	1980	48,098,460	50.2	49.8	37.3
Pitcairn Island	1.8	4.5	214	51	215	28.3	11.3	−0.4	1987	68	54.7[13]	45.3[13]	—
Poland	120,727	312,683	64	37,864,000	26	313.6	121.1	0.7	1978	35,061,450	48.7	51.3	57.5
Portugal	35,672	92,389	106	10,349,000	63	290.1	112.0	0.7	1981[3]	9,833,014	48.2	51.8	29.7
Puerto Rico	3,515	9,104	148	3,301,000	108	939.1	362.6	0.2	1980	3,196,520	48.7	51.3	66.8
Qatar	4,400	11,400	143	420,000	147	95.5	36.8	8.0	1986	369,079	67.2	32.8	88.0[4]
Réunion	982	2,544	156	575,000	140	585.5	226.0	1.7	1982[3]	515,798	49.1	50.9	52.8
Romania	91,699	237,500	79	23,014,000	37	251.0	96.9	0.4	1977	21,559,910	49.3	50.7	47.5
Rwanda	10,169	26,338	131	6,709,000	84	659.8	254.7	3.4	1978	4,830,984	48.9	51.1	4.5
St. Helena and Ascension	159	412	181	7,300	206	45.9	17.7	1.4	1976[41]	5,866	52.0	48.0	25.8
St. Kitts and Nevis	104	269	190	43,200	189	415.4	160.6	−0.3	1980	43,309	48.1	51.9	37.1
St. Lucia	238	617	171	145,000	167	609.2	235.0	2.0	1980	120,300	47.2	52.8	...
St. Pierre and Miquelon	93	242	193	6,200	208	66.7	25.6	0.4	1982	6,041	49.4	50.6	...
St. Vincent and the Grenadines	150	389	182	113,000	170	753.3	290.5	1.2	1980	97,845	48.5[2]	51.5[2]	25.7[2]
San Marino	24	61	205	22,800	196	950.0	373.8	0.6	1976	19,149	50.4	49.6	90.1[42]
São Tomé and Príncipe	386	1,001	163	117,000	169	303.1	116.9	2.9	1981	96,611	49.7	50.3	...
Saudi Arabia	865,000	2,240,000	12	12,972,000	55	15.0	5.8	4.0	1974	6,726,466	53.2	46.8	65.9[2]
Senegal	75,955	196,722	82	7,187,000	80	94.6	36.5	2.9	1976	4,907,057	49.5	50.5	26.7
Seychelles	175	453	178	66,900	181	382.3	147.7	0.8	1977	61,898	50.4	49.6	37.2
Sierra Leone	27,699	71,740	112	3,883,000	101	140.2	54.1	1.9	1985	3,517,530	49.6	50.4	28.3[4]
Singapore	240	622	170	2,641,000	115	11,004.2	4,246.0	1.1	1980	2,413,945	51.0	49.0	100.0
Solomon Islands	10,954	28,370	127	301,000	154	27.5	10.6	3.5	1986	285,176	51.9	48.1	9.3[20]
Somalia	246,000	637,000	41	6,334,000	87	25.7	9.9	2.8	1975	3,253,024[1]	49.4[2]	50.6[2]	30.2[2]
South Africa[43]	473,290	1,225,815	23	36,840,000	27	77.8	30.1	2.6	1985[44]	27,722,100	51.2	48.8	55.9[45]
Bophuthatswana	16,988	44,000	—	2,005,000	—	118.0	45.6	6.8	1980	1,287,814	46.9[24]	53.1[24]	14.2[24]
Ciskei	2,996	7,760	—	946,000	—	315.8	121.9	4.1	1985	831,636	47.3	52.7	49.8
Transkei	16,855	43,653	—	3,714,000	—	220.4	63.3	4.2	1980	2,334,946	41.2[24]	58.8[24]	3.2[24]
Venda	2,771	7,176	—	547,000	—	197.4	76.2	5.9	1985	459,986	41.0[39]	59.0[39]	2.1[39]
South West Africa/Namibia	317,818	823,144	34	1,228,000	129	3.9	1.5	2.4	1981	1,040,708	49.2	50.8	26.0
Spain	194,898	504,783	48	38,996,000	25	200.1	77.3	0.4	1981	37,746,260	49.1	50.9	72.8[2]
Sri Lanka	25,332	65,610	114	16,606,000	46	655.5	253.1	1.5	1981	14,848,364	50.8	49.2	21.5
Sudan, The	966,757	2,503,890	9	26,263,000	31	27.2	10.5	3.8	1983	20,564,364	50.8	49.2	20.6[4]
Suriname	63,251	163,820	87	425,000	145	6.7	2.6	2.7	1980	354,860	49.5	50.5	44.8[2]
Swaziland	6,704	17,364	139	716,000	139	106.8	41.2	3.2	1986	681,059	47.2	52.8	22.8
Sweden	173,732	449,964	52	8,415,000	73	48.3	18.6	0.2	1986[16]	8,381,515	49.4	50.6	83.1[39]
Switzerland	15,943	41,293	121	6,626,000	85	415.6	160.5	0.4	1980[46]	6,365,960	48.9	51.1	57.1
Syria	71,498	185,180	84	11,338,000	58	158.6	61.2	3.4	1981	9,052,628	51.1	48.9	47.0
Taiwan	13,900	36,000	123	19,813,000	41	1,425.4	550.4	1.4	1980[3]	17,968,797	52.2	47.8	70.6[2]
Tanzania	364,881	945,037	30	23,996,000	33	65.8	25.4	3.3	1978	17,512,611	49.0	51.0	13.8
Thailand	198,115	513,115	47	54,862,000	18	276.9	106.9	2.1	1980	44,824,540	49.8	50.2	17.0
Togo	21,925	56,785	115	3,486,000	106	159.0	61.4	4.1	1981	2,705,250	48.7	51.3	15.2
Tokelau	4.7	12.2	212	1,700	213	361.7	139.3	1.2	1986	1,690	49.2	50.8	—
Tonga	301	780	166	95,300	174	316.6	122.2	0.5	1986	94,535	50.3	49.7	24.7[20]
Trinidad and Tobago	1,978	5,124	151	1,258,000	128	636.0	245.5	2.0	1980	1,079,791	50.0	50.0	56.9[2]
Tunisia	59,664	154,530	88	7,877,000	75	132.0	51.0	2.9	1984	6,975,450	50.8	49.2	52.8
Turkey	300,948	779,452	36	54,176,000	19	180.0	69.5	2.5	1985	50,664,458	50.4	49.6	45.9
Turks and Caicos Islands	193	500	174	10,500	203	54.4	21.0	5.9	1980	7,413	48.3	51.7	—
Tuvalu	9.3	24.0	208	8,700	204	935.5	362.5	0.9	1985	8,229	47.4	52.6	...
Uganda	93,070	241,040	77	15,990,000	49	171.8	66.3	2.9	1980	12,636,179	49.5	50.5	8.1
U.S.S.R.	8,649,500	22,402,200	1	285,796,000	3	33.0	12.8	1.0	1979	262,436,227	46.6	53.4	62.3
United Arab Emirates	30,000	77,700	110	1,774,000	124	59.1	22.8	6.4	1985	1,622,464	64.9	35.1	80.8[13]
United Kingdom	94,251	244,110	76	57,006,000	16	604.8	233.5	0.2	1981[48]	56,379,000	48.6	51.4	89.6
United States	3,679,192	9,529,063	4	246,113,000	4	66.9	25.8	0.9	1980[49]	226,545,805	48.6	51.4	73.7
Uruguay	68,037	176,215	86	2,981,000	110	43.8	16.9	0.5	1985	2,940,200	48.7	51.3	86.2
Vanuatu	4,707	12,190	141	149,000	166	31.7	12.2	3.1	1979	111,251	53.1	46.9	17.8
Venezuela	352,144	912,050	32	18,757,000	42	53.3	20.6	2.7	1981	14,516,735	50.0	50.0	85.7
Vietnam	128,052	331,653	60	63,807,000	12	498.3	192.4	2.1	1979	52,741,766	48.5	51.5	19.2
Virgin Islands (U.S.)	136	352	185	107,000	171	786.8	304.0	0.6	1980	96,569	47.8	52.2	29.6
Wallis and Futuna	106	274	189	15,700	199	148.1	57.3	4.5	1983	12,408	50.5	49.5	...
West Bank	2,270	5,900	149	865,000	134	381.1	146.6	2.6	1985[16]	793,400	49.8	50.2	...
Western Sahara	97,344	252,120	73	189,000	160	1.9	0.7	2.5	1970	76,425	...	...	...
Western Samoa	1,093	2,831	154	162,000	164	148.2	57.2	0.6	1981	156,349	51.8	48.2	21.2
Yemen (Aden)	130,066	336,869	59	2,345,000	118	18.0	7.0	2.6	1973	1,590,275	49.5	50.5	33.3
Yemen (Şan'ā')	75,300	195,000	83	8,614,000	71	114.4	44.2	2.6	1986	9,274,173[50]	47.3[13]	52.7[13]	10.2[13]
Yugoslavia	98,766	255,804	72	23,591,000	36	238.9	92.2	0.7	1981	22,424,711	49.4	50.6	47.3
Zaire	905,365	2,344,885	11	32,559,000	28	36.0	13.9	2.3	1984	29,671,407	49.2	50.8	36.6[4]
Zambia	290,586	752,614	38	7,384,000	79	25.4	9.8	3.5	1980	5,679,808	49.0	51.0	43.0
Zimbabwe	150,873	390,759	55	8,878,000	69	58.8	22.7	2.8	1982	7,532,000	49.3	50.7	23.0

[1]Settled population only. [2]1980 estimate. [3]Data are for de jure population. [4]1985 estimate. [5]1977 census. [6]Includes residents abroad; excludes visitors. [7]Excludes institutional population. [8]1982 estimate. [9]Excludes institutional population, residents abroad, and visitors. [10]1975 census. [11]Includes residents abroad and visitors. [12]Excludes visitors. [13]1981 census. [14]1973 census. [15]1974 census. [16]Civil register; not a census. [17]1986 register. [18]1983 estimate. [19]Excludes the Sinai and residents abroad. [20]1976 census. [21]1980 census. [22]Excludes visitors, transients, and family members of British servicemen. [23]1984 estimate. [24]1970 census. [25]Data exclude Alderney (population 2,130) and Sark (population 604). [26]1976 census. [27]Excludes residents abroad, visitors, and Vietnamese refugees. [28]Excluding territory occupied after 1967. [29]Includes East Jerusalem and Israeli residents in the occupied territories. [30]Excluding West Bank. [31]1962 census.

0–14	15–29	30–44	45–59	60–74	75 and older	1930	1940	1950	1960	1970	1980	1990 projection	2000 projection	country
		age distribution (%)							population (by decade, '000s)					
19.4	23.3	21.7	14.3	14.6	6.7	2,807	2,973	3,265	3,581	3,877	4,086	4,232	4,383	Norway
44.3[4]	24.8[4]	18.0[4]	8.9[4]	3.5[4]	0.6[4]	...	...	390	494	657	984	1,457	1,973	Oman
														Pacific Is., Trust Territory of the
50.5	25.2	12.1	7.0	4.2	1.0	10	...	11	15	22	31	46	67	Marshall Islands
46.4	26.8	12.6	8.5	4.5	1.1	32	...	30	40	57	77	109	153	Micronesia, Federated States of
40.6	27.9	17.8	9.2	3.8	0.8	19	48	6	9	10	17	23	31	Northern Mariana Islands
35.0	29.6	17.9	9.6	6.0	1.9	8	25	6	9	11	12	15	20	Palau
44.5	23.9	15.4	9.3	5.3	1.6	23,600	28,300	36,450	45,851	64,449	86,143	114,071	143,672	Pakistan
39.1	28.1	16.7	9.5	5.1	1.5	523	620	800	1,082	1,458	1,956	2,418	2,893	Panama
43.0	25.9	17.0	10.4	3.5	0.2	1,306	1.308	1,613	1,920	2,419	2,999	3,727	4,706	Papua New Guinea
41.1	28.1	15.4	9.1	4.8	1.5	880	1,111	1,371	1,778	2,290	3,168	4,231	5,405	Paraguay
41.2	27.9	15.6	9.3	4.4	1.6	5,752	6,784	7,975	9,993	13,248	17,295	22,332	27,952	Peru
42.0	28.5	15.6	8.6	4.3	1.0	13,094	16,459	20,988	27,561	36,850	48,316	61,483	74,057	Philippines
32.1[13]	13.2[13]	18.9[13]	13.2[13]	9.4[13]	13.2[13]	0.19	0.20	0.14	0.14	0.09	0.06	...	...	Pitcairn Island
23.9	27.4	18.5	16.9	9.9	3.4	29,500	31,500	24,824	29,561	32,657	35,578	38,257	39,866	Poland
25.5	23.5	18.0	17.2	11.9	3.9	6,804	7,696	8,405	8,826	9,040	9,781	10,493	10,838	Portugal
31.6	26.4	18.5	12.3	8.3	2.9	1,552	1,880	2,219	2,358	2,718	3,206	3,316	3,389	Puerto Rico
27.8	29.3	32.3	8.6	1.6	0.4	...	...	47	59	151	225	467	639	Qatar
35.6	29.8	——27.6——		——6.9——		198	221	244	338	447	507	595	707	Réunion
25.7	23.7	19.6	17.1	10.9	3.0	14,141	15,907	16,311	18,407	20,799	22,201	23,206	24,189	Romania
47.7[2]	25.7[2]	14.2[2]	8.4[2]	3.4[2]	0.6[2]	1,600	1,910	2,189	2,740	3,679	5,144	7,179	10,123	Rwanda
34.0	27.5	16.7	10.8	8.4	2.6	4	5	5	5	5	7	8	9	St. Helena and Ascension
37.2	30.4	9.5	9.4	10.0	4.3	38	43	49	51	46	43	43	40	St. Kitts and Nevis
49.6	21.3	11.6	9.8	5.5	2.2	60	70	79	94	100	124	151	185	St. Lucia
28.7	26.0	20.4	13.2	8.5	3.2	4	4	5	5	5	6	6	7	St. Pierre and Miquelon
41.7[2]	33.3[2]	11.5[2]	7.3[2]	5.2[2]	1.0[2]	53	61	67	80	86	103	116	131	St. Vincent and the Grenadines
24.4	23.0	19.9	17.4	11.4	3.9	10	10	13	15	19	21	23	25	San Marino
46.3	25.0	11.6	10.0	5.3	1.8	...	60	60	64	74	94	124	163	São Tomé and Príncipe
46.7	23.9	15.2	7.9	——6.3——		...	...	3,200	4,175	6,120	9,372	13,988	19,824	Saudi Arabia
43.1	26.2	15.3	9.1	4.6	1.5	...	...	2,600	3,076	4,267	5,711	7,618	10,193	Senegal
39.6	26.3	14.0	10.8	6.8	2.1	27	32	34	42	54	63	68	73	Seychelles
40.7[15]	24.8[15]	17.4[15]	9.2[15]	——7.9[15]——		1,600	1,700	1,809	2,165	2,692	3,336	4,033	4,874	Sierra Leone
27.0	34.7	19.8	11.3	5.9	1.3	596	751	1,022	1,639	2,075	2,414	2,699	3,008	Singapore
47.3	25.7	13.9	8.1	——4.9——		94	94	104	125	163	229	323	455	Solomon Islands
44.1[2]	25.5[2]	15.8[2]	9.5[2]	4.3[2]	0.7[2]	...	...	1,826	2,226	2,790	5,074	6,695	8,833	Somalia
37.1	28.5	18.1	10.1	4.7	1.5	8,541	10,353	12,458	15,925	22,460	29,799	38,604	48,916	South Africa[43]
52.6[24]	21.3[24]	10.4[24]	——13.6[24]——		2.1[24]	...	...	...	...	880	1,335	2,152	3,065	Bophuthatswana
44.9	26.2	15.0	6.9	5.5	1.5	...	...	...	...	530	682	1,027	1,543	Ciskei
43.7[24]	21.5[24]	13.3[24]	——20.3[24]——		1.2[24]	...	...	...	...	1,746	2,336	3,940	5,296	Transkei
43.3[24]	20.3[24]	12.4[24]	——22.7[24]——		1.3[24]	...	...	...	...	269	345	613	1,091	Venda
44.0[2]	26.0[2]	15.5[2]	9.3[2]	4.3[2]	0.9[2]	283	336	405	522	761	989	1,288	1,640	South West Africa/ Namibia
25.6[3]	23.2[3]	17.9[3]	17.6[3]	11.4[3]	4.2[3]	23,445	25,757	27,868	30,303	33,779	37,424	39,322	40,747	Spain
35.3	29.6	17.9	10.6	5.2	1.4	5,253	5,972	7,678	9,889	12,514	14,747	17,108	19,227	Sri Lanka
45.1[4]	26.1[4]	15.6[4]	8.7[4]	3.8[4]	0.7[4]	7,500	8,500	9,322	11,256	14,090	19,449	28,311	37,315	Sudan, The
39.3	29.5	13.8	10.0	4.5	2.8	170	193	215	247	292	357	448	579	Suriname
47.3	26.6	13.4	7.4	3.4	1.3	139	154	253	320	409	558	763	1,042	Swaziland
17.9	20.7	22.2	16.1	15.5	7.6	6,142	6,371	7,041	7,498	8,081	8,310	8,450	8,625	Sweden
19.2	23.1	22.0	17.4	12.7	5.6	4,066	4,234	4,715	5,429	6,270	6,385	6,680	6,957	Switzerland
47.5[2]	27.4[2]	12.4[2]	7.9[2]	3.6[2]	1.1[2]	...	2,597	3,495	4,561	6,305	8,704	12,112	16,854	Syria
32.1	32.1	16.5	12.6	5.7	1.0	4,614	5,987	7,619	10,792	14,676	17,642	20,323	23,072	Taiwan
46.2	24.9	14.4	8.5	4.5	1.6	...	...	7,892	10,073	13,273	18,580	25,635	36,008	Tanzania
38.3	30.1	16.1	10.1	4.3	1.1	11,838	15,296	20,010	26,392	35,745	46,961	56,677	64,348	Thailand
44.4[2]	25.8[2]	15.6[2]	9.1[2]	4.3[2]	0.8[2]	750	834	1,201	1,465	1,954	2,600	3,764	5,113	Togo
42.9[13]	22.5[13]	12.7[13]	10.2[13]	7.2[13]	4.5[13]	1.1	1.3	1.5	1.8	1.7	2	2	2	Tokelau
44.4[20]	26.2[20]	14.8[20]	9.5[20]	4.0[20]	1.1[20]	28	37	50	65	80	92	96	101	Tonga
34.2	30.9	16.3	10.0	6.2	1.7	408	503	668	828	941	1,082	1,321	1,608	Trinidad and Tobago
39.7	28.8	14.2	10.7	5.4	1.2	2,381	2,887	3,530	4,221	5,137	6,392	8,313	10,878	Tunisia
37.1	26.3	17.1	12.6	——6.9——		14,448	17,723	20,809	27,509	35,321	44,438	56,941	73,029	Turkey
41.4	26.7	11.8	11.0	7.0	2.2	5	6	6	6	6	7	11	14	Turks and Caicos Islands
31.8[47]	31.7[47]	15.2[47]	13.2[47]	6.3[47]	1.7[47]	4	4	5	5	6	8	9	11	Tuvalu
47.8[2]	26.0[2]	14.0[2]	8.0[2]	3.5[2]	0.6[2]	...	...	5,969	7,551	9,806	12,786	16,928	22,399	Uganda
24.3[2]	26.6[2]	19.0[2]	16.9[2]	9.6[2]	3.4[2]	179,000	195,000	180,075	214,335	241,700	265,542	290,939	311,637	U.S.S.R.
31.9[4]	24.9[4]	32.1[4]	8.7[4]	1.9[4]	0.5[4]	...	...	70	90	223	980	1,881	2,518	United Arab Emirates
20.6	22.8	19.4	16.9	14.4	5.8	46,038	48,226	50,290	52,372	55,632	56,330	57,291	58,859	United Kingdom
22.6	27.4	19.1	15.2	11.3	4.4	123,616	132,594	152,271	180,671	204,879	227,757	250,800	270,794	United States
26.6	22.8	18.3	16.5	11.4	4.3	1,734	1,974	2,194	2,531	2,824	2,862	3,011	3,168	Uruguay
45.3	27.5	15.0	7.7	3.4	1.1	...	43	52	65	86	118	159	215	Vanuatu
40.5	29.9	15.8	8.7	4.0	1.1	2,980	3,740	5,009	7,502	10,604	15,024	19,735	24,715	Venezuela
42.5[2]	28.6[2]	13.2[2]	9.6[2]	5.0[2]	1.1[2]	...	...	24,600	30,200	40,064	53,722	66,573	82,310	Vietnam
36.0	24.2	21.5	11.1	5.7	1.4	22	25	27	32	75	98	108	114	Virgin Islands (U.S.)
45.8	24.8	13.8	9.0	5.7	0.9	...	...	7	8	9	11	17	26	Wallis and Futuna
46.6	30.1	9.5	8.2	——5.7——		...	...	...	608	721	906	1,142		West Bank
42.9	27.2	16.3	7.4	4.4	1.8	...	...	14	32	76	155	199	254	Western Sahara
44.3	29.1	12.2	9.0	3.8	1.0	45	61	82	111	143	155	164	173	Western Samoa
47.3	20.8	15.8	8.6	——6.6——		...	...	907	1,109	1,436	1,910	2,468	3,191	Yemen (Aden)
45.7[13]	23.2[13]	15.1[13]	10.5[13]	4.7[13]	0.8[13]	...	...	3,622	4,429	4,840	6,933	9,060	11,660	Yemen (Ṣanā')
24.5	25.0	19.8	18.3	8.3	3.5	14,360	16,425	16,346	18,402	20,371	22,304	23,915	25,608	Yugoslavia
45.2[4]	25.9[4]	15.5[4]	8.7[4]	3.9[4]	0.7[4]	8,764	10,370	13,055	16,151	21,368	27,406	34,138	42,980	Zaire
46.9[2]	25.7[2]	14.7[2]	8.3[2]	3.6[2]	0.7[2]	1,272	1,484	2,473	3,219	4,295	5,648	7,912	11,237	Zambia
51.0	26.3	13.4	6.5	1.2	1.6	1,100	1,461	2,276	3,538	5,308	7,100	9,369	11,943	Zimbabwe

[32]No census ever taken. [33]1967 census. [34]Island of Mauritius only. [35]1978 census. [36]Including 163,868 in Western Sahara. [37]Indigenous population only. [38]A census was taken in 1973, but the results were repudiated. [39]1980 census. [40]Excludes Afghan refugees and residents of Pakistani-occupied Jammu and Kashmir. [41]Excludes the island of Tristan da Cunha and military personnel. [42]1987 estimate. [43]Includes Black states shown separately. [44]Excludes Bophuthatswana, Ciskei, Transkei, and Venda. [45]1985 estimate; includes Bophuthatswana, Ciskei, Transkei, and Venda. [46]Includes resident aliens; excludes seasonal workers. [47]1979 census. [48]Includes residents abroad and foreign military personnel; excludes visitors. [49]Excludes 515,000 armed forces overseas. [50]Includes 1,168,199 national abroad.

Major cities and national capitals

The following table lists the principal cities or municipalities (those exceeding 100,000 in population) of the countries of the world, together with figures for each national capital (indicated by a ★), regardless of size.

Most of the populations given refer to a so-called city proper, that is, a legally defined, incorporated or chartered area defined by administrative boundaries and by national or state law as a "city" (in some cases, only as a locality that is "urban" in nature, or perhaps, in the smallest countries, simply as "the settlement"). There are many variations on this basic concept, however. One that is encountered frequently is the municipality, or commune, similar to the medieval city-state in that the city is governed together with its immediately adjoining, economically dependent areas, whether urban or rural in nature. Some countries define no other demographic or legal entities within such communes or municipalities, but many identify a centre, seat, head (*cabecera*), or locality that corresponds to the most densely populated, compact, contiguous core of the municipality. Secondary centres may also be defined, and in certain countries these may be places of considerable size, depending on how long the municipality's boundaries have gone unchanged. Because the amount of work involved in defining these "centres" carefully may be considerable, the necessary manpower, employment and commuting data, and cartographic resources usually exist only at the time of a national census (generally five or ten years apart). Between censuses, therefore, it may be possible only to track the growth of the municipality as a whole. Thus, in order to provide the most up-to-date data for cities in this table, figures referring to municipalities or communes may be given (identified by the abbreviation "MU"), even though the country itself may define a smaller, more closely knit city proper. Specific identification of municipalities is provided in this table *only* when the country also publishes data for a more narrowly defined city proper; it is *not* provided when the sole published figure is the municipality, whether or not this is the proper local administrative term for the entity.

Since many national capitals are first-order administrative subdivisions (equivalent to a U.S. state) in their national hierarchy of local government, care has been taken to provide data referring to the actual urban core of the subdivision (the demographic "city proper"). Thus, data are provided for the city of Brasília, or Kuala Lumpur, but not for the national or federal capital areas that contain them. Problems also exist in the identification of cities in terms of named legal entities. There is, for example, a single municipality (*commune*) named Brussel (Brussels) at the centre of the Brussels agglomeration in Belgium; the *commune* numbers only about 137,000 population, while the agglomeration, which is understood by most people to constitute the city, numbers nearly a million. Both are shown so as to apprise the reader of the existence of a problem.

For certain countries, more than one form of the name of the city is given, usually to permit recognition of recent place name changes or of *forms* of the place name likely to be encountered in press stories if the title of the city's entry in the *Encyclopædia Britannica* is spelled according to a different romanization or spelling policy. One such case is China, for which city names are spelled first according to a long-established scholarly system called Wade–Giles, while current press references are likely to be spelled according to the more recent Chinese romanization system, Pinyin. (Peking in Wade–Giles, for example, would be spelled Pei-ching; in Pinyin, Beijing.) The use of the conventional Western spelling Peking in this table is supplemented by provision of the Pinyin alternative spelling.

Sources for this data were usually the national census and statistical abstracts of the countries concerned, supplemented by correspondence with most national statistical offices to solicit data not yet issued as part of the national publishing program.

Major cities and national capitals

country city	population
Afghanistan (1984 est.)	
Herāt	159,804
★ Kābul	1,179,341
Mazār-e Sharīf	117,723
Qandahār	203,177
Albania (1985 est.)	
★ Tiranë	215,900
Algeria (1987)	
★ Algiers	1,483,000
Annaba	310,000
Batna	182,000
Bejaïa	124,122[1]
Blida (el-Boulaida)	165,000
Boufarik	112,000[2]
ech-Cheliff	118,996[1]
Constantine (Qacentina)	438,000
Oran (Wahran)	590,000
Sétif	168,000
Sidi bel Abbes	146,653[1]
Skikda	141,159[1]
Tizi Ouzou	100,749[1]
Tlemcen (Tilimsen)	146,089[1]
American Samoa (1985 est.)	
★ Pago Pago	3,400
Andorra (1986)	
★ Andorra la Vella	15,639
Angola (1987 est.)	
★ Luanda	1,134,000
Lubango	105,000[3]
Anguilla (1984)	
★ The Valley	1,042
Antigua and Barbuda (1982 est.)	
★ Saint John's	30,000
Argentina (1980)	
Almirante Brown	332,548
Avellaneda	330,654
Bahía Blanca	220,765
Berazategui	200,926
★ Buenos Aires	2,922,829
Caseros	340,343
Córdoba	968,829
Corrientes	180,612
Esteban Echeverría	187,969
Florencio Varela	172,654
General San Martín	384,306
General Sarmiento	499,648
Godoy Cruz	141,553
Guaymallén	157,334
La Plata	454,884
Lanús	465,891
Lomas de Zamora	508,620
Mar del Plata	407,024
Mendoza	118,427
Merlo	282,828
Moreno	193,626
Morón	596,769
Paraná	161,638
Posadas	143,889
Quilmes	441,780
Resistencia	218,438
Río Cuarto	110,254
Rosario	875,664
Salta	260,744
San Fernando	134,156
San Isidro	287,048
San Juan	117,731
San Justo	946,715
San Miguel de Tucumán	392,888
San Salvador de Jujuy	124,950
Santa Fe	287,240
Santiago del Estero	148,758
Tigre	205,926
Vicente López	289,815
Aruba (1986 est.)	
★ Oranjestad	19,800
Australia (1986 est.)[4]	
Adelaide	1,003,800
Brisbane	1,196,000
★ Canberra	281,000
Geelong	145,900
Gold Coast	233,900
Hobart	178,900
Melbourne	2,931,900
Newcastle	416,100
Perth	1,050,400
Sydney	3,472,700
Townsville	106,300
Wollongong	232,500
Austria (1981)	
Graz	243,166
Innsbruck	117,287
Linz	199,910
Salzburg	139,426
★ Vienna	1,531,346
Bahamas, The (1980)	
★ Nassau	110,000
Bahrain (1987 est.)	
★ al-Manāmah	146,994
Bangladesh (1981)	
Barisāl	172,905
Chittagong	980,000
Comilla	184,132
★ Dhākā (Dacca)	2,365,695
Jessore	148,927
Khulna	646,359
Mymensingh	190,911
Pābna	109,065
Rājshāhi	253,740
Rangpur	153,174
Saidpur	126,608
Sirājganj	106,774
Sylhet	168,371
Barbados (1980)	
★ Bridgetown	7,552
Belgium (1987 est.)	
Antwerp	479,748
Brugge (Bruges)	117,755
★ Brussels	136,920
Agglomeration	973,499
Charleroi	209,395
Ghent	233,856
Liège (Luik)	200,891
Namur	102,670
Schaerbeek	104,919
Belize (1986 est.)	
★ Belmopan	3,500
Benin (1982 est.)	
★ Cotonou (official)	487,020
★ Porto-Novo (de facto)	208,258
Bermuda (1985 est.)	
★ Hamilton	1,676
Bhutan (1985 est.)	
★ Paro (administrative)	3,000
★ Thimphu (official)	20,000
Bolivia (1986 est.)	
Cochabamba	329,941
★ La Paz (administrative)	1,033,288
Oruro	184,101
Potosí	117,010
Santa Cruz	457,619
★ Sucre (judicial)	88,774
Botswana (1986 est.)	
★ Gaborone	95,163
Brazil (1980)	
Americana	121,794
Anápolis	160,520
Aracaju	288,106
Araçatuba	113,486
Barra Mansa	123,421
Bauru	178,861
Belém	758,117
Belo Horizonte	1,442,483
Blumenau	144,819
★ Brasília	411,305
Campina Grande	222,229
Campinas	566,517
Campo Grande	282,844
Campos	174,218
Canoas	214,115
Carapicuíba	185,763
Caruaru	137,636
Cascavel	100,351
Caxias do Sul	198,824
Contagem	111,697
Cuiabá	167,894
Curitiba	843,733
Diadema	228,594
Divinópolis	108,344
Duque de Caxias	306,057
Feira de Santana	225,003
Florianópolis	153,547
Fortaleza	648,815
Franca	143,630
Goiânia	703,263
Governador Valadares	173,699
Guarulhos	395,117
Imperatriz	111,818
Ipatinga	105,083
Itabuna	129,938
Jacareí	103,652
João Pessoa	290,424
Joinville	217,074
Juàzeiro do Norte	125,248
Juiz de Fora	299,728
Jundiaí	210,015
Lages	108,768
Limeira	137,812
Londrina	258,054
Maceió	376,479
Manaus	613,068
Marília	103,904
Maringá	158,047
Mauá	205,817
Mogi das Cruzes	122,265
Montes Claros	151,881
Mossoró	118,007
Natal	376,552
Nilópolis	103,033
Niterói	386,185
Nova Iguaçu	491,802
Novo Hamburgo	132,066
Olinda	266,392
Osasco	473,856
Passo Fundo	103,121
Pelotas	197,092
Petrópolis	149,427
Piracicaba	179,395
Ponta Grossa	171,111
Porto Alegre	1,108,883
Porto Velho	101,644
Presidente Prudente	127,623
Recife	1,184,215
Ribeirão Prêto	300,704
Rio Claro	103,174
Rio de Janeiro	5,090,700
Rio Grande	124,706
Salvador	1,506,602
Santa Maria	151,202
Santarém	101,534
Santo Andre	549,278
Santos	411,023
São Bernardo do Campo	381,261
São Caetano do Sul	163,030
São Carlos	109,231
São Gonçalo	221,278
São João de Meriti	210,548
São José do Rio Prêto	171,982
São José dos Campos	268,073
São Luís	182,466
São Paulo	7,033,529
São Vicente	192,770
Sorocaba	254,718
Taubaté	155,371
Teresina	339,264
Uberaba	180,296
Uberlândia	230,400
Vitória	144,143
Vitória da Conquista	125,717
Volta Redonda	177,772
British Virgin Islands (1980)	
★ Road Town	2,525
Brunei (1985 est.)	
★ Bandar Seri Begawan	55,000
Bulgaria (1987 est.)	
Burgas	186,369
Pleven	132,206
Plovdiv	349,148
Ruse	186,428
Shumen	102,886
★ Sofia	1,119,152
Sliven	104,345
Stara Zagora	153,538
Tolbukhin	110,471
Varna	303,071
Burkina Faso (1985)	
Bobo Dioulasso	231,162
★ Ouagadougou	442,223
Burma (1983)	
Bassein	144,092
Mandalay	532,895
Monywa	106,873
Moulmein	219,991
Pegu	150,447
★ Rangoon	2,458,712
Sittwe (Akyab)	107,907
Taunggye	107,607
Burundi (1986 est.)	
★ Bujumbura	272,622
Cameroon (1987 est.)	
Douala	1,116,872
Garoua	102,057
Maroua	106,242
Nkongsamba	112,454
★ Yaoundé	712,089
Canada (1986)	
Brampton	188,498
Burlington	116,675
Burnaby	145,161
Calgary	636,104
East York	101,085
Edmonton	573,982
Etobicoke	302,973
Halifax	113,577
Hamilton	306,728
Kitchener	150,604
Laval	284,164
London	269,140
Longueuil	125,441
Markham	114,597
Mississauga	374,005
Montreal	1,015,420
North York	556,297
Oshawa	123,651
★ Ottawa	300,763
Quebec	164,580
Regina	175,064
Richmond	108,492
Saint Catharines	123,455
Saskatoon	177,641
Scarborough	484,676
Surrey	181,447
Thunder Bay	112,272
Toronto	612,289
Vancouver	431,137
Windsor	193,111
Winnipeg	594,551
York	135,401
Cape Verde (1985 est.)	
★ Praia	49,500
Cayman Islands (1987 est.)	
★ George Town	11,500
Central African Republic (1985 est.)	
★ Bangui	473,817

country city	population
Chad (1986 est.)	
★ N'Djamena	511,700
Sarh	100,000
Chile (1987 est.; MU)	
Antofagasta	204,577
Arica	169,774
Calama	109,645
Chillán	148,805
Concepción	294,375
Coquimbo	105,252
Iquique	132,948
La Serena	106,617
Los Angeles	126,122
Osorno	122,462
Puente Alto	165,534
Puerto Montt	113,488
Punta Arenas	111,724
Quilpué	103,004
Rancagua	172,489
San Bernardo	168,534
★ Santiago	421,900
Greater Santiago	4,858,342
Talca	164,482
Talcahuano	231,356
Temuco	217,789
Valdivia	117,205
Valparaíso	278,762
Viña del Mar	297,294
China (1987 est.)[5]	
A-K'o-su (Aksu)	140,791
An-ch'ing (Anqing)	229,782
An-shan (Anshan)	1,121,889
An-shun (Anshun)	130,767
An-ta (Anda)	130,641
An-yang (Anyang)	363,151
Canton (Guangzhou)	2,649,861
Chan-chiang	
(Zhanjiang)	351,612
Ch'ang-chi (Changji)	113,119
Chang-chia-k'ou	
(Zhangjiakou)	499,354
Ch'ang-chih	
(Changzhi)	285,138
Ch'ang-chou	
(Changzhou)	462,479
Chang-chou	
(Zhangzhou)	165,292
Ch'ang-ch'un	
(Changchun)	1,511,537
Ch'ang-sha	
(Changsha)	1,000,823
Ch'ang-shu (Changshu)	144,145
Ch'ang-te (Changde)	184,705
Chao-ch'ing (Zhaoqing)	151,710
Ch'ao-chou	
(Chaozhou)	270,070
Ch'ao-hu (Chaohu)	112,041
Chao-tung (Zhaodong)	163,059
Ch'ao-yang (Chaoyang)	187,522
Chen-chiang	
(Zhenjiang)	328,529
Chen-chou (Chenzhou)	153,354
Cheng-chou	
(Zhengzhou)	1,024,433
Ch'eng-te (Chengde)	234,724
Ch'eng-tu (Chengdu)	1,572,279
Chi-an (Ji'an)	136,027
Chi-hsi (Jixi)	643,217
Chi-lin (Jilin)	940,493
Chi-nan (Jinan)	1,188,457
Chi-ning (Jining)	
(*Inner Mongolia*)	148,427
Chi-ning (Jining)	
(*Shantung*)	220,330
Ch'i-t'ai-ho (Qitaihe)	173,095
Chia-hsing (Jiaxing)	204,350
Chia-mu-ssu	
(Jiamusi)	437,627
Chiang-men	
(Jiangmen)	177,237
Chiao-tso (Jiaozuo)	344,651
Ch'ih-feng (Chifeng)	300,864
Chin-ch'eng (Jincheng)	107,906
Chin-chou (Jinzhou)	625,854
Chin-hsi (Jinxi)	228,639
Chin-hua (Jinhua)	124,817
Ch'in-huang-tao	
(Qinhuangdao)	320,202
Ching-men (Jingmen)	192,794
Ch'ing-tao (Qingdao)	1,176,578
Ching-te-chen	
(Jingdezhen)	308,750
Chiu-chiang (Jiujiang)	257,833
Chou-k'ou (Zhoukou)	119,910
Ch'ü-ching (Qujing)	147,962
Chu-chou (Zhuzhou)	358,131
Ch'u-hsien (Chuxian)	108,870
Chu-ma-tien (Zhumadian)	107,625
Ch'üan-chou	
(Quanzhou)	161,425
Chungking	
(Chongqing)	2,128,191
Chung-shan	
(Zhongshan)	245,201
Fo-shan (Foshan)	254,204
Fu-chou (Fuzhou)	
(*Kiangsi*)	108,713
Fu-chou (Fuzhou)	805,546
Fu-hsin (Fuxin)	593,578
Fu-shun (Fushun)	1,126,369
Fu-yang (Fuyang)	157,857
Ha-mi (Hami)	149,373
Hai-ch'eng (Haicheng)	198,871
Hai-k'ou (Haikou)	218,013
Hai-la-erh (Hailar)	158,819
Han-chung	
(Hanzhong)	150,612
Han-tan (Handan)	767,562
Hang-chou	
(Hangzhou)	1,025,933
Harbin	2,289,896
Heng-yang	
(Hengyang)	431,480
Ho-fei (Hefei)	645,207
Ho-kang (Hegang)	484,896
Ho-pi (Hebi)	173,701
Ho-tse (Heze)	140,498
Hsi-ch'ang (Xichang)	119,913
Hsi-ning (Xining)	518,816
Hsia-men (Xiamen)	351,138
Hsiang-fan (Xiangfan)	333,946
Hsiang-t'an	
(Xiangtan)	400,853
Hsiao-kan (Xiaogan)	137,712
Hsien-ning (Xianning)	122,956
Hsien-t'ao (Xiantao)	201,365
Hsien-yang (Xianyang)	294,693
Hsin-hsiang	
(Xinxiang)	419,656
Hsin-t'ai (Xintai)	162,749
Hsin-yang (Xinyang)	170,832
Hsin-yu (Xinyu)	137,943
Hsing-t'ai (Xingtai)	270,426
Hsü-ch'ang	
(Xuchang)	176,702
Hsü-chou (Xuzhou)	738,393
Hu-chou (Huzhou)	212,160
Hu-ho-hao-t'e	
(Hohhot)	586,290
Huai-hua (Huaihua)	106,502
Huai-nan (Huainan)	633,539
Huai-pei (Huaibei)	275,361
Huai-yin (Huaiyin)	197,278
Huang-shih	
(Huangshi)	410,522
Hui-chou (Huizhou)	121,844
Hun-chiang	
(Hunjiang)	453,792
I-ch'ang (Yichang)	346,983
I-ch'un (Yichun)	765,107
I-ch'un (Yichun) (*Kiangsi*)	142,015
I-ning (Yining)	157,081
I-pin (Yibin)	220,434
I-yang (Yiyang)	158,441
K'ai-feng (Kaifeng)	464,746
K'ai-li (Kaili)	100,598
Kan-chou (Ganzhou)	196,971
Kashgar (Kashi)	151,194
Ko-chiu (Gejiu)	201,129
K'o-la-ma-i (Karamay)	174,161
K'u-erh-le (Korla)	133,689
Kuang-yüan (Guangyuan)	164,247
Kuei-lin (Guilin)	332,226
K'uei-t'un (Kuytun)	111,684
Kuei-yang (Guiyang)	915,875
K'un-ming (Kunming)	1,111,487
Kung-chu-ling	
(Gongzhuling)	192,188
Lai-wu (Laiwu)	140,717
Lan-chou (Lanzhou)	1,096,660
Lang-fang (Langfang)	128,338
Lao-ho-k'ou (Laohekou)	107,204
Le-shan (Leshan)	324,198
Leng-shui-chiang	
(Lengshuijiang)	113,836
Liao-ch'eng	
(Liaocheng)	134,581
Liao-yang (Liaoyang)	450,265
Liao-yüan (Liaoyuan)	320,270
Lien-yün-kang	
(Lianyungang)	294,046
Lin-fen (Linfen)	166,279
Lin-ho (Linhe)	104,750
Lin-i (Linyi)	177,092
Liu-chou (Liuzhou)	539,187
Liu-p'an-shui	
(Liupanshui)	353,115
Lo-ho (Luohe)	103,681
Lo-yang (Luoyang)	668,726
Long-yen (Longyan)	119,547
Lu-an (Lu'an)	128,479
Lu-chou (Luzhou)	242,486
Ma-an-shan	
(Ma'anshan)	269,810
Man-chou-li	
(Manzhouli)	108,959
Mao-ming (Maoming)	140,107
Mei-ho-k'ou (Meihekou)	187,641
Mei-hsien (Meixian)	173,645
Mien-yang (Mianyang)	234,465
Mu-tan-chiang	
(Mudanjiang)	513,050
Nan-ch'ang (Nanchang)	941,171
Nan-ch'ung	
(Nanchong)	161,261
Nan-ning (Nanning)	627,899
Nan-p'ing (Nanping)	160,639
Nan-t'ung (Nantong)	292,634
Nan-yang (Nanyang)	201,782
Nanking (Nanjing)	1,918,836
Nei-chiang (Neijiang)	197,657
Ning-po (Ningbo)	507,738
Pai-ch'eng	
(Baicheng)	200,552
Pai-yin (Baiyin)	179,387
Pang-pu (Bengbu)	410,289
Pao-chi (Baoji)	291,676
Pao-ting (Baoding)	441,456
Pao-t'ou (Baotou)	912,953
Pei-an (Bei'an)	200,716
Pei-pïao (Beipiao)	183,070
★ Peking (Beijing)	5,350,783
Pen-hsi (Benxi)	710,290
P'ing-hsiang	
(Pingxiang)	391,996
P'ing-ting-shan	
(Pingdingshan)	380,834
P'u-ch'i (Puqi)	106,486
P'u-ling (Puling)	164,452
P'u-yang (Puyang)	153,634
San-ming (Sanming)	147,451
Sha-shih (Shashi)	229,698
Shan-t'ou (Shantou)	500,154
Shao-hsing (Shaoxing)	163,546
Shao-kuan (Shaoguan)	315,735
Shao-yang (Shaoyang)	220,611
Shang-ch'iu	
(Shangqiu)	139,263
Shang-jao (Shangrao)	116,139
Shanghai	6,987,253
Shen-chen (Shenzhen)	215,615
Shen-yang	
(Shenyang)	3,335,059
Shih-chia-chuang	
(Shijiazhuang)	958,457
Shih-ho-tzu (Shihezi)	299,128
Shih-tsui-shan	
(Shizuishan)	237,763
Shih-yen (Shiyan)	235,753
Shuang-ya-shan	
(Shuangyashan)	357,148
Sian (Xi'an)	1,776,761
Ssu-p'ing (Siping)	287,294
Su-chou (Suzhou)	
(*Anhwei*)	125,468
Su-chou (Suzhou)	634,815
Sui-chou (Suizhou)	179,698
Sui-hua (Suihua)	205,115
Sui-ning (Suining)	125,383
Ta-ch'ing (Daqing)	559,501
Ta-hsien (Daxian)	152,530
Ta-li (Dali)	116,338
Ta-lien (Dalian)	1,421,881
Ta-t'ung (Datong)	723,905
T'ai-an (Tai'an)	206,987
T'ai-chou (Taizhou)	133,888
T'ai-yüan (Taiyuan)	1,439,792
Tan-tung (Dandong)	479,513
T'ang-shan	
(Tangshan)	958,633
Te-chou (Dezhou)	163,776
Te-yang (Deyang)	177,334
T'ieh-fa (Tiehfa)	116,350
T'ieh-ling (Tieling)	220,045
T'ien-shui (Tianshui)	219,076
Tientsin (Tianjin)	4,244,065
Tsa-lan-t'un	
(Zalantun)	114,403
Ts'ang-chou	
(Cangzhou)	202,480
Tsao-chuang	
(Zaozhuang)	270,935
Tsitsihar (Qiqihar)	997,749
Tsun-i (Zunyi)	242,790
Tu-k'ou (Dukou)	371,917
Tu-yün (Duyun)	126,756
Tun-hua (Dunhua)	219,696
T'ung-ch'uan	
(Tongchuan)	280,718
T'ung-hua	
(Tonghua)	295,954
Tung-kuan (Dongguan)	264,768
T'ung-liao (Tongliao)	197,322
T'ung-ling	
(Tongling)	200,353
Tung-ying (Dongying)	193,587
Tzu-hsing (Zixing)	100,801
Tzu-kung (Zigong)	368,406
Tzu-po (Zibo)	752,493
Wa-fang-tien	
(Wafangdian)	232,090
Wan-hsien (Wanxian)	141,692
Wei-fang (Weifang)	317,600
Wei-nan (Weinan)	112,664
Wen-chou (Wenzhou)	375,645
Wu-chou (Wuzhou)	199,830
Wu-hai (Wuhai)	240,634
Wu-han (Wuhan)	3,023,892
Wu-hsi (Wuxi)	724,589
Wu-hu (Wuhu)	403,457
Wu-lan-hao-t'e (Ulanhot)	134,424
Wu-lu-mu-ch'i (Ürümqi)	958,196
Wu-wei (Wuwei)	119,044
Ya-k'o-she (Yakeshe)	351,526
Yang-chou	
(Yangzhou)	267,955
Yang-ch'üan	
(Yangquan)	327,117
Yen-ch'eng (Yancheng)	193,017
Yen-chi (Yanji)	185,647
Yen-t'ai (Yantai)	354,844
Yin-ch'uan	
(Yinchuan)	291,638
Ying-k'ou (Yingkou)	378,885
Yü-lin (Yulin)	122,922
Yü-men (Yumen)	106,634
Yü-tz'u (Yuci)	174,997
Yü-yao (Yuyao)	117,832
Yüeh-yang	
(Yueyang)	254,056
Yung-an (Yong'an)	104,850
Christmas Island	
(1980 est.)	
★ The Settlement at Flying	
Fish Cove	1,200
Cocos (Keeling) Islands	
(1985 est.)	
★ West Island	233
Colombia (1985)	
Armenia	180,221
Barrancabermeja	137,406
Barranquilla	896,649
Bello	206,297
★ Bogotá	3,974,813
Bucaramanga	341,513
Buenaventura	160,342
Cali	1,323,944
Cartagena	491,368
Cúcuta	357,026
Floridablanca	137,975
Ibagué	269,495
Itagüí	135,797
Manizales	275,067
Medellín	1,418,554
Montería	157,466
Neiva	178,130
Palmira	175,186
Pasto	197,407
Pereira	233,271
Popayán	141,964
Santa Marta	177,922
Sincelejo	120,537
Soledad	164,494
Valledupar	142,771
Villavicencio	161,166
Comoros (1986 est.)	
★ Moroni	21,000
Congo (1984)	
★ Brazzaville	585,812
Pointe-Noire	294,203
Cook Islands (1986)	
★ Rarotonga Island	9,678
Costa Rica (1984)	
★ San José	241,464
Côte d'Ivoire	
(1984 est.)	
★ Abidjan	1,850,000
Bouaké	220,000
Yamoussoukro	120,000
Cuba (1987 est.)	
Bayamo	108,716
Camagüey	265,588
Cienfuegos	112,225
Guantánamo	179,091
Holguín	199,861
★ Havana	2,036,799
Matanzas	106,954
Pinar del Río	108,109
Santa Clara	182,349
Santiago de Cuba	364,554
Cyprus (1986 est.)	
Limassol	113,600
★ Nicosia	163,700[6]
Czechoslovakia	
(1987 est.)	
Bratislava	427,500
Brno	387,400
Košice	227,600
Liberec	103,000
Olomouc	106,300
Ostrava	329,800
Plzen	174,800
★ Prague	1,203,700
Denmark (1986)	
Ålborg	113,650
Århus	195,152
★ Copenhagen	1,351,999[4]
Odense	137,286
Djibouti (1987 est.)	
★ Djibouti	250,000
Dominica (1981)	
★ Roseau	8,346
Dominican Republic	
(1983 est.)	
La Romana	101,000
Santiago de los	
Caballeros	285,000
★ Santo Domingo	1,410,000
Ecuador (1987 est.)	
Ambato	126,067
Cuenca	201,490
Guayaquil	1,572,615
Machala	144,396
Portoviejo	141,568
★ Quito	1,137,705
Egypt (1986 est.)	
Alexandria	2,917,327[7]
Aswān	195,700
Asyūt	291,300
Banhā	120,200
Bani Suwayf	162,500
Būr Sa'īd (Port Said)	382,000
★ Cairo	6,052,836[7]
Damanhūr	225,900
Damyāt	121,200
al-Fayyūm	227,300
Hulwan (Helwan)	352,300
al-Ismā'īlīyah	236,200
al-Jīzah (Giza)	1,670,800
Kafr ad-Dawwar	160,554[1]
Kafr ash-Shaykh	104,200
al-Maḥallah al-Kubrā	385,300
al-Manṣūrah	357,800
al-Minya	203,300
Qinā	141,700
Sawhāj	141,500
Shibīn al-Kawm	135,900
Shubrā al-Khaymah	533,300
as-Suways (Suez)	265,000
Ṭanṭa	373,500
al-Uqṣur (Luxor)	147,900
az-Zaqāziq	274,400
El Salvador (1985 est.)	
★ San Salvador	459,902
Santa Ana	137,879
Equatorial Guinea	
(1983)	
★ Malabo	30,710
Ethiopia (1985 est.)	
★ Addis Ababa	1,464,901
Asmera	284,748
Faeroe Islands	
(1987 est.)	
★ Tórshavn	15,287
Falkland Islands	
(1986)	
★ Stanley	1,200
Fiji (1986)	
★ Suva	69,481
Finland (1988 est.)	
Espoo	166,925
★ Helsinki	490,478
Tampere	170,073
Turku	160,486
Vantaa	148,728
France (1982)	
Aix-en-Provence	100,221
Amiens	130,302
Angers	135,293
Besançon	112,023
Bordeaux	201,965
Boulogne-Billancourt	102,582
Brest	154,110
Caen	112,332
Clermont-Ferrand	145,901
Dijon	139,188
Grenoble	156,437
Le Havre	198,700
Le Mans	145,976
Lille	167,791
Limoges	137,809
Lyon	410,455
Marseille	868,435
Metz	113,236
Montpellier	190,423
Mulhouse	111,742
Nantes	237,789
Nice	331,165
Nîmes	120,515
★ Paris	2,165,892
Perpignan	107,812
Reims	176,419
Rennes	190,861
Roubaix	101,488
Rouen	100,696
Saint-Étienne	193,938
Strasbourg	247,068
Toulon	177,443
Toulouse	344,917
Tours	131,265
Villeurbanne	115,378
French Guiana (1982)	
★ Cayenne	37,097
French Polynesia (1983)	
★ Papeete	23,496
Gabon (1985 est.)	
★ Libreville	235,700
Port Gentil	124,400
Gambia, The (1986)	
★ Banjul	44,188[1]
Serekunda	102,600
Gaza Strip (1979 est.)	
Gaza (Ghazzah)	120,000
Germany, East	
(1987 est.)	
★ Berlin (East)	1,236,248
Cottbus	126,592
Dessau	103,538
Dresden	519,810
Erfurt	217,134

Major cities and national capitals (continued)

country city	population
Gera	132,319
Halle	236,148
Jena	107,610
Karl-Marx-Stadt	313,799
Leipzig	550,641
Magdeburg	288,975
Potsdam	141,231
Rostock	249,349
Schwerin	128,328
Zwickau	120,923
Germany, West (1987 est.)	
Aachen	239,170
Augsburg	245,962
Bergisch Gladbach	101,776
Berlin (West)	1,879,225
Bielefeld	299,360
Bochum	381,216
★ Bonn	291,439
Bottrop	112,256
Braunschweig	247,836
Bremen	521,976
Bremerhaven	132,194
Cologne (Köln)	914,336
Darmstadt	133,572
Dortmund	568,164
Duisburg	514,628
Düsseldorf	560,572
Erlangen	100,200
Essen	615,421
Frankfurt am Main	592,411
Freiburg im Breisgau	186,156
Gelsenkirchen	283,560
Göttingen	133,796
Hagen	206,070
Hamburg	1,571,267
Hamm	165,957
Hannover	505,718
Heidelberg	136,227
Heilbronn	111,713
Herne	171,274
Hildesheim	100,558
Karlsruhe	268,309
Kassel	184,353
Kiel	243,626
Koblenz	110,277
Krefeld	216,598
Leverkusen	154,703
Lübeck	209,159
Ludwigshafen	152,162
Mainz	189,005
Mannheim	294,648
Mönchengladbach	255,087
Mülheim an der Ruhr	170,392
Munich (München)	1,274,716
Münster	267,628
Neuss	143,832
Nürnberg	467,392
Oberhausen	221,542
Offenbach am Main	107,078
Oldenburg	139,256
Osnabrück	153,776
Paderborn	110,296
Pforzheim	104,452
Recklingshausen	117,585
Regensburg	123,821
Remscheid	121,005
Saarbrücken	184,353
Salzgitter	105,392
Siegen	107,319
Solingen	157,401
Stuttgart	565,486
Ulm	100,745
Wiesbaden	266,542
Witten	102,232
Wolfsburg	121,951
Wuppertal	376,217
Würzburg	127,050
Ghana (1988 est.)	
★ Accra	949,113
Kumasi	385,192
Sekondi-Takoradi	103,653
Tamale	151,069
Tema	109,975
Gibraltar (1988 est.)	
★ Gibraltar	29,692[8]
Greece (1981)	
★ Athens	885,737
Iráklion	102,398
Kallithéa	117,319
Larissa	102,426
Pátrai (Patras)	142,163
Peristérion	140,858
Piraiévs (Piraeus)	196,389
Thessaloníki	406,413
Greenland (1987 est.)	
★ Nuuk (Godthåb)	11,209
Grenada (1986 est.)	
★ Saint George's	7,500
Guadeloupe (1982)	
★ Basse-Terre	13,397
Guam (1980)	
★ Agana	896
Guatemala (1981)	
★ Guatemala City	754,243
Guernsey (1986)	
★ St. Peter Port	16,085
Guinea (1983)	
★ Conakry	705,280
Guinea-Bissau (1979)	
★ Bissau	109,214
Guyana (1985 est.)	
★ Georgetown	200,000
Haiti (1987 est.)	
★ Port-au-Prince	472,895
Honduras (1986 est.)	
San Pedro Sula	399,700
★ Tegucigalpa	604,600[9]
Hong Kong (1988 est.)	
Hong Kong	5,683,000[8]
Hungary (1988 est.)	
★ Budapest	2,104,700
Debrecen	217,364
Györ	130,703
Kecskemét	105,107
Miskolc	209,807
Nyíregyháza	119,040
Pécs	181,356
Szeged	187,800
Székesfehérvár	113,442
Iceland (1986 est.)	
★ Reykjavík	91,394
India (1981)	
Ādoni	108,939
Agartala	132,186
Āgra	694,191
Ahmadābād	2,059,725
Ahmadnagar	143,937
Ajmer	375,593
Akola	225,412
Aligarh	320,861
Allahābād	616,051
Alleppey	169,940
Alwar	145,795
Ambāla	104,565
Ambattur	114,915
Amrāvati	261,404
Amritsar	594,844
Amroha	112,682
Anantapur	119,531
Arrah	125,111
Asansol	183,375
Aurangābād	284,607
Avadi	124,574
Bally	147,735
Bālurghāt	104,648
Bangalore	2,476,355
Baranagar	170,343
Bareilly	386,734
Barrackpur	115,253
Belgaum	274,430
Bellary	201,579
Bhāgalpur	225,062
Bharatpur	105,274
Bharūch	110,070
Bhatinda	124,453
Bhātpāra	260,761
Bhavnagar	307,121
Bhilai (Nagar)	290,090
Bhīlwāra	122,625
Bhīmavaram	101,894
Bhiwandi	115,298
Bhiwāni	101,277
Bhopāl	671,018
Bhubaneswar	219,211
Bhusāwal	123,133
Bihār	151,343
Bijāpur	147,313
Bikaner	253,174
Bilāspur	147,218
Bokaro Steel City	224,099
Bombay (Greater)	8,243,405
Brahmapur	162,550
Bulandshahr	103,436
Burdwān	167,364
Burhānpur	140,986
Calcutta	3,305,006
Chandernagore	101,925
Chandīgarh	373,789
Chandrapur	115,777
Chāpra	111,564
Cochin	513,249
Coimbatore	704,514
Cuddalore	127,625
Cuddapah	103,125
Cuttack	269,950
Darbhanga	176,301
Dāvangere	196,621
Dehra Dūn	211,416
Delhi	4,884,234
Dhānbād	120,221
Dhārwār-Hubli	527,108
Dhūlia	210,759
Dindigul	164,103
Dombivli	103,222
Durg	114,637
Durgāpur	311,798
Elūru	168,154
Erode	142,252
Etāwah	212,174
Faizābād	101,873
Farīdābād	330,864
Farrukhābād-Fatehgarh	145,793
Fīrozābād	202,338
Gadag-Betigeri	117,368
Gangānagar	123,692
Garden Reach	191,107
Gaya	247,075
Ghāziābād	271,730
Gondia	100,423
Gorakhpur	290,814
Gulbarga	221,325
Guntūr	367,699
Gwalior	539,015
Hāpur	102,837
Hardwār	114,180
Hissār	131,309
Howrah (Haora)	744,429
Hugli Chinsurah	125,193
Hyderābād	2,150,580
Ichalkaranji	133,751
Imphāl	156,622
Indore	829,327
Jabalpur	614,162
Jadabpur	251,968
Jaipur	977,165
Jālgaon	145,335
Jālna	122,276
Jammu	206,135
Jāmnagar	277,615
Jamshedpur	438,385
Jaunpur	105,140
Jhānsi	246,172
Jodhpur	506,345
Jullundur	408,196
Junāgadh	118,646
Kākināda	226,409
Kalyān	136,052
Kāmārhāti	234,951
Kānchipuram	130,926
Kānpur	1,481,789
Karnāl	132,107
Katihār	104,781
Khandwa	114,725
Kharagpur	150,475
Kolhāpur	340,625
Kota	358,241
Kozhikode (Calicut)	394,447
Kumbakonam	132,832
Kurnool	206,362
Lātūr	111,986
Lucknow	895,721
Ludhiāna	607,052
Madras	3,276,622
Madurai	820,891
Mālegaon	245,883
Mandya	100,285
Mangalore	172,252
Masulipatam	138,530
Mathura	147,493
Meerut	417,395
Miraj	105,455
Mirzāpur-cum-Vindhyachal	127,787
Monghyr	129,260
Morādābād	330,051
Muzaffarnagar	171,816
Muzaffarpur	190,416
Mysore	441,754
Nabadwīp	109,108
Nadiād	142,689
Nāgercoil	171,648
Nāgpur	1,219,461
Naihāti	114,607
Nānded	191,269
Nāsik (Nashik)	262,428
Navsāri	106,793
Nellore	237,065
★ New Delhi	273,036
Nizāmābād	183,061
Pālghāt	111,245
Pānihāti	205,718
Pānipat	137,927
Parbhani	109,364
Pathānkot	110,039
Patiāla	205,141
Patna	776,371
Pimpri-Chinchwad	220,966
Pondicherry	162,639
Porbandar	115,182
Proddatūr	107,070
Pune	1,203,351
Puri	100,942
Quilon	137,943
Raichūr	124,762
Raipur	338,245
Rājahmundry	203,358
Rājapālaiyam	101,640
Rājkot	445,076
Rāmpur	204,610
Rānchi	489,626
Ratlām	142,319
Raurkela Steel Township	206,821
Rewa	100,641
Rohtak	166,767
Sāgar	160,392
Sahāranpur	295,355
Salem	361,394
Sambalpur	110,282
Sambhal	108,232
Sāngli	152,389
Secunderābād (Cantonment)	135,994
Shāhjahānpur	185,396
Shillong	109,244
Shimoga	151,783
Sholāpur (Solapur)	511,103
Shrīrāmpur	127,304
Sīkar	102,970
Silīguri	154,378
Sītāpur	101,210
Sonepat	109,369
South Dum-Dum	230,266
South Suburban	378,765
Srīnagar	586,038
Surat	776,583
Tamkūr	108,670
Tenāli	119,257
Thāna (Thane)	309,897
Thanjāvūr	184,015
Tiruchchirāppalli	362,045
Tirunelveli	128,850
Tirupati	115,292
Tiruppūr	165,223
Tiruvottiyūr	134,014
Titāgarh	104,534
Trivandrum	483,086
Tumkūr	108,670
Tuticorin	192,949
Udaipur	232,588
Ujjain	278,454
Ulhāsnagar	273,668
Vadodara (Baroda)	734,473
Valparai	115,452
Vārānasi (Benares)	708,647
Vellore	174,247
Vijayawāda	454,577
Vishākhapatnam	565,321
Vizianagaram	114,806
Warangal	335,150
Yamunānagar	109,304
Indonesia (1980)	
Ambon	208,898
Balikpapan	280,675
Bandung	1,462,637
Banjarmasin	381,286
Bogor	247,409
Cirebon	223,776
★ Jakarta	6,503,449
Jambi	230,373
Jember	122,712
Kediri	221,830
Madiun	150,562
Magelang	123,484
Malang	511,780
Manado	217,159
Medan	1,378,955
Padang	480,922
Pakanbaru	186,262
Palembang	787,187
Pekalongan	132,558
Pematangsiantar	150,376
Pontianak	304,778
Probolinggo	100,296
Samarinda	264,718
Semarang	1,026,671
Sukabumi	109,994
Surabaya	2,027,913
Surakarta	469,888
Tanjung Karang-Telukbetung	284,275
Tegal	131,728
Ujung Pandang	709,038
Yogyakarta	398,727
Iran (1985 est.)	
Ahvāz	508,500
Āmol	106,500
Arāk	244,300
Ardabīl	258,100
Bakhtarān	536,500
Bandar 'Abbās	212,300
Borūjerd	162,800
Dezfūl	123,000
Gorgān	113,200
Hamadān	262,200
Isfahan (Eşfahān)	1,121,200
Karaj	431,900
Kāshān	136,000
Kermān	266,800
Khorramābād	235,600
Meshed (Mashhad)	1,103,300
Orūmīyeh	298,400
Qazvīn	205,900
Qom	637,700
Rasht	266,300
Sabzevār	129,600
Sanandaj	207,500
Shīrāz	834,800
Tabrīz	929,200
★ Tehrān	5,751,500
Yazd	223,300
Zāhedān	220,500
Zanjān	205,900
Iraq (1985 est.)	
al-Amārah	131,758
★ Baghdad	4,648,609
Ba'qūbah	114,516
Basra	616,700
al-Ḥillah	215,249
Irbīl	333,903
Karbalā'	184,574
Kirkūk	207,900[10]
Mosul	570,926
an-Najaf	242,603
an-Nasiriyah	138,842
ar-Ramādī	137,388
as-Sulaymaniyah	279,424
Ireland (1986)	
Cork	133,271
★ Dublin	502,749
Isle of Man (1986)	
★ Douglas	20,368
Israel (1986 est.)	
Bat Yam	131,200
Beersheba (Be'er Sheva')	115,000
Bene Beraq	102,400
Haifa (Ḥefa)	224,600
Ḥolon	138,800
★ Jerusalem (Yerushalayim, Al-Quds)	457,700
Netanya	109,600
Petaḥ Tiqwa	129,300
Ramat Gan	116,000
Rishon le-Ẕiyyon	112,300
Tel Aviv–Yafo	322,800
Italy (1987 est.; MU)	
Ancona	104,409
Bari	362,524
Bergamo	118,959
Bologna	432,406
Bolzano	101,151
Brescia	199,286
Cagliari	222,574
Catania	372,486
Catanzaro	102,558
Cosenza	106,026
Ferrara	143,950
Florence (Firenze)	425,835
Foggia	159,051
Forlì	110,482
Genoa (Genova)	727,427
La Spezia	108,937
Lecce	100,981
Livorno	174,065
Messina	268,896
Milan (Milano)	1,495,260
Modena	176,880
Monza	122,476[3]
Naples (Napoli)	1,204,211
Novara	102,742
Padua (Padova)	225,769
Palermo	723,732
Parma	175,842
Perugia	146,713
Pescara	131,027
Piacenza	105,626
Pisa	104,384
Prato	161,705[3]
Ravenna	136,016
Reggio di Calabria	178,821
Reggio nell'Emilia	130,086
Rimini	129,506[3]
★ Rome (Roma)	2,815,457
Salerno	154,848
Sassari	120,152
Siracusa	122,857
Taranto	244,997
Terni	111,157
Torre del Greco	104,654[3]
Turin (Torino)	1,035,565
Trieste	239,031
Udine	100,211
Venice (Venezia)	331,454
Verona	259,151
Vicenza	110,449
Jamaica (1982)	
★ Kingston	104,041
Japan (1987 est.)	
Abiko	115,006
Ageo	185,003
Aizuwakamatsu	118,780
Akashi	263,124
Akishima	101,143
Akita	298,794
Amagasaki	505,618
Anjō	136,579
Aomori	293,712
Asahikawa	365,441
Ashikaga	168,156
Atsugi	184,829
Beppu	133,458
Chiba	805,607
Chigasaki	193,052
Chōfu	195,825
Daitō	124,382
Fuchu	206,824
Fuji	217,782
Fujieda	115,006
Fujinomiya	114,336
Fujisawa	337,084
Fukui	252,794
Fukuoka	1,190,551

country city	population
Fukushima	273,515
Fukuyama	363,432
Funabashi	519,772
Gifu	410,367
Habikino	112,658
Hachinohe	242,609
Hachiōji	440,907
Hadano	148,469
Hakodate	315,579
Hamamatsu	523,292
Higashi-Kurume	522,787
Higashi-Murayama	128,895
Higashi-Ōsaka	522,787
Himeji	453,974
Hino	160,376
Hirakata	388,766
Hiratsuka	234,759
Hirosaki	175,877
Hiroshima	1,065,201
Hitachi	204,870
Hōfu	118,526
Ibaraki	254,574
Ichihara	244,643
Ichikawa	415,073
Ichinomiya	260,391
Ikeda	103,112
Imabari	123,916
Iruma	127,406
Ise	105,184
Isesaki	113,276
Ishinomaki	123,536
Itami	185,295
Iwaki	352,347
Iwakuni	111,559
Iwatsuki	102,743
Izumi (*Miyagi Pref.*)	135,247
Izumi (*Osaka Pref.*)	142,870
Joetsu	130,879
Kadoma	141,496
Kagoshima	533,592
Kakamigahara	127,504
Kakogawa	232,807
Kamakura	176,358
Kanazawa	434,708
Kariya	115,860
Kashihara	113,793
Kashiwa	289,734
Kasugai	262,168
Kasukabe	178,653
Katsuta	105,914
Kawagoe	294,658
Kawaguchi	416,808
Kawanishi	140,147
Kawasaki	1,126,485
Kiryū	129,471
Kisarazu	121,103
Kishiwada	187,259
Kita-Kyūshū	1,045,560
Kitami	107,527
Kobe	1,432,462
Kochi	314,924
Kodaira	159,793
Kofu	201,871
Koganei	105,014
Komaki	116,847
Komatsu	106,077
Koriyama	307,023
Koshigaya	269,705
Kumagaya	146,320
Kumamoto	565,685
Kurashiki	415,058
Kure	222,965
Kurume	225,535
Kushiro	213,325
Kyōto	1,479,386
Machida	336,194
Maebashi	281,804
Matsubara	136,606
Matsudo	440,155
Matsue	142,086
Matsumoto	199,211
Matsusaka	117,535
Matsuyama	433,968
Minakoyojō	131,781
Minō	119,720
Misato	115,522
Mishima	102,060
Mitaka	166,680
Mito	232,116
Miyazaki	283,541
Moriguchi	158,944
Morioka	232,304
Muroran	134,005
Musashino	139,321
Nagano	341,296
Nagaoka	184,305
Nagareyama	131,120
Nagasaki	449,149
Nagoya	2,142,896
Naha	306,430
Nara	339,809
Narashino	143,800
Neyagawa	258,896
Niigata	479,803
Niihama	131,247
Niiza	133,018
Nishinomiya	424,798
Nobeoka	134,640
Noda	108,684
Numazu	211,228
Obihiro	166,044
Ōdawara	188,977
Ōgaki	147,011
Ōita	398,573
Okayama	582,924
Okazaki	293,949
Ōkinawa	103,784
Ōme	116,073
Ōmiya	383,452
Ōmuta	156,079
Ōsaka	2,648,621
Ōta	136,246
Ōtaru	172,540
Ōtsu	242,296
Oyama	136,545
Saga	169,851
Sagamihara	501,126
Sakai	817,512
Sakata	101,136
Sakura	128,627
Sapporo	1,594,914
Sasebo	249,403
Sayama	151,209
Sendai	700,790
Seto	124,531
Shimizu	241,479
Shimonoseki	267,047
Shizuoka	471,792
Sōka	197,139
Suita	352,706
Suzuka	169,309
Tachikawa	150,144
Takamatsu	329,316
Takaoka	176,200
Takarazuka	199,761
Takasaki	234,141
Takatsuki	355,623
Tama	134,276
Tokorozawa	289,762
Tokushima	260,576
Tokuyama	112,371
★ Tokyo	8,354,459
Tomakomai	159,332
Tondabayashi	104,773
Tottori	139,014
Toyama	317,177
Toyohashi	328,394
Toyokawa	108,975
Toyonaka	417,182
Toyota	318,611
Tsu	151,942
Tsuchiura	121,815
Ube	175,404
Ueda	117,346
Uji	171,621
Urawa	390,872
Urayasu	102,526
Utsunomiya	415,355
Wakayama	400,143
Yachiyo	143,776
Yaizu	110,153
Yamagata	247,284
Yamaguchi	126,767
Yamato	184,428
Yao	276,721
Yatsushiro	109,351
Yokkaichi	268,077
Yokohama	3,110,273
Yokosuka	428,646
Yonago	131,696
Zama	103,785
Jersey (1986)	
★ St. Helier	27,083
Jordan (1986 est.)	
★ Amman	833,500
az-Zarqā'	285,000
Irbid	150,000
Kampuchea (1988 est.)	
★ Phnom Penh	750,000
Kenya (1984 est.)	
Kisumu	167,100
Mombasa	425,600
★ Nairobi	1,103,600
Nakuru	101,700
Kiribati (1985)	
★ Bairiki	21,393
Korea, North (1981 est.)	
Ch'ŏngjin	490,000
Haeju	213,000[1]
Hamhŭng-Hungnam	775,000
Kaesŏng	240,000
Kimch'aek (Songjin)	490,000[1]
★ P'yŏngyang	1,283,000
Sinŭiju	200,000
Wŏnsan	240,000
Korea, South (1985)	
Andong	114,216
Anyang	361,577
Ch'angwŏn	173,508
Chech'ŏn	102,274
Cheju	202,911
Chinhae	121,341
Chinju	227,309
Ch'ŏnan	170,196
Ch'ŏngju	350,256
Chŏnju	426,473
Ch'unch'ŏn	162,988
Ch'ungju	113,331
Inch'ŏn	1,386,911
Iri	192,269
Kangnŭng	132,897
Kumi	142,094
Kunsan	185,649
Kwangju	905,896
Kwangmyŏng	219,611
Kyŏngju	127,544
Masan	448,746
Mokp'o	236,085
P'ohang	260,691
Puch'ŏn	456,292
Pusan	3,514,798
Sŏngnam	447,692
★ Seoul (Sŏul)	9,639,110
Sunch'ŏn	121,958
Suwŏn	430,752
T'aebaek	113,997
Taegu	2,029,853
Taejŏn	866,148
Ŭijŏngbu	162,700
Ulsan	551,014
Wŏnju	151,165
Yŏsu	171,933
Kuwait (1985)	
Ḥawallī	145,215
★ Kuwait (al-Kuwayt)	44,224
as-Sālimīyah	153,220
Laos (1985)	
★ Vientiane	377,410
Lebanon (1985 est.)	
★ Beirut (Bayrūt)	1,500,000
an-Nabaṭīyah	100,000
Sidon (Ṣaydā)	100,000
Tripoli (Ṭarābulus)	500,000
Zaḥlah	200,000
Lesotho (1986)[4]	
★ Maseru	109,382
Liberia (1984 est.)	
★ Monrovia	425,000
Libya (1981 est.)	
Banghāzi	367,600
Misrātah	116,900
★ Tripoli (Ṭarābulus)	858,500
Liechtenstein (1987 est.)	
★ Vaduz	4,891
Luxembourg (1986 est.)	
★ Luxembourg	86,200
Macau (1986 est.)	
★ Macau (Santo Nome de Deus)	416,200
Madagascar (1985 est.)	
★ Antananarivo	662,600
Malaŵi (1987 est.)	
Blantyre	402,500
★ Lilongwe	220,300
Mzuzu	115,000
Malaysia (1980)	
Ipoh	293,849
Johor Baharu	246,395
Kelang	192,080
Kota Baharu	167,872
★ Kuala Lumpur	565,329
Kuala Terengganu	180,296
Kuantan	131,547
Petaling Jaya	207,805
Pinang (George Town)	248,241
Port Kelang	192,080
Seremban	132,911
Taiping	146,002
Maldives (1985)	
★ Male	46,334
Mali (1987)	
★ Bamako	646,163
Malta (1987 est.)	
★ Valletta	9,263
Martinique (1982)	
★ Fort-de-France	96,649
Mauritania (1984 est.)	
★ Nouakchott	350,000
Mauritius (1987 est.)	
★ Port Louis	139,730
Mayotte (1985)	
★ Dzaoudzi	5,425
Mamoudzou (★ designate)	7,325
Mexico (1980)	
Acapulco	301,902
Aguascalientes	293,152
Atizapán de Zaragoza (Ciudad López Mateos)	188,497
Campeche	128,434
Celaya	141,675
Chihuahua	385,603
Ciudad Madero	132,444
Ciudad Obregón	165,572
Ciudad Victoria	140,161
Coatzacoalcos	127,170
Cuernavaca	192,770
Culiacán	304,826
Ensenada	120,483
Durango	257,915
Gómez Palacio	116,967
Guadalajara	1,626,152
Guadalupe	370,524
Hermosillo	297,175
Irapuato	170,138
Jalapa	204,594
Juárez	544,496
León	593,002
Los Mochis	122,531
Matamoros	188,745
Mazatlán	199,830
Mérida	400,142
Mexicali	341,559
★ Mexico City	8,831,079
Minatitlán	106,765
Monclova	115,786
Monterrey	1,090,009
Morelia	297,544
Nezahualcóyotl	1,341,230
Nuevo Laredo	201,731
Oaxaca	154,223
Orizaba	114,848
Pachuca	110,351
Poza Rica	166,799
Puebla	835,759
Querétaro	215,976
Reynosa	194,693
Saltillo	284,937
San Luis Potosí	362,371
San Nicolás de los Garza	280,696
Tampico	267,957
Tepic	145,741
Tijuana	429,500
Tlaquepaque	133,500
Toluca	199,778
Torreón	328,086
Tuxtla	131,096
Uruapan	122,828
Veracruz	284,822
Villahermosa	158,216
Zapopan	345,390
Monaco (1982)	
★ Monaco	27,063[8]
Mongolia (1986 est.)	
★ Ulaanbaatar (Ulan Bator)	500,200
Montserrat (1980)	
★ Plymouth	1,568
Morocco (1982)	
Agadir	110,479
Casablanca (Dar el-Beida)	2,139,204
Fès (Fez)	448,823
Kenitra	188,194
Khouribga	127,181
Marrakech	439,728
Meknès	319,783
Mohammedia	105,120
Oujda	260,082
★ Rabat	518,616
Safi	197,309
Salé	289,391
Tanger	266,346
Tétouan	199,615
Mozambique (1986 est.)	
Beira	269,700
★ Maputo (Lourenço Marques)	882,814
Nampula	182,553
Nauru (1983)	
★ Yaren	559
Nepal (1981)	
★ Kāthmāndu	235,160
Netherlands, The (1987 est.)	
★ Amsterdam (capital)	682,702
Apeldoorn	145,696
Arnhem	127,671
Breda	119,427
Dordrecht	106,987
Eindhoven	190,962
Enschede	144,227
Groningen	168,019
Haarlem	149,099
Leiden	106,808
Maastricht	115,272
Nijmegen	146,639
Rotterdam	572,642
★ The Hague (seat of government)	445,127
Tilburg	153,625
Utrecht	229,326
Zaanstad	128,388
Netherland Antilles (1985 est.)[4]	
★ Willemstad	125,000
New Caledonia (1983; MU)	
★ Nouméa	60,112
New Zealand (1987 est.)	
Auckland	148,400
Christchurch	167,700
Manukau	181,000
★ Wellington	136,000
Nicaragua (1985 est.)	
León	100,982
★ Managua	682,111
Niger (1983 est.)	
★ Niamey	399,100
Nigeria (1988 est.)	
Aba	244,700
Abeokuta	349,800
Ado-Ekiti	294,300
Akure	132,800
Benin City	187,900
Bida	103,000
Calabar	142,800
Deba	113,400
Ede	251,400
Effon-Alaiye	128,200
Enugu	258,700
Gusau	129,300
Ibadan	1,172,000
Ife	242,900
Ijebu-Ode	128,000
Ikare	115,300
Ikerre	200,300
Ikire	100,900
Ikirun	148,600
Ikorodu	151,400
Ila	216,100
Ilawe-Ekiti	151,000
Ilesha	309,700
Ilobu	162,900
Ilorin	389,500
Iseyin	177,800
Iwo	296,200
Jos	168,900
Kaduna	280,100
Kano	551,800
Katsina	169,100
Kumo	121,200
Lafia	100,200
★ Lagos	1,243,000
Maiduguri	262,000
Makurdi	100,800
Minna	112,000
Mushin	272,800
Offa	161,400
Ogbomosho	597,500
Oka	117,200
Ondo	138,900
Onitsha	304,500
Oshogbo	390,400
Owo	159,300
Oyo	209,900
Port Harcourt	335,600
Sapele	114,200
Shaki	142,500
Shomolu	120,900
Sokoto	167,800
Zaria	310,500
Niue (1984)	
★ Alofi	894
Norfolk Island	
★ Kingston	...
Norway (1987 est.; MU)	
Bergen	209,299
★ Oslo	451,484
Trondheim	135,005
Oman (1981 est.)	
★ Muscat	50,000
Pacific Islands, Trust Territory of the	
Marshall Is. (1985 est.)	
★ Majuro	14,267
Micronesia, Federated States of (1980)	
★ Kolonia	5,549
Northern Mariana Is. (1985 est.)	
★ Saipan	17,840
Palau (1986)	
★ Koror	9,442
Pakistan (1981)	
Bahāwalpur	180,263
Chiniot	105,559
Dera Ghāzi Khān	102,007
Faisalābād (Lyallpur)	1,104,209
Gujrānwāla	658,753
Gujrāt	155,058
Hyderābād	751,529
★ Islāmābād	204,364
Jhang	195,558
Jhelum	106,462
Karāchi	5,208,132
Kasūr	155,523
Lahore	2,952,689
Lahore Cantonment	237,000
Lārkāna	123,890
Mardān	147,977
Mirpur Khās	124,371
Multān	730,070
Nawābshāh	102,139
Okāra	153,483
Peshāwar	566,248
Quetta	285,719
Rahīm Yār Khān	119,036
Rāwalpindi	794,843
Sāhiwāl	150,954
Sargodha	291,362
Sheikhūpura	141,168
Siālkot	302,009

Major cities and national capitals (continued)

country city	population
Sukkur	190,551
Wāh Cantonment	122,335
Panama (1987 est.)	
★ Panama City	439,996
San Miguelito	231,920
Papua New Guinea (1987 est.)	
★ Port Moresby	152,100
Paraguay (1985 est.)	
★ Asunción	477,065
Peru (1987 est.)	
Arequipa	572,000
Callao	545,000
Chiclayo	379,000
Chimbote	270,000
Cuzco	245,000
Huancayo	195,000
Ica	140,000
Iquitos	237,000
★ Lima	375,957[11]
Metro Lima-Callao	5,875,900
Piura	284,000
Pucallpa	134,000
Tacna	131,000
Trujillo	476,000
Philippines (1988 est.)	
Angeles	239,585
Bacolod	311,966
Bago	123,551
Baguio	148,555
Batangas	172,242
Butuan	215,070
Cabanatuan	167,732
Cadiz	139,373
Cagayan de Oro	328,792
Calbayog	121,003
Caloocan	593,362[12]
Cebu	609,859
Cotabato	102,192
Dagupan	110,494
Davao	810,818
General Santos	220,003
Iligan	194,290
Iloilo	280,611
Lapu-Lapu	124,088
Las Piñas	194,064[12]
Legaspi	116,491
Lipa	144,762
Lucena	139,543
Makati	441,411[12]
Malabon	233,469[12]
Mandaluyong	223,084[12]
Mandaue	166,230
★ Manila	1,987,055[12]
Metro Manila	7,211,753[12]
Marikina	318,251[12]
Muntilupa	170,282[12]
Naga	100,000
Navotas	145,050[12]
Olongapo	189,069
Ormoc	127,280
Parañaque	371,450[12]
Pasay	321,210[12]
Pasig	318,853
Quezon City	1,322,907[12]
San Carlos	115,491
San Juan del Monte	156,568[12]
San Pablo	152,329
Silay	129,309
Tacloban	131,819
Tagig	165,742[12]
Toledo	112,590
Valenzuela	260,450[12]
Zamboanga	414,016
Pitcairn Island (1987 est.)	
★ Adamstown	51[8]
Poland (1987 est.)	
Białystok	255,700
Bielsko-Biała	176,900
Bydgoszcz	369,500
Bytom	239,500
Chorzów	140,500
Czestochowa	250,700
Dąbrovo Górnicza	138,900
Elbląg	119,600
Gdańsk	468,400
Gdynia	248,200
Gliwice	211,200
Gorzów Wielkopolski	117,600
Jastrzębie-Zdrój	101,400
Kalisz	105,000
Katowice	367,300
Kielce	205,900
Koszalin	103,300
Kraków	744,000
Łódź	847,400
Lublin	329,700
Olsztyn	152,200
Opole	127,500
Płock	116,300
Poznań	578,100
Radom	219,100
Ruda Śląska	167,200
Rybnik	139,200
Rzeszów	144,900
Sosnowiec	258,100
Szczecin	395,000

country city	population
Tarnów	117,100
Toruń	194,600
Tychy	185,900
Wałbrzych	140,400
★ Warsaw (Warszawa)	1,644,700
Włocławek	117,800
Wodzislaw Śląskie	110,500
Wrocław	640,000
Zabrze	198,900
Zielona Góra	112,200
Portugal (1986 est.)	
★ Lisbon	829,600
Porto	347,300
Puerto Rico (1984 est.; MU)	
Bayamón	202,500
Caguas	121,100
Carolina	165,700
Ponce	190,900
★ San Juan	428,900
Qatar (1986)	
★ Doha	217,294
Réunion (1982)	
★ Saint-Denis	84,400
Romania (1986 est.)	
Arad	187,744
Bacău	179,877
Baia Mare	139,704
Botoşani	108,775
Brăila	235,620
Braşov	351,493
★ Bucharest	1,989,823
Buzău	136,080
Cluj-Napoca	310,017
Constanţa	327,676
Craiova	281,044
Galaţi	295,372
Iaşi	313,060
Oradea	213,846
Piatra Neamţ	109,393
Piteşti	157,190
Ploieşti	234,886
Reşiţa	105,914
Satu Mare	130,082
Sibiu	177,511
Timişoara	325,272
Tirgu Mureş	158,998
Rwanda (1981 est.)	
★ Kigali	156,700
St. Helena and Ascension (1987)	
★ Jamestown	1,413
St. Kitts and Nevis (1985 est.)	
★ Basseterre	18,500
St. Lucia (1986 est.)	
★ Castries	52,868
St. Pierre and Miquelon (1982)	
★ Saint-Pierre	5,415
St. Vincent and The Grenadines (1987 est.)	
★ Kingstown	18,830
San Marino (1988 est.)	
★ San Marino	2,359
São Tomé and Príncipe (1984 est.)	
★ São Tomé	34,997
Saudi Arabia (1980 est.)	
ad-Dammām	200,000
Jiddah	1,500,000[1]
Mecca (Makkah)	550,000
Medina (al-Madinah)	290,000
★ Riyadh (ar-Riyad)	1,308,000[11]
aṭ-Ṭā'if	300,000
Senegal (1985 est.)	
★ Dakar	1,382,000
Kaolack	132,400
Thiès	156,200
Ziguinchor	106,500
Seychelles (1977)	
★ Victoria	23,012
Sierra Leone (1985)	
★ Freetown	469,776
Singapore (1988 est.)[8]	
★ Singapore	2,641,000
Solomon Islands (1986 est.; MU)	
★ Honiara	30,499
Somalia (1981 est.)	
★ Mogadishu	500,000
South Africa (1985)	
★ Bloemfontein (judicial)	104,381
Boksburg	110,832
★ Cape Town (legislative)	776,617
Metro Cape Town	1,911,521
Durban	634,301
Metro Durban	982,075
Germiston	116,718
Johannesburg	632,369
Metro Johannesburg	1,609,408
Pietermaritzburg	133,809
Port Elizabeth	272,844
★ Pretoria (executive)	443,059
Metro Pretoria	822,925
Roodepoort	141,764
Soweto	864,000[13]

country city	population
Bophuthatswana	
★ Mmabatho	...
Ciskei (1986 est.)	
★ Bisho	2,850
Mdantsane	242,823
Transkei (1978 est.)	
★ Umtata	30,000
Venda (1985)	
★ Thohoyandou	10,166
South West Africa/Namibia (1986 est.)	
★ Windhoek	129,000
Spain (1986 est.; MU)	
Albacete	126,594
Alcalá de Henares	142,862[11]
Alcorcón	140,657[11]
Alicante	258,707
Almería	154,242
Badajoz	119,220
Badalona	227,744[11]
Barcelona	1,699,231
Bilbao	379,107
Burgos	158,610
Cádiz	155,219
Castellón de la Plana	127,578
Córdoba	296,075
Coruña, La	239,505
Gerona	126,030[11]
Getafe	127,060[11]
Gijón	255,969[11]
Granada	256,528
Hospitalet de Llobregat	294,033[11]
Huelva	135,576
Jaén	103,291
La Laguna	112,635[11]
Leganés	163,426[11]
León	135,014
Lérida	107,787
Logroño	115,922
★ Madrid	3,053,101
Málaga	566,480
Móstoles	149,649[11]
Murcia	304,185
Orense	100,430
Oviedo	185,920
Palma (de Mallorca)	295,351
Palmas de Gran Canaria, Las (Is. Canarias)	356,730
Pamplona	184,340
Sabadell	194,943[11]
Salamanca	152,766
San Sebastián	175,267
Santa Coloma de Gramanet	140,588[11]
Santa Cruz de Tenerife	212,523
Santander	186,456
Sevilla (Seville)	651,299
Tarragona	106,361
Terrassa	155,360[11]
Valencia	728,622
Valladolid	327,786
Vigo	258,724[11]
Vitoria	199,936
Zaragoza (Saragossa)	573,711
Sri Lanka (1985 est.)	
★ Colombo	664,000
Dehiwala-Mount Lavinia	188,000
Galle	102,000
Jaffna	138,000
Kandy	125,000
Kotte	102,000
Moratuwa	138,000
Sudan, The (1983)	
★ Khartoum	476,218
Khartoum North	341,146
Port Sudan	206,727
Omdurman	526,287
Suriname (1986 est.)	
★ Paramaribo	77,558
Swaziland (1986 est.)	
★ Mbabane	48,000
Sweden (1988 est.; MU)	
Borås	100,395
Göteborg	431,521
Helsingborg	106,982
Jönköping	108,962
Linköping	118,602
Malmö	230,838
Norrköping	119,001
Örebro	119,066
★ Stockholm	666,810
Uppsala	159,962
Västerås	117,563
Switzerland (1988 est.)	
Basel (Bâle)	173,582
★ Bern (Berne)	137,606
Geneva (Genève)	164,423
Lausanne	125,646
Zürich	351,086
Syria (1987 est.)	
Aleppo (Halab)	1,216,000
★ Damascus (Dimashq)	1,292,000
Hamāh	214,000
Homs (Hims)	431,000

country city	population
Latakia (al-Ladhiqiyah)	241,000
Taiwan (1987 est.)	
Chang-hua	203,541
Chi-lung (Keelung)	349,616
Chia-i	254,001
Chung-ho	334,663
Chung-li	241,476
Feng-shan (Kao-hsiung-hsien)	271,738
Fêng-yüan	142,552
Hsin-chu	306,088
Hsin-chuang	243,706
Hsin-tien	198,125
Hua-lien	106,265
Kao-hsiung	1,320,552
Pan-ch-'iao (T'ai-pei-hsien)	491,721
P'ing-tung	202,079
San-chu'ung	358,812
T'ai-chung	695,562
T'ai-nan	646,298
T'ai-tung	110,461
★ Taipei (T'ai-pei)	2,575,180
T'ao-yuan	210,753
Yung-ho	238,677
Tanzania (1978)	
★ Dar es Salaam	769,445
Mwanza	110,553
Tanga	103,399
Zanzibar	110,506
Thailand (1983 est.)	
★ Bangkok	5,018,327
Chiang Mai	150,499
Hat Yai	113,964
Khon Kaen	115,515
Nakhon Ratchasima	190,692
Ubon Ratchathani	100,255
Togo (1983)	
★ Lomé	366,476
Tokelau	
—	—
Tonga (1986)	
★ Nuku'alofa	28,899
Trinidad and Tobago (1986 est.)	
★ Port-of-Spain	57,400
Tunisia (1984)	
Ṣafāqis (Sfax)	231,911
★ Tunis	596,654
Turkey (1985)	
Adana	777,554
Adapazari	155,041
★ Ankara	2,235,000
Antakya	109,233
Antalya	258,139
Balıkesir	152,402
Batman	114,210
Bursa	612,500
Denizli	171,360
Diyarbakır	305,259
Elaziğ	181,523
Erzurum	252,648
Eskişehir	367,328
Gaziantep	466,302
İçel	314,105
İskenderun	173,607
Isparta	101,784
İstanbul	5,475,982
İzmir	1,489,772
İzmit	236,144
Kahramanmaraş	212,206
Kayseri	378,458
Konya	438,839
Kütahya	120,354
Malatya	251,257
Manisa	126,319
Osmaniye	107,748
Samsun	280,068
Sivas	197,266
Trabzon	155,960
Urfa (Şanlıurfa)	206,385
Van	121,306
Zonguldak	119,125
Turks and Caicos Islands (1980)	
★ Cockburn Town	3,124
Tuvalu (1985 est.)	
★ Funafuti	2,810
Uganda (1980)	
★ Kampala	458,503
Union of Soviet Socialist Republics (1987 est.)	
Abakan	151,000
Achinsk	121,000
Aktyubinsk	248,000
Alma-Ata	1,108,000
Almalyk	119,000
Almetyevsk	128,000
Andizhan	288,000
Andropov	254,000
Angarsk	262,000
Angren	131,000
Anzhero-Sudzhensk	112,000
Arkhangelsk	416,000
Armavir	172,000
Arzamas	108,000

country city	population
Ashkhabad	382,000
Astrakhan	509,000
Baku	1,115,000
Balakovo	188,000
Balashikha	132,000
Baranovichi	154,000
Barnaul	596,000
Batumi	135,000
Belaya Tserkov	194,000
Belgorod	293,000
Belovo	118,000
Beltsy	157,000
Bendery	130,000
Berdyansk	133,000
Berezniki	200,000
Biysk	231,000
Blagoveshchensk	202,000
Bobruysk	232,000
Borisov	140,000
Bratsk	249,000
Brest	238,000
Bryansk	445,000
Bukhara	220,000
Chardzhou	166,000
Cheboksary	414,000
Chelyabinsk	1,119,000
Cherepovets	315,000
Cherkassy	287,000
Cherkessk	107,000
Chernigov	291,000
Chernovtsy	254,000
Chimkent	389,000
Chirchik	160,000
Chita	349,000
Daugavpils	128,000
Dimitrovgrad	121,000
Dneprodzerzhinsk	279,000
Dnepropetrovsk	1,182,000
Donetsk	1,090,000
Dushanbe	582,000
Dzerzhinsk	281,000
Dzhambul	315,000
Dzhezkazgan	105,000
Ekibastuz	141,000
Elektrostal	150,000
Engels	182,000
Fergana	203,000
Frunze	632,000
Gomel	488,000
Gorky	1,425,000
Gorlovka	345,000
Grodno	263,000
Grozny	404,000
Guryev	150,000
Irkutsk	609,000
Ivano-Frankovsk	225,000
Ivanovo	479,000
Izhevsk	631,000
Kalinin	447,000
Kaliningrad	394,000
Kaliningrad (*Moscow obl.*)	146,000
Kaluga	307,000
Kamensk-Uralsky	204,000
Kamenets-Podolsky	101,000
Kamyshin	119,000
Kansk	108,000
Karaganda	633,000
Karshi	141,000
Kaunas	417,000
Kazan	1,068,000
Kemerovo	520,000
Kerch	173,000
Khabarovsk	591,000
Kharkov	1,587,000
Kherson	358,000
Khimki	128,000
Khmelnitsky	230,000
Kiev	2,544,000
Kineshma	105,000
Kirov	421,000
Kirovabad	270,000
Kirovakan	169,000
Kirovograd	269,000
Kiselevsk	128,000
Kishinyov	663,000
Kislovodsk	110,000
Klaipėda	201,000
Kokand	173,000
Kokchetav	127,000
Kolomna	159,000
Kolpino	134,000
Kommunarsk	126,000
Komsomolsk-na-Amure	316,000
Konstantinovka	115,000
Kostroma	276,000
Kovrov	158,000
Kramatorsk	198,000
Krasnodar	623,000
Krasnoyarsk	899,000
Krasny Luch	112,000
Kremenchug	230,000
Krivoy Rog	698,000
Kurgan	354,000
Kursk	434,000
Kustanay	212,000
Kutaisi	220,000

country / city	population
Kuybyshev	1,280,000
Kzyl-Orda	189,000
Leninabad	157,000
Leninakan	228,000
Leningrad	4,393,000
Leninsk-Kuznetsky	169,000
Liepāja	114,000
Lipetsk	465,000
Lisichansk	124,000
Lutsk	185,000
Lvov	767,000
Lyubertsy	162,000
Magadan	148,000
Magnitogorsk	430,000
Makeyevka	455,000
Makhachkala	320,000
Margilan	127,000
Maykop	145,000
Melitopol	174,000
Mezhdurechensk	104,000
Miass	163,000
Michurinsk	103,000
Minsk	1,543,000
Mogilyov	359,000
★ Moscow	8,614,000
Murmansk	432,000
Murom	124,000
Mytishchi	152,000
Naberezhnye Chelny	480,000
Nakhodka	152,000
Nalchik	236,000
Namangan	291,000
Navoi	106,000
Nevinnomyssk	116,000
Nikolayev	501,000
Nikopol	157,000
Nizhnekamsk	183,000
Nizhnevartovsk	212,000
Nizhny Tagil	427,000
Noginsk	122,000
Norilsk	181,000
Novgorod	228,000
Novocheboksarsk	109,000
Novocherkassk	188,000
Novokuybyshevsk	112,000
Novokuznetsk	589,000
Novomoskovsk (*Tula obl.*)	147,000
Novorossiysk	179,000
Novoshakhtinsk	106,000
Novosibirsk	1,423,000
Novotroitsk	105,000
Nukus	152,000
Odessa	1,141,000
Odintsovo	120,000
Oktyabrsky	106,000
Omsk	1,134,000
Ordzhonikidze	313,000
Orekhovo-Zuyevo	137,000
Orenburg	537,000
Orsha	123,000
Orsk	273,000
Oryol	335,000
Osh	209,000
Panevėžys	122,000
Pavlodar	331,000
Pavlograd	126,000
Penza	540,000
Perm	1,075,000
Pervouralsk	139,000
Petropavlovsk	233,000
Petropavlovsk-Kamchatsky	252,000
Petrozavodsk	264,000
Pinsk	116,000
Podolsk	209,000
Poltava	309,000
Prokopyevsk	278,000
Pskov	202,000
Pyatigorsk	121,000
Riga	900,000
Rostov-na-Donu	1,004,000
Rovno	233,000
Rubtsovsk	168,000
Rudny	118,000
Rustavi	147,000
Ryazan	508,000
Salavat	153,000
Samarkand	588,000
Saransk	323,000
Sarapul	111,000
Saratov	918,000
Semipalatinsk	330,000
Serov	103,000
Serpukhov	142,000
Sevastopol	350,000
Severodonetsk	127,000
Severodvinsk	239,000
Shakhty	225,000
Shchelkovo	107,000
Shevchenko	161,000
Šiauliai	140,000
Simferopol	338,000
Slavyansk	144,000
Smolensk	338,000
Sochi	317,000
Solikamsk	108,000
Stakhanov	112,000
Stary Oskol	167,000
Stavropol	306,000
Sterlitamak	251,000
Sukhumi	130,000
Sumgait	234,000
Sumy	268,000
Surgut	227,000
Sverdlovsk (*Sverdlovsk obl.*)	1,331,000
Syktyvkar	224,000
Syzran	174,000
Taganrog	295,000
Taldy-Kurgan	113,000
Tallinn	478,000
Tambov	305,000
Tartu	113,000
Tashauz	110,000
Tashkent	2,124,000
Tbilisi	1,194,000
Temirtau	228,000
Ternopol	197,000
Tiraspol	173,000
Tolyatti (Togliatti)	627,000
Tomsk	489,000
Tselinograd	276,000
Tula	538,000
Tyumen	456,000
Ufa	1,092,000
Ukhta	105,000
Ulan-Ude	351,000
Ulyanovsk	589,000
Uralsk	201,000
Urgench	123,000
Usolye-Sibirskoye	108,000
Ussuriysk	158,000
Ust-Ilimsk	105,000
Ust-Kamenogorsk	321,000
Uzhgorod	111,000
Velikiye Luki	113,000
Vilnius	566,000
Vinnitsa	383,000
Vitebsk	347,000
Vladimir	343,000
Vladivostok	615,000
Volgodonsk	179,000
Volgograd	988,000
Vologda	278,000
Volzhsky	257,000
Vorkuta	112,000
Voronezh	872,000
Voroshilovgrad	509,000
Votkinsk	101,000
Yakutsk	188,000
Yaroslavl	634,000
Yelets	119,000
Yenakiyevo	117,000
Yerevan	1,168,000
Yevpatoriya	106,000
Yoshkar-Ola	243,000
Yuzhno-Sakhalinsk	166,000
Zagorsk	113,000
Zaporozhye	875,000
Zelenograd	148,000
Zhdanov	529,000
Zhitomir	287,000
Zlatoust	206,000
United Arab Emirates (1980)	
★ Abu Dhabi (Abū Ẓaby)	243,000
Al-'Ayn	102,000
Dubai (Dubayy)	266,000
Sharjah (ash-Shāriqah)	125,000
United Kingdom (1981)	
Aberdeen	190,465
Belfast	354,400
Birmingham	1,024,118
Blackburn	110,254
Blackpool	149,012
Bolton	143,921
Bournemouth	148,382
Bradford	295,048
Brighton	137,985
Bristol	420,234
Cardiff	266,267
Coventry	322,573
Derby	220,681
Dudley	187,367
Dundee	174,345
Edinburgh	420,169
Glasgow	765,030
Gloucester	108,150
Huddersfield	148,544
Ipswich	131,131
Kingston upon Hull	325,485
Leeds	451,841
Leicester	328,835
Liverpool	544,861
★ London	6,677,928
Luton	164,743
Manchester	448,604
Middlesbrough	159,421
Newcastle upon Tyne	203,591
Newport	116,658
Northampton	155,694
Norwich	173,286
Nottingham	277,203
Oldbury/Smethwick	153,461
Oldham	107,830
Oxford	119,909
Peterborough	114,733
Plymouth	242,560
Poole	124,974
Portsmouth	177,905
Preston	168,405
Reading	198,341
Rotherham	123,312
St. Helens	114,822
Sheffield	477,257
Slough	106,822
Southampton	214,802
Southend-on-Sea	156,969
Stockport	136,792
Stoke-on-Trent	275,168
Sunderland	195,896
Sutton Coldfield	103,097
Swansea	175,172
Swindon	128,493
Walsall	178,852
West Bromwich	154,531
Wolverhampton	265,631
York	126,377
United States (1987 est.)	
Abilene (*Tex.*)	113,160
Akron (*Ohio*)	227,550
Albuquerque (*N.M.*)	371,760
Alexandria (*Va.*)	109,990
Allentown (*Pa.*)	104,770
Amarillo (*Tex.*)	166,910
Amherst Town (*N.Y.*)	104,190
Anaheim (*Calif.*)	246,820
Anchorage (*Alsk.*)	231,040
Ann Arbor (*Mich.*)	108,340
Arlington (*Tex.*)	251,370
Arlington (*Va.*)	161,920
Atlanta (*Ga.*)	429,950
Aurora (*Colo.*)	219,900
Austin (*Tex.*)	469,540
Bakersfield (*Calif.*)	154,200
Baltimore (*Md.*)	764,890
Baton Rouge (*La.*)	242,540
Beaumont (*Tex.*)	120,670
Berkeley (*Calif.*)	106,740
Birmingham (*Ala.*)	282,100
Boise City (*Idaho*)	107,900
Boston (*Mass.*)	575,880
Bridgeport (*Conn.*)	142,850
Brownsville (*Tex.*)	102,770
Buffalo (*N.Y.*)	325,790
Cedar Rapids (*Iowa*)	107,730
Charlotte (*N.C.*)	356,600
Chattanooga (*Tenn.*)	163,930
Chesapeake (*Va.*)	137,120
Chicago (*Ill.*)	3,018,300
Chula Vista (*Calif.*)	121,840
Cincinnati (*Ohio*)	371,590
Clearwater (*Fla.*)	100,430
Cleveland (*Ohio*)	548,170
Colorado Springs (*Colo.*)	275,100
Columbus (*Ga.*)	183,650
Columbus (*Ohio*)	567,800
Concord (*Calif.*)	108,660
Corpus Christi (*Tex.*)	265,590
Dallas (*Tex.*)	1,009,900
Dayton (*Ohio*)	181,700
Denver (*Colo.*)	509,520
Des Moines (*Iowa*)	190,930
Detroit (*Mich.*)	1,091,500
Durham (*N.C.*)	115,340
El Paso (*Tex.*)	494,950
Elizabeth (*N.J.*)	107,270
Erie (*Pa.*)	115,720
Eugene (*Ore.*)	106,430
Evansville (*Ind.*)	130,130
Flint (*Mich.*)	146,300
Fort Lauderdale (*Fla.*)	153,050
Fort Wayne (*Ind.*)	172,900[12]
Fort Worth (*Tex.*)	432,310
Fremont (*Calif.*)	157,460
Fresno (*Calif.*)	291,900
Fullerton (*Calif.*)	111,500
Garden Grove (*Calif.*)	138,260
Garland (*Tex.*)	177,640
Gary (*Ind.*)	137,470
Glendale (*Ariz.*)	131,320
Glendale (*Calif.*)	157,540
Grand Rapids (*Mich.*)	187,440
Greensboro (*N.C.*)	178,920
Hampton (*Va.*)	128,550
Hartford (*Conn.*)	138,950
Hayward (*Calif.*)	104,090
Hialeah (*Fla.*)	166,580
Hollywood (*Fla.*)	124,520
Honolulu (*Ha.*)	832,610
Houston (*Tex.*)	1,740,000
Huntington Beach (*Calif.*)	188,260
Huntsville (*Ala.*)	164,660
Independence (*Mo.*)	113,780
Indianapolis (*Ind.*)	778,690
Inglewood (*Calif.*)	105,140
Irving (*Tex.*)	129,350
Jackson (*Miss.*)	280,410
Jacksonville (*Fla.*)	629,890
Jersey City (*N.J.*)	220,980
Kansas City (*Kan.*)	163,100
Kansas City (*Mo.*)	444,380
Knoxville (*Tenn.*)	175,090
Lakewood (*Colo.*)	123,240
Lansing (*Mich.*)	129,610
Laredo (*Tex.*)	117,810
Las Vegas (*Nev.*)	193,240[12]
Lexington (*Ky.*)	212,930
Lincoln (*Neb.*)	182,620
Little Rock (*Ark.*)	182,290
Livonia (*Mich.*)	101,030
Long Beach (*Calif.*)	406,300
Los Angeles (*Calif.*)	3,341,700
Louisville (*Ky.*)	286,520
Lubbock (*Tex.*)	187,600
Macon (*Ga.*)	120,700
Madison (*Wis.*)	176,640
Manchester (*N.H.*)	100,130
Memphis (*Tenn.*)	659,720
Mesa (*Ariz.*)	262,430
Miami (*Fla.*)	385,090
Milwaukee (*Wis.*)	607,890
Minneapolis (*Minn.*)	359,370
Mobile (*Ala.*)	204,800
Modesto (*Calif.*)	136,300
Montgomery (*Ala.*)	195,760
Nashville (*Tenn.*)	487,100
New Haven (*Conn.*)	124,310
New Orleans (*La.*)	549,540
New York City (*N.Y.*)	7,284,300
Newark (*N.J.*)	318,400
Newport News (*Va.*)	164,980
Norfolk (*Va.*)	280,370
Oakland (*Calif.*)	366,000
Oceanside (*Calif.*)	101,650
Odessa (*Tex.*)	101,860
Oklahoma City (*Okla.*)	441,410
Omaha (*Neb.*)	374,930
Ontario (*Calif.*)	117,210
Orange (*Calif.*)	103,290
Orlando (*Fla.*)	150,250
Oxnard (*Calif.*)	130,190
Pasadena (*Calif.*)	133,180
Pasadena (*Tex.*)	118,810
Paterson (*N.J.*)	140,080
Peoria (*Ill.*)	110,610
Philadelphia (*Pa.*)	1,649,400
Phoenix (*Ariz.*)	933,200
Pittsburgh (*Pa.*)	389,020
Plano (*Tex.*)	111,740
Pomona (*Calif.*)	118,460
Portland (*Ore.*)	390,850
Portsmouth (*Va.*)	113,250
Providence (*R.I.*)	158,980
Pueblo (*Colo.*)	102,150
Raleigh (*N.C.*)	182,750
Reno (*Nev.*)	115,320
Richmond (*Va.*)	222,110
Riverside (*Calif.*)	201,720
Roanoke (*Va.*)	103,970
Rochester (*N.Y.*)	236,670
Rockford (*Ill.*)	135,760[12]
Sacramento (*Calif.*)	331,700
St. Louis (*Mo.*)	429,410
St. Paul (*Minn.*)	265,550
St. Petersburg (*Fla.*)	246,550
Salt Lake City (*Utah*)	159,840
San Antonio (*Tex.*)	920,220
San Bernardino (*Calif.*)	142,120
San Diego (*Calif.*)	1,040,900
San Francisco (*Calif.*)	767,900
San Jose (*Calif.*)	730,100
Santa Ana (*Calif.*)	242,800
Santa Rosa (*Calif.*)	100,070
Savannah (*Ga.*)	149,630
Scottsdale (*Ariz.*)	116,000
Seattle (*Wash.*)	494,430
Shreveport (*La.*)	218,410
South Bend (*Ind.*)	107,720
Spokane (*Wash.*)	175,820
Springfield (*Mass.*)	150,000
Springfield (*Ill.*)	100,580
Springfield (*Mo.*)	140,380
Stamford (*Conn.*)	101,790
Sterling Heights (*Mich.*)	112,510
Stockton (*Calif.*)	188,070
Sunnyvale (*Calif.*)	114,960
Syracuse (*N.Y.*)	161,230
Tacoma (*Wash.*)	161,640
Tallahassee (*Fla.*)	123,010
Tampa (*Fla.*)	285,860
Tempe (*Ariz.*)	142,450
Toledo (*Ohio*)	344,960
Topeka (*Kan.*)	119,330
Torrance (*Calif.*)	139,000
Tucson (*Ariz.*)	374,550
Tulsa (*Okla.*)	369,960
Virginia Beach (*Va.*)	340,160
Waco (*Tex.*)	105,900
Warren (*Mich.*)	150,530
★ Washington D.C.	622,000
Waterbury (*Conn.*)	103,020
Wichita (*Kan.*)	290,770
Winston-Salem (*N.C.*)	149,980
Worcester (*Mass.*)	158,400
Yonkers (*N.Y.*)	186,630
Youngstown (*Ohio*)	108,360
Uruguay (1985 est.)	
★ Montevideo	1,246,000
Vanuatu (1987 est.)	
★ Vila	15,100
Venezuela (1988 est.)	
Acarigua	123,320
Barcelona	226,805
Barinas	165,417
Barquisimeto	681,961
Baruta	264,068
Cabimas	163,454
★ Caracas	1,261,116
Ciudad Bolívar	249,590
Ciudad Guayana (San Felix de Guayana)	484,061
Coro	127,745
Cumaná	222,980
Guarenas	165,496
Los Teques	154,031
Maracaibo	1,151,933
Maracay	510,926
Maturín	212,810
Mérida	193,006
Petare	507,260
San Cristóbal	238,650
Turmero	187,230
Valencia	889,228
Valera	134,508
Vietnam (1979)	
Bien Hoa	190,086
Can Tho	182,856
Da Nang	318,655
Haiphong	330,755
★ Hanoi	819,913
Ho Chi Minh City (Saigon)	2,441,185
Hon Gai	115,312
Hue	165,865
Long Xuyen	112,488
My Tho	101,496
Nam Dinh	161,180
Nha Trang	172,663
Quy Nhon	130,534
Tha Nguyen	138,023
Thanh Hoa	103,981
Vinh	154,040
Virgin Islands (U.S.) (1980)	
★ Charlotte Amalie	11,842
Wallis and Futuna (1983)	
★ Matautu	815
West Bank	
★ —	—
Western Sahara (1982)	
★ El Aaiún (Laayoune)	93,875
Western Samoa (1981)	
★ Apia	33,170
Yemen (Aden) (1984 est.)	
★ Aden	318,000
Yemen (Ṣan'ā') (1986)	
Al-Ḥudaydah	155,110
★ Ṣan'ā'	427,185
Ta'izz	178,430
Yugoslavia (1981)	
Banja Luka	123,937
★ Belgrade (Beograd)	1,087,915
Ljubljana	224,817
Maribor	106,113
Niš	161,376
Novi Sad	170,020
Osijek	104,775
Priština	108,083
Rijeka	159,433
Sarajevo	319,017
Skopje (Skoplje)	408,143
Split	169,322
Subotica	100,516
Zagreb	649,586
Zaire (1984)	
Bukavu	171,064
Kananga	290,898
Kikwit	146,784
★ Kinshasa	2,653,558
Kisangani	282,650
Likasi	194,465
Lubumbashi	543,268
Matadi	144,742
Mbandaka	125,263
Mbuji-Mayi	423,363
Zambia (1987 est.)	
Chingola	187,310
Kabwe	190,752
Kitwe	449,442
Luanshya	160,667
★ Lusaka	818,994
Mufulira	192,323
Ndola	418,142
Zimbabwe (1983 est.)	
Bulawayo	429,000
Chitungwiza	202,000
★ Harare	681,000

[1]1983. [2]1977. [3]1984. [4]Population refers to widest officially-defined agglomeration or metropolitan area. [5]Excludes the agricultural population of the named civil division. [6]Excludes population of Lefkoşe (Turkish-occupied Nicosia), estimated at 37,400 in 1985. [7]1986 census. [8]No separate areas within the state are distinguished administratively as cities. [9]Population is for the "central district," which includes Comayagüela. [10]1970. [11]1981. [12]1986. [13]1980.

Language

This table presents data on the principal language communities of each of the countries of the world. The countries, and the principal languages used in each, are listed alphabetically; a bullet (●) indicates those languages that are designated as official by each country. The sum of the estimated populations for each language community and of the "Other" group equals the 1988 estimated de facto population of the country given in the *Area and population* table.

The estimates represent, so far as national data collection systems permit, the distribution of mother tongues (a mother tongue being the language spoken first and, usually, most fluently by an individual). Many countries do not collect data on this basis, however, and for these countries a variety of techniques have been used to approximate mother-tongue distribution. Some countries compile data on ethnic or "national" groups; for such countries ethnic distribution was often assumed to conform roughly to the distribution of language communities. This approach, however, must be used with caution, because a minority population is not always free to educate its children in its own language and because better economic opportunities often draw minority group members into the majority-language community. For some countries, a given individual may only be visible in national statistics as a passport-holder of a foreign nation, however long he may remain resident. Such persons, often guest workers, have sometimes had to be assumed to be speakers of the principal language of their home country. For example, since The Netherlands does not collect language data, holders of Moroccan passports were assumed to be speakers of Arabic (although perhaps a quarter of them might be of Berber heritage). For other countries, the language mosaic may be so complex, the language communities so minute in size, scholarly study so inadequate, and the census base so obsolete that it was possible only to assign percentages to groups of related languages, despite their mutual unintelligibility (Papuan and Melanesian languages in Papua New Guinea, for instance). For some countries in the Americas, so few speakers of any single indigenous language remain that it was necessary to combine these groups as *Amerindian* so as to give a fair impression of their aggregate size within their respective countries.

No systematic attempt has been made to account for populations that may legitimately be described as bilingual, unless the country itself collects data on that basis, as does Bolivia or the Comoros, for example. Where a nonindigenous official or excolonial language constitutes a lingua franca of the country, however, speakers of the language as a second tongue are shown in italics, even though very few may speak it as a mother tongue. No comprehensive attempt has been made to distinguish between degrees of dialectal variance among communities *usually* classified as belonging to the same language though this *was* possible for some countries—*e.g.,* between French and Occitan (the dialect of southern France), or among the various dialects of Chinese.

In giving the names of Bantu languages, grammatical particles specific to a language's autonym (name for itself) have been omitted (the form *Rwanda* is used here, for example, rather than *kinyaRwanda,* and *Tswana* instead of *seTswana*). Parenthetical alternatives are given for a number of languages that differ markedly from the name of the people speaking them (such as Kurukh, spoken by the Oraon tribes of India) or that may be combined with other groups sometimes distinguishable in national data but appearing here under the name of the largest member—*e.g.,* "Tamil (and other Indian languages)" combining data on South Asian Indian populations in Singapore. The term *creole* as used here refers to distinguishable dialectal communities related to a national, official, or former colonial language (such as the French creole that survives in Grenada from the end of French rule in 1783).

Language

Major languages by country	Number of speakers	Major languages by country	Number of speakers	Major languages by country	Number of speakers	Major languages by country	Number of speakers	Major languages by country	Number of speakers
Afghanistan[1]		**Australia**		**Benin**[1]		Fulani	710,000	**Cape Verde**	
● Dari (Persian), of which		Aboriginal and Torres		Bariba	430,000	Grusi	440,000	Crioulo (Portuguese	
Chahar Aimaq	420,000	Strait Islander		Fon	2,910,000	Gurma	410,000	Creole)	359,000
Ḥazāra	1,260,000	languages	180,000	● French	690,000	Lobi	590,000	● Portuguese	...
Tadzhik	2,940,000	Chinese Languages		Fulani (Peul)	180,000	Mande	750,000		
● Pashto	7,570,000	(Hakka, Hokkien, and		Somba	240,000	Mossi	4,090,000	**Cayman Islands**	
Turkmen	290,000	Cantonese dialects,		Yoruba (Nago)	390,000	Senufo	450,000	● English	23,000
Uzbek	1,260,000	and Standard Chinese		Other	290,000	Tuareg	280,000		
Other (including		[Mandarin])	120,000			Other	220,000	**Central African Republic**[1]	
other Dari)	730,000	Dutch	110,000	**Bermuda**				Banda	810,000
		● English	14,640,000	● English	54,000	**Burma**[1]		Baya (Gbaya)	700,000
Albania[1]		German	150,000	Other	4,000	● Burmese	27,170,000	● French	330,000
● Albanian	3,047,000	Greek	180,000			Karen	2,640,000	Kare	70,000
Greek	59,000	Italian	310,000	**Bhutan**[1]		Rakhine		Mbaka	120,000
Macedonian	11,000	Yugoslavian languages		Assamese	180,000	(Arakanese)	1,760,000	Mbum	120,000
Montenegrin	5,000	(Croatian, Macedonian,		● Dzongkha (Bhutia)	850,000	Shan	3,560,000	Ngbandi	300,000
Romanian	16,000	Serbian, and		Gurung	210,000	Other	4,830,000	Sango (lingua franca)	...
Other	11,000	Slovenian)	170,000	Other	120,000			Sara	200,000
		Other	600,000			**Burundi**[1]		Zande (Azande)	280,000
Algeria[1]				**Bolivia**		● French	350,000	Other	250,000
● Arabic	19,690,000	**Austria**		● Aymara	530,000	● Rundi	5,000,000		
Berber	4,040,000	Czech	1,000	● Quechua	960,000	Hutu	4,200,000	**Chad**[1]	
French	30,000	● German	7,489,000	● Spanish	2,540,000	Tutsi	690,000	● Arabic	1,410,000
Other	80,000	Hungarian	3,000	Aymara-Quechua	90,000	Twa	50,000	Dagu	120,000
		Serbo-Croatian	12,000	Spanish-Aymara	1,150,000	Other[3]	140,000	● French	320,000
American Samoa		Slovene	9,000	Spanish-Quechua	1,460,000			Hausa	120,000
● English	1,000	Other	63,000	Spanish-Aymara-		**Cameroon**[1]		Kanuri	120,000
● Samoan	34,000			Quechua	170,000	Bamileke-Widekum-		Kotoko	110,000
Other	3,000	**Bahamas, The**		Spanish-others	80,000	Bamum	2,080,000	Masa	120,000
		● English	...	Other	10,000	Duala-Lunda-Basa	1,650,000	Masalit, Maba, and Mimi	340,000
Andorra		English Creole	208,000			● English	...	Mbum	350,000
Castilian Spanish	31,000	French (Haitian) Creole	25,000	**Botswana**[1]		Fang	2,200,000	Mubi	230,000
● Catalan	15,000	Other	12,000	● English	...	● French	1,690,000	Sara, Bagirmi,	
French	3,000			Khoikhoin (Hottentot)	30,000	Fulani	1,080,000	and Kreish	1,640,000
Other	2,000	**Bahrain**		Ndebele	16,000	Maka	440,000	Tama	340,000
		● Arabic	300,000	San (Bushmen)	42,000	Mandara	640,000	Teda (Tubu)	390,000
Angola[1]		Other	120,000	Shona	150,000	Tikar	830,000	Other	90,000
Ambo (Ovambo)	230,000			Tswana	914,000	Other	2,300,000		
Chokwe	390,000	**Bangladesh**[1]		Other	59,000			**Chile**[1]	
Herero	70,000	● Bengali	105,310,000			**Canada**		Amerindian languages	
Kongo	1,240,000	Chakma	400,000	**Brazil**[1]		● English	15,652,000	(mostly Araucanian)	870,000
Luchazi	230,000	Garo	100,000	Amerindian languages	250,000	● French	6,286,000	● Spanish	11,680,000
Luimbe-Nganguela	510,000	Khasi	90,000	German	790,000	English-French	339,000	Other	200,000
Lunda	110,000	Magh	200,000	Italian	610,000	English-other	536,000		
Luvale (Luena)	340,000	Santal	80,000	Japanese	690,000	French-other	36,000	**China**[1]	
Mbunda	110,000	Tippera	80,000	● Portuguese	140,580,000	English-French-other	47,000	Achang	20,000
Mbundu	2,030,000	Other	1,510,000	Other	1,340,000	Aboriginal (Amerindian		Bulan (Blang)	60,000
Nyaneka-Humbe	510,000					and Eskimo [Inuktitut])		Ch'iang (Qiang)	110,000
Ovimbundu	3,490,000	**Barbados**		**British Virgin Islands**		languages	186,000	Chinese (Han)	1,015,320,000
● Portuguese	...	● English	20,000	● English	...	Arabic	41,000	Cantonese	
Other	150,000	English Creole	232,000	English Creole	11,000	Chinese	272,000	(Yüeh [Yue])	50,800,000
		Other	2,000	Other	1,000	Dutch	127,000	Hakka	37,600,000
Anguilla						Filipino (Pilipino)	44,000	Hsiang (Xiang)	48,700,000
● English	...	**Belgium**[1]		**Brunei**[1]		Finnish	26,000	Kan (Gan)	24,400,000
English Creole	7,000	● Dutch	5,850,000	Chinese	46,000	German	448,000	● Mandarin	726,000,000
		● French	3,250,000	● English	77,000	Greek	114,000	Min	41,600,000
Antigua and Barbuda		● German	90,000	Indian	9,000	Hungarian	70,000	Wu	86,300,000
● English	...	Italian	280,000	● Malay	172,000	Italian	466,000	Chingpo (Jingpo)	100,000
English Creole	80,000	Other	390,000	Other indigenous	13,000	Polish	127,000	Chuang (Zhuang)	14,510,000
Other	3,000			Other	10,000	Portuguese	158,000	Daghur (Daur)	100,000
		Belize				Punjābi	65,000	Evenk (Ewenki)	20,000
Argentina		Black Carib (Garífuna)	12,000	**Bulgaria**[1]		Russian	26,000	Gelo	60,000
Amerindian languages	350,000	● English	...	● Bulgarian	7,660,000	Spanish	85,000	Hani (Woni)	1,150,000
Italian	560,000	English Creole	90,000	Romany	220,000	Ukrainian	212,000	Hui	7,840,000
● Spanish	30,690,000	German	3,000	Turkish	760,000	Vietnamese	41,000	Kazakh	980,000
Other	350,000	Mayan (Kekchi)	17,000	Other	330,000	Yiddish	23,000	Kirgiz	120,000
		Spanish	56,000			Other	453,000	Korean	1,910,000
Aruba				**Burkina Faso**[1, 2]				Lahu	330,000
● Dutch	...			Bobo	580,000			Li	960,000
Papiamento	59,000			● French	510,000				
Other	7,000								

Major languages by country	Number of speakers
Lisu	520,000
Manchu	4,670,000
Maonan	40,000
Miao	5,440,000
Mongol	3,700,000
Mulam	100,000
Nakhi (Naxi)	270,000
Nu	30,000
Pai (Bai)	1,230,000
Pumi	30,000
Puyi (Chung-chia)	2,300,000
Salar	80,000
She	400,000
Shui	310,000
Sibo (Xibe)	90,000
Tadzhik	30,000
Tai (Dai)	910,000
Tibetan	4,170,000
Tu	170,000
T'u-chia (Tujia)	3,080,000
T'ung (Dong)	1,550,000
Tung-hsiang (Dongxiang)	300,000
Uighur	6,460,000
Wa (Va)	320,000
Yao	1,530,000
Yi	5,910,000
Other	970,000
Christmas Island	
Chinese	900
● English	400
Malay	500
Other	100
Cocos (Keeling) Islands[1]	
● English	200
Malay	400
Colombia[1]	
Amerindian languages	260,000
Arawakan	30,000
Cariban	20,000
Chibchan	130,000
Other	80,000
English Creole	40,000
● Spanish	30,360,000
Comoros	
● Arabic	...
Comorian	325,000
Comorian-French	56,000
Comorian-Malagasy	24,000
Comorian-Arabic	7,000
Comorian-Swahili	2,000
Comorian-French-other	17,000
● French	*20,000*
Other	2,000
Congo[1]	
Bubangi	30,000
● French	*660,000*
Kongo	1,170,000
Kota	20,000
Lingala (lingua franca)	...
Maka	40,000
Mbete	110,000
Mboshi	260,000
Monokutuba (lingua franca)	...
Punu	70,000
Sanga	60,000
Teke	390,000
Other	120,000
Cook Islands	
● English	...
● Maori	16,000
Other	1,000
Costa Rica	
Chibchan	5,000
Chinese	5,000
English Creole	53,000
● Spanish	2,597,000
Spanish-Chibchan	11,000
Côte d'Ivoire[1]	
Akan	4,820,000
● French	*3,050,000*
Kru	1,940,000
Malinke	1,730,000
Southern Mande	1,190,000
Voltaic (including Senufo)	1,830,000
Other	140,000
Cuba	
● Spanish	10,421,000
Cyprus[1]	
● Greek	530,000
● Turkish	170,000
Other	30,000
Czechoslovakia[1]	
● Czech	9,860,000
German	56,000
Hungarian	596,000
Polish	72,000
Russian	8,000
● Slovak	4,914,000
Ukrainian	47,000
Other	51,000

Major languages by country	Number of speakers
Denmark[1]	
● Danish	5,002,000
English	15,000
German	8,000
Norwegian	10,000
Swedish	8,000
Turkish	23,000
Other	64,000
Djibouti[1]	
Afar	180,000
● Arabic	30,000
● French	*40,000*
Issa	230,000
Other	40,000
Dominica	
● English	...
French Creole	56,000
French Creole-English	24,000
Dominican Republic	
French (Haitian) Creole	140,000
● Spanish	6,710,000
Ecuador	
Quechuan (and other Indian languages)	710,000
● Spanish	9,490,000
Egypt[1]	
● Arabic	49,670,000
Other	600,000
El Salvador	
● Spanish	5,083,000
Equatorial Guinea[1]	
Bubi	49,000
Duala	9,000
Fang	241,000
Ibibio	4,000
Maka	4,000
● Spanish	...
Other[4]	27,000
Ethiopia	
● Amharic	17,910,000
Gurage	1,550,000
Oromo (Galla)	16,780,000
Tigrinya	4,090,000
Other	7,160,000
Faeroe Islands	
● Danish	...
● Faeroese	47,000
Falkland Islands	
● English	2,000
Fiji[1]	
● English	...
Fijian	342,000
Hindi	362,000
Other	39,000
Finland	
● Finnish	4,636,000
● Swedish	302,000
Other	15,000
France	
Arabic[5]	1,460,000
● French[5, 6, 7]	52,070,000
Basque	*80,000*
Breton	*550,000*
Catalan (Rousillonais)	*200,000*
Corsican	*160,000*
Dutch (Flemish)	*100,000*
German (Alsatian)	*1,270,000*
Occitan	*1,510,000*
Italian[5]	340,000
Polish[5]	70,000
Portuguese[5]	790,000
Spanish[5]	330,000
Turkish[5]	130,000
Other[5]	670,000
French Guiana	
Amerindian languages	3,000
English Creole	1,000
● French	...
French Creoles	84,000
Other	4,000
French Polynesia	
● French[8]	12,000
Tahitian[8]	130,000
Other[9]	46,000
French speakers	*160,000*
Gabon[1]	
Fang	430,000
● French	*410,000*
Mbete	170,000
Mpongwe	180,000
Punu	140,000
Other	290,000
Gambia, The	
Dyola	80,000
● English	...
Fulani	150,000
Malinke	330,000
Soninke	70,000
Wolof	120,000
Other	60,000

Major languages by country	Number of speakers
Gaza Strip	
Arabic	562,000
Hebrew	...
Other	9,000
Germany, East[1]	
● German	16,540,000
Other	50,000
Germany, West[1]	
Dutch	110,000
● German	56,470,000
Greek	280,000
Italian	530,000
Portuguese	80,000
Spanish	150,000
Turkish	1,430,000
Yugoslavian languages	590,00
Other	1,140,000
Ghana[1]	
Akan	7,210,000
● English	...
Ewe	1,630,000
Ga-Adangme	1,070,000
Mossi	2,180,000
Other	1,660,000
Gibraltar	
● English	10,000
Spanish	11,000
Other	9,000
Greece[1]	
Albanian	60,000
● Greek	9,610,000
Macedonian	150,000
Turkish	90,000
Other	140,000
Greenland	
● Danish	5,000
● Greenlandic	49,000
Grenada	
● English	...
English Creole	102,000
Other	4,000
Guadeloupe	
French Creole-French	323,000
● French	...
Other	17,000
Guam	
Chamorro	43,000
● English	45,000
Japanese	2,000
Palauan	1,000
Philippine languages	21,000
Other	13,000
Guatemala	
Black Carib (Garífuna)	20,000
Mayan languages	2,930,000
Cakchiquel	550,000
Kekchí	350,000
Quiché	1,160,000
● Spanish	5,730,000
Guernsey	
English	59,300
French	...
Guinea[1]	
● French	*550,000*
Fulani (Peul)	2,530,000
Kissi	390,000
Mande, of which	3,330,000
Malinke	1,520,000
Susu	720,000
Other	1,100,000
Other	290,000
Guinea-Bissau[1]	
Balante	250,000
Fulani	210,000
Malinke	110,000
Mandyako	100,000
Pepel	90,000
● Portuguese	...
Other	160,000
Guyana	
Amerindian languages	14,000
Arawakan	5,000
Cariban	9,000
● English	...
English Creole	591,000
Other (includes Caribbean Hindi and English)	151,000
Haiti	
● French	50,000
French-Haitian (French) Creole	660,000
● Haitian (French) Creole	4,750,000
Honduras	
Black Carib (Garífuna)	98,000
English Creole	15,000
Miskito	14,000
● Spanish	4,673,000
Other	2,000

Major languages by country	Number of speakers
Hong Kong[1]	
● Chinese (Cantonese)[10]	5,512,000
● English	...
Filipino (Pilipino)	38,000
Other	134,000
Hungary[1]	
German	170,000
● Hungarian	10,230,000
Romanian	20,000
Slovak	120,000
Southern Slav	30,000
Other	20,000
Iceland[1]	
● Icelandic	240,000
Other	8,000
India	
Anga (Angika)	590,000
Assamese	13,120,000
Baghēlkhaṇḍī	340,000
Bāgṛī	1,550,000
Banjārī	690,000
Barel	340,000
Bengali	65,220,000
Bhīlī (Bhilali)	360,000
Bhīlī (Bhilodi)	1,830,000
Bhojpurī	21,010,000
Boḍo	750,000
Bundēlkhaṇḍī	550,000
Chhattisgaṛhī	9,800,000
Ḍōgrī	1,900,000
● English	*20,000,000*
Gaṛhwālī	1,870,000
Gārō	600,000
Gojri	480,000
Gōṇḍī	2,270,000
Gujarātī	37,580,000
Halabī	510,000
Hāṛautī	490,000
● Hindī	225,190,000
Hō	1,100,000
Kachchī	690,000
Kannaḍa	31,600,000
Kashmiri	3,550,000
Khāsī	560,000
Khortha (Khotta)	740,000
Kōṅkaṇī	2,230,000
Kōrkū	420,000
Kōyā	310,000
Kui	510,000
Kumaunī	1,810,000
Kurukh (Oraon)	1,820,000
Lamani (Banjārī)	1,760,000
Lushai (Mizo)	400,000
Maghī (Magadhī)	9,720,000
Maithilī	8,970,000
Malayāḷam	32,110,000
Mālvī	940,000
Manḍeālī	350,000
Marāṭhī	61,120,000
Mārwāṛī	6,910,000
Meithei (Manipurī)	1,140,000
Mēwāṛī	1,200,000
Mikir	290,000
Muṇḍā	320,000
Muṇḍārī	1,130,000
Nagpurī	490,000
Nepali (Gōrkhālī)	1,890,000
Nīmāḍī	1,160,000
Oṛiyā	28,900,000
Pahāṛī	1,860,000
Punjābī	20,360,000
Rajāsthānī	3,070,000
Sadānī (Sadrī)	1,180,000
Santālī	5,410,000
Savara (Sōrā)	320,000
Sindhī	1,760,000
Surgujia	790,000
Tamil	55,070,000
Telugu	65,490,000
Tripuri	390,000
Tuḷu	1,700,000
Urdū	41,900,000
Other	11,340,000
Indonesia	
● Bahasa Indonesia	21,140,000
Balinese	3,590,000
Banjarese	2,360,000
Batak	3,750,000
Bugi	3,380,000
Javanese	70,540,000
Madurese	8,460,000
Minang	4,430,000
Sundanese	26,830,000
Other	31,430,000
Iran[1]	
Armenian	250,000
Iranian languages	37,950,000
Bakhtyārī (Lurī)	860,000
Baluchi	1,170,000
● Farsī (Persian)	23,370,000
Gilaki	2,700,000
Kurdish	4,680,000
Lurī	2,210,000
Māzandarānī	1,840,000
Other	1,110,000

Major languages by country	Number of speakers
Semitic languages	1,230,000
Arabic	1,110,000
Other	120,000
Turkic languages	11,420,000
Afshari	580,000
Azerbaijani	8,610,000
Qashqa'i	650,000
Shahsavani	310,000
Turkish (mostly Pishagchi, Bayat, and Qajar)	370,000
Turkmen	800,000
Other	100,000
Other	380,000
Iraq[1]	
● Arabic	12,820,000
Assyrian	140,000
Kurdish	3,150,000
Persian	140,000
Turkish	60,000
Turkmen	230,000
Other	100,000
Ireland	
● English	3,380,000
● Irish	180,000
Isle of Man	
● English	64,000
Israel	
● Arabic	829,000
English	54,000
French	37,000
German	30,000
● Hebrew	3,103,000
Hungarian	25,000
Romanian	70,000
Russian	78,000
Spanish	38,000
Yiddish	97,000
Other	150,000
Italy[1]	
Albanian	120,000
Catalan	30,000
French	300,000
German	300,000
Greek	40,000
● Italian	53,990,000
Rhaetian	730,000
Friulian	710,000
Ladin	20,000
Sardinian	1,520,000
Slovene	120,000
Other	240,000
Jamaica	
Chinese	22,000
● English	645,000
English Creoles	1,685,000
Hindi and other Indian languages	50,000
Spanish	6,000
Japan[1]	
Chinese	60,000
● Japanese	121,890,000
Korean	580,000
Other	90,000
Jersey	
English	82,000
● French	...
Jordan[1]	
● Arabic	2,940,000
Other	20,000
Kampuchea[1]	
Chinese	370,000
● Khmer	6,930,000
Vietnamese	370,000
Other[11]	210,000
Kenya[1]	
Arabic	60,000
Bajun (Rajun)	60,000
Basuba	90,000
Boran	100,000
Degodia	140,000
Embu	270,000
Gabbra	50,000
Gurreh	120,000
Gusii (Kisii)	1,410,000
Kalenjin	2,470,000
Kamba	2,580,000
Kikuyu	4,790,000
Kuria	130,000
Luhya	3,170,000
Luo	2,920,000
Masai	360,000
Mbere	90,000
Meru	1,260,000
Nyika (Mijikenda)	1,100,000
Ogaden	40,000
Orma	50,000
Pokomo	60,000
Sambur	110,000
Somali	230,000
Swahili	10,000
● Swahili (lingua franca)	*13,800,000*
Taita	230,000

Language (continued)

Major languages by country	Number of speakers
Teso	200,000
Turkana	310,000
Other[12]	510,000
Kiribati[1]	
• English	...
Kiribati (Gilbertese)	67,400
Tuvaluan (Ellice)	500
Other	400
Korea, North[1]	
• Korean	21,860,000
Chinese	40,000
Korea, South[1]	
• Korean	42,550,000
Other	40,000
Kuwait[1]	
• Arabic	1,530,000
Other	430,000
Laos[1]	
• Lao	2,580,000
Miao (Hmong)-Man (Yao)	200,000
Mon-Khmer	180,000
Palaung-Wa	460,000
Tai	300,000
Other[13]	130,000
Lebanon[1]	
• Arabic	2,573,000
Armenian	20,000
French	680,000
Kurdish	14,000
Other	221,000
Lesotho[1]	
• English	...
• Sotho	1,666,000
Other	5,000
Liberia[1]	
• English	360,000
Kwa (Kru)	
Bassa	336,000
Belle	12,000
Dey	9,000
Grebo	217,000
Krahn	92,000
Kru	178,000
Mande (Northern)	
Gbandi	68,000
Kpelle	471,000
Loma	137,000
Mandingo	124,000
Mende	19,000
Vai	87,000
Mande (Southern)	
Gio	190,000
Mano	172,000
West Atlantic (Mel)	
Gola	96,000
Kissi	98,000
Other	120,000
Libya[1]	
• Arabic	3,910,000
Berber	230,000
Other[14]	180,000
Liechtenstein[1]	
• German	25,500
Other	2,300
Luxembourg[1]	
Belgian	10,000
• French	15,000
• German	10,000
Italian	22,000
Luxembourgish	262,000
Portuguese	32,000
Other	22,000
Macau	
Chinese	456,000
• Portuguese	...
Other	10,000
Madagascar[1]	
• French	1,120,000
Malagasy	10,800,000
Other	110,000
Malaŵi[1]	
• Chewa (Maravi)	4,790,000
• English	...
Lomwe	1,510,000
Ngoni	550,000
Yao	1,090,000
Other	280,000
Malaysia	
Bajau	110,000
Chinese	980,000
Chinese and others	560,000
Dusan	180,000
English	80,000
English and others	190,000
Iban	400,000
Iban and others	70,000
• Malay	7,310,000
Malay and others	2,600,000
Tamil	660,000
Tamil and others	10,000
Other	3,820,000
Maldives	
• Divehi (Maldivian)	202,000
Mali[1]	
Bambara	2,480,000
Bobo	190,000
Dogon	310,000
Dyula	230,000
• French	620,000
Fulani	1,090,000
Malinke	520,000
Senufo	930,000
Songhai	560,000
Soninke	680,000
Tuareg	570,000
Other	230,000
Malta[1]	
• English	7,000
• Maltese	332,000
Other	8,000
Martinique	
French Creole-French	325,000
• French	...
Other	11,000
Mauritania[1]	
• Arabic	...
• French	110,000
Fulani	20,000
Hassānīyah Arabic	1,540,000
Soninke	50,000
Tukulor	100,000
Wolof	130,000
Other	50,000
Mauritius	
Bhojpuri	207,000
• English	2,000
French	38,000
French Creole	582,000
Hindi	117,000
Tamil	37,000
Urdū	25,000
Other	42,000
Mayotte[15]	
Maharais (local dialect of Comoroian Swahili)	69,100
Other Comoroian Swahili dialects	28,600
Malagasy	32,200
• French	24,700
Arabic	1,900
Other	3,100
Mexico	
Amerindian languages	7,450,000
Aztec (Nahuatl)	1,980,000
Chinantec	110,000
Chol	140,000
Huastec	150,000
Huichol	70,000
Mazahua	280,000
Mazatec	180,000
Mayo	80,000
Mixe	110,000
Mixtec	460,000
Otomi	440,000
Tarahumara	90,000
Tarasco	170,000
Tlapanec	80,000
Totonac	280,000
Tzeltal	310,000
Tzotzil	190,000
Yucatec (Mayan)	960,000
Zapotec	610,000
Other	760,000
• Spanish	75,210,000
Spanish-Amerindian languages	5,320,000
Monaco[1]	
English	1,000
• French	17,000
Italian	5,000
Monegasque	4,000
Other	2,000
Mongolia[1]	
Bayad	40,000
Buryat	38,000
Dariganga	31,000
Dörbed	58,000
Dzakhchin	25,000
Kazakh	108,000
• Khalkha (Mongolian)	1,584,000
Ould	11,000
Torgut	11,000
Uryankhai	24,000
Other	113,000
Montserrat	
• English	...
English Creole	12,000
Morocco[1]	
• Arabic	17,710,000
Berber	5,980,000
Other[11]	120,000
Mozambique[1]	
Makua	7,050,000
Malaŵi	1,790,000
• Portuguese	...
Shona	1,680,000
Tsonga	3,470,000
Yao	560,000
Other	350,000
Nauru	
Chinese	700
English	600
Kiribati (Gilbertese)	1,400
• Nauruan	4,700
Tuvaluan (Ellice)	700
Nepal	
Bhojpuri	1,370,000
Bhutia (Sherpa)	90,000
Gurung	210,000
Hindī (Awadhi dialect)	280,000
Limbu	150,000
Magar	260,000
Maithili	2,000,000
• Nepālī	10,510,000
Newari	540,000
Rai, Kirati	260,000
Tamang	630,000
Thārū	650,000
Other	1,050,000
Netherlands, The[1]	
Arabic	127,000
• Dutch	14,169,000
Dutch and Frisian	400,000
Turkish	162,000
Other	285,000
Netherlands Antilles	
• Dutch	...
English	14,000
Papiamento	152,000
Other	11,000
New Caledonia	
• French	56,000
Melanesian languages	65,000
Polynesian languages (mostly Wallisian)	26,000
Other	9,000
New Zealand	
• English	3,133,000
• Maori	107,000
Other	114,000
Nicaragua	
English Creole	36,000
Misumalpan languages	
Miskito	143,000
Sumo	9,000
• Spanish	3,431,000
Other	3,000
Niger[1]	
• French	340,000
Fulani	720,000
Hausa	3,610,000
Kanuri	600,000
Songhai	560,000
Tuareg	200,000
Zerma and Dendi	1,020,000
Other	220,000
Nigeria[1]	
Arabic	300,000
Bura	1,800,000
Edo	3,800,000
• English (lingua franca)	17,000,000
English Creole (lingua franca)[16]	39,000,000
Fulani	12,600,000
Hausa	24,000,000
Hausa (lingua franca)	36,000,000
Ibibio	6,300,000
Igbo (Ibo)	20,200,000
Ijaw	2,000,000
Kanuri	4,700,000
Nupe	1,400,000
Tiv	2,500,000
Yoruba	24,000,000
Other	8,800,000
Niue	
• English	...
Niuean	2,000
Norfolk Island	
• English	2,000
Norway[1]	
Danish	17,000
English	24,000
• Norwegian	4,092,000
Swedish	11,000
Other	58,000
Oman[1]	
• Arabic (Omani)	1,060,000
Bengali	30,000
Indian	210,000
Pakistani (mostly Baluchi)	50,000
Other	30,000
Pacific Islands, Trust Territory of the	
Marshall Islands	
• English	700
• Marshallese	38,600
Other	2,900
Micronesia, Federated States of	
• English	500
Kosraean	7,400
Mortlockese	7,700
Palauan	400
Pohnpeian	24,000
Trukese	42,000
Woleaian	3,700
Yapese	5,900
Other	9,500
Northern Mariana Islands	
Chamorro	12,000
• English	1,200
Palauan	800
Philippine languages	3,000
Woleaian	2,500
Other	2,400
Palau	
• English	100
• Palauan	12,400
Other	2,200
Pakistan	
Baluchi	3,290,000
Brahui	1,310,000
Pashto	14,380,000
Punjābī, of which	55,370,000
Punjābī	52,710,000
Hindko	2,660,000
Sindhī, of which	23,640,000
Sindhī	12,880,000
Siraiki	10,760,000
• Urdū	8,320,000
Other[12]	3,120,000
Panama	
Amerindian languages	109,000
Chibchan	97,000
Cuna	42,000
Guaymí	55,000
Choco	11,000
Chinese	7,000
English	...
English Creoles	325,000
• Spanish	1,878,000
Other	3,000
Papua New Guinea[1]	
• English	...
Melanesian languages	540,000
Papuan languages	2,990,000
Other[17]	30,000
Paraguay	
German	34,000
Guaraní	1,608,000
Guaraní-Spanish	1,949,000
Portuguese	127,000
• Spanish	260,000
Other	29,000
Peru	
Aymara	620,000
• Quechua	5,650,000
• Spanish	14,450,000
Other	540,000
Philippines	
Aklanon	570,000
Bicol	4,090,000
Bolinao (Zambal)	250,000
Cebuano	14,320,000
Chavacano	300,000
Chinese	150,000
Davaweno	170,000
• English	20,000
• Filipino (Pilipino; Tagalog)	13,980,000
Hamtikanon	480,000
Hiligaynon/Ilongo	5,870,000
Ibanag	340,000
Ifugao	180,000
Ilocano	6,540,000
Kangkanai	220,000
Maguindanao	700,000
Manobo	180,000
Maranao	840,000
Masbate	430,000
Pampango	2,010,000
Pangasinan	1,320,000
Romblon	240,000
Samal	340,000
Samar-Leyte (Waray-Waray)	2,710,000
Subanon	190,000
Sulu-Moro (Tau Sug)	460,000
Other	1,770,000
Pitcairn Island	
• English	51
Poland	
Belorussian	190,000
• Polish	37,370,000
Ukrainian	230,000
Other	80,000
Portugal[1]	
• Portuguese	10,260,000
Other	90,000
Puerto Rico	
• English	13,000
• Spanish	1,873,000
Spanish-English	1,370,000
Other	46,000
Qatar[1]	
• Arabic	380,000
Other	40,000
Réunion	
• French	170,000
French Creole	520,000
Other[18]	60,000
Romania[1]	
Bulgarian	10,000
German	365,000
Hebrew	26,000
Hungarian	1,772,000
• Romanian	20,352,000
Romany	233,000
Russian	32,000
Serbian	34,000
Slovak	22,000
Tatar	23,000
Turkish	23,000
Ukrainian	56,000
Other	65,000
Rwanda	
• French	460,000
• Rwanda	6,710,000
St. Helena and Ascension	
• English	7,000
St. Kitts and Nevis	
• English	...
English Creole	43,000
St. Lucia	
• English	...
French/English Creole	137,000
Other	8,000
St. Pierre and Miquelon[1]	
• French	6,100
Other	100
St. Vincent and the Grenadines	
• English	...
English Creole	112,000
Other	1,000
San Marino[1]	
• Italian	23,000
São Tomé and Príncipe	
Crioulo (Portuguese Creole)	117,000
• Portuguese	...
Saudi Arabia[1]	
• Arabic	12,320,000
Other	650,000
Senegal[1]	
Dyola	490,000
• French	360,000
Fulani (Peul)	900,000
Malinke (Mandingo)	390,000
Maure	90,000
Sarakole (Soninke)	120,000
Serer	1,030,000
Tukulor	760,000
Wolof	3,010,000
Other	400,000
Seychelles	
• English	...
• French	10,000
French Creole	64,000
Other	3,000
Sierra Leone[1]	
Bullom	150,000
• English	...
Fulani	150,000
Kissi	90,000
Kono	200,000
Koranko	130,000
Krio (English Creole [lingua franca])	...
Limba	320,000
Mende	1,340,000
Temne	1,230,000
Yalunka	130,000
Other	140,000
Singapore[1]	
• Bahasa Malaysia	398,000
Chinese	2,010,000
• English	...
• Mandarin Chinese	...
• Tamil (and other Indian languages)	171,000
Other	62,000

Major languages by country	Number of speakers
Solomon Islands[1]	
● English	...
Melanesian languages	258,000
Papuan languages	26,000
Polynesian languages	11,000
Other[19]	6,000
Somalia[1]	
● Arabic	...
English	...
● Somali	6,230,000
Other	110,000
South Africa[20]	
● Afrikaans[21]	5,880,000
● English[21]	3,350,000
Nguni	11,410,000
North Ndebele	200,000
South Ndebele	350,000
Swazi	780,000
Xhosa	2,580,000
Zulu	7,500,000
Sotho	6,960,000
North Sotho	2,980,000
South Sotho	2,340,000
Tswana (Western Sotho)	1,640,000
Tsonga	1,110,000
Venda	200,000
Other	720,000
Bophuthatswana	
● Afrikaans	...
● English	...
● Tswana	1,360,000
Other	650,000
Ciskei	
● English	...
● Xhosa	930,000
Other	20,000
Transkei	
● English	...
● Xhosa	3,500,000
Other	220,000
Venda	
● Afrikaans	...
● English	...
● Venda	490,000
Other	60,000
South West Africa/Namibia[1]	
● Afrikaans	...
Bergdama (Damara)	92,000
East Caprivian (mostly Lozi)	46,000
● English	131,000
German	...
Herero	92,000
Kavango (Okavango)	114,000
Nama	59,000
Ovambo (Ambo [Kwanyama])	609,000
San (Bushmen)	35,000
Other	180,000
Spain	
Basque	900,000
● Castilian Spanish	28,390,000
Catalan	6,400,000
Galician	3,200,000
Other	120,000
Sri Lanka	
English	10,000
English-Sinhalese	910,000
English-Tamil	190,000
English-Sinhalese-Tamil	600,000
● Sinhalese	10,020,000
Sinhalese-Tamil	1,550,000
Tamil	3,260,000
Other	60,000
Sudan, The[1]	
● Arabic	12,960,000
Azande	710,000
Bari	650,000
Beja	1,680,000
Dinka	3,030,000
Fur	540,000
Lotuko	390,000
Nubian	2,130,000
Nuer	1,290,000
Shilluk	450,000
Other	2,440,000

Major languages by country	Number of speakers
Suriname	
● Dutch	...
English	...
Sranantonga	170,000
Sranantonga-other	170,000
Other (mostly Hindi, Javanese, and Saramacca)	90,000
Swaziland[1]	
● English	...
● Swazi	600,000
Zulu	70,000
Other[22]	40,000
Sweden[1]	
Finnish	261,000
● Swedish	7,657,000
Other	497,000
Switzerland	
● French	1,221,000
● German	4,310,000
● Italian	647,000
Romansh	53,000
Other	395,000
Syria[1]	
● Arabic	10,070,000
Armenian	320,000
Kurdish	710,000
Other	240,000
Taiwan[1]	
South Fukien Chinese	13,270,000
Hakka and Hokkien Chinese	1,980,000
● Mandarin Chinese	4,140,000
Other	420,000
Tanzania[1]	
Chagga (Chaga), Pare	1,180,000
● English	...
Gogo	940,000
Ha	830,000
Haya	1,410,000
Hehet	1,650,000
Iramba	680,000
Luguru	1,180,000
Luo	200,000
Makonde	1,410,000
Masai	240,000
Ngoni	320,000
Nyakyusa	1,300,000
Nyamwezi (Sukuma)	5,060,000
Shambala	1,020,000
● Swahili	2,120,000
Tatoga	180,000
Yao	590,000
Other	3,690,000
Thailand[1]	
Chinese	6,650,000
Karen	200,000
Malay	2,000,000
Mon-Khmer languages	1,480,000
Khmer	700,000
Kuy	590,000
Other	190,000
Thai languages	43,970,000
Lao	14,750,000
● Thai (Siamese)	28,840,000
Other	380,000
Other	570,000
Togo[1]	
● French	600,000
Gur (Voltaic) languages	
Gurma	560,000
Tem-Kabre	930,000
Kwa languages	
Ana-Ife (Yoruba)	110,000
Ewe-Adja	1,500,000
Kebu-Akposo	130,000
Other	250,000
Tokelau	
● English	...
Tokelauan	1,700
Tonga	
● English	...
● Tongan	94,000
Other	2,000

Major languages by country	Number of speakers
Trinidad and Tobago	
● English	...
English Creole	1,258,000
French Creole	...
Hindi	...
Spanish	...
Tunisia	
● Arabic	5,510,000
Arabic-French	2,070,000
Arabic-French-English	250,000
Arabic-other	10,000
Other-no Arabic	20,000
Other	20,000
Turkey[1]	
Arabic	860,000
Kurdish	5,730,000
● Turkish	46,410,000
Other	1,180,000
Turks and Caicos Islands	
● English	...
English Creole	8,400
Haitian (French) Creole	2,100
Tuvalu	
● English	...
Kiribati (Gilbertese)	600
Tuvaluan (Ellice)	8,100
Uganda[1]	
Acholi	740,000
Chiga (Kiga)	1,090,000
● English	...
Ganda (Luganda)	2,840,000
Gisu	1,150,000
Gwere	460,000
Karamojong	330,000
Lango	960,000
Lugbara	610,000
Nkole	1,310,000
Nyoro	520,000
Rundi	490,000
Rwanda	930,000
Soga	1,310,000
Teso	1,420,000
Toro	510,000
Other[3]	1,290,000
U.S.S.R.	
Armenian	4,110,000
Avar	510,000
Azerbaijani	5,850,000
Bashkir	1,000,000
Belorussian	7,660,000
Bulgarian	270,000
Buryat	350,000
Chechen	810,000
Chuvash	1,560,000
Dargin	310,000
Estonian	1,060,000
Gagauz	170,000
Georgian	3,830,000
German	1,200,000
Greek	140,000
Hebrew	280,000
Hungarian	180,000
Ingush	200,000
Kabardinian	340,000
Kara-Kalpak	320,000
Kazakh	6,970,000
Kirgiz	2,030,000
Komi	270,000
Komi-Permyak	130,000
Korean	230,000
Kumyk	240,000
Lak	100,000
Latvian	1,490,000
Lezgian	380,000
Lithuanian	3,040,000
Mari	590,000
Moldavian	3,020,000
Mordovian	940,000
Ossetian	520,000
Polish	370,000
● Russian	167,390,000
Tadzhik	3,090,000
Tatar	5,920,000
Turkmenian	2,180,000
Tuvinian	180,000
Udmurt	600,000
Uighur	200,000
Ukrainian	38,240,000
Uzbek	13,380,000
Yakut	340,000
Other	3,820,000

Major languages by country	Number of speakers
United Arab Emirates[1]	
● Arabic	1,550,000
Other	230,000
United Kingdom	
● English	52,980,000
Scots-Gaelic	70,000
Welsh	520,000
Other	3,430,000
United States	
American Indian or Alaska Native languages	420,000
Arabic	270,000
Armenian	120,000
Asian Indian languages	310,000
Chinese	750,000
Czech	140,000
Dutch	180,000
● English	218,260,000
Finnish	80,000
French	1,850,000
German	1,850,000
Greek	470,000
Hungarian	200,000
Italian	1,850,000
Japanese	390,000
Korean	330,000
Lithuanian	80,000
Norwegian	130,000
Persian	130,000
Philippine languages	590,000
Polish	930,000
Portuguese	420,000
Russian	200,000
Serbo-Croatian	170,000
Slovak	100,000
Spanish	13,760,000
Swedish	110,000
Thai	110,000
Ukrainian	140,000
Vietnamese	240,000
Yiddish	360,000
Other	1,180,000
Uruguay	
● Spanish	2,880,000
Other	100,000
Vanuatu	
● Bislama (English Creole)	120,000
● English	...
● French	50,000
Melanesian languages	141,000
Other	8,000
Venezuela	
● Amerindian languages	180,000
Goajiro (Guajiro)	70,000
Warrau (Waroa)	20,000
Other	90,000
● Spanish	18,170,000
Other	410,000
Vietnam[1]	
Bahnar	130,000
Chinese	1,060,000
Jarai	220,000
Khmer	870,000
Muong	500,000
Nung	680,000
Rhadé	170,000
Tai	940,000
Tay (Tho)	1,100,000
● Vietnamese	55,820,000
Yao	420,000
Other	1,890,000
Virgin Islands (U.S.)	
● English	87,000
French	3,000
Spanish	14,000
Other	3,000
Wallis and Futuna	
● French	...
Wallisian	16,000
West Bank	
Arabic	835,000
Hebrew	30,000

Major languages by country	Number of speakers
Western Sahara	
Arabic	189,000
Western Samoa	
● English	1,000
● Samoan	77,000
Samoan-English	84,000
Yemen (Aden)[1]	
● Arabic	2,240,000
Other	100,000
Yemen (Şan'ā')[1]	
● Arabic	8,480,000
Other	140,000
Yugoslavia	
Albanian	1,850,000
Hungarian	430,000
● Macedonian	1,450,000
Romany	150,000
● Serbo-Croatian	17,190,000
● Slovenian	1,850,000
Vlach	140,000
Other	530,000
Zaire[1]	
Azande	1,990,000
Boa	760,000
Chokwe	600,000
● French	2,530,000
Kongo	5,230,000
Luba	5,850,000
Lugbara	520,000
Mongo	4,390,000
Ngala and Bangi	1,880,000
Rundi	1,250,000
Rwanda	3,340,000
Teke	890,000
Other	5,850,000
Zambia[1]	
Barotze group	610,000
Lozi (Barotze)	440,000
Luyana (Luyi)	110,000
Nkoya	40,000
Other	10,000
Bemba group	2,680,000
Bemba	1,840,000
Bisa	110,000
Lala	210,000
Lamba	170,000
Ushi (Aushi)	130,000
Other	220,000
● English	...
Mambwe group	340,000
Lungu	70,000
Mambwe	120,000
Mwanga (Winawanga)	140,000
Other	10,000
Maravi (Nyanja) group	1,300,000
Chewa	390,000
Maravi (Nyanja)	380,000
Ngoni	140,000
Nsenga	340,000
Other	40,000
North-Western group	740,000
Chokwe	50,000
Kaonde	200,000
Luchazi	50,000
Lunda	190,000
Luvale (Luena)	150,000
Mbunda	110,000
Tonga (Ila-Tonga) group	1,110,000
Ila	60,000
Lenje	130,000
Soli	60,000
Tonga	810,000
Other	60,000
Tumbuka group	340,000
Senga	60,000
Tumbuka	280,000
Other	270,000
Zimbabwe	
● English	690,000
Ndebele (Nguni)	1,400,000
Nyanja	460,000
Shona	6,290,000
Other	40,000

[1]Figures given represent ethnolinguistic groups. [2]Majority of population speak Moré (language of the Mossi); Dyula is language of commerce. [3]Swahili also spoken. [4]Pidgin English and Portuguese Creole also spoken. [5]Based on "nationality" at 1982 census. [6]Includes naturalized citizens. [7]French is the universal language throughout France; traditional dialects and minority languages are retained regionally in the approximate numbers shown, however. [8]Mother tongue. [9]Mostly non-Tahitian Polynesian and Chinese languages bilingual or multilingual with French or Tahitian. [10]Includes some Kan-Hakka and Mandarin speakers. [11]French also spoken. [12]English also spoken. [13]English and French also spoken. [14]English and Italian also spoken. [15]Data reflect ability to speak the language, not mother tongue. 1988 population estimate is 77,600. [16]Includes speakers of standard English. [17]About half the population also speaks Pisin (Pidgin English); English and Hiri (Police Motu) also spoken. [18]Gujarāti and Chinese also spoken. [19]Solomon Islands Pidgin (English) is the lingua franca. [20]Excludes the Black states shown separately. [21]White, Coloured, and Asian speakers only. [22]Afrikaans and Portuguese also spoken.

Religion

The following table presents statistics on religious affiliation for each of the countries of the world. An assessment was made for each country of the available data on distribution of religious communities within the total population; the best available figures, whether originating as census data, membership figures of the churches concerned, or estimates by external analysts in the absence of reliable local data, were applied as percentages to the estimated 1988 midyear population of the country to obtain the data shown below.

Several concepts govern the nature of the available data, each useful separately but none the basis of any standard of international practice in the collection of such data. The word "affiliation" was used above to describe the nature of the relationship joining the religious bodies named and the populations shown. This term implies some sort of formal, usually documentary, connection between the religion and the individual (a baptismal certificate, a child being assigned the religion of its parents on a census form, maintenance of one's name on the tax rolls of a state religion, etc.) but says nothing about the nature of the individual's personal religious practice, in that the individual may have lapsed, never been confirmed as an adult, joined another religion, or may have joined an organization that is formally atheist.

The user of these statistics should be careful to note that not only does the nature of the affiliation (with an organized religion) differ greatly from country to country, but the social context of religious practice does also. A country in which a single religion has long been predominant will often show more than 90% of its population to be *affiliated,* while in actual fact, no more than 10% may actually *practice* that religion on a regular basis. Such a situation often leads to undercounting of minority religions (where someone [head of household, communicant, child] is counted at all), blurring of distinctions seen to be significant elsewhere (a Hindu country may not distinguish Protestant [or even Christian] denominations; a Christian country may not distinguish among its Muslim or Buddhist citizens), or double-counting in countries where an individual may conscientiously practice more than one "religion" at a time.

Communist countries consciously attempt to ignore, suppress, or render invisible religious practice within their boundaries. Countries with large numbers of adherents of traditional, often animist, religions and belief systems usually have little or no formal methodology for defining the nature of local religious practice. On the other hand, countries with strong missionary traditions, or good census organizations, or few religious sensitivities may have very good, detailed, and meaningful data.

The most authoritative work available is DAVID B. BARRETT (ed.), *World Christian Encyclopedia* (1982); it examines both the theoretical and practical problems of collecting and analyzing religious statistics, assembles a mine of national detail, and establishes a basis for further study.

Religion

Religious affiliation	1988 population
Afghanistan	
Sunnī Muslim	10,720,000
Shī'ī Muslim	3,620,000
other	140,000
Albania	
Muslim	650,000
Christian[1]	170,000
atheist	590,000
nonreligious	1,740,000
Algeria	
Sunnī Muslim	23,630,000
other	220,000
American Samoa	
Congregational	20,000
other	18,000
Andorra	
Roman Catholic	48,000
other	3,000
Angola	
Christian[1]	8,450,000
traditional beliefs	890,000
other	50,000
Anguilla	
Anglican	2,700
Methodist	2,200
other	1,700
Antigua and Barbuda	
Anglican	37,000
other Protestant	35,000
Roman Catholic	8,000
other	3,000
Argentina	
Roman Catholic	29,670,000
other	2,290,000
Aruba	
Roman Catholic	58,000
other	7,500
Australia[2]	
Anglican	4,300,000
Roman Catholic	4,280,000
Uniting Church	810,000
Presbyterian	720,000
Methodist	560,000
Orthodox	480,000
other Protestant	1,330,000
nonreligious	1,780,000
other	2,210,000
Austria	
Roman Catholic	6,390,000
Protestant	420,000
atheist and nonreligious	450,000
other	310,000
Bahamas, The	
Anglican	50,000
other Protestant	120,000
Roman Catholic	60,000
other	10,000
Bahrain	
Shī'ī Muslim	250,000
Sunnī Muslim	110,000
other	60,000
Bangladesh	
Muslim	93,370,000
Hindu	13,070,000
other	1,310,000
Barbados	
Anglican	101,000
other Protestant	65,000
other	88,000
Belgium	
Roman Catholic	8,970,000
other	990,000
Belize	
Roman Catholic	110,000
Anglican	21,000
other	47,000
Benin	
traditional beliefs	2,730,000
Roman Catholic	820,000
Muslim	680,000
other	220,000
Bermuda	
Anglican	22,000
Methodist	10,000
Roman Catholic	8,000
other	18,000
Bhutan	
Buddhist	950,000
Hindu	340,000
other	80,000
Bolivia	
Roman Catholic	6,570,000
other	420,000
Botswana	
Christian[1]	610,000
traditional beliefs	600,000
other	10,000
Brazil	
Roman Catholic	126,660,000
Protestant	8,800,000
Afro-American Spiritist	2,890,000
Spiritist	2,450,000
atheist and nonreligious	2,020,000
other	1,300,000
British Virgin Islands	
Methodist	6,000
Anglican	3,000
other	4,000
Brunei	
Muslim	159,000
Buddhist	35,000
other	56,000
Bulgaria	
Eastern Orthodox	2,400,000
Muslim	670,000
atheist	5,790,000
other	110,000
Burkina Faso	
traditional beliefs	3,820,000
Muslim	3,670,000
Christian[1]	1,040,000
Burma	
Buddhist	35,730,000
Christian	1,960,000
Muslim	1,530,000
other	720,000
Burundi	
Roman Catholic	4,020,000
traditional beliefs	690,000
other	430,000
Cameroon	
Roman Catholic	3,920,000
Protestant	2,300,000
traditional beliefs	2,420,000
Muslim	2,470,000
other	100,000
Canada	
Roman Catholic	12,030,000
Protestant	10,660,000
Eastern Orthodox	390,000
Jewish	310,000
Muslim	100,000
Sikh	80,000
Hindu	80,000
nonreligious	1,920,000
other	310,000
Cape Verde	
Roman Catholic	351,000
Protestant	8,000
Cayman Islands	
Presbyterian	8,000
Church of God	5,000
other	10,000
Central African Republic	
Protestant	1,420,000
Roman Catholic	940,000
traditional beliefs	340,000
other	140,000
Chad	
Muslim	2,370,000
Christian[1]	1,780,000
traditional beliefs	1,230,000
other	10,000
Chile	
Roman Catholic	10,100,000
other	2,660,000
China	
nonreligious	644,200,000
Chinese folk-religionist	218,700,000
atheist	130,600,000
Buddhist	65,300,000
Muslim	26,100,000
other	3,300,000
Christmas Island	
Buddhist	700
Muslim	500
Christian	300
other	400
Cocos (Keeling) Islands	
Muslim	340
Christian	130
other	120
Colombia	
Roman Catholic	29,070,000
other	1,590,000
Comoros	
Sunnī Muslim	432,000
Christian	1,000
Congo	
Roman Catholic	1,220,000
Protestant	560,000
African Christian	320,000
other	170,000
Cook Islands	
Congregational	11,300
other	5,600
Costa Rica	
Roman Catholic	2,470,000
other	200,000
Côte d'Ivoire	
traditional beliefs	5,100,000
Christian[1]	3,720,000
Muslim	2,790,000
other	20,000
Cuba	
Roman Catholic	4,130,000
nonreligious	5,080,000
atheist	670,000
other	560,000
Cyprus	
Greek Orthodox	549,000
Muslim	133,000
other	38,000
Czechoslovakia	
Roman Catholic	10,240,000
atheist	3,140,000
Czechoslovak Church	690,000
other	1,540,000
Denmark	
Evangelical Lutheran	4,650,000
other	490,000
Djibouti	
Sunnī Muslim	455,000
Christian[1]	29,000
Dominica	
Roman Catholic	61,000
other	18,000
Dominican Republic	
Roman Catholic	6,420,000
other	430,000
Ecuador	
Roman Catholic	9,400,000
other	810,000
Egypt	
Sunnī Muslim	47,310,000
Christian	2,950,000
other	10,000
El Salvador	
Roman Catholic	4,660,000
other	420,000
Equatorial Guinea	
Roman Catholic	270,000
other	70,000
Ethiopia	
Ethiopian Orthodox	24,940,000
Muslim (mostly Sunni)	14,920,000
traditional beliefs	5,420,000
other	2,240,000
Faeroe Islands	
Evangelical Lutheran	35,000
other	12,000
Falkland Islands	
Anglican	1,000
other	900
Fiji	
Christian	393,000
Hindu	283,000
Muslim	58,000
other	8,000
Finland	
Lutheran	4,420,000
other	530,000
France	
Roman Catholic	42,680,000
nonreligious	6,810,000
atheist	1,900,000
Muslim	1,680,000
other	2,790,000
French Guiana	
Roman Catholic	71,000
other	21,000
French Polynesia	
Protestant	103,000
Roman Catholic	74,000
other	11,000
Gabon	
Roman Catholic	790,000
other	430,000
Gambia, The	
Muslim (mostly Sunni)	774,000
other	37,000
Gaza Strip	
Muslim	562,000
other	9,000
Germany, East	
Protestant	7,800,000
Roman Catholic	1,160,000
unaffiliated and other	7,630,000
Germany, West	
Protestant	28,750,000
Roman Catholic	26,620,000
other Christian	1,040,000
nonreligious	2,250,000
Muslim	1,460,000
atheist	550,000
other	120,000
Ghana	
Christian[1]	8,610,000
traditional beliefs	2,940,000
Muslim	2,160,000
other	40,000
Gibraltar	
Roman Catholic	22,000
other	8,000
Greece	
Greek Orthodox	9,810,000
Muslim	150,000
other	40,000
Greenland	
Evangelical Lutheran	53,000
other	1,000
Grenada	
Roman Catholic	68,000
Anglican	22,000
other	16,000
Guadeloupe	
Roman Catholic	307,000
other	33,000
Guam	
Roman Catholic	100,000
Protestant	22,000
other	4,000
Guatemala	
Roman Catholic	6,500,000
Protestant	2,200,000
Guernsey	
Anglican	39,000
other	20,000
Guinea	
Muslim	4,510,000
traditional beliefs	1,930,000
other	100,000
Guinea-Bissau	
traditional beliefs	610,000
Muslim	280,000
Christian	50,000
Guyana	
Hindu	260,000
Christian[1]	390,000
Muslim	70,000
other	30,000
Haiti	
Roman Catholic	4,380,000
Baptist	530,000
other (mostly Protestant)	550,000
Honduras	
Roman Catholic	4,620,000
other	190,000
Hong Kong	
Buddhist (some Confucianist and Taoist)	5,190,000
Christian	490,000
Hungary	
Roman Catholic	5,710,000
Protestant	2,290,000
nonreligious	920,000
atheist	760,000
other	910,000
Iceland	
Lutheran	240,000
other	8,000
India[3]	
Hindu	643,360,000
Muslim	88,360,000
Christian	18,920,000
Sikh	15,310,000
Buddhist	5,520,000
Jain	3,750,000
other	3,310,000
Indonesia	
Muslim	152,900,000
Protestant	11,360,000
Roman Catholic	5,510,000
Hindu	3,410,000
Buddhist	1,720,000
other	1,000,000

Religious affiliation	1988 population
Iran	
Shi'i Muslim	47,640,000
Sunni Muslim	2,560,000
other	1,020,000
Iraq	
Shi'i Muslim	8,900,000
Sunni Muslim	7,030,000
other	700,000
Ireland	
Roman Catholic	3,306,000
other	247,000
Isle of Man	
Anglican	40,000
other	24,000
Israel	
Jewish	3,710,000
Muslim (mostly Sunni)	620,000
other	190,000
Italy	
Roman Catholic	47,760,000
nonreligious	7,810,000
atheist	1,490,000
other	340,000
Jamaica	
Protestant	1,351,000
Roman Catholic	119,000
other	937,000
Japan	
Shintoist[4]	114,220,000
Buddhist[4]	90,640,000
Christian	1,690,000
other	14,650,000
Jersey	
Anglican	51,000
Roman Catholic	19,000
other	13,000
Jordan	
Sunni Muslim	2,760,000
other	210,000
Kampuchea	
Buddhist	6,960,000
other	920,000
Kenya	
Roman Catholic	6,050,000
Anglican	1,650,000
other Protestant	4,420,000
African Christian	4,030,000
traditional beliefs	4,330,000
Muslim	1,380,000
other	1,060,000
Kiribati	
Roman Catholic	36,000
Congregational	28,000
other	5,000
Korea, North	
atheist and nonreligious	14,870,000
traditional beliefs	3,420,000
Ch'ŏndogyo	3,040,000
other	570,000
Korea, South	
Buddhist	15,470,000
Protestant	9,940,000
Confucian	10,410,000
Roman Catholic	2,200,000
Ch'ŏndogyo	980,000
Wonbulgyo	1,110,000
other	2,480,000
Kuwait	
Sunni Muslim	1,430,000
Shi'i Muslim	360,000
other	170,000
Laos	
Buddhist	2,230,000
traditional beliefs	1,290,000
other	340,000
Lebanon	
Shi'i Muslim	900,000
Maronite Christian	690,000
Sunni Muslim	590,000
Druze	200,000
other	430,000
Lesotho	
Roman Catholic	730,000
Protestant	500,000
other	440,000
Liberia	
Christian	1,640,000
traditional beliefs	450,000
Muslim	340,000
Libya	
Sunni Muslim	4,190,000
other	130,000
Liechtenstein	
Roman Catholic	24,300
other	3,500
Luxembourg	
Roman Catholic	346,000
other	26,000
Macau	
Buddhist and Taoist	210,000
Roman Catholic	34,000
nonreligious	214,000
other	9,000
Madagascar	
Christian[1]	5,570,000
traditional beliefs	5,130,000
other	220,000
Malaŵi	
Christian[1]	5,300,000
traditional beliefs	1,560,000
Muslim	1,330,000
other	20,000
Malaysia	
Muslim	8,970,000
Buddhist	2,930,000
Chinese folk-religionist	1,970,000
Hindu	1,190,000
Christian	1,090,000
other	810,000
Maldives	
Sunni Muslim	202,000
Mali	
Muslim	7,000,000
traditional beliefs	700,000
Christian	80,000
Malta	
Roman Catholic	338,000
other	9,000
Martinique	
Roman Catholic	307,000
other	29,000
Mauritania	
Sunni Muslim	1,880,000
other	10,000
Mauritius	
Hindu	550,000
Roman Catholic	270,000
Muslim	140,000
other	90,000
Mayotte	
Sunni Muslim	75,000
Christian	2,000
Mexico	
Roman Catholic	76,560,000
Protestant	2,720,000
nonreligious	2,580,000
other	800,000
Monaco	
Roman Catholic	26,000
other	2,700
Mongolia	
atheist and nonreligious	1,340,000
traditional beliefs	630,000
other	70,000
Montserrat	
Anglican	4,400
Methodist	2,500
other	5,000
Morocco	
Muslim (mostly Sunni)	23,500,000
other	310,000
Mozambique	
traditional beliefs	7,120,000
Muslim	1,940,000
Roman Catholic	4,680,000
other	1,150,000
Nauru	
Congregational	4,400
Roman Catholic	1,900
other	1,700
Nepal	
Hindu	16,110,000
Buddhist	950,000
Muslim	490,000
other	450,000
Netherlands, The	
Roman Catholic	5,340,000
Dutch Reformed Church	2,670,000
Reformed Churches	1,220,000
nonreligious	5,120,000
other	400,000
Netherlands Antilles[5]	
Roman Catholic	154,000
other	23,000
New Caledonia	
Roman Catholic	98,000
Sunni Muslim	6,000
other (mostly Protestant)	52,000
New Zealand	
Anglican	810,000
Presbyterian	600,000
Roman Catholic	510,000
Methodist	160,000
nonreligious	550,000
other	720,000
Nicaragua	
Roman Catholic	3,150,000
other	480,000
Niger	
Sunni Muslim	6,760,000
other	170,000
Nigeria	
Muslim	50,520,000
Protestant	29,520,000
Roman Catholic	13,580,000
African Christian	11,900,000
traditional beliefs	6,290,000
other	460,000
Niue	
Congregational	1,800
other	600
Norfolk Island	
Anglican	800
other	1,100
Norway	
Lutheran	3,694,000
other	508,000
Oman	
Muslim	1,180,000
Hindu	180,000
other	10,000
Pacific Islands, Trust Territory of the[6]	
Protestant	88,000
Roman Catholic	82,000
other	9,000
Pakistan	
Muslim (mostly Sunni)	105,930,000
other	3,500,000
Panama	
Roman Catholic	2,067,000
other	255,000
Papua New Guinea	
Protestant	2,270,000
Roman Catholic	1,170,000
other	120,000
Paraguay	
Roman Catholic	3,847,000
other	160,000
Peru	
Roman Catholic	19,650,000
other	1,610,000
Philippines	
Roman Catholic	49,390,000
Aglipayan	3,640,000
Protestant	2,290,000
Muslim	2,530,000
other	880,000
Pitcairn Island	
Seventh-day Adventist	51
Poland	
Roman Catholic	35,670,000
other	2,200,000
Portugal	
Roman Catholic	9,780,000
other	570,000
Puerto Rico	
Roman Catholic	2,820,000
other	490,000
Qatar	
Muslim (mostly Sunni)	388,000
other	33,000
Réunion	
Roman Catholic	489,000
other	86,000
Romania	
Romanian Orthodox	16,110,000
Greek Orthodox	2,300,000
atheist	1,610,000
nonreligious	2,070,000
other	920,000
Rwanda	
Roman Catholic	3,760,000
Protestant	810,000
Muslim	600,000
traditional beliefs	1,540,000
St. Helena and Ascension	
Anglican	6,400
other	900
St. Kitts and Nevis	
Anglican	17,000
Methodist	15,000
other	14,000
St. Lucia	
Roman Catholic	125,000
other	20,000
St. Pierre and Miquelon	
Roman Catholic	6,100
other	100
St. Vincent and the Grenadines	
Anglican	41,000
Methodist	23,000
Roman Catholic	22,000
other	27,000
San Marino	
Roman Catholic	21,700
other	1,100
São Tomé and Príncipe	
Roman Catholic	90,000
Protestant	20,000
Saudi Arabia	
Muslim (mostly Sunni)	12,820,000
other	150,000
Senegal	
Sunni Muslim	6,540,000
other	610,000
Seychelles	
Roman Catholic	60,800
other	6,000
Sierra Leone	
traditional beliefs	2,000,000
Sunni Muslim	1,530,000
other	354,000
Singapore	
Taoist	774,000
Buddhist	705,000
Muslim	430,000
Christian	272,000
nonreligious	349,000
other	111,000
Solomon Islands	
Protestant	233,000
Roman Catholic	58,000
other	10,000
Somalia	
Sunni Muslim	6,321,000
other	12,000
South Africa[7]	
Dutch (Afrikaans) Reformed	4,600,000
Roman Catholic	2,850,000
Black independent churches	6,170,000
other Christian churches	9,530,000
Hindu	620,000
Muslim	410,000
nonreligious[8]	5,250,000
other	220,000
Bophuthatswana	
Christian	1,810,000
traditional beliefs	190,000
Ciskei	
Christian	690,000
traditional beliefs	260,000
Transkei	
Christian	2,600,000
traditional beliefs	1,100,000
Venda	
traditional beliefs	430,000
Christian	130,000
South West Africa/Namibia	
Lutheran	629,000
Roman Catholic	243,000
other	356,000
Spain	
Roman Catholic	37,826,000
other	1,170,000
Sri Lanka	
Buddhist	11,510,000
Hindu	2,570,000
Muslim	1,250,000
Roman Catholic	1,140,000
other	130,000
Sudan, The	
Sunni Muslim	19,170,000
traditional beliefs	4,390,000
Christian[1]	2,390,000
other	320,000
Suriname	
Hindu	116,000
Roman Catholic	97,000
Muslim	83,000
Protestant	80,000
other	49,000
Swaziland	
Christian[1]	550,000
traditional beliefs	150,000
other	20,000
Sweden	
Church of Sweden (Lutheran)	7,673,000
other	742,000
Switzerland	
Roman Catholic	3,154,000
Protestant	2,937,000
other	535,000
Syria	
Muslim (mostly Sunni)	10,160,000
Christian	1,010,000
other	170,000
Taiwan	
Chinese folk-religionist	9,610,000
Buddhist	8,520,000
Christian[1]	1,470,000
other	220,000
Tanzania	
Christian	8,160,000
Muslim	7,920,000
traditional beliefs	7,920,000
Thailand	
Buddhist	52,120,000
Muslim	2,080,000
other	650,000
Togo	
traditional beliefs	2,050,000
Roman Catholic	750,000
Sunni Muslim	420,000
other	270,000
Tokelau	
Congregational	1,200
other	500
Tonga	
Free Wesleyan	45,000
Roman Catholic	15,000
other	34,000
Trinidad and Tobago	
Roman Catholic	414,000
Protestant	356,000
Hindu	313,000
other	174,000
Tunisia	
Sunni Muslim	7,830,000
other	50,000
Turkey	
Muslim (mostly Sunni)	53,740,000
other	430,000
Turks and Caicos Islands	
Baptist	4,300
Methodist	2,000
Anglican	1,900
other	2,300
Tuvalu	
Congregational	8,400
other	200
Uganda	
Roman Catholic	7,930,000
Protestant	4,570,000
traditional beliefs	2,010,000
Muslim (mostly Sunni)	1,060,000
other	420,000
U.S.S.R.	
Christian	104,030,000
Orthodox	90,000,000
Protestant	8,860,000
Roman Catholic	5,140,000
Muslim	32,010,000
Jewish	3,140,000
nonreligious	84,880,000
atheist	61,160,000
other	570,000
United Arab Emirates	
Sunni Muslim	1,350,000
Shi'i Muslim	340,000
other	90,000
United Kingdom	
Christian[1]	49,540,000
Church of England	32,380,000
Roman Catholic	7,470,000
nonreligious	5,020,000
Muslim	800,000
Jewish	460,000
other	1,190,000
United States	
Christian[1]	214,370,000
Protestant	135,520,000
Roman Catholic	72,970,000
Eastern Orthodox	5,320,000
Jewish	7,890,000
Muslim	4,690,000
Hindu	540,000
atheist and nonreligious	16,640,000
other	1,990,000
Uruguay	
Roman Catholic	1,770,000
other	1,220,000
Vanuatu	
Presbyterian	55,000
Anglican	22,000
Roman Catholic	22,000
other	49,000
Venezuela	
Roman Catholic	17,010,000
other	1,750,000
Vietnam	
Buddhist	35,290,000
atheist and nonreligious	11,800,000
Roman Catholic	4,470,000
other	12,250,000
Virgin Islands (U.S.)	
Protestant	69,000
Roman Catholic	36,000
other	2,000
Wallis and Futuna	
Roman Catholic	15,500
West Bank	
Muslim (mostly Sunni)	690,000
Jewish	100,000
Christian and other	70,000
Western Sahara	
Sunni Muslim	189,000
Western Samoa	
Congregational	77,000
Roman Catholic	35,000
other	50,000
Yemen (Aden)	
Muslim (mostly Sunni)	2,333,000
other	11,000
Yemen (Ṣan'ā')	
Shi'i Muslim	5,170,000
Sunni Muslim	3,450,000
Yugoslavia	
Orthodox	8,160,000
Roman Catholic	6,130,000
Crypto-Christian	2,670,000
Muslim	2,450,000
atheist and nonreligious	3,940,000
other	240,000
Zaire	
Roman Catholic	15,760,000
Protestant	9,440,000
African Christian	5,570,000
traditional beliefs	1,110,000
other	690,000
Zambia	
Christian[1]	5,320,000
traditional beliefs	1,990,000
other	70,000
Zimbabwe	
Christian[1]	5,150,000
traditional beliefs	3,600,000
other	130,000

[1]Includes affiliated and nominal Christians. [2]Based on self-identification of respondent at 1981 census. [3]Excludes Assam. [4]Many Japanese adhere to both Shintoism and Buddhism. [5]Includes Aruba. [6]Includes the Marshall Is., the Fed. States of Micronesia, N. Mariana Is., and Palau. [7]Excludes Black republics listed separately. [8]Includes traditional beliefs and religion not known.

Vital statistics, marriage, family

This table provides some of the basic measures of the factors that influence the size, direction, and rates of population change within a country. The accuracy of these data depends on the effectiveness of each respective national system for registering vital and civil events (birth, death, marriage, etc.) and on the sophistication of the analysis that can be brought to bear upon the data so compiled.

Data on birth rates, for example, depend not only on the completeness of registration of births in a particular country but also on the conditions under which those data are collected: Do all births take place in a hospital? Are the births reported comparably in all parts of the country? Are the records of the births tabulated at a central location in a timely way with an effort to eliminate inconsistent reporting of birth events, perinatal mortality, etc.? Similar difficulties attach to death rates but with the added need to identify "cause of death." Even in a developed country such identifications are often left to non-medical personnel, and in a developing country with, say, only one physician for every 10,000 population there will be too few physicians to perform autopsies to assess accurately the cause of death after the fact and also too few to provide ongoing care at a level where records would permit inference about cause of death based on prior condition or diagnosis.

Calculating natural increase, which at its most basic is simply the difference between the birth and death rates, may be affected by the differing degrees of completeness of birth and death registration for a given country. The total fertility rate may be understood as the average number of children that would be borne per woman if all childbearing women lived to the end of their childbearing years and bore children at each age at the average rate for that age. Calculating a meaningful fertility rate requires analysis of changing age structure of the female population over time, changing mortality rates among mothers and their infants, and changing medical practice at births, each improvement of natural survivorship or medical support leading to greater numbers of live-born children and greater numbers of children who survive their first year (the basis for measurement of infant mortality, another basic indicator of demographic conditions and trends within a population).

As indicated above, data for causes of death are not only particularly difficult to obtain, since many countries are not well equipped to collect the data, but are also difficult to assess, as their accuracy may be suspect and their meaning may be subject to varying interpretation. Take the case of a citizen of a less developed country who dies of what is clearly a lung infection: Was the death complicated by chronic malnutrition, itself complicated by a parasitic infestation, these last two together so weakening the subject that he died of an infection that he might have survived had his general health been better? Similarly, in a developed country: Someone may die from what is identified in an autopsy as a cerebrovascular accident, but if that accident occurred in a vascular system that was weakened by diabetes, what was the actual cause of death? Statistics on causes of death seek to identify the "underlying" cause (that which sets the final train of events leading to death in motion) but often must settle for the most proximate cause or symptom. Even this kind of analysis may be misleading for those charged with interpreting the data with a view to ordering health-care priorities for a particular country. The eight groups of causes of death utilized here include most, but not all, of the

Vital statistics, marriage, family

country	vital rates						causes of death (rate per 100,000 population)								
	year	birth rate per 1,000 population	death rate per 1,000 population	infant mortality rate per 1,000 live births	rate of natural increase per 1,000 population	total fertility rate	year	infectious and parasitic diseases	malignant neoplasms (cancers)	endocrine and metabolic disorders	diseases of the nervous system	diseases of the circulatory system	diseases of the respiratory system	diseases of the digestive system	accidents, poisoning, and violence
Afghanistan	1980–85	48.9	27.3	194.0	21.6	6.9	...	...	...	...	...	...	...	...	...
Albania	1985	26.2	5.8	44.0[2]	20.4	3.6[3]	...	...	...	...	...	...	...	...	...
Algeria	1985	39.5	8.4	81.2[4]	31.1	6.1[4]	...	...	...	...	...	...	...	...	...
American Samoa	1986	41.7	4.7	9.9	37.0	4.2[5]	1986	2.8[6]	66.2	19.3[7]	...	110.3[8]	44.1[9]	...	38.6[10]
Andorra	1986	11.6	3.8	3.7	7.8	...									
Angola	1984	47.0	25.0	200.0[11]	22.0	6.4	1973	73.2	6.5	4.9	3.6	19.2	24.6	3.6	89.0
Anguilla	1986	22.2	9.0	19.5	13.2	1.9[12]	1981–85[13]	45.0	111.0	30.0	18.0	414.0	135.0	9.0	...
Antigua and Barbuda	1987	18.0	6.0	10.0	12.0	1.7	1983	21.7	62.6	34.5	26.4[15]	171.3	40.3[15]	18.1[15]	31.1[16]
Argentina	1985	25.0	9.0	36.0[4]	16.0	3.4	1982	24.5	141.0	22.2	9.4	360.8	43.7	41.5	53.3
Aruba	1983	16.9	5.1	10.0[17]	11.8	1.8[17]									
Australia	1987	15.2	7.5	8.8[18]	7.7	1.9[18]	1985	3.9	175.2	15.5	11.8	364.4	58.0	25.3	49.5
Austria	1986	11.5	11.5	10.3[17]	0.0	1.4	1986	4.8	247.1	21.3	15.0	617.9	57.7	57.1	81.8
Bahamas, The	1985	24.1	5.8	22.8[19]	18.3	3.1[4]	1985	19.8	93.5	26.3	14.7	166.8	57.3	27.2	70.3
Bahrain	1986	36.8	5.8	50.0	31.0	5.2	1985	6.5	35.0[20]	9.5[21]	2.8	102.1	19.5	7.5	31.3
Bangladesh	1986	42.7	16.3	133.0	26.4	5.7	1976	15.5	19.8	...	...	5.9	25.7	...	...
Barbados	1987	15.1	8.1	12.7	7.0	1.9[4]	1984	20.6	142.1	56.0	12.7	364.7	38.9	21.0	36.9
Belgium	1987	11.9	11.3	9.4[5]	0.6	1.6[5]	1984	7.7	273.5	27.0	22.1	480.0	81.2	43.0	74.8
Belize	1986	36.1	4.1	22.0[22]	32.0	4.9[5]	1982–84[13]	42.9	34.0	19.2	8.3	123.1	50.6	15.4	33.3
Benin	1984	49.0	17.0	116.0	32.0	6.5	1977	...	...	...	...	...	206.5	200.7	...
Bermuda	1986	15.5	7.2	10.6[22]	8.3	1.7[3]	1985	3.5[4]	185.0	50.0[16]	7.0[16]	397.0	26.0	19.6[15]	54.0
Bhutan	1986	37.8	17.3	137.0	20.5	5.5									
Bolivia	1980–85	44.0	15.9	110.0[5]	28.1	6.3									
Botswana	1986	45.6	11.1	68.4[23]	34.5	6.8									
Brazil	1985–90	28.6	7.9	63.2	20.7	3.5	1983[24]	44.0	61.8	9.9[7]	2.6[25]	155.0	32.0	10.0	60.0
British Virgin Islands	1986	17.7	6.8	23.5	10.9	...	1986	—	91.5	16.6[7]	...	241.3	108.2	16.6	33.3
Brunei	1986	30.6	3.2	7.4	27.4	4.4[12]	1985	48.0	64.0	...	...	132.0	25.0	...	21.0
Bulgaria	1986	13.4	11.6	15.4	1.8	2.0[5]	1985	7.1	163.8	17.3	6.0	721.1	92.3	36.8	63.5
Burkina Faso	1980–85	47.8	20.1	137.0[5]	27.7	6.5									
Burma	1987	32.6	13.2	102.0	19.4	4.3	1978	32.6	6.5	6.1	...	14.1	19.8	1.7	7.3
Burundi	1986–87	45.7	17.4	114.0	28.4	6.3									
Cameroon	1985–86	42.8	15.5	94.0	27.3	5.9[17]									
Canada	1986	14.8	7.3	7.9[5]	7.5	1.7[5]	1985	7.9	182.7	18.3	13.5	309.6	55.4	26.7	52.9
Cape Verde	1986	32.0	8.7	76.5[5]	23.3	2.6[26]	1980	153.7	43.8	20.6	16.5	135.8	72.3	27.7	30.1
Cayman Islands	1987	16.0	5.2	11.1[11]	10.8	...	1979	18.2	60.1	52.0	...	204.6	54.1	...	102.1
Central African Republic	1980–85	44.6	21.8	142.0	22.8	5.9	1978	59.0	...						
Chad	1985	44.2	19.9	139.0[4]	24.3	5.9									
Chile	1986	22.1	5.9	19.1	16.2	3.0[23]	1984	22.7	100.9	13.3	7.8	177.7	66.0	54.6	77.4
China	1987	21.0	6.7	33.0	14.3	2.4	1981[27]	23.7	113.0	6.3	9.4	251.1	43.0	25.9	31.3
Christmas Island	1985	15.4	1.8	...	13.6	...									
Cocos (Keeling) Islands	1981	14.4	1.8	—	12.6	...									
Colombia	1983–88	27.9	7.4	40.0[29]	20.5	3.4[30]	1977[31]	89.0	53.3	7.4[7]	6.1[25]	132.4	62.3	10.1	71.8
Comoros	1987	47.0	14.0	96.0	33.0	7.0									
Congo	1980–85	44.5	18.6	81.0	25.9	6.0									
Cook Islands	1986	24.0	5.2	21.7	18.8	4.1[5]	1976–78	54.0	38.0	27.0	0.0	197.0	110.0	18.0	49.0
Costa Rica	1985	33.3	4.3	18.9[4]	29.0	3.3[4]	1984	15.2	81.0	8.9	9.2	117.7	38.6	17.0	42.9
Côte d'Ivoire	1985–86	45.5	15.3	100.0	30.2	6.6									
Cuba	1986	16.3	6.2	13.3[17]	10.1	1.8[17]	1985	11.3	116.9	17.1	10.3	277.8	65.8	22.9	71.4
Cyprus	1986	19.5	7.9	11.6	12.0	2.4									
Czechoslovakia	1986	14.2	11.9	13.9	2.3	2.0	1986	...	238.8	...	8.8	651.4	86.7	47.0	78.0
Denmark	1986	10.8	11.3	8.2	-0.5	1.5	1985	4.9	283.9	19.5[21]	11.6	523.8	89.3	37.1	78.3
Djibouti	1980–85	49.2	18.3	c. 200	30.9	6.8									
Dominica	1984	20.8	5.2	16.3[32]	15.6	3.2[17]	1984	13.4	88.6	26.7	14.6	197.8	27.9	9.7	8.5
Dominican Republic	1985	34.0	9.0	74.0	25.0	4.0[4]	1982	47.0	26.8	14.9	10.6	85.6	29.4	22.1	34.7
Ecuador	1986	36.8	5.3	50.6[5]	31.5	4.8[5]	1984	87.5	45.9	9.8	10.5	85.6	71.0	24.8	66.8
Egypt	1985	37.5	9.1	70.5	28.4	5.3	1982	168.9	21.8	7.3[7]	1.7[25]	186.3	106.3	8.8	39.7

detailed causes classified by the World Health Organization and would not, thus, aggregate to the country's crude death rate for the same year. Among the lesser causes excluded by the present classification are: benign neoplasms; nutritional disorders; anemias; mental disorders; kidney and genitourinary diseases not classifiable under the main groups; maternal deaths (for which data *are* provided, however, in the "Health services" table); diseases of the skin and musculoskeletal systems; congenital and perinatal conditions; and general senility and other ill-defined (ill-diagnosed) conditions, a kind of "other" category.

Expectation of life is probably the most accurate single measure of the quality of life in a given society. It summarizes in a single number all of the natural and social stresses that operate upon individuals in that society. The number may range from as few as 40 years of life in the least developed countries to as much as 80 years for women in the most developed nations. The lost potential in the years separating those two numbers is prodigious, regardless of how the loss arises—wars and civil violence, poor public health services, or poor individual health practice in matters of nutrition, exercise, stress management, and so on.

Data on marriages and marriage rates probably are less meaningful in terms of international comparisons than some of the measures mentioned above because the number, timing, and kinds of social relationships that substitute for marriage depend on many kinds of social variables—income, degree of social control, heterogeneity of the society (race, class, language communities), or level of development of civil administration (if one must travel for a day or more to obtain a legal civil ceremony, one may forgo it). Nevertheless, the data for a single country say specific things about local practice in terms of the age at which a man or woman typically marries, and the overall rate will at least define the number of legal civil marriages, though it cannot say anything about other, less formal arrangements (here the figure for the legitimacy rate for children in the next section may identify some of the societies in which economics or social constraints may operate to limit the number of marriages that are actually confirmed on civil registers). The available data usually include both first marriages and remarriages after annulment, divorce, widowhood, or the like.

The data for families provide information about the average size of a family unit (individuals related by blood or civil register) and the average number of children under a specified age (set here at 15 to provide a consistent measure of social minority internationally, though legal minority depends on the laws of each country). When well-defined family data are not collected as part of a country's national census or vital statistics surveys, data for households are substituted on the assumption that most households worldwide represent families in some conventional sense. In the older countries of Europe and North America increasing numbers of households are composed of unrelated individuals (unmarried heterosexual couples, aged [or younger] groups sharing limited [often fixed] incomes for reasons of economy, or homosexual couples); such arrangements are not yet so common in the rest of the world that they represent great numbers overall. Very few census programs, even in developed countries, make adequate provision for distinguishing these households.

expectation of life at birth (latest year)		marriages			age at marriage (latest) — groom (percent)			bride (percent)			families (households)		children		induced abortions		country
male	female	year	total number	rate per 1,000 population	19 and under	20-29	30 and over	19 and under	20-29	30 and over	total ('000)	size	number under age 15	percent legitimate	number	ratio per 100 live births	
36.6	37.3	1970	6,212	0.4	...	...	...	...	...	...	H 2,110	H 6.2	H 2.8[1]	...	...	...	Afghanistan
67.9	72.9	1985	25,271	8.5	1.3	81.2	17.5	21.4	74.6	4.0	...	F 5.4	...	...	...	...	Albania
61.6	63.3	1985	123,688	5.7	3.4	68.3	28.3	37.7	53.5	8.8	...	H 6.9	...	...	...	...	Algeria
67.5	73.1	1982	362	10.7	5.6	65.5	28.8	24.5	60.5	15.0	H 4	H 7.1	H 2.9	86.0	...	...	American Samoa
——70.0——		1984	130	3.1	...	...	...	...	...	...	...	...	...	...	...	...	Andorra
40.4	43.6	1972	26,278	4.5	...	...	...	...	...	...	...	H 4.8	...	...	...	...	Angola
68.6	71.9	1986	154	22.2	1.7[14]	56.7[14]	41.6[14]	10.7[14]	58.0[14]	31.3[14]	H 1.6	H 4.1	H 1.8	34.4	...	...	Anguilla
70.0	74.0	1986	309	3.8	0.5	41.1	58.5	10.6	54.8	34.6	H 15	H 4.2	H 1.9	17.1	...	...	Antigua and Barbuda
68.6	73.3	1983	177,010	6.0	5.6	71.5	22.9	26.0	58.6	15.4	H 7,104	H 3.9	H 1.2	70.2	...	...	Argentina
71.6	76.8	1983	490	7.5	...	...	...	...	...	...	...	H 3.6	...	41.3	...	...	Aruba
72.8	79.1	1986	114,900	6.9	1.4	62.6	36.0	9.1	65.4	25.5	F 4,140	F 3.1	F 0.5	83.2	...	...	Australia
69.2	76.4	1986	45,821	6.1	2.4	67.8	29.8	11.2	70.4	18.4	F 2,057	F 3.6	F 0.6	76.7	...	...	Austria
66.9	70.9	1985	1,980	8.5	1.5	55.3	43.2	8.2	57.7	34.1	H 40	H 4.3	H 1.8	37.9	...	...	Bahamas, The
65.0	68.4	1985	2,656	6.6	3.7	77.0	19.3	37.1	56.6	6.3	H 67	H 4.9	H 3.0	...	...	...	Bahrain
50.2	49.2	1986	...	15.9	...	...	...	...	...	...	...	H 5.6	...	...	...	...	Bangladesh
70.0	75.4	1984	1,163	4.6	0.9	42.2	56.9	4.2	54.9	40.9	H 67	H 3.7	H 1.5	27.9	...	...	Barbados
70.0	76.8	1987	56,783	5.8	4.3	79.8	15.9	22.1	67.1	10.8	F 3,613	F 2.7	F 0.5	94.3	...	...	Belgium
66.0	71.0	1986	1,025	6.0	...	...	...	...	...	...	H 33	H 5.2	H 2.4	45.1	...	...	Belize
47.0	51.0	1980-85	...	12.8	...	...	...	...	...	...	...	H 5.4	...	...	...	...	Benin
68.8	76.3	1986	769	13.5	—	42.4	57.5	2.1	53.1	44.9	H 18	H 2.7	H 0.7	70.9	92	11.0	Bermuda
47.7	46.3	...	...	...	...	...	...	...	...	...	...	H 5.4	...	...	...	...	Bhutan
48.6	53.0	1980	26,990	4.8	8.3	75.1	16.6	26.1	55.4	18.5	H 1,050	H 4.4	H 1.8	80.9	...	...	Bolivia
54.7	61.2	...	...	...	...	...	...	...	...	...	H 125	H 5.7	H 2.0	28.0	17	0.1	Botswana
62.3	67.6	1985	952,294	7.0	7.5	70.3	22.2	33.8	52.3	13.9	F 31,076	F 4.1	F 1.6	...	...	...	Brazil
68.6	71.9	1986	139	11.6	—	39.6	60.4	0.7	52.5	46.8	H 3	H 3.3	H 1.1	44.2	...	...	British Virgin Islands
70.1	72.7	1985	1,898	8.5	10.0	72.8	17.2	18.4	71.5	10.1	H 23	H 5.8	H 2.5	99.6	...	...	Brunei
68.4	73.6	1986	64,965	7.3	6.1	73.8	20.1	37.4	50.0	12.6	F 2,627	F 3.3	F 0.7	88.6	132,041	111.0	Bulgaria
43.7	46.8	1975	...	9.4	...	...	...	...	...	...	...	H 4.9	...	...	...	...	Burkina Faso
51.9	55.0	...	...	...	...	...	...	...	...	...	...	H 5.2	...	...	...	...	Burma
46.9	50.2	...	...	...	...	...	...	...	...	...	...	H 4.9	...	...	...	...	Burundi
49.0	52.0	...	...	...	...	...	...	...	...	...	...	H 5.2	...	...	...	...	Cameroon
72.9	79.8	1986	190,680	7.4	1.7	64.9	33.4	8.4	68.2	23.4	F 6,735	F 3.1	F 0.8	83.8	60,956	16.2	Canada
60.3	64.0	1975	1,604	5.4	...	...	...	...	...	...	F 59	F 5.1	...	55.2	...	...	Cape Verde
——74.5——		1987	279	12.4	...	...	...	...	...	...	H 4	H 3.8	H 1.1	62.3	...	...	Cayman Islands
41.4	44.6	...	...	...	...	...	...	...	...	...	...	H 4.3	...	...	...	...	Central African Republic
43.4	46.6	...	...	...	...	...	...	...	...	...	...	H 3.9	...	...	...	...	Chad
68.1	75.1	1985	91,099	7.5	6.5	74.4	19.1	26.4	60.7	12.9	F 1,690	F 4.5	F 2.0	68.2	2,346	1.0	Chile
67.8	70.7	1985	8,290,588	8.0	...	...	...	...	...	...	H 241.3[28]	H 4.3	...	...	...	...	China
63.0	66.5	1982	25	8.3	—	90.9	9.1	45.5	36.4	18.1	...	H 5.8	H 1.5	97.1	...	...	Christmas Island
63.0	66.5	1981	6	10.8	—	100.0	—	—	100.0	—	...	H 6.3	H 2.6	93.3	2	40.0	Cocos (Keeling) Islands
63.4	69.2	1977	88,401	3.5	5.6	69.5	24.9	33.6	55.3	11.1	F 4,772	F 5.4	F 2.5	75.2	...	...	Colombia
53.0	57.0	1964	1,959	8.5	...	...	...	...	...	...	...	H 5.6	...	...	...	...	Comoros
44.9	48.1	...	...	...	...	...	...	...	...	...	H 326	H 4.7	H 2.0	...	...	...	Congo
64.0	70.0	1986	105	6.1	1.2	63.4	35.4	22.0	51.2	26.8	H 3	H 5.6	H 2.4	...	...	...	Cook Islands
70.5	75.7	1985	19,747	7.8	9.2	69.3	21.5	36.2	51.1	12.7	F 472	F 5.0	F 1.7	62.8	...	...	Costa Rica
51.0	54.0	...	...	...	...	...	...	...	...	...	...	H 4.5	...	...	...	...	Côte d'Ivoire
72.6	76.1	1986	84,274	8.3	10.6	57.9	31.5	29.5	48.3	22.2	F 2,002	F 4.2	H 1.6	...	138,671	76.2	Cuba
72.3	77.0	1986	6,255	9.3	1.3	75.5	23.2	18.2	70.2	11.6	H 160	H 3.5	H 1.1	99.6	...	...	Cyprus
67.4	74.8	1986	119,927	7.7	6.7	73.1	20.2	27.3	57.4	15.3	H 5,288	H 0.9	H 0.9	93.0	124,188	56.5	Czechoslovakia
71.6	77.5	1986	30,773	6.0	0.6	47.4	52.0	3.0	60.9	36.1	F 2,675	F 1.9	F 0.3	56.1	20,067	36.3	Denmark
——45.0——		1982	2,500	6.7	...	...	...	...	...	...	...	H 5.6	...	96.8	...	...	Djibouti
73.0	79.0	1969	234	3.3	...	...	...	...	...	...	H 18	H 4.3	H 2.2	35.0	...	...	Dominica
60.7	64.6	1985	21,301	3.4	8.0	63.0	29.0	29.7	51.0	19.3	H 753	H 5.1	H 2.5	32.8	...	...	Dominican Republic
59.8	63.6	1986	60,205	6.2	12.8	65.4	21.8	38.2	49.1	12.7	...	H 5.1	...	67.9	...	...	Ecuador
59.0	62.1	1985	442,280	9.1	8.5	61.5	30.0	46.9	42.3	10.8	H 9,619	H 5.0	H 2.1	100.0	...	...	Egypt

Vital statistics, marriage, family (continued)

country	vital rates						causes of death (rate per 100,000 population)								
	year	birth rate per 1,000 population	death rate per 1,000 population	infant mortality rate per 1,000 live births	rate of natural increase per 1,000 population	total fertility rate	year	infectious and parasitic diseases	malignant neoplasms (cancers)	endocrine and metabolic disorders	diseases of the nervous system	diseases of the circulatory system	diseases of the respiratory system	diseases of the digestive system	accidents, poisoning, and violence
El Salvador	1987	37.0	10.0	88.0	27.0	4.9	1984	60.0	21.6	9.9	9.0	63.9	34.8	26.1	124.6
Equatorial Guinea	1980–85	42.5	21.0	137.0[29]	21.5	5.7[18]	...	...	...	...	...	...	...	...	...
Ethiopia	1985	49.7	23.1	155.0	26.6	6.7	1978	39.5	3.8	24.6	2.7	5.6	16.3	28.9	15.8
Faeroe Islands	1986	17.1	8.0	6.4	9.1	2.4	1986	13.0	162.9	8.7[21]	—	451.6	45.6	15.2	67.3
Falkland Islands	1981	15.0	5.0	...	10.0	...	...	...	...	...	...	...	...	...	...
Fiji	1987	28.0	5.2	19.0	22.8	3.2	1985	31.3	53.3	29.1[7]	2.7[25]	190.8	43.1	13.3	48.5
Finland	1986	12.3	9.6	5.8	2.7	1.6	1986	7.8	193.9	11.8[21]	11.1	505.1	65.9	26.6	80.8
France	1987	13.8	9.5	7.6	4.3	1.8[18]	1985	13.2	239.2	22.0	16.1	366.7	70.9	57.1	90.2
French Guiana	1987	30.4	6.3	22.2[33]	24.1	3.1[34]	1984	55.2	62.7	10.1[7]	3.8[25]	152.9	25.1	33.8	104.0
French Polynesia	1987	28.0	5.1	20.2[33]	22.9	3.5	1984	21.2	67.7	10.0	19.4	120.1	36.5	17.7	58.9
Gabon	1980–85	33.8	18.1	121.6	15.7	4.5	...	...	...	...	...	...	...	...	...
Gambia, The	1980–85	48.4	29.0	174.0	19.4	6.4	...	...	...	...	...	...	...	...	...
Gaza Strip	1985	45.4	7.0	...	38.4		...	...	...	...	...	...	...	...	...
Germany, East	1986	13.4	13.4	9.2	0.0	1.6[5]	1985	4.9	211.6	38.1	9.8	797.2	84.3	31.1	37.9
Germany, West	1986	10.2	11.5	8.9	-1.3	1.3[4]	1986	8.1	267.0	22.3	13.7	575.7	76.5	51.9	56.3
Ghana	1980–85	46.9	14.6	98.0	32.3	6.5	...	...	...	...	...	...	...	...	...
Gibraltar	1986	17.4	9.9	...	7.5	...	...	...	...	...	...	...	...	...	...
Greece	1986	11.3	9.2	12.2	2.1	2.2	1986	5.8	184.0	11.5	12.2	460.3	50.5	30.0	46.2
Greenland	1986	20.0	8.3	23.4	11.7	2.1	1986	9.3	140.0	1.9	5.6	203.5	61.6	5.6	242.7
Grenada	1986	32.5	7.2	48.0[17]	25.3	3.1[17]	1981	26.7	90.9	48.3[21]	...	186.3	41.5	31.4	30.0
Guadeloupe	1986	19.1	6.7	15.2	12.4	2.4	1983	13.0	105.8	31.2	16.4	243.0	22.7	33.9	80.0
Guam	1986	26.7	3.6	9.4	23.1	3.2[3]	1986	5.7	46.0[20]	17.0[21]	10.5	143.7	36.3	13.7	58.1
Guatemala	1987	36.5	9.5	66.0	27.0	5.1	1984	211.5	29.8	29.6	9.0	57.2	145.7	21.7	52.0
Guernsey	...	...	...	...	...	...	...	...	...	...	...	...	...	...	...
Guinea	1980–85	46.8	23.5	159.0	23.3	6.2	...	...	...	...	...	...	...	...	...
Guinea-Bissau	1980–85	40.7	21.7	143.0	19.0	5.4	...	...	...	...	...	...	...	...	...
Guyana	1985	25.5	7.6	41.0	17.9	3.34	1977	88.1	45.6	46.4	10.4	236.2	69.3	35.9	67.3
Haiti	1985	36.0	13.0	107.0	23.0	4.54	...	...	...	...	...	...	...	...	...
Honduras	1985	41.0	8.0	73.0	33.0	6.2[4]	1981	80.9	14.9	4.9	9.8	53.1	31.9	21.6	53.9
Hong Kong	1987	12.5	4.8	7.5	7.7	1.4	1986	14.1	145.5	4.7	3.2	135.9	74.3	19.3	28.9
Hungary	1987	11.8	13.4	17.4	-1.6	1.74	1986	9.8	277.2	21.2	11.2	739.3	72.4	75.7	122.2
Iceland	1986	15.6	6.8	5.7[5]	8.8	1.9[5]	1985	5.0	163.3	3.7	10.0	325.5	86.6	15.8	41.9
India	1986	32.4	11.1	96.0[17]	21.3	4.1[17]	...	...	...	...	...	...	...	...	...
Indonesia	1986	29.8	11.7	77.0	18.1	3.7	...	...	...	...	...	...	...	...	...
Iran	1985–90	38.5	10.8	109.0[17]	27.7	5.2[17]	...	...	...	...	...	...	...	...	...
Iraq	1986	45.1	8.6	63.3	36.5	7.1	...	...	...	...	...	...	...	...	...
Ireland	1986	17.4	9.5	10.1[4]	7.9	3.2[12]	1984	6.2	188.9	12.2	17.2	451.0	115.8	25.2	40.4
Isle of Man	1987	11.4	14.4	15.5[11]	-3.0	...	1986	4.7	364.0	12.4[7]	—[25]	793.4	161.8	21.8	54.4
Israel	1987	22.7	6.7	11.2[18]	16.0	2.9[5]	1985	13.5	118.5	13.2	7.8	273.5	46.2	17.3	45.2
Italy	1986	9.7	9.5	10.3[5]	0.2	1.6[26]	1984	5.9	226.0	36.1	14.1	429.7	60.5	54.7	45.8
Jamaica	1986	23.1	5.7	18.0[17]	17.4	3.1[17]	1978	39.3	74.8	40.5[21]	12.0	210.9	41.7	21.4	28.0
Japan	1987	11.2	6.1	5.3[18]	5.1	1.8[18]	1986	9.0	157.8	8.9	5.1	239.5	61.3	30.9	47.6
Jersey	1986	11.8	10.9	...	0.9	...	...	...	...	...	...	...	...	...	...
Jordan	1986	34.7	5.8	48.6	27.9	6.6	...	...	...	...	...	...	...	...	...
Kampuchea	1987	41.8	16.9	133.0	24.9	4.8	...	...	...	...	...	...	...	...	...
Kenya	1980–85	55.1	14.0	92.0[4]	41.1	7.7[4]	...	...	...	...	...	...	...	...	...
Kiribati	1981–85	37.5	13.9	82.0	23.6	4.9	...	...	...	...	...	...	...	...	...
Korea, North	1980–85	30.5	6.0	29.7	24.5	3.8	...	...	...	...	...	...	...	...	...
Korea, South	1987	19.4	6.1	27.0	13.3	2.1	1985	19.9	73.5	6.4	5.7	155.0	22.6	43.9	56.5
Kuwait	1986	29.5	2.4	34.2	27.1	5.1	1986	8.8	29.5	8.5	6.3	75.7	13.7	5.1	37.8
Laos	1987	42.7	14.1	111.0	28.6	6.0	...	...	...	...	...	...	...	...	...
Lebanon	1986	30.4	7.7	49.2	22.7	3.8	...	...	...	...	...	...	...	...	...
Lesotho	1980–85	41.8	16.5	109.0[29]	25.3	5.8	...	...	...	...	...	...	...	...	...
Liberia	1984–89	46.8	12.6	122.0	34.2	6.9	...	...	...	...	...	...	...	...	...
Libya	1980–85	47.3	12.7	107.0	34.6	7.4	...	...	...	...	...	...	...	...	...
Liechtenstein	1987	13.2	6.5	15.4[35]	6.7	...	1987	7.3	152.4[20]	21.8[7]	...	221.4	18.1	25.4	58.1
Luxembourg	1986	11.7	10.7	7.9	1.0	1.4	1986	4.6	254.6	25.5	14.9	521.2	70.0	54.3	68.4
Macau	1986	17.9	3.2	7.2	14.7	3.8[26]	1983	31.4	80.8	12.2	2.4	138.7	40.2	21.0	36.9
Madagascar	1985–90	44.1	15.2	67.0	28.9	6.5[5]	...	...	...	...	...	...	...	...	...
Malawi	1984	54.0	22.0	152.0[5]	32.0	7.6[5]	1982[39]	45.9	3.6	16.0	4.7	3.6	18.6	2.8	6.1
Malaysia	1986	30.6	5.7	27.0	24.9	3.8	1981[40]	19.2	18.6	2.7	1.5	43.5	10.6	3.3	21.0
Maldives	1987	42.8	10.4	77.0	32.4	6.4	...	...	...	...	...	...	...	...	...
Mali	1985–86	50.5	22.2	169.0	28.0	6.7	...	...	...	...	...	...	...	...	...
Malta	1987	15.4	8.4	7.3	7.0	2.0	1986	4.7	147.9	20.5	4.1	523.8	47.9	21.0	17.8
Martinique	1987	19.0	6.4	11.9[33]	12.6	2.0	1985	11.6	129.6	22.9	10.7	234.8	35.1	36.3	52.4
Mauritania	1985–90	50.0	19.2	133.0[4]	30.8	6.9	...	...	...	...	...	...	...	...	...
Mauritius	1986	18.0	6.6	26.3	11.4	1.9	1986	17.8	51.6	45.0	7.5	286.1	61.2	31.7	45.7
Mayotte	1987	51.0	13.0	96.0	38.0	6.9	...	...	...	...	...	...	...	...	...
Mexico	1987	32.0	5.1	53.0[5]	26.9	3.4[11]	1982	68.4	40.3	30.9	8.7	95.1	66.3	44.9	92.5
Monaco	1983	19.6	16.6	...	3.0	...	...	...	...	...	...	...	...	...	...
Mongolia	1985	36.0	9.2	46.0[17]	26.8	5.0[17]	...	...	...	...	...	...	...	...	...
Montserrat	1985	21.0	11.5	17.0	9.5	2.2	1985	67.5	75.9	8.4	8.4	615.9	59.1	67.5	33.7
Morocco	1980–85	44.1	11.7	97.0	32.4	6.4	...	...	...	...	...	...	...	...	...
Mozambique	1980–85	45.1	19.7	153.0	25.4	6.1	...	...	...	...	...	...	...	...	...
Nauru	1983	31.2	5.8	31.2[23]	25.4	...	1976–81[13]	33.0	38.0	24.0	13.0	89.0	16.0	53.0	116.0
Nepal	1986	42.2	16.0	111.5	26.2	6.0	...	...	...	...	...	...	...	...	...
Netherlands, The	1986	12.7	8.6	6.4	4.1	1.6	1985	4.3	229.2	20.2	15.5	375.3	62.7	29.1	38.4
Netherlands Antilles	1982	20.7	5.5	8.4	15.2	3.4[4,42]	1983	20.8	128.6	17.9	5.2	206.0	27.1	31.2	57.1
New Caledonia	1985	23.5	5.7	13.8	17.8	3.5[4]	...	...	...	...	...	...	...	...	...
New Zealand	1986	16.1	8.3	11.2	7.8	1.9[17]	1984	4.7	180.7	13.4	11.9	368.8	79.6	21.1	54.3
Nicaragua	1985	44.2	9.7	76.4	34.5	5.2[17]	1978	52.3	13.5	2.9	4.5	62.1	18.6	14.2	59.2
Niger	1980–85	51.0	22.9	146.0	28.1	7.1	...	...	...	...	...	...	...	...	...
Nigeria	1980–85	50.4	17.1	114.0	33.3	7.1	...	...	...	...	...	...	...	...	...
Niue	1984	22.5	7.2	19.1[45]	15.3	...	...	...	...	...	...	...	...	...	...
Norfolk Island	1986	11.6	5.1	...	6.5	...	...	...	...	...	...	...	...	...	...

male	female	year	total number	rate per 1,000 population	groom 19 and under	groom 20-29	groom 30 and over	bride 19 and under	bride 20-29	bride 30 and over	families (households) total ('000)	size	children number under age 15	percent legitimate	induced abortions number	ratio per 100 live births	country
61.7	65.3	1984	16,727	3.5	7.2	57.2	35.6	27.1	49.1	23.8	H 686	H 5.4	H 2.4	32.6	...	...	El Salvador
44.0	48.0	1966	209	0.8	...	...	...	...	...	...	...	H 4.5	...	...	...	...	Equatorial Guinea
39.5	42.6										...	H 4.5					Ethiopia
73.3	79.6	1986	222	4.8	—	65.3	34.7	8.1	69.4	22.5	F 14	F 3.0	F 0.9	60.0	26	3.3	Faeroe Islands
...	...	1980	11								H 1	H 0.9	H 0.9	75.0			Falkland Islands
68.0	72.4	1985	6,593	10.1	7.3	72.5	20.2	14.4	75.0	10.6	F 97	F 6.0	F 2.5	82.7			Fiji
70.5	78.7	1986	25,820	5.3	2.5	68.5	29.0	10.6	69.4	20.0	F 1,163	H 2.5	F 0.9	82.0	13,642	21.0	Finland
71.0	79.2	1987	265,400	4.8	0.8	70.0	29.2	7.4	72.0	20.6	H 20,899	H 2.7	H 1.0	80.4	173,300	22.6	France
63.4	69.7	1987	365	4.1							H 12	H 3.3	H 1.4	19.8	388	16.8	French Guiana
70.0	74.0	1987	971	5.3	11.3[14]	75.8[14]	12.9[14]	41.5[14]	52.5[14]	6.0[14]	H 32	H 5.0	H 2.0	41.1			French Polynesia
48.0	51.4										H 136	H 4.0					Gabon
40.9	44.1										H 123	H 4.9	H 3.4				Gambia, The
...	...																Gaza Strip
69.6	75.4	1985	131,514	7.8	2.9	70.7	26.4	13.9	67.9	18.2	F 4,781	F 3.5	F 0.7	66.2	80,100	35.0	Germany, East
71.2	77.8	1986	371,900	6.1	1.9	63.7	34.4	10.1	69.1	20.8	F 22,882	F 2.7	F 0.5	90.4	85,538	14.6	Germany, West
50.3	53.8										H 2,355	H 4.9	H 2.2				Ghana
71.4	75.5	1986	177	6.1							H 7	H 3.8	H 1.0	97.1			Gibraltar
72.2	76.4	1986	58,933	5.9	1.7	64.5	33.8	25.8	58.6	15.6	F 2,990	H 3.3	H 0.7	98.1	180	0.2	Greece
60.4	66.3	1986	349	6.5	1.4	46.4	52.2	6.0	61.3	32.7	F 28	F 1.9	F 0.5	26.8	539	51.3	Greenland
65.4	69.4	1979	360	3.9							H 20	H 4.7	H 2.2	22.5			Grenada
69.0	76.0	1986	1,709	5.1	0.6	56.8	42.6	8.8	67.5	23.7	H 70	H 3.7	H 1.9	43.4	561	8.7	Guadeloupe
69.6	74.5	1986	1,522	12.3	4.7	62.1	33.2	12.0	65.8	22.2	H 25	H 3.7	H 1.5	68.6			Guam
58.0	62.0	1985	38,489	4.8	15.9	55.8	28.3	41.5	38.0	20.5	H 1,102	H 5.5	H 2.7	34.8			Guatemala
...	...										H 18	H 2.9		83.6			Guernsey
38.7	41.8										H 1,064	H 4.7					Guinea
41.4	44.6										H 124	H 4.1	H 2.8	11.3			Guinea-Bissau
66.9	70.9	1968	2,760	4.2							H 178	H 5.0	H 2.5	61.4			Guyana
51.2	54.4	1980		0.7							H 1,147	H 4.4	H 1.8				Haiti
60.2	63.9	1983	19,875	4.9	7.7	65.1	27.2	27.9	58.5	13.6	H 463	H 5.7	H 2.8				Honduras
73.0	78.5	1987	48,561	9.0	0.9	59.6	39.5	4.8	73.0	22.2	H 1,453	H 3.7	H 0.9	94.5	10,600	12.0	Hong Kong
65.3	73.2	1987	66,037	6.2	6.4	69.4	24.2	29.8	53.0	17.0	F 3,058	F 2.9	F 0.8	90.8	84,500	67.0	Hungary
74.7	80.2	1986	1,230	5.1	2.6	68.8	28.6	7.6	73.7	18.7	H 49	H 3.3	H 1.3	52.9	687	15.7	Iceland
56.7	57.6										H 97,093	H 5.6	H 2.4		561,033	2.2	India
53.9	56.7	1984–85	1,110,328	6.8							H 30,263	H 4.6	H 2.0				Indonesia
58.0	58.3	1984–85	384,876	8.9							H 8,125	H 5.0	H 2.2				Iran
61.0	64.5	1982	56,440	4.0	4.0	49.1	46.9	23.9	47.2	28.9	H 2,128	H 6.9	H 3.2				Iraq
70.1	75.6	1985	18,590[4]	5.2	5.2	77.1	17.7	14.9	75.2	9.9	H 726	H 3.9	H 1.3	92.2			Ireland
		1987	435	6.8	3.7	52.6	43.7	8.9	58.9	32.2				78.2			Isle of Man
73.5	77.0	1987	30,141	6.9	3.3	75.4	21.3	24.0	65.2	10.8	H 1,026	H 3.7	H 1.3	99.0	18,406	18.5	Israel
71.4	78.1	1986	296,539	5.2	1.7	75.2	23.1	18.7	70.1	11.2	F 17,615	F 3.2	F 0.7	94.4	227,809	38.9	Italy
68.1	72.6	1985	11,800	5.1							H 509	H 4.3	H 2.0	15.7			Jamaica
75.2	80.9	1985	735,850	6.1	1.0[14]	63.5[14]	35.5[14]	3.3[14]	81.7[14]	15.0[14]	F 22,240	F 5.4	F 1.2	99.0	598,100	37.9	Japan
											H 29	H 2.6		88.1			Jersey
65.0	68.8	1984	18,189	7.1	6.0	71.6	22.4	46.7	47.8	5.5	H 375	H 6.9	H 3.4				Jordan
46.5	49.4											H 5.6					Kampuchea
51.2	54.7										H 1,938	H 6.2	H 2.7				Kenya
50.6	55.6	1973	213	4.5	9.9	66.7	23.5	34.7	54.5	10.8	H 10	H 6.1	F 2.0				Kiribati
65.0	72.0											H 5.7					Korea, North
65.6	71.8	1983	355,056	8.9	1.5	83.1	15.4	8.9	85.8	3.8	F 7,969	F 4.8	F 1.6	99.5			Korea, South
70.3	73.0	1985	9,426	5.3	5.3	69.3	25.4	39.9	50.0	10.1	H 246	H 7.4	H 1.6				Kuwait
50.3	53.3											H 5.3					Laos
64.7	68.8	1973	18,601	7.0							H 405	H 5.3	H 2.2				Lebanon
46.3	52.3										H 242	H 4.4	H 2.0				Lesotho
53.9	56.3										H 474	H 5.0					Liberia
56.6	60.0	1979	17,236	6.0							F 383	F 5.4	F 2.9				Libya
77.6	82.6	1987	165	6.0	—[36]	59.4[37]	40.6[38]	4.8[36]	77.6[37]	17.6[38]	H 8	H 3.0	H 0.7	94.8			Liechtenstein
70.0	76.7	1986	1,892	5.1	2.0	64.5	33.5	8.6	70.9	20.5	H 128	H 2.8	H 0.5	89.8			Luxembourg
68.0	73.0	1986	2,900	4.8	0.3	60.6	39.1	4.2	81.6	14.2	H 50	H 4.8	H 1.8	99.3			Macau
48.9	50.4	1975	19,800	2.6	14.5	60.3	25.2	49.5	36.9	13.6	H 1,709	H 4.7	H 2.0				Madagascar
44.0	46.0	1977	4,300	7.8								H 4.5					Malawi
67.0	71.2											H 5.2					Malaysia
58.0	59.0										H 23	H 6.1	H 2.7				Maldives
42.4	45.6	1983	21,785	2.8							H 1,254	H 5.1					Mali
72.2	76.8	1986	2,619	7.6	1.5	78.2	20.3	9.7	79.1	11.2	H 76	H 3.6	H 1.2	98.5			Malta
71.0	77.0	1987	1,537	4.6	0.5	54.7	44.8	5.0	65.1	29.9	H 71	H 3.8		34.6	1,753	30.6	Martinique
44.0	47.0										H 246	H 5.0					Mauritania
64.4	71.2	1986	10,337	10.3	1.5	58.3	40.2	23.9	59.0	17.1	F 155	F 5.3	F 2.0	72.8			Mauritius
53.0	57.0										H 10	H 4.7	H 2.3	89.2			Mayotte
65.9	72.3	1985	553,000	7.1	17.3	63.5	19.2	40.7	46.9	12.4	H 14,796	H 5.1	H 2.3	72.5			Mexico
...	...	1981	190	7.3							H 10	H 2.3	H 0.3	96.8			Monaco
61.4	65.5	1985	12,500	6.3							F 311	F 5.1					Mongolia
68.6	71.9	1985	55	4.6	—	41.8	58.2	9.1	45.5	45.5	H 4	H 3.1		23.4			Montserrat
56.1	59.4										H 2,819	H 5.8	H 2.5				Morocco
44.4	46.2	1974	6,037	0.7							F 1,860	F 4.4	F 2.0	73.1			Mozambique
48.9	62.1	1977	43[41]	6.3							H 1	H 8.0	H 2.6				Nauru
53.4	50.6											F 5.8	H 2.2				Nepal
73.1	79.6	1985	87,337	6.0	0.5	66.0	33.5	3.7	74.1	22.2	H 5,598	H 2.6	H 0.6	91.2	18,700	10.7	Netherlands, The
71.1[43]	75.7[43]	1982	959	5.6	4.0	77.0	18.9	22.2	61.1	16.7	H 41	H 3.7	H 2.1	52.3			Netherlands Antilles
64.6	68.5	1983	831	5.7	3.6	70.2	26.2	31.4	53.4	15.2		H 4.1		53.0			New Caledonia
72.0	78.0	1986	24,037	7.3	1.3	62.8	35.9	7.7	67.2	25.1	H 1,078	H 3.1	H 0.8	73.0	7,130	13.8	New Zealand
58.7	61.0	1985	11,822	3.6	—	18.1[36]	81.9[44]	—	48.2[36]	51.8[44]		H 6.9					Nicaragua
40.9	44.1										H 1,029	H 5.2	H 2.4				Niger
46.9	50.2										H 14,441	H 5.0					Nigeria
63.0	66.5	1982	12	3.8							F 1	F 4.1	F 1.9	58.2			Niue
58.0	59.9	1986	17	8.6	—	56.3	43.7	6.3	50.0	43.7				100.0			Norfolk Island

Vital statistics, marriage, family (continued)

country	vital rates						causes of death (rate per 100,000 population)								
	year	birth rate per 1,000 population	death rate per 1,000 population	infant mortality rate per 1,000 live births	rate of natural increase per 1,000 population	total fertility rate	year	infectious and parasitic diseases	malignant neoplasms (cancers)	endocrine and metabolic disorders	diseases of the nervous system	diseases of the circulatory system	diseases of the respiratory system	diseases of the digestive system	accidents, poisoning, and violence
Norway	1986	12.6	10.5	8.5	2.1	1.7	1985	7.5	231.9	13.0[21]	16.1	518.5	105.2	30.4	65.0
Oman	1986	44.2	13.0	110.5	31.2	7.0	...								
Pacific Is., Trust Terr. of the															
Marshall Islands	1985	38.7	5.2	30.3	33.5	5.1[3]	1985	35.5	32.7	38.2	27.3	70.9	109.1	13.6	49.1
Micronesia, Fed. States of	1984	29.4	2.7	95.0	26.7	...	1984	20.4	27.1	6.8	4.5	53.2	47.5	5.7	23.8
Northern Mariana Islands	1985	34.3	4.7	20.1	29.6	...	1985	...	73.7[20]	...	...	157.2	54.1	24.6	29.5
Palau	1986	25.0	6.3	25.9	18.7	3.2	1985–86	15.3	92.1[20]	19.2[21]	11.5	176.5	99.8	34.5	95.9
Pakistan	1987	41.9	14.1	120.0	27.8	5.5	...								
Panama	1985–90	26.7	5.2	22.7	21.5	3.1	1986[46]	21.3	50.0	9.0[7]	1.9[25]	104.1	19.9	7.5	45.0
Papua New Guinea	1987	35.6	12.9	63.0	22.7	5.2	...								
Paraguay	1985–90	34.9	6.6	48.9	28.3	4.5	1984	40.5	25.6	14.3	6.5	95.7	31.4	13.4	26.1
Peru	1988	34.2	9.0	85.8	25.2	4.4	1982	88.2	33.5	13.5	10.5	58.0	97.9	24.1	30.5
Philippines	1987	34.6	7.9	56.0	26.7	4.6	1984	179.8	30.2	13.4	...	100.6	...	...	16.8
Pitcairn Island	1982	—	—	—	...	...									
Poland	1986	17.0	10.1	17.3	6.9	2.3	1986	9.6	181.8	16.6	9.1	515.4	53.5	31.7	70.3
Portugal	1986	12.4	9.4	11.6	3.0	2.3[26]	1986	8.6	159.1	23.0	8.4	411.6	64.2	48.0	68.0
Puerto Rico	1986	19.4	7.1	14.9[5]	12.3	2.4	1983	11.6	105.3	35.0	9.1	260.7	72.5	43.6	54.8
Qatar	1986	26.9	2.1	37.4	24.8	4.9	1986	9.3	20.4[20]	6.9[21]	2.4	50.0	10.6	6.1	41.0
Réunion	1986	23.1	5.6	10.3[5]	17.5	2.9[4]	1984	9.5	46.4	22.4	...	174.0	38.7	36.5	71.1
Romania	1985	15.8	10.9	25.6	4.9	2.4[2]	1984	8.4	128.4	7.4	8.3	603.7	115.4	50.0	66.3
Rwanda	1985	52.0	19.0	127.0	33.0	8.0	...								
St. Helena and Ascension	1986	9.0	3.6	29.7	5.4	...	...								
St. Kitts and Nevis	1985	22.3	9.6	30.2	12.7	2.8[17]	1984	35.1	114.0	37.9[29]	6.8[3]	462.7	41.7	6.6	28.5
St. Lucia	1986	28.0	6.0	20.8[22]	22.0	3.8	1986	24.4	65.2	19.4	15.8	203.5	55.9	30.8	39.4
St. Pierre and Miquelon	1984	21.0	9.5	12.3[29]	11.5	...	1977	72.9	108.3	102.1	25.0	366.7	45.8	39.6	39.6
St. Vincent and the Grenadines	1986	24.5	5.9	23.8[22]	18.6	3.2[4]	1986	17.2	65.9	39.7	9.0	118.3	27.1	27.1	30.7
San Marino	1983–87	9.6	7.5	8.4	2.1	1.3[4]	1983–87[13]	—	256.3	8.1	4.5	325.3	29.6	19.7	54.7
São Tomé and Príncipe	1985	36.3	8.8	61.7	27.5	5.0	...								
Saudi Arabia	1986	37.3	12.8	108.6	24.5	7.2	...								
Senegal	1984	48.6	18.5	141.0[26]	30.1	7.0	...								
Seychelles	1986	26.2	7.6	17.4	18.6	3.5[4]	1985	40.2	115.0	6.1	19.9	200.8	64.4	35.2	69.0
Sierra Leone	1980–85	47.4	29.7	134.0[4]	17.7	6.1	...								
Singapore	1987	16.8	5.0	7.4	11.8	1.4[11]	1986	15.5	111.6	19.3	3.4	173.3	76.3	12.6	39.6
Solomon Islands	1982	44.6	11.7	46.0	32.9	7.3	...								
Somalia	1985	47.9	23.2	152.0	24.7	6.6[12]	...								
South Africa	1985	33.4	10.4	59.2	23.0	5.1[26]	...								
Bophuthatswana	1982	...	...	89.0	...	...	...								
Ciskei	1982	...	...	89.0	...	...	...								
Transkei	1982	...	...	89.0	...	...	...								
Venda	1982	...	...	89.0	...	...	...								
South West Africa/ Namibia	1980–85	44.9	11.5	110.0[5]	33.5	6.0	...								
Spain	1984	11.9	7.7	9.2	4.2	2.1[26]	1982	14.2	153.7	20.5	11.8	361.2	67.4	42.7	43.2
Sri Lanka	1986	23.9	6.2	23.5[5]	17.7	2.8	1982	50.4	24.6	10.4[23]	43.2[23]	84.7	43.2[23]	12.1[23]	64.9
Sudan, The	1980–85	45.9	17.4	118.0	28.5	6.6	...								
Suriname	1985	29.7	6.8	27.6	22.9	3.2[17]	1985	34.5	48.0	25.1	6.3	149.1	42.2	28.2	67.6
Swaziland	1980–85	47.3	17.2	129.2	30.1	7.0[5]	...								
Sweden	1987	12.5	11.1	5.9[11]	1.4	1.8[11]	1986	7.9	255.1	19.1[21]	10.6	609.2	87.8	28.7	59.8
Switzerland	1986	11.7	9.2	6.8	2.5	1.8	1986	7.2	240.1	24.0[21]	14.1	414.9	62.3	28.9	75.8
Syria	1986	42.4	7.5	48.1	34.9	7.1	1981	15.1	8.4	5.0	4.0	60.7	13.2	4.5	20.0
Taiwan	1987	16.0	4.9	6.3[11]	11.1	1.7[11]	1986	...	85.6	15.3[7]	...	145.5[49]	26.0[50]	16.6[51]	74.6[10]
Tanzania	1980–85	50.3	16.8	111.0[4]	33.5	7.0[5]	...								
Thailand	1986	25.3	7.4	52.0	17.9	3.0	1985	17.3[52]	27.0	...	...	36.4[53]	7.4[54]	2.9[55]	28.9
Togo	1980–85	45.2	15.7	102.0	29.5	6.1	...								
Tokelau	1982	27.7	10.3	—	17.4	4.3	...								
Tonga	1985	28.9	3.5	26.0[29]	25.4	4.3[26]	1980	53.5	46.9	13.1	3.3	61.1	41.5	17.5	14.2
Trinidad and Tobago	1984	27.0	6.7	14.1[32]	20.3	2.8	1983	16.3	74.5	71.8	10.2	271.1	48.5	29.3	59.4
Tunisia	1986	31.1	6.4	71.0[12]	24.7	4.3[4]	...								
Turkey	1980–85	33.6	9.3	84.0[5]	24.3	4.5	1983	16.8	25.2	2.3	1.4	107.3	19.8	3.9	7.4
Turks and Caicos Islands	1983	27.5	3.9	10.2[2]	23.6	...	...								
Tuvalu	1985	23.8	10.7	54.0	13.1	2.7	1985	40.0	70.0	20.0	120.0	150.0	120.0	170.0	...
Uganda	1980–85	50.3	16.8	110.0[4]	33.5	7.0[17]	...								
U.S.S.R.	1986	20.0	9.8	25.4	10.2	2.3[4]	1983	...	148.1	...	...	554.3	...	...	...
United Arab Emirates	1986	33.5	3.9	39.9	29.6	6.0	...								
United Kingdom	1986	13.3	11.6	9.5	1.7	1.8	1986	4.9	277.1	19.1	21.4	560.6	128.8	35.9	39.4
United States	1988	15.3	9.4	10.2[17]	5.9	1.8[17]	1987–88	17.7	196.9	16.0[7]	0.5[25]	400.1	63.4[60]	17.2	60.2
Uruguay	1985	17.8	9.5	29.5	8.3	2.6[2]	1985	23.7	219.9	25.8	14.4	391.0	65.6	37.3	52.1
Vanuatu	1985	42.8	9.2	94.0[4]	33.6	5.8[17]	1985[46]	69.3	22.9	16.2	11.8	37.6	60.5	12.5	23.6
Venezuela	1986	28.3	4.4	25.8	23.9	3.4	1983	47.4	54.3	17.4	10.0	132.0	35.6	19.0	71.4
Vietnam	1987	33.1	10.0	68.0	23.1	4.3	1979	48.0	54.0	...	...	123.8	...	...	...
Virgin Islands (U.S.)	1985	21.6	4.9	20.2[29]	16.7	2.9[5]	1981	6.1	83.5	25.5	5.1	209.8	20.4	34.6	84.5
Wallis and Futuna	1978	41.1	10.6	40.5	30.5	...	...								
West Bank	1985	41.3	7.6	...	33.7	...	...								
Western Sahara	1980–85	29.0	4.5	5.3	24.5	...	...								
Western Samoa	1985	12.1[46]	1.5[46]	52.0[11]	10.6[46]	4.4[11]	1985[46]	8.8	18.2	5.6[7]	0.6[25]	42.0	13.2	6.9	8.8
Yemen (Aden)	1986	49.7	17.8	133.3	31.9	7.5	...								
Yemen (Şan'ā')	1986	49.1	20.8	140.2	28.3	7.5	...								
Yugoslavia	1986	15.4	9.1	27.1	6.3	2.1[4]	1983	15.8	136.4	12.4	7.4	486.4	64.8	43.1	59.9
Zaire	1980–85	45.1	15.8	107.0	29.3	6.1	...								
Zambia	1980–85	48.1	15.1	88.0	33.0	6.8	...								
Zimbabwe	1983–87	37.9	11.2	61.0[5]	26.7	4.9[17]	1979	7.3	152.9	7.0	1.6	310.6	64.7	6.6	102.4

expectation of life at birth (latest year) male	female	nuptiality, family, and family planning — marriages: year	total number	rate per 1,000 population	age at marriage (latest) groom 19 and under	groom 20–29	groom 30 and over	bride 19 and under	bride 20–29	bride 30 and over	families (F), households (H) (latest) families (households) total ('000)	size	children number under age 15	percent legitimate	induced abortions number	ratio per 100 live births	country
72.8	79.5	1985	20,221	4.8	1.5	68.0	30.5	9.2	72.2	18.6	F 1,684	F 2.4	F 0.6	74.2	14,599	28.0	Norway
51.0	53.7	...	...	...	...	...	...	...	...	...	H 350	H 3.7	...	...	...	...	Oman
																	Pacific Is., Trust Terr. of the
											H 4	H 8.0	...	...			Marshall Islands
65.0	70.0										H 11	H 7.0	...	...			Micronesia, Fed. States of
59.0	64.0										H 3	H 5.4					Northern Mariana Islands
62.7	70.4										H 2	H 5.9					Palau
52.4	50.6	1971	62,900	10.7[34]													Pakistan
70.2	74.1	1986	10,091	4.5	4.2[47]	56.1[47]	39.7[47]	18.7[47]	54.0[47]	27.3[47]	F 347	F 4.9	...	28.1	12	—	Panama
53.0	54.6	...	...	...	...	...	...	...	...	...	H 674	H 4.6					Papua New Guinea
63.7	68.6	1985	18,370	5.8	3.1	62.5	34.4	31.2	46.5	22.3	H 345	H 5.2	...	68.7			Paraguay
60.1	64.0	1982	109,200	6.0	5.5	60.4	34.1	25.9	51.4	22.6	H 2,772	H 4.8	...	57.8			Peru
61.7	64.9	1983	351,663	6.8	10.4	70.3	19.3	30.0	58.0	12.0	F 9,566	F 5.7	F 2.4	93.9			Philippines
63.0	66.5	1972	2														Pitcairn Island
66.8	75.1	1986	257,887	6.9	3.6	78.3	18.1	19.2	67.8	13.0	F 9,435	F 3.6	F 0.9	95.0	135,564	20.0	Poland
69.3	76.2	1986	69,271	6.8	5.5	75.8	18.7	23.2	64.3	12.5	H 2,954	H 3.8	H 0.8	87.2			Portugal
71.0	79.0	1984	29,499	9.1	11.0	57.7	31.3	25.7	51.1	23.2	F 563	F 4.1	F 1.8	75.6			Puerto Rico
65.2	67.6	1986	1,181	3.1	6.4	73.2	20.4	39.5	54.7	5.8	H 61	H 6.4	...	...			Qatar
64.6	68.2	1985	3,185	5.8	2.3	73.6	24.1	29.0	56.6	14.4	H 121	H 4.2	H 2.3	56.3	3,838	32.5	Réunion
67.0	72.6	1985	161,094	7.1	3.1	75.1	21.8	34.2	51.0	14.8	H 7,115	H 3.1	...	...	404,000	99.0	Romania
46.0	49.0	1982	14,313	2.6							H 894	H 5.2	...	94.9			Rwanda
		1982	29	5.2	8.3	58.4	33.3	38.9	44.4	16.7	H 1	H 4.4	H 1.6	56.4			St. Helena and Ascension
63.0	67.0	1977	150	3.5							H 11	H 3.7	H 1.9	19.2			St. Kitts and Nevis
68.0	74.8	1986	432	3.1	0.7	46.9	52.4	8.8	53.6	37.6	H 27	H 4.6	...	15.0			St. Lucia
65.8	71.6	1985	32	5.2							H 2	H 3.3	H 0.9	83.0			St. Pierre and Miquelon
67.5	71.4	1984	394	3.6	0.7	44.2	55.1	11.1	57.2	31.7	H 20	H 5.0	...	...			St. Vincent and the Grenadines
70.7	76.2	1985	202	9.0	2.8	80.8	16.4	19.9	72.6	7.5	F 8	F 2.9	F 0.8	95.2			San Marino
41.7	44.9	...	...	...	...	...	...	...	...	...				9.8			São Tomé and Príncipe
54.8	57.7										H 1,513	H 6.6					Saudi Arabia
45.0	48.0										H 1,167	H 4.8					Senegal
66.2	73.5	1984	390	6.0	1.8	55.9	42.3	15.6	60.8	23.6	H 13	H 4.8	H 1.9	29.8	188	10.9	Seychelles
46.7	50.0										H 749	H 4.7					Sierra Leone
69.9	76.2	1987	23,404	9.0	0.6	68.6	30.8	7.0	78.3	14.7	H 510	H 5.9	H 1.3	...	23,512	55.3	Singapore
54.0	54.0										F 41	F 5.6	F 2.3	...			Solomon Islands
40.3	43.5											H 4.9					Somalia
51.8	55.2	1977	64,979[48]	...	3.5[48]	69.4[48]	27.1[48]	22.1[48]	58.6[48]	19.3[48]	F 1,403	H 5.1	...	75.9			South Africa
—57.0—																	Bophuthatswana
—57.0—											H 144	H 6.2					Ciskei
—57.0—																	Transkei
—57.0—											H 70	H 5.4					Venda
46.6	49.9											H 4.8					South West Africa/Namibia
71.3	77.5	1983	183,068	4.8	5.7	80.8	13.5	20.8	71.7	7.5	F 10,665	F 3.5	...	97.9			Spain
68.0	71.2	1985	128,034	7.8	0.5	71.1	28.4	16.9	73.0	10.1	H 2,721	H 5.2	H 1.9	94.6			Sri Lanka
46.6	49.0										H 3,471	H 5.3	...	...			Sudan, The
65.0	70.0	1985	2,400	6.1								H 3.9					Suriname
45.3	52.2										H 112	H 5.0	...	...	1,145	...	Swaziland
73.6	79.5	1987	41,064	4.9	0.4	42.7	56.9	2.3	56.4	41.3	H 3,670	H 2.3	H 0.5	51.6	30,838	31.3	Sweden
72.8	79.7	1986	40,234	6.1	0.3	57.6	42.1	3.4	70.4	26.2	H 2,500	H 2.5	...	94.4			Switzerland
64.3	67.9	1985	96,326	7.7							F 1,151	F 6.2	F 2.4	...			Syria
71.0	75.9	1987	146,075	7.5	2.4	76.6	21.0	11.2	81.5	7.3	H 4,427	H 4.5	H 1.5	98.0			Taiwan
47.4	50.7	1967	3,475	9.8							H 3,435	H 5.1	H 2.3	...			Tanzania
61.3	67.3	1985	343,134	6.6							H 8,419	H 5.3	H 2.0	...			Thailand
48.8	52.2	1979[56]	5,753	2.3							H 479	H 5.6	...	...			Togo
63.0	66.5	1981	9	6.0	—	83.3	16.7	—	100.0	—		H 5.5	...	90.7			Tokelau
61.0	64.8	1985	645	6.6							F 15	F 6.1	F 2.7	80.6			Tonga
66.2	71.3	1985	7,842	6.6	3.5	64.5	32.0	21.8	59.7	18.5	H 193	H 4.2	H 2.1	56.9	...	...	Trinidad and Tobago
60.1	61.1	1986	47,914	6.4	1.4	72.5	26.1	35.9	54.7	9.4	H 1,313	H 5.5	...	99.8	20,500	9.5	Tunisia
62.5	65.8	1983	308,256	6.4	7.1[57]	74.0[57]	18.9[57]	35.7[57]	53.5[57]	10.8[57]	H 8,601	H 5.2	H 2.0	...			Turkey
68.6	71.9	1980	27	3.6							H 1	H 4.3	H 2.0	82.4			Turks and Caicos Islands
59.0	62.0										H 1	H 6.4	H 2.2	82.2			Tuvalu
49.0	53.0										H 2,766	H 4.8	...	...			Uganda
65.0	73.6	1986	2,753,100	9.8	3.7	73.6	22.7	24.8	56.3	18.9	F 66,307	F 3.9	...	...	10,000,000	230.0	U.S.S.R.
68.4	71.7										H 247	H 6.8					United Arab Emirates
71.5	77.4	1986	393,938	6.9	6.6[36]	59.3[58]	34.1	18.4[36]	56.7[58]	24.9	H 21,672	H 2.7	H 1.7	79.0	180,983[59]	25.0[59]	United Kingdom
71.3	78.3	1986	2,433,000	9.7	8.5	59.5	32.0	21.1	55.8	23.1	F 63,558	F 2.6	F 1.0	76.6	1,157,776	34.7	United States
69.1	73.8	1985	22,336	7.6	8.3	62.7	29.0	28.3	51.7	20.0	H 863	H 3.3	...	73.8			Uruguay
61.1	59.3										H 23	H 5.0					Vanuatu
66.7	72.8	1986	100,002	5.6	11.3	63.2	25.5	33.6	51.0	15.4	H 2,707	H 5.3	...	47.0			Venezuela
58.5	62.9																Vietnam
66.7	70.7	1983	1,341	12.9	3.1	44.6	52.3	12.7	50.9	36.4	H 28	H 3.4	H 1.3	48.7			Virgin Islands (U.S.)
59.2	62.9	1980	60	5.6								H 6.6	H 3.0	78.3			Wallis and Futuna
																	West Bank
		1972	459	4.9													Western Sahara
62.6	65.6	1984	555	5.0	0.9	58.7	40.4	7.2	68.8	24.0	F 20	F 7.8	F 3.8	43.5			Western Samoa
47.1	50.9										H 392	H 5.6					Yemen (Aden)
45.6	48.9										H 1,456	H 5.6	...	...			Yemen (Şan'ā')
66.0	74.0	1984	167,789	7.3	2.7	75.0	22.3	26.2	61.4	12.4	H 6,187	H 3.6	H 0.9	91.6	288,100	74.0	Yugoslavia
48.3	51.7	1975	185,300	7.5								H 6.0					Zaire
49.6	53.1										H 1,370	H 4.4	H 2.1	...			Zambia
57.9	61.4											H 5.8	...	95.8			Zimbabwe

[1]Excludes nomadic tribes. [2]1982. [3]1980. [4]1984. [5]1985. [6]Septicemia only. [7]Diabetes mellitus only. [8]Diseases of the heart and cerebrovascular disease only. [9]Chronic obstructive pulmonary diseases, pneumonia, and influenza only. [10]Suicide and accidents only. [11]1986. [12]1985–90. [13]Average annual rates for the period. [14]First marriages only. [15]1977. [16]1978. [17]1987. [18]1986. [19]1983–85 average. [20]Includes benign neoplasms. [21]Includes nutritional disorders. [22]1984–86 average. [23]1981. [24]Data exclude deaths of unknown cause. [25]Meningitis only. [26]1980–85. [27]Estimates based on rural survey. [28]Millions of households. [29]1983. [30]1981–86. [31]Based on burial permits. [32]1982–84 average. [33]1985–87 average. [34]1975–80. [35]1982–86 average. [36]Under 21 years of age. [37]21–30 years of age. [38]Over 31 years of age. [39]Reported inpatient deaths only. [40]Medically certified deaths only. [41]1973. [42]Includes Aruba. [43]Curaçao only. [44]Over 21 years of age. [45]1981–85 average. [46]Registered events only. [47]Excludes tribal Indians. [48]Whites, Asians, and Coloureds only. [49]Cerebrovascular disease, heart disease, and hypertensive disease only. [50]Pneumonia, bronchitis, emphysema, and asthma only. [51]Chronic liver disease and cirrhosis only. [52]Malaria, diarrhea, and tuberculosis only. [53]Heart disease only. [54]Pneumonia only. [55]Diseases of the stomach and duodenum only. [56]African population only. [57]Urban areas only. [58]21–29 years of age. [59]Excludes Northern Ireland. [60]Bronchitis, pneumonia, influenza, and chronic obstructive pulmonary diseases only.

National product and accounts

The national product and accounts table furnishes, for most of the countries of the world, breakdowns of (1) total and per capita gross national product (GNP); (2) nominal and real gross domestic product (GDP); (3) principal accounting and industrial components of national GDP; (4) growth rates of real GDP during the last two decades; and (5) principal elements of each country's balance of payments, including international goods trade, invisibles, and tourism payments.

Measures of national output. The two most commonly used measures of national output (except for certain centrally planned economies) are GDP and GNP. Each of these measures represents an aggregate value of goods and services produced by a specific country. The GDP, the more basic of these, is a measure of the total value of goods and services produced entirely within a given country. The GNP, the more comprehensive value, is composed of both domestic production, GDP, *and* the net income from current (short-term) transactions with other countries. When the income received from other countries is greater than payments to them, a country's GNP is greater than its GDP. In theory, if all national accounts could be equilibrated, the global summation of GDP would equal GNP.

In the first section of the table, data are provided for the nominal GNP (value in current prices for the year indicated), together with the per capita value of this product, both denominated in U.S. dollars for ease of comparison. Beside these are given figures for GDP denominated in the national currency, first as a nominal value, then as a "real" value (adjusted, that is, to eliminate the effect of recent inflation [most often] or, occasionally, of deflation). The real values are obtained by dividing the nominal GDP by a GDP deflator (essentially a consumer price index

that covers price changes in the whole economy) and are adjusted to a common base year of 1980. GNP per capita provides a rough measure of annual national income per person, but values should be compared cautiously, as they are subject to a number of distortions, notably purchasing power parity (the differing ability [by more than a simple exchange rate] of any two currencies to purchase comparable goods in their respective domestic markets) and in the existence of elements of national production that do not enter the monetary economy in such a way as to be visible to fiscal authorities (*e.g.,* food, clothing, or housing produced and consumed within families or communal groups; services exchanged; criminal transactions; and the like).

In a number of countries with centrally planned economies the conventional concept for the aggregated national income/product is net material product (NMP), which includes only material goods and "productive" services. These NMP accounts are not directly comparable to the GDP values presented in this table for free market economies. The GDP value is more comprehensive and includes a number of sectors (especially personal and financial services) excluded from the NMP value. Estimated GNPs have been supplied for most countries (including the centrally planned), based either on the country's own, or on external, analysis.

The internal structure of the national product. Even though GDP/GNP values allow comparison of the relative size of national economies, more information is provided when these aggregates are analyzed according to their component kinds of expenditure, cost components, and industrial sectors of origin.

There are three major domestic components of GDP expenditure: pri-

National product and accounts

country	gross national product (GNP), 1986 nominal ('000,000 U.S.$)	per capita (U.S.$)	gross domestic product (GDP), 1986 nominal ('000,000,000 national currency)	real (constant prices of 1980; '000,000,000 national currency)	GDP by type of expenditure, 1985 (%) consumption private	government	gross domestic investment	foreign trade exports	imports	cost components of GDP, 1985 (%) indirect taxes net of subsidies	consumption of fixed capital	compensation of employees	net operating surplus
Afghanistan	3,520[1]	230[1]	...	112.9[2]	...	...	...	...	...	...	...	...	...
Albania	2,800	880	...	...	...	...	...	...	...	...	...	...	...
Algeria	58,040	2,570	289.2[1]	...	47	16	34	24	-21	20[7]	8[7]	37[7]	35[7]
American Samoa	190[1]	5,340[1]	...	...	...	...	...	...	...	...	...	...	...
Andorra	360[5]	9,000[5]	...	...	...	...	...	...	...	...	...	...	...
Angola	6,930[8]	830[8]	178.9[1]	...	49	22	7	45	-24	...	...	...	...
Anguilla	...	...	0.047	0.037[10]	53	17	29	49	-49	...	...	...	...
Antigua and Barbuda	190	2,380	0.510	0.366	68[8]	19[8]	27[8]	91[8]	-104[8]	...	...	...	...
Argentina	72,920	2,350	74.309	0.027	72[8]	14[8]	14[8]	13[8]	-9[8]	8[5]	12	34[5]	57[5,12]
Aruba	...	...	0.817[1]	...	13	13	13	13	13	13	13	13	13
Australia	190,470	11,910	250.7	146.2	61	17	25	16	-20	12	16	50	21
Austria	75,540	10,000	1,441.1	1,095.2	57	19	24	40	-40	14	12	52	21
Bahamas, The	1,700	7,190	2.216	...	61	13	20	61	-55	...	...	...	...
Bahrain	3,670	8,530	1.876[1]	...	30[5]	17[5]	45[5]	78[5]	-70[5]	4[5]	10[5]	30[5]	56[5]
Bangladesh	16,070	160	481.6	252.0	88	8	13	6	-15	...	...	...	...
Barbados	1,310	5,140	2.677	...	60	19	16	65	-60	14[15]	6[15]	57[15]	24[15]
Belgium	91,010	9,230	5,011.2	3,665.6	66	18	15	72	-70	10	9	55	26
Belize	200	1,170	0.425	0.409	68	24	22	52	-66	12[8]	9[8]	——79[8]——	
Benin	1,140	270	499.8[1]	290.0[1]	81	8	15	21	-26	6[5]	10[5]	21[5]	63[5]
Bermuda	1,140	20,420	1.148	0.622	67	12	18	58	-55	...	...	...	...
Bhutan	200	160	2.678	2.452[18]	...	...	...	...	...	...	...	...	...
Bolivia	3,540	540	10.559	0.106	81	8	9	19	-18	10[15]	6[15]	36[15]	47[15]
Botswana	930	840	2.145	1.316	45	27	30	58	-60	13[5]	12[5]	37[5]	38[5]
Brazil	25,520	1,810	3,687.470	14.876	67	10	18	12	-7	10[9]	5[9]	——85[9]——	
British Virgin Islands	...	8,170[21]	0.098	...	43[5]	18[5]	38[5]	114[5]	-115[5]	12[22]	12	53[22]	36[12,22]
Brunei	3,590[21]	15,400[21]	7.529[1]	3.568[1]	...	...	...	...	...	...	...	...	...
Bulgaria	60,618	6,770	26.851[2]	25.923[2]	58[8]	11[8]	24[8]	——78——		...	...	...	...
Burkina Faso	1,240	150	363.8[8]	260.0[8]	86	16	28	17	-48	7[8]	6[8]	25[8]	61[8]
Burma	7,450	200	58.452	51.677	——89——		15	5	-9	7	9	38	45
Burundi	1,140	240	147.733	104.233	82	13	14	11	-19	11[9]	2[9]	21[9]	66[9]
Cameroon	9,580	910	3,838.9[8]	2,398.7[8]	62	10	26	19	-17	13[5]	5[5]	27[5]	54[5]
Canada	361,720	14,100	505.2	362.4	58	20	20	29	-26	10	11	54	24
Cape Verde	150	460	17.9[1]	...	97	11	23	9	-40	...	...	...	...
Cayman Islands	...	12,900[21]	0.230	...	...	...	...	...	...	...	...	...	...
Central African Republic	770	290	318.7[1]	202.7[1]	84	20	8	23	-34	12[27]	—	24[27]	64[27]
Chad	560[8]	110[8]	465.7[1]	...	82	22	7	19	-30	6[25]	7[25]	13[25]	75[25]
Chile	16,200	1,320	3,258.6	1,114.3	69	14	14	29	-26	14[9]	11[9]	42[9]	34[9]
China	314,800	300	779.0[2]	...	60[2]	9[2]	38[2]	——6[2]——		...	...	...	...
Christmas Island	...	...	...	...	...	...	...	...	...	...	...	...	...
Cocos (Keeling) Islands	...	...	...	...	...	...	...	...	...	...	...	...	...
Colombia	35,530	1,230	6,701.4	1,842.7	70	11	18	14	-13	9[8]	12	44[8]	47[8,12]
Comoros	130	280	48.750[1]	...	65	20	36	20	-41	...	...	...	...
Congo	2,020	1,040	920.1[8]	...	40	16	30	55	-42	16[8]	18[8]	27[8]	39[8]
Cook Islands	20[15]	1,110[15]	...	...	80[27]	32[27]	26[27]	32[27]	-71[27]	...	...	...	...
Costa Rica	3,790	1,420	242.118	44.037	62	16	24	32	-33	14	3	48	36
Côte d'Ivoire	7,730	740	2,827.8[1]	...	60	14	13	46	-33	19[9]	8[9]	35[9]	38[9]
Cuba	26,920[8]	2,690[8]	12,853.9[2]	14,475.5[2]	80[2]	9[2]	27[2]	——15[2]——		...	...	...	...
Cyprus	2,920	4,360	1.585	1.028	63	16	31	52	-62	8	11	——81——	
Czechoslovakia	142,550	9,180	562.2[2]	580.7[2]	68[2]	8[2]	19[2]	——52——		...	...	...	...
Denmark	64,610	12,640	662.2	434.6	55	25	20	37	-37	16	9	54	22
Djibouti	302[8]	740[8]	74.0[1]	...	77	36	23	42	-77	——17[28]——		35[28]	48[28]
Dominica	100	1,210	0.231[8]	0.203[8]	71[8]	25[8]	39[8]	37[8]	-72[8]	13[30]	3[30]	37[30]	47[30]
Dominican Republic	4,680	710	15.604	7.344	74	8	19	9	-11	7[8]	6[8]	——87[8]——	
Ecuador	11,200	1,160	1,366.3	335.8	64	11	18	27	-21	12	12	18	70[12]
Egypt	37,700	760	38.295	...	69	18	23	20	-29	6[9]	12	36[9]	59[9,12]

vate consumption (analyzed in greater detail in the "Household budgets and consumption" table), government spending, and gross domestic investment. The fourth, nondomestic, component of GDP expenditure is net foreign trade; values are given for both exports (a positive value) and imports (a negative value, representing obligations to other countries). The sum of these five percentages, excluding statistical discrepancies and rounding, should be 100% of the GDP.

The structure of GDP as accounted by cost components here comprises four general categories: indirect taxes (excise or value-added taxes), net of subsidies; consumption of fixed capital (depreciation); and two income categories: (a) compensation of employees (salaries, wages, etc.) and (b) net operating surplus ("profits," interests, rent, etc.).

The distribution of GDP for ten industrial sectors is aggregated into three major industrial groups:

1. The primary sector, composed of agriculture (including forestry and fishing) and mineral production (including fossil fuels).
2. The secondary sector, composed of manufacturing, construction, and public utilities.
3. The tertiary sector, which includes transportation and communications, trade (wholesale and retail), financial services (including banking, real estate, etc.), other (personal and business) services, and government.

Percentages in this section of the table may not add to 100 because the value of each industry is calculated as a percentage of the total GDP, which may contain significant monetary adjustments that are not distributable to all industries.

Average annual growth rate of real GDP. These columns show average annual growth rates of real product for the decade from 1970 to 1980, as well as for the six years from 1980 to 1986. Real GDP growth rates indicate the change in total output achieved by each country during the periods indicated excluding inflation.

Balance of payments (external account transactions). The external account records the sum (net) of all economic transactions of a current nature between one country and the rest of the world. The account shows a country's net of overseas receipts and obligations, including not only the trade of goods and services but also such invisible items as interest and dividends, short- and long-term investments, tourism, transfers to or from overseas residents, etc. Each transaction gives rise either to a foreign claim for payment, recorded as a deficit (e.g., from imports, capital outflows), or a foreign obligation to pay, recorded as a surplus (e.g., from exports, capital inflows) or a domestic claim on another country. Any international transaction automatically creates a deficit in the balance of payments of one country and a surplus in that of another. Values are given in U.S. dollars for comparability.

Tourist trade. Net income or expenditure from tourism is often a significant element in a country's balance of payments. Receipts from foreign nationals reflect payments for goods and services from foreign currency resources by tourists in the given country. Expenditures by nationals abroad are also payments for goods and services, but in this case made by the residents of the given country as tourists abroad. The U.S. dollar is used as the common currency for comparability by the World Tourism Organization.

origin of GDP by economic sector, 1985 (%)										avg. annual growth rate of real GDP (%)		balance of payments, 1987 (current external transactions; '000,000 U.S.$)			tourist trade, 1986 ('000,000 U.S.$)		country
primary		secondary			tertiary					1970–1980	1980–1986	net transfers		current balance of payments	receipts from foreign nationals	expenditures by nationals abroad	
agriculture	mining	manufacturing	construction	public utilities	transp., communications	trade	financial svcs.	other svcs.	govt.			goods-merchandise	invisibles				
65[2]	3	16[2,3]	4[2]	3	3[2]	10[2]	2[2]			2.1[2]	2.0[2]	−604[4]	48[4]	−556[4]	1	...	Afghanistan
34[2,5]	3	43[2,3,5]	8[2,5]	3	15[2,5]					6.3[2]	5.7[2,6]	...	...	...	...	...	Albania
9[8]	28[8]	13[8]	17[8]		5[8]	14[8]	14[8]			7.8	4.6	177[4]	−2,407[4]	−2,230[4]	137	446	Algeria
...	...	...	...		...	...	...			...	...	−60[4]			7	...	American Samoa
...	...	...	...		...	...	...			...	...	...	...	...	...	...	Andorra
46	23	3	2		27					−2.2	3.1	−34[9]	−175[9]	−209[9]	...	...	Angola
7	1	1	12	2	13	36	14	2	18	...	10.1[11]	...	...	...	9	...	Anguilla
44	24	64	8[4]	4[4]	22[4]	27[4]	23[4]		9[4]	2.3	4.5	−157[4]	81[4]	−76[4]	114	14	Antigua and Barbuda
16	3	23	3	5	12	13	8	18		2.4	−0.9	1,000	−5,285	−4,285	545	853	Argentina
...	...	...	...		...	...	...			...	...	...	...	...	110	17	Aruba
4	5	17	8	4	9	13	21	17	5	3.3	3.0	−512	−8,164	−8,676	1,371	1,932	Australia
3	14	28[14]	7	3	6	16	15	3	14	3.7	1.6	−4,471	4,268	−203	6,076	3,257	Austria
44	3	10[4]	3[4]	3	11[4]	26[4]	12[4]	16[4]	17[4]	6.3	...	−882	716	−166	1,114	131	Bahamas, The
1[8]	19[8]	11[8]	10[8]	18	10[8]	10[8]	15[8]	13[8]	10[8]	4.6	5.3[6]	177[4]	−142[4]	35[4]	100	112	Bahrain
52	14	8[14]	5	1	6	8	2	15	4	4.5	4.1	−1,381	1,043	−338	15	50	Bangladesh
6[4]	1[4]	9[4]	5[4]	3[4]	8[4]	27[4]	12[4]	18[4]		4.3	−0.5[16]	−278[4]	273[4]	−5[4]	327	23	Barbados
2	1	23	5	4	8	20	6	28		3.3	1.0	−156[17]	3,076[17]	2,920[17]	2,271[17]	2,889[17]	Belgium
21	—	10	6	3	9	15	35			4.9	3.0	−30	56	26	12	6	Belize
36	14	9[14]	5	1	9	19	21			3.9	3.4[16]	−156[7]	104[7]	−52[7]	10	4[8]	Benin
1[7]	—	4[7]	5[7]	2[7]	77	33[7]	22[7]	18[7]	8[7]	3.0	−0.1	−366[4]	436[4]	70[4]	407	19	Bermuda
50		4	11	—	3	11	20			4.1	6.3[19]	−63[20]	−32[20]	−95[20]	2	...	Bhutan
27	7	19	4	1	6	15	10	3	7	4.5	−2.4	−188	−300	−488	35	38	Bolivia
44	47[4]	64	3[4]	24	24	18[4]	5[4]	24	13[4]	15.8	11.1	730	−133	597	28	21	Botswana
10	1	28	6	4	8	16	10	11	7	8.6	2.8	8,348[4]	−12,825[4]	−4,477[4]	1,527	1,464	Brazil
5[23]		3[23]	10[23]	24	82[23,24]					3.7	−0.4[6]	−14[25]	13[25]	−1[25]	121	...	British Virgin Islands
1	54	10	4	—	3	12	15			8.9	−3.5[16]	...	...	...	...	...	Brunei
13[2]	3	60[2,3]	10[2]	3	7[2]	7[2]	32.2[6]			6.7[2]	4.0[2]	...	...	...	345	...	Bulgaria
43[8]		14[8]	1[8]	18	6[8]	12[8]	22[8]			5.3	2.8	−129[8]	125[8]	−4[8]	7	30	Burkina Faso
48	1	10	2	1	4	24	11			4.3	5.0	−202[1]	−4[1]	−206[1]	14	0.4	Burma
63[4]	1[4]	10[4]	5[4]		2[4]	7[4]		1[4]	10[4]	4.0	3.9	−60			35	18	Burundi
25	17	11	6	1	5	28			8	4.5	8.3	443[4]	−1,037[4]	−594[4]	47	130	Cameroon
4[4]	6[4]	20[4]	7[4]	3[4]	8[4]	12[4]	14[4]	20[4]	6[4]	4.1	2.6	8,755	−15,990	−7,235	3,860	4,294	Canada
24	1	5	21		49					−0.2	7.4	−667	647	−27	...	...	Cape Verde
...	...	...	...		...	...	...			...	...	−96[5]	153[5]	57[5]	94	...	Cayman Islands
41	2	7	2	1	4	21	20			2.6	1.5[16]	−72[4]	−15[4]	−87[4]	3[28]	33	Central African Republic
46	1	9	2		42					0.5	−2.8	−150	67	−83	12	20	Chad
10[4]	8[4]	21[4]	6[4]	3[4]	6[4]	17[4]	30[4]			2.8	0.6	1,230	−2,041	−811	172	319	Chile
41[29]	...	41[29]	6[29]	...	3[29]	8[29]	...			5.8	9.8[16]	−9,140[4]	2,106[4]	−7,034[4]	1,530	314	China
...	...	...	...		...	...	...			...	...	...	...	...	...	...	Christmas Island
...	...	...	...		...	...	...			...	...	...	...	...	...	...	Cocos (Keeling) Islands
21[4]	3[4]	22[4]	4[4]	1[4]	10[4]	12[4]	7[4]	13[4]	8[4]	5.5	2.6	1,826	−1,571	255	220	340	Colombia
37	...	4	10		4	25		20		2.0	3.8	−35	12	−23	2	13	Comoros
8[8]	43[8]	5[8]	7[8]	18	7[8]	11[8]	18[8]			4.7	5.1	160[4]	−761[4]	−601[4]	7	67	Congo
26[15]	...	11[15]	9[15]	2[15]	7[15]	14[15]	3[15]	...	...	−2.6	3.2[6]	−20[4]			16	...	Cook Islands
20	1[4]	22[14]	5	3	7	16	13	4	10	5.7	1.0	36[4]	−201[4]	−165[4]	133	60	Costa Rica
28[8]	3[8]	12[8]	2[8]	18	7[8]	47[8]				6.5	1.3	1,546[4]	−1,684[4]	−138[4]	70	96	Côte d'Ivoire
10[2]	3	36[2,3]	10[2]	3	7[2]	37[2]	12.2[6]			5.8[2]	6.6[2]	...	...	...	80	...	Cuba
74		15[4]	10[4]	24	10[4]	19[4]	14[4]	10[4]	7[4]	4.2	5.2	−777	869	92	497	103	Cyprus
8[2]	3	60[2,3]	11[2]	3	5[2]	16[2]	12.2[6]			4.6[2]	3.1[2]	...	...	...	307	229	Czechoslovakia
6	1	21	6	1	8	14	3	21	22	2.4	2.5	812	−3,792	−2,980	1,759	2,119	Denmark
4[8]	—	8[8]	7[8]	3[8]	10[8]	16[8]	11[8]	2[8]	27[8]	0.9	1.4	−100[9]	75[9]	−25[9]	6	...	Djibouti
29[4]	14	9[4]	7[4]	24	9[4]	14[4]	12[4]		21[4]	2.9	6.2[6]	−114	74	−44	11	3	Dominica
17	4	17	6	2	8	16	10	20		7.0	1.7	−544[4]	425[4]	−119[4]	464	90	Dominican Republic
14	17	19	5	—	9	16	4	8	7	9.1	2.3	−33	−1,155	−1,188	135	210	Ecuador
16[4]	14	33[4,14]	5[4]	14	8[4]	13[4]	5[4]	4[4]	15[4]	7.1	7.1	−4,011[4]	2,141[4]	−1,870[4]	785	106	Egypt

National product and accounts   (continued)

country	gross national product (GNP), 1986		gross domestic product (GDP), 1986		GDP by type of expenditure, 1985 (%)					cost components of GDP, 1985 (%)			
	nominal ('000,000 U.S.$)	per capita (U.S.$)	nominal ('000,000,000 national currency)	real (constant prices of 1980; '000,000,000 national currency)	consumption private	government	gross domestic investment	foreign trade exports	imports	indirect taxes net of subsidies	consumption of fixed capital	compensation of employees	net operating surplus
El Salvador	4,000	820	19.763	8.166	81	15	11	22	-30	9	4	—87—	
Equatorial Guinea	107[21]	330[21]	34.540	...	54	32	15	28	-30	...	...	...	...
Ethiopia	5,400	120	10.804	8.959	80	19	11	11	-22	...	...	...	...
Faeroe Islands	550	12,180	5.460	...	61[4]	20[4]	39[4]	45[4]	-65[4]	9[4]	12	62[4]	29[4,12]
Falkland Islands	...	...	...	...									
Fiji	1,280	1,810	1.340[1]	1.046[1]	63	19	17	44	-44	10	7	46	38
Finland	60,040	12,180	357.2	228.5	54	21	25	29	-28	11	14	55	20
France	595,180	10,740	5,018.8	3,086.0	61	20	19	24	-23	13	12	54	21
French Guiana	180[5]	2,340[5]	...	...									
French Polynesia	1,370[1,21]	7,830[1,21]	136.953[9]	104.446[9]	68[9]	34[9]	32[9]	12[9]	-45[9]	6[9]	17[9]	46[9]	31[9]
Gabon	3,150	3,020	1,537.0[9]	...	30	17	34	59	-40	18[7]	14[7]	30[7]	37[7]
Gambia, The	180	230	0.990	...	74	21	26	69	-91				
Gaza Strip	544	1,020	0.495	0.002	152[4]	14[4]	34[4]	47[4]	-148[4]				
Germany, East	187,751	11,170	252.2[2,32]	...	57[8]	11[8]	18[8]	—138—		10[2,9]	9[2,9]	40[2,9]	41[2,9]
Germany, West	735,940	12,080	1,936.9	1,608.5	57	20	20	35	-31	10	13	54	23
Ghana	5,130	390	373.0[1]	41.9[1]	82	10	10	10	-12	5[22]	3[22]	—91[22]—	
Gibraltar	130[1]	4,550[1]	0.074[1]	...									
Greece	36,690	3,680	5,564.6	1,850.6	69	21	22	22	-35	10	9	42	39
Greenland	470	8,790	...	...									
Grenada	120	1,240	0.348	0.257	80	22	30	45	-77				
Guadeloupe	1,100[1,21]	3,300[1,21]	9.884[1]	...	96[5]	33[5]	24[5]	7[5]	-60[5]	11[15]	12	70[15]	19[12,15]
Guam	670	5,660	...	...									
Guatemala	7,640	930	15.785	7.448	83	7	12	18	-20				
Guernsey	1,350[1,35]	9,900[1,35]	...	...									
Guinea	1,950[1]	320[1]	857.4[1]	...	67	16	14	24	-22				
Guinea-Bissau	150	170	21.2[1]	...	79	33	37	14	-65				
Guyana	400	500	2.219	...	58[8]	32[8]	23[8]	55[8]	-68[8]	17[8]	7[8]	—76[8]—	...
Haiti	1,990	330	11.218	6.867	—94—		17	24	-35	10[9]	3[9]	—87[9]—	
Honduras	3,360	740	7.477	5.506	72	15	18	26	-30	12	5	—84—	
Hong Kong	37,360[21]	6,720[21]	295.348	199.634	65	7	21	106	-99	—78—		48[8]	45[8]
Hungary	83,806	7,890	1,088.8	798.9	63	10	25	42	-40				
Iceland	3,260	13,370	158.993	18.031	63	17	19	42	-41	22[8]	13[8]	—65[8]—	
India	213,440	270	2,927.9	1,854.8	68[8]	11[8]	25[8]	7[8]	-9[8]	12	7	—81—	
Indonesia	82,110	500	94,492.0[1]	56,543.0[1]	56	12	31	23	-21	3	5	—92—	
Iran	188,200	4,170	15,305.8[1]	9,044.3[1]	57	16	27	8	-7	2[8]	7[8]	—91[8]—	
Iraq	34,470[8]	2,310[8]	14.547[1]	...	—91[9]—		42[9]	24[9]	-57[9]	—	12[9]	34[9]	53[9]
Ireland	18,190	5,080	18.239	10.227	58	19	21	62	-60	10	9	55	26
Isle of Man	340[41]	5,280[41]	0.200[41]	0.156[41]									
Israel	26,730	6,210	41.044	0.127	59	38	18	46	-61	14	13	46	27
Italy	489,880	8,570	894,362.0	434,681.0	63	17	23	21	-23	9	10	55	27
Jamaica	1,980	880	13.328	4.873	70	15	25	58	-68	12	9	44	35
Japan	1,559.720	12,850	330,116.0	297,736.0	58	10	29	16	-13	7	14	55	24
Jersey	1,230	15,330	0.998	...									
Jordan	4,220	1,540	1.614	1.241	90	26	28	49	-93	13	8	43	36
Kampuchea	600[28]	90[28]	...	...									
Kenya	6,470	300	116.635	...	61	18	22	27	-28	13	12	37	50[12]
Kiribati	21[21]	330[21]	0.032	0.023	93[15]	36[15]	44[15]	23[15]	-96[15]	5[15]	5[15]	30[15]	61[15]
Korea, North	17,400	860	11.8[9]	...									
Korea, South	98,370	2,370	86,653.0	61,063.0	59	10	30	36	-36	12	9	41	38
Kuwait	24,650	13,890	4.998	6.475	45	25	21	59	-49				
Laos	765[8]	220[8]	...	...									
Lebanon	5,000[5]	1,900[5]	12.599[9]	...	—110[7]—		18[7]	—28[7]—		8[30]	5[30]	—88[30]—	
Lesotho	660	410	0.647	0.329	187	39	45	23	-195	22[5]	3[5]	40[5]	35[5]
Liberia	1,030[1]	450[1]	1.057[1]	0.797[1]	46	18	17	58	-39	14[9]		—86[9]—	
Libya	26,980[1]	7,170[1]	6.473	...	39	33	24	46	-42	4[9]	5[9]	30[9]	61[9]
Liechtenstein	450	16,500	...	...									
Luxembourg	5,830	15,920	239.0[1]	170.2[1]	53	13	19	101	-86	13	11	58	18
Macau	1,030	2,680[1]	...	...									
Madagascar	2,390	230	1,806.9	...	73	18	15	11	-17	12[7]	1[7]	—87[7]—	
Malawi	1,180	160	2.301	1.132	70	17	18	23	-28	9[7]	7[7]	27[7]	57[7]
Malaysia	29,500	1,850	71.731	69.127	52	15	28	55	-50	16[22]	12	32[22]	52[12,22]
Maldives	60	310	0.537[8]	0.511[8]	59	18	33	68	-78				
Mali	1,330	170	470.2[8]	...	78	12	31	20	-41	8[9]	7[9]	25[9]	60[9]
Malta	1,240	3,470	0.512	0.443	70	18	28	73	-88	9	4	47	39
Martinique	1,400[1,21]	4,280[1,21]	12.577[1]	...	87	33	17	12	-49	10[15]	12	66[15]	24[12,15]
Mauritania	760	440	44.500[8]	36,059[8]	65	27	20	57	-69	9[25]	6[25]	27[25]	58[25]
Mauritius	1,240	1,2000	19.240	...	67	12	22	54	-56	16	12	42	42[12]
Mayotte	...	...	...	...									
Mexico	149,110	1,850	77,778.0	4,460.4	61[8]	10[8]	22[8]	18[8]	-10[8]	10[8]	6[8]	28[8]	56[8]
Monaco	280[9]	10,260[9]	...	...									
Mongolia	1,911[1]	1,010[1]	...	...									
Montserrat	30[1]	2,530[1]	0.114	0.076	96	20	26	12	-54				
Morocco	13,160	590	134.3	...	71	16	22	27	-35	14[15]	12	33[15]	53[12,15]
Mozambique	3,030	210	88.5	...	87	18	12	5	-21				
Nauru	160[8]	20,000[8]	...	...									
Nepal	2,640	160	50.124	29.408	80	8	21	13	-22	6[8]	5[8]	—89[8]—	
Netherlands, The	146,200	10,050	429.6	361.2	59	16	20	64	-59	9	10	52	29
Netherlands Antilles	860[1]	6,020[1]	2.558[9,13]	...	55[13,15]	24[13,15]	21[13,15]	110[13,15]	-109[13,15]	5[9,13]	8[9,13]	73[9,13]	14[9,13]
New Caledonia	1,210[5]	8,300[5]	114.2[5]	...	60[5]	35[5]	17[5]	27[5]	-39[5]	3[5]	9[5]	59[5]	29[5]
New Zealand	23,300	7,110	53.382	...	59	16	27	32	-34	10	8	49	33
Nicaragua	2,670	790	435.742	21.335	48	36	23	15	-22	9[22]	4[22]	56[22]	31[22]
Niger	1,690	260	682.3[1]	...	76	10	16	31	-33	9[15]	7[15]	16[15]	68[15]
Nigeria	66,210	640	...	39.886	75	8	9	18	-11	4[5]	2[5]	29[5]	65[5]
Niue	4[15]	1,160[15]	...	...									
Norfolk Island	...	...	...	...									

agri-culture	mining	manu-factur-ing	con-struc-tion	public util-ities	transp., commu-nications	trade	finan-cial svcs.	other svcs.	govt.	1970–1980	1980–1986	goods-merchan-dise	invisibles	current balance of payments	receipts from foreign nationals	expendi-tures by nationals abroad	country
24	—	18	3	4	6	17	8	7	13	3.4	-1.5	-216[1]	187[1]	-29[1]	22	89	El Salvador
59	—	1	9	2	2	4	—23—			-9.4	2.9	-15[28]	-3[28]	-18[28]	...	...	Equatorial Guinea
44	—	11	4	1	7	11	4	7	9	2.6	0.8	-508[1]	614[1]	106[1]	5	4	Ethiopia
16[4]	...	24[4]	9[4]	3[4]	11[4]	14[4]	9[4]	—22[4]—		...	...	-107[4]	46[4]	-61[4]	...	...	Faeroe Islands
...	...																Falkland Islands
17	1	10	6	3	10	17	14	—24—		3.9	1.2[16]	-122[4]	127[4]	5[4]	185	24	Fiji
9	1	28	7	3	8	11	16	4	15	3.7	2.9	1,323	-3,262	-1,949	596	1,060	Finland
4	2	26	6	3	5	9	12	19	14	3.6	1.6	-9,820	4,729	-5,091	9,704	6,504	France
57	...	4[7]	8[7]	-17	7[7]	12[7]	9[7]	—56[7]—		2.9	-4.8[6]	-260[4]	...	...	...	...	French Guiana
5[8]	...	10[8]	12[8]	71[8]	7[8]	14[8]	—53[8]—			5.4	5.3[6]	-379[9]	337[9]	-42[9]	146	...	French Polynesia
7[4]	24[4]	5[4]	9[4]	2[4]	5[4]	13[4]	1[4]	11[4]	14[4]	7.5	-1.7	555	-998	-443	4	83	Gabon
26	—	4	3	1	9	27	6	2	13	2.2	2.6	-26	40	14	2	11	Gambia, The
22[4]	14	13[4,14]	22[4]	24	—43[4,24]—					7.1[31]	1.6	-237[4]	295[4]	58[4]	41	81	Gaza Strip
8[2]	3	70[2,3]	6[2]	3	4[2]	9[2]	—32,26—			4.9[2]	4.5[2]	...	...	...	...	...	Germany, East
2	4[33]	33	5	33	—14—		—26—		11	2.7	1.4	70,160	-24,930	45,230	7,826	20,664	Germany, West
41	1	11	3	1	7	28	—8—			1.3	0.7	-125	28	-97	2	11	Ghana
...	...	...	...	...	...	...	...	...	...			-95[4]	...	...	18	...	Gibraltar
17[4]	2[4]	18[4]	6[4]	3[4]	8[4]	—16[4]—		8[4]	17[4]	4.8	1.3	-5,498	4,200	-1,298	1,834	494	Greece
16[7]	14	32[7,14]	27[7]	34	3[4]	8[7]	—127,34—			...	...	-103	...	...	...	...	Greenland
17[4]	—	5[4]	9[4]	2[4]	14[4]	20[4]	—16[4]—		22[4]	3.4	4.1	-47[4]	37[4]	-10[4]	27	5	Grenada
7[15]	1[4]	6[14,15]	4[15]	—	4[15]	18[15]	11[15]	20[15]	29[15]	5.2	1.2[6]	-627[15]	458[15]	-169[15]	98	...	Guadeloupe
—	...	13[9]	8[9]	...	6[9]	52[9]	10[9]	—12[9]—		...	...	...	...	...	308	304	Guam
26	—	16	2	2	7	25	9	6	7	5.7	-0.9	-383	-87	-470	77	24	Guatemala
...	...	...	...														Guernsey
40	13	2	6	—	1	21	3	—12—		2.7	-3.5						Guinea
58	...	4	3	...	—14—		—2—		19	1.4	2.5	-65[1]	15[1]	-50[1]	...	...	Guinea-Bissau
26	9	11	7	36	7	7	7	3	23[36]	1.8	-5.6[37]	5[1]	-102[1]	-97[1]	4	11[5]	Guyana
32	—	17	6	1	2	18	6	11	7	4.8	-0.7	-109	78	-31	58	38	Haiti
24	2	12	5	2	7	12	11	8	5	4.8	1.3	-31	-162	-183	26	30	Honduras
1	—	22	5	3	8	23	27	—17—		9.6	6.5	11	...	...	2,211	...	Hong Kong
12[2]	14	39[2,14]	10[2]	12	7[2]	12[2]	—19[2,26]—			5.0	1.7	166	-746	-580	611	241	Hungary
22[4]	—	13[4]	8[4]	38	10[4]	21[4,38]	38	—27[4]—		4.9	2.6	-52	-139	-191	60	114	Iceland
31	3	17	5	2	7	15	8	6	5	3.3	5.1[19]	-5,438[4]	811[4]	-4,627[4]	1,390	354	India
24	16	14	5	1	7	15	—19—			8.0	4.5[16]	4,968	-6,646	-1,678	591	699	Indonesia
19	10	8	7	1	7	20	—29—			3.6	5.7[16]	2,358[8]	-2,772[8]	-414[8]	28	488	Iran
16	25	10	8	1	5	11	—25—			9.3	-3.1[6]	...	...	...	100	...	Iraq
11	39	36[39]	39	39	—19—		—28—		7	4.6	1.5	2,615	-2,215	400	634[40]	685	Ireland
3	—	16	10	3	11	12	30	24	8	3.7	-4.1	...	...	...	36	...	Isle of Man
5	14	23[14]	4	2	8	14	—43—			3.4	2.3	-3,806	2,807	-999	969	847	Israel
5	3	23	7	5	7	16	12	9	14	3.2	1.8	95	-1,173	-1,078	9,855	2,758	Italy
6	5	20	8	3	8	24	—25—			-0.7	0.4	-358	261	-97	516	32	Jamaica
3	—	30	7	3	6	14	15	20	5	4.7	3.7	96,460	-9,460	87,000	1,463	7,229	Japan
4[4]	—	—2[4]—			—94[4]—					...	...	-328[15]	...	...	293	...	Jersey
7	3	14	8	2	11	17	—38—			7.1	3.9	-1,467	1,115	-352	534	443	Jordan
...	...	...	...	...	...	...	...			-8.8	-2.1[6]	...			...	...	Kampuchea
27	—	11	5	2	6	11	13	3	13	6.1	2.9	-291[4]	189[4]	-102[4]	313	21	Kenya
27[4]	—	2[4]	5[4]	3[4]	14[4]	11[4]	6[4]	2[4]	25[4]	0.6	0.0	...	...	...	...	...	Kiribati
...	...	...	...	...	...	...	...			5.9[2]	8.5[2,6]	...			...	...	Korea, North
14	1	31	8	3	8	13	11	5	6	8.3	8.3	7,659	2,195	9,854	1,550	613	Korea, South
—	46	6	3	3	4	10	10	—19—		2.3	-2.9	3,545	869	4,414	86	1,222	Kuwait
75[8]	3	5[3,8]	5	3	18	12[8]	—18—			0.8	2.4[6]	...	...	...	...	...	Laos
9[25]	14	13[14,25]	3[25]	5[25]	8[25]	28[25]	—23[25]—		10[25]	1.5	-8.6[6]	...	...	...	...	...	Lebanon
18	—	10	9	1	2	15	12	24	10	9.0	2.3	-316[4]	299[4]	-17[4]	7	5	Lesotho
17	17	7	3	2	6	6	—41—			0.6	-3.8	149[4]	-57[4]	92[4]	6	...	Liberia
4	56	4	—9—		—27—					7.5	-3.3	1,248[4]	-1,302[4]	-54[4]	4	409	Libya
...		...	...	...	...	...	...	...	...	...	...				...	...	Liechtenstein
3	—	30	5	3	6	16	13	13	12	4.4	2.6[16]	17	17	17	...	...	Luxembourg
...	...	...	...	...	...	...	...			...	...				...	...	Macau
42	39	16[39]	39	39	—42—					0.7	-0.2	-19[8]	-16[48]	-183[8]	5.6	21	Madagascar
36	—	12	4	2	6	18	7	4	13	5.1	1.9	63[4]	-63[4]	—4	8	7	Malawi
21[4]	11[4]	21[4]	4[4]	2[4]	7[4]	12[4]	8[4]	—	12[4]	8.1	4.4	5,825	-3,489	-2,336	612	1,192	Malaysia
35	1	4[42]	6	42	5	8	—25—		16	13.2	9.5[6]	-36[1]	271	-91	42	5	Maldives
52	3	7	—6—		—32—					0.3	2.1	-115[4]	-344	-149[4]	16	25	Mali
5	43	29	5[43]	5	6	15	5	16	14	10.6	2.1	-393	404	11	150	33	Malta
89	14	6[9,14]	4[9]	19	4[9]	17[9]	—55[9]—			3.9	0.1[6]	-736[15]	581[15]	-155[15]	92	...	Martinique
19[8]	10[8]	9[8,42]	8[8]	42	7[8]	—135—		18[8]	6[8]	2.2	1.5	18[4]	-204[4]	-186[4]	7	22[5]	Mauritania
14	—	20	5	3	11	13	16	6	11	5.9	4.4	58[4]	36[4]	94[4]	89	26	Mauritius
...	...	...	...														Mayotte
9	4	25	5	2	8	24	9	12	4	6.6	0.7	8,433	-4,549	3,884	2,984	2,132	Mexico
...	...	...	...														Monaco
16[2]	14	33[2,14]	—5[2]—		11[2]	33[2]	—22,26—			6.1[2]	6.4[2]	...	...	...	...	...	Mongolia
4	1	6	7	3	11	17	—51—			4.6	2.6	-8[1]	7[1]	-1[1]	8	...	Montserrat
18	7	17	7	2	5	13	3	16	12	5.6	2.8	-1,067[4]	855[4]	-212[4]	800	100	Morocco
44[4]	14	26[4,14]	11[4]	...	8[4]	—10[4]—				-0.6	-8.2	-372[5]	178[5]	-194[5]	...	...	Mozambique
...	...	...	...	...	...	...	...			...	...				...	...	Nauru
58[8]	—	4[8]	7	—	6[8]	4[8]	—21[8]—			2.1	3.9	-350	227	-123	43	29	Nepal
4	10	19	6	2	7	15	—29—		14	3.4	1.2	5,237	-1,848	3,389	2,228	4,970	Netherlands, The
1	—	13	10	3	12	18	16	6	24	...	...	-690	640	-50	255	107[5]	Netherlands Antilles
2[5]	55	10[5]	5[5]	25	4[5]	27[5]	—17[5]—		28[5]	0.7	-2.0[6]	-106[5]	273[5]	167[5]	40	...	New Caledonia
11	1	24	5	3	8	18	15	5	11	2.4	2.5	578	-2,251	-1,673	277	400	New Zealand
23	—	27	4	1	5	17	6	4	11	1.8	-0.4	-479[4]	-214[4]	-693[4]	5	7[5]	Nicaragua
45	8	4	3	2	4	—13—		13	8	3.9	0.6	-39	-31	-70	8	13	Niger
27	20	9	5	1	3	20	4	4	8	4.9	-3.6	2,535[4]	-2,170[4]	365[4]	175	109	Nigeria
...	...	...	...	...	...	...	...			...	...				0.6	...	Niue
...	...	...	...	...	...	...	...			...	...				...	...	Norfolk Island

National product and accounts   (continued)

country	gross national product (GNP), 1986		gross domestic product (GDP), 1986		GDP by type of expenditure, 1985 (%)						cost components of GDP, 1985 (%)			
	nominal ('000,000 U.S.$)	per capita (U.S.$)	nominal ('000,000,000 national currency)	real (constant prices of 1980; '000,000,000 national currency)	consumption		gross domestic invest-ment	foreign trade		indirect taxes net of subsidies	consump-tion of fixed capital	compen-sation of employ-ees	net operating surplus
					private	govern-ment		exports	imports				
Norway	64,440	15,480	516.0	351.1	49	18	24	47	−39	13	14	48	25
Oman	6,440	4,990	3.457[1]	4.167[1]	33	25	27	48	−33	1[28]	99[28]		
Pacific Is., Trust Terr. of the	160[8]	1,030[8]	...	...	...	...	...	...	...	...	...	...	...
Marshall Islands	...	...	0.046	...	...	...	...	...	...	10[8]	4[8]	51[8]	36[8]
Micronesia, F.S. of	...	...	0.107	...	...	...	...	...	...	...	...	...	...
Northern Mariana Is.	...	...	0.256	...	...	...	...	...	...	...	...	...	...
Palau	...	...	0.032	...	...	...	...	...	...	5	5	62	28
Pakistan	34,690	350	539.5	346.8	83	12	17	10	−22	9	6	85	
Panama	5,190	2,330	5.121	4.214	63	21	15	35	−35	8	8	51	33
Papua New Guinea	2,470	690	2.472	...	62	24	23	44	−53	8	9	38	45
Paraguay	3,360	880	1,833.8	627.2	76	6	22	35	−40	5	10	31	54
Peru	21,540	1,130	157,977[1]	4.842[1]	68	11	14	26	−19	9[5]	7[5]	31[5]	53[5]
Philippines	31,820	570	626.7	259.5	77	7	14	21	−18	8	11	81	
Pitcairn Island	...	...	...	...	...	...	...	...	...	...	...	...	...
Poland	259,524	6,930	12,953.0	...	62	10	28	18	−17	...	...	...	...
Portugal	22,880	2,230	3,524.8[1]	1,319.6[1]	68	14	20	39	−41	10	4	45	41
Puerto Rico	17,190	5,190	21.109[1]	17.657[1]	74	15	10	58	−56	6	6	44	43
Qatar	4,180	12,520	18.018	...	31	44	22	40	−37	...	...	...	...
Réunion	2,120[21]	3,940[21]	18.857	...	87	32	21	7	−47	10[9]	12	63[9]	27[9, 12]
Romania	137,346	6,020	871.8	...	58	6	32	4		...	...	...	...
Rwanda	1,820	290	161.9	...	75	17	17	9	−17	8[8]	4[8]	19[8]	69[8]
St. Helena	...	...	...	...	...	...	...	...	...	...	...	...	...
St. Kitts	70	1,700	0.167[8]	0.154[8]	78[8]	22[8]	32[8]	56[8]	−87[8]	17[47]	4[47]	67[47]	13[47]
St. Lucia	180	1,320	0.408[8]	0.348[8]	62[8]	25[8]	35[8]	64[8]	−86[8]	...	...	...	...
St. Pierre and Miquelon	...	...	...	...	...	...	...	...	...	...	...	...	...
St. Vincent	110	960	0.274[1]	0.201[1]	57[8]	29[8]	31[8]	71[8]	−89[8]	17[7]	8[7]	49[7]	26[7]
San Marino	188[48]	8,590[48]	...	...	...	...	...	...	...	...	...	...	...
São Tomé and Príncipe	40	340	1.912[1]	...	70	48	27	33	−79	10[49]	4[49]	46[49]	40[49]
Saudi Arabia	83,270	6,930	286.7	322.6	44	35	28	41	−48	—	12	17[9]	83[9, 12]
Senegal	2,840	420	1,186.9[1]	763.1[1]	77	19	15	30	−41	17[28]	6[28]	77[28]	
Seychelles	160[1]	2,450[1]	1.163[1]	0.963[1]	63	32	23	47	−64	18[8]	6[8]	39[8]	37[8]
Sierra Leone	1,170	310	5.932	...	67	8	31	20	−27	4[5]	10[5]	26[5]	60[5]
Singapore	19,160	7,410	37.774	34.270	45	13	44	3		10[5]	14[5]	29[5]	47[5]
Solomon Islands	150	530	0.193[1]	...	...	...	...	...	...	10[5]	14[5]	29[5]	47[5]
Somalia	1,560	280	82.1[1]	...	48	19	24	51	−41	...	...	...	...
South Africa	59,910	1,800	139.695	65.646	53	17	20	33	−23	8	16	52	23
Bophuthatswana	1,736[8, 51]	950[8, 51]	1.207[1]	...	...	...	...	...	...	...	...	...	...
Ciskei	377[1]	490[1]	0.397[1]	...	...	...	...	...	...	...	...	...	...
Transkei	1,471[8, 51]	470[8, 51]	1.458[1]	...	...	...	...	...	...	...	...	...	...
Venda	201[8, 51]	490[8, 51]	0.245[1]	...	...	...	...	...	...	...	...	...	...
S.W. Africa/Namibia	1,150	1,020	2.929	1.393	53[4]	29[4]	12[4]	63[4]	−57[4]	7[4]	5[4]	46[4]	42[4]
Spain	188,030	4,840	32,085.0	16,845.0	65	14	19	23	−21	7	12	47	34
Sri Lanka	6,460	400	179.474	...	78	10	24	26	−38	14	5	45	35
Sudan, The	7,290	320	10.421[1]	...	70	18	21	16	−25	7[28]	9[28]	40[28]	44[28]
Suriname	1,010	2,510	1.751	1.572	48	34	17	37	−35	12[8]	10[8]	68[8]	9[8]
Swaziland	470	600	0.957	...	94	27	30	86	−137	20[28]	6[28]	44[28]	30[28]
Sweden	109,950	13,170	933.7	580.6	51	28	19	35	−33	12	11	58	19
Switzerland	115,360	17,840	243.6	187.1	62	14	24	39	−39	6	10	62	22
Syria	16,980	1,560	98.374	65.319	62	25	24	11	−22	4	3	93	
Taiwan	73,270	3,790	2,701.8	2,597.0	51	17	18	56	−42	11	9	50	30
Tanzania	5,370	240	149.467	44.936	87	9	13	7	−17	10	2	13	75
Thailand	42,440	810	1,098.4	904.7	65	13	23	26	−27	11	9	27	54
Togo	780	250	281.3[5]	209.4[5]	76	15	23	35	−48	14[9]	7[9]	28[9]	51[9]
Tokelau	0.9[15]	560[15]	...	...	...	...	...	...	...	...	...	...	...
Tonga	70	740	0.073[5]	0.073[5]	96[5]	18[5]	28[5]	41[5]		11[5]	3[5]	37[5]	48[5]
Trinidad and Tobago	6,170	5,120	18.140[1]	12.468[1]	51	23	21	33	−29	—	8	61	32
Tunisia	8,340	1,140	7.025	...	63	16	27	33	−39	14[8]	10[8]	76[8]	
Turkey	57,120	1,110	39,155.0	5,914.9	79[8]	10[8]	20[8]	12[8]	−21[8]	7	5	88	
Turks and Caicos Is.	...	4,490[21]	0.045	...	...	...	...	...	...	...	...	...	...
Tuvalu	5[28]	680[28]	0.004[5]	...	...	...	...	...	...	...	...	...	...
Uganda	3,290[8]	230[8]	2,855.1[1]	...	111	19	16	6	−52	16[25]	8[25]	26[25]	49[25]
U.S.S.R.	2,356,700	8,410	576.0	563.1[2]	72[2, 5]		26[2, 5]	22[2, 5]		...	...	...	...
United Arab Emirates	20,590	14,410	78.3	78.1	27	20	25	59	−31	−3[8]	17[8]	24[8]	61[8]
United Kingdom	504,850	8,920	373.4	258.7	61	21	17	29	−28	14	12	56	20
United States	4,221,750	17,500	4,185.5	3,215.2	66	18	19	7	−10	8	13	60	19
Uruguay	5,630	1,860	945.037	83.942	75	13	8	23	−20	13	2	84	
Vanuatu	118[1]	880[1]	9.442[9]	...	...	...	...	...	...	...	...	...	...
Venezuela	51,940	2,930	403.9	250.5	62	13	15	27	−17	7	8	38	46
Vietnam	18,100[8]	310[8]	...	...	...	...	...	...	...	...	...	...	...
Virgin Islands (U.S.)	...	10,050[21]	1.070	...	...	...	...	...	...	...	...	...	...
Wallis and Futuna	10[9]	920[9]	...	...	...	...	...	...	...	...	...	...	...
West Bank	1,438	1,740	1.826	0.005	97[4]	9[4]	31[4]	21[4]	−57[4]	...	...	...	...
Western Sahara	...	...	...	...	...	...	...	...	...	...	...	...	...
Western Samoa	110	680	...	...	...	...	...	...	...	...	...	...	...
Yemen (Aden)	1,030	480	0.311[9]	...	106[15]	42[15]	49[15]	14[15]	−111[15]	19[9]	7[9]	57[9]	17[9]
Yemen (San'ā')	4,510	550	19.297[8]	14.996[8]	93	22	21	5	−41	15[9]	2[9]	31[9]	52[9]
Yugoslavia	144,825	6,220	25,083.2[52]	1,662.8[52]	48	13	40	21	−22	7	11	82	
Zaire	5,070	160	203.416	18.779	48	12	29	72	−61	9[25]	7[25]	84[25]	
Zambia	2,060	300	12.098	3.209	59	24	15	37	−35	12	13	45	30
Zimbabwe	5,410	620	8.880	4.286	58	19	23	26	−26	12[8]	12	53[8]	31[8, 12]

[1]1985. [2]Net material product. [3]Manufacturing includes mining and public utilities. [4]1986. [5]1983. [6]1980–84. [7]1979. [8]1984. [9]1982. [10]At prices of 1984. [11]1984–87. [12]Net operating surplus includes consumption of fixed capital. [13]Netherlands Antilles includes Aruba. [14]Manufacturing includes mining. [15]1980. [16]1980–85. [17]Data refer to the Belgium–Luxembourg Economic Union (BLEU) and exclude transactions between the two countries. [18]At prices of 1981. [19]1981–86. [20]1986–87. [21]GDP. [22]1978. [23]1983–85 average. [24]Tertiary sector includes public utilities. [25]1977. [26]Activities in the material sphere not elsewhere specified. [27]1970. [28]1981. [29]National income. [30]1973. [31]1968–80. [32]At prices of 1985. [33]Mining includes public utilities.

origin of GDP by economic sector, 1985 (%); avg. annual growth rate of real GDP (%); balance of payments, 1987 (current external transactions; '000,000 U.S.$) — net transfers; tourist trade, 1986 ('000,000 U.S.$)

primary		secondary			tertiary					avg. annual growth rate of real GDP (%)		balance of payments, 1987 — net transfers		current balance of payments	tourist trade, 1986		country
agri-culture	mining	manu-facturing	con-struction	public utilities	transp./commu-nications	trade	finan-cial svcs.	other svcs.	govt.	1970–1980	1980–1986	goods-merchan-dise	invisibles		receipts from foreign nationals	expendi-tures by nationals abroad	
4	20	14	5	4	9	12	7	8	18	4.8	3.5	−869	−3,268	−4,137	991	2,426	Norway
3	48	3	7	1	3	13	9	1	15	3.6	15.1[16]	607[4]	−1,576[4]	−969[4]	...	47	Oman
...	...	...	...	...	...	...	...	...	...	...	...	...	...	...	...	...	Pacific Is., Trust. Terr. of
...	...	...	...	...	...	...	...	...	...	...	...	...	...	...	...	...	Marshall Islands
...	...	...	...	...	...	...	...	...	...	...	...	...	...	...	...	...	Micronesia, F.S of
...	...	...	...	...	...	...	...	...	...	...	...	...	...	...	140	...	Northern Mariana Is.
16	—	—	11	1	3	19	4	2	36	...	...	−27[1]	...	...	...	...	Palau
25	2	17	5	2	8	17	6	8	9	4.7	6.7	−2,310	1,756	−554	180	228	Pakistan
9	—	9	5	4	13	14	46			5.6	2.9	−586[4]	1,041[4]	455[4]	210	66	Panama
33[5]	11[5]	9[5]	4[5]	1[5]	4[5]	8[5]	10[5]	13[5]	8[5]	4.0	1.3[16]	−10	−315	−325	12	26	Papua New Guinea
29	...	16	6	2	4	26	16			8.6	1.9	−162[4]	−197[4]	−359[4]	111	49	Paraguay
15	9	23	5	4[4]	4[4]	41[44]	4[4]	8		3.5	−0.3[16]	−16[4]	−1,014[4]	−1,030[4]	247	188	Peru
26	2	25	4	1	6	21	14			6.1	−0.3	1,017	478	−539	647	56	Philippines
...	...	...	...	...	...	...	...	...	...	...	...	...	...	...	...	...	Pitcairn Island
16[2]	3	49[2,3]	12[2]	3	7[2]	14[2]	2[2,26]			5.6[2]	5.0[2]	790	−1,162	−372	136	186	Poland
9[8]	14	32[8,14]	6[8]	2[8]	20[8]		6[8]	13[8]	12[8]	4.8	1.0[16]	−3,375	4,015	640	1,574	332	Portugal
2	43	39	2[43]	4[5]	8[45]	14	13	9	12	4.9	2.2[16]	−720[8]	−1,668[8]	−2,388[8]	720	491	Puerto Rico
1[4]	31[4]	10[4]	7[4]	1[4]	2[4]	10[4]	31[4]			4.0	−2.2[6]	1,842[5]	−1,432[5]	410[5]	...	...	Qatar
7[9]	...	10[9]	4[9]	6[9]	5[9]	15[9]	24[9]	32[9]		6.0	4.4[6]	−699[9]	696[9]	−39[9]	...	...	Réunion
15[2]	3	63[2,3]	8[2]	3	6[2]	8[2]				9.2[2]	4.4[2,16]	1,917[4,46]	−509[4,46]	1,408[4,46]	178	57	Romania
45	—	16	5	1	3	14	18			3.0	2.8	−146	12	−134	6	11[8]	Rwanda
...	...	...	...	...	...	...	...	...	...	...	...	...	...	...	...	...	St. Helena
10	...	13	9	1	13	18	36			3.0	4.6	−28[5]	14[5]	−14[5]	34	3	St. Kitts
15	1	8	7	4	10	23	11	5	22	5.8	4.2	−62[1]	49[1]	−13[1]	68	52	St. Lucia
...	...	...	...	...	...	...	...	...	...	...	...	...	...	...	...	...	St. Pierre and Miquelon
17	—	9	11	3	21	15	11		15	2.8	5.2[16]	−10[4]	14[4]	4[4]	25	8	St. Vincent
...	...	...	...	...	...	...	...	...	...	...	...	...	...	...	...	...	San Marino
54[8]	—	10[8]	9[8]	3[8]	11[8]	10[8]	1[8]	...	29[8]	−1.1	−3.6	−6[5]	−2[5]	−8[5]	...	...	São Tomé and Príncipe
4	33	5	12	—	7	8	8	12	10	11.1	−2.9	5,340	−14,910	−9,570	2,000	3,152[5]	Saudi Arabia
21	3	19	8		50					2.0	3.3	−221[8]	−53[8]	−274[8]	118	42	Senegal
7	14	9[14]	5	3	41	9	8	3	16	6.2	0.0	−87[4]	55[4]	−32[4]	56	10	Seychelles
39[5]	5[5]	7[5]	3[5]	1[5]	17[5]	11[5]	18[5]			2.0	−2.3	15[4]	−20[4]	−5[4]	3	3	Sierra Leone
1[4]	—	25[4]	8[4]	2[4]	14[4]	17[4]	28[4]	12[4]		9.2	5.3	−2,540	3,079	539	1,842	652	Singapore
59[50]	3	13[50]	2[50]	3	2[50]	8[50]	8[50]		14[50]	8.6	4.7[6]	11	−20[1]	−19[1]	2[22]	...	Solomon Islands
58	...	5	3	—	6	9	6	6	6	1.7	2.5	−295[4]	207[4]	−88[4]	8	13[5]	Somalia
6[4]	16[4]	22[4]	3[4]	4[4]	9[4]	12[4]	12[4]	4[4]	13[4]	3.4	1.0	7,163	−4,161	3,002	388	543	South Africa
6[15]	39	69[15,39]	39	39	25[15]					...	...	...	...	...	...	...	Bophuthatswana
8[8]	—	13[8]	10[8]	—	9[8]	3[8]	7[8]	50[8]		9.1	9.6[16]	...	...	...	...	...	Ciskei
27[15]	39	12[15,39]	39	39	61[15]					...	...	...	...	...	...	...	Transkei
...	...	...	...	...	...	...	...	...	...	...	...	...	...	...	...	...	Venda
8[4]	36[4]	5[4]	2[4]	2[4]	7[4]	11[4]	6[4]	2[4]	18[4]	4.8	−0.6	48	29	77	46[28]	...	S.W. Africa/Namibia
6	14	27[14]	7	3	6	20	30			3.8	1.7	−6,322[4]	10,473[4]	4,151[4]	12,058	1,513	Spain
28	2	15	8	1	11	20	7	9		4.7	5.1[16]	−472	128	−344	75	55	Sri Lanka
28	14	9[14]	6	2	10	23	...	10	12	2.2	0.2	−447	198	−249	31	37	Sudan, The
9	6	13	6	4	8	17	15	1	25	5.2	−0.3	65	10	75	6	11	Suriname
25[5]	3[5]	23[5]	4[5]	1[5]	6[5]	9[5]	7[5]	4[5]	17[5]	6.9	2.9	−7	47	40	28	15	Swaziland
3[4]	1[4]	24[4]	7[4]	3[4]	7[4]	13[4]	14[4]	4[4]	23[4]	2.0	1.7	4,466	−5,339	−873	1,540	2,811	Sweden
...	...	...	...	...	...	...	...	...	...	1.3	1.6	−4,844[4]	9,381[4]	4,537[4]	4,227	3,368	Switzerland
16	14	29[14]	11	...	9	14	4	2	15	9.9	4.1	−1,951[1]	999[1]	−952[1]	395	302	Syria
6	1	41	4	4	6	14	9	7	10	9.7	6.8	20,662	−2,605	18,057	1,066[8]	1,229[5]	Taiwan
58	—	5	2	1	7	13	13			5.4	1.1	−566[4]	393[4]	−173[4]	15	12	Tanzania
17	3	20	5	2	9	18	10	11	4	6.9	4.7	−386	−143	−529	1,421	296	Thailand
48	...	13	6		35					3.2	−1.1	−46	−27	−73	41	28	Togo
...	...	...	...	...	...	...	...	...	...	...	...	...	...	...	...	...	Tokelau
41[5]	—	5[5]	4[5]	—	6[5]	15[5]	6[5]	22[5]		4.1	8.6[6]	−21[1]	15[1]	−6[1]	7	4	Tonga
3	24	7	11	2	10	9	10	8	15	4.4	−4.1[16]	355	−624	−269	190	165	Trinidad and Tobago
15	10	12	6	2	5	22	4	13	12	7.1	3.8	−728	669	−59	488	107	Tunisia
16	14	30[4]	4	3[6]	9	17	6	5	6[36]	5.2	5.3	−3,234	2,250	−984	1,215	314	Turkey
...	...	...	...	...	...	...	...	...	...	5.6	−0.2[6]	...	...	...	12	...	Turks and Caicos Is.
16[7]	—	17	13[7]	...	4[7]	34[7]	32[7]			...	...	...	...	...	...	...	Tuvalu
73	—	4	1		21					−1.6	1.2	854[4]	−89[4]	−4[4]	8	10	Uganda
19[2]	3	46[2,3]	11[2]	3	6[2]	18[2]	...	...	...	5.1[2]	3.7[2]	...	...	...	...	...	U.S.S.R.
1	45	9	9	2	4	9	20			15.1	−5.5	...	...	...	...	...	United Arab Emirates
2	14	25[14]	6	11	7	13	20	14	7	2.0	2.0	−15,800	13,136	−2,664	7,921	8,686	United Kingdom
2	3	20	5	3	6	16	16	16	12	2.5	3.0	−160,280	6,330	−153,950	12,913	17,627	United States
10	14	24[14]	2	3	7	10	11	11	9	3.1	−1.6	109	−233	−124	259	174	Uruguay
20[9]	8[9,33]	5[9]	2[9,33]	3[9]	10[9]	52[9]				3.5	7.6[6]	−38[4]	35[4]	−34[4]	71	2	Vanuatu
7	7	21	3	4	13	9	22		14	4.1	−0.2	2,057	−2,374	−317	190	307	Venezuela
58[2]	3	24[2,3]	3[2]	3	2[2]	12[2]	2[2,26]			0.5[2]	10.7[2,6]	...	...	...	...	...	Vietnam
...	...	...	...	...	...	...	...	...	...	3.1	−3.2[6]	...	...	...	509	...	Virgin Islands (U.S.)
...	...	...	...	...	...	...	...	...	...	...	...	...	...	...	...	...	Wallis and Futuna
33[4]	14	8[4,14]	14[4]	2[4]	46[4,24]					10.2[31]	3.6	−269[4]	383[4]	114[4]	71	35[1]	West Bank
...	...	...	...	...	...	...	...	...	...	...	...	...	...	...	...	...	Western Sahara
...	...	...	...	...	...	...	...	...	...	3.0	−3.2[37]	−44	50	6	9	2	Western Samoa
10[15]	—	12[15]	8[15]	1[15]	10[15]	13[15]	11[15]	1[15]	23[15]	1.2	1.6[16]	−380	257	−123	7	12[5]	Yemen (Aden)
20[4]	2[4]	13[4]	4[4]	1[4]	13[4]	13[4]	13[4]	20[4]		8.0	4.5[16]	−781[4]	656[4]	−125[4]	15	23	Yemen (Şan'ā')
11	11	34	7	2	7	11	24			5.7[52]	1.1[52]	−702[4]	1,802[4]	1,100[4]	1,105	86	Yugoslavia
32[8]	25[8]	2[8]	5[8]	—	18	19[8]	15[8]			0.5	1.8	561[4]	−163[4]	398[4]	16	43	Zaire
14	14	22	2	1	7	13	26			1.4	0.8	1724	−474[4]	−302[4]	7	31	Zambia
11[4]	7[4]	30[4]	3[4]	6[4]	6[4]	13[4]	6[4]	15[4]	6[4]	3.5	3.9	315[4]	−262[4]	53[4]	45	38	Zimbabwe

[34]Services includes public utilities and transportation and communications. [35]Guernsey and Jersey. [36]Government includes public utilities. [37]1980–83. [38]Trade includes public utilities and finance. [39]Manufacturing includes mining, construction, and public utilities. [40]Includes Northern Ireland. [41]1985–86. [42]Manufacturing includes public utilities. [43]Construction includes mining. [44]Trade includes public utilities, transportation and communications, and finance. [45]Transportation and communications includes public utilities. [46]Transactions in convertible currencies only. [47]1975. [48]1987. [49]1974. [50]1972. [51]At prices of 1978. [52]Gross material product.

Employment and labour

This table provides international comparisons of the world's national labour forces—giving their size; composition by demographic component and employment status; and structure by industry.

The table focuses on the concept of "economically active population," which the International Labour Organisation (ILO) defines as persons of all ages who are either employed or looking for work. In general, "economically active population" does not include students, persons occupied solely in domestic duties, retired persons, persons living entirely on their own means, and persons wholly dependent on others. Persons engaged in illegal economic activities—smugglers, prostitutes, drug dealers, bootleggers, black marketeers, and others—also fall outside the purview of the ILO definition. Countries differ markedly in their treatment, as part of the labour force, of such groups as members of the armed forces, inmates of institutions, the unemployed (both persons seeking their first job and those previously employed), seasonal and international migrant workers, and persons engaged in informal, subsistence, or part-time economic activities. Some countries include all or most of these groups among the economically active, while others may treat the same groups as inactive.

Three principal structural comparisons of the economically active total are given in the first part of the table: (1) participation rate, or the proportion of the economically active who possess some particular characteristic, is given for women and for those working age (usually ages 15 to 64); (2) activity rate, the proportion of the total population who *are* economically active, is given for both sexes and as a total; and (3) employment status, usually (and here) grouped as employers, self-employed, employees, family workers (usually unpaid), and others.

Each of these measures indicates certain characteristics in a given national labour market; none should be interpreted in isolation, however, as the meaning of each is influenced by a variety of factors—demographic structure and change, social or religious customs, educational opportunity, sexual differentiation in employment patterns, degree of technological development, and the like. Participation and activity rates, for example, may be high in a particular country because it possesses an older population with few children, hence a higher proportion of working age, or because, despite a young population with many below working age, the economy attracts eligible immigrant workers, themselves almost exclusively of working age. At the same time, low activity and participation rates might be characteristic of a country having a young population with poor employment possibilities or of a country with a good job market distorted by the presence of large numbers of "guest" or contract workers who are not part of the domestic labour force. An illiterate woman in a strongly sex-differentiated labour force is likely to begin and end as a family or traditional agricultural worker. Loss of working-age men to war, civil violence, or emigration for job opportunities may also affect the structure of a particular labour market.

Employment and labour

country	year	total ('000)	participation rate (%) female	participation rate (%) ages 15–64	activity rate (%) total	activity rate (%) male	activity rate (%) female	employment status (%) employers, self-employed	employment status (%) employees	employment status (%) unpaid family workers	employment status (%) other	agriculture, forestry, fishing number ('000)	agriculture, forestry, fishing % of econ. active	manufacturing; mining, quarrying; public utilities number ('000)	manufacturing; mining, quarrying; public utilities % of econ. active
Afghanistan	1979	3,946	7.9	49.1	30.2	54.1	4.9	...	...	...	...	2,369	60.1	494	12.5
Albania	1985	1,398	41.0	74.5	45.8	53.5	38.1	...	...	...	...	152[3,4]	21.8[3,4]	253[3,4]	36.2[3,4]
Algeria	1985[5]	4,498	11.6	40.0	18.0[4]	33.8[4]	2.4[4]	21.0[6]	72.2[6]	6.4[6]	0.4[6]	999[7]	25.7[7]	595[7]	15.3[7]
American Samoa	1980	9	39.2	46.1	26.4	31.6	21.0	2.4	97.3	0.2	0.1	0.1[8]	1.4[8]	2.6[8,9]	31.4[8,9]
Andorra	1986	21	...	...	46.8	...	...	...	...	...	...	0.1	0.6	2.8	13.0
Angola	1985	3,719	39.7	71.8	42.5	52.1	33.2	...	...	...	...	2,672	71.8	361[13]	9.7[13]
Anguilla	1984	2.8	40.5	73.6	41.6	50.8	32.9	17.2	56.6	—	26.2	0.2	6.3	0.1	3.4
Antigua and Barbuda	1983	31	39.6	56.2[17]	39.4	49.6	30.0	12.3[18]	69.9[18]	0.6[18]	17.2[18]	2.1[19,20]	9.0[19,20]	2.1[19,20]	9.1[19,20]
Argentina	1985	11,452	26.8	59.2	37.5	55.3	19.9	25.1[21]	71.2[21]	3.3[21]	0.4[21]	1,201[21]	12.0[21]	2,136[21]	21.3[21]
Aruba	1981	26	36.7	62.0	43.2	56.1	30.9	...	...	...	...	0.04[7]	0.2[7]	2.5[7]	10.6[7]
Australia	1986[5]	7,481	39.5	70.2	46.8	56.8	36.9	14.6	76.6	0.9	8.0	415	5.5	1,360	18.2
Austria	1986	3,388	39.6	65.9	44.8	56.9	33.8	10.4	85.1	4.5	—	285	8.4	1,011	29.8
Bahamas, The	1980	87	44.5	70.5	41.6	47.4	36.0	81.4	3.4	0.5	14.8	4.5	5.2	6.6	7.6
Bahrain	1986	183	14.2	65.3	42.1	61.9	14.4	9.8[23]	88.7[23]	0.1[23]	1.4[23]	4	2.0	25	13.4
Bangladesh	1984	28,493	8.9	49.4	29.9	53.5	5.4	38.1	44.1	15.6	2.2	16,448	57.7	2,593	9.1
Barbados	1987	119	47.2	75.4[25]	47.1	51.9	42.6	8.8[19]	76.4[19]	0.2[19]	14.6[19]	9[25]	7.7[25]	27[13,25]	22.9[13,25]
Belgium	1986	4,212	39.8[26]	65.4[23,27]	42.6[26]	52.6[26]	33.1[26]	12.1[26]	71.8[26]	3.3[26]	12.8[26]	103	2.5	853	20.3
Belize	1983–84	47	32.5	63.0[21]	29.6	39.5	19.5	23.4	55.1	7.5	14.0	13.1	27.6	4.9	10.3
Benin	1985	1,964	48.3	86.6	48.5	51.1	46.0	...	...	...	...	1,246[21]	70.2[21]	118[13,21]	6.7[13,21]
Bermuda	1986	33	46.8	82.1[21,28]	58.3	63.5	53.3	7.7[21]	88.6[21]	0.5[21]	3.2[21]	0.3	0.9	1.7	5.0
Bhutan	1985	632	32.9	69.0	46.8	58.0	30.3	...	...	...	...	531[21]	92.5[21]	16[13,21]	2.8[13,21]
Bolivia	1986	2,077	23.4	54.0	31.4	48.7	14.6	48.9[29]	38.2[29]	9.1[29]	3.8[29]	693[29]	46.2[29]	208[29]	13.9[29]
Botswana	1985[5]	368	53.0	72.7	37.0	38.1	36.0	3.1[23]	41.0[23]	45.4[23]	10.5[23]	159	43.2	20	5.4
Brazil	1985[30]	55,098	33.5	66.8[31]	41.9	56.2	27.9	27.0[21]	65.3[21]	5.2[21]	2.5[21]	15,190	28.5	8,687	16.3
British Virgin Islands	1980	5	38.5	72.8	45.4	54.6	35.8	13.1	82.1	0.7	4.1	0.3	5.3	0.9	17.3
Brunei	1981	71	23.8	61.1	36.7	52.3	18.7	7.4	88.4	0.6	3.6	3.4	4.9	8.6	12.2
Bulgaria	1985	4,802	47.6	75.3[32]	53.7	56.8	50.6	...	99.2	...	0.8	816	17.0	1,778	37.0
Burkina Faso	1985	3,765	47.0	88.6	54.2	58.0	50.5	...	...	...	...	2,964[21]	86.7[21]	146[13,21]	4.3[13,21]
Burma	1983	13,726	35.3	64.2	40.2	52.4	28.2	...	...	...	...	9,268[33]	67.5[33]	1,196	8.7
Burundi	1986	2,654	52.7	88.7	55.5	54.0	56.9	35.7[35]	5.6[35]	58.5[35]	0.2[35]	2,246[35]	93.1[35]	40[35]	1.7[35]
Cameroon	1982	3,543	37.5	65.6	39.9	50.0	29.8	60.2	14.6	18.0	7.1	2,595	73.2	164	4.6
Canada	1986[5]	12,870	42.9	74.3	50.9	58.8	43.1	8.6	89.8	0.8	0.8	590	4.6	2,321	18.0
Cape Verde	1980	63	29.9	60.0[26]	21.9	33.3	12.1	24.1	65.1	1.1	9.6	20.9	33.1	2.7	4.3
Cayman Islands	1985	10	43.8	...	48.7[35]	58.1[35]	39.8[35]	12.1	87.9	—	—	—	0.4	0.3	3.4
Central African Republic	1985	1,282	47.0	81.6	49.8	54.5	45.3	...	...	...	...	969	67.8	54[13]	4.2[13]
Chad	1985	1,790	21.7	57.4	35.7	56.7	15.3	...	...	...	...	1,454	81.2	93[13]	5.2[13]
Chile	1986	4,269	30.0	54.8	35.1	50.2	20.6	23.7	63.7	3.9	8.8	826	19.4	696	16.3
China	1987[5]	521,506[19]	43.7[19]	83.7[19]	52.3[19]	57.3[19]	47.0[19]	...	...	...	...	313,110[38]	61.1[38]	95,890[38]	18.7[38]
Christmas Island	1981	1.6	9.8	75.9[39]	56.3	76.0	16.6	...	...	...	...	—	0.1	1.1	68.8
Cocos (Keeling) Islands	1981	0.3	33.5	70.5[39]	51.2	63.4	37.0	...	...	...	...	0.1	21.8	—	3.2
Colombia	1985	9,558	32.8	49.4[40]	34.3	46.6	22.3	...	...	...	...	2,412[21]	28.5[21]	1,231[21]	14.5[21]
Comoros	1985	117	26.2	53.1	29.6	43.5	15.6	47.6[21]	25.6[21]	—26.8[21]—		53[21]	53.3[21]	4.1[21]	4.2[21]
Congo	1985	710	39.3	69.4	40.8	50.2	31.6	...	...	...	...	405[21]	62.5[21]	77[13,21]	11.9[13,21]
Cook Islands	1981	5.8	30.3	63.1	33.7	45.6	21.1	11.0	65.7	3.7	19.6	1.7	29.2	5.5	9.5
Costa Rica	1985	887	26.1	55.8[41]	35.7	53.2	18.5	20.0	69.1	4.1	6.8	238	26.8	142[42]	16.1[42]
Côte d'Ivoire	1985	4,053	34.7	71.4	41.3	52.8	29.3	...	...	...	...	2,452	60.5	409[13]	10.1[13]
Cuba	1986	3,541[23]	31.3[23]	57.2[23]	36.4[23]	49.5[23]	23.0[23]	4.8[23]	94.1[23]	0.2[23]	0.9[23]	602[23]	18.4[3]	726[3]	22.2[3]
Cyprus	1985[43]	249	35.2	67.2[21]	46.0	59.9	32.3	24.2	70.6	1.5	3.7	36	14.8	47	19.4
Czechoslovakia	1986	7,750	46.0	78.9[21]	49.8	55.2	44.7	0.1[21]	91.2[21]	8.5[21]	0.2[21]	989	12.8	3,027	39.1
Denmark	1985	2,753	45.6	79.6	53.9	59.4	48.6	9.3	87.9	2.3	0.5	176	6.4	574	20.8
Djibouti	1985	161	39.1	65.2[44]	44.5	52.5	36.0	...	...	...	...	125	77.5	12[13]	7.3[13]
Dominica	1981	25	34.1	61.7	34.3	45.4	23.3	29.4	49.8	1.9	18.9	7.8	31.0	1.7	6.6
Dominican Republic	1981	1,915	28.9	53.6	33.9	48.1	19.7	36.5	51.3	3.3	8.9	420	22.0	243	12.7
Ecuador	1982	2,346	20.6	49.6	29.1	46.3	12.0	37.3	47.6	5.8	9.3	787	33.5	307	13.1
Egypt	1986	12,095	14.6	45.1	25.3	42.3	7.6	26.0[4]	51.5[4]	16.0[4]	6.6[4]	5,161	42.7	2,002	16.6

The distribution of the economically active population by employment status reveals that a large percentage of economically active persons in some less developed countries falls under the heading "employers, self-employed." This occurs because the countries involved have poor, largely agrarian economies in which the average worker is a farmer who tills his own small plot of land. In countries with well-developed economies, "employees" will usually constitute the largest portion of the economically active.

Caution should be exercised when using the economically active data to make intercountry comparisons, as countries often differ in their choices of classification schemes, definitions, and coverage of groups and in their methods of collection and tabulation of data. The population base containing the economically active population, for example, may range, in developing countries, from age 9 or 10 with no upper limit to, in developed countries, age 18 or 19 upward to a usual retirement age of from 55 to 65, with sometimes a different range for each sex. Data on female labour-force participation, in particular, often lack comparability. In many less developed countries, particularly those dominated by the Islamic faith, a cultural bias favouring traditional roles for women results in the undercounting of economically active women. In other, less developed countries, particularly those in which subsistence workers are deemed economically active, the role of women may be overstated.

The second major section of the table provides data on the distribution

by economic (also conventionally called industrial) sector of the "economically active population." The data usually include such groups as unpaid family workers, members of the armed forces, and the unemployed, the last distributed by industry as far as possible.

The categorization of industrial sectors is based on the divisions listed in the International Standard Industrial Classification of All Economic Activities. The "other" category includes persons whose activities were not adequately defined and the unemployed who were not distributable by industrial sector.

A substantial part of the data presented in this table is summarized from various issues of the ILO's *Yearbook of Labour Statistics,* which compiles its statistics both from official publications and from information submitted directly by national census and labour authorities. The editors have supplemented and updated ILO statistical data with information from Britannica's holdings of relevant official publications and from direct correspondence with national authorities.

construction		transportation, communications		trade, hotels, restaurants		finance, real estate		public administration, defense		services		other		country
number ('000)	% of econ. active	number ('000)	% of econ. active	number ('000)	% of econ. active	number ('000)	% of econ. active	number ('000)	% of econ. active	number ('000)	% of econ. active	number ('000)	% of econ. active	
51	1.3	66	1.6	138	3.5	1	1	1	1	749[1]	19.0[1]	78[2]	2.0[2]	Afghanistan
81[3,4]	11.6[3,4]	33[3,4]	4.8[3,4]	54[3,4]	7.7[3,4]	...	...	...	...	87[3,4]	12.5[3,4]	38[3,4]	5.4[3,4]	Albania
670[7]	17.3[7]	202[7]	5.2[7]	311[7]	8.0[7]	1	1	1	1	1,107[1,7]	28.5[1,7]	—	—	Algeria
0.6	7.4	9	9	0.9	11.2	0.2	2.6	10	10	3.6[10]	43.6[10]	0.2[11]	2.4[11]	American Samoa
1.8	8.2	1.8	8.5	5.8[12]	26.9[12]	1.3	6.0	0.7	3.0	5.2[12]	24.3[12]	2.0	9.4	Andorra
13	13	14	14	14	14	14	14	14	14	686[14]	18.5[14]	—	—	Angola
0.4	15.5	0.2	5.8	0.4	14.6	15	15	0.6	22.7	0.1[15]	4.6[15]	0.8[16]	27.2[16]	Anguilla
2.6[19,20]	11.1[19,20]	2.6[19,20]	11.1[19,20]	5.2[19,20]	22.4[19,20]	0.8[19,20]	3.4[19,20]	10	10	7.9[10,19,20]	33.9[10,19,20]	0.8[16]	27.2[16]	Antigua and Barbuda
1,003[21]	10.0[21]	460[21]	4.6[21]	1,702[21]	17.0[21]	396[21]	3.9[21]	10	10	2,399[10,21]	23.9[10,21]	736[22]	7.3[22]	Argentina
1.9[7]	8.0[7]	1.3[7]	5.4[7]	7.7[7]	32.7[7]	1.0[7]	4.4[7]	10	10	9.1[7,10]	38.5[7,10]	0.0[27]	0.1[7]	Aruba
491	6.6	542	7.2	1,384	18.5	699	9.3	324	4.3	1,671	22.3	596[11]	8.0[11]	Australia
284	8.4	223	6.6	624	18.4	190	5.6	10	10	754[10]	22.2[10]	16	0.5	Austria
6.7	7.7	6.2	7.1	24.5	28.1	6.4	7.4	10	10	24.1[10]	27.7[10]	8.1[16]	9.3[16]	Bahamas, The
38	21.0	17	9.4	25	13.4	7	4.2	10	10	67[10]	36.5[10]	—	—	Bahrain
487	1.7	1,088	3.8	3,255	11.4	136	0.5	10	10	2,294[10]	8.1[10]	2,188[24]	7.7[24]	Bangladesh
13	13	6[25]	6[25]	25[25]	5.1[25]	25[25]	21.7[25]	3[25]	2.9[25]	10	10	41[10,25]	35.3[10,25]	5[25]	4.4[25]	Barbados
205	4.9	261	6.2	713	16.9	302	7.2	10	10	1,262[10]	30.0[10]	514[16]	12.2[16]	Belgium
2.0	4.2	2.0	4.3	4.6	9.6	0.6	1.2	6.3	13.2	7.3	15.5	6.6[11]	14.0[11]	Belize
13	13	14	14	14	14	14	14	14	14	410[14,21]	23.1[14,21]	—	—	Benin
2.1	6.3	2.4	7.1	11.9	35.5	4.3	13.0	10	10	10.8[10]	32.2[10]	—	—	Bermuda
13	13	14	14	14	14	14	14	14	14	27[14,21]	4.7[14,21]	—	—	Bhutan
82[29]	5.5[29]	56[29]	3.7[29]	107[29]	7.1[29]	13[29]	0.9[29]	10	10	282[10,29]	18.8[10,29]	60[10,22]	4.0[10,22]	Bolivia
9	2.5	3	0.7	16	4.3	3	0.8	10	10	65[10]	17.7[10]	93[16]	25.3[16]	Botswana
3,097	5.8	1,916	3.6	5,815	10.9	15	15	2,347	4.4	14,439[15]	27.1[15]	1,747	3.3	Brazil
0.1	1.2	0.1	2.8	0.4	8.1	0.3	5.8	0.9	17.3	1.9	36.8	0.3	5.5	British Virgin Islands
12.6	17.9	4.5	6.4	7.4	10.4	2.0	2.8	10	10	29.3[10]	41.4[10]	2.8[16]	4.0[16]	Brunei
377	7.9	326	6.8	397	8.2	1	1	1	1	1,035[1]	21.6[1]	73	1.5	Bulgaria
13	13	14	14	14	14	14	14	14	14	310[14,21]	9.1[14,21]	—	—	Burkina Faso
157	1.1	345	2.5	1,362	9.9	26	0.2	393	2.9	388	2.8	591[34]	4.3[34]	Burma
15[35]	0.6[35]	6[35]	0.3[35]	21[35]	0.9[35]	1.3[35]	0.1[35]	6[35]	0.2[35]	75[35]	3.1[35]	—	—	Burundi
63	1.8	47	1.3	141	4.0	8	0.2	10	10	271[10]	7.7[10]	253[36]	7.1[36]	Cameroon
627	4.9	777	6.0	2,082	16.2	654	5.1	800	6.2	3,783	29.4	1,236[11]	9.6[11]	Canada
17.8	28.2	3.3	5.2	3.9	6.1	0.2	0.4	2.1	3.4	7.3	11.6	4.9	7.8	Cape Verde
1.1	10.7	1.1	10.8	3.6	35.6	1.8	17.7	1.1	11.3	1.0	10.1	—	—	Cayman Islands
13	13	14	14	14	14	14	14	14	14	359[14]	28.0[14]	—	—	Central African Republic
13	13	14	14	14	14	14	14	14	14	243[14]	13.6[14]	—	—	Chad
227	5.3	246	5.8	708[37]	16.6[37]	165	3.9	10	10	1,321[10,37]	31.0[10,37]	78[36]	1.8[36]	Chile
22,720[38]	4.4[38]	13,020[38]	2.5[38]	24,850[38]	4.8[38]	1,520[38]	0.3[38]	8,720[38]	1.7[38]	19,580[38]	3.8[38]	13,380[38]	2.6[38]	China
0.1	3.3	0.1	4.5	0.1	4.0	—	1.5	—	2.0	0.2	9.7	0.1[24]	6.2[24]	Christmas Island
0.1	24.6	—	5.3	—	4.6	—	0.7	—	11.6	0.1	22.2	—	6.0	Cocos (Keeling) Islands
242[21]	2.9[21]	353[21]	4.2[21]	1,262[21]	14.9[21]	278[21]	3.3[21]	10	10	1,998[10,21]	23.6[10,21]	691[21,22]	8.2[21,22]	Colombia
3.3[21]	3.3[21]	2.1[21]	2.1[21]	1.9[21]	1.9[21]	0.2[21]	0.2[21]	2.4[21]	2.4[21]	4.6[21]	4.7[21]	28[21]	27.8[21]	Comoros
13	13	14	14	14	14	14	14	14	14	166[14,21]	25.6[14,21]	—	—	Congo
0.3	5.3	0.6	10.0	0.7	12.3	0.1	2.3	10	10	1.6[10]	27.1[10]	0.3	4.3	Cook Islands
47	5.3	53[42]	6.0[42]	165	18.6	1	1	1	1	223[1]	25.1[1]	18[36]	2.1[36]	Costa Rica
13	13	14	14	14	14	14	14	14	14	1,192[14]	29.4[14]	—	—	Côte d'Ivoire
322[3]	9.9[3]	224[3]	6.9[3]	371[3]	11.4[3]	21[3]	0.6[3]	169[3]	5.2[3]	777[3]	23.8[3]	52[3]	1.6[3]	Cuba
21	8.6	12	5.0	44	18.1	11	4.5	10	10	45[10]	18.6[10]	27[24]	10.9[24]	Cyprus
781	10.1	516	6.7	867	11.2	15	15	174	2.2	1,396[15]	18.0[15]	—	—	Czechoslovakia
189	6.9	188	6.8	419	15.2	199	7.2	164	6.0	804	29.2	40[22]	1.5[22]	Denmark
13	13	14	14	14	14	14	14	14	14	24[14]	15.2[14]	—	—	Djibouti
2.3	9.1	0.9	3.6	1.6	6.4	0.3	1.0	10	10	5.0[10]	19.7[10]	5.8[16]	22.7[16]	Dominica
81	4.3	40	2.1	192	10.0	22	1.2	10	10	363[10]	18.9[10]	553[22]	28.9[22]	Dominican Republic
158	6.7	101	4.3	272	11.6	44	1.9	10	10	555[10]	23.7[10]	122[36]	5.2[36]	Ecuador
571	4.7	596	4.9	1,027	8.5	122	1.0	10	10	2,616[10]	21.6[10]	—	—	Egypt

Employment and labour (continued)

country	year	economically active population						employment status (%)				distribution by economic sector			
		total ('000)	participation rate (%)		activity rate (%)			employers, self-employed	employees	unpaid family workers	other	agriculture, forestry, fishing		manufacturing; mining, quarrying; public utilities	
			female	ages 15–64	total	male	female					number ('000)	% of econ. active	number ('000)	% of econ. active
El Salvador	1980[5]	1,593	34.8	62.4	35.4	47.5	24.0	28.2	59.2	10.9	1.7	637	40.0	262	16.4
Equatorial Guinea	1983	101	...	...	34.0	...	...	...	...	...	...	86.5	85.7	0.9	0.9
Ethiopia	1985	19,182	38.4	73.5	44.0	54.5	33.7	...	...	...	...	14,982	78.1	1,630[13]	8.5[13]
Faeroe Islands	1977	17.6	27.2	64.2[45]	41.9	58.2	23.9	11.9	86.1	...	2.0	3.3	18.8	3.9	21.9
Falkland Islands	1980	0.95	22.5	70.3[39]	52.5	74.3	26.1	...	...	...	...	...	...	...	...
Fiji	1986	241	21.2	54.6[39]	33.7	52.4	14.5	33.6	42.2	16.3	7.9	106	44.1	22	9.0
Finland	1986	2,596	47.1	76.9	52.8	57.6	48.2	12.8	85.1	1.3	0.8	279	10.7	619	23.9
France	1986[5]	24,318	42.0	65.8	43.9	52.3	36.0	14.2[26, 46]	75.6[26]	[46]	10.3[26]	1,583[26]	6.7[26]	5,163[26]	21.9[26]
French Guiana	1982	32	35.8	69.8	44.3	54.1	33.5	14.9	65.5	——19.6——		4	11.4	2	5.9
French Polynesia	1983	62	32.0	60.8[47]	37.4	48.9	25.0	15.3	72.0	5.2	7.6	8.0	12.8	4.5	7.3
Gabon	1985	518	38.4	68.2	45.0	56.4	34.0	...	...	...	...	379[21]	75.5[21]	54[13, 21]	10.8[13, 21]
Gambia, The	1983	326	46.3	78.2	47.3	51.1	43.6	...	...	...	...	240	73.7	9	2.9
Gaza Strip	1986	96	4.6	33.4[48]	17.5	...	...	...	...	...	...	17.3	18.8	16.5[49]	17.3[49]
Germany, East	1986	8,548	49.1	...	51.4	55.0	48.1	...	...	...	...	927	10.8	3,473	40.6
Germany, West	1986	29,623	39.7	67.2[26]	47.6[26]	60.3[26]	35.9[26]	8.2	82.1	2.9	6.9	1,369	4.6	9,114	30.8
Ghana	1984	5,580	51.2	82.5[39]	44.9	44.9	45.8	67.7	15.7	12.2	4.4	3,311	59.3	631	11.3
Gibraltar	1986	12.2[26]	29.7[26]	64.1[23, 39]	42.2[26]	58.2[26]	25.6[26]	5.9[23]	93.8[23]	...	0.3[23]	—	—	2.9[50]	24.7[50]
Greece	1986	4,048	36.0	57.5[26]	39.2[26]	51.4[26]	27.3[26]	31.4	43.8	13.7	11.1	1,031	25.5	810	20.0
Greenland	1976	21.4	33.4	...	43.1	53.0	31.4	12.6	82.5	0.4	4.5	3.2	15.1	3.5	16.4
Grenada	1981[7]	28	...	...	31.3	...	...	21.3	77.7	1.0	—	8.0	28.7	2.0	7.2
Guadeloupe	1982	124	42.5	63.7	37.9	44.5	31.6	...	...	...	...	13	10.5	7.3	5.9
Guam	1980	44	34.8	66.6[17]	42.0	52.4	30.6	2.3	96.6	0.1	1.0	0.3	0.7	1.6[42]	3.6[42]
Guatemala	1981	1,696	14.6	49.1	28.0	48.0	8.1	42.5	47.2	6.8	3.5	909	53.6	188	11.1
Guernsey	1976	25.6	...	...	47.7	62.4	34.0	17.9	82.1	—	—	4.5	17.7	2.2	8.7
Guinea	1985	2,846	40.8	76.2	46.8	56.1	40.0	...	...	...	...	2,236	78.6	268[13]	9.4[13]
Guinea-Bissau	1979	213	3.6	41.0	38.7	78.4	2.6	...	...	...	...	153	71.9	3	1.5
Guyana	1980[51]	239	24.8	57.3	31.5	47.9	15.5	19.8[18]	77.6[18]	2.1[18]	0.5[18]	49	20.3	40	16.8
Haiti	1983	2,264	42.9	69.1	44.2	52.1	36.9	59.3	16.6	10.5	13.6	1,299	57.4	152	6.7
Honduras	1984	1,256	16.7	53.6	29.7	49.3	9.9	...	...	...	...	719	57.2	177	14.1
Hong Kong	1986[5]	2,754	37.7	71.5	51.0	61.9	39.5	10.3	83.9	1.8	4.0	49	1.8	1,004	36.5
Hungary	1986	4,893	46.0	72.5[21]	46.0	51.4	40.9	3.4	80.5	2.4	13.6	986	20.2	1,615	33.0
Iceland	1984[52]	117	31.5[4]	79.1[53]	48.7	60.6[53]	44.5[53]	...	...	...	...	24	20.4	28	23.9
India	1981[54]	244,605	26.0	57.4[39]	36.8	52.7	19.8	10.0[55]	17.1[55]	3.3[55]	69.6[55]	153,015	62.6	27,381	11.2
Indonesia	1985	63,826	36.0	62.1[39]	38.9	50.0	27.9	29.4	45.2	23.2	2.2	34,142	53.5	6,281	9.8
Iran	1976	9,796	14.8	50.2	29.1	48.1	8.9	30.5	48.4	10.4	10.6	3,615	36.9	1,834	18.7
Iraq	1986	4,307	18.2	50.6	26.9	42.5	10.1	25.4[57]	59.5[57]	11.4[57]	3.7[57]	1,193	27.7	483	11.2
Ireland	1985	1,299	29.5	59.8	36.7	51.7	21.7	18.0	77.0	2.2	2.8	173	13.3	269	20.7
Isle of Man	1981	27.6	38.2	67.7	42.6	55.1	31.2	14.0	79.8	—	6.2	1.4	5.1	4.0	14.4
Israel	1986[5]	1,472	38.6	56.2	34.2	42.1	26.4	17.9	73.7	1.3	7.1	72	4.9	348	23.6
Italy	1986[5]	23,617	35.9	58.5[45]	41.5	54.6	29.0	21.4	62.9	4.7	11.1	2,241	9.5	4,939	20.9
Jamaica	1986	1,056	46.3	78.0[19, 45]	45.1	48.9	41.4	32.8	44.8	—	22.4	267	25.3	122[42]	11.5[42]
Japan	1987	60,840	39.9	68.7	49.8	60.9	39.0	15.0	72.8	9.0	3.2	4,890	8.0	14,640	24.1
Jersey	1986	45	41.6	65.7[39]	55.6	67.2	44.7	13.3	84.1	...	2.6	2.5	5.6	4.3	9.6
Jordan	1986	524	10.9	39.0	19.6	33.6	4.5	22.8[35]	67.2[35]	0.8[35]	9.2[35]	33	6.2	40	7.7
Kampuchea	1985	3,602	40.5	71.4	49.5	59.2	39.8	...	...	...	...	2,454[21]	74.4[21]	220[13, 21]	6.7[13, 21]
Kenya	1985	8,389	40.9	76.2	40.7	48.4	33.2	...	...	...	...	6,635	79.1	596[13]	7.1[13]
Kiribati	1985	26	36.1	67.8[39]	41.2	53.1	29.5	71.0	26.5	...	2.5	19.2	72.9	0.4	1.4
Korea, North	1985	9,084	46.0	75.3	44.6	48.6	40.6	...	...	...	...	3,355[21]	42.8[21]	2,373[13, 21]	30.3[13, 21]
Korea, South	1986[5]	16,116	39.1	57.3	38.9	46.8	30.6	30.2	52.3	13.7	3.8	3,662	22.7	4,053	25.1
Kuwait	1986	712	20.6	63.5	39.0	54.8	18.5	10.0[21]	88.4[21]	0.1[21]	1.5[21]	14	1.9	69	9.7
Laos	1985	2,014	45.3	84.2	48.9	53.1	44.6	...	...	...	...	1,393[21]	75.7[21]	130[13, 21]	7.1[13, 21]
Lebanon	1986	694	21.7	39.9[39]	25.1	40.7	10.6	...	...	...	...	132	19.1	131	18.9
Lesotho	1976	424	32.3	56.1	34.8	48.9	21.7	7.5	49.9	36.8	5.8	99	23.3	141	33.2
Liberia	1984	669	31.2[26]	64.7[26]	31.8	...	...	...	...	...	...	481	71.9	31	4.6
Libya	1985	1,062	8.1	47.6	24.1[58]	42.3[58]	3.5[58]	23.7[58]	69.6[58]	4.2[58]	2.6[58]	178	16.8	162	15.2
Liechtenstein	1987	13	35.9	67.9	48.1	63.2	33.7	8.1	89.3	2.5	—	0.4	2.8	4.7	35.6
Luxembourg	1981	154	33.3	61.3	42.2	57.7	27.4	9.4	85.1	3.5	2.0	7	4.9	36	23.3
Macau	1981	127	37.1	61.5[44]	48.6	59.0	37.5	9.7	84.9	3.4	2.0	8	5.9	57	45.0
Madagascar	1985	4,510	40.4	74.9	45.1	54.2	36.1	...	...	...	...	3,590	79.6	284[13]	6.3[13]
Malawi	1985	3,074	42.6	74.3	44.3	51.9	36.9	79.9[57]	17.8[57]	0.3[57]	2.0[57]	2,502	81.4	206[13]	6.7[13]
Malaysia	1980	4,924	33.7	62.1	37.5	49.6	25.3	28.7	54.3	10.2	6.7	1,855	37.7	652	13.2
Maldives	1985	79	37.2[57]	78.3[57]	47.2[57]	56.2[57]	37.1[57]	86.4[57]	13.4[57]	...	0.2[57]	36	45.5	20	25.0
Mali	1976	2,266	17.0	53.2	35.4	60.2	11.8	45.8	4.1	42.5	7.5	1,862	82.2	27	1.2
Malta	1986	124	24.4	...	36.0	55.2	17.3	14.1[4]	77.4[4]	...	8.5[4]	3	2.7	37	30.2
Martinique	1982	131	44.7	62.5	39.9	45.6	34.6	12.3	57.4	0.3	30.0	10	7.5	7	5.3
Mauritania	1985	590	21.0	55.7	31.2	49.8	13.0	...	...	...	...	389	66.0	59[13]	10.0[13]
Mauritius	1983[59]	359	25.9	58.2	37.1	55.2	19.1	9.0	60.8	0.6	29.6	62	17.2	58	16.1
Mayotte	1978	15.1	35.9	65.0	32.1	41.0	23.1	48.1	26.3	19.8	5.8	9.3	61.6	1.0	6.5
Mexico	1980	22,066	27.8	57.2	33.0	48.2	18.2	27.0	44.3	6.6	22.1	5,700	25.8	3,168	14.4
Monaco	1975	11	40.8	64.6	44.3	57.3	33.3	18.6	76.4	1.7	3.3	...	0.2	2.0[13]	17.8[13]
Mongolia	1985	894	45.5	82.2	46.9	50.9	42.8	...	...	...	...	544	60.8	108	12.1
Montserrat	1980	5.1	41.6	74.1	44.0	53.4	35.3	20.4[18]	78.0[18]	1.6[18]	—	0.5	9.3	0.6	10.9
Morocco	1982	5,999	19.7	48.9	29.3	47.1	11.6	27.1	40.5	17.6	14.8	2,352	39.2	1,016	16.9
Mozambique	1980	5,671	52.4	87.3[39]	48.6	47.6	49.5	44.4[18]	40.0[18]	14.5[18]	1.1[18]	4,755	83.8	347	6.1
Nauru	1977	2.2	8.8[60]	69.8[60]	30.5	...	...	...	...	...	...	...	...	...	...
Nepal	1986	7,760	34.7	82.5	45.5	57.8	32.5	86.2[23]	9.1[23]	2.5[23]	2.2[23]	6,244[23]	91.1[23]	37[23]	0.5[23]
Netherlands, The	1987	5,862	35.1	58.1	40.2	52.8	27.8	8.0[26]	79.2[26]	2.1[26]	10.8[26]	268[26]	4.7[26]	1,049[26]	18.2[26]
Netherlands Antilles	1981	70	40.6	63.5	40.9	50.3	32.2	...	...	...	...	0.3[7]	0.5[7]	7.8[7]	13.6[7]
New Caledonia	1983	58	...	63.6[29]	40.0	...	...	...	...	...	...	20	33.9	8[13]	13.5[13]
New Zealand	1986	1,605	41.7	74.5	49.2	57.9	40.7	15.9	74.7	1.2	8.2	144[23]	10.8[23]	331[23]	24.8[23]
Nicaragua	1987	1,126	21.6[21]	48.2[44]	32.2	...	...	...	...	...	...	365	32.4	101	9.0
Niger	1985	3,203	47.4	89.7	52.4	55.6	49.2	...	...	...	...	2,870	89.6	64[13]	2.0[13]
Nigeria	1983	29,453	31.9	59.4	32.0	43.1	20.6	55.9	28.0	8.9	7.2	9,296	31.6	1,764	6.0
Niue	1984	1.0	35.7	57.3[39]	35.4	44.5	25.9	9.1	71.5	10.9	8.5	0.2	19.5	0.1	11.5
Norfolk Island	1986	1.2	45.3	79.2[39]	61.6	66.5	56.5	...	...	...	...	0.037	3.0	0.048	3.9

construction number ('000)	construction % of econ. active	transportation, communications number ('000)	transportation, communications % of econ. active	trade, hotels, restaurants number ('000)	trade, hotels, restaurants % of econ. active	finance, real estate number ('000)	finance, real estate % of econ. active	public administration, defense number ('000)	public administration, defense % of econ. active	services number ('000)	services % of econ. active	other number ('000)	other % of econ. active	country
80	5.0	66	4.1	256	16.1	16	1.0	[10]	[10]	250[10]	15.7[10]	27[36]	1.7[36]	El Salvador
1.0	1.0	...	...	2.6	2.6	...	...	7.4	7.3	2.5	5.2	—	—	Equatorial Guinea
[13]	[13]	[14]	[14]	[14]	[14]	[14]	[14]	[14]	[14]	2,570[14]	13.4[14]	—	—	Ethiopia
2.0	11.1	1.9	11.1	2.1	11.9	0.3	1.9	[10]	[10]	3.5[10]	20.1[10]	0.6	3.2	Faeroe Islands
...	...	...	...	...	...	...	...	...	...	...	...	...	...	Falkland Islands
12	4.9	13	5.5	26	10.8	6	2.5	[10]	[10]	37[10]	15.2[10]	20[16]	8.2[16]	Fiji
208	8.0	190	7.3	371	14.3	162	6.3	123	4.7	619	23.8	26[36]	0.8[36]	Finland
1,517[26]	6.4[26]	1,369[26]	5.8[26]	3,484[26]	14.7[26]	1,689[26]	7.2[26]	[10]	[10]	6,084[10,26]	25.8[10,26]	2,730[16,26]	11.6[16,26]	France
3	8.8	1.3	4.2	2	6.2	4	11.3	[10]	[10]	10[10]	31.3[10]	7[16]	20.9[16]	French Guiana
6.2	10.0	3.4	5.5	9.7	15.5	2.6	4.1	[10]	[10]	23.4[10]	37.4[10]	4.6[16]	7.4[16]	French Polynesia
[13]	[13]	[14]	[14]	[14]	[14]	[14]	[14]	[14]	[14]	69[14,21]	13.7[14,21]	—	—	Gabon
4	1.3	8	2.5	17	5.1	1	1	1	1	22[1]	6.8[1]	25	7.7	Gambia, The
23.5	24.6	4.8	5.0	13.3	13.9	15	15	12.0	12.6	5.9[15,49]	6.2[15,49]	1.4[11]	1.5[11]	Gaza Strip
574	6.7	627	7.3	878	10.3	1	1	1	1	2,069[1]	24.2[1]	—	—	Germany, East
1,805	6.1	1,573	5.3	4,153	14.0	1,740	5.9	[10]	[10]	7,443[10]	25.1[10]	2,436[16]	8.2[16]	Germany, West
65	1.2	123	2.2	792	14.2	27	0.5	98	1.7	376	6.7	158[11]	2.8[11]	Ghana
2.2[50]	18.5[50]	0.5[50]	4.5[50]	2.5[50]	20.7[50]	0.7[50]	5.5[50]	1.3[50]	11.0[50]	1.8[50]	15.1[50]	—	—	Gibraltar
252	6.2	255	6.3	580	14.3	143	3.5	[10]	[10]	637[10]	15.7[10]	340[16]	8.4[16]	Greece
3.1	14.6	1.8	8.6	2.2	10.1	15	15	1.5	7.1	5.4[15]	25.5[15]	0.6	2.8	Greenland
2.9	10.3	1.7	6.1	3.9	14.0	0.4	1.3	1.7	6.0	2.6	9.2	4.8	17.2	Grenada
10	8.1	4.8	3.9	10	8.1	15	12.2	[10]	[10]	28[10]	22.7[10]	35[16]	28.6[16]	Guadeloupe
3.0	6.8	3.3[42]	7.5[42]	7.3	16.4	1.6	3.5	16.0	35.9	9.7	21.8	1.7[16]	3.8[16]	Guam
86	5.1	43	2.5	147	8.7	21	1.2	[10]	[10]	215[10]	12.7[10]	88[22]	5.2[22]	Guatemala
2.7	10.7	1.3	5.2	5.8	22.5	1.1	4.2	3.0	12.0	4.5	17.5	0.4	1.4	Guernsey
[13]	[13]	[14]	[14]	[14]	[14]	[14]	[14]	[14]	[14]	342[14]	12.0[14]	—	—	Guinea
2	0.8	2	1.1	5	2.4	0.2	0.1	[10]	[10]	26[10]	12.3[10]	21	10.0	Guinea-Bissau
7	2.7	9	3.8	15	6.1	3	1.2	[10]	[10]	57[10]	24.0[10]	60[16]	25.0[16]	Guyana
23	1.0	18	0.8	303	13.4	5	0.2	[10]	[10]	134[10]	5.9[10]	331[36]	14.6[36]	Haiti
43	3.5	38	3.0	107	8.5	12	1.0	[10]	[10]	160[10]	12.8[10]	—	—	Honduras
173	6.3	219	7.9	617	22.4	175	6.3	[10]	[10]	498[10]	18.1[10]	19	0.7	Hong Kong
348	7.1	401	8.2	509	10.4	15	15	229	4.7	757[15]	15.5[15]	49	1.0	Hungary
12	10.0	...	...	17	14.5	...	...	...	...	28	23.9	9	7.5	Iceland
3,565	1.5	6,069	2.5	12,165	5.0	1,764	0.7	[10]	[10]	18,557[10]	7.6[10]	22,088[56]	9.0[56]	India
2,096	3.3	1,958	3.1	9,345	14.6	250	0.4	[10]	[10]	8,317[10]	13.0[10]	1,436[16]	2.2[16]	Indonesia
1,202	12.3	433	4.4	672	6.9	101	1.0	[10]	[10]	1,524[10]	15.6[10]	415[36]	4.2[36]	Iran
521	12.1	260	6.0	330	7.0	50	1.2	[10]	[10]	1,470[10]	34.1[10]	—	—	Iraq
105	8.0	73	5.6	214	16.5	82	6.3	73	5.6	200	15.4	112[22]	8.6[22]	Ireland
2.9	10.6	2.3	8.3	5.5	20.1	1.5	5.5	1.6	5.9	6.3	22.7	2.0[16]	7.3[16]	Isle of Man
70	4.8	90	6.1	187	12.7	139	9.4	[10]	[10]	506[10]	34.4[10]	61[36]	4.1[36]	Israel
1,882	8.0	1,120	4.7	4,407	18.7	749	3.2	[10]	[10]	5,668[10]	24.0[10]	2,611[11]	11.1[11]	Italy
35	3.4	38[42]	3.6[42]	125	11.9	15	15	80	7.6	150[15]	14.2[15]	238[16]	22.5[16]	Jamaica
5,330	8.8	3,480	5.7	13,660	22.5	2,340	3.8	1,980	3.3	12,550	20.6	1,970[16]	3.2[16]	Japan
3.9	8.8	2.6	5.8	10.6	23.9	5.8	12.9	2.9	6.6	10.8	24.1	1.2[16]	2.8[16]	Jersey
56	10.7	45	8.6	55	10.5	17	3.3	[10]	[10]	278[10]	53.1[10]	—	—	Jordan
[13]	[13]	[14]	[14]	[14]	[14]	[14]	[14]	[14]	[14]	625[14,21]	18.9[14,21]	—	—	Kampuchea
[13]	[13]	[14]	[14]	[14]	[14]	[14]	[14]	[14]	[14]	1,158[14]	13.8[14]	—	—	Kenya
0.4	1.7	1.1	4.0	1.1	4.3	0.1	0.4	1.6	6.1	1.8	6.8	0.6[16]	2.5[16]	Kiribati
[13]	[13]	[14]	[14]	[14]	[14]	[14]	[14]	[14]	[14]	2,110[14,21]	26.9[14,21]	—	—	Korea, North
889	5.5	733	4.5	3,480	21.6	614	3.8	[10]	[10]	2,074[10]	12.9[10]	611[11]	3.8[11]	Korea, South
130	18.3	39	5.5	80	11.3	22	3.1	[10]	[10]	357[10]	50.1[10]	—	—	Kuwait
[13]	[13]	[14]	[14]	[14]	[14]	[14]	[14]	[14]	[14]	316[14,21]	17.2[14,21]	—	—	Laos
43	6.2	48	7.0	115	16.5	24	3.5	[10]	[10]	200[10]	28.8[10]	—	—	Lebanon
12	2.9	4	1.1	8	2.0	0.3	0.1	[10]	[10]	74[10]	17.6[10]	84	19.9	Lesotho
4	0.6	14	2.1	47	7.0	2	0.3	[10]	[10]	61[10]	9.1[10]	29	4.3	Liberia
257	24.2	93	8.7	41	3.9	13	1.2	69	6.5	184	17.3	66	6.2	Libya
1.1	8.1	0.4	3.0	1.6	12.0	0.9	6.5	0.6	4.7	3.4	25.3	0.3[24]	2.0[24]	Liechtenstein
14	9.3	11	6.9	30	19.3	12	7.9	[10]	[10]	39[10]	25.3[10]	5[16]	3.2[16]	Luxembourg
10	7.8	6	4.5	23	18.1	2	1.7	5	3.2	15	11.9	2[36]	1.8[36]	Macau
[13]	[13]	[14]	[14]	[14]	[14]	[14]	[14]	[14]	[14]	636[14]	14.1[14]	—	—	Madagascar
[13]	[13]	[14]	[14]	[14]	[14]	[14]	[14]	[14]	[14]	366[14]	11.9[14]	—	—	Malawi
208	4.2	161	3.3	560	11.4	80	1.6	306	6.2	666	13.5	438[16]	8.9[16]	Malaysia
4.7	5.9	4.8	6.1	2.5	3.2	1	1	1	1	11.3[1]	14.3[1]	—	—	Maldives
8	0.3	12	0.5	45	2.0	0.2	—	49	2.1	124	5.5	139	6.1	Mali
6	4.5	8	6.6	12	9.7	4	2.9	31	25.3	14	11.2	8[11]	6.9[11]	Malta
8	6.0	5	4.0	10	7.6	18	13.7	[10]	[10]	29[10]	22.5[10]	44[16]	33.4[16]	Martinique
[13]	[13]	[14]	[14]	[14]	[14]	[14]	[14]	[14]	[14]	142[14]	24.0[14]	—	—	Mauritania
19	5.4	16	4.4	27	7.5	6	1.8	[10]	[10]	64[10]	18.0[10]	106[16]	29.6[16]	Mauritius
1.4	9.0	0.3	1.9	0.7	4.5	0.2	1.5	0.2	1.4	1.2	7.8	0.9[11]	5.8[11]	Mayotte
1,296	5.9	672	3.0	1,729	7.8	406	1.8	[10]	[10]	2,418[10]	11.0[10]	6,676[24]	30.3[24]	Mexico
[13]	[13]	0.6	5.4	2.6	23.6	0.9	8.5	2.1	18.8	2.4	21.7	0.5[16]	4.1[16]	Monaco
29	3.3	36	4.1	42	4.7	1	1	1	1	106[1]	11.8[1]	29	3.2	Mongolia
0.7	13.3	0.2	4.5	0.4	8.1	0.1	1.7	[10]	[10]	2.0[10]	39.8[10]	0.6	12.4	Montserrat
437	7.3	141	2.3	498	8.3	15	15	533	8.9	474[15]	7.9[15]	548[2]	9.1[2]	Morocco
42	0.7	7.7	1.4	112	2.0	1	1	1	1	243[1]	4.3[1]	95[11]	1.7[11]	Mozambique
...		...		...		...		...		...		...		Nauru
2[23]	—	7[23]	0.1[23]	109[23]	1.6[23]	10[23]	0.1[23]	[10]	[10]	314[10,23]	4.6[10,23]	127	1.9	Nepal
386[26]	6.7[26]	323[26]	5.6[26]	907[26]	15.7[26]	457[26]	7.9[26]	[10]	[10]	1,176[10,26]	29.8[10,26]	660[16,26]	11.4[16,26]	Netherlands, The
5.1[7]	9.0[7]	4.6[7]	8.0[7]	14.1[7]	24.7[7]	3.9[7]	6.8[7]	[10]	[10]	21.2[7,10]	37.0[7,10]	0.1[7]	0.3[7]	Netherlands Antilles
[13]	[13]	3	[14]	4[37]	7.5[37]	1	1	[10]	[10]	19[10,37]	32.5[10,37]	4[16]	6.3[16]	New Caledonia
86[23]	6.4[23]	108[23]	8.1[23]	218[23]	16.4[23]	92[23]	6.9[23]	77[23]	5.8[23]	230[23]	17.3[23]	46[22,23]	3.4[22,23]	New Zealand
17	1.5	21	1.8	95	8.4	19	1.7	77	6.9	149	13.2	283[56]	25.1[56]	Nicaragua
[13]	[13]	[14]	[14]	[14]	[14]	[14]	[14]	[14]	[14]	269[14]	8.4[14]	—	—	Niger
909	3.1	1,123	3.8	6,534	22.2	204	0.7	[10]	[10]	7,081[10]	24.0[10]	2,542[16]	8.6[16]	Nigeria
0.1	9.6	—	4.2	0.1	8.7	—	0.1	[10]	[10]	0.4[10]	37.0[10]	0.1[11]	8.5[11]	Niue
0.092	7.6	0.070	5.8	0.275[37]	22.6[37]	0.062	5.1	0.202	16.6	0.325[37]	26.7[37]	0.106	8.7	Norfolk Island

Employment and labour (continued)

country	year	economically active population										distribution by economic sector			
		total ('000)	participation rate (%)		activity rate (%)			employment status (%)				agriculture, forestry, fishing		manufacturing; mining, quarrying; public utilities	
			female	ages 15–64	total	male	female	employers, self-employed	employees	unpaid family workers	other	number ('000)	% of econ. active	number ('000)	% of econ. active
Norway	1986[5]	2,111	44.5	77.4[28]	50.7	56.8	44.6	9.2	86.6	2.2	1.9	144	6.8	422	20.0
Oman	1986	468	7.5	60.9	35.7	57.6	6.2	...	...	...	...	109	23.3	15	3.3
Pacific Is., Trust Terr. of the															
Marshall Islands	1980	4.4	25.2	30.0[17]	14.3	20.8	7.4	3.3	78.1	0.3	18.4	0.1	1.0	0.4[9]	9.4[9]
Micronesia, Fed. States of	1980	9.8	29.8	26.1[17]	13.4	18.4	8.2	2.7	74.4	0.1	22.7	0.2	2.0	0.6[9]	6.0[9]
Northern Mariana Islands	1980	6.1	34.3	63.6[17]	36.4	45.5	26.3	2.0	95.2	—	2.8	0.1	2.1	0.6[9]	10.3[9]
Palau	1980	2.9	34.3	41.6[17]	23.9	30.3	17.0	3.0	89.1	—	7.9	0.1	2.9	0.3[9]	10.6[9]
Pakistan	1985[5]	28,872	9.4	50.6	29.6	51.7	5.8	44.7	26.0	25.6	3.7	14,054	48.7	4,039	14.0
Panama	1986[61]	720	31.8[26]	58.7[26,41]	32.1[21]	45.8[21]	18.2[21]	25.2	60.0	4.3	10.5	185	25.6	73	10.2
Papua New Guinea	1980[62]	733	39.8	35.2[44]	24.6	28.3	20.5	72.7	26.4	—	0.9	564	77.0	21	2.9
Paraguay	1982	1,039	19.7	57.5	34.3	54.8	13.6	43.1	37.7	9.2	9.9	446	42.9	129	12.4
Peru	1987	6,990	25.4[23]	56.2[39]	33.7	...	...	39.8[23]	41.8[23]	8.4[23]	10.0[23]	2,460	35.2	909	13.0
Philippines	1985[5]	21,643	38.1	65.4	39.6	48.8	30.3	36.3	42.1	15.5	6.1	10,085	46.6	2,134	9.9
Pitcairn Island	1981	0.035	...	...	66.0	...	...	...	...	...	...	0.003	8.6	0.002	5.7
Poland	1986	18,005	45.7	82.5[63]	47.9	53.4	42.7	13.2[53]	74.0[53]	12.1[53]	0.7[53]	5,059	28.1	5,123	28.5
Portugal	1986	4,681	41.4	67.2	45.7	55.5	36.5	24.0	62.8	4.8	8.4	940	20.1	1,094	23.4
Puerto Rico	1987[5]	994	36.1	48.9	30.2	39.6	21.2	13.2	84.5	0.9	1.3	29	2.9	165	16.6
Qatar	1986	201	9.8	75.5[39]	54.5	73.3	16.2	...	...	...	...	0.3	0.1	43.3	21.5
Réunion	1982	176	35.3	57.5[28]	34.0	44.9	23.6	10.4	56.3	1.1	32.2	17	10.1	8	4.7
Romania	1986	10,670	45.6[57]	75.6[57]	50.1[57]	55.2[57]	45.1[57]	...	...	...	...	3,062	28.7	3,980	37.3
Rwanda	1978	2,661	51.5	94.3	55.1	54.6	55.6	38.8	7.2	53.8	0.2	2,472	92.9	49	1.8
St. Helena and Ascension	1976	2.4	26.3	...	40.8	57.7	22.4	3.3	84.1	...	12.6	...	...	...	...
St. Kitts and Nevis	1984	17[21]	41.0[21]	69.5[21]	39.5[21]	48.5[21]	31.3[21]	12.4[18]	86.6[18]	1.1[18]	—	4.4[7]	29.6[7]	3.2[7]	21.6[7]
St. Lucia	1980	49	55.2	54.4[18]	41.1	39.0	43.0	27.3[18]	70.8[18]	2.0[18]	—	...	33.9[7]	...	11.1[7]
St. Pierre and Miquelon	1982	2.4	31.8	60.6	39.4	54.5	24.7	12.5	76.8	———10.7—		0.1	2.8	0.3	12.1
St. Vincent	1970	24	35.9	58.9[45]	27.5	37.6	18.7	16.0	82.5	1.5	—	6.9	29.0	2.1	8.9
San Marino	1987	12	41.0	71.2[25]	52.1	59.7	42.2	19.9	73.6	0.9	5.7	0.3	2.9	4.2[65]	35.5[65]
São Tomé and Príncipe	1981	31	32.4	61.1	31.7	43.1	20.4	15.8	79.4	0.1	4.7	16	53.9	1.9	6.2
Saudi Arabia	1986	3,032	3.2	51.5	29.8	48.4	2.3	...	...	...	...	432	14.3	452	14.9
Senegal	1985	3,095	41.8	78.1	47.1	55.3	39.1	...	...	...	...	1,119[19,50]	9.1[19,50]	36[19,50]	30.8[19,50]
Seychelles	1985	28	42.4	66.8[39]	42.4	49.0	35.9	10.7[23]	76.6[23]	0.3[23]	12.4[23]	2.3[66]	9.5[66]	2.3[66]	9.6[66]
Sierra Leone	1985	1,352	33.7	62.9	37.5	50.8	24.8	...	...	...	...	904	66.9	204[13]	15.1[13]
Singapore	1986[5]	1,229	37.1	65.9	47.5	59.8	35.2	12.9	78.9	1.8	6.5	10	0.8	299	24.4
Solomon Islands	1986[50]	39	25.6	24.9[48]	13.7	19.7	7.3	29.6	68.6	...	1.8	18	46.0	3.4	8.7
Somalia	1985	1,999	39.7	72.8	43.0	52.5	33.7	...	...	...	...	1,475	73.8	176[13]	8.8[13]
South Africa	1985	8,692	36.4	65.4[21,27]	37.2	47.9	26.7	4.0[21]	89.4[21]	...	6.6[21]	1,180	13.6	2,215	25.5
Bophuthatswana	1979	405	...	...	31.5	...	...	...	...	...	...	36	8.9	12[67,68]	3.1[67,68]
Ciskei	1984	90	41.3[21]	...	20.4[21]	25.5[21]	15.9[21]	12.1[35]	77.0[35]	10.9[35]	—	9.9	10.9	27.3	30.2
Transkei	1977	121	...	...	...	...	...	...	...	...	...	2.5	2.1	16	13.1
Venda	1980	30	38.5	...	8.6	12.9	5.6	...	...	...	...	7.2	24.2	1.7	5.7
South West Africa/Namibia	1985	477	23.9	55.4	30.8	47.3	14.6	...	...	...	...	185[21]	43.4[21]	93[13,21]	21.8[13,21]
Spain	1986	13,781	30.8	56.9[28]	34.0[23]	52.1[23]	16.5[23]	18.0	67.6	5.2	9.2	1,997	14.5	3,094	22.5
Sri Lanka	1985	5,972	32.8	61.0	37.7	50.1	25.0	24.4	50.1	11.5	14.1	2,531	42.4	737	12.3
Sudan, The	1985	6,991	20.8	55.6	32.4	51.2	13.5	59.2[58]	25.3[58]	9.9[58]	5.6[58]	4,786	68.5	587[13]	8.4[13]
Suriname	1980	98	...	38.7[70]	27.5	...	...	...	...	...	...	7.6	7.8	14.1	14.4
Swaziland	1985	273	39.9	72.1	42.0	51.2	33.1	...	...	...	...	194	71.0	25[13]	9.1[13]
Sweden	1986[5]	4,385	47.6	83.0[28]	52.4	55.6	49.2	6.1	91.0	0.2	2.7	179	4.1	1,030	23.5
Switzerland	1980	3,092	36.2	70.7	48.6	63.4	34.4	9.7	90.3	...	...	191	6.2	976	31.6
Syria	1986	2,488	12.8	46.7	23.2	39.6	6.1	34.0[4]	56.2[4]	7.4[4]	2.4[4]	746	30.0	360	14.5
Taiwan	1986	9,392	36.6	71.0	48.3	59.0	36.7	20.9	66.3	10.6	2.2	2,148	22.9	2,740	29.2
Tanzania	1985	10,913	48.9	85.7	48.5	50.2	46.8	...	...	...	...	9,091	83.3	469[13]	4.3[13]
Thailand	1986	26,970	45.5	79.1[39]	52.1	56.5	47.7	31.4	28.1	27.6	12.9	14,995[33]	55.6[33]	2,929	10.9
Togo	1985	1,244	37.5	69.5	42.0	53.3	31.1	...	...	...	...	579[23]	64.3[23]	59[23]	6.6[23]
Tokelau	1981	0.8	51.2	88.3	48.5	47.9	49.2	...	...	...	...	0.1	16.1	—	...
Tonga	1976	21	15.7	43.7	23.8	39.3	7.6	32.7	33.3	13.1	20.9	9.5	44.5	0.5	2.4
Trinidad and Tobago	1985	465	33.3	64.5	39.4	52.6	26.2	18.0	74.5	5.3	2.2	44	9.5	65[65]	14.1[65]
Tunisia	1984	2,137	21.3	52.9	30.6	48.7	13.3	21.4	54.9	5.4	18.3	475	22.2	383	17.9
Turkey	1980	19,212	36.1	68.2	42.9	54.1	31.4	23.2	32.1	40.9	3.8	11,105	57.8	2,141	11.1
Turks and Caicos Islands	1980	2.9	42.8	69.4	39.2	46.5	32.5	...	...	...	...	0.4	13.9	—	1.0
Tuvalu	1979[71]	4.0	51.3	81.1[39]	55.2	57.6	53.1	0.3	22.2	———77.5—		—	1.0	0.1	1.9
Uganda	1985[5]	7,054	41.9	78.9	45.6	53.4	37.9	...	...	...	...	5,940	84.2	317[13]	4.5[13]
U.S.S.R.	1986[5]	130,905	50.8	72.7[21]	51.7[35]	55.7[35]	48.1[35]	...	82.8[32]	...	17.2[32,73]	24,940	19.1	43,220	33.0
United Arab Emirates	1986	891	6.6	76.7	53.2	73.1	11.0	6.8[21]	92.7[21]	0.1[21]	0.5[21]	44	5.0	92	10.4
United Kingdom	1986	27,774	40.9	68.7[23]	48.9	59.4	39.0	9.5	78.9	...	11.6	603	2.2	5,991	21.6
United States	1986	119,540	44.0	72.9[28]	49.6	57.1	42.5	8.0	90.8	0.4	0.9	3,605	3.0	25,043	20.9
Uruguay	1985	1,172	33.1	71.3[27]	39.9	54.8	25.7	22.7	70.6	1.7	5.0	179	15.3	231	19.7
Vanuatu	1979	51	43.4	84.3	46.0	49.0	42.5	...	...	...	...	39.3	76.8	1.1	2.2
Venezuela	1986	6,107	27.4	57.9	34.1	49.0	18.9	26.7	59.8	3.1	10.3	859	14.1	1,134	18.6
Vietnam	1985	28,755	47.2	80.1	48.2	52.3	44.2	...	...	...	...	17,502	60.9	907	3.2
Virgin Islands (U.S.)	1980	38	45.5	65.1	39.4	44.9	34.4	7.1	86.4	0.3	6.2	0.5	1.2	3.8	10.0
Wallis and Futuna	1976	3.4	35.8	65.1[48]	36.5	46.9	26.1	42.2	18.3	39.5	—	2.7	79.2	0.2[13]	5.5[13]
West Bank	1986	174	14.3	37.8[48]	20.8	...	...	...	...	...	...	38.5	22.2	27.3[49]	15.7[49]
Western Sahara	...	...	...	...	...	...	...	...	...	...	...	...	...	...	...
Western Samoa	1981	42	15.0	48.6	26.5	43.5	8.3	21.1	43.5	35.0	0.4	25	60.4	1.2	2.9
Yemen (Aden)	1986	551	10.9	50.8	25.0	45.0	5.4	29.8[58]	34.2[58]	15.1[58]	20.9[58]	257	46.6	69	12.6
Yemen (Şan'ā')	1986	1,492	12.5	38.5	18.2	33.6	4.3	45.2[35]	34.0[35]	19.1[35]	1.7[35]	895	59.9	70	4.7
Yugoslavia	1981	9,359	38.7	68.7[27]	43.4	54.3	32.9	17.2	65.7	10.5	6.6	2,683	28.7	2,210	23.6
Zaire	1985	11,666	36.6	66.8	39.0	50.2	28.1	...	...	...	...	7,939	68.1	1,692[13]	14.5[13]
Zambia	1985	2,221	28.2	60.1	33.6	48.6	18.8	...	...	...	...	1,587	71.5	227[13]	10.2[13]
Zimbabwe	1982	2,484	39.2	63.5[39]	33.1	41.1	25.4	...	...	...	...	277[26,50]	26.1[26,50]	233[26,50]	22.0[26,50]

[1]Services includes finance, real estate and public administration, defense. [2]Unemployed, not previously employed only. [3]State sector only. [41]1983. [5]Excludes armed forces. [61]1984. [7]Employed persons only. [8]Agriculture includes mining, quarrying. [9]Manufacturing; mining, quarrying; public utilities includes transportation, communications. [10]Services includes public administration, defense. [11]Unemployed only. [12]Services includes hotels. [13]Manufacturing; mining, quarrying; public utilities includes construction. [14]Services includes transportation, communications; trade, hotels, restaurants; finance, real estate; and public administration, defense. [15]Services includes finance, real estate. [16]Mostly unemployed. [17]Over age 16. [18]1970. [19]1982. [20]Wage earners and self-employed only. [21]1980. [22]Includes unemployed, not previously employed. [23]1981. [24]Includes unemployed. [25]1986. [26]1985. [27]Ages 20–64. [28]Ages 16–64. [29]1976. [30]Distribution by economic sector excludes persons not working regularly on a weekly basis. [31]Ages 15–59. [32]1975. [33]Includes unemployed seasonal agricultural workers. [34]Includes unemployed seasonal nonagricultural workers. [35]1979. [36]Mostly unemployed, not previously employed. [37]Services includes hotels and restaurants. [38]Excludes unemployed.

construction number ('000)	construction % of econ. active	transportation, communications number ('000)	transportation, communications % of econ. active	trade, hotels, restaurants number ('000)	trade, hotels, restaurants % of econ. active	finance, real estate number ('000)	finance, real estate % of econ. active	public administration, defense number ('000)	public administration, defense % of econ. active	services number ('000)	services % of econ. active	other number ('000)	other % of econ. active	country
157	7.4	177	8.4	375	17.8	146	6.9	116	5.5	558	26.4	16[22]	0.8[22]	Norway
128	27.5	6	1.4	124	26.4	8	1.7	10	10	77[10]	16.5[10]	—	—	Oman
														Pacific Is., Trust Terr. of the
0.4	8.4	9	9	0.5	12.3	—	0.7	0.6	13.4	1.6	36.4	0.8[16]	18.4[16]	Marshall Islands
0.9	9.6	9	9	0.9	8.8	0.1	1.2	1.8	18.0	3.1	31.5	2.2[16]	22.8[16]	Micronesia, Fed. States of
1.0	16.4	9	9	0.9	15.1	0.2	2.7	1.3	20.7	1.8	30.1	0.2[16]	2.7[16]	Northern Mariana Islands
0.5	16.4	9	9	0.3	11.6	—	1.6	0.5	16.2	1.0	32.8	0.2[16]	8.0[16]	Palau
1,556	5.4	1,445	5.0	3,207	11.1	245	0.8	10	10	3,077[10]	10.7[10]	1,249	4.3	Pakistan
35	4.8	38	5.2	93	13.0	27	3.7	10	10	179[10]	24.9[10]	90[16]	12.5[16]	Panama
22	2.9	1.7	2.4	25	3.4	4	0.6	10	10	77[10]	10.5[10]	2	0.2	Papua New Guinea
70	6.7	31	2.9	86	8.3	18	1.7	10	10	174[10]	16.8[10]	86[22]	8.3[22]	Paraguay
252	3.6	308	4.4	1,034	14.8	175	2.5	10	10	1,852[10]	26.5[10]	—	—	Peru
678	3.1	913	4.3	2,650	12.2	351	1.6	10	10	3,515[10]	16.2[10]	1,317[16]	6.1[16]	Philippines
—	—	0.005	14.3	0.002	5.7	0.016	45.7	10	10	0.007[10]	20.0[10]	—	—	Pitcairn Island
1,317	7.3	1,023	5.7	1,477	8.2	444	2.5	276	1.5	2,409	13.4	878[64]	4.9[64]	Poland
352	7.5	185	3.9	630	13.5	131	2.8	10	10	954[10]	20.4[10]	394[16]	8.4[16]	Portugal
41	4.1	38	3.9	154[12]	15.5[12]	32	3.2	10	10	369[10,12]	37.1[10,12]	165[11]	16.6[11]	Puerto Rico
36.1	17.9	6.1	3.0	30.8	15.3	7.8	3.9	10	10	74.9[10]	37.3[10]	2.0[11]	1.0[11]	Qatar
11	6.5	6	3.4	14	8.3	16	9.4	10	10	45[10]	25.8[10]	55[16]	31.9[16]	Réunion
790	7.4	736	6.9	619	5.8	15	15	53	0.5	1,280[15]	12.0[15]	149	1.4	Romania
25	0.9	7	0.3	26	1.0	1	—	10	10	74[10]	2.8[10]	8	0.3	Rwanda
...	...	...	...	...	...	...	...	10	10	...	...	...	...	St. Helena and Ascension
0.4[7]	2.7[7]	0.5[7]	3.0[7]	0.9[7]	6.3[7]	0.3[7]	1.9[7]	10	10	4.7[7,10]	31.7[7,10]	0.5[7]	3.1[7]	St. Kitts and Nevis
...	8.1[7]	...	4.6[7]	...	8.7[7]	...	1.5[7]	10	7.4[7]	...	24.7[7]	—	—	St. Lucia
0.1	5.4	0.2	8.5	0.6	26.1	—	2.1	10	10	0.8[10]	32.5[10]	0.3[16]	10.5[16]	St. Pierre and Miquelon
2.9	12.1	1.1	4.5	2.9	12.1	1	1	1	1	7.2[1]	30.3[1]	0.7	3.1	St. Vincent
0.965	7.4[65]	0.1	1.2	1.7	14.4	0.2	1.9	1.9	16.2	0.7	5.8	1.7[24]	14.7[24]	San Marino
1.8	5.9	1.0	3.4	2.0	6.5	0.2	0.5	10	10	5.8[10]	19.0[10]	1.4[11]	4.6[11]	São Tomé and Príncipe
568	18.7	210	6.9	374	12.3	94	3.1	10	10	902[10]	29.8[10]	—	—	Saudi Arabia
8[19,50]	7.2[19,50]	25[19,50]	21.3[19,50]	15[19,50]	12.6[19,50]	8[19,50]	6.8[19,50]	10	10	14[10,19,50]	12.3[10,19,50]	—	—	Senegal
1.1[66]	4.4[66]	2.3[66]	9.4[66]	3.1[66]	12.8[66]	0.8[66]	3.4[66]	10	10	3.6[10,66]	15.0[10,66]	8.6[24,66]	35.8[24,66]	Seychelles
13	13	14	14	14	14	14	14	14	14	2431[14]	18.0[14]	—	—	Sierra Leone
100	8.1	114	9.3	266	21.7	100	8.1	10	10	259[10]	21.1[10]	81[16]	6.6[16]	Singapore
2.2	5.6	2.0	5.1	3.3	8.4	0.6	1.4	10	10	9.4[10]	23.9[10]	0.3	0.8	Solomon Islands
13	13	14	14	14	14	14	14	14	14	384[14]	17.4[14]	—	—	Somalia
556	6.4	418	4.8	942	10.8	339	3.9	446	5.1	1,520	17.5	1,077[16]	12.4[16]	South Africa
...	...	...	...	68	68	...	...	29	7.2	226[8]	5.5[68]	306[24,69]	75.4[24,69]	Bophuthatswana
5.1	5.6	4.8	5.3	12.5	13.8	1.1	1.2	10	10	29.9[10]	33.0[10]	—	—	Ciskei
9.3	7.7	1.0	0.8	7.9	6.5	1.0	0.8	59	48.3	25	20.8	—	—	Transkei
1.5	5.1	0.8	2.8	2.6	8.6	0.1	0.4	10	10	8.4[10]	28.2[10]	7.4[16]	25.0[16]	Venda
13	13	14	14	14	14	14	14	14	14	1481[14,21]	34.7[14,21]	—	—	South West Africa/Namibia
1,194	8.7	672	4.9	2,374	17.2	526	3.8	10	10	2,695[10]	19.6[10]	1,228[36]	8.9[36]	Spain
227	3.8	220	3.7	514	8.6	65	1.1	10	10	631[10]	10.6[10]	1,047[16]	17.5[16]	Sri Lanka
13	13	14	14	14	14	14	14	14	14	1,618[14]	23.1[14]	—	—	Sudan, The
3.9	4.0	2.9	3.0	11.4	11.7	2.0	2.0	10	10	38.0[10]	38.9[10]	17.7[16]	18.1[16]	Suriname
13	13	14	14	14	14	14	14	14	14	541[14]	19.9[14]	—	—	Swaziland
257	5.9	302	6.9	594	13.5	328	7.5	204	4.7	1,371	31.3	120[16]	2.7[16]	Sweden
222	7.2	183	5.9	551	17.8	271	8.8	259	8.4	387	12.5	52[24]	1.7[24]	Switzerland
386	15.5	158	6.3	258	10.4	23	0.9	10	10	559[10]	24.4[10]	—	—	Syria
373	4.0	424	4.5	1,310	13.9	214	2.3	1,398	14.9	580	6.2	206[16]	2.2[16]	Taiwan
13	13	14	14	14	14	14	14	14	14	1,353[14]	12.4[14]	—	—	Tanzania
764	2.8	604	2.2	2,808	10.4	1	1	1	1	2,767[1]	10.3[1]	2,102[16]	7.8[16]	Thailand
21[23]	2.3[23]	21[23]	2.3[23]	105[23]	11.6[23]	2[23]	0.2[23]	10	10	64[10,23]	7.1[10,23]	50[23,36]	5.6[23,36]	Togo
—	—	—	0.9	—	3.0	—	—	0.1	10.0	0.4	55.2	0.1	14.8	Tokelau
1.2	5.4	0.8	3.9	0.8	3.8	0.1	0.3	1.4	6.4	2.7	12.6	4.4[36]	20.7[36]	Tonga
102[65]	21.8[65]	30	6.5	105	22.6	1	1	1	1	108[1]	23.2[1]	113[36]	2.3[36]	Trinidad and Tobago
237	11.1	87	4.1	154	7.2	13	0.6	130	6.1	212	9.9	446[16]	20.9[16]	Tunisia
765	4.0	531	2.8	1,084	5.6	294	1.5	1,293	6.7	1,132	5.9	867[16]	4.5[16]	Turkey
0.3	9.7	0.1	3.7	0.1	4.3	—	1.0	0.7	24.8	0.5	17.1	0.7[16]	24.0[16]	Turks and Caicos Islands
0.2	5.6	0.1	2.7	0.1	2.4	—	0.3	0.2	4.4	0.2	4.2	3.1[24,72]	77.5[24,72]	Tuvalu
13	13	14	14	14	14	14	14	14	14	797[14]	11.3[14]	—	—	Uganda
11,659	8.9	12,513	9.6	10,108	7.7	670	0.5	2,375	1.8	23,774	18.1	1,646	1.3	U.S.S.R.
221	24.8	66	7.4	121	13.6	28	3.1	10	10	318[10]	35.7[10]	—	—	United Arab Emirates
1,487	5.4	1,454	5.2	4,988	18.0	2,456	8.8	2,309	8.3	5,257	18.9	3,229[11]	11.6[11]	United Kingdom
8,169	6.8	6,519	5.5	24,565	20.5	12,317	10.3	18,399	15.4	18,132	15.2	1,084[74]	0.9[74]	United States
63	5.4	59	5.0	137	11.7	42	3.6	10	10	362[10]	30.9[10]	99[22]	8.5[22]	Uruguay
1.1	2.2	1.3	2.6	2.2	4.3	0.3	0.6	10	10	5.5[10]	10.7[10]	0.3	0.6	Vanuatu
555	9.1	374	6.1	1,181	19.3	312	5.1	10	10	1,579[10]	25.8[10]	112[36]	1.8[36]	Venezuela
517	1.8	188	0.7	447	1.6	1	1	1	1	9,194[1]	32.0[1]	—	—	Vietnam
3.7	9.7	2.8	7.4	9.0	23.8	2.6	6.7	4.1	10.8	9.2	24.2	2.3[11]	6.2[11]	Virgin Islands (U.S.)
13	13	—	1.2	0.1	1.5	1	1	1	1	0.4[1]	12.5[1]	—	—	Wallis and Futuna
40.8	23.5	8.2	4.7	23.1	13.3	15	15	21.0	12.1	8.2[15,49]	4.7[15,49]	6.6[11]	3.8[11]	West Bank
...	...	...	...	...	...	...	...	...	...	...	...	...	...	Western Sahara
2.3	5.5	1.4	3.3	1.8	4.4	1.3	3.1	1.8	4.4	6.4	15.4	0.3	0.6	Western Samoa
39	7.0	32	5.8	47	8.6	0.6	0.1	10	10	106[10]	19.3[10]	—	—	Yemen (Aden)
122	8.2	76	5.1	202	13.5	8	0.5	10	10	120[10]	8.0[10]	—	—	Yemen (Ṣan'ā')
689	7.4	445	4.8	828	8.8	205	2.2	10	10	1,585[10]	16.9[10]	714[16]	7.6[16]	Yugoslavia
13	13	14	14	14	14	14	14	14	14	2,035[14]	17.4[14]	—	—	Zaire
13	13	14	14	14	14	14	14	14	14	407[14]	18.3[14]	—	—	Zambia
46[26,50]	4.3[26,50]	50[26,50]	4.8[26,50]	79[26,50]	7.4[26,50]	16[26,50]	1.5[26,50]	92[26,50]	8.7[26,50]	266[26,50]	25.2[26,50]	—	—	Zimbabwe

[39]Over age 15. [40]Over age 12. [41]Ages 15–69. [42]Transportation, communications includes public utilities. [43]Republic of Cyprus only. [44]Over age 10. [45]Ages 14–64. [46]Employers, self-employed includes unpaid family workers. [47]Ages 14–59. [48]Over age 14. [49]Services includes public utilities. [50]Wage earners only. [51]Data are for persons aged 15–64 only. [52]Workers covered by compulsory social insurance only. [53]1978. [54]Excludes Assam. [55]1971. [56]Mostly underemployed informal workers. [57]1977. [58]1973. [59]Island of Mauritius only. [60]1966. [61]Excludes indigenous areas, former Canal Zone, and institutional households. [62]Citizens over age 10 involved in money-raising activities only. [63]Ages 18–64 (male) and ages 18–59 (female). [64]Mostly employed abroad. [65]Construction includes public utilities. [66]Excludes self-employed and domestic workers. [67]Mining only. [68]Services includes trade and manufacturing. [69]Mostly migrant workers. [70]Ages 10–64. [71]De facto indigenous population only. [72]Mostly workers in the noncash economy. [73]Includes communal workers and their families. [74]Unemployed not previously employed and persons whose last job was in the armed forces only.

Agriculture and land use

This table provides data on the structure of national agricultural sectors from the perspective of farms and farmland use. The data are taken mainly from national agricultural censuses and surveys, supplemented by reports of the United Nations Food and Agriculture Organization's (FAO's) *World Census of Agriculture*. Many of these national censuses, of course, are taken under guidelines established by the FAO for the *World Census of Agriculture* programs (the 1990 census is the fifth and will include national censuses taken during the decade 1986–95). It represents a cooperative effort by FAO member countries to collect agricultural data within a general framework that permits international harmonization of concepts and definitions; transfer of technical expertise; and increased effectiveness in the collection, analysis, publication, and policy-related use of such statistics. Some 92 countries participated in the 1980 round; more than 100 countries were expected to participate in the 1990 round of censuses.

All agricultural statistics are subject to quality-control problems, including errors or biases arising from such factors as incomplete or inaccurate lists of holdings, ambiguous questions, respondents who inadvertently or willfully give inaccurate information, failure to record data for all parts of fragmented holdings, respondents' misunderstandings of the definitions of land use and cropping methods, or a failure to report livestock tem-

porarily absent from the holding on public or common pasture land or in transit. Frequently subjects studied, classificational schemes, and definitions vary from the FAO guidelines from country to country (economic planners need different information about a commercial, high-technology, multicrop agricultural sector than they do for a family-subsistence, low-technology, one-crop sector). When a complete census of agriculture is impossible, a sample survey may be taken. This is a limited census of a predetermined number of carefully screened holdings. From these results, nationwide projections may be prepared, but these are often of uncertain reliability.

With respect to the first section of the table, number and size of farms, many countries impose a minimum size limit for holdings that may be covered in their census reports, and this cutoff, if not sufficiently low, can result in a substantial undercount of smaller holdings; conversely Soviet bloc nations often publish statistics only on state collective or cooperative farms and exclude privately held plots of land, even though in some instances these provide a significant fraction of agricultural output.

The land tenure statistics classify farms according to the rights under which the farmer holds the land. Owner-operated includes two types of ownership: outright ownership in which the holder has title and has the right to determine use and transfer of the land; and ownerlike possession

Agriculture and land use

country	farms (latest census of agriculture)[a]											tenure (% of farms)					
	year	number of farms ('000)	size of holding									owner-operated			rented (including share-croppers)	tribal/ com-munal	other[b]
			average (ha)	size class (%)								individual/ family	corporate/ state	socialized/ collective			
				under 1 ha	1–5 ha	5–10 ha	10–20 ha	20–50 ha	50–200 ha	over 200 ha						
Afghanistan	1981	126[1]	3.5[1]	44.8[1]	35.2[1]	—	—	20.0[1]	—	—		55.1[1]	—	—	25.1[1]	—	19.8[1]
Albania	1983	0.4	1,686	...	...	...	...	...	...	...		—	—100.0—		—	...	...
Algeria	1973	899	6.2	1.1	12.7	15.8	21.7	25.6	18.0	5.1		...	...	...	...	...	...
American Samoa	1980	1.3	1.8	49.2[5]	45.5[6]	—4.9[7]—		—	0.4[8]	—		85.9	...	...	5.0	—	9.1
Andorra	...	...	...	...	...	...	...	...	...	...		...	...	...	...	...	...
Angola	1970	1,067	3.9	3.3	13.5	9.3	11.3	13.7	19.2	29.7		80.5	1.1	—	—	18.2	0.2
Anguilla	...	...	...	...	...	...	...	...	...	...		...	...	...	...	...	...
Antigua and Barbuda	1981	2.1	0.8	53.5	—46.5—		...	...	...	...		...	...	...	...	...	...
Argentina	1974	510	399	—19.4—		8.2	9.5	16.7	25.1	21.1		73.8[9]	...	—	11.7[9]	—	14.5[9]
Aruba	...	...	...	...	...	...	...	...	...	...		...	...	...	...	...	...
Australia	1985–86	173	2,834	0.7[10]	7.2[10]	5.2[10]	6.3[10]	11.9[10]	26.2[10]	42.6[10]		90.9	6.4	—	—	—	2.7
Austria	1980[11]	303	24.2	3.7	31.0	17.3	21.0	21.2	5.2	0.6		59.0	—	—	2.3	—	38.7
Bahamas, The	1978	4.2	8.5	55.25	30.16	—12.3[7]—		1.1[12]	0.4[13]	1.0[14]		74.9	0.6	—	4.0	—	20.5
Bahrain	1980	0.8	4.4	19.4	52.9	17.4	8.2	2.0	—0.1—			37.9	0.1	—	62.0	—	—
Bangladesh	1983–84	10,045	0.9	70.3	24.7[15]	—	—	5.0[16]	—	—		53.2[17]	...	...	0.5[17]	...	46.3[17]
Barbados	1969	0.2	95.8	...	...	...	...	...	...	...		...	...	...	...	...	...
Belgium	1985	100	13.9	2.4	37.7	15.4	21.0	20.1	—4.4—			27.7[9, 18]	...	0.8[9, 18]	71.5[9, 18]	—	—
Belize	1974	8.9	26.7	—69.4—			16.7	8.6	4.4	0.9		43.6	56.4	—	—	—	—
Benin	1983	...	...	...	...	...	...	...	...	...		...	...	...	...	...	...
Bermuda	1981	...	...	...	...	...	...	...	...	...		...	...	...	...	...	...
Bhutan	1984	...	1.6[20]	51.3[5, 20]	42.9[6, 20]	—	—	5.8[20, 21]	—	—		...	...	...	...	...	...
Bolivia	1980	700	25.0[22]	...	...	...	...	...	...	...		80.0[22]	...	...	...	...	20.0[22]
Botswana	1985	81.0	3.2	32.1	49.9	12.6	—	—5.4—				—	0.6	—	—	99.4	—
Brazil	1980	5,160	70.7	9.1	27.5	13.8	15.0	16.6	12.6	5.4		61.3	—	—	17.2	—	21.5[25]
British Virgin Islands	1981	0.3	...	...	...	...	...	...	...	...		...	...	...	...	...	...
Brunei	1964	6.3	2.6	44.1[5]	40.4[6]	—	—	15.5[21]	—	—		52.3	1.0	—	22.0	—	24.7
Bulgaria	1982	0.296[27]	12,431[27]	...	...	...	...	...	...	...		...	...	...	...	...	...
Burkina Faso	...	...	...	...	...	...	...	...	...	...		...	...	...	...	...	...
Burma	1981	4,285[22]	2.3[22]	61.2[22, 28]	—	—	38.8[22, 29]			—		...	...	...	...	...	...
Burundi	1983	...	...	...	...	...	...	...	...	...		...	...	...	...	...	...
Cameroon	1973	926	1.6	42.7	53.8	3.2	0.3	—	—	—		2.4	—	—	5.2	59.5	32.9
Canada	1986	293	231	1.6[5]	3.4[6]	12.1[32]	29.7[33]	14.6[34]	—38.6[35]—			—	—63.7[9]—		36.3[9]	—	—
Cape Verde	1979	...	...	...	...	...	...	...	...	...		...	...	...	...	...	...
Cayman Islands	1984	0.2	...	—	5.0	80.0	—	10.0	3.0	2.0		—	—90.0—		—	—10.0—	
Central African Republic	1974	283	1.7	32.2	65.2	2.5	—	—	—	—		0.3[9]	—	—	0.1[9]	98.6[9]	1.2[9]
Chad	1973	366	2.6	19.7	69.5	10.0	—0.8—		—	—		...	...	...	...	...	...
Chile	1976	306	94.1	...	...	...	...	...	...	...		...	...	...	...	...	...
China	1985	1,650[38]	...	...	...	...	...	...	...	...		—	10.0[10]	90.0[10]	—	—	—
Christmas Island	...	...	...	...	...	...	...	...	...	...		...	...	...	...	...	...
Cocos (Keeling) Islands	...	...	...	...	...	...	...	...	...	...		...	...	...	...	...	...
Colombia	1971	1,177	26.3	22.8	36.7	13.6	10.0	8.5	6.3	2.1		68.7	—	—	5.8	4.1	21.4
Comoros	1982	...	...	...	...	...	...	...	...	...		...	...	...	...	...	...
Congo	1986	143[39]	1.4[39]	37.3[39]	62.2[39]	0.5[39]	—	—	—	—		91.7[9]	8.3[9]	—	—	—	—
Cook Islands	1975[40]	1.1	2.3	...	...	...	...	...	...	...		...	...	...	...	...	...
Costa Rica	1973	82	38.3	23.3	25.5	11.2	10.8	15.2	10.7	3.3		97.9	1.7	—	0.1	—	0.3
Côte d'Ivoire	1975	550	5.0	9.5	54.4	24.9	9.4	1.7	0.1	—		...	...	...	...	...	...
Cuba	1985	...	...	...	...	...	...	...	...	...		...	...	...	...	...	...
Cyprus	1985	48.0	3.8	24.4	56.8	15.0	2.9	—0.9—				—	—79.0—		9.4	—	11.6[41]
Czechoslovakia	1980	1,391	8.1	89.9[42]	—	—9.9[43]—		0.0[44]	0.2[45]			6.0[9]	30.8[9]	63.2[9]	—	0.6	—
Denmark	1987	87	32.2	—3.0—		16.0	25.0	39.0	—17.0—			...	...	...	...	...	...
Djibouti	...	...	...	...	...	...	...	...	...	...		...	...	...	...	...	...
Dominica	1986	...	...	...	...	...	...	...	...	...		...	...	...	...	...	...
Dominican Republic	1981	385	6.3	16.0	65.7	8.5	5.4	2.6	1.5	0.3		53.2	18.5	4.5	1.6	—	17.4
Ecuador	1974	517	15.4	27.8	38.8	10.6	8.0	8.2	5.6	0.9		70.3	0.3	—	7.7	7.4	14.3
Egypt	1983	...	...	...	...	...	...	...	...	...		...	...	...	...	...	...
El Salvador	1970–71	271	5.4	48.9	37.9	5.8	3.4	2.6	1.2	0.2		41.5	—	—	28.2	6.3	24.1
Equatorial Guinea	...	...	...	...	...	...	...	...	...	...		...	...	...	...	...	...
Ethiopia	1976–77	4,893	1.4	49.9	46.5	3.4	0.2	—	—	—		98.4	1.6	—	—	—	—
Faeroe Islands	...	...	...	...	...	...	...	...	...	...		...	...	...	...	...	...
Falkland Islands	1982	0.041	32,586[46]	—	—	—	—	—	—	100.0		—	75.0[46]	—	—	—	25.0[46]

in which the holder lacks the legal title but uses it under perpetual lease, hereditary tenure, or leases of 30 years or more with nominal, or no, rent. Farms classed as owner-operated are divided into individual and family, corporate or state, and socialized or collective proprietorships. Rented includes sharecropping; communal/tribal includes types of customary or traditional arrangements in which title or goods do not change hands. "Other" usually includes farms held under multiple forms of tenure.

Statistics on types of farms by commodities produced refer to FAO categories. The terms "mainly crops" and "mainly livestock" indicate that more than half of the for-sale production was that indicated, and farms not fitting either category were defined as mixed.

The section on technology provides some principal measures of the extent to which modern technology plays a role in the farm activities of each country (although, of course, irrigation may employ technology developed in ancient times).

The classification of farmland by economic use is also subject to differing treatment internationally. For purposes of this table, "cropland" comprises: (1) land under temporary crops (those requiring replanting after each harvest), (2) land under permanent crops (those *not* requiring replanting, including tree, bush and shrub, and vine crops), and (3) land temporarily (less than five years) fallow (unused, but capable of being returned to cultivation with no special preparation). "Meadows and pastures" includes land (both permanent and temporary use) whose principal purpose is the raising of animal fodder or forage. "Woodland and forest" includes both natural and planted tracts of timber, whether harvested or not. "Other" comprises: (1) mixed and multiple use lands, (2) residue of farmland holdings not classifiable according to categories listed above (including areas of farm buildings, roads, ornamental gardens, flooded land, wasteland, etc.), (3) land not classified by respondents in census, or (4) detail not distinguishable as one of categories above by reason of its summarization in a published source.

Measurements of area are given in hectares (1 hectare is equal to 2.4711 acres). The following notes further define the column headings:
a. All properties used wholly or partly for agricultural production. A property need not have agricultural land to be considered a farm; piggeries, hatcheries, and poultry batteries are farms because they engage in agricultural production, *i.e.,* raise livestock and produce livestock products.
b. All forms of tenure not included in the preceding categories. Includes land operated by schools, religious bodies, squatters, seasonally by nomads, and built-on, waste, and similar types of alienation.
... Not available, or no agricultural census or survey ever taken.
—None, less than half the smallest unit shown, or not applicable.

activity (% of farms)			technology (% of farms using)				land in farms		land use (%) — cropland							country
mainly crops	mainly live-stock	mixed/ other	tractor	electri-city	irriga-tion works	artificial fertilizer (kg/ha)	total ('000 ha)	% of total land area	perma-nent crops	tempo-rary crops	fallow	total crop-land	mead-ows and pastures	wood-land and forest	other	
...	...	...	...	...	33[2]	2.5	39,810	61.0	1.8	46.3	51.9	19.9	75.4	4.8	...	Afghanistan
...	...	...	...	...	...	...	710	24.7	27.2	—72.8—		62.6	...	—37.4—	...	Albania
...	...	...	8[3]	...	4[2]	29[4]	5,544	2.3	4.1	65.1	30.8	93.9	2.3	3.9	...	Algeria
5.6	1.0	93.4	...	39.7	...	...	2.4	12.2	—89.3—		10.7	78.0	5.1	...	16.9	American Samoa
...	...	...	...	...	...	...	...	...	...	...	...	...	...	...	...	Andorra
...	...	...	3[3]	...	89.3	2[4]	4,180	3.4	36.8	63.2	—	1.7	82.0	...	16.2	Angola
...	...	...	...	...	...	...	...	...	...	...	...	...	...	...	...	Anguilla
...	...	...	...	...	...	...	1.5	3.4	...	...	...	...	...	...	...	Antigua and Barbuda
10.6	78.9	10.5	6[3]	...	5[2]	4[4]	203,345	73.1	...	...	...	10.6	78.9	4.8	5.7	Argentina
...	...	...	...	...	...	...	...	...	...	...	...	...	...	...	...	Aruba
30.5	52.6	16.9	7[3]	...	3[2]	26[4]	485,200	63.2	0.3	—99.7—		10.0	90.0	...	...	Australia
...	...	...	71	...	...	256[4]	7,326	87.4	6.6	87.4	6.0	21.3	26.0	41.5	11.2	Austria
...	...	...	...	...	10.3	...	36.2	2.6	23.3	59.9	16.8	23.3	6.9	25.7	44.0	Bahamas, The
...	...	...	...	21.3	...	...	3.5	5.2	50.7	49.3	—	45.9	...	...	54.1	Bahrain
91.3[17]	8.7[17]	—	0.5[17]	...	43.3	51.0[17]	9,117	63.5	2.1[17]	96.3[17]	1.5[17]	88.7[17]	...	—11.3[17]—		Bangladesh
...	...	...	18[3]	...	...	200[4]	19.8	45.9	...	...	...	13.7	—86.3—			Barbados
...	...	...	146[3,19]	...	...	517[4,19]	1,390	45.5	7.4[18]	92.6[18]	—	62.8[18]	34.2[18]	0.7[18]	2.3[18]	Belgium
...	...	...	17[3]	...	4[2]	37[4]	233	10.0	13.1	81.1	5.8	36.5	15.9	36.1	11.6	Belize
...	...	...	...	...	1[2]	4[4]	3,300	29.3	...	...	...	100.0	...	...	...	Benin
...	...	...	...	...	...	...	0.3	6.6	24.2	63.0	12.7	83.8	10.8	5.4	...	Bermuda
...	...	...	...	...	...	2[4]	156	3.4	11.7	—88.3—		100.0	...	...	...	Bhutan
...	...	...	...	...	5[2]	2[4]	84,060	76.3	19.3	80.7	—	1.4	49.4	49.2	...	Bolivia
13.6	27.9	58.5	63	...	1[2]	1.7[23]	343[24]	5.9[24]	—	100.0[24]	—	83.5[24]	...	...	...	Botswana
80.0[26]	16.2[26]	3.8[26]	10[3]	4.1[26]	3[2]	45[4]	364,854	42.9	18.2	66.9	14.9	15.8	47.8	24.2	12.2	Brazil
...	...	...	...	...	...	...	...	...	...	...	...	...	...	...	...	British Virgin Islands
...	...	...	10[3]	...	14[2]	...	16.4	2.8	78.0	22.0	—	54.8	0.1	16.4	28.7	Brunei
...	...	...	14[3]	...	29[2]	233[4]	6,182	55.7	7.0	—93.0—		75.3	24.7	...	...	Bulgaria
...	...	...	...	...	...	4[4]	...	...	...	...	...	...	...	...	...	Burkina Faso
...	...	...	1[3]	...	11[2]	19[4]	10,300	15.2	—80.2[30]—		19.8[30]	14.8[30]	...	14.0[30]	71.2[30]	Burma
...	...	...	...	...	...	1	2,388	85.8	—73.8—		26.2	56.7	37.7	5.6	...	Burundi
...	...	...	...	...	...	60.0[31]	1,490	3.3	...	...	...	100.0	...	...	...	Cameroon
52.2	44.4	3.4	14[3]	...	6.5	51[4]	67,826	7.4	—79.6—		20.4	61.5	5.2	—33.3—		Canada
...	...	...	...	...	5[2]	—	25[36]	6.2[36]	20.8[36]	79.1[36]	—	100.0[36]	...	...	...	Cape Verde
2.4	7.1	90.5	90.0	...	85.0	...	...	...	...	...	...	...	...	...	...	Cayman Islands
...	...	...	...	...	...	1[4]	491	0.8	11.8	88.2	—	100.0	...	...	...	Central African Republic
...	...	...	...	...	...	2[4]	23,877[37]	45.8[37]	50.0[37]	—50.0[37]—		23.7[37]	76.3[37]	...	...	Chad
...	...	...	6[3]	...	23[2]	33	28,800	39.1	6.1	65.5	28.4	11.5	42.3	20.7	25.4	Chile
...	...	...	9[3]	...	44[2]	194[4]	143,600	15.0	2.6	—97.4—		100.0	...	...	...	China
...	...	...	...	...	...	...	...	...	...	...	...	...	...	...	...	Christmas Island
...	...	...	...	...	...	...	...	...	...	...	...	...	...	...	...	Cocos (Keeling) Islands
...	...	...	5[3]	...	6[2]	64[4]	30,993	27.0	30.6	27.6	41.8	24.7	56.4	...	18.9	Colombia
...	...	...	...	...	...	...	83	44.3	56.4	—43.6—		100.0	...	...	...	Comoros
...	...	...	1[3]	...	1[2]	4[4]	226	0.7	14.8	85.2	—	100.0	...	...	...	Congo
...	...	...	...	...	...	...	...	...	55.9	21.9	22.2	100.0	...	...	...	Cook Islands
...	...	...	10[3]	...	13[2]	149[4]	3,122	60.0	42.2	57.8	—	15.7	49.9	22.9	11.4	Costa Rica
...	...	...	1[3]	...	2[2]	10[4]	2,753	8.6	65.9	34.1	—	100.0	...	...	...	Côte d'Ivoire
...	...	...	20[3]	...	32[2]	179[4]	8,679	78.3	...	...	...	33.9	32.1	31.9	2.1	Cuba
72.7	27.3	—	25.5	...	17.3[9]	41[4]	210	35.6	34.7	54.3	11.0	74.9	—	—25.1—		Cyprus
34.3	24.4	41.3	26[3]	100.0	4[2]	339[4]	6,924	54.1	2.6	—97.4—		75.3	24.7	...	...	Czechoslovakia
51.6	23.1	25.3	85.5[18]	...	15[2]	251[4]	2,798	65.2	1.0	98.9	0.1	92.5	7.5	...	...	Denmark
...	...	...	...	...	...	...	...	...	...	...	...	...	...	...	...	Djibouti
...	...	...	5[3]	...	...	147[4]	20	26.3	...	...	...	...	...	...	...	Dominica
44.0	56.0	—	80.0	60.0	18.2	40[4]	2,412	49.8	38.0	40.2	21.8	34.1	51.6	13.0	0.9	Dominican Republic
67.8	12.4	19.8	3[3]	...	21[2]	29[4]	7,955	29.6	32.8	51.5	15.7	32.8	32.2	29.0	6.0	Ecuador
...	...	...	17[3]	...	100[2]	344[4]	2,731	3.0	3.5	96.5	...	100.0	...	...	...	Egypt
95.3	4.7	—	5[3]	...	15[2]	76[4]	1,452	69.0	25.1	58.6	16.4	44.9	38.2	11.6	5.3	El Salvador
...	...	...	...	...	...	...	...	...	...	...	...	...	...	...	...	Equatorial Guinea
...	...	...	...	...	1[2]	2[4]	6,971	5.7	7.4	76.8	15.8	86.9	9.1	...	4.0	Ethiopia
...	...	...	...	...	...	...	...	...	...	...	...	...	...	...	...	Faeroe Islands
...	...	...	...	...	...	...	1,173[46]	96.4[46]	...	...	...	...	...	...	...	Falkland Islands

Agriculture and land use (continued)

country	year	number of farms ('000)	average (ha)	under 1 ha	1–5 ha	5–10 ha	10–20 ha	20–50 ha	50–200 ha	over 200 ha	individual/ family	corporate/ state	socialized/ collective	rented (including share-croppers)	tribal/ communal	other[b]
Fiji	1978–79	66	4.2	64.3	20.6	8.1	3.7	2.1	—1.2—		—	—	—	3.5	95.1	1.4
Finland	1985	200	60.0	—	15.2	25.6	30.2	23.2	—5.8—		79.9	0.7	—	19.3	—	0.1
France	1980	1,263	26.6	9.5	18.8	13.2	19.3	27.5	—11.7—		65.2[10]	—	—	33.5[10]	—	1.2[10]
French Guiana	1981	2.2	3.3	50.4	41.2	4.4			—4.0—							
French Polynesia	...	...	...	...	...	...	...	...	...	...	...	...	...	...	...	...
Gabon	1975	71	1.0	68.0	—32.0—		—	—	—	—	81.8	—	—	0.3	5.3	12.5
Gambia, The	...	...	...	...	...	...	...	...	...	...	...	...	...	...	...	...
Gaza Strip	1980	...	...	...	...	...	...	...	...	...	...	...	...	...	...	...
Germany, East	1982[48]	4.8	...	...	...	...	...	...	...	...	...	9.7	90.3	...	...	...
Germany, West	1983	887	13.6	16.0	26.4	15.4	18.8	19.5	3.9	—	39.5	—	—	6.7	—	53.8
Ghana	1970	805	3.2	36.6	48.7	9.0	3.9	1.8	—	—	...	...	...	...	...	...
Gibraltar		...	...	...	...	...	...	...	...	...	...	...	...	...	...	...
Greece	1981	999	3.5	24.7	54.2	15.0	4.7	1.2	—0.2—		...	...	...	...	...	...
Greenland		...	...	...	...	...	...	...	...	...	...	...	...	...	...	...
Grenada	1981	8	1.7	88.3[28]	6.9[49]	3.3[50]	0.7	0.4[12]	—0.3[51]—		—73.2—			14.1	—	12.7
Guadeloupe	1981	19	3.7	32.1	58.6	7.1			—2.2—		46.6[52]	—	—	19.1[52]	—	34.3[52]
Guam	1982	2.0	5.3	81.8[5]	12.2[6]	4.8[7]	1.2[8]	—	—	—	79.4	—	—	6.8	—	13.8
Guatemala	1979	600	6.8	39.7[54]	49.8[55]	8.2[56]	2.0[57]		—0.2[58]—		—74.0[59]—			6.3[59]	5.8[59]	13.9[59]
Guernsey	1987	0.106	18.6	6.7[60]	24.0[60]	23.1[60]	—46.1[60]—		—		31.1[9]	—	—	68.9[9]	—	—
Guinea		...	...	...	...	...	...	...	...	...	...	...	...	...	...	...
Guinea-Bissau	1961	87	3.0	13.4	73.3	10.0	3.0	0.3	—	—	...	...	...	...	...	...
Guyana	1964	...	...	...	...	...	...	...	...	...	...	90.0	...	...	—	10.0
Haiti	1971	617	1.4	58.7	37.5	—3.8—		—	—	—	66.6	—	—	25.0	—	8.4
Honduras	1974	195	13.5	17.3	46.6	14.5	9.8	7.8	3.3	0.8	99.7	0.1	—	—	0.2	—
Hong Kong	1986	11	0.3	97.5	2.3	0.1	—0.1—		—	—	—	—	9.0	77.0	—	14.0
Hungary	1981	798	8.3	...	...	...	...	...	...	...	6.8	13.3	74.5	...	...	...
Iceland	1981	7.0	...	15.7	9.3	11.7	23.7	35.8	—3.7—		...	...	...	...	...	...
India	1976–77	81,569	2.0	54.6	35.8	6.6	2.4	0.5	—0.1—		92.7	—	—	1.2	—	6.1
Indonesia[62]	1973	14,374	1.0	70.4	27.4	1.6	0.6	—	—	—	74.8	—	—	3.2	—	22.1
Iran	1973	...	...	...	...	...	...	...	...	...	...	...	...	...	...	...
Iraq	1971	591	9.7	20.2	29.3	21.4	18.5	9.0	1.3	0.3	52.5	—	—	40.9	—	6.6
Ireland	1986	279[26]	25.0[63]	2.7[26]	—37.8[26]—		—52.4[26]—		7.1[26]		72.0	—	—	28.0	—	—
Isle of Man	1987	0.8	59.7	25.8[64]	14.0[65]	18.2[12]	23.4[13]	—18.5[14]—		—	...	...	...	...	...	...
Israel	1981	52	11.3	26.5	57.6	8.3	4.0	2.0	—1.8—		84.0	—	1.4	—	—	14.6
Italy	1982	3,269	7.2	18.0[46]	30.2[46]	37.7[46]	3.1[46]	9.2[46]	1.8[46]	—	81.5[26]	—	—	6.7[26]	—	11.8[26]
Jamaica	1978–79	184	2.9	32.5[66]	60.7[67]	4.8[50]	0.9	0.4[12]	0.3[13]	0.4[14]	99.5[68]	0.2[68]	—	—	—	0.3[68]
Japan	1987	4,270	1.2	68.1	29.7	—2.2—					79.4[26]	—	—	...	...	20.6[26]
Jersey	1986	0.7	9.4	—45.6—		18.0	21.9	—14.5—			31.4[20]	—	—	68.6[20]	—	—
Jordan	1983	57	6.3	25.3	44.6	15.6	8.6	4.5	1.3	0.1	80.5	—	—	13.1	0.3	6.1
Kampuchea	...	...	...	...	...	...	...	...	...	...	...	...	...	...	...	...
Kenya	1976–79	2,750	2.5	65.5	27.3	2.7[70]	—4.4[71]—		—	—	...	...	...	...	...	...
Kiribati		...	...	...	...	...	...	...	...	...	...	...	...	...	...	...
Korea, North		...	...	...	...	...	...	...	...	...	...	...	...	...	...	...
Korea, South	1984	1,974	1.1	66.6	—33.4—		—	—	—	—	82.5[26]	—	—	17.4[26]	—	0.1[26]
Kuwait	1985–86	1.9	2.4	48.6[26]	25.4[26]	10.2[26]	8.7[26]	4.0[26]	3.1[26]	—	95.3	...	...	...	...	4.7
Laos	1983	...	...	...	...	...	...	...	...	...	...	...	...	...	...	...
Lebanon	1970	143	4.3	47.7	—44.5—		—6.5—		1.2	0.1	...	...	...	...	...	...
Lesotho	1970	187	2.0	27.0	67.5	—5.5—		—3.7—		—0.5—		...	...	...	...	...	...
Liberia[73]	1971	122	3.0	52.8	31.0	12.0	—42.0[75, 76]—		—13.0[75, 77]—		40.0[9]	—	—	—	43.3[9]	16.7[9]
Libya	1977	170	11.0	5.0[75]	—40.0[75]—						...	...	...	...	...	...
Liechtenstein	1985	0.45	8.7	30.8	27.9	13.4	13.2	13.6	—1.1—		85.5	—	—	11.7	—	2.8
Luxembourg	1987	4.2	33	8.4	17.3	9.1	11.4	29.8	—24.0—		51.7[9]	—0.6[9]—		47.7[9]	—	—
Macau		...	...	...	...	...	...	...	...	...	...	...	...	...	...	...
Madagascar	1984–85	1,544	1.3	65.0[10]	35.0[10]	—	—	—	—	—	...	...	...	...	...	...
Malawi	1980–81	1,136	1.2	54.9	40.1[15]	—5.0[16]—					...	...	...	...	...	...
Malaysia[78]	1980	920[79]	2.2[79, 80]	...	...	...	...	...	...	...	53.2[26, 79]	18.2[26, 81]	—	19.6[26, 79]	...	9.0[26, 79]
Maldives	1985	...	...	...	...	...	...	...	...	...	...	...	...	...	...	...
Mali	1982–83	562	4.0	20.1	54.1	17.4	—8.4—		—	—	96.8[83]	3.2	—	...	...	...
Malta	1983	12	1.1	67.8	30.0	2.0	—0.2—		—	—	16.0	—	—	70.4	—	13.6[41]
Martinique	1981	19.6	3.1	67.5	26.4	3.4	—2.1—		—0.6—		...	...	...	...	...	...
Mauritania	1985	...	...	...	...	...	...	...	...	...	...	...	...	...	...	...
Mauritius	1980	32.5	1.1	61.3	36.2	1.9	0.3	0.2	—0.1—		95.8	—	—	4.2	—	—
Mayotte	1978	4.8	1.7	...	...	...	...	...	...	...	...	...	...	...	...	...
Mexico	1970[84]	2,848	49	23.5	39.4	21.1	8.8	2.7	2.9	1.5	—97.6—			1.0	—	1.5
Monaco		...	...	...	...	...	...	...	...	...	...	...	...	...	...	...
Mongolia	1985	0.3	385,000	...	...	...	...	...	...	...	—	16.0[85]	84.0[85]	—	—	—
Montserrat	1979	0.8	1.2	62.5[66]	28.0[86]	—9.5[29]—					14.6	—	—	84.4	—	1.0
Morocco	1985–86	1,900[53]	3.9[53]	—75.0[53]—		—25.0[53]—					...	...	...	...	...	...
Mozambique	1973	1,605	3.1	—89.7[87]—		—10.0[88]—				—0.3—		0.2	0.1	—	—	99.7	—
Nauru		...	...	...	...	...	...	...	...	...	...	...	...	...	...	...
Nepal	1981–82	2,194	1.1	66.7	29.9	2.7	—0.7—				97.5	—	—	1.6	—	0.9
Netherlands, The	1987	132	15.3	11.2	22.1	16.4	22.2	24.2	—3.9—		—47.0[89]—		—	12.9[89]	—	40.1[41, 89]
Netherlands Antilles		...	...	...	...	...	...	...	...	...	...	...	...	...	...	...
New Caledonia	1983–84	12.7	23	71.2[28]	13.8[91]	3.7	2.3	2.5	3.8	2.8	...	...	...	...	...	...
New Zealand	1987	80.8	220	—12.5[89]—		10.3[89]	8.4[89]	—46.5[89]—		22.3[89]	85.7[89]	10.9[89]	—	—	—	3.4[89]
Nicaragua		...	...	...	...	...	...	...	...	...	...	...	...	...	...	...
Niger	1980[92]	699	4.9	3.8	54.1	37.8	—4.3—		—	—	...	...	...	...	...	...
Nigeria	1971	...	...	92	7.8	0.2	—	—	—	—	...	...	...	...	...	...
Niue	1985	...	...	...	...	...	...	...	...	...	100.0	—	—	—	—	—
Norfolk Island		...	...	...	...	...	...	...	...	...	...	...	...	...	...	...
Norway	1987	98	9.4	10.8[28]	24.8[91]	27.9	25.9	9.8	—0.8—		97.4[9, 18]	1.8[9, 18]	—	—	—	0.8[9, 18]
Oman	1978–79	65	1.3	...	...	...	...	...	...	...	...	...	...	...	...	...
Pacific Is., Trust Terr. of	1970	4.0	10.3	7.4	53.4	22.4	7.8	5.5	3.6	—	90.8	—	—	1.4	—	7.8
Marshall Islands		...	...	...	...	...	...	...	...	...	...	...	...	...	...	...
Micronesia, F.S. of		...	...	...	...	...	...	...	...	...	...	...	...	...	...	...

							farm land use									
activity (% of farms)			technology (% of farms using)				land in farms		land use (%)							country
									cropland							
mainly crops	mainly live-stock	mixed/ other	tractor	electri-city	irriga-tion works	artificial fertilizer (kg/ha)	total ('000 ha)	% of total land area	perma-nent crops	tempo-rary crops	fallow	total crop-land	meadows and pastures	wood-land and forest	other	
...	...	...	20[3]	...	3[2]	66[4]	277	15.2	...	...	...	...	...	...	...	Fiji
...	...	...	102[3]	100.0[26]	...	217[4]	12,025	39.5	0.3[26]	97.6[26]	2.1[26]	20.1	1.1	58.1	20.7	Finland
...	...	...	74.8	...	10.4	307[4]	33,649	61.8	7.4	90.6	2.0	53.6	34.1	8.2	4.1	France
...	...	...	32[3]	...	...	117[4]	7.3	0.1	10.4	52.5	37.3	89.6	10.4	...	...	French Guiana
...	...	...	2[3]	...	...	24[4]	...	...	...	...	...	...	...	...	...	French Polynesia
...	...	...	3[3]	...	...	6[4]	73.0	0.3	...	...	...	...	...	...	...	Gabon
...	...	...	...	...	20[2]	13[4]	...	...	...	...	...	...	...	...	...	Gambia, The
30.0	68.5	1.5	...	...	52.8[47]	...	19.3	53.2	74.6	25.4	...	100.0	...	...	...	Gaza Strip
...	...	...	31[3]	...	3[2]	314[4]	6,208	57.3	...	...	...	75.9	20.1	...	4.0	Germany, East
...	...	...	199[3]	...	4[2]	427[4]	12,026	48.4	1.2[18]	—97.8[18]—		51.7[18]	32.6[18]	11.5[18]	4.2[18]	Germany, West
...	...	...	1[3]	...	...	3[4]	2,574	10.8	61.4	38.6	—	100.0	...	...	...	Ghana
...	...	...	...	...	...	...	...	...	...	...	...	...	...	...	...	Gibraltar
...	...	...	43[3]	...	57.3	168[4]	3,546	26.9	29.2	61.1	9.7	98.1	1.9	...	...	Greece
...	...	...	...	...	...	...	...	...	...	...	...	...	...	...	...	Greenland
...	...	...	2[3]	...	...	...	13.9	40.2	...	...	...	...	...	...	...	Grenada
84.2	15.8	—	3.2	...	5[2]	255	70	39.6	23.0	73.3	3.7	56.2	25.2	7.6	11.0	Guadeloupe
...	...	...	9.7	88.4[53]	...	...	10.8	19.9	—51.2—		48.8	17.8	34.3	—47.9—		Guam
...	...	...	2[3]	...	4[2]	50[4]	4,147	38.1	27.6	—72.4—		42.0	27.3	27.2	3.4	Guatemala
—	100.0	—	...	...	4[2]	...	2	31.2	—	100.0	—	7.6	92.4	...	...	Guernsey
...	...	...	...	...	...	...	...	...	...	...	...	...	...	...	...	Guinea
...	...	...	...	...	...	...	169	4.7	...	...	...	...	...	...	...	Guinea-Bissau
...	...	...	7[3]	...	26[2]	30[4]	10,652	26.2	...	...	...	8.4	91.6	...	...	Guyana
...	...	...	1[3]	...	8[2]	4[4]	1,579	57.0	...	...	...	54.4	33.3	12.3	...	Haiti
56.3	37.3	6.4	2[3]	...	5[2]	21[4]	2,630	23.5	15.4[18]	34.6[18]	50.0[18]	52.0[18]	48.0[18]	...	...	Honduras
...	...	...	22.7	...	90.0	100.0[23]	7.3	6.8	7.4	37.0	55.6	100.0	...	...	...	Hong Kong
...	...	...	10[3]	...	4[2]	288[4]	7,413	79.7	11.8	86.1	2.1	71.7	17.3	...	11.0	Hungary
...	...	...	1,750[3]	87.0[37]	...	3,330[4]	...	...	...	...	...	...	...	...	...	Iceland
86.8	—	13.2	3[3]	...	24[2]	47[4]	163,343	49.7	—88.3[61]—		11.7[61]	96.0[61]	1.5[61]	—2.5[61]—		India
...	...	...	1[3]	...	26[2]	90[4]	14,168	7.4	21.6	71.1	7.3	89.5	0.6	1.4	8.5	Indonesia[62]
...	...	...	7[3]	...	39[2]	62[4]	20,235	12.3	...	...	...	...	...	...	...	Iran
87.9	11.2	0.8	7[3]	...	32[2]	22[4]	5,732	13.1	3.0	62.4	34.6	87.2	0.7	0.2	11.9	Iraq
...	...	...	159[3]	...	...	697[4]	5,692	82.6	0.5	99.5	...	9.5	69.5	—21.0—		Ireland
...	...	...	...	...	...	...	48	83.3	3.5	—96.5—		12.8	87.2	...	...	Isle of Man
...	...	...	30.9	...	64[2]	229[4]	584	28.2	22.0	—78.0—		70.5	19.1	...	10.4	Israel
...	...	...	52.6	...	25.5	171[4]	23,632	78.4	26.3[46]	73.7[46]	...	52.4[46]	21.2[46]	17.1[46]	9.3[46]	Italy
80.8[24]	—19.2[24]—		11[3]	...	13[2]	86[4]	603[68]	54.8[68]	22.2[68]	72.2[68]	5.6[68]	41.3[68]	21.6[68]	13.5[68]	23.6[68]	Jamaica
85.1[53]	14.9[53]	—	345[3]	...	68[2]	440[4]	5,340	14.1	10.3	—89.7—		95.5	—	...	4.5	Japan
...	...	...	...	...	...	...	6.5	56.2	—98.9—		1.1	63.4	—	—36.6—		Jersey
58.2[46,69]	14.9[46,69]	26.9[46,69]	5.0	1.5	19.2	35.5[23]	364	4.1	13.3	63.0	23.7	87.7	1.0	0.3	11.0	Jordan
...	...	...	...	...	3[2]	1[4]	...	...	...	...	...	...	...	...	...	Kampuchea
...	...	...	3[3]	...	2[2]	34[4]	6,922	11.9	11.5	—88.5—		71.0	23.8	1.9	3.3	Kenya
...	...	...	...	...	...	...	...	...	...	...	...	...	...	...	...	Kiribati
...	...	...	29[3]	...	46[2]	335[4]	...	...	...	...	...	...	...	...	...	Korea, North
94.0[68]	0.4[68]	5.6[68]	0.4	10.3[72]	55[2]	359[4]	2,152	21.7	5.9	—94.1—		100.0	...	...	...	Korea, South
36.7	61.8	1.5	100.0	100.0	100	150[4]	44.7	2.5	...	...	...	100.0	...	...	...	Kuwait
77.0[69]	8.1[69]	14.9[69]	1[3]	...	13[2]	...	1,680	7.1	2.3	—97.7—		52.4	47.6	...	...	Laos
...	...	...	10[3]	...	29[2]	170[4]	275[24]	27.0[24]	36.7[24]	39.7[24]	23.6[24]	100.0[24]	...	...	...	Lebanon
5.3[69]	93.3[69]	1.4[69]	5[3]	...	...	15[4]	372	12.3	—	89.6	10.4	98.8	...	...	1.2	Lesotho
...	...	...	1[3]	...	1[2]	3[4]	370[74]	3.8[74]	66.2[74]	33.8[74]	...	98.3[74]	...	1.7[74]	...	Liberia[73]
...	...	...	13[3]	...	11[2]	55[4]	8,800[74]	5.1[74]	—33.3[74]—		66.7[74]	20.5[74]	79.5[74]	...	...	Libya
23.9	61.6	14.5	...	...	...	...	3.7	23.1	1.6	—98.4—		30.4	66.0	2.5	1.1	Liechtenstein
27.6	58.3	14.1	...	...	...	19	139	53.7	2.5	97.1	0.4	41.2	49.9	8.0	0.9	Luxembourg
...	...	...	...	...	...	...	...	...	...	...	...	...	...	...	...	Macau
...	...	...	1[3]	...	33[2]	24	2,044	3.5	15.4	84.6	—	100.0	...	...	...	Madagascar
22.1	...	77.9	1[3]	...	0.2[47]	32.7[23]	1,332	14.1	0.2	99.8	—	94.8	...	5.2	...	Malawi
...	...	...	2[3,82]	...	8[2,82]	140[4,82]	4,100[20]	31.2[20]	84.8[20]	15.2[20]	—	100.0[20]	...	...	...	Malaysia[78]
...	...	...	...	...	...	...	19	63.5	—	100.0	—	100.0	...	...	...	Maldives
...	...	...	...	...	17[2]	11[4]	2,277	1.8	...	...	...	...	...	...	...	Mali
...	...	...	12.9	...	8[2]	86[4]	13.0	41.2	5.0	—95.0—		87.5	...	—12.5—		Malta
...	...	...	50[3]	...	30[2]	530[4]	75.4	71.1	39.6	60.0	0.4	36.9	33.6	10.0	19.5	Martinique
...	...	...	2[3]	...	4[2]	2[4]	194	0.2	—	56.2	43.8	100.0	...	...	...	Mauritania
...	...	...	3[3]	...	16[2]	253[4]	171	91.5	5.9	94.1	—	62.2	4.4	33.4	...	Mauritius
...	...	...	...	...	...	...	8.0	21.0	...	...	...	...	...	...	...	Mayotte
88.8	8.3	2.9	6[3]	...	20[2]	67[4]	139,868	72.7	6.3	58.1	35.6	16.5	53.3	14.2	16.0	Mexico
...	...	...	...	...	...	...	...	...	...	...	...	...	...	...	...	Monaco
...	...	...	8[3]	...	3[2]	13[4]	124,587	79.6	—	66.8	33.2	0.9	99.1	...	...	Mongolia
...	...	...	...	...	...	...	1.6[38]	15.3[38]	32.1[38]	67.9[38]	—	46.9[38]	53.1[38]	...	...	Montserrat
...	...	...	4[3]	...	6[2]	30[4]	8,062	17.6	6.6	72.9	20.5	100.0	...	...	...	Morocco
...	...	...	2[3]	...	3[2]	1[4]	13,626	17.8	—44.9—		55.1	55.0	45.0	...	...	Mozambique
...	...	...	...	...	...	...	...	...	...	...	...	...	...	...	...	Nauru
31.4[90]	55.6[90]	13.0[90]	1[3]	...	39	18[4]	2,464	16.7	1.3	97.1	1.6	94.0	1.7	0.6	3.7	Nepal
...	...	...	217[3]	...	59[2]	786[4]	2,014	48.1	—98.4—		0.6	45.9	54.1	...	...	Netherlands, The
...	...	...	...	...	...	...	...	...	...	...	...	...	...	...	...	Netherlands Antilles
13.1	67.9	19.0	7.3	...	...	5.6[23]	293	15.8	51.7	34.8	13.5	6.5	93.5	...	...	New Caledonia[53]
...	...	...	152[3]	...	1.2[47,89]	1,042[4]	17,795	66.4	13.0	87.0	...	1.9	98.1	...	...	New Zealand
...	...	...	2[3]	...	7[2]	38[4]	3,407	2.9	...	...	...	...	...	...	...	Nicaragua
...	...	...	...	...	...	...	...	...	...	...	...	...	...	...	...	Niger
...	...	...	...	...	4[2]	9[4]	34,290	37.1	—20.0—		80.0	31.4	27.5	41.1	...	Nigeria
...	...	...	5.0	...	—	80.0[23]	7.5	29.1	43.9	35.1	21.0	98.3	1.7	...	...	Niue
...	...	...	...	...	...	...	...	...	...	...	...	...	...	...	...	Norfolk Island
...	...	...	171[3]	...	10[2]	201	958	3.0	...	...	...	45.1	54.9	...	...	Norway
...	...	...	2[3]	...	87[2]	20[4]	83	0.3	68.6	31.4	...	49.2	—50.8—		...	Oman
...	...	...	...	...	...	...	40	21.1	54.2	9.8	36.0	68.7	17.5	...	13.7	Pacific Is., Trust Terr. of
...	...	...	...	...	...	...	...	...	...	...	...	...	...	...	...	Marshall Islands
...	...	...	...	...	...	...	...	...	...	...	...	...	...	...	...	Micronesia, F.S. of

Agriculture and land use (continued)

country	farms (latest census of agriculture)[a]															
	year	number of farms ('000)	size of holding								tenure (% of farms)					
			average (ha)	size class (%)							owner-operated			rented (including share-croppers)	tribal/com-munal	other[b]
				under 1 ha	1–5 ha	5–10 ha	10–20 ha	20–50 ha	50–200 ha	over 200 ha	individual/ family	corporate/ state	socialized/ collective			
Northern Mariana Is.	1980	0.3	16.5	32.8[28]	34.1[49]			33.1[21]			75.6	...	...	12.4	...	12.0
Palau				...	...	...		...		...	...	...	...	...	...	...
Pakistan	1980	4,070	4.7	17.2	56.2	17.4	6.5		2.7		64.1[9]	0.3[9]	—	35.6[9]	—	...
Panama	1980	153	14.7	41.0	25.0	9.3	9.0	9.0	5.6	1.0	23.2	—	—	2.0	—	74.8[25]
Papua New Guinea[93]	1985	0.8	483			26.8[94]			28.3[94]	44.9[94]	26.9[9, 94]	71.0[9, 94]	—	2.1[9, 94]	—	...
Paraguay	1981	249	88	8.6	27.4	19.9	22.7	14.5	4.4	2.5	54.5	0.4	—	9.2	—	35.9[25]
Peru	1984	1,574	9.5	24.1	47.7	13.2	6.7	5.5	2.8		75.5	—	—	0.8	6.8	16.9
Philippines	1980	3,420	2.6	22.7	63.3	10.5		3.5			58.3	—	—	27.4	—	14.3
Pitcairn Island	...	...	...	...	...	...		...		...	...	...	...	...	...	...
Poland	1986	3,952	4.8	52.0[28]	19.5[91]	17.5		10.9		0.1	76.5[9]	—	23.5[9]			
Portugal	1979	784	6.6	44.5	41.9	7.7	3.3	1.5	0.7	0.4	68.1	—	—	8.7	—	23.2
Puerto Rico	1982	22	17.7	5.3[5, 53]	28.0[53, 95]	20.4[53]	20.3[53]	12.8[53]	10.8[53]	2.5[53]	79.3	—	—	7.4	—	13.3
Qatar	1986	0.8[94]	42.5[94]		79.1[24, 96]			20.9[24, 97]			...	...	...	...	...	...
Réunion	1981	21	3.6	50.9	41.6	5.3	1.8		0.3		46.1[98]	—	—	22.5[98]	—	31.4[98]
Romania	1985	4.8[48]	3,141[48]	...	...	...	...	...	...	...	...	13.7[9]	60.8[9]	—	—	25.5[9]
Rwanda	1984	1,112	1.2	56.8	26.8[99]		16.4[29]				50.9	—	—	1.4	—	47.7[41]
St. Helena	1983	...	...	...	...	...	...	...	...	...	—	—	—	100.0	—	...
St. Kitts and Nevis	1981	...	...	...	...	...	...	...	...	...	46.8[9]	48.0[9]	—	5.2[9]	—	...
St. Lucia	1973–74	11	2.7	47.8[66]	44.9[67]	4.3[50]	1.8	0.5[12]	0.2[13]	0.8[14]	69.1	—	—	18.3	—	12.6
St. Pierre and Miquelon	...	...	...	...	...	...	...	...	...	...	...	...	...	...	...	...
St. Vincent	1983	8[52]	1.8[52]	48.0[52, 66]	40.7[52, 86]	8.5[49, 52]	2.4[7, 52]		0.5[8, 52]		62.0[52]	—	—	8.8[52]	—	19.2[52]
San Marino	1975	0.7	7.0	21.3	47.8		24.7	5.1	1.1		39.9[9]	15.5[9]	—	29.9[9]	—	14.7[9]
São Tomé and Príncipe	1964	11.1	8.7	88.5	9.8	0.7	0.2	0.2	0.2	0.4	77.2	—	—	20.5	—	2.3
Saudi Arabia	1983	212	10.1	36.6	35.8	11.3	8.2	5.0	2.6	0.5	85.9	—	—	2.6	—	11.5
Senegal	1976	362	7.0			99.4			0.6		...	...	0.6	...	...	99.4
Seychelles	1977	4.9	1.5	...	...	...	...	...	...	...	...	...	...	...	...	...
Sierra Leone	1971	286	1.8	38.8	55.0		6.1		0.1		93.6	—	—	6.4	—	...
Singapore	1973	16	0.8	77.4	22.2	0.3		0.1			7.4	—	—	88.8	—	3.8
Solomon Islands	1975[79]	92	1.0	...	...	...	...	...	...	...	—	—	—	—	100.0	...
Somalia	1984	198	3.6	...	...	...	...	...	...	...	99.9	0.1	—	...	...	...
South Africa	1978	72	1,193	...	...	...	...	...	...	...	...	...	...	...	...	...
Bophuthatswana	1976	...	...	...	...	...	...	...	...	...	...	...	...	...	...	...
Ciskei	1986	...	...	...	...	...	...	...	...	...	...	...	...	...	...	...
Transkei	1976	...	...	...	...	...	...	...	...	...	...	...	...	...	...	...
Venda	1976	53.3	9.3	...	...	...	...	...	...	...	...	...	...	...	...	...
S.W. Africa/Namibia	1983	...	...	...	...	...	...	...	...	...	...	...	...	...	...	...
Spain	1982	2,375	18.7	26.4	37.1	14.0	10.2	7.1	3.9	1.3	75.4	—	—	4.0	—	20.6
Sri Lanka	1982	1,817	1.1	77.5[5]	22.2[100]		0.1[101]	0.1[12]	0.1[102]		77.1[98]	6.4[98]	0.1[98]	14.4[98]	—	2.0[98]
Sudan, The	1982	...	...	...	...	...	...	...	...	...	22.3	2.2	—	28.0	42.0	5.5
Suriname	1981	22	7.5	21.9[68]	61.2[68]	11.1[68]	3.6[68]	1.6[68]	0.3[68]	0.3[68]	20.2[68]	0.9[68]	—	49.5[68]	—	29.4[68]
Swaziland	1972	39	19.5	26.2	60.4		12.0			1.4	86.1	—	—	3.4	—	10.5
Sweden	1987	104[103]	27.9[103]	...	16.1[92, 103]	20.0[103]	21.9[103]	27.6[103]	13.7[103]	0.7[103]	47.5[103]	—	—	15.8[103]	—	36.7[41, 103]
Switzerland	1985	119	9.1	23.1	18.7	14.6	27.5	15.2	0.9	—	36.2[24]	—	0.8[24]	58.5[24]	—	4.5[24]
Syria	1986	485[74]	11.5[74]		51.0[74, 96]		42.0[74, 104]		6.2[74, 105]	0.8[74, 106]	65.8[9, 83]	1.8[9]	32.5[9]			
Taiwan	1985	791	1.1	73.2[24]	26.2[24]	0.5[24]	0.1[24]	—	—	—	93.5	—	—	6.5	—	—
Tanzania	1972	2,489	3.0	59.7	37.7	2.1	0.4	0.1		0.2	87.3	—	—	3.6	—	9.1
Thailand	1983	4,471	3.6	14.7	70.2[107]		15.1[108]				72.4	—	—	5.5	—	22.1
Togo	1982–83	263	1.5	48.8	38.6[15]		12.7[16]				70.7[9]	—	—	21.1[9]	8.2[9]	—
Tokelau	1987	0.2	6.1	...	...	...	...	...	...	...	...	...	...	...	...	...
Tonga	1976	9.1	7.6	0.7	37.7		1.6				8.4	8.4	—	83.2	...	...
Trinidad and Tobago	1982	30.6	4.3	35.1	50.7	9.6	4.1	—	0.4	0.1	52.1	—	—	36.5	—	11.4
Tunisia	1986	...	...	...	...	...	...	...	...	...	...	...	...	...	...	...
Turkey	1980	3,651	6.2	15.8	46.3	20.2	11.6	5.3	0.8	—	88.6	—	—	12.1	—	1.2
Turks and Caicos Is.	...	...	...	...	...	...	...	...	...	...	...	...	...	...	...	...
Tuvalu	1976	1.5	1.7	...	...	...	...	...	...	...	99.9	—	—	...	0.1	...
Uganda	1964	1,171	3.9	20.7	59.8	11.2		8.3			97.4	—	—	—	—	2.6
U.S.S.R.	1987	49.6[48]	12,300[48]	—	—	—	—	—	—	100.0[48]	—	46.2	53.8	—	—	110
United Arab Emirates	1985–86	5.3[111]	2.6[111]	...	...	...	...	...	...	...	...	...	...	...	...	...
United Kingdom	1986	260	71.9	5.7[28]	8.3[91]	13.0	16.5	25.0	25.7	5.7		71.2[112]		28.8[112]	—	...
United States	1982	2,241	180.0		8.4[67]	20.0[7]		31.8[113]	23.5[114]	16.3[115]	75.2	12.7	—	11.6	—	0.5
Uruguay	1980	68	234.4	—	12.2	14.4	14.6	16.6	21.0	21.2		59.1		17.3	—	23.6
Vanuatu	1983–84	27	6.9	...	...	...	...	...	...	...	65.3[24]	34.7[24]	—	...	...	...
Venezuela	1971	288	91.9	5.8	37.7	17.2	14.4	11.3	7.9	5.7	61.5	—	—	6.1	—	31.3[25]
Vietnam	1983	...	...	...	...	...	...	...	...	...	...	...	...	...	...	...
Virgin Islands (U.S.)	1978	0.4	26.1	24.1[5]	41.8[95]	15.1	5.3	5.6	6.0	2.1	84.7	—	—	7.4	—	7.9
Wallis and Futuna	1983	...	...	...	...	...	...	...	...	...	...	...	...	...	...	...
West Bank	1980	...	...	...	...	...	...	...	...	...	...	...	...	...	...	...
Western Sahara	1983	...	...	...	...	...	...	...	...	...	...	...	...	...	...	...
Western Samoa	1975	...	...	...	...	...	...	...	...	...	...	...	...	...	86.0	14.0
Yemen (Aden)	1977	0.08[48]	604[48]	...	...	...	...	...	...	...	...	44.3[48]	55.7[48]	...	...	...
Yemen (San'ā')	1977–83	591	2.3	57.5	30.9	7.4	3.3	0.8	0.1		90.3[9]	—	—	9.4[9]	—	0.3[9]
Yugoslavia	1981	2,680	4.2	30.4	48.4	16.4	3.8	0.9	0.1		99.9	—	0.1	...	—	...
Zaire	1970	2,538	2.3	41.6	57.3	1.0	0.2	—	—	—	4.2	0.1	—	...	95.6	0.1
Zambia	1971	768	3.1	50.5	45.2		3.8		0.5			—	—	—	98.0	—
Zimbabwe	1974	765	38.7		16.7[116]		52.8[117]	29.8[118]	0.7[77]			2.0		—	98.0	—

[1]1967. [2]Irrigated land as percentage of area of arable land, not percentage of number of farms; 1984. [3]Tractors per 1,000 hectares of arable land; 1984. [4]Kilograms per hectare of arable land; 1984. [5]Less than 1.2 hectares. [6]1.2 to 4.0 hectares. [7]4.0 to 20 hectares. [8]20 hectares or more. [9]Based on area, not number of holdings. [10]1971. [11]Excludes holdings without land. [12]20 to 40 hectares. [13]40 to 81 hectares. [14]81 hectares or more. [15]1.0 to 3.0 hectares. [16]3.0 hectares or more. [17]1977. [18]1979. [19]Belgium includes Luxembourg. [20]1982. [21]4.0 hectares or more. [22]Family farms only. [23]Percentage of farms using artificial fertilizer. [24]1980. [25]Almost all squatters. [26]1970. [27]Government agro-industrial complexes. [28]Less than 2.0 hectares. [29]2.0 hectares or more. [30]1976. [31]1981. [32]4.0 to 28 hectares. [33]28 to 100 hectares. [34]100 to 160 hectares. [35]160 hectares or more. [36]Irrigated land only. [37]1968. [38]1984. [39]1973. [40]Rarotonga only. [41]Owned and rented holdings. [42]Less than 0.5 hectare. [43]0.5 to 50 hectares. [44]50 to 1,000 hectares. [45]1,000 hectares or more. [46]1975. [47]Irrigated land as percentage of all farmland. [48]State farms and cooperatives only. [49]2.0 to 4.0 hectares. [50]4.0 to 10 hectares. [51]40 hectares or more. [52]1972. [53]1978. [54]Less than 0.7 hectare. [55]0.7 to 7.1 hectares. [56]7.1 to 45 hectares. [57]45 to 452 hectares. [58]452 hectares or more. [59]Excludes holdings of 0.04 hectare (400 square metres) or less. [60]1974. [61]Excludes state of Punjab. [62]Excludes estates, collective farms, and traditional farms. [63]1980.

mainly crops	mainly livestock	mixed/ other	tractor	electricity	irrigation works	artificial fertilizer (kg/ha)	total ('000 ha)	% of total land area	permanent crops	temporary crops	fallow	total cropland	meadows and pastures	woodland and forest	other	country
...	...	...	...	...	...	...	...	...	...	...	...	...	...	...	...	Northern Mariana Is.
...	...	...	...	...	...	...	...	...	...	...	...	...	...	...	...	Palau
...	...	...	35.8	...	32.4	61[4]	19,109	24.0	---83.7---		16.3	93.8	...	0.6	5.6	Pakistan
...	...	...	3.9[10]	0.5[10]	5[2]	50[4]	2,259	29.3	21.6	43.3	35.0	24.6	57.4	15.6	2.4	Panama
...	...	...	3[3]	...	...	18[4]	386	0.8	100.0	—	—	33.7	26.4	...	39.9	Papua New Guinea[93]
33.0	---67.0---		4.5	...	56.2	5.4[23]	21,941	53.9	4.2	76.6	19.2	12.6	47.5	38.5	1.4	Paraguay
4.9	93.0	2.1	8.1	6.5	38.8	25.0[23]	14,893	11.6	24.1	75.9	—	27.1	47.5	19.8	5.6	Peru
98.2	1.5	0.3	4.0[10]	...	21.2[10]	33[4]	9,034	30.1	57.5	42.5	—	86.3	6.8	---6.9---		Philippines
...	...	...	...	...	...	...	...	...	...	...	...	...	...	...	...	Pitcairn Island
...	...	...	54[3]	...	1[2]	222[4]	18,804	60.1	1.6	---98.4---		86.7	13.3	...	...	Poland
...	...	...	58	...	79	78[4]	5,183	56.1	26.1	44.6	29.3	52.6	3.2	34.5	9.7	Portugal
...	...	...	6.2	...	3.7	...	386	43.6	---74.0---		26.0	28.7	49.6	16.8	4.9	Puerto Rico
99.7	0.3	—	21[3]	...	100.0	151[4]	65	5.7	36.1	63.9	—	6.5	...	...	93.5	Qatar
...	...	...	3.0	...	15.6[47, 98]	127[4]	74	29.1	5.0	86.3	8.7	61.2	11.6	13.8	13.4	Réunion
...	...	...	16[3]	...	20.4[47]	159[4]	15,038	63.3	6.0	94.0	—	70.7	29.3	...	...	Romania
...	...	...	...	...	0.2[47]	2[4]	1,350	51.3	---85.6---		14.4	63.7	10.6	5.2	20.5	Rwanda
...	...	...	...	...	—		4.0	12.9	—	---100.0---		50.0	50.0	...	...	St. Helena
...	...	...	...	...	...		12	45.3	31.5	---68.5---		58.1	---41.9---			St. Kitts and Nevis
25.0	---75.0---		...	...	5.8		29	47.3	68.5	---31.5---		57.9	10.2	26.4	5.5	St. Lucia
...	...	...	...	...	...	...	...	...	...	...	...	...	...	...	...	St. Pierre and Miquelon
...	...	...	...	...	2.2[52]		11	28.8	75.0	---25.0---		82.1	17.9	...	...	St. Vincent
...	...	...	...	...	...		4.7	76.5	60.9	6.5	32.6	69.2	6.2	8.2	16.4	San Marino
...	...	...	3[3]	...	6.2[47]	...	96	100.0	99.4	---0.6---		38.3	...	59.7	2.0	São Tomé and Príncipe
...	...	...	60.3	...	43.8	190[4]	2,135	1.0	4.1	18.7	77.2	88.5	---11.5---			Saudi Arabia
...	...	...	...	...	5.9[47]	4[4]	11,338	59.1	0.1	---99.9---		22.4	77.6	...	...	Senegal
1.8	32.4	65.8	5[3]	...	...		7.5	27.8	89.6	---10.4---		100.0	...	...	...	Seychelles
50.3	---49.7---		...	...	0.4[47]	1[4]	2,732	38.1	20.7	---79.3---		19.3	80.7	...	...	Sierra Leone
12.5	6.2	81.3	1.4	...	100.0	833[4]	5.6[38]	9.0[38]	75.0	25.0	—	66.7	...	33.3	...	Singapore
43.4	---56.6---		...	...	...		93	3.4	40.0	45.2	14.8	100.0	...	...	...	Solomon Islands
20.0	60.0	20.0	0.5	...	40.0	4[4]	...	...	...	...	...	...	...	...	...	Somalia
...	...	...	14[3]	...	12.4	73[4]	85,447	70.2	5.9	---94.1---		11.9	79.7	1.3	7.1	South Africa
...	...	...	...	...	1.1[47]		3,839	94.8		87.1	—	2.4	97.6	...	...	Bophuthatswana
...	...	...	...	...	0.3[47]		770	95.3	9.7	80.3	—	10.0	90.0	...	...	Ciskei
...	...	...	...	...	2.8[47]		622	14.9				100.0	...	...	...	Transkei
...	...	...	0.3	...	0.5[47]	4.8	500	64.9	25.4	63.6	11.0	9.2	90.8	...	...	Venda
...	...	...	4[3]	...	0.2[47]	...	662	0.8	0.3	---99.7---		100.0	...	...	...	S.W. Africa/Namibia
...	...	...	19	...	45	80[4]	44,312	87.8	23.8	55.8	20.4	40.9	12.5	21.7	24.9	Spain
...	...	...	12[3]	...	25[2]	87[4]	1,967	30.0	62.4[98]	37.6[98]		88.3[98]	0.4[98]	2.1[98]	9.2[98]	Sri Lanka
...	...	...	1[3]	...	14[2]	4[4]	31,500	13.3	0.8	88.7	10.5	23.8	76.2	...	...	Sudan, The
33.0[68]	12.5[68]	54.5[68]	28[3]	...	78[2]	199[4]	165	1.0	15.0	53.0	32.0	40.4	23.1	19.1	17.4	Suriname
39.7	---60.3---		26[3]	...	42[2]	59[4]	766,775	44.6	2.0	81.1	16.9	19.7	60.6	12.0	7.7	Swaziland
49.7[103]	---50.3[103]---		93.9	...	1.8[47, 94]	477	8,375	20.4	---92.3---		7.7	34.5	4.0	50.4	11.0	Sweden
35.5[24]	---64.5[24]---		251[3]	...	4.3[47]	437[4]	1,203	29.1	6.7	66.2	27.1	36.1	53.4	10.5	...	Switzerland
...	...	...	0.37[4]	...	14.8[38]	39[4]	6,135	33.1	10.9	58.5	30.6	91.7	...	...	8.3	Syria
...	...	...	...	...	37.6[47]	400[53]	1,334[53]	37.1[53]	8.6[53]	91.4[53]		67.0[53]	---33.0[53]---			Taiwan
56.2	---43.8---		0.3	...	0.8[47]	7[4]	7,545	8.5	19.1	72.5	8.4	49.8	10.2	24.7	15.3	Tanzania
...	...	...	51	...	28.5	244[4]	15,916	31.0	10.6	---89.4---		94.0	---4.3---		1.7	Thailand
...	...	...	...	...	0.4[26, 47]	6[4]	406	7.1	17.3[17]	---82.7[17]---		71.0[17]	29.0[17]	...	...	Togo
95.0	5.0	—	1.0	85.0	...	3.0	1.2	100.0	99.9	—	0.1	98.4	0.1	1.6	—	Tokelau
8.4	...	91.6	1[3]	...	...	2[4]	58	83.6	57.0	---43.0---		93.1	6.9	...	...	Tonga
63.7[109]	---36.3[109]---		22[3]	40.7	0.6[47, 94]	52[4]	132	25.8	55.9	---44.1---		62.3	4.4	6.1	27.2	Trinidad and Tobago
...	...	...	6[3]	...	2.3[47]	18[4]	4,696	30.4	38.7	38.0	23.3	100.0	...	...	...	Tunisia
11.5	2.5	86.0	20[3]	...	46.9	56[4]	27,483[90]	35.3[90]	10.6[90]	68.4[90]	21.0[90]	100.0[90]	...	...	...	Turkey
...	...	...	...	...	...	...	...	...	...	...	...	...	...	...	...	Turks and Caicos Is.
...	...	...	...	...	...	...	...	...	...	...	...	...	...	...	...	Tuvalu
...	...	...	1[3]	...	2.2[47, 94]	...	2,262	11.3	29.8	70.2	—	100.0	...	...	...	Uganda
—	—	100.0	12[3]	...	3.1[4]	99[4]	608,000	27.2	---92.2---		7.8	37.5	61.6	---0.9---		U.S.S.R.
...	...	...	...	...	28.6[47]	235[4]	17.5[53]	0.25[3]	64.8[53]	18.2[53]	17.1[53]	97.6[53]		1.3[53]	1.1[53]	United Arab Emirates
...	...	...	77[3]	...	0.8[47, 94]	370[4]	18,676	76.5	0.9	98.4	0.7	37.5	59.6	1.7	1.2	United Kingdom
43.4	52.6	4.0	85.7	66.2	12.4	104[4]	416,707	43.7	1.5	86.4	12.1	45.1	42.4	8.8	3.7	United States
37.1	58.7	4.2	23[3]	...	0.5[47]	37[4]	16,025	90.9	3.8	75.2	21.0	7.6	86.5	2.8	3.1	Uruguay
92.2	7.2	0.6	1[3]	...	...	...	183	15.0	62.5	3.0	34.5	84.9	15.1	...	...	Vanuatu
39.8	12.1	48.1	11[3]	...	1.2[47, 94]	71[4]	26,470	30.0	19.0	59.0	22.0	13.2	57.0	22.8	7.0	Venezuela
...	...	...	6[3]	...	22.8[47]	60[4]	7,857	24.1	8.4	---91.6---		65.4	34.6	...	...	Vietnam
53.4	---46.6---		12.2	...	...		9.9	29.1	63.7	5.9	30.4	7.0	77.6	9.9	5.5	Virgin Islands (U.S.)
...	...	...	...	...	...		5.0	25.0	80.0	---20.0---		100.0	...	...	...	Wallis and Futuna
...	...	...	...	...	4.7[47]		185	31.4	62.2	37.8	—	100.0	...	...	...	West Bank
...	...	...	...	...	...		5,002	18.8	—	—	—		100.0	...	...	Western Sahara
...	...	...	...	...	...		70	24.8	71.2	28.8	—	93.8	6.2	...	...	Western Samoa
...	...	...	7[3]	...	53.8[47]	14[4]	108	0.3	3.9	85.1	11.0	95.7	4.3	...	...	Yemen (Aden)
35.5[9, 30]	56.9[9, 30]	7.6[9, 30]	39.2	...	4.4	13[4]	1,351	0.1	6.7	69.7	23.6	98.8	...	...	1.2	Yemen (Ṣan'ā')
12.7[68]	---87.3[68]---		16.5	4.8[72]	2[2]	125[4]	12,462[68]	48.8[68]	8.5[68]	84.7[68]	6.8[68]	52.8[68]	26.4[68]	16.2[68]	4.6[68]	Yugoslavia
92.3	---9.7---		0.4	...	...	2[4]	5,897	2.6	7.7	---92.3---		70.6	20.1	2.0	7.3	Zaire
15.8	9.7	74.5	1[3]	...	0.3[47]	11[4]	938	1.3	4.5	---95.5---		14.2	38.1	...	47.7	Zambia
1.8[9, 53]	26.7[9, 53]	71.5[9, 53]	3[3]	...	1.5[53]	54[4]	29,620	76.6	2.5	---97.5---						Zimbabwe

[64]Less than 8.0 hectares. [65]8.0 to 20 hectares. [66]Less than 0.4 hectare. [67]0.4 to 4.0 hectares. [68]1969. [69]Farms producing mainly for cash sales. [70]5.0 to 8.0 hectares. [71]Over 8.0 hectares. [72]Percentage of farms having electric motors. [73]Excludes temporary bushland available for agricultural use to subsistence farms. [74]1981. [75]Western Libya only. [76]10 to 100 hectares. [77]100 hectares or more. [78]Peninsular Malaysia only; excludes shifting cultivators. [79]Smallholder farms only. [80]Average size of estate farm is 400 hectares. [81]Based on total number of households on estates. [82]All Malaysia. [83]Includes rented farms. [84]Includes 1,828,000 holdings on 22,700 communes (ejidos). [85]In area, state lands constitute 80.6% of Mongolia's farmland, agricultural cooperatives 19.4%. [86]0.4 to 2.0 hectares. [87]Less than 3.0 hectares. [88]3.0 to 50 hectares. [89]1985. [90]1986. [91]2.0 to 5.0 hectares. [92]Data refer to cultivated area only. [93]Large holdings only. [94]1983. [95]1.2 to 5.0 hectares. [96]Less than 7.0 hectares. [97]7.0 hectares or more. [98]1973. [99]1.0 to 2.0 hectares. [100]1.2 to 12 hectares. [101]2.0 to 5.0 hectares. [102]0.4 to 2.0 hectares. [103]Holdings of arable land only. [104]7.0 to 25 hectares. [105]25 to 300 hectares. [106]300 hectares or more. [107]1.0 to 6.4 hectares. [108]6.4 hectares or more. [109]1963. [110]24,600,000 farm households with small plots constitute 8% of total farmland. [111]Abu Dhabi only. [112]Excludes Northern Ireland. [113]20 to 72 hectares. [114]72 to 202 hectares. [115]202 hectares or more. [116]Less than 8.0 hectares. [117]8.0 to 16 hectares. [118]16 to 100 hectares.

Crops and livestock

This table provides comparative data for selected categories of agricultural production for the countries of the world. The data are taken mainly from the United Nations Food and Agriculture Organization's (FAO) annual *Production Yearbook*.

The FAO depends largely on questionnaires supplied to each country for its statistics, but, where no official or semiofficial responses are returned, the FAO makes estimates, using incomplete, unofficial, or other similarly limited data. And, although the FAO provides standardized guidelines upon which many nations have organized their data collection systems and methods, persistent, often traditional, variations in standards of coverage, methodology, and reporting periods reduce the comparability of statistics that *can* be supplied on such forms. FAO data are based on calendar-year periods; that is, data for any particular crop refer to the calendar year in which the harvest (or the bulk of the harvest) occurred.

In spite of the often tragic food shortages in a number of countries in recent years, worldwide agricultural production is probably more often underreported than overreported. Many countries do not report complete domestic production; the Soviet bloc, for example, excepting Czechoslo-vakia, publishes, initially at least, statistics only for collective or cooperative production and excludes the production of privately held plots of land that in some instances represent a significant part of total agricultural production. Some countries report only crops that are sold commercially and ignore crops produced for family or communal subsistence.

Methodological problems attach to much smaller parts of the agricultural whole, however. The FAO's cereals statistics relate, ideally, to weight or volume of crops harvested for dry grain (excluding cereal crops used for grazing; harvested for hay; or harvested green for food, feed, or silage). Some countries, however, collect the basic data they report to the FAO on sown or cultivated areas instead and calculate production statistics from estimates of yield. Millet and sorghum, which in many European and North American countries are used primarily as livestock or poultry feed, may be reportable by such countries as animal fodder only, while the U.S.S.R. and many African and Asian nations use the same grains for human consumption and report them as cereals. Statistics for tropical fruits are frequently not compiled by producing countries, and coverage is not uniform, with some countries reporting only commercial fruits and others including those consumed for subsistence as well. Figures on

Crops and livestock

country	grains production ('000 metric tons) 1975–77 average	grains production 1987	grains yield (kg/hectare) 1975–77 average	grains yield 1987	roots and tubers[a] production ('000 metric tons) 1975–77 average	roots production 1987	roots yield (kg/hectare) 1975–77 average	roots yield 1987	pulses[b] production ('000 metric tons) 1975–77 average	pulses production 1987	pulses yield (kg/hectare) 1975–77 average	pulses yield 1987	fruits[c] production ('000 metric tons) 1975–77 average	fruits production 1987	vegetables[d] production ('000 metric tons) 1975–77 average	vegetables production 1987
Afghanistan	4,417	4,463	1,301	1,333	250	350	13,282	14,000	33	40	1,563	1,633	860	791	611	798
Albania	800	1,088	2,307	3,048	113	142	7,312	9,161	18	25	320	409	140	209	163	188
Algeria	2,045	3,053	649	984	513	832	7,201	6,809	72	63	747	360	1,538	1,207	704	1,647
American Samoa	...	...	...	...	4	4	5,913	5,620	...	...	...	...	2	1	...	...
Andorra																
Angola	520	382	722	530	1,937	2,190	13,507	14,175	68	40	569	364	416	425	204	227
Anguilla																
Antigua and Barbuda	—	—	1,788	2,000	...	...	3,695	5,652	...	...	...	...	8	10	1	3
Argentina	23,168	23,758	2,008	2,433	2,149	2,707	12,696	16,698	205	232	1,076	862	6,615	6,097	2,337	2,869
Aruba[3]																
Australia	16,553	19,520	1,250	1,413	725	1,015	20,620	27,166	102	1,855	639	1,514	2,046	2,428	939	1,365
Austria	4,065	4,816	4,006	4,810	1,559	901	23,042	26,394	5	1	2,226	2,250	986	816	562	487
Bahamas, The	1	1	1,021	1,262	1	2	8,644	9,368	1	1	1,427	1,294	11	13	26	28
Bahrain	...	...	...	...	...	...	23,000	17,313	...	...	...	...	36	49	19	11
Bangladesh	19,001	23,372	1,841	2,346	1,595	1,617	10,052	10,299	228	176	718	746	1,404	1,343	1,051	1,212
Barbados	2	2	2,614	2,500	12	6	10,637	8,257	1	1	1,199	1,254	2	3	6	5
Belgium[4]	1,772	1,988	3,939	5,204	1,286	1,957	32,131	46,595	11	11	2,677	4,041	337	410	1,083	1,431
Belize	22	23	1,366	1,762	2	4	19,389	21,875	1	3	541	771	56	104	2	4
Benin	302	399	736	719	1,200	1,424	7,914	8,167	28	46	419	512	134	158	86	142
Bermuda	...	...	...	...	1	1	17,082	17,825	...	...	...	...	1	—	2	2
Bhutan	145	205	1,417	1,693	37	69	6,642	8,903	2	4	556	717	38	58	10	11
Bolivia	594	912	1,134	1,336	1,141	1,094	6,733	5,792	17	27	950	1,124	570	662	352	310
Botswana	87	12	500	226	6	7	4,821	5,385	18	14	611	467	8	11	15	16
Brazil	29,431	43,849	1,419	1,868	29,152	28,052	11,892	12,086	2,204	2,071	496	386	15,005	25,929	3,518	5,184
British Virgin Islands													—	1	...	...
Brunei	7	2	2,062	1,267	2	1	6,530	2,368	...	...	...	...	4	6	6	9
Bulgaria	7,926	6,465	3,518	3,266	350	505	11,326	12,536	82	82	784	980	2,249	1,921	1,911	1,824
Burkina Faso	1,120	1,637	529	643	93	89	5,544	3,652	172	180	376	368	43	70	58	128
Burma	9,527	14,492	1,795	2,783	88	288	5,189	10,070	274	650	461	774	1,069	905	1,734	2,188
Burundi	303	482	1,100	1,199	1,102	1,346	7,465	7,272	365	353	1,003	878	974	1,517	131	188
Cameroon	928	904	929	963	2,170	2,232	2,362	2,443	98	126	600	555	1,039	1,209	408	437
Canada	41,352	52,450	2,198	2,425	2,359	2,972	21,744	26,420	127	929	1,305	1,606	666	749	1,493	1,903
Cape Verde	4	18	467	900	16	15	4,496	2,863	1	6	189	600	10	10	5	6
Cayman Islands	...	...	...	...	—	—	4,533	4,513	...	...	...	...	1	1	...	...
Central African Republic	94	143	526	789	1,100	651	3,225	4,657	6	7	500	492	154	177	39	52
Chad	600	617	538	574	348	598	4,191	5,302	54	58	398	420	88	117	49	77
Chile	1,685	2,824	1,768	3,219	743	734	9,639	12,503	116	134	912	763	1,595	2,171	1,148	1,259
China	242,557	358,950	2,497	3,977	144,743	147,762	13,020	16,091	6,183	5,838	1,066	1,322	9,905	14,334	69,076	109,808
Christmas Island	...	...	...	...	...	...	...	...	...	...	...	...	...	...	...	...
Cocos (Keeling) Islands																
Colombia	2,800	3,642	2,302	2,663	3,541	3,885	9,626	11,541	126	143	597	656	3,308	4,405	1,223	1,518
Comoros	17	23	1,183	1,082	95	113	3,434	3,189	2	3	547	600	31	40	2	3
Congo	21	11	652	700	604	684	5,921	6,620	7	8	604	705	189	253	28	39
Cook Islands	...	...	...	...	11	12	29,790	32,237	...	...	...	...	15	15	2	2
Costa Rica	283	265	1,889	2,094	38	56	8,482	7,115	15	31	527	557	1,376	1,196	52	76
Côte d'Ivoire	810	1,084	775	868	3,284	4,704	4,635	6,008	8	8	625	667	1,635	1,894	257	391
Cuba	547	562	2,253	2,430	695	1,020	5,622	6,559	25	28	705	786	591	1,322	386	568
Cyprus	129	134	1,298	2,514	182	153	20,392	21,594	8	5	853	1,164	432	362	111	119
Czechoslovakia	9,594	11,777	3,585	4,699	3,846	3,072	15,944	17,187	120	228	1,445	2,066	657	650	1,025	1,196
Denmark	6,511	7,271	3,663	4,774	752	942	21,632	32,483	11	440	2,926	2,842	153	71	221	340
Djibouti	...	...	...	...	...	...	...	...	...	...	...	...	...	...	1	15
Dominica	...	...	1,311	1,405	23	26	9,813	9,792	1	1	500	500	65	78	5	6
Dominican Republic	357	563	2,516	3,559	352	227	6,031	7,708	63	81	999	1,026	1,270	1,509	195	284
Ecuador	721	836	1,379	1,994	814	647	10,450	9,339	50	48	512	582	3,854	3,165	297	345
Egypt	7,925	9,968	3,948	4,825	1,017	1,790	17,271	21,059	347	411	2,030	2,480	3,520	3,155	6,506	8,895
El Salvador	591	640	1,529	1,540	18	33	10,326	14,145	38	24	703	415	269	252	92	161
Equatorial Guinea	...	...	...	...	80	91	2,722	2,329	...	...	...	...	14	19	...	...
Ethiopia	4,408	5,350	987	1,141	1,187	1,320	3,283	2,876	640	885	769	956	186	215	442	560
Faeroe Islands	...	...	...	...	1	1	13,671	13,508	...	...	...	...	...	...	...	...
Falkland Islands																

wild fruits and berries are seldom included in national reports at all. FAO vegetable statistics include vegetables and melons grown for human consumption only. Some countries do not make this distinction in their reports, and some exclude the production of kitchen gardens and small family plots, although in certain countries, such small-scale production may account for 20 to 40 percent of total ouput.

Livestock statistics may be distorted by the timing of country reports. Ireland, for example, takes a livestock enumeration in December that is reported the following year and that appears low against data for otherwise comparable countries because of the slaughter and export of animals at the close of the grazing season. It balances this, however, with a June enumeration, when numbers tend to be high. Milk production as defined by the FAO includes whole fresh milk, excluding milk sucked by young animals but including amounts fed by farmers or ranchers to livestock, but national practices vary. Certain countries do not distinguish between milk cows and other cattle, so that yield per dairy cow must be estimated. Some countries do not report egg production statistics (here given in metric tons), and external estimates must be based on the numbers of chickens and reported or assumed egg-laying rates. Other countries report egg production by number, and this must be converted to weight, using conversion factors specific to the makeup by species of national poultry flocks.

Metric system units used in the table may be converted to English system units as follows:

metric tons × 1.1023 = short tons
kilograms × 2.2046 = pounds
kilograms per hectare × 0.8922 = pounds per acre.

The notes that follow, keyed by references in the table headings, provide further definitional information.
a. Includes such crops as potatoes and cassava.
b. Includes beans and peas harvested for dry grain only. Does not include green beans and green peas.
c. Excludes melons.
d. Includes melons, green beans, and green peas.
e. From milk cows only.
f. From chickens only.

livestock														country
cattle		sheep		hogs		chickens		milk e				eggs f		
stock ('000 head)		stock ('000 head)		stock ('000 head)		stock ('000 head)		production ('000 metric tons)		yield (kg/animal)		production (metric tons)		
1975–77 average	1987	1975–77 average	1987	1975–77 average	1987	1975–77 average	1987	1975–77 average	1987	1975–77 average	1987	1975–77 average	1987	
3,663	3,760	20,620	20,000	...	...	6,233	7,000	569	610	532	500	13,447	14,200	Afghanistan
490	619	1,163	1,238	133	229	3,067	5,000	254	346	1,441	1,410	7,347	13,200	Albania
1,049	1,597	9,803	15,000	4	5	16,528	23,000	453	551	964	966	16,700	120,000	Algeria
...	...	...	...	10	11	49	50[1]	—	—	800	800	33	30	American Samoa
...	1[2]	...	9[2]	...	...	...	...	...	...	...	...	...	...	Andorra
2,817	3,390	205	260	360	475	5,000	6,000	140	148	500	502	3,450	3,900	Angola
...	...	...	...	...	...	...	...	...	...	...	...	...	...	Anguilla
8	18	10	13	3	4	62	80[1]	8	6	1,230	1,000	128	164	Antigua and Barbuda
58,645	55,684	34,799	28,998	3,960	4,036	32,800	46,000	5,586	6,296	1,905	2,179	191,893	285,000	Argentina
...	...	...	...	...	...	...	...	...	...	...	...	...	...	Aruba[3]
32,587	23,260	145,219	159,177	2,200	2,640	42,339	54,000	6,344	6,333	2,767	3,460	195,547	186,000	Australia
2,528	2,637	166	256	3,693	3,801	12,856	14,000	3,301	3,700	3,247	3,776	88,585	106,000	Austria
4	5	31	40	17	20	748	1,000	2	3	1,000	1,000	330	460	Bahamas, The
5	6	3	8	...	...	350	1,000	6	6	2,800	2,619	1,750	4,750	Bahrain
26,060	23,500	1,138	1,130	...	...	50,992	69,000	759	950	250	264	32,954	53,000	Bangladesh
20	17	49	56	38	49	525	1,000	6	11	1,112	1,325	1,681	1,300	Barbados
3,045	3,100	101	150	4,809	5,800	31,807	31,000	3,861	4,100	3,655	3,905	235,500	165,000	Belgium[4]
48	51	3	4	18	25	310	1,000	4	4	1,018	1,024	623	1,250	Belize
720	950	856	1,200	380	620	8,533	23,000	10	16	117	130	6,120	17,100	Benin
—	1	...	...	1	2	56	50[1]	1	2	3,036	3,056	318	580	Bermuda
272	395	39	25	61	62	125	...	24	28	257	257	145	240	Bhutan
3,407	5,380	7,970	9,500	1,227	1,690	7,270	8,000	75	99	1,404	1,414	16,893	27,500	Bolivia
2,840	2,300	230	215	15	9	650	1,000	71	100	350	350	489	720	Botswana
100,489	131,503	17,946	19,200	34,979	32,000	327,477	520,000	10,166	12,350	780	718	537,891	1,100,000	Brazil
2	2	7	8	2	3	...	...	...	...	...	...	...	...	British Virgin Islands
3	3	...	...	11	14	618	2,000	...	...	...	...	1,420	2,230	Brunei
1,644	1,678	9,843	9,563	3,589	4,050	35,304	38,000	1,480	2,196	2,274	3,506	105,002	158,002	Bulgaria
2,550	3,170	1,650	2,300	153	206	10,200	21,000	74	89	175	175	5,724	14,700	Burkina Faso
7,542	9,912	194	300	1,771	2,988	16,783	33,000	217	580	245	245	23,182	48,420	Burma
785	360	310	390	36	80	2,700	4,000	47	21	350	350	2,052	2,945	Burundi
2,756	4,400	2,083	2,500	900	1,200	8,983	11,000	37	48	500	500	7,040	10,800	Cameroon
14,993	11,691	595	697	5,906	10,476	86,488	109,000	7,731	8,000	3,840	4,857	312,427	336,770	Canada
11	13	2	1	22	50	59	230[1]	1	—	500	500	48	176	Cape Verde
4	5	...	...	...	...	16	21[1]	...	...	...	...	82	86	Cayman Islands
925	2,224	68	116	160	371	1,352	3,000	3	5	110	110	890	997	Central African Republic
3,535	5,148	2,295	2,700	6	12	2,700	4,000	108	113	270	270	2,430	3,240	Chad
3,474	3,580	5,691	6,050	896	1,100	16,267	19,000	1,100	1,100	1,393	1,618	57,516	91,800	Chile
55,087	71,347	94,245	99,009	276,399	344,248	690,000	1,796,000	870	3,305	1,286	1,774	2,320,000	6,170,000	China
...	...	...	...	...	...	...	...	...	...	...	...	...	...	Christmas Island
...	...	...	...	...	...	...	...	...	...	...	...	...	...	Cocos (Keeling) Islands
23,831	23,971	2,028	2,652	1,876	2,511	25,760	36,000	2,225	3,142	961	952	119,498	226,000	Colombia
74	88	7	9	...	...	243	362[1]	3	4	500	500	519	615	Comoros
58	71	53	64	43	45	885	1,000	2	3	1,500	1,500	662	1,088	Congo
...	...	...	...	14	18	63	...	...	...	...	...	82	112	Cook Islands
1,850	2,360	2	6	218	238	6,100	6,000	279	410	1,041	1,367	16,087	15,568	Costa Rica
503	965	1,010	1,500	253	450	10,733	16,000	9	19	112	122	4,800	11,500	Côte d'Ivoire
5,531	5,007	339	382	1,472	2,400	19,320	26,000	830	1,150	1,342	1,513	82,906	111,930	Cuba
32	44	460	320	147	225	3,200	2,000	24	75	3,380	4,162	4,790	6,138	Cyprus
4,592	5,073	804	1,104	6,741	6,833	39,765	47,000	5,464	6,921	2,920	3,857	227,157	277,216	Czechoslovakia
3,085	2,347	59	69	7,769	9,685	14,993	15,000	5,034	4,900	4,582	5,904	71,367	79,000	Denmark
28	51	367	410	...	...	...	...	...	...	...	...	...	...	Djibouti
4	4	3	4	8	9	98	117[1]	1	2	1,067	1,063	234	279	Dominica
1,925	2,058	51	84	719	2,637	7,433	17,000	348	350	1,517	1,556	21,933	21,000	Dominican Republic
2,576	3,847	2,142	2,100	2,737	4,160	16,367	42,000	814	1,000	1,365	1,316	22,682	42,000	Ecuador
2,076	1,900	1,875	1,160	†5	15	26,375	30,000	632	970	673	674	74,258	142,000	Egypt
1,141	1,024	4	5	453	398	3,510	5,000	258	250	1,007	781	30,697	33,980	El Salvador
4	4	32	36	4	5	120	195[1]	...	...	...	...	100	162	Equatorial Guinea
25,662	30,000	23,081	23,200	16	19	51,200	57,000	554	780	203	207	70,249	77,970	Ethiopia
2	2	70	73	...	...	...	...	...	...	...	...	...	...	Faeroe Islands
9	7	642	705	...	...	3	2[1]	1	2	1,000	1,000	...	...	Falkland Islands

Crops and livestock (continued)

country	grains production ('000 metric tons) 1975–77 average	1987	grains yield (kg/hectare) 1975–77 average	1987	roots and tubers[a] production ('000 metric tons) 1975–77 average	1987	roots and tubers yield (kg/hectare) 1975–77 average	1987	pulses[b] production ('000 metric tons) 1975–77 average	1987	pulses yield (kg/hectare) 1975–77 average	1987	fruits[c] production ('000 metric tons) 1975–77 average	1987	vegetables[d] production ('000 metric tons) 1975–77 average	1987
Fiji	21	26	2,160	2,274	20	58	8,115	6,976	2	1	1,644	1,600	13	17	13	10
Finland	3,452	2,183	2,670	1,920	788	491	15,957	11,763	11	4	2,080	1,682	98	97	98	159
France	35,926	52,588	3,730	5,659	6,257	7,200	21,530	36,679	147	1,955	1,973	4,042	13,514	14,217	6,418	7,271
French Guiana	1	10	1,671	3,112	14	13	10,766	11,498	...	...	...	...	2	2	1	9
French Polynesia	...	...	...	...	18	13	12,582	8,333	...	...	...	...	6	5	5	8
Gabon	8	11	1,465	1,459	343	407	5,827	6,599	—	—	400	600	154	192	18	29
Gambia, The	70	158	834	1,362	9	6	3,278	3,000	4	4	250	267	4	4	7	8
Gaza Strip	...	5	...	2,807	3	16	17,751	18,000	...	1	...	2,571	257	197	50	81
Germany, East	8,599	11,461	3,406	4,531	8,267	11,300	14,099	24,565	71	106	1,392	1,857	577	893	1,059	1,392
Germany, West	20,666	23,693	3,912	5,052	10,676	7,150	26,057	32,500	60	323	2,731	3,123	3,946	3,477	1,823	2,470
Ghana	666	913	828	986	3,315	4,593	6,264	6,344	16	11	102	88	1,298	838	365	717
Gibraltar	...	...	...	...	...	...	...	...	...	...	...	...	...	...	...	...
Greece	3,625	5,349	2,365	3,709	974	907	15,210	19,771	98	53	1,137	1,414	4,137	3,450	3,127	3,887
Greenland	...	...	...	...	...	...	...	...	...	...	...	...	...	...	...	...
Grenada	1	—	899	1,000	3	4	4,984	4,998	1	1	1,157	1,390	28	24	2	2
Guadeloupe	—	—	1,400	1,200	34	23	11,536	11,220	—	—	676	531	163	179	22	26
Guam	...	...	1,500	1,500	1	2	14,075	12,966	...	...	...	...	1	1	1	1
Guatemala	1,004	1,108	1,431	1,541	62	53	3,917	4,565	84	125	594	651	560	980	222	287
Guernsey	...	...	...	...	...	...	...	...	...	...	...	...	...	...	...	...
Guinea	565	593	829	790	778	663	7,122	7,053	40	50	667	769	587	677	384	420
Guinea-Bissau	85	240	706	980	33	40	5,128	6,154	2	2	544	567	40	42	23	20
Guyana	277	353	2,170	3,739	23	31	6,826	7,045	1	1	622	522	37	46	8	11
Haiti	413	475	1,092	1,267	721	863	4,386	4,190	82	96	494	525	917	1,086	255	324
Honduras	474	517	1,006	1,569	19	26	3,372	7,461	31	22	413	1,000	1,297	1,380	70	115
Hong Kong	3	—	1,854	1,250	1	—	16,964	23,750	...	...	...	...	3	3	182	141
Hungary	11,970	14,068	3,899	4,964	1,562	1,047	12,697	15,927	132	236	1,681	1,996	2,415	2,113	1,837	1,972
Iceland	...	...	...	...	7	11	9,069	11,100	...	...	...	...	...	...	1	2
India	129,165	148,065	1,264	1,465	15,022	17,759	12,139	14,706	11,642	11,176	504	490	17,858	23,951	36,753	48,265
Indonesia	25,887	43,480	2,397	3,430	15,312	16,555	8,654	10,225	275	334	1,001	819	3,645	5,855	2,258	3,343
Iran	8,653	12,485	1,135	1,313	606	2,210	14,356	16,371	214	370	1,139	705	3,675	3,628	3,431	4,176
Iraq	1,642	1,653	874	866	61	120	9,687	16,000	38	32	780	871	1,721	1,271	1,811	2,872
Ireland	1,488	2,028	4,189	5,733	1,243	770	26,216	25,413	—	1	3,222	3,500	23	13	276	242
Isle of Man	...	...	...	...	...	...	...	...	...	...	...	...	...	...	...	...
Israel	276	345	1,961	2,844	185	211	32,861	38,471	8	11	1,462	1,180	2,014	1,902	736	911
Italy	15,942	18,321	3,236	3,906	2,992	2,680	16,588	19,654	365	257	1,236	1,395	19,957	19,603	12,104	13,902
Jamaica	12	13	1,957	2,117	207	248	9,994	12,222	5	8	690	961	319	362	84	121
Japan	16,964	14,531	5,720	5,700	5,508	6,323	22,429	25,101	167	134	1,375	1,659	7,970	5,924	14,964	15,506
Jersey	...	...	...	...	...	...	...	...	...	...	...	...	...	...	...	...
Jordan	74	156	408	841	7	23	14,826	15,000	10	13	396	648	102	114	350	505
Kampuchea	1,740	1,805	1,280	1,040	110	164	8,195	8,000	18	40	574	909	175	233	457	466
Kenya	3,164	2,332	1,590	1,176	1,188	1,650	7,680	10,185	295	460	486	920	480	735	382	467
Kiribati	...	...	...	...	10	13	8,546	8,823	...	...	...	...	4	5	4	5
Korea, North	7,295	11,574	3,702	4,591	1,645	2,444	12,557	13,355	260	305	796	876	727	1,235	1,944	3,020
Korea, South	8,970	8,247	4,559	5,466	2,364	1,395	17,243	23,077	56	48	848	1,124	1,002	1,579	7,044	8,545
Kuwait	—	1	1,908	3,384	—	1	13,467	19,143	...	...	...	...	5	2	26	106
Laos	786	1,219	1,278	2,358	97	259	9,500	9,904	13	29	1,444	2,200	91	161	149	244
Lebanon	66	22	1,114	1,052	38	241	5,524	21,804	11	11	877	1,017	689	758	279	399
Lesotho	175	147	950	603	5	6	13,061	15,000	19	6	876	411	13	15	19	26
Liberia	243	280	1,222	1,217	316	384	3,910	4,041	3	3	489	550	114	130	59	77
Libya	238	296	407	698	89	114	5,469	7,150	8	12	1,104	1,182	320	278	483	594
Liechtenstein	...	...	...	...	10	12	18,703	18,951	...	...	...	...	...	...	...	...
Luxembourg[4]	...	...	...	...	3	4	10,000	10,100	...	...	...	...	4	5	1	2
Macau	...	...	...	...	...	...	...	...	...	...	...	...	...	...	...	...
Madagascar	2,154	2,385	1,767	1,762	1,960	3,279	6,217	5,989	71	62	871	914	871	788	278	300
Malawi	1,333	1,414	1,141	1,074	517	476	4,519	4,139	194	220	612	593	334	403	185	221
Malaysia	1,983	1,902	2,650	2,904	525	503	9,843	9,384	...	...	...	...	897	1,133	448	466
Maldives	1	—	839	789	6	9	5,138	5,147	—	—	600	597	7	8	15	18
Mali	1,188	1,485	725	784	93	143	9,185	8,938	34	57	1,098	1,036	10	12	110	245
Malta	5	9	2,540	3,855	20	13	8,509	6,842	1	2	1,885	2,389	10	14	46	48
Martinique	...	...	...	...	32	40	9,097	8,832	...	...	...	...	278	252	30	27
Mauritania	42	107	470	718	6	6	1,173	2,001	20	24	365	319	16	14	4	9
Mauritius	2	4	2,590	3,607	11	17	15,281	18,775	1	1	476	650	7	10	24	28
Mayotte	...	...	...	...	...	...	...	...	...	...	...	...	...	...	...	...
Mexico	17,024	21,484	1,751	1,764	849	1,081	12,213	14,021	1,072	1,268	590	503	6,758	8,701	2,870	4,705
Monaco	...	...	...	...	...	...	...	...	...	...	...	...	...	...	...	...
Mongolia	423	910	937	1,422	40	136	8,316	11,333	2	4	518	1,050	3	—	21	50
Montserrat	—	—	1,000	1,667	—	—	2,363	3,250	...	...	...	...	...	...	...	...
Morocco	4,110	4,325	886	850	222	560	10,793	12,446	363	376	666	730	1,587	1,540	1,308	1,478
Mozambique	679	513	720	574	2,783	3,470	4,784	5,827	73	60	611	480	303	358	186	196
Nauru	...	...	...	...	...	...	...	...	...	...	...	...	...	...	...	...
Nepal	3,707	4,042	1,701	1,498	363	550	5,495	5,294	110	150	401	435	125	156	215	270
Netherlands, The	1,121	1,132	4,674	6,517	5,234	7,478	32,531	44,805	27	198	2,813	4,266	508	549	2,391	3,150
Netherlands Antilles[3]	1	2[1]	653	714[1]	...	...	...	...	...	...	...	...	...	...	...	...
New Caledonia	1	2	2,500	2,564	18	22	5,865	5,837	—	—	722	667	8	7	3	4
New Zealand	818	992	3,767	4,472	255	289	25,662	28,716	49	118	2,481	2,873	267	601	323	476
Nicaragua	319	486	1,085	1,837	25	88	4,058	12,097	47	34	753	680	334	315	44	51
Niger	1,242	1,460	400	352	221	234	7,322	7,326	225	256	270	158	32	43	106	165
Nigeria	7,660	10,560	888	1,094	28,049	35,402	10,003	11,157	711	1,050	279	495	2,035	3,100	2,490	3,960
Niue	...	...	...	...	2	2	2,503	2,518	...	...	...	...	2	2	...	...
Norfolk Island	...	...	...	...	...	...	...	...	...	...	...	...	...	...	...	...
Norway	897	1,055	2,988	3,158	536	360	22,363	21,176	...	...	...	...	113	116	165	166
Oman	4	2	1,177	1,880	—	2	1,111	4,306	...	...	...	...	87	128	36	226
Pacific Is., Trust Territory of the	—	—	1,091	1,216	11	14	8,339	8,832	—	—	600	600	3	3	3	3
Marshall Islands	...	...	...	...	...	...	...	...	...	...	...	...	...	...	...	...
Micronesia, Fed. States of	...	...	...	...	...	...	...	...	...	...	...	...	...	...	...	...

cattle stock ('000 head)		sheep stock ('000 head)		hogs stock ('000 head)		chickens stock ('000 head)		milk[e] production ('000 metric tons)		milk yield (kg/animal)		eggs[f] production (metric tons)		country
1975–77 average	1987	1975–77 average	1987	1975–77 average	1987	1975–77 average	1987	1975–77 average	1987	1975–77 average	1987	1975–77 average	1987	
157	159	...	...	17	29	787	2,000	48	51	1,700	1,700	1,850	2,400	Fiji
1,807	1,485	113	66	1,123	1,309	8,769	7,000	3,222	2,938	4,261	5,062	83,833	80,800	Finland
23,986	22,803	10,806	10,580	11,664	12,002	166,037	188,000	29,814	32,400	2,911	3,375	755,667	900,000	France
2	17	—	1	4	10	121	100[1]	—	1	503	500	311	250	French Guiana
6	7	3	2	20	51	419	1,000	2	2	2,833	2,533	624	920	French Polynesia
3	9	73	83	127	153	1,020	2,000	—	1	250	250	617	1,410	Gabon
288	300	135	195	9	13	280	349[1]	5	5	175	175	359	618	Gambia, The
2	5	69	67	...	...	717	1,000	9	7	5,290	6,000	1,657	2,525	Gaza Strip
5,529	5,804	1,866	2,647	11,437	12,840	47,699	50,000	8,042	9,348	3,772	4,600	305,418	332,000	Germany, East
14,473	15,305	1,073	1,383	20,209	24,503	88,729	72,000	22,097	24,200	4,092	4,792	875,325	745,000	Germany, West
830	1,248	1,810	2,400	379	703	11,661	11,000	7	10	55	55	11,029	11,660	Ghana
...	...	...	...	...	...	...	...	...	...	...	...	...	...	Gibraltar
1,180	743	8,311	11,412	763	1,226	29,620	31,000	701	635	1,512	1,825	111,546	130,000	Greece
...	...	18	22	...	...	...	...	...	...	...	...	...	...	Greenland
6	4	9	17	11	11	252	260[1]	1	2	800	800	930	1,000	Grenada
83	76	3	4	37	44	420	390[1]	10	21	518	500	457	1,210	Guadeloupe
2	2	...	...	10	14	127	218[1]	...	...	...	...	1,191	1,600	Guam
1,472	2,300	583	690	616	865	10,880	15,000	310	375	894	938	33,017	42,500	Guatemala
4	4	...	...	...	...	...	...	8	9	3,075	3,854	...	...	Guernsey
1,546	1,800	410	460	34	50	5,313	13,000	36	42	185	185	5,565	13,860	Guinea
266	340	146	205	210	290	357	1,000	8	10	170	170	252	552	Guinea-Bissau
265	210	108	120	125	185	10,100	15,000	12	23	771	793	3,583	4,200	Guyana
850	1,474	81	93	1,700	700	4,450	8,000	23	22	230	238	1,835	3,900	Haiti
1,839	2,859	5	7	519	567	3,885	6,000	241	295	650	886	16,100	21,700	Honduras
10	2	...	...	429	353	4,488	7,000	5	2	2,363	2,200	2,792	2,140	Hong Kong
1,936	1,725	2,137	2,337	7,700	8,687	56,072	63,000	1,961	2,773	2,768	4,819	232,123	235,000	Hungary
63	70	865	770	7	13	247	307[1]	128	123	3,491	3,806	2,808	3,600	Iceland
180,031	199,300	40,722	55,482	7,416	8,800	147,957	175,000	11,396	17,700	513	644	495,667	961,000	India
6,324	6,470	3,614	5,300	2,878	6,216	102,783	400,000	66	230	735	1,045	73,980	348,000	Indonesia
7,283	8,350	34,333	34,500	52	...	60,000	105,000	1,260	1,700	771	723	204,667	240,000	Iran
1,835	1,500	9,960	8,700	...	...	15,433	75,000	320	280	750	751	24,617	90,000	Iraq
6,308	5,626	2,649	2,917	888	980	8,249	7,000	4,543	5,450	3,228	4,037	39,095	35,000	Ireland
...	32	...	147	...	8	...	71	...	...	...	...	...	...	Isle of Man
304	319	205	281	83	130	19,000	23,000	656	880	6,289	8,421	92,410	101,400	Israel
8,446	8,819	8,197	9,799	8,933	9,278	106,667	112,000	9,597	10,900	3,307	3,604	658,400	643,700	Italy
279	290	5	3	203	246	4,300	5,000	49	50	1,000	1,000	13,500	17,600	Jamaica
3,747	4,694	11	27	7,758	11,354	246,031	351,000	5,319	7,380	4,159	5,264	1,858,000	2,355,000	Japan
...	6[1]	...	...	...	...	...	...	...	...	...	...	...	...	Jersey
33	33	732	1,000	...	...	24,000	35,000	11	26	898	1,368	9,413	27,000	Jordan
1,050	1,600	2	1	433	1,300	4,133	6,000	18	16	170	170	6,100	10,200	Kampuchea
9,537	9,500	3,168	7,200	63	100	16,527	22,000	920	1,001	456	450	17,864	34,848	Kenya
...	...	...	...	10	10	154	220[1]	...	...	...	...	101	120	Kiribati
850	1,200	268	368	1,700	3,050	17,316	19,000	31	83	2,000	2,441	75,473	135,000	Korea, North
1,684	2,807	6	4	1,561	3,347	26,829	56,000	205	1,100	4,546	5,000	189,920	378,000	Korea, South
10	25	127	265	...	...	5,353	23,000	13	53	2,332	3,419	2,365	24,000	Kuwait
327	593	...	...	669	1,565	4,225	8,000	5	8	200	200	18,333	28,750	Laos
40	50	150	140	17	21	3,867	11,000	47	95	1,799	2,346	17,317	58,500	Lebanon
505	520	1,197	1,430	78	70	824	1,000	17	23	290	290	775	812	Lesotho
35	42	176	240	93	140	2,100	4,000	1	1	100	100	1,928	3,840	Liberia
188	212	4,147	5,700	...	...	4,692	26,000	56	71	1,188	1,464	9,015	17,050	Libya
8	9	1	2	8	10	43	...	15	20	3,213	3,362	250	250	Liechtenstein
...	...	...	...	7	6	353	450[1]	...	...	...	...	...	...	Luxembourg[4]
2	3	...	...	...	...	...	...	...	...	...	...	535	618	Macau
8,799	10,565	606	611	601	1,361	13,018	20,000	31	41	700	700	10,078	11,820	Madagascar
689	940	84	185	174	250	7,783	8,000	30	40	415	460	9,967	11,570	Malawi
449	620	50	75	1,503	2,200	44,448	57,000	23	24	680	550	112,967	174,000	Malaysia
...	...	...	...	...	...	...	...	...	...	...	...	...	...	Maldives
4,014	4,476	5,310	5,700	30	59	12,500	15,000	80	94	200	200	6,750	8,280	Mali
14	14	7	5	23	95	999	1,000	28	28	3,688	3,889	6,625	6,600	Malta
49	43	41	88	35	47	1,117	2,000	4	3	679	750	1,020	850	Martinique
1,147	1,000	4,170	3,950	...	...	2,850	4,000	69	95	350	350	2,422	3,570	Mauritania
53	38	3	7	5	10	1,100	2,000	24	25	2,377	2,510	2,347	4,200	Mauritius
...	...	...	...	...	...	...	...	...	...	...	...	...	...	Mayotte
25,286	31,156	6,309	5,800	14,030	18,662	145,247	210,000	6,145	7,500	1,180	1,339	464,090	860,000	Mexico
...	...	...	...	...	...	...	...	...	...	...	...	...	...	Monaco
2,403	2,480	14,289	13,194	14	80	165	300[1]	208	240	409	421	453	1,530	Mongolia
8	9	3	4	1	1	30	33[1]	2	2	750	750	41	60	Montserrat
3,547	2,850	14,457	15,000	8	9	20,000	37,000	506	850	552	567	55,433	84,000	Morocco
1,366	1,350	100	117	117	155	14,092	21,000	58	65	170	170	7,867	12,700	Mozambique
...	...	...	...	2	2	3	...	...	...	...	...	7	10	Nauru
6,634	6,374	690	821	329	467	7,450	10,000	181	225	325	326	13,300	13,100	Nepal
4,616	4,895	780	900	7,691	14,349	68,832	95,000	10,441	11,650	4,725	5,601	319,076	597,000	Netherlands, The
8	9	8	10	6	7	100	135[1]	4	4	1,286	1,281	477	560	Netherlands Antilles[3]
115	122	5	3	22	43	166	1,000	3	4	600	600	480	1,300	New Caledonia
9,016	8,250	56,942	66,400	447	470	7,278	9,000	6,436	7,100	3,165	3,498	55,762	50,000	New Zealand
2,662	2,100	2	3	670	749	4,097	6,000	457	125	1,123	625	25,008	31,500	Nicaragua
2,676	3,358	2,356	3,626	27	38	8,000	15,000	76	108	177	200	5,440	7,990	Niger
11,267	12,200	10,400	13,200	910	1,300	90,000	175,000	310	360	275	295	125,300	270,000	Nigeria
1	1	...	...	1	1	15	20[1]	—	—	772	715	35	20	Niue
...	...	...	...	...	...	...	...	...	...	...	...	...	...	Norfolk Island
927	965	1,696	2,350	689	742	3,796	4,000	1,854	1,969	4,816	5,531	38,205	51,400	Norway
132	130	65	215	...	...	800	1,000	16	34	420	420	483	1,600	Oman
7	12[c]	...	...	21	29	164	...	...	...	...	...	135	159	Pacific Is., Trust Territory of the Marshall Islands
...	...	...	...	...	...	...	...	...	...	...	...	...	...	Micronesia, Fed. States of

Crops and livestock (continued)

country	crops — grains production ('000 metric tons) 1975–77 average	1987	grains yield (kg/hectare) 1975–77 average	1987	roots and tubers[a] production ('000 metric tons) 1975–77 average	1987	roots and tubers yield (kg/hectare) 1975–77 average	1987	pulses[b] production ('000 metric tons) 1975–77 average	1987	pulses yield (kg/hectare) 1975–77 average	1987	fruits[c] production ('000 metric tons) 1975–77 average	1987	vegetables[d] production ('000 metric tons) 1975–77 average	1987
Northern Mariana Islands	...	...	...	...	...	...	...	...	...	...	...	...	...	...	...	...
Palau	...	...	...	...	321	612	11,435	9,932	852	874	525	569	2,124	3,857	1,925	2,739
Pakistan	14,169	18,384	1,441	1,628	75	87	8,234	8,549	5	6	296	446	1,206	1,024	34	61
Panama	241	275	1,237	1,455	1,046	1,195	6,951	6,979	1	2	500	512	981	1,120	230	283
Papua New Guinea	3	3	1,588	1,545	...	...	...	...	...	...	...	...	...	...	...	...
Paraguay	445	1,231	1,401	1,572	1,690	3,508	14,021	14,784	71	59	815	815	713	990	207	244
Peru	1,592	2,382	1,901	2,552	2,375	2,387	6,987	7,765	103	129	824	823	1,608	1,170	736	742
Philippines	9,571	12,960	1,398	1,841	2,261	2,845	5,554	6,612	32	38	631	795	3,413	6,683	824	808
Pitcairn Island	...	...	...	...	...	...	...	...	...	...	...	...	...	...	...	...
Poland	19,940	26,043	2,532	3,107	45,843	36,252	18,378	18,744	232	512	1,146	1,709	1,648	1,161	4,005	5,315
Portugal	1,426	1,725	1,057	1,646	1,200	1,277	8,682	9,029	85	81	230	313	1,790	1,804	1,710	1,760
Puerto Rico	5	6	6,652	8,750	39	31	5,785	6,409	4	4	738	715	286	283	23	37
Qatar	—	2	3,108	3,091	—	—	9,792	8,333	...	...	...	...	3	7	6	21
Réunion	13	14	5,316	5,385	12	10	15,050	11,088	1	—	2,781	1,778	23	34	10	13
Romania	17,890	31,706	2,838	4,949	3,904	7,800	12,854	24,000	98	327	121	499	2,795	4,211	3,704	6,397
Rwanda	235	265	1,094	986	1,297	1,428	8,354	7,304	219	150	803	544	1,838	2,168	150	192
St. Helena and Ascension	...	...	...	...	3	3	3,411	3,446	—	...	1,000	1,000	2	2	1	1
St. Kitts and Nevis	...	...	...	...	10	11	4,484	4,180	—	...	2,000	2,500	98	185	1	1
St. Lucia	—	—	700	769	...	...	...	...	...	...	...	...	...	...	...	...
St. Pierre and Miquelon	...	...	...	...	...	...	...	...	...	...	...	...	...	...	...	...
St. Vincent and the Grenadines	—	1	3,214	3,380	21	63	7,674	6,500	—	—	845	1,000	30	57	1	1
San Marino	...	...	...	...	...	...	...	...	...	...	...	...	4	4	2	3
São Tomé and Príncipe	1	1	1,522	1,556	13	16	12,197	13,913	6	7	1,717	2,000	693	643	686	1,213
Saudi Arabia	289	2,201	750	3,433	—	25	2,545	20,417	16	37	267	509	63	84	71	102
Senegal	687	1,000	641	795	95	71	3,262	4,789	...	...	...	...	...	...	...	...
Seychelles	—	—	...	...	...	...	5,766	5,000	...	...	...	...	2	2	1	2
Sierra Leone	615	545	1,448	1,436	120	152	4,309	3,326	28	35	564	633	114	153	146	186
Singapore	...	...	...	...	2	—	11,556	11,190	...	...	...	...	17	5	38	17
Solomon Islands	4	2	2,750	1,000	76	96	13,450	16,400	1	2	788	1,150	11	13	5	6
Somalia	260	491	637	592	33	43	11,001	10,750	10	29	330	338	231	252	26	33
South Africa[5]	11,192	10,907	1,375	1,579	759	1,130	12,304	12,697	96	95	883	1,092	2,602	3,431	1,510	1,826
Bophuthatswana[5]	...	...	...	...	...	...	...	...	...	...	...	...	...	...	...	...
Ciskei[5]	...	...	...	...	...	...	...	...	...	...	...	...	...	...	...	...
Transkei[5]	...	...	...	...	...	...	...	...	...	...	...	...	...	...	...	...
Venda[5]	...	...	...	...	...	...	...	...	...	...	...	...	...	...	...	...
South West Africa/Namibia	88	98	488	489	187	240	9,333	9,600	6	6	945	985	29	33	25	28
Spain	13,642	20,320	1,889	2,607	5,675	5,428	14,296	18,388	432	309	689	729	11,193	13,715	8,226	9,479
Sri Lanka	1,414	2,178	1,865	3,017	890	864	5,019	9,684	15	43	566	692	1,049	756	648	921
Sudan, The	2,724	1,603	669	358	287	201	3,516	2,634	89	112	1,237	1,128	792	828	768	943
Suriname	184	279	3,771	3,927	3	4	5,510	6,251	—	—	820	800	56	56	3	6
Swaziland	94	98	1,404	1,442	13	9	3,652	1,889	3	3	582	609	106	130	11	13
Sweden	5,332	5,415	3,394	3,964	1,058	1,050	23,363	26,992	20	112	1,868	2,670	205	168	235	315
Switzerland	748	937	4,268	5,173	797	720	32,562	37,306	2	1	2,983	3,814	730	772	269	374
Syria	2,252	2,319	823	827	140	314	13,129	15,956	217	173	752	717	1,386	984	2,232	2,855
Taiwan	3,565	3,303[1]	4,264	5,272[1]	2,341	5,430[1]	15,146	13,889[1]	32	401[1]	944	1,887[1]	1,639	2,165[1]	2,387	3,531[1]
Tanzania	2,488	3,967	1,062	1,101	5,980	6,059	9,179	10,674	218	385	459	541	1,730	2,931	911	1,062
Thailand	17,341	20,641	1,789	1,952	10,072	19,934	14,587	14,109	206	371	658	666	4,525	5,562	2,758	3,118
Togo	252	382	882	725	804	775	11,351	7,542	23	28	344	215	37	48	58	79
Tokelau	...	...	...	...	—	—	18,269	17,635	...	...	...	...	...	...	7	7
Tonga	...	...	...	...	94	100	6,720	6,834	...	...	...	...	11	14	7	...
Trinidad and Tobago	25	8	2,864	2,548	21	8	11,891	9,391	3	2	1,514	1,258	65	58	32	20
Tunisia	1,017	1,937	744	1,255	97	190	9,323	12,338	79	81	588	730	693	685	920	1,300
Turkey	23,664	29,312	1,741	2,123	2,713	4,300	14,955	22,163	749	2,204	1,188	1,070	10,553	7,957	10,924	16,884
Turks and Caicos Islands	...	...	...	...	—	—	...	...	...	...	...	...	...	...	—	1
Tuvalu	...	...	...	...	...	...	...	...	...	...	...	...	...	...	...	...
Uganda	1,651	1,225	1,258	1,375	5,090	7,380	4,543	7,235	382	528	671	788	8,965	8,494	251	319
U.S.S.R.	179,383	202,509	1,454	1,863	85,819	75,900	11,685	12,086	7,150	8,510	1,352	1,254	18,027	13,897	27,322	33,463
United Arab Emirates	—	5	6,691	3,855	—	5	17,359	11,538	...	...	...	...	36	95	35	327
United Kingdom	14,642	21,399	3,975	5,433	5,399	6,788	24,526	38,135	189	577	2,590	2,828	510	558	3,705	3,947
United States	257,983	279,122	3,561	4,725	16,228	18,050	27,780	32,414	943	1,451	1,451	1,754	26,757	25,198	24,785	27,939
Uruguay	953	1,020	1,178	2,018	198	187	4,989	6,188	5	6	892	1,016	292	347	149	196
Vanuatu	1	1	500	515	30	30	20,001	20,000	...	...	...	...	5	7	6	8
Venezuela	1,129	2,351	1,692	2,035	553	629	7,685	8,184	38	56	447	524	1,886	2,200	318	404
Vietnam	11,469	15,900	2,061	2,592	3,425	5,355	6,468	5,758	95	152	487	768	2,103	3,828	2,251	3,096
Virgin Islands (U.S.)	...	...	...	...	...	...	...	...	...	...	...	...	...	...	...	...
Wallis and Futuna	...	...	...	...	6	6	10,326	10,161	...	...	...	...	8	9	—	1
West Bank	...	...	...	...	...	...	...	...	...	...	...	...	...	...	...	...
Western Sahara	1	2[1]	708	741[1]	...	...	...	...	...	...	...	...	...	...	...	1
Western Samoa	...	...	...	...	35	45	6,861	7,139	...	...	...	529	53	59	...	...
Yemen (Aden)	112	122	1,628	1,714	4	8	13,187	15,000	—	—	...	...	115	51	107	117
Yemen (Ṣan'ā')	931	665	841	824	82	110	11,243	12,791	76	39	1,046	1,625	106	265	187	455
Yugoslavia	15,936	15,016	3,419	3,680	2,752	2,210	8,816	8,155	231	192	1,236	1,201	3,281	3,262	2,636	2,613
Zaire	770	1,167	744	897	12,557	16,802	6,878	7,047	147	127	611	634	2,457	2,589	464	542
Zambia	1,699	1,039	1,397	1,447	191	256	3,423	3,848	8	6	412	393	62	93	182	254
Zimbabwe	2,187	1,474	1,408	881	73	116	3,951	4,987	28	48	606	681	93	132	128	145

livestock														country
cattle		sheep		hogs		chickens		milk[e]				eggs[f]		
stock ('000 head)		stock ('000 head)		stock ('000 head)		stock ('000 head)		production ('000 metric tons)		yield (kg/animal)		production (metric tons)		
1975–77 average	1987	1975–77 average	1987	1975–77 average	1987	1975–77 average	1987	1975–77 average	1987	1975–77 average	1987	1975–77 average	1987	
...	...	...	...	...	...	...	...	...	...	...	...	...	...	Northern Mariana Islands
...	...	...	...	...	...	...	...	...	...	...	...	...	...	Palau
14,855	16,951	18,979	26,640	...	...	31,571	140,000	2,163	2,700	888	968	51,700	230,000	Pakistan
1,361	1,490	...	...	182	205	4,134	8,000	78	109	961	1,023	12,914	20,500	Panama
129	123	1	2	1,327	1,500	1,052	3,000	1	—	179	200	1,597	2,640	Papua New Guinea
5,470	7,332	370	398	1,083	1,690	9,501	15,000	128	194	1,905	1,898	18,393	33,800	Paraguay
4,153	3,850	15,017	13,500	2,099	2,240	36,838	44,000	818	840	1,218	1,273	53,674	72,500	Peru
1,753	1,695	30	30	6,395	7,000	45,820	50,000	13	15	1,027	1,034	183,982	231,000	Philippines
...	...	...	...	...	...	...	...	...	...	...	...	...	...	Pitcairn Island
13,051	10,523	3,513	4,739	20,070	18,546	81,354	53,000	16,610	15,400	2,754	2,958	445,391	450,000	Poland
1,110	1,087	3,850	5,150	1,879	2,920	16,593	18,000	684	900	2,274	2,344	47,226	76,000	Portugal
559	593	6	6	282	210	5,341	8,000	408	363	2,130	1,782	19,574	19,100	Puerto Rico
8	8	38	120	...	...	207	1,000	5	9	1,545	1,500	...	1,000	Qatar
22	19	2	3	104	74	2,634	4,000	5	3	495	314	1,920	1,800	Réunion
5,938	7,017	14,042	18,762	9,191	14,711	70,700	131,000	3,832	4,150	1,837	2,075	273,950	435,000	Romania
651	673	253	350	76	86	762	1,000	30	77	340	513	583	1,100	Rwanda
1	1	1	2	1	1	12	15[1]	...	...	...	...	...	...	St. Helena and Ascension
6	7	14	15	9	10	74	85[1]	...	...	...	...	255	370	St. Kitts and Nevis
8	12	11	15	8	12	128	250[1]	1	1	1,317	1,378	460	530	St. Lucia
...	...	...	...	...	...	...	...	...	...	...	...	...	...	St. Pierre and Miquelon
7	8	11	14	6	7	139	178[1]	1	2	1,348	1,364	450	585	St. Vincent and the Grenadines
...	...	...	...	...	...	...	...	...	...	...	...	...	...	San Marino
2	3	1	2	5	3	70	100[1]	—	—	170	170	132	172	São Tomé and Príncipe
306	530	2,221	3,800	...	...	5,933	36,000	153	410	1,000	1,139	15,807	150,000	Saudi Arabia
2,379	2,200	1,734	2,200	174	210	6,524	12,000	84	79	353	360	5,219	10,000	Senegal
2	2	...	...	10	15	109	290[1]	—	—	512	524	394	1,530	Seychelles
323	330	280	330	28	50	3,360	6,000	17	17	350	350	3,864	6,325	Sierra Leone
1	—	...	...	1,127	459	12,600	7,000	...	...	...	...	24,787	16,008	Singapore
24	23	...	...	41	51	133	143[1]	1	1	600	600	269	289	Solomon Islands
3,848	5,500	9,679	11,500	8	10	2,500	3,000	154	221	351	350	2,000	2,680	Somalia
12,845	11,799	31,317	29,728	1,350	1,455	26,000	36,000	2,515	2,600	2,753	2,826	143,518	185,000	South Africa[5]
...	...	...	...	...	...	...	...	...	...	...	...	...	...	Bophuthatswana[5]
...	...	...	...	...	...	...	...	...	...	...	...	...	...	Ciskei[5]
...	...	...	...	...	...	...	...	...	...	...	...	...	...	Transkei[5]
...	...	...	...	...	...	...	...	...	...	...	...	...	...	Venda[5]
2,850	2,040	5,200	6,300	33	47	435	1,000	65	69	399	412	120	175	South West Africa/Namibia
4,442	4,954	15,864	17,177	8,486	14,000	52,280	54,000	5,344	6,341	2,872	3,337	605,517	725,059	Spain
1,716	1,807	28	28	35	97	5,739	9,000	161	164	428	256	16,904	46,423	Sri Lanka
15,289	20,490	14,830	19,000	...	...	23,000	32,000	860	1,760	500	499	22,967	40,500	Sudan, The
26	66	4	3	18	23	907	6,000	8	10	1,606	1,538	3,100	3,400	Suriname
630	655	32	35	19	18	507	1,000	33	39	246	255	265	300	Swaziland
1,873	1,665	382	405	2,571	2,370	11,398	11,000	3,221	3,350	4,853	5,816	107,000	128,500	Sweden
1,991	1,880	370	365	2,011	1,973	6,104	6,000	3,439	3,700	3,886	4,684	41,905	45,100	Switzerland
590	738	6,456	12,669	1	1	7,038	12,000	301	650	1,141	2,008	34,283	88,000	Syria
130	105[1]	...	...	3,267	6,674[1]	24,760	59,313[1]	46	92[1]	3,426	5,000[1]	59,462	178,500[1]	Taiwan
11,590	14,500	3,498	4,500	141	182	14,167	29,000	333	440	160	160	25,470	59,566	Tanzania
4,268	4,931	34	73	3,409	4,200	53,352	80,000	7	75	2,004	2,063	87,700	180,000	Thailand
222	290	796	950	260	300	2,364	4,000	6	8	225	225	1,700	4,560	Togo
...	...	...	...	1	1	3	...	...	...	...	...	5	4	Tokelau
7	8	...	...	59	65	121	130[1]	—	—	1,500	1,500	293	411	Tonga
73	77	9	12	55	83	6,700	8,000	7	12	1,726	1,696	7,540	8,000	Trinidad and Tobago
895	610	5,913	5,800	3	4	12,667	17,000	222	360	856	1,500	19,767	55,000	Tunisia
14,790	12,400	41,137	40,400	15	12	41,300	58,000	3,039	3,400	589	590	161,327	275,000	Turkey
...	...	...	...	...	...	...	...	...	...	...	...	...	...	Turks and Caicos Islands
...	...	...	...	6	9	10	21[1]	...	...	...	...	8	15	Tuvalu
4,877	5,200	993	1,720	167	260	12,333	19,000	283	367	350	350	11,924	19,000	Uganda
110,167	122,103	142,192	142,210	64,409	79,501	741,000	1,130,000	91,129	102,880	2,173	2,415	3,202,000	4,519,000	U.S.S.R.
21	48	90	400	...	...	199	5,000	6	12	609	480	1,137	16,000	United Arab Emirates
14,182	12,476	25,524	25,976	7,886	7,955	129,763	119,000	14,518	15,400	4,383	4,936	833,333	736,000	United Kingdom
127,606	102,000	13,516	10,334	52,965	53,795	919,267	1,200,000	54,163	64,833	4,908	6,214	3,810,200	4,115,230	United States
10,676	10,323	15,560	25,560	452	190	5,217	6,000	747	980	1,698	1,786	13,099	22,100	Uruguay
102	103	...	...	63	73	131	180[1]	2	2	197	200	208	256	Vanuatu
9,346	12,654	257	422	1,797	3,351	31,113	54,000	1,222	1,593	1,175	1,259	96,111	153,945	Venezuela
1,531	2,755	12	22	9,008	11,796	56,300	70,000	18	35	800	800	52,667	86,700	Vietnam
7	11	4	3	3	3	57	49[1]	3	2	3,709	2,769	175	202	Virgin Islands (U.S.)
...	...	...	...	9	29	20	36[1]	—	—	1,500	1,500	29	44	Wallis and Futuna
...	...	...	...	...	...	...	...	...	...	...	...	...	...	West Bank
...	...	17	25[1]	...	...	...	1,000[1]	...	...	...	...	...	...	Western Sahara
26	27	...	...	50	65	487	1,000	1	1	1,000	1,000	130	180	Western Samoa
83	96	855	930	...	...	1,403	2,000	13	16	398	425	1,468	2,300	Yemen (Aden)
863	1,023	1,604	2,604	...	...	2,497	18,000	56	80	200	230	9,991	12,500	Yemen (Ṣan'ā')
5,756	5,030	7,830	7,819	7,511	8,459	51,232	74,000	3,857	4,650	1,429	1,722	190,933	240,000	Yugoslavia
1,143	1,431	722	777	680	792	11,500	19,000	6	7	792	868	6,561	7,800	Zaire
1,963	2,850	28	80	185	221	19,404	14,000	53	77	300	300	29,493	31,600	Zambia
6,356	5,500	712	570	212	180	8,400	10,000	145	220	1,160	1,560	9,543	12,600	Zimbabwe

[1]1986. [2]1982. [3]Netherlands Antilles includes Aruba. [4]Belgium includes Luxembourg. [5]South Africa includes Bophuthatswana, Ciskei, Transkei, and Venda.

Extractive industries

Extractive industries are generally defined as those exploiting *in situ* natural resources and include such activities as mining, forestry, fisheries, and agriculture; the definition is often confined, however, to nonrenewable resources only. For the purposes of this table, agriculture is excluded; it is covered in the two tables immediately preceding.

Extractive industries are divided here into three parts: mining, forestry, and fisheries. These major headings are each divided into two main subheadings, one that treats production and one that treats foreign trade. The production sections are presented in terms of volume except for mining, and the trade sections are presented in terms of U.S. dollars. Volume of production data usually imply output of primary (unprocessed) raw materials only, but, because of the way national statistical information is reported, the data may occasionally include some processed and manufactured materials as well, since these are often indistinguishably associated with the extractive process (sulfur from petroleum extraction, cured or treated lumber, or "processed" fish). This is also the case in the trade sections, where individual national trade nomenclatures may not distinguish some processed and manufactured goods from unprocessed raw materials.

Mining. In the absence of a single international source publication or standard of practice for reporting volume or value of mineral production, single-country sources predominantly have been used to compile mining production figures, supplemented by U.S. Bureau of Mines data and industry sources, especially *Mining Journal*'s *Mining Annual Review*. Each country has its own methods of classifying mining data, which do not always accord with the principal mineral production categories adopted in this table—namely, "metals," "nonmetals," and "energy." The available data have therefore been adjusted to make them accord better with the definition of each group. Included in the "metal" category are all ferrous and nonferrous metallic ores, concentrates, and scrap; the "nonmetal" group includes all nonmetallic minerals (stone, clay, precious gems, etc.) except the mineral fuels; the last group, "energy," is composed predominantly of the natural hydrocarbon fuels, though it may also include manufactured gas.

The contribution (value) of each national mineral sector to its country's gross domestic product is given, as is the distribution by group of that contribution (to gross domestic product and to foreign trade), although statistics regarding the value of mineral production are less readily available in country sources than those regarding trade or volume of minerals produced. Figures for value added by mineral output, though not always available, were sought first, as they provide the most consistent standard to compare the importance of minerals both within a particular national economy and among national mineral sectors worldwide. Where value added to the gross domestic product was not available, gross value of production or sales was substituted and the exception footnoted. Figures for value of production are reported here in millions of U.S. dollars to permit comparisons to be made from country to country. Comparisons can also be made as to the relative importance of each mineral group within a given country.

Extractive industries

Columns: **mining** — % of GDP, 1986; **mineral production (value added)**: year, total ('000,000 U.S.$), by kind (%) [metals[a] | non-metals[b] | energy[c]]; **trade (value)**: year, exports total ('000,000 U.S.$), exports by kind (%) [metals[a] | non-metals[b] | energy[c]], imports total ('000,000 U.S.$), imports by kind (%) [metals[a] | non-metals[b] | energy[c]].

country	% of GDP, 1986	prod. year	total ('000,000 U.S.$)	metals[a]	non-metals[b]	energy[c]	trade year	exports total ('000,000 U.S.$)	exp. metals[a]	exp. non-metals[b]	exp. energy[c]	imports total ('000,000 U.S.$)	imp. metals[a]	imp. non-metals[b]	imp. energy[c]
Afghanistan	...	1982–83	283.8[1]	—	0.1[1]	99.9[1]	1986	272.6[2]	—	—	100.0[2]	0.3	—	100.0	—
Albania	...	...	...				...	...				...			
Algeria	25.5	1983	13,021.3	—	1.3[3]	98.7[3]	1985	6,093.9	0.2	0.3	99.5	142.1	0.5	46.5	53.0
American Samoa	...	1985	...	—	100.0	—	1985	—				0.3	—	6.8	93.2
Andorra	...	...	...				1986	...			100.0[6]	1.8	...	100.0	...
Angola	17.4[5]	1985	764.0	...	...	...	1986	1,753.3	—	—	100.0	—	—	—	—
Anguilla	1.6[8]	1987	0.3	—	100.0	—	1981	[9]	...	...	...	...	...	...	...
Antigua and Barbuda	1.2[10]	1984	1.0	—	100.0	—	1984	...	...	...	...	1.1	—	—	100.0
Argentina	2.8[5]	1986	632.6	3.3	7.2	89.4	1985	83.8	4.6	6.6	88.8	597.9	22.7	4.2	73.1
Aruba[12]	...	...	...				...	...				...			
Australia	6.4	1985–86	9,112.0	28.1	5.5	66.4	1986	7,664.9	43.1	2.1	54.8	574.5	2.9	37.1	60.0
Austria	0.5[5]	1985	314.2	8.0[13]	14.7[13]	77.3[13]	1986	195.9	42.5	56.4	1.1	2,055.0	16.1	8.9	75.0
Bahamas, The	...	1986	13.4[14]	—	100.0	—	1986	23.8	—	85.1	14.9	333.2	—	—	100.0
Bahrain	19.0[13]	1984	947.1	—	0.9	99.1	1985	90.0	42.5	4.1	53.4	108.9	5.4	5.9	88.7
Bangladesh	0.1	1985–86	22.0	—	0.6	99.4	1985	—	—	—	—	243.0	—	11.2	88.8
Barbados	1.2	1985	21.9	—	100.0	—	1986	0.2	—	100.0	—	1.3[6]	—	—	100.0[6]
Belgium	0.4	1986	501.4	—	49.8[6]	50.2[6]	1986[15]	4,672.1	5.0	92.0	3.0	10,235.5	13.0	42.9	44.1
Belize	0.2	1985	0.4	—	100.0	—	1985	0.1	—	100.0	—	1.1	—	—	100.0
Benin	0.2[5]	1985	2.0	—	100.0[16]	—	1986	56.6	—	3.8	96.2	2.0[7]	—	100.0[7]	—
Bermuda	0.3[17]	1978–79	1.3	—	100.0	—	1984	0.3[6]	73.2[6]	26.8[6]	—	1.1	—	—	100.0
Bhutan	0.5	1986	1.1	—	100.0	—	1982	—	—	—	—	1.2	...	100.0	...
Bolivia	4.9	1986	268.6	—	35.9	64.1	1985	465.9	16.9	3.3	79.8	1.2	—	100.0	—
Botswana	44.1[8]	1985–86	530.6	12.5[7,14]	86.6[7,14]	0.9[7,14]	[19]	...	...	...	...	...	...	...	...
Brazil	0.8	1984	3,061.7	25.3[6,14]	22.1[6,14]	52.6[6,14]	1986	2,860.0	90.8	8.8	0.4	1,341.8	14.9	20.1	65.0
British Virgin Islands	0.2[10]	1985	0.8	—	100.0	—	1982	—	—	—	—	0.8[11]	10.3[11]	89.7[11]	—
Brunei	54.3[5]	1985	1,918.3	...	...	...	1986	1,961.6	—	—	100.0	8.4	7.9	92.1	—
Bulgaria	0.4	1986	113.3	...	...	...	...	...	...	...	...	...	...	...	...
Burkina Faso	0.1[13]	1984	0.7	—	100.0	—	1983	—	—	—	—	2.3	—	100.0	—
Burma	1.2	1984–85	72.4[20]	...	...	...	1986	37.2	65.3	34.7	—	...	...	...	...
Burundi	0.5	1982	5.6	...	...	...	1985	0.7	—	100.0	—	1.9	—	100.0	—
Cameroon	17.2[5]	1983–84	1,247.1[16]	...	...	...	1986	380.7	—	—	100.0	29.9[7]	66.6[7]	33.4[7]	—
Canada	5.8[8]	1984	20,024.7	13.4[6]	4.3[6]	82.3[6]	1986	10,334.9	24.3	13.8	61.9	4,674.0	30.3	9.3	60.4
Cape Verde	1.0[5]	1981	0.2	—	100.0	—	1982	1.1	1.8	98.2	—	0.8[21]	—	—	100.0[21]
Cayman Islands	1.5[10]	...	...				1983	3.8[22]	—	14.1[22]	85.9[22]	0.4[21]	—	—	100.0[21]
Central African Republic	6.9[5]	1985	17.4[23]	—	100.0[23]	—	1986	43.8	—	100.0	—	1.4[21]	—	100.0[21]	—
Chad	0.5[5]	1985	3.0	—	100.0	—	1984	—	—	100.0[7]	—	0.8	—	100.0	—
Chile	8.4	1986	2,372.0	...	...	...	1986	854.4	94.4	5.5	0.1	403.8	3.8	6.1	90.1
China	...	1985	19,866.5[24]	9.7[24]	...	90.3[24]	1982	3,923.9	4.1	4.2	91.7	773.4	76.4	15.7	7.9
Christmas Island	...	1985	...	—	100.0	—	1986	27.5	—	100.0	—	...	...	...	...
Cocos (Keeling) Islands	...						1986	2.9	20.6	79.4	—	0.2[6]	100.0[6]	—	—
Colombia	2.6	1986	1,008.0	...	...	...	1985	148.3	—	17.4	82.6	222.4	4.3	14.3	81.4
Comoros	...	1985	...	—	100.0	—	1983	0.1	—	100.0	—	...	...	...	...
Congo	43.0[13]	1984	905.9[16]	...	...	...	1986	785.6	1.7	5.9	92.4	3.8[21]	—	100.0[21]	—
Cook Islands	—						1984	—	—	—	—	0.1[21]	—	42.1[21]	57.9[21]
Costa Rica	1.9[6]	1979	75.9	23.6[3]	76.4[3]	—	1983	0.9	100.0	—	—	110.3[7]	0.1[7]	3.9[7]	96.0[7]
Côte d'Ivoire	2.9[13]	1984	192.5[16]	...	...	...	1985	37.2	6.4	0.9	92.7	313.1	0.2	3.6	96.2
Cuba	1.0[26]	...	...				1985	886.5	40.5	0.7	58.8	41.4	3.4	69.5	27.1
Cyprus	0.4	1985	12.4	12.5	87.5	—	1986	10.5	25.0	75.0	—	89.4	—	9.8	90.2
Czechoslovakia	2.3[6]	1985	4,415.7	7.9	7.7	84.4	1985	264.5	...	20.4	79.6	5,712.6	9.1	2.8	88.1
Denmark	0.9	1985	586.5	—	13.9[13]	86.1[13]	1986	313.4	22.7	16.5	60.8	1,161.0	2.2	8.8	89.0
Djibouti	—[5]	1983	—	—	100.0	—	1983					22.9[27]	—	6.8	93.2[27]
Dominica	0.8[5]	1984	0.6	—	100.0	—	1985					0.6	—	16.9	83.1
Dominican Republic	3.7	1986	327.0	94.1[6]	5.9[6]	—	1985	1.3	20.8	79.2	—	367.2	14.7	—	85.3
Ecuador	10.8	1986	1,256.7	—	6.5	93.5	1986	838.4	—	—	100.0	10.6	1.4	53.8	44.8
Egypt	18.5[5]	1985	10,311.0	0.3[11]	1.1[11]	98.6[11]	1986	1,145.7	0.4	0.1	99.5	216.8	3.6	18.5	77.9

Since the data for value of mineral production are obtained mostly from country sources, there is some variation (from a standard calendar year) in the time periods to which the data refer. In addition, the time period for which production data are available does not always correspond with the year for which mineral trade data are available.

The Standard International Trade Classification (SITC), Revision 3, was used to determine the commodity groupings for foreign trade statistics. The actual trade data for these groups is taken largely from the United Nations annual *Yearbook of International Trade Statistics* and national sources.

Forestry. Data for the production and trade sections of forestry are based on the United Nations annual *Yearbook of Forest Products.* Production of roundwood (all wood obtained in removals from forests) is the principal indicator of the volume of each country's forestry sector; this total is broken down further (as percentages of the roundwood total) into its principal components: fuelwood and charcoal, and industrial roundwood. The latter group was further divided to show its principal component, sawlogs and veneer; lesser categories of industrial roundwood could not be shown for reasons of space. These included pitprops (used in mining, a principal consumer of wood) and pulpwood (used in papermaking and plastics). Value of trade in forest products is given for both imports and exports, although exports alone tend to be the significant indicator for producing countries, while imports of wood are rarely a significant fraction of the trade of most importing countries.

Fisheries. Data for nominal (live weight) catches of fish, crustaceans, mollusks, etc., in all fishing areas (inland waters and marine areas) are taken from the United Nations annual *Yearbook of Fishery Statistics* (*Catches and Landings*). Total catch figures are given in metric tons; the catches in inland waters and marine areas are given as percentages of the total catch. The principal fishery commodities excluded are marine mammals, such as whales and seals; frogs; turtles; jellyfish; and such aquatic animal products as corals, sponges, and pearls.

Figures for trade in fishery products (including processed products and preparations like oils, meals, and animal feeding stuffs) are taken from the United Nations annual *Yearbook of Fishery Statistics* (*Fishery Commodities*). Value figures for trade in fish products are given for both imports and exports.

The following notes further define the column headings:
a. Includes ferrous and nonferrous metallic ores and scraps, such as bauxite, copper, gold (except unwrought or semimanufactured), iron ore, lead, uranium, or zinc.
b. Includes natural fertilizers; stone, sand, and aggregate; and pearls, precious and semiprecious stones, worked and unworked.
c. Includes hydrocarbon solids, liquids, and gases.
1 cubic metre = 35.3147 cubic feet
1 metric ton = 1.1023 short tons

forestry, 1986						fisheries, 1986								country
production of roundwood				trade (value '000 U.S.$)		catch (nominal)						trade (value, '000 U.S.$)		
total ('000 cubic metres)	fuelwood, charcoal (%)	industrial roundwood (%)		exports	imports	total ('000 metric tons)	by source (%)		by kind of catch (%)			exports	imports	
		total	sawlogs, veneer				marine	fresh-water	fish	crusta-ceans	mollusks			
6,730	76.7	23.3	12.7	...	29,018	1.5	—	100.0	100.0	—	—	...	...	Afghanistan
2,330	69.0	31.0	31.0	710	445	13.7	73.7	26.3	84.7	—	15.3	...	...	Albania
1,944	87.9	12.1	1.0	...	285,672	70.0	100.0	—	95.4	4.6	—	200	31,600	Algeria
...	...	...	...	...	1,801[4, 5]	0.4	100.0	—	76.0	0.9	—	253,620	1,241	American Samoa
...	...	...	...	...	...	...	...	...	...	...	...	...	...	Andorra
5,009	80.0	20.0	2.2	98[7]	256	58.4	86.4	13.6	99.9	0.1	—	...	41,570	Angola
...	...	...	...	...	...	—	100.0	—	100.0	—	—	49[7]	...	Anguilla
...	...	...	...	...	2,596[11]	2.2	100.0	—	99.2	0.8	—	—	...	Antigua and Barbuda
12,562	56.9	43.1	15.4	35,262	100,672	420.3	98.0	2.0	94.9	1.7	3.4	183,000	6,675	Argentina
...	...	...	...	...	...	0.8	100.0	—	100.0	—	—	...	...	Aruba[12]
19,999	14.4	85.6	40.7	206,627	794,682	156.6	98.6	1.4	51.8	24.1	24.1	321,758	225,718	Australia
13,622	10.4	89.6	59.2	1,784,249	801,423	4.6	—	100.0	—	—	—	2,175	93,014	Austria
115	—	100.0	13.0	1,061[5]	17,660	5.9	100.0	—	31.8	60.6	7.2	21,375	563	Bahamas, The
—	—	—	—	...	45,907	8.3	100.0	—	76.3	23.3	0.4	—	4,360	Bahrain
27,840	97.0	3.0	1.7	7,688	14,916	794.0	26.1	73.9	93.5	6.5	—	107,110	...	Bangladesh
3,403[15]	15.8[15]	84.2[15]	55.5[15]	...	12,705	4.2	100.0	—	100.0	—	—	—	2,500	Barbados
...	...	...	...	825,712[15]	1,502,897[15]	39.5	98.6	1.4	93.9	3.9	2.2	126,192[15]	427,694[15]	Belgium
155	81.3	18.7	18.7	657	3,193	1.4	99.7	0.3	36.9	53.7	9.4	7,193	514	Belize
4,538	95.0	5.0	0.4	...	1,869	23.5	31.7	68.1	100.0	—	—	760	3,420	Benin
...	...	...	...	...	2,434[5, 18]	0.7	100.0	—	92.3	7.7	—	—	4,130	Bermuda
3,224	91.4	8.6	7.4	286	143[11]	1.0	—	100.0	100.0	—	—	—	...	Bhutan
1,348	88.9	11.1	10.1	5,923	4,300	4.8	—	100.0	100.0	—	—	...	1,800	Bolivia
1,225	93.8	6.2	—	...	9,415	1.9	—	100.0	100.0	—	—	...	1,500	Botswana
237,774	72.2	27.8	16.8	936,349	204,538	847.9	74.6	25.4	85.7	13.3	1.0	153,848	130,528	Brazil
...	...	...	...	...	...	0.3	100.0	—	92.1	7.9	—	69[11]	55[11]	British Virgin Islands
293	27.0	73.0	70.3	30	6,721	2.8	95.3	4.7	80.5	18.2	1.3	210	6,370	Brunei
4,525	39.1	60.9	24.1	21,550	168,785	109.2	87.1	12.9	93.1	—	6.9	14,250	10,490	Bulgaria
6,931	95.5	4.5	—	...	2,242	7.0	—	100.0	100.0	—	—	...	1,170	Burkina Faso
19,096	84.6	15.4	9.5	139,672	9,000	643.8	77.2	22.8	98.9	1.1	—	21,600	...	Burma
3,742	98.8	1.2	0.2	...	1,342	6.8	—	100.0	100.0	—	—	—	24	Burundi
12,166	77.2	22.8	17.2	89,801	5,400	84.0	76.2	23.8	84.7	15.3	—	4,560	38,265	Cameroon
180,491	3.4	96.6	72.4	12,140,039	1,141,218	1,466.6	96.9	3.1	88.2	6.4	5.4	1,744,189	433,113	Canada
...	...	...	...	...	963	10.2	100.0	—	99.3	0.7	—	2,900	25	Cape Verde
3,417	87.5	12.5	5.8	23,085	280	13.0	—	100.0	100.0	—	—	6,120	1,260	Cayman Islands
...	...	...	...	...	...	...	100.0	—	100.0	—	—	...	210	Central African Republic
3,654	85.9	14.1	0.1	...	591	110.0	—	100.0	100.0	—	—	...	...	Chad
16,364	37.7	62.3	35.1	370,321	41,600	5,571.6	100.0	—	97.2	0.5	1.8	516,043	200	Chile
268,385[25]	64.9[25]	35.1[25]	20.3[25]	525,879[25]	2,658,721[25]	8,000.1	58.0	42.0	80.0	8.6	11.0	645,813	76,312	China
...	...	...	...	...	...	—	100.0	—	100.0	—	—	...	...	Christmas Island
...	...	...	...	...	...	—	...	...	100.0	—	—	...	...	Cocos (Keeling) Islands
17,522	84.7	15.3	11.2	14,052	133,551	80.4	31.8	68.2	90.5	8.2	1.3	41,250	42,300	Colombia
...	...	...	...	...	...	5.3	100.0	—	99.0	1.0	—	10	110	Comoros
2,574	63.2	36.8	27.8	62,430	3,762	30.0	60.0	40.0	99.7	0.3	—	3,200	30,200	Congo
...	...	...	...	...	...	0.8	100.0	—	68.5	0.7	28.4	...	140	Cook Islands
3,127	83.7	16.3	10.0	16,942	66,231	20.9	98.6	1.4	55.7	42.8	0.6	32,260	5,270	Costa Rica
11,865	69.5	30.5	25.1	191,744	26,660	97.2	78.4	21.6	96.5	3.5	—	61,316	79,370	Côte d'Ivoire
3,278	84.0	16.0	1.5	...	252,747	244.6	93.4	6.6	89.1	8.3	1.9	123,080	39,780	Cuba
81	28.4	71.6	42.0	60	46,733	2.6	98.0	2.0	93.9	0.1	6.0	295	11,401	Cyprus
18,959	7.3	92.7	51.3	401,666	91,460	20.7	—	100.0	100.0	—	—	2,879	89,252	Czechoslovakia
2,191	18.0	82.0	42.9	229,383	1,185,929	1,871.3	98.7	1.3	93.5	0.9	5.6	1,381,460	595,950	Denmark
...	...	...	...	...	1,587	0.4	100.0	—	97.4	2.6	—	...	240	Djibouti
...	...	...	...	...	602	0.5	100.0	—	100.0	—	—	...	700	Dominica
982	99.4	0.6	0.4	17[11]	48,996	17.2	95.1	4.9	85.9	4.3	9.5	2,180	15,855	Dominican Republic
8,687	71.8	28.2	26.3	15,342	107,690	1,019.3	99.9	0.1	94.3	5.4	0.3	383,565	5	Ecuador
2,057	95.4	4.6	—	...	892,582	138.8	19.1	80.9	97.0	2.2	0.8	4,685	82,881	Egypt

Extractive industries (continued)

country	mining % of GDP, 1986	mineral production (value added) year	total ('000,000 U.S.$)	metals[a]	non-metals[b]	energy[c]	trade (value) year	exports total ('000,000 U.S.$)	metals[a]	non-metals[b]	energy[c]	imports total ('000,000 U.S.$)	metals[a]	non-metals[b]	energy[c]
El Salvador	0.1	1985	8.2	—100.0—			1982	2.4	8.7	91.3	—	227.0	—	2.1	97.9
Equatorial Guinea	—	...	...	...	...	...	1983	1.3	100.0	—	—	...	...	...	...
Ethiopia	0.2[28]	1984–85	7.9	—100.0—		—	1985	...	...	...	...	136.0	1.4	0.4	98.2
Faeroe Islands	—	1986	—	—	—	—	1983	2.1[29]	1.3	87.2	11.5[29]				
Falkland Islands	...	...	...	...	...	...	1983	...	...	...	...	...	...	...	...
Fiji	0.9	1986	10.4	87.1[6]	12.9[6]	—	1984	15.3[21]	100.0[21]	—	—	4.6[29]	—	32.8	67.2[29]
Finland	0.4	1986	150.0	50.7[5]	49.3[5]	—	1986	113.3	8.6	33.5	57.9	1,936.4	10.6	7.6	81.8
France	1.7[5]	1985	3,583.7	4.7	30.4	64.9	1986	1,479.0	46.7	34.9	18.4	13,918.2	7.1	6.2	86.7
French Guiana	...	1986	...	—100.0—		—	1986	...	100.0	—	—	1.2	—	—	100.0
French Polynesia	...	...	...	...	...	...	1986	21.0	—	98.1	—	3.5[6]	—	—	100.0[6]
Gabon	24.0	1983	1,589.5	8.9	0.1	91.0	1986	1,285.1	7.5	—	92.5	6.5[6]	—	100.0[6]	—
Gambia, The	—	1982–83	0.3	—	100.0	—	1986	3.3	—	100.0	—	...	...	...	...
Gaza Strip	...	...	...	...	...	...	32	32	...	...	...	...	...	...	...
Germany, East	...	...	...	...	...	...	1986	2,683.0	27.6	30.8	41.6	17,857.7	17.9	7.2	74.9
Germany, West	1.0[13]	1984	6,149.2	0.5[14]	16.6[14]	82.9[14]									
Ghana	1.0[5]	...	...	...	...	...	1986	51.2	37.8	62.2	—	331.0[21]	20.7[21]	1.6[21]	77.7[21]
Gibraltar	...	...	...	...	...	...	1986	1.0	—	100.0	—	0.3	—	100.0	—
Greece	1.6	1985	605.0	25.0[13]	25.4[13]	49.5[13]	1986	297.1	26.8	37.0	36.2	1,859.0	4.3	3.6	92.1
Greenland	...	1985	...	—100.0—		—	1986	22.0	63.8	36.2	—	1.3	—	100.0	—
Grenada	0.4	1985	1.1	—	100.0	—	1984	—	—	—	—	0.1[21]	2.7[21]	—	97.3[21]
Guadeloupe	...	1980	...	—	100.0	—	1986	0.3	100.0	—	—	3.9	—	—	100.0
Guam	...	1984	...	—	100.0	—	1986[33]	...	100.0[33]	—	—	...	...	...	...
Guatemala	0.3	1986	30.0[16]	...	...	...	1986	13.6	—	1.3	98.7	97.5[6]	—	3.8[6]	96.2[6]
Guernsey	...	...	...	...	...	...	...	...	...	...	...	...	...	...	...
Guinea	13.4[5]	1983	299.0[35]	—100.0[35]—		—	1986	410.9	91.9	8.1	—	0.3[5]	100.0[5]	—	—
Guinea-Bissau	1.3[6]	1983	1.0	—	100.0	—	1986	1.0	—	100.0	—	1.3[21]	—	89.5[21]	10.5[21]
Guyana	7.9	1986	45.0[36]	—100.0—		...	1986	75.6	98.7	1.3	—	1.1	—	100.0	—
Haiti	0.1	1986	2.0	—100.0—		—	1983	8.5[22]	100.0[22]	—	—	...	...	...	...
Honduras	1.8	1986	67.0	—100.0—		—	1984	38.4	100.0	—	—	54.2	0.5	4.6	94.9
Hong Kong	0.1	1985	45.7	—	100.0	—	1986	506.8	26.5	72.7	0.8	1,318.5	2.6	76.4	21.0
Hungary	8.1[6]	1985	1,312.3	3.3	3.0	93.7	1986	404.7[27]	18.4	—	81.6[27]	1,895.1[27,29]	3.3	5.0	91.7[27,29]
Iceland	...	1986	...	—	100.0	—	1986	10.9	—	100.0	—	37.0	61.0	24.5	14.5
India	3.0	1984–85	5,216.6	6.0	8.6	85.4	1986	2,541.4	25.1	65.9	9.0	1,775.5	16.1	75.5	8.4
Indonesia	16.2[5]	1985	14,054.8	—4.1—		95.9	1985	12,207.8	2.2	0.2	97.6	1,064.6	9.6	10.3	80.1
Iran	11.3[13]	1983–84	22,601.3	—8.2[14,37]—		91.8[14,37]	1986	9,044.1	—0.1—		99.9	28.4	10.4	19.1	70.5
Iraq	24.7[5]	1985	11,569.3[16]	...	...	...	1986	8,784.3	—	0.4	99.6	4.6	23.5	74.9	1.6
Ireland	1.2[11]	1983	284.2[38]	23.9	74.6	1.5[38]	1986	291.6	63.2	27.8	9.0	505.2	12.7	8.9	78.4
Isle of Man	...	1983	...	—	100.0	—	...	...	...	...	...	...	...	...	...
Israel	0.7[39]	1982–83	195.4	5.7[39,40]	94.3[39]	[39,40]	1986	2,015.2	0.1	99.9	—	2,553.3	0.2	72.5	27.3
Italy	0.9	1982	2,593.0	3.8	14.8	81.4	1986	432.9	23.7	61.7	14.6	16,085.9	9.8	4.8	85.4
Jamaica	6.8	1985	102.4	97.2	2.8	—	1986	261.2	98.9	1.1	—	5.1	—	38.2	61.8
Japan	0.4	1985	5,139.6	10.9[13]	24.1[13]	65.0[13]	1986	378.0	37.8	61.2	2.0	39,830.3	14.5	5.8	79.7
Jersey	...	...	...	...	...	...	1985	249.7	1.0	99.0	—	519.2	—	5.2	94.8
Jordan	3.3	1986	154.0	—	—100.0—		1982	3.8	100.0	—	—	...	...	...	...
Kampuchea	...	1985	...	—	100.0	...	...	...	...	...	...	...	...	...	...
Kenya	0.2	1985	12.2	0.8[7]	99.2[7]	—	1986	22.1	—	98.1	1.9	262.6	...	1.1	98.9
Kiribati	—	1982	...	...	...	...	1983	...	...	...	...	0.2[11]	100.0[11]	—	—
Korea, North	...	...	...	...	...	...	...	...	...	...	...	...	...	...	...
Korea, South	1.3	1985	1,251.6	5.9[13]	23.5[13]	70.6[13]	1986	82.0	22.4	77.6	—	5,779.3	17.0	5.4	77.6
Kuwait	36.9	1986	6,313.4	—	0.1	99.9	1986	4,048.1	0.5	0.4	99.1	10.5	30.8	68.3	0.9
Laos	...	1985	...	—100.0—		—	1983	0.7[22]	100.0[22]	—	—	...	...	...	...
Lebanon	...	...	...	...	...	...	1986	45.8	28.3	71.7	—	28.9	2.2	78.3	19.5
Lesotho	0.3	1984–85	1.4	—	100.0	—	19	...	...	...	...	...	...	...	...
Liberia	19.2[5]	1985	134.9	—100.0[42]—		—	1986	193.3	86.3	13.7	—	...	...	...	...
Libya	37.5[5]	1985	9,710.0	—	0.7[21]	99.3[21]	1986	6,521.8	—	—	100.0	86.7[6]	80.1[6]	19.9[6]	—
Liechtenstein	...	...	...	...	...	...	15	...	...	...	...	...	...	...	...
Luxembourg	0.1[5]	1985	2.6	—	100.0	—	1985	1.0	29.6	70.4	—	4.2	17.6	—	82.4
Macau	...	1984	1.4	—	100.0	—	1985	14.5	35.8	64.2	—	43.1	—	2.1	97.9
Madagascar	0.2[5]	1985	5.0	—100.0—		—	1983	...	...	...	...	5.9[11]	—	45.8[11]	54.2[11]
Malawi	—	1984	0.27	—	100.0	—									
Malaysia	10.9[8]	1987	2,555.6	...	100.0	...	1986	3,716.0	2.9	1.1	96.0	234.9	38.4	29.8	31.8
Maldives	1.1	1985	0.9	...	100.0	...	1985	—	...	...	...	...	...	...	...
Mali	0.2[13]	1984	2.6[44]	—100.0—		...	1986	11.5	—	100.0	—	1.5	—	100.0	—
Malta	...	1985	44.5	—	100.0	—	1986	4.1	11.6	88.4	—	4.7	—	98.2	1.8
Martinique	...	1984	...	—	100.0	—	1986	3.3[6]	14.1[6]	—	85.9[6]	63.9	0.1	—	99.9
Mauritania	9.9[5]	1984	69.4	—100.0—		—	1986	150.6	100.0	—	—	0.3	—	100.0	—
Mauritius	0.1	1986	1.5	—	100.0	—	1986	13.7	—	100.0	—	17.0	—	100.0	—
Mayotte	...	...	...	...	...	...	...	...	...	...	...	...	...	...	...
Mexico	7.2	1984	17,210.9	5.6	4.4	90.0	1986	5,865.2	1.8	7.3	90.9	302.2	28.1	28.1	43.8
Monaco	...	...	...	...	...	...	...	...	...	...	...	...	...	...	...
Mongolia	...	...	...	...	...	...	1986	0.4	—	—	100.0	5.1	—	100.0	...
Montserrat	1.3[10]	1985	0.4	—100.0—		—									
Morocco	3.6	1986	525.8	—97.1[11,14]—		2.9[11,14]	1985	573.0	10.9	88.0	1.1	1,287.7	0.1	18.0	81.9
Mozambique	0.3[5]	1985	6.0	...	...	...	1984	1.7	71.6	—	28.4	21.0	—	100.0	—
Nauru	...	1984	...	—	100.0	—	1986	69.0	—	100.0	—	...	...	...	...
Nepal	0.3[13]	1983–84	6.4	...	...	...	1985	0.2	—	100.0	—	2.8	17.7	75.3	7.0
Netherlands, The	5.9	1985	10,537.7	—	2.1[6]	97.9[6]	1986	5,452.8	10.7	7.1	82.2	7,764.3	10.0	7.8	82.2
Netherlands Antilles[12]	...	1983	...	—	100.0	—	1986	114.9	2.3	13.8	83.9	3,331.5[13]	—	—	100.0[13]
New Caledonia	4.6[6]	1983	36.0	100.0	—	—	1986	101.5	100.0	—	—	9.2[6]	—	5.4[6]	94.6[6]
New Zealand	1.7	1985–86	296.6	5.4[46]	16.5[46]	78.1[46]	1986	71.5	39.1	7.7	53.2	316.8	26.4	18.3	55.3
Nicaragua	0.6	1986	16.0	—100.0—		—	1984	3.2	100.0	—	—	152.1[7]	—	1.5[7]	98.5[7]
Niger	7.8[5]	1985	115.1	97.9[21]	2.9[21]	-0.8[21]	1984	363.2[22]	99.3[2]	0.4[2]	0.3[2,29]	9.6[11]	—	100.0[11]	—
Nigeria	19.8[5]	1985	8,104.2	0.1[46]	7.2[46]	92.7[46]	1984	11,340.4	—0.1—		99.9	128.1	14.2	85.8	—
Niue	—	1983	...	—	100.0	—	1984	...	...	...	...	—	—	100.0	—
Norfolk Island	...	...	...	...	...	...	1985	...	...	...	...	—	—	100.0	—

forestry, 1986						fisheries, 1986								country
production of roundwood				trade (value '000 U.S.$)		catch (nominal)						trade (value, '000 U.S.$)		
total ('000 cubic metres)	fuelwood, charcoal (%)	industrial roundwood (%)		exports	imports	total ('000 metric tons)	by source (%)		by kind of catch (%)			exports	imports	
		total	sawlogs, veneer				marine	fresh-water	fish	crusta-ceans	mollusks			
4,899	98.3	1.7	1.1	2,597	25,370	12.5	86.4	13.6	25.0	73.5	1.5	19,080	1,220	El Salvador
607	73.6	26.4	26.4	17,835	...	4.4	89.8	10.2	83.0	10.2	3.4	—	2,640	Equatorial Guinea
38,918	95.3	4.7	0.3	...	13,266	4.1	14.6	85.4	100.0	—	—	20	50	Ethiopia
...	...	...	...	...	...	353.7	100.0	—	96.3	3.1	0.6	222,073	3,885	Faeroe Islands
...	...	...	...	...	...	—	100.0	—	37.5	62.5	—	—	—	Falkland Islands
249	14.9	85.1	82.3	5,916	8,450	27.0	88.4	11.6	79.3	5.4	13.2	16,235	13,918	Fiji
41,289	7.7	92.3	41.2	5,491,486	325,516	158.6	79.6	20.4	100.0	—	—	6,803	106,455	Finland
39,115	26.7	73.3	48.4	1,892,636	3,650,048	850.0	96.5	3.5	69.8	3.2	27.0	501,233[30]	1,510,431[30]	France
254	26.0	74.0	70.5	2,169	1,087	3.1	100.0	—	64.3	35.7	—	23,792	14,479	French Guiana
...	...	...	...	...	14,695	1.9	...	—	99.8	0.2	—	7	3,975	French Polynesia
4,056	63.4	36.6	36.6	90,967	3,655	20.4	91.2	8.8	92.2	7.8	—	8,130	9,320	Gabon
856	97.5	2.5	1.6	...	235	10.7[31]	74.8[31]	25.2[31]	95.5[31]	4.5[31]	...	1,000	3,100	Gambia, The
...	...	...	...	...	...	0.5	—	—	100.0	—	—	...	...	Gaza Strip
10,868	5.2	94.8	36.9	108,100	522,500	208.9	90.6	9.4	97.5	0.5	2.0	...	31,937	Germany, East
30,411	12.5	87.5	54.7	3,587,102	6,404,293	202.4	88.0	12.0	76.4	8.4	15.2	358,433	1,113,211	Germany, West
9,668	87.3	12.2	8.2	30,460	4,079	309.2	87.1	12.9	99.2	0.4	0.4	27,290	12,600	Ghana
...	...	...	...	...	...	...	...	...	...	...	...	...	...	Gibraltar
2,893	66.2	33.8	21.3	31,425	378,978	116.0	91.6	8.4	90.5	4.0	5.5	46,463	107,309	Greece
—	—	—	—	...	...	155.4	100.0	—	58.6	41.2	0.2	211,020	1,123	Greenland
...	...	...	...	...	...	2.3	100.0	—	98.9	0.1	0.6	...	800	Grenada
17	88.2	11.8	11.8	...	14,254	8.5	100.0	—	96.0	1.4	3.5	243	10,736	Guadeloupe
...	...	...	...	77[6]	1,935[6]	0.7	86.2	13.8	100.0	—	—	1,039[6]	6,613[6]	Guam
6,983	98.4	1.6	1.5	9,458	43,822	2.1	94.3	5.7	36.5	63.5	—	7,600	750	Guatemala
...	...	...	...	...	...	34	34	34	34	34	34	...	...	Guernsey
4,350	85.9	14.1	4.1	800	1,056	30.0	93.3	6.7	100.0	—	—	...	3,265	Guinea
561	75.2	24.8	7.1	350	310	3.6	100.0	—	72.2	27.2	0.6	850	250	Guinea-Bissau
209	8.6	91.4	81.3	4,142	2,710	44.6	98.2	1.8	88.8	11.2	—	5,835	—	Guyana
6,056	96.1	3.9	3.7	...	4,584	8.0	96.2	3.8	96.9	3.1	—	...	5,290	Haiti
5,490	85.3	14.7	14.4	28,251	24,876	13.4	98.7	1.3	9.9	85.3	4.8	25,531	1,425	Honduras
186	100.0	—	—	78,239	702,382	213.6	97.3	2.7	83.9	9.1	7.0	396,868	624,726	Hong Kong
6,929	44.1	55.9	28.5	110,380	298,065	36.1	—	100.0	100.0	—	—	9,095	36,870	Hungary
—	—	—	—	...	36,820	1,657.1	100.0	—	96.7	2.3	1.0	857,994	1,607	Iceland
250,256	90.4	9.6	7.3	15,088	196,529	2,925.3	58.8	41.2	91.3	8.0	0.7	362,541	—	India
157,768	82.1	17.9	16.1	1,535,238	172,806	2,521.2	75.9	24.1	90.3	6.7	2.6	340,619	26,315	Indonesia
6,757	35.2	64.8	5.5	38[13]	181,006	152.1	80.1	19.9	95.5	3.4	1.1	21,776	32,200	Iran
143	65.0	35.0	14.0	...	114,456	20.6	24.3	75.7	100.0	—	—	...	...	Iraq
1,245	3.7	96.3	52.9	29,581	266,972	228.9	100.0	—	89.2	4.5	6.3	139,857	50,588	Ireland
...	...	...	...	...	...	5.8	100.0	—	18.4	2.7	78.9	3,460[6]	...	Isle of Man
118	9.3	90.7	22.0	11,134	165,992	22.0	32.7	67.3	99.3	0.7	—	2,505	49,622	Israel
9,623	51.7	48.3	33.3	918,024	3,317,913	547.6	92.0	8.0	63.6	5.4	31.0	167,594[41]	1,264,513[41]	Italy
93	14.0	86.0	72.0	1,452	43,907	10.5	86.7	13.3	100.0	—	—	2,000	18,650	Jamaica
32,639	1.7	98.3	56.4	962,905	6,551,948	11,966.8	98.3	1.7	86.6	1.7	10.7	897,851	6,593,515	Japan
...	...	...	...	...	...	2.3[34]	100.0[34]	—	10.5[34]	82.0[34]	7.5[34]	3,599	...	Jersey
9	55.6	44.4	—	9,267	60,949	—	100.0	—	100.0	—	—	—	9,264	Jordan
5,422	89.5	10.5	2.0	94	100	70.0	9.3	90.7	99.3	0.7	—	...	...	Kampuchea
33,763	95.3	4.7	1.3	2,539	17,522	102.5	5.8	94.2	99.6	0.3	0.1	3,105	752	Kenya
...	...	...	...	...	...	33.6	100.0	—	89.6	0.4	10.0	910	100	Kiribati
4,595	86.9	13.1	13.1	...	24,750	1,700.0	94.1	5.9	100.0	—	—	35,850	—	Korea, North
8,564	72.1	27.9	12.0	226,396	928,229	3,102.5	98.2	1.8	71.3	3.0	24.6	1,188,391	117,079	Korea, South
—	—	—	—	20,152	102,443	7.0	100.0	—	86.0	14.0	—	6,050	26,400	Kuwait
4,213	92.5	7.5	5.1	10,251	200	20.0	—	100.0	100.0	—	—	—	—	Laos
486	94.9	5.1	5.1	2,451	71,174	1.6	93.7	6.3	100.0	—	—	...	...	Lebanon
539	100.0	—	—	...	...	—	—	100.0	100.0	—	—	...	2,400	Lesotho
4,752	85.7	14.3	11.4	48,599	2,028	16.1	75.1	24.9	97.3	2.6	—	1,020	8,833	Liberia
635	84.4	15.6	9.9	...	75,754	7.8	100.0	—	100.0	—	—	—	17,540	Libya
8[5]	—	100.0[5]	...	...	...	—	—	100.0	100.0	—	—	43	43	Liechtenstein
15	15	15	15	15	15	—	—	—	—	—	—	15	15	Luxembourg
...	...	...	...	399	7,981	8.0	100.0	—	30.8	67.0	2.2	7,348	10,414	Macau
7,066	88.6	11.4	6.6	46	6,959	63.6	27.7	72.3	87.8	12.0	0.1	25,870	660	Madagascar
6,722	95.4	4.6	0.7	600[13]	8,103	72.9	—	100.0	100.0	—	—	210	149	Malawi
38,137	20.3	79.7	76.5	1,740,118	262,532	616.3	98.5	1.5	73.6	14.5	10.7	132,547	126,598	Malaysia
...	...	...	...	...	1,915	45.8	100.0	—	100.0	—	—	16,138	—	Maldives
5,051	93.7	6.3	0.2	...	...	61.0	—	100.0	100.0	—	—	550	700	Mali
...	...	...	...	...	17,458	1.1	100.0	—	96.8	1.8	1.4	140	6,237	Malta
11	90.9	9.1	9.1	...	13,834	5.0	100.0	—	97.0	2.1	—	107	17,242	Martinique
12	58.3	41.7	8.3	...	...	104.1	94.2	5.8	53.2	1.2	45.6	177,256	270	Mauritania
24	70.8	29.2	12.5	...	15,508	13.0	99.8	0.2	96.1	0.6	3.3	10,055	7,865	Mauritius
...	...	...	...	...	...	0.8	...	...	...	...	...	...	...	Mayotte
21,228	66.8	33.2	18.6	13,884	324,005	1,303.7	92.9	7.1	87.8	6.4	5.6	423,879	8,220	Mexico
...	...	...	...	...	1.5	1.5	100.0	—	100.0	—	—	30	30	Monaco
2,390	56.5	43.5	43.5	70[13]	6,800	0.4	—	100.0	100.0	—	—	—	2,000	Mongolia
...	...	...	...	...	367[4, 11]	0.1	100.0	—	100.0	—	—	—	178[21]	Montserrat
2,006	64.4	35.6	6.5	18,594	132,301	595.9	99.8	0.2	94.3	0.2	5.5	306,724	833	Morocco
15,255	93.5	6.5	0.6	1,299	396	31.9	97.6	2.4	80.6	18.9	0.5	31,000	7,340	Mozambique
...	...	...	...	...	...	—	...	...	100.0	—	—	...	...	Nauru
16,127	96.5	3.5	3.5	12,000	300	9.4	—	100.0	100.0	—	—	...	...	Nepal
1,113	8.6	91.4	44.0	1,307,572	2,717,576	454.8[45]	99.1[45]	0.9[45]	80.9	...	19.1	766,379	387,935	Netherlands, The
...	...	...	...	...	11,636	1.1	100.0	—	100.0	—	—	...	6,340	Netherlands Antilles[12]
12	—	100.0	91.7	...	5,936	4.2	100.0	—	36.1	2.8	0.5	500	1,570	New Caledonia
9,341	0.5	99.5	52.9	426,078	122,446	339.6[47]	...	—	81.9[47]	1.6[47]	16.5[47]	344,392[48]	22,379[48]	New Zealand
3,674	76.0	24.0	22.6	2,569	9,866	2.4	97.7	2.3	23.9	76.1	—	8,688	—	Nicaragua
4,039	93.8	6.2	—	...	2,383	2.3	—	100.0	100.0	—	—	—	1,640	Niger
98,567	92.0	8.0	5.7	6,091	177,376	268.5	60.2	39.8	97.2	2.8	—	2,000	90,309	Nigeria
...	...	...	...	...	...	—	100.0	—	100.0	—	—	—	—	Niue
...	...	...	...	...	...	—	100.0	—	100.0	—	—	...	...	Norfolk Island

Extractive industries (continued)

country	% of GDP, 1986	mining — year	mineral production total ('000,000 U.S.$)	metals[a]	non-metals[b]	energy[c]	trade — year	exports total ('000,000 U.S.$)	exports metals[a]	exports non-metals[b]	exports energy[c]	imports total ('000,000 U.S.$)	imports metals[a]	imports non-metals[b]	imports energy[c]
Norway	18.7[5]	1985	10,731.4	0.4	0.8	98.8	1986	7,703.4	2.5	1.1	96.4	1,076.8	46.0	11.6	42.4
Oman	35.6	1986	2,610.4	0.4	0.5	99.1	1985	3,976.8[2]	—	—	100.0[2]	12.4	6.0	60.9	33.1
Pacific Is., Trust Terr. of the	...	...	...	...	...	...	1984	1.6	100.0	—	—				
Marshall Islands							1982					3.7[7]	—	—	100.0[7]
Micronesia, Fed. States of	—	—	—	—	—	—	...								
Northern Mariana Islands	—	—	—	—	—	—									
Palau							1983					2.1[6]	—	—	100.0[6]
Pakistan	2.3[8]	1985–86	674.2	—22.0[14]—		78.0[14]	1986	17.2	27.4	72.6	—	564.4	11.6	4.0	84.4
Panama	0.1	1985	5.8	—100.0—		—	1985	136.9	18.4	81.6	—	314.9	2.6	11.8	85.6
Papua New Guinea	10.7[6]	1983	252.7	100.0	—	—	1985	265.1	99.9	0.1	—	0.5	—	100.0	—
Paraguay	0.5	1985	18.6	—	100.0	—	1984	...	...	...	...	70.0	—	4.2	95.8
Peru	9.2	1986	2,320.0	51.5[21]	8.2[21,50]	40.3[21,50]	1984	671.9	71.6	0.6	27.8	31.9	55.1	32.1	12.8
Philippines	1.6	1985	736.6	69.0[13]	2.8[13]	28.2[13]	1985	262.8	92.5	1.9	5.6	1,421.3	0.4	2.4	97.2
Pitcairn Island															
Poland	5.4[6]	1985	2,780.2	10.4	13.2	76.3	1985	1,927.6	1.5	20.8	77.7	2,289.2	10.9	7.6	81.5
Portugal	0.6[21]	1984	112.5	20.8	71.8	7.4	1986	91.3	16.9	80.4	2.7	1,259.7	2.7	7.2	90.1
Puerto Rico	1.7[8]	1984–85	12.1	—	100.0	—	1986[33]	50.7	2.4	95.9	1.7	52.1	0.4	28.8	70.8
Qatar	30.9	1986	1,527.5	...	...	...	1985	3,034.2	—	—	100.0	4.8	58.3	41.7	—
Réunion	...	1984	...	—	100.0	—	1986	0.2	100.0	—	—	8.1	—	—	100.0
Romania	...	...	...	...	...	...	...	...	...	...	...	...	...	...	...
Rwanda	0.3[13]	1984	5.7	—100.0—		—	1984	10.4[2]	100.0	—	—	0.3	—	100.0	—
St. Helena and Ascension		1984	1.4	—	100.0	—						0.4[7]	—	100.0[7]	—
St. Kitts and Nevis	0.3[5]	1985	0.2	—	100.0	—	1985	12.9	—	—	100.0	0.1[13]	100.0[13]	—	—
St. Lucia	0.6	1985	0.9	—	100.0	—	1983	...	...	...	...	...	...	...	...
St. Pierre and Miquelon	...	1985	...	—	100.0	—	1985	1.3	—	—	100.0	0.1[13]	—	—	100.0[13]
St. Vincent	0.3	1985	0.3	—	100.0	—	1983	—	—	—	—	0.6[21]	—	—	100.0[21]
San Marino															
São Tomé and Príncipe	0.3[13]	1982	0.1	—	100.0	—	1983	...	...	...	...	...	...	...	...
Saudi Arabia	28.9	1985–86	22,759.3	—2.1—		97.9	1986	22,750.0	0.2	0.3	99.5	109.7	32.9	64.4	2.7
Senegal	1.2[5]	1985	25.0	—	100.0	—	1986	66.9	4.0	96.0	—	258.9[13]	0.1[13]	5.4[13]	94.5[13]
Seychelles		1985		—	100.0	—	1985	0.3[13]	0.4[13]	99.6[13]	—	0.2	1.0	—	99.0
Sierra Leone	5.9[5]	1985	43.0	—100.0—		—	1986	112.6	57.0	43.0	—	0.1	—	100.0	—
Singapore	0.2[8]	1986	42.9	—	100.0	—	1986	193.2	55.1	16.7	28.2	3,933.8	1.8	2.2	96.0
Solomon Islands	0.3[6]	1984	...	—100.0—		—	1984	0.6[53]	100.0[53]	—	—	...	...	...	...
Somalia	0.3[5]	1985	3.3	—	100.0	—	1983	...	...	...	...	0.8[21]	—	74.8[21]	25.2[21]
South Africa	16.4	1986	9,189.4	—87.3[5]—		12.7[5]	1986[19]	2,999.4[54]	30.0	29.8	40.2[54]	224.2[54]	36.2	63.8	—[54]
Bophuthatswana	52.6[21]	...	...	...	...	...	...	...	...	...	...	...	...	...	...
Ciskei	0.1[21]	...	...	...	...	...	...	...	...	...	...	...	...	...	...
Transkei	...	...	...	...	...	...	...	...	...	...	...	...	...	...	...
Venda	...	...	...	...	...	...	...	...	...	...	...	...	...	...	...
South West Africa/Namibia	36.1	1986	467.8	—100.0—		—	1983	593.0	64.0	36.0	—	[19]	[19]	[19]	[19]
Spain	1.4[13]	1983	1,759.0	11.9	16.0	72.1	1986	275.7	31.6	61.8	6.6	6,949.1	12.4	5.1	82.5
Sri Lanka	2.2[5]	1984	47.5	—100.0[56]—		—	1986	84.8	14.2	85.8	—	82.0	1.4	54.8	43.8
Sudan, The	0.1[5]	1985	6.0	—100.0—		—	1981	1.2[2]	100.0[2]	—	—	162.7	—	0.1	99.9
Suriname	7.3	1985	53.2	99.8[13,14]	0.2[13,14]	—	1986	178.3	99.6	—	0.4	4.4	—	—	100.0
Swaziland	2.6[5]	1985	9.0	9.4[21]	77.3[21]	13.3[21]	1986	17.2	—	70.0	30.0	[19]	[19]	[19]	[19]
Sweden	0.5	1985	532.3	88.6	11.4	—	1986	661.3	81.5	14.3	4.2	2,610.5	14.2	7.6	78.2
Switzerland	...	1984	...	—	100.0	—	1986	1,683.9	3.9	95.7	0.4	2,776.4	3.4	70.0	26.6
Syria	7.4[5]	1985	1,503.4	—	—100.0[16]—		1986	466.1	—	7.9	92.1	22.1	2.0	1.9	96.1
Taiwan	0.5	1986	392.0	0.4	62.6	37.1	1986	8.8	—	—100.0—		2,993.2	—	—13.1—	86.9[29]
Tanzania	0.3[5]	1985	15.2	...	...	...	1982	15.3	50.4	49.6	—	159.6[11]	—	3.0[11]	97.0[11]
Thailand	2.1	1986	888.8	18.9[13]	39.6[13]	41.5[13]	1986	434.5	10.7	89.2	0.1	1,124.3	7.3	16.0	76.7
Togo	13.7[13]	1984	92.2	—	100.0	—	1986	208.7	—	100.0	—	83.2[21]	—	1.4[21]	98.6[21]
Tokelau	—	1985	...	—	100.0	—	1983	—	—	—	—	...	...	...	...
Tonga	0.5[6]	1983	0.4	—	100.0	—	1983	...	...	...	...	0.4[7]	—	73.2[7]	26.8[7]
Trinidad and Tobago	16.6	1986	801.1	—	—	100.0	1986	561.8	—	1.1	98.9	25.2	64.3	33.9	1.8
Tunisia	8.6	1986	765.7	—9.1—		90.9	1986	444.0	0.7	9.9	89.4	283.6	1.0	65.1	33.9
Turkey	2.2	1986	1,150.5	22.6[1]	13.7[1]	63.7[1]	1986	781.5	8.0	35.0	57.0	3,820.8[5]	5.7[5]	1.8[5]	92.5[5]
Turks and Caicos Is.	2.1[10]	1983	1.0	—	100.0	—	1983	0.4	—	100.0	—	...	...	...	...
Tuvalu	—	1985					1983					...	—	—	100.0
Uganda	0.1[5]	1985	2.0	...	...	...	1984	1.6	100.0	—	—	...	...	...	...
U.S.S.R.	...	1984	63,099.0	—31.8[14]—		68.2[14]	1984	52,690.0[57]	10.3	1.4	88.3[57]	10,070.0[57]	59.3	2.7	38.0[57]
United Arab Emirates	46.6[13]	1985	7,569.2[58]	—	0.2[58]	99.8[58]	1986	9,043.3	0.3	0.1	99.6	33.3	19.7	79.5	0.8
United Kingdom	7.0[13]	1984	29,958.5	0.1[6,14]	5.2[6,14]	94.7[6,14]	1986	13,424.4	5.9	21.3	72.8	10,993.8	15.2	27.4	57.4
United States	1.9[8]	1986	95,300.0	2.4[6]	4.5[6]	93.1[6]	1986	9,345.6	30.3	20.6	49.1	35,020.7	6.5	15.3	78.2
Uruguay	1.1[5]	1985	55.8	—	100.0	—	1984	1.1	—	100.0	—	267.0	—	2.3	97.7
Vanuatu	...	1984	—	—	100.0	—	1983	—	—	—	—	2.2[7]	—	75.6[7]	24.4[7]
Venezuela	7.0	1985	7,816.4	7.5	4.1	88.5	1986	6,016.3	3.4	0.4	96.2	168.1	65.5	29.0	5.5
Vietnam	...	...	...	...	...	...	...	...	...	...	...	...	...	...	...
Virgin Islands (U.S.)	...	1985	...	—	100.0	—	1986[33]	0.3	18.3	81.7	—	966.5	—	0.2	99.8
Wallis and Futuna	...	...	...	...	...	...	...	...	...	...	...	...	...	...	...
West Bank							1986[32]	11.8[32,60]	...	...	...	...	...	...	...
Western Sahara	...	...	...	...	61		...	...	...	...	...	...	...	...	...
Western Samoa	...	1984	...	...	...	...	1983	—[2]	100.0[2]	—	—	0.2	—	100.0	—
Yemen (Aden)	0.1[6]	1983	1.4	—	100.0	—	1983	29.2[22]	—	—	100.0[22]	160.2	—	—	100.0
Yemen (Ṣanʿāʾ)	2.0	1986	53.7	—	—100.0—		1983	—	—	—	—	3.9[11]	—	—	100.0[11]
Yugoslavia	2.8[5]	1985	1,317.0	24.1	14.0	61.8	1986	97.4	52.0	15.4	32.6	693.5	24.9	16.0	59.1
Zaire	24.8[13]	1984	684.0	65.2[62]	27.8[63]	7.0[64]	1986	278.0	9.7	45.4	44.9	1.7[21]	4.9[21]	95.1[21]	—
Zambia	15.3[8]	1987	311.0	96.5[6]	3.5[6]	...	1986	13.6	40.4	59.6	—	...	...	...	...
Zimbabwe	6.9	1986	342.9	68.8[14]	18.5[14]	12.7[14]	1986	75.2	20.8	79.2	—	10.3[7]	98.5[7]	1.5[7]	—

[1]Gross value of sales. [2]1983–84 average. [3]1978. [4]Lumber only. [5]1985. [6]1983. [7]1982. [8]1987. [9]Salt exports valued at U.S.$33,000. [10]1984–86 average. [11]1981. [12]Netherlands Antilles includes Aruba, except fish-catch data. [13]1984. [14]Gross value of production (output). [15]Belgium includes Luxembourg. [16]Mostly crude petroleum. [17]1978–79. [18]Wood, lumber, and cork only. [19]South Africa includes Botswana, Lesotho, South West Africa/Namibia, and Swaziland. [20]Mostly crude petroleum and natural gas. [21]1980. [22]1982–83 average. [23]Mostly diamonds; some gold. [24]Excludes nonmetals. [25]China includes Taiwan. [26]1980–83 average percentage of social products. [27]Includes petroleum products. [28]1984–85. [29]Includes coke and briquettes. [30]France includes Monaco. [31]Excludes mollusks. [32]West Bank includes Gaza Strip. [33]Trade with United States only. [34]Jersey includes Guernsey. [35]Mostly bauxite and diamonds. [36]Mostly bauxite. [37]1982–83. [38]Excludes crude petroleum and natural gas. [39]1979–80. [40]Metals includes energy. [41]Italy includes San Marino. [42]Of which iron ore 97.4%. [43]Switzerland includes

forestry, 1986						fisheries, 1986								country
production of roundwood				trade (value '000 U.S.$)		catch (nominal)						trade (value, '000 U.S.$)		
total ('000 cubic metres)	fuelwood, charcoal (%)	industrial roundwood (%)		exports	imports	total ('000 metric tons)	by source (%)		by kind of catch (%)			exports	imports	
		total	sawlogs, veneer				marine	fresh-water	fish	crusta-ceans	mollusks			
10,330	7.7	92.3	43.8	881,121	598,931	1,898.4	100.0	—	96.1	3.1	0.8	1,171,170	105,217	Norway
...	...	...	...	352[7,18]	62,322	96.3	100.0	—	97.2	2.4	0.4	26,250	2,840	Oman
...	...	...	...	...	...	5.5	100.0	—	100.0	—	—	800	350	Pacific Is., Trust Terr. of the
...	...	...	...	...	...	...	...	...	...	...	...	...	...	Marshall Islands
														Micronesia, Fed. States of
...	...	...	...	...	...							17[33]	...	Northern Mariana Islands
						0.6[13]	100.0[13]	...	99.0[13]	...	...	149[13]	...	Palau
21,395	93.7	6.3	4.7	...	103,172	414.9	80.0	20.0	93.4	6.5	0.1	97,037	102	Pakistan
2,047	83.4	16.6	13.6	521	54,799	129.0	100.0	—	89.3	10.5	0.2	88,730[49]	7,790[49]	Panama
7,623	72.6	27.4	24.6	76,119	5,504	6.3	100.0	—	67.2	32.8	—	10,784	21,350	Papua New Guinea
8,210	60.5	39.5	34.7	67,005	8,638	13.0	—	100.0	100.0	—	—	—	—	Paraguay
7,735	84.4	15.6	14.4	3,355	57,109	5,609.6	99.5	0.5	99.1	0.1	0.8	256,127	170	Peru
35,690	84.1	15.9	8.6	206,541	78,863	1,916.3	71.9	28.1	82.5	5.8	11.4	200,099	19,019	Philippines
...	...	...	...	...	...				100.0	—	—			Pitcairn Island
24,296	18.3	81.7	41.4	158,585	173,743	645.2	95.4	4.6	93.7	0.3	6.0	103,879	59,571	Poland
9,038	6.6	93.4	44.3	626,373	175,144	389.6[47]	...	...	96.6[47]	0.5[47]	2.9[47]	142,845	256,373	Portugal
						1.3[47]	...	...	85.4[47]	7.7[47]	6.9[47]	51	51	Puerto Rico
—	—	6.1	—	...	18,015	2.0	100.0	—	93.8	5.5	0.7	—	1,060	Qatar
33	93.9	6.1	—	...	15,298	1.9	100.0	—	68.4	31.6	—	4,628	18,532	Réunion
24,629	18.6	81.4	36.2	290,050	115,160	271.1	75.7	24.3	...	...	...	—	20,580	Romania
5,842	95.9	4.1	0.5	...	1,362	1.5	—	100.0	100.0	—	—	—	—	Rwanda
...	...	...	...	...	...	0.6	100.0	—	44.9	55.1	—	25	—	St. Helena and Ascension
...	...	...	...	11[11]	857[11]	1.5	100.0	—	100.0	—	—	—	—	St. Kitts and Nevis
...	...	...	...	5,227[7,52]	6,385[6]	0.8	100.0	—	99.9	0.1	—	—	1,125	St. Lucia
...	...	...	...	...	...	12.5[13]	100.0	—	100.0[13]	—	—	16,362	230	St. Pierre and Miquelon
...	...	...	...	...	2,984	0.5	100.0	—	100.0	—	—	180	580	St. Vincent
...	...	...	...	...	...							41	41	San Marino
6	—	100.0	100.0	...	...	2.8	100.0	—	99.1	0.1	0.8	—	—	São Tomé and Príncipe
...	...	...	...	...	390,659	45.5	100.0	—	87.1	12.5	0.4	3,150	59,065	Saudi Arabia
4,098	86.3	13.7	0.5	...	21,920	255.4	94.1	5.9	93.5	2.3	4.2	259,110	20,640	Senegal
...	...	...	...	...	...	4.0	100.0	—	97.5	—	1.2	2,060	250	Seychelles
7,919	98.2	1.8	0.3	...	1,162	53.0	69.8	30.2	96.5	1.6	1.9	7,300	1,900	Sierra Leone
...	...	...	...	431,717	363,315	20.5	98.9	1.1	84.4	11.7	3.9	204,268	257,666	Singapore
636	33.0	67.0	67.0	20,530	2,292	54.9	100.0	—	99.8	—	—	29,985	775	Solomon Islands
4,532	98.5	1.5	0.6	...	2,170	16.5	100.0	—	97.0	3.0	—	1,300	—	Somalia
19,022[55]	37.2[55]	62.8[55]	21.7[55]	298,950[55]	225,234[55]	628.7	99.9	0.1	98.1	1.0	0.9	91,282[19]	71,600[19]	South Africa
...	...	...	...	...	...	...	...	...	...	...	...	...	...	Bophuthatswana
...	...	...	...	...	...	...	...	...	...	...	...	...	...	Ciskei
...	...	...	...	...	...	...	...	...	...	...	...	...	...	Transkei
...	...	...	...	...	...	...	...	...	...	...	...	...	...	Venda
55	55	55	55	55	55	201.3	100.0	—	99.4	0.6	—	19	19	South West Africa/Namibia
16,457	13.7	86.3	24.9	505,524	934,259	1,303.5	97.9	2.1	78.0	2.3	19.7	398,703	721,977	Spain
8,687	92.3	7.7	1.5	600	26,179	176.9	80.0	20.0	97.2	2.8	—	16,900	21,775	Sri Lanka
20,095	90.6	9.4	0.2	...	30,890	23.9	5.0	95.0	100.0	—	—	—	48	Sudan, The
196	7.1	92.9	79.6	2,666	8,310	3.1	93.6	6.4	71.8	28.2	—	28,650	200	Suriname
2,223	25.2	74.8	14.3	83,424	730	—	—	100.0	100.0	—	—	19	19	Swaziland
51,834	8.5	91.5	44.2	5,796,858	813,176	214.7	98.5	1.5	98.7	1.3	—	96,851	333,058	Sweden
4,861	17.9	82.1	61.2	534,362	1,045,917	4.7	—	100.0	100.0	—	—	6,431[43]	264,921[43]	Switzerland
48	31.2	68.8	31.2	113	115,500	4.9	10.4	89.6	99.8	0.2	—	—	9,320	Syria
537[5]	11.6[5]	88.4[5]	...	...	...	1,094.6	75.7	24.3	...	...	...	395,961	47,115	Taiwan
23,882	93.7	6.3	1.4	1,665	15,700	309.9	14.2	85.8	99.6	0.2	0.2	1,230	210	Tanzania
36,896	87.9	12.1	5.5	74,123	244,322	2,119.1	92.1	7.9	78.1	7.8	12.2	1,011,896	283,658	Thailand
789	78.7	21.3	2.3	...	2,525	14.8	95.3	4.7	100.0	—	—	900	5,500	Togo
...	...	...	...	...	...	—	—	—	100.0	—	—	...	...	Tokelau
5	—	100.0	100.0	...	2,166	2.0	100.0	—	100.0	—	—	320	225	Tonga
57	38.6	61.4	57.9	351[13]	94,918	3.0	100.0	—	87.3	12.7	—	2,076	13,404	Trinidad and Tobago
2,845	96.0	4.0	0.1	81[21]	117,235	92.6	100.0	—	85.7	2.4	11.9	59,086	70	Tunisia
16,229	64.7	35.3	23.1	50,770	96,371	579.8	93.1	6.9	96.7	1.1	2.2	74,230	551	Turkey
						1.6	100.0	—	24.9	10.9	64.2	3,780	—	Turks and Caicos Is.
						0.8	100.0	—	100.0	—	—	—	57[11]	Tuvalu
12,932	87.0	13.0	0.6	38[21]	1,166	212.2	—	100.0	100.0	—	—	...	...	Uganda
377,600	23.0	77.0	42.8	2,858,775	777,400	11,260.0	91.8	8.2	94.9	3.8	1.2	587,081	155,909	U.S.S.R.
						72.4	100.0	—	99.8	0.2	—	1,700	15,000	United Arab Emirates
4,861	3.0	97.0	63.0	876,890	6,207,544	847.8	98.4	1.6	89.7	4.8	5.5	481,669	1,216,042	United Kingdom
484,511	21.0	79.0	50.5	6,286,203	11,111,064	4,943.2	98.5	1.5	75.4	7.6	16.7	1,480,990[51]	4,748,692[51]	United States
2,668	90.4	9.6	3.5	7,066	12,358	141.3	99.5	0.5	97.9	0.5	1.6	65,150	850	Uruguay
38	63.2	36.8	36.8	376	380	2.9	100.0	—	53.1	16.8	30.1	7,500	7,050	Vanuatu
1,174	58.3	41.7	39.5	...	274,605	283.6	94.4	5.6	90.5	3.6	5.9	188,452	617	Venezuela
25,352	87.1	12.9	6.4	...	8,707	800.0	71.2	28.8	87.3	8.8	3.9	90,044	—	Vietnam
						0.6	100.0	—	90.6	6.3	3.1	356[59]	2,067[59]	Virgin Islands (U.S.)
...	...	...	...	...	...	1.0	100.0	—	100.0	—	—	...	...	Wallis and Futuna
														West Bank
—						—	100.0	...	...	...	...	...	...	Western Sahara
131	53.4	46.6	44.3	1,478	2,369	3.7	100.0	—	97.2	1.4	1.4	—	1,230	Western Samoa
294	100.0	—	—	29	10,499	91.2	100.0	—	93.0	1.5	5.5	14,850	380	Yemen (Aden)
...	...	...	...	...	...	22.3	100.0	—	98.1	1.9	—	340	3,500	Yemen (Ṣan'ā')
16,084	26.9	73.1	52.8	386,871	270,982	77.5	66.3	33.7	96.9	0.5	2.6	16,423	51,547	Yugoslavia
31,418	91.8	8.2	1.4	17,846	4,225	101.0	1.0	99.0	100.0	—	—	—	58,724	Zaire
9,946	94.7	5.3	1.3	...	7,390	68.2	—	100.0	100.0	—	—	—	381	Zambia
7,320	81.8	18.2	4.2	8,059	14,529	17.5	—	100.0	100.0	—	—	71	1,514	Zimbabwe

Liechtenstein. [44]Includes cement. [45]Excludes crustaceans. [46]1983–84. [47]Marine catch only. [48]Excludes trade with Cook Islands, Niue, and Tokelau. [49]Excludes the Free Zone of Colón and the Canal Zone. [50]Nonmetals includes coal mining. [51]United States includes Puerto Rico. [52]Paper and paperboard only. [53]Mostly gold. [54]Excludes crude petroleum. [55]South Africa includes South West Africa/Namibia. [56]Mostly precious and semiprecious stones. [57]Includes refined petroleum and electricity. [58]Abu Dhabi only. [59]Trade with U.S. and Puerto Rico only. [60]Exports of stone and marble to Jordan only. [61]Accounts for 4% to 5% of 1986 phosphate production of Morocco. [62]Includes coal and nonmetals other than diamonds. [63]Diamonds only. [64]Crude petroleum only.

Manufacturing industries

This table summarizes the activity of the manufacturing sectors of the countries of the world, providing figures for value added, number of establishments, and the distribution of value added by size of establishment (as reckoned by number of employees). The data are organized to show the relative importance of six principal sectors for each country and the concentration of activity within each sector. Manufacturing activity is classified according to the scheme outlined in the International Standard Industrial Classification (ISIC), revision 2, published by the United Nations.

The sectors for which data have been provided include: (1) food, beverages, and tobacco; (2) textiles, apparel, and leather; (3) wood, paper, chemicals, and related products; (4) primary and fabricated metals and processed minerals; (5) machinery (except electrical) and transport equipment; (6) electrical and electronic machinery. For each of these sectors (for which ISIC definitions are provided below), data are given for their respective share of total manufacturing value added (or, occasionally, some other measure of value, when value added was not reported); for the number of establishments with fewer than and more than 100 employees, and, where it was known, for the share of the sectoral value added represented by these two groups of establishments; and, finally, for the total value added in U.S.$ by all manufacturing.

The collection and publication of national manufacturing data is usually carried out by one of three methods: a full census of manufacturing (usually done every five to ten years for a given country), a periodic survey of manufacturing (usually taken at annual or other regular intervals between censuses), and the onetime sample survey (often limited in geographical, sectoral, or size-of-enterprise coverage). The full census is, naturally, the most complete, but since up to ten years may elapse between such censuses, it has often been necessary to substitute a survey of more recent date, but less complete coverage, in order to provide more timely data. For each country the initial date indicates the year of the survey.

To permit international comparisons U.S. dollar figures for total value added by manufacturing have been given, but should be used only with caution, because of inherent uncertainties with respect to national accounting methods, purchasing power parities, price structures and preferments, exchange rates, and so on.

The majority of countries collect data for establishments, generally referring to each separate physical facility, regardless of the number of separately incorporated legal entities (companies, partnerships, parastatal organizations), any of which may operate more than one facility. Other countries collect data only for enterprises, focusing on the corporate legal entity but often combining data for several separate, and smaller, estab-

Manufacturing industries

country	year	food, beverages, and tobacco (group 1) — percent of total value added	group 1 — 1–99 employees: number	group 1 — 1–99 employees: percent of value added	group 1 — 100 or more emp.: number	group 1 — 100 or more emp.: percent of value added	textiles, apparel, and leather (group 2) — percent of total value added	group 2 — 1–99 employees: number	group 2 — 1–99 employees: percent of value added	group 2 — 100 or more emp.: number	group 2 — 100 or more emp.: percent of value added	wood, paper, chemicals, and related products (group 3) — percent of total value added	group 3 — 1–99 employees: number	group 3 — 1–99 employees: percent of value added	group 3 — 100 or more emp.: number	group 3 — 100 or more emp.: percent of value added
Afghanistan[1]	1983	52.0	67	...	...	...	20.2	...	...	78	...	25.5	...	...	*55*	...
Albania	1984	...	...	...	...	...	....	...	...	...	...	...	...	...	...	...
Algeria[3]	1985	11.0	...	...	...	...	16.6	...	...	...	...	14.8	...	...	...	...
American Samoa	1982[4]	...	...	...	...	...	...	...	...	...	...	...	...	...	...	...
Andorra	1972	...	*142*	...	...	...	...	*104*	...	...	...	...	*49*	...	...	...
Angola[3]	1985	...	...	...	...	...	...	...	...	...	...	...	...	...	...	...
Anguilla		...	...	...	...	...	...	...	...	...	...	...	...	...	...	...
Antigua and Barbuda[5]	1986	...	14	100.0	—	—	...	12	100.0	—	—	...	15	100.0	—	—
Argentina[3,6]	1986	25.1	1,188	...	92	...	9.3	1,059	...	75	...	23.7	1,394	...	101	...
Aruba[8]		...	...	...	...	...	...	...	...	...	...	...	...	...	...	...
Australia[9]	1984	17.8	2,986	32.8	401	67.2	7.0	2,414	44.7	253	55.3	32.4	7,463	55.3	419	44.7
Austria[11]	1983	16.7	453	...	132	...	9.0	857	...	220	...	23.0	4,270	...	300	...
Bahamas, The[13,14]	1987	11.2	...	...	...	...	...	...	...	...	...	88.4	...	...	...	...
Bahrain	1982	...	...	...	...	...	...	...	...	...	...	92.5	...	...	...	...
Bangladesh[15,16]	1985	22.8	*550*	...	...	...	34.2	...	...	*1,606*	...	24.6	*729*	...	...	...
Barbados	1984	30.8	40	47.2	10	52.8	11.4	37	25.1	7	74.9	20.3	76	80.3	3	19.7
Belgium[16]	1984	20.0	6,964	...	...	...	7.3	3,728	...	...	...	20.8	5,883	...	...	...
Belize	1984	...	...	...	...	...	...	...	...	...	...	...	...	...	...	...
Benin[3]	1985	45.6	...	...	...	...	—	...	...	...	...	9.9	...	...	...	...
Bermuda	1979	...	...	...	...	...	...	...	...	...	...	...	...	...	...	...
Bhutan	1985	...	*30*	...	...	...	...	*16*	...	...	...	...	*47*	...	...	...
Bolivia[11,18]	1984	52.1	*201*	...	...	...	9.5	*145*	...	...	...	13.3	*256*	...	...	...
Botswana[3]	1984	54.3	*43*	...	...	...	7.4	*58*	...	...	...	8.5	*67*	...	...	...
Brazil[11]	1980	17.0	26,226	38.6	1,272	61.4	10.9	14,325	23.8	1,913	76.2	30.8	27,752	30.5	1,925	69.5
British Virgin Islands	1978	...	1	100.0	—	—	...	—	—	—	—	...	2	100.0	—	—
Brunei[20]	1980	...	29	100.0	—	—	...	76	100.0	—	—	...	60	100.0	—	—
Bulgaria[21]	1985	11.0	...	...	308	...	4.3	...	...	244	...	14.1	...	...	381	...
Burkina Faso[22,23]	1982	63.9	14	...	2	...	14.9	4	...	2	...	8.2	27	...	...	...
Burma	1984	37.0	...	...	...	...	12.0	...	...	...	...	51.0[24]	...	...	25	...
Burundi	1984	78.0	...	...	...	...	22.0[25]	...	...	...	...	...	...	...	...	...
Cameroon[3]	1985	35.0	...	...	...	...	17.2	...	...	...	...	12.8	...	...	...	...
Canada	1985	13.9	3,038	27.9	519	72.1	6.0	3,381	37.2	517	62.8	34.6	12,818	28.1	1,132	71.9
Cape Verde	1983	100.0	...	...	...	...	—	...	...	...	...	...	...	...	...	...
Cayman Islands	1985[19]	...	...	...	...	...	...	...	...	...	...	...	...	...	...	...
Central African Republic[3,16,22]	1985	20.3	*15*	...	...	...	39.5	...	...	4	...	27.9	...	...	*16*	...
Chad[3]	1985	...	...	...	...	...	...	...	...	...	...	...	...	...	...	...
Chile[11,26]	1984	26.9	...	...	315	...	6.8	...	...	187	...	30.2	...	...	303	...
China[22,27,28]	1985	13.5	79,286	...	...	...	14.3	29,366	...	...	...	26.1	76,820	...	—	—
Christmas Island		..	...	...	...	...	...	...	...	...	...	...	...	...	...	...
Cocos (Keeling) Islands		...	...	...	...	...	...	...	...	...	...	...	...	...	...	...
Colombia	1985	36.1	1,012	19.6	222	80.4	13.8	1,538	21.6	208	78.4	27.1	1,347	21.9	242	78.1
Comoros	1985	...	...	...	...	...	...	...	...	...	...	...	...	...	...	...
Congo[3]	1985	47.7	...	...	...	...	18.9	...	...	...	...	22.4	...	...	...	...
Cook Islands	1985	*29*	...	...	...	...	*29*	...	...	...	...	...	...	...	...	...
Costa Rica[11]	1984	46.8	...	...	...	...	9.8	...	...	...	...	30.6	...	...	...	...
Côte d'Ivoire[3,22,31]	1985	36.1	*281*	...	...	...	16.6	...	...	75	...	26.8	*172*	...	...	...
Cuba[22]	1985	63.4[32]	...	...	334[32]	...	4.3	...	...	44	...	11.7	...	...	84	...
Cyprus[11]	1985	27.7	950	46.5	16	53.5	24.6	1,737	71.5	25	28.5	26.7	2,133	82.4	6	17.6
Czechoslovakia[22]	1986	9.0	...	...	119	...	10.7	...	...	86	...	28.8	...	...	179	...
Denmark[34]	1985	23.1	877[35]	...	...	...	5.3	753[35]	...	...	...	27.9	2,277[35]	...	...	...
Djibouti	1984	...	...	...	...	...	...	...	...	...	...	...	...	...	...	...
Dominica	1986	...	...	...	...	...	...	...	...	...	...	...	...	...	...	...
Dominican Republic[11,36,37]	1983	60.6	...	...	1,069	...	6.9	225	...	...	...	21.3	346	...	...	...
Ecuador[15,31]	1986	54.8	*357*	...	...	...	16.7	*240*	...	...	...	11.7	*399*	...	...	...
Egypt[3,6,38]	1985	39.5	*2,521*	...	...	...	26.5	...	...	1,309	...	18.4	...	...	643	...
El Salvador[16]	1985	55.0	*100*	...	...	...	11.3	...	...	107	...	19.9	...	...	92	...
Equatorial Guinea[3]	1985	...	...	...	...	...	...	...	...	...	...	...	...	...	...	...
Ethiopia[11,15]	1984	49.6	...	...	158	...	20.7	...	...	88	...	23.7	...	...	93	...
Faeroe Islands	1986	...	...	...	...	...	...	...	...	...	...	...	...	...	...	...
Falkland Islands	1986	*29*	...	...	...	...	*29*	...	...	...	...	...	...	...	...	...

lishments. When only a single sectoral enterprise or establishment total was available, the *average* size of these establishments was calculated (since the total number of employees in the sector was known), and the figure for number of establishments was placed in the table above or below the 100-employee cutoff accordingly. Such figures are given in italics.

Another impediment to international comparability in terms of size of establishment is the limit each country establishes as the minimum reporting unit for such surveys. "Size" is usually determined either by number of employees or by value of sales. Employees may include owners, partners, or unpaid family workers. For a small country, it may be both feasible and desirable to survey all establishments, however small. For larger countries, the cost to collect and analyze data for all establishments may be prohibitively high, and, moreover, interest from a development point of view may be exclusively in middle and large-scale industry, that needed to permit replacement of imported goods with domestic manufactures. Thus, when the distributions of number of establishments are examined, it should be noted (and has been footnoted wherever possible) when such limits in coverage may be applicable.

In terms of the industrial groups implied by the names of the manufacturing sectors used here, the content of each sector is usually defined by the two- or three-digit level of classification in the ISIC system:

group	EB category	ISIC code (-s)	remarks
1.	Food, beverages, and tobacco	31	
2.	Textiles, apparel, and leather	32	
3.	Wood, paper, chemicals, and related products	33	wood and furniture
		34	paper and products; printing and publishing
		35	industrial chemicals, pharmaceuticals, petroleum and products, rubber, plastics
4.	Primary and fabricated metals and processed minerals	36	pottery, china, glass
		37	iron; steel; nonferrous metals
		381	metal products
5.	Machinery (except electrical) and transport equipment	382 + 384 minus 3825	machinery and transport equipment minus office equipment and computers
6.	Electrical and electronic machinery	383 + 3825	electrical and electronic equipment, plus office equipment and computers

It should be noted that these groups do not account for ISIC groups 385 and 390 (professional goods and other industries, respectively).

G4 % total value added	G4 1–99 emp: number	G4 1–99 emp: % VA	G4 100+ emp: number	G4 100+ emp: % VA	G5 % total value added	G5 1–99 emp: number	G5 1–99 emp: % VA	G5 100+ emp: number	G5 100+ emp: % VA	G6 % total value added	G6 1–99 emp: number	G6 1–99 emp: % VA	G6 100+ emp: number	G6 100+ emp: % VA	total manufacturing value added (U.S.$'000,000)	country
2.3[2]	...	...	17[2]	...	2	...	...	2	...	2	...	...	2	...	202	Afghanistan
...	...	...	...	...	...	...	...	...	...	...	...	...	...	...	1,100	Albania
57.6[2]	...	...	...	...	2	...	...	...	...	...	...	...	...	...	4,756	Algeria
...	...	...	...	...	...	...	...	...	...	...	...	...	...	...	...	American Samoa
...	*38*	...	...	...	...	*25*	...	...	...	...	*83*	...	...	...	...	Andorra
...	...	...	...	...	...	...	...	...	...	...	...	...	...	...	127	Angola
...	...	...	...	...	...	...	...	...	...	...	...	...	...	...	...	Anguilla
...	10	100.0	—	—	...	—	—	—	—	...	—	—	—	—	11	Antigua and Barbuda
10.6	206	...	21	...	24.5[7]	...	...	151	...	7	...	...	29	...	15,724	Argentina
...	...	...	...	...	...	...	...	...	...	...	...	...	...	...	...	Aruba
23.2	6,020	35.0	357	65.0	26.6[10]	6,744[10]	34.1[10]	5,544[10]	65.9[10]	10	10	10	10	10	31,670	Australia
25.0	759	...	155	...	13.6[12]	965	...	202	...	10.4[12]	300	...	114	...	13,516	Austria
0.4	...	...	...	...	—	...	...	...	...	—	...	...	...	...	14[13]	Bahamas, The
7.5	...	...	...	...	...	...	...	...	...	...	...	...	...	...	400	Bahrain
6.2	381	...	...	...	8.7	160	...	...	...	3.4	...	...	60	...	841	Bangladesh
36.0[2]	50[2]	62.4[2]	7[2]	37.6[2]	2	2	2	2	2	2	2	2	2	2	116	Barbados
47.3[2]	*4,651*	...	...	...	2	*1,343*	...	...	...	2	...	...	628	...	18,735	Belgium
12.6[2]	...	...	...	...	2	...	...	...	...	—	...	...	...	...	17	Belize
...	...	...	...	...	2	...	...	...	...	2	...	...	...	...	53	Benin
...	...	...	...	...	...	...	...	...	...	...	...	...	...	...	20	Bermuda
...	*10*	...	...	...	...	—	—	—	—	...	—	—	—	—	7[17]	Bhutan
24.1	*121*	...	...	...	0.3[12]	21	...	—	—	0.4[12]	13	...	—	—	1,068	Bolivia
10.1[2]	*68[2]*	...	...	...	2	2	...	...	...	2	2	...	...	...	64	Botswana
17.9	25,084	25.3	1,641	74.7	15.6	9,268	18.0	1,651	82.0	5.3	2,245	48.7	558	51.3	77,648	Brazil
...	4	100.0	—	—	—	—	—	—	—	—	—	—	—	—	2.5[19]	British Virgin Islands
...	*70[2]*	*100.0[2]*	—	—	...	2	2	—	—	...	2	2	—	—	382[17]	Brunei
17.1	...	...	*157*	...	41.4	...	...	450	...	12.0	...	...	165	...	1,530	Bulgaria
2.8[2]	9	...	...	...	2	...	...	...	...	2	...	...	...	...	129	Burkina Faso
24	...	...	...	...	24	...	...	...	...	24	...	...	...	...	871	Burma
25	...	...	...	...	25	...	...	...	...	25	...	...	...	...	127	Burundi
29.6[2]	...	...	...	...	2	...	...	...	...	2	...	...	...	...	790	Cameroon
17.4	6,980	31.7	524	68.3	18.5	2,783	13.7	503	86.3	7.0	1,102	15.7	277	84.3	70,213	Canada
—	...	...	...	...	...	...	...	...	...	—	...	...	...	...	5	Cape Verde
...	...	...	...	...	...	...	...	...	...	...	...	...	...	...	9	Cayman Islands
12.3[2]	*4[2]*	...	...	...	2	2	...	...	...	2	2	...	...	...	44	Central African Republic
...	...	...	...	...	...	...	...	...	...	...	...	...	...	...	50	Chad
32.1	...	...	*171*	...	2.5	...	...	52	...	1.4	...	...	23	...	5,196	Chile
18.2	*42,325*	...	...	...	23.8[12]	*57,153[12]*	...	...	...	4.1[12]	*4,010[12]*	...	...	...	143,822[17]	China
—	...	...	...	...	—	...	...	...	...	—	...	...	...	...	...	Christmas Island
—	—	—	—	—	—	—	—	—	—	—	—	—	—	—	...	Cocos (Keeling) Islands
13.2	806	15.9	149	84.1	4.9	439	26.2	60	73.8	3.2	150	20.8	38	79.2	6,711	Colombia
8.1[2]	...	...	...	...	2	...	...	...	...	...	...	...	...	...	5	Comoros
...	...	...	...	...	...	...	...	...	...	2	...	...	...	...	127	Congo
...	...	...	...	...	...	...	...	...	...	...	...	...	...	...	0.9[30]	Cook Islands
6.3	...	...	...	...	3.5[12]	...	...	...	...	2.9[12]	...	...	...	...	701	Costa Rica
17.4[2]	*21*	...	...	...	2	*59[7]*	...	...	...	2	7	...	...	...	631	Côte d'Ivoire
5.6	...	...	87	...	10.1[12]	...	...	142[12]	...	1.1[12]	...	...	17[12]	...	4,315[33]	Cuba
13.1	1,072	73.9	6	24.1	4.2	300	81.0	2	19.0	1.7	63	65.5	1	34.5	417	Cyprus
11.6	...	...	129	...	32.1[12]	...	...	222[12]	...	6.6[12]	...	...	52[12]	...	37,526[33]	Czechoslovakia
14.3	*1,296[35]*	...	...	...	18.8[12]	*1,233[35]*	...	...	...	6.0[12]	*314[35]*	...	...	...	10,413	Denmark
...	...	...	...	...	...	...	...	...	...	—	—	—	—	—	28	Djibouti
...	...	...	...	...	...	...	...	...	...	...	...	...	...	...	8	Dominica
9.7	*138*	...	...	...	0.5[12]	*10[12]*	...	...	...	0.8[12]	*17[12]*	...	...	...	1,503	Dominican Republic
12.0	*243*	...	...	...	2.5[7]	*58*	...	...	...	7	*47*	...	...	...	2,193	Ecuador
15.5[2]	...	...	*1,125*	...	2	...	...	*118*	...	2	...	...	*48*	...	8,270	Egypt
9.0	*43*	...	...	...	1.1	*14*	...	...	...	1.7	*10*	...	...	...	938	El Salvador
...	...	...	...	...	...	...	...	...	...	...	...	...	...	...	2	Equatorial Guinea
5.9	...	...	57	...	—	—	—	—	—	0.1	*3*	...	...	...	578	Ethiopia
...	...	...	...	...	...	...	...	...	...	...	...	...	...	...	148	Faeroe Islands
...	...	...	...	...	...	...	...	...	...	...	...	...	...	...	...	Falkland Islands

Manufacturing industries (continued)

country	year	food, beverages, and tobacco (group 1) — percent of total value added	1–99 employees: number	1–99 employees: percent of value added	100 or more emp.: number	100 or more emp.: percent of value added	textiles, apparel, and leather (group 2) — percent of total value added	1–99 employees: number	1–99 employees: percent of value added	100 or more emp.: number	100 or more emp.: percent of value added	wood, paper, chemicals, and related products (group 3) — percent of total value added	1–99 employees: number	1–99 employees: percent of value added	100 or more emp.: number	100 or more emp.: percent of value added
Fiji	1984	54.3	100	...	10	...	5.3	132	...	1	...	25.5	153	...	5	...
Finland[39]	1986	12.6	915	...	141	...	6.6	749	...	159	...	38.4	2,141	...	405	...
France	1986	11.5	...	...	...	...	6.7	...	...	...	...	31.4	...	...	...	...
French Guiana[38]	1982	...	2	...	1	...	...	8[42]	...	1[42]	...	...	...[42]	...	...[42]	...
French Polynesia	1980	20.3	...	...	...	...	...	...	...	...	...	...	...	...	...	...
Gabon[3]	1985	21.1	...	...	...	...	2.3	...	...	...	...	55.5	...	...	...	...
Gambia, The[11,37]	1982	74.4	...	...	13	...	3.6	2	...	...	...	1.7	4	...	...	...
Gaza Strip[44]	1985	13.9	107	...	...	...	20.4	536	...	...	...	65.7[24]	986[24]	...	...	...
Germany, East[1,22]	1985	13.5	...	...	557	...	86.5[25]	...	...	2,969[25]	...	[25]	...	...	25	...
Germany, West	1984	11.9	3,360	...	1,165	...	4.7	3,746	...	1,287	...	21.3	8,105	...	2,990	...
Ghana[11,45]	1983	53.1	...	...	74	...	5.7	55	...	...	...	24.6	...	...	164	...
Gibraltar		...	...	...	...	...	...	...	...	...	...	...	...	...	...	...
Greece	1984	18.6	22,118	...	...	...	24.7	31,114	...	...	...	22.2	33,228	...	...	...
Greenland[1]	1986	99.3	...	...	...	...	0.6	...	...	...	...	...	...	...	...	...
Grenada[1]	1984	76.2	16	...	...	...	15.9	7	...	...	...	7.9[24]	11[24]	...	...	...
Guadeloupe[31,38]	1980	68.1	17	...	4	...	31.9[25]	29[25]	...	—	—	[25]	25	...	1	...
Guam	1982[24]	...	...	...	...	...	...	...	...	...	...	...	...	...	...	...
Guatemala[11,37]	1984	38.7	577	...	...	...	11.7	388	...	...	...	34.5	545	...	...	...
Guernsey		...	...	...	...	...	...	...	...	...	...	...	...	...	...	...
Guinea[3]	1985	...	...	...	...	...	...	...	...	...	...	...	...	...	...	...
Guinea-Bissau[3]	1985	...	...	...	...	...	...	...	...	...	...	[25]	...	...	...	...
Guyana[23,37]	1981	36.7	31	...	...	...	63.3[25]	8	...	...	...	44.6[24]	20	...	...	...
Haiti[11]	1985	40.9	472	...	...	...	14.5	126	...	...	...	44.6[24]	110	...	...	...
Honduras	1975	56.1	233	...	...	...	9.9	198	...	...	...	23.0	280	...	...	...
Hong Kong	1985	4.8	877	...	...	...	41.0	15,451	...	...	...	19.6	14,100	...	...	...
Hungary[22]	1985	7.8	—	...	199	...	11.3	...	...	305	...	24.3	...	...	295	...
Iceland[3]	1984	48.8	901	...	...	...	7.7	253	...	...	...	17.3	781	...	...	...
India[3,47]	1982	10.4	25,597	...	...	...	15.6	...	...	13,426	...	25.5	17,053	...	...	...
Indonesia[39,48]	1985	11.0	...	...	2,356	...	5.5	...	...	1,979	...	71.6	...	...	2,047[49]	...
Iran	1985	14.8	725	...	151	...	23.1	992	...	208	...	15.9	1,416	...	146	...
Iraq	1981	27.9	3,775	...	...	...	15.1	7,797	...	...	...	17.2	4,769	...	...	...
Ireland[50]	1984	25.7	773	39.8	131	60.2	5.8	530	48.1	76	51.9	26.6	1,323	36.8	74	63.2
Isle of Man		...	...	...	...	...	...	...	...	...	...	...	...	...	...	...
Israel[3,34,51]	1985	14.0[37]	977	...	...	...	11.2[37]	1,808	...	...	...	23.2[37]	3,327	...	...	...
Italy[18,22]	1982	5.7	...	...	2,056	...	12.6	5,973	...	...	...	25.4	...	...	5,834	...
Jamaica[39,52]	1985	44.4	325	...	...	...	5.7	135	...	...	...	30.2	329	...	...	...
Japan	1983	9.6	51,856	50.1	1,836	49.9	5.9	73,142	70.1	1,578	29.9	26.1	95,585	54.3	2,453	45.7
Jersey	1986	...	...	...	...	...	...	...	...	...	...	...	...	...	...	...
Jordan	1985	29.3	918	...	...	...	5.8	1,061	...	...	...	31.4	1,462	...	...	...
Kampuchea[28]	1983	...	10	...	...	...	...	9	...	...	...	...	11	...	...	...
Kenya	1977	37.4	432	14.0	71	86.0	10.7	1,010	24.5	41	75.5	32.5	930	30.6	71	69.4
Kiribati	1984	...	...	...	...	...	...	...	...	...	...	...	...	...	...	...
Korea, North		...	...	...	...	...	...	...	...	...	...	...	...	...	...	...
Korea, South[11,37,53]	1985	16.1	4,164	13.0	281	87.0	18.1	8,950	20.7	1,309	79.3	25.4	19,642[24]	18.2[24]	1,817[24]	81.8[24]
Kuwait[39]	1986	13.9	406	...	...	...	7.1	2,150	...	...	...	54.0	436	...	...	...
Laos		...	...	...	...	...	...	...	...	...	...	...	...	...	...	...
Lebanon	1984	...	...	...	...	...	...	...	...	...	...	...	...	...	...	...
Lesotho	1983	74.1	5	...	6	...	9.0	6	...	4	...	8.0	9	...	2	...
Liberia[3]	1985	...	...	...	...	...	...	...	...	...	...	...	...	...	...	...
Libya[3]	1985	38.1	...	...	...	...	26.1	...	...	...	...	26.1	...	...	...	...
Liechtenstein	1987	...	...	...	1	...	2.0	9	...	...	...	26.3[55]	...	...	4	...
Luxembourg[16,48]	1985	7.8	31	...	...	...	69.2	389	23.2	155	76.8	13.9	235	36.0	16	64.0
Macau	1982	1.8	101	100.0	—	—	48.1	...	...	56	...	13.7[24]	113[24]	...	...	...
Madagascar[11]	1984	35.9	...	...	130	...	13.4	...	...	22	...	27.1	...	...	34	...
Malawi[13,56]	1983	49.0	...	...	37	...	...	...	...	...	...	27.1	...	...	...	...
Malaysia[3]	1984	21.5	1,326	...	...	...	5.4	...	...	461	...	35.2	2,173	...	...	...
Maldives	1985	...	...	...	...	...	...	...	...	...	...	...	...	...	...	...
Mali[22]	1981	24.4	51	...	...	...	57.4	...	...	16	...	2.6	17	...	...	...
Malta	1985	20.7	362	...	6	...	31.0	163	...	36	...	18.7	507	...	5	...
Martinique[38,57]	1982	37.5	22	...	3	...	62.5[25]	20[25]	...	1[25]	...	[25]	25	...	...	...
Mauritania	1983	59.4[58]	...	...	...	...	...	...	...	...	...	...	...	...	...	...
Mauritius[15]	1985	31.1	198	...	...	...	45.0	...	...	285	...	11.5	113	...	...	...
Mayotte		...	...	...	...	...	...	...	...	...	...	...	...	...	...	...
Mexico	1985	25.4	...	...	...	...	11.6	...	...	...	...	32.8	...	...	...	...
Monaco		...	...	...	...	...	...	...	...	...	...	...	...	...	...	...
Mongolia[13,22]	1985	26.8	...	...	45	...	43.2	...	...	56	...	23.4	...	...	90	...
Montserrat	1980	...	7	...	—	—	...	5	...	—	—	...	7	...	—	—
Morocco[6]	1983	24.3	5,481	...	...	...	14.2	21,312	...	...	...	28.8	9,092	...	...	...
Mozambique[13]	1985	39.1	...	...	...	...	27.1	...	...	...	...	15.9	...	...	...	...
Nauru	1985	—	...	...	...	...	—	...	...	...	...	—	...	...	...	...
Nepal	1982	69.8	3,715	...	58	...	11.5	256	...	16	...	12.2	477	...	13	...
Netherlands, The[23]	1984	22.2	1,242	...	313	...	3.4	1,039	...	265	...	32.1[49]	1,444	...	322	...
Netherlands Antilles[8]	1980	...	...	...	...	...	...	...	...	...	...	...	...	...	...	...
New Caledonia	1983	15.8	...	...	...	...	...	...	...	...	...	...	...	...	...	...
New Zealand	1984	27.0	1,643	...	...	...	10.2	1,988	...	...	...	27.8	4,164	...	...	...
Nicaragua[11,45]	1984	49.8	...	...	84	...	12.9	...	...	59	...	27.8	90	...	...	...
Niger	1980	32.5	...	...	26.2	...	...	...	...	...	...	27.1	...	...	...	...
Nigeria[11,15]	1983	27.2	676	...	...	...	11.4	...	...	152	...	32.7	...	...	737	...
Niue		...	...	...	...	...	...	...	...	...	...	...	...	...	...	...
Norfolk Island		...	...	...	...	...	...	...	...	...	...	...	...	...	...	...
Norway	1985	14.8	2,230	45.1	94	54.9	2.7	780	72.3	26	27.7	33.2	4,434	45.5	188	54.5
Oman	1986	...	...	...	...	...	...	...	...	...	...	47.0[59]	...	...	...	...
Pacific Is., Trust Terr. of the Marshall Islands[1]	1981	39.7	...	...	...	...	...	...	...	...	...	60.3	...	...	...	...
Micronesia, Fed. States of		...	...	...	...	...	...	...	...	...	...	...	...	...	...	...

primary and fabricated metals; proc. minerals (group 4)					machinery (except elec.) and transport equip. (group 5)					electrical and electronic machinery (group 6)					total manufac-turing value added (U.S.$'000,000)	country
percent of total value added	establishments 1–99 employees number	percent of value added	100 or more emp. number	percent of value added	percent of total value added	establishments 1–99 employees number	percent of value added	100 or more emp. number	percent of value added	percent of total value added	establishments 1–99 employees number	percent of value added	100 or more emp. number	percent of value added		
11.2	61	...	2	...	3.0[7]	28[7]	...	1[7]	...	7	7	...	—[7]	...	95	Fiji
15.2	1,222	...	155	...	17.8	914	...	186	...	8.5[40]	173	...	57	...	14,813	Finland
13.7	...	...	...	...	16.4[41]	...	...	...	...	9.2[41]	...	...	...	...	186,956	France
...	42	...	42	...	—	...	...	...	...	—	—	—	...	...	9[43]	French Guiana
...	...	...	...	...	49.6[7]	...	...	...	...	7	...	...	...	...	107	French Polynesia
21.1[2]	...	...	...	...	2	...	...	...	...	2	...	...	...	...	175	Gabon
−0.8	2	...	...	...	—	...	...	—	...	—	...	...	—	...	8	Gambia, The
24	24	...	...	...	24	24	...	...	...	24	24	...	...	...	31	Gaza Strip
25	...	...	25	...	25	...	...	25	...	25	...	...	25	...	...	Germany, East
21.2	8,137	...	2,481	...	23.5	5,536	...	2,532	...	14.8	1,879	...	1,458	...	200,567	Germany, West
14.5	...	...	38	...	1.4	...	...	12	...	0.4	11	...	...	...	1,615	Ghana
...	...	...	...	...	...	...	...	...	...	...	...	...	...	...	...	Gibraltar
32.5[2]	53,746[2]	...	...	...	2	2	...	...	...	2	2	...	...	...	4,684	Greece
...	...	...	...	...	...	...	...	...	...	...	...	...	...	...	90	Greenland
24	24	...	...	...	24	24	...	...	...	24	24	...	...	...	12	Grenada
25	25	...	—	—	25	25	...	—	—	25	25	...	—	—	95	Guadeloupe
...	...	...	...	...	...	...	...	...	...	...	...	...	...	...	...	Guam
11.5	293	...	...	...	1.1	53	...	...	...	1.8	30	...	...	...	880	Guatemala
...	...	...	...	...	...	...	...	...	...	...	...	...	...	...	...	Guernsey
...	...	...	...	...	...	...	...	...	...	...	...	...	...	...	71	Guinea
...	...	...	...	...	...	...	...	...	...	...	...	...	...	...	2	Guinea-Bissau
25	...	...	...	...	25	...	...	...	...	25	1	...	...	...	53	Guyana
24	57	...	...	...	24	...	...	34[7]	...	24	...	...	7	...	162	Haiti
9.0	98	...	...	...	0.6	11	...	...	...	1.1	9	...	...	...	419[46]	Honduras
8.5	7,625	...	...	...	4.8	4,509	...	...	...	12.9	2,017	...	...	...	6,447	Hong Kong
13.9	...	...	188	...	20.1[12]	...	...	343[12]	...	14.2[12]	...	...	125[12]	...	5,360	Hungary
24.4[2]	630[2]	...	...	...	2	2	...	...	...	2	2	...	...	...	475	Iceland
20.9	18,056	...	...	...	17.7	9,901	...	...	...	8.7	3,763	...	...	...	14,788	India
7.4	...	...	1,055	...	2.7[12]	...	...	326	...	1.6[12]	...	...	115	...	15,275	Indonesia
22.4	2,534	...	343	...	14.7	675	...	143	...	6.7	95	...	49	...	9,873	Iran
17.3	3,534	...	...	...	8.7	98	...	...	...	4.6	17	...	...	...	6,055	Iraq
10.7	940	39.2	121	60.8	5.3	349	41.1	35	58.9	20.2	228	15.2	59	84.8	5,734	Ireland
...	...	...	...	...	...	...	...	...	...	...	...	...	...	...	...	Isle of Man
21.9[37]	2,918	...	...	...	10.5[37]	365[12]	...	...	...	18.9[37]	460[12]	...	...	...	4,733[37]	Israel
21.9	...	...	5,890	...	21.9[12]	...	...	3,230[12]	...	9.3[12]	...	...	1,127[12]	...	75,078	Italy
18.7[2]	361[2]	...	...	...	2	2	...	...	...	2	2	...	...	...	412	Jamaica
18.2	82,626	43.9	2,126	56.1	20.1	55,266	27.3	2,596	62.7	16.8	29,639	19.1	2,705	80.9	360,987	Japan
...	...	...	...	...	...	...	...	...	...	...	...	...	...	...	20	Jersey
22.7	942	...	...	...	6.3	1,466	...	...	...	0.4	12	...	...	...	568	Jordan
...	...	...	...	...	...	11	...	...	...	...	...	...	...	...	...	Kampuchea
12.7	290	17.0	37	83.0	3.2	184	42.1	10	57.9	2.6	26	13.8	4	86.2	532	Kenya
...	...	...	...	...	...	...	...	...	...	—	—	—	—	—	0.5	Kiribati
...	...	...	...	...	...	...	...	...	...	...	...	...	...	...	...	Korea, North
16.9	24	24	24	24	20.5[17]	24	24	24	24	17	24	24	24	24	28,609	Korea, South
24.6[2]	741	...	...	...	2	47	...	...	...	2	25	...	...	...	1,116	Kuwait
...	...	...	...	...	...	...	...	...	...	...	...	...	...	...	196	Laos
8.9[2]	11[2]	...	—	...	2	2	...	—	...	2	2	...	—	...	21	Lebanon
...	...	...	...	...	...	...	...	...	...	...	...	...	...	...	55	Lesotho
9.3[2]	...	...	...	...	2	...	...	...	...	2	...	...	...	...	1,375	Libya
...	...	...	20[54]	...	...	...	...	54	...	...	...	...	54	...	...	Liechtenstein
52.7	...	...	50[40]	...	8.1[12]	...	...	26[12]	...	2.3[12]	7[12]	...	7[12]	...	1,226	Luxembourg
1.9	107	72.5	2	27.5	2.1[12]	49[12]	60.3	1	39.7	3.0[12]	24[12]	36.1	10	63.9	143	Macau
24	24	...	...	...	24	24	...	...	...	24	24	...	...	...	146	Madagascar
9.0	...	...	16	...	0.8	...	...	2	...	0.7	4	...	...	...	100	Malawi
13.0	1,099	...	...	...	7.1	653	...	...	...	16.5	...	...	235	...	5,248	Malaysia
...	...	...	...	...	...	...	...	...	...	...	...	...	...	...	4[55]	Maldives
6.5	...	...	3	...	9.1	19	...	...	...	—	—	—	—	—	188	Mali
7.0	217	...	1	...	4.3[12]	56[12]	...	2[12]	...	11.8[12]	33[12]	...	5[12]	...	266	Malta
25	25	...	25	...	25	25	...	25	...	25	25	...	25	...	75	Martinique
...	...	...	...	...	...	...	...	...	...	...	...	...	...	...	67	Mauritania
7.7[2]	95[2]	...	...	...	2	2	...	...	...	2	2	...	...	...	172	Mauritius
...	...	...	...	...	...	...	...	...	...	...	...	...	...	...	...	Mayotte
12.9	...	...	...	...	8.8[12]	...	...	...	...	2.2[12]	...	...	...	...	43,183	Mexico
...	...	...	...	...	...	...	...	...	...	...	...	...	...	...	...	Monaco
6.7[2,40]	...	...	24[2,40]	...	2	...	...	2	...	2	...	...	2	...	...	Mongolia
...	4[2]	...	—	—	2	2	...	—	...	2	2	...	—	...	2.4[19]	Montserrat
22.1	5,817[2]	...	...	...	6.4	2	...	...	...	3.8	2	...	...	...	1,626	Morocco
9.5	...	...	...	...	2.4	...	...	...	...	3.6	...	...	...	...	359	Mozambique
...	...	...	...	...	...	...	...	...	...	...	...	...	...	...	—	Nauru
3.3	201	...	57	...	1.2	42	...	3	...	—	—	—	—	—	178	Nepal
15.6	552	...	134	...	12.2	2,513[7]	...	441[7]	...	13.8	7	...	7	...	19,983[49]	Netherlands, The
...	...	...	...	...	...	...	...	...	...	...	...	...	...	...	302	Netherlands Antilles
47.3	...	...	...	...	15.9[7]	...	...	...	...	7	...	...	...	...	80	New Caledonia
17.2	2,976	...	...	...	11.4	2,437	...	...	...	5.0	613	...	...	...	4,430	New Zealand
1.9	19	...	...	...	1.4	19	...	...	...	0.8	10	...	...	...	1,335	Nicaragua
14.2[2]	...	...	...	...	2	...	...	...	...	2	...	...	...	...	28	Niger
11.2	...	...	459	...	15.6	...	...	40	...	1.8	...	...	33	...	7,223	Nigeria
...	...	...	...	...	...	...	...	...	...	...	...	...	...	...	...	Niue
...	...	...	...	...	...	...	...	...	...	...	...	...	...	...	...	Norfolk Island
20.4	2,189	34.7	98	65.3	21.4[12]	2,038[12]	34.7[12]	144[12]	65.3[12]	6.4[12]	399[12]	28.6[12]	46[12]	71.4[12]	7,973	Norway
...	...	...	...	...	...	...	...	...	...	...	...	...	...	...	467	Oman
...	...	...	...	...	...	...	...	...	...	...	...	...	...	...	0.2	Pacific Is., Trust Terr. of the Marshall Islands
...	...	...	...	...	...	...	...	...	...	...	...	...	...	...	...	Micronesia, Fed. States of

Manufacturing industries (continued)

country	year	food, beverages, and tobacco (group 1) percent of total value added	1–99 employees number	1–99 employees percent of value added	100 or more emp. number	100 or more emp. percent of value added	textiles, apparel, and leather (group 2) percent of total value added	1–99 employees number	1–99 employees percent of value added	100 or more emp. number	100 or more emp. percent of value added	wood, paper, chemicals, and related products (group 3) percent of total value added	1–99 employees number	1–99 employees percent of value added	100 or more emp. number	100 or more emp. percent of value added
Northern Mariana Islands	1982[4]	...	...	...	...	...	...	...	...	...	...	...	...	...	...	...
Palau	1983	...	...	...	...	...	...	...	...	...	...	...	...	...	...	...
Pakistan	1981	35.2	380	11.8	169	88.2	21.3	1,067	25.8	244	74.2	23.6	537	13.0	126	87.0
Panama[39,60]	1986	47.1	324	...	...	...	11.0	91	...	...	...	27.4	285	...	...	...
Papua New Guinea	1985	60.9	147	...	...	...	0.6	16	...	...	...	17.0	157	...	...	...
Paraguay	1984	44.4	...	...	...	...	12.8	...	...	...	...	26.2	...	...	...	...
Peru[11,5]	1982	23.2[61]	6,236	...	82	...	11.3	8,613	...	106	...	34.9	7,476	...	148	...
Philippines[38]	1984	42.8	...	...	1,541	...	12.1	...	...	894	...	28.5	1,568	...	...	...
Pitcairn Island	...	...	...	...	...	...	...	...	...	...	...	...	...	...	...	...
Poland	1986	16.8	1,600	...	880	...	15.1	6,224	...	186	...	18.9	3,977	...	922	...
Portugal	1985	16.7	3,212	...	...	...	23.6	2,163	...	...	...	28.2	4,932	...	...	...
Puerto Rico	1982	11.2	296	22.7	37	77.3	8.4	286	25.6	131	74.4	47.5	578	25.2	68	74.8
Qatar	1985	4.2	104	...	...	...	3.2	536	...	...	...	69.7	278	...	...	...
Réunion	1983	45.8	48	...	...	...	2.2	9	...	...	...	23.3	46	...	...	...
Romania[22,62]	1985	11.0	...	...	301	...	15.0	...	...	227	...	74.0[24]	...	...	196	...
Rwanda[22,23]	1981	75.7	...	...	17	...	10.1	...	...	3	...	5.8	...	...	17	...
St. Helena and Ascension	...	...	...	...	...	...	...	...	...	...	...	...	...	...	...	...
St. Kitts and Nevis	1986	...	...	...	...	...	...	...	...	...	...	...	...	...	...	...
St. Lucia	1986	...	...	...	...	...	...	...	...	...	...	...	...	...	...	...
St. Pierre and Miquelon	...	...	...	...	...	...	...	...	...	...	...	...	...	...	...	...
St. Vincent	1986	...	...	...	...	...	...	...	...	...	...	...	...	...	...	...
San Marino	1978	7.2	31	100.0	—	—	9.5	3	...	2	...	22.2	112	100.0	—	—
São Tomé and Príncipe[3]	1985	...	...	...	...	...	...	...	...	...	...	...	...	...	...	...
Saudi Arabia[6,63]	1986	...	2,145	...	26	...	...	8,019	...	2	...	58.8[59]	2,751	...	37	...
Senegal[11]	1984	48.2[61]	...	...	52[61]	...	16.0	...	...	33	...	15.4	72	...	...	...
Seychelles	1984	79.1	14	...	...	...	2.0	2	...	...	...	12.0	10	...	...	...
Sierra Leone[3]	1985	...	...	...	...	...	...	...	...	...	...	...	...	...	...	...
Singapore[3,15]	1986	6.1	304	...	...	...	4.2	506	...	...	...	23.2	1,053	...	...	...
Solomon Islands	...	...	...	...	...	...	...	...	...	...	...	...	...	...	...	...
Somalia[3,23]	1985	83.0	75	...	...	...	6.1	58	...	...	...	8.3	37	...	...	...
South Africa	1979	14.8	1,722	16.5	457	83.5	9.8	1,733	14.9	556	85.1	27.4	3,666	20.7	649	79.3
Bophuthatswana	1985	...	...	...	...	...	...	...	...	...	...	...	...	...	...	...
Ciskei	1984	...	...	...	5	...	...	...	...	30	...	...	...	...	13	...
Transkei	...	...	...	...	...	...	...	...	...	...	...	...	...	...	...	...
Venda[1]	1985	70.7	...	...	8	...	19.4	...	...	12	...	4.9	...	...	6	...
South West Africa/Namibia	1986	62.2	...	...	...	...	...	...	...	...	...	...	...	...	...	...
Spain[3]	1983	17.2	44,399	...	...	...	9.3	15,209	...	...	...	29.1	44,746	...	...	...
Sri Lanka[6]	1985	45.6	204	...	...	...	19.2	...	...	332	...	18.5	365	...	...	...
Sudan, The[3]	1985	...	...	...	...	...	...	...	...	...	...	...	...	...	...	...
Suriname	1985	...	...	...	...	...	...	...	...	...	...	...	...	...	...	...
Swaziland[3]	1983	55.1	...	...	13	...	1.8	34	...	67	...	32.9	...	...	38	...
Sweden	1985	10.0	685	...	152	...	2.5	559	...	67	...	33.5	2,772	...	423	...
Switzerland	1985	...	3,352	...	149	...	...	2,699	...	131	...	...	15,395	...	318	...
Syria[65]	1984	3.3	8,029	...	...	...	20.5	15,126	...	...	...	25.1	12,783	...	...	...
Taiwan[3,31]	1985	7.8	8,770	...	81	...	19.8	9,583	...	1,066	...	27.9	26,140	...	1,071	...
Tanzania[3,15]	1983	30.9	...	...	165	...	25.5	...	...	175	...	20.8	253	...	...	...
Thailand[18]	1984	44.8	...	...	1,667	...	12.7	...	...	761	...	22.1	...	...	1,684	...
Togo[11,22]	1979	62.1	...	...	12	...	7.4	3	...	...	...	13.6	26	...	...	...
Tokelau	...	...	...	...	...	...	...	...	...	...	...	...	...	...	...	...
Tonga	1981	73.8	33	100.0	—	—	1.1	11	100.0	...	...	11.7	23	100.0	—	—
Trinidad and Tobago[3]	1984	27.2	...	...	...	...	4.1	...	...	...	...	68.7[24]	...	...	...	...
Tunisia	1981	14.1	283	35.9	35	64.1	16.9	276	26.4	124	73.6	22.2	253	26.8	49	73.2
Turkey[11,66]	1984	20.5	1,595	16.3	304	83.7	15.9	1,521	18.3	326	81.7	29.4	1,432	9.2	242	90.8
Turks and Caicos Islands	1985[19]	...	...	...	...	...	...	...	...	...	...	...	...	...	...	...
Tuvalu	1979	...	...	...	...	...	...	...	...	...	...	...	...	...	...	...
Uganda[3]	1985	50.2	...	...	...	...	24.8	...	...	...	...	7.0	...	...	...	...
U.S.S.R.[13,22]	1983	20.3	...	...	9,491	...	17.4	...	...	7,842	...	15.7	...	...	4,057	...
United Arab Emirates[6,38,67]	1985	2.5	73	...	...	...	—	67	...	...	...	92.3	209	...	...	...
United Kingdom[3]	1985	13.4	8,887	7.7	1,491	92.3	6.7	16,434	29.2	1,744	70.8	27.4	40,118	23.8	3,787	76.2
United States[53]	1985	11.6	18,523	20.3	3,770	79.7	5.3	28,446	33.3	5,310	66.7	29.9	121,107	27.0	9,339	73.0
Uruguay	1985	31.8	2,712[30]	36.7[30]	70[30]	63.3[30]	19.1	1,878[30]	37.9[30]	117[30]	62.1[30]	36.0	2,858[30]	33.3[30]	48[30]	66.7[30]
Vanuatu	1984	51.5	...	...	...	...	1.9	...	...	...	...	20.8	...	...	...	...
Venezuela[11,37]	1985	21.5	2,138[68]	25.2[68]	161[68]	74.8[68]	7.7	1,778[68]	44.1[68]	132[68]	55.9[68]	46.0	2,085[68]	34.7[68]	191[68]	65.3[68]
Vietnam	...	...	...	...	...	...	...	...	...	...	...	...	...	...	...	...
Virgin Islands (U.S.)	1982[4]	...	...	...	...	...	...	...	...	...	...	...	...	...	...	...
Wallis and Futuna	...	...	...	...	...	...	...	...	...	...	...	...	...	...	...	...
West Bank	1985	46.6	233	...	...	...	10.8	685	...	...	...	20.8	584	...	...	...
Western Sahara	...	...	...	...	...	...	...	...	...	...	...	...	...	...	...	...
Western Samoa	1983	...	25	...	...	...	...	3	...	—	—	...	31	...	...	...
Yemen (Aden)[23,27]	1984	36.7[37]	488	...	...	...	11.7[37]	...	...	13	...	30.6[37]	...	...	14	...
Yemen (Şan'ā')[37,69]	1980	34.2	442	...	...	...	7.9	536	...	...	...	13.6	659	...	...	...
Yugoslavia[22,70]	1985	11.8	...	...	1,355	...	16.8	...	...	1,563	...	23.4	...	...	2,796	...
Zaire	1980	39.5	...	...	...	...	16.0	...	...	...	...	17.3	...	...	...	...
Zambia	1983	47.5	...	...	...	...	12.5	...	...	...	...	14.8	...	...	...	...
Zimbabwe	1983	35.9	...	...	...	...	13.0	...	...	...	...	21.1	...	...	...	...

[1]Percentages in value-added columns are based on gross output in value of sales. [2]Group 4 includes groups 5 and 6. [3]Value added calculated in factor values. [4]Census data insufficiently detailed. [5]Establishments data are for 1980. [6]Establishments data are for 1981. [7]Group 5 includes group 6. [8]Netherlands Antilles includes Aruba. [9]4 or more employees only. [10]Group 5 includes group 6 and 385 and 390. [11]Value added calculated in producer's prices. [12]Group 5 includes, and group 6 excludes, ISIC 3825 (office machinery and computing equipment). [13]Data in value-added columns refer to gross output in producer's prices. [14]Data refer to foreign-owned manufactures of rum, pharmaceuticals, and cement only. [15]10 or more employees only. [16]Establishments data are for 1983. [17]1984. [18]20 or more employees only. [19]1984–86 average. [20]Establishments data are incomplete. [21]State enterprises only. [22]Establishments data refer to enterprises. [23]Establishments data are for 1979. [24]Group 3 includes groups 4, 5, and 6. [25]Group 2 includes groups 3, 4, 5, and 6. [26]50 or more employees only. [27]Percentages in value-added columns are based on 1984 gross output of production. [28]Average enterprise size not available. [29]Most manufacturing is in food and apparel industries. [30]1978. [31]Establishments data are for 1982. [32]Includes sugarcane cropping; excludes fish processing. [33]Conversion into U.S.$ based on official (not commercial or tourist) exchange rate. [34]Value-added data are for 1984. [35]6 or more employees only. [36]Includes sugarcane cropping. [37]5 or more employees only. [38]Establishments data are for 10 or more employees. [39]Establishments data are for 1984.

primary and fabricated metals; proc. minerals (group 4)					machinery (except elec.) and transport equip. (group 5)					electrical and electronic machinery (group 6)					total manufac-turing value added (U.S.$'000,000)	country
percent of total value added	establishments				percent of total value added	establishments				percent of total value added	establishments					
	1–99 employees		100 or more emp.			1–99 employees		100 or more emp.			1–99 employees		100 or more emp.			
	number	percent of value added	number	percent of value added		number	percent of value added	number	percent of value added		number	percent of value added	number	percent of value added		
...	...		...		...	...		...		...	...		...		...	Northern Mariana Islands
...					...					...					0.1	Palau
11.5	528	17.2	69	82.8	4.2	358	14.0	37	86.0	3.5	154	15.9	31	84.1	2,898	Pakistan
12.3	126	...	...	...	0.6	23	...	...	...	0.4	13	...	...	...	422	Panama
21.5[2,54]	145[2,54]	...	...	...	[2]	[2]	...	...	...	[2]	[2]	...	...	...	267	Papua New Guinea
7.6[2]	...	...	...	...	[2]	...	...	...	...	[2]	...	...	...	...	856	Paraguay
15.9	98	...	11	...	9.6	1,774	...	83	...	3.7	524	...	5	...	4,810[61]	Peru
14.3[2]	636	...	[2]	...	[2]	462	...	[2]	...	[2]	...	...	146	...	8,219	Philippines
—	...		...		—	...		...		—	...		...		...	Pitcairn Island
15.9	4,594	...	877	...	21.1	1,819	...	865	...	7.2	1,065	...	324	...	23,881	Poland
15.8	1,953	...	...	...	7.8	...	...	527	...	7.2	...	...	194	...	4,192	Portugal
3.1	351	53.0	16	47.0	6.7[12]	104	13.9	12	86.1	13.2[12]	112	18.5	69	81.5	8,606	Puerto Rico
22.7	267	...	...	...	—	[2]	...	...	...	—	[2]	...	...	...	486	Qatar
25.1[2]	31[2]	...	...	...	[2]	[2]	...	...	...	[2]	[2]	...	...	...	105	Réunion
[24]	...	...	472[2]	...	[24]	...	...	[2]	...	[24]	...	...	[2]	...	...	Romania
3.8		...	10[2]	...	4.4	...	...	[2]	...	0.1	...	...	[2]	...	134	Rwanda
...	...	...	...	...	...	...	...	...	...	...	...	...	...	...	...	St. Helena and Ascension
...	...		...		...	...		...		...	...		...		8	St. Kitts and Nevis
—	...		...		—	...		...		—	...		...		13	St. Lucia
...	...		...		...	...		...		...	...		...		...	St. Pierre and Miquelon
...	...		...		...	...		...		...	...		...		9	St. Vincent
38.5	136	...	4	...											47	San Marino
...	...		...		...	...		...		...	...		...		3	São Tomé and Príncipe
...	6,361	...	...		...	609[12]	...			...	2,287[12]	...			7,124	Saudi Arabia
20.4[54]	45[54]	...			[54]	[54]	...			[54]	[54]	...			205[61]	Senegal
6.9	4	...			—	—				—	—				14	Seychelles
—					—					...					30	Sierra Leone
10.2	568	...			16.0	561	...			37.1	...	...	323	...	5,145	Singapore
...					...					...					...	Solomon Islands
1.5[2]	37	...			[2]	—				[2]	—				112	Somalia
27.3	3,585	15.9	577	84.1	13.7	2,117	23.5	312	76.5	5.2	638	16.7	117	83.3	13,409	South Africa
...					...					...					120	Bophuthatswana
...	8[2]	...			[2]	[2]	...			[2]	[2]	...			36[64]	Ciskei
...					...					...					...	Transkei
5.0	9	...			—	—				—	—				12	Venda
...					...					...					58	South West Africa/Namibia
20.9	26,190	...			14.9	16,076	...			7.2	2,641	...			32,232	Spain
16.3[2]	...	...	201	...	[2]	61	...	[2]	...	[2]	31	...	[2]	...	498	Sri Lanka
...	...		...		...	...		...		...	...		...		394	Sudan, The
...	...		...		...	...		...		...	...		...		115	Suriname
7.6	31	...	...	...	2.4[7]	...	...	4[7]	...	7	...	...	7	...	81	Swaziland
17.4	1,843	...	255	...	24.7	1,311	...	315	...	9.9	343	...	121	...	24,487	Sweden
...	7,973	...	228	...	...	2,983	...	280	...	...	2,676[40]	...	224[40]	...	...	Switzerland
44.9[2]	18,254[2]	...			[2]	[2]	...	[2]	...	[2]	[2]	...			1,659	Syria
14.0	24,861	...	490	...	9.3	11,552[12]	...	322[12]	...	13.0	4,597[12]	...	509[12]	...	19,498	Taiwan
14.1	...	...	69	...	6.3	...	...	40	...	1.6	...	...	25	...	321	Tanzania
13.2	...	...	917	...	3.8	...	...	285	...	2.7	...	...	181	...	14,012	Thailand
16.5	...	...	9	...	—	—				—	—				52	Togo
...					...					...					...	Tokelau
12.8[2]	19	100.0	—	—	[2]	7	100.0	—	—	[2]	2	100.0	—	—	4	Tonga
[24]	...	...			[24]	...				[24]	...				809	Trinidad and Tobago
46.8[54]	...	...			[54]	...				[54]	...				840	Tunisia
18.3	1,519	16.0	285	84.0	10.4	835	13.9	165	86.1	5.0	452	10.1	85	89.9	9,706	Turkey
—					—					—					0.3	Turks and Caicos Islands
—	—	—			—					—					0.04	Tuvalu
17.9[2]	...	...			[2]	...				[2]	...				165	Uganda
46.6[54]	...	...	16,093[54]	...	[54]	...				[54]	...				...	U.S.S.R.
5.2	285	...			—	5				—	9				2,210	United Arab Emirates
13.6	5,656	31.7	1,620	68.3	23.6	25,396	17.9	2,572	82.1	12.6	9,318	12.2	1,281	87.8	98,686	United Kingdom
13.6	53,491	29.6	5,675	70.4	20.4	55,566	17.0	4,620	83.0	13.7	14,839	9.7	3,783	90.3	999,066	United States
6.5	1,504[30]	49.3[30]	37[30]	50.7[30]	3.6	796[30]	55.8[30]	14[30]	44.2[30]	2.5	349[30]	57.1[30]	12[30]	42.9[30]	1,340	Uruguay
13.7															7	Vanuatu
16.7	2,063[68]	35.0[68]	126[68]	65.0[68]	5.2	408[68]	26.1[68]	65[68]	73.9[68]	2.2	163[68]	30.5[68]	40[68]	69.5[68]	14,071	Venezuela
...	...		...		...	...		...		...	...		...		...	Vietnam
...	...		...		...	...		...		...	...		...		...	Virgin Islands (U.S.)
—					—					—					...	Wallis and Futuna
15.4	813	...			—					—					142	West Bank
—	—				—					—					...	Western Sahara
	11[2]	...			[2]	[2]					[2]				5	Western Samoa
21.1[2,37]	112[2]	...			[2]	[2]				[2]	[2]				127	Yemen (Aden)
27.9[2]	1,324[2]	...			[2]	[2]				[2]	[2]				172	Yemen (Şan'ā')
22.0	...	...	2,005	...	15.9[12]	...	...	1,167[12]	...	9.0[12]	...	...	543[12]	...	1,369	Yugoslavia
9.6	...	...			6.4	...				1.7	...				664	Zaire
24.2[2]	...	...			[2]	[2]				[2]	[2]					Zambia
25.1[71]	...	...			[71]					3.3	...				1,609	Zimbabwe

[40]Includes professional goods.   [41]Group 5 includes, and group 6 excludes, ISIC 3825 (office machinery and computing equipment). Group 6 includes professional goods.   [42]Group 2 includes groups 3 and 4.   [43]1979.   [44]Value-added data are "revenue."   [45]30 or more employees only.   [46]1985.   [47]All data refer to either establishments with electric power and 10 or more employees or establishments without electric power and 20 or more employees.   [48]Establishments data are for 20 or more employees.   [49]Excludes petroleum refining.   [50]Data in value-added columns refer to net output.   [51]Excludes diamond industry.   [52]Value added calculated in purchaser's values.   [53]Percent of value added by establishment size and number of establishments data refer to 1982.   [54]Group 4 includes groups 5 and 6; professional goods (385) and other industries (390) are also included.   [55]Includes electricity.   [56]Establishments data refer to establishments with annual sales of 100,000 kwachas or more.   [57]Value-added data are for 1980.   [58]Fish processing.   [59]Petroleum refining.   [60]Establishments data are for 5 or more employees.   [61]Excludes fish processing.   [62]Value-added data are for 1982.   [63]Privately owned establishments only.   [64]1980.   [65]Establishments data are for private sector only.   [66]Excludes private establishments with fewer than 10 employees.   [67]Value-added data are for Abu Dhabi only.   [68]1977.   [69]Includes a 10% sample of establishments with fewer than 5 employees.   [70]Socialized sector only.   [71]Group 4 includes group 5.

Energy

This table provides data about the commercial energy supplies (reserves, production, consumption, and trade) of the various countries of the world, together with data about oil pipeline networks and traffic. Many of the data and concepts used in this table are adopted from the United Nations' *Energy Statistics Yearbook*.

Electricity. Total installed electrical power capacity comprises the sum of the rated power capacities of all main and auxiliary generators in a country. 'Total installed capacity' (kW) is multiplied by 8,760 hours per year to yield 'Total production capacity' (kW-hr).

Production of electricity comprises the total gross production of electricity by publicly or privately owned enterprises and also that generated by industrial establishments for their own use, but usually excludes consumption by the utility itself. Measured in 1,000,000s of kilowatt-hours (kW-hr), annual production of electricity ranges generally between 30% and 40% of total production capacity. The data are further analyzed by type of generation: fossil fuels, hydroelectric power, and nuclear fuel.

The great majority of the world's electrical and other energy needs are met by the burning of fossil hydrocarbon solids, liquids, and gases, either for thermal generation of electricity or in internal combustion engines. Many renewable and nontraditional sources of energy are being developed worldwide (wood, biogenic gases and liquids, tidal, wave, and wind power, geothermal and photothermal [solar] energy, and so on), but collectively these sources are still negligible in the world's total energy consumption.

For this reason only hydroelectric and nuclear generation are considered here separately with fossil fuels.

Trade in electrical energy refers to the transfer of generated electrical output via an international grid. Total electricity consumption (residential and nonresidential) is equal to total electricity requirements less transformation and distribution losses.

Coal. The term coal, as used in the table, comprises all grades of anthracite, bituminous, subbituminous, and lignite that have acquired or may in the future, by reason of new technology or changed market prices, acquire an economic value. These types of coal may be differentiated according to heat content (density) and content of impurities. Most coal reserve data are based on proved recoverable reserves only, of all grades of coal. Exceptions are footnoted, with proved in-place reserves reported only when recoverable reserves are unknown. Production figures include deposits removed from both surface and underground workings as well as quantities used by the producers themselves or issued to the miners. Wastes recovered from mines or nearby preparation plants are excluded from production figures.

Natural gas. This term refers to any combustible gas (usually chiefly methane) of natural origin from underground sources. The data for production cover, to the extent possible, gas obtained from gas fields, petroleum fields, or coal mines that is actually collected and marketed. (Much natural gas in Middle Eastern and North African oil fields is

Energy

country	electricity installed capacity, 1986 ('000 kW)	production, 1986 capacity ('000,000 kW-hr)	production, 1986 amount ('000,000 kW-hr)	power source, 1986 fossil fuel (%)	power source, 1986 hydro-power (%)	power source, 1986 nuclear fuel (%)	trade, 1986 exports ('000,000 kW-hr)	trade, 1986 imports ('000,000 kW-hr)	consumption amount, 1986 ('000,000 kW-hr)	consumption per capita, 1986 (kW-hr)	consumption resi-dential, 1984 (%)	consumption non-resi-dential, 1984 (%)	coal reserves, latest ('000,000 metric tons)	coal pro-duction, 1986 ('000 metric tons)	coal con-sump-tion, 1986 ('000 metric tons)
Afghanistan	470	4,117	1,171	38.5	61.5	—	—	—	1,171	68	...	...	66	160	160
Albania	760	6,658	3,880	12.4	87.6	—	650	—	3,230	1,037	24.1[3]	75.9[3]	15[1]	2,300	2,530
Algeria	3,736	32,727	12,746	94.8	5.2	—	85	169	12,830	572			43	9	1,109
American Samoa	32	280	75	100.0	—	—	—	—	75	2,143	27.5[5]	72.5[5]			
Andorra	...	...	...	...	...	...	...	...	...	...	...	...	...	...	...
Angola	600	5,256	1,790	25.4	74.6	—	—	—	1,790	199	27.5[4]	72.5[4]	...	—	...
Anguilla	—	...	—	...	...	...	...	...	—	—	...	...	...	...	...
Antigua and Barbuda	26	228	77	100.0	—	—	—	—	77	951	42.4	57.6	...	—	...
Argentina	16,255	142,394	48,984	45.4	42.9	11.7	6	—	48,978	1,578	25.7	74.3	130	365	1,525
Aruba[6]	...	...	...	...	...	...	...	...	...	...	...	...	...	...	...
Australia	33,478	293,267	127,659	87.2	12.1	0.7[7]	—	—	127,659	8,029	30.1[4]	69.9[4]	75,900	169,451	76,743
Austria	15,784	138,268	44,134	29.4	70.6	—	7,426	5,962	42,670	5,688	23.1[4]	83.4[4]	64	2,969	5,850
Bahamas, The	357	3,127	865	100.0	—	—	—	—	865	3,697	33.6	66.4	...	...	...
Bahrain	1,099	9,627	2,970	100.0	—	—	—	—	2,970	6,600	...	...	...	—	...
Bangladesh	1,339	11,730	5,125	91.2	8.8	—	—	—	5,125	49	25.7	74.3	1,054[1]	—	148
Barbados	95	832	390	100.0	—	—	—	—	390	1,535	25.5	74.5	...	—	...
Belgium	14,168	124,112	57,621	31.0	0.6	68.4	5,521	5,308	57,408	5,791	26.9[8]	73.1[8]	410	5,625	13,165
Belize	21	184	62	100.0	—	—	—	—	62	371	...	...	...	—	...
Benin	15	131	5	100.0	—	—	—	190	195	47	...	...	...	—	...
Bermuda	150	1,314	400	100.0	—	—	—	—	400	4,938	41.4[5]	58.6[5]	...	—	—
Bhutan	19	166	21	61.9	38.1	—	—	10	31	21	29.2[5]	69.8[5]	...	—	1
Bolivia	532	4,660	1,625	28.0	72.0	—	—	2	1,627	249	45.1	54.9	...	—	1
Botswana	10	10	522[10,11]	10	10	10	10	82[10,11]	10	10	...	...	3,500	400[8,10]	10
Brazil	44,749	392,001	201,618	9.3	90.6	0.1	9	10,568	212,177	1,532	20.1	79.9	2,343	7,391	17,131
British Virgin Islands	5	44	30	100.0	—	—	—	—	30	2,308	...	...	...	—	...
Brunei	285	2,497	958	100.0	—	—	—	—	958	3,926	55.3	44.7	...	—	—
Bulgaria	10,243	89,729	41,817	65.6	5.6	28.8	1,470	5,427	45,774	5,025	41.2[5]	58.8[5]	3,730	35,222	42,190
Burkina Faso	56	491	123	100.0	—	—	—	—	123	17	...	...	...	—	...
Burma	945	8,278	2,217	51.6	48.4	—	—	—	2,217	59	...	59.1[4,12]	2	98	278
Burundi	9	79	2	100.0	—	—	—	72	74	15	...	...	...	—	...
Cameroon	605	5,300	2,385	2.7	97.3	—	—	—	2,385	235	...	...	...	1	1
Canada	98,400	861,984	468,571	18.5	66.3	15.2	38,934	4,957	434,594	16,914	28.8	71.2	6,846	57,047	44,854
Cape Verde	5	44	28	100.0	—	—	—	—	28	84	...	...	...	—	...
Cayman Islands	35	307	137	100.0	—	—	—	—	137	6,850	55.4[5]	44.6[5]	...	—	...
Central African Republic	43	377	93	17.2	82.8	—	—	—	93	35	17.5[13]	82.5[13]	4	—	...
Chad	31	272	51	100.0	—	—	—	—	51	10	...	...	...	—	...
Chile	3,987	34,926	14,820	23.7	76.3	—	—	—	14,820	1,212	19.7	80.3	1,181	1,668	1,893
China	87,000	762,120	444,130	77.5	22.5	—	42	1,208	445,296	423	6.1[11]	93.9[11]	737,100[1]	880,000	873,920
Christmas Island	11	96	38	100.0	—	—	—	—	34	16,940	...	...	...	—	...
Cocos (Keeling) Islands	...	...	...	...	...	...	...	...	...	...	...	...	...	...	...
Colombia	5,854	51,281	27,000	27.0	73.0	—	10	8	26,998	921	45.1	54.9	1,035	10,700	4,800
Comoros	3	26	12	100.0	—	—	—	—	12	26	...	...	...	—	...
Congo	149	1,305	235	0.9	99.1	—	—	57	292	163	...	...	...	—	...
Cook Islands	6	53	12	100.0	—	—	—	—	12	600	...	...	...	—	...
Costa Rica	909	7,963	2,918	1.5	98.5	—	100	177	2,995	1,123	43.9	56.1	...	—	...
Côte d'Ivoire	1,163	10,188	1,817	22.6	77.4	—	—	—	1,817	179	15.4	84.6	...	—	...
Cuba	3,305	28,952	13,167	99.6	0.4	—	—	—	13,167	1,301	29.4	70.6	...	—	100
Cyprus	389	3,408	1,423	100.0	—	—	—	—	1,423	2,105	21.2	78.8	...	—	55
Czechoslovakia	20,371	178,450	84,775	74.2	4.7	21.1	8,620	10,077	86,232	5,518	23.6[5]	76.4[5]	5,560	126,429	126,870
Denmark	8,621	75,520	30,720	99.4	0.1	0.5[7]	2,083	2,165	30,802	6,015	32.5[8]	67.5[8]	63[1]	—	11,721
Djibouti	40	350	165	100.0	—	—	—	—	165	439	...	...	...	—	...
Dominica	7	61	18	11.1	88.9	—	—	—	18	234	53.5	46.5	...	—	...
Dominican Republic	960	8,410	4,614	80.5	19.5	—	—	—	4,614	723	...	...	...	—	1[11]
Ecuador	1,790	15,680	5,301	18.6	81.4	—	—	10	5,311	551	41.2	58.8	18	—	...
Egypt	5,850	51,246	25,100	57.6	42.4	—	—	—	25,100	523	28.3	71.1	53	—	1,200

flared [burned] because it is often not economical to capture and market it.) Manufactured gas is generally a by-product of industrial operations such as gasworks, coke ovens, and blast furnaces. It is usually burned at the point of production and rarely enters the marketplace. Production of manufactured gas is, therefore, only reported as a percentage of domestic gas consumption.

Crude petroleum. Crude petroleum is the liquid product obtained from oil wells; the term also includes shale oil, tar sand extract, and field or lease condensate. Production and consumption data in the table refer, so far as possible, to the same year so that the relationship between national production and consumption patterns can be clearly seen; both are given in barrels.

Proved reserves are that oil remaining underground in known fields whose existence has been "proved" by the evaluation of nearby producing wells or by seismic tests in sedimentary strata known to contain crude petroleum, and that is judged recoverable within the limits of present technology and economic conditions (prices). The published proved reserve figures do not necessarily reflect the true reserves of a country, because government authorities or corporations often have political or economic motives for withholding or altering such data.

The estimated exhaustion rate of petroleum reserves is an extrapolated ratio of published proved reserves to the current rate of withdrawal/production. Present world published proved reserves will last about 30 years at the present rate of withdrawal, but there are large country-to-country variations above or below the average.

Data on petroleum and product pipelines are provided because of the great importance to both domestic and international energy markets of this means of bringing these energy sources from their production or transportation points to refineries, intermediate consumption and distribution points, and final consumers. Their traffic may represent a very significant fraction of the total movement of goods within a country. Available data for petroleum pipelines are often incomplete and their basis varies internationally, some countries reporting only international shipments, others reporting domestic shipments of 50 kilometres or more, and so on.

For data in the hydrocarbons portions of the table (coal, natural gas, and petroleum), extensive use has been made of a variety of international sources, such as those of the United Nations, the International Energy Agency (of the Organization for Economic Cooperation and Development), and the World Energy Conference; of the resources of the U.S. Department of Energy; and of various industry surveys, such as those published by British Petroleum (BP *Statistical Review of World Energy*), the *International Petroleum Encyclopedia*, the *Oil and Gas Journal*, the *Petroleum Economist*, and *World Oil*.

a. Includes refined petroleum products pipelines.

natural gas — published proved reserves, 1988 ('000,000,000 cu m)	natural gas — production: natural gas, 1987 ('000,000 cu m)	natural gas — production: manufactured gas 1986 (% of total gas consumption)	natural gas — consumption: amount, 1986 ('000,000 cu m)	natural gas — consumption: residential, 1984 (%)	natural gas — consumption: non-residential, 1984 (%)	crude petroleum — reserves 1988: published proved ('000,000 barrels)	crude petroleum — reserves 1988: years to exhaust proved reserves	crude petroleum — production, 1987 ('000,000 barrels)	crude petroleum — consumption, 1987 ('000,000 barrels)	crude petroleum — refining capacity, 1988 ('000 barrels per day)	pipelines (latest)[a] — length (km)	pipelines (latest)[a] — traffic ('000,000 metric ton-km)	country
61	2,800	...	626	...	...			—	—	—	—	—	Afghanistan
6	450	...	384	...	...	200	8	26	20[2]	40	182	...	Albania
2,999	43,170	23.4	13,851	26.8[4]	73.2[4]	4,900	13	385	175[2]	465	6,910	...	Algeria
...	...	...	...	...	...	...	...	...	...	...	...	...	American Samoa
...	...	...	...	...	...	...	...	...	...	...	...	...	Andorra
48	450	11.7	128			2,000	15	133	11[2]	32	179	...	Angola
...	...	...	...	...	...	...	...	—	...	—	—	—	Anguilla
...	...	...	...	...	...	...	...	—	...	—	—	—	Antigua and Barbuda
693	15,410	11.7	18,114	36.1	63.9	2,265	15	155	158[2]	682	6,290	...	Argentina
...	...	...	...	...	...	...	...	—	...	—	—	—	Aruba[6]
845	13,870	32.2	15,332	...	...	2,195	11	200	224	637	2,975	...	Australia
9	839	25.6	5,169	25.7[4]	74.3[4]	102	15	7	76	204	725	5,003	Austria
...	—	...	...			...	...	—	27[5]	—	—	...	Bahamas, The
198	6,130	5.8	4,312	...	...	126	8	15	88[2]	250	72	...	Bahrain
360	3,720	0.4	3,325	31.7	68.3	—	—	—	7[2]	31	—	...	Bangladesh
—	22	...	26	55.6	44.4	3.6	7	0.5	2[2]	3	—	—	Barbados
—	29[2]	31.7	8,613	43.4[8]	56.6[8]	...	...	—	172[9]	631	1,328	709	Belgium
...	...	...	...	...	...	...	...	—	—	—	—	—	Belize
—	...	...	...			100	25	4	...	—	—	—	Benin
...	...	...	...	...	...	...	...	—	—	—	—	—	Bermuda
...	...	...	...	...	...	...	...	—	—	—	—	—	Bhutan
142	2,810	45.3	238	—	100.0	176	25	7	8[2]	47	2,250	...	Bolivia
...	...	[10]	...	...	...	...	...	—	[10]	—	—	—	Botswana
105	2,880	69.8	2,671	23.4[11]	76.6[11]	2,551	12	215	425[2]	1,407	5,804	...	Brazil
...	...	...	...	...	...	...	...	—	...	—	—	—	British Virgin Islands
331	8,710	10.5	343	...	...	1,600	28	57	—	10	553	...	Brunei
5	150	9.7	6,473	...	...	13	43	0.3	94[2]	300	611	...	Bulgaria
...	...	...	...	...	...	...	...	—	...	—	—	—	Burkina Faso
268	1,190	0.5	1,084	—	100.0	200	33	6	10[2]	26	1,343	...	Burma
...	...	...	...	...	...	...	...	—	...	—	—	—	Burundi
110	—	100.0	...	...	...	500	8	61	16[2]	43	—	—	Cameroon
2,725	85,426	23.0	56,670	20.6[4]	79.4[4]	4,820	9	561	517	1,869	23,564	99,700	Canada
...	...	...	...	...	...	...	...	—	—	—	—	—	Cape Verde
...	...	...	...	...	...	...	...	—	—	—	—	—	Cayman Islands
...	...	...	...	...	...	...	...	—	—	—	—	—	Central African Republic
...	...	...	...	...	...	...	...	—	...	...	—	—	Chad
120	2,005	48.8	879	49.3	50.7	200	18	11	31[2]	141	1,540	...	Chile
856	20,499	...	14,023	...	...	22,300	23	978	761	2,200	7,600	...	China
...	...	...	...	...	...	...	...	—	—	—	—	—	Christmas Island
...	...	...	...	...	...	...	...	—	—	—	—	—	Cocos (Keeling) Islands
112	5,108	15.4	4,249	0.8	99.2	2,028	14	141	77[2]	226	4,935	...	Colombia
...	...	...	...	...	...	...	...	—	...	—	—	—	Comoros
70	34[2]	30.8	2	...	...	695	16	44	4	21	25	...	Congo
—	...	...	...			...	...	—	—	—	—	—	Cook Islands
...	—	33.4	—	...	...	...	...	—	3[2]	16	95	...	Costa Rica
100	—	52.6	—	—	—	125[14]	21	6	13[2]	60	—	—	Côte d'Ivoire
—	24	93.6	5	...	...	...	...	—	45[2]	160	—	—	Cuba
—	—	62.1	...			...	...	—	4[2]	16	—	—	Cyprus
9	744	33.1	11,404	...	...	18	18	1	116[2]	455	2,948	9,016	Czechoslovakia
82	2,427	27.8	1,225	...	...	555	16	34	77	177	688	1,005	Denmark
...	...	...	...	...	...	...	...	—	—	—	—	—	Djibouti
...	...	...	...	...	...	...	...	—	—	—	—	—	Dominica
...	...	32.4	...	...	...	...	...	—	11[2]	49	104	...	Dominican Republic
114	106	45.2	87	—	100.0	1,595	23	69	34[2]	123	2,158	...	Ecuador
266	5,527	11.8	4,190	25.3	74.7	4,685	14	328	153[2]	489	1,767	...	Egypt

Energy (continued)

country	installed capacity, 1986 ('000 kW)	production, 1986 capacity ('000,000 kW-hr)	production, 1986 amount ('000,000 kW-hr)	power source, 1986 fossil fuel (%)	power source, 1986 hydro-power (%)	power source, 1986 nuclear fuel (%)	trade, 1986 exports ('000,000 kW-hr)	trade, 1986 imports ('000,000 kW-hr)	consumption amount, 1986 ('000,000 kW-hr)	consumption per capita, 1986 (kW-hr)	consumption residential, 1984 (%)	consumption non-residential, 1984 (%)	coal reserves, latest ('000,000 metric tons)	coal production, 1986 ('000 metric tons)	coal consumption, 1986 ('000 metric tons)
El Salvador	500	4,380	1,790	6.7	52.5	40.8[7]	—	—	1,790	313	45.5	54.5	...	...	...
Equatorial Guinea	5	44	16	87.5	12.5	—	—	—	16	40	...	...	...	...	...
Ethiopia	335	2,935	802	19.3	80.7	—	—	—	802	18	...	...	11	—	—
Faeroe Islands	68	596	178	71.9	28.1	—	—	—	178	4,238	...	...	—	—	—
Falkland Islands	1	9	3	100.0	—	—	—	—	3	1,500	...	...	...	...	...
Fiji	197	1,726	406	18.2	81.8	—	—	—	406	578	19.8[2]	80.2[2]	...	—	15
Finland	11,456	100,355	46,855	35.5	26.1	38.4	492	6,212	52,575	10,708	18.6[4]	81.3[4]	...	—	5,002
France	92,100[15]	806,796[15]	343,045[15]	11.9[15]	17.7[15]	70.4[15]	33,000[15]	7,800[15]	317,845[15]	5,798[15]	30.3[8]	69.7[8]	381	18,451[15]	32,900[15]
French Guiana	75	657	220	100.0	—	—	—	—	220	2,619	...	58.7[4,12]	...	...	...
French Polynesia	79	692	225	84.4	15.6	—	—	—	225	1,355	...	...	...	...	...
Gabon	200	1,752	867	22.5	77.5	—	—	—	867	740	37.5	62.5	...	...	...
Gambia, The	11	96	42	100.0	—	—	—	—	42	64	...	...	...	...	...
Gaza Strip	...	...	...	...	...	...	...	...	...	...	...	...	...	...	...
Germany, East	22,059	193,237	115,291	89.0	1.5	9.5	3,873	4,872	116,290	6,928	31.7[11]	68.3[11]	21,000	311,260	317,955
Germany, West	82,660	724,102	406,386	66.5	4.1	29.4	15,461	20,592	411,517	6,774	26.3[8]	73.7[8]	59,069	201,485	206,089
Ghana	1,185	10,381	3,749	2.1	97.9	—	275	—	3,474	247	...	...	...	...	2
Gibraltar	21	184	65	100.0	—	—	—	—	65	2,097	...	...	...	...	...
Greece	7,525	65,919	28,237	88.1	11.9	—	297	1,583	29,523	2,977	30.6[8]	69.4[8]	3,000	38,096	39,835
Greenland	88	771	185	100.0	—	—	—	—	185	3,426	34.1[2]	65.9[2]	...	...	...
Grenada	8	70	25	100.0	—	—	—	—	25	221	46.8	53.2	...	...	...
Guadeloupe	103	902	462	100.0	—	—	—	—	462	1,375	...	32.9[12]	...	...	...
Guam	302	2,646	1,100	100.0	—	—	—	—	1,100	9,483	36.9[8]	63.1[8]	...	...	...
Guatemala	780	6,833	1,760	61.4	38.6	—	—	—	1,760	215	27.0[4]	73.0[4]	...	...	...
Guernsey	...	...	...	...	...	...	...	...	...	...	...	...	...	...	...
Guinea	176	1,542	497	66.8	33.2	—	—	—	497	80	...	...	...	...	...
Guinea-Bissau	7	61	14	100.0	—	—	—	—	14	15	...	...	...	...	...
Guyana	168	1,472	390	98.7	1.3	—	—	—	390	402	32.5[16]	67.5[16]	...	...	...
Haiti	146	1,279	438	27.4	72.6	—	—	—	438	65	...	...	13[1]	...	...
Honduras	285	2,497	1,075	18.1	81.9	—	2	160	1,233	273	29.7	70.3	21[1]	...	...
Hong Kong	5,953	52,148	21,412	100.0	—	—	1,208	—	20,204	3,578	19.9	80.1	...	—	6,393
Hungary	6,242	54,680	28,063	72.8	0.5	26.5	1,346	11,862	38,579	3,610	30.7[5]	69.3[5]	4,661	23,129	25,348
Iceland	947	8,296	4,098	0.1	95.3	4.6[7]	—	—	4,098	16,727	20.9[4]	79.1[4]	...	—	74
India	54,689	479,076	202,574	71.0	26.5	2.5	100	15	202,489	262	12.3	87.7	1,581	174,124	176,374
Indonesia	8,470	74,197	29,850	75.7	23.6	0.7[7]	—	—	29,850	176	24.9	75.1	23,232[1]	1,725	2,221
Iran	13,404	117,419	36,800	83.2	16.8	—	—	—	36,800	801	21.1[11]	78.9[11]	193	800	950
Iraq	2,600	22,776	18,850	96.8	3.2	—	—	—	18,850	1,146	28.9[18]	71.1[18]	...	—	—
Ireland	3,915	34,295	12,307	89.7	10.3	—	—	—	12,307	3,369	41.4[8]	58.6[8]	15	54	2,307
Isle of Man	...	...	188[19]	100.0	—	—	—	—	172	2,530	48.1[8]	51.9[8]	...	...	...
Israel	4,275	37,449	16,277	100.0	—	—	369	—	15,908	3,678	27.1	72.9	...	—	3,222
Italy	56,205[20]	492,356[20]	188,989[20]	72.1[20]	21.8[20]	4.6[20]	1,814[20]	23,928[20]	211,103[20]	3,681[20]	25.0[8]	75.0[8]	39	1,554[20]	22,111[20]
Jamaica	740	6,482	2,400	93.8	6.2	—	—	—	2,400	1,012	18.1	81.9	...	—	...
Japan	173,329	1,518,362	671,770	61.8	12.9	25.1	—	—	671,770	5,533	20.8[4]	79.2[4]	1,015	16,012	104,665
Jersey	...	...	337[19]	...	...	...	...	...	303[19]	3,940[19]	...	...	...	...	...
Jordan	979	8,576	2,955	99.9	0.1	—	233	...	2,722	745	35.3	64.7	...	...	...
Kampuchea	55	482	155	58.1	41.9	—	—	—	155	21	...	...	...	...	—
Kenya	559	4,897	2,500	19.2	67.2	13.6[7]	—	220	2,720	127	27.6	72.4	...	—	85
Kiribati	2	18	6	100.0	—	—	—	—	6	92	...	...	...	...	...
Korea, North	8,700	76,212	50,000	42.0	58.0	—	—	—	50,000	2,394	...	...	600	52,000	54,450
Korea, South	19,607	171,757	69,763	53.6	5.8	40.6	—	—	69,763	1,663	16.8[8]	83.2[8]	132	24,253	41,153
Kuwait	6,144	53,821	17,216	100.0	—	—	—	—	17,216	9,075	70.4	29.6	...	...	...
Laos	225	1,971	1,050	4.8	95.2	—	756	17	311	74	...	...	...	...	...
Lebanon	668	5,852	1,370	59.1	40.9	—	—	30	1,400	517	...	...	...	...	...
Lesotho	10	10	10	10	10	10	10	10	10	10	...	...	...	10	10
Liberia	325	2,847	819	61.2	38.8	—	—	—	819	362	...	...	...	...	...
Libya	1,580	13,841	9,000	100.0	—	—	—	—	9,000	2,405	...	...	—	—	2
Liechtenstein	21	21	21	21	21	21	21	21	21	21	...	...	...	...	21
Luxembourg	1,238	10,845	572	85.7	14.3	—	434	3,915	4,053	11,165	15.3[8]	84.7[8]	...	—	184
Macau	135	1,183	513	100.0	—	—	—	42	555	1,354	75.0	25.0	...	...	...
Madagascar	102	894	500	46.4	53.6	—	—	—	500	49	...	...	1,075[1]	—	9
Malawi	160	1,402	528	2.5	97.5	—	1	—	527	73	14.5[5]	85.5[5]	12	—	28
Malaysia	4,390	38,456	16,099	74.7	25.3	—	—	—	16,099	1,012	20.3	79.7	7	—	390
Maldives	4	35	13	100.0	—	—	—	—	13	69	50.9[5]	49.1[5]	...	...	...
Mali	82	718	172	24.4	75.6	—	—	—	172	21	...	...	—	—	...
Malta	205	1,796	850	100.0	—	—	—	—	850	2,208	25.1[11]	74.9[11]	...	—	146
Martinique	65	569	275	100.0	—	—	—	—	275	836	...	40.9[12]	...	...	...
Mauritania	53	464	92	100.0	—	—	—	—	92	47	...	...	...	...	5
Mauritius	274	2,400	518	78.8	21.2	—	—	—	518	485	...	...	...	...	56
Mayotte	3	26	...	...	...	...	...	...	...	...	...	...	...	...	...
Mexico	24,085	210,985	97,518	70.1	28.1	1.8[7]	1,468	126	96,176	1,188	17.4[11]	82.6[11]	1,917	8,450	8,800
Monaco	15	15	15	15	15	15	15	15	15	15	...	...	...	15	15
Mongolia	760	6,658	2,800	100.0	—	—	—	200	3,000	1,530	29.8[5]	70.2[5]	24,000[1]	6,000	5,750
Montserrat	4	35	12	100.0	—	—	—	—	12	1,000	38.6	61.4	...	...	...
Morocco	2,284	20,008	7,156	93.2	6.8	—	...	—	7,156	318	28.5	71.5	45	800	980
Mozambique	1,803	15,794	497	88.3	11.7	—	—	103	600	42	...	...	240	4	66
Nauru	10	88	29	100.0	—	—	—	—	29	3,625	...	...	...	...	...
Nepal	190	1,664	427	6.6	93.4	—	21	56	462	27	46.7	53.3	...	8	158
Netherlands, The	17,157	150,295	67,123	94.0	—	6.0	12	2,383	69,494	4,774	25.0	75.0	497	—	9,816
Netherlands Antilles[6]	400	3,504	1,485	100.0	—	—	—	—	1,485	5,562	...	...	...	...	...
New Caledonia	367	3,215	1,109	63.8	36.2	—	—	—	1,109	7,109	...	...	2	—	175
New Zealand	7,388	64,719	28,160	18.4	77.4	4.2[7]	—	—	28,160	8,411	37.5	62.5	243	2,295	1,945
Nicaragua	395	3,460	1,063	46.6	25.2	28.2[7]	10	200	1,253	370	41.7	58.3	...	...	...
Niger	63	552	156	100.0	—	—	—	131	287	46	4.9	95.1	5[1]	50	50
Nigeria	4,040	35,390	9,875	77.7	22.3	—	100	—	9,775	99	37.9	62.1	169	144	104
Niue	1	9	3	100.0	—	—	—	—	3	1,000	...	...	...	...	...
Norfolk Island	...	...	...	...	...	...	...	...	...	...	...	...	...	...	...

natural gas — published proved reserves, 1988 ('000,000,000 cu m)	production — natural gas, 1987 ('000,000 cu m)	production — manufactured gas, 1986 (% of total gas consumption)	consumption — amount, 1986 ('000,000 cu m)	consumption — residential, 1984 (%)	consumption — non-residential, 1984 (%)	crude petroleum reserves, 1988 — published proved ('000,000 barrels)	reserves, 1988 — years to exhaust proved reserves	production, 1987 ('000,000 barrels)	consumption, 1987 ('000,000 barrels)	refining capacity, 1988 ('000 barrels per day)	pipelines (latest)[a] — length (km)	pipelines — traffic ('000,000 metric ton-km)	country
—	—	92.6	—	—	—	...	...	—	5[2]	17	—	—	El Salvador
...	...	...	...	...	...	...	...	—	...	—	—	—	Equatorial Guinea
—	—	100.0	—	...	...	...	...	—	6[2]	18	—	—	Ethiopia
...	...	...	—	...	...	...	...	—	—	—	—	—	Faeroe Islands
...	...	...	...	...	...	...	...	—	—	—	—	—	Falkland Islands
...	...	100.0	...	...	...	...	...	—	—	—	—	—	Fiji
—	—	33.0	1,087	0.6[8]	99.4[8]	...	...	—	82	241	—	—	Finland
33	5,495	22.5[15]	30,183[15]	32.4[8]	67.6[8]	216	9	24	631	1,940	7,546	25,859	France
...	...	...	...	...	...	...	...	—	—	—	—	—	French Guiana
...	...	...	...	...	...	...	...	—	—	—	—	—	French Polynesia
15	68	3.2	210	—	100.0	960	17	56	9[2]	23	284	...	Gabon
...	...	...	...	...	...	...	...	—	—	—	—	—	Gambia, The
...	...	...	...	...	...	...	...	—	—	—	—	—	Gaza Strip
187	13,000	35.7	8,239	...	...	4	20	0.2	164[2]	470	1,801	4,300	Germany, East
272	19,172	25.0	56,764	36.6[8]	63.4[8]	438	16	27	831	1,648	5,732	8,676	Germany, West
—	—	100.0	—	...	...	1	10	0.1[2]	8[2]	28	3	...	Ghana
...	...	...	...	...	...	...	...	—	—	—	—	—	Gibraltar
0.5	102	97.2	117	...	...	22	3	8	90	385	573	...	Greece
...	...	...	...	...	...	...	...	—	—	—	—	—	Greenland
...	...	...	...	...	...	...	...	—	—	—	—	—	Grenada
...	...	100.0	...	...	...	...	...	—	—	—	—	—	Guadeloupe
...	...	...	...	...	...	...	...	—	11[2]	—	...	...	Guam
0.6	17	8.3	—	...	...	42	42	1	8[2]	16	275	...	Guatemala
...	...	...	...	...	...	...	...	—	—	—	—	—	Guernsey
...	...	...	...	...	...	...	...	—	—	—	—	—	Guinea
...	...	...	...	...	...	...	...	—	—	—	—	—	Guinea-Bissau
...	...	...	...	...	...	...	...	—	—	—	—	—	Guyana
—	—	30.7	—	—	—	...	...	—	—	—	—	—	Haiti
—	—	55.1	—	...	...	...	...	—	2[2]	14	—	—	Honduras
...	...	...	...	...	...	...	...	—	—	—	—	—	Hong Kong
125	7,116	10.7	10,808	14.0[8]	86.0[8]	290	21	14	58[2]	220	1,804	2,819	Hungary
—	—	—	—	—	—	—	—	—	4	—	—	—	Iceland
504	7,055	31.5	5,566	55.0[17]	45.0[17]	4,400	19	233	342[2]	1,059	5,325	...	India
2,464	34,966	15.9	7,086	—	100.0	8,500	19	444	243[2]	714	2,961	...	Indonesia
14,074	18,992	12.3	8,537	—	100.0	35,612	40	895	212[2]	530	9,800	...	Iran
745	1,696	46.0	615	...	...	100,000	132	758	111[2]	319	5,075	...	Iraq
54	1,657	2.7	1,590	13.9[8]	86.1[8]	...	...	—	31	56	—	—	Ireland
...	...	...	...	...	...	...	...	—	—	—	—	—	Isle of Man
1	59	98.4	40	—	100.0	0.7	18	0.04	47[2]	180	998	...	Israel
289	16,218	20.6[20]	31,743[20]	45.6[8]	54.4[8]	925	36	26	615	2,581	3,851	11,315	Italy
—	—	52.7	—	...	...	...	...	—	7[2]	36	10	—	Jamaica
30	2,134	45.5	40,376	61.3[16]	38.7[16]	55	18	3	1,516	4,567	406	...	Japan
...	...	...	...	...	...	...	...	—	—	—	—	—	Jersey
—	—	92.6	—	...	...	...	...	—	17[2]	100	209	...	Jordan
...	...	...	...	...	...	...	...	—	—	—	—	—	Kampuchea
—	—	105.3	—	—	—	...	...	—	15[2]	90	483	...	Kenya
...	...	...	...	...	...	...	...	—	—	—	—	—	Kiribati
...	...	...	...	...	...	...	...	—	20[2]	42	37	...	Korea, North
...	...	56.5	74	100.0	...	...	...	—	210[2]	820	294	...	Korea, South
1,062	4,420	42.9	6,699	21.7	78.3	95,500	253	377	217[2]	628	917	...	Kuwait
—	—	28.6	...	...	...	...	...	—	8[2]	37	136	—	Laos
—	—	10	—	...	...	...	...	—	10	—	72	...	Lebanon
—	—	10	—	...	...	...	...	—	—	—	—	—	Lesotho
—	—	50.5	—	...	...	...	...	—	5[5]	15	—	—	Liberia
726	6,660	17.6	3,024	...	...	22,570	65	346	65[2]	329	4,826	...	Libya
—	—	21	21	...	...	...	...	—	—	—	—	—	Liechtenstein
...	—	53.0	360	48.0[8]	52.0[8]	...	...	—	9	—	48	—	Luxembourg
...	...	...	...	...	...	...	...	—	—	—	—	—	Macau
—	—	100.0	—	...	...	...	...	—	2[2]	16	—	—	Madagascar
...	—	100.0	—	...	...	...	...	—	—	—	—	—	Malawi
1,478	13,051	24.2	2,096	33.8	66.2	3,300	18	182	56[2]	212	1,307	...	Malaysia
...	...	...	...	...	...	...	...	—	—	—	—	...	Maldives
—	...	...	...	...	...	...	...	—	—	—	—	...	Mali
—	—	—	...	...	...	...	...	—	—	—	—	—	Malta
—	—	200.0	...	...	...	...	...	—	3[2]	13	—	—	Martinique
...	...	...	...	...	...	...	...	—	—	—	—	—	Mauritania
...	...	...	...	...	...	...	...	—	—	—	—	—	Mauritius
											—	—	Mayotte
2,119	11,947	30.5[15]	16,469[15]	3.9[11]	96.1[11]	54,110	58	927	412[2]	1,354	12,726	...	Mexico
...	...	...	...	...	...	...	...	—	—	—	—	—	Monaco
...	...	...	...	...	64.6[4,12]	...	...	—	—	—	—	—	Mongolia
											—	—	Montserrat
2	59	45.3	86	—	100.0	2	10	0.2	35[2]	155	362	...	Morocco
62	—	—	...	...	...	...	...	—	...	...	289	...	Mozambique
...	...	...	...	...	...	...	...	—	—	—	—	—	Nauru
...	...	...	...	...	...	...	...	—	—	—	—	—	Nepal
1,770	74,247	13.8	47,980	46.8	53.4	189	6	34	219	1,381	1,383	4,287	Netherlands, The
—	—	50.0	...	...	...	...	...	—	61[2]	320	—	—	Netherlands Antilles[6]
...	...	...	...	...	...	...	...	—	—	—	—	—	New Caledonia
115	3,983	1.7	3,288	4.8	95.2	157	14	11	35	82	310	...	New Zealand
—	—	92.9	—	—	—	...	...	—	4[2]	15	56	...	Nicaragua
...	...	...	...	...	...	...	...	—	—	—	—	—	Niger
1,290	2,798	1.8	3,150	—	100.0	15,845	34	465	78[2]	270	5,042	...	Nigeria
...	...	...	...	...	...	...	...	—	—	—	—	—	Niue
...	...	...	...	...	...	...	...	—	—	—	—	—	Norfolk Island

Energy (continued)

country	electricity installed capacity, 1986 ('000 kW)	production, 1986 capacity ('000,000 kW-hr)	production, 1986 amount ('000,000 kW-hr)	power source, 1986 fossil fuel (%)	power source, 1986 hydro-power (%)	power source, 1986 nuclear fuel (%)	trade, 1986 exports ('000,000 kW-hr)	trade, 1986 imports ('000,000 kW-hr)	consumption amount, 1986 ('000,000 kW-hr)	consumption per capita, 1986 (kW-hr)	consumption residential, 1984 (%)	consumption non-residential, 1984 (%)	coal reserves, latest ('000,000 metric tons)	coal production, 1986 ('000 metric tons)	coal consumption, 1986 ('000 metric tons)
Norway	23,672	207,367	96,359	0.4	99.6	—	2,169	4,212	98,402	23,706	27.0[4]	73.0[4]	30	580	1,273
Oman	1,111	9,732	2,906	100.0	—	—	—	—	2,906	2,256	...	...	...	...	...
Pacific Is., Trust Territory of the	57	499	168	82.1	17.9	—	—	—	168	1,063	...	...	...	...	...
Marshall Islands	...	...	...	...	...	...	...	...	...	...	...	...	...	...	...
Micronesia, Fed. States of	...	...	...	...	...	...	...	...	...	...	...	...	...	...	...
Northern Mariana Islands	...	...	...	...	...	...	...	...	...	...	...	...	...	...	...
Palau	...	...	...	...	...	...	...	...	...	...	...	...	...	...	...
Pakistan	5,427	47,541	25,768	45.0	53.6	1.4	—	—	25,768	250	28.8	71.2	102	2,086	2,906
Panama	894	7,831	2,736	23.4	76.6	—	—	—	2,736	1,229	26.8[11]	73.2[11]	...	—	5
Papua New Guinea	505	4,424	1,575	73.0	27.0	—	—	—	1,575	438	8.9	91.1	...	...	...
Paraguay	900	7,884	1,644	0.2	99.8	—	50	2	1,596	421	...	...	...	...	...
Peru	3,575	31,317	12,818	22.3	77.7	—	—	—	12,818	634	20.4[11]	79.6[11]	28[1]	150	105
Philippines	6,462	56,607	22,320	52.4	27.1	20.5[7]	—	—	22,320	400	19.7	80.3	82	1,243	1,890
Pitcairn Island	...	...	...	...	...	...	...	...	...	...	...	...	...	...	...
Poland	29,773	260,811	140,294	97.3	2.7	—	7,796	7,833	140,331	3,744	33.5[5]	66.5[5]	42,700	259,338	225,874
Portugal	6,458	56,572	20,225	58.4	41.6	—	989	2,874	22,110	2,152	36.4[4]	63.6[4]	52	212	1,963
Puerto Rico	4,100	35,916	12,300	98.8	1.2	—	—	—	12,300	3,512	31.0[11]	69.0[11]	...	—	40
Qatar	1,005	8,804	3,565	100.0	—	—	—	—	3,565	10,642	69.0[17]	31.0[17]	...	...	...
Réunion	151	1,323	615	1.0	99.0	—	—	—	615	1,143	...	...	...	...	...
Romania	19,682	172,414	71,580	83.1	16.9	—	—	3,000	74,580	3,218	23.6[5]	76.4[5]	3,970[1]	46,700	52,000
Rwanda	60	526	170	2.4	97.6	—	3	20	187	30	...	...	...	...	...
St. Helena and Ascension	2	18	2	100.0	—	—	—	—	2	333	...	...	...	...	...
St. Kitts and Nevis	15	131	35	100.0	—	—	—	—	35	745	...	...	...	...	...
St. Lucia	20	175	73	100.0	—	—	—	—	73	553	26.6[5]	73.4[5]	...	...	...
St. Pierre and Miquelon	25	219	40	100.0	—	—	—	—	40	6,667	...	...	...	...	...
St. Vincent and the Grenadines	10	88	30	40.0	60.0	—	—	—	30	286	45.3	54.7	...	...	...
San Marino	20	20	20	20	20	20	20	20	20	20	...	...	...	20	20
São Tomé and Príncipe	6	53	12	58.3	41.7	—	—	—	12	120	...	...	...	...	...
Saudi Arabia	14,120	123,691	32,900	100.0	—	—	—	—	32,900	2,740	67.4[17]	32.6[17]	...	...	...
Senegal	207	1,813	758	100.0	—	—	—	—	758	115	...	...	...	...	...
Seychelles	19	166	66	100.0	—	—	—	—	66	835	...	...	...	...	...
Sierra Leone	110	964	184	100.0	—	—	—	—	184	50	...	...	...	...	...
Singapore	2,741	24,011	10,577	100.0	—	—	—	—	10,577	4,089	18.0	82.0	...	—	1
Solomon Islands	13	114	30	100.0	—	—	—	—	30	107	26.6	73.4	...	...	...
Somalia	60	526	143	100.0	—	—	—	—	143	30	...	...	...	...	...
South Africa	24,727[10]	216,609[10]	122,320[10]	96.2[10]	0.6[10]	3.2[10]	300[10]	—	122,020[10]	3,195[10]	...	...	58,404	175,671[10]	132,671[10]
Bophuthatswana	...	...	...	...	...	...	...	...	...	...	...	...	...	...	...
Ciskei	...	...	...	...	...	...	...	...	...	...	...	...	...	...	...
Transkei	...	...	...	...	...	...	...	...	...	...	...	...	...	...	...
Venda	...	...	...	...	...	...	...	...	...	...	...	...	...	...	...
South West Africa/Namibia	10	10	10	10	10	10	10	10	10	10	...	...	...	10	10
Spain	35,079	307,292	127,713	50.1	20.6	29.3	4,152	2,896	126,457	3,262	16.7[4]	83.2[4]	883	38,582	47,308
Sri Lanka	1,065	9,329	2,652	0.3	99.7	—	—	—	2,652	161	16.9	83.1	...	—	1
Sudan, The	460	4,030	1,052	50.9	49.1	—	—	—	1,052	47	...	...	...	—	—
Suriname	415	3,635	1,325	29.8	70.2	—	—	—	1,325	3,487	...	...	...	—	1
Swaziland	10	10	10	10	10	10	10	10	10	10	18.7[16]	81.3[16]	1,820	10	10
Sweden	33,100	289,956	138,023	5.1	44.0	50.9	6,451	1,819	133,391	15,979	26.4[4]	73.6[4]	1	12	4,230
Switzerland	15,210[21]	133,240[21]	54,857[21]	1.8[21]	59.4[21]	38.8[21]	23,098[21]	14,512[21]	46,271[21]	7,220[21]	26.6[8]	73.4[8]	...	—	549[21]
Syria	2,940	25,754	7,032	63.8	36.2	—	130	—	6,902	633	21.2[8]	78.8[8]	200	...	—
Taiwan	16,594	145,363	59,031	43.7	12.5	43.8	—	—	53,813	2,780	26.0[2]	74.0[2]	...	...	...
Tanzania	439	3,846	880	29.5	70.5	—	—	—	880	38	...	...	200	4	4
Thailand	7,570	66,313	25,932	78.6	21.4	—	17	756	26,671	510	24.4	75.6	879	5,476	5,648
Togo	34	298	35	88.6	11.4	—	—	230	265	87	...	...	...	...	...
Tokelau	...	...	...	...	...	...	...	...	...	...	...	...	...	...	...
Tonga	6	53	12	100.0	—	—	—	—	12	108	...	...	...	...	...
Trinidad and Tobago	765	6,701	3,313	100.0	—	—	—	—	3,313	2,752	24.7	75.3	...	...	...
Tunisia	1,414	12,387	4,202	98.8	1.2	—	7	15	4,210	582	32.7	67.3	...	—	12
Turkey	10,113	88,590	39,695	70.0	29.9	0.1	—	777	40,472	804	14.2[11]	85.8[11]	4,857	45,734	49,028
Turks and Caicos Islands	8	70	9	100.0	—	—	—	—	9	1,125	...	...	...	...	...
Tuvalu	...	...	...	...	...	...	...	...	...	...	...	...	...	...	...
Uganda	163	1,428	656	1.4	98.6	—	110	—	546	34	...	...	...	...	...
U.S.S.R.	321,671	2,817,838	1,598,890	76.4	13.5	10.1	29,000	300	1,570,190	5,582	21.6[5]	78.4[5]	244,700	704,683	689,391
United Arab Emirates	2,480	21,725	6,745	100.0	—	—	—	—	6,745	4,874	...	...	...	...	...
United Kingdom	66,512	582,645	298,156	78.8	1.4	19.8	189	4,444	302,411	5,366	35.4[8]	64.6[8]	4,600	108,092	112,396
United States	719,444	6,302,329	2,582,510	72.1	11.4	16.0	4,816	40,713	2,618,407	10,906	34.9[8]	65.1[8]	263,843	805,721	723,837
Uruguay	1,457	12,763	7,429	1.8	98.2	—	3,151	—	4,278	1,410	43.4	56.6	...	...	—
Vanuatu	11	96	26	100.0	—	—	—	—	26	177	...	...	...	...	...
Venezuela	12,499	109,491	46,724	54.4	45.6	—	8	—	46,716	2,626	22.7	77.3	372	57	307
Vietnam	1,260	11,038	5,200	61.5	38.5	—	—	—	5,200	85	36.4[5]	63.6[5]	150	5,500	5,000
Virgin Islands (U.S.)	341	2,987	900	100.0	—	—	—	—	900	8,411	40.2	59.8	...	...	...
Wallis and Futuna	...	...	...	...	...	...	...	...	...	...	...	...	...	...	...
West Bank	...	...	...	...	...	...	...	...	...	...	...	...	...	...	...
Western Sahara	56	491	78	100.0	—	—	—	—	78	488	...	...	...	...	...
Western Samoa	17	149	45	55.6	44.4	—	—	—	45	274	...	...	...	...	...
Yemen (Aden)	160	1,402	420	100.0	—	—	—	—	420	191	...	...	...	...	...
Yemen (San'ā')	125	1,095	310	100.0	—	—	—	—	310	44	...	...	1[1]	...	...
Yugoslavia	16,132	141,316	77,381	56.8	34.6	5.2	2,178	2,664	77,867	3,340	26.1[4]	73.9[4]	16,570	68,788	73,274
Zaire	2,166	18,974	4,619	2.9	97.1	—	110	12	4,521	147	...	89.1[4,12]	600	127	167
Zambia	1,729	15,146	10,100	0.3	99.7	—	3,100	20	7,020	1,018	13.6	86.4	72	564	554
Zimbabwe	1,539	13,482	5,988	47.3	52.7	—	—	3,000	8,988	988	16.3	83.7	734	4,047	4,034

natural gas						crude petroleum							country
published proved reserves, 1988 ('000,000,000 cu m)	production natural gas, 1987 ('000,000 cu m)	production manufactured gas, 1986 (% of total gas consumption)	consumption amount, 1986 ('000,000 cu m)	consumption residential, 1984 (%)	consumption non-residential, 1984 (%)	reserves, 1988 published proved ('000,000 barrels)	reserves, 1988 years to exhaust proved reserves	production, 1987 ('000,000 barrels)	consumption, 1987 ('000,000 barrels)	refining capacity, 1988 ('000 barrels per day)	pipelines (latest)[a] length (km)	pipelines (latest)[a] traffic ('000,000 metric ton-km)	
2,285	29,235	50.9	1,083	...	...	12,500	33	375	74	240	53	4,511	Norway
264	1,767	79.9	1,796	...	...	4,105	19	213	17[2]	77	1,300	...	Oman
...	...	...	...	...	...	...	...	—	—	...	—	—	Pacific Is., Trust Territory of the Marshall Islands
...	...	...	...	...	...	...	...	—	—	...	—	—	Micronesia, Fed. States of
													Northern Mariana Islands
													Palau
634	11,887	1.0	9,255	25.8	74.2	144	10	15	44[2]	130	1,135	...	Pakistan
—	—	40.5	—	—	—	...	...	—	9[2]	100	130	...	Panama
28	—	100.0	—	—	—	200	...	—	—	—	—	—	Papua New Guinea
—	—	10.0	...	...	...	...	...	—	2[2]	8	—	—	Paraguay
18	1,303	26.7	589	...	71.4[12]	480	8	60	60[2]	182	800	...	Peru
0.5	—	76.7	—	—	—	17	9	2	58[2]	286	357	—	Philippines
...	...	...	...	...	...	...	...	...	...	...	...	...	Pitcairn Island
118	5,746	34.4	12,625	...	...	12	12	1	106[2]	385	2,346	16,996	Poland
—	—	64.4	...	...	...	...	...	—	69	294	69	...	Portugal
—	—	78.1	...	...	...	...	...	—	33[2]	123	...	...	Puerto Rico
4,437	4,655	18.7	4,134	—	100.0	3,516	33	107	11[2]	62	235	...	Qatar
...	...	...	...	...	...	...	...	—	—	—	—	—	Réunion
136	35,900	8.1	39,936	...	...	1,286	16	78	191[2]	617	4,229	4,481	Romania
50	—	—	1	...	...	...	...	—	—	—	—	—	Rwanda
...	...	...	...	...	...	...	...	—	—	—	—	—	St. Helena and Ascension
...	...	...	...	...	...	...	...	—	—	—	—	—	St. Kitts and Nevis
...	...	...	...	...	...	...	...	—	—	—	...	...	St. Lucia
...	...	...	...	...	...	...	...	—	—	—	...	...	St. Pierre and Miquelon
...	...	...	...	...	...	...	...	—	—	—	—	—	St. Vincent and the Grenadines
...	...	...	...	...	...	...	...	—	—	—	—	—	San Marino
...	...	20	20	...	...	...	...	—	—	—	—	—	São Tomé and Príncipe
4,017	20,980	119.9	7,469	11.1[17]	88.9[17]	167,400	115	1,457	280[2]	1,375	6,550	—	Saudi Arabia
—	—	15.8	...	...	...	...	...	—	4[2]	30	—	—	Senegal
...	...	...	...	...	...	...	...	—	—	—	...	...	Seychelles
...	...	...	...	...	...	...	...	—	2[2]	10	—	—	Sierra Leone
—	—	157.2	—	—	—	...	...	—	256[2]	858	—	—	Singapore
—	—	—	—	—	—	...	...	—	—	—	—	—	Solomon Islands
6	...	...	...	...	...	...	...	—	3[2]	10	15	—	Somalia
28	—	100.0[10]	—	—	—	115[14]	...	...	117[2,10]	434	2,679	...	South Africa
...	...	...	...	...	...	...	...	—	—	—	...	...	Bophuthatswana
...	...	...	...	...	...	...	...	—	—	—	...	...	Ciskei
...	...	...	...	...	...	...	...	—	—	—	...	...	Transkei
...	...	...	...	...	...	...	...	—	—	—	...	...	Venda
...	...	10	...	...	...	...	...	...	10	—	—	—	South West Africa/Namibia
17	736	58.2	3,035	...	...	42	4	12	324	1,305	2,059	3,165	Spain
—	—	98.2	...	...	...	...	...	—	12[2]	50	62	...	Sri Lanka
—	—	44.4	...	...	...	300	...	—	7[2]	21	815	—	Sudan, The
...	...	...	...	...	...	27	34	0.8	1[2]	—	—	—	Suriname
...	...	10	...	...	...	...	...	...	10	—	—	—	Swaziland
—	—	60.1	215	...	...	...	...	—	138	437	—	—	Sweden
—	—	18.8[21]	1,547[21]	38.3[8]	61.7[8]	...	...	...	91	132	314	1,161	Switzerland
144	476	40.4	179	...	...	1,720	20	84	75[2]	229	1,819	...	Syria
20	1,011	...	...	...	...	9	10	0.9	...	600	615	...	Taiwan
116	—	100.0	...	...	...	...	...	...	4[2]	14	982	...	Tanzania
105	5,120	16.8	3,498	—	100.0	120	9	13	55[2]	192	67	...	Thailand
—	...	...	...	...	...	...	...	...	...	20	—	—	Togo
...	...	...	...	...	...	...	...	...	...	—	—	—	Tokelau
...	...	...	...	...	...	...	...	...	...	—	—	—	Tonga
289	3,837	8.9	2,974	—	100.0	528	9	59	38[2]	300	1,051	...	Trinidad and Tobago
84	319	5.2	650	4.4	95.6	1,725	45	38	12[2]	34	883	...	Tunisia
29	396	68.9	461	...	...	380	20	19	153	676	4,059	31,936	Turkey
...	...	...	...	...	...	...	...	...	...	—	—	—	Turks and Caicos Islands
...	...	...	...	...	...	...	...	...	...	—	—	—	Tuvalu
...	...	...	...	...	...	...	...	...	...	—	—	—	Uganda
41,003	727,005	10.0	614,473	...	...	58,700	13	4,554	3,222	12,260	89,000	1,312,500	U.S.S.R.
5,763	16,282	295.1	859	...	...	56,139	105	534	51[2]	180	830	...	United Arab Emirates
644	47,648	13.5	62,524	52.7[8]	47.3[8]	5,152	6	884	561	1,803	3,926	10,561	United Kingdom
5,338	502,080	20.3	472,939	33.4[11]	66.6[11]	25,300	8	3,034	5,691	15,328	275,834	827,541	United States
—	—	89.2	—	—	—	...	...	—	8[2]	45	—	—	Uruguay
...	...	...	...	...	...	...	...	...	...	...	—	—	Vanuatu
2,837	19,264	10.9	19,545	8.2	91.8	56,781	92	620	304[2]	1,201	6,850	...	Venezuela
...	...	...	...	...	...	...	...	...	...	...	150	...	Vietnam
...	...	100.0	...	...	...	...	...	...	114[2]	545	...	...	Virgin Islands (U.S.)
...	...	...	...	...	...	...	...	...	...	—	—	—	Wallis and Futuna
...	...	...	...	...	...	...	...	...	...	—	—	—	West Bank
...	...	...	...	...	...	...	...	...	...	—	—	—	Western Sahara
...	...	...	...	...	...	...	...	...	...	—	—	—	Western Samoa
...	...	100.0	...	...	...	...	...	...	24[2]	170	32	—	Yemen (Aden)
105	...	...	...	...	...	550	92	6	3	10	424	...	Yemen (Şan'ā')
84	2,283	25.9	5,091	...	...	220	8	28	111[2]	608	1,523	2,504	Yugoslavia
0.8	—	100.0	—	—	—	112	9	12	2[2]	17	390	...	Zaire
...	—	100.0	—	—	—	...	...	...	4[2]	24	1,724	...	Zambia
...	—	89.8	—	—	—	...	...	...	...	...	8	...	Zimbabwe

[1]Estimated reserves in place. [2]1986. [3]1972. [4]1981. [5]1985. [6]Netherlands Antilles includes Aruba. [7]Geothermally generated electricity. [8]1983. [9]Belgium includes Luxembourg. [10]South Africa includes Botswana, Lesotho, South West Africa/Namibia, and Swaziland. [11]1982. [12]Transportation and industry only; excludes agricultural, commercial, and public service sectors. [13]1978. [14]1987. [15]France includes Monaco. [16]1980. [17]Residential includes agriculture. [18]1977. [19]1984. [20]Italy includes San Marino. [21]Switzerland includes Liechtenstein.

Transportation

This table presents data on the transportation infrastructure of the various countries and dependencies of the world and on their commercial passenger and cargo traffic. Most states have roads and airports, with services corresponding to the prevailing level of economic development. A number of states, however, lack railroads or inland waterways, because of either geographic constraints or lack of development capital and technical expertise. Pipelines, one of the oldest means of bulk transport if aqueducts are considered, are today the least developed transportation mode worldwide for shipment of bulk materials. Because the principal contemporary application of pipeline technology is to facilitate the shipment of hydrocarbon liquids and gases, coverage of pipelines will be found in the "Energy" table. However, it is also true that pipelines now find increasing application for slurries of coal or other raw materials.

While the United Nations' *Statistical Yearbook* and *Monthly Bulletin of Statistics* provide much data on infrastructure and traffic and have established basic categories and classifications for transportation statistics, the number of countries covered is limited. Several commercial publications maintain substantial data bases and publishing programs for their particular areas of interest: Highway and vehicle statistics are provided by the International Road Federation's annual *Road and Motor Vehicle Statistics* and *World Road Statistics;* the International Union of Railways' *International Railway Statistics* and Jane's *World Railways* provide similar data for railways; Lloyd's *Register of Shipping Statistical Tables* summarizes

the world's merchant marine; the *Official Airline Guide,* the International Civil Aviation Organization's *Digest of Statistics: Commercial Air Carriers,* and the International Air Transport Association's *World Air Transport Statistics* have also been used to supplement and update data collected by the UN. Because several of these agencies are commercially or insurance-oriented, their data tend to be more complete, accurate, and timely than those of intergovernmental organizations, which depend on periodic responses to questionnaires or publication of results in official sources. All of these international sources have been extensively supplemented by national statistical sources to provide additional data. Such diversity of sources, however, imposes limitations on the comparability of the statistics from country to country because the basis and completeness of data collection and the frequency and timeliness of analysis and publication may vary greatly. Data more than five years old are shown in italic.

The categories adopted in the table also have special problems of comparability. Total road length is subject to wide international variation of interpretation, as "roads" can mean anything from mere tracks to highly developed highways. Each country also has individual classifications that differ according to climate, availability of road-building materials, traffic patterns, administrative responsibility, and so on. "Paved roads," by contrast, is a much more tightly definable category, but the proportion of paved to total roads may be distorted by the less comparable total road statistics. Automobile and truck and bus fleet statistics, which are usually

Transportation

country	roads and motor vehicles (latest)								railroads (latest)					
	roads			motor vehicles			cargo		track length		traffic			
	length		paved (per-cent)	auto-mobiles	trucks and buses	persons per vehicle	short ton-mi ('000,-000)	metric ton-km ('000,-000)	mi	km	passengers		cargo	
	mi	km									passen-ger-mi ('000,000)	passen-ger-km ('000,000)	short ton-mi ('000,000)	metric ton-km ('000,000)
Afghanistan	11,789	18,974	42	34,908	30,800	214	*1,993*	*2,910*	6	10	...	...	...	...
Albania	7,456	12,000	40	3,500	11,200	146	...	...	277	445	*181*	*291*	*87*	*127*
Algeria	27,688	44,560	...	712,700	471,500	18	*2,148*	*3,136*	2,337[2]	3,761[2]	1,265	2,035	2,010	2,934
American Samoa	217	350	43	—4,818—		7.4	...	...	—	—	—	—	—	—
Andorra	137	220	55	25,000	6,250	1.5	...	...	—	—	—	—	—	—
Angola	45,877	73,830	51	56,625	29,000	97	...	...	1,834[2]	2,952[2]	...	...	...	...
Anguilla	55	88	80	973	239	5.4	...	...	—	—	—	—	—	—
Antigua and Barbuda	341	548	44	11,188	3,321	5.6	...	...	—	—	—	—	—	—
Argentina	131,338	211,369	27	3,898,000	1,434,700	5.8	...	...	21,233[2]	34,172[2]	7,740	12,456	6,000	8,760
Aruba	236	380	100	23,409	582	2.5	...	...	—	—	—	—	—	—
Australia	530,020	852,986	50	8,770,899	1,231,359	1.6	32,964	48,127	24,389[2, 8]	39,251[2, 8]	1,359	2,187	27,018	39,448
Austria	67,791	109,100	100	2,609,390	221,672	2.7	5,949	8,685	4,128	6,643	4,556	7,332	7,743	11,305
Bahamas, The	2,548	4,100	40	88,000	5,600	2.4	...	...	—	—	—	—	—	—
Bahrain	96	155	100	81,872	24,720	3.9	...	...	—	—	—	—	—	—
Bangladesh	*98,522*	*158,551*	12	39,688	23,887	1,618	...	...	1,797[2]	2,892[2]	3,731	6,005	419	612
Barbados	1,020	1,642	79	34,850	5,282	6.3	...	...	—	—	—	—	—	—
Belgium	79,600	128,100	96	3,379,180	326,879	2.7	13,099	19,124	2,248[2]	3,618[2]	3,788	6,096	4,981	7,272
Belize	1,639	2,637	16	3,707	1,855	29	...	...	—	—	—	—	—	—
Benin	4,626	7,445	11	2,740	567	1,191	...	...	360	580	85.5	137.6	121.1	176.8
Bermuda	150	240	100	17,852	2,768	2.8	...	...	—	—	—	—	—	—
Bhutan	1,345	2,165	79	1,587	916	524	...	...	—	—	—	—	—	—
Bolivia	25,468	40,987	4	69,836	130,796	33	*1,133*	*1,654*	2,263[2]	3,642[2]	491	790	364	532
Botswana	8,388	13,500	15	16,426	24,786	27	...	...	442	712	...	...	0.9	1.3
Brazil	881,349	1,418,396	9	10,516,000	1,067,000	12	158,085	230,800	18,503[2]	29,777[2]	10,167	16,362	68,401	99,863
British Virgin Islands	66	107	62	—3,589—		3.3	...	...	—	—	—	—	—	—
Brunei	1,156	1,860	50	84,527	11,051	2.4	...	...	12[15]	19[15]	—	—	—	—
Bulgaria	23,237	37,397	91	1,030,090	587,400	5.5	7,071	10,324	2,668	4,294	4,973	8,004	12,553	18,327
Burkina Faso	6,979	11,231	12	21,182	6,647	238	...	...	342	550	422	680	322	470
Burma	14,416	23,200	17	*43,300*	*44,700*	386	...	...	1,949[2]	3,137[2]	2,707	4,356	378	552
Burundi	3,196	5,144	7	8,977	7,342	297	...	...	—	—	—	—	—	—
Cameroon	32,408	52,157	5	72,449	41,301	90	*175*	*255*	729[2]	1,173[2]	291	468	427	624
Canada	549,445	884,249	81	11,118,071	3,095,243	1.8	29,033	42,388	74,600	120,000	1,297	2,088	161,866	236,320
Cape Verde	1,398	2,250	29	3,000	1,343	70	...	...	—	—	—	—	—	—
Cayman Islands	110	177	68	7,800	1,200	2.3	...	...	—	—	—	—	—	—
Central African Republic	12,600	20,278	2	1,035	827	1,453	...	...	—	—	—	—	—	—
Chad	*24,855*	*40,000*	*1*	7,000	5,000	390	...	...	—	—	—	—	—	—
Chile	49,144	79,089	12	638,000	263,000	14	...	...	5,037[2]	8,107[2]	790	1,272	1,701	2,484
China	584,000	940,000	20	794,452	2,231,981	341	24,315	35,500	35,200[2]	56,600[2]	176,700	284,300	648,700	947,100
Christmas Island	20	32	...	759	383	2.9	...	...	15	24	...	...	...	...
Cocos (Keeling) Islands	15	24	...	...	...	...	...	...	—	—	—	—	—	—
Colombia	66,001	106,218	10	840,776	391,433	24	6,745	9,848	2,023[2]	3,255[2]	112	180	477	696
Comoros	466	750	53	*3,600*	*2,000*	68	...	...	—	—	—	—	—	—
Congo	6,835	11,000	5	30,500	78,600	15	*46*	*67*	498	802	268	432	353	516
Cook Islands	174	280	...	689	728	12	...	...	—	—	—	—	—	—
Costa Rica	21,942	35,313	14	119,067	76,287	13	...	...	435[2]	700[2]	56	90	102.7	150.0
Côte d'Ivoire	34,175	55,000	9	182,956	52,491	41	...	...	816[2]	1,314[2]	533[18]	858[18]	363[18]	530[18]
Cuba	21,100	34,000	30	200,100	164,500	27	*1,116*	*1,630*	3,033	4,881	1,374	2,212	1,693	2,472
Cyprus	7,441	11,975	49	127,300	54,600	3.9	...	...	—	—	—	—	—	—
Czechoslovakia	45,556	73,316	100	2,694,994	425,174	5.0	8,357	12,201	8,150	13,116	12,387	19,935	47,536	69,401
Denmark	43,614	70,190	100	1,617,832	216,365	2.8	6,400	9,400	1,535	2,471	2,818	4,535	1,227	1,791
Djibouti	1,799	2,895	7	12,049	951	33	...	...	66	106	...	...	90.1	131.6
Dominica	489	787	60	*2,713*	*1,250*	21	...	...	—	—	—	—	—	—
Dominican Republic	10,788	17,362	29	101,979	61,307	39	...	...	88	142	—	—	—	—
Ecuador	22,486	36,187	16	256,812	36,691	33	...	...	600[2]	965[2]	18	29	5	7
Egypt	19,661[21]	31,641[21]	51[21]	757,925	354,139	43	14,641	21,375	3,335	5,367	16,300	26,232	1,912	2,792

based upon registration, are relatively accurate, though some countries round off figures, and unregistered vehicles may cause substantial undercount. There is also inconsistent classification of vehicle types; in some countries a vehicle may serve variously as an automobile, a truck, or a bus, or even as all three on certain occasions. Relatively few countries collect and maintain commercial road traffic statistics.

Data on national railway systems are generally given for railway track length rather than the length of routes, which may be multitracked. Siding tracks usually are not included, but some countries fail to distinguish them. The United States data include only class 1 railways, which account for about 94 percent of total track length. Passenger traffic is usually calculated from tickets sold to fare-paying passengers. Such statistics are subject to distortion if there are large numbers of nonpaying passengers, such as military personnel, or if season tickets are sold and not all the allowed journeys are utilized. Railway cargo traffic is calculated by weight hauled multiplied by the length of the journey. Changes in freight load during the journey should be accounted for but sometimes are not, leading to discrepancies.

Merchant fleet and tonnage statistics collected by Lloyd's registry service for vessels over 100 gross tons are quite accurate. Cargo statistics, however, reflect the port and customs requirements of each country and the reporting rules of each country's merchant marine authority (although these, increasingly, reflect the recommendations of the International Mar-

itime Organization); often, however, they are only estimates based on customs declarations and the count of vessels entered and cleared. Even when these elements are reported consistently, further uncertainties may be introduced because of ballast, bunkers, ships' stores, or transshipped goods included in the data.

Airport data are based on scheduled flights reported in the commercial *Official Airline Guide* and are both reliable and current. The comparability of civil air traffic statistics suffers from differing characteristics of the air transportation systems of different countries; data for an entire country may be two to three years behind those for a single airport.

Outside of Europe, where standardization of data on inland waterways is necessitated by the volume of international traffic, comparability of national data declines markedly. Calculations as to both the length of a country's waterway system (or route length of river, lake, and coastal traffic) and the makeup of its stock of commercially significant vessels (those for which data will be collected) are largely determined by the nature and use of the country's hydrographic net—its seasonality, relief profile, depth, access to potential markets—and inevitably differ widely from country to country. Data for coastal or island states may refer to scheduled coastwise or interisland traffic.

merchant marine				air							canals and inland waterways (latest)				country
fleet, 1987 (vessels over 100 gross tons)	total dead-weight tonnage, 1987 ('000)	international cargo (latest)		airports with sched-uled flights, 1988	traffic (latest)						length		cargo		
		loaded metric tons ('000)	off-loaded metric tons ('000)		passengers		cargo				mi	km	short ton-mi ('000,000)	metric ton-km ('000,000)	
					passenger-mi ('000,000)	passenger-km ('000,000)	short ton-mi ('000,000)	metric ton-km ('000,000)							
—	—	—	—	1	87[1]	140[1]	5.1[1]	7.4[1]			750	1,200	...	...	Afghanistan
20	79.9	1,077	626	1	...	...	...	...			27	43	...	...	Albania
148	1,043.0	50,543	15,450	22	1,518[3]	2,433[3]	3.5[3]	5.2[3]			...	...	...	...	Algeria
2	4	195	574	3	...	...	...	...			...	...	...	...	American Samoa
—	—	—	—	—	—	—	—	—			...	...	—	—	Andorra
108	125.3	10,140	980	18	606[5]	975[5]	23.2[5]	33.9[5]			805	1,295	...	...	Angola
13	5.5	...	18	1	...	...	...	...			...	...	...	—	Anguilla
55	102.7	33	104	2	...	...	...	...			...	...	...	...	Antigua and Barbuda
434	2,853.3	37,724	5,375	63	5,420	8,722	674	984			6,800	11,000	19,326	28,215	Argentina
79[6]	7	...	...	1	...	...	...	...			...	...	...	...	Aruba
690	3,701.3	224,182	23,582	441	20,585	33,129	2,640	3,855			5,200	8,368	...	...	Australia
29	337.9	1,916	5,190	6	857	1,380	16.1	23.5			277	446	5,941	8,674	Austria
469	15,695.8	9,325	8,710	21	245[9]	394[9]	...	...			...	...	...	...	Bahamas, The
94	52.0	12,258	3,261	1	721[10]	1,160[10]	21.5[10]	31.4[10]			...	...	...	...	Bahrain
283	574.6	1,116	7,572	8	1,022	1,644	151.1	220.7			5,000	8,046	...	...	Bangladesh
37	8.6	211	460	1	93[11]	149[11]	0.8[12]	1.1[12]			...	...	...	...	Barbados
350	3,653.8	46,032	81,024	3	3,452	5,556	407.0	594.0			1,269	2,043	3,468	5,063	Belgium
3	0.8	136	144	8	...	...	...	...			513	825	...	...	Belize
13	4.8	137	1,030	5	144.2[13]	232.1[13]	27.4[13]	40.0[13]			300	500	...	...	Benin
105	3,131.5	112	462	1	...	...	...	...			...	...	...	...	Bermuda
—	—	—	—	10	2.7	4.4	...	...			...	...	—	—	Bhutan
2	22.2	...	...	22	567	912	18.4	26.9			6,214	10,000	90	132	Bolivia
—	—	—	—	8	14[14]	22[14]	0.1[14]	0.1[14]			...	...	...	...	Botswana
718	10,437.9	140,380	61,872	110	15,176	24,423	840	1,226			31,069	50,000	60,960	89,000	Brazil
32	8.5	2	52	3	...	...	...	...			...	...	...	...	British Virgin Islands
24	343.6	13,312	920	1	153.5	247.0	3.0	4.4			130	209	...	...	Brunei
205	2,302.9	3,930	25,377	13	1,840	2,961	29.5	43.1			293	471	40,167	58,643	Bulgaria
—	—	—	—	3	147.6	237.6	26.3	38.5			...	...	...	...	Burkina Faso
117	363.3	720	720	21	142	229	16	23			7,954	12,800	...	...	Burma
1	0.4	39	182	2	...	...	...	...			...	...	...	...	Burundi
47	71.8	1,040	3,188	9	360	580	76	111			1,299	2,090	...	...	Cameroon
1,238	3,502.9	143,421	60,669	61	29,963	48,222	860	1,255			1,860	3,000	...	...	Canada
29	22.1	108	286	8	16.1	26.0	1.6	2.3			...	...	...	...	Cape Verde
249	1,050.6	677	671	3	...	...	...	...			...	...	...	...	Cayman Islands
—	—	—	—	1	132.8[16]	213.7[16]	24.7[16]	36.1[16]			500	800	...	...	Central African Republic
—	—	—	—	1	147.6	237.6	26.3	38.5			1,240	2,000	...	...	Chad
264	824.9	12,632	4,480	17	1,218	1,960	94.0	137.2			450	725	5,629	8,218	Chile
1,773	18,484.2	59,580	70,680	80	11,600	18,600	450	660			68,040	109,500	518,639	757,200	China
—	—	1,202	44	1	...	...	...	...			...	...	...	...	Christmas Island
—	—	...	...	1	...	...	...	...			...	...	...	...	Cocos (Keeling) Islands
93	597.4	7,410	6,909	101	1,227	1,975	172.6	252.0			8,900	14,300	1,921	2,804	Colombia
5	2.8	10	95	3	...	...	...	...			...	...	...	...	Comoros
21	10.8	8,369	660	14	147.6	237.6	26.3	38.5			696	1,120	...	...	Congo
—	—	10	28	6	...	...	...	...			...	...	...	...	Cook Islands
24	13.6	1,532	1,653	6	347[17]	558[17]	20.1[17]	29.4[17]			454	730	...	...	Costa Rica
56	149.3	4,658	4,874	15	198.9[16]	320.1[16]	35.8[16]	52.2[16]			609	980	...	...	Côte d'Ivoire
422	1,291.1	2,196	2,232	12	1,639	2,637	23.8	34.8			149	240	...	...	Cuba
1,341	27,322.9	2,268	3,648	3	872	1,404	19.3	28.1			...	...	...	...	Cyprus
18	220.4	...	...	14	1,369	2,203	39.9	58.3			295	475	3,305	4,825	Czechoslovakia
983	6,961.1[19]	11,269	33,069	13	4,596[20]	7,397[20]	566[20]	826[20]			259	417	1,438	2,100	Denmark
7	2.7	382	1,060	3	...	...	...	...			...	...	...	...	Djibouti
6	2.5	33	51	2	...	...	...	...			...	...	...	...	Dominica
37	70.8	2,234	3,844	5	393.8	633.8	42.9	62.7			...	...	...	...	Dominican Republic
156	588.2	13,543	2,458	14	555	893	29.2	42.6			932	1,500	...	...	Ecuador
428	1,515.2	12,804	39,612	11	2,500	4,023	76.4	111.5			2,088	3,360	1,287	1,879	Egypt

Transportation (continued)

country	roads and motor vehicles (latest)								railroads (latest)					
	roads			motor vehicles			cargo		track length		traffic			
	length		paved (per-cent)	auto-mobiles	trucks and buses	persons per vehicle	short ton-mi ('000,000)	metric ton-km ('000,000)	mi	km	passengers		cargo	
	mi	km									passen-ger-mi ('000,000)	passen-ger-km ('000,000)	short ton-mi ('000,000)	metric ton-km ('000,000)
El Salvador	7,558	12,164	14	136,163	19,461	32	...	...	374[2]	602[2]	2.9	4.7	17.4	25.4
Equatorial Guinea	1,715	2,760	12	4,000	3,000	40	...	...	—	—	—	—	—	—
Ethiopia	23,532	37,871	34	41,250	19,159	720	...	...	485[23]	781[23]	217	350	86	125
Faeroe Islands	124	200	...	13,211	3,146	2.8	...	...	—	—	—	—	—	—
Falkland Islands	317	510	6	1,000	500	1.3	...	...	—	—	—	—	—	—
Fiji	2,564	4,127	13	34,380	24,318	12	...	...	660[15]	1,062[15]	...	...	...	...
Finland	47,362	76,223	57	1,619,848	196,631	2.7	13,767	20,100	5,544	8,923	1,931	3,108	5,071	7,404
France	500,055	804,765	92	21,250,000	3,406,000	2.2	75,344	110,000	21,524[2]	34,640[2]	37,222	59,904	36,165	52,800
French Guiana	691	1,112	65	27,010	1,120	3.2	...	...	—	—	—	—	—	—
French Polynesia	495	797	33	—44,000—		4.0	...	...	—	—	—	—	—	—
Gabon	4,682	7,535	8	16,093	10,503	43	...	...	416	670	12	19	71	103
Gambia, The	1,484	2,388	21	5,200	720	129	...	...	—	—	—	—	—	—
Gaza Strip			...	17,969	4,572	24	...	...	—	—	—	—	—	—
Germany, East	77,434	124,615	...	3,462,184	425,049	4.3	5,177	7,559	8,702	14,005	13,920	22,402	40,328	58,881
Germany, West	305,242	491,240	99	27,908,200	1,375,500	2.1	94,591	138,100	41,965	67,536	28,976	46,632	40,373	58,944
Ghana	17,600	28,300	20	52,864	23,375	163	...	...	592	953	126.0	201.1	50.5	73.8
Gibraltar	31	50	100	13,049	1,005	2.1	...	...	—	—	—	—	—	—
Greece	64,191	103,306	83	1,444,850	680,762	4.7	...	...	1,540[2]	2,479[2]	1,184	1,905	481.1	702.4
Greenland	96	154	41	2,037	1,320	16	...	...	—	—	—	—	—	—
Grenada	621	1,000	66	4,784	981	16	...	...	—	—	—	—	—	—
Guadeloupe	1,297	2,087	80	95,962	28,134	2.7	...	...	—	—	—	—	—	—
Guam	419	674	100	60,804	17,569	1.5	...	...	—	—	—	—	—	—
Guatemala	11,200	18,000	16	188,100	58,500	31	...	...	467[2]	751[2]	...	...	...	...
Guernsey														
Guinea	17,600	28,400	4	12,000	12,000	253	...	...	584[2]	940[2]	...	...	...	...
Guinea-Bissau	3,143	5,058	8	3,000	2,000	175	...	...	—	—	...	...	...	...
Guyana	5,524	8,890	9	25,541	7,648	24	...	...	65	109	...	...	...	...
Haiti	2,299	3,700	17	34,669	11,658	113	...	...	—	—	—	—	—	—
Honduras	10,831	17,431	12	66,666	18,759	51	...	...	571[2]	919[2]	...	...	...	...
Hong Kong	867	1,395	100	183,787	115,320	19	...	...	21	34	1,327	2,136	49	72
Hungary	18,514	29,796	98	1,660,300	201,890	5.7	6,655	9,716	8,160	13,133	6,974	11,224	15,131	22,092
Iceland	7,069	11,376	13	112,760	13,366	1.9	318	464	—	—	—	—	—	—
India	1,101,000	1,772,000	47	1,517,000	952,000	306	55,500	81,000	38,423[2]	61,836[2]	160,621	258,495	148,847	217,312
Indonesia	136,572	219,791	39	1,059,851	1,132,658	77	17,000	25,000	4,061	6,536	4,556	7,332	995	1,452
Iran	84,740	136,380	41	2,246,143	434,944	17	46,750	68,250	2,837[2]	4,567[2]	1,570	2,526	2,645	3,861
Iraq	20,653	33,238	74	491,800	246,700	21	...	...	1,268[2]	2,041[2]	624	1,005	886	1,294
Ireland	57,354	92,303	94	711,087	106,285	4.3	...	...	1,848	2,975	675	1,086	393	574
Isle of Man	357	574	58	33,404	4,302	1.7	...	...	37[2]	59[2]	...	...	...	...
Israel	7,968	12,823	100	655,827	129,033	5.6	...	...	537	865	452	727	1,276	1,863
Italy	187,223	301,307	100	22,398,000	1,863,250	2.4	98,720	144,129	12,257	19,726	25,165	40,500	11,967	17,472
Jamaica	7,680	12,360	39	42,888	26,060	34	...	...	215	346	24	40	89	129
Japan	700,600	1,127,500	58	28,653,692	19,091,587	2.6	144,058	205,941	16,016	25,776	208,032	334,796	14,121	20,617
Jersey			...	57,175	6,451	1.3	...	...	—	—	—	—	—	—
Jordan	3,519	5,663	100	158,892	73,469	12	19,133	27,934	385[2]	619[2]	3.7	6.0	864	1,262
Kampuchea	8,296	13,351	20	700	1,800	2,600	...	...	380	612	34	54	6.8	10
Kenya	33,700	54,200	12	126,188	103,844	88	...	...	1,649[2]	2,654[2]	422.5	680.0	1,252	1,828
Kiribati	398	640	...	—163—		344	...	...	—	—	—	—	—	—
Korea, North	13,670	22,000	2				...	...	2,779	4,473	...	...	...	...
Korea, South	32,475	52,264	50	664,226	627,228	32	4,955	7,234	3,914	6,299	14,641	23,563	8,789	12,831
Kuwait	1,208	1,944	100	420,643	114,607	3.5	...	...	—	—	—	—	—	—
Laos	8,067	12,983	31	15,800	3,000	200	...	...	—	—	—	—	—	—
Lebanon	4,579	7,370	85	473,372	49,560	5.0	...	...	235	378	5.3	8.6	29	42
Lesotho	2,640	4,250	12	5,129	11,962	82	...	...	1	2	—	—	—	—
Liberia	4,138	6,659	7	12,747	8,288	100	...	...	304[2]	490[2]	...	...	2,154[15]	3,145[15]
Libya	15,954	25,675	56	415,509	334,405	4.3	...	...	—	—	—	—	—	—
Liechtenstein	201	323	...	15,229	1,651	1.6	...	...	12	19	...	...	...	...
Luxembourg	3,244	5,220	99	162,481	14,869	2.1	136	198	168[2]	270[2]	171	276	414	604
Macau	56	90	100	19,513	4,773	17	...	...	—	—	—	—	—	—
Madagascar	11,560	18,610	30	21,860	14,542	283	...	...	580[2]	933[2]	129	208	129	188
Malawi	7,590	12,215	21	15,339	15,755	246	...	...	515[2]	829[2]	64	103	67	98
Malaysia	24,276	39,069	80	1,173,968	138,343	12	...	...	1,018[2]	1,639[2]	850.4[36]	1,368.5[36]	714[36]	1,042[36]
Maldives			...	336	338	270	...	...	—	—	—	—	—	—
Mali	9,756	15,700	11	22,020	6,422	280	...	...	401	646	107	173	165	241
Malta	909	1,463	93	85,598	17,824	3.3	...	...	—	—	—	—	—	—
Martinique	1,156	1,861	85	135,269	7,328	2.3	...	...	—	—	—	—	—	—
Mauritania	4,557	7,335	22	15,017	2,188	96	...	...	428[2]	689[2]	4.4	7.0	4,207	6,142
Mauritius	1,108	1,783	92	33,607	11,433	23	...	...	—	—	—	—	—	—
Mayotte	143	230	49	—1,528—		40	...	...	—	—	—	—	—	—
Mexico	140,233	230,375	45	5,028,604	2,167,000	11	...	...	16,244[2]	26,142[2]	3,868	6,225	30,283	44,212
Monaco	29	47	100	15,709	3,260	1.5	...	...	1	2	...	...	...	...
Mongolia	29,000	46,700	2	...	...	...	1,401	2,046	1,086	1,748	290	467	4,338	6,333
Montserrat	180	290	73	1,217	215	8.3	...	...	—	—	—	—	—	—
Morocco	36,784	59,198	47	527,437	247,722	29	830	1,212	1,105[2]	1,779[2]	1,216.7	1,958.1	3,392.2	4,952.6
Mozambique	12,420	19,990	25	99,400	24,700	100	...	...	2,182	3,512	163.8	263.6	207.7	303.3
Nauru	12	19	100	—1,788—		4.0	...	...	3	5	—	—	—	—
Nepal	3,918	6,306	44	14,201	9,988	574	984	1,437	33[2]	53[2]	...	...	...	...
Netherlands, The	69,996	112,648	87	4,950,000	408,711	2.7	13,184	19,249	1,755	2,824	5,542	8,919	2,089	3,050
Netherlands Antilles	510	820	...	24,000	855	9.3	...	...	—	—	—	—	—	—
New Caledonia	3,422	5,507	14	42,000	2,500	3.3	...	...	—	—	—	—	—	—
New Zealand	57,769	92,971	55	1,552,988	334,316	1.8	...	...	2,692	4,332	285	458	2,168	3,165
Nicaragua	9,319	14,997	11	46,184	30,535	44	...	...	214	344	38	60	3.2	4.7
Niger	11,806	19,000	17	23,102	9,052	189	...	...	—	—	—	—	—	—
Nigeria	77,000	124,000	48	262,550	90,731	241	...	...	2,178	3,505	1,212	1,950	1,048	1,530
Niue	142	229	54	264	64	12	...	...	—	—	—	—	—	—
Norfolk Island	50	80	66	1,802	90	1.1	...	...	—	—	—	—	—	—

merchant marine fleet, 1987 (vessels over 100 gross tons)	total deadweight tonnage, 1987 ('000)	international cargo (latest) loaded metric tons ('000)	off-loaded metric tons ('000)	air airports with scheduled flights, 1988	traffic (latest) passengers passenger-mi ('000,000)	passenger-km ('000,000)	cargo short ton-mi ('000,000)	metric ton-km ('000,000)	canals and inland waterways (latest) length mi	km	cargo short ton-mi ('000,000)	metric ton-km ('000,000)	country
14	3.3	288	1,920	1	238.7[22]	384.1[22]	1.2[22]	1.8[22]	...	...	...	...	El Salvador
2	6.7	144	51	2	4	7	0.7	1.0	104	167	...	...	Equatorial Guinea
25	94.1	711	1,955	37	346.9	558.3	71.1	103.8	70	113	...	...	Ethiopia
202	[24]	257	340	1	...	...	...	...	...	...	...	...	Faeroe Islands
5	4.1	4	6	1	...	...	...	...	...	...	...	...	Falkland Islands
60	32.4	480	576	17	317	509	4.4	6.4	126	203	...	...	Fiji
257	1,400.6	22,440	31,284	21	1,812	2,916	63.6	92.9	4,148	6,675	3,082	4,500	Finland
857	8,406.7[25]	55,968	177,348	67	24,383[26]	39,240[26]	2,188.7[26]	3,195.5[26]	9,278	14,932	4,110	6,000	France
1	[27]	27	249	7	...	...	...	...	286	460	...	...	French Guiana
34	[27]	12	523	32	...	...	...	...	...	...	...	...	French Polynesia
22	29.3	5,868	968	25[28]	...	...	...	...	994	1,600	...	...	Gabon
8	5.1	78	167	1	...	...	...	...	250	400	...	...	Gambia, The
—													Gaza Strip
377	1,880.0	11,982	13,141	2	1,646	2,649	48.4	70.7	1,441	2,319	1,669	2,437	Germany, East
1,414	5,659.1	41,868	89,484	27	19,370	31,752	2,319.7	3,386.7	3,245	5,222	35,744	52,185	Germany, West
138	143.0	1,036	2,496	4	168.4	271.0	23.1	33.7	803	1,293	...	...	Ghana
113	5,293.3	5	405	1	...	...	...	...	...	...	...	...	Gibraltar
1,948	42,775.9	22,872	29,544	29	3,967	6,384	69.4	101.4	50	80	585	854	Greece
71	[24]	291	280	21	9	14	0.16	0.24	...	...	...	...	Greenland
3	0.8	27	52	2	...	...	...	...	...	...	...	...	Grenada
9	[27]	432	1,068	7	...	...	...	...	...	...	...	...	Guadeloupe
5	[4]	87	169	1	...	...	...	...	...	...	...	...	Guam
5	6.5	1,546	2,098	2	85	136	4.9	7.1	162	260	...	...	Guatemala
—	...	...	...	1	...	...	...	...	...	...	...	...	Guernsey
19	2.9	10,106	489	2	17.9	28.8	1.7	2.5	805	1,295	...	...	Guinea
17	2.8	33	129	1	6	9	0.7	1.0	...	...	...	...	Guinea-Bissau
100	20.4	1,548	636	18	104	168	12	18	3,700	6,000	...	...	Guyana
2	0.2	169	680	2	...	...	...	...	60	100	...	...	Haiti
503	741.7	1,392	1,138	5	242.6[29]	390.5[29]	9.8[29]	14.3[29]	289	465	...	...	Honduras
409	13,471.0	22,872[30]	47,664[30]	1	...	...	...	...	...	...	...	...	Hong Kong
16	109.4			4	799	1,286	10.9	15.9	1,008	1,622	1,311	1,914	Hungary
396	151.0	943	1,565	31	1,719	2,767	193.1	281.9	...	...	58	84	Iceland
803	10,890.8	24,668	39,490	95	10,655	17,148	459.8	671.2	10,054	16,180	...	...	India
1,734	2,963.2	147,552	40,596	130	5,704	9,180	155.0	226.2	13,409	21,579	17,000	25,000	Indonesia
370	7,222.8	78,667	12,205	13	2,963	4,768	90.4	132.0	626	1,008	...	...	Iran
142	1,683.1	97,830	8,638	2	746	1,200	36	52	631	1,015	...	...	Iraq
153	162.9	5,373	13,316	5	1,551	2,496	54.1	79.0	454	731	...	...	Ireland
—		3	183	1	...	...	...	...	...	...	...	...	Isle of Man
62	612.6	8,052	11,323	5	4,526[31]	7,284[31]	443.9[31]	648.1[31]	...	...	...	...	Israel
1,571	12,178.3	38,832	200,184	30	8,694[32]	13,992[32]	589.0[32]	859.0[32]	994	1,600	192	280	Italy
14	18.5	5,485	3,672	6	1,316	2,118	18.3	26.7	...	...	...	...	Jamaica
9,822	54,669.4	83,736	621,108	65	44,076	70,934	2,450	3,650	1,100	1,770	140,974	205,818	Japan
—	—	...	...	1	...	...	...	...	...	...	...	...	Jersey
4	47.7	11,268	8,748	2	2,230	3,589	113.6	165.9	...	...	19,202	28,035	Jordan
3	3.8	10	100	1	...	...	...	...	2,300	3,700	...	...	Kampuchea
28	4.8	1,628	3,792	16	652.5[33]	1,050.0[33]	93.7[33]	136.8[33]	...	...	...	...	Kenya
7	2.8	12	29	18	6.2	10.0	0.03	0.04	3	5	...	...	Kiribati
73	603.0	609	4,640	3	52	84	1.4	2.0	1,400	2,250	...	...	Korea, North
1,899	11,452.8	41,760	112,056	5	8,329	13,404	1,005.2	1,467.5	1,000	1,600	8,928	13,034	Korea, South
236	3,183.6	43,973	7,253	1	2,304	3,708	235.0	343.2	...	...	...	...	Kuwait
—	—	—	—	7	6	9	0.7	1.0	2,850	4,587	...	...	Laos
214	729.5	151	1,053	1	516	831	334	488	...	...	...	...	Lebanon
—		—		15	7.8	12.5	0.07	0.10	—	—	—	—	Lesotho
1,574	97,957.9	14,640	1,729	1	11	17	0.07	0.10	230	370	...	...	Liberia
102	1,447.5	47,172	6,975	12	1,139[34]	1,672[34]	3.7[34]	5.4[34]	—	—	...	...	Libya
—	—	—	—						17	27	...	...	Liechtenstein
—				1	57	92	0.2	0.3	23	37	208	304	Luxembourg
6	[35]	313	502	—	...	...	...	...	...	...	...	...	Macau
72	82.2	348	768	35	262.6	422.6	26.0	38.0	727	1,170	...	...	Madagascar
1	0.3	...	...	5	74	119	0.7	1.1	891	1,434	...	...	Malawi
498	2,388.3	44,816	22,809	35	4,727	7,608	242.9	354.7	4,534	7,296	...	...	Malaysia
38	159.9	20	70	2	...	...	...	...	...	...	...	...	Maldives
—	—	—	—	9	68	110	0.4	0.6	1,128	1,815	18	27	Mali
271	2,852.6	192	1,668	1	462	744	3.0	4.5	...	...	...	...	Malta
6	[27]	338	1,014	1	...	...	...	...	...	...	...	...	Martinique
94	13.9	9,956	486	9	147.6	237.6	26.3	38.5	500	800	...	...	Mauritania
33	240.7	892	1,165	2	472.6	760.6	61.7	90.0	...	...	...	...	Mauritius
—				1	...	...	...	...	...	...	...	...	Mayotte
651	2,173.0	89,580	11,244	74	10,491[37]	16,884[37]	109.5[37]	159.8[37]	1,800	2,900	...	...	Mexico
—	—	...	...	1	—	1					...	...	Monaco
				1	200	322	4.9	7.1	247	397	2.9	4.3	Mongolia
1	1.0	5	42	1	...	...	...	...	...	...	...	...	Montserrat
315	579.9	26,840	14,097	14	1,283	2,064	26.6	38.8	600	1,000	2,622	3,828	Morocco
105	29.0	2,110	2,427	7	306	492	7.6	11.1	2,330	3,750	...	...	Mozambique
7	92.9	1,483	59	1	148[38]	238[38]	1.1[38]	1.6[38]	...	...	...	...	Nauru
—	—	—	—	5	186[34]	300[34]	4.2[34]	6.2[34]	...	...	...	...	Nepal
1,228	5,122.9[39]	82,716	249,576	6	12,106[40]	19,483[40]	2,390[40]	3,490[40]	3,939	6,340	22,455	32,784	Netherlands, The
41	[7]	12,032	11,529	5	234[42]	377[42]	1.2[42]	1.8[42]	...	...	...	...	Netherlands Antilles
12	[27]	1,936	713	10	154[43]	244[43]	...	...	...	...	...	...	New Caledonia
124	371.3	9,648	7,368	36	5,598	9,009	242.5	354.0	1,000	1,609	1,503	2,195	New Zealand
22	17.0	333	1,453	1	47	76	3.8	5.5	1,379	2,220	...	...	Nicaragua
—				1	147.6	237.6	26.3	38.5	186	300	...	...	Niger
213	855.0	62,830	11,490	16	1,405	2,261	23.2	33.9	5,328	8,575	...	...	Nigeria
—				1	...	...	...	...	...	...	...	...	Niue
—	—	—	—	1	...	...	...	...	...	...	...	...	Norfolk Island

Transportation (continued)

country	roads length mi	km	paved (per-cent)	auto-mobiles	trucks and buses	persons per vehicle	cargo short ton-mi ('000,000)	metric ton-km ('000,000)	track length mi	km	passenger-mi ('000,000)	passenger-km ('000,000)	cargo short ton-mi ('000,000)	metric ton-km ('000,000)
Norway	53,529	86,147	68	1,592,195	282,805	2.2	4,514	6,590	2,622[2]	4,219[2]	1,379	2,220	2,065	3,015
Oman	13,781	22,179	15	120,367	106,097	5.9	...	—	—	—	—	—	—	—
Pacific Is., Trust Terr. of the	1,000	1,600	25	4,206	2,311	20	...	...	—	—	—	—	—	—
Marshall Islands	...	...		...	...	...			—	—	—	—	—	—
Micronesia, Fed. States of	140	226	17	...	...	...			—	—	—	—	—	—
Northern Mariana Islands	186	300	...						—	—	—	—	—	—
Palau	16	26	...	—1,687—		7.2			—	—	—	—	—	—
Pakistan	67,437	108,530	43	500,163	154,537	158	...		7,842	12,620	10,513	16,919	5,356	7,819
Panama	6,039	9,719	33	120,995	41,753	13			354[2]	569[2]	—	—	...	...
Papua New Guinea	12,263	19,736	6	18,748	30,497	69			—	—	—	—	—	—
Paraguay	9,186	14,783	13	84,986	41,986	26			274[2]	441[2]	14	22	24	34
Peru	42,479	68,363	11	377,208	226,533	33			2,144[2]	3,451[2]	301.4	485.1	704.1	1,028
Philippines	101,156	162,325	13	773,242	110,192	63			658[2]	1,059[2]	104	168	41	60
Pitcairn Island	4	6	—	3		18			—	—	—	—	—	—
Poland	158,000	254,000	61	3,961,953	912,984	7.7	25,363	37,029	16,683	26,848	30,153	48,526	82,681	120,712
Portugal	32,282	51,953	86	1,958,872	502,267	4.1	4,950	7,220	2,241[2]	3,607[2]	3,606	5,803	992	1,448
Puerto Rico	5,813	9,355	86	1,102,155	197,012	2.5			—	—	—	—	—	—
Qatar	671	1,080		131,044	3,710	2.8			—	—	—	—	—	—
Réunion	1,684	2,710	81	138,081	45,017	2.1			—	—	—	—	—	—
Romania	45,235	72,799	64	250,000	130,000	58	4,080	5,957	6,972	11,221	19,313	31,082	50,830	74,215
Rwanda	7,500	12,070	5	7,396	10,357	353	140	200	—	—	—	—	—	—
St. Helena and Ascension	109	175	74	—1,250[47]—		4.7[47]			—	—	—	—	—	—
St. Kitts and Nevis	190	305	41	3,540	690	11			—	—	—	—	...	...
St. Lucia	460	740	78	7,049	2,084	22			—	—	—	—	—	—
St. Pierre and Miquelon	75	120	50	1,932	637	2.4			—	—	—	—	—	—
St. Vincent and the Grenadines	463	745	58	5,069	2,279	15			—	—	—	—	—	—
San Marino	147	237	...	17,387	1,809	1.2			—	—	—	—	—	—
São Tomé and Príncipe	199	320	66	1,774	265	41			—	—	—	—	—	—
Saudi Arabia	52,573	84,866	36	2,165,675	1,966,172	2.7			544[2]	875[2]	44	71	220	321
Senegal	9,315	15,000	30	76,142	37,105	58	375	547	562[2]	905[2]	18.9	30.5	287.1	462.3
Seychelles	164	264	61	3,531	1,277	14			—	—	—	—	—	—
Sierra Leone	4,635	7,459	16	23,500	6,763	121	36	53	52	84	...	...	...	...
Singapore	1,643	2,644	95	236,120	113,671	7.5			16	26	...	...	...	...
Solomon Islands	1,300	2,100	12	1,350	1,708	92			—	—	—	—	—	—
Somalia	10,697	17,215	15	17,754	9,533	204			—	—	—	—	—	—
South Africa	114,243	183,851	28	3,130,288	1,203,383	6.6			14,669[2]	23,607[2]	11,077	17,826	63,603	92,859
Bophuthatswana	3,900	6,300	13						165	265	...	...	...	...
Ciskei	2,203	3,546	9.1						60	96	...	...	...	...
Transkei	5,468	8,800	...						174	280	...	...	...	...
Venda	762	1,226	4.1						8	13	...	...	...	...
South West Africa/Namibia	34,230	55,088	9	—103,715—		11			1,454[2]	2,340[2]	...	...	1,300	1,900
Spain	198,211	318,991	56	9,761,968	1,727,172	3.4	80,000	116,800	7,917[2]	12,742[2]	9,567	15,396	7,858	11,472
Sri Lanka	53,573	86,218	35	165,224	138,253	53			1,208	1,944	1,225	1,972	139.5	203.6
Sudan, The	4,100	6,599	59	99,400	17,211	203			2,974[2]	4,786[2]	714	1,149	1,096	1,600
Suriname	5,541	8,917	26	35,052	14,600	8.1			54	87	...	...	...	...
Swaziland	1,692	2,723	23	18,830	10,843	22			230[2]	370[2]			73	107
Sweden	81,296	130,834	74	3,253,601	243,696	2.4	14,505	21,177	7,279	11,715	3,954	6,363	12,707	18,552
Switzerland	43,855	70,578	96	2,678,911	231,934	2.3	4,552	6,646	3,128	5,034	5,719	9,204	4,772	6,967
Syria	18,440	29,677	93	111,455	129,270	44	1,075	1,570	1,272	2,047	559	900	970	1,416
Taiwan	12,356	19,885	84	1,254,955	472,708	11	6,410	9,359	2,983	4,800	5,256	8,459	1,706	2,490
Tanzania	50,887	81,895	4	—84,190—		250			1,615	2,600	737[55]	1,186[55]	527[55]	770[55]
Thailand	51,740	83,268	40	545,479	856,375	37			2,321[2]	3,735[2]	5,950	9,576	1,866	2,724
Togo	4,349	7,000	24	41,122	20,241	53			250	403	65	105	11	16
Tokelau	...	...	...						—	—	—	—	—	—
Tonga	269	433	65	1,561	3,397	19			—	—	—	—	—	—
Trinidad and Tobago	4,909	7,900	46	241,595	82,361	3.6			—	—	—	—	—	—
Tunisia	16,584	26,689	56	271,133	182,679	16	637	930	1,314[2]	2,115[2]	492	792	1,323	1,932
Turkey	235,039	378,259	16	1,087,234	590,581	31	29,232	42,678	5,076[2]	8,169[2]	3,833	6,168	4,973	7,260
Turks and Caicos Islands	75	121	20	—1,563—		5			—	—	—	—	—	—
Tuvalu	5	8	—			...			—	—	—	—	—	—
Uganda	17,605	28,332	22	32,155	5,646	400			799[2]	1,286[2]	...	...	...	...
U.S.S.R.	604,000	971,500	84	8,255,000	7,254,000	17	97,000	142,000	90,471	145,600	242,000	390,000	2,626,250	3,834,500
United Arab Emirates	2,709	4,360	61	61,146	16,618	18			—	—	—	—	—	—
United Kingdom	217,733	350,407	100	16,981,000	2,932,000	2.9	69,933	102,100	23,645[58]	38,053[58]	19,126[58]	30,780[58]	10,915[58]	15,936[58]
United States	3,879,538	6,243,340	88	135,431,112	40,760,227	1.4	672,000	981,000	184,235	296,497	12,000	19,200	867,722	1,266,852
Uruguay	30,952	49,813	20	281,275	49,813	8.8	500	730	1,859[2]	2,991[2]	206	332	140	204
Vanuatu	660	1,062	24	3,087	2,500	8.4			—	—	—	—	—	—
Venezuela	62,492	100,571	33	2,300,000	1,248,000	5.0			273[2]	439[2]	10.7	17.1	7.9	11.6
Vietnam	37,282	60,000	17	100,000	200,000	163	5,664	8,269	1,568	2,523	2,087	3,359	595	869
Virgin Islands (U.S.)	660	1,062	100	—48,800—		2.2			—	—	—	—	—	—
Wallis and Futuna	62	100	...						—	—	—	—	—	—
West Bank	...	...		38,326	13,629	16			—	—	—	—	—	—
Western Sahara	3,790	6,100	8	6,284	424	20			—	—	—	—	...	...
Western Samoa	1,296	2,085	14	1,757	2,593	37			—	—	—	—	—	—
Yemen (Aden)	3,500	5,600	30	17,800	19,400	53			—	—	—	—	—	—
Yemen (Ṣanʿāʾ)	23,129	37,223	6	121,015	176,203	28			—	—	—	—	—	—
Yugoslavia	74,192	119,401	59	2,957,116	283,180	7.2	15,753	22,999	5,745	9,246	7,704	12,398	18,886	27,573
Zaire	28,379	45,671	18	89,471	16,807	268			3,623	5,252	181[63]	292[63]	1,339[63]	1,954[63]
Zambia	23,135	37,232	17	105,783	94,780	30			1,340	2,157	347	558	1,072	1,565
Zimbabwe	48,421	77,927	17	253,470	28,839	29			2,109[2]	3,394[2]	...	...	9,390	13,710

[1]Bakhtar Afghan Airlines only. [2]Route length. [3]Air Algérie international flights only. [4]Included with the United States. [5]TAAG airline only. [6]Includes Netherlands Antilles. [7]Included with The Netherlands. [8]Government railways only. [9]Bahamasair only. [10]Apportionment of ¼ of international flights of Gulf Air (jointly run by Bahrain, Oman, Qatar, and United Arab Emirates) only. [11]Caribbean Airways only. [12]Caribbean Air Cargo only. [13]Cotonou airport only. [14]Air Botswana only. [15]For industrial purposes only. [16]Air Afrique only. [17]Lasca only. [18]Traffic between Ouagadougou, Burkina Faso, and Abidjan, Côte d'Ivoire. [19]Includes Faeroe Islands and Greenland. [20]Apportionment of ²/₇ of SAS operations only. [21]National roads only. [22]TACA airline only; data for nine months only. [23]Includes 100 km of the Chemin de Fer Djibouti-Ethiopien in (CDE) Djibouti. [24]Included with Denmark. [25]Includes French overseas territories. [26]Air France, UTA, and Air Inter only. [27]Included with France. [28]Includes airfields. [29]TAN and SAHSA airlines only. [30]Includes transshipments. [31]El Al only. [32]Alitalia only. [33]Kenya Airways only. [34]International

merchant marine				air					canals and inland waterways (latest)				country
fleet, 1987 (vessels over 100 gross tons)	total dead-weight tonnage, 1987 ('000)	international cargo (latest)		airports with scheduled flights, 1988	traffic (latest)				length		cargo		
		loaded metric tons ('000)	off-loaded metric tons ('000)		passengers		cargo		mi	km	short ton-mi ('000,000)	metric ton-km ('000,000)	
					passenger-mi ('000,000)	passenger-km ('000,000)	short ton-mi ('000,000)	metric ton-km ('000,000)					
1,979	9,656.3	58,379	20,121	48	5,485[20]	8,828[20]	622.4[20]	908.6[20]	980	1,577	7,860	11,476	Norway
31	16.4	22,143	4,028	6	553[10]	890[10]	16.3[10]	23.8[10]	...	...	...	...	Oman
22	[4]	26	117	11	188	302	3.9	5.6	...	...	...	...	Pacific Is., Trust Terr. of the
...	...	...	...	2	...	...	...	...	...	...	...	...	Marshall Islands
...	...	...	...	5	...	...	...	...	...	...	...	...	Micronesia, Fed. States of
...	...	2	56	3	...	...	...	...	...	...	...	...	Northern Mariana Islands
...	...	...	...	1	...	...	...	...	...	...	...	...	Palau
74	565.7	4,248	15,936	29	4,554	7,329	219.7	320.7	...	...	...	...	Pakistan
5,136	70,435.8	1,120	2,023	6	342	551	38.2	55.8	497	800	...	...	Panama
92	44.9	2,052	1,749	177	291	468	7.0	10.2	6,798	10,940	...	...	Papua New Guinea
40	49.2	...	...	1	290	466	1.4	2.0	1,900	3,100	...	...	Paraguay
635	1,036.2	11,789	3,456	22	1,314	2,114	183.2	267.4	5,300	8,600	...	...	Peru
1,394	14,827.7	12,624	20,736	42	5,734[44]	9,228[44]	168.9[44]	246.6[44]	2,000	3,219	...	...	Philippines
...	...	...	...	...	...	...	...	...	...	...	...	...	Pitcairn Island
719	4,728.4	31,608	17,388	12	1,365	2,196	8.2	12.0	2,479	3,989	1,110	1,620	Poland
286	1,048.2[45]	6,168	18,561	18	2,781[46]	4,476[46]	91.1[46]	133.0[46]	510	820	...	...	Portugal
29	[4]	[4]	[4]	8	...	...	...	...	...	...	...	...	Puerto Rico
61	460.9	13,527	2,127	1	721[10]	1,160[10]	21.4[10]	31.4[10]	...	...	...	...	Qatar
6	[27]	336	1,128	1	...	...	...	...	...	...	...	...	Réunion
430	4,893.3	11,863	31,055	15	2,115	3,403	50.0	73.0	1,071	1,724	1,655	2,417	Romania
...	...	...	...	2	...	...	...	...	...	...	...	...	Rwanda
2	2.8	1	32	1	...	...	...	...	...	...	...	...	St. Helena and Ascension
2	0.6	33	37	2	...	...	...	...	...	...	...	...	St. Kitts and Nevis
7	2.5	195	281	2	...	...	...	...	...	...	...	...	St. Lucia
5	[27]	20	56	1	...	...	...	...	...	...	...	...	St. Pierre and Miquelon
145	1,132.8	67	109	4	...	...	...	...	...	...	...	...	St. Vincent and the Grenadines
—	—	—	—	—	—	—	—	—	—	—	—	—	San Marino
3	1.2	11	19	1	...	...	...	...	...	...	...	...	São Tomé and Príncipe
349	4,588.3	163,766	37,521	21	9,332	15,018	299.4	437.2	...	...	...	...	Saudi Arabia
149	36.0	2,327	2,733	12	207.8[34]	253.0[34]	12.6[34]	18.4[34]	935	1,505	...	...	Senegal
6	2.5	6	215	6	...	...	...	...	...	...	...	...	Seychelles
34	3.4	1,216	607	1	76[48]	122[48]	1.3[48]	1.9[48]	500	800	447	652	Sierra Leone
700	11,924.6	46,992	71,304	1	14,212	22,872	791.4	1,155.4	...	...	...	...	Singapore
29	5.4	250	305	21	74[49]	114[49]	0.02[49]	0.04[49]	...	...	...	...	Solomon Islands
27	18.9	233	1,006	14	181.4	291.9	2.7	3.9	...	...	...	...	Somalia
247	570.4	81,529	10,587	37	5,674[50]	9,132[50]	281.9[50]	411.5[50]	...	...	...	...	South Africa
—	—	—	—	1	—	—	—	—	...	...	...	...	Bophuthatswana
—	—	—	—	1	—	—	—	—	...	...	...	...	Ciskei
—	—	—	—	1	...	...	...	...	...	...	...	...	Transkei
—	—	—	—	—	—	—	—	—	...	...	...	...	Venda
—	—	—	—	8	...	...	...	...	...	...	...	...	South West Africa/Namibia
2,350	8,387.5	40,260	97,008	29	12,683	20,412	386.6	564.4	649	1,045	21,836[51]	31,880[51]	Spain
99	908.5	3,324	5,400	1	1,208	1,944	34.7	50.6	267	430	...	...	Sri Lanka
25	127.7	663	2,286	10	292.5[52]	470.7[52]	6.4[52]	9.3[52]	3,300	5,310	...	...	Sudan, The
23	13.7	6,000	1,435	5	248.9[53]	400.0[53]	33.9[53]	49.5[53]	746	1,200	...	...	Suriname
—	—	—	—	1	14	22	1.5	2.2	...	...	...	...	Swaziland
642	2,402.5	43,512	59,496	36	3,342[54]	5,378[54]	130.8[54]	190.9[54]	1,275	2,052	6,200	9,000	Sweden
30	579.9	...	...	5	8,000	12,875	496.8	725.3	40	65	108	158	Switzerland
57	93.2	6,504	6,864	5	585	942	10.7	15.7	418	672	...	...	Syria
594	6,887.0	16,300	65,765	9	9,009	14,498	2,017	2,945	...	...	...	...	Taiwan
39	32.9	635	2,602	19	155	249	1,709	2,495	726	1,168	...	...	Tanzania
254	758.4	20,892[56]	16,440[56]	22	7,009	11,280	322.8	485.9	2,500	4,000	...	...	Thailand
13	92.1	208	856	1	150	241	12.5	18.6	30	50	...	...	Togo
—	—	—	—	—	—	—	—	—	...	...	...	...	Tokelau
19	23.4	12	55	6	4.3	6.9	0.01	0.01	...	...	...	...	Tonga
50	12.5	8,327	4,267	2	1,339[57]	2,155[57]	8.6[57]	12.6[57]	...	...	...	...	Trinidad and Tobago
71	449.7	4,176	7,860	5	849	1,367	13.2	19.3	...	...	...	...	Tunisia
852	5,516.1	58,476	37,692	14	1,627	2,618	31.1	45.5	750	1,200	35	51	Turkey
13	4.3	164	156	5	...	...	...	...	...	...	...	...	Turks and Caicos Islands
2	0.5	...	...	1	...	...	...	...	...	...	...	...	Tuvalu
3	8.6	...	...	5	59.7	96.1	16.0	23.4	...	...	...	...	Uganda
6,705	28,555.7	164,670	84,830	52	121,800	196,000	2,317	3,384	76,550	123,200	175,081	255,630	U.S.S.R.
240	1,159.9	57,865	7,097	2	2,213[10]	3,562[10]	65.3[10]	95.3[10]	...	...	...	...	United Arab Emirates
2,165	11,676.5	153,696	147,504	47	31,697	51,012	1,286.9	1,878.8	1,424	2,291	28,600	41,700	United Kingdom
6,366	29,111.3[59]	324,132[60]	424,668[60]	824	381,728	614,333	8,181	11,944	25,482	41,009	421,000	615,000	United States
90	218.1	596[61]	1,518[61]	7	241.9	389.3	25.3	37.0	1,000	1,600	...	...	Uruguay
88	982.2	59	61	24	...	...	...	...	...	...	...	...	Vanuatu
283	1,418.1	72,267	14,902	39	1,531	2,464	147.4	215.2	4,400	7,100	...	...	Venezuela
162	537.8	304	1,359	3	183	295	4.1	6.0	11,000	17,702	...	...	Vietnam
3	[4]	105.5	648.3	6	...	...	...	...	...	...	...	...	Virgin Islands (U.S.)
8	[27]	—	—	2	...	...	...	...	...	...	...	...	Wallis and Futuna
—	—	...	...	—	...	...	...	...	...	...	...	...	West Bank
—	—	42	15	1	...	...	...	...	...	...	...	...	Western Sahara
6	34.8	43	87	3	...	...	...	...	...	...	...	...	Western Samoa
26	13.2	1,299	4,659	7	62	100	1.2	1.7	...	...	...	...	Yemen (Aden)
12	414.6	237	2,426	5	358[62]	577[62]	43.5[62]	63.6[62]	...	...	...	...	Yemen (Şan'ā')
498	4,939.9	9,888	25,380	17	4,355	7,008	75.8	110.7	1,243	2,001	2,689	3,926	Yugoslavia
30	75.9	2,057	779	22	237[64]	382[64]	8.3[64]	12.2[64]	9,300	15,000	678	990	Zaire
—	—	—	—	11	380	612	18.0	26.3	1,398	2,250	...	...	Zambia
—	—	—	—	8	388	624	10.1	14.8	...	...	...	...	Zimbabwe

flights only.   [35]Included with Portugal.   [36]Peninsular Malaysia and Singapore.   [37]Aeronaves de Mexico and Mexicana only.   [38]Air Nauru only.   [39]Includes Netherlands Antilles and Aruba.   [40]KLM only.   [41]Included with Aruba.   [42]Antillean Airlines only.   [43]Air Caledonie only.   [44]PAL only.   [45]Includes Macau.   [46]TAP only.   [47]St. Helena only.   [48]Sierra Leone Airlines international traffic only.   [49]Solair only.   [50]SAA only.   [51]Coastal shipping only.   [52]Sudan Airways only.   [53]Suriname Airways only.   [54]Apportionment of 3/7 of SAS operations only.   [55]Tanzania Railways Corporation only.   [56]Port of Bangkok only.   [57]BWIA international traffic only.   [58]British Railways only; excludes Northern Ireland.   [59]Includes American Samoa, Guam, Trust Territory of the Pacific Islands, Puerto Rico, and U.S. Virgin Islands.   [60]Includes Puerto Rico.   [61]Port of Montevideo only.   [62]Yemen Airways only.   [63]Zaire National Railways only.   [64]Air Zaire only.

Communications

Virtually all the states of the world have a variety of communications services available to their citizens: newspapers (although only daily papers are included in this table), radio broadcast systems, and telephone, post office, and telegraph facilities; most also have television and telex. The focus of this table, therefore, is on the relative density and distribution of communications services. Unfortunately, the availability of information about the infrastructure and traffic volume of these national systems often runs behind the capabilities of the systems themselves. Certain countries publish no information about themselves; others publish data analyzed according to a variety of fiscal, calendar, religious, or other years; still others, while they possess such data almost simultaneously with the end of the business year, may not see them published except in company reports of limited distribution. Even when they are published in national statistical summaries, it may be only after a delay of up to several years.

The data also differ in their completeness and reliability. Data for some kinds of communications apparatus and traffic are relatively easy to collect; telephones, for example, even mobile, must be installed, and service recorded so that it may be charged. But in most countries radios may be purchased by anyone and turned on whenever desired; car radios are seldom enumerated or licensed separately. As a result, data on distribution and use of radio and television apparatus may be collected in a variety

of ways—on the basis of numbers of subscribers, licenses issued, periodic sample surveys, census or housing surveys, or private consumer surveys.

The United Nations Educational, Scientific and Cultural Organization (Unesco) publishes in its *Statistical Yearbook* extensive data on newspapers, radio, and television that have been collected from standardized questionnaires. The quality and recency of its data, however, depend on the completion and timely return of each questionnaire by national authorities, and response rates depend on a variety of factors. In general, however, response rates for inquiries by international organizations in communications are better than in other fields because these organizations and the responsible authorities in each country must conduct day-to-day business and, hence, have a better ongoing relationship.

Newspaper statistics are especially difficult to collect and compare. Newspapers continually are founded, cease publication, merge, or change frequency of publication. Data on circulation, sales, and readership are often incomplete, slow to be aggregated at the national level, or regarded as proprietary for either private or governmental publications. In some countries circulation data are virtually nonexistent. In others no daily newspaper exists.

The commercially published annual *World Radio TV Handbook* (A. G. Sennitt, editor) is a valuable source of information on broadcast media

Communications

country	daily newspapers (latest)			radio, 1986			television, 1987			telephones, 1986		traffic ('000 calls)		
	number	total circulation ('000)	circulation per 1,000 population	transmitters (latest)	receivers (all types) ('000)	persons per receiver	transmitters (latest)	receivers (all types) ('000)	persons per receiver	receivers ('000)	persons per receiver	local	long-distance	international
Afghanistan	12	107	7	5	150	93	1	20	709	31[1]	443[1]	——————110[2]		18[2]
Albania	2	145	52	32	210	15	216	52	59	4.8[5]	580[5]	...	...	...
Algeria	4	480	23	55	3,250	6.9	44	1,550	15	822	28	——————1,488,957[6]		962,386[6]
American Samoa	2	9	243	1	40[4]	0.9[4]	3	8.0[8]	4.5[8]	7.3	5.0	...	...	798
Andorra	—	—	—	9	8.0	5.8	54	4.0[8]	12[8]	21[1]	1.9[1]	...	...	...
Angola	4	112	14	73	400	22	3	33	276	40[5]	202[5]	66,140[10]	260[10]	320[10]
Anguilla	—	—	—	4	6.3	1.1	—	...	...	1.4	4.8	——————1,211		58
Antigua and Barbuda	1	6	66	5[12]	35	2.3	2	27	3.0	11[1]	7.2[1]	36,400[1, 6]	3,600[1, 6]	3,223[4, 13]
Argentina	227	...	...	175	19,866	1.6	183	5,950	5.3	3,206	9.8	16,698,605[6, 9]	30,969[18]	5,864
Aruba	2	9	131	4	12[19]	5.1[19]	1	19	3.4	22	3.0	——————67,565[13]		5,749[13]
Australia	61	4,740	308	284	30,000[4]	0.5[4]	386	6,500[4]	2.3[4]	8,727[4]	1.8[4]	7,363,533	1,250,729	40,388
Austria	33	...	...	604	2,639	2.9	951	2,660	2.8	3,843	2.0	——————26,064,267[4, 13]		321,017[13]
Bahamas, The	3	28	118	6	120	2.0	1	50	4.8	108	2.2	——————3,161[4]		3,642[4]
Bahrain	5	21	50	5	142	2.9	2	135	3.1	119	3.5	——————215,265[6]		35,296[13]
Bangladesh	54	554	6	22	775[4]	130[4]	11	311[4]	324[4]	151[4]	664[4]	——————347,600[22]		84[13, 22]
Barbados	2	41	162	4	335	0.8	1	62	4.1	91	2.8	——————483,000[9]		1,182[4]
Belgium	37	2,500	250	41	4,516	2.2	32	2,984[8]	3.3[8]	4,556	2.2	2,289,315[6]	2,538,153[6]	106,896
Belize	—	—	—	11	88	1.9	1	12	15	9.7[4]	17[4]	...	...	844[4, 13]
Benin	1	12	3	7	300	14	2	16	276	15	274	...	7,103[4, 13]	2,382[13]
Bermuda	1	18	314	6	100	0.6	2	67	0.9	52[1]	1.1[1]	...	...	18,397[4, 13]
Bhutan	—	—	—	1	13[19]	104[19]	—	0.2[9]	6,180[9]	1.8[4]	684[4]	...	...	...
Bolivia	13	311	50	184	3,700[4]	1.7[4]	42	390	17	182	37	...	44,509[13]	3,795[13]
Botswana	1	30	22	9	140[4]	7.8[4]	...	...	...	19[4]	57[4]	77,580[6]	1,031[13]	6,984[13]
Brazil	279	8,528	62	1,729	50,540	2.7	137	36,000	4.0	12,580	11	18,000,000	1,623,000	13,100
British Virgin Islands	—	—	—	1	7.0[4]	1.7[4]	1	2.7	4.4	3.7[4]	3.2[4]	——————4,000[1, 6]		2,150[4, 13]
Brunei	—	—	—	8	74	3.1	2	48	5.0	36	6.6	...	22,720[6, 10]	8,275[13]
Bulgaria	17	2,834	316	39	1,997	4.5	744	1,693[8]	5.3[8]	1,876	4.8	25,800[9]	600[9]	6,130[9]
Burkina Faso	2	7	0.8	9	311	26	2	42	198	17	482	——————16,132[1, 6]		1,130[1, 13]
Burma	6	533	14	6	800	48	2	68	581	51[9]	723[9]	——————65,000[22]		72[9]
Burundi	1	20	4	13	230	21	1	4.5	1,110	7.9	622	1,205[9]	533[9]	635[13]
Cameroon	1	66	6	26	800	12	21	5.0	2,172	49[1]	210[1]	...	...	22,905[4, 13]
Canada	110	5,700	225	1,607	28,800[4]	0.9[4]	2,002	15,709	1.6	19,598	1.3	34,672,867	1,959,151	28,235[26]
Cape Verde	—	—	—	5	50	6.8	...	0.5[4]	668[4]	4.44	76[4]	——————126[1]		377[1]
Cayman Islands	2	14	624	4	20	1.1	...	1.2[8]	19[8]	14	1.6	——————16,353[1, 6]		4,412[4, 13]
Central African Republic	1	0.2	0.1	4	125	22	...	1.4[9]	1,817[9]	7.0[4]	380[4]	16	1[13]	61
Chad	1	2	0.3	7	100	51	...	...	...	4.7	1,114	4,379[13]	109[13]	269[13]
Chile	33	1,145	91	295	14,000	1.1	131	2,330	5.4	796	16	1,544,966[4]	62,919[4]	13,585[4]
China	222	...	...	571	253,900[19]	4.2[19]	c. 5,400	92,140	12	7,059	149	——————903,200		17,660
Christmas Island	—	—	—	1	2.5[4]	0.9[4]	1	...	...	...	...	...	...	...
Cocos (Keeling) Islands	—	—	—	1	0.25[4]	2.5[4]	—	...	...	0.18[9]	3.1[9]	...	...	...
Colombia	30	1,862	61	439	7,980	3.5	49	5,500	5.5	2,289	13	17,061,200[13]	1,200,600[13]	49,869[13]
Comoros	—	—	—	4	100[19]	4.2[19]	...	...	...	0.50[9]	740[9]	——————940[3]		14[3]
Congo	3	24	11	10	200	10	1	5.5	396	19	115	7,245	2,940	425
Cook Islands	1	2	116	5	4.5	3.8	...	...	...	2.8[4]	6.2[4]	...	...	270[4, 13]
Costa Rica	5	201	78	123	200	13	14	470	5.5	344	7.5	787,652[13]	445,062[13]	17,708[13]
Côte d'Ivoire	2	130	12	25	1,210	8.8	11	625	18	88[2]	97[2]	...	...	1,500
Cuba	17	1,290	126	160	3,232	3.2	78	2,000	5.2	543	19	——————125,800		1,500
Cyprus	12	78	144	6	171	3.9	29	164	4.3	244	2.7	——————795,730[6]		1,094,309[6]
Czechoslovakia	30	4,372	280	126	4,209[4]	3.7[4]	81	4,368[8]	3.5[8]	3,707	4.2	5,651,000	415,000	7,770
Denmark	47	1,855	363	49	2,052	2.5	32	1,954	2.6	4,195	1.2	2,547,000	1,594,000	68,000
Djibouti	—	—	—	2	32	14	1	14	34	8.3	56	——————16,709[6]		2,431[13]
Dominica	—	—	—	4	35	2.5	...	...	...	6.9[4]	12[4]	——————6,000[1, 6]		779[4, 13]
Dominican Republic	8	294	44	126	800	8.2	19	425	16	186[1]	34[1]	...	...	...
Ecuador	7	538	57	370	2,750[4]	3.4[4]	27	600	17	352	28	...	...	12,700[13]
Egypt	17	...	...	154	12,000	3.9	74	3,860	13	1,394	35	4,353,000[13]	253,000[13]	27,300[13]
El Salvador	5	253	52	79	1,200	4.1	5	425	12	129	39	390,217[6]	260,144[6]	19,710[13]
Equatorial Guinea	2	1	3	5	35	9.1	1	2.5	131	1.4[5]	209[5]	...	...	...
Ethiopia	3	47	1	9	2,000	22	18	70	659	132	344	308,208[6]	4,647	2,393[13]
Faeroe Islands	—	—	—	4	18	2.6	23	10	4.7	20[1]	2.3[1]	...	...	445
Falkland Islands	—	—	—	2	1	1.9	1	...	...	0.44[4]	4.4[4]	——————4[5]		1,151[4, 13]

and has complete and timely coverage. It depends on data received from broadcasters, but because some do not respond, local correspondents and monitors are used in many countries, and some unconfirmed or unofficial data are included as estimates. Data on transmitters may be complicated by new or changing technology in areas like the use of low-powered relays (secondary, or repeater installations) for local rebroadcast or use of satellite relays.

The statistics on telephones, telegraph, and telex are derived mainly from the UN-affiliated International Telecommunication Union's (ITU's) *Yearbook of Common Carrier Telecommunication Statistics* with additional statistics from national and regional intergovernmental sources. A number of countries report incomplete telephone data: the national total may exclude figures for some telephone companies, or some portion of the national territory; some countries supply statistics only on telephone exchange lines; some island states report only radio telephones. A number of countries omit data on public coin-box telephones; their statistics, thus, reflect an undercount. The traffic data for telephone calls may represent any one of three quantities: "pulses," a measure of mechanical activity rather than an enumeration of actual conversations; minutes of connect time; or "calls," the practical equivalent of a conversation between individuals. Depending on a country's metering system, multiple counting

of a single call may occur. Telegraph traffic is reported predominantly as "messages," or sometimes in words; telex traffic is usually reported in minutes of connect time, but, depending on the national metering system, it may also be given as "pulses," or minutes.

Post office statistics are compiled mainly from the Universal Postal Union's annual summary *Statistique des services postaux*. Postal services, unlike the other media discussed above, tend most often to be operated by a single national service, to cover a country completely, and to record traffic data according to broadly similar schemes (although the details of *classes* of mail handled may differ). Some countries do not enumerate domestic traffic or may record only international traffic requiring handling charges.

Unesco surveys, the diverse industry sources cited above, and scores of national statistical sources have also been used in the compilation of this table because no single source is complete.

... Not available.

—None, nil, or not applicable.

post offices, 1986			telegraph, 1986			telex, 1986				country
number	persons per office	pieces of mail handled ('000)	total traffic ('000)	national traffic ('000)	international outgoing traffic ('000)	subscriber lines	traffic ('000 minutes)			
							total	national	international outgoing	
349[3]	36,447[3]	11,218[3]	183[2]	95[2]	88[2]	125[4]	...	...	169[4]	Afghanistan
292[3]	7,328[3]					...				Albania
2,185[4]	10,516[4]	358,480[4]	2,402[7]	2,173[7]	229[7]	7,759	31,658	23,243	8,415	Algeria
...	...		14	—	14	80	101	...	...	American Samoa
...	...	3,483[9]				...	...	...	...	Andorra
133	64,662	8,223	198[10]	154[10]	44[10]	587[10]	...	...	1,599[10]	Angola
22	318	435	0.9[9]	0.004[9]	334,[7]	36	...	...	10[11]	Anguilla
153	5,333[3]	2,262[14, 15, 16, 17]	...	...	315[4,7]	108[4]	...	...	189[4]	Antigua and Barbuda
5,690	5,371	677,978	14,051	13,822	229	11,620	...	135,982[2, 6]	9,190[9]	Argentina
20	20	20	8.7	3.3	5.4	21	304	17	287	Aruba
4,537	3,449	3,396,433	3,048	2,665	383	45,025	64,797[11]	49,416[11]	15,318[11]	Australia
2,650[4, 21]	2,851[4, 21]	2,915,155[4]	1,366	1,148	218	25,774	113,344[4]	76,321[4]	36,642	Austria
127	1,650	48,485	25	12	13	544	1,127	76	1,052	Bahamas, The
10	35,080	47,100	125	18	107	2,092	10,160	2,273	7,887	Bahrain
7,684	13,206	514,335	3,998[22]	3,470[22]	528[22]	1,090[4]	...	90[11, 22]	2,437[4]	Bangladesh
16	15,875	18,392[15]	...	...	29[4]	353[4]	741[4]	2.6[4]	738[4]	Barbados
1,842[21]	5,352[21]	2,993,473	809	592	216	27,570	135,813	62,392	73,421	Belgium
112	1,518	3,096	209[9]	10[9]	270[4,7]	974	..	..	138[4]	Belize
178	24,011	5,980	...	53[4]	...	284	14,294[6]	76[4]	330	Benin
153	3,333[3]	...	...	...	572[4,7]	530[4]	...	...	1,616[4]	Bermuda
										Bhutan
81[3]	16,728[3]	2,266[23]	...	...	...	...	...	...	...	Bolivia
458[3]	11,572[3]	54,609[3]	197	173	24	1,170	2,743	1,496	1,248	Botswana
150	7,519	39,685	...	...	292[7]	651	2,672	1,159	1,513	Brazil
11,631	11,899	3,474,867[24]	27,715	27,624	91	88,390	420,300	400,200	20,100	British Virgin Islands
9	1,222	9[4, 25]	...	...	77[4,7]	58[1]	...	...	77[4]	
13	16,923	4,785	...	1.5	25[7]	500	...	...	811	Brunei
2,857[3]	3,101[3]	...	7,593[9]	7,393[9]	199[9]	6,030[9]	30,733[9]	27,463[9]	3,270[9]	Bulgaria
216[4]	37,037[4]	22,891	...	...	221	313	...	...	501[1]	Burkina Faso
1,114	33,707	79,737	1,028[9]	997[9]	31[9]	130	...	...	472	Burma
17[4]	266,088[4]	1,616[4, 14]	5.1	1.6	3.5	191	...	...	293	Burundi
261[4]	33,823[4]	64,248[4, 23]	917[1]	889[1]	28[1]	1,650[4]	...	...	3,002[4]	Cameroon
13,153	1,962	7,843,109[24]	...	...	574[4, 26]	42,000	...	...	14,962	Canada
59[21]	5,733[21]	2,210	52[1]	41[1]	11[1]	80[4]	170[1]	0.6[1]	210[4]	Cape Verde
12	1,667	4,281	...	...	396[4,7]	246	...	...	463[4]	Cayman Islands
76	32,310	...	73	48	25	154	...	...	380	Central African Republic
32	161,875	1,501	750[7]	71[7]	679[7]	110	292	11	282	Chad
1,061	10,627	172,723[15]	2,391	2,332	59	6,915	16,665	11,517	5,148	Chile
50,969	20,799	4,959,433[15, 17, 24]	198,595	197,498	1,097	5,391	...	...	12,360	China
2[9]	1,600[9]	...	...	...	...	...	...	...	...	Christmas Island
4[9]	154[9]	...	...	...	...	...	...	...	...	Cocos (Keeling) Islands
1,622	17,163	191,000	20,438	20,366	72	6,251	31,898	26,097	5,801	Colombia
9[3]	38,889[3]	1,732[27]	...	173	...	61[4]	...	...	83[4]	Comoros
133[4]	14,394[4]	19,770[4]	115	89	25	468	...	...	809	Congo
12	1,458	1,815	36[1]	26[1]	10[1]	72[4]	...	115[5]	91[4]	Cook Islands
330[4]	7,879[4]	29,039[4]	272[4]	227[4]	45[4]	1,623	2,553	583	1,970	Costa Rica
1,135	8,590	63,824[14]	581[2]	508[2]	73[2]	1,821[4]	...	...	3,304[4]	Côte d'Ivoire
826	12,348	1,060,099[28]	...	17,376	7,671[7]	3,945	35,039	33,353	1,686	Cuba
720	935	37,098[14, 15]	144	98	46	3,479	6,689	2,378	4,310	Cyprus
6,634	2,340	77,288[25]	9,366	9,095	271	11,119	...	70,805[6]	6,481	Czechoslovakia
1,287	3,982	1,697,771	309	196	113	13,367	59,611	18,138	41,473	Denmark
5[9]	60,000[9]	1,623[9]	1.9	0.2	19	195	560	24	535	Djibouti
63[9]	1,274[9]	2,051[9]	...	...	244[4,7]	494	...	...	82[4]	Dominica
154[3]	25,807[3]	21,741[29]	...	...	...	...	...	...	...	Dominican Republic
526	18,341	26,634	...	...	48	3,030	6,971[9]	3,882[9]	3,563	Ecuador
8,843	5,451	461,582	10,587	9,880	707	6,081	17,985	8,300	9,685	Egypt
394	13,548	28,961	1,658	1,640	18	879	4,778	3,806	972	El Salvador
19	20,474	...	...	...	...	...	...	...	...	Equatorial Guinea
483	86,957	32,389[14, 15, 17]	306	292	14	727	2,169	971	1,198	Ethiopia
...	...	...	28	...	28	200	...	...	...	Faeroe Islands
...	...	233[30]	...	...	1.5[4]	17[4]	72[4]	1.1[4]	71[4]	Falkland Islands

Communications (continued)

country	daily newspapers (latest)			radio, 1986			television, 1987			telephones, 1986		traffic ('000 calls)		
	number	total circulation ('000)	circulation per 1,000 population	transmitters (latest)	receivers (all types) ('000)	persons per receiver	transmitters (latest)	receivers (all types) ('000)	persons per receiver	receivers ('000)	persons per receiver	local	long-distance	international
Fiji	2	53	76	14	400	1.8	...	...	...	58	12	—166,917[6]—		3,507[13]
Finland	66	2,665	542	115	2,515	2.0	214	1,822	2.7	3,028[4]	1.6[4]	2,040,200	426,660	20,440
France	95	11,369	205	840	58,000[19]	1.0[19]	10,670	18,168	3.1	34,346[4]	1.6[4]	—87,606,000[6]—		
French Guiana	2	17	191	15	44	1.9	14	6.5	14	28	3.1	—112,080[6]—		
French Polynesia	3	23	129	14	84	2.1	15	27	6.9	41	4.4	—48,200[6]—		3,600[13]
Gabon	2	33	35	34	145	8.1	8	37	32	14[1]	81[1]	13,560[6,9]	34,800[6,9]	288,000[6,9]
Gambia, The	1	2	3	7	110	7.0	...	...	...	3.5[4]	215[4]	3,700[4]	475[4]	350[4]
Gaza Strip	—	—	—	...	...	...	...	...	...	...	...	...	...	...
Germany, East	39	9,300	559	130	6,699[19]	2.5[19]	576	6,182	2.7	3,755	4.4	1,351,300	776,779	13,321
Germany, West	660	25,439	417	469[32]	25,916	2.4	5,718	23,011	2.6	39,128	1.6	18,057,434	10,463,446	468,198
Ghana	4	460	35	17	3,000	4.4	6	175	77	73	182	187[18]	105[18]	105[18]
Gibraltar	1	3	103	3	10	2.8	4	7.0	4.2	12	2.5	...	...	2,550[4, 13]
Greece	130	...	...	67	4,000	2.5	372	1,750	5.7	3,579[19]	2.8[19]	7,719,198	687,659	30,345
Greenland	—	...	...	38	14	3.9	7	12	4.5	12[1]	4.4[1]	...	...	...
Grenada	—	—	—	1	50	2.0	1	...	...	6.6[19]	16[19]	—148[9]—		1,124[4, 13]
Guadeloupe	1	25	75	20	100[19]	3.4[19]	21	70	4.8	107	3.1	—369,570[6]—		
Guam	1	18	149	5	102	1.2	2	83	1.5	31[1]	3.7[1]	...	...	...
Guatemala	9	...	...	104	500	16	24	475	18	128[4]	63[4]	8,583[4]	12,468[4]	2,301[4]
Guernsey	1	16	277	1	...	...	1	...	...	51	1.1	—43,446—		442
Guinea	—	—	—	9	200	31	1	12	532	16[10]	310[10]	...	96[9, 13]	986[9, 13]
Guinea-Bissau	1	6	7	2	26	34	...	...	...	3.0	297	...	...	...
Guyana	2	78	98	13	350	2.3	...	...	...	33	24	—88,458[4, 6]—		289[4]
Haiti	6	22	4	35	200	27	4	25	215	82	65	...	452[5]	818[5]
Honduras	7	293	65	209	300	15	39	140	33	50	91	254,100[13]	159,600[13]	14,200[13]
Hong Kong	68	3,189	602	24	2,740	2.0	52	1,357	4.1	2,654[19]	2.1[19]	—4,100,000[4]—		184,203[13]
Hungary	29	2,511	236	51	5,500[4]	1.9[4]	109	2,958[8]	3.5[8]	1,609[19]	6.6[19]	...	...	...
Iceland	6	100	415	34	73	3.3	130	71	3.5	125[1]	1.9[1]	...	...	1,716
India	1,423	...	...	191	50,000	15	174	9,300	84	4,057	192	13,824,000[6]	218,000	5,736
Indonesia	97	3,049	18	745	32,800[4]	5.1[4]	207	8,948[8]	198	764	221	4,949,040[5, 6]	...	2,481[5]
Iran	13	...	...	349	10,000	4.8	585	2,100[8]	23[8]	1,884	26	11,340,148	276,970	5,716
Iraq	6	324	20	46	2,800	5.6	35	610	26	886[4]	17[4]	—1,518,817[5, 6]—		13,329[4, 13]
Ireland	7	709	200	26	2,050[4]	1.7[4]	77	795	4.5	942[4]	3.8[4]	—2,286,467[6]—		37,238[13, 34]
Isle of Man	—	—	—	1	22[10]	3.0[10]	...	22[9]	3.0[9]	...	...	...	...	...
Israel	25	1,148	263	63	700	6.2	56	655	6.8	1,935[19]	2.2[19]	2,200,000[6]	4,300,000[6]	53,300[13]
Italy	99	...	...	2,179	14,817	3.9	2,711	14,605[8]	3.9[8]	26,874	2.1	13,090,435	5,705,802	141,138
Jamaica	2	90	38	20	910	2.6	8	387	6.1	152	15	...	...	55,725[1, 13]
Japan	124	70,669	578	1,134	94,700	1.3	13,119	31,509[8]	3.9[8]	66,636[4]	1.8[4]	—42,000,000[22]—		320,000[13]
Jersey	1	24	300	1	...	...	1	...	...	73	1.1	49,006	8,882	654
Jordan	5	195	71	17	700	3.9	46	250	11	114[1]	22[1]	...	...	21,412[13]
Kampuchea	10	...	...	6	200	37	2	30	256	7.3[10]	790[10]	...	...	...
Kenya	5	269	13	33	2,100	10	4	192	117	292	74	6,841[18]	7,221[18]	150[18]
Kiribati	—	—	—	10	10	6.6	...	115	5.5[5]	1.1[4]	57[4]	6[5, 13]	17[4, 13]	434[4, 13]
Korea, North	11	...	...	32	1,920	11	11	180	119	109	2,009[9]	...	...	...
Korea, South	26	11,000	265	214	38,605[4]	1.1[4]	144	8,643	4.9	9,288	4.5	40,302,000[6]	104,000[6]	15,424
Kuwait	8	453	253	14	500	3.6	10	700	2.7	310	5.9	...	...	9,400
Laos	3	13	4	18	367[19]	10[19]	2	32	118	8.1[4]	450[4]	3,879[4]	2[4]	23[4]
Lebanon	38	583	215	22	2,000	1.4	18	500	5.5	150[5]	18[5]	...	...	...
Lesotho	3	44	28	3	100	16	3	1.5	1,085	14[4]	112[4]	...	...	...
Liberia	5	...	...	14[36]	500	4.6	5	43	55	7.7[5]	263[5]	...	...	...
Libya	1	40	10	30	500	7.9	13	236	18	102[5]	33[5]	...	...	...
Liechtenstein	2	15	546	...	9.2	3.0	...	8.7[8]	3.2[8]	27	1.0	7,266[5]	12,727[5, 13]	5,242[5, 13]
Luxembourg	6	130	365	7	228	1.6	3	92	4.0	157	2.3	—165,917[4]—		80,865[4, 13]
Macau	14	242	568	5	84	5.0	4	70	6.3	61	7.1	—123,852—		6,299
Madagascar	5	116	11	29	2,020	5.1	41	100	106	44	240	23,540	4,890	318
Malawi	2	32	5	16	1,060	7.2	...	...	...	45	174	—134,700[3, 6]—		3,290[13]
Malaysia	42	...	...	83	6,600[4]	2.4[4]	65	1,565	11	1,381	12	—8,490,642[6]—		25,796[13]
Maldives	2	...	...	2	21[19]	9.2[19]	2	3.8	51	2.5[4]	75[4]	3,600[4]	68[4]	260[4]
Mali	1	40	5	14	300	25	1	0.9	8,497	9.6[1]	760[1]	...	90[5]	97[5]
Malta	4	81	235	3	92[4]	3.7[4]	1	128[4]	2.7[4]	140	2.4	—75,000—		1,651
Martinique	1	30	90	46	55	6.0	10	45	7.4	120	2.8	—298,729[6]—		
Mauritania	1	...	...	4	200	8.5	1	1.1	1,676	4.8[9]	350[9]	7,712[6, 9]	85[9, 13]	310[9, 13]
Mauritius	8	77	74	5	200	5.2	4	128	8.1	62	17	—60,059[9]—		2,600[4, 13]
Mayotte	1	...	...	1	30	2.3	...	...	...	...	...	...	...	...
Mexico	392	11,256	142	887	25,278	3.2	430	9,500	8.5	8,237[19]	10[19]	2,909,921	672,110	39,961
Monaco	2	11	408	12	9.7[4]	2.9[4]	5	18	1.6	37[4]	0.8[4]	—13,200[4, 6]—		208,700[4, 6]
Mongolia	2	96	85	22	194	9.7	20	888	21[8]	49	38	...	...	...
Montserrat	—	—	—	5[37]	9.0[4]	1.3[4]	1	1.2[8]	9.9[8]	3.5[4]	3.4[4]	—4,674[4, 6]—		688[4, 13]
Morocco	8	282	12	34	3,000	7.5	77	1,206	19	325	70	—779,314[6]—		
Mozambique	2	81	6	40	500	28	1	10	1,452	62	232	101,317[1, 13]	2,635[5]	317
Nauru	...	...	...	1	5.5[1]	1.5[1]	...	...	...	1.6	5.1	—1,800—		300
Nepal	58	...	...	4	2,012	8.5	1	27	651	24[1]	650[1]	—4,432[1, 13]—		1,002[4, 13]
Netherlands, The	43	4,579	315	50	4,809	3.0	29	4,633	3.2	9,080	1.6	3,378,000	2,721,000	140,187
Netherlands Antilles	5	66	375	18[38]	149	1.2	3	32	5.5	504[4, 20]	5.8[4, 20]	681,133[9, 13]	8,848[9, 13]	11,671[9, 13]
New Caledonia	2	24	158	25	85	1.8	35	36	4.3	321	4.6[1]	—25,680[6]—		3,230[13]
New Zealand	32	1,055	324	90	2,800[4]	1.2[4]	567	940[8]	3.5[8]	2,194	1.5	—829,210[13]—		66,082[13]
Nicaragua	4	219	62	44	300	11	7	175	20	50[1]	64[1]	—272,503[1, 6]—		5,069[1, 13]
Niger	1	5	0.7	17	300	22	12	25	280	12[4]	563[4]	—57,366[5, 6]—		2,231[4, 13]
Nigeria	26	...	...	77	15,680	6.7	41	2,000	54	265	397	86,947[4, 6]	1,140[4, 18]	25,257[4, 13]
Niue	—	—	—	1	0.91	3.2[1]	—	—	—	0.50[1]	5.9[1]	...	...	...
Norfolk Island	—	—	—	2	1.5[19]	1.3[19]	1	0.4[1]	4.7[1]	1.02	2.0	402[13]		23[13]
Norway	63	2,008	482	764	1,510	2.8	1,389	1,454	2.9	2,579[1]	1.6[1]	—6,745,470[6]—		203,944[13]
Oman	3	30	24	14	500	2.6	34	400[8]	3.2[8]	74	18	—386,282[6]—		13,634[13]
Pacific Is., Trust Terr. of the	—	—	—	...	...	...	...	...	...	9.2[5]	165[5]	...	...	...
Marshall Islands	—	—	—	2	...	...	...	...	...	...	...	...	...	...
Micronesia, Fed. States of	...	...	...	4	17	5.4	3	1.13	87	...	...	...	...	...
Northern Mariana Islands	—	—	—	3	10.4	2.0	1	4.1	5.2	...	...	...	...	...
Palau	...	...	...	1	...	...	1	1.6	9.0	0.85[1]	15[1]	...	...	...
Pakistan	126	1,220	12	51	5,250	20	19	1,880	57	613	168	—3,182,630[6]—		2,130
Panama	9	197	89	85	900	2.5	14	476	4.8	232	9.6	742,952	140,118	3,529
Papua New Guinea	1	28	8	54	225	15	10	230[4]	14[4]	63	54	—64,762—		2,740[4]

post offices, 1986			telegraph, 1986			telex, 1986	traffic ('000 minutes)			country
number	persons per office	pieces of mail handled ('000)	total traffic ('000)	national traffic ('000)	international outgoing traffic ('000)	subscriber lines	total	national	international outgoing	
225	3,179	28,253[15]	132	125	7	681	...	1,143[6]	1,232	Fiji
3,632[9]	1,340[9]	1,098,005[9]	536	477	59	8,300	25,150	9,900	15,250	Finland
17,297[31]	3,196[31]	16,804,900[31]	12,156	10,681	1,475	134,293	541,612	392,792	148,820	France
...	...	...	19	16	3	284	664	570	94	French Guiana
91	1,857	12,533	79	59	20	232	716	39	677	French Polynesia
...	...	13,435[3]	272[9]	146[9]	126[9]	801[4]	2,721[9]	876[9]	2,286[4]	Gabon
...	...	...	11[4]	3[4]	8[4]	85[4]	122[4]	12[4]	110[4]	Gambia, The
...	...	...	...	...	...	...	...	...	...	Gaza Strip
11,972	1,390	1,453,628	13,333	10,967	2,366	16,724	...	...	9,353	Germany, East
17,826	3,423	15,291,212	5,471	3,831	1,640	164,952	561,961	373,263	188,698	Germany, West
997	12,243	102,053	154	33	121	406	1,081	98	983	Ghana
4	7,300	5,175	10[4]	4[4]	6[4]	188[4]	436[4]	8[4]	428[4]	Gibraltar
1,221[21]	8,162[21]	425,515	2,862	2,646	216	21,643	52,923	34,088	20,834	Greece
...	...	...	...	...	...	...	...	...	...	Greenland
51[3]	2,157[3]	...	...	0.2[5]	29[4]	53[4]	...	...	117[4]	Grenada
44[3]	7,500[3]	...	106	101	5	689	990	862	128	Guadeloupe
...	...	...	...	...	...	...	...	...	...	Guam
...	...	54,301[33]	...	...	2,907[4,7]	1,182[4]	...	...	597[4,11]	Guatemala
22	2,545	12,418[24]	1.3	0.8	0.5	324	...	...	...	Guernsey
...	...	30,809[16]	50[9]	21[9]	29[9]	195[9]	...	...	415[9]	Guinea
...	...	...	...	...	...	...	...	...	...	Guinea-Bissau
131	6,489	32,272	...	...	...	142	365[11]	52[11]	313[11]	Guyana
132[3]	33,106[3]	1,046,472[16]	...	...	...	...	...	...	...	Haiti
508[3]	7,264[3]	60,689[3]	19[1]	1[1]	18[1]	806	3,639	2,525	1,113	Honduras
147	38,184	617,454	936	8	928	28,813	83,592	36,607	46,985	Hong Kong
3,218	3,301	1,821,847	12,371	11,944	427	11,345	172,017[2,6]	73,654[6]	9,008	Hungary
137	1,781	38,823[9]	590	576	14	520	1,685	271	1,414	Iceland
144,396	4,745	12,193,669	61,294	59,584	1,710	30,180	...	281,341[6]	50,663	India
16,950	9,939	431,937	7,281[5]	7,142[5]	139[5]	10,407[4]	...	440,683[5,6]	10,450[4]	Indonesia
3,815[4]	12,389[4]	256,751[4,14,15,17]	5,768	5,701	67	4,764	22,746[4]	16,272[4]	6,424	Iran
288[9]	48,995[9]	193,996[9]	...	844[9]	426[4]	2,187[4]	7,668[4]	1,652[4]	6,016[4]	Iraq
2,096[3]	1,662[3]	482,153[15,16]	152	122	30	7,143	34,319	21,008	13,311	Ireland
37	1,748	26,944	...	...	...	...	...	...	...	Isle of Man
1,404[4]	3,050[4]	410,000[4]	528	380	148	6,080	22,852	16,500	6,352	Israel
14,373	3,986	7,481,940	24,050	22,016	2,034	69,363	371,433	212,882	158,551	Italy
788[4]	2,779[4]	...	273[1]	195[1]	78[1]	506[4]	...	...	1,007[4]	Jamaica
23,698	5,134	18,108,732	40,649	40,050	599	45,000	165,822[10]	111,103[10]	51,181	Japan
24	3,358	41,193	...	...	...	512	...	...	1,525[1]	Jersey
783	3,571	101,174	...	...	152	2,612	...	...	3,914	Jordan
...	...	10,320[27]	...	...	...	...	...	...	...	Kampuchea
853	20,938	210,639	1,368	1,212	156	2,290	4,981	1,371	3,610	Kenya
5[3]	10,800[3]	374[30,35]	38[4]	35[4]	3[4]	28[4]	107[1]	57[1]	72[4]	Kiribati
...	...	...	...	...	...	...	...	...	...	Korea, North
2,830	14,545	1,349,458	11,384	11,251	133	10,000	11,423[4,11]	3,125[4,11]	8,229[11]	Korea, South
57	31,579	122,261[14,15,17]	548	114	435	3,271	10,907	3,835	7,072	Kuwait
...	...	4,496[3]	5,066[4,7]	4,894[4,7]	172[4,7]	37[4]	...	...	47[4]	Laos
...	...	...	156[4]	91[4]	65[4]	...	...	...	...	Lebanon
130	11,538	18,377[15]	56[1]	7[1]	49[1]	219[1]	287[1]	142[9]	166[9]	Lesotho
50	30,427	13,960[15,17]	...	...	...	...	...	...	...	Liberia
317	10,943	92,348[4]	...	...	...	...	...	...	...	Libya
12	2,283	15,574[24]	...	...	...	...	...	...	...	Liechtenstein
106	3,471	158,781	46[4]	18[4]	28[4]	2,391[4]	10,474[4]	2,105[4]	8,369[4]	Luxembourg
8	50,000	6,718	31	0.6	30	641	977	189	788	Macau
8,844	1,228	40,683	183	172	11	387	988	127	861	Madagascar
263[4]	23,828[4]	113,975[4]	221	200	21	549	...	...	853	Malawi
5,698	2,827	852,739	...	873	4,315[7]	11,383	...	...	9,639	Malaysia
264	6,978[4]	1,367[4]	...	...	6[4]	150[4]	...	...	256[4]	Maldives
122	66,308	8,578	...	...	...	928	2,692	342	2,350	Mali
16[3]	22,500[3]	37,366[3]	45[4]	22[4]	23[4]	562	1,153	953	200	Malta
443[3]	7,273[3]	...	98	93	5	...	...	...	...	Martinique
...	...	3,035[3]	42[9]	28[9]	14[9]	231[4]	...	3,560[6,9]	192[4]	Mauritania
109	9,546	31,435	...	...	41[4]	444[4]	1,315[4]	141[4]	1,174[4]	Mauritius
...	...	...	0.026	0.022	0.004	35	...	...	...	Mayotte
7,075	10,948	628,601	13,190	12,962	228	23,916	186,932[10]	171,343[10]	13,306[4]	Mexico
...	...	...	12[4]	7[4]	5[4]	672[4]	...	...	2,338[4]	Monaco
382[3]	3,900[3]	...	...	...	...	...	...	...	...	Mongolia
114	1,090[4]	394[4]	...	...	...	33[4]	...	...	31[4]	Montserrat
1,130	20,091	175,307	1,072	953	119	6,729	4,222[11]	2,185[11]	2,037[11]	Morocco
328	43,783	22,694	...	117[22]	40[4]	722	...	782[6]	1,679	Mozambique
1[4]	7,000[4]	168[4]	...	...	22	17	54	0.3	54	Nauru
...	...	...	1,196[4]	1,111[4]	85[4]	230[4]	...	...	581[4]	Nepal
2,878	5,078	5,529,200	723	415	308	40,200	...	375,705[4,6]	88,064	Netherlands, The
144[4,20]	19,458[4,20]	14,045[4,20]	...	...	978[9,20]	635	...	...	1,307	Netherlands Antilles
267	562	18,914	34	9	25	195	512[1]	21[1]	491[1]	New Caledonia
1,242	2,553	838,656[14]	1,226	928	298	6,471	19,753	11,453	8,299	New Zealand
...	...	35,890[27]	770[1]	755[1]	15[1]	391[10]	1,572[1]	425[1]	1,147[1]	Nicaragua
255	28,059	3,995	621[4]	598[4]	23[4]	297[4]	...	...	529[4]	Niger
3,466	28,444	1,111,452[15]	484[4]	431[4]	53[4]	4,848[4]	...	11,502[4,6]	3,661[4]	Nigeria
...	...	...	9[4]	...	...	...	...	...	...	Niue
1	2,000	919	0.7	—	0.7	24	2	—	2	Norfolk Island
2,738	1,524	1,737,835	351	252	99	11,026	40,009	19,565	20,444	Norway
103	14,563	19,886[14]	178	11	167	1,805	4,717	2,215	2,502	Oman
6[3]	...	...	...	...	...	...	...	...	...	Pacific Is., Trust Terr. of the
										Marshall Islands
										Micronesia, Fed. States of
...	...	...	...	...	...	...	...	...	...	Northern Mariana Islands
										Palau
12,006	8,135	650,750[24]	2,994	2,650	344	6,940	...	305[5,11]	2,960[11]	Pakistan
268	6,834	27,820	356	336	20	1,737	3,485	881	2,603	Panama
114	34,182	40,202	804[4]	61[4]	17	1,376	3,412[4]	1,800[4]	1,553	Papua New Guinea

Communications (continued)

country	daily newspapers (latest)			radio, 1986			television, 1987			telephones, 1986		traffic ('000 calls)		
	number	total circulation ('000)	circulation per 1,000 population	transmitters (latest)	receivers (all types) ('000)	persons per receiver	transmitters (latest)	receivers (all types) ('000)	persons per receiver	receivers ('000)	persons per receiver	local	long-distance	international
Paraguay	4	123	32	48	624	6.1	5	350	11	93	41	228,533[6]	91,841[6]	6,527[13]
Peru	66	...	...	413	3,969	5.1	138	1,600	13	600[4]	33[4]	1,804,270[4, 13]	165,568[4, 13]	19,469[4, 13]
Philippines	25	2,379	44	295	7,500	7.5	43	4,114	14	820[4]	67[4]	—17,463[1]—		4,378[1]
Pitcairn Island	—	...	...	—	...	...	—	...	...	0.02[5]	2.7[5]	...		...
Poland	45	7,480	200	107	10,512[19]	3.5[19]	118	9,692	3.9	4,418	8.5	—1,139,248[1]—		4,103
Portugal	30	...	...	92	2,165	4.7	23	1,618	6.4	1,936	5.3	1,794,121[4, 6]	3,244,194[4, 6]	55,334[4, 13]
Puerto Rico	5	599	183	68	2,000	1.6	19	830	4.0	772[4]	4.3[4]	1,135,406[5]	68,538[5]	1,375[5]
Qatar	5	52	147	11	120	3.1	9	160	2.5	115	3.4	...		27,000[13]
Réunion	3	62	113	15	123	4.5	32	90	6.3	131	4.3	—310,315[6]—		
Romania	36	3,109	136	83	3,192[19]	7.1[19]	344	3,856	5.9	1,963[4]	11[4]	...		...
Rwanda	1	...	...	8[37]	250	25	...	...	—	9.1	700	8,129[6]	487[13]	453[13]
St. Helena and Ascension	—	—	—	2	3.3	2.1	—	—	—	1.0[4]	7.0[4]	...		...
St. Kitts and Nevis	—	—	—	1	22	2.0	1	7.0	6.6	3.8[4]	12[4]	...		1,065[4, 13]
St. Lucia	—	—	—	3	92	1.5	...	5.0[8]	28[8]	14	10	—13,073[1, 6]—		353[4]
St. Pierre and Miquelon	—	—	—	5	3.0	2.0	8	2.0	3.1	4.1	1.5	—12,949[6]—		
St. Vincent and the Grenadines	—	—	—	2	66	1.7	1	10	11	8.5[4]	13[4]	—5,500[1, 6]—		1,169[4, 13]
San Marino	—	—	—	1	119	2.0[9]	...	68	3.7[8]	13	1.7	—6,840[4]—		2,201[4]
São Tomé and Príncipe	—	—	—	5	28	4.0	...	...	...	2.2	50	2,384[1]	24[1]	18[1]
Saudi Arabia	10	488	41	14	3,230	3.7	64	3,750	3.3	1,382[4]	8.5[4]	2,092,778[6]	229,956	41,738
Senegal	1	31	5	19	450	15	3	57	119	34[4]	192[4]	...		10,666[13]
Seychelles	1	3	48	1	19	3.5	7	5.5	12	11[4]	5.8[4]	—3,955[4]—		671[4, 13]
Sierra Leone	1	10	3	3	225	17	2	25	152	15	253	...		637[13]
Singapore	7	698	270	21	593	4.4	8	517	5.1	1,116	2.3	3,220,000	25,270	21,611
Solomon Islands	—	—	—	5	60	4.7	...	...	...	5.0	58	3,400[4]	400[4]	613[13]
Somalia	1	...	...	4	250	24	1	...	...	6.0[4]	971[4]	...		...
South Africa	21	1,162	41	301	8,550[39]	4.1[39]	465	2,629[39]	14[39]	4,058	7.1	—12,058,861[6]—		17,491
Bophuthatswana	—	—	—	16	39	39	9	39	39	24[1]	62[1]	...	716[5]	...
Ciskei	—	—	—	2	39	39	...	39	39	6.7[1]	135[1]	4,344[5, 6]	1,281[5]	...
Transkei	—	—	—	14	39	39	...	39	39	...	...	...		...
Venda	—	—	—	6	39	39	...	39	39	...	...	...		...
South West Africa/Namibia	3	21	18	c. 40	200	5.8	8	25	48	69	17	...	29,146[4, 13]	1,017[4, 13]
Spain	102	3,053	80	264	10,810	3.6	1,027	14,871	2.6	14,748	2.6	...	2,997,571	99,327
Sri Lanka	15	850	53	59	2,073	7.8	12	500	33	125	130	—660,000[4]—		4,005[1, 13]
Sudan, The	6	105	5	6	1,500	16	20	240	105	78[4]	307[4]	...		...
Suriname	2	...	...	14	246	1.6	6	48	8.6	38	11	—121,638[6]—		3,037[13]
Swaziland	2	16	24	8	96	7.0	11	13	56	20	34	18,255[13]	25,435[13]	1,146[13]
Sweden	186	4,902	586	340	3,330	2.5	683	3,283	2.6	7,410[1]	1.1[1]	—25,497,660[6]—		7,533,344[6]
Switzerland	102	3,229	491	196	2,512	2.6	1,077	2,270	2.9	5,623	1.2	5,241,000[13]	6,200,000[13]	802,000[13]
Syria	9	201	19	29	2,000	5.3	40	405	27	637	17	664,000	83,000[13]	15,000[13]
Taiwan	29	4,917	259	...	13,500[4]	1.4[4]	28	6,085	3.2	6,078	3.2	...	9,300	77,063[13]
Tanzania	3	101	5	15	2,000	11	2	8	2,902	117	195	5,663[18]	3,863[18]	625
Thailand	31	...	...	382	7,916	6.5[4]	48	4,122[4]	13[4]	1,000	53	1,576,153	75,000	4,698
Togo	2	...	...	6	250	13	4	23	146	12[1]	241[1]	4,572[5, 6]	750[13]	1,040[13]
Tokelau	—	—	—	...	...	...	...	...	...	0.003[5]	525[5]	...		...
Tonga	—	—	—	2	50	1.9	...	...	...	4.0[1]	24[1]	1,566[1]	60[1]	716[1]
Trinidad and Tobago	4	175	146	5	552	2.2	6	345	3.6	109[1]	11[1]	2,700[9]	8,200[9]	550[9]
Tunisia	6	272	36	12	1,160	6.1	20	500	15	291	26	—721,128[6]—		479,580[6]
Turkey	338	4,188	81	55	8,227	6.3	325	5,015	11	4,222	12	—8,946,281[6]—		76,027[13]
Turks and Caicos Islands	—	—	—	2	4.8[4]	1.8[4]	...	...	...	1.6[4]	5.2[4]	—4,564[4, 6]—		587[4, 13]
Tuvalu	—	—	—	1	2.2	3.7	...	...	...	0.15	57	—	39[13]	3[13]
Uganda	2	49	3	8	600	25	9	90	173	54[9]	259[9]	...		196[9]
U.S.S.R.	727	96,414	345	...	182,790	1.5	2,882	90,000	3.1	31,000	9.0	...	1,454,400[5]	2,130[5]
United Arab Emirates	12	291	174	15[41]	434	3.9	15[41]	150	11	358	4.7	...	335,249[13]	119,965[13]
United Kingdom	107	25,159	443	705	63,528	0.9	1,643	18,953	3.0	29,518[1]	1.91[1]	20,315,000[1]	4,328,000[1]	199,400[1]
United States	1,657	62,502	259	11,561	478,000	0.5	6,837	145,000[4]	1.74	181,091[1]	1.3[1]	372,296,473	42,320,812	478,770
Uruguay	21	...	...	115	1,800	1.6	33	500	5.9	399	7.4	638,684	53,075	5,380
Vanuatu	—	...	...	4	18	7.8	...	...	...	3.2	44	—4,329[4, 6]—		719[13]
Venezuela	61	2,739	172	221	6,747	2.6	63	2,760	6.6	1,581	11	11,309,269[13]	1,535,827[13]	74,837[13]
Vietnam	4	...	...	38	6,045	10	20	505	124	115	537	—7,528[10]—		1,239[13]
Virgin Islands (U.S.)	2	19	165	8	85	1.3	2	32	3.5	52[4]	2.1[4]	96,371[5]	3,670[5]	91[5]
Wallis and Futuna	—	—	—	2	...	...	...	...	...	0.34[4]	40[4]	—255[4]—		101[4, 13]
West Bank	—	—	—	—	...	...	...	...	...	...	...	...		...
Western Sahara	—	—	—	...	...	...	...	...	...	1.05	143[5]	...		...
Western Samoa	—	—	—	6	70[4]	2.3[4]	...	5.0[4]	32[4]	6.3[4]	25[4]	...	785	208[5]
Yemen (Aden)	2	25	11	7	300	7.9	5	47	49	23[9]	94[9]	40[5]	18[5]	71[5]
Yemen (San'ā')	2	...	...	5	200	35	17	150	56	90[5]	70[5]	...	...	1,474
Yugoslavia	28	2,498	107	919	4,794	4.9	1,061	4,126[8]	5.7[8]	3,598	6.5	3,845,000[1]	7,978,000[1]	2,970,000[1]
Zaire	4	45	1.6	13	525	59	18	16	1,988	39[4]	791[4]	788[4]	1,020[4]	3,685[4]
Zambia	2	105	15	31	1,000	7.0	9	200	36	85	82	320[13]	3,654[13]	5,829[13]
Zimbabwe	3	191	23	50	315	27	9	112	77	256	33	126,913[13]	112,031[13]	17,957[13]

post offices, 1986			telegraph, 1986			telex, 1986				country
number	persons per office	pieces of mail handled ('000)	total traffic ('000)	national traffic ('000)	international outgoing traffic ('000)	subscriber lines	traffic ('000 minutes)			
							total	national	international outgoing	
405	7,481	6,461	261	222	39	931	1,161	11	1,150	Paraguay
2,633	7,675	53,307	11,765[4]	11,724[4]	41[4]	3,519	22,521[4]	128,954[6]	4,033	Peru
2,096	26,718	777,197	13,457[1]	13,243[1]	214[1]	8,792[4]	11,782[1]	3,463[1]	7,435[4]	Philippines
1	64	...	...	...	...	...	...	...	...	Pitcairn Island
8,297	4,528	1,679,062	18,651	17,943	708	30,733	...	...	9,236	Poland
7,932	1,290	527,140	1,166	1,068	98	20,898	77,070	54,803	22,267	Portugal
124[3]	24,677[3]	...	...	...	...	...	...	...	...	Puerto Rico
24	10,417	29,423[25]	117	8	109	1,055	2,679	852	1,827	Qatar
50[3]	10,340[3]	...	47	39	8	597	1,400	1,098	302	Réunion
5,046[3]	4,429[3]	795,199[16]	5,393[22]	5,150[22]	243[22]	6,750[10]	...	...	3,683[10]	Romania
26	243,485	13,552	29	27	2	100	625[10]	522[10]	276	Rwanda
10[4]	600[4]	128[4]	5[4]	...	...	11[4]	...	...	41[4]	St. Helena and Ascension
93	5,000[3]	6,381[3]	...	10[4]	172[4,7]	59[4]	...	...	118[4]	St. Kitts and Nevis
54	1,852	18,315	19[10]	...	285[4,7]	166	...	...	233[4]	St. Lucia
...	...	1,714[15,16]	1.1	0.7	0.4	45	86	60	26	St. Pierre and Miquelon
50	2,580	...	...	...	208[4,7]	93[4]	...	...	127[4]	St. Vincent and the Grenadines
10	2,300	...	...	4.9	...	94	103	8	95	San Marino
10	9,600	229	0.5[1]	0.2[1]	0.3[1]	46[4]	55[1]	0.1[1]	70[4]	São Tomé and Principe
443	15,831	477,066	1,493	803	690	15,793	14,800[11]	8,175[11]	6,625[11]	Saudi Arabia
136[21]	48,286[21]	44,391[9]	328	198	130	915	...	...	2,124	Senegal
...	...	1,618[30]	...	...	2	172[4]	325[4]	78[4]	247[4]	Seychelles
98[21]	38,469[21]	29,986	...	20[2]	11	320	703	47	656	Sierra Leone
131	19,847	362,047	285	14	271	17,604	62,749	32,566	30,183	Singapore
999[9]	2,121[9]	5,595[9]	20[4]	15[4]	4	118	264[4]	15[4]	257	Solomon Islands
...	...	...	...	...	...	...	...	...	...	Somalia
2,227[3,39]	13,529[3,39]	1,678,751[3,39]	8,172[4]	7,900[4]	272[4]	32,542	...	283,921[6]	16,226	South Africa
39	39	39	...	...	...	...	...	...	...	Bophuthatswana
34[1,39]	39	39	...	...	...	...	...	...	...	Ciskei
39	39	39	...	...	...	...	...	...	...	Transkei
39	39	39	...	...	...	...	...	...	...	Venda
813[3]	12,914[3]	...	...	...	...	...	...	...	...	South West Africa/Namibia
12,938	2,968	4,538,487	6,565	6,207	358	39,958	117,222	71,443	45,779	Spain
3,751	4,294	596,783	2,084[5]	1,870[5]	146	1,330	1,826[1,11]	252[1,11]	4,749	Sri Lanka
792	27,265	71,129	...	...	...	775[5]	...	...	1,379[5]	Sudan, The
...	...	...	62[1]	6[1]	564[4]	315	1,361	152	1,209	Suriname
72[9]	8,405[9]	17,267[9]	...	107[7]	27	351	2,008	352	1,655	Swaziland
4,883	1,716	3,347,767[40]	233	110	123	18,408	48,649	16,890	31,759	Sweden
3,784	1,737	4,351,993	1,637	1,018	619	40,129	159,146	85,320	73,826	Switzerland
556	19,086	25,748	241	159	82	2,141	...	...	1,992	Syria
12,553	1,542	1,446,694	949	826	123	...	...	...	...	Taiwan
738	30,302	183,604	...	1,199	...	1,231	7,684	2,970	4,714	Tanzania
4,017	13,081	433,584	7,168	7,072	96	5,806	12,364	4,899	7,465	Thailand
389	8,094	...	33	9	24	430	1,719	231	1,488	Togo
...	...	...	...	...	...	...	...	...	...	Tokelau
...	...	1,063[25,27]	152[1]	81[1]	71[1]	80[4]	...	...	89[4]	Tonga
230	5,214	17,064[24]	...	217[5]	...	267[9]	...	...	1,053[9]	Trinidad and Tobago
593	11,973	179,726	455	371	84	3,082	5,452	1,733	3,719	Tunisia
63,116	341	1,086,851	8,194	8,094	100	17,550	...	122,955[6]	18,204	Turkey
7	1,324	354[14,15]	...	0.1[4]	40[4,7]	70[4]	...	...	90[4]	Turks and Caicos Islands
9	973	733[25]	16	5	11	5	...	...	23	Tuvalu
360	36,111	13,609	57[9]	52[9]	5[9]	419[9]	262[9,11]	114[9,11]	148[9,11]	Uganda
94,750	2,973	58,831,000[24]	541,012[5]	540,110[5]	902[5]	1,704[4]	...	...	9,581[1]	U.S.S.R.
104	15,601	119,550	489	60	429	6,141	18,683	7,933	10,750	United Arab Emirates
21,211	2,659	13,035,400	2,836[9]	886[9]	836	111,505	218,746[9,11]	110,296[9,11]	345,095	United Kingdom
39,270	5,769	146,827,627[24]	22,269	20,040	2,229	100,515	...	...	179,235	United States
1,277[3]	2,323[3]	35,356[16]	1,137	1,092	45	1,600	2,593	170	2,424	Uruguay
6[9]	20,833[9]	3,000[9]	...	...	4	98	264	23	240	Vanuatu
633	27,731	64,526[15]	3,244[4]	2,928[4]	316[4]	18,000	11,305	1,842	9,463	Venezuela
...	...	...	...	5[10]	275	...	...	10[10,11]	788	Vietnam
5[3]	23,200[3]	...	...	...	...	...	...	...	...	Virgin Islands (U.S.)
6[4]	2,065[4]	233[4]	9[4]	4[4]	5[4]	4[4]	...	...	5[4]	Wallis and Futuna
...	...	...	...	...	...	...	...	...	...	West Bank
...	...	...	...	...	...	...	...	...	...	Western Sahara
47[4]	3,326[4]	2,087[4,14,25]	...	...	...	100[4]	...	...	43[4]	Western Samoa
111	20,523	2,757	...	0.1[4]	433[4,7]	100[4]	371[5]	45	433[4]	Yemen (Aden)
141	65,774	15,995	...	...	55	965	504	75	429	Yemen (Şan'ā')
3,892	6,001	1,232,839	12,388	11,504	884	12,999	...	298,733[6]	17,344	Yugoslavia
362[9]	83,592[9]	...	53[4]	43[4]	10[4]	1,697[4]	2,068[4]	66[4]	2,002[4]	Zaire
422	15,213	28,160	24,912[4,7]	23,212[7]	2,004[4,7]	1,478	4,997	3,311	1,685	Zambia
311	24,264	170,362	823	793	30	2,102	3,621	1,577	2,044	Zimbabwe

[1]1984. [2]1980. [3]1978. [4]1985. [5]1982. [6]Number of pulses ('000). [7]Number of words ('000). [8]1986. [9]1983. [10]1981. [11]Number of calls ('000). [12]Excludes transmitters of the BBC, "Deutsche Welle," and Voice of America. [13]Number of minutes ('000). [14]Excludes postcards. [15]Excludes small packets. [16]1977. [17]Excludes printed matter. [18]Operator-controlled calls only. [19]1987. [20]Netherlands Antilles includes Aruba. [21]Permanent post offices only. [22]1979. [23]1972. [24]Domestic and foreign sent only. [25]Foreign received and foreign sent only. [26]Excludes traffic to the U.S. [27]1973. [28]Domestic letters and foreign printed matter only. [29]1975. [30]1971. [31]Includes overseas departments. [32]Excludes foreign armed services network transmitters. [33]1976. [34]Excludes traffic to the U.K. [35]Includes Tuvalu. [36]Excludes eight Voice of America transmitters. [37]Excludes transmitters of "Deutsche Welle." [38]Excludes transmitters of Transworld Radio and "Radio Nederland." [39]South Africa includes Bophuthatswana, Ciskei, Transkei, and Venda. [40]Domestic letters only. [41]Abu Dhabi only.

Trade: external

The following table presents comparative data on the international, or foreign, trade of the countries of the world. The table analyzes data for both imports and exports in two ways: (1) into several major commodity groups defined in accordance with the United Nations system called the Standard International Trade Classification (SITC) and (2) by direction of trade for each country with major world trading blocs and partners. These commodity groupings are defined by the SITC code numbers beneath the column headings. The single-digit numbers represent broad SITC categories (in the SITC, called "sections"); the double-digit numbers represent subcategories ("divisions") of the single-digit categories (27 is a subcategory of 2), the three-digit is a subcategory ("group") of the double-digit (667 is a subcategory of 66). Where a plus or minus sign is used before one of these SITC numbers, the SITC category or subcategory is being added to or subtracted from the aggregate implied by the total of the preceding sections. The SITC commodity aggregations used here are listed in the table at the end of this headnote. The full SITC commodity breakdown—some 3,118 basic headings—is presented in the 1986 United Nations publication *Standard International Trade Classification, Revision 3* (though most countries still report according to revision 2).

The SITC was developed by the United Nations through its Statistical Commission as an outgrowth of the need for a standard system of aggregating commodities of external trade to provide international comparability of foreign trade statistics. All member nations of the United Nations are urged to use the SITC system as far as possible in reporting their external trade statistics. The United Nations Statistical Commission has defined external merchandise trade as "all goods whose movement into or out of the customs area of a country compiling the statistics adds to or subtracts from the material resources of the country." Goods passing through a country for transport only are excluded, but goods entering for reexport, or deposited (as in a bonded warehouse, or free trade area) for reimport, are included. Statistics in this table refer only to goods and exclude purely financial transactions that are covered in the "Finance" and "National product and accounts" tables.

For purposes of comparability of data, total value of imports and exports is given in this table in U.S. dollars; conversions from other currencies are determined according to International Monetary Fund (IMF) average rates for the year for which data are supplied. The commodity categories are given in terms of percentages of the total value of the country's import or export trade (with the exclusions noted above). Value is based on transaction value: for imports, the value at which the goods were

Trade: external

country	year	imports													
		total value U.S.$ (000,000)	Standard International Trade Classification (SITC) categories (percent)							direction of trade (percent)					
			food and agricultural raw materials (0+1+2 −27−28 +4)	mineral ores and concentrates (27+28 +667)	fuels and other energy (3)	manufactured goods				from European Economic Community (EEC)[b]	from United States	from U.S.S.R. and Eastern Europe[c]	from Japan	from all other[d]
						total[a] (5+6 −667 +7+8 +9)	of which chemicals and related products (5)	of which machinery and transport equipment (7)	of which other[a] (6−667 +8+9)					
Afghanistan	1986[1]	1,403.5	16.4[2]	0.5[2]	18.0[2]	65.1[2]	4.5[2]	24.8[2]	35.8[2]	6.7	0.4	50.5	10.7	31.7
Albania	1985[3]	274.3	...	...	33.3[2]	...	16.6[2]	22.2[2]	...	28.0	4.3	42.4	0.1	25.2
Algeria	1986	9,234.4	25.3	0.8	3.0	70.9	10.7	33.2	26.9	63.2	7.7	2.7	4.6	21.9
American Samoa	1984[4]	284.1	——54.5[5]——		17.2	28.3[6]	0.7	7.0	20.7[6]	—[7]	81.2[7]	—[7]	5.6[7]	13.2[7]
Andorra	1986	530.6	...	...	...	...	...	...	...	...	...	...	...	100[8]
Angola	1981	1,678.4	31.7	0.2	0.8	67.3	12.1	20.9	34.3	56.8	9.8	5.2	4.5	23.7
Anguilla	1984	6.6	...	...	...	...	...	...	...	...	...	...	...	...
Antigua and Barbuda	1984	131.9	24.6	—	25.0	50.4	6.4	21.8	22.2	10.6	37.8	—	—	51.6
Argentina	1986	4,723.5	11.6	4.3	9.0	75.1	24.0	32.7	18.4	29.1	17.6	2.1	7.1	44.0
Aruba	1984	2,126.2	3.1	—	88.1	8.7	2.3	2.8	3.6	1.9	7.6	—	0.8	89.8
Australia	1986	24,448.7	7.3	0.9	4.7	87.0	8.7	41.9	36.4	24.2	22.0	0.3	21.8	31.7
Austria	1987	32,674.2	9.6	1.6	7.2	81.6	10.3	34.7	36.5	68.0	3.5	6.8	4.4	17.4
Bahamas, The	1985	3,081.1	6.5	—	73.7	19.8	3.9	6.5	9.4	3.6	27.3	—	1.4	67.6
Bahrain	1986	2,426.6	11.2	0.5	48.4	39.9	5.8	13.4	20.7	23.1[3]	8.8[3]	...	5.5[3]	62.6[3]
Bangladesh	1986	1,983.9	23.1	1.2	18.9	56.8	9.6	21.1	26.1	13.1	6.9	4.4	13.1	62.5
Barbados	1986	593.2	17.6	0.5	10.2	71.6	8.7	35.9	27.0	20.6	40.0	0.1	5.6	33.7
Belgium[10]	1987	83,229.3	14.0	8.4	9.3	68.3	10.5	29.4	28.5	72.4	4.7	2.2	2.7	18.0
Belize	1986	122.0	27.4	0.1	13.9	58.6	8.4	18.0	32.2	16.4	57.4	0.1	2.4	23.7
Benin	1982	475.5	25.4	0.4	4.7	69.4	5.3	22.2	41.9	60.5	5.1	2.3	5.5	26.7
Bermuda	1985	402.5	20.5	0.1	14.3	65.1	9.2	19.9	36.0	16.5	60.1	0.2	3.4	19.8
Bhutan	1983	39.0[11]	14.5	0.3	21.4	63.9	3.4	29.7	30.8	12.0	0.3	—	4.6	83.1[12]
Bolivia	1984	416.6	19.5	0.3	0.5	79.7	12.7	41.0	26.0	15.3	19.9	5.2	6.7	53.0
Botswana	1984	706.8	20.8	1.9	10.3	67.1	6.8	29.2	31.0	...	1.9	...	0.3	97.8[14]
Brazil	1987	16,578.6	10.4	2.9	32.5	54.2	15.6	26.0	12.5	21.9	20.7	2.8	5.7	49.0
British Virgin Islands	1982	58.5	28.2	0.4	10.6	60.8	4.3	33.0	23.6	7.8	42.9	—	0.1	49.2
Brunei	1985	610.5	20.8	0.9	1.8	76.5	7.2	34.1	35.2	17.6	15.7	—	19.9	46.8
Bulgaria	1986	15,249.0	8.5	——43.9[17]——		47.5[18]	5.4	37.4	4.7[18]	9.7	0.9	74.3	0.7	14.4
Burkina Faso	1983	287.5	27.6	0.8	17.1	54.5	10.0	23.7	20.7	44.9	9.4	0.3	4.3	41.1
Burma	1984[1]	640.7	——19.2——			80.8	...	47.6	...	25.8	...	16.2	33.7	24.3
Burundi	1985	193.4	16.2	1.0	17.7	65.2	8.4	28.2	28.6	50.1	5.7	0.2	6.3	37.8
Cameroon	1982	1,243.2	10.2	2.4	3.7	83.7	13.2	34.8	35.7	67.6	7.6	1.1	6.1	17.6
Canada	1987	87,577.9	7.9	2.0	4.9	85.3	6.1	54.7	24.4	11.6	68.1	0.3	6.5	13.5
Cape Verde	1984	70.5	44.8[19]	—[19]	9.1[19]	46.0[19]	6.6[19]	13.9[19]	25.5[19]	70.1	2.1	3.3	1.7	22.8
Cayman Islands	1986	160.8	——22.3[5]——		10.0	67.7[6]	6.6	25.3	36.7[6]	...	70.3	—	7.6	22.1
Central African Republic	1985	112.8	21.8[19]	1.7[19]	1.8[19]	74.7[19]	11.8[19]	33.9[19]	29.1[19]	63.5	2.8	0.2	3.3	30.2
Chad	1984	171.2	15.9[22]	0.6[22]	14.2[22]	69.3[22]	16.4[22]	28.8[22]	24.1[22]	39.3[3]	11.2[3]	...	0.1[3]	49.4[3]
Chile	1986	2,964.0	8.4	1.3	14.9	75.4	16.4	35.7	23.3	22.7	21.6	0.3	10.0	45.3
China	1987	43,393.0	13.4	1.3[5]	1.2	84.0[6]	11.6	33.9	38.5[6]	16.8	11.1	7.1	23.4	41.6
Christmas Island	...	...	...	...	...	...	...	...	...	...	...	...	...	...
Cocos (Keeling) Islands	...	...	...	...	...	...	...	...	...	...	...	...	...	...
Colombia	1986	3,852.1	12.7	1.1	4.0	82.2	22.0	36.7	23.5	23.2	36.1	1.6	9.1	30.1
Comoros	1985	36.7	——47.1[5, 23]——		13.1[23]	39.8[6, 23]	3.5[23]	17.6[23]	18.8[6, 23]	53.2[3]	3.4[3]	...[3]	0.8[3]	42.6[3]
Congo	1985	580.2	19.5	0.5	3.1	76.8	8.4	35.4	33.0	72.1	6.6	1.1	3.4	16.7
Cook Islands	1987	33.7	——29.3[5]——		11.4	59.3[6]	7.0	18.3	34.0[6]	7.2[24]	4.2[24]	—[24]	10.4[24]	78.1[24]
Costa Rica	1984	1,086.2	11.4	0.7	15.3	72.5	22.9	20.3	29.3	14.0	36.2	0.3	7.5	41.9
Côte d'Ivoire	1985	1,733.8	18.2	0.7	22.0	59.1	12.8	22.2	24.0	54.1	6.9	1.1	5.0	33.0
Cuba	1985	8,692.6	15.5	0.3[5]	33.2	51.0[6]	5.5	30.2	15.2	6.8	—	80.4	2.7	10.0
Cyprus	1987	1,479.9	15.2	0.7	12.3	71.8	9.6	24.5	37.7	56.9	4.5	5.9	10.2	22.4
Czechoslovakia	1986	21,088.9	10.6	3.7	30.4	55.4	6.7	32.2	16.5	9.8	0.2	74.5	0.4	15.1
Denmark	1987	25,348.2	16.0	0.5	7.9	75.5	10.9	29.9	34.7	51.9	5.1	2.5	4.4	36.1
Djibouti	1983	221.0	42.8	1.1	9.4	46.7	5.1	22.5	19.1	52.2	1.8	—	7.6	38.4
Dominica	1985	55.3	28.0	0.2	10.9	60.9	11.4	22.5	27.0	23.4	24.5	0.1	7.4	44.7
Dominican Republic	1985	1,247.9	13.7	0.3	35.2	50.7	11.7	23.2	15.9	10.3	34.7	—	6.3	48.6
Ecuador	1983	1,506.2	12.9	0.7	1.6	84.7	19.2	35.5	30.0	21.5	36.2	1.4	9.3	31.6
Egypt	1986	11,502.3	34.9	0.4	3.4	61.2	9.4	25.7	26.2	38.3	15.3	12.5	5.4	28.5
El Salvador	1984	1,314.0	14.5	0.4	37.8	47.3	16.9	10.5	19.8	7.6	23.9	0.2	3.1	65.1
Equatorial Guinea	1984	33.2[3]	...	...	22.4[21]	...	...	17.4[21]	...	73.8[3]	0.7[3]	—[3]	0.8[3]	24.7[3]
Ethiopia	1985	988.6	32.8	0.3	14.8	52.2	7.4	28.7	16.1	35.6	16.1	20.0	6.0	22.3
Faeroe Islands	1986	329.2	14.6	0.7	9.7	75.0	4.8	38.5	31.8	65.2	2.3	0.8	4.8	26.9
Falkland Islands	1986	13.9	...	...	...	...	...	...	...	100.0	—	—	—	—

purchased by the importer plus the cost of transportation and insurance to the frontier of the importing country (c.i.f. [cost, insurance, and freight] valuation); for exports, the value at which the goods were sold by the exporter, including the cost of transportation and insurance to bring the goods onto the transporting vehicle at the frontier of the exporting country (f.o.b. [free on board] valuation).

The largest part of the information presented here comes from the United Nations' *Commodity Trade Statistics* (including microfiche format) and *International Trade Statistics Yearbook*. These publications, however, cannot always provide the most recent data for all countries listed in this table and must be supplemented by national and regional sources.

a. Also includes any unallocated commodities.
b. EEC of twelve countries (Belgium, Denmark, France, West Germany, Greece, Ireland, Italy, Luxembourg, The Netherlands, Portugal, Spain, and the United Kingdom).
c. Includes Albania, Bulgaria, Czechoslovakia, East Germany, Hungary, Poland, and Romania.
d. May include value of trade shown as not available (...) in any of the four preceding columns.
... Not available.

— None, less than 0.05%, or not applicable.
Detail may not add to 100.0 or indicated subtotals because of rounding.

SITC category codes:

0	food and live animals.
1	beverages and tobacco.
2	crude materials, inedible, except fuels.
27	crude fertilizers and crude minerals (excluding coal, petroleum, and precious stones).
28	metalliferous ores and metal scrap.
3	mineral fuels, lubricants, and related materials (including coal, petroleum, natural gas, and electric current).
4	animal and vegetable oils, fats, and waxes.
5	chemicals and related products not elsewhere specified.
6	manufactured goods classified chiefly by material.
667	pearls, precious and semiprecious stones, unworked or worked.
7	machinery and transport equipment.
8	miscellaneous manufactured articles.
9	commodities and transactions not classified elsewhere.

exports

total value U.S.$ (000,000)	food and agricultural raw materials (0+1+2-27-28+4)	mineral ores and concentrates (27+28+667)	fuels and other energy (3)	manufactured goods total[a] (5+6-667+7+8+9)	of which chemicals and related products (5)	of which machinery and transport equipment (7)	of which other[a] (6-667+8+9)	to EEC[b]	to United States	to U.S.S.R. and Eastern Europe[c]	to Japan	to all other[d]	country
551.9	44.4[2]	—[2]	39.3[2]	16.3[2]	1.7[2]	—[2]	14.6[2]	16.4	1.1	66.2	0.4	16.0	Afghanistan
252.4	...	26.2[2]	40.3[2]	...	...	...	...	22.9	1.5	43.6	4.8	27.2	Albania
7,830.6	0.3	0.5	97.6	1.6	0.8	0.1	0.7	73.4	17.4	1.1	1.3	6.8	Algeria
212.0	95.8	—	—	4.2	—	—	4.2	...	92.1	...	...	7.9	American Samoa
16.6	...	...	...	...	...	...	...	...	...	...	...	100[9]	Andorra
1,874.5	5.4	12.1	82.1	0.4	...	...	0.4	26.6	37.2	2.0	1.3	32.9	Angola
0.6	...	...	...	...	...	...	...	...	...	...	...	...	Anguilla
17.6	6.2	—	11.5	82.3	7.5	30.1	44.7	3.4	17.9	—	—	78.7	Antigua and Barbuda
6,852.2	69.6	0.2	2.4	27.8	4.7	7.2	15.9	28.8	10.3	7.8	5.7	47.4	Argentina
2,088.6	0.2	0.7	98.9	0.3	0.1	0.1	—	7.9	63.4	—	—	28.6	Aruba
22,478.6	38.3	15.5	21.4	24.8	1.8	6.1	17.0	14.0	8.5	3.7	25.3	48.6	Australia
27,171.0	7.9	0.9	1.8	89.4	9.0	33.4	47.0	63.4	3.6	9.0	1.2	22.9	Austria
3,033.1	—1.8[5]—		89.3	8.8[6]	7.9	0.5	0.4[6]	5.0	84.9	—	1.8	8.3	Bahamas, The
2,343.9	0.2	0.1	86.7	13.0	0.1	0.9	12.0	4.1[3]	3.4[3]	—	11.4[3]	81.1[3]	Bahrain
954.5	32.5	—	0.9	66.6	0.1	2.4	64.2	23.2	27.6	4.6	7.7	36.9	Bangladesh
277.4	15.6	0.4	16.2	67.8	5.4	47.7	14.7	13.7	44.8	1.4	1.2	39.0	Barbados
83,188.1	11.9	6.6	3.8	77.7	12.6	27.0	38.1	74.4	5.2	1.3	1.0	18.0	Belgium[10]
92.6	69.7	—	2.9	27.4	0.9	3.6	23.0	16.4	57.4	0.1	2.4	23.7	Belize
42.6	48.4	—	3.9	47.7	0.4	3.7	43.5	32.9	—	—	6.9	60.2	Benin
23.1	1.8	—	—	98.2	57.1	1.2	39.9	34.2	22.7	—	—	43.1	Bermuda
13.9[11]	32.1	—	—	67.9	16.5	—	51.4	0.4	—	—	0.2	99.4[13]	Bhutan
781.4	3.5	20.2	49.8	26.6	—	—	26.5	23.3	18.6	2.4	1.1	54.7	Bolivia
673.9	10.2	80.2	—	9.5	0.5	2.3	6.7	...	8.2	...	0.1	91.8[15]	Botswana
26,225.0	39.5[16]	7.5[16]	6.3[16]	46.7[16]	6.6[16]	15.2[16]	24.9[16]	26.9[16]	27.2[16]	4.0[16]	5.5[16]	36.4[16]	Brazil
1.2	78.1	2.7	1.5	17.7	0.1	10.2	7.4	4.6	57.4	—	—	38.0	British Virgin Islands
2,972.0	0.2	—	98.5	1.3	0.1	0.8	0.4	0.1	7.3	—	61.2	31.4	Brunei
14,192.0	17.1	—8.0[17]—		74.9[18]	5.4	57.8	11.7[18]	4.9	0.4	79.8	0.1	14.8	Bulgaria
57.0	89.4	0.1	—	10.5	0.1	4.1	6.3	28.8	0.1	—	4.3	66.8	Burkina Faso
421.5	81.6	14.7	—	3.7	...	...	...	12.3	...	—	6.7	81.1	Burma
109.6	91.0	—	—	9.0	—	—	9.0	41.7	5.9	—	1.2	51.2	Burundi
1,028.9	43.8	—	47.0	9.2	1.3	0.9	7.0	47.6	40.1	0.4	1.2	10.7	Cameroon
94,402.4	20.1	4.5	10.0	65.3	5.0	38.1	22.3	7.4	75.5	0.8	5.4	10.9	Canada
49.7	4.5	0.5	86.1	8.9	—	7.3	1.6	2.5	—	—	—	97.5[20]	Cape Verde
2.6	2.1[21]	2.2[21]	—[21]	95.8[21]	94.1[21]	0.5[21]	1.2[21]	—[21]	100.0[21]	—[21]	—[21]	—[21]	Cayman Islands
91.7	71.2[19]	25.0[19]	—[19]	3.8[19]	—[19]	—[19]	3.8[19]	91.4	—	...	—	8.5	Central African Republic
111.1	83.1[22]	0.8[22]	7.9[22]	8.2[22]	0.5[22]	5.4[22]	2.3[22]	64.4[3]	0.1[3]	...	4.3[3]	31.3[3]	Chad
4,165.5	37.7	20.5	0.1	41.7	2.5	1.6	37.7	34.7	20.0	1.0	10.2	34.0	Chile
39,541.4	20.4	1.6[5]	11.5	66.5[6]	5.7	4.4	56.4[6]	9.8	7.7	7.2	16.2	59.0	China
...	...	...	...	...	...	...	...	...	...	...	...	...	Christmas Island
...	...	...	...	...	...	...	...	...	...	...	...	...	Cocos (Keeling) Islands
5,107.9	71.1	0.8	13.0	15.0	2.7	1.2	11.1	39.7	30.0	3.5	4.9	22.0	Colombia
15.7	64.5[19]	—[19]	—[19]	35.5[19]	18.1[19]	—[19]	17.4[19]	53.6[3]	39.7[3]	...[3]	...[3]	6.6[3]	Comoros
1,087.2	3.1	1.1	93.3	2.5	—	0.2	2.3	34.5	60.0	0.2	—	5.2	Congo
7.1	24.3	—	—	75.7	0.1	4.4	71.2	1.8	0.1	—	9.5	88.5	Cook Islands
951.3	74.0	—	1.9	24.1	6.3	3.1	14.6	25.6	37.6	3.3	0.5	32.9	Costa Rica
2,670.0	79.8	0.1	9.7	10.3	2.5	1.8	6.1	57.5	12.6	5.8	1.1	22.9	Côte d'Ivoire
6,484.5	82.4	5.5[5]	10.4	1.7[6]	0.3	0.4	1.0[6]	4.8	—	86.1	1.3	7.8	Cuba
619.9	33.2	2.0	5.2	59.6	4.7	9.8	45.2	41.0	1.8	5.0	0.5	51.6	Cyprus
20,457.0	5.5	0.4	3.5	90.5	6.0	54.2	30.3	9.8	0.4	72.0	0.2	17.7	Czechoslovakia
24,708.3	34.9	0.6	3.0	61.5	9.1	24.2	28.1	46.8	7.0	1.4	3.7	41.1	Denmark
10.8	6.1[25]	—[25]	...	93.9[25]	0.1[25]	1.4[25]	92.5[25]	42.1[21]	5.9[21]	0.1[21]	—[21]	52.0[21]	Djibouti
28.4	59.8	—	—	40.1	28.6	5.4	6.1	50.4	3.4	—	—	46.2	Dominica
738.5	75.7[24]	0.3[24]	—[24]	24.1[24]	4.0[24]	4.5[24]	15.6[24]	13.4	77.1	3.0	2.4	4.2	Dominican Republic
2,225.6	25.1	—	73.9	1.0	0.3	0.1	0.6	2.7	58.2	0.7	1.2	37.2	Ecuador
2,934.3	22.9	0.1	51.3	25.7	1.4	0.1	24.1	35.5	2.9	23.4	2.7	35.5	Egypt
615.0	70.4	0.3	2.7	26.7	6.0	1.6	19.1	24.4	34.9	2.5	5.4	32.8	El Salvador
32.3[3]	98.7[21]	—[21]	—[21]	1.3[21]	—[21]	—[21]	1.3[21]	83.8[3]	2.3[3]	—[3]	1.1[3]	12.8[3]	Equatorial Guinea
337.5	88.9	0.2	9.8	1.1	0.6	—	0.5	48.9	10.5	8.7	10.3	21.7	Ethiopia
242.2	93.7	—	—	6.3	—	6.3	—	68.6	14.0	0.5	2.0	15.0	Faeroe Islands
17.9	100.0	—	—	—	—	—	—	100.0	—	—	—	—	Falkland Islands

Trade: external   (continued)

country	year	total value U.S.$ (000,000)	food and agricultural raw materials (0+1+2 -27-28 +4)	mineral ores and concentrates (27+28 +667)	fuels and other energy (3)	manufactured goods total[a] (5+6 -667 +7+8 +9)	of which chemicals and related products (5)	of which machinery and transport equipment (7)	of which other[a] (6-667 +8+9)	from European Economic Community (EEC)[b]	from United States	from U.S.S.R. and Eastern Europe[c]	from Japan	from all other[d]
Fiji	1985	441.6	19.0	0.3	22.7	58.0	7.6	18.0	32.3	9.3	4.1	0.1	15.1	71.4
Finland	1987	19,867.6	8.9	2.3	13.5	75.3	10.4	36.6	28.3	44.2	5.2	16.5	7.1	27.0
France[26]	1987	157,914.1	14.2	1.3	10.8	73.7	10.7	31.6	31.4	61.1	7.2	2.8	3.8	25.2
French Guiana	1987	394.4	22.4	0.1	10.1	67.4	5.9	31.9	29.6	74.9	4.3	0.4	3.2	17.3
French Polynesia	1983	538.3	21.4	0.3	11.9	66.3	5.3	30.1	30.9	57.9	15.8	0.1	4.3	21.9
Gabon	1983	685.6	18.5	1.0	1.8	78.8	7.5	38.5	32.7	74.6	11.0	0.4	7.4	6.6
Gambia, The	1986[4]	100.2	—37.8[5]—		10.0	52.2[6]	6.0	17.2	29.0[6]	52.9[3]	9.2[3]	3.3[3]	2.9[3]	31.7[3]
Gaza Strip	1986	378.0	...	...	...	...	...	...	...	...	...	...	...	100.0[27]
Germany, East	1986	27,413.7	—55.4—			44.6	8.6	29.5	6.5	13.0[29]	0.4[29]	63.3[29]	0.7[29]	22.6[29]
Germany, West[30]	1987	228,219.4	15.5	2.0	9.6	72.8	9.4	28.0	35.4	52.7	6.2	3.9	6.2	31.0
Ghana	1982	1,016.4	12.0	0.2	35.4	52.4	10.9	20.7	20.8	30.1	15.3	1.0	2.5	51.0
Gibraltar	1987	231.0	22.6	0.7[5]	21.6	55.0[6]	4.4	16.9	33.7[6]	72.8[31]	3.7[31]	...[31]	8.8[31]	14.7[31]
Greece	1986	11,304.5	20.9	1.3	17.7	60.1	10.5	25.8	23.8	58.3	3.0	5.2	6.1	27.4
Greenland	1986	359.7	21.8	0.4	6.9	70.9	3.7	29.4	37.8	77.2	2.7	0.3	4.6	15.2
Grenada	1982	56.5	—35.5[5]—		13.3	51.2[6]	10.0	14.8	26.4[6]	23.3	20.2	0.9	4.6	50.6
Guadeloupe	1987	1,040.2	24.2	0.2	4.7	70.9	9.2	29.6	32.0	80.1	3.3	0.4	2.7	13.6
Guam	1983	610.7	16.9	0.1	46.9	36.2	2.3	19.1	14.8	...	23.4	...	19.9	56.6
Guatemala	1984	1,472.2	8.9	0.2	33.0	57.8	21.7	15.2	20.9	12.0	28.8	0.4	4.6	54.2
Guernsey[34]	...	...	...	...	...	...	...	...	...	...	...	...	...	...
Guinea	1980	204.4	—10.0[5]—		30.3	59.7[6]	3.0	39.8	16.9[6]	71.0[3]	10.2[3]	5.8[3]	1.7[3]	11.3[3]
Guinea-Bissau	1984	38.7	20.1[19]	2.2[19]	6.2[19]	71.5[19]	5.6[19]	36.4[19]	29.5[19]	51.9	8.8	15.2	0.2	23.8
Guyana	1983	246.1	5.6	0.5	43.2	50.7	9.4	23.2	18.1	20.1	21.6	0.7	1.6	56.0
Haiti	1986[35]	397.1	—30.2[5]—		12.8	57.0[6]	9.1	15.9	32.1[6]	16.1[3]	47.4	0.3[3]	7.0	29.2[3]
Honduras	1984	813.4	11.7	0.3	12.4	75.6	20.3	24.9	30.5	14.9	39.9	0.4	5.4	39.5
Hong Kong	1987	48,503.3	12.0	2.9	2.5	82.6	8.1	26.0	48.6	11.1	8.5	0.4	19.0	61.0
Hungary	1986	9,583.6	12.4	1.6[5]	20.4	65.6[6]	13.7	28.3	23.6[6]	22.8	2.0	50.9	1.5	22.9
Iceland	1987	1,581.5	10.1	2.0	7.4	80.5	7.1	38.3	35.0	52.1	7.1	5.8	8.2	26.8
India	1983[11]	14,859.8	10.2	7.9	40.2	41.7	6.9	18.0	16.8	23.9	10.0	12.0	7.6	46.6
Indonesia	1987	12,370.3	12.0	2.1	9.2	76.7	18.8	39.0	18.9	19.0	11.4	0.7	29.1	39.8
Iran	1985	11,635.0	15.4[36]	0.4[36]	—[36]	83.9[36]	7.2[36]	44.3[36]	32.5[36]	38.5[3]	0.7[3]	7.2[3]	12.9[3]	40.8[3]
Iraq	1985	10,556.0	—24.3[5,37]—		0.3[37]	75.4[6,37]	7.2[37]	30.6[37]	37.6[6,37]	29.9[37]	5.6[37]	3.3[37]	15.5[37]	45.7[37]
Ireland	1987	13,621.5	14.2	0.9	7.4	77.5	12.3	33.5	31.7	65.6	17.0	1.4	4.3	11.7
Isle of Man[34]	...	...	...	...	...	...	...	...	...	...	...	...	...	...
Israel	1987	11,899.5[38]	10.1	18.8	8.7	62.4	8.7	29.6	24.1	53.3	16.2	0.4	3.4	26.8
Italy[39]	1987	125,075.8	20.2	2.0	13.7	64.2	10.9	27.2	26.1	56.5	5.3	4.1	2.1	31.9
Jamaica	1987	1,234.3	19.8	0.2	19.2	60.8	9.7	20.0	31.2	12.4	47.6	0.8	4.1	35.1
Japan	1987	146,048.0	25.8	6.3	27.1	40.8	7.8	11.4	21.6	11.9	21.7	1.6	—	64.7
Jersey	1980	537.1	23.9	0.4	9.3	66.5	6.5	24.8	35.2	...	...	...	...	100.0[40]
Jordan	1986	2,445.4	23.5	1.2	14.2	61.1	8.8	20.6	31.7	35.0	8.8	5.2	7.8	43.1
Kampuchea	...	...	...	...	...	...	...	...	...	...	...	...	...	...
Kenya	1986	1,649.0	11.3	0.4	18.2	70.1	16.5	37.6	16.1	48.4	4.9	1.0	10.9	34.8
Kiribati	1985	15.1	33.4	0.1	15.0	51.5	5.0	29.4	17.0	6.2	2.6	—	21.2	70.0
Korea, North	1986	1,760.0[3]	...	...	...	...	...	...	...	4.4[3]	—[3]	64.8[3]	8.8[3]	22.0[3]
Korea, South	1986	31,583.9	14.5	4.1	16.1	65.3	11.1	34.2	20.1	10.2	20.7	—	34.4	34.7
Kuwait	1984	6,896.4	18.2	0.6	0.6	80.7	4.8	38.7	37.2	36.4	9.4	1.3	23.8	29.1
Laos	1982	115.0	32.1[43]	0.2[43]	11.2[43]	56.4[43]	6.1[43]	25.7[43]	24.7[43]	10.0[3]	0.4[3]	...	9.3[3]	80.3[3]
Lebanon	1987	1,929.7[3]	21.0[36]	7.0[36]	6.6[36]	65.5[36]	4.6[36]	21.1[36]	39.8[36]	40.6[3]	5.5[3]	...	3.1[3]	50.9[3]
Lesotho	1981	504.9	25.1	0.8[5]	9.6	64.5[6]	6.4	17.0	41.1[6]	1.5	0.2	—	—	98.2[44]
Liberia	1984	363.2	25.5	0.9	19.8	53.9	6.7	26.8	20.5	40.0	22.3	1.1	8.1	28.5
Libya	1982	7,175.5	17.1	0.4	1.4	81.1	3.9	36.8	40.4	63.5	4.2	5.4	5.1	21.9
Liechtenstein	1986	265.4	5.1	0.3[5]	0.4	94.3[6]	4.9	32.1	57.3[6]	...	...	...	...	...
Luxembourg	1984	2,770.0	13.4	3.8[5]	13.6	69.1[6]	14.1	20.6	34.5[6]	90.0	2.9	...	0.3	6.8
Macau	1986	909.1	17.3	0.3	5.2	77.2	4.7	12.6	59.9	6.6	6.1	0.2	9.9	77.2
Madagascar	1986	373.6	17.0	0.4	23.1	59.5	11.7	28.8	19.0	48.6	10.7	10.3	6.5	23.8
Malawi	1984	270.1	—10.8[5]—		16.5	72.7[6]	22.0	23.3	27.3[6]	23.8	4.2	—	8.2	63.9
Malaysia	1987	12,693.5	12.9	2.0	7.5	77.7	10.4	44.9	22.5	13.4	18.7	0.4	21.7	45.9
Maldives	1985	52.7	37.4	1.8	15.5	45.4	7.3	17.5	20.6	10.4[3]	—[3]	—[3]	25.4[3]	64.1[3]
Mali	1982	401.8	21.3	0.7	27.5	50.4	9.2	18.4	22.8	43.8	2.4	0.9	1.3	51.6
Malta	1986	879.7	15.9	1.1	6.1	76.9	8.1	28.0	40.9	75.2	5.3	3.1	2.1	14.4
Martinique	1987	1,120.1	21.8	0.2	8.2	69.9	8.7	31.1	30.1	83.6	2.2	0.2	2.5	11.5
Mauritania	1984	207.6	30.3[19]	4.5[17,19]	14.0[19]	51.2[18,19]	4.3[19]	27.0[19]	19.9[19]	70.0[3]	8.6[3]	...	1.5[3]	19.9[3]
Mauritius	1987	1,012.8	15.7	1.5	7.5	75.3	6.4	22.1	46.8	64.0	1.7	...	9.8	24.4
Mayotte	1985	21.8	—34.0—		11.9	54.2	10.0	18.4	25.7	...	...	...	...	100.0[45]
Mexico	1985	16,151.8	16.6	2.6	4.4	76.5	13.9	43.5	19.2	11.8	69.6	0.3	5.2	13.1
Monaco[26]	...	...	...	...	...	...	...	...	...	...	...	...	...	...
Mongolia	1985	1,447.7[3]	10.4	—28.7[17]—		59.5[18]	6.0	36.2	17.3[18]	...	—[3]	96.8[3]	0.1[3]	3.0[3]
Montserrat	1985	18.4	—31.2[5]—		11.8	57.0[6]	6.6	21.1	29.3[6]	19.6[47]	38.5[47]	—[47]	4.7[47]	37.1[47]
Morocco	1985	3,849.6	22.7	6.1	28.0	43.3	8.1	17.9	17.3	47.2	6.1	6.2	2.4	38.1
Mozambique	1984	487.2	—25.0[5]—		18.7	56.4[6]	4.6	17.3	34.4[6]	32.1	5.8	25.7	3.2	33.2
Nauru	1981[48]	17.7	—34.4[5]—		1.9	63.8[6]	5.3	14.8	43.7[6]	...	...	...	...	...
Nepal	1985[4]	442.1	16.2	0.6	11.6	71.6	13.4	19.6	38.6	7.0	1.3	0.7	11.8	79.2
Netherlands, The	1987	91,316.5	17.5	1.6	11.3	69.7	10.6	28.7	30.5	64.1	7.2	2.5	3.3	22.9
Netherlands Antilles	1984[49]	1,898.2	5.5	0.1	81.8	12.6	2.3	3.7	6.7	6.2	9.5	0.1	1.0	83.3
New Caledonia	1983	303.4	23.7	0.2	23.1	53.0	6.0	20.6	26.4	48.0	10.2	0.1	5.6	36.1
New Zealand	1987	7,255.1	8.1	2.4	6.7	82.8	12.4	39.8	30.5	23.1	16.1	0.3	18.8	41.8
Nicaragua	1984	825.9	14.1	0.2	17.7	68.0	20.7	27.8	19.5	16.3	16.2	21.3	2.9	43.2
Niger	1981	509.7	24.8	1.9	14.8	58.4	6.9	25.7	25.8	48.0	3.7	0.4	2.5	45.4
Nigeria	1986	4,436.2	17.3	1.7	0.5	80.5	17.4	38.1	25.0	57.8	11.9	6.0	5.2	19.1
Niue	1985	1.9	40.5	0.1	19.9	39.5	3.7	19.6	16.2	—	0.1	—	13.3	86.6
Norfolk Island	1986[4]	16.3	20.1	0.1	9.6	70.2	5.4	14.4	50.4	...	...	...	...	100.0[50]
Norway	1987	22,584.8	8.7	3.0	5.3	83.0	7.3	39.2	36.6	49.6	6.4	2.0	5.7	36.3
Oman	1986	2,384.1	17.2	0.4	2.9	79.6	4.7	41.2	33.7	41.0	7.6	—	14.4	37.0
Pacific Is., Trust Territory of the	1978[4]	38.9	—46.2[5]—		12.9	40.9[6]	4.8	12.5	23.5[6]	—[36]	34.7[36]	—[36]	25.2[36]	40.1[36]
Marshall Islands	1983	17.4	—36.2[2,5]—		18.2[2]	45.5[2,6]	3.4[2]	9.7[2]	32.4[2,6]	...	...	...	...	...
Micronesia, Fed. States of	...	...	...	...	...	...	...	...	...	...	...	...	...	...

total value U.S.$ (000,000)	food and agricultural raw materials (0+1+2 −27−28 +4)	mineral ores and concen- trates (27+28 +667)	fuels and other energy (3)	total[a] (5+6 −667 +7+8 +9)	of which chemicals and related products (5)	of which machinery and transport equipment (7)	of which other[a] (6−667 +8+9)	to European Economic Community (EEC)[b]	to United States	to U.S.S.R. and Eastern Europe[c]	to Japan	to all other[d]	country
236.5	58.1	0.1	20.0	21.8	0.9	3.4	17.5	31.6	4.7	—	2.3	61.3	Fiji
20,059.4	14.7	0.3	2.2	82.7	5.4	26.9	50.5	41.6	5.1	16.8	1.4	35.1	Finland
143,401.5	18.3	0.9	2.3	78.5	14.3	35.4	28.8	60.4	7.3	2.2	1.5	28.6	France[26]
53.8	77.0	0.1	0.1	22.9	0.9	5.6	16.3	40.9	21.9	—	10.7	26.4	French Guiana
41.2	14.4	15.2	—	70.4	2.4	17.2	50.7	70.4	12.6	—	4.9	12.1	French Polynesia
1,475.4	7.5	7.0	79.5	6.0	1.2	0.6	4.1	54.6	25.6	1.8	0.3	17.6	Gabon
44.7	78.0[19]	—[19]	—[19]	22.0[19]	—[19]	—[19]	22.0[19]	32.4[3]	1.0[3]	...[3]	18.0[3]	48.6[3]	Gambia, The
139.7	...	...	...	...	...	...	...	...	...	...	...	100.0[28]	Gaza Strip
27,728.8	—23.7—			76.3	13.2	46.7	16.4	...[29]	...[29]	...[29]	...[29]	...[29]	Germany, East
294,263.2	6.0	0.7	1.3	92.0	13.0	48.4	30.5	52.8	9.5	3.4	2.0	32.4	Germany, West[30]
717.6	63.0	1.7	9.7	25.6	—	0.1	25.5	46.6	22.1	7.9	8.1	15.4	Ghana
84.8	8.7	—[5]	62.2	29.1[6]	2.5	13.2	13.4[6]	28.3	0.2	...	...	71.5[32]	Gibraltar
5,660.4	33.3	3.3	6.6	56.8	3.3	2.9	50.5	63.6	7.1	4.9	0.7	23.7	Greece
236.1	89.4	5.9	1.4	3.3	—	2.6	0.7	95.5	0.2	...	...	4.3	Greenland
18.6	84.5[33]	—[33]	—[33]	15.5[33]	—[33]	—[33]	15.5[33]	57.5[33]	2.4[33]	3.9[33]	—[33]	36.2[33]	Grenada
91.7	78.2	0.3	0.2	21.3	3.0	9.8	8.5	68.7	0.4	...	—	30.9	Guadeloupe
39.2	23.5	2.7	3.5	70.3	5.6	11.5	53.2	...	24.9	...	4.8	70.4	Guam
1,094.6	73.9	0.2	2.4	23.5	9.8	1.1	12.6	15.0	38.3	0.1	4.5	42.1	Guatemala
...	...	...	...	...	...	...	...	...	...	...	...	...	Guernsey[34]
466.7	3.0	96.8	—	0.2	—	—	0.2	45.4[3]	23.5[3]	21.4[3]	—[3]	9.6[3]	Guinea
18.9	87.1[19]	0.3[19]	—[19]	12.6[19]	0.3[19]	—[19]	12.3[19]	64.4	—	—	—	35.6	Guinea-Bissau
188.7	52.9	36.4	0.2	10.5	2.7	3.4	4.4	37.1	17.3	4.0	8.0	33.6	Guyana
193.9	30.8[2]	10.5[2]	—[2]	58.7[2]	3.5[2]	...	55.2[2]	43.2[3]	53.2	0.1[3]	0.4	3.1[3]	Haiti
703.7	87.2	5.5	0.7	6.7	2.1	0.2	4.4	21.7	52.8	2.1	7.9	15.5	Honduras
48,501.8	5.9	1.4	0.5	92.3	4.7	23.5	64.1	16.1	27.9	0.3	5.1	50.7	Hong Kong
9,157.3	22.5	0.9[5]	4.0	72.6[6]	10.9	35.1	26.6[6]	17.5	2.3	54.1	0.5	25.6	Hungary
1,375.1	80.0	0.9	—	19.1	—	1.5	17.5	57.3	18.3	4.7	7.8	11.9	Iceland
9,143.5	28.3	16.4	14.1	41.2	4.0	6.6	30.6	16.7	10.5	23.0	9.5	40.3	India
17,135.6	21.2	2.0	50.1	26.7	1.5	0.3	24.9	9.0	19.5	0.9	43.1	27.4	Indonesia
13,328.0	...	...	98.0	...	...	...	...	35.5[3]	5.2[3]	5.2[3]	17.2[3]	36.9[3]	Iran
10,357.0	—0.4[5]—		99.6[3]	0.1[6]	...	...	—[6]	43.8[3]	4.3[3]	0.2[3]	5.5[3]	46.2[3]	Iraq
15,972.2	29.2	2.0	0.7	68.1	12.0	31.4	24.7	73.7	7.8	0.6	1.7	16.3	Ireland
...	...	...	...	...	...	...	...	...	...	...	...	...	Isle of Man[34]
8,476.8	12.7	28.8	—	58.5	14.2	17.9	26.4	32.4	32.5	0.2	5.8	29.1	Israel
116,602.1	7.7	0.4	2.4	89.5	7.5	34.8	47.1	56.1	9.6	3.1	1.6	29.6	Italy[39]
708.4	26.7	47.8	2.0	23.5	3.0	2.2	18.3	29.6	36.9	4.2	1.2	28.1	Jamaica
229,054.5	1.3	0.2	0.4	98.2	5.0	70.6	22.6	16.6	36.8	1.4	—	45.2	Japan
209.2	27.6	4.3[41]	—	68.0	1.2	31.1	35.7	...	...	...	...	100.0[42]	Jersey
731.6	18.7	38.1	0.1	43.1	21.4	6.7	15.0	11.3	0.6	6.0	2.7	79.4	Jordan
...	...	...	...	...	...	...	...	...	...	...	...	...	Kampuchea
1,216.7	74.5	2.0	11.1	12.4	3.2	1.5	7.7	44.6	8.7	0.8	0.9	45.1	Kenya
4.2	94.7	—	—	5.3	—	—	5.3	30.1	8.2	—	1.7	60.1	Kiribati
1,490.0[3]	...	...	...	...	...	...	...	5.4[3]	—[3]	48.4[3]	13.7[3]	32.6[3]	Korea, North
34,714.5	5.5	0.3	1.9	92.3	3.1	33.6	55.6	12.4	40.1	—	15.6	31.9	Korea, South
12,274.6	1.1	0.2	82.8	15.9	8.8	3.5	3.6	24.4	2.6	0.2	16.5	56.4	Kuwait
40.0	84.0[43]	11.9[43]	—[43]	4.1[43]	—[43]	—[43]	4.1[43]	2.4[3]	3.6[3]	...	2.6[3]	91.4[3]	Laos
600.6	20.1[36]	0.5[36]	—[36]	79.2[36]	9.6[36]	11.4[36]	58.2[36]	15.2[3]	5.2[3]	...	0.3[3]	79.3[3]	Lebanon
49.6	28.8	42.6	0.1	28.5	0.9	3.3	24.3	10.3	0.1	—	—	89.6	Lesotho
449.1	34.1	64.8	—	1.1	0.1	0.3	0.8	70.5	20.2	1.9	1.3	6.1	Liberia
13,953.7	—	—	99.9	0.1	...	...	...	65.5[3]	3.5[3]	2.3[3]	0.3[3]	28.5[3]	Libya
688.8	0.3	0.1[5]	0.2	99.5[6]	5.7	46.5	47.3[6]	40.1	...	...	...	59.9	Liechtenstein
2,519.0	6.2	1.5[5]	0.4	91.9[6]	16.8	13.3	61.7[6]	74.4	5.8	...	0.1	19.7	Luxembourg
1,072.1	2.1	0.1	—	97.7	0.6	5.0	92.1	36.5	33.3	0.5	1.5	28.2	Macau
316.6	84.6	5.7	2.2	7.5	1.3	1.9	4.4	58.2	14.8	3.6	10.9	12.4	Madagascar
311.8	—95.1[5]—		—	4.9[6]	0.5	1.7	2.7[6]	57.2	8.6	—	3.0	31.2	Malawi
17,929.7	37.3	1.1	19.7	41.9	1.6	25.9	14.4	14.3	16.6	1.1	19.5	48.5	Malaysia
23.0	67.4	0.1	—	32.5	—	—	32.5	3.4	24.3	—	10.1	62.2	Maldives
233.5	97.2	—	—	2.8	—	—	2.7	29.4	—	—	1.6	69.0	Mali
497.0	5.6	0.9	2.2	91.3	1.5	26.8	63.1	66.7	7.6	6.3	0.2	19.2	Malta
193.5	69.1	0.3	14.5	16.1	3.4	3.9	8.8	70.3	0.3	—	—	29.4	Martinique
291.2	50.2	49.1	—	0.7	—	—	0.7	64.7[3]	0.3[3]	...	12.5[3]	22.5[3]	Mauritania
934.5	—40.9—		—	59.1	0.6	0.6	57.9	79.3	14.6	0.3	0.1	5.7	Mauritius
0.6	24.6	—	—	75.4	41.5	—	33.9	...	...	...	...	100.0[46]	Mayotte
24,364.5	8.9	2.1	60.1	28.9	3.1	15.9	9.9	16.6	65.1	0.2	7.1	11.0	Mexico
...	...	...	...	...	...	...	...	...	...	...	...	...	Monaco[26]
568.8[3]	39.9	—42.6[17]—		17.5[18]	...	0.1	17.4[18]	...	0.7[3]	90.7[3]	1.3[3]	7.3[3]	Mongolia
2.9	5.8	—	0.3	93.9	0.2	20.5	73.2	...	55.6[33]	...	...	44.4[33]	Montserrat
2,165.1	27.9	26.2	3.9	42.0	21.1	1.1	19.9	58.6	1.4	7.8	4.3	27.9	Morocco
86.4	79.3	1.4[5]	6.3	13.0[6]	—	—	13.0[6]	26.9	14.6	15.4	11.9	31.2	Mozambique
89.2	—	100.0	—	—	—	—	...	...	...	...	...	...	Nauru
128.5	40.7	0.2	—	59.1	3.5	—	55.6	15.2	21.7	4.2	0.5	58.4	Nepal
92,881.8	25.9	1.2	11.1	61.7	18.0	20.9	22.8	74.9	4.3	1.4	0.8	18.6	Netherlands, The
1,639.6	—	0.1	97.6	2.2	1.6	0.3	0.3	15.6	17.4	—	0.4	66.6	Netherlands Antilles
155.1	1.6	15.9	0.1	82.3	0.3	4.5	77.5	47.1	6.9	—	23.7	22.3	New Caledonia
6,963.6	71.0	0.5	0.9	27.6	4.7	4.2	18.7	22.5	15.4	1.9	16.6	43.6	New Zealand
386.7	91.7	—	—	8.3	4.6	—	3.7	36.2	12.6	3.0	24.7	23.4	Nicaragua
454.8	17.1	79.7	0.9	2.3	—	0.5	1.8	46.6	—	—	17.7	35.7	Niger
6,717.8	5.5	—	93.1	1.3	—	—	1.3	51.8	35.0	0.1	0.2	12.9	Nigeria
0.1	61.9	—	—	38.1	—	—	38.1	...	1.3	—	—	98.7	Niue
1.8	24.0	—	—	76.0	1.0	12.0	63.0	...	...	...	...	100.0[51]	Norfolk Island
21,459.4	10.7	1.5	40.5	47.3	7.5	17.1	22.7	64.4	5.7	1.0	1.2	27.7	Norway
2,539.1	2.3	0.2	88.6	8.9	0.2	6.1	2.6	5.8[3]	1.5[3]	—[3]	58.8[3]	33.9[3]	Oman
19.3	—96.5[5]—		—	3.5[6]	—	—	3.5[6]	...	...	...	...	...	Pacific Is., Trust Territory of the
3.1	99.1	...	...	0.9	...	...	0.9	...	...	...	...	...	Marshall Islands
...	...	...	...	...	...	...	...	...	...	...	...	...	Micronesia, Fed. States of

Trade: external   (continued)

country	year	imports total value U.S.$ (000,000)	Standard International Trade Classification (SITC) categories (percent)							direction of trade (percent)				
			food and agricultural raw materials (0 + 1 + 2 − 27 − 28 + 4)	mineral ores and concentrates (27 + 28 + 667)	fuels and other energy (3)	manufactured goods				from European Economic Community (EEC)[b]	from United States	from U.S.S.R. and Eastern Europe[c]	from Japan	from all other[d]
						total[a] (5 + 6 − 667 + 7 + 8 + 9)	of which chemicals and related products (5)	of which machinery and transport equipment (7)	of which other[a] (6 − 667 + 8 + 9)					
Northern Mariana Islands	...	...	...	...	...	...	...	...	...	...	...	...	...	...
Palau	1984	25.1	——29.1——		0.9	70.0[6]	4.0	24.5	41.5[6]	...	...	...	...	...
Pakistan	1986	5,377.0	21.8	1.6	14.3	62.3	15.1	32.0	15.2	26.4	13.2	2.3	16.2	41.9
Panama	1985	1,383.3	12.5	0.2	21.2	66.1	12.3	23.5	30.3	8.3	31.7	0.2	8.9	50.9
Papua New Guinea	1984	968.4	——20.3[5]——		18.0	61.6[6]	7.9	28.1	25.7[6]	6.7[3]	10.3	—[3]	15.7	67.2[3]
Paraguay	1986	578.1	10.0	0.6	21.4	67.9	8.7	32.6	26.6	18.0	13.6	0.1	6.0	62.4
Peru	1984	1,881.4	26.5	1.5	3.4	68.7	16.3	32.8	19.6	20.2	34.0	1.0	8.9	36.0
Philippines	1987	7,187.6	12.0	1.4	18.2	68.4	14.0	16.6	37.8	11.6	22.1	0.7	16.6	49.0
Pitcairn Island	...	...	...	...	...	...	...	...	...	...	...	...	...	...
Poland	1986	11,208.4	14.3	3.4	20.7	61.6	9.6	32.3	19.8	19.3	0.6	46.2	1.1	32.9
Portugal	1987	13,441.2	18.2	1.0	11.6	69.1	10.6	33.4	25.1	63.4	4.9	0.8	4.0	27.0
Puerto Rico	1984[4]	9,528.5	——20.3[5]——		22.2	57.5[6]	12.0	16.6	28.9[6]	6.7	57.3	0.1	5.9	30.1
Qatar	1984	1,162.0	22.6	2.4	0.9	74.1	5.8	35.3	32.9	39.3	9.1	0.5	19.2	32.0
Réunion	1987	1,464.6	22.2	0.2	4.5	73.0	9.3	30.3	33.4	80.2	0.3	—	2.6	16.8
Romania	1985	11,266.9	10.6	——56.1[17]——		33.3[18]	6.8	22.2	4.3[18]	10.2	3.1	43.1	1.1	42.6
Rwanda	1982	286.3	——17.6[5]——		11.9	70.5[6]	6.4	26.0	38.1[6]	39.7	4.2	0.7	13.0	42.4
St. Helena and Ascension	1984	4.3	39.0	—	11.7	49.2	6.8	15.7	26.7	57.0	—	—	0.2	42.8
St. Kitts and Nevis	1983	51.9	25.1	0.1	10.0	64.8	8.5	19.2	37.1	20.7	40.5	—	3.4	35.4
St. Lucia	1986	154.8	25.7	0.2	7.7	66.5	12.2	19.8	34.5	24.4	34.1	0.2	6.9	34.4
St. Pierre and Miquelon	1984	43.9	19.4	0.1	29.9	50.6	4.3	27.4	18.8	46.1	0.3	—	—	53.5
St. Vincent and the Grenadines	1986	87.3	27.1	0.2[5]	6.6	66.0[6]	13.3	18.1	34.6[6]	25.6	34.1	0.3	4.1	36.0
San Marino[39]	...	...	...	...	...	...	...	...	...	...	...	...	...	...
São Tomé and Príncipe	1984	11.0	46.5[36]	3.0[17, 36]	1.9[36]	45.7[18, 36]	10.1[36]	12.8[36]	22.8[18, 36]	69.3[3]	—[3]	5.0[3]	3.3[3]	22.4[3]
Saudi Arabia	1985	23,622.4	15.6	0.4	0.5	83.5	6.5	35.8	41.3	35.2	17.0	0.6	19.0	28.2
Senegal	1984	1,009.7	29.6	—	28.0	42.4	8.4	16.8	17.3	44.1	5.1	0.7	1.7	48.5
Seychelles	1985	99.3	18.7	0.1	26.2	55.0	5.9	25.4	23.7	45.2	4.5	—	4.8	44.7
Sierra Leone	1983	165.7	28.5	0.4	34.7	36.4	5.5	14.9	15.9	40.7	3.5	0.7	4.6	50.5
Singapore	1987	32,557.4	10.7	0.6	18.3	70.4	6.0	40.2	24.2	12.0	14.7	0.3	20.5	52.4
Solomon Islands	1985	82.7	21.3	0.4	20.3	58.0	6.0	26.3	25.7	6.1	2.1	—	19.6	72.2
Somalia	1981	512.9	26.6	—	2.3	71.1	2.0	50.0	19.1	66.0	4.3	0.1	1.8	27.8
South Africa[52]	1985	10,311.7	5.6[2]	1.5[2]	0.4[2, 53]	92.4[2, 54]	8.6[2]	42.9[2]	41.0[2, 54]	42.4	14.0	0.1	10.0	33.4
Bophuthatswana[52]	...	...	...	...	...	...	...	...	...	...	...	...	...	...
Ciskei[52]	...	...	...	...	...	...	...	...	...	...	...	...	...	...
Transkei[52]	...	...	...	...	...	...	...	...	...	...	...	...	...	...
Venda[52]	...	...	...	...	...	...	...	...	...	...	...	...	...	...
South West Africa/Namibia[52]	1986	652.0	...	...	...	...	...	...	...	...	...	...	...	...
Spain	1987	49,075.4	15.9	2.7	16.4	65.1	10.7	34.8	19.6	54.6	8.3	2.6	4.5	30.1
Sri Lanka	1987	2,029.2	16.8[47]	0.8[47]	25.7[47]	56.7[47]	8.3[47]	24.3[47]	24.1[47]	17.2	5.6	0.9	15.0	61.3
Sudan, The	1983	1,354.4	18.6	0.3	26.6	54.6	11.0	26.6	17.0	38.3	9.1	1.5	3.2	47.9
Suriname	1986	317.0	11.9[23]	2.3[17, 23]	27.2[23]	57.7[18, 23]	11.5[23]	29.8[23]	16.4[18, 23]	29.2	32.4	0.4	2.0	36.1
Swaziland	1986[11]	328.5	11.7	0.8	25.7	61.8	4.9	21.4	35.5	9.2	1.2	—	1.0	88.6[56]
Sweden	1987	40,644.7	9.3	1.6	9.0	80.1	9.6	38.4	32.1	57.3	6.9	4.1	6.0	25.7
Switzerland	1987	50,609.5	9.6	4.8	4.5	81.2	11.3	31.6	38.3	72.1	5.3	1.4	4.6	16.5
Syria	1985	3,967.0	21.5	0.6	29.3	48.6	9.5	18.8	20.3	33.9	6.1	12.5	2.8	44.6
Taiwan	1987	33,977.0	15.0	2.3	10.7	72.0	13.6	35.1	23.4	12.3	22.1	—	34.3	31.3
Tanzania	1985	1,016.8	7.6[21]	0.6[21]	30.8[21]	61.0[21]	10.0[21]	35.0[21]	16.1[21]	43.0	3.6	1.2	9.5	42.7
Thailand	1986	9,139.0	11.4	3.3	13.5	71.8	15.4	30.4	25.9	15.1	14.4	1.3	26.4	42.8
Togo	1984	271.2	——30.0——		11.4	58.6	10.8	20.0	27.9	63.3	4.3	0.7	5.3	26.5
Tokelau	1982	0.6	55.7	—	33.4	11.1	5.7	1.1	4.3	—	—	—	—	100.0[57]
Tonga	1986	40.0	31.6	0.7	12.3	55.4	8.7	15.3	31.4	4.0	3.8	—	11.4	80.7
Trinidad and Tobago	1987	1,218.7	23.6	2.7	4.3	69.3	12.2	29.2	27.9	21.7	41.9	0.1	5.3	31.0
Tunisia	1986	2,900.6	18.2	6.6	6.8	68.4	9.6	25.1	33.7	67.7	7.0	3.9	1.6	19.9
Turkey	1987	14,162.6	11.2	3.1	22.4	63.3	15.2	28.6	19.5	40.0	9.7	5.5	6.1	38.7
Turks and Caicos Islands	1984[11]	26.3	——32.1[5]——		11.6	56.3[6]	...	...	...	...	74.7	...	...	25.3
Tuvalu	1983	2.7	36.8	0.2	14.0	49.0	6.9	12.3	29.7	2.5	0.5	—	2.1	94.9
Uganda	1986	344.1[3]	8.7[23]	0.7[23]	29.6[23]	61.0[23]	11.1[23]	26.8[23]	23.0[23]	37.6[3]	1.3[3]	...	5.0[3]	56.1[3]
U.S.S.R.	1987	97,185.3	——18.6[5]——		2.7	78.8[6]	7.9	41.4	29.5[6]	11.4	1.5	56.5	2.7	27.9
United Arab Emirates	1984	7,062.1	16.1	1.2	7.7	74.9	5.6	32.1	37.2	34.9	12.0	0.7	17.8	34.5
United Kingdom[34]	1987	154,082.3	15.2	3.4	6.5	75.0	8.9	34.9	31.2	52.8	9.7	1.8	5.8	29.9
United States[59]	1987	424,037.2	8.6	1.8	11.0	78.6	3.9	43.2	31.5	20.0	—	0.5	20.8	58.7
Uruguay	1986	870.0	13.9	1.2	19.4	65.5	22.7	25.6	17.2	19.9	8.5	1.8	3.4	66.4
Vanuatu	1983	51.2	26.5	0.2	11.0	62.2	6.3	21.0	34.9	14.2	1.1	—	12.2	72.5
Venezuela	1985	8,234.2	16.4	2.8	2.4	78.4	14.2	42.3	21.9	24.0	46.3	0.4	5.8	23.6
Vietnam	1986	2,639.0[3]	...	...	...	...	...	...	...	2.4[3]	1.3[3]	76.0[3]	7.9[3]	12.4[3]
Virgin Islands (U.S.)	1978	667.4	11.9	—	58.5	29.6	3.7	8.2	17.6	0.9	58.0	0.1	0.2	40.7
Wallis and Futuna	1984	8.1	——34.9[5]——		11.8	53.2[6]	...	17.5	35.7[6]	...	...	...	...	...
West Bank	1986	512.0	...	...	...	...	...	...	...	...	...	...	...	100.0[61]
Western Sahara	...	...	...	...	...	...	...	...	...	...	...	...	...	...
Western Samoa	1983	52.6	24.3	0.3	17.5	57.9	7.4	22.9	27.6	5.5	11.0	—	11.4	72.2
Yemen (Aden)	1977	544.0	——18.1[5]——		46.6	35.2[6]	2.0	22.7	10.6[6]	18.4	—	4.0	11.3	66.4
Yemen (Şan'ā')	1981	1,608.8	32.2	0.1	8.3	59.4	5.6	25.4	28.4	30.8	2.8	1.2	17.7	47.5
Yugoslavia	1987	16,094.4	12.4	2.8	17.4	67.4	16.3	30.5	20.6	40.0	5.7	29.6	1.4	23.4
Zaire	1983	931.0	22.4[63]	1.2[63]	7.6[63]	68.8[63]	10.3[63]	31.7[63]	26.9[63]	50.8	6.9	0.3	3.0	39.0
Zambia	1984	740.8	6.9	0.6	29.7	62.7	13.6	28.7	20.4	24.5	6.4	0.3	3.3	65.4
Zimbabwe	1984	959.4	10.8	0.3	21.4	67.5	14.8	31.1	21.6	28.9	9.3	—	5.3	56.5

[1]Year ending March.   [2]1982.   [3]Estimated based on trading partners' information.   [4]Year ending June 30.   [5]Excluding precious stones, etc. (667).   [6]Including precious stones, etc. (667).   [7]Excluding fish imported for canneries.   [8]Includes 42.4% from France and 27.0% from Spain.   [9]Includes 54.3% to France and 32.8% to Spain.   [10]Figures for Belgium–Luxembourg Economic Union (Luxembourg is also shown separately).   [11]1986: imports $88.0, exports $25.3.   [12]Includes 82.1% from India.   [13]Includes 97.5% to India.   [14]Includes 78.1% from rest of Customs Union of Southern Africa.   [15]Includes 71.9% to Switzerland.   [16]1985.   [17]Including metals.   [18]Excluding metals.   [19]1980.   [20]94.7% for ships' bunkers and stores.   [21]1981.   [22]1975.   [23]1976.   [24]1983.   [25]1979.   [26]Figures for France include Monaco.   [27]Includes 91.7% from Israel.   [28]Includes 85.0% to Israel.   [29]Import figures refer to total trade turnover (figures are not available separately for imports and for exports).   [30]Excluding trade with East Germany (1.6% of total imports and 1.4% of total exports in 1986).   [31]Excluding petroleum products.   [32]Includes 62.2% for ships' bunkers.   [33]Domestic exports only.   [34]Figures for United Kingdom include Guernsey, Isle of Man, and Jersey (the latter is also shown separately).   [35]Year ending September 30.   [36]1977.   [37]Commercial imports only (excluding oil

total value U.S.$ (000,000)	food and agricultural raw materials (0+1+2 −27−28 +4)	mineral ores and concentrates (27+28 +667)	fuels and other energy (3)	manufactured goods total[a] (5+6 −667 +7+8 +9)	of which chemicals and related products (5)	of which machinery and transport equipment (7)	of which other[a] (6−667 +8+9)	to European Economic Community (EEC)[b]	to United States	to U.S.S.R. and Eastern Europe[c]	to Japan	to all other[d]	country
...	...	...	...	...	...	...	...	...	...	...	...	...	Northern Mariana Islands
0.5	69.1	...	...	30.9	...	...	30.9	...	...	...	...	...	Palau
3,384.0	31.4	0.5	0.7	67.4	0.8	2.9	63.7	28.0	10.8	4.0	9.8	47.4	Pakistan
301.2	78.2	1.1	7.2	13.5	3.3	0.1	10.1	16.1	64.1	0.2	0.1	19.5	Panama
899.0	40.1[2]	50.5[2]	0.1[2]	9.3[2]	0.1[2]	1.8[2]	7.4[2]	45.4[3]	2.7	0.7[3]	29.3	21.9[3]	Papua New Guinea
232.5	90.9	—	—	9.1	3.3		5.7	20.5	4.0		0.8	74.7	Paraguay
2,525.1	20.3	19.2	25.8	34.7	1.3	1.4	31.9	18.3	44.1	2.5	9.3	25.7	Peru
5,720.2	28.3	4.1	1.7	65.9	4.3	10.5	51.1	18.9	36.1	0.5	17.2	27.4	Philippines
...													Pitcairn Island
12,073.7	12.0	3.4	13.2	71.4	6.4	34.7	30.2	21.3	2.1	39.0	0.3	37.3	Poland
9,167.0	16.6	1.3	1.9	80.2	5.4	16.4	58.3	71.2	6.5	1.0	0.7	20.7	Portugal
9,146.0	—17.6[5]—		5.8	76.6[6]	27.7	21.4	27.5[6]	4.4	82.7	—	0.2	12.8	Puerto Rico
4,512.6	—[21]	—[21]	93.9[21]	6.1[21]	3.9[21]	—[21]	2.2[21]	43.2[21]	0.2[21]	—[21]	33.3[21]	23.4[21]	Qatar
148.3	88.8	0.1	0.2	10.9	2.9	4.6	3.3	89.3	0.2	—	2.7	7.8	Réunion
12,167.3	12.6	—28.3[17]—		59.0[18]	10.7	29.9	18.4[18]	24.1	5.8	36.1	0.6	33.5	Romania
90.5	—98.9—		—	1.1			1.1	48.1	33.3		1.4	17.3	Rwanda
0.04	100.0	—	—					...	...	...	...	...	St. Helena and Ascension
18.4	67.9	—	—	32.1	0.4	10.1	21.6	19.6	51.7	—	0.3	28.5	St. Kitts and Nevis
82.9	75.6	—	0.1	24.4	0.3	4.7	19.3	69.2	12.1	—	—	18.7	St. Lucia
7.8	99.9	—	—	0.1			0.1	7.7	74.3	—	—	18.0	St. Pierre and Miquelon
63.8	85.9	—[5]	—	14.1[6]	1.0	3.8	9.3[6]	31.2	9.4	—	—	59.4	St. Vincent and the Grenadines
...													San Marino[39]
12.2	99.8[36]	—[36]	...[36]	0.2[36]	—[36]	0.1[36]	0.1[36]	56.6[3]	—[3]	34.7[3]	—[3]	8.7[3]	São Tomé and Príncipe
27,487.1	0.5	0.1	94.4	5.0	2.8	1.4	0.8	22.3[3]	6.7[3]	1.7[3]	34.1[3]	35.2[3]	Saudi Arabia
534.4	—63.3—		18.5	18.2	9.0	2.6	6.7	48.0	0.2	—	1.6	50.2	Senegal
27.9	10.8	—	82.2	7.1		3.5	3.5	3.8	2.5	—	3.4	90.3	Seychelles
91.5	33.1	62.0	3.9	1.1	0.1	—	1.0	91.0	2.4	—	—	6.6	Sierra Leone
28,685.8	10.9	0.6	16.2	72.3	6.2	43.6	22.4	12.2	24.4	0.9	9.0	53.5	Singapore
70.1	96.3	—	—	3.7	—		3.7	28.0	2.5	—	52.3	17.1	Solomon Islands
152.0	99.4	—	0.2	0.4		0.1	0.2	6.2	—	—	—	93.7	Somalia
16,420.1	12.4[2]	10.7[2]	6.5[2]	70.4[2,55]	2.5	2.6	65.4[2,55]	21.4	8.4	0.1	7.8	62.4	South Africa[52]
...	...	...	...	...	...	...	...	...	...	...	...	...	Bophuthatswana[52]
...	...	...	...	...	...	...	...	...	...	...	...	...	Ciskei[52]
...	...	...	...	...	...	...	...	...	...	...	...	...	Transkei[52]
...	...	...	...	...	...	...	...	...	...	...	...	...	Venda[52]
877.5	9.7	82.6	...	7.7	...	...	7.7	...	...	...	...	...	South West Africa/Namibia[52]
34,118.0	20.4	1.1	6.2	72.3	8.7	31.2	32.4	63.8	8.1	1.6	1.1	25.4	Spain
1,353.7	63.0[47]	2.5[47]	9.0[47]	25.5[47]	0.5[47]	1.4[47]	23.5[47]	22.2	26.6	3.2	5.0	43.1	Sri Lanka
623.5	93.9	0.3	2.7	3.1		2.2	0.9	25.2	2.0	7.7	5.4	59.7	Sudan, The
329.4	21.6[23]	32.7[17,23]	—[23]	45.7[18,23]	43.1[23]	0.5[23]	2.1[18,23]	34.9	16.4	—	12.7	36.0	Suriname
176.8	82.3	0.1	1.6	15.9	0.4	0.1	15.5	...	...	...	...	...	Swaziland
44,446.7	9.7	1.5	2.9	85.8	6.8	43.3	35.7	51.0	10.8	2.1	1.5	34.7	Sweden
45,487.2	3.9	4.4	0.1	91.6	21.9	33.1	36.6	55.8	8.8	3.3	3.8	28.3	Switzerland
1,637.3	12.5	1.2	74.1	12.2	3.1	0.9	8.2	45.8	—	44.9	0.1	9.2	Syria
52,631.9	6.8	0.2	0.8	92.2	2.6	32.3	57.3	13.0	44.2	—	12.9	29.8	Taiwan
254.9	82.4[21]	10.1[21]	0.2[21]	7.3[21]	0.7[21]	2.5[21]	4.1[21]	64.2	2.0	1.2	4.2	28.4	Tanzania
8,835.6	52.4	4.2	0.8	42.7	1.6	10.9	30.2	21.4	18.1	1.2	14.2	45.2	Thailand
191.3	41.0	49.0	1.4	8.6	0.5	2.3	5.8	62.5	0.8	10.6	0.7	25.4	Togo
0.1	100.0	—	—	—	—	—	—	...	...	...	...	...	Tokelau
6.4	77.8	—	—	22.2	0.2	3.6	18.4	2.1	16.5	—	0.2	81.2	Tonga
1,462.4	4.5	0.6	71.2	23.7	14.1	1.4	8.2	12.4	58.3	—	2.3	26.9	Trinidad and Tobago
1,759.6	13.0	2.7	24.3	60.1	20.0	5.3	34.8	73.8	0.7	3.6	0.1	21.8	Tunisia
10,189.7	27.6	2.7	2.3	67.4	6.6	10.7	50.1	47.8	7.0	3.1	1.5	40.6	Turkey
3.0	100.0	—	—					—	100.0	—	—	—	Turks and Caicos Islands
0.1	78.8	—	—	21.2			21.2	—	—	—	—	100.0[58]	Tuvalu
429.7[3]	96.6[23]	0.2[23]	0.8[23]	2.4[23]	—[23]	—[23]	2.4[23]	56.3[3]	29.5[3]	...	3.9[3]	10.3[3]	Uganda
109,026.9	6.7	2.3[5]	46.4	44.5[6]	3.0	15.5	26.0[6]	14.4	0.4	50.4	1.4	33.3	U.S.S.R.
13,869.2	1.7	0.2	87.5	10.6	0.5	3.4	6.7	15.2[3]	6.3[3]	—[3]	38.2[3]	40.3[3]	United Arab Emirates
130,868.5	8.8	3.2	11.0	77.1	13.2	36.1	27.9	49.5	13.8	1.4	1.9	33.5	United Kingdom[34]
254,356.2	16.0	2.1	3.1	78.8	10.2	45.3	23.3	23.5	—	0.9	10.9	64.7	United States[59]
1,082.1	53.1	0.2	0.5	46.3	5.5	2.4	38.4	26.1	12.0	4.7	1.5	55.7	Uruguay
29.6	99.3[33]	—[33]	—[33]	0.7[33]	—[33]	—[33]	0.7[33]	46.2	18.2	—	12.6	23.0	Vanuatu
12,272.0	0.7[24]	1.2[24]	94.4[24]	3.8[24]	0.4[24]	0.2[24]	3.1[24]	21.4[24]	32.6[24]	2.8[24]	2.8[24]	43.1[24]	Venezuela
815.0[3]	...	...	...	...	...	...	...	4.2[3]	—[3]	60.2[3]	9.3[3]	26.3[3]	Vietnam
2,512.1	—	—	91.3	8.7	6.2	...	2.5	1.0	96.8	1.3	0.1	0.8	Virgin Islands (U.S.)
0.02	100.0	—	—	—	—	—	—	—	—	—	—	100.0[60]	Wallis and Futuna
238.6	...	...	...	...	...	...	...	...	...	...	...	100.0[62]	West Bank
...													Western Sahara
18.6	90.6	—	—	9.4	—	5.8	3.6	11.6	31.7	—	3.6	53.1	Western Samoa
180.8	—15.5—		84.0	0.5[6]	—	0.4	0.1[6]	1.8	—	—	9.6	88.6	Yemen (Aden)
47.5	23.8	—	—	76.2	1.6	64.5	10.2	24.6	3.0	0.1	0.1	72.3	Yemen (Şan'ā')
14,542.7	12.8	1.0	1.9	84.3	11.3	30.4	42.6	34.8	6.4	34.2	0.3	24.2	Yugoslavia
1,559.5	13.0	70.8	11.1	5.0				51.8[3]	22.0[3]	—[3]	4.9[3]	21.3[3]	Zaire
659.6	0.4[25]	0.6[25]	1.2[25]	97.7[25]	0.2[25]	0.3[25]	97.2[25]	32.2	9.6	0.7	23.5	34.0	Zambia
1,004.3	47.9	7.3	1.3	43.4	1.9	1.8	39.8	34.7	6.2	—	5.2	53.8	Zimbabwe

companies' imports). [38]Excluding imported military goods of $2,480.9 million. [39]Figures for Italy include San Marino. [40]Includes 84.9% from United Kingdom. [41]Including coins. [42]Includes 67.3% to United Kingdom. [43]1974. [44]Includes 97.1% from rest of Customs Union of Southern Africa. [45]Includes 56.1% from France. [46]Includes 70.2% to France. [47]1984. [48]Based on trade with Hong Kong, Australia, and New Zealand only; year ending June 30. [49]Curaçao only. [50]Includes 49.2% from Australia. [51]Includes 62.6% to Australia. [52]Figures for South Africa refer to Customs Union of Southern Africa (includes South Africa, Botswana, Lesotho, and Swaziland, also shown separately; also South West Africa/Namibia, Bophuthatswana, Ciskei, Transkei, and Venda). [53]Excluding crude oil. [54]Including crude oil (included in "special transactions" accounting in total for 23.4%). [55]Including gold (included in "special transactions" accounting in total for 54.4%). [56]Includes 81.1% from rest of Customs Union of Southern Africa. [57]All from South Pacific countries [58]All to Fiji. [59]Figures for United States include American Samoa, Guam, Puerto Rico, and Virgin Islands (U.S.), also shown separately. [60]All to Northern Mariana Islands. [61]Includes 88.1% from Israel. [62]Includes 65.3% to Israel, 34.3% to Jordan. [63]1978.

Trade: domestic

The following table presents data relating to domestic wholesale and retail trade for the countries of the world. The section on wholesale trade is based for the most part on establishments engaged primarily in selling goods to retailers and distributors for resale or to purchasers who buy for business and farm uses. The retail trade section is based on businesses engaged in selling merchandise for personal or household consumption; restaurants are, when possible, included, hotels excluded.

The data presented here are based on information received from a variety of direct country and international sources. The direct country sources include such items as correspondence, statistical abstracts, annual reports, and censuses of business and trade. Among the more useful international sources are the various compilations of the United Nations dealing with domestic trade and Euromonitor's *Retail Trade International* (2 vols.).

Since there is no single published source or common international methodology for the compilation of data on wholesale and retail trade, nor a single current year on which, by common agreement, the various national reports would be based, allowance must be made for variations in the meaning and recency of the information provided for any single country and for its comparability internationally. Variations occur in part because of the ways in which countries define wholesale and retail trade; the conventional capitalist, or free-enterprise, distinctions between wholesale and retail activity (of a single enterprise or an entire national trade sector) may not exist in the business practice of some countries, and data may overlap in their final reports. Variations also exist in the kind and level of detail reported. For example, countries may design surveys differently according to the size (number of employees, sales, surface area) of establishments surveyed, their profitability, or other less direct criteria, such as ownership or location. The depth of analysis to which the data are subjected may also vary. The structure of a national trade sector is also affected by the degree of government involvement, which may range from total control of wholesale distribution in some socialist countries, to partial involvement in some strategic sectors, or to relative noninvolvement in fully private trade sectors of capitalist countries. In some smaller countries data may refer to a single trading enterprise.

At the table's extreme left, preceding the year to which the trade data refer, the combined value of the country's wholesale and retail trade as a percentage of gross domestic product or net material product is given. Unless otherwise noted, GDP data include restaurants and exclude hotels.

Both the wholesale and retail sections of the table provide similar detail: establishments or outlets, employees, sales, and derived values for relationships among these measures; the retail section provides an additional breakdown of sales by an end-use classification of retail sales outlets.

Although all sales figures are given in U.S. dollars, the comparability of these dollar figures may differ considerably; for instance, the purchasing power of various national currencies in domestic transactions may bear only a distant relationship to the exchange rate of the same currency in international transactions. The price of goods may also vary, depending on the degree to which they are subject to direct subsidies and artificial cost controls such as tax, investment, or free-trade preferences by a central government seeking to influence social or economic conditions.

Trade: domestic

country	domestic trade as percentage of GDP, 1985	year	wholesale trade					retail trade		
			establishments[a]	employees[b]	sales[c] $'000,000	employees per establishment	sales per establishment $'000	outlets[a]	employees[b]	sales[c] $'000,000
Afghanistan	10.2[1,2]	1979–80	...	3	...	...	...	...	146,075[3,4]	...
Albania	9.5[5]	1983	...	...	...	...	...	10,585[6]	...	994[6]
Algeria	15.5	1971	...	3	...	...	...	3,600[7]	65,917[3,8]	12,607[9]
American Samoa	...	1985	40	77[10]	...	...	...	300	499[10]	...
Andorra	25.2[11]	1972	...	...	...	...	...	592	2,264	...
Angola	4.8[12]	1973	3	...	...	3	...	29,138[3]	...	...
Anguilla	...	1984	3	3	...	3	...	92[3]	403[3]	...
Antigua and Barbuda	27.6[2,13]	1980	25	350	...	14.0	...	199	1,000	23[9]
Argentina	12.7	1974	45,700	275,000[4]	10,922[14]	6.0[4]	...	445,798[15]	930,000[4,15]	15,540[9]
Aruba	...	1983	...	3	...	...	...	3,192[3,16]		17
Australia	15.7	1987	39,319[18]	361,000[4,18]	84,798[18]	9.2[4,18]	2,157[18]	110,500[10]	737,378[4,10]	58,975
Austria	16.0[2]	1984	15,330[9]	168,572[4,9]	34,819[9]	11.0[4,9]	2,271[9]	42,491[9]	249,646[4,9]	17,015[9]
Bahamas, The[19]	26.2[2,13]	1980	23	1,066	143	46.3	6.235	132	4,059	257[11]
Bahrain	14.8[13]	1983	3	3	...	3	...	255[3]	12,551[3]	1,601
Bangladesh	8.5[2]	1983	...	3	...	...	...	...	146,000[3,20]	4,800
Barbados	27.9[2]	1979	...	3	...	...	...	1,911	5,800[3,15]	264[9]
Belgium	16.7[2]	1984	57,079[11]	166,900[12]	65,286[11]	3.0[12]	1,144[11]	121,690[11]	159,848[11]	26,497
Belize	15.2[2]	1983	...	...	...	...	...	...	...	23
Benin	19.3[2]	1979	...	...	...	...	...	1707	1,910[4,7]	150[9]
Bermuda	32.8[21]	1985	60[21]	820	...	...	...	310[7,12]	4,342[15]	116[13,15]
Bhutan	11.3[2]	1982	...	3	...	...	...	...	9,000[3,4]	...
Bolivia	17.2[2]	1983	...	3	...	...	...	...	17,414[3,22]	1,818
Botswana	21.3[2]	1982–83	117[13]	1,800	494	...	...	3,248[13]	5,200	165
Brazil	13.4[2]	1984	45,969[10]	370,000[10]	91,331[10]	8.0[10]	1,987[10]	1,030,000	3,450,000	40,090
British Virgin Islands	26.7[2,5]	1982	...	...	...	...	...	...	366	5[12]
Brunei	12.2[2]	1986	3	3	...	3	...	833[3,26]	4,261[3,26]	...
Bulgaria	7.1[1,2]	1986	...	7,600[9]	...	...	...	41,354[15]	79,231[15]	35,500[15]
Burkina Faso	11.6[2,13]	1975	...	3	...	...	...	...	19,354[3,4]	...
Burma	24.3[2]	1983	...	...	...	...	...	...	...	2,116
Burundi	7.1[27]	1981	...	...	...	...	...	...	1	445
Cameroon	14.7[2,13]	1980	...		...	...	...	1,312[7]	13,776[4,7]	753[9]
Canada	11.7[27]	1985	...	451,665[10]	139,110[13]	...	...	...	1,138,500[15]	103,410
Cape Verde	...									
Cayman Islands	17.0[16]	1979	...	3	...	...	...	...	1,518[3]	...
Central African Republic	21.3[2]	1978[2]	3	3	3	...	3	102[3,7]	26,659[3,4,28]	252[3,7]
Chad	30.1[2,8]	1983	...	3	3	...	...	...	1,661[3,7,22]	497[3]
Chile	16.7[2]	1983	561[7]	15,300[7]	2,312[7]	27.2[7]	4,121[7]	1,125[7,15]	21,700[7,15]	1,403[7,15]
China	10.2[2]	1985	67,000	1,067,000[4]	...	15.9[4]	...	7,783,000[15]	17,960,000[4,15]	145,534[13,15]
Christmas Island	...	1981	—	3	...	—	—	5	65[3]	...
Cocos (Keeling) Islands	...	1981	—	3	...	...	...	1	13[3]	...
Colombia	13.7[2]	1983	...	...	...	...	...	...	...	6,285
Comoros	25.0[2]	1974	...	3	...	...	...	...	983[3,7,30]	...
Congo	10.9[2,13]	...	...	...	...	...	...	...	...	...
Cook Islands	24.0[5]	1982[31]	3	3	3	3	3	109[3]	369[3]	31[3]
Costa Rica	19.3[2]	1975	332[32]	4,073[32]	35[32]	12.3[32]	104[32]	9,713	26,486	475[9]
Côte d'Ivoire	17.1[2,10]	1981	...	...	3	...	...	2,023[7]	16,720[7]	1,548[3,9]
Cuba	36.4[1,2]	1986	...	...	11,541	...	...	56,916[33]	220,100[4,9]	11,388
Cyprus	18.7[2]	1986	1,538[9]	12,400	225	5.2[9]	733[9]	8,312[9]	20,100[4,15]	268[15]
Czechoslovakia	16.4[1,2]	1986	...	...	...	...	...	63,050	254,552	16,608
Denmark	13.1[2]	1983	5,692	124,000	27,028[13]	21.8	4,907	50,826[12]	116,000[12]	12,397[13]
Djibouti	15.6[2]	1985	28	37[11]	...	...	...	431	1,877[11]	...
Dominica	13.5[2,27]	1983	...	...	...	...	...	...	1,597[3,12]	4
Dominican Republic	15.8[2]	1983	670	...	3,136	...	4,681	11,220[11]	...	1,259[11]
Ecuador	15.7[2]	1980[2]	2,450	15,591[4]	2,805	6.4[4]	1,145	102,981	179,847[4]	5,922
Egypt	13.2[2,34]	1980–81[7]	1,766	42,300[4]	3,216	24.0[4]	1,821	2,136	48,200[4]	2,015

The data on distribution of retail sales by kind of consumer goods may have their origin in several different types of data or analysis: One country may aggregate sales data by kind of establishment only (this may be perfectly satisfactory in a country of small, independent outlets); another may aggregate data directly by kind of goods (most easily done in a country with well-developed statistical, tax-reporting, and commercial systems). Other countries may find it impolitic to publish data that reflect the poverty of their distribution network or their supply of consumer goods and may aggregate or publish data for only a few sectors: food or nonfood goods, for example. For countries with only a few trading enterprises in a particular sector, detail must often be withheld to preserve the confidentiality of individual businesses.

The notes that follow further define the various headings.

a. The number of establishments or outlets refers to economic units that operate at a single physical location in one principal kind of activity, whether singly owned or part of a multiunit firm. Such units are not necessarily identical with a company or enterprise.

b. Number of employees refers to full-time and part-time paid workers, including salaried managers and officers; it usually excludes owner-operators, partners, vendors, and unpaid relatives.

c. Total sales (also called turnover) includes the value of merchandise sold for cash or credit; amounts received from customers for layaway purchases; receipts from rental or leasing of vehicles, equipment, tools, instruments, etc.; receipts for delivery, installation, maintenance, repair, alteration, storage, and other services.

d. Outlets engaged primarily in the sale of food and nonalcoholic beverages, such as grocery stores, meat and fish markets, and bakeries.

e. Outlets engaged primarily in the sale of clothing and shoes; also includes outlets that sell accessory items, such as millinery, furs, and leather goods.

f. Outlets engaged primarily in the sale of home furnishings, including furniture, draperies, floor coverings, household appliances, and home entertainment equipment.

g. Outlets that primarily serve food and drink, including restaurants, lunchrooms, cafeterias, social caterers, refreshment places, contract feeders, ice cream parlors, and bars and taverns.

h. Outlets engaged primarily in the sale of pharmaceuticals, cosmetics, and perfumes.

i. Outlets engaged primarily in the sale of building materials, hardware, garden supplies, paint, electrical supplies, and farm equipment.

j. Outlets engaged primarily in the sale of motor vehicles, motorcycles, bicycles, and tires, batteries, and other automotive supplies and parts; includes service stations.

k. Outlets engaged in the sale of multiple lines of merchandise, such as department stores, variety stores, and rural general stores.

l. Miscellaneous specialized outlets such as those engaged primarily in the sale of liquors, sporting goods, books, jewelry, photographic and optical goods, gifts, flowers, tobacco products, home fuels, and newspapers.

retail trade (continued)									employees per outlet	sales per outlet $'000	population per outlet	country
percent breakdown of sales												
food[d]	clothing, shoes[e]	home furnishings[f]	eating, drinking[g]	drugs, pharma-ceuticals[h]	building materials[i]	automobile parts[j]	general merchandise[k]	other[l]				
...	...	...	...	...	...	...	...	...	...	...	...	Afghanistan
61.5	...	...	...	38.5	...	...	...	...	...	93[6]	268[6]	Albania
...	...	...	...	...	...	...	...	...	5.0[7]	...	5,146[7]	Algeria
...	...	...	...	...	...	...	...	...	...	...	119	American Samoa
...	...	...	...	...	...	...	...	...	3.8	...	39	Andorra
...	...	...	...	...	...	...	...	...	...	...	...	Angola
...	...	...	...	...	...	...	...	...	4.3[3]	...	73[3]	Anguilla
...	...	...	...	...	...	...	...	...	5.0	100	378	Antigua and Barbuda
...	...	...	...	...	...	...	...	...	2.1[4, 15]	...	58[15]	Argentina
...	...	...	...	...	...	...	...	...	...	...	...	Aruba
41.4	10.6	11.4	11.5[2]	4.2	...	...	12.3	8.6	6.7[4, 10]	398[10]	132[10]	Australia
30.0	14.5	10.3	...	4.8	...	13.7	10.1	16.6	5.9[4, 9]	400[9]	178[9]	Austria
24.4[11]	7.7[11]	7.1[11]	—	3.7[11]	8.4[11]	30.1[11]	7.6[11]	11.0[11]	30.8	1,881	1,026	Bahamas, The[19]
...	...	...	...	...	...	...	...	...	49.2[3]	...	1,507[3]	Bahrain
...	...	...	...	...	...	...	...	...	...	...	...	Bangladesh
...	...	...	...	...	...	...	...	...	...	...	130	Barbados
35.1	...	...	...	64.9	...	...	...	...	1.2[11]	218[11]	81[11]	Belgium
...	...	...	...	...	...	...	...	...	...	...	...	Belize
...	...	...	...	...	...	...	...	...	11.3[4, 7]	...	19,871[7]	Benin
...	...	...	...	...	...	...	...	...	11.0[9, 15]	...	178[7, 12]	Bermuda
...	...	...	...	...	...	...	...	...	...	...	...	Bhutan
...	...	...	...	...	...	...	...	...	...	...	...	Bolivia
...	...	...	...	...	...	...	...	...	2.7[21]	120[21]	322[13]	Botswana
15.0[23]	7.2	13.0[24]	...	4.7	24	27.3[25]	19.3	13.5	3.4	39	129	Brazil
...	...	...	...	...	...	...	...	...	...	...	...	British Virgin Islands
...	...	...	...	...	...	...	...	...	5.1[3, 26]	...	2793[3, 26]	Brunei
51.1	10.7	2.0	...	5.9	...	...	0.2	30.1	1.9[15]	858[15]	217[15]	Bulgaria
...	...	...	...	...	...	...	...	...	...	...	...	Burkina Faso
...	...	...	...	...	...	...	...	...	...	...	...	Burma
...	...	...	...	...	...	...	...	...	...	...	...	Burundi
...	...	...	...	...	...	...	...	...	10.5[4, 7]	...	6,481[7]	Cameroon
22.8	5.1	2.3	8.3	3.8	0.8	29.8	12.8	14.3	...	...	...	Canada
...	...	...	...	...	...	...	...	...	...	...	...	Cape Verde
...	...	...	...	...	...	...	...	...	...	...	...	Cayman Islands
...	...	...	...	...	...	...	...	...	...	2,471[3, 7]	21,774[3, 7]	Central African Republic
...	...	...	...	...	...	...	...	...	...	...	...	Chad
28.3[11]	29	5.0[11]	1.6[11]	5.4[11]	4.7[11]	18.0[11]	17.1[11, 29]	19.9[11]	19.3[7, 15]	1,247[7, 15]	10,210[7, 15]	Chile
45.8[13]	16.9[13]			37.3[13]					2.4[4, 15]	22[13, 15]	134[15]	China
...	...	...	...	...	...	...	...	...	...	...	662	Christmas Island
...	...	...	...	...	...	...	...	...	...	...	569	Cocos (Keeling) Islands
...	...	...	...	...	...	...	...	...	...	...	...	Colombia
...	...	...	...	...	...	...	...	...	...	...	...	Comoros
...	...	...	...	...	...	...	...	...	...	...	...	Congo
...	...	...	...	...	...	...	...	...	3.4[3]	284[3]	84[3]	Cook Islands
37.7	13.5	6.9	...	8.2	7.0	15.1	5.9	5.7	2.7	59	202	Costa Rica
...	...	...	...	...	...	...	...	...	8.3[7]	...	4,257[7]	Côte d'Ivoire
35.8	...	...	29.0	3.4	...	2.9	...	28.9	...	150[33]	177[33]	Cuba
21.9[23, 33]	17.7[33]	8.6[33]	...	3.2[33]	9.0[33]	29.7[33]	...	9.9[33]	1.0[9]	126[9]	78[9]	Cyprus
48.2	16.4	9.8	...	3.5	4.3	7.0	...	10.8	4.0	263	246	Czechoslovakia
48.9[11]	6.7[11]	7.7[11]	—[11]	0.6[11]	2.6[11]	15.0[11]	8.6[11]	9.9[11]	2.3[12]	311[12]	101[12]	Denmark
...	...	...	...	...	...	...	...	...	...	...	998	Djibouti
...	...	...	...	...	...	...	...	...	...	...	...	Dominica
...	...	...	...	...	...	...	...	...	...	112[11]	519[11]	Dominican Republic
24.2	29.1	8.1	3.0	4.8	4.0	17.8	3.4	5.6	1.7[4]	58	79	Ecuador
...	...	...	...	...	...	...	...	...	22.6[4]	943	20,036	Egypt

Trade: domestic (continued)

country	domestic trade as percentage of GDP, 1985	year	wholesale trade					retail trade		
			establishments[a]	employees[b]	sales[c] $'000,000	employees per establishment	sales per establishment $'000	outlets[a]	employees[b]	sales[c] $'000,000
El Salvador	29.1[2]	1982	384	6,800	629	17.7	1,638	1,435	10,900	930[9]
Equatorial Guinea	3.6[2]	...	...	...	...	...	...	...	...	...
Ethiopia	9.7[2]	1973[7,36]	375	3,200	[3]	8.5	...	7,416	17,100	201
Faeroe Islands	11.7[2,10]	1984	87	[3]	...	...	...	570[2]	1,484[2,3,10]	...
Falkland Islands	...	1976	2	...	...	...	...	21	...	...
Fiji	15.5[2]	1983	138[7]	2,000[7]	248[7]	14.5[7]	1,797[7]	578[7]	6,000[7]	351[7]
Finland	10.3[2]	1984	8,186[11]	85,900[4,11]	27,300[11]	10.5[4,11]	3,335[11]	36,333	143,336	16,160
France	11.8[2,13]	1987	133,235	994,044[27]	251,108[27]	6.5[13]	1,368[13]	599,217	1,215,867[27]	166,136[27]
French Guiana	12.3[21]	1981	[3]	[3]	...	...	...	113[3,7]	372[3,7]	...
French Polynesia	24.1[2,9]	1983	[3]	...	...	...	...	...	1,535[3]	...
Gabon	8.2[9]	1982	...	...	...	...	...	...	12,683[3,4,12]	...
Gambia, The	27.0[2]	1983	...	1,900	...	...	...	...	500	...
Gaza Strip	...	1985	...	[3]	...	...	...	...	1,000[3]	...
Germany, East	8.9[1,2]	1986	...	...	...	...	...	102,900[9]	878,600	58,053
Germany, West	10.6[2]	1985	41,215	965,800[4]	287,563	23.4[4]	6,977	142,184	1,931,500[4]	147,312
Ghana	28.4[2]	1977[7]	460	1,100	115	2.4	250	2,182	5,700	237
Gibraltar	...	1981	...	552	...	...	...	...	1,443	...
Greece	11.7[2]	1984	23,218	73,812	...	3.2	...	184,892	301,318	12,263[13]
Greenland	8.0[21]	1986	...	[3]	126	...	...	...	2,153[3,4,22]	94
Grenada	19.9[2,27]	1983	...	[3]	[3]	...	...	...	2,813[3,12]	6[3]
Guadeloupe	17.5[2,10]	1983	...	[3]	...	...	...	...	2,994[3,12]	212
Guam	51.5[11]	1982	89	981	165	11.0	1,853	802	5,400	413
Guatemala	25.3	1982	...	[3]	...	...	...	88,200	51,700[3,4,10]	712[9]
Guernsey	...	1976	...	[3]	...	...	...	...	2,805[3]	...
Guinea	21.5	1979	...	[3]	...	...	...	...	12,808[3,30]	...
Guinea-Bissau	...	1977	[3]	[3]	...	...	...	685[3]	516[3]	44[3,22]
Guyana	7.4	1980[7]	...	...	...	...	...	147	...	93[9]
Haiti	17.9	1983	...	[3]	...	...	...	653[7,28]	3,900[3,4,16]	174
Honduras	12.1[2]	1983	...	...	...	...	...	...	45,900[8]	401
Hong Kong	20.1[2]	1983	11,729	44,613	6,829	3.8	582	51,810	250,267	10,873[34]
Hungary	12.0[1,2]	1987	206[11]	122,600[11]	13,121[12]	595[11]	...	37,539[38]	168,700[38]	10,973[38]
Iceland	9.5[2]	1984	1,509[9,39]	5,132[12]	598[9,39]	...	396[39]	1,801[39]	8,500[39,40]	951[39]
India	13.1[2]	1980	[3]	[3]	...	...	...	3,132,000[3,15]	3,615,000[3,15]	108,300[9]
Indonesia	15.4[2]	1983	...	[3]	...	...	...	...	1,000,063[3,11]	44,816
Iran	19.9[2]	1972–73	18,210	31,688	2,429	1.7	133	218,132	80,055	27,814[9]
Iraq	11.0[2]	1975–76	1,532[26]	2,700[26]	...	1.8[26]	...	77,766[26]	106,800[26]	11,378[9]
Ireland	11.8[2,13]	1984	3,073[8]	40,584[8]	4,593[8]	13.2[8]	1,495[8]	32,332[8]	79,870[8]	5,110
Isle of Man	12.0[10]	1981	...	775	...	...	...	...	3,146	...
Israel	14.4[2]	1983	3,836[8]	44,700[27]	...	8.7[8]	...	43,112	91,200[27]	10,578
Italy	19.3[2]	1983	...	[3]	...	...	...	1,033,725	1,369,200[3]	122,978
Jamaica	24.3[2]	1979	...	1,830[7]	...	...	...	10,150[10]	11,230[7]	1,457[9]
Japan	13.7[2]	1985	413,016	3,998,000[4]	2,221,892	9.7[4]	5,379	1,628,620[15]	6,329,000[4,15]	426,423[4,15]
Jersey	...	1981	...	909[4]	...	...	...	...	4,415[4]	...
Jordan	17.8[2]	1977	78[7]	1,075[7]	...	13.8[7]	...	189[7]	2,436[7]	2,210[9]
Kampuchea	...	...	...	...	...	...	...	...	...	...
Kenya	11.1[2]	1985	2,018	27,481	[3]	13.6	...	4,969	34,628	638[2,3]
Kiribati	15.8[11]	1985	...	440[4]	...	...	...	35[22]	569[3]	7[22]
Korea, North	...	...	...	...	...	...	...	...	...	...
Korea, South	12.9[2]	1982	45,568	173,156	9,693	3.8	213	749,538	1,467,286	20,889
Kuwait	9.3[2]	1984	3,020	25,753[4]	4,543	8.5[4]	1,504	14,131	57,211[4]	6,555
Laos	12.1[13]	...	...	...	...	...	...	...	...	...
Lebanon	28.0[13]	1983	...	...	...	...	...	...	...	1,662
Lesotho	14.5	...	...	...	...	...	...	...	...	...
Liberia	6.4[2]	...	...	...	...	...	...	...	...	...
Libya	5.9[2,11]	1973	1,126	4,148[4]	...	3.7[4]	...	26,825	44,605[4]	9,205[9]
Liechtenstein	...	1975	67	216	...	3.2	...	228	740	...
Luxembourg	16.0[2]	1985	1,184	7,830[11]	2,319	6.8[11]	1,959	3,704	12,867[11]	1,587
Macau	...	1981	...	482[4]	...	...	...	...	13,652[4]	...
Madagascar	29.0[2]	1976	1,104	...	...	...	...	1,570	...	696[12]
Malawi	18.2[2]	1983	588[7]	17,300[7]	429[7,12]	29[7]	1,039[7,12]	708[7]	7,500[7]	206[7,22]
Malaysia	12.7	1980	19,663	116,200	15,461	5.9	786	95,993	73,000	6,099
Maldives	8.1	1977	...	[3]	...	...	...	...	1,341[3,4]	...
Mali	15.5[13]	1979	...	[3]	...	...	...	...	5,200[3]	...
Malta	14.0[2]	...	...	...	...	...	...	...	...	...
Martinique	17.4[2,11]	1983	...	[3]	...	...	...	...	3,518[3,12]	234
Mauritania	12.8[2,13]	1971[7]	23	100	102	4.3	4,445	59	700	103
Mauritius	11.0[2]	1986	[3]	[3]	...	[3]	...	207[2,3,7]	10,107[2,3,7]	164[2,3,7]
Mayotte	...	1983	[3]	...	[3]	...	[3]	41[3]	...	27[3]
Mexico	23.1[2]	1975	11,652	130,939[4]	6,739	11.2[4]	578	463,612	987,089[4]	17,062[9]
Monaco	...	...	...	...	...	...	...	...	...	...
Mongolia	33.0[1,13]	1983[3,42]	...	...	...	...	...	4,828	21,100	1,088
Montserrat	17.0[2]	1980	...	...	...	...	...	160	200	11[12]
Morocco	13.4[2]	1972	...	[3]	...	...	...	4,000[7]	20,000[7]	4,727[9]
Mozambique	...	1980	...	...	...	...	...	...	63,058[3]	...
Nauru	...	...	...	...	...	...	...	...	...	...
Nepal	3.9[2,33]	1983	...	[3]	...	...	...	...	119,000[3,4,12]	736
Netherlands, The	12.8[2]	1985	...	255,300[9]	...	...	...	87,832	336,000[9]	25,251
Netherlands Antilles	25.6[2,10]	1983	...	[3]	...	...	...	...	7,810[3,16,43]	149[17]
New Caledonia	26.7[2,9]	1981	...	[3]	...	...	...	324	4,524[3]	...
New Zealand	19.0[2]	1984	8,263[44]	76,664[44]	16,295[44]	9.3[44]	1,972[44]	29,961[15,44]	116,301[15,44]	11,263
Nicaragua	17.4	1983	...	...	...	...	...	20,610[11]	92,100[21]	356
Niger	13.5[2,13]	...	...	...	...	...	...	...	...	...
Nigeria	19.7[2]	1982[7]	...	...	...	...	...	22,190	266,280	...
Niue	...	1982	[3]	[3]	...	...	...	22[3]	82[3]	...
Norfolk Island	...	1986	...	[3]	...	...	...	...	275[3]	...

retail trade (continued)									employees per outlet	sales per outlet $'000	population per outlet	country
percent breakdown of sales												
food[d]	clothing, shoes[e]	home furnishings[f]	eating, drinking[g]	drugs, pharmaceuticals[h]	building materials[i]	automobile parts[j]	general merchandise[k]	other[l]				
11.9[8,35]	7.6[8,35]	16.2[8,35]	...	7.9[8,35]	6.3[8,35]	12.4[8,35]	28.2[8,35]	9.5[8,35]	7.6	600	3,249	El Salvador
...	...	...	...	...	...	...	...	...	...	...	...	Equatorial Guinea
...	...	...	...	...	...	...	...	...	2.3	27	...	Ethiopia
...	...	...	...	...	...	...	...	...	...	...	...	Faeroe Islands
...	...	...	...	...	...	...	...	...	...	...	95	Falkland Islands
27.8[22]	10.4[22]	1.7[22]	...	1.0[22]	2.6[22]	17.1[22]	22.7[22]	16.7[22]	10.4[7]	607[7]	1,163[7]	Fiji
22.8	5.4	1.9	...	2.5	8.2	27.5	20.6	11.1	3.9	445	134	Finland
40.9[33]	15.9[33]	17.6[33]	...	5.8[33]	...	4.0[33,37]	...	15.9[33]	2.0[13]	209[13]	93	France
...	...	...	...	...	...	...	...	...	34[3,7]	...	648[3,7]	French Guiana
...	...	...	...	...	...	...	...	...	...	...	...	French Polynesia
50.5	9.6	...	...	...	33.8	6.1	...	...	...	...	...	Gabon
...	...	...	...	...	...	...	...	...	...	...	...	Gambia, The
...	...	...	...	...	...	...	...	...	...	...	...	Gaza Strip
49.6	15.6	5.8	—	5.6	6.9	...	...	16.5	8.7[4,9]	380[9]	162[9]	Germany, East
32.0	10.9	...	—	5.9	...	14.5	26.3	10.3	13.6[4]	1,036	429	Germany, West
...	...	...	...	...	...	...	...	...	2.6	108	4,738	Ghana
...	...	...	...	...	...	...	...	...	...	...	...	Gibraltar
60.0[13]	18.1[13]	9.5[13]	...	...	...	...	...	12.4[13]	1.6	...	54	Greece
...	...	...	...	...	...	...	...	...	...	...	...	Greenland
...	...	...	...	...	...	...	...	...	...	...	...	Grenada
...	...	...	...	...	...	...	...	...	...	...	...	Guadeloupe
16.3	4.3	3.1	9.2	0.6	4.2	32.6	7.4	22.3	6.7	515	138	Guam
...	...	...	...	...	...	...	...	...	...	...	83	Guatemala
...	...	...	...	...	...	...	...	...	...	...	...	Guernsey
...	...	...	...	...	...	...	...	...	...	...	...	Guinea
...	...	...	...	...	...	...	...	...	0.8[3]	...	1,080[3]	Guinea-Bissau
9.7	18.9	13.8	4.5	2.8	17.7	18.6	...	14.0	...	743	5,884	Guyana
...	...	...	...	...	...	...	...	...	...	...	7,034[7,28]	Haiti
...	...	...	...	...	...	...	...	...	...	...	...	Honduras
23.7[13]	8.8[13]	...	...	...	...	...	5.0[13]	62.5[13]	4.8	210	103	Hong Kong
32.5	7.4	12.7	...	0.8	7.8	8.0	12.6	18.2	4.5[38]	292[38]	283[38]	Hungary
24.6[9]	8.8[9]	10.1[9]	—	5.6[9]	—	—	31.1[9]	19.8[9]	4.7[39,40]	528[39]	133[39]	Iceland
...	...	...	...	...	...	...	...	...	1.2[3,15]	...	2,193[3,15]	India
...	...	...	...	...	...	...	...	...	...	...	...	Indonesia
...	...	...	...	...	...	...	...	...	0.4	...	141	Iran
...	...	...	...	...	...	...	...	...	1.4[26]	...	148[26]	Iraq
40.0	12.4	...	15.8	3.4	...	6.0	6.0	16.4	2.5[8]	129[8]	99[8]	Ireland
...	...	...	...	...	...	...	...	...	...	...	...	Isle of Man
22.0	7.0	11.0	...	...	...	10.0	6.0	44.0	2.1	245	95	Israel
50.8	15.1	...	...	3.4	...	...	...	30.7	...	119	55	Italy
...	...	...	...	...	...	...	...	...	...	...	214[10]	Jamaica
26.3	10.5	7.2	—	2.5	3.8	21.0[25]	13.6	15.1	3.9[4,15]	262[15]	74[15]	Japan
...	...	...	...	...	...	...	...	...	...	...	...	Jersey
...	...	...	...	...	...	...	...	...	12.9[7]	...	792[7]	Jordan
...	...	...	...	...	...	...	...	...	...	...	...	Kampuchea
...	...	...	...	...	...	...	...	...	7.0	128[2,3]	4,092	Kenya
...	...	...	...	...	...	...	...	...	...	189[22]	1,571[22]	Kiribati
...	...	...	...	...	...	...	...	...	...	...	...	Korea, North
29.4[21,23]	13.1[21]	8.9[21]	18.9[21]	5.0[21]	2.4[21]	5.4[21]	1.2[21]	15.6[21]	2.0	28	53	Korea, South
13.4	12.6	15.4	...	1.6	6.4	25.9	22.0	2.7	4.0[4]	464	116	Kuwait
...	...	...	...	...	...	...	...	...	...	...	...	Laos
...	...	...	...	...	...	...	...	...	...	...	...	Lebanon
...	...	...	...	...	...	...	...	...	...	...	...	Lesotho
...	...	...	...	...	...	...	...	...	...	...	...	Liberia
...	...	...	...	...	...	...	...	...	1.7[4]	...	84	Libya
...	...	...	...	...	...	...	...	...	3.2	...	105	Liechtenstein
30.4[23]	11.9	10.1	...	3.4	...	36.4	2.1	5.7	3.3[11]	428	99	Luxembourg
...	...	...	...	...	...	...	...	...	...	...	...	Macau
...	...	...	...	...	...	...	...	...	...	...	4,977	Madagascar
...	...	...	...	...	...	...	...	...	10.6[7]	...	9,668[7]	Malawi
32.9[41]	7.3[41]	10.8[41]	...	2.5[41]	1.1[41]	33.3[25,41]	4.4[41]	7.7[41]	0.8	64	143	Malaysia
...	...	...	...	...	...	...	...	...	...	...	...	Maldives
...	...	...	...	...	...	...	...	...	...	...	...	Mali
...	...	...	...	...	...	...	...	...	...	...	...	Malta
...	...	...	...	...	...	...	...	...	...	...	...	Martinique
...	...	...	...	...	...	...	...	...	11.9	1,742	20,300	Mauritania
...	...	...	...	...	...	...	...	...	48.8[2,3,7]	792[2,3,7]	4,976[2,3,7]	Mauritius
...	...	...	...	...	...	...	...	...	...	652[3]	1,477[3]	Mayotte
17.8	7.3	5.8	...	2.8	7.3	24.5	16.6	17.9	2.1[4]	41	138	Mexico
...	...	...	...	...	...	...	...	...	...	...	...	Monaco
...	...	...	...	...	...	...	...	...	4.3	225	372	Mongolia
...	...	...	...	...	...	...	...	...	1.2	c. 70	73	Montserrat
...	...	...	...	...	...	...	...	...	5.0[7]	...	c. 4,000[7]	Morocco
...	...	...	...	...	...	...	...	...	...	...	...	Mozambique
...	...	...	...	...	...	...	...	...	...	...	...	Nauru
...	...	...	...	...	...	...	...	...	...	...	...	Nepal
42.6	11.2	5.5	...	1.8	...	6.0	5.2	27.7	3.7[9]	288	165	Netherlands, The
...	...	...	...	...	...	...	...	...	...	...	...	Netherlands Antilles
...	...	...	...	...	...	...	...	...	...	...	439	New Caledonia
17.9	4.7	7.1	4.0[45]	2.3	1.6	41.4	5.4	15.7[46]	3.9[15,44]	346[15,44]	106[15,44]	New Zealand
...	...	...	...	...	...	...	...	...	...	...	143[11]	Nicaragua
...	...	...	...	...	...	...	...	...	...	...	...	Niger
...	...	...	...	...	...	...	...	...	12.0	...	4,016	Nigeria
...	...	...	...	...	...	...	...	...	3.7[3]	...	144[3]	Niue
...	...	...	...	...	...	...	...	...	...	...	...	Norfolk Island

Trade: domestic (continued)

country	domestic trade as percentage of GDP, 1985	year	wholesale trade					retail trade		
			establishments[a]	employees[b]	sales[c] $'000,000	employees per establishment	sales per establishment $'000	outlets[a]	employees[b]	sales[c] $'000,000
Norway	11.0[2]	1986	14,851	109,352[4]	39,274	7.4[4]	2,644	38,075	133,258[4]	22,158
Oman	12.4[2]	1983	...	3	...	...	...	4,731[2, 3, 5]	...	2,449
Pacific Is., Trust Terr. of the										
Marshall Islands	...	1980	...	148[4]	...	...	...	...	395[2, 4]	...
Micronesia, Fed. States of	29.6[9]	1980	...	348[4]	...	...	...	...	489[2, 4]	...
Northern Mariana Islands	...	1982	11	364	29	33	2,595	258	1,490	57
Palau	...	1983	...	114[4]	...	...	...	...	226[2, 4]	...
Pakistan	15.0[2]	1983	...	...	...	...	...	276,701[28]	501,773[4, 28]	12,848
Panama	14.2[2]	1982[47]	560	13,115	1,491	23.4	2,662	7,561	15,765[7]	1,334
Papua New Guinea	7.9[9]	1985	...	...	...	...	...	...	...	669[2]
Paraguay	25.9[2]	1983	...	...	...	...	...	...	91,900[4, 8]	1,186
Peru	16.7[2, 13]	1973	4,210	34,100	2,163	8.1	514	103,010	72,200	2,015
Philippines	20.6[2]	1981	20,642	122,717	4,538	5.9	220	279,968	241,872	4,836
Pitcairn Island	...	1982	—	—	—	—	—	1	...	...
Poland	15.5[1, 2]	1983	...	124,100	34,652	...	...	214,330	441,800	31,247
Portugal	22.0[2, 12]	1981[7]	7,719	163,500[4]	12,860	21.2[4]	1,666	15,290	114,600[4]	5,108
Puerto Rico	15.6[2]	1983	2,635	26,000[4]	7,346	11.6	2,789	43,848	140,000[4]	8,077
Qatar	6.4[27]	1983	268	...	...	...	...	2,848	...	1,943
Réunion	15.6[9]	1988	3	3	...	...	...	6,409[3]	11,132[3, 13]	...
Romania	6.3[1, 9]	1985	...	...	...	...	...	82,707	457,800	16,164
Rwanda	13.6[2]	1978	...	3	...	...	...	...	8,014[2, 3]	...
St. Helena and Ascension	...	1976	...	3	...	...	...	...	95[3, 4]	...
St. Kitts and Nevis	18.1[2]	1983	...	3	...	...	...	...	568[3]	...
St. Lucia	22.7[2]	1980	...	3	...	...	...	...	4,770[2, 3, 4]	...
St. Pierre and Miquelon	...	1982	...	3	...	...	...	...	279[2, 3, 4]	...
St. Vincent	12.2	...	...	...	...	...	...	...	...	...
San Marino	...	1986	102	3	...	...	...	867	838[3]	...
São Tomé and Príncipe	9.2[11]	...	...	...	...	...	...	...	...	...
Saudi Arabia	9.5[13]	1981	4,460	31,481[4]	...	7.1[4]	...	80,266	174,187[4]	36,574[9]
Senegal	38.1[2]	1982	...	4,600[21]	...	...	...	510[8]	5,610[7]	664[9]
Seychelles	24.7[2]	1985	3	3	...	3	...	186[3, 13]	1,298	...
Sierra Leone	13.0[2, 11]	1977	...	2,521[7]	...	...	...	...	2,293[7]	177[9]
Singapore	18.5[2]	1983	20,103	115,149[4]	30,772	5.7[4]	1,531	16,029[15]	66,096[4]	4,741
Solomon Islands	7.7[15, 16]	1984	...	272	...	...	...	...	1,709	...
Somalia	5.6	...	...	...	...	...	...	...	...	...
South Africa	11.1[3, 49]	1987	10,106[8, 49]	232,478[8, 49]	35,008	23.0[8, 49]	1,878[8, 49]	58,100[9, 49]	373,200[9, 49]	22,276
Bophuthatswana	[49]	1979[3]	...	...	...	...	...	1,248	4,195	110
Ciskei	[49]	1979[3]	...	...	...	...	...	682	1,632	36
Transkei	[49]	1977[3]	...	...	...	...	...	...	5,580[4]	...
Venda	[49]	1978[3]	...	...	...	...	...	485	...	...
South West Africa/Namibia	11.2[27]	1977	222	5,035	377	22.7	1,698	1,284	7,569	254
Spain	20.0[2]	1984	40,000[21]	...	...	...	...	710,865[21]	1,400,000[21]	54,777
Sri Lanka	18.4[2]	1982	239[7]	21,400[7]	3	89.5[7]	...	1,400[7]	60,000[7]	1,116[3, 13]
Sudan, The	23.4	1981	...	...	...	...	...	...	...	3,278
Suriname	15.4[2]	1983	...	...	...	...	...	...	12,700[4, 8]	189
Swaziland	8.9[9]	1983	79	1,100	...	13.9	...	646	4,200	23[27]
Sweden	11.2[2]	1983	27,913	163,000	38,685	5.8	1,386	75,389[33]	219,058[33]	26,821[33]
Switzerland	...	1985	15,019	143,470	...	9.6	...	53,465	259,674	23,620[13]
Syria	22.2[2]	1983	2,827[28]	...	...	...	...	75,865[28]	110,000[4, 28]	5,696
Taiwan	13.9[2]	1986	55,654[9]	169,200	7,572[33]	2.9[9]	101[9]	355,760[9]	180,300	14,291[33]
Tanzania	12.2[2]	1983	...	...	...	...	...	1,620[7]	16,524[7]	945
Thailand	22.2[2]	1980[7, 52]	5,647	187,737	21,693	33.2	3,842	11,280	113,408	3,945
Togo	22.0[9]	1980	...	...	...	...	...	181[7]	1,815[7]	112
Tokelau	...	1984	...	...	...	...	...	3	8[12]	...
Tonga	14.8[2, 9]	1976	...	14[4]	...	...	...	...	654[4]	...
Trinidad and Tobago	14.3[2]	1977	124	6,786	509	54.7	4,102	370	15,986	812[9]
Tunisia	18.4[2]	1983	...	...	...	...	...	...	106,300[3, 4, 11]	2,814
Turkey	17.3[2]	1980	24,592	46,071	8,049	0.5	327	281,949	85,059	8,686
Turks and Caicos Islands	...	...	...	...	...	...	...	...	...	...
Tuvalu	34.0[21]	1979	...	3	...	...	...	...	113[3, 4]	...
Uganda	6.6[12]	1977	226	4,100	...	18.1	...	251	3,200	5,285[12]
U.S.S.R.	18.2[1, 2]	1984	...	2,358,000[9]	240,800[9]	...	...	1,030,400	7,592,000	363,512
United Arab Emirates	8.8[2]	1983	3	3	...	...	3	13,906[2, 3, 8]	74,332[2, 3, 4, 10]	5,093
United Kingdom	11.5[2]	1987	104,688[9, 54]	877,000[9, 54]	214,596[9, 54]	8.4[9, 54]	2,050[9, 54]	343,153[13, 54]	2,326,000[4, 13, 15, 54]	168,800[15, 34, 54]
United States	16.5[2]	1986	415,829[11]	4,984,880[11]	1,997,895[11]	12.0[11]	4,805[11]	1,923,228[11]	16,877,000[13]	1,437,497
Uruguay	14.2[2, 13]	1984	...	...	...	...	...	...	...	5,397[15]
Vanuatu	...	1983[55]	18	187[4]	...	10.4[4]	...	256	1,439[4]	...
Venezuela	11.2[2]	1979	...	...	...	...	...	...	161,596	13,366[9]
Vietnam	11.7[1, 9]	1979	2,400[56]	...	...	...	...	2,000[56]	50,000[56]	7,485[8]
Virgin Islands (U.S.)	...	1982	104	1,363	197	13.1	1,196	1,191	6,980	489
Wallis and Futuna	...	1983	...	3	...	...	...	...	123[3, 4]	...
West Bank	...	1985	...	3	...	...	...	...	2,400[3]	...
Western Sahara	...	...	...	...	...	...	...	...	...	...
Western Samoa	9.5[2, 16]	1975	...	3	...	...	...	...	1,172[2, 3]	...
Yemen (Aden)	13.9[2, 12]	...	...	...	...	...	...	...	...	...
Yemen (Şan'ā')	16.7[2, 11]	1983	...	3	...	...	...	...	71,100[3, 12]	2,195
Yugoslavia	10.8[2]	1986	9,146	54,818	6,332	6.0	692	41,751	219,775	16,994
Zaire	18.6[13]	1981	...	...	...	...	...	3,036[7]	33,398[7]	3,300[9]
Zambia	8.7[2]	1974	494[7]	15,500[7]	977[7]	31.4[7]	1,978[7]	1,636[7]	13,700[7]	768[9]
Zimbabwe	11.8[2]	1983	...	3	...	...	...	...	80,600[2, 3]	693

[1]Percent of net material product. [2]Includes hotels. [3]Retail trade data include wholesale trade. [4]All persons engaged including proprietors. [5]1978. [6]Excludes retail trade network of the agricultural cooperatives. [7]Data refer to larger establishments only. [8]1977. [9]1983. [10]1980. [11]1982. [12]1981. [13]1984. [14]1973. [15]Excludes restaurants (eating and drinking establishments). [16]1972. [17]Netherlands Antilles includes Aruba. [18]1981–82. [19]Data refer to New Providence Island only. [20]1974. [21]1979. [22]1976. [23]Includes alcohol and tobacco. [24]Home furnishings includes building materials. [25]Includes all fuels. [26]Privately owned establishments only. [27]1986. [28]1975. [29]General merchandise includes clothing, shoes. [30]Includes wage earners in finance and insurance. [31]Rarotonga only. [32]Wholesalers selling directly to the public only. [33]1985. [34]1987. [35]Selected outlets in urban areas only. [36]Excludes Addis Ababa and Asmera. [37]Motorcycles, bicycles,

retail trade (continued)

food[d]	clothing, shoes[e]	home furnishings[f]	eating, drinking[g]	drugs, pharmaceuticals[h]	building materials[i]	automobile parts[i]	general merchandise[k]	other[l]	employees per outlet	sales per outlet $'000	population per outlet	country
30.1[23]	9.6	7.2	...	...	4.8	34.2	4.9	9.2	3.5[4]	582	109	Norway
...	...	...	...	...	...	...	...	...	...	...	188[2,3,5]	Oman
...	...	...	...	...	...	...	...	...	...	...	...	Pacific Is., Trust Terr. of the Marshall Islands
...	...	...	...	...	...	...	...	...	...	...	...	Micronesia, Fed. States of
25.1	1.4	1.0	10.4	...	6.2	20.5	6.6	28.8	5.8	220	71	Northern Mariana Islands
...	...	...	...	...	...	...	...	...	...	...	...	Palau
64.0	12.0	4.0	...	...	...	...	...	20.0	1.8[4,28]	...	273[28]	Pakistan
33.5[48]	10.9[48]	9.5[48]	...	...	...	...	...	46.1[48]	13.9[7]	176	270	Panama
...	...	...	7.1[2]	...	...	26.0	...	66.9	...	...	...	Papua New Guinea
...	...	...	...	...	...	...	...	...	...	...	...	Paraguay
...	...	...	...	...	...	...	...	...	0.7	20	145	Peru
25.4[23]	12.3	6.7	...	...	11.3	29.5[25]	...	14.8	0.9	17	177	Philippines
...	...	...	...	...	...	...	...	...	...	...	54	Pitcairn Island
31.1[38]	9.9[38]	11.1[38]	...	2.0[38]	4.9[38]	6.7[38]	...	34.3[38]	2.1	146	171	Poland
21.5[5]	14.1[5]	11.2[5]	...	3.3[5]	5.6[5]	35.2[5]	—9.1[5]—		7.5[4]	334	645	Portugal
30.5[11]	9.9[11]	4.5[11]	7.5[11]	4.3[11]	5.9[11]	23.2[11]	8.9[11]	5.3[11]	3.2	184	74	Puerto Rico
...	...	...	...	...	...	...	...	...	...	682	99	Qatar
...	...	...	...	...	...	...	...	...	1.7[3,13]	...	83[3,13]	Réunion
30.0	10.0	5.9	25.0	1.6	0.8	...	...	26.7	5.5	195	275	Romania
...	...	...	...	...	...	...	...	...	...	...	...	Rwanda
...	...	...	...	...	...	...	...	...	...	...	...	St. Helena and Ascension
...	...	...	...	...	...	...	...	...	...	...	...	St. Kitts and Nevis
...	...	...	...	...	...	...	...	...	...	...	...	St. Lucia
...	...	...	...	...	...	...	...	...	...	...	...	St. Pierre and Miquelon
...	...	...	...	...	...	...	...	...	...	...	26	St. Vincent
...	...	...	...	...	...	...	...	...	...	...	...	San Marino
...	...	...	...	...	...	...	...	...	...	...	120	São Tomé and Príncipe
...	...	...	...	...	...	...	...	...	2.2[4]	...	120	Saudi Arabia
...	...	...	...	...	...	...	...	...	11.0[7]	...	11,839[7]	Senegal
...	...	...	...	...	...	...	...	...	7.8[3,13]	...	348[3,13]	Seychelles
...	...	...	...	...	...	...	...	...	...	...	...	Sierra Leone
1.2	4.3	10.2	10.5	0.7	0.3	22.1	—50.7—		4.1[4]	296	156	Singapore
...	...	...	...	...	...	...	...	...	...	...	...	Solomon Islands
...	...	...	...	...	...	...	...	...	...	...	...	Somalia
42.4	13.9	8.2	2.6	3.5	...	8.7	13.6	7.0	6.4[3,49]	383[9,49]	c. 540[9,49]	South Africa
...	...	...	...	...	...	...	...	...	3.4	88	1,041	Bophuthatswana
...	...	...	...	...	...	...	...	...	2.4	53	972	Ciskei
...	...	...	...	...	...	...	...	...	...	...	...	Transkei
...	...	...	...	...	...	...	...	...	...	...	621	Venda
31.4	11.9	5.3	...	2.8	1.7	...	41.9	5.0	5.9	198	713	South West Africa/Namibia
39.2	10.5	16.7	...	...	...	4.2[50]	...	29.4	2.0[21]	119[21]	52[21]	Spain
...	...	...	...	...	...	...	...	...	42.9[7]	...	10,814[7]	Sri Lanka
...	...	...	...	...	...	...	...	...	...	...	...	Sudan, The
...	...	...	...	...	...	...	...	...	...	...	...	Suriname
52.5[27]	25.1[27]	22.4[27]	...	...	...	...	...	...	6.5	...	948	Swaziland
30.7	8.0	8.6	—	2.3	2.3	21.2	10.5	16.3	2.9	356	111	Sweden
46.4[13]	13.5[13]	8.6	...	4.0[13]	...	...	...	36.1[13]	4.9	...	122	Switzerland
16.0	2.5	...	...	3.5	12.3	39.5[51]	3.5	22.7	1.4[4,28]	...	97[28]	Syria
21.5[12]	3.2[12]	8.8[12]	...	4.1[12]	3.1[12]	8.7[12,25]	3.1[12]	47.5[12]	0.3[9]	33[9]	52[9]	Taiwan
...	...	...	...	...	...	...	...	...	10.0[7]	...	12,600[7]	Tanzania
2.6	2.7	10.8	...	1.3	10.8	57.8	5.5	8.5	10.1	350	4,163	Thailand
...	...	...	...	...	...	...	...	...	10.0[7]	...	15,600[7]	Togo
...	...	...	...	...	...	...	...	...	...	...	533	Tokelau
...	...	...	...	...	...	...	...	...	...	...	...	Tonga
18.6	...	8.5	2.7	...	10.7	28.2	15.3	15.9	43.2	1,467	2,798	Trinidad and Tobago
...	...	...	...	...	...	...	...	...	...	...	...	Tunisia
24.8	12.3	15.4	...	3.7	8.8	11.2[53]	0.6	23.2[25]	0.3	30	158	Turkey
...	...	...	...	...	...	...	...	...	...	...	...	Turks and Caicos Islands
...	...	...	...	...	...	...	...	...	...	...	...	Tuvalu
...	...	...	...	...	...	...	...	...	12.7	...	47,200	Uganda
42.6	23.9	7.4	8.7	1.2	1.1	5.6	...	9.5	7.4	353	267	U.S.S.R.
...	...	...	...	...	...	...	...	...	...	...	49[2,3,8]	United Arab Emirates
37.8	9.8	17.2[24]	...	1.4	[24]	...	18.3	16.0	6.8[4,13,15,54]	321[15,54]	165[13,15,54]	United Kingdom
21.0	5.2	5.6	9.4	3.6	5.3	28.7	11.5	9.7	7.5[11]	554[11]	121[11]	United States
...	...	...	...	...	...	...	...	...	...	...	...	Uruguay
...	...	...	...	...	...	...	...	...	5.6[4]	...	484	Vanuatu
50.2	10.1	7.6	...	...	...	5.0	...	27.1	...	...	...	Venezuela
...	...	...	...	...	...	...	...	...	25.0[56]	...	26,300[56]	Vietnam
26.5	7.1	3.7	8.6	2.2	3.8	13.1	4.6	30.4	5.9	411	97	Virgin Islands (U.S.)
...	...	...	...	...	...	...	...	...	...	...	...	Wallis and Futuna
...	...	...	...	...	...	...	...	...	...	...	...	West Bank
...	...	...	...	...	...	...	...	...	...	...	...	Western Sahara
...	...	...	...	...	...	...	...	...	...	...	...	Western Samoa
...	...	...	...	...	...	...	...	...	...	...	...	Yemen (Aden)
...	...	...	...	...	...	...	...	...	...	...	...	Yemen (Şan'ā')
35.1	16.1	...	...	...	5.8	...	...	43.1	5.3	407	557	Yugoslavia
...	...	...	...	...	...	...	...	...	11.0[7]	...	9,676[7]	Zaire
...	...	...	...	...	...	...	...	...	8.4[7]	359[7]	2,873[7]	Zambia
...	...	...	...	...	...	...	...	...	...	...	...	Zimbabwe

motor fuel, lubricants, and tires only.   [38]Socialist sector only.   [39]Excludes fuels, automobiles, alcohol and tobacco, and building materials.   [40]Full-time equivalents.   [41]Peninsular Malaysia only.   [42]State- and cooperative-owned establishments including public catering.   [43]Curaçao only.   [44]1982–83.   [45]Excludes bars.   [46]Includes bars and hotels.   [47]Excludes Colón Free Trade Zone.   [48]1971.   [49]South Africa includes Bophuthatswana, Ciskei, Transkei, and Venda.   [50]Motor vehicles only.   [51]Includes machinery, transport equipment, and petroleum products.   [52]Excludes combined wholesale/retail outlets.   [53]Excludes all fuels.   [54]Excludes motor vehicles.   [55]Urban establishments only.   [56]State sector only.

Finance

This table presents major statistical aggregates comprising national financial structure or constituting a basis for certain international financial comparisons. It includes such data as international reserves, money supply, central banking activity and discount rates, commercial (or "deposit money") banking activity, and external indebtedness of the central government. The country models are broadly similar and permit comparison of internal structure and external position at a high level of generalization.

One of the principal financial criteria of the relative economic position of a country is the size of its international reserves. International reserves as represented in this table comprise the sum of a country's (1) reserve position in the International Monetary Fund (IMF), a quota subscribed in the country's own currency, constituting a level up to which transactions may be effected within the IMF system; (2) holdings of foreign exchange; (3) holdings of gold; and (4) holdings of Special Drawing Rights (SDRs; an unconditional credit allocation, within a quota system set by the IMF, of currency needed by a country to maintain stability of foreign exchange transactions or markets). At appropriate accounting intervals these four elements are valued in a single unit of account (the SDR) and summed. The portion of this reserve total comprised by foreign exchange is very significant as an indication of the country's international liquidity (ability to pay its debts immediately in hard currencies). The ratio of external debt to total reserves, however, is less susceptible of interpretation in isolation: a low ratio, for example, may characterize the situation of a country with little need to borrow or of one with substantial debt but also the means

to repay it. Much higher ratios, on the other hand, may be manageable, despite small reserves, if a country's export earnings are also high.

The section on money supply for the country, both as a total and as a per capita amount, refers to one particular measure of money in circulation: M1, the sum of money in private sector demand deposit accounts and outside banks in circulation; it is distinguished from a broader measure of supply, M2, which is roughly M1 plus "quasi-money" (the time, savings, and foreign-currency deposits of residents).

The section of the table outlining banking activity and the principal monetary aggregates encompasses both central bank authorities and commercial (deposit) banks. For both, the principal component aggregates are grouped under assets and liabilities. For certain countries, the four principal aggregates under assets and liabilities do not comprise the entire total, and the percentages shown, therefore, may add to less than 100% (occasionally more, when the net of other liabilities [capital, reserves, undistributed profits, checks, and other transit items] is negative, reducing the total against which these percentages are calculated). The items excluded by the choice of categories are the least significant worldwide but may be important locally; they include such items as quasi-money, money seasonally adjusted, unused bank overdrafts, and so on. In the case of the central bank authority, data are also provided for the central bank discount rate, generally the controlling interest rate for banking and commercial activity in the country.

The largest share of assets in the case of both central and commercial

Finance

country	international reserves, 1988[a]			money supply, 1987[b]		central bank authority, 1987[b]								central bank discount rate, 1988[a]
						assets (%)				liabilities (%)				
	total ('000,000 SDRs)	% foreign exchange	ratio of external debt to total reserves, 1986[b]	stock ('000,000,000 national currency)	M1 per capita	claims on government	claims on private sector	claims on banks	claims on foreign assets	reserve money	government deposits	foreign liabilities	capital accounts	
Afghanistan	230	85.7	4.3[1]	85.1[2]	5,960[2]	87.9[2,3]	0.5[2]	1.8[2]	9.8[2]	72.5[2]	6.8[2]	0.3[2]	10.4[2]	...
Albania	...	...	...	...	...	...	...	...	...	...	...	...	...	...
Algeria	969	79.9	7.8	223.869	9,530	74.8	0.1	16.5	8.6	93.0	0.4	0.2	—	...
American Samoa	...	...	...	...	...	...	...	...	...	...	...	...	...	...
Andorra	...	...	...	...	...	...	...	...	...	...	...	...	...	...
Angola	...	...	...	...	...	...	...	...	...	...	...	...	...	...
Anguilla	...	...	...	...	...	...	...	...	...	...	...	...	...	...
Antigua and Barbuda	20	100.0	4.6[1]	0.111	1,330	34.5	—	—	65.5	103.6	—	—	—	6.5[6]
Argentina	1,293[7]	88.27	13.2	5.600[2]	180[2]	31.2[8]	—	35.2[8]	33.6[8]	39.2[8]	0.3[8]	21.6[8]	8.9[8]	357.0[6,7]
Aruba	62	100.0		0.156	2,380	—	—	—	100.0	72.1	8.3	—	9.2	9.5
Australia	9,773	97.2	...	31.218	1,910	31.5	—	—	68.5	61.6	—	—	—	12.5
Austria	6,394	88.4	...	213.5	28,200	3.0	—	35.0	62.0	73.1	0.1	—	30.4	3.0
Bahamas, The	159	100.0	0.9	0.278	1,150	22.4	—	5.1	72.6	63.1	8.3	—	27.4	9.0
Bahrain	725	99.3	0.5[1]	0.247	590	—	—	—	100.0	29.0	39.7	—	34.2	5.0[6]
Bangladesh	690	99.9	17.7	49.996[2]	480[2]	27.9[3]	—	37.2	35.4	55.1	0.7	35.9	4.8	11.2[2]
Barbados	112	100.0	3.0	0.470	1,850	25.3	7.0	0.5	67.2	67.7	27.8	21.8	7.1	8.0
Belgium	7,808	84.9	...	1,038.9[2]	105,000[2]	20.1	—	—	79.9	93.3	—	—	—	6.5
Belize	44	100.0	3.6	0.084	470	40.1	—	—	59.9	57.8	—	19.8	—	12.0
Benin	3	100.0	159.5	62.0	14,200	23.7	—	74.8	1.5	36.0	3.1	55.7	—	8.5
Bermuda	...	...	...	0.040[2]	690[2]	...	...	...	...	...	...	...	...	...
Bhutan	...	...	...	0.305[2]	230[2]	...	...	...	...	...	...	...	...	11.0[7,10]
Bolivia	59	47.5	17.5	0.502	70	66.9	—	12.4	20.6	11.8	78.4	30.2	—	149.0[8]
Botswana	1,535	100.0	0.3	0.312	260	—	—	—	100.0	8.8	57.8	—	11.9	6.5
Brazil	4,525[7]	98.1[7]	14.0	106.19	770[9]	32.3[3,9]	17.3[9]	4.3[9]	46.1[9]	14.1[9]	23.7[9]	67.1[9]	—	330.6
British Virgin Islands	...	...	...	0.024[2,11]	1,990[2,11]	...	...	...	...	...	...	...	...	5.2[2,10]
Brunei	...	...	...	1.350[8]	6,100[8]	...	...	...	...	...	...	...	...	...
Bulgaria	...	...	...	...	...	...	...	...	...	...	...	...	...	...
Burkina Faso	249	99.6	2.6	90.7	10,800	15.0	—	7.3	77.7	78.1	3.7	16.0	—	8.5
Burma	61	85.2	83.2	16.337[2]	420[2]	−26.5[2]	—	124.7[2]	1.8[2]	69.5[2]	—	5.3[2]	—	1.5[6,8]
Burundi	47	100.0	7.6	19.596	3,870	68.0[3]	0.5	0.6	30.8	47.6	16.8	11.5	18.6	7.0[7]
Cameroon	46	97.8	37.8	387.0	35,400	20.1	—	75.3	4.6	43.3	19.0	32.3	—	8.0
Canada	12,394	94.4	...	85.1	3,320	56.7	—	—	43.3	97.4	—	—	—	9.1
Cape Verde	...	...	...	...	...	...	...	...	...	...	...	...	...	...
Cayman Islands	...	...	...	0.027[2]	1,290[2]	...	...	...	...	...	...	...	...	...
Central African Republic	81	98.8	5.9	54.8	19,500	34.1	—	21.4	44.5	70.7	3.2	23.9	—	9.0
Chad	58	98.3	10.8	70.6	13,200	17.6	—	58.9	23.4	79.6	6.3	10.0	—	8.0
Chile	1,922	97.2	6.3	199.6	15,800	14.6[8]	11.0[8]	48.1[8]	26.3[8]	5.8[8]	1.8[8]	35.3[8]	11.3[8]	28.9[6,9]
China	14,230	96.9	1.4	421.5[2]	400[2]	11.3[2]	0.9[2]	82.2[2]	5.5[2]	84.0[2]	9.6[2]	1.2[2]	6.3[2]	...
Christmas Island	...	...	...	...	...	...	...	...	...	...	...	...	...	...
Cocos (Keeling) Islands	...	...	...	...	...	...	...	...	...	...	...	...	...	...
Colombia	2,754	99.1	4.1	545.3[9]	18,600[9]	31.5[9]	4.4[9]	23.9[9]	40.2[9]	49.1[9]	9.0[9]	10.6[9]	6.3[9]	30.0
Comoros	15[7]	100.0[7]	9.1	7.232[2]	17,500[2]	17.9[2]	—	—	82.1[2]	74.1[2]	2.3[2]	2.8[2]	24.7[2]	8.5[7]
Congo	4	75.0	389.8	102.3	46,000	56.4	—	41.3	2.3	57.5	5.7	32.0	—	8.0
Cook Islands	...	...	...	...	...	...	...	...	...	...	...	...	...	...
Costa Rica	395	99.5	6.8	42.611	16,100	46.9[3]	—	19.0	34.2	27.6	2.5	149.9	5.0	31.4
Côte d'Ivoire	11	90.9	295.2	598.6	52,500	36.1	—	63.6	0.3	51.5	4.1	40.1	—	8.5
Cuba	...	...	...	...	...	...	...	...	...	...	...	...	...	...
Cyprus	687	97.7	1.5	0.314	570	20.0	—	11.6	68.5	84.2	3.1	0.8	—	6.0
Czechoslovakia	...	...	...	...	...	...	...	...	...	...	...	...	...	...
Denmark	8,820	99.4	...	235.4	45,900	0.6	22.2	16.1	61.1	21.6	51.8	0.7	—	7.0
Djibouti	...	...	...	26.084[9]	58,900[9]	...	...	...	...	...	...	...	...	...
Dominica	13	100.0	14.5[1]	0.059	650	51.4	—	—	48.6	67.4	—	30.8	—	5.0[6]
Dominican Republic	129	100.0	6.9	2.609	380	42.1[3]	—	29.1	28.8	62.7	—	265.9	−2.9	...
Ecuador	363	96.1	12.0	265.737	26,400	42.1[3]	3.8	39.4	14.7	36.8	22.7	110.7	2.3	11.0[8]
Egypt	1,138	92.5	24.4	18.241	370	78.9[3]	—	11.5	9.7	68.3	5.9	24.0	—	13.0

banks is usually either claims on government and government agencies or foreign assets and holdings, though some of the latter, such as the large outstanding loans to socialist and less developed countries, have become the chief liabilities. The chief liability of a central bank is usually reserve money (the currency and notes issued by the bank). When government deposits represent a substantial share, budgetary surpluses have usually been deposited by the central government. Large foreign liabilities imply extensive foreign investment. Among the deposit money banks, loans to the private sector normally represent the largest share of assets; occasionally, a trade- or banking-oriented country such as Belgium or Hong Kong will show major foreign assets. The chief liabilities of these banks will usually be savings deposits. If the country commands a high degree of confidence internationally, foreign liabilities may comprise a substantial share of liabilities.

Because the majority of the world's countries are in the less developed bloc, and because their principal financial concern is external debt and its service, data are given for outstanding external public and publicly guaranteed long-term debt rather than for total public debt, which is the major concern in the developed countries. For comparability, the data are given in U.S. dollars. The volume of debt by itself does not create external payment problems. If the country's external debt service (interest payments plus principal repayment) needs can be met by a strong, dependable export market, by export of services, or, occasionally, by direct remittances from abroad (by residents working abroad and sending wages

home in foreign currencies, for example), no debt problem need exist. Countries whose debt service ratio (total debt service as a percent of exports of goods and services) is relatively high, however, must often base their external borrowing policy on maintenance of domestic conditions of strict efficiency and, sometimes, austerity. The failure to adhere to such policies may lead to eventual crises of financial liquidity, deflation, and slower growth.

Ideally, the data presented here should be obtained by utilizing a single international methodology to provide a universally comparable set of international statistics. No international agency, however, can collect such data for all countries because of differences, both overall and in detail, in national definitions of financial aggregates, in accounting methodology, and in the completeness with which it is possible to survey a country's financial activity. The greater part of the data presented in the table comes from the IMF's *International Financial Statistics* and the World Bank's *World Debt Tables*. These sources are supplemented by other recent data from national, regional, or other international sources. In a few cases the desired data are negligible or unavailable, as noted.

Detailed percentages may not add to 100.0 because of rounding, statistical discrepancy, or nonaccounting of negligible quantities.
—None, less than 0.5 of the last significant figure, or not applicable.
... Not available.
a. Latest month.
b. Year-end.

deposit money banks, 1987[b]										external public debt outstanding (long-term, disbursed only), 1986[b]							country
assets (%)				liabilities						total ('000,000 U.S.$)	creditors (%)		debt service				
loans to govern-ment	loans to private sector	re-serves	foreign assets	deposits ('000,000,000 national currency)	composition (%)						offi-cial	private	total ('000,000 U.S.$)	repayment (%)		debt service ratio (%)	
					demand depos.	savings depos.	govt. depos.	foreign liabilities						princi-pal	inter-est		
4.4[2,3]	44.1[2]	11.9[2]	39.7[2]	18.944[2]	21.8[2]	48.7[2,4]	0.2[2]	2.6[2]		1,424[1]	...	...	46[1]	56.5[1]	43.5[1]	6.6[1]	Afghanistan
																	Albania
9.8	87.0	2.6	0.6	207.54[1]	50.0	16.4	5.0	19.8		14,777.0	20.4	79.6	5,155.0	68.0	32.0	51.5	Algeria
...	...	...	...	...	...	...	...	...		...	...	...	...	...	...	...	American Samoa
...	...	...	...	...	...	...	...	...		...	...	...	...	...	...	...	Andorra
...	38.9[5]	1.9[5]	51.8[5]	0.063[5]	13.2[5]	67.1[5]	...	13.4[5]		1,106[1]	...	...	348[1]	79.2[1]	20.8[1]	13.2[1]	Angola
14.1[3]	61.1	10.3	14.5	0.576	11.9	58.8	—	24.1		76[1]	...	...	6[1]	...	...	4.7[1]	Anguilla
21.5[2]	62.0[2]	11.5[2]	5.0[2]	26.593[2]	6.0[2]	45.7[2,4]	14.9[2]	31.0[2]		38,453.2	12.3	87.7	4,615.4	31.1	68.9	50.4	Antigua and Barbuda
2.7	63.0	13.0	21.3	0.546	22.1	50.3	2.7	21.1			...	...	...	...	...	...	Argentina
																	Aruba
16.3[3]	74.5	2.9	6.2	163.815	12.4	57.6	0.4	10.2		...	...	...	...	...	...	...	Australia
34.9[3]	36.5	2.1	26.5	2,471.9	4.9	43.8	2.8	28.4		...	...	...	...	...	...	...	Austria
15.8[3]	90.3	6.3	−12.3	0.936	21.7	67.1[4]	2.3	—		199.1	12.0	88.0	42.6	48.8	51.2	2.6	Bahamas, The
14.7	34.1	3.7	47.5	1.462	11.1	49.4	21.8	10.0		847[1]	...	...	164[1]	78.0[1]	22.0[1]	4.3[1]	Bahrain
31.7[2,3]	56.0[2]	6.8[2]	5.5[2]	152.340[2]	20.3[2]	54.3[2]	3.5[2]	2.4[2]		7,281.7	98.6	1.4	271.0	60.0	40.0	25.1	Bangladesh
22.2	55.4	7.5	14.9	1.622	17.2	56.0	5.9	20.9		453.8	45.0	55.0	55.1	56.1	43.9	7.5	Barbados
26.2[3]	17.1	0.2	56.5	8,756.8	7.8	17.0[4]	—	70.0			...	...	...	...	...	...	Belgium
23.4[3]	59.7	10.4	6.6	0.245	15.0	64.1	6.7	9.1		96.6	87.8	12.2	12.3	63.4	36.6	8.9	Belize
6.4	85.4	3.3	5.0	110.2	35.3	31.7	10.4	27.1		780.6	55.3	44.7	57.6	62.2	37.8	9.2[9]	Benin
...	...	...	...	6.344[2]	...	...	...	...		284[1]	...	...	108[1]	71.3[1]	28.7[1]	95.8[1]	Bermuda
				1.128						5[1]	...	...	8[1]	...	...	23.5[1]	Bhutan
—	78.5	15.9	5.6	1.437	7.3	47.3[4]	—	13.8		3,522.6	66.7	33.3	160.8	46.1	53.9	23.6	Bolivia
4.2[3]	49.4	37.2	9.2	0.531	45.8	41.6	—	7.6		355.1	88.9	11.1	44.4	39.2	60.8	4.3	Botswana
20.9[3]	47.1	25.2	6.8	3,760.2	15.1	14.4	3.2	24.6		82,522.8	22.7	77.3	8,408.6	27.9	72.1	33.2	Brazil
—	30.9[2]	1.2[2]	65.6[2]	0.212[2]	8.2[2]	47.6[2]	—	39.2[2]		9[1]	...	...	0[1]	...	...	...	British Virgin Islands
—28.5[8]—		0.5[8]	...	3.864[8]	—69.5[8]—			...		2[1]	...	...	1[1]	...	...	...	Brunei
										4,880[12]	...	...	...	...	...	...	Bulgaria
3.6	63.1	27.2	6.0	154.0	28.6	23.6	34.5	8.8		615.7	94.3	5.7	34.3	65.6	34.4	14.8	Burkina Faso
93.1[2,3]	5.7[2]	1.2[2]	...	52.909[2]	2.1[2]	14.1[2,4]	9.1[2]	14.5[2]		3,664.5	90.7	9.3	246.7	64.4	35.6	55.4	Burma
46.1[3]	40.6	9.8	3.5	19.273	48.3	30.4	6.6	5.5		527.7	94.9	5.1	31.1	61.1	38.9	19.0	Burundi
8.6	83.2	2.1	6.1	1,219.7	17.6	23.8	18.2	9.6		2,267.3	80.6	19.4	299.6	59.7	40.3	11.2	Cameroon
5.6[3]	73.2	2.0	19.2	333.6	20.3	46.8[4]	0.5	26.2		...	...	...	...	...	...	...	Canada
										107.4	97.2	2.8	4.2	54.8	45.2	...	Cape Verde
—	—	—	99.9[8]	143.939[8]	—	—	—	99.9[8]		145[1]	...	...	39[1]	...	...	...	Cayman Islands
0.6	77.4	1.1	20.9	38.1	33.9	17.0	4.2	5.8		392.6	94.1	5.9	17.9	49.7	50.3	9.4	Central African Republic
0.7	87.0	6.4	5.8	85.3	27.8	5.6	8.6	4.3		171.8	80.2	19.8	3.2	50.0	50.0	7.5[9]	Chad
9.7[8]	81.6[8]	2.6[8]	6.0[8]	1,331.0[8]	3.9[8]	29.1[8]	7.0[8]	64.2[8]		15,108.7	18.5	81.5	1,621.6	16.7	83.3	30.8	Chile
—80.9[2]—		16.0[2]	3.1[2]	1,005.1[2]	26.6[2]	24.4[2]	—	3.1[2]		17,192.5	40.5	59.5	2,381.6	57.4	42.6	7.9	China
...	...	...	...	...	...	...	...	...		...	...	...	...	...	...	...	Christmas Island
...	...	...	...	...	...	...	...	...		...	...	...	...	...	...	...	Cocos (Keeling) Islands
4.6[9]	65.1[9]	23.4[9]	3.9[9]	1,148.7[9]	29.7[9]	36.4[9]	—	16.4[9]		11,436.9	53.2	46.8	1,795.3	51.5	48.5	27.6	Colombia
5.6[2]	58.1[2]	26.3[2]	9.9[2]	6.854[2]	42.4[2]	20.9[2]	5.1[2]	18.0[2]		156.0	99.9	0.1	1.8	55.6	44.4	6.4	Comoros
10.9	83.3	1.2	4.6	225.2	18.6	16.1	22.3	9.6		2,860.7	44.1	55.9	310.9	74.7	25.3	43.5	Congo
...	...	...	...	...	...	...	...	...		21	...	...	0[1]	...	...	...	Cook Islands
8.2[3]	65.8	18.5	7.6	79.655	34.7	80.5[4]	2.0	4.8		3,582.2	47.2	52.8	377.9	48.2	51.8	26.3	Costa Rica
6.9	81.8	7.6	3.6	1,416.8	20.6	23.4	11.6	14.6		6,500.2	45.8	54.2	785.3	32.3	67.7	21.2	Côte d'Ivoire
...	...	...	...	...	...	...	...	...		5,937[1]	...	...	412[1]	51.2[1]	48.8[1]	5.5[1]	Cuba
11.8	63.6	18.0	6.6	1.542	11.1	59.1	2.3	17.1		1,170.1	53.5	46.5	189.9	58.8	41.2	12.1	Cyprus
										4,480[12]	...	...	...	...	...	...	Czechoslovakia
6.3	63.7	0.8	29.2	573.5	38.5	31.8	—	27.7		...	...	...	...	...	...	...	Denmark
5.0[3]	40.9	20.3	33.8	0.232	16.6	57.8	—	17.7		119.1	95.8	4.2	7.3	58.9	41.1	...	Djibouti
16.0[3]	67.4	14.4	2.2	5.651	22.8	41.4	8.6	1.6		48[1]	...	...	1[1]	...	...	4.1[1]	Dominica
—	82.8	13.6	3.6	414.451	39.4	27.9	—	...		2,609.2	69.9	30.1	293.3	41.6	58.4	20.6	Dominican Republic
28.4[3]	28.0	18.3	25.3	57.670	12.9	46.2[4]	2.1	14.2		7,918.6	29.1	70.9	845.4	24.3	75.7	32.3	Ecuador
										22,788.2	74.5	25.5	1,736.3	59.5	40.5	21.3	Egypt

Finance (continued)

country	international reserves, 1988[a]			money supply, 1987[b]		central bank authority, 1987[b]								central bank discount rate, 1988[a]
	total ('000,000 SDRs)	% foreign exchange	ratio of external debt to total reserves, 1986[b]	stock ('000,000,000 national currency)	M1 per capita	assets (%)				liabilities (%)				
						claims on government	claims on private sector	claims on banks	claims on foreign assets	reserve money	government deposits	foreign liabilities	capital accounts	
El Salvador	112	85.7	7.7	3.147	630	41.3[3]	0.9	34.7	23.1	44.2	13.7	33.1	8.7	...
Equatorial Guinea	—		57.6	9.0	27,200	53.8	—	44.5	1.7	80.9	7.6	70.0	—	8.0
Ethiopia	104	93.3	7.7	3.341	70	51.5	—	40.0	8.5	65.4	7.9	4.9	9.0	3.0
Faeroe Islands	...	...	...	...	...	...	...	...	...	...	...	...	...	...
Falkland Islands	...	...	...	...	...	...	...	...	...	...	...	...	...	...
Fiji	127	100.0	1.7	0.179[2]	250[2]	1.1[2, 3]	—	—	98.9[2]	58.9[2]	6.7[2]	—	35.3[2]	17.7[7]
Finland	5,752	98.8	...	30.342	6,140	2.4	12.8	9.0	75.8	65.9	2.2	0.3	16.6	8.0
France	25,919	88.9	...	1,317.0	23,600	7.9	—	29.1	63.1	51.1	—	2.0	—	9.5
French Guiana	...	...	...	2.583	28,600	...	...	...	...	...	...	...	...	...
French Polynesia	...	...	...	39.773	214,000	...	...	...	...	...	...	...	...	...
Gabon	10	90.0	8.6	133.2	110,000	66.2	—	28.9	4.9	57.2	14.2	33.5	—	8.0
Gambia, The	19[7]	100.0[7]	16.9	0.198	250	23.8[3]	—	29.3	46.9	43.9	57.7	198.5	19.8	20.0
Gaza Strip	...	...	...	...	...	...	...	...	...	...	...	...	...	...
Germany, East	...	...	...	...	...	...	...	...	...	...	...	...	...	...
Germany, West	52,767	93.7	...	365.7	6,010	9.1	—	33.5	57.4	81.2	1.9	7.7	—	3.0
Ghana	134	94.0	2.7	55.156[2]	4,170[2]	49.7[2, 3]	—	2.0[2]	48.3[2]	24.9[2]	3.6[2]	76.6[2]	—	23.5[7]
Gibraltar	...	...	...	...	...	...	...	...	...	...	...	...	...	...
Greece	1,788	93.5	9.0	875.6[2]	87,700[2]	55.2	0.3	16.5	28.0	80.5	3.3	—	—	19.0
Greenland	...	...	...	...	...	...	...	...	...	...	...	...	...	...
Grenada	13	100.0	0.7	0.074	710	36.2	—	—	63.8	91.0	—	5.7	—	6.0[6]
Guadeloupe	...	...	...	4.949	14,700	...	...	...	...	...	...	...	...	...
Guam	...	...	...	...	...	...	...	...	...	...	...	...	...	...
Guatemala	209	91.4	5.7	1.766	210	73.4[3]	—	6.8	19.8	79.9	34.6	62.7	6.8	9.0
Guernsey	...	...	...	...	...	...	...	...	...	...	...	...	...	...
Guinea	...	...	...	22.5[2]	3,660[2]	...	...	...	...	...	...	...	...	...
Guinea-Bissau	...	...	...	...	...	...	...	...	...	...	...	...	...	...
Guyana	2	100.0	90.2	1.324	1,640	98.8	—	—	1.2	36.4	—	81.1	9.7	14.0
Haiti	15	93.3	34.1	1.400[8]	270[8]	83.6[3, 8]	9.7[8]	2.3[8]	4.5[8]	44.1[8]	6.7[8]	37.1[8]	8.8[8]	...
Honduras	42	97.6	20.8	1.119	240	44.3[3]	—	43.4	12.3	29.1	17.0	56.2	15.5	24.0
Hong Kong	...	...	...	81.902	14,500	...	...	...	...	...	...	...	...	...
Hungary	1,405	96.0	4.3	306.1	28,900	17.9	—	61.5	20.6	38.3	3.6	88.8	2.3	10.5
Iceland	205	99.5	...	34.374	139,000	43.9	1.5	7.9	46.7	58.5	14.1	3.3	—	44.4
India	4,972	92.7	4.7	523.2	660	76.9	—	11.5	11.7	71.8	0.1	7.3	7.1	10.0
Indonesia	4,009	97.3	7.6	12,705.0	73,000	10.7[3]	5.0	46.8	37.5	27.2	29.5	10.0	11.2	12.2[7, 13]
Iran	...	...	...	3,922.0[14]	89,400[14]	85.0[3, 14]	—	2.1[14]	12.8[14]	68.2[14]	17.9[14]	1.6[14]	3.9[14]	...
Iraq	...	...	...	...	...	...	...	...	...	...	...	...	...	...
Ireland	4,154	99.7	...	2.640	740	13.3	—	—	86.7	62.2	19.6	—	26.1	8.0
Isle of Man	...	...	...	...	...	...	...	...	...	...	...	...	...	...
Israel	4,338	99.2	3.4	3.346	750	43.1	—	6.5	50.4	75.9	18.6	0.2	—	31.4[7]
Italy	22,980	89.8	...	358,312.0	6,428,000	63.8	—	0.9	35.4	70.0	—	—	—	12.0
Jamaica	143	100.0	30.6	2.252	940	75.3	—	—	24.7	72.8	60.2	171.5	8.5	21.0
Japan	67,146	98.7	...	102,973.0	841,000	35.2	—	31.0	33.8	100.0	17.4	—	—	2.5
Jersey	...	...	...	...	...	...	...	...	...	...	...	...	...	...
Jordan	56	37.5	6.4	0.980	340	47.3	—	—	52.7	104.9	0.2	—	—	6.2
Kampuchea	...	...	...	...	...	...	...	...	...	...	...	...	...	...
Kenya	182	98.9	8.2	18.917	840	75.3	—	—	24.7	62.8	—	34.9	4.7	12.5
Kiribati	...	...	...	...	...	...	...	...	...	...	...	...	...	...
Korea, North	...	...	...	...	...	...	...	...	...	...	...	...	...	...
Korea, South	6,866	99.8	8.7	10,107.0	239,000	13.7[3]	—	72.6	13.7	36.4	16.6	2.1	—	7.0
Kuwait	2,804	96.8	0.1[1]	1.036	540	—	—	—	100.0	60.0	41.7	—	27.2	6.0
Laos	...	...	...	...	...	...	...	...	...	...	...	...	...	...
Lebanon	1,028	68.6	0.2	30.326[2]	11,100[2]	30.9[2]	0.4[2]	1.2[2]	67.5[2]	22.3[2]	71.7[2]	—	—	21.8
Lesotho	40	100.0	3.0	0.157	100	28.9	—	—	71.1	84.4	−4.0	3.4	12.2	12.5
Liberia	—	—	409.5	0.170	70	98.8[3]	0.2	0.9	0.1	37.9	3.4	64.8	4.0	5.6[6]
Libya	3,902	96.8	0.2[1]	3.041[2]	750[2]	28.2	1.5	—	70.3	97.6	32.8	—	—	5.0[7]
Liechtenstein	...	...	...	...	...	...	...	...	...	...	...	...	...	...
Luxembourg	...	...	...	53.6	145,000	...	...	...	...	...	...	...	...	4.2[6]
Macau	...	...	...	...	...	...	...	...	...	...	...	...	...	...
Madagascar	123[7]	100.0[7]	22.9	289.6[2]	27,700[2]	90.4[2, 3]	—	—	9.5[2]	20.6[2]	33.4[2]	112.0[2]	1.0[2]	11.5[7]
Malawi	44	100.0	35.4	0.298	40	84.4[3]	—	—	15.6	65.2	12.0	45.8	—	11.0
Malaysia	4,495	98.2	2.7	16.375	980	9.1	—	—	90.9	49.7	4.9	0.4	—	3.3
Maldives	6	100.0	8.1	0.204	1,030	75.0[3]	—	0.3	24.7	78.7	35.4	2.8	5.3	7.0[13]
Mali	10	100.0	64.0	109.3	15,000	71.1	—	25.5	3.4	61.9	—	29.1	—	8.5
Malta	959	98.3	0.1	0.351	1,020	—	—	—	100.0	80.8	6.3	—	—	5.5
Martinique	...	...	...	4.514	13,500	...	...	...	...	...	...	...	...	...
Mauritania	38	100.0	33.5	11.393[2]	6,260[2]	33.5[2]	—	38.7[2]	27.8[2]	38.7[2]	3.2[2]	71.3[2]	28.5[2]	6.5[7]
Mauritius	288	99.7	3.1	3.241	3,100	30.1	—	1.2	68.7	44.4	—	30.0	5.0	10.0
Mayotte	...	...	...	0.254	3,360	...	...	...	...	...	...	...	...	...
Mexico	10,558	99.2	13.0	13,517.0	165,000	28.5	—	0.4	71.1	33.8	—	26.8	—	150.4[13]
Monaco	...	...	...	...	...	...	...	...	...	...	...	...	...	...
Mongolia	...	...	...	...	...	...	...	...	...	...	...	...	...	...
Montserrat	...	...	...	0.009[5, 11]	800[5, 11]	...	...	...	...	...	...	...	...	...
Morocco	262	90.5	60.6	54.489	2,320	43.0	21.1	25.0	10.9	73.6	1.4	30.2	—	8.5[7]
Mozambique	...	...	...	...	...	...	...	...	...	...	...	...	...	...
Nauru	...	...	...	...	...	...	...	...	...	...	...	...	...	...
Nepal	189	97.4	7.6	8.682	490	62.3[3]	1.4	8.7	27.6	55.6	23.7	11.5	—	11.0
Netherlands, The	12,682	87.9	...	103.7	7,050	4.5	—	10.3	85.3	53.6	4.5	—	—	3.3
Netherlands Antilles	192	90.1	4.2[1]	0.565	3,200	21.2	0.1	—	78.7	73.0	10.6	—	9.4	6.0
New Caledonia	...	...	...	39.012	255,000	...	...	...	...	...	...	...	...	...
New Zealand	2,828	100.0	...	6.711	2,000	28.8	0.9	—	70.3	22.9	39.7	27.8	—	17.0
Nicaragua	171[14]	97.7[14]	...	10.937[14]	3,520[14]	74.3[14]	—	17.9[14]	7.8[14]	34.9[14]	−0.9[14]	84.5[14]	1.3[14]	...
Niger	173	100.0	5.4	73.2	10,300	32.9	—	21.1	46.0	45.2	22.0	25.6	—	8.5
Nigeria	689	96.5	19.4	12.663[2]	110[2]	63.0[2]	5.7[2]	15.6[2]	15.8[2]	38.1[2]	12.3[2]	0.4[2]	3.8[2]	15.0[7]
Niue	...	...	...	...	...	...	...	...	...	...	...	...	...	...
Norfolk Island	...	...	...	...	...	...	...	...	...	...	...	...	...	...

deposit money banks, 1987[b] assets (%)				liabilities	composition (%)				external public debt outstanding (long-term, disbursed only), 1986[b] total ('000,000 U.S.$)	creditors (%)		debt service total ('000,000 U.S.$)	repayment (%)		debt service ratio (%)	country
loans to govern-ment	loans to private sector	re-serves	foreign assets	deposits ('000,000,000 national currency)	demand depos.	savings depos.	govt. depos.	foreign liabilities	total ('000,000 U.S.$)	offi-cial	private	total ('000,000 U.S.$)	princi-pal	inter-est	debt service ratio (%)	country
6.5	71.9	16.1	5.5	7.433	22.5	61.7[4]	—	1.1	1,463.3	92.4	7.6	181.8	63.0	37.0	18.0	El Salvador
—	80.7	1.1	18.1	11.1	22.7	4.4	1.0	—	141.0	91.6	8.4	4.5	68.9	31.1	...	Equatorial Guinea
59.2[3]	15.2	22.7	2.9	3.749	42.6	37.7	3.5	3.1	1,989.1	86.2	13.8	176.8	70.8	29.2	21.5	Ethiopia
...	...	...	...	...	...	...	...	...								Faeroe Islands
									0[1]	...	...	0[1]	...	...	...	Falkland Islands
19.5[2,3]	53.9[2]	7.8[2]	18.8[2]	0.683[2]	16.9[2]	59.8[2]	2.6[2]	18.5[2]	293.1	78.9	21.1	56.0	55.4	44.6	10.0	Fiji
0.8[2]	73.6[2]	3.7[2]	21.9[2]	313.653[2]	6.8[2]	46.6[2]	3.2[2]	31.4[2]	...	...	...	...	...	...	...	Finland
4.7[2]	60.0[2]	1.4[2]	34.0[2]	3,997.0[2]	18.2[2]	27.6[2]	—	32.2[2]	...	...	...	...	...	...	...	France
									18[1]	...	...	1[1]	...	...	1.7[1]	French Guiana
									127[1]	...	...	11[1]	36.4[1]	63.6[1]	4.5[1]	French Polynesia
22.3	73.2	1.8	2.6	400.6	20.7	26.3	12.8	9.8	1,094.7	35.7	64.3	209.1	70.7	29.3	17.2	Gabon
31.0[3]	47.4	13.2	8.5	0.388	25.8	37.5	—	2.4	228.0	88.1	11.9	10.6	50.0	50.0	11.3	Gambia, The
...	...	...	...	...	...	...	...	...								Gaza Strip
									16,750[12]	...	...	...	...	...	...	Germany, East
18.7[3]	64.5	3.1	13.7	2,678.2	9.0	31.6	7.6	7.8	...	...	...	...	...	...	...	Germany, West
21.2[2,3]	37.4[2]	40.6[2]	0.8[2]	49.585[2]	35.8[2]	28.1[2]	2.6[2]	5.2[2]	1,412.9	95.1	4.9	88.7	68.1	31.9	10.8	Ghana
—17.4[2]—		0.9[2]	...	0.401[2]	—79.0[2]—			...	85[1]	...	...	19[1]	71.1[1]	28.9[1]	...	Gibraltar
33.2[2]	40.9[2]	19.2[2]	6.7[2]	3,838.9[2]	5.3[2]	64.4[2]	—	24.2[2]	15,014.9	23.8	76.2	2,171.7	50.2	49.8	27.6	Greece
...	...	...	...	...	...	...	...	...								Greenland
12.9[3]	58.5	16.7	11.9	0.322	12.8	55.7	—	15.2	52.8	94.5	5.5	5.6	67.9	32.1	9.1	Grenada
									62[1]	...	...	8[1]	50.0[1]	50.0[1]	4.2[1]	Guadeloupe
...	...	...	...	...	...	...	...	...								Guam
6.3	71.7	20.0	2.0	3.782	21.4	63.5	—	3.5	2,186.9	66.8	33.2	281.1	47.6	52.4	23.3	Guatemala
...	...	...	...	...	...	...	...	...								Guernsey
									1,421.1	85.8	14.2	103.0	81.7	18.3	...	Guinea
									293.8	71.9	28.1	8.7	77.0	23.0	54.1	Guinea-Bissau
16.3[3]	22.8	56.8	4.1	4.297	13.9	57.4	—	3.4	772.0	77.6	22.4	26.3	43.0	57.0	9.5[9]	Guyana
—	54.1[8]	36.8[8]	9.1[8]	1.635[8]	24.2[8]	60.6[8]	—	2.7[8]	584.7	88.2	11.8	18.8	60.1	39.9	6.1	Haiti
23.6	71.9	4.2	0.3	2.964	19.7	45.7[4]	—	3.5	2,341.7	78.4	21.6	190.7	42.1	57.9	18.5	Honduras
—	—	...	83.3	2,752.5	...	...	...	82.5	3,978[1]	...	...	954[1]	...	...	2.4[1]	Hong Kong
46.5[3]	32.9	17.2	3.4	863.4	16.8	32.9[4]	—	9.4	13,567.1	10.6	89.4	3,943.5	71.8	28.2	35.9	Hungary
3.5	81.3	11.5	3.7	100.117	32.1	36.0	—	23.0	...	...	...	...	...	...	...	Iceland
22.2	63.5	14.3	—	1,347.1	15.2	71.9	—	—	31,913.4	84.3	15.7	2,696.3	58.7	41.3	18.1	India
13.0[3]	62.2	7.6	17.2	45,264.0	15.0	46.2[4]	3.9	1.7	31,901.2	55.4	44.6	4,431.7	53.8	46.2	29.3	Indonesia
19.3[8]	44.6[8]	33.6[8]	2.5[8]	6,117.88	37.5[8]	48.8[8]	—	1.0[8]	2,494[1]	...	...	1,049[1]	86.5[1]	13.5[1]	6.2[1]	Iran
...	...	...	...	...	...	...	...	...	7,150[1]	...	...	1,982[1]	75.7[1]	24.3[1]	13.2[1]	Iraq
18.9	60.0	5.4	15.6	11.333	10.6	52.0	0.7	25.3	...	...	...	...	...	...	...	Ireland
...	...	...	...	...	...	...	...	...								Isle of Man
37.2	38.1	14.0	10.7	92.896	2.1	37.2	5.1	17.0	15,937.6	71.9	28.1	2,189.4	38.1	61.9	18.9	Israel
21.7	54.2	13.7	10.3	691,686.0	43.8	32.7	—	15.0	...	...	...	...	...	...	...	Italy
29.1	50.6	15.8	4.5	7.999	17.6	65.9	2.6	7.2	2,993.2	82.3	17.7	430.6	50.1	49.9	31.7	Jamaica
11.7[3]	77.4	1.3	9.7	500,867.0	14.9	53.9	—	16.0	...	...	...	...	...	...	...	Japan
...	...	...	...	...	...	...	...	...								Jersey
14.9	58.0	7.8	19.4	2.329	13.9	59.7	5.5	16.4	3,078.6	67.8	32.2	540.3	66.7	33.3	28.7	Jordan
...	...	...	...	...	...	...	...	...	507[1]	...	...	12[1]	...	...	45.8[1]	Kampuchea
26.3[3]	63.5	8.6	1.6	40.407	27.9	51.4[4]	4.0	2.2	3,437.9	81.4	18.6	429.8	59.5	40.5	23.2	Kenya
...	...	...	...	...	...	...	...	...	10[1]	...	...	0[1]	...	...	3.1[1]	Kiribati
...	...	...	...	...	...	...	...	...	796[1]	...	...	69[1]	39.9[1]	60.1[1]	...	Korea, North
5.9	70.9	10.0	13.2	74,781.0	7.8	40.3[4]	4.3	12.3	29,107.6	35.9	64.1	6,995.7	66.7	33.3	16.7	Korea, South
—	69.6	2.0	28.4	8.040	8.7	46.3	2.3	15.0	686[1]	...	...	1,057[1]	92.8[1]	7.2[1]	6.3[1]	Kuwait
...	...	...	...	...	...	...	...	...	457[1]	...	...	21[1]	13.6[1]	86.4[1]	28.8[1]	Laos
9.0[2]	30.7[2]	2.3[2]	57.9[2]	413.453[2]	3.8[2]	71.0[2,4]	0.2[2]	15.7[2]	211.0	92.7	7.3	28.4	56.0	44.0	...	Lebanon
32.2[3]	25.5	26.8	15.4	0.443	27.9	52.0	4.4	3.0	182.1	95.6	4.4	13.8	69.6	30.4	4.2	Lesotho
25.5[3]	28.6	40.4	5.5	0.262	35.7	21.6	5.0	15.0	1,001.8	81.8	18.2	27.7	47.3	52.7	6.0	Liberia
—	66.0[2]	29.2[2]	4.9[2]	3.094[2]	62.2[2]	35.8[2]	11.2[2]	1.7[2]	1,177[1]	...	...	614[1]	92.1[1]	8.0[1]	5.9[1]	Libya
...	...	...	...	...	...	...	...	...								Liechtenstein
—	2.5	—	97.5	7,738.7	1.3	6.3	—	85.1	...	...	...	...	...	...	...	Luxembourg
...	...	...	...	...	...	...	...	...	91[1]	...	...	14[1]	46.7[1]	53.3[1]	1.3[1]	Macau
1.9[2]	76.9[2]	13.9[2]	7.3[2]	552.0[2]	31.9[2]	14.1[2]	6.1[2]	4.4	2,634.5	86.2	13.8	113.3	44.9	55.1	29.9[9]	Madagascar
22.3[3]	31.0	45.8	1.0	0.663	23.6	55.9	—	8.6	909.7	92.9	7.1	108.0	66.7	33.3	40.0	Malawi
14.4	75.6	3.4	6.6	73.416	11.4	54.4	8.8	6.8	16,758.8	22.0	78.0	2,227.9	47.4	52.6	13.7	Malaysia
23.1[3]	39.8	22.2	15.0	0.454	12.5	35.6	0.4	36.9	59.8	85.5	14.5	12.9	86.0	14.0	8.7[9]	Maldives
2.1	79.3	13.1	5.5	132.1	34.0	15.6	8.4	17.7	1,565.7	96.5	3.5	35.2	64.2	35.8	14.2	Mali
8.5	53.7	22.0	15.8	0.514	6.9	77.2	—	9.0	113.5	100.0	—	16.5	86.7	13.3	1.6	Malta
...	...	...	...	...	...	...	...	...	27[1]	...	...	6[1]	50.0[1]	50.0[1]	1.7[1]	Martinique
1.1[2]	89.7[2]	4.9[2]	4.3[2]	19.168[2]	35.8[2]	18.1[2]	0.8[2]	29.9[2]	1,637.2	90.8	9.2	77.2	59.8	40.2	17.0	Mauritania
28.5	55.5	8.3	7.7	12.675	12.4	79.4	—	0.5	426.8	78.8	21.2	64.4	56.1	43.9	7.3	Mauritius
...	...	...	...	...	...	...	...	...								Mayotte
47.4[3]	37.2	8.2	7.2	71,414.0	7.9	52.4[4]	0.2	22.8	74,961.8	14.3	85.7	8,753.6	28.7	71.3	36.8	Mexico
...	...	...	...	...	...	...	...	...								Monaco
									4,396[1]	...	...	95[1]	—	100.0[1]	...	Mongolia
—	71.7[5]	2.9[5]	17.6[5]	0.0435	18.8[5]	61.4[5]	—	13.9[5]	4.1[1]	...	...	0[1]	—	100.0[1]	5.9[1]	Montserrat
38.6[9]	52.7[9]	1.6[9]	7.1[9]	43.934[9]	54.4[9]	37.8[9]	—	1.1[9]	14,610.3	67.4	32.6	1,441.5	48.5	51.5	40.8	Morocco
...	...	...	...	...	...	...	...	...	1,224[1]	...	...	149[1]	63.1[1]	36.9[1]	81.0[1]	Mozambique
									27[1]	...	...	14[1]	...	...	...	Nauru
33.0[3]	44.6	9.2	13.2	14.780	15.6	70.0	—	3.8	711.1	95.1	4.9	30.6	58.8	41.2	9.2	Nepal
14.5[3]	50.9	0.3	34.3	601.9	11.7	39.8[4]	—	32.1	...	...	...	...	...	...	...	Netherlands, The
0.2[3]	51.1	11.3	37.4	1.923	16.3	45.8[4]	1.1	33.2	816[1]	...	...	146[1]	63.7[1]	36.3[1]	5.8[1]	Netherlands Antilles
									125[1]	...	...	13[1]	42.9[1]	57.1[1]	3.5[1]	New Caledonia
19.9	73.6	0.9	5.6	24.883	22.4	58.1	—	6.3	...	...	...	...	...	...	...	New Zealand
—	84.4[14]	13.8[14]	1.8[14]	20.709[14]	26.2[14]	20.5[4,14]	21.6[14]	6.5[14]	5,343.1	74.9	25.1	32.0	32.8	67.2	13.0	Nicaragua
13.5	64.2	20.2	2.1	144.2	24.9	28.6	13.9	26.6	1,026.2	80.3	19.7	92.1	60.3	39.7	24.8	Niger
30.1[2]	56.0[2]	5.5[2]	6.3[2]	27.461[2]	22.6[2]	39.8[2]	3.6[2]	3.0[2]	21,496.3	39.0	61.0	1,624.4	75.9	24.1	23.0	Nigeria
...	...	...	...	...	...	...	...	...	...	...	...	...	...	...	...	Niue
...	...	...	...	...	...	...	...	...	...	...	...	...	...	...	...	Norfolk Island

Finance (continued)

country	international reserves, 1988[a] total ('000,000 SDRs)	% foreign exchange	ratio of external debt to total reserves, 1986[b]	money supply, 1987[b] stock ('000,000,000 national currency)	M1 per capita	central bank authority, 1987[b] assets (%) claims on government	claims on private sector	claims on banks	claims on foreign assets	liabilities (%) reserve money	government deposits	foreign liabilities	capital accounts	central bank discount rate, 1988[a]
Norway	11,186	99.6	...	153.7	37,000	12.6	—	40.2	47.2	17.6	62.8	—	—	8.0[2]
Oman	849	98.8	2.6	0.325	240	—	—	—	100.0	34.9	17.8	0.3	19.7	9.56, 9
Pacific Is., Trust Terr. of the	...	...	...	...	...	...	...	...	...	...	...	...	...	...
Marshall Islands	...	...	...	...	...	...	...	...	...	...	...	...	...	...
Micronesia, Fed. States of	...	...	...	...	...	...	...	...	...	...	...	...	...	...
Northern Mariana Islands	...	...	...	...	...	...	...	...	...	...	...	...	...	...
Palau	...	...	...	...	...	...	...	...	...	...	...	...	...	...
Pakistan	566	88.0	14.9	172.622	1,600	59.93	—	24.6	15.5	66.1	13.4	12.7	—	10.0
Panama	55	100.0	20.2	0.4109	1909	70.43	23.5	—	6.1	14.2	25.2	54.5	9.4	...
Papua New Guinea	312	99.4	2.7	0.281	80	15.0	—	—	85.0	25.5	32.9	2.1	29.5	8.87
Paraguay	363	99.7	3.9	243.667	61,700	32.23	1.2	19.3	47.3	82.3	6.6	7.4	10.1	...
Peru	362	87.8	7.3	42.7132	2,0902	35.72, 3	—	25.52	38.72	72.22	12.32	21.12	11.52	72.09
Philippines	576	81.6	10.9	52.4	900	42.63	—	20.5	36.8	52.4	37.4	49.8	—	9.1
Pitcairn Island	...	...	...	...	...	...	...	...	...	...	...	...	...	...
Poland	1,236	98.6	49.0	2,989.12	79,6002	24.92	—	69.82	5.32	73.12	21.62	4.12	1.22	4.07
Portugal	3,985	85.9	6.0	1,413.42	138,0002	53.32, 3	—	4.52	42.32	29.62	0.62	5.52	17.62	13.5
Puerto Rico	...	...	...	...	...	...	...	...	...	...	...	...	...	...
Qatar	440	93.2	0.41	4.778	11,700	—	—	0.2	99.8	70.3	12.8	—	4.0	7.06
Réunion	...	...	...	6.802	11,900	...	...	...	...	...	...	...	...	...
Romania	5397	84.87	7.4	179.72	7,8602	—	42.12	55.92	2.12	28.22	28.72	2.92	—	...
Rwanda	88	100.0	2.5	17.791	2,700	34.83	1.1	5.8	58.3	58.6	15.0	8.6	—	9.0
St. Helena and Ascension	...	...	...	...	...	...	...	...	...	...	...	...	...	...
St. Kitts and Nevis	7	100.0	...	0.0235, 11	5205, 11	...	...	...	...	...	...	...	...	...
St. Lucia	22	100.0	2.61	0.126	870	30.8	—	—	69.2	98.9	—	—	—	5.06
St. Pierre and Miquelon	...	...	...	0.209	33,800	...	...	...	...	...	...	...	...	...
St. Vincent and the Grenadines	13	100.0	1.1	0.053	470	25.6	—	—	74.4	98.2	—	—	—	4.06
San Marino	...	...	...	...	...	...	...	...	...	...	...	...	...	...
São Tomé and Príncipe	...	...	...	...	...	—	—	—	100.0	18.0	34.4	—	—	...
Saudi Arabia	15,113	98.9	0.21	86.32	6,7802	51.7	—	47.5	0.7	40.2	2.9	53.7	—	8.5
Senegal	9	88.9	223.1	214.2	31,100	...	...	...	...	...	...	...	...	...
Seychelles	10	100.0	9.2	0.155	2,350	61.7	—	6.1	32.2	46.8	41.6	—	6.2	6.0
Sierra Leone	97	100.07	34.1	1.8522	4902	89.52	—	—	10.52	64.12	0.62	400.42	—	16.0
Singapore	11,319	100.0	0.2	11.031	4,200	—	—	—	100.0	26.0	20.5	—	—	4.013
Solomon Islands	24	100.0	2.3	0.037	120	11.0	—	8.4	80.6	26.6	29.1	9.8	41.0	10.76, 7
Somalia	57	80.07	105.1	12.1432	2,0002	65.12, 3	—	24.82	10.12	49.92	13.82	139.22	9.12	12.07
South Africa	712	78.9	...	32.026	1,090	7.3	—	11.7	81.0	80.4	29.2	11.4	—	11.5
Bophuthatswana	...	...	...	...	...	...	...	...	...	...	...	...	...	...
Ciskei	...	...	...	...	...	...	...	...	...	...	...	...	...	...
Transkei	...	...	...	...	...	...	...	...	...	...	...	...	...	...
Venda	...	...	...	...	...	...	...	...	...	...	...	...	...	...
South West Africa/Namibia	...	...	...	...	...	...	...	...	...	...	...	...	...	...
Spain	25,265	98.1	9.7	8,899.0	229,000	39.1	—	17.4	43.5	97.7	3.1	—	6.3	8.0
Sri Lanka	268	98.9	9.7	24.901	1,510	66.8	—	8.2	25.0	53.7	6.1	5.4	34.7	10.0
Sudan, The	8	100.0	120.2	5.8492	2402	96.43	—	2.8	0.8	81.6	—	96.2	1.5	...
Suriname	12	83.3	1.71	1.562	3,720	96.7	—	—	3.3	86.0	0.8	—	3.0	...
Swaziland	81	100.0	2.1	0.125	180	5.6	—	—	94.4	73.2	13.0	7.5	8.5	10.0
Sweden	6,610	96.8	...	112.22	13,4002	64.9	—	1.6	33.6	46.5	—	0.3	—	8.5
Switzerland	21,508	86.5	...	84.0	12,700	6.4	—	9.9	83.7	77.9	2.7	—	—	2.5
Syria	1472	80.32	17.0	61.2142	5,6702	95.72, 3	—	1.42	2.82	75.62	11.02	13.52	0.22	5.08
Taiwan				1,568.2	79,300	0.13	—	2.5	97.4	28.4	4.1	—	—	4.5
Tanzania	50	100.0	59.7	35.8102	1,5702	61.1	—	34.3	4.6	48.3	—	68.0	—	12.5
Thailand	3,832	97.7	3.8	132.4	2,430	33.2	—	20.0	46.8	41.9	3.2	8.8	48.8	8.0
Togo	247	100.0	2.7	91.0	26,600	29.9	—	3.6	66.4	80.8	0.4	15.4	—	8.5
Tokelau	...	...	...	...	...	...	...	...	...	...	...	...	...	...
Tonga	...	...	...	...	...	...	...	...	...	...	...	...	...	...
Trinidad and Tobago	68	97.1	2.4	2.187	1,760	50.5	—	—	49.5	54.7	17.4	—	44.5	7.5
Tunisia	425	98.6	16.0	2.035	260	5.5	—	64.8	29.8	61.5	5.5	17.2	20.1	9.27
Turkey	1,487	91.0	14.3	8,381.0	157,000	69.73	—	5.7	24.6	22.9	0.6	73.9	1.1	54.0
Turks and Caicos Islands	...	...	...	...	...	...	...	...	...	...	...	...	...	...
Tuvalu	...	...	...	...	...	...	...	...	...	...	...	...	...	...
Uganda	26	100.0	31.6	6.0622	4002	92.12, 3	—	—	7.92	91.02	47.32	69.32	—	32.0
U.S.S.R.	...	...	...	...	...	...	...	...	...	...	...	...	...	...
United Arab Emirates	3,371	99.1	0.41	10.096	5,770	—	—	5.6	94.4	61.1	25.1	—	13.5	...
United Kingdom	31,509	97.9	...	92.3	1,620	6.3	—	—	93.7	56.7	—	38.1	—	9.013
United States	32,034	71.4	...	765.9	3,130	83.6	—	—	16.4	95.7	5.1	0.1	—	6.5
Uruguay	450	79.8	4.7	84.22	28,5002	48.7	5.5	15.6	30.1	12.3	46.5	47.0	—	65.06
Vanuatu	32	100.0	0.4	4.364	29,700	—	—	—	100.0	30.6	54.3	0.1	12.6	9.013
Venezuela	4,190	90.4	3.5	133.779	7,230	6.8	—	3.3	89.9	51.1	21.3	—	25.7	12.9
Vietnam	...	...	...	...	...	...	...	...	...	...	...	...	...	...
Virgin Islands (U.S.)	...	...	...	...	...	...	...	...	...	...	...	...	...	...
Wallis and Futuna	...	...	...	0.602	39,200	...	...	...	...	...	...	...	...	...
West Bank	...	...	...	...	...	...	...	...	...	...	...	...	...	...
Western Sahara	...	...	...	...	...	...	...	...	...	...	...	...	...	...
Western Samoa	25	100.0	2.8	0.027	170	1.9	—	14.2	83.9	52.0	17.4	21.3	—	12.06
Yemen (Aden)	71	98.6	13.8	0.452	200	94.8	—	—	5.2	95.1	—	1.8	—	...
Yemen (Şan'ā')	238	100.0	4.8	26.641	3,130	87.43	—	—	12.6	78.9	8.9	1.5	0.5	9.56
Yugoslavia	776	91.5	8.6	7,643.7	325,000	8.2	8.0	47.6	36.3	216.7	1.7	89.6	—	131.07
Zaire	136	87.5	18.8	68.549	2,130	70.63	0.7	3.5	25.2	30.6	1.5	70.4	−54.6	26.07
Zambia	76	98.7	50.4	2.3042	3302	86.22	2.12	—	11.72	22.22	0.12	202.52	—	14.0
Zimbabwe	114	87.7	13.2	1.1182	1302	35.32, 3	—	—	64.72	77.32	0.12	59.42	—	9.0

deposit money banks, 1987[b]									external public debt outstanding (long-term, disbursed only), 1986[b]							country
assets (%)				liabilities					total ('000,000 U.S.$)	creditors (%)		debt service				
loans to govern-ment	loans to private sector	re-serves	foreign assets	deposits ('000,000,000 national currency)	composition (%)					offi-cial	private	total ('000,000 U.S.$)	repayment (%)		debt service ratio (%)	
					demand depos.	savings depos.	govt. depos.	foreign liabilities					princi-pal	inter-est		
10.9[3]	78.5	0.7	9.9	562.3	20.3	33.6[4]	0.8	21.9	...	...	...	...	...	...	...	Norway
5.4	67.4	5.4	21.8	1.074	13.4	51.9	11.2	10.0	2,501.2	16.5	83.5	394.6	56.5	43.5	11.3	Oman
...	...	...	...	...	...	...	...	...	32[1]	...	...	29[1]	86.7[1]	13.3[1]	...	Pacific Is., Trust Terr. of the Marshall Islands
...	...	...	...	...	...	...	...	...	...	...	...	...	...	...	...	Micronesia, Fed. States of
...	...	...	...	...	...	...	...	...	...	...	...	...	...	...	...	Northern Mariana Islands
...	...	...	...	...	...	...	...	...	...	...	...	...	...	...	...	Palau
27.8[3]	58.9	8.0	5.3	273.324	32.6	31.8	0.7	11.6	11,764.5	93.3	6.7	1,062.7	66.6	33.4	26.8	Pakistan
1.4[9]	9.0[9]	—	89.6[9]	25.184[9]	1.4[9]	5.5[9]	...	88.9[9]	3,438.7	35.8	64.2	466.4	31.0	69.0	7.6	Panama
15.9	79.0	2.8	2.4	0.893	19.3	67.5	2.1	6.7	1,147.0	47.9	52.1	148.8	55.8	44.2	12.4	Papua New Guinea
—	52.9	42.8	4.2	406.400	28.0	47.0	...	1.2	1,752.3	68.1	31.9	197.3	55.4	44.6	19.2	Paraguay
1.0[2]	50.1[2]	44.3[2]	4.6[2]	49.383[2]	32.0[2]	43.9[2,4]	...	3.2[2]	11,048.6	44.1	55.9	490.2	53.4	46.6	14.4	Peru
17.6[3]	50.9	10.1	21.4	215.7	7.8	48.1	4.0	27.5	19,827.7	39.5	60.5	1,581.4	39.2	60.8	18.3	Philippines
...	...	...	...	...	...	...	...	...	...	...	...	...	...	...	...	Pitcairn Island
52.0[2,3]	33.8[2]	9.3[2]	4.9[2]	13,722.0[2]	13.3[2]	19.1[2]	0.2[2]	44.7[2]	35,200.4	66.1	33.9	2,610.1	51.6	48.4	18.5	Poland
33.3[2,3]	50.4[2]	7.5[2]	8.8[2]	3,836.9[2]	26.1[2]	93.3[3]	5.9[2]	5.8[2]	13,928.5	16.3	83.7	3,143.0	61.7	38.3	31.5	Portugal
...	...	...	...	20.667[15]	...	...	...	...	...	...	...	...	...	...	...	Puerto Rico
—	47.8	2.5	49.7	18.289	19.3	48.5	1.8	14.6	211[1]	...	...	126[1]	78.6[1]	21.4[1]	2.8[1]	Qatar
...	...	...	...	...	...	...	...	...	55[1]	...	...	13[1]	38.5[1]	61.5[1]	4.3[1]	Réunion
30.4[2]	66.1[2]	1.1[2]	2.5[2]	670.2[2]	6.5[2]	25.0[2]	...	14.2[2]	5,308.5	48.5	51.5	1,602.5	66.1	33.9	11.9	Romania
23.8[3]	57.3	9.8	9.1	23.110	34.3	47.1	9.1	2.9	411.9	97.7	2.3	17.9	70.9	29.1	7.6	Rwanda
...	...	...	...	...	...	...	...	...	...	...	...	...	...	...	...	St. Helena and Ascension
2.4[5]	60.2[5]	2.8[5]	14.8[5]	0.206[5]	9.5[5]	68.0[5]	1.4[5]	5.5[5]	12[1]	...	...	0[1]	...	...	1.1[1]	St. Kitts and Nevis
8.7[3]	58.3	12.4	20.6	0.532	13.8	67.1	...	9.5	34[1]	...	...	1[1]	...	...	1.0[1]	St. Lucia
...	...	...	...	...	...	...	...	...	...	...	...	...	...	...	...	St. Pierre and Miquelon
19.9[3]	42.8	14.8	22.4	0.304	9.8	62.8	—	15.5	28.8	98.6	1.4	2.7	51.9	48.1	2.2[14]	St. Vincent and the Grenadines
...	...	...	...	...	...	...	...	...	...	...	...	...	...	...	...	San Marino
—	32.7	10.4	56.9	179.6	28.8	42.7[4]	0.8	13.6	74.2	99.2	0.8	1.8	66.7	33.3	36.9[9]	São Tomé and Príncipe
3.5	86.9	7.2	2.4	445.4	24.6	26.6	7.2	12.2	3,947[1]	...	...	1,785[1]	88.9[1]	11.1[1]	4.1[1]	Saudi Arabia
71.7[3]	17.7	4.5	6.1	0.501	14.4	57.1	9.6	5.1	2,456.2	88.4	11.6	208.8	53.1	46.9	10.9[9]	Senegal
31.4[2,3]	20.1[2]	21.6[2]	26.8[2]	1.837[2]	45.4[2]	23.6[2]	—	9.2[2]	67.3	83.7	16.3	9.0	68.9	31.1	6.9	Seychelles
7.1	49.6	3.3	39.9	73.955	7.6	35.2	3.0	41.5	459.1	64.3	35.7	14.5	72.4	27.6	8.4	Sierra Leone
26.6	59.1	7.4	6.9	0.096	21.0	62.3	2.1	5.7	2,120.1	15.1	84.9	420.3	58.7	41.3	1.4	Singapore
5.7[2,3]	32.5[2]	20.3[2]	41.5[2]	12.597[2]	47.6[2]	36.3[2]	—	—	68.8	77.5	22.5	5.3	66.0	34.0	2.6[9]	Solomon Islands
7.3	86.8	2.7	3.2	65.421	41.1	41.0	—	6.7	1,414.8	95.2	4.8	72.0	74.9	25.1	44.4	Somalia
...	...	...	...	...	...	...	...	...	...	...	...	...	...	...	...	South Africa
...	...	...	...	...	...	...	...	...	...	...	...	...	...	...	...	Bophuthatswana
...	...	...	...	...	...	...	...	...	...	...	...	...	...	...	...	Ciskei
...	...	...	...	...	...	...	...	...	...	...	...	...	...	...	...	Transkei
...	...	...	...	...	...	...	...	...	...	...	...	...	...	...	...	Venda
0.2[8]	50.5[8]	23.0[8]	—	0.810[8]	—64.7[8]—		24.6[8]	0.4[8]	...	...	...	...	...	...	...	South West Africa/Namibia
25.5[3]	54.5	13.1	6.9	40,356.0	14.4	37.5	3.5	9.0	...	...	...	...	...	...	...	Spain
20.5[3]	57.7	8.3	13.5	68.697	16.4	50.5	4.9	11.2	3,448.2	79.8	20.2	277.8	59.2	40.8	...	Sri Lanka
1.7[2]	39.5[2]	40.3[2]	18.5[2]	6.680[2]	39.5[2]	28.1[2]	9.9[2]	6.2[2]	7,057.0	87.0	13.0	55.4	42.6	57.4	14.1[9]	Sudan, The
6.7	42.3	49.9	1.1	1.829	49.7	36.6	0.6	5.6	43[1]	...	...	5[1]	40.1[1]	60.0[1]	1.3[1]	Suriname
1.4	49.9	40.3	8.5	0.406	23.4	59.2	1.5	3.0	207.7	95.3	4.7	24.8	60.1	39.9	7.1	Swaziland
8.0[9]	79.2[9]	1.3[9]	11.4[9]	594.8[9]	9.4[9]	54.4[9]	—	24.4[9]	...	...	...	...	...	...	...	Sweden
2.3	62.2	3.0	32.5	624.0	6.9	38.4	—	22.5	...	...	...	...	...	...	...	Switzerland
41.3[2,3]	13.8[2]	43.2[2]	1.6[2]	54.895[2]	41.8[2]	18.0[2]	6.5[2]	9.0[2]	3,060.3	94.7	5.3	297.0	70.8	29.2	15.6	Syria
8.0	51.6	36.7	3.6	4,084.7	31.4	47.3[4]	5.4	10.5	5,669[1]	...	...	2,218[1]	74.8[1]	25.2[1]	...	Taiwan
79.0[2,3]	10.0[2]	4.1[2]	6.9[2]	29.742[2]	58.8[2]	48.7[2]	2.5[2]	26.1[2]	3,649.7	89.4	10.6	69.2	61.8	38.2	15.1	Tanzania
15.2[3]	77.4	3.0	4.5	861.2	5.2	78.5	2.7	4.3	11,022.6	59.6	40.4	1,942.9	61.3	38.7	16.7	Thailand
0.5	52.1	37.8	9.7	177.9	23.5	40.9	22.9	15.7	882.0	90.5	9.5	128.3	67.0	33.0	32.3	Togo
...	...	...	...	...	...	...	...	...	...	...	...	...	...	...	...	Tokelau
...	...	...	...	...	...	...	...	...	24[1]	...	...	1[1]	...	...	7.0[1]	Tonga
14.8[3]	72.3	9.5	3.5	8.491	16.0	75.8	1.7	2.0	1,154.1	16.2	83.8	228.3	59.5	40.5	15.8	Trinidad and Tobago
12.5[2]	82.5[2]	1.0[2]	4.0[2]	4.541[2]	29.1[2]	26.6[2]	—	7.9[2]	5,001.3	68.9	31.1	793.2	63.9	36.1	29.0	Tunisia
26.7[3]	52.2	12.0	9.2	27,032.0	22.4	30.4	8.3	23.4	23,308.9	60.5	39.5	3,395.9	55.0	45.0	31.3	Turkey
...	...	...	...	...	...	...	...	...	32[1]	...	...	0[1]	...	...	...	Turks and Caicos Islands
...	...	...	...	...	...	...	...	...	...	...	...	...	...	...	...	Tuvalu
0.5	44.9	31.9	22.8	7.872	95.9	25.9	2.0	4.0	928.8	92.6	7.4	28.7	56.1	43.9	6.5	Uganda
...	...	...	...	...	...	...	...	...	36,700[12]	...	...	...	...	...	...	U.S.S.R.
7.8[3]	38.5	7.9	45.9	105.507	6.2	42.5	5.3	16.7	1,335[1]	...	...	704[1]	81.5[1]	18.5[1]	4.5[1]	United Arab Emirates
1.9[3]	34.2	0.5	63.4	727.2	10.7	17.9[4]	—	65.3	...	...	...	...	...	...	...	United Kingdom
10.3[3]	81.0	3.0	5.7	4,072.5	13.8	50.1	1.1	6.6	...	...	...	...	...	...	...	United States
13.1[2,3]	47.3[2]	18.0[2]	21.5[2]	760.2[2]	5.4[2]	46.8[2,4]	2.2[2]	27.5[2]	2,759.3	18.1	81.9	333.4	25.4	74.6	20.9	Uruguay
1.4[3]	12.2	0.8	85.6	33.431	10.1	39.8[4]	1.1	48.1	8.9	83.1	16.9	1.1	63.6	36.4	2.1	Vanuatu
4.8[3]	77.6	12.5	5.1	264.640	35.8	58.2[4]	9.4	2.1	24,485.2	0.5	99.5	3,096.5	43.0	57.0	28.5	Venezuela
...	...	...	...	...	...	...	...	...	5,302[1]	...	...	154[1]	7.8[1]	92.2[1]	...	Vietnam
...	...	...	...	...	...	...	...	...	...	...	...	...	...	...	...	Virgin Islands (U.S.)
...	...	...	...	...	...	...	...	...	...	...	...	...	...	...	...	Wallis and Futuna
...	...	...	...	...	...	...	...	...	...	...	...	...	...	...	...	West Bank
...	...	...	...	...	...	...	...	...	3[1]	...	...	0[1]	...	...	...	Western Sahara
16.8[3]	37.3	34.1	11.8	0.087	19.3	59.4	2.2	1.5	65.4	96.3	3.7	5.9	74.6	25.4	24.0	Western Samoa
7.9[3]	3.7	75.7	12.7	0.410	37.2	40.8	12.9	8.5	1,927.1	100.0	—	99.2	78.0	22.0	44.5	Yemen (Aden)
2.0[3]	28.3	61.1	8.5	14.830	31.3	47.6	1.4	12.3	2,051.6	96.2	3.8	99.1	57.5	42.5	44.9	Yemen (Şan'ā')
0.1	55.8	38.4	5.7	44,633.0	12.1	47.7[4]	—	32.8	13,173.9	39.5	60.5	1,985.8	47.0	53.0	11.4	Yugoslavia
3.8[3]	34.2	37.4	24.6	66.971	46.2	10.2[4]	2.0	9.5	5,429.9	86.6	13.4	369.7	38.3	61.7	18.2	Zaire
28.3[2]	36.2[2]	19.9[2]	15.6[2]	4.942[2]	34.6[2]	35.6[2]	2.7[2]	11.3[2]	3,574.7	83.7	16.3	123.6	55.9	44.1	7.6	Zambia
45.3[2,3]	44.2[2]	8.7[2]	1.7[2]	2.487[2]	29.2[2]	53.8[2]	—	4.2[2]	1,711.6	47.8	52.2	338.6	65.4	34.6	19.9	Zimbabwe

[1]1985; includes external long-term private debt not guaranteed by the government. [2]1986. [3]Includes claims on nonfinancial government (public) enterprises and/or local governments. [4]Includes foreign currency deposits. [5]1982. [6]Short-term deposit rate. [7]1987. [8]1984. [9]1985. [10]Long-term deposit rate. [11]Cash and demand deposits at local banks only. [12]Gross hard currency debt to the West. [13]Money market rate. [14]1984. [15]June 30.

Housing and construction

The present table summarizes data about the housing stock and the construction industries of the countries of the world. The principal focus is on the elements that are most comparable internationally: the age of the housing (by decade, so far as possible), the legal tenure of the householder, construction of exterior walls, principal physical amenities, sanitary arrangements, and the amount of space both absolutely (total area of the average dwelling in square metres [1 square metre equals 1.20 square yards, or 10.76 square feet]) and relatively (persons per room). The data on construction characterize the industry in number of new units constructed annually, their area, and the portion of the gross domestic product (GDP) represented by each country's construction industry.

Because housing patterns differ greatly from country to country, the portion of each country's housing stock for which data are compared is defined as specifically as possible. In general, the numbers refer to permanent, private dwelling units that are usually occupied year-round, whether or not actually occupied on the date of the housing census or survey. That definition implies the exclusion of certain housing that is often part of national housing censuses: vacation homes, second homes occupied less than half the year, collective or communal dwellings, and so on. The housing unit to which the data on tenure refer may be either the individual dwelling or the household, according to the reporting practice of the country concerned.

The data are collected mostly from national housing censuses and surveys. The majority of countries combine the housing census with the population census at five- to ten-year intervals. Some countries, however, can conduct a meaningful housing census only in the capital city or in the few largest cities; others may be able to collect and process data for only a few of the most important housing characteristics even when national coverage is complete. These choices may be dictated by the lack of funding to collect data for the entire country or by the perception, particularly in a tropical, rural country where adequate dwellings can be built by hand, that no urgent housing problem exists. These choices may be complex, however, as planners are always aware that much housing is physically inadequate to protect dwellers from the elements, is disadvantageously placed in relation to tainted or disease-infested water supply or to the outfall of unprocessed sewage, or is built of materials (mud,

Housing and construction

country	housing stock year	dwelling units[a]	median age[b] (years)	decade built (%) 1939 or earlier	1940–49	1950–59	1960–69	1970 or later	tenure[c] (%) owned	rented	collective, vacant, other	exterior walls (%) traditional materials	sawn/framed wood	masonry or cement	other
Afghanistan	1979	3,940,000[1]	...	...	...	...	...	...	55.2	23.5	21.3	...	...	...	...
Albania	...	...	...	...	...	...	...	...	...	...	...	...	...	...	...
Algeria	1977	2,208,712[5]	...	...	...	...	23.7	...	56.7	29.4	13.9	...	...	...	...
American Samoa	1980	4,688	13.4	4.2	4.8	7.7	38.4	44.9	71.2	25.1	3.7	4.1	56.3	34.9	4.7
Andorra	...	...	...	...	...	...	...	...	...	...	...	...	...	...	...
Angola	...	...	...	...	...	...	...	...	...	...	...	—	8.1	91.2	0.7
Anguilla	1984	1,840	...	...	...	...	...	...	...	...	...	—	8.1	91.2	0.7
Antigua and Barbuda	1970	15,405[5]	11.1	13.8	9.7	31.4	46.1	—	55.9	40.4	3.7	...	...	...	...
Argentina	1980	7,103,853	21.6	9.1	14.9	17.3	22.0	36.7	67.7	14.8	17.5	6.1	6.7	84.2	3.0
Aruba	1981	14,929	29.0	28.2	—34.2—		14.9	22.7	49.0	51.0	—	—	9.4	87.7	2.9
Australia	1981	5,285,571[11]	26.1	—37.9—		10.4	18.6	33.1	61.6	22.6	15.8	...	...	...	...
Austria	1981	3,150,600[11]	63.6	—44.5—		13.3	19.4	22.8	47.7	36.2	16.1	...	...	...	...
Bahamas, The	1980	54,308	30.7		—54.7—		25.6	19.7	51.4	37.4	11.2	4.0[14]	32.3	54.7	9.0
Bahrain	1981	52,810	15.2	41.2	17.1	14.5	—27.2—		60.6[13]	33.6[13]	5.8[13]	2.1[13]	...	95.1[13]	2.8[13]
Bangladesh	1981	14,790,000	...	...	...	...	...	...	89.7	5.0	5.3	20.0	11.6	5.0	63.4
Barbados	1980	67,138	18.9		—51.3—		20.6	28.1	70.2	21.5	8.3	0.1	68.9[15]	26.3	4.7
Belgium	1981	3,997,100[16]	35.2	48.4[17]	—17.2[18]—		14.2	16.0	59.2	38.1	2.7	...	...	...	...
Belize	1980	27,298	...		—24.6—		30.0	41.0	56.1	27.2	16.7	7.5	73.4	14.0	5.1
Benin	1975	644,000	...						...	...	...	...	...	...	...
Bermuda	1980	20,350	31.2		—67.9—		16.6	15.5	39.4	53.7	6.9	...	1.7[15]	95.1	3.2
Bhutan	...	...	...	...	...	...	...	...	...	...	...	...	...	...	...
Bolivia	1976	1,040,704	...	...	...	...	47.4	...	69.3	15.1	15.6	...	...	...	...
Botswana	1981	170,262	...						59.9	17.1	23.0	65.5	—	28.0	6.5
Brazil	1984	29,163,724	...						63.4	22.3	14.3	...	...	...	...
British Virgin Islands	1980	3,287	21.6	—39.8—		—31.2—		29.0	47.4	43.0	9.6	—	21.6	68.0	10.4
Brunei	1981	28,676	...						83.8	11.8	4.4	0.2	54.8	36.5	8.5
Bulgaria	1975	3,214,500[11]	17.9	47.0	—34.9—		11.1	7.0	77.3	22.7	—	...	...	...	...
Burkina Faso	...	...	...	...	...	...	...	...	...	...	...	...	...	...	...
Burma	1983	6,750,884	...						98.7	1.1	0.2	83.5	14.8	—	1.7
Burundi	1979[24]	938,000	...						...	...	...	...	...	...	...
Cameroon	1976	1,390,896	...						83.4	11.2	5.4	75.5	13.9	9.5	1.1
Canada	1981	9,057,533[11]	14.6	—41.2—		13.8	17.9	27.1	62.1	37.9		...	...	...	...
Cape Verde	1980	59,006	...									1.0	24.0	74.0	1.0
Cayman Islands	1979	4,426	...		—52.0—			48.0	67.8	32.2	—	82.2	7.1	2.5	8.2
Central African Republic	1975	405,399	...						...	...	...	...	...	...	...
Chad	...	...	...	...	...	...	...	...	...	...	...	...	...	...	...
Chile	1982	2,510,275	20.4		—46.2—		21.1	32.7	63.1	18.7	18.2	13.0	44.4	41.6	1.0
China	1982	220,100,775	...						18.5[2]	81.5[2]		...	...	...	...
Christmas Island	1984	1,231	14.0[8]		—32.8—		27.2	40.6[8]	—	86.4[25]	13.6[25]	—	1.7[25]	74.7[25]	23.6[25]
Cocos (Keeling) Islands	1981	150	...					33.3	—80.7—		19.3	—	6.0	52.0	42.0
Colombia	1985	5,266,581	20.6[27]	46.7[27]	7.9[27]	26.2[27]	19.2[27]	...	67.6	23.6	8.8	16.7	7.0	75.6	0.7
Comoros	1980	81,791	...	—5.3—		7.7	21.3	63.7	87.4	3.1	9.5	73.5	1.8	16.9	7.8
Congo	1984	363,140	...						61.0	34.6	4.4	15.0	20.0	52.8	12.2
Cook Islands	1981	3,153[5]	14.0	5.9	5.7	16.8	48.6	23.0	85.3[12]	9.4[12]	5.3[12]	1.1	60.1	35.6	3.2
Costa Rica	1984	500,788	...	...	...	...	36.4[27]	...	65.8	20.7	13.5	...	...	...	...
Côte d'Ivoire	1985	1,146,370[28]	...						...	...	...	1.4	37.1	61.5	—
Cuba	1981	2,363,364	24.6	15.0[29]	8.2[30]	21.3[31]	21.6	25.6	...	...	...	11.9	—	87.6	0.5
Cyprus	1982	194,300[11]	22.8		—39.9—		15.4	44.7	60.0	16.5	23.5	—	2.9	93.8	3.3
Czechoslovakia	1980	5,747,000[11]	36.7	—40.0[17]—		15.1[18]	20.3	24.6	44.7	41.7	13.6	...	...	...	...
Denmark	1985	2,120,549	30.8	40.0	6.7	10.8	17.9	24.6	55.3	43.2	1.5	...	...	...	...
Djibouti	1982	25,000	27.6						64.7[19]	26.6[19]	8.7[19]	—	73.0[32]	22.5	4.5
Dominica	1981	17,307	...	—58.4[19]—		16.9[19]	21.1[19]	3.6[19]	72.0	17.0	11.0	0.2[19]	88.8[19]	10.2[19]	0.8[19]
Dominican Republic	1981	1,114,833[5]	...	—12.4—			—87.6—		66.7	22.9	10.4	31.8[19]	46.2[19]	15.3[19]	6.7[19]
Ecuador	1982	1,576,441	...	...	...	...	...	...	64.0	27.2	8.8	46.9	9.3	41.4	2.4
Egypt	1986	9,732,728	...	17.2[2]	—19.9[2]—		—62.9[2]—		...	...	...	...	...	...	...
El Salvador	1971	680,456	...						56.7[22]	22.3[22]	21.0[22]	37.9	9.6	46.9	5.6
Equatorial Guinea	...	...	...	...	...	...	...	...	...	...	...	...	...	...	...
Ethiopia	1984	9,300,000	...									—	43.9	53.5	2.6
Faeroe Islands	1977	11,172	32.5	33.7	—26.4—		21.8	15.0	84.5	9.9	5.6	—	86.4	10.9	2.7
Falkland Islands	1980	589	...						38.9	16.6	44.5	...	...	...	...
Fiji	1986	124,098	...						74.4	14.6	11.0	9.0	26.4	29.8	34.8
Finland	1985	1,887,710	17.0	19.1	5.8	13.7	18.1	43.3	69.0	26.0	5.0	14.0[38]	81.8[38]	—4.2[38]—	
France	1982	19,590,400	31.0[22]		—71.9[22]—		12.7[22]	15.4[22]	50.7	41.0	8.3	...	...	...	...
French Guiana	1982	21,063	...						34.5	54.0	11.5	29.4[40]	—70.6—		
French Polynesia	1983	...	13.6	—5.0—		9.0	30.0	56.0	...	...	...	38.0	—62.0—		

skins, thatch, etc.) that may harbour pests or disease. In the developed countries, median age and the distribution of physical amenities provide strong indicators of the quality and availability of housing.

The data for construction industries refer to new construction for the most recent year in which a broad range of countries could be surveyed. The scope of the data may be limited in several respects. It may be confined to activity capable of being surveyed in the national capital region only, may be limited to private new construction only or to government and government-financed activity only, or may refer to construction mortgaged or financed through certain organizations only. Depending on national data-collection systems, it usually excludes remodeling of old premises but may include extensions or enlargements of existing buildings. The data for construction are usually taken either from the UN's *Construction Statistics Yearbook* or from official national sources that report two principal types of data: authorized new construction or certification after construction that newly built structures meet building and fire codes and the like. The figures for completed construction are naturally more meaningful but are not available for many countries, necessitating

the provision of authorized construction data, which are usually available only for areas regulated by certain types of governmental authorities.

A more complete indication of total activity in a national construction industry is its contribution to the national gross domestic product, since that figure also includes civil-engineering projects, such as dams, roads and other transportation infrastructure, recreational facilities, irrigation and land reclamation works, and the like. The predominance within the "new residential" sector of multiunit housing usually indicates (in a developed country) a particularly mobile society or (in a developing country) one in which limited development resources obliges planners to concentrate available physical and manpower resources in collective projects.

a. Data refer to permanent, private dwelling units that are usually occupied year-round, whether or not occupied on the census date.
b. Data are estimates unless specifically provided by a country source.
c. Data may be either for dwellings or for households, depending on country reporting practice.
d. Data may be either for construction completed or for construction authorized, depending on country reporting practice.

physical amenities (percent)			sewage disposal (percent)			space[b]			construction industry (1985)							country
piped water	electricity	inside toilet or WC	closed public sewer or septic tank	open public sewer	other	average area (sq m)	rooms per dwelling unit	persons per room	percent of GDP	new residential[d]			new nonresidential[d]			
										1- or 2-unit dwellings	multiunit dwellings	floor area ('000 sq m)	number of units	floor area ('000 sq m)		
25.3[2]	66.5[2]	5.5[2]	5.5	77.9	16.6	...	5.5	2.1	4.0[3]	—224[4]—		...	4	...		Afghanistan
...	...	...	...	...	...	...	...	...	7.8[1]	...	...	...	...	...		Albania
45.8	49.2	...	54.1	—45.9—		...	2.2[6]	2.8[6]	15.1[1]	...	...	...	...	...		Algeria
77.4	96.2	...	83.5	—	16.5	...	3.0	2.3	...	—187[4]—		...	4	...		American Samoa
—	...	—	...	...	...	...	...	...	13.4[7]	—95[8]—		91.3[8]	14[8]	47.5[8]		Andorra
36.9	64.1	30.1[9]	55.7	—44.3—		...	4.8	0.8	1.7[1]	—1,587[8]—		585.2[8]	210[8]	164.5[8]		Angola
85.4	...	...	17.0	—83.0—		...	3.1	...	...	...	...	...	...	...		Anguilla
72.9	86.8	95.1	77.1	—22.9—		...	3.9	1.3	5.2[10]	...	...	...	...	...		Antigua and Barbuda
98.7	98.7	89.2	...	...	...	...	4.3	1.1	3.8	—81,323[4, 10]—		10,607[4, 10]	4	4		Argentina
										—84[1]—		...	102[1]	...		Aruba
97.1[12]	98.4[13]	92.2	99.0	—1.0—		...	5.1	0.6	6.9	122,500	37,900	21,360	23,340	8,123		Australia
95.0	...	85.5	94.3	—	5.7	76.5	4.3[11]	0.6[11]	6.5	14,100	1,300	2,900	500	100		Austria
63.9	77.9	...	63.2	2.2	34.6	...	4.0	1.2	3.1[11]	—1,409—		...	92	...		Bahamas, The
97.5	98.2	...	44.7	—	55.3	...	3.0[13]	2.3[13]	9.9[10]	—2,124[1]—		...	2,445[1]	...		Bahrain
56.8	...	...	1.3	—98.7—		...	2.0	2.9	5.7	...	...	...	...	...		Bangladesh
82.4	83.0	43.6	95.8	0.7	3.5	...	4.2	0.8	4.9	—753[12]—		...	35[12]	...		Barbados
95.3	100.0	79.0	62.5[19]	—37.5[19]—		82.1	5.5[16]	0.4[16]	5.3	24,344	443	17,776[20]	6,198	22,422[20]		Belgium
60.1	59.4	19.7	21.1	—78.9—		...	2.5[21]	1.9[21]	5.7	...	...	...	...	...		Belize
...	...	...	...	...	...	...	...	...	4.7	...	...	...	...	...		Benin
97.4	...	96.7	96.7	—3.3—		...	3.2	0.7	4.9[10]	148[22]	12[22]	20.1[22]	15[22]	15.0[22]		Bermuda
...	...	...	...	...	...	...	...	...	10.5	—101—		...	1[1]	...		Bhutan
37.9	33.0	...	12.5	—87.5—		...	...	...	4.7	...	...	...	...	...		Bolivia
56.1	5.4	25.4	8.6	20.4	71.0	...	...	...	2.9[11]	—756—		81.9	472	97.6		Botswana
66.2	79.4	...	47.9	—52.1—		...	5.1[8]	0.9[8]	6.1	—62,164—		12,069	5,017	3,771		Brazil
62.3	90.2	65.1	65.1	25.3	9.6	...	3.9	1.1	10.1[23]	...	...	...	...	...		British Virgin Islands
90.3	64.2	94.2	57.4	—42.6—		...	4.2	1.6	3.4	—195[10]—		...	5[10]	...		Brunei
74.6	99.8	33.2	33.2	—67.8—		...	2.5[11]	1.1[11]	9.8[3]	9,109	1,541	5,174	...	...		Bulgaria
...	...	...	...	...	...	...	...	...	1.4[10]	...	...	...	...	...		Burkina Faso
...	...	...	...	...	...	...	...	...	1.7	...	...	...	...	...		Burma
11.0	0.6	...	1.6	—98.4—		...	...	...	5.3[11]	...	...	...	...	...		Burundi
22.0	5.9	2.2	2.2	70.4	27.6	...	4.1	1.2	6.0[10]	780[1]	201[1]	230.4[1]	53[1]	51.1[1]		Cameroon
99.5	100.0	98.9	98.9	—1.1—		...	5.7	0.5	7.0[11]	...	2,818	...	14,846	...		Canada
...	...	...	...	...	...	...	...	...	20.3[25]	—2427—		30.5[7]	37	0.5[7]		Cape Verde
99.0	96.0	83.7	57.0	—43.0—		...	4.0	1.1	...	...	...	...	...	...		Cayman Islands
...	...	...	...	...	...	...	1.1[26]	3.4[26]	2.5	—103[10]—		6.5[10]	16[10]	...		Central African Republic
...	...	...	...	...	...	...	...	...	1.3[1]	...	...	...	...	...		Chad
81.4	84.7	...	63.2	36.4	0.4	...	3.6	1.3	5.5[11]	...	...	29.9	...	93.8		Chile
89.4[2]	...	25.2[2]	47.0[2]	—53.0[2]—		37.0	2.2	1.8	5.6[3]	...	...	95,651	...	75,761		China
100.0	100.0	100.0	100.0	—	—	...	5.7	1.0	...	...	...	...	...	...		Christmas Island
35.6	100.0	100.0	100.0	—	—	...	6.1	0.6	...	...	...	...	...	...		Cocos (Keeling) Islands
70.5	78.5	77.9	69.6	—30.4—		...	3.3	1.6	5.8	7,739	7,952	7,404	1,442	1,224		Colombia
12.9	5.7	...	2.1	—97.9—		33.7	2.5	2.1	11.5[7]	...	...	...	...	...		Comoros
30.5	8.8	16.6	—86.2[2]—		13.8[2]	...	3.7[2]	1.7[2]	7.5[10]	...	...	...	...	...		Congo
88.3[12]	60.6[12]	...	36.7[12]	—63.3[12]—		...	4.0[12]	0.7[12]	4.5[22]	—68—		...	24	...		Cook Islands
86.9	97.3	...	66.5	—33.5—		...	4.0	1.4	3.5	—9,470—		760	2,868	178		Costa Rica
23.0	39.6	23.9	—68.5—		31.5	...	...	...	2.2[10]	...	...	...	...	...		Côte d'Ivoire
74.1	82.9	45.2	60.9	9.0	30.1	...	4.1	1.0	9.4[3]	31,773	710	4,819	469	1,803		Cuba
100.0	98.1	74.5	95.6	—4.4—		...	4.6	0.8	10.0	3,656	461	1,077	1,103	411		Cyprus
91.6	100.0	70.8	91.2	—8.8—		68.0	3.5	0.9	11.0[3]	26,838	...	8,100	...	...		Czechoslovakia
100.0	100.0	99.2	98.6[25]	—1.4[25]—		108.0	5.1[11]	0.6[11]	4.9	—23,324—		2,446	15,309	4,111		Denmark
45.0	58.0	82.0	26.0	23.0	51.0	...	1.9	6.9	7.5[10]	—110—		32.2	46	21.7		Djibouti
91.1[1]	...	12.3[19]	12.3[19]	—87.7[19]—		...	2.8[19]	1.7[19]	7.7[10]	...	...	...	...	...		Dominica
49.3	36.7[19]	14.1	52.1[19]	22.6[19]	25.3[19]	...	2.8[19]	1.5[19]	8.5[10]	2,899	1,059	641	471	229		Dominican Republic
51.8	47.3	32.7	34.9	13.3	51.8	...	2.8	1.8	4.4	18,609	6,384	3,825	596	412.7		Ecuador
73.1	87.0	...	...	...	...	...	3.3	1.5	4.8[33]	...	...	...	...	...		Egypt
48.0[34]	34.1	6.3[13]	20.0[34]	—80.0[34]—		...	1.5[22]	3.3[22]	3.0	7,626	309	340.7	8	0.7		El Salvador
...	...	...	...	...	...	...	...	...	9.4	...	...	...	...	...		Equatorial Guinea
...	...	...	...	...	...	...	...	2.7[35]	3.2	—2,016[1]—		157.7[1]	921	46.9[1]		Ethiopia
99.7	99.5	95.0	89.7	8.1	2.2	...	5.5	1.1	10.2[8]	...	...	...	...	...		Faeroe Islands
98.8	...	98.8	98.0[36]	—2.0[36]—		...	7.4[36]	0.4[36]	...	...	...	...	...	...		Falkland Islands
73.7	48.5	56.0	35.4[37]	—64.6[37]—		...	3.3	1.8	5.8	—797—		79	102	39		Fiji
93.9	95.9[38]	91.1	95.9	—4.1—		73.9	3.6	0.7	6.8	25,517	1,028	16,473[20]	32,886	28,265[20]		Finland
99.2	98.8[39]	85.0	73.8[28]	—26.2[28]—		77.0[22]	3.8[10]	0.6[10]	5.9[10]	164,665[10]	3,675[10]	...	...	17,682[10]		France
67.7	80.4	59.1	34.3	—65.7—		...	2.8	1.3	...	...	...	16.9[1]	...	28.5		French Guiana
86.0	76.0	76.0	2.0	67.0	31.0	...	3.4	1.7[37]	9.4[7]	—562—		97.6[4]	214	4		French Polynesia

Housing and construction (continued)

country	year	dwelling units[a]	median age[b] (years)	1939 or earlier	1940–49	1950–59	1960–69	1970 or later	owned	rented	collective, vacant, other	traditional materials	sawn/framed wood	masonry or cement	other
				decade built (percent)					tenure[c] (percent)			construction of exterior walls (percent)			
Gabon	1967[41]	15,886	...	...	...	...	...	...	—87.0—		13.0[42]	...	...	...	...
Gambia, The	1983	202,199	...	...	...	...	...	...	63.9	21.9	14.2	82.9	—	12.9	4.2
Gaza Strip	1985	66,819[43]	...	...	...	...	...	...	89.1[44]	7.6[44]	3.3[44]	...	...	...	...
Germany, East	1981	6,910,700[11]	...	—62.4—		6.1	10.1	21.4	36.3	63.7	—	...	...	...	...
Germany, West	1982	27,317,600[11]	...	—53.7—			20.5	25.8	36.0[22]	64.0[22]	—	...	...	...	...
Ghana	1970	1,216,677[10]	...	...	...	...	...	...	47.7[28]	25.3[28]	27.0	...	...	...	...
Gibraltar	1986	7,846	...	...	...	...	...	...	5.9	94.1	—	...	...	...	...
Greece	1981	3,999,332	29.2	—30.2[17]—		27.4[18]	20.7	21.5	73.1[9]	26.9[9]	—	...	...	...	...
Greenland	1985	16,096	10.8[12]	—11.9[12]—		18.8[12]	46.5[12]	22.8[12]	39.3	—60.7—		...	...	...	...
Grenada	1970	19,642	18.3	—48.0—		29.0	22.2	0.8	76.5	14.0	9.5	0.4	80.8	17.8	1.0
Guadeloupe	1982	85,629	...	...	...	...	8.1[9]	...	64.3	29.9	5.8	29.5[40]	—70.5—		
Guam	1980	28,091	...	...	...	...	...	44.6	40.8	47.6	11.6[42]	...	...	...	...
Guatemala	1981	1,259,598	12.5	—62.0—			10.0	28.0	64.7	11.3	24.0	55.6	21.1	19.3	4.0
Guernsey	1976	17,824	...	...	...	...	...	...	63.5	33.5	3.0	...	...	...	...
Guinea	...	...	...	...	...	...	...	...	...	...	...	...	...	...	...
Guinea-Bissau	1979	123,936	...	...	...	...	...	...	...	...	...	95.7	0.1	2.3	1.9
Guyana	1970	129,722	...	—45.8—			31.6	.1.0	56.8	29.8	13.4	3.1	87.2	7.1	2.6
Haiti	1982	1,130,795	...	...	...	...	...	24.1	82.9[12]	4.8[12]	12.3[12]	...	...	...	...
Honduras	1974	526,566	...	—43.1—			37.9	14.2	71.8	16.5	12.7	61.0	26.4	11.7	0.9
Hong Kong	1986	1,205,900	...	...	...	...	13.6[25]	38.3[25]	35.1	58.1	6.8	...	...	...	...
Hungary	1984	3,890,600[11]	36.2	—40.6[17]—		12.8[31]	16.9	29.7	75.1	24.7	0.2	30.8	14.3	54.8	0.1
Iceland	1984	82,200[11]	25.6	18.5	—27.5—		—54.1—		70.3[21]	—29.7[21]—		...	...	71.9[21]	...
India	1981	142,954,921	...	...	...	...	...	...	84.6[13]	15.4[13]	—	...	...	...	...
Indonesia	1980	30,263,273	...	...	...	...	...	...	87.0[13]	5.0[13]	8.0[13]	...	...	...	...
Iran	1976	5,331,220	...	—82.5—				17.5	70.2	15.0	14.8	...	...	...	...
Iraq	1956	741,000	...	...	...	...	...	...	83.0	12.8	4.2	...	...	...	...
Ireland	1981	985,300[16]	47.2	44.6	—16.4—		12.8	26.2	67.9	20.9	11.2	...	...	...	...
Isle of Man	1981	24,348[45]	...	...	...	...	...	...	62.5	36.5	1.0	...	...	...	...
Israel	1983	1,104,270	...	—9.5[46]—			—90.5[47]—		72.9	24.6	2.5	...	...	...	...
Italy	1981	17,542,000	19.4	—30.8[17]—		19.7[18]	27.5[48]	22.0	58.9	35.5	5.6	...	...	...	...
Jamaica	1982	517,297	...	—33.6—			26.8	39.6	46.7	29.5	23.8	7.1	28.4	54.4	10.1
Japan	1983	34,704,500	13.0	—13.5—		9.7	24.0	52.1	62.4	37.3	0.3	—	77.4	21.5	1.1
Jersey	1981[45]	26,674	...	...	...	...	...	...	48.8	49.2	2.0	...	...	...	...
Jordan	1979	378,815[50]	...	...	...	...	...	...	62.6	30.8	6.6	...	...	...	...
Kampuchea	...	...	...	...	...	...	...	...	...	...	...	...	...	...	...
Kenya	1962[2]	137,000[5]	...	...	...	...	...	...	...	...	...	64.4	—35.6—		
Kiribati	1978	10,093[16,45]	...	...	...	...	...	...	68.2	17.9	13.9	...	...	...	...
Korea, North	...	...	...	...	...	...	...	...	...	...	...	...	...	...	...
Korea, South	1985	6,104,210	19.0[8]	—26.1[8]—		15.8[8]	18.2[8]	39.9[8]	83.8	12.8	3.4	11.8[8]	38.8[8]	49.2[8]	0.2[8]
Kuwait	1985	228,781	14.5[8]	—12.2[8]—			38.8[8]	34.5[8]	38.2	53.6	8.2	46.5[38]	—	36.5[38]	17.0[38]
Laos	...	...	...	...	...	...	...	...	...	...	...	...	...	...	...
Lebanon	1970	483,908[5]	...	—30.1[51]—		40.2[52]	29.4	—	...	...	...	...	...	...	...
Lesotho	1986[45]	330,035	...	...	...	...	...	...	...	...	...	...	...	...	...
Liberia	1974[41]	263,333	...	...	...	...	...	...	...	...	...	...	...	...	...
Libya	1984	569,679	...	...	...	...	...	...	62.5[27]	28.0[27]	9.5[27]	...	...	...	...
Liechtenstein	1980	8,421	29.4	—27.1[51]—		15.0[52]	27.1	30.8	53.6	41.7	4.7	...	...	...	...
Luxembourg	1981	128,281[45]	...	—62.1[46]—		11.8[53]	7.8	18.3	59.2	—40.8—		...	...	...	...
Macau	1981	45,158	...	...	...	...	...	...	71.8[19]	28.2[19]	—	—	0.5[19]	99.3[19]	0.2[19]
Madagascar	...	...	...	...	...	...	...	...	...	...	...	...	...	...	...
Malawi	1977	1,834,118	...	...	...	...	...	...	39.6	—60.4—		...	...	...	...
Malaysia	1980	2,332,563	...	...	...	...	...	...	64.0	23.0	13.0	...	...	...	...
Maldives	1985	29,818	...	...	...	...	...	...	...	...	...	...	...	...	...
Mali	1976[45]	1,253,802	...	...	...	...	...	...	...	...	...	...	...	...	...
Malta	1985	101,509	...	—81.8[55]—			18.2[56]	—	53.9	43.0	3.1	93.0[43]	...	92.9[43]	0.21[43]
Martinique	1982	85,265	...	...	...	...	...	...	64.1	31.3	7.3	20.4[40]	—79.6—		
Mauritania	...	...	...	...	...	...	...	...	...	...	...	...	...	...	...
Mauritius	1983[57]	158,215	...	—19.7—			24.3[58]	56.0[59]	73.2	12.5	14.3	—	4.2	66.8	28.9
Mayotte	1985	13,142	...	...	...	...	...	...	88.1[22]	6.2[22]	5.7[22]	67.7	—16.7—		15.6
Mexico	1980	12,216,462	...	—51.4—			15.4	33.2	66.8	—33.2—		28.2	9.6	56.2	6.0
Monaco	1975	12,625	28.5	—51.4—		22.7	—25.8—		...	...	...	...	...	...	...
Mongolia	1969	242,000	...	...	...	...	...	...	100.0	—	—	...	...	...	...
Montserrat	1980	3,706	...	—47.4—			24.5	28.1	69.2	21.9	8.8	...	60.9	39.0	0.1
Morocco	1982[45]	3,419,282	...	...	...	...	...	...	40.8[2]	43.7[2]	15.5[2]	24.5	...	73.5	1.8
Mozambique	1980	2,712,439	...	...	...	...	...	...	...	...	...	86.5	2.3	8.3	2.9
Nauru	1977	508[60]	...	—88.6[60]—				11.4[60]	11.0[35]	80.6[35]	8.4[35]	...	...	...	...
Nepal	1961[61]	37,122	...	...	...	...	...	...	75.3	10.7	14.0	...	...	...	...
Netherlands, The	1977	5,384,100[16]	20.0	22.0[62]	—29.0[63]—		24.6	24.4	45.3	54.7	—	...	21.6	75.7	2.7
Netherlands Antilles	1981	41,101	21.0	22.4	—27.4—		19.7	30.5	53.0	31.1	15.9	6.3	21.0	58.1	14.6
New Caledonia	1983	35,107	15.8	—9.8—		11.2	32.1	46.9	74.1	23.1	2.8	...	...	...	...
New Zealand	1986	1,167,826	...	—64.6[25]—			19.2[25]	16.2[30]	...	...	...	...	...	...	...
Nicaragua	1971	330,422	...	...	...	...	...	...	64.4	20.3	15.3	30.8	45.6	21.8	1.8
Niger	1960	611,070[45]	...	...	...	...	...	...	...	...	...	66.5	...	...	...
Nigeria	1961[41]	92,900	...	...	...	...	...	...	8.0	80.9	11.1	...	...	...	...
Niue	1986	549	...	...	...	...	...	...	75.2	7.5	17.3	...	...	...	...
Norfolk Island	1986	787	14.8[25]	—32.8[25]—			32.5[25]	34.7[25]	55.0	34.1	10.9	—	46.4	3.8	49.8
Norway	1980	1,720,000[11]	25.3	35.1	6.9	16.8	18.7	22.5	66.6	23.5	9.9	...	...	...	...
Oman	1982	2,469	...	...	...	...	...	...	...	...	...	...	...	...	...
Pacific Is., Trust Terr. of the															
Marshall Islands	1980	4,163	...	3.4	3.1	13.3	24.7	55.5	60.0	33.0	7.0	10.7	63.5	15.9	9.9
Micronesia, Fed. States of	1980	11,562	...	1.7	2.1	5.2	21.3	69.7	51.8	39.2	9.0	6.0	41.8	14.6	37.6
Northern Mariana Islands	1980	3,373	...	0.8	3.7	8.4	29.4	57.7	53.6	36.1	10.3	0.0	6.1	33.4	60.5
Palau	1980	2,265	...	2.5	3.1	8.6	29.8	56.0	78.0	12.1	9.9	0.7	23.1	16.7	59.5
Pakistan	1980	12,587,648	17.2[64]	...	17.1[51,64]	36.7[64,65]	24.9[64,66]	21.3[64,67]	78.4[64]	7.7[64]	13.9[64]	49.2[64]	2.4[64]	41.4[64]	7.1[64]
Panama	1980	364,726	18.0	—47.4—		12.8	18.1	21.7	70.1	21.1	8.8	37.1	—	52.2	10.7
Papua New Guinea	1980	556,519[45]	...	...	...	...	...	...	40.0[28]	—60.0[28]—		...	...	...	...

physical amenities (percent)			sewage disposal (percent)			space[b]			construction industry (1985)						country
									percent of GDP	new residential[d]			new nonresidential[d]		
piped water	electricity	inside toilet or WC	closed public sewer or septic tank	open public sewer	other	average area (sq m)	rooms per dwelling unit	persons per room		1- or 2-unit dwellings	multiunit dwellings	floor area ('000 sq m)	number of units	floor area ('000 sq m)	
...	50.5	...	...	...	...	...	3.0	1.3	7.3[1]	—445[28]—		216.1[28]	75[28]	119.4[28]	Gabon
21.9	...	...	...	...	...	...	2.0	2.0	3.3[11]	120[28]	76[28]	...	14[28]	...	Gambia, The
97.2	93.5	97.3	...	...	...	...	2.6	2.4	...	—1,402[11]—		246.8[11]	...	32.8[11]	Gaza Strip
98.2	100.0	60.1	90.8	—9.2—		63.0	2.8[11]	0.9[11]	5.9	...	...	7,207	...	...	Germany, East
99.2[36]	99.7[36]	97.1	97.1	—2.9—		...	4.6[11]	0.5[11]	5.1	117,702	14,523	154,283[20]	29,974	123,491[20]	Germany, West
34.0[34]	...	...	...	...	...	...	...	...	2.6	...	...	...	...	...	Ghana
96.7[25]	100.0[25]	98.8[25]	100.0[25]	—	—	...	3.2[25]	1.2[25]	...	...	...	...	...	...	Gibraltar
81.3[13]	89.0[13]	93.0[13]	...	...	...	138.4[11]	3.3[11]	0.9[13]	5.7	28,940	4,958	23,361[20]	11,471	12,887[20]	Greece
62.7[12]	84.2[12]	39.1[12]	39.1[12]	—60.9[12]—		...	2.8	1.2	27.4[34]	—561—		41.5	...	12.3	Greenland
86.5	...	23.0	23.0	—77.0—		...	2.9	1.6	9.0[11]	...	...	...	...	...	Grenada
69.4	77.2	55.4	24.6	—75.4—		...	3.5	1.1	4.4[8]	460[25]	10[25]	91.9[25]	31[25]	40.9[25]	Guadeloupe
99.5	...	96.5	97.5	—2.5—		...	4.7	0.7	7.9[7]	369[38]	16[38]	...	1,101[38]	...	Guam
52.0	37.0	14.3	20.1	3.4	76.5	...	2.4	2.2	1.8	—3,969[4]—		269.0	4	144.0	Guatemala
96.5	...	88.8	49.3	—50.7—		...	5.5	0.5	...	...	...	...	...	...	Guernsey
...	...	...	...	...	...	...	...	...	6.4	...	...	...	...	...	Guinea
3.7	3.9	25.6	25.8	—74.2—		...	1.4	4.5	2.6[1]	...	...	...	...	...	Guinea-Bissau
81.0	...	26.3	13.0	—87.0—		...	2.7	2.1	5.9[10]	—1,259[8]—		...	56[8]	...	Guyana
12.0[34]	1.1[13]	...	2.0[34]	—98.0[34]—		...	2.2[13]	2.1[13]	5.6	—464[4]—		...	4	...	Haiti
55.0[34]	25.0	13.0	14.4	—85.6—		...	2.4	2.3	5.2	1,130	...	149.9	112	86.1	Honduras
85.7[25]	...	69.2[27]	65.4[27]	—34.6[27]—		53.2[13]	3.1[27]	2.8[27]	4.6	—684—		1,643	238	1,262	Hong Kong
81.2	98.8	65.9	79.5	—20.5—		65.0	3.6[11]	0.8[11]	10.2[3]	35,033	1,474	24,038[20]	3,433	21,886[20]	Hungary
99.1[21]	94.6[21]	93.6[21]	86.5[21]	—13.5[21]—		...	4.8[21]	0.9[21]	6.1	...	...	756.0[20]	...	926.5[10,20]	Iceland
67.0[27]	53.5[2,27]	20.0[27]	...	...	...	...	2.0[13]	2.6[13]	4.8	—73,729[10]—		...	13,908[10]	...	India
11.0	14.2	26.6	22.8[13]	—77.2[13]—		59.0	3.3	1.7[13]	5.6	—167,837[10]—		...	...	...	Indonesia
46.8	48.3	26.7	...	...	...	60.0	2.7	2.0	7.3	106,122	2,098	18,608	5,235	1,466	Iran
20.8	17.1	...	...	...	...	...	2.4	...	7.5	—53,890—		8,330	11,799	1,960	Iraq
94.8	94.7[13]	93.0	72.3[13]	—27.7[13]—		...	3.7[16]	1.0[16]	6.4[10]	...	...	2,265	...	...	Ireland
...	...	96.8	...	...	...	...	...	0.4	...	...	...	...	...	...	Isle of Man
96.5[13]	96.5[13]	98.8	99.0[9]	—1.09—		...	3.0	1.2	3.9	1,087	1,222	3,070	...	1,380	Israel
98.7	99.0[13]	94.0	95.7[13]	—4.3[13]—		85.3	4.0[16]	0.8	6.0	—39,383—		82,700[20]	24,061	85,000[20]	Italy
76.9	48.6	35.2	...	...	...	...	2.4[19]	4.3	8.5	—3,132[10]—		...	235[28]	...	Jamaica
94.0	...	58.2	61.2	—38.8—		85.9	4.7	0.7	7.4	609,200	207,600	114,848	211,300	84,712	Japan
91.0[49]	...	93.0	91.0[49]	...	...	...	...	0.5	...	—349[1]—		...	...	...	Jersey
77.2	77.3	55.4[35]	15.7	—84.3—		...	...	...	7.7	—6,354[4]—		1,515[4]	4	4	Jordan
...	...	...	...	...	...	...	...	...	5.3[6]	...	...	...	...	...	Kampuchea
...	...	...	...	...	...	...	1.9	2.5	4.6	—577—		97	73	83	Kenya
21.3	23.7	15.5	...	...	...	...	...	...	2.7[10]	...	...	...	...	...	Kiribati
...	...	...	...	...	...	...	...	...	...	...	...	...	...	...	Korea, North
34.0	49.9[19]	33.1	...	...	...	73.0	3.5	1.8	8.3[10]	—61,252—		20,606	34,166	17,609	Korea, South
53.9[8]	99.5[8]	...	35.9[8]	—64.1[8]—		...	4.0[8]	1.8[8]	3.4	—647—		1,375	71	1,358	Kuwait
...	...	...	...	...	...	...	...	...	5.3[10]	...	...	...	...	...	Laos
...	93.4	82.9	...	...	...	...	...	...	8.8	...	...	...	...	...	Lebanon
...	...	...	...	...	...	...	2.3[45]	1.7	3.3	...	...	...	...	...	Lesotho
...	...	...	...	...	...	...	...	...	...	...	...	...	...	...	Liberia
70.1[27]	72.1[27]	40.6[27]	40.6[27]	—59.4[27]—		...	3.3[27]	1.8[27]	10.9[10]	...	...	...	...	...	Libya
96.5	96.6	86.7	90.2	—9.8—		102.0	3.0	1.4	...	...	...	202.1[16,20]	...	373.8[16,20]	Liechtenstein
99.4[19]	...	97.2	93.0[19]	—7.0[19]—		86.4[19]	5.4	0.5	5.8[10]	948[10]	73[10]	331.2[10]	88[10]	126.2[10]	Luxembourg
95.7	99.3	68.9	...	...	...	...	3.2[10]	2.5[10]	...	—164—		216.2	25	184.9	Macau
...	...	...	...	...	...	...	...	...	4.5[1]	—354[4]—		15.6	4	9.7	Madagascar
12.4	15.7[43]	33.0[43]	33.0[43]	—67.0[43]—		...	2.1	1.7	4.1[11]	—102—		...	77	...	Malawi
65.0	64.4	...	56.4	4.4	39.2	...	2.3[19,54]	2.6[19,54]	4.3[11]	...	...	...	...	...	Malaysia
...	9.8[37]	...	2.5[37]	—97.5[37]—		...	2.3[37]	2.7[37]	7.6[10]	...	...	...	...	...	Maldives
...	...	...	...	...	...	...	...	...	4.9[10]	...	...	...	...	...	Mali
98.0	98.0	98.8	98.0	15.4[43]	6.1[43]	...	3.2[43]	1.3[43]	3.0[8]	—2,881—		...	1,013	...	Malta
55.4	70.5	41.8	41.8	—58.2—		...	3.4	1.1	3.6[7]	...	...	...	...	56.2	Martinique
...	...	...	...	...	...	...	...	...	7.9[10]	...	...	...	...	...	Mauritania
79.7	92.6	51.1	51.1	—48.9—		...	5.4	...	4.7	—4,012—		376	563	131	Mauritius
27.4[22]	...	4.4	54.7[22]	—45.3[22]—		...	4.1	2.5	...	...	...	...	...	...	Mayotte
66.2	74.6	45.0	49.2	—50.8—		...	2.3	2.5	5.0	—285,681[25]—		...	61,386[25]	...	Mexico
100.0	100.0	98.4	98.4	—1.6—		...	2.8	0.4	...	...	...	...	...	...	Monaco
0.3	47.5	...	...	...	...	...	...	...	5.1[7]	...	...	378.7	...	113.3[8]	Mongolia
78.6	72.1	49.3	49.3	30.4	20.4	...	3.5	0.9	7.1	...	...	...	...	...	Montserrat
30.5	37.2	50.2	...	...	...	...	2.7	2.2	6.5	21,200	2,156	5,461	1,014	457	Morocco
12.7	4.2	...	...	...	...	...	...	...	11.0[11]	—145[28]—		51.7[28]	20[28]	25.0[28]	Mozambique
...	49.2	...	...	...	...	...	3.6[35]	1.6[35]	...	...	...	...	...	...	Nauru
47.7	30.2	6.1	...	...	...	...	3.7	2.0	6.6[10]	...	...	...	...	...	Nepal
95.7[2,13]	94.8[2,13]	89.8[2,13]	89.8[2,13]	—10.2[2,13]—		...	3.4[1]	0.8[1]	5.0	—17,766—		35,616[20]	15,091	49,968[20]	Netherlands, The
79.6	96.9	79.6	...	...	...	...	4.2	1.0	9.0[8]	—358—		...	467	...	Netherlands Antilles
85.1	79.0[23]	68.3	69.2	—30.8—		...	3.3	1.3	4.6[1]	—286[10]—		45.9	1[10]	...	New Caledonia
92.7[13]	...	97.1[13]	...	...	...	...	5.6	0.5	5.6	...	...	2,848	8,398	3,228	New Zealand
27.9	40.9	19.3	19.2	—80.8—		...	2.2	2.1	4.3	—842[10]—		43.2[10]	28[10]	19.6[10]	Nicaragua
...	...	...	...	...	...	...	...	...	2.8	...	...	...	...	...	Niger
...	81.3	7.0	...	...	...	...	1.4	3.0	5.1	2,175[8]	2,197[8]	...	1,592[8]	...	Nigeria
93.0	98.0	44.0	14.1	—85.9—		...	4.0[25]	1.2[25]	...	6	...	...	...	...	Niue
8.0	98.3	...	94.2	—	5.8	...	6.2	2.5	...	...	...	...	...	...	Norfolk Island
97.5[19]	...	86.8	86.8	—13.2—		83.5	5.1[11]	0.5[11]	5.4	18,702	350	4,808	4,954	2,709	Norway
...	...	...	...	...	...	...	...	...	7.0	2,362	152	...	477	...	Oman
46.3	48.9	...	28.6	—71.4—		...	...	...	...	...	...	...	...	...	Pacific Is., Trust Terr. of the — Marshall Islands
40.0	28.3	...	8.0	—92.0—		...	...	...	...	...	...	...	...	...	Micronesia, Fed. States of
92.5	94.1	...	54.8	—45.2—		...	...	...	...	...	...	...	...	...	Northern Mariana Islands
70.8	75.7	...	19.6	—80.4—		...	...	...	...	...	...	...	...	...	Palau
20.3[64]	30.6[64]	25.1[64]	...	...	...	...	1.9[64]	3.3[64]	5.6	...	...	...	...	...	Pakistan
80.7	65.7	74.3	43.9	—56.1—		...	2.6	1.8	4.7	991	197	341.4	90	142.5	Panama
50.0	56.0	40.0	...	...	...	...	...	...	4.3[1]	—657—		...	...	...	Papua New Guinea

Housing and construction (continued)

country	housing stock			decade built (percent)					tenure[c] (percent)			construction of exterior walls (percent)			
	year	dwelling units[a]	median age[b] (years)	1939 or earlier	1940–49	1950–59	1960–69	1970 or later	owned	rented	collective, vacant, other	traditional materials	sawn/ framed wood	masonry or cement	other
Paraguay	1982	580,810[5]	21.1	——————56.0——————			17.0	27.0	80.4	10.5	9.1	21.5	29.7	47.6	1.2
Peru	1981	3,257,100	...	——————30.9——————			——69.1——		68.5	14.8	14.8	47.4	7.0	33.1	12.5
Philippines	1980	8,607,187	...	...	...	...	21.5[19]	...	80.2	12.4	7.4	36.3	33.6	23.8	6.3
Pitcairn Island	1986	15	...	46.7	20.0	13.3	—	20.0	100.0	—	—	—	100.0	—	—
Poland	1978	10,834,300[11]	...	42.1[68]		——38.8[69]——		19.1	...	...	...	——14.1——		——85.9——	
Portugal	1981	3,235,630	33.7	——————53.3——————			17.5	29.2	56.7	38.8	4.6	—	0.7	61.0	38.3
Puerto Rico	1980	969,611	15.8	5.7	6.5	15.0	31.6	41.2	65.7	23.8	10.5	—	19.7	77.4	2.9
Qatar	...	...	...	...	...	...	...	...	...	...	...	...	...	...	...
Réunion	1982	141,123	...	...	...	...	21.2[9]	...	54.6	34.5	10.9	...	...	...	...
Romania	1966	5,380,299	...	...	...	...	...	...	...	...	...	...	...	...	...
Rwanda	...	...	...	...	...	...	...	...	...	...	...	...	...	...	...
St. Helena and Ascension	1976	1,147	23.4	...	...	...	...	...	57.7	30.1	12.2	...	...	...	...
St. Kitts and Nevis	1980	11,445	24.2	——————66.9——————			18.2	14.9	52.7	32.7	14.6	—	51.3	21.6	27.1
St. Lucia	1980[45]	26,919	...	——41.1[70]——			24.0[70]	34.9[70]	64.7	26.0	9.3	0.1	83.6[15]	12.8	3.5
St. Pierre and Miquelon	1982	1,760	11.3	——————69.0——————			13.8	17.2	77.3	17.8	4.9	...	...	...	...
St. Vincent and the Grenadines	1970	16,940	...	—	...	...	...	...	74.7	16.5	7.9	8.9	64.1	26.1	0.8
San Marino	1979	7,000	...	...	...	...	...	...	73.5	21.9	4.6	...	...	...	...
São Tomé and Príncipe	1970	819[45, 71]	...	...	...	...	...	...	...	...	...	...	...	...	...
Saudi Arabia	...	...	...	...	...	...	...	...	...	...	...	...	...	...	...
Senegal	1955[41, 72]	13,000	...	...	...	...	...	...	——84.6——		15.4	...	...	...	...
Seychelles	1977	12,315	...	...	...	...	...	...	46.6	——53.4——		4.1	57.2	38.7	—
Sierra Leone	...	...	...	...	...	...	...	...	...	...	...	...	...	...	...
Singapore	1980	513,224	...	——————63.2——————				36.8	55.0	39.6	5.4	4.7	——95.3——		
Solomon Islands	1979[41]	3,423	...	...	...	...	...	...	27.4[12]	43.0[12]	29.6[12]	...	...	...	...
Somalia	...	...	...	...	...	...	...	...	...	...	...	...	...	...	...
South Africa	1970	1,354,520	18.6	24.6	16.0	24.2	35.2	—	...	...	...	...	...	...	...
Bophuthatswana	...	...	...	...	...	...	...	...	...	...	...	...	...	...	...
Ciskei	...	...	...	...	...	...	...	...	...	...	...	...	...	...	...
Transkei	...	...	...	...	...	...	...	...	...	...	...	...	...	...	...
Venda	...	...	...	...	...	...	...	...	...	...	...	...	...	...	...
South West Africa/Namibia	...	...	...	...	...	...	...	...	...	...	...	...	...	...	...
Spain	1984	15,332,900	39.4[8, 38]	39.2[8, 38]	——23.4[8, 38]——		18.5[8, 38]	18.9[8, 38]	57.2[38]	24.4[38]	18.3[38]	...	...	...	...
Sri Lanka	1981	2,811,406	...	...	...	...	11.1[13]	...	69.4	10.1	20.5	...	...	...	...
Sudan, The	1966[2]	253,060	...	...	...	...	...	...	59.2	28.3	12.6	76.5	4.4	16.7	2.4
Suriname	1980	77,658	...	——————52.4——————				47.6	...	...	...	38.9[73]	——61.1[73]——		
Swaziland	1976	86,847	...	...	...	...	...	...	...	...	...	39.9	——60.1——		
Sweden	1985	3,863,439	24.0	25.9	10.4	15.2	23.1	25.4	38.9[8]	56.0[8]	5.1[8]	98.7[8]	...	...	...
Switzerland	1980	2,969,000[11]	...	——————58.1——————			22.6	19.3	29.9	67.1	3.0	...	...	...	...
Syria	1983	1,642,809	...	...	...	...	8.7[19]	...	81.6[19]	15.5[19]	2.8[19]	...	...	...	...
Taiwan	1980	3,171,876[5]	15.3	——13.8[17]——		14.0[18]	42.4[74]	29.8[75]	79.1	11.8	9.1	...	...	...	...
Tanzania	1978	3,554,793	...	——————17.0——————			——83.0——		75.4	19.4	5.2	83.0	—	16.3	0.7
Thailand	1980	8,414,648	...	——22.0[19]——		25.0[19]	53.0[19]	—	83.4	9.1	7.5	15.1	70.0	6.3	8.6
Togo	1958–60[2]	22,274	...	...	...	...	...	...	...	...	...	...	...	...	...
Tokelau	1981	284	...	...	...	...	...	...	97.7[36]	2.3[36]	—	49.6	28.2	12.3	9.9
Tonga	1976	13,908	22.5	52.7	——6.7[76]——		20.3[77]	20.3[78]	85.1	2.5	12.4	35.1	45.4	15.3	4.2
Trinidad and Tobago	1980	231,436	...	——————56.3——————			14.5	29.2	64.6	34.0	1.4	3.3	32.6	53.8	10.3[15]
Tunisia	1984	1,313,200	...	...	...	...	...	...	78.9	12.6	8.5	...	...	...	...
Turkey	1986	10,855,495	...	...	...	...	...	...	76.2[79]	22.0	1.8	0.7[45]	——99.3[45]——		
Turks and Caicos Islands	1980	1,644	20.0	——————45.1——————			15.5	39.4	68.6	22.8	8.6	—	36.8	59.9	3.3
Tuvalu	1979	1,079	...	...	...	...	...	...	81.6	12.1	6.6	64.9	4.2	31.0	—
Uganda	...	...	...	...	...	...	...	...	...	...	...	...	...	...	...
U.S.S.R.	1984	79,285,700[45]	...	...	...	...	...	...	42.1	57.9	—	...	...	...	...
United Arab Emirates	1980	153,009	15.0	—	0.8	1.3	11.4	86.5	36.2	45.2	18.6	2.9	7.3	87.3	2.5
United Kingdom	1981[80]	22,611,700[11]	32.6	——54.0——		13.0	16.6	16.4	51.1	40.3	8.6	...	...	...	...
United States	1983	99,888,000[11]	22.7	29.9	9.0	15.6	19.7	25.8	64.7	32.6	2.7	...	...	...	...
Uruguay	1985	852,400	...	...	...	...	...	...	59.0[79]	23.9	17.1	...	...	...	...
Vanuatu	1979	22,513	...	...	...	...	...	...	40.9[41]	25.7[41]	33.4[41]	61.4	7.7	13.6	17.2
Venezuela	1981	2,708,674	...	...	...	...	...	...	75.1	17.8	7.1	11.8	2.1	78.9	7.2
Vietnam	1962[81]	204,000[5]	...	...	...	...	...	...	68.4	28.0	3.6	...	...	...	...
Virgin Islands (U.S.)	1980	32,650	14.7	6.5	3.5	8.9	42.7	38.4	34.6	52.2	13.2	...	...	...	...
Wallis and Futuna	1983	1,389	14.4	——8.0——		11.0	24.0	57.0	94.4[12]	0.6[12]	5.0[12]	67.0	——31.0——		2.0
West Bank	1985	119,165[43]	...	...	...	...	...	...	86.2[44]	11.5[44]	2.3[44]	...	...	...	...
Western Sahara	1974	4,000	...	...	...	...	...	...	32.2[39]	62.3[39]	5.5[39]	...	...	...	...
Western Samoa	1976	32,938	...	...	...	...	...	...	93.4	2.1	4.5	75.6	——24.4——		
Yemen (Aden)	1973	74,261[38]	...	...	...	...	...	...	...	...	...	...	...	...	...
Yemen (Şan'ā')	1975	863,109	...	...	...	...	...	...	85.3	7.0	7.7	...	...	...	...
Yugoslavia	1981	6,786,700[16]	...	——31.1——		12.7	26.8	29.4	67.1	25.0	7.9	...	——82.6——		17.4
Zaire	1967[41]	168,000	...	...	...	...	...	...	47.4	38.3	14.3	...	...	...	...
Zambia	1980	1,128,300	...	...	...	...	...	...	78.8[82]	21.1[82]	...	...	...	...	...
Zimbabwe	1969	925,581	...	...	...	...	...	...	65.1[83]	32.6[83]	2.3[83]	55.9[84]	——44.1[84]——		

[1]1983. [2]Urban areas only. [3]Percent of net material product. [4]Residential includes nonresidential. [5]Occupied dwellings only; may include seasonal and temporary housing. [6]1966. [7]1982. [8]1980. [9]1974. [10]1984. [11]1986. [12]1976. [13]1971. [14]Stucco. [15]Includes wood and brick, and wood and concrete. [16]1985. [17]1945 and earlier. [18]1946–1960. [19]1970. [20]Volume ('000 cubic metres). [21]1960. [22]1978. [23]1983–85 average. [24]Data refer to rugos, which usually contain two or three houses each. [25]1981. [26]1959–1960; data refer to households and are based on a demographic survey of the African population excluding Bangui town, East Dubangi, and the nomad population. [27]1973. [28]1975. [29]1933 and earlier. [30]1934–45. [31]1946–59. [32]Includes corrugated steel. [33]1987. [34]1979. [35]1961. [36]1972. [37]1977. [38]Data refer to buildings, not dwellings. [39]1968. [40]Traditional houses (usually constructed of fragile tropical materials and lacking modern conveniences). [41]Capital city only. [42]Vacant dwellings only. [43]1967. [44]Excludes refugee camps. [45]Data refers to households. [46]1947 and earlier. [47]1948–83. [48]1961–71. [49]Minimum.

physical amenities (percent)			sewage disposal (percent)			space[b]			construction industry (1985)						country
									percent of GDP	new residential[d]			new nonresidential[d]		
piped water	electricity	inside toilet or WC	closed public sewer or septic tank	open public sewer	other	average area (sq m)	rooms per dwelling unit	persons per room		1- or 2-unit dwellings	multiunit dwellings	floor area ('000 sq m)	number of units	floor area ('000 sq m)	
...	...	26.4	...	...	...	...	2.2[36]	2.4[36]	5.9	208	10	60.8	1,221	163.2	Paraguay
73.4	89.5	78.0	58.1	—41.9—	...	42.4	2.6	2.0	4.6[11]	...	...	951.5	...	...	Peru
41.4	46.0	35.0	44.1	—55.9—	...	...	2.4[36]	2.3[36]	4.5	—20,244—		2,124	2,807	2,170	Philippines
100.0	100.0	—	...	—100.0—	...	100.0	5.0	0.4	...	...	...	...	...	...	Pitcairn Island
69.7	96.2	41.4	67.0	—33.0—	...	53.9	4.0[11]	0.9[11]	12.3[3]	56,467	4,342	72,573[20]	62,041	62,526[20]	Poland
73.4	77.6	67.7	75.5	—24.5—	...	...	5.0[10]	0.8	6.2[10]	16,366	1,534	5,692	5,873	1,535	Portugal
95.2	97.4	89.7	89.6	—10.4—	...	...	4.8	0.8	1.6	3,941	47	1,798	900	41.0	Puerto Rico
...	...	...	...	...	...	...	...	...	6.9[11]	—515—		...	147	...	Qatar
70.6	81.6	50.7	52.4	—47.6—	...	...	3.6	1.2	4.7[8]	...	...	...	...	...	Réunion
...	48.6	...	12.2	—87.8—	...	...	2.6	1.4	7.8[3]	...	...	8,591	...	...	Romania
...	...	...	...	...	...	...	...	...	4.8	—435[10]—		...	63[10]	...	Rwanda
58.0	62.6	46.9	...	...	...	...	4.1	1.1	...	...	...	...	...	...	St. Helena and Ascension
96.6	58.3	33.5	31.8[19]	—68.2[19]—		...	3.0	1.3	9.0	...	...	...	...	...	St. Kitts and Nevis
79.5[19]	36.1[19]	...	11.0[19]	—89.0[19]—		...	2.7[19]	1.7[19]	6.9	—339[37]—		...	46[37]	...	St. Lucia
99.7	99.8	99.2	97.6	—2.4—	...	...	4.6	0.7	...	...	...	...	...	...	St. Pierre and Miquelon
95.0[1]	...	...	22.0[1]	—78.0[1]—		...	2.8	1.8	9.2	...	...	...	...	...	St. Vincent and the Grenadines
99.8	100.0	98.3	98.3	—1.7—	...	...	4.5	0.8	...	—161—		...	38	...	San Marino
...	...	...	...	...	...	...	...	...	3.3[1]	...	...	...	...	...	São Tomé and Príncipe
...	...	...	...	...	...	...	...	...	14.1[10]	—59,033[4,10]—		...	4	...	Saudi Arabia
87.7	95.9	...	...	...	...	...	2.3	1.5	6.6	—886—		228.0	44	37.0	Senegal
77.5	46.8	33.1	33.1	—66.9—	...	...	3.6	1.4	6.1	—4,802[4,37]—		...	4	...	Seychelles
...	...	...	...	...	...	...	...	...	2.6[1]	...	...	...	...	...	Sierra Leone
90.6[19]	98.3	63.6[19]	63.6[19]	—36.4[19]—		...	1.8[19]	2.5[19]	10.9	—933—		9,222	992	2,202	Singapore
92.7[12]	79.6[12]	89.2	89.2[12]	—10.8[12]—		41.8[12]	2.3[12]	2.0[12]	3.2	1,174[8]	...	...	...	...	Solomon Islands
...	...	...	...	...	...	...	...	...	...	...	...	...	...	...	Somalia
...	...	...	...	...	...	...	3.4	...	3.3	24,159	790	...	...	...	South Africa
...	...	...	...	...	...	...	...	...	...	...	...	...	...	...	Bophuthatswana
...	...	...	...	...	...	...	...	...	...	...	...	...	...	...	Ciskei
...	...	...	...	...	...	...	...	...	...	...	...	...	...	...	Transkei
...	...	...	...	...	...	...	...	...	...	...	...	...	...	...	Venda
...	...	...	...	...	...	...	...	...	2.2[11]	...	...	...	...	...	South West Africa/Namibia
90.5[8,38]	94.7[8,38]	...	87.9[8,38]	—12.1[8,38]—		...	4.4[19]	...	6.8	—41,554—		119,874	...	...	Spain
18.2	14.9	4.7	4.7	—95.3—	...	18.6[19]	2.5	2.1	7.6	—8,914—		833.2	...	...	Sri Lanka
63.9	26.4	70.2	2.6	—97.4—	...	...	2.2	2.5	5.5	—1,522—		355.0[20]	...	...	Sudan, The
62.9	82.0	40.4	19.6[73]	—80.4[73]—		...	2.1	1.9	5.6	...	...	...	161	...	Suriname
33.4	...	20.0	...	...	...	...	...	...	4.3[1]	—48[10]—		...	28[10]	...	Swaziland
100.0	96.2[8]	98.0	96.3[8]	—3.7[8]—		...	3.2	0.7	6.2	15,755	1,206	3,087	...	3,818[10]	Sweden
100.0	...	93.3	92.2	—	7.8	86.0	3.8[11]	0.6[11]	...	13,212[7]	4,466[7]	...	9,058[7]	...	Switzerland
40.2	41.7	...	36.0	—64.0—	...	90.6	3.0	2.0	6.8	—23,072—		6,112	1,113	682	Syria
79.4	99.7	94.2	69.3	...	...	85.9	3.7	1.5	4.1[11]	...	...	...	...	...	Taiwan
37.2	6.3	...	...	...	...	...	2.5	1.9	1.9	...	...	...	...	...	Tanzania
17.3	43.0	40.9	40.9[12]	9.8[12]	49.3[12]	...	1.9[12]	...	5.2	...	...	5,391	...	4,868	Thailand
4.1	10.3	...	—	—100.0—		...	1.8	3.4	2.9[1]	—153[8]—		43.2[8]	12[8]	...	Togo
2.3[36]	60.9	2.3[36]	...	...	...	...	...	...	...	...	...	...	...	...	Tokelau
61.3	20.9	42.3	11.2	—88.8—	...	...	...	...	3.9[1]	—738[7,8]—		668[7,8]	4	4	Tonga
64.3	83.3	41.1	41.0	—59.0—	...	...	3.3	1.4	12.5	2,376	14	388.0	58	38.0	Trinidad and Tobago
26.4	63.4	43.3	51.8	—41.2—	...	...	1.9	2.4	5.7	—17,208[7]—		2,679[7]	...	...	Tunisia
68.0	56.8[28]	70.6	42.0	52.0	6.0	...	2.4[16]	2.2[19]	3.4	20,425	28,955	12,457	2,803	3,032	Turkey
19.9	47.6	...	70.5	—29.5—	...	...	3.5	1.1	...	...	...	...	...	...	Turks and Caicos Islands
65.4	7.4	37.3	...	...	...	...	...	...	13.0[34]	...	...	...	...	...	Tuvalu
...	...	...	...	...	...	...	...	...	0.3[7]	—179[36]—		37.3[36]	65[36]	26.8[36]	Uganda
90.8[2]	100.0[2]	88.7[2]	88.7[2]	—11.3[2]—		...	...	...	10.8[3]	—2,008,000[10]—		112,510[10]	...	...	U.S.S.R.
30.9[39]	24.2[39]	84.5	...	...	...	...	2.8	1.8	8.9	—3,197[10]—		...	133[10]	...	United Arab Emirates
...	...	99.0	...	...	...	...	3.8	0.6	5.3	...	...	...	...	...	United Kingdom
97.6	100.0[2]	98.1	98.1	—1.9—	...	...	5.1	0.6	4.7	...	...	214,900	...	140,100	United States
88.9	84.7	73.3	...	92.0	...	...	3.4	1.7	1.8	—2,168—		160.1	105	21.4	Uruguay
13.7	11.7	19.1	...	...	...	...	...	...	2.0[7]	...	...	7.2	...	7.3	Vanuatu
85.3	88.6	84.4	71.3	—28.7—	...	...	3.9[13]	1.5[13]	3.0	1,930	334	2,319	547	787.8	Venezuela
23.7	71.0	...	...	...	...	...	...	...	3.0[3,1]	—400[27]—		212.3[27]	53[27]	59.3[27]	Vietnam
96.3	98.1	86.0	93.6	—6.4—	...	...	4.2	0.8	...	833[34]	75[34]	...	262[34]	...	Virgin Islands (U.S.)
23.0	...	9.0	24.0	—	7.6	...	1.8[12]	4.0[12]	...	...	...	...	...	...	Wallis and Futuna
75.2	91.2	90.1	...	...	...	...	...	2.7	2.4[10]	—5,136[11]—		680.5[11]	...	143.2[11]	West Bank
78.5	95.3	...	...	...	...	...	4.5	1.2	...	...	...	...	...	...	Western Sahara
9.2[72]	18.8[72]	...	...	...	...	...	3.9[72]	1.5[72]	13.2[7]	—97[10]—		...	140[10]	...	Western Samoa
...	...	...	...	...	...	...	2.0	3.0	10.2[1]	...	...	...	...	...	Yemen (Aden)
5.7	4.6	...	...	...	...	...	2.0	2.8	4.2[11]	—6,911—		1,988	...	...	Yemen (Șan'ā')
67.8	95.7	53.3	...	...	...	60.7	2.6[16]	1.3[16]	6.8	60,190	1,848	13,598	19,489	6,403	Yugoslavia
...	...	...	...	...	...	...	...	...	5.1[10]	—111—		20	73	39	Zaire
12.4[82]	27.5[21]	15.1[82]	...	82.3[82]	...	...	1.9[82]	2.6[82]	2.1	...	...	...	...	...	Zambia
...	9.3[84]	...	...	...	...	...	2.8	1.9	...	—1,440—		...	...	...	Zimbabwe

[50]Includes nonconventional housing units. [51]1946 and earlier. [52]1947–60. [53]1948–60. [54]Peninsular Malaysia only. [55]1957 and earlier. [56]1958–67. [57]Excluding Rodrigues Island and lesser outlying islands. [58]1960–68. [59]1969–83. [60]Nauruan dwellings only. [61]Data are for the cities of Kāthmāndu, Lalitpur, Bhaktapur, Birātnagar, Nepālganj, and Birgani only. [62]1930 and earlier. [63]1931–59. [64]Excludes Islāmābād, North-West Frontier, and Federally Administered Tribal Areas. [65]1947–65. [66]1966–75. [67]1976–80. [68]1944 and earlier. [69]1945–70. [70]Proportional distribution of known data. [71]Principe only. [72]European-style dwellings only. [73]1964. [74]1961–75. [75]1976 and later. [76]1939–56. [77]1956–66. [78]1966–70. [79]Includes squatters. [80]Data exclude Northern Ireland. [81]Data refer to Ho Chi Minh City (Saigon) only. [82]1969. [83]Data refer to dwellings occupied by Europeans, Asians, and Coloureds only. [84]Data refer to dwellings occupied by Africans only.

Household budgets and consumption

This table provides international data on household income, on the consumption expenditure of households for goods and services, and on the principal object of such expenditure (in most countries), food consumption (by kind). For purposes of this compilation, income comprises pretax monetary payments and payment in kind. The first part of the table provides data on distribution of income by households and by sources of income; the second part analyzes the largest portion of income use—consumption expenditure. Such expenditure is defined as the purchase of goods and services to satisfy current wants and needs. This definition excludes income expended on taxes, debts, savings and investments, and insurance policies. The third and last part of the table focuses on food, which usually, and often by a wide margin, represents the largest share of consumer spending worldwide. The data provided include daily available calories per capita and consumption of major food groups.

For both sources of income and consumption expenditure, the primary basis of analysis for most countries is the household, an economic unit that can be as small as a single person or as large as an extended family. For some of the countries that do not compile information by household, the table provides data on personal income and personal expenditure; *i.e.,* the income and expenditure of all the individuals constituting a society's households. When no expenditure data at all is available, the table reports the weights of each major class of goods and services comprising a given country's consumer (or retail) price index (CPI). The weighting of the components of the CPI usually reflects household spending patterns within the country, its principal urban or rural areas, though sometimes only in the country's major city.

The data on distribution of income show, collectively for an entire country, the proportion of total income earned by households comprising the lowest quintile and highest decile (poorest 20% and wealthiest 10%) within the country. These figures show the degree to which either group represents a disproportionate share of poverty or wealth.

The data on sources of income illuminate patterns of economic structure in the gaining of an income. They indicate, for example, that in poor, agrarian countries income often derives largely from self-employment (usually farming) or that in industrial countries, with well-developed systems of salaried employment and social welfare, income derives mainly from wages and salaries and secondarily from transfer payments (see headnote a). Because household sizes and numbers of income earners vary so greatly internationally, and because the frequency and methodology of household and CPI surveys do not permit single-year comparisons for more than a few countries at once, no summary of total *household* income or expenditure was possible. Instead, U.S. dollar figures are supplied for *per capita* private final consumption expenditure (for a single, recent year) that are more comparable internationally and refer to the same date. The figures on distribution of consumption expenditure by end use reveal patterns of personal and family use of disposable income and indicate, inter alia, that in developing countries food may absorb 50% or more of disposable income, while in the larger household budgets of the developed countries, by contrast, food purchases may account for only 20–30% of spending. In either type of country, the cost of transportation often rivals that of housing, once the more basic need. Each category of expenditure betrays similar complexities of local habit, necessity, and aspiration.

The reader should exercise caution when using these data to make inter-country comparisons. Most of the information comes from single-country surveys, which often differ markedly in their coverage of economically or demographically stratified groups, in sample design, or in the methods

Household budgets and consumption

country	income (latest)						consumption expenditure						
	percent received by		by source (percent)				per capita private final, U.S.$ 1986	by kind or end use (percent of household or personal budget; latest)					
	lowest 20% of households	highest 10% of households	wages, salaries	self-employment	transfer payments[a]	other[b]		food[c]	housing[d]	clothing[e]	health care	energy, water	education
Afghanistan	...	...	20.7	28.0	8.2	43.1	100[1]	33.9	3.0	...	1.1	0.7	...
Albania	...	...	...	...	...	...		...	...	...	...	...	...
Algeria	...	...	...	...	...	...	1,080[2]	55.7	11.7	9.2	3.1	...	[3]
American Samoa	...	...	...	...	...	...		41.3	22.2[4]	5.1	...	...	1.3
Andorra	...	...	...	...	...	...	...	...	...	...	...	...	...
Angola	...	...	...	...	...	...	360[2]	...	...	...	...	...	...
Anguilla	...	...	...	...	...	...		...	...	...	...	...	...
Antigua and Barbuda	...	...	...	...	...	...	1,380[5]	46.5	23.3	7.5	...	5.5	...
Argentina	4.4	35.2	...	...	...	...	1,410[6]	...	...	...	...	...	...
Aruba	...	...	...	...	...	...	[7]	27.4[8]	18.4	8.4	2.9	...	[3]
Australia	4.7	28.4	60.3	7.4	25.7	6.6	6,550	20.8	21.9	6.2	6.4	2.4	[3]
Austria	4.0	28.7	56.1	19.6	24.3	—	6,940	20.4	12.4	10.8	4.4	4.9	0.3
Bahamas, The	3.6	32.1	...	...	...	...	4,250	20.5	14.1	4.0	3.2	3.6	0.1
Bahrain	...	...	...	...	...	...	2,150	...	...	...	...	...	...
Bangladesh	6.6	29.5	19.6	60.6	1.2	18.6	150	66.1	8.9	7.9	1.1	6.9	1.2
Barbados	6.8	...	...	...	...	...	3,180	51.6[8]	13.1	5.1	...	6.2	...
Belgium	7.9[9]	21.5[9]	51.9	10.4	20.7	17.0	7,230	23.5	16.7	8.4	...	6.3	...
Belize	...	...	84.1	——15.9——			790[2]	51.5[8]	2.3	11.1	3.4	6.0	1.5
Benin	8.0	39.0	...	...	...	...	220[2]	...	...	...	...	...	...
Bermuda	7.2	24.7	72.2	6.7	2.4	18.7	12,690[2]	17.3	20.8	5.3	4.1	4.0	2.8
Bhutan	...	...	...	...	...	...		72.3	...	21.2	...	3.7	...
Bolivia	4.0	...	...	...	...	...	640	41.7	12.6	9.8	4.6	0.7	1.2
Botswana	4.3[9,10]	42.0[9,10]	65.6	14.8	19.6	—	390	40.1[8]	13.6[11]	10.8	1.3	[11]	
Brazil	2.3	48.3	...	...	...	...	330	49.0[8,12]	8.6[12]	6.4[12]	5.3[12]	11.7[12]	2.2[12]
British Virgin Islands	...	...	...	...	...	...	2,880[6]	34.1	21.0	8.2	3.1	4.5	3.2
Brunei	...	...	...	...	...	...		45.1	5.0[11]	6.1	...	[11]	[3]
Bulgaria	9.7	22.5	53.8	11.0	18.8	16.4	1,420	44.3	7.1	10.1	2.1	[11]	[3]
Burkina Faso	...	...	...	...	...	...	110[2]	47.7[13]	5.1[13]	4.4[13]	5.2[13]	13.7[13]	[3]
Burma	8.0	...	...	...	...	...	180	49.1[13]	10.4[13]	15.3[13]	2.4[13]	4.0[13]	5.9[13]
Burundi	...	...	...	...	...	...	190	59.6[13]	4.4[13]	11.1[13]	...	5.8[13]	...
Cameroon	...	...	...	...	...	...	510[2]	33.6[13]	14.6[13]	16.3[13]	5.0[13]	...	15
Canada	6.0	30.1	65.4	6.9	15.3	12.4	8,430	19.8	24.0	8.6	2.6	5.7	1.1
Cape Verde	...	...	...	...	...	...	330[2]	70.1[8,13]	...	9.2[13]	...	...	...
Cayman Islands	...	...	...	...	...	...		...	...	...	...	...	...
Central African Republic	...	...	...	...	...	...	200[2]	70.5[13]	0.6[13]	9.5[13]	1.0[13]	6.5[13]	...
Chad	8.0	30.0	...	...	...	...	100[2]	45.3[13]	...	3.5[13]	11.9[13]	5.8[13]	...
Chile	4.4	34.8	40.8	...	8.1	51.2	940	41.9	13.3	7.6	...	...	[3]
China	8.5[16]	37.7[16,17]	81.2[18]	...	15.2[18]	3.6[18]	130	56.3[16]	14.4[16]	9.5[16]	...	5.2[16]	3,[16]
Christmas Island	...	...	...	...	...	...	...	...	...	...	...	...	...
Cocos (Keeling) Islands	...	...	...	...	...	...	...	...	...	...	...	...	...
Colombia	4.0	43.5	49.3	36.6	6.2	7.9	760	35.9	11.3	6.0	6.0	1.8	1.7
Comoros	...	...	25.6	64.5	8.7	1.2	170[2]	56.0	...	10.0	5.0	14.4	...
Congo	7.0	43.5	...	...	...	...	400[2]	...	...	...	...	...	...
Cook Islands	...	...	...	...	...	...		65.2[8,13]	3.1[13]	12.4[13]	...	...	...
Costa Rica	3.9[18]	39.8[18]	...	...	...	...	1,040	40.8[13,19]	12.3[13,19]	10.0[13,19]	—	6.6[13,19]	[3]
Côte d'Ivoire	2.4	43.7	44.9	49.9	——5.2——		540	51.1	11.6	8.4	...	8.1	...
Cuba	...	...	57.3	...	...	42.7	1,460	26.9	...	...	...	...	...
Cyprus	7.9[18]	...	...	...	...	...	2,650	25.1	6.8	12.3	2.4	2.0	0.7
Czechoslovakia	10.0[20]	21.8[20]	62.8	—	20.1	17.1	4,170	26.4	...	8.5	...	...	...
Denmark	3.8	25.2	65.5	8.8	12.4	13.3	8,810	21.3	19.3	5.8	1.9	6.2	1.5
Djibouti	...	...	51.6	36.0	10.5	1.9	610[2]	50.3	6.4	1.7	2.4	13.1	...
Dominica	...	...	...	...	...	...	730[5]	43.1	16.1[4]	6.5	...	5.4	...
Dominican Republic	4.5[9]	41.7[9]	41.7	31.8	1.5	25.0	620	51.7[8]	23.9	6.0	...	...	...
Ecuador	2.9	51.5	26.2	65.8	4.8	3.2	780	37.6[8]	...	11.1	3.8	6.7	...
Egypt	5.8	33.2	...	...	...	...	810	49.7[18]	8.8[18]	14.2[18]	1.8[18]	3.6[18]	2.1[18]

employed for collection, classification, and tabulation of data. Further, the reference period of the data varies greatly; while a significant portion of the data is from 1979 or later, information for some countries dates from the early and mid-1970s. This older information is typeset in italic. Finally, intercountry comparisons of annual personal consumption expenditure may be misleading because of the distortions of price and purchasing power present when converting a national currency unit into U.S. dollars.

The table's food consumption data include total daily available calories per capita (food supply), which amounts to domestic production and imports minus exports, animal feed, and nonfood uses, and a percentage breakdown of the major food groups that make up food supply.

The data for daily available calories per capita provide a measure of the nutritional adequacy of each nation's food supply. The following list, based on estimates from the United Nations Food and Agriculture Organization (FAO), indicates the regional variation in recommended daily minimum nutritional requirements, which are defined by factors such as climatic ambience and average body weight: Africa (2,320 calories), Centrally Planned Asia (2,300 calories), Far East (2,240 calories), Latin America (2,360 calories), Near East (2,440 calories).

The breakdown of diet by food groups describes the character of a nation's food supply. A typical breakdown for a low-income country might show a diet with heavy intake of vegetable foods, such as cereals, potatoes, or cassava. In the high-income countries, a relatively larger portion of total calories derives from animal products (meat, eggs, and milk). The reader should note, however, that these data refer to total national *supply* and do not reflect the dietary differences that often exist between socioeconomic groups within a single country.

In compiling this table, Britannica editors rely on both numerous national reports and principal secondary sources such as the International Bank for Reconstruction and Development's *World Development Report* (annual), the International Labour Organisation's *Household Income and Expenditure Statistics 1968–1976* and *Statistical Sources and Methods, vol. 1 Consumer Price Indices* (2nd ed.); the UN's *Yearbook of National Accounts Statistics* (annual) and *National Accounts Statistics: Compendium of Income Distribution Statistics;* and the FAO's *Food Balance Sheets 1979–81* and *1984–86*.

The following terms further define the column headings:
a. Includes pensions, family allowances, unemployment payments, remittances from abroad, and social security and related benefits.
b. Includes interest and dividends, rents and royalties, and all other income not reported under the three preceding categories.
c. Includes alcoholic and nonalcoholic beverages. Excludes tobacco except as noted.
d. Rent, maintenance of dwellings, and taxes only; excludes energy and water (heat, light, power, and water) and household durables (furniture, appliances, utensils, and household operations), shown separately.
e. Includes footwear.
f. Furniture, appliances, and utensils; usually includes expenditure on household operation.
g. Includes expenditure on cultural activities other than education.
h. May include data not shown separately in preceding categories, including meals away from home.
i. Represents pure fats and oils only.
j. Consists mainly of peas, beans, and lentils; spices; stimulants; sugars and honey; and nuts and oilseeds.

				food consumption									country
				daily available calories per capita	percent of total calories derived from								
transpor-tation, com-munications	household durable goods[f]	recrea-tion[g]	personal effects, other[h]		cereals	potatoes, cassava	meat, poultry	fish	eggs, milk	fruits, vegeta-bles	fats, oils[i]	other[j]	
...	...	...	61.3	1,896	81.5	1.4	3.3	—	3.6	2.4	3.1	4.7	Afghanistan
...	...	...	...	2,657	66.4	2.6	5.2	0.1	6.2	4.7	6.4	8.4	Albania
6.7	6.4	3.4[3]	3.9	2,688	57.1	2.1	2.2	0.3	7.5	4.2	13.5	13.1	Algeria
12.4	4	1.6	16.1	...	...	...	...	...	...	...	...	...	American Samoa
...	...	...	...	...	...	...	...	...	...	...	...	...	Andorra
...	...	...	...	2,141	35.3	33.8	3.2	0.9	1.9	4.2	7.2	13.5	Angola
...	...	...	...	...	...	...	...	...	...	...	...	...	Anguilla
10.0	...	...	7.2	2,089	35.3	0.4	9.6	2.4	11.7	7.2	12.8	20.7	Antigua and Barbuda
...	...	...	...	3,191	30.9	2.7	20.7	0.3	8.6	4.3	11.9	19.5	Argentina
17.4	9.1	5.0[3]	11.4	7	7	7	7	7	7	7	7	7	Aruba
13.4	6.7	3.9[3]	18.3	3,326	23.3	2.7	18.0	0.8	11.7	4.8	15.1	23.5	Australia
16.5	7.3	5.4	17.6	3,416	20.0	3.3	14.5	0.5	11.2	5.7	22.7	22.1	Austria
15.1	6.0	6.5	26.9	2,609	24.5	2.2	19.2	0.8	7.1	8.4	10.3	27.5	Bahamas, The
...	...	...	...	...	...	...	...	...	...	...	...	...	Bahrain
0.9	...	...	7.0	1,922	83.9	0.9	0.7	0.8	1.4	1.3	5.1	6.0	Bangladesh
4.6	9.6	...	9.8	3,181	30.1	2.4	15.1	2.1	7.1	2.6	12.8	27.9	Barbados
12.8	9.3	9.8	13.2	3,850	19.4	5.0	19.4	0.7	8.9	4.8	23.4	18.6	Belgium
6.5	10.1	2.2	5.4	2,585	34.9	0.7	9.2	0.6	9.3	7.2	10.5	27.5	Belize
...	...	...	...	2,181	32.4	20.9	2.7	0.6	1.0	3.2	11.5	27.7	Benin
10.6	11.9	5.4	17.8	2,545	26.7	1.4	20.2	2.4	10.8	8.1	11.4	19.1	Bermuda
...	0.7	...	2.1	2,028	85.2	2.4	0.4	0.1	0.6	1.4	5.3	4.6	Bhutan
12.6	8.9	3.1	4.8	2,128	46.2	9.4	8.7	0.1	2.8	6.2	7.1	19.5	Bolivia
10.5	13.7	...	10.0	2,230	60.9	0.3	4.8	0.3	7.4	1.4	5.1	19.9	Botswana
6.3[12]	...	2.1[12]	8.4[12]	2,644	39.4	7.0	5.7	0.4	6.1	4.9	10.5	26.1	Brazil
2.3	13.1	1.6	8.9	...	...	...	...	...	...	...	...	...	British Virgin Islands
17.2	8.3	8.9[3]	9.4	2,850	45.7	1.3	10.3	1.6	6.9	4.3	7.2	22.7	Brunei
7.2	4.4	10.5[3]	14.3	3,634	40.6	1.6	9.6	0.5	8.9	5.3	14.7	18.9	Bulgaria
18.6[13]	3.0[13]	2.3[3, 13]	—	2,049	68.0	0.6	2.3	0.1	2.0	1.0	4.6	21.3	Burkina Faso
3.8[13]	0.5[13]	1.1[13]	7.5[13]	2,592	77.1	0.5	2.0	1.7	1.1	2.5	6.7	8.3	Burma
...	6.0[13]	...	13.1[13, 14]	2,270	26.5	8.2	1.0	0.3	0.9	7.9	1.5	53.8	Burundi
10.5[13]	...	5.1[13]	14.9[13, 15]	2,040	35.5	7.2	3.4	0.6	0.8	9.7	10.2	32.7	Cameroon
16.0	7.2	4.7	10.3	3,425	20.2	3.2	16.7	1.0	10.0	5.7	18.9	24.3	Canada
...	...	...	20.7	2,729	53.4	1.6	1.9	1.7	2.5	2.7	12.8	23.4	Cape Verde
...	...	...	...	...	...	...	...	...	...	...	...	...	Cayman Islands
4.1[13]	0.8[13]	1.3[13]	5.7[13]	1,940	18.7	33.3	7.0	0.5	0.4	5.6	7.1	27.4	Central African Republic
...	...	...	33.5[13]	1,762	57.2	11.2	3.2	1.6	2.6	2.9	3.3	18.0	Chad
11.8	7.8	8.2[3]	9.4	2,573	49.2	4.0	6.8	0.8	6.2	4.5	8.7	19.9	Chile
...	...	7.3[3, 16]	7.3[16]	2,628	71.3	0.9	6.5	0.4	1.1	2.3	4.6	12.9	China
...	...	...	...	...	...	...	...	...	...	...	...	...	Christmas Island
...	...	...	...	...	...	...	...	...	...	...	...	...	Cocos (Keeling) Islands
14.2	5.3	3.9	13.9	2,550	33.1	8.6	7.0	0.2	5.8	8.6	9.1	27.5	Colombia
6.6	...	3.0	5.0	2,110	42.5	26.0	2.0	1.2	1.4	6.5	4.8	15.7	Comoros
5.7[13]	9.6[13]	...	4.0[13]	2,599	19.5	37.9	2.4	3.3	1.1	7.6	13.0	15.4	Congo
...	...	...	...	...	...	...	...	...	...	...	...	...	Cook Islands
6.5[13, 19]	8.2[13, 19]	9.2[3, 13, 19]	6.4[13, 19]	2,781	37.3	0.8	5.9	0.2	8.5	6.2	11.5	29.4	Costa Rica
...	7.3	...	13.5	2,550	40.3	8.5	2.9	1.0	1.8	7.9	9.1	28.6	Côte d'Ivoire
...	...	...	73.1	3,107	36.5	3.2	7.4	1.2	8.4	3.9	8.9	30.5	Cuba
16.8	11.8	5.5	16.6	3,054	40.0	2.5	13.7	0.4	7.9	7.0	10.1	18.4	Cyprus
...	5.0	...	60.1	3,473	30.2	4.2	13.7	0.4	9.8	4.0	17.0	20.7	Czechoslovakia
16.5	6.9	7.9	12.6	3,512	20.4	3.8	22.2	1.3	9.5	4.0	17.3	21.4	Denmark
...	1.5	...	24.6	...	...	...	...	...	...	...	...	...	Djibouti
...	4	...	34.3	2,649	28.8	0.8	7.8	1.0	5.9	9.6	6.6	39.6	Dominica
...	...	...	18.4	2,464	32.3	1.7	4.9	0.4	6.3	14.7	12.9	26.8	Dominican Republic
12.0	7.1	...	25.5	2,058	34.1	4.9	5.8	1.9	7.9	9.7	12.6	23.1	Ecuador
5.2[18]	3.6[18]	1.3[18]	9.7[18]	3,313	61.5	1.4	2.7	0.3	2.2	5.7	13.0	13.2	Egypt

Household budgets and consumption   (continued)

| country | income (latest) | | | | | | consumption expenditure | | | | | | |
| | percent received by | | by source (percent) | | | | per capita private final, U.S.$ 1986 | by kind or end use (percent of household or personal budget; latest) | | | | | |
	lowest 20% of households	highest 10% of households	wages, salaries	self-employment	transfer payments[a]	other[b]		food[c]	housing[d]	clothing[e]	health care	energy, water	education
El Salvador	5.5[9]	29.5[9]	...	...	...	...	610	42.7	6.0	9.8	4.1	2.1	1.2
Equatorial Guinea	...	...	...	...	...	...	180	...					
Ethiopia	...		...	...	...	...	90	57.4[13]	21	7.8[13]	2.1[13]	...	
Faeroe Islands	...		...	...	...	...	...	43.8	8.5	8.0	...	18.9	
Falkland Islands	...		...	...	...	...	...	46.0[13]	10.0[13]	13.0[13]	...	5.0[13]	
Fiji	3.7	37.8	81.5	9.1	—	9.4	1,020	40.3[8]	18.6	6.3	...	4.9	...
Finland	3.0	26.8	66.4	16.8	14.2	2.6	7,800	23.7	14.5	5.6	2.4	4.1	3
France	5.5	26.4	52.2	21.5	26.3	—	7,900	19.7	28.6[11]	7.4	10.9	11	3
French Guiana			74.6		—25.4—			50.0	7.3	10.4	2.2	4.1	
French Polynesia	...	...	48.0	40.9	9.4	1.6	4,660[1]	36.5	5.9	9.0	1.0	8.6	3
Gabon	3.3	54.4					890[2]	54.7[8,13]	13.0[13]	17.5[13]	1.9[13]		
Gambia, The							190[2]	58.0[22]	5.1[22]	17.5[22]		5.4[22]	
Gaza Strip	...						720[5]						
Germany, East	12.2[9,23]	17.5[9,23]	68.3	...	31.7	...	6,000	41.1[8]	3.2	15.4	...	2.0	4.3
Germany, West	6.0	24.0	57.2	24	22.0	20.7[24]	8,160	21.8	15.6	9.0	3.2	6.0	3
Ghana	...	...	41.6[25]	47.1[25]	—	11.3[25]	280[2]	57.4	11.5[11]	14.3	1.3	11	3
Gibraltar								39.1[8]	12.6	11.0			
Greece			42.8	24	17.3	39.9[24]	2,650	38.6	8.9	8.4	3.4	3.3	0.6
Greenland							...	33.6	8.9	9.2	1.7	7.8	—
Grenada							940	61.5[8]	6.5	8.0	...	6.0	
Guadeloupe	...	...	—76.8—		—23.2—		3,250[6]	36.7[8]	13.0	7.7	1.1	4.5	1.0
Guam								24.1	28.6	10.6	4.8		
Guatemala	5.3	42.1	76.8	...	...	23.2	840	57.3[18]	12.7[11,18]	10.4[18]	2.1[18]	11	1.0[18]
Guernsey			...	...	...	...	...	23.7	12.2	7.5	...	8.2	
Guinea	...	...					280[2]	61.5	7.3[11]	7.9	11.1	11	...
Guinea-Bissau	...	...					230[2]						
Guyana			73.0	...	6.3	20.7	310	42.5[8]	21.4	8.6	...	5.2	3
Haiti							400	77.9	8.3	3.2			
Honduras	3.2	50.6	52.7	...	1.7	45.6	600	44.4	22.3[11]	9.1	6.9	11	3
Hong Kong	4.3[20]	37.3[20]					4,470	20.6	15.4[11]	19.4	6.2	11	1.1
Hungary	6.9[9]	20.5[9]	65.9		—34.1—		1,290	39.5	8.7	10.5	...	4.7	...
Iceland	4.7	27.2		—80.0—		—20.0—	9,810	25.3	11.0	8.8	1.7	5.5	0.4
India	5.0	34.9	42.2	39.7	...	18.1	200	56.8	2.7	10.8	1.9	4.8	2.2
Indonesia	6.6	34.0	42.1	41.5	2.5	13.9	290	63.3[8]	17.4[11]	4.6	...	11	...
Iran	3.8	41.7	40.8	28.2	3.7	27.3	2,070	43.3[8]	22.8[11]	9.6	4.3	11	3
Iraq	2.1	...					930[27]	55.4	7.9	10.3	2.4	4.1	—
Ireland	4.6	26.5	60.3	14.4	20.2	5.1	2,220	38.1	6.2	6.4	...	6.2	3
Isle of Man	...						...	29.1	8.3	6.3	...	11.2	
Israel	8.4	23.2	90.8	0.8	—8.4—		4,020	30.3[8]	18.0	5.6	...	3.6	
Italy	6.2	28.1	49.5	19.9	20.6	10.0	6,550	25.5	13.7	8.4	2.0	5.1	3
Jamaica	2.2	...	70.9	27.3	1.8	3.6	680	36.8	8.5	2.3	2.5	4.6	0.2
Japan	9.1[20]	22.7[20]	57.5	12.3	19.0	11.1	9,374	26.8	4.7	7.1	2.5	6.3	3.9
Jersey								28.3	14.9	8.3	...	6.5	
Jordan							1,380	38.8	6.5[11]	6.0	4.0	11	3.4
Kampuchea								53.0	23.0	9.0			
Kenya	2.6	45.8	22.4	...	...	77.6	200	46.5	10.0	7.7	2.2	2.6	1.0
Kiribati			69.7	21.4	6.0	2.9	370[27]	64.0[8]	1.0	8.0	...	3.6	
Korea, North								46.5[28]	0.6[28]	29.5[28]	29	3.3[28]	29
Korea, South	8.0[18,30]	24.5[18,30]	57.8	18.5	4.7	19.0	1,290	36.1	5.2	7.5	6.5	7.6	12.3
Kuwait			53.8	20.8	—25.4—		4,950	26.5[8]	27.2[11]	7.7	0.7	11	3
Laos													
Lebanon	5.0	45.0	27.9	...	3.0	69.1	1,410[27]	42.0[13]	16.8[13]	8.6[13]	7.2[13]	4.5[13]	3.9[13]
Lesotho	...	...	42.0	51.6	—6.4—		270	34.0[18]	9.7[18]	19.3[18]	1.8[18]	4.8[18]	4.1[18]
Liberia	5.3	...					300	40.1[8,13]	14.9[13]	13.8[13]	...	5.0[13]	3
Libya	10.1						2,930[2]	37.2	32.2[11]	6.9	3.3	11	3
Liechtenstein			92.9[31]	7.1[31]	...	...		21.3[8]	18.0	6.6	7.7	4.4	3
Luxembourg	...	...	88.1	9.4	2.5	—	7,980	17.4	11.7	6.4	6.8	8.5	3
Macau								44.2[8]	22.8	7.3	...	4.8	
Madagascar	5.2	...	58.8[13,32]	14.1[13,32]	—	27.1[13,32]	180	35.8		12.0	...		
Malawi	10.4	40.1	83.3	6.0	—	11.7	100	39.3[8,33]	13.3[33]	10.7[33]	...	...	...
Malaysia	3.5	39.8					890	37.1	10.6[11]	5.7	2.2	11	0.5
Maldives	...	...					260						
Mali	...	...					120[2]						
Malta			51.4	18.7	14.7	15.2	2,590	32.0	3.9[34]	9.1	...	2.1[34]	3
Martinique	...	...	74.2	...		25.8	4,770[2]	34.8	5.3	10.2	16.1	1.9	
Mauritania	...	...					260[2]	61.0[13]	24.0[13]	5.2[13]	...		
Mauritius	4.0	46.7	53.1	32.4	4.3	10.3	870	50.4[8]	4.0	10.5	3.0	6.4	2.9
Mayotte													
Mexico	2.9	40.6	52.4	23.6	5.6	18.4	1,360[5]	35.8[8]	8.2[11]	10.3	5.0	11	3
Monaco	...												
Mongolia													
Montserrat	...						3,200	54.1[8]	0.7	17.9	...	1.8	
Morocco	4.0						630	54.0	7.0	8.5	...	3.0	
Mozambique	...						120[2]						
Nauru	...												
Nepal	3.1	50.7	39.2[13]		—60.8[13]—		110	57.4[13]	11.4[6,13]	10.5[13]	4.2[13]	11	3
Netherlands, The	8.3	21.5	40.0	19.6	28.2	12.2	7,150	19.1	19.4[11]	7.3	12.7	11	3
Netherlands Antilles	...	...					3,520[7,27]	22.1[8,35]	18.8[35]	8.7[35]	2.2[35]	—	3
New Caledonia			63.1	23.9	13.0	—	2,840[5]	27.5	13.3	6.2	2.7	3.9	1.3
New Zealand	5.1[20]	28.7[20]	68.1	9.1	12.7	10.1	4,950	19.7	20.4	5.7	1.6	2.4	0.5
Nicaragua	3.1[16]	...					1,070	68.4[8,13]	12.2[4,11,13]	11.6[13]	...	11	...
Niger	...	...					210[2]	50.5	19.1[4]	7.3			
Nigeria	...	...	36.2	49.4	4.3	10.1	490	53.0[8]	6.0	...	11.4		
Niue	...	...						54.5[8]	5.0	5.0			
Norfolk Island	...	...	...	...	...	...		...					

transportation, communications	household durable goods[f]	recreation[g]	personal effects, other[h]	daily available calories per capita	cereals	potatoes, cassava	meat, poultry	fish	eggs, milk	fruits, vegetables	fats, oils[i]	other[j]	country
11.2	13.2	3.4	6.3	2,048	56.9	0.9	2.4	0.2	5.3	4.7	8.4	21.3	El Salvador
...	...	...	...	...	...	...	...	...	...	...	...	...	Equatorial Guinea
5.3[13]	17.1[13]	3.0[13]	7.3[13]	1,793	68.8	3.9	4.2	—	2.9	0.8	2.2	17.2	Ethiopia
...	6.6	...	14.2	3,135	29.3	5.5	15.8	3.9	7.0	3.3	18.0	17.2	Faeroe Islands
...	5.0[13]	...	21.0[13]	...	...								Falkland Islands
11.3	7.6	...	11.0	2,901	38.8	7.3	4.5	2.5	3.0	1.8	8.9	33.2	Fiji
17.3	7.3	9.9[3]	15.2	3,080	23.1	6.1	16.1	2.5	15.2	3.8	14.6	18.8	Finland
10.4	8.5	6.8[3]	7.7	3,273	23.1	4.3	14.0	1.1	12.9	5.3	18.1	21.2	France
7.5	6.7	4.9	6.9	2,748	35.3	2.8	16.4	2.6	7.0	5.5	7.6	22.8	French Guiana
13.1	9.2	8.6[3]	8.1	2,896	35.8	3.5	10.4	2.2	5.0	3.6	16.4	23.2	French Polynesia
6.3[13]	...	...	6.6[13]	2,428	24.2	24.3	6.2	1.9	2.8	13.8	8.3	18.5	Gabon
...	...	...	14.0[22]	2,367	60.8	1.2	2.7	1.5	2.1	0.6	11.3	19.9	Gambia, The
...	...	...	...	2,596	50.4	1.6	4.2	0.2	4.9	9.0	13.8	15.9	Gaza Strip
1.4	4.1	...	28.5	3,800	25.1	7.1	14.6	0.9	9.2	4.2	18.3	20.6	Germany, East
15.1	9.4	9.7[3]	10.2	3,475	21.2	4.1	15.4	0.6	10.5	5.9	19.3	23.1	Germany, West
3.3	3.8	3.9[3]	4.5	1,733	27.8	27.0	2.3	2.3	0.4	8.3	8.5	23.4	Ghana
13.3	10.0	...	14.0	...									Gibraltar
13.4	7.8	3.6	12.0	3,686	30.5	3.4	12.7	0.9	10.3	8.9	17.1	16.2	Greece
7.8	5.9	4.3	20.8[26]	...									Greenland
4.0	6.5	...	7.5	2,409	32.7	0.6	6.9	1.1	10.2	7.9	7.7	32.8	Grenada
16.4	6.5	5.2	8.9	2,674	34.6	1.5	11.3	3.4	9.0	7.6	10.4	22.3	Guadeloupe
18.0	...	5.1	8.8	...									Guam
5.8[18]	6.0[18]	1.8[18]	3.2[18]	2,297	58.0	0.6	2.2	0.1	4.6	3.7	7.0	24.0	Guatemala
15.7	8.3	...	24.6	...									Guernsey
5.1	2.9	4.1	...	1,782	41.2	12.5	1.8	0.7	1.2	15.9	12.8	13.9	Guinea
...	...	...	...	2,326	57.7	8.2	3.9	0.3	2.3	5.4	12.6	9.6	Guinea-Bissau
4.8	2.9	6.4[3]	8.2	2,456	56.0	0.0	3.7	2.9	3.7	2.9	5.6	25.2	Guyana
...	4.0	...	6.6	1,902	39.5	3.4	3.1	0.4	1.5	10.1	5.7	36.4	Haiti
3.0	8.3	2.4[3]	3.5	2,078	55.6	0.4	3.3	0.1	5.8	7.9	8.2	18.8	Honduras
8.0	13.3	7.9	8.1	2,779	36.3	0.6	20.2	3.4	4.3	4.7	14.4	16.1	Hong Kong
10.3	8.0	8.0	10.3	3,540	30.2	2.6	13.7	0.3	8.2	4.3	19.1	21.7	Hungary
18.8	8.8	10.1	9.6	3,146	18.4	3.6	15.6	6.3	18.7	2.9	11.8	22.6	Iceland
11.0	4.5	0.7	4.6	2,204	64.2	1.6	0.3	0.3	4.4	3.3	7.2	18.8	India
...	3.1	...	11.6	2,513	66.4	6.5	1.0	1.1	0.5	2.3	6.7	15.6	Indonesia
6.0	6.3	1.0[3]	6.7	2,986	64.1	1.2	3.8	—	2.8	4.7	8.4	15.0	Iran
5.3	6.2	1.2	7.2	2,155	60.6	0.5	3.9	0.2	3.6	6.3	5.9	19.0	Iraq
13.0	6.5	9.1[3]	14.5	3,689	24.0	6.6	17.3	1.3	10.6	3.5	15.2	21.7	Ireland
15.0	6.7	...	23.3	...									Isle of Man
...	7.2	...	35.3	3,037	33.2	2.1	8.2	0.8	10.5	8.3	17.9	19.1	Israel
15.7	7.5	6.0[3]	16.1	3,494	32.3	2.0	11.1	0.9	10.4	6.9	19.3	17.2	Italy
13.2	5.3	3.3	23.3	2,581	36.4	0.9	5.5	0.4	5.4	8.2	13.0	30.3	Jamaica
9.0	4.1	9.0	26.6	2,858	42.1	1.8	7.0	6.2	5.8	4.4	12.2	20.5	Japan
13.9	7.1	...	21.0	...									Jersey
5.9	5.0	2.8	27.6	2,107	61.8	1.6	3.7	0.3	5.2	2.9	9.1	15.4	Jordan
...	...	...	15.0	1,925	80.5	1.1	3.7	1.2	0.4	3.6	1.9	7.6	Kampuchea
8.4	9.4	3.1	9.1	2,140	60.3	5.0	2.8	0.4	3.7	2.7	5.1	20.0	Kenya
8.0	2.9	...	12.5	2,936	25.1	0.0	2.3	5.9	0.8	5.4	10.2	50.2	Kiribati
29	3.8[28]	29	15.9[29]	3,199	68.4	4.0	2.9	3.4	0.9	4.1	2.5	13.9	Korea, North
6.2	5.0	...	13.6	2,876	62.3	0.5	4.8	3.0	1.7	6.1	6.4	15.1	Korea, South
13.0	10.5	4.9[3]	9.5	3,076	38.0	1.2	11.1	0.4	10.1	7.5	12.7	18.9	Kuwait
...	...	...	...	1,929	83.4	1.4	5.5	0.6	1.3	2.5	1.1	4.2	Laos
5.4[13]	2.6[13]	1.9[13]	6.3[13]	2,495	52.7	2.0	3.6	0.2	3.9	6.0	8.0	23.6	Lebanon
9.5[18]	6.9[18]	3.1[18]	6.8[18]	2,296	74.4	0.0	3.8	0.3	2.5	1.7	3.2	14.2	Lesotho
...	6.1[13]	...	20.1[13]	2,358	46.8	18.8	2.4	1.2	0.9	5.1	15.5	9.3	Liberia
9.4	4.6	8.5[3]	2.5	3,611	42.1	1.4	7.7	0.1	6.8	7.8	18.2	15.9	Libya
13.3	5.8	16.3[3]	6.6	...									Liechtenstein
17.1	9.1	3.6[3]	19.4	3,950	19.4	5.0	19.4	0.7	8.9	4.8	23.4	18.6	Luxembourg
4.9	2.9	...	13.1	2,205	40.2	0.6	17.9	2.1	5.2	4.8	11.8	17.6	Macau
9.7	...	...	42.5	2,413	59.6	16.0	6.3	0.4	0.5	4.1	2.6	10.5	Madagascar
17.6[33]	9.6[33]	...	9.5[33]	2,372	67.8	4.3	1.6	0.7	0.7	4.2	2.8	17.9	Malawi
18.0	7.7	6.0	12.2	2,723	47.3	2.6	6.2	3.0	5.2	3.9	13.7	18.2	Malaysia
...	...	...	...	1,765	42.5	6.4	0.8	12.4	—	6.3	7.7	23.9	Maldives
...	...	...	...	2,021	78.5	1.3	3.9	0.7	2.2	0.9	3.7	8.9	Mali
15.0	8.8	6.2[3]	19.3	2,878	32.3	1.3	12.2	1.0	11.5	5.8	15.4	20.6	Malta
9.7	8.1	...	13.9	2,780	33.7	1.1	10.3	2.9	5.5	7.6	7.1	31.9	Martinique
...	...	...	9.8[13]	2,283	48.5	0.1	4.4	8.2	16.3	2.2	7.0	13.4	Mauritania
10.0	6.4	—	6.4	2,736	52.3	1.3	2.4	1.1	6.3	1.2	11.3	24.1	Mauritius
...	...	...	...	...									Mayotte
12.4	12.0	4.9[3]	11.5	3,148	48.7	0.6	8.5	0.6	5.9	3.5	10.5	21.8	Mexico
...	...	...	...	...									Monaco
...	...	...	...	2,830	56.6	2.7	21.9	0.1	3.3	0.6	5.8	9.1	Mongolia
...	10.2	...	15.3	...									Montserrat
6.9	3.6	...	17.0	2,864	65.6	1.1	2.5	0.6	2.0	2.9	9.6	15.8	Morocco
...	...	...	...	1,607	34.1	42.0	1.8	0.5	1.0	2.0	10.9	7.8	Mozambique
...	...	...	...	...									Nauru
2.1[13]	—	7.9[3,13]	6.5[13]	2,050	81.5	1.6	1.5	0.0	4.2	0.9	4.3	6.0	Nepal
10.9	7.5	9.5	13.6	3,258	19.7	4.7	11.9	0.8	13.0	5.2	23.3	21.4	Netherlands, The
19.4[35]	10.0[35]	5.9[3,35]	10.7[35]	2,922[27]	29.2[27]	2.1[7]	16.5[7]	1.4[7]	11.4[7]	7.0[7]	13.2[7]	19.2[7]	Netherlands Antilles
15.1	11.4	6.4	12.2	2,984	35.8	2.2	10.2	1.9	7.5	4.3	12.4	25.8	New Caledonia
19.6	10.9	5.2	14.0	3,405	22.0	2.7	16.8	1.6	14.4	5.4	15.5	21.6	New Zealand
...	4	...	7.8[13]	2,446	40.5	1.2	6.1	0.4	7.7	5.1	9.7	29.3	Nicaragua
...	4	...	23.1	2,349	69.4	3.4	3.6	0.1	2.6	1.7	4.4	14.9	Niger
4.7	3.8	...	21.1	2,115	40.9	12.0	1.7	0.5	0.8	3.7	10.9	29.5	Nigeria
17.5	13.0	...	5.0	...									Niue
...	...	...	...	...									Norfolk Island

Household budgets and consumption   (continued)

country	income (latest)						consumption expenditure						
	percent received by		by source (percent)				per capita private final, U.S.$ 1986	by kind or end use (percent of household or personal budget; latest)					
	lowest 20% of households	highest 10% of households	wages, salaries	self-employment	transfer payments[a]	other[b]		food[c]	housing[d]	clothing[e]	health care	energy, water	education
Norway	4.0	25.1	61.8	11.7	20.8	5.8	9,080	26.0[8]	17.1[11]	8.2	3.7	11	3
Oman	...	...	...	...	...	...	2,730[2]	...	...	...	...	...	...
Pacific Is., Trust Territory of the													
Marshall Islands	...	...	...	...	...	...	...	...	...	...	...	...	...
Micronesia, Federated States of	...	...	...	...	...	...	...	73.5					
Northern Mariana Islands	...	...	...	...	...	...	...	36.9	7.4	...	3.1	6.3	3.7
Palau	...	...	...	...	...	...	...	...	...	...	...	...	...
Pakistan	8.0	...	28.9	49.1	1.6	20.4	250	48.6[8]	11.2	7.5	...	5.6	3
Panama	2.0	44.2	85.3	...	9.2	5.5	1,320	47.3	12.7[11]	4.8	4.9	11	3
Papua New Guinea	...	...	72.7	2.5	...	24.8	470	40.3[8]	18.6	6.3	...	4.9	...
Paraguay	...	...	38.1	...	2.6	59.3	1,110	48.7	16.4	9.7	3.4	—	1.5
Peru	5.9[18]	28.4[18]	...	...	...	...	400[2]	38.1[8, 13]	15.6[11, 13]	7.3[13]	2.6[13]	11	3
Philippines	5.2	37.0	44.8	40.3	2.1	12.8	420	54.1	...	6.2	...	4.4	...
Pitcairn Island	...	...	...	...	...	...	...	...	...	...	...	...	...
Poland	10.1[19]	20.6[19]	74.8	...	11.7	13.5	970	44.6	10.8	12.8	3.0	2.5	...
Portugal	5.2	33.4	42.4	24	21.8	35.8[24]	1,570	34.8	3.2	11.2	4.3	2.7	0.8
Puerto Rico	3.2	34.7	56.0	6.4	28.0	9.6	5,100	30.2	16.1[11]	9.0	5.1	11	2.2
Qatar	...	...	...	...	...	...	4,430[2]	39.1	10.7	4.4	0.2	0.8	1.6
Réunion	3.1[20]	51.4[20]	66.4	17.1	12.4	3.8	3,700[2]	38.9	7.1	11.5	...	7.4	...
Romania	...	...	62.6	...	—37.4—		1,390	62.7[36]	—	13.8[36]	0.7[36]	9.2[36]	3
Rwanda	...	...	16.5	71.0	9.5	3.0	210	...	...	...	...	...	...
St. Helena and Ascension	...	...	...	...	...	...	...	77.9[8]	1.0	1.0	8.2	...	...
St. Kitts and Nevis	...	...	...	...	...	...	1,050[5]	55.6[8]	7.6	7.5	...	6.6	...
St. Lucia	...	...	...	...	...	...	740[5]	49.6[8]	13.5	6.5	2.3	4.5	3
St. Pierre and Miquelon	...	...	...	...	...	...	...	...	...	...	...	...	...
St. Vincent and the Grenadines	...	...	...	...	...	...	560[2]	62.6[8]	6.3	7.7	...	6.2	...
San Marino	...	...	...	...	...	...	240[2]	30.4[8]	9.7[11]	8.8	5.1	11	3
São Tomé and Príncipe	...	...	...	...	...	...	2,750	52.2[18, 37]	17.2[18, 37]	6.6[18, 37]	2.1[18, 37]	1.8[18, 37]	1.1[18, 37]
Saudi Arabia	...	...	...	...	...	...							
Senegal	5.5	45.4	51.6	...	—48.4—		310	56.0[13]	8.7[13]	11.9[13]	...	5.8[13]	...
Seychelles	4.1	35.6	77.2	3.8	3.2	15.8	1,190	53.9	13.6	4.2	0.4	9.1	...
Sierra Leone	5.6	37.8	27.9	61.6	...	10.5	140[2]	55.1[8]	7.4[11]	12.9	1.3	11	3
Singapore	6.5	34.4	75.4	18.7	2.0	3.9	3,180	22.7	9.6[11]	8.1	3.1	11	0.9
Solomon Islands	...	...	74.1	...	—25.9—		550[1]	56.5[8, 13]	15.5[11, 13]	5.0[13]	...	11	...
Somalia	...	...	...	...	...	...	170[2]	62.3[8, 13]	15.3[13]	5.6[13]	...	4.3[13]	...
South Africa	1.9	39.4	82.9	...	4.8	12.3	970[38]	32.2	11.7[11]	8.1	4.2	11	—
Bophuthatswana	...	...	...	...	...	...	...	...	...	...	...	...	...
Ciskei	...	...	...	...	...	...	...	38.6[8]	10.8	12.2	2.8	...	1.8
Transkei	3.4	43.8	...	...	...	...	...	...	...	...	...	...	...
Venda	...	...	56.2	4.8	32.9	6.1	...	51.2	4.3	11.2	0.5	4.5	1.9
South West Africa/Namibia	...	...	76.0	...	3.6	20.4	38	...	...	...	...	...	...
Spain	6.9[9]	24.5[9]	52.3	28.6	16.8	2.3	3,760	30.2[8]	12.9[11]	8.9	5.9	11	2.0
Sri Lanka	5.9	35.2	50.8	...	12.8	36.4	310	54.2	2.7	6.3	1.4	3.2	0.6
Sudan, The	4.0	34.6	35.8	53.0	...	11.2	150[2]	66.5[8]	12.4	5.9	...	...	...
Suriname	9.3	...	74.6	...	3.2	22.2	1,270	40.0[13]	4.4[13]	11.0[13]	3.6[13]	6.9[13]	2.6[13]
Swaziland	2.8	54.5	...	...	...	...	390	39.3[8, 39]	...	10.0[39]	8.0[39]	6.5[39]	...
Sweden	5.3	22.9	61.5	11.2	21.4	5.9	8,130	24.0[8]	25.8[11]	7.7	1.6	11	3
Switzerland	6.0[40]	27.0[40]	63.9	24	14.8	21.3[24]	12,300	21.3[8]	18.0	6.6	7.7	4.4	3
Syria	6.0	...	...	...	...	...	1,530	48.8[8]	17.7	9.1	...	4.6	3
Taiwan	8.4	22.8	66.4	5.4	0.9	27.3	1,590	37.4[8]	23.3[11]	5.8	5.4	11	3
Tanzania	5.8	35.6	33.8	59.8	...	6.4	180	54.3[8]	8.6	10.8	4.5	6.6	0.8
Thailand	5.1	42.8	36.7	29.7	6.0	27.6	510	43.7[8]	25.0[11]	6.9	...	11	3
Togo	8.0	30.5	...	...	...	...	170[2]	60.9	9.9[11]	7.7	1.6	11	0.6
Tokelau	...	...	...	...	...	...	...	...	...	...	...	...	...
Tonga	...	...	...	...	...	...	860[5]	63.6[8]	3.8	6.2	...	...	...
Trinidad and Tobago	2.6	33.6	...	...	...	...	2,160	27.7	22.7	15.5	2.2	1.1	1.5
Tunisia	4.1	37.6	...	...	...	...	790	42.8	9.3	10.9	3.7	5.6	1.7
Turkey	3.5[9]	41.5[9]	38.9[18]	46.8[18]	9.4[18]	4.9[18]	810[5]	41.2[18]	25.2[18]	14.8[18]	3.3[18]	...	...
Turks and Caicos Islands	...	...	...	...	...	...	...	...	...	...	...	...	...
Tuvalu	...	...	17.9	76.1	...	6.0	...	56.0[8]	11.5	7.5	...	...	...
Uganda	6.2	...	88.3[13, 41]	1.8[13, 41]	—9.9[13, 41]—		310[2]	58.0[13, 37]	...	14.0[13, 37]	...	6.0[13, 37]	...
U.S.S.R.	...	...	67.1	3.0	22.9	7.0	2,160	39.1	3.2[42]	19.3	42	0.3[42]	42
United Arab Emirates	...	...	...	...	...	...	4,870	...	...	...	...	...	...
United Kingdom	5.8	24.8	65.1	6.8	17.7	10.4	6,010	25.0	16.4	7.3	...	6.1	...
United States	3.7	46.1	59.5	8.2	14.5	17.8	11,590	17.5	15.5	7.4	13.4	4.2	7.5
Uruguay	6.0[9, 18]	29.3[9, 18]	53.5	20.8	—30.1—		1,610	39.9	17.6[11]	7.0	9.3	11	1.3
Vanuatu	...	...	59.0	33.7	...	7.3	...	36.3[43]	21.5[43]	4.8[43]	...	6.8[43]	...
Venezuela	3.0	35.7	...	...	...	...	2,360	54.3	9.3[11]	4.1	4.4	11	3
Vietnam	...	...	...	...	...	...	...	...	...	...	...	...	...
Virgin Islands (U.S.)	...	...	65.7	2.6	13.0	12.7	...	25.3[44]	24.9[44]	5.4[44]	...	6.5[44]	...
Wallis and Futuna	...	...	...	...	...	...	...	...	...	...	...	...	...
West Bank	...	...	...	...	...	...	1,080[5]	...	...	...	...	...	...
Western Sahara	...	...	...	...	...	...	...	...	...	...	...	...	...
Western Samoa	...	...	49.4	22.8	...	27.8	590[5]	58.8	5.1[4]	4.2	...	5.0	...
Yemen (Aden)	...	...	...	...	...	...	...	...	...	...	...	...	...
Yemen (Ṣan'ā')	...	...	12.2	74.1	13.4	0.3	370	65.0[8]	6.1	5.8	4.0	7.2	0.9
Yugoslavia	7.2	24.7	56.9	...	18.9	24.2	650	49.4[8]	8.5[11]	10.2	3.6	11	3
Zaire	...	...	...	...	...	...	50	60.6	17.1[4, 11]	9.5	2.5	11	0.8
Zambia	3.4	46.4	79.9	17.8	1.3	1.0	150	37.7[8]	11.0	8.3	1.0	...	2.1
Zimbabwe	3.0	55.5	...	...	...	...	340	35.3[8]	7.3	12.2	1.6	8.7	3.2

[1]1982. [2]1985. [3]Recreation includes education. [4]Housing includes household durable goods. [5]1984. [6]1983. [7]Netherlands Antilles includes Aruba. [8]Includes tobacco. [9]Based on post-tax income. [10]Rural wage earners only. [11]Housing includes energy, water. [12]Middle-income families in São Paulo. [13]Capital city only. [14]Includes wage taxes. [15]Personal effects, other includes education. [16]Rural only. [17]Highest 20%. [18]Urban areas only. [19]Low and middle-income families only. [20]Based on post-tax per capita income. [21]Consumer price index excludes rent. [22]Low-income population in Banjul and Kombo St. Mary only. [23]Excludes property income and pensions. [24]Other includes self-employment. [25]Urban areas of eastern region only. [26]Includes

transportation, communications	household durable goods[f]	recreation[g]	personal effects, other[h]	daily available calories per capita	cereals	potatoes, cassava	meat, poultry	fish	eggs, milk	fruits, vegetables	fats, oils[i]	other[j]	country
													food consumption
							percent of total calories derived from						
17.6	8.1	8.7[3]	10.6	3,215	24.4	4.6	11.3	3.1	14.9	4.5	18.5	18.7	Norway
...	...	...	...	...	...	...	...	...	...	...	...	...	Oman
...	...	...	...	...	...	...	...	...	...	...	...	...	Pacific Is., Trust Territory of the
...	...	...	26.5	...	...	...	...	...	...	...	...	...	Marshall Islands
													Micronesia, Federated States of
18.2	7.5	4.0	12.9										Northern Mariana Islands
...	...	...	...	...	...	...	...	...	...	...	...	...	Palau
4.5	2.0	2.8[3]	17.8	2,245	60.1	0.4	2.2	0.2	5.5	2.7	13.6	15.3	Pakistan
6.8	8.5	5.8[3]	9.2	2,439	39.9	1.8	9.0	0.4	5.6	4.5	12.8	25.9	Panama
11.3	7.6	...	11.0	2,269	15.4	34.5	6.3	1.9	0.6	23.7	4.4	13.2	Papua New Guinea
4.5	6.2	2.3	7.3	2,843	32.2	14.0	13.4	0.1	4.1	8.6	7.0	20.7	Paraguay
9.8[13]	7.0[13]	7.4[13]	12.2[13]	2,192	46.7	7.5	4.8	1.5	4.6	4.7	7.2	23.1	Peru
3.3	14.0		18.0	2,354	62.2	3.0	5.0	3.2	1.4	6.5	4.2	14.6	Philippines
...	...	...	...										Pitcairn Island
5.6	...	9.0	11.7	3,298	34.7	6.0	9.6	1.3	12.3	3.5	14.6	18.1	Poland
14.6	10.0	3.9	14.5	3,134	39.7	5.5	10.7	2.4	5.1	4.9	14.4	17.4	Portugal
16.2	6.6	4.7	9.9										Puerto Rico
3.7	24.4	—15.1—											Qatar
7.2	6.2	...	21.8	3,011	46.3	1.1	10.2	1.5	4.8	3.5	12.3	20.4	Réunion
3.7[36]	4.7[36]	3.0[3, 36]	2.2[36]	3,358	43.2	3.9	8.8	0.7	9.1	6.5	12.0	15.9	Romania
...	...	...	...	1,880	12.9	13.2	1.4	—	1.8	13.3	2.0	55.3	Rwanda
0.8	0.7	...	10.4										St. Helena and Ascension
4.3	9.4	...	9.0	2,349	26.3	1.0	11.0	2.0	11.2	2.9	10.2	35.3	St. Kitts and Nevis
6.3	5.8	3.2[3]	8.3	2,499	26.9	1.1	13.3	1.5	7.0	12.3	9.7	28.3	St. Lucia
...	...	...	...										St. Pierre and Miquelon
3.7	6.6	...	6.9	2,776	38.0	1.8	7.7	0.6	3.6	3.7	9.0	35.6	St. Vincent and the Grenadines
14.5	7.5	8.1[3]	15.9										San Marino
				2,385	36.4	3.9	1.6	2.8	1.0	3.0	18.2	33.1	São Tomé and Príncipe
4.5[18, 37]	5.9[18, 37]	...	8.6[18, 37]	3,031	41.9	0.5	8.8	0.5	8.7	10.5	13.5	15.7	Saudi Arabia
5.4[13]	1.7[13]		10.5[13]	2,336	68.9	0.4	3.0	1.3	2.5	1.2	11.8	11.0	Senegal
6.4	6.6	1.4	4.4										Seychelles
9.2	8.0	3.8[3]	2.3	1,868	56.3	4.8	1.2	1.8	0.5	3.9	18.1	13.4	Sierra Leone
13.9	9.2	11.0	21.5	2,854	36.0	1.9	16.9	2.5	6.1	6.9	5.2	24.5	Singapore
11.0[13]	...	...	12.0[13]	2,163	23.0	0.5	3.7	5.5	0.8	3.1	8.0	55.6	Solomon Islands
...	...	...	12.1[13]	2,088	44.2	0.9	11.7	0.5	16.0	2.4	12.1	12.3	Somalia
17.3	10.0	5.4	11.1	2,941	53.0	1.5	8.1	0.6	4.7	2.4	8.3	21.4	South Africa
													Bophuthatswana
8.5	7.7	1.2	16.3										Ciskei
				2,450	...	...	...	...	...	...	...	...	Transkei
5.4	11.9	0.9	8.2										Venda
...	...	...	...	2,183	47.7	14.2	13.8	—	4.8	1.8	10.0	7.7	South West Africa/Namibia
11.6	7.5	4.6	16.4	3,365	25.1	5.8	15.2	1.5	9.8	7.0	17.2	18.4	Spain
16.9	3.6	3.0	8.1	2,436	58.3	3.2	0.3	1.4	2.2	4.2	5.2	25.1	Sri Lanka
...	...	...	15.2	2,077	46.0	0.9	7.3	0.1	13.2	3.5	11.0	17.9	Sudan, The
9.5[13]	12.3[13]	5.8[13]	3.9[13]	2,713	52.6	1.7	6.1	1.8	4.8	2.7	8.2	22.1	Suriname
15.3[39]	9.0[39]	9.9	11.9[39]	2,550	51.9	0.5	6.6	—	4.0	2.9	7.6	26.6	Swaziland
16.4	6.6	9.9[3]	8.4	3,048	22.3	4.3	10.4	2.1	16.2	4.4	19.1	21.2	Sweden
13.3	5.8	16.3[3]	6.6	3,431	19.6	2.6	19.0	0.6	13.7	6.5	17.1	21.0	Switzerland
3.8	5.1	3.1[3]	7.8	3,259	46.6	1.6	3.8	0.1	6.3	8.3	12.9	20.5	Syria
8.2	4.3	10.0[3]	5.6	2,749	...	...	...	...	...	...	...	...	Taiwan
6.4	6.3	1.6	0.1	2,214	46.2	18.4	2.4	1.0	2.1	8.2	5.0	16.7	Tanzania
11.6	...	4.7[3]	8.1	2,329	63.4	2.0	4.0	1.5	1.4	6.3	2.6	19.0	Thailand
8.2	3.9	0.4	6.8	2,224	45.7	16.8	2.4	1.0	0.6	1.5	6.8	25.4	Togo
...	...	...	...										Tokelau
6.1	12.4	...	7.9	2,942	15.5	—	10.4	1.4	1.1	4.2	6.1	61.3	Tonga
13.2	8.8	1.4	5.9	3,058	34.3	1.8	7.1	1.0	9.7	4.4	13.8	28.0	Trinidad and Tobago
8.0	5.7	6.1	6.2	2,941	57.5	1.3	3.0	0.7	4.2	5.8	13.1	14.4	Tunisia
5.5[18]	...	6.1[18]	3.9[18]	3,148	52.7	3.5	2.9	0.5	3.7	9.1	13.0	14.6	Turkey
...	...	...	...										Turks and Caicos Islands
10.5	...	...	14.5	...	...	...	...	...	...	...	...	...	Tuvalu
10.0[13, 37]	...	...	12.0[13, 37]	2,225	22.0	23.4	2.6	1.2	1.9	13.1	1.3	34.5	Uganda
42	11.0	10.8	16.3	3,394	37.2	5.8	9.9	2.0	8.6	3.8	12.7	19.9	U.S.S.R.
...	...	...	...	3,714	34.4	0.6	7.4	2.7	7.4	12.2	14.2	21.1	United Arab Emirates
15.1	7.2	...	22.9	3,218	19.9	5.9	15.4	0.8	11.6	4.2	19.1	23.0	United Kingdom
12.4	7.9	7.4	6.8	3,642	18.8	2.7	18.5	0.8	11.3	5.2	17.4	25.4	United States
10.4	6.3	3.1	5.1	2,676	33.0	2.6	19.3	0.3	11.5	3.9	10.5	18.9	Uruguay
8.6[43]	5.5[43]	...	16.5[43]	2,344	26.3	0.1	13.6	2.6	2.4	3.5	8.2	43.5	Vanuatu
10.8	5.1	5.9[3]	6.1	2,532	37.9	1.7	9.1	1.1	9.1	6.1	11.9	23.1	Venezuela
...	...	...	...	2,135	72.9	8.6	4.8	2.2	0.1	2.6	2.0	6.8	Vietnam
11.7[44]	4.3[44]	...	21.9[44]	...	...	...	...	...	...	...	...	...	Virgin Islands (U.S.)
...	...	...	...										Wallis and Futuna
...	...	...	...	2,905	44.4	1.9	6.1	0.1	6.2	11.0	12.5	17.8	West Bank
...	...	...	...										Western Sahara
9.0	4	...	17.9	2,463	18.9	0.4	11.5	4.0	1.0	13.1	7.8	43.3	Western Samoa
...	...	...	...	2,275	63.4	0.7	3.1	2.4	5.7	4.0	6.7	14.0	Yemen (Aden)
3.2	7.8	—	—	2,331	63.5	2.4	4.4	0.3	4.4	3.6	6.7	14.8	Yemen (San'ā')
11.8	8.2	3.9[3]	4.4	3,542	46.0	2.7	7.8	0.3	8.2	3.7	15.6	15.8	Yugoslavia
5.7	4	2.0	1.7	2,160	16.2	54.0	2.1	0.6	0.2	7.4	7.2	12.4	Zaire
4.3	—	—	35.6	2,125	62.9	4.3	2.6	1.0	1.5	1.6	4.5	12.9	Zambia
4.0	9.3	1.4	17.0	2,120	62.9	1.5	2.4	0.2	1.7	1.2	8.7	21.4	Zimbabwe

shooting, hunting, and fishing. [27]1980. [28]Workers and clerical workers only. [29]Includes health, education, transportation, communications, and cultural activities. [30]Excludes single-person households and self-employed. [31]Earned income only. [32]Malagasy households only. [33]Blantyre and Lilongwe only. [34]Housing includes water. [35]Curaçao and Bonaire only. [36]Rural cooperatives only. [37]Middle-income population only. [38]South Africa includes South West Africa/Namibia. [39]Middle- to high-income families only. [40]Excludes transfers and property income. [41]Unskilled African workers only. [42]Mostly paid by state subsidies. [43]Urban, low-income households only. [44]St. Thomas only.

Health services

The provision of health services in most countries is both a principal determinant of the quality of life and a large and growing sector of the national economy. This table summarizes the basic indicators of: health manpower; hospitals, by kind and utilization; mortality rates that are most indicative of general health services; external controls on health (adequacy of food supply and availability of safe drinking water); and sources and amounts of expenditure on health care. Each datum refers more or less directly to the availability or use of a particular health service in a country, and, while each may be an accurate measure at a national level, each may also conceal considerable differences in availability of the particular service to different segments of a population or regions of a country. In the United States, for example, the availability of physicians ranges from about one per 900 persons in the least well-served state to one per 350 in the best-served, with a rate of one per 185 in the national capital. These disparities are even more pronounced in most other countries, unless the government has made some special effort to achieve a more even distribution of manpower and facilities. In addition, even when trained manpower exists and facilities have been created, the country may lose health professionals via the "brain drain" to foreign countries; or low levels of financial support at the national level may leave facilities underserved; or lack of good transportation may prevent those most in need from reaching a clinic or hospital that could help them.

Definitions and limits of data have been made as specific as possible in the compilation of this table. For example, despite wide variation worldwide in the nature of the qualifying or certifying process that permits an individual to represent himself as a physician, organizations such as the World Health Organization (WHO) try to institute international standards for training and qualification. International statistics presented here for "physicians" refer to persons qualified according to WHO standards and exclude traditional health practitioners, whatever the local custom with regard to the designation "doctor." Statistics for health manpower in this table uniformly include all those actually working in the health service field, whether in the actual provision of services or in teaching, administration, research, or other tasks. One group of practitioners for whom this type of guideline works less well is that of midwives, whose training and qualifications vary enormously from country to country but who must be included, as they represent, after nurses, perhaps the largest and most important category of health auxiliary worldwide. The statistics here refer to those midwives working in some kind of institutional setting (a hospital, clinic, community health-care centre, or the like) and exclude rural noninstitutional midwives and traditional birth attendants.

Hospitals also differ considerably worldwide in terms of staffing and services. In this tabulation, the term hospital refers generally to a permanent facility offering inpatient services and/or nursing care and staffed by at least one physician. Establishments offering only outpatient or custodial care are excluded. These statistics are broken down into data for general hospitals (those providing care in more than one specialty), specialized facilities (with care in only one specialty), local medical centres, and rural health-care centres; the last two generally refer to institutions that provide a more limited range of medical or nursing care, often less than full-time. Hospital data are further analyzed into three categories of administrative classification: public, private nonprofit, and private for profit. Statistics on

Health services

country	health personnel							hospitals									hospital beds per 10,000 pop.
	year	physicians	dentists	nurses	pharmacists	midwives	population per physician	year	number	kinds (%) general	specialized	medical centres	rural	ownership (%) government	private nonprofit	private for profit	
Afghanistan	1982	1,160	110[1]	1,054	206	529	12,172	1982	68	66.2	16.2	—	17.6	86.8	13.2	—	5
Albania	1982	3,861	900[4]	6,801[5]	532[5]	5,098[5]	720	1977	928	5.2	3.1	82.4	9.3	100.0	—	—	62[6]
Algeria	1986	15,361	3,754	24,700[9]	1,584	3,800[9]	1,468	1984	447	—44.3—		55.7	—	85.3[10]	4.4[10]	10.3[10]	23
American Samoa	1983	27	7	141	1	1	1,270	1986	1	100.0	—	—	—	100.0	—	—	37
Andorra	1984	53	...	...	2	...	784	1984	1	100.0	—	—	—	100.0	—	—	31
Angola	1986	655	...	9,528	...	1,237	13,489	1986	24	...	...	...	...	...	...	...	15
Anguilla	1987	4	1	16[15]	1[16]	11[16]	1,683	1987	1	—	—	—	100.0	100.0	—	—	36
Antigua and Barbuda	1986	45	7	194	27	160[5]	1,695	1986	2	50.0	50.0	—	—	100.0	—	—	54
Argentina	1984	81,260	6,620	14,150	...	...	370	1980	3,189	84.2	15.8	—	—	41.9	3.6	54.5	54
Aruba	1985	59	16	189	9	...	1,043	1985	1	100.0	—	—	—	100.0	—	—	45
Australia	1982	27,500	5,721	106,600[1]	9,800[1]	5,900[1]	552	1987	1,053[17]	...	...	...	...	68.4[17]	—31.6[17]—		54
Austria	1987	20,228	3,062	27,458	2,003	776	374	1987	342	38.6	61.4	—	—	60.0	—40.0—		110
Bahamas, The	1985	218	31[20]	952	37[20]	120[20]	1,031	1985	5	60.0	20.0	20.0	—	60.0	—40.0—		43
Bahrain	1985	518	35[15]	2,374[15]	68[15]	276[15]	839	1982	12	42.7	58.3	—	—	75.0	16.7	8.3	34[9]
Bangladesh	1986	17,062	447	6,912	...	5,199	6,028	1986	415	68.9	5.1	23.1	2.9	60.5	—39.5—		2
Barbados	1984	213	30[15]	1,050[15]	...	36[15]	1,183	1982	11	27.3	18.2	—	54.5	81.8	—	18.2	84[11]
Belgium	1986	29,776	5,760	91,263[15]	10,792	4,920[15]	331	1982	531	53.3	46.7	—	—	36.3	—63.7—		92[19]
Belize	1986	75	12[11]	209[11]	17[11]	179[1]	2,260	1986	12[10]	58.3[10]	25.0[10]	—	16.7[10]	100.0[10]	—	—	34
Benin	1982	270	13[20]	1,294[20]	55[20]	312[20]	13,570	1980	131	4.6	9.9	80.9	4.6	87.8	12.2	—	13[15]
Bermuda	1987	70	20	561	31	...	826	1986	2	50.0	50.0	—	—	50.0	50.0	—	45
Bhutan	1986	134	...	252	63	17[15]	9,791	1986	28	...	...	...	...	...	...	...	7
Bolivia	1984	4,032	1,182[26]	1,552[26]	1,902[26]	...	1,551	1983	400[27]	18.0[27]	5.5[27]	42.5[27]	34.0[27]	...	...	...	18
Botswana	1986	156	14	1,530	10[20]	714[20]	7,218	1984	22	—63.6—		36.4	—	72.7	—27.3—		23
Brazil	1981	103,000	56,015[20]	306,411[20]	5,129[20]	2,526[20]	1,200	1986	23,314[15]	22.6[15]	13.3[15]	—64.1[15]—		64.0[15]	—36.0[15]—		34
British Virgin Islands	1986	7	1[20]	46[20]	2[4]	1[4]	1,720	1987	1	100.0	—	—	—	100.0	—	—	41
Brunei	1986	171	28	779	8	185	1,323	1986	8	87.5	—	—	12.5	87.5	12.5	—	39
Bulgaria	1986	26,451	5,844	58,961	4,150	7,769	331	1986	250	74.8	25.2	—	—	...	...	...	97
Burkina Faso	1984[28]	180	14[1]	1,927[1]	46[1]	281[1]	42,128	1984	445	4.5[5]	—	88.7[5]	6.8[5]	100.0[5]	—	—	7
Burma	1986	10,031	410[1]	6,978[1,28]	80[1,28]	15,543[1]	3,797	1986	614[15]	49.7[15]	2.4[15]	—	47.9[15]	100.0[15]	—	—	7
Burundi	1985[28]	178	9	559	9	73[10]	26,494	1985[21]	220	—13.6—		—86.4—		...	...	...	12
Cameroon	1982	604	17	3,216	96	399	14,800	1984	1,003[5]	5.8[5]	0.5[5]	87.5[5]	6.2[5]	70.1[5]	23.5[5]	6.4[5]	27
Canada	1985	51,966	13,027	250,458	18,813	...	491	1978	1,226	65.8	26.9	7.3	—	93.4	—	6.6	75[20]
Cape Verde	1980	51[28]	3	187[28]	7[28]	232[28]	5,820[28]	1980	21	9.5	4.8	61.9	23.8	100.0	—	—	21
Cayman Islands	1987	33	8[19]	59[9]	3[10]	119	682	1987	2	50.0	—	—	50.0	100.0	—	—	28
Central African Republic	1984	112	6	710	16	168	22,997	1984	104	19.2	4.8	76.0	—	74.0	—	26.0	15
Chad	1980	94	44[28]	933[4,28]	94[28]	96[4,28]	47,640	1978	4	100.0	—	—	—	—	—	100.0	8
Chile	1986	12,334	1,774[28]	26,389[28]	202[28]	2,021[28]	983	1986	219	51.4[15]	19.0[15]	—	29.6[15]	82.2	—17.8—		27
China	1987	1,482,000[30]	...	718,000	33,800[9]	76,000[9]	724[30]	1987	60,429	14.7[9]	5.6[9]	—	79.5[9]	100.0[9]	—	—	22
Christmas Island	1985	2	1	5[1]	1	...	1,100	1985	1	100.0	—	—	—	100.0	—	—	133
Cocos (Keeling) Islands	1985	1	—	4	—	...	621	1984	2	50.0	—	50.0	—	100.0	—	—	86
Colombia	1983	21,778	7,990	28,020	...	...	1,288	1983	946	—79.6—		—20.4—		82.1[20]	17.9[20]	—	17
Comoros	1982	20	1[4]	108[20]	2[4]	13[20]	17,200	1980	17	17.7	—	23.5	58.8	100.0	—	—	22
Congo	1980	278	2[4]	1,915[4]	28[4]	413[4]	5,986	1978	473	0.6	0.2	97.3	1.9	94.9	5.1	—	45
Cook Islands	1982	18	8[28]	65[28]	21[28]	81[28]	939	1981	8	12.5	—	—	87.5	100.0	—	—	87
Costa Rica	1982	1,929	239[10]	1,192[10]	123[5,28]	...	1,198	1980	39	48.7	28.2	—23.1—		92.3	—	7.7	29[16]
Côte d'Ivoire	1982	502	36[4]	3,052[4]	76[4]	615[4]	17,847	1978	61[16]	13.1[16]	3.3[16]	—	83.6[16]	98.4	—1.6—		11[15]
Cuba	1986	25,567	5,752	48,339	650	...	399	1986	261	28.0	—47.1—		24.9	100.0	—	—	53
Cyprus	1986[32]	911	330	2,211[33]	337[15]	33	601	1986[32]	124[15]	3.2[15]	—89.5[15]—		7.3[15]	12.1[15]	0.8[15]	87.1[15]	62
Czechoslovakia	1987	48,414	8,307	146,952	7,375	6,792[15]	321	1987	377	61.0	39.0	—	—	100.0	—	—	99
Denmark	1986	13,144	4,795	31,757	1,476	915[9]	390	1986	127[15]	87.4[15]	12.6[15]	—	—	91.3[15]	8.7[15]	—	69
Djibouti	1985	68	4	288[1,34]	4	19[1,34]	6,323	1984	29	6.9	3.5	75.8	13.8	100.0	—	—	30[9]
Dominica	1986	27	4	153[6]	5	47[4]	2,983	1983	48	2.1	2.1	91.6	4.2	100.0	—	—	40[19]
Dominican Republic	1984	3,555	...	2,431[35]	...	...	1,782	1973	339	80.5	6.8	—	12.7	40.7	0.3	59.0	16[20,21]
Ecuador	1984	11,000	795[10]	...	505[10]	...	829	1984	337	16.6	7.1	49.6	26.7	53.7[10]	1.9[10]	44.4[10]	17
Egypt	1984	73,300	8,218[15]	34,371[1]	18,860[15]	9,004[15,28]	635	1982	1,521	32.3	13.2	15.9	38.6	83.1	3.8	13.1	18[11]

number of beds refer to beds that are maintained and staffed on a full-time basis for a succession of inpatients to whom care is provided.

Data on hospital utilization refer to institutions defined as above. Admission and discharge, the two principal points at which statistics are normally collected, are the basis for the data on the amount and distribution of care by kind of facility. The data on numbers of patients exclude babies born during a maternal confinement but include persons who die before being discharged. The bed-occupancy and average length-of-stay statistics depend on the concept of a "patient-day," which is the annual total of daily censuses of inpatients. The bed-occupancy rate is the ratio of total patient-days to potential days based on the number of beds; the average length-of-stay rate is the ratio of total patient-days to total admissions. Bed-occupancy rates may exceed 100% because stays of partial days are counted as full days.

Two measures that give health planners and policy makers an excellent indication of the level of ordinary health care are those for mortality of children under age five and for maternal mortality. The former is the probability of a newborn infant dying before age five. The latter refers to deaths attributable to delivery or complications of pregnancy, childbirth, the puerperium (the period immediately following birth), or abortion. Levels of nutrition and access to safe drinking water are two of the most basic limitations imposed by the physical environment in which health-care activities take place. The nutritional data are based on recommendations of the United Nations' Food and Agriculture Organization for the necessary daily intake (in calories) for a moderately active person of average size in a climate of a particular kind (fewer calories are needed

in a hot climate) to remain in average *good* health. Excess intake in the most developed countries ranges to more than 150% of what is required to maintain health (the excess usually being construed to diminish, rather than raise, health). The range of deficiency is less dramatic numerically but far more critical to the countries in which deficiencies are chronic, because the deficiencies lead to overall poor health (raising health service needs and costs), to decreased productivity in nearly every area of national economic life, and to the loss of social and economic potential through early mortality. By "safe" water is meant only water that has no substantial quantities of chemical or biological pollutants, *i.e.*, quantities sufficient to cause "immediate" health problems.

Two principal kinds of public health-care finance data are given: health insurance and central government expenditure. The data on insurance refer to public programs only and identify the mandated basis or extent of responsibility for costs or funding required under the relevant law of the principal participants (individuals, employers, and government). Data on public health-care expenditure refer to a consolidated statement of expenditure, budgetary and otherwise, by all elements of the central government but exclude expenditure by other levels (state, city, etc.). In a number of countries significant governmental expenditures for health-care services are made at these other levels, amounting to 2, 10, and sometimes 20 times the level of central government expenditure. These expenditures may include costs for national health insurance, family-planning programs, and workmen's compensation. Expenditures at the national level for social security are excluded.

admissions or discharges					bed occu-pancy rate (%)	aver-age length of stay (days)	mortality		popu-lation with access to safe water (latest) (%)	food supply (% of FAO require-ment) 1984	financing of public health care, latest year				public health expendi-tures (% of natl. budget)	public health expendi-tures per capita (U.S.$)	country
rate per 10,000 pop.	by kinds of hospital (%)						under age 5 per 1,000 live newborn 1985–90	maternal mortality per 100,000 live births 1980–84			health-care insurance						
	general	special-ized	medical centres	rural							indiv. (% of earn-ings)	em-ployer (% of payroll)	govt. (% of covered earnings)				
76[2]	52.8[2]	46.7[2]	—	0.5[2]	58.0[2]	8[2]	318	640.0	22	91	—	—	—		...	2.10[3]	Afghanistan
	...	...	...	...			48		92	121[6]	—	8.0[7]	8		...	43.10[3]	Albania
568[11]	...	...	...	...	64.1[10, 12]	10[10, 12]	105	129.0	85	112	4.5[7]	5.5[7]	—		...	35.40[3]	Algeria
1,253	100.0	—	—	—	40.0	4.3	30[13]	...	100		...	...	...		17.6	237.10	American Samoa
							17[13]	...			...	...	...		...	...	Andorra
260	...	...	...	...	44.5[14]	16[14]	232		31	84		...	...		...	10.10[3]	Angola
1,097[15]	—	—	—	100.0[15]	52.3[4]	6[4]	27[13]	...	...	...		...	...		8.3	88.00	Anguilla
63[17]	...	...	...	...	49.9[17]	7[17]	27[13]	...	100	81[6]	3.0[7]	5.0[7]	—		13.1	66.60[3]	Antigua and Barbuda
	...	...	...	...			38	69.0	67	122	3.0	4.5	—		1.3	6.50	Argentina
	...	...	...	...			27[13]	...				...	...		...	...	Aruba
	...	...	...	...			10	8.9	99	127	18	—	8		9.5	289.00	Australia
2,148[19]	...	...	...	...	87.4[19]	16[19]	12	10.9	100	134	3.2[18]	3.2[18]	...		12.0	599.60	Austria
979[21]	77.0	—23.0—					27[13]	19.3[11]	98	85[6]	1.7[7, 22]	7.37.[23]	—		13.4	274.40	Bahamas, The
1,104	74.0	26.0	—	—	72.6[17]	9[17]	32	...	100		—	—	—		6.4	205.40	Bahrain
	...	...	...	...			188	600.0	41	86		...	...		6.2	1.00	Bangladesh
842	93.9	4.6	—	1.5	89.8[21]	34[21]	14	22.3	98	129	1.0	1.0	—		11.5	180.80	Barbados
1,552	91.0	9.0	—	—	85.3	19	12	7.5	95	140	1.8	3.8	—		1.7	78.10	Belgium
	...	...	...	...			...	34.0	80	114	3.0[7]	4.1[7]	8		9.0	30.70	Belize
	...	...	...	...			184	1,680.0	20	94	—	0.2[24]	—		5.6	3.80[3]	Benin
1,272	96.6	3.4	—	—	76.0	9.4[17]	11[13]	...				...	...		20.7	761.30[3]	Bermuda
4,149[25]	...	...	...	...			196	...	8	90[20]		...	...		5.6	3.00	Bhutan
	...	...	...	...			171	480.0	43	90	2.0	8.0	—		1.5	5.10	Bolivia
691[20]	89.1[20]	6.7[20]	4.2[20]	—	90.0[17]	10[17]	92	300.0	77	96	—	—	—		5.0	55.60	Botswana
	...	...	...	...			86	154.0	77	110	18	18	18		6.4	26.80	Brazil
868[20]	100.0[20]	—	—	—	75.0[20]	8[20]	27[13]	...	90			...	...		10.3	198.70	British Virgin Islands
1,069[15]	98.5[15]	—	—	1.5[15]	38.0[15]	4[15]	...	...	90	126		...	...		2.2	175.90	Brunei
2,118[15]	...	...	...	...	84.4[15]	16[15]	19	20.1	96	147	—	30.0[7]	8		...	197.50[3]	Bulgaria
665,[12]	...	...	...	...	63.7[5, 12]	12[5, 12]	235	1,500.0	35	81	—	11.5[29]	—		5.8	2.10	Burkina Faso
289[15]	75.7[15]	10.1[15]	—	14.2[15]	78.1[15]	9[15]	85	135.0	26	118	1.0	2.0	1.0		7.7	2.20	Burma
109	...	...	...	...			191	...	24	91	—	—	—		2.4	2.00[3]	Burundi
	...	...	...	...			153	141.0	36	90	—	7.0[29]	—		5.1	9.10	Cameroon
1,677	93.9	6.0	0.1	—	75.7[15]	13[15]	9	4.8	100	129	18	18	18		6.1	207.60	Canada
279[14]	...	...	...	...	71.7[14]	11[14]	86	107.3[20]	50	112	8.0	15.0	—		...	...	Cape Verde
1,160	91.7	—	—	8.3	74.1[19]	7[19]	27[13]	...	99	...		...	...		12.2	357.30	Cayman Islands
326	43.9[10]	1.0[10]	37.9[10]	17.2[10]	41.9	7	223	600.0	18	91	—	12.0[24, 29]	—		5.1	3.30	Central African Republic
	...	...	...	...			223	...	31	63	—	6.0[29]	...		4.2	0.80[3]	Chad
1,039[9]	84.9[20]	9.3[20]	—	5.8[20]	75.2[9]	8[9]	24	53.5	86	107	6.0	—	...		6.0	24.40	Chile
182[9]	...	...	...	...	82.7[9]	16[9]	44	44.0	50	110	—	31	—		...	4.30[3]	China
	...	...	...	...			10[13]	...	100	...		...	...		...	...	Christmas Island
445	84.6	—	15.4	—			10[13]	...	100	...		...	...		...	...	Cocos (Keeling) Islands
385[15]	88.9[4]	11.1[4]	—	—	59.3[15]	6[15]	68	126.0	92	111	2.3	4.7	...		4.4	9.00	Colombia
510[4]	63.7[4]	—	—	36.3[4]	67.9[4]	11[4]	127	...	...	90	—	—	—		5.6	8.30	Comoros
	...	...	...	...			115	...	30	115	—	0.2	—		...	21.60	Congo
1,352	70.7	—	—	29.3	43.6[17]	9[17]	30[13]	...				...	...		...	...	Cook Islands
1,192	77.8	16.7	—5.5—		75.7	8	22	27.4	91	125	5.5	9.3	1.3		19.3	88.40	Costa Rica
171[16]	...	...	...	...			148	...	66	108	—	5.5[29]	...		4.0	8.40	Côte d'Ivoire
1,619	32.3	—64.2—		3.5	74.4[15]	11[15]	18	51.6	61	135	—	10.0	8		...	66.00[3]	Cuba
759	94.3	1.5	—	4.2	77.7[17]	7[17]	16	...	100	140	6.0[7, 32]	6.07.[32]	8, 32		6.5[32]	110.20[32]	Cyprus
1,809	95.7	4.3	—	—	81.3	13	16	10.2	74	140	—	20.0[7]	8		...	329.30[3]	Czechoslovakia
2,032	97.9	2.1	—	—	81.9	10	9	5.6	100	132	—	—	8		1.1	49.50	Denmark
	...	...	...	...			188[13]	...	45	...		...	...		5.8	19.50	Djibouti
729	...	...	...	...			33[13]	57.5	77	109	3.0[7]	5.0[7]	—		8.8	22.70	Dominica
	73.1[21]	16.7[21]	—	10.2[21]	59.8[21]	7[21]	82	56.0	62	109	2.5[7]	7.0[7]	2.5[7]		9.0	8.90	Dominican Republic
471	—85.0[10, 36]—		15.0[10]	36	60.4	8	87	162.0	59	90	5.0[7]	1.0	—		7.3	18.80	Ecuador
	...	...	...	...			124	80.0	90	130	1.0	4.0	—		2.4	12.50	Egypt

Health services (continued)

country	year	physicians	dentists	nurses	pharmacists	midwives	population per physician	year	number	general (%)	specialized (%)	medical centres (%)	rural (%)	government (%)	private non-profit (%)	private for profit (%)	hospital beds per 10,000 pop.
El Salvador	1984	1,592[27]	600[1]	1,350[27]	597[10]	...	3,002[27]	1979	82	15.8	17.1	15.9	51.2	69.5	1.2	29.3	14[11,27]
Equatorial Guinea	1975	5	...	248	...	2	62,000	1982	65[5]	...	...	...	...	...	...	...	105
Ethiopia	1984	539	16[20]	7,547[20,33]	216	33	78,740	1984	85	32.6[20]	18.6[20]	—	48.8[20]	88.4[20]	9.3[20]	2.3[20]	3
Faeroe Islands	1986	79	37	221	8	18	583	1986	3	33.3	—	—	66.7	100.0	—	—	81
Falkland Islands	1987	4	1	12	—	5	50	1987	1	100.0	—	—	—	100.0	—	—	145
Fiji	1986	385	67	1,572	44[20]	...	1,859	1984	27	11.1	33.3	—	55.6	92.6	7.4	—	24[19]
Finland	1986	10,556	4,027	45,531[33]	7,060	33	467	1985	367	79.8	20.2	—	—	94.9	—5.1—		124
France	1985	132,138	34,744	286,703	43,965	9,147	417	1985	3,696	—90.7—			9.3	28.6	—71.4—		130
French Guiana	1986	149	44	442	32	26	574	1984	6	16.7[15]	—	66.7[15]	16.7[15]	33.3	—66.7—		125
French Polynesia	1983	174	51[15]	424[15,28]	24[15]	10[15,28]	950	1981	34	8.8	5.9	52.9	32.4	94.1	—	5.9	55[6]
Gabon	1980	265	20[5]	823[5]	28[5]	99[38]	4,053	1981	103	—15.5—			84.5	100.0	—	—	44
Gambia, The	1981	60	6[4]	179[4]	2[4]	90[4]	10,900	1978	16	18.8	12.5	—	68.7	87.5	12.5	...	12[1]
Gaza Strip	...	...	...	...	...	...	...	1986	7	...	...	...	...	85.7	14.3	...	17
Germany, East	1987	39,157	12,185		3,871	...	424	1986	542	...	...	...	...	85.2	—14.8—		102
Germany, West	1987	165,015	38,055	315,090	33,025	5,518	370	1987	3,071	44.7[20]	55.3[20]	—	—	35.4	34.0	30.6	110
Ghana	1984	1,900	95[1]	17,758[1]	611[1]	6,728[1]	6,640	1979	329	2.7	4.9	54.7	37.7	78.4	13.1	8.5	18[1]
Gibraltar	1987	25	5[15]	246[11]	13[15]	14[15]	1,117	1986	3	100.0	—	—	—	100.0	—	—	90
Greece	1985	29,103	8,737	22,560	...	1,907	341	1985	552	50.0	50.0	—	—	23.0	—77.0—		55
Greenland	1986	61	29	535	...	13	878	1986	16	6.3	—	—	93.7	100.0	—	—	106
Grenada	1986	38	7[1]	337[1]	1[4]	107[4]	2,687	1982	39	7.7	7.7	69.2	15.4	100.0	—	—	33[19]
Guadeloupe	1985	416	127	1,131	127	70	800	1985	29	60.0[4]	30.0[4]	—	10.0[4]	37.9	—62.1—		125
Guam	1982	83	23	396	30	...	1,363	1982	4	25.0	25.0	50.0	—	50.0	—50.0—		21[10]
Guatemala	1984	3,544	275[1]	4,345[10,28]	15	...	2,256	1982	159[40]	38.4[40]	25.8[40]	32.7[40]	3.1[40]	76.7[40]	—	23.3[40]	14
Guernsey	1982	53	21	592	16	31	1,094	1982	5	20.0	80.0	—	—	100.0	—	—	91
Guinea	1980	301	21[35]	1,533[35]	159[35]	394[35]	17,000	1976	314	1.9	—	87.9	10.1	100.0	—	—	17
Guinea-Bissau	1980	108	2	...	3	...	7,287	1981	17	11.8	—	—	88.2	100.0	—	—	19[6]
Guyana	1987	142	19	881[10]	32[10]	546[10]	5,307	1979	55	20.0	12.7	27.3	40.0	87.3	3.6	9.1	53
Haiti	1985	803	92	657	6[10,28]	100[10]	6,539	1981	72	—77.8—		22.2		61.1	—38.9—		7[9]
Honduras	1986	2,087	394	3,545[20]	551	...	2,163	1986	46	59.1[15]	11.4[15]	—	29.5[15]	45.7	—54.3—		14
Hong Kong	1987[34]	5,484	1,240	17,215	623	981	1,024	1982	71	43.7	15.5	39.4	1.4	50.7	26.8	22.5	44[41]
Hungary	1987	30,924	4,499	43,579	4,506	2,605	343	1987	...	...	...	...	...	...	...	...	99
Iceland	1985	626	197	2,868[33]	178	33	385	1985	46[20]	54.3[20]	41.4[20]	4.3[20]	—	...	—28.4—		111
India	1985[34]	297,200	8,648[1]	165,000	155,621[1]	217,981[1]	2,522	1981	25,452	26.7	0.3	65.8	7.2	71.6	—28.4—		8[19]
Indonesia	1985	18,947	1,292[6]	62,615[15]	1,800[10]	16,928[15]	8,717	1985	1,367	14.7	8.3[4]	39.4	37.6[4]	30.2	23.0[4]	46.8[4]	7
Iran	1983	15,945	2,340	29,486	2,650	2,202	2,582	1982	581	71.1	15.5	9.8	3.6	66.4	13.9	19.7	16
Iraq	1984	4,428	984	6,082[15]	952	2,267[15]	3,324	1982	230[9]	48.3	33.8	2.1	15.8	95.7	—	4.3	18[11]
Ireland	1984	4,250	990	24,390[10,33]	2,068[1]	33	830	1982	238	33.5[20]	37.8[20]	1.4[20]	27.3[20]	63.2[20]	21.5[20]	15.3[20]	55
Isle of Man	1988	86	19[15,28]	750[15,28]	30[15]	61[15,28]	745	1986	3	33.3	33.3	—	33.3	—	—	—	109[1]
Israel	1983	11,895	2,900	14,785	2,540	12,110	345	1986	150	29.3	70.7	—	—	30.0	30.0	40.0	63
Italy	1981	190,196[30]	...	186,335[33]	43,500[20]	33		1985	1,798	73.5	26.5	—	—	63.2	—36.8—		82
Jamaica	1986[28]	365	57	2,560	116	477	6,401	1986	37	83.8	16.2	—	—	83.8	—16.2—		25
Japan	1986	191,346	66,797	621,451	135,990	24,056	635	1986	9,699	88.8	11.2	—	—	15.3	—84.7—		125
Jersey	1986	85	41[15]	646[15]	22[15]	27[15]	944	1986	6	16.7	83.3	—	—	100.0	—	—	94
Jordan	1986	3,114	486[11]	830[11]	800[11]	266[11]	881	1986	41[11]	80.0[11]	20.0[11]	—	—	39.0[11]	—61.0[11]—		19
Kampuchea	1984	200	...	...	130	...	36,000	1984	146	84.9	15.1	—	—	...	...	...	23
Kenya	1985	2,752	384	19,815[11]	131[11]	...	7,387	1984	506	—42.1—		57.9		...	...	...	15[9]
Kiribati	1986	16	1[9]	129[9]	3[9]	213[15]	4,094	1982	34	2.9	—	97.1	—	100.0	—	—	43[19]
Korea, North	1983	46,600	...	...	...	...	417	1982	7,924	19.3	12.4	—68.3—		...	...	...	130
Korea, South	1986	31,616	5,995	64,270	31,334	6,513	1,315	1986	9,081	—5.6—		94.4		...	...	...	19
Kuwait	1986	2,802	327	8,768	805	109	639	1985	24	40.0[15]	36.7[15]	23.3[15]	—	66.7	—33.3—		35
Laos	1985	558	15[35]	1,028[35]	16[35]	352[35]	6,495	1985	38[16]	...	...	...	...	...	...	...	27
Lebanon	1982	3,000	730[10]	3,681[10]	1,002[10]	614[10]	1,000	1982	130[40]	...	...	...	...	...	...	...	38
Lesotho	1982	114	6	452	7	...	12,265	1985	136	—14.7—		—85.3—		40.9[5]	59.1[5]	—	16
Liberia	1985	89	5	908	4[20]	443	24,600	1981	85[20]	...	...	...	...	60.0[20]	—40.0[20]—		15
Libya	1982[28]	5,210	384	9,495	514	1,218	637	1982	64	68.8	31.2	—	—	100.0	—	—	48
Liechtenstein	1986	26	7	...	2	...	1,048	1985	1	...	...	...	...	...	...	...	37
Luxembourg	1986	686	181	86	262	107	537	1985	33	60.6	39.4	—	—	...	...	...	125
Macau	1986	697	105[1]	605[1]	5[1]	1,357	612	1986	4[5]	50.0[5]	50.0[5]	—	—	...	...	...	30
Madagascar	1982	940	94[1]	3,779[1]	871	1,423[1]	9,851	1978	749	0.8	1.1	75.7	22.4	100.0	—	—	23[15]
Malawi	1983	161	12	2,149[33]	12	33	41,108	1986	371	12.9	0.8	—86.3—		67.7	—32.3—		17
Malaysia	1986	5,394	1,050[11]	29,358[6]	815[11]	14,525[6]	2,986	1981[45]	163	20.2	50.4	—	29.4	39.9	—	60.1	20
Maldives	1985	23	...	74	13	141	7,957	1985	4	100.0	—	—	—	100.0	—	—	7
Mali	1983	283	14[4]	2,058	24[4]	305	25,248	1983	162	0.5[5]	81.3[5]	—	18.2[5]	100.0	—	—	6
Malta	1982	413	57	2,962	369	225	799	1983	7	28.6	71.4	—	—	...	...	...	101
Martinique	1985	472	117	1,871[15]	111	106[15]	701	1984	19	17.6[10]	11.9[10]	17.6[10]	52.9[10]	78.9	—21.1—		128
Mauritania	1984	170	8	582	16	129	9,547	1984	13	8.3[5]	—	—	91.7[5]	100.0	—	—	8
Mauritius	1986	761	106	2,019[28,33]	100	33	1,353	1986	19	36.8	21.1	31.6	10.5	89.5	—10.5—		28[21]
Mayotte	1980	9	1	51	1	2	5,567	1985	2	...	...	...	...	...	...	...	15
Mexico	1982	66,373	1,879[26]	40,998[26]	112[26]	634[26]	1,102	1974	1,575	47.3	10.6	26.2	15.9	...	...	...	9[11]
Monaco	1986	53	32[15]	391[15]	56[15]	6[15]	538	1982	1	100.0	—	—	—	100.0	—	—	152[16]
Mongolia	1986[25]	4,400	200	7,932[6]	300	963[1]	356	1981	1,659	2.1	5.4	71.9	20.6	100.0	—	—	112[19]
Montserrat	1985	8	1[15]	73	2[4]	32[1]	1,482	1986	1	100.0	—	—	—	100.0	—	—	58
Morocco	1986	3,945	198[11]	22,147[1]	1,030[11]	74[1]	5,755	1986[27]	169	52.7	—	47.3	—	100.0	—	—	11
Mozambique	1986	279	96[20,28]	2,694	82[20,28]	971	50,817	1986	250	4.0	0.8	84.4	10.8	100.0	—	—	11
Nauru	1980	11	2[38]	61[33,38]	1[38]	33	700	1980	2[38]	100.0[38]	—	—	—	50.0[38]	50.0[38]	—	250
Nepal	1987	863[30]	...	742[19]	427[19]	1,845	20,356[30]	1987	91	88.2[20]	11.8[20]	—	—	82.4[20]	17.6[20]	—	2
Netherlands, The	1987	33,330	7,405	34,500[4]	1,991	1,014	438	1986	309	64.1	35.9	—	—	...	...	...	64
Netherlands Antilles	1985	184	35	...	21	12	950	1985	11	—100.0—				...	...	...	85
New Caledonia	1985	194	33	283[1]	42	27	772	1981	38	10.5	7.9	39.5	42.1	92.1	—	7.9	66[9]
New Zealand	1986	8,312[34]	1,259	40,950	3,283	2,600[15]	398[34]	1986	346	...	...	...	...	51.4	—48.6—		93
Nicaragua	1984	2,172	222	5,649	...	...	1,456	1985	52	55.1	8.2	36.7	—	46.2[35]	—	53.8[35]	16
Niger	1980	136	10[4]	1,080[4]	12[4]	88[4]	40,209	1978	212	1.9	0.5	94.8	2.8	97.2	2.8	—	6[10]
Nigeria	1981	10,399	379	36,464	2,609	30,190	8,326	1981	2,374[20]	25.2[20]	—	74.8[20]	—	70.2[47]	—29.8[47]—		9
Niue	1986[28]	3	3	27	...	7	858	1986	1	100.0	—	—	—	100.0	—	—	97
Norfolk Island	1987[28]	2	1	8[1]	19	11	1,002	1987	1	100.0	—	—	—	100.0	—	—	110

rate per 10,000 pop.	general	special- ized	medical centres	rural	bed occu- pancy rate (%)	aver- age length of stay (days)	under age 5 per 1,000 live newborn 1985–90	maternal mortality per 100,000 live births 1980–84	popu- lation with access to safe water (latest) (%)	food supply (% of FAO require- ment) 1984	indiv. (% of earn- ings)	em- ployer (% of payroll)	govt. (% of covered earnings)	public health expendi- tures (% of natl. budget)	public health expendi- tures per capita (U.S.$)	country
378[17]	...	...	...	...	77.1[17]	7[17]	84	72.5	55	94	2.5	6.3	...	5.9	13.00	El Salvador
...	...	...	...	...	...	...	214	...	...	...	...	...	...	...	...	Equatorial Guinea
...	...	...	...	...	33.2[37]	11[37]	252	...	15	72	—	—	...	3.6	1.00	Ethiopia
1,812	76.6	—	—	24.3	89.7	11	10[13]	...	...	...	...	...	...	...	...	Faeroe Islands
1,790[1]	100.0[1]	...	...	...	41.7[1]	8[1]	...	...	...	...	...	...	...	...	...	Falkland Islands
997[1]	59.4[1]	10.2[1]	—	30.4[1]	77.1[1]	8[1]	31	41.1[9]	83	110	...	—	—	8.5	39.40	Fiji
2,139	58.9[20]	40.8[20]	—0.3[20]—		84.6	18	7	3.1	84	112	1.0	1.4	[8]	10.6	352.40	Finland
2,027[11]	...	...	...	...	80.4[11]	19[11]	10	14.3	99	133	5.5	8.0	...	14.5	611.80	France
2,081	82.2[15,21]	—	—	17.8[15,21]	79.4	10	...	...	...	...	...	...	...	...	...	French Guiana
1,472	70.9	—	3.2	25.9	51.7	8	30[13]	...	...	109	...	...	...	...	...	French Polynesia
258	...	...	...	...	23.6	13	169	124.0	50	104	—	4.0	...	...	44.20[3]	Gabon
437[17]	...	...	...	...	...	...	281	...	49	93	—	—	...	8.0	8.20	Gambia, The
1,312	...	...	...	...	68.4	3	100[13]	...	...	...	...	...	...	...	...	Gaza Strip
1,383[6]	42.8[4]	57.2[4]	—	—	74.0[6]	21[6]	12	15.6	90	145	10.0[7]	12.5[7,39]	[8]	...	234.50[3]	Germany, East
1,871[11]	80.5[6]	19.5[6]	—	—	84.8[11]	18[11]	11	16.3	100	130	3.5[22]	3.5[22]	...	18.7	579.10	Germany, West
...	...	...	...	...	...	...	145	1,074.0	52	76	5.0[7]	11.5[7]	—	8.2	1.60	Ghana
1,464	100.0	—	—	—	46.2	10	17[13]	...	...	...	...	...	...	10.4	308.50	Gibraltar
1,190	67.3	32.7	—	—	69.3	12	16	13.1	95	149	3.7	3.7	...	10.5	160.80	Greece
2,525[9]	23.1[9]	—	—	76.9[9]	61.9[9]	10[9]	...	...	...	...	...	...	...	...	...	Greenland
749[12]	...	...	...	...	...	...	33[13]	...	85	98	4.0[7]	4.0[7]	—	15.6	21.90	Grenada
2,420[11]	58.1[21]	41.9[21]	—	...	87.1[11]	15[11]	17	106.4[4]	...	111	...	...	...	...	...	Guadeloupe
738[10]	97.6[10]	2.4[10]	—	...	78.8[10]	8[10]	...	...	100	...	...	...	...	12.9	177.70	Guam
317	...	...	...	...	70.8	11	99	92.0	52	105	2.0	4.0	...	7.6	8.90	Guatemala
977	89.0	11.0	—	...	83.9	28	10[13]	...	...	...	...	...	...	...	...	Guernsey
...	...	...	...	...	...	...	249	...	20	75	—	3.2	...	...	3.90[3]	Guinea
326	59.8	—	—	40.2	57.5	11	223	400.0	33	84	...	...	...	...	...	Guinea-Bissau
...	...	...	...	...	...	...	37	104.0	80	110	4.9[7]	7.4[7]	...	5.7	28.00	Guyana
123	...	...	...	...	...	...	170	156.0	34	82	2.0[22]	4.0[23]	1.2	...	3.70[3]	Haiti
429[20]	75.6[20]	16.7[20]	—	7.7[20]	70.2[20]	8[20]	106	82.0	69	98	2.5	5.0	2.5	8.0	9.80	Honduras
1,494	93.6	3.2	3.2	—	82.4	8	10	6.0	100	118	—	3[1]	...	...	...	Hong Kong
2,091	...	...	...	...	76.7	13	19	19.2	84	132	3.0[22]	24.0	[8]	3.6	36.70	Hungary
2,087	84.0[20]	14.2[20]	1.8[20]	—	101.0	19[15]	7	0.0	100	116	2.0	—	[8]	23.0	690.00	Iceland
...	...	...	...	...	...	...	148	500.0	55	99	2.2	4.4	25.0	2.1	1.00	India
66[4,17]	...	...	...	...	55.1[4,17]	9[4,17]	117	800.0	33	117	2.0	5.0	—	1.9	2.10	Indonesia
...	...	...	...	...	...	...	155	...	71	130	7.0[7]	20.0[7]	3.0[7]	8.1	68.90	Iran
592	65.5	26.4	7.0	1.1	60.3	6	94	...	84	121	5.0[7]	12.0[7,42]	—	...	15.20[3]	Iraq
1,764[43]	...	...	...	...	96.[43]		11	7.2	97	153	1.0	1.0	[8]	13.2	339.50	Ireland
1,274[1]	83.9[1]	7.0[1]	—	9.1[1]	81.2[1]	25[1]	10[13]	...	...	...	...	...	...	24.6	646.40	Isle of Man
1,688	96.0	4.0	—	—	88.5	13	16	3.1	98	119	0.8	5.7	—	3.4	133.70	Israel
1,660	91.1	8.9	—	—	69.1	12	12	11.3	99	140	1.2	11.9[22]	...	9.9	517.30	Italy
647[9]	81.0[9]	19.0[9]	—	—	77.0	7	23	102.0	96	115	2.5[7]	2.5[7]	—	7.8	44.40	Jamaica
643[15]	97.9[15]	2.1[15]	—	—	83.3[15]	56[15]	8	17.8	98	122	4.3	4.3	16.4	...	473.90[3]	Japan
1,782	82.0	18.0	—	—	86.8[6]	24[6]	10[13]	...	...	...	...	...	...	19.0	533.30	Jersey
1,061	93.6[15]	6.4[15]	—	—	61.8	4	57	...	97	120	—	—	—	3.8	25.90	Jordan
...	...	...	...	...	...	...	192	...	44	95	—	—	—	...	...	Kampuchea
633	47.6	...	52.4	...	58.0	15	113	168.0	28	93	...	—	—	6.4	5.00	Kenya
...	...	...	...	...	...	...	36[13]	...	44	...	—	—	—	...	...	Kiribati
...	...	...	...	...	...	...	31	41.0	100	135	...	...	...	...	10.10[3]	Korea, North
279[9,44]	97.8[9,44]	2.2[9,44]	—	—	60.0	12[9,44]	31	12.1[9]	83	121	1.5[22]	1.5[22]	...	2.6	12.90	Korea, South
1,082[21]	66.4[15]	28.5[15]	5.1[15]	—	71.7[15]	8[15]	23	11.3	100	...	—	—	...	7.1	401.80	Kuwait
96[16]	...	...	...	...	19.7[16]	7[16]	160	...	21	100	—	—	—	...	...	Laos
...	...	...	...	...	...	...	49	...	92	121	1.5	5.5	...	...	28.00[3]	Lebanon
410[5]	20.8[5]	0.4[5]	6.2[5]	72.6[5]	79.6[5,17]	10[5,17]	135	...	14	103	...	...	...	6.9	5.30	Lesotho
...	...	...	...	...	...	...	206	...	40	100	—	—	—	5.7	7.00	Liberia
719	...	...	...	...	52.7	13	118	80.0	96	153	1.0	1.4	1.6	...	105.10[3]	Libya
...	...	...	...	...	...	...	10[13]	...	...	...	...	...	...	...	...	Liechtenstein
1,880	93.3	6.7	—	—	80.9	20	10	0.0	100	140	4.1	4.1	...	2.2	97.30	Luxembourg
...	...	...	...	...	...	...	31[13]	...	...	107[6]	...	...	...	...	...	Macau
699[17]	...	...	...	...	57.9[17]	2[17]	90	...	23	109	—	8.3[29]	—	...	6.50[3]	Madagascar
420[6]	...	...	...	...	53.0[6]	8[6]	263	250.0	65	106	...	...	...	6.9	3.30	Malawi
635[21]	...	...	...	...	...	...	35	59.0	80	120	—	—	[8]	4.4	29.90	Malaysia
291	100.0	—	—	—	57.5[46]	5[46]	17	...	17	92	—	—	—	5.8	8.30	Maldives
178[5]	54.9[5]	37.5[5]	—	7.6[5]	58.8[5]	7[5]	291	...	16	76	—	2.0	—	1.7	0.80	Mali
1,569[15]	...	...	...	...	83.7[15]	19[15]	13	17.9	100	103	8.3[7]	8.3[7]	8.3[7]	8.9	106.90	Malta
1,722	69.0[10]	6.0[10]	11.3[10]	13.7[10]	75.9	15	19	...	...	116	...	...	...	...	...	Martinique
115[5]	...	...	...	...	97.8[5]	5[5]	214	...	37	90	—	2.0	—	2.8	4.50	Mauritania
1,139[9,21]	...	...	...	...	84.5[20,21]	8[20,21]	28	52.0	99	121	...	...	...	7.5	30.00	Mauritius
778	100.0	—	—	—	74.8	6	...	...	...	...	...	...	...	...	...	Mayotte
...	...	...	...	...	...	...	68	92.0	76	136	2.3	5.6	...	1.4	8.10	Mexico
2,630	100.0	...	...	...	77.6	14	10[13]	...	...	...	...	...	...	...	...	Monaco
2,508	25.9	33.0	1.1	40.0	89.1	14	58	140.0	100	116	...	...	...	...	14.70[3]	Mongolia
718[1]	100.0[1]	—	—	—	30.7[1]	5[1]	27[13]	...	100	...	...	...	...	...	...	Montserrat
233	92.8[47]	—	7.2[47]	—	59.8	10	118	327.0	60	111	0.2	0.4	—	2.8	5.00	Morocco
92[17,20]	...	...	...	...	70.2[17,20]	9[17,20]	241	300.0	9	72	...	...	...	...	3.40[3]	Mozambique
2,660[38]	100.0[38]	...	...	...	...	...	36[13]	...	...	...	—	—	[8]	14.2	178.50	Nauru
46[17,20]	...	...	...	...	61.5[17,20]	7[17,20]	196	850.0	16	92	—	—	—	5.0	1.30	Nepal
1,091	97.8	2.2	—	—	83.0	18	9	7.4	100	124	5.9	14.1	...	10.8	732.20	Netherlands, The
...	...	...	...	...	...	...	27[13]	...	...	112[6]	...	...	...	...	...	Netherlands Antilles
1,468	77.9	3.0	3.2	15.9	57.6	16	39[13]	...	...	110	...	...	...	...	...	New Caledonia
1,268[9,21]	...	...	...	...	77.7[9,21]	11[9,21]	12	11.8	100	128	—	—	[8]	12.5	345.80	New Zealand
634	—91.7—		8.3	...			93	65.0	58	108	4.0	11.0	0.5	14.6	33.10	Nicaragua
83[17]	...	...	...	...	62.0[17]	9[17]	228	420.0	36	96	...	11.0[24,29]	...	4.1	3.50	Niger
...	...	...	...	...	...	...	173	1,500.0	37	86	6.0[7]	6.0[7]	...	2.5	2.50	Nigeria
1,674[9]	100.0[9]	—	...	...	56.7[20]	14[20]	10[13]	...	...	...	...	...	...	9.6	136.10	Niue
...	...	...	...	...	37.7[9]	9[9]	10[13]	...	...	...	...	...	...	8.4	124.90	Norfolk Island

Health services (continued)

country	year	physicians	dentists	nurses	pharmacists	midwives	population per physician	year	number	general	specialized	medical centres	rural	government	private non-profit	private for profit	hospital beds per 10,000 pop.
										kinds (%)				ownership (%)			
Norway	1985	10,110	4,397	44,353[33]	3,041[6]	[33]	411	1985	1,192	6.2	91.9	...	1.9	...	...	...	165
Oman	1986	1,096	80	2,533	224	33[6]	1,175	1986	45	—100.0—	—	—	100.0	—	—	22
Pacific Is., Trust Terr. of the																	
Marshall Islands	1985	17	2	51	...	...	2,111	1985	2	100	—	—	—	100	—	—	15
Micronesia, Fed. States of	1985	36	13	257	7	...	2,542	1985	4	100	—	—	—	100	—	—	36
Northern Mariana Islands	1986	23	4	103	2	2	898	1986	3	33.3	—	—	67.7	100	—	—	36
Palau	1986[28]	10	3	82	1	...	1,397	1986	1	100	—	—	—	100	—	—	49
Pakistan	1987	51,020	1,539[19]	16,661	2,785[19]	10,650	2,086	1987	895[12,15]	62.3[15]	6.1[15]	...	31.6[15]	82.2[15]	1.1[15]	16.7[15]	6
Panama	1986	2,596	519	2,357	157[4]	...	858	1986	58	...	...	...	...	85.7[47]	—14.3[47]—	35
Papua New Guinea	1986	283	16[20]	3,228[20,33]	9[20]	33	12,015	1980	390	5.1	—	53.6	41.2	46.2	53.8	—	45[11]
Paraguay	1982	2,201	855[10]	2,636[10]	860[10]	783[10]	1,379	1985	143[16]	63.6[16]	4.9[16]	...	31.5[16]	91.6[16]	8.4[16]	—	9
Peru	1986	19,237	4,641	14,728	4,758	3,303	1,051	1985	349	—100.0—	—	—	49.9	—50.1—	15
Philippines	1982	46,579	1,090[1,28]	9,644[1,28]	539[1,28]	9,470[1,28]	1,090	1984	1,602	...	...	...	...	25.2	—74.8—	13
Pitcairn Island	1985	...	...	1[28]	—	—	...	...	...	...	...	...	...	...	...	...	...
Poland	1987	75,473	17,391	178,387	16,109	20,773	498	1986	706	60.8	39.2	...	...	...	...	53
Portugal	1987	25,696	1,078	29,525[9]	5,199	824[9]	400	1986	590	24.4	14.1	61.5	—	84.9	—15.1—	47
Puerto Rico	1984	7,560	741[20]	14,392[20]	1,436[20]	199[20]	433	1980	111	72.1	27.9	—	—	48.6	19.8	31.5	38[11]
Qatar	1986	543	66	1,161[28]	135[28]	70[1,28]	696	1985	3	33.0	67.0	—	—	100.0	—	—	29[19]
Réunion	1987	959	244	1,942[19]	184	102[19]	589	1984	21	36.4[5]	18.1[5]	—	45.5[5]	74.2[47]	—25.8[47]—	64[9]
Romania	1987[28]	40,706	7,356	81,031[15]	6,471	12,248[15]	567	1987	437[1]	56.8[1]	32.5[1]	—	10.8[1]	...	...	94
Rwanda	1985[28]	178	9	559	9	616[1]	21,943	1985[21]	220	—13.6—	—86.4—	100.0	—	—	9
St. Helena and Ascension	1986	3	1	30[10]	...	7[10]	2,367	1986	8	12.5	12.5	75.0	—	100.0	—	—	76
St. Kitts and Nevis	1987	22	5	231	79	123[20]	2,090	1987	4	...	...	...	...	...	...	...	56
St. Lucia	1985	43	5	225[33]	16[6]	33	3,185	1986	5	20.0	20.0	—	60.0	...	...	...	36
St. Pierre and Miquelon	1986	13	3	20[5]	...	1[5]	473	1986	1	100.0	—	—	—	100.0	—	—	163
St. Vincent	1987	39	2	236	...	...	2,874	1987	9	11.1	22.2	11.1	55.6	88.9	—11.1—	41
San Marino	1987	60	—	...	...	...	378	1987	...	...	...	...	...	...	...	...	66
São Tomé and Príncipe	1985	53	—	157[1]	1[1]	131[1]	2,016	1978	16	12.5	—	87.5	—	...	...	...	78
Saudi Arabia	1986	12,707	1,084	24,955	479	...	945	1986	181	...	...	...	...	77.9	—22.1—	24
Senegal	1984	470[15]	50	2,360[1,28]	167	451	12,987[15]	1984	87	18.4	29.9	51.7	—	100.0	—	—	10[15]
Seychelles	1985	35	8	288	3	131[10]	1,864	1985	6	16.7	16.7	66.7	—	100.0	—	—	51
Sierra Leone	1983	197	30[20]	1,758[20,33]	8[20]	33	17,906	1984	109	5.5	5.5	54.1	34.9	89.9	—10.1—	13
Singapore	1985	2,631	496	8,395	436	650	972	1987	21	...	...	...	...	42.9	—57.1—	37
Solomon Islands	1986	32	15[9]	487	...	556	8,790	1986	8	100.0	—	—	—	75.0	25.0	—	52
Somalia	1986	450	2	1,834	180	556	13,315	1985	...	...	...	...	...	...	...	...	9
South Africa	1986[34]	22,525	3,704	88,795	7,557	...	1,510	1980	595	...	...	...	...	40.7	—59.3—	41
Bophuthatswana	1987	106	...	2,672	...	...	18,300	1987	163	—6.7—	—93.3—	...	...	...	33
Ciskei	1986[28]	283	7	3,855	10	54	3,080	1986	97	5.2	1.0	92.8	1.0	99.0	1.0	—	41
Transkei	1985	240	...	4,112[4]	...	...	14,200	1987	31	...	...	...	...	...	...	21
Venda	1985	25	...	839	...	...	18,400	1985	54	5.5	1.9	—92.6—	...	...	...	34
South West Africa/Namibia	1986	276	41	3,916	...	...	4,238	1986	61	...	...	...	...	...	...	57
Spain	1986	131,080	5,722	147,462	31,118	6,103	295	1983	976	43.2	56.8	—	—	40.1	15.1	44.8	47
Sri Lanka	1986[28]	2,222	275[15]	8,019	441[15]	3,808[15]	7,253	1982	493	5.9	31.4	20.7	42.0	100.0	—	—	28[19]
Sudan, The	1981[28]	2,169	334	13,693	58	376	9,369	1981	160	21.9	5.6	—	72.5	...	...	9
Suriname	1985	219	21[4]	660[4]	134	88[4]	1,798	1980	17	29.4	17.6	47.1	5.9	58.8	29.4	11.8	50[9]
Swaziland	1984	80	13	84[4]	10[4]	731[4]	7,971	1984	23	30.4	8.7	—60.9—	56.5	—43.5—	25
Sweden	1985	21,000	9,243	72,386[9,33]	4,234	33	398	1985	1,000[6]	10.36	89.7[6]	—	—	...	...	137
Switzerland	1985	15,090	3,117	26,998[11]	1,366	1,650[10]	433	1983	372	52.7	47.3	—	—	...	...	102
Syria	1987	8,146	2,456	9,786	2,960	3,049	1,347	1987	206	79.6	20.4	—	—	22.8	—77.2—	11
Taiwan	1987	17,045	3,750[19]	30,174	8,528[19]	2,380	1,148	1987	1,086	6.3	5.5	88.2	—	...	...	44
Tanzania	1984	1,065	18[4]	8,291[15]	25[5]	2,887[15]	19,775	1982	3,032	4.9	—	87.2	7.9	...	...	11[11]
Thailand	1985	8,650	1,451	60,691	3,371	7,716	5,988	1985	923	89.4	3.4	—7.3—	75.5	—24.5—	16
Togo	1985	230	4[20]	1,116	50	559[20]	12,992	1979	65	10.8	4.6	61.5	23.1	96.9	3.1	—	13[15]
Tokelau	1987[28]	3	1	...	...	...	567	1987	3	—	—	—	100.0	100.0	—	—	212
Tonga	1987	47	11	216	2	27	2,017	1982	9	44.4	—	55.6	—	100.0	—	—	30
Trinidad and Tobago	1985	1,103	129	3,344[33]	496	33	1,071	1985	31	8.0[10]	16.0[10]	40.0[10]	36.0[10]	60.0[10]	—	40.0[10]	35
Tunisia	1987	3,474	550[10]	9,778	1,264	...	2,198	1987	148	—16.9—	—83.1—	100.0	—	—	21
Turkey	1986	37,142	8,410	32,392	12,866	19,127	1,388	1986	736	—87.2—	—12.8—	84.6	—15.4—	21
Turks and Caicos Islands	1987[28]	5	1[11]	36[33]	...	33	2,063	1987	5	20.0	—	—	80.0	100.0	—	—	27
Tuvalu	1985[28]	4	2	36[33]	1	33	2,075	1985	8	11.1	—	—	88.9	100.0	—	—	36
Uganda	1984	700	17[1]	6,778[1,33]	27[1]	33	20,300	1981	485	15.5	1.2	83.3	—	84.5	15.5	—	15[6]
U.S.S.R.	1988	1,232,600[30]	30	2,880,000[15,33]	86,000[11]	33	229[32]	1988	23,700	...	...	...	...	100.0	—	—	131
United Arab Emirates	1984[28]	1,840	95[15]	2,814[15]	89[15]	...	666	1984	20[6]	50.0[1]	27.3[1]	4.5[1]	18.2[1]	95.5[1]	4.5[1]	—	40
United Kingdom	1985	84,700	22,988	284,116[33]	15,108[15]	33	668	1985	2,501[1]	...	...	...	...	100.0	—	—	74
United States	1986	576,700	156,000	1,531,000	156,960[9]	2,700	419	1986	6,841	84.9	15.1	—	—	32.3	51.4	16.3	53
Uruguay	1986	6,529	2,799	15,200[10]	560	282	397	1986	48[21]	—29.2—	—	70.8	100.0	—	—	30
Vanuatu	1986	27	2[15]	303	3[15]	5[15]	5,191	1980	21	14.3	—	52.4	33.3	47.6	52.4	—	35[6]
Venezuela	1986	24,626	6,666	53,882	4,063[10]	...	722	1986	534	...	...	...	...	42.9	—57.1—	27
Vietnam	1986	19,100[30]	...	44,080[1]	11,900[28]	13,700[1,28]	3,162[30]	1984	10,768	14.6	6.5	78.9	—	100.0	—	—	35[19]
Virgin Islands (U.S.)	1985	167	...	241[26]	...	...	622	1985	...	...	...	...	...	...	...	...	49
Wallis and Futuna	1981[25]	4	1	27	1	5	2,800	1982	3	33.3	—	—	66.7	100.0	—	—	77
West Bank	...	...	...	...	...	...	...	1986	17	...	...	...	...	52.9	—47.1—	16
Western Sahara[49]	...	...	...	...	...	...	...	1982[27]	2	50.0	—	50.0	—	100.0	—	—	9
Western Samoa	1982	11	—	...	2	...	13,000	1984	30	3.3	—	—	96.7	100.0	—	—	37[41]
Yemen (Aden)	1981	63	7	344	4	42[28]	2,476	1986	54	12.2[20]	16.4[20]	34.7[20]	36.7[20]	98.0[20]	2.0[20]	—	20
Yemen (Şan'ā')	1986	652	18[11]	1,733[11]	29[11]	261[11]	3,416	1984	34	63.3[15]	3.3[15]	—	33.3[15]	86.7[15]	13.3[15]	—	6
Yugoslavia	1984	1,069	41	2,440	114	113	6,435	1985	425[20]	32.5[20]	30.3[20]	37.2[20]	—	...	...	61
Zaire	1986	40,329	9,278	67,468[11]	5,047[11]	7,747[11]	577	1982	942[10]	37.3[10]	38.9[10]	23.8[10]	—	40.9[10]	44.6[10]	14.5[10]	26
Zambia	1982	2,000	58[10]	14,661[10]	414[10]	3,043[10]	14,092	1987	965	8.2	0.3	19.0	72.5	80.9	19.1	—	32[11]
Zimbabwe	1984	798	42	5,167	44	1,392	8,076	1984	1,202	3.7	1.3	—95.0—	72.5	—27.5—	23
	1986	1,257	124	12,391	313	2,320	6,687										

[1]1981. [2]Excludes four specialized hospitals. [3]May include expenditures at the intermediate and local levels of government and/or the costs of additional services such as national health insurance and family-planning programs. [4]1978. [5]1977. [6]1983. [7]Includes funds for old-age retirement, incapacitating disability, work injury, and death insurance. [8]Government provides remainder of the cost of benefits. [9]1985. [10]1979. [11]1984. [12]Excludes medical centres. [13]Regional average. [14]1972. [15]1982. [16]1975. [17]General hospitals only. [18]Amounts vary internally. [19]1986. [20]1980. [21]Government hospitals only. [22]Minimum on a graduated scale. [23]Maximum on a graduated scale. [24]Employed women only. [25]Includes outpatients. [26]1974. [27]Public sector only. [28]Government-employed health personnel only. [29]Includes family allowances. [30]Includes physicians practicing dentistry. [31]Employer provides entire cost. [32]Republic of Cyprus only.

rate per 10,000 pop.	general	specialized	medical centres	rural	bed occu-pancy rate (%)	aver-age length of stay (days)	under age 5 per 1,000 live newborn 1985–90	maternal mortality per 100,000 live births 1980–84	popu-lation with access to safe water (latest) (%)	food supply (% of FAO require-ment) 1983	indiv. (% of earn-ings)	em-ployer (% of payroll)	govt. (% of covered earnings)	public health expendi-tures (% of natl. budget)	public health expendi-tures per capita (U.S.$)	country
1,663	87.1	—12.9—			84.0	9	9	3.9	99	121	4.4[7]	16.8[7]	4.9[7]	10.5	542.00	Norway
1,179	...	...	...	...	86.7	5	157	...	23	...	...	...	...	5.0	162.00	Oman
																Pacific Is., Trust Terr. of the
							36[13]	...	...	...	...	...	...	26.1	120.20	Marshall Islands
2,171	100	—	—	—			36[13]	...	...	...	...	...	...		100.00	Micronesia, Fed. States of
1,170	93.3	—	—	6.7			36[13]	...						...	511.60	Northern Mariana Islands
1,233	...	...	...	...			36[13]	...							229.00	Palau
							165	600.0	44	93	—	7.0	—	1.0	0.60	Pakistan
692			·		64.5[6]	7[6]	33	66.0	63	105	1.0	8.0	0.8[7]	15.8	114.20	Panama
253[17]							84	1,000.0	16	82				9.6	21.90	Papua New Guinea
							61	469.0	25	121	9.5[7]	16.5[7]	1.5[7]	5.8	9.40	Paraguay
416[15]					88.2[15]	14[15]	122	314.0	55	92	2.5	5.0	—	5.3	13.00	Peru
							72	80.0	64	104	1.3	1.3	8	4.8	3.80	Philippines
							...	...						15.4	303.00	Pitcairn Island
1,272					80.5[15]	17[15]	19	14.2	67	125	—	33.0[7]	8	...	182.30[3]	Poland
846	—92.8—	7.2	—		65.7	14	20	18.7	92	129	8.0[7]	21.0[7]	...	...	71.10[3]	Portugal
1,227	95.0	5.0	—	—	64.8	8	17	10.4	...	...				...	...	Puerto Rico
1,328[1]	54.3[1]	45.7[1]	—	—			38	...	95	...				...	...	Qatar
836[5,17]					82.0[5,17]	12[5,17]	14	...	...	129				...	...	Réunion
							28	152.0	77	128	—	7.0[22]	8	0.8	5.00	Romania
85[44]					42.8[44]	7[44]	205	210.0	60	83				4.5	1.50	Rwanda
							...	...						...	...	St. Helena and Ascension
1,028[17,20]					58.9[17,20]	10[17,20]	27[13]	90.9[1]	75	...				...	...	St. Kitts and Nevis
916							33[13]	...	70	102[6]	5.0[7]	5.0[7]		...	...	St. Lucia
							11[13]	...	...	...				...	...	St. Pierre and Miquelon
629[17,19]					64.5[17,19]	7[17,19]	33[13]	...	75	100[6]	—	—	—	12.7	43.10	St. Vincent
1,435[20]					69.5	11[20]	17[13]	...						...	...	San Marino
1,733	76.1	—	23.9	—	68.7	12	178[13]	...	52	104				...	...	São Tomé and Príncipe
757[21]							98	...	93	129				...	472.60[3]	Saudi Arabia
378[4,5]	34.2[5]	—	54.8[5]	11.0[5]	75.1[4,5]	9.6[4,5]	222	530.0	45	98	3.0[23]	3.0[23]	—	4.7	5.00	Senegal
1,451[17]					66.6[17]	6[17]	188[13]	...	82	...	5.0[7]	10.0[7]	—	13.1	37.20	Seychelles
13[17,20]					77.1[17,20]	18[17,20]	291	450.0	24	79	—	—	—	7.5	3.70	Sierra Leone
1,200					73.0[1]	10[1]	11	9.6	100	120	—	—	8	6.5	121.50	Singapore
							39[13]	...	27	80	—	—	—	9.1	11.50	Solomon Islands
							252	1,100.0	36	90				3.2	2.20	Somalia
							96	...	...	122			8	13.40[3]	...	South Africa
							103[13]	...						5.4	26.00	Bophuthatswana
488					79.0	16	103[13]	...						...	...	Ciskei
							103[13]	...						...	...	Transkei
1,130					102.4	11	103[13]	...						...	...	Venda
							176	...	...	83				...	...	South West Africa/Namibia
914[1]	91.7[1]	8.3[1]	—	—	73.0[1]	15	11	10.0	95	136	4.8[7]	25.8[7]	—	13.1	170.30	Spain
1,623	39.9	15.0	0.8	44.3	88.3	6	43	90.0	37	107	—	—	8	6.1	7.60	Sri Lanka
81[17]							175	...	51	74	—	—	—	1.3	1.30	Sudan, The
820	83.6	2.4	8.0	6.0	41.6	15	37	75.0	98	119				3.7	47.60	Suriname
506							173	...	38	111	—	—	—	8.6	19.30	Swaziland
2,002					85.2	21	7	4.3	100	115	—	9.5	...	1.1	76.50	Sweden
1,278	85.9	14.1	—	—	80.8	24	8	6.7	99	128	—	—	—	13.1	384.70	Switzerland
456					55.7	5	63	280.0	80	128	—	—	—	1.1	7.80	Syria
							...	...	...	...	1.4[7]	5.6[7]	3.2[7]	...	80.60[3]	Taiwan
706	66.5	—	13.1	20.4			174	370.0	52	101	5.0[7]	5.0[7]	—	4.9	3.50	Tanzania
							49	270.0	70	111	—	2.0[24]	—	5.7	8.80	Thailand
							152	84.0	35	97				3.6	3.20	Togo
965[15]	—	—	—	100.0[15]	12.0[15]	11[15]								4.8	50.60	Tokelau
718	97.6	—	2.4	—	56.8	10	30[13]	...	75	108				...	...	Tonga
980[10,48]					88.6[10,48]	5[10,48]	23	56.3	99	124	2.8[7]	5.6[7]	8	5.9	113.90	Trinidad and Tobago
652[11]					65.5[11]	8[11]	99	...	89	119	5.0	15.0	—	6.5	29.20	Tunisia
515	78.3[1]	19.1[1]	—	2.6[1]	44.1[1]	9[1]	92	207.0	78	126	5.0	6.0	—	2.2	5.20	Turkey
							27[13]	...						9.1	137.00	Turks and Caicos Islands
1,368	40.9	—	—	59.1	51.5[17]	12.2[17]	36[13]	...						...	...	Tuvalu
							169	300.0	16	89	—	—	—	2.4	51.60	Uganda
							27	...	100	134	—	4.4[22]	—	...	227.90[3]	U.S.S.R.
1,032[15]	78.4[1]	15.4[1]	0.8[1]	5.4[1]	69.6[15]	7[15]	38	...	100	...				6.2	185.00	United Arab Emirates
1,216					75.8	10	11	7.0	100	124	9.0	11.45	—	12.6	410.50	United Kingdom
1,458	96.9[11]	3.1[11]	—	—	68.4	7	12	8.3	100	139	1.3	1.3	...	11.6	493.60	United States
442					70.8	18	30	44.8	83	101	3.0	4.0	...	4.8	23.70	Uruguay
912	40.5	—	14.0	45.5	33.6	8	39[13]	...	55	88	—	—	1.5[7]	...	...	Vanuatu
							43	56.8	83	105	2.0	4.25[22]	1.5[22]	8.1	58.60	Venezuela
1,587	12.4	8.1	56.6	22.9	80.7	7	91	110	41	104				...	...	Vietnam
							27[13]	...						...	...	Virgin Islands (U.S.)
1,100	76.0	—	—	24.0	49.4	13	30[13]	...						...	...	Wallis and Futuna
901					73.9	5	100[13]	...						...	...	West Bank
226	98.2	—	1.8	—	36.9	5	105[13]	...						...	...	Western Sahara[49]
823	62.0	—	—	38.0	25.4	7	30[13]	...	95	94[6]	—	—	—	9.3	18.50	Western Samoa
277[11]							196	100.0	53	97				...	...	Yemen (Aden)
95	89.0	0.4	—	10.6	73.4	18	196	...	37	93				4.7	5.60	Yemen (Şan'ā')
1,275	52.1[50]	23.5[50]	24.4[50]		85.9	15	28	21.0	68	142	8.7	—	—	—	123.30[3]	Yugoslavia
474[10,17]					71.6[10,17]	12[10,17]	161	800.0	22	97				3.2	2.10	Zaire
1,249	—75.7—	—24.3—			68.5	7	127	109.0	49	93	5.0[23]	5.0[22]	—	7.2	9.00	Zambia
867	35.4	24.8	—39.8—		69.7	7	113	145.0	52	86				6.2	12.30	Zimbabwe

[33]Nurses includes midwives. [34]Registered personnel; all may not be present and working in the country. [35]1976. [36]General hospitals includes specialized and rural hospitals. [37]Rural hospitals only. [38]1971. [39]Excludes hazardous occupations such as mining. [40]1973. [41]1987. [42]Excludes oilfield operations. [43]Public general and specialized hospitals only. [44]General and specialized hospitals only. [45]Peninsular Malaysia only. [46]Central Hospital only. [47]Based on bed ownership. [48]Excludes specialized hospitals and medical centres. [49]Settlements of Smara, Boujdour, and El Aaiun only. [50]Based on patient-days.

Social protection

This table summarizes the principal social protective activities of the countries of the world. Because the administrative structure, financing, manning, and scope of programmed tasks vary so greatly from country to country, the basis of the comparisons is most often either manpower or finance.

The provision of social security programs for specific social needs, however, is summarized simply in terms of the existence or nonexistence of a specific benefit program because of the great complexity of national programs in terms of eligibility, coverage, term, age limits, financing, payments, and so on. Activities connected with a particular type of benefit often take place at more than one governmental level or through more than one agency at the same level. The data shown here are summarized from the U.S. Social Security Administration's *Social Security Programs Throughout the World* (biennial). A bullet symbol (●) indicates that a country has at least one program within the defined area; in some cases it may have several. A blank space indicates that no program existed providing the benefit shown; ellipses [...] indicate that no information was available as to whether a program existed.

Data given for social security expenditure as a percentage of total central governmental expenditure are taken from the International Monetary Fund's *Government Finance Statistics Yearbook,* which provides the most

comparable analytical series on the consolidated accounts of the central governments, governmentally administered social security funds, and independent national agencies, all usually separate accounting entities, through which these services may be provided in a given country.

Data on the finances of social security programs are taken in large part from the International Labour Office's *The Cost of Social Security* (triennial), supplemented by national data sources.

Figures for manpower in police and fire services are from a variety of national sources, principally census and manpower surveys, from the 1976–86 census period. The relative scarcity of international sources and data on these topics is in part a reflection of the fact that in many countries these functions are viewed as matters of merely local concern and, as they are not conducted or directly funded by the central government, tend to be ignored in the data collection and publication programs of the central government. The manpower figures refer, for the most part, to full-time, paid professional staff, excluding clerical support and volunteer staff. Fire fighters employed by private companies are included. Personnel in military service who perform either police or fire functions are presumed to be employed in their principal activity, military service. Figures for criminal offenses known to police, usually excluding civil offenses and minor traffic

Social protection

country	social security																
	programs available, 1987					expenditures, 1985 (% of total central govt.)	finances										
							year	receipts					expenditures			
	old-age invalidity, death	sickness and maternity[a]	work injury	unemployment	family allowances			total ('000,000 natl. cur.)	insured persons (%)	employers (%)	government (%)	other (%)	total ('000,000 natl. cur.)	benefits (%)	administration (%)	other (%)
Afghanistan			●			...	...	...	...	...	...	...	...	...	...	...
Albania	●	●	●		●	...	...	...	...	...	...	...	...	...	...	...
Algeria	●	●	●		●	...	1984	11,086.0	...	...	...	...	11,417.0	...	...	...
American Samoa	●	...	...	...	...	...	1980	2.3	29.3	40.9	...	29.7	0.6	100.0	—	—
Andorra	...	...	...	...	...	...	...	...	...	...	...	...	...	...	...	...
Angola						...	...	...	...	...	...	...	...	...	...	...
Anguilla	●		●			...	1986	...	...	...	...	...	0.1	...	...	...
Antigua and Barbuda	●		●			...	1983	13.0	29.2	48.7	—	22.1	4.2	66.1	33.9	...
Argentina	●	●	●	●	●	32.6[6]	1983	60.5	29.5	23.2	30.8	16.5	58.9	78.9	3.4	17.7
Aruba	●					[8]	...	...	...	...	...	...	...	...	...	...
Australia	●	●	●	●	●	26.0	1982–83	25,638.4	13.5	13.3	69.3	3.9	23,084.9	95.6	4.0	0.4
Austria	●	●	●	●	●	45.8[6]	1983	303,603.0	28.6	46.5	21.5	3.4	295,799	95.2	2.5	2.3
Bahamas, The	●	●	●			10.9	1983	48.5	23.2	38.0	5.1	33.7	19.9	77.0	21.8	1.2
Bahrain	●		●			1.4[6]	1983	47.1	24.9	49.9	—	25.2	9.3	61.5	16.5	22.0
Bangladesh	...	...	●			2.0[5, 6]	1983	29.0	19.4	43.4	4.3	32.9	13.0	94.9	5.1	—
Barbados	●	●	●	●		16.2	1983	135.5	35.0	36.2	3.3	25.5	78.3	92.7	4.6	2.7
Belgium	●	●	●	●	●	39.5	1983	1,180,799.7	19.6	38.1	38.0	4.4	1,172,396.4	94.6	4.3	1.2
Belize	●	●	●			5.5	1983	11.5	7.3	77.3	3.0	12.3	5.7	89.1	10.7	0.2
Benin	●	●	●		●	8.7[6, 9]	1983	7,001.7	21.3	78.6	—	0.1	6,200.2	95.0	5.0	—
Bermuda	●					...	...	...	...	...	...	...	...	...	...	...
Bhutan	...	...	...	...	...	...	...	...	...	...	...	...	...	...	...	...
Bolivia	●	●	●		●	4.9[2]	1983	41,325.3	25.5	34.8	24.2	15.5	31,679.2	84.8	14.6	0.7
Botswana			●			2.8[6]	1983	—	...	...	...	...	11.06	...	...	...
Brazil	●	●	●		●	20.7	1983	6,823,360.0	15.2	74.7	8.0	2.2	6,753,246.0	93.0	6.9	0.1
British Virgin Islands	...	●					1982	...	...	...	...	...	0.2	...	...	...
Brunei	●	...	...	...	...	...	1981	...	...	...	...	...	2.5[11]	...	...	...
Bulgaria	●	●	●		●	...	1983	2,953.7	...	...	...	...	2,953.7	100.0	...	...
Burkina Faso	●	●	●		●	8.2	1983	9,322.8	23.4	74.1	0.1	2.4	5,891.2	67.3	27.2	5.5
Burma	●	●	●			0.3	1983	37.1	19.9	59.8	17.8	2.4	25.5	70.2	18.5	11.4
Burundi	●		●		●	0.7[11]	1983	890.0	32.1	41.0	11.2	15.7	502.5	77.9	18.4	3.7
Cameroon	●		●		●	4.2	1983	42,817.0	11.1	69.0	—	19.9	16,536.0	91.2	—	8.8
Canada	●	●	●	●	●	27.2	1983	65,451.7	11.3	15.3	63.7	9.7	60,701.0	96.5	2.6	0.9
Cape Verde	●	●	●		●	...	...	...	...	...	...	...	...	...	...	...
Cayman Islands	●	...	●			2.1[6]	...	...	...	...	...	...	...	...	...	...
Central African Republic	●		●		●	6.2[6, 12]	1983	2,283.5	9.9	88.7	—	1.4	1,922.0	55.8	35.9	8.3
Chad	●		●		●	1.9[13]	1983	230.9	13.8	84.8	—	1.4	203.5	23.1	75.3	1.6
Chile	●	●	●	●	●	48.5	1983	262,412.6	30.8	2.1	48.5	18.6	224,473.7	90.3	8.2	1.5
China	●	●	●			...	...	...	...	...	...	...	...	...	...	...
Christmas Island	●	●	●	●	●	...	...	...	...	...	...	...	...	...	...	...
Cocos (Keeling) Islands	●	●	●	●	●	...	1985	0.2	...	...	...	...	0.2	...	...	...
Colombia	●	●	●		●	19.3[5, 6]	1983	78,006.0	22.9	49.3	10.8	17.0	67,996.0	88.3	11.6	0.1
Comoros	...	...	...	...	...	...	1983	40.7	100.0	—	—	—	54.3	17.4	62.3	20.3
Congo	●		●		●	0.4[7]	1983	15,272.8	12.1	80.2	—	7.7	7,256.7	66.6	21.3	12.1
Cook Islands						...	...	...	...	...	...	...	...	...	...	...
Costa Rica	●	●	●		●	22.9	1983	11,702.1	28.4	47.0	18.5	6.1	7,780.5	88.8	5.1	6.1
Côte d'Ivoire	●		●		●	3.1[6, 17]	1983	29,125.0	61.9	17.7	—	20.4	16,337.7	78.4	9.1	12.5
Cuba	●	●	●			...	1983	1,491.5	—	44.3	55.7	—	1,491.5	96.6	—	3.4
Cyprus[18]	●	●	●	●		17.6	1983	95.0	28.6	42.4	20.4	8.6	56.6	98.1	1.7	0.2
Czechoslovakia	●	●	●		●	...	1983	105,190.0	—	3.7	94.6	1.7	105,190.0	99.7	0.3	—
Denmark	●	●	●	●	●	33.8[5]	1983	149,307.6	3.3	8.1	85.9	2.7	143,850.2	97.1	2.9	—
Djibouti	●		●		●	8.3[9]	1979	1,352.2	...	...	...	...	1,115.7	...	...	...
Dominica	●	●	●			1.4[9]	1983	7.1	27.4	45.6	—	27.0	2.0	56.7	43.3	—
Dominican Republic	●	●	●			7.0	1980	136.8	...	...	43.6	4.4	123,852	87.2	8.0	4.8
Ecuador	●	●	●		●	0.9[6]	1983	30,616.0	28.9	39.9	0.8	30.4	23,344.0	64.6	22.5	12.9
Egypt	●	●	●	●		11.6	1984	2,796.6	...	...	...	...	1,435.1	...	...	...
El Salvador	●	●	●			2.4	1983	288.7	27.9	35.9	12.2	24.2	178.0	86.3	13.7	—
Equatorial Guinea	...	...	...	...	...	...	1983	43.0	4.7	95.3	—	—	20.0	30.0	70.0	—
Ethiopia	●		●			3.4[17]	1983	126.5	31.6	65.3	—	3.1	106.3	98.1	1.9	—
Faeroe Islands	●	...	...	...	●	...	...	...	...	...	...	...	...	...	...	...
Falkland Islands	●	...	...	...	●	...	...	...	...	...	...	...	...	...	...	...

violations, are taken in part from Interpol's *International Crime Statistics* (biennial) and a variety of national sources; supplemental information about the constitution of various national police forces may be found in JOHN ANDRADE, *World Police & Paramilitary Forces* (1985). Criminal offense data for certain countries refer to cases disposed of in court, rather than to complaints. Virtually all data on fire alarms and on expenditure for police and fire services are taken from national statistical sources. Data for fire alarms usually exclude nonemergency calls, medical emergencies, and fire code inspection visits but may include false fire alarms to which a normal response with personnel and equipment was made.

The figures for military manpower refer to full-time, active-duty military service and exclude reserve, militia, paramilitary, and similar organizations. Because of the difficulties attached to the analysis of data on military manpower and budgets (including problems such as data withheld on national security grounds, or the publication of budgetary data specifically intended to hide actual expenditure, or the complexity of long-term financing of purchases of military matériel [how much was actually spent as opposed to what was committed, offset by nonmilitary transfers, etc.]), extensive use is made of the principal international analytical tools: publications such as those of the International Institute for Strategic Studies

(*The Military Balance* and *Strategic Survey*), the Stockholm International Peace Research Institute (*World Armaments and Disarmament,* SIPRI *Yearbook*), and the U.S. Arms Control and Disarmament Agency (*World Military Expenditures and Arms Transfers*).

The data on military expenditures are from the sources identified above, as well as from the IMF's *Government Finance Statistical Yearbook* and country statistical publications.

a. Sickness and maternity refers to cash benefits for sickness and maternity. Countries must provide both benefits to be included. In many countries medical care and hospital coverage are also provided for sickness and maternity.

b. A police officer is a full-time, paid professional, performing domestic security functions. Data include administrative staff, but exclude clerical employees, volunteers, and members of paramilitary groups.

c. A fire fighter is a full-time, paid, professional. Data include administrative staff, but exclude clerical employees and volunteers.

d. Includes all active-duty personnel, regular and conscript, performing national security functions. Excludes reserves, paramilitary forces, border patrols, and gendarmeries.

e. Constant prices of 1984.

police protection (latest)			fire protection (latest)			military protection								arms trade, 1986 ('000,000 U.S.$)		country
offenses (reported to police) per 100,000 population	population per police officer[b]	government expenditure per 1,000 population (U.S.$)	fire alarms per 100,000 population	population per fire fighter[c]	government expenditure per 1,000 population (U.S.$)	manpower, 1988[d]		expenditure, 1985								
						total ('000)	per 1,000 population	total '000,000 U.S.$	per capita[e]	% of central government expenditure	% of GDP or GNP	imports	exports	
...	540[1]	...	...	...	...	55.0	3.8	287[2]	21[2]	64.4[2]	7.7[2]	600	0	Afghanistan
...	550	...	...	...	...	42.0	13.3	143	47	10.9	5.3	0	0	Albania
1,673	840	...	...	...	...	139.0	5.8	1,364	60	6.2	2.5	575	0	Algeria
5,386	460	17,676	180	850	8,126	—	3	—	—	—	—	0	...	American Samoa
3,009	220	...	...	...	...	—	—	...	...	...	...	...	...	Andorra
240	14[4]	...	...	...	...	100.0	10.7	690[5]	99[5]	25.0[5]	8.7[5]	1,200	0	Angola
2,102	100	24,233	...	...	...	—	3	...	...	...	...	...	...	Anguilla
2,718	120	41,624	...	...	...	0.75	8.9[5]	...	...	...	...	...	...	Antigua and Barbuda
1,102	1,270	8,429[7]	...	...	...	95.0	3.0	2,368	76	12.9	3.3	30	5	Argentina
1,631	...	...	...	...	...	—	3	—	—	—	—	...	...	Aruba
6,699	450	16,132	...	...	...	70.5	4.3	5,105	315	9.2	2.9	800	0	Australia
5,646	470	...	...	...	...	54.7	7.2	849[2]	112[2]	3.3[2]	1.3[2]	10	330	Austria
5,781	150	...	...	...	...	0.6	2.4	9[2]	40[2]	2.5[2]	0.5[2]	...	...	Bahamas, The
348	180	...	236	...	...	2.9	6.8	151	338	10.7	4.0	50	0	Bahrain
21	2,560	453	...	...	...	101.5	0.9	253	2	13.1	1.7	70	0	Bangladesh
3,336	280	...	...	...	...	—	—	10	31	2.3	0.8	0	0	Barbados
2,350	640	...	...	...	...	88.3	9.0	2,414	237	5.6	3.0	80	20	Belgium
1,882	290	...	...	...	...	0.7	3.9	4[2]	25[2]	4.0[2]	2.0[2]	...	...	Belize
1,234	3,250	1,138	...	...	...	4.4	1.0	24[2]	6[2]	10.2[2]	2.6[2]	10	0	Benin
6,441	370	290,191	...	1,030	471	—	3	—	—	—	—	...	...	Bermuda
...	...	...	...	...	...	4.0[10]	3.1[10]	—	—	—	—	...	...	Bhutan
...	...	...	...	...	...	27.6	3.9	171[2]	29[2]	5.4[2]	2.2[2]	10	0	Bolivia
5,046	750	...	...	21,300	...	3.3	2.7	25	22	5.1	2.7	0	0	Botswana
116	...	...	13	3,450	...	319.2	2.2	2,307	16	3.6	1.0	70	120	Brazil
1,865	190	...	...	...	...	—	3	—	—	—	—	...	...	British Virgin Islands
5,779	100	126,103	279	...	33,195	4.0	16.0	305[2]	1,398[2]	24.5[2]	8.1[2]	...	...	Brunei
...	...	...	...	...	...	157.8	17.6	4,638	503	18.5	8.0	725	370	Bulgaria
...	...	...	...	...	...	8.7	1.0	27[2]	3[2]	17.6[2]	2.7[2]	30	0	Burkina Faso
40	650	...	...	...	191	186.0	4.7	209	5	21.2	3.0	10	0	Burma
82	...	...	...	...	...	7.2	1.4	33	7	12.5	3.2	10	0	Burundi
...	1,170	...	...	...	...	11.6	1.0	156	16	8.3	2.0	10	0	Cameroon
8,640	471	...	283	...	...	84.6	3.3	7,902	302	8.6	2.3	120	120	Canada
...	105	...	...	...	...	1.2	3.3	12[12]	47[12]	13.5[12]	11.8[12]	5	0	Cape Verde
11,681	110	33,287	1,764	313	...	—	3	—	—	—	—	...	...	Cayman Islands
...	2,740[1]	...	...	...	...	6.5	2.3	11[5]	5[5]	10.8[5]	2.0[5]	0	0	Central African Republic
...	990	...	...	...	...	17.0	3.2	12	3	32.3	1.9	10	0	Chad
1,373	470	6,459	...	...	...	101.0	7.9	760	61	11.4	4.1	0	10	Chile
...	1,360[14]	...	...	...	...	3,200.0	2.9	24,870	23	33.6	6.7	140	1,100	China
790[15]	190	...	...	...	...	—	3	—	—	—	—	...	...	Christmas Island
...	...	...	...	...	...	—	3	—	—	—	—	...	...	Cocos (Keeling) Islands
622	420	...	...	...	...	86.3	2.8	447	15	7.8	1.2	20	0	Colombia
...	960	...	...	...	...	—	16	...	...	...	...	...	...	Comoros
10	870	...	...	...	...	8.8	3.9	69	34	8.0	3.4	20	0	Congo
...	...	...	...	...	...	—	3	...	...	...	...	...	...	Cook Islands
558	480	...	...	953,000	...	9.5	3.6	33	12	4.0	1.0	5	0	Costa Rica
295	4,640	...	...	...	...	7.1	0.6	76[2]	8[2]	4.4[2]	1.2[2]	0	0	Côte d'Ivoire
...	650	2,503	...	...	...	180.5	17.3	1,600	154	...	5.4	1,500	0	Cuba
671	180	35,383	...	...	...	13.0	18.1	31	45	4.1	1.3	0	0	Cyprus[18]
...	640	...	...	...	...	197.0	12.6	7,923	495	17.9	5.8	460	1,100	Czechoslovakia
10,050	600	67,601	...	...	13,548	29.3	5.7	1,269	241	5.2	2.3	40	5	Denmark
...	...	...	...	...	...	4.2	8.7	27[2]	67[2]	22.4[2]	8.1[2]	...	...	Djibouti
18,328	300	29,740	...	...	...	—	—	...	...	...	...	...	...	Dominica
295	580	...	...	...	...	20.8	3.0	142	21	11.7	1.4	5	0	Dominican Republic
292	260	...	...	...	...	40.0	3.9	193[2]	21[2]	11.3[2]	1.6[2]	10	0	Ecuador
2,378	580	...	...	...	...	445.0	8.9	6,294	124	28.1	14.2	825	50	Egypt
...	1,000	...	...	...	...	55.0	10.8	254	49	29.1	5.5	80	0	El Salvador
...	190	...	...	...	...	1.4	4.2	2[17]	9[17]	21.0[17]	...	0	0	Equatorial Guinea
324	1,100	...	...	...	...	315.8	6.7	411	9	26.5	9.1	310	0	Ethiopia
...	...	49	...	...	...	—	3	—	—	—	—	...	...	Faeroe Islands
...	330	38,723	...	—	—	—	3	—	—	—	—	...	...	Falkland Islands

Social protection (continued)

country	programs available, 1987 — old-age invalidity, death	sickness and maternity[a]	work injury	unemployment	family allowances	expenditures, 1985 (% of total central govt.)	year	receipts total ('000,000 natl. cur.)	insured persons (%)	employers (%)	government (%)	other (%)	expenditures total ('000,000 natl. cur.)	benefits (%)	administration (%)	other (%)
Fiji	•		•			7.6	1983	92.7	26.5	26.8	9.1	37.6	33.1	74.3	4.6	21.1
Finland	•	•	•	•	•	33.9[6]	1983	61,869.5	7.1	39.6	46.5	6.8	56,564.8	96.0	4.0	—
France	•	•	•	•	•	44.0[5,6]	1983	1,246,605.6	20.5	48.0	24.2	7.3	1,216,861.4	90.4	4.0	5.6
French Guiana	•	...	•	...	•	...	...	...	...	...	...	...	...	...	...	...
French Polynesia	•	...	•	...	•	...	...	...	...	...	...	...	...	...	...	...
Gabon	•	...	•	...	•	...	1983	39,632.0	16.0	65.1	12.8	6.1	33,350.0	81.0	12.1	6.9
Gambia, The	•	...	•		•	3.5[19]	1978	—								
Gaza Strip	...	...	...	...	...	—	...									
Germany, East	•	•	•	•	•	...	1983	30,829.5	23.1	29.5	47.3	0.1	30,829.5	99.7	0.3	—
Germany, West	•	•	•	•	•	50.2[2,6]	1983	408,738.0	35.5	33.9	27.2	3.4	409,569.0	96.6	2.6	0.8
Ghana	•	...	•	•		4.0	1984	—								
Gibraltar	•	•	...	•	•	...	...	...	...	...	...	...	...	...	...	...
Greece	•	•	•	•	•	28.8[12]	1983	572,741.0	28.2	41.9	23.0	6.9	542,909.0	93.4	6.0	0.6
Greenland	•	•	...	...		...	...									
Grenada	•	•				5.0[6,11]	1983	8.6	20.2	64.7	5.5	9.6	5.2	82.8	3.8	13.4
Guadeloupe	•	...	...	...	•	...	...	...	...	...	...	...	...	...	...	...
Guam	•	...	•	...		...	...	...	...	...	...	...	...	...	...	...
Guatemala	•	•	•	...		2.6[9]	1983	124.2	29.5	51.0	3.6	15.9	90.2	88.7	11.3	—
Guernsey	...	...	...	...	...	...	...									
Guinea	•	•	•	...	•	...	1983	166.3	78.7	21.3	—	...	44.7	74.6	25.4	...
Guinea-Bissau	...	...	...	...	...	...	1983	28.2	25.5	44.1	—	30.4	47.8	3.4	19.3	77.3
Guyana	•	•	•	...		3.7[5]	1983	136.3	22.7	28.0	1.0	48.3	26.6	71.9	26.2	1.9
Haiti	•	•	•	...		5.1[2]	1977	60.5	—26.6—		69.9	3.5	52.4	92.7	7.3	—
Honduras	•	•	•	...		4.5[9]	1983	77.5	25.6	47.2	7.1	20.1	54.8	81.5	17.9	0.6
Hong Kong	•	...	•	...	•	...	1985						895.6			
Hungary	•	•	•	•	•	23.9	1983	138,375.0	14.9	47.1	38.0	—	138,375.0	99.5	0.5	—
Iceland	•	•	•	•	[21]	14.2[2]	1981	932.0	—	14.8	85.2	—	...	...	...	...
India	•	•	•	•		...	1983	46,228.3	14.1	67.0	2.1	16.8	24,262.5	97.4	1.9	0.7
Indonesia	•	...	•	...		...	1983	56.3	16.5	48.4	—	35.1	15.9	29.8	64.0	6.2
Iran	•	•	•	•	•	8.1	1983	301,532.0	17.4	49.8	25.9	6.9	107,519.0	93.3	6.7	...
Iraq	•	•	•	...		...	1977	107.8	9.9	55.6	21.9	12.6	71.0	94.0	2.4	3.6
Ireland	•	•	•	•	•	24.9[2]	1983	3,384.4	13.1	24.6	60.6	1.7	3,426.0	94.6	4.9	0.5
Isle of Man	•	•	•	•	•	17.2	1985						14.4			
Israel	•	•	•	•	•	20.2	1983	100,258.8	18.9	37.5	34.1	9.5	91,205.3	86.6	8.9	4.5
Italy	•	•	•	•	•	27.5	1983	143,008.0	15.3	48.0	33.8	2.9	139,511.0	93.0	3.6	3.4
Jamaica	•	...	•	...		3.2[11]	1983	191.7	18.6	22.3	31.9	27.3	96.8	87.1	12.8	0.1
Japan	•	•	•	•	•	...	1983	40,946,872.0	26.2	28.7	29.0	16.0	32,661,494.0	90.1	1.8	8.1
Jersey	•	•	•	...	•	9.9	1984	31.3	—58.9—		30.3	10.8	27.1[20]			
Jordan	•	...	•	...		7.3	1983	30.3	30.7	59.0	—	10.3	3.4	74.6	24.5	0.9
Kampuchea	...	...	•	...	...	...	...	...	...	...	...	...	...	...	...	...
Kenya	•	...	•	...		0.1	1983	600.4	25.3	25.3	—	49.4	55.5	72.8	27.2	—
Kiribati	•	...	•	...		...	...									
Korea, North	...	•	...	...	...	...	...									
Korea, South	•	•	•	...		5.4	1984	157,400.0	...	...	...	...	...	...	...	...
Kuwait	•	...	...	...		6.6	1983	213.0	9.0	17.7	39.9	33.4	92.8	95.1	4.6	0.3
Laos	...	...	•	...	...	...	...									
Lebanon	•	•	•	...	•	...	...									
Lesotho	...	...	•	...	...	1.0	1983	...	...	...	...	...	...	...	...	...
Liberia	•	•	•	...		0.6	1983	2.9	—	69.0	13.8	17.2	2.6	54.4	45.6	—
Libya	•	...	•	...		...	1977	192.9	9.1	28.7	58.7	3.5	128.2	96.2	3.2	0.5
Liechtenstein	•	•	•	•	•	...	...	...	...	...	...	...	...	...	...	...
Luxembourg	•	•	•	•	•	48.2[2]	1983	51,234.3	24.3	32.0	25.8	17.9	48,230.8	85.5	2.4	12.1
Macau	•	...	...	...		...	1981	...	...	...	...	...	...	...	...	...
Madagascar	•	...	•	...	•	10.3[24]	1983	9,536.1	5.3	69.6	—	25.1	6,609.0	100.0	—	—
Malawi	...	...	•	...	...	0.8	...	...	...	...	...	...	...	...	...	...
Malaysia	•	...	•	...		2.6[12]	1983	4,376.6	24.3	45.4	0.6	29.7	3,138.4	96.3	3.6	0.1
Maldives	...	...	...	...	...	1.3	1983	—								
Mali	•	•	•	...	•	6.1[6]	1983	5,781.6	10.8	59.5	1.5	28.2	5,628.9	50.9	27.3	21.8
Malta	•	•	•	•	•	35.8	1983	70.1	27.6	33.2	39.2	—	67.2	99.1	0.9	—
Martinique	•	...	...	...	•	...	...	...	...	...	...	...	...	...	...	...
Mauritania	•	...	•	...	•	3.7[9]	1983	1,210.3	9.2	56.9	29.7	4.2	1,076.3	87.8	6.0	6.2
Mauritius	•	•	•	...	•	15.5[6]	1983	454.4	10.1	20.2	54.3	15.4	262.1	95.4	4.5	0.1
Mayotte	...	...	...	...	...	...	...	...	...	...	...	...	...	...	...	...
Mexico	•	•	•	...		9.6	1983	526,385.0	21.7	57.5	8.1	12.7	471,840.0	66.6	17.1	16.3
Monaco	•	•	•	•	•	...	...	...	...	...	...	...	...	...	...	...
Mongolia	•	•	•	...	•	...	...									
Montserrat	•	...	•	...		...	...	...	...	...	...	...	...	...	...	...
Morocco	•	•	•	...	•	5.6[6]	1983	1,451.6	8.4	78.4	—	13.2	818.1	93.3	6.7	—
Mozambique	•	...	•	...		...	1983	154.0	99.8	—	—	0.2	83.0	21.4	37.0	41.6
Nauru	•	...	...	...		...	...	...	...	...	...	...	...	...	...	...
Nepal	•	...	•	...		0.7	1982									
Netherlands, The	•	•	•	•	•	1.7	1983	146,960.0	38.0	30.5	17.6	13.9	126,547.0	92.2	3.3	4.5
Netherlands Antilles	•	•	•	...	...	8.7[8,9]	1982	124.4	...	...	...	...	...	...	...	...
New Caledonia	•	...	•	...	•	...	...	...	...	...	...	...	...	...	...	...
New Zealand	•	•	•	•	•	29.6	1983	5,822.1	2.2	4.4	91.6	1.8	5,711.2	98.1	1.8	0.1
Nicaragua	•	•	•	...		3.3[17]	1983	832.9	20.4	53.5	10.4	15.7	427.5	65.5	28.5	6.0
Niger	•	...	•	...	•	1.7[6,17]	1983	6,116.3	8.4	80.6	—	11.0	4,619.9	38.3	18.2	43.5
Nigeria	•	...	•	...		2.5[27]	1983	78.4	28.2	20.1	—	51.7	11.3	45.6	54.4	...
Niue	...	...	...	...	...	...	...	...	...	...	...	...	...	...	...	...
Norfolk Island	•	...	...	...		...	...	...	...	...	...	...	...	...	...	...
Norway	•	•	•	•	•	35.1[6]	1983	91,154.6	20.9	32.1	45.1	1.9	87,863.0	97.6	2.4	—
Oman	...	...	•	...	...	—	1984						—	...	...	...
Pacific Is., Trust Territory of the Marshall Islands	•	...	...	...	...	...	...	...	...	...	...	...	...	...	...	...
Micronesia, Fed. States of	•	...	•	...	...	...	...	...	...	...	...	...	...	...	...	...

police protection (latest)			fire protection (latest)			military protection								country
						manpower, 1988[d]		expenditure, 1985				arms trade, 1986 ('000,000 U.S.$)		
offenses (reported to police) per 100,000 population	population per police officer[b]	government expenditure per 1,000 population (U.S.$)	fire alarms per 100,000 population	population per fire fighter[c]	government expenditure per 1,000 population (U.S.$)	total ('000)	per 1,000 population	total '000,000 U.S.$	per capita[e]	% of central government expenditure	% of GDP or GNP	imports	exports	
2,002	440	24,800	...	2,600	...	3.5	4.7	16[2]	23[2]	4.6[2]	1.4[2]	0	0	Fiji
5,948	640	44,927	10	1,300	4,478	35.2	7.1	772	158	5.0	1.5	100	0	Finland
5,252	630	...	...	2,840	...	456.9	8.2	20,800	365	8.9	4.1	170	3,800	France
...	...	...	...	...	...	—	[3]	—	—	—	—	...	...	French Guiana
...	...	...	...	...	...	—	[3]	—	—	—	—	...	...	French Polynesia
134	1,290	...	...	...	...	3.0	2.5	67[2]	69[2]	4.9[2]	2.0[2]	0	0	Gabon
...	3,310	...	...	...	...	0.6	0.7	2[12]	3[12]	3.6[12]	1.3[12]	10	0	Gambia, The
4,355	...	...	...	...	...							...	...	Gaza Strip
666	...	...	...	...	...	172.0	10.4	11,290	657	10.7	6.4	525	220	Germany, East
7,154	...	...	...	...	...	488.7	8.0	20,800	330	10.5	3.2	260	410	Germany, West
...	620	...	...	4,330	...	10.6	0.8	76	6	7.2	0.9	5	0	Ghana
8,140	170	...	814	220	...	—	[3]					...	...	Gibraltar
3,562	380	501,048	...	...	...	214.0	21.3	2,506	244	16.0	7.2	110	0	Greece
12,460	340	109,098	...	3,580	117,380[20]	—	[3]	—	—	—	—	...	...	Greenland
1,457	230	15,202	...	...	...	—	—	...	...	...	...	...	...	Grenada
...	...	...	...	...	...	—	[3]	—	—	—	—	...	...	Guadeloupe
3,454	...	...	...	...	...	—	[3]	—	—	—	—	...	...	Guam
...	670	...	...	...	...	42.0	4.8	174	21	15.9	1.8	0	0	Guatemala
...	...	...	...	...	...	—	[3]	—	—	—	—	...	...	Guernsey
...	1,140	...	...	...	...	9.9	1.5	60[2]	10[2]	...	3.2[2]	80	0	Guinea
...	...	...	...	...	...	9.2	9.9	6[19]	7[19]	8.4[19]	4.6[19]	20	0	Guinea-Bissau
5,287	190	...	...	...	...	5.5	7.3	34	43	5.9[5]	8.9	0	0	Guyana
701	400	...	...	...	...	7.6	1.4	30	5	8.4	1.6	0	0	Haiti
...	1,040	...	...	...	...	18.7	3.9	120	26	12.9	3.8	60	0	Honduras
2,800	220	76,780	437	900	9,589	—	[3]	—	—	—	—	...	...	Hong Kong
1,180	710	...	94	...	...	99.0	9.4	3,536	322	8.1	4.4	100	200	Hungary
1,550	940	...	...	...	...	—	—	—	—	—	—	0	0	Iceland
206	820	...	...	...	...	1,362.0	1.7	7,493	9	17.3	3.8	2,800	0	India
70	1,340	766	...	...	...	284.0	1.6	2,181	12	11.0	2.5	190	0	Indonesia
...	...	21,088	...	...	...	604.5	11.8	11,690[2]	257[2]	29.9[2]	7.2[2]	1,800	0	Iran
518	140	...	...	...	...	1,000.0	60.1	15,920[2]	1,044[2]	50.8[19]	42.5[2]	4,900	0	Iraq
2,320	314	63,050	...	...	...	13.2	3.7	308	84	3.0	1.9	20	0	Ireland
...	...	...	...	...	...	—	[3]					...	...	Isle of Man
4,335	210	23,099	425	...	...	141.0	31.3	3,678	875	26.1[2]	13.9	450	20	Israel
2,451	680	...	...	...	...	386.0	6.7	10,010	170	4.8	2.7	170	250	Italy
1,845	434	18,841	...	...	2,915	2.5	1.0	18	7	1.8	0.9	0	0	Jamaica
1,565	480	55,594	61	960	25,990	245.0	2.0	13,080	108	5.5	1.0	675	20	Japan
...	...	...	...	...	...	—	[3]					...	...	Jersey
505	630	27,536	...	...	...	85.3	28.8	719	272	31.7	17.4	330	0	Jordan
...	1,980	...	...	...	...	60.0	7.62	68[22]	18[22]	...	11.0[22]	150	0	Kampuchea
363	1,500	...	...	...	...	23.0	1.0	223	11	12.6	3.6	10	0	Kenya
2,472	330	...	...	63,980	...	—	—					...	...	Kiribati
...	460	...	...	...	...	842.0	38.4	5,400	257	...	22.2	410	200	Korea, North
1,588	420	...	19	5,650	...	629.0	14.8	4,891	115	26.6	5.5	500	30	Korea, South
287	80	...	90	...	...	20.3	5.3	1,513	857	13.6	6.3	130	0	Kuwait
...	280	...	...	...	...	55.5	14.4	55	15	21.3[2]	10.5[2]	80	0	Laos
489	530	...	...	...	...	—	—	429[5]	135[5]	20.0[5]	8.2[5]	10	0	Lebanon
1,643	1,130	...	...	...	...	—	—	47[2]	32[2]	28.5[2]	6.5[2]	0	0	Lesotho
...	1,570	...	...	...	...	5.8	2.4	28	12	8.8	2.7	10	0	Liberia
1,022	...	26,667	...	...	...	71.5	16.6	5,225[2]	1,441[2]	40.0[2]	17.8[2]	1,200	60	Libya
...	660	...	...	...	...	—	[23]	—	—	—	—	...	...	Liechtenstein
3,947	730	15,067	299	3,220	...	0.8	2.2	39	102	2.2	0.8	5	0	Luxembourg
823	...	...	17	1,380	...	—	[3]	...	...	...	...	...	...	Macau
...	2,900	...	...	...	...	21.0	1.9	56	5	8.0	2.4	20	0	Madagascar
1,005	1,670	...	...	...	...	5.3	0.6	19[2]	3[2]	5.7[2]	1.7[2]	5	0	Malawi
595	760	...	...	...	...	113.0	6.7	1,227	77	9.3	3.8	40	0	Malaysia
3,989	35,710	2,003	...	—	...			...	...	...	...	...	...	Maldives
...	160	...	...	...	...	7.3	0.9	27	3	7.9[5]	2.5	0	0	Mali
1,385	225	34,223	...	...	...	1.2	3.5	11[2]	30	2.6[2]	1.0[2]	0	0	Malta
...	...	...	...	...	...	—	[3]	—	—	—	—	...	...	Martinique
...	710	...	...	...	...	11.0	5.8	47	26	25.0	6.6	0	0	Mauritania
2,366	240	...	...	...	...	—	—	2	2	0.8	0.2	0	0	Mauritius
...	...	...	...	...	...	—	[3]	—	—	—	—	...	...	Mayotte
315	...	...	21	...	...	138.0	1.7	1,052	13	4.4	0.6	60	0	Mexico
3,392	...	...	...	...	...	—	—	...	...	...	...	...	...	Monaco
...	120	...	...	...	...	24.5	12.0	...	...	...	...	10	0	Mongolia
5,626[15]	110	16,901	...	...	...	—	[3]	—	—	—	—	...	...	Montserrat
589	840	...	...	...	...	203.5	8.6	780	33	15.0	6.5	80	0	Morocco
...	...	...	...	...	...	36.7	2.5	164	12	38.0	7.4	170	0	Mozambique
...	110	...	...	...	...	...	—	—	—	—	—	...	...	Nauru
29	1,000	497	...	...	...	35.0	1.9	32	2	6.2	1.2	0	0	Nepal
6,725	506	72,251	262	...	...	106.1	7.2	4,051	271	5.4	3.1	370	140	Netherlands, The
4,684[25]	330	...	...	...	...	—	[3]	—	—	—	—	...	...	Netherlands Antilles
...	...	...	...	...	...	—	[3]	—	—	—	—	...	...	New Caledonia
12,509	630	38,418	652	1,260	...	12.8	3.8	451	134	4.5	2.0	40	0	New Zealand
...	90[4]	...	...	...	...	77.0	21.3	702	215	22.5	16.8	575	0	Nicaragua
32	2,350[26]	...	...	...	...	3.3	0.5	12	2	5.0	0.8	10	0	Niger
312	1,140	...	...	...	...	94.5	0.8	1,088	10	7.9	1.4	320	5	Nigeria
...	270	20,727	...	—	...	—	[3]					...	...	Niue
...	746	27,358	1,117	...	...	—	[3]					...	...	Norfolk Island
3,536	660	97,765	...	1,660	27,931	35.8	8.5	1,853	432	7.5	3.2	160	10	Norway
162	430	...	...	...	...	25.5	18.6	2,157	1,813	42.3	24.4	10	5	Oman
...	320[28]	...	...	...	...	—	[29]	—	—	—	—	...	...	Pacific Is., Trust Territory of the Marshall Islands
2,273	400	...	...	...	...	—	[29]	—	—	—	—	...	...	Micronesia, Fed. States of

Social protection (continued)

country	social security — programs available, 1987					expenditures, 1985 (% of total central govt.)	finances — year	receipts — total ('000,000 natl. cur.)	insured persons (%)	employers (%)	government (%)	other (%)	expenditures — total ('000,000 natl. cur.)	benefits (%)	administration (%)	other (%)
	old-age invalidity, death	sickness and maternity[a]	work injury	unemployment	family allowances											
Northern Mariana Islands	•	...	...	...	...		...	...	...	...	...	...	...	...	...	...
Palau																
Pakistan	•	•	•			0.2	1983	2,587.2	—	62.8	33.1	4.1	2,249.7	97.8	1.7	0.5
Panama	•	•	•			12.8	1983	455.8	27.3	43.3	3.2	26.2	339.9	86.0	7.8	6.2
Papua New Guinea	•		•			0.4	1983	45.0	40.5	32.1	8.0	19.4	9.4	82.3	9.7	8.0
Paraguay	•	•	•			30.3[2]	1982	14,660.0	...	...	...	...	11,278.0	...	...	...
Peru	•	•	•			0.2[5]	1983	567.3	—88.4—		—	11.6	605.2	88.5	11.5	—
Philippines	•	•	•			1.6	1983	6,762.8	26.0	36.1	—	37.9	2,850.3	83.6	14.0	2.4
Pitcairn Island	...	...	...	...	...											
Poland	•	•	•		•	...	1980	325,454.0	2.1	52.2	44.2	1.5	304,600.0	98.8	0.5	0.7
Portugal	•	•	•	•	•	26.8[6,22]	1983	228,867.6	27.9	61.6	10.1	0.4	231,782.7	94.7	5.3	—
Puerto Rico	•		•			...	1980	...	...	...	...	...	1,041.3	100.0	—	—
Qatar	...	...	...	...	...											
Réunion	•	...	•	...	•											
Romania	•	•	•		•	21.8	1983	72,064.9	—	54.0	46.0	—	63,927.5	100.0	—	—
Rwanda	•		•		•	2.9[6,19]	1977	1,440.5	26.9	44.8	—	28.3	384.9	58.3	41.7	—
St. Helena and Ascension	•	...	•		...											
St. Kitts and Nevis	•	•	•			...											
St. Lucia	•		•			...	1983	6.9	43.5	43.5	—	13.0	2.2	45.5	54.5	—
St. Pierre and Miquelon	...	...	...	...	...											
St. Vincent and the Grenadines	•	•	•			2.4[6]	1983	...	...	...	...	...	...	...	...	...
San Marino	•	•	...	...	•	...	1983	51,673.0	12.0	48.7	36.1	3.2	46,179.0	95.7	3.7	0.6
São Tomé and Príncipe	•	•				...	1983	82.9	40.0	59.7	—	0.3	19.7	100.0	—	—
Saudi Arabia	•		•			...											
Senegal	•	...	•		•	2.6[2,6]	1983	7,914.0	—	93.2	—	6.8	6,085.0	79.0	19.4	1.6
Seychelles	•	•	•			5.3[11]	1983	69.1	30.1	60.2	—	9.7	42.7	69.6	4.9	25.5
Sierra Leone	•		•			1.7	1977	10.5	—26.7—		73.3	—	10.0	100.0	—	—
Singapore	•		•			1.4	1983	4,935.1	38.7	42.7	0.1	18.6	2,226.3	59.7	0.9	39.4
Solomon Islands	•		•			0.9[6]	1983	7.5	30.3	45.5	—	24.2	1.5	78.2	21.8	—
Somalia	•		•			1.7[6,27]	1978	...	...	...	...	...	...	...	...	...
South Africa	•	•	•	•	•		1982	243.0					310.0	...	...	...
Bophuthatswana	...	...	...	...	...		...						...			
Ciskei	...	...	...	...	...		1984	...					21.9			
Transkei	...	...	...	...	...											
Venda	...	...	...	...	...											
South West Africa/Namibia	•	...														
Spain	•	•	•	•	•	43.0[2]	1983	4,021,128.7	16.1	59.1	22.9	2.0	4,044,425.8	96.0	2.6	1.4
Sri Lanka	•	•	•			11.4[6]	1983	4,800.0	19.1	20.4	37.8	22.7	2,695.3	97.9	1.8	0.3
Sudan, The	•		•			2.2[19]	1983	33.2	16.8	37.4	—	45.8	7.5	35.8	64.2	—
Suriname	•					6.0[31]	1983	125.8	35.8	26.5	36.6	1.1	106.3	98.1	1.9	—
Swaziland	•		•			—	1983	11.1	29.5	40.8	—	29.7	4.6	52.6	24.6	22.8
Sweden	•	•	•	•	•	46.4[6]	1983	252,244.1	1.0	43.8	46.0	9.2	234,574.4	97.8	2.2	—
Switzerland	•	•	•	•	•	49.9[2]	1983	33,854.7	41.4	25.8	23.9	8.9	29,831.6	93.3	2.9	3.8
Syria	•	•	•			8.2[6,12]	1981	...	...	...	...	...	...	...	...	...
Taiwan	•	•	•			18.2[2,6]										
Tanzania	•		•			0.5	1983	394.7	32.2	32.2	—	35.6	201.3	32.1	22.2	45.7
Thailand	•		•			2.9	1983	1,832.5	—	93.1	0.7	6.2	1,609.4	99.2	0.8	—
Togo	•		•		•	7.4[6]	1983	7,167.0	9.7	73.5	—	16.8	3,315.0	69.7	26.3	4.0
Tokelau	...	...	...	...	...											
Tonga	...	...	...	...	...											
Trinidad and Tobago	•	•	•			5.3[12]	1983	680.5	12.6	27.3	47.1	13.0	456.9	91.3	8.7	—
Tunisia	•	•	•			6.2[2]	1977	124.5	25.6	53.9	3.7	16.8	67.8	90.0	6.1	3.9
Turkey	•	•	•			0.9	1983	556,419.0	32.1	41.6	7.6	18.7	432,858.0	96.1	3.4	0.5
Turks and Caicos Islands	...	...	...	...	...											
Tuvalu	•						1981	...	...	...	...	...	0.1	67.6	32.4	—
Uganda	•		•			1.6[6]	1983	171.0	24.3	24.3	—	51.4	56.2	5.7	94.3	—
U.S.S.R.	•	•	•		•	...	1983	75,789.0	—	—	97.2	2.8	75,789.0	100.0	—	—
United Arab Emirates	...	...	...	...	...	3.8[2,6]	1981	...	...	...	...	...	...	...	...	...
United Kingdom	•	•	•	•	•	28.6[6]	1983	58,456.0	17.9	23.9	55.6	2.6	56,523.0	95.3	2.9	1.8
United States	•	•	•	•	•[35]	24.1	1983	517,050.0	22.5	34.1	34.7	8.7	454,283.0	95.3	3.1	1.6
Uruguay	•	•	•		•	42.0	1983	23,129.0	24.7	24.6	47.9	2.8	20,424.0	92.5	5.5	2.0
Vanuatu	...	...	...	...	...											
Venezuela	•	•	•			6.7[6]	1983	5,109.0	—67.9—		13.7	18.4	4,449.0	82.4	17.6	—
Vietnam	•	•	•			...										
Virgin Islands (U.S.)	•	...		•	...											
Wallis and Futuna	...	...	...	...	...											
West Bank																
Western Sahara																
Western Samoa	•		•			—										
Yemen (Aden)	...	...	...	...	...											
Yemen (San'ā')						—	1983	...	...	...	...	...	...	...	...	...
Yugoslavia	•	•	•	•	•	6.8	1983	488,529.9	63.2	23.2	6.9	6.7	486,099.8	86.8	2.8	10.4
Zaire	•		•		•		1983	145.9	...	...	...	...	...	...	...	...
Zambia	•		•			2.2[2]	1983	94.3	38.5	28.5	—	33.0	44.0	70.3	29.7	—
Zimbabwe			•			3.1	1983	167.0	25.9	7.6	64.2	2.3	112.2	93.7	6.2	0.1

offenses (reported to police) per 100,000 population	population per police officer[b]	government expenditure per 1,000 population (U.S.$)	fire alarms per 100,000 population	population per fire fighter[c]	government expenditure per 1,000 population (U.S.$)	manpower, 1988[d] total ('000)	per 1,000 population	expenditure, 1985 total '000,000 U.S.$	per capita[e]	% of central government expenditure	% of GDP or GNP	arms trade, 1986 ('000,000 U.S.$) imports	exports	country
...	...	...	323	...	...	—[3]		—	—	—	—	...	...	Northern Mariana Islands
						—[29]								Palau
224	720	1,954	...	...	...	480.6	4.4	2,378	23	28.1	6.4	290	0	Pakistan
448	180	...	...	...	...	7.3	3.1	102	45	3.7	2.2	10	0	Panama
834	720	...	...	...	...	3.2	0.9	38	11	4.1	1.5	0	0	Papua New Guinea
...	310	...	...	...	...	16.0	4.0	65	16	18.3	1.1	0	0	Paraguay
424	730	...	...	...	...	118.0	5.6	1,388	68	37.1	6.9	150	0	Peru
334	1,160	2,423	...	9,090	...	147.5	2.5	400	7	9.5	1.3	30	0	Philippines
						—[3]								Pitcairn Island
1,292	370	...	56	...	...	406.0	10.7	14,610	381	22.6	6.0	650	1,100	Poland
492	660	...	...	...	...	73.9	7.1	650	62	8.4	3.3	30	200	Portugal
5,484	380	...	229	2,870	...	—						...	...	Puerto Rico
213	...	...	...	...	...	7.0	16.7	2,308	7,678	53.7	46.9	70	0	Qatar
...	220	...	...	...	...	—[3]						...	...	Réunion
...	...	...	...	...	...	179.5	7.8	5,473	233	18.0	4.3	320	180	Romania
359	4,650	...	...	...	...	5.2	0.8	31	5	9.4	1.7	0	0	Rwanda
...	170	8,368	...	5,150	—	—[3]						...	...	St. Helena and Ascension
...	300	...	...	...	...	—	—					...	...	St. Kitts and Nevis
...	430	...	...	...	...							...	...	St. Lucia
...	...	...	...	...	...	—[3]						...	...	St. Pierre and Miquelon
...	250	18,008	...	...	...	—	—					...	...	St. Vincent and the Grenadines
...	...	...	...	...	...							...	...	San Marino
...	400	...	...	...	...	—	—	1[17]	717	2.5[17]	1.6[17]	5	0	São Tomé and Príncipe
123	280	131,140	60	...	...	72.3	5.6	22,900	1,651	27.0	24.4	2,900	0	Saudi Arabia
105	730	...	...	...	...	9.7[30]	1.4[30]	65	9	8.8	2.8	5	0	Senegal
6,369	120	...	...	2,420	...	1.3	19.4	8[2]	124[2]	7.4[2]	5.6[2]	...	...	Seychelles
...	600	...	...	...	...	3.1	0.8	10	3	5.0	0.9	0	0	Sierra Leone
1,413	230	474,409	321	2,840	...	55.5	21.0	1,196	453	23.6	6.2	240	30	Singapore
...	620	5,112	...	...	...							...	...	Solomon Islands
...	540	...	...	...	...	65.0	10.3	89[2]	12[2]	27.5[2]	2.8[2]	20	0	Somalia
...	870	28,460	...	...	...	103.5	2.8	2,978[2]	93[2]	13.2[2]	4.2[2]	0	0	South Africa
...	...	...	...	...	...							...	...	Bophuthatswana
...	...	...	...	...	...							...	...	Ciskei
...	...	...	...	...	...							...	...	Transkei
...	...	...	...	...	...							...	...	Venda
...	...	...	...	...	...	—[3]						...	...	South West Africa/Namibia
2,172	580	...	...	...	...	309.5	7.9	3,502[2]	91[2]	6.5[2]	2.3[2]	190	150	Spain
...	860	...	...	...	...	22.0	1.3	167	10	7.7	2.7	0	0	Sri Lanka
1,771	740	12,049	...	...	...	57.7	2.2	144	6	12.9	2.0	50	5	Sudan, The
...	...	...	...	...	...	3.0	7.1	25	64	5.4	2.5	0	0	Suriname
...	610	21,249	...	...	...			8	12	5.2	1.5	0	0	Swaziland
9,711	330	176,110	189	1,230	...	67.0	8.0	2,932	340	6.1	3.0	60	190	Sweden
5,134	640	135,820	...	...	...	3.5	0.5	2,244	333	11.2	2.2	60	30	Switzerland
1,568	1,970	...	...	...	...	404.0	35.6	4,512	422	42.0	22.8	1,100	20	Syria
481	720	...	...	1,040	...	405.5	20.4	4,740	238	50.0	7.6	340	0	Taiwan
64	1,330	1,953	...	...	...	40.1	1.7	193	9	13.8	3.4	30	0	Tanzania
214	530	4,262	...	...	...	256.0	4.8	1,892	35	19.7	4.4	110	0	Thailand
11	1,970	...	...	...	...	5.9	1.7	20	6	6.9	2.9	5	0	Togo
...	210	...	...	...	...	—[3]						...	...	Tokelau
1,278	330	7,139	...	...	...	—[32]						...	...	Tonga
2,530	280	142,083	...	...	...	2.8	2.2	204[2]	175[2]	6.0[2]	2.7[2]	0	0	Trinidad and Tobago
1,408	340	...	...	...	...	38.0	4.8	301	40	7.4	3.6	30	0	Tunisia
179	1,570	...	...	...	...	635.3	11.7	2,416	46	17.9	4.6	600	0	Turkey
...	90	20,611	...	—	...	—[3]						...	...	Turks and Caicos Islands
...	290	13,069	...	...	...	—	—	...	...	...	...	...	...	Tuvalu
...	1,090	1,173	...	...	...	35.0	2.2	53[2]	4[2]	16.6[2]	1.1[2]	10	0	Uganda
...	1,050[33]	...	42	...	...	5,096.0	17.8	275,000	956	49.6	12.5	1,100	18,000	U.S.S.R.
1,297	140	...	...	...	...	43.0	24.2	1,385	855	42.0	5.7	30	0	United Arab Emirates
8,360	420	93,570[34]	...	1,460	20,920[34]	316.7	5.6	24,200	414	12.7[2]	5.3	575	700	United Kingdom
5,468	345	87,940	989	755	27,469	2,163.2	8.8	265,800	1,077	26.5	6.6	450	7,600	United States
...	170	...	79	...	...	24.4	8.2	134	44	10.6	2.7	0	0	Uruguay
...	450	...	...	...	...	—	—					...	...	Vanuatu
837	320	...	...	...	...	69.0	3.7	682	38	4.7	1.4	80	0	Venezuela
...	240	...	...	...	...	1,252.0	19.6	1,300[2]	222	50.0[2]	7.2[2]	1,600	0	Vietnam
3,798	...	126,972	980	680	...	—[3]						...	...	Virgin Islands (U.S.)
...	...	...	...	...	...	—[3]						...	...	Wallis and Futuna
2,226	...	...	...	...	...							...	...	West Bank
...	...	...	...	...	...	—[3]						...	...	Western Sahara
...	...	6,997	...	...	...	—[32]						...	...	Western Samoa
...	1,440	...	...	...	...	27.5	11.7	193	85	21.0[5]	17.6	280	0	Yemen (Aden)
...	500	1,905	...	...	...	36.6	4.3	424	67	28.5	10.0	240	0	Yemen (Şan'ā')
1,116	140	...	...	...	...	188.0	8.0	1,690	71	54.8	3.7	20	60	Yugoslavia
...	910	...	...	...	...	51.0	1.6	81	3	9.8	1.7	5	0	Zaire
2,569	540	3,960	...	...	...	16.2	2.2	167[2]	262	20.9[2]	6.6[2]	0	0	Zambia
1,425	750	12,457	...	...	...	47.0	5.3	322[2]	40[2]	15.0[2]	6.3[2]	50	0	Zimbabwe

[1]Rural areas only. [2]1984. [3]Political dependency; defense is the responsibility of the administering country. [4]Includes civilian militia. [5]1983. [6]Includes welfare. [7]1971. [8]Netherlands Antilles includes Aruba. [9]1979. [10]1985. [11]1977. [12]1981. [13]1976. [14]Local officers only. [15]Offenses disposed of in court. [16]Military defense is the responsibility of France. [17]1980. [18]Republic of Cyprus only. [19]1982. [20]Benefits paid only. [21]Coverage is through tax system. [22]1975. [23]Military defense is the responsibility of Switzerland. [24]1974. [25]Curaçao only. [26]Includes paramilitary forces. [27]1978. [28]Marshall Islands and Palau only. [29]Military defense is the responsibility of the United States. [30]Includes The Gambia. [31]1986. [32]Military defense is the responsibility of New Zealand. [33]MVD (internal security) only. [34]England and Wales only. [35]Federal–state system.

Education

This table presents international data on education analyzed to provide maximum comparability among the different educational systems in use among the nations of the world. The principal data are, naturally, numbers of schools, teachers, and students, arranged by four principal levels of education—the first, or primary; general second level (secondary); vocational second level; and third level (higher). The ratio of students to teachers is calculated for each level. These data are supplemented at each level by a figure for enrollment ratio, an indicator of each country's achieved capability to educate the total number of children potentially educable in the age group usually represented by that level. At the first and second levels this is given as a net enrollment ratio and at the third level as a gross enrollment ratio. Two additional comparative measures are given at the third level: students per 100,000 population and proportion (percent) of adults age 25 and over who have achieved some level of higher or postsecondary education. Data in this last group are confined as far as possible to those who have completed their educations and are no longer in school. No enrollment ratio is provided for vocational training at the second level because of the great variation worldwide in the academic level at which vocational training takes place, in the need of countries to encourage or direct students into vocational programs (to support national development), and, most particularly, in the age range of students who normally constitute a national vocational system (some will be as young as 14, having just completed a primary cycle; others will be much older).

At each level of education, differences in national statistical practice, in national educational structure, public-private institutional mix, training and deployment of teachers, and timing of cycles of enrollment or completion of particular grades or standards all contribute to the problems of comparability among national educational systems.

Reporting the number of schools in a country is not simply a matter of counting permanent red-brick buildings with classrooms in them. Often the resources of a less developed country are such that temporary or outdoor facilities are all that can be afforded, while in a developed but sparsely settled country students might have to travel 80 km (50 mi) a day to find a classroom with 20 students of the same age, leading to the institution of measures such as traveling teachers, radio or televisual instruction at home under the supervision of parents, or similar systems. According to UNESCO definitions, therefore, a "school" is defined only as "a body of students . . . organized to receive instruction . . . ."

Such difficulties also limit the comparability of statistics on numbers of teachers, with the further complications that many at any level must work part-time, or that the institutions in which they work may perform a mixture of functions that do not break down into the tidy categories required by a table of this sort. In certain countries teacher training is confined to higher education, in others as a vocational form of secondary training, and so on. For purposes of this table, teacher training at the secondary level has been treated as vocational education. At the higher level, teacher training is classified as one more specialization in higher education itself.

The number of students may conceal great variation in what each country defines as a particular educational "level." Many countries do, indeed,

Education

country	year	first level (primary) schools	teachers[c]	students[d]	student/teacher ratio	net enrollment ratio	general second level (secondary) schools	teachers[c]	students[d]	student/teacher ratio	net enrollment ratio	vocational second level[a] schools	teachers[c]
Afghanistan	1985	792	15,581	580,499	37.3	15[1]	332	5,715	105,032	18.4	...	16[2]	666[2]
Albania	1984	1,631	27,387	540,332	19.7	...	204	1,552	35,643	23.0	...	313[4]	5,405
Algeria	1987	11,692	113,250	3,635,000	27.3	86[1]	1,959[5]	95,113	1,877,000	19.7	45[1]	71[6]	2,528
American Samoa	1986	33	454[1]	7,725	17.0[1]	...	7	203[1]	3,187	16.5[1]	...	1[8]	4[8]
Andorra	1987	13	214[7]	5,344	24.8[7]	...	10	53[7]	2,253	20.5[7]	...	5	37[7]
Angola	1984	6,308[4]	32,004[44]	870,410	...	66[3]	...	3,870[3]	151,759	...	...	...	410[3]
Anguilla	1986	6	66	1,483	22.5	...	1	39	634	16.3	...	...	...
Antigua and Barbuda	1983	48	426	9,933	23.3	...	16	331	4,197	12.7	...	2[7]	...
Argentina	1985	20,700	229,715	4,589,291	20.0	96[10]	1,987[2, 11]	93,675[11]	715,518[11]	7.6[11]	42[10]	3,117[2, 11]	136,418[11]
Aruba	1988	31	327	6,341	19.4	...	11	173	3,011	17.4	...	15	225
Australia	1986	8,466	95,606	1,711,932	17.9	97[1]	1,619	101,115	1,289,457	12.8	86[1]	234[1]	52,587[1]
Austria	1987	3,395	28,454	342,378	12.0	86[2]	2,067	57,177	483,167	8.5	68[12]	1,392	22,662
Bahamas, The	1985	183	1,757	37,181	21.2	...	38	1,472	23,563	16.0	...	...	...
Bahrain	1985	114	2,963	49,644	16.8	95	21	951	32,927	34.6	68	5	233
Bangladesh	1986	43,712	184,668	10,776,000	58.4	54[1]	8,793	99,016	2,745,000	27.7	17[1]	157	2,151
Barbados	1985	130	1,464	30,792	21.0	99[3]	36	1,449	28,815	19.9	89[2]	3	154
Belgium	1986	4,790[1]	45,261	758,260	...	94[1]	2,272[1]	56,719[4]	855,704	...	87[1]	209[4]	6,864[4]
Belize	1986	225	1,582[1]	39,190	24.3[1]	...	24	504[1]	6,853	13.2[1]	...	5[14]	62[1, 14]
Benin	1985	2,715	13,452	444,163	33.1	51	133[3]	2,409[2]	112,267[2]	46.6[2]	...	30[3]	609[4]
Bermuda	1988	22	313	5,334	17.0	...	12	335	3,778	11.3	...	1	55
Bhutan	1986	147	1,321	36,998	28.0	8[15]	30	613	15,454	25.2	...	8[1]	103[1]
Bolivia	1984	8,038	47,224	1,181,246	25.0	81	845[4]	8,091[4]	199,944	...	25	...	...
Botswana	1986	537	7,324	235,941	32.2	88[1]	73	1,619	35,966	22.2	22[1]	22	317
Brazil	1985	187,274	1,040,566	24,769,736	23.8	83[2]	9,260	206,111	3,016,138	14.6	15[2]	...	...
British Virgin Islands	1986	27	135	2,399	17.8	...	4	76	1,140	15.0	...	—	—
Brunei	1986	146	2,225	36,983	16.6	...	29	1,636	18,714	11.4	...	8	414[14]
Bulgaria	1987	3,501[17]	62,188[17]	1,097,437[17]	17.6[17]	97[2]	17	17	17	17	78[2]	528	18,692
Burkina Faso	1986	1,758	6,091	351,807	57.8	27[1]	107	1,519	48,875	32.2	4[1]	18	421
Burma	1988	31,499	188,417	5,369,641	28.5	65[12]	2,429	61,556	1,591,927	25.9	16[12]	146	1,536
Burundi	1986	1,023	7,245	387,710	53.5	41[1]	62	795	13,037	16.4	3[1]	47	1,064
Cameroon	1987	5,920	35,431	1,723,024	48.6	75[15]	388	9,289	288,515	31.1	15[8]	220	4,449
Canada	1988	15,512[17]	273,190[017]	4,959,000[17]	18.1[17]	97[2]	17	17	17	17	92[2]	...	...
Cape Verde	1987	347	1,464	49,703	34.0	92[1]	16	321	10,304	32.1	...	3	53
Cayman Islands	1987	16	123	2,094	17.0	...	7	159	2,278	14.3	...	1	9
Central African Republic	1985	986	4,502	294,312	65.4	60[3]	41	914	45,166	49.4	...	4	127
Chad	1984	1,231	4,494	288,479	64.2	25[18]	...	590[12]	43,053	...	...	...	...
Chile	1984	8,862	62,746[3]	2,099,413[1]	...	92	1,401	...	588,123[1]	...	46[4]	369	...
China	1986	820,846	5,414,000	131,825,000	24.3	...	92,967	2,758,000	48,899,000	17.7	...	15,751	550,000
Christmas Island	1985	2	30	261	8.7	...	1	12	114	9.5	...	1	7
Cocos (Keeling) Islands	1986	2	8	105	13.1	...	1	5	30	6.0	...	1	1
Colombia	1986	36,979	135,924	4,002,543	29.4	75[1]	6,336[19]	107,084[19]	2,136,239[19]	19.9[19]	...	19	19
Comoros	1981	236	1,671[4]	61,469[4]	38.0[4]	69[3]	32	432	13,528	31.3	...	4	17
Congo	1985	1,522	7,612	458,338	60.2	...	247	5,188	199,073	38.4	...	19	1,073
Cook Islands	1986	30	165	3,183	19.3	...	8	146	2,156	14.8	...	...	...
Costa Rica	1985	3,091	11,526	362,877	31.5	87	...	...	87,038	...	35	...	...
Côte d'Ivoire	1984	5,976	28,561	1,179,456	41.3	...	218[8]	4,569[8]	245,043	...	...	38[8]	1,947[6]
Cuba	1987	9,837	61,490	1,000,971	16.3	94[1]	1,275	64,859	800,732	12.3	69[1]	798	33,246
Cyprus[20]	1987	373	2,225[7]	54,254	22.9[7]	...	94	2,639	40,627	15.4	...	10	458
Czechoslovakia	1987	6,274	97,385	2,088,750	21.4	...	343	9,723	134,103	13.8	...	561	17,044
Denmark	1986	2,556	34,541[1]	402,707	12.0[1]	...	3,251	36,105[1]	336,754	9.4[1]	84[2]	288	...
Djibouti	1987	59	559	27,136	48.5	...	21[19]	302[19]	8,003[19]	26.5[19]	...	19	19
Dominica	1986	66	642[17]	12,340	30.3[17]	...	17	17	7,111	17	...	...	35[2]
Dominican Republic	1985	6,299	27,952	1,219,681	43.6	68	...	11,754	438,922	37.3	...	...	107[2, 21]
Ecuador	1986	15,969	58,584	1,973,445	33.7	87[15]	2,056[19]	49,641[19]	860,419[19]	17.3[19]	28[10]	19	19
Egypt	1985	13,223	194,929	6,002,850	30.8	...	20,106	128,616	2,704,371	21.0	...	519[4]	48,605[4]

have a primary system comprised of grades 1 through 6 (or 1 through 8) that passes students on to some kind of post-primary education. But the age of intake, the ability of parents to send their children or to permit them to finish that level, or the need to withdraw the children seasonally for agricultural work all make even a simple enrollment figure difficult to assess in isolation. All of these difficulties are compounded when a country has instruction in more than one language, or when its educational establishment is so small that higher, sometimes even secondary, education cannot take place within the country. Enrollment figures in this table may, therefore, include students enrolled outside the country.

Student-teacher ratio, however, usually provides a good measure of the ratio of trained educators to the enrolled educable. In general, at each level of education both students and teachers have been counted on the basis of full-time enrollment or employment, or full-time equivalent when country statistics permit. At the primary and secondary levels, net enrollment ratio is the ratio of the number of children within the usual age group for a particular level who are actually enrolled to the total number of children in that age group (× 100). This ratio is usually less than (occasionally, equal to) 100 and is the most accurate measure of the completeness of enrollment at that particular level. It is not always, however, the best indication of utilization of teaching staff and facilities. Utilization, provided here for higher education only, is best seen in a gross enrollment ratio, which compares total enrollment (of all ages) to the population within the normal age limits for that level. For a country with substantial adult literacy or general educational programs, the difference

may be striking: typically, for a less developed country, even one with a good net enrollment ratio of 90 to 95, the gross enrollment ratio may be 20, 25, even 30% higher, indicating the heavy use made by the country of facilities and teachers at that level.

Literacy data provided here have been compiled as far as possible from data for the population age 15 and over for the best comparability internationally. Standards as to what constitutes literacy may also differ markedly; sometimes completion of a certain number of years of school is taken to constitute literacy; elsewhere it may mean only the ability to read or write at a minimal level testable by a census taker; in other countries studies have been undertaken to distinguish among degrees of functional literacy.

Finally, the data provided for public expenditure on education are complete in that they include all levels of public expenditure (national, state, local) but are incomplete for certain countries in that they do not include data for private expenditure; in some countries this fraction of the educational establishment may be of significant size. Occasionally data for external aid to education may be included in addition to domestic expenditure.

a. Usually includes teacher training at the second level.
b. Latest.
c. Full-time.
d. Full-time; may include students registered in foreign schools.

| students[d] | student/teacher ratio | third level (higher) | | | | | | | literacy[b] | | | | public expenditure on education (percent of GNP)[b] | country |
		institutions	teachers[c]	students[d]	student/teacher ratio	gross enroll-ment ratio	students per 100,000 popula-tion[b]	percent of population age 25 and over with post-secondary education[b]	over age	total (%)	male (%)	female (%)		
7,360[2]	11.1[2]	5[2]	1,283[2]	13,450[2]	10.5[2]	1.4[3]	120	3.0	15	20.0	33.2	5.8	1.8	Afghanistan
123,797	22.9	8[4]	1,502	21,285	14.2	7.1[1]	721		15	71.5	79.9	63.1		Albania
98,000	38.8	15[3]	11,464[7]	143,300	...	5.8[2]	529	0.3	15	44.7	57.3	31.7	6.1	Algeria
45[8]	11.2[8]	1	48[2]	802	35.7[2]	...	...	12.6	25	98.5	98.8	98.3	8.2	American Samoa
1,248	18.7[7]	...	...	...	...	...	...	...	15	100.0	...	...		Andorra
7,147	...	1[4]	316[4]	4,493	...	0.6[2]	53	...	15	28.0	36.2	19.3	5.2	Angola
...	...	...	...	...	...	...	...	6.8[9]	15	94.7	94.6	94.8		Anguilla
631[7]	...	...	...	...	...	...	...	1.3	15	90.0	...	...	3.0	Antigua and Barbuda
1,084,531[11]	8.0[11]	1,251[2]	70,699	846,145	12.0	36.4	2,768	6.1	15	94.9	95.5	94.4	4.2	Argentina
2,807	12.5	—	—	—	—	—	—		15	95.0	...	...		Aruba
859,195[1]	16.3[1]	95	26,036	390,706	15.0	28.7[7]	2,464	21.5	15	99.5	...	...	6.5	Australia
364,264	16.1	18	10,352	175,924	16.4	26.9[1]	2,309	3.3	15	99.0	100.0	100.0	5.8	Austria
		1	135	2,000	14.8	...	...		15	89.0	...	...	5.1	Bahamas, The
2,846	12.2	2	159	3,650	22.9	10.0	967	3.8	15	75.1	82.0	63.5	3.5	Bahrain
34,840	16.2	43	3,774	44,464	11.8	5.2[1]	462	1.3	15	33.1	43.3	22.2	1.9	Bangladesh
3,592	23.3	1	108	1,617	15.0	19.4[2]	2,065	3.3	15	98.0[13]	98.3[13]	97.7[13]	6.1	Barbados
218,813	...	17[1]	...	103,598	...	31.0[1]	2,449		15	100.0	...	...	6.1	Belgium
834[14]	12.3[1,14]	14	14	14	14	...	...	2.3	15	93.0	...	...	...	Belize
6,784[2]	...	1[4]	803[4]	6,818[4]	8.5[4]	2.1[4]	179	0.3	15	27.9	39.8	16.6	5.1	Benin
475	8.6	1	14	86	6.1	...	...	7.4	15	96.9	96.7	97.0	3.2	Bermuda
688[1]	6.7[1]	2	184	422	...	0.05[4]	25	...	15	18.0	31.0	9.0	...	Bhutan
		25[4]	1,487[4]	79,836	...	19.5	1,693	5.0	15	63.2	75.8	51.4	0.5	Bolivia
3,217	10.1	1	249	1,700	6.8	1.4[1]	130	0.5	15	70.8	72.6	69.5	8.4	Botswana
...	...	859	122,486	1,367,609	11.2	11.3[4]	1,140	5.0	15	79.3	80.4	78.3	2.9	Brazil
—	—	—	—	—	—	—	—	8.5	15	98.3	98.1	98.5	4.7	British Virgin Islands
1,688[14]	4.1[14]	1[16]	33[16]	176[16]	5.3[16]	...	...	9.4	15	80.3	86.5	72.8	2.0	Brunei
228,620	12.2	30	16,453	109,291	6.6	18.4[1]	1,255	5.2	15	95.5	...	...	7.0	Bulgaria
4,808	11.4	1	325	3,869	11.9	0.7[2]	57	...	15	13.2	20.7	6.1	2.7	Burkina Faso
17,000	11.1	35	7,191	255,866	35.6	5.1[6]	489	0.2	15	78.5	85.8	71.6	1.6	Burma
12,902	12.1	8	468	2,783	5.9	0.7[1]	55	...	10	33.8	42.8	25.7	2.7	Burundi
93,857	21.1	5	975	19,586	20.1	2.2[2]	185	0.3	15	55.2	70.2	41.0	2.9	Cameroon
...	...	266	59,300	795,730	13.4	55.4[1]	5,090	37.4	14	95.6	95.6	95.7	7.2	Canada
211	4.0			—		—	—		15	49.3	55.3	43.4	2.8	Cape Verde
122	13.6	1	10	105	10.5	...	...	2.9	15	97.5	97.5	97.6	...	Cayman Islands
2,233	17.6	...	105[2]	2,133[2]	20.3[2]	1.2	101	...	15	40.0	53.0	29.0	5.5	Central African Republic
2,559	...	1	141	1,643	11.6	0.4	34	...	15	17.8	35.6	0.5	1.9	Chad
143,788[1]	...	24	15,131	197,437[1]	...	15.8[1]	1,636	7.2	12	94.4	95.0	93.8	4.4	Chile
6,074,000	11.0	1,054	372,000	1,880,000	5.1	1.7[1]	168	1.0	15	72.6	83.5	61.2	2.9	China
60	8.6	...	...	...	...	...	...		15	80.0	...	...	...	Christmas Island
9	9.0	...	...	...	...	...	...	...	...	...	...	...	...	Cocos (Keeling) Islands
19	19	231	43,447	402,438	9.3	13.0[1]	1,402	3.3	18	69.1	...	...	2.9	Colombia
270	15.9	—	—	—	—	...	...	...	15	46.3	54.2	39.0	5.2	Comoros
5,477	22.2	1	...	9,385	...	6.9[3]	572	...	15	62.9	71.4	55.4	5.4	Congo
		...	41[8]	360[8]	8.8[8]	...	...	2.1	...	91.8	92.1	91.4	...	Cook Islands
25,493	...	14[4]	...	63,771	...	23.0	2,453	5.8	15	92.6	92.6	92.6	4.9	Costa Rica
21,758	...	1[8]	1,204[3]	19,660	...	2.5	208	...	15	57.3	...	...	7.2	Côte d'Ivoire
352,927	10.6	35	21,573	256,619	11.9	21.4[1]	2,343	5.9	15	91.1	91.1	91.1	6.9	Cuba
4,094	8.9	15	282	3,006	10.7	...	469	...	15	93.1	...	...	3.9	Cyprus[20]
257,968	15.1	36	19,459	169,011	8.7	15.5[1]	1,087	6.0	15	100.0	100.0	100.0	5.1	Czechoslovakia
150,772	...	96[4]	10,411[4]	116,319	...	29.1[2]	2,236	...		100.0	100.0	100.0	6.6	Denmark
19	19	—	—	161[2]	...	...	...		14	11.9	...	...	3.9	Djibouti
436[2]	12.5[2]	...	17[1]	601	3.5[1]	...	...	1.7	15	94.9	...	...	...	Dominica
1,932[2,21]	18.1[2,21]	67[,16]	3,107[7,16]	88,024[7,16]	28.3[7,16]	10.1[10]	900	1.9	15	77.3	77.7	76.8	1.8	Dominican Republic
19	19	21	11,186	172,649	15.4	33.1[2]	3,078	7.6	15	69.1	86.8	56.9	3.6	Ecuador
765,057[4]	15.7[4]	12	33,200[4]	739,017	...	22.8	2,057	3.4	15	44.9	57.6	31.8	5.2	Egypt

Education (continued)

country	year	first level (primary)					general second level (secondary)					vocational second level[a]	
		schools	teachers[c]	students[d]	student/ teacher ratio	net enroll- ment ratio	schools	teachers[c]	students[d]	student/ teacher ratio	net enroll- ment ratio	schools	teachers[c]
El Salvador	1985	2,883	24,295	940,963	38.7	62[2]	285	3,880	90,288	23.3	14[2]	174	667[4]
Equatorial Guinea	1981	511	647	40,110	62.0	...	14[19]	288[19]	3,013[19]	10.5[19]	...	19	19
Ethiopia	1986	7,900	50,922	2,448,778	48.1	...	1,209	15,218	655,517	43.1	...	...	390[1]
Faeroe Islands	1987	71[17,22]	...	5,550	...	...	17	...	2,904	...	...	10	...
Falkland Islands	1987	8	19	222	11.7	...	1	11	130	11.8	...	—	—
Fiji	1986	672	4,315	131,221	30.4	100[1]	140	2,551	42,200	16.5	...	44	257
Finland	1986	4,233	25,140	380,509	15.1	...	1,093	22,360	300,748	13.4	...	593[14]	22,869[14]
France	1986	67,504	331,040	6,944,849	21.0	96[2]	11,589[19]	373,605[19]	5,584,233[19]	14.9[19]	83[2]	19	19
French Guiana	1983	51	409	9,780	23.9	...	11[1]	470[1]	6,468[7]	...	...	...	177[1]
French Polynesia	1985	198	1,337	27,401	20.5	...	24	804	13,611	16.9	...	17	362
Gabon	1985	940	3,837	178,811	46.6	...	51	1,894	25,815	13.6	...	29	720
Gambia, The	1985	189	2,640	66,257	25.1	68	8	235	4,348	18.5	17	16	502
Gaza Strip	1987	305[17]	4,087[17]	107,809	40.8[17]	...	17	17	58,993	17	...	17	17
Germany, East	1985	5,649	58,406	859,830	14.7	...	5,711	112,076	1,140,391	10.2	...	4,500	55,234
Germany, West	1987	24,282	302,097	4,221,948	14.0	82[2]	5,312	188,541	2,670,458	14.2	69[2]	7,568	89,829
Ghana	1986	9,180	67,261	1,567,778	23.3	...	5,702	44,518	768,347	17.2	...	137	2,887
Gibraltar	1986	14	181	2,931	16.2	...	2	122	1,728	14.2	...	1	25
Greece	1985	9,229	36,093	904,426	25.1	91[4]	2,613	36,851	701,711	19.0	77[4]	601	8,427
Greenland	1988	94	...	7,259	...	...	37[8]	1,131[19]	1,740	...	...	5[8]	19
Grenada	1987	59	...	19,984	...	...	20	...	6,462	...	...	...	...
Guadeloupe	1986	230	1,927	42,734	22.2	...	...	...	38,510	...	...	...	...
Guam	1987	31	822	14,471	17.6	...	24	944	15,281	16.2	...	3	117
Guatemala	1985	8,121	28,467	1,046,043	36.7	62[4]	1,310[19]	14,629[19]	204,049[19]	13.9[19]	14[3]	19	19
Guernsey	1984	23	224	4,260	19.0	...	9	297	4,095	13.8	...	1	47
Guinea	1987	2,204	7,493	270,140	36.0	24[1]	225	3,577	76,493	21.4	7[1]	31	758
Guinea-Bissau	1985	668	3,153	81,444	25.8	53[2]	12	650	11,710	18.0	34	4	107
Guyana	1983	423[6]	3,257	121,869	37.4	90[6]	88	3,334	64,518	19.4	...	15[8]	348[8]
Haiti	1985	3,677	20,311	819,565	40.4	44[2]	314[2]	6,106	154,271	25.3	...	...	...
Honduras	1986	6,710	20,732	805,504	38.9	87[2]	428	6,945	130,247	18.8	20[2]	...	...
Hong Kong	1987	714	19,368	531,993	27.5	95[2]	397	18,323	434,145	23.7	64[2]	27	1,174
Hungary	1988	3,540	90,925	1,277,300	14.0	97[1]	186	8,368	125,811	15.0	69[1]	758	22,467
Iceland	1983	187	2,600	25,000	9.6	...	157	...	21,800	...	...	44	...
India	1986	528,079	...	86,465,189	...	92[2]	195,388	...	43,230,690	...	41[2]	5,494[14]	19
Indonesia	1986[24]	139,511	1,037,174	26,550,015	25.6	98[2]	22,086	480,464	7,680,417	16.0	17[10]	2,774	75,158
Iran	1986	48,982	268,606	6,343,300	23.6	92[1]	13,818	167,769	2,922,576	17.4	...	1,325	20,683
Iraq	1986	8,142	118,442	2,816,326	23.8	86[1]	2,109[1]	35,143	1,038,627	29.6	44[2]	228[1]	7,855
Ireland	1986	3,384	21,144	567,086	26.8	89[3]	563	14,284	252,896	17.7	98[2]	256	5,173
Isle of Man	1987	33	240[4]	5,063	...	...	5[25]	276[4]	4,531	...	...	17,[25]	32[10]
Israel	1987	1,832	44,409	621,393	14.0	92[4]	57[2]	39,242[26]	249,040[26]	6.3[26]	...	373	...
Italy	1987	27,188	222,160	3,530,825	15.9	98[10]	10,031	128,210	2,714,038	21.2	66[10]	7,624	116,119
Jamaica	1985[25]	785	...	337,231	...	94[4]	132	7,435	228,241	30.7	57[8]	11	501
Japan	1987	24,933	448,978	10,226,325	22.8	100[1]	16,738	566,976	11,456,437	20.2	96[1]	...	...
Jersey	1986	38[4]	294	5,611	19.1	...	6[4]	378	4,682	12.4	...	1[1]	...
Jordan	1986	1,239	16,979	530,906	31.3	88[4]	1,671	17,074	305,046	17.9	71[3]	52[21]	1,012[21]
Kampuchea	1984	3,629[3]	36,520	1,504,840	41.2	...	207	4,494	145,730	32.4	...	13	278
Kenya	1984	12,539	122,788	4,380,232	35.7	86[8]	2,396	19,368	510,943	26.4	8[10]	40	1,551
Kiribati	1986	112	457	13,331	29.2	...	8	128	2,167	16.9	...	3	43
Korea, North	1982	4,700[18]	...	2,500,000	...	...	...	100,000[19]	2,500,000[19]	25.0[19]	...	...	19
Korea, South	1987	6,535	126,677	4,798,323	37.9	92[7]	3,408	114,658	4,111,043	35.9	76[3]	736	34,189
Kuwait	1987	282	9,704	175,767	18.1	85[1]	401	19,158	245,865	12.8	74[3]	67	788[7]
Laos	1984	7,470	18,070	4953751	27.4	...	419[4]	5,815	91,356	15.7	...	117[7]	2,326
Lebanon	1985	1,116	28	329,340	...	...	1,405[3]	53,450[3,28]	230,934	...	...	181[3]	3,506
Lesotho	1985[25]	1,141	5,663	314,003	55.4	72[2]	143	1,676	35,423	21.1	13[2]	9	221
Liberia	1980	1,232	9,099	208,045[1]	...	...	419	1,129	52,514[1]	...	...	6	63
Libya	1983	2,744	42,202	741,502	17.6	...	1,555	25,044	301,415	12.0	...	195	3,883
Liechtenstein	1988	14	102	1,754	17.2	...	9	98	1,707	17.4	...	1	30[29,30]
Luxembourg	1986	74	1,745	24,424	14.0	88[2]	...	3,482[4,29,31]	7,951	...	60[2]	...	31
Macau	1986	...	1,080	31,669	29.3	...	31	769	13,849	18.0	...	2[21]	13[21]
Madagascar	1984	13,973	42,462	1,625,216	38.3	...	104[32]	10,383	288,543	27.8	...	126	1,302
Malawi	1986	2,520	15,440	942,539	61.0	44[2]	75	1,141	24,894	22.8	...	7	314
Malaysia	1986	6,652	98,061	2,232,575	22.8	...	1,136	58,223	1,297,734	22.3	...	54	1,909
Maldives	1986	243	1,138	41,812	36.7	...	9	291	3,581	12.3	...	10	52
Mali	1983	1,558	10,912	348,373	31.9	15	20	3,870	64,148	16.6	...	11	890
Malta	1987	210[17,22]	3,776[17,22]	36,322	...	89[2]	17	17	21,248	...	72[2]	26	661
Martinique	1984	224	2,024	39,050	19.3	...	...	2,416	31,912	13.2	...	...	653[4]
Mauritania	1986	878	2,629[2]	140,871	45.4[2]	...	44	1,013[2]	34,674	27.6[2]	...	6	372[2]
Mauritius	1986	273	6,161	138,765	22.5	97[1]	125	3,572	68,604	19.2	34[10]	7[2]	69[3]
Mayotte	1985	72	429[7]	15,625[7]	36.4[7]	...	3[19]	66[19]	...	13.4[19]	20.8[19]	19	19
Mexico	1988	80,518	455,693	14,875,000	32.6	98[1]	16,999	224,732[7]	4,401,000	...	45[1]	5,811[7]	139,391[7]
Monaco	1982	6	1,354	...	...	...	...	1,914	...	...	...	...	...
Mongolia	1986	28	28	28	28	99[3]	678[28]	17,000[28]	428,000[28]	25.2[28]	84[15]	40	1,200
Montserrat	1985	14	66	1,090	16.5	...	4	67	1,050	15.7	...	1	13
Morocco	1987	3,703	79,678[25]	2,227,960	28.0	64[1]	1,239	59,860[25]	1,278,855	21.4	24[1]	17[21]	674[21]
Mozambique	1986	4,382	20,756	1,251,391	60.3	49[1]	208	3,422	144,012	42.1	4[6]	34	864
Nauru	1985	7	102	1,451	14.2	...	2	36	465	12.9	...	1	4
Nepal	1987	12,186	53,405	1,857,658	34.8	56[2]	5,140	21,785	540,049	24.8	18[2]	5[7]	117[7]
Netherlands, The	1986	9,388	102,388	1,568,265	15.3	87[2]	1,382	53,361	803,782	15.1	87[2]	2,002	55,931
Netherlands Antilles	1983	91	1,248	24,578	19.7	...	22	633	8,623	13.6	...	3	79
New Caledonia	1987	276	1,564	32,205	20.6	...	47	1,179	13,540	11.5	...	28	200
New Zealand	1986	2,408	18,384	441,028	24.0	100[2]	420	13,310	226,116	17.0	79[10]	28	3,130
Nicaragua	1985	4,102	15,273	524,020	34.3	76	431[19]	4,778[19]	151,269[19]	31.7[19]	20[2]	19	19
Niger	1985	1,976	7,690	293,512	38.2	27	546	1,963	51,448	26.2	4[8]	8[6]	120[6]
Nigeria	1984	37,692[4]	424,717[4]	15,021,100[4]	35.4[4]	...	5,498[4]	82,749	3,169,624	38.3	...	475[4]	15,738
Niue	1987	8	31	392	12.6	...	1	21	310	14.8	...	—	—
Norfolk Island	1987	2	18[17]	122	13.2[17]	...	1	17	115	17	...	—	—

students[d]	student/ teacher ratio	third level (higher) institutions	teachers[c]	students[d]	student/ teacher ratio	gross enrollment ratio	students per 100,000 population[b]	percent of population age 25 and over with post-secondary education[b]	literacy[b] over age	total (%)	male (%)	female (%)	public expenditure on education (percent of GNP)[b]	country
9,505	...	34	3,404	60,994	17.9	13.8	1,270	...	15	69.0	73.2	65.3	3.0	El Salvador
19	19				—	3.8	324	...	...	31.5	46.0	17.0	...	Equatorial Guinea
4,969[1]	12.7[1]	11[2]	1,314[1]	18,436	...	0.7[1]	63	...	...	3.7	...	...	3.6	Ethiopia
1,422	...	1		94	...	...	...	...	15	99.0	...	...	...	Faeroe Islands
—	—	—	—	—	—	—	...	...	15	99.5	...	...	...	Falkland Islands
3,793	14.8	5[4]	...	1,877	...	3.0	272	3.3	15	85.5	90.2	80.9	6.7	Fiji
114,183	...	14	14	127,976	...	32.7[1]	2,616	5.5	15	100.0	100.0	100.0	5.5	Finland
19	19	1,094[6]	46,648[1]	1,163,903[1]	25.0	29.3[2]	2,362	...	15	98.8	98.9	98.7	5.8	France
2,623	...	...	...	...	...	...	...	6.4	16	82.0	82.5	81.3	19.2	French Guiana
3,441	9.5	...	...	180[2]	...	...	...	...	15	95.0	94.9	95.0	9.7	French Polynesia
13,529	18.8	1[2]	616[2]	3,228[2]	5.2[2]	3.6[4]	290	...	15	77.0	...	...	4.9	Gabon
10,102	20.1	9	177	1,489	8.4	—	...	0.2	15	24.9	35.6	15.1	4.3	Gambia, The
831	17	1[4]	30[3]	2,387[4]	...	...	...	9.5[23]	...	...	...	...	...	Gaza Strip
378,761	6.9	54	42,336	432,672	10.2	30.5	2,581	17.3	15	100.0	100.0	100.0	5.4	Germany, East
2,600,822	30.0	110	336,996	1,366,057	4.0	29.8[1]	2,546	4.3	15	100.0	100.0	100.0	4.6	Germany, West
40,485	14.0	9	1,316	10,225	7.8	1.5[2]	125	0.4	15	53.2	64.1	42.8	2.3	Ghana
352	14.1	—	—	—	—	—	...	...	10	99.0	99.0	99.0	6.0	Gibraltar
101,558	12.0	102	11,735	167,957	14.3	20.9[4]	1,518	7.6	14	93.8	97.3	90.6	2.4	Greece
1,469[7]	...	—	—	—	—	...	...	...	15	100.0	100.0	100.0	...	Greenland
...	...	2	195	850	4.4	...	...	1.5	15	85.0	...	...	5.6	Grenada
...	...	1	92	5,212	56.7	...	...	5.2	15	90.1	89.7	90.5	15.2	Guadeloupe
2,410	20.6	1	206	2,208	10.7	...	...	34.4	15	96.4	96.4	96.5	8.0	Guam
19	19	12, 16	3,043[2, 16]	45,552[2, 14]	15.0[2, 14]	8.6[7]	779	1.2	15	55.0	62.8	47.4	1.8	Guatemala
134	2.9	—	—	—	—	...	...	...	15	100.0	100.0	100.0	...	Guernsey
4,929	6.5	23	946	7,470	7.9	1.7[1]	145	...	15	28.3	39.7	17.2	3.3	Guinea
1,027	9.6	...	...	...	...	—	...	0.1	15	31.4	46.2	17.3	3.4	Guinea-Bissau
4,647[8]	13.4[8]	17	258[7]	1,626[7]	6.3[7]	2.1[2]	245	1.8	15	95.5	97.1	94.0	8.7	Guyana
3,210	...	...	818[2]	5,492[2]	6.7[2]	1.1[2]	101	0.7	15	34.7	37.1	32.5	1.2	Haiti
81,920	...	7[1]	2,692[1]	34,478[1]	14.0[1]	9.5[1]	838	3.3	15	59.5	60.7	58.4	4.3	Honduras
21,593	18.4	11	3,530	34,434	9.8	12.8[2]	1,410	7.1	15	88.1	94.7	80.9	2.8	Hong Kong
373,187	16.6	54	15,302	99,025	6.5	15.4[1]	929	7.0	15	98.9	99.2	98.6	7.0	Hungary
4,280	...	4	280	4,780	17.1	22.1[1]	2,040	3.7	15	100.0	100.0	100.0	4.1	Iceland
3,196,963[14]	...	14	14	14	...	8.7[15]	776	2.5	15	40.8	54.8	25.7	3.7	India
1,106,106	14.7	478[2]	74,044[2]	806,470[2]	10.9[2]	6.5[2]	600	0.8	15	74.1	83.0	65.4	2.0	Indonesia
277,609	13.4	114[4]	13,698	145,809	10.6	4.7[1]	439	...	15	42.8	55.4	30.1	3.8	Iran
152,206	19.4	25[4]	7,176[2]	126,715[2]	17.7[2]	10.0[4]	856	...	15	45.9	65.9	26.0	3.8	Iraq
83,938	16.2	25	3,690[2]	51,341	...	21.6[2]	1,888	7.9	15	100.0	100.0	100.0	6.7	Ireland
450[7]	...	...	...	...	...	...	...	...	...	...	...	...	...	Isle of Man
102,739	...	7[16]	8,112[7]	98,821[27]	...	34.2[2]	2,769	23.1	15	91.8	95.0	88.3	8.5	Israel
2,658,588	21.2	...	...	1,179,851[7]	...	26.3[2]	2,065	4.1	15	97.0	97.9	96.3	5.7	Italy
7,856	15.7	17	...	14,581	...	5.9[3]	659	2.0	14	88.6	88.2	89.1	5.7	Jamaica
...	...	1,097	138,587	2,597,073	18.7	29.6[2]	2,006	14.3	15	100.0	100.0	100.0	5.6	Japan
...	...	...	...	...	...	...	...	...	...	...	...	...	4.1	Jersey
27,042[21]	26.7[21]	3	1,295	26,711	20.6	37.4[4]	1,590	0.8	15	79.4	...	...	4.7	Jordan
7,334	26.4	2[4]	...	586[4]	...	...	...	...	15	48.0	...	...	...	Kampuchea
24,984	16.1	4	...	19,798	...	1.3[1]	106	...	15	59.2	69.6	49.2	6.7	Kenya
534	12.4	...	...	...	...	...	...	...	15	90.0	...	...	8.7	Kiribati
19	19	175	9,244	200,000	21.6	...	...	...	...	90.0	...	...	3.6	Korea, North
1,007,272	29.5	459	35,573	1,332,455	37.5	32.9[7]	3,672	8.9	15	92.7	97.5	87.9	4.9	Korea, South
12,272[7]	15.6[7]	1	887	17,414	19.6	15.5[1]	1,307	10.1	15	75.1	78.7	69.6	4.6	Kuwait
19,358	8.3	8	452[4]	6,400[7]	...	1.4[4]	122	...	15	45.2	52.8	37.6	...	Laos
37,036	10.6	18[3]	7,460	70,510	9.4	27.4[2]	2,634	3.1	15	77.0	85.7	68.9	...	Lebanon
2,221	10.0	1	146	1,119	7.7	1.8[2]	158	0.1	15	73.6	62.4	84.5	3.3	Lesotho
2,322	36.9	3	190	3,955[1]	...	2.5[15]	203	1.5	15	22.4	27.4	18.4	5.7	Liberia
50,363	12.9	8[3]	1,340[8]	25,700[3]	...	10.6[1]	832	1.0	10	74.4	85.0	62.0	5.7	Libya
117[30]	...	—	—	—	—	—	...	5.4	15	100.0	100.0	100.0	...	Liechtenstein
15,785	...	...	31	934[1]	...	2.9[2]	232	...	15	100.0	100.0	100.0	5.6	Luxembourg
52[21]	4.0[21]	5	75	5,840	77.9	—	...	1.4	10	61.3	76.4	46.2	...	Macau
11,041	8.5	3	1,059	37,746	35.6	4.6[1]	383	...	15	67.5	73.7	61.6	3.5	Madagascar
2,441	7.8	4	278	1,974	7.1	0.7[9]	58	0.2	15	41.2	...	...	3.7	Malawi
21,337	11.2	41[1]	8,415[1]	96,212[1]	11.4[1]	6.0[1]	599	...	15	72.6	82.2	63.2	6.6	Malaysia
462	8.9	—	—	—	—	...	...	0.4	15	81.1	80.2	82.0	0.6	Maldives
12,612	14.2	7	499	5,792	11.6	1.1	93	0.2	15	10.1	18.6	1.8	3.3	Mali
6,610	10.0	1	142	1,449	10.2	4.7[1]	385	2.4	15	96.0	96.2	95.9	3.4	Malta
15,410[4]	23.6[4]	1	40	1,220	30.5	...	...	...	15	92.5	91.8	93.2	13.9	Martinique
4,336	9.6[2]	7[2]	256[4]	4,434	...	...	...	...	15	28.0	38.0	17.0	7.4	Mauritania
444[2]	...	2[2]	184[3]	344	...	0.7[1]	91	3.6	15[33]	81.8[33]	89.0[33]	74.8[33]	3.8	Mauritius
19	19	—	—	—	—	...	...	...	15	31.8	...	...	...	Mayotte
2,088,292[7]	15.0[7]	1,347[7]	98,061[7]	1,072,764[7]	13.7[7]	16.0[1]	1,529	4.9	15	90.3	92.3	88.3	2.6	Mexico
1,218	...	...	...	...	...	...	...	6.8	...	...	...	...	...	Monaco
27,700	23.1	8	1,500	24,500	16.4	25.5[6]	2,297	...	15	89.5	93.4	85.5	7.0	Mongolia
60	4.6	...	...	...	...	...	...	5.8	15	90.0	...	...	3.5	Montserrat
7,432[21]	11.0[21]	28	5,753	157,374	27.4	8.8[1]	820	...	15	70.7	82.4	58.7	7.9	Morocco
10,485	12.2	2	330	1,569	4.8	0.1[1]	10	...	15	16.6	20.0	13.3	1.2	Mozambique
60	15.0	—	—	88[34]	—	...	...	...	15	99.0	...	...	...	Nauru
648[7]	5.5[7]	116[7]	4,165[7]	67,555[7]	16.2	4.6[2]	397	6.8	15	20.7	31.9	9.2	3.0	Nepal
635,493	11.4	453	30,952	307,537	9.9	31.0[2]	2,704	7.2	15	100.0	100.0	100.0	6.9	Netherlands, The
732	9.3	1	53	677	12.8	...	...	4.4	15	95.0	...	...	10.1	Netherlands Antilles
5,887	29.4	6	40	853	21.3	...	...	...	14	89.4	90.1	88.7	13.4	New Caledonia
131,655[35]	42.1	7[16]	2,974[16]	35,177[16]	11.8[16]	35.1[1]	3,255	30.6	15	100.0	100.0	100.0	4.5	New Zealand
19	19	16	2,527	29,001	11.5	9.8	886	...	15	88.0	...	...	5.6	Nicaragua
2,351[6]	19.6[6]	16	314[2]	2,863[2]	9.1[2]	0.6[2]	48	...	15	9.8	14.0	5.8	3.3	Niger
391,588	24.9	80[4]	...	101,558	...	2.9	239	...	15	42.4	53.8	31.5	1.3	Nigeria
—	—	—	—	—	—	—	...	1.9	15	99.8	99.7	99.9	...	Niue
—	—	—	—	—	—	...	...	...	15	100.0	100.0	100.0	...	Norfolk Island

Education (continued)

country	year	first level (primary)					general second level (secondary)					vocational second level[a]	
		schools	teachers[c]	students[d]	student/ teacher ratio	net enroll- ment ratio	schools	teachers[c]	students[d]	student/ teacher ratio	net enroll- ment ratio	schools	teachers[c]
Norway	1986	3,525	31,459	534,000	17.0	97[2]	937[19]	18,156[19]	192,000[19]	10.6[19]	97[2]	19	19
Oman	1987	354	7,517	194,996	25.9	77[1]	304	3,734	50,749	13.6	14[6]	23	551
Pacific Is., Trust Territory of the													
Marshall Islands	1986	89	507[17]	9,906	22.9[17]	...	7	17	1,727	17	...	...	...
Micronesia, Fed. States of	1984	151	1,051	23,345	22.2	...	14	314	4,159	13.2	...	...	...
Northern Mariana Islands	1986	18	367	7,597	20.7	...	8	235	3,915	16.7	...	...	...
Palau	1987	26	289[17]	2,784	13.1[17]	...	6	17	1,009	17	...	1[2]	36[2]
Pakistan	1987	88,734	207,800	8,081,000	38.9	...	11,436	158,300	2,661,000	16.8	...	296	4,346
Panama	1986	2,574	14,176	341,914	24.1	89[1]	334	10,113	187,312	18.5	47[1]	70	644
Papua New Guinea	1986	2,461	12,318	374,950	30.4	...	122	2,025	49,974	24.7	...	112	745
Paraguay	1985	3,993	22,764	570,775	25.1	86	740[19]	9,044[19]	172,132[19]	19.0[19]	21[15]	19	19
Peru	1986	31,186	123,000	4,060,000	33.0	97[1]	4,831	74,000	1,676,000	22.6	...	288	7,000
Philippines	1986	33,104	289,251	8,925,959	30.9	95[1]	5,388[1]	99,468	3,214,159	32.3	50[1]	36	36
Pitcairn Island	1986	1[17]	1[17]	15	18.0[17]	...	17	17	3	17	...	...	...
Poland	1987	17,553	262,500	5,007,800	19.1	99[1]	898	21,100	353,100	16.7	73[1]	6,635	78,500
Portugal	1986	12,741	73,343	1,238,112	16.9	97[4]	1,509	53,881	647,391	12.0	28[10]	345[2]	2,971[2]
Puerto Rico	1986	1,542	18,359	427,582	23.3	...	395	13,612	334,661	24.6	...	52	...
Qatar	1986[25]	90	2,764	31,844	11.5	100[1]	68	2,250	19,506	8.7	57[1]	3	105
Réunion	1986	349	3,811	73,985	19.4	...	851,[19]	3,984[19]	46,550	17.5[19]	...	19	19
Romania	1987	14,046	144,878	3,017,339	20.8	...	981	46,124	1,196,949	25.9	...	747	12,420
Rwanda	1985	1,594	14,896	836,877	56.2	61	...	1,331[19]	7,252	...	2	...	19
St. Helena and Ascension	1983	8	32	589	18.4	...	4	33	507	15.4	...	2	10
St. Kitts and Nevis	1987	32	266[25]	7,805	24.7[25]	...	6	268	4,153	15.5	...	1	18
St. Lucia	1987	78[25]	1,103[25]	32,400[25]	29.4[25]	...	12[25]	337[25]	5,934[25]	17.6[25]	...	4	...
St. Pierre and Miquelon	1985	5	39	612	15.7	...	3[15]	56[4]	535[4]	9.6[4]	...	2[15]	15[4]
St. Vincent and the Grenadines	1986	62[4]	1,263	24,561	19.4	...	19[4]	368	6,535	17.8	...	5[4]	...
San Marino	1987	13	171	1,363	8.0	...	5	179	1,222	6.8	...	...	...
São Tomé and Príncipe	1985	63	517	19,086	36.9	...	11	300	6,186	20.6	...	2	35
Saudi Arabia	1986	7,566	77,480	1,285,433	16.6	55[1]	2,946	37,096	524,738	14.1	29[1]	31	2,350
Senegal	1986	2,171	11,513	583,507	41.2	44[1]	162	2,346[2]	113,653	...	...	5	...
Seychelles	1988	26[7]	702	14,522	20.7	...	47	162	2,643	16.3	...	1[7]	147
Sierra Leone	1985	1,219	10,451	350,160	33.5	...	171	3,829	81,879	21.4	...	12	406
Singapore	1987	298	11,259	280,889	24.9	100[2]	157	9,301	201,125	21.6	58[15]	18	2,029
Solomon Islands	1986	430	1,849	39,563	21.4	...	20	276	5,553	20.1	...	2[2]	63[2]
Somalia	1985	1,121	14,521	274,610	18.9	18[4]	80	2,522	65,186	25.8	7[6]	23	725
South Africa	1987	19,310[17]	227,700[17]	5,045,000	29.8[17]	...	17	17	1,747,000	17	...	132[1]	18,290
Bophuthatswana	1982	802	7,221	373,653	51.7	...	310	4,391	115,737	26.4	...	18	360
Ciskei	1986	538	4,559	194,921	42.8	...	157	1,875	45,783	24.4	...	2	32
Transkei	1983	...	...	582,090	...	...	...	...	150,720	...	...	...	...
Venda	1984	375	3,638	132,042	36.3	...	134	1,544	41,253	26.7	...	1	33
South West Africa/Namibia	1986	1,074[17]	11,121[17]	273,500	31.5[17]	...	17	17	76,580	17	...	5	81
Spain	1986	23,105[4]	193,455	5,594,285	28.9	100[4]	2,635	75,550	1,234,874	16.3	75[3]	2,248	49,408
Sri Lanka	1985	9,349	144,707	2,242,645	15.5	...	5,629[4]	113,148[4]	2,930,070[4]	25.9[4]	...	27	1,101
Sudan, The	1985	6,707	47,750	1,653,491	34.6	...	2,167	17,591	490,583	27.9	...	98	1,513[2]
Suriname	1985	...	2,809	71,454	25.4	98[2]	63	1,047	18,612	17.8	...	64	1,283
Swaziland	1987	477	4,462	147,743	33.1	85[2]	113	1,760	32,942	18.7	21[10]	7	181
Sweden	1987	4,667	98,920	920,780	9.3	96[6]	534	28,550	243,971	8.5	81[6]	...	...
Switzerland	1987	...	...	405,800	...	...	...	...	368,600	...	...	...	...
Syria	1987	9,315	85,583	2,158,594	25.2	97[1]	1,922	52,074	855,453	16.4	53[1]	143	7,245
Taiwan	1987	2,461	74,433	2,356,304	31.7	...	839	60,796	1,247,774	20.5	...	203	16,613
Tanzania	1986	10,147	93,000	3,160,000	34.0	54[1]	193[1]	4,329[1]	83,098[1]	19.2[1]	...	41	1,277
Thailand	1985	32,359	369,822	7,150,489	19.3	...	1,437[8]	100,218[25]	1,870,360[25]	18.7[25]	...	1,528[8]	17,893[2]
Togo	1987	2,345	10,229	474,998	46.5	67[2]	248[3]	3,985[2]	88,327	...	...	18	198
Tokelau	1983	3[8]	39	482	15.8	...	3[8]	6[8]	80[8]	13.3[8]	...	...	12[8]
Tonga	1985	112	744	17,019	22.9	...	50[2]	770	14,644	19.0	...	12[2]	70
Trinidad and Tobago	1985	468	7,627	168,308	22.1	90	95	4,744	92,595	19.5	50	...	...
Tunisia	1988	3,605	43,189	1,338,905	31.0	95[1]	428	22,373	480,245	21.5	32[2]	...	...
Turkey	1986	47,630	212,717	6,635,821	31.2	84[1]	5,734	93,384	2,282,537	24.4	33[1]	2,075	44,298
Turks and Caicos Islands	1985	17	1,540	74	20.8	...	3	51	707	13.9	...	—	—
Tuvalu	1984	11	61	1,349	22.1	100[3]	1	15[4]	243	16.7[4]	...	8[4]	16[4]
Uganda	1984	6,420	58,377	1,908,564	32.7	40[3]	297	5,603	114,828	20.5	...	118	1,039
U.S.S.R.	1987	65,500	2,668,000[17]	36,800,000	13.8[17]	...	62,000	17	4,600,000	17	...	4,506	246,000[1]
United Arab Emirates	1986	327[17]	5,278[25]	152,125	...	77[1]	17	3,967[25]	61,468	17	...	9[2]	273[2]
United Kingdom	1986[25]	24,756	205,800	4,520,800	22.0	100[2]	5,161	260,500	4,080,000	15.7	81[4]	753[37]	93,000[1, 37]
United States	1988	101,050[17]	1,517,000	31,704,000	20.9	96[1]	17	1,075,000[19]	13,734,000[19]	12.8[19]	89[1]	19	19
Uruguay	1987	2,371	16,212	352,459	21.7	91[1]	268	9,045	169,932	18.8	55[2]	94	...
Vanuatu	1983	265[7]	934	23,856[7]	...	...	9	126[3]	2,186	...	...	2	40[3]
Venezuela	1986	19,868	130,227	3,332,366	25.6	86[1]	2,277[19]	60,112[19]	1,037,950[19]	17.3[19]	38[1]	19	19
Vietnam	1986	13,596[17]	414,000[17]	12,203,000[17]	29.5[17]	86[1]	17	17	17	17	...	298	11,400
Virgin Islands (U.S.)	1987[38]	41	781[39]	14,723	...	...	10	506[39]	10,903	...	...	3[2]	27[2]
Wallis and Futuna	1983	13[26]	134[3]	3,962	...	...	...	...	1503,[34]	...	...	—	—
West Bank	1987[40]	1,142[17]	8,972[17]	181,804	31.7[17]	...	17	17	102,659	17	...	17	17
Western Sahara	1985	24	428	13,943	32.6	...	7	237	4,560	19.2	...	...	...
Western Samoa	1983	164	1,502[41]	31,447	20.9	...	38[2]	520	20,404	39.2	...	4	69
Yemen (Aden)	1984	924	11,281	294,028	26.1	...	51	1,493	29,205	19.6	...	29	453
Yemen (Şan'ā')	1986	5,824	15,092	904,487	59.9	22[10]	942	5,298	121,922	23.0	3[10]	73	445[2]
Yugoslavia	1986	12,148	137,201	2,846,845	20.7	80[8]	1,212	62,797	952,904	15.2	76[8]	20[42]	...
Zaire	1986	10,065[2]	112,077[2]	4,993,523	44.6	75[4]	3,972[2]	49,459[2]	3,198,051	...	49[2]	20[42]	...
Zambia	1986	3,164	29,841	1,442,133	48.3	86[4]	276	5,627	150,298	26.8	...	28	1,055
Zimbabwe	1986	4,297	57,823	2,260,367	39.1	100[2]	1,262[19]	19,560	545,841	27.9	...	14[21]	1,031[21]

[1]1985. [2]1984. [3]1982. [4]1983. [5]Excludes lycées for general education. [6]1981. [7]1986. [8]1980. [9]Age 30 and over. [10]1975. [11]General second level includes teacher training at the second level. [12]1977. [13]National literacy standard based solely on school attendance. [14]Vocational second level includes third level. [15]1979. [16]Universities only. [17]First level includes second level. [18]1976. [19]General second level includes vocational second level. [20]Republic of Cyprus only. [21]Teacher training only. [22]Includes preschool. [23]Includes East Jerusalem. [24]Schools under the Department of Education and Culture only. [25]Public schools only. [26]Includes intermediate education (ages 12–14). [27]Includes post-secondary teacher training. [28]General second level includes

students[d]	student/ teacher ratio	third level (higher) institutions	teachers[c]	students[d]	student/ teacher ratio	gross enrollment ratio	students per 100,000 population[b]	percent of population age 25 and over with post-secondary education[b]	literacy[b] over age	total (%)	male (%)	female (%)	public expenditure on education (percent of GNP)[b]	country
19	19	228	7,025	94,503	13.4	30.8[1]	2,339	11.9	15	100.0	100.0	100.0	6.7	Norway
2,963	5.4	1	123	520	4.0	0.5[1]	40	...	6	38.0	55.0	20.0	4.4	Oman
								7.8	25	86.3	89.1	83.2	...	Pacific Is., Trust Territory of the Marshall Islands
				920				8.0	15	76.7	67.0	87.2	...	Micronesia, Fed. States of
		1	20	534	26.7	...	...	21.9	25	94.9	96.0	93.5		Northern Mariana Islands
382[2]	10.6[2]							16.8	25	92.7	94.4	91.0		Palau
61,000	14.0	595	22,601	550,308	24.4	5.1[1]	488	1.9	15	25.6	36.0	15.2	2.1	Pakistan
10,548	16.4	8	4,650	56,227	12.1	25.9[1]	2,536	8.4	15	88.2	89.0	87.7	5.4	Panama
10,078	13.5	2	400	3,029	7.6	1.7[1]	144	...	15	42.3	52.4	31.3	7.7	Papua New Guinea
19	19	2	2,694	29,154	10.8	9.7[2]	929	2.0	15	85.7	88.7	82.9	1.6	Paraguay
151,000	21.6	46	22,000	394,000	17.9	24.0[1]	2,271	10.1	15	81.6	89.9	73.5	2.9	Peru
36	36	1,178[1,36]	33,935[1,36]	1,127,968[1,36]	33.2[1,36]	38.0[1]	3,621	15.2	15	88.7	89.9	87.5	1.3	Philippines
—	—	—	—	—	—				15	100.0	100.0	100.0		Pitcairn Island
1,327,300	16.9	92	57,700	261,100	4.5	16.5[1]	1,221	5.7	15	99.2	...	...	4.7	Poland
27,946[2]	9.4[2]	51[1]	10,505	107,650	10.2	12.6[2]	1,112	1.6	15	79.4	84.8	74.6	4.2	Portugal
149,191	...	45	9,045	156,818	17.3	48.1[6]	4,100	18.4	15	89.1	89.7	88.5	8.2	Puerto Rico
700	6.7	1[30]	452[30]	4,931[30]	10.9[30]	19.3[1]	1,697	...	15	74.7	76.8	72.5	5.6	Qatar
23,313	19	1[30]	90[30]	3,515[30]	39.1	...	...	...	15	78.6	76.5	80.5	15.3	Réunion
257,196	20.7	44	12,504	157,174	12.6	11.2[1]	694	4.6	15	95.8	...	...	2.1	Romania
10,881	...	3	305[4]	1,705[4]	5.6[4]	0.3[4]	30	0.3	15	49.4	62.2	37.2	3.1	Rwanda
48	4.8								15	97.1	96.8	97.5	...	St. Helena and Ascension
166	9.2	1[25]	9[25]	55[25]	6.1[25]	...	...	2.1	15	90.0	...	...	6.9	St. Kitts and Nevis
817	...	1	16	123	7.7	...	...	1.3	15	59.7	...	...	7.8	St. Lucia
216[4]	14.4[4]	—	—	—	—	...	...	7.5	15	99.5	99.5	99.5	...	St. Pierre and Miquelon
275	...	1[4]	19[4]	105[4]	5.5[4]	...	...	1.4	15	85.0	...	...	5.0	St. Vincent and the Grenadines
744[34]	—	—	...	332[34]	...	...	...	...	15	98.0	98.2	97.7	...	San Marino
370	10.6	...	...	700[4,34]	...	...	...	0.3	15	54.2	70.2	39.1	6.4	São Tomé and Príncipe
21,110	8.9	77	9,724	102,709	10.6	10.8[1]	905	...	12	57.2	69.7	35.1	8.9	Saudi Arabia
3,515	...	7	497[2]	13,450	...	2.4[1]	206	...	15	22.5	31.0	14.2	4.7	Senegal
1,405	9.6							2.6	15	57.3	54.9	59.6	9.0	Seychelles
4,774	11.8	2	296	2,445	8.3	0.6[8]	55	...	15	23.6	31.2	16.5	3.8	Sierra Leone
27,001	13.3	6	3,961	44,746	11.3	11.8[4]	1,406	3.4	15	82.9	91.6	74.0	4.4	Singapore
1,142[2]	18.1[2]	—	—	—	—	...	...	1.6	15	54.1	62.4	44.9	5.5	Solomon Islands
10,203	14.1	1	262[6]	3,405	...	0.9[15]	72	...	10	54.8	60.9	47.9	1.4	Somalia
151,131	8.3	84[1]	27,352	247,694	9.1	...	...	3.7	15	79.3	80.6	78.0	3.8	South Africa
6,053	16.8	1	36[8]	816	...	...	...	...	15	75.0	...	...	...	Bophuthatswana
240	7.5	4	76[2]	1,383	...	...	...	...	15	72.0	...	...	...	Ciskei
		...	...	560	...	...	...	...						Transkei
358	10.8	4	119	2,857	24.0	...	...	...						Venda
1,200	14.8	3	137	537	3.9	...	...	...	15	72.5	74.2	70.8	1.9	South West Africa/Namibia
738,340	14.9	33[1]	34,378[1]	784,173[1]	22.8[1]	26.7[2]	2,167	7.1	15	92.8	95.9	89.9	3.3	Spain
20,796	18.9	8[16]	2,792	56,020	20.1	4.6	432	1.1	15	86.1	90.8	81.2	3.1	Sri Lanka
30,973	...	16	1,464[4]	35,648	...	2.0[4]	175	...	15	21.6	36.5	6.5	4.8	Sudan, The
15,996	12.5	...	373	2,914	7.8	6.9[2]	783	...	15	79.2	83.8	74.8	8.6	Suriname
1,280	7.1	1	178	1,270	7.1	3.3[4]	278	...	15	67.0	69.0	65.0	5.2	Swaziland
			24,990	341,712	13.7	38.1[2]	2,650	...	15	100.0	100.0	100.0	7.7	Sweden
249,900	...	...	...	117,000	...	22.6[7]	1,790	...	15	100.0	100.0	100.0	4.9	Switzerland
56,664	7.8	4[16]	...	138,743[16]	...	16.8[2]	1,616	1.3	15	61.1	76.5	45.5	5.9	Syria
436,276	26.3	105	21,769	442,648	20.3	...	2,225	...	15	90.8	95.8	85.4	3.6	Taiwan
13,956	10.9	2	877[1]	3,342	...	0.4[2]	26	...	15	85.0	...	...	4.3	Tanzania
390,640[2]	21.8[2]	628[1]	30,905	1,026,952	33.2	19.6	1,998	2.9	15	88.8	93.2	84.5	3.9	Thailand
5,050	25.5	1	308	4,500	14.6	1.8[2]	156	1.3	15	39.1	51.7	27.5	5.4	Togo
197[8]	16.4[8]	—	—	32[34]	—	...	...	...	15	99.8	99.8	99.8	...	Tokelau
591	8.4	1[3]		705		...	...	...	15	92.8	92.9	92.8	4.5	Tonga
3,802	...	1	...	2,684	...	4.2	464	2.9	15	95.1	96.7	93.6	5.9	Trinidad and Tobago
			5,171[30]	43,797	...	5.8[1]	587	2.8	15	48.2	60.4	35.7	4.7	Tunisia
635,847	14.4	310	22,968	449,416	19.6	8.9[2]	863	3.6	15	65.6	81.3	49.8	2.3	Turkey
								7.7	15	86.7	85.0	88.0	...	Turks and Caicos Islands
354[4]	22.1[4]	—	—	—	—	—	...	...	15	95.5	95.5	95.5	...	Tuvalu
23,335	22.5	14	934	8,216	8.8	0.6	55	0.1	15	57.3	69.7	45.3	1.3	Uganda
2,880,000	...	896	377,000[1]	2,688,000	...	21.3[1]	1,667	11.5	15	99.0	...	...	6.6	U.S.S.R.
2,442[2]	8.9[2]	...	449[1]	6,326[1]	14.1[1]	8.4[1]	576	6.0	15	73.0	74.5	68.4	1.9	United Arab Emirates
506,600[37]	...	46[16]	31,412	352,419	11.2	22.4[2]	1,795	...	15	100.0	100.0	100.0	5.2	United Kingdom
19	19	3,406	722,000	7,117,000	9.9	57.4[1]	5,145	31.9	15	95.5	95.7	95.3	6.8	United States
54,727	...	1	...	91,580	...	31.7[1]	3,040	6.3	10	95.3	94.8	95.8	2.6	Uruguay
718	...	—	—	—	—	...	...	...	15	52.9	57.3	47.8	...	Vanuatu
19	19	82	31,735	444,450	14.0	26.4[1]	2,559	7.0	15	89.0	90.7	87.2	6.6	Venezuela
128,000	11.2	97	18,800	88,600	4.7	2.2[8]	212	3.0	15	94.0	...	...	3.0	Vietnam
775[2]	28.7[2]	1	97	757	8.3	...	...	17.6	15	90.0	...	...	7.4	Virgin Islands (U.S.)
								1.0[9]	20	48.9	51.4	46.6	...	Wallis and Futuna
1,225	17	4[4]	483[15]	7,066[4]	—	...	...	8.1	...	...	...	...	...	West Bank
									15	...	...	...	...	Western Sahara
651	9.4	6	37	562	15.2	...	...	2.2	15	97.8	97.8	97.9	5.9	Western Samoa
5,602	12.4	1	486[4]	6,256[7]	...	2.3[6]	177	...	15	38.9	66.6	10.9	7.4	Yemen (Aden)
11,616	...	1[2]	245[2]	9,024[2]	36.8[2]	1.2[8]	76	...	15	18.9	38.5	3.1	7.5	Yemen (Şan'ā')
	...	103	25,629	349,013	13.6	19.5[2]	1,571	...	15	89.6	95.5	83.9	3.6	Yugoslavia
319,805	...	36	3,072	37,706	12.3	1.6	137	...	15	61.2	78.6	44.7	3.4	Zaire
9,687	9.2	11	613[1]	4,860[1]	7.9[1]	1.6[1]	132	0.4	15	68.6	79.3	58.3	5.4	Zambia
30,935	...	1	431[2]	5,866	...	3.9[7]	342	0.6	15	76.0	81.5	66.8	8.1	Zimbabwe

first level. [29]Includes part-time teachers. [30]1987. [31]General second level includes vocational second level and third level. [32]1972. [33]Island of Mauritius only. [34]Students registered abroad. [35]Includes part-time students. [36]Third level includes vocational second level. [37]Third level vocational and teacher training. [38]Excludes 19 combined primary-secondary schools. [39]Public school teachers only. [40]Excludes East Jerusalem. [41]Includes some secondary teachers. [42]1978.

Cultural institutions

This table supplies worldwide statistics for the principal and most comparable elements of cultural activity: publishing, libraries, cinema, performing arts, museums, and nature preservation. For the most part, the data that can be compiled and compared are those measures produced as a result of governmental activity or expenditure, such as copyright and deposit, public funding, taxation, and land-use policy.

International comparisons of such data, however, should be approached with caution. In older, more prosperous nations, where the physical necessities of life are in secure supply, more money is available for cultural activities—and, indeed, for collecting data on them—than in less developed countries. Yet a developing country with an embryonic statistical system may have a flourishing cultural life that includes theatrical performance, live music, or the practice of arts no longer central to the Western experience, such as oral storytelling, ceremonial dance, traditional community ritual, or puppetry. Such activities may be more fully integrated into the life of the people than the more measurable cultural pursuits of a developed society.

The statistics actually reported may include books published (copyrighted), cultural facilities, library holdings, seating capacities of theatres and cinemas, attendance (tickets sold), and so on. Even when these figures are recalculated on a per capita basis, apparent differences among countries may be more a function of each country's statistical reporting system than of differences in the cultural habits and preferences of the people.

Furthermore, some kinds of data cannot be given meaningfully. For example, available data on government expenditures for cultural activities represent a wide variety of government policies. Some governments provide no support for cultural activities at any level; others subsidize or support them directly. Some offer tax incentives; others employ artists as teachers, performers, scholars, or archivists. Most national data on manpower engaged in cultural activities are collected on the basis of the individual's main source of income, without regard for his or her aspirations or avocations, part-time paid or unpaid activities, or other less convenient measures. A substantial part of the data presented were obtained from periodic surveys by Unesco, and they refer to a wide range of years. Throughout the table, data given in roman type are from 1984 or later; those in italic are from before 1984.

Figures for book production generally include all works published in separate bindings except advertising works, timetables, telephone directories, price lists, catalogs of businesses or exhibitions, musical scores, maps, atlases, and the like. The figures include government publications, school texts, theses, offprints, series works, and illustrated works, even those consisting principally of illustrations. Figures refer to works actually published during the year of survey, usually by a registered publisher, and deposited for copyright. A book is defined as a work of 49 or more pages, a pamphlet as a work of from 5 to 48 pages. A work published simultaneously in more than one country is counted as having been published in each. Data for newspapers are given in the Communications table beginning on page 818.

Data on libraries are for public libraries and exclude other types of collections, such as national (except when it is the sole *public* library), school

Cultural institutions

country	book publishing								public libraries			
	number of titles				number of copies ('000)				number	volumes ('000)	registered borrowers ('000)	loans per 1,000 population
	books		periodicals	pamphlets	books		periodicals	pamphlets				
	total	of which school textbooks			total	of which school textbooks						
Afghanistan	415[3]	108[3]	51	...	5,981[3]	...	1,094	...	55	350	11	...
Albania	844	555	8	95	5,410	3,456	2,894	300	45	3,723	...	...
Algeria	551	39	27	167	1,300[5]	1,194	476	...	35	165	...	...
American Samoa	98[3]	24[3]	16	7[3]	333.8	...	8	13	1	251	...	5,400
Andorra	...	...	15	...	...	...	15	...	1	...	...	631
Angola	35[3]	...	...	12[3]	338[3]	...	81	191[3]	2	41	...	...
Anguilla	...	...	...	...	...	...	...	...	...	...	...	...
Antigua and Barbuda	...	...	...	...	...	...	...	...	1	...	...	...
Argentina	4,216[10]	243[10]	...	10	13,526[10]	1,289[10]	...	10	1,528	9,532	4,201	360
Aruba	12	...	...	12	...	...	...	...	12	12	12	12
Australia	1,954	165	3,534	649	...	...	...	...	350	24,500	...	...
Austria	8,008	637	2,273	1,141	...	...	...	...	2,042	6,916	768	1,880
Bahamas, The	...	...	...	...	...	...	...	...	37	60	...	...
Bahrain	46	46	...	...	858	858	237	49	13	204	315	722
Bangladesh	1,209	...	255	...	...	...	558	...	69	500	...	...
Barbados	18	...	120	69	...	...	...	...	1[14]	173	64	2,212
Belgium	6,527[10]	...	11,256	10	...	...	...	...	2,351	24,140	1,731	4,300
Belize	—	—	...	12[5]	—	—	...	156[5]	1	100	...	...
Benin	13	...	—	—	18	...	...	—	1	32	1	...
Bermuda	...	...	...	...	...	...	...	...	1	149	3	...
Bhutan	...	...	...	...	...	...	...	...	—	—	—	—
Bolivia	274	4[3]	106	27	...	...	...	...	99[18]	125	1,120	37
Botswana	70[3]	...	...	273	35	...	...	33	1	108	30	190
Brazil	15,845	...	3,907	5,339	178,813	...	900,332	114,289	3,291	9,600	2,744	58
British Virgin Islands	20	...	20	...	3	...	23	—	1[14]	35	10	2,939
Brunei	25[3]	25[3]	19	—	263.10	249[3]	128	10	1	97	6	230
Bulgaria	4,322	1,026	1,758	849	54,843	12,145	10,211	8,263	5,699	52,100	2,225	5,800
Burkina Faso	4	...	—	—	9	...	...	...	—	—	...	...
Burma	673	...	26	—	...	...	823	—	6	154	...	...
Burundi	...	...	...	...	...	...	...	...	2	34	...	...
Cameroon	22[3]	7[3]	41	...	94[3]	7[3]	...	...	5	6	...	...
Canada	8,600	...	1,382	429	...	...	59,071	...	770	53,673	...	6,347
Cape Verde	10	...	4	...	13	...	...	...	—	—	...	...
Cayman Islands	5	...	—	—	...	...	...	—	1	6	2	2,300
Central African Republic	...	...	...	...	...	...	...	...	...	...	...	...
Chad	...	...	4	...	...	...	...	...	1	4	0.2	—
Chile	1,304	116	89	334	15,118	1,500	...	4,770	179	783	18	367
China	52,000[10]	6,159[10]	3,100	10	5,280,000[10]	2,488,460[10]	2,380,000	10	2,406	261,000	117,000	154
Christmas Island	...	...	...	...	...	...	...	...	1	13	3	8,000
Cocos (Keeling) Islands	...	...	...	...	...	...	...	...	1	...	...	...
Colombia	6,500	2,570	1,034	8,541	48,005	25,750	...	70,749	...	...	...	...
Comoros	...	...	...	...	...	...	...	...	2	8	...	...
Congo	9	...	...	118	285	...	...	1,471	1	11	14	22
Cook Islands	...	...	...	...	...	...	...	...	1	15	3	1,100
Costa Rica	1,759	825	274	—	641	...	163	...	18	707	...	...
Côte d'Ivoire	46	11	...	...	3,766	3,517	...	...	1	25	2	3
Cuba	1,713	863	47	455	41,623	22,027	2,279	5,420	318	5,377	554	1,258
Cyprus	72[30]	71	35	110[30]	603[30]	597	93	7[30]	130[18]	180	...	230
Czechoslovakia	8,718	3,157[3, 31]	1,080	1,126	76,268	21,811[3, 31]	22,983	11,953	9,453	56,577	2,908	6,447
Denmark	7,297	939[32]	3,564	3,660	...	...	...	...	250	34,122	...	16,600
Djibouti	...	...	2	...	...	...	1	...	2	16	...	64
Dominica	...	...	...	...	...	...	...	...	1	15	4	660
Dominican Republic	1,504	...	...	715	3,017	...	...	1,320	15	9	533	120
Ecuador	...	...	284	...	...	...	...	...	97	324	...	...
Egypt	1,192	286	216	85	57,716	45,332	2,188	2,404	223	1,329	6	10

and university, private, professional, business, or government libraries, even though these may play a significant role locally or nationally. Public libraries were thought to provide the most representative set of figures. Data for "volumes" may reflect either actual holdings or an estimate based on length of occupied shelving.

Statistics on commercial cinema attendance may originate from a variety of screening facilities, including fixed, mobile, or drive-in facilities. Seating capacity is given for fixed facilities only. The data on long (or feature) films may refer to prints with a length of from 1,000 to 3,000 metres, depending on the reporting practices of the individual country. However, there is some consensus among reporting countries on a standard length (for classification purposes) of 2,000 metres.

In the performing arts, many countries (if they report such data at all) include not only the familiar Western performance modes—music, theatre, opera, musical theatre, dance—but also other types of live performance, such as traditional, ceremonial, seasonal, festival, or holiday observances and such entertainments as circuses and puppet and shadow theatre. Data on number of performances and attendance refer to both amateur and professional performances unless footnoted. Statistics on the number of theatres refer to theatre buildings and open-air theatres intended mainly for theatrical and other dramatic performances. Premises only occasionally or partly used for performances of this type, such as cultural centres, cultural houses, youth centres, sports establishments, concert halls, cinemas, university and school premises, open-air grounds, antique theatres, historic buildings, and ancient sites, are excluded.

Museum data are derived in large part from surveys by Unesco and the International Council of Museums (ICOM). The number of museums and museum attendance refer to public and private institutions whose exhibits and collections are devoted primarily to art, archaeology and history, natural history and natural science and technology, or ethnology and anthropology; they may be specialized (single theme), regional, or general. National parks and nature reserves, zoos, aquariums, and botanical gardens have not been counted with museums since they are included in the nature conservation section of the table.

Data on nature preservation facilities generally refer to those operated by the national conservation authority (though in some countries, particularly those with federal systems, authority may be lodged with other governmental levels). The data on number of facilities cover all types of facilities operated by the relevant authority, including national parks and monuments, scientific reserves, game reserves, protected landscapes, resource and anthropological reserves, and multiple-use management areas. Data on surface extent usually include only those facilities with an area of more than 10 sq km (4 sq mi).

The data on national parks and nature reserves are derived from information compiled by the International Union for Conservation of Nature and Natural Resources (IUCN) and from Britannica's holdings of published and unpublished national data. The data on zoos, aquariums, and botanical gardens are mainly from the International Species Inventory System (zoos and aquariums) and the International Association of Botanical Gardens.

cinema					performing arts				museums			nature preservation			country
annual attendance (all cinemas)		fixed cinemas		number of long films produced	number of facilities	number of performances	annual attendance		number	annual attendance		national parks and nature reserves		zoos, botanical gardens, etc. (number[2])	
number ('000,000)	per 1,000 population	number	seating capacity ('000)				number ('000)	per 1,000 population		number ('000)	per 1,000 population	number	square metres per capita[1]		
4.9	300	34	19	3	...	...	...	...	7	7	0.5	6	120	1	Afghanistan
...	1,300	103[4]	28[4]	14	29	25,280	8,654	2,884	2,034	...	...	6	110	1	Albania
20.5[6]	900[6]	216	110	2	...	...	...	...	11[7]	391[7]	18[7]	5	100	3	Algeria
0.1	3,200	6	6	...	...	...	...	...	1	52	1,700	1	4,300	...	American Samoa
0.2	6,900	5	2	...	—	14	6	190	2	9	300	—	...	...	Andorra
3.2	400	44	33	1	3	6[9]	3[9]	...	10	...	...	5	1,800	1	Angola
...	...	...	...	...	...	...	...	...	...	...	...	...	...	...	Anguilla
...	...	3	...	...	...	...	...	...	3	...	...	1	250	...	Antigua and Barbuda
49.9[4,6]	1,700[4,6]	919[4]	622[4]	15	399	330	4,136[9]	160[9]	318	5,215[11]	200[11]	29	850	16	Argentina
...	...	...	...	...	...	...	...	12	...	...	...	—	—	12	Aruba
...	...	703	333	34	...	1,419[9]	...	...	15	5,279[13]	360[13]	580	22,500	41	Australia
16.1[6]	2,100[6]	472	114	18	36	6,858[9]	...	...	209	8,943	1,200	27	390	21	Austria
...	...	13	6	...	...	...	...	...	7	...	...	4	5,300	1	Bahamas, The
1.1	3,000	313	...	...	...	...	...	...	2	99	250	...	...	...	Bahrain
...	...	608	343	68	...	...	...	...	38	...	...	3	3	1	Bangladesh
1.2	5,200	6	5	...	5	118[15]	12[15]	47[15]	1	30	120	1	10	...	Barbados
20.5[6]	2,100[6]	472	...	14	30	6,000[9]	1,430[9]	145[9]	132[16]	3,454[16]	350[16]	4	12	12	Belgium
...	...	...	...	...	...	...	...	...	5	9	64	2	320	...	Belize
0.9[6]	300[6]	4[4]	4[4]	...	...	...	...	...	5	8[17]	2[17]	2	2,100	...	Benin
0.2	2,700	4	2	...	3	63[15]	15[15]	280[15]	14	...	...	10	5	1	Bermuda
...	...	12	5	...	...	...	...	...	1	16	13	11	6,700	...	Bhutan
31.1[6]	5,700[6]	209	160	2	13	500[9]	123[9]	22[9]	28	...	...	12	7,300	4	Bolivia
0.1[4]	200[4]	1[4]	0.8[4]	...	...	29	...	...	2	52	59	8	107,000	...	Botswana
91.3	700	1,397	708	79	253	1,563	...	...	647	15,656	121	50	880	31	Brazil
35.3[19]	3,300	1	0.4	...	...	3	4	330	1	1	85	7	800	...	British Virgin Islands
2.6	13,000	7	6	...	—	78	9	41	3	112	510	...	...	1	Brunei
96.4	10,800	3,314	717	40	65	18,469[9]	6,026[9]	670[9]	206	15,426	1,700	12	62	4	Bulgaria
4.0	600	12	14	...	...	...	...	...	1	...	...	6	1,000	...	Burkina Faso
...	...	175[4]	136[4]	45	...	...	...	...	12	...	...	5	87	2	Burma
0.1	24	7	3	...	13	79[15]	77[15]	19[15]	2[20]	6[20]	1[20]	7	210	...	Burundi
...	...	52	29	1	...	44[21]	39[21]	5	12	4,641	560	15	2,300	2	Cameroon
79.7	3,200	860	568	32	476	30,720[9,22]	9,468[9,22]	374[9,22]	661	16,165[23]	640[23]	78	9,000	104	Canada
...	...	...	...	...	...	...	...	...	...	...	...	...	...	...	Cape Verde
0.2[6]	11,700[6]	4	1	...	...	...	...	...	...	...	...	...	...	...	Cayman Islands
...	...	...	...	...	...	...	...	...	65	...	...	4	15,000	...	Central African Republic
25.2	6,000	13	12	...	4	120[24]	7[24]	1[24]	5	3[25]	0.6[25]	1	230	...	Chad
12.6[6]	1,000[6]	177	107	2	20	2,513[9]	872[9]	72[9]	69	...	...	64	10,500	10	Chile
18,250	18,100	143,650[26]	...	130	1,756	743,891[9]	723,222[9]	690[9]	900	...	...	62	22	47	China
...	...	2	...	...	...	...	...	...	...	...	...	1	7,000	...	Christmas Island
...	...	...	...	...	...	...	...	...	...	...	...	...	...	...	Cocos (Keeling) Islands
56.1[6]	2,000[6]	586	277	9	14	159[9]	90[9]	3[9]	73	1,442[27]	57[27]	30	1,400	8	Colombia
...	...	...	...	...	...	...	...	...	...	...	...	...	...	...	Comoros
...	...	...	...	1	1	74	...	...	5[20]	57[28]	29[28]	10	7,800	1	Congo
...	...	...	...	...	...	...	...	...	1	6	320	1	7,800	...	Cook Islands
0.2[6]	100[6]	104	...	2	9	347[9]	50[9]	24[9]	16	473[29]	200[29]	21	1,700	1	Costa Rica
7.0	900	72	42	2	...	...	...	...	1	...	...	10	1,800	2	Côte d'Ivoire
76.5	7,600	510	276	17	42	51,638	25,600	2,559	241	8,159	816	4	24	7	Cuba
...	...	...	...	2	10	793	206	330	26	95	150	—	—	1	Cyprus
76.6[6]	4,900[6]	2,787	...	63	81	21,361[9]	8,549[9]	550[9]	314	21,335	1,400	28	750	42	Czechoslovakia
11.3	2,200	428	76	10	89[33]	10,317[9,33]	2,583[9,33]	486[9,33]	286	8,158	1,020	23	250	19	Denmark
0.6	5,200	4	6	...	...	...	...	...	...	...	...	—	—	...	Djibouti
...	...	3	...	...	...	...	...	...	...	...	...	1	810	1	Dominica
7.0[4,6]	1,500[4,6]	834	46[4]	...	2	41	74	14	6	...	...	5	350	1	Dominican Republic
...	...	330	...	...	75	148	...	...	23	...	...	12	3,000	1	Ecuador
31.9	700	185	164	52	...	1,941	364	9	51	2,755	62	1	4	9	Egypt

Cultural institutions (continued)

country	book publishing number of titles books total	of which school textbooks	periodicals	pamphlets	number of copies ('000) books total	of which school textbooks	periodicals	pamphlets	public libraries number	volumes ('000)	registered borrowers ('000)	loans per 1,000 population
El Salvador	37[3]	6[3]	...	8	170	...	66	...	113	111	...	...
Equatorial Guinea									3[18]	12	...	...
Ethiopia	100	60	1	127	270	180	2	381	3	80	...	...
Faeroe Islands	113	9	...	...	11	1	...	...	13	135	7	3,238
Falkland Islands	...	...	3	...	...	...	2	...	...	...	...	...
Fiji	10[3]	6[3]	13	3	20[3]	12[3]	...	6	9	91	33	520
Finland	8,930	533	4,275	2,180	...	...	...	...	461	30,469	2,021	15,933
France	29,068	4,218	13,716	11,741	366	59	183,379	...	1,141	64,379	6,094	1,957
French Guiana	1[3]	—	7	...	2[3]	—	6	1	1	19	0.7	210
French Polynesia	56	8	17	16	92	40	25	10	1	17	1	220
Gabon												
Gambia, The	65[3]	30[3]	3	7	40[3]	...	...	5	1	89	2	29
Gaza Strip												
Germany, East	5,655	179	541	937	112,976	19,552	21,410	20,783	6,912	46,631	3,964	5,470
Germany, West	47,033	650	6,183	7,409	268,332	...	...	...	14,123[18]	75,660	6,174	3,195
Ghana	338	27	74	12	163	...	254	91	9	1,119	55	54
Gibraltar	...	...	15	...	...	...	4	...	1	20	6	1,541
Greece	4,651[10]	114	868	430	10	...	...	...	498[18]	...	...	...
Greenland	...	...	...	...	...	...	...	...	72[36]	308[36]	...	5,740[36]
Grenada	2[3]	...	...	8[3]	2[3]	...	...	9[3]	1	15	0.8	...
Guadeloupe	...	...	45	...	...	...	142	...	1	90	15	410
Guam	12[3]	...	28	...	2[3]	...	...	...	8	188	17	...
Guatemala	312	...	...	181	...	...	...	...	1	27	...	...
Guernsey												
Guinea	...	...	1	...	...	...	...	...	1	12	...	...
Guinea-Bissau												
Guyana	16	1[3]	65	39	...	...	53	...	1	10	...	—
Haiti	...	...	...	...	...	...	...	...	1	12	...	...
Honduras	...	...	...	...	...	...	...	...	1	20	...	5
Hong Kong	3,642	538	495	2,039	27,483	7,771	...	16,829	48	2,277	1,601	1,900
Hungary	8,206	1,457	1,678	1,374	95,600	26,700	13,278	14,688	9,647[40]	49,405[40]	2,261[40]	5,370[40]
Iceland	1,121	...	...	...	...	...	...	...	238	1,426	...	...
India	9,954	362	19,937	...	...	...	50,094	...	17,024[18]	...	...	...
Indonesia	5,254	265	1,767	1,234	...	...	...	...	275	468	2,768	...
Iran	5,568	...	180	...	...	...	...	...	385	2,161	...	8
Iraq	82	...	...	...	452	...	...	...	15	240	17	...
Ireland	609	20	252	190	...	...	2,958	...	31	8,221	651	4,254
Isle of Man												
Israel	4,161	1,189	890	243	8,872[10]	5,263[10]	...	10	983[42]	12,603	1,063	4,776
Italy	13,943	1,168	8,786	1,602	129,675	45,485	9,144	11,604	8,686	16,133	3,436	...
Jamaica	23[3]	3[3]	...	48	...	...	...	380	14	1,170	656	980
Japan	37,016[3]	1,676	2,503	...	717,269	218,190	36,293	—	1,028	103,968	10,367	1,579
Jersey												
Jordan	...	...	41	...	...	...	211	...	65	70	1	6
Kampuchea	...	...	3	...	...	...	...	...	...	...	...	...
Kenya	238[3]	30[3]	...	...	331[3]	60[3]	...	...	2	511	98	34
Kiribati	...	...	...	...	...	...	...	...	1	40	...	...
Korea, North												
Korea, South	33,743	3,396	870	2,094	114,971	50,293	...	9,151	159	3,255	13,565	200
Kuwait	329[5]	113	45	60[5]	8,404	3,724	982	368	25	421	600	45
Laos												
Lebanon	...	...	...	...	...	...	...	...	6	94	...	...
Lesotho	...	...	2	...	...	...	10	...	1	...	3	14
Liberia	...	...	...	...	...	...	...	...	3	78	...	...
Libya	481[10]	...	...	10	2,405[10]	...	...	10	5	100	...	...
Liechtenstein									1	...	10	1,000
Luxembourg	333	12	427	44	...	...	...	...	...	...	...	...
Macau	...	...	...	...	...	...	...	...	4	250	120	...
Madagascar	242	44	...	79	335	100	...	158	56	76	69	2
Malawi	75	38	43	59	1,500	1,160	166	1,605	6	130	20	51
Malaysia	1,657	389	1,631	897	7,009	1,945	1,689	3,459	20	2,785	811	329
Maldives	3[3]	...	...	...	...	...	...	—	1	8	...	...
Mali	—	...	...	160[5]	—	—	...	92[5]	46	552	...	...
Malta	246	14[3]	264	111	...	...	...	...	2	274	44	2,000
Martinique	3[3]	...	8	18	10[3]	...	17	33	1	120	...	...
Mauritania	21	21	...	20	...	...	...	...	1	26	...	...
Mauritius	58	23[3]	...	36	188	153	...	55	4	210	...	...
Mayotte												
Mexico	5,482	...	1,964	...	...	...	...	...	557	3,720	8,492	174
Monaco	105[10]	...	105	10	792[10]	...	792	10	1	150	...	...
Mongolia	861[10]	...	38	10	6,009[10]	...	6,200	10	397	8,700	...	...
Montserrat	...	...	...	...	...	...	...	...	1	...	...	...
Morocco	...	...	63	...	...	...	145	...	8	448	...	...
Mozambique	29	19	...	37	3,130	3,085	...	360	2	105	...	...
Nauru	...	...	...	...	...	...	...	...	...	...	...	...
Nepal	43	—	94	—	70	—	...	—	400[18]	...	...	...
Netherlands, The	12,629[10]	2,055	...	10	...	...	...	...	471	42,919	4,177	12,029
Netherlands Antilles	28[12]	...	...	24[12]	...	...	...	...	1[12]	100[12]	10[12]	99[12]
New Caledonia	15	...	15	7	7	...	27	1	1	60	...	...
New Zealand	1,601	14	5,788	1,851	...	...	...	...	209	6,062	2,666	8,000
Nicaragua	26	...	...	...	146	...	...	...	41	...	...	...
Niger	...	4	...	...	8	8	...	0.1	—	...	...	...
Nigeria	1,836	360	...	896	...	...	...	...	18	481	206	2
Niue	...	...	2	1	...	...	...	...	1	6	1	3.359
Norfolk Island	—	—	2	1	—	—	3	1	1	5	0.2	6,000

cinema annual attendance number ('000,000)	per 1,000 population	fixed cinemas number	seating capacity ('000)	number of long films produced	performing arts number of facilities	number of performances	annual attendance number ('000)	per 1,000 population	museums number	annual attendance number ('000)	per 1,000 population	national parks and nature reserves number	square metres per capita[1]	zoos, botanical gardens, etc. (number[2])	country
15.9[6]	3,700[6]	79	52.1	...	6	620	341	65	20	1,333	290	—	—	1	El Salvador
0.5	1,600	10	4	...	...	219	169[9]	479[9]	1	...	...	...	...	...	Equatorial Guinea
...	...	46	38	...	3	705	808	17	17	67	0.17	10	700	3	Ethiopia
...	1,000	5	1	...	...	...	...	...	3	14	308	...	...	...	Faeroe Islands
18.9[19]	10,500	2	0.5	...	...	...	...	...	1	...	...	...	...	...	Falkland Islands
0.3	500	50	40	...	3	255	57	90	1	40	58	2	76	1	Fiji
7.6[6]	1,400[6]	378	89	22	44	11,041[9]	2,618[9]	533[9]	57[34]	2,897	590	33	1,600	7	Finland
172.2	3,200	7,139	1,276	151	...	20,394[9,35]	6,042[9,35]	110[9,35]	1,434[20]	13,237[7]	239[7]	26	270	79	France
...	...	...	...	...	1	...	...	...	1	12	190	—	—	...	French Guiana
0.1[6]	600[6]	3	1	...	2	33[9]	14[9]	99[9]	3	...	...	2	220	...	French Polynesia
1.1	2,100	18	7	...	...	...	...	...	1	...	...	5	14,000	...	Gabon
...	...	...	...	...	...	...	...	...	...	...	...	1	32	...	Gambia, The
...	...	...	...	...	...	...	...	...	...	...	...	...	...	...	Gaza Strip
70.8	4,260	2,163	346	16	200	84,693[9]	29,155[9]	582[9]	714	34,322	2,070	13	12	119	Germany, East
104.2	1,700	3,418	723	71	286	61,300[9]	29,500[9]	480[9]	2,025	60,779	996	45	87	126	Germany, West
3.9[6]	340[6]	7	9	1	8	3,672	653	61	8	69	6	8	920	3	Ghana
0.2	5,900	4	2	...	3	39	15	450	1	17	590	...	...	...	Gibraltar
57.4	5,900	...	...	33	88	8,500[9]	2,000[9]	200[9]	83	3,174	321	14	63	3	Greece
...	...	...	...	...	...	...	...	...	11	...	...	2	37	...	Greenland
1.2	12,500	6	4	...	1	4[15]	10[15]	104[15]	1	8	86	1	140	2	Grenada
0.8	2,650	...	...	...	...	92	44	130	5	31[25]	95[25]	1	680	...	Guadeloupe
...	...	...	...	...	1	...	...	...	4	...	...	1	510	...	Guam
7.9[6]	1,000[6]	115	72	3	1	206[38]	50[38]	7[38]	18	58[39]	7[39]	2	75	2	Guatemala
...	...	...	...	...	...	...	...	...	9	...	...	...	...	1	Guernsey
2.6[6]	400[6]	29	61.2	...	...	...	...	...	5	21	4	1	24	...	Guinea
...	...	...	...	...	17	181	167	191	...	...	...	...	...	...	Guinea-Bissau
13.3[6]	14,700[6]	50	40	4	3	...	...	...	2	97[25]	130[25]	1	120	2	Guyana
2.1[6]	400[6]	28	14	...	...	...	...	...	4	73[17]	16[17]	2	10	...	Haiti
...	...	...	...	...	...	...	...	...	3	22	7	4	970	3	Honduras
58.0	10,700	90	103	105	8	556[9]	297[9]	60[9]	5	565	130	...	...	3	Hong Kong
68.0	6,600	3,600	558	23	41	12,960[9]	5,957[9]	560[9]	661	19,572	1,840	36	500	14	Hungary
2.6[6]	11,400[6]	47[4]	12[4]	4	4	528	154	658	16	108	462	21	32,000	2	Iceland
4,920.0	6,500	12,696	6,030	840	...	...	...	...	422	...	...	239	140	42	India
144.9[6]	1,000[6]	1,833[4]	959[4]	63	22	20,695	2,084	12	100	7,171	45	140	830	12	Indonesia
28[6]	600[6]	294[4]	167[4]	60	19	84[9]	...	...	44	...	...	24	680	3	Iran
...	...	84	65	1	132	743[9]	228[9]	19[9]	13	63	4	...	...	1	Iraq
11.6	3,200	125	53	2	14	10,260[9]	...	...	49	...	...	3	57	5	Ireland
...	...	...	...	...	...	...	...	...	4	...	...	...	...	2	Isle of Man
24.2	6,600	214	152	19	5	275[9,11]	...	...	83	8,085	1,900	5	79	13	Israel
123.1	2,100	4,885	...	80	313	64,238[9]	18,055[9]	320[9]	1,122	22,912[43]	410[43]	34	91	57	Italy
...	...	...	...	...	16	868[15]	1,143	540	5	44[17]	22[17]	2[44]	2	5	Jamaica
161	1,300	2,109[4]	...	311	543	39,768[9]	...	...	571	57,386	480	50	180	105	Japan
...	...	...	...	...	...	...	...	...	5	...	...	...	...	1	Jersey
15.0	4,900	41	20	...	5	64	180	84	16	147[45]	58[45]	2	130	...	Jordan
...	...	...	...	...	...	...	...	...	2	...	...	1	15	...	Kampuchea
9.2	600	40	20	...	...	...	...	...	6	531	27	28	1,500	5	Kenya
...	...	...	...	...	—	23[15]	...	...	...	...	...	2	870	...	Kiribati
187	9,200	1,178	653	37	3[46]	...	...	...	17	...	...	...	...	2	Korea, North
48.1[6]	1,200[6]	482	...	81	16	3,449	402	10	146	665[47]	16[47]	14	120	4	Korea, South
1.0	600	12	15	...	3	...	95	66	3	383	214	...	...	1	Kuwait
...	...	...	...	...	...	...	...	...	...	...	...	...	...	...	Laos
...	...	...	...	...	...	...	...	...	7	...	...	...	...	1	Lebanon
...	...	...	...	...	...	...	...	...	1	...	...	1	45	...	Lesotho
1.5	800	13	9	...	...	...	...	...	7	...	...	1	590	1	Liberia
10.2	3,500	49	22	2	14	439	160	51	26	50	16	2	340	2	Libya
...	...	...	...	...	...	...	...	...	4	41	1,500	6	410	...	Liechtenstein
1.1	3,000	...	...	...	3	394[48]	244[48]	618[48]	14	225	630	4	3,100	...	Luxembourg
3.0	9,300	8	9	...	4	84	...	...	1	18	55	...	...	...	Macau
...	...	...	...	...	70[15]	140[15]	60[15]	7[15]	47	217[17]	26[17]	14	670	3	Madagascar
1.5	300	4	2	...	2	...	...	...	2	80	12	9	1,500	...	Malawi
34.0	2,700	425	...	8	10	1,303	312	25	16	...	...	34	1,000	6	Malaysia
...	...	7	3	...	11	...	...	...	1	3	17	...	...	...	Maldives
...	...	...	...	1	...	...	...	...	...	...	...	6	1,100	1	Mali
1.0	2,600	22	16	...	...	...	...	...	18	562	1,700	2	1.1	2	Malta
1.1	3,450	...	...	...	...	...	...	...	5	...	...	1	2,100	...	Martinique
...	...	19	8	...	...	136	36	38	...	...	...	2	9,000	...	Mauritania
10.0	9,500	44	40	...	6	136	36	38	3	237	236	3	39	1	Mauritius
...	...	...	...	...	2	...	...	...	...	...	...	...	...	...	Mayotte
292.4	3,900	2,172	...	88	11	17,069[49]	6,549[49]	97[49]	216	13,070	170	29	120	11	Mexico
0.1	3,800	3	1	...	3	31	13	500	2	154	6,200	...	...	4	Monaco
17.7	9,400	59	...	6	21	...	3,600	1,700	4	7,400	4,400	4	24,000	...	Mongolia
...	...	1	...	...	1	16	4	360	1	2	170	...	...	...	Montserrat
39.0[6]	1,900[6]	267	162	12	...	...	...	12	11	1,580	74	2	17	5	Morocco
9.6[6]	700[6]	70	27	...	...	...	...	9	...	...	...	6	1,300	4	Mozambique
...	...	...	...	...	...	...	...	...	...	...	...	...	...	...	Nauru
...	...	...	...	1	16	65	...	5	...	...	...	10	590	1	Nepal
14.9	1,023	451	108.5	12	451	36,125	8,600	590	538	15,879	1,096	47	100	36	Netherlands, The
...	...	...	...	...	...	...	...	7[12]	...	...	...	3	625	2[12]	Netherlands Antilles
0.3	2,000	8	2	...	2	61	22	147	1	30	220	7	3,300	1	New Caledonia
...	...	172	103	9	...	2,287[9]	515[9]	120[9]	110	...	...	147	8,300	15	New Zealand
5.2	1,800	127	74	1	1	...	...	...	9	...	...	2	53	1	Nicaragua
...	...	...	...	...	...	...	...	...	1[6]	600[7]	110[7]	3	590	...	Niger
8.6	100	240	...	20	23	...	...	...	18	...	...	3	90	8	Nigeria
...	...	...	...	...	...	...	...	...	...	...	...	...	...	...	Niue
10[19]	5,000	1	0.1	...	1	7	2	1,000	1	20	10,000	1	...	1	Norfolk Island

Cultural institutions (continued)

country	book publishing								public libraries			
	number of titles				number of copies ('000)				number	volumes ('000)	registered borrowers ('000)	loans per 1,000 population
	books		periodicals	pamphlets	books		periodicals	pamphlets				
	total	of which school textbooks			total	of which school textbooks						
Norway	2,991[50]	...	4,010	568[50]	...	...	...	...	1,375	16,811	1,198	4,472
Oman	...	...	14	...	...	...	...	...	1	20	...	...
Pacific Is., Trust Terr. of the	93[3]	26	...	40[3]	47	11	...	80	5[18]	16	...	...
Marshall Islands	...	...	...	...	...	...	...	...	...	...	...	...
Micronesia, Fed. States of	...	...	...	...	...	...	...	...	...	...	...	...
Northern Mariana Islands												
Palau	...	...	...	...	...	...	...	...	...	...	...	...
Pakistan	1,600	...	1,470	...	...	...	1,537	...	98	1,340	...	6
Panama	114	93	...	57	38[3]	...	...	53	18	26	...	29
Papua New Guinea	...	...	72	...	...	...	...	...	24	186	...	...
Paraguay	...	...	...	...	...	...	...	...	15	45	...	...
Peru	475	16	507	43	...	...	...	...	557	1,950	...	123
Philippines	265	175	...	277	14,516[5]	14,464	...	202[5]	507[18]	...	194	...
Pitcairn Island												
Poland	7,920	373	2,986	1,961	181,351	40,703	39,426	68,095	10,000	124,266	7,674	4,124
Portugal	9,140	698[32]	1,012	1,153	65,290	6,869[32]	...	2,002	178	7,546	...	513
Puerto Rico	...	...	...	...	...	...	...	...	121[40]	715	...	...
Qatar	316	219	8	21	2,100	1,533	191	105	7	273	10	53
Réunion	41	13	53	32	...	...	110	...	3	315	...	...
Romania	5,276[10]	...	422	10	69,266[10]	...	227,000	10	6,920	67,379	4,661	2,050
Rwanda	13	13	8	1	204	204	2	3	5	...	...	...
St. Helena and Ascension	...	...	2	...	...	...	...	...	2	...	...	...
St. Kitts and Nevis	2[3]	—	...	3[3]	...	...	...	2[3]	2	...	...	...
St. Lucia	44	25	...	19	89	84	7	18	4	...	...	...
St. Pierre and Miquelon	...	...	...	...	...	...	...	...	3	15	...	...
St. Vincent	...	...	...	...	...	...	...	...	1	...	...	...
San Marino	14	...	14	1	...	...	...	...	...	...	...	...
São Tomé and Príncipe	...	...	...	...	...	...	...	...	1	...	...	...
Saudi Arabia	207	—	58	11	...	...	...	...	28	36	...	...
Senegal	42[3,10]	8[3,10]	...	10	169[3,10]	70[3,10]	...	10	1	7	...	...
Seychelles	2[3]	...	4	31[3]	...	...	...	...	1	35	...	1,672
Sierra Leone	17[3]	16	...	44[3]	9[3]	4[3]	...	123	11	392	...	...
Singapore	1,524[56]	389	1,786	403[56]	8,947[56]	4,081	...	2,179[56]	1	2,162	655	2,372
Solomon Islands	...	...	2	...	...	...	4	...	8	22	5	...
Somalia	...	...	...	...	...	...	...	...	...	...	...	...
South Africa	...	...	...	...	...	...	...	...	85	7,857	...	...
Bophuthatswana	...	...	...	...	...	...	...	...	...	...	...	...
Ciskei	...	...	...	...	...	...	...	...	...	...	...	...
Transkei	...	...	...	...	...	...	...	...	...	...	...	...
Venda	...	...	...	...	...	...	...	...	1	10	3	11
South West Africa/Namibia	...	...	3	...	...	...	18	...	8	157	...	...
Spain	29,276	2,300	5,508	5,408	206,873	28,003	55,352	33,363	1,396	11,730	1,308	170
Sri Lanka	707	111	454	1,244	12,340	10,895	42,511	5,273	650	36	197	...
Sudan, The	...	138[59]	25	...	...	12,905[59]	195	—	7	36	...	...
Suriname	...	...	22	...	...	...	44	...	2	268	54	2,100
Swaziland	...	...	1	...	...	...	2,600	...	1	51	...	...
Sweden	9,532[10]	...	3,690	10	...	...	...	...	394	44,699	...	9,230
Switzerland	11,822[10]	218[10]	1,533	10	...	...	31,773	...	79[60]	24,000[60]	...	1,400
Syria	119	13	48	—	553	...	454	—	...	...	...	...
Taiwan	9,256	...	2,661	...	...	...	...	...	139	1,084	...	...
Tanzania	166	12[3]	69	197	...	...	646	...	19	454	10	9
Thailand	7,136	560	1,189	153	...	...	...	...	375	1,599	31	...
Togo	...	...	...	...	...	...	...	...	1	8	...	...
Tokelau	...	...	...	...	...	...	...	...	1	0.2	...	...
Tonga	33	5	...	287	0.4	0.1	...	...	...	...	...	...
Trinidad and Tobago	101	7	...	85	...	...	...	...	3	246	73	345
Tunisia	336	38	230	204	...	6,000	...	...	280	1,315	65	174
Turkey	6,794	212	2,670	654	...	...	...	...	686	6,631	486	40
Turks and Caicos Islands	...	...	...	...	...	...	...	...	1	26	3	1,641
Tuvalu	...	...	...	...	...	...	...	...	...	...	...	...
Uganda	...	...	...	...	...	...	...	...	1	73	157	31
U.S.S.R.	55,565	2,697[32]	5,275	28,411	1,530,337	289,331[32]	3,690,800	620,397	134,165	2,138,179	148,000	11,500
United Arab Emirates	41	41	8	—	2,215	2,215	25	16	7	15	...	...
United Kingdom	59,837	1,241	6,408	3,964	...	...	...	...	167	131,338	...	11,300
United States	45,401[65]	841	3,731	...	...	...	...	...	9,170	509,250	...	4,300
Uruguay	1,206	152	351	495	...	...	...	...	72	166	...	...
Vanuatu	...	...	...	...	...	...	...	...	1	12	0.7	...
Venezuela	3,596	...	160	604	1,194	...	4,649	...	23	1,130	66	160
Vietnam	2,060[10]	300[10]	173	10	42,800[10]	10	323	10	427	8,900	...	...
Virgin Islands (U.S)	...	...	...	...	...	...	...	...	1	90	10	707
Wallis and Futuna	...	...	...	...	...	...	...	...	...	...	...	...
West Bank	...	...	...	...	...	...	...	...	...	...	...	...
Western Sahara	...	...	...	...	...	...	...	...	...	...	...	...
Western Samoa	79	...	...	156	39	...	...	43	1	61	...	...
Yemen (Aden)	...	...	...	...	...	...	...	...	2	40	...	...
Yemen (Şan'ā')												
Yugoslavia	8,682	1,456	1,613	2,493	48,039	20,191	4,473	10,417	1,972	26,424	...	1,200
Zaire	194[3]	53	106	373	...	...	225	...	11	177	9	1
Zambia	454	215[3]	...	—	235[68]	...	...	...	11	240	18	28
Zimbabwe	276	119	...	268	2,017	...	...	134	6	523	18	74

[1]Calculations based on statutory areas, whether of land or water. [2]Excludes zoological and aquatic collections in museums. [3]First editions only. [4]16-millimetre data not available. [5]School textbooks, university theses, and government publications only. [6]Excludes drive-ins, mobile units, or both. [7]National museums only. [8]Excludes school textbooks and children's books. [9]Professional only. [10]Books include pamphlets. [11]214 reporting. [12]Netherlands Antilles includes Aruba. [13]14 reporting. [14]The public library also serves as the national library. [15]Amateur only. [16]Ministry of Flemish culture museums only. [17]3 reporting. [18]Library service points. [19]Attendance in '000's. [20]National and public museums only. [21]Drama, ballet, and dance only. [22]Drama, opera, ballet, and dance only. [23]644 reporting. [24]Amateur ballet, dance, and drama only. [25]1 reporting. [26]Film projection units. [27]57 reporting. [28]4 reporting. [29]11 reporting. [30]Excludes some Turkish publications. [31]Includes university theses. [32]Includes school pamphlets. [33]Royal theatre and regional theatres only. [34]263 reporting. [35]Drama and opera only. [36]Includes national library and school libraries. [37]13,400,000 square metres per capita; a single national park comprises about one-third of the area of Greenland. [38]Drama only. [39]12 reporting. [40]Public educational libraries include

cinema		fixed cinemas		number of long films produced	performing arts		annual attendance		museums number	annual attendance		nature preservation		zoos, botanical gardens, etc. (number[2])	country
annual attendance (all cinemas)		number	seating capacity ('000)		number of facilities	number of performances	number ('000)	per 1,000 population		number ('000)	per 1,000 population	national parks and nature reserves number	square metres per capita[1]		
number ('000,000)	per 1,000 population														
12.9[6]	2,000[6]	448	125	12	10	5,024[9]	1,149[9]	280[9]	434	4,768	1,150	55	2,900	7	Norway
0.9	1,100	24	—	...	...	35[51]	5[51]	5[51]	1	...	...	1	190	...	Oman
...	...	52	...	...	...	...	...	...	5	...	...	1	93	...	Pacific Is., Trust Terr. of the Marshall Islands
...	...	...	...	...	...	...	...	...	...	...	...	—	—	...	Micronesia, Fed. States of
...	...	...	...	...	...	...	...	...	...	...	...	2	370	...	Northern Mariana Islands
...	...	...	...	...	...	...	...	...	...	...	...	—	—	...	Palau
182.0	2,200	650[4]	455	92	11	...	153[9]	2[9]	18	2,245	23	52	650	6	Pakistan
7.1	4,800	...	...	...	1	55	...	...	10	...	...	6	3,000	2	Panama
...	...	...	...	...	7	122	265	91	2	100	32	2	9	3	Papua New Guinea
...	...	...	...	...	...	...	...	...	18	...	...	9	3,300	1	Paraguay
33.0	1,900	425	...	1	28	134[21]	185[21]	9[21]	12	201	10	11	1,200	2	Peru
...	...	...	...	152	6[52]	121[52]	29[52]	0.6[52]	61	...	...	26	72	5	Philippines
...	...	...	...	...	...	...	...	...	...	...	...	...	...	...	Pitcairn Island
94.3	2,500	1,757	469	39	149	127,184[9]	32,965[9]	877[9]	537	21,556	574	15	30	26	Poland
40.4	1,900	350[4]	180[4]	5	37	3,707	1,126	120	139	3,800[53]	380[53]	12[54]	380[54]	10	Portugal
...	...	165	...	...	...	...	...	...	24	...	...	2	1	8	Puerto Rico
0.2	580	4	3.8	1	8	12[55]	1	5	1	60	300	1	...	1	Qatar
...	...	...	...	...	...	654	122	220	2	79	150	...	...	...	Réunion
191.5	8,300	5,454	257	27	154	49,400[9]	17,900[9]	788[9]	459	17,108	750	9	43	9	Romania
0.5	100	34	9.3	1	9	311[15]	58[15]	12[15]	4	...	...	2	430	...	Rwanda
53.0[19]	8,800	2	1	...	...	1	1	170	1	...	...	...	...	...	St. Helena and Ascension
...	...	3	...	...	1	6[15]	...	...	1	...	...	...	...	...	St. Kitts and Nevis
...	...	6	...	...	...	...	...	...	1	7	58	1	120	...	St. Lucia
...	...	...	...	...	...	...	...	...	1	4	640	...	...	...	St. Pierre and Miquelon
...	...	2	...	...	...	...	...	...	...	...	...	...	...	1	St. Vincent
0.1	4,500	7	3	...	1	26[9]	10[9]	460[9]	11	741	35,000	...	...	...	San Marino
...	...	...	...	...	...	...	...	...	...	...	...	...	...	...	São Tomé and Príncipe
...	...	...	...	...	94	141[15]	18[15]	2[15]	1	40	4	1	400	2	Saudi Arabia
3.6[6]	700[6]	60[4]	...	...	105	122[9]	52[9]	9[9]	4	55	10	9	3,300	4	Senegal
...	...	...	...	...	2	6[15]	3[15]	40[15]	1	8	130	3	3,400	...	Seychelles
...	...	...	...	...	...	...	...	...	19	178[25]	55[25]	1	250	1	Sierra Leone
27.4	10,800	51	58	25	3	523	645	270	3	940	390	1	10	4	Singapore
0.1[6]	300[6]	2	1	...	—	3	1	5	1	29	150	1	46	...	Solomon Islands
...	...	...	...	...	...	...	...	...	1	...	...	1	570	...	Somalia
31.2	1,200	260	...	12	51	3,597[57]	1,348[57]	54[57]	22[58]	2,477[58]	96[58]	136	2,000	35	South Africa
...	...	...	...	...	...	...	...	...	...	...	...	2	380	...	Bophuthatswana
...	...	...	...	...	...	...	...	...	...	...	...	8	360	...	Ciskei
...	...	...	...	...	...	...	...	...	...	...	...	2	22	...	Transkei
...	...	...	...	...	...	...	...	...	1	...	...	1	75	...	Venda
...	...	9	...	...	...	...	...	...	9	...	...	9	60,000	1	South West Africa/Namibia
101.1[6]	2,600[6]	3,109	...	69	301	18,862	6,702	180	554	11,697	320	56	440	22	Spain
36.5	2,300	318	201	18	22	1,002[15]	600[15]	41[15]	9	466	34	37	400	4	Sri Lanka
13.0	600	56	97	2	...	...	...	...	7	221	10	3	810	2	Sudan, The
...	...	...	...	...	7	333	134	340	3	...	...	9	15,000	1	Suriname
...	...	4	...	...	...	...	...	...	1	...	...	4	610	...	Swaziland
18.0	2,200	1,165	315	24	27	12,009	2,335	280	181	15,800	1,900	67	1,800	18	Sweden
19.0	2,300	437	128	44	67	12,617	1,747[9]	270[9]	585	...	...	19	190	32	Switzerland
12.0	1,100	140	48	1	9	281	61	6	16	327[61]	42[61]	...	...	...	Syria
128.0	6,500	602	516	235	...	...	...	...	10	...	...	28	84	3	Taiwan
4.0	200	34	15	...	5	21	15	1	6	119[62]	7[62]	15	4,900	...	Tanzania
...	...	651[14]	439[14]	80	...	...	...	...	64	...	...	45	530	3	Thailand
...	...	...	...	...	...	...	...	...	1	48	21	7	1,600	...	Togo
...	...	...	...	...	...	...	...	...	...	...	...	...	...	...	Tokelau
0.1	1,000	3	2	...	—	...	...	...	...	...	...	5	320	...	Tonga
...	...	72	57	...	...	49[15]	...	...	1	8	7	8	140	1	Trinidad and Tobago
4.4	700	79	38	...	22	781	164	26	35	367[63]	52[63]	3	46	3	Tunisia
40.2	800	675	402	96	38	3,660[9,64]	1,224[9,64]	26[9,64]	133	6,637	129	15	58	7	Turkey
...	...	3	1	...	...	3	0.6	100	...	...	...	...	...	...	Turks and Caicos Islands
...	...	...	...	...	...	...	...	...	...	...	...	...	...	...	Tuvalu
2.3[6]	200[6]	17[4]	10[4]	...	...	...	...	...	16	...	...	18	900	2	Uganda
3,882.0	13,700	143,027	25,847	321	640[9]	281,800[9]	126,000[9]	449[9]	1,932	195,800	660	163	660	144	U.S.S.R.
7.1	10,300	74	29	...	18	37[38]	40[38]	31[38]	2	...	...	...	...	2	United Arab Emirates
62.0	1,100	1,327	505	39	404	...	40,242[9,22]	720[9,22]	1,768	52,000	920	57	270	155	United Kingdom
1,053.1	4,500	16,032	5,611	396	...	21,596	40,200	170	4,440	329,083	1,500	200	1,309	532	United States
6.2	2,100	120	80	1	25	3,097	...	...	19	17[66]	6[66]	6	100	4	Uruguay
0.1	1,000	3	1	...	...	...	...	...	...	...	...	...	...	...	Vanuatu
13.2[6]	800[6]	437	169	16	38	4,445	868	50	133	...	...	34	4,300	12	Venezuela
375.0	6,300	430	178	35	81	...	57,400[9]	1,000[9]	9	1,918[67]	37[67]	12	27	2	Vietnam
...	...	...	...	...	...	...	...	...	5	811	7,700	2	660	1	Virgin Islands (U.S.)
...	...	...	...	...	...	...	...	...	...	...	...	...	...	...	Wallis and Futuna
...	...	...	...	...	...	...	...	...	...	...	...	4	...	...	West Bank
...	...	...	...	...	...	...	...	...	...	...	...	...	...	...	Western Sahara
0.5	3,200	6	6	...	...	9	2	11	...	...	...	1	180	1	Western Samoa
3.9[6]	2,000[6]	24	24	...	...	...	...	...	5	...	...	...	...	...	Yemen (Aden)
14.5[6]	2,500[6]	35	28	...	...	...	...	...	...	...	...	...	...	...	Yemen (Şan'ā')
78.1	3,500	1,271	437	24	123	19,496	5,610	240	379	10,649	497	20	140	19	Yugoslavia
...	...	...	...	...	4	72[9]	217[9]	17[9]	4	...	...	9	2,700	4	Zaire
1.6	300	12	4	...	...	...	...	...	3	12	2	19	10,000	1	Zambia
2.5	600	32	...	...	...	...	...	...	9	162[69]	20[69]	17	3,400	4	Zimbabwe

service points and trade union libraries.   [41]Opera and ballet only.   [42]Includes 9 mobile libraries.   [43]1,083 reporting.   [44]Marine parks only.   [45]10 reporting.   [46]Opera only.   [47]58 reporting.   [48]Two facilities only.   [49]Excludes amateur opera and musical comedy.   [50]Excludes school text material.   [51]Drama and folk dance only.   [52]Metropolitan Manila only.   [53]139 reporting.   [54]Excludes the Azores and Madeira.   [55]Folk dance only.   [56]Excludes government publications.   [57]Performances of state-subsidized regional performing arts councils only.   [58]Museums designated "declared cultural institutions" only.   [59]Includes children's books.   [60]Public libraries with 50,000 or more volumes only.   [61]13 reporting.   [62]5 reporting.   [63]32 reporting.   [64]State theatres only.   [65]Excludes government publications, books sold only by subscription, dissertations, and pamphlets.   [66]2 reporting.   [67]8 reporting.   [68]School textbooks and government publications only.   [69]6 reporting.

BIBLIOGRAPHY AND SOURCES

The following list indicates the principal sources used in the compilation of *Britannica World Data*. It is by no means a complete list, either for international or for national sources, but is indicative only of the range of materials to which reference has been made in preparing this compilation. For example, in addition to the kinds of works cited below, reference has also been made to the constitutions of each country, to the publications of its central or commercial banks, to unpublished information received in correspondence from the countries, and to other more specialized sources.

International Statistical Sources

Africana Publishing Co. *Africa Contemporary Record* (Colin Legum, ed. [annual]).
Asian Development Bank. *Key Indicators of Developing Member Countries of ADB* (annual, with supplements).
Billboard Ltd. *World Radio TV Handbook* (annual).
British Petroleum. *BP Statistical Review of World Energy* (annual).
Caribbean Community and Common Market. *Caricom Statistics Digest* (annual).
Council for Mutual Economic Assistance (Comecon). *Statistichesky Yezhegodnik Stran-Chlenov Soveta Economicheskoy Vzaimopomoshchi* (Statistical Yearbook of the Council for Mutual Economic Assistance).
Eastern Caribbean Central Bank. *Report and Statement of Accounts* (annual).
Europa Publications Ltd. *Africa South of the Sahara* (annual); *The Europa Year Book* (2 vol.); *The Far East and Australasia* (annual); *The Middle East and North Africa* (annual); *South America, Central America, and the Caribbean* (annual).
Food and Agriculture Organization. *Food Balance Sheets* (irreg.); *Production Yearbook; Trade Yearbook; World Census of Agriculture* (decennial); *Yearbook of Fishery Statistics; Yearbook of Forest Products.*
Her Majesty's Stationery Office. *The Commonwealth Yearbook.*
Holmes & Meier Publishers. *Latin America and Caribbean Contemporary Record* (Abraham F. Lowenthal, ed. [annual]); *Middle East Contemporary Survey* (Itamar Rabinovich and Haim Shaked, eds. [annual]).
Instituts d'Émission d'Outre-Mer et des Départements d'Outre-Mer (France). *Rapports d'Activité* (annual), *Bulletin trimestriel* (quarterly).
Inter-American Development Bank. *Economic and Social Progress in Latin America* (annual).
Inter-Parliamentary Union. *World Directory of Parliaments* (annual).
International Air Transport Association. *World Air Transport Statistics* (annual).
International Bank for Reconstruction and Development/The World Bank. *World Bank Atlas* (annual); *World Debt Tables* (annual); *World Development Report* (annual); *World Tables* (irreg.).
International Civil Aviation Organization. *Civil Aviation Statistics of the World* (annual); *Digest of Statistics.*
International Institute for Strategic Studies. *The Military Balance* (annual).
International Labour Organisation. *Year Book of Labour Statistics; The Cost of Social Security: Basic Tables* (triennial).
International Monetary Fund. *Exchange Arrangements and Exchange Restrictions* (annual); *Government Finance Statistics Yearbook; International Financial Statistics* (monthly, with supplements and yearbook).

International Road Federation. *Road and Motor Vehicle Statistics* (annual); *World Road Statistics* (annual).
Jane's Publishing Co., Ltd. *Jane's World Railways* (annual).
Lloyd's Register of Shipping. *Lloyd's Register of Shipping: Statistical Tables* (annual).
Longman Group U.K. Ltd. *Keesing's Record of World Events* (monthly).
Macmillan Press Ltd. *The Statesman's Year-Book.*
Middle East Economic Digest Ltd. *Africa Economic Digest* (semimonthly); *Middle East Economic Digest* (semimonthly).
Mining Journal. *Mining Annual Review.*
Nordic Council. *Yearbook of Nordic Statistics.*
Official Airline Guides, Inc. *Official Airline Guide* (monthly).
Organization of Eastern Caribbean States. *Annual Digest of Statistics.*
Organization for Economic Cooperation and Development. *Economic Surveys* (annual); *Financing and External Debt of Developing Countries* (annual); *National Accounts of Developing Countries* (irreg.).
Oxford University Press. *World Christian Encyclopedia* (David B. Barrett, ed. [1982]).
Pacific Publications. *Pacific Islands Year Book* (irreg.).
PennWell Publishing Co. *International Petroleum Encyclopedia* (annual).
René Moreux et Cie. *Marchés tropicaux & Méditerranéens* (semimonthly).
South Pacific Commission. *Key Economic Indicators* (occasional); *South Pacific Economies: Statistical Summary* (biennial).
United Nations (UN). *Compendium of Human Settlements Statistics* (irreg.); *Construction Statistics Yearbook; Demographic Yearbook; International Trade Statistics Yearbook; Energy Statistics Yearbook; Industrial Statistics Yearbook* (2 vol.); *Monthly Bulletin of Statistics; Population Studies* (irreg.); *National Accounts Statistics* (3 vol.; annual); *Population and Vital Statistics Report* (quarterly); *Statistical Yearbook; Supplement to the Statistical Yearbook and the Monthly Bulletin of Statistics* (quinquennial); *World Population Prospects, Estimates and Projections as Assessed in 1984.*
UN: Conference on Trade and Development. *Handbook of International Trade and Development Statistics* (annual); *The Least Developed Countries, 1985 Report* (2 vol.; 1987).
UN: Economic Commission for Africa. *African Socio-Economic Indicators* (annual); *African Statistical Yearbook; Demographic and Related Socio-Economic Data Sheets for ECA Member States* (1982); *Survey of Economic and Social Conditions in Africa* (irreg.).
UN: Economic Commission for Europe. *Annual Bulletin of Housing and Building Statistics for Europe; Annual Bulletin of Transport Statistics for Europe.*
UN: Economic Commission for Latin America. *Economic Survey of Latin America* (2 vol.; annual); *Statistical Yearbook for Latin America.*
UN: Economic and Social Commission for Asia and the Pacific. *Foreign Trade Statistics of Asia and the Pacific* (annual); *Statistical Indicators for Asia and the Pacific* (quarterly); *Statistical Yearbook for Asia and the Pacific.*
UN: Economic and Social Commission for Western Asia. *Demographic and Related Socio-Economic Data Sheets* (irreg.); *Population Bulletin* (irreg.); *The Population Situation in the ECWA Region* (irreg.); *Statistical Abstract of the Region of the Economic and Social Commission for Western Asia* (annual).
UN: Educational, Scientific, and Cultural Organization. *Statistical Yearbook.*
United States: Central Intelligence Agency, *The World Factbook* (annual); Dept. of Commerce, *Foreign Economic Trends* (irreg.), *Overseas Business Reports* (annual), *World Population* (annual);

Dept. of Energy, *International Energy Annual;* Dept. of Health and Human Services, *Social Security Programs Throughout the World* (biennial); Dept. of Interior, *Minerals Yearbook* (3 vol.); Dept. of State, *Background Notes* (irreg.).
Vatican (Central Statistics Office of the Church). *Statistical Yearbook of the Church.*
West India Committee and FT International. *The Caribbean Handbook* (annual).
World Health Organization. *World Health Statistics Annual.*
World Tourism Organization. *World Tourism Statistics* (annual).

National Statistical Sources

Afghanistan. *First Seven-Year Economic and Social Development Plan, 1355–1361* (March 1976–March 1983); *Preliminary Results of the First Afghan Population Census, 1979; Review of the General Socio-economic Situation in the Democratic Republic of Afghanistan During 1358* (21 March 1979–20 March 1980).
Albania. *Report on the Directives of the 9th Congress of the Party for the 8th Five-Year Plan (1986–1990) of the Development of the Economy and Culture of the People's Socialist Republic of Albania; Portrait of Albania* (1982); *Vjetari statistikor R P SH* (Statistical Yearbook of the People's Republic of Albania [annual]); *40 années d'Albanie socialiste* (1984).
Algeria. *Annuaire statistique; Recensement général de la population et de l'habitat, 1987.*
American Samoa. *American Samoa Statistical Digest* (annual); *Population of American Samoa* (ESCAP; Country Monograph Series No. 7.1 [1979]); *1980 Census of Population and Housing* (U.S.).
Andorra. *Recull Estadístic* (1985).
Angola. *Anuário Estatístico; Recenseamento Geral da População, 1960; Situação Economica e Financeira de Angola* (annual).
Anguilla. *Abstract of Statistics, 1960–1982; Anguilla Census of Population 1984.*
Antigua. *Statistical Yearbook.*
Argentina. *Anuario estadístico de la República Argentina; Boletín estadístico trimestral* (quarterly); *Censo nacional de población y vivienda, 1980; Encuesta permanente de hogares* (irreg.).
Aruba. *Monthly Statistical Report: International Tourism to Aruba.*
Australia. *Census of Manufacturing Establishments: Summary of Operations by Industry Subdivision, Australia* (annual); *Monthly Summary of Statistics, Australia; National Income and Expenditure* (annual); *Foreign Trade Australia: Comparative and Summary Tables* (annual); *Social Indicators* (irreg.); *Year Book Australia; 1986 Census of Population and Housing.*
Austria. *Österreichisches Jahrbuch* (annual); *Sozialstatistische Daten 1986; Statistisches Handbuch* (annual); *Volkserzählung, 1981.*
Bahamas, The. *Quarterly Statistical Summary; Statistical Abstract* (annual); *Vital Statistics Report* (annual); *1980 Census of Population and Housing.*
Bahrain. *Statistical Abstract* (annual); *1981 Census of Bahrain.*
Bangladesh. *Bangladesh Population Census, 1981; Population of Bangladesh* (ESCAP; Country Monograph Series No. 8 [1981]); *Statistical Pocketbook of Bangladesh* (annual); *Statistical Yearbook of Bangladesh.*
Barbados. *Barbados Economic Report* (annual); *Monthly Digest of Statistics; Report on the Census of Production, 1981.*
Belgium. *Annuaire statistique de la Belgique; Bulletin de statistique* (monthly); *Recensement de la population et des logements au 1er mars 1981; Statistiques demographiques* (quarterly).
Belize. *Abstract of Statistics* (annual); *Belize Economic Survey* (annual); *Labour Force Survey* (1983–84); *1980–81 Population Census of the Commonwealth Caribbean, Belize.*

Benin. *Annuaire statistique; Recensement des Entreprises 1980* (2 parts); *Recensement général de la population et de l'habitation* (1979).

Bermuda. *Bermuda Digest of Statistics* (annual); *Report of the Population Census, 1980; Report of the Registrar General* (annual).

Bhutan. *Development in a Himalayan Kingdom* (A World Bank Country Study [1983]); *Statistical Yearbook of Bhutan* (annual).

Bolivia. *Bolivia en cifras, 1980; Censo Nacional de población y vivienda de 1976; Compendio Estadístico* (annual); *Resumen estadístico* (annual).

Botswana. *National Development Plan 1985–91; 1981 Population and Housing Census; Statistical Abstract* (annual).

Brazil. *Anuário Econômico-Fiscal; Anuário Estatístico do Brasil; Brazil: A Country Study* (1983); *Foreign Trade of Brazil* (annual); *IX Recenseamento Geral do Brasil, 1980.*

British Virgin Islands. *Census of the British Virgin Islands, 12th May 1980 (Provisional); Statistical Abstract* (irreg.).

Brunei. *Annual Report; Brunei Statistical Yearbook; Report on the Census of Population, 1981.*

Bulgaria. *Prebroyavane—1975; resultati, perspektivi* (Census of Population—1975: Results, Perspectives); *Statisticheskii yezhgodnik* (Statistical Yearbook).

Burkina Faso. *Annuaire Statistique; Recensement général de la population du 10 au 20 decembre 1985; Statistiques Sociales* (annual).

Burma. *Burma: A Country Study* (1983); 1983 *Population Census; Statistical Abstract* (irreg.).

Burundi. *Annuaire statistique; Recensement général de la population, 16–30 août 1979.*

Cameroon. *Note annuelle de statistique; Recensement général de la population et de l'habitat d'avril 1976; Tableaux économiques du Cameroun* (1983).

Canada. *Canada Year Book* (irreg.); *Census of Agriculture, 1981; National Income and Expenditure Accounts* (quarterly); *Census Canada 1986: Population.*

Cape Verde. *Boletim Trimestral Estatística* (quarterly); *I.º Recenseamento Geral da População e Habitação—1980.*

Cayman Islands. *Cayman Islands Population Census 1979; Statistical Abstract of the Cayman Islands* (annual).

Central African Republic. *Annuaire statistique; Recensement général de la population de décembre 1975.*

Chad. *Annuaire statistique.*

Chile. *Chile XV censo nacional de población y de vivienda, 21 de abril 1982; Compendio estadístico* (annual); *Cuentas nacionales de Chile, 1960–1980; Plan nacional indicativo de desarrollo* (quinquennial).

China, People's Republic of. *Almanac of China's Economy* (irreg.); *China: A Statistical Survey in 19*** (annual); *People's Republic of China Year-Book; Major Figures by 10 Percent Sampling on the 1982 Census of the People's Republic of China; Statistical Yearbook of China; Yearbook of the Encyclopedia of China.*

Christmas Island. *Annual Report; Census of Population and Housing, 30 June 1981.*

Cocos (Keeling) Islands. *Annual Report; Census of Population and Housing, 30 June 1981.*

Colombia. *Colombia estadística* (annual); *Cuentas nacionales de Colombia, 1970–1981; Industria manufacturera* (annual); *XV Censo nacional de población y IV de vivienda* (1985).

Comoros. *Plan interimaire de développement économique et sociale (1983–1986); Recensement général de la population et de l'habitat 15 septembre 1980.*

Congo, People's Republic of the. *Annuaire statistique; Recensement général de la population de 1974.*

Cook Islands. *Cook Islands Census of Population and Dwellings, 1986; Cook Islands Quarterly Statistical Bulletin.*

Costa Rica. *Anuario estadístico; Censos Nacionales de 1973; Costa Rica: A Country Study* (1984).

Côte d'Ivoire. *Annuaire statistique; La Côte d'Ivoire en chiffres* (annual); *L'Économie Ivoirienne* (annual); *Enquête permanente aupres des menages: resultats provisoires 1985.*

Cuba. *Anuario estadístico; Censo de población y viviendas, 1981; Compendio estadístico de Cuba* (annual); *Cuba Quarterly Economic Report.*

Cyprus. *Census of Industrial Production* (annual); *Economic Report* (annual); *Statistical Abstract* (annual).

Czechoslovakia. *Statistická ročenka Československé Socialistické Republiky* (Statistical Yearbook of the Czechoslovak Socialist Republic); *Sčítání lidu, domů a bytů 1980* (Census of Population and Housing).

Denmark. *Folke- og boligtaellingen, 1981* (Population and Housing Census); *Statistisk årbog* (Statistical Yearbook).

Djibouti. *Annuaire statistique de Djibouti.*

Dominica. *Statistical Digest.*

Dominican Republic. *República Dominicana en cifras* (annual); *VI Censo nacional de población y vivienda, 1981.*

Ecuador. *Encuesta anual de manufactura y minería; Serie estadística* (quinquennial); *IV Censo de población: III de vivienda resultados anticipados por muestreo* (1982).

Egypt. *Census of Population and Housing, 1976; Egypt: A Country Study* (1982); *Statistical Yearbook.*

El Salvador. *Anuario estadístico; Censos económicos, 1979 (Manufactura diversa; Agroindustrias; Comercio y servicios; Electricidad, construcción, transporte comercial); El Salvador en cifras* (annual).

Equatorial Guinea. *Censos Nacionales, I de Población y I de Vivienda—4 al 17 de Julio de 1983.*

Ethiopia. *Ethiopia: A Country Study* (1980); *Ethiopia 1984 Population and Housing Census; Ethiopia Statistical Abstract* (annual).

Faeroe Islands. *Árbog for Faerøerne* (Yearbook for the Faeroe Islands).

Fiji. *Annual Employment Survey; Census of Industries* (annual); *Current Economic Statistics* (quarterly); *1986 Census of the Population.*

Finland. *Annual Statistics of Agriculture; Economic Survey* (annual); *Population and Housing Census, 1980; Statistical Yearbook of Finland.*

France. *Annuaire statistique de la France; Données sociales* (triennial); *Recensement général de la population de 1982; Métropole; Tableaux de l'Economie Française* (annual).

French Guiana. *Annuaire statistique de la Guyane; Bulletin trimestriel de statistique; Recensement général de la population dans les Départements d'outre-mer en 9 mars 1982, Guyane.*

French Polynesia. *Bilan statistique de l'année; Comptes économiques* (quadrennial); *Résultats du recensement de la population de la Polynésie Française, 15 Octobre 1983; Te avei'a: Bulletin d'information statistique* (quarterly).

Gabon. *Situation économique, financière et sociale de la République Gabonaise* (annual).

Gambia, The. *The Gambia since Independence: 1965–1980, 15 years of Nationhood.*

Gaza Strip. *Judaea, Samaria, and Gaza Area Statistics Quarterly; Palestinian Statistical Abstract* (annual).

Germany, East. *Statistisches Jahrbuch der Deutschen Demokratischen Republik.*

Germany, West. *Federal Republic of Germany: A Country Study* (1983); *Statistisches Jahrbuch für die Bundesrepublik Deutschland; Volkszählung vom 27 Mai 1970* (Census of Population).

Ghana. *Economic Survey* (annual); *Ghana: An Official Handbook* (1977); *Industrial Statistics* (annual); *Population Census of Ghana, 1984.*

Gibraltar. *Abstract of Statistics* (annual); *Census of Gibraltar, 1981.*

Greece. *Recensement des industries manufacturières: Artisanat, du commerce et autres services* (1978); *Recensement de la population et des habitations, 1981; Statistical Yearbook of Greece.*

Greenland. *Grønland* (annual); *Grønlands befolkning* (Greenland Population [annual]).

Grenada. *Abstract of Statistics* (annual).

Guadeloupe. *Annuaire statistique de la Guadeloupe; Recensement général de la population dans les Departements d'Outre-mer en 9 mars 1982, Guadeloupe.*

Guam. *Guam Annual Economic Review; 1980 Census of Population and Housing.*

Guatemala. *Anuario estadístico; Censos nacionales, 1981: IX de población—IV de habitación; Guatemala: A Country Study* (1983).

Guernsey. *Guernsey Census 1976.*

Guinea, Republic of. *Situation Économique et Conjoncturelle au 31 decembre 1985 et éléments sur la mise en oeuvre de la réform économique au cours du première trimestre 1986.*

Guinea-Bissau. *Boletim Trimestral de Estatística; Recenseamento Geral da População e da Habitação, 16 de Abril de 1979.*

Guyana. *Annual Statistical Abstract.*

Haiti. *Bulletin trimestriel de statistique; Haiti: A Country Profile* (1981); *Résultats préliminaires du recensement général (Septembre 1982).*

Honduras. *Anuario estadístico; Censo nacional de Población, 1974; Honduras: A Country Profile* (1981); *Honduras en cifras* (annual).

Hong Kong. *Annual Digest of Statistics; Hong Kong* (annual); *Hong Kong 1986 By-Census; Hong Kong in Figures* (annual); *Hong Kong Social and Economic Trends* (irreg.).

Hungary. *Statisztikai évkönyv* (Statistical Yearbook); *1980, Évi népszámlálás* (Census of Population).

Iceland. *Tölfraedihandbók* (Statistical Abstract of Iceland [irreg.]); *Verslunarskýrslur* (External Trade [annual]).

India. *Census of India, 1981; Economic Survey* (annual); *India: A Reference Annual; Statistical Abstract* (annual).

Indonesia. *Indikator ekonomi* (monthly); *Indonesia: An Official Handbook* (1984); *Sensus penduduk Indonesia, 1980* (Census of Population); *Statistical Yearbook of Indonesia.*

Iran. *General Census of Population and Housing, November 1976; A Statistical Reflection of the Islamic Republic of Iran* (annual); *Statistical Yearbook of the Islamic Republic of Iran.*

Iraq. *Iraq: A Country Study* (1979); *Statistical Abstract* (annual).

Ireland. *Census of Population of Ireland, 1986; National Income and Expenditure* (annual); *Statistical Abstract* (annual).

Isle of Man. *Isle of Man 1981 Census Report; Isle of Man Digest of Economic and Social Statistics* (annual).

Israel. *1983 Census of Population and Housing; Statistical Abstract* (annual).

Italy. *Annuario di statistica agraria: Annuario di statistiche demografiche; Annuario di statistiche industriali; Annuario statistico dell'istruzione; Annuario statistico Italiano; Statistiche forestale* (annual); *Statistiche sociali* (1981); *12 Censimento general della popolazione, 1981.*

Jamaica. *Economic and Social Survey* (annual); *Statistical Abstract* (annual); *Statistical Yearbook of Jamaica.*

Japan. *Establishment Census of Japan, 1981; Japan: A Country Study* (1983); *Japan Statistical Yearbook; Statistical Indicators on Social Life* (annual); *1985 Population Census of Japan.*

Jersey. *Report of the Census for 1986; Statistical Digest* (annual).

Jordan. *Census 1979; Family Expenditure Survey* (1980); *National Accounts* (irreg.); *Statistical Yearbook.*

Kenya. *Economic Survey* (annual); *Kenya Statistical Digest* (quarterly); *Statistical Abstract* (annual).

Kiribati. *National Development Plan, 1979–1982; Report on the 1985 Census of Population.*

Korea, North. *North Korea: A Country Study* (1981).

Korea, South. *Korea Statistical Yearbook; Social Indicators in Korea* (irreg.); *South Korea: A Country Study* (1982); *The 5th Five-Year Economic and Development Plan, 1982–1986; 1980 Population and Housing Census.*

Kuwait. *Statistical Abstract; Economic Report* (annual); *General Census of Population and Housing and Buildings 1985.*

Lesotho. *Annual Statistical Bulletin; 1976 Population Census Report.*

Liberia. *Economic Survey* (annual); *1974 Census of Population and Housing.*

Libya. *The Five-Year Development Plan 1981–85; Libya Population Census, 1973; Statistical Abstract for Libya* (annual).

Liechtenstein. *Statistisches Jahrbuch; Volkszählung, 2 Dezember 1980* (Census of Population).

Luxembourg. *Annuaire statistique; Bulletin du STATEC* (monthly); *Recensement général de la population du 31 mars 1981.*

Macau. *Anuário Estatístico; Inquerito Industrial* (annual); *XII Recenseamento Geral da População, 1981.*

Madagascar. *Recensement général de la population et des habitats, 1975; Situation économique* (annual).

Malawi. *Malawi Population and Housing Census, 1987; Malawi Statistical Yearbook; Malawi Yearbook.*

Malaysia. *Fifth Malaysia Plan, 1986–1990; Malaysia: A Country Study* (1985); *Malaysian Annual Statistical Bulletin; 1980 Population and Housing Census.*

Maldives. *National Development Plan 1985–1987* (2 vols.); *Population and Housing Census, 1985; Statistical Year Book of Maldives.*

Mali. *Annuaire statistique du Mali; Recensement de la population, 1–16 décembre 1976.*

Malta. *Annual Abstract of Statistics; Census of Industrial Production Report for 19*** (annual); *Malta Year Book* (annual); *Trade Statistics* (quarterly).

Martinique. *Annuaire statistique de la Martinique; Bulletin de statistique* (quarterly); *Comptes*

économiques de la Martinique (irreg.); *Recensement de la population dans les départements d'outre-mer, 9 mars 1982—Martinique.*

Mauritania. *Annuaire Statistique; Area Handbook.*

Mauritius. *Bi-annual Digest of Statistics; 1983 Housing and Population Census of Mauritius; 1980–1982 Two-Year Plan for Economic and Social Development.*

Mayotte. *Recensement général de la population, 1978.*

Mexico. *Anuario estadístico; X Censo general de población y vivienda, 1980; La Economia Mexicana en Cifras* (1986); *Informe de Gobierno: Estadístico* (annual).

Mongolia. *National Economy of the MPR, 1921–86* (1986; quinquennial?).

Montserrat. *Caribbean Population Census, May 12, 1980; Statistical Digest* (annual).

Morocco. *Annuaire statistique du Maroc; Economic and Social Development Report, 1981; Morocco: A Country Study* (1985); *Recensement général de la population et de l'habitat de 1982.*

Mozambique. *Anuário Estatístico; Informação Estatística* (annual); *Mozambique: A Country Study* (1985); *1º Recenseamento Geral da População, 1980.*

Nepal. *Census of Manufacturing Establishments of Nepal, 1981–82; Economic Survey* (annual); *Population Monograph of Nepal* (1987); *The Sixth Plan (1980–85); Statistical Pocket Book* (irreg.); *Statistical Yearbook of Nepal.*

Netherlands, The. *Landbouwcijfers* (Agricultural Data [annual]); *Statistical Yearbook of the Netherlands; 14e Algemene volkstelling, 28 februari 1971* (14th General Population Census).

Netherlands Antilles. *Tweede Algemene Volks- en Woningtelling Nederlandse Antillen: toestand per 1 Februari 1981; Statistical Yearbook of the Netherlands Antilles.*

New Caledonia. *Annuaire statistique; Enquête socio-économique, 1980–1981; Resultats du Recensement de la population, 15 Avril 1983.*

New Zealand. *1986 New Zealand Census of Population and Dwellings; New Zealand Official Yearbook.*

Nicaragua. *Anuario estadístico de Nicaragua; Nicaragua: A Country Study* (1982); *Plan Económico, 1987* (irreg.).

Niger. *Annuaire statistique; Les comptes de la nation: années 1978–1979–1980* (1984); *Données de base* (1979).

Nigeria. *Annual Abstract of Statistics; Fourth National Development Plan* (1981); *Nigeria: A Country Study* (1981).

Niue. *Abstract of Statistics* (annual); *Census of Population and Housing, 1976; Niue National Development Plan, 1980–1985.*

Norfolk Island. *Annual Report; Census of Population and Housing, 30 June 1986.*

Norway. *Folke- og boligtelling 1980* (Population and Housing Census); *Industristatistikk* (annual); *Statistisk årsbok* (Statistical Yearbook).

Oman. *Statistical Year Book; The Second Five-Year Plan of Development, 1981–1985.*

Pacific Islands, Trust Territory of the. *Report of the Trusteeship Council to the Security Council on the Trust Territory of the Pacific Islands* (annual); *Report to the United Nations* (annual).

Pakistan. *Economic Survey* (annual); *Pakistan Year Book; Pakistan Statistical Yearbook; Population Census of Pakistan, 1981; Some Socio-Economic Trends* (annual); *10 Years of Pakistan in Statistics, 1972–1982* (1983).

Panama. *Indicadores económicos y sociales* (annual); *Octavo censo de población: Cuarto censo de vivienda, 11 de mayo de 1980; Panama en cifras* (annual); *Situacion económica: Cuentas nacionales* (annual); *Situacion económica: Industria* (annual).

Papua New Guinea. *Abstract of Statistics* (quarterly); *National Accounts Statistics—Statistical Bulletin* (quarterly); *Papua New Guinea: Selected Development Issues* (A World Bank Country Study [1982]); *Population of Papua New Guinea (ESCAP;* Country Monograph Series No. 7.2 [1982]); *Rural Industries* (annual); *Summary of Statistics* (annual); *1980 National Population Census.*

Paraguay. *Anuario estadístico del Paraguay; Censo nacional de población y viviendo, 1982.*

Peru. *Censos nacionales; VIII de población: III de vivienda, 12 de julio de 1981; Compendio estadístico* (annual); *Informe estadístico* (annual); *Peru: A Country Study* (1980).

Philippines. *Philippine Statistical Yearbook; Philippine Yearbook; 1980 Census of Population.*

Poland. *Narodowy spis powszechny z dnia 7 XII 1978 r.* (Census of Population); *Poland: A Country Study* (1984); *Rocznik statystyczny* (Statistical Yearbook).

Portugal. *Anuário Estatístico; Estatísticas Agricolas* (annual); *Estatísticas do Comercio Externo* (annual); *Estatísticas Demograficas* (annual); *Estatísticas Industriais* (2 vol.; annual); *Estatísticas Monetarias e Financeiras* (annual); *Recenseamento Agricola, 1979; XII Recenseamento Geral da População: II Recenseamento Geral da Habitação, 1981.*

Puerto Rico. *Anuario estadístico; Compendio estadísticas sociales* (annual); *Informe económico al gobernador* (Economic Report to the Governor [annual]); *1980 Census of Population* (U.S.).

Qatar. *Annual Statistical Abstract; Economic Survey of Qatar* (annual); *Qatar Year Book.*

Réunion. *Annuaire statistique de la Réunion; Comptes économiques de la Réunion* (irreg.); *Panorama de l'Économie de la Réunion* (annual); *Faits et chiffres réunionnaise* (1985); *Recensement général de la population en 1974: Départements d'outre-mer—Réunion.*

Romania. *Anuarul statistic al Republicii Socialiste România; Recensămîntul populației și al locuințelor, din 5 ianuarie 1977; Romania Yearbook.*

Rwanda. *Bulletin de Statistique: Supplement Annuel; IIIème Plan de Developpement Economique, Social et Culturel 1982–86.*

St. Kitts and Nevis. *Annual Digest of Statistics; St. Christopher and Nevis: Economic Report* (World Bank Country Study) (1985).

St. Lucia. *Annual Statistical Digest.*

St. Pierre and Miquelon. *Résultats du recensement de la population dans les départements d'outremer, 9 mars 1982.*

St. Vincent and the Grenadines. *Digest of Statistics* (annual).

San Marino. *Annuario statistico, 1981–84* (4 vol.?; irreg.); *3 Censimento generale dell agricoltura* (1977); *5 Censimento generale della popolazione* (1979).

Saudi Arabia. *Saudi Arabia: A Country Study* (1985); *The Statistical Indicator* (annual); *Statistical Summary* (Saudi Arabian Monetary Agency [annual]); Statistical Year Book.

Senegal. *Le Sénégal en chiffres* (annual); *Situation économique du Senegal* (annual).

Seychelles. *National Development Plan, 1985–89; Statistical Abstract* (annual); *1977 Census Report.*

Sierra Leone. *Sierra Leone: 12 Years of Economic Achievement and Political Consolidation under the APC and Dr. Siaka Stevens, 1968–80.*

Singapore. *Census of Population, 1980; Economic and Social Statistics, 1960–1982; Report on the Census of Industrial Production* (annual); *Singapore Yearbook; Yearbook of Statistics Singapore.*

Solomon Islands. *Solomon Islands 1986 Population Census; Statistical Yearbook.*

Somalia. *Statistical Abstract* (annual).

South Africa. *Population Census 1985; South Africa: Official Yearbook of the Republic of South Africa; South African Statistics* (biennial).

South West Africa/Namibia. *Budget 19**–19*** (annual); *Statistical/Economic Review* (annual).

Spain. *Anuario estadístico; Censo de población de 1981.*

Sri Lanka. *Census of Population and Housing, 1981; Report on the Survey on Manufacturing Industries, 1979; Sri Lanka Year Book; Statistical Pocketbook of the Democratic Socialist Republic of Sri Lanka* (annual).

Sudan, The. *Third Population Census, 1983.*

Swaziland. *Annual Statistical Bulletin; Report on the 1976 Swaziland Population Census.*

Sweden. *Folk- och bostadsräkningen, 1980* (Population and Housing Census); *Jordbruksstatistisk årsbok* (Yearbook of Agricultural Statistics); *Statistisk årsbok för Sverige* (Statistical Abstract of Sweden [annual]).

Switzerland. *Recensement fédéral de la population, 1980; Statistisches Jahrbuch* (Statistical Yearbook).

Syria. *Census of Agriculture, 1981; General Census of Housing and Inhabitants, 1981; Statistical Abstract* (annual).

Taiwan. *Industry of Free China* (monthly); *Social Indicators of the Republic of China* (annual); *Statistical Abstract* (annual); *Statistical Yearbook of the Republic of China; Taiwan Statistical Data Book* (annual); *Yearbook of Labor Statistics; 1980 Census of Population and Housing.*

Tanzania. *Tanzania Statistical Abstract* (annual); *1978 Population Census.*

Thailand. *Report of the Survey of Business Trade and Services* (biennial); *Foreign Trade Statistics* (monthly); *Report of the Industrial Survey, Whole Kingdom* (biennial); *Report of the Labor Force Survey: Whole Kingdom* (quarterly); *Statistical Handbook of Thailand* (annual); *Statistical Yearbook; 1980 Population and Housing Census.*

Togo. *Annuaire statistique; Plan de développement économique & social, 1981–1985; Recensement général de la population, 1970.*

Tokelau. *Census of Population, 1981; Report of the Administrator of Tokelau for the Year Ended: 31 March 19*** (annual).

Tonga. *Population Census, 1986; Statistical Abstract* (irreg.).

Trinidad and Tobago. *Population Census, 1980; Annual Statistical Digest.*

Tunisia. *Annuaire statistique de la Tunisie; Recensement général de la population et des logements, 30 mars 1984.*

Turkey. *Diş Ticaret İstatistikleri* (Annual Foreign Trade Statistics); *Genel Sanayi ve İşyerleri Sayımı* (Census of Industry and Business Establishments [1980]); *Genel Nüfus Sayımı, 12. 10. 1985* (Census of Population); *Genel Tarım Sayımı, 1980* (Census of Agriculture); *İnşaat İstatistikleni* (Construction Statistics [annual]); *Türkiye İstatistik Yilliği* (Statistical Yearbook of Turkey).

Turks and Caicos. *Pocket Digest of Statistics* (irreg.).

Tuvalu. *Abstract of Statistics* (annual); *Census of the Population, 1979.*

Union of Soviet Socialist Republics. *Narodnoye Khozyaystvo SSSR* (National Economy of the U.S.S.R. [annual]).

United Arab Emirates. *Statistical Yearbook* (Abu Dhabi) (annual).

United Kingdom. *Agricultural Statistics United Kingdom* (annual); *Annual Abstract of Statistics; Britain: An Official Handbook* (annual); *National Income and Expenditure* (annual); *Census 1981; Report on the Census of Production: Summary Tables* (annual).

United States. *Agricultural Statistics* (annual); *Annual Energy Review; Current Population Reports* (Series P-20, P-23, P-25, P-26, P-27, P-28, P-60); *Digest of Education Statistics* (annual); *Minerals Yearbook* (3 vol.; annual); *National Transportation Statistics* (annual); *Statistical Abstract* (annual); *U.S. Exports: SIC-Based Products* (annual); *U.S. Imports: SIC-Based Products* (annual); *Vital and Health Statistics* (series 1–20); *1982 Census of Construction Industries; 1982 Census of Manufacturing; 1982 Census of Mineral Industries; 1982 Census of Retail Trade; 1982 Census of Wholesale Trade; 1982 Census of Agriculture; 1980 Census of Population and Housing.*

Uruguay. *Anuario Estadístico; Encuesta Nacional de Hogares* (annual).

Vanuatu. *Recensement de la population, 1979; Vanuatu Statistical Yearbook.*

Venezuela. *Anuario estadístico; Encuesta de hogares por muestreo* (annual); *Encuesta industrial* (annual); *IX Censo general de población y vivienda, 20 de octubre 1981.*

Virgin Islands of the United States. *Annual Report; Economic Review, 1986; 1980 Census of Population* (U.S.).

Wallis and Futuna. *Résultats du Recensement de la Population, 15 Février 1983.*

West Bank. *Judaea, Samaria, and Gaza Area Statistics Quarterly; Palestinian Statistical Abstract* (annual).

Western Sahara. *Recensement General de la Population et de l'Habitat* (1982 [Morocco]).

Western Samoa. *Annual Statistical Abstract; Census of Population and Housing, 1976.*

Yemen, People's Democratic Republic of. *The Yemens: Country Studies* (1986).

Yemen Arab Republic. *The Housing and Population Census, February 1975; Statistical Year Book.*

Yugoslavia. *Popis stanovištva i stanova od 31. marta 1981* (Census of Population and Housing as of March 31, 1981); *Statistički godišnjak Jugoslavije* (Statistical Yearbook of Yugoslavia).

Zaire. *Annuaire statistique;* Conjoncture Economique (annual); *Recensement Scientifique de la Population du 1er juillet 1984.*

Zambia. *Country Profile: Zambia 1985; Monthly Digest of Statistics; Third National Development Plan, 1979–83; 1980 Census of Population and Housing.*

Zimbabwe. *1982 Population Census: Main Demographic Features of the Population of Zimbabwe; Statistical Year-book.*

A. C. Nielson / Amis 881

Index

This index covers both *Britannica Book of the Year* (cumulative for ten years) and *Britannica World Data.*

Entries in dark type are titles of articles in the *Book of the Year;* an accompanying year in dark type gives the year the reference appears, and the accompanying page number in light type shows where the article appears. For example, "Archaeology 89:125; 88:125; 87:141; 86:164; 85:165; 84:176; 83:177; 82:183; 81:183; 80:181" indicates that the article "Archaeology" appeared every year from 1980 through 1989. Other references that appear with a page number but without a year refer to references from the current yearbook.

Indented entries in light type that follow dark type article titles refer by page number to other places in the text where the subject of the article is discussed. Light type entries that are not indented refer by page number to subjects that are not themselves article titles. Names of people covered in biographies and obituaries are followed by the abbreviation "(biog.)" or "(obit.)" with the year in dark type and a page number in light type, *e.g.,* Bellisario, Marisa (obit.) **89**:89, or Reagan, Ronald Wilson (biog.) **89**:82; **88**:80; **87**:93; **86**:108; **85**:110; **84**:95; **83**:89; **82**:90; **81**:88. In cases where a person has both a biography and an obituary, the words appear as subentries under the main entry and are alphabetized accordingly, *e.g.,*:

Belushi, John
biography **80**:71
obituary **83**:100

References to illustrations are by page number and are preceded by the abbreviation *il.*

The index uses word-by-word alphabetization (treating a word as one or more characters separated by a space from the next word). Names beginning with "Mc" and "Mac" are alphabetized as "Mac"; "St." is treated as "Saint."

A

A. C. Nielsen Co. (Am. co.)
special report **80**:659
television and radio 363
A. H. Robins (Am. co.)
Dalkon Shield lawsuit 142
"A cor et à cri" (Leiris)
French literature 247
ABB (Swed./Swiss co.)
electrical industry 217
nuclear industry 223
Abbado, Claudio (biog.) **80**:70
classical music 272
Abbas, Mahmoud Abul
Palestine Liberation Organization 405
Abboud, Albert Robert (biog.) **81**:70
ABC: *see* American Broadcasting Corporation
Abdul-Jabar, Kareem *il.* 312
Abdullah, Sheikh Muhammad (obit.) **83**:99
Abdurabi, Ali Jusuf
Tanzania 401
Abel, Iorwith Wilbur (obit.) **88**:87
"Abgang" (Boock)
German literature 248
ABM: *see* antiballistic missile
Abokor, Ismail Ali
Somalia 397
abortion
Canada 481
RU 486 drug 205
state governments 489
Abreu, Caio Fernando
Brazilian literature 251
ABRI: *see* Indonesian Armed Forces
Abruzzo, Ben (obit.) **86**:120
ABT: *see* American Ballet Theatre
Abu Musa
Middle Eastern affairs 405
Abubakr III (obit.) **89**:88
Abul-Dahab, Galal
Egypt 408
abuse
women's mental health 206
Academy Award, *or* Oscar
motion pictures 266
Academy Chicago
Cheever publication dispute 287
Acción Democrática, *or* AD (pol. party, Venez.)
Venezuelan elections 511
Ace, Goodman (obit.) **83**:99
ACGB: *see* Arts Council of Great Britain
Acheampong, Ignatius Kutu (obit.) **80**:103
acid rain
environmental damage 197
Acland, Sir Hugh John Dyke (obit.) **82**:100
acquired immune deficiency syndrome: *see* AIDS
acquisition
paint industry 223
rubber industry 224
"Acrobat and Young Harlequin" (paint.)
record art sale 134
ACTS (cable network)
television ministry 292
AD (pol. party, Venez.): *see* Acción Democrática
Adami, Eddie Fenech
Malta 458
Adams, Ansel Easton (obit.) **85**:120
Adams, Harriet Stratemeyer (obit.) **83**:99
Adams, Sir John Bertram (obit.) **85**:120
Adams, John Michael Geoffrey Manningham (obit.) **86**:120
Adams, Michael
chess 316
Adamson, Joy (obit.) **81**:101
Addams, Charles Samuel (obit.) **89**:88
Aden: *see* Yemen, People's Democratic Republic of
"Adieu. . .je pars pour Viazmal!" (Basile)
French-Canadian literature 248
Adler, Lawrence James (obit.) **89**:88
Adler, Mortimer J.
"The Real American Bicentennial" (feature article) **87**:16
Adriatic Sea
marine biology studies 239
Adventist Development and Relief Agency, *or* ADRA
Seventh-day Adventist programs 295
advertising 210
television and radio 365
"Advertising Age" (mag.)
national advertisers ranking 210
aerial sports **89**:306; **88**:308; **87**:346; **86**:380; **85**:374; **84**:150; **83**:150; **82**:154; **81**:154; **80**:156
aerospace 210
Aerospace Museum (Los Angeles, Calif., U.S.)
architectural design 129
AERP: *see* African Economic Recovery Plan
AFDC: *see* Aid to Families with Dependent Children
"Affairs of State" (Anderson)
Canadian literature 246
Afghanistan **89**:429; **88**:429; **87**:471; **86**:502; **85**:506; **84**:151; **83**:151; **82**:155; **81**:155; **80**:157
international law 233
Islam 299
Pakistan 434
refugees 283
Soviet withdrawal 255, 375, 478
United Nations 376
see also WORLD DATA
African affairs **89**:382; **88**:382; **87**:421; **86**:453; **85**:456; **84**:153; **83**:153; **82**:157; **81**:157; **80**:158
AIDS epidemic 203
consumer affairs 141
demography 280
economic affairs 169, 174
education 184
hydrology 158
insurance 220
libraries 235
locust plague 114
Lutheran Communion 294
military affairs 262
Reformed churches 295
roads and highways 192
special reports **85**:457; **82**:161, 520; **81**:160
tourism 227
see also individual countries by name
African Development Bank
Zaire 402
African Economic Recovery Plan, *or* AERP
African affairs 382
African National Congress, *or* ANC
South Africa 398
African Unity, Organization of, *or* OAU
African affairs 382
Africanized bee
entomological studies 238
Agassi, Andre
tennis 338
Agca, Mehmet Ali (biog.) **84**:75
"Age of Chivalry: Art in Plantagenet England 1200–1400, The" (art exhibit) 132
Ager, Milton (obit.) **80**:103
Agfa-Gevaert, Inc. (Ger. co.)
new photographic films 277
Aggett, Neil Hutchin (obit.) **83**:99
Agricole de Céréales (Fr. co.)
food processing 123
Agriculture and Food Supplies 89:113; **88**:113; **87**:127; **86**:150; **85**:150; **84**:155; **83**:156; **82**:163; **81**:163; **80**:161
consumer affairs 141
see also WORLD DATA *and* individual countries by name
Ahlers, Conrad (obit.) **81**:101
Ahrens, Thomas
geology 156
Aid to Families with Dependent Children, *or* AFDC
children in poverty 302
social security and welfare services 303
AIDS, *or* acquired immune deficiency syndrome
dentistry 207
Guinea-Bissau 390
Middle Eastern affairs 406
protest *il.* 202
religious controversy 291
research 202
Seventh-day Adventist committee 295
special report **88**:206
state governments 489
United Nations 378
United States 486
Aiken, George David (obit.) **85**:120
Ailuropoda melanoleuca: *see* giant panda
air bag (automobile)
automobile industry 213
consumer affairs 142
Air Canada
partial privatization 481
Air Defense Command, *or* VVO (U.S.S.R.)
military affairs 259
air pollution
environmental standards 196
air-traffic control
aerospace 210
aviation 372, *il.*
Airbus A320 (aircraft)
aerospace industry 211
Airbus A330 (aircraft)
aerospace industry 211
Airbus A340 (aircraft)
aerospace industry 211
Airbus Industrie (Eur. co.)
aerospace industry 210
Aitken, Sir John William Maxwell (obit.) **86**:120
Akhmatova, Anna
Soviet literature 251
Akhmilovskaya, Yelena
chess 317
Akhromeyev, Sergey (biog.) **85**:89
Akihito, Crown Prince (biog.) **89**:65
Japan 423
Akoun, Laurent
Côte d'Ivoire 387
Aksyonov, Vasily
Soviet literature *il.* 251
Akuffo, Fred W. K. (obit.) **80**:103
"Alabama Journal" (news.) 285
Alaska
oil 522
"Alaska Construction and Oil"
oil-production statistics 522
Alban Gate (U.K.)
architectural design 131
Albania **89**:468; **88**:468; **87**:513; **86**:541; **85**:547; **84**:168; **83**:169; **82**:175; **81**:176; **80**:174
Yugoslavia 479
see also WORLD DATA
Albers, Josef
art exhibition 134
Albertson, Jack (obit.) **82**:100
Albery, Sir Donald Arthur Rolleston (obit.) **89**:88
Alboreto, Michele
automobile racing 307
Albright, Ivan Le Lorraine (obit.) **84**:106
Alda, Alan (biog.) **80**:70
Aldrich, Robert (obit.) **84**:106
Alebua, Ezekiel
Solomon Islands 517
Aleixandre, Vicente (obit.) **85**:120
Alekseyef, Aleksandr (obit.) **83**:99
Alemán, Miguel (obit.) **84**:106
Alessandri Rodríguez, Jorge (obit.) **87**:100
Alexander, Kelly Miller, Sr. (obit.) **86**:120
Alexander, Lincoln (biog.) **86**:89
Alexandrovitch, Prince Andrew (obit.) **82**:100
Alfa-Laval (Swed. co.)
food processing 123
Alfonsín, Raúl (biog.) **84**:75
Argentina 493, *il.* 510
algae
environmental concerns 460, 463
Algeria **89**:407; **88**:407; **87**:448; **86**:479; **85**:483; **84**:168; **83**:170; **82**:176; **81**:176; **80**:174
dams 190
Islam 299
North African affairs 406
Morocco 416
Western Sahara 377
see also WORLD DATA
Algiers declaration
Palestine Liberation Organization 405
Ali, Salim (obit.) **88**:87
Alia, Ramiz (biog.) **86**:89
Albanian politics 468
Alianza Popular, *or* AP (pol. party, Sp.)
Far Right (special report) 445
Spain 462
Alice, Princess, Countess of Athlone (obit.) **82**:100
alitame
soft drinks 215
All-Star game (baseball) 310
All-Union Party Conference (U.S.S.R.)
Soviet literature 251
Allais, Maurice (biog.) **89**:65
Allan of Kilmahew, Robert Alexander Allan, Baron (obit.) **80**:103
Allégret, Yves Edouard (obit.) **88**:87
Allen, Clabon Walter (obit.) **88**:87
Allen, William Ernest Chesney (obit.) **83**:99
Allen-Bradley (Am. co.)
electrical industry 217
Allen of Fallowfield, Alfred Walter Henry Allen (obit.) **86**:120
alleopathy, *or* alleochemics
botanical research 240
Alliance of Motion Picture and Television Producers (U.S.)
television and radio 365
Alliance of Young Democrats, *or* FIDESZ
Hungary 472
Allon, Yigal (obit.) **81**:101
Almirante, Giorgio (obit.) **89**:88
ALP: *see* Australian Labor Party
Alpine World Cup
skiing 335
Alston, Walter Emmons (obit.) **85**:120
aluminum
Venezuelan production 264
aluminum oxide
ceramics 216
Alva, Walter
Peruvian archaeological finds 127
Alvarez, Luis Walter (obit.) **89**:88
Álvarez Armelino, Gregorio Conrado (biog.) **82**:68
Alvin, Juliette (obit.) **83**:99
Alysheba
horse racing 327
AMA (Am. org.): *see* American Medical Association
Amal
Lebanon 415
Amalrik, Andrey Alekseyevich (obit.) **81**:101
Amara, Roy C.
"1985" (feature article) **80**:138
amateur radio
television and radio 367
amber
geologic research 156
Ambrose, C. E. L.
cricket 318
Ambystoma opacum: *see* marble salamander
Ameche, Alan Dante (obit.) **89**:88
Amendola, Giorgio (obit.) **81**:101
American Association of Zoological Parks and Aquariums
panda dispute 138
American Ballet Theatre, *or* ABT
dance developments 148, *il.* 151
American Bowling Congress 314
American Broadcasting Corporation, *or* ABC (N.Y., N.Y., U.S.)
television and radio 364
American Council on Education
college graduate survey 185
American Furniture Hall of Fame (Wash., D.C., U.S.)
furniture 218
American Home Products
consumer boycott 142
American Indian Dance Theatre (Am. dance co.)
performance in Italy 151
"American Ingenuity—Does It Still Thrive?" (feature article) **81**:137
American International Toy Fair (N.Y., N.Y., U.S.) 219
American literature 244
American Medical Association, *or* AMA (Am. org.)
smokeless cigarette 227
American Music Festival, *or* AMF (Am. production)
dance 149
"American Potential: The Human Dimension" (U.S. educ. report)
education reforms 184
American Samoa
political corruption 520
American Stock Exchange, *or* Amex
stock exchanges 177
American Telephone and Telegraph, *or* AT&T
telecommunications 225
Unix standardization 229
American Tuna Boat Association (Am. org.)
Oceanian affairs 512
America's Cup
sailing 334
Amex: *see* American Stock Exchange
AMF (Am. production): *see* American Music Festival
Amin, Idi
special report **87**:441
Amis, Kingsley
literature 244

882 *Amnesty / Babaquara*

Amnesty International
Islamic activities 299
Amoroso, Emmanuel Ciprian (obit.) **83**:99
Amory, Derick Heathcoat Amory, 1st Viscount (obit.) **82**:100
Amsterdam (Neth.)
chess tournaments 316
Amsterdam, Ajax
soccer 320
Amsterdam, Jane
newspaper publishing 285
Amsterdam Stock Exchange (Neth.)
stock exchanges 180
"Anatomie d'un scandale" (Fédier)
French literature 247
ANC: *see* African National Congress
Andean Group
South America 492
"Anders" (Burmeister)
German literature 248
Andersch, Alfred (obit.) **81**:101
Anderson, Doris
literature 246
Anderson, John Bayard (biog.) **81**:70
Anderson, Ken (biog.) **82**:68
Anderson, Maxie Leroy (obit.) **84**:106
Anderson, Ottis (biog.) **80**:70
Anderson, Sparky (biog.) **85**:89
Andersson, Sven Olof Morgan (obit.) **88**:87
Andorra **89**:446; **88**:445; **87**:489; **86**:518; **85**:523; **84**:169; **83**:171; **82**:176; **81**:178; **80**:176
see also WORLD DATA
Andrew, Prince: *see* York, Duke and Duchess of
Andrews, Eamonn (obit.) **88**:87
Andrews, Tommie Lee
DNA fingerprinting 139
Andropov, Yury Vladimirovich
biography **83**:70
obituary **85**:120
Androsch, Hannes
Austrian politics 447
Andrzejewski, Jerzy (obit.) **84**:106
"Anfitrión, El" (Edwards)
Latin-American literature 250
Anga, Pierre
Congolese affairs 387
"angélique, L' " (Robbe-Grillet)
French literature 247
Angeloz, Eduardo
Argentina 493
Anghelis, Odysseus (obit.) **88**:87
Anglican Communion 293
Anglican Roman Catholic International Commission, *or* ARCIC 296
Angola **89**:383; **88**:383; **87**:422; **86**:455; **85**:459; **84**:170; **83**:171; **82**:177; **81**:178; **80**:176
international affairs
Africa 382
Mozambique 394
South Africa 399
Cuba 499
United Nations 377
Zaire 402
military affairs 262, *il.* 384
peace talks 234, 376
special report **86**
see also WORLD DATA
anilox flexo (news press)
printing 224
animal
embryo cloning 139
marine biology 239
animal rights
fur production 218
special report **86**:301
anisoylated plasminogen streptokinase activator, *or* APSAC (drug)
heart attack treatment 204
"Änkan" (Belblanc)
Swedish literature 249
Anouilh, Jean-Marie-Lucien-Pierre (obit.) **88**:87
Anquetil, Jacques (obit.) **88**:88
Ansett, Sir Reginald Myles (obit.) **82**:100
Antarctic Treaty (1961)
Antarctic mineral regulation 520
Antarctica **89**:520; **88**:520; **87**:568; **86**:600; **85**:606; **84**:171; **83**:172; **82**:178; **81**:180; **80**:177
environmental concerns 196
ozone layer 160
Anthropology 89:124; **88**:124; **87**:140; **86**:163; **85**:163; **84**:173; **83**:175; **82**:180; **81**:181; **80**:180
anti-indecency rule (U.S.)
television and radio 363
anti-Semitism
West Germany 289
antiballistic missile, *or* ABM
Soviet military affairs 259
Antigua and Barbuda **89**:492; **88**:492; **87**:538; **86**:569; **85**:600; **84**:175; **83**:176; **82**:182; **81**:300; **80**:300
see also WORLD DATA
antiques
special report **81**:424
Antonov, Oleg Konstantinovich (obit.) **85**:121
anxiety
mental health 206
"Anything for Billy" (McMurtry)
American literature 245
Aoki, Isao (biog.) **84**:75
Aoki, Rocky (biog.) **83**:70
Aoun, Michel
Lebanon 414
AP (pol. party, Sp.): *see* Alianza Popular
apartheid
African affairs 382
Commonwealth of Nations 378
crime and law enforcement 143
refugees 282
South Africa 288, 397
special report **86**:471
Appelgren, Mikael
table tennis 338
Apple Computer Inc. (Am. co.)
Microsoft lawsuit 229
Appleton, Dave
rodeo 333
application specific integrated circuits, *or* ASIC
microelectronics 222
APSAC (drug): *see* anisoylated plasminogen streptokinase activator
APV (Br. co.)
food processing 123
Aqsa Mosque, al-, *or* Temple Mount
Islam 299
Aquino, Corazon (biog.) **87**:76
Philippines 435, 440
Arab-Israeli conflict: *see* Middle Eastern and North African affairs
Arabic literature 243
Hebrew translations 252
Arabica (coffee brand)
production 118
Arabidopsis thaliana
botanical research 240, *il.* 239
Arafat, Yasir (biog.) **84**:76; **83**:71
Geneva speech 234, 404, *il.* 36
Israel 413
Jordan 413
meeting with Mubarak *il.* 409
Palestine Liberation Organization 377
Syria 418
Aragon, Louis (obit.) **83**:99
Aral Sea (U.S.S.R.)
hydrology 159
aramid
man-made fibres 226
Arbitration and Conciliation Commission
Australian economy 515
Arbitron ratings
special report **80**:659
Archaeology 89:125; **88**:125; **87**:141; **86**:164; **85**:165; **84**:176; **83**:177; **82**:183; **81**:183; **80**:181
special reports **85**:167; **83**:181
Archaeopteryx
fossil studies 237
Archer, Jeffrey Howard (biog.) **86**:89
archery **88**:345; **87**:347; **86**:381; **85**:376; **84**:650; **83**:648; **82**:653; **81**:647; **80**:652
Architecture 89:128; **88**:128; **87**:144; **86**:167; **85**:169; **84**:179; **83**:183; **82**:186; **81**:186; **80**:185
ARCIC: *see* Anglican Roman Catholic International Commission
Arctic Regions **89**:522; **88**:522; **87**:570; **86**:602; **85**:607; **84**:182; **83**:187; **82**:190; **81**:190; **80**:189
Arden, John
literature 244
Ardito Barletta Vallarina, Nicolás (biog.) **85**:89
Ardizzone, Edward Jeffrey Irving (obit.) **80**:103
Ardrey, Robert (obit.) **81**:101
ARENA (pol. party, El Sal.): *see* Nationalist Republican Alliance
Argentina **89**:493; **88**:492; **87**:539; **86**:569; **85**:580; **84**:185; **83**:188; **82**:192; **81**:191; **80**:191
Falkland Islands 518
foreign debt 174
motion pictures 268
roads and highways 191
sports
polo 333
rugby 321
volleyball 344
trade 492
see also WORLD DATA
Argüello, Alexis (biog.) **83**:71
Ariane (rocket)
space exploration 306
Arias Madrid, Arnulfo (obit.) **89**:89
Panama 508
Arias Sánchez, Oscar (biog.) **88**:65; **87**:76
Central American peace plan 262, 491
Aringo, Peter Aloo
sex education proposal 184
Ariyoshi, Sawako (obit.) **85**:121
Arizona
state government 489
Arizona State University (Tempe, Ariz.)
wrestling 344
Arkell, the Rev. Anthony John (obit.) **81**:101
Arkoff, Samuel Z. (biog.) **80**:71
Arland, Marcel (obit.) **87**:100
Arlen, Harold (obit.) **87**:100
Armenia (state, U.S.S.R.) *map* 477
earthquake 157, *il.* 154
Islam 299
protests 476
Armitage, John (obit.) **81**:101
arms control
military affairs 261
Armstrong, Henry (obit.) **89**:89
Armstrong, John Ward (obit.) **88**:88
Armstrong of Sanderstead, William Armstrong, Baron (obit.) **81**:102
Arnaud, Claude
French literature 247
Arnaz, Desi (obit.) **87**:100
Aron, Raymond-Claude-Ferdinand (obit.) **84**:106
Aronson, Boris (obit.) **81**:102
Arosemena Gómez, Otto (obit.) **85**:121
Arout, Gabriel (obit.) **83**:100
Arpino, Giovanni
Italian literature 249
Arron, Henck
Suriname 510
"Art Centres and Artists in Northern Europe" (art exhibit) 132
Art Deco
gemstones 219
Art Exhibitions and Art Sales 89:131; **88**:131; **87**:147; **86**:170; **85**:172; **84**:187; **83**:190; **82**:193; **81**:193; **80**:193
museums 269
special report **80**:199
Art Gallery of New South Wales (Sydney, Austr.)
art exhibition 132
Art Gallery of South Australia
art exhibition 132
Art Institute of Chicago (Chicago, Ill., U.S.)
art exhibition 131
museum expansion 270
Thai religious art controversy *il.* 292
Arthur Guinness (Irish co.)
food processing 123
Arthur M. Sackler Gallery (Wash., D.C., U.S.) 129
Arts and Libraries, Office of, *or* OAL (U.K.)
theatre 367
Arts Council of Great Britain, *or* ACGB
theatre 367
Arturo Ramos, Luis
"Este era un gato" 250
Artyomov, Vladimir
gymnastics 326
Aru Basin (Indon.)
marine biology studies 239
Ärzt für das Leben (law case)
European Commission on Human Rights 232
ASEAN: *see* Southeast Asian Nations, Association of
Ashdown, Paddy (biog.) **89**:65
British politics 466
Ashley, Laura (obit.) **86**:120
Ashton, Sir Frederick William Mallandaine (obit.) **89**:89
Ashton-Warner, Sylvia **85**:121
ASIC: *see* application specific integrated circuits
Askey, Arthur Bowden (obit.) **83**:100
aspartame
soft drinks 215
Assad, Hafez al- (biog.) **85**:90
Syria 418
association football, *or* soccer 320
Dutch championship 459
Association of...: *see under* substantive word; *e.g.*, Southeast Asian Nations, Association of
Astaire, Adele Marie (obit.) **82**:100
Astaire, Fred (obit.) **88**:88
Asther, Nils (obit.) **82**:100
Astor, Mary (obit.) **88**:88
Astor of Hever, Gavin Astor, 2nd Baron (obit.) **85**:121
Astorga, Nora (obit.) **89**:89
Astronauts Memorial (Fla., U.S.)
architectural design 131
Astronomy 89:135; **88**:135; **87**:151; **86**:174; **85**:176; **84**:193; **83**:196; **82**:200; **81**:198; **80**:201
earth sciences 156
special report **87**:152
"At the Core of the Problem of Peace—Israel and the West Bank: Two Views" (feature article) **84**:8
AT&T (Am. co.): *see* American Telephone and Telegraph
Athanasiadis-Novas, Georgios (obit.) **88**:88
Athenagoras, Theodoritos (obit.) **80**:103
athletes
television advertising 210
Atkinson, Justin Brooks (obit.) **85**:121
"Atlantic" (mag.)
magazine awards 286
Atlantic Ocean
hydrothermal vents 161
"Atlantis" (space shuttle)
space exploration 305
atmosphere pack
food processing 123
Atsuko Asai
bowling 313
Attenborough, Sir Richard Samuel (biog.) **84**:76
Attorney General v. The Observer Ltd.
"Spycatcher" injunction 232
Atwood, Margaret Eleanor (biog.) **88**:65
literature 246
Auburn University (Auburn, Ala., U.S.)
college football 323
women's collegiate basketball 311
Auchinleck, Sir Claude John Eyre (obit.) **82**:100
Audi (W.Ger. co.)
automobile industry 213
sudden-acceleration problem 142
Auric, Georges (obit.) **84**:107
Australia **89**:512; **88**:511; **87**:558; **86**:590; **85**:594; **84**:195; **83**:198; **82**:202; **81**:201; **80**:203
agriculture 116
fishing industry 121
archaeological finds 125
arts
art exhibitions 132
literature 248
motion pictures 266
botanical gardens 138
education 183
gold mining *il.* 265
industry
automobile industry 212
gemstones 219
wine production 215
wool market 226
international affairs
Kiribati 515
Nauru 515
New Zealand 516
Oceania 511
Solomon Islands 517
international law 234
international migration 282
labour-management relations 231
1987 stock market crash (special report) 176
race relations 287
roads and highways 191, 374
social security and welfare services 303
special reports **85**:596; **84**:199; **83**:202; **82**:206; **81**:205; **80**:207
sports
cricket 317
harness racing 329
horse racing 329
polo 333
rowing 334
rugby 321
squash rackets 335
stock exchanges 181
wildlife conservation 199
see also WORLD DATA
Australian Aborigines
race relations 287
"Australian Bicentennial"
art exhibition 132
Australian Labor Party, *or* ALP
referendum 512
Australian National Gallery (Canberra, Austr.)
art exhibition 132
Australian Open
tennis 338
Australian Wool Corporation, *or* AWC
wool 226
"Australia's Bicentennial Year" (feature article) **88**:20
australopithecus
anthropology 124
Australopithecus robustus
anthropology 125
Austria **89**:446; **88**:446; **87**:489; **86**:518; **85**:524; **84**:201; **83**:204; **82**:208; **81**:208; **80**:209
Liechtenstein 458
special report **87**
stock exchanges 181
see also WORLD DATA
Auteuil, Daniel
theatre 369
"Authorized by Memory" (Tvardovsky)
Soviet literature 251
autism
mental health 207
autofocus camera
photography 276
automobile 211
consumer affairs 142
solar power 188
special report **87**:411
automobile insurance
state governments 490
automobile racing **89**:307; **88**:308; **87**:347; **86**:381; **85**:376; **84**:541; **83**:540; **82**:548; **81**:547; **80**:545
aviation 372
advertising 490
disasters 152
Avineri, Shlomo
"At the Core of the Problem of Peace—Israel and the West Bank: Two Views" (feature article) **84**:8
Avril, Prosper
Haiti 503, *il.*
AWC: *see* Australian Wool Corporation
Awolomo, Chief Obafemi (obit.) **88**:88
Ayer, A. J.
literature 244
Aykhenrand, Leyzer
"The Eternal Moment" 253
Aylmer, Sir Felix (obit.) **80**:103
Azcona Hoyo, José Simón (biog.) **87**:76
Honduras 504
Azerbaijan (state, U.S.S.R.)
protests 476
AZT, or zidovudine, or Retrovir
AIDS treatment 203

B

B-52 (bomber)
U.S. military affairs 257
Babangida, Maj. Gen. Ibrahim (biog.) **86**:90
Babaquara Dam (Braz.)
plan abandonment 190

Julien / Laker 895

Julien, Claude Norbert (biog.) **81**:81
Jumblatt, Walid (biog.) **84**:85
Jumping World Cup
skiing 335
"June 1941" (Vorzoger)
Yiddish literature 253
Jupiter
special report **80**:631
Jurgens, Curt (obit.) **83**:113
Justice Department, U.S.
crime statistics 143
ethical misconduct 232
International Brotherhood of Teamsters 231
Jusuf, Mohammad (obit.) **80**:82
Jutra, Claude (obit.) **88**:100

K

Kabalevsky, Dmitry Borisovich (obit.) **88**:100
Kadar, Jan (obit.) **80**:114
Kadar, Janos (biog.) **83**:82
Kadosa, Pal (obit.) **84**:121
Kadota, Hiromitsu
Japanese baseball 310
Kaempfert, Berthold (obit.) **81**:113
Kagin, Vladimir
furniture 218
Kahane, Meir (biog.) **85**:102
Kahn, Alfred (biog.) **80**:83
Kahn, Herman (obit.) **84**:121
Kahnweiler, Daniel-Henry (obit.) **80**:114
Kalambay, Sumbu
boxing 315
Kaldor, Mary
"Flourishing, Worldwide, Deadly—The Open Market in Arms" (feature article) **84**:35
Kaldor, Nicholas Kaldor, Baron (obit.) **87**:112
Kalgoorlie (Austr.)
gold mining *il.* 265
Kalikow, Peter
newspaper publishing 285
"kamalatta" (Geissler)
German literature 248
Kamanin, Nikolay Petrovich (obit.) **83**:113
Kamina (Zaire)
military affairs 402
"Kammerherr und König" (Jaeck)
German literature 248
Kampelman, Max (biog.) **86**:100
Kampuchea **89**:438; **88**:438; **87**:480; **86**:510; **85**:516; **84**:467; **83**:468; **82**:474; **81**:226; **80**:228
refugees 282
Sino-Soviet relations 423
Southeast Asian affairs 434
Thailand 442
Vietnam 443
United Nations 377
see also WORLD DATA
Kanai, Mieko
"Oh, Tama" 253
Kanak, *or* Melanesian (people)
independence struggle 451, 519
Oceanian affairs 511
Kanellopoulos, Kanellos
man-powered flight 306
Kanellopoulos, Panayotis (obit.) **87**:112
Kania, Stanislaw (biog.) **81**:81
Kansas, University of (Lawrence, Kansas, U.S.)
basketball championship 311
Kant, Hermann
German literature 248
Kante, Mory
kora playing 274
Kantorovich, Leonid Vitalyevich (obit.) **87**:112
KANU (pol. party, Ken.): *see* Kenya African National Union
Kapitsa, Pyotr Leonidovich (obit.) **85**:134
Kaplan, Mordecai Menahem (obit.) **84**:121
Kapoor, Raj (obit.) **89**:99
Kapwepwe, Simon Mwansa (obit.) **81**:113
Karajan, Herbert von (biog.) **85**:103
Karami, Rashid Abdul Hamid
biography **85**:103
obituary **88**:100
Karandash (obit.) **84**:121
Karas, Anton (obit.) **86**:133
Karayev, Kara Abulpaz (obit.) **83**:113
Kardelj, Edvard (obit.) **80**:114
Kardiner, Abram (obit.) **82**:112
"Karin B" (ship)
waste removal 198
Kariuki, Julius
track and field 342
Karle, Jerome (biog.) **86**:100
Karmal, Babrak (biog.) **81**:82
Karolyi, Bela (biog.) **87**:87
Karpov, Anatoly
chess 316
Kasparov, Garry (biog.) **86**:100
chess 316
Kastler, Alfred (obit.) **85**:134
Katanyan, Vasily Abgarovich (obit.) **81**:113
Katayev, Valentin Petrovich (obit.) **87**:112
Kathmandu (Nepal)
stampede 433
katydid
entomological research 237
Kaunda, Kenneth
Zambia 403
Kautner, Helmut (obit.) **81**:113
Kawamata, Katsuji (obit.) **87**:112
Kaye, Danny (obit.) **88**:100
Kaye, Nora (obit.) **88**:100
Kaye, Sammy (obit.) **88**:100
Keating, Paul John (biog.) **88**:75
Australia 514
Keating, Tom (obit.) **85**:134
Kedourie, Elie
"Islam Resurgent" (feature article) **80**:58
Keefer, Janice Kulyk
literature 246
Keillor, Garrison (biog.) **86**:101
"Kein näheres Zeichen" (Czechowski)
literature 248
Kekkonen, Urho Kaleva (obit.) **87**:112
Kelly, Emmett Lee (obit.) **80**:114
Kelly, Patsy (obit.) **82**:112
Kelly, Petra Karin (biog.) **83**:82
Kemp, Jack (biog.) **83**:82
U.S. presidential election (special report) 483
Kemper, James Scott (obit.) **82**:112
Kempf, Hippolyt
skiing 335
Kempowski, Walter
literature 248
Kennan, George Frost
Britannica Awards 15
Kennedy, Anthony (biog.) **89**:76
swearing-in ceremony *il.* 485
Kennedy, Daisy (obit.) **82**:113
Kennedy, Edward Moore (biog.) **80**:83
Kennedy, John F.
television and radio 366
Kennedy, William
American literature 245
Kenner, Hugh
literary criticism 243
Kent, Msgr. Bruce (biog.) **84**:86
Kenton, Stanley Newcombe (obit.) **80**:114
Kenya **89**:390; **88**:391; **87**:430; **86**:461; **85**:467; **84**:469; **83**:469; **82**:475; **81**:475; **80**:473
sex education 184
social security 300
track and field 342
wildlife conservation 199
world cross country championship 343
see also WORLD DATA
Kenya African National Union, *or* KANU (pol. party, Ken.)
Kenyan elections 390
Keon Jong Yul
bowling 313
Kerans, John Simon (obit.) **86**:133
Kérékou, Mathieu
Benin 384
Kerley, Sir Peter James (obit.) **80**:114
Kerpestein, LeRoy: *see* Loring, Eugene
Kertész, André (obit.) **86**:133
Kessel, Joseph (obit.) **80**:114
Kettlewell, Henry Bernard Davis (obit.) **80**:114
Keynes, Sir Geoffrey Langdon (obit.) **83**:113
Keyserling, Leon H. (obit.) **88**:100
keystone buffet *il.* 217
Khalid ibn Abd al-'Aziz Al Saud (obit.) **83**:114
Khalifah, Khalifah ibn Ahmad al-Bahrain 407
Khama, Sir Seretse (obit.) **81**:113
Khamenei, Hojatoleslam Sayyed Ali (biog.) **82**:81
Khan, Fazlur Rahman (obit.) **83**:114
Khan, Ghulam Ishaq
Pakistan 433
Khan, Inamullah
Islam 299
Khindaria, Brij
"Foundation for Survival" (feature article) **81**:65
Khmer Rouge, *or* KR (pol. party, Kamp.)
Kampuchean affairs 438
Khomeini, Ayatollah Ruhollah (biog.) **80**:83
Iran-Iraq war 410
Khrushchev, Nina Petrovna (obit.) **85**:134
Kidder, Margot (biog.) **84**:86
Kiehl, Marina
skiing 335
Kieseritzsky, Ingomar
German literature 248
Kiesinger, Kurt Georg (obit.) **89**:99
West Germany 453
Kil, Chung Young
boxing 315
Killian, James Rhyne, Jr. (obit.) **89**:99
Kim Chong Il (biog.) **85**:103
Korean affairs 426
Kim Dae Jung (biog.) **86**:101; **84**:86
South Korea 427
Kim Hyon Hui
Korea 426
terrorism 142
Kim Il Sung
North Korea 427
Kim Young Sam
South Korea 427
Kimball, Spencer W. (obit.) **86**:133
Kimbell Art Museum (museum, Ft. Worth, Tex.)
art exhibition 133
King, Cecil Harmsworth (obit.) **88**:101
King, Clarence
National Mining Hall of Fame 263
King, Henry (obit.) **83**:114
King, the Rev. Martin Luther, Sr. (obit.) **85**:134
King, Stephen (biog.) **81**:82
"King Ludd" (Sinclair)
British literature 244
Kingdom, Roger
track and field 342
Kingman committee (U.K.)
education report 183
Kinmonth, John Bernard (obit.) **83**:114
Kinnear, Roy Mitchell (obit.) **89**:99
Kinnock, Neil Gordon (biog.) **84**:87
British politics 466
Kinshasa (Zaire)
inflation 402
Kinugasa, Sachio (biog.) **88**:75
Kipphardt, Heinar (obit.) **83**:114
Kiribati **89**:515; **88**:515; **87**:562; **86**:594; **85**:600; **84**:470; **83**:470; **82**:476; **81**:476; **80**:474
see also WORLD DATA
Kirk, Hans
Danish literature 248
Kirkland, Joseph Lane (biog.) **80**:84
Kirkpatrick, Jeane J. (biog.) **85**:103; **82**:81
"Kiro—The Final Stand" (photograph)
World Press Photo of the Year Award *il.* 276
Kirochi, Wilfred
cross country running 343
Kishi, Nobusuke (obit.) **88**:101
Kissinger, Henry Alfred (biog.) **84**:87
Kiszczak, Czeslaw
Polish politics 473
Kitaro (biog.) **88**:75
Kivengere, Festo
Anglican Communion 293
KKR: *see* Kohlberg, Kravis, Roberts and Co. (investment firm)
Kleffens, Eelco Nicolaas van (obit.) **84**:121
Klier, Freya
East Germany 471
Klindt-Jensen, Ole (obit.) **81**:113
Klitzing, Klaus von (biog.) **86**:101
Kluszewski, Ted (obit.) **89**:99
KMT, Nationalist Party (pol. party, Tai.): *see* Kuomintang
Knight, Bobby (biog.) **80**:84
Knight, George Richard Wilson (obit.) **86**:133
Knight, John Shively (obit.) **82**:113
Knight-Ridder (news. chain)
newspaper publishing 285
knitwear
fashion and dress 200
Knopf, Alfred A. (obit.) **85**:134
Knowles, John Hilton (obit.) **80**:115
Koch, Erich (obit.) **87**:113
Kodak: *see* Eastman Kodak Co.
Kodama, Yoshio (obit.) **85**:135
Koenigswald, G. H. Ralph von (obit.) **83**:114
Koeppler, Sir Heinz (obit.) **80**:115
Koestler, Arthur (obit.) **84**:121
Kogan, Leonid Borisovich (obit.) **83**:114
Kohl, Helmut (biog.) **86**:102; **83**:83
France 451
West Germany 452, *il.* 444
Kohlberg, Kravis, Roberts and Co., *or* KKR (investment firm)
book publishing 286
Köhlmeier, Michael
German literature 248
Koirala, Bisheshwar Prasad (obit.) **83**:114
Koivisto, Mauno Henrik (biog.) **83**:83
Finland 449, *il.*
Kokoschka, Oskar (obit.) **81**:113
Kolingba, André (biog.) **82**:81
Central African Republic 386
Kollsman, Paul (obit.) **83**:114
Kolman, Arnost Ernst (obit.) **80**:115
Kolmogorov, Andrey Nikolayevich (obit.) **88**:101
Kolodin, Irving (obit.) **89**:99
Kolvenbach, Peter-Hans (biog.) **84**:87
Komeito (pol. party, Japan): *see* Clean Government Party
Komori Printing Machinery (Japanese co.)
printing 224
Kondrashin, Kyril (obit.) **82**:113
"Kontrolliert" (Goetz)
German literature 248
Koop, Charles Everett (biog.) **88**:75
cigarette smoking report 206
Koopmans, Tjalling Charles (obit.) **86**:133
Koornhof, Pieter Gerhardus Jacobus (biog.) **82**:81
Koppel, Ted (biog.) **84**:87
Korea **89**:426; **88**:426; **87**:469; **86**:499; **85**:504; **84**:470; **83**:471; **82**:477; **81**:476; **80**:474
military affairs 262
North
Olympic boycott 339
Olympic terrorism 142
South
automobile industry 212
badminton 308
China 423
economic affairs 169
iron and steel 221
Japan 425
Kiribati 515
Olympic security 142
shipbuilding 225
social security and welfare services 300
strike *il.* 231
tourism 227
wrestling competition 344
see also WORLD DATA
Korner, Alexis (obit.) **85**:135
Koruturk, Fahri S. (obit.) **88**:101
Koskotas, George
Greek scandal 454
Kosovo (prov., Yugos.)
Yugoslavia 479, *il.* 35
Kostelanetz, Andre (obit.) **81**:113
Kosygin, Aleksey Nikolayevich (obit.) **81**:114
Kotani, Mikako
synchronized swimming 337
Kotarbinski, Tadeusz Marian (obit.) **82**:113
Koun, Karolos (obit.) **88**:101
Kountché, Gen. Seyni (obit.) **88**:101
Kouprey, *or* Bos sauveli
wildlife conservation 199
Kowarski, Lew (obit.) **80**:115
Kpolleh, William Gabriel
Liberia 392
KR (pol. party, Kamp.): *see* Khmer Rouge
Kraft Inc. (Am. co.)
food processing 123
Kraftwerk Union (elec. co.)
electrical industry 217
Krasner, Lee (obit.) **85**:135
Krasnoyarsk (U.S.S.R.)
radar installation 261
Kratochvilova, Jarmila (biog.) **84**:88
Krawczyk, Stephan
East Germany 471
Krebs, Sir Hans Adolf (obit.) **82**:113
Kreisky, Bruno (biog.) **80**:84
Krige, Uys (obit.) **88**:101
Krishnamurti, Jiddu (obit.) **87**:113
Kristallnacht
West Germany 453
Kristiansen, Ingrid (biog.) **87**:87
Krleza, Miroslav (obit.) **82**:113
Kroc, Ray Albert (obit.) **85**:135
Kuenn, Harvey Edward (obit.) **89**:99
Kulle, Jarl
Royal Dramatic Theatre 369
Kunstsammlung Nordrhein-Westfalen (Ger.)
art exhibition 131
Kuomintang, *or* KMT, Nationalist Party (pol. party, Tai.)
Taiwan 428
Kurd (people)
Iraq 406, 411
Turkey 419
Kurlovich, Aleksandr
Olympic weight-lifting competition 344
Kuron, Jacek (biog.) **82**:82
Kurosawa, Akira (biog.) **80**:84
Kurtinaitis, Rimas
basketball 312
Kuwait **89**:414; **88**:414; **87**:454; **86**:486; **85**:490; **84**:473; **83**:473; **82**:479; **81**:479; **80**:477
engineering projects 190
see also WORLD DATA
Kuwait Airways
hijacking 143, 234
Algeria 407
Kuwait 414
terrorism 405
Kuznets, Simon Smith (obit.) **86**:134
Kuznetsov, Anatoly Vasilievich (obit.) **80**:115
Kwangju (S.Kor.)
riot investigation 427
Kyocera Corporation (Jap. co.)
Yashica Samurai camera 277
Kyprianou, Spyros
Greece 407
Kyser, Kay (obit.) **86**:133

L

La Guma, Alex (obit.) **86**:134
La Malfa, Ugo (obit.) **80**:115
La Natividad (anc. colony, Haiti)
archaeological finds 127
La Salle Plaza (Minneapolis, Minn., U.S.)
architectural design 130
Labour-Management Relations 89:230; **88**:232; **87**:263; **86**:288; **85**:286; **84**:429; **83**:427; **82**:431; **81**:434; **80**:434
South Africa 398
special reports **85**:288; **82**:435; **81**:436
Labour Party (pol. party, Isr.)
elections 405, 412
Labour Party (pol. party, Nor.)
economic policies 459
Labour Party (pol. party, U.K.)
politics 464
Lacan, Jacques (obit.) **82**:113
Lacasa, A.
zoological research 237
Lacaze, Jeannon (Fr. mil. of.)
Zaire 403
Lacouture, Jean
television and radio 366
Lacroix, Christian (biog.) **88**:76
Ladd, Alan, Jr. (biog.) **80**:85
Ladefense-Isey Plaine
Parisian mass transit 374
Ladies International
polo 333
"Lady Pepa" (Ferrero)
Spanish literature 250
Laguerre, André (obit.) **80**:115
LAIA: *see* Latin American Integration Association
Laing, Hugh (obit.) **89**:99
Laker, Jim (obit.) **87**:113

P&O / pluralism 901

P

P&O (cruise co.)
shipping and ports 373
Paasio, Rafael (obit.) **81**:120
PAC: *see* political action committee
Pacific Ocean
hydrothermal vents 161
Page, George (biog.) **82**:87
Page, Geraldine (obit.) **88**:106
Pagnani, Andreina (obit.) **82**:118
Paige, Leroy Robert (obit.) **83**:118
"Painters by Painters: Portraits from the Uffizi Gallery" (art exhibit) 131
paints and varnishes 223
Pakistan **89**:433; **88**:434; **87**:476; **86**:506; **85**:512; **84**:558; **83**:559; **82**:566; **81**:564; **80**:563
Afghanistan 233, 429
military affairs 261
sports
cricket 317
squash rackets 335
see also WORLD DATA
Pakistan People's Party, *or* PPP
elections 434
Pal, George (obit.) **81**:120
Palacio de Bellas Artes (Mex. City, Mex.)
art exhibition 133
Palacio Villahermosa (Madrid, Sp.)
art exhibition 132
Palaemon elegans: *see* shrimp
Palar, Lambertus Nicodemus (obit.) **82**:118
Palatine Hill (It.)
archaeological finds *il.* 126
Palau
U.S. relations 519
Paleckis, Justas (obit.) **81**:120
paleoclimatology
geological studies 156
Palestine
Japan 425
Jordan 413
Palestine Liberation Organization, *or* PLO
Middle Eastern affairs 405
Egypt 409
Israel 375, 412
Jordan 413
Lebanon 415
Syria 418
Netherlands 459
terrorism 143
United Nations 377
United States office 234
Palewski, Gaston (obit.) **85**:140
Palme, Sven Olof Joachim
biography **83**:86
crime and law enforcement 147
obituary **87**:118
Palmer, Leonard Robert (obit.) **85**:140
Palmer, Lilli (obit.) **87**:119
Pálsson, Thorsteinn (biog.) **88**:78
Iceland 455
PAN (pol. party, Mex.): *see* Partido Acción Nacional
Pan American World Airways
explosion 143, *il.* 37
Panama **89**:507; **88**:506; **87**:553; **86**:584; **85**:579; **84**:560; **83**:561; **82**:568; **81**:566; **80**:564
international law 234
Latin-American affairs 491
see also WORLD DATA
Panduro, Leif
Danish literature 248
Panhellenic Socialist Movement, *or* Pasok (pol. party, Gr.)
Greece 454
pants
fashion and dress 200
"Pão e Sangue" (Trevisan)
Brazilian literature 251
PAP (pol. org., Sing.): *see* People's Action Party
Papandreou, Andreas (biog.) **82**:88
Greece 454, *il.* 448
Turkey 419
Papiernikov, Yoysef
"Tree and Forest" 253
Papua New Guinea **89**:517; **88**:516; **87**:563; **86**:595; **85**:601; **84**:560; **83**:562; **82**:568; **81**:566; **80**:565
Solomon Islands 517
see also WORLD DATA
parabolic superposition (physiol.)
zoological research 237
Paraguay **89**:508; **88**:506; **87**:553; **86**:585; **85**:588; **84**:561; **83**:562; **82**:569; **81**:567; **80**:566
see also WORLD DATA
Paray, Paul (obit.) **80**:120
Paris (Fr.)
urban mass transit 374
Paris Bourse (Fr.)
French economy 451
stock exchanges 179
Paris Club of Western creditor nations
Brazil 496
Zaire 402
Paris Opéra Ballet (Fr. dance co.)
dance 150
"Paris Trout" (Dexter)
American literature 245
Park Chung Hee (obit.) **80**:120
Park Joon Kyu *il.* 427
Park Si Hun *il.* 314
Parker, Charlie
jazz 272
Parker, James Stewart (obit.) **89**:105
Parkinson, Cecil Edward (biog.) **88**:78
coal industry privatization 465
Parodi, Alexandre (obit.) **80**:120
Parrington, Francis Rex (obit.) **82**:119
Parrot, André (obit.) **81**:120
Parrott, Sir Cecil Cuthbert (obit.) **85**:140
Parry, Clive (obit.) **83**:119
Parry, Sir Thomas (obit.) **86**:140
Parshin, A. N.
mathematics 254
Parsons, Talcott (obit.) **80**:120
Parti Démocratique Gabonais, *or* PDG (pol. party, Gab.)
Gabon 389
Parti Démocratique Sénégalais, *or* PDS (pol. party, Sen.)
Senegal 396
Parti Socialist (pol. party, Fr.): *see* Socialist Party
Parti Socialiste (pol. party, Sen.)
Senegal 396
Partido Acción Nacional, *or* PAN, *or* National Action Party (pol. party, Mex.)
Mexican elections 505
Partido Justicialista, *or* Peronists (pol. party, Arg.)
Argentina 493
Partido Movimento Democratico Brasileiro (pol. party, Braz): *see* Brazilian Democratic Movement Party
Partido Revolucionario Institucional, *or* PRI, *or* Institutional Revolutionary Party (pol. party, Mex.)
Mexican presidential election 491, 505
"Partners in the Mystery of Redemption" (letter)
women ordination 291
Partridge, Eric Honeywood (obit.) **80**:121
Pascal, Pierre (obit.) **84**:126
Paskai, Laszlo Cardinal
papal invitation 296
Paso, Fernando del
Mexican literature 250
Pasok (pol. party, Gr.): *see* Panhellenic Socialist Movement
passport
Dutch controversy 459
Pasternak, Boris
house *il.* 270
Soviet literature 251
Pastora Gómez, Edén (biog.) **85**:110
Patent and Trademark Office (U.S.)
animal patent 241
paternal sex ratio, *or* psr (chromosome)
entomological research 238
Paternoster Square (London, U.K.)
architectural controversy 128
Paton, Alan Stewart (obit.) **89**:105
Patrick, Nigel (obit.) **82**:119
Patterson, Frederick Douglass (obit.) **89**:105
Patterson, William Allan (obit.) **81**:120
Pattison, Jim (biog.) **87**:92
Paul, Jean-Claude (obit.) **89**:105
Pavarotti, Luciano (biog.) **81**:87
Pavilion for Japanese Art (Calif., U.S.)
opening 270
Pawley, Howard (biog.) **83**:86
payments, balance of
world economy 162, 173
Payne, the Rev. Ernest Alexander (obit.) **81**:121
Paynter, Thomas William (obit.) **85**:140
Paz, Octavio
Latin-American literature 250
Paz Estenssoro, Víctor (biog.) **86**:106
Bolivia 495
PBS (U.S.): *see* Public Broadcasting Service
PC: *see* personal computer
PDG (Gab.): *see* Parti Démocratique Gabonais
PDM (Turks and Caicos Isls.): *see* People's Democratic Movement
PDS (pol. party, Sen.): *see* Parti Démocratique Sénégalais
Peace and Democracy, Party for, *or* PPD (pol. party, S.Kor.)
South Korea 427
Peacekeeper (missile)
U.S. military affairs 258
Peacock, Andrew Sharp (biog.) **82**:88
Pears, Sir Peter Neville Luard (obit.) **87**:119
Pearson (Br. co.)
newspaper publishing 284
Peary, Robert
North Pole claim 523, *il.*
Peccei, Aurelio (obit.) **85**:140
Peckford, Alfred Brian (obit.) **80**:90
Peckinpah, Sam (obit.) **85**:140
Pecsi, Kalman
Comecon reform 171
Pedersen, Charles John (biog.) **88**:79
Peduzzi, Richard
theatre 369
Peerce, Jan (obit.) **85**:141
"Pelicano" (freighter)
waste disposal 198
"Pelle the Conqueror" (film)
Scandinavian motion pictures 267
Pelshe, Arvid Yanovich (obit.) **84**:126
Pendleton, Clarence
biography **86**:106
obituary **89**:105
Pène du Bois, Raoul (obit.) **86**:140
Peng Zhen (P'eng Chen) (biog.) **84**:94
Penhaligon, David Charles (obit.) **87**:119
Penn Nouth, Samdech (obit.) **86**:140
penology: *see* prisons and penology
Penrose, Sir Roland Algernon (obit.) **85**:141
Pentagon
crime and law enforcement 147
Pentecostal Church of Chile
United Church of Christ 296
Pentecostal Churches 294
fundamentalism (special report) 290
People of the Year 89:65; **88**:65; **87**:76; **86**:89; **85**:89; **84**:75; **83**:70; **82**:68; **81**:70; **80**:70
People That Love (U.S.): *see* PTL
People's Action Party, *or* PAP (pol. org., Sing.)
Singapore 441
People's Democratic Movement, *or* PDM (pol. party, Turks and Caicos Isls.)
election results 519
People's Liberation Front (pol. org., Sri Lanka)
Tamil separatist war 434
People's United Party, *or* PUP (pol. party, Belize)
elections 495
Pepper, Art (obit.) **83**:119
Pepper, Claude Denson (biog.) **84**:94
PepsiCo (Am. co.)
Soviet advertising 210
Percival, Edgar Wikner (obit.) **85**:141
Pereira, Aristides
Cape Verde 386
Pereira, William Leonard (obit.) **86**:140
Perelman, Sidney Joseph (obit.) **80**:121
Peres, Shimon (biog.) **85**:110
Israel 405, 413
perestroika
centrally planned economies 171
East Germany 470
Eastern Europe 468
Soviet literature 251
Soviet military affairs 259
special report **88**:474
U.S.S.R. 375, 474
Peretz, Yitzhak *il.* 412
Pérez, Carlos Andrés
Venezuela 511
Pérez Alfonso, Juan Pablo (obit.) **80**:121
Pérez de Cuéllar, Javier (biog.) **89**:81; **83**:87
United Nations 376
Perham, Dame Margery (obit.) **83**:119
Périer, François
theatre 369
Perkins, Carl Dewey (obit.) **85**:141
Perkins, Richard Marlin (obit.) **87**:119
Perón, María Estela Martínez de, *or* Isabelita
Argentina 493
Peronists (pol. party, Arg.): *see* Partido Justicialista
Perroux, François (obit.) **88**:106
Perry, William (biog.) **86**:106
Persichetti, Vincent (obit.) **88**:107
personal computer, *or* PC
microelectronics 222
printing 224
special report **86**:286
Personal Ensign
horse racing 327
Peru **89**:508; **88**:507; **87**:553; **86**:585; **85**:500; **84**:562; **83**:563; **82**:569; **81**:567; **80**:566
archaeological finds 126, *il.* 127
drug trade (special report) 144
see also WORLD DATA
pesticide
consumer affairs 141
PET: *see* polyethylene terephthalate
Peterson, David (biog.) **86**:107
Peterson, Roger Tory (biog.) **83**:87
"Petite Danseuse de 14 ans" (sculp.)
record art sale 135
Petri, Elio (obit.) **83**:119
Petrillo, James Caesar (obit.) **85**:141
Petrobia latens: *see* brown wheat mite
petrochemical industry
Saudi production 417
petroleum
Arctic Regions 522
developing nations 168
1987 stock market crash (special report) 176
OPEC price levels 186
special report **87**:211
stock exchanges 181
see also individual countries by name
Petroleum Exporting Countries, Organization of, *or* OPEC
Middle Eastern affairs 406
Iraq 411
Saudi Arabia 417
oil prices 186
Petrosian, Tigran Vartanovich (obit.) **85**:141
Pettersson, Allan Gustaf (obit.) **81**:121
Peurala, Alice (biog.) **80**:90
Pevsner, Sir Nikolaus Bernard Leon (obit.) **84**:126
PGA: *see* Professional Golfers' Association
Pham Hung (obit.) **89**:105
"Phantom of the Opera" (play)
theatre 370, *il.* 367
pharmaceuticals 223
pheasant
Chinese research work 238
"Phera" (film)
Indian motion pictures 268
Philately and Numismatics 89:274; **88**:277; **87**:312; **86**:343; **85**:342; **84**:563; **83**:564; **82**:570; **81**:568; **80**:567
Philby, Kim (obit.) **89**:105
crime and law enforcement 147
Philip Morris, Lorillard and Liggett Group (Am. co.)
advertising 210
smoking lawsuit 142
Philippines **89**:440; **88**:440; **87**:482; **86**:513; **85**:518; **84**:564; **83**:565; **82**:572; **81**:570; **80**:569
economic affairs 169
Southeast Asia 435
see also WORLD DATA
"Philippines: Is Democracy Restored?, The" (feature article) **87**:5
Phillips, Jason
college football 322
Phillips, Marjorie Acker (obit.) **86**:140
Phillips Collection (U.S.)
art exhibition 131
Phipps, Ogden
horse racing 327
Phobos
space exploration 306
Phoenix, Pat (obit.) **87**:119
Phoenix Cardinals
football 324
Photography 89:276; **88**:278; **87**:313; **86**:344; **85**:343; **84**:565; **83**:566; **82**:573; **81**:571; **80**:570
Phoumi Nosavan (obit.) **86**:140
PHWR: *see* pressurized-heavy-water reactor
Physics 89:278; **88**:280; **87**:315; **86**:346; **85**:345; **84**:567; **83**:568; **82**:575; **81**:573; **80**:571
special report **80**:573
Piaget, Jean (obit.) **81**:121
Piasecki, Lech
cycling 319
"Piave" (It. ship)
toxic waste disposal 198
Picasso, Pablo
record art sale 134
Piccard, Franck
skiing 334
Piccard, the Rev. Jeanette Ridlon (obit.) **82**:119
Pickens, Slim (obit.) **84**:126
Pickens, T. Boone, Jr. (biog.) **86**:107
Pickford, Mary (obit.) **80**:121
Picot Report (N.Z. educ. report)
school administration policies 183
Pidgeon, Walter (obit.) **85**:141
Pierpont Morgan Library (N.Y.C., N.Y., U.S.)
expansion 270
Pieske, Manfred 248
Pignedoli, Sergio Cardinal (obit.) **81**:121
pilgrimage
Saudi-Iranian controversy 299, 417
Pilinszky, Janos (obit.) **82**:119
Pilkington, William Henry Pilkington, Baron (obit.) **84**:126
"Pillow Book" (Sei)
record book sale 135
Pilyugin, Nikolay Alekseyevich (obit.) **83**:119
Pima Indians
obesity research 205
Pinheiro de Azevedo, José Batista (obit.) **84**:126
Pink Lady (biog.) **80**:91
Pinochet Ugarte, Augusto
Chilean plebiscite 491, 496, *il.* 497
television and radio 366
Pinto Balsemão, Francisco José Pereira (biog.) **82**:88
Pioneer
space exploration 306
pipeline 373
Piper Alpha
insurance 219, *il.* 220
Piquet, Nelson
automobile racing 307
Pit Theatre (U.K.)
productions 368
Pitchfork, Colin
DNA fingerprinting 139
Pitman, Sir Isaac James (obit.) **86**:140
Pitterman, Bruno (obit.) **84**:127
PKI: *see* Indonesian Communist Party
Plaisted, Ralph
North Pole claim 523
Planinc, Milka (biog.) **83**:87
Plante, Jacques (obit.) **87**:120
plants
molecular biology 240
plastics 224
plate tectonics
geological research 156
Play the King
horse racing 328
Plaza Lasso, Galo (obit.) **88**:107
Pleistocene Era
archaeological finds 125
Plimsoll, Sir James (obit.) **88**:107
PLO: *see* Palestine Liberation Organization
Plomley, Francis Roy (obit.) **86**:141
Plotkin, Manuel D.
"The Changing Face of America" (feature article) **82**:137
Plugge, Leonard Frank (obit.) **82**:119
pluralism
socialist societies 5

906 *Spanish literature / Taborski*

Far Right (special report) 445
hydrology 159
stock exchanges 181
see also WORLD DATA
Spanish literature 250
Spark, Muriel
British literature 244
Sparkman, John Jackson (obit.) **86**:145
Sparteca: *see* South Pacific Regional Trade and Economic Cooperation Agreement
Späth, Lothar
West German elections 452
Special Air Service (U.K.)
crime and law enforcement 143
IRA shootings 467
Spectre, Jay
furniture 218
speech, freedom of
court decisions 232
speed skating 331
"Speed-the-Plow" (play)
theatre 370, *il.*
Speelman, Jon
chess 316
Speer, Albert (obit.) **82**:122
Speidel, Hans (obit.) **85**:146
Spencer, 2nd Earl
book collection sale 135
Spender, Sir Percy Claude (obit.) **86**:145
Spender, Stephen
British literature 244
sperm
DNA fingerprinting 139
sperm whale 140
Sphinx
archaeology 125
Spielberg, Steven (biog.) **83**:92
"Spielplatz der Helden" (Köhlmeier)
German literature 248
spin (particle phys.)
superconductivity 279
Spinelli, Altiero (obit.) **87**:123
Spinks, Michael
boxing 314
"Spirit of the Dead Watching, The" (Gauguin)
art exhibition *il.* 133
spirits 214
Spivak, Charlie (obit.) **83**:124
spongiform encephalopathy, *or* BSE
cattle infestation 208
Sport Recife (Braz. sports team)
soccer 321
Sports and Games 89:306; **88**:308; **87**:346; **86**:380; **85**:374
special reports **89**:340; **87**:392; **85**:428, 422; **81**:728
television and radio 365
see also specific sports or games, *e.g.*, baseball
Sporting Record 89:345
Spratly Islands
rival claims 436
Vietnam 443
Springer, Axel (obit.) **86**:145
Springsteen, Bruce (biog.) **86**:113; **82**:92
Spry, Graham (obit.) **84**:131
"Sputnik" (Sov. mag.)
Soviet publishing 283
"Spycatcher" (Wright)
British literature 243
censorship attempt 283, 465
court ruling 232
Spychalski, Marian (obit.) **81**:125
squash rackets **89**:335; **88**:338; **87**:385; **86**:420; **85**:415; **84**:590; **83**:588; **82**:595; **81**:593; **80**:591
Squyres, Steven
geological research 156
Sraffa, Piero (obit.) **84**:131
Sri Lanka **89**:434; **88**:434; **87**:477; **86**:507; **85**:513; **84**:633; **83**:631; **82**:637; **81**:631; **80**:636
gemstones 219
race relations 287
see also WORLD DATA
Sri Venkatesvara (temple, Malibu, Calif., U.S.)
Hindu celebration 298
SSBN: *see* ballistic missile nuclear submarine
Städtische Kunsthalle (Ger.)
art exhibition 131
Stafford, Jean (obit.) **80**:125
Stalin, Joseph
Russo-Finnish War 449
Stalinism
Soviet literature 251
Stallone, Sylvester (biog.) **86**:113
stamp: *see* Philately and Numismatics
Standard & Poor
stock exchanges 177
Stanford-Tuck, Robert Rolland (obit.) **88**:110
Stanford University (Stanford, Calif. U.S.)
liberal arts education 185
Stankiewicz, Richard Peter (obit.) **84**:131
Stanner, William Edward Hanley (obit.) **82**:123
star
supernova SN 1987A 136, *il.*
Star Wars: *see* Strategic Defense Initiative
starfish, *or* Leptsasterias
marine biology 239
Stargell, Willie (biog.) **80**:95
Stark, Koo
newspapers 283
Starling, Marlon
boxing 315
"Stars & Stripes" (U.S. boat)
sailing 334, *il.* 362
START: *see* Strategic Arms Reduction Talks Treaty
starvation: *see* famine
state government 488
State Russian Museum (museum, Leningrad, U.S.S.R.)
art exhibition 131
State Tretyakov Gallery (museum, Moscow, U.S.S.R.)
art exhibition 131
Staten Island Midland Beach (U.S.)
pollution *il.* 196
"Stationen der Moderne"
art exhibition 132
Staunton, Imelda
theatre 368
Stazewski, Henryk (obit.) **89**:109
Stead, Christina Ellen (obit.) **84**:131
Stealth bomber (aircraft): *see* Northrop B-2
steel: *see* iron and steel
Steele-Perkins, Chris
photography 278
Stein, John (obit.) **86**:145
Stein, Jules Caesar (obit.) **82**:123
Stein, William Howard (obit.) **81**:125
Stein & Day (Am. co.)
book publishing 287
Steinberger, Jack (biog.) **89**:84
stele
archaeological finds 126
Stephanopoulos, Stephanos (obit.) **83**:124
Stephen, Sir Ninian Martin (biog.) **83**:92
Steptoe, Patrick Christopher (obit.) **89**:109
sterling (U.K.): *see* pound sterling
Sterling, John Ewart Wallace (obit.) **86**:145
Stern, Irwin
"Dictionary of Brazilian Literature" 251
Stern, Sholom
Holocaust 297
Stevens, Bernard George (obit.) **84**:131
Stevens, Jimmy Moli (biog.) **81**:92
Stevens, Siaka Probyn
biography **81**:92
obituary **89**:110
Stewart, Donald Ogden (obit.) **81**:125
Stewart, Ella Winter (obit.) **81**:125
Stewart, Michael (obit.) **88**:110
Stewart, Potter (obit.) **86**:145
Stewart, Monsignor Richard Louis (obit.) **86**:145
Stikker, Dirk Uipko (obit.) **80**:125
Still, Clyfford (obit.) **81**:125
Stinus, Erik
Danish literature 249
Stirling, James Frazer (biog.) **81**:93
Stitt, Edward (obit.) **83**:124
stock exchanges **89**:174; **88**:176; **87**:192; **86**:220; **85**:219; **84**:634; **83**:632; **82**:638; **81**:632; **80**:637
Bahrain 407
crime and law enforcement 146
1987 crash **89**:176, 208
special report **88**:144
Stockman, David (biog.) **82**:93
Stockton, Maurice Harold Macmillan (obit.) **87**:123
Stokes, Ralph Shelton Griffin (obit.) **80**:125
Stoltenberg, Gerhard
West German economy 452
Stone, John
Australia 514
Stone, Michael
terrorism 143
Stone, Oliver (biog.) **88**:82
"Stones" (Findley)
Canadian literature 247
"Stories of Nara" (Shibaki)
Japanese literature 253
"Story of My Life" (McInerney)
American literature 245
Stout, Alan Ker (obit.) **84**:131
Stow Hill, Frank Soskice (obit.) **80**:125
"strade di polvere, Le" (Loy)
Italian literature 250
Straight, Whitney Willard (obit.) **80**:125
Strange, Curtis
golf 324
Strasberg, Lee (obit.) **83**:124
Strategic Air Command, *or* SAC (U.S.)
military affairs 257
Strategic Arms Limitation Treaty II, *or* SALT II
special report **80**:289
Strategic Arms Reduction Talks Treaty, *or* START
military affairs 261
Strategic Defense Initiative, *or* SDI, *or* Star Wars (U.S.)
military affairs 260
special report **85**:320
Strategic Nuclear Forces Command
Soviet military affairs 259
Stratford Festival (Stratford, Can.)
theatre 371
Stratton, Monty Franklin Pierce (obit.) **83**:124
Strauss, Franz-Josef
biography **80**:95
obituary **89**:110
West Germany 452
Strauss, Robert (biog.) **80**:95
Strawberry, Darryl
baseball 310
Streatfield, Mary Noel (obit.) **87**:123
Streep, Meryl (biog.) **81**:93
Streibl, Max
West Germany 453
Strelcyn, Stefan (obit.) **82**:123
"Stresses in the Western Alliance" (feature article) **83**:65
Strickland, Earl
pocket billiards 313
strike
Poland 473
South Africa 398
South Korea 427
special report **81**:436
Yugoslavia 479
Stroessner, Alfredo
Paraguay politics 508
Strolz, Hubert
skiing 334
Strong, Sir Kenneth William Dobson (obit.) **83**:124
Strong Pass
contract bridge 317
Strougal, Lubomir
Czechoslovakian political leadership 470
Strout, Richard Lee (biog.) **84**:99
"Structural Unemployment: The Reality Behind the Myth" (feature article) **84**:29
"Struggling for Nationhood: The Birth of Zimbabwe" (feature article) **82**:8
Stuck, Hans
automobile racing 308
Stuschinski, Osher
Yiddish literature 253
Stypulkowski, Zbigniew (obit.) **80**:125
Suau, Anthony
photography 278
Suazo Córdova, Roberto (biog.) **83**:92
substrates
ceramics industry 216
subway: *see* urban mass transit
sucralose
soft drinks 215
Sudan, The **89**:400; **88**:400; **87**:439; **86**:472; **85**:477; **84**:639; **83**:639; **82**:644; **81**:638; **80**:643
African affairs 382
Ethiopia 388
famine relief efforts 378
flooding *il.* 400
refugees 282
Uganda 402
see also WORLD DATA
Sudets, Vladimir (obit.) **82**:123
Sudharmono
Indonesia 437
Suez Canal
Egyptian economy and development 409
sugar
Belize 495
production 117
Saint Kitts and Nevis 509
Sugar, Alan Michael (biog.) **87**:97
Suharto
Indonesia 436, 437
suit
fashion and dress 201
Suleymanoglu, Naim (biog.) **89**:84
Olympic weight-lifting competition 344, *il.* 343
Turkish immigration 420
sulfide oxidation
energy source 240
sulfur dioxide
environmental hazard 197
Sullivan, Danny
automobile racing 308
Sullivan, Maxine (obit.) **88**:110
Sultan, Fouad
Egyptian tourism 409
"Summe, Die" (Kant)
German literature 248
Summerskill, Edith Clara Summerskill, Baroness (obit.) **81**:125
Sumpter, Donald
theatre 368
Sun
solar flares *il.* 137
Sun Microsystems (Am. co.)
Unix standardization 229
Sun Yat-sen, Madame (obit.) **82**:123
Sunay, Cevdet (obit.) **83**:124
"Sunday Times" (Br. news.)
newspaper publishing 284
Sunette
food processing 124
sunlight
molecular biology 240
"Sunrise on the Summit of Mount Huang" (painting)
art sale *il.* 134
Sunshine Skyway Bridge (Fla., U.S.)
suspension bridge *il.* 189
Sununu, John
government relations 488
Middle Eastern affairs 405
Super Bowl
advertising 210
football 323
Super Channel
television and radio 364
supercomputer
information systems 230
superconductivity
applications 188
ceramics 216, *il.* 279
high-temperature research 278
Superconductor Super Collider
Texas 490
Superman (biog.) **89**:85
supernova
SN 1987A 136, *il.*
Superset
food processing 123
Supreme Court of the United States
decisions 232
education 182
state governments 488
surimi
fishing industry 121
Suriname **89**:510; **88**:508; **87**:555; **86**:587; **85**:587; **84**:640; **83**:639; **82**:644; **81**:638; **80**:643
see also WORLD DATA
Surkov, Aleksey Aleksandrovich (obit.) **84**:132
surrogate motherhood 490
"Survey of the '70s" (feature article) **80**:129
Suslov, Mikhail Andreyevich (obit.) **83**:124
Susskind, David (obit.) **88**:110
Sutherland, Graham Vivian (obit.) **81**:125
Sutherland, Dame Lucy Stuart (obit.) **81**:125
Sutter, Bruce (biog.) **83**:92
Sutton, Willie (obit.) **81**:125
Suzuki, Zenko (biog.) **81**:93
Svan, Gunde
skiing 335
Svavarsdottir, Hlif
dance 151
Svestka, Oldrich (obit.) **84**:132
Svoboda, Ludvik (obit.) **80**:125
Swaggart, Jimmy
sex scandal 292, 294
Swakara Karakul
fur production 218
Swanson, Gloria (obit.) **84**:132
Swart, Charles Robberts (obit.) **83**:124
Swaziland **89**:401; **88**:400; **87**:439; **86**:473; **85**:477; **84**:640; **83**:640; **82**:645; **81**:639; **80**:644
see also WORLD DATA
Swearingen, John Eldred, Jr. (biog.) **85**:113
Sweden **89**:463; **88**:462; **87**:507; **86**:535; **85**:541; **84**:641; **83**:641; **82**:645; **81**:639; **80**:644
arts
literature 249
motion pictures 267
television and radio 364
theatre 370
crime and law enforcement 147
environmental concerns 194
international affairs
Baltic zones dispute 235
North Atlantic Treaty Organization 460
nuclear power 188
political pluralism 13
skiing 335
stock exchanges 180
see also WORLD DATA
Swedenborg, Emanuel
Swedish literature 249
Swedish literature 249
swimming **89**:336; **88**:338; **87**:386; **86**:421; **85**:416; **84**:642; **83**:642; **82**:646; **81**:641; **80**:645
Swinnerton, Frank Arthur (obit.) **83**:125
Switzerland **89**:463; **88**:463; **87**:508; **86**:536; **85**:542; **84**:644; **83**:643; **82**:648; **81**:642; **80**:647
freight traffic 373
Liechtenstein 458
literature 248
motion pictures 267
social security 300
stock exchanges 180
theatre 369
see also WORLD DATA
Symington, William Stuart (obit.) **89**:110
Symonette, Sir Roland Theodore (obit.) **81**:122
symphony
classical music 271
synchronized swimming
Olympic games 337
Syria **89**:418; **88**:418; **87**:461; **86**:490; **85**:496; **84**:645; **83**:645; **82**:649; **81**:643; **80**:648
archaeological finds 125
Lebanon 414
military affairs 261
see also WORLD DATA
Szabo, Laszlo Csekefalvi (obit.) **85**:146
Szarkowski, John
photographic retrospective 277
Szent-Györgyi, Albert (obit.) **87**:123
Szentkuthy, Miklos (obit.) **89**:110
Szeryng, Henryk (obit.) **89**:110
Szmuness, Wolf (obit.) **83**:125

T

t-Pa (drug): *see* tissue plasminogen activator
"T. S. Eliot and Prejudice" (Hicks)
British literature 244
Taba strip (Sinai penin.)
international adjudication 234
Tabai, Ieremia (biog.) **80**:96
table tennis **89**:337; **88**:339; **87**:388; **86**:422; **85**:417; **84**:647; **83**:646; **82**:650; **81**:644; **80**:649
tabloid (pub.)
newspapers 283
Taborski, Boleslaw
theatre 370

Tabucchi / Tumbledown 907

Tabucchi, Antonio
Italian literature 250
tagging
prisons and penology 147
Tahiti
strikes 519
Taipei (Tai.)
Taiwan political leadership 428
Taiwan **89**:428; **88**:428; **87**:470; **86**:501; **85**:506; **84**:648; **83**:646; **82**:651; **81**:645; **80**:650
American cigarettes *il.* 227
economic affairs 169
literature 253
military affairs 262
motion pictures 269
see also WORLD DATA
Takakura, Ken (biog.) **86**:113
Takamatsu, Prince (obit.) **88**:110
Takamiyama (biog.) **85**:114
Takemitsu, Toru (biog.) **82**:93
takeover
stock exchanges 175
Takeshita, Noboru (biog.) **88**:83; **86**:114
crime and law enforcement 146
Japan 423
Talking Heads (rock group)
popular music 274
Talmon, Jacob Leib (obit.) **81**:126
Talyzin, Nikolay
U.S.S.R. 475
Tamayo, Rufino
art exhibition 133
Tambimuttu, Meary James Thurairajah (obit.) **84**:132
Tambo, Oliver (biog.) **86**:114
Tamil (people)
refugees 282
Sri Lankan race relations 287, 434
Tamil Nadu (India)
government changes 431
Tamil Tigers (pol. org., Sri Lanka): *see* Liberation Tigers of Tamil Eelam
Tamil United Liberation Front (pol. org., Sri Lanka)
Sri Lanka 434
Tan Liangde
Olympic diving competition 337
Tanaka, Kakuei (biog.) **84**:99
Tanaka, Miyako
synchronized swimming 337
Tandy Corp. (Am. co.)
Micro Channel replication 230
Tange, Kenzo (biog.) **88**:83
Tanglewood Summer Festival (Berkshire Hills, Mass.)
classical music 271
tango 268
Taniguchi Masaharu (obit.) **86**:146
Tank, Kurt (obit.) **84**:132
Tanzania **89**:401; **88**:400; **87**:440; **86**:473; **85**:477; **84**:649; **83**:647; **82**:652; **81**:646; **80**:651
see also WORLD DATA
Taraki, Nur Mohammad (obit.) **80**:126
tariff
agricultural products 120
Tarkovsky, Andrey Arsenyevich
biography **85**:114
obituary **87**:123
Tarradellas i Joan, Josep (obit.) **89**:110
Tarsis, Valery Yakovlevich (obit.) **84**:132
Tasmania (Austr.)
Australia 513
special report **83**
Tatarkiewicz, Wladyslaw (obit.) **81**:126
Tate, John Orley Allen (obit.) **80**:126
Tate Gallery (museum, London, U.K.)
art exhibition 134
expansion 270
Tati, Jacques (obit.) **83**:125
Taurog, Norman (obit.) **82**:123
Taussig, Helen Brooke (obit.) **87**:124
taxation
Australia 514
state governments 488
Taya, Maaouya Ould Sidi Ahmed
Mauritania 393
Taylor, D. J.
British literature 243
Taylor, David
magazine publishing 285
Taylor, Gordon Rattray (obit.) **82**:123
Taylor, Kenneth (biog.) **81**:93
Taylor, Lawrence (biog.) **87**:97
Taylor, Maxwell Davenport (obit.) **88**:110
Tchicaya U Tam'si (obit.) **89**:110
Te Kanawa, Dame Kiri (biog.) **84**:99
teaching
U.S. school problems 184
Teare, Robert Donald (obit.) **80**:126
Tebbit, Norman Beresford (biog.) **86**:114; **82**:93
"Technology & Teamwork" (auto exhibit)
automobile industry 212
Tekere, Edgar
Zimbabwe 404
telecommunications 225
television and radio 363
televangelism
scandals 292
special report **88**:294
Television and Radio **89**:363; **88**:363; **87**:399; **86**:432; **85**:435; **84**:651; **83**:650; **82**:654; **81**:648; **80**:653
advertising 210
special reports **83**:656; **82**:487, 659; **80**:659
writers' strike *il.* 363
TEM: *see* Trans-European North-South Motorway
"Temple, The" (Spender)
British literature 244
Temple Mount: *see* al-Aqsa Mosque
Templer, Sir Gerald Walter Robert (obit.) **80**:126
"Tenants of Time, The" (Flanagan)
American literature 244
Teng Hsiao-p'ing: *see* Deng Xiaoping
Tennant, Kylie (obit.) **89**:110
tennis **89**:338; **88**:340; **87**:388; **86**:423; **85**:417; **84**:657; **83**:658; **82**:661; **81**:653; **80**:662
tenpins: *see* bowling
Tenzing Norgay (obit.) **87**:124
Teragon (Swed. co.)
printing systems 224
Terayama, Shuji (obit.) **84**:132
terrorism 142
Greece 455
Middle Eastern affairs 405
Kuwait 414
Lebanon 415
special report **81**:487
Zimbabwe 404
Terry, Fernando Belaúnde: *see* Belaúnde Terry, Fernando
Terry, Quinlan
architecture 128
Terry, Walter (obit.) **83**:125
Terzieff, Laurent
theatre 369
"Tetris"
games and toys *il.* 218
Texaco Inc. (Am. co.)
oil refining 188
textbook
school controversy 182
textiles
trade restructuring 226
Tewson, Sir Harold Vincent (obit.) **82**:123
Tezza, Cristóvao
"Trapo" 251
TF1 (TV channel)
television and radio 366
Thailand **89**:441; **88**:441; **87**:484; **86**:514; **85**:519; **84**:659; **83**:660; **82**:663; **81**:655; **80**:664
bridges 373
demography 281
Laos relations 439
refugees 282
roads and highways 191
wildlife conservation 199
see also WORLD DATA
thallium
superconductivity 278
Thames (London ITV co.)
television and radio 366
Thani, Hamad ibn Khalifah ath-
Qatar 417
Tharp, Twyla
American Ballet Theatre choreography 149
Thatcher, Margaret Hilda (biog.) **89**:85; **88**:83; **87**:97; **86**:115; **84**:100; **83**:93; **82**:93; **81**:94; **80**:96
capitalism 9
international affairs
European Communities 444, *il.*
United Kingdom 464, *il.*
visits
Nigeria 395
Poland 473
Spain 462
Turkey 419
West Germany 454
television and radio 366
Theatre **89**:367; **88**:367; **87**:403; **86**:436; **85**:439; **84**:660; **83**:661; **82**:664; **81**:656; **80**:665
special report **85**:229
Theatre Nuclear Forces, *or* TNF
North Atlantic Treaty Organization 260
Theismann, Joe (biog.) **84**:100
Theorell, Axel Hugo Teodor (obit.) **83**:125
Thériault, Yves (obit.) **84**:133
Thill, Georges (obit.) **85**:146
"Things Change" (film)
motion pictures 266
"thirtysomething" (TV program)
television and radio 365
Thomas, Derrick
college football 323
Thomas, Franklin (biog.) **80**:96
Thomas, Gwyn (obit.) **82**:123
Thomas, Henri
French literature 247
Thomas, Horatio Oritsejolmi (obit.) **80**:126
Thomas, Isiah
basketball 312
Thomas, Kurt (biog.) **80**:96
Thomas, Lowell (obit.) **82**:123
Thomas, Michael Tilson
classical music 272
Thomas, Philip Michael (biog.) **86**:99
Thomas, William Miles Webster Thomas, Baron (obit.) **81**:126
Thomas Cup
badminton 308
"Thomas Paine" (Ayer)
British literature 244
Thompson, Daley (biog.) **85**:114; **81**:94
Thomson, Virgil (biog.) **82**:94
Thorburn, Cliff (biog.) **84**:100
Thorn, Gaston (biog.) **81**:94
Thornton, Charles Bates (obit.) **82**:124
Thornton, Willie Mae (obit.) **85**:146
Thoroddsen, Gunnar (obit.) **84**:133
thoroughbred racing 327
Thorsteinsdóttir, Sigrún
Icelandic politics 455
Thranhardt, Carlo
track and field 342
three-cushion billiards
competition results 312
Thurman, Howard (obit.) **82**:124
Thuy, Xuan (obit.) **86**:146
Thyssen-Bornemisza Museum (Switz.)
art loan 132
Tian Jiyun (biog.) **86**:115
Tibet
anti-Chinese riots 421
Buddhism 298
Tidyman, Ernest R. (obit.) **85**:146
Tierno Galván, Enrique (obit.) **87**:124
Tigrai People's Liberation Front, *or* TPLF
African affairs 382
Ethiopia 388
Tikhonov, Nikolay Aleksandrovich (biog.) **81**:94
Tikhonov, Viktor
ice hockey 331
Tikhonova, Tamara
skiing 335
Tikkoo, Ravi
shipping and ports 373
Tillstrom, Burr (obit.) **86**:146
timber
wood products 228
Timerman, Jacobo (biog.) **82**:94
"Times, The" (U.K. news.)
chess puzzle 317
Timmermann, Ulf
track and field 342
tin
mining 263
Tinbergen, Nikolaas (obit.) **89**:111
Tinker, Grant (biog.) **82**:94
Tiomkin, Dmitri (obit.) **80**:126
Tippet, Clark
dance 149
Tisch, Laurence Alan (biog.) **87**:98
tissue plasminogen activator, *or* t-PA (drug)
heart attack treatment 204
pharmaceutical industry 224
Tito (obit.) **81**:126
Titusville (U.S.)
archaeological finds 127
Tjibaou, Jean-Marie (biog.) **86**:115
referendum *il.* 519
TNF: *see* Theatre Nuclear Forces
"To a Safer Place" (film) 269
"To Midnight and After" (TV program)
television and radio 366
tobacco 227
tobacco hornworm, *or* Manduca sexta
botanical research 240
Todman, William Seldon (obit.) **80**:126
Tofilau Eti Alesana
Western Samoan politics 518
Togo **89**:401; **88**:401; **87**:440; **86**:473; **85**:478; **84**:666; **83**:666; **82**:668; **81**:660; **80**:670
see also WORLD DATA
Toivo Ja Toivo, Andimba (biog.) **85**:114
Tojo, Teruo (biog.) **82**:94
Tokyo Stock Exchange (Japan)
1987 crash (special report) 176
stock exchanges 181
Tolbert, William Richard, Jr. (obit.) **81**:126
toll road
Norway 374
U.S. 191
Tomás, Americo De Deus Rodrigues (obit.) **88**:110
Tomasek, Frantisek
Czechoslovakia 470
Tomba, Alberto
skiing 335, *il.*
Tomonaga, Shinichiro (obit.) **80**:126
Ton Duc Thang (obit.) **81**:126
Tonegawa, Susumu (biog.) **88**:83
Tonga **89**:517; **88**:517; **87**:564; **86**:596; **85**:602; **84**:666; **83**:667; **82**:669; **81**:661; **80**:670
see also WORLD DATA
Tony Bin
horse racing 328
"Torn-up Roots" (Stuschinski)
Yiddish literature 253
Toronto Stock Exchange (Can.)
stock exchanges 178
Torrejón (air base, Sp.)
Spain 462
Torrelio Villa, Celso (biog.) **82**:95
Torrijos Herrera, Omar (obit.) **82**:124
Torvill, Jayne, and Dean, Christopher (biog.) **84**:100
Tosh, Peter (obit.) **88**:110
Tosoh Corp. (Japanese co.)
food processing 123
"Touch of Genius, A" (Brown and Cave)
British literature 244
Tour de France
cycling 319
Touré, Ahmed Sékou (obit.) **85**:146
tourism 227
Antarctica 521
Bhutan 430
Cuba 500
Egypt 408
India 298
Saint Kitts and Nevis 509
San Marino 461
Seychelles 396
toxic waste
consumer affairs 141
environmental hazard 197, *il.* 194
Guinea-Bissau 390
special report **84**:364
toy: *see* games and toys
toy gun
games and toys 219
Toynbee, Theodore Philip (obit.) **82**:124
Toyoda, Eiji (biog.) **81**:95
Toyota Motor Co. (Japanese co.)
automobile industry 212
TPA: *see* tissue plasminogen activator
TPLF: *see* Tigrai People's Liberation Front
track and field sports **89**:339; **88**:341; **87**:390; **86**:425; **85**:419; **84**:666; **83**:667; **82**:669; **81**:661; **80**:671
special report **81**:665
"Tracks" (Erdrich)
American literature 245
trade: *see* international trade
Trader Vic (obit.) **85**:146
Trades Union Congress, *or* TUC (U.K.)
labour-management relations 230
traffic
disasters 155
Trans-African Highway
construction 192
Trans-Canada Highway
renovation 191
Trans-European North-South Motorway, *or* TEM
construction 192
Transkei 400
Transnuklear (Eur. co.)
nuclear industry 223
Transpolar Ski Expedition
Canadian participation 482
Transportation **89**:371; **88**:371; **87**:408; **86**:411; **85**:443; **84**:669; **83**:671; **82**:672; **81**:668; **80**:674
special report **87**:411
see also WORLD DATA
Transrapid (train)
magnetic train development *il.* 374
Traoré, Moussa
Mali 393
"Trapo" (Tezza)
Brazilian literature 251
Trapp, Maria von (obit.) **88**:111
"trappola amorosa, La" (Arpino)
Italian literature 249
"Traumfrau, Die" (Pieske)
German literature 248
travel
magazines 286
Travers, Ben (obit.) **81**:126
Travis, Merle (obit.) **84**:133
"Treasures from the Royal Collection"
art exhibition 132
"Tree and Forest" (Papiernikov)
Yiddish literature 253
Trefil, James
American literature 246
Trelford, Donald Gilchrist (biog.) **85**:115
Trend, Burke St. John Trend (obit.) **88**:111
Trepper, Leopold (obit.) **83**:125
tretinoin (drug): *see* Retin-A
Trevelyan, Humphrey Trevelyan, Baron (obit.) **86**:146
Trevelyan, John (obit.) **87**:124
Trevelyan, Julian Otto (obit.) **89**:111
Trevisan, Dalton
"Pão e Sangue" 251
Trident (missile)
U.S. military affairs 258
Trifonov, Yury Valentinovich (obit.) **82**:124
trimetrexate (drug)
AIDS treatment 203
Trinidad and Tobago **89**:510; **88**:509; **87**:556; **86**:587; **85**:594; **84**:674; **83**:675; **82**:677; **81**:673; **80**:679
see also WORLD DATA
Trippe, Juan Terry (obit.) **82**:124
TRNC: *see* Turkish Republic of Northern Cyprus
"Troga, La" (Rugarli)
Italian literature 249
"Trois Hommes qui marchent" (sculp.)
record art sale 135
Troisgros, Jean (obit.) **84**:133
Trottier, Bryan (biog.) **83**:93
truck
sales 213
Trudeau, Pierre Elliott (biog.) **81**:95
special report **84**:225
Truffaut, François (obit.) **85**:147
Truman, Bess (obit.) **83**:125
Truman, Harry
newspaper publishing history 284
Trump, Donald John (biog.) **88**:84
Truong Chinh (obit.) **89**:111
Tsarapkin, Semyon Konstantinovich (obit.) **85**:147
Tsatsos, Konstantinos (obit.) **88**:111
Tshisekedi, Etienne wa Mulumba
Zaire 403
"Tsipor Kelu'a" (Hurvitz)
Hebrew literature 252
"Tsutaya Juzaburo" (Matsumoto)
Japanese literature 253
Tsvigun, Semyon Kuzmich (obit.) **83**:125
Tubb, Ernest Dale (obit.) **85**:147
TUC (U.K.): *see* Trades Union Congress
Tuchman, Barbara (biog.) **80**:97
literature *il.* 245
Tudor, Anthony (obit.) **88**:111
"Tumbledown" (TV program)
television and radio 366